FOR REFERENCE

Do Not Remove From This Room

3 1243 00179 9369

Library Use Only

PROPERTY OF
LAKE FOREST
LIBRARY

W9-BQZ-500

Baker's Biographical Dictionary of Musicians

EIGHTH EDITION

Baker's Biographical Dictionary of Musicians

EIGHTH EDITION

Revised by
Nicolas Slonimsky

SCHIRMER BOOKS
A Division of Macmillan, Inc.
NEW YORK

MAXWELL MACMILLAN CANADA
TORONTO

MAXWELL MACMILLAN INTERNATIONAL
NEW YORK · OXFORD · SINGAPORE · SYDNEY

Copyright © 1900, 1905, 1919, 1940, 1958, 1971 by G. Schirmer, Inc.
Copyright © 1978, 1984, 1992 by Schirmer Books
A Division of Macmillan, Inc.

All rights reserved. No part of this book may be reproduced or transmitted
in any form or by any means, electronic or mechanical, including photocopying,
recording, or by any information storage and retrieval system, without permission
in writing from the Publisher.

Schirmer Books
A Division of Macmillan, Inc.
866 Third Avenue, New York, NY 10022

Maxwell Macmillan Canada, Inc.
1200 Eglinton Avenue East, Suite 200, Don Mills, Ontario M3C 3N1

Macmillan, Inc. is part of the Maxwell Communication Group of Companies.

Library of Congress Catalog Card Number: 91-24591

Printed in the United States of America

Printing number
 2 3 4 5 6 7 8 9 10

Library of Congress Cataloging-in-Publication Data

Baker, Theodore, 1851–1934.
    [Biographical dictionary of musicians]
    Baker's biographical dictionary of musicians. — 8th ed. / revised
by Nicolas Slonimsky.
        p. cm.
    Includes bibliographical references.
    ISBN 0-02-872415-1
    1. Music—Bio-bibliography. 2. Musicians—Biography—
Dictionaries. I. Slonimsky, Nicolas, 1894–
    ML105.B16 1991
780′.92′2—dc20   91-24591
[B]   CIP
                                            MN

REFERENCE 780.92 BAK
Baker, Theodore, 1851-1934.
Baker's biographical
dictionary of musicians

The paper used in this publication meets the minimum requirements of American
National Standard for Information Sciences—Permanence of Paper for Printed Library Materials. ANSI Z39.48–1984.

Preface to the Eighth Edition

My life as a diaskeuast is connected by an invisible but substantial thread with the illustrious German-educated American lexicographer Theodore Baker. He was the one who published the first edition of this eternally famous (in musicological circles) *Baker's Biographical Dictionary of Musicians*. He published it first in 1900 as a modest, slim compilation that paid tribute to a number of his contemporaries in the field that only then evolved as musicology, a science of music. Whether the biography of musicians can be called a science is a moot question. What is scientific about discovering that Beethoven jotted down an instruction to his charwoman to purchase for him in the store—among sundry daily articles—a piece of soap? But what kind of soap? Of what color? Beethoven's handwriting was well-nigh indecipherable. (His copyist said he would rather transcribe ten pages of Rossini's original manuscripts than a single page of Beethoven's.) But, after years of meticulous chirography, a German-born English music scholar ascertained that Beethoven's indecipherable word was *gelb*, yellow. Problem solved: the soap Beethoven preferred for his toilette was *gelb*. (He left the dishwashing to his well-informed menial.) Is this musicology?

But, from the ridiculous to the sublime. Is the contemplation of Beethoven's famous, but probably mythical, "immortal beloved" musicology? A prosaic lexicographer like my spectral Theodore Baker would not have philosophized about Beethoven's absent (alas!) sex life. He attended to facts. But mere facts are so jejune, so unappealing, so paltry. How much more exciting to speculate about the identity of Beethoven's imaginary flame! Accordingly, a number of musicographers squandered their expendable energies in endless conjecture. And what about Beethoven's possessive affection for his fatherless nephew? Some otherwise normal and serious Germans wasted their time worrying about the nature of Beethoven's desire to replace the missing parent. The adoption plan had to be submitted to the Austrian court, which was an extremely severe legal institution. Beethoven himself had a peculiar sense of legality, naively believing that he could overcome the strictures of the established state law. He tried to prove that he was a fit guardian by claiming noble social descent evidenced by the nobiliary particle, "van", attached to his name. But the court disagreed, rendering the judgment that "van" was a common Dutch particle not to be confused with the truly noble "von".

So much stuff has been written and so much paper wasted on the controversy connected with Beethoven's abortive dedication of his so-called Eroica Symphony that it may not be irrelevant to point out that Napoleon and Beethoven were nearly the same age; Napoleon was older by a year and four months. And thereby hangs a tale. When Napoleon was safely put away in the inaccessible island of St. Helena, his English custodians were well aware of his continuous hold on the imagination of Europeans, who had been at different times conquered by him. Indeed, the responsibility that the English felt over the care, feeding, and psychological welfare of their famous prisoner went so far as to compel them to commission the composition of an oratorio for a special performance at St. Helena. The name of a little-known Austrian composer was suggested, but a music publisher proposed in a conversation with Beethoven, recorded in Beethoven's famous conversation books (Beethoven's deafness was a positive factor in the preservation of such discussions), that the commission should be made to Beethoven himself. Beethoven reacted with interest, even expressing the view that had he elected to study military science, he would have been as great on the field of battle as he was on the pages of a symphony. Nothing came of this project and Napoleon died without benefit of a musical consecration.

Incidentally, and perhaps irrelevantly, I am against capital punishment, but I would gladly pull the switch on a member of a publishing management who was introduced to me as a specialist in German, on the strength, I understand, of his having taken a quickie course at a respectable New York university. Going over the page proofs of the 6th edition of *Baker's Biographical Dictionary of Musicians*, he found an obvious error, the famous nobiliary particle spelled "van." He crossed it out and in dark red pencil wrote on the margin in very large letters, "V-O-N." The referent was Beethoven. I restrained my murderous feelings towards the aforesaid expert in German, but asked my publisher not to let him near my final page proofs.

Artists are perpetually in need of money. Mozart was woefully short of funds sufficient to provide for his family, and periodically wrote pathetic begging letters to a friendly banker for loans that he never bothered to repay. Many such letters are extant and, as manuscripts, are worth much more than the original donation so humbly entreated. Thus, a recipe for a musical genius to raise money is rather simple: write a begging letter to a rich friend, wait a century or so, and sell the letter for an imposing sum of money. Mozart's fame, however, was such that extravagant capital gains are not needed to sustain his immortality. Many immortals of music have streets and theaters named in their honor, but who has a whole town named for him? Mozart has, in the Canadian province of Saskatchewan.

Contemplating the laws of probability in the lives of great composers, we could let our imaginations run. Mozart died at a tragically young age, but what if he had lived as long as Verdi? He could have been a drinking companion of Berlioz, and, who knows, even a mentor to Wagner and Liszt. Continuing in this vein, we could imagine Schubert playing four-hand piano with Chopin. We could visualize Tchaikovsky at the age of 73, attending a performance of Stravinsky's *Rite of Spring*. He would have thought that music had become the handmaiden of hell. Yet Rachmaninoff, whose concept of music was so close to Tchaikovsky's, actually studied Stravinsky's score with interest. Shall we go on in this chronological phantasmagory? All we have to do is to read what great composers said about each other when they were contemporaries. Or, worse still, read reviews by supposedly enlightened journalists about composers of their own time. Can it be believed that an intelligent English music critic would have written the following review of Chopin's recital in London: "The entire works of Chopin present a motley surface of ranting hyperbole and excruciating cacophony." But avaunt the stormy clouds of artistic incomprehension! Let us return to the clear weather of today's music. Or is it cloudless? No, this is a book of biographical events and we must try not to confuse facts with opinion. In his essay "What is art?," Tolstoy tried to solve esthetic problems, but even he, the titan of universal comprehension, failed.

Now I must recollect myself and reaffirm the formal and prosaic *raison d'être* of the present 8th edition of *Baker's*, which represents a gathering of information that has come since the publication of the previous edition. Any new edition of a biographical dictionary of musicians aims to augment, refine, and update the contents of the previous edition, and the present work is no exception. For the first time since the 5th edition, substantial rewrites of entries on several major figures have been undertaken, incorporating the latest in research.

The 8th edition is also chock-full of new entries. A significant constituency is reflected in the number of non-European musicians who have risen to fame on the world scene during the second half of the 20th century. One has to abandon patronizing condescension to so-called Third World artists. Indeed, the classification "Third World," traditionally used to represent the vast territories of Asia and Africa, may have to be redefined. Who would have imagined that one of the greatest contemporary cellists would be a Chinese called Yo-Yo Ma? Or that the youthful Korean conductor Myung-Whun Chung would be selected to head the newly formed Bastille Opera in Paris? *Tempora mutantur et nos mutamur in illis.* It would have been unimaginable a scant half century ago that two of the most important American symphony orchestras—the Boston Symphony Orchestra and the New York Philharmonic—would be led by Asian musicians: Seiji Ozawa of Japan and Zubin Mehta of India! The art of symphonic conducting had been for many years preponderantly Germanic. Henry Lee Higginson, founder of the Boston Symphony Orchestra, specified in his contracts of financial support that the conductor must be a German. It was a great shock to him when Karl Muck was interned as an enemy alien toward the end of the First World War. Distressed, Higginson withdrew all financial support from the Boston Symphony Orchestra.

But *revenons à nos moutons*, as the French say, lest the aforesaid muttons get stranded in the columns of our dictionary. Indeed, new lambs arrive from all over the world and a significant number of them have wandered in from Japan. Their biographies were supplied by the Japanese Union of Composers, an organization that issues periodical catalogues remarkable in their completeness and in some respects excelling music dictionaries and catalogues by music publishers in Europe and America. Another national group of musicians well represented in *Baker's* for the first time is the Koreans, who were individually and personally responsive to requests for biographical information.

Music history knows many women who adorned the opera stage and became celebrated under the colorful Italian definition of *diva*, "the divine one." Popular books on opera tell stories, not always verifiable, about worshipful admirers who unharnessed the carriage horses of the current diva to pay homage by pulling the carriage to the house, palace, hotel, or wherever the object of their adoration was making her temporary habitation. Envious rivals to such *prime donne* suggested that these adulatory excesses were remunerated. Anyway, the custom went into desuetude with the advent of the automobile.

From its inception, *Baker's* listed biographies of great female singers dating from the beginning of opera, but what was missing in previous editions was a rightful place for women composers. And yet there were such, worthy of note, long before *Baker's* saw its first light of day. In the 18th century, ladies with a compositional bent confined their efforts to songs and occasional harp pieces, but in the 19th century women were writing orchestral music and even operas. The names of most of them have been duly tabulated in previous editions of *Baker's*, but many more musical suffragettes, if such a borrowing from the world of politics can be allowed, have since made their appearance on symphony programs. One such modern musical woman, Ellen Zwilich, was awarded the Pulitzer Prize in Music, the first to be received by a woman composer. Thea Musgrave has emerged as an important composer of symphonies and operas. The Soviet composer Sofia Gubaidulina has acquired fame on par with any of her male colleagues.

The new *Baker's* has increased not only its coverage of women, but also of ethnomusicologists, a term of relatively recent origin which has now acquired its proper place in new dictionaries of musical terminology. But though we can catch up with the sedentary academic ethnomusicologists, the more elusive ethnic musicians sometimes escape our net. Multi-media composers and performance artists have also attained a legitimate place among practicing musicians. They freely combine the arts of speech, dance, and even gymnastics with lighting effects, all of which are written into the score. Many of these novel effects have been anticipated by earlier composers. In his *Poem of Fire*, Scriabin introduced an instrument listed as "*luce*," using the Italian word for light, but technical problems still frustrate the realization of the effect that Scriabin visualized in his futuristic dream.

Modern technology enables the artisans of new sonorities to perform scales and harmonies independent of the established division of the octave into 12 chromatic intervals. The Russian electrical engineer Theremin constructed an instrument that produced any fractional interval by the wave of the hand, but the results were rarely accurate. It was not until the invention of electronic keyboard instruments that accurate fractional intervals could be achieved and that an octave could be divided into any number of equal intervals, causing Bach's "equal temperament" to be no longer a *conditio sine qua non* of intervallic equality. The Mexican composer Julián Carrillo claimed to have constructed instruments that produced sounds divisible into any number of equal intervals down to 1/64 of an octave, but the accurate division of the octave could never be achieved. With the accession of musical electronics, any desired effect of fractional tonality can be achieved. But is this extension of musical means welcome? Is a new Bach even now creating an electronic masterpiece? The availability of new means of sonic production has not yet occasioned the appearance of a creator of surpassing genius.

When we speak of forward leaps, we invariably encounter the phenomenon of John Cage, the primary experimenter with chance. When he first met his audience in the 1940s, he was an object of derision as an intruder into the sacred temple of the Muses. But, as has happened to visionaries from Pythagoras to Schoenberg, he eventually proved the validity of his innovations. The *Encyclopaedia Britannica* unreservedly states that he is the single greatest influence on composers of the second half of the 20th century. He even began collecting the world's most prestigious appointments and most opulent prizes, from Harvard to Kyoto. His mind-boggling, syllable-tossing stage work entitled *Europeras 1 & 2* garnered sensational headlines all over the world.

One of the most laborious aspects in the preparation of the present edition has been the compiling of a world necrology of musicians, which I have inelegantly tabulated in a list entitled "Stiffs." As the present edition went to press, the number of stiffs exceeded 600. *Morituri te salutant.* Such spirits cannot be gathered merely by scanning obituary notices in major newspapers or music magazines, but demand luck and persistence equal to that of Hamlet's gravedigger who produced the skull of "poor Yorick." A properly compiled biography of a stiff must include place and date of death, but it ought also to contain a sort of mournful coda about a musician's life and career as well as reference to the cause of death. Unfortunately, published death notices rarely mention the specific cause of a person's demise. Difficulties abound in chasing down those extravagant spirits, to quote Hamlet addressing his father's ghost. ("Extravagant" meaning, of course, walking beyond the proper limits for the dead, not being careless about money. One American production of *Hamlet*, not trusting the verbal expertise of its audience, replaced the Shakespearean word with the common adjective "restless.")

Specific causes of death are occasionally suppressed in obituary notices because of purely social considerations. Unesthetic illnesses such as gout, which was a frequent affliction of large, fat men of power in 18th-century England, were considered unfit for print. The proverbial illness of 19th-century artistic poverty was tuberculosis, which took many young lives; it was euphemistically replaced in print with "consumption." Cancer as a cause of death was also unmentionable. In Tolstoy's short novel *The Death of Ivan Ilych*, the progressive symptoms of the protagonist's disease plainly point to a cancerous condition, but the ominous word itself is nowhere to be found in the text. And then came AIDS, a cruel and ironic acronym for Acquired Immune Deficiency Syndrome.

In simpler days there were simpler answers for disease. Scrofula, common from the Middle Ages well into the 19th century, affected the sufferer with painful glandular swellings that came to be known as the King's Evil. The cure was simplicity itself. All you had to do was to petition an anointed sovereign to touch the diseased area. Belief in the healing power of crowned royalty was so widely accepted that the kings of England and France set aside certain days of the year when those afflicted could come for a cure. Charles II of England lent his healing touch to some 90,000 of his subjects. In 1712 Queen Anne freely administered the cure for the King's Evil to hundreds of Englishmen; among them was Samuel Johnson who was touched as a small child. In France, on Easter Sunday, 1686, Louis XIV touched 1,600 persons while giving credit to God, saying: "Le Roi te touche; le Dieu te guérisse."

Nothing in the history of musical biography can compare in sheer ferocity to the witch's sabbath that descended upon the world of music at the death of Tchaikovsky in 1893. Despite unequivocal and unimpeachable testimony to the reality of Tchaikovsky's fatal illness of cholera, the apparently irresistible rumor of suicide splashed the world's newspapers with sensational headlines. The glamour attached to the name Tchaikovsky caused other deviations from truth about his life and death.

Tchaikovsky is an icon in Russia, second only to Lenin. The primacy of Tchaikovsky's genius and of his name led to the elimination of all mention of his homosexuality from all biographical material published in Russia. Censorship extended also to Russian translations of books in foreign languages. Tchaikovsky himself tried to cover up his preference for the inverted mode of love by contracting a nominal marriage to a young conservatory student, but this desperate ploy collapsed when Tchaikovsky explained the situation to her on their wedding night. They were never divorced, and Tchaikovsky arranged to pay her annual stipends as long as their marriage was in force. It ought to be mentioned that homosexuality was a criminal offense in the Czarist Russian legal code and remained so even after the revolution.

Mental disease was long taboo in musical biographies, since it was often connected with paresis, a final stage of syphilis. Schumann contracted syphilis as a young man, and, as his condition worsened, tried to commit suicide by jumping into the Rhine. (He was rescued.) He also suffered an auricular nightmare, tinnitus, which caused him to hear the tone of middle A ringing constantly in his ears. His distraction was such that he began to lose his grip on reality; he no longer wished to see his cherished Clara, the "Chiara" as he tenderly called her in his *Carnaval*, nor did he ask about his seven children. (Apparently two of his three daughters died insane.) Seems that old Professor Wieck, Clara's father, who opposed their marriage so bitterly that the young couple had to go to court to overcome his objections, might have been right after all in suspecting Schumann of pathological instability.

Another syphilitic composer was Hugo Wolf, who eventually had to be confined to an insane asylum. Mahler suffered from an extreme case of neurasthenia; at one time he consulted Freud for help. On the margin of his unfinished 10th Symphony he scrawled: "Devil take me away with you!" Edward MacDowell, American nationalist composer, succumbed totally to the insanity of paresis, falling into a state of childhood, unable to take care of his physiological functions. A charitable subscription in his behalf had to be circulated in New York City to enable him to end his life in peace.

What has all this to do with the factual preoccupation of a musical biographer? Nothing, except a warning, *cave canem*, which may mean either "careful of the dog" or "caution, I may sing!" There is a clan of musical biographers who believe that to qualify as a genius, a musician has to possess a countervailing sin leading to either murder or self-destruction. A most attractive example of such a violent life is that of Don Carlo Gesualdo, who wrote elegant madrigals, but also (so the story goes) hired assassins to do away with his erring spouse and her lover. Some modern musicologists positively salivate over Gesualdo's supposed darksome deed, but, unfortunately, trustworthy documentation of the event is lacking.

But why was Schubert, the modest, inoffensive Schubert, classified a perennial misfit? In one frothy little movie he was depicted as the hopeless suitor of a worldly aristocratic lady to whom he played the first movement of his *Unfinished Symphony*. She liked the tunes, but their disparity of social rank made it impossible for her to consider his as yet unspoken offer of marriage. "If so," Schubert said in this silly movie, "I will let my symphony remain incomplete, just as my love for you must be." More recently, one speculative writer proposed an alternate solution for Schubert's celibacy: he preferred men. Proof? Schubert addressed a classmate using the second person singular, *du*. But what about Brahms and other unmarried men of music? Brahms liked women but he never went beyond kissing their hands in a fine Viennese manner. Musical biographers who should have known better claimed that he proposed marriage to Clara Schumann, but there is not one scintilla of evidence that he did. Why can't biographers admit that there are some men who simply never get around to contracting a marriage?

One of the values of *Baker's* to music scholars is the inclusion of luminary obscurities (can such oxymorons be allowed in a supposedly scholarly volume?). Let us consider the case of Joseph Paul Johannes Hoch, the wealthy businessman who founded the famous conservatory in Frankfurt, Germany, which counted among its graduates such famous musicians as Pfitzner, Hindemith, and MacDowell, and had among its distinguished faculty the likes of Raff and Humperdinck. The biographies of these illustrious persons dutifully cite their connection with Hoch's conservatory, but who was Hoch? Unexpectedly, his biography turned up in the business section of a 19th-century almanac, complete with dates.

In my stubborn search for facts, particularly funerary facts, I conducted a special hunt for the once-famous Spanish wunderkind Pepito Arriola. He was of my own generation, and I remember attending his concert in St. Petersburg early in the century. He played Schumann and Chopin and he wore blue velvet pants. And then he disappeared into the Lethe of musical oblivion. There was a long article with illustrations of Pepito in a Spanish dictionary published in the 1920s, but no mention of what happened to him after he ceased to be a wunderkind. I finally located him in an obscure German volume dealing with child prodigies. He had died unknown, unnoticed, unwept.

Dramatic circumstances surrounding the demise of celebrated musicians have been given due note in the present edition. Herbert von Karajan, who believed that he could attain physical immortality by cryogenics, succumbed to a heart attack when the helicopter that he owned and operated arrived too late to take him to the hospital. The former concertmaster of the Boston Symphony Orchestra, Richard Burgin, suddenly interrupted a bridge game, of which he was an enthusiast, and said in great distress, "What color are hearts?" He ceased to distinguish colors and died a few weeks later.

Different geographical locations and dates for the birth of identical twins surely deserve attention. The Bulgarian composer Pantcho Vladigerov was born in Switzerland but his twin brother Luben had emerged on the previous day in Bulgaria. It seems their mother was distrustful of Bulgarian obstetrics and, after giving birth to the first twin, decided to take the train to Switzerland to bear the second, hours later, in improved medical circumstances.

One adventure in musical sleuthing that I cannot forbear to relate occurred when I came upon the name of João Gomes de Araújo, a Brazilian opera composer, who, according to biographical notes available in my sources, was born in 1846 and served as inspector of the Conservatory of São Paulo. That was reason enough for me to write, in 1940, to the administration of the aforesaid conservatory for information about his life and death. To my delighted astonishment, I received in reply a message from the ancient man himself, which said, in quaint but clear English: "It is a fact that I was born on the fifth of August, 1846, but in spite of this being quite a long existence, I should say that I am still healthy and fit for anything." São Paulo was the second stop after Rio de Janeiro on my Latin American trip of musical discovery, and I notified Gomes of my traveling plans. Sure enough, he met me at the railroad station. He wore no glasses and walked briskly without the aid of a cane. He accompanied me to his humble house where he introduced me to an old man, confined to a wheelchair. "This is my son," he said. Alas, Gomes did not live to be 100; he died in 1942.

Another fantastic search for a potential spirit was that for an English composer and music theorist, Edward Maryon, the author of an unusual book entitled *Marcotone*. I wrote to the American publisher of that book and inquired whether the author was still alive (the opus in question having been published in 1919). I received a reply that Maryon must have died long ago, but when and where, his publisher did not know. I persevered, writing to various bibliographers and music editors in London, but none was even aware of Edward Maryon's existence. Then I wrote to the owner of the house where Maryon was known to have lived, only to learn that the house itself had been destroyed during the London blitz early in World War II. I finally wrote to Scotland Yard, the ultimate in matters of natural and unnatural deaths. I received a courteous reply, which explained that the famous police institution kept track only of deaths due to criminal activity, and that there was no record of Maryon having been a victim of crime. And then, quite unexpectedly, I got a letter from an English music scholar who knew Maryon personally. Maryon was apparently very much alive, and I was given his address. Losing no time, I wrote to Maryon, who expressed astonishment that anyone in the United States would be interested in his productions. He complained that no one in England took the slightest note of his music. We had a lively correspondence until he died in 1954.

Shortly after his death, I received notice that a trunk had arrived for me care of the Boston Public Library. A letter from the executors of Maryon's estate accompanied the package, which explained that they had acted at the deceased's explicit instruction to send all his musical manuscripts and personal documents to me since I was the only person who had taken any interest in his work. The trunk contained not only music manuscripts but also the original patents of nobility conferred upon Maryon's forebears by British monarchs going back to Henry V. What was I to do with this extraordinary bequest? Eventually the whole collection went to the Library of Congress, where it presumably still resides.

Several Russian musicians who left Europe after the revolution simply disappeared. Seeking clues as to their whereabouts, I addressed a letter to the editor of a Russian newspaper published in New York in the hope of finding their relatives. To my great satisfaction I received a reply from a relative of Vasili Sapelnikov, informing me that his last known residence was in San Remo, Italy. I wrote at once to the municipal authorities of San Remo and obtained the exact date of the composer's death, which I duly communicated to my Russian lexicographical colleagues (and also added to Sapelnikov's entry in the 6th edition of *Baker's*). Yet, try as I might, I could not find out what happened to multiconsonantal Nikolai Shcherbachev, a composer anointed by Mussorgsky as a "young genius," who was associated with the nationalist group of St. Petersburg musicians in the second half of the 19th century. According to a brief notice which appeared in the last issue of a Russian music magazine published in Petrograd in 1918, Shcherbachev had left Russia after the revolution and was employed in Europe in various capacities including that of a croupier in the casino of Monaco. I lost no time writing to the directorate of that famous gambling house and in due time received a polite reply: after thorough investigation, no Russian employee could be found with a name even remotely resembling that of Shcherbachev. Subsequently, I came upon an obituary notice of a man of the same name who died in Paris. I immediately wrote to the family asking whether there was any connection. There was none. Nor was there any connection between Mussorgsky's "young genius" and one Vladimir Shcherbachev, a composer active in Leningrad. And, although several of Nikolai Shcherbachev's songs and instrumental pieces had been published by Belaiev, its Paris office had no information about him. However, a tantalizing notice had appeared in a little bulletin of composers published in France, listing the name of Nikolai S., who, according to this bulletin, died in Cannes in 1920. Oh, yes, I wrote there. Wrong town, wrong number, wrong name. I decided not to draw the saga of inquiry out any longer and left him out of *Baker's* altogether.

Among biomusical curiosa, the case of two Russian cellists, Gregor Piatigorsky, who emigrated and earned world fame, and his younger brother Alexander, who remained in Moscow, deserves telling. To avoid confusion, Alexander Piatigorsky changed his name to Stogorsky. Now, *piat* in Russian means five, and *sto* means one hundred. The story goes that the younger brother claimed that he was 20 times more important than his sibling. The second part of their names, *gorsky*, means "of the mountain". So, the lesser known cellist was worth one hundred mountains against five for his celebrated brother.

Serge Koussevitzky is a magical name. Famous first as a double bass player, he later achieved renown as a conductor. Koussevitzky had a nephew who also played the double bass and then became a conductor. They both began their careers in Russia. Such coincidence of name and career could not be tolerated, and the uncle ordered his nephew to amputate the first syllable of his surname. The younger Koussevitzky became Sevitzky. Both wound up in the United States, and, as fate would have it, both received positions as conductors in Boston, the uncle with the great Boston Symphony Orchestra and the nephew, much later, with a minor local orchestra. Rather than keep a low profile, Sevitzky had the temerity to announce a performance of Beethoven's Ninth Symphony at an Easter concert during the same week that Koussevitzky had scheduled it with the Boston Symphony Orchestra. The uncle summoned his ambitious nephew to his apartment and ordered him to cancel his performance. "How dare you lift your stick over Beethoven!" he thundered. But his irrepressible nephew dared to invoke American freedom as the right to conduct anything he chose. Koussevitzky threw him out of the house. Then Koussevitzky died, and Sevitzky decided to claim part of his estate, perhaps as compensation for a life spent under the shadow cast by his famous uncle. He had no chance to win and blackened his name forever with millions of Koussevitzky worshippers. Eventually, he obtained a post with another provincial American orchestra, but failed to retain it. Stubborn to the end, he decided to go on a European tour as conductor, paying his own way. He died during a rehearsal in Greece.

The sempiternal begetter of the original edition of the present dictionary, Theodore Baker, was an American-born scholar who went to Germany early in his twenties to acquire knowledge of the science and history of music. He settled in Leipzig, where he published a worthwhile investigation of the music of American Indians. So totally engrossed did he become in German culture and in the German language itself that his first American edition of *Baker's* was full of German idioms. Thus, in describing Berlioz (whose music he did not particularly appreciate) Baker conceded that Berlioz was undoubtedly "genial," which did not refer to his easy-going nature, but, in the German sense, to his "possessing genius."

Baker's method of selecting entrants for his dictionary was sometimes idiosyncratic; many he included were musicians with whom he had been personally and professionally connected. In this way, Baker followed the example of that great man of musical information, Hugo Riemann, who was himself an amateur performer on the violin and liked to assemble and play in string quartets at his residence. As a result, early editions of Riemann's famous *Musiklexikon* are filled to the brim with obscure German string players. It took the efforts of several editors of both Riemann's and Baker's volumes to cleanse the originals of perfectly deserving but utterly unknown practicing musicians.

It is awkward for me to describe my own labors on the biographies contained in Theodore Baker's monumental compilation. But since nobody applied himself to the task of selecting proper entrants, I have to take the honor and the blame for the contents of Baker's tome beginning with the 5th edition. Moreover, I had the gall (if not the more colloquial *chutzpah*) to find errors even in the sublime lexicographical edifice of Hugo Riemann's *Musiklexikon*.

And it is with some measure of pride that I quote the acknowledgement of my contributions in Riemann's 12th edition, thanking me for my "numerous valuable biographical dates and materials." In his preface to the 1940 edition of *Baker's*, Carl Engel called me "that lexicographic beagle of keen scent and sight." Eric Blom in his 5th edition of *Grove's Dictionary of Music and Musicians* said, "To none do I owe a greater debt than to Nicolas Slonimsky, who never ceases to undertake arduous detective work all over Europe and America in order to rectify mistakes made by his colleagues." Catherine Drinker Bowen, author of several biographies of musicians, remarked that my "hawk-like, lie-detecting eye brings terror to all writers on musical subjects." In his *Oxford Companion to Music*, Percy A. Scholes referred to me as "the world's most ingenious and pertinacious musicological detective."

I cannot deny that I was peculiarly amused and delighted by more recent responses of two music critics. Martin Bernheimer of the *Los Angeles Times* greeted the appearance of the 6th edition of *Baker's* with a shout (how else can I describe this?): "Do not walk, run to the nearest bookstore and get the latest edition of *Baker's Biographical Dictionary of Musicians* edited by Nicolas Slonimsky!" Robert Commanday of the *San Francisco Chronicle* offered the elegant commendation: "I appreciate Slonimsky's verbal acuity."

It now behooves me to sing the praises of my helpers in the present and previous editions of *Baker's*. The first to catch me on errors and inadequacies was Steve Ellis who castigated me for various sins of omission and commission. I was woefully remiss in covering the list of works of the Rumanian composer Mihalovici. Was I ignorant of the supplement to the Rumanian dictionary that listed all anyone could wish to know about Mihalovici? I was. But by far the greatest debt of gratitude I owe is to the formidable historiographer of Indianapolis, Dennis McIntire. He deserves a special medal for bravery beyond the call of duty for compiling a mass of information gathered from all points of the globe, amounting to more than two thousand typewritten pages, unimpeachable in accuracy. A further word for Bakerology is due to Michael Keyton of Dallas, a professor of mathematics who contributed information about musicians who were also mathematicians. Unstinted praise goes to Samuel Sprince of Massachusetts whose determination in establishing facts calls for a maximum of musicological savoir-faire. Am I running out of words of praise? The crowning contribution to the present edition came from Laura Kuhn, a lady of exquisite learning, a seeded (to use a tennis term for top-notch quality) musicologist, who has already commended herself by numerous contributions of enlightened musical criticism to musicological publications; she also possesses the precious gift of communicating this knowledge in clear language to classes of college students and to participants in public conferences on music. She has the all-important ability to collate and to edit the immensity of materials that has come to hand from various sources during the process of preparing this 8th edition.

To conclude, I offer a Latin sentence that appeared in some early published books of the 16th century: "Igitur eme, lege, fruere." Therefore buy, read, enjoy.

Nicolas Slonimsky
St. Petersburg–Paris–Boston–Los Angeles
8 August 1990

Acknowledgments

The following individuals and institutions have lent their most valuable assistance in preparing the present edition of *Baker's:*

Natalia Alexeyeva, Editor-in-Chief, *Music in the U.S.S.R.*
Charles Amirkhanian, Music Director, KPFA-FM, Berkeley, California
Paul Attinello, University of California, Los Angeles
Australia Music Centre, Ltd., Sydney

Herbert Barrett Management, N.Y.
Harry Beall Management, Inc., N.Y.
John Beckwith, Institute for Canadian Music, University of Toronto
Dr. Finn Benestad, University of Oslo
Boosey & Hawkes, N.Y.
Breitkopf & Härtel, Wiesbaden
Herbert H. Breslin, Inc., N.Y.

Philip Caggiano, Press Department, Metropolitan Opera, N.Y.
Canadian Music Centre/Centre de musique canadienne, Toronto
CeBeDeM (Belgian Centre for Music Documentation), Brussels
Maria Fernanda Cidrais, Assistant Director, Music Department, Gulbenkian Foundation, Lisbon
Columbia Artists Management, Inc., N.Y.
David Cummings, ed., *The New Everyman Dictionary of Music,* and co-consultant ed., *The International Who's Who in Music and Musicians' Directory,* London

Dallas Public Library: Jane Holahan, Sharon Herfurth, and Dr. Gleaniece Robinson
Kenneth DeKay, Esperance, N.Y.
Pierre Delièvre, Paris
Jody Diamond, Dartmouth College, Hanover, N.H.
Orhan Doğan, President, Turkish National Library, Ankara
Donemus, Amsterdam

Edition Wilhelm Hansen, Copenhagen

Finnish Music Information Centre, Helsinki
R. Michael Fling, The Music Library, Indiana University, Bloomington
Francesca Franchi, Archivist, The Royal Opera House, Covent Garden, London
Richard D. Freed, Rockville, Md.

Harrison/Parrott, Ltd., London
Dr. Phil. Habil. Dieter Härtwig, Dresden
John Holzaepfel, Port Jefferson, N.Y.
Prof. Carol Hughes, Music Department, Southern Methodist University, Dallas

ICM Artists, Ltd., N.Y.
Icelandic Music Information Centre, Reykjavík
Indianapolis-Marion County Public Library, Central Library, Dan Gann, Head, Arts Division; and Newspaper and Periodicals Division
Israel Music Institute, Tel Aviv

Mary Johnson, John F. Kennedy Center for the Performing Arts, Washington, D.C.
The Juilliard School, N.Y.

Helmut Kallmann, former Chief, Music Division, National Library of Canada/Bibliothèque nationale du Canada, Ottawa
Dr. János Kárpáti, Franz Liszt Academy of Music, Budapest
Knud Ketting, Director, Danish Music Information Centre, Copenhagen

Dr. François Lesure, former Chief, Music Department, Bibliothèque Nationale, Paris
Library of Congress, Washington, D.C.

Audrey Michaels, N.Y.
Dr. Karl Miller, Univ. of Texas Library, Austin
Music Information Centre of the Czech Music Fund, Prague

New York Philharmonic Orchestra
Bendt Viinholt Nielsen, Director, Danish Music Information Centre, Copenhagen
Norwegian Music Information Centre, Oslo

Dr. Kurt Oehl, Mainz
Steve Olem (deceased), Dallas
Oxford University Press, Music Department, London

A.J. Heward Rees, Director, Welsh Music Information Centre, Cardiff
Klaus G. Roy, Cleveland
Royal Academy of Music, London
Royal College of Music, London
Dr. H.J. van Royen, General Manager, Royal Concertgebouw Orchestra, Amsterdam

Dr. Dag Schjelderup-Elbe, Oslo
B. Schotts Söhne, Mainz
Shaw Concerts, Inc., N.Y.
Bob Skinner, Head, Fine Arts Library, Southern Methodist University, Dallas
George Sturm, Executive Director, Music Associates of America, Englewood, N.J.
SUISA (Schweizerische Gesellschaft für die Rechte der Urheber musikalischer Werke), Zürich
Swedish Music Information Centre, Stockholm

Jane Terry, Indianapolis Symphony Orchestra
Jacinto Torres, Director, Center of Musical Documentation, Madrid
Prof. Stanislav Tuksar, Zagreb

Union of Bulgarian Composers, Sofia
University of North Texas Library: Morris Martin, Head Librarian, and Dr. Donna Arnold
Yvonne K. Unrath, Alumni Liaison Officer, The Curtis Institute of Music, Philadelphia

Dr. Vasile Văcaru, Director, Scientific and Encyclopaedic Publishing House, Bucharest
Bálint András Varga, Head of Promotion, Editio Musica Budapest
Haris Vrondos, Athens

Joachim E. Wenzel, former Archivist, Hamburg State Opera

Barbara Zwolska-Stęszewska, Manager, Polish Music Centre, Warsaw

Preface to the Sixth Edition

If I were to write an autobiography (which God forbid!) I would call it *I am a footnote,* or *I am a parenthesis.* I am a footnote in the entry on Carl Maria von Weber in the Fifth Edition of *Grove's Dictionary* and a parenthesis in the article on Lully in *Die Musik in Geschichte und Gegenwart.* And I am a paragraph in the Fifteenth Edition of the *Encyclopedia Britannica* under Pandiatonicism, which is my polysyllabic brainchild.

Dr. Samuel Johnson defines a lexicographer in his famous dictionary as "a harmless drudge." Harmless? Not necessarily. In fact, lexicography, when practiced in excess, may well be harmful to the lexicographer's psyche. Consider the melancholy case of John Wall Callcott (1766–1821) as related in *Baker's Biographical Dictionary of Musicians:* "His mind gave way from overwork on a projected biographical dictionary of musicians, . . . He recovered, but not sufficiently to continue his work." Callcott reached the letter Q, associated with such disturbing images as queer, quaquaversal, and quagmire, and then quit.

One of my predecessors in editing *Baker's* jotted down these words in the margin of the galley proofs: "I will go mad if I have to continue this for a long time." Another music editor, working on another dictionary, deliberately rented a room on the ground floor lest he should be tempted to jump out the window in despair over the contents of the book.

Although most of my friends regard me as an eccentric, I am not given to suicidal impulses while working on a dictionary. But I am rather paranoiac in my suspicions about melodrama, except in opera librettos. I never believed that Salieri poisoned Mozart, even though I memorized, as part of my school assignments in St. Petersburg, Salieri's monologue in Pushkin's play *Mozart and Salieri,* in which Salieri explains his reason for poisoning Mozart lest his blazing genius should eclipse the work of such humble votaries in the divine art of harmony as himself. In another tale of Mozart, I became suspicious of the reports in practically every reference work and every biography that a fierce snowstorm was raging in Vienna on the day of his funeral in December 1791, which made it impossible for his friends to follow his body to the cemetery (the snowballs were as large as tennis balls, the top Vienna Mozartologist, Erich Schenk, asserts). Why wasn't this meteorological phenomenon as much as mentioned in early Mozart biographies? It would have at least explained why Mozart's widow did not attend the funeral, if not her failure to pay dues for keeping Mozart's grave in perpetuity, which was the reason why he was eventually moved to the place of common burial. The snowstorm episode appears for the first time in Otto Jahn's monumental biography of Mozart, and the only source to substantiate it was an anonymous article published in a Vienna newspaper on the occasion of Mozart's centennial in 1856. Some Mozartologists identified the writer (who signed his report as "a man of the people") as the bartender of Mozart's favorite Vienna tavern, although by the time of Mozart's centennial he himself, if still living, would have been about a hundred years old. To resolve my puzzlement, I wrote to the Vienna Weather Bureau for a report on the climatic conditions on that December day in 1791. Great was my malicious sense of gratification when I received a report that the temperature on that day was well above freezing and that a gentle Zephyr wind blew from the West. No snowballs. No frigid weather which frightened away Mozart's friends. No melodrama, except the tragedy of Mozart's death so young. Encouraged by the prompt response of the Vienna Weather Bureau (which had kept records for more than two centuries), I inquired about another melodramatic episode: an electric storm on the afternoon of Beethoven's death. Yes, there was an electric storm, even though it was hardly likely that Beethoven in his debilitated physical condition could have lifted his clenched first toward heaven in a gesture of defiance of *Jupiter tonans.*

Not every melodramatic report is necessarily a pabulum for the gullible. I became incredulous of the tale told in *Baker's* about the French singer Alexandre Taskin, who reportedly displayed an untenorlike bravery during a conflagration at the Opéra-Comique in Paris on the night of May 25, 1887, when he sang in *Mignon*. The lives of hundreds of panic-stricken opera-goers were supposedly saved thanks to his *sang-froid*. Well, it turns out that there was a rather horrendous fire at the Opéra-Comique on that night, and that "le beau Taskin," as he was known to his admirers, did display courage in calming down the audience, and was commended for it by the French government.

I was smugly confident of the accuracy of the report that the Italian conductor Gino Marinuzzi was assassinated by the anti-Fascist partisans in Milan on August 17, 1945, as duly noted in *Baker's,* and also in *Grove,* in Riemann's *Musik-Lexikon* ("ermordet") and in the Italian ency-clopedia *La Musica* ("morì assassinato"). But why did the anti-Fascist partisans wait so long after the end of the Mussolini regime to shoot him? True, he was the author of a triumphal ode on the occasion of the historic meeting between Hitler and Mussolini in an Alpine tunnel, but many other Italian composers expressed a similar lack of precognition in glorifying the Fascist regime. I received many letters from Italian composers during the fascist years, dated E.F. XV, E.F. XVIII, etc, i.e., Era Fascista followed by the year, in Roman numerals, since Mussolini's march on Rome ("tough on Jesus Christ," a witty Bostonian remarked when I showed him these letters), and they remained unscathed. However that might be, the publishers of *Baker's* received an irate letter from a Milan lawyer, acting on behalf of the Marinuzzi family, protesting that the account of the assassination was false and demanding an immediate rectification. Gino Marinuzzi, the letter said, died peacefully in a Milan hospital on the date correctly given in *Baker's,* succumbing not to a bullet wound but to hepatic anemia. Fortunately, *Baker's* VI was still in a fluid state, and the publishers were able to pacify the Marinuzzi family lawyer, promising to make a correction. But why did the Marinuzzis wait all these years to fire their salvo, and why zero in on *Baker's* rather than on their own Italian dictionaries? And where did the original report of assassination come from? The *Corriere della Sera,* Milan's major newspaper, carried an *R.I.P.* notice of Marinuzzi's death, with no mention of the cause. The case was clinched eventually by the Servizio Mortuario of the city of Milan, stating that Marinuzzi had indeed died of acute atrophy of the liver. No bullets, no assassination, no melodrama.

Beware of false suspicions! Could two musicians with identical last names (except for a nobiliary particle), Victor Alessandro of Texas and Raffaele d'Alessandro of Switzerland, have died on their respective, albeit mutually different, birthdays? They could, and they did. Could Raselius have written a book on Roselius? He could, and he did. Could Gabriel Faure (no accent) have written a monograph on Gabriel Fauré (accent)? He could and he did. Was Schubart really the author of the words of *Die Forelle* by Schubert? Yes, he was. Could two composers, each named Victor Young, have been active in the movies in Hollywood during the same period? They were. Could I myself have had a classmate, in a St. Petersburg high school, called Nicolas Slonimsky? I had, and since I joined the class after him, my name was registered as Nicolas II, which was the official name of the then reigning Czar of all the Russians.

Among the many persistent errors plaguing musical biography is the belief that Wagner originated the term *Leitmotiv*. He did not; it was first proposed by Friedrich Wilhelm Jähns in the preface to his book on Weber published in 1871. Bizet did not write the famous *Habanera* in *Carmen*. He took it from a collection of Spanish songs by Sebastián Yradier, without any alteration of key, harmonization, tempo, rhythm, and dynamics.

The Russians have a marvelously expressive word for a story unsupported by evidence— "nyebylitsa," an "un-was-ity." Famous last words by historic personages are almost all such un-was-ities. Madame Roland's exclamation on her way to the guillotine, "Liberty, how many crimes are committed in thy name!" first appeared in print in Lamartine's *Histoire de la Révolution française,* or so it is cited in *Bartlett's Familiar Quotations*. But browsing through the 1793 volume of *The Annual Register* of London, I came upon a Paris dispatch quoting the famous phrase. Is one to suppose then the British Paris correspondent actually followed the tumbril taking Madame Roland to the place of execution and actually heard her utter the famous apostrophe? Not bloody likely.

"Lexicographis secundus post Herculem labor" was the judgment pronounced by Joseph Justus Scaliger (1540–1609), himself a lexicographer of stature. The mythological reference is, of course, to the labor performed by Hercules in cleaning up the manure-filled stables of King Augeus, son of the sun god Helius. Hercules did the job in twenty-four hours; to clean up a clogged music dictionary takes a little longer. But sanitation must be done with circumspection; one never knows what shining gems, what bits of fascinating tektite, are embedded in rejected debris. Take the story of the Italian singer Giulio Rossi as related by *Baker's*. He started out as a tenor, but unintentionally plunged into the Tiber on a cold day and as a consequence became a *basso profondo*. Incredible? Yes, incredible, but what lexicographer would have the heart to throw it into the pile of refuse? I couldn't. So—*stet!*

There should be no such spirit of acceptance for the purple prose that some editors indulged in while describing the life and works of admired persons. I had to deflate somewhat the verbal effusions in the original *Baker's* entry on A.W. Thayer, biographer of Beethoven. Here is a sample: "Unhappily, his wonderful capacity for work was overtaxed, and volume IV of his nobly conceived Beethoven biography, executed with a painstaking thoroughness and scrupulous fidelity beyond praise, was left unfinished. Though he lived for years in straitened circumstances, he resolutely refused offers from firms like Novello & Co. and G. Schirmer, Inc., hoping to recast entirely the English version of his *Beethoven*." Suffocating! Give us air to breathe!

A biographical dictionary ought to be a democratic assembly of factual information. Great masters are by right to be given preferential treatment, but opaque luminaries, e.g., Bibl, Kittl, Lickl, or Titl, ought to be tendered hospitality, if not lavish accommodations. Ay, there's the rub! Proportionate representation is the ideal desideratum, but availability of information and productivity of work determine the space allowance. One would fain wish that there were more biographical information on Shakespeare than on Pepys, on Josquin Des Prez than on a whole gallery of later madrigalists, on Bach than on Reger. As it is, an unhappy editor must gather every bit of information on the great masters of the past and make a judicious selection of biographical data and a list of works of *dii minores* in the arts.

One must also beware of lexicographical zombies, typographical clones and monsters. The great Eitner, who spent a lifetime tabulating manuscripts in European libraries, was also a progenitor of such teratological creatures. Working on a pile of anonymous French songs, he apparently mistook the nouns in their titles for names of composers. Thus we learn from Eitner that "La Chanson d'un gai Berger" was a song by Ungay Berger, and that "La Chanson de l'Auberge Isolée" was composed by Mlle. Isolée L'Auberge. There must be a number of desperate music researchers trying to find out who Mr. Gay Shepherd and Miss Isolated Tavern were in life. *Cobbett's Cyclopedia of Chamber Music* is responsible for spawning D. Michaud (a misprint for D. Milhaud), Marcel Babey (for Marcel Labey), and, most intriguing, a famous violinist, Heinrich Wehtan, generated through the transliteration of the Russian spelling in Cyrillic letters of the name of Henri Vieuxtemps via a German translation of an article originally written in Russian by a contributor to *Cobbett*.

To exorcise such vampires and to drive a stake through their hideous hearts I myself decided to create a monster as the last entry of the 1958 edition of *Baker's*. Never fear: I killed it in page proofs. But here it is *à titre documentaire*:

Zyžík, Krsto, Czech composer; b. Pressburg, Feb. 29, 1900. [1900 was not a leap year in the West.] He traveled widely to Pozsony and Bratislava [Pozsony and Bratislava are respectively the Hungarian and Slovak names of Pressburg], and back to Pressburg. He attracted attention with his oratorio *Dieta Wormsová*, written for the quadricentennial of the Diet of Worms in a vermicular counterpart [the Diet of Worms was an actual historic assembly, held in the city of Worms in 1521; it condemned Luther as a heretic]; then brought out a bel canto work, *Strč prst skrz krk* (a Czech tongue twister, meaning *put your finger on your throat*), using only consonants in consonant harmony. His works include *Pinč mj šuga* (*Pinch me, Sugar*, or *Pinch Meshuga* in phonetical transcription) for chorus and pinched strings; *Smyccový Kvartet* (string quartet) for woodwind quintet; *Sappho LXIX* for 2 female participants (Lesbos Festival, 1955): *Macho* for large secular organ (male player), etc. In 1979, after many years of aggravated floccillation and severe dyscrasia, he was committed to a dissident asylum. See Sol Mysnik [rather obvious anagram of Slonimsky], *A Czech Checkmate: The Story of Krsto Zyžik* (Los Angeles, 1979).

The most authentic sources of information ought to be diaries and autobiographies, correspondence, and reminiscences of friends and relatives. But much too frequently, at least in musical biography, accounts by musicians themselves are tainted by a desire for self-glorification hidden behind a mask of assumed modesty. "Look at me," they seem to tell the reader, "and marvel at my accomplishments; starting out in poverty, privations, and need, and by dint of faith in my destiny and hard work, rising to the top of the pyramid of fame, recognition, and even wealth." Wagner's autobiography abounds in trivia, including some tedious pages about his pet dogs, but he never mentions the episode of his incarceration at the Clichy prison in Paris from October 28 to November 17, 1840, for non-payment of debt. True, it was one of those permissive jailings, with easy family furloughs, but still the episode is a legitimate part of Wagner's biography. Naturally, Wagner never gave an account in his autobiography of his cavalier treatment of the women in his life, nor did he make clear the circumstances of the birth of his natural daughter Isolde, born to Cosima on April 10, 1865, while she was still married to Hans von Bülow. In 1914 Isolde petitioned the Bavarian Civil Court to grant her a share in Wagner's royalties; her claim was rejected on the ground that there was no evidence that Cosima had ceased all communication with her legitimate husband, Hans von Bülow, within the period of ten months before Isolde's birth, a legal maximum for the length of gestation. The court also overruled the evidence submitted by Isolde's lawyer husband, based on the phrenological and hemological similarities between Wagner and Isolde.

It was fashionable among artists of the nineteenth century to claim paternity from celebrated or titled persons. Was the French cellist François Servais actually a bastard child of Liszt, as was claimed for him in various sources, including *Baker's*? He was born in St. Petersburg, or so the dictionaries said, in 1846, a date that fits the chronology of Liszt's liaison with Princess Sayn-Wittgenstein. But nothing in the voluminous correspondence between her and Liszt during that period indicated that she was a prospective mother. My earnest inquiries in Russia brought no results. The verdict in this case, therefore, must remain unproven.

A more involved claim of desirable paternity concerns the once famous pianist Sigismond Thalberg, who apparently authorized the report that he was the son of a Prince Dietrichstein and a baroness. Further inquiries were discouraged by a footnote in the 1954 edition of *Grove's Dictionary* stating that Thalberg's birth certificate (he was born in Geneva) was unobtainable. Distrustful of this notice, I wrote to Geneva and obtained a copy of the certificate by airmail within a matter of days. I discovered later that the document had been previously published in a Belgian magazine on the occasion of Thalberg's centenary in 1912. The certificate stated that Thalberg was a legitimate son of Joseph Thalberg and Fortunee Stein, both of Frankfurt am Main, and that he was born in Geneva on January 8, 1812. The case was further complicated by the publication in various sources of a letter allegedly written by Thalberg's natural mother to Prince Dietrichstein at the time of Thalberg's birth, suggesting that he should be given the name Thalberg, so that he would grow as peacefully as a Thal (valley) and would tower over humanity as high as a Berg (mountain). Just who fabricated this letter and for what purpose remains unclear. The Supplement to Riemann's *Musik-Lexikon,* published in 1975, adds the intriguing bit of information that Thalberg was indeed adopted by Prince Dietrichstein later in life.

The strange lure of aristocratic birth seems to be undiminished even in our own century. An English singer who was active in recital and on the light-opera stage in the early 1900s under the name Louis Graveure declared in an interview published in the *New York Times* in 1947 that he was of royal or possibly imperial birth, and that it would be worth a fortune to him to find out who he really was. Well, for the modest sum of two shillings and sixpence I obtained from London a copy of his birth certificate which dispelled the mystery. His real name was Wilfrid Douthitt, and he used it in his early appearances in England as a baritone; later he changed to tenor and gave concerts as Louis Graveure, which was his mother's maiden name.

Much more honest was the search for true paternity undertaken by the American folk songster and poet Rod McKuen. He knew he was illegitimate, and his mother never told him who his father was. He undertook a long quest, almost epic in its simple grandeur, and in the end established the identity of his father, a backwoods lumberjack.

The desire to recreate one's life according to one's fancy is universal, and artists are particularly apt to imagine, and at times consciously to contrive, the tales of might-have-been. Was Liszt actually kissed on the brow by Beethoven at the concert he played in Vienna as a child?

There is a charming lithograph of the supposed event, which is reproduced in several Liszt biographies. But the evidence of Beethoven's archives suggests that Beethoven was annoyed by Liszt's father's bringing the child Liszt to Beethoven's quarters, and that he never went to the concert, despite Schindler's efforts to persuade him to attend. Liszt did play for Beethoven in private, but whether he was kissed on the brow or not remains uncertain.

Working on a biographical dictionary of musicians, I have found myself in the uncomfortable position of private detective. Some years back I received a letter from a Russian woman living in Rome. She asked my help to find out whether her father, the Russian violinist Bezekirsky, who emigrated to American when she was a child, was still alive. Since Bezekirsky was in *Baker's*, I had to search for him anyway to bring him up to date, dead or alive. Tracking him down through several music schools where he taught violin, I finally reached him in a small locality in upstate New York. Delighted that I could restore a missing father to an anxious daughter, I wrote to both, giving their mutual addresses. Frankly, I expected letters full of emotional gratitude for my humanitarian endeavor, but I got none from either father or daughter. I do not relish unfinished human symphonies, so I wrote to Bezekirsky again, asking him to let me know whether he had established contact with his long-lost offspring. Great was my shock when I received from him a postcard scribbled in English in a senile hand, saying as follows: "Your mission was successful, if you call several unpleasant and demanding letters from my daughter a success. I am in no position to help her in any way." I never heard from the daughter.

One of the sharpest rebukes I ever received for trying to obtain information was administered by the remarkable English composer Kaikhosru Sorabji. I made the terrible *faux pas* of describing him as an Indian composer. "Do not dare to call me an Indian," he thundered in reply. "We are Parsi, followers of Zarathustra." He flatly refused to supply biographical data about himself, but he sent me a signed copy of his formidable *Opus Clavicembalisticum,* and pointed out for my information that it is the greatest polyphonic work since Bach's *Kunst der Fuge.* For all I know, it may be exactly that, at least in the grandeur of conception and extraordinary skill of its structure. But his rebuke to me was mild in comparison with the eruption of invective he poured on Percy Scholes for what he deemed to be an undignified and inadequate entry on himself in the *Oxford Companion to Music.* Scholes sent the letter to me with the inscription "For your delectation." It is worth reproducing *in toto:*

Corfe Castle, Dorset, XXII.II.MCMLII A.D.

My Good Sir:

A valued friend draws my attention to a lucubration of yours under the entry of my name in a recently published book of reference. One is hard put to it at which to marvel the more, the exiguity of your sense of proportion or the poverty of your taste in devoting double the amount of space to cheap impertinences regarding the place and date of my birth (which is as little business of yours as of any other prying nosey busybody) to that which is devoted to my work, which is all that concerns anyone and which carefully conveys inaccurate and false information by leaving our material facts. Formerly I used to consider it enough when dealing with these stupid and impudent enquiries from lexicographical persons, deliberately to mislead them as to dates and places. This is a mistake: their enquiries should either be ignored or refused. And the sooner folk of their kidney grasp the fact that one is under no moral obligation to provide them with accurate, or indeed any information at all just because they choose to ask for it, the very much better for all concerned.

I have the honor to be, Sir, Yours very faithfully,
Kaikhosru Shapurji Sorabji

Sorabji is a unique figure in music, and his full biography would be fascinating. Erik Chisholm, who knew him personally, told me that the gate of Sorabji's castle in Dorset bears this legend: "Visitors Unwelcome. Roman Catholic Nuns in Full Habit May Enter Without An Appointment." In reckless disregard of Sorabji's demurrer at biographical information about himself, I wrote to the London registry of birth to find out at least when and where he was born. To my surprise the document stated that his real name was Leon Dudley Sorabji; Kaikhosru was apparently his Parsi name assumed later in life. I informed Eric Bloom, who was then working on the Fifth Edition of *Grove,* of my findings. His response was prompt. "I knew right along," he wrote, "that Sorabji's name was Leon Dudley, but if you value your life I would not advise you to put it in print, for I fear that if you do he would take the next plane to America and assassinate you personally." And Samuel Johnson said that a lexicographer is a "harmless drudge"!

Once in a while in a beleaguered lexicographer's life the subject of an entry in a biographical dictionary voices his gratitude for the honor. A letter I received from Walter Stockhoff, an American composer whose music was praised by Busoni as "a fresh voice from the New World that could revitalize the tired art of Europe," certainly warmed the cockles of my heart. "As pure, cool, crystal-clear water," he wrote me, "revives one thirsting in the desert, so intelligence, understanding, sympathy and sense of values come to brighten one's pathway. There is a noble generosity in your giving thought to my work. Through the greatness of your nature you strengthen others."

Chronological memory is treacherous. Casals owned the manuscript of the B-flat major string quartet, op. 67, of Brahms, given to him by a Vienna collector. It was, he told me, mysteriously connected with his life, for he was conceived when Brahms began the composition of the quartet, and was born when Brahms completed it. Leaving aside the problem of knowing the date of one's conception, the chronology does not support this fancy. Brahms wrote the work during the summer and fall of 1875, and it was first performed in Berlin on October 30, 1876. Casals was born two months after its performance and could not have been conceived fourteen or fifteen months previously.

Lexicographical cross-pollination of inaccurate information in similar wording is a hazard. Philip Hale used to say that when several mutually independent reference works vouchsafe identical data, he deems the information reliable. Not necessarily so. If we consider the case of Mascagni, one comes upon a curious iteration of idiom that arouses suspicion. The 1906 edition of *Grove's* states that Mascagni was compelled to study music "by stealth" because his father, a baker, wanted him to be a lawyer. The *Oxford Companion to Music* paraphrases *Grove's:* "Mascagni was the son of a baker who took music lessons by stealth." The 1940 edition of *Baker's* echoes: "Mascagni's father (a baker) wished him to study jurisprudence, but he learned piano-playing by stealth." What is this obsession with the quaint locution "by stealth" in all these reference works? In point of fact, Mascagni's father was quite proud of his son's achievement as a musician and eagerly supported his studies at the conservatory of Milan, as attested by their published correspondence.

If autobiographies are inevitably images of one's life as refracted through a prism resulting in an attractive and colorful spectrum, it is nevertheless strange that a composer would alter the history of the creation of a particular work. Berlioz did so paraleptically in his most famous score, *Symphonie fantastique,* by leaving out of its program the fact that one of the movements was taken from his early school work and that he implanted the unifying *idée fixe* surgically in a vacant measure containing a fermata, in order to justify its inclusion. And yet this manipulation creates the false impression of coherence. Of course, composers need not apologize to their biographers and analysts for revising their works in the light of later wisdom. Mahler denied the programmatic intent of several of his symphonies even though the descriptive titles appeared in the manuscripts. Beethoven carefully disavowed the pictorial nature of his *Pastoral Symphony* by stating that the music represented an impression rather than a description of a day in the country, and this despite the birdcalls and the electric storm in the score. Schoenberg, who was opposed to representational music, nevertheless yielded to the importunities of his publishers in authorising romantic titles for the individual movements of his *Five Orchestral Pieces.*

On the other hand, Stravinsky's latter-day denial that his early *Scherzo fantastique* was inspired by his reading of Maeterlinck's *La Vie des Abeilles* is puzzling. In Robert Craft's *Conversations with Igor Stravinsky,* in reply to the question about the subject matter of the work, Stravinsky replies unequivocally: "I wrote the *Scherzo* as a piece of pure symphonic music. The bees were a choreographer's idea . . . Some bad literature about bees was published on the fly-leaf of the score to satisfy my publisher who thought a 'story' would help to sell the music." This declaration was most unfair to the publisher and to the choreographer. In his own letters to Rimsky-Korsakov at the time of composition of the score (1907), published in Moscow in 1973, Stravinsky writes: "I intended to write a scherzo already in St. Petersburg, but I lacked subject matter. It so happens that I have been reading *La Vie des Abeilles* by Maeterlinck, a half-philosophical, half-poetic work, which captivated me completely. At first, I intended to use direct quotations so as to make the program of my piece quite clear, but then I realized that it would not do because in the book the scientific and poetic elements are closely interwoven. I decided therefore to guide myself by a definite programmatic design without actual quotations, and to entitle the work simply *The Bees*, after Maeterlinck, a fantastic scherzo."

In the nineteenth century America was, to all practical purposes, a German colony in instrumental music and an Italian colony in opera. Lillian Norton would never have made a singing career had she not changed her name to Nordica. Conductors had to be German or Austrian (Damrosch, Muck, Henschel, Nikisch, Mahler). Pianists prospered when their last names ended with "sky" or "ski." Paderewski was a shining example of grandeur and glory. (I myself profited peripherally when I entered the United States in 1923 exempt from the rigid quota imposed by the Immigration Office on Slavs and such, exception being made for "artists," particularly those whose names looked and sounded artistic.) Ethel Liggins, an Englishwoman intent on making an American career, was advised to change her name to Leginska ("ska" being the feminine counterpart of "ski"). She told me interesting stories about herself; among her many memories, she said that as a child she was bounced by Winston Churchill on his knee after his return as a hero from the Boer War. She volunteered her own date of birth, April 13, 1886, and I checked on it by securing her birth certificate; it was correct. Now, Churchill came home in glory in 1899, and since it is unlikely that he proceeded right away to bounce Liggins (not yet Leginska) on his knee, she must have reached a nubile adolescence at the time, and the whole episode assumed a totally different complexion. "Botheration!" she exclaimed when I pointed out the embarrassing chronology to her. "How do you know when Churchill returned to England from South Africa? You are not British!"

No greater splendor among contemporary orchestral conductors surrounded the career of Leopold Stokowski, who lived to be 95, working in music to the last days of his life. And his name ended in "ski"! Invidious rumors had it that his real name was Stokes, and that he polonized it as many other artists did. False! He was born in London, the son of a Polish cabinetmaker named Kopernik Joseph Boleslaw Stokowski and an Irishwoman, Annie Marion Moore-Stokowski, on April 18, 1882. Not satisfied with his true half-Polish origin, he for some reason chose to maintain that he was totally Polish, born in Cracow in 1887 (rather than 1882), and that his name was Leopold Boleslawowicz Stokowski. This bit of fantasy appears in the main volume of Riemann's *Musik-Lexikon*. When I sounded the alarm, pointing out that the patronymic ending on "which" or "wicz" or "witch" is possible in Russian, but not in Polish, the Riemann's editors sent me a photostat copy of the original questionnaire in Stokowski's own hand embodying all this fanciful information. By way of rebuttal, I forwarded to the Riemann's people a copy of Stokowski's birth certificate which I had obtained from London. The 1975 supplement to Riemann's carries a corresponding correction.

Among many fantastic tales that accompany musical biographies there is one concerning Werner Egk. The name sounded like a manufactured logogriph, or an acronym for "ein guter Künstler," and even more self-anointed, "ein genialer Künstler." I wrote to the director of the archives of the city of Augsburg where Egk was born, and elicited the information that his real name was Mayer. If so, whence Egk? The composer himself came forward with an explanation that was more puzzling than the original riddle: he changed his name from Mayer to Egk after his marriage to Elisabeth Karl; the initials of her first and last name formed the outer letters of Egk, and the middle "g" was added "for euphony." Guttural euphony?

No experience in my "harmless drudgery" equaled the Case of Walter Dahms, an obscure German author of musical biographies. According to musical lexica that listed his name, including *Baker's*, he went to Rome in 1922, and promptly vanished. I did not care to leave him dangling like an unshriven ghost, an elusive zombie. I used to mention Dahms to every musicologist I met as a disappearing act, and one of them told me that there was nothing mysterious about Dahms, that he went to Lisbon, adopted a Portuguese-sounding pseudonym, and continued publishing books on music. I inserted this seemingly innocuous bit of information in my 1965 Supplement to *Baker's*, but unbeknownst to myself it unleashed a fantastic chain of events. The editors of the Supplement to Riemann's *Musik-Lexikon*, who were also interested to bring Dahms up to date, seized upon my addendum and inquired through Santiago Kastner, a London-born German-educated music scholar resident in Lisbon, to find out facts about Dahms. But no one in the rather flourishing German colony in Lisbon, not even anyone at the German embassy, knew anything about Dahms. The Riemann editors would not be pacified. "Baker (really Slonimsky)," they wrote Kastner again, "is greatly valued here because of its reliability. Behind the bland statement that Dahms was still in Lisbon in 1960 must lie a lot of painstaking research." Kastner volunteered a guess that Dahms might be a German-speaking Portuguese citizen named Gualterio Armando, Gualterio being a Portuguese form of Walter, and Armando containing three letters of the name Dahms. He addressed the question directly to Dahms, whether he was or was not Dahms. All hell broke loose thereafter. "I am not identical with anyone but myself," replied Gualterio Armando. "I have absolutely nothing to say about Herr W. D. mentioned in your letter because I know nothing about him. I hope that this will put an end to this whole business once and for all." Kastner reported his failure to the Riemann's editors, and announced that he was through with his investigation, but voiced his conviction that Dahms "must be identical with that asshole Gualterio Armando after all." Why was he so vehement in denying his real identity? He died on October 5, 1973, carrying the secret to his grave.

Among the unburied musical ghosts that haunted me through the years was Alois Minkus, an Austrian composer of operas and ballets who spent most of his career in Russia. For a hundred years, first under the Czars, then under the Soviets, his ballets never ceased to be the favorite numbers in the Russian ballet repertory. Not a year passed without my receiving an insistent inquiry from Russia and abroad as to the fate of Minkus after he left Russia in 1891. Some reference works have him dead in that year; others prolong his life until 1907, with the date accompanied by a parenthetical question mark. I must have written a dozen letters to various registries of vital statistics in Vienna on the supposition that Minkus returned to Vienna, where he was born, and died there. I did obtain his birth certificate ascertaining that he was born on March 23, 1826, rather than 1827 as most Russian and other music reference sources have it, but the Vienna archivists could tell me nothing as to his date of death. Then in the summer of 1976 I made one more half-hearted inquiry in Vienna. To my astonishment I got a clue that all death notices before 1939 were moved from the Stadtarchiv, the Landesarchiv, and the Vienna Rathaus and its numerous subdivisions to the corresponding parochial registries. Hot on the scent, I wrote to the proper Lutheran parish, and to my absolute joy of discovery I received a document certifying that Alois Minkus died at Gentzgasse 92 in Vienna, on December 7, 1917, in the 92nd year of his life, from pneumonia, and that his mortal remains were deposed at the cemetery of Döbling. I immediately rushed this information and the pertinent documentation to the editors of the big Russian musical encyclopedia, which had just reached the letter M, and the date got in at the last moment before going to press, with an appropriate proud parenthetical clause testifying to its authenticity.

One of the most fantastic episodes in my hunt for missing musical persons was the search for Heinrich Hammer, a German conductor and composer who emigrated to the United States about the turn of the century, and then vanished from the musical scene. I appealed for help to William Lichtenwanger, who combines profound erudition with a detective flair that would have made him a rich man had he dedicated himself to the search for missing heirs and holders of unused bank accounts. Quick as a panther, he produced a clipping from the *Los Angeles Times* of October 25, 1953, which carried on its society page a photograph of Heinrich Hammer, 91, and his young bride Arlene, 22. Their address was given in the story, but when I wrote to him my letter came back with the notation "Deceased." But when and where? Lichtenwanger got on the telephone, and after a few inquiries got hold of Hammer's son, a repair worker of the California telephone company. Unbelievably, contact was established with him atop a telephone pole, and he gave Lichtenwanger the needed information. Hammer had moved to Phoenix, Arizona, where he died on October 28, 1954, just a year after his marriage.

How much of personal life ought to be reported in a dignified biographical dictionary? Volumes have been written speculating about the identity of Beethoven's "Immortal Beloved," even though the famous letter addressed to her was never sent off. Should a biographer be so bold as to doubt a great man's own confession of love? A conscientious biographer took exception to Goethe's declaration that he had never loved anyone as much as Lili Schönemann. "Here the great Goethe errs," he commented: "His greatest love was Frederike Brion." From the sublime to contemporary love lore. The formidable Hungarian pianist Nyiregyházi was married nine times, and admitted to 65 extramarital liaisons. Is this proper information in a biographical dictionary? The marriages, perhaps; the liaisons, only famous ones, like Liszt's and Chopin's.

It was only recently that the known homosexuality of Tchaikovsky became a matter of open discussion in his biographies; the first inkling of it appeared in the preface to the 1934 edition of Tchaikovsky's correspondence with his benefactress Madame von Meck. In 1940 a collection of his letters to the family, including those to his brother and biographer Modest, who was also a homosexual, was published in Russia, but it was soon withdrawn from publication and became a sort of bibliographical phantom; an expurgated edition was published later. In subsequent books on Tchaikovsky published in Russia the matter is unmentioned. But a strange mass of unfounded rumors began circulating both in Russia and abroad shortly after Tchaikovsky's death that he committed "suicide by cholera," that he deliberately drank unboiled water during a raging cholera epidemic in St. Petersburg, and this despite his fear of cholera, which had been the cause of his mother's death. The stories that I heard during my visit to Russia in 1962 were right out of Gothic horror tales. It seems that Tchaikovsky became involved in a homosexual affair with a young member of the Russian Imperial family, and that when Czar Alexander III got wind of it, he served the Tchaikovsky family an ultimatum: either have Tchaikovsky take poison, or have him tried for sodomy and sent to Siberia. Tchaikovsky accepted the verdict, and with the connivance of his personal physician, Dr. Bertenson, was given a poison that produced symptoms similar to those of cholera. As additional evidence that Tchaikovsky did not die of cholera, the proponents of this theory argue, is the fact that his body was allowed to lie in state and that several of his intimates kissed him on the mouth, as the Russian death ritual allows, whereas cholera victims were buried in zinc-lined sealed coffins to prevent contagion.

Dramatic deaths should rightly be noted in biographies, but grisly details had better be left out. It is not advisable to follow the type of reporting exemplified in an obituary of Sir Armine Woodhouse in *The Annual Register of London* for the year 1777, noting that his death "was occasioned by a fishbone in his throat."

Percy Scholes took credit for sending the British writer on music, Arthur Eaglefield Hull, to his death under the wheels of a train. He wrote me: "Hull's suicide was the result of my exposure of his thefts in his book *Music, Classical, Romantic and Modern.* He threw himself under a train."

A suicide directly connected with a musical composition was that of Rezsö Seress, Hungarian author of the sad, sad song "Gloomy Sunday." At one time the playing of the tune was forbidden in Central Europe because it drove several impressionable people to suicide. Seress himself jumped out the window, on a Monday, not a gloomy Sunday.

Musical murders are surprisingly few; singers are occasionally murdered out of jealousy, but not famous singers. The most spectacular murder, never conclusively solved, was that of the French eighteenth-century musician Jean Marie Leclair, stabbed to death in his own house. Since nothing was taken, it could not have been a burglary. I proposed a theory that he was done to death by his estranged wife, who was a professional engraver and publisher of some of Leclair's music, and had sharp tools at her disposal, but my painstaking argumentation in favor of this theory was pooh-poohed by the foremost French music historian Marc Pincherle and others.

Dementia, insanity, and bodily disintegration are scourges that hit many composers, and in most cases they were caused by syphilis. Undoubtedly, the tragic illnesses of Schumann, Smetana, Hugo Wolf, and MacDowell were all caused by the lues, the *morbus gallicus*, as it was usually described in the past centuries. In his book on Delius, Sir Thomas Beecham remarks ruefully that the goddess Aphrodite Pandemos repaid Delius cruelly for his lifelong worship at her altar. Delius died blind and paralyzed.

In light of recent disclosures, free from displaced piety for a great man, it appears that Beethoven, too, was a victim of syphilis. His deafness was only a symptom (as in the case of Smetana) which does not necessarily indicate a venereal infection. But there are too many other circumstances that lead to this sad conclusion, recounted in the recent study by Dieter Kerner, *Krankheiten grosser Musiker.*

Even the worshipful speculation as to psychological causes of physical decline and death, so cherished in old-fashioned biography, has no place in a book of reference. I brushed aside such probings into a person's psyche as were found in an old entry on the eighteenth-century French composer Isouard, to the effect that he was so deeply "mortified" by his failure to be elected to the French Academy that "although a married man" he abandoned work, "plunged into dissipation, and died."

Triskaidecaphobia, an irrational fear of the number 13, demonstrably affected the state of mind of two great composers, Rossini and Schoenberg. In addition to his superstition about the malevolent character of 13, Rossini was also fearful of Friday. He died on November 13, 1868, which was a Friday. Numerologists could cite his case to prove predestination. Schoenberg's case is remarkable because there is so much recent evidence that his triskaidecaphobia was not a whimsical pose. He was born on the 13th of the month of September in 1874, and he regarded this as ominous in his personal destiny. He sometimes avoided using 13 in numbering the bars of his works. When he realized that the title of his work *Moses und Aaron* contained 13 letters, he crossed out the second "a" in Aaron, even though the spelling Aron cannot be substantiated either in German or in English. When someone thoughtlessly remarked to him on his 76th birthday that $7 + 6 = 13$, he seemed genuinely upset; he died at the age of 76. On his last day of life, July 13, 1951, he remarked to his wife that he would be all right if he would survive the ominous day, but he did not, and died.

Going over my list of *morituri,* centenarians or near-centenarians, I came upon the name of Victor Küzdö, a Hungarian-American violinist born, or so the old edition of *Baker's* said, in 1869. I wrote to Küzdö at his last known address, which I found in an old musical directory, in effect asking him whether he was living or dead. A few days later I received from him a dictated postcard saying that, although practically blind, he was still alive and well, in Glendale, California. Furthermore, he took the opportunity to correct his death of birth: he was born in 1863, not in 1869, and had shortly before celebrated his 100th anniversary! But this was not the end of the story; soon afterwards I got a letter from a real-estate man in Glendale notifying me that Küzdö was in the habit of diminishing his age, and that he was actually 103, not 100! How could he be sure? Simple: he was a numerologist. When the inevitable end came to Küzdö on February 24, 1966, his death certificate gave his age as 106. He was born in 1859, not in 1863, not in 1869.

The most remarkable woman centenarian on my list was Margaret Ruthven Lang, of the Boston musical dynasty of Lang, who died at the age of 104 in 1972. She was a regular symphony-goer since the early days of the Boston Symphony. On her 100th birthday the orchestra played the hymn *Old Hundred* in her honor. The Russian-French singer Marie Olénine d'Alheim lived to be 100. Among other recent centenarians was the French conductor and composer Henri-Paul Busser, who died in 1973 at the age of 101.

It would be most interesting to compile actuarial tables of the life expectancy of musicians according to their specialties. One thing appears certain: great musicians die young; consider Mozart, Schubert, Chopin, Mendelssohn, Scriabin. It is a fascinating speculation to project Mozart's life from 1756 into 1840, and Schubert's life to an even later date! One may indulge in a revery that very great musicians are summoned to Heaven because they would be more at home there.

Statistically speaking, organists live the longest lives, perhaps because their sedentary occupation keeps them from wasting their energy on idle pastimes. Scholars and pedagogues come next in longevity; conductors are fairly durable, too; among instrumentalists, those handling big instruments, like the double bass or trombone, live longer than violinists, who in turn live longer than flutists and oboe players, who are apt to be frail in physique. Among singers, tenors dissipate their vitality faster than bass singers. In all musical categories mediocrities outlive great artists by a large margin.

In addition to all the troubles involved in the compilation of a biographical dictionary, there are people who concoct sinister plots to further bamboozle the proverbial "harmless drudge." Mikhail Goldstein, a respectable Russian violinist, annoyed by his unfair treatment by the Soviet Music Publishing House in systematically rejecting his compositions, decided to take revenge on them. He invented a Russian composer named Ovsianiko-Kulikovsky, furnished him with a plausible biography, obtained a quantity of old manuscript paper, and composed a symphony in his name, pretending that he had found the score in the archives of the Odessa Conservatory, where he was librarian at the time. The Soviets swallowed the bait and published the score, proclaiming it to be a major discovery; it was also recorded, and greeted with enthusiastic reviews, not only in Russia but elsewhere. (Shall I confess, blushingly? I reviewed the recording for the *Musical Quarterly,* and announced with some reservations that if the work were genuine it would be the first Russian symphony ever written.) A doctoral dissertation was published on the work. When Goldstein admitted the hoax, he was accused of trying to appropriate an important piece of the national legacy. The situation degenerated into a farce, and Goldstein got out of Russia as soon as he could get an exit visa. But, as in Prokofiev's *Lieutenant Kije,* it was too late to kill off Ovsianiko-Kulikovsky, and his symphony is still listed in some record catalogues and is kept on the shelves of music libraries.

An even more dangerous mystification was perpetrated by the eminent Italian music scholar Alberto Cametti, who claimed discovery of an important biographical notebook of Palestrina, which established the elusive exact date of Palestrina's birth. He said he had purchased the document from one Telemaco Bratti, and even went to the trouble of reproducing, or rather forging, part of the manuscript in an article he wrote on the subject. Another Italian music scholar, Raffaele Casimiri, embraced the "discovery" as a gift of God to all true Palestrinologists. Then Alberto Cametti let it pass through various channels that the name of the alleged discoverer of the document, Telemaco Bratti, was an anagram of Alberto Cametti. A great inner storm ensued in the confined company of Italian music scholars, but in the meantime the hoax found its way into reputable bibliographies. (It was thanks to a knowledgeable friend that I myself did not fall into the trap in giving the exact date of Palestrina's birth in my edition of *Baker's;* this date remains unknown to this day.)

It is amazing that grown men and women would deliberately falsify their vital statistics, particularly their dates of birth, in order to appear younger in a reference work. The gambit is understandable among actresses and prima donnas; and it has been said that a woman has the privilege of improvising her age. It would also be understandable for men in their dotage who marry girls in their nonage, but both men and women of music rejuvenate themselves lexicographically even when they are not stage performers.

The Spanish composer Oscar Esplá produced his passport to prove to me that he was born in 1888 and not in 1886 as I had it in *Baker's.* But I had obtained a copy of his birth certificate which confirmed the accuracy of the earlier date.

Mabel Daniels, the Boston composer, once included in a piece a C-sharp against C, explaining that she "had to use a dissonance," since she was living in the same town with me. She petulantly accused me of being "no gentleman" in putting her down as born in 1878 rather than 1879, her own chosen year. She was born in November 1878, just a few weeks away from 1879, so why should I not accept the later year, she pleaded. Poor Mabel! She lived a full life until well into her tenth decade, dying in 1971.

A desire to appear young, if only on paper, is not a modern phenomenon. Since time immemorial, musicians, poets, painters, actors, even politicians, have exercised their unquestionable prerogative to fib about their age. Johann Jakob Froberger gave the date of May 18, 1620, as that of his birth to his physician, but his certificate of baptism reveals that he was baptized on May 19, 1616. It is a reasonable assumption that the day and the month of his birth, as given by himself, were correct, and that he was baptized on the next day, in 1616, not 1620.

In his handwritten autobiographical note for Mattheson's *Grundlage einer Ehrenpforte,* Telemann stated that he was born in 1682, whereas he was born a year earlier; as in many such cases, the day and the month of his birth, March 14, were given correctly.

The Italian composer and conductor Angelo Mariani, who was born on October 11, 1821, insisted in his communications to Francesco Regli, editor of an Italian biographical dictionary, that he was born on October 11, 1824. Mariani's birth certificate proves that he was born in 1821.

It was common practice in Catholic families to give identical Christian names to infants born after the death of a previous son, or a daughter, so as to perpetuate the memory of the lost child. This has led to a number of mistaken identities. The bicentennial of Giovanni Battista Viotti was widely celebrated in 1953, commemorating the birth in Fontanetto, Italy, of an infant of that name born on May 23, 1753, who died in the following year, on July 10, 1754. On May 12, 1755, another child was born to the Viottis and was given the names Giovanni Battista Guglielmo Domenico, retaining the first two names from those of their deceased son. This second similarly named child was the composer, whose bicentennial was celebrated two years early.

Biographical notices for Giacomo Insanguine found in old music dictionaries list his year of birth variously between 1712 and 1742. I applied for a copy of his birth certificate from the registries of his native town of Monopoli, and received a document purporting to show that he was born in 1712, a date that did not seem to agree with the known facts of his education and career. I pressed for a further search, which revealed that a Giacomo Insanguine who was born in 1712 died in 1726 at the age of 14. On March 22, 1728, a boy was born to the bereaved parents, and was given the names Giacomo Antonio Francesco Paolo Michele. This was the composer Insanguine.

Beethoven was eager to prove that he was born in 1772, not in 1770, and that he had an older brother who was born in 1770. It was discovered that a Ludwig Maria van Beethoven was born on April 1, 1769, but he died a few days later. The great Beethoven was born in the following year.

Next to birth certificates, the best sources of information are family Bibles, marriage certificates, and school registries. The date of birth of Kaspar Othmayr—March 12, 1515—is verified by his astrological chart, and one can be sure that in those remote times no one would hoodwink one's own astrologer. Even in modern times there are practicing astrologers among composers; of these, Dane Rudhyar is professionally the most successful.

In one famous event the correct age of the protagonist became a matter of life or death. On June 28, 1914, Gavrilo Princip, a young Serbian patriot, assassinated Crown Prince Franz Ferdinand of Austria. His act precipitated World War I, which precipitated the Russian Revolution, which precipitated the rise of Hitler, which precipitated World War II, etc., etc., etc. According to the Austrian law of the time no person less than twenty years of age could be executed for a capital crime. Gavrilo Princip was born on July 25, 1894, according to the Gregorian calendar, and was not quite twenty when he turned the world upside down. This saved him from execution, and he died in prison of tuberculosis of the bone marrow on April 28, 1918.

Oscar Wilde was not so lucky in his own chronology. He had whittled two years off his true age, claiming that he was born in 1856, whereas his real year of birth was 1854. Owing to a peculiar twist of English law, persons under forty indicted for immorality were granted leniency. Oscar Wilde was arrested for sodomy in 1895, and would have benefited by the law had it not been for the prying investigation of the court clerk, who secured Wilde's birth certificate proving that he was over forty at the time of his offense. This precluded leniency, and Wilde got a severe sentence. Despite the availability of the correct date, the *Encyclopaedia Britannica* carried the 1856 date in its article on Oscar Wilde right through its thirteenth edition. The *Century Cyclopedia* still gives the wrong date.

Much confusion is created in musical biography by the discrepancy in dating past events according to the Russian and Western calendars. The Greek Orthodox Church refused to accept the Gregorian calendar, and continued to use the Julian calendar until 1918. The Julian calendar was also in force in Bulgaria and Rumania during the same period. As a result, the dating of Russian births and deaths lagged behind the Western calendar, by 11 days in the 18th century, 12 days in the 19th century and 13 days in the 20th century. (The increase in discrepancy was caused by the fact that the years 1800 and 1900 were leap years in Russia but not in the West.) Stravinsky was born on June 5, 1882, according to the Julian calendar, which corresponded to June 17 of the Western calendar. But after 1900, when the difference between the two calendars increased by a day, he began celebrating his birthday on June 18. As his 80th anniversary approached in June 1962, he let it be known that he was going to celebrate it on June 18, which gave occasion to the *New York Times* to say that the faces of some lexicographers would be red on June 18, Stravinsky's preferred date for his birth, seeing that most dictionaries, including two edited by me, gave this date as June 17. I sent a rebuttal explaining my reasons for sticking to the June 17 date, and the *New York Times* published it under the caption, "It Is All Clear Now." This aroused Stravinsky's anger, and he shot off a wire to the paper reasserting his prerogative to celebrate his birthday on any date he wished. He declared his intention to mark the date in the twenty-first century on June 19, assuming that the difference between the two calendars would continue to increase a day each century, but he overlooked the fact that the year 2000 will be a leap year according to both the Gregorian and Julian calendars, because Pope Gregory ruled, on the advice of learned astronomers, that a year divisible by 400 must be reckoned as a leap year.

Are trivia worth mentioning in a biographical dictionary? It all depends. If such trivia have significant bearing on the subject's life and career, they should be given consideration. The unique case of the male castrato Tenducci, who eloped with a young girl and subsequently married her, deserves comment to dispel incredulity. He was a triorchis, and was therefore capable of marriage even after he was two-thirds castrated. His wife wrote a book of memoirs on the affair.

There remain a few categories that ought to be dealt with in separate rubrics.

INCLUSION AND EXCLUSION. *Baker's Biographical Dictionary of Musicians* must necessarily include men and women active in music who were not professional musicians, such as aristocratic patrons and patronesses, wealthy promoters of musical events, impresarios, music publishers, ballet masters who played important roles in commissioning and performing works from composers, and of course music critics. A practical criterion for including names of little-known composers, performers, and pedagogues should be the degree of likelihood that a music student, or a concertgoer, or a person who wants to know who is who in music would look it up in a dictionary. Thousands of names hover in the periphery of the music world and many more populate the index pages of biographies of famous composers. Still more are modest members of world orchestras who have distinguished themselves in various ways. Hugo Leichtentritt told me that Riemann, with whom he studied, used to play chamber music with amateurs and professionals at his home in Leipzig, and after each session, would ask them to fill out questionnaires for inclusion in his *Musik-Lexikon*. Theodore Baker, the compiler of the original edition of the present dictionary, collected biographical data from his friends who played in the Boston Symphony Orchestra. As a result, the early editions of both lexica became overpopulated with individuals who were perfectly honorable practitioners of their art, but who failed to leave an indelible, or even delible, mark on the sands of music. Most of these long-dead servants of music, whether borrowed by Baker from Riemann and other collectors of musical flesh, or installed anew by Baker and his successors out of personal friendship, have been allowed in the present edition to remain under their individual lexicographical tombstones for humanitarian reasons, rather than relegated to the common graves of crumbling newspaper clippings in public libraries; still, the paragraphs devoted to them originally have been mercifully cut down to commensurate size. No more will the impatient user of the dictionary be offered long lines of printed matter dealing with this or that obscure orchestral player, church organist, or provincial music teacher, relating in stultifying detail the advancement of their dull careers. But musical, or even unmusical, figures that multidentally smile on us from huge posters or gold-rimmed record albums, the glamorized purveyors of popular subculture of whatever degree of vulgarity, the Beatles and other singing coleoptera, are welcomed to this edition of *Baker's* even more liberally than they were to the 1958 edition and to the 1965 and 1971 Supplements. When, overcoming a natural revulsion, I dictated to my California secretary a paragraph on Humperdinck, the pop singer whose manager had the supreme *chutzpah* to appropriate the honored name of the composer of *Hänsel und Gretel* because it sounded "funny" and would attract attention, she was genuinely surprised at my liberality, but revealed her complete ignorance as to the existence of an earlier musician of the same name as the glorified rock singer.

DATES OF PERFORMANCE. A determined effort has been made in the present edition to list as many exact dates as possible of first performances of major works, especially operas and symphonies, not only by celebrated masters but also by modern composers. Care had to be taken to avoid duplication, for many composers are, and have been, in the habit of changing the titles of their works and then presenting them as new compositions. For instance, Don Emilio Arrieta y Corera wrote an opera, *La Conquista de Granada*, which was produced in Madrid in 1850 and revived under the title *Isabel la Católica* in 1855. The opera got a double billing in the valuable compilation *Cronica de la Opera italiana en Madrid*, published in 1878, the index of which correctly lists the two titles interchangeably, but this precaution has failed to deter other publications from duplicating the work. Quite often, composers append an optional descriptive title to an earlier work, which is apt to be duplicated in the catalogue.

SPELLING OF NAMES. Variants of spelling of celebrated musical names cause uncertainty, and choice had to be made in the present edition of *Baker's* guided by common usage; alternative spellings are then cross-referenced. Spanish, Portuguese, and Latin American names commonly include both the paternal and maternal surname; a selection has to be made according to the preferred usage. Thus, Alejandro García Caturla is listed under Caturla, the name he used in his published works; Oscar Lorenzo Fernandez is listed under Fernandez. In some instances, a musician changes the form of his name in the middle of his career. In the earlier editions of this dictionary the main entry on Edmund Rubbra appeared under Duncan-Rubbra; Duncan was the name of his first wife, which he adopted in some of his works; later he reverted to the legal name Rubbra, which is therefore used in the present edition of *Baker's*. Philip Heseltine published most of his music under the witching surname Peter Warlock, but Heseltine would seem preferable for a biographical dictionary. Americanization had produced several changes in the spelling of names; Arnold Schoenberg changed the spelling of his last name from Schönberg to Schoenberg when he emigrated to the United States. Carlos Salzedo dropped the acute accent that marked the antepenultimate letter of his original name. Eugen Zádor dropped the accent and changed his first name to Eugene when he came to America. Aladár Szendrei made his career in Europe under his original Hungarian name and surname, but changed it phonetically to Sendrey when he emigrated to the United States; a cross-reference has been made in the present edition under Sendrey to his original name. Edgar Varèse was baptized as Edgard Varèse, but most of his works were published with the first name spelled Edgar; in 1940 or thereabouts he changed it back to his legal name, Edgard. However, the present edition of *Baker's* keeps the familiar form Edgar. The existence of the alternate spellings Carl and Karl in many German names creates considerable confusion. The 1958 edition of *Baker's* modernized virtually all Carls to Karls, with some curious results, such as the spelling Karl Philipp Emanuel Bach instead of the standard Carl; the traditional spelling has been restored in the present edition. A curious case is that of Carl Ruggles, the American composer, whose real first name was Charles. He changed it to Carl as a youth when he decided to devote himself to music; he hoped that the Germanic form of the name would give him a better chance to succeed in the highly German-minded musical world of early twentieth-century America.

NOBILIARY PARTICLES. Early in this century it was common in American and British usage to put the nobiliary particle "von" in front of German names, such as "von Bülow" and the like. In the wake of World War I the "von" became unpopular among the Allied nations. The original full name of the English composer Gustav Holst, who was of Swedish ancestry, was von Holst. During the war, at the suggestion of Percy Scholes, he dropped the objectionable "von" from his name. Anton von Webern eliminated the "von" after the fall of the Austro-Hungarian Empire in 1918; the present edition lists his name under Webern, Anton von, in appreciation of the fact that he used the full name in the titles of many of his early works. A more difficult problem is encountered in the Dutch and Flemish nobiliary particle "van." Beethoven was very proprietary about his own "van" and regarded it as a proof of his noble origin, an important claim at the time when he tried to assure the guardianship of his nephew. The French and Spanish "de" and the Italian "di" often become coalesced with the last name. Debussy was Bussy to friends in his youth; Madame von Meck, the patroness of Tchaikovsky, who employed Debussy as a house musician and teacher in Moscow, referred to him as Bussy. No book of reference would list Bussy as an alternative for Debussy, but in some other names, not necessarily French, this nobiliary particle retains its independent existence. De Koven is an example. But De Falla is improper; his name should be listed under Falla, Manuel de.

RUSSIAN NAMES. The Russian alphabet has two intractable letters: one is represented by the Cyrillic symbol "ы," the other by a fence of three sticks with a line underneath it, and a wriggle, or a cedilla, on the right of the protracted horizontal line. Only Turkish has the phonetic equivalent of "ы," represented by an undotted "i" in the new Turkish alphabet. As for the second Cyrillic symbol aforementioned, it can be very adequately represented by the coalescence of the sounds "sh" and "ch" in a compound word such as fish-chips. The Russian sound for "e" is palatalized into "yeh" as in the new accepted English spelling of Dostoyevsky. English and American music dictionaries have inherited the spelling of Russian names of composers and performers from German, which has no "ch" sound, and in which the Russian (and English) "v" sound is represented by "w." As a result, we had Tschaikowsky for at least half a century. British and American librarians, realizing that Tsch = Ch, began spelling Tchaikovsky as Chaikovsky. But if we follow phonetics, then why do we need the diphthong "ai"? Why not plain "i" as in China? Here we come to the antinomy of sound, sight, and audiovisual association: Chikovsky has an impossible look. A compromise is necessary: hence, Tchaikovsky in *Baker's*. "Ch" in Rachmaninoff has a guttural German sound that English does not possess. The spelling Rachmaninoff is part-German ("ch") and part-French ("ff"), but this is the way he signed his name, familiar from printed music and concert programs. Most British sources prefer Rakhmaninov.

Once we start on the road to phonetics we will be bound for disaster. The name of the poet Evtushenko is pronounced Yevtushenko, but the eye rebels against its aspect. Besides, an unpalatalized "e" in such an initial sound is not necessarily un-Russian; some people from the northern provinces or from Siberia would say Evtushenko, just as if it were written in English. Another thing: the final diphthong "iy," as it is often represented phonetically in names like Tchaikovsky (or for that matter in Slonimsky), is nearest to the French "ille" in "volaille," but it is not as emphatically articulated. There is no reason to add ugliness to a name like Tchaikovsky by spelling it Tchaikovskiy. Then there is the vexing problem of transliterating Russian names of French or German origin back into their original languages. Some music dictionaries transliterate Cui as Kyue, a visual monstrosity. Cui was the son of a Napoleonic soldier who remained in Russia after the campaign of 1812 and married a Russian woman. His French name Cui ought to stay. The Soviet composer Shnitke (spelled phonetically in English) was of German origin, and his father signed his name in German as Schnittke; this spelling ought to remain even in an English reference work. The same consideration holds for names like Schneerson (Jewish-German) or Steinpress (pronounced Shteinpress in Russian) and Steinberg (for Shteinberg). If we try to transliterate foreign names in Russian back and forth, we will arrive at mutations such as Betkhoven and (yes, unbelievable but true) Poochcheenee, used for a time in the bibliography of *Notes*. I am proud to say that I opened such a vigorous letter-writing campaign against this practice that it was stopped. To conclude, the transliteration of Russian names and Russian titles of works should be guided by ear and by sight. There are seasonal changes and fashions for some Russian names. It used to be Sergey, Bolshoy Theater, etc. Now it is Sergei, Bolshoi, etc. Both visually and phonetically, these altered spellings are fine. In this edition of *Baker's* the paternal names have been omitted in listings of Russian composers, except in that of Piotr Ilyich Tchaikovsky, which has become traditional. The pronunciation of Russian names has been indicated only when mispronunciation is common, as for instance in Balakirev (stress on the second syllable, not the third), Borodin (stress on the last syllable). The pronunciation of Khachaturian's name with the accent on the third syllable has become so common that it would be idle to try to change it to the proper pronunciation, with the accent on the last syllable; equally futile would it be to persuade people to compress the last two vowels into one: "yan." The doubling of "s" between vowels in Russian names such as Mussorgsky is admittedly Germanic in origin; but in seeking to avoid the vocalization of the middle "s" in Mussorgsky the doubling of "s" becomes essential. Thus it is Mussorgsky rather than Musorgsky; but in less familiar names like Stasov, a single "s" is postulated. Illogical? So is the language itself.

GEOGRAPHIC NAMES. Place names have been playing musical chairs during the wars and revolutions of the first half of the present century. I was born in St. Petersburg, left Petrograd in 1918, and revisited Leningrad in 1962. One can travel from Pressburg to Bratislava to Pozsony without budging an inch. A person born in Klausenburg finds himself nominally transferred to Kolozsvàr and then to Cluj without moving from one's house. Sometimes a town renamed to honor a current revolutionary figure resumes its original name when the eponymous hero falls into disfavor. Perm was renamed Molotov after the Soviet Revolution, but became Perm once more when Molotov faded out in 1956. In Poland, Katowice was named Stalinogorod in 1953 but became Katowice once more in 1956 when Stalin was posthumously disfranchised. Then there is Liège. For over a century it bore an unnatural acute accent over its middle letter. In 1946 its Municipal Council resolved that the accent should be changed to the grave one. A Belgian musician born in a town with an acute accent may die there with a grave.

ABBREVIATIONS. All abbreviations except the obvious ones, like vol., prof., symph. orch., etc., and the names of the months (except March and April, which remain unabbreviated), have been eliminated from this edition. No more the impenetrable jungle of Ztsch., Vsch., vcs., mvt., or Kgl.

BIBLIOGRAPHY. In listing sources of information pertaining to the subject of an entry, a conscientious bibliographer ought to use common sense. It would serve no rational purpose to cite general histories of music for references to Bach, Mozart, or Beethoven in the bibliographical section; obviously each of such books will have extended chapters on great masters of music. But in bibliographies on modern composers, it is worthwhile to mention collections of articles containing informative material relating to such composers. The same consideration would apply to books on great conductors, great instrumentalists, or great singers; they ought to be listed if they contain useful biographical information. Magazine articles of extensive length are also proper bibliographical material. Title pages are sometimes deceptive. A brochure on Louis-Gilbert Duprez by A. A. Elwart bears the claim on its title page "avec une biographie authentique de son maître A. Choron." Upon examination, it turns out that it contains only a couple of pages on Choron. On the other hand, there are books modestly titled that provide a wealth of biographical information not available in special monographs on the subject. Since it is patently impractical to append an evaluation of each bibliographical item in a book of general reference, a reader's attention can be called to a particularly valuable publication by a word or two, such as "important," "of fundamental value," etc. Conversely, a warning should be given against worthless publications of a biographical nature that for some reason have become widely read. A famous, or infamous, example is a purported book of memoirs attributed to the nineteenth-century German prima donna Wilhelmina Schröder-Devrient and duly listed under her name in the bibliography of a number of respectable music dictionaries. It is a mildly pornographic (as pornography went at the time of its publication a hundred years ago) volume recounting her amours with famous people. It was made available in German and French; there is even a French edition in existence illustrated with erotic drawings. Less obvious in intent, but much more harmful in its effect, is the notorious correspondence between Chopin and Potocka manufactured by a Polish woman in 1945 and broadcast over Warsaw Radio during the first months after the liberation of Poland from Nazi occupation. Respectable music scholars and Chopinologists eagerly accepted these letters, which portrayed Chopin as a sex maniac given to verbal obscenities, as genuine. In one of Chopin's alleged letters he is made to use a sexual pun on a vulgar Polish word that was not in use until 1900; and there were other indecencies. The poor woman who concocted these letters committed suicide, but even then some people refused to give up their faith in the authenticity of this clumsy forgery.

Archaic spelling of the titles of old books is preserved in the present edition of *Baker's*. Martin Agricola's work *Ein kurtz deudsche Musica* retains its ancient title. Varieties of spelling in different editions of old English books are indicated, as in Christopher Simpson's *Practicall Musick*. Inordinately long book titles are abbreviated unless they contain some specific limiting clauses. For instance, Karl Grunsky's volume *Die Technik des Klavierauszuges entwickelt am dritten Akt von Wagners Tristan und Isolde* treats the problem of piano reduction only of the third act of *Tristan,* and it would be misleading to list it as *Die Technik des Klavierauszuges* plain and simple. In all such cases, practical sense rather than pedantic considerations should guide the compiler.

POLTERGEIST. Typographical errors are not just human failures of perception. They are acts of a malevolent mischievous spirit that lays its eggs in the linotype ribbon. Or else how are we to account for alterations that are obviously intended as mockery? Such fanciful conceits as "scared music," "pubic rectal," or "anals of music" cannot be accidents endemic to the typesetter. Avaunt! Avaunt! (Memo to proofreader: typos intentional to illustrate the dreadful dangers in writing books; do not change to "sacred music," "public recital" and "annals of music.")

I have a recurrent dream: I am in the dock facing a trio of stern judges vaguely resembling my schoolteachers of long ago, about to hear a sentence pronounced upon me for incompetence, negligence, dereliction of duty, fraudulent pretense at lexicographical expertise. The judges exhibit grotesquely enlarged entries from my edition of Baker's, engraved on huge slabs of granite, as evidence against me. In my anguish I plead extenuating circumstances. Yes, I was guilty of procrastination, sloth, accidie, pigritude (a lovely old word for laziness), stupidity perhaps, but did I not try? Did I not get from Naples the birth certificates of thirteen Enrico Carusos before giving up? Did I not locate Edward Maryon in England after his publisher told me he had been dead for years? Maryon bequeathed to me his manuscripts and other memorabilia, going back to the seventeenth century (he was of the nobility; his full name was Maryon d'Aulby), which were sent to me in a huge trunk by his executors after his death. I donated the materials to the Boston Public Library.

At least one living composer showed kindness to me in appreciation of my efforts to get his biography right (and failing), Ezra Sims of Massachusetts. I got his string quartets all mixed up in my 1971 Supplement to *Baker's,* and created a nonexistent String Quartet No. 2, composed, according to my mistaken impression, in 1962. In an unparalleled act of forgiveness, Sims composed a piece scored for a quintet of winds and strings, called it String Quartet No. 2, dated it 1962, although he wrote it in 1974, and dedicated it to me so that I "may be now less in error."

De minimis non curat lex, says an old legal maxim. But still there are minutiae that ought to be attended to in a reference work. The title of Leoncavallo's most famous opera is *Pagliacci,* without the definite article, not *I Pagliacci*. The original manuscript score is in the Library of Congress in Washington, D.C., and the title page can be examined by any doubting person. But the bronze plaque underneath the precious relic bears the wrong title *I Pagliacci!* Aaron Copland's best-known work, *Lincoln Portrait,* was listed in *Baker's* 1958 as *A Lincoln Portrait,* and Copland specifically pointed out to me that the score has no such indefinite article in its title. And yet the program of its very first performance carried an intrusive "A," and many symphony programs repeated the error.

My medulla oblongata, or whatever part of the brain controls lexicographical reflexes, overflows with gratitude to many unselfish people who have helped me in putting together the 1958 edition of *Baker's,* its two Supplements, of 1965 and 1971, and, most importantly, the present swollen edition. First to be thanked are the multitudinous registrars, clerks, and keepers of city or state archives all over the habitable world who have provided me with copies of birth and death certificates that have made it possible to establish correct chronology in the lives of thousands of musicians represented in *Bakers*. The editors of the Riemann *Musik-Lexikon* have most generously let me have hundreds of documents pertaining to musical biography and copies of a number of birth and death certificates which I had not had in my possession—a most extraordinary example of scholarly cooperation. Boris Steinpress, editor of the Soviet musical encyclopedia, patiently collected for me dates of first performances of Russian operas and symphonies and corrected numerous errors encountered in the articles on Russian composers in the previous editions of *Bakers*. Grigori Schneerson of Moscow was a great lexicographical and personal friend during the many years of our correspondence. And there were many others in Russia and in other countries in Europe.

How can I thank William Lichtenwanger, that magus of musical, and not only musical, encyclopedias, the polynomial scholar who possesses in his head a cross-reference to all subjects biographical, historical, and lexicographical? A polymath, a polyglot at home in all European languages, an enlightened opsimath in Russian and a philological connoisseur of Turkish and Japanese, he was willing to read and to critically annotate the galley proofs of the entire bulk of the present edition of *Baker's;* he got for me precious biographical data on *Baker* inmates who dwelt in the lexicographical nirvana for decades. To quote from James Joyce's passage in *Finnegans Wake*, written in bird language, "Nobirdy aviar soar anywing to eagle it." Lichtenwanger is unique.

Much as I welcome people volunteering corrections in *Baker's* and other lexicographical publications of which I have been in charge, I admit that I was somewhat startled when in August 1972 I received a letter from Stephen W. Ellis of Glenview, Illinois, in which he tore to pieces my 1971 Supplement to *Baker's*, sideswiping also at the basic 1958 volume. "Grossly incomplete," "flagrantly inaccurate," "absurd," "shockingly out of date," "sadly inadequate," "ridiculous," "disgraceful," and even "criminal," were some of his expletives. The 1971 Supplement must have been a "one-man job," he correctly surmised. But who *was* Stephen W. Ellis? I had never heard of him, and I could not find his name in any index of articles on music. Yet the man exhibited such precise knowledge of many obscure items of music history and musical biography that he could not have been just an amateur. My first impulse was to respond with lofty indignation: "Sirrah! Do you realize that you are addressing one whom the *Penguin Dictionary of Music* called 'a modern prince of musical lexicography,' and for whom Percy A. Scholes invoked, in a personal letter (*rubesco referens*), the famous lines of Goldsmith, 'and still the wonder grew that one small head could carry all he knew'? One, who . . ." But I quickly cooled down, realizing how valuable Ellis could be for the completely new edition of *Baker's*. I wrote him with genuine curiosity, asking how on earth he could have collected such a mountain of information on music and musicians, which he dispensed with such certainty of his sources. I was sure he was not an academic person, I wrote him, but I guessed that he was a record collector, that he was about 42 years old, married, and had two children. I was right, as it turned out, that he was not a professional musicologist (no professional musicologist would possess such a variety of knowledge), that he was an ardent collector of records, and subscribed to bulletins issued by unions of composers all over the world. He was not 42, but only 30 years old at the time; yes, he was married, but had only one child (a second child came along soon). By profession, he was a copy reader for a small publishing house. A fortunate publishing house it was indeed! It did not take me long to persuade Ellis to help me in putting together the present edition of *Baker's*; in fact he was eager to help. His proofreading ability, I soon found out, was prodigious, but what was most remarkable, and what still astounds me, is his uncanny knack for digging up information about contemporary composers, in precise detail, and his perseverance in getting these data for *Baker's* from reluctant, recalcitrant, and unwilling musicians. The wealth of information about modern Finns, Swedes, Norwegians, and Danes which he was able to gather for me was truly comprehensive; he was comparably "teeming with the news," to borrow a phrase from Gilbert and Sullivan, about composers of Iceland, Japan, Belgium, Holland, Spain, and Portugal; he seemed to be able to get more information about the musicians of Rumania than I could after my trip to Rumania in 1963; he was equally successful with Poles, Yugoslavs, Czechs, and Bulgarians, not to mention Americans. His special contribution was information on hard-to-get Australians. All told, he sent me about 1,250 biographies, each having a very complete list of works. I could not use all this material, and I had to cut down drastically on some catalogues of works. Inevitably, I had to use my own verbiage for the introductory paragraphs of each entry, but the hard core of information on hundreds of these contemporary composers from all lands under the lexicographical sun was furnished by Ellis.

My effusive thanks are owed to Samuel Sprince of Boston, Massachusetts. Like the Canadian Royal Mounties, he never failed to get his man; in this context, the man (or the woman) was some obscure musician whose opaque name made an insignificant blur on a page in an old edition of *Baker's* and who somehow remained unnoticed by subsequent editors. Still, such unfortunates had to be taken care of, dead or alive, to preserve the continuity of the *Baker's* heritage. Sprince tracked down for me quite a number of such personages, most of them hovering between uncertain life and certain death in some wretched nursing home. Several of them met their Maker without the benefit of an obituary, and were lost until some relative could be found to supply the missing obit. It is unfortunate that so many musicians die out of alphabetical order, so that when a dictionary is already half-printed, a *revenant* from the early part of the alphabet is apt to make a belated appearance. The entries under the early letters of the alphabet in the present edition of *Baker's* already constitute a sizable mortuary.

The following individuals and institutions have lent their most valuable assistance in preparing the present edition of *Baker's:*

Patsy Felch, Head Reference Librarian, and Don Roberts, Head Music Librarian, Northwestern University Music Library, Evanston, Illinois

Centre Belge de Documentation Musicale, Brussels

Per Olof Lundahl, Executive Secretary, Swedish Music Information Center, Stockholm

Bálint András Varga, Head of Promotion, Editio Musica Budapest, Budapest

Jarmo Sermilä, former Executive Secretary, Finnish Music Information Center, Helsinki

Kimiko Shimbo, Secretary General, The Japan Federation of Composers, Tokyo

Rina Smits-Westhof, Librarian, Foundation Donemus, Amsterdam

Canadian Music Centre, Toronto

Timothy Rice, Faculty of Music, University of Toronto

Czechoslovak Music Information Center, Prague

Magnhild Stoveland, Society of Norwegian Composers, Oslo

Secretaria de Estado da Comunicação Social, Lisbon

Union of Rumanian Composers, Bucharest

Icelandic Music Information Center, Reykjavik

Dimiter Christoff, Secretary General of the UNESCO International Music Council in Sofia, Bulgaria

Teresa Mochtak, Head of the Music Department, Polski Wydawnictwo Muzyczne Edition, Warsaw

James Murdoch, National Director, Australia Music Centre, Ltd., Sydney

Wilhelm Hansen Edition, Copenhagen

Esperanza Pulido, editor, *Heterofonía*, Mexico City

Hellenic Association for Contemporary Music, Athens

Instituto de Cultura Puertorriqueña, San Juan

Benjamin Bar-Am, Secretary, League of Composers in Israel, Tel Aviv

I conclude this rather inflated preface, as I did in my 1971 Supplement to *Baker's*, with a cherished quotation from a letter I received from Alfred Einstein shortly before his death. In his characteristic mood of gentle humor, he wondered "ob wir, und natürlich vor allem Sie, im Himmel einmal dafür belohnt werden, dass wir einige Ungenauigkeiten aus der Welt geschafft haben. . . ." Onward to a heavenly reward!

Nicolas Slonimsky
Los Angeles, California
September 1978

List of Abbreviations

A.B.	Bachelor of Arts
ABC	American Broadcasting Company
A.M.	Master of Arts
ASCAP	American Society of Composers, Authors, and Publishers
B.A.	Bachelor of Arts
BBC	British Broadcasting Corporation
B.M.	Bachelor of Music
CBC	Canadian Broadcasting Corporation
CBS	Columbia Broadcasting System
cons./Cons.	conservatory/Conservatory
diss.	dissertation
D.M.A.	Doctor of Musical Arts
ed(s).	edit(ed), editor(s), edition(s)
enl.	enlarged
IRCAM	Institut de Recherche et de Coordination Acoustique/Musique
ISCM	International Society for Contemporary Music
inst./Inst.	institute/Institute
M.A.	Master of Arts
M.M.	Master of Music
MS(S)	manuscript(s)
Mus.B.	Bachelor of Music
Mus.D.	Doctor of Music
Mus.M.	Master of Music
NAACP	National Association for the Advancement of Colored People
NBC	National Broadcasting Company
n.d.	no date
NEA	National Endowment for the Arts
no(s).	number(s)
op(p).	opus (opera)
orch(s).	orchestra(s); orchestral
Orch.	Orchestra; Orchestre
p(p).	page(s)
PBS	Public Broadcasting Service
perf.	performance, performed
Ph.D.	Doctor of Philosophy
phil.	philharmonic
posth.	posthumously
prof.	professor
publ.	publish(ed)
RAI	Radiotelevisione Italiana
rev.	revised
RIAS	Radio in the American Sector
S.	San, Santo, Santa
Ss.	Santi, Sante
St(e).	Saint(e)
sym(s).	symphony (-ies)
tr.	translate(d), translation
vol(s).	volume(s)
WDR	Westdeutscher Rundfunk (West German Radio)

Aaltonen, Erkki, Finnish composer; b. Hämeenlinna, Aug. 17, 1910. He studied violin at the Helsinki Cons. and composition privately with Väinö Raitio and Selim Palmgren. From 1966 to 1973 he was director of the Kemi Music Inst. His music often reflects topical subjects.

WORKS: 5 syms.: No. 1 (1947); No. 2, *Hiroshima* (1949); No. 3, *Popular* (1952); No. 4 (1959); No. 5 (1964); *Hämeenlinna,* rhapsody for Orch. (1945); 2 piano concertos (1948, 1954); *Folk Music* for Orch. (1953–60); 2 ballet suites from *Lapponia* (1956, 1959); Violin Concerto (1966); Piano Sonata (1932; rev. 1972); Oboe Sonata (1945); 5 string quartets; piano pieces; songs.

Aarne, Els, Estonian pianist and composer; b. Makeyevka, Ukraine, March 30, 1917. She studied piano with Lemba at the Tallinn Cons. in Estonia and composition with A. Kapp. She subsequently joined the faculty of the Tallinn Cons. as an instructor in piano and theory.

WORKS: ORCH.: Sym. No. 1 (1961); Sym. No. 2 (1966); *Baltic Sea, the Sea of Peace* for Wind Orch. (1958); Piano Concerto (1945); Horn Concerto (1958); Double-bass Concerto (1968). CHAMBER: Wind Quintet (1965); Nocturne for Cello and Piano (1970). VOCAL: *Fatherland,* cantata for Chorus and Orch. (1939); *Sing, Free People,* cantata (1949); numerous songs.

Aaron, abbot of the monasteries of St. Martin and St. Pantaleon at Cologne, where he died on Nov. 18, 1052. He was the author of 3 historically important treatises: *De utilitate cantus vocalis, De modo cantandi et psallendi,* and *De regulis tonorum et symphoniarum.* He is believed to be the 1st cleric to introduce the Gregorian evening service (nocturns) into Germany.

Aaron, Pietro, Italian music theorist; b. Florence, c.1480; d. probably in Bergamo, c.1550. He was cantor at the Cathedral of Imola in 1521, and at the Rimini Cathedral in 1523. In 1525 he was "maestro di casa" in a Venetian house; in 1536 he entered the Order of Jerusalem. He publ. *Libri tres de institutione harmonica* (Bologna, 1516); *Thoscanello de la musica* (Venice, 1523; 4 rev. eds., 1529–62); *Trattato della natura et cognitione di tutti gli tuoni di canto figurato* (Venice, 1525; reproduced in part, in an Eng. tr., in O. Strunk's *Source Readings in Music History,* N.Y., 1950); *Lucidario in musica di alcune opinione antiche e moderne* (Venice, 1545); *Compendiolo di molti dubbi, segreti, et sentenze intorno al canto fermo et figurato* (Milan, posthumous; title page bears the inscription: "In memoria eterna erit Aron").

BIBL.: J. Link, Jr., *Theory and Tuning: A.'s Meantone Temperament and Marpurg's Temperament "I"* (Boston, 1963); P. Bergquist, "Mode and Polyphony around 1500; Theory and Practice," *Music Forum,* I (1967).

Aav, Evald, Estonian composer; b. Reval, Feb. 22, 1900; d. there, March 21, 1939. He studied composition in Reval with Arthur Kapp; he wrote mostly vocal music to words in the Estonian language. In 1928 he composed the 1st national Estonian opera, *The Vikings* (Tallinn, Sept. 8, 1928). He also wrote a Sym. (1939) and the tone poem *Life.* In his style of composition he followed the model of Tchaikovsky.

Aavik, Juhan, Estonian composer; b. Holstre, near Reval, Jan. 29, 1884; d. Stockholm, Nov. 26, 1982. He studied at the St. Petersburg Cons.; was a conductor in Tartu (1911–23); settled in Reval (Tallinn; 1925–44) as prof. and director of the Cons. there. In 1944 he went to Sweden; he was conductor of the Estonian song festivals there from 1948 to 1961 before retirement. A highly prolific composer, he wrote about 200 numbered works, among them 2 syms.; a Cello Concerto (1949); Double-bass Concerto (1950); Piano Trio (1957); Requiem (1959); and numerous choral works, songs, and pieces of chamber music. He publ. a history of Estonian music in 4 vols. (Stockholm, 1965–69). He died at the age of 98.

Abaco, Evaristo Felice dall', Italian composer, father of **Joseph Marie Clément dall'Abaco;** b. Verona, July 12, 1675; d. Munich, July 12, 1742. He came from a well-placed family in Verona, and studied violin and cello there. He was in Modena from 1696 to 1701. In 1704 he was at the Bavarian court in Munich; then he followed the Duke of Bavaria to Belgium and France, where he became acquainted with French music, which left some influence on his later works. In 1715 he returned to Munich, and was active as leader of the Court Orch. He wrote 12 Violin Sonatas, with Cello or Cembalo, op. 1 (1706); *Concerti da chiesa* for 4 String Instruments, op. 2 (1714); *6 sonate da chiesa* and *6 sonate da camera* for 3 String Instruments, op. 3 (1715); *12 sonate da camera* for Violin and Cello, op. 4 (1716; arranged by Chédeville for Musette, Flute, Oboe, and Continuo); *6 concerti* for 7 Instruments (4 Violins, Viola, Bassoon or Cello, and Bass), op. 5 (1717); Concerto for Violin Solo with Instruments, op. 6 (1730; his most important work). Sandberger publ. a biographical sketch and a selection from opp. 1–4 in vol. 1 of Denkmäler der Tonkunst in Bayern, and a 2nd selection in vol. 16 (9.i); Riemann ed. 3 trio sonatas.

BIBL.: R. Brenzoni, "Un grande musicista veronese, E.F. d.'A.," *Note d'Archivio,* XII (1935).

Abaco, Joseph Marie Clément dall', Netherlands cellist and composer, son of **Evaristo Felice dall'Abaco;** b. Brussels (baptized), March 27, 1710; d. Arbizzano di Valpolicella, near Verona, Aug. 31, 1805. He received his musical training from his father, and as a youth of 19 entered the service of the Prince Elector at Bonn; played in the Court Orch.; in 1738 he was appointed music director. He was in England in 1740; in 1753 he went to Verona; he was given the title of baron by Prince Maximilian of Bavaria (1766). His works include more than 30 cello sonatas and other compositions.

Abbadia, Natale, Italian composer; b. Genoa, March 11, 1792; d. Milan, Dec. 25, 1861. He composed the opera *Giannina di Pontieu* (1812); the musical farce *L'Imbroglione ed il castigamatti;* masses, motets, and other religious music.

Abbado, Claudio, outstanding Italian conductor, brother of **Marcello Abbado;** b. Milan, June 26, 1933. If the genealogical record of his family is to be trusted, he is a direct descendant of a Moorish chieftain, Abdul Abbad, who was expelled from Spain in 1492. Abbado received his early training in music from his father, a professional violinist; he then enrolled in the Milan Cons., graduating in 1955 in piano. He also received instruction in conducting from Antonino Votto and took piano lessons in Salzburg with Friedrich Gulda (1955). From 1956 to 1958 he attended the conducting classes of Hans Swarowsky at the Vienna Academy of Music, spending the summers working with Carlo Zecchi and Alceo Galliera at the Accademia Chigiana in Siena. In 1958 he made his conducting debut in Trieste; he also won the Koussevitzky conducting prize at the Berkshire Music Center in Tanglewood, and, in 1963, was 1 of 3 winners of the Mitropoulos Competition in N.Y. He made his American conducting debut with the N.Y. Phil. on April 7, 1963. In 1965 he appeared as a sym. conductor at La Scala in Milan; he also began conducting the Vienna Phil., leading it in Salzburg, in Vienna, and on tour. He joined the opera at La Scala in 1967, and, in 1972, became principal guest conductor of the London Sym. Orch. In 1972–73 he took the Vienna Phil. to Japan and China; in 1974 he conducted concerts in Russia with the La Scala company; in 1976 he led appearances in the U.S. with both the Vienna Phil. and the La Scala company, which had its American debut during the celebrations of the Bicentennial. In 1978 he founded the European

Community Youth Orch.; from 1981 he was principal conductor of the Chamber Orch. of Europe, which was composed of the former's members. In 1979 he was appointed principal conductor of the London Sym. Orch., and in 1982 was named principal guest conductor of the Chicago Sym. Orch., which post he held until 1986. He founded La Filarmonica della Scala in Milan in 1982. From 1983 to 1988 he was music director of the London Sym. Orch. In 1986 he became chief conductor of the Vienna State Opera; that same year he founded Vienna's Mahler Orch. In 1988 he conducted the famous New Year's Day Concert of the Vienna Phil., and in 1989 was named artistic director of the Berlin Phil. in succession to Karajan. Abbado's conducting engagements have taken him all over the globe. A fine technician, he is capable of producing distinguished performances ranging from the Classical era to the cosmopolitan avant-garde. Among his honors are the Mozart Medal of the Mozart-Gemeinde of Vienna (1973), the Golden Nicolai Medal of the Vienna Phil. (1980), the Gran Croce of his homeland (1984), and the Mahler Medal of Vienna (1985); in 1986 he was made a member of the Légion d'honneur of France.

BIBL.: J. von Rhein, "C. A.," *Ovation* (May 1984).

Abbado, Marcello, Italian pianist and composer, brother of **Claudio Abbado;** b. Milan, Oct. 7, 1926. He studied at the Cons. in Milan with Gavazzeni (piano) and Ghedini (composition), graduating in 1947. In 1951 he was appointed instructor at the Cons. of Venice; from 1958 to 1966 he was director of the Liceo Musicale in Piacenza; in 1966 he was appointed director of the Rossini Cons. in Pesaro; in 1972 he became director of the Milan Cons. He has written a cantata, *Ciapo* (1945); *Lento e Rondo* for Violin and Piano (1949); *Costruzioni* for 5 Small Orchs. (1964); Double Concerto for Violin, Piano, and 2 Chamber Orchs. (1967); Quadruple Concerto for Piano, Violin, Viola, Cello, and Orch. (1969); 3 string quartets (1947, 1953, 1969); piano pieces.

Abbatini, Antonio Maria, Italian composer; b. Tiferno (Città di Castello), c.1597; d. there, c.1679. He served as maestro di cappella at the Lateran (1626–28) and other Roman churches; he was at the church of Loreto from March to Oct. 1667. In 1672 he was employed at S. Maria Maggiore. He wrote 3 operas; the 1st, *Dal male al bene,* written in 1653, is of historical importance because it introduced a final ensemble. His other operas were *Ione* (Vienna, 1664) and *La Comica del cielo* or *La Baltasara* (Rome, 1668). He also composed a dramatic cantata, *Il pianto di Rodomonte* (Orvieto, 1633). He publ. 3 books of masses, 4 books of Psalms, various antiphons (1630, 1638, 1677), and 5 books of motets (1635).

BIBL.: H. Goldschmidt, *Studien zur Geschichte der italienischen Oper im 17. Jahrhundert* (Leipzig, 1901–4); F. Coradini, *A.M. A. e Lorenzo Abbattini: Notizie biografiche* (Arezzo, 1922); K. Andrae, *Ein römischer Kapellmeister im 17. Jahrhundert: A.M. A. (ca. 1600–1679). Studien zu Leben und Werk* (diss., Univ. of Hamburg, 1985).

Abbey, John, noted English organ builder; b. Whilton, Northamptonshire, Dec. 22, 1785; d. Versailles, Feb. 19, 1859. He went to Paris in 1826 at the invitation of Sébastien Érard to construct an organ for the Paris Exposition. He remained in France and built organs for the cathedrals of many French cities. In 1831 he installed an organ at the Paris Opéra. His innovations in the English type of bellows were adopted by many French organ builders.

Abbott, Emma, American soprano; b. Chicago, Dec. 9, 1850; d. Salt Lake City, Jan. 5, 1891. Her father was a singer and her brother a violinist; as a young woman she filled engagements with them in hotels and clubs. Her 1st regular employment was with Chapin's choir in N.Y. (1870–72) at a salary of $1,500 a year. In March 1872 she went to Europe, where she took voice lessons with Sangiovanni in Milan and with Marchesi, Wartel, and Delle Sedie in Paris. She made her professional debut as an opera singer in London on May 2, 1876, in the role of Maria in Donizetti's *La Fille du régiment;*

returning to America, she sang the same role in N.Y. on Feb. 8, 1877. She was in many ways an American primitive, traveling with her own small opera company across the country; at her performances she was prone to interpolate her "specialties" in the opera scores, such as singing the hymn *Nearer My God to Thee* in *Faust*.

BIBL.: S.E. Martin, *The Life and Professional Career of E. A.* (Minneapolis, 1891).

Abe, Kōmei, Japanese composer; b. Hiroshima, Sept. 1, 1911. He studied cello at the Tokyo Academy of Music, graduating in 1933, and took postgraduate composition courses there with Klaus Pringsheim (1933–36) and conducting with Joseph Rosenstock (1935–39). He then became a prof. at the Elizabeth Music College at Kyoto; he was from 1969 to 1974 a prof. at Kyoto Municipal Univ. of Arts.

WORKS: *Theme and Variations* for Orch. (Tokyo, Feb. 8, 1936); *Kleine Suite* for Orch. (Tokyo, Feb. 27, 1937); Cello Concerto (Tokyo, March 31, 1942); Piano Concerto (1945; Tokyo, March 27, 1947); 2 syms.: No. 1 (Tokyo, May 9, 1957) and No. 2 (Tokyo, Oct. 10, 1960); *Serenade* for Orch. (Tokyo, Oct. 7, 1963); Sinfonietta (Tokyo, Jan. 14, 1965); 11 string quartets (1935, 1937, 1939, 1943, 1946, 1948, 1950, 1952, 1955, 1978, 1982); 2 flute sonatas (1942, 1949); Clarinet Quintet (1942); *Divertimento* for Saxophone and Piano (1951; orchestrated 1953); *Divertimento* for 9 Instruments (1954); Sextet for Flute, Clarinet, Violin, Viola, Cello, and Piano (1964); *A Picture Book for Children* for Piano (1967); Piano Sonatina (1970); 3 piano sonatinas for children (1971); *Variation on a Subject by Grieg* for 4 Trumpets, 4 Horns, 3 Trombones, and Tuba (1972); choral music; songs; film music.

Abeille, Johann Christian Ludwig, German organist and composer; b. Bayreuth, Feb. 20, 1761; d. Stuttgart, March 2, 1838. He was educated at Stuttgart; in 1782 he joined the private orch. of the Duke of Württemberg; in 1802 he became Konzertmeister, serving in this capacity until 1832. He publ. several albums of songs that found their way into vocal anthologies; wrote 2 light operas, *Amor und Psyche* (1800) and *Peter und Ännchen* (1809); and composed harpsichord pieces and concerted music for small groups.

Abejo, Rosalina, Filipino pianist and composer; b. Tagoloan, Oriental Misamis, July 13, 1922. She studied at the Philippine Women's Univ., receiving her M.M. in 1957; then went to Cincinnati, where she studied composition with Felix Labunski; she later took courses with Wayne Barlow at the Eastman School of Music in Rochester, N.Y. She joined the Order of the Virgin Mary, and was the 1st nun to conduct a sym. orch. An exceptionally prolific composer, she wrote a number of sacred works, among them *Thanatopsis* for Orch. (1956) and *The Trilogy of Man* for Orch. (1971), and also several secular works on political themes, including a symphonic poem entitled *Guerrilla*, dedicated to President Marcos of the Philippines (1971). Other works include a Guitar Concerto, a Marimba Concerto, divers chamber music pieces, piano compositions, and song cycles. She also publ. several teaching manuals.

Abel, Carl Friedrich, German viola da gamba player and composer; b. Cöthen, Dec. 22, 1723; d. London, June 20, 1787. He studied with his father, a player on the gamba; then moved to Leipzig, where he enrolled in the Thomasschule; he then lived for many years in Dresden, where he joined the Court Orch. (1743–58). In 1759 he went to London, making it his permanent home; in 1764 he became court musician to Queen Charlotte, a position he held until his death. He also became associated with Bach's son, the "London Bach," John (Johann) Christian, and with him organized a series of concerts, which gained renown as the Bach-Abel Concerts (1765–81). Abel composed a number of instrumental works, among them 23 syms., a *Sinfonia concertante*, several piano concertos, string quartets, trio sonatas, piano sonatas, violin sonatas, and pieces for the viola da gamba. In his style of composition he followed the Mannheim School, emphasizing symmetric instrumental forms and diversified dynamics. His Sym. in E-flat major was

erroneously ascribed to Mozart and even listed as K. 18; A51, which testifies, however obliquely, to the intrinsic worth of his music. Abel was the last great virtuoso on the viola da gamba of the Classical period, until the revival of original instruments in the 20th century by Dolmetsch and others. Abel's compositions have been publ. in a collected ed. by W. Knape, *K.F. Abel: Kompositionen* (Cuxhaven, 1958–74); Knape also prepared a *Bibliographisch-thematisches Verzeichnis der Kompositionen von Karl Friedrich Abel* (Cuxhaven, 1971).

BIBL.: S. Helm, *C.F. A., Symphonist: A Biographical, Stylistic and Bibliographical Study* (diss., Univ. of Michigan, 1953); P. Young, "Johann Christian, der englische Bach," in H. Wegener, ed., *Musa—Mens—Musici: Im Gedenken an Walther Vetter* (Leipzig, 1969); G. Beechey, "C.F. A.'s Six Symphonies, op. 14," *Music & Letters* (July 1970); M. Charters, "A. in London," *Musical Times,* CXIV (1973); W. Knape, *K.F. A.: Leben und Werk eines frühklassischen Komponisten* (Bremen, 1973); M. Charters, *The Bach-A. Concerts* (diss., Univ. of London, 1978).

Abell, Arthur M., American music critic; b. Norwich, Conn., April 6, 1868; d. Hastings-on-Hudson, N.Y., Feb. 8, 1958. He studied in Weimar with Carl Halir (violin), Wilhelm Saal (piano), and Fritz Hartmann (theory); he remained in Europe for 28 years (1890–1918) as a correspondent for the *Musical Courier* and other publications. He knew Brahms, and was a friend of Richard Strauss, Max Bruch, Joseph Joachim, and other celebrated musicians. Upon his return to the U.S., he lived in retirement in Hastings-on-Hudson. In 1955 he publ. a book of memoirs, *Talks with Great Composers.*

Abell, John, celebrated Scottish lute player; b. Aberdeenshire, 1652; d. Cambridge, 1724. He was a chorister in the Chapel Royal in London; in 1679 he received a stipend from Charles II that enabled him to study in Italy. He returned to London in 1681; suspected of Roman Catholic adherence, he was compelled to seek employment on the Continent. He served as Intendant of music at Kassel (1698–99), and was back in London shortly afterward, able to resume his career (he was described in a contemporary report as "a harmonious vagabond"). He gave his last London concert in 1716. He publ. *A Collection of Songs in Several Languages, A Collection of Songs in English, A Choice Collection of Italian Ayres.*

BIBL.: H.G. Farmer, "J. A.," in *Hinrichsen's Musical Year Book,* VII (1952).

Abendroth, Hermann, notable German conductor; b. Frankfurt am Main, Jan. 19, 1883; d. Jena, May 29, 1956. He studied music in Munich with Thuille and Mottl (1900–1905); in 1907 he was named chief conductor of the Städtische Oper in Lübeck; in 1911 he became music director in Essen; in 1915 he assumed the post of director of the Cologne Cons. and conductor of the Gürzenich Orch.; in 1918 he became Generalmusikdirektor in Cologne; he also appeared as a sym. conductor in a number of cities in Germany. Arriving at a tenuous modus vivendi with the Nazi regime, he was appointed Kapellmeister of the Gewandhaus Orch. of Leipzig in 1934; he also served as director of the Leipzig Cons.; in 1945 he became music director of the National Theater in Weimar and its Generalmusikdirektor in 1946. Abendroth was regarded as a model interpreter of German music and a faithful keeper of its traditions.

Abendroth, Walter, German musicologist; b. Hannover, May 29, 1896; d. Hausham, Sept. 30, 1973. He studied music in Berlin and was active mainly in Hamburg. He publ. monographs on Pfitzner (Munich, 1935), Brahms (Berlin, 1939), and Bruckner (Berlin, 1940); he also put out *Kleine Geschichte der Musik* (Frankfurt, 1959). He also publ. an amusing pamphlet, *Ich warne Neugierige* (I Warn the Curious; Munich, 1966). Like so many earnest writers on music, he composed a number of uninteresting, unperformed, and unlamented instrumental pieces.

Aber, Adolf, German musicologist; b. Apolda, Jan. 28, 1893; d. London, May 21, 1960. He studied with Kretzschmar, Stumpf, Wolf, and Friedlaender. From 1919 to 1933 he served as chief music critic for the *Leipziger Neueste Nachrichten;* he then left Germany and settled in London, where he became an editorial adviser with the Novello publishing firm.

WRITINGS: *Handbuch der Musikliteratur* (1922); *Die Musikinstrumente und ihre Sprache* (1924); *Die Musik im Schauspiel, Geschichtliches und Ästhetisches* (1926); *Verzeichnis der Werke von Brahms* (1928).

Abert, Anna Amalie, distinguished German musicologist, daughter of **Hermann Abert;** b. Halle, Sept. 19, 1906. She studied musicology with her father, with Blume, and with Sachs at the Univ. of Berlin (Ph.D., 1934, with the diss. *Die stilistischen Voraussetzungen der "Cantiones sacrae" von Heinrich Schütz*); she then joined the staff of the Univ. of Kiel. She completed her Habilitation there in 1943 with *Claudio Monteverdi und das musikalische Drama* (publ. in Lippstadt, 1954); in 1950 she became a prof. there, and also a research fellow in 1962; she retired in 1971. From 1949 to 1958 she was an ed. of *Die Musik in Geschichte und Gegenwart.* She contributed important articles to the *Mozart-Jahrbuch;* her writings include *Christoph Willibald Gluck* (Munich, 1959); *Die Opern Mozarts* (Wolfenbüttel, 1970; in Eng. in *The New Oxford History of Music,* vol. VII, London, 1973); *Richard Strauss: Die Opern* (Velber, 1972).

BIBL.: K. Hortschansky, ed., *Opernstudien: A.A. A. zum 65. Geburtstag* (Tutzing, 1975).

Abert, Hermann, eminent German musicologist, son of **Johann Joseph Abert** and father of **Anna Amalie Abert;** b. Stuttgart, March 25, 1871; d. there, Aug. 13, 1927. He studied with his father; then with Bellermann, Fleischer, and Friedlaender in Berlin; he received his Ph.D. from the Univ. of Berlin in 1897 with the dissertation *Die Lehre vom Ethos in der griechischen Musik* (publ. in Leipzig, 1899); completed his Habilitation in 1902 at the Univ. of Halle with *Die ästhetischen Grundsätze der mittelalterlichen Melodiebildung* (publ. in Halle, 1902); was named honorary prof. there in 1909 and lecturer in 1911. In 1920 he became prof. at the Univ. of Leipzig (succeeding Hugo Riemann) and in 1923, at the Univ. of Berlin (succeeding August Kretzschmar). He was one of the outstanding scholars of his time, noted for his wide-ranging musicological interests. Among his important writings, his exhaustively rewritten and revised ed. of Jahn's biography of Mozart is still valuable; it was publ. as *Wolfgang Amadeus Mozart: Neu bearbeitete und erweiterte Ausgabe von Otto Jahns "Mozart"* (2 vols., Leipzig, 1919–21; it was further rev. by his daughter and publ. in 1955–56). Other books include *Robert Schumann* (Berlin, 1903; 4th ed., 1920); *Die Musikanschauung des Mittelalters und ihre Grundlagen* (Halle, 1905); *Niccolo Jommelli als Opernkomponist* (Halle, 1908); *Goethe und die Musik* (Engelhorn, 1922); he also wrote a biography of his father (Leipzig, 1916). His collected writings were posthumously ed. by F. Blume as *Gesammelte Schriften und Vorträge* (Halle, 1929).

BIBL.: F. Blume, ed., *Gedenkschrift für H. A. von seinen Schülern* (Halle, 1928); H. Brockhaus, *H. A.s Konzeption der musikalischen Historiographie* (Habilitationsschrift, Humboldt Univ. of Berlin, 1966); A. Abert, "H. A.s Weg zur Musikwissenschaft," in *Musa—Mens—Musici: Im Gedenken an Walther Vetter* (Leipzig, 1969).

Abert, Johann Joseph, German composer, father of **Hermann Abert;** b. Kochowitz, Sept. 20, 1832; d. Stuttgart, April 1, 1915. He studied double bass and composition at the Prague Cons. (1846–53), then played the double bass in the Court Orch. at Stuttgart; in 1867 he became its conductor, and held this post until 1888. Abert's style, greatly influenced by Mendelssohn and Schumann, represents the German Romantic tradition at its most typical among worthy epigones. His composing technique was flawless, however. His son wrote a detailed biography: *J.J. A., 1832–1915: Sein Leben und seine Werke* (Leipzig, 1916).

WORKS: OPERAS: *Anna von Landskron* (1858); *König Enzio* (1862); *Astorga,* based on the life of the composer Emanuele d'Astorga (Stuttgart, May 27, 1866; quite successful at the time); *Ekkehard* (Berlin, Oct. 11, 1878). He also wrote *Columbus,* a "musical sea picture" in the form of a sym. (Stuttgart, Jan. 26, 1864), 6 syms., several overtures, chamber music, and pieces for double bass.

Abos, Girolamo (baptismal name, **Geronimo**), Maltese composer; b. La Valetta, Nov. 16, 1715; d. Naples, Oct. 1760. He was a student of Francesco Durante and Gerolimo Ferraro in Naples; served as secondo maestro at the Cons. Poveri di Gesù Cristo (1742–43); and was also secondo maestro at the Cons. della Pietà dei Turchini (1754–59). Among his pupils was Paisiello. Abos wrote 14 operas which were produced in Naples and Rome; of these, *Tito Manlio* (Naples, May 30, 1751) was successful. He also wrote 7 masses and other church music.

Abraham, Gerald, able English writer on musical subjects; b. Newport, Isle of Wight, March 9, 1904; d. Midhurst, March 18, 1988. A man of many and varied interests, he studied philology and mastered the complications of the Russian language. He publ. several books of some lasting value dealing with Russian music as well as studies on Schubert, Sibelius, Schumann, and Handel, and a readable book of essays under the fanciful title *This Modern Stuff* (1933), later issued under the more specific heading *This Modern Music* (1952). He further contributed vols. of a more embracing character, among them *Slavonic and Romantic Music* (1968), *The Tradition of Western Music* (1974), and *The New Oxford History of Music* (vol. III, 1960; vol. IV, 1968; vol. VIII, 1982; vol. IX, 1990).

Abraham, Max, German music publisher; b. Danzig, June 3, 1831; d. Leipzig, Dec. 8, 1900. He became a partner in C.F. Peters's "Bureau de Musique" in 1863, and sole proprietor in 1880. On Jan. 1, 1894, his nephew, Heinrich Hinrichsen, of Hamburg, entered the firm; upon Abraham's death, he became its head. The famous "Edition Peters" was inaugurated by Abraham.

Abraham, Otto, German specialist in tone psychology; b. Berlin, May 30, 1872; d. there, Jan. 24, 1926. He studied medicine, and served as an assistant to Stumpf at the Berlin Psychological Inst.; he also collaborated with Hornbostel in building up the Archive of Phonographic Recordings in Berlin. He publ. several valuable treatises on acoustics and primitive music, among them *Wahrnehmung kürzester Töne und Geräusche* (1898); "Studien über das Tonsystem und die Musik der Japaner," publ. in *Sammelbände der internationalen Musikgesellschaft* (1902–3); "Phonographierte Indianermelodien aus British Columbia," in the *Festschrift* for Franz Boas (N.Y., 1906). He also wrote studies on recorded Turkish, Siamese, and Hindu melodies, and a paper on Chinese musical notation.

Ábrahám, Paul, Hungarian composer of light operas; b. Apatin, Nov. 2, 1892; d. Hamburg, May 6, 1960. He studied in Budapest and wrote chamber music before turning to light opera. His most successful operetta was *Viktoria und ihr Husar* (Vienna, Dec. 23, 1930); his other popular productions were *Die Blume von Hawaii* (Leipzig, July 24, 1931) and *Ball im Savoy* (Berlin, Dec. 23, 1932). In 1938 Abraham went to the U.S., but suffered a mental breakdown and in 1955 was committed to a sanatorium in Hamburg, where he died.

BIBL.: G. Sebestyén, *P. A.: Aus dem Leben eines Operettenkomponisten* (Vienna, 1987).

Abrahamsen, Hans, Danish composer; b. Copenhagen, Dec. 23, 1952. He studied horn, theory, and music history at the Royal Danish Cons. (1969–71), then studied composition at the Jutland Academy of Music in Århus with Gudmundsen-Holmgreen and Nørgård. His music presents an effective blend of folkloric Scandinavian elements and modernistic devices often veering off into atonal melos, viralized by polyrhythmic dynamic contrasts.

WORKS: ORCH.: *Skum* (Foam; 1970); Sym. in C (1972); 2 syms.: No. 1 (1974) and No. 2 (1982); *Stratifications* (1973–75); *Nacht und Trompeten* (1981; Berlin, March 25, 1982);

Märchenbilder for 14 Players (1984; London, Feb. 7, 1985); Cello Concerto (1987). **CHAMBER:** *Fantasy Pieces after Hans-Jørgen Nielsen* for Flute, Horn, Cello, and Piano (1969; rev. 1976); *October* for Piano left hand (1969; rev. 1976); *Herbst* for Tenor, Flute, Guitar, and Cello (1970–72; rev. 1977); *Round and In Between* for Brass Quintet (1972); 2 woodwind quintets: No. 1, *Landscapes* (1972); No. 2, *Walden* (1978); *Nocturnes*, 4 pieces for Flute and Piano (1972); *Flowersongs* for 3 Flutes (1973); *Scraps* for Cello and Piano (1973); 2 string quartets: No. 1, *10 Preludes* (1973); No. 2 (1981); *Flush* for Solo Saxophone (1974; rev. 1979); *Songs of Denmark* for Soprano and 5 Instruments (1974; rev. 1976); *Double* for Flute and Guitar (1975); *Winternacht* for 7 Instruments (1976–79); *Canzone* for Solo Accordion (1978); *Aria* for Soprano and 4 Instruments (1979); *Geduldspiel* for 10 Instruments (1980); *6 Pieces* for Violin, Horn, and Piano (1984); *10 Studies* for Piano (1983–87). **VOCAL:** *Universe Birds* for 10 Sopranos (1973).

Abramsky, Alexander, Russian composer; b. Lutsk, Jan. 22, 1898; d. Moscow, Aug. 29, 1985. He studied at the Moscow Cons., graduating in 1926, then was commissioned to do research in the Asian Soviet republics and produced an opera based on the native themes of Uzbekistan. He also wrote choral music of indefinite characteristics.

Ábrányi, Cornelius, Hungarian pianist, composer, and writer on music, grandfather of **Emil Ábrányi;** b. Szentgyörgy-Ábrányi, Oct. 15, 1822; d. Budapest, Dec. 20, 1903. He came of an ancient Magyar family whose name was orig. **Eördögh.** He was 1st destined to a legal profession, but in 1834 a meeting with the Hungarian national composer Erkel made him decide to study music. In 1843 Ábrányi went abroad; in Munich he met Liszt, and became his lifelong friend. He went to Paris and took lessons with Chopin and Kalkbrenner for a short time, returning to Hungary in 1845. He took a leading part in the formation and encouragement of the Hungarian national school of composition. His own compositions (130 opus numbers) emphasize the Hungarian national elements, the most ambitious of these works being his *Hungarian Millennial Sonata*, op. 103. His books (all in Hungarian) include: *Art and Revolution* (1867); *Biography of Franz Liszt and Survey of His Oratorio Christus* (1873); *General History of Music* (1886); *History of Hungarian Music in the Nineteenth Century* (1900). He also wrote an autobiography, *From My Life and Memories* (1897).

Ábrányi, Emil, Hungarian composer and conductor; b. Budapest, Sept. 22, 1882; d. there, Feb. 11, 1970. His father was Emil Ábrányi, the poet, and his grandfather was **Cornelius Ábrányi,** the composer and pianist. In 1902 Emil Ábrányi went to Germany, where he had instruction in conducting in Leipzig with Nikisch. He subsequently held posts as conductor at the Municipal Theater in Cologne (1904) and at Hannover (1907). Returning to Budapest in 1911, he became conductor at the Royal Opera House; he was also director of the Budapest Municipal Theater (1921–26). As a composer, Ábrányi was a convinced Wagnerian, building his operas on a series of leading themes.
WORKS: OPERAS: *Monna Vanna* (Budapest, March 2, 1907); *Paolo e Francesca* (Budapest, Jan. 13, 1912); *Don Quixote* (Budapest, Nov. 30, 1917); *Singing Dervishes* (1935); *The Prince with the Lilies* (1938); *Byzantium* (1945); and *The Cantor of St. Thomas Church* (1947; the 1st opera written on the life of Bach).

Abravanel, Maurice, distinguished Greek-born American conductor; b. Saloniki (of Spanish-Portuguese parents; an ancestor is reputed to have been chancellor to Ferdinand and Isabella of Spain), Jan. 6, 1903. He was taken to Switzerland at the age of 6, and studied general subjects at the Univ. of Lausanne; in 1922 he went to Berlin, where he took composition lessons with Kurt Weill; with the advent of the Nazi regime in 1933, Abravanel moved to Paris, where he conducted ballet; in 1934–35 he toured Australia; in 1936 he received an offer to join the staff of the Metropolitan Opera in N.Y.; he made

his debut there on Dec. 26, 1936, conducting *Samson et Dalila;* generally adverse reviews compelled him to leave the Metropolitan in 1938. He turned to leading Broadway musicals, and conducted a season with the Chicago Opera Co. (1940–41). In 1947 he became conductor of the Utah Sym. Orch. at Salt Lake City, and revealed a great talent for building up the orch.; in the 32 years of his conductorship it became one of the finest sym. orchs. in the U.S.; he also introduced many modern works into its repertoire. In 1976 he underwent open-heart surgery; in 1979 he retired as music director of the Utah Sym. Orch.

Abreu (Rebello), Sergio (b. Rio de Janeiro, June 5, 1948) and **Eduardo** (b. Rio de Janeiro, Sept. 19, 1949), sibling Brazilian guitarists. They 1st studied with their grandfather, Antonio Rebello, and then with Adolfina Raitzin Távora; they began their career in 1963 with concerts throughout South America; they made their European debut in London in 1968, and their U.S. debut in N.Y. in 1970; they later toured extensively all over the world.

Absil, Jean, eminent Belgian composer; b. Bonsecours, Oct. 23, 1893; d. Brussels, Feb. 2, 1974. He studied organ and composition at the Brussels Cons., and later took lessons in advanced composition with Gilson. He won the Prix Agniez for his 1st Sym. (1921); in 1922 he won a 2nd Prix de Rome for the cantata *La Guerre;* he also received the Prix Rubens in 1934. His 1st Piano Concerto was commissioned by the 1938 Concours Ysaÿe in Brussels as the compulsory work for the 12 finalists in the contest eventually won by Emil Gilels. He was music director of the Academy of Etterbeek in Brussels (1922–64); taught at the Brussels Cons. (1930–59); and was one of the founders of the *Revue Internationale de Musique.* Absil evolved an individual style, characterized by rhythmic variety, free tonality, and compact counterpoint.
WORKS: STAGE: *Peau d'âne,* lyrical poem in 3 acts (1937); *Ulysse et les sirènes,* radio play (1939); *Fansou ou Le Chapeau chinois,* musical comedy (1944); *Le Miracle de Pan,* ballet (1949); *Pierre Breughel l'Ancien,* radio play (1950); *Épouvantail,* ballet (1950); *Les Voix de la mer,* opera (1951; Brussels, March 26, 1954); *Les Météores,* ballet (1951). **ORCH.:** 5 syms. (1920, 1936, 1943, 1969, 1970); *La Mort de Tintagiles,* symphonic poem (1923–26); *Rapsodie flamande* (1928; also for Wind Ensemble); *Berceuse* for Small Orch., and Cello or Saxophone (1932); 2 violin concertos (1933, 1964); *Petite suite* for Small Orch. (1935; also for Wind Ensemble); 3 piano concertos (1937, 1967, 1973); *Rapsodie No. 2* (1938); *Hommage à Lekeu* (1939); Cello Concertino (1940); *Sérénade* (1940); *Variations symphoniques* (1942); Viola Concerto (1942); *Rapsodie roumaine* for Violin and Orch. (1943); *Concerto grosso* for Wind Quintet and Orch. (1944); *Jeanne d'Arc,* symphonic poem (1945); *Rites,* triptych for Wind Ensemble (1952); *Rapsodie brésilienne* (1953); *Mythologie,* suite (1954); *Croquis sportifs* for Wind Ensemble (1954); *Divertimento* for Saxophone Quartet and Chamber Orch. (1955); *Introduction et Valses* (1955); *Legend* for Wind Ensemble (1956); *Suite,* after Rumanian folklore (1956); *Suite bucolique* for Strings (1957); *Fantaisie concertante* for Violin, and Orch. or Piano (1959); *Danses bulgares* (1959; also for Wind Quintet or Piano); *Rapsodie bulgare* (1960); 2 *Danses rituelles* for Small Orch. (1960); *Triptyque* for Small Orch. (1960); *Fantaisie-humoresque* for Clarinet, and Strings or Piano (1962); *Rapsodie No. 6* for Horn, and Orch. or Piano (1963); Viola Concertino (1964); *Nymphes et faunes* for Wind Orch. (1966); *Allegro brillante* for Piano and Orch. (1967); *Fantaisie-caprice* for Saxophone and Strings (1971); Guitar Concerto (1971); *Ballade* for Saxophone, Piano, and Small Orch. (1971); *Déités,* suite (1973). **VOCAL:** *La Guerre,* cantata (1922); *Philatélie,* chamber cantata (1940); *Les Bénédictions,* cantata (1941); *Les Chants du mort,* cantata for Vocal Quartet and Small Orch., to texts from old Rumanian ritual chants lamenting the death of a person (1941); *Le Zodiaque,* symphonic variations with Chorus and Piano Concertante (1949); *Phantasmes* for Contralto, Saxophone, Piano, and Percussion (1950); *Le Cirque volant,* cantata (1953); *Petites poly-*

phonies for 2 Voices and Orch. (1966); *À cloche-pied* for Children's Chorus and Orch. (1968). **CHAMBER:** 4 string quartets (1929, 1934, 1935, 1941); 2 piano trios (1931, 1972); 2 string trios (1935, 1939); *Fantaisie rapsodique* for 4 Cellos (1936); Cello Quartet (1937); Quartet for Saxophones (1937); Piano Quartet (1938); *Fantaisie* for Piano Quartet (1939); *Concert à cinq* for Flute, Violin, Viola, Cello, and Harp (1939); 2 suites for Cello and Piano (1942, 1968); *Chaconne* for Solo Violin (1949); 3 *Contes* for Trumpet and Piano (1951); Suite for Trombone and Piano (1952); *Sonatine en duo* for Violin and Viola (1962); Saxophone Sonata (1963); 3 *Pièces* for Organ (1965); Quartet for Clarinets (1967); Solo Violin Sonata (1967); *Croquis pour un carnaval* for 4 Clarinets and Harp (1968); *Suite mystique* for 4 Flutes (1969); Violin Sonata (1970); *Esquisses* for Wind Quartet (1971); *Images stellaires* for Violin and Cello (1973). **PIANO:** 3 *Impromptus* (1932); 3 sonatinas (1937, 1939, 1965); 3 *Marines* (1939); Bagatelles (1944); 2 *Grand Suites* (1944, 1962); *Sketches on the 7 Capital Sins* (1954); Variations (1956); *Chess Game*, suite (1957); *Passacaglia* (1959); *Rapsodie No. 5* for 2 Pianos (1959); *Humoresques* (1965); Ballade (1966); *Asymétries* for 2 Pianos (1968); *Alternances* (1968); *Féeries* (1971); *Poésie et vélocité,* 20 pieces (1972); also numerous pieces for guitar, a cappella choral works, songs.
BIBL.: J. Dopp, "J. A.," *La Revue Musicale* (Oct./Dec. 1937); R. de Guide, *J. A.* (Tournai, 1965).

Abt, Franz (Wilhelm), German songwriter and conductor; b. Eilenburg, Dec. 22, 1819; d. Wiesbaden, March 31, 1885. His father, a clergyman, sent him to the Leipzig Thomasschule to study theology; he later obtained an excellent musical education both there and at the univ. He became a choral conductor in Zürich (1841). In 1852 he was appointed 2nd conductor at the Braunschweig Court; in 1855 he became 1st conductor. In 1869 he traveled, as a choral conductor, to Paris, London, and Russia; in 1872 he made a highly successful tour in America. He retired on a pension from Braunschweig in 1882. Abt wrote over 600 works, comprising more than 3,000 numbers; the largest are the 7 secular cantatas. His popularity as a songwriter is due chiefly to the flowing, easy, and elegant style of his vocal melodies, some of which (*Wenn die Schwalben heimwärts zieh'n; Gute Nacht, du mein herziges Kind; So viele Tausend Blumen;* etc.) have become so well known as to be mistaken for genuine folk songs.
BIBL.: B. Rost, *Vom Meister des volkstümlichen deutschen Liedes, F. A.* (Chemnitz, 1924).

Accardo, Salvatore, outstanding Italian violinist; b. Turin, Sept. 26, 1941. He studied with Luigi d'Ambrosio at the Conservatorio S. Pietro a Majella in Naples and with Yvonne Astruc at the Accademia Musicale Chigiana in Siena. He won the Vercelli (1955), Geneva (1956), and Paganini (Genoa, 1958) competitions, then pursued a remarkable career, appearing both as soloist with major orchs. of the world and as recitalist. He was also active in later years as a conductor. He publ. *L'arte del violino* (ed. by M. Delogu; Milan, 1987). As a violin virtuoso, he excels in a vast repertoire; in addition to the standard literature, he performs many rarely heard works, including those by Paganini. His playing is marked by a fidelity to the classical school of violin playing, in which virtuosity is subordinated to stylistic propriety.
BIBL.: B. Schwarz, *Great Masters of the Violin* (N.Y., 1983).

Achron, Isidor, Russian-American pianist, brother of **Joseph Achron;** b. Warsaw, Nov. 24, 1892; d. N.Y., May 12, 1948. He studied at the St. Petersburg Cons. with Anna Essipoff (piano) and Liadov (composition). In 1922 he settled in the U.S.; he was naturalized in 1928. From 1922 to 1933 he was accompanist to Jascha Heifetz and was active as a piano teacher in N.Y. He was also a composer; he played his Piano Concerto with the N.Y. Phil. on Dec. 9, 1937; his *Suite Grotesque* for Orch. was 1st performed in St. Louis, Jan. 30, 1942. He also wrote a number of piano pieces, all in a moderate Romantic manner in the prevalent tradition of the time.

Achron, Joseph, Russian-born American violinist and composer, brother of **Isidor Achron;** b. Losdseje, near Suwalki, Poland, May 13, 1886; d. Los Angeles, April 29, 1943. In 1890 the family moved to Warsaw. He studied violin there, and gave his 1st public concert at the age of 7. In 1898 he entered the St. Petersburg Cons. as a student of Leopold Auer in violin and Liadov in music theory. Graduating in 1904, he went to Berlin, where he appeared as a soloist with orchs. In 1907 he returned to St. Petersburg to continue his studies in theory and orchestration at the Cons. there. In 1911 he organized, along with several Jewish musicians, a society for Jewish folklore. One of the products of his research was the popular *Hebrew Melody* for Violin and Piano (1911), based on a Hasidic theme. During World War I he was a member of the music corps of the Russian army. From 1919 to 1921 he was active as composer for the Hebrew Chamber Theater in Petrograd; in 1922 he went again to Berlin; in 1924 he was in Palestine, and in 1925 emigrated to the U.S.; he became a naturalized American citizen in 1930. He lived in N.Y. until 1934, then went to Hollywood, where he earned his living as a violinist in film studios, and continued to compose energetically. His early compositions are marked by characteristic Russian harmonies with a distinctly Romantic aura, but under the impact of modern techniques he developed a strong idiom based on purely structural principles employing atonal and polytonal devices. Schoenberg wrote about him in the program book of a memorial concert of Achron's compositions given in Los Angeles in 1945: "Joseph Achron is one of the most underestimated of modern composers, but the originality and profound elaboration of his ideas guarantee that his works will last." Achron's major compositions include a suite for Chamber Orch., *Golem* (1932), the last section of which is the exact retrograde movement of the 1st section, to symbolize the undoing of the monster Golem; 3 violin concertos in which he appeared as soloist: No. 1 (Boston, Jan. 24, 1927); No. 2 (Los Angeles, Dec. 19, 1936); No. 3 (Los Angeles, March 31, 1939); *4 tableaux fantastiques* for Violin and Piano (1907); *Chromatic String Quartet* (1907); 2 violin sonatas (1910, 1918); *Hazan* for Cello and Orch. (1912); 2 *Hebrew Pieces* for Violin and Piano (1912); *Suite bizarre* for Violin and Piano (1916); *Scher* for Violin and Piano (1916); *Elegy* for String Quartet (1927); *Statuettes* for Piano (1929); *Sextet* for Flute, Oboe, Clarinet, Bassoon, Horn, and Trumpet (1938); Piano Concerto (1941); *Evening Service for the Sabbath* (1930); songs and choruses.
BIBL.: P. Moddel, *J. A.* (Tel Aviv, 1966).

Achucarro, Joaquín, Spanish pianist; b. Bilbao, Nov. 1, 1936. He began to play the piano as a child; he made his public debut in Bilbao at the age of 12. At 17 he won 1st prize in the Viotti Competition in Vercelli, Italy; he subsequently continued his studies with Gieseking, Magaloff, Seidlhofer, and Kabós. In 1959 he won 1st prize in the Liverpool International Pianoforte Competition, which marked the beginning of a successful career as a concert pianist.

Acker, Dieter, German composer and pedagogue; b. Sibiu, Rumania (of German parents), Nov. 3, 1940. He studied piano, organ, and theory with Franz Dressler in Sibiu (1950–58), then composition with Sigismund Toduţă at the Cluj Cons. (1959–64), where he subsequently served on the faculty (1964–69). He then settled in West Germany and taught at the Robert Schumann Cons. in Düsseldorf (1969–72); he later joined the faculty at the Munich Hochschule für Musik.
WORKS: 3 string trios (1963, 1983, 1987); 4 string quartets (1964; 1965–66; *Cantus lugubris,* 1966–68; 1971–75); *Texturae* for Orch. (1970); *Quodlibet II* for Chamber Orch. (1975); 2 syms.: No. 1, *Lebensläufe* (1977–78); No. 2, *Sinfonia concertante* (1982); Bassoon Concerto (1979–80); Violin Concerto (1981); Concerto for String Orch. (1984); Piano Concerto (1984); *Kammerspiel* for 12 Solo Instruments (1985); *Musik for Strings and Harp* (1987); Clarinet Quintet (1973); Piano Trio No. 2 (1984); Sonata for Viola and Piano (1985); 2 piano quartets (1986); Trio for Flute, Viola, and Harp (1987); Trio for 2 Flutes and Piano (1988); several piano pieces, including

Hölderlin Sonata (1978); organ pieces, including *Myriaden I* (1971) and *II* (1972); choral works; songs.

Ackerman, William, phenomenally successful American composer, guitarist, and entrepreneur; b. in Germany, Nov. 16, 1949. He was orphaned, and was subsequently adopted at the age of 9 by a Stanford Univ. (Palo Alto, Calif.) prof.; he soon began playing guitar, eventually mastering folk, classical, and rock styles. He studied at Stanford Univ., dropping out just before graduation to become a carpenter; as an avocation, he composed guitar pieces for theater productions. He eventually invested $300 to make a record, initiating a business that grew in 13 years to become the $3,000,000 Windham Hill Records Corp. He is the most important businessman and also one of the best composers in the "New Age" style, which was created and popularized by his record company; it has been termed "neo-impressionism," and generally involves folk and modal elements performed by guitar, piano, or electronics. His company also produces recordings of jazz and folk music and children's stories, in addition to videos. Among his most popular recordings are *Passage* (1981), *Past Light* (1983), *Conferring with the Moon* (1986), and *Imaginary Roads* (1988).

Ackermann, Otto, Rumanian conductor; b. Bucharest, Oct. 18, 1909; d. Wabern, near Bern, March 9, 1960. He was educated at the Royal Academy of Music in Bucharest and at the Hochschule für Musik in Berlin, then held numerous posts as an opera conductor at Düsseldorf (1927–32), Brno (1932–35), Bern (1935–46), Zürich (1948–53), Cologne (1953–58), and again Zürich (1958–60). He was noted for his authoritative interpretations of the operatic repertoire, but was also successful as an operetta conductor.

Ackté (real name, **Achté**), **Aïno,** Finnish soprano; b. Helsinki, April 23, 1876; d. Nummela, Aug. 8, 1944. She studied at the Paris Cons. and made her debut at the Paris Opéra as Marguerite (Oct. 8, 1897). She sang the same role at her 1st appearance in the U.S. at the Metropolitan Opera in N.Y. (Feb. 20, 1904). Her performance of Salomé in Strauss's opera at Covent Garden (Dec. 8, 1910) led to an invitation from Richard Strauss to sing the part in Dresden and Paris. Her other roles were Juliette, Ophélie, Gilda, Nedda, Elsa, Elisabeth, and Sieglinde. Her memoirs are publ. in Finnish, Swedish, and German.

Acuff, Roy (Claxton), American country-music singer, guitarist, and songwriter; b. Maynardville, Tenn., Sept. 15, 1903. He learned to play the fiddle, and later appeared as a singer and guitarist with local musicians; in 1938 he and his Smoky Mountain Boys became featured artists on the "Grand Ole Opry" radio program in Nashville; he gained fame with his renditions of such songs as *The Great Speckled Bird, Wabash Cannonball,* and *Night Train to Memphis.* He also composed songs, including the very popular *Precious Jewel,* and was active as a music publisher (with Fred Rose). In 1962 he became the 1st living musician to be elected to the Country Music Hall of Fame. He publ. *Roy Acuff's Nashville: The Life and Good Times of Country Music* (with W. Neely; N.Y., 1983). In 1988 he celebrated his 50th anniversary as a regular member of the "Grand Ole Opry."
BIBL.: E. Schlappi, *R. A.: The Smoky Mountain Boy* (Gretna, La., 1978).

Adam, Adolphe (-Charles), celebrated French opera composer, son of **(Jean) Louis Adam**; b. Paris, July 24, 1803; d. there, May 3, 1856. He studied piano with his father, a professional pianist, and with Lemoine; then went to the Paris Cons., where he became a student of Benoist in organ playing, of Reicha in counterpoint, and of Boieldieu in composition. Boieldieu exercised the greatest influence on Adam's development as an opera composer; another powerful influence was that of Hérold. Adam devoted his entire career exclusively to the music of the theater; he obtained his 1st success with a short comic opera, *Le Châlet,* produced at the Opéra-Comique in Paris on Sept. 25, 1834, which held the stage for 1,400 performances through the years; a far greater success was the production of *Le Postillon de Longjumeau* at the Opéra-Comique on Oct. 13, 1836, an opera that achieved permanence in the operatic repertoire all over the world. There followed a long series of stage works; at times Adam produced 2 or more operas in a single season. In the process of inevitable triage, most of them went by the board, but a considerable number remained in the repertoire; among these was the comic opera *Si j'étais roi* (Paris, Sept. 4, 1852). Adam wrote 53 operas in all, an astonishing example of fecundity, since his entire life comprised not quite 53 years. Perhaps his most durable work was not an opera but a ballet, *Giselle* (Paris Opéra, June 28, 1841), a perennial in choreographic history which continues to be performed with no sign of decline in popularity. His song *Cantique de Noël* also became popular. Unfortunately, Adam was a poor businessman; in 1847 he ventured into the field of management with an operatic enterprise, the Opéra-National, which failed miserably and brought him to the brink of financial ruin. In 1849 he was appointed prof. at the Paris Cons.; he also traveled widely in Europe, visiting London, Berlin, and St. Petersburg. As one of the creators of French opera, Adam ranks with Auber and Boieldieu in the expressive power of his melodic material and a sense of dramatic development. Adam's memoirs were publ. posthumously in 2 vols., *Souvenirs d'un musicien* (1857) and *Derniers souvenirs d'un musicien* (1859).
WORKS: OPERAS (1st perf. in Paris, most of them at the Opéra-Comique): *Le Mal du pays, ou La Batelière de Brientz* (Dec. 28, 1827); *Pierre et Catherine* (Feb. 9, 1829); *Danilowa* (April 23, 1830); *Trois jours en une heure* (Aug. 21, 1830); *Le Morceau d'ensemble* (March 10, 1831); *Le Grand Prix* (July 9, 1831); *Casimir* (Dec. 1, 1831); *Le Proscrit* (Sept. 18, 1833); *Une Bonne Fortune* (Jan. 23, 1834); *Le Châlet* (Sept. 25, 1834); *La Marquise* (Feb. 28, 1835); *Micheline* (June 29, 1835); *Le Postillon de Longjumeau* (Oct. 13, 1836); *Le Fidèle Berger* (Jan. 6, 1838); *Régine* (Jan. 17, 1839); *La Reine d'un jour* (Sept. 19, 1839); *Le Brasseur de Preston* (Oct. 31, 1839); *La Rose de Péronne* (Dec. 12, 1840); *La Main de fer* (Oct. 26, 1841); *Le Roi d'Yvetôt* (Oct. 13, 1842); *Richard en Palestine* (Oct. 7, 1844, and on the same bill, *Cagliostro*); *La Bouquetière* (May 31, 1847); *Le Toréador* (May 18, 1849); *Giralda* (July 20, 1850); *La Poupée de Nuremberg* (Feb. 21, 1852); *Le Farfalet* (March 19, 1852); *Si j'étais roi* (Sept. 4, 1852; extremely successful); *Le Sourd* (Feb. 2, 1853); *Le Roi des Halles* (April 11, 1853); *Le Bijou perdu* (Oct. 6, 1853); *Le Muletier de Tolède* (Dec. 16, 1854); *À Clichy* (Dec. 24, 1854); *Le Houzard de Berchiny* (Oct. 17, 1855); *Falstaff* (Jan. 18, 1856); *Les Pantins de Violette* (April 29, 1856).
BIBL.: J. Halévy, *Notice sur la vie et les ouvrages d'A. A.* (Paris, 1859); A. Pougin, *A. A.* (Paris, 1877); P. Hering, "L.J.P. Hérold, A. A., E. Waldteufel," *La Musique en Alsace hier et aujourd'hui* (Paris, 1970).

Adam, Claus, American cellist and composer; b. on a kapok plantation in Central Sumatra, of Austrian parents, Nov. 5, 1917; d. N.Y., July 4, 1983. His father was an ethnologist; the family moved to Austria in 1923, and Adam received his early musical training at the Mozarteum in Salzburg. In 1929 they emigrated to the U.S., and settled in Brooklyn. Adam studied cello with E. Stoffnegen, D.C. Dounis, and Emanuel Feuermann; also took lessons in conducting with Leon Barzin. In 1940 he was engaged as a cellist with the Minneapolis Sym. Orch. He served in the U.S. Air Force; returning to N.Y., he studied composition with Stefan Wolpe. From 1948 to 1955 he was a founding member of the New Music Quartet; from 1955 to 1974 he was the cellist of the prestigious Juilliard String Quartet; in 1975 he held a Guggenheim Foundation grant, and was composer-in-residence at the American Academy in Rome in 1976. During all that time he was engaged in serious composition. His works are marked by pragmatic modernism free from doctrinaire adherence to any particular technique. He wrote mostly chamber music. His Concerto-Variations for Orch. were performed in N.Y. on April 5, 1977.

He suffered a stroke on June 8, 1983, and never recovered.

Ádám, Jenö, Hungarian conductor and educator; b. Sziget-szentmiklós, Dec. 12, 1896; d. Budapest, May 15, 1982. He studied composition in Budapest with Kodály (1921–25) and conducting in Basel with Felix Weingartner (1933–35); subsequently was associated with Kodály in reorganizing the system of musical education in Hungary. He was on the faculty of the Academy of Music in Budapest (1939–59).

WORKS: 2 operas: *Magyar Karácsony* (Hungarian Christmas; 1930; Budapest, Dec. 22, 1931) and *Mária Veronika* (1934–35; Budapest, Oct. 27, 1938); *Dominica Suite* for Orch. (1925; transcribed as *My Village*, 1963); *Lacrima Sonata* for Baritone and Orch. (1927); 2 string quartets (1924, 1930); Cello Sonata (1926); choral works; songs.

Adam, (Jean) Louis, Alsatian pianist, teacher, and composer, father of **Adolphe (-Charles) Adam;** b. Müttersholz, Dec. 3, 1758; d. Paris, April 8, 1848. He went to Paris in 1775; later was a prof. of piano at the Paris Cons. (1797–1842). He was the teacher of Kalkbrenner and Hérold, and was also known as a composer of virtuoso piano pieces, some of which (especially variations on *Le Roi Dagobert*) were very popular. He was the author of a standard manual for piano: *Méthode nouvelle pour le piano* (5 eds., 1802–32), which he wrote for his pupils at the Paris Cons.

Adam, Theo, distinguished German bass-baritone; b. Dresden, Aug. 1, 1926. As a boy, he sang in the Dresdner Kreuzchor; he studied voice in his native city with Rudolf Dittrich (1946–49). On Dec. 25, 1949, he made his operatic debut as the hermit in *Der Freischütz* at the Dresden State Opera, and in 1952 made his 1st appearance at the Bayreuth Festival, quickly rising to prominence as one of the leading Wagnerian heroic bass-baritones of his time. He was a principal member of the Berlin State Opera from 1953, and made guest appearances at London's Covent Garden, the Vienna State Opera, the Paris Opéra, the Salzburg Festivals, the San Francisco Opera, and the Chicago Lyric Opera. On Feb. 7, 1969, he made his debut at the Metropolitan Opera in N.Y. as Hans Sachs in *Die Meistersinger von Nürnberg*. In addition to his Wagnerian roles, he also sang in operas by Mozart, Verdi, and Richard Strauss with notable success; he appeared in various contemporary works as well, creating the leading roles in Cerha's *Baal* (1981) and Berio's *Un Re in ascolto* (1984). In 1979 he was made an Austrian Kammersänger. He publ. *Seht, hier ist Tinte, Feder, Papier . . .* (1980) and *Die hundertste Rolle, oder, Ich mache einen neuen Adam* (1987).

Adamberger, (Josef) Valentin, noted German tenor; b. Munich, July 6, 1743; d. Vienna, Aug. 24, 1804. He studied in Italy with Valesi, and made appearances there using the name **Adamonti.** He went to Munich in 1772; sang in London in 1777; settled in Vienna in 1780. He created the role of Belmonte in *Die Entführung aus dem Serail* (July 16, 1782); also sang the part of Herr Vogelsang in *Der Schauspieldirektor* (Feb. 7, 1786). In 1789 he became a member of the Italian Opera in Vienna, and remained there until his retirement in 1793. He then devoted himself to teaching voice.

Adam (or Adan) de la Halle (or Hale), called "Le Bossu d'Arras" ("Hunchback of Arras"); b. Arras, c.1237; d. Naples, c.1287. Adam was a famous trouvère, many of whose works have been preserved; the most interesting is a dramatic pastoral, *Le Jeu de Robin et de Marion* (1285), written for the Anjou court at Naples and resembling an opéra comique in its plan. He was gifted in the dual capacity of poet and composer. Both monodic and polyphonic works of his survive. A facsimile reprint of one of the important MS sources of Adam's works was issued as *Le Chansonnier d'Arras*, introduction by A. Jeanroy (Paris, 1925). For transcriptions of most of the extant music, see E. de Coussemaker, *Œuvres complètes du trouvère Adam de la Halle* (1872); F. Gennrich, *Rondeaux, Virelais und Balladen* (Dresden; I, 1921; II, 1927); J. Chailley, *Adam de la Halle: Rondeaux* (Paris, 1942); F. Gennrich, *Le Jeu de Robin et de Marion*, in Musikwissenschaftliche Studienbibliothek (Langen,

1962); N. Wilkins, *The Lyric Works of Adam de la Halle: Chansons, Jeux-Partis, Rondeaux, Motets* (Dallas, 1967). Transcriptions of the texts only: R. Berger, *Canchons und Partures des altfranzösischen Trouvère Adan de la Halle le Bochu d'Arras* (1900); L. Nicod, *Les Partures Adan: Les Jeux-partis d'Adam de la Halle* (Paris, 1917); E. Langlois, *Le Jeu de la Feuillée* (Paris, 1923); idem, *Le Jeu de Robin et de Marion* (Paris, 1924); A. Langfors, *Recueil général des jeux-partis français* (2 vols., Paris, 1926). A new ed. of the complete works, using all known music and text sources, including those never before transcribed, is being prepared by a consortium of music and language specialists at City Univ. of N.Y.

BIBL.: H. Guy, *Essai sur la vie et les œuvres littéraires d'A. d.l.H.* (Paris, 1898); J. Tiersot, *Sur le Jeu de Robin et Marion* (1897); R. Barth-Wehrenalp, *Studien zu A. d.l.H.* (Tutzing, 1982).

Adam de St. Victor, celebrated French churchman and poet who flourished in the 1st half of the 12th century. By 1107 he was precentor at Notre Dame Cathedral in Paris, where he served as a high official for more than 2 decades. In 1133 he donated his prebend to the Abbey of St. Victor in Paris, where he subsequently lived and later served as a canon until his death (c.1148). He played a major role in the development of the late sequence. It is possible that he was also a composer. For eds. of texts attributed to Adam de St. Victor, see L. Gautier, *Œuvres poétiques d'Adam de St.-Victor, précédées d'un essai sur sa vie et ses ouvrages* (Paris, 1858–59; 3rd ed., 1894); M. Legrain, ed., *Proses d'Adam de Saint-Victor* (Rome, 1899); E. Misset and P. Aubry, eds., *Les Proses d'Adam de Saint-Victor: Texte et musique* (Paris, 1901); H. Prévost, ed., *Recueil complet des célèbres séquences du maître Adam le breton, chanoine régulier de l'abbaye royale de Saint-Victor de Paris (XIIe siècle) d'après les manuscrits de la même abbaye* (Ligugé, 1901); C. Blume, G. Dreves, and H. Bannister, eds., *Analecta hymnica medii aevi*, LIV–LV (Leipzig, 1915, 1922); D. Wrangham, ed., *The Liturgical Poetry of Adam of St. Victor from the Text of Gautier, with Translations into English in the Original Metres and Short Explanatory Notes* (London, 1939); G. Vecchi, ed., *Adam de S. Victor: Liriche sacre* (Bologna, 1953); and F. Wellner, ed. and translator, *Adam de Saint-Viktor: Sämtliche Sequenzen, lateinisch und deutsch* (Munich, 1955).

BIBL.: M.-J.-J. Brial, "A. d.S.V.," *Histoire littéraire de la France* (vol. XV, Paris, 1820); P. LeJay, "Les Traités attribués à A. d.S.-V.," *Revue d'histoire et de littérature religieuses*, IV (1899); D. Morin, "Un Traité faussement attribué à A. d.S.-V.," *Revue Bénédictine*, XVI (1899); H. Spanke, "Die Kompositionskunst der Sequenzen A. v.S.V.," *Studi medievali*, XIV (1941); H. Husmann, "Notre-Dame und S. V.: Repertoire-Studien zur Geschichte der gereimten Prosen," *Acta Musicologica*, XXXVI (1964); E. Hegener, *Studien zur "zweiten Sprache" in der religiösen Lyrik des zwölften Jahrhunderts: A. v.S.V., Walter von Châtillon* (Ratingen, 1971); M. Fassler, *Musical Exegesis in the Sequences of A. and the Canons of St. Victor* (diss., Cornell Univ., 1983); idem, "Who Was A. of S.V.?: The Evidence of the Sequence Manuscripts," *Journal of the American Musicological Society* (Summer 1984).

Adamis, Michael, Greek composer of ultramodern music; b. Piraeus, May 19, 1929. While studying theology at Athens Univ. (1948–54), he took music courses at the Athens Cons. (1947–51) and courses on Byzantine music and harmony at Piraeus Cons. (1951–56); studied composition with Papaioannou at the Hellikon Cons. in Athens (1956–59), followed by advanced studies in electronic music and Byzantine musical paleography at Brandeis Univ. in Waltham, Mass. (1962–65). His works are derived from a universal spectrum of musical techniques and sonorous resources: dodecaphonic, electronic, liturgical, neo-Baroque, choreographic.

WORKS: *Liturgikon Concerto* for Oboe, Clarinet, Bassoon, and String Orch. (1955); *2 Pieces* for Violin and Piano (1958); Variations for String Orch. (1958); *Suite in ritmo antico* for Piano (1959); *Sinfonia da camera* for Flute, Clarinet, Horn, Trumpet, Percussion, Piano, and String Orch. (1960–61); Duo for Violin and Piano (1961); *3 Pieces* for Double Bass and Piano (1962); *Anakyklesis* for Flute, Oboe, Celesta, Violin, and Cello (1964); *Perspective* for Flute, Piccolo, and Percussion (1965); *Apocalypse* (*6th Seal*) for Chorus, Narrator, Piano, and Tape (1967); *Byzantine Passion* for 6 Soloists, Chorus, and Percussion (1967); *Genesis* for 3 Choirs, Narrator, Tape, Painting, Projection, and Dance (1968); *Lamentation* for 2 Chanters, 2 Drone Chanters, Percussion, and Tape (1970); *Tetelestai* for Narrator, 3 Choirs, Tape, and Bells (1971); *Iketirion* for Women's Choir, Percussion, and Tape (1971); *Kratima* for Narrator, Oboe, Tuba, and Tape (1971); *The Fiery Furnace* for Chanters' Choir and 3 Children (1972; based on a 15th-century MS that is the only extant specimen of Byzantine liturgical drama); *Orestes* for Baritone, Percussion, and Tape (1972); *Photonymon* for Narrator, Chorus, and Percussion (1973). He also has numerous pieces for tape alone, and tape and voice, and has produced electronic stage music for plays by Aeschylus, Euripides, Shakespeare, and others.

Adamowski, Joseph, American cellist, brother of **Timothée Adamowski;** b. Warsaw, July 4, 1862; d. Cambridge, Mass., May 8, 1930. He studied at the Warsaw Cons. (1873–77) with Goebelt, and at the Moscow Cons. with Fitzenhagen; also attended Tchaikovsky's classes there. He gave concerts from 1883 to 1889 in Warsaw. From 1889 to 1907 he played in the Boston Sym. Orch. In 1896 he married the pianist **Antoinette Szumowska.** With his wife and his brother Timothée, he formed the Adamowski Trio.

Adamowski, Timothée, American violinist, brother of **Joseph Adamowski;** b. Warsaw, March 24, 1857; d. Boston, April 18, 1943. He studied in Warsaw and at the Paris Cons.; in 1879 gave concerts in the U.S. with Maurice Strakosch and Clara Louise Kellogg, and settled in Boston, where he taught at the New England Cons. (until 1933). In 1888 he organized the Adamowski String Quartet, which gave about 30 concerts annually; he also conducted several summer seasons of popular concerts given by the Boston Sym. Orch. (1890–94; 1900–1907). He publ. songs and violin pieces (*Barcarolle, Polish Dance,* etc.).

Adams, Charles, American dramatic tenor; b. Charlestown, Mass., Feb. 9, 1834; d. West Harwich, Mass., July 4, 1900. He studied music in Boston; then went to Vienna, where he took voice lessons with Barbieri; was subsequently a member of the Royal Opera in Berlin and of the Court Opera in Vienna (1867–76). He also sang at La Scala, Milan; Covent Garden, London; and in the U.S. He settled in Boston as a vocal teacher in 1879.

Adams, John (Coolidge), prominent American composer; b. Worcester, Mass., Feb. 15, 1947. He spent the tender years of his life in the healthy atmosphere of Vermont and New Hampshire; his father taught him clarinet, and he later took clarinet lessons with Felix Viscuglia, a member of the Boston Sym. Orch. He subsequently entered Harvard College, receiving his B.A. (magna cum laude) in 1969 and his M.A. in music composition in 1971. At Harvard his principal teacher was Leon Kirchner; he also worked in composition with David Del Tredici and had some sessions with Sessions. While still in college he conducted the Bach Soc. Orch. and was a substitute clarinetist with the Boston Sym. and the Boston Opera Co. In 1969 he played the solo part in Walter Piston's Clarinet Concerto at Carnegie Hall in N.Y. In 1971 he moved to San Francisco, where he found a congenial environment for his activities as a conductor and composer. He was appointed head of the composition dept. at the San Francisco Cons. (1971–81). In 1978 he became adviser on new music to the San Francisco Sym. Orch., and subsequently was its composer-in-residence (1982–85). His own music covers a wide spectrum of media, including works for video, tape, and live electronics; he also wrote the musical film score for *Matter of Heart,* a psychological documentary dealing with the life and theories of Carl G. Jung. In 1982 he was awarded a Guggenheim fellowship. In his compositions he reveals himself as an apostle of the idea that a maximum effect can be achieved with a minimum of practical means, a notion usually described by the somewhat inaccurate term "minimalism," wherein a composer postulates harmonic and melodic austerity with audacious repetitiveness, withal electing to use the simplest time-honored units of the musical structure, to wit, major triads in the fundamental positions, with the tonic in the bass. Adams is a modernist among minimalists, for he allows for a constant flow of divergent tonalities in his works, but he also succeeds in exploiting such elementary harmonic progressions as the serenely cadential alternations of the tonic and the dominant, achieving a desired effect. Typical of such works are his *Harmonium* for Chorus and Orch. and the grandiose popular score titled *Grand Pianola Music.* Many of his works have been performed by leading U.S. orchs. His topical opera *Nixon in China* (1987) brought him international attention.
WORKS: OPERAS: *Nixon in China* (Houston, Oct. 22, 1987); *The Death of Klinghoffer* (Brussels, March 19, 1991). **ORCH.:** *Common Tones in Simple Time* (1979); *Harmonium* for Chorus and Orch., after John Donne and Emily Dickinson (1980; San Francisco, April 15, 1981); *Grand Pianola Music* for 2 Sopranos, 2 Pianos, and Small Orch. (1981–82; San Francisco, Feb. 20, 1982); *Shaker Loops* for String Orch. (1983; also for String Septet, 1978); *Harmonielehre* (1984–85; San Francisco, March 21, 1985); *Fearful Symmetries* (N.Y., Oct. 29, 1988); *The Wound-Dresser* for Baritone and Chamber Orch. (1989); *Eros Piano* for Piano and Chamber Orch. (1989). **CHAMBER:** Piano Quintet (1970); *American Standard* for Unspecified Ensemble (1973); *Grounding* for 3 Solo Voices, Instruments, and Electronics (1975); *Onyx* for Tape (1976); *Shaker Loops* for String Septet (1978; also for String Orch., 1983). **PIANO:** *Ragamarole* (1973); *China Gates* (1977); *Phrygian Gates* (1977).
BIBL.: N. Malitz, "J. A.'s Revolutionary New Opera *Nixon in China,*" *Ovation* (Oct. 1987); *Current Biography* (May 1988); M. Swed, "J. A.," *Musical Times* (Nov. 1989).

Adams, Suzanne, American soprano; b. Cambridge, Mass., Nov. 28, 1872; d. London, Feb. 5, 1953. She studied with Bouhy in N.Y.; in 1889 went to Paris, where she took lessons with Mathilde Marchesi. She made her professional debut at the Paris Opéra as Juliette in Gounod's opera on Jan. 9, 1895; continued to sing there for 3 more seasons; in 1898 she sang at Covent Garden, London. Returning to the U.S., she made her debut at the Metropolitan Opera in N.Y. as Juliette on Jan. 4, 1899. After the death of her husband, the cellist Leo Stein, in 1904, she retired from the stage.

Adams, Thomas, eminent English organist; b. London, Sept. 5, 1785; d. there, Sept. 15, 1858. He studied with Thomas Busby, and was organist at various London churches. His publ. organ works include fugues, voluntaries, 90 interludes, and variations on popular airs.

Adam von Fulda, German music theorist and composer; b. Fulda, c.1440; d. (of the plague) Wittenberg, 1505. After some years at Vormbach's Benedictine monastery, he entered the service of Friedrich the Wise of Saxony as a singer (1490); became prof. of music at the Univ. of Wittenberg (1502). His treatise *De musica* was publ. in Gerbert's *Scriptores ecclesiastici* (1784); he wrote a Mass and a Magnificat (ed. by W. Ehmann in the *Kirchenmusikalisches Jahrbuch,* XVII, 1902); 7 hymns, 2 antiphons, and a respond are in Das Erbe Deutscher Musik, 1st series, XXXII–XXXIII (1956–60).
BIBL.: H. Moser, "Leben und Lieder des A. v.F.," *Jahrbuch der Staatlichen Akademie für Kirchen- und Schulmusik,* I (1929); W. Ehmann, *A. v.F. als Vertreter der ersten deutschen Komponistengeneration* (Berlin, 1936); C. Petzsch, "Die rhythmische Struktur der Liedtenores des A. v.F.," *Archiv für Musikwissenschaft,* XV (1958).

Adaskin, Murray, Canadian violinist and composer; b. Toronto, March 28, 1906. He studied violin with his older brother Harry; then went to Paris, where he took lessons with Marcel Chailley. Returning to Toronto, he continued his lessons with Luigi von Kunits and Kathleen Parlow. He subsequently played violin in the Toronto Sym. Orch. (1923–36). He studied composition with John Weinzweig (1944–48), and took a course with Darius Milhaud (1949–50; 1953). In 1952 he became head of the music dept. at the Univ. of Saskatchewan; from 1966 to 1972 was composer-in-residence there. He writes music in a facile laissez-faire manner, enlivened by a rhythmic pulse.

Works: Chamber opera, *Grant, Warden of the Plains* (Winnipeg, July 18, 1967); *Ballet Symphony* (1950–51); Violin Concerto (1956); *Algonquin Symphony* (1957–58); *Saskatchewan Legend* for Orch. (1959); Bassoon Concerto (1960); *Qalala and Nilaula of the North*, symphonic poem based on Eskimo tunes (1969); *Fanfare* for Orch. (1970); *There Is My People Sleeping*, symphonic poem (1970); *Nootka Ritual* for Small Orch. (1972); *Adagio* for Cello and Orch. (1973–75); Violin Sonata (1946); Piano Sonata (1950); *Sonatine Baroque* for Solo Violin (1952); 4 divertimentos: No. 1 for 2 Violins and Piano (1956); No. 2 for Violin and Harp (1964); No. 3 for Violin, Horn, and Bassoon (1965); No. 4 for Trumpet and Orch. (1970); *Introduction and Rondo* for Piano Quartet (1957); String Quartet (1963); *Calisthenics* for Violin and Piano (1968); Trio for Flute, Cello, and Piano (1970); *2 Pieces* for Viola da Gamba (1972); *2 Portraits* for Violin and Piano (1973); Wind Quintet (1974); songs.

Adderley, Julian Edwin ("Cannonball"), black American jazz alto saxophone player; b. Tampa, Fla., Sept. 15, 1928; d. Gary, Ind., Aug. 8, 1975. He began his career as a member of a jazz group at a Greenwich Village club in N.Y.; in 1956 he formed his own combo with his brother **Nat Adderley** (b. Tampa, Nov. 25, 1931), who plays the cornet. He achieved fame mainly through his recordings, beginning with *African Waltz* in 1961. He received an academic education, graduating from Florida A. & M. with a B.A. in music. For 2 years (1948–50) he was a band director at Dillard High School in Fort Lauderdale. After leaving his school position, he lectured frequently in colleges on the subject of his "black experience in music." He owes his nickname, "Cannonball," to the mispronunciation of *cannibal*, a slurring reference to his voracious eating habits. He suffered a stroke during a concert engagement in Gary, Ind. Among his most successful recordings were *Dis Here; Sermonette; Work Song; Jive Samba; Mercy, Mercy, Mercy; Walk Tall*. He also wrote *Suite Cannon*, its title alluding both to his academic background and to his popular nickname.

Addinsell, Richard (Stewart), English composer of theater and film music; b. London, Jan. 13, 1904; d. there, Nov. 14, 1977. He studied law at Oxford Univ. and music at the Royal College of Music in London. His 1st theater score was for Clemence Dane's play *Come of Age* (1928). In 1929 he went to Berlin and Vienna for further musical study. In 1933, Eva Le Gallienne commissioned him to write the music for her production of *Alice in Wonderland*. He then wrote a series of successful film scores, among them *A Tale of Two Cities, Blithe Spirit, Fire over England,* and *Dark Journey*. During World War II he wrote film music for several patriotic documentaries, among them *Siege of Tobruk* and *We Sail at Midnight*. He achieved fame with a score for the film *Dangerous Moonlight* (released in the U.S. as *Suicide Squadron*), containing a movement for piano and orch. which became immensely popular under the title *Warsaw Concerto*. While the music is a feeble imitation of Rachmaninoff's 2nd Piano Concerto, it possesses a popular flair that made it a classic of pop music.

Addison, Adele, black American soprano; b. N.Y., July 24, 1925. She studied at Westminster Choir College, Princeton, and the Berkshire Music Center at Tanglewood, and also took lessons with Povla Frijsh. She made her N.Y. debut at Town Hall in 1952, then sang with the New England Opera and the N.Y. City Opera; she made numerous appearances with major American orchs. Her extensive repertoire included works from the Baroque era to the 20th century.

Addison, John, English composer; b. Chobham, Surrey, March 16, 1920. He was educated at Wellington College, and in 1938 entered the Royal College of Music. His studies were interrupted by World War II, during which he served in a cavalry regiment. After the war he continued his musical education with Gordon Jacob in composition, Leon Goossens in oboe, and Frederick Thurston in clarinet. In 1951 he joined the staff of the Royal College of Music, remaining there until 1958, when he decided to devote himself mainly to composition for films. He wrote music for more than 60 motion pictures, both in England and the U.S., including such popular productions as *Tom Jones* (1963), which won for him an Academy Award; *The Loved One* (1965); *Torn Curtain* (1966); *The Charge of the Light Brigade* (1968); *Sleuth* (1972); *The Seven Per Cent Solution*, a comedy involving Sherlock Holmes and Freud (1976). His film music is particularly effective in epical subjects with understated humor. Apart from film music, he wrote *Variations* for Piano and Orch. (1948); Concerto for Trumpet, Strings, and Percussion (1949); Woodwind Sextet (1949); Trio for Oboe, Clarinet, and Bassoon (1950); Trio for Flute, Oboe, and Piano; *Serenade and Conversation Piece* for 2 Soprano Voices, Harpsichord, Organ, and Harp. He also wrote music for television documentaries. Since 1975 Addison has divided his time between Los Angeles and a small village in the French Alps, where he does some skiing and mountaineering.

Adelburg, August, Ritter von, Austrian violinist and composer; b. Pera, Nov. 1, 1830; d. Vienna, Oct. 20, 1873. He studied violin with Mayseder in Vienna (1850–54) and composition with Hoffmann, then toured Europe as a violinist. He wrote 3 operas: *Zrinyi* (Budapest, June 23, 1868; his most successful work); *Martinuzzi* (1870); *Wallenstein* (on Schiller's drama); an oratorio, *War and Peace*; 5 string quartets; *School of Velocity* for Violin.

Adgate, Andrew, American church organist and choral conductor; b. Norwich, Conn., March 22, 1762; d. Philadelphia, of yellow fever, Sept. 30, 1793. In 1784 he organized, in Philadelphia, the Institution for the Encouragement of Church Music; in 1785 he founded there the Free School for Spreading the Knowledge of Vocal Music, reorganized in 1787 as The Uranian Academy, the purpose of which was to urge the incorporation of musical study with general education. On May 4, 1786, he presented in Philadelphia "A Grand Concert of Sacred Music," with a chorus of 230 voices and an orch. of 50, featuring works by Handel, Billings, and others. Adgate compiled several publications: *Lessons for the Uranian Society* (1785); *Select Psalms and Hymns* (1787); *Rudiments of Music* (1788); *Selection of Sacred Harmony* (1788).

Adkins, Cecil (Dale), American musicologist; b. Red Oak, Iowa, Jan. 30, 1932. He studied at the Univ. of Omaha (B.F.A., 1953), the Univ. of South Dakota (M.M., 1959), and the Univ. of Iowa (Ph.D., 1963). In 1963 he was appointed prof. of musicology at North Texas State Univ., Denton. There he established a series devoted to reviving performances of Renaissance works. His publications include an important ed. and tr. of Orazio Vecchi's *L'Amfiparnaso* (1977) and numerous technical papers in American music magazines.

Adler, Clarence, American pianist, father of **Richard Adler;** b. Cincinnati, March 10, 1886; d. N.Y., Dec. 24, 1969. He studied at the Cincinnati College of Music (1898–1904); then in Berlin with Godowsky (1905–9). He toured in Europe as a pianist with the Hekking Trio. Returning to America in 1913, he settled in N.Y.; made his American debut with the N.Y. Sym. Orch. (Feb. 8, 1914). In 1941 he broadcast all of Mozart's piano concertos. He publ. an album of piano pieces, as well as arrangements of works by Dvořák and Franck.

Adler, F. Charles, American conductor; b. London, July 2, 1889; d. Vienna, Feb. 16, 1959. He studied piano with August Halm, theory with Beer-Walbrunn, and conducting with Mahler. He was assistant to Felix Mottl at the Royal Opera in Munich (1908–11); in 1913 he became 1st conductor of the Municipal Opera in Düsseldorf; conducted sym. concerts in Europe (1919–33). He was owner of Edition Adler in Berlin until 1933, when he went to America. In 1937 he founded the Saratoga Springs Music Festivals in N.Y.

Adler, Guido, eminent Austrian musicologist; b. Eibenschütz, Moravia, Nov. 1, 1855; d. Vienna, Feb. 15, 1941. He studied at the Vienna Cons. under Bruckner and Dessoff; entered Vienna Univ. in 1874 and founded, in cooperation with Felix Mottl and K. Wolf, the academical Wagner Soc.; took the degree of Dr.Jur. in 1878, and in 1880 that of Dr.Phil. (diss., *Die historischen Grundklassen der christlich-abendländischen Musik bis 1600*), and in 1882 qualified as an instructor, lecturing on musical science (thesis, *Studie zur Geschichte der Harmonie*). With Chrysander and Spitta he founded, in 1884, the *Vierteljahrsschrift für Musikwissenschaft*. In 1885 he was appointed prof. of musicology at the German Univ. at Prague. In 1892 he was elected president of the Central Committee of the Internationale Ausstellung für Musik und Theater. In 1895 he succeeded Hanslick as prof. of music history at the Univ. of Vienna, retiring in 1927. Important books by Adler are *Methode der Musikgeschichte* (1919); *Der Stil in der Musik* (1911; 2nd ed., 1929); *Gustav Mahler* (1916); *Handbuch der Musikgeschichte* (1 vol., 1924; 2nd ed. in 2 vols., 1930); *Wollen und Wirken*, memoirs (Vienna, 1935). He was also ed. of the monumental collection Denkmäler der Tonkunst in Österreich from its inception (the 1st vol. appeared in 1894) until 1938 (83 vols. in all). He contributed many articles to music periodicals.

WRITINGS: *Richard Wagner: Vorlesungen* (Leipzig, 1904); *Joseph Haydn* (Vienna and Leipzig, 1909); *Der Stil in der Musik* (Leipzig, 1911; 2nd ed., 1929); *Gustav Mahler* (Vienna, 1916); *Methode der Musikgeschichte* (Leipzig, 1919); ed. *Handbuch der Musikgeschichte* (Frankfurt am Main, 1924; 2nd ed., rev., 1930); *Wollen und Wirken: Aus dem Leben eines Musikhistorikers* (Vienna, 1935).

BIBL.: C. Engel, "G. A. in Retrospect," *Musical Quarterly* (July 1941); R. Heinz, "G. A.'s Musikhistorik als historistisches Dokument," in W. Wiora, ed., *Die Ausbreitung des Historismus über die Musik* (Regensburg, 1969); E. Reilly, *Gustav Mahler und G. A.* (Vienna, 1978).

Adler, Kurt, American pianist and conductor; b. Neuhaus, Bohemia, March 1, 1907; d. Butler, N.J., Sept. 21, 1977. He studied musicology with Guido Adler and Robert Lach at Vienna Univ. He served as assistant conductor of the Berlin State Opera (1927–29) and at the German Opera in Prague (1929–32). In 1933, with the advent of the Nazi regime, he went to Russia, where he was principal conductor of the Kiev State Opera (1933–35), then organized and conducted the Phil. Orch. of Stalingrad (1935–37). In 1938 he went to the U.S., first appearing as a pianist, then conducted in Canada and Mexico. In 1943 he joined the staff at the Metropolitan Opera in N.Y. as choirmaster and assistant conductor; made his conducting debut at the Metropolitan on Jan. 12, 1951, in Mozart's *Die Zauberflöte*, and led about 20 different operas there until he resigned in 1973. He ed. *Operatic Anthology; The Prima Donna Album; Arias from Light Operas; Famous Operatic Choruses*. He also brought out *The Art of Accompanying and Coaching* (Minneapolis, 1965) and *Phonetics and Diction in Singing* (Minneapolis, 1967). He was no relation to Kurt Herbert Adler.

Adler, Kurt Herbert, notable Austrian-born American conductor and operatic administrator; b. Vienna, April 2, 1905; d. Ross, Calif., Feb. 9, 1988. He studied at the Vienna Academy of Music and the Univ. of Vienna; made his debut as a conductor at the Max Reinhardt Theater there in 1925, and subsequently conducted at the Volksoper, as well as in Germany, Italy, and Czechoslovakia. He served as assistant to Toscanini at the Salzburg Festival in 1936. As the dark cloud of Nazidom descended upon central Europe, he moved to the U.S., and from 1938 to 1943 was guest conductor of the Chicago Opera; he subsequently was choirmaster (1943), artistic director (1953), and general director of the San Francisco Opera. After his retirement in 1981, he was made general director emeritus. Under his direction the San Francisco Opera prospered greatly, advancing to the foremost ranks of American opera theaters. He was not related to Kurt Adler.

Adler, Larry (Lawrence Cecil), American harmonica player; b. Baltimore, Feb. 10, 1914. He won a harmonica contest at 13 for the best rendition of Beethoven's Minuet in G. He has appeared in numerous revues, and also gave concerts as a soloist with piano and with orch., as well as command performances for King George VI, King Gustav of Sweden, and presidents Roosevelt and Truman. In 1940, determined to learn to read music, he took lessons with Ernst Toch. In 1949 he was viciously attacked by a wolf pack of right-wing agitators who accused him of Communistic leanings and un-American thoughts. Unable to get any engagements from frightened American managers, he went to England. When the winds of national hysteria subsided, he returned to the U.S. and resumed his concert career. He wrote some film scores and other works. His autobiography was publ. as *It Ain't Necessarily So* (London, 1984).

Adler, Peter Herman, conductor; b. Jablonec, Czechoslovakia, Dec. 2, 1899; d. Ridgefield, Conn., Oct. 2, 1990. He studied in Prague with Fidelio Finke, Vítězslav Novák, and Alexander von Zemlinsky. In 1923 he was appointed opera conductor in Brno; from 1929 to 1932 he conducted at the Bremen State Theater. In 1932 he went to Russia, where he served as the chief conductor of the Ukrainian State Orch. in Kiev; in 1937 he returned to Prague. With the Nazi occupation of Czechoslovakia, he went to the U.S. in 1939; made his American debut as conductor at a concert for Czech relief in N.Y., Jan. 24, 1940, and later filled guest engagements with several American orchs. From 1959 to 1967 he was music director of the Baltimore Sym. Orch. In 1972 he made his 1st conducting appearance at the Metropolitan Opera in N.Y.

Adler, Richard, American composer of popular music, son of **Clarence Adler;** b. N.Y., Aug. 3, 1921. He was educated at the Univ. of North Carolina; served in the U.S. Navy (1943–46); then became a producer; staged shows at the White House during the Kennedy and Johnson administrations. He wrote his own musicals in collaboration with Jerry Ross. Of these the most popular were *The Pajama Game*, with its striking hit song *Hernando's Hideaway*, and *Damn Yankees* (1955). He also wrote *The Lady Remembers* (*The Statue of Liberty Suite*) for Soprano and Orch. (Detroit, Oct. 28, 1985).

Adler, Samuel (Hans), German-born American composer and pedagogue; b. Mannheim, March 4, 1928. His father was cantor in the Mannheim Synagogue, and his mother was an amateur pianist. Adler began to study the violin as a child with Albert Levy; in 1939 the family left Germany and settled in Worcester, Mass., where his father was appointed music director of the local temple. He took lessons with Herbert Fromm in Boston (1941–46); later attended Boston Univ. (1946–48), where his teachers were Hugo Norden, Karl Geiringer, and Paul Pisk; after receiving a B.M. in 1948 he entered Harvard Univ., where he attended the classes of Walter Piston, Randall Thompson, and Irving Fine (1948–50); he also took summer courses at the Berkshire Music Center at Tanglewood where he studied composition with Aaron Copland and conducting with Serge Koussevitzky. He earned his master's degree in music from Harvard in 1950; then joined the U.S. Army, and served as conductor of the 7th Army Sym. in Germany. Returning to the U.S., he held the post of music director of Temple Emanu-El in Dallas (1953–56); then was prof. of composition at North Texas State Univ. at Denton (1957–66). In 1966 he was appointed prof. of composition at the Eastman School of Music in Rochester, N.Y., and in 1973 was named chairman of the music dept. there. He has received many honors and awards, including grants from the NEA, the ASCAP–Deems Taylor Award (1983) for his book *The Study of Orchestration*, and a Guggenheim fellowship (1984–85). His idiom of composition may be described as midstream modernism, in which densely interwoven contrapuntal lines support the basically tonal harmonic complex, with a frequent incidence of tangential atonal episodes. Much of his music is inspired by the liturgical cantilena of traditional Jewish music; oriental inflections also occur.

WORKS: OPERAS: 1-act opera, *The Outcasts of Poker Flat,* after Bret Harte (1959; Denton, Tex., June 8, 1962); sacred opera, *The Wrestler* (Dallas, June 22, 1972); *The Lodge of Shadows,* music drama for Baritone Solo, Dancers, and Orch. (1973); *The Disappointment,* reconstruction of an early American ballad opera of 1767 (Washington, D.C., April 7, 1976). **ORCH.:** Sym. No. 1 (Dallas, Dec. 7, 1953); Sym. No. 2 (Dallas, Feb. 12, 1958); Sym. No. 3, *Diptych,* for Wind Orch. (1960); Sym. No. 4, *Geometrics* (1967); Sym. No. 5, *We Are the Echoes,* for Mezzo-soprano and Orch. (Fort Worth, Texas, Nov. 10, 1975); Sym. No. 6 (1985); *Toccata* (1954); *Rhapsody* for Violin and Orch. (1961); *Song and Dance* for Viola and Orch. (1965); *City by the Lake,* "a portrait of Rochester, N.Y." (1968); Organ Concerto (1970); Sinfonietta (1970); Concerto for Orch. (1971); Flute Concerto (1977); Piano Concerto (1983; Washington, D.C., Jan. 3, 1985). **CHAMBER:** 7 string quartets (1945, 1950, 1953, 1963, 1969, 1975, 1981); 5 *Vignettes* for 12 Trombones (1968); Concerto for Winds, Brass, and Percussion (1968); *Brass Fragments* for 20 Brass Instruments (1970); *Histrionics* for Brass and Percussion (1971); *Déjà Vu* for 6 Recorders (1975); Piano Trio (1964); 3 violin sonatas (1948, 1956, 1965); Sonata for Horn and Piano (1948); Sonata for Cello Unaccompanied (1966); 7 *Epigrams* for Woodwind Quintet (1966); *Intrada* for Woodwind (1967); 11 pieces, each titled *Canto,* most of them for a single unaccompanied instrument (trumpet, bass trombone, violin, saxophone, double bass, tuba, piano, cello), composed between 1970 and 1984; also 1 for Soprano, Flute, Cello, and Percussion; *4 Dialogues* for Euphonium and Marimba (1974); also 2 concertinos for String Orch. (1975–76); *Line Drawings* for Saxophone Quartet (1978); *Aeolus* for Clarinet and Piano Trio (1977); *A Little Night and Day Music* for Wind Ensemble (1978); *Trumpet Triptych* (1979). **SACRED VOCAL:** *From Out of Bondage,* biblical cantata (Temple Sinai, Brookline, Mass., April 4, 1969); *The Vision of Isaiah* for Bass, Chorus, and Orch. (1963); *The Binding* (1968); *High Flight* for Chorus and Chamber Orch. (1986); *Choose Life,* oratorio for Mezzo-soprano, Tenor, Chorus, and Orch. (1986); an untold number of vocal pieces with organ, songs, and piano pieces. **WRITINGS:** *Anthology for the Teaching of Choral Conducting* (N.Y., 1971; 2nd ed., 1985); *Singing and Hearing* (N.Y., 1979); *The Study of Orchestration* (N.Y., 1982).

Adlgasser, Anton Cajetan, German organist and composer; b. Inzell, Bavaria, Oct. 1, 1729; d. Salzburg, Dec. 22, 1777. He studied with Johann Eberlin in Salzburg; on Dec. 11, 1750, was appointed organist at Salzburg Cathedral and held this post until his death (he died of a stroke while playing the organ). Adlgasser enjoyed a great reputation as a musical scholar and was admired by the young Mozart. He wrote an opera, *La Nitteti* (Salzburg, 1766); several oratorios and school dramas; 7 syms.; keyboard sonatas and concertos; and church works.

Adlung, Jakob, German organist and music scholar; b. Bindersleben, near Erfurt, Jan. 14, 1699; d. Erfurt, July 5, 1762. He studied with Christian Reichardt; in 1727 became organist at the Erfurt Lutheran Church; in 1741 was named prof. at the town school. A man of wide erudition, Adlung gave language lessons as well as musical instruction. He built 16 clavichords with his own hands. Of his writings, 3 have historical value: *Anleitung zu der musikalischen Gelehrtheit* (Erfurt, 1758; 2nd ed., rev. by J.A. Hiller, 1783; facsimile ed. by H.J. Moser, Kassel, 1953); *Musica mechanica organoedi* (1768; facsimile ed. by C. Mahrenholz, Kassel, 1931); *Musikalisches Siebengestirn* (1768). His autobiographical sketch was publ. by Marpurg (*Kritische Briefe,* II). **BIBL.:** E. Valentin, s.v., *Die Musik in Geschichte und Gegenwart.*

Adolphus, Milton, productive American composer; b. N.Y., Jan. 27, 1913; d. Hyannis, Mass., Aug. 16, 1988. In 1935 he moved to Philadelphia, where he took composition lessons with Rosario Scalero; in 1938 he relocated to Harrisburg, where he took a job in the Dept. of Labor and Industry of the Commonwealth of Pennsylvania. Although he never practiced music

vocationally, he became extremely prolific, writing 13 syms. and 31 string quartets, in addition to other forms. Some of his works show a measure of sophisticated humor, exemplified by *Bitter Suite* for Oboe, 4 Clarinets, and Strings (1955) and *Petits fours* for Cello and Piano (1960), or his op. 147 for Violin, Horn, and Piano, entitled *Trio prosaico.* In 1980 he wrote a Concerto for Percussion and Orch.

Adomián, Lan, Russian-born Mexican composer; b. near Mogilev, April 29, 1905; d. Mexico City, May 9, 1979. He studied violin, emigrated to the U.S. in 1923, and studied at the Peabody Cons. of Music in Baltimore (1924–26) and at the Curtis Inst. of Music in Philadelphia (1926–28), where his teachers were Bailly (viola) and R.O. Morris (composition). He moved to N.Y. in 1928; conducted working-class choruses and bands; in 1936 he joined the Abraham Lincoln Brigade and went to Spain to fight on the Republican side during the Spanish Civil War. Upon his return to America, he wrote music for documentary films. In 1952 his radical politics made it prudent for him to leave the U.S. He moved to Mexico and became a Mexican citizen. Adomián was uncommonly prolific as a composer. He wrote 8 syms.; an opera, *La Macherata* (1969–72); a dramatic scene, *Auschwitz,* for Baritone and Instruments (1970); and numerous choruses and songs. **BIBL.:** *La voluntad de crear* (2 vols., Mexico City, 1980, 1981; vol. 2 contains a complete list of works).

Adorno (real name, **Wiesengrund**), **Theodor,** significant German musician and philosopher; b. Frankfurt am Main, Sept. 11, 1903; d. Visp, Switzerland, Aug. 6, 1969. He studied music with Sekles in Frankfurt and with Alban Berg in Vienna; for several years he was a prof. at the Univ. of Frankfurt. Devoting himself mainly to music criticism, he was ed. of the progressive music journal *Anbruch* in Vienna (1928–31). In 1934 he went to Oxford, and later emigrated to the U.S., where he became connected with radio research at Princeton Univ. (1938–41); subsequently lived in California. He returned to Germany in 1949 and became director of the Institut für Sozialforschung in Frankfurt. He publ. numerous essays dealing with the sociology of music, among them *Philosophie der neuen Musik* (Tübingen, 1949); *Dissonanzen: Musik in der verwalteten Welt* (Göttingen, 1956); *Arnold Schönberg* (Berlin, 1957); *Klangfiguren* (Berlin, 1959); *Einleitung in die Musiksoziologie* (Frankfurt, 1962); *Moments musicaux* (Frankfurt, 1964); *Form in der Neuen Musik* (Mainz, 1966); *Impromptus* (Frankfurt, 1968); *Alban Berg, der Meister des kleinsten Übergangs* (Vienna, 1968). Adorno advised Thomas Mann in the musical parts of his novel *Doktor Faustus.* He exercised a deep influence on the trends in musical philosophy and general esthetics, applying the sociological tenets of Karl Marx and the psychoanalytic techniques of Freud. In his speculative writings he introduced the concept of "cultural industry," embracing all types of musical techniques, from dodecaphony to jazz. A Festschrift was publ. in honor of his 60th birthday under the title *Zeugnisse* (Frankfurt, 1963). Numerous articles in several languages have been publ. on Adorno's theories in various music journals. In his early writings he used the hyphenated name Wiesengrund-Adorno. **WRITINGS:** *Philosophie der neuen Musik* (Tübingen, 1949; 3rd ed., 1967; Eng. tr., 1973); *Versuch über Wagner* (Berlin, 1952; 2nd ed., 1964); *Dissonanzen: Musik in der verwalteten Welt* (Göttingen, 1956; 3rd ed., augmented, 1963); *Klangfiguren: Musikalische Schriften I* (Berlin, 1959); *Mahler: Eine musikalische Physiognomik* (Frankfurt, 1960; 2nd ed., 1963); *Alban Berg: Der Meister des kleinsten Übergangs* (Vienna, 1968). **BIBL.:** R. Stephan, "T. W.A. (1903–1969)," *Die Musikforschung* (July/Sept. 1969); W. Gramer, *Musik und Verstehen: Eine Studie zur Musikästhetik T. W.A.s* (Mainz, 1976); M. Jay, A. (London, 1984); H. Blumenfeld, "Ad vocem A.," *Musical Quarterly* (Fall 1984); G. Zabel, "A. on Music: A Reconsideration," *Musical Times* (April 1989).

Adriaensen (Adrianssen, Adriansen, Adriaenssen, Hadrianus), Emanuel (Emmanuel), South Netherlands lutenist, teacher, and composer; b. Antwerp, c. 1554; d. there (buried),

Feb. 27, 1604. He pursued his studies in Rome (from 1574); returning to Antwerp, he set up a school for lutenists; was highly regarded as a teacher and composer. He publ. *Pratum musicum* . . . (Antwerp, 1584; 2nd ed., rev., 1600) and *Novum pratum musicum* . . . (Antwerp, 1592) in French lute tablature; these collections contain 5 fantasias, about 50 vocal pieces, and some 30 dances by such composers as Cipriano de Rore, Orlando di Lasso, J. de Berchem, and H. Waelrant.

BIBL.: G. Spiessens, "E. A. et son Pratum Musicum," *Acta Musicologica*, XXXVI (1964); J. Myers, "Performance Practice Indications in E. A.'s Lute Ensemble Music," *Journal of the Lute Society of America*, II (1969); G. Spiessens, *Leven en werk van de Antwerpse luitcomponist E. A. (ca. 1555–1604)* (Brussels, 1974–76).

Adrio, Adam, German musicologist; b. Essen, April 4, 1901; d. Ritten, Bozen, Sept. 18, 1973. He studied at the Univ. of Berlin (1923–25; 1927–31; Ph.D., 1934) and served as a lecturer there from 1932 to 1945. In 1951 he joined the faculty of the Free Univ. of Berlin; was prof. of musicology there from 1953 to 1967. He was regarded as a foremost authority on Protestant church music. Among his publications of importance is the dissertation *Die Anfänge des geistlichen Konzerts* (Berlin, 1935).

Afanasiev, Nikolai, Russian composer; b. Tobolsk, Jan. 12, 1821; d. St. Petersburg, June 3, 1898. He studied violin with his father, an amateur musician, and joined the orch. of the Moscow Opera at the age of 17. Later he conducted Italian opera in Moscow and St. Petersburg. He traveled in Europe in 1857. Afanasiev was regarded as the 1st Russian composer to write a string quartet (1860), but this is refuted by the discovery of 3 string quartets by Aliabiev. He further wrote a cantata, *The Feast of Peter the Great;* 4 operas: *Ammalat-Bek,* which was produced at the Imperial Opera in St. Petersburg on Dec. 5, 1870; and 3 others, *Stenka Razin, Vakula the Smith,* and *Taras Bulba,* which were never performed. He also wrote some children's songs.

Afranio de Pavia (family name, **Albonese**), Italian theologian, reputed inventor of the bassoon; b. Pavia, c.1465; d. Ferrara, c.1540, as canon of Ferrara. His claim to the invention of the bassoon is based on the attribution to him of the instrument Phagotus, in the book by his nephew Teseo Albonese *Introductio in chaldaicam linguam* (Pavia, 1539).

Agazzari, Agostino, Italian organist, theorist, and composer; b. Siena, Dec. 2, 1578; d. there, April 10, 1640. He was maestro di cappella in Rome at the Collegio Germanico and its adjoining church of S. Apollinare (1602–3), and then at the Seminario Romano (1606–7); he adopted Viadana's innovation in sacred vocal music (writing church concertos for 1 or 2 voices with instrumental harmonic support). In 1607 he went to Siena; by 1613 he was organist at the cathedral there, and may have later served as its maestro di cappella. His works, variously reprinted in Germany and the Netherlands, were numerous and in great favor. His treatise *La musica ecclesiastica* (Siena, 1638) is a theoretical endeavor to bring the practice of church music into accord with the Resolution of the Council of Trent; he was also among the 1st to give written instructions for performing the basso continuo, presented in the tract *Del sonare sopra 'l basso con tutti li Stromenti e dell'uso loro nel Conserto* (Siena, 1607; in Eng., O. Strunk, *Source Readings in Music History*, N.Y., 1950). His pastoral drama *Eumelio* (Rome, 1606) is one of the earliest operas.

BIBL.: G. Barblan, "Contributo a una biografia critica di A. A.," *Collectanea Historiae Musicae*, II (1957); G. Rose, "A. and the Improvising Orchestra," *Journal of the American Musicological Society*, XVIII (1965); M. Johnson, "A.'s *Eumelia*, a 'dramma pastorale,' " *Musical Quarterly* (July 1971); idem, *A. A. (1578–1640); The Motets for 1 to 4 Voices* (diss., Tulane Univ., 1972).

Ager, Milton, American composer of popular music; b. Chicago, Oct. 6, 1893; d. Inglewood, Calif., May 6, 1979. He began his career as a pianist in silent film theaters and accompanist to singers in vaudeville. He served in the U.S. Army Morale Division during World War I. His song *Happy Days Are Here Again* was selected by Franklin D. Roosevelt as his campaign song in 1932, and became an anthem of the Democratic Party in subsequent election campaigns. Ager also wrote the greatly popular ballads *Ain't She Sweet; Crazy Words, Crazy Tune;* and *Hard-Hearted Hannah.*

AgghÁzy, KÁroly, Hungarian pianist, composer, and teacher; b. Pest, Oct. 30, 1855; d. Budapest, Oct. 8, 1918. He studied at the National Cons. in Pest (1867–70) and at the Vienna Cons. (1870–73); then had piano lessons with Liszt and took a course in composition with Volkmann at the Budapest Academy of Music (1875–78). From 1878 to 1881 he toured in duo recitals with the violinist Jenö Hubay. From 1881 to 1883 he was a prof. of piano at the National Cons. in Budapest; from 1883 to 1889 taught at the Stern and Kullak conservatories in Berlin; in 1889 returned to Budapest and resumed his post at the National Cons. He composed some 100 piano pieces in a prevalent salon manner, and also wrote 2 operas, choral pieces, and songs.

Agnesi, Maria Teresa, Italian harpsichordist, singer, and composer; b. Milan, Oct. 17, 1720; d. there, Jan. 19, 1795. She made appearances in Milan as a harpsichordist and singer; wrote a successful pastorale, *Il ristoro d'Arcadia,* which was produced in Milan at the Teatro Ducale in 1747, and an opera, *Ciro in Armenia,* to her own libretto (Milan, Dec. 26, 1753). Her other stage works were *Sofonisba* (Naples, 1765); *Insubria consolata* (Milan, 1766); and *Nitocri* (Venice, 1771). She also composed pieces for the keyboard.

Agnew, Roy (Ewing), Australian composer and pianist; b. Sydney, Aug. 23, 1893; d. there, Nov. 12, 1944. He went to London and studied with Gerrard Williams (1923–28); gave concerts in England (1931–34). He then returned to Australia, was appointed director of Australian Radio (1938–43), and taught at the Sydney Cons.

WORKS: *Breaking of the Drought* for Mezzo-soprano and Orch. (1928); many piano works, including *Dance of the Wild Men* (1920); *Fantasia Sonata* (1927); *Sonata Poem* (1935); *Sonata Ballade* (1936); *Sonata Legend "Capricornia"* (1940).

Agosti, Guido, Italian pianist and teacher; b. Forlì, Aug. 11, 1901; d. Milan, June 2, 1989. He studied piano with Busoni at the Bologna Cons. He began his professional career as a pianist in 1921; subsequently taught piano at the Venice Cons. (1933–40) and at the Rome Cons. (1941–45). In 1947 he was appointed prof. of piano at the Accademia Chigiana in Siena; subsequently went abroad in 1963 and taught at Weimar until 1970, when he joined the faculty of the Sibelius Academy of Music in Helsinki; eventually he returned to Italy. Apart from teaching, he also wrote some acceptable pieces for piano solo.

Agostini, Lodovico, Italian singer and composer; b. Ferrara, 1534; d. there, Sept. 20, 1590. He became a priest; was at the cappella of Ferrara Cathedral (from 1572); served as maestro di cappella to Duke Alfonso II of Este of Ferrara (1578–90). A number of his sacred and secular vocal works were publ. in Milan, Ferrara, and Venice between 1567 and 1586.

Agostini, Mezio, Italian composer, pianist, conductor, and pedagogue; b. Fano, Aug. 12, 1875; d. there, April 22, 1944. He studied with his father and with Carlo Pedrotti at the Liceo Rossini in Pesaro (1885–92). He was a prof. of harmony there from 1900 to 1909, and then director of the Liceo Benedetto Marcello in Venice (1909–40). He was active as an opera conductor in Venice and other Italian cities, and gave chamber music concerts as a pianist. His *Trio* won 1st prize at the international competition in Paris in 1904. He wrote the operas *Iovo e Maria* (1896); *Il Cavaliere del Sogno* (Fano, Feb. 24, 1897); *La penna d'Airone* (1896); *Alcibiade* (1902); *America* (also entitled *Hail Columbia,* after Longfellow, 1904); *L'ombra* (1907); *L'agnello del sogno* (1928); *La Figlio del navarca* (Fano, Sept. 3, 1938). He also wrote a Sym., 4 orch. suites, a Piano Concerto, 2 string quartets, 2 piano trios, a Cello Sonata, a

Violin Sonata, the cantata *A Rossini,* numerous piano pieces, and songs.

Agostini, Paolo, Italian organist and composer; b. Vallerano, 1583; d. Rome, Oct. 3, 1629. He was a member of the choir school of S. Luigi dei Francesi in Rome, where he studied with G.B. Nanino. After serving as organist and maestro di cappella at S. Maria del Ruscello in Vallerano, he returned to Rome as organist at S. Maria in Trastevere; later was vice-maestro di cappella there and concurrently maestro di cappella at Ss. Trinita dei Pellegrini. He was also vice-maestro at S. Lorenzo in Damaso (1619–26) and maestro di cappella at the Cappella Giulia at St. Peter's (from 1626). His music displays great ingenuity of contrapuntal structure; some of his choral works are written for 48 independent parts.
   Works (all publ. in Rome): *Salmi della madonna, Magnificat, Ave maris stella, antifone, motetti, lib. 1* for 1 to 3 Voices and Basso Continuo (1619); *Liber secundus missarum* for 4 Voices (1626); *Spartitura delle messe del primo libro* for 4 to 5 Voices (1627); *Spartitura del secondo libro delle messe e motetti* for 4 Voices (1627); *Partitura del terzo libro della messa sine nomine, con 2 Resurrexit* for 4 Voices (1627); *Libro quarto delle messe in spartitura* (1627); *Spartitura della messa et motetto Benedicam Dominum ad canones* for 4 Voices (1627); *Partitura delle messe et motetti con 40 esempi di contrapunti* for 4 to 5 Voices (1627); *Missarum liber posthumus* (1630).

Agrell, Johan Joachim, Swedish violinist, harpsichordist, and composer; b. Löth, Feb. 1, 1701; d. Nuremberg, Jan. 19, 1765. He studied at Uppsala Univ.; later was active in Kassel (1723–46) and in Nuremberg (from 1746). Among his publ. works are 5 concertos for Cembalo and Strings, 2 sonatas for Violin and Cembalo, 6 sonatas for Cembalo Solo, and pieces for cembalo in dance forms. His syms. and cantatas are preserved in various European libraries.

Agricola, Alexander, composer of the Netherlands school, sometimes said to have been of German extraction, but referred to as a Belgian in his epitaph; b. Flanders, c.1446; d. Valladolid, Spain, 1506. He entered the service of the Duke of Milan in 1471; then went to Cambrai; in 1476 he is mentioned as "petit vicaire" at Cambrai Cathedral. He later traveled in Italy; entered the service of Philip I of Burgundy in 1500 and followed him to Spain in 1502, returning to Belgium in 1505. He went to Spain again in January 1506 and died shortly afterward. Thirty-one of Agricola's songs and motets were printed by Petrucci (Venice, 1501–3), who also publ. a vol. of 5 masses based on chanson material: *Le Serviteur, Je ne demande, Malheur me bat, Primi toni, Secundi toni* (Venice, 1503).

Agricola, Benedetta Emilia (née **Molteni**), Italian soprano; b. Modena, 1722; d. Berlin, 1780. She studied with Porpora, Hasse, and Salimbeni; made her operatic debut at the Berlin Royal Opera in 1743 in C.H. Graun's *Cesare e Cleopatra*. She was married to **Johann Friedrich Agricola,** director of the Royal Chapel in Berlin; her connection with the court ceased upon his death in 1774, and she disappeared from the music scene.

Agricola, Johann Friedrich, German organist and composer; b. Dobitzschen, near Altenburg, Jan. 4, 1720; d. Berlin, Dec. 2, 1774. He entered the Univ. of Leipzig as a law student in 1738, studying music meanwhile with J.S. Bach, and later (1741) with Johann Quantz in Berlin. In 1751 Agricola was appointed court composer to Frederick the Great; in 1759 he succeeded C.H. Graun as director of the Royal Chapel. Agricola wrote 11 operas (produced between 1750 and 1772 at Berlin and Potsdam) and church music; he also made arrangements of the King's compositions. He taught singing and in 1757 tr. Pier Tosi's *Opinioni de' cantori.* Under the pseudonym **Flavio Amicio Olibrio** Agricola printed some polemical pamphlets directed against the theorist Friedrich Marpurg; he was also a collaborator with Jakob Adlung in the latter's *Musica mechanica organoedi* (1768). His wife was **Benedetta Emilia** (née **Molteni) Agricola.**
   Bibl.: H. Wucherpfennig, *J.F. A.* (diss., Univ. of Berlin, 1922).

Agricola, Martin, important German music theorist and writer; b. Schwiebus (Brandenburg), Jan. 6, 1483; d. Magdeburg, June 10, 1556. His real name was **Sore,** but he adopted the Latin name Agricola to indicate his peasant origin. Mattheson says that he was the 1st to abandon the old tablature for modern notation, but this is not quite accurate; Agricola merely proposed an improved system for lute tablature. From 1519 he was a private music teacher in Magdeburg; in 1525 he was cantor at the 1st Lutheran church there. His friend and patron, Rhaw of Wittenberg, publ. most of Agricola's works, the magnum opus being *Musica instrumentalis deudsch* (i.e., "Set in German"; 1st ed., Wittenberg, 1529; 4th ed., considerably rev., 1545; modern reprint, Leipzig, 1896). This work, although derived from Virdung's *Musica getutscht,* contains much new material and is set in couplet verse in the German vernacular. Further works are: *Ein kurtz deudsche Musica* (1529; 3rd ed. as *Musica choralis deudsch,* 1533); *Musica figuralis deudsch,* with the supplement *Büchlein von den proportionibus* (1532); *Scholia in musicam planam Venceslai Philomatis* (1538); *Rudimenta musices* (1539); *Quaestiones vulgatiores in musicam* (1543); *Duo libri musices* (posthumous; Wittenberg, 1561; includes reprints of *Musica choralis* and *Musica figuralis*; and 54 *Instrumentische Gesänge* as a supplement). Compositions: *Ein Sangbüchlein aller Sonntags-Evangelien* (1541); *Neue deutsche geistliche Gesänge* (1544); *Hymni aliquot sacri* (1552); *Melodiae scholasticae* (1557).
   Bibl.: H. Funck, *M. A.* (Wolfenbüttel, 1933).

Aguado (y García), Dionisio, Spanish guitarist and composer; b. Madrid, April 8, 1784; d. there, Dec. 29, 1849. He went to Paris in 1825, and attracted the attention of Rossini and Paganini by his virtuosity. Returning to Madrid in 1838, he taught guitar playing. He wrote *Estudio para la guitarra* (Madrid, 1820); *Escuela o método de guitarra* (Madrid, 1825); also 45 waltzes, 6 minuets, and other minor pieces.

Aguilera de Heredia, Sebastian, Spanish organist and composer; b. Saragossa (baptized), Aug. 15, 1561; d. there, Dec. 16, 1627. He was organist at Huesca (1585–1603) and then maestro de musica at Saragossa Cathedral. He publ. there his collection *Canticum Beatissimae Virginis Deiparae Mariae octo modis seu tonis compositum, quaternisque vocibus, quinis, senis et octonis concionandum* (1618). It contains sacred choruses in 4, 5, 6, and 8 parts, derived from 8 church modes. His music is notable for skillful use of dissonances ("falsas").
   Bibl.: H. Anglès, "Orgelmusik der Schola Hispanica von XV–XVII. Jahrhunderte," in *Peter Wagner-Festschrift* (Leipzig, 1926).

Aguirre, Julián, Argentine composer; b. Buenos Aires, Jan. 28, 1868; d. there, Aug. 13, 1924. He was taken to Spain as a child, and studied at the Madrid Cons., returning to Buenos Aires in 1887. His works are mostly miniatures for piano in the form of stylized Argentine dances and songs. He wrote 61 opus numbers; *Gato* and *Huella* (op. 49), his most popular pieces, were orchestrated by Ansermet, who performed them in Buenos Aires (April 6, 1930); the *Huella* was also arranged for Violin and Piano by Jascha Heifetz. Other notable works are *Aires nacionales argentinos* (op. 17) and *Zamba* (op. 40).
   Bibl.: J. Giacobbe, *J. A.* (Buenos Aires, 1945); C. García Muñoz, *J. A.* (Buenos Aires, 1970).

Agujari, Lucrezia (called **La Bastardina,** or **Bastardella,** being the natural daughter of a nobleman), brilliant Italian singer; b. Ferrara, 1743; d. Parma, May 18, 1783. Her father entrusted her instruction to P. Lambertini; in 1764 she made a triumphant debut at Florence, followed by a succession of brilliant appearances in Milan and other Italian cities; also in London. Mozart wrote of her that she had "a lovely voice, a flexible throat, and an incredibly high range." In 1780 she married the Italian composer Giuseppe Colla, whose songs she constantly performed at her concerts. Her compass was phenomenal, embracing 3 octaves (C^1–C^4).

Ahern, David (Anthony), Australian composer; b. Sydney, Nov. 2, 1947. He played piano and violin as a child; studied composition with Butterley and Meale; then took courses with Stockhausen in Cologne; also was in London, where he became a disciple of Cardew, exploring the outer regions of the art of hypermusical speculations. He formed an avant-garde performing group called Teletopa Improvisation in Sydney (1970). His early works are rigidly serial, but after 1965 he began employing random theatrical effects. His works include a Sonata for Solo Violin (1963); *After Mallarmé* for Orch. (1966); *Annunciations* for Orch. (1966); *Auriga* for Wind Quartet (1966); *Arabesques* for 48 Solo Strings (1967); *Music for 9* (Piano, Flute, Clarinet, String Quartet, and 2 Percussionists, 1967); *Ned Kelly Music* for Orch. (1967); *Journal* for 6 Actors and Actresses, Didjeridu, Electric Bass, Violin, and Ring Modulator (1968); a symbolic score, *Stereo/Mono* (1971); *Cinemusic* (1972); *Hilo* for 6 Trumpets, 4 Tubas, 4 Percussionists, Harp, Piano, 16 Violins, and 8 Double Basses (1975).

Ahle, Johann Georg, German organist, writer on music, and composer, son of **Johann Rudolf Ahle;** b. Mühlhausen (baptized), June 12, 1651; d. there, Dec. 2, 1706. He succeeded his father as organist in Mühlhausen, and was made poet laureate by Emperor Leopold I. Among Ahle's works publ. during his lifetime are *Musikalische Frühlings-, Sommer-, Herbst-, und Wintergespräche* (1695–1701; written to illustrate his method of composition); *Instrumentalische Frühlingsmusik* (1676; publ. in 2 vols., 1675–76); *Anmuthige zehn vierstimmige Viol-di-gamba Spiele* (1681); many vols. of dances, sacred and secular songs.

Ahle, Johann Rudolf, German organist, writer on music, and composer, father of **Johann Georg Ahle;** b. Mühlhausen, Dec. 24, 1625; d. there, July 9, 1673. From 1646 he was cantor in Erfurt. He was organist of St. Blasius, Mühlhausen, in 1654, and in 1661 was elected burgomaster of the town. Ahle was a diligent composer of church music and writer of theoretical works. His *Compendium pro tonellis* (1648) ran through 4 eds., 2nd as *Brevis et perspicua introductio in artem musicam* (1673), 3rd and 4th as *Kurze und deutliche Anleitung* (1690 and 1704); His principal compositions include: *Geistlich Dialoge,* songs in several parts (1648); *Thüringischer Lustgarten* (1657); *Geistliche Fest- und Communionandachten* (posthumous). Many of his songs are still popular in Thuringia. A selection from his works was publ. by J. Wolf in Denkmäler Deutscher Tonkunst (1901).
BIBL.: J. Wolf, "J.R. A.: Eine bio-bibliographische Skizze," *Sammelbände der Internationalen Musik-Gesellschaft,* II (1900–1901); A. Adrio, s.v., *Die Musik in Geschichte und Gegenwart.*

Ahlersmeyer, Mathieu, German baritone; b. Cologne, June 29, 1896; d. Garmisch-Partenkirchen, July 23, 1979. He studied voice in Cologne; made his debut in Mönchen as Wolfram in *Tannhäuser* (1929); then sang with the Kroll Opera in Berlin (1930–31) and at the Hamburg State Opera (1931–33). He was subsequently on the staff of the Dresden State Opera, and again with the Hamburg State Opera (1946–61); also sang in Berlin, Vienna, Milan, and London until his retirement in 1973. He created the role of the Barber in Strauss's *Die schweigsame Frau* (Dresden, June 24, 1935).

Ahlstrom, David, American composer; b. Lancaster, N.Y., Feb. 22, 1927. He studied composition with Henry Cowell and Bernard Rogers; became interested in Asian philosophy and took lessons with Haridas Chaudhuri. He obtained a Ph.D. in composition from the Eastman School of Music in Rochester, N.Y., in 1961; he then taught music theory at Northwestern Univ. (1961–62), Southern Methodist Univ. in Dallas (1962–67), and Eastern Illinois Univ. in Charleston (1967–76). In 1976 he moved to San Francisco, and became active in the production of new American stage music. Among his own works, the most significant is his opera *America, I Love You,* to a libretto by e.e. cummings, first produced in its entirety, composer conducting, in San Francisco on June 25, 1983; other operas are *Doctor Faustus Lights the Lights,* after Ger-

trude Stein (San Francisco, Oct. 29, 1982), and *3 Sisters Who Are Not Sisters,* also derived from Gertrude Stein's text, produced under Ahlstrom's direction in San Francisco, Sept. 17, 1982. He also wrote several syms. and clarinet sonatas, and a number of theater works employing electronic sound and dance.

Ahna, Heinrich Karl Herman de. See **De Ahna, Heinrich Karl Herman.**

Aho, Kalevi, Finnish composer; b. Forssa, March 9, 1949. He studied composition with Rautavaara at the Sibelius Academy in Helsinki, graduating in 1971; he then went to Berlin and took lessons in composition with Boris Blacher. In 1974 he was appointed to the music faculty at Helsinki Univ. His early music was influenced by Prokofiev and Shostakovich; he later diverged from his Russian antecedents and adopted a free-flowing cosmopolitan style, neo-classical in form and atonal in melodic structure. His later works evolved into an advanced postmodern style.
WORKS: STAGE: Scenic monologue, *Avain* (The Key), for Baritone and Chamber Orch. (1978–79); *Hyönteiselämää* (Insect Life), opera (1985–87). ORCH.: 7 syms.: No. 1 (1969); No. 2 (1970); No. 3, *Sinfonia concertante,* for Violin and Orch. (1973); No. 4 (1973); No. 5 (1976); No. 6 (1980); No. 7, *Hyönteissinfonia* (Insect Sym.; Helsinki, Oct. 26, 1988); Chamber Sym. for Strings (1976); Violin Concerto (1981); *Hiljaisuus* (Silence; 1982); Cello Concerto (1983–84); *Fanfare for YS* (Helsinki, April 18, 1986); Piano Concerto (1988–89). CHAMBER: 3 string quartets: No. 1 (suppressed); No. 2 (1970); No. 3 (1971); Sonata for Solo Violin (1974); Quintet for Oboe and String Quartet (1974); Quintet for Bassoon and String Quartet (1977); *Ludus solemnis* for Organ (1978); Piano Sonata (1980); Quartet for Flute, Saxophone, Guitar, and Percussion (1982); Accordion Sonata (1984); *Inventions* for Oboe and Cello (1986); also songs and choral works.

Ahrens, Joseph Johannes Clemens, eminent German organist and composer; b. Sommersell, Westphalia, April 17, 1904. He displayed an early talent for improvisation on the organ; after studying with Wilhelm Middelschulte, he was appointed an organist at St. Hedwigs-Kathedrale in Berlin; later he was prof. of Catholic church music at the Berlin Hochschule für Musik. In 1968 he received a silver pontifical medal from the Vatican in appreciation of his accomplishments in sacred music. He composed almost exclusively for organ and chorus, maintaining the strict form of the Gregorian chorale within the framework of complex polyphony, and applying advanced melodic and harmonic formulas, including the 12-tone technique. His compositions, couched in a modern Baroque style, were highly esteemed by professional organists.
WORKS: *Missa choralis* (1945); *Missa dorica* (1946); *Missa gotica* (1948); *Missa hymnica* (1948); *Missa Salvatoris* (1949); *Missa pro unitate* (1963); *Missa dodekaphonica* (1966, in which Gregorian chant is combined with 12-tone melodic patterns); *Passion of St. Matthew* (1950); *Passion of St. John* (1961); *Fantasie und Ricercare* for Organ (1967).

Ahronovich, (Georgi) Yuri, Russian conductor; b. Leningrad, May 13, 1932. He studied conducting with Kurt Sanderling and Nathan Rachlin. He then appeared with leading opera houses and orchs. in the Soviet Union. In 1974 he conducted at the Cologne Opera and at Covent Garden in London. From 1975 to 1986 he was chief conductor of the Gürzenich Orch. in Cologne, and from 1982 to 1987 of the Stockholm Phil.

Aibl, Joseph, founder of a music publishing house, established in Munich in 1824; his successors were **Eduard Spitzweg** (from 1836) and his sons, **Eugen** and **Otto.** In 1904 Universal Edition bought the firm.

Aiblinger, Johann Kaspar, German conductor and composer; b. Wasserburg, Bavaria, Feb. 23, 1779; d. Munich, May 6, 1867. He studied music in Munich, then at Bergamo under Simon Mayr (1802); lived at Vicenza (1803–11), then became 2nd maestro di cappella to the viceroy at Milan; founded the

Odeon (a society for the cultivation of Classical vocal music) at Venice, in collaboration with Abbé Trentino; was engaged (1819) for the Italian opera in Munich as maestro al cembalo; returned in 1833 to Bergamo, and amassed a fine collection of early classical music, now in the Staatsbibliothek at Munich. He wrote many sacred compositions (masses, Requiems, liturgies, Psalms, etc.), which were very popular. He also wrote 2 operas, including the popular *Rodrigo e Ximene* (Munich, 1821), and 3 ballets.

Aichinger, Gregor, important German church composer; b. Regensburg, 1564; d. Augsburg, Jan. 21, 1628. At the age of 13 he went to Munich, where he was under the tutelage of Orlando Lasso, then entered the Univ. of Ingolstadt. He made 2 journeys to Rome; visited Venice, where he mastered the art of Venetian polyphony. He eventually settled in Augsburg as choirmaster and vicar of the Cathedral. He wrote almost exclusively for voices, to Latin texts; his sacred works are remarkable for their practical value and for the excellence of their musical content. Among his many publ. works are 3 books of *Sacrae cantiones* (Venice, 1590; Augsburg, 1595; Nuremberg, 1597); *Tricinia Mariana* (Innsbruck, 1598); *Divinae laudes* (Augsburg, 1602); etc. His publication *Cantiones ecclesiasticae cum basso generali et continuo* (Dillingen, 1607) is noteworthy as one of the earliest works in which the term "basso continuo" appears in the title. A selection of Aichinger's works is included in vol. 18 (formerly 10.i) of Denkmäler der Tonkunst in Bayern, prefaced with a biographical article by the ed., Theodor Kroyer.

Aitken, Hugh, American composer; b. N.Y., Sept. 7, 1924. He received his primary training at home; his father was an accomplished violinist, and his paternal grandmother was a pianist. He took lessons in clarinet playing and also enrolled in a chemistry class at N.Y. Univ. From 1943 to 1945 he served as a navigator in the U.S. Army Air Corps. Returning from the war, he entered the Juilliard School of Music in N.Y. as a student in composition of Bernard Wagenaar, Vincent Persichetti, and Robert Ward (M.S., 1950); in 1960 he joined the faculty there; in 1970 became a prof. of music at William Paterson College in Wayne, N.J. In his music he professes a moral dedication to the Classical ideals and regards any deviation from the natural melodic flow and harmonic euphony as unjustifiable tonicide.

WORKS: STAGE: *Fables,* chamber opera after La Fontaine (1975); *Felipe,* opera after Cervantes (1981). **ORCH.:** Chamber Concerto for Piano, Winds, Brass, and String Quintet (1947; rev. 1977); *Toccata* (1950); Piano Concerto (1953); *Short Suite* for String Orch. (1954); *Partita I* (1957); *7 Pieces* for Chamber Orch. (1957); *Serenade* for Chamber Orch. (1958); *Partita II* (1959); *Partita* for String Orch. and Piano (1960); *Partita III* and *IV* (1964); *Partita* for String Quartet and Orch. (1964); *Rameau Remembered* for Flute, 2 Oboes, Bassoon, and Strings (1980); *In Praise of Ockeghem* for String Orch. (1981); 2 violin concertos (1984, 1988); *Happy Birthday* for the 40th anniversary of the Aspen Music Festival (1988). **CHAMBER:** *Short Suite* for Wind Quintet and Piano (1948); String Trio (1951); *Suite* for Clarinet (1955); *Partita* for 6 Instruments (1956); Quintet for Oboe and Strings (1957); *8 Studies* for Wind Quintet (1958); *Partita* for Violin (1958); Quartet for Clarinet and Strings (1959); *Trombone Music* (1961); *Suite* for Solo Bass (1961); *Montages* for Bassoon (1962); *Serenade* for Oboe and String Trio (1965); Trios for 11 Players (1970); *Trumpet!* (1974); *Oboe Music* (1975); *Tromba* for Trumpet and String Quartet (1976); *Johannes* for 5 Renaissance Instruments (N.Y., Oct. 27, 1977); *For the Violin* (1978); *For the Cello* (1980); *Op. 95 Revisited* for String Quartet (1980); *Flute Music* (1981); *5 Short Pieces* for 3 Clarinets (1982); Trio for Flute, Clarinet, and Cello (1984); Concertino for Contrabass and String Trio (1984); *Music for the Horn* (1985). **VOCAL:** 8 cantatas (1958–87); oratorio, *The Revelation of St. John the Divine, Part I* for Soloists, Chorus, and Orch. (1965), *Part II* for Soloists, Chorus, and Orch. (1986); choruses; songs. Also piano and organ pieces; band music.

Aitken, Robert, noted Canadian flutist and composer; b. Kentville, Nova Scotia, Aug. 28, 1939. He studied flute with Marcel Moyse, Julius Baker, and Jean-Pierre Rampal; took courses in composition with Barbara Pentland at the Univ. of British Columbia in Vancouver and with John Weinzweig at the Univ. of Toronto; also received instruction in electronic music from Myron Schaeffer. He then was principal flutist of several Canadian orchs. and taught flute playing at the Royal Cons. in Toronto; he held the degrees of B.M. in composition (1961) and M.M. (1964). In 1971 he organized the New Music Concerts in Toronto; in 1972 he was appointed to the faculty of the Univ. of Toronto. In his music he explores unusual instrumental combinations and spatial concepts of antiphonal groupings.

WORKS: *Rhapsody* for Orch. (1961); Quartet for Flute, Oboe, Viola, and Double Bass (1961); *Music* for Flute and Electronic Tape (1963); *Noēsis* for Electronic Tape (1963); Concerto for 12 Solo Instruments (1964); *Spectra* for 4 Chamber Groups (1969); *Kebyar* for Flute, Clarinet, 2 Double Basses, Percussion, and Tape (1971); *Shadows I: Nekuia* for Orch. (1971); *Shadows II: Lalitá* for Flute, 3 Cellos, 2 Percussionists, and 2 Harps (1972); *Shadows III: Nira* for Solo Violin, Flute, Oboe, Viola, Double Bass, Piano, and Harpsichord (1974–88); *Spiral* for Orch., with Amplified Flute, Oboe, Clarinet, and Bassoon (1975); *Icicle* for Solo Flute (1977); *Plainsong* for Solo Flute (1977); *Folia* for Woodwind Quintet (1980); *Monody* for Chorus (1983).

Aitken, Webster, American pianist; b. Los Angeles, June 17, 1908; d. Santa Fe, N.Mex., May 11, 1981. He studied piano in Europe with Artur Schnabel and Emil von Sauer; in 1929 he made his professional debut in Vienna. Returning to America, he gave a concert in N.Y. (Nov. 17, 1935); in 1938 he presented a series of recitals in N.Y. in programs featuring all of Schubert's piano works. He subsequently devoted himself mainly to teaching.

Ajmone-Marsan, Guido, Italian-born American conductor; b. Turin, March 24, 1947. He was taken to the U.S. as a child and became an American citizen in 1962. He studied clarinet and piano; continued his studies in Salzburg, Venice, and Siena. He took a course in conducting with Franco Ferrara at the Accademia di Santa Cecilia in Rome. His conducting career received its decisive impetus in 1973, when he won 1st prize in the Solti Competition in Chicago; subsequently he appeared as a guest conductor with the Chicago, Philadelphia, and Cleveland orchs., and with various orchs. abroad. After serving as music director of Arnhem's Het Gelders Orch. (1982–86), he was Generalmusikdirektor of the Essen City Theater (1986–90).

Akeroyde, Samuel, English composer of songs; b. Yorkshire, c.1650; d. London, after 1706. He was in the service of James II in 1687 as Musician in Ordinary, and wrote songs for at least 11 plays produced in London between 1685 and 1706. His songs were printed in several contemporary collections: Durfey's *Third Collection of Songs* (1685); *The Theatre of Musick* (1685–87); *Vinculum Societatis* (1687); *Comes Amoris* (1687–94); *The Banquet of Musick* (1688); *Thesaurus Musicus* (1693–96).

Akimenko (real name, **Yakimenko**), **Fyodor,** Russian composer; b. Kharkov, Feb. 20, 1876; d. Paris, Jan. 3, 1945. He studied with Balakirev at the Court Chapel in St. Petersburg (1886–90), then with Liadov and Rimsky-Korsakov at the St. Petersburg Cons. (1895–1900). He was the 1st composition teacher of Stravinsky, whom he taught privately. After the Russian Revolution he emigrated to Paris, where he remained until his death. He wrote mostly for piano in the manner of the Russian lyric school, and had the good fortune of having his pieces and songs publ. by Belaiev; some of them were included in anthologies of Russian music. He wrote an opera, *The Fairy of the Snows* (1914); a concert overture, which was conducted by Rimsky-Korsakov in St. Petersburg on Nov. 20,

1899; an orch. fantasy, conducted by Glazunov in St. Petersburg on Oct. 28, 1900; *Petite ballade* for Clarinet and Piano; *Pastorale* for Oboe and Piano; Piano Trio; Violin Sonata; Cello Sonata; 2 *Sonata-Fantasias* for Piano; numerous character pieces for piano; and songs.

Akiyama, Kazuyoshi, Japanese conductor; b. Tokyo, Jan. 2, 1941. He attended the Toho School of Music, studying conducting with Hideo Saito. In 1964 he became conductor of the Tokyo Sym. Orch. His other posts include: principal guest conductor, New Japan Phil., Tokyo; principal conductor, Osaka Phil.; resident conductor and music director, Vancouver Sym. Orch. (1972–85); music director, American Sym. Orch., N.Y. (1973–78). In 1985 he became music director of the Syracuse (N.Y.) Sym. Orch.

Akses, Necil Kâzim, Turkish composer; b. Constantinople, May 6, 1908. He studied at the Constantinople Cons.; in 1926 went to Vienna, where he had instruction with Joseph Marx; subsequently moved to Prague and took lessons with Alois Hába and Josef Suk (1931–34). Returning to Turkey in 1935, he was appointed to the Teachers College in Ankara; he also attended classes of Paul Hindemith, who was teaching in Ankara at the time. In 1936 Akses was appointed prof. of composition at the Ankara State Cons. His music incorporates elements of Turkish folk songs, but the contrapuntal and harmonic formulation is entirely modern.

WORKS: *Mete*, opera (1933); *Bayönder*, opera (Ankara, Dec. 27, 1934); *Ankara Castle*, tone poem (Ankara, Oct. 22, 1942); *Poem* for Cello and Orch. (Ankara, June 29, 1946); *Ballade* for Orch. (Ankara, April 14, 1948); *Allegro feroce* for Saxophone and Piano (1931); Flute Sonata (1939); Sym. (1966); piano pieces.

Akutagawa, Yasushi, noted Japanese composer; b. Tokyo, July 12, 1925; d. there, Jan. 31, 1989. He was a son of the famous Japanese writer who wrote *Rashomon*. He studied composition, conducting, and piano playing at the Tokyo Academy of Music and was active in Tokyo as a conductor and composer. He was an ardent believer in the cause of autochthonous Japanese music and organized musical groups for this purpose. His opera *Orpheus in Hiroshima* was produced on Tokyo television on Aug. 27, 1967. He furthermore composed several ballets; of these the following were produced in Tokyo: *The Dream of the Lake* (Nov. 6, 1950), *Paradise Lost* (March 17, 1951), *Kappa* (July 21, 1957), and *Spider's Web* (March 17, 1969). He also composed several syms. and a number of other instrumental works. His film score *Gate of Hell* received a prize.

Alain, Jehan (Ariste), French organist and composer, brother of **Marie-Claire** and **Olivier Alain;** b. St.-Germain-en-Laye, Feb. 3, 1911; d. in action at Petits-Puis, near Saumur, June 20, 1940. He studied organ with his father and piano with Augustin Pierson; then entered the Paris Cons. (1927), where he studied composition with Dukas and Roger-Ducasse and organ with Dupré; was organist at St. Nicolas Cathedral in Maisons-Lafitte, near Paris (1935–39). His death at 29, while leading a motorcycle patrol in the early months of World War II, was a great loss to French music. In addition to many works for organ and piano, he wrote choral pieces, chamber music, and songs. His works for organ have proved to be the most enduring; among the most frequently performed are the *Fantaisies* Nos. 1 and 2 (1934, 1936) and the *Litanies* (1937).

BIBL.: B. Gavoty, *J. A., musicien français (1911–1940)* (Paris, 1945); M.-C. Alain, "L'Œuvre d'orgue de J. A.," *L'organo*, VI (1968); F. Sabatier, "À propos de l'œuvre d'orgue de J. A.," *Jeunesse et Orgue* (1973); G. Beechey, "The Organ Music of J. A.," *Musical Times*, CXV (1974); J. Welch, "Chronological Dating of the Organ Works of J. A.," *Music—the A.G.O.- R.C.C.O. Magazine* (July 1978).

Alain, Marie-Claire, noted French organist, sister of **Jehan (Ariste)** and **Olivier Alain;** b. St. Germain-en-Laye, Aug. 10, 1926. She was educated at the Paris Cons., studying harmony with Duruflé, counterpoint and fugue with Plé-Caussade, and organ with Dupré. She made her debut in Paris in 1950;

later gave successful organ recitals in Europe and the U.S.; she became particularly noted for her authoritative renditions of the organ music of the Baroque period.

Alain, Olivier, French pianist, musicologist, and composer, brother of **Jehan (Ariste)** and **Marie-Claire Alain;** b. St. Germain-en-Laye, Aug. 3, 1918. He studied organ and piano in his youth; then took courses in composition with Aubin and Messiaen at the Paris Cons. From 1950 to 1964 he served as director of the Cons. in St. Germain-en-Laye; in 1961 he was appointed to the faculty of the École César Franck in Paris. He composed an oratorio, *Chant funèbre sur les morts en montagne* (1950); also wrote motets and pieces for organ and piano. He publ. the manual *L'Harmonie* (Paris, 1965) and the monograph *Bach* (Paris, 1970).

Alaleona, Domenico, Italian music theorist and composer; b. Montegiorgio, Nov. 16, 1881; d. there, Dec. 28, 1928. He studied organ and clarinet in his native town; in 1901 went to Rome, where he studied piano with Sgambati, organ with Renzi, and theory with De Sanctis at the Accademia di Santa Cecilia; was then active as a choral conductor in Leghorn and Rome; in 1911 obtained the post of prof. of musical esthetics at the Accademia di Santa Cecilia. He wrote an opera, *Mirra* (1912; produced in Rome, March 31, 1920, with critical acclaim, but not revived); a Requiem; *Sinfonia italiana*; 12 *Canzoni italiane*; and 4 *Laudi italiane* for various Instrumental Groups; a cycle of 18 songs, *Melodie Pascoliane*; etc. However, his importance lies in his theoretical writings. His valuable book *Studi sulla storia dell'oratorio musicale in Italia* (Turin, 1908) was reprinted in Milan (1945) as *Storia dell'oratorio musicale in Italia* and is now a standard work. A believer in musical progress, he contributed several original ideas to the theory of modern music, notably in his article "L'armonia modernissima," *Rivista Musicale Italiana* (1911), and originated the term "dodecafonia."

BIBL.: G. Cardi, *D. A.: Musicista e musicologo* (Ascoli Piceno, 1957).

Alard, Jean-Delphin, distinguished violinist of the French school; b. Bayonne, March 8, 1815; d. Paris, Feb. 22, 1888. He was a student of Habeneck at the Paris Cons. He succeeded Baillot as a violin teacher there in 1843, and as leader of the royal orch. teaching in the Cons. till 1875. A fine instructor (Sarasate was his pupil), he publ. *Violin School*, a manual of high merit; *Les Maîtres classiques du violon*, a selection from 18th-century classics; and numerous brilliant and popular pieces for violin (concertos, études, fantasias, etc.).

BIBL.: B. Schwarz, *Great Masters of the Violin* (N.Y., 1983).

Alarie, Pierrette, Canadian soprano; b. Montreal, Nov. 9, 1921. She studied in Montreal and later with Elisabeth Schumann in Philadelphia; made her debut in Montreal in 1940. After winning the Metropolitan Opera Auditions of the Air, she made her debut with the company on Dec. 8, 1945, as Oscar in *Un ballo in maschera*; remained on its roster until 1948. She made her Paris Opéra debut in 1949; also sang at La Scala in Milan, the Vienna State Opera, the Aix-en-Provence Festival, and the Salzburg Festival; in addition, she made concert appearances. She was married to the Canadian tenor **Léopold Simoneau.**

Alary, Jules (Giulio) Eugène Abraham, Italian-French composer; b. Mantua, March 16, 1814; d. Paris, April 17, 1891. He studied at the Cons. of Milan; then played the flute at La Scala. In 1838 he settled in Paris as a successful voice teacher and composer. He wrote numerous operas, among them *Rosamunda* (Florence, June 10, 1840); *Le tre nozze* (Paris, March 29, 1851; a polka-duet from it, sung by Henrietta Sontag and Lablache, was highly popular); and *Sardanapalo* (St. Petersburg, Feb. 16, 1852). His opera *La Voix humaine* had the curious distinction of being staged at the Paris Opéra (Dec. 30, 1861) with the sole purpose of making use of the scenery left over after the fiasco of *Tannhäuser* (the action of Alary's opera takes place in Wartburg, as does that of *Tannhäuser*). It held the stage for 13 performances (*Tannhäuser* had 3).

Alary also wrote a mystery play, *Redemption* (Paris, April 14, 1850), much sacred music, and some chamber works.

Albanese, Licia, noted Italian-born American soprano; b. Bari, July 22, 1909. She studied with Emanuel De Rosa in Bari and with Giuseppina Baldassare-Tedeschi in Milan. She made her operatic debut in 1934 under unusual circumstances at the Teatro Lirico in Milan, when she was urgently summoned to sing the 2nd part of *Madama Butterfly* as Cio-Cio-San to substitute for a soprano who was taken ill during the 1st act. In 1935 she won 1st prize for best singing in a national Italian contest, and made her official debut in Parma on Dec. 10, 1935, again as Cio-Cio-San. Her success was so great that she was offered a contract with the San Carlo Opera in Naples, and subsequently became a member of La Scala in Milan. She received a number of high honors, among them the Order of Merit in Italy and the award of the Lady Grand Cross of the Equestrian Order of the Holy Sepulchre, which was given to her by Pope Pius XI. On Feb. 9, 1940, she made a brilliant debut at the Metropolitan Opera in N.Y. in her favorite role as Cio-Cio-San; she continued to sing with the Metropolitan for 26 years; altogether she sang there 286 times in N.Y. and 115 times on tour, in 17 roles; besides Cio-Cio-San, which she performed 72 times, she sang Mimi in *La Bohème*, Marguerite in *Faust*, Violetta in *La Traviata*, Desdemona in *Otello*, and Tosca. She gave her final performance at the Metropolitan on April 16, 1966. She returned to the stage for a recital at Carnegie Hall on Feb. 22, 1970, in a program of operatic arias; she sang again at a benefit of the Puccini Foundation in Town Hall, N.Y., on Feb. 5, 1975. She married in 1945 an Italian-American businessman, Joseph Gimma.

BIBL.: D. Ewen, *Musicians Since 1900* (N.Y., 1978).

Albani, Dame Emma (real name, **Marie Louise Cécile Emma Lajeunesse**), Canadian dramatic soprano; b. Chambly, near Montreal, Nov. 1, 1847; d. London, April 3, 1930. She sang in a Catholic church in Albany, N.Y., in 1864; was then sent to Europe for study, first in Paris with Duprez, and then in Milan with Lamperti, who dedicated to her his treatise on the trill. She made her debut as Amina in *La Sonnambula* in Messina in 1870, under the name of Albani, taken from an old Italian family. After further appearances in Italy, she made her London debut, again as Amina (Covent Garden, April 2, 1872). In 1873 she sang in Moscow and St. Petersburg. Her American operatic debut was in the same role at the N.Y. Academy of Music, in Max Strakosch's company (Oct. 21, 1874). It paved the way for later successes with the Metropolitan Opera, where she made her 1st appearance as Gilda (Dec. 23, 1891). Her last important operatic engagement was as Isolde at Covent Garden (June 26, 1896). She sang in concerts, however, for several years longer. Her farewell concert took place at the Royal Albert Hall in London on Oct. 14, 1911. Her repertoire included the roles of Marguerite, Mignon, Ophelia, Elsa, Elisabeth, Lucia, and Desdemona. Albani married Ernest Gye, the lessee of Covent Garden, in 1878. In her singing, she combined high technical skill with profound feeling. She was equally successful on the operatic stage and in oratorio. In appreciation of her services to British art, she was made a Dame of the Order of the British Empire (1925). She publ. her memoirs, *Forty Years of Song* (London, 1911).

BIBL.: C. Macdonald, *E. A.: Victorian Diva* (Toronto, 1984).

Albani, Mattia (real name, **Mathias Alban**), violin maker; b. S. Niccolo di Kaltern (Alto Adige), March (baptized, March 28) 1621; d. Bolzano, Feb. 7, 1712. He was a pupil of Jakob Stainer. Violins of Albani's are extant dating from as early as the end of 1644. His best examples date from 1680 onward. The great vogue his violins enjoyed spawned many forgeries; false Albani labels have been discovered on violins dating from as early as 1640; the original labels appeared from 1690. A son, **Giuseppe**, his pupil, worked from 1680 to 1722 at Bolzano, and another son, **Michele** (1677–1730), at Graz. Other violin makers named Albani, or at least using the name on their instruments (perhaps for its commercial value), are the following, none appearing to have been connected with the family of the original Mattia: Mattia (Rome, c.1650–1715); Nicola (worked at Mantua, c.1763); Filippo (active c.1773); Francesco (active at Graz, c.1724); Michele (at Palermo, 18th century); and Paolo (at Palermo and Cremona, 1630–70).

Albéniz, Isaac (Manuel Francesco), eminent Spanish composer; b. Camprodón, May 29, 1860; d. Cambô-les-Bains (Pyrénées), May 18, 1909. Endowed with exceptionally precocious musical gifts, he was exhibited as a child pianist at a tender age; soon he began taking formal piano lessons with Narciso Oliveros in Barcelona. His sister **Clementine Albéniz** was also a precocious pianist, and they gave concerts together. When he was 7, his mother took him to Paris, where he was accepted as a private pupil by the famous prof. Marmontel, the teacher of Bizet and Debussy. Returning to Spain he studied with Mendizábal at the Madrid Cons., but possessed by the spirit of adventure, he stowed away on a ship bound for Puerto Rico; from there he made his way to the southern states of the U.S., where he earned a living by playing at places of entertainment. He finally returned to Spain and, having acquired a considerable technique as a serious pianist, he traveled in Europe, and enrolled at the Leipzig Cons. as a student of Jadassohn and Reinecke. Once again in Spain, he was befriended by Count Guillermo Morphy, who sent him to the Brussels Cons., where he studied piano with Brassin and composition with Gevaert and Dupont; he won 1st prize in 1879; in 1880 he met Liszt in Budapest. After a trip to South America he settled in Barcelona in 1883; there he married Rosina Jordana; one of their daughters, Laura Albéniz, became a well-known painter. A meeting with the eminent musicologist and folk-song collector Felipe Pedrell influenced Albéniz in the direction of national Spanish music. Still anxious to perfect his technique of composition, he went to Paris for studies with Paul Dukas and Vincent d'Indy. Abandoning his career as concert pianist, he spent several years in London (1890–93), and in 1893 settled in Paris; there he taught piano at the Schola Cantorum; from 1900 to 1902 he was in Barcelona, and then returned once more to Paris; in 1903 he moved to Nice; later he went to Cambô-les-Bains in the Pyrénées, where he died shortly before his 49th birthday. Almost all of the works of Albéniz are written for piano, and all without exception are inspired by Spanish folklore. He thus established the modern school of Spanish piano literature, derived from original rhythms and melodic patterns, rather than imitating the imitations of national Spanish music by French and Russian composers. His piano suite *Iberia*, composed between 1906 and 1909, is a brilliant display of piano virtuosity.

WORKS: PIANO: *Iberia*, suite of 12 pieces (1906–9): *Evocación, El puerto, Fête-Dieu à Séville, Rondeña, Almería, Triana, El Albaicín, El polo, Lavapiés, Málaga, Jérez, Eritaña*; other piano works are *Suite española; La vega; Cantos de España;* several sonatas; 2 pieces left unfinished: *Azulejos* (completed by Granados); *Navarra* (completed by de Séverac). Fernández Arbós made effective orch. transcriptions of *Evocación, Triana,* and *Fête-Dieu à Séville* (also orchestrated by Leopold Stokowski). Among other piano pieces, the *Seguidillas, Córdova,* and the *Tango in D* have attained great popularity. ORCH.: *Catalonia; Rapsodia española*; Piano Concerto. OPERAS: *The Magic Opal* (London, Jan. 19, 1893); *Enrico Clifford* (Barcelona, May 8, 1895); *Pepita Jiménez* (Barcelona, Jan. 5, 1896); *San Antonio de la Florida* (Madrid, Oct. 26, 1894); *Merlin,* 1st part of an uncompleted operatic trilogy on the legend of King Arthur.

BIBL.: F. Pedrell, "I. A.," *Revista Musical Catalana,* VI (1909); J. de Marliave, "I. A.," *Études Musicales* (Paris, 1917); G. Jean-Aubry, "I. A. (1860–1909)," *Musical Times* (Dec. 1917); H. Klein, "A.'s Opera, *Pepita Jiménez,*" ibid. (March 1918); G. Jean-Aubry, *La Musique et les nations* (Paris, 1922; Eng. tr., London, 1923); H. Collet, *A. et Granados* (Paris, 1926; 2nd ed., 1948); E. Istel, "I. A.," *Musical Quarterly* (Jan. 1929); R. Moragas, "Epistolario inédito de I. A.," *Música,* I (1938); A. de las Heras, *Vida de A.* (Barcelona and Madrid, 1940); V. Ruiz Albéniz, *I. A.* (Madrid, 1948); M. Raux Deledicque, *A., Su vida inquieta y ardorosa* (Buenos Aires, 1950); A. Sagardia,

I. A. (Madrid, 1951); G. Laplane, *A.: Sa vie, son œuvre* (Paris, 1956).

Albéniz, Mateo (Antonio Pérez de), Spanish composer, father of **Pedro Albéniz y Basanta;** b. in the Basque region of Spain, c.1755; d. San Sebastián, June 23, 1831. He was a church organist; publ. *Instrucción melódica especulativa y practica para enseñar a cantar y a tañer la música antigua* (San Sebastián, 1802). His Sonata for Piano was publ. by Joaquín Nín in *16 Sonates anciennes d'auteurs espagnols* (Paris, 1925).

Albéniz y Basanta, Pedro, Spanish organist and composer, son of **Mateo (Antonio Pérez de) Albéniz;** b. Logroño, April 14, 1795; d. Madrid, April 12, 1855. He studied with his father; from his early youth, played the organ in various Spanish towns; later studied piano in Paris with Kalkbrenner and Henri Herz. In 1830 he was appointed prof. of piano at the Madrid Cons.; in 1834, became court organist. He was an energetic promoter of modern methods of piano playing in Spain. He publ. a manual (1840), which was adopted at the Madrid Cons.; also wrote some 70 piano pieces in a highly developed technical style (rondos, variations, medleys, etc.).

Albergati Capacelli, Pirro, Conte d', Italian composer; b. Bologna, Sept. 20, 1663; d. there, June 22, 1735. He wrote 2 operas, *Gli amici* (Bologna, Aug. 16, 1699) and *Il Principe selvaggio* (Bologna, 1712), and numerous oratorios, which were regularly performed at various churches in Bologna (1686–1732): *Nabuccodonosor; Giobbe; S. Orsola; Il convito di Baldassare; L'innocenza di S. Eufemia; S. Catarina; S. Eustachio; Maria annunciata dall'angelo; La morte di Cristo;* etc. Besides these works, Albergati publ. during his lifetime 15 opus nos., consisting of vocal and instrumental music, among them *Balletti; Correnti; Cantate morali; Cantate spirituali; Messa e salmi; Cantate da camera; Motetti et antifone; Capricci;* 12 sonatas for 2 Violins and Bass; etc.

Alberghi, Paolo Tommaso, Italian violinist, composer, and teacher; b. Faenza (baptized), Dec. 31, 1716; d. there, Oct. 11, 1785. He studied violin with Tartini; then was a violinist at the Faenza Cathedral, where his brother Don Francesco Alberghi was maestro di cappella; was named 1st violinist in 1755; upon the death of his brother in 1760, he was appointed maestro di cappella. He was highly esteemed as a violinist and a teacher; among his pupils was Giuseppe Sarti. He composed mostly instrumental works; wrote some 20 violin concertos, which are notable for their late Baroque virtuosity; also composed sonatas and trios; his sacred works include a Magnificat and a Mass.

Albert, Prince Consort of Queen Victoria; b. Rosenau, Coburg, Aug. 26, 1819; d. Windsor, Dec. 14, 1861. He married Queen Victoria on Feb. 10, 1840; lent energetic support to musical activities in England, sponsoring orchs. and choral societies. He studied organ and theory, and acquired an estimable technique of composition; wrote *Invocazione alla armonia* for Chorus and Orch. His songs were publ. in 1881 under the title *The Collected Compositions of His Royal Highness the Prince Consort.* They reveal a Romantic musical temper, influenced by Mendelssohn.

d'Albert, Eugène (Francis Charles), Scottish-born German pianist and composer; b. Glasgow, April 10, 1864; d. Riga, March 3, 1932. His father, **Charles Louis Napoléon d'Albert** (b. Nienstetten, near Hamburg, Feb. 25, 1809; d. London, May 26, 1886), was a dancing master who wrote popular music; it was from him that d'Albert received his early instruction in music. At the age of 10 he entered the National Training School in London, where he studied piano with Pauer and theory with Stainer, Prout, and Arthur Sullivan. He made extraordinary progress as both a pianist and a composer, and after several appearances at the Popular Concerts, was the soloist in Schumann's Concerto at the Crystal Palace in London (Feb. 5, 1881). On Oct. 24, 1881, when only 17, he played his own piano concerto at one of Hans Richter's concerts, arousing great enthusiasm; the press compared him to Mozart and Mendelssohn. He received a Mendelssohn fellowship and went to Vienna; later he studied with Liszt, who was greatly impressed by his technique and often referred to him as "the young Tausig." In 1895, d'Albert was appointed conductor at Weimar; in 1907, he became director of the Hochschule für Musik in Berlin. In the wake of his success, he repudiated his English birth, adopting German citizenship, and made repeated statements derogatory to English culture and even to his former English teachers; he further changed his 1st name to a German form, **Eugen.** During the 1st World War, he was vocal in his enmity toward England, which led in turn to an understandable repugnance among British musicians to accept his music. Despite a brilliant beginning, Eugène d'Albert did not justify his early promise, and his operas and other works are rarely revived. His musical idiom oscillates between the Italian melodic style and German contrapuntal writing, and fails to achieve originality. A considerable corpus of his autograph music MSS, including 11 of his operas (though not *Tiefland*), was acquired in 1963 by the Library of Congress. Eugène d'Albert's personal life was a stormy one. He was married 6 times; his 1st wife (1892–95) was Teresa Carreño; his 2nd was the singer Hermine Finck. D'Albert composed industriously. He publ. 2 piano concertos (in B minor and E); Cello Concerto in C; 2 overtures: *Hyperion* and *Esther;* Sym. in F (1886); Orch. Suite in 5 movements (1924); Piano Sonata; Piano Suite in 5 movements; 2 string quartets; *Der Mensch und das Leben* for 6-part Chorus and Orch. (op. 14); 4 piano pieces, op. 16 (Waltz, Scherzo, Intermezzo, Ballade); minor piano pieces and songs. Of his 20 operas, the most successful were *Tiefland,* 1st staged at the German opera in Prague (Nov. 15, 1903), and *Die toten Augen* (Dresden, March 5, 1916). His other operas are: *Der Rubin* (Karlsruhe, Oct. 12, 1893); *Ghismonda* (Dresden, Nov. 28, 1895); *Gernot* (Mannheim, April 11, 1897); *Die Abreise* (Frankfurt, Oct. 20, 1898); *Kain* (Berlin, Feb. 17, 1900); *Der Improvisator* (Berlin, Feb. 20, 1902); *Flauto solo* (Prague, Nov. 12, 1905); *Tragaldabas,* or *Der geborgte Ehemann* (Hamburg, Dec. 3, 1907); *Izeÿl* (Hamburg, Nov. 6, 1909); *Die verschenkte Frau* (Vienna, Feb. 6, 1912); *Liebesketten* (Vienna, Nov. 12, 1912); *Der Stier von Olivera* (Leipzig, March 10, 1918); *Revolutions-hochzeit* (Leipzig, Oct. 26, 1919); *Scirocco* (Darmstadt, May 18, 1921); *Mareike von Nymwegen* (Hamburg, Oct. 31, 1923); *Der Golem* (Frankfurt, Nov. 14, 1926); *Die schwarze Orchidee* (Leipzig, Dec. 1, 1928); *Mister Wu* (unfinished; completed by Leo Blech; Dresden, Sept. 29, 1932).
BIBL.: W. Raupp, *E. d'A.: Ein Künstler- und Menschenschicksal* (Leipzig, 1930); H. Heisig, *D'A.s Opernschaffen* (diss., Univ. of Leipzig, 1942).

Albert, Heinrich, German composer; b. Lobenstein, Saxony, July 8, 1604; d. Königsberg, Oct. 6, 1651. In 1622 he went to Dresden to study music with his cousin Heinrich Schütz; then studied law at the Univ. of Leipzig; traveled to Warsaw with a peace delegation in 1627, but was seized as a prisoner of war by the Swedes. Upon his release in 1628, he settled in Königsberg; was appointed cathedral organist in 1631; took courses with Johann Stobäus. He publ. in Königsberg 8 books of arias (1638–50); a cantata, *Musikalische Kürbs-Hütte* (1645), consisting of a cycle of 12 terzets to Albert's own texts (a modern reprint was issued by J.M. Müller-Blattau in 1932). A selection of his songs is found in the *Neudrucke deutscher Litteraturwerke* (Halle, 1883); the arias in vols. XII and XIII of Denkmäler Deutscher Tonkunst.
BIBL.: L.H. Fischer, *Gedichte des Königsberger Dichterkreises* (Halle, 1883); G. Kraft, ed., *Festschrift zur Ehrung von H. A. (1604–1651)* (Weimar, 1954).

Albert, Karel, Belgian composer; b. Antwerp, April 16, 1901; d. Liedekerke, May 23, 1987. He studied at the Flemish Cons. and became associated with the Belgian Radio and Television Co., retiring in 1961. He composed 4 syms., numerous overtures and suites, and some chamber music suitable for performance without requiring particular effort.
WORKS: Opera buffa, *Europa ontvoerd* (1950); 2 ballets: *De*

toverlantaarn (The Magic Lantern; 1942) and *Tornooi* (1953); 4 syms. (1941, 1943, 1945, 1966); Sinfonietta (1968); *Pieta* (1933); *Wilde jacht* (1933); overture, *Ananke* (1934); *Lentewandeling* (1935); *Humoresque* (1936); *Het Land* (1937); *Impulsions* (1939); *Suite flamande* (1947); *De Nacht* (1956); Suite (1958); *Dansende beeldekens* (1959); *3 Constructions* for Strings (1959); *In the Beginning Was the Word* for Baritone and Orch. (1962); Chamber Sym. (1932); 2 string quartets (1929, 1941); Trio for Oboe, Clarinet, and Bassoon (1930); Quintet for Flute, Oboe, Violin, Viola, and Cello (1954); *Étude* for Alto and Wind Quintet (1958); Quartet for 4 Saxophones (1960); Brass Quartet (1964). He publ. *De evolutie van de muziek van de Oudheid tot aan Beethoven aan de hand van fonoplaten* (Brussels, 1947).

Albert, Stephen (Joel), American composer; b. N.Y., Feb. 6, 1941. He played trumpet, French horn, and piano in the school band in Great Neck, N.Y.; also took private lessons in composition with Elie Siegmeister, who made his home there. In 1958 he enrolled in the Eastman School of Music in Rochester, N.Y., in the class of Bernard Rogers. In 1960 he went to Stockholm to study with Karl-Birger Blomdahl; returning to the U.S., he took courses at the Philadelphia Musical Academy with Roy Harris and Joseph Castaldo. In 1962 he studied counterpoint with George Rochberg at the Univ. of Pa. in Philadelphia. From 1965 to 1967 he lived in Rome on an American Prix de Rome grant. In 1968–69 he held a Guggenheim fellowship; in 1970–71 he was a lecturer at Stanford Univ.; from 1974 to 1976 he was on the faculty at Smith College in Northampton, Mass. In 1985 he won the Pulitzer Prize in music for his sym., *RiverRun*. From 1985 to 1987 he was composer-in-residence of the Seattle Sym. Orch. Albert's style of composition reflects his geographical wanderings and intellectual wonderings, resulting in a pragmatic and unprejudiced selection of fitting idioms. Thus, while refusing to renounce tonality, he espouses the quaquaversality of modern moods and modes without blundering into the crepuscular regions of serialistic glossolalia. *Musicus sum; musicae nil a me alienum puto*, seems to be his motto: nothing that is of music is alien to him.

WORKS: ORCH.: *Illuminations* for Brass, Pianos, Harps, and Percussion (1962); *Supernatural Songs* for Soprano and Chamber Orch. (1963); *Imitations* for String Quartet (1964); *Winter Songs* for Tenor and Orch. (1965); *Wedding Songs* for Soprano and Piano (1965); *Bacchae* for Narrator, Chorus, and Orch. (1967–68); *Wolf Time* for Soprano and Chamber Orch. (1968); *Letters from the Golden Notebook* for Orch. (1971); *Cathedral Music* for amplified Flutes, amplified Cellos, amplified Guitar, amplified Harpsichord, Brass, Percussion, Electronic Piano, Electronic Organ, and 2 Grand Pianos (1972); *Voices Within* for a Concertino Ensemble encased in an Orch. (1975); *RiverRun*, sym. (1983–84); *Flower of the Mountain* for Soprano and Chamber Orch. (N.Y., May 17, 1986); *Concerto in 1 Movement* for Violin and Orch. (1986); *Anthem and Processionals* (1987). **CHAMBER:** *To Wake the Dead* for Soprano, Flute, Clarinet, Violin, Cello, and Piano, to a text from James Joyce's *Finnegans Wake* (N.Y., March 21, 1979); *Winterfire* for 7 Players (1979); *Music from the Stone Harp* for 8 Players (1980); *Into Eclipse* for Tenor and 12 Instruments (1983–84); *TreeStone* (1983–84); Trio for Violin and Piano (Washington, D.C., Oct. 28, 1988).

BIBL.: D. Ewen, *American Composers* (N.Y., 1982).

Alberti, Domenico, Italian singer, harpsichordist, and composer; b. Venice, 1710; d. Formio (or Rome), c.1740. He studied with Lotti, and won considerable renown as a singer and harpsichord player; wrote 3 operas, *Endimione, Galatea,* and *Olimpiade*. In 1737 he was a member of the Venetian Embassy in Rome, and made several appearances there as a singer and player. His fame in music history rests on his reputed invention of the arpeggio style of keyboard accompaniment, which became known as the "Alberti Bass." His set of 8 sonatas, publ. by Walsh in London, gives many illustrations of this device.

Alberti, Gasparo, Italian composer; b. Padua, c.1480; d. Bergamo, c.1560. He became a singer at S. Maria Maggiore in Bergamo in 1508; periodically he served as its maestro di cappella (until 1554). He is regarded as one of the most significant composers of sacred polyphonic vocal music in Italy in the early Renaissance. His works include 2 8-voice Magnificat settings; Psalms; 5 masses; Lamentations; canticles.

BIBL.: G. d'Alessi, "Precursors of Adriano Willaert in the Practice of Coro spezzato," *Journal of the American Musicological Society*, V (1952); K. Jeppesen, "A Forgotten Master of the Early 16th Century: G. d.A.," *Musical Quarterly*, XLIV (1958); K. Jeppesen, ed., *Italia sacra musica* (Copenhagen, 1962); A. Carver, "The Psalms of Willaert and His North Italian Contemporaries," *Acta Musicologica*, XLVII (1975).

Alberti, Giuseppe Matteo, Italian violinist and composer; b. Bologna, Sept. 20, 1685; d. there, Feb. 18, 1751. He studied violin with C. Manzolini and P.M. Minelli, and took lessons in counterpoint with F. Arresti; then played violin in the orch. of S. Petronio in Bologna; he was also a member of the Accademia Filarmonica there, and was its president from 1721. He composed violin concertos, sonatas, sinfonias, and vocal works, several of which were publ. in his lifetime.

BIBL.: M. Talbot, "A Thematic Catalogue of the Orchestral Works of G.M. A. (1685–1751)," *RMA Research Chronicle*, XIII (1976).

Alberti, Johann Friedrich, German organist and composer; b. Tönning, Schleswig, Jan. 11, 1642; d. Merseburg, June 14, 1710. He studied theology in Rostock, and jurisprudence at the Univ. of Leipzig; also took courses in music with Werner Fabricius and Vincenzo Albrici. He spent most of his life as cathedral organist in Merseburg. Some of his chorales, publ. in modern eds., testify to his aptitude.

Albertini, Joachim (Gioacchino), Italian-born Polish composer; b. Pesaro, 1749; d. Warsaw, March 27, 1812. He was a conductor to Prince Karol Radziwill in Neiświez, later serving as maître de chapelle to King Stanislaw August Poniatowski in Warsaw (from 1782). In 1795 he received Poland's life pension.

WORKS: STAGE: *La Cacciatrice brillante*, intermezzo (Rome, Feb. 1772); *Don Juan albo Ukarany libertyn* (Don Juan or The Rake Punished), opera (Warsaw, Feb. 23, 1783); *Virginia*, opera seria (Rome, Jan. 7, 1786); *Circe und Ulisses*, opera seria (Hamburg, Jan. 30, 1786); *Scipione Africano*, opera seria (Rome, 1789); *La Virgine vestale*, opera seria (Rome, Carnival, 1803); *Kapelmajster polski* (Polish Kapellmeister), intermezzo (Warsaw, Oct. 28, 1808); masses and other sacred works.

Albertsen, Per Hjort, Norwegian organist and composer; b. Trondheim, July 27, 1919. He studied organ at the Oslo Cons., graduating in 1946; took lessons in composition with Sven Erik Tarp in Copenhagen, Ralph Downes in London, and Hanns Jelinek in Vienna. He was an organist in Trondheim (1947–68); then lectured in the music dept. of the univ. there (1968–72). Much of his music has been written for performance in schools.

WORKS: School opera, *Russicola* (1956); Flute Concertino (1948); *Villemann og Magnill*, folk ballad for Soprano, Baritone, Male Chorus, and Orch. (1951); *Symphonic Prelude* (1951); *Gunnerus Suite* for String Orch. (1952); *Little Suite* for String Orch. (1955); *Presentation*, overture (1958); *Notturno e Danza* for Orch. (1960); *Concerto piccolo* for Violin or Clarinet, and Amateur String Orch. (1961); Concerto for Piano and School Orch. (1969); *Tordenskioldiana* for Orch. (1972); *Bendik og Årolilja*, folk ballad for Tenor, Chorus, and Piano (1943; orchestrated 1979); *Slåttesonata* for Piano (1946); Clarinet Sonatina (1950); *4 Religious Folksongs* for Violin, Cello, and Organ (1974); *Toccata, Chaconne and Fugue* for Organ (1976); *Suite* for String Quartet (1984); Sonatine for Violin and Piano (1985); numerous choral works.

Albicastro, Henricus (real name, **Heinrich Weissenburg**), Swiss violinist and composer; b. Switzerland at an uncertain date; d. c.1738 in the Netherlands, where he was a court musician. His works for string instruments were publ. in Amsterdam between 1700 and 1706; of these, 12 concertos *a 4*, a Trio

Sonata, and several violin sonatas with Basso Continuo are available in modern eds.

BIBL.: W.S. Newman, *The Sonata in the Baroque Era* (Chapel Hill, 1959; 4th ed., rev., 1983); M. Talbot, "The Concerto Allegro in the Early Eighteenth Century," *Music & Letters* (Jan., April 1971).

Albinoni, Tomaso (Giovanni), Italian violinist and composer; b. Venice, June 8, 1671; d. there, Jan. 17, 1751. Between 1694 and 1740 he produced 53 operas, most of them in Venice. He rarely absented himself from Venice, but it is known that he attended the premiere of his opera *Griselda* in Florence (1703), serving as concertmaster in the orch.; in 1722 he was in Munich, where he presented his festive opera *I veri amici.* It is, however, as a composer of instrumental music that he is significant. Bach, his close contemporary, admired Albinoni's music; he made arrangements of 2 fugues from Albinoni's trio sonatas. The famous *Adagio* for Strings and Organ is almost totally the work of R. Giazotto, the Italian musicologist. For his instrumental works, see W. Kolneder, ed., *T.G. A.: Gesamtausgabe der Instrumentalmusik* (Berg, 1974–).

BIBL.: M. Talbot, "A.: The Professional Dilettante," *Musical Times* (June 1971); idem, "Vivaldi and A.," *Informations de la Société Int. Antonio Vivaldi* (1972); idem, "A.'s Oboe Concertos," *Consort* (July 1973); J. Solie, "Aria Structure and Ritornello Form in the Music of A.," *Musical Quarterly* (Jan. 1977).

Alboni, Marietta (real name, **Maria Anna Marzia Alboni**), famous Italian contralto; b. Città di Castello, March 6, 1823; d. Ville d'Avray, France, June 23, 1894. She studied in Bologna with Mombelli; in 1841 was introduced to Rossini, who agreed to give her lessons. She made her debut in Bologna, in Pacini's opera *Saffo* (Oct. 3, 1842); shortly afterward sang at La Scala in Rossini's *Assedio di Corinto* (*Le Siège de Corinthe*; Dec. 30, 1842). She then sang in Russia and obtained great success during the season of 1844–45 in St. Petersburg, appearing at the Italian opera with Tamburini, Rubini, and Mme. Viardot. After appearances in Prague, Berlin, and Hamburg, she appeared in the spring of 1847 in Rome and at Covent Garden, where she became a rival of Jenny Lind with the public. So successful were her London appearances that her fees were increased to 2,000 pounds a season. She gave 4 "concerts-spectacles" in Paris in Oct. 1847; made her Paris opera debut in Rossini's *Semiramide* (Dec. 2, 1847). Auber wrote the opera *Zéline ou La Corbeille d'oranges* for her and she sang at its premiere (May 16, 1851). She made an American tour from June 1852 till May 1853 in concert and opera, appearing in N.Y., Boston, and other cities. On July 21, 1853, Alboni married Count Pepoli, who died on Oct. 10, 1867; on Jan. 22, 1877, she married Charles Ziéger, a French officer, and settled in France. Suffering from excessive obesity, she gradually retired from the stage, but continued to appear occasionally in concert, singing while sitting in a large chair. Her vocal range was exceptional, from the contralto G to high soprano C, enabling her to sing soprano parts. She bequeathed a large sum of money to the city of Paris. In appreciation, the City Council, on Oct. 15, 1895, named a street in Passy after her. Arthur Pougin's monograph *Marietta Alboni* (Paris, 1912) quotes many of her autobiographical notes and presents a documented outline of her career.

Albrecht, Alexander, Slovak composer; b. Arad, Rumania, Aug. 12, 1885; d. Bratislava, July 30, 1958. He studied piano with Thomán and Bartók and composition with Koessler at the Budapest Academy of Music; after graduation, he settled in Bratislava. He wrote a number of orch. works for chamber ensemble, including *Šípková ružička* (Sleeping Beauty; 1919); a symphonic poem, *Spomienky a túžby* (Memories and Desires; 1932); *Symphonic Variations* for Trumpet and Orch. (1947); chamber music, cantatas, and choruses.

BIBL.: F. Klinda, *A. A.* (Bratislava, 1959).

Albrecht, Evgeni, Russian violinist, son of **Karl Albrecht** and brother of **Konstantin Albrecht;** b. St. Petersburg, July 16, 1842; d. there, Feb. 9, 1894. He studied violin with Ferdi-

nand David at the Leipzig Cons. (1857–60). Upon his return to Russia, he conducted the Italian opera in St. Petersburg (1860–77); he was also music director of military schools there (1872–77). In 1877 he became inspector of the Imperial Orchs.; in 1892 was music librarian of the Imperial Theaters. He publ. 3 albums of Russian folk songs and a book of 128 children's songs.

Albrecht, Gerd, German conductor, son of **Hans Albrecht;** b. Essen, July 19, 1935. He studied at the Univs. of Kiel and Hamburg. He then conducted opera in Stuttgart (1958–61), Mainz (1961–63), Lübeck (1963–66), and Kassel (1966–72). From 1972 to 1979 he held the post of chief conductor of the German Opera in West Berlin; concurrently he also served, from 1975 on, as conductor of the Tonhalle Orch. in Zürich. In 1981 he made his U.S. operatic debut conducting the American premiere of Reimann's *Lear* at the San Francisco Opera. In 1986 he made his 1st appearance as a guest conductor of a U.S. orch. when he led the Houston Sym. Orch. He served as chief conductor of the Hamburg State Opera and the Phil. State Orch. from 1988.

Albrecht, Hans, German music scholar, father of **Gerd Albrecht;** b. Magdeburg, March 31, 1902; d. Kiel, Jan. 20, 1961. He studied music at the Essen Cons. and later at the Univ. of Münster; then went to the Univ. of Berlin (1921–25); in 1925 he joined the faculty of the Essen Cons., and taught there until 1937. During World War II he was prof. at the State Inst. in Berlin. In 1947 he became director of the Landesinstitut für Musikforschung in Kiel; also was on the faculty of the Univ. of Kiel, being appointed prof. there in 1955. He ed. several music journals; publ. a valuable monograph, *Caspar Othmayr, Leben und Werke* (Kassel, 1943).

BIBL.: W. Brennecke and H. Haase, eds., *H. A. in Memoriam* (Kassel, 1962).

Albrecht, Johann Lorenz, German music scholar; b. Görmar, Thuringia, Jan. 8, 1732; d. Mühlhausen, Nov. 29, 1768. He studied at Leipzig; ed. Adlung's *Musica mechanica* and *Siebengestirn* (Berlin, 1768); wrote the essay *Abhandlung über die Frage: Ob die Musik beim Gottesdienst zu dulden sei oder nicht* (1764), the manual *Gründliche Einleitung in die Anfangslehren der Tonkunst* (1761), and the treatise *Vom Hasse der Musik* (1765); contributed articles to Marpurg's *Kritische Beiträge,* etc. He also composed several cantatas.

Albrecht, Karl, German-Russian conductor, father of **Konstantin** and **Evgeni Albrecht;** b. Posen, Aug. 27, 1807; d. Gatchina, near St. Petersburg, March 8, 1863. He studied harmony and counterpoint with Josef Schnabel in Breslau; also learned to play on string and wind instruments. In 1825 he joined the Breslau Theater Orch. as 1st violinist; in 1835 he went to Düsseldorf, where he was engaged as répétiteur in the opera theater. In 1838 he went to St. Petersburg, where he conducted a German opera troupe; from 1840 to 1850 he conducted the Russian Opera there. In 1842 he conducted the 1st performance of Glinka's opera *Ruslan and Ludmila.*

Albrecht, Konstantin, Russian cellist, son of **Karl Albrecht** and brother of **Evgeni Albrecht;** b. Elberfeld, Oct. 4, 1835; d. Moscow, June 26, 1893. He was brought to Moscow by his father at the age of 2 and received his musical education from him. In 1854 he became a member of the orch. of the Moscow Opera. In 1860 he collaborated with Nikolai Rubinstein in organizing the Moscow Cons.; in 1866 he was appointed inspector there; also taught elementary theory. He was an intimate friend of Tchaikovsky and was a notable figure in the Moscow music world. He publ. a manual on solfeggio and compiled several collections of choral works.

Albrecht, Otto Edwin, eminent American musicologist; b. Philadelphia, July 8, 1899; d. there, July 6, 1984. He studied at the Univ. of Pa. (A.B., 1921; M.A., 1925; Ph.D., 1931, with the diss. *Four Latin Plays of St. Nicholas from the 12th Century Fleury Play-book,* publ. in Philadelphia and London, 1935); was an instructor in French at his alma mater (1935–38); in 1937 became curator of the Music Library there; from 1938 was also a lecturer in the music dept.; retired in 1970 and was made emeritus prof. of music.

WRITINGS: *A Census of Autograph Music Manuscripts of European Composers in American Libraries* (Philadelphia, 1953); *The Mary Flagler Cary Music Collection* (N.Y., 1970). **BIBL.:** J. Hill, ed., *Studies in Musicology in Honor of O.E. A.* (Kassel, 1977; Clifton, N.J., 1980).

Albrechtsberger, Johann Georg, famous Austrian organist, music theorist, pedagogue, and composer; b. Klosterneuburg, near Vienna, Feb. 3, 1736; d. Vienna, March 7, 1809. He studied organ and figured bass with Leopold Pittner, the dean of the Augustinians in Klosterneuburg, then was a choirboy at the Melk Abbey (1749–54), where he received instruction in organ and composition from Marian Gurtler, its regens chori, and from Joseph Weiss, its organist; he subsequently spent a year in Vienna at the Jesuit seminary before commencing his career as an organist in small towns. He was organist in Melk (1759–65), during which period his outstanding playing brought him to the attention of Emperor Joseph. In 1772 he was called to Vienna to serve as regens chori to the Carmelites; in 1791 he became assistant Kapellmeister at St. Stephen's Cathedral, and in 1793, Kapellmeister, holding the position with great distinction. In addition to his renown as an organist, he was widely esteemed as a teacher of composition. Haydn sent Beethoven to him for study in 1794–95. His important theoretical writings include *Gründliche Anweisung zur Composition . . .* (Leipzig, 1790; 3rd ed., augmented, 1821; Eng. tr., 1844), *Kurzgefaste Methode, den Generalbass zu erlernen* (Vienna, c.1791; 2nd ed., augmented, 1792; Eng. tr., 1815), and *Clavierschule für Anfänger* (Vienna, c.1800); for his complete writings, see I. von Seyfried, ed., *Johann Georg Albrechtsbergers sämmtliche Schriften über Generalbass, Harmonie-Lehre, und Tonsetzkunst* (Vienna, 1826; 2nd ed., 1837; Eng. tr., 1834). He was a prolific composer; his sacred music includes 35 masses, 48 graduals, 42 offertories, and 6 oratorios; his secular works include numerous quintets, quartets, and trios. For his instrumental works, see F. Brodsky and O. Biba, eds., *Johann Georg Albrechtsberger: Instrumentalwerke* in Documenta Musicologica (1968–75). **BIBL.:** O. Kappelmacher, *J.G. A.: Sein Leben und seine Instrumentalwerke* (diss., Univ. of Vienna, 1907); A. Weissenbäck, "J.G. A. als Kirchenkomponist," *Studien zur Musikwissenschaft*, XIV (1927); G. Uebele, *J.G. A., der Theoretiker* (diss., Univ. of Vienna, 1932); A. Schramek-Kirchner, *J.G. A.s Fugenkompositionen in seinen Werken für Tasteninstrumente* (diss., Univ. of Vienna, 1954); U. Thomson, *Voraussetzungen und Artung der österreichischen Generalbasslehre zwischen A. und Sechter* (diss., Univ. of Vienna, 1960); R. Harpster, *The String Quartets of J.G. A.* (diss., Univ. of Southern Calif., 1975); E. Paul, *J.G. A.: Ein Klosterneuburger Meister der Musik und seine Schule* (Klosterneuburg, 1976); D. Schröder, *Die geistlichen Vokalkompositionen J.G. A.s* (2 vols., 1987); A. Weinmann, *J.G. A.: Thematischer Katalog seiner weltlichen Kompositionen* (Vienna, 1987).

Albrici (or **Alberici**), **Vincenzo,** Italian organist, harpsichordist, and composer; b. Rome, June 26, 1631; d. Prague, Aug. 8, 1696. He was born into a musical family; his father, Domenico, was an alto singer; his brother, Bartolomeo, was also a musician. Vincenzo Albrici was a boy soprano at the German College in Rome, where he studied with Carissimi (1641–46); he then accompanied his father and brother to Lombardy, Germany, Flanders, and Sweden; was in the service of Queen Christina of Sweden (1652–53); in 1654 he became a Kapellmeister at the Dresden court, where he served with Schütz and Bontempi; in 1660 he was once more in the service of Queen Christina; in 1662–63 he was again in Dresden. He subsequently went to England, where he entered the service of King Charles II. He returned to Dresden about 1668; was named director of the Italian musicians at the court in 1676; after the Italian musicians were dismissed in 1680, he became organist at the Thomaskirche in Leipzig in 1681 (he was briefly converted to the Protestant faith). In 1682 he be-

came organist at St. Augustus in Prague, a post he held until his death. He composed about 40 Latin motets, Italian solo cantatas, and some other vocal works. **BIBL.:** C.-A. Moberg, "V. A. (1631–1696): Eine biographische Skizze mit besonderer Berücksichtigung seiner schwedischen Zeit," *Festschrift Friedrich Blume zum 70. Geburtstag* (Kassel, 1963).

Albright, William (Hugh), American composer, pianist, and organist; b. Gary, Ind., Oct. 20, 1944. He studied piano with Rosetta Goodkind and music theory with Hugh Aitken at the Juilliard Preparatory Dept. in N.Y. (1959–62); then took courses in composition with Ross Lee Finney and Leslie Bassett at the Univ. of Michigan; also studied organ with Marilyn Mason there (1963–70). In 1968 he went to France and studied composition with Olivier Messiaen at the Paris Cons.; also took private lessons with Max Deutsch. In 1970 he joined the faculty of the Univ. of Michigan to teach composition; also served as associate director of its Electronic Music Studio. He received a Guggenheim fellowship in 1976; was composer-in-residence at the American Academy in Rome in 1979. In his compositions he pursues quaquaversal methods of experimental music, using varied techniques according to need. He has also made a concert career as a pianist in programs of ragtime and jazz.

WORKS: **MULTIMEDIA AND STAGE:** *Tic* for Soloist, 2 Jazz-rock Improvisation Ensembles, Film, and Tape (1967); *Beulahland Rag* for Narrator, Jazz Quartet, Improvisation Ensemble, Tape, Film, and Slide Projections (1967–69); *Cross of Gold* for Actors, Chorus, and Instruments (1975). **ORCH.:** *Alliance,* suite (1967–70); *Night Procession* for Chamber Orch. (1972); *Heater* for Saxophone and Sym. Band (1977); *Bacchanal* for Organ and Orch. (Univ. of Nebraska, Nov. 16, 1981). **CHAMBER:** *Foils* for Wind Instruments and Percussion (1963–64); *2 pieces* for 9 Instruments (1966); *Caroms* for 7 Instruments (1966); *Marginal Worlds* for Winds, Strings, Piano, and Percussion (1970); *Take That* for Percussion (1972); *Gothic Suite* for Organ, Percussion, and Strings (1973); *Introduction, Passacaglia and Rondo Capriccioso* for Piano and Winds (1974); *7 Deadly Sins* for Flute, Clarinet, String Quartet, Piano, and Optional Narrator (1974). **PIANO:** *Pianoàgogo* (1965–66); *Grand Sonata in Rag* (1968); *5 Chromatic Dances* (1976). **ORGAN:** *Chorale Partita in Old Style* (1963); *Juba* (1965); *Pneuma* (1966); 3 organ collections (1967, 1971, 1978); *Stipendium Peccati,* with Piano and Percussion (1973); *Jericho Battle Music,* with Trumpet (1976); *Halo,* with Metal Instruments (1978); *King of Instruments,* with Narrator (1978). **CHORAL:** *An Alleluia Super-Round* (1973); *Mass in D major* (1974); *The Chichester Mass* (1974).

Alcaide, Tomáz, Portuguese tenor; b. Estremoz, Feb. 16, 1901; d. Lisbon, Nov. 9, 1967. He studied at the Univ. of Coimbra; took voice lessons in Lisbon, and later in Milan; in 1925 he made his debut at the Teatro Carcano in Milan as Wilhelm Meister in *Mignon.* He subsequently sang principal roles in Italian and French operas at La Scala in Milan, at the Paris Opéra, at the Vienna State Opera, at the Salzburg Festival, and at the Rome Opera; also made concert tours of Europe and the U.S. After his retirement from the stage in 1948, he settled in Lisbon. He wrote an autobiography, *Um cantor no palco e na vida* (Lisbon, 1961).

Alcantara, Theo, Spanish conductor; b. Cuenca, April 16, 1941. He studied at the Madrid Cons.; then took courses in conducting at the Mozarteum in Salzburg. He began his career as a conductor with the Frankfurt Opera Orch. (1964–66); then came to the U.S., where he served as director of orchs. at the Univ. of Michigan in Ann Arbor (1968–73), and then music director of the Grand Rapids Sym. Orch. (1973–78). From 1978 to 1989 he was music director of the Phoenix Sym. Orch.; he was also artistic director of the Music Academy of the West in Santa Barbara from 1981 to 1984. In 1987 he became principal conductor of the Pittsburgh Opera.

Alcock, John, Sr., English organist and composer; b. London, April 11, 1715; d. Lichfield, Feb. 23, 1806. He served as a chorister at St. Paul's Cathedral and took lessons with the blind organist Stanley; subsequently he held positions as organist at St. Andrew's Church in Plymouth (1737), at St. Laurence's Church in Reading (1742), and at Lichfield Cathedral (1750). In 1766 he took his degree of D.Mus. at Oxford. He publ. several suites for harpsichord, collections of anthems, and sacred choral works; also wrote numerous glees, for which he obtained prizes from the Catch Club. His son, **John Alcock, Jr.** (baptized in Plymouth, Jan. 28, 1740; d. Walsall [buried], March 27, 1791), was organist at various churches and composer of anthems.

Alda, Frances (real name, **Frances Jeanne Davies**), New Zealand–born American soprano; b. Christchurch, May 31, 1883; d. Venice, Sept. 18, 1952. She studied with Marchesi in Paris, and made her debut as Manon at the Opéra-Comique (April 15, 1904). She later sang in Brussels, London, Milan, Warsaw, and Buenos Aires. Her debut at the Metropolitan Opera was on Dec. 7, 1908 (opposite Caruso in *Rigoletto*); her farewell appearance there, on Dec. 28, 1929, in *Manon Lescaut*. She also made numerous recital tours in the U.S. Her principal roles included Louise, Mimi, Manon, Marguerite, Juliette, Gilda, Violetta, and Aida. She married Giulio Gatti-Casazza, manager of the Metropolitan Opera, on April 3, 1910; they divorced in 1928; she married Ray Vir Den in 1941. In 1939 she became an American citizen. She wrote an autobiography, *Men, Women and Tenors* (Boston, 1937).

Aldrich, Henry, English music scholar; b. Westminster, Jan. 1648; d. Oxford, Dec. 14, 1710. A man of versatile talents, excelling in music, he was also distinguished as an architect, theologian, linguist, and logician. He was educated at Christ Church, Oxford, receiving the degree of M.A. in 1669; in 1681 he became a canon, and in 1689, dean of Christ Church, and exercised decisive influence on the teaching of music and other arts. He wrote the learned works *On the Commencement of Greek Music, Theory of Organ-building,* and *Theory of Modern Instruments;* composed several services (one of which, in G, is still sung); in a lighter vein, glees and catches (among them the popular *Catches on Tobacco*). The collections of Boyce, Arnold, and Page contain numerous pieces by Aldrich.
BIBL.: W.G. Hiscock, *H. A. of Christ Church* (Oxford, 1960).

Aldrich, Putnam (Calder), American harpsichord player and music scholar; b. South Swansea, Mass., July 14, 1904; d. Cannes, France, April 18, 1975. He studied at Yale Univ. (B.A., 1926); then took piano lessons with Tobias Matthay in London (1926–27) and harpsichord lessons with Wanda Landowska in Paris (1929–33); later took his Ph.D. at Harvard Univ. (1942). From 1950 to 1969 he was on the faculty at Stanford Univ. in California. He publ. an important treatise, *Ornamentation in J.S. Bach's Organ Works* (N.Y., 1950), as part of a much larger and very valuable work on Baroque ornamentation, orig. submitted as his doctoral dissertation at Harvard; the work still awaits publication. He also publ. *Rhythm in 17th-century Italian Monody* (London, 1965).

Aldrich, Richard, American music critic; b. Providence, July 31, 1863; d. Rome, June 2, 1937. He studied with Paine at Harvard Univ., graduating in 1885. He then was music critic of the *Providence Journal* (1885–89) and the *Evening Star* (1889–91). From 1891 to 1901 he was assistant to H.E. Krehbiel on the *New York Tribune*, then became music ed. of the *New York Times* (1902–23). A selection of his articles from the *Times* was publ. in *Musical Discourse* (1928) and, posth., in *Concert Life in New York, 1902–1923* (1941). He also wrote *Guide to Parsifal* (1904) and *Guide to the Ring of the Nibelung* (1905). His critical writings were urbane and witty; while liberal-minded in regard to milder types of modern music, he vehemently opposed its extreme trends.

Aldrovandini, Giuseppe (Antonio Vincenzo), Italian composer; b. Bologna, June 8, 1671; d. there, Feb. 9, 1707, when, under the influence of alcohol, he fell into a canal and was drowned. He studied with Giacomo Perti at the Bologna Phil. Academy. In 1695 he was appointed to teach at his alma mater, and in 1702 became its head. He wrote 15 operas; among

them the following were produced in Bologna: *Gli inganni amorosi* (Jan. 28, 1696); *Dafne* (Aug. 10, 1696); *Le due Auguste* (Aug. 16, 1700); *I tre rivali in soglio* (posth., Jan. 2, 1711). He also wrote instrumental music and a great many sacred works, among them 6 oratorios, cantatas, motets, etc., some of which were publ. during his lifetime.

d'Alembert, Jean-le-Rond, French philosopher and encyclopedist; b. Paris, Nov. 16, 1717; d. there, Oct. 29, 1783. He was the illegitimate child of one Mme. de Tencin and an artillery officer named Destouches; his mother abandoned him on the steps of the church of St. Jean-le-Rond, which name was subsequently attached to him. Later his father acknowledged him, and enabled him to study. He was sent to the Mazarin College, and progressed rapidly in mathematics. He also was interested in theoretical musical subjects, and publ. several treatises on acoustics and on the theory of music: *Recherches sur la courbe, que forme une corde tendue mise en vibration* (1749); *Recherches sur les vibrations des cordes sonores* and *Recherches sur la vitesse du son* (both in *Opuscules mathématiques,* Paris, 1761–80); *Reflexions sur la musique en général et sur la musique française en particulier* (1754); *Reflexions sur la théorie de la musique* (1777). His best-known work on music was *Éléments de musique, théorique et pratique, suivant les principes de M. Rameau* (1752), which went into 6 eds. He contributed several articles on music to the famous *Encyclopédie,* which he ed. with Diderot.
BIBL.: J. Bertrand, *d'A.* (Paris, 1889).

Alemshah, Kourkene M., Armenian composer; b. Erevan, May 22, 1907; d. Detroit, Dec. 14, 1947. He studied in Milan with Pizzetti (1924–30); in 1931 he settled in Paris. He died during an American tour, which he undertook as a choral conductor. His music is strongly permeated with Armenian melos, and the settings are impressionistic. A memorial festival of his music was presented in Paris on Feb. 19, 1950.
WORKS: Symphonic poems: *Légende* (Paris, June 19, 1932) and *La Bataille d'Avarayr* (Paris, June 2, 1934); *Danses populaires arméniennes* for Orch. (Paris, June 2, 1934).

Aler, John, American tenor; b. Baltimore, Oct. 4, 1949. He studied voice at the Catholic Univ. of America (M.M., 1972); also took courses at the Berkshire Music Center at Tanglewood; in 1977 he won 1st prize for men at the Concours International de Chant in Paris, and also 1st prize for interpretation of French art songs. As an opera singer he appeared with the N.Y. City Opera, the Glyndebourne Festival, the Netherlands Opera, and the Vienna State Opera.

Alessandrescu, Alfred, eminent Rumanian composer and conductor; b. Bucharest, Aug. 14, 1893; d. there, Feb. 18, 1959. He studied piano and theory at the Bucharest Cons. with Kiriac and Castaldi (1903–11); then went to Paris, where he took composition courses with Vincent d'Indy at the Schola Cantorum and with Paul Vidal at the Paris Cons. (1913–14). Returning to Bucharest, he was active as a pianist. In 1921 he was appointed conductor of the Rumanian Opera in Bucharest, retaining this post until his death; also conducted the Bucharest Phil. Orch. (1926–40) and was artistic director of the Bucharest Radio (1933–59); appeared as a conductor in Germany and France; was piano accompanist to Georges Enesco, Jacques Thibaud, and others.
WORKS: *Amurg de toamnă* (The Twilight of Autumn) for String Orch. (1910); *Didona,* symphonic poem (1911); *Fantezie română* for Orch. (1913); *Violin Sonata* (1914); *Acteon,* symphonic poem (Bucharest, Dec. 20, 1915); *Pièce pour quatuor à cordes* (1921); songs; also orchestrated many works by Rumanian composers, as well as classical compositions.
BIBL.: V. Tomescu, *A. A.* (Bucharest, 1962).

Alessandri, Felice, Italian opera composer; b. Rome, Nov. 24, 1747; d. Casinalbo, Aug. 15, 1798. He studied music in Naples; then lived in Paris (1765–68) and in London (1768). From 1784 to 1789 he was in Russia; then in Berlin as 2nd conductor at the Royal Opera (1789–92); finally returned to Italy. Alessandri wrote about 30 operas in all; 2 were produced in London: *La Moglie fedele* (1768) and *Il Re alla caccia* (1769); and 2 at La Scala in Milan: *Calliroe* (Dec. 26, 1778) and *Ezio* (1st given in Verona for Carnevale, 1767; staged at La Scala Feb. 1, 1782). In Potsdam he produced *Il ritorno di Ulisse a Penelope* (Jan. 25, 1790); *Dario* (1791); and the comic opera *La compagnia d'opera a Nanchino* (1790), which exhibited the colorful effects of pseudo-Chinese music. His opera *Virginia* was given in Venice (Dec. 26, 1793). He also wrote an oratorio, *Betulia liberata* (1781); 6 sinfonie in 8 parts; 6 trio sonatas for 2 Violins and Basso Continuo; etc.; all in the then-prevalent Italian manner.

BIBL.: L. Valdrighi, *F. A.: Maestro di cappella di Federico Guglielmo II re di Prussia (1790–92)* (Modena, 1896).

d'Alessandro, Raffaele, Swiss composer; b. St. Gallen, March 17, 1911; d. Lausanne, March 17, 1959 (on his 48th birthday). He studied music with Victor Schlatter and Willi Schuh in Zürich; then went to Paris, where he studied composition with Nadia Boulanger and organ with Marcel Dupré. In 1940 he returned to Switzerland and settled in Lausanne, where he became active as a pianist, organist, and composer.

WORKS: BALLET: *Isla persa* (1952). **ORCH.:** *Rumba sinfonica* (1940); *Conga contrapuntique* (1941); *Thème et Variations* (1944); Sym. No. 1 (1948); Sym. No. 2 (1953); *Tema variato* (1957); Piano Concerto No. 1 (1939); Violin Concerto (1941); Flute Concerto (1943); Piano Concerto No. 2 (1945); Piano Concerto No. 3 (1951); Bassoon Concerto (1955); Oboe Concerto with String Orch. (1958). **CHAMBER:** 2 violin sonatas (1936, 1953); Cello Sonata (1937); Piano Trio (1940); Flute Sonata (1943); 2 string quartets (1947, 1952); Oboe Sonata (1949); Sonatina for Oboe Solo (1953); Sonatina for Clarinet and Piano (1953); Bassoon Sonata (1957); Sonata for Flute, Viola, and Piano (1958). **PIANO:** Sonatina for left hand alone (1939); 24 Preludes (1940); Sonatina for 2 Pianos (1943); 12 études (1952); *Contes drolatiques* (1952); 6 *Klavierstücke* for left hand alone (1958); also many pieces for organ; choruses; several songs with orch., organ, or piano.

Alessandro, Victor (Nicholas), American conductor; b. Waco, Texas, Nov. 27, 1915; d. San Antonio, Nov. 27, 1976 (on his 61st birthday). He studied French horn with his father; then took composition courses with Howard Hanson and Bernard Rogers at the Eastman School of Music in Rochester, N.Y.; subsequently attended classes at the Accademia di Santa Cecilia in Rome. Returning to the U.S., he was conductor of the Oklahoma Sym. Orch. (1938–51); in 1951 was appointed conductor of the San Antonio Sym. Orch., a position which he held until his death.

Alexander, Haim, German-born Israeli composer; b. Berlin, Aug. 9, 1915. He studied piano at the Stern Cons.; emigrated to Palestine in 1936; then studied piano and composition with Irma and Stefan Wolpe at the Palestine Cons. and Academy of Music; subsequently was active as a teacher. His compositions encompass both traditional and avant-garde idioms. His *6 Israeli Dances* (1950) acquired considerable popularity; he also composed chamber works, cantatas, and many piano pieces, including *Patterns* (1973).

Alexander, John, American tenor; b. Meridian, Miss., Oct. 21, 1923; d. there, Dec. 8, 1990. He studied at the Cincinnati Cons. of Music; made his operatic debut in Cincinnati in 1952. In 1957 he sang at the N.Y. City Opera; he made his Metropolitan Opera debut as Ferrando in *Così fan tutte* on Dec. 19, 1961; also made appearances with the Vienna State Opera (1968) and the Royal Opera at Covent Garden in London (1970). In 1974 he joined the faculty of the Univ. of Cincinnati–College Cons. of Music. He became particularly adept in lyric tenor roles; he also gained success as a concert artist.

Alexander, Josef, American composer; b. Boston, May 15, 1907; d. Seattle, Dec. 23, 1989. The only musical connection in his family was the fact that the paternal grandfather of his paternal grandfather played the clarinet in the Russian military band during the Crimean War (which ended inconclusively). He studied piano at the New England Cons. in Boston, graduating in 1925; then entered Harvard Univ., where

he took a course in composition with Walter Piston and in orchestration with Edward B. Hill; received his B.A. in 1938 and his M.A. in 1941. In 1939 he went to Paris, where he studied with Nadia Boulanger; returning to the U.S., he attended a class in composition with Aaron Copland and in conducting with Serge Koussevitzky at the Berkshire Music Center in Tanglewood in 1940. In 1943 he was appointed to the music faculty at Brooklyn College; retired in 1977 as prof. emeritus. In his compositions he adopted a facile, laissez-faire idiom marked by a pleasurable admixture of euphonious dissonances.

WORKS: ORCH.: Symphonic poem, *The Ancient Mariner* (Boston, June 8, 1940); 4 syms.: No. 1, subtitled *Clockwork* (N.Y., Nov. 28, 1949); No. 2 (1954); No. 3 (1961; N.Y., April 27, 1970); No. 4 (1968); Piano Concerto (1938; Boston, June 8, 1940); *A New England Overture* (St. Louis, Feb. 12, 1943); *Williamsburg Suite* for Orch. (N.Y., Aug. 19, 1944); *Epitaphs* for Orch. (1947; N.Y., March 8, 1951); *Andante and Allegro* for String Orch. (1952; St. Louis, Feb. 20, 1953); *Concertino* for Trumpet and Strings (1959); *Celebrations* for Orch. (1960); *Quiet Music* for Strings (1966). **CHAMBER:** String Quartet (1940); Piano Quintet (1942); Piano Trio (1944); Wind Quintet (1949); Piano Quartet (1952); Violin Sonata (1953); Cello Sonata (1953); Flute Sonata (1954); Clarinet Sonata (1957); *Songs of Eve*, cycle of 15 songs for Soprano and Instruments (1957); 4 Movements for Brass (1958); Trombone Sonata (1959); *Nocturne and Scherzo* for Violin and Piano (1963); *3 Pieces* for 8 Instruments (1965); *Triptych* for Cornet, Marimba, and Guitar (1968); *Playthings of the Wind* for Voices, Brass, and Piano (1970); Brass Trio (1971); *Gitanjali* for Soprano, Harpsichord, and Percussion, based on texts from Rabindranath Tagore (N.Y., Nov. 14, 1975); *Symphonic Odes* for Male Chorus and Orch. (1975); Horn Sonata (1979); *Dyad* for 4 Tubas (1979); *Escapades* for Marimba (1988); hundreds of solo piano pieces, including some in collections such as *Signs of the Zodiac: 12 Astral Preludes* (1966).

BIBL.: D. Ewen, *American Composers* (N.Y., 1982).

Alexander, Meister, German Minnesinger and composer who flourished in the 2nd half of the 13th century, known as **Der wilde Alexander.** He was a significant composer of Sprüche; see R. Taylor, ed., *The Art of the Minnesinger* (Cardiff, 1968).

BIBL.: R. Haller, *Der wilde A.* (Wurzburg, 1935); J. Biehl, *Der wilde A.: Untersuchungen zur literarischen Technik eines Autors im 13. Jahrhundert* (diss., Univ. of Hamburg, 1970); N. Wagner, "Die Lebenszeit des wilden A.," *Zeitschrift für deutsches Altertum und deutsche Literatur,* CIV (1975).

Alexander, Roberta, black American soprano; b. Lynchburg, Va., March 3, 1949. She was reared in a musical family; then studied at the Univ. of Michigan in Ann Arbor (1969–71; M.Mus., 1971). She appeared as Pamina at the Houston Grand Opera in 1980, as Daphne in Santa Fe (1981), and as Elettra in *Idomeneo* in Zürich (1982). Following a tour of Europe, she made a successful debut at the Metropolitan Opera in N.Y. as Zerlina on Nov. 3, 1983; later sang Bess in *Porgy and Bess* and the title role in Janáček's *Jenůfa*, a role she repeated at the Glyndebourne Festival in 1989. In 1984 she made her 1st appearance at the Aix-en-Provence Festival in Mozart's *La finta giardiniera*. She made her debut in Vienna as Cleopatra in Handel's *Giulio Cesare* at the Theater an der Wien in 1985. In 1986 she was a soloist with the Vienna Phil. at the Salzburg Festival and in 1988 she appeared with the English Chamber Orch. at the London Promenade Concerts.

Alexandra, Liana, Rumanian composer; b. Bucharest, May 27, 1947. She studied at the Porumbescu Academy of Music in Bucharest (1965–71) and in Darmstadt; subsequently lectured in orchestration and analysis at the Bucharest Academy of Music. She won many honors for her compositions, including the von Weber Prize (Dresden, 1979), 1st prize from the Gaudeamus Foundation (Netherlands, 1980), and the Rumanian State Prize (1980).

WORKS: OPERA: *The Snow Queen* for children (1979). **ORCH.:**

Sym. No. 1 (1971); Sym. No. 2, *Hymns* (1978); Sym. No. 3, *Diacronies* (1981); Sym. No. 4 (1984); Sym. No. 5 (1986); *Valences* (1973); *Resonances* for Piano and Orch. (1973); Clarinet Concerto (1974); Music for 5 Soloists (Clarinet and Piano Quartet) and Orch. (1975); Concerto for Flute, Viola, and Chamber Orch. (1980). **CHAMBER:** Music for Clarinet, Harp, and Percussion (1972); Sonata for Solo Flute (1973); Lyric Sequence for Clarinet, Trumpet, and Piano (1974); *Collages* for Brass Quintet (1977); 2 *Incantations:* No. 1 for Mezzo-soprano, Flute, Percussion, and Harpsichord (1978); No. 2 for Clarinet and Piano Quartet (1978); 5 *Consonances:* No. 1 for 4 Trombones (1978); No. 2 for Clarinet and Piano (1979); No. 3 for Organ (1979); No. 4 for Clarinet and Tape (1980); No. 5 for Organ (1980). **VOCAL:** 4 cantatas (1971, 1977, 1977, 1978); 2 Sequences for Soprano and Chamber Orch. (1976).

Alexandrov, Alexander, Russian composer; b. Plakhino, April 13, 1883; d. Berlin, July 8, 1946, during a concert tour. He studied with Rimsky-Korsakov and Glazunov at the St. Petersburg Cons. (1899–1901) and later at the Moscow Cons. with Vasilenko (1909–13). In 1928 he organized the Red Army Ensemble and conducted it on numerous tours in Russia and abroad. His song *Hymn of the Bolshevik Party*, with a new set of words, was proclaimed the Soviet national anthem on March 15, 1944.

Alexandrov, Anatoli, eminent Russian pianist and composer; b. Moscow, May 25, 1888; d. there, April 16, 1982. He studied with Taneyev at the Moscow Cons. (1907–10); also studied composition there with Vasilenko and piano with Igumnov, graduating in 1916. In 1923 he became a prof. at the Moscow Cons. He composed mainly for piano; wrote 14 piano sonatas (1914–71); in his style of composition he followed the main lines of Rachmaninoff and Scriabin. His other works include 2 operas, *Bela* (Moscow, Dec. 10, 1946) and *Wild Bara* (Moscow, March 2, 1957); 4 string quartets (1914–53); *Classical Suite* for Orch. (1926); *Dithyramb* for Double Bass and Piano (1959); Sym. No. 1 (1965); several song cycles; and incidental music for theatrical plays.

Alexanian, Diran, noted Armenian cellist and pedagogue; b. Constantinople, 1881; d. Chamonix, July 27, 1954. While studying with Grützmacher, he had the honor of playing chamber music with Brahms and Joachim; he commenced his career as a virtuoso at age 17. In 1901 he went to Paris, where he later taught at the École Normale de Musique (1921–37); then settled in the U.S. Among his outstanding students were Maurice Eisenberg and Antonio Janigro. With Casals, he wrote the treatise *Traité théorique et pratique du violoncelle* (1922); also prepared a critical ed. of the Bach solo cello suites (1929).

Alexeev, Dmitri, talented Russian pianist; b. Moscow, Aug. 10, 1947. He entered Moscow's Central Music School at the age of 6; then studied with Bashkirov in Moscow, winning 2nd prize at the Long-Thibaud Competition in Paris (1969) and becoming the 1st Russian pianist to win 1st prize at the Leeds Competition (1975); subsequently gave recitals in Europe, Japan, and Australia. He made his American debut as a soloist with the Chicago Sym. Orch. in 1976, and in 1978 he appeared at Carnegie Hall. He further played duo-piano recitals with his wife, Tatiana Sarkissova. As a soloist he was notable in the Romantic piano repertoire.

Alfano, Franco, eminent Italian composer; b. Posilippo (Naples), March 8, 1875; d. San Remo, Oct. 27, 1954. He studied composition with Paolo Serrao in Naples, and with Jadassohn and Hans Sitt in Leipzig. From the beginning of his musical career, Alfano was interested in opera. His 1st stage work, *Miranda*, was written when he was barely 20; another opera, *La fonte di Enchir*, followed (Breslau, Nov. 8, 1898). In 1899 he went to Paris and became fascinated by light theater music. While in Paris he wrote *Napoli*, a ballet in the folk manner, which was staged at the Folies-Bergères (Jan. 28, 1901), proving so successful that it ran for 160 successive performances. Returning to Italy, he began work on an opera based on Tolstoy's novel *Resurrection*. It was produced as *Risurrezione* in Turin (Nov. 4, 1904) with sensational acclaim; the American pre-

miere (Chicago, Dec. 31, 1925) was equally successful; there were also numerous performances in Germany and France. The opera was widely praised for its dramatic power and melodic richness in the best tradition of realistic Italian opera. Alfano continued to compose industriously for another half-century, but his later operas failed to equal the success of *Risurrezione*. They are: *Il Principe Zilah* (Genoa, Feb. 3, 1909); *L'ombra di Don Giovanni* (La Scala, April 3, 1914); *La leggenda di Sakuntala* (Bologna, Dec. 10, 1921); *Madonna Imperia*, lyric comedy (Turin, May 5, 1927; Metropolitan Opera, N.Y., Feb. 8, 1928); *L'Ultimo Lord* (Naples, April 19, 1930); *Cyrano de Bergerac* (Rome, Jan. 22, 1936); *Il Dottor Antonio* (Rome, April 30, 1949). Alfano also wrote 3 syms. (1909, 1932, 1934), 3 string quartets, a Violin Sonata, a Cello Sonata, and a ballet, *Vesuvius* (1938; a symphonic poem was drawn from it in 1946). One of Alfano's signal achievements was that he completed Puccini's last opera, *Turandot*, adding the last scene. His *Hymn to Bolivar* for Chorus and Orch., written for the centennial of Bolivar's death, was performed in Caracas, Venezuela, on Dec. 22, 1930. He was also active in the field of musical education; was successively director of the Liceo Musicale in Bologna (1918–23); director of the Turin Cons. (1923–39); superintendent of the Teatro Massimo in Palermo (1940–42); and (1947–50) acting director of the Rossini Cons. in Pesaro.

BIBL.: G.M. Gatti, "F. A.," *Musicisti moderni d'Italia e di fuori* (Bologna, 1920; also in the *Musical Times*, March 1921); G. Cesàri, "La leggenda di Sakuntala di F. A.," *Rivista Musicale Italiana* (1921); Andrea della Corte, *Ritratto di F. A.* (Turin, 1935).

Alfarabi (or **Alpharabius,** properly **Al Farabi**), **Abu Nasr,** so named from his birthplace, Farab (now transoxine Othrâx), Arabian music theorist; b. c.870; d. Damascus, c.950. Of Turkish descent, he was a Greek scholar and attempted unsuccessfully to introduce the Greek musical system into his country. He was renowned for his writings on philosophy, political science, and the arts; his principal work is *Kitab al-Musiqi al-Kabir* (Greater Book about Music; reprint with commentary, Cairo, 1967), dealing with acoustics, intervals, scales, instruments, and rhythm. The 2nd vol. of this work was lost. Excerpts from this book are contained in Kosegarten's *Alii Ispahanis Liber Cantilenarum Magnus* (1840) and in J. Land's *Recherches sur l'histoire de la gamme arabe* (Leyden, 1884). Another treatise, *Kitab al-Iqua'at*, was tr. into German by E. Neubauer in *Oriens* (1968/69).

BIBL.: M. Steinschneider, *Al Farabi* (St. Petersburg, 1869); Baron d'Erlanger, *La Musique arabe*, vol. I (Paris, 1930); E.A. Beichert, *Die Wissenschaft der Musik bei Al-Farabi* (Regensburg, 1931); H.G. Farmer, *Al-Farabi's Arabic-Latin Writings on Music* (Glasgow, 1934).

Alferaki, Achilles, Russian composer of Greek extraction; b. Kharkov, July 3, 1846; d. Petrograd, Dec. 27, 1919. He studied philology at the Univ. of Moscow; simultaneously he took lessons in piano and music theory. He joined the group of composers whose works were publ. by Belaiev, and wrote numerous songs and piano pieces in the manner of the Russian national school, many of them also publ. by Belaiev. He furthermore wrote an opera, *St. John's Eve*, which remains in MS.

Alfieri, Pietro, Italian music scholar; b. Rome, June 29, 1801; d. there, June 12, 1863. He was a member of the Camaldolese Order; taught Gregorian music at the English College in Rome. His major work is *Raccolta di musica sacra* (1841–46), a collection of 16th-century church music in 7 vols., which includes virtually all representative works of Palestrina; other collections are *Excerpta ex celebrioribus de musica viris* (Rome, 1840), containing works by Palestrina, Victoria, and Allegri; *Raccolta di motetti* (1841); etc. His essays on Gregorian chant are very valuable: *Ristabilimento del canto e della musica ecclesiastica* (1843); *Saggio storico del canto gregoriano* (1855); *Prodromo sulla restaurazione de' libri di canto ecclesiastico detto gregoriano* (1857); etc. He also publ. a biography of N. Jommelli (1845) and contributed articles on musical subjects to Italian periodicals.

Alford, Kenneth J. See **Ricketts, Frederick J.**

Alfvén, Hugo (Emil), outstanding Swedish composer; b. Stockholm, May 1, 1872; d. Falun, May 8, 1960. He studied violin at the Stockholm Cons. (1887–91); continued these studies with Lars Zetterquist until 1896 while taking composition lessons from Johan Lindegren. He was then sent by the government to Brussels to complete his violin studies with César Thomson (1896–99). Government scholarships in 1896, 1897, and 1899, as well as the Jenny Lind stipend (1900–1903), enabled him to study composition in many European countries. In 1910 he became music director at the Univ. of Uppsala and conductor of the student chorus until his retirement in 1939; continued to conduct various mixed choruses. The music of Alfvén represents the best traits of Scandinavian national art, along the lines of Grieg and Sibelius. He publ. 4 vols. of memoirs: *Första satsen* (Stockholm, 1946); *Tempo furioso* (1948); *I dur och moll* (1949); *Finale* (1952).

WORKS: His best-known work is *Midsommarvaka* (Midsummer Vigil; Stockholm, May 10, 1904), the 1st of his 3 Swedish rhapsodies for Orch. It was produced as a ballet, *La Nuit de Saint-Jean*, by the Ballets Suédois in Paris, Oct. 25, 1920, and had over 250 performances in 4 years. His other works include the 2nd and 3rd Swedish rhapsodies: *Uppsala* (1907) and *Dalecarlian* (1937); 5 syms.: No. 1 (1896–97; Stockholm, Feb. 9, 1897); No. 2 (1898–99; Stockholm, May 2, 1899); No. 3 (1905–6; Göteborg, Dec. 5, 1906); No. 4, with Soprano and Tenor (1918–19; Stockholm, Nov. 4, 1919); No. 5 (1942–52; 1st complete perf., Stockholm, April 30, 1952; Alfvén withdrew the work except for the 1st movement, which subsequently had frequent perfs. as a separate piece); 2 ballet pantomimes: *Bergakungen* (The Mountain King; 1923) and *Den förlorade sonen* (The Prodigal Son; 1957); *En skärgårdssägen* (A Tale of the Skerries), symphonic poem (1905); *Festspiel* (Festival Music) for Orch. (1907); suite of incidental music to the play *Gustaf II Adolf* (1932); *Synnöve Solbakken*, suite for Small Orch. (1934); 10 cantatas, many contributed for various occasions, such as 1 celebrating the 450th anniversary of the founding of Uppsala Univ. (1927) and another on the 500th jubilee of the Swedish Parliament (1935); Violin Sonata (1896); *Elegie* for Horn and Organ (1897); *Skärgårdsbilder* (Pictures from the Skerries) for Piano (1902); a ballad on Gustaf Vasa for Soloists, Mixed Chorus, and Organ (1920); numerous male choruses and folk-song arrangements.

BIBL.: S.E. Svensson, *H. A., Som människa och konstnär* (Uppsala, 1946); J.O. Rudén, *H. A.s kompositioner. Käll-och verkförteckning* (thematic index; Stockholm, 1972).

Algarotti, Francesco, Italian musician and scholar; b. Venice, Dec. 11, 1712; d. Pisa, May 3, 1764. The fame of his great knowledge reached Frederick the Great, who invited him to Berlin in 1740 and gave him the title of Count, and in 1747, that of "Chevalier de l'ordre pour le mérite." In 1753 Algarotti returned to Italy. His musical monument is the *Saggio sopra l'opera in musica*, publ. in 1755; also in many later eds., including German and French trs. The English text of the *Saggio . . .* is reproduced in part in O. Strunk's *Source Readings in Music History* (N.Y., 1950).

BIBL.: D. Michelessi, *Memorie intorno alla vita ed agli scritti del F. A.* (Venice, 1770); R. Northcott, *F. A., A Reprint of His "Saggio . . ." and a Sketch of His Life* (London, 1917).

Aliabiev, Alexander (Nikolaievich), Russian composer; b. Tobolsk, Siberia, Aug. 15, 1787; d. Moscow, March 6, 1851. His father was the governor of Tobolsk, and Aliabiev spent his childhood there. The family went to St. Petersburg in 1796, and in 1804 settled in Moscow. He studied music in Moscow and had his 1st songs publ. in 1810. During the War of 1812, he served in the Russian army, and participated in the entry of the Russian army into Dresden and Paris. Returning to Russia, he lived in St. Petersburg, in Voronezh, and in Moscow. In 1825 he was arrested on suspicion of murder after a card game, was sentenced to prison, and in 1828 was deported to his birthplace in Siberia. There he organized concerts of popular music and also composed. In 1831 he was allowed to return to European Russia and lived in the Caucasus and in Orenburg. In 1843 he returned to Moscow, but was still under police surveillance. He wrote more than 100 songs, of which *The Nightingale* became extremely popular; it is often used in the music-lesson scene in Russian productions of Rossini's opera *The Barber of Seville*; Glinka and Liszt made piano arrangements of it. He also wrote a Sym., 3 string quartets, 2 piano trios, a Piano Quintet, a Violin Sonata, a Quartet for 4 Flutes, a Quintet for Wind Instruments, a Piano Sonata, and choruses. Among his works for the theater are scores of incidental music to *The Prisoner of the Caucasus* and to Shakespeare's plays; also stage ballads: *The Village Philosopher*, *The Moon Night*, and *Theatrical Combat* (with Verstovsky and Mauer).

BIBL.: I. Ilyin, "A. in Siberia" (with a facsimile reproduction of the registry of Aliabiev's birth), *Sovietskaya Muzyka* (Aug. 1952); B. Steinpress, *A. in Exile* (Moscow, 1959); B. Dobrohotov, *A. A.* (Moscow, 1966).

Ali Akbar Khan, Indian instrumentalist; b. Shibpore, Bengal, April 14, 1922. He studied dhrupad, dhamar, khayal, and sarod with his father; pakhawaj and tabla with his uncle. He founded the Ali Akbar College of Music in Calcutta in 1956; toured widely in Europe, America, and Japan as a virtuoso; held the post of court musician in Jodhpur. He has written a number of new ragas. Several of his students achieved prominence as Indian instrumentalists in their own right.

Aliprandi, Bernardo, Italian cellist and composer; b. Milan, c.1710; d. Frankfurt am Main, c.1792. On Oct. 1, 1731, he became a member of the Court Orch. in Munich, retiring in 1778. He wrote 3 theatrical works with music: *Apollo tra le Muse in Parnasso* (Munich, Aug. 6, 1737); *Mitridate* (Munich, 1738); *Semiramide riconosciuta* (Munich, 1740); and a *Stabat Mater* (1749).

Alkan (real name, **Morhange**), **Charles-Valentin,** eccentric French pianist and composer; b. Paris, Nov. 30, 1813; d. there, March 29, 1888. His father, Alkan Morhange (1780–1855), operated a music school in Paris; his brothers, Ernest (1816–76), Maxime (1818–91), Napoleon (1826–1906), and Gustave (1827–86), all became well-known musicians; all 5 adopted their father's 1st name as their surname. Charles-Valentin entered the Paris Cons. in 1819; then studied harmony with V. Dourlen and piano with P.J.G. Zimmerman. He made his public debut as pianist and composer in Paris on April 2, 1826. In 1831 he played in a trio with A. Franchomme and J. Alard, for whom he wrote 3 chamber works. He visited London in 1833 and 1835, the only times he left Paris; in Paris, he developed friendships with leading musicians, artists, and literati, including Alexandre Dumas, Victor Hugo, George Sand, Eugène Delacroix, and his neighbor, F. Chopin. On March 3, 1838, he appeared in a concert with Chopin; then, despite the favorable reception, inexplicably he did not appear again until 1844. Following several concerts in 1845, he again enigmatically interrupted his solo piano career for 28 years. Several laudatory articles by Schumann, Fétis, and Léon Kreutzer appeared during the interim concerning his compositions. One article by Kreutzer is significant as it also discusses a Sym. for Orch., which has subsequently disappeared. His piano work *Le Chemin de fer*, op. 27 (1844), is the earliest work descriptive of the railroad. In 1848 Zimmerman retired as prof. of piano at the Paris Cons. and suggested Alkan as his successor. Despite intercessions on his part by Sand, the position was given to A. Marmontel; this event propelled Alkan even further into seclusion. After Chopin's death, he moved away from his contingent of artistic companions and became a virtual recluse. In 1857 a deluge of compositions were publ., including the remarkable *12 études dans les tons mineurs*, op. 39; *Études 4–7* constitute a *Symphony for Piano Solo*, *Études 8–10* a *Concerto for Piano Solo*. In 1859 one of his rare non-pianistic works, the grotesque *Marche funèbre sulla morte d'un papagallo* for Voices, 3 Oboes, and Bassoon, appeared. About this time he also became interested in the pédalier, a pedal board that attaches to a piano, on which he played organ works of Bach and for which he wrote many compositions, including the unique *Bombardo-carillon* for 4 feet alone.

Evidence is strong that his student Elie Delaborde was his natural son, although there is no formal documentation to substantiate the claim. Other students included I. Cervantes, F. Stockhausen, Jr., and J. Wieniawski. During his lifetime, Alkan was an enigma; his pianistic skills were highly praised, even compared to those of Chopin and Liszt, and yet his aberrant behavior and misanthropy caused his name not to remain in the foreground. Judging from the scores of his difficult works, his skills must have been formidable. Since his death several pianists, notably Busoni, Petri, Lewenthal, and Smith, have kept his works alive. Creating an accurate catalog of his voluminous works would be extremely difficult, since several works were publ. with as many as 3 different opus numbers in eds. by different publishers; some works were printed using different names, some opus numbers are missing (or possibly were never assigned), and some works were never publ.

BIBL.: A. Marmontel, *Les Pianistes célèbres* (Paris, 1887); A. de Bertha, "C.-V. A. aîné; Étude psycho-musicale," *Bulletin Français de la Société Internationale de Musique* (Feb. 1909); H.H. Bellamann, "The Piano Works of C.-V. A.," *Musical Quarterly* (1924); K.S. Sorabji, *Around Music* (London, 1932); B. van Dieran, *Down among the Dead Men* (London, 1935); H. Searle, "A Plea for A.," *Music & Letters* (1937); J. Bloch, *C.-V. A.* (Indianapolis, 1941); R. Lewenthal, *The Piano Music of A.* (N.Y., 1964); R. Smith, "C.-V. A.," *Listener* (1971); H. Macdonald, "The Death of A.," *Musical Times* (Jan. 1973); D. Henning, *C.-V. A.* (diss., Oxford Univ., 1975); R. Smith, *A., Vol. I: The Enigma* (London, 1976) and *A., Vol. II: The Music* (N.Y., 1987); H. Macdonald, "The Enigma of A.," *Musical Times* (1976); B. Schilling, *Virtuose Klaviermusik des 19. Jahrhunderts am Beispiel von C.V. A., 1813–1888* (Regensburg, 1986); H. Macdonald, "More on A.'s Death," *Musical Times* (March 1988).

Allanbrook, Douglas, American composer; b. Melrose, Mass., April 1, 1921. He studied with Nadia Boulanger at the Longy School of Music in Cambridge, with Walter Piston at Harvard College (B.A., magna cum laude, 1948), and again with Boulanger in Paris. During World War II he served in the infantry in Italy, receiving a Bronze Star Medal. In 1950 he received a Fulbright fellowship to study harpsichord and early keyboard music with Ruggero Gerlin in Naples; returning to the U.S. in 1952, he taught at St. John's College in Annapolis.

WORKS: STAGE: 2 operas: *Ethan Frome* (1952); *Nightmare Abbey* (1960). ORCH.: Sym. No. 1 (1958); Sym. No. 2, *An Elegy*; Sym. No. 3, *Orchestral Landscapes* (1966); Sym. No. 4; Sym. No. 5 for Brass Quintet and Orch. (1977); Sym. No. 6, *5 Heroic Attitudes* (1968); Sym. No. 7, *Music from the Country* (1979); Concerto for Harpsichord and Small Orch. (1957); Violin Concerto (1959); Serenade for Piano and Orch. (1982). VOCAL: Songs to Shakespeare Sonnets for Medium Voice and Orch. (1951); *3 Noble Love Songs* for Baritone and Orch. (1960); *The 7 Last Words* for Mezzo-soprano, Baritone, Chorus, and Orch. (1970); *Te Deum* (1948); *Ash Wednesday* for Soprano, Chorus, and Orch. (1947). CHAMBER: 2 piano sonatas (1948, 1949); 4 string quartets; Quintet for Oboe, Clarinet, Violin, Viola, and Cello; *5 Transcendental Studies* for Piano (1980); *5 Night Pieces* for Piano (1986); other chamber works.

Alldahl, Per-Gunnar, Swedish composer; b. Solna, Oct. 11, 1943. He studied organ and composition at the Stockholm Musikhögskolan (1968–71); later joined its staff as an instructor. In his music, he pursues the twin goals of total freedom of realization and strict observance of minuscule tonal data.

WORKS: *Nulla ars . . .* for String Orch. (1966; Helsinki, Feb. 24, 1967); *Biceps* for Chamber Orch. and Tape (1968–69; Swedish Radio, Dec. 7, 1969); *Music* for Solo Cello (1968); *Light Music* for 5 Flutes, Hammond Organ, and Vibraphone (1968); *Play* for Orch. (Bollnäs, April 4, 1970); *Ad lib* for Any Instruments, though orig. for Bass Clarinet, Trombone, and Cello (1971); *Bruspolska* for Nyckelharps (1972); *Stämma*

blod for Chorus and Percussion (1972); *Unisona* for Alto Voice, Flute, Trombone, Double Bass, and Vibraphone (1972); *Från när och fjärran* for Jazz Quartet (1973); *Mot värk* for Chorus and Percussion (1973; a sequel to *Stämma blod*); *Knaver-lik* for Nyckelharp and String Orch. (1974); *. . . ljudens dikt sjunger i venden . . .* for Narrator, Chorus, and Small Orch. (1974); *Till flöjten, ordern och kärleken* for Chorus and Chamber Ensemble (1980); *Var och en av oss* for Chorus and Organ (1986).

Alldis, John, English choral conductor; b. London, Aug. 10, 1929. He was educated at King's College, Cambridge. In 1962 he joined the faculty of the Guildhall School of Music in London; founded the John Alldis Choir, which soon achieved prominence. Later he conducted the London Sym. Orch. Chorus (1966–69), the London Phil. Orch. Chorus (1969–82), the Danish Radio Chorus in Copenhagen (1972–77), and the Groupe Vocal de France (1978–83).

Allegri, Domenico, Italian composer; b. Rome, 1585; d. there, Sept. 5, 1629. He was maestro di cappella at S. Maria Maggiore from 1610 to 1629, and was one of the 1st to provide vocal music with an independent instrumental accompaniment. A few of his motets are extant (a soprano solo, a tenor duet, and a bass solo, each accompanied by 2 violins).

Allegri, Gregorio, Italian composer; b. Rome, c.1582; d. there, Feb. 7, 1652. He was a choirboy in Rome from 1591 to 1596; then studied with Giovanni Maria Nanino (1600–1607). He entered the Papal Chapel in 1630 after serving for some years as chorister and composer for the Cathedral at Fermo. He is chiefly known as the composer of the celebrated *Miserere* in 9 parts (i.e., for 2 Choirs, one singing 4 parts and one 5), regularly sung during Holy Week at the Sistine Chapel; Mozart wrote this out after hearing it twice, though surreptitiously, since its publication was forbidden on pain of excommunication; since then it has been frequently publ. Many other works by Allegri are preserved in MS; 1 book of *concertini* and 2 books of *mottetti* have been printed; also a 4-part Sonata for Strings, which might be regarded as the prototype of the string quartet.

BIBL.: A. Cametti, "La scuola dei pueri cantus di S. Luigi dei Francesi in Roma," *Rivista Musicale Italiana* (1915); J. Amann, *A.s Miserere und die Aufführungspraxis in der Sixtina* (Regensburg, 1935).

Allegri, Lorenzo, Italian lutenist and composer; b. c.1573; d. Florence, July 15, 1648. He became a lutenist at the Medici court in Florence in 1604; remained at the court until his death. He publ. *Primo libro delle musiche* (Venice, 1618), a collection which contains mostly instrumental music.

BIBL.: H. Bellermann, "L. A.," *Allgemeine Musikalische Zeitung*, IV (1869).

Allen, Betty, black American mezzo-soprano; b. Campbell, Ohio, March 17, 1930. She attended Wilberforce Univ. (1944–46); then studied at the Hartford School of Music (1950–53); among her teachers were Paul Ulanowsky and Zinka Milanov. She sang in the N.Y. City Opera in 1954; also sang opera in San Francisco, Houston, Boston, and Santa Fe. On Feb. 20, 1973, she made her Metropolitan Opera debut in N.Y. She taught at the Manhattan School of Music in N.Y., the North Carolina School of the Arts in Winston-Salem (1978–87), and the Philadelphia Musical Academy (1979). She also served as executive director of the Harlem School of the Arts (from 1979).

Allen, Henry (James, Jr.) "Red," black American jazz trumpeter; b. New Orleans, Jan. 7, 1908; d. N.Y., April 17, 1967. His father, **Henry Allen** (1877–1952), was director of the New Orleans Brass Band; after studying the violin and alto horn, he turned to the trumpet; gained experience in his father's band; then played with King Oliver, Fletcher Henderson, and later Louis Armstrong (1937–40). In 1940 he formed his own group, Red's Sextet, and toured with it; also made solo appearances in the U.S. and Europe.

Allen, Sir Hugh Percy, eminent English organist and educator; b. Reading, Dec. 23, 1869; d. Oxford, Feb. 20, 1946. He studied with Dr. F. Read in Reading, and at Oxford Univ. (Mus.Doc., 1898). At the age of 11 he acted as church organist in Reading. Thereafter he was an organist at various churches and cathedrals until the turn of the century. He was organist at New College, Oxford (1901–18), and later (1908–18) director of music at Univ. College in Reading. In 1918 he became prof. of music at Oxford, and in the same year, director of the Royal College of Music in London, from which he resigned in 1937. He was knighted in 1920. For many years he conducted the London and the Oxford Bach choirs; he was an ardent promoter of British music.
  BIBL.: C. Bailey, *H.P. A.* (London, 1948).

Allen, Paul Hastings, American composer; b. Hyde Park, Mass., Nov. 28, 1883; d. Boston, Sept. 28, 1952. He studied at Harvard Univ. (A.B., 1903); then went to Italy. During World War I he was in the American diplomatic service in Italy; returning to the U.S. in 1920, he settled in Boston. He learned to play virtually all the orch. instruments as well as piano, and acquired fluent knowledge in Italian, German, and French, as well as a smattering of Russian. His music reflected the Italian techniques in operatic composition, while his instrumental works were written largely in a Romantic manner. He wrote much chamber music for unusual combinations, such as a Quartet for 2 Clarinets, Basset Horn, and Bass Clarinet.
  WORKS: OPERAS: *Il filtro* (Genoa, Oct. 26, 1912); *Milda* (Venice, June 14, 1913); *L'ultimo dei Mohicani* (Florence, Feb. 24, 1916); *Cleopatra* (1921); *La piccola Figaro* (1931); *Pilgrim Symphony* (1910; received the Paderewski prize); piano pieces; choral works; songs.

Allen, Terry, American singer, songwriter, and pianist; b. Wichita, Kans., May 7, 1943. He was raised in Lubbock, Texas, beginning his career as a sculptor and painter; then achieved cult fame in music. His albums are largely composed of story-songs, many involving humorous texts about U.S. locales and mores; most notable are *Lubbock (On Everything)* (1978), *Smokin the Dummy* (1980), and *Bloodlines* (1983). He also composed music for the film *Amerasia* (1986).

Allen, Thomas, distinguished English baritone; b. Seaham, Sept. 10, 1944. He was educated at the Royal College of Music in London; after singing in the Glyndebourne Chorus, he made his debut with the Welsh National Opera in 1969; from 1971 he sang at Covent Garden; also at the Aldeburgh and Glyndebourne festivals, and in Paris, Florence, and Buenos Aires. In 1989 he was made a Commander of the Order of the British Empire. He is generally regarded as one of the best European baritones, praised for both his lyric and his dramatic abilities.

Allende (-Sarón), (Pedro) Humberto, eminent Chilean composer; b. Santiago, June 29, 1885; d. there, Aug. 16, 1959. He studied violin and music theory at the National Cons. in Santiago (1889–1908); then taught in public schools there. In 1918 he visited France and Spain; in 1928 served as Chilean delegate to the Congress of Popular Arts in Prague, under the auspices of the League of Nations; in 1929 he took part in the Festival of Ibero-American Music in Barcelona. Returning to Santiago, he taught composition at the National Cons. (1930–50). He received the National Arts Prize in appreciation of his work in musical ethnology. His music is marked with an exquisite sense of authentic Chilean folk song, while the purely formal structure follows the impressionistic manner akin to that of Debussy, Ravel, and Granados.
  WORKS: Sym. (1910; awarded Chilean Centennial Prize); *Escenas campesinas chilenas* for Orch. (1913); Cello Concerto (1915); *La voz de las calles,* symphonic poem utilizing street cries of Chilean cities (Santiago, May 20, 1921); *La despedida* for 2 Sopranos, Contralto, and Orch. (Santiago, May 7, 1934); Violin Concerto (Santiago, Dec. 4, 1942); Piano Concerto (1945); String Quartet (1945); 3 piano sonatas (1906–15); *12 tonadas de carácter popular chileno* for Piano (1918–22); his

most distinctive work in a national style; also arranged for Orch.); songs; a teaching manual, *Método original de iniciación musical* (Santiago, 1937).
  BIBL.: N. Slonimsky, "H. A., First Modernist of Chile," *Musical America* (Aug. 1942); special issue of *Revista Musical Chilena* (Sept. 1945); V.S. Viu, *La creación musical en Chile* (Santiago, 1952).

Allers, Franz, Czech conductor; b. Karlovy Vary, Aug. 6, 1905. He studied violin; went to Berlin in 1926 and conducted theater orchs. He left Germany at the advent of the Nazis and held engagements conducting ballet performances in London, South America, and Canada. Eventually he settled in the U.S. He made his debut at the Metropolitan Opera in N.Y. as conductor on Nov. 30, 1963. From 1973 to 1976 he served as chief conductor of the Gärtnerplatz State Theater in Munich.

Allin, Norman, English bass; b. Ashton-under-Lyne, Nov. 19, 1884; d. Hereford, Oct. 27, 1973. He studied at the Royal Manchester College of Music (1906–10); made his operatic debut with the Beecham Opera Co. in London in 1916. In 1922 he became a director and leading bass of the British National Opera Co. in London, remaining with it until 1929; from 1942 to 1949 he was a member of the Carl Rosa Opera Co. He led vocal classes at the Royal Academy of Music in London (1935–60) and the Royal Manchester College of Music (1938–42).

Allison, Mose, American singer, songwriter, and pianist; b. Tippo, Miss., Nov. 11, 1927. After serving in the U.S. Army, he formed his own trio; then played with Stan Getz and Gerry Mulligan. His mature songs, marked by satirical and cynical lyrics, have been performed by such notables as The Who, John Mayall, Georgie Fame, and Bonnie Raitt. Successful albums include *Mose Alive, Western Man, Your Mind's on Vacation, Middle Class White Boy,* and *Lessons in Living.*

Almeida, Antonio (Jacques) de, conductor and music editor; b. Paris, Jan. 20, 1928. The son of a Portuguese diplomat and an American mother, he was taken by the family to Buenos Aires, where he studied with Alberto Ginastera. He also took an interest in science and applied for a scholarship at the Mass. Inst. of Technology; there he attended courses in nuclear chemistry, and also conducted the student orch. He subsequently enrolled in the class of Paul Hindemith in advanced music theory at Yale Univ.; during the summers he attended the Berkshire Music Center in Tanglewood, where he received training as a conductor with Koussevitzky and Bernstein. He then went to England, where he became associated with Sir Thomas Beecham, who gave him an opportunity to conduct the Royal Phil. He made his American debut in N.Y. on Nov. 1, 1960, conducting Gluck's *Orfeo ed Euridice* with the American Opera Soc.; on Feb. 24, 1982, he gave a concert performance in N.Y. of Wagner's early opera *Die Feen.* His other engagements included several seasons in Lisbon (beginning in 1956), along with the posts of principal conductor of the Stuttgart Phil. (1960–64), guest conductor at the Paris Opéra (1964–68) and the Houston Sym. Orch. (1969–71), and music director of the Nice Phil. (1976–78). While thus preoccupied, he devoted a great deal of eager attention to rescuing from oblivion little-known operas and operettas of Offenbach; from contacts with Offenbach's descendants he was able to recover the original uncut version of *Les Contes d'Hoffmann;* another find was the original score of Offenbach's comic opera *La Belle Hélène.* On April 15, 1982, he conducted at the N.Y. City Opera a newly restored version of Offenbach's operetta *La Grande Duchesse de Gérolstein.* In 1982 he assumed the general editorship of the multivolume ed. of Offenbach's collected works, including his instrumental music, along with the publication of a catalogue raisonné of the entire Offenbach oeuvre.

d'Almeida, Fernando, Portuguese composer; b. Lisbon, c.1600; d. Tomar, March 21, 1660. He was a distinguished pupil of Duarte Lobo; in 1638, entered the Order of Christ at Tomar. Of his many church compositions, only 1 folio vol. in

MS is known: *Lamentacões, Responsorias e Misereres das tres officias da Quarta, Quinta e Sexta-feria da Semana Santa.*

Almeida, Laurindo, Brazilian guitarist; b. São Paulo, Sept. 2, 1917. After mastering the guitar, he settled in Rio de Janeiro and made appearances on the radio; also led his own orch. at the Casino da Urca. In 1947 he moved to the U.S.; was a soloist with Stan Kenton's jazz band; subsequently gave numerous recitals and was a soloist with sym. orchs.; also appeared in recital with his wife, the soprano Deltra Eamon.

Almenräder, Carl, German bassoon virtuoso and composer; b. Ronsdorf, near Düsseldorf, Oct. 3, 1786; d. Biebrich, Sept. 14, 1843. He was a prof. of bassoon at Cologne, a theater conductor in Frankfurt, and a regimental bandmaster; started a factory for wind instruments (1820) at Cologne, but gave it up in 2 years, entering the Nassau Court Orch. at Biebrich. He materially improved the bassoon; wrote a treatise on it (Mainz, 1824) and a method for it. He also publ. a Bassoon Concerto; Variations for Bassoon and Quartet; duettinos for 2 Bassoons; etc.; and the popular ballad *Des Hauses letzte Stunde.*

Almquist, Carl Jonas Love, Swedish composer; b. Stockholm, Nov. 28, 1793; d. Bremen, Nov. 26, 1866. He studied at Uppsala Univ., and composed songs to his own words, but refused to study music theory for fear that his instinct for simple melodic writing might be destroyed by learning. His life was an adventurous one; he was forced to leave Sweden after an accusation of murder was leveled against him. From 1851 to 1865 he lived in America; then went to Germany, where he died. His publications included the song collection *Törnrosens bok* (Stockholm, 1832–42); he also publ. *Fria Fantasier* for Piano (1847–49).

Alnaes, Eyvind, Norwegian composer; b. Fredriksstad, April 29, 1872; d. Oslo, Dec. 24, 1932. He studied in Christiania with Ivar Holter (1889–92) and in Leipzig with Carl Reinecke (1892–95). From 1895 he occupied various positions as a church organist in Norway.
    Works: 2 syms. (1898, 1923); *Variations symphoniques* (1898); Piano Concerto (Christiania, Feb. 7, 1914); *Marche symphonique* for 2 Pianos; several choruses and songs. He also publ. a collection of Norwegian folk songs (1922).

Alnar, Hasan Ferit, Turkish composer; b. Constantinople, March 11, 1906; d. Ankara, July 27, 1978. From his earliest studies he became fascinated with indigenous Turkish percussion instruments and even composed an operetta using native instruments. He then went to Vienna, where he studied composition with Joseph Marx and conducting with Oswald Kabasta. He returned to Turkey in 1932 and developed a career as a conductor and teacher in Ankara. He wrote a cello concerto in an acceptable European manner and also a native-colored concerto for the kanun, a Turkish psaltery.

Alpaerts, Flor, Belgian composer, father of **Jef Alpaerts;** b. Antwerp, Sept. 12, 1876; d. there, Oct. 5, 1954. He studied composition with Benoit and Blockx and violin at the Flemish Cons. in Antwerp; in 1903 he joined its staff; was its director from 1934 to 1941. He conducted the local orch. at the Zoological Gardens (1919–51); was in charge of the ed. of works by Peter Benoit. His own music is marked by an intense feeling for the modalities of Flemish folk songs. His 5-vol. treatise *Muzieklezen en Zingen* was adopted as the official textbook in all Flemish music institutions.
    Works: Opera, *Shylock,* after Shakespeare (Antwerp, Nov. 22, 1913); *Symphonie du printemps* (1906); symphonic poems: *Psyche* (1900); *Herleving* (1903); *Cyrus* (1905); *Pallieter* (1921); *Thijl Uilenspiegel* (1927); *Avondindruk* (1928); *Zomeridyll* (1928). Other symphonic works include *Poème symphonique* for Flute and Orch. (1903); *Karakterstuk* for Trumpet and Strings (1904); *Bosspeling* (1904); *Salomé danse,* theme and variations (1907; based on incidental music to the Wilde play); *Vlaamse Idylle* (1920); *Romanza* for Violin and Small Orch. (1928); *James Ensor Suite* for Orch. (1929); 2 suites for Small Orch. (1932); *Humor* (1936); *Serenade* for Cello and Orch.

(1936); *Small Suite* for Strings (1947); Violin Concerto (1948); *Capriccio* (1953). He also wrote *Kolonos* for Soloists, Chorus, and Orch. (1901); a cantata, *Het schoner vaderland* (1912); 2 *Pieces* for Piano Trio (1906); *Avondmuziek* for 8 Woodwinds (1915); 4 string quartets (1943, 1944, 1945, 1950); 3 *petites pièces* for Violin and Piano (1944); 4 *Bagatelles* for String Quartet (1953); incidental music to 6 plays; *Kinderleideren,* in 4 sets (1915–16).

Alpaerts, Jef, Belgian conductor and pianist, son of **Flor Alpaerts;** b. Antwerp, July 17, 1904; d. there, Jan. 15, 1973. He received his primary education at the Royal Flemish Cons. in Antwerp; then went to Paris, where he studied piano with Isidor Philipp and with Cortot, and composition with Vincent d'Indy at the Schola Cantorum. Returning to Belgium in 1936, he was appointed to the faculty of the Antwerp Cons.; retired in 1969. In 1938 he inaugurated the Collegium Musicum Antverpiense for performances of early music.

Alpenheim, Ilse von, Austrian pianist; b. Innsbruck, Feb. 11, 1927. She studied with Franz Ledwinka and Winfried Wolf at the Salzburg Mozarteum; then appeared in recital and chamber music concerts; toured Europe, Japan, Australia, and the U.S. as a soloist; played with the Cleveland Orch., Philadelphia Orch., National Sym. of Washington, D.C., Detroit Sym., and Boston Sym. She was a sensitive interpreter of the Haydn and Mozart piano works. She was married to the conductor **Antal Dorati.**

Alsina, Carlos Roqué, Argentine composer; b. Buenos Aires, Feb. 19, 1941. He studied music theory with various local teachers; joined the modern society Agrupación de Nueva Música in Buenos Aires (1959–64); from 1964 to 1966 he worked in Berlin on a Ford Foundation grant; there he took instruction with Luciano Berio, who inculcated him in the arcana of ultramodern compositional techniques. From 1966 to 1968 he lived in Buffalo, where he taught at the State Univ. of N.Y.; in 1969 he founded, along with Vinko Globokar, Jean-Pierre Drouet, and Michel Portal, the improvisatory group New Phonic Art, which toured Europe. He subsequently spent several years in Berlin, and eventually settled in Paris. His music is of a functional nature, peculiar to the cosmopolitan avant-garde; it presents a colorful synthesis of quaquaversal idioms, ranging from stark, cloistered dissonance to overt, triadic formalism. Aleatory techniques are in evidence in his improvisatory performances.
    Works: STAGE: *Texts 1967,* theater piece for Soprano, Flute, Trombone, Violin, Cello, Double Bass, Percussion, and Piano (1967); *Fusion,* choreographic music for Dancer, 2 Pianos, and 2 Percussionists (1974); *Encore,* musical spectacle to a text by Arie Dzierlatka (1976); *La Muraille,* opera (Avignon, 1981); *Del Tango,* azione scenica (Paris, 1982). **ORCH.:** 3 *Pieces* for String Orch. (1964); *Symptom* (1969); *Dispersion 1969* for Chamber Orch. (1969); *Überwindung* (Conquest) for 4 Instrumental Soloists and Orch. (1970; Donaueschingen, Oct. 18, 1970; New Phonic Art group soloists); *Omnipotenz* for Chamber Orch. (1971); *Schichten* (Layers) I for Chamber Orch. (1971) and *Schichten II* for Chamber Ensemble (1972); *Approach* for Piano, Percussion, and Orch. (1972; West Berlin, March 14, 1973); *Thema II* for Solo Percussion and String Orch. (1974–75; Royan, France, March 26, 1975); *Stücke* (1977; Royan, April 4, 1977); *Señales* for Piano and Chamber Orch. (1977; La Rochelle, July 3, 1977); *Decisions* for Chamber Orch. (1977); *Études* for Orch. and Tape (1979; Metz, Nov. 17, 1979); *Prima sinforian* for Flute, Soprano, Cello, and Orch. (1983); Piano Concerto (1985). **CHAMBER:** *Quinteto de Maderas* for Wind Quintet (1961); *Funktionen* for Flute, Clarinet, Bassoon, Trumpet, Violin, Cello, Piano, and 2 Percussionists (1965); *Consecuenza* for Solo Trombone (1966); *Auftrag* for 9 Players (1966); *Trio 1967* for Cello, Trombone, and Percussion (1967); *Rendez-vous* for 4 Players (1970); *Unity* for Clarinet and Cello (1973); *A Letter* for Wind Quintet (1973); *Étude* for Solo Zarb (1973); *Thema* for Percussion (1974). **VOCAL:** *Requiem y aleluya* for Soprano, 5 Instruments, and Percussion (1960); *Oratorio* for 3 Soloists, 4 Actors, and 3 Small Instrumen-

tal Ensembles (1964); *Text*, scene for Trombone, 3 Percussion Instruments, and Chorus (1966); *Consecuenza II* for Solo Voice (1971); Cantata for Tenor, Chorus, and Orch. (Radio France, April 22, 1977); *Harmonies* for Children's Chorus, 2 Lectors, Narrator, 4 Soloists, Tape, and Orch. (1979; Paris Radio, Dec. 22, 1979); *Hinterland* for Piano, Percussion, and Tape (1982); *Voice avec voice* for String Quartet (1984).

Altenburg, Johann Ernst, German trumpet player and composer; b. Weissenfels, June 15, 1734; d. Bitterfeld, May 14, 1801. He served as a field trumpeter during the 7 Years' War; returning to civilian life, he became an organist at Bitterfeld. He wrote the 1st specialized manual on playing the trumpet and kettledrums, *Versuch einer Anleitung zur heroisch-musikalischen Trompeter- und Paukerkunst* (Halle, 1795; reprinted, Dresden, 1911); also pieces for 2, 4, 6, and 8 trumpets, and a Concerto for 7 Trumpets and Kettledrums.
BIBL.: A. Werner, "J.E. A.: Der letzte Vertreter der heroischen Trompeter- und Paukerkunst," *Zeitschrift für Musikwissenschaft*, XV (1932–33).

Altenburg, Michael, German church musician; b. Alach, near Erfurt, May 27, 1584; d. Erfurt, Feb. 12, 1640. He studied theology in Erfurt (1598–1603); in 1610 he moved to Tröchtelborn, where he was a pastor; then went to Gröss-Sommerda in 1621, and finally to Erfurt in 1637, remaining there until his death. He publ. a Wedding Motet in 7 parts; a collection of songs "for Church and Home" in 5, 6, and 8 voices (3 vols., Erfurt, 1620–21); 16 instrumental *Intraden* in 6 parts (Erfurt, 1620); and numerous church anthems, some of which have been permanently incorporated in the Lutheran service.
BIBL.: K. Ameln, "M. A.," *Jahrbuch für Liturgik und Hymnologie*, VIII (1963).

Altenburger, Christian, German violinist; b. Heidelberg, Sept. 5, 1957. He began to study violin with his father; at the age of 7 he made his 1st public appearance; he subsequently enrolled at the Vienna Academy of Music, graduating at 16; then went to the U.S. as a scholarship student at the Juilliard School of Music in N.Y., where he studied with Dorothy DeLay; graduated in 1978. In 1976 he made his professional debut in a recital at the Musikverein in Vienna; then appeared as soloist with the Berlin Phil., Vienna Phil., Concertgebouw Orch. of Amsterdam, London Sym., Chicago Sym., and other orchs.

Altès, Ernest-Eugène, French violinist, conductor, and composer, brother of **Joseph-Henri Altès;** b. Paris, March 28, 1830; d. St.-Dyé, near Blois, July 8, 1899. He studied with Habeneck at the Paris Cons., where he won 1st prize for violin playing in 1848. In 1871 he joined the staff of the Paris Opéra as conductor, retiring in 1887. He composed a Sym., chamber music, and an orch. *Divertissement* on ballet airs by Auber on the occasion of Auber's centennial (1882).

Altès, Joseph-Henri, French flutist, brother of **Ernest-Eugène Altès;** b. Rouen, Jan. 18, 1826; d. Paris, July 24, 1895. He studied at the Paris Cons.; then became a flutist at the Paris Opéra. He was appointed prof. of flute at the Paris Cons. in 1868, holding this post to the end of his life. He publ. a number of flute pieces.

Altglass, Max, Polish-born American tenor; b. Warsaw, Feb. 16, 1886; d. N.Y., Feb. 13, 1952. He studied in Berlin; made his operatic debut in Frankfurt in 1913; then went to the U.S.; appeared with the Metropolitan Opera in N.Y. on Nov. 6, 1924, remaining on its roster until 1940. Subsequently he was active as a vocal teacher.

Althouse, Paul (Shearer), American tenor; b. Reading, Pa., Dec. 2, 1889; d. N.Y., Feb. 6, 1954. He studied with Oscar Saenger; made his debut as Dimitri in the American premiere of *Boris Godunov* at the Metropolitan Opera on March 19, 1913; continued on its roster until 1920, and joined it again in 1923; sang Wagnerian roles as a Heldentenor at the Metropolitan from 1934 to 1940; was a soloist with Toscanini and the N.Y. Phil. in Beethoven's 9th Sym.; also toured in Europe, Australia, and New Zealand as a concert singer; subsequently

was chiefly active as a vocal teacher in N.Y. Among his most prominent students were Eleanor Steber and Richard Tucker.

Altman, Ludwig, German-American organist and composer; b. Breslau, Sept. 2, 1910; d. San Francisco, Nov. 27, 1990. He studied at the Univ. of Breslau with Arnold Schmitz and Peter Epstein; from 1929 to 1933 he attended courses of Hans Joachim Moser, Arnold Schering, Johannes Wolf, and Friedrich Blume at the State Academy for Sacred Music in Berlin; also took private lessons in organ playing with Arthur Zubke. He remained in Berlin for 3 years after Hitler's advent to power, serving as organist at the Neue Synagoge, the largest Jewish synagogue still in operation (1933–36). In 1936 he emigrated to America; settled in San Francisco; in 1937 became organist and choral director at Temple Emanu-El; from 1940 to 1973 was organist of the San Francisco Sym. Orch. From 1948 to 1965 he was also organist of the Bach Festivals in Carmel, Calif.; in 1952 he became Municipal Organist of San Francisco. He composed numerous scores of sacred music, among them *Sabbath Music* for Cantor, Choir, and Organ (1963); *The Blessing of Moses* for Baritone Solo, Choir, and Organ (1977); several Psalms for Voices and Organ; and works for organ solo. He furthermore ed. Beethoven's organ works, Telemann's *Suite Baroque*, pieces by C.P.E. Bach for Organ Clock, and some organ compositions by Mendelssohn. As a concert organist he appeared in solo recitals in London, Berlin, Hamburg, Munich, Stuttgart, Frankfurt, Bern, Lausanne, and Zürich, as well as in San Francisco, in programs of Baroque and Classical music with a generous inclusion of ultramodern works by contemporary composers, receiving undiluted praise in the press.

Altmann, Wilhelm, German music scholar; b. Adelnau, near Posen, April 4, 1862; d. Hildesheim, March 25, 1951. He studied philology and government in Marburg and Berlin, and in 1885 received his Dr.Phil. He served as librarian in Greifswald (1889–1900). In 1900 he was appointed a librarian of the Prussian State Library in Berlin; in 1915 he became director of the music dept., retiring in 1927. In 1906 he founded, in cooperation with Breitkopf & Härtel, the Deutsche Musiksammlung at the Berlin library. From 1945 he lived in Hildesheim. Altmann compiled a number of valuable bibliographical works, among them *Chronik des Berliner Phil. Orchesters* (1902); *Richard Wagners Briefe* (1905; a list of 3,143 letters with brief synopses); *Brahms' Briefwechsel* (1908); *Wagners Briefwechsel mit seinen Verlegern* (2 vols., 1911); *Kammermusik-Literatur-Verzeichnis*, a list of chamber music publ. since 1841 (1910; 6 revisions up to 1945); *Max-Reger-Katalog* (1917, 1923); a catalog of music for viola and viola d'amore (1937) and a catalog of music for piano, 4- and 6-hands, and for 2 pianos (1943). He also ed. Paul Frank's *Tonkünstler-Lexikon* (1926, 1927, 1936, 1949). Furthermore, he publ. bibliographies of books on instruments and made arrangements of classical works.

Altmeyer, Jeannine (Theresa), American soprano; b. La Habra, Calif., May 2, 1948. She received instruction from Martial Singher and Lotte Lehmann in Santa Barbara, Calif.; later took courses at the Salzburg Mozarteum. She made her debut as the Heavenly Voice in *Don Carlos* at the Metropolitan Opera (N.Y., Sept. 25, 1971); then sang Freia in *Das Rheingold* at the Chicago Lyric Opera (1972), in Salzburg (1973), and at London's Covent Garden (1975). From 1975 to 1979 she was a member of the Württemberg State Theater in Stuttgart; subsequently appeared widely in Europe. She is notably successful in Wagnerian roles, including Elisabeth, Gutrune, Eva, Brünnhilde, Elsa, and Sieglinde.

Altmeyer, Theo(dor David), German tenor; b. Eschweiler, March 16, 1931. He was educated in Cologne; in 1956 he joined the Berlin Städtische Oper, remaining on its roster until 1960; then became a member of the Hannover Opera; later appeared at the Stuttgart Opera and the Vienna State Opera; also toured North America. In 1974 he joined the faculty of the Hochschule für Musik in Hannover; continued to appear in opera and concerts.

Altnikol, Johann Christoph, German organist and composer; b. Berna, Silesia, Dec. 1719 (baptized, Jan. 1, 1720); d. Naumburg, July 25, 1759. He was a pupil of Bach during the period 1744–48; then served as an organist at St. Wenzel's Church in Naumburg. On Jan. 20, 1749, Altnikol married Bach's daughter Elisabeth. In a letter of recommendation Bach described him as "quite skillful in composition." Furthermore, Altnikol acted as Bach's copyist and was instrumental in establishing authentic texts of several of Bach's works. Only a few of his works are extant.
  BIBL.: H. David and A. Mendel, eds., *The Bach Reader* (N.Y., 1945; rev. ed., 1966).

Altschuler, Modest, Russian-born American cellist and conductor; b. Mogilev, Feb. 15, 1873; d. Los Angeles, Sept. 12, 1963. He studied cello at the Warsaw Cons. as a child; then went to Moscow, where he took courses in composition with Arensky and Taneyev and in piano and conducting with Safonov at the Cons., graduating in 1890. After touring Russia as a cellist, he emigrated to America, and in 1903 organized in N.Y. the Russian Sym. Soc. He conducted its 1st concert on Jan. 7, 1904; for some 12 years the concerts of this organization became an important cultural medium for performances of Russian music in America. One of Altschuler's signal accomplishments was the world premiere of Scriabin's *Le Poème de l'extase*, which he gave in N.Y. on Dec. 10, 1908, in advance of its Russian performance. At the same concert Mischa Elman made his American debut as a concert violinist. Altschuler also conducted the 1st American performance of Scriabin's *Prométhée*, in N.Y. on March 20, 1915, at which he made an unsuccessful attempt to include the part of *Luce* (a color organ), prescribed by Scriabin in the score. Among other Russian composers whose works Altschuler presented for the 1st time in America were Rachmaninoff, Liadov, Vasilenko, and Ippolitov-Ivanov. Altschuler eventually retired to Los Angeles; he wrote an autobiography which remains unpubl.

Alva, Luigi (real name, **Luis Ernesto Alva Talledo**), noted Peruvian tenor; b. Lima, April 10, 1927. He studied voice in Lima; made his operatic debut there in 1950; then continued his vocal studies in Milan. In 1954 he embarked on a European tour; sang at La Scala in Milan, at Edinburgh, at Salzburg, and at the Vienna State Opera; in 1960 he made his debut at Covent Garden in London; on March 6, 1964, he appeared at the Metropolitan Opera as Fenton in Verdi's *Falstaff*. As a leading lyric tenor, he excelled primarily in the Italian repertoire.

Alvarez (real name, **Gourron**), **Albert (Raymond),** French tenor; b. Cenon, near Bordeaux, May 16, 1861; d. Nice, Feb. 1, 1933. He started his musical career as the leader of a military band in France; then began his vocal studies in Paris; made his debut at the Paris Opéra in 1892. He made successful appearances at Covent Garden in London; made his American debut at the Metropolitan Opera in N.Y. on Dec. 18, 1899, remaining with the company until 1903, when he returned to Paris to become a singing teacher. His repertoire included about 60 roles.

Alvary, Lorenzo, Hungarian-born American bass; b. Debrecen, Feb. 20, 1909. He studied law at the Univ. of Budapest and in Geneva; then took voice lessons in Milan and Berlin. In 1937 he made his 1st appearance at the Vienna State Opera; in 1939 he came to the U.S., where he sang with the San Francisco Opera. He made his Metropolitan Opera debut in N.Y. on Nov. 26, 1942, as Zuñiga in *Carmen*; subsequently became a regular member of the company; also gave solo recitals.

Alvary (real name, **Achenbach**), **Max,** German tenor; b. Düsseldorf, May 3, 1856; d. near Gross-Tabarz, Thuringia, Nov. 7, 1898. His father was a noted painter. Alvary studied with Julius Stockhausen in Frankfurt; later took voice lessons with Lamperti in Milan. He made his debut in Weimar in 1879, and lived in Weimar until 1885. On Nov. 25, 1885, he made

his American debut at the Metropolitan Opera in N.Y. as Don José in *Carmen*, singing the role in German; he remained with the Metropolitan until 1889; then made guest appearances in Munich, Hamburg, and Bayreuth. He was particularly noted for his Wagnerian roles.

Alwin, Karl (real name, **Alwin Oskar Pinkus**), German conductor; b. Königsberg, April 15, 1891; d. Mexico City, Oct. 15, 1945. He studied composition in Berlin with Humperdinck and Hugo Kaun; later he dedicated himself mainly to conducting. He was Kapellmeister in Halle (1913), Posen (1914), Düsseldorf (1915–17), and Hamburg (1917–20). From 1920 to 1938 he served as conductor of the Vienna State Opera. He left Austria in 1938, after the Anschluss, and went to Mexico, where he conducted opera from 1941 until his death. He was married to **Elisabeth Schumann** (1920–36).

Alwyn, Kenneth, English conductor; b. Croydon, July 28, 1925. He received his musical training at the Royal Academy of Music in London; then conducted ballet at the Sadler's Wells Theatre; was an assistant conductor at the Royal Ballet (1957–61) and from 1961 a conductor at the Western Theatre Ballet; he served as its music director from 1967 to 1969. He was also active in broadcasting and films; was a conductor with the BBC Concert Orch. from 1968; in 1969 he became principal conductor of the BBC Northern Ireland Orch.

Alwyn, William, English composer; b. Northampton, Nov. 7, 1905; d. Southwold, Sept. 11, 1985. He studied at the Royal Academy of Music, and although he failed to graduate, he was appointed to the faculty there, teaching composition from 1926 to 1956. In 1976 he was named Commander of the Order of the British Empire. He acquired a peculiar knack for writing effective film music, and wrote scores for *Desert Victory* (1943), *Odd Man Out* (1947), *Fallen Idol* (1949), *The Magic Box* (1951), *The Silent Enemy* (1958), *Swiss Family Robinson* (1960), *The Naked Edge* (1961), *In Search of the Castaways* (1961), and *The Running Man* (1963). He also wrote some workable pieces for various instrumental combinations, such as *Dance* for Harp, Guitar, and Harpsichord (1977), Octet (1977), a Double-bass Concerto (1981), stage music and multimedia works, vocal scores for various combinations, and some fanciful productions that include audience participation.

Alypios, Greek music theorist who flourished in the middle of the 4th century. His *Introduction to Music* is the chief source of specific information regarding ancient Greek notation; it contains a summary of Greek scales in all their transpositions, for both voices and instruments. This treatise was publ. by Meursius (Leyden, 1616); by Meibom in his *Antiquae musicae auctores septem* (Amsterdam, 1652); and reprinted by F. Bellermann in *Die Tonleitern und Musiknoten der Griechen* (Berlin, 1847). A new critical ed. is found in Jan's *Musici scriptores graeci* (1895). A graphic explanation of the notation of Alypios is presented by A. Samoiloff in his article "Die Alypiusschen Reihen der altgriechischen Tonbezeichnung," *Archiv für Musikwissenschaft* (1924).

Åm, Magnar, Norwegian composer; b. Trondheim, April 9, 1952. He studied composition, organ, and singing at the Bergen Cons. (1968–71); then took a course in advanced composition in Stockholm with Lidholm (1971–72); later joined the music faculty of the Bergen Cons. His music expands classical forms and conventional harmony to conceptual grandiosity.
  WORKS: 2 *Movements* for String Quartet (1970); *Lydar i løynd* (Sounds in Secret), 7 poems for Piano (1971); *Poem* for 2 Horns and Hardanger Fiddle (1971); *Bøn* (Prayer) for Soprano, Chorus, and String Orch. (1972); *Mot dag* (Dawn Is Breaking) for Chorus and Orch. (1972); *Song* for Brass and Percussion (1974); *Intermezzo* for 3 Woodwinds (1976); *Dance* for Harp, Guitar, and Harpsichord (1977); *Octet* (1977); *Punkt null* (Zero), version A for Soprano, Alto, Chorus, Children's Chorus, and Amateur Orch. (1979); version B for Chorus (1978; rev. 1983); version C for Solo Voice, Chorus, Audience, and Organ (1982); *Du, bli her!* (You Stay Here!) for Viola and Cello (1979); *Farewell, Limits* for Piano (1980); *Agamemnon,*

choral drama for 5 Dancers, 8 Actors, Solo Voice, Women's Chorus, and 2 Clarinets (1981); *Veinje* for Mixed Chorus, Women's Chorus, Men's Chorus, 3 Clarinets, Bass Clarinet, and Cello (1981); *På Glytt . . .* (Ajar . . .), double-bass concerto (1981); *Burfugls Draum* (Dream of a Caged Bird), multimedia score (1982); *Utenkjelege Far* (Inconceivable Father) for Child Soprano, Children's Chorus, Bass Clarinet, Timpani, Double Bass, and Organ (1982); *Min klode, mi sjel* (My Planet, My Soul), sym. (1982); *Water Music*, electronic score (1984); *Tvers Gjennom Alt Dette* for Orch. (1985).

Amacher, Maryanne, American composer, performer, sound architect, and mixed-media artist; b. Kates, Pa., Feb. 25, 1943. She studied with George Rochberg at the Univ. of Pa. (B.F.A., 1964) and with Stockhausen; then became involved in computer science at the Univs. of Pa. and Illinois, the Mass. Inst. of Technology, and Radcliffe College, Harvard. In 1967 she initiated the *City-Links* series, sound-displacement experiments in which she transmitted, via microphone installations, the sounds of distant locations to her own studio or performance space; then developed theories about the psychoacoustical effects of sound on daily life patterns, which have informed all subsequent work. Since 1980 she has been developing a form of music theater utilizing the "virtual environment" (3D simulated reality), to which the Vivarium Group at M.I.T. is similarly directed. Her *Music for Sound-joined Rooms*, in which various architectural features of a building are used as sound structures, are complex mixed-media works incorporating video, 3D graphics, projected images, lighting, furniture, sculpture, photography, and texts. One current project is *Fake Ears*, programmable software that means to enhance the capabilities of the human ear. Because of the extreme technological sophistication of her work, public access is currently quite limited; live performances are rare.

WORKS: *City-Links*, mixed media (1967–79); *Lecture on the Weather* (with John Cage, 1975); *Remainder*, dance music (for Merce Cunningham; 1976); *Close Up* (for Cage's *Empty Words;* 1979); *Music for Sound-joined Rooms*, mixed media (1980–82); *Sound House*, Mini-Sound Series (1985); *The Music Rooms*, Mini-Sound Series (1987); other electronic and mixed-media scores.

BIBL.: T. Johnson, "M. A.: Acoustics Joins Electronics," *Village Voice* (Dec. 15, 1975); L. Durner, "M. A.: Architect of Aural Design," *Ear Magazine*, XIII, no. 10 (Feb. 1989).

Amadei, Filippo, Italian opera composer; b. Reggio, c.1670; d. probably in Rome, c.1729. His claim to attention is that under the name of **Signor Pippo** (diminutive of Filippo) he wrote the 1st act of the opera *Muzio Scevola*, for which Bononcini wrote the 2nd act and Handel the 3rd, and which was produced at the Royal Academy of Music in London on April 15, 1721. His other works are the opera *Teodosio il Giovane* (Rome, 1711), the oratorio *Il trionfo di Tito* (Rome, 1709), and the cantata *Il pensiero* (Rome, 1709). Amadei's name was erroneously converted into **Filippo Mattei** by Mattheson in his *Critica musica*, and the mistake was carried into reference works and Handel's biographies.

Amaducci, Bruno, Italian conductor; b. Lugano-Viganello, Jan. 5, 1925. He studied at the École Normale de Musique in Paris and at the Verdi Cons. of Music in Milan; then began his conducting career. He appeared with many of the leading opera houses of Europe; also conducted at the Metropolitan Opera and the N.Y. City Opera.

Amalia Catharina, Countess of Erbach; b. Arolsen, Aug. 8, 1640; d. Cuylenburg, the Netherlands, Jan. 4, 1697. She was the daughter of Count von Waldeck; in 1664 she married Count Georg Ludwig von Erbach; of her 16 children only a few survived perilous infancy. She merits attention of musical biographers as one of the few women of the German nobility who actually composed all by themselves a number of singable religious anthems.

Amalia Friederike, Princess of Saxony who wrote comedies under the name of **Amalie Heiter;** b. Dresden, Aug. 10, 1794;

d. there, Sept. 18, 1870. She composed several light operas (*Una Donna, Le tre cinture, Die Siegesfahne, Der Kanonenschuss,* etc.) and church music.

Amani, Nikolai, Russian composer; b. St. Petersburg, April 4, 1872; d. Yalta, Oct. 17, 1904. He studied piano with Anne Essipova and composition with Rimsky-Korsakov and Liadov at the St. Petersburg Cons. (1890–1900); then went to Italy and played a concert of his piano works at Naples (July 29, 1900); in 1901–2 he traveled in Germany. Tuberculosis forced him to stop working; he lived his last 2 years in the Crimea. Amani's music is close in style to Tchaikovsky's, but he wrote only in small forms. He composed a String Trio (1900) and a number of harmonious piano pieces and songs, many of them publ. A memoir of his short life was publ. in Italian by S. Gentile, *Breve ricordo della vita e opere di N. A., musicista russo* (Palermo, 1911).

Amar, Licco, Hungarian violinist; b. Budapest, Dec. 4, 1891; d. Freiburg im Breisgau, July 19, 1959. He studied with Henri Marteau in Berlin and in 1912 joined the Marteau Quartet as 2nd violinist. He subsequently was appointed concertmaster of the Berlin Phil. (1915–20) and at the National Theater in Mannheim (1920–23). In 1921 he organized the Amar Quartet, with Paul Hindemith as the violist, Walter Caspar as 2nd violinist, and Maurits Frank as cellist. In 1933 he was compelled to leave Germany; in 1935 he was engaged as a prof. at the Cons. of Ankara in Turkey. In 1957 he returned to Germany and taught at the Hochschule für Musik in Freiburg im Breisgau.

Amara (real name, **Armaganian**), **Lucine,** American soprano; b. Hartford, Conn., March 1, 1927, of Armenian parentage. She studied violin; began her vocal training in San Francisco after her parents moved west. She made her operatic debut at the Metropolitan Opera in N.Y. on Nov. 6, 1950, as the Heavenly Voice in Verdi's *Don Carlos;* although criticized for the lack of celestial quality in that part, she made progress in her career; in 1954 she sang at the Glyndebourne Festival, and at the Vienna State Opera in 1960. She made a world tour in 1968, which included several appearances in Russia. She also made a cameo appearance in a movie, as the female interest in *The Great Caruso*, opposite Mario Lanza.

Amat, Juan Carlos (real name, **Joan Carles y Amat**), Spanish physician and writer on guitar playing; b. Monistrol de Montserrat, c.1572; d. there, Feb. 10, 1642. His book *Guitarra española en cinco ordenes* (Barcelona, 1596) has been reprinted many times.

BIBL.: E. Pujol, "Significación de J.C. A. (1572–1642) en la historia de la guitarra," *Anuario Musical*, vol. V (Barcelona, 1950); M. Hall, "The 'Guitar española' of J.C. A.," *Early Music*, VI (1978).

Amati, renowned Italian family of violin makers working at Cremona. (1) **Andrea** (b. between 1500 and 1505; d. before 1580) was the 1st violin maker of the family. He established the prototype of Italian instruments, with characteristics found in modern violins. His sons were (2) **Antonio** (b. c.1538; d. c.1595), who built violins of varying sizes; and (3) **Girolamo** (b. c.1561; d. Nov. 2, 1630), who continued the tradition established by his father, and worked together with his brother, Antonio. (4) **Nicola,** or **Niccolò** (b. Dec. 3, 1596; d. April 12, 1684), was the most illustrious of the Amati family. He was the son of Girolamo Amati, and signed his labels "Nicolaus Amati Cremonens, Hieronimi filius Antonii nepos." He built some of the "grand Amatis," large violins of powerful tone surpassing in clarity and purity those made by his father and his grandfather, Andrea. In Nicola's workshop both Andrea Guarneri and Antonio Stradivari received their training. (5) **Girolamo** (b. Feb. 26, 1649; d. Feb. 21, 1740), son of Nicola and the last of the family, produced violins inferior to those of his father, his grandfather, and his great-grandfather. In his work he departed from the family tradition in many respects and seemed to be influenced by Stradivari's method without equaling his superb workmanship.

BIBL.: G. de Picolellis, *Genealogia degli A. e dei Guarneri* (Florence, 1886); W.L. von Lütgendorff, *Die Geigen- und Lautenmacher vom Mittelalter bis zur Gegenwart* (2 vols.; Frankfurt, 1904; 4th ed., 1922); D.D. Boyden, *The History of Violin Playing from Its Origins to 1761* (London, 1965).

Amato, Pasquale, Italian baritone; b. Naples, March 21, 1878; d. N.Y., Aug. 12, 1942. He studied at the Cons. of Naples (1896–99); made his debut in *La Traviata* in Naples in 1900. He later sang at leading European opera houses, and in Russia, England, Egypt, and Argentina. He made his American debut at the Metropolitan Opera in *La Traviata* (Nov. 20, 1908) with Sembrich and Caruso; remained a member of the Metropolitan until 1918, then again from 1919 to 1921; eventually settled in N.Y. as a voice teacher. He greatly distinguished himself in Italian roles; created the role of Jack Rance in *La Fanciulla del West* at the Metropolitan (Dec. 10, 1910).

BIBL.: P. Kenyon and C. Williams, "P. A.," *Record Collector*, XXI (1973; with discography).

Ambros, August Wilhelm, eminent Austrian music historiographer; b. Mauth, near Prague, Nov. 17, 1816; d. Vienna, June 28, 1876. He studied law and music; rapidly rose in the legal profession; was appointed public prosecutor in Prague (1850), but continued to devote much time to music; publ. his *Die Grenzen der Musik und Poesie* (Leipzig, 1856; Eng. tr., N.Y., 1893) as a reply to Hanslick's views on esthetics, followed by a brilliant collection of essays under the title *Culturhistorische Bilder aus dem Musikleben der Gegenwart* (Leipzig, 1860); also publ. 2 collections of articles, *Bunte Blätter* (1872–74; 2nd ed. by E. Vogel, 1896). In 1869 Ambros was appointed prof. of music at Prague Univ. and Prague Cons.; in 1872 received a post in the Ministry of Justice in Vienna; he also taught at the Vienna Cons. His major work was the monumental *Geschichte der Musik* commissioned by the publisher Leuckart in 1860. Ambros spent many years of research in the libraries of Munich, Vienna, and several Italian cities for this work, but died before completing the 4th vol., which was ed. from his notes by C.F. Becker and G. Nottebohm; a 5th vol. was publ. in 1882 by O. Kade from newly collected materials. W. Langhans wrote a sequel in a more popular style under the title *Die Geschichte der Musik des 17., 18. und 19. Jahrhunderts*, bringing the work up to date (2 vols., 1882–86). A list of names and a general index were issued by W. Bäumker (1882). A 2nd ed. of the original 4 vols. (Leipzig, 1880) contains the following: vol. I, *The Beginnings of Music*; vol. II, *From the Christian Era to the First Flemish School*; vol. III, *From the Netherlands Masters to Palestrina*; vol. IV, *Palestrina, His Contemporaries and Immediate Successors*. Vol. I has been rewritten, not always for the better, by B. Sokolovsky; vol. II was reprinted in a new revision by Riemann (1892), vol. IV by Leichtentritt (1909); vol. V was revised and enl. by O. Kade (1911). Ambros was also an excellent practical musician, a proficient pianist, and a composer. He wrote an opera in Czech, *Bretislaw a Jitka*; overtures to *Othello* and *Magico prodigioso*; numerous songs; and religious music.

BIBL.: G. Adler, "A.W. A.," *Musical Quarterly* (July 1931).

Ambros, Vladimír, Czech composer; b. Prostějov, Moravia, Sept. 18, 1890; d. there, May 12, 1956. He studied at the Brünn Organ School (1908–10) and at the Frankfurt Cons., later becoming active as a conductor with the Carl Rosa Opera Co. in England. After World War I he returned to Prostějov. His works include the operas *Ukradené štěstí* (Stolen Happiness; 1924) and *Maryla* (1951); 3 syms. (1941; 1944; 1946–51); Symphonietta (1938); a cantata, *Veliký navrat* (Grand Return; 1951); chamber music and songs.

BIBL.: V. Gregor, *V. A.* (Prostějov, 1969).

Ambrose (Ambrosius), Christian saint and creator of "Ambrosian Chant"; b. Trier (Trèves), c.333; d. Milan, April 4, 397. He was elected Bishop of Milan in 374; canonized after his death. In 384 he became responsible for the regulation and development of singing in the Western Church by the introduction and cultivation of ritual song (antiphonal and congregational) as practiced at the time in the Eastern Church. His indisputable authorship of several sacred songs has earned him the title of "Father of Christian Hymnology," but his reputed composition of the Ambrosian Chant *Te Deum laudamus* (said to have been sung by St. Ambrose and St. Augustine at the baptism of the latter) is mythical.

BIBL.: L. Biraghi, *Inni sinceri e carmi di S. Ambrogio* (Milan, 1862); G.M. Dreves, *Aurelius Ambrosius, der Vater des Kirchengesanges* (Freiburg, 1893); A. Mocquereau, *Notes sur l'influence de l'accent et du cursus tonique latins dans le chant ambrosien* (Paris, 1897); A. Steier, *Untersuchungen über die Echtheit der Hymnen des Ambrosius* (Leipzig, 1903); P. Wagner, *Introduction to the Gregorian Melodies*, part 1, *Origin and Development of the Forms of Liturgical Chant* (London, 1907); E. Garbagnati, *Riviste sull'antica salmodia ambrosiana* (Rome, 1912); A.S. Parodi, *S. Ambrogio e la sua età* (Milan, 1941).

d'Ambrosio, Alfredo, Italian violinist and composer; b. Naples, June 13, 1871; d. Nice, Dec. 29, 1914. He studied composition with Enrico Bossi at the Cons. of Naples; then went to Madrid, where he took violin lessons with Sarasate; later continued his violin study with Willhelmj in London. He then went to Nice, where he was active mainly as a violin teacher. He wrote an opera, *Pia de Tolomei*; a ballet, *Ersilia*; a String Quintet; a String Quartet; and 2 violin concertos (1904, 1913); also numerous concert numbers for violin (*Romanza, Canzonetta*, etc.).

Ambrosius, Hermann, German composer; b. Hamburg, July 25, 1897; d. Engen am Hegau, Oct. 25, 1983. He studied at the Univ. of Leipzig; later took private lessons in composition with Pfitzner. In 1925 he joined the faculty of the Leipzig Cons.; eventually settled in Engen. A prolific composer, he wrote 12 syms. (1920–63); 3 piano concertos (1926–52); 2 cello concertos (1928–38); 2 guitar concertos (1953–62); an orch. suite entitled *Iskusstvo* (the Russian word for "art"), inspired by Russian paintings; and an astonishing number of pieces for accordion; not to mention pieces for the electronic instrument Trautonium. His fecundity was noted in an admiring Festschrift, ed. by F. Hirtler, publ. on his 70th birthday.

Ameling, Elly (Elisabeth Sara), outstanding Dutch soprano; b. Rotterdam, Feb. 8, 1934. After studies in Rotterdam and The Hague, she completed her training with Pierre Bernac in Paris; won the 's Hertogenbosch (1956) and Geneva (1958) competitions, then made her formal recital debut in Amsterdam (1961). Subsequent appearances with the Concertgebouw Orch. in Amsterdam and the Rotterdam Phil. secured her reputation. In 1966 she made her London debut and in 1968 her N.Y. debut; her 1st appearance in opera was as Ilia in *Idomeneo* with the Netherlands Opera in Amsterdam in 1973, but she chose to concentrate upon a career as a concert artist. She gained renown for her appearances with many major European orchs. and her lieder recitals. In 1971 she was made a Knight of the Order of Oranje Nassau by the Dutch government. She established the Elly Ameling Lied Prize to be awarded at the 's Hertogenbosch competition.

Amellér, André (Charles Gabriel), French composer; b. Arnaville, Jan. 2, 1912; d. Garenne-Colombes, near Paris, May 14, 1990. He studied composition with Roger-Ducasse and Gaubert at the Paris Cons.; also violin and double bass. He was taken prisoner of war in Germany in 1940; after the war he returned to France, and from 1953 to 1981 was director of the Dijon Cons. He wrote operas: *La Lance de Fingal* (1947); *Sampiero Corso, Monsieur Personne* (1957); *Cyrnos* (Nancy, April 6, 1962); ballets: *La Coupe de sang* (1950) and *Oiseaux du vieux Paris* (1967); Cello Concerto (1946); *Jeux de table* for Saxophone and Piano (1955); *Terre secrète*, 6 poems for Voice and Orch. (1956); *Airs hétérogènes* for Wind Ensemble (1966); *Hétérodoxes* for 2 Flutes, 2 Trumpets, String Quartet, and String Orch. (1969); *Suite Florentine* for Cello (1986); *Uranie* for Flute and Piano (1986); Duo Concertant for Double Basses (1987).

Amengual (-Astaburuaga), René, Chilean composer; b. Santiago, Sept. 2, 1911; d. there, Aug. 2, 1954. He studied with Humberto Allende at the National Cons. in Santiago. His compositions are few, and mostly in small forms; their style shows influences of the modern French school. He wrote: Piano Sonatina (1938); *Introduction and Allegro* for 2 Pianos (1939); Piano Concerto (Santiago, June 30, 1942); *El Vaso* for Voice and Chamber Orch. (Santiago, Aug. 25, 1944); etc. His *Burlesca* for Piano is included in the album *Latin American Art Music for the Piano* (N.Y., 1942).

Amfitheatrov, Daniele, Russian-born American composer; b. St. Petersburg, Oct. 29, 1901; d. Rome, June 7, 1983. He was a son of a famous Russian journalist. The family left Russia after the Revolution; once abroad, Amfitheatrov studied composition in Prague, then moved to Italy, where he took lessons with Ottorino Respighi. In 1937 he moved to the U.S., where he became active as a conductor. In 1941 he went to Hollywood and wrote some music for films; he became an American citizen in 1944. Eventually he returned to Italy. Among his compositions are *Poema del mare* for Orch. (1925), *American Panorama* for Orch. (1939), and a Requiem (1960).

Amicis, Anna Lucia de, Italian soprano; b. Naples, 1733; d. there, 1816. She went to London in 1763; there she appeared in concert with Bach's son, the "London Bach." Returning to Naples, she married the physician Francesco Buonsollazzi (1768) and thenceforth appeared under the name De Amicis Buonsollazzi; she continued her active career as an opera singer until 1786. Her talent was appreciated by Mozart, who often mentioned her name in his correspondence.

Amiot, Père Jean Joseph Marie, French ecclesiastic; b. Toulon, Feb. 8, 1718; d. Peking, Oct. 9, 1793. He was a Jesuit missionary to China; while there, he tr. Li Koang Ti's work on Chinese music: *Commentaire sur le livre classique touchant la musique des anciens;* also wrote *Mémoires sur la musique des Chinois, tant anciens que modernes* (vol. VI of *Mémoires concernant l'histoire, les sciences, les arts . . . des Chinois;* Paris, 1780, ed. by Abbé Roussier).

Amirkhanian, Charles (Benjamin), American avant-garde composer and influential radio producer of Armenian extraction; b. Fresno, Calif., Jan. 19, 1945. He studied English literature at Calif. State Univ. at Fresno (B.A., 1967), interdisciplinary creative arts at San Francisco State College (M.A., 1969), and electronic music and sound recording at Mills College (M.F.A., 1980). In his early percussion compositions he experimented with the potentialities of sound phenomena independent of traditional musical content; his *Composition No. 1* is a solo for an acoustically amplified Ratchet (1965), and his *Symphony I* (1965) is scored for 12 Players and 200-odd nonmusical objects, ranging from pitchpipes to pitchforks. In collaboration with the painter Ted Greer, he developed a radical system of notation in which visual images are transduced by performers into sound events. Representative of this intermedia genre are *Micah, the Prophet,* a cantata for 4 Intoning Males, 2 Accordions, 2 Drummers, and 2 Painters (1965), and, particularly, *Mooga Pook,* a tetraphallic action for Dancers, realistically notated on graph paper (San Francisco, Dec. 12, 1967). He also evolved the art of "text-sound composition," in which the voice, percussively intoning and articulating decontextualized words and phrases, is featured; to this category belong *Words* (1969), *Oratora konkurso rezulto: Auturo de la Jaro,* an Esperanto recitation (1970), *If In Is* (1971), *Spoffy Nene* (1971), *Just* (1972), *Heavy Aspirations* (1973), *Seatbelt Seatbelt* (1973), *MUGIC* (1973), *Muchrooms* (1974), *Beemsterboer* (1975), *Mahogany Ballpark* (1976), and *Dutiful Ducks* (1977). His compositions since the early 1980s make extensive use of sampled ambient sounds created and manipulated by a Synclavier digital synthesizer; among these are *Gold and Spirit* (for the Los Angeles Summer Olympics; 1984), *The Real Perpetuum Mobile* (on the occasion of N. Slonimsky's 90th birthday; Los Angeles, April 27, 1984), *Metropolis San Francisco* (for WDR/Köln Studio 3 Hörspiel; 1985–86), *Walking Tune* (a tribute to Percy Grainger; 1986–87), and *Pas de voix* ("Portrait of Samuel Beckett"; 1987). Amirkhanian is music director at the radio station KPFA in Berkeley, Calif. (since 1969), producer and host of the "Speaking of Music" series held at San Francisco's Exploratorium Science Museum (since 1983), and co-founder and co-director, with John Lifton, of the "Composer-to-Composer" Inst. in Telluride, Colo. (since 1988).

BIBL.: P. Kresh, "An Art between Speech & Music," *N.Y. Times* (April 3, 1983); S. Cahill, "C. A.," *Ear Magazine* (July 1989).

Amirov, Fikret Dzhamil, Azerbaijani composer; b. Gyandzha, Nov. 22, 1922; d. Baku, Feb. 20, 1984. He received his early musical instruction from his father, who was a singer and guitarist; he then studied composition at the Cons. of Azerbaijan, graduating in 1948. His compositions reflect the melorhythmic patterns of popular Azerbaijani music, marked by characteristic oriental inflections, while retaining a classical format and development, particularly in variation form. Among his works are a symphonic poem, *To the Memory of the Heroes of the Great National War* (1944); Double Concerto for Violin, Piano, and Orch. (1948); *The Pledge of the Korean Guerrilla Fighter* for Voice and Orch. (1951); several symphonic suites based on the national modes ("mugamas"), of which *Shur* is the best known; and the opera *Sevil* (Baku, Dec. 25, 1953). He also wrote a Piano Concerto on Arab themes (1957; in collaboration with Nazirova). In 1959 he visited the U.S. as a member of the Soviet delegation of composers under the auspices of the State Dept.

BIBL.: D. Danilov, *F. A.* (Moscow, 1958).

Ammann, Benno, Swiss composer; b. Gersau, June 14, 1904; d. Rome, March 14, 1986. He studied composition at the Leipzig Cons.; later proceeded to Paris, where he took private lessons with Honegger, Milhaud, and Albert Rousseau. Returning to Switzerland, he was engaged as chorus leader and theater conductor in Basel and, later, in Rome. Among his more important works are a Mass entitled *Defensor pacis* (Rome, 1947), *Vision pastorale* for Orch. (1954), and various pieces for solo flute, for bass clarinet and 2 guitars, single movements for double bass, and short solos for oboe and other instruments.

Ammerbach, Elias Nicolaus, German organist; b. Naumburg, c.1530; d. Leipzig (buried), Jan. 29, 1597. On Jan. 1, 1561, he became organist of the Thomaskirche in Leipzig, remaining at that post until 1595. He publ. *Orgel oder Instrument Tabulatur* (Leipzig, 1571; reprinted 1583), a work of importance detailing the practice of tuning, the fingering of keyboard instruments, execution of ornaments, etc., and *Ein neu künstlich Tabulaturbuch* (Leipzig, 1575; 2nd ed., 1582). He further publ. several vols. of keyboard music.

Ammons, "Jug" (Eugene), black American jazz tenor saxophonist; b. Chicago, April 14, 1925; d. there, Aug. 6, 1974. After working with Billy Eckstine (1944–47) and Woody Herman (1949), he formed a combo with Sonny Stitt (1950–52); subsequently led his own groups until drug dependency led to total dissipation. He was principally known as a practitioner of so-called soul jazz.

Amner, John, English organist and composer; b. Ely (baptized), Aug. 24, 1579; d. there (buried), July 28, 1641. He studied music in Oxford; in 1610 he became "informator choristarum" at Ely Cathedral; subsequently was ordained to the diaconate; later was made "vicarius" (minor canon), and thus received remuneration as both organist and prebendary; obtained his B.Mus. from Cambridge in 1640. He publ. *Sacred Hymnes of 3. 4. 5 and 6 parts for Voyces and Vyols* (London, 1615).

Amon, Blasius, Austrian composer; b. Hall, Tirol, 1558; d. Vienna, June 1590. He was a choirboy in the service of Archduke Ferdinand of Austria, who sent him to Venice for his musical education. In 1578 he returned to Innsbruck and joined the Franciscan order. In 1587 he went to the Franciscan monastery in Vienna, where he entered the priesthood. He printed a book of 5-part introits (Vienna, 1582); a book of 4-part masses (Vienna, 1588); 2 books of 4-, 5-, and 6-part motets (Munich, 1590). A number of works in MS are in the libraries of Munich and Vienna. A vol. containing his church music was publ. by Caecilianus Huigens in Denkmäler der Tonkunst in Österreich, 73 (38.i).

Amorevoli, Angelo (Maria), Italian tenor; b. Venice, Sept. 16, 1716; d. Dresden, Nov. 15, 1798. He began his career in Rome in 1730; sang in Venice (1730), in Milan (1731–35), in Naples (1736–40), and in Florence (1741); he then went to London, where he was on the staff of the King's Theatre (1741–43). In 1745 he settled in Dresden, where he served as a chamber and church singer at the court.

Amoyal, Pierre, French violinist; b. Paris, June 22, 1949. He studied at the Paris Cons.; won the Ginette Neveu prize in 1963, the Paganini prize in 1964, and the Enesco prize in 1970; took sporadic lessons with Jascha Heifetz in Los Angeles (1966–71). He subsequently played concertos with the Orch. de Paris, the BBC Sym. of London, the Hallé Orch. of Manchester, and the Berlin Phil.; also toured in Russia, Japan, and South Africa. In the U.S. he was a soloist with the Boston Sym., the Cleveland Orch., the Detroit Sym., and the Houston Sym. From 1977 to 1986 he was a member of the faculty of the Paris Cons.

Amram, David (Werner, III), American instrumentalist, conductor, and composer; b. Philadelphia, Nov. 17, 1930, of Jewish parents. He played a bugle in school; then studied trumpet at the Settlement Music School, and also played piano. When he was 12, the family moved to Washington, D.C.; soon he played trumpet in school bands; later switched to the horn. In 1948 he enrolled at the Oberlin (Ohio) College Cons., and continued his practicing on the horn; later shifted to George Washington Univ., graduating in 1952. He then enlisted in the U.S. Army, and played the horn in the 7th Army Sym. Orch., which was stationed in Germany. In 1955 he returned to the U.S. and studied composition with Vittorio Giannini at the Manhattan School of Music. He also studied privately with Charles Mills. Very soon he found his way into the inviting world of public theater. He wrote incidental music for off-Broadway productions of Shakespeare's plays, and finally landed lucrative jobs in the films; he composed sound tracks for such hits as *Splendor in the Grass* (1961), *The Manchurian Candidate* (1962), and *The Arrangement* (1969). He also wrote jazz music, sacred services for the Park Avenue Synagogue in N.Y., and straight concert pieces, braving somehow the danger of cross-pollination of these quaquaversal activities. On May 8, 1960, he gave an evening of his works in N.Y., among them a *Shakespearean Concerto*; presented another pan-Amram concert in N.Y. on Feb. 20, 1962. There followed a cornucopia of cantatas, and in 1965, a radio opera, *The Final Ingredient*. In 1966–67 he received an exclusive appointment as composer-in-residence of the N.Y. Phil. As a sign of public recognition of his music, the National Educational Television network broadcast on April 17, 1969, a documentary, proudly entitled *The World of David Amram*. Amram was also the recipient of several grants by the State Dept. and U.S. Information Agency for travel abroad. He visited some 25 countries; he also joined a jazz group to play in Cuba in 1977. He eagerly absorbed the varicolored ethnic materials, which he used, in metamorphosis, in some of his own compositions. In 1979 he received an honorary doctorate from Moravian College, Bethlehem, Pa. He publ. an autobiography, *Vibrations: The Adventures and Musical Times of David Amram* (N.Y., 1968).

Works: STAGE AND SCREEN: Opera, *The Final Ingredient,* to a story set in a Nazi concentration camp (ABC-TV network, April 11, 1965, composer conducting); *12th Night,* after Shakespeare (Lake George Opera Festival, Aug. 1, 1968); incidental music for 28 off-Broadway productions. **FILMS:** *The Young Savages* (1961); *Splendor in the Grass* (1961); *The Manchurian Candidate* (1962); *The Arrangement* (1969). **ORCH.:** *Autobiography for Strings* (1959); *Shakespearean Concerto* for Oboe, 2 Horns, and Strings (N.Y., May 8, 1960); *King Lear Variations*

for Woodwinds, Brass, Percussion, and Piano (N.Y. Phil., March 23, 1967); *Elegy* for Violin and Orch. (1970); Horn Concerto (1966); Concerto for Jazz Quintet and Orch. (N.Y., Jan. 10, 1971); Bassoon Concerto (Washington, D.C., March 21, 1972); *The Trail of Beauty* for Mezzo-soprano, Oboe, and Orch. (Philadelphia, March 4, 1977); Violin Concerto (1980); *Across the Wide Missouri: A Musical Tribute to Harry S. Truman* (1984); *American Dance Suite* (1986). **CHAMBER:** Trio for Saxophone, Horn, and Bassoon (1958); *Overture and Allegro* for Solo Flute (1959); Violin Sonata (1960); *3 Songs for Marlboro* for Horn and Cello (1961); *Discussion* for Flute, Cello, Piano, and Percussion (1961); String Quartet (1961); *Dirge and Variations* for Piano Trio (1962); *The Wind and the Rain* for Viola and Piano (1963); Sonata for Solo Violin (1964); *3 Dances* for Oboe and Strings (1966); Wind Quintet (1968); *Triptych* for Solo Viola (1969); *Native American Portraits* for Violin, Piano, and Percussion (1976); *Zohar* for Flute Solo (1978). **VOCAL:** *Sacred Service for Sabbath Eve* for Tenor, Chorus, and Organ (1961); *The American Bell,* cantata (Philadelphia, July 4, 1962); *A Year in Our Land,* cantata (N.Y., May 13, 1964); *Let Us Remember,* cantata (San Francisco, Nov. 15, 1965); *By the Rivers of Babylon* for Soprano and Female Choir (1966); *Songs from Shakespeare* for Voice and Piano (1968); *3 Songs for America* for Baritone and String Quintet (1969). He also wrote a Piano Sonata and minor piano pieces. **BIBL.:** D. Ewen, *American Composers* (N.Y., 1982).

Amy, Gilbert, French conductor, music educator, and composer; b. Paris, Aug. 29, 1936. He studied composition with Milhaud and Messiaen and piano with Loriod at the Paris Cons.; also received instruction in counterpoint and fugue from Plé-Caussade in Paris and attended the Darmstadt summer courses in new music given by Boulez. In 1962 he began his conducting career; was director of the Domaine Musical in Paris (1967–73) and founder-conductor of the Nouvel Orch. Philharmonique de Radio France in Paris (1976–81). After teaching briefly at Yale Univ. (1982), he returned to France and became director of the Lyons Cons. (1984). His early compositions reflect the influence of Boulez; after experimenting with doctrinaire serial procedures, he adopted greater freedom in his later works.

Works: ORCH.: *Mouvements* (1958); *Diaphonies* (1962); *Antiphonies* for 2 Orchs. (1964); *Triade* (1965); *Trajectoires* for Violin and Orch. (1966); *Chant* (1968–69; rev. 1980); *Jeux et formes* for Oboe and Chamber Orch. (1971); *Refrains* (1972); *7 Sites* for 14 Instruments (1975); *Echos XIII* for 13 Instruments (1976); *Adagio et Stretto* (1977–78); *Orchestrale* (1985). **CHAMBER:** *Variations* for Flute, Clarinet, Cello, and Piano (1956); Piano Sonata (1957–60); *Inventions* for Flute, Vibraphone or Marimbaphone, Harp, and Piano or Celesta (1959–61); *Cahier d'épigrammes* for Piano (1964); *Alpha-beth* for Wind Sextet (1963–64); *Cycle* for Percussion Sextet (1964–66); *Relais* for Brass Quintet (1967); *Quasi Scherzando* for Cello (1981); *Quasi una toccata* for Organ (1981). **VOCAL:** *Oeil de fumée* for Soprano and Piano (1955); orchestrated 1957; *Cette étoile enseigne à s'incliner* for Men's Chorus and Instruments (1970); *. . . d'un désastre obscur* for Mezzo-soprano and Clarinet (1971); *D'un espace déployé* for Soprano, 2 Pianos, and 2 Orch. Groups (1972–73); *Sonata pian'e forte* for Soprano, Mezzo-soprano, and 12 Instruments (1974); *Après ". . . d'un désastre obscur"* for Mezzo-soprano and Small Ensemble (1976); *Messe* for Soprano, Alto, Tenor, Bass, Children's Chorus ad libitum, Chorus, and Orch. (1982–83); *Écrits sur toiles* for Reciter and Small Ensemble (1983).

Anacker, August Ferdinand, German cantor and composer; b. Freiberg, Saxony, Oct. 17, 1790; d. there, Aug. 21, 1854. He studied at the Univ. of Leipzig; returned to Freiberg in 1821 and served as cantor at the Cathedral; in 1823 he founded the Singakademie of Freiberg. He was closely acquainted with Beethoven, Mendelssohn, and Wagner. His oratorio, *Bergmannsgruss* (1831–32), was widely performed in his lifetime; but his music sank irretrievably into the bottomless pit of oblivion after his death.

Ančerl, Karel, Czech conductor; b. Tučapy, April 11, 1908; d. Toronto, July 3, 1973. He studied at the Prague Cons., taking courses in composition with Alois Hába and Křička and percussion playing with Šourek; at the same time he practiced conducting. He devoted himself mainly to the modern repertoire, and conducted several concerts at the festivals of the ISCM. He held the post of music director of the Prague Radio, but as a Jew, was removed from this position when Czechoslovakia was occupied by the Nazis in 1939. In 1942 he was deported to the Jewish ghetto camp in Theresienstadt, and was later transported to Auschwitz; his entire family was put to death there but, providentially, he was spared. After the war he resumed his activities as a conductor; was at the Prague Opera from 1945 to 1947 and also with the Radio Orch. (1945–50); from 1950 to 1968 was conductor of the Czech Phil., with which he traveled through Europe, Canada, the U.S., Australia, and Japan. In 1969 he was appointed conductor of the Toronto Sym. Orch., and lived in Toronto until his death. He was distinguished mainly for his congenial interpretation of music by Czech composers; in appreciation of his service he was named a People's Artist in 1966.
BIBL.: K. Šrom, *K. A.* (Prague, 1968).

Anchieta, Juan de, Spanish composer; b. probably in Urrestilla, near Azpeitia, 1462; d. Azpeitia, July 30, 1523. In 1489 he entered the service of Queen Isabella as a singer in the court chapel; upon the Queen's death in 1504, he entered the service of her daughter, Joanna, consort of Philip the Fair; he accompanied them to Flanders and England. In addition to his duties as Joanna's chaplain and singer, he was made a benefice-holder (in absentia) at Villarino in 1499; was also named rector of the parish church of S. Sebastian de Soreasu in Azpeitia in 1500; became Abbot of Arbos in 1518. He was pensioned by the court of Charles V in 1519. Anchieta composed sacred and secular vocal works, most of them for large choirs; several of these were publ. in modern eds. in *Monumentos de la música española,* vols. I (1941), V (1947), and X (1951).
BIBL.: A. Cohen, *The Vocal Polyphonic Style of J. d.A.* (diss., N.Y. Univ., 1953); R. Stevenson, *Spanish Music in the Age of Columbus* (The Hague, 1960).

Ancina, (Giovanni) Giovenale, Italian composer of sacred music; b. Fossano, Oct. 19, 1545; d. Saluzzo, Aug. 31, 1604. He was a student of medicine and theology, but became deeply interested in sacred services in music after he met Filippo Neri, the creator of the oratorio. On Oct. 1, 1580, he joined the Congregazione dei Preti dell'Oratorio, founded by Neri. He began writing music for the church; publ. *Tempio armonico della beata Vergine* (Rome, 1599).
BIBL.: P.I. Bacci, *Vita del servo di Dio G. A.* (Rome, 1671); P. Damilano, *G.G. A. e la lauda cinquecentesca* (Milan, 1953).

Ancona, Mario, Italian baritone; b. Livorno, Feb. 28, 1860; d. Florence, Feb. 22, 1931. He studied jurisprudence and was briefly engaged in a diplomatic career; then began to study voice; made his professional debut in Trieste in 1889. On May 19, 1893, he sang the part of Tonio in *Pagliacci* at Covent Garden, London; made regular appearances there during the period 1895 to 1905. He made his debut as Tonio at the Metropolitan Opera in N.Y. on Dec. 11, 1893, and remained on the roster of the Metropolitan until 1897; from 1906 to 1908 he was a member of the Manhattan Opera House; was also on the roster of the Chicago Opera (1915–16). He appeared as a guest artist in Spain, Portugal, Argentina, and Russia. After retiring from the stage he was active as a vocal teacher in Florence.

Ancot, family of Belgian musicians. (1) **Jean,** *père* (b. Bruges, Oct. 22, 1779; d. there, July 12, 1848), violin virtuoso, pianist, and composer. He studied (1799–1804) in Paris under Baillot, Kreutzer, and Catel; then settled in Bruges as a teacher; publ. 4 violin concertos, overtures, marches, sacred music, etc.; most of his works are lost. He taught his sons, Jean and Louis. (2)

Jean, *fils* (b. Bruges, July 6, 1799; d. Boulogne, June 5, 1829). He finished his education at the Paris Cons. under Pradher and Berton; an accomplished pianist, he was successful in London (1823–25); eventually settled in Boulogne. Considering that he died short of his 30th birthday, he was an astonishingly prolific composer (225 works, among them a Piano Concerto, sonatas, études, 4-hand fantasias, and violin concertos). (3) **Louis** (b. Bruges, June 3, 1803; d. there, 1836). For a time, he was pianist to the Duke of Sussex in London; made extended continental tours, taught at Boulogne and Tours, and finally returned to Bruges. He wrote piano music in salon style.

Anda, Géza, eminent Hungarian-born Swiss pianist; b. Budapest, Nov. 19, 1921; d. Zürich, June 13, 1976. He studied with Dohnányi at the Royal Academy of Music in Budapest; won the Liszt Prize. During World War II he went to Switzerland; became a Swiss citizen in 1955. He made his American debut with the Philadelphia Orch. on Oct. 21, 1955. He was an ardent champion of the music of Béla Bartók, and performed all of Bartók's 3 piano concertos numerous times; he also was a congenial interpreter of the music of Brahms. Later on he made a specialty of Mozart, acting as both soloist and conductor in all of Mozart's piano concertos. He publ. a vol. of Mozart cadenzas (Berlin and Wiesbaden, 1973). Apart from his concerts he also held seminars in Switzerland.

Anderberg, Carl-Olof, Swedish composer; b. Stockholm, March 13, 1914; d. Malmö, Jan. 4, 1972. He studied composition with Broman in Stockholm, piano in Copenhagen, and conducting with Weingartner in Salzburg. His early compositions are permeated with a romantic "Scandinavian" idiom; among them was an opera, *Hilde.* In the 1950s he joined various avant-garde groups active in Sweden. These associations led to a radical change in his style of composition toward advanced forms of musical expression.
WORKS: *Music I* and *II* for Chamber Orch. (1947, 1948); Sym. (1948); *Cyclus Stellarum I* and *II* for Strings (1949, 1957); *Episode,* chamber opera (1952); 3 piano sonatas (1950, 1952, 1956); *3 estampies* for Piano, Percussion, and Violins (1953); 2 string quartets (1955, 1957); Cello Sonata (1956); *4 Serious Caprices* for Clarinet and Piano (1956); *Fyra legeringar* (4 Alloys) for Soprano and 5 Instruments (1958); Duo I for Flute and Piano (1958); *Teater,* suite for Orch. (1958); *Höstens Hökar,* metamorphoses for Narrator and 5 Instruments (1959); *Triad* for Solo Violin (1959); *Variationer över Variationer* for Clarinet, Bassoon, Violin, Cello, and Harp (1959); *Transfers* for Symphonic Groups (1960); *Di Mi Se Mai* for Soprano, Narrator, and Orch. (1963); *Hexafoni* for 6 Instruments (1963); *Execution I* for Clarinet, Piano, and Percussion (1963); *Strändernas svall* (The Surge of the Seaside), cantata for Soprano, Baritone, Narrator, and Instrumental Ensemble (1963–64); *Acroama I* and *II* for Orch. (1965–66); Duo II and III for Violin and Piano (1968); *Klangskap I* (Soundscape) for Piano (1968); Piano Concerto (Malmö, March 18, 1969); *Concerto for a Ballet* for Piano, Winds, Percussion, and Double Basses (1969–70; Swedish Radio, March 4, 1972); *Orkesterspel I* and *II* (Orchestral Game; 1969–70); *Music for Piano, Winds, and Tape* (1970); *Dubbelspel* (Double Play) for Soprano, Baritone, Clarinet, Cello, Piano, and Tape (1971); piano pieces; songs.

Anders, Peter, German tenor; b. Essen, July 1, 1908; d. Hamburg, Sept. 10, 1954 (as a result of injuries sustained in an automobile accident). He studied at the Berlin Hochschule für Musik; began his professional appearances as an opera singer in 1932; from 1939 to 1948 was a member of the Berlin Staatsoper. On Nov. 29, 1936, he appeared with the Hamburg State Opera in the role of Tamino in Mozart's opera *Die Zauberflöte;* another appearance with the Hamburg Opera took place on Dec. 19, 1937. Anders was a distinguished interpreter of Wagnerian roles as well.

Andersen, (Carl) Joachim, Danish flute player and composer; b. Copenhagen, April 29, 1847; d. there, May 7, 1909. From 1869 to 1877, he was a member of the Royal Orch.; in

1881 he was in Berlin, where he was co-founder and, for 10 years, 1st flutist and assistant conductor of the Phil. Orch.; from 1893, was conductor of the Palace Orch. at Copenhagen. He wrote solo works for Flute; also pieces with Orch.: *Hungarian Fantasia; Ballade; Dance of the Sylphs;* 24 easy and 24 difficult études; etc. His brother, **Vigo** (b. Copenhagen, April 21, 1852; d. [suicide] Chicago, Jan. 28, 1895), was an eminent flute player; he was 1st flutist in the Theodore Thomas Orch. in Chicago.

Andersen, Karl August, Norwegian composer and cellist; b. Christiania, Sept. 29, 1903; d. there (Oslo), Aug. 15, 1970. He studied cello and composition in Christiania and later cello with Hugo Becker in Berlin (1921–22); then became a cellist in the Oslo Phil. (1924).

WORKS: 3 string quartets (No. 1, 1934; No. 3, 1961–67); Sym. for Chamber Orch. (1936); Suite for Orch. (1937); Trio for Flute, Clarinet, and Cello (1939); *Vårdagen* for Male Chorus (1942); *Allegro festivo e solenne Norwegese (Festforspill)* for Orch. (1950); *Variations over Theme and Rhythm* for Wind Quintet (1966).

Andersen, Karsten, Norwegian conductor; b. Christiania, Feb. 16, 1920. He began his career as a violinist. In 1945 he was named music director in Stavanger. In 1965 he became music director of the Bergen Harmonien Soc., leading the concerts of the Bergen Sym. Orch. until 1985. He was a founder of the noted Bergen Music Festival. From 1973 to 1980 he also was chief conductor of the Iceland Sym. Orch. in Reykjavík.

Anderson, Beth, inventive American composer, performance artist, and astrologer; b. Lexington, Ky., Jan. 3, 1950. She moved to California and joined a group of the extreme avant-garde musicians at various places and in various points in time. She took advice in composition from John Cage, Robert Ashley, Larry Austin, Terry Riley, Helen Lipscomb, Richard Swift, Kenneth Wright, John B. Chance, and Nathan Rubin, but went on a diagonal tangent in her own original practices. Her resources were manifold, passing through the entire spectrum of sound, sight, and motion in specially designed multimedia productions. She espoused the method of composition known as text-sound as propounded by Charles Amirkhanian, which allows total freedom of improvisation while observing a minimum of controlling serialism of sounds, rhythms, and harmonic combinations. As a professional astrologer, she made an earnest attempt to connect ideas of harmony with cosmic consciousness, extrasensory perception, and numerology. She also applied the techniques of collage and cut-ups. She became co-ed. of *Ear Magazine,* and publ. poetry as well. Among her ascertainable works are an opera, *Queen Christina,* produced at Mills College in Oakland, Calif., on Dec. 1, 1973; an oratorio, *Joan,* performed at the Cabrillo Festival on Aug. 22, 1974; *Soap Tuning,* theater piece (1976); *Elizabeth Rex,* musical (1983); *Revel* for Orch. (1985); *Music for Charlemagne Palestine* (1973), *Pennyroyal Swale* (1985), and *Rosemary Swale* (1986) for String Quartet; piano pieces; tape works; several text-sound pieces, including the opera *Riot Rot* (1984).

Anderson, "Cat" (**William Alonzo**), black American jazz trumpeter; b. Greenville, S.C., Sept. 12, 1916; d. Norwalk, Conn., April 29, 1981. He was reared in Charleston's Jenkins Orphanage, where he organized a jazz group, the Carolina Cotton Pickers; later worked with Claude Hopkins, Lionel Hampton, and Duke Ellington. A gifted musician, he became best known for his high-note virtuosity. He publ. *The Cat Anderson Trumpet Method: Dealing with Playing in the Upper Register* (Los Angeles, 1973).

Anderson, Emily, Irish musicologist; b. Galway, March 17, 1891; d. London, Oct. 26, 1962. She went to Germany for her education, and attended the univs. of Berlin and Marburg. Returning to England, she was employed in the British Foreign Office while pursuing her interest in music history and biography as an avocation. Of value are her trs. of the correspondence of Mozart and Beethoven: *Letters of Mozart and His Family*

(3 vols., London, 1938; 2nd ed., rev. by A. Hyatt King and M. Carolan, 1966; 3rd ed., rev., 1985); *The Letters of Beethoven* (3 vols., London, 1961).

Anderson, June, American soprano; b. Boston, Dec. 30, 1952. She was a pupil of Robert Leonard in N.Y., and on Oct. 26, 1978, made her operatic debut as the Queen of the Night at the N.Y. City Opera, where she remained until 1981; then made her European debut as Semiramide in Rome (1982). During the 1985–86 season, she appeared as Amina at La Scala in Milan and as Isabelle in *Robert le Diable* at the Paris Opéra. Among her other roles are Rossini's Desdemona, Bellini's Elvira, Lucia, Violetta, and Gilda.

Anderson, Laurie, imaginative representative of American performance art in a decidedly avant-garde tradition; b. Chicago, June 5, 1947. Renouncing the tradition of conventional modernism, she set for herself a goal of uniting all arts as they once existed in ancient theatrical practice; in doing so, she made use of all available modern techniques, from topical pop to electronics, even making her own body a part of the instrumental combination, playbacking with herself on magnetic tape and projecting images on a screen. In her performances, she combines speech, song, and bodily exertions. She also uses a variety of instrumentations, including a homemade violin activated by a luminous bow made of electronic tape. She has become particularly famous for her multimedia cyberpunk projections, extending the principles of cybernetics to deliberately commonplace movements, behavior, and language. Her programmed compositions are mostly improvisations in which she alters her natural voice electronically, making use of vocal glissando, crooning, panting, and heavy aspiration. Her satirical piece *New York Social Life* uses oriental drum effects; another piece, *Time to Go,* scored for guitar, violin, and organ, portrays the repeated exhortation of a museum guard to visitors to leave at the closing time. In 1976 she gave a successful exhibition of psychomusicurgy at the Berlin Akademie der Kunst, and in 1983 she produced her grandiose collage epic entitled simply *United States,* on themes of travel, politics, money, and love. Her book *United States* was publ. in N.Y. in 1984. On Oct. 3, 1989, she presented a new solo work, *Empty Places,* at the Brooklyn Academy of Music.

BIBL.: J. Kardon, ed., *L. A.: Works from 1969 to 1983* (Philadelphia, 1983).

Anderson, Leroy, American composer of light instrumental music; b. Cambridge, Mass., June 29, 1908; d. Woodbury, Conn., May 18, 1975. He received his 1st musical training from his mother, an organist, and studied double bass with Gaston Dufresne in Boston. He then took courses in theory of composition with Walter Spalding, Edward Ballantine, and Walter Piston at Harvard Univ., obtaining his B.A. magna cum laude in 1929 and his M.A. in 1930. From 1932 to 1935 he was conductor of the Harvard Univ. Band. In 1935 he became an arranger for the Boston Pops. In 1942 he entered the U.S. Army and was stationed in Iceland. A linguist, he acted as translator, particularly in Scandinavian languages (Anderson was of Swedish extraction). In 1939 he wrote a piece for String Orch. called *Jazz Pizzicato,* which was played at the Boston Pops and became an immediate hit. This was followed by a number of similar inventive instrumental novelties, among them *Jazz Legato, The Syncopated Clock* (1950), *Fiddle Faddle, Sleigh Ride* (1950), *Serenata, A Trumpeter's Lullaby, China Doll, A Bugler's Holiday, Blue Tango* (his greatest success, 1952), *The Typewriter.* He also wrote a musical, *Goldilocks* (N.Y., Oct. 11, 1958).

Anderson, Lucy (née **Philpot**), English pianist; b. Bath, Dec. 12, 1797; d. London, Dec. 24, 1878. Her father, John Philpot, was a prof. of music; she settled in London; was the 1st woman to be engaged as piano soloist by the Phil. Soc. She married George Frederick Anderson (b. London, 1793; d. there, 1876) in 1820; he became Master of the Queen's Musick (1848–70); Lucy Anderson taught piano to Queen Victoria and her children.

Anderson, Marian, celebrated black American contralto; b. Philadelphia, Feb. 17, 1899, into a poor family; her father sold ice and coal; her mother helped eke out the family income by taking in laundry. Marian Anderson sang in a choir at the Union Baptist Church in South Philadelphia. Funds were raised for her to study voice with Giuseppe Boghetti; in 1923 she won 1st prize at a singing contest in Philadelphia, and in 1925 she received 1st prize at a contest held by the N.Y. Phil. at Lewisohn Stadium, appearing as a soloist there on Aug. 27, 1925. In 1929 she gave a recital at Carnegie Hall. In 1930 she made her 1st European appearance, in London; she soon extended her European tours to include Sweden, Norway, and Finland; she also gave successful concerts in Paris, Vienna, Brussels, Geneva, and Salzburg; also made a tour of Russia. Her singing of Negro spirituals produced a sensation wherever she sang in Europe. Returning to the U.S., she gave a concert in Town Hall, N.Y. (Nov. 30, 1935), and in Carnegie Hall (Jan. 30, 1936). In Feb. 1939, she became a center of national attention when the Daughters of the American Revolution refused to let her appear at Constitution Hall in Washington, D.C., citing the organization's rules of racial segregation. The resulting publicity only contributed to her success; Eleanor Roosevelt sent her resignation to the DAR, and the secretary of the interior, Harold L. Ickes, invited Marian Anderson to sing at the Lincoln Memorial on Easter Sunday, April 9, 1939: a huge audience attended; the concert was broadcast. She was given the prestigious Spingarn Award for the "highest and noblest achievement by an American Negro" during the year. Another landmark in the history of freedom was established when she sang the role of Ulrica in *Un ballo in maschera* at the Metropolitan Opera on Jan. 7, 1955, breaking the unspoken prohibition against black artists' singing there. In 1958 she was designated by President Eisenhower to be a delegate to the General Assembly of the United Nations. Honors piled upon honors in her life. She was awarded 24 honorary degrees from various colleges and univs., and received medals from the governments of Sweden, Finland, Japan, and other countries. President Johnson awarded her the American Freedom Medal. She sang at the inaugural ball for President Kennedy in 1961. On the occasion of her 75th birthday, a resolution was passed by the U.S. Congress to strike a gold medal in her honor. In 1986 she was awarded the National Medal of Arts. She publ. her autobiography, *My Lord, What a Morning* (N.Y., 1956).

BIBL.: K. Vehanen, *M. A.* (N.Y., 1941); J. Sims, *M. A.: An Annotated Bibliography and Discography* (Westport, Conn., 1981); C. Patterson, *M. A.* (N.Y., 1988); A. Tedards, *M. A.* (N.Y., 1988).

Anderson, (Evelyn) Ruth, American flutist and composer; b. Kalispell, Mont., March 21, 1928. She studied flute (B.A., 1949) and composition (M.A., 1951) at the Univ. of Washington in Seattle; then studied electronic music and composition with Ussachevsky and Kim at Columbia Univ. and Princeton Univ.; also studied composition privately with Boulanger and Milhaud and flute with John Wummer and Rampal. She was active as an orch. player and as an orchestrator for Broadway and television before becoming a teacher at Hunter College of the City Univ. of N.Y. (1966), where she designed and installed its electronic music studio (1968–70).

WORKS: MIXED MEDIA: *Centering* for Dancer, 4 Performers, and Live Electronics (1979). **TEXT PIECES:** *Naming* (1975); *A Long Sound* (1976); *Sound Portraits I–II* (1977); *Silent Sound* (1978); *Greetings from the Right Hemisphere* (1979); *Communications* (1980). **TAPE:** *The Pregnant Dream* (1968); *ES II* (1969); *DUMP*, collage (1970); *3 Studies* (1970); *3 Pieces* (1970–71); *So What, Nos. 1 and 2* (1971); *SUM (State of the Union Message)*, collage (1973); *Conversations* (1974); *Points* (1974); *Dress Rehearsal* (1976); *I Come Out of Your Sleep* (1979). **SOUND SCULPTURES:** *Sound Environment* (1975); *Time and Tempo* (1984).

Anderson, T(homas) J(efferson, Jr.), black American composer; b. Coatesville, Pa., Aug. 17, 1928, a son of schoolteachers.

He attended classes in Washington, D.C., and Cincinnati; played in a school orch.; then entered West Virginia State College; received his bachelor of music degree at Pa. State Univ.; then taught music at High Point, N.C. (1951–54). In 1954 he attended composition classes with Scott Huston at the Cincinnati Cons. of Music and with Philip Benzanson and Richard Hervig at the Univ. of Iowa in Iowa City, obtaining his Ph.D. in 1958. In 1964 he took a summer course in composition with Darius Milhaud at Aspen, Colo. From 1958 to 1963 he was prof. of music at Langston Univ., Oklahoma; from 1963 to 1969 he taught at the Tennessee State Univ., Nashville; and from 1968 to 1971 he was composer-in-residence with the Atlanta Sym. Orch.; then taught at Morehouse College in Atlanta (1971–72), and in 1972 was appointed chairman of the Tufts Univ. music dept. in Medford, Mass., serving until 1980; and continued to teach there. He served as chairman of the Advisory Board of the Black Music Center at Indiana Univ. (1969–71). In 1976 he went to Brazil under the aegis of the Office of Cultural Relations of the U.S. Dept. of State. He played a major role in the revival of interest in the music of Scott Joplin, and arranged Joplin's opera *Treemonisha* for its production in Atlanta (Jan. 28, 1972). His own style of composition is audaciously modern, while preserving a deeply felt lyricism in melodic patterns; his harmonies are taut and intense without abandoning the basic tonal frame; his contrapuntal usages suggest folklike ensembles, but he freely varies his techniques according to the character of each particular piece. His resources are quaquaversal, and he excludes none in his creative process.

WORKS: STAGE: Opera, *Soldier Boy, Soldier*, to a story of a Vietnam veteran (Bloomington, Oct. 23, 1982); operetta, *The Shell Fairy* (1977). **ORCH.:** *Pyknon* (1958); *Introduction and Allegro* (1959); *New Dances* (1960); *Classical Symphony* (1961); *Symphony in 3 Movements*, in memory of John F. Kennedy (1964; Oklahoma City, April 10, 1964); *Squares* (Chickasha, Okla., Feb. 25, 1966); *Rotations* for Symphonic Band (1967); Chamber Sym. (Nashville, Nov. 24, 1969); *Intervals*, 7 orch. sets (1970–71); Concerto for 2 Violins and Chamber Orch. (Chicago, May 29, 1988); *Remembrances*, chamber concerto (Cleveland, Oct. 30, 1988). **VOICES AND ORCH.:** *Personals*, cantata in commemoration of the centennial of Fisk Univ. (Nashville, April 28, 1966); *Beyond Silence* for Tenor and Instruments (1973); *In Memoriam Malcolm X* (N.Y., April 7, 1974); *Horizons '76* for Soprano and Orch., a U.S. Bicentennial commission, for 3 Speakers, Dancer, and Instruments (Chicago, June 11, 1978); *Messages, a Creole Fantasy* for Voices and Orch. (1979). **CHAMBER:** String Quartet No. 1 (1958); 5 *Bagatelles* for Oboe, Violin, and Harpsichord (1963); 5 *Études and a Fancy* for Woodwind Quintet (1964); *Connections* for String Quintet (1966); *Swing Set*, duo for Clarinet and Piano (1973); 5 *Easy Pieces* for Violin, Piano, and Jew's Harp (1974); *Variations on a Theme by Alban Berg* for Viola and Piano (1977); *Bridging and Branching* for Flute and Double Bass (1986); *Ivesiana* for Violin, Cello, and Piano (Weston, Mass., April 10, 1988); also piano pieces, among them 5 *Portraitures of 2 People* for Piano, 4-hands (1965), and *Watermelon* (1971); organ works; many vocal settings.

BIBL.: B. Thompson, "T.J. A.: Composer," *Sinfonian Newsletter* (Feb. 1975); D. Ewen, *American Composers* (N.Y., 1982); B. Thompson, "The Influence and Use of Jazz and Blues in the Music of T.J. A.," *Jazzforschung* (1987).

d'Andrade, Francesco, Portuguese baritone; b. Lisbon, Jan. 11, 1859; d. Berlin, Feb. 8, 1921. He studied in Italy; made his debut in San Remo (1882); then lived in Berlin. He was well known as a successful singer in Europe; his most famous role was that of Don Giovanni.

Andrašovan, Tibor, Slovak composer and conductor; b. Slovenská Lupča, April 3, 1917. He studied with E. Suchon, A. Moyzes, A. Kafendová, and others at the Bratislava Cons., later serving as artistic director of the Slovak Folk Artistic Ensemble (1955–58; 1969–74). He received many awards, including

Merited Artist (1971). He was active in unifying folk elements with concert music and in promoting Slovak stage works. His opera *Gelo the Joker* was the 1st Slovak comic opera.

WORKS: STAGE: *Orpheus and Euridice*, ballet (1948); *The Song of Peace*, ballet (1949); *Gelo the Joker*, opera (1957); *The Quadrille*, operetta (1960); *The White Disease*, music drama (1967); *The Gamekeeper's Wife*, opera (1973–74); *The King of Fools*, musical (1982); *The Festival of Solstice*, ballet (1985). **ORCH.:** Concerto for Cembalo and Strings (1977). **CHAMBER:** String Quartet, *Folklorica* (1976). **VOCAL:** *Tokajik*, cantata for Soprano, Chorus, and Orch. (1975); *The Echoes of the Uprising Mountains*, song cycle for Narrator, Soprano, Tenor, and Piano (1979).

André, (Johann) Anton, German music publisher, 3rd son of **Johann André;** b. Offenbach, Oct. 6, 1775; d. there, April 6, 1842. A precocious talent, he studied with Karl Vollweiler in Mannheim (1792–93); was a fine pianist, violinist, and composer before entering the Univ. of Jena; after completing his studies, he made extensive travels; on his father's death, took charge of the business, adding particular luster to its good name by the purchase, in 1799, of Mozart's entire musical remains. He publ. Mozart's autograph thematic catalog, and supplemented it by a list of the works so acquired. By accepting the application of the lithographic process to music engraving (1799), he took another long stride toward placing his firm in the front rank. He was also a composer (2 operas, syms., songs, etc.), a successful teacher, and a noteworthy theorist. He wrote 2 vols. on harmony, counterpoint, canon, and fugue (1832–42; new rev. ed., abridged, 1874–78); and *Anleitung zum Violinspiele.* His sons were: (1) **Carl August** (b. Offenbach, June 15, 1806; d. Frankfurt, Feb. 15, 1887), head (from 1835) of the Frankfurt branch opened in 1828, and founder of a piano factory ("Mozartflügel"); author of *Der Klavierbau und seine Geschichte* (1855). (2) **Julius** (b. Offenbach, June 4, 1808; d. there, April 17, 1880), a fine organist and pianist, pupil of Aloys Schmitt (his grandfather's pupil), author of a *Praktische Orgelschule,* composer of several interesting organ compositions, and arranger of Mozart's works for piano, 4-hands. (3) **Johann August** (b. Offenbach, March 2, 1817; d. there, Oct. 29, 1887), his father's successor (1839) in the publishing establishment. His 2 sons, **Karl** (b. Aug. 24, 1853; d. June 29, 1914) and **Adolf** (b. April 10, 1855; d. Sept. 10, 1910), succeeded to the business. (4) **Jean Baptiste** (**de St.-Gilles;** b. Offenbach, March 7, 1823; d. Frankfurt, Dec. 9, 1882), pianist and composer of various pieces for piano and voice, a pupil of A. Schmitt, Taubert (piano), and Kessler and Dehn (harmony); lived for years in Berlin; had the honorary title of "Herzoglich Bernbergischer Hofkapellmeister."

André, Franz, Belgian conductor; b. Brussels, June 10, 1893; d. there, Jan. 20, 1975. He studied violin with César Thomson at the Brussels Cons., and conducting with Weingartner in Berlin. He was mobilized at the advent of World War I, and spent the years 1914–18 on the crucial front in the trenches at Ypres. After the war he began teaching violin; was on the faculty of the Brussels Cons. from 1920 to 1944. In 1935 he organized the Belgian Radio Sym. Orch. and led it until 1958. He trained the orch. in difficult modern works which he insisted on reading *à livre ouvert* at rehearsals; he cultivated the works of modern French and Belgian composers, and conducted several orch. scores by Schoenberg.

André, Johann, German composer, publisher, and father of a musical family; b. Offenbach, March 28, 1741; d. there, June 18, 1799. He founded (Sept. 1, 1774) at Offenbach a music publishing house under his name and had publ. 1,200 compositions by the time of his death. For 7 years (1777–84) he was Kapellmeister of Döbbelin's Theater in Berlin. He was a prolific composer, author of 19 singspiels and 14 miscellaneous scores for the stage, among them *Der Töpfer* (Hanau, Jan. 22, 1773) and *Der Liebhaber als Automat* (Berlin, Sept. 11, 1782). Bretzner wrote the libretto of *Die Entführung aus dem Serail,* or *Belmont und Constanze,* for him; the opera was produced in Berlin, May 25, 1781. The same text was used the following year by Mozart for his celebrated work, which elicited Bretzner's haughty protest against "a certain man named Mozart" for the unauthorized use of his libretto. Among André's songs, the *Rheinweinlied* ("Bekränzt mit Laub") was widely performed. André is credited with being the composer of the 1st "durchkomponierte Ballade," *Die Weiber von Weinsberg* (1783).

André, Maurice, French trumpet virtuoso; b. Alès, near Nîmes, May 21, 1933. He was apprenticed as a coal miner, the trade he plied from his 14th through his 18th year; his father was also a coal miner, but he played the trumpet in his free hours. André practiced on the trumpet, too, and enrolled in the class of Barthélémy; received the Prix d'Honneur and joined the Paris Radio Orch.; was later the 1st trumpet in the Lamoureux Orch.; also played in jazz groups. In 1956 he won an international competition in Geneva, and in 1963 won the International Music Competition of the German Radio; then played in chamber orchs. In 1974 he made his American debut as a soloist with the Württemberg Chamber Orch. on tour. Soon he became well known as a proponent of the Baroque repertoire; he also performed modern trumpet concertos, some written especially for him; he made some 260 recordings, including 30 different trumpet concertos. An ardent collector, he owns 80 trumpets of different types and national origins; as a trumpet virtuoso, he tours all over the world; in 1983 he made one of his frequent visits to America.

Andreae, Marc, Swiss conductor, grandson of **Volkmar Andreae;** b. Zürich, Nov. 8, 1939. He studied piano and conducting at the Zürich Cons.; then went to Paris for studies in composition with Nadia Boulanger. Subsequently he took lessons in conducting with Franco Ferrara at the Accademia di Santa Cecilia in Rome. Eventually he became conductor of the Orch. del Radio della Svizzera Italiana in Lugano.

Andreae, Volkmar, eminent Swiss conductor and accomplished composer, grandfather of **Marc Andreae;** b. Bern, July 5, 1879; d. Zürich, June 18, 1962. He studied music with Karl Munzinger in Bern and later with Wüllner at the Cologne Cons.; was then répétiteur at the Royal Opera in Munich; in 1902 he became conductor of the municipal chorus of Zürich, and in 1904 of the male chorus there; in 1906 was appointed to lead the Tonhalle Orch. of Zürich, a post he held until 1949; during his long tenure there, he championed the music of Bruckner, Strauss, Mahler, and Debussy. From 1914 until 1941 he served as director of the Zürich Cons. In his own compositions, Andreae reflected the post-Romantic tendencies of German music.

WORKS: 2 operas: *Ratcliff* (Duisburg, May 25, 1914) and *Abenteuer des Casanova* (Dresden, June 17, 1924); *Das Göttliche* for Tenor, Chorus, and Orch., to Goethe's poem (1902); *Charons Nachen* for Soloists, Chorus, and Orch. (1903); *Symphonic Fantasy* for Tenor Solo, Tenor Chorus, Organ, and Orch. (1904); *Vater unser* for Mezzo-soprano, Female Chorus, Mixed Chorus, and Organ (1911); *Li-tai-pe,* 8 Chinese songs for Tenor and Orch. (1931); *La Cité sur la montagne* for Tenor, Male Chorus, and Orch. (1942); *Little Suite* for Orch. (1916); Sym. in F major; *Notturno and Scherzo* for Orch. (1919); Sym. in C major (Zürich, Nov. 3, 1919); *Rhapsody* for Violin and Orch. (1920); *Music for Orchestra* (Zürich, Nov. 12, 1929); Violin Concerto (1940); Oboe Concertino (1942); 2 piano trios (1901, 1908); Violin Sonata (1903); 2 string quartets (1905, 1922); String Trio (1919); Divertimento for Flute and String Trio (1945); *6 Piano Pieces* (1912); choruses; songs.

BIBL.: F. Seiler, *Dr. V. A. . . . zum Jubiläum seiner 25-jährigen Tätigkeit* (Zürich, 1931); R. Schoch, *Hundert Jahre Tonhalle Zürich* (Zürich, 1968); M. Engeler and E. Lichtenhahn, eds., *Briefe an V. A.: Ein halbes Jahrhundert Züricher Musikleben, 1902–1959* (Zürich, 1986).

Andrée, Elfrida, Swedish organist and composer; b. Visby, Feb. 19, 1841; d. Göteborg, Jan. 11, 1929. She studied at the Stockholm Cons., and later took lessons with Niels Gade in

Copenhagen; at the same time she studied telegraphy and was the 1st woman telegraph operator in Sweden. In 1867 she was appointed organist at the Göteborg Cathedral. She established a series of popular concerts and presented about 800 programs. In consideration of her achievements, she was elected a member of the Swedish Academy of Music. She was a pioneer among Swedish women as an organist and composer. She wrote 4 syms., and a Swedish Mass, which had frequent performances.

Andreis, Josip, eminent Croatian musicographer; b. Split, March 19, 1909; d. Zagreb, Jan. 16, 1982. He studied philology in Zagreb and Rome; also took courses in composition. In 1945 he was appointed to the faculty of the Music Academy in Zagreb, retiring in 1972. He publ. an encyclopedia of music in the Croatian language, issued in Zagreb in 2 vols. (1958, 1963), another work of importance was a 3-vol. ed., also in the Croatian language, on music history (Zagreb, 1951–54; 2nd ed., 1966). Other publications were *Yugoslav Music* (in Eng.; Belgrade, 1959) and a monograph on the Yugoslav composer Gotovac (Split, 1957).

Andreoli, Carlo, Italian pianist, conductor, and composer; b. Mirandola, Jan. 8, 1840; d. Reggio Emilia, Jan. 22, 1908. He studied with his father, Evangelista Andreoli; then was a student of Antonio Angeleri at the Milan Cons. (1852–58). He made his debut as a pianist in Milan in 1858; subsequently appeared as a virtuoso throughout Italy and Europe. With his brother Guglielmo Andreoli (1862–1932), he organized the Società dei Concerti Sinfonica Popolari of Milan, serving as its conductor from 1877 to 1887. He became insane in 1891, and lingered in this condition for many years until his death.

BIBL.: G. Tebaldini, *In memoria di C. A.* (Milan and Mirandola, 1910).

Andrésen, Ivar, noted Norwegian bass; b. Christiania, July 27, 1896; d. Stockholm, Nov. 25, 1940. He studied at the Royal Opera School in Stockholm; made his debut there in 1919; in 1925 he joined the Dresden State Opera; then sang with the Berlin State Opera (1934–36), and concurrently at the Bayreuth Festivals (1927–36). On Nov. 1, 1930, he made his Metropolitan Opera debut in N.Y. as Daland in *Der Fliegende Holländer*; continued on its roster until 1932. He was particularly distinguished in Wagnerian roles.

Andreví y Castellar, Francisco, prominent Spanish church music composer; b. Sanahuja, near Lérida, Nov. 7, 1786; d. Barcelona, Nov. 23, 1853. He started as a choirboy, and from his earliest years devoted himself to the study of church music. At the age of 22 he became music director at the Cathedral of Segorbe; then held similar posts at the churches at Barcelona, Valencia, and Seville. During the civil war in Spain he was in Bordeaux (1832–42); later (1845–49) in Paris, where he publ. his *Traité d'harmonie et de composition* (1848; in the same year it was also publ. in Spanish). Andreví returned to Barcelona in 1849. He wrote a sacred drama, *Juicio universal;* also much choral music, most of which is in MS; 2 of his sacred choruses (*Nunc dimittis* and *Salve regina*) are included in Eslava's *Lira Sacra-Hispana.*

Andrews, Julie (née **Julia Elizabeth Wells**), English singer of popular music and actress; b. Walton-on-Thames, Oct. 1, 1935. Her mother was a pianist and her stepfather was a music-hall singer; she adopted her stepfather's surname for professional purposes. She gained attention when she sang in the Broadway musical *The Boy Friend* (1954), displaying considerable vocal range and technique; then followed her outstanding portrayal of Eliza Doolittle in *My Fair Lady* (1956–60), for which she received the Drama Critics Award; subsequently appeared in *Camelot* (1960–62). Turning her attention to films, she appeared in the whimsical *Mary Poppins* (1964), for which she won an Academy Award for best actress, and *The Sound of Music* (1966); in later years she was also active as a dramatic actress.

BIBL.: J. Cottrell, *J. A.* (London, 1970); R. Windeler, *J. A.* (N.Y., 1983).

Andrews, Patti, American popular singer; b. Minneapolis, Minn., Feb. 16, 1920. With her sisters LaVerne and Maxene, she formed the Andrews Sisters, which became the most successful "girl group" in history, selling over 60 million records. Among their most popular songs were *Bei Mir Bist Du Schön* (1937), *Rum and Coca Cola* (1944), and *Winter Wonderland* (1947). They were also successful with boogie-woogie renditions, performed in close 3-part harmony, which included *Beat Me Daddy 8 to the Bar* and *Boogie Woogie Bugle Boy*; the latter was released in a new interpretation by Bette Midler in 1973 (with Midler doing all 3 vocal parts), which set off a resurgence of interest in their music.

Andricu, Mihail, Rumanian composer; b. Bucharest, Jan. 3, 1895; d. there, Feb. 4, 1974. He studied at the Bucharest Cons. (1903–9); later became a teacher there (1926–59). For many years he was an accompanist for Georges Enesco.

WORKS: BALLETS: *Cenuşăreasa* (Cinderella; 1929); *Taina* (The Secret; 1933; Bucharest, Feb. 8, 1936); *Luceafărul* (The Morning Star; Bucharest, Sept. 24, 1951). ORCH.: 11 syms. (1944; 1947; 1950; 1954; 1955; 1957; 1958; 1960; 1962; 1968; No. 11, *In Memoriam,* 1970); 3 chamber syms. (1927, 1961, 1965); 11 sinfoniettas (1945–71); 9 suites (1924–58); *Poem* for Piano and Orch. (1923); 3 *Symphonic Pictures* (1925); *Serenade* (1928); 2 sets of 3 *Symphonic Sketches* (1936, 1951); *Fantezie* for Piano and Orch. (1940); 3 *Symphonic Pieces* (1950); *Rapsodie* (1952); Violin Concerto (1960); Cello Concerto (1961); 6 *Portraits* (1969); *Evocation* (1971); *Miniatures and Images* (1971). PIANO: 4 *Novelettes* for Piano Quartet (1925); Octet (1928); Sextet (1932); 2 quintets (1938, 1956); Sonata for Piano, 4-hands (1946); Sonata (1949); 3 *Pieces* for Piano and Winds (1964). Also wrote String Quartet (1931); Violin Sonata (1941); choral pieces and songs.

Andries, Jean, Belgian musician; b. Ghent, April 25, 1798; d. there, Jan. 21, 1872. He played violin in a local theater orch. from 1817 to 1852; from 1835 he also taught at the Ghent Cons.; in 1851 he became its director; retired in 1859. He publ. several valuable treatises, among them *Aperçu historique de tous les instruments de musique actuellement en usage* (1856); *Précis de l'histoire de la musique depuis les temps les plus reculés* (1862); *Instruments à vent: La Flûte* (1866); *Remarques sur les cloches et les carillons* (1868).

Andriessen, Hendrik, eminent Dutch organist and composer, brother of **Willem Andriessen** and father of **Jurriaan** and **Louis Andriessen;** b. Haarlem, Sept. 17, 1892; d. Heemstede, April 12, 1981. He studied music with his brother; then took piano and organ lessons with Louis Robert and J.B. de Pauw; studied composition with Bernard Zweers at the Amsterdam Cons. (1914–16); subsequently taught harmony there (1926–34). He succeeded his father as organist at St. Joseph's Church in Haarlem (1913–34); was then organist at Utrecht Cathedral (1934–49). He was director of the Royal Cons. in The Hague (1949–57) and special prof. at the Catholic Univ. in Nijmegen (1952–63). His music is Romantically inspired; some of his instrumental works make use of modern devices, including melodic atonality and triadic polytonality. He was particularly esteemed for his ability to revive the authentic modalities of Gregorian chant; his choral works present a remarkable confluence of old usages with modern technical procedures.

WORKS: OPERAS: *Philomela* (Holland Festival, June 23, 1950) and *De Spiegel uit Venetië* (The Mirror from Venice; 1964; Dutch Television, Oct. 5, 1967). ORCH.: 4 syms. (1930, 1937, 1946, 1954); *Variations and Fugue on a Theme of Kuhnau* for String Orch. (1935); *Capriccio* (1941); *Variations on a Theme of Couperin* for Flute, Harp, and Strings (1944); *Ballet Suite* (1947); *Ricercare* (1949); *Wilhemus van Nassouwe,* rhapsody (1950); Organ Concerto (1950); *Symphonic Étude* (1952; The Hague, Oct. 15, 1952); *Libertas venit,* rhapsody (1954); *Mascherata,* fantasy (1962); *Symphonie concertante* (1962); Violin Concerto (1968–69); Concertino for Oboe and String Orch. (1969–70); Concertino for Cello and Orch. (1970); *Chro-*

matic Variations for Flute, Oboe, Violin, Cello, and Strings (1970); *Canzone* (1971); *Chantecler,* overture (1972). **CHAMBER:** Cello Sonata (1926); Violin Sonata (1932); *3 Inventions* for Violin and Cello (1937); Piano Trio (1939); Suite for Violin and Piano (1950); Solo Cello Sonata (1951); Suite for Brass Quintet (1951); Wind Quintet (1951); Ballade for Oboe and Piano (1952); Theme and Variations for Flute, Oboe, and Piano (1953); *Quartetto in stile antico,* string quartet (1957); *Il peniero,* string quartet (1961); *Pezzo festoso* for Organ, 2 Trumpets, and 2 Trombones (1962); *Canzonetta* for Harpsichord (1963); *Canzone,* Trio No. 2 for Flute, Oboe, and Piano (1965); Viola Sonata (1967); *Concert spirituel* for Flute, Oboe, Violin, and Cello (1967); *Haydn Variations* for English Horn and Piano (1968); *L'Indifférent,* string quartet (1969); Clarinet Sonata (1971); *Choral varié* for 3 Trumpets and 3 Trombones (1973). **SOLO SONG CYCLES** (most with Organ or Orch.): *L'Aube spirituelle* (1916); *L'Invitation au voyage* (1918); *Magna res est amor* (1919); *L'Attente mystique* (1920); *Miroir de peine* (1923); *Cantique spirituel* (1924); *La Vièrge à midi* (1966). **CHORAL:** *Missa Simplex,* a cappella (1927); *Missa Sponsa Christi* for Male Chorus with Organ (1933); *Missa Christus Rex* for Double Chorus and Organ (1938); *2 Madrigals,* with Strings (1940); *Te Deum Laudamus I,* with Organ or Orch. (1943–46), and *II,* with Orch. (1968); *De Zee en het land (Declamatorium),* with Speaker and Orch. (1953); *Veni Creator,* with Orch. (1960); *Psalm IX,* with Tenor and Orch. (1968); *Lux Jocunda,* with Tenor or Orch. (1968); *Carmen Saeculare (Horatius),* with Soprano, Tenor, Winds, Harpsichord, and Double Bass (1968). **ORGAN:** 4 chorales (1913, c.1918, 1920, 1952); Toccata (1917); *Fête-Dieu* (1918); *Sonata de Chiesa* (1927); Passacaglia (1929); *Sinfonia* (1940); *Intermezzi* (1943); Theme and Variations (1949); 4 Studies (1953). **PIANO:** 2 sonatas (1934, 1966); Pavane (1937); Serenade (1950).

Andriessen, Jurriaan, Dutch composer, son of **Hendrik Andriessen;** b. Haarlem, Nov. 15, 1925. He studied theory with his father; took lessons in conducting with Willem van Otterloo at the Utrecht Cons. After graduating in 1947, he went to Paris to study film music; a Rockefeller Foundation fellowship enabled him to come to the U.S., where he studied composition with Copland at the Berkshire Music Center in Tanglewood during the summers of 1949 and 1950. Returning to the Netherlands, he was active mainly as a music consultant to the national radio and television.

WORKS: He wrote the 1st television opera to be produced in the Netherlands, *Kalchas* (June 28, 1959); an opera buffa, *Het Zwarte Blondje* (The Black Blonde) (1964); Piano Concertino (1943); Concerto for 2 Pianos Alone (1944); *Hommage à Milhaud* for 11 Instruments (1945; also for Flute and String Quartet, 1948); Violin Sonata (1946); *Symphonietta concertante* for 4 Trumpets and Orch. (1947); Piano Concerto (1948); *Het wonderlijk uur* (The Strange Hour), Suite No. 1 for Orch. (1948); *Octet Divertissement* for Winds (1948); 5 syms.: No. 1, *Berkshire Symphonies* (1949; produced as a ballet under the title *Jones Beach,* N.Y., March 12, 1950; No. 2 for Wind Orch. (1962); No. 3, *Symphonyen fan Fryslàn* (1963); No. 4, *Aves* (The Birds), after Aristophanes, with Chorus (1963); No. 5, *Time Spirit,* after M.C. Escher's prints, for Clarinet, Orch., Pop Group, and 6 Dancers (Rotterdam, Nov. 19, 1970); *Magnificat* for Soprano, Chorus, and Orch. (1950); Flute Concerto (1951); *Les Otaries* (The Seals), classic ballet fantasy (1951); *Cymbeline,* overture (1954); *Rouw past Electra* (Mourning Becomes Electra), suite for 11 Winds and Percussion (1954); 2 piano sonatas; 5 trios: No. 1 for Flute, Oboe, and Piano (1955); No. 2 for Flute, Viola, and Piano (1955); No. 3 for 3 Recorders (1957); No. 4 for Flute, Oboe, and Bassoon (1957); No. 5, *Sonata da camera,* for Flute, Viola, and Guitar (1959); *L'incontro di Cesare e Cleopatra,* sextet for Winds and Piano (1956); *Astrazione* for Piano (1957); *Inno della Tecnica,* introduction and scherzo for Orch. (1957); *Ritratto di una città (Ouverture Den Haag)* (1957); *Duo* for 2 Violins (1958); *Balocco* for Solo Oboe (1960); *Thai,* symphonic rhapsody based on jazz tunes by King Bhumibol Adulyadej of Thailand, written for a special

performance during the King's visit in the Netherlands (The Hague, Oct. 25, 1960); Concertino for Bassoon and Winds (1962); *Fantasy* for Piano, 4-hands (1962); *Respiration,* suite for Double Wind Quintet (1962); *Sciarada spagnuola* for Wind Quintet (1962); *Movimenti I* for Trumpet, Horn, Trombone, Strings, and Timpani (1965), *II* for Oboe, Clarinet, Bassoon, Strings, and Percussion (1972), and *III* for Violin, Viola, Cello, Winds, and Percussion (1974); Trio for Clarinet, Cello, and Piano (1965); *Concerto Rotterdam* for Jazz Combo and Orch. (Rotterdam, June 20, 1966); *Entrata festiva* for Brass and Timpani (1966); *Antifono e Fusione* for Wind Quintet, Brass Quartet, and Timpani (1966); *In pompa magna* for Brass and Percussion (1966); *Summer-Dances* for 7 Percussionists, Harp, and Guitar (1966); *Les Bransles érotiques,* pantomime of the 16th century for 8 Performers (1967); *Contra-bande,* "rapsodia interrotta" for Sousaphone and Orch. (1967); *Il divorcio di Figaro,* variations for Amateur Orch. (1967); *Omaggio à Sweelinck* for Harpsichord and 24 Strings (1968); *Trelleborg Concerto* for Harpsichord and 3 Orch. Groups (Amsterdam, Sept. 27, 1969); *Antifona dell'Aja* for Orch. (1969); *Beestenkwartet* (Animal Quartet) for Amateur Orch. (1972); *Een Prince van Oraengien (Wilhelmus-Phantasy)* for Chorus and Orch. (1973); *Pasticcio-Finale* for Orch., Dixieland Band, and Tape (1974); *Quartetto buffo* for Clarinet and String Trio (1974); *The Cave* for Solo Cello, 12 Winds, 4 Keyboard Instruments, and Electronics (1976); *Monomania e policromia* for Orch. (1984); *Serenade* for Horn (1985); *Musica per clavicembalo* (1987); incidental music for more than 60 plays.

Andriessen, Louis, Dutch composer, son of **Hendrik Andriessen;** b. Utrecht, June 6, 1939. He 1st studied with his father and with Kees van Baaren at the Royal Cons. in The Hague (1957–62); also took lessons with Luciano Berio in Milan (1962–63). He was a co-founder of a Charles Ives Soc. in Amsterdam. His works are conceived in an advanced idiom.

WORKS: Flute Sonata (1956); *Séries* for 2 Pianos (1958); *Percosse* for Flute, Trumpet, Bassoon, and Percussion (1958); Nocturnes for Soprano and Chamber Orch. (1959); *Aanloop en sprongen* for Flute, Oboe, and Clarinet (1961); *Ittrospezione I* for 2 Pianos (1961), *II* for Orch. (1963), and *III* for 2 Pianos, and Chamber Ensemble or Saxophone (1964); *A Flower Song I* for Solo Violin (1963), *II* for Solo Oboe (1963), and *III* for Solo Cello (1964); *Sweet* for Recorder or Flute (1964); *Double* for Clarinet and Piano (1965); *Paintings* for Recorder or Flute, and Piano (1965); *Souvenirs d'enfance* for Piano and Tape (1966); *Anachronie,* to the memory of Charles Ives, *I* for Orch. (1965–66; Rotterdam, Jan. 18, 1968) and *II* for Solo Oboe, 4 Horns, Piano, Harp, and String Orch. (1969); *Contra-tempus* for 23 Musicians (1968); the anti-imperialist collective opera *Reconstructie* (1968–69; Holland Festival, June 29, 1969; in collaboration with Reinbert de Leeuw, Misha Mengelberg, Peter Schat, and Jan van Vlijmen); *Hoe het is* (What It's Like) for Live-Electronic Improvisers and 52 Strings (Rotterdam, Sept. 14, 1970); *Spektakel* (Uproar) for 16 Winds, 6 Percussionists, and Electronic Instruments (1970); *The 9 Symphonies of Beethoven* for Promenade Orch. and Ice Cream Bell (1970); *De Volharding* (The Persistence) for Piano and Winds (1972); *On Jimmy Yancey* for Chamber Ensemble (1973); *Il Principe,* after Machiavelli, for 2 Choirs, Winds, Piano, and Bass Guitar (1974); *Symphonieën der Nederlanden* for Brass Band (1974); *De Statt* (The State) for 4 Women's Voices and 27 Instruments (1972–76); *Workers' Union,* symphonic movement for any loud-speaking group of Instruments (1975); *Hoketus* for 2 Panpipes, 2 Pianos, and Electronics (1977); *Orpheus,* for theater (1977); Sym. for Open Strings (1978); *De tijd* (Time) for Choir and Orch. (1981); *De snelheid* (Velocity) for Orch. (1983; San Francisco, Jan. 11, 1984); *De Stijl* for Orch. (1985).

Andriessen, Willem, Dutch pianist and composer, brother of **Hendrik Andriessen;** b. Haarlem, Oct. 25, 1887; d. Amsterdam, March 29, 1964. He studied piano and composition at the Amsterdam Cons. (1903–8); taught piano at The Hague Cons. (1910–17) and at the Rotterdam Cons.; from 1937 to 1953 was director of the Amsterdam Cons. He was a professional pianist of a high caliber. He wrote a Piano Concerto (1908); *3 Songs* for Voice and Orch. (1911); *Hei, 't was de Mei*, scherzo for Orch. (1912); Piano Sonata (1938); Piano Sonatina (1945).

Anerio, Felice, Italian composer, brother of **Giovanni Francesco Anerio;** b. Rome, c.1560; d. there, Sept. 26, 1614. He studied with G.M. Nanino; was a chorister at S. Maria Maggiore in Rome (1568–75); then sang at St. Peter's under Palestrina (from May 1575 to March 1579). In 1584 he became maestro di cappella of the English College in Rome. After Palestrina's death, Anerio was appointed by Pope Clement VIII to succeed him as composer to the Papal Chapel (April 3, 1594). His eminence as a composer is best attested by the fact that several of his compositions were for a long time supposed to be Palestrina's own. Besides MSS in Roman libraries, many of Anerio's works are extant in printed collections. They include: *Madrigali spirituali a 5* (1585; reprinted 1598); *Canzonette a 4* (1586; reprinted 1603, 1607); *Madrigali a 5* (1587); *Madrigali a 6,* book I (1590; reprinted 1599); *Concerti spirituali a 4* (1593); *Sacri hymni e cantica a 8,* book I (1596); *Madrigali a 3* (1598); *Madrigali a 6,* book II (1602); *Responsorii per la Settimana Santa a 4* (1602); *Sacri hymni e cantica a 8,* book II (1602); *Responsoria a 4* (1606).

BIBL.: L. Torri, "Nei parentali di F. A.," *Rivista Musicale Italiana* (1914); A. Cametti, "Nuovi contributi alle biografie de F. A.," ibid. (1915).

Anerio, Giovanni Francesco, Italian composer, younger brother of **Felice Anerio;** b. Rome, c.1567; d. Graz (buried), June 12, 1630. He served as a chorister at St. Peter's from 1575 to 1579, and sang, with his brother, under Palestrina. From 1600 to 1603 he was maestro di cappella at the Lateran church. In 1607 he was at the court of King Sigismund III of Poland in Krakow; in 1608 he returned to Rome; then became choirmaster at the Cathedral of Verona, and later held similar positions at the Seminario Romano (1611–12) and at the Jesuit Church of S. Maria dei Monti in Rome (1613–20). In 1616 he was ordained a priest. In 1624 he visited Treviso, near Venice; then became choirmaster at the Polish Court in Warsaw. He was a prolific composer; several of his works were printed in Italy. He also arranged Palestrina's 6-part *Missa Papae Marcelli* for 4 voices (Rome, 1600).

BIBL.: G. Liberali, "G.F. A.," *Note d'Archivio* (Dec. 1940); G. Dixon, "G.F. A. (1567–1630) and the Roman School," *Musical Times* (June 1980).

Anet, Baptiste (actually, **Jean-Jacques-Baptiste**), French violinist, son of **Jean-Baptiste Anet, père;** b. Paris (baptized), Jan. 2, 1676; d. Lunéville, Aug. 14, 1755. He was a pupil of Corelli in Rome; upon returning to France, he was a member of the Royal Chapel in Paris; in 1737 he went to Lunéville as a court musician to the former Polish King Stanislas Leszczynski. He publ. 3 sets of sonatas for violin with basso continuo (1729) and 3 collections of duets for musettes (1726, 1730, 1734).

BIBL.: L. de La Laurencie, *L'École française de violon de Lully à Viotti* (vol. 1, Paris, 1922).

Anet, Jean-Baptiste, père, French violinist; b. Paris, June 20, 1650; d. there, April 28, 1710. He was active as a teacher in Paris; in 1699 he became a member of the 24 Violons du Roi. He was the father of **Baptiste Anet.**

Anfossi, Pasquale, Italian composer; b. Taggia, near Naples, April 5, 1727; d. Rome, Feb. 1797. He studied composition with Piccinni, and began writing operas in the prevalent Italian manner. His 3rd opera, *L'Incognita perseguitata,* produced in Rome in 1773, won popular approval; its subject was the same as Piccinni's previously staged opera, but if contemporary reports are to be trusted, Anfossi's opera was more successful than that of his erstwhile master. Encouraged by his success, Anfossi proceeded to write one opera after another; according to some accounts, he wrote 76 operas; a more plausible computation credits him with no fewer than 60, but no more than 70 operas. In 1779 he was in Paris; from Dec. 1782 to 1786

he was at the King's Theater in London as director of the Italian opera there. He then traveled in Germany; returning to Italy, he was appointed maestro di cappella at the Lateran church in 1791, and turned his attention to sacred compositions; he composed at least 12 oratorios, and a number of masses and Psalms. Mozart wrote 2 arias for use in Anfossi's opera *Il Curioso indiscreto* (Vienna, 1783) and for *Le Gelosie fortunate* (Vienna, 1788).

Angeles, Victoria de Los (real name, **Victoria Gómez Cima**), famous Spanish soprano; b. Barcelona, Nov. 1, 1923. She studied at the Barcelona Cons., and made her concert debut there in 1944. In 1946 she made her 1st operatic appearance at the Teatro Lírico in Barcelona. In 1947 she won 1st prize at the International Singing Contest in Geneva. Returning to Barcelona, she sang Elsa in *Lohengrin,* Marguerite in *Faust,* and other important roles. In 1949 she performed at the Paris Opéra as Marguerite; in 1950 she appeared at Covent Garden in London as Mimi in *La Bohème.* Her American debut took place in a recital at Carnegie Hall in N.Y., on Oct. 24, 1950. On March 17, 1951, she appeared at the Metropolitan Opera in N.Y. as Marguerite in *Faust.* She continued to sing at the Metropolitan from 1951 through 1961. In 1953 she gave concerts in South Africa, and in 1956, in Australia. In 1957 she sang at the Vienna State Opera; in 1961–62 she was a guest artist at the Bayreuth Festival. She retired from the stage in 1969 but continued to give occasional recitals; she excelled particularly in Spanish and French songs. Her extensive operatic repertoire included such admired roles as Manon, Donna Anna, Nedda, Mélisande, Cio-Cio-San, and Carmen.

d'Angeli, Andrea, Italian composer and writer on music; b. Padua, Nov. 9, 1868; d. S. Michele, near Verona, Oct. 28, 1940. He studied at the Univ. of Padua; then was an instructor at the Liceo Rossini in Pesaro. He wrote several operas: *L'Innocente; Il Negromante; Al Ridotto di Venezia; Fiori e Colombi; Maurizio e Lazzaro;* also a number of libretti. He publ. monographs on Verdi (Milan, 1924) and Benedetto Marcello (Milan, 1930), and numerous essays on music in *La Cronaca Musicale,* of which he was ed. (1907–14).

Angelini, Bontempi Giovanni Andrea. See **Bontempi, Giovanni Andrea.**

d'Angelo, Louis, Italian-born American baritone; b. Naples, May 6, 1888; d. Jersey City, N.J., Aug. 9, 1958. He was taken to the U.S. as a child, and was 1st apprenticed as a glove cutter in Gloversville, N.Y.; then sang in a local church choir. He went to N.Y. City at the age of 18 and appeared in vaudeville; he made his Metropolitan Opera debut as Wagner in Faust (Nov. 17, 1917), and remained on its roster until 1946. He had more than 300 operatic roles in his repertoire and was particularly successful in his interpretation of Bartolo in *Il Barbiere di Siviglia.*

Angeloni, Carlo, Italian composer; b. Lucca, July 16, 1834; d. there, Jan. 13, 1901. He wrote a number of operas, several of which were performed in Lucca: *Carlo di Viana* (1855); *Asraele degli Abenceragi* (1871); *Dramma in montagna* (posth., 1902).

BIBL.: L. Landucci, *C. A.* (Lucca, 1905).

Angerer, Paul, Austrian conductor, teacher, and composer; b. Vienna, May 16, 1927. He received violin and piano lessons as a child; later he studied violin, piano, and composition at the Vienna Academy of Music. He was made a violist in the Vienna Sym. Orch. (1947), Zürich's Tonhalle Orch. (1948), and Geneva's Orch. de la Suisse Romande (1949); then was 1st violist of the Vienna Sym. Orch. (1953–57). After serving as director and chief conductor of the Vienna Chamber Orch. (1956–63), he was 1st conductor at the Bonn Stadttheater (1964–66); then was music director of the Ulm Theater (1966–68), chief conductor of the Salzburg Landestheater (1967–72), and director of the South West German Chamber Orch. in Pforzheim (1971–82). In 1983 he was awarded the Vienna culture prize.

WORKS: STAGE: *Das verräterische Herz,* pantomime and ballet (1956); *Die Passkontrolle*, television opera (1958); *Hotel Comedie*, musical (1970). ORCH.: *Musica ad pulsum et impulsum* for Strings and Percussion (1955); *Musica fera* (1956); *Concerto pour la jeunesse* (1956); *Gloriatio* for Double Bass and Chamber Orch. (1957); Concerto for Piano and String Orch. (1962); Viola Concerto (1962); *Ire in orbem* for Strings (1975); *Luctus et gaudium* for Trumpet and String Orch. (1977). CHAMBER: *Musica pro organo* (1946); Quartet for Oboe, Horn, Viola, and Cello (1951); Trio for Recorder, Viola d'Amore, and Lute (1953); Quintet for Flute, Oboe, Clarinet, Horn, and Bassoon (1956); *Chanson gaillarde* for Oboe, Cello, and Harpsichord (1963); *Cogitatio* for 9 Instruments (1964); *Musica articolata* for 13 Winds (1970); Quartet for Recorder, Viola da Gamba, Guitar, and Percussion (1971); *Syngrapha* for Violin, Viola, and Cello (1975); *Obolus* for 6 Oboes (1983–84); *Hilasatio* for Viola d'Amore, Flute, Violin, and Double Bass (1987).

Angermüller, Rudolph (Kurt), German musicologist and editor; b. Gadderbaum, Bielefeld, Sept. 2, 1940. He studied musicology in Mainz and Münster; received his Ph.D. in 1970 from the Univ. of Salzburg with the dissertation *Antonio Salieri: Sein Leben und seine weltlichen Werke* (publ. in Munich, 1971). In 1968 he joined the faculty of the Univ. of Salzburg. In 1973 he was named ed. in chief of the Neue Mozart-Ausgabe. His writings include *Untersuchungen zur Geschichte des Carmen-Stoffes* (1967) and *W.A. Mozarts Musikalische Umwelt in Paris (1777–78): Eine Dokumentation* (1982).

d'Anglebert, Jean-Henri, French clavecin player; b. Paris, probably in 1628; d. there, April 23, 1691. He studied with Champion de Chambonnières; in 1662 he succeeded his teacher as clavecinist to Louis XIV. In 1689 he publ. a collection, *Pièces de clavecin avec la manière de les jouer*, containing original suites, arrangements of airs from Lully's operas, and 22 variations on *Folies d'Espagne* (the theme later used by Corelli); the same vol. contains instruction on figured bass. D'Anglebert contributed greatly to the establishment of the French method of performance on the harpsichord. His extant compositions were publ. in 1934 by Marguerite Roesgen-Champion in *Publications de la Société Française de Musicologie*, also containing biographical information. His son **Jean-Baptiste Henri d'Anglebert** (b. Paris, Sept. 5, 1661; d. there, Nov. 1735) succeeded him as court musician.

BIBL.: C. Bouvet, "Les Deux d'A.," *La Revue de Musicologie* (May 1928).

Anglès, Higini (Catalan form; in Spanish, **Higinio Anglès**), distinguished Catalonian musicologist; b. Maspujols, Jan. 1, 1888; d. Rome, Dec. 8, 1969. He studied philosophy at Tarragona (1900–1913); musicology with Felipe Pedrell and composition with V.M. Gibert in Barcelona (1913–19). In 1917 he became head of the music dept. of the Barcelona library. In 1923 he went to Germany and studied with W. Gurlitt at Freiburg and F. Ludwig at Göttingen. In 1924 he returned to Barcelona, and in 1927 became prof. of music history at the Cons. With the outbreak of the Spanish Civil War in 1936, he went to Munich; returned to Barcelona in 1939. In 1943 he was appointed director of the Instituto Español de Musicología; in 1947 he became director of the Pontifical Inst. of Sacred Music in Rome. His most important publication is *El Códex Musical de Las Huelgas* (3 vols., 1928–31), containing facsimiles and transcriptions of Spanish music of the 13th and 14th centuries. Part of the text of this ed. was publ. in the *Musical Quarterly* (Oct. 1940). He publ. the following books: *Cantigas del Rei N'Anfos el Savi* (Barcelona, 1927); *Historia de la música española* (Barcelona, 1935); *La música a Catalunya fins al segle XIII* (Barcelona, 1935); *La música española desde la edad media hasta nuestros días* (Barcelona, 1941); and many smaller works. He ed. the collected works of J. Pujol (1925); the organ works of Cabanilles (1926); *La música en la corte de los reyes católicos* (2 vols.; Madrid, 1941; Barcelona, 1947); *Recopilación de sonetos*, etc., by Juan Vásquez (Barcelona, 1946); *El cancionero musical de Palacio* (Barcelona, 1947). Anglès contributed to many music journals and wrote articles on Spanish music for *Die Musik in Geschichte und Gegenwart*. He was regarded as an outstanding expert on Spanish music of the Middle Ages.

Anglès, Rafael, Spanish organist and composer; b. Rafales (Teruel), 1731; d. Valencia, Feb. 19, 1816. He was organist at Valencia Cathedral from 1762 until his death. He devoted his life to liturgical music; also wrote keyboard pieces, 4 of which are printed by J. Nín in his collection *17 Sonates et pièces anciennes d'auteurs espagnols* (Paris, 1929); 2 sonatas were publ. by J. Climent (Madrid, 1970).

Anhalt, István, Hungarian-born Canadian composer and teacher; b. Budapest, April 12, 1919. He studied composition with Kodály at the Budapest Academy of Music (1937–41); then received training in composition from Boulanger, in conducting from Fourestier, and in piano from S. Stravinsky in Paris (1946–49). In 1949 he went to Montreal and joined the faculty of McGill Univ., where he was founder-director of its electronic music studio (1964–71); in 1969 he also was Slee Prof. at the State Univ. of N.Y. in Buffalo. From 1971 to 1981 he was head of the music dept. at Queen's Univ. in Kingston, Ontario, where he was made prof. emeritus in 1984. In 1982 he was awarded an honorary D.Mus. from McGill Univ. He publ. the vol. *Alternative Voices: Essays on Contemporary Vocal and Choral Composition* (Toronto, 1984). In a number of his works he utilizes synthetic sounds.

WORKS: MUSIC THEATER AND MULTIMEDIA: *Arc en ciel*, ballet "in 3 nights" for 2 Pianos (1951); *Foci* for Amplified Soprano, Instrumental Ensemble, and Electronics (1969); *La Tourangelle* for 3 Sopranos, Tenor, Bass, Instrumental Ensemble, and Tapes (1972–74; Toronto, July 17, 1975); *Thisness*, duodrama for Mezzo-soprano and Piano (1985; Vancouver, Jan. 19, 1986); *Winthrop* for Solo Voices, Chorus, Boy's Chorus, and Orch. (Kitchener, Sept. 6, 1986). ORCH.: *Concerto in stilo di Handel* for 2 Oboes, 2 Horns, and Strings (1946); *Interludium* for Strings, Piano, and Timpani (1950); *Funeral Music* (1951); Sym. (1954–58); *Symphony of Modules* (1967); *Simulacrum* (Ottawa, Oct. 1987); *Sparkskraps* (1988); *Sonance-Resonance: Welche Töne?* (Toronto, Sept. 13, 1989). CHAMBER: Piano Sonata (1951); Trio for Violin, Cello, and Piano (1953); *Fantasia* for Piano (1954); Sonata for Violin and Piano (1954). ELECTROACOUSTIC: *Sine Nomine I* (1959) and *II* (1959); *Birds and Bells* (1960); *On the Beach* (1961); also many choral works; songs.

Anievas, Agustin, American pianist and teacher; b. N.Y., June 11, 1934. He commenced piano lessons at age 4 with his mother; following appearances as a child pianist, he pursued formal training with Steuermann, Samaroff, and Marcus at N.Y.'s Juilliard School of Music. In 1952 he made his formal debut as soloist with the Little Orch. Soc. of N.Y.; after winning the Concert Artists Guild Award in 1959 and capturing 1st prize in the Mitropoulos Competition in 1961, he toured widely; served as prof. of piano at Brooklyn College of the City Univ. of N.Y. (from 1974).

Animuccia, Giovanni, Italian composer of sacred music; b. Florence, c.1500; d. Rome, March 20, 1571. In 1555 he was appointed maestro di cappella at St. Peter's as successor to Palestrina (who returned to that post after Animuccia's death in 1571). He worked with Filippo Neri, for whom he composed his *Laudi spirituali* (2 vols.; 1563 and 1570), which were performed by Neri in his "oratorian." These are contrapuntal hymnlike songs of praise, rather than forerunners of true oratorio. Other publ. works are 4 books of madrigals (1547, 1551, 1554, 1565), a book of masses (1567), and a book of Magnificats (1568). Animuccia's compositions mark a gradual emancipation from the involved formalism of the Flemish School in the direction of a more practical style, which approached that of Palestrina. Animuccia possessed a great skill in polyphony, demonstrated especially in his ingenious canonic writing.

BIBL.: L. Cervelli, "Le Laudi spirituali di G. A.," *Rassegna Musicale* (1950); G. Reese, *Music in the Renaissance* (N.Y., 1954; 2nd ed., rev., 1959).

Anka, Paul, popular Canadian singer and composer; b. Ottawa, July 30, 1941, of Syrian parentage. He began improvising songs as a child; at the age of 15 he recorded his song *Diana*, to his own lyrics, and it became a substantial hit. He then embarked on a highly successful career as a ballad singer; acquired considerable musical ability, and wrote some 300 songs. In 1962 he incorporated himself to manage his growing fortune. He had his nose remodeled in 1958 for television appearances.

Anna Amalia, Princess of Prussia, sister of Frederick the Great; b. Berlin, Nov. 9, 1723; d. there, Sept. 30, 1787. She received her general musical training from her brother; then studied with the cathedral organist Gottlieb Hayne, and with Johann Philipp Kirnberger. She wrote music to Ramler's *Tod Jesu,* which was later set also by Graun; she also composed some instrumental works and many chorales. Her Sonata for Flute, a Trio Sonata, and 4 military marches have been publ. She assembled a great library of MSS, including some of Bach's; a catalog was publ. by Eitner (Berlin, 1884).

Anna Amalia, Duchess of Saxe-Weimar; b. Wolfenbüttel, Oct. 24, 1739; d. Weimar, April 10, 1807. She was the mother of the Grand Duke Charles Augustus, who was Goethe's protector. Goethe supplied her with a libretto for *Erwin und Elmire,* a singspiel; 1st performed at the Weimar Court (May 24, 1776), it had numerous revivals. Max Friedländer publ. its vocal score in 1921. She also wrote some instrumental music (*Divertimento* for Piano, Clarinet, Viola, and Cello; etc.).
BIBL.: W. Bode, *Amalie, Herzogin von Weimar* (3 vols.; Berlin, 1908); O. Heuschele, *Herzogin A. A.* (Munich, 1947).

Annibale (Il Padovano, from his birthplace, Padua), Italian organist and composer; b. Padua, c.1527; d. Graz, March 15, 1575. He was organist at San Marco (1552–64); in 1567 was appointed "Obrister Musicus" to the Archduke Carl at Graz; in 1570 named Kapellmeister.
WORKS: A book of ricercari *a* 4 (1556; modern ed. by N. Pierront and J.P. Hennebains, 1934); a book of madrigals *a* 5 (1564); a book of motets *a* 5–6 (1567); a book of masses *a* 5 (1573); a book of *Toccate e Ricercari* for Organ (1604). Two ricercari for Organ are reprinted in vol. III of Torchi's *L'arte musicale in Italia.*
BIBL.: G. del Valle de Paz, *A. I. P., Nella storia della musica del cinquecento* (Turin, 1933; contains complete bibliography and musical examples).

Anosov, Nikolai, Russian conductor and pedagogue, father of **Gennadi Rozhdestvensky;** b. Borisoglebsk, Feb. 18, 1900; d. Moscow, Dec. 2, 1962. He conducted orchs. in Rostov-on-Don (1937–38) and Baku (1938–39); studied piano and composition at the Moscow Cons. (graduated 1943), where he later joined the faculty. He appeared as a guest conductor in Germany, Hungary, Poland, and China; was noted for reviving old Russian operas by Bortniansky and Fomin. He wrote a textbook on reading orch. scores, and composed a few works, including a Concertino for Piano and Orch. and a Quartet for Woodwinds. He was married to the soprano Natalia Rozhdestvenskaya; their son Gennadi assumed his mother's name as Rozhdestvensky.

Anrooy (properly, **Anrooij**), **Peter van,** Dutch conductor and composer; b. Zalt-Bommel, Oct. 13, 1879; d. The Hague, Dec. 31, 1954. He studied with Johan Wagenaar in Utrecht; in 1899 he went to Moscow, where he studied violin and conducting with Willem Kes and Taneyev. He played the violin in the orchs. of Glasgow and Zürich (1902); then was active as a conductor in Groningen (1905) and Arnhem (1910); in 1917 became conductor of the Residentie Orch. in The Hague, retiring in 1935. He wrote an orch. rhapsody on Dutch themes, *Piet Hein* (1901); Ballade for Violin and Orch. (1902); several pieces of chamber music.

Anschütz, Karl, German conductor; b. Koblenz, Feb. 1815; d. N.Y., Dec. 30, 1870. He studied with Friedrich Schneider. In 1844 he assumed the directorship of the music school founded by his father; in 1848 went to London, where he conducted the Wednesday Concerts for a time. In 1857 he went to America and settled in N.Y. as an opera conductor. He was a cultivated musician; apart from his activity as a conductor, he publ. several piano pieces.

Anselmi, Giuseppe, noted Italian tenor; b. Catania, Nov. 16, 1876; d. Zoagli, May 27, 1929. He studied voice with Luigi Mancinelli; made his operatic debut in Athens in 1896; then sang in Naples, London, Buenos Aires, St. Petersburg, Warsaw, and Madrid; he retired in 1917. He was a remarkable bel canto stylist, winning acclaim for his Verdi and Puccini roles. His love for Madrid, where he was particularly successful, prompted him to bequeath his heart to that city; the rest of his body was deposed in Catania Cathedral.

Ansermet, Ernest, celebrated Swiss conductor; b. Vevey, Nov. 11, 1883; d. Geneva, Feb. 20, 1969. He studied mathematics with his father, who was a schoolteacher, and received his musical training from his mother. He became himself a mathematics teacher, and taught school in Lausanne (1906–10). At the same time he took courses in music with Denéréaz, Barblan, and Ernest Bloch; he also studied conducting with Mottl in Munich and with Nikisch in Berlin. From then on he devoted himself mainly to conducting. He led the summer concerts in Montreux (1912–14), and from 1915 to 1918 was conductor of the sym. concerts in Geneva. In 1918 he organized the prestigious Orch. de la Suisse Romande in Geneva, at which he performed a great deal of modern French and Russian music; he retired from conducting in 1967. He met Stravinsky, who introduced him to Diaghilev, and subsequently conducted Diaghilev's Ballets Russes. On Sept. 28, 1918, he presented in Lausanne the 1st performance of Stravinsky's *L'Histoire du soldat.* He made numerous guest appearances as conductor with the Ballets Russes in Paris, London, Italy, Spain, South America, and the U.S., and also conducted performances with major American and European orchs., attaining the reputation of a scholarly and progressive musician capable of fine interpretations of both Classical and modern works. He himself composed a symphonic poem, *Feuilles de printemps;* orchestrated Debussy's *6 épigraphes antiques,* and 2 Argentine dances by Julian Aguirre. He publ. *Le Geste du chef d'orchestre* (Lausanne, 1943) and *Les Fondements de la musique dans la conscience humaine* (2 vols., Neuchâtel, 1961), making use of mathematical formulations to demonstrate the lack of validity in 12-tone technique and other advanced methods of composition.
BIBL.: *E. A.: 1883–1969* (Lausanne, 1983); F. Hudry, *E. A.: Pionnier de la musique* (1983).

Ansorge, Conrad (Eduard Reinhold), German pianist; b. Buchwald, near Löbau, Silesia, Oct. 15, 1862; d. Berlin, Feb. 13, 1930. He studied at the Leipzig Cons. (1880–82) and was one of the last pupils of Liszt in Weimar (1885). He toured in Russia and America; then lived in Weimar (1893–95) and in Berlin (from 1895). From 1898 he taught at the Klindworth-Scharwenka Cons. In 1920 he gave courses at the German Cons. in Prague. Ansorge excelled as an interpreter of Romantic compositions; he was called "a metaphysician among pianists" for his insight into the inner meaning of the music of Beethoven, Schubert, and Schumann. He wrote a Piano Concerto, a String Sextet, 2 string quartets, and a Cello Sonata; *Ballade, Traumbilder, Polish Dances,* and 3 sonatas for Piano; and a Requiem.

Antegnati, Costanzo, Italian organist and composer; b. Brescia (baptized), Dec. 9, 1549; d. there, Nov. 14, 1624. He was descended from a family of organ builders, and served as an apprentice to his father. In 1584 he became organist at Brescia Cathedral. His madrigals and sacred compositions (masses, motets, Psalms, and canzoni) were publ. in Venice (1571–1608) with pieces in organ tablature; he also publ. an important treatise, *L'arte organica* (Brescia, 1608; new ed. by Renato Lunelli, Mainz, 1938). His *3 ricercari* for Organ are reprinted in vol. III of Luigi Torchi's *L'arte musicale in Italia.*
BIBL.: D. Muoni, *Gli A.* (Milan, 1883).

Antes, John, American Moravian (*Unitas Fratrum*) minister; b. Frederickstownship, Pa., March 24, 1740; d. Bristol, England, Dec. 17, 1811. He left America in 1764, and was a missionary in Egypt, where he was beaten and crippled by order of a bey who tried to extort money from him. He spent the rest of his life in England. A watchmaker by trade, he was an inventive artisan. He constructed several string instruments; one violin made by him in Bethlehem, Pa., in 1759 is preserved in the Museum of the Moravian Historical Soc. at Nazareth, Pa. A contribution by Antes to the *Allgemeine musikalische Zeitung* in 1806 describes a device for better violin tuning, as well as improvements of the violin bow and of the keyboard hammer. Antes also invented a machine with which one could turn pages while playing. He wrote about 25 melodious short anthems to German or English words for Chorus, Winds, Strings, and Organ. All of his MS compositions are in the Archives of the Moravian Church at Bethlehem, and at Winston-Salem, N.C.; compositions in MS are also found in the Archiv der Brüder-Unität in Herrnhut, Germany. His 3 string trios were discovered in 1949. They are the earliest known chamber works by a native American. His interesting autobiography was publ. in *Nachrichten aus der Brüder-Gemeinde* (1845). **BIBL.:** D.M. McCorkle, "J. A., 'American Dilettante,' " *Musical Quarterly* (Oct. 1956; reprinted as No. 2 in the series Moravian Music Foundation Publications, Winston-Salem, N.C.).

Antheil, George (Georg Johann Carl), remarkable American composer who cut a powerful swath in the world of modern music by composing dissonant and loud pieces glorifying the age of the machine; b. Trenton, N.J., July 8, 1900; d. N.Y., Feb. 12, 1959. He studied music theory with Constantin Sternberg in Philadelphia; then went to N.Y. to take lessons in composition with Ernest Bloch. Defying the norms of flickering musical conservatism, Antheil wrote piano pieces under such provocative titles as *Sonate sauvage, Mechanisms,* and *Airplane Sonata.* In 1922 he went to Europe and gave a number of concerts featuring his own compositions as well as some impressionist music. He spent a year in Berlin and then went to Paris, which was to become his domicile for several years; he was one of the 1st American students of the legendary Nadia Boulanger, who was to be the *nourrice* of a whole generation of modernistically minded Americans. In Paris he also made contact with such great literary figures as James Joyce and Ezra Pound; in the natural course of events, Antheil became the self-styled *enfant terrible* of modern music. Naively infatuated with the new world of the modern machine, he composed a *Ballet mécanique* with the avowed intention to "épater les bourgeois." The culmination of Antheil's Paris period was marked by the performance of an orch. suite from his *Ballet mécanique* (June 19, 1926), with musical material taken from a score he wrote for a film by Fernand Léger. He then returned to America as a sort of conquering hero of modern music, and staged a spectacular production of the *Ballet mécanique* at Carnegie Hall in N.Y. on April 10, 1927, employing a set of airplane propellers, 8 pianos, and a large battery of drums, creating an uproar in the audience and much publicity in the newspapers. A revival of the *Ballet mécanique* took place in N.Y. on Feb. 20, 1954, with a recording of the noise of a jet plane replacing the obsolescent propellers, but the piece was received by the public and press as merely a curiosity of the past. Abandoning all attempts to shock the public by extravaganza, Antheil turned to composition of operas. His 1st complete opera, *Transatlantic,* to his own libretto, portraying the turmoil attendant on the presidential election, and employing jazz rhythms, was staged on May 25, 1930, in Frankfurt, Germany, arousing a modicum of interest. Another opera, *Mr. Bloom and the Cyclops,* based on James Joyce's novel *Ulysses,* never progressed beyond fragmentary sketches. A 2nd opera, *Helen Retires,* with a libretto by John Erskine, was produced in N.Y. on Feb. 28, 1934. In 1936, Antheil moved to Hollywood, where he wrote some film music and ran a syndicated column of advice to perplexed lovers; another of his whimsical diversions was working on a torpedo device, in collaboration with the motion picture actress Hedy Lamarr; they actually filed a patent, No. 2,292,387, dated June 10, 1941, for an invention relating to a "secret communication system involving the use of carrier waves of different frequencies, especially useful in the remote control of dirigible craft, such as torpedoes." It is not known whether the Antheil-Lamarr device was ever used in naval warfare. He continued to write syms., operas, and other works, but in the spirit of the times, reduced his musical idiom to accessible masses of sound. These works were rarely performed, and in the light of musical history, Antheil remains a herald of the avant-garde of yesterday. He publ. an autobiography, *Bad Boy of Music* (N.Y., 1945). He was married to Elizabeth ("Böski") Markus, a niece of the Austrian dramatist and novelist Arthur Schnitzler; she died in 1978. Antheil was the subject of a monograph by Ezra Pound entitled *Antheil and the Treatise on Harmony, with Supplementary Notes* (Chicago, 1927), which, however, had little bearing on Antheil and even less on harmony.

WORKS: OPERAS: *Transatlantic* (Frankfurt, May 25, 1930); *Helen Retires* (N.Y., Feb. 28, 1934); *Volpone,* after Ben Jonson (Los Angeles, Jan. 9, 1953); *The Brothers* (Denver, July 28, 1954); *The Wish* (Louisville, Ky., April 2, 1955); *Cabeza de vaca,* opera cantata (CBS Television, June 10, 1962). **BALLETS:** *Ballet mécanique* (Paris, June 19, 1926; N.Y., April 10, 1927); *The Capital of the World* (N.Y., Dec. 27, 1953). **ORCH.:** *Zingareska* (Berlin, Nov. 21, 1922); a "sym." for 5 Instruments, also referred to as "Quintet" (1923); Sym. No. 1, in F major (1926; N.Y., April 10, 1927; a finale from it was orig. labeled *Jazz Symphonietta,* and later rescored and renamed *Jazz Symphony*); Sym. No. 2 (1937); Sym. No. 3, subtitled *American Symphony* (1942); Sym. No. 4 (NBC Sym. Orch., N.Y., Stokowski conducting, Feb. 13, 1944); Sym. No. 5, subtitled *The Joyous* (Philadelphia, Dec. 21, 1948); Sym. No. 6 (San Francisco, Feb. 10, 1949); Piano Concerto (1926); *McKonkey's Ferry,* orch. overture (1948); *Over the Plains* (1948); *Serenade* for String Orch. (1948); *Tom Sawyer: A Mark Twain Overture* (1950). **CHAMBER:** 3 string quartets (1924, 1928, 1948); 4 violin sonatas (1923–48); Piano Trio (1950); 5 piano sonatas (1922–50); a group of pieces for Piano Solo under the title *La Femme: 100 têtes,* inspired by Max Ernst's book of collages of that title (1933); *8 Fragments* from Shelley, for Chorus (1951); *Songs of Experience* for Voice and Piano (1948). **FILM MUSIC:** *The Plainsman* (1937); *Specter of the Rose* (1946); *Knock on Any Door* (1949); *The Juggler* (1953); *Not as a Stranger* (1955); *The Pride and the Passion* (1957). **BIBL.:** L. Whitesitt, *The Life and Music of G. A., 1900–1959* (Ann Arbor, Mich., 1983).

Anthony, James R(aymond), American musicologist; b. Providence, R.I., Feb. 18, 1922. He studied at Columbia Univ. (B.S., 1946; M.A., 1948), the Univ. of Paris (diploma, 1951), and the Univ. of Southern Calif. (Ph.D., 1964, with the diss. *The Opera-ballets of André Campra: A Study of the First Period French Opera-ballet*); taught at the Univ. of Montana (1948–50) and the Univ. of Arizona (from 1952). He publ. the study *French Baroque Music from Beaujoyeul to Rameau* (London, 1973; 2nd ed., rev., 1978); contributed articles to *The New Grove Dictionary of Music and Musicians* (1980). **BIBL.:** J. Heyer, ed., *Jean-Baptist Lully and the Music of the French Baroque: Essays in Honour of J. A.* (Cambridge, 1988).

Anthony, Ray (real name, **Raymond Antonini**), American trumpeter and bandleader; b. Bentleyville, Pa., Jan. 20, 1922. He studied trumpet with his father; then played in the Glenn Miller orch. (1940–41); subsequently served in the U.S. Navy during World War II, leading a band in the Pacific; after the war, formed his own band and toured widely with it in the U.S.

Antico (also **Anticho, Antiquo, Antiquus,** etc.), **Andrea,** Italian music publisher and composer; b. Montona, Istria, c.1480; d. probably in Venice, after 1539. He was a music publisher in Rome (1510–18) and Venice (1520–21; 1533–39). He was apparently also a competent composer. His collection of *Canzoni, sonetti, strambotti et frottole, libro tertio* was brought out by Alfred Einstein (Northampton, Mass., 1941).

BIBL.: C. Chapman, *A. A.* (diss., Harvard Univ., 1964); M. Picker, "The Motet Anthologies of A. A.," *A Musical Offering: Essays in Honor of Martin Bernstein* (N.Y., 1977).

Antill, John (Henry), notable Australian composer; b. Sydney, April 8, 1904; d. there, Dec. 29, 1986. He studied with Alfred Hill at the Sydney Cons. and simultaneously worked as a mechanical draftsman; among other things, he designed a steam whistle capable of producing a major ninth-chord for the use of the New South Wales Government Railways. Abandoning such mechanical endeavors, he sang in a provincial opera and also served as musical program maker of the Australian Broadcasting Commission; he received the Order of the British Empire in 1971. He also displayed interest in aboriginal music and attended festivals of popular music in the outback of Australia. As a testimony of his interest in indigenous music he produced a ballet, *Corroboree,* which was produced in Sydney on July 3, 1950. He further composed 3 operas: *Endymion* (Sydney, 1953), *The Music Critic* (Sydney, 1953), and *The 1st Christmas* (Sydney, Dec. 25, 1969). He also wrote a number of pageants and choral works on Australian themes.

Antoine, Georges, Belgian composer; b. Liège, April 28, 1892; d. Bruges, Nov. 15, 1918 (of an ailment acquired during World War I). He studied at the Cons. of Liège (1902–13) with Sylvain Dupuis; joined the Belgian army in 1914. He wrote: Piano Concerto (1914); *Vendanges* for Voice and Orch. (1914); *Veillée d'armes,* symphonic poem (1918); Piano Quartet (1916); Violin Sonata (1912–15); songs.
BIBL.: M. Paquot, *G. A.* (Brussels, 1935).

Antoni, Antonio d', Italian conductor and composer; b. Palermo, June 25, 1801; d. (suicide) Trieste, Aug. 18, 1859. He studied with his grandfather and with his father, both of whom were musicians; appeared as conductor of his own Mass for St. Cecilia's Day when he was 12. He also conducted the premiere of his 1st opera, *Un duello,* in Palermo at the age of 16, and, after touring as a conductor in Italy, France, and England, scored notable success with his opera *Amina ossia L'Orfanella di Ginevra* (Trieste, Carnival 1825). He settled in Trieste and became conductor of the Società Filarmonico-Dramatica (1829).

Antoniou, Theodore, Greek-American avant-garde composer; b. Athens, Feb. 10, 1935. He studied violin, voice, and music theory at the National Cons. in Athens, where his teachers were Manolis Kalomiris and Yannis Papaioannou (1947–61). In 1961 he went to Germany, where he studied composition with Günther Bialas at the Hochschule für Musik in Munich (1961–65); also attended summer seminars on new music in Darmstadt (1963–65). In 1966 he traveled in the U.S. on a State Dept. grant. Returning to Greece, he served as director of the Orch. of the City of Athens (1967); in 1968 took part in organizing the Hellenic Week of Contemporary Music. In 1969 he emigrated to America and was engaged as composer-in-residence at Stanford Univ. in Palo Alto, Calif., and at the Berkshire Center in Tanglewood; in the summers of 1970 and 1972 held a similar post at the Univ. of Utah in Salt Lake City. In 1970 he was appointed prof. of composition at the Philadelphia College of Performing Arts, and concurrently was engaged as conductor of the Sym. Orch. at the Philadelphia Musical Academy. In 1979 he was appointed prof. of composition at Boston Univ. Also in 1979 he received a Guggenheim fellowship. His music is remarkably compendious in its integration of quaquaversal layers of sound; folk elements in Greek modalities are also in evidence, and many titles have Greek philosophic or literary connotations.
WORKS: STAGE: *Riders without Horses* (Athens, April 26, 1961); *Rhinoceros,* after Ionesco's play (Athens, May 4, 1962); *Philoctet,* after Sophocles (Epidaurus, June 25, 1967); *Juno and the Peacock,* after O'Casey (Athens, Oct. 16, 1969); *Birds,* after Aristophanes (Nuremberg, Feb. 8, 1970); *Autopsy,* after G. Michaelidis (Athens, Dec. 14, 1970); *Midsummer Night's Dream,* after Shakespeare (Athens, Oct. 15, 1971); *Romeo and Juliet* (Athens, March 17, 1971); *Wozzeck,* after Büchner

(Athens, July 30, 1972); *Sunday Walk,* after G. Michel (Athens, Sept. 29, 1972); *Oedipus at Colonus,* after Sophocles (Epidaurus, July 6, 1975); *7 against Thebes,* after Aeschylus (Athens, July 25, 1975); *Oresteia,* after Aeschylus (Stanford Univ., Feb. 24, 1976); *Medea,* after Euripides (Saloniki, Aug. 16, 1976); *Bacchae,* after Euripides (Comédie Française, Paris, April 14, 1976); *News from the New World Discovered in the Moon,* after Ben Jonson (Athens, Nov. 30, 1978); *Periander,* mixed-media opera (1979); *Bacchae,* ballet for Chamber Orch. and Tape (1980); *The Magic World,* ballet (1984). **MULTIMEDIA:** *Clytemnestra,* sound-action for Actress, Dancers, Instruments, and Tape (Kassel, June 4, 1968); *Katharsis* for Flute, Orch., Tape, and Projections (Athens, Dec. 22, 1968); *Cassandra,* sound-action for Dancers, Actors, Chorus, Orch., Tapes, Lights, and Projections (Barcelona, Nov. 14, 1970); *Cheironomiai* (Gestures), improvisation by conductor and any combination of Instruments and Voices (Kassel, Oct. 31, 1971); *Chorochronos I* (Philadelphia, May 11, 1973); *Chorochronos II* (Reitlingwest, Germany, Oct. 29, 1973); *Chorochronos III* (Berlin, Jan. 26, 1975). **VOCAL:** *Greek Folk Songs* for Mixed Choir (1961); *Epilogue,* after *The Odyssey,* for Voice and Orch. (Munich, March 10, 1964); *Kontakion* for Voices, Chorus, and String Orch. (Berlin, May 7, 1965); *Melos,* cantata after Sappho for Medium Voice and Orch. (Athens, April 2, 1967); *Climate of Absence* for Voice and Orch. (Munich, Nov. 12, 1968); *Die weisse Rose,* cantata (Philadelphia, April 25, 1976); *Circle of Thanatos and Genesis,* cantata (Boston, Jan. 23, 1981); *Oneiro Mega* for Soprano, Tenor, Narrator, and Chamber Orch. (1984). **ORCH.:** Triple Concerto for Violin, Trumpet, Clarinet, and Orch. (1959); *Concertino* for Piano, String Orch., and Percussion (Athens, Dec. 16, 1962); *Antithesis* for Orch. (Hannover, Jan. 20, 1966); *Concertino* for Piano, 9 Wind Instruments, and Percussion (Philadelphia, Dec. 4, 1973); *Jeux* for Cello and String Orch. (March 4, 1968); Violin Concerto (Athens, Aug. 16, 1965); *Kinesis ABCD* for 2 Groups of Strings (Athens, July 13, 1966); *Op Overture* for Orch. and Tape (1966); *Micrographies* (Kassel, April 3, 1968); *Events I* for Violin, Piano, and Orch. (Hagen, June 10, 1968); *Events II* for Orch. (Tanglewood, Aug. 30, 1969); *Events III* for Orch. with Tape (Barcelona, Oct. 8, 1969); *Synthesis* for Oboe, Organ, Percussion, Double Bass, and 4 Synthesizers (1971); *Threnos* for Wind Orch. (Tanglewood, Aug. 7, 1974); *Fluxus I* (Basel, Dec. 18, 1979); *Fluxus II* (Philadelphia, April 4, 1976); *Circle of Accusation* (Lemesos, Cyprus, Aug. 8, 1977); *Parastasis I* for Percussion and Tape (1977); *Parastasis II* for Percussion and Instruments (1978); Double Concerto for Percussion and Orch. (Philadelphia, April 26, 1978); *The GBYSO Music* (1982). **CHAMBER:** Trio for Flute, Viola, and Cello (1961); *Dialogues* for Flute and Guitar (1962); *Quartetto giocoso* for Oboe, Violin, Cello, and Piano (West Berlin, June 8, 1968); *6 Likes* for Solo Tuba (1967); *Lyrics* for Violin and Piano (1967); *5 Likes* for Solo Oboe (1969); *4 Likes* for Solo Violin (1972); *3 Likes* for Solo Clarinet (1973); *2 Likes* for Solo Double Bass (1976); *Stichomythia II* for Solo Guitar (1977); *The Do Quintet* for 2 Trumpets, Horn, Trombone, and Tuba (1978). **PIANO:** *Aquarelle* (1958); *Syllables* (1965); *Entrata* (1983).

Antony, Franz Joseph, German organist and writer on music; b. Münster, Westphalia, Feb. 1, 1790; d. there, Jan. 7, 1837. He was appointed music director at Münster Cathedral in 1819; in 1832 succeeded his father, Joseph Antony (1758–1836), as organist. He publ. *Archäologisch-liturgisches Gesangbuch des Gregorianischen Kirchengesangs* (1829) and *Geschichtliche Darstellung der Entstehung und Vervollkommnung der Orgel* (1832).

Anzaghi, Davide, Italian composer; b. Milan, Nov. 29, 1936. He studied piano, conducting, and composition at the G. Verdi Cons. in Milan, graduating in 1957; then took courses in composition with Ghedini and Donatoni in Venice. He subsequently joined the faculty of his alma mater at the G. Verdi Cons.
WORKS: ORCH.: *Riturgia* (Venice, Sept. 15, 1972); *Limbale* (Bologna, Nov. 10, 1973); *Ausa* (La Rochelle, France, July 5, 1974); *Egophonie* (1974; Milan, Feb. 3, 1975); *Aur'ore* for Cho-

rus and Orch. (1975–76; Milan, Feb. 4, 1977); *Ermosonio* (1978; Milan, Nov. 30, 1979); *Anco* (1984; Milan, March 30, 1985); Piano Concerto (1987–88; Milan, March 30, 1989). **CHAMBER:** *Limine* for String Trio (1971); *Aulografia* for Solo Flute (1975); *In-Chiostro* for 2 Violins and Viola (1975); *Alena* for 10 Wind Instruments (1976); *Remota* for 7 Players (1977); *Alia* for Bass Clarinet and Piano (1980); *Oiseau triste* for Piccolo and Piano (1980); *Soavodia* for Clarinet and Piano (1980); *Làbia* for String Quartet (1982); *Élan* for 9 Instruments (1984); *Tremes* for Viola (1988). **PIANO:** *Segni* (1968); *Ritografia* (1971); *Revenants*, 8 prelude-variations (1981).

Apel, Willi, eminent German musical scholar and encyclopedist; b. Konitz, Oct. 10, 1893; d. Bloomington, Ind., March 14, 1988. He studied mathematics at the univs. of Bonn (1912), Munich (1913), and Berlin (Ph.D., 1932, with the diss. *Accidentien und Tonalität in den Musikdenkmälern des 15. und 16. Jahrhunderts;* publ. as vol. 24 in the *Collection d'études musicologiques,* Strasbourg, 1937; 2nd ed., augmented, Baden-Baden, 1972); concurrently he studied music and took piano lessons. He taught mathematics and music in Germany until 1936, when he was forced to emigrate; settling in the U.S., he gave lectures at Harvard Univ. (1938–42). In 1950 he became prof. of music at Indiana Univ. in Bloomington, retiring in 1964 as prof. emeritus. While in Germany, he ed. 2 vols. of early piano music, *Musik aus früher Zeit für Klavier* (Mainz, 1934); he also publ. *Die Fuge* (1932). In America he publ. the extremely valuable treatises and compilations *The Notation of Polyphonic Music, 900–1600* (Cambridge, Mass., 1942; 5th ed., rev., 1961); *The Harvard Dictionary of Music,* a prime reference work of musical terminology (Cambridge, Mass, 1944; 2nd ed., rev. and enl., 1969); *Historical Anthology of Music,* 2 vols. (with A.T. Davison; Cambridge, Mass., 1946 and 1950); *Masters of the Keyboard* (Cambridge, Mass., 1947); and *Gregorian Chant* (Bloomington, Ind., 1958). A Festschrift in his honor, *Essays in Musicology,* ed. by H. Tischler (Bloomington, Ind., 1968), contains a bibliography of his writings. Apel acknowledged his lack of interest in opera or modern developments in music; he was a musical purist who regarded the developments of musical composition after the era of Bach as of passing significance to music history.

Aperghis, Georges, avant-garde Greek composer; b. Athens, Dec. 23, 1945. He studied music privately with Yannis Papaioannou in Athens; in 1963 went to Paris and became a student of Xenakis, who initiated him into the mysteries of ultramodern techniques involving such arcana as musical indeterminacy and audiovisual coordinates in spatial projection. **WORKS: THEATER:** *Bis, spectacle musical* for 10 Actors and 10 Instruments (1968); *The Tragic Story of the Necromancer Hieronimo and His Mirror* for Puppets, Voice, Guitar, and Piano (1971); *Histoires de loup,* opera (Avignon, 1976); *Fragments (Journal d'un opéra)* for 7 Singers, Piano, and 2 Vibraphones (1977; Strasbourg, Jan. 11, 1978); *Liebestod,* opera (1981). **OTHER WORKS:** *2 Movements* for String Quartet (1964); *Dialogues* for Flute, Harpsichord, and Xylophone (1965); *Antistixis A* for 3 String Quartets (1964–65), *B* for 4 Flutes, 4 Percussionists, Celesta, Harp, Ondes Martenot, and Double Bass (1965), and *C* for Orch. (1966); *Contrepoint* for Orch. (1967); *Libretto* for Orch. in 4 groups (1968); *Anacrusis* for Chamber Ensemble (1967); *Eluding Game* for Instrumental Ensemble (1968); *Freak Map* for 6 Instruments and 3 Percussionists (1968); *Contrepoint* for 3 String Quartets, Piano, Trombone, and Percussion (1968); *Plastic Piece* for 2 Orchs. (1968); *Music for an Orange Girl* for Chamber Ensemble and Tape (1968); *Color Music* for 19 Instruments (1966–69); *Musique automatique,* suite of 6 pieces for Female Voice and Chamber Ensemble (1969); *Boogie-Woogie* for Chamber Ensemble (1969); *Variations* for 10 Musicians (1969); *B.A.C.H.* for Chorus and Orch. (1969); *4 pièces superposables* for Conductor, Percussion, Voice, and Strings (1969); *La Création* for Speaker and Instrumental Ensemble (1969); *Variations sur un portrait de Bach* for Any Instrument (1970); *Le Fil d'Ariane* for Ondes Martenot (1970); *Variations 1 and 2* for 5 Percussionists and 5 Xylophones

(1970); *Variations 3 and 4* (Awake) for 6 Oboes (1970); *Music Box* for Harpsichord (1970); *Vesper,* oratorio (1970); Quartet for 4 Double Basses (1970); Quartet for 4 Percussionists (1970); *Symplexis* for 22 Jazz Soloists and Orch. (Paris, Nov. 3, 1970); *Puzzles* for 5 Woodwinds, 5 Brass, and Percussion (1971); *Die Wände haben Ohren* (The Walls Have Ears) for Orch. (Metz, France, Nov. 26, 1972); *BWV* for 6 Singers and Instrumental Ensemble (1973); *Sports et rebondissements* for 6 Voices, Actors, 2 Trombones, Tuba, Percussion, and Tape (1974); *Les Lauriers sont coupés* for Voice and Chamber Ensemble (1975); *Mouvement* for Violin, Viola, Cello, Clarinet, and Piano (1975); *Parenthèses* for Ensemble (1977); *Ilios* for 10 Instruments (1978); *Graffitis* for Percussionist (1980).

ApIvor, Denis, Irish-born English composer; b. Collinstown, West Meath, April 14, 1916. He studied music theory privately in London with Patrick Hadley and Alan Rawsthorne (1937–39); adopted a fairly advanced technique of composition while adhering to tradition in formal design; his pieces are quite playable, and the associations he brings out with extramusical elements (painting, etc.) are most ingenious. **WORKS: OPERAS:** *She Stoops to Conquer,* after Goldsmith's play (1943–47; rev. 1976–77); *Yerma,* after García Lorca's play (1955–58); *Ubu roi,* after Alfred Jarry's play (1965–66); *Bouvard and Pecuchet,* after Flaubert (1970). **BALLETS:** *The Goodman of Paris* (1951); *A Mirror for Witches* (1951); *Blood Wedding,* after Lorca (1953); *Saudades* (1954); *Corporal Jan* (1967); cantata, *The Hollow Men,* after T.S. Eliot's poem (1939; BBC Radio, London, Feb. 21, 1950); *Cantata,* to poems by Dylan Thomas (1960); Piano Concerto (1948); Concerto for Violin and 15 Instruments (1950); 4 syms. (1952; 1963; 1978–79; 1985); Guitar Concertino (1953); *Overtones,* 9 short pieces for Orch., based on Paul Klee's paintings (1961–62); *String Abstract,* concerto for String Trio and Orch. (1967); *Tarot,* variations for Chamber Orch. (1968); *Neumes,* variations for Orch. (1969); *The Tremulous Silence* for Guitar and Chamber Orch. (1972); *Exotics Theater,* 10 pieces for Chamber Ensemble (1972; Klee pieces: iii); *Resonance of the Southern Flora* for wordless Chorus and Orch. (1972; Klee pieces: iv); *Fern Hill,* after Thomas, for Tenor and 11 Instruments (1973); Violin Concerto (1975); Violin Sonata (1944–45); *Concertante* for Clarinet, Piano, and Percussion (1944–45); *Variations* for Solo Guitar (1958); Wind Quintet (1960); *Mutations* for Cello and Piano (1962); 2 String Quartets (1964, 1976); *Crystals* for Percussion, Hammond Organ, Guitar, and Double Bass (1964–65); *Harp, Piano, Piano-Harp* (1966); *10 String Design* for Violin and Guitar (1967); *Discanti,* 5 pieces for Solo Guitar (1970); *Saeta* for Solo Guitar (1972); *Psycho-pieces,* 8 pieces for Clarinet and Piano (1973; Klee pieces: v); *Studies for Wind,* 7 pieces, 1 each for Flute, Oboe, Clarinet, Bassoon, Horn, Trumpet, and Trombone (1974); Clarinet Quintet (1975); *Liaison,* duo for Guitar and Keyboard (1976); *Animalcules,* 12 piano pieces (1962); *5 Piano Pieces* (1968); *Orgelberg* for Organ (1971; Klee pieces: ii); songs.

Aponte-Ledée, Rafael, Puerto Rican composer; b. Guayama, Oct. 15, 1938. He studied composition with Cristóbal Halffter at the Madrid Cons. (1957–64); then took courses with Ginastera at the Latin American Center of Advanced Musical Studies at the Di Tella Inst. in Buenos Aires (1965–66). Returning to Puerto Rico, he founded in San Juan, with the collaboration of Francis Schwartz, the Fluxus group for the promotion of new music (1967); taught composition and theory at the Univ. of Puerto Rico (1968–74). His music is highly advanced, employing nearly every conceivable technique of the cosmopolitan avant-garde. **WORKS:** *Tema y 6 Diferencias* for Piano (1963); *Dialogantes 1* for Flute and Violin (1965); *Elejía* for 13 Strings (1965; version for 50 Strings, 1967); *Presagio de Pájaros muertos* for Narrator and Tape (1966); *Epíthasis* for 3 Oboes, 2 Trombones, Double Bass, and 3 Percussionists (1967); *Dialogantes 2* for 3 Flutes, 3 Trombones, and 3 Clarinets (1968); *La ventana abierta* for 3 Mezzo-sopranos, 3 Flutes, Clarinet, Trumpet, 2 Percussionists, Celesta, Piano, Violin, Cello, and Double Bass (1968; version for 3 Mezzo-sopranos, Flutes, Clarinet, 2 Trumpets, Horn, 2 Percussionists, Guitar, Piano, and 2 String Quartets, 1969); *Streptomicyne* for Soprano, Flute, Clarinet, Trumpet, and Piano (1970); *SSSSSS²* for Double-bass Solo, 3 Flutes, Trumpet, and Percussion (1971); *Volúmenes* for Piano (1971); *Elvira en sombras* for Piano and Orch. (1973); *Estravagario, In memoriam Salvador Allende* for Orch. and Tape (1973); *Cuídese de los angeles que caen*, musique concrète (1974); *Los huevos de Pandora* for Clarinet and Tape (1974); *El palacio en sombras* for Orch. without Violins and Cellos (1977).

Apostel, Hans (Erich), German-born Austrian composer; b. Karlsruhe, Jan. 22, 1901; d. Vienna, Nov. 30, 1972. After early studies in Karlsruhe he went to Vienna in 1921, and became a pupil in composition of Schoenberg and Alban Berg. He served as an ed. at Universal Edition and in that capacity prepared for publication the posthumous works of Berg. He was also active as a teacher. Apostel received numerous prizes for his own works, among them the Grand Prize of the City of Vienna (1948) and the Grand Prize of the Republic of Austria (1957). In 1951 he adopted the method of composition with 12 tones according to Schoenberg's precepts, without, however, avoiding tonal combinations. He experimented in Klangfarben effects, and applied audible overtones in his piano pieces by holding down the keys without striking them. His music was often performed at international festivals, but it rarely penetrated beyond the confines of Central Europe.
Works: Piano Sonata (1929); *Requiem*, to Rilke's words, for Chorus and Orch. (1933; Vienna Radio, May 3, 1958); *Sonatina ritmica* for Piano (1934); 2 string quartets (1935, 1956); *Adagio* for String Orch., 2 Harps, Celesta, and Piano (1937); 5 *Songs*, after Hölderlin, for Low Voice and Orch. (1939–40); *Kubiniana*, 10 piano pieces (1945–50); Quartet for Flute, Clarinet, Horn, and Bassoon (1947–49); *Variations on a Theme of Joseph Haydn* for Orch. (1949; Zürich, May 10, 1951); 3 *Songs*, after Trakl, for Low Female Voice, 4 Violins, 2 Cellos, and Double Bass (1951); Solo Flute Sonatina (1951); Solo Clarinet Sonatina (1951); Solo Bassoon Sonatina (1951); 5 *Bagatelles* for Flute, Clarinet, and Bassoon (1952); *Intrada* for Brass and Percussion (1954); *Ballade* for Orch. (1955); *Suite concise*, 7 pieces for Piano (1955); *Variations on 3 Folk Songs* for Small Orch. (1956); *Rondo ritmico* for Orch. (1957); Piano Concerto (1958; Venice, Sept. 24, 1959); *Fantasie* for Piano (1959); 5 *Austrian Miniatures* for Orch. (1959); 6 *épigrammes* for String Quartet (1962); Cello Sonata (1962); *Ode* for High Voice and Orch. (1961–62); *Kleine Kammerkonzert* for Flute, Viola, and Guitar (1964); Solo Oboe Sonatina (1964); Solo Horn Sonatina (1964); *Kammersymphonie* (1965–67; Vienna, June 4, 1968); *Epitaph* for String Orch. (1969); *Paralipomena dodekaphonika* (*Haydn Variations, Part II*) for Orch. (1969–70; Donawitz, Oct. 29, 1970); *Fischerhaus-Serenade* for 4 Woodwinds, 3 Brasses, and String Quartet (1971); *Passacaglia* for Orch. (2nd movement of an uncompleted Concerto for Orch., 1972; posthumous, London, July 10, 1974).

Appeldoorn, Dina, Dutch composer; b. Rotterdam, Feb. 26, 1884; d. The Hague, Dec. 4, 1938. She was the composer of several works in the Romantic style, including 2 symphonic poems, *Noordzee* and *Volkfeest*; also wrote chamber music and songs.

Appenzeller (Appencellers, Appenzelder, Appenzelders), Benedictus, Franco-Flemish composer of the 1st half of the 16th century. Possibly a pupil of Josquin, he served Mary of Hungary as court musician and master of choirboys at her chapel in Brussels (1537–c.1554) and probably accompanied her on her visit to Germany (1551). Appenzeller's works were formerly attributed to Benedictus Ducis. Among Appenzeller's extant compositions are a book of chansons (1542; 2 of the chansons from this collection had been publ. by Attaignant in 1529 without being ascribed to Appenzeller); a lament on the death of Josquin (1521), which uses half of the *Musae Jovis* text; and a double canon on *Sancta Maria* embroidered on a tablecloth for Mary of Hungary (1548). Pieces by him are included in the 2nd *Musyckboexken* of Susato; the *Hortus*

Musarum, part I (1552), publ. by Phalese, contains a transcription for 2 lutes of a piece by Appenzeller.
Bibl.: E. van der Straeten, *La Musique aux Pays-Bas* (Brussels, 1867–68; vols. 3, 7, and 8); D. Bartha, *Benedictus Ducis und Appenzeller* (Wolfenbüttel, 1930); G. Reese, *Music in the Renaissance* (N.Y., 1954; 2nd ed., rev., 1959).

Appia, Edmond, Italian-Swiss violinist and conductor; b. Turin, May 7, 1894; d. Geneva, Feb. 12, 1961. He studied violin with Henri Marteau at the Cons. of Geneva, in Paris with Lucien Capet, and at the Brussels Cons., obtaining the Premier Prix in 1920; toured Europe (1920–35); taught violin in Geneva and Lausanne. In 1935 he became a conductor of Radiodiffusion Suisse in Lausanne; in 1938 was appointed conductor of the Geneva Radio Orch. He also wrote articles on Swiss music for the *Musical Quarterly* and many European publications.

Applebaum, Edward, American composer; b. Los Angeles, Sept. 28, 1937. He studied piano as a youth; later studied with Henri Lazarof and Lukas Foss at the Univ. of Calif. at Los Angeles (Ph.D., 1966). In 1969 he was composer-in-residence of the Oakland Sym. Orch.; in 1971, became a prof. of theory and composition at the Univ. of Calif. at Santa Barbara. From 1985 to 1987 he was composer-in-residence of the Santa Barbara Sym. Orch., and then of the Music Academy of the West in Santa Barbara (1988). In 1989 he became prof. of composition and director of the new-music ensemble at Florida State Univ. in Tallahassee.
Works: Piano Sonata (1965); String Trio (1966); Concerto for Viola and Chamber Orch. (1967); *Montages* for Clarinet, Cello, and Piano (1968); *Shantih* for Cello and Piano (1969); Sym. No. 1 (1970); *Foci* for Viola and Piano (1971); *The Face in the Cameo* for Clarinet and Piano (1973); *The Frieze of Life*, 1-act chamber opera (1974); *To Remember*, trio for Clarinet, Cello, and Piano (1976); *The Garden* for Soprano, Chamber Ensemble, and Tape (1979); Sym. No. 2 (St. Louis, Oct. 6, 1983); *Prelude* for String Quartet (1984); *And with, and to* for Men's Chorus (1984); *The Princess in the Garden* for String Orch. (1985); *Dreams and Voyage*, piano concerto (1986); *Night Waltz*, guitar concerto (1987); *The Waltz in 2* for Narrator and Orch. (1988); *Whispers of Yesterday* for Woodwind Quintet (1988).

Applebaum, Louis, Canadian composer; b. Toronto, April 3, 1918. He studied with Healy Willan, Leo Smith, and Sir Ernest MacMillan at the Toronto Cons., but did not graduate; then studied with Bernard Wagenaar and Roy Harris in N.Y. (1940–41). He returned to Canada in 1941 and was a member of the board of directors of the Composers, Authors and Publishers Assoc. of Canada (1956–68) and then its music executive (1968–72); from 1970 to 1979 he was executive director of the Ontario Arts Council.
Works: Musical comedy, *Ride a Pink Horse* (1960); 3 ballets: *Dark of the Moon* (1953; rev. as *Barbara Allen*, 1960; concert suite, 1965); *Legend of the North* (1957); *Homage* (1969); *East by North* for Orch. (1947); *Variations on a Theme from a Film Score* for Oboe, Piano, and String Trio (1948; rev. 1953); *Christmas Overture* (1951); *Suite of Miniature Dances* for Orch. (1958; arranged for Band, 1964); 3 *Greek Dances* for Orch. (1958); *Moments from "Romeo and Juliet"* for Wind Quintet, Cello, Harp, and Percussion (1961); *Action Stations* for Orch. (1962); *Concertante* for Small Orch. (1967); *Fanfare and Anthem* for Orch. (1969); incidental music for plays and more than 100 films; piano pieces; songs.

Appledorn, Mary Jeanne van. See **van Appledorn, Mary Jeanne.**

Appleton, Jon (Howard), American composer; b. Los Angeles, Jan. 4, 1939. He studied at Reed College (B.A., 1961), with Imbrie in Berkeley, Calif. (1961–62), with Homer Keller at the Univ. of Oregon (M.A., 1965), and with Ussachevsky, Davidovsky, and William Mitchell at the Columbia-Princeton Center for Electronic Music (1965–66); held Guggenheim and Fulbright fellowships (1970). He taught at Oakland Univ. in

Rochester, Mich. (1966–67) and at Dartmouth College, where he founded the Bregman Electronic Music Center; also helped to develop the Dartmouth Digital Synthesizer and the Synclavier, a polyphonic digital synthesizer. He wrote many articles on electronic music, and with Perera ed. *The Development and Practice of Electronic Music* (1975).

WORKS: ORCH.: *After "Nude Descending a Staircase"* (1965). **CHAMBER:** *2 Movements* for Woodwind Quintet (1963); *6 Movements* for Woodwind Quintet (1964); *4 Explorations* for Violin and Piano (1964); *4 Inventions* for 2 Flutes (1965); *Winesburg, Ohio* for Flute, Clarinet, Violin, Cello, and Piano (1972); String Quartet (1976). **VOCAL:** *This Is America* for Chorus (1976); *Sonaria* for 4 Voices and Live Electronics (1978); *The Lament of Kamuela* for 4 Voices, Live Electronics, Rock Band, String Quartet, Shamisen, Slides, Film, and Video (1983); also electronic scores.

Aprile, Giuseppe, Italian castrato soprano; b. Martina Franca, Apulia, Oct. 28, 1731; d. there, Jan. 11, 1813. He studied voice with his father, and since he showed signs of excellence, his father had him evirated at the age of 11. He then studied singing in Naples and appeared as a soprano at the Naples Royal Chapel in 1751. He made his professional debut as a singer at the Teatro San Carlo in Naples in 1753; he subsequently sang at the Court of Württemberg in Stuttgart (1756), and remained in that service for 13 years. He later was active as a teacher in Naples; among his pupils was Cimarosa. Aprile's vocal treatise *The Modern Italian Method of Singing, with 36 Solfeggi* was publ. by Broderip in London in 1791 and was reprinted in several eds. and tr. into several languages.

Apthorp, William Foster, American music critic; b. Boston, Mass., Oct. 24, 1848; d. Vevey, Switzerland, Feb. 19, 1913. A graduate of Harvard Univ. (1869), he studied music with Paine. He taught music at the New England Cons. and lectured on music history at Boston Univ. He wrote music criticism for the *Atlantic Monthly* (1872–77); was music and drama critic on the *Boston Evening Transcript* (1881–1903). In his criticisms Apthorp violently opposed new Russian, French, and German music (his intemperate attacks on Tchaikovsky elicited protests from his readers). Apthorp was also the annotator of the Boston Sym. programs (1892–1901). He publ. several books: *Musicians and Music Lovers* (N.Y., 1894); *By the Way,* a collection of short essays in 2 vols.: I, *About Music,* and II, *About Musicians* (Boston, 1898); *The Opera, Past and Present* (N.Y., 1901). He was co-ed. of *Scribner's Cyclopedia of Music and Musicians* (N.Y., 1888–90).

Ara, Ugo, Italian violinist and member of the Flonzaley Quartet; b. Venice, July 19, 1876; d. Lausanne, Switzerland, Dec. 10, 1936. He studied violin with Tirindelli in Venice; at the age of 13 played in theater orchs. In 1894 he went to Liège, where he studied with César Thomson; he then took lessons in composition with R. Fuchs at the Vienna Cons. When the Flonzaley Quartet was established, he joined it as a viola player (1903–17); later returned to Italy.

Aragall (y Garriga), Giacomo (Jaime), Spanish tenor; b. Barcelona, June 6, 1939. He won the Busseto singing competition in 1963; then sang the role of Gastone in Verdi's *Gerusalemme* in Venice; during the 1963–64 season he appeared at La Scala in Milan; in 1965 sang at the Holland Festival and in Edinburgh. In 1966 he made his London debut at Covent Garden as the Duke of Mantua; in the 1982–83 season he attracted favorable publicity when he replaced Luciano Pavarotti as Cavaradossi on short notice. He made his Metropolitan Opera debut in N.Y. in 1968 as the Duke in *Rigoletto;* from 1973 to 1977 he sang opera in Chicago and San Francisco.

Araiza, Francisco, Mexican tenor; b. Mexico City, Oct. 4, 1950. He studied at the Univ. of Mexico City, where he sang in the univ. choir; made his concert debut in Mexico City in 1969, and subsequently sang in opera there; then went to Europe, where he joined the Karlsruhe Opera in 1974; also

took lessons in Munich with Richard Holm and Erik Werba. He subsequently made appearances with opera houses in Zürich, Düsseldorf, Stuttgart, and Munich; also sang at the Bayreuth Festival. He received praise for his performances in Mozart's operas.

Araja, Francesco, Italian composer; b. Naples, June 25, 1709; d. Bologna, 1770. He produced his 1st opera, *Lo matremmonejo pe' mennetta,* in the Neapolitan dialect (Naples, 1729); his subsequent operas were *Berenice* (Florence, 1730); *La forza dell'amore e dell'odio* (Milan, 1734); *Lucio Vero* (Venice, Jan. 4, 1735). In 1735 he was engaged as music director and court composer in St. Petersburg. There he wrote annual pieces for court occasions, beginning with the cantata *La gara dell'amore e del zelo* (April 28, 1736). Among his operas given at the Russian court were *La Semiramide riconosciuta* (Feb. 9, 1737); *Artaserse* (1738); *Seleuco* (1744); *Scipione* (1745); *Mitridate* (1747); *L'asilo della pace* (1748); *Bellerofonte* (1750); *Eudossa incoronata* (1751). He wrote 17 operas; *La clemenza di Tito,* attributed to him by some, was the work of Hasse. On Feb. 27, 1755, Araja presented in St. Petersburg the 1st opera ever composed to a libretto in the Russian language, on the story of Cephalus and Procris, written by the famous Russian dramatist Sumarokov. Araja was in Italy from 1740 to 1742, and again from 1759 to 1762; in 1762 he revisited Russia briefly at the summons of Peter III, his great admirer, returning to Italy after the Czar's death. Nothing is known of Araja's last years.

BIBL.: R.A. Mooser, *Annales de la musique et des musiciens en Russie au XVIIIᵉ siècle* (vol. I, Geneva, 1948).

Arakishvili, Dmitri, Russian composer; b. Vladikavkaz, Feb. 23, 1873; d. Tbilisi, Aug. 13, 1953. He studied composition at the Moscow Phil. Inst. with Ilyinsky and also took private lessons with Gretchaninov. At the same time he studied archaeology and ethnic sciences; in 1901 he became a member of the Musical Ethnographic Commission at the Univ. of Moscow. In 1906 he took part in the organization of the Moscow People's Cons., which offered free music lessons to impecunious students. He was ed. of the Moscow publication *Music and Life* (1908–12). In 1918 he moved to Tiflis, where he was active as a teacher and conductor. He composed one of the earliest national Georgian operas, *The Legend of Shota Rustaveli* (Tiflis, Feb. 5, 1919); a comic opera, *Dinara* (1926); 3 syms. (1934, 1942, 1951); *Hymn of the New East* for Orch. (1933); and film music. But his best compositions are some 80 art songs in a lyrico-dramatic manner reflecting the Georgian modalities.

Arangi-Lombardi, Giannina, Italian soprano; b. Marigliano, near Naples, June 20, 1891; d. Milan, July 9, 1951. She studied at the Naples Cons.; made her debut as a mezzo-soprano in 1920 at the Teatro Costanzi in Rome; sang soprano roles from 1923; appeared at La Scala in Milan (1924–30). In 1928 she accompanied Melba on an Australian tour; also sang in South America. After retiring from the stage she taught voice at the Milan Cons. (1937–47) and later at Ankara, Turkey. She was at her best in the lyrico-dramatic roles of the Italian repertoire.

d'Arányi, Jelly (in full, **Jelly Eva Arányi de Hunyadvar**), Hungarian violinist, grandniece of **Joachim** and sister of **Adila Fachiri;** b. Budapest, May 30, 1893; d. Florence, March 30, 1966. She studied violin with Hubay in Budapest; after some concerts in Europe, she went to America and made her debut in a solo recital in N.Y. on Nov. 26, 1927; made her 2nd American tour in 1932. She frequently appeared in joint recitals with Myra Hess. A pioneer in modern music, she gave 1st performances of many new works. Béla Bartók's 1st Violin Sonata, Ravel's *Tzigane,* and the *Concerto accademico* for Violin and Orch. by Vaughan Williams are dedicated to her. She attracted considerable attention in 1937 when she proclaimed that Schumann's spirit appeared to her during a séance and revealed the secret of his unpubl. Violin Concerto; but Schumann's ghost spoke ungrammatical German, which aroused suspicion concerning the authenticity of the phenomenon; besides, it had long been known that the MS of the concerto was preserved at the Berlin State Library; the 1st performance of the piece was eventually given in Germany by another violinist. D'Arányi was given a chance, however, to perform it with the BBC Sym. Orch. in London on Feb. 16, 1938.

BIBL.: J. Macleod, *The Sisters d'A.* (London, 1969).

Arapov, Boris (Alexandrovich), eminent Russian composer and pedagogue; b. St. Petersburg, Sept. 12, 1905. He was a scion of an intellectual family; his grandfather was a lawyer; his father was a naturalist. He spent his childhood in Poltava, where he received his early musical training; in 1921 the family returned to St. Petersburg (now renamed Petrograd); he studied composition with Shcherbachev at the Cons. there, graduating in 1930; was then appointed to its faculty as an instructor (1930) and later prof. (1940). Among his pupils were many Soviet composers of stature, including Dmitri Tolstoy, Falik, Uspensky, Banshchikov, Knaifel, and Sergei Slonimsky. The years 1941–44 Arapov spent in Tashkent, in Uzbekistan, where the entire faculty of the Leningrad Cons. was evacuated during the siege of Leningrad. There he studied indigenous folklore, and wrote an Uzbeki opera, *Khodja Nasreddin.* After the siege was lifted, Arapov returned to Leningrad, resumed his pedagogical duties, and continued to compose. In 1955–56 he was in China, where he wrote several works on Chinese themes. In 1959 he visited Korea, and composed a sym. using the pentatonic Korean modes. During the years 1950–73 he also traveled in Europe. Arapov's compositions represent to perfection the evolutionary character of Soviet music, taking their source in the Russian traditions of the previous centuries, making ample use of ethnic materials of the constituent regions of the immense territory of the U.S.S.R., and integrating the native homophonic melorhythms in an increasingly complex tapestry of colorful fabrics, richly ornamented with occasional application of such modern devices as dodecaphonic melodic structures. But Arapov was also able to produce a virtuoso display of instrumental techniques for piano and other instruments.

WORKS: STAGE: OPERAS: *Khodja Nasreddin,* on Uzbeki motifs (Tashkent, 1944); *Frigate Victory,* after Pushkin's novella *The Moor of Peter the Great* (radio premiere, Leningrad, Oct. 12, 1959); *Rain,* after Somerset Maugham's short story (Leningrad, April 25, 1968). **BALLET:** *The Picture of Dorian Gray* (Leningrad, April 20, 1973). **ORCH.:** *Fugato* (Leningrad, Feb. 2, 1928); *Tadzhikistan Suite* (Leningrad, Feb. 13, 1939); Sym. No. 1 (1947; unperf.); *Russian Suite* (Leningrad, March 11, 1950); Sym. No. 2 (Leningrad, Oct. 2, 1959); Sym. No. 3 (Leningrad, March 28, 1963); Sym. No. 4 for Mezzo-soprano, Baritone, Narrator, 2 Mixed Choirs, and Orch. (Leningrad, July 29, 1977); Violin Concerto (Leningrad, April 18, 1965); Concerto for Orch. (Leningrad, Dec. 29, 1969); Concerto for Violin, Piano, Percussion, and Chamber Orch., in memory of Stravinsky (Copenhagen, Feb. 21, 1974); Sym. No. 5 (1981; Leningrad, Nov. 1, 1982); Sym. No. 6 for Soloists, Chorus, and Orch. (1983; Leningrad, Sept. 14, 1985). **VOCAL:** Vocal symphonic cycle to Pushkin's texts (Leningrad, Dec. 27, 1940); *Dzhelal Eddin,* oratorio (Tashkent, Dec. 26, 1944); *Songs of Protest,* suite for Bass Singer and Jazz Orch. (radio premiere, Feb. 12, 1940); *4 Songs* to texts by Alexander Blok (1948); *Monologue* for Voice, Piano, Trumpet, and Percussion (1969); *Sonnets of Petrarca,* song cycle for Mezzo-soprano and Piano (1975); *4 Seasons,* song cycle for Soprano, Tenor, and 9 Instruments, to text from Japanese haiku (1977); *2 Monologues* for Voice and Piano, to texts by Boris Pasternak (1979); Vocal Cycle for Mezzo-soprano and Instruments, after Russian poets (1988). **CHAMBER:** Sonata for Solo Violin (1930); Quintet for Oboe, Horn, Harp, Viola, and Cello (1979); Sonata for Horn and Piano (1981); Sonata for Cello and Piano (1985); *Decimet* for 10 Instruments (1986). **PIANO:** *Variations* (1929); *Humoresque* (1938); 6 Pieces on Chinese themes (1955); *Étude-Scherzo* (1969); 2 piano sonatas (1971, 1978); 3 Pieces (1976). He also composed film scores.

BIBL.: L. Danke, *B. A.* (Leningrad, 1980).

Arauxo (or **Arauxo**), **(Francisco).** See **Correa de Araujo, (Francisco).**

Arban, (Joseph) Jean-Baptiste (Laurent), renowned French cornet player and pedagogue; b. Lyons, Feb. 28, 1825; d. Paris, April 9, 1889. He studied trumpet at the Paris Cons. with Dauverné (1841–45); then was engaged as a leader of Parisian salon orchs. In 1857 he became a prof. of saxhorn at the École Militaire in Paris; in 1869 he joined the faculty of the Paris Cons. as a teacher of cornet; then traveled to Russia as a conductor; returning to Paris in 1880, he resumed his post as a teacher. Arban is acknowledged as the founder of the modern school of trumpet playing. He publ. the standard manual *Grande méthode complète pour cornet à pistons et de saxhorn* (Paris, 1864); also made arrangements for cornet.

BIBL.: J.-P. Mathez, *J.J.-B.L. A. (1825–1889)* (Moudon, 1977).

Arbeau, Thoinot (anagram of real name, **Jehan Tabourot**), French writer; b. Dijon, March 17, 1520; d. Langres, July 23, 1595. He owes his fame to his didactic treatise in dialogue form, *Orchésographie, et traité en forme de dialogue par lequel toutes personnes peuvent facilement apprendre et pratiquer l'honnête exercice des danses* (Langres, 1588; 2nd ed., 1589), which contains not only instructions for dancing (indicating dance steps by a simple system of initial letters), but also valuable observations on the dance music of his time. It was publ. in Eng. tr. by C.W. Beaumont (London, 1925) and M. Evans (N.Y., 1948).

Arbós, Enrique Fernández, Spanish violinist and conductor; b. Madrid, Dec. 24, 1863; d. San Sebastián, June 2, 1939. He studied violin with Monasterio in Madrid, with Vieuxtemps in Brussels, and with Joachim in Berlin. After successful tours in Europe, he returned to Spain in 1888; taught violin at the Madrid Cons. In 1889 he was concertmaster of the Glasgow Sym. Orch.; from 1894 to 1916 he held the post of honorary prof. at the Royal College of Music in London. He was appointed conductor of the new Madrid Sym. Orch. in 1904; conducted in the U.S. (1928–31), then in Europe. At the outbreak of the Spanish Civil War in 1936 he retired to San Sebastián. Arbós was the author of a comic opera, *El centro de la tierra* (Madrid, Dec. 22, 1895). He was a brilliant orchestrator; his arrangement of the music from *Iberia* by Albéniz is very popular.

BIBL.: V. Espinós Moltó, *El Maestro A.* (Madrid, 1942).

Arbuckle, Matthew, American cornet player and bandmaster; b. 1828; d. N.Y., May 23, 1883. He publ. a manual, *Complete Cornet Method.*

Arbuthnot, John, Scottish physician and musical amateur; b. Arbuthnot, Scotland, 1667; d. London, Feb. 27, 1735. He was one of the founders of the Scriblerus Club in London (1714), and was friendly with Handel during the composer's difficulties with his opera company. Arbuthnot's *Miscellaneous Works* throws sharp sidelights on various persons of interest at the time. He wrote several anthems, glees, etc.

Arcadelt, Jacob (or **Jachet Arkadelt, Archadet, Arcadet, Harcadelt**), great Flemish composer; b. probably in Liège, c.1505; d. Paris, Oct. 14, 1568. He was "magister puerorum" to the Papal Chapel (1539), and choirmaster (1540). In 1544 he held the office of "camerlingo." He went to France in 1546; returned to Rome in May 1547. In 1555 he again went to France, this time with the Duc de Guise. Arcadelt is mentioned in Paris as "Regis musicus" in 1557. In the domain of secular music, his Roman period was, in the main, devoted to the madrigal; his Paris period, to the French chanson. He wrote 24 motets, 126 French chansons, and over 200 madrigals. Of his extant works, the most important are 6 books of 5-part madrigals (Venice, 1538–56; his finest and most characteristic compositions) and 3 books of masses in 3–7 parts (Paris, 1557).

BIBL.: W. Klefisch, *A. als Madrigalist* (Cologne, 1938); F. Lesure, "Notes et Documents," *Revue de Musicologie* (Dec. 1961).

d'Archambeau, Iwan, Belgian cellist and member of the Flonzaley Quartet; b. Hervé, Sept. 28, 1879; d. Villefranche-sur-Mer, France, Dec. 29, 1955. He studied music at home; played in a family quartet with his father and 2 brothers. He then studied cello with A. Massau in Verviers and with Hugo Becker in Frankfurt. In 1903 he became a member of the Flonzaley Quartet, until it disbanded in 1929; in 1935 he joined the Stradivarius Quartet in N.Y. From 1939 to 1950 he lived in Cambridge, Mass.; then returned to Belgium.

Archangelsky, Alexander, Russian choral conductor; b. near Penza, Oct. 23, 1846; d. Prague, Nov. 16, 1924. He studied singing and music theory at the Court Chapel in St. Petersburg. In 1880 he organized a chorus there; toured Russia with it in 1899–1900, presenting 110 concerts; also gave concerts in western Europe (1907 and 1912). He was the 1st choir leader in Russia to include women's voices in performances of sacred works. He supported (with Gretchaninov) the reform movement in Russian church music; wrote choral pieces for his organization and made transcriptions of Russian church hymns. In 1923 he went to Prague as conductor of a students' choir, and died there the following year.

Archer, Frederick, English-American organist, conductor, and composer; b. Oxford, June 16, 1838; d. Pittsburgh, Oct. 22, 1901. He studied organ in Leipzig, and in 1873 was appointed organist of Alexandra Palace in London; then became conductor of a Glasgow choir (1878–80). In 1881 he came to America; was active as a church organist in Brooklyn and, from 1895, at Carnegie Inst. in Pittsburgh. He was the 1st conductor of the Pittsburgh Sym. Orch., from Feb. 27, 1896, until 1898, when he was succeeded by Victor Herbert. A prolific composer, he publ. a cantata, *King Witlaf's Drinking-horn;* also organ and piano pieces and songs. The bulk of his music remains in MS. He was the author of the manuals *The Organ* (1875) and *A Complete Method for the American Reed Organ* (1899), and founder and ed. of the magazine *Keynote* (1883).

Archer, Violet, prolific Canadian pianist and composer; b. Montreal, April 24, 1913. She studied composition with Champagne, and piano at the McGill Cons. in Montreal (1932–36); took private lessons with Bartók in N.Y. (1942) and attended courses in composition with Hindemith at Yale Univ. (1948–49). She taught at McGill (1944–47), North Texas State College (1950–53), and the Univ. of Oklahoma (1953–61), and served (1962–78) as chairman of the composition dept. at the Univ. of Alberta, Edmonton. Her music is structurally strong, polyphonically disciplined, and generally kept within organized tonality, with occasional dodecaphonic episodes.
WORKS: OPERAS: *Sganarelle* (Edmonton, Feb. 5, 1974); *The Meal* (1983). ORCH.: Timpani Concerto (1939); *Scherzo Sinfonico* (1940); *Poem* (1940); *Fantasia concertante* for Flute, Oboe, Clarinet, and Strings (1941); *Britannia, a Joyful Overture* (1941); Fantasy for Clarinet and Strings (1942); Clarinet Concertino (1946); Sym. (1946); *Fantasy on a Ground* (1946); *Fanfare and Passacaglia* (1949); Piano Concerto (1956); Divertimento (1957); Violin Concerto (1959); *3 Sketches* (1961); *Prelude-Incantation* (1964); *Sinfonietta* (1968); *Sinfonia* (1969; Edmonton, Oct. 24, 1970); *Little Suite* for Strings (1970); Clarinet Concerto (1971); *Divertimento* for Piano and Strings (1985); *Evocations* for 2 Pianos and Orch. (1987). VOCAL: *Choruses from "The Bacchae"* for Chorus and Orch. (1938); *Leaves of Grass,* after Whitman, for Chorus and Orch. (1940); *Lamentations of Jeremy* for Chorus and Orch. (1947); *The Bell,* cantata (1949); *Apocalypse* for Soprano, Chorus, Brass, and Timpani (1958); *Cantata Sacra* for 5 Soloists and Small Orch. (1966); songs, choruses, anthems. CHAMBER: *6 Pieces* for Piano and Timpani (1939); 2 string quartets (1940; 1948–49); Theme and Variations for String Quartet (1942); Sonata for Flute, Clarinet, and Piano (1944); Quartet for Wind Instruments (1945); Divertimento No. 1 for Oboe, Clarinet, and Bassoon (1949); *Fugue Fantasy* for String Quartet (1949); 2 string trios

(1953, 1961); 2 piano trios (1954, 1957); *Prelude and Allegro* for Violin and Piano (1954); Cello Sonata (1956); Violin Sonata (1956); Divertimento No. 2 for Oboe, Violin, and Cello (1957); Divertimento for Brass Quintet (1963); Horn Sonata (1965); Clarinet Sonata (1970); Suite for 4 Violins (1971); Fantasy for Violin and Piano (1971); Saxophone Sonata (1972); Oboe Sonata (1973); Sonata for Solo Cello (1980); *Celebration,* fanfare for Brass Quintet (1983); *If the Stars Are Burning* for Clarinet, Mezzo-soprano, and Piano (1987). PIANO: 3 sonatinas (1945, 1946, 1973); Sonata (1945); *3 Sketches* for 2 Pianos (1947); 6 preludes (1947); Fantasy (1947); Suite (1947); *11 Short Pieces* (1960); Theme and Variations (1963); *Improvisations* (1968); *Lydian Mood* (1971).

Ardévol, José, Cuban composer; b. Barcelona, March 13, 1911; d. Havana, Jan. 7, 1981. He studied with his father, conductor of an orch. in Barcelona; at the age of 19 he went to Havana, where he organized a chamber group; he also ed. the magazine *La Música.* He became active in musical politics after the revolution of 1959, and served in various capacities in Cuba and elsewhere; was appointed national director for music, a post which he held until 1965. Several of his works have distinct revolutionary connotations.
WORKS: *Cantos de la revolución* (1962); *Por Viet-Nam,* to words by Fidel Castro (1966); *Cantata Ché comandante* (glorifying the revolutionary role of Ché Guevara, 1968); *Cantata Lenin* (1970); Concerto for 3 Pianos and Orch. (1938); 3 syms. (1943, 1945, 1946); several string quartets; numerous piano pieces and songs; *Música para pequeña orquesta* (Washington, D.C., April 19, 1958); *Triptico de Santiago* for Orch. (Cologne, May 25, 1953).

Arditi, Luigi, Italian composer and conductor; b. Crescentino, Piedmont, July 16, 1822; d. Hove, near Brighton, England, May 1, 1903. He studied violin, piano, and composition at the Milan Cons., where he also produced his 1st opera, *I Briganti* (1841). He then embarked on a career as an operatic conductor. From 1846 he traveled in Cuba, where he produced his opera *Il Corsaro* (Havana, 1846); also visited N.Y. and Philadelphia. In N.Y. he produced his opera *La Spia* (March 24, 1856). He finally settled in London (1858) as a conductor and vocal teacher, while making annual tours with the Italian Opera in Germany and Austria. He conducted in St. Petersburg in 1871 and 1873. His operas and other works were never revived, but he created a perennial success with his vocal waltz *Il bacio.* He wrote his autobiography, *My Reminiscences* (N.Y., 1896).

Arel, Bülent, Turkish-born American composer; b. Constantinople, April 23, 1918; d. Stony Brook, N.Y., Nov. 24, 1990. He studied composition with Necil Kâzim Akses, piano with Ferhunde Erkin, conducting with Ernst Praetorius, and 20th-century music with Edward Zuckmayer at the Ankara State Cons. (1940–47); then took courses in sound engineering in Paris (1951). He taught in Ankara at the State Cons. and at the Teachers College (1947–59); was also a sound engineer and director of Western music programming at the Ankara Radio (1951–59). In 1959 he went to the U.S. on a Rockefeller research grant and worked at the Columbia-Princeton Electronic Music Center until 1963; was also an instructor in electronic music at Yale Univ. (1961–62). After again working at the Ankara Radio (1963–65), he returned to teach at Yale Univ. (1965–70) and Columbia Univ. (1970–71). He was prof. of music and director of the electronic music studio at the State Univ. of N.Y. at Stony Brook (from 1971). In 1973 he became a naturalized U.S. citizen. In his early works he explored Turkish folk songs; then wrote pieces alternatively in a neo-Classical and impressionistic manner while experimenting with serial techniques, eventually turning to electronic composition.
WORKS: Piano Concerto (1946); *Suite intime* for Orch. (1949); *Masques* for Winds and Strings (1949); 2 syms. (1951, 1952); *6 Bagatelles* for Strings (1958); *Short Piece* for Orch. (1967); electronic pieces: *Short Study* (1960); *Fragment* (1960);

Electronic Music No. 1 (1960); *Stereo Electronic Music I* (1960); *Impressions of Wall Street* (1961); *Music for a Sacred Service* (1961); *Capriccio for T.V.* (1969); *Stereo Electronic Music No. 2* (1970); dance scores: *Mimiana I* (1968), *II* (1969), and *III* (1973).

Arens, Franz Xavier, German-American composer; b. Neef (Rhenish Prussia), Oct. 28, 1856; d. Los Angeles, Jan. 28, 1932. His family came to the U.S. and settled in Milwaukee when he was very young; he studied with his father and later in Germany with Rheinberger. Upon his return to America, he was active as a conductor of various choral and instrumental groups. He led the Gesangverein in Cleveland (1885–88); from 1890 to 1892 he was again in Europe; he was the 1st to present complete programs of orch. works by American composers in Germany. He was president of the Indianapolis College of Music (1892–96), and later settled in N.Y. as a vocal teacher. In 1900 he established a series of People's Sym. Concerts, with low admission prices (from 5 to 50 cents). He wrote orch. music, a String Quartet, and numerous songs.

Arensky, Anton (Stepanovich), Russian composer; b. Novgorod, July 12, 1861; d. Terijoki, Finland, Feb. 25, 1906. He studied at the St. Petersburg Cons. with Johanssen and Rimsky-Korsakov (1879–82); then taught harmony at the Moscow Cons. (1882–94). Returning to St. Petersburg, he conducted the choir of the Imperial Chapel (1895–1901); a victim of tuberculosis, he spent his last years in a sanatorium in Finland. In his music he followed Tchaikovsky's lyric style. He composed 3 operas: *A Dream on the Volga* (Moscow, Jan. 2, 1891); *Raphael* (Moscow, May 18, 1894); *Nal and Damayanti* (Moscow, Jan. 22, 1904); 2 syms. (Moscow, Nov. 24, 1883, and Dec. 21, 1889). He was more successful in his works for smaller forms; his *Variations* for String Orch. on Tchaikovsky's song *The Christ Child Had a Garden* (orig. the *Variations* formed the slow movement of Arensky's Quartet, op. 35, in A minor for Violin, Viola, and 2 Cellos) became a standard work. His Piano Trio also retains its popularity. His 4 suites for 2 Pianos, expertly written, are often heard; he also arranged these suites for orch. Some of his songs are included in vocal anthologies. Other works are: music to Pushkin's poem *The Fountain of Bakhtchissaray;* ballet, *Egyptian Nights* (St. Petersburg, 1900); *The Diver,* ballad for Voices and Orch.; *Coronation Cantata; Marche solennelle* for Orch.; *Intermezzo* for String Orch.; Piano Concerto; Violin Concerto in A minor; a Fantasy on epic Russian songs, for Piano and Orch.; Piano Quintet in D; String Quartet in G, op. 11; pieces for cello; works for violin; many pieces for piano solo. He publ. *Manual of Harmony* (tr. into German) and *Handbook of Musical Forms.*
Bibl.: G. Tzypin, *A.S. A.* (Moscow, 1966).

Aretz (de Ramón y Rivera), Isabel, Argentine-born Venezuelan folklorist and composer; b. Buenos Aires, April 13, 1909. She studied piano and composition at the National Cons. of Music in Buenos Aires; subsequently dedicated herself to research in Argentine folklore at the Museo de Ciencias Naturales de Buenos Aires (1938–44); she received her Ph.D. in musicology in 1967 at the Argentine Catholic Univ. in Buenos Aires with the dissertation *Música tradicional argentina: La Rioja.* She served as an associate member of the Instituto Argentino de Musicología (1938–50); then was the 1st prof. of ethnomusicology at the Escuela Nacional de Danzas de Argentina (1950–52). In 1953 she settled in Caracas, Venezuela, as a research fellow in ethnomusicology and folklore at the Instituto Nacional de Folklore de Venezuela; in 1965 she became director of the folklore dept. of the Instituto Nacional de Cultura y Bellas Artes; in 1970 she became director of the Instituto Interamericano de Etnomusicología y Folklore. As a composer, her music reflects her interest in folk music and contemporary European trends.
Writings: *Música tradicional argentina: Tucumán, historia y folklore* (Buenos Aires, 1946); *El folklore musical argentino* (Buenos Aires, 1953); *Manual de folklore venezolano* (Caracas, 1957; 3rd ed., 1972); *Cantos navideños en el folklore venezolano* (Caracas, 1962); *Instrumentos musicales de Venezuela* (Cumaná, 1967); *La artesania en Venezuela* (Caracas, 1967); *El traje en Venezuela* (Caracas, 1972); *El tamunangue* (Barquisimeto, 1976).

d'Arezzo, Guido. See Guido d'Arezzo.

Argenta (Maza), Ataulfo, Spanish conductor; b. Castro Urdiales, Santander, Nov. 19, 1913; d. Los Molinos, near Madrid, Jan. 21, 1958. He studied at the Madrid Cons.; then went to Germany, where he took lessons in conducting with Carl Schuricht. Returning to Spain in 1939, he conducted various small groups; in 1945 he was appointed director of the National Orch. in Madrid.
Bibl.: A. Fernandez-Cid, *A. A.* (Madrid, 1958).

Argento, Dominick, greatly talented American composer excelling especially in opera; b. York, Pa., Oct. 27, 1927. He played the piano, but had no formal instruction in music theory; after high school he enlisted in the U.S. Army as a cryptographer (1945–47). In 1947 he enrolled at the Peabody Cons. of Music in Baltimore, where he took courses with Nicolas Nabokov and Hugo Weisgall, graduating in 1951 with a B.A. degree. He then went to Italy on a Fulbright fellowship and studied piano with Pietro Scarpini and composition with Luigi Dallapiccola at the Conservatorio Cherubini in Florence. Upon returning to the U.S., he attended classes of Henry Cowell in composition at the Peabody Cons. in Baltimore; eager to pursue his studies further, he entered the Eastman School of Music in Rochester, N.Y., where his teachers were Howard Hanson and Bernard Rogers; in 1957 he received his doctorate in music there. In 1957 he was awarded a Guggenheim fellowship, which enabled him to go once more to Florence and work on his opera *Colonel Jonathan the Saint;* in 1964 he obtained his 2nd Guggenheim fellowship. In 1958 he was appointed to the music faculty of the Univ. of Minnesota in Minneapolis; in 1964 he became a founder of the Center Opera in Minnesota, later renamed the Minnesota Opera. The connection gave Argento an opportunity to present his operas under his own supervision. In 1980 he was elected a member of the American Academy and Inst. of Arts and Letters. In the pantheon of American composers Argento occupies a distinct individual category, outside any certifiable modernistic trend or technical idiom. He writes melodious music in a harmonious treatment, so deliberate in intent that even his apologists profess embarrassment at its unimpeded flow; there is also a perceptible ancestral strain in the bel canto style of his Italianate opera scores; most important, audiences, and an increasing number of sophisticated critics, profess their admiration for his unusual songfulness. Yet an analysis of Argento's productions reveals the presence of acerb harmonies and artfully acidulated melismas.
Works: operas: *Sicilian Limes* (N.Y., Oct. 1, 1954); *The Boor,* after Chekhov's short comedy (Rochester, May 6, 1957); *Colonel Jonathan the Saint* (1958–61; Denver, Dec. 31, 1971); *Christopher Sly,* a scene from Shakespeare's play *The Taming of the Shrew* (Minneapolis, May 31, 1963); *The Masque of Angels* (Minneapolis, Jan. 9, 1964); *Shoemaker's Holiday* (Minneapolis, June 1, 1967); *Postcard from Morocco* (Minneapolis, Oct. 14, 1971); *The Voyage of Edgar Allan Poe* (St. Paul, April 24, 1976; achieved great critical acclaim); *Miss Havisham's Fire* (1978), opera buffa (St. Paul, April 12, 1985); *The Aspern Papers* (Dallas, Nov. 19, 1988). **other vocal:** Oratorio, *Jonah and the Whale* (Minneapolis, March 9, 1974); *Song about Spring,* song cycle for Soprano and Orch. (1950; rev. in 1954 and 1960); *Ode to the West Wind,* concerto for Soprano and Orch. (1956); *6 Elizabethan Songs* for Voice and Piano (1962); *The Revelation of St. John the Divine,* rhapsody for Tenor, Men's Chorus, Brass, and Percussion (1966); *A Nation of Cowslips* for Chorus (1968); *Letters from Composers,* song cycle for Tenor and Guitar (1968); *Tria carmina paschalia,* 3 songs to Latin verses for Women's Voices, Harp, and Guitar (1970); *To Be Sung upon the Water* for Voice, Clarinet, and Piano (1973); *A Water Bird Talk,* monodrama (1974); *From the Diary of Virginia Woolf* for Voice and Piano

(1974; awarded the Pulitzer Prize); *In Praise of Music*, 7 songs for Orch. (1977). **BALLET:** *Resurrection of Don Juan* (Rochester, May 5, 1956). **ORCH.:** *A Ring of Time*, preludes and pageants for Orch. and Bells (Minneapolis, Oct. 5, 1972); *Le Tombeau d'Edgar Poe* (1985; Baltimore, Feb. 27, 1986); *Capriccio: Rossini in Paris* for Clarinet and Orch. (St. Louis, May 16, 1986). **CHAMBER:** *Divertimento* for Piano and Strings (Rochester, July 2, 1958); String Quartet (1956); *Royal Invitation (or Homage to the Queen of Tonga)* for Chamber Orch. (St. Paul, March 22, 1964); *Variations (The Mask of Night)* for Orch. with Soprano Solo in the final variations (Minneapolis, Jan. 26, 1966); *Bravo Mozart!*, concerto for Oboe, Violin, Horn, and Orch. (1969).
BIBL.: *Current Biography* (May 1977).

Argerich, Martha, Argentine pianist; b. Buenos Aires, June 5, 1941. She studied with Gulda, Magaloff, and Madeleine Lipatti; made her debut in Buenos Aires in 1949. After taking part in several piano competitions, she became successful as a soloist, both in Europe and America. She was married for some years to the Swiss conductor **Charles Dutoit.**

Aribon (Aribo Scholasticus, Aribon de Liège, Aribon de Freising, Aribon d'Orléans), medieval scholar; b. probably in Liège, c.1000; d. Orléans, c.1078. In 1024 he was chancellor to the Bishop of Liège; after a short period of service he went to Italy, where he acquired a knowledge of the methods of Guido d'Arezzo. From 1060 to 1070 he was again in Liège as preceptor at the Cathedral school; then went to Orléans. Aribon was the author of the important treatise *De musica*, written in Liège c.1065. It is reproduced in Gerbert's *Scriptores* (vol. II, pp. 197–230) and in J. Smits van Waesberghe's *Corpus scriptorum de musica* (vol. II, Rome, 1951).
BIBL.: J. Smits van Waesberghe, *Muziekgeschiedenis der Middeleeuwen* (Tilburg, 1936).

d'Arienzo, Nicola, Italian composer; b. Naples, Dec. 22, 1842; d. there, April 25, 1915. He composed an opera in the Neapolitan dialect at the age of 18; a series of Italian operas followed: *I due mariti* (Naples, Feb. 1, 1866); *Il Cacciatore delle Alpi* (Naples, June 23, 1870); *Il Cuoco* (Naples, June 11, 1873); *I Viaggi* (Milan, June 28, 1875); *La Figlia del diavolo* (Naples, Nov. 16, 1879; his most successful opera, which aroused considerable controversy for its realistic tendencies); *I tre coscritti* (Naples, Feb. 10, 1880); etc. He also wrote 2 syms. and much choral music. He publ. a treatise, *Introduzione del sistema tetracordale nella moderna musica*, favoring pure intonation; a historical essay, *Dell' opera comica dalle origini a Pergolesi* (1887; German tr., 1902); several monographs on Italian composers and numerous articles in periodicals.

Ariosti, Attilio, Italian composer; b. Bologna, Nov. 5, 1666; d. c.1729. He joined the Servite Order in 1688, but later abandoned it. He served as organist in Bologna in 1693; in 1697 he was in Berlin as court musician. From 1703 to 1711 he was in Vienna, then returned to Bologna. He was in London in 1716 and again from 1723 to 1727. A vol. of his cantatas and "lessons" for viola d'amore, on which he was an accomplished performer, was publ. in London in 1724. Ariosti then disappeared, the most probable conjecture being that he returned to Italy and died there in obscurity. Burney's attribution to Ariosti of 1 act of the opera *Muzio Scevola* (produced in London on April 15, 1721) is an anachronism, for Ariosti was not in London at the time.
WORKS: A list of his known operas includes the following: *Tirsi* (erroneously named *Dafne* by many music historians; Venice, 1696, in collaboration with Lotti and Caldara); *Mars und Irene* (Berlin, July 12, 1703); *Marte placato* (Vienna, March 19, 1707); *Artaserse* (London, Dec. 1, 1724); *Dario* (London, April 10, 1725); *Lucio Vero, Imperator di Roma* (London, Jan. 7, 1727). He also wrote 5 oratorios, some instrumental works, and numerous cantatas (many of which are preserved in various European libraries).
BIBL.: G. Weiss, "57 unbekannte Instrumentalstücke (15

Sonaten) von A. A. . . .," *Die Musikforschung* (April–June 1970).

Aristakesian, Emin, Armenian composer; b. Erevan, Nov. 19, 1936. He studied composition with Yegiazarian at the Erevan Cons., graduating in 1961; then taught in various Armenian institutes. Much of his music is, in its melorhythmic structure, derived from Armenian folk songs.
WORKS: Ballet, *Prometheus* (Erevan, 1967); *Armenia*, oratorio (1961); 2 syms. (1962, 1975); Viola Concerto (1963); Sinfonietta for Strings, Piano, and Xylophone (1969); *Suite* for String Quintet (1955); *Poem* for Piano Quintet (1959); *Polyphonic Variations* for String Quartet (1960); *Fantastic Variations* for Piano (1964); *Capriccio* for Piano (1965); *Poem about Lenin* for Chorus and Piano (1970); Piano Sonata (1971); *5 Sharageans of Saak Parteva* for Voice and Piano (1972); other songs.

Aristides Quintilianus, Greek writer on music; lived A.D. c.200 in Smyrna. His treatise *De musica libri VII* was printed in Meibom's *Antiquae musicae auctores septem* (1652) and by A. Jahn (1882); R. Schäfke publ. it in German (1937) with a commentary; T. Mathiesen prepared an annotated Eng. tr. as *On Music, in Three Books* (New Haven, 1983). Despite the dubious authenticity of some of his descriptions of Greek scales, the work is one of the basic sources of our knowledge of ancient Greek music.

Aristotle, famous Greek philosopher, pupil of Plato; b. Stagira, 384 B.C.; d. Chalcis, 322 B.C. The 19th section of the *Problems*, once ascribed to him, is the product of a much later follower of his theories; the Eng. tr., by E.S. Forster, is found in *The Works of Aristotle*, vol. 7 (Oxford, 1927); the Greek text with French tr. and commentary by F.A. Gevaert and C. Vollgraff is publ. in *Les Problèmes musicaux d'Aristote* (3 vols., 1899–1902). Aristotle's actual writings on music are reproduced by K. von Jan in his *Musici scriptores Graeci* (1895). The name Aristotle was also used by a writer on mensurable music of the 12th–13th centuries, whose treatise is publ. by E. de Coussemaker in his *Scriptores*, vol. I.

Aristoxenus, one of the earliest Greek writers on music; b. Tarentum, 354 B.C.; place and date of death unknown. His *Harmonic Elements* (complete) and *Rhythmical Elements* (fragmentary) are among the most important treatises on Greek music theory that have come down to us. They have been publ. by R. Westphal and F. Saran (2 vols.; 1883, 1893); also by H.S. Macran, with English and Greek text and a commentary (1902). The *Harmonic Elements* are included, in an Eng. tr., in O. Strunk's *Source Readings in Music History* (N.Y., 1950). See also L. Laloy, *Aristoxène de Tarente* (1904); C.F.A. Williams, *The Aristoxenian Theory of Musical Rhythm* (Cambridge, 1911).

Arizaga, Rodolfo, Argentine composer; b. Buenos Aires, July 11, 1926; d. there, 1985. He studied philosophy at the Univ. of Buenos Aires and composition with Luis Gianneo; then went to Paris, where he took lessons with Nadia Boulanger and Messiaen. Beginning with folkloric composition of the traditional Latin American type, he traversed the entire gamut of modern techniques, including 12-tone structures and aleatory composition, and applied these diverse methods liberally according to need and intention. Arizaga also publ. the monographs *Manuel de Falla* (Buenos Aires, 1961) and *Juan José Castro* (Buenos Aires, 1963) and ed. *Enciclopedia de la música argentina* (Buenos Aires, 1971).
WORKS: Cantatas: *Martirio de Santa Olalla* (1952) and *Delires* (1957; rev. 1970); *Prometeo 45*, opera (1958); Piano Concerto (1963); *Tientos para Santa Maria* for Orch. (1965); *Música para Christóbal Colón* for Orch. (1966); *Sonata breve* for Ondes Martenot and Piano (1958); *Diferenzas del tercer tiento* for Organ (1966); 2 string quartets (1968, 1969); various vocal works and piano pieces.

Arkas, Nikolai, Ukrainian composer and writer on music; b. Nikolayev, Jan. 7, 1853; d. there, March 26, 1909. He collected and compiled many Ukrainian folk songs; also wrote one of the earliest Ukrainian operas, *Katerina*, based on a poem by Shevchenko, a modern version of which was prepared from the publ. piano score by G. Taranov. He publ. a history of the Ukraine and Russia (St. Petersburg, 1904).

BIBL.: L. Kaufman, *N. A.* (Kiev, 1958).

Arkhipova, Irina (Konstantinovna), outstanding Russian mezzo-soprano; b. Moscow, Dec. 2, 1925. She attended vocal classes at the Moscow Architectural Inst., graduating in 1948; then continued vocal training with Leonid Savransky at the Moscow Cons., graduating in 1953. She sang with the Sverdlovsk Opera (1954–56); then made her debut as Carmen at Moscow's Bolshoi Theater (1956), where she quickly rose to prominence; traveled with it outside Russia, garnering praise for her appearances at Milan's La Scala (1965) and at the Montreal EXPO (1967). She appeared as Amneris at the San Francisco Opera in 1972 and as Azucena at London's Covent Garden in 1975. In 1966 she was made a People's Artist of the U.S.S.R. She excelled particularly in the Russian repertoire, but also distinguished herself in French and Italian music.

Arkor, André d', Belgian tenor; b. Tilleur, near Liège, Feb. 23, 1901; d. Brussels, Dec. 19, 1971. He studied at the Liège Cons.; made his operatic debut in 1925 in *Lakmé* at the Liège Théâtre Royal; then sang in Ghent and Lyons; in 1930 he joined the Théâtre de la Monnaie in Brussels, where he remained as a leading tenor until 1945; from 1945 to 1965 he was director of the Liège Théâtre Royal.

Arlen, Harold (real name, **Hyman Arluck**), American composer of popular music; b. Buffalo, Feb. 15, 1905; d. N.Y., April 23, 1986. The son of a cantor, he joined the choir of a synagogue where his father was chorus master. He quickly learned music and found employment as a pianist on lake steamboats and in nightclubs. Then he went to N.Y., where he became engaged in a variety of professions, as a singer with jazz bands, as an arranger, and, finally, as a composer. Possessing a natural gift for melody, he created several song hits, among them *Stormy Weather*, which became a classic of American popular music. He subsequently wrote a number of Broadway musicals, among them *Bloomer Girl* (1944) and *House of Flowers* (1954). He further contributed several film scores, including *The Wizard of Oz* (1939).

BIBL.: E. Jablonski, *H. A.: Happy with the Blues* (Garden City, 1961); A. Wilder, *American Popular Song* (N.Y., 1972).

Arlt, Wulf (Friedrich), German musicologist; b. Breslau, March 5, 1938. He studied musicology at the Univ. of Cologne; then received his Ph.D. in 1966 from the Univ. of Basel with the dissertation *Ein Festoffizium des Mittelalters aus Beauvais in seiner liturgischen Bedeutung* (publ. in Cologne, 1970); subsequently completed his Habilitation there in 1970 with his *Praxis und Lehre der "Ars subtilior": Studien zur Geschichte der Notation im Spätmittelalter.* He joined the faculty of the Univ. of Basel as a lecturer in 1965; became a prof. there in 1972. In 1971 he also became director of the Schola Cantorum Basiliensis. Arlt further devoted his critical capacities to elucidating the problems of music in the Middle Ages, and contributed important articles on the subject to music journals.

Arma, Paul (real name, **Imre Weisshaus**), Hungarian composer; b. Budapest, Oct. 22, 1904; d. Paris, Nov. 28, 1987. From 1921 to 1924 he attended classes of Béla Bartók at the Budapest Academy of Music, then went to N.Y., where he became associated with radical political and musical groups and contributed highly complex pieces to Henry Cowell's publication *New Music Quarterly*. A composer of empiric persuasion, he explored quaquaversal paths of modern techniques in contrasting sonorities. In 1930 he went to Paris and worked under the pseudonym Paul Arma. In 1947 he publ. in Paris a modernistically planned *Nouveau dictionnaire de musique*. Typical of his modernistic techniques, reflected in the titles of some of his works, are Concerto for String Quartet and Orch. (1947); Violin Sonata (1949); *31 instantanés* for Woodwind, Percus-

sion, Celesta, Xylophone, and Piano (1951); *Polydiaphonie* for Orch. (1962); *Structures variées* for Orch. (1964); *Prismes sonores* for Orch. (1966); *6 transparences* for Oboe and String Orch. (1968); *Résonances* for Orch. (1971); numerous experimental pieces for various instrumental combinations.

Armatrading, Joan, West Indies–born English singer and songwriter; b. St. Kitts, Dec. 9, 1950. Her family moved to Birmingham in 1956; after relocating to London in the early 1970s, she paired up with Pam Nestor, producing 2 moderately successful albums, *Whatever's for Us* (1974) and *Back to the Night* (1975); her subsequent solo album, *Joan Armatrading* (1976), was extremely well received, reaching No. 12 on the U.K. pop charts. With the decline of interest in the singer/songwriter genre in the 1980s, Armatrading's popularity declined; many of her songs, however, acoustic-based and with mature lyrics, have had lasting appeal, especially among feminists.

Armbruster, Karl, German conductor; b. Andernach-am-Rhein, July 13, 1846; d. London, June 10, 1917. He studied piano in Cologne; at the age of 17 settled in London, where he made propaganda for Wagner by means of numerous lectures. He was Hans Richter's assistant at the Wagner concerts in London in 1884; later conducted operas at London theaters. He was also one of the conductors of the Wagner cycles at Bayreuth (1884–94).

Armin, Georg (real name, **Herrmann**), German singer and pedagogue; b. Braunschweig, Nov. 10, 1871; d. Karlslunde Strand, Denmark, Feb. 16, 1963. He studied architecture; then turned to singing. He settled in Berlin as a voice teacher; from 1925 to 1942 he ed. the periodical *Der Stimmwart*. His home in Berlin was destroyed in an air raid during World War II; in 1949 he settled in Denmark. He publ. several papers on voice production, among them *Das Stauprinzip* (1905) and *Von der Urkraft der Stimme* (1921).

BIBL.: J. Berntsen, *Ein Meister der Stimmbildungskunst* (Leipzig, 1936).

Armingaud, Jules, French violinist; b. Bayonne, May 3, 1820; d. Paris, Feb. 27, 1900. He began his career as a member of the orch. at the Paris Opéra. In 1855 he organized a string quartet, which he later enlarged by adding wind instruments and named the Société Classique. He publ. some violin pieces and 2 musico-philosophical books of essays: *Consonances et dissonances* and *Modulations*.

Armstrong, Karan, American soprano; b. Horne, Mont., Dec. 14, 1941. She studied at Concordia College in Moorhead, Minn. (B.A., 1963). In 1969 she won both the San Francisco Opera and Metropolitan Opera auditions; then appeared with the N.Y. City Opera, Baltimore Opera, Houston Opera, Seattle Opera, and others. In 1976 she made her European debut as Salome with the Strasbourg Opera; in 1979 she sang Elsa at the Bayreuth Festival, and returned there in subsequent seasons. She made her debut at Covent Garden in London as Lulu in Alban Berg's opera in 1981. She also appeared with the Vienna State Opera, Bavarian Opera, Paris Opéra, and Hamburg State Opera. Her finest roles include Violetta, Tosca, Mimi, Alice Ford, Countess Almaviva, and Eva. She married **Götz Friedrich.**

Armstrong, Louis, famous black American jazz trumpeter, singer, bandleader, and entertainer, familiarly known as "Satchmo" (for "Satchel Mouth," with reference to his spacious and resonant oral cavity); b. New Orleans, probably in 1898 (there is no documentation to substantiate his claim that he was born on July 4, 1900); d. N.Y., July 6, 1971. He grew up in Storyville, New Orleans's brothel district, and in his youth was placed in the Colored Waifs' Home, where he played cornet in its brass band. After his release, he learned to play jazz in blues bands in local honky-tonks; also received pointers on cornet playing from "King" Oliver and played in "Kid" Ory's band (1918–19). In 1922 he went to Chicago to play in Oliver's Creole Jazz Band, with which he made his 1st recordings in 1923; then was a member of Fletcher Henderson's band in

N.Y. (1924–25). Returning to Chicago, he organized his own jazz combo, the Hot 5, in 1925; made a series of now historic recordings with it, with the Hot 7, and with other groups he led until 1928. From about 1926 he made the trumpet his principal instrument. In 1929 he went to N.Y. again, where he became notably successful through appearances on Broadway, in films, and on radio. From 1935 to 1947 he led his own big band, and in 1947 organized his All Stars jazz combo. In succeeding years he made innumerable tours of the U.S., and also toured widely abroad. He became enormously successful as an entertainer; made many television appearances and several hit recordings, including his best-selling version of *Hello, Dolly* in 1964. Although he suffered a severe heart attack in 1959, he continued to make appearances until his death. Armstrong was one of the greatest figures in the history of jazz and one of the most popular entertainers of his time. His style of improvisation revolutionized jazz performance in the 1920s. His unique gravelly-voiced renditions of jazz and popular songs became as celebrated as his trumpet virtuosity. He was married 4 times. In 1924 he married his 2nd wife, the jazz pianist Lil(lian) Hardin (b. Memphis, Tenn., Feb. 3, 1898; d. while playing in a memorial concert for Armstrong in Chicago, Aug. 27, 1971), who was the pianist for both Oliver and Armstrong in Chicago; they divorced in 1938. Armstrong publ. *Swing the Music* (N.Y., 1936) and *Satchmo: My Life in New Orleans* (N.Y., 1954).

BIBL.: R. Goffin, *Horn of Plenty, the Story of L. A.* (N.Y., 1947); H. Panassié, *L. A.* (Paris, 1947; N.Y., 1971); M. Jones et al., *Salute to Satchmo* (London, 1970); M. Jones and J. Chilton, *L.: The L. A. Story, 1900–1971* (Boston and Toronto, 1971); R. Merryman, *L. A.—A Self Portrait* (N.Y., 1971); J. Jespen, *L. A. Discography, 1923–1971* (Rugsted Vyst, Denmark, 1973); J. Collier, *L. A., an American Genius* (N.Y., 1983); M. Pinfold, *L. A.: His Life and Times* (N.Y., 1987); S. Tanenhaus, *L. A.* (N.Y., 1989).

Armstrong, Richard, English conductor; b. Leicester, Jan. 7, 1943. He studied at Corpus Christi College, Cambridge. In 1966 he joined the staff of the Royal Opera House, Covent Garden; in 1968 he became assistant conductor of the Welsh National Opera, Cardiff; from 1973 to 1986 he was its music director. He also appeared as a guest conductor of various operatic and symphonic units.

Armstrong, Sheila, English soprano; b. Ashington, Northumberland, Aug. 13, 1942. She was educated at the Royal Academy of Music in London, winning the 1965 Kathleen Ferrier Memorial Scholarship; made her operatic debut as Despina at the Sadler's Wells Theatre in 1965; then sang at the Glyndebourne Festival from 1966 and at the Royal Opera House, Covent Garden, from 1973. She was also active as an oratorio singer.

Arndt, Günther, German choral conductor; b. Berlin-Charlottenburg, April 1, 1907; d. Berlin, Dec. 25, 1976. He was educated at the Academy for School and Church Music in Berlin; also studied musicology at the Univ. of Berlin; then was engaged as lecturer at the Volkshochschule in Berlin (1932–40). After the war he headed the chamber music dept. of the Berlin Radio RIAS; also conducted the Berlin Motet Choir (1950–60) and the RIAS Chamber Choir (1955–72); served as deputy head of music for the RIAS (1964–72). He gained distinction as a conductor of modern choral music.

Arne, Michael, English composer, illegitimate son of **Thomas Augustine Arne;** b. London, c.1740; d. there, Jan. 14, 1786. He was trained as an actor and a singer, and made his debut in a concert in London on Feb. 20, 1750. He also acquired considerable skill as a harpsichord player. In 1771–72 he traveled in Germany as a conductor of stage music; from 1776 he was in Dublin; at some time prior to 1784 he returned to London. He was known for his eccentricities; among his vagaries was an earnest preoccupation with alchemy in search of the philosopher's stone to convert base metals into gold, a quest which proved a disappointment.

WORKS: 9 operas (all perf. in London), including *Hymen* (Jan. 20, 1764); *Cymon* (Jan. 2, 1767); *The Artifice* (April 14, 1780); *The Choice of Harlequin* (Dec. 26, 1781); *Vertumnus and Pomona* (Feb. 21, 1782); also collaborations with other composers in about 14 productions.

BIBL.: J. Parkinson, *An Index to the Vocal Works of Thomas Augustine Arne and M. A.* (Detroit, 1972).

Arne, Thomas, Augustine, famous English dramatic composer, natural father of **Michael Arne;** b. London, March 12, 1710; d. there, March 5, 1778. His father, an upholsterer, sent him to Eton; he then spent 3 years in a solicitor's office. He studied music on the side, much against his father's wishes, and acquired considerable skill on the violin. He soon began to write musical settings, "after the Italian manner," to various plays. His 1st production was Addison's *Rosamond* (March 7, 1733). He renamed Fielding's *Tragedy of Tragedies* as *Opera of Operas,* and produced it at the Haymarket Theatre (Oct. 29, 1733); a masque, *Dido and Aeneas,* followed (Jan. 12, 1734). His most important work was the score of *Comus* (Drury Lane, March 4, 1738). On Aug. 1, 1740, he produced at Clivedon, Buckinghamshire, the masque *Alfred,* the finale of which contains the celebrated song *Rule Britannia,* which became a national patriotic song of Great Britain. In the meantime, on March 15, 1737, Arne married Cecilia Young, daughter of the organist Charles Young, and herself a fine singer. In 1742 he went with her to Dublin, where he also stayed in 1755 and 1758. Of his many dramatic productions the following were performed at Drury Lane in London: *The Temple of Dullness* (Jan. 17, 1745); *Harlequin Incendiary* (March 3, 1746); *The Triumph of Peace* (Feb. 21, 1748); *Britannia* (May 9, 1755); *Beauty and Virtue* (Feb. 26, 1762); *The Rose* (Dec. 2, 1772). The following were staged at Covent Garden: *Harlequin Sorcerer* (Feb. 11, 1752); *The Prophetess* (Feb. 1, 1758); *Thomas and Sally* (Nov. 28, 1760); *Love in a Village* (Dec. 8, 1762); *The Fairy Prince* (Nov. 12, 1771). He further contributed separate numbers to 28 theatrical productions, among them songs to Shakespeare's *As You Like It;* "Where the Bee Sucks" in *The Tempest;* etc. He wrote 2 oratorios: *The Death of Abel* (Dublin, Feb. 18, 1744) and *Judith* (Drury Lane, Feb. 27, 1761), the latter remarkable for the introduction of female voices into the choral parts. He also wrote numerous glees and catches, and miscellaneous instrumental music. He received the honorary degree of D.Mus. from Oxford Univ. (July 6, 1759), which accounts for his familiar appellation of "Dr. Arne."

BIBL.: J. Parkinson, *An Index to the Vocal Works of T.A. A. and Michael Arne* (Detroit, 1972); J. Rowntree, "Lulworth Chapel and a Missing A. Mass," *Musical Times* (June 1987).

d'Arneiro, (José Augusto) Ferreira Veiga, Viscount, distinguished Portuguese composer; b. Macao, China, Nov. 22, 1838; d. San Remo, July 7, 1903. He studied with Botelho, Schira, and Soares in Lisbon. The production of his ballet *Gina* (Lisbon, 1866) attracted attention; he then produced an opera, *L'Elisire di Giovinezza* (Lisbon, March 31, 1876), followed by *La Derelitta* (Lisbon, 1885). His *Te Deum,* performed in Lisbon and in London in 1871, was very successful; it was later given in Paris under the somewhat affected title of "Symphonie-Cantate."

Arnell, Richard (Anthony Sayer), English composer; b. London, Sept. 15, 1917. He studied with John Ireland at the Royal College of Music in London (1935–39). In 1939 he went to America; when Winston Churchill had a reception at Columbia Univ. in 1946, Arnell wrote *Prelude and Flourish* for Brass Instruments, performed at the occasion. In 1948 Arnell returned to London. His music may be described as festive without pomposity, and very English.

WORKS: STAGE: OPERAS: *Love in Transit* (London, Feb. 27, 1958); *The Petrified Princess* (London, May 5, 1959); *Moonflowers* (Kent, July 23, 1959); *Combat Zone* (Hempstead, Hofstra College, April 27, 1969). **BALLETS:** *Harlequin in April,* suggested by T.S. Eliot's *The Waste Land* (London, May 8, 1951); *The Great Detective,* about Sherlock Holmes (1953).

Also 7 syms.; overture, *The New Age* (N.Y., Jan. 13, 1941); *Quasi variazioni* (N.Y., March 15, 1942); Violin Concerto (N.Y., April 22, 1946); 2 piano concertos (1946, 1966); *Abstract Forms*, suite for Strings (Bath, June 2, 1951); *Lord Byron*, symphonic portrait (London, Nov. 19, 1952); 5 string quartets; other chamber music; piano pieces.

Arnestad, Finn (Oluf Bjerke), Norwegian composer; b. Christiania, Sept. 23, 1915. He studied violin and piano in Oslo and, briefly, composition with Bjarne Brustad; in 1952 he studied African and oriental folk music in Paris; after returning to Oslo he was active as a music critic. His music is influenced by French Impressionism, with tangential use of dodecaphony.
WORKS: ORCH.: *Constellation*, intermezzo (1948); *Conversation*, concert intermezzo for Piano and Orch. (1950); *Meditation*, intermezzo (1952); *I.N.R.I.*, 2 concert suites from a symphonic mystery play (1952–55); Violin Concerto (1957); *Aria appassionata* (1962); *Cavatina cambiata* (1965; orig. titled *Dopplersonance*); *Overture* (1970); *Væsletjennet* for Norwegian Recorder and Orch. (1970; based on a 1938 piano piece); *Toccata* (1972); *Arabesque* (1975); Piano Concerto (1976); *Mouvement concertant*, concert piece for Double Bass and Orch. (1978). **CHAMBER:** String Quartet (1947); Sextet for Flute, Clarinet, Bassoon, Violin, Cello, and Piano (1959); Quintet for Flute and Strings (1962); *Suite in Old Dance Rhythms* for Flute, Oboe, Harpsichord, and Strings (1966); Trombone Sonata (1971); Solo Violin Sonata (1980); Solo Double-bass Sonata (1980). **PIANO:** 2 sonatas: No. 1 (1967) and No. 2, *Ritagliata* (1967); *Tango*, 3-part canon (1981). **VOCAL:** *Missa Brevis* for Chorus and 6 Instruments (1951); *Amen* for Chorus a cappella (1959); *Smeden og Bageren* (The Blacksmith and the Baker) for Baritone, Flute, Oboe, Harpsichord, and Strings (1966).

Arnič, Blaž, Slovenian composer; b. Luče, Jan. 31, 1901; d. Ljubljana, Feb. 1, 1970. He studied organ and music theory at the Cons. of Ljubljana (1925–29) and at the New Vienna Cons. (1929–32). In 1945 he was appointed prof. at the Music Academy of Ljubljana. Most of his music is of programmatic content; all of his syms. bear descriptive titles; the melodic and rhythmic material of his music reflects the folk motifs of Slovenia.
WORKS: *Symphonic Rhapsody* (1933); syms.: *Resurrection* (1935); *Reverie* (1940); *The Whirlwind of War* (1941); *Pioneer* (1948); *Symphony of Labor* (1950); *In the Fatherland's Soul* (1951); *War and Peace* (1960); symphonic poems, *Memento mori* (1934) and *Witch Dance* (1951); Organ Concerto (1931); Cello Concerto (1960); Clarinet Concerto (1963); 3 violin concertos (1953, 1953, 1966); Viola Concerto (1967); chamber music; piano pieces; songs.

Arnold, Byron, American composer of experimental music; b. Vancouver, Wash., Aug. 15, 1901; d. Oscoda, Mich., Dec. 25, 1971. He studied composition with Bernard Rogers and Howard Hanson at the Eastman School of Music in Rochester, N.Y. Upon graduation, he filled various teaching posts in Alabama and elsewhere. He created a certain stir in musical circles by writing a symphonic suite entitled 5 *Incapacitated Preludes*, each portraying a serious neurological ailment affecting sight, hearing, and muscular structures; in the deaf prelude the players are instructed to make an outward pretense at playing, blowing, and soundless drumbeating. It was performed in Rochester on April 19, 1937. He also wrote 3 *Fantasticisms* for Orch. Among his normal contributions is his *Folksongs of Alabama* (1950).

Arnold, Denis (Midgley), English musicologist; b. Sheffield, Dec. 15, 1926; d. Budapest, April 28, 1986. He was educated at Sheffield Univ. (B.A., 1947; B.Mus., 1948; M.A., 1950). From 1951 to 1960 he was a lecturer and from 1960 to 1964 a reader in music at Queen's Univ., Belfast; in 1964 he was made senior lecturer at the Univ. of Hull; in 1969 he became prof. of music at the Univ. of Nottingham; from 1975 was Heather Prof. of Music at Oxford Univ. From 1976 to 1980

he was joint ed. of *Music & Letters*. From 1979 to 1983 he was president of the Royal Musical Assoc. In 1983 he was made a Commander of the Order of the British Empire. He was regarded as one of the foremost authorities on Italian music of the Renaissance and the early Baroque period.
WRITINGS: *Monteverdi* (London, 1963); *Marenzio* (London, 1965); *Monteverdi Madrigals* (London, 1967); ed., with N. Fortune, *The Monteverdi Companion* (London, 1968; 2nd ed., rev., 1985, as *The New Monteverdi Companion*); ed., with N. Fortune, *The Beethoven Companion* (London, 1971); *Giovanni Gabrieli* (London, 1974); *Giovanni Gabrieli and the Music of the Venetian High Renaissance* (Oxford, 1979); *Monteverdi Church Music* (London, 1982); ed., *The New Oxford Companion to Music* (2 vols., Oxford, 1983); *Bach* (Oxford, 1984); with E. Arnold, *The Oratorio in Venice* (London, 1986).
BIBL.: Special issue of the *Journal of the Royal Musical Association*, 113/2 (1988).

Arnold, Eddy (Richard Edward), American singer of country-western music; b. Henderson, Tenn., May 15, 1918. He took up the guitar and had some lessons with a traveling musician, but did not learn to read music; played in night spots; then became a favorite singer on the "Grand Ole Opry" radio program in Nashville, billing himself as the "Tennessee Plowboy." He gained fame with such songs as *That's How Much I Love You*, *Bouquet of Roses*, and *Anytime*. After the 1st wave of rock-'n'-roll had subsided, he became a leading figure in the movement toward the urbanized country-music genre (country pop or Nashville sound); in 1966 he was the 1st country-western musician to lead a concert at Carnegie Hall in N.Y.; that earned him election to the Country Music Hall of Fame. His later successes included his renditions of *What's He Doing in My World*, *Make the World Go Away*, *Misty Blue*, *Turn the World Around*, *Here Comes Heaven*, etc. His autobiography, *It's a Long Way from Chester County*, was publ. in 1969.

Arnold, Johann Gottfried, German cellist and composer, father of **Karl Arnold**; b. Niedernhall, near Öhringen, Feb. 1, 1773; d. Frankfurt am Main, July 26, 1806. He studied with Willmann and Bernhard Romberg; after a brief concert career he became a theater cellist in Frankfurt. He wrote *Symphonie concertante* for 2 Flutes and Orch.; several cello concertos; 6 sets of variations for cello; and various pieces for the guitar and other instruments.

Arnold, Karl, German organist and conductor, son of **Johann Gottfried Arnold**; b. Neukirchen, near Mergentheim, Württemberg, May 6, 1794; d. Christiania (Oslo), Norway, Nov. 11, 1877. He studied with J.A. André and Vollweiler; then occupied various positions in St. Petersburg, Russia (1818), in Berlin (1824), and in Münster (1835). In 1847 he went to Norway, where he became conductor of the Phil. Soc. in Christiania, and also was a church organist there. He wrote an opera, *Irene* (Berlin, 1832), a Piano Sextet, and numerous works for piano solo.

Arnold, Malcolm, prolific and versatile English composer; b. Northampton, Oct. 21, 1921. He studied trumpet, conducting, and composition at the Royal College of Music in London (1938–40); played 1st trumpet with the London Phil. (1941–42; 1946–48). He then devoted himself chiefly to composition, developing a melodious and harmonious style of writing that possessed the quality of immediate appeal to the general public while avoiding obvious banality; many of his works reveal modalities common to English folk songs, often invested in acridly pleasing harmonies. His experience as a trumpeter and conductor of popular concerts provided a secure feeling for propulsive rhythms and brilliant sonorities. He had a knack for composing effective background music for films. In his sound track for *The Bridge on the River Kwai* he popularized the rollicking march *Colonel Bogey*, orig. composed by Kenneth Alford in 1914. In 1970 Arnold was made a Commander of the Order of the British Empire.
WORKS: STAGE: OPERAS: *The Dancing Master* (1951) and

The Open Window (London, Dec. 14, 1956). *BALLETS: Homage to the Queen* (Covent Garden, London, in the presence of Queen Elizabeth II, on June 2, 1953); *Rinaldo and Armida* (1954); *Sweeney Todd* (1958); *Electra* (1963). *OTHER STAGE WORKS:* Nativity play, *Song of Simeon* (1958); children's spectacle, *The Turtle Drum* (1967). *ORCH.:* Sym. for Strings (1946); 8 numbered syms.: No. 1 (Cheltenham Festival, July 6, 1951); No. 2 (Bournemouth, May 25, 1953); No. 3 (1954–57; London, Dec. 2, 1957); No. 4 (London, Nov. 2, 1960); No. 5 (Cheltenham Festival, 1961); No. 6 (Sheffield, June 28, 1968, composer conducting); No. 7 (London, May 1974, composer conducting); No. 8 (N.Y., May 5, 1979); solo concertos: 2 for Horn (1945, 1956); 2 for Clarinet (1948, 1974); 1 for Piano Duet (1951); 1 for Oboe (1952); 2 for Flute (1954, 1972); 1 for Harmonica (London, Aug. 14, 1954; Larry Adler, soloist); 1 for Organ (1954); 1 for Guitar (1958); 1 for 2 Violins (1962); 1 for 2 Pianos, 3-hands (1969); 1 for Viola (1970); 1 for Trumpet (1981); 1 for Cello (London, March 9, 1989); 10 overtures: *Beckus the Dandipratt* (1943); *Festival Overture* (1946); *The Smoke* (1948); *A Sussex Overture* (1951); *Tam O'Shanter* (1955); *A Grand, Grand Overture* for 3 Vacuum Cleaners, 1 Floor Polisher, 4 Rifles, and Orch. (1956; London, Nov. 13, 1956); *Commonwealth Christmas Overture* (1957); *Peterloo* (1968); *Anniversary Overture* (1968); *The Fair Field* (1972); tone poem, *Larch Trees* (1943); Serenade for Small Orch. (1950); 8 *English Dances* in 2 sets (1950–51); *The Sound Barrier*, rhapsody (1952); 3 sinfoniettas (1954, 1958, 1964); 2 *Little Suites* (1955, 1962); Serenade for Guitar and Strings (1955); 4 *Scottish Dances* (1957); 4 *Cornish Dances* (1966); Concerto for 28 Players (1970); *Fantasy for Audience and Orchestra* (1970); *A Flourish for Orchestra* (1973); *Fantasy for Brass Band* (1974); *Philharmonic Concerto* (1977); Sym. for Brass Instruments (1979). *CHAMBER:* Trio for Flute, Viola, and Bassoon (1943); 3 *Shanties* for Wind Quintet (1944); Duo for Flute and Viola (1945); 2 violin sonatas (1947, 1953); Viola Sonata (1947); Flute Sonatina (1948); 2 string quartets (1949, 1976); Oboe Sonatina (1951); Clarinet Sonatina (1951); Recorder Sonatina (1953); Piano Trio (1955); Oboe Quartet (1957); *Toy Symphony* for 12 Toy Instruments, Piano, and String Quartet (1957); Brass Quintet (1961); 5 pieces for Violin and Piano (1965); 9 solo fantasies: for Bassoon, Clarinet, Horn, Flute, Oboe, Trumpet, Trombone, Tuba, and Guitar (1966–70); *Trevelyan Suite* for Wind Instruments (1968); piano pieces; songs. *FILM MUSIC: The Captain's Paradise* (1953); *I Am a Camera* (1955); *Trapeze* (1956); *Island in the Sun* (1957); *The Bridge on the River Kwai* (1957); *Inn of the Sixth Happiness* (1958); *Roots of Heaven* (1958); *Nine Hours to Rama* (1962).

BIBL.: A. Poulton;, *M. A.: A Catalogue of His Music* (London, 1986); R. Preston, "Light and Shade—A Profile of M. A.," *Music and Musicians International* (April 1989).

Arnold, Maurice (real name, **Maurice Arnold Strothotte**), American violinist and composer; b. St. Louis, Jan. 19, 1865; d. N.Y., Oct. 23, 1937. He studied in Cincinnati; then in Germany with several teachers, including Max Bruch. The performance of his orch. work *American Plantation Dances* (N.Y., 1894) aroused the interest of Dvořák, because of the Negro melodies used in it, and he engaged Arnold to teach at the National Cons., of which Dvořák was then head. Arnold subsequently was active as a conductor of light opera, and as a violin teacher. He wrote a comic opera, *The Merry Benedicts* (Brooklyn, 1896); a grand opera, *Cleopatra*; a Sym.; a cantata, *The Wild Chase; Minstrel Serenade* for Violin and Piano; and a Fugue for Piano, 8-hands.

Arnold, Richard, German-American violinist; b. Eilenberg, Prussia, Jan. 10, 1845; d. N.Y., June 21, 1918. He emigrated to the U.S. in 1853, but returned to Germany in 1864 to study with Ferdinand David in Leipzig. He was a violinist in the Theodore Thomas Orch. (1869–76), and concertmaster of the N.Y. Phil. Orch. (1880–1909); then lived in N.Y., teaching violin.

Arnold, Samuel, celebrated English composer, organist, and music scholar; b. London, Aug. 10, 1740; d. there, Oct. 22,

1802. He received his musical training from Gates and Nares as a chorister of the Chapel Royal. He showed a gift for composition early on, and was commissioned to arrange the music for the play *The Maid of the Mill*; for this he selected songs by some 20 composers, including Bach, and added several numbers of his own; the resulting pasticcio was produced with success at Covent Garden (Jan. 31, 1765). This was the 1st of his annual productions for Covent Garden and other theaters in London, of which the following were composed mainly by Arnold: *Harlequin Dr. Faustus* (Nov. 18, 1766); *The Royal Garland* (Oct. 10, 1768); *The Magnet* (June 27, 1771); *A Beggar on Horseback* (June 16, 1785); *The Gnome* (Aug. 5, 1788); *New Spain, or Love in Mexico* (July 16, 1790); *The Surrender of Calais* (July 30, 1791); *The Enchanted Wood* (July 25, 1792); *The 63rd Letter* (July 18, 1802). He also wrote several oratorios, among them *The Cure of Saul* (1767); *Abimelech; The Resurrection; The Prodigal Son;* and *Elisha* (1795; his last oratorio). On the occasion of a performance of *The Prodigal Son* at Oxford Univ. in 1773, Arnold was given the degree of D.Mus. In 1783, he became the successor of Nares as composer to the Chapel Royal, for which he wrote several odes and anthems. In 1789 Arnold was engaged as conductor of the Academy of Ancient Music; in 1793 he became organist of Westminster Abbey. He was buried in Westminster Abbey, near Purcell and Blow. Arnold's ed. of Handel's works, begun in 1786, was carried out by him in 36 vols., embracing about 180 numbers; it is, however, incomplete and inaccurate in many respects. His principal work is *Cathedral Music* (4 vols., 1790); its subtitle describes its contents: "A collection in score of the most valuable and useful compositions for that Service by the several English Masters of the last 200 years." It forms a sequel to Boyce's work of the same name. A new ed. of Arnold's *Cathedral Music* was issued by Rimbault (1847).

Arnold, Yuri, Russian composer and music theorist; b. St. Petersburg, Nov. 13, 1811; d. Karakash, Crimea, July 20, 1898. He was of German extraction; studied at the German Univ. of Dorpat, Estonia; from 1863 to 1871 he lived in Leipzig; then returned to Russia; he lived in Moscow until 1894, when he moved to St. Petersburg. He wrote a comic opera, *Treasure Trove* (St. Petersburg, Feb. 1, 1853), the MS of which was lost in a fire at the St. Petersburg Opera Theater in 1859, together with the MS of his other opera, *St. John's Eve.* He further composed an overture, *Boris Godunov.* Arnold was the author of the 1st book in the Russian language dealing with the theory of composition (1841); also publ. *Theory of Old Russian Religious Dance* (Moscow, 1880) and many articles on Russian music for German periodicals. Among his publications in German was *Der Einfluss des Zeitgeistes auf die Entwicklung der Tonkunst* (Leipzig, 1867). He tr. into German the librettos of operas by Tchaikovsky and Glinka, and publ. historically valuable memoirs (3 vols., Moscow, 1893).

Arnoldson, Sigrid, Swedish soprano; b. Stockholm, March 20, 1861; d. there, Feb. 7, 1943. She was the daughter of the celebrated tenor **Oscar Arnoldson** (1830–81). She studied voice with Maurice Strakosch and Désirée Artôt; made her professional debut in Prague in 1885; in 1886 she was a guest artist in Moscow, and in 1887 appeared in London; subsequently sang in Paris, Nice, and Rome. In 1888 she was engaged as a regular member at Covent Garden in London. On Nov. 29, 1893, she made her debut at the Metropolitan Opera in N.Y., but remained on its roster for only 1 season. In 1910 she was elected a member of the Royal Swedish Academy of Music in Stockholm; in 1922 she was in Vienna as a singing teacher; later also taught voice in Berlin. On June 16, 1888, she married the Austrian impresario Alfred Fischhof, a nephew of Maurice Strakosch.

Arnould, (Madeleine) Sophie, French soprano; b. Paris, Feb. 13, 1740; d. there, Oct. 22, 1802. She studied singing with Mme. Fel and acting with Mlle. Clairon; made her debut at the Paris Opéra on Dec. 15, 1757. She created the title role in Gluck's *Iphigénie en Aulide* (April 19, 1774), and after a highly successful career, retired in 1778 with a pension of

2,000 livres. Gabriel Pierné wrote a 1-act "lyric comedy," *Sophie Arnould* (1926), based on incidents of her life.

BIBL.: *A.iana*, a large collection of anecdotes, publ. anonymously (Paris, 1813; real author, A. Deville); E. and J. de Goncourt, *S. A. d'après sa correspondance et ses mémoires* (Paris, 1857); R.B. Douglas, *S. A., Actress and Wit* (Paris, 1898).

Aronowitz, Cecil (Solomon), English violist; b. King William's Town, South Africa, March 4, 1916; d. Ipswich, Sept. 7, 1978. He was of Russian descent. He studied at the Royal College of Music in London, where his principal teachers were Vaughan Williams and Jacob (composition) and Rivarde (violin). He turned to viola playing later in life, and served as 1st violist in the Boyd Neel Orch., in the Goldsborough (later English) Chamber Orch., and in the London Mozart Players; also was a member of the Melos Ensemble and the Pro Arte Piano Quartet. From 1950 to 1975 he taught viola and chamber music at the Royal College of Music in London.

Arrau, Claudio, eminent Chilean-born American pianist; b. Chillán, Feb. 6, 1903; d. Mürzzuschlag, Austria, June 9, 1991. He received his early training from his mother, an amateur pianist, and as a child played a program of pieces by Mozart, Beethoven, and Chopin at a public performance in Santiago. In 1910 he was sent by the Chilean government to Berlin, where he took lessons with Martin Krause. In 1914–15 he gave piano recitals in Germany and Scandinavia, attracting attention by his precocious talent. In 1921 he returned to Chile, making his 1st professional appearances there and elsewhere in South America. In 1924 he made his 1st American tour, as a soloist with the Boston Sym. Orch. and the Chicago Sym. In 1924 he was appointed to the faculty of the Stern Cons. in Berlin. He won the Grand Prix International des Pianistes at Geneva in 1927; in 1929 he made a tour of Russia, returning for a 2nd tour the following year. During the season 1935–36 he presented in Berlin the complete keyboard works of Bach in 12 recitals; in 1936 he performed all the keyboard works of Mozart in 5 recitals in Berlin. In 1938 he played all 32 piano sonatas and all 5 piano concertos of Beethoven in Mexico City, and in 1939 repeated this series in Buenos Aires and Santiago. In 1941 he settled permanently in N.Y., devoting himself to concert appearances and teaching. In 1947 he made a tour of Australia, and in 1949 gave a series of concerts in South Africa; in 1951 toured in Israel; in 1956 played in India; in 1958 gave concerts in Prague and Bucharest; in 1965 made his 1st tour in Japan. From 1962 to 1969 he made a complete recording of Beethoven's sonatas. He also supervised the ed. of the Urtext of Beethoven's piano sonatas. In 1978 he gave up his Chilean citizenship in protest against the military regime in his homeland, and became a naturalized U.S. citizen in 1979. He nevertheless remained a revered figure in Chile; in 1983 he was awarded the Chilean National Arts Prize. He returned to Chile for a tour in 1984, after an absence of 17 years. In his playing, Arrau combined a Classical purity and precision of style with a rhapsodic éclat.

BIBL.: J. Horowitz, *Conversations with A.* (N.Y., 1982); I. Harden, *C. A.: Ein Interpretenportrait* (Frankfurt, 1983); *Current Biography* (Nov. 1986); D. Cameron, "C. A.: A Continuing Quest," *Ovation* (April 1988).

Arregui Garay, Vicente, Spanish composer; b. Madrid, July 3, 1871; d. there, Dec. 1, 1925. He studied in Paris and Rome; was active in Madrid as a music critic; wrote a symphonic poem, *Historia de una madre* (after H.C. Andersen, 1910); *Sinfonia vasca* for Orch.; the operas *Yolanda, La Maya,* and *El Cuento de Barba Azul*; a cantata, *El Lobo ciego*; chamber music and choral works. His music follows the Romantic school of programmatic writing.

Arriaga (y Balzola), Juan Crisóstomo (Jacobo Antonio de), precocious Spanish composer; b. Rigoitia, near Bilbao, Jan. 27, 1806; d. Paris, Jan. 17, 1826 (10 days before his 20th birthday). At the age of 11, he wrote an Octet for French Horn, Strings, Guitar, and Piano, subtitled *Nada y mucho*; at 13, a 2-act opera, *Los esclavos felices.* On the strength of these

works he was accepted at the Paris Cons., where he studied with Baillot and Fétis. In Paris he wrote a Sym.; a biblical scene, *Agar*; 3 string quartets; several fugues; piano pieces; songs. On Aug. 13, 1933, a memorial to him was unveiled in Bilbao and a Comisión Permanente Arriaga was formed to publ. his works. Under its auspices, the vocal score of the opera and the full scores of his Sym. and Octet were printed. A bibliographical pamphlet, *Resurgimiento de las obras de Arriaga,* by Juan de Eresalde was also publ. (Bilbao, 1953).

Arrieta y Corera, Pascual Juan Emilio, Spanish composer; b. Puente la Reina, Oct. 21, 1823; d. Madrid, Feb. 11, 1894. He studied at the Milan Cons. (1839–45) with Vaccai; returned to Spain in 1846; was a prof. at the Madrid Cons. in 1857; became its director in 1868. He wrote more than 50 zarzuelas and several grand operas in Italian. Of these productions the most important is *La conquista de Granada,* produced in Madrid (Oct. 10, 1850) with Arrieta himself conducting, and revived 5 years later under the title *Isabel la Católica* (Madrid, Dec. 18, 1855). Other successful zarzuelas and operas are *Ildegonda* (Milan, Feb. 28, 1845); *El Domino Azul* (Madrid, Feb. 19, 1853); *El Grumete* (Madrid, June 17, 1853; its sequel, *La Vuelta del Corsario,* perf. in Madrid, Feb. 18, 1863); *Marina* (Madrid, Sept. 21, 1855; rev. and produced as a grand opera, Madrid, Oct. 4, 1871); *S. Francesco da Siena* (Madrid, Oct. 27, 1883).

Arrieu, Claude, French pianist and composer; b. Paris, Nov. 30, 1903; d. there, March 7, 1990. She studied piano with Marguerite Long, and took courses in composition at the Paris Cons. with Roger-Ducasse and Noël Gallon, graduating with the Premier Prix in 1932. She achieved her best successes writing for the theater.

WORKS: *Noë,* music drama (Strasbourg, Jan. 29, 1950); *Cadet Roussel,* comic opera (Marseilles, Oct. 2, 1953); *La Cabine téléphonique,* radio sketch (Paris, March 15, 1959); *La Princesse de Babylone,* comic opera (Rheims, March 4, 1960); *The Love of Don Perlimplin and Belisa in His Garden,* opera enl. from incidental music to Lorca's play (Tours, March 1, 1980).

Arrigo, Girolamo, Italian composer; b. Palermo, April 2, 1930. He studied at the Palermo Cons., and later in Rome and Paris. His works are mostly in small forms, and virtually all with programmatic connotations. The most important among them are *3 occasioni* for Soprano and 32 Instruments (1958); *Quarta occasione* for 7 Voices, Horn, Viola, Mandolin, Guitar, and Celesta (1959); *Fluxus* for 9 Instruments (1959); *Episodi* for Soprano and Flute, to texts by ancient Greek poets (1963); *Shadows* for Orch. (1965); and *Infrarosso* (Infrared) for 16 Instruments (1967). He also wrote a "collage opera" entitled *Orden* (1969), consisting of several not necessarily related numbers, to texts in French, Italian, and Spanish, and an "épopée musicale," *Addio Garibaldi* (Paris, Oct. 10, 1972).

Arrigoni, Carlo, Italian composer; b. Florence, Dec. 5, 1697; d. there, Aug. 19, 1744. He left Italy as a young man; in 1728 he was in Brussels. In 1732 he was invited to London by a group favorable to Italian composers in opposition to Handel; there he produced an opera, *Fernando* (Feb. 5, 1734). Arrigoni then went back to Italy through Vienna, where he produced an oratorio, *Esther* (1738); returning to Florence, he staged his new operas *Sirbace* and *Scipione nelle Spagne* (1739). His 10 *Cantate da camera* were publ. in London (1732). Several airs from his opera *Fernando* are preserved in the British Museum; Burney mistakenly attributed the music of this opera to Porpora.

Arriola, Pepito (José Rodriguez), Spanish *wunderkind* of the piano; b. Betanzos, Feb. 28, 1896; d. Barcelona, Oct. 24, 1954. Even dismissing tales of his incredible precocity (he was reported as playing in public at the age of 6), the fact remains that he made successful European tours as a child prodigy in programs of adult difficulty. He also composed piano pieces in a Spanish manner. However, as happens in so many pathetic cases of premature development, poor Arriola lost his glamour as soon as he had to drop his baby pet name Pepito, doff his velvet pants, and dress in grown-up clothes. He ceased to attract attention and lingered in utter obscurity and abject poverty.

Arro, Elmar, Estonian musicologist; b. Riga, July 2, 1899; d. Vienna, Dec. 14, 1985. He studied musicology at the Univ. of Vienna, where he received his Ph.D. in 1928 with the dissertation *Über das Musikleben in Estland im 19. Jahrhundert;* in 1933 he joined the faculty of the German Luther Academy in Dorpat; in 1939 he went to Germany; taught at the Univ. of Heidelberg (from 1955) and the Univ. of Kiel (from 1968). He was instrumental in helping to found the Ost-Europa Institut (now the J.G. Herder Forschungsstelle für Musikgeschichte). He subsequently made his home in Vienna. He contributed valuable articles on the music of Russia and Eastern Europe to various music journals; he also founded and served as ed. of the 1st 4 vols. of *Musik des Ostens* (1962–67).

Arroyo, João Marcellino, eminent Portuguese composer, writer, and statesman; b. Oporto, Oct. 4, 1861; d. Colares, near Lisbon, May 18, 1930. A member of a musical family, he first took lessons with his father; at the same time he studied law. From 1884 to 1904 he was a member of the Portuguese parliament; in 1900–1901 he held the posts of minister of foreign affairs and minister of public education. A royalist, he abandoned politics after the revolution of 1910, and received a professorship of law at the Univ. of Coimbra.

WORKS: 2 operas: *Amor de Perdição* (Lisbon, March 2, 1907; Hamburg, Jan. 25, 1910), regarded as the 1st modern Portuguese opera, and *Leonor Teles;* 2 symphonic poems; several choral works and songs; also compiled a manual of solfeggio for primary schools.

BIBL.: C.A. Dos Santos, *J. A.* (Lisbon, 1941).

Arroyo, Martina, American soprano; b. N.Y., Feb. 2, 1936. She is of partly Hispanic, partly black origin. Her voice teacher was Marinka Gurewich, who remained her principal mentor throughout her professional career. After graduation from Hunter College (B.A., 1956), she sang in the American premiere of Pizzetti's *Assassinio nella cattedrale* at Carnegie Hall in N.Y., on Sept. 17, 1958. In 1959 she married an Italian viola player, Emilio Poggioni, but their marriage ended in divorce. On March 14, 1959, she made her debut with the Metropolitan Opera as the Celestial Voice in *Don Carlos;* then sang incidental parts in Wagner's tetralogy. In 1963 she toured Europe; made appearances with the Vienna State Opera, at the Berlin State Opera, and in Zürich. Returning to the U.S., she was a soloist with the N.Y. Phil. and other orchs. She demonstrated her professional mettle when on Feb. 6, 1965, she was suddenly called to substitute for Birgit Nilsson as Aida at the Metropolitan Opera, a challenge she carried off brilliantly; after that she was given major roles at the Metropolitan; she sang Elvira in *Ernani,* Leonora in *Il Trovatore,* Elsa in *Lohengrin,* Donna Anna in *Don Giovanni,* and Aida, all with excellent success. What is even more remarkable, she proved herself technically equal to the complex soprano parts in the works of such avant-garde composers as Varèse, Dallapiccola, and Stockhausen, which she selflessly performed at special concerts.

Artaria, music publishing house in Vienna, founded by the cousins **Carlo** (1747–1808) and **Francesco Artaria** (1744–1808). They opened a music shop on Kohlmarkt in 1769, and in 1778 began printing music; they introduced the method of zinc plating for the 1st time in Vienna. In 1779 the firm acquired some of Haydn's works, which brought it fame; music of Clementi, Salieri, and Boccherini was publ. later. Artaria publ. Mozart's 6 violin sonatas (K. 296, 376–80), the *Haffner-Sinfonie,* and 6 string quartets dedicated to Haydn, among other works, thus becoming Mozart's most important publisher in his lifetime. Other 1st eds. in Artaria's catalog were several songs by Schubert; Beethoven's C-major Quintet, op. 29, and string quartets, opp. 130 and 133. The last owners were **Carl August** (d. 1919), **Dominik** (d. 1936), and **Franz Artaria** (d. 1942). After 1932, the old house became an art gallery and an auction bureau, preserving the name Artaria.

BIBL.: F. Artaria and H. Botstiber, *Joseph Haydn und das Verlagshaus A.* (Vienna, 1909); D. MacArdle, "Beethoven, A., and the C major Quintet," *Musical Quarterly* (Oct. 1948); A. Weinmann, *Vollständiges Verlagsverzeichnis, A. & Comp.* (Vienna, 1952).

Arteaga, Esteban de, Spanish writer on music; b. Moraleja de Coca, Segovia, Dec. 26, 1747; d. Paris, Oct. 30, 1799. He joined the Jesuit Order at 16, and was banished to Corsica when the Jesuits were proscribed in Spain. He left the Order in 1769; from 1773 to 1778 he studied philosophy at the Univ. of Bologna; there he formed a friendship with Padre Martini, and at his behest undertook a history of the musical theater in Italy. The resulting work, *Le rivoluzioni del teatro musicale italiano dalla sua origine fino al presente,* was publ. in 3 vols. in Bologna and Venice (1783–86; the materials in the Bologna ed. partly overlap, partly supplement those in the Venice ed.); it was brought out in German by J. Forkel (2 vols., Leipzig, 1789); a summary was publ. in French (1802). Arteaga's strong and often critical opinions expressed in this work antagonized many Italian writers who resented the intrusion of a foreigner into their own field. A polemical exchange of considerable acrimony followed; Arteaga's views were attacked by Matteo Borsa in the tract *Del gusto presente in letteratura italiana* . . . and by Vincenzo Manfredini in *Difesa della musica moderna* . . . (Bologna, 1786). After a sojourn in Venice (1785), Arteaga lived in Rome (1786–87); in 1796 he went to Florence and later to Paris. In addition to his magnum opus, he publ. a book on esthetics, *Investigaciones filosóficas sobre la belleza ideal* . . . (Madrid, 1789; new ed., Madrid, 1943). A book of essays, *Lettere musico-filologiche,* and the treatise *Del ritmo sonoro e del ritmo muto nella musica degli antichi* (long regarded as lost) were publ. in Madrid in 1944, with an extensive biographical account by the ed. Miguel Batllori, who also gives the bibliographical synopsis of the Bologna and Venice eds. of *Rivoluzioni.*

BIBL.: E. Rudat, *The Aesthetic Ideas of E. d.A.: Origin, Meaning and Current Value* (diss., Univ. of Calif., Los Angeles, 1969).

Artôt, Alexandre-Joseph Montagney, Belgian violinist and composer; b. Brussels, Jan. 25, 1815; d. Ville-d'Avray, July 20, 1845. He studied with his father, **Maurice Montagney Artôt,** and with Snel; then took lessons from Rodolphe and Auguste Kreutzer at the Paris Cons., obtaining 1st prize (1828). He then played concerts on the Continent; made his debut in London (June 3, 1839) in his own *Fantaisie* for Violin and Orch. In 1843 he embarked on an American concert tour. He wrote a Violin Concerto, several sets of variations for violin, and some chamber music.

Artôt, Désirée (baptismal name, **Marguerite-Joséphine Désiré Montagney**), Belgian mezzo-soprano, daughter of **Jean-Désiré Artôt;** b. Paris, July 21, 1835; d. Berlin, April 3, 1907. She studied with Mme. Viardot-Garcia; sang in Belgium, the Netherlands, and England (1857). Meyerbeer engaged her to sing in *Le Prophète* at the Paris Opéra (Feb. 5, 1858); she was greatly praised by Berlioz and other Paris musicians and critics. In 1858 she went to Italy; then made appearances in London. In 1868 she was in Russia, where she was briefly engaged to Tchaikovsky; however, this engagement was quickly disrupted by her marriage (on Sept. 15, 1869) to the Spanish baritone **Mariano Padilla y Ramos.** Their daughter was **Lola Artôt de Padilla.**

Artôt, Jean-Désiré, Belgian horn player and composer; b. Paris, Sept. 23, 1803; d. Brussels, March 25, 1887. He was a pupil and successor of his father, **Maurice Montagney Artôt.** From 1843 he taught at the Brussels Cons.; also played in the Court Orch. He publ. fantasias and études for horn, and quartets for cornets à pistons.

Artôt, Maurice Montagney, ancestor of a celebrated line of musicians (the true family name being Montagney); b. Gray, Haute-Saône, Feb. 3, 1772; d. Brussels, Jan. 8, 1829. He was a bandmaster in the French army; then went to Brussels, where he became 1st horn player at the Théâtre de la Monnaie. A versatile musician, he also played the guitar and taught singing.

Artusi, Giovanni Maria, Italian composer and writer on music; b. Bologna, c.1540; d. there, Aug. 18, 1613. He became canon-in-ordinary at S. Salvatore in Bologna in Feb. 1562. A capable musician and writer who studied with Zarlino, Artusi was reactionary in his musical philosophy. His 1st publication, *L'arte del contrappunto* (in 2 parts; Venice, 1586 and 1598), has considerable theoretical value. He then publ. several polemical essays directed mainly against the innovations of Monteverdi and others: the characteristically named vol. *L'Artusi, ovvero Delle imperfettioni della moderna musica* (Venice, 1600; reproduced in part in Eng. by O. Strunk in *Source Readings in Music History*, N.Y., 1950); a posthumous attack on his teacher Zarlino in *Impresa del R.P. Gioseffo Zarlino* (Bologna, 1604); *Considerazioni musicali* (1603; as part II of *L'Artusi,* etc.); *Discorso musicale . . .* (1606) and *Discorso secondo musicale* (both attacking Monteverdi); and further polemical essays against Bottrigari and Vincenzo Galileo. Monteverdi replied to Artusi in a leaflet entitled *Ottuso accademico* and in the preface to his 5th book of madrigals; this reply is reproduced in Strunk's *Source Readings in Music History*. Bottrigari replied in a pamphlet entitled *Ant' Artusi.* As a composer, Artusi followed the old school; he publ. a set of 4-part *Canzonette* (1598) and an 8-part motet, *Cantate Domino* (1599).

Artyomov, Viacheslav, Russian composer; b. Moscow, June 29, 1940. He studied composition with Pirumov and then at the Moscow Cons. with Sidelnikov, graduating in 1968. Together with Gubaidulina and Suslin, he formed the folk-instrument improvisatory group Astrea in 1975. In his compositions he applies euphonious dissonances over the basic lines of simulated Russian folk modalities, with asymmetrical rhythms in spasmodically lyric melos.

WORKS: String Quartet (1960); 3 pieces for String Quartet (1960); Piano Concerto (1961); *Chamber Suite* for Wind Quintet (1966); 2 clarinet sonatas (1966, 1971); *Northern Songs* for Mezzo-soprano, Percussion, and Piano (1966); *Jubilee Overture* (1967); *Concerto 13* for instrumental and vocal ensemble (1967); Violin Concerto (1968); *Tempo constante* for Orch. (1970); Accordion Concerto (1971); *Variations* for Flute and Piano (1974); *Capriccio for 1975* for Soprano Saxophone, Baritone Saxophone, and Vibraphone (1975); *Totem* for Percussion Ensemble (1976); *Elegiac Symphony* for 2 Violins, Percussion, and Strings (1977); *Awakening* for 2 Violins (1978); *The Road to Olympus* for Orch. (1978; Moscow, Oct. 11, 1979); *Invocations* for Soprano and Percussion (1979–80); *Recitations* for Various Solo Instruments (1976–80); songs.

Artzibushev, Nikolai, Russian composer, music editor, and pedagogue; b. Tsarskoe-Selo, March 7, 1858; d. Paris, April 15, 1937. He studied with Rimsky-Korsakov and Soloviev; in 1908 was elected president of the St. Petersburg Royal Music Soc. After the Revolution he went to Paris, where he was in charge of the Belaiev publishing house. As a composer, he is chiefly known for his melodious piano pieces and songs in a distinct style of the Russian national school; he also wrote a *Valse fantasia* for Orch. and was one of the group of composers who contributed to the collection *Variations on a Russian Theme* for String Quartet; other variations were by Rimsky-Korsakov, Glazunov, Liadov, and Scriabin.

Artzt, Alice (Josephine), American guitarist; b. Philadelphia, March 16, 1943. She first studied piano and flute, turning to the classical guitar when she was 13 and later studying with Ida Presti and Alexandre Lagoya in France and with Julian Bream in England; also took courses with Paul Henry Lang and Otto Luening at Columbia Univ. (B.A., 1967), and studied composition with Darius Milhaud. She made her formal debut in London in 1969, and subsequently toured throughout the world; she was also active as a teacher, serving on the faculties of the Mannes College of Music in N.Y. (1966–69) and Trenton (N.J.) State College (1977–80).

Arundell, Dennis, English opera producer and writer on music; b. London, July 22, 1898; d. there, Dec. 10, 1988. He studied with C.B. Rootham, Henry Moule, and Stanford at St. John's College, Cambridge. He also pursued a career as an actor and singer, and was a regular producer with the Sadler's Wells Opera in London. In 1978 he was made a Member of the Order of the British Empire. Among his books are the valuable biography *Henry Purcell* (London, 1927) and the historical survey *The Story of Sadler's Wells* (London, 1965).

Arutiunian, Alexander, Armenian composer; b. Erevan, Sept. 23, 1920. He studied piano and composition at the local cons.; later went to Moscow, where he took a course in composition with Litinsky; back in Armenia, he was appointed music director of the Armenian Phil. Soc. In his works he utilizes authentic folk-song inflections of Armenian popular music; his *Cantata of the Fatherland* on native themes (1948) achieved considerable success. His other important works are Piano Concerto (1941); Trumpet Concerto (1950); Piano Concertino (1951); Sym. (1957); *Chronicle of the Armenian People,* symphonic poem (1961); Horn Concerto (1962); Concerto for 5 Wind Instruments and Orch. (1964); opera, *Sayat-Nova* (1967); *Ode to Lenin* (1967); *Hymn to Brotherhood* (1970); cycle for Chorus a cappella, *My Armenia* (1971); chamber music. A monograph on him was publ. in the Armenian language in Erevan (1962).

Asafiev, Boris (Vladimirovich), Russian composer and writer on music; b. St. Petersburg, July 29, 1884; d. Moscow, Jan. 27, 1949. He studied with Kalafati and Liadov at the St. Petersburg Cons., graduating in 1910; at the same time he studied philology and history at St. Petersburg Univ. He then became a ballet coach at the Opera. In 1914 he began writing music criticism under the pseudonym **Igor Glebov.** Subsequently he publ. his literary writings under that name, sometimes indicating his real name as well. He always signed his musical works, however, with the name Asafiev. In 1920 he was appointed dean of the dept. of music of the Inst. of History of Arts in Petrograd. He was also an ed. of the journal *Novaya Muzyka* (1924–28); within a few years he publ. brief monographs on Mussorgsky, Scriabin, Rimsky-Korsakov, Liszt, Chopin, etc.; tr. articles from German, French, and Italian. He was a prof. of history, theory, and composition at the Leningrad Cons. (1925–43); then was director of the research section at the Moscow Cons.; at the same time he continued to compose, mostly for the stage. The following ballets by him were performed in Leningrad: *Flames of Paris* (Nov. 7, 1932); *The Fountain of Bakhtchisaray,* after Pushkin (Sept. 28, 1934; very popular); *The Partisan Days* (May 16, 1937); *The Prisoner of the Caucasus* (April 14, 1938). Altogether he wrote 11 operas, 28 ballets, works for orch., including 5 syms. (No. 1, *In Memory of Lermontov,* 1938; No. 2, *From the Age of the Peasant Uprisings,* 1938; No. 3, *Homeland,* 1938–42; No. 4, *Welcome,* 1938–42; No. 5, *The Seasons,* 1942, unfinished), and chamber music. But it was as a historian of Russian music that Asafiev-Glebov was especially important. He continued the tradition of Vladimir Stasov in his ardent advocacy of the national Russian style. He publ. *The Russian Poets in Russian Music* (with a valuable catalog of Russian vocal works; 1921); *Symphonic Études,* an account of the evolution of the Russian operatic style (1922); *Stravinsky,* a comprehensive analysis of Stravinsky's works (1929; later he repudiated the favorable view of Stravinsky expressed in this book); *Russian Music from the Beginning of the Nineteenth Century* (1930; Eng. tr. by A. Swan; American Council of Learned Societies, 1953); *Musical Form as a Process* (2 vols., 1930 and 1947); *Glinka* (Moscow, 1947; the only book on music to receive the Stalin Prize). A 7-vol. ed. of Asafiev's collected writings was begun in Moscow in 1952.

Aschaffenburg, Walter (Eugene), German-born American composer; b. Essen, May 20, 1927. He came to America when he was 11; served in the U.S. Army in Germany in 1947; upon returning to America, he studied music at Oberlin College (B.A., 1951) and at the Eastman School of Music in Rochester,

N.Y. (M.A., 1952). In 1952 he was appointed to the faculty of the Oberlin Cons.; in 1968 became chairman of the dept. of composition there. He retired in 1987.

WORKS: Opera, *Bartleby* (Oberlin, Nov. 12, 1964); *Ozymandias,* "symphonic reflections after Shelley" (Rochester, N.Y., April 22, 1952); *Oedipus Rex,* overture (1952); Piano Trio (1951); *Divertimento* for Trumpet, Horn, and Trombone (1951); Cello Sonata (1954); Sonata for Solo Violin (1954); String Quartet (1955); Woodwind Quintet (1967); *Libertatem appellant* for Tenor, Baritone, and Orch. (1974–76); Concertino for Violin, 10 Winds, and Contrabass (1979–81); *Carrousel,* 24 little pieces for Piano (1980).

Aschenbrenner, Christian Heinrich, German violinist and composer; b. Altstettin, Dec. 29, 1654; d. Jena, Dec. 13, 1732. He studied music with his father; then took composition lessons with Johann Theile; went to Vienna and had some further studies with J.H. Schmelzer. He was active as a violinist at Zeitz (1677–82) and Merseburg (1683–95); served as music director to the Duke of Zeitz (1695–1713) and later to the Duke of Merseburg (1713–19); finally retired on a pension to Jena. His only known work is *Gast- und Hochzeitsfreude, bestehend in Sonaten, Präludien, Allemanden, Couranten, Balletten, Arien, Sarabanden mit 3, 4 und 5 Stimmen, nebst dem Basso continuo* (1673).

Ascher, Joseph, Dutch pianist and composer; b. Groningen, June 4, 1829; d. London, June 20, 1869. He studied with Moscheles; went to Paris in 1849 and was court pianist to the Empress Eugénie. He wrote numerous pieces of salon music (études, nocturnes, galops, etc.).

Ascher, Leo, Austrian composer of light operas; b. Vienna, Aug. 17, 1880; d. N.Y., Feb. 25, 1942. His 1st successful operetta was *Vergeltsgott* (Vienna, Oct. 14, 1905); *Soldat der Marie* and *Hoheit tanzt Walzer* followed. Altogether he composed some 50 stage works, and film music. In 1938 he left Austria to live in N.Y.

Ascone, Vicente, Uruguayan composer of Italian extraction; b. Siderno, Aug. 16, 1897; d. Montevideo, March 5, 1979. He was taken to Uruguay as a child; studied trumpet and composition. Most of his music is rooted in Uruguayan folk songs, while stylistically he followed the traditional Italian formulas. He wrote 5 operas, of which *Paraná Gauzú,* based on an Indian subject, was produced in Montevideo on July 25, 1931. He further wrote 3 syms. (1945, 1955, 1959); *Politonal* for Piano and Orch. (1967); a Trumpet Concerto (1969); a Violin Concerto (1970); a symphonic poem, *Sobre el Río Uruguay* (1946); and numerous songs.

Ashforth, Alden (Banning), American composer and writer on music; b. N.Y., May 13, 1933. He studied at Oberlin College (A.B., 1958) and composition with Joseph Wood and Richard Hoffmann at its Cons. (Mus.B., 1958); subsequently took courses with Roger Sessions, Milton Babbitt, and Earl Kim at Princeton Univ. (M.F.A., 1960; Ph.D., 1971). He taught at Princeton Univ. (1961), Oberlin College (1961–65), N.Y. Univ. (1965–66), the City College of the City Univ. of N.Y. (1966–67), and the Univ. of Calif. at Los Angeles (from 1967). He was active as a jazz researcher and as a recorder/producer of many jazz recordings; contributed articles to the *Annual Review of Jazz Studies* and to *The New Grove Dictionary of Jazz.*

WORKS: **STAGE:** *The Quintessential Zymurgistic Waffle,* musical comedy (1975; in collaboration with P. Reale). **CHAMBER:** Piano Sonata (1955); Sonata for Flute and Harpsichord (1956); Variations for Orch. (1958); *Fantasy-Variations* for Violin and Piano (1959); *Episodes,* chamber concerto for 8 Instruments (1962–68). **VOCAL:** *The Unquiet Heart* for Soprano, and Chamber Orch. or Piano (1959–68). **ELECTRONIC:** *Cycles* (1965); *Mixed Brew* (1968); *Byzantia: 2 Journeys after Yeats* for Organ and Tape (1971–73).

Ashkenazy, Vladimir (Davidovich), greatly gifted Russian pianist and conductor; b. Gorki, July 6, 1937. His parents were professional pianists and taught him to play at an early age; subsequently he took regular lessons with Anaida Sumbatian

at the Central Music School in Moscow, and in 1955 entered the class of Lev Oborin at the Moscow Cons. In 1955 he won 2nd prize at the International Chopin Competition in Warsaw. A great turning point in his career was reached when in 1956, at the age of 19, he won 1st prize in the Queen Elisabeth of Belgium International Competition in Brussels; in 1958 he made his 1st tour of the U.S.; in 1962 he and John Ogdon were both awarded 1st prizes in the Tchaikovsky International Competition in Moscow. In 1961 he married a young pianist, Sofia Johannsdottir of Iceland, who was studying in Moscow at the time. In 1963 they went to England while retaining their common Soviet citizenship. In 1968 they moved to Reykjavík, and in 1972 Ashkenazy became a citizen of Iceland; their 4 children speak English and Icelandic. He was also drawn into conducting, and in 1981 was appointed principal guest conductor of the Philharmonia Orch. of London. From 1987 he was music director of the Royal Phil. in London; was also principal guest conductor of the Cleveland Orch. (from 1987) and chief conductor of the (West) Berlin Radio Sym. Orch. (from 1989). With J. Parrott, he brought out the book *A.: Beyond Frontiers* (London, 1984). As a piano virtuoso he has gained an international reputation for his penetrating insight and superlative technique; his mastery extends from Haydn to the contemporary era. As a conductor, he has demonstrated an affinity for the 19th- and 20th-century repertoire. He has prepared and conducted his own effective orchestration of Mussorgsky's *Pictures at an Exhibition.*

Ashley, Robert (Reynolds), American composer; b. Ann Arbor, Mich., March 28, 1930. He studied composition with Ross Lee Finney, Leslie Bassett, and Roberto Gerhard at the Univ. of Michigan (B.Mus., 1952) and with Wallingford Riegger at the Manhattan School of Music in N.Y. (M.Mus., 1954); also took courses in psychoacoustics and cultural speech patterns at the Speech Research Laboratories at the Univ. of Michigan, where he was employed as a research assistant in acoustics at the Architectural Research Laboratory. He was active with Milton Cohen's Space Theater (1957–64), the ONCE Festival and ONCE Group (1958–69), and the Sonic Arts Union (1966–76), touring widely with them in the U.S. and Europe; served as director of the Center for Contemporary Music at Mills College in Oakland, Calif. (1969–81). In his independent compositions he pursues the ideal of "total musical events," which absorbs gesticulation, natural human noises, and the entire planetary environment.

WORKS: **OPERAS:** *In Memoriam . . . Kit Carson* (1963); *That Morning Thing* (1967; Ann Arbor, Mich., Feb. 8, 1968); *Music with Roots in Aether,* television opera (1976); *Perfect Lives* (1978–80); *The Lessons,* television opera (1981); *Atalanta (Acts of God)* (1982); *Atalanta Strategy,* television opera (1984); *When Opportunity Knocks* (1984–85); *Foreign Experiences* (1984–85); *El Aficionado* (1987); *My Brother Called* (1989). **ELECTRONIC MUSIC THEATER:** *Public Opinion Descends upon the Demonstrators* (1961); *The Lecture Series* (1964; in collaboration with Mary Ashley); *Combination Wedding and Funeral* (1964); *Unmarked Interchange* (1965); *Night Train* (1966; in collaboration with Mary Ashley); *The Wolfman Motorcity Revue* (1968); *What She Thinks* (1976); *Title Withdrawn* (1976). **FILM MUSIC:** *The Image in Time* (1957); *The Bottleman* (1960); *The House* (1961); *Jenny and the Poet* (1964); *My May* (1965); *Overdrive* (1968); *Dr. Chicago* (1968–70); *Portraits, Self-Portraits and Still Lifes* (1969); *Battery Davis* (1970); numerous chamber works, many involving electronics.

BIBL.: T. DeLio, *Circumscribing the Open Universe: Essays on Cage, Feldman, Wolff, A. and Lucier* (Washington, D.C., 1984).

Ashrafi, Mukhtar, Russian composer; b. Bukhara, June 11, 1912; d. Tashkent, Dec. 15, 1975. He studied at the Moscow Cons. (1934–37) and later at the Leningrad Cons. (1941–43). As the war situation led to a siege of Leningrad, he was evacuated to Tashkent. Since he never acquired comprehensive technique of composition, his operas were orchestrated by his teacher at the Moscow Cons., Vasilenkov; 2 of these were produced in Tashkent: *Buran* (June 12, 1939) and *The Grand Canal* (Jan. 12, 1941). He further wrote several ballets and 2 syms. on patriotic themes, several orch. suites on central Asian themes, and a number of songs.

Ashton, Algernon (Bennet Langton), English composer; b. Durham, Dec. 9, 1859; d. London, April 10, 1937. His family moved to Leipzig, and he studied at the Leipzig Cons. with Reinecke and Jadassohn (1875–79); later took lessons with Raff in Frankfurt (1880). Returning to England, he obtained the post of piano teacher at the Royal College of Music (1885–1910). He was a prolific composer, having written more than 160 opus numbers, mostly in a conventional German style: 5 syms.; 3 overtures; a Piano Concerto; a Violin Concerto; 3 piano quintets; 3 piano quartets; 3 piano trios; Trio for Clarinet, Viola, and Bassoon; Trio for Piano, Horn, and Viola; 5 violin sonatas; 5 cello sonatas; a Viola Sonata; and more than 200 piano works (among them a Sonata, 3 fantasias, and various picturesque pieces such as *Idyls* and *Roses and Thorns*); also more than 200 songs, choral pieces, and organ works. Many of his chamber music compositions were publ., but he was never given recognition as a composer; however, he acquired notoriety by his curious letters in the English press dealing with a variety of subjects. Many of these letters he collected in his vols. *Truth, Wit and Wisdom* (London, 1904) and *More Truth, Wit and Wisdom* (London, 1905).

Asioli, Bonifazio (or **Bonifacio**), Italian composer; b. Correggio, Aug. 30, 1769; d. there, May 18, 1832. He began writing music at a very early age. He studied with Angelo Morigi in Parma (1780–82); then lived in Bologna and Venice as a harpsichord player. His 1st opera, *La Volubile*, was produced in Correggio (1785) with marked success; it was followed by *Le nozze in villa* (Correggio, 1786); *Cinna* (Milan, 1793); and *Gustavo al Malabar* (Turin, 1802). From 1787 he was private maestro to the Marquis Gherardini, in Turin, then in Venice (1796–99); subsequently he went to Milan and taught at the Cons. (1808–14). Asioli wrote 6 operas; an oratorio, *Giuseppe in Galaad*; many cantatas; instrumental music; sacred choral works; etc. He was the author of several textbooks: *Principi elementari di musica* (Milan, 1809; also in Eng., German, and French); *Trattato d'armonia e d'accompagnamento* (1813); also manuals for harpsichord, voice, and double bass. His theoretical book *Il Maestro di composizione* was publ. posth. (1836).
BIBL.: A. Coli, *Vita di B. A.* (Milan, 1834); O.S. Ancarani, *Sopra alcune parole di Carlo Botta intorno al metodo musicale di B. A.* (1836); A. Amadei, *Intorno allo stile della moderna musica di chiesa* (1841).

Askenase, Stefan, Polish-born Belgian pianist; b. Lemberg, July 10, 1896; d. Bonn, Oct. 18, 1985. In Vienna he studied piano with Emil von Sauer and composition with Joseph Marx. He traveled as a concert pianist; then taught in Rotterdam and Brussels. In 1950 he adopted Belgian citizenship.

Asola (Asula), Giammateo (Giovanni Matteo), Italian composer; b. Verona, c.1532; d. Venice, Oct. 1, 1609. He entered the congregation of secular canons at S. Giorgio in Alga in 1546; held benefices at S. Stefano in Verona from 1566; subsequently served as a secular priest. He became maestro di cappella at Treviso Cathedral in 1577; then served in a similar capacity at Vicenza Cathedral in 1578. In 1588 he became one of the chaplains at S. Severo in Venice. He was active as a teacher; among his pupils was Leone Leoni. He wrote much sacred music in the style of Palestrina. The *Opera omnia*, ed. by G. Vecchi, began to appear in 1963.
BIBL.: F. Caffi, *Della vita e delle opere G. A.* (Padua, 1862); D. Fouse, *The Sacred Music of G. A.* (diss., Univ. of North Carolina, 1960).

Asow, Erich Hermann Müller von. See Mueller von Asow, Erich Hermann.

Aspa, Mario, Italian opera composer; b. Messina, 1799; d. there, Dec. 14, 1868. He studied with Zingarelli in Naples. He produced 42 operas, of which the most successful were *Paolo e Virginia* (Rome, April 29, 1843) and *Il Muratore di Napoli* (Naples, Oct. 16, 1850). His last opera, *Piero di Calais*, was produced posth. (Messina, March 6, 1872).

Aspestrand, Sigwart, Norwegian opera composer; b. Fredrikshald, Nov. 13, 1856; d. Oslo, Dec. 31, 1941. He studied at Leipzig and Berlin and spent 30 years of his life (1885–1915) in Germany. Of his 7 operas, *Die Seemansbraut*, produced in Gotha (March 29, 1894), was the most successful. His other operas, all in German, are: *Der Recke von Lyrskovsheid, Freyas Alter, Die Wette, Der Kuss auf Sicht, Robin Hood,* and *Pervonte.*

Asplmayr, Franz, Austrian composer; b. Linz (baptized), April 2, 1728; d. Vienna, July 29, 1786. He studied violin with his father; wrote ballets for the Austrian court. Historically, Asplmayr was important as one of the earliest Austrian composers to adopt the instrumental style, rich in dynamics, as established by the Mannheim school.
WORKS: Ballets: *Agamemnon* vengé (1771), *Ifigenie* (1772), and *Acis et Galathée*; singspiel, *Die Kinder der Natur*; music for Shakespeare's *Macbeth* (1777) and *The Tempest* (1781); chamber works; 6 *Serenate*, op. 1; 6 *Quatuors concertants*, op. 2; 6 *Trios*, op. 5; 6 *Quatuors*, op. 6.

Aspull, George, precocious English pianist and composer; b. Manchester, June 1813; d. Leamington, Aug. 19, 1832. He 1st gained notice as a youthful pianist in Paris (1825); then toured in England with notable success before his promising career was cruelly cut short by tuberculosis at the age of 19. His father, Thomas Aspull, ed. and publ. the vol. *George Aspull's Posthumous Works for the Pianoforte* (London, 1837).
BIBL.: M. Silburn, "The Most Extraordinary Creature in Europe," *Music & Letters,* III (1922).

Asriel, André, Austrian composer; b. Vienna, Feb. 22, 1922. He enrolled in the Vienna Academy of Music at the age of 13; in 1938 he went to England, where he took courses at the Royal College of Music in London. In 1946 he went to East Berlin and studied piano and composition at the Hochschule für Musik in Berlin-Charlottenburg; he also took lessons with Hanns Eisler at the Academy of the Arts. In 1951 he was appointed instructor at the newly founded Deutsche Hochschule für Musik; from 1967 to 1984 he was a prof. there. He wrote a number of songs on socialist themes, among them *Freundschaft, Einheit, Frieden, Das neue Deutschland*; he further composed music for film documentaries; also became interested in jazz as a type of American folk music. He wrote a cycle of choral pieces a cappella to the texts of Aesop's fables. Among his purely instrumental works are 4 *Inventions* for Trumpet, Trombone, and Orch. (1963) and *Serenade* for 9 Instruments (1969). He publ. a book, *Jazz Analysen und Aspekte* (Berlin, 1966; 4th ed., 1984).

Assmayer, Ignaz, Austrian composer; b. Salzburg, Feb. 11, 1790; d. Vienna, Aug. 31, 1862. He studied piano, organ, and theory with A. Brunmayrs in Salzburg and later with T. Gerls. In 1815 he moved to Vienna, where he took lessons with Salieri. In 1846 he was appointed 1st Kapellmeister in Vienna, succeeding Eybler. He wrote several oratorios, among them *Saul und David, Sauls Tod,* and *Das Gelübde*, which he performed with the Vienna Tonkünstler Soc. He further wrote 21 masses, 2 Requiems, and other sacred works, as well as some 60 instrumental compositions, many of which were publ.

Astaire, Fred (real name, **Frederick Austerlitz**), charismatic American dancer, choreographer, singer, and actor; b. Omaha, May 10, 1899; d. Los Angeles, June 22, 1987. With his sister Adele (b. Omaha, Sept. 10, 1897; d. Phoenix, Jan. 25, 1981), he appeared in dance and comedy routines from the age of 7; after working on the vaudeville circuit, they starred in revues and musicals. Following his sister's retirement from the stage, he went to Hollywood; teaming up with the dancer Ginger Rogers, he gained renown through such films as *The Gay Divorcee* (1934), *Roberta* (1935), *Top Hat* (1935), *Swing Time* (1936), and *The Story of Vernon and Irene Castle* (1939). His mastery of the dance, ably abetted by his insouciant singing style, contributed greatly to the development of the musical film, earning him a special Academy Award in 1949. He publ. *Steps in Time* (N.Y., 1959).

BIBL.: A. Croce, *The F. A. and Ginger Rogers Book* (N.Y., 1972); S. Green and B. Goldberg, *Starring F. A.* (N.Y., 1973); B. Thomas, *A.: The Man, the Dancer* (N.Y., 1984).

Astor, Peter (George), English conductor and composer; b. Birmingham, Oct. 5, 1938. He studied composition and conducting at the Birmingham School of Music, completing his education at the Univ. of York (Ph.D., 1970, with the diss. *George Jeffreys and the English Baroque*). He devoted himself mainly to conducting English Baroque ensembles; conducted the Aldeburgh Festival Singers (from 1975). He also occupied various teaching positions in English univs. As a composer, he produced mostly sacred vocal music; among his particularly interesting works are *My Dancing Day*, cantata for Soprano, Tenor, Flute, Clarinet, and String Quartet (1966); *Sacrapant, the Sorcerer*, children's opera (1967); *A Mass for All Saints* for Chorus and Organ (1987); and *Great Is the Lord* for Chorus and Organ (1988).

d'Astorga, Baron Emanuele (Gioacchino Cesare Rincón), Italian composer of operas; b. Augusta, Sicily, March 20, 1680; d. probably in Madrid, after 1757. Of a noble Spanish family which had settled in Augusta early in the 17th century, he was a baron in his own right, from his estate Ogliastro, nearby. Later in life he moved to Palermo; during the revolution of 1708 he was an officer in the municipal guard. In 1712 he went to Vienna, and was in Znaim in 1713; he left Vienna in 1714 and returned to Palermo, where he became a senator. It is known that he sold his Sicilian estate in 1744 and went to Spain, where he was in the service of the King. D'Astorga was widely known as a versatile and highly educated person; he was also adept as a singer and harpsichordist, but never regarded music as his primary profession. He composed at least 3 operas: the 1st, *La Moglie nemica*, was produced at Palermo in 1698; the 2nd and most notable, *Dafni*, was staged at Genoa on April 21, 1709, and was probably also heard in Barcelona (1709) and in Breslau (1726); the 3rd, *Amor tirannico*, was given in Venice in 1710. He also wrote numerous chamber cantatas and himself publ. 12 of them in 1 vol. (Lisbon, 1726). His best-known work is *Stabat Mater* for 4 Voices; it was 1st heard in Oxford in 1752; a new ed. of it was publ. by R. Franz in 1878. In his 2-vol. biography of d'Astorga (Leipzig, 1911 and 1919), Hans Volkmann refutes the unsupported statement of R. Pohl in the 1st ed. of *Grove's Dictionary* that d'Astorga died at Raudnitz on Aug. 21, 1736; Volkmann also exposes the romantic account of d'Astorga's life publ. by Rochlitz in vol. II of *Für Freunde der Tonkunst* (1825) as a fanciful invention. *Astorga*, an opera based on his life, was written by J.J. Abert (1866). See also O. Tiby, "E. D'Astorga," *Acta Musicologica* (1953).

Åstrand, (Karl) Hans (Vilhelm), Swedish music historian and lexicographer; b. Bredaryd, Feb. 5, 1925. He studied organ, double bass, and cello; also took courses in Romance languages at the Univ. of Lund (Licentiate, 1958). He was music critic of the Malmö newspaper *Kvällsposten* (from 1950), founder-director of the Chamber Choir '53 (1953–62), and founder (1960) and director (1965–71) of the Ars Nova Soc. for New Music. He served as ed. in chief of the fundamental Swedish musical encyclopedia, *Sohlmans musik-lexikon* (5 vols., Stockholm, 1975–79). He was a board member (from 1966) and perpetual secretary (from 1973) of the Royal Swedish Academy of Music in Stockholm.

Asuar, José Vicente, Chilean composer; b. Santiago, July 20, 1933. He studied electrical engineering and music, 1st in Santiago and later in Berlin. From 1963 to 1965 he was prof. of acoustics and contemporary music at the Santiago National Cons.; from 1965 to 1968 he led a studio for electronic music in Caracas; he composed and performed there a multimedia work, *Imagen de Caracas*, employing synchronized projectors of 8 films plus chorus and orch.; from 1968 to 1972 he directed a course in sound technology at the Univ. of Chile.

He composed mostly for electronic tape; his *Estudio aleatorio* (1962) makes use of random devices. Among his purely instrumental works are *Heterophonías* for Orch. (1965), *Octet* for 4 Flutes and 4 Percussion Players (1966), and *Guararia repano* for Indigenous Indian Instruments (1968).

Atanasov, Georgi, Bulgarian composer; b. Plovdiv, May 18, 1881; d. Fasano, Italy, Nov. 17, 1931. He went to Italy in 1901, and took lessons in composition with Mascagni at the Pesaro Cons. Returning to Bulgaria, he became active as a military bandleader, as well as a composer. He wrote 2 of the earliest operas on national Bulgarian subjects, *Borislav* (Sofia, March 4, 1911) and *Gergana* (Sofia, June 19, 1917); other operas were *Zapustialata vodenitza* (The Abandoned Mill; Sofia, March 31, 1923), *Altzek*, and *Tzveta*; he also wrote 2 children's operas, *The Sick Teacher* and *About Birds*.

BIBL.: I. Sagaev, *Maestro G. A.* (Sofia, 1961).

Atanasov, Nikola, Bulgarian conductor, teacher, and composer; b. Kyustendil, Oct. 25, 1886; d. Sofia, Sept. 30, 1969. He studied with F. Dugan at the Croatian Cons. in Zagreb; returning to Bulgaria, he taught at the Sofia Cons. (from 1929). He composed 3 syms. (1912, 1922, 1950); *Christo Botev* (1928) and *Forest Murmurs* (1931) overtures; chamber music; piano pieces; songs.

BIBL.: P. Londev, *N. A.* (Sofia, 1963).

Atherton, David, English conductor; b. Blackpool, Jan. 3, 1944. He studied at Cambridge Univ. In 1967 he founded the London Sinfonietta, serving as its music director until 1973. In 1968 he became a conductor at the Royal Opera House, Covent Garden. In 1978 he had several engagements at the San Francisco Opera. In 1980 he became principal conductor of the Royal Liverpool Phil. Orch.; from 1981 to 1987 he was music director of the San Diego Sym. Orch., but continued his association with the Liverpool Phil. as a principal guest conductor. In 1989 he became music director of the Hong Kong Phil.

Atkins, Chet (Chester Burton), American guitarist of country-western and popular music; b. Luttrell, Tenn., June 20, 1924. He began to play the guitar as a child, mastering it without formal instruction; from 1941 appeared on various radio programs, including the "Grand Ole Opry" in Nashville. In 1957 he became an executive for RCA Victor, managing its recording studio in Nashville; as such he became the leader in the movement toward popular country-western music (country pop or Nashville sound), emphasizing electronic instruments and techniques. A versatile guitarist, he felt at ease in the performance of many popular genres; he also played jazz and made successful tours to Europe, the Far East, and Africa. He was elected to the Country Music Hall of Fame in 1973. His autobiography, *Country Gentleman*, was publ. in 1974.

Atlantov, Vladimir, Russian tenor and baritone; b. Leningrad, Feb. 19, 1939. He was brought up in a musical atmosphere; his father was a professional singer. He studied voice at the Leningrad Cons., graduating in 1963; continued his vocal studies at the La Scala Opera School in Milan (1963–65). In 1967 he became a regular member of the Bolshoi Theater in Moscow; also gave concert recitals in Italy, Austria, Hungary, France, and Japan. He is especially effective in lyrico-dramatic parts; his interpretations of Don José in *Carmen*, Alfredo in *La Traviata*, Cavaradossi in *Tosca*, and Lensky in *Eugene Onegin* are especially fine. In 1977 he extended his repertoire to include baritone roles.

Atlas, Allan W(arren), American musicologist; b. N.Y., Feb. 19, 1943. He was educated at Hunter College (B.A., 1964) and N.Y. Univ. (M.A., 1966; Ph.D., 1971, with the diss. *The Cappella Giulia Chansonnier and the Dissemination of the Franco-Netherlandish Chanson in Italy, c.1460–c.1520*); in 1971, was appointed to the faculty of Brooklyn College. He contributed numerous articles to *The New Grove Dictionary of Music and Musicians* (1980); publ. *Music in the Classic Period: Essays in Honor of Barry S. Brook* (N.Y., 1985) and *Music at the Aragonese Court of Naples* (Cambridge, 1985).

Attaignant (also **Attaingnant, Atteignant**), **Pierre,** French printer of music; b. c.1494; d. Paris, 1552. He was probably the earliest printer in France to employ movable type in music printing. His 1st publication was a *Breviarium Noviomense* (1525). He publ. a great many works, including 18 dances in tablature for the Lute (1529); 25 pavans (1530); a folio ed. of 7 books of masses (1532); 13 books of motets (1534–35); and a series of 35 books of chansons (1539–49) containing 927 part-songs by French and Flemish composers. Reprints: E. Bernoulli, facsimile ed. of 4 books under the title *Chansons und Tänze* (Munich, 1914); 31 chansons in Henry Expert's *Les Maîtres Musiciens de la Renaissance française* (1894–1908); D. Heartz, *Preludes, Chansons, Dances for Lute (1529–30)* (1964); *Danseries à 4 parties,* in Le Pupitre, 9 (Paris, 1969).

BIBL.: Y. Rihouet (Rokseth), "Note bibliographique sur Attaignant," *Revue de Musicologie* (1924); F. Lesure, "P. Attaignant, Notes et documents," *Musica Disciplina,* III (1949); D. Heartz, *P. Attaignant, Royal Printer of Music* (Berkeley, Calif., 1969).

Attenhofer, Karl, Swiss conductor and composer; b. Wettingen, May 5, 1837; d. Zürich, May 22, 1914. He studied at the Leipzig Cons. with Richter and Dreyschock; went to Zürich in 1866, and in 1870 was appointed director of music at the Univ. of Zürich; also held the post of 2nd director of the Zürich Cons. (the post of 1st director was held by Friedrich Hegar). Attenhofer wrote mainly for chorus; his cantatas *Hegelingenfahrt* (1890), *Frühlingsfeier,* and *Der deutsche Michel* for men's voices have achieved considerable popularity. For women's voices he wrote *Beim Rattenfänger im Zauberberg, Das Kind der Wüste, Prinzessin Wunderhold,* and *Rütlifahrt;* he also compiled a manual, *Liederbuch für Männergesang* (1882).

BIBL.: E. Isler, *K. A.* (Zürich, 1915).

Atterberg, Kurt, eminent Swedish composer; b. Göteborg, Dec. 12, 1887; d. Stockholm, Feb. 15, 1974. He studied engineering and was employed in the wireless service; then took courses in composition at the Stockholm Cons. with Hallén, and in Berlin with Schillings (1910–12). In 1913 he was appointed conductor at the Drama Theater in Stockholm, holding this post until 1922; in 1919 he began writing music criticism and continued to contribute to Stockholm newspapers until 1957; concurrently he was also employed at the Swedish patent office (1912–68) and served as secretary of the Royal Swedish Academy of Music in Stockholm (1940–53). He was one of the founders of the Soc. of Swedish Composers in 1924, and was on its board until 1947. During all this time he continued to compose with inexhaustible energy, producing works in all genres: operas, ballets, syms., concertos, choruses, and chamber music, all with preordained precision of form and technique. It is ironic that his music remained hermetically sealed within the confines of Sweden, rarely if ever performed beyond its borders. Atterberg's name attracted unexpected attention when he was declared winner of the ill-conceived Schubert Centennial Contest organized in 1928 by the Columbia Phonograph Co., with the declared intention to finish Schubert's *Unfinished Symphony.* The entire venture was severely criticized in musical circles as an attempt to derive commercial advantage under the guise of an homage to a great composer. Rumors spread that Atterberg had deliberately imitated the style of composition of some members of the jury (Glazunov, Alfano, Nielsen) in order to ingratiate himself with them so as to secure the prize, but Atterberg denied any such suggestion, pointing out that he knew the names only of those in the jury from the Nordic zone, whereas the international membership comprised 10 national zones. Furthermore, the sym. he had submitted was written in a far more advanced style than Atterberg's previous symphonic works and was certainly much more modern than any music by the jury members, using as it did such procedures as polytonality. There can be no doubt, however, that Atterberg was a master technician of his craft, and that his music had a powerful appeal. That it never gained a wider audience can be ascribed only to an unfathomable accident of world culture.

WORKS: STAGE: OPERAS (1st perf. in Stockholm): *Härvard Harpolekare* (Harvard the Potter; 1915–17; Sept. 29, 1919; rev. as *Härvard der Harfner* and produced in German at Chemnitz, 1936; a later version with new 3rd act produced in Linz, June 14, 1952); *Bäckahästen* (1923–24; Jan. 23, 1925); *Fanal* (1929–32; Jan. 27, 1934); *Aladdin* (1936–41; March 18, 1941); *Stormen,* after Shakespeare's *Tempest* (1946–47; Sept. 19, 1948). **BALLETS:** *Per Svinaherde* (Peter the Swineherd; 1914–15); ballet-pantomime, *De fåvitska jungfrurna* (The Wise and Foolish Virgins; 1920; Paris, Nov. 18, 1920). **ORCH.: SYMS.:** No. 1 (1909–11; Stockholm, Jan. 10, 1912); No. 2 (1911–13; Stockholm, Feb. 11, 1912); No. 3 (1914–16; Stockholm, Nov. 28, 1916); No. 4, *Sinfonia piccola* (1918; Stockholm, March 27, 1919); No. 5, *Sinfonia funèbre* (1919–22; Stockholm, Jan. 6, 1923); No. 6 (1927–28; won the Schubert Centennial Prize; Stockholm, Oct. 15, 1928); No. 7, *Sinfonia romantica* (1942; Frankfurt, Feb. 14, 1943); No. 8 (1944; Helsinki, Feb. 9, 1945); No. 9, *Sinfonia visionaria,* with Mezzo-soprano, Baritone, and Chorus (1955–56; Helsinki, Feb. 26, 1957); also a *Sinfonia* for Strings (1952–53); *Varmlandsrhapsodi* on northern Swedish folk tunes, written in honor of Selma Lagerlöf's 75th birthday (Swedish Radio, Nov. 20, 1933). **OTHER ORCH. WORKS:** 9 suites, among them No. 3, for Violin, Viola, and Strings (1917); No. 4, *Turandot* (1921); No. 5, *Suite barocco* (1922); and No. 8, *Suite pastorale* (1931); Rhapsody for Piano and Orch. (1909); Violin Concerto (1913; Göteborg, Feb. 11, 1914); Cello Concerto (1917–22; Berlin, Jan. 6, 1923); 2 Suites for the play *Stormen,* after Shakespeare's *Tempest:* No. 1 (1921; rev. 1962–63); No. 2 (1964–65); *Rondeau rétrospectif* for Orch. (1926); Horn Concerto (1926; Stockholm, March 20, 1927); *Älven* (The River), symphonic poem (1929–30); Piano Concerto (1927–35; Stockholm, Jan. 12, 1936); *Ballad and Passacaglia* for Orch. (1936); *Rondeau caractéristique* (1939–40); *Indian Tunes* for Orch. (1950); *Ballad utan ord* (Ballad without Words) for Orch. (1957–58); Concerto for Violin, Cello or Viola, and Orch. (1959–60; version with String Orch., 1963); *Vittorioso* for Orch. (1962); *Adagio amoroso* for Flute and Strings (1967); a *Requiem* (1913); a cantata, *Järnbäraland* (1919). **CHAMBER:** 2 string quartets (1915, 1937); Cello Sonata (1925); Piano Quintet (1927); *Variations and Fugue* for String Quartet (1943); *Trio concertante* for Violin, Cello, and Harp (1959–60; rev. 1965).

Attwood, Thomas, English organist and composer; b. London, Nov. 23, 1765; d. there, March 24, 1838. He was a chorister at the Chapel Royal under Nares and Ayrton from the age of 9. Following a performance before the Prince of Wales (afterward George IV), he was sent to Italy for further study; there he received instruction in Naples from Filippo Cinque and Gaetano Latilla. He then went to Vienna, where Mozart accepted him as a pupil; his notes from these theory and composition lessons are printed in the *Neue Mozart Ausgabe,* X/30/1. In 1787 he returned to London and held various posts as an organist. He was also music tutor to the Duchess of York (1791) and to the Princess of Wales (1795). A founder of the London Phil. Soc. (1813), he conducted some of its concerts. He occupied an important position in the English music world; when Mendelssohn came to London as a young man, Attwood lent him enthusiastic support. Attwood was a prolific composer of operas, of which many were produced in London, including *The Prisoner* (Oct. 18, 1792); *The Mariners* (May 10, 1793); *The Packet Boat* (May 13, 1794); *The Smugglers* (April 13, 1796); *The Fairy Festival* (May 13, 1797); *The Irish Tar* (Aug. 24, 1797); *The Devil of a Lover* (March 17, 1798); *The Magic Oak* (Jan. 29, 1799); *True Friends* (Feb. 19, 1800); *The Sea-Side Story* (May 12, 1801). In all, Attwood wrote 28 operas, in some of which he used material from other composers (he included music by Mozart in *The Prisoner* and *The Mariners*). He also wrote church music, piano sonatas, songs, and glees.

BIBL.: C. Oldman, "T. A., 1765–1838," *Musical Times* (Nov. 1965).

Auber, Daniel-François-Esprit, prolific French composer of comic operas; b. Caen, Normandy, Jan. 29, 1782; d. Paris,

May 12, 1871. His father, an art dealer in Paris, sent him to London to acquire knowledge of business. Auber learned music as well as trade and wrote several songs for social entertainment in London. Political tension between France and England, however, forced him to return to Paris in 1803; there he devoted himself exclusively to music. His pasticcio *L'Erreur d'un moment*, a resetting of an old libretto, was produced by an amateur group in Paris in 1806; his next theatrical work was *Julie*, performed privately, with an accompaniment of 6 string instruments, in 1811. Cherubini, who was in the audience, was attracted by Auber's talent and subsequently gave him some professional advice. Auber's 1st opera to be given publicly in Paris was *Le Séjour militaire* (1813); 6 years later the Opéra-Comique produced his new work *Le Testament et les billets-doux* (1819). These operas passed without favorable notice, but his next production, *La Bergère châtelaine* (1820), was a definite success. From that time until nearly the end of his life, hardly a year elapsed without the production of a new opera. Not counting amateur performances, 45 operas from Auber's pen were staged in Paris between 1813 and 1869. He was fortunate in having the collaboration of the best librettist of the time, Scribe, who wrote (alone, or with other writers) no fewer than 37 libretti for Auber's operas. Auber's fame reached its height with *Masaniello, ou La Muette de Portici*, produced at the Opéra, Feb. 29, 1828. Its success was enormous. Historically, it laid the foundation of French grand opera with Meyerbeer's *Robert le Diable* and Rossini's *Guillaume Tell*. Its vivid portrayal of popular fury stirred French and Belgian audiences; revolutionary riots followed its performance in Brussels (Aug. 25, 1830). Another popular success was achieved by him with his Romantic opera *Fra Diavolo* (Opéra-Comique, Jan. 28, 1830), which became a standard work. Despite these successes with grand opera, Auber may be rightfully regarded as a founder of the French comic opera, a worthy successor of Boieldieu and at least an equal of Adam and Hérold. The influence of Rossini was noted by contemporary critics, but on the whole, Auber's music preserves a distinctive quality of its own. Rossini himself remarked that although Auber's music is light, his art is profound. Auber was greatly appreciated by the successive regimes in France; in 1829 he succeeded Gossec at the Academy; in 1842 he was appointed director of the Paris Cons. by Louis Philippe, and retained this post until his death. In 1852 Napoleon III made him imperial maître de chapelle. At the age of 87 he produced his last opera, *Rêve d'amour*. Auber lived virtually all his life in Paris, remaining there even during the siege by the Germans. He died, during the days of the Paris Commune, at the age of 89. His memory was honored by the Academy. Among his operas (most of which were produced at the Opéra-Comique) are also the following: *Le Cheval de bronze* (March 23, 1835); *Le Domino noir* (Dec. 2, 1837); *Les Diamants de la couronne* (March 6, 1841); *Manon Lescaut* (Feb. 23, 1856); *Le Premier Jour de bonheur* (Feb. 15, 1868).

BIBL.: A. Pougin, *A.* (Paris, 1873); A. Kohut, *A.* (Leipzig, 1895); C. Malherbe, *A.* (Paris, 1911); J. Klein, "D.-F. A. (1782–1871)," *Opera* (Aug. 1971).

Aubert, Jacques (called **"le vieux"**), celebrated French violinist and composer; b. Paris, Sept. 30, 1689; d. Belleville, near Paris, (buried), May 19, 1753. He was a pupil of Senaillé; in 1719 he became bandleader to the Duke of Bourbon; in 1727 was one of the King's 24 violinists; he played in the orch. of the Grand Opéra as 1st violinist from 1728 to 1752, and took part in the Concert Spirituel (1729–40). He publ. 33 separate instrumental works; was also the 1st in France to publ. instrumental concertos (scored for 4 violins and a bass). His music, distinguished by elegance, contributed to the formation of the French *style galant*.

BIBL.: L. La Laurencie, *L'École française de violon de Lully à Viotti* (Paris, 1922–23).

Aubert, Louis-François-Marie, French composer; b. Paramé, Ille-et-Vilaine, Feb. 19, 1877; d. Paris, Jan. 9, 1968. Of precocious talent, he entered the Paris Cons. as a child,

and studied piano with Diémer, theory with Lavignac, and advanced composition with Gabriel Fauré; he also sang in church choirs. His song *Rimes tendres* was publ. when he was 19. His *Fantaisie* for Piano and Orch. was performed in Paris by the Colonne Orch. with his teacher Diémer as soloist (Nov. 17, 1901). His *Suite brève* for 2 Pianos was presented at the Paris Exposition in 1900; an orch. version of it was performed for the 1st time in Paris on April 27, 1916. Aubert's major work is an operatic fairy tale, *La Forêt bleue* (Geneva, Jan. 7, 1913); a Russian production was given in Boston on March 8, 1913, attracting considerable attention. The Paris production of *La Forêt bleue*, delayed by the war, took place on June 10, 1924, at the Opéra-Comique. Aubert's style is largely determined by the impressionistic currents of the early 20th century; like Debussy and Ravel, he was attracted by the music of Spain and wrote several pieces in the Spanish idiom, of which the symphonic poem *Habanera* (Paris, March 22, 1919) was particularly successful. The list of Aubert's works further includes: *La Légende du sang* for Narrator, Chorus, and Orch. (1902); 3 ballets: *La Momie* (1903); *Chrysothémis* (1904); *La Nuit ensorcélée* (1922); *6 poèmes arabes* for Voice and Orch. (1907); a song cycle, *Crépuscules d'automne* (Paris, Feb. 20, 1909); *Nuit mauresque* for Voice and Orch. (1911); *Dryade* for Orch. (1921); *Caprice* for Violin and Orch. (1925); *Feuilles d'images*, symphonic suite (Paris, March 7, 1931); *Saisons* for Chorus and Orch. (1937); *Offrande aux victimes de la guerre* for Orch. (1947); *Le Tombeau de Châteaubriand* for Orch. (1948); *Cinéma*, ballet (1953); *Improvisation* for 2 Guitars (1960); a set of 3 piano pieces, *Sillages* (1913); a Piano Quintet; songs; etc.

BIBL.: L. Vuillemin, *L. A. et son œuvre* (Paris, 1921); M. Landowski and G. Morançon, *L. A.* (Paris, 1967).

Aubéry du Boulley, Prudent-Louis, French composer; b. Verneuil, Eure, Dec. 9, 1796; d. there, Jan. 28, 1869. He studied at the Paris Cons. with Momigny, Méhul, and Cherubini. He wrote much chamber music, in which he used the guitar; publ. a guitar method and a textbook, *Grammaire musicale* (Paris, 1830). He was an active teacher in his native province, and contributed much to the cultivation of music there.

BIBL.: J. de L'Avre, *A.d.B.* (Paris, 1896).

Aubin, Tony (Louis Alexandre), French composer, conductor, and pedagogue; b. Paris, Dec. 8, 1907; d. there, Sept. 21, 1981. He studied at the Paris Cons. with Samuel-Rousseau, Noël Gallon, and Paul Dukas; in 1930 he won the 1st Grand Prix de Rome. Upon his return to Paris from Rome, he studied conducting with Philippe Gaubert, and later was in charge of the music division at the Paris Radio until the collapse of France in 1940; from 1945 to 1960 he served as conductor with the French Radio; concurrently he taught at the Paris Cons. In 1968 he was elected member of the Académie des Beaux-Arts. A pragmatic composer, Aubin cultivated an eclectic idiom calculated to impress professionals and please common music-lovers.

WORKS: *Symphonie romantique* (1937); *Suite éolienne* for Clarinet, Flute, and Strings (1958); *Concertinetto dell'amicizia* for Flute and Piano (1964); *Concertinetto* for Violin and Piano (1964); *Brughiera* for Bassoon and Piano (1966); opera, *Goya* (1970).

Aubry, Pierre, French music scholar; b. Paris, Feb. 14, 1874; d. (following a fencing accident) Dieppe, Aug. 31, 1910. He began his education as a philologist; studied oriental languages, and traveled to Turkestan on a research project. He then became interested in medieval music; was, for a time, lecturer on music history at the École des Hautes Études Sociales. His theories of notation are based on a plausible interpretation of medieval writers.

WRITINGS: His many publications, distinguished by profound scholarship, include: *8 chants héroïques de l'ancienne France* (1896); *Mélanges de musicologie critique*, in 4 vols.: I, *La Musicologie médiévale* (1899); II, *Les Proses d'Adam de Saint-Victor* (1900, with Abbé Misset); III, *Lais et Descorts* *français du XIIIᵉ siècle* (1901, with Jeanroy and Brandin); IV, *Les Plus Anciens Monuments de la musique française* (1903, with 24 facsimiles); *Essais de musicologie comparée*, 2 vols.: I, *Le Rhythme tonique dans la poésie liturgique et dans le chant des églises chrétiennes au Moyen-Age* (1903); II, *Esquisse d'une bibliographie de la chanson populaire en Europe* (1905); *Les Caractères de la danse: Histoire d'un divertissement pendant la première moitié du XVIIIᵉ siècle* (1905); *Au Turkestan: Notes sur quelques habitudes musicales chez les Tadjikes et chez les Sartes* (1905); *La Musique et les musiciens d'église en Normandie au XIIIᵉ siècle* (1906); *Estampies et Danses royales: Les Plus Anciens Textes de musique instrumentale au Moyen-Age* (1907); *Recherches sur les ténors français dans les motets du XIIIᵉ siècle* (1907); *Recherches sur les ténors latins dans les motets du XIIIᵉ siècle* (1907; facsimile ed. of the Parisian MS, with index and editorial explanations); *Cent motets du XIIIᵉ siècle* (1908; 3 vols.; photographic facsimile of Bamberg Codex E. d. IV. 6, with annotations; a most important work); *Refrains et Rondeaux du XIIIᵉ siècle* (1909, in the Riemann Festschrift); *Trouvères et troubadours* (1909; Eng. ed., N.Y., 1914); and a number of essays on kindred topics, publ. in *Mercure Musical* (1903–8).

Auda, Antoine, French-Belgian organist and music scholar; b. St. Julien-en-Jarez, Loire, Oct. 28, 1879; d. Brussels, Aug. 19, 1964. He studied music at Marseilles; then established himself at Liège as an organist; publ. important studies on the musical history of the region: *Étienne de Liège* (1923); *La Musique et les musiciens de l'ancien pays de Liège* (1930); and valuable theoretical works: *Les Modes et les tons* (1931) and *Les Gammes musicales* (1947).

Audran, Edmond, French composer of light opera, son of **Marius-Pierre Audran;** b. Lyons, April 12, 1840; d. Tierceville, Aug. 17, 1901. He studied at the École Niedermayer in Paris (graduated in 1859). In 1861 he was appointed organist at St. Joseph's Church in Marseilles, where he produced his 1st operetta, *L'Ours et le Pacha* (1862). He wrote a funeral march on Meyerbeer's death (1864). After the production of *Le Grand Mogol* (Marseilles, Feb. 24, 1877), he returned to Paris, and staged *Les Noces d'Olivette* (Nov. 13, 1879). With the production of *La Mascotte* (Bouffes-Parisiens, Dec. 28, 1880), Audran achieved fame; this operetta became immensely popular; thousands of performances were given in Paris and all over the world. He continued to produce new operettas almost annually; of these, the following were successful: *Gillette de Narbonne* (1882); *La Cigale et la fourmi* (1886); *Miss Hélyett* (1890); *Sainte Freya* (1892); *Madame Suzette* (1893); *Mon Prince* (1893); *La Duchesse de Ferrare* (1895); *Photis* (1896); *La Poupée* (1896); *Monsieur Lohengrin* (1896); *Les Petites Femmes* (1897).

Audran, Marius-Pierre, French tenor and composer of songs, father of **Edmond Audran;** b. Aix, Provence, Sept. 26, 1816; d. Marseilles, Jan. 9, 1887. He began his career in the provinces (Marseilles, Bordeaux, Lyons); then became 1st tenor at the Opéra-Comique in Paris. After a period of travel (1852–61), he settled in Marseilles and in 1863 became a prof. of voice and director of the Marseilles Cons.

Auer, Leopold, celebrated Hungarian violinist and pedagogue; b. Veszprém, June 7, 1845; d. Loschwitz, near Dresden, July 15, 1930. He studied with Ridley Kohné at the Budapest Cons.; after making his debut in the Mendelssohn Concerto in Budapest, he continued his training with Jacob Dont in Vienna and then with Joachim in Hannover (1861–63). He was concertmaster in Düsseldorf (1864–66) and Hamburg (1866–68). In 1868 he was called to St. Petersburg as soloist in the Imperial Orch., and prof. of violin at the newly founded Cons. He became one of the most famous violin teachers in Russia; among his pupils were Elman, Zimbalist, and Heifetz. Tchaikovsky orig. dedicated his Violin Concerto to him, but was offended when Auer suggested some revisions and changed the dedication to Brodsky. Nevertheless, the Concerto became Auer's favorite work, and he made it a *pièce de résis-*

tance for all his pupils. He was active as a teacher in London (1906–11), Dresden (1912–14), and Norway (1915–17). In the summer of 1917 he left Russia, never to return. On March 23, 1918, he played a concert in N.Y.; settling permanently in America, he devoted himself mainly to teaching, first at the Inst. of Musical Art in N.Y. (from 1926) and then at the Curtis Inst. of Music in Philadelphia (from 1928). He publ. the manuals *Violin Playing as I Teach It* (N.Y., 1921) and *Violin Master Works and Their Interpretation* (1925), and an autobiography, *My Long Life in Music* (1923). Auer's performances were marked by an assured technique, exemplary taste, and nobility of expression. He was the great-uncle of **György (Sándor) Ligeti.**

BIBL.: B. Schwarz, *Great Masters of the Violin* (N.Y., 1983).

Auer, Max, Austrian writer on music; b. Vöcklabruck, May 6, 1880; d. Vienna, Sept. 24, 1962. He studied in Vienna; later taught in provincial public schools in Austria. He was one of the foremost authorities on Bruckner. He publ. *Anton Bruckner, Sein Leben und Werk* (Vienna, 1923) and *Anton Bruckner als Kirchenmusiker* (Regensburg, 1927); completed vols. 2–4 (1928, 1932, 1937) of Göllerich's monumental biography, *Anton Bruckner, Ein Lebens- und Schaffensbild.*

Augener, George, English publisher, founder of Augener & Co.; b. Germany, 1830; d. London, Aug. 25, 1915. He organized the firm in 1853 (incorporated Oct. 11, 1904), and was its head until he retired in 1910. In 1870 Augener started publishing the music periodical *Monthly Musical Record.* In 1896 the firm purchased the catalog of Robert Cocks & Co.

Augér, Arleen (Joyce), esteemed American soprano; b. Los Angeles, Sept. 13, 1939. She majored in education at Calif. State Univ. in Long Beach (B.A., 1963); then studied voice with Ralph Errolle in Chicago. She made her European operatic debut as the Queen of the Night in *Die Zauberflöte* at the Vienna State Opera (1967), remaining on its roster until 1974; also chose that role for her N.Y. City Opera debut (March 16, 1969). She appeared with the conductor Helmuth Rilling on a tour of Japan in 1974, and subsequently gained prominence through a major series of recordings of the music of Bach under his direction; also devoted increasing attention to a concert career. On Oct. 2, 1978, she made her Metropolitan Opera debut in N.Y. as Marzelline in *Fidelio,* and, in 1984, made a notably successful N.Y. recital debut. Her appearance in the title role of Handel's *Alcina* in London (1985) and Los Angeles (1986) elicited further critical accolades. In 1986 she was chosen to sing at the royal wedding of Prince Andrew and Sarah Ferguson in London. During the 1986–87 season, she made an extensive concert tour of the U.S. and Europe.

BIBL.: H. Waleson, "A. A.: You Can Go Home Again," *Ovation* (March 1987); *Current Biography* (Feb. 1989).

Augustine (Augustinus), Aurelius (known as **St. Augustine**), b. Tagaste, Numidia, Nov. 13, 354; d. as bishop, at Hippo, Aug. 28, 430. St. Augustine was one of the 4 great fathers of the Latin Church. He was educated at Madaura and Carthage. He became a Christian in 387, receiving his baptism from St. Ambrose. His writings contain valuable information concerning Ambrosian song; the book entitled *De musica* treats largely of meter. It is printed in Migne, *Patrologiae cursus* (vol. 32); German tr. by C.J. Perl (Strasbourg, 1937); Eng. tr. by R. Catesby Taliaferro in *The Classics of the St. John's Program* (1939). A synopsis of *De musica* in Eng. (with commentaries and tr. by W.F. Jackson Knight) was publ. by the Orthological Inst. (London, 1949).

BIBL.: J. Huré, *Saint Augustin Musicien* (1924); H. Edelstein, *Die Musikanschauung Augustins* (Freiburg, 1928); W. Hoffmann, *Philosophische Interpretation der Augustin-Schrift De musica* (Freiburg, 1930); H. Davenson, *Traité de la musique selon l'esprit de Saint Augustin* (Neuchâtel, 1944).

Auletta, Pietro, Italian composer; b. S. Angelo, Avellino, c.1698; d. Naples, Sept. 1771. He studied at the Cons. of S. Onofrio in Naples; gained renown with his comic opera *Orazio* (Naples, Carnival 1737). Only a few of his stage works are extant, but *La Locandiera* (Naples, July 10, 1738) survives as a testimony to his abilities as a dramatic composer.

Aulin, Tor (Bernhard Vilhelm), Swedish violinist, conductor, and composer; b. Stockholm, Sept. 10, 1866; d. Saltsjöbaden, March 1, 1914. He studied with C.J. Lindberg in Stockholm (1877–83) and with Sauret and P. Scharwenka in Berlin (1884–86). In 1887 he established the Aulin String Quartet, and traveled with it in Germany and Russia. He was concertmaster at the Stockholm Opera from 1889 to 1902, but continued his concert career, and was considered the greatest Scandinavian violinist since Ole Bull. Aulin was appointed conductor of the Stockholm Phil. Soc. in 1902; was concertmaster of the Göteborg Orch. from 1909 to 1912. As a conductor and violinist, he made determined propaganda for Swedish composers. He wrote incidental music to Strindberg's *Mäster Olof*, 3 violin concertos, several suites of Swedish dances for Orch., a Violin Sonata, a violin method, and songs. His sister, **Laura Valborg Aulin** (b. Gävle, Jan. 9, 1860; d. Örebro, Jan. 11, 1928), was a well-known pianist; she also composed chamber and piano music.

Aurelianus Reomensis, French scholar and monk at Réomé in the 9th century. His treatise *Musica disciplina* (publ. by Gerbert in *Scriptores,* I) contains the earliest information on the melodic character of the church modes.
   BIBL.: H. Riemann, *Handbuch der Musikgeschichte,* I (Leipzig, 1919).

Auriacombe, Louis, French conductor; b. Paris, Feb. 22, 1917; d. Toulouse, March 12, 1982. He studied at the Toulouse Cons., then with Igor Markevitch (conducting) in Salzburg. In 1953 he founded the Toulouse Chamber Orch., with which he made many tours; he was particularly noted for his performances of Baroque and 20th-century music.

Auric, Georges, notable French composer; b. Lodève, Hérault, Feb. 15, 1899; d. Paris, July 23, 1983. He 1st studied music at the Cons. of Montpellier; then went to Paris, where he was a student of Caussade at the Cons. and of Vincent d'Indy and Albert Roussel at the Schola Cantorum. While still in his early youth (1911–15) he wrote something like 300 songs and piano pieces; at 18 he composed a ballet, *Les Noces de Gamache.* At 20 he completed a comic opera, *La Reine de cœur;* however, he was dissatisfied with this early effort and destroyed the MS. In the aftermath of continental disillusion following World War I he became a proponent of the anti-Romantic movement in France, with the apostles of this age of disenchantment, Erik Satie and Jean Cocteau, preaching the new values of urban culture, with modern America as a model. Satie urged young composers to produce "auditory pleasure without demanding disproportionate attention from the listener," while Cocteau elevated artistic ugliness to an esthetic ideal. Under Satie's aegis, Auric joined several French composers of his generation in a group described as *Les Nouveaux Jeunes,* which later became known as *Les Six* (the other 5 were Milhaud, Honegger, Poulenc, Durey, and Germaine Tailleferre). Auric soon established an important connection with the impresario Serge Diaghilev, who commissioned him to write a number of ballets for his Paris company; Auric's facile yet felicitous manner of composing, with mock-Romantic connotations, fit perfectly into Diaghilev's scheme; particularly successful were Auric's early ballets, *Les Fâcheux* (1924) and *Les Matelots* (1925). He also wrote music for the movies, of which *À nous la liberté* (1932) achieved popular success as a symphonic suite. Auric's familiarity with the theater earned him important administrative posts; from 1962 to 1968 he acted as general administrator of both the Grand Opéra and the Opéra-Comique in Paris. From 1954 to 1977 he served as president of the French Union of Composers and Authors. In 1962 he was elected to the membership of the Académie des Beaux-Arts.
   WORKS: BALLETS: *Les Fâcheux* (Monte Carlo, Jan. 19, 1924); *Les Matelots* (Paris, June 17, 1925); *La Pastorale* (Paris, May 26, 1926); *Les Enchantements d'Alcine* (Paris, May 21,

1929); *Les Imaginaires* (Paris, May 31, 1934); *Le Peintre et son modèle* (Paris, Nov. 16, 1949); *Phèdre* (Paris, May 23, 1950); *La Pierre enchantée* (Paris, June 23, 1950); *Chemin de lumière* (Munich, March 27, 1952); *Coup de feu* (Paris, May 7, 1952); *La Chambre* (Paris, 1955); *Le Bal des voleurs* (Paris, 1960); also (in collaboration with Milhaud and others), *Les Mariés de la Tour Eiffel,* to the scenario of Jean Cocteau (Paris, June 15, 1921). **FILM:** *Le Sang d'un poète* (1930); *À nous la liberté* (1932); *Les Mystères de Paris* (1936); *La Belle et la bête* (1946); *Symphonie pastorale* (1946); *Les Parents terribles* (1949); *Orphée* (1950); *Moulin Rouge* (1952); *Gervaise* (1956); *Bonjour tristesse* (1957). **CHAMBER:** Piano Sonata (1932); Violin Sonata (1937); Partita for 2 Pianos (1958); *Suite symphonique* (1960); Flute Sonata (1964).
   BIBL.: A. Goléa, *G. A.* (Paris, 1958).

Aus der Ohe, Adele, German pianist; b. Hannover, Dec. 11, 1864; d. Berlin, Dec. 7, 1937. She studied as a child with Kullak in Berlin; at the age of 12 became a pupil of Liszt for 7 years. She then played concerts in Europe; made her American debut with Liszt's 1st Piano Concerto in N.Y. (Dec. 23, 1886) and continued her American tours for 17 consecutive years. She played 51 times with the Boston Sym. Orch. between 1887 and 1906. One of the highlights of her career was her appearance as soloist in Tchaikovsky's 1st Piano Concerto under Tchaikovsky's own direction at his last concert (St. Petersburg, Oct. 28, 1893). Because of a crippling illness, she was forced to abandon her concert career; she lost her accumulated earnings in the German currency inflation in the 1920s, and from 1928 till her death, subsisted on a pension from the Bagby Music Lovers Foundation of N.Y.

Austin, Ernest, English composer, brother of **Frederic Austin;** b. London, Dec. 31, 1874; d. Wallington, Surrey, July 24, 1947. He had no formal musical education; began to compose at the age of 33 after a business career. His compositions, therefore, acquired an experimental air; he was particularly interested in a modern treatment of old English tunes. He publ. a book, *The Fairyland of Music* (1922).
   WORKS: *The Vicar of Bray* for String Orch. (1910); *Hymn of Apollo* for Chorus and Orch. (Leeds, 1918); *Stella Mary Dances* (London, 1918); *Ode on a Grecian Urn,* after Keats (1922); 14 sonatinas on English folk songs for children; a cycle of organ works in 12 parts (inspired by Bunyan's *Pilgrim's Progress*); chamber music and songs.

Austin, Florence, American violinist; b. Galesburg, Mich., March 11, 1884; d. (in a railroad accident) Fairchild, Wis., Sept. 1, 1927. She studied with Schradieck in N.Y., and with Musin at the Liège Cons., winning 1st prize (the 1st American to do so). Upon her return to N.Y. (1901), she appeared in recitals, then settled in Newark, N.J., as a violin teacher.

Austin, Frederic, English baritone and composer, brother of **Ernest Austin;** b. London, March 30, 1872; d. there, April 10, 1952. He studied with his uncle, Dr. W.H. Hunt; was employed as an organist in Liverpool; in 1902 he appeared as a singer in London; made his operatic debut there at Covent Garden as Gunther in the *Ring* cycle in 1908; also became known in England as a composer; wrote a Sym. and an Overture. His most successful contribution was, however, not an original composition but a practical arrangement of *The Beggar's Opera* for its revival in London in 1920; he also wrote a modern version of its sequel, *Polly,* produced in London, Dec. 30, 1922.

Austin, Henry Richter, English-American organist, music publisher, and editor; b. London, May 17, 1882; d. Marblehead, Mass., May 13, 1961. He was organist at the English Royal Church in Berlin (1904–6); settled in the U.S.; held positions as a church organist in and around Boston until 1948. He conducted experiments with the acoustical characteristics of non-tempered scales and devised a keyboard, Novaton, of 16 keys (8 white, 8 black) providing the true 7th partial tone. He became president of the Arthur P. Schmidt Co. in 1954, after many years with the firm; after his death the firm was bought out by Summy-Birchard, Inc., of Evanston, Ill.

Austin, John Turnell, English-American organist; b. Podington, Bedfordshire, May 16, 1869; d. Hartford, Conn., Sept. 17, 1948. He went to the U.S. in 1889 and worked for various organ-building firms. On March 3, 1899, he founded an organ company under his own name in Hartford, retiring in 1937. He patented the Austin Universal Air Chest. The Austin Organ Co. supplied organs for many concert halls in the U.S.

Austin, Larry (Don), American avant-garde composer; b. Duncan, Okla., Sept. 12, 1930. He studied music with Violet Archer at North Texas State Univ., Denton (B.M.E., 1951; M.M., 1952); with Darius Milhaud at Mills College, Oakland, Calif. (1955); and with Andrew Imbrie and Seymour Shifrin at the Univ. of Calif., Berkeley (1955–58). In 1969 he took a special course in computer-generated music systems at Stanford Univ. From 1958 to 1972 he served as prof. of music at the Univ. of Calif., Davis; this sojourn was especially significant, since it was on the Davis campus that Austin became a co-founder of a unique modern music unperiodical, *Source,* which counted among its contributors the *crème de la crème* of the world's most intransigent modernists, who were given total freedom to express their innermost personalities in graphic notation and in verbal annotations. (Alas, *Source* dried out at its 13th issue, and became, in 1971, a collector's item.) In 1963, Austin and his colleagues at Davis formed the New Music Ensemble, exploring free group improvisation. This period was followed by further experimentation in synthetic arts in so-called event/complexes, combining a quadrastereophonic tape with various instruments and voices. In the meantime, Austin was active as a lecturer and conductor. He made 3 European concert and lecture tours (1964–65; 1967; 1973), 2 in South America (1969, 1973), and several in the U.S. and Canada. In 1972 he was appointed chairman of the dept. of music, Univ. of South Florida, Tampa; also served as director of systems complex for the Studio of Performing Arts at the univ. there. In 1978 he received a professorship at his alma mater, North Texas State Univ.; also was director of its Electronic Music Center (1981–82) and co-director of its Center for Experimental Music and Intermedia (from 1982). He was a recipient of numerous grants and several commissions from various prestigious organizations. Most of Austin's compositions are cast for mixed media, in which theatrical, acoustical, and dynamic elements are integrated into manifestations of universal vitality. In order to attain a maximum impact with a minimum of anarchy, he introduced the concept of coordinated improvisation, which he termed "open styles." His research projects include the development of software for hybrid computer systems for electronic music. With T. Clark he publ. the textbook *Learning to Compose: Modes, Materials, and Models of Musical Invention* (Dubuque, 1988).

WORKS: Woodwind Quartet (1948); Woodwind Quintet (1949); Brass Quintet (1949); String Trio (1952); Concertino for Flute, Trumpet, and Strings (1952); *Prosody* for Orch. (1953); *Improvisations for Orchestra and Jazz Soloists* (1961); *Collage* for Assorted Instruments (1963); *Continuum* for 2, 3, 4, 5, 6, or 7 Instruments (1964); *In Memoriam J.F. Kennedy* for Band (1964); Piano Variations (1964); *A Broken Consort* for 7 Instruments (1964); *Open Style* for Orch. and Piano Soloists (1965); *The Maze,* theater piece in Open Style (1967); *Catharsis,* in Open Style, for 2 Improvisation Ensembles, Tapes, and Conductor (1967; Oakland, Nov. 11, 1969); *Accidents* for Electronically Prepared Piano, Magnetic Tape, Mirrors, Actions and Counteractions, and Black Light (1967); *Piano Set,* in Open Style (1968); *Current* for Clarinet and Piano (1968); *Transmission 1,* video-audio electronic composition for Color Television (1969); *Agape,* celebration for Priests, Musicians, Dancers, Rock Band, Actors, and Poets (Buffalo, Feb. 25, 1970); *Plastic Surgery* for Electric Piano, Percussion, Magnetic Tape, and Film (N.Y., March 1, 1970); *Heaven Music* for a Condominium of Flutes (Tampa, Fla., June 3, 1975); *Phoenix* for Tape (1976); *Catalogo sonoro* for Viola and Tape

(1979); *Phantasmagoria,* conjectural construction and fantasies on Ives's *Universe Symphony* for Narrator, Digital Synthesizer, Tape, and Orch. (Denton, Texas, Feb. 18, 1982); *Stars*,* computer music on tape (1982); *Sonata concertante* for Piano and Computer (1983–84); *Clarini!* for 20 Trumpets (1985); *Sinfonia concertante: A Mozartean Episode* for Chamber Orch. and Computer Music Narrative (Cleveland, Oct. 19, 1986); *Concertante cybernetica,* "interactions" for Performer and Synclavier Digital Music System (1987); *Transmission 2,* radiophonic composition (1988–89).

Austin, William W(eaver), American musicologist; b. Lawton, Okla., Jan. 18, 1920. He studied at Harvard Univ., obtaining his Ph.D. in 1951. In 1947 he was appointed to the faculty of Cornell Univ. In 1961–62 he was the recipient of a Guggenheim fellowship.

WRITINGS: *Music in the 20th Century from Debussy through Stravinsky* (N.Y., 1966); "Susanna," "Jeanie" and "The Old Folks at Home": The Songs of Stephen C. Foster from His Time to Ours (N.Y., 1975); ed. *New Looks at Italian Opera* (Ithaca, N.Y., 1968); tr. *Musikästhetik* by Carl Dahlhaus into Eng. as *Esthetics of Music* (Cambridge, 1982).

Austral (real name, **Wilson**), **Florence,** Australian soprano; b. Richmond, near Melbourne, April 26, 1892; d. Newcastle, New South Wales, May 15, 1968. She studied at the Melbourne Cons. (1914–18); made her operatic debut as Brünnhilde at Covent Garden in London, under the auspices of the newly formed British National Opera Co. (May 16, 1922); later she sang the roles of Isolde and Aida. She toured the U.S. between 1925 and 1931 with her husband, the flutist John Amadeo; eventually returned to Australia.

Auteri Manzocchi, Salvatore, Italian opera composer; b. Palermo, Dec. 26, 1845; d. Parma, Feb. 21, 1924. He studied in Palermo with Platania, and with Mabellini in Florence. His 1st opera, *Marcellina,* was never performed; his 2nd, *Dolores* (Florence, Feb. 23, 1875), enjoyed considerable success, as did *Stella* (Piacenza, May 22, 1880). His other operas are *Il Negriero* (Milan, 1878); *Il Conte di Gleichen* (Milan, 1887); *Graziella* (Milan, Oct. 23, 1894); and *Severo Torelli* (Bologna, April 25, 1903).

Autori, Franco, Italian-born American conductor; b. Naples, Nov. 29, 1903; d. Tulsa, Oct. 16, 1990. After study in Italy, he emigrated to America in 1928; became a naturalized citizen in 1936. He conducted the Chicago Civic Opera Co. (1928–32) and the summer series of the Dallas Sym. Orch. (1932–34); was staff conductor of the Federal Music Project in N.Y. (1934–36); then held the post of conductor of the Buffalo Phil. (1936–45); subsequently was active as guest conductor in Poland and Argentina; from 1949 to 1959 served as associate conductor of the N.Y. Phil. From 1961 to 1971 he was conductor of the Tulsa Phil.

Avdeyeva, Larissa (Ivanovna), Russian mezzo-soprano; b. Moscow, June 21, 1925. She studied at the Stanislavsky Opera Studio in Moscow; in 1947 she joined the Stanislavsky Music Theater; in 1952 she became a member of the Bolshoi Theater, where she distinguished herself as an outstanding interpreter in operas by Tchaikovsky, Borodin, Mussorgsky, and Rimsky-Korsakov; she also made tours of Europe, the U.S., and Japan. She was made a People's Artist of the R.S.F.S.R. in 1964. She married the Russian conductor **Evgeny Svetlanov.**

Avenary, Hanoch (real name, **Herbert Loewenstein**), Israeli musicologist; b. Danzig, May 25, 1908. He studied musicology and other subjects at the univs. of Leipzig, Munich, and Frankfurt; then received his Ph.D. in 1931 from the Univ. of Königsberg with the dissertation *Wort und Ton bei Oswald von Wolkenstein* (publ. in Königsberg, 1932). He went to Palestine in 1936; there he was active as a publisher of Jewish art books. He also served in the Israeli air force; in 1965 he joined the faculty of Hebrew Univ., where he remained until 1972; from 1966 he was also a lecturer at the Univ. of Tel Aviv. His books include *Studies in the Hebrew, Syrian and Greek*

Liturgical Recitative (Tel Aviv, 1963); *Hebrew Hymn Tunes: The Rise and Development of a Musical Tradition* (Tel Aviv, 1971); *The Ashkenazi Tradition of Biblical Chant between 1500 and 1900* (Tel Aviv, 1976).

Aventinus (real name, **Turmair**), **Johannes,** German music theorist; b. Abensberg (whence Aventinus), July 4, 1477; d. Regensburg, Jan. 9, 1534. His treatise *Annales ducum boiariae* (publ. in 1554) contains considerable information (not always trustworthy) about musical matters. He also ed. Nicolaus Faber's *Musica rudimenta admodum brevia* (1516).

Averkamp, Anton, Dutch choral conductor and composer; b. Willige Langerak, Feb. 18, 1861; d. Bussum, June 1, 1934. He studied with Daniel de Lange in Amsterdam, with Friedrich Kiel in Berlin, and with Rheinberger in Munich. In 1890 he founded the famous chorus Amsterdam A Cappella Coor, with which he traveled in Europe, presenting programs of early polyphonic music. He wrote an opera, *De Heidebloem* (not produced); a symphonic poem, *Elaine und Lancelot;* 2 choral works with Orch., *Decora Lux* and *Die versunkene Burg;* a Sym.; a *Te Deum;* a Violin Sonata; and songs. He contributed numerous historical articles to music periodicals; publ. a manual for singers, *Uit mijn practijk* (Groningen, 1916), and the book *De Koordirigent* (1933).

Avidom (real name, **Mahler-Kalkstein**), **Menahem,** Polish-born Israeli composer; b. Stanislawow, Jan. 6, 1908. He studied at the American Univ. in Beirut (1926–28) and at the Paris Cons. (1928–31). In 1935 he settled in Tel Aviv, teaching music theory at the Cons. there until 1946. From 1955 to 1970 he was the chairman of the Israeli Composers' League; in 1984 he was made its honorary president-for-life; also was head of the Israeli performing rights society and was active as a music critic. His early works reflect the influences of Expressionism; in several of them he made explicit use of dodecaphonic techniques. After settling in Israel, he turned to the exploration of authentic Israeli folkways.

WORKS: STAGE: *Alexandra,* opera (Tel Aviv, Aug. 15, 1959); *In Every Generation,* opera (Ein-Gev Passover Festival, 1955); *The Crook,* comic opera (Tel Aviv, April 22, 1967); *The Farewell,* radiophonic opera (1969; broadcast perf., Nov. 1971); *The Pearl and the Coral,* ballet for 12 Instruments (1972); *The Emperor's New Clothes,* comic opera (Israel Festival, 1976); *Yodfat's Cave,* musical drama (1977); *The End of King Og,* children's opera (1979); *The 1st Sin,* satirical opera (1980); children's ballet for Chamber Orch. (1984). ORCH.: 10 syms.: No. 1, *A Folk Symphony* (Prague Spring Festival, 1946); No. 2, *David Symphony* (Tel Aviv, Dec. 1, 1949); No. 3, *Mediterranean Sinfonietta* (1951); No. 4 (1955); No. 5, *The Song of Eilät,* for Voice and Orch. (1956–57); No. 6 (1960); No. 7, *Philharmonic* (1961); No. 8, *Festival Sinfonietta* (Jerusalem, July 27, 1966); No. 9, *Symphonie variée,* for Chamber Orch. (1968); No. 10, *Sinfonia brevis* (1980); Concerto for Flute and Strings (1946); *Music for Strings* (1949); *Jubilee Suite* (1959); *Triptyque symphonique* (1966); *Spring,* overture (Jerusalem, Dec. 13, 1973); *Movements* for String Orch. or String Quartet (1979). CHAMBER: Concertino for Violin and Piano (1950; also with Chamber Orch., 1972); *Concertino for Piatigorsky* for Cello and Piano (1952); String Quartet No. 1 (1953); String Quartet No. 2, *Metamorphoses* (1960); *Adagio* for Harp (1962); *Enigma* for 5 Wind Instruments, Percussion, and Piano (1962); *Reflexions* for 2 Flutes (1963); Brass Quartet (1963); *B-A-C-H,* suite for Woodwinds, Strings, Piano, and Percussion (1964); *Triptyque* for Solo Violin (1967); *Monothema,* sonatina for String Quartet (1982). PIANO: 2 sonatinas (1939, 1945); *12 Changing Preludes* (1965); *6 Inventions on the Name of Artur Rubinstein* (1973); *Yemenite Wedding Suite* (1973); *Piece on the Name of SCHoEnBerG* (1974); *Triptic* (1981); Sonatine for Piano, 4-hands (1982). VOCAL: *12 Hills,* cantata (1976); *Beyond,* cantata for Voice and 13 Instruments (1977).

Avison, Charles, English organist and composer; b. Newcastle-upon-Tyne, 1709 (old style; baptized, Feb. 16); d. there, May 9, 1770. He acquired the rudiments of music at home; he

was appointed organist at St. John's church in Newcastle on Oct. 13, 1735; took up his post in 1736. An enterprising musician, he organized in Newcastle a series of subscription concerts, one of the earliest musical presentations of its kind in Great Britain; was music director of the Newcastle Musical Soc. in 1738; held this post until his death. He wrote a large number of concertos employing various combinations of strings with harpsichord continuo, and sonatas in which the keyboard instrument is given a predominant function. These works were publ. between 1740 and 1769; in 1758 Avison collected 26 concertos in 4 books, arranged in score, for strings *a* 7 (4 violins, viola, cello, bass), with harpsichord; other works were 12 keyboard concertos with string quartet, 18 quartets for keyboard with 2 violins and cello, and 3 vols. of trio sonatas for keyboard with 2 violins. His *Essay on Musical Expression* (London, 1752) is historically important as an early exposition of relative musical values by an English musician. His views were opposed by an anonymous pamphlet, *Remarks on Mr. Avison's Essay . . . in a Letter from a Gentleman in London,* which was probably written by Prof. William Hayes of Oxford (London, 1753). Not to be thus thwarted, Avison publ. a rebuttal that same year, reinforced by a statement of worth contributed by a Dr. Jortin. A posthumous ed. appeared in 1775, which renewed the polemical exchange. Among his scholarly publications is Marcello's *Psalm-Paraphrases* with an English text, containing a biography of Marcello (jointly with John Garth, 1757).

BIBL.: A. Milner, "C. A.," *Musical Times* (Jan. 1954); C. Cudworth, "A. of Newcastle," ibid. (May 1970); L. Lipking, "C. A. and the Founding of English Criticism of Music," chapter 8 of *The Ordering of the Arts in Eighteenth-Century England* (Princeton, 1970); O. Edwards, "C. A.: English Concerto-Writer Extraordinary," *Musical Quarterly* (July 1973).

Avni, Tzvi (Jacob), German-born Israeli composer, teacher, and writer on music; b. Saarbrücken, Sept. 2, 1927. He emigrated to Palestine in 1935; studied with Abel Ehrlich and Mordecai Seter at the Tel Aviv Academy of Music (diploma, 1958), and also received private instruction in orchestration from Paul Ben-Haim. He was a student of Aaron Copland and Lukas Foss at the Berkshire Music Center in Tanglewood (summer 1963), later pursuing studies in electronic music with Ussachevsky and in music librarianship at Columbia Univ. He also studied with Myron Schaeffer at the Univ. of Toronto (1964). He was director of the AMLI Central Music Library in Tel Aviv (1961–75), served as ed. of the journal *Gitit* (1966–80), was director of the electronic music studio (from 1971) and a prof. (from 1976) at the Rubin Academy of Music in Jerusalem, and was chairman of the Israel League of Composers (1978–80) and of the music committee of the National Council for Culture and Art (1983–87). In 1986 he was awarded the ACUM Prize for his life's work. In many of his mature compositions he utilized advanced techniques; he later pursued neo-tonal writing.

WORKS: BALLETS: *Requiem for Sounds* (1969); *Ein Dor* (1970); *I Shall Sing to Thee in the Valley of the Dead My Beloved* (1971); *Lyric Episodes* (1972); *Frames* (1974); *He and She* (1976); *Genesis Reconsidered* (1978); incidental music for plays. ORCH.: *Holiday Metaphors* (1970); *By the Rivers of Babylon* (1971); *2 Movements from Sinfonia sacra* (1977); *Programme Music* (1980); *Mizmor* for Santour (a traditional Persian instrument) and Orch. (1982); *Introduction and Capriccio* (1983); *Metamorphoses on a Bach Chorale* (1985); *Kaddish* for Cello and Strings (1987); *Mashav,* concertino for Xylophone, 10 Winds, and Percussion (1988). CHAMBER: *Prayer* for Strings (1961; rev. 1969); *Meditations on a Drama* (1966); *The Binding* for Viola and 4 Chamber Groups (1969); *De Profundis* for Strings (1972); *On This Cape of Death* (1974); *2 Psalms* for Oboe and Strings (1975); *Michtam of David* for Harp and Strings (1975; rev. 1978; also for Harp and String Quartet); *Mobile* for Clarinet and Harp (1977); *Beyond the Curtain* for Piano Quartet (1979); *Tandu* for 2 Flutes (1982); *5 Variations for Mr. K.* for Percussion and Tape (1983); choral pieces; piano pieces; songs.

d'Avossa, Giuseppe, Italian composer; b. Paola, Calabria, 1708; d. Naples, Jan. 9, 1796. He studied with Gaetano Greco and Francesco Durante in Naples; later held the position of maestro di cappella at S. Maria Verticelli, Naples, and at Pesaro, where he also conducted the orch. of the municipal theater. He wrote 4 operas, the most popular being *La Pupilla* (Naples, Carnival 1763), and much sacred music.

Avshalomov, Aaron, Russian-American composer, father of **Jacob (David) Avshalomov;** b. Nikolayevsk, Siberia, Nov. 11, 1894; d. N.Y., April 26, 1965. He studied at the Zürich Cons.; in 1914 he went to China, where he wrote a number of works on Chinese subjects, making use of authentic Chinese themes. On April 24, 1925, he conducted the 1st performance in Peking of his 1st opera, on a Chinese subject, *Kuan Yin;* his 2nd opera, also on a Chinese subject, *The Great Wall,* was staged in Shanghai on Nov. 26, 1945, and also was presented in Nanking under the sponsorship of Mme. Chiang Kai-Shek, the wife of the powerful generalissimo. His other works composed in China were also performed for the 1st time in Shanghai, among them: *Peiping Hutungs,* symphonic sketch (Feb. 7, 1933; also given by Stokowski with the Philadelphia Orch., Nov. 8, 1935); *The Soul of the Ch'in,* ballet (May 21, 1933); *Incense Shadows,* pantomime (March 13, 1935); Piano Concerto (Jan. 19, 1936); Violin Concerto (Jan. 16, 1938); 1st Sym. (March 17, 1940, composer conducting); *Buddha and the 5 Planetary Deities,* choreographic tableau (April 18, 1942). In 1947 Avshalomov went to America, where he continued to compose works in large forms, among them his 2nd Sym. (Cincinnati, Dec. 30, 1949); 3rd Sym. (1950); 4th Sym. (1951).

Avshalomov, Jacob (David), Russian-born American composer and conductor, son of **Aaron Avshalomov;** b. Tsingtao, China, March 28, 1919. His mother was American; his father, Russian. He studied music in Peking; in 1936 he was in Shanghai, where material circumstances forced him to work for a time in a slaughterhouse. In 1937 he went to the U.S.; studied with Ernst Toch in Los Angeles, then with Bernard Rogers in Rochester, N.Y. From 1943 to 1945 he was in the U.S. Army as an interpreter. From 1947 to 1954 he was an instructor at Columbia Univ.; received a Guggenheim fellowship in 1952; in 1954 he was appointed permanent conductor of the Portland (Oreg.) Junior Sym. His music reflects the many cultures with which he was in contact; while the form is cohesive, the materials are multifarious, with tense chromatic harmonies and quasi-oriental inflections.
Works: *Sinfonietta* (1946; N.Y., Nov. 29, 1949); *Evocations* for Clarinet and Chamber Orch. (1947; Saratoga Springs, N.Y., Aug. 17, 1950); Sonatina for Viola and Piano (1947); *Prophecy* for Cantor, Chorus, and Organ (1948); *Taking of T'ung Kuan* for Orch. (1948; Detroit, Nov. 20, 1953); *Tom o' Bedlam* for Chorus (N.Y., Dec. 15, 1953; received the N.Y. Music Critics Award); *The Plywood Age* for Orch., commissioned for the 50th anniversary of the Fir Plywood Corp. (Portland, June 20, 1955); *Psalm 100* for Chorus and Wind Instruments (1956); *Inscriptions at the City of Brass* for Chorus, Narrator, and Large Orch., to a text from the *Arabian Nights* (1956); *Quodlibet Montagna* for Brass Sextet (1975).

Ax, Emanuel, outstanding Polish-born American pianist; b. Lwow, June 8, 1949. He began to play the violin at age 6; soon took up the piano and studied with his father, who was a coach at the Lwow Opera House. The family moved to Warsaw when he was 8, and then to Winnipeg, Canada, when he was 10; in 1961 they settled in N.Y., where he enrolled at the Juilliard School of Music as a student of Mieczyslaw Munz; he also received a bachelor's degree in French from Columbia Univ., in 1970. He made a concert tour of South America in 1969; became a U.S. citizen in 1970. He competed at the Chopin (1970) and Queen Elisabeth (1972) competitions; in both placed only 7th; in 1971 won 3rd place in the Vianna

da Motta Competition in Lisbon; then made his N.Y. debut at Alice Tully Hall on March 12, 1973. A long-awaited victory came in 1974, when he won 1st place in the Artur Rubinstein International Piano Master Competition in Tel Aviv; among its awards was a contract for an American concert tour; there followed numerous appearances throughout the U.S. and Europe. He was awarded the Avery Fisher Prize in 1979. In addition to his fine interpretations of the standard repertoire, he has also distinguished himself as a champion of contemporary music.
Bibl.: *Current Biography* (March 1984); K. Monson, "E. A.," *Ovation* (April 1985).

Axman, Emil, Czech composer; b. Rataje, June 3, 1887; d. Prague, Jan. 25, 1949. Of a musical family, he began to compose at an early age. He studied musicology with Nejedlý at Prague Univ., obtaining his Ph.D. in 1912; took private composition lessons with Novák (1908–10) and Ostrčil (1920). In 1913 he was appointed keeper of the musical archives at the National Museum in Prague. He participated in the modern musical movement typified by Janáček but was not attracted to any spirit of experimentation, his music remaining highly lyrical. His musicological writings include *Moravian Operas of the 18th Century* (1912) and *Moravia in Czech Music of the 19th Century* (1920).
Works: 6 syms.: No. 1, *Tragic* (1925–26); No. 2, *Giocosa* (1926–27; ISCM Festival, Frankfurt am Main, July 3, 1927); No. 3, *Spring* (1928); No. 4, *Eroica* (1932); No. 5, *Dithyrambic* (1936); No. 6, *Patriotic* (1942); symphonic poems: *Sorrows and Hopes* (1919–20) and *A Bright Sky* (1921–22); 5 cantatas: *My Mother* (1926); *A Ballad on the Eyes of a Stoker* (1927); *Ilonka Beniačová* (1930); *The Cemetery of Sobotka* (1933); *Stabat Mater* (1938); *From the Beskids* for Chamber Orch. (1934); Violin Concerto (1936); Piano Concerto (1939); Cello Concerto (1940); Double Concerto for Violin, Cello, and Orch. (1944); Suite in the Form of Variations for Orch. (1948); Violin Sonata (1923); Cello Sonata (1924); 4 string quartets (1924, 1925, 1929, 1946); Piano Trio (1924–25); Wind Quintet (1938); Suite for String Quartet (1940); *Divertimento* for Nonet (1944); *3 Moravian Dances* for Nonet (1944); Variations for String Quartet (1944); 3 piano sonatas: No. 1, *Appassionata* (1922); No. 2, *To the Memory of a Great Man* (1922); No. 3 (1924); *Sonatina charakeristicka* for Piano (1922); *Moravia Sings* for Piano (1925; orchestrated 1935); several choruses and song cycles.
Bibl.: F. Pala, *E. A. Žídot a dílo* (Prague, 1966).

Ayala Perez, Daniel, Mexican (Indian) composer; b. Abalá, Yucatán, July 21, 1906; d. Veracruz, June 20, 1975. He went to Mérida, Yucatán, to study music; entered the National Cons. in Mexico City in 1927; studied violin with Ezequiel Sierra and Revueltas, composition with Ponce, Huízar, and Carrillo. He played in nightclubs in Mexico City; in 1931, became a violinist with the Orquesta Sinfónica de México; in 1934, together with Moncayo, Contreras, and Galindo, formed the Grupo de los Cuatro (Group of the 4). He became conductor of the Banda de Policía in Mérida in 1940 and in 1942 founded the Yucatán Orch. His music, inspired by ancestral melos of the Mayan civilization and legends, is cast in pentatonic modes and possesses a vigorous rhythmic pulse.
Works: 2 ballets: *El Hombre Maya* (as a symphonic suite, Mexico City, Nov. 21, 1940) and *La gruta diabólica* for Chamber Orch. (1940); symphonic poems: *Tribú* (Mexico City, Oct. 18, 1935); *Paisaje* (Landscape; 1935; Mexico City, June 2, 1936); *Panoramas de México* (1936; Dallas, Dec. 1, 1940); *Mi viaje a Norte America* (1947). Voice: *4 Canciones,* with Piano (1932); *Uchben X'Coholte* (Ancient Cemetery) for Soprano and Chamber Orch. (Mexico City, Oct. 13, 1933; ballet version, 1936; Mexico City, March 6, 1936); *El grillo* (Cricket) for Soprano, Clarinet, Violin, Timbrel, and Piano (1933); *U Kayil Chaac,* an incantation for rain, for Soprano, Mexican Percussion Instruments, and Chamber Orch. (1934); *Brigadier de Choque* for Chorus and Percussion (1935); *Suite infantil* for Soprano and Chamber Orch. (1937); *Los Yaquis y los Seris,* 2 suites for Voice, Chamber Ensemble, and Mexican Percussion Instru-

ments (1938; Mérida, July 31, 1942); *Radiograma* for Piano, imitating radio code signals (1931).

Ayers, Roy (E., Jr.), appealing American vibes player and singer; b. Los Angeles, Sept. 10, 1940. He played piano as a child, later joining the bands of Curtis Amy, Hampton Hawes, and Herbie Mann. In the early 1970s he formed his own group, Roy Ayers Ubiquity, which was noted for its use of Latin percussion instruments; later dropped "Ubiquity," and, as simply Roy Ayers, produced a number of successful albums, including *Starbooty, Let's Do It, Step into Our Life,* and the treasured *You Send Me,* with tantalizing vocals by both Ayers and Carla Vaughn. Perennial favorites at his invariably well-attended performances include the songs *Get On Up, Get On Down; And Don't You Say No; (Let Me Kiss You on Your) Poo Poo La La;* and *You Send Me.* Recent albums include *In the Dark* (1984) and *I'm the One (For Your Love Tonight)* (1987).

Ayestarán, Lauro, Uruguayan musicologist; b. Montevideo, July 9, 1913; d. there, July 22, 1966. He studied voice and music history; became an instructor of choral music in municipal schools in Montevideo. He is the author of the important monograph *Domenico Zipoli, El gran compositor y organista romano en el Rio de la Plata* (Montevideo, 1941); also wrote *El folklore musical Uruguayo* (Montevideo, 1967).

Ayler, Albert, black American jazz saxophonist; b. Cleveland, July 13, 1936; d. (body found in the East River) N.Y., Nov. 25, 1970. He began playing the alto saxophone in his father's band; took up the tenor saxophone, and subsequently became a leading figure in avant-garde jazz circles in N.Y.; he also toured in Europe. He was highly regarded as an innovative jazz musician. His accidental death remained unexplained.

Ayres, Frederic (real name, **Frederick Ayres Johnson**), American composer; b. Binghamton, N.Y., March 17, 1876; d. Colorado Springs, Nov. 23, 1926. He studied with Edgar S. Kelley (1897–1901) and Arthur Foote (1899). His works include an overture, *From the Plains;* 2 string quartets; 2 piano trios; 2 violin sonatas; a Cello Sonata; and numerous songs. In his later music he showed a tendency toward Impressionism and used moderately complex harmonic combinations.
    Bibl.: W.T. Upton, "Frederick A.," *Musical Quarterly* (Jan. 1932).

Ayrton, Edmund, English organist and composer, father of **William Ayrton;** b. Ripon, Yorkshire, baptized on Nov. 19, 1734, probably born the day before; d. London, May 22, 1808. He studied organ with Nares; from 1755 was organist in various churches; in 1764 was appointed Gentleman of the Chapel Royal, and in 1780 was appointed lay vicar at Westminster Abbey. He was in charge of the Chapel Royal from 1780 to 1805. In 1784, he was given the degree of D.Mus. at Trinity College in Cambridge, and in 1788, D.Mus. at Oxford. He wrote a number of anthems, of which *Begin unto My God with Timbrels,* scored for 4 vocal soloists, mixed choir, 2 oboes, 2 bassoons, 2 trumpets, timpani, and strings, obtained great success at its performance on June 29, 1784, in St. Paul's Cathedral in London. His glee *An Ode to Harmony* (1799) was also popular. He was admittedly a faithful imitator of Handel, but the judgment of Wesley, who described Ayrton as "one of the most egregious blockheads under the sun," seems unduly severe.

Ayrton, William, English organist, music critic, and editor, son of **Edmund Ayrton;** b. London, Feb. 24, 1777; d. there, March 8, 1858. He received a fine education; was one of the founders of the London Phil. Soc. in 1813; wrote music criticism for the *Morning Chronicle* (1813–26) and for the *Examiner*

(1837–51). In 1823 he started the publication of the historically important London music periodical *Harmonicon,* and was its ed.; from 1834 to 1837 ed. *The Musical Library,* which publ. vocal and instrumental music. He also compiled a practical collection, *Sacred Minstrelsy* (2 vols., 1835).

Azanchevsky, Mikhail, Russian music educator and composer; b. Moscow, April 5, 1839; d. there, Jan. 24, 1881. He studied composition with Richter and Hauptmann at the Leipzig Cons. (1861–64), and piano with Liszt in Rome. After a sojourn in Paris (1866–70) he returned to Russia, where he became executive director of the St. Petersburg Cons. (1871–76). A disciplinarian by nature, he raised the minimal requirements for acceptance of new pupils and engaged important teachers, among them Rimsky-Korsakov. In Paris he purchased the important music library of Anders, which he later presented, together with other acquisitions, to the St. Petersburg Cons. He composed a concert overture, 2 string quartets, 2 piano trios, a Cello Sonata, a *Festival polonais* for 2 Pianos, and numerous piano solo pieces and songs.

Azevedo, Alexis-Jacob, French writer on music; b. Bordeaux, March 18, 1813; d. Paris, Dec. 21, 1875. He was a prolific contributor to *Le Ménestrel* and other French music magazines; publ. monographs on Félicien David (1863) and Rossini (1864); a pamphlet, *La Vérité sur Rouget de Lisle et la Marseillaise* (Dieppe, 1864); *La Transposition par les nombres* (Paris, 1874); a collection of articles, *Les Doubles-croches malades* (1874); etc.

Azkué (Aberasturi), Resurrección María de, Spanish composer and musicologist; b. Lequeitio, Aug. 5, 1864; d. Bilbao, Nov. 9, 1951. He studied theology in Spain, then went to Paris and studied music at the Schola Cantorum. He wrote 2 operas to Basque texts: *Ortzuri* (Bilbao, 1911) and *Urlo* (Bilbao, 1913); an oratorio, *Daniel;* a *Te Deum;* several zarzuelas. He publ. a valuable collection, *Cancionero popular Vasco* (11 vols.), and *Literatura popular del país Vasco* (4 vols., the last containing musical examples).

Azmayparashvili, Shalva, Georgian composer; b. Tiflis, Jan. 7, 1903; d. there (Tbilisi), May 17, 1957. He studied trumpet and kettledrums; then was engaged as conductor at the local opera theater. Among his compositions are an opera, *The Village Elder* (Tbilisi, Jan. 21, 1951); a musical comedy, *Times Are Different* (Tbilisi, Feb. 12, 1952); and a number of mass choruses on Georgian themes.

Aznavour (real name, **Aznavurian**), **Charles,** French chansonnier; b. Paris, May 22, 1924. A son of an Armenian baritone from Tiflis, he received his early musical training at home; acted in Paris variety shows at the age of 5; learned to play the guitar. He made several American tours as a nightclub entertainer with a valuable French accent; also acted in films. He composed a great number of songs, of the genre of "tristesse chansons" and frustration ballads, among them the popular tunes *On ne sait jamais, Comme des étrangers,* and *Ce jour tant attendu.* His operetta *Monsieur Carnaval* was produced in Paris on Dec. 17, 1965. He wrote an autobiography, entitled *Aznavour par Aznavour* (Paris, 1970).

Azzopardi, Francesco, Italian (Maltese) music theorist and composer; b. Rabat, Malta, May 5, 1748; d. there, Feb. 6, 1809. His fame rests on the school manual *Il musico prattico* (1760), publ. by Framéry in French tr. (Paris, 1786) and quoted by Cherubini in his course on counterpoint and fugue, and by Grétry. He also composed sacred music, including an oratorio, *La Passione di Cristo.*
    Bibl.: P. Pullicino, *Notizia biografica di F. A.* (1876).

B

Baaren, Kees van, Dutch composer; b. Enschede, Oct. 22, 1906; d. Oegstgeest, Sept. 2, 1970. He studied at the Hochschule für Musik in Berlin and later for 4 years with Willem Pijper in Rotterdam. His early works are in the lyric tradition of Grieg. However, he destroyed his early works in 1933 and started afresh in the direction of structural techniques, following the precepts of Schoenberg and Anton von Webern. His Trio (1936) shows traces of serialism, and his Septet (1952) is the 1st work by a Dutch composer written in an integral serial style, in which not only the 12 tones of the chromatic scale, but durations, dynamics, and meters, are organized according to a unifying thematic set. Baaren was director of the Amsterdam Music Academy (1948–53), the Cons. of Utrecht (1953–57), and the Royal Cons. of The Hague (1958–70).

WORKS: Piano Concertino (1934); cantata, *The Hollow Men,* after T.S. Eliot (1948); *Sinfonia* (1956–57); 5 *Variazioni* for Orch. (1959); Piano Concerto (1964); *Musica* for Orch. (Rotterdam, May 18, 1966); 2 string quartets (1932–33; *Sovraposizioni I,* 1962); Trio for Flute, Clarinet, and Bassoon (1936); Piano Sonatina (1948); Septet for Concertante Violin, Wind Quintet, and Double Bass (1952); *Sovraposizioni II,* wind quintet (1963); *Musica* for Solo Flute (1965); *Musica* for 72 Carillons (1964–68; alternate version for 47 Carillons, 1964–69); *Musica* for Organ (1968–69).

Babadzhanian, Arno, Armenian pianist and composer; b. Erevan, Jan. 22, 1921; d. Moscow, Nov. 15, 1983. He studied at the Erevan Cons.; after graduation in 1947, he went to Moscow, where he took courses in piano with Igumnov at the Cons. and in composition with Litinsky at the Armenian Culture Center; graduated from both in 1948. In 1950 he returned to Armenia and joined the piano faculty at the Erevan Cons. His music is derived from the folk-song patterns of Armenia, continuing the line cultivated by Khachaturian, with emphasis on rhythmic coloration in a characteristic quasi-oriental manner. His most ambitious works are a Violin Concerto (1949) and a Cello Concerto (1962); he also wrote *Heroic Ballad* for Piano and Orch. (1950), 2 string quartets (1942, 1947), Piano Trio (1952), Violin Sonata (1959), and a number of popular ballads under such appealing titles as *The Song of 1st Love* and *Make a Wish.* A monograph on Babadzhanian by A. Grigorian was publ. in Moscow in 1961.

Babayev, Andrei, Russian composer; b. Azerbaijan, Dec. 27, 1923; d. Moscow, Oct. 21, 1964. He studied in Baku; played native instruments; then entered the Baku Cons., where he was a student in composition of Gadzhibekov and Karayev, graduating in 1950; later took advanced courses with Shaporin at the Moscow Cons. His music is inspired mainly by Armenian folk melodies; he also arranged songs of Central Asia and India; some of his original songs (*I Met a Girl, Lovely Eyes,* etc.) acquired popularity.

WORKS: *Eagles' Bastion,* opera (1957); *October,* cantata (1947); Sym. (1950); *Indian Fantasy* for Orch. (1958); pieces for native instruments.

Babbi, (Pietro Giovanni) Cristoforo (Bartolomeo Gasparre), Italian violinist and composer, son of **Gregorio Babbi;** b. Cesena, May 6, 1745; d. Dresden, Nov. 19, 1814. He studied violin, counterpoint, and composition with Paolo

Alberghi in Faenza; subsequently was primo violino at the festas there (1766, 1769, 1770, 1772); also played in the orch. of the Rimini Opera (1773). In 1774 he was elected a member of the Accademia Filarmonica of Bologna; then was maestro di cappella at the Teatro Comunale there (1775–78); in 1779 he became primo violino and direttore d'orchestra in Forlì. He was called to Dresden in 1781 as provisional Konzertmeister; received a permanent appointment in 1782, and proceeded to reorganize the Kapelle; he held an equal place with J.G. Naumann, the Dresden Kapellmeister. He composed syms., operas, concertos, and other works.

Babbi, Gregorio (Lorenzo), famous Italian tenor, father of **Cristoforo Babbi;** b. Cesena, Nov. 16, 1708; d. there, Jan. 2, 1768. He made his operatic debut in Florence in 1730; in 1741 he entered the service of Charles III, King of Naples; in 1748 he was engaged by the Teatro San Carlo of Naples, where his wife, **Giovanna Guaetta,** was also a singer; he was pensioned in 1759.

Babbitt, Milton (Byron), prominent American composer, teacher, and theorist; b. Philadelphia, May 10, 1916. He received his early musical training in Jackson, Miss.; at the same time he revealed an acute flair for mathematical reasoning; this double faculty determined the formulation of his musical theories, in which he promulgated a system of melodic and rhythmic sets ultimately leading to integral serialism. His academic studies included courses with Philip James and Marion Bauer at N.Y. Univ. (B.A. 1935) and at Princeton Univ. (M.A. 1942); he also had private sessions with Sessions. From 1942 to 1945 he taught mathematics at Princeton Univ., then music (1948–84). He held a Guggenheim grant in 1961; was elected a member of the National Inst. of Arts and Letters in 1965. At Princeton and Columbia Univs. he inaugurated an experimental program of electronic music, with the aid of a newly constructed synthesizer. He also taught at the Juilliard School in N.Y. (from 1973) and at various other venues in the U.S. and Europe. Taking as the point of departure the Schoenbergian method of composition with 12 different tones, Babbitt extended the serial principle to embrace 12 different note values, 12 different time intervals between instrumental entries, 12 different dynamic levels, and 12 different instrumental timbres. In order to describe the potential combinations of the basic 4 aspects of the tone-row, he introduced the term "combinatoriality," with symmetric parts of a tone-row designated as "derivations." His paper "Twelve-Tone Invariants as Compositional Determinants," publ. in the *Musical Quarterly* of April 1960, gives a résumé of his system of total serialism. The serial application of rhythmic values is expounded in Babbitt's paper "Twelve-Tone Rhythmic Structure and the Electronic Medium," publ. in *Perspectives of New Music* (Fall 1962). A general exposition of his views on music is found in S. Dembski and J. Straus, eds., *M. B.: Words about Music* (*The Madison Lectures*) (Madison, Wis., 1987).

Babbitt's scientific-sounding theories have profoundly influenced the musical thinking of young American composers; a considerable literature, both intelligible and unintelligible, arose in special publications to penetrate and, if at all possible, to illuminate Babbitt's mind-boggling speculations. His original music, some of it aurally beguiling, can be fully understood only after a preliminary study of its underlying compositional plan. In 1982 he won a special citation of the Pulitzer Committee for "his life's work as a distinguished and seminal American composer."
Works: 3 *Compositions for Piano* (1947); *Composition for 4 Instruments* (1948); *Composition* for 12 Instruments (1948); *Composition* for Viola and Piano (1950); *The Widow's Lament in Springtime* for Voice and Piano (1950); *Du,* a song cycle (1951); *Quartet* for Flute, Oboe, Clarinet, and Bassoon (1953); String Quartet No. 1 (1954); String Quartet No. 2 (1954); 2 *Sonnets* for Voice and 3 Instruments (1955); *Semisimple Variations* for Piano (1956); *All Set* for Jazz Ensemble (1957); *Sounds and Words,* to a text of disparate syllables for Voice and Piano (1958); *Composition* for Voice and 6 Instruments (1960); Com-

position for Synthesizer (1961); *Vision and Prayer,* song for Soprano and Synthesized Magnetic Tape (1961); *Philomel* for Voice and Magnetic Tape (1964); *Ensemble* for Synthesizer (1964); *Relata I* for Orch. (1965); *Post-Partitions* for Piano (1966); *Sextets* for Violin and Piano (the title refers to the sextuple parameters of the work; 1966); *Correspondences* for String Orch. and Synthesized Magnetic Tape (1967); *Relata II* for Orch. (1968); *Occasional Variations,* a compost collated by Synthesizer (1969); String Quartet No. 3 (1970); *Phonemena* for Soprano and Piano (1970); *Arie da Capo* for 5 Players, "models of similar, interval-preserving, registrally uninterpreted pitch-class and metrically-durationally uninterpreted time-point aggregate arrays" (1974); *Reflections* for Piano and Synthesized Tape (1975); *Concerti* for Violin, Small Orch., and Synthesized Tape (N.Y., March 13, 1976); *Paraphrases* for 9 Wind Instruments and Piano (1979); *A Solo Requiem* for Soprano and 2 Pianists (N.Y., Feb. 10, 1979); *Dual* for Cello and Piano (1980); *Elizabethan Sextette,* 6 poems for 6 Unaccompanied Voices (1981); Piano Concerto (1985; N.Y., Jan. 19, 1986); *Transfigured Notes* for String Orch. (1986); *Beaten Paths* for Marimba (1988); *The Crowded Air* for 11 Instruments (1988); *Consortini* for 5 Instruments (1989).
Bibl.: Special issue of *Perspectives of New Music,* XIV/2–XV/1 (1976); A. Mead, "Recent Developments in the Music of M. B.," *Musical Quarterly* (Summer 1984).

Babell, William, English harpsichordist, violinist, organist, and composer; b. probably in London, c.1690; d. there, Sept. 23, 1723. He studied music with his father and with Pepusch; was then active in London concert life as an instrumentalist; was also organist of All Hallows. He composed a number of works for the harpsichord; also concertos for violin and for flute.

Babin, Victor, Russian-born American pianist and composer; b. Moscow, Dec. 13, 1908; d. Cleveland, March 1, 1972. He studied at the Cons. of Riga, Latvia, graduating in 1927; in 1928 went to Berlin, where he took lessons in piano with Artur Schnabel and in composition with Franz Schreker at the Berlin Hochschule für Musik. On Aug. 31, 1933, he married the pianist **Vitya Vronsky;** they emigrated to the U.S. in 1937. From 1943 to 1946, Babin served in the U.S. Army; became a naturalized American citizen in 1944. From 1951 to 1954 he taught at the Aspen Music School in Colorado. In 1961 he was appointed director of the Cleveland Inst. of Music, a post he held until his death. He composed 2 concertos for 2 pianos and orch. and several pieces for duo-pianos, which he performed with his wife.

Babini, Matteo, famous Italian tenor; b. Bologna, Feb. 19, 1754; d. there, Sept. 22, 1816. He studied with Cortoni; made his debut in 1780; then toured England, Russia, Germany, and Austria with great acclaim. He settled in Paris as a court favorite until the Revolution forced him to leave France; he was in Berlin in 1792 and in Trieste in 1796. Brighenti publ. an "Elogio" in his memory (Bologna, 1821).

Babitz, Sol, American violinist; b. N.Y., Oct. 11, 1911; d. Los Angeles, Feb. 18, 1982. In 1932 he went to Berlin, where he studied violin with Carl Flesch and composition with Paul Juon; also took a course in musicology with Curt Sachs. In 1933 he proceeded to Paris and continued violin instruction with Marcel Chailley. Shortly afterward he returned to the U.S., and became a violinist in the Los Angeles Phil. Orch. (1933–37). From 1942 to 1961 he played violin in studio orchs. in Hollywood. He publ. *Principles of Extensions in Violin Fingering* (N.Y., 1947); also ed. for publication violin works by contemporary composers.

Bacarisse, Salvador, Spanish composer; b. Madrid, Sept. 12, 1898; d. Paris, Aug. 5, 1963. He studied at the Madrid Cons. with Conrado del Campo; received the Premio Nacional de Música in 1923, 1930, and 1934. During the Spanish Civil War he was active in the music section of the loyalist army, and after its defeat in 1939 went to Paris, where he remained until his death. He wrote music in all genres; among his works are an opera, *Charlot* (1933); the symphonic poem *La tragedia de Doña Ajada* (1929); *Corrida de feria*, a ballet (1930); 3 piano concertos (1933, 1957, 1958); *Tres movimientos concertantes* for String Trio and Orch. (1934); a cantata, *Por la paz y felicidad de las naciones* (1950); Concerto for Guitar and Orch. (Paris, Oct. 22, 1953); 3 string quartets; piano pieces; songs.

Baccaloni, Salvatore, Italian bass; b. Rome, April 14, 1900; d. N.Y., Dec. 31, 1969. He sang as a child in the Sistine Chapel at the Vatican; for some years studied architecture; then began his career as an opera singer. He made his debut in Rome in 1922; in 1926 he appeared at La Scala in Milan. In 1930 he went to the U.S.; was on the roster of the Chicago Civic Opera (1930–32); made his debut with the Metropolitan Opera in N.Y. on Dec. 7, 1940, as Bartolo in *Le nozze di Figaro;* remained on its staff until his final appearance there on Feb. 14, 1962. He specialized in buffo roles; his repertoire consisted of some 150 roles in several languages.

Baccusi, Ippolito, Italian composer; b. Mantua, 1550; d. Verona, Sept. 2, 1608. He served as maestro di cappella at S. Marco in Venice. In 1570 he was in Ravenna as an organist and in 1572 in Verona; from 1584 to 1587 he was maestro di cappella in Mantua; in 1591 went to Verona. He publ. 5 books of masses (1570–96); 7 books of madrigals (1570–1605); also numerous other choral works. His music shows the influence of the Venetian school; his motets have considerable expressive power.

Bacewicz, Grażyna, significant Polish composer; b. Lodz, Feb. 5, 1909; d. Warsaw, Jan. 17, 1969. She studied composition and violin at the Warsaw Cons., graduating in 1932; continued her study of composition with Nadia Boulanger in Paris (1933–34); upon her return to Poland, she taught at the Lodz Cons.; in 1966 she was appointed prof. at the State Academy of Music in Warsaw. A prolific composer, she adopted a neo-Classical style, characterized by a firm rhythmic pulse and crisp dissonant harmonies. **WORKS:** Comic radio opera, *Przygody króla Artura* (The Adventures of King Arthur; 1959); 3 ballets: *Z chlopa Król* (A Peasant Becomes King; 1953), *Esik in Ostende* (1964), *Poządanie* (Desire; 1968); *Sinfonietta* (1937); 7 violin concertos (1938, 1946, 1948, 1952, 1954, 1957, 1965); Overture (1943); 4 numbered syms. (1942–45; 1950; 1952; 1953); an unnumbered Sym. for String Orch. (1943–46); *Olympic Cantata* (1948); Concerto for String Orch. (1948); Piano Concerto (1949); 2 cello concertos (1951, 1963); *Polish Overture* (1954); Partita for Orch. (1955); Variations for Orch. (1957); *Muzyka* for Strings, 5 Trumpets, and Percussion (Warsaw, Sept. 14, 1959); *Pensieri notturni* for Chamber Orch. (1961); Concerto for Orch. (1962); *Cantata,* after Wyspiański's "Acropolis" (1964); *Musica Sinfonica* (1965); Divertimento for String Orch. (1965); *Incrustations* for Horn and Chamber Ensemble (1965); *Contradizione* for Chamber Orch. (1966; Dartmouth College, Hanover, N.H., Aug. 2, 1967); 2-piano Concerto (1966); *In una parte* for Orch. (1967); Viola Concerto (1967–68); Wind Quintet (1932); Trio for Oboe, Violin, and Cello (1935); 7 string quartets (1938, 1942, 1947, 1950, 1955, 1960, 1965); 5 violin sonatas (1945, 1946, 1947, 1951, 1955); Quartet for 4 Violins (1949); 2 piano quintets (1952, 1965); solo Violin Sonata (1958); Quartet for 4 Cellos (1964); Trio for Oboe, Harp, and Percussion (1965); *4 Caprices* for Solo Violin (1968); 3 piano sonatas (1935, 1949, 1952); *10 Concert Studies* for Piano (1957); *Esquisse* for Organ (1966). **BIBL.:** J. Rosen, *G. B.: Her Life and Works* (Los Angeles, 1984).

Bach is the name of the illustrious German family which, during 2 centuries, gave to the world a number of musicians and composers of distinction. History possesses few records of such remarkable examples of hereditary art, which culminated in the genius of Johann Sebastian Bach. In the Bach genealogy, the primal member was Johannes or Hans Bach, who is mentioned in 1561 as a guardian of the municipality of Wechmar, a town near Gotha. Also residing in Wechmar

was his relative **Veit Bach;** a baker by trade, he was also skillful in playing on a small cittern. Another relative, **Caspar Bach,** who lived from 1570 to 1640, was a Stadtpfeifer in Gotha who later served as a town musician in Arnstadt. His 5 sons, **Caspar, Johannes, Melchior, Nicolaus,** and **Heinrich,** were all town musicians. Another Bach, **Johann(es Hans) Bach** (1550–1626), was known as "der Spielmann," that is, "minstrel," and thus was definitely described as primarily a musician by vocation. His 3 sons, **Johann(es Hans), Christoph,** and **Heinrich,** were also musicians. J.S. Bach took great interest in his family history, and in 1735 prepared a genealogy under the title *Ursprung der musicalisch-Bachischen Familie. The Bach Reader,* compiled by H. David and A. Mendel (N.Y., 1945; rev. ed., 1966), contains extensive quotations from this compendium. Karl Geiringer's books *The Bach Family: Seven Generations of Creative Genius* (N.Y., 1954) and *Music of the Bach Family: An Anthology* (Cambridge, Mass., 1955) give useful genealogical tables of Bach's family. Bach's father, **Johann Ambrosius,** was a twin brother of Bach's uncle; the twins bore such an extraordinary physical resemblance that, according to the testimony of Carl Philipp Emanuel Bach, their own wives had difficulty telling them apart after dark. To avoid confusion, they had them wear vests of different colors. A vulgar suggestion that because of this similarity Bach may have been begotten by his uncle is too gross to require a refutation.

When the family became numerous and widely dispersed, its members agreed to assemble on a fixed date each year. Erfurt, Eisenach, and Arnstadt were the places chosen for these meetings, which are said to have continued until the middle of the 18th century, as many as 120 persons of the name of Bach then assembling. At these meetings, a cherished pastime was the singing of "quodlibets," comic polyphonic potpourris of popular songs. An amusing example attributed to J.S. Bach is publ. in *Veröffentlichungen der Neuen Bach-Gesellschaft* (vol. XXXII, 2).

Entries for Bach family members follow immediately. Entries for other musicians named Bach begin on page 87.

Bach, Carl Philipp Emanuel (the "Berlin" or "Hamburg" Bach), 3rd (and 2nd surviving) son of **Johann Sebastian;** b. Weimar, March 8, 1714; d. Hamburg, Dec. 14, 1788. He was educated under his father's tuition at the Thomasschule in Leipzig; then studied jurisprudence at the Univ. of Leipzig and at the Univ. of Frankfurt-an-der-Oder. Turning to music as his chief vocation, he went to Berlin in 1738; in 1740 he was confirmed as chamber musician to Frederick the Great of Prussia. In that capacity he arranged his father's visit to Potsdam. In March 1768 he assumed the post of cantor at the Johanneum (the Lateinschule) in Hamburg, and also served as music director for the 5 major churches. He held these posts until his death. Abandoning the strict polyphonic style of composition of his great father, he became an adept of the new school of piano writing, a master of "Empfindsamkeit" ("intimate expressiveness"), the North German counterpart of the French Rococo. His *Versuch über die wahre Art das Clavier zu spielen* . . . (2 parts, 1753–62; re-edited by Schelling in 1857; new, but incomplete, ed. by W. Niemann, 1906) became a very influential work which yielded much authentic information about musical practices of the 2nd half of the 18th century. An Eng. tr. of the *Versuch* . . . , entitled *Essay on the True Art of Playing Keyboard Instruments,* was publ. by W. Mitchell (N.Y., 1949). His autobiography was reprinted by W. Kahl in *Selbstbiographien deutscher Musiker des XVIII. Jahrhunderts* (Cologne, 1948); an Eng. tr. was made by W. Newman, "Emanuel Bach's Autobiography," *Musical Quarterly* (April 1965). His compositions are voluminous (see E. Helm, *A New Thematic Catalog of the Works of C.P.E. B.* [1987]). **WORKS:** For clavier, numerous solo pieces, concertos with orch.; quartets; trios; duets; 20 orch. syms.; many miscellaneous pieces for wind instruments; trios for flute, violin, and double bass; flute, oboe, and cello concertos; soli for flute, viola da gamba, oboe, cello, and harp; duets for flute and violin and for 2 violins; also pieces for clarinet. Vocal music: 2 oratorios: *Die Israeliten in der Wüste* and *Die Auferstehung und Himmelfahrt Jesu;* 22 Passions; cantatas; about 300 songs; etc. Editions of his various works include the following: C. Krebs, ed., *Die Sechs Sammlungen von Sonaten, freien Fantasien und Rondos für Kenner und Liebhaber* (Leipzig, 1895; rev. ed. by L. Hoffmann, Erbrecht, 1953); O. Vrieslander, *Kleine Stücke für Klavier* (Hannover, 1930); O. Vrieslander, *Vier leichte Sonaten* (Hannover, 1932); K. Herrman, ed., *Sonaten und Stücke* (Leipzig, 1938); V. Luithlen and H. Kraus, eds., *Klavierstücke* (Vienna, 1938); K. Herrman, ed., *Leichte Tänze und Stücke für Klavier* (Hamburg, 1949); P. Friedheim, ed., *Six Sonatas for Keyboard* (N.Y., 1967); H. Ferguson, ed., *Keyboard Works of C.P.E. B.* (4 vols., London, 1983).

BIBL.: C. Bitter, *C.P.E. B. und Wilhelm Friedemann Bach und deren Brüder* (2 vols., Berlin, 1868); M. Fleuler, *Die norddeutsche Symphonie zur Zeit Friedrichs des Grossen, und besonders die Werke P.E. B.s* (Berlin, 1908); H. Schenker, *Ein Beitrag zur Ornamentik; Als Einführung zu P.E. B.s Klavierwerke* (Vienna, 1908); O. Vrieslander, *C.P.E. B.* (Munich, 1923); H. Wien-Claudi, *Zum Liedschaffen C.P.E. B.s* (Reichenberg, 1928); H. Miesner, *P.E. B. in Hamburg* (Leipzig, 1929); E. Schmid, *C.P.E. B. und seine Kammermusik* (Kassel, 1931); A.-E. Cherbuliez, *C.P.E. B. 1714–1788* (Zürich and Leipzig, 1940); D. Plamenac, "New Light on the Last Years of C.P.E. B.," *Musical Quarterly* (Oct. 1949); E. Beurmann, *Die Klaviersonaten C.P.E. B.s* (diss., Univ. of Göttingen, 1952); K. Geiringer, *The Bach Family: Seven Generations of Creative Genius* (N.Y., 1954); C. Haag, *The Keyboard Concertos of K.P.E. B.* (diss., Univ. of Calif., Los Angeles, 1956); G. Busch, *C.P.E. B. und seine Lieder* (Regensburg, 1957); P. Barford, *The Keyboard Music of C.P.E. B.* (London, 1965); E. Suchalla, *Die Orchestersinfonien C.P.E. B.s nebst einem thematischen Verzeichnis seiner Orchesterwerke* (Augsburg, 1968); H.-G. Ottenberg, *C.P.E. B.* (Leipzig, 1982; Eng. tr., 1988); S. Clark, ed., *C.P.E. B. Studies* (Oxford, 1988); E. Helm, "The editorial transmission of C.P.E. B.'s music," *Early Music* (Feb. 1989).

Bach, Christoph, 2nd son of **Johann(es Hans)** "der Spielmann" and grandfather of **Johann Sebastian;** b. Wechmar, April 19, 1613; d. Arnstadt, Sept. 12, 1661. He was a court musician in Weimar; from 1642 he was a town musician in Erfurt; from 1654, court and town musician in Arnstadt. The only known musical item by him is publ. in the *Bach-Jahrbuch* (1928).

Bach, Georg Christoph, eldest son of **Christoph;** b. Erfurt, Sept. 6, 1642; d. Schweinfurt, April 24, 1697. He was cantor in Themar from 1668; in Schweinfurt from 1684. A cantata of his is publ. in *Das Erbe deutscher Musik* (vol. II, Leipzig, 1935).

Bach, Heinrich, 3rd son of **Johann(es Hans)** "der Spielmann"; b. Wechmar, Sept. 16, 1615; d. Arnstadt, July 10, 1692. He was a town musician in Schweinfurt from 1629, in Erfurt from 1635, and in Arnstadt from 1641; from 1641, was also organist at the Liebfrauenkirche in Arnstadt, a post he held for 51 years, until his death. M. Schneider publ. a thematic index of his works in the *Bach-Jahrbuch* (1907, pp. 105–9). A cantata of his is found in *Das Erbe deutscher Musik* (vol. II, Leipzig, 1935); also 3 organ chorales in D. Hellmann, ed., *Orgelwerke der Familie Bach* (Leipzig, 1967).

Bach, Johann(es Hans), eldest son of **Johann(es Hans)** "der Spielmann"; b. Wechmar, Nov. 26, 1604; d. Erfurt, May 13, 1673. He was apprenticed to Christoph Hoffmann, Stadtpfeifer in Suhl; was a town musician in Erfurt; from 1636, was organist at the Predigerkirche there. Several of his compositions are extant.

Bach, Johann Aegidius, 2nd son of **Johann(es Hans);** b. Erfurt, Feb. 9, 1645; d. there (buried), Nov. 22, 1716. He succeeded his father as municipal music director in Erfurt in 1682; was also organist at the Michaeliskirche there from 1690, succeeding Pachelbel.

Bach, Johann Ambrosius, 2nd son of **Christoph,** twin brother of **Johann Christoph,** and father of **Johann Sebastian;** b. Erfurt, Feb. 22, 1645; d. Eisenach, Feb. 20, 1695. As a boy, he went to Arnstadt; was trained as a Stadtpfeifer. In 1667 he became a member of the town band in Erfurt; from 1671 was court trumpeter and director of the town band in Eisenach. He was married twice: on April 8, 1668, to Maria Elisabeth Lämmerhirt (b. Erfurt, Feb. 24, 1644; d. Eisenach, May 3, 1694), the mother of Johann Sebastian; and on Nov. 27, 1694, to the widow of his cousin Johann Günther Bach.

BIBL.: F. Rollberg, "J.A. B., Stadtpfeifer zu Eisenach von 1671–1695," *Bach-Jahrbuch* (1927).

Bach, Johann Bernhard, son of **Johann Aegidius,** one of the best organists and composers of his generation; b. Erfurt, Nov. 23, 1676; d. Eisenach, June 11, 1749. He was an organist at Erfurt and Magdeburg, and the successor to **Johann Christoph** as organist at Eisenach (1703); also served the Duke of Saxe-Eisenach. He wrote harpsichord pieces; also a number of organ chorales: 2 of these have been publ. in *Das Erbe deutscher Musik* (vol. IX, Leipzig, 1937); 2 more in D. Hellmann, ed., *Orgelwerke der Familie Bach* (Leipzig, 1967). He also wrote 4 orch. suites; one was publ. by A. Fareanu (Leipzig, 1920); another by K. Geiringer, *Music of the Bach Family: An Anthology* (Cambridge, Mass., 1955).

BIBL.: S. Orth, "Zu den Erfurter Jahren J.B. B.s (1676–1749)," *Bach-Jahrbuch* (1971).

Bach, Johann (John) Christian (the "London" Bach), 11th and youngest surviving son of **Johann Sebastian;** b. Leipzig, Sept. 5, 1735; d. London, Jan. 1, 1782. He received early instruction in music from his father, after whose death in 1750 he went to Berlin to study with his brother **Carl Philipp Emanuel.** In 1754 he went to Italy, where he continued his studies with Padre Martini; he also found a patron in Count Agostino Litta of Milan. He converted to the Roman Catholic faith in order to be able to obtain work, and became one of the organists at the Cathedral in Milan (1760–62); he also traveled throughout the country and composed several successful operas during his stay in Italy. In 1762 he went to England; his highly acclaimed opera *Orione* was given its premiere in London on Feb. 19, 1763; in 1764 he was appointed music master to the Queen. From 1764 to 1781 he gave, together with C.F. Abel, a series of London concerts. When child Mozart was taken to London in 1764, J.C. Bach took great interest in him and improvised with him at the keyboard; Mozart retained a lifelong affection for him; he used 3 of J.C. Bach's piano sonatas as thematic material for his piano concertos. J.C. Bach was a highly prolific composer; he wrote about 90 syms., several piano concertos, 6 quintets, a Piano Sextet, violin sonatas, and numerous piano sonatas. In his music he adopted the *style galant* of the 2nd half of the 18th century, with an emphasis on expressive "affects" and brilliance of instrumental display. He thus totally departed from the ideals of his father, and became historically a precursor of the Classical era as exemplified by the works of Mozart. Although he was known mainly as an instrumental composer, J.C. Bach also wrote successful operas, most of them to Italian librettos; among them were *Artaserse* (Turin, Dec. 26, 1760); *Catone in Utica* (Naples, Nov. 4, 1761); *Alessandro nell' Indie* (Naples, Jan. 20, 1762); *Orione, ossia Diana vendicata* (London, Feb. 19, 1763); *Zanaida* (London, May 7, 1763); *Adriano in Siria* (London, Jan. 26, 1765); *Carattaco* (London, Feb. 14, 1767); *Temistocle* (Mannheim, Nov. 4, 1772); *Lucio Silla* (Mannheim, Nov. 4, 1774); *La clemenza di Scipione* (London, April 4, 1778); *Amadis de Gaule* (Paris, Dec. 14, 1779). See E. Warburton, general ed., *J.C. B., 1735–1782: The Collected Works* (48 vols., N.Y., 1988–90).

BIBL.: M. Schwarz, "J.C. B.," *Sammelbände der Internationalen Musik-Gesellschaft* (1900–1901); idem, *J.C. B.: Sein Leben und seine Werke* (Leipzig, 1901); G. de Saint-Foix, "À propos de Jean-Chrétien B.," *Revue de Musicologie* (1926); H. Schökel, *J.C. B. und die Instrumentalmusik seiner Zeit* (Wolfenbüttel, 1926); F. Tutenberg, *Die Sinfonik J.C. B.* (Wolfenbüttel, 1928); C. Terry, *John C. B.* (London, 1929; 2nd ed. by H.C. Robbins Landon, 1967); A. Wenk, *Beiträge zur Kenntnis des Opernschaffens von J.C. B.* (diss., Univ. of Frankfurt am Main, 1932); E. Reeser, *De zonen van Bach* (Amsterdam, 1941; in Eng., 1949); K. Geiringer, *The Bach Family: Seven Generations of Creative Genius* (N.Y., 1954); R. Seebandt, *Arientypen J.C. B.s* (diss., Humboldt Univ., Berlin, 1956); E. Downes, *The Operas of J.C. B. as a Reflection of the Dominant Trends in Opera Seria 1750–1780* (diss., Harvard Univ., 1958); J. White, Jr., *The Concerted Symphonies of J.C. B.* (diss., Univ. of Michigan, 1958); W. Haacke, *Die Söhne Bachs* (Königstein im Taunus, 1962); B. Mekota, *The Solo and Ensemble Keyboard Works of J.C. B.* (diss., Univ. of Michigan, 1969); M. Vos, *The Liturgical Choral Works of J.C. B.* (diss., Washington Univ., St. Louis, 1969); E. Warburton, *A Study of J.C. B.'s Operas* (diss., Oxford Univ., 1969); I. Baierle, *Die Klavierwerke von J.C. B.* (diss., Univ. of Graz, 1974); S. Roe, "J.C. B., 1735–1782: Towards a New Biography," *Musical Times* (Jan. 1982); R. Maunder, "J.C. B.'s Endimione," ibid. (July 1982); E. Warburton, "J.C. B.'s Latin Church Music," ibid. (Nov. 1982); S. Roe, "J.C. B.'s Vauxhall Songs: A New Discovery," ibid. (Nov. 1983).

Bach, Johann Christoph, eldest son of **Heinrich,** organist and composer of the highest distinction among the earlier Bachs; b. Arnstadt, Dec. 3, 1642; d. Eisenach, March 31, 1703. From 1663 to 1665 he was an organist in Arnstadt; from 1665, in Eisenach; from 1700, was court musician there. A thematic catalogue of his compositions was publ. by M. Schneider in the *Bach-Jahrbuch* (1907, pp. 132–77). C.P.E. Bach described him as a "great and expressive composer"; his works are printed in *Das Erbe deutscher Musik* (vols. I and II, Leipzig, 1935); several of his motets were publ. by V. Junk (Leipzig, 1922); 44 chorales with preludes for organ were ed. by M. Fischer (Kassel, 1936); 3 additional such works attributed to him were ed. by C. Wolff in *The Neumeister Collection of Chorale Preludes from the Bach Circle* (Yale University Manuscript LM 4708) (facsimile ed., New Haven, 1986); his *Praeludium und Fuge* for Organ is in D. Hellmann, ed., *Orgelwerke der Familie Bach* (Leipzig, 1967).
BIBL.: M. Fischer, "Die organistische Improvisation bei J.C. B.," *Königsberger Studien zur Musikwissenschaft,* V (1928); F. Rollberg, "J.C. B.: Organist zu Eisenach 1665–1703," *Zeitschrift für Musikwissenschaft,* XI (1929); C. Freyse, "J.C. B.," *Bach-Jahrbuch* (1956).

Bach, Johann Christoph, twin brother of **Johann Ambrosius;** b. Erfurt, Feb. 22, 1645; d. Arnstadt, Aug. 25, 1693. He was a Stadtpfeifer in Erfurt from 1666; in Arnstadt, from 1671. The physical resemblance between him and his twin brother (father of **Johann Sebastian**) was such that, according to the testimony of C.P.E. Bach, even their wives had difficulty distinguishing between them.

Bach, Johann Christoph, brother of **Johann Sebastian** and eldest son of **Johann Ambrosius;** b. Erfurt, June 16, 1671; d. Ohrdruf, Feb. 22, 1721. He was a pupil of Pachelbel; served as organist at the Thomaskirche in Erfurt and for a short time at Arnstadt; from 1690 he was organist at the Michaeliskirche in Ohrdruf, where Johann Sebastian stayed with him for almost 5 years.
BIBL.: C. Freyse, *Die Ohrdrufer Bache in der Silhouette: J.S. Bachs ältester Bruder J.C. und seine Nachkommen* (Eisenach, 1957).

Bach, Johann Christoph Friedrich (the "Bückeburg" Bach), 9th son of **Johann Sebastian;** b. Leipzig, June 21, 1732; d. Bückeburg, Jan. 26, 1795. He studied music with his father; then attended the Univ. of Leipzig, where he took courses in jurisprudence. Adopting music as his principal vocation, he became a chamber musician in Bückeburg, a post he held until his death. Although less known as a composer than his brothers, he was a fine musician. A selected edition of his works was ed. by G. Schünemann and sponsored by the Fürstliches Institut für Musikwissenschaftliche Forschung (1920–

22). Schünemann also ed. several oratorios in Denkmäler Deutscher Tonkunst (vol. 56, 1917). G. Walter ed. the cantata *Die Amerikanerin* (Berlin, 1919), and L. Duttenhofer, a set of 6 quartets (Paris, 1922); several other chamber works may be found in K. Geiringer, *Music of the Bach Family: An Anthology* (Cambridge, Mass., 1955); 3 syms. have been ed. in facsimile by H. Wohlfarth (Bückeburg, 1966).
BIBL.: G. Schünemann, "J.C.F. B.," *Bach-Jahrbuch* (1914); H. Wohlfarth, *J.C.F. B.* (Bern, 1971; includes a catalogue of his works).

Bach, Johann Ernst, only son of **Johann Bernhard;** b. Eisenach, Jan. 28, 1722; d. there, Sept. 1, 1777. He was a pupil of his uncle **Johann Sebastian.** After studying law at the Univ. of Leipzig, he returned to Eisenach and practiced as an advocate. In 1748 he became assistant organist to his father at the Georgenkirche; succeeded him as organist in 1749. In 1756 he became Court Kapellmeister to the fused courts of Weimar, Gotha, and Eisenach. When this arrangement was dissolved in 1758, he retained his position and worked in the administration of the ducal finances in Eisenach. He publ. *Sammlung auserlesener Fabeln mit Melodeyen* (ed. by H. Kretzschmar in Denkmäler Deutscher Tonkunst, vol. 42, 1910) and other works. Only a small part of his works has been publ.; his Passion oratorio, *O Seele, deren Sehen,* is in Denkmäler Deutscher Tonkunst, vol. 48, 1914. A sonata is in K. Geiringer, *Music of the Bach Family: An Anthology* (Cambridge, Mass., 1955). Two fantasies and fugues for organ are found in D. Hellmann, ed., *Orgelwerke der Familie Bach* (Leipzig, 1967).

Bach, Johann Ludwig, son of Johann Jacob (I) and a great-grandson of Lips Bach (d. Oct. 10, 1620); b. Thal (baptized), Feb. 6, 1677; d. Meiningen (buried), March 1, 1731. In 1699 he became a court musician in Meiningen; was appointed cantor in 1703, and Court Kapellmeister in 1711. He wrote numerous vocal compositions; also orch. works, but few have been preserved.
BIBL.: A. Jaffé, *The Cantatas of J.L. B.* (diss., Boston Univ., 1957); W. Scheide, "J.S. B.s Sammlung von Kantaten seines Vetters J.L. B.," *Bach-Jahrbuch* (1959, 1961, 1962).

Bach, Johann Michael, brother of **Johann Christoph** and father of Maria Barbara, 1st wife of **Johann Sebastian;** b. Arnstadt, Aug. 9, 1648; d. Gehren, May 17, 1694. From 1673 he was organist and town clerk of Gehren; also worked as a maker of instruments. His works are listed in the *Bach-Jahrbuch* (1907, pp. 109–32); many of them are included in *Das Erbe deutscher Musik* (vol. I, Leipzig, 1935); motets of his are publ. in Denkmäler Deutscher Tonkunst (vols. 49 and 50, 1915). Some of his organ compositions are found in *Das Erbe deutscher Musik* (vol. IX, Leipzig, 1937); 72 organ chorales are included in D. Hellmann, ed., *Orgelwerke der Familie Bach* (Leipzig, 1967); 25 such works, including 13 recently discovered pieces, are included in C. Wolff, ed., *The Neumeister Collection of Chorale Preludes from the Bach Circle* (Yale University Manuscript LM 4708) (facsimile ed., New Haven, 1986).

Bach, Johann Nicolaus, eldest son of **Johann Christoph;** b. Eisenach, Oct. 10, 1669; d. Jena, Nov. 4, 1753. He was educated at the Univ. of Jena; in 1694 he became organist at Jena, and in 1719 was also at the Univ. He was an expert on organ building and also made keyboard instruments. He wrote a fine *Missa* (Kyrie and Gloria; ed. by A. Fareanu and V. Junk, Leipzig, 1920); a comic cantata, *Der Jenaische Wein- und Bier-rufer,* a scene from life at Jena Univ. (ed. by F. Stein, Leipzig, 1921); suites for keyboard, which are not preserved; and organ chorales, of which only 1 is known.
BIBL.: H. Koch, "J.N., der 'Jenaer' B.," *Die Musikforschung,* XXI (1968).

Bach, Johann Sebastian, supreme arbiter and lawgiver of music, a master comparable in greatness of stature with Aristotle in philosophy and Leonardo da Vinci in art; b. Eisenach, March 21 (baptized, March 23), 1685; d. Leipzig, July 28, 1750. He was a member of an illustrious family of musicians who were active in various capacities as performing artists, composers, and teachers. That so many Bachs were musicians lends support to the notion that music is a hereditary faculty, that some subliminal cellular unit may be the nucleus of musicality. The word "Bach" itself means "stream" in the German language; the rhetorical phrase that Johann Sebastian Bach was not a mere stream but a whole ocean of music ("Nicht Bach aber Meer haben wir hier") epitomizes Bach's encompassing magnitude. Yet despite the grandeur of the phenomenon of Bach, he was not an isolated figure dwelling in the splendor of his genius apart from the zeitgeist, the spirit of his time. Just as Aristotle was not only an abstract philosopher but also an educator (Alexander the Great was his pupil), just as Leonardo da Vinci was not only a painter of portraits but also a practical man of useful inventions, so Bach was a mentor to young students, a master organist and instructor who spent his life within the confines of his native Thuringia as a teacher and composer of works designed for immediate performance in church and in the schoolroom. Indeed, the text of the dedication of his epoch-making work *Das wohltemperierte Clavier oder Praeludia und Fugen* emphasizes its pedagogical aspect: "The Well-tempered Clavier, or Preludes and Fugues in all tones and semitones, both with the major third of Ut Re Mi, and the minor third of Re Mi Fa, composed and notated for the benefit and exercise of musical young people eager to learn, as well as for a special practice for those who have already achieved proficiency and skill in this study." The MS is dated 1722. Bach's system of "equal temperament" (which is the meaning of "well-tempered" in the title *Well-tempered Clavier*) postulated the division of the octave into 12 equal semitones, making it possible to transpose and to effect a modulation into any key, a process unworkable in the chaotic tuning of keyboard instruments before Bach's time. Bach was not the 1st to attempt the tempered division, however. J.C.F. Fischer anticipated him in his collection *Ariadne musica* (with the allusion to the thread of Ariadne that allowed Theseus to find his way out of the Cretan labyrinth); publ. in 1700, it contained 20 preludes and fugues in 19 different keys. Undoubtedly Bach was aware of this ed.; actually, the subjects of several of Bach's preludes and fugues are similar to the point of identity to the themes of Fischer's work. These coincidences do not detract from the significance of Bach's accomplishment, for it is the beauty and totality of development that makes Bach's work vastly superior to those of any of his putative predecessors.

It is interesting to note that Bach shared the belief in numerical symbolism held by many poets and artists of his time. By summing up the cardinal numbers corresponding to the alphabetical order of the letters of his last name, he arrived at the conclusion that the number 14 had a special significance in his life (B = 2, A = 1, C = 3, H = 8; 2 + 1 + 3 + 8 = 14). That the number of buttons on his waistcoat in one of his portraits is 14 may be an indication of the significance he attached to this number. The theme of Bach's chorale *Von deinen Thron tret' ich hiermit*, which he wrote shortly before his death, contains 14 notes, while the notes in the entire melody number 43, comprising the sum total of the alphabetical index of letters in J.S. Bach (10 + 19 + 2 + 1 + 3 + 8 = 43). In Bach's chorale prelude *Wenn wir in höchsten Nöten sein*, the principal melody contains 166 notes, which represents the alphabetical sum of the full name JOHANN SEBASTIAN BACH (10 + 15 + 8 + 1 + 14 + 14 + 19 + 5 + 2 + 1 + 19 + 20 + 9 + 1 + 14 + 2 + 1 + 3 + 8 = 166). The symbolism of melodies and harmonies in Baroque music, expressing various states of mind, joy or sadness, has been accepted as a valid "doctrine of affects" by musical philosophers, among them Albert Schweitzer. Indeed, there seems to be little doubt that a natural connection exists between such a line as "Geh' auf! Geh' auf!" and an ascending major arpeggio in a Bach cantata, or that, generally speaking, major modes represent joy and exhilaration, and minor keys suggest melancholy and sadness. We find numerous instances in the choral works of Baroque composers of the use of a broken diminished-seventh-chord in a precipitous downward movement to depict the fall from grace and regression to Hell. The chromatic weaving around a thematic tone often represents in Bach's cantatas and Passions the thorny crown around the head of Jesus Christ. An ascending scale of several octaves, sung by basses, tenors, altos, and sopranos in succession, is found to accompany the words "We follow you." A hypothesis may be advanced that such tonal patterns were used by Baroque composers to facilitate the comprehension of the meaning of the text by the congregation in church performances. Indeed, such word painting has become an accepted procedure in the last 2 or 3 centuries; composers equated major keys with joy and virtue, and minor keys with melancholy and sin. Similarly, fast tempos and duple time are commonly used by composers to express joy, while slow movements are reserved for scenes of sadness.

The term "Baroque" had a humble origin; it was probably derived from *barroco*, the Portuguese word for a deformed pearl; originally it had a decidedly negative meaning, and was often applied in the 17th century to describe a corrupt style of Renaissance architecture. Through the centuries the word underwent a change of meaning toward lofty excellence. In this elevated sense, "Baroque" came to designate an artistic development between the years 1600 and 1800. The advent of Bach marked the greatest flowering of Baroque music; his name became a synonym for perfection. Max Reger was told by Hugo Riemann that he could be the 2nd Bach, and his skill in composition almost justified his aspiration; Ferruccio Busoni was described by his admirers as the Bach of the modern era; a similar honor was claimed for Hindemith by his disciples. Yet the art of Bach remains unconquerable. Although he wrote most of his contrapuntal works as a didactic exercise, there are in his music extraordinary visions into the remote future; consider, for instance, the A-minor Fugue of the 1st book of the *Well-tempered Clavier*, in which the inversion of the subject seems to violate all the rules of proper voice-leading in its bold leap from the tonic upward to the 7th of the scale and then up a third. The answer to the subject of the F minor Fugue of the 1st book suggests the chromatic usages of later centuries. In the art of variations, Bach was supreme. A superb example is his set of keyboard pieces known as the *Goldberg Variations*, so named because it was commissioned by the Russian diplomat Kayserling through the mediation of Bach's pupil Johann Gottlieb Goldberg, who was in Kayserling's service as a harpsichord player. These variations are listed by Bach as the 4th part of the *Clavier-Übung;* the didactic title of this division is characteristic of Bach's intention to write music for utilitarian purposes, be it for keyboard exercises, for church services, or for chamber music. A different type of Bach's great musical projections is exemplified by his *Concerts à plusieurs instruments*, known popularly as the *Brandenburg Concertos*, for they were dedicated to Christian Ludwig, margrave of Brandenburg. They represent the crowning achievement of the Baroque. Nos. 2, 4, and 5 of the *Brandenburg Concertos* are essentially concerti grossi, in which a group of solo instruments—the concertino—is contrasted with the accompanying string orch. Finally, *Die Kunst der Fuge*, Bach's last composition, which he wrote in 1749, represents an encyclopedia of fugues, canons, and various counterpoints based on the same theme. Here Bach's art of purely technical devices, such as inversion, canon, augmentation, diminution, double fugue, triple fugue, at times appearing in fantastic optical symmetry so that the written music itself forms a balanced design, is calculated to instruct the musical mind as well as delight the aural sense. Of these constructions, the most extraordinary is represented by *Das musikalische Opfer* (The Musical Offering), composed by Bach for Frederick the Great of Prussia. Bach's 2nd son, **Carl Philipp Emanuel,** who served as chamber musician to the court of Prussia, arranged for Bach to visit Frederick's palace in Potsdam; Bach arrived there, accompanied by his son **Wilhelm Friedemann,** on May 7, 1747. The ostensible purpose of Bach's visit was to test the Silbermann pianos installed in the palace. The King, who liked to flaunt his love for the arts and sciences, gave Bach a musical theme of his own invention and asked him to compose a fugue upon it. Bach also presented an organ recital at the Heiliggeistkirche in Potsdam and attended a chamber music concert held by the King; on that occasion he improvised a fugue in 6 parts on a theme of his own. Upon his return to Leipzig, Bach set to work on the King's theme. Gallantly, elegantly, he inscribed the work, in scholastic Latin, "Regis Iussu Cantio et Reliqua Canonica Arte Resoluta" ("At the King's command, the cantus and supplements are in a canonic manner resolved"). The initials of the Latin words form the acronym RICERCAR, a technical term etymologically related to the word "research" and applied to any study that is instructive in nature. The work is subdivided into 13 sections; it includes a puzzle canon in 2 parts, marked "quaerendo invenietis" ("you will find it by seeking"). Bach had the score engraved, and sent it to the King on July 7, 1747. Intellectually independent as Bach was, he never questioned the immanent rights of established authority. He was proud of the title Royal Polish and Electoral Saxon Court Composer to the King of Poland and Elector of Saxony, bestowed upon him in 1736 while he was in the service of Duke Christian of Weissenfels, and he even regarded the position of cantor of the Thomasschule in Leipzig as inferior to it. In his dedications to royal personages he adhered to the customary humble style, which was extended even to the typography of his dedicatory prefaces. In such dedications the name of the exalted commissioner was usually printed in large letters, with conspicuous indentation, while Bach's own signature, preceded by elaborate verbal genuflection, appeared in the smallest type of the typographer's box.

Bach's biography is singularly lacking in dramatic events. He attended the Latin school in Eisenach, and apparently was a good student, as demonstrated by his skill in the Latin language. His mother died in 1694; his father remarried and died soon afterward. Bach's school years were passed at the Lyceum in the town of Ohrdruf; his older brother **Johann Christoph** lived there; he helped Bach in his musical studies; stories that he treated Bach cruelly must be dismissed as melodramatic inventions. Through the good offices of Elias Herda, cantor of the Ohrdruf school, Bach received an opportunity to move, for further education, to Lüneburg; there he was admitted to the Mettenchor of the Michaeliskirche. In March of 1703 he obtained employment as an attendant to Johann Ernst, Duke of Weimar; he was commissioned to make tests on the new organ of the Neukirche in Arnstadt; on Aug. 9, 1703, he was appointed organist there. In Oct. 1705 he obtained a leave of absence to travel to Lübeck to hear the famous organist Dietrich Buxtehude. The physical mode of Bach's travel there leaves much to be explained. The common versions found in most biographies tell that Bach made that journey on foot. But the distance between Arnstadt and Lübeck is 212 miles (335 km) and the route lies through the forbidding Harz Mountain chain, with its legendary peak Brocken, which, according to common superstition, was the site of the midnight gathering of a coven of witches. Assuming that Bach had about a month to spend in Lübeck to attend Buxtehude's concerts (or else the journey would not have been worthwhile), he had about 45 days to cover 424 miles (670 km) for a round trip: he would have had to travel on the average of 20 miles a day. The actual travel time between Arnstadt and Lübeck, considering the absence of good roads, must have been much longer. Not only would it have been exhausting in the extreme, even for a young man of 19 (Bach's age at the time), but it would have necessitated a change of 3 or 4 pairs of heavy boots that would wear out in the generally inclement weather during the months of Nov. and Dec. A query for information from the office of the Oberbürgermeister of Arnstadt elicited the suggestion that Bach (and Handel, who made a similar journey before) must have hired himself out as a valet to a coach passenger, a not uncommon practice among young men of the time. The impetus of Bach's trip was presumably the hope of obtaining Buxtehude's position as organist upon his retirement, but there was a peculiar clause attached to the contract for such a candidate: Buxtehude had 5 unmarried daughters; his successor was expected to marry the eldest of them. Buxtehude himself obtained his post through such an expedient, but Bach apparently was not prepared for matrimony under such circumstances.

On June 15, 1707, Bach became organist at the Blasiuskirche in Mühlhausen. On Oct. 17, 1707, he married his cousin Maria Barbara Bach, who was the daughter of **Johann Michael Bach.** On Feb. 4, 1708, Bach composed his cantata *Gott ist mein König* for the occasion of the installation of a new Mühlhausen town council. This was the 1st work of Bach's that was publ. Although the circumstances of his employment in Mühlhausen were seemingly favorable, Bach resigned his position on June 25, 1708, and accepted the post of court organist to Duke Wilhelm Ernst of Weimar. In Dec. 1713 Bach visited Halle, the birthplace of Handel; despite its proximity to Bach's own place of birth in Eisenach, the 2 great composers never met. On March 2, 1714, Duke Wilhelm Ernst offered Bach the position of Konzertmeister. In Sept. 1717 Bach went to Dresden to hear the famous French organist Louis Marchand, who resided there at the time. It was arranged that Bach and Marchand would hold a contest as virtuosos, but Marchand left Dresden before the scheduled event. This anecdote should not be interpreted frivolously as Marchand's fear of competing; other factors may have intervened to prevent the meeting. Johann Samuel Drese, the Weimar music director, died on Dec. 1, 1716; Bach expected to succeed him in that prestigious position, but the Duke gave the post to Drese's son. Again, this episode should not be interpreted as the Duke's lack of appreciation for Bach's superior abilities; the appointment may have merely followed the custom of letting such administrative posts remain in the family. In 1717 Bach accepted the position of Kapellmeister and music director to Prince Leopold of Anhalt in Cöthen, but a curious contretemps developed when the Duke of Weimar refused to release Bach from his obligation, and even had him held under arrest from Nov. 6 to Dec. 2, 1717, before Bach was finally allowed to proceed to Cöthen. The Cöthen period was one of the most productive in Bach's life; there he wrote his great set of *Brandenburg Concertos,* the *Clavierbüchlein für Wilhelm Friedemann Bach,* and the 1st book of *Das Wohltemperierte Clavier.* In Oct. 1719 Bach was in Halle once more, but again missed meeting Handel, who had already gone to England. In 1720 Bach accompanied Prince Leopold to Karlsbad. A tragedy supervened when Bach's devoted wife was taken ill and died before Bach could be called to her side; she was buried on July 7, 1720, leaving Bach to take care of their 7 children. In 1720 Bach made a long journey to Hamburg, where he met the aged Reinken, who was then 97 years old. It is a part of the Bach legend that Reinken was greatly impressed with Bach's virtuosity and exclaimed, "I believed that the art of organ playing was dead, but it lives in you!" Bach remained a widower for nearly a year and a half before he married his 2nd wife, Anna Magdalena Wilcken, a daughter of a court trumpeter at Weissenfels, on Dec. 3, 1721. They had 13 children during their happy marital life. New avenues were opened to Bach when Johann Kuhnau, the cantor of Leipzig, died on June 5, 1722. Although Bach applied for his post, the Leipzig authorities offered it 1st to Telemann of Hamburg, and when he declined, to Christoph Graupner of Darmstadt; only when Graupner was unable to obtain a release from his current position was Bach given the post. He traveled to Leipzig on Feb. 7, 1723, for a trial performance, earning a favorable reception. On April 22, 1723, Bach was elected to the post of cantor of the city of Leipzig and was officially installed on May 31, 1723. As director of church music, Bach's duties included the care of musicians for the Thomaskirche, Nicolaikirche, Matthaeikirche, and Petrikirche, and he was also responsible for the provision of the music to be performed at the Thomaskirche and Nicolaikirche. There were more mundane obligations that Bach was expected to discharge, such as gathering firewood for the Thomasschule, about which Bach had recurrent disputes with the rector; eventually he sought the intervention of the Elector of Saxony in the affair. It was in Leipzig that Bach created his greatest sacred works: the St. *John Passion,* the Mass in B minor, and the *Christmas Oratorio.* In 1729 he organized at the Thomasschule the famous Collegium Musicum, composed of professional musicians and univ. students with whom he gave regular weekly concerts; he led this group until 1737, and again from 1739 to 1741. He made several visits to Dresden, where his eldest son, Wilhelm Friedemann, served as organist at the Sophienkirche. In June 1747 Bach joined the Societät der Musikalischen Wissenschaften, a scholarly organization founded by a former member of the Collegium Musicum, Lorenz C. Mizler, a learned musician, Latinist, and mathematician who spent his life confounding his contemporaries and denouncing them as charlatans and ignorant pretenders to knowledge. The rules of the society required an applicant to submit a sample of his works; Bach contributed a triple canon in 6 parts and presented it, along with the canonic variations *Vom Himmel hoch da komm' ich her.* This was one of Bach's last works. He suffered from a cataract that was gradually darkening his vision. A British optician named John Taylor, who plied his trade in Saxony, operated on Bach's eyes in the spring of 1749; the operation, performed with the crude instruments of the time, left Bach almost totally blind. The same specialist operated also on Handel, with no better results. The etiology of Bach's last illness is unclear. It is said that on July 18, 1750, his vision suddenly returned (possibly when the cataract receded spontaneously), but a cerebral hemorrhage supervened, and a few days later Bach was dead. Bach's great contrapuntal work, *Die Kunst der Fuge,* remained unfinished. The final page bears this inscription by C.P.E. Bach: "Upon this Fugue, in which the name B-A-C-H is applied as a countersubject, the author died." Bach's widow, Anna Magdalena, survived him by nearly 10 years; she died on Feb. 27, 1760. In 1895 Wilhelm His, an anatomy prof. at the Univ. of Leipzig, performed an exhumation of Bach's body, made necessary because of the deterioration of the wooden coffin, and took remarkable photographs of Bach's skeleton, which he publ. under the title *J.S. Bach, Forschungen über dessen Grabstätte, Gebeine und Antlitz* (Leipzig, 1895). On July 28, 1949, on the 199th anniversary of Bach's death, his coffin was transferred to the choir room of the Thomaskirche.

Of Bach's 20 children, 10 reached maturity. His sons Wilhelm Friedemann, Carl Philipp Emanuel, **Johann Christoph Friedrich,** and **Johann (John) Christian** (the "London" Bach) made their mark as independent composers. Among Bach's notable pupils were Johann Friedrich Agricola, Johann Christoph Altnikol, Heinrich Nicolaus Gerber, Johann Gottlieb Goldberg, Gottfried August Homilius, Johann Philipp Kirnberger, Johann Christian Kittel, Johann Tobias Krebs, and Johann Ludwig Krebs. It is historically incorrect to maintain that Bach was not appreciated by his contemporaries; Bach's sons Carl Philipp Emanuel and the "London" Bach kept his legacy alive for a generation after Bach's death. True, they parted from Bach's art of contrapuntal writing; Carl Philipp Emanuel turned to the fashionable *style galant,* and wrote keyboard works of purely harmonic content. The 1st important biography of Bach was publ. in 1802, by J.N. Forkel.

Dramatic accounts of music history are often inflated. It is conventional to say that Bach's music was rescued from oblivion by Mendelssohn, who conducted the *St. Matthew Passion* in Berlin in 1829, but Mozart and Beethoven had practiced Bach's preludes and fugues. Bach's genius was never dimmed; he was never a prophet without a world. In 1850 the centennial of Bach's death was observed by the inception of the Leipzig Bach-Gesellschaft, a society founded by Carl Becker, Moritz Hauptmann, Otto Jahn, and Robert Schumann. Concurrently, the publishing firm of Breitkopf & Härtel inaugurated the publication of the complete ed. of Bach's works. A Neue Bach-Gesellschaft was founded in 1900; it supervised the publication of the important *Bach-Jahrbuch,* a scholarly journal begun in 1904. The bicentennial of Bach's death, in 1950, brought about a new series of memorials and celebrations. With the development of recordings, Bach's works were made available to large masses of the public. Modern composers, even those who champion the total abandonment of all conventional methods of composition and the abolition of musical notation, are irresist-

ibly drawn to Bach as a precursor; suffice it to mention Alban Berg's use of Bach's chorale *Es ist genug* in the concluding section of his Violin Concerto dedicated to the memory of Alma Mahler's young daughter. It is interesting to note also that Bach's famous acronym B-A-C-H consists of 4 different notes in a chromatic alternation, thus making it possible to use it as an element of a 12-tone row. Bach's images have been emblazoned on popular T-shirts; postage stamps with his portrait have been issued by a number of nations in Europe, Asia, and Africa. The slogan "Back to Bach," adopted by composers of the early 20th century, seems to hold true for every musical era.

In the list of Bach's works given below, each composition is identified by the BWV (Bach-Werke-Verzeichnis) number established by W. Schmieder in his *Thematisch-systematisches Verzeichnis der musikalischen Werke von J.S. B. Bach-Werke-Verzeichnis* (Leipzig, 1950; 3rd ed., 1961).

WORKS: CHURCH CANTATAS: About 200 are extant. The following list gives the BWV number, title, and date of 1st performance: 1, *Wie schön leuchtet der Morgenstern* (March 25, 1725); 2, *Ach Gott, vom Himmel sieh darein* (June 18, 1724); 3, *Ach Gott, wie manches Herzeleid* (Jan. 14, 1725); 4, *Christ lag in Todesbanden* (c.1707–8); 5, *Wo soll ich fliehen hin* (Oct. 15, 1724); 6, *Bleib bei uns, denn es will Abend werden* (April 2, 1725); 7, *Christ unser Herr zum Jordan kam* (June 24, 1724); 8, *Liebster Gott, wann werd ich sterben?* (Sept. 24, 1724); 9, *Es ist das Heil uns kommen her* (c.1732–35); 10, *Meine Seel erhebt den Herren* (July 2, 1724); 11, *Lobet Gott in seinen Reichen* (Ascension oratorio; May 19, 1735); 12, *Weinen, Klagen, Sorgen, Zagen* (April 22, 1714); 13, *Meine Seufzer, meine Tränen* (Jan. 20, 1726); 14, *Wär' Gott nicht mit uns diese Zeit* (Jan. 30, 1735); 16, *Herr Gott, dich Loben wir* (Jan. 1, 1726); 17, *Wer Dank opfert, der preiset mich* (Sept. 22, 1726); 18, *Gleichwie der Regen und Schnee vom Himmel fällt* (c.1714); 19, *Es erhub sich ein Streit* (Sept. 29, 1726); 20, *O Ewigkeit, du Donnerwort* (June 11, 1724); 21, *Ich hatte viel Bekümmernis* (c.1714); 22, *Jesus nahm zu sich die Zwölfe* (Feb. 7, 1723); 23, *Du wahrer Gott und Davids Sohn* (Feb. 7, 1723); 24, *Ein ungefärbt Gemüte* (June 20, 1723); 25, *Es ist nicht Gesundes an meinem Leibe* (Aug. 29, 1723); 26, *Ach wie flüchtig, ach wie nichtig* (Nov. 19, 1724); 27, *Wer weiss, wie nahe mir mein Ende!* (Oct. 6, 1726); 28, *Gottlob! nun geht das Jahr zu Ende* (Dec. 30, 1725); 29, *Wir danken dir, Gott, wir danken dir* (Aug. 27, 1731); 30, *Freue dich, erlöste Schar* (c.1738); 31, *Der Himmel lacht! die Erde jubilieret* (April 21, 1715); 32, *Liebster Jesu, mein Verlangen* (Jan. 13, 1726); 33, *Allein zu dir, Herr Jesu Christ* (Sept. 3, 1724); 34, *O ewiges Feuer, O Ursprung der Liebe* (based upon 34a; early 1740s); 34a, *O ewiges Feuer, O Ursprung der Liebe* (part of score not extant; 1726); 35, *Geist und Seele wird verwirret* (Sept. 8, 1726); 36, *Schwingt freudig euch empor* (based upon secular cantata 36c; Dec. 2, 1731); 37, *Wer da gläubet und getauft wird* (May 18, 1724); 38, *Aus tiefer Not schrei ich zu dir* (Oct. 29, 1724); 39, *Brich dem Hungrigen dein Brot* (June 23, 1726); 40, *Dazu ist erschienen der Sohn Gottes* (Dec. 26, 1723); 41, *Jesu, nun sei gepreiset* (Jan. 1, 1725); 42, *Am Abend aber desselbigen Sabbats* (April 8, 1725); 43, *Gott fähret auf mit Jauchzen* (May 30, 1726); 44, *Sie werden euch in den Bann tun* (May 21, 1724); 45, *Es ist dir gesagt, Mensch, was gut ist* (Aug. 11, 1726); 46, *Schauet doch und sehet* (Aug. 1, 1723); 47, *Wer sich selbst erhöhet* (Oct. 13, 1726); 48, *Ich elender Mensch, wer wird mich erlösen* (Oct. 3, 1723); 49, *Ich geh und suche mit Verlangen* (Nov. 3, 1726); 50, *Nun ist das Heil und die Kraft* (date unknown); 51, *Jauchzet Gott in allen Landen!* (Sept. 17, 1730); 52, *Falsche Welt, dir trau' ich nicht* (Nov. 24, 1726); 54, *Widerstehe doch der Sünde* (July 15, 1714); 55, *Ich armer Mensch, ich Sündenknecht* (Nov. 17, 1726); 56, *Ich will den Kreuzstab gerne tragen* (Oct. 27, 1726); 57, *Selig ist der Mann* (Dec. 26, 1725); 58, *Ach Gott, wie manches Herzeleid* (Jan. 5, 1727); 59, *Wer mich liebet, der wird mein Wort halten* (c.1723–24); 60, *O Ewigkeit, du Donnerwort* (Nov. 7, 1723); 61, *Nun komm, der Heiden Heiland* (1714); 62, *Nun komm, der Heiden Heiland* (Dec. 3, 1724); 63, *Christen, ätzet diesen*

Tag (c.1716); 64, *Sehet, welch eine Liebe* (Dec. 27, 1723); 65, *Sie werden aus Saba alle kommen* (Jan. 6, 1724); 66, *Erfreut euch, ihr Herzen* (based upon lost secular cantata 66a; April 10, 1724); 67, *Halt' im Gedächtnis Jesum Christ* (April 16, 1724); 68, *Also hat Gott die Welt geliebt* (May 21, 1725); 69, *Lobe den Herrn, meine Seele* (based upon 69a; 1740s); 69a, *Lobe den Herrn, meine Seele* (Aug. 15, 1723); 70, *Wachet! betet! betet! wachet!* (based upon 70a; Nov. 21, 1723); 70a, *Wachet! betet! betet! wachet!* (music not extant; Dec. 6, 1716); 71, *Gott ist mein König* (Feb. 4, 1708); 72, *Alles nur nach Gottes Willen* (Jan. 27, 1726); 73, *Herr, wie du willst, so schick's mit mir* (Jan. 23, 1724); 74, *Wer mich liebet, der wird mein Wort halten* (based partly upon 59; May 20, 1725); 75, *Die Elenden sollen essen* (May 30, 1723); 76, *Die Himmel erzählen die Ehre Gottes* (June 6, 1723); 77, *Du sollst Gott, deinen Herren, lieben* (Aug. 22, 1723); 78, *Jesu, der du meine Seele* (Sept. 10, 1724); 79, *Gott der Herr ist Sonn und Schild* (Oct. 31, 1725); 80, *Ein' feste Burg ist unser Gott* (based upon 80a; Oct. 31, 1724); 80a, *Alles, was von Gott geboren* (music not extant; 1715); 80b, *Ein' feste Burg ist unser Gott* (Oct. 31, 1723); 81, *Jesus schläft, was soll ich hoffen?* (Jan. 30, 1724); 82, *Ich habe genug* (Feb. 2, 1727); 83, *Erfreute Zeit im neuen Bunde* (Feb. 2, 1724); 84, *Ich bin vergnügt mit meinem Glücke* (Feb. 9, 1727); 85, *Ich bin ein guter Hirt* (April 15, 1725); 86, *Wahrlich, wahrlich, ich sage euch* (May 14, 1724); 87, *Bisher habt ihr nichts gebeten* (May 6, 1725); 88, *Siehe, ich will viel Fischer aussenden* (July 21, 1726); 89, *Was soll ich aus dir machen, Ephraim?* (Oct. 24, 1723); 90, *Es reisset euch ein schrecklich Ende* (Nov. 14, 1723); 91, *Gelobet seist du, Jesu Christ* (Dec. 25, 1724); 92, *Ich hab in Gottes Herz und Sinn* (Jan. 28, 1725); 93, *Wer nur den lieben Gott lässt walten* (July 9, 1724); 94, *Was frag ich nach der Welt* (Aug. 6, 1724); 95, *Christus, der ist mein Leben* (Sept. 12, 1723); 96, *Herr Christ, der ein'ge Gottessohn* (Oct. 8, 1724); 97, *In allen meinen Taten* (1734); 98, *Was Gott tut, das ist wohlgetan* (Nov. 10, 1726); 99, *Was Gott tut, das ist wohlgetan* (Sept. 17, 1724); 100, *Was Gott tut, das ist wohlgetan* (c.1732–35); 101, *Nimm von uns, Herr, du treuer Gott* (Aug. 13, 1724); 102, *Herr, deine Augen sehen nach dem Glauben* (Aug. 25, 1726); 103, *Ihr werdet weinen und heulen* (April 22, 1725); 104, *Du Hirte Israel* (April 23, 1724); 105, *Herr, gehe nicht ins Gericht* (July 25, 1723); 106, *Gottes Zeit ist die allerbeste Zeit* (c.1707); 107, *Was willst du dich betrüben* (July 23, 1724); 108, *Es ist euch gut, dass ich hingehe* (April 29, 1725); 109, *Ich glaube, lieber Herr, hilf meinem Unglauben!* (Oct. 17, 1723); 110, *Unser Mund sei voll Lachens* (Dec. 25, 1725); 111, *Was mein Gott will, das g'scheh allzeit* (Jan. 21, 1725); 112, *Der Herr ist mein getreuer Hirt* (April 8, 1731); 113, *Herr Jesu Christ, du höchstes Gut* (Aug. 20, 1724); 114, *Ach, lieben Christen, seid getrost* (Oct. 1, 1724); 115, *Mache dich, mein Geist, bereit* (Nov. 5, 1724); 116, *Du Friedefürst, Herr Jesu Christ* (Nov. 26, 1724); 117, *Sei Lob und Ehr dem höchsten Gut* (c.1728–31); 119, *Preise, Jerusalem, den Herrn* (Aug. 30, 1723); 120, *Gott, man lobet dich in der Stille* (c.1728–29); 120a, *Herr Gott, Beherrscher aller Dinge* (based upon 120; part of score not extant; c.1729); 120b, *Gott, man lobet dich in der Stille* (based upon 120; music not extant; 1730); 121, *Christum wir sollen loben schon* (Dec. 26, 1724); 122, *Das neugebor'ne Kindelein* (Dec. 31, 1724); 123, *Liebster Immanuel, Herzog der Frommen* (Jan. 6, 1725); 124, *Meinen Jesum lass ich nicht* (Jan. 7, 1725); 125, *Mit Fried' und Freud' ich fahr dahin* (Feb. 2, 1725); 126, *Erhalt' uns, Herr, bei deinem Wort* (Feb. 4, 1725); 127, *Herr Jesu Christ, wahr'r Mensch und Gott* (Feb. 11, 1725); 128, *Auf Christi Himmelfahrt allein* (May 10, 1725); 129, *Gelobet sei der Herr, mein Gott* (c.1726–27); 130, *Herr Gott, dich loben alle wir* (Sept. 29, 1724); 131, *Aus der Tiefen rufe ich, Herr, zu dir* (1707); 132, *Bereitet die Wege, bereitet die Bahn!* (1715); 133, *Ich freue mich in dir* (Dec. 27, 1724); 134, *Ein Herz, das seinen Jesum lebend weiss* (based upon secular cantata 134a; April 11, 1724); 135, *Ach Herr, mich armen Sünder* (June 25, 1724); 136, *Erforsche mich, Gott, und erfahre mein Herz* (July 18, 1723); 137, *Lobe den Herren, den mächtigen König*

der Ehren (Aug. 19, 1725); 138, *Warum betrübst du dich, mein Herz?* (Sept. 5, 1723); 139, *Wohl dem, der sich auf seinen Gott* (Nov. 12, 1724); 140, *Wachet auf, ruft uns die Stimme* (Nov. 25, 1731); 144, *Nimm, was dein ist, und gehe hin* (Feb. 6, 1724); 145, *Ich lebe, mein Herze, zu deinem Ergötzen* (c.1729); 146, *Wir müssen durch viel Trübsal* (c.1726–28); 147, *Herz und Mund und Tat und Leben* (based upon 147a; July 2, 1723); 147a, *Herz und Mund und Tat und Leben* (not extant; Dec. 20, 1716); 148, *Bringet dem Herrn Ehre seines Namens* (Sept. 19, 1723); 149, *Man singet mit Freuden vom Sieg* (c.1728–29); 150, *Nach dir, Herr, verlanget mich* (c.1708–9); 151, *Süsser Trost, mein Jesus kommt* (Dec. 27, 1725); 152, *Tritt auf die Glaubensbahn* (Dec. 30, 1714); 153, *Schau, lieber Gott, wie meine Feind* (Jan. 2, 1724); 154, *Mein liebster Jesus ist verloren* (Jan. 9, 1724); 155, *Mein Gott, wie lang, ach lange* (Jan. 19, 1716); 156, *Ich steh' mit einem Fuss im Grabe* (Jan. 23, 1729); 157, *Ich lasse dich nicht, du segnest mich denn* (Feb. 6, 1727); 158, *Der Friede sei mit dir* (date unknown); 159, *Sehet, wir geh'n hinauf gen Jerusalem* (Feb. 27, 1729); 161, *Komm, du süsse Todesstunde* (Oct. 6, 1715); 162, *Ach! ich sehe, jetzt, da ich zur Hochzeit gehe* (Nov. 3, 1715); 163, *Nur jedem das Seine* (Nov. 24, 1715); 164, *Ihr, die ihr euch von Christo nennet* (Aug. 26, 1725); 165, *O heil'ges Geist- und Wasserbad* (June 16, 1715); 166, *Wo gehest du hin?* (May 7, 1724); 167, *Ihr Menschen, rühmet Gottes Liebe* (June 24, 1723); 168, *Tue Rechnung! Donnerwort* (July 29, 1725); 169, *Gott soll allein mein Herze haben* (Oct. 20, 1726); 170, *Vergnügte Ruh', beliebte Seelenlust* (July 28, 1726); 171, *Gott, wie dein Name, so ist auch dein Ruhm* (c.1729); 172, *Erschallet, ihr Lieder* (May 20, 1714); 173, *Erhöhtes Fleisch und Blut* (based upon secular cantata 173a; May 29, 1724); 174, *Ich liebe den Höchsten von ganzem Gemüte* (June 6, 1729); 175, *Er rufet seinen Schafen mit Namen* (May 22, 1725); 176, *Es ist ein trotzig, und versagt Ding* (May 27, 1725); 177, *Ich ruf zu dir, Herr Jesu Christ* (July 6, 1732); 178, *Wo Gott der Herr nicht bei uns hält* (July 30, 1724); 179, *Siehe zu, dass deine Gottesfurcht* (Aug. 8, 1723); 180, *Schmücke dich, o liebe Seele* (Oct. 22, 1724); 181, *Leichtgesinnte Flattergeister* (Feb. 13, 1724); 182, *Himmelskönig, sei willkommen* (1714); 183, *Sie werden euch in den Bann tun* (May 13, 1725); 184, *Erwünschtes Freudenlicht* (based upon lost secular cantata 184a; May 30, 1724); 185, *Barmherziges Herze der ewigen Liebe* (July 14, 1715); 186, *Ärg're dich, o Seele, nicht* (based upon 186a; July 11, 1723); 186a, *Ärgre dich o Seele, nicht* (not extant; Dec. 13, 1716); 187, *Es wartet alles auf dich* (Aug. 4, 1726); 188, *Ich habe meine Zuversicht* (c.1728); 190, *Singet dem Herrn ein neues Lied!* (part of score not extant; Jan. 1, 1724); 190a, *Singet dem Herrn ein neues Lied!* (based upon 190; not extant; 1730); 191, *Gloria in excelsis Deo* (based upon 232, Mass in B minor; c.1740); 192, *Nun danket alle Gott* (part of score not extant; 1730); 193, *Ihr Tore zu Zion* (c.1727); 194, *Höchsterwünschtes Freudenfest* (based upon lost secular cantata 194a; Nov. 2, 1723); 195, *Dem Gerechten muss das Licht* (c.1737); 196, *Der Herr denket an uns* (c.1708); 197, *Gott ist uns're Zuversicht* (c.1742); 197a, *Ehre sie Gott in der Höhe* (part of score not extant; c.1728); 199, *Mein Herze schwimmt im Blut* (Aug. 12, 1714); 200, *Bekennen will ich seinen Namen* (fragment only extant; c.1742). BWV numbers have been assigned to the following lost or incomplete cantatas: 223, *Meine Seele soll Gott loben* (not extant; date unknown); 224a, *Klagt, Kinder, klagt es aller Welt* (music not extant; March 24, 1729); Anh. 1, *Gesegnet ist die Zuversicht* (not extant; date unknown); Anh. 2, fragment only; Anh. 3, *Gott, gib dein Gerichte dem Könige* (music not extant; 1730); Anh. 4, *Wünschet Jerusalem Glück* (music not extant; c.1727); Anh. 4a, *Wünschet Jerusalem Glück* (music not extant; 1730); Anh. 5, *Lobet den Herrn, alle seine Heerscharen* (music not extant; Dec. 10, 1718); Anh. 14, *Sein Segen fliesst daher wie ein Strom* (music not extant; Feb. 12, 1725); Anh. 15, *Siehe, der Hüter Israel* (not extant; April 27, 1724); Anh. 17, *Mein Gott, nimm die gerechte Seele* (not extant; date unknown); 1,045, title unknown (autograph fragment only extant; c.1742); also the following without BWV numbers:

Herrscher des Himmels, König der Ehren (final chorus only, based upon secular cantata 208, extant; Aug. 29, 1740); *Ich bin ein Pilgrim auf der Welt* (fragment of 4th movement only extant; April 18, 1729); *Ihr wallenden Wolken* (not extant; date unknown); *Leb' ich oder leb' ich nicht* (music not extant; May 19, 1715); *Sie werden euch in den Bann tun* (6-bar sketch only); etc. BWV numbers have been assigned to the following doubtful and spurious cantatas: 15, *Denn du wirst meine Seele* (by J.L. Bach); 53, *Schlage doch, gewünschte Stunde* (by G.M. Hoffmann); 141, *Das ist je gewisslich wahr* (by Telemann); 142, *Uns ist ein Kind geboren* (doubtful); 143, *Lobe den Herrn, meine Seele* (doubtful); 160, *Ich weiss, dass mein Erlöser lebt* (by Telemann); 189, *Meine Seele rühmt und preist* (doubtful); 217, *Gedenke, Herr, wie es uns gehet* (spurious); 218, *Gott der Hoffnung erfülle euch* (by Telemann); 219, *Siehe, es hat überwunden der Löwe* (by Telemann); 220, *Lobt ihn mit Herz und Munde* (spurious); 221, *Wer sucht die Pracht, wer wünscht den Glanz* (spurious); 222, *Mein Odem ist schwach* (by J.E. Bach); Anh. 16, *Schliesset die Gruft! ihr Trauerglocken* (not extant; doubtful); also without BWV number, *Siehe, eine Jungfrau ist schwanger* (doubtful).

SECULAR CANTATAS: 22 are extant in full: 30a, *Angenehmes Wiederau, freue dich* (Sept. 28, 1737); 36b, *Die Freude reget sich* (c.1735); 36c, *Schwingt freudig euch empor* (1725); 134a, *Die Zeit, die Tag und Jahre macht* (Jan. 1, 1719); 173a, *Durchlaucht'ster Leopold* (c.1722); 198, *Trauer Ode: Lass, Fürstin, lass noch einen Strahl* (Oct. 17, 1727); 201, *Der Streit zwischen Phoebus und Pan: Geschwinde, ihr wirbeln den Winde* (c.1729); 202, *Weichet nur, betrübte Schatten* (c.1718–23); 203, *Amore traditore* (date unknown); 204, *Ich bin in mir vergnügt* (c.1726–27); 205, *Der zufriedengestellte Äolus: Zerreisset, zerspringet, zertrümmert die Gruft* (Aug. 3, 1725); 206, *Schleicht, spielende Wellen* (Oct. 7, 1736); 207, *Vereinigte Zwietracht der wechselnden Saiten* (Dec. 11, 1726); 207a, *Auf, schmetternde Töne* (Aug. 3, 1735); 208, *Was mir behagt, ist nur die muntre Jagd!* (c.1713); 209, *Non sa che sia dolore* (c.1734); 210, *O holder Tag, erwünschte Zeit* (c.1740); 211, *Schweigt stille, plaudert nicht* (Coffee Cantata; c.1734–35); 212, *Mer hahn en neue Oberkeet* (Peasant Cantata; Aug. 30, 1742); 213, *Hercules auf dem Scheidewege: Lasst uns sorgen, lasst uns wachen* (Sept. 5, 1733); 214, *Tönet, ihr Pauken! Erschallet, Trompeten!* (Dec. 8, 1733); 215, *Preise dein Glücke, gesegnetes Sachsen* (Oct. 5, 1734). BWV numbers have been assigned to the following lost or incomplete cantatas: 36a, *Steigt freudig in die Luft* (music not extant; Nov. 30, 1726); 66a, *Der Himmel dacht auf Anhalts Ruhm und Glück* (music not extant; Dec. 10, 1718); 184a, title unknown (not extant); 193a, *Ihr Häuser des Himmels, ihr scheinenden Lichter* (music not extant; Aug. 3, 1727); 194a, title unknown (not extant); 205a, *Blast Lärmen, ihr Feinde!* (based upon 205; music not extant; Feb. 19, 1734); 208a, *Was mir behagt, ist nur die muntre Jagd!* (music not extant; c.1740–42); 210a, *O angenehme Melodei!* (music not extant; c.1738–40); 216, *Vergnügte Pleissenstadt* (only partially extant; Feb. 5, 1728); 216a, *Erwählte Pleissenstadt* (music not extant; c.1728); 249a, *Entfliehet, verschwindet, entweichet, ihr Sorgen* (music not extant; Feb. 23, 1725); 249b, *Die Feier des Genius: Verjaget, zerstreuet, zerrüttet, ihr Sterne* (music not extant; Aug. 25, 1726); Anh. 6, *Dich loben die lieblichen Strahlen* (music not extant; Jan. 1, 1720); Anh. 7, *Heut ist gewiss ein guter Tag* (music not extant; Dec. 10, 1720); Anh. 8, title unknown (not extant); Anh. 9, *Entfernet euch, ihr heitern Sterne* (music not extant; May 12, 1727); Anh. 10, *So kämpfet nur, ihr muntern Töne* (music not extant; Aug. 25, 1731); Anh. 11, *Es lebe der König, der Vater im Lande* (music not extant; Aug. 3, 1732); Anh. 12, *Frohes Volk, vergnügte Sachsen* (based upon Anh. 18; music not extant; Aug. 3, 1733); Anh. 13, *Willkommen! Ihr herrschenden Götter* (music not extant; April 28, 1738); Anh. 18, *Froher Tag, verlangte Stunden* (music not extant; June 5, 1732); Anh. 19, *Thomana sass annoch betrübt* (music not extant; Nov. 21, 1734); Anh. 20, title unknown (not extant); also, without BWV number, *Auf! süss entzückende Gewalt* (music not extant; Nov. 27, 1725).

OTHER CHURCH MUSIC: 232, Mass in B minor (assembled c.1747–49 from music previously composed by Bach); 233, 233a, 234–36, 4 *missae breves:* F major (Kyrie in F major), A major, G minor, G major (late 1730s); 237–41, 5 settings of the Sanctus: C major, D major, D minor, G major, D major (although preserved in Bach's own hand, these appear to be arrangements of works by other composers, 238 excepted); 243a, Magnificat in E-flat major (including 4 Christmas texts: *Vom Himmel hoch, Freut euch und jubiliert, Gloria in excelsis, Virga Jesse floruit;* Dec. 25, 1723); 243, a revision of the preceding, without Christmas texts, as Magnificat in D major (c.1728–31); 244, *Matthäuspassion* (St. Matthew Passion; 1st perf. April 11, 1727, or April 15, 1729); 245, *Johannespassion* (St. John Passion; April 7, 1724; later rev.); 248, *Weihnachtsoratorium* (Christmas Oratorio), 6 cantatas for Christmas to Epiphany: *Jauchzet, frohlocket, auf preiset die Tage* (Dec. 25, 1734), *Und es waren Hirten in derselben Gegend* (Dec. 26, 1734), *Herrscher des Himmels, erhöre das Lallen* (Dec. 27, 1734), *Fallt mit Danken, fallt mit Loben* (Jan. 1, 1735), *Ehre sei dir, Gott, gesungen* (Jan. 2, 1735), *Herr, wenn die stolzen Feinde schnauben* (Jan. 6, 1735); 249, *Easter Oratorio* (1st perf. as a cantata, April 1, 1725; rev. as an oratorio 1732–35); motets, including 225, *Singet dem Herrn ein neues Lied* (May 12, 1727), 226, *Der Geist hilft unsrer Schwachheit auf* (Oct. 24, 1729), 227, *Jesu, meine Freude* (July 18, 1723), 228, *Fürchte dich nicht* (Feb. 4, 1726), 229, *Komm, Jesu, komm!* (March 26, 1730), 230, *Lobet den Herrn alle Heiden* (date unknown). Also 247, St. Mark Passion (score and parts not extant; March 23, 1731; partial reconstruction from other works made by D. Hellmann, Stuttgart, 1964); 246, St. Luke Passion (spurious).

CHORALES: 3 wedding chorales for 4 Voices: 250, *Was Gott tut das ist wohlgetan;* 251, *Sei Lob und Ehr' dem höchsten Gut;* 252, *Nun danket alle Gott.* Also, 186 arrangements for 4 Voices: 253, *Ach bleib bei uns, Herr Jesu Christ;* 254, *Ach Gott, erhör' mein Seufzen;* 255, *Ach Gott und Herr;* 256, *Ach lieben Christen, seid getrost;* 259, *Ach, was soll ich Sünder machen;* 260, *Allein Gott in der Höh' sei Ehr';* 261, *Allein zu dir, Herr Jesu Christ;* 262, *Alle Menschen müssen sterben;* 263, *Alles ist an Gottes Segen;* 264, *Als der gütige Gott;* 265, *Als Jesus Christus in der Nacht;* 266, *Als vierzig Tag nach Ostern;* 267, *An Wasserflüssen Babylon;* 268, *Auf, auf, mein Herz, und du mein ganzer Sinn;* 269, *Aus meines Herzens Grunde;* 270, *Befiehl du deine Wege;* 271, *Befiehl du deine Wege;* 272, *Befiehl du deine Wege;* 273, *Christe, der du bist Tag und Licht;* 274, *Christe, der du bist Tag und Licht;* 275, *Christe, du Beistand deiner Kreuzgemeinde;* 276, *Christ ist erstanden;* 277, *Christ lag in Todesbanden;* 278, *Christ lag in Todesbanden;* 279, *Christ lag in Todesbanden;* 280, *Christ, unser Herr, zum Jordan kam;* 281, *Christus, der ist mein Leben;* 282, *Christus, der ist mein Leben;* 283, *Christus, der uns selig macht;* 284, *Christus ist erstanden, hat überwunden;* 285, *Da der Herr Christ zu Tische sass;* 286, *Danket dem Herren;* 287, *Dank sei Gott in der Höhe;* 288, *Das alte Jahr vergangen ist;* 289, *Das alte Jahr vergangen ist;* 290, *Das walt' Gott Vater und Gott Sohn;* 291, *Das walt' mein Gott, Vater, Sohn und heiliger Geist;* 292, *Den Vater dort oben;* 293, *Der du bist drei in Einigkeit;* 294, *Der Tag, der ist so freudenreich;* 295, *Des heil'gen Geistes reiche Gnad';* 296, *Die Nacht ist kommen;* 297, *Die Sonn' hat sich mit ihrem Glanz;* 298, *Dies sind die heil'gen zehn Gebot';* 299, *Dir, dir, Jehova, will ich singen;* 300, *Du grosser Schmerzensmann;* 301, *Du, o schönes Weltgebäude;* 302, *Ein' feste Burg ist unser Gott;* 303, *Ein' feste Burg ist unser Gott;* 304, *Eins ist Not! ach Herr, dies Eine;* 305, *Erbarm' dich mein, o, Herre Gott;* 306, *Erstanden ist der heil'ge Christ;* 307, *Es ist gewisslich an der Zeit;* 308, *Es spricht der Unweisen Mund wohl;* 309, *Es stehn vor Gottes Throne;* 310, *Es wird schier der letzte Tag herkommen;* 311, *Es woll' uns Gott genädig sein;* 312, *Es woll' uns Gott genädig sein;* 327, *Für deinen Thron tret' ich hiermit;* 313, *Für Freuden lasst uns springen;* 314, *Gelobet seist du, Jesu Christ;* 315, *Gib dich zufrieden und sei stille;* 316, *Gott, der du selber bist das Licht;* 317, *Gott, der Vater, wohn' uns bei;* 318, *Gottes Sohn ist kommen;* 319, *Gott hat das Evangelium;* 320, *Gott lebet noch;* 321, *Gottlob, es geht nunmehr zu Ende;* 322, *Gott sei gelobet und gebenedeiet;* 323, *Gott sei uns* gnädig; 325, Heilig, heilig; 326, Herr Gott, dich loben alle wir; 328, Herr, Gott, dich loben wir; 329, Herr, ich denk' an jene Zeit; 330, Herr, ich habe missgehandelt; 331, Herr, ich habe missgehandelt; 332, Herr Jesu Christ, dich zu uns wend'; 333, Herr Jesu Christ, du hast bereit't; 334, Herr Jesu Christ, du höchstes Gut; 335, Herr Jesu Christ, mein's Lebens Licht; 336, Herr Jesu Christ, wahr'r Mensch und Gott; 337, Herr, nun lass in Frieden; 338, Herr, straf mich nicht in deinem Zorn; 339, Herr, wie du willst, so schick's mit mir; 340, Herzlich lieb hab ich dich, o Herr; 341, Heut' ist, o Mensch, ein grosser Trauertag; 342, Heut' triumphieret Gottes Sohn; 343, Hilf, Gott, dass mir's gelinge; 344, Hilf, Herr Jesu, lass gelingen; 345, Ich bin ja, Herr, in deiner Macht; 346, Ich dank' dir, Gott, für all' Wohltat; 347, Ich dank' dir, lieber Herre; 348, Ich dank' dir, lieber Herre; 349, Ich dank' dir schon durch deinen Sohn; 350, Ich danke dir, o Gott, in deinem Throne; 351, Ich hab' mein' Sach' Gott heimgestellt; 352, Jesu, der du meine Seele; 353, Jesu, der du meine Seele; 354, Jesu, der du meine Seele; 355, Jesu, der du selbsten wohl; 356, Jesu, du mein liebstes Leben; 357, Jesu, Jesu, du bist mein; 358, Jesu, meine Freude; 359, Jesu meiner Seelen Wonne; 360, Jesu meiner Seelen Wonne; 361, Jesu, meines Herzens Freud'; 362, Jesu, nun sei gepreiset; 363, Jesus Christus, unser Heiland; 364, Jesus Christus, unser Heiland; 365, Jesus, meine Zuversicht; 366, Ihr Gestirn', ihr hohlen Lüfte; 367, In allen meinen Taten; 368, In dulci jubilo; 369, Keinen hat Gott verlassen; 370, Komm, Gott Schöpfer, heiliger Geist; 371, Kyrie, Gott Vater in Ewigkeit; 372, Lass, o Herr, dein Ohr sich neigen; 373, Liebster Jesu, wir sind hier; 374, Lobet den Herren, denn er ist freundlich; 375, Lobt Gott, ihr Christen, allzugleich; 376, Lobt Gott, ihr Christen, allzugleich; 377, Mach's mit mir, Gott, nach deiner Güt'; 378, Meine Augen schliess' ich jetzt; 379, Meinen Jesum lass' ich nicht, Jesus; 380, Meinen Jesum lass' ich nicht, weil; 322, Meine Seele erhebet den Herrn; 381, Meines Lebens letzte Zeit; 382, Mit Fried' und Freud' ich fahr' dahin; 383, Mitten wir im Leben sind; 384, Nicht so traurig, nicht so sehr; 385, Nun bitten wir den heiligen Geist; 386, Nun danket alle Gott; 387, Nun freut euch, Gottes Kinder all'; 388, Nun freut euch, lieben Christen, g'mein; 389, Nun lob', mein' Seel', den Herren; 390, Nun lob', mein' Seel', den Herren; 391, Nun preiset alle Gottes Barmherzigkeit; 392, Nun ruhen alle Wälder; 393, O Welt, sieh hier dein Leben; 394, O Welt, sieh dein Leben; 395, O Welt, sieh hier dein Leben; 396, Nun sich der Tag geendet hat; 397, O Ewigkeit, du Donnerwort; 398, O Gott, du frommer Gott; 399, O Gott, du frommer Gott; 400, O Herzensangst, o Bangigkeit; 401, O Lamm Gottes, unschuldig; 402, O Mensch, bewein' dein' Sünde gross; 403, O Mensch, schau Jesum Christum an; 404, O Traurigkeit, o Herzeleid; 405, O wie selig seid ihr doch, ihr Frommen; 406, O wie selig seid ihr doch, ihr Frommen; 407, O wir armen Sünder; 408, Schaut, ihr Sünder; 409, Seelen-Bräutigam; 410, Sei gegrüsset, Jesu gütig; 411, Singet dem Herrn ein neues Lied; 412, So gibst du nun, mein Jesu, gute Nacht; 413, Sollt' ich meinem Gott nicht singen; 414, Uns ist ein Kindlein heut' gebor'n; 415, Valet will ich dir geben; 416, Vater unser im Himmelreich; 417, Von Gott will ich nicht lassen; 418, Von Gott will ich nicht lassen; 419, Von Gott will ich nicht lassen; 257, Wär' Gott nicht mit uns diese Zeit; 420, Warum betrübst du dich, mein Herz; 421, Warum betrübst du dich, mein Herz; 422, Warum sollt' ich mich denn grämen; 423, Was betrübst du dich, mein Herze; 424, Was bist du doch, o Seele, so betrübet; 425, Was willst du dich, o meine Seele; 426, Weltlich Ehr' und zeitlich Gut; 427, Wenn ich in Angst und Not; 428, Wenn mein Stündlein vorhanden ist; 429, Wenn mein Stündlein vorhanden ist; 430, Wenn mein Stündlein vorhanden ist; 431, Wenn wir in höchsten Nöten sein; 432, Wenn wir in höchsten Nöten sein; 433, Wer Gott vertraut, hat wohl gebaut; 434, Wer nur den lieben Gott lässt walten; 435, Wie bist du, Seele, in mir so gar betrübt; 436, Wie schön leuchtet der Morgenstern; 437, Wir glauben all' an einen Gott; 258, Wo Gott der Herr nicht bei uns hält; 438, Wo Gott zum Haus nicht gibt sein' Gunst.

SACRED SONGS: 69 for 1 Voice with Basso Continuo only: 439, Ach, dass nicht die letzte Stunde; 440, Auf, auf! die rechte Zeit ist hier; 441, Auf, auf! mein Herz, mit Freuden; 422, Beglückter Stand getreuer Seelen; 443, Beschränkt, ihr Weisen dieser Welt; 444, Brich entzwei, mein armes Herze; 445, Brunnquell aller Güter; 446, Der lieben Sonnen Licht und Pracht; 447, Der Tag ist hin, die Sonne gehet nieder; 448, Der Tag mit seinem Lichte; 449, Dich bet' ich an, mein höchster Gott; 450, Die bittre Leidenszeit beginnet abermal; 451, Die goldne Sonne, voll Freud' und Wonne; 452, Dir, dir Jehovah, will ich singen (melody by Bach); 453, Eins ist Not! ach Herr, dies Eine; 454, Ermuntre dich, mein schwacher Geist; 455, Erwürgtes Lamm, das die verwahrten Siegel; 456, Es glänzet der Christen; 457, Es ist nun aus mit meinem Leben; 458, Es ist vollbracht! vergiss ja nicht; 459, Es kostet viel, ein Christ zu sein; 460, Gieb dich zufrieden und sei stille; 461, Gott lebet noch; Seele, was verzagst du doch?; 462, Gott, wie gross ist deine Güte; 463, Herr, nicht schicke deine Rache; 464, Ich bin ja, Herr, in deiner Macht; 465, Ich freue mich in dir; 466, Ich halte treulich still und liebe; 467, Ich lass' dich nicht; 468, Ich liebe Jesum alle Stund'; 469, Ich steh' an deiner Krippen hier; 476, Ihr Gestirn', ihr hohen Lüfte; 471, Jesu, deine Liebeswunden; 470, Jesu, Jesu, du bist mein; 472, Jesu, meines Glaubens Zier; 473, Jesu, meines Herzens Freud'; 474, Jesus ist das schönste Licht; 475, Jesus, unser Trost und Leben; 477, Kein Stündlein geht dahin; 478, Komm, süsser Tod, komm, sel'ge Ruh'! (melody by Bach); 479, Kommt, Seelen, dieser Tag; 480, Kommt wieder aus der finstern Gruft; 481, Lasset uns mit Jesu ziehen; 482, Liebes Herz, bedenke doch; 483, Liebster Gott, wann werd' ich sterben?; 484, Liebster Herr Jesu! wo bleibest du so lange?; 485, Liebster Immanuel, Herzog der Frommen; 488, Meines Lebens letzte Zeit; 486, Mein Jesu, dem die Seraphinen; 487, Mein Jesu! was für Seelenweh; 489, Nicht so traurig, nicht so sehr; 490, Nur mein Jesus ist mein Leben; 491, O du Liebe meine Liebe; 492, O finstre Nacht; 493, O Jesulein süss, o Jesulein mild; 494, O liebe Seele, zieh' die Sinnen; 495, O wie selig seid ihr doch, ihr Frommen; 496, Seelen-Bräutigam, Jesu, Gottes Lamm!; 497, Seelenweide, meine Freude; 499, Sei gegrüsset, Jesu gütig; 498, Selig, wer an Jesum denkt; 500, So gehst du nun, mein Jesu, hin; 501, So giebst du nun, mein Jesu, gute Nacht; 502, So wünsch' ich mir zu guter Letzt; 503, Steh' ich bei meinem Gott; 504, Vergiss mein nicht, dass ich dein nicht; 505, Vergiss mein nicht, vergiss mein nicht (melody by Bach); 506, Was bist du doch, o Seele, so betrübet; 507, Wo ist mein Schäflein, das ich liebe. BWV numbers have been assigned to the following sacred songs, which are most likely spurious: 519, Hier lieg' ich nun; 520, Das walt' mein Gott; 521, Gott mein Herz dir Dank; 522, Meine Seele, lass es gehen; 523, Ich gnüge mich an meinem Stande.

ORGAN: 525–30, 6 trio sonatas: E-flat major, C minor, D minor, E minor, C major, G major; 531, Prelude and Fugue in C major; 532, Prelude and Fugue in D major; 533, Prelude and Fugue in E minor; 534, Prelude and Fugue in F minor; 535, Prelude and Fugue in G minor; 536, Prelude and Fugue in A major; 537, Fantasia and Fugue in C minor; 538, Toccata and Fugue in D minor, "Dorian"; 539, Prelude and Fugue in D minor; 540, Toccata and Fugue in F major; 541, Prelude and Fugue in G major; 542, Fantasia and Fugue in G minor; 543, Prelude and Fugue in A minor; 544, Prelude and Fugue in B minor; 545, Prelude and Fugue in C major; 546, Prelude and Fugue in C minor; 547, Prelude and Fugue in C major; 548, Prelude and Fugue in E minor; 549, Prelude and Fugue in C minor; 550, Prelude and Fugue in G major; 551, Prelude and Fugue in A minor; 552, Prelude and Fugue in E-flat major, "St. Anne"; 562, Fantasia and Fugue in C minor; 563, Fantasia in B minor; 564, Toccata, Adagio, and Fugue in C major; 565, Toccata and Fugue in D minor; 566, Prelude and Fugue in E major; 568, Prelude in G major; 569, Prelude in A minor; 570, Fantasia in C major; 572, Fantasia in G major; 573, Fantasia in C major; 574, Fugue in C minor (on a theme by Legrenzi); 575, Fugue in C minor; 578, Fugue in G minor; 579, Fugue in B minor (on a theme by Corelli); 582, Passacaglia in C minor; 583, Trio in D minor; 586, Trio in G major (Bach's organ transcription of a work by Telemann); 587, Aria in F major (transcription from Couperin); 588, Canzona in D minor;

590, Pastorale in F major; 592–97, 6 concertos: G major (arrangement of a concerto by Duke Johann Ernst of Saxe-Weimar), A minor (arrangement of Vivaldi's op. 3, no. 8), C major (arrangement of Vivaldi's op. 7, no. 5), C major (arrangement of a concerto by Duke Johann Ernst of Saxe-Weimar), D minor (arrangement of Vivaldi's op. 3, no. 11), E-flat major (arrangement of a concerto by an unknown composer); 598, Pedal-Exercitium; 802–5, 4 duettos: E minor, F major, G major, A minor; 1,027a, Trio in G major (transcription from final movement of sonata 1,027). BWV numbers have been assigned to the following doubtful and spurious works: 131a, Fugue in G minor (spurious); 561, Fantasia and Fugue in A minor (spurious); 567, Prelude in C major (spurious); 571, Fantasia in G major (spurious); 576, Fugue in G major (spurious); 577, Fugue in G major (spurious); 580, Fugue in D major (spurious); 581, Fugue in G major (spurious); 584, Trio in G minor (doubtful); 585, Trio in C minor (by J.F. Fasch); 589, Allabreve in D major (doubtful); 591, Kleines harmonisches Labyrinth (doubtful); also 8 brief preludes and fugues: C major, D minor, E minor, F major, G major, G minor, A minor, B-flat major (doubtful).

OTHER ORGAN MUSIC: 45 Chorales in Das Orgel-Büchlein: 599, *Nun komm, der Heiden Heiland*; 600, *Gott, durch deine Güte*; 601, *Herr Christ, der ein'ge Gottes-Sohn*; 602, *Lob sei dem allmächtigen Gott*; 603, *Puer natus in Bethlehem*; 604, *Gelobet seist du, Jesu Christ*; 605, *Der Tag, der ist so freudenreich*; 606, *Vom Himmel hoch, da komm' ich her*; 607, *Vom Himmel kam der Engel Schar*; 608, *In dulci jubilo*; 609, *Lobt Gott, ihr Christen, allzugleich*; 610, *Jesu, meine Freude*; 611, *Christum wir sollen loben schon*; 612, *Wir Christenleut'*; 613, *Helft mir Gottes Güte preisen*; 614, *Das alte Jahr vergangen ist*; 615, *In dir ist Freude*; 616, *Mit Fried' und Freud' ich fahr dahin*; 617, *Herr Gott, nun schleuss den Himmel auf*; 618, *O Lamm Gottes unschuldig*; 619, *Christe, du Lamm Gottes*; 620, *Christus, der uns selig macht*; 621, *Da Jesus an dem Kreuze stund'*; 622, *O Mensch, bewein' dein' Sünde gross*; 623, *Wir danken dir, Herr Jesu Christ*; 624, *Hilf Gott, dass mir's gelinge*; 625, *Christ lag in Todesbanden*; 626, *Jesus Christus, unser Heiland*; 627, *Christ ist erstanden*; 628, *Erstanden ist der heil'ge Christ*; 629, *Erschienen ist der herrliche Tag*; 630, *Heut' triumphieret Gottes Sohn*; 631, *Komm, Gott Schöpfer, heiliger Geist*; 632, *Herr Jesu Christ, dich zu uns wend'*; 633, *Liebster Jesu, wir sind hier*; 635, *Dies sind die heil'gen zehn Gebot'*; 636, *Vater unser im Himmelreich*; 637, *Durch Adams Fall ist ganz verderbt*; 638, *Es ist das Heil uns Kommen her*; 639, *Ich ruf zu dir, Herr Jesu Christ*; 640, *In dich hab' ich gehoffet, Herr*; 641, *Wenn wir in höchsten Nöten sein*; 642, *Wer nur den lieben Gott lässt walten*; 643, *Alle Menschen müssen sterben*; 644, *Ach wie nichtig, ach wie flüchtig*; 6 chorales publ. by J.G. Schübler, hence the name Schübler-Chorales: 645, *Wachet auf, ruft uns die Stimme* (based upon Cantata 140, 4th movement); 646, *Wo soll ich fliehen hin* (source unknown); 647, *Wer nur den lieben Gott lässt walten* (based upon Cantata 93, 4th movement); 648, *Meine Seele erhebet den Herren* (based upon Cantata 10, 5th movement); 649, *Ach bleib' bei uns, Herr Jesu Christ* (based upon Cantata 6, 3rd movement); 650, *Kommst du nun, Jesu, vom Himmel herunter* (based upon Cantata 137, 2nd movement); 651, *Fantasia super Komm, Heiliger Geist*; 652, *Komm, Heiliger Geist*; 653, *An Wasserflüssen Babylon*; 654, *Schmücke dich, o liebe Seele*; 655, *Trio super Herr Jesu Christ, dich zu uns wend*; 656, *O Lamm Gottes, unschuldig*; 657, *Nun danket alle Gott*; 658, *Von Gott will ich nicht lassen*; 659, *Nun komm, der Heiden Heiland*; 660, *Trio super Nun komm, der Heiden Heiland*; 661, *Nun komm, der Heiden Heiland*; 662, *Allein Gott in der Höh' sei Ehr*; 663, *Allein Gott in der Höh' sei Ehr*; 664, *Trio super Allein Gott in der Höh' sei Ehr*; 665, *Jesus Christus, unser Heiland*; 666, *Jesus Christus, unser Heiland*; 667, *Komm, Gott Schöpfer, Heiliger Geist*; 668, *Wenn wir in höchsten Nöten sein* (Vor deinen Thron tret ich). Chorale preludes in the 3rd part of the *Clavier-Übung*: 669, *Kyrie, Gott Vater in Ewigkeit*; 670, *Christe, aller Welt Trost*; 671, *Kyrie, Gott heiliger Geist*; 672, *Kyrie, Gott Vater in Ewigkeit*; 673, *Christe, aller Welt Trost*; 674, *Kyrie, Gott heiliger*

Geist; 675, *Allein Gott in der Höh' sei Ehr*; 676, *Allein Gott in der Höh' sei Ehr*; 677, *Fughetta super Allein Gott in der Höh' sei Ehr*; 678, *Dies sind die heil'gen zehn Gebot'*; 679, *Fughetta super Dies sind die heil'gen zehn Gebot'*; 680, *Wir glauben all an einen Gott*; 681, *Fughetta super Wir glauben all' an einen Gott*; 682, *Vater unser im Himmelreich*; 683, *Vater unser im Himmelreich*; 684, *Christ, unser Herr, zum Jordan kam*; 685, *Christ, unser Herr, zum Jordan kam*; 686, *Aus tiefer Not schrei ich zu dir*; 687, *Aus tiefer Not schrei ich zu dir*; 688, *Jesus Christus, unser Heiland, der von uns den Zorn Gottes wandt*; 689, *Fuga super Jesus Christus unser Heiland*. Further chorales: 690, *Wer nur den lieben Gott lässt walten*; 691, *Wer nur den lieben Gott lässt walten*; 694, *Wo soll ich fliehen hin*; 695, *Fantasia super Christ lag in Todesbanden*; 696, *Christum wir sollen loben schon*; 697, *Gelobet seist du, Jesu Christ*; 698, *Herr Christ, der ein'ge Gottes-Sohn*; 699, *Nun komm, der Heiden Heiland*; 700, *Vom Himmel hoch, da komm ich her*; 701, *Vom Himmel hoch, da komm ich her*; 703, *Gottes Sohn ist kommen*; 704, *Lob sei dem allmächtigen Gott*; 706, *Liebster Jesu, wir sind hier*; 709, *Herr Jesu Christ, dich zu uns wend*; 710, *Wir Christenleut' haben jetzt Freud*; 711, *Allein Gott in der Höh' sei Ehr*; 712, *In dich hab ich gehoffet, Herr*; 713, *Fantasia super Jesu, meine Freude*; 714, *Ach Gott und Herr*; 715, *Allein Gott in der Höh' sei Ehr*; 717, *Allein Gott in der Höh' sei Ehr*; 718, *Christ lag in Todesbanden*; 720, *Ein' feste Burg ist unser Gott*; 721, *Erbarm' dich mein, o Herre Gott*; 722, *Gelobet seist du, Jesu Christ*; 724, *Gott, durch deine Güte (Gottes Sohn ist kommen)*; 725, *Herr Gott, dich loben wir*; 726, *Herr Jesu Christ, dich zu uns wend*; 727, *Herzlich tut mich verlangen*; 728, *Jesus, meine Zuversicht*; 729, *In dulci jubilo*; 730, *Liebster Jesu, wir sind hier*; 731, *Liebster Jesu, wir sind hier*; 732, *Lobt Gott, ihr Christen, allzugleich*; 733, *Meine Seele erhebet den Herren (Fuge über das Magnificat)*; 734a, *Nun freut euch, lieben Christen g'mein*; *O Lamm Gottes, unschuldig*; 735, *Fantasia super Valet will ich dir geben*; 736, *Valet will ich dir geben*; 737, *Vater unser im Himmelreich*; 738, *Vom Himmel hoch, da komm ich her*; 739, *Wie schön leucht't uns der Morgenstern*; 741, *Ach Gott vom Himmel sieh darein*; 753, *Jesu, meine Freude*; 764, *Wie schön leuchtet uns der Morgenstern*; 766, *Christ, der du bist der helle Tag*; 767, *O Gott, du frommer Gott*; 768, *Sei gegrüsset, Jesu gütig*. BWV numbers have been assigned to the following doubtful and spurious works: 691a, *Wer nur den lieben Gott lässt walten* (doubtful); 692, *Ach Gott und Herr* (by J.G. Walther); 693, *Ach Gott und Herr* (by J.G. Walther); 695a, *Fantasia super Christ lag in Todesbanden* (doubtful); 702, *Das Jesulein soll doch mein Trost* (doubtful); 705, *Durch Adam's Fall ist ganz verderbt* (doubtful); 707, *Ich hab' mein' Sach' Gott heimgestellt* (doubtful); 708, *Ich hab' mein' Sach' Gott heimgestellt* (doubtful); 713a, *Fantasia super Jesu, meine Freude* (doubtful); 716, *Fuga super Allein Gott in der Höh' sei Ehr* (doubtful); 719, *Der Tag, der ist so freudenreich* (doubtful); 723, *Gelobet seist du, Jesu Christ* (doubtful); 734, *Nun freut euch, lieben Christen g'mein* (doubtful); 740, *Wir glauben all' an einen Gott, Vater* (doubtful); 742, *Ach Herr, mich armen Sünder* (spurious); 743, *Ach, was ist doch unser Leben* (spurious); 744, *Auf meinen lieben Gott* (doubtful); 745, *Aus der Tiefe ruf ich* (doubtful); 746, *Christ ist erstanden* (doubtful); 747, *Christus, der uns selig macht* (spurious); 748, *Gott der Vater wohn' uns bei* (doubtful); 749, *Herr Jesu Christ, dich zu uns wend'* (spurious); 750, *Herr Jesu Christ, mein's Lebens Licht* (spurious); 751, *In dulci jubilo* (spurious); 752, *Jesu, der du meine Seele* (spurious); 754, *Liebster Jesu, wir sind hier* (spurious); 755, *Nun freut euch, lieben Christen* (spurious); 756, *Nun ruhen alle Wälder* (spurious); 757, *O Herre Gott, dein göttlich's Wort* (spurious); 758, *O Vater, allmächtiger Gott* (doubtful); 759, *Schmücke dich, o liebe Seele* (by G.A. Homilius); 760, *Vater unser im Himmelreich* (doubtful); 761, *Vater unser im Himmelreich* (doubtful); 762, *Vater unser im Himmelreich* (spurious); 763, *Wie schön leuchtet der Morgenstern* (spurious); 765, *Wir glauben all' an einen Gott* (spurious); 770, *Ach, was soll ich Sünder machen?* (doubtful); 771, *Allein Gott in der Höh sei Ehr'* (nos. 3 and 8 by A.N. Vetter).

OTHER KEYBOARD MUSIC: 772–86, 15 2-part inventions in the *Clavier-Büchlein für Wilhelm Friedemann Bach:* C major, C minor, D major, D minor, E-flat major, E major, E minor, F major, F minor, G major, G minor, A major, A minor, B-flat major, B minor; 787–801, 15 3-part inventions, called sinfonias, in the *Clavier-Büchlein für Wilhelm Friedemann Bach:* C major, C minor, D major, D minor, E-flat major, E major, E minor, F major, F minor, G major, G minor, A major, A minor, B-flat major, B minor; 806–11, 6 English suites: A major, A minor, G minor, F major, E minor, D minor; 812–17, 6 French suites: D minor, C minor, B minor, E-flat major, G major, E major; 825–30, 6 partitas in part 1 of the *Clavier-Übung:* B-flat major, C minor, A minor, D major, G major, E minor; 831, *Ouvertüre nach französischer Art,* a partita in B minor in part 2 of the *Clavier-Übung;* 846–93, *Das wohltemperierte Clavier* (The Well-Tempered Clavier), in 2 parts: 24 preludes and fugues in each part in all the major and minor keys; 971, *Concerto nach italiänischem Gusto* (Concerto in the Italian Style) in part 2 of the *Clavier-Übung;* 988, *Aria mit verschiedenen Veränderungen* (the so-called *Goldberg Variations*), part 4 of the *Clavier-Übung.* Further keyboard works: 818, Suite in A minor; 819, Suite in E-flat major; 820, Ouvertüre in F major; 821, Suite in B-flat major; 822, Suite in G minor; 823, Suite in F minor; 832, Partie in A major; 833, Prelude and Partita in F major; 836 and 837, 2 allemandes in G minor (1 unfinished); 841–43, 3 minuets: G major, G minor, G major; 894, Prelude and Fugue in A minor; 896, Prelude and Fugue in A major; 900, Prelude and Fughetta in E minor; 901, Prelude and Fughetta in F major; 902, Prelude and Fughetta in G major; 903, Chromatic Fantasia and Fugue in D minor; 904, Fantasia and Fugue in A minor; 906, Fantasia and Fugue in C minor; 910, Toccata in F-sharp minor; 911, Toccata in C minor; 912, Toccata in D major; 913, Toccata in D minor; 914, Toccata in E minor; 915, Toccata in G minor; 916, Toccata in G major; 944, Fugue in A minor; 946, Fugue in C major; 950, Fugue in A major (on a theme by Albinoni); 951, Fugue in B minor (on a theme by Albinoni); 953, Fugue in C major; 954, Fugue in B-flat major; 955, Fugue in B-flat major; 958, Fugue in A minor; 959, Fugue in A minor; 963, Sonata in D major; 965, Sonata in A minor (based upon a sonata by J.A. Reinken); 966, Sonata in C major (based upon part of a sonata by J.A. Reinken); 967, Sonata in A minor (based upon the 1st movement of a sonata by an unknown source); 989, Aria variata in A minor; 991, Air with variations in C minor (fragment); 992, *Capriccio sopra la lontananza del suo fratello dilettissimo* (Capriccio on the Departure of His Most Beloved Brother), in B-flat major; 993, Capriccio in E major; also 924–29, 6 works from the *Clavier-Büchlein für Wilhelm Friedemann Bach:* Praeambulum in C major, Prelude in D minor, Praeambulum in F major, Prelude in F major, Trio in G minor, Praeambulum in G minor; 933–38, 6 preludes: C major, C minor, D minor, D major, E major, E minor; 939–43, 5 preludes: C major, D minor, E minor, A minor, C major; 994, Applicatio in C major, the 1st piece in the *Clavier-Büchlein für Wilhelm Friedemann Bach;* several pieces in the 2 parts of the *Clavier-Büchlein für Anna Magdalena Bach;* and 972–87, 16 concertos: D major (arrangement of Vivaldi's op. 3, no. 9), G major (arrangement of Vivaldi's op. 8/II, no. 2), D minor (arrangement of Oboe Concerto by A. Marcello), G minor (arrangement of Vivaldi's op. 4, no. 6), C major (arrangement of Vivaldi's op. 3, no. 12), C major (source unknown), F major (arrangement of Vivaldi's op. 3, no. 3), B minor (source unknown), G major (arrangement of Vivaldi's op. 4, no. 1), C minor (source unknown), B-flat major (arrangement of a concerto by Duke Johann Ernst of Saxe-Weimar), G minor (source unknown), C major (arrangement of a concerto by Duke Johann Ernst of Saxe-Weimar), G minor (arrangement of Violin Concerto by Telemann), G major (source unknown), D minor (arrangement of a concerto by Duke Johann Ernst of Saxe-Weimar). BWV numbers have been assigned to the following doubtful and spurious works: 824, Suite in A major (fragment; by Telemann); Allemande in C minor (spurious); 835, Allemande in A minor (by Kirnberger); 838, Allemande and Courante in A major (by C. Graupner); 839, Sarabande in G minor (spurious); 840, Courante in G major (by Telemann); 844, Scherzo in D minor (by W.F. Bach); 845, Gigue in F minor (spurious); 895, Prelude and Fugue in A minor (doubtful); 897, Prelude and Fugue in A minor (partly doubtful; prelude by C.H. Dretzel); 898, Prelude and Fugue in B-flat major (doubtful); 899, Prelude and Fughetta in D minor (doubtful); 905, Fantasia and Fugue in D minor (doubtful); 907, Fantasia and Fughetta in B-flat major (doubtful); 908, Fantasia and Fughetta in D major (doubtful); 909, Concerto and Fugue in C minor (doubtful); 917, Fantasia in G minor (doubtful); 918, Fantasia on a rondo in C minor (doubtful); 919, Fantasia in C minor (doubtful); 920, Fantasia in G minor (doubtful); 921, Prelude in C minor (doubtful); 922, Prelude in A minor (doubtful); 923, Prelude in B minor (doubtful); 945, Fugue in E minor (spurious); 947, Fugue in A minor (doubtful); 948, Fugue in D minor (doubtful); 949, Fugue in A major (doubtful); 952, Fugue in C major (doubtful); 956, Fugue in E minor (doubtful); 957, Fugue in G major (doubtful); 960, Fugue in E minor (unfinished; spurious); 961, Fughetta in C minor (doubtful); 962, Fugato in E minor (by Albrechtsberger); 964, Sonata in D minor (doubtful; arrangement of Violin Sonata 1,003); 968, Adagio in G major (doubtful; arrangement of 1st movement of Violin Sonata 1,005); 969, Andante in G minor (spurious); 970, Presto in D minor (by W.F. Bach); 990, Sarabande con partite in C major (spurious); etc.

LUTE: 995, Suite in G minor; 996, Suite in E minor; 997, Partita in C minor; 998, Prelude, Fugue, and Allegro in E-flat major; 999, Prelude in C minor; 1,000, Fugue in G minor; 1,006a, Partita in E major (arrangement of 1,006).

CHAMBER: 1,001–6, sonatas and partitas for Solo Violin: Sonata No. 1 in G minor, Partita No. 1 in B minor, Sonata No. 2 in A minor, Partita No. 2 in D minor, Sonata No. 3 in C major, Partita No. 3 in E major; 1,007–12, 6 suites for Solo Cello: G major, D minor, C major, E-flat major, C minor, D major; 1,013, Partita in A minor for Flute; 1,014–19, 6 sonatas for Violin and Harpsichord: No. 1 in B minor, No. 2 in A major, No. 3 in E major, No. 4 in C minor, No. 5 in F minor, No. 6 in G major; 1,021, Sonata in G major for Violin and Basso Continuo; 1,023, Sonata in E minor for Violin and Basso Continuo; 1,027–29, 3 sonatas for Harpsichord and Viola da Gamba: G major, D major, G minor; 1,030, Sonata in B minor for Flute and Harpsichord; 1,032, Sonata in A major for Flute and Harpsichord; 1,034, Sonata in E minor for Flute and Basso Continuo; 1,035, Sonata in E major for Flute and Basso Continuo; 1,039, Sonata in G major for 2 Flutes and Basso Continuo; 1,040, Trio in F major for Violin, Oboe, and Basso Continuo. BWV numbers have been assigned to the following doubtful and spurious works: 1,020, Sonata in G minor for Violin and Harpsichord (doubtful); 1,022, Sonata in F major for Violin and Harpsichord (most likely spurious); 1,024, Sonata in C minor for Violin and Basso Continuo (doubtful); 1,025, Suite in A major for Violin and Harpsichord (doubtful); 1,026, Fugue in G minor for Violin and Harpsichord (doubtful); 1,037, Sonata in C major for 2 Violins and Harpsichord (most likely spurious); 1,031, Sonata in E-flat major for Flute and Harpsichord (doubtful); 1,033, Sonata in C major for Flute and Basso Continuo (doubtful); 1,036, Sonata in D minor for 2 Violins and Harpsichord (most likely spurious); 1,038, Sonata in G major for Flute, Violin, and Basso Continuo (most likely spurious).

ORCH.: 1,041, Concerto in A minor for Violin; 1,042, Concerto in E major for Violin; 1,043, Concerto in D minor for 2 Violins; 1,044, Concerto in A minor for Flute, Violin, and Harpsichord; 1,046–51, 6 *Brandenburg Concertos:* No. 1 in F major, No. 2 in F major, No. 3 in G major, No. 4 in G major, No. 5 in D major, No. 6 in B-flat major; 1,052, Concerto in D minor for Harpsichord; 1053, Concerto in E major for Harpsichord; 1,054, Concerto in D major for Harpsichord; 1,055, Concerto in A major for Harpsichord; 1,056, Concerto in F minor for Harpsichord; 1,057, Concerto in F major for Harpsichord; 1,058, Concerto in G minor for Harpsichord; 1,059, Concerto in D minor for Harpsichord; 1,060, Concerto in C minor for

2 Harpsichords; 1,061, Concerto in C major for 2 Harpsichords; 1,062, Concerto in C minor for 2 Harpsichords; 1,063, Concerto in D minor for 3 Harpsichords; 1,064, Concerto in C major for 3 Harpsichords; 1,065, Concerto in A minor for 4 Harpsichords (arrangement of Vivaldi's op. 3, no. 10); 1,066–69, 4 suites or *ouvertures*: No. 1 in C major, No. 2 in B minor, No. 3 in D major, No. 4 in D major. Also 1,045, concerto movement in D major for Violin (fragment); 1,046a, Sinfonia in F major (early version of 1,046); 1,070, Overture in G minor (most likely spurious).

OTHER WORKS: 769, *Einige canonische Veränderungen über das Weynacht Lied, Vom Himmel hoch da komm' ich her* for Organ (composed for his membership in the Societät der Musikalischen Wissenschaften); 1,079, *Musikalisches Opfer* (Musical Offering); 1,080, *Die Kunst der Fuge* (The Art of the Fugue).

BIBL.: COLLECTED EDITIONS., SOURCE MATERIAL: *J.S. B.'s Werke*, the 1st major ed. of his collected works, was publ. by the Bach-Gesellschaft (46 vols., Leipzig, 1851–99; vol. 47, supplement, 1932). The Johann-Sebastian-Bach-Inst. of Göttingen and the Bach-Archiv of Leipzig are now preparing a completely new ed., the *Neue Ausgabe sämtlicher Werke* (the *Neue B.-Ausgabe*, or NBA). It began publication in 1954; a *Kritischer Bericht* accompanies each vol.; in addition, facsimile reproductions of Bach's original MSS and documents may be found in the *Faksimile-Reihe B.scher Werke und Schriftstücke*. When this monumental ed. is completed, it will contain over 80 vols. There are also innumerable reprints of many of Bach's compositions.

The standard thematic catalogue of Bach's works is to be found in W. Schmieder, *Thematisch-systematisches Verzeichnis der musikalischen Werke von J.S. B. Bach-Werke-Verzeichnis* (Leipzig, 1950; 3rd ed., 1961); it includes bibliographical information on each composition. See also M. McAll, ed., *Melodic Index to the Works of J.S. B.* (N.Y., 1962); U. Balestrini, ed., *Catalogo Tematico (Incipit) delle Opere di J.S. B. (BWV 1–1080)* (Milan, 1988).

Other important sources are as follows: J. Schreyer, *Beiträge zur B.-Kritik* (vol. 1, Dresden, 1910; vol. 2, Leipzig, 1912); E. Müller von Asow, ed., *J.S. B., Gesammelte Briefe* (Regensburg, 1938; 2nd ed., with H. Müller von Asow, as *J.S. B., Briefe, Gesamtausgabe*, Regensburg, 1950); H. David and A. Mendel, eds., *The B. Reader: A Life of J.S. B. in Letters and Documents* (N.Y., 1945; rev. ed., 1966); K. Matthaei, ed., *B.-Gedenkschrift* (Zürich, 1950); P. Kast, *Die B.-Handschriften der Berliner Staatsbibliothek*, Tübinger B-Studien, II–III (Trossingen, 1958); G. von Dadelsen, "Originale Daten auf den Handschriften J.S. B.s," *Hans Albrecht in Memoriam* (Kassel, 1962); W. Neumann and H.-J. Schulze, eds., *Schriftstücke von der Hand J.S. B.s*, Bach-Dokumente, I (Leipzig, 1963); P. Krause, ed., *Handschriften der Werke J.S. B.s in der Musikbibliothek der Stadt Leipzig* (Leipzig, 1964); M. Geck, ed., *B.-Interpretationen* (Göttingen, 1969); H.-J. Schulze, ed., *Fremdschriftliche und gedruckte Dokumente zur Lebensgeschichte J.S. B.s 1685–1750*, Bach-Dokumente, II (Leipzig, 1969); P. Krause, ed., *Originalausgaben und ältere Drucke der Werke J.S. B.s in der Musikbibliothek der Stadt Leipzig* (Leipzig, 1970); H.-J. Schulze, ed., *Dokumente zum Nachwirken J.S. B.s 1750–1800*, Bach-Dokumente, III (Leipzig, 1972); K.-H. Köhler, "Die B.-Sammlung der Deutschen Staatsbibliothek—Überlieferung und Bedeutung," *Bach-Studien*, V (1975); W. Neumann, ed., *Bilddokumente zur Lebensgeschichte J.S. B.s*, Bach-Dokumente, IV (Leipzig, 1978); R. Leaver, *B.s theologische Bibliothek: Eine kritische Bibliographie—B.'s Theological Library: A Critical Bibliography* (Neuhausen-Stuttgart, 1983); H. Raupach, *Das wahre Bildnis des J.S. B.: Bericht und Dokumente* (Munich, 1983); G. Herz, ed., *B.-Quellen in Amerika—B. Sources in America* (Kassel, 1984); M. Cyr, "B.'s Music in France: A New Source," *Early Music* (May 1985); D. Franklin, ed., *B. Studies* (Cambridge, 1989).

BIOGRAPHICAL: C.P.E. Bach and J. Agricola publ. an obituary (*Nekrolog*) in L. Mizler's *Neu eröffnete musikalische Bibliothek* (Leipzig, 1754; reprint ed. by B. Richter in the *Bach-Jahrbuch*, 1920; Eng. tr. in H. David and A. Mendel, eds., *The B. Reader:*

A Life of J.S. B. in Letters and Documents, N.Y., 1945; rev. ed., 1966, pp. 213–24); Bach's 1st biographer was J. Forkel, *Über J.S. B.s Leben, Kunst und Kunstwerke* (an invaluable source based on information provided by C.P.E. Bach; Leipzig, 1802; Eng. tr., London, 1820; new Eng. tr. with notes by C. Terry, London, 1920); C. Hilgenfeldt, *J.S. B.'s Leben, Wirken und Werke; Ein Beitrag zur Kunstgeschichte des achtzehnten Jahrhunderts* (Leipzig, 1850); C. Bitter, *J.S. B.* (2 vols., Berlin, 1865; 2nd ed., 4 vols., Dresden, 1880); P. Spitta, *J.S. B.* (the standard source on Bach's life and work; although in error concerning some details, it remains an essential study; 2 vols., Leipzig, 1873–80; Eng. tr. by C. Bell and J. Fuller Maitland, with many additions, 3 vols., London, 1884–85; 2nd ed., 1899; reprint, 2 vols., N.Y., 1951); A. Schweitzer, *J.S. B., Le Musicien-poète* (an important biography, which places special emphasis on esthetic problems; Paris, 1905; augmented German eds., 1908, 1915; Eng. tr. by E. Newman, 2 vols., London, 1911); C. Abdy Williams, *B.* (London, 1900; rev. ed., 1934); A. Pirro, *J.-S. B.* (Paris, 1906; Eng. tr., N.Y., 1957); P. Wolfrum, *J.S. B.* (vol. 1, Berlin, 1906; 2nd ed., 1910; vol. 2, Leipzig, 1910); C. Parry, *J.S. B.: The Story of the Development of a Great Personality* (N.Y. and London, 1909; rev. ed., 1934); J. Tiersot, *J.-S. B.* (Paris, 1912; 2nd ed., 1934); H. Kretzschmar, *B.-Kolleg* (Leipzig, 1922); W. Dahms, *J.S. B., Ein Bild seines Lebens* (Munich, 1924); T. Gérold, *J.-S. B.* (Paris, 1925); C. Terry, *B.: A Biography* (a major study based on extensive research; London, 1928; rev. ed., 1933); R. Boughton, *B., the Master: A New Interpretation of His Genius* (N.Y. and London, 1930); H. Besseler, "J.S. B.," *Die grossen Deutschen* (Berlin, 1935; new ed., 1956); T. Scott Buhrmann, *B.'s Life Chronologically as He Lived It* (illustrated chronological tables; N.Y. 1935); H. Moser, *J.S. B.* (Berlin, 1935; 2nd ed., 1943); J. Müller-Blattau, *B.* (Leipzig, 1935; 2nd ed., Stuttgart, 1950); H. Preuss, *B., der Lutheraner* (Erlangen, 1935); R. Steglich, *J.S. B.* (richly illustrated; Potsdam, 1935); P. Collaer, *J.S. B.* (Brussels, 1936); W. Gurlitt, *J.S. B.: Der Meister und sein Werk* (an important study; Berlin, 1936; 3rd ed., 1949; Eng. tr., St. Louis, 1957); W. Vetter, *J.S. B.* (Leipzig, 1938; 2nd ed., 1943); K. Hasse, *J.S. B.* (Cologne and Krefeld, 1941; 2nd ed., 1948); R. Pitrou, *J.-S. B.* (Paris, 1941; 2nd ed., 1949); W. Cart, *J.S. B.: 1685–1750* (Lausanne, 1946); A.-E. Cherbuliez, *J.S. B.: Sein Leben und sein Werk* (Olten, 1946; 2nd ed., 1947); H. Gadamer, *B. und Weimar* (Weimar, 1946); E. and S. Grew, *B.* (London, 1947); H. Keller, *J.S. B.* (Lorch, 1947); E. Fischer, *J.S. B.* (Bern, 1948); H. Engel, *J.S. B.* (Berlin, 1950); G. Fock, *Der junge B. in Lüneburg* (Hamburg, 1950); B. Paumgartner, *J.S. B.: Leben und Werk* (vol. I, Zürich, 1950); R. Petzoldt, *J.S. B., Sein Leben in Bildern* (Leipzig, 1950); F. Wiegand, *J.S. B. und seine Verwandten in Arnstadt* (Arnstadt, 1950); F. Smend, *B. in Köthen* (Berlin, 1951); H. Löffler, "Die Schüler J.S. B.s," *Bach-Jahrbuch* (1953); W. Neumann, *Auf den Lebenswegen J.S. B.s* (Berlin, 1953; 4th ed., 1962); K. Geiringer, *The B. Family: Seven Generations of Creative Genius* (N.Y., 1954); H. Franck, *J.S. B.: Die Geschichte seines Lebens* (Berlin, 1960); A. Mendel, "Recent Developments in B. Chronology," *Musical Quarterly* (July 1960); W. Neumann, *B.: Eine Bildbiographie* (Munich, 1960; Eng. tr. as *B.: A Pictorial Biography*, N.Y., 1961; rev. ed. as *B. and His World*, N.Y., 1970); R. Miles, *J.S. B.* (Englewood Cliffs, N.J., 1962); F. Blume, "Outlines of a New Picture of B.," *Music & Letters* (July 1963); E. Buchet, ed., *J.-S. B., L'Œuvre et la vie* (Paris, 1963); I. Holst, *B.* (London, 1965); K. Geiringer, *J.S. B.: The Culmination of an Era* (an important 1-vol. study of Bach's life and works, especially valuable for its critical survey of his compositions; N.Y., 1966); F. Blume, *Der junge B.* (Wolfenbüttel, 1967; Eng. tr. as "J.S. B.'s Youth," *Musical Quarterly* [Jan. 1968]); E. Buchet, *J.-S. B., Après deux siècles d'études et de témoignages* (Paris, 1968); B. Schwendowius and W. Dömling, eds., *J.S. B.: Zeit, Leben, Wirken* (Kassel, 1976; tr. as *J.S. B.: Life, Times, Influence*, London, 1978); M. Boyd, *B.* (London, 1983); D. Arnold, *B.* (Oxford, 1984); R. de Candé, *J.-S. B.* (Paris, 1984); G. Stiller, *J.S. B. and Liturgical Life in Leipzig* (St. Louis, 1984); H. Wohlfarth, *J.S. B.* (Freiburg, 1984; Eng. tr. in Philadelphia and Cambridge, 1985); P. Buscaroli, *B.* (Milan, 1985); W. Felix, *J.S. B.* (London, 1985); S. Sadie, "J.S. B., 1685–1750," *Ovation* (Feb. 1985).

CRITICAL, ANALYTICAL: In addition to the following writings, numerous articles of importance may be found in the *Bach-Jahrbuch* (1904–). F. Rochlitz, *Wege zu B.* (extracted from *Für Freunde der Tonkunst*, Leipzig, 1824–37, by J. Müller-Blattau, Augsburg, 1926); M. Hauptmann, *Erläuterungen zu J.S. B.s Kunst der Fuge* (Leipzig, 1841; 2nd ed., 1861); H. Riemann, *Handbuch der Fugenkomposition* (vols. I and II [analysis of *Das Wohltemperierte Klavier*; Berlin 1890–91; 3rd ed., 1914; Eng. tr. by J. Shedlock, 2 vols., London, 1893]; vol. III [analysis of the *Kunst der Fuge*; Berlin, 1894; 3rd ed., 1921]); A. Pirro, *L'Orgue de J.-S. B.* (Paris, 1895; Eng. tr., London, 1902); F. Iliff, *The 48 Preludes and Fugues of J.S. B.* (London, 1897); A. Pirro, *L'Esthétique de J.-S. B.* (Paris, 1907); A. Heuss, *J.S. B.s Matthäuspassion* (Leipzig, 1909); R. Wustmann, *J.S. B.s Kantatentexte* (Leipzig, 1913; 2nd ed., 1967); J. Fuller Maitland, "The Toccatas of B.," *Sammelbände der Internationalen Musik-Gesellschaft* (1915); C. Terry, *B.'s Chorals* (3 vols., Cambridge, 1915, 1917, 1921); idem, *B.'s Mass in B Minor: A Study* (Glasgow, 1915); E. Kurth, *Grundlagen des linearen Kontrapunkts. Einführung in Stil und Technik von B.s melodischer Polyphonie* (Bern, 1917; 5th ed., 1956); H. Grace, *The Organ Works of B.* (London, 1922); C. Terry, *J.S. B.'s Original Hymn-Tunes for Congregational Use* (London, 1922); W. Werker, *Studien über die Symmetrie im Bau der Fugen und die motivische Zusammengehörigkeit der Präludien und Fugen des Wohltemperierten Klaviers von J.S. B.* (Leipzig, 1922); C. Terry, *A B. Hymn Book for the Church's Seasons* (London, 1923); W. Werker, *Die Matthäus-Passion* (Leipzig, 1923); C. Terry, *B.: The Mass in B Minor* (London, 1924; rev. ed., 1931); W. Whittaker, *Fugitive Notes on Certain Cantatas and the Motets of J.S. B.* (London, 1924); F. Franke, *B.s Kirchen-Kantaten* (Leipzig, 1925); J. Fuller Maitland, *The "48": B.'s Wohltemperiertes Clavier* (London, 1925); idem, *The Keyboard Suites of J.S. B.* (London, 1925); C. Terry, *B.: The Cantatas and Oratorios* (2 vols., London, 1925); idem, *J.S. B.: Cantata Texts, Sacred and Secular, with a Reconstruction of the Leipzig Liturgy of His Period* (London, 1926); M. Zulauf, *Die Harmonik J.S. B.s* (Bern, 1927; 2nd ed., 1937); H. David, "Zu B.s Kunst der Fuge," *Peters-Jahrbuch* (1928); C. Terry, *B.: The Passions* (London, 1926; 2nd ed., 1935); P. Wackernagel, *B.s Brandenburgische Konzerte* (Berlin, 1928); H. Abert, *B.s Matthäuspassion* (Halle, 1929); F. Atkins, *B.'s Passions* (London,1929); H. David, "Zur Gesamtgestalt von B.s H-moll Messe," *Festschrift für Johannes Wolf* (1929); J. Fuller Maitland, *B.'s "Brandenburg" Concertos* (London, 1929; 2nd ed., 1945); A. Hull, *B.'s Organ Works* (London, 1929); C. Terry, *The Four-Part Chorales of J.S. B.* (5 vols., London, 1929); idem, *The Magnificat, Lutheran Masses and Motets* (London, 1929); idem, *B.: The Historical Approach* (London, 1930); K. Ziebler, *Das Symbol in der Kirchenmusik J.S. B.s* (Kassel, 1930); E. Schwebsch, *J.S. B. und die Kunst der Fuge* (Stuttgart, 1931; 2nd ed., 1955); D. Tovey, *A Companion to the Art of Fugue* (London, 1931); C. Terry, *B.'s Orchestra* (London, 1932; 2nd ed., 1958); C. Freyse, *Eisenacher Dokumente um J.S. B.* (Leipzig, 1933); L. Landshoff, *Revisionsbericht zur Urtextausgabe von J.S. B.s Inventionen und Sinfonien* (Leipzig, 1933); C. Terry, *The Music of B.: An Introduction* (London, 1933); C. Terry, "The Spurious B. 'Lukas-Passion,' " *Music & Letters* (July 1933); H. Huggler, *J.S. B.s Orgelbüchlein* (Bern, 1935); A. Dickinson, *The Art of J.S. B.* (London, 1936; rev. ed., 1950); G. Herz, *J.S. B. im Zeitalter des Rationalismus und der Frühromantik* (Bern, 1936); L. Landshoff, *Musikalisches Opfer* (Leipzig, 1936); A. Schering, *J.S. B.s Leipziger Kirchenmusik* (Leipzig, 1936; 2nd ed., 1954); E. Thiele, *Die Chorfugen J.S. B.s* (Bern and Leipzig, 1936); H. Besch, *J.S. B., Frömmigkeit und Glaube* (Gütersloh, 1938; 2nd ed., Kassel, 1950); C. Gray, *The 48 Preludes and Fugues of J.S. B.* (London, 1938); W. Neumann, *J.S. B.'s Chorfuge* (Leipzig, 1938); C. Freyse, "Das Bach-Haus zu Eisenach," *Bach-Jahrbuch* (1939; 1940–48); G. Frotscher, *J.S. B. und die Musik des 17. Jahrhunderts* (Wadenswil, 1939); W. Korte, *Musik und*

Weltbild (Leipzig, 1940); A. Schering, *Das Zeitalter J.S. B.s und Johann Adam Hillers* (Leipzig, 1940); B. Martin, *Untersuchungen zur Struktur der Kunst der Fuge* (Regensburg, 1941); H. Rutters, *J.S. B. en onze tijd* (Amsterdam, 1941); A. Schering, *Das Symbol in der Musik* (Leipzig, 1941); idem, *J.S. B. und das Musikleben Leipzigs im 18. Jahrhundert* (Leipzig, 1941); H. Boetticher, "B.s Kunst der Bearbeitung," *Festschrift zu Peter Raabes 70. Geburtstag* (Leipzig, 1942); H. Drinker, *Texts of the Choral Works of J.S. B. in English Translation* (4 vols., N.Y., 1942–43); A. Schering, *Über Kantaten J.S. B.s* (Leipzig, 1942; 3rd ed., 1950); F. Smend, "Neue B.-Funde," *Archiv für Musikforschung* (1942); S. Taylor, *The Chorale Preludes of J.S. B.* (London, 1942); H. David, *J.S. B.'s Musical Offering: History, Interpretation and Analysis* (N.Y., 1945); G. Herz, "B.'s Religion," *Journal of Renaissance and Baroque Music* (June 1946); M. Mayer, *J.-P. Rameau: J.S. B.* (Chambery, 1946); L. Schrade, "B.: The Conflict between the Sacred and Secular," *Journal of the History of Ideas* (April 1946); J. Barbour, "B. and 'The Art of Temperament,' " *Musical Quarterly* (Jan. 1947); F. Blume, *J.S. B. im Wandel der Geschichte* (Kassel, 1947; Eng. tr., 1950); F. Florand, *J.S. B.: L'Œuvre d'orgue* (Paris, 1947); W. Neumann, *Handbuch der Kantaten J.S. B.s* (Leipzig, 1947; 4th ed., 1971); F. Smend, *J.S. B.: Kirchen-Kantaten* (6 vols., Berlin, 1947–49; 3rd ed., 1966); idem, *Luther und B.* (Berlin, 1947); M. Dehnert, *Das Weltbild J.S. B.s* (Leipzig, 1948; 2nd ed., 1949); N. Dufourcq, *J.S. B., Le Maître de l'orgue* (Paris, 1948); H. Keller, *Die Orgelwerke B.s: Ein Beitrag zu ihrer Geschichte, Form, Deutung und Wiedergabe* (Leipzig, 1948; Eng. tr., 1967); W. Emery, "B.'s Symbolic Language," *Music & Letters* (Oct. 1949); R. Steglich, *Wege zu B.* (Regensburg, 1949); H. Besseler and G. Kraft, *J.S. B. in Thüringen* (Weimar, 1950); W. Blankenburg, *Einführung in B.s h-moll Messe* (Kassel and Basel, 1950; 3rd ed., 1973); H. Dräger and K. Laux, eds., *B.-Probleme* (Leipzig, 1950); I. Finlay, "B.'s Secular Cantata Texts," *Music & Letters* (July 1950); K. Geiringer, "Artistic Interrelations of the B.s," *Musical Quarterly* (July 1950); H. Keller, *Die Klavierwerke B.s* (Leipzig, 1950); C. Mahrenholz, *J.S. B. und der Gottesdienst seiner Zeit* (Kassel and Basel, 1950); R. Petzoldt and L. Weinhold, eds., *J.S. B.: Das Schaffen des Meisters im Spiegel einer Stadt* (Leipzig, 1950); A. Schmitz, *Die Bildlichkeit der wortgebundenen Musik J.S. B.s* (Mainz, 1950); W. Vetter, *Der Kapellmeister B.: Versuch einer Deutung* (Potsdam, 1950); P. Aldrich, *Ornamentation in J.S. B.'s Organ Works* (N.Y., 1951); W. David, *J.S. B.s Orgeln* (Berlin, 1951); A. Davison, *B. and Handel: the Consummation of the Baroque in Music* (Cambridge, Mass., 1951); A. Dürr, *Studien über die frühen Kantaten J.S. B.s* (Leipzig, 1951; rev. ed., Wiesbaden, 1977); R. Gerber, *B.s Brandenburgische Konzerte* (Kassel and Basel, 1951); F. Hamel, *J.S. B.: Geistige Welt* (Göttingen, 1951); P. Hindemith, *J.S. B.: Heritage and Obligation* (New Haven, 1952); W. Scheide, *J.S. B. as a Biblical Interpreter* (Princeton, 1952); W. Emery, *B.'s Ornaments* (London, 1953; 2nd ed., 1961); idem, *Notes on B.'s Organ Works: A Companion to the Revised Edition* (London, 1953–57); F. Rothschild, *The Lost Tradition in Music: Rhythm and Tempo in J.S. B.'s Time* (N.Y., 1953); K. Geiringer, *Symbolism in the Music of B.* (Washington, D.C., 1955); L. Czaczkes, *Analyse des Wohltemperierten Klaviers* (Vienna, 1956–65); A. Dickinson, *B.'s Fugal Works* (London, 1956); H. Engel, *J.S. B.s Violinkonzerte* (Leipzig, 1956); J. Krey, *B.s Orgelmusik in der Weimarer Periode* (diss., Univ. of Jena, 1956); W. Neumann, ed., *J.S. B.: Sämtliche Kantatentexte* (Leipzig, 1956; 2nd ed., 1967); L. Tagliavini, *Studi sui testi delle cantate sacre di J.S. B.* (Padua, 1956); G. von Dadelsen, *Bemerkungen zur Handschrift J.S. B.s, seiner Familie und seines Kreises*, Tübinger Bach-Studien, I (Trossingen, 1957); J. David, *Die zweistimmigen Inventionen von J.S. B.* (Göttingen, 1957); A. Dürr, "Zur Chronologie der Leipziger Vokalwerke J.S. B.s," *Bach-Jahrbuch* (1957; rev. and publ. separately, Kassel, 1976); W. Reich, ed., *J.S. B., Leben und Schaffen* (Zürich, 1957); G. von Dadelsen, *Beiträge zur Chronologie der Werke J.S. B.s*, Tübinger B.-Studien, IV–V (Trossingen, 1958); J. David, *Die dreistimmigen Inventionen* von J.S. B. (Göttingen, 1959); W. Whittaker, *The Cantatas of J.S. B., Sacred and Secular* (2 vols., London, 1959; 2nd ed., 1964); E. Bodky, *The Interpretation of B.'s Keyboard Works* (Cambridge, Mass., 1960); R. Donington, *Tempo and Rhythm in B.'s Organ Music* (London, 1960); W. Neumann, "Das 'Bachische Collegium Musicum,'" *Bach-Jahrbuch* (1960); J. Day, *The Literary Background to B.'s Cantatas* (London, 1961); J. David, *Das wohltemperierte Klavier* (Göttingen, 1962); R. Davis, *Self Parody among the Cantatas of J.S. B.* (diss., Boston Univ., 1962); R. Steglich, *Tanzrhythmen in der Musik J.S. B.s* (Wolfenbüttel, 1962); P. Aldrich, "On the Interpretation of B.'s Trills," *Musical Quarterly* (July 1963); N. Carrell, *B.'s Brandenburg Concertos* (London, 1963); J. Chailley, *Les Passions de J.-S. B.* (Paris, 1963; 2nd ed., rev., 1984); D. Johnston, "B. and the Bible," *Proceedings of the Renaissance Music Association,* XC (1963–64); H. Keller, *Das Wohltemperierte Klavier von J.S. B.: Werk und Wiedergabe* (Kassel, 1965); F. Neumann, "A New Look at B.'s Ornamentation," *Music & Letters* (April 1965); W. Siegmund-Schultze, "B. und Händel," *Händel-Jahrbuch* (1966); J. Westrup, *B. Cantatas* (London, 1966); N. Carrell, *B. the Borrower* (London, 1967); M. Geck, *Die Wiederentdeckung der Matthäuspassion im 19. Jahrhundert* (Regensburg, 1967); G. Kraft, *B. in Eisenach* (Jena, 1967); C. Wolff, *Der stile antico in der Musik J.S. B.s* (Wiesbaden, 1968); P. Brainard, "B.'s Parody Procedure and the St. Matthew Passion," *Journal of the American Musicological Society,* XXII (1969); A. Dürr, *Die Kantaten von J.S. B.* (Kassel and Munich, 1971; 5th ed., rev., 1985); C. Wolff, "New Research on B.'s Musical Offering," *Musical Quarterly* (July 1971); J. Chailley, *L'Art de la fugue de J.-S. B.* (Paris, 1971–72); R. Marshall, *The Compositional Process of J.S. B.: A Study of the Autograph Scores of the Vocal Works* (Princeton, 1972); A. Robertson, *The Church Cantatas of J.S. B.* (London, 1972); J. Rifkin, "The Chronology of B.'s Saint Matthew Passion," *Musical Quarterly* (July 1975); C. Wolff et al., "B.'s 'Art of Fugue'; An Examination of the Sources," *Current Musicology,* 19 (1975); N. Kenyon, "A Newly Discovered Group of Canons by B.," *Musical Times* (May 1976); R. Marshall, "B. the Progressive: Observations on His Later Works," *Musical Quarterly* (July 1976); W. Kolneder, *Die Kunst der Fuge: Mythen des 20. Jahrhunderts* (Wilhelmshaven, 1977); P. Williams, *The Organ Music of J.S. B.* (3 vols., Cambridge, 1980–84); W.H. Mellers, *B. and the Dance of God* (N.Y., 1980); S. Daw, *The Music of J.S. B.: The Choral Works* (East Brunswick, N.J., 1981); H. Klotz, *Streifzüge durch die Bachsche Orgelwelt* (Wiesbaden, 1981); R. Azekus, *J.S. B. und die Aufklärung* (Leipzig, 1982); J. Rifkin, "B.'s 'Choruses,' The Record Cleared," *High Fidelity* (Dec. 1982); A. Heinich, *B.'s Die Kunst der Fuge: A Living Compendium of Fugal Procedures* (Washington, D.C., 1983); G. Krapf, *Improvised Ornamentation and Keyboard Cadenzas: An Approach to Creative Performance* (Dayton, 1983); R. Kirkpatrick, *Interpreting B.'s "Well-Tempered Clavier": A Performer's Discourse of Method* (New Haven and London, 1984); P. Williams, ed., *B., Handel and Scarlatti: Tercentenary Essays* (Cambridge, 1985); J. Pelikan, *B. among the Theologians* (Philadelphia, 1986); G. Stauffer and E. May, eds., *J.S. B. as Organist: His Instruments, Music and Performance Practices* (Bloomington, Ind., 1986); H. Vogt, *J.S. B.'s Chamber Music* (1988); R. Marshall, *The Music of J.S. B.: The Sources, the Style, the Significance* (N.Y., 1989); H.-J. Schulze, "J.S. B.'s orchestra: some unanswered questions," *Early Music* (Feb. 1989); W. Young, *The Cantatas of J.S. B.: An Analytical Guide* (Jefferson, N.C., 1989); J. Butt, *B. Interpretation: Articulation Marks in Primary Sources of J.S. B.* (Cambridge, 1990); R. Tatlow, *B. and the Riddle of the Number Alphabet* (Cambridge, 1990); E. Chafe, *Tonal Allegory in the Vocal Music of J.S. B.* (Berkeley, 1991).

ICONOGRAPHY: W. His., *J.S. B., Forschungen über dessen Grabstätte, Gebeine und Antlitz* (dealing with the state of Bach's skull and bones at the time of his exhumation and reinterment; Leipzig, 1895); M. Schneider, "Verzeichnis von Bildnissen B.s," *Bach-Jahrbuch* (1905); A. Kurzwelly, "Neues über das Bachbildnis der Thomasschule und andere Bildnisse J.S. B.s," *Bach-Jahrbuch* (1914); J. Müller, "B. Portraits," *Musical Quar-*

terly (April 1935); G. Herz, "A 'New' B. Portrait," *Musical Quarterly* (April 1943); K. Geiringer, *The Lost Portrait of J.S. B.* (N.Y., 1950); H. Raupach, *Das wahre Bildnis J.S. B.s* (Wolfenbüttel, 1950); F. Smend, *J.S. B. bei seinem Namen gerufen* (Kassel, 1950); H. Besseler, *Fünf echte Bildnisse J.S. B.s* (Kassel, 1956); H. van Tuyll van Serooskerken, *Probleme des Bachporträts* (Bilthoven, 1956); C. Freyse, *B.s Antlitz. Betrachtungen und Erkenntnisse zur B.-Ikonographie* (Eisenach, 1964).

Bach, Wilhelm Friedemann (the "Halle" Bach), eldest son of **Johann Sebastian;** b. Weimar, Nov. 22, 1710; d. Berlin, July 1, 1784. He was a pupil of his father; studied at the Thomasschule in Leipzig (1723–29); also studied violin with J.G. Graun in Merseburg (1726); in 1729 he enrolled at the Univ. of Leipzig, where he took courses in mathematics, philosophy, and law. In 1733 he became organist of the Sophienkirche in Dresden; in 1746 he was appointed organist of the Liebfrauenkirche in Halle, a post he held until 1764. In 1774 he went to Berlin. As a composer, he was highly gifted; his music reflects the influences of the Baroque and Rococo styles. An ed. of selected works was begun by the Abteilung für Musik der Preussischen Akademie der Künste; vol. I contains 4 trios (Leipzig, 1935). His Sinfonias opp. 64 and 65 have been ed. by W. Lebermann (Mainz, 1971), opp. 67–71 by M. Schneider (Leipzig, 1914). His piano compositions have been ed. by W. Rehberg in *Die Söhne Bachs* (1933); 3 excerpts are in K. Geiringer, *Music of the Bach Family: An Anthology* (Cambridge, Mass., 1955). His organ works are printed in E. Power Biggs and G. Weston, eds., *W.F. Bach: Complete Works for Organ* (N.Y., 1947).

BIBL.: C. Bitter, *Carl Philip Emanuel und W.F. B. und deren Brüder* (2 vols., Berlin, 1868); M. Falck, *W.F. B.: Sein Leben und seine Werke* (Leipzig, 1913); K. Stabenow, *J.S. Bachs Sohn* (Leipzig, 1935); K. Geiringer, *The Bach Family: Seven Generations of Creative Genius* (N.Y., 1954); H. Franck, *F., der Sohn J.S. Bachs* (Berlin, 1963).

Bach, Wilhelm Friedrich Ernst, son of **Johann Christoph Friedrich,** and grandson and last male descendant of **Johann Sebastian;** b. Bückeburg, May 23, 1759; d. Berlin, Dec. 25, 1845. He studied with his father and with his uncle **Johann Christoph** in London. In 1787 he became music director at Minden; in 1788 he was named Kapellmeister and harpsichordist to Queen Friedrike of Prussia; in 1797 he was appointed to a similar position to Queen Luise; also served as music master to the royal princes. He attended the dedication of the J.S. Bach monument in Leipzig on April 23, 1843. See K. Geiringer, *Music of the Bach Family: An Anthology* (Cambridge, Mass., 1955).

Bach (real name, **Bak**), **Albert,** Hungarian singer; b. Gyula, March 24, 1844; d. Edinburgh, Nov. 19, 1912. He studied at the Vienna Cons.; gave his 1st concert there in 1871; continued his studies in Italy. He sang opera in Italy, Russia, Germany, and England. In his recitals he always performed Loewe's songs. He was a member of the Loewe-Verein in Berlin and ed. 3 vols. of Loewe's ballades with Eng. trs.; also publ. several papers on music.

Bach, August Wilhelm, German organist; b. Berlin, Oct. 4, 1796; d. there, April 15, 1869. After a period of organ playing in churches and in concert, he became a teacher at and later director (1832) of the Royal Inst. for Church Music in Berlin. Mendelssohn was his pupil in organ playing.

Bach, Jan (Morris), American composer; b. Forrest, Ill., Dec. 11, 1937. He studied composition at the Univ. of Illinois (B.Mus., 1959; D.M.A., 1971); also took courses with Copland and Musgrave. In 1966 he was appointed to the faculty at Northern Illinois Univ. in De Kalb.

WORKS: OPERAS: *The System* (1973; N.Y., March 5, 1974); *The Student from Salamanca* (1979; N.Y., Oct. 9, 1980). ORCH.: *Toccata* (1959); *Burgundy Variations* (1968); Piano Concerto (1975; Chicago, July 8, 1981); *The Happy Prince* for Narrator, Violin, and Orch. (1978; Omaha, March 18, 1980); *Sprint* (1982; Greenwich, Conn., March 26, 1983); Horn Concerto

(Chicago, June 4, 1983); *Dompes and Jompes* for String Orch. (London, April 17, 1986); Harp Concerto (1986; Indianapolis, Feb. 6, 1987). **BAND OR WIND**: *The Eve of St. Agnes* for Wind Ensemble (1976); *Praetorius Suite* (1977). **CHAMBER**: String Trio (1956); Quartet for Strings (1957); Quintet for Oboe and Strings (1958); *Partita* for Flute, Harpsichord, and Cello (1958); *4 2-Bit Contraptions* for Flute and Horn (1964); *Skizzen* for Woodwind Quintet (1967); *Turkish Music* for Multi-percussion Solo (1967); *Eisteddfod* for Flute, Viola, and Harp (1972); *Concert Variations* for Euphonium and Piano (1977); *Lowlands* for Contrabass and Piano (1981); *Gypsy Rock* for String Quartet (1984); *Lazy Blues* for 5 Bassoons (1985). **VOCAL**: *My Wilderness* (1974); *Hair Today* (1977); *Laudate Dominum* for Chorus, Children's Chorus, and Organ (1981); *A Solemn Music* (1987); songs.

Bach, Leonhard Emil, German pianist and composer; b. Posen, March 11, 1849; d. London, Feb. 15, 1902. He studied with T. Kullak (piano) and with Kiel (theory); in 1869 became a teacher at Kullak's Academy in Berlin. He settled in London; from 1882 taught at the Guildhall School of Music. He wrote several short operas: *Irmengard* (London, 1892); *The Lady of Longford* (London, 1894); *Des Königs Garde* (Cologne, 1895). These were fairly successful at their 1st productions.

Bacharach, Burt, American composer of popular songs; b. Kansas City, May 12, 1928. He was raised in a cultural atmosphere (his father was a newspaper columnist). He played jazz piano in nightclubs; then studied music seriously at McGill Univ. in Montreal; also attended courses of Darius Milhaud and Henry Cowell at the New School for Social Research in N.Y. From 1958 to 1961 he traveled with Marlene Dietrich as her accompanist. In 1962 he joined forces with the lyricist Hal David with felicitous results; together they produced such fine songs as *Reach Out for Me, Trains and Boats and Planes, Make It Easy on Yourself, Blue on Blue, Walk on By, Always Something There to Remind Me, What the World Needs Now Is Love, Do You Know the Way to San Jose?, Raindrops Keep Fallin' on My Head, The Look of Love, I'll Never Fall in Love Again, Our Little Secret, She Likes Baseball.* He wrote the title songs for the films *What's New Pussycat?, Wives and Lovers, Alfie, Send Me No Flowers, Promise Her Anything,* and *Butch Cassidy and the Sundance Kid.* With Hal David again as his lyricist, he produced the highly successful Broadway musical *Promises, Promises* (1968).

Bachauer, Gina, eminent Greek pianist; b. Athens, May 21, 1913; d. there, Aug. 22, 1976. Her father was of Austrian descent; her mother, Italian. She showed her aptitude as a pianist at the age of 5; entered the Athens Cons., where her teacher was Waldemar Freeman. She then went to Paris, where she took lessons with Alfred Cortot at the École Normale de Musique. In 1933 she won the Medal of Honor at the International Contest for Pianists in Vienna; between 1933 and 1935 she received occasional instructions from Rachmaninoff in France and Switzerland; in 1935 she made her professional debut with the Athens Sym. Orch. under the direction of Mitropoulos; she was also piano soloist in Paris in 1937 with Monteux. During World War II she lived in Alexandria, Egypt, and played several hundred concerts for the Allied Forces in the Middle East. On Jan. 21, 1946, she made her London debut with the New London Orch. under the direction of Alec Sherman, who became her 2nd husband. Her 1st American appearance took place in N.Y. on Oct. 15, 1950. Only 35 people attended this concert, but she received unanimous acclaim from the critics, and her career was assured. The uncommon vigor of her technique suggested comparisons with Teresa Carreño; her repertoire ranged from Mozart to Stravinsky; in both classical and modern works she displayed impeccable taste. She died suddenly of a heart attack in Athens on the day she was to appear as soloist with the National Sym. Orch. of Washington at the Athens Festival.

Bache, Constance, English writer and musician; b. Birmingham, March 11, 1846; d. Montreux, Switzerland, June 28, 1903. She was the sister of the English pianists **Francis Edward Bache** (1833–58) and **Walter Bache** (1842–88). She studied at the Munich Cons. and later with Klindworth; planned a piano career, but was forced to abandon it owing to an accident to her hand. In 1883 she settled in London. She publ. a vivid book of memoirs, *Brother Musicians* (London, 1901), describing the lives of her brothers; tr. the letters of Hans von Bülow and Franz Liszt, and Heintz's analyses of Wagner's operas; also tr. the libretto of Humperdinck's *Hänsel und Gretel*.

Bachelet, Alfred, French composer; b. Paris, Feb. 26, 1864; d. Nancy, Feb. 10, 1944. He studied at the Paris Cons.; received the Grand Prix de Rome for his cantata, *Cléopâtre* (1890). From his earliest works, Bachelet devoted himself mainly to opera. In his youth, he was influenced by Wagnerian ideas, but later adopted a more national French style. During World War I he conducted at the Paris Opéra; in 1919 became director of the Nancy Cons.; in 1939 was elected a member of the Académie des Beaux Arts.

WORKS: Lyric dramas: *Scémo* (Paris Opéra, May 6, 1914) and *Un Jardin sur l'Oronte* (Paris Opéra, Nov. 3, 1932); *Quand la cloche sonnera*, 1-act music drama, his most successful work (Opéra-Comique, Nov. 6, 1922); ballets: *La Fête chez la Pouplinière* and *Castor et Pollux* by Rameau (adapted and rewritten); orch. works with voices: *L'Amour des Ondines, Joie, Le Songe de la Sulamith, Noël; Surya* for Tenor, Chorus, and Orch. (1940); *Ballade* for Violin and Orch.; songs.

Bachmann, Alberto Abraham, violinist and composer; b. Geneva, March 20, 1875; d. Neuilly-sur-Seine, Nov. 24, 1963. He studied violin at the Cons. of Lille, then took courses in succession with Ysaÿe, César, Thomson, Hubay, and Adolf Brodsky. He was in the U.S. from 1916 to 1926; then lived near Paris. He composed 3 violin concertos (the last of which is called *American Concerto*); 12 improvisations for solo violin; about 250 various pieces and as many transcriptions for violin. He publ. *Le Violon* (1906); *Les Grands Violonistes du passé* (1913); *Gymnastique à l'usage des violonistes* (1914); *L'École du violoniste* (in 4 parts); and *Encyclopedia of the Violin* (N.Y., 1925).

Bachofen, Johann Caspar, Swiss composer; b. Zürich, Dec. 26, 1695; d. there, June 23, 1755. He studied in Zürich at the Cathedral school; received the title of V.D.M. (verbi divini minister) in 1720; in 1742 was named cantor at the Grossmünster Cathedral there; concurrently served as Kapellmeister at the German School there (from 1739). He is best known for his popular collection of sacred songs for home use, publ. as *Musicalisches Hallelujah* (1727; many subsequent reprints).

BIBL.: B. Arnold, *The Life and Works of J.C. B.* (diss., Univ. of Southern Calif., 1956).

Bachrich, Sigmund (real name, **Sigismund**), Hungarian violist and composer; b. Zsambokreth, Jan. 23, 1841; d. Vienna, July 16, 1913. He studied violin in Vienna; spent several years in Paris, where he was viola player with the Hellmesberger and Rosé quartets. From 1869 to 1899 he was a member of the viola section in the Vienna Phil. He wrote several operas, among them *Muzzedin* (1883), *Heini von Steier* (1884), and *Der Fuchs-Major* (1889), as well as a ballet, *Sakuntala.* His memoirs were publ. posthumously under the title *Aus verklungenen Zeiten* (Vienna, 1914). In his professional activities he adopted Sigmund as his 1st name.

Bacilly, Bénigne de, French composer and teacher; b. c.1625; d. Paris, Sept. 27, 1690. He composed a number of sacred and secular vocal works; however, he is best known for an important vocal treatise, *Remarques curieuses sur l'art de bien chanter* (Paris, 1668; Eng. ed., 1968).

Bäck, Sven-Erik, significant Swedish composer; b. Stockholm, Sept. 16, 1919. He studied violin at the Stockholm Musikhögskolan (1938–43); composition with Hilding Rosenberg (1940–45); then went to Switzerland and took courses in medieval music at the Schola Cantorum in Basel (1948–50); later studied advanced composition with Petrassi in Rome (1951).

Returning to Sweden, he played violin and also viola in 2 local string quartets and conducted the "Chamber Orch. 1953" until 1957. In 1959 he was appointed director of the Swedish Radio music school at Edsberg Castle outside Stockholm. As a composer, he at 1st embraced the Scandinavian Romantic manner, but soon began experimentation in serial procedures, later annexing electronic sound. His 1st important work which attracted merited praise was the radio opera *Tranfjädrarna* (The Crane Feathers), a symbolist subject from Japanese Noh drama (1956; Swedish Radio, Feb. 28, 1957; 1st stage perf., Stockholm, Feb. 19, 1958). His other works include a scenic oratorio, *Ett spel om Maria, Jesu Moder* (A Play about Mary, Mother of Jesus; Swedish Radio, April 4, 1958); a chamber opera, *Gästabudet* (The Feast; Stockholm, Nov. 12, 1958); a radio opera, *Fågeln* (The Birds; Swedish Radio, Feb. 14, 1961; later versions for stage and commercial recording, 1969); a ballet, *Ikaros* (Stockholm, May 1963); a television ballet, *Movements* (Swedish Television, Feb. 27, 1966); a ballet, *Kattresan* (Cat's Journey; 1969; original version was a "concerto per bambini" for Children's Chorus, 2 Recorders, Violin, and Percussion, 1952); 2 electronic ballets, *Mur och port* (Wall and Gate; Stockholm, Jan. 17, 1971) and *Genom Jorden genom havet* (Through the Earth, Through the Sea; 1971; Stockholm, June 17, 1972); also, 4 string quartets (1945, 1947, 1962, 1984); string quintet, *Exercises* (1948); Solo Flute Sonata (1949); *Expansive Preludes* for Piano (1949); *Sonata alla ricercare* for Piano (1950); *Sinfonia per archi* (1951); *Sinfonia Sacra* for Chorus and Orch. (1953); Trio for Viola, Cello, and Double Bass (1953); *Sinfonia da camera* (1954); Sonata for 2 Cellos (1957); Violin Concerto (1957); *Impromptu* for Piano (1957); *A Game around a Game* for Strings and Percussion (Donaueschingen, Oct. 17, 1959); *Arkitektur* for 2 Wind Orchs. and Percussion (1960); *Favola* for Clarinet and Percussion (1962); *Intrada* for Orch. (Stockholm, April 26, 1964); Cello Concerto (1965); *O Altitudo I* for Organ (1966; orch. version, *O Altitudo II*, 1966); *5 Preludes* for Clarinet and Percussion (1966); *Humlan* for Chorus, Cello, Piano, and Percussion (1968); *. . . in principio . . .* for Tape (1969); String Trio (1970); *For Eliza* for Organ or Tape ad lib. (1971); *Aperio* for 3 Orch. Groups, each including Electronic Sound (1973); *Decet* for Wind Quintet, String Quartet, and Double Bass (1973); *Där fanns en brunn* for Chorus, Flute, Clarinet, Cello, Percussion, and Piano or Organ (1973); *Just da de langsta skuggorna . . .* for 4 Singers and 10 Instruments (1974); *Tollo I* for Piano Duet (1974) and *II* for 2 Pianos and Microphones (1975); *Time Present* for 2 Violins, Echo Filter, and Feedback Systems (1975); *Sumerki*, serenade for String Orch. (1976–77); *Ciclos*, concerto for Orch. (1977); *Ekvator*, ballad for Orch. and Tape (1988); String Octet (1988); *Pro Musica Vitae*, concerto for Strings (1989); many motets and religious cantatas; short electronic pieces.

Backer-Grøndahl, Agathe (Ursula), Norwegian composer and pianist; b. Holmestrand, Dec. 1, 1847; d. Ormöen, near Christiania, June 16, 1907. She studied in Norway with Kjerulf and Lindeman, in Florence with Hans von Bülow, and in Weimar with Liszt; married the singing teacher Grøndahl (1875). Among her piano works, *Études de concert, Romantische Stücke,* and *Trois morceaux* became well known and have been frequently reprinted. She also wrote a song cycle, *Des Kindes Frühlingstag.*
BIBL.: I. Hoegsbro, *Biography of the Late A. B.-G.* (N.Y., 1913); O. Sandvik, *A. B.-G.* (Oslo, 1948).

Backers, Cor, Dutch music historian and composer; b. Rotterdam, June 5, 1910. He studied piano with Dirk Schäfer and composition at the Rotterdam Cons. He gave piano recitals in the Netherlands; also traveled through Europe and East Africa; conducted the chamber choir Haags Kamerkoor (1950–60), specializing in the forgotten masterpieces of the past. He publ. a valuable compendium, *Nederlandse componisten van 1400 tot op onze tijd* (The Hague, 1941; 2nd enl. ed., 1948), which details the evolution of music in the Netherlands, with particular emphasis on modern Dutch music; he

also publ. monographs on Handel, Puccini, Gershwin, and others. He composes mostly for voices and organ; among his works are a "declamatorio," *Joost de Decker,* for Narrator and Piano; Piano Sonata (1935); *6 Goethe-Lieder* for Chorus a cappella (1969); *Missa Sancta* for Soloists, Chorus, and Organ (1973–74); *Te Deum Laudamus* for Chorus, and Organ or Orch. (1973–75).

Backhaus, Wilhelm, eminent German-born Swiss pianist and pedagogue; b. Leipzig, March 26, 1884; d. Villach, Austria, July 5, 1969. He studied with Reckendorf in Leipzig (1891–99); made his debut there at the age of 8. After studying briefly with Eugène d'Albert in Frankfurt (1899), he began his career with a major tour in 1900; soon acquired a fine reputation in Europe as both a pianist and a teacher. He made his U.S. debut on Jan. 5, 1912, as soloist in Beethoven's 5th Piano Concerto with Walter Damrosch and the N.Y. Sym. Orch. In 1930 he settled in Lugano, where he continued to teach, and became a Swiss citizen. Following World War II, he resumed his concert tours; made his last appearance in the U.S. at a recital in N.Y. in 1962, at the age of 78, displaying undiminished vigor as a virtuoso. He died while visiting Austria for a concert engagement. He was particularly distinguished in his interpretations of the works of Beethoven and Brahms.
BIBL.: F. Herzog, *W. B.* (Berlin, 1935); A.H. Eichmann, *W. B.* (Ghent, 1957; Eng. tr., 1958).

Bacon, Ernst, remarkable American composer; b. Chicago, May 26, 1898; d. Orinda, Calif., March 16, 1990. He studied music theory at Northwestern Univ. with P.C. Lutkin (1915–18), and later at the Univ. of Chicago with Arne Oldberg and T. Otterstroem (1919–20); also took private piano lessons in Chicago with Alexander Raab (1916–21). In 1924 he went to Vienna, where he took private composition lessons with Karl Weigl and Franz Schmidt. Returning to America, he studied composition with Ernest Bloch in San Francisco, and conducting with Eugene Goossens in Rochester, N.Y.; completed his education at the Univ. of Calif. (M.A., 1935). From 1934 to 1937 he was supervisor of the Federal Music Project in San Francisco; simultaneously deployed numerous related activities, as a conductor and a music critic. He was on the faculty of Converse College in South Carolina (1938–45) and Syracuse Univ. (1945–63). In 1939 and 1942 he held Guggenheim fellowships. He also engaged in literary pursuits—wrote poetry and publ. a book of aphorisms—and espoused radical politics. A musician of exceptional inventive powers, he publ. a brochure, *Our Musical Idiom* (Chicago, 1917), when he was 19; in it he outlines the new resources of musical composition. He later publ. *Words on Music* (1960) and *Notes on the Piano* (1963). In some of his piano works he evolved a beguiling technique of mirror reflection between the right and the left hand, exact as to the intervals, with white and black keys in 1 hand reflected respectively by white and black keys in the other hand. However, Bacon is generally regarded as primarily a composer of lyric songs. In 1963 he went to California and lived in Orinda, near San Francisco.
WORKS: 4 syms.: No. 1 for Piano and Orch. (1932); No. 2 (1937; Chicago, Feb. 5, 1940); No. 3, *Great River,* for Narrator and Orch. (1956); No. 4 (1963); a musical play, *A Tree on the Plains* (Spartanburg, S.C., May 2, 1942); a folk opera, *A Drumlin Legend* (N.Y., May 4, 1949); *By Blue Ontario,* oratorio to words by Walt Whitman (1958); *The Last Invocation,* a Requiem, to poems by Walt Whitman, Emily Dickinson, and others (1968–71); *Nature,* a cantata cycle (1968); ballets: *Jehovah and the Ark* (1968–70) and *The Parliament of Fowls* (1975); songs to words by Emily Dickinson and Walt Whitman: *From Emily's Diary* for Soprano, Alto, Women's Chorus, and Orch. (1945); *The Lord Star,* cantata (1950); *Songs of Eternity* (1932); *Black and White Songs* for Baritone and Orch. (1932); *Twilight,* 3 songs for Voice and Orch. (1932); *Midnight Special,* 4 songs for Voice and Orch. (1932); Piano Quintet (1946); Cello Sonata (1946); String Quintet (1951); *Riolama* for Piano and Orch., in 10 short movements (1964); *Spirits and Places,* a cycle

with geographical connotations for Organ (1966); *Saws*, a suite of canons for Chorus and Piano (1971); *Dr. Franklin*, music play for the bicentennial (1976), to text by Cornel Lengyel. Among Bacon's publ. books are *Words on Music* (1960) and *Notes on the Piano* (1963). A collection of his songs, *Grass Roots* for Soprano, Alto, and Piano, was publ. in 2 vols. in 1976.

Bacon, Richard Mackenzie, English writer on music; b. Norwich, May 1, 1776; d. Cossey, Nov. 27, 1844. He publ. *Elements of Vocal Science* (London, 1824) and *Art of Improving the Voice and Ear* (London, 1825); was the founder and ed. of the *Quarterly Musical Magazine and Review* (1818–30), the 1st music periodical in England. He was also instrumental in organizing the triennial Music Festivals at Norwich.

Bacquier, Gabriel (-Augustin-Raymond-Théodore-Louis), noted French baritone; b. Béziers, May 17, 1924. He studied at the Paris Cons. His 1st notable success came in 1953, when he sang the role of Figaro in Rossini's *The Barber of Seville* in Brussels. On Oct. 17, 1964, he made his appearance at the Metropolitan Opera House in N.Y. In 1975 he was made a Chevalier of the Légion d'honneur. A fine singing artist, he was especially notable in dramatic roles.

Badarzewska, Thekla, Polish composer of salon music; b. Warsaw, 1834; d. there, Sept. 29, 1861. At the age of 17 she publ. in Warsaw a piano piece, *Molitwa dziewicy* (A Maiden's Prayer), which was republ. as a supplement to the Paris *Revue et Gazette Musicale* in 1859, and unaccountably seized the imagination not only of inhibited virgins, but of sentimental amateur pianists all over the world. More than 100 eds. of this unique piece of salon pianism, dripping maudlin arpeggios, were publ. in the 19th century, and the thing was still widely sold even in the 20th century. Badarzewska wrote 34 more piano pieces in the salon style, but none of them matched *A Maiden's Prayer*. An ungentlemanly German critic opined in an obituary that "Badarzewska's early death saved the musical world from a veritable inundation of intolerable lachrymosity."

Badea, Christian, Rumanian-born American conductor; b. Bucharest, Dec. 10, 1947. He studied violin and composition at the Bucharest Cons.; subsequently took courses in Brussels, in Salzburg, and at the Juilliard School of Music in N.Y. He conducted at the Spoleto Festival of Two Worlds in Charleston, S.C., and Spoleto, Italy; also served as music director of the Savannah (Ga.) Sym. Orch. and the Columbus (Ohio) Sym. Orch. (from 1983).

Baden, Conrad, Norwegian composer, organist, teacher, and music critic; b. Drammen, Aug. 31, 1908; d. June 12, 1989. After studies in his hometown, he took advanced training in Leipzig (1931–32) and later in Paris with Honegger and Rivier (1951–52). He was organist in Drammen from 1943 and in Oslo from 1961; also taught at the Oslo Cons. (1948–73). His style of composition moved from neo-Romanticism to basically modern.

WORKS: Mass for Soloists, Chorus, and Orch. (1949); Divertimento for Orch. (1950); *Overtura Gioia* (1951); 6 syms. (1952, 1957, 1959, 1970, 1976, 1980); Concertino for Clarinet and Strings (1953); *Pastorale and Fugue* for Chamber Orch. (1957); 3 anniversary cantatas: for the city of Skien's 600th (1958), for Strömsö Church's 300th (1966–67), and for Dröbak Church's 200th (1973); *Eventyr-Suite* (Fairy-tale Suite) for Orch. (1960); *Fantasia Brevis* for Orch. (1965); Concerto for Orchestra (1968); *Intrada Sinfonica* for Orch. (1969); *Mennesket* (The Human Being), cantata for Chorus and Orch. (1971); Violin Sonata (c.1942); 3 string quartets (1944, 1946, 1961); 2 trios for Flute, Oboe, and Clarinet (1957, 1964); Sonata for Solo Flute (1958); Divertimento for Flute, Oboe, and Clarinet (1964); *Hymnus* for Alto Voice, Flute, Oboe, and Viola (1966); Wind Quintet; Piano Trio; piano pieces; *Sonata Sacra* for Organ (1974); choral works.

BIBL.: H. Herresthal, "Kirckemusikeren og komponisten C. B.," *Norsk musiktidsskrift* (1971/72).

Badescu, Dinu (Constantin), Rumanian tenor; b. Craiova, Oct. 17, 1904. He studied in Bucharest; made his debut as a baritone in 1931 in Cluj; later began singing tenor roles. He was a leading member of the Bucharest Opera (1936–61); also sang at the Vienna Volksoper (1941–44) and made appearances at the Vienna State Opera (from 1948); was highly successful as a guest artist with the Bolshoi Theater in Moscow, in Leningrad, Budapest, Prague, etc. He made a specialty of lyrico-dramatic roles in Verdi's operas.

Badia, Carlo Agostino, Italian composer; b. probably in Venice, 1672; d. Vienna, Sept. 23, 1738. His 1st known work was his oratorio *La sete di Cristo in croce* (Innsbruck, 1691); soon thereafter he was made a court composer at Innsbruck. In 1694 he was called to Vienna, where he became Musik-Compositeur of the Imperial Court; he held that post for the rest of his life. His 1st wife was **Anna Maria Elisabetta Nonetti,** a prominent singer at the Viennese court (d. 1726). Badia was an important composer in his day, producing some 25 works for the stage, about 40 oratorios, and over 50 chamber cantatas and duets.

WORKS: STAGE: *La Ninfa Apollo* (1692); *Amor che vince lo sdegno, ovvero Olimpia placata* (Rome, Carnival 1692); *La Rosaura ovvero Amore figlio della gratitudine* (Innsbruck, 1692); *L'Amazone corsara, ovvero L'Alvilda, regina de' Goti* (Innsbruck, 1692); *Bacco, vincitore dell'India* (Vienna, Carnival 1697); *La pace tra i numi discordi nella rovina di Troia* (Vienna, May 21, 1697); *L'idea del felice governo* (Vienna, June 9, 1698); *Lo squittinio dell'eroe* (Vienna, July 26, 1698); *Imeneo trionfante* (Vienna, Feb. 28, 1699); *Il Narciso* (Vienna, June 9, 1699); *Il commun giubilo del mondo* (Vienna, July 26, 1699); *Cupido fuggitivo da Venere e ritrovato a' piedi della Sacra Reale Maestà d'Amalia* (Vienna, Carnival 1700); *Le gare dei beni* (Vienna, Feb. 21, 1700); *Diana rappacificata con Venere e con Amore* (Vienna, April 21, 1700); *La costanza d'Ulisse* (Vienna, June 9, 1700); *L'amore vuol somiglianza* (Vienna, Jan. 7, 1702); *L'Arianna* (Vienna, Feb. 21, 1702); *Il Telemacco, ovvero Il valore coronato* (Vienna, March 19, 1702); *La concordia della Virtù e della Fortuna* (Vienna, April 21, 1702); *Enea negli Elisi* (Vienna, July 26, 1702); *La Psiche* (Vienna, Feb. 21, 1703); *Napoli ritornata ai Romani* (Vienna, Oct. 1, 1707); *Ercole, vincitore di Gerione* (Vienna, Nov. 4, 1708); *Gli amori di Circe con Ulisse* (Dresden, June 20, 1709); *Il bel genio dell'Austria ed il Fato* (Vienna, Nov. 1723).

BIBL.: C. Nemeth, "Zur Lebensgeschichte von C.A. B. (1672–1738)," *Anzeiger der phil.-hist. Klasse der Österreichischen Akademie der Wissenschaften* (1955).

Badia, Conchita (Conxita), noted Spanish soprano; b. Barcelona, Nov. 14, 1897; d. there, May 2, 1975. She studied piano and voice with Granados; also had lessons with Casals and Manuel de Falla. She made her debut in Barcelona as a concert singer in 1913 in the 1st performance of *Canciónes amatorias* by Granados, with the composer as piano accompanist. She subsequently devoted herself to concert appearances, excelling as an interpreter of Spanish and Latin American music; often appeared in performances with Casals and his orch. in Barcelona. In later years she taught voice in Barcelona, where her most famous pupil was Montserrat Caballé.

BIBL.: J. Alavedra, *Conxita B.: Una vida d'artista* (Barcelona, 1975).

Badings, Henk, prominent Dutch composer; b. Bandung, Indonesia (of Dutch parents), Jan. 17, 1907; d. Maarheeze, June 26, 1987. He was orphaned at an early age and taken to the Netherlands, where he became a mining engineer while pursuing composition as an avocation. His Sym. was performed in Amsterdam on July 6, 1930; he then began taking instruction in composition with Willem Pijper. During the German occupation of the Netherlands he taught music at the Royal Cons. of The Hague, and after the end of the war he was accused of collaboration. He was able to exonerate himself, however, and resumed his work as a composer and teacher. His mature style of composition may be described as Romantic Modernism marked by intense dynamic quality. In his melodic foundation he often employed the scale of alternating major and minor seconds, a progression also favored by his teacher Pijper. After

1950, he began experimenting with electronic sound and also adapted some of his works to the scale of 31 melodic divisions orig. devised by the Dutch physicist Adriaan Fokker. In time he became extremely prolific. Among his major compositions were several operas: *De nachtwacht* (1942; Antwerp, May 13, 1950); *Liefde's listen* (1944–45; Hilversum, Jan. 6, 1948); a radio opera, *Orestes* (Florence, Sept. 24, 1954); a radio opera, *Asterion* (Johannesburg, South Africa, April 11, 1958); *Salto mortale*, chamber opera for television (Netherlands Television, Eindhoven, June 19, 1959; 1st opera to be accompanied exclusively by electronic sound); and *Martin Korda, D.P.* (Amsterdam, June 15, 1960). He also wrote several ballets, including one for electronic sound, *Kain* (The Hague, June 21, 1956); *Evolutionen* (Hannover, Sept. 28, 1958); and *Genèse* for 5 Studio-frequency Oscillators in quadraphonic sound placement (Brussels, Oct. 7, 1958). Furthermore, he wrote oratorios, among them *Apocalypse* (1948; Rotterdam, Nov. 25, 1959) and *Jonah* (Adelaide, Australia, Sept. 30, 1963); *St. Mark's Passion* for 4 Voices and Electronic Tape (Rotterdam, May 18, 1972); 14 syms., widely performed; 4 violin concertos; 2 cello concertos; 6 overtures; 2 piano concertos; a Saxophone Concerto; 2 organ concertos; 2 concertos for 2 Violins tuned in the 31-tone temperament; 2 flute concertos; numerous other orch. works with soloists; a considerable amount of chamber music; 6 piano sonatas; a lot of piano pieces and compositions for electronic tape. Badings was the author of a book on contemporary Dutch music, publ. in Amsterdam in 1936, and a treatise on electronic music (Amsterdam, 1958). A complete catalog of his works, publ. in German and in Eng., was issued in 1965, with a supplement following in 1970. Badings was surely an exceptional phenomenon in modern music, considering the fact that he began his musical study after engaging in engineering; his productivity was almost unparalleled among modern composers, and he was greatly renowned during his lifetime. However, his music, quaquaversal as it was, lacked the quality of permanence, so that despite the numerous publications of his work, it failed to earn universal recognition. After his death his works lapsed into innocuous desuetude. **BIBL.:** J. Wouters, "H. B.," *Sonorum Speculum*, 32 (1967); R. de Beer, "An odour of taboo: H. B., 1907–1987," *Key Notes*, 24 (1987).

Badini, Ernesto, Italian baritone; b. San Colombano al Lambro, Sept. 14, 1876; d. Milan, July 6, 1937. He studied at the Milan Cons.; made his debut in 1895; sang in many of the regional opera houses of Italy. In 1913 Toscanini chose him for the Verdi centennial celebrations in Parma; then invited him to La Scala in Milan; Badini remained on its roster until 1931. In addition to buffo roles, Badini also sang in a number of contemporary operas.

Badinski, Nicolai, Bulgarian-born German violinist, teacher, and composer; b. Sofia, Dec. 19, 1937. From 1963 to 1976 he lived in East Berlin; then moved to West Berlin, obtaining his German citizenship in 1980. After study at the Sofia Academy of Music, he took courses at the Accademia Musicale in Siena; in Germany worked with Ligeti, Stockhausen, Xenakis, and Kagel at the Darmstadt International Courses for New Music. Besides composition, he was active as a concert violinist. In his music he follows practical modernistic trends, avoiding extreme applications of experimental techniques. **WORKS:** 3 syms. (1967, 1978, 1981); 3 violin concertos (1971, 1972, 1972); Viola Concerto (1975); Harpsichord Concerto (1977); *Homage to Stravinsky* for String Orch. (1979); *Klavieriada* for Piano and Orch. (1981); *The Ruins under Sofia,* octet (1972); *Silenzio disturbato* for Sextet (1976); 3 string quartets (1965, 1973, 1978); Wind Quintet (1969); *Imaginable Trio* for Computer (1980); numerous pieces of electronic music: *Rotation,* in memory of a Soviet cosmonaut, for Electronic Sound (1974); *Musik mit Papier* and *Luftmusik* for Electronics (1980–81); *Traumvisionen* for Electronic Sound (1982).

Badura-Skoda (real name, **Badura**), **Paul,** eminent Austrian pianist, music editor, and pedagogue; b. Vienna, Oct. 6, 1927. He was brought up by his stepfather, Skoda, whose name he

adopted professionally. He studied science as well as music; graduated from the Vienna Cons. in 1948 as a piano pupil of Edwin Fischer. A scholarly musician, he won several prizes for excellence. He had a successful career as a concert pianist; gave recitals in Europe; made his N.Y. debut on Jan. 10, 1953. From 1966 until 1971 he was artist-in-residence at the Univ. of Wisconsin. On Sept. 19, 1951, he married Eva Halfar (b. Munich, Jan. 15, 1929), who collaborated with him on his various eds. He publ. *Mozart-Interpretation* (with his wife; Vienna, 1957; in Eng. as *Interpreting Mozart on the Keyboard,* N.Y., 1962; also in Japanese, Tokyo, 1963) and *Die Klaviersonaten von Ludwig van Beethoven* (with J. Demus, Wiesbaden, 1970); also contributed valuable articles on Chopin, Schubert, and others to German music journals.

Baervoets, Raymond, Belgian composer; b. Brussels, Nov. 6, 1930; d. Rome, Aug. 19, 1989. He studied composition at the Brussels Cons., and later took a course with Petrassi in Rome. Virtually all of his compositions followed the classical form, while the contents evolved in an ultra-chromatic coloristic idiom with occasional use of quarter-tones. **WORKS:** 2 ballets, *Métamorphose* (1963) and *La Chasse fantastique* (Antwerp, Sept. 28, 1968); Guitar Concerto (1958); Violin Concerto (1961); *Constellations* for Orch. (1966); *Erosions I* and *Erosions II* for Alto and 6 Performers and for Female Chorus and Orch. (both 1965); *Les Dents de la terre* for Narrator, Soloists, Chorus, and 2 Orchs. (1968); a variety of pieces for instrumental combinations; miscellaneous compositions for piano solo.

Baeyens, August, Belgian composer; b. Antwerp, June 5, 1895; d. there, July 17, 1966. He studied at the Royal Flemish Cons. in Antwerp; beginning in 1911, he was a viola player in Belgian orchs. In 1932 he became secretary of the Royal Flemish Opera, later serving as director (1944–48 and 1953–58). Despite his intimate association with the Flemish currents in the music of Belgium, he turned away from the dominant national direction and wrote music of a distinctly expressionistic type, rooted in a quasi-atonal chromaticism. **WORKS:** 2 operas, *De Ring van Gyges* (1943) and *De Triomferende Min* (1948); a radio opera, *Coriolanus,* after Shakespeare (1941); a ballet, *De Dode Dichter* (The Dead Poet; 1920); *De Liefde en de Kakatoes* (Love and the Cockatoos), a "grotesque" in 1 act (1928); 8 syms. (1923, 1939, 1949, 1952, 1954, 1955, 1958, 1961); a *Sinfonia Breve* (1928); *Arkadia,* chamber sym. for 19 Soloists (1951); 6 orch. scores: *Entrata* (1917), *Niobé* (1918), *4 Small Pieces* (1923), *Arlequin* (1924), *Cyclops* (1925), *Notturno* (1953); Viola Concerto (1956); Trumpet Concerto (1959); Horn Concerto (1960); *Rhapsodie* for Clarinet and Orch. (1966); *Lofzang aan de haven* (Hymn of Praise for the Port), cantata (1929); *Barabbas* for Narrator and Orch. (1949); 6 string quartets (1922, 1925, 1927, 1949, 1951, 1962); Wind Quintet (1950); Concertino for Oboe, Clarinet, and Bassoon (1951); *Piranesi Suite* for Flute and Cello (1951); Violin Sonata (1952); Piano Sonata (1930); songs.

Baez, Joan (Chandos), politically active American folksinger, guitarist, and songwriter of English, Irish, and Mexican descent; b. Staten Island, N.Y., Jan. 9, 1941. She played the guitar by ear; then studied drama at Boston Univ. She made her 1st impact on American mass consciousness in 1959 when she appeared at the Newport Folk Festival. In 1965 she founded the Inst. for the Study of Non-Violence; joined the struggle against the Vietnam War and supported the organizing fight of the United Farm Workers' Union. Accompanying herself on the guitar, she appeared at numerous concerts promoting topical humanitarian causes. She publ. the autobiographical books *Daybreak* (N.Y., 1968) and *And a Voice to Sing With: A Memoir* (N.Y., 1987).

Bagge, Selmar, German composer and pedagogue; b. Coburg, June 30, 1823; d. Basel, July 16, 1896. He studied in Vienna; from 1851 to 1855 was on the faculty of the Vienna Cons.; then went to Germany, and became the ed. of the *Allgemeine Musikzeitung* in Leipzig (1863–68). In 1868 he was appointed director of the Basel Music School, retaining this post until his death. He composed 4 syms., piano pieces, and other works; he publ. *Lehrbuch der Tonkunst* (1873), *Die geschichtliche Entwickelung der Sonate* (1880), *Die Symphonie in ihrer historischen Entwickelung* (1884). A biographical sketch of Bagge was publ. by Eglinger (Basel, 1897).

Baggiani, Guido, Italian composer; b. Naples, March 4, 1932. He studied composition at the Accademia di Santa Cecilia in Rome; then attended courses given by Stockhausen in Cologne, which were crucial for his further development. In Rome he organized a group for propagandizing contemporary music with the meaningful name of Nuova Consonanza. In 1970 he was appointed prof. of composition at the Cons. of Pesaro. In 1972 he formed a group with the curious Italian-American name Gruppo Team Roma for performances of electronic music. His principal works are *Mimesi* for Strings and Woodwinds (1967); *Metafora* for Solo Strings (1968); *UBU-ng* for Soprano, Piano, Vibraphone, Electric Guitar, and 6 Chinese Gongs (of indeterminate duration; 1970); *Twins* for Piano and Magnetic Tape (1971); *Memoria* for Chamber Orch. and 2 Magnetic Tapes (1972); *Accordo Presunto* for 2 Instrumental Groups and Electronic Media (1973); *ContriAzione* for 2 Orchs. (1975); *Double* for Chamber Ensemble (1977); *Il crudo e il cotto* for 4 Female Voices, 2 Flutes, 2 Clarinets, and Electronic Media (1982).

Bahner, Gert, German conductor; b. Neuwiese, March 26, 1930. He was educated at the Leipzig Hochschule für Musik. In 1957 he made his debut at the Berlin Komische Oper; from 1958 to 1962 he was music director in Potsdam; then Generalmusikdirektor of Karl-Marx-Stadt (1962–65). In 1965 he became 1st conductor of the Berlin Komische Oper; in 1969 its music director. In 1973 he became music director of the Leipzig Opera. In 1983 he settled in (East) Berlin as an opera conductor; also taught at the Hochschule für Musik.

Bähr, (Franz) Josef, noted Austrian clarinetist; b. Feb. 19, 1770; d. Vienna, Aug. 7, 1819. He was in the service of Prince Kraft Ernst of Oettingen-Wallerstein (1787–94); he settled in Vienna in 1797, and then became a court musician in the service of Count Johann Joseph Liechtenstein. Beethoven was impressed by his talent, and during the period 1796–1802 wrote his major solo clarinet parts with Bähr in mind.

Bibl.: P. Weston, *Clarinet Virtuosi of the Past* (London, 1971).

Bai (also **Baj**), **Tommaso,** Italian singer and composer; b. Crevalcuore, near Bologna, c.1650; d. Rome, Dec. 22, 1714. He was a tenor at the Vatican, where he became maestro di cappella on Nov. 19, 1713. The best-known composition by Bai, follower of Palestrina, is a 5-part *Miserere* sung during Holy Week in the Papal Chapel alternately with those by Allegri and Baini. It is reprinted in various collections (Choron, Burney, Peters); other works of Bai are included in C. Proske's *Musica Divina* (1853–63).

Baïf, Jean-Antoine de, French poet; b. Venice, Feb. 19, 1532; d. Paris, Sept. 19, 1589. He was taken to Paris as a child, and formed a friendship with Ronsard and other eminent poets. In 1570, with the musician Joachim Thibault de Courville, he founded the Académie de Poésie et de Musique, which met in Baïf's home (1571–74); it pursued the aim of reviving the music and poetry of ancient Greece. He developed a system of "musique mesurée," which he believed would possess a moral force similar to the Greek ideas of "ethos." Settings of his early sonnets and chansons were composed by Arcadelt, F. Roussel, and Cereau, and of his chansonnettes mesurées and Psalms by Lassus, Le Jeune, Mauduit, and others.

Bibl.: M. Auge-Chiquet, *La Vie, les idées et l'œuvre de J.-A. d.B.* (Paris, 1909); W. Müller-Blattau, "Chanson, Vaudeville, und Air de cour," *Volks- und Hochkunst in Dichtung und Musik* (Saarbrücken, 1968).

Bailey, "Buster" (William C.) outstanding black American jazz clarinetist; b. Memphis, July 19, 1902; d. N.Y., April 12, 1967. He played in W.C. Handy's orch. in his youth. In 1919 he went to Chicago, where he worked with Erskine Tate and King Oliver. He subsequently settled in N.Y., where he was a member of Fletcher Henderson's band (1924–37), and later worked with John Kirby's sextet (1937–46). In his last years he was a member of the Saints and Sinners Orch. (1961–65) and Louis Armstrong's All Stars (1965–67).

Bailey, Lillian. See **Henschel, Lillian June.**

Bailey, Mildred, American blues singer; b. Tekoa, Wash., Feb. 27, 1907; d. Poughkeepsie, N.Y., Dec. 12, 1951. After appearing on radio programs, she joined Paul Whiteman in 1929, remaining with his orch. until 1933; subsequently appeared with the bands of Red Norvo, Benny Goodman, and others. She married Red Norvo in 1933 and divorced him in 1945.

Bailey, Norman (Stanley), English baritone; b. Birmingham, March 23, 1933. He received a B.Mus. degree from Rhodes Univ. in South Africa; then studied at the Vienna Academy of Music; his principal teachers there were Julius Patzak, Adolf Vogel, and Josef Witt. He made his operatic debut with the Vienna Chamber Opera in 1959; was then a member of the Linz Landestheater (1960–63), the Wuppertal Opera (1963–64), the Deutsche Oper am Rhein in Düsseldorf (1964–67), and the Sadler's Wells Opera Co. in London (1967–71). On Oct. 23, 1976, he made his Metropolitan Opera debut in N.Y. as Hans Sachs. In 1977 he was made a Commander of the Order of the British Empire. He was particularly noted for his performances in Wagner's operas. In 1985 he married **Kristine Ciesinski.**

Bailey, Pearl (Mae), black American singer of popular music; b. Newport News, Va., March 29, 1918; d. Philadelphia, Aug. 17, 1990. After winning an amateur contest in Philadelphia at 15, she quit school to pursue a career as an entertainer; worked as a dancer and a singer in various nightclubs in Washington, D.C., Baltimore, and N.Y. She made her Broadway debut in 1946 in *St. Louis Woman* and subsequently appeared in *Arms and the Girl* (1950), *Bless You All* (1950), and *House of Flowers* (1954); her greatest success came in 1967, when she starred in the all-black version of the hit musical *Hello, Dolly!* She also appeared in films, including *Carmen Jones* (1954), *St. Louis Blues* (1958), and *Porgy and Bess* (1959), and had her own television show (1970–71). She gained fame with her renditions of *Birth of the Blues; Toot Toot Tootsie, Goodbye; Takes 2 to Tango;* and *Row, Row, Row.* She publ. 3 entertaining accounts of her life and career, *The Raw Pearl* (N.Y., 1968), *Talking to Myself* (N.Y., 1971), and *Between You and Me: Loving Reminiscences* (N.Y., 1989).

Baillie, Dame Isobel, esteemed Scottish soprano; b. Hawick, Roxburghshire, March 9, 1895; d. Manchester, Sept. 24, 1983. She was educated in Manchester; then went to Italy and began to take voice lessons in Milan. She made her concert debut in London in 1923, and through the years established herself as a successful singer, particularly in oratorio. It is said that she sang the *Messiah* more than 1,000 times. In 1978 Queen Elizabeth II made her a Dame Commander of the Order of the British Empire. Her autobiography was aptly titled *Never Sing Louder Than Lovely* (London, 1982).

Baillot, Pierre (-Marie-François de Sales), celebrated French violinist; b. Passy, near Paris, Oct. 1, 1771; d. Paris, Sept. 15, 1842. The son of a lawyer, he received an excellent education; at the age of 9 he became a pupil of the French violinist Sainte-Marie; he later was sent to Rome, where he studied under Pollani; returned to Paris in 1791. He met Viotti, who obtained for him a position in the orch. of the Théâtre Feydeau; he served as a clerk in the Ministry of Finance. In 1795 he received the important appointment as violin teacher at the newly opened Paris Cons.; but continued to study composition with Cherubini, Reicha, and Catel. In 1802 he joined Napoleon's private instrumental ensemble; toured Russia with the cellist Lamarre (1805–8). Upon his return to Paris, he organized chamber music concerts, which enjoyed excellent success; also gave concerts in Belgium, the Netherlands, and England. In 1821 he became 1st violinist at the Paris Opéra; from 1825 he was also solo violinist in the Royal Orch. Baillot's musical compositions, rarely performed, comprise 9 violin concertos, 3 string quartets, 15 trios, a Sym. Concertante for 2 Violins with Orch., 6 violin duos, etc. Baillot's name is chiefly remembered through his manual *L'Art du violon* (1834); with Rode and Kreutzer, he wrote a *Méthode de Violon*, adopted by the Paris Cons. and republished in numerous editions and languages; he also ed. the *Méthode de violoncelle* by Levasseur, Catel, and Baudiot.

Bailly, Louis, French violist and pedagogue; b. Valenciennes, June 13, 1882; d. Cowansville, Quebec, Nov. 21, 1974. He studied violin and viola at the Paris Cons., graduating with 1st prize in 1899; was subsequently the violist in the Capet, Flonzaley (1917–24), Elman, and Curtis quartets; served as head of the viola and chamber music dept. at the Curtis Inst. of Music in Philadelphia; in 1954 went to Canada and taught in Montreal.

Bain, Wilfred, American music educator and administrator; b. Shawville, Quebec, Jan. 20, 1908. He was educated at Houghton College (A.B., 1929) and York Univ. (M.A., 1936; Ed.D., 1938). He was head of the music dept. at Central College, S.C. (1929–30); then of voice and choral music at Houghton College (1931–38). He was dean of music at North Texas State Univ. (1938–47). In 1947 he was appointed dean of the Indiana Univ. School of Music; he retired in 1973.

Bainbridge, Simon (Jeremy), English composer and conductor; b. London, Aug. 30, 1952. He learned to play the recorder and the clarinet as a child, later studying composition with John Lambert at the Royal College of Music in London (1969–72) and with Gunther Schuller at the Berkshire Music Center in Tanglewood (1973–74). Subsequently he was active as a conductor of modern works.

Works: *Heterophony* for Orch. (1970); *Spirogyra* for 7 Instruments (1971; rev. and used in *3 Pieces* for Chamber Ensembles, 1982); Wind Quintet (1971); String Quartet (1972); *Flugal* for 10 Instruments (1973; rev. and used in *3 Pieces* for Chamber Ensembles, 1982); Wind Quartet (1974); *People of the Dawn* for 3 Clarinets, Soprano Saxophone, Piano or Celesta, Percussion, and Soprano (1975); Viola Concerto (1976); *Landscapes and Magic Words* for Soprano and Ensemble (1981); *Voicing* for Ensemble (1982); *Devil's Punchbowl* for Chamber Orch., Children, and Instrumental Ensemble (1987); *Trace,* dance score for Instrumental Ensemble and Electronics (1987); *Metamorphosis* for 13 Instruments (Amsterdam, June 6, 1988).
Bibl.: D. Wright, "An Introduction to B.," *Musical Times* (June 1988).

Baines, Anthony, English music scholar; b. London, Oct. 6, 1912. He studied at the Royal College of Music in London; for several seasons (1935–39 and 1946–48) played the bassoon in the London Phil. Orch. In 1949 he became associate conductor of the International Ballet Co., and in 1970 was appointed curator of the Bate Collection of Historical Wind Instruments of the Faculty of Music at Oxford Univ. He publ. *Woodwind Instruments and Their History* (London, 1957; 3rd ed., rev., 1967); *Bagpipes* (Oxford, 1960); *European and American Musical Instruments* (London, 1966); edited *Musical Instruments through the Ages* (Baltimore, 1961; 2nd ed., rev., 1976).

Baini, Giuseppe (also known as **Abbate Baini**), Italian writer on music and composer; b. Rome, Oct. 21, 1775; d. there, May 21, 1844. He received rudimentary training from his uncle, Lorenzo Baini; then entered the Seminario Romano, where his instructor, Stefano Silveyra, indoctrinated him with the spirit of Palestrina's music. In 1795 he became a member of the papal choir at St. Peter's; he continued his studies there with Bianchini; in 1802 he took courses with Jannaconi, whom he succeeded as maestro di cappella at St. Peter's (1818). In 1821 he wrote his masterpiece, a 10-part *Miserere,* which was accepted for singing at the Sistine Chapel during Holy Week, in alternation with the *Misereres* of Allegri and Bai. He also wrote many Psalms, hymns, masses, and motets. His great ambition was to publ. a complete ed. of Palestrina's works, but he was able to prepare only 2 vols. for publication. The

monument of his devotion to Palestrina was his exhaustive biography, *Memorie storico-critiche della vita e delle opere di Giovanni Pierluigi da Palestrina* (Rome, 1828; German tr. by Kandler, with notes by Kiesewetter, 1834), which remains extremely valuable despite its occasional inaccuracies. He also wrote a *Saggio sopra l'identità de' ritmi musicali e poetici* (1820). Haberl publ. an essay on Baini in the *Kirchenmusikalisches Jahrbuch* (1894).

Bainton, Edgar Leslie, English composer; b. London, Feb. 14, 1880; d. Sydney, Australia, Dec. 8, 1956. He studied piano and composition at the Royal College of Music with Walford Davies and Charles Stanford. He taught piano and composition at the Cons. of Newcastle upon Tyne from 1901 until 1914. The outbreak of World War I found him in Berlin, and he was interned as an enemy alien. After the end of the war he resumed his pedagogical activities as director of the Newcastle Cons. In 1934 he went to Australia and was director of the State Cons. at Sydney until 1947. In his style he followed the tenets of the British national school, writing in broad diatonic expanses with a Romantic élan.

Works: 3 syms. (1903–56); *Before Sunrise* for Voice, Chorus, and Orch. (1917); symphonic poem, *Paracelsus* (1921); *Concerto-Fantasia* for Piano and Orch. (Carnegie Award, 1917; London, Jan. 26, 1922); 2 operas: *Oithona,* after Ossian (Glastonbury, Aug. 11, 1915), and *The Pearl Tree* (Sydney, May 20, 1944); chamber music; and songs.
Bibl.: H. Bainton, *Remembered on Waking: E.L. B.* (Sydney, 1960).

Baird, Martha, American pianist and music patroness; b. Madera, Calif., March 15, 1895; d. N.Y., Jan. 24, 1971. She studied at the New England Cons. and with Artur Schnabel in Berlin; appeared as soloist with Beecham in London and Koussevitzky in Boston. In 1957 she married John D. Rockefeller, Jr., and became a benefactress of opera and concert music.

Baird, Tadeusz, prominent Polish composer; b. Grodzisk Mazowiecki, July 26, 1928; d. Warsaw, Sept. 2, 1981. He studied music privately in Lodz with Sikorski and Woytowicz (1943–44); then at the Warsaw Cons. with Rytel and Perkowski (1947–51); had piano lessons with Wituski (1948–51); also studied musicology with Zofia Lissa at the Univ. of Warsaw (1948–52). In 1949, together with Jan Krenz and Kazimierz Serocki, he founded a progressive society of composers under the name Group 49. In 1956 he became active in initiating the 1st International Festival of Contemporary Music, during the "Warsaw Autumn." In 1977 he was appointed prof. of composition at the Chopin Academy of Music in Warsaw. As a composer, Baird won numerous awards, among them the Fitelberg Competition of 1958, 3 prizes of the Tribune Internationale des Compositeurs in Paris (1959, 1963, 1966), and the Polish State Awards for his 3 syms. (1951, 1964, 1969). He also was awarded the Commander's Cross of the Order of Poland's Revival (1964) and the Order of the Banner of Labor, 2nd and 1st Class (1974, 1981). His early music followed the neo-Romantic modalities characteristic of Polish music; further evolution was marked by complex structures in the manner of dynamic expressionism, with occasional applications of serialism.

Works: OPERA: *Jutro* (Tomorrow), after a short story by Conrad (1964–66). ORCH.: Sinfonietta (1949); 3 syms. (1950; *Sinfonia quasi una fantasia,* 1952; 1969); *Overture in Old Style* (1950); *Colas Breugnon,* suite for Flute and String Orch. (1951); *Overture giocosa* (1952); *Concerto for Orchestra* (1953); *Cassazione* (1956); 4 *Essays* (1958); *Espressioni varianti* for Violin and Orch. (1958–59); *Variations without a Theme* (1961–62); *Epiphany Music* (1963); 4 *Dialogues* for Oboe and Chamber Orch. (1966); 4 *Novelettes* for Chamber Orch. (1967; Hanover, N.H., July 16, 1967); *Sinfonia breve* (1968); *Psychodrama* (1971–72); Concerto for Oboe and Orch. (1973; Warsaw, Sept. 23, 1973); *Elegy* (1973); *Concerto lugubre* for Viola and Orch. (1974–75; Nuremberg, May 21, 1976); Double Concerto for Cello, Harp, and Orch. (1976). CHAMBER: 4 *Preludes* for Bassoon and Piano (1954); *Divertimento* for Flute, Oboe, Clarinet, and Bassoon (1956); String Quartet (1957); *Play* for String

Quartet (1971). VOCAL: *Lyrical Suite*, 4 songs for Soprano and Orch. (1953); *4 Love Sonnets*, after Shakespeare, for Baritone and Chamber Ensemble (1956; 2nd version with Strings and Harpsichord, 1969); *Exhortations* on old Hebrew texts, for Narrator, Chorus, and Orch. (1959–60); *Erotyki* (Love Songs), cycle of 6 songs for Soprano and Orch. (1961); *Study* for 28 Mixed Voices, 6 Percussion Players, and Piano (1967); *4 songs* for Mezzo-soprano and Chamber Orch. (1966); *5 Songs* for Mezzo-soprano and Chamber Orch. (1968); *Goethe-Briefe*, cantata (1970; Dresden, June 6, 1971); *Voices from Afar*, 3 songs for Baritone and Orch. (1981).
BIBL.: T. Zielinski, *T. B.* (Krakow, 1966).

Bairstow, Sir Edward (Cuthbert), English organist and composer; b. Huddersfield, Aug. 22, 1874; d. York, May 1, 1946. He studied organ and music theory at Durham Univ. (Mus.D., 1901); was organist at Wigan (1899–1906), at Leeds (1906–13), and at the York Minster. He composed church music, anthems, part-songs, and an organ sonata (1937); he publ. *Counterpoint and Harmony* (1937) and *The Evolution of Musical Form* (1943).
BIBL.: E. Bradbury, "Sir E. B.: A Birthday Tribute," *Musical Times* (Aug. 1944).

Bajoras, Feliksas, Lithuanian composer; b. Alytus, Oct. 7, 1934. He studied violin and composition at the State Cons. in Vilnius (1957–63); in 1965 was appointed music director of the Lithuanian State Youth Theater. In his compositions he employs melorhythmic features of Lithuanian folklore in a modern harmonic dressing.
WORKS: ORCH.: 3 syms.: No. 1 (1964; rev. 1968–70); No. 2, *Stalactites*, for String Orch. (1970); No. 3 (1972; rev. 1976); *Intermezzo and Postlude* for Chamber Orch. (1964); *Suite of Verbs* for Chamber Orch. (1966); *Prelude and Toccata* for Strings (1966); *Legends*, symphonic poem (1969); *Mourning Music* for Wind Orch. (1972); *Rondo* (1976). CHAMBER: Violin Sonatina (1961); Variations for Double Bass and String Quartet (1968); *4 Pieces* for String Quartet (1968); *Cycle of 15 Pieces* for Violin and Piano (1973); 2 string quartets (1974, 1975); Suite for Septet (1975); Violin Sonata (1979). PIANO: *3 Pieces* (1958); Variations (1959); *Variations on a Folk Theme* (1971).

Bakala, Břetislav, Czech organist, conductor, and composer; b. Fryšták, Feb. 12, 1897; d. Brno, April 1, 1958. He studied organ in Brno (1912–15); then entered the Brno Cons., studying with Vilem Kurz (piano) and with Neumann (conducting); also attended the master class of Janáček there. In 1920–25 he was a répétiteur and chorus director at the Brno City Theater. He was also, for a season, an organist in Philadelphia (1925–26). Returning to Czechoslovakia, he served as pianist and conductor at the State Radio (1926–36) and later conductor of the Radio Orch. (1937–55). In 1956 he was appointed conductor-in-chief and music director of the State Phil. in Brno; also taught a conducting class at the Janáček Academy in Brno (1951–58). He wrote a Scherzo for Orch. (1923), a *Fantasy* for String Quartet, and numerous choruses and songs. His chief merit was editing works by early Czech composers and arranging vocal scores of several operas by Janáček.

Bakaleinikov, Vladimir, Russian-American viola player and conductor; b. Moscow, Oct. 12, 1885; d. Pittsburgh, Nov. 5, 1953. He studied violin with Michael Press; graduated from the Moscow Cons. in 1907; subsequently played the viola in the Grand Duke of Mecklenburg Quartet (1910–20); taught at the Cons. of St. Petersburg (1913–20); conducted opera at the Musicalnaya Drama in St. Petersburg (1914–16). Returning to Moscow, he taught at the Moscow Cons. (1920–24); was in charge of the opera branch of the Moscow Art Theater (1920–27). He went to America in 1927; was associate conductor of the Cincinnati Sym. Orch.; eventually settled in Pittsburgh as a conductor and teacher; among his pupils was Lorin Maazel. He wrote a Viola Concerto (1937) and a suite of oriental dances for Orch.; publ. several arrangements of works by Bach and Beethoven; also *Elementary Rules of Conducting* (1937); *The Instruments of the Band and Orchestra* (with M. Rosen,

N.Y., 1940); and an autobiography, *A Musician's Notes* (N.Y., 1943; in Russian).

Bake, Arnold Adriaan, Dutch music scholar; b. Hilversum, May 19, 1899; d. London, Oct. 8, 1963. He studied oriental languages at the Univ. of Leiden; received his Ph.D. in 1930 from the Univ. of Utrecht with the dissertation *Bytrage tot de Kennis der Voor-Indische musiek* (publ. in Paris, 1930). He subsequently went to India, where he studied Indian music and languages at Tagore's school in Santiniketan; he also served as music adviser to the All India Radio in Delhi and as director of European music of the Calcutta Radio. In 1948 he went to London, where he became a lecturer on Sanskrit and Indian music at the School of Oriental and African Studies. His interests also included Indian philosophy, tribal music, and dance.

Baker, Benjamin Franklin, American music pedagogue; b. Wenham, Mass., July 10, 1811; d. Boston, March 11, 1889. He was a singer in various churches in Salem, Boston, and Portland, Maine; in 1841 he succeeded Lowell Mason as teacher of music in the public schools; sang with the Handel and Haydn Soc. He founded the Boston Music School (1851–68) and ed. the *Boston Musical Journal;* composed 3 cantatas: *The Storm King, The Burning Ship,* and *Camillus;* publ. a textbook, *Thorough-Bass and Harmony* (1870).

Baker, Chet (Chesney), American jazz trumpeter; b. Yale, Okla., Dec. 23, 1929; d. in a suicidal defenestration in Amsterdam, May 13, 1988. He played in jazz bands in Los Angeles and San Francisco, and was associated with Charlie Parker. Everything seemed to foretell a successful career, but the demon of drugs crushed him during a European engagement, leading to imprisonment in Italy (1960–61). He returned to the U.S., but fate was implacable; in 1968 he was beaten by hoodlums in San Francisco and lost all his teeth. His life was also plagued by broken marriages.
BIBL.: M. Hawthorn, "C. B.," *Down Beat,* XLVIII/10 (1981).

Baker, David (Nathaniel), black American composer and jazz musician; b. Indianapolis, Ind., Dec. 21, 1931. He graduated from Indiana Univ. in 1953; also studied music theory privately with Heiden, Schuller, Orrego-Salas, William Russo, and George Russell. He subsequently taught music in small colleges and public school; in 1966 became chairman of the dept. of jazz studies at Indiana Univ. As a jazz performer, he played the trombone with Stan Kenton, Lionel Hampton, and Quincy Jones. His own compositions fuse jazz improvisation with ultramodern devices, including serial procedures. He has written many articles on jazz; among his books are *Jazz Improvisation: A Comprehensive Method of Study for All Players* (1969) and *Techniques of Improvisation* (1971); with L. Belt and H. Hudson, he ed. *The Black Composer Speaks* (1978).
WORKS: ORCH.: *Reflections* for Orch. and Jazz Ensemble (1969); Concerto for Violin and Jazz Band (1969; Indiana Univ., April 5, 1970); Concerto for Flute, Jazz Ensemble, and String Quartet (1971); Concerto for Double Bass, Jazz Ensemble, String Quartet, and Solo Violin (1972); Concerto for Trombone, Jazz Band, and Chamber Orch. (1972); *Kosbro* (1973; rev. 1975); *Levels*, concerto for Double Bass, Jazz Band, Flute Quartet, Horn Quartet, and String Quartet (1973); *Le Chat qui pêche* for Orch., Jazz Quartet, and Soprano (1974); *2 Improvisations* for Orch. and Jazz Combo (1974); Concerto for Tuba, Jazz Band, Percussion, Chorus, Dancers, Slide Projections, and Tape Recorders (1975); Concerto for Cello and Chamber Orch. (1975–76); Concerto for 2 Pianos, Jazz Band, Chamber Orch., and Percussion (1976); Clarinet Concerto (1985).
VOCAL: *Psalm* 22, jazz oratorio (1966); *Lutheran Mass* for Chorus and Jazz Septet (1967); *The Beatitudes* for Chorus, Soloists, Narrator, Jazz Ensemble, String Orch., and Dancers (1968); *Black America: To the Memory of Martin Luther King,* jazz cantata (1968); *Catholic Mass for Peace* for Chorus and Jazz Ensemble (1969); *A Song of Mankind* for Chorus, Orch., Jazz Ensemble, Rock Band, Lights, and Sound Effects (1970); *Songs of the Night* for Soprano, String Quartet, and Piano

(1972); *Give and Take* for Soprano and Chamber Ensemble (1975).

CHAMBER: String Quartet No. 1 (1962); Viola Sonata (1966); *Ballade* for Horn, Saxophone, and Cello (1967); Violin Sonata (1967); *Salute to Beethoven* for Piccolo, Wind Quintet, Flute Choir, Jazz Ensemble, and Tape (1970); Sonata for Brass Quintet and Piano (1970); Sonata for Piano and String Quintet (1971); Sonata for Tuba and String Quartet (1971); Sonata for Viola, Guitar, and Double Bass (1973); Cello Sonata (1973); Sonata for Violin and Cello (1974); Suite for Solo Violin (1975); *Contrasts* for Piano Trio (1976); *Ethnic Variations on a Theme of Paganini* for Violin and Piano (1976); *Roots* for Piano Trio (1976); Sonata for Violin, Cello, and 4 Flutes (1980); *Calypso* for Violin Ensemble and Piano (1985); Quintet for Jazz Violin and String Quartet (1987; Washington, D.C., March 13, 1988); *Impressions* for 2 Cellos (Bloomington, Ind., Sept. 8, 1989); numerous works for jazz ensembles of various instrumentations; also Piano Sonata (1968) and a 2-piano Sonata (1971).

Baker, Dame Janet (Abbott), celebrated English mezzo-soprano; b. Hatfield, Yorkshire, Aug. 21, 1933. Her parents were music-lovers and she grew up in an artistic atmosphere from her early childhood. She took academic courses at the College for Girls in York, and also began to take singing lessons in London, where her teachers were Helene Isepp and Meriel St. Clair. She won a prize in 1956 which made it possible for her to travel to Salzburg and attend singing classes at the Mozarteum there. Later she enrolled in a master class of Lotte Lehmann in London. She sang in the chorus at the Glyndebourne Festival (1956) and also filled engagements in opera productions in Oxford and London. In 1960 she gave a recital at the Edinburgh Festival. In 1961 she had a part in Bach's *St. John Passion* in Copenhagen, and later sang in Bach's B-minor Mass in Zürich. A decisive turn in her career came with her membership in the English Opera Group, directed by Benjamin Britten; on May 16, 1971, she appeared in the leading role in Britten's opera *Owen Wingrave* on television. She made her 1st American appearance in 1966 as soloist with the San Francisco Sym. in Mahler's *Das Lied von der Erde.* On Dec. 2, 1966, she presented a solo recital in N.Y., with excellent reviews. Her subsequent engagements took her all over Europe; her fame as an artist of intellectual brilliance grew. In 1970 she was named a Commander of the Order of the British Empire, and in 1976 Queen Elizabeth II made her a Dame Commander of the Order of the British Empire. She gave her last operatic appearance in 1982. An account of her final operatic season was publ. in her book *Full Circle* (London, 1982). Baker was one of the outstanding singers of her era. Her operatic repertoire was extensive, ranging from Monteverdi and Handel to R. Strauss and Britten. She was also one of the great lieder artists of her day, excelling in Schubert and Schumann.

BIBL.: A. Blyth, *J. B.* (London, 1973).

Baker, Josephine, black American-born French dancer, singer, and actress; b. St. Louis, June 3, 1906; d. Paris, April 12, 1975. She became a street musician when she was 13, and after touring with the Dixie Steppers on the vaudeville circuit, gained recognition in the show *Chocolate Dandies* (1924). Making her way to Paris, she starred in *La Revue nègre* (1925). Her exotic, erotic, quixotic stage persona gained her rapid recognition. She became a naturalized French citizen in 1937, and was active in the Résistance during the occupation of France by the German army in 1940–44. After the war, she turned to humanitarian causes, adopting orphans from various countries. She was also active in the U.S. civil rights movement. With J. Bouillon she penned the vol. *Josephine* (N.Y., 1977).

BIBL.: L. Haney, *Naked at the Feast: A Biography of J. B.* (N.Y., 1981); P. Rose, *Jazz Cleopatra* (N.Y., 1989).

Baker, Julius, distinguished American flutist; b. Cleveland, Sept. 23, 1915. He studied at the Eastman School of Music in Rochester, N.Y., and at the Curtis Inst. of Music in Philadelphia. In 1937 he joined the Cleveland Orch.; then was principal flutist of the Pittsburgh Sym. (1941–43), of the CBS Sym. (1943–51), and of the Chicago Sym. (1951–53). In 1954 he was appointed to the faculty of the Juilliard School of Music. From 1947 to 1965 he was a member of the Bach Aria Group, with which he made several concert tours. In 1965 he became principal flutist of the N.Y. Phil.; retired in 1983. He also taught at the Curtis Inst. of Music (from 1980).

Baker, Michael, American-born Canadian composer; b. West Palm Beach, Fla., March 13, 1937. He moved to Canada in 1958; studied composition with J. Coulthard and E. Weisgarber at the Univ. of British Columbia in Vancouver (1962–66); later took private lessons with Lennox Berkeley during a year in London (1974–75). Returning to Vancouver, he devoted himself to pedagogical work as well as composition. His works follow along tonal lines with effective utilization of contemporary techniques.

WORKS: BALLET: *The Letter* (1974). **ORCH.:** *Dialogues* for Orch., Chorus, and Solo Baritone (1971); *Counterplay* for Viola and String Orch. (1971; also for Viola and Piano); *Okanagan Landscapes* for Piano and Orch. (1972); *Contours* for Double Bass, Harpsichord, and String Orch. (1973); Concerto for Flute and String Orch. (1974); *Point No Point* for Viola and String Orch. (1975); Concerto for Piano and Chamber Orch. (1976); *Duo Concertante* for Violin, Viola, and String Orch. (London, Aug. 19, 1976); *A Struggle for Dominion* for Piano and Orch. (Vancouver, Sept. 26, 1976); Sym. No. 1 (1977); *Baroque Diversions* for Chamber Orch. (Mannheim, Oct. 18, 1981); *Evocations* for Orch. (Winnipeg, Feb. 3, 1982); *Rita Joe*, tone poem (1983); *Capriccio* for Solo Voices, Instruments, and Orch. (1986); *Chanson joyeuse* (1987). **CHAMBER:** *Ballade* for Cello and Piano (1961); Flute Sonata (1963); *5 Epigrams* for Woodwind Trio (1965); Wind Quintet (1965); Piano Quartet (1966); Scherzo for Trumpet and Organ (1967); String Quartet (1969); *Concert Piece* for Organ, Piano, and Timpani (1969–70); Piano Trio (1972); *Elegy* for Flute and Organ (1972); *Music for 6 Players* for Flute, Oboe, Harpsichord, and String Trio (1973); *Combinations* for Double Bass and Harpsichord (1974); *En rapport* for 2 Guitars (1974); *4 Views from a Nursery Tune* for Violin, Horn, and Piano (1975); *Dance Sequences* for Solo Cello (1975); *Capriccio* for 2 Pianos (1964); *Mirage* for Trumpet, Horn, and Organ (1981); *Red on White* for Flute and String Trio (1981); *Rainforest Suite* for Piano (1987); organ music; vocal works; film scores.

Baker, Theodore, American writer on music, and the compiler of the original edition of the present dictionary bearing his name; b. N.Y., June 3, 1851; d. Dresden, Oct. 13, 1934. As a young man, he was trained for business pursuits; in 1874 he decided to devote himself to musical studies; he went to Leipzig, where he took courses with Oskar Paul; he received his Ph.D. there in 1882 for his dissertation *Über die Musik der nordamerikanischen Wilden,* the 1st serious study of American Indian music. He lived in Germany until 1890; then returned to the U.S., and became literary ed. and translator for the publishing house of G. Schirmer, Inc. (1892); he retired in 1926 and went back to Germany. In 1895 he publ. *A Dictionary of Musical Terms,* which went through more than 25 printings and sold over a million copies; another valuable work was *A Pronouncing Pocket Manual of Musical Terms* (1905). He also issued *The Musician's Calendar and Birthday Book* (1915–17). In 1900 G. Schirmer, Inc., publ. *Baker's Biographical Dictionary of Musicians,* which became Baker's imperishable monument. The 1st ed. included the names of many American musicians not represented in musical reference works at the time; a 2nd ed. was publ. in 1905; the 3rd ed., revised and enl. by Alfred Remy, was issued in 1919; the 4th ed. appeared in 1940 under the general editorship of Carl Engel. A Supplement in 1949 was compiled by Nicolas Slonimsky, who undertook in 1958 a completely revised 5th ed. of the Dictionary and compiled the Supplements of 1965 and 1971. In 1978 Slonimsky edited the 6th ed., in 1984 the 7th ed., and in 1991 the 8th ed.

Bakfark, Valentin (or **Bálint**), celebrated Hungarian lutenist; b. Kronstadt, 1507; d. Padua, Aug. 15, 1576. He was brought up by the family of his brother's wife, **Greff** (or **Graew**), and used that name in conjunction with his own; the spelling **Bacfarc** or **Bekwark** is also encountered. As a youth he was in the service of the King of Hungary (1526–40) in Buda, where he studied lute. He was later attached to the court of Sigismund II Augustus of Poland in Wilno (1549–66). He subsequently traveled in Germany, France, and Italy, eventually settling in Padua, where he died of the plague. He publ. works for the lute in tablature: *Intabulatura* (Lyons, 1552; reprinted as *Premier Livre de Tablature de Luth,* Paris, 1564). A 2nd book, *Pannonii Harmonicarum Musicarum . . . tomus primus,* appeared in Krakow in 1564, and was reprinted in Antwerp in 1569. Some of his works are included in Denkmäler der Tonkunst in Österreich (vol. XVIII, 2).

Baklanov, George, Russian baritone; b. Riga, Jan. 17, 1881; d. Basel, Dec. 6, 1938. His real name was **Bakkis,** but he changed it to create the necessary euphony for professional appearances. He studied voice at the Kiev Cons.; also went to Milan for advanced voice lessons. He made his operatic debut with the Kiev Opera in 1903 as A. Rubinstein's Demon; subsequently sang at the Bolshoi Theater in Moscow (1905–9). He made several tours in Europe and America; sang at Covent Garden, London (1910), with the Boston Opera (1911–14), and with the Chicago Opera (1917–26). He was particularly successful in dramatic roles, such as Rigoletto and Boris Godunov.

Balada, Leonardo, Spanish composer; b. Barcelona, Sept. 22, 1933. He was apprenticed to his father's tailoring shop in Barcelona, and also took piano at the Conservatorio del Liceo there. In 1956 he went to the U.S.; studied at the N.Y. College of Music (1956–57); then enrolled in the Juilliard School of Music (1958–60) to study composition; later attended classes at the Mannes College of Music (1961–62). His principal instructors in composition were Aaron Copland and Vincent Persichetti. He also studied conducting in Paris with Igor Markevitch. He eked out a living by working at odd jobs in the garment district in N.Y.; subsequently he obtained musical employment as a teacher at the United Nations International School; then was composer-in-residence at the Aspen Inst. In 1970 he was appointed to the faculty of Carnegie-Mellon Univ. in Pittsburgh. His music retains much of his Spanish heritage, while its formal elements are Classical in structure. **WORKS: STAGE:** *Hangman, Hangman!,* chamber opera, based on a traditional cowboy song (Barcelona, Oct. 10, 1982); *Zapata!,* based on the story of the famous Mexican revolutionary leader (1982); *Cristóbal Colón,* opera (1987; Barcelona, Sept. 24, 1989). **ORCH.:** *Musica tranquila* for String Orch. (1960); Piano Concerto (1964); Guitar Concerto (1965); *Guernica* (1966; New Orleans, April 25, 1967); *Sinfonia en negro* in homage to Martin Luther King (1968); Concerto for Bandoneon and Orch. (1970); Sinfonia Concertante for Guitar and Orch. (1972); *Sinfonia de acero* (Steel Sym; Pittsburgh, Jan. 12, 1973); *Auroris* (1973); *Ponce de Leon* for Narrator and Orch. (New Orleans, Oct. 9, 1973); Concerto for Piano, Winds, and Percussion (1974); *Homage to Casals* (Pittsburgh, May 7, 1976); *Homage to Sarasate* (Pittsburgh, May 7, 1976); Concerto for 4 Guitars and Orch. (Barcelona, Dec. 17, 1977); *3 Anecdotes,* concertino for Castanets and Chamber Orch. (Pittsburgh, Nov. 8, 1978); *Sardana* (1979; Pittsburgh, Oct. 21, 1982); Violin Concerto (1982; Pittsburgh, Nov. 11, 1982); *Quasi un pasodoble* (N.Y., Nov. 24, 1982); *Fantasias sonoras* (Pittsburgh, Oct. 4, 1987); *Alegrias* (Exuberance) for Flute and String Orch. (1988). **CHAMBER:** Violin Sonata (1960); Concerto for Cello and 9 Players (1962); *Geometrias No. 1* for Flute, Oboe, Clarinet, Bassoon, Trumpet, and Percussion (1966); *Geometrias No. 2* for String Quartet (1967); *Cuatris* for Instrumental Ensemble (1969); *Mosaico* for Brass Quintet (1970); *Tresis* for Flute, Guitar, and Cello (1973); *Apuntes* for Guitar Quartet (1974); Sonata for 10 Winds (1980); *Music* for String Quartet and Flute (1988); numerous pieces for guitar solo and piano

solo; also *End and Beginning* for Rock Music Ensemble (1970). **CHORAL:** *Maria Sabina* for Narrators, Chorus, and Orch. (1969); *Las moradas* for Mixed Chorus and Instrumental Ensemble (1970); *No-Res,* cantata (1974); *Torquemada,* cantata (1980).

Balakauskas, Osvaldas, Lithuanian composer; b. Ukmerge, Dec. 19, 1937. He graduated from the Vilna State Pedagogical Inst. in 1961; in 1969 took composition courses from Liatoshinsky at the Kiev Cons. In his music he adopts a colorful manner, often sharply modernistic in melodic curvature, rhythmic angularity, and harmonic heterophony, while retaining the generic classical definitions of form. **WORKS: ORCH.:** Piano Concertino (1966); *Rhapsody* (1967); *Ludus modorum,* cello concerto (1972); Sym. (1973); Suite for Strings (1973); *The Mountain Sonata,* sym. for Piano and Orch. (1975); *Ad astra* (1976). **CHAMBER:** *Dance Suite* for Violin and Piano (1964); Variations for Flute, Oboe, and Bassoon (1965); Suite for Cello and Violin (1965); *Auletika* for Flute and Oboe (1966); *Extrema* for Piccolo, English Horn, Bass Clarinet, Double Bassoon, Trumpet, Xylophone, and Harp (1966); *Aerophonia* for Wind Quintet (1968); Violin Sonata (1969); *Quartetto concertante* for Flute, Violin, Cello, and Piano (1970); 2 String Quartets (1971, 1971); *Les Musiques* for Cello and Wind Quintet (1972); Violin Sonatina (1972); *Impresonata* for Flute and Piano (1974); *Suite of the Globe* for Violin and Piano (1974); *Retrospectives* for Cello and Piano (1974); *9 Sources* for Oboe and Harpsichord (1974); *Like a Touch of a Sea Wave,* 3 pieces for Violin and Piano (1975); *A Tree and a Bird,* viola sonata (1976). **PIANO:** *3 Caprices* (1964); *Cascades* (1967); *Studi sonori* for 2 Pianos (1971); also Organ Sonata (1973).

Balakirev, Mily (**Alexeievich;** the last name is pronounced "Balákirev," with the stress on the 2nd syllable, not the 3rd), greatly significant Russian composer, protagonist of the Russian national school of composition; b. Nizhny-Novgorod, Jan. 2, 1837 (new style; Dec. 21, 1836, old style); d. St. Petersburg, May 29, 1910. His mother gave him his 1st piano lessons; he was then sent to Moscow, where he took piano lessons with Alexandre Dubuque, and studied music theory with a German musician named Karl Eisrich, who put Balakirev in touch with Oulibishev, author of a book on Mozart (who owned an estate in Nizhny-Novgorod). Balakirev often took part in private musical evenings at Oulibishev's estate, playing piano. In 1853–54 he attended classes in mathematics at the Univ. of Kazan. In 1855 he went to St. Petersburg, where he was introduced to Glinka, who encouraged him to continue his musical studies. On Feb. 24, 1856, Balakirev made his 1st appearance as a composer in St. Petersburg, playing the solo part in the 1st movement of his Piano Concerto; his *Overture on the Theme of 3 Russian Songs* was performed in Moscow on Jan. 2, 1859, and his overture *King Lear,* at a concert of the Univ. of St. Petersburg on Nov. 27, 1859. In 1860 he took a boat ride down the Volga River from his birthplace of Nizhny-Novgorod to the delta at the Caspian Sea; during this trip he collected, notated, and harmonized a number of Russian songs; his collection included the universally popular *Song of the Volga Boatmen,* also known as *Song of the Burlaks* (peasants who pulled large boats loaded with grain upstream on the Volga). In 1863 Balakirev organized in St. Petersburg a musical group which became known as the Balakirev Circle. Its avowed aim was to make national propaganda of Russian music to oppose the passive imitation of classical German compositions, which at the time exercised a commanding influence in Russia. Simultaneously, he founded the Free Music School in St. Petersburg, and gave concerts which included works by Russian musicians as well as those of recognized German masters. These activities coincided with the rise of a Slavophile movement among patriotic Russian writers and artists, based on the realization of a kinship of blood and the similarity of the Slavic languages (Czech, Serbian, Polish, Bulgarian) and further stimulated by a series of wars against Turkey, aimed at the liberation of Bulgaria; a dream of uniting all Slavic nations under the loving domination of Mother Russia animated Balakirev and other musicians. In 1866 he went to Prague with the intention of conducting Glinka's operas there, but the outbreak of the Austro-Prussian War forced the cancellation of these plans. He repeated his visit to Prague in 1867 and was able to conduct *Ruslan and Ludmila* there on Feb. 16, 17, and 19, 1867; then he conducted *A Life for the Czar*, on Feb. 22, 1867. He took this opportunity to invite several Czech musicians to take part in a concert of music by Russian and Czech composers conducted by Balakirev at his Free Music School on May 24, 1867; the program included, besides the works by the Czech guests, compositions by Borodin, Cui, Mussorgsky, Rimsky-Korsakov, and Balakirev himself. The occasion proved to be of historical importance, for it moved the critic Vladimir Stasov to write an article in which he proudly declared that Russia, too, had its "mighty little company" (*moguchaya kuchka*) of fine musicians; the phrase became a catchword of Russian musical nationalism; in general music histories it came to be known as "The Mighty Five." But the spiritual drive toward the union with the Western Slavic nations was not the only animating force in the music of "The Mighty Five." It combines, somehow, with the historical drive toward the exotic Moslem lands through the Caucasus to Persia in the South and to Central Asia in the East. Balakirev became fascinated with the quasi-oriental melodies and rhythms of the Caucasus during his several trips there. In 1869 he wrote a brilliant oriental fantasy for piano entitled *Islamey*; its technical difficulties rival the transcendental studies of Liszt. His associates, especially Rimsky-Korsakov and Borodin, also paid tribute to the colorful glories of the East, the 1st in his *Scheherazade*, and the 2nd in his symphonic movement *In the Steppes of Central Asia*. Among his comrades, Balakirev was always a leader; when Rimsky-Korsakov went on a prolonged cruise as a midshipman in the Russian Imperial Navy, he maintained a remarkable correspondence with Balakirev, who gave him specific advice in composition. Unaccountably, Balakirev slackened the tempo of his work as a composer, conductor, and teacher; he seems to have had trouble completing his scores. In 1872 he discontinued his concerts at the Free Music School, and took a clerical job in the railroad transport administration; in 1873 he became music inspector in a women's educational inst. in St. Petersburg; in 1875 he took another administrative job in a women's school. In 1881 he returned to musical activities, and on March 29, 1882, he conducted at the Free Music School the premiere of the 1st sym. by the 16-year-old Glazunov; he also began to work on the revision of his early scores. His *2nd Overture on Russian Themes*, orig. performed in St. Petersburg on April 18, 1864, and retitled *One Thousand Years* to commemorate the millennium of Russia observed in 1862, was revised by Balakirev in 1882 and renamed *Russia*. It took Balakirev many years to complete his symphonic poem *Tamara*, which he conducted in St. Petersburg on March 19, 1883; the score, inspired by Lermontov's poem and permeated by Caucasian melodic inflections, was dedicated to Liszt. Balakirev spent 33 years (1864–97) working intermittently on his Sym. in C, which he conducted at a concert at the Free Music School on April 23, 1898; this was his last appearance as a conductor. He completed his 2nd Sym. in D minor between 1900 and 1908; it was performed in St. Petersburg on April 23, 1909. He worked on his 1st Piano Concerto in 1855 and began the composition of his 2nd Piano Concerto in 1861, but laid it aside until 1909; it was completed after his death by Liapunov. In 1883 he became director of music of the Imperial Chapel, resigning from this post in 1894. During his last years, Balakirev was increasingly unsociable and morose; he became estranged from Rimsky-Korsakov when the latter became chief adviser to Belaiev, the wealthy publisher who ceased to support the Free School headed by Balakirev and instead sponsored a series of Russian Sym. Concerts in 1886, attracting a number of younger Russian composers, among them Glazunov, Liadov, Arensky, and Ippolitov-Ivanov. Their quarrel reached such lamentable extremes that they did not even greet each other at public places or at concerts. Still, Rimsky-Korsa-

kov continued to perform Balakirev's music at his concerts. Balakirev made a tremendous impact on the destinies of Russian music, particularly because of his patriotic conviction that Russia could rival Germany and other nations in the art of music. But he left fewer works than his long life would have justified, and they are rarely performed. Among his lesser compositions are *Spanish Overture* (1886); *Czech Overture* (1867); Octet for Flute, Oboe, French Horn, Violin, Viola, Cello, Double Bass, and Piano (1850–56); 2 Piano Sonatas (1857, 1905); and a Piano Sonatina (1909). He made an effective piano transcription of Glinka's song *The Lark* and wrote about 35 original songs; he further publ. an important collection of Russian folk songs (1865). A complete ed. of Balakirev's piano works was publ. in Moscow in 1952; a collection of all of his songs was publ. in Moscow in 1937.

BIBL.: Balakirev's *Autobiography* was publ. in *Russkaya Musykalnaya Gazeta* in 1910. See also M.D. Calvocoressi, ed., "M. B.: Lettres inédites à M.D. Calvocoressi," *Revue Musicale Mensuelle*, VII (1911); S. Lyapunov, ed., *M.A. B.'s Correspondence with P.I. Tchaikovsky* (St. Petersburg, 1912); M.D. Calvocoressi and G. Abraham, "M. B.," *Masters of Russian Music* (London, 1936; rev. ed., 1958); G. Kiselev, *B.* (Moscow, 1938); V. Muzalevsky, *M.A. B.: Critical-biographical Essay* (Leningrad, 1938); G. Abraham, *On Russian Music* (London, 1939); J. Leyda and S. Bertensson, *The Mussorgsky Reader* (N.Y., 1947); A. Kandinsky, *Symphonic Works of M. B.* (Moscow and Leningrad, 1950); G. Fedorova, *B.* (Moscow, 1951); V. Kiselyov, *M.A. B.: Correspondence with N.G. Rubinstein and M.P. Belaiev* (Moscow, 1956); V. Kiselyov and S. Lyapunova, eds., *M.A. B.'s Correspondence with P. Jurgenson's Publishing House* (Moscow, 1958); M. Gordeyeva, *The Mighty Company* (Moscow, 1960); E. Fried, ed., *M.A. B.: Essays and Articles* (Leningrad, 1961); E. Fried, general ed., *M.A. B.: Reminiscences and Letters* (Leningrad, 1962); A. Lyapunova, ed., *N. Rimsky-Korsakov: Complete Works* (vol. 5 includes the complete correspondence between Balakirev and Rimsky-Korsakov; Moscow, 1963); E. Garden, *B.: A Critical Study of His Life and Works* (the most detailed work in Eng.; London, 1967); I. Kunin, *M.A. B.: Life and Works in Letters and Documents* (Moscow, 1967); A. Lyapunova and E. Yazovitskaya, *M.A. B.: Chronicle of His Life and Works* (Leningrad, 1967); E. Garden, "B.'s Personality," *Proceedings of the Royal Musical Association*, XCVI (1969–70); A. Lyapunova, ed., *M.A. B.–V.V. Stasov: Correspondence* (2 vols., Moscow, 1970–71).

Balanchine, George, celebrated Russian-American choreographer, son of **Meliton (Antonovich)** and brother of **Andrei (Melitonovich) Balanchivadze;** b. St. Petersburg, Jan. 22, 1904; d. N.Y., April 30, 1983. He attended the Imperial Theater School in St. Petersburg, where he learned the rudiments of classical dance. He also took piano lessons at the Petrograd Cons., and acquired a certain ability to read scores. In 1924 he undertook a tour through Germany and England; then joined Diaghilev's Ballets Russes in Paris and created a number of works for it. In 1933, at the invitation of the American dance specialist Lincoln Kirstein, he went to N.Y.; together they formed the School of American Ballet, which opened in Manhattan on Jan. 2, 1934. In 1935 it was incorporated as the American Ballet; Balanchine was the chief choreographer. The group was renamed Ballet Soc. in 1946, and in 1948 it was reorganized as the N.Y. City Ballet, and became part of the City Center. In 1962 Balanchine made a tour of Russia with this company. He was distinguished for his modern productions, with music by Stravinsky, Ives, and other contemporary composers. In 1983 he received the Presidential Medal of Freedom. Early in that year he was hospitalized with an ailment diagnosed as "progressive cerebral disintegration." As a gesture of devotion, he was named director emeritus of the N.Y. City Ballet, but had to abandon all active work, and soon died of pneumonia. Balanchine adored women; he used to say, "Ballet is woman." He was married 5 times; all of his brides were dancers: the 1st was Tamara Geva, whom he married in Russia when he was 18 and she was 15; his 2nd wife was Alexandra Danilova, whom he married in 1927; his 3rd and most famous one was Vera Zorina, whom he married in 1938; then followed Maria Tallchief and finally Tanaquil Le-Clercq, from whom he was divorced in 1969. In his long life as a choreographer he created nearly 200 ballets to musical scores ranging from the Baroque to the avant-garde; he said once: "Music must be seen, and dance must be heard."

BIBL.: G. B. and F. Mason, *B.'s Complete Stories of the Great Ballets* (Garden City, N.Y., 1954); B. Taper, *B.* (N.Y. 1963); H. Koegler, *B. und das moderne Ballet* (Hannover, 1964); L. Kirstein, *The New York City Ballet* (N.Y., 1973); *Choreography by G. B.: A Catalogue of Works* (N.Y., 1983).

Balanchivadze, Andrei (Melitonovich), Russian composer, son of **Meliton (Antonovich) Balanchivadze** and brother of **George Balanchine;** b. St. Petersburg, June 1, 1906. He studied with his father; then entered the Tiflis Cons., where he took courses in piano, and in composition with Ippolitov-Ivanov. In 1935 he joined its staff, and in 1962 became chairman of the composition dept.; numerous Georgian composers have studied under him. In his music he makes use of Georgian folk motifs in a tasteful harmonic framework characteristic of the Russian national school of composition. Among his works is the 1st Georgian ballet, *The Heart of the Mountains* (1936); another ballet, *Mtsyri*, after Lermontov, was produced in Tbilisi in 1964. His other works include 3 syms. (1944, 1959, 1984); symphonic poem, *The Ocean* (1952); 4 piano concertos (1944, 1946, 1952, 1968); choruses and songs.

BIBL.: G. Ordzhonikidze, *A. B.* (Tbilisi, 1967).

Balanchivadze, Meliton (Antonovich), noted Russian composer, father of **George Balanchine Andrei (Melitonovich) Balanchivadze;** b. Banodzha, Dec. 24, 1862; d. Kutaisi, Nov. 21, 1937. He was educated in the ecclesiastical seminary in Tiflis, where he sang in a chorus. In 1880 he became a member of the local opera theater; in 1882 he organized a chorus and arranged Georgian folk songs. In 1889 he went to St. Petersburg, where he took vocal lessons, and in 1891 entered Rimsky-Korsakov's class in composition. In 1895 he organized a series of choral concerts of Georgian music. After the Revolution he returned to Georgia, where he continued his work of ethnic research. He composed a national Georgian opera, *Tamara the Treacherous* (1897), and a number of songs in the manner of Georgian folk music.

BIBL.: P. Khuchua, *M. B.* (Tbilisi, 1964).

Balart, Gabriel, Spanish composer; b. Barcelona, June 8, 1824; d. there, July 5, 1893. He studied at the Paris Cons.; composed various pieces of salon music, which enjoyed some success. In 1849 he went to Milan as a theater conductor; in 1853 was appointed music director of the Teatro del Liceo in Barcelona. He wrote 5 syms. in a Romantic vein, which he conducted in Spain; for a time his light opera *Amor y Arte* enjoyed considerable success.

Balasanian, Sergei, Tadzhik composer; b. Ashkhabad, Aug. 26, 1902; d. Moscow, June 3, 1982. He studied at the Moscow Cons., graduating in music history in 1935. From 1936 to 1943 he was mainly active in Tadzhikistan; then was in charge of radio programming there. In 1948 he joined the faculty of the Moscow Cons.; in 1962–71 was chairman of the composition dept. He was one of the founders of the national school of composition in Tadzhikistan; in his works he made use of native folk motifs, in ingenious harmonic coloration.

WORKS: OPERAS: *The Revolt of Vose* (1939; rev. 1959); *The Blacksmith Kova* (1941); *Bakhtyor and Nisso* (1954). **BALLETS:** *Leyly and Medzhnun* (1947) and *Shakuntala* (1963). **ORCH.:** 4 symphonic suites on Central Asian folk motifs; *Armenian Rhapsody* (1944); *The Islands of Indonesia* (1960); numerous choruses, songs, and various instrumental pieces.

Balassa, Sándor, Hungarian composer; b. Budapest, Jan. 20, 1935. He studied at the Béla Bartók Cons. in Budapest (1952–56), then with Endre Szervánszky at the Budapest Academy of Music (1960–65). Upon graduation he joined the staff of Hungarian Radio and also taught at the Budapest Academy

of Music. In 1983 he was made a Merited Artist by the Hungarian government. His music is pragmatic in its structure and effect, with a fine veneer of impressionistic colors.

WORKS: *Bagatelles and Sequences* for Piano (1957); *Locks,* monologue for Soprano and Chamber Ensemble (1963); Violin Concerto (1964); Septet for Brass (1965); *Golden Age,* cantata (1965); 3 *Songs* for Soprano and String Trio (1965); *Dimensioni* for Flute and Viola (1966); Wind Quintet (1966); *Zenith* for Soprano and Orch. (1967); *Antinomia* for Soprano, Clarinet, and Cello (1968); Quartet for Percussion (1969); Trio for Violin, Viola, and Harp (1970); *Xénia,* nonet (1970); *Iris* for Orch. (1971); *Lupercalia,* concerto in memory of Stravinsky, for Woodwinds and Brass (1972); *Tabulae* for Chamber Ensemble (1972); opera, *Az ajtón kívül* (Beyond the Threshold; 1973–76); *Calls and Cries* for Orch. (Boston, Oct. 21, 1982); songs and motets.

Balatka, Hans, Czech conductor and composer; b. Hoffnungsthal, Moravia, Feb. 26, 1825; d. Chicago, April 17, 1899. After studying music in Vienna, he emigrated to America in 1849; settled in Milwaukee, where he organized the German Musikverein, and in 1860 became conductor of the Chicago Phil. Soc., which was the nucleus of the Theodore Thomas Orch. (later Chicago Sym. Orch.). He was an important figure in carrying German musical culture to the American Midwest. He also composed some insignificant choral works.

Balbastre (or **Balbâtre**), **Claude (-Bénigne),** French organist and composer; b. Dijon, Jan. 22, 1727; d. Paris, May 9, 1799. In about 1750 he began studying with Jean-Philippe Rameau. Between 1755 and 1782 he served as organist in concerts held by the Concert Spirituel. In 1756 he was named organist at St. Roch in Paris; in 1760 he was organist at Notre-Dame de Paris, serving there 3 months a year. He wrote 14 piano suites based on the motifs of French Christmas songs; also composed numerous organ pieces.

Balbi (Balbus), Lodovico, Italian composer; b. Venice, 1545; d. there, Dec. 15, 1604. He was a pupil of Costanzo Porta; sang in the choir of S. Marco in Venice (1570); then was maestro di cappella at the Franciscan monastery there (1578), and at S. Antonio in Padua (1585–91); later returned to Venice. He publ. masses, motets, canzoni, madrigals, sacred songs, etc.; compiled a collection of graduals and antiphons by celebrated Italian masters, publ. by Gardano (Venice, 1591).

Balbi, Melchiore, Italian theorist and composer; b. Venice, June 4, 1796; d. Padua, June 21, 1879. He was a pupil of Nini, Valeri, and Calegari in Padua; was theater conductor there (1818–53); from 1854 was maestro di cappella at the Basilica San Antonio. He wrote 3 operas, all produced in Padua: *La notte perigliosa* (1820), *L'abitator del bosco* (1821), *L'alloggio militare* (1825); a Requiem (for Rossini, 1868); masses; Psalms; ed. Calegari's *Trattato del sistema armonico* (Padua, 1829); and wrote *Grammatica ragionata della musica considerata sotto l'aspetto di lingua* (Milan, 1845) and *Nuova scuola basata sul sistema semitonato equabile* (1872).

Baldi, João José, Portuguese composer; b. Lisbon, 1770; d. there, May 18, 1816. He studied at the Seminário Patriarcal in Lisbon; in 1789 he became mestre de capela at Guarda Cathedral; in 1794 he went to Faro Cathedral in a similar capacity, and then returned to Lisbon in 1800 to become 2nd mestre de capela at the Royal Chapel of Bemposta; he was made 1st mestre de capela there and at the Lisbon Cathedral in 1806, holding these posts until his death. He composed mostly sacred works; also wrote some piano music.

Bales, Richard (Henry Horner), American conductor and composer; b. Alexandria, Va., Feb. 3, 1915. He studied at the Eastman School of Music in Rochester, N.Y. (Mus.B., 1936), at the Juilliard Graduate School in N.Y. (1938–41), and with Koussevitzky at the Berkshire Music Center in Tanglewood (1940). In 1935 he made his conducting debut with the National Sym. Orch. in Washington, D.C.; then was conductor of the Virginia–North Carolina Sym. Orch. (1936–38). In 1942 he became the 1st music director of the National Gallery of

Art in Washington, D.C., and in 1943 founded the National Gallery Orch., which he conducted until his retirement in 1985. He also was music director of the Washington, D.C., Cathedral Choral Soc. (1945–46). In 1960 he received the Alice M. Ditson Award. During his long tenure at the National Gallery of Art, he introduced numerous works by American composers, both old and new.

WORKS: ORCH.: *Music* for Strings (1940); *From Washington's Time* for Strings (1941); *National Gallery Suites: I* (1943), *II* (1944), *III* (1957), and *IV* (1965); *Theme and Variations* for Strings (1944); *Music of the American Revolution*, Suite No. 2 for Strings (1952); *Stony Brook Suite* for Strings (1968); *Fitzwilliam Suite* for Strings (1972); *The Spirit of Engineering*, suite (1984). **CHAMBER:** *Sarcasms* for Violin, Viola, and Cello (1937); String Quartet (1944); *Reverie* and *Virginia Reels* for Violin and Piano (1989); piano pieces, including the suite *To Elmira with Love* (1972; orchestrated, 1983), *Diary Pages* for 2 Pianos (1978), and *Aaronesque* (for Aaron Copland's 80th birthday; 1980); various vocal scores, choral pieces, and songs; also film scores and many transcriptions and arrangements.

Balfe, Michael William, notable Irish composer; b. Dublin, May 15, 1808; d. Rowney Abbey, Hertfordshire, Oct. 20, 1870. He was the son of a dancing master, and as a small child played the violin for his father's dancing classes. He subsequently took violin lessons with O'Rourke. After his father's death on Jan. 6, 1823, Balfe went to London, where he studied violin with Charles Edward Horn and composition with Carl Friedrich Horn. In 1824 he was engaged as a violinist at the Drury Lane Theatre; also sang in London and in the provinces. His patron, Count Mazzara, took him to Italy in 1825; there he took composition lessons with Federici in Milan and voice lessons with Filippo Galli; there also he produced his 1st ballet, *La Pérouse* (1826). He met Rossini, who advised him to continue singing lessons with Bordogni; in 1828 he was engaged as principal baritone at the Italian Opera in Paris. In Italy he married the Hungarian vocalist **Lina Rosa** (b. 1808; d. London, June 8, 1888). Returning to England in 1833, he devoted himself to the management of opera houses and to composition. He was manager of the Lyceum Theatre during the 1841–42 season. He made London his principal residence, with occasional visits to Vienna (1846), Berlin (1848), St. Petersburg, and Trieste (1852–56). Apart from his administrative duties, he displayed great energy in composing operas, most of them to English librettos; of these, *The Bohemian Girl*, produced at the Drury Lane Theatre in London on Nov. 27, 1843, obtained an extraordinary success and became a perennial favorite on the English stage; it was also tr. into French, German, and Italian. In 1864 he retired to his country seat at Rowney Abbey. His daughter, Victoire, made her debut as a singer at the Lyceum Theatre in London in 1857.

WORKS: OPERAS: 3 early operas in Italian, *I rivali di se stessi* (Palermo, 1829), *Un avertimento ai gelosi* (Pavia, 1830), *Enrico IV al Passo della Marna* (Milan, Feb. 19, 1833); in French, *L'Étoile de Séville* (Paris Opéra, Dec. 17, 1845). The following operas were produced in English at Drury Lane and Covent Garden in London and other theaters: *The Siege of Rochelle* (Drury Lane, London, Oct. 29, 1835); *The Maid of Artois* (May 27, 1836); *Catherine Grey* (May 27, 1837); *Joan of Arc* (Nov. 30, 1837); *Diadeste, or The Veiled Lady* (May 17, 1838); *Falstaff* (in Italian, July 19, 1838); *Këolanthe, or The Unearthly Bride* (March 9, 1841); *Le Puits d'amour* (Opéra-Comique, Paris, April 20, 1843; in Eng. as *Geraldine*, Princess's Theatre, London, Aug. 14, 1843); *The Bohemian Girl*, Balfe's most famous work (Drury Lane Theatre, London, Nov. 27, 1843); *Les Quatre Fils Aymon* (Opéra-Comique, Paris, July 9, 1844; in Eng. as *The Castle of Aymon*, Princess's Theatre, London, Nov. 20, 1844); *The Daughter of St. Mark* (Nov. 27, 1844); *The Enchantress* (May 14, 1845); *The Bondman* (Dec. 11, 1846); *The Maid of Honour* (Dec. 20, 1847); *The Sicilian Bride* (March 6, 1852); *The Devil's in It* (July 26, 1852); *Moro, the Painter of Antwerp* (Jan. 28, 1882; orig. produced as *Pittore e duca*, Trieste, Nov. 21, 1854); *The Rose of Castille* (Oct. 29, 1857);

Satanella, or The Power of Love (Dec. 20, 1858); *Bianca, or The Bravo's Bride* (Dec. 6, 1860); *The Puritan's Daughter* (Nov. 30, 1861); *Blanche de Nevers* (Nov. 21, 1863); *The Armourer of Nantes* (Feb. 12, 1863); *The Sleeping Queen*, operetta (Aug. 31, 1864); *The Knight of the Leopard* (Liverpool, Jan. 15, 1891; orig. produced in London as *Il talismano*, June 11, 1874). **VOCAL:** *Mazeppa*, a cantata, and 2 other cantatas; ballads, glees, songs.

BIBL.: C. Kenney, *A Memoir of M.W. B.* (London, 1875); W.A. Barrett, *B.: His Life and Work* (London, 1882).

Balfoort, Dirk Jacobus, Dutch musicologist; b. Utrecht, July 19, 1886; d. The Hague, Nov. 11, 1964. He studied with Evert Cornelis; played violin in various German orchs.; then held teaching posts in the Netherlands; also organized concerts of old music by Dutch composers. He publ. valuable books (in Dutch) on music making in the Netherlands: *De Hollandsche vioolmakers* (Amsterdam, 1931); *Het Muziekleven in Nederland in de 17e en 18e eeuw* (Amsterdam, 1938); a monograph on Stradivarius (Amsterdam, 1945; also in German and Eng.); etc.

Balin, Marty, American pop musician, singer, and songwriter; b. Cincinnati, Jan. 30, 1942. His real name was **Martyn Jerel Buchwald.** He materialized in San Francisco, performing with a folk group; then formed a band under a puzzling name, The Jefferson Airplane, which specialized in a fusion of hard rock and soft folk music. Other members of the band were the guitarists **Paul Kantner** and Jorma Kaukonen, the vocalist Singe Toly, the string-bass player Bob Harvey, and the drummer Jerry Pelequin. The group gave its 1st performance in San Francisco on Aug. 13, 1965. There were inevitable changes in personnel, and the vocalist **Grace Slick** joined the group. Their 1st album, under the proud name *Jefferson Airplane Takes Off*, inaugurated the so-called San Francisco sound. There followed the highly successful albums *Surrealistic Pillow, After Bathing at Baxter's, Volunteers,* and *Bless Its Pointed Head.* The Jefferson Airplane cultivated calculated absurdity in the titles of its songs and a total stylistic heterogeneity, covering the spectrum from the beatnik era through the hippie period and ending in psychedelic abstraction. Among Balin's contributions were a romantic ballad, *Comin' Back to Me*; a kinetic, frenetic, psychedelic song, *3/5 of a Mile in 10 Seconds*; and the surreal *Plastic Fantastic Lover.* In 1968 the Jefferson Airplane made a successful European tour, but soon personal discords and political divergencies in their common social radicalism led to a gradual dissolution of the group. They got together again in 1975 with the successful *Red Octopus*, which included Balin's hit *Miracles*, disbanded again, and reassembled for another psychedelic flight in 1980 with the self-denigrating collection *The Worst of The Jefferson Airplane.*

Balkwill, Bryan (Havell), English conductor; b. London, July 2, 1922. After private studies, he won a scholarship to the Royal Academy of Music in London. He then was conductor with the New London Opera. In 1950 he conducted at Glyndebourne, eventually becoming associate conductor. He also served as music director of the Festival Ballet (London). From 1959 to 1965 he was resident conductor at the Royal Opera House, Covent Garden. He was music director of the Welsh National Opera (1963–67) and of the Sadler's Wells Opera (1966–69). He then conducted widely in both opera and sym. In 1978 he was appointed a prof. of music at the Indiana Univ. School of Music.

Ball, Ernest R., American composer of popular songs; b. Cleveland, July 21, 1878; d. Santa Ana, Calif., May 3, 1927. He studied at the Cleveland Cons.; moved to N.Y., where he earned his living as a vaudeville pianist. His 1st success came with the song *Will You Love Me in December as You Do in May?* to the words of James J. Walker (later, mayor of N.Y.). No less successful were his sentimental songs *Mother Machree, When Irish Eyes Are Smiling, Little Bit of Heaven, Dear Little Boy of Mine, Till the Sands of the Desert Grow Cold, Love Me and the World Is Mine*, etc., sung by John McCormack and other famous artists. Ball was a charter member of ASCAP (1914).

Ball, Michael, English composer; b. Manchester, Nov. 10, 1946. He began writing music at an early age, producing an opera for children when he was 11. In 1964 he entered the Royal College of Music in London, where he studied with Herbert Howells, Humphrey Searle, and John Lambert; later he went to Italy, where he attended the master classes of Luciano Berio and György Ligeti. In his own works he pursued stylizations of British Renaissance music. Among his notable compositions are his *Resurrection Symphonies* (1982; Manchester, May 23, 1984), *Danses vitales: Danses macabres* for Orch. (1987), and *The Pentecost Castle* for Chorus (1988).

Ballantine, Edward, American composer; b. Oberlin, Ohio, Aug. 6, 1886; d. Oak Bluffs, Mass., July 2, 1971. He studied with Walter Spalding at Harvard Univ.; graduated with highest honors in 1907; took piano courses with Artur Schnabel and Rudolph Ganz in Berlin (1907–9). In 1912 he was appointed instructor at Harvard; became assistant prof. in 1926, associate prof. in 1932; retired in 1947. His 1st publ. work was a musical play, *The Lotos Eaters* (1907); 3 of his orch. pieces were performed by the Boston Sym. Orch.: *Prelude to The Delectable Forest* (Dec. 10, 1914), *The Eve of St. Agnes* (Jan. 19, 1917), *From the Garden of Hellas* (Feb. 9, 1923); and 1, *By a Lake in Russia,* by the Boston Pops (June 27, 1922). He also wrote a Violin Sonata and songs. His most striking work is a set of piano variations on *Mary Had a Little Lamb* (1924) in the styles of 10 composers; a 2nd series of variations on the same tune (1943) includes stylizations of Stravinsky, Gershwin, and others.

Ballard, family of French music printers. The establishment was founded on Aug. 14, 1551, by Robert Ballard, whose patent from Henri II made him "Seul imprimeur de la musique de la chambre, chapelle, et menus plaisirs du roy"; the patent was renewed to various members of the family until 1776, when it expired. The firm enjoyed a virtual monopoly on French music printing, and continued under the management of the Ballard family until 1788. Until c.1750, the movable types invented in 1540 by Guillaume le Bé were used; the Ballards printed Lully's operas in this style (from 1700); later printings were from engraved copperplates.

Ballard, Louis W(ayne), American Indian composer of Quapaw-Cherokee extraction (his Indian name is **Hunka-No-Zhe,** which means Grand Eagle); b. Miami, Okla., July 8, 1931. He studied piano and composition at Oklahoma Univ. and Tulsa Univ.; obtained his B.A. in music in 1954, and M.M. in composition in 1962. He subsequently took private lessons with Darius Milhaud, Castelnuovo-Tedesco, and Carlos Surinach. In 1964 he traveled in Europe under the auspices of the State Dept.; was awarded a Ford Foundation grant in 1971. He was subsequently appointed program director at the Bureau of Indian Affairs in Washington, D.C. (1971–79). He wrote 2 books on American Indian music: *My Music Reaches to the Sky* (1973) and *Music of North American Indians* (1975). Virtually all his compositions are musical realizations of authentic Indian melodies and rhythms. **Works:** *Koshare,* ballet on Hopi themes (Barcelona, May 16, 1966); *The God Will Hear,* cantata (1966); *The 4 Moons,* ballet commemorating the 60th anniversary of the statehood of Oklahoma (Tulsa, Oct. 28, 1967); *Devil's Promenade* for Orch. (Tulsa, May 20, 1973); *Incident at Wounded Knee* for Orch. in 4 sections, dramatizing the rebellion of the Sioux Indians at the locality known as Wounded Knee in South Dakota (partial perf., St. Paul, Minn., April 16, 1974); *Ritmo Indio* for Woodwind Quintet and a Sioux Flute (1968); *Katcina Dances* for Cello and Piano (1970); *Desert Trilogy* for Winds, Strings, and Percussion (1971); *Cacega Ayuwipi* (The Decorative Drums) for Percussion Ensemble of 35 instruments and Standard Drums (Washington, D.C., July 27, 1973); *Thus Spake Abraham,* cantata (1976); *City of Fire* for Piano (1981); *Xactce'oyan* (Companion of Talking God) for Orch. (1982);

Fantasy Aborigine III for Orch. (1984). He publ. a collection of percussion pieces, *Pan-Indian Rhythms.*

Ballif, Claude, French composer; b. Paris, May 22, 1924. He studied composition at the Paris Cons. with Tony Aubin, Noël Gallon, and Messiaen, and later in Berlin with Blacher and Rufer. For several years he was connected with various pedagogical insts. in Paris; he was associated with the Groupe de Recherches Musicales of the French Radio and Television (1959–61), and in 1964 he was appointed to the staff of the Rheims Cons. From 1971 he taught at the Paris Cons. He has also written articles on subjects dealing with modern musical techniques. Among his publications are *Introduction à la métatonalité* (Paris, 1956) and *Économie musicale—Souhaits entre symboles* (Paris, 1979). **Works:** Several works bearing surrealist titles, e.g., *Airs comprimés* for Piano (1953); *Voyage de mon oreille* for Orch. (1957); *Ceci et cela* for Orch. (1959); *À cor et à cri* for Orch. (1962); and several pieces under the generic title *Imaginaire* for Various Ensembles; also Quintet for Flute, Oboe, and String Trio (1958); Double Trio for Flute, Oboe, Cello, Violin, Clarinet, and Horn (1961); *Un Coup de dés* for Choir, Instruments, and Tape (1980).

Balling, Michael, German conductor; b. Heidingsfeld, near Würzburg, Aug. 27, 1866; d. Darmstadt, Sept. 1, 1925. He began his career as an orch. viola player. In 1892 he went to Nelson, New Zealand, where he organized a music school, an orch., and a choral society. Returning to Europe, he conducted Wagner's operas in Bayreuth, Hamburg, and Lübeck. In 1912 he succeeded Hans Richter as conductor of the renowned Hallé Orch. in Manchester, leading it until 1914. In 1919 he went to Darmstadt, where he remained until his death.

Ballista, Antonio, Italian pianist; b. Milan, March 30, 1936. He studied piano and composition at the Milan Cons., graduating in 1955; subsequently pursued a successful career as a soloist; is particularly noted for his discerning performances of avant-garde music; he also appeared in duo recitals with the pianist Bruno Canino.

Ballou, Esther Williamson, American composer; b. Elmira, N.Y., July 17, 1915; d. Chichester, England, March 12, 1973. She studied at Bennington College in Vermont and at Mills College in Oakland, Calif.; subsequently obtained a graduate degree in composition at the Juilliard School of Music in N.Y. as a student of Bernard Wagenaar. She also took private lessons with Otto Luening and Wallingford Riegger. From 1959 to 1973 she was on the faculty of the American Univ. in Washington, D.C. **Works:** ORCH.: Piano Concerto (1964); *Konzertstücke* for Viola and Orch. (1969); *Beguine* for Percussion and Strings; also arranged for 2 Pianos, 4-hands, and for 4 Pianos, 8-hands; alternate title, *40-Finger Beguine* (1960). CHAMBER: *Suite* for Double Wind Quintet (1957); *Sextette* for Brass and Piano (1962); Piano Trio (1956); *Prism* for String Trio (1969); *Capriccio* for Violin and Piano (1963); *A Plaintive Note* for Cello and Piano (1951); *A Cheerful Note* for Cello and Piano (1962); *Suite* for Cello and Piano (1952); 2 piano sonatas; *Street Scenes* for Piano (1960); a number of choruses and solo songs. BIBL.: J. Heintze, *E.W. B.: A Bio-Bibliography* (Westport, Conn., 1987).

Balmer, Luc, Swiss conductor and composer; b. Munich, July 13, 1898. He studied piano and composition with Hans Huber, Egon Petri, and Ernst Levy at the Basel Cons., and took a course with Busoni in Berlin in 1922. Returning to Switzerland, he devoted himself to conducting; from 1941 to 1964 he conducted the Musical Soc. of Bern. He composed symphonic and chamber music in a healthy romantic manner; a Piano Concerto; a Violin Concerto; and a comic opera, after Tirso de Molina, *Die drei gefoppten Ehemänner* (1969).

Balogh, Ernö, Hungarian pianist; b. Budapest, April 4, 1897; d. Mitchellville, Md., June 2, 1989. He played in public as an infant; later entered the Royal Academy of Music in Budapest as a pupil of Béla Bartók in piano and Kodály in theory.

In 1924 he emigrated to the U.S. and earned his living as a piano teacher. He also composed some amiable instrumental pieces of brief dimensions. Fritz Kreisler performed his *Caprice antique* and *Arabesque*.

Baloković, Zlatko, eminent Yugoslav violinist; b. Zagreb, March 21, 1895; d. Venice, March 29, 1965. He studied at the Zagreb Cons. as a child; then in Vienna with Sevčik. He appeared as a soloist all over the world, including Australia, where he received a state prize. He gave the 1st performance of John Alden Carpenter's Violin Concerto with the Chicago Sym. Orch. on Nov. 18, 1937. From that time on he divided his activities between America and Europe.

Balsam, Artur, Polish-born American pianist and pedagogue; b. Warsaw, Feb. 8, 1906. He studied in Lodz; made his debut there at the age of 12; then went to Berlin and enrolled at the Berlin Hochschule für Musik; in 1930 obtained the prestigious Mendelssohn Prize; in 1932 he made a U.S. tour with Yehudi Menuhin. With the advent of the anti-Semitic Nazi regime in 1933, he settled in America, where he became a superlative accompanist to celebrated artists; also played much chamber music and gave occasional solo recitals. He served on the faculties of the Eastman School of Music in Rochester, N.Y., Boston Univ., and the Manhattan School of Music; also composed cadenzas for several piano concertos of Mozart.

Balsis, Eduardas, Lithuanian composer; b. Nikolayev, Dec. 20, 1919; d. 1984. He studied composition with Račiunas at the Vilnius Cons., graduating in 1950; then took music courses at the Leningrad Cons. (1953). In 1953 he joined the faculty of the Vilnius Cons.; in 1960 was appointed chairman of the composition dept. In his music he adheres to classical forms but makes experimental use of modern techniques, including dodecaphonic progressions. **WORKS: STAGE:** *Eglè žalčiu karalienė* (Egle, Queen of Grass Snakes), ballet (Vilnius, 1960; orch. suite, 1961; 4 fragments for Violin and Piano, 1963). **ORCH.:** *Vilnius,* a sym. (1950); *Heroic Poem* (1953); 2 violin concertos (1954, 1958); *Folk Dance Suite* (1958); *Dramatic Frescoes* for Violin, Piano, and Orch. (1965); *Symphony-Concerto* for Organ, Percussion, and Orch. (1977). **VOCAL:** 3 cantatas: *Song for My Land* for Chorus and Orch. (1962), *Saulę nešantis* (He Who Carries the Sun) for High Voice, Chorus, Organ, and Percussion (1972), *Glory to Lenin* for Mixed Chorus, Male Chorus, and Children's Chorus (1976); an oratorio, *Nelieskite mėlyno gaublio* (Don't Touch the Blue Globe) for Soloists, Children's Chorus, 2 Pianos, Double Bass, and Percussion (1969). **CHAMBER:** Piano Sonata (1947); *Variations* for Piano (1948); String Quartet (1953).

Baltsa, Agnes, Greek mezzo-soprano; b. Lefkas, Nov. 19, 1944. She was educated in Athens, Munich, and Frankfurt. In 1968 she made her debut at the Frankfurt Opera, remaining there until 1972; also sang at the Deutsche Oper in West Berlin. In 1976 she made her debut at the Vienna State Opera; in 1977 she sang at Salzburg. On Dec. 13, 1979, she made her debut with the Metropolitan Opera in N.Y. as Octavian in *Der Rosenkavalier*.

Baltzar, Thomas, German violinist and composer; b. Lübeck, c.1630; d. London (buried), July 27, 1663. He was a member of a family of German musicians; in 1653 he was made a chamber violinist to Queen Christina of Sweden; about 1655 he went to England, where he established himself as a soloist at private musical gatherings. In 1661 he was named a musician-in-ordinary for the violin in the King's Private Musick. He also composed several works for violin. **BIBL.:** C. Stiehl, "Thomas Baltzar, Ein Paganini seiner Zeit," *Monatshefte für Musikgeschichte,* XX (1888); D. Boyden, *The History of Violin Playing from Its Origins to 1761* (London, 1965).

Bal y Gay, Jesús, Spanish composer and musicologist; b. Lugo, June 23, 1905. He studied in Madrid. After the outbreak of the Spanish Civil War he went to England, and eventually to Mexico, where he was appointed to the staff of the Instituto Nacional de Bellas Artes. He publ. a number of valuable essays

on Spanish music, among them *Tientos ensayos de estética musical* (Mexico City, 1960), which traces the development of the Ricercare in Spain. He composed some symphonic and chamber music.

Bamberger, Carl, Austrian conductor; b. Vienna, Feb. 21, 1902; d. N.Y., July 18, 1987. He studied at the Univ. of Vienna, then conducted opera in Germany. He went to Russia as the tide of Hitlerism became a storm, and in 1937 emigrated to the U.S. and devoted himself mainly to teaching. From 1938 to 1975 he was a member of the staff of the Mannes College of Music in N.Y. After the war he filled several conducting engagements in West Germany. He publ. a useful manual, *The Conductor's Art* (N.Y., 1965).

Bamboschek, Giuseppe, Italian-American conductor; b. Trieste, June 12, 1890; d. N.Y., June 24, 1969. He studied at the Trieste Cons., graduating in 1907. In 1913 he went to the U.S. as accompanist for Pasquale Amato; in 1919 he joined the staff at the Metropolitan Opera in N.Y., specializing in the Italian repertoire. After 1929 he was active mainly as a conductor for radio and motion pictures.

Bamert, Matthias, Swiss composer and conductor; b. Ersigen, July 5, 1942. He studied in Bern, Zürich, Darmstadt, Salzburg, and Paris. His principal teachers in composition were Jean Rivier and Pierre Boulez. He was 1st oboist of the Salzburg Mozarteum Orch. (1965–69); then became assistant conductor to Leopold Stokowski with the American Sym. Orch. of N.Y. (1970–71). He received the 1st George Szell Memorial Award, joining the conducting staff of the Cleveland Orch. in 1971. In 1977 he was appointed music director of the Swiss Radio Orch. in Basel; then was principal guest conductor of the Scottish National Orch. in Glasgow (from 1985). **WORKS:** Concertino for English Horn, String Orch., and Piano (1966); *Mantrajana* for Orch. (1971); *Ol-Okun* for String Orch. (1976); *Circus Parade* for Narrator and Orch. (1979); *Snapshots* for Orch. (1989).

Bampton, Rose, American soprano; b. Lakewood, Ohio, Nov. 28, 1908. She studied with Queena Mario at the Curtis Inst. of Music in Philadelphia; also took academic courses at Drake Univ. in Des Moines, Iowa, where she obtained a doctorate of fine arts. She sang as contralto with the Philadelphia Opera (1929–32), then changed to mezzo-soprano and finally to soprano, so that she could sing the roles of both Amneris (mezzo-soprano) and Aida (soprano). She made her debut at the Metropolitan Opera in N.Y. on Nov. 28, 1932, as Laura in *La Gioconda,* and continued on its staff until 1945; she was again with the Metropolitan Opera from 1947 to 1950. She made annual appearances at the Teatro Colón in Buenos Aires from 1942 to 1948; then returned to N.Y. She was married to the conductor **Wilfrid Pelletier.**

Banchieri, Adriano (Tomaso), eminent Italian organist and composer; b. Bologna, Sept. 3, 1568; d. there, 1634. He studied with Lucio Barbieri and Giuseppe Guami. On Sept. 8, 1589, he took Holy Orders and entered the monastery of Monte Oliveto. In 1592 he was at the monastery of S. Bartolomeo in Lucca; in 1593, in Siena; was organist at S. Maria in Regola di Imola in 1600. In 1608 he returned to Bologna, remaining there until his death. Despite his clerical rank (he became abbot in 1620), Banchieri never abandoned music, and was active in the Accademia Filarmonica in Bologna (where he was known as "Il dissonante"). He wrote numerous stage works, historically important in the evolution of early opera. Among these dramatic works were *La pazzia senile* (1598); *Il zabaione musicale* (1604); *La barca da Venezia per Padova* (1605); *La prudenza giovanile* (1607); *Tirsi, Filli e Clori* (1614). He wrote a number of masses for 3 to 8 voices, and other sacred vocal works; also several groups of instrumental works: *I canzoni alla francese a 4 voci per sonar* (1595); *Dialoghi, concentus e sinfonie* (1625); *Il virtuoso ritrovato accademico* (1626); etc. As a theorist, he advocated the extension of the hexachord and proposed to name the 7th degree of the scale by the syllables *ba* and *bi* (corresponding to B-flat and B). Banchieri's theoretical work *L'organo suonarino* (Venice, 1605) gives instructions for accompaniment with figured bass; his *Moderna prattica musicale* (Venice, 1613) contains further elaborations of the subject. Banchieri was the 1st to use the signs *f* and *p* for loudness and softness (in his *Libro III di nuovi pensieri ecclesiastici*, 1613). He also wrote dramatic plays under the name of **Camillo Scaligeri della Fratta**. A reprint of his *Sinfonia d'istromenti* (1607) is found in A. Schering's *Geschichte der Musik in Beispielen* (No. 151); the organ pieces from *L'organo suonarino* are reprinted in Torchi's *Arte musicale in Italia* (vol. III). Banchieri further publ. the treatises *Cartella musicale del canto figurato, fermo e contrappunto* (Venice, 1614); *Direttorio monastico di canto fermo* (Bologna, 1615); and *Lettere armoniche* (Bologna, 1628).

BIBL.: M. Schneider, *Die Anfänge des Basso continuo* (1918); F. Vatielli, "Il madrigale drammatico e A. B.," in *Arte e vita musicale a Bologna* (1927); F.T. Arnold, *The Art of Accompaniment from a Thorough Bass* (London, 1931); E. Capaccioli, "Precisazioni biografiche su A. B.," *Rivista Musicale* (Oct.–Dec. 1954); H.J. Wilbert, *Die Messen des A. B.* (Mainz, 1969); O. Mischiati, *A. B.* (Bologna, 1972).

Bandrowska-Turska, Eva, Polish soprano; b. Krakow, May 20, 1897; d. Warsaw, June 25, 1979. She studied with her uncle, **Alexander Bandrowski-Sas;** then took further instruction with Helena Zboinska-Ruszkowska. She made her debut as a concert singer in 1919, and subsequently appeared in opera; in later years she gained distinction as a solo singer; she excelled as a congenial interpreter of the songs of Debussy, Ravel, Roussel, and Szymanowski.

Bandrowski-Sas, Alexander, noted Polish tenor; b. Lubaczów, April 22, 1860; d. Krakow, May 28, 1913. He made his stage debut as a baritone in an operetta production in Lemberg in 1881, using the name **Barski;** then studied voice with Sangiovanni in Milan and Salvi in Vienna; subsequently pursued a successful career as a tenor, using the name **Brandt;** sang in Vienna (1890), in Berlin (1896, 1898), and in Dresden and Munich, and at La Scala in Milan (1896, 1899); was a member of the Frankfurt Opera (1889–1901); also filled engagements in N.Y., Philadelphia, Chicago, and Boston. He retired from the stage in 1904, and then taught voice in Krakow.

Bandy, "Mo" (Marion F., Jr.), American country-music singer and guitarist; b. Meridian, Miss., Feb. 12, 1944. He learned to play guitar from his father, the leader of a country-music band; after 1972 made regular appearances on the "Grand Ole Opry" in Nashville and toured the U.S. and Europe. He upheld the cause of traditional country music against the inroads of country pop, regaling his public with songs of honky-tonk provenance.

Banevich, Sergei, Soviet composer; b. Okhansk, near Perm, Dec. 2, 1941. He studied composition at the Leningrad Cons., graduating in 1966. As a composer he devoted himself mainly to the musical theater; also wrote children's pieces for various instruments.

WORKS: *White Is the Lonely Sail,* opera (1972); *Ferdinand the Magnificent,* opera (1974); *Goodbye, Arbat!,* operetta (1976); *The Cat That Walked by Himself,* musical play after Kipling (1977); songs.

Banister, Henry Charles, English music theorist, teacher, and composer; b. London, June 13, 1831; d. Streatham, near London, Nov. 20, 1897. He studied music with his father, a cellist; then with Cipriani Potter at the Royal Academy of Music, where he twice gained the King's scholarship (1846 and 1848); was appointed assistant prof. (1853) of harmony and composition at the Royal Academy of Music; taught harmony at Guildhall School (from 1880) and at the Royal Normal College for the Blind (from 1881). He publ. *Textbook of Music* (London, 1872; 15 eds. since); *Some Musical Ethics and Analogies* (1884); *Lectures on Musical Analysis* (1887); *Musical Art and Study* (1888); *George Alexander Macfarren* (1892); *Helpful Papers for Harmony Students* (1895); *The Harmonising of Melodies* (1897); and *The Art of Modulating* (1901). A collection of his lectures, *Interludes,* ed. by Macpherson, appeared in 1898.

Banister composed 4 syms. and 5 overtures, chamber music, cantatas, piano pieces, and songs.

Banister, John, English violinist and composer, father of **John Banister, Jr.;** b. London, c.1625; d. there, Oct. 3, 1679. After he had received some musical instruction from his father, his skill earned him the patronage of King Charles II, who sent him to France for further study; was later a member of Charles's band, until an outspoken preference for the English over the French musicians playing in it caused his expulsion. Banister was director of a music school, and established the 1st public concerts not associated with taverns or other gathering places in which music was of only incidental importance, in London (1672–78); was a prominent figure in the English musical life of his day. He wrote music for Davenant's *Circe* and Shakespeare's *The Tempest* (both 1676); composed *New Ayres and Dialogues* for Voices and Viols (London, 1678); contributed to Playford's *Courtly Masquing Ayres* (1662), and to Lock's *Melothesia* (1673); also wrote music for plays by Dryden, Shadwell, and Wycherley.

Banister, John, Jr., English violinist and composer, son of **John Banister;** b. London, c.1663; d. there, c.1725. He studied violin with his father; served as concertmaster at the Italian Opera in London. He composed mostly for the theater; contributed to Playford's *Division Violin* (1685), the 1st violin manual publ. in England.

Bank, Jacques, Dutch composer; b. Borne, April 18, 1943. He studied with Jos Kunst and Ton de Leeuw at the Amsterdam Cons., graduating in 1974. Apart from his musical activities, he taught English in Amsterdam schools.

WORKS: *Blind Boy Fuller I* for Recorder, Piano, and optional Voice, being a recording of *Thousand Women Blues,* sung by Blind Boy Fuller in 1940 in Chicago (1966); *The Memoirs of a Cyclist* for 2 Recorders (1967–70); *Emcée* for Voices (1969); *Put Me on My Bike I* for Solo Baritone, Recorder, and Chorus (1971); *Fan It* for Orch. (1973); *Song of Sitting Bull* for Recorder Player possessing a Baritone Voice, and Organ (1974); *Monk's Blues* for Piano, 14 Voices, and 12 Winds (1974); *Blue Mosque* for Bass Recorder (1974); *Die Ouwe* (The Old One) for Bass Recorder, Bass Clarinet, and Piano (1975); *Hitch* for Piano (1975); *Last Post* for Bass Clarinet and Piano (1975); *Thomas* for the recorded Voice of poet Dylan Thomas reading his "Lament," and 19 Instruments (1975); *Pathétique* for Orch. (1976); *Alexandre's Concerto* for Piano and Orch. (1978); *Coda* for Choir and Orch. (1983); *Requiem voor een levende* for Reciter, Chorus, and Chamber Ensemble (1985); *Een Tanthologie,* opera (1986–87).

Banks, Don(ald Oscar), Australian composer; b. Melbourne, Oct. 25, 1923; d. Sydney, Sept. 5, 1980. He took piano lessons as a child; played in dance bands as a youth; served in the Australian Army (1941–46). After World War II, he studied composition with Le Gallienne at the Melbourne Cons. (1947–49); went to England, where he studied composition privately in London with Mátyás Seiber (1950–52), then in Florence with Luigi Dallapiccola (1953). He remained in England and worked as an arranger and composer of film and television music; was music director of Goldsmiths' College of the Univ. of London (1965–70). In 1971 he went back to Australia and became head of the dept. of composition and electronic music at the Canberra School of Music. In some of his works he applied serial methods, modified so as not to destroy the sense of tonality; he also made effective use of electronics.

WORKS: ORCH.: *4 Pieces* (1953; London, June 1, 1954); *Episode* for Chamber Orch. (1958); *Elizabethan Miniatures* for Lute, Viola da Gamba, and Strings (1962); *Divisions* (Cheltenham Festival, July 12, 1965); Horn Concerto (1965; London, Feb. 27, 1966; Barry Tuckwell, soloist); *Assemblies* (1966; Melbourne, Dec. 3, 1966); Violin Concerto (1966; London, Aug. 12, 1966); *Intersections* for Orch. and Tape (1969; London, Jan. 1970); *Meeting Place* for Chamber Orch., Jazz Group, and 2 Synthesizers (London, June 15, 1970); *Nexus* for Jazz Quintet and Orch. (1970; Kassel, April 8, 1971); *Music for Wind Band* (1971); *Prospects* (1974); *Trilogy* (1977).

CHAMBER: *Duo* for Violin and Cello (1951–52); *Divertimento* for Flute and String Trio (1951–52); Violin Sonata (1953); *Sonata da Camera,* in memory of Seiber, for 8 Instruments (1961); *Equation I* for 12 Players (1963), *II* for 12 Players (1969), and *III* for Chamber Group, Jazz Quartet, and Synthesizers (1972); Trio for Violin, Horn, and Piano (1962); *Sequence* for Solo Cello (1967); *Prelude, Night Piece and Blues for 2* for Clarinet and Piano (1968); *4 Pieces* for String Quartet (1971); *Take 8* for String Quartet and Jazz Quartet (1973); String Quartet (1976); *4 × 2* for Clarinet(s) and Tape (1977).

VOCAL: *Psalm 70* for Voice and Chamber Orch. (1954); *5 North Country Folk Songs* for Voice, and String Orch. or Piano (1953–54); *Settings from Roget* for Voice and Jazz Quartet (1966); *Tirade,* triptych for Soprano, Harp, Piano, and 3 Percussionists (1968); *Findings Keepings* for Chorus and Percussion (1969); *Limbo,* cantata for 3 Singers, 8 Instruments, and 2-channel Tape (1971); *Benedictus* for Voices, Jazz Quartet, 5 Synthesizers, Fender Electric Piano, and Tape (1976).

PIANO: *Pezzo dramatico* (1956); *Commentary* for Piano and Tape (1971).

BIBL.: W. Mann, "The Music of D. B.," *Musical Times* (Aug. 1968).

Bannister, Henry (-Marriott), English music editor and bibliographer; b. Oxford, March 18, 1854; d. there, Feb. 16, 1919. He studied theology; was ordained priest in 1878; publ. the valuable editions *Monumenti Vaticani di paleografia musicale latina* (Leipzig, 1913; also in Italian tr. by R. Baralli, a catalogue of the music MSS in the Vatican Library, including 141 plates; *Anglo-French Sequelae* (ed. by Dom Anselm Hughes and publ. by The Plainsong and Medieval Music Soc. in 1934); co-ed. vols. 47, 49, 53, and 54 of *Analecta Hymnica Medii Aevi* (1886–1922); also publ. some MSS of the Abbey of Coupar-Angus in Scotland, with a brief description (Rome, 1910); ed. a Gallican sacramentary, *Missale Gothicum,* with introduction and liturgical notes (London, 1917–19). He was for many years librarian of the Bodleian Library at Oxford.

Banshchikov, Gennadi, Soviet composer; b. Kazan, Nov. 9, 1943. He studied composition with Balasanian at the Moscow Cons. (1961–64) and with Arapov at the Leningrad Cons. (1965–66); in 1973 he was appointed to the faculty of the Leningrad Cons. In his works he adopts a fairly progressive, even aggressive, modern idiom, making an occasional use of serial techniques.

WORKS: STAGE: *The Legend Remained,* radio opera for children (1967); *Lyubov and Silin,* chamber opera (1968); *The Stolen Sun,* television opera (1969); *Vestris,* ballet (1969); *Opera about How Ivan Ivanovich Quarreled with Ivan Nikiforovich,* comic opera after the Gogol tale (1971); *The Death of Cornet Klauzov,* 1-act opera after Chekhov's "The Brimstone Match" (1976). **ORCH.:** *Triade* (1962); 5 cello concertos: No. 1 (1962); No. 2 (1963); No. 3 for Cello Solo (1965); No. 4, *Duodecimet,* for Cello and 11 Instruments (1966); No. 5 (1970); Piano Concerto (1963; rev. 1978); Trumpet Concertino (1963); 2 syms.: No. 1 (1967) and No. 2 for Strings (1977). **VOCAL:** Song cycle for Soprano and Piano, to poems by García Lorca (1962); 3 cantatas: *Architects* for Bass, Male Chorus, and Orch. (1964); *To the Memory of García Lorca* for Chorus and Chamber Orch. (1965); *Ashes in the Palms,* chamber cantata to poems by César Vallejo (1978). **CHAMBER:** *4 Impressions* for Cello and Piano (1963; rev. 1978); *Small Duet* for Violin and Piano (1965); *4 Pieces* for Clarinet and Piano (1968); Cello Sonata (1970); *Trio-Sonata* for Violin, Viola, and Cello (1972); Clarinet Sonata (1972); Flute Sonata (1975); Accordion Sonata (1977). **PIANO:** *Concert Allegro* (1963); *Syllogisms* (1964); 3 sonatas (1968, 1973, 1974).

Banti, Brigida (née **Giorgi**), famous Italian soprano; b. Monticelli d'Ongina, 1759; d. Bologna, Feb. 18, 1806. She sang in Paris cafés, where she attracted the attention of de Vismes, director of the Paris Opéra, who engaged her to sing there. She made her debut on Nov. 1, 1776, singing a song during the intermission. She then studied with Sacchini. In 1779 she went to London for a season; then sang in Vienna (1780),

Venice (1782–83), Warsaw (1789), and Madrid (1793–94). Paisiello wrote for her his opera *Giuochi di Agrigento,* and she sang at its premiere (Venice, May 16, 1792). From 1794 to 1802 she sang at King's Theatre in London; then retired. She married the dancer Zaccaria Banti; her son wrote her biography.

BIBL.: G. Banti, *Vita di B. B.-G.* (Bologna, 1869); C. Lozzi, "B. B., regina del teatro lirico nel secolo XVIII," *Rivista Musicale Italiana,* XI (1904).

Bantock, Sir Granville, eminent English composer; b. London, Aug. 7, 1868; d. there, Oct. 16, 1946. He studied at the Royal Academy of Music in London, graduating in 1892; was the 1st holder of the Macfarren Scholarship. His earliest works were presented at the Academy concerts: an Egyptian ballet suite, *Rameses II;* overture, *The Fire Worshippers;* and a short opera, *Caedmar,* which was later presented at the Crystal Palace (Oct. 18, 1893). He then developed varied activities; he was founder and ed. of *New Quarterly Musical Review* (1893–96); toured as a musical comedy conductor (1894–95); organized and conducted concerts devoted to works by young British composers; conducted a military band and later a full orch. at New Brighton (1897–1901). At the same time he was engaged in teaching activities; in 1907 he succeeded Sir Edward Elgar as prof. of music at Birmingham Univ., a post he retained until 1934, when he became chairman of the board of Trinity College of Music. In 1938, at the age of 70, he undertook a journey to India and Australia, returning to England on the eve of World War II. He was married in 1898 to Helen von Schweitzer, daughter of the poet Hermann von Schweitzer. Bantock was knighted in 1930. As a composer, he was attracted to exotic subjects with mystical overtones; his interests were cosmopolitan and embraced all civilizations, with a particular predilection for the Celtic and oriental cultures; however, his music was set in Western terms. He was a strong believer in the programmatic significance of musical images, and most of his works bear titles relating to literature, mythology, or legend. Yet he was a typically British composer in the treatment of his materials. His works are brilliantly scored and effective in performance, but few of them have been retained in the repertoire of musical organizations.

WORKS: 3 Celtic operas: *Caedmar* (1892), *The Pearl of Iran* (1894), and *The Seal-Woman* (Birmingham, Sept. 27, 1924); ballets: *Egypt* (1892), *Lalla Rookh* (1902), *The Great God Pan* (1902); 5 tone poems: *Thalaba the Destroyer* (1900), *Dante* (1901; rev. 1910), *Fifine at the Fair* (1901), *Hudibras* (1902), *The Witch of Atlas* (1902); overture, *The Pierrot of the Minute* (1908); *Hebridean Symphony* (Glasgow, Jan. 17, 1916); *Pagan Symphony* (1923–28); *Celtic Symphony* for Strings and 6 Harps (1940); *2 Heroic Ballads* (1944); *The Funeral* (1946); choral works with Orch.: *The Time Spirit* (1902); *Sea Wanderers* (1906); *Omar Khayyám* (in 3 parts; 1906–9; Bantock's most ambitious work); *The Pilgrim's Progress* (1928); *Prometheus Unbound* (1936); numerous works for Unaccompanied Chorus, among them 3 "choral syms.": *Atalanta in Calydon* (1911), *Vanity of Vanities* (1913), *A Pageant of Human Life* (1913); also *The Golden Journey to Samarkand* (1922); choral suites to words from the Chinese; children's songs to the poems of Helen Bantock; works for brass band, cello, and orch. and for voice and orch.; 2 string quartets; 3 violin sonatas; viola sonatas; cello sonatas; several sets of piano pieces; *Songs of the East* (6 cycles of 6 songs each); several sets of *Songs from the Chinese Poets;* sets of Celtic songs; etc. Bantock also ed. albums of keyboard pieces by Byrd.

BIBL.: H.O. Anderton, *G. B.* (London, 1915); H. Antcliffe, "A Brief Survey of the Works of G. B.," *Musical Quarterly* (July 1918); P.J. Pirie, "B. and His Generation," *Musical Times* (Aug. 1968); M. Bantock, *G. B.: A Personal Portrait* (London, 1972).

Banwart, Jakob, German composer; b. Sigmaringen, May 19, 1609; d. Konstanz, c.1657. He studied with Daniel Bollius, the court organist in Sigmaringen; then (1629–31) continued his education at Dillingen Univ., where he received a master's degree; he was ordained in Konstanz in 1632, and subsequently was active as a musician at the court there; in 1641 he became Kapellmeister of the Cathedral. He composed mostly music for the church, but also took time off to write a collection of humorous dialogues, quodlibets, and other pieces which were publ. in his lifetime.

Bar-Illan, David (Jacob), Israeli pianist; b. Haifa, Feb. 7, 1930. He 1st studied piano in his native city; then continued his studies at the Juilliard School of Music and the Mannes College of Music in N.Y. After playing in his native Israel, he made his 1st appearance with the N.Y. Phil. in 1960; in subsequent seasons he appeared with all of the major orchs. of the U.S.; also played with many orchs. of Europe. From 1980 he taught at the Mannes College of Music.

Baranović, Krešimir, eminent Croatian composer; b. Šibenik, July 25, 1894; d. Belgrade, Sept. 17, 1975. He studied piano and theory in Zagreb and in Vienna. He was subsequently a theater conductor in Zagreb (1915–27); then traveled with Anna Pavlova's ballet group (1927–28). Returning to Yugoslavia, he was music director of the Zagreb Opera (1929–40); then served as a prof. at the Belgrade Academy (1946–61); was also conductor of the Belgrade Phil. (1952–61). A prolific composer, he was successful mostly in music for the theater. **WORKS: COMIC OPERAS:** *Striženo-Košeno* (Clipped and Mowed; Zagreb, May 4, 1932, composer conducting) and *Nevjesta od Cetingrada* (The Bride from Cetingrad; Belgrade, May 12, 1951, composer conducting). **BALLETS:** *Kineska priča* (Chinese Tale), in which he made use of the pentatonic scale for local color (Belgrade, April 30, 1955); *The Gingerbread Heart* (Edinburgh Festival, 1951). **ORCH.:** *Pjesma guslara* (Song of the Minstrel; Zagreb, Jan. 25, 1947); *Pan* for Narrator, Voices, and Orch. (Belgrade, March 10, 1958); *Oblaci* (The Clouds) for Mezzo-soprano and Orch. (Belgrade, Oct. 31, 1964).

Barati, George, Hungarian-born American cellist, conductor, and composer; b. Györ, April 3, 1913. After initial training at the Györ Music School (graduated, 1932), he studied at the Franz Liszt Academy of Music in Budapest (graduated, 1935; teacher's diploma, 1937; artist diploma, 1938); he also was a member of the Budapest Concert Orch. (1933–36) and 1st cellist of the Budapest Sym. Orch. and Municipal Opera orch. (1936–38). In 1939, he emigrated to the U.S., becoming a naturalized citizen in 1944; he then studied composition with Georges Couvreur and Henri Switten at Westminster Choir College in Princeton, N.J. (1938–39), and with Roger Sessions at Princeton Univ. (1939–43). He played cello in the Pro Ideale (later Westminster) String Quartet (1936–39), then taught at Princeton Univ. (1939–43). He also conducted the Princeton Ensemble and Choral Union (1941–43) and the Alexandria (La.) Military Sym. Orch. (1944–46). He was a cellist in the San Francisco Sym. Orch. and the California String Quartet (1946–50); he also was music director of the Barati Chamber Orch. of San Francisco (1948–52). From 1950 to 1968 he was music director of the Honolulu Sym. Orch. and Opera, leaving to become executive director of the Montalvo Center for the Arts and conductor of the Montalvo Chamber Orch. in Saratoga, Calif. From 1971 to 1980 he was music director of the Santa Cruz County Sym. Orch. in Aptos, Calif.; he then was music director of the Barati Ensemble (from 1989). As a composer, he writes fine music in a modern European tradition. During his stay in Hawaii, he studied native melodic and rhythmic patterns of exotic South Sea islands, and these found reflection in some of his works of the period. **WORKS: STAGE:** *OPERA: Noelani* (1968). **BALLET:** *The Love of Don Perlimplin* (1947). **INCIDENTAL MUSIC:** *30 Pieces of Silver* for Narrator and Chamber Orch. (1951). **FILM SCORES:** *The Ugly Duckling* (1981; arranged as a suite for Narrator, and Chamber Orch. or Band, 1982–83); *What Do 2 Rights Make?* (1983). **ORCH.:** *2 Symphonic Movements* (1941); *Lamentoso* (1943); *Scherzo* (1946); *Configuration* (1947); Chamber Concerto for Flute, Oboe, Clarinet, Bassoon, and String Orch. (1952); Cello Concerto (1953; rev. 1957); *The Dragon and*

the Phoenix (1960); Sym. (1963); *Polarization* (1965); *Festival Hula,* symphonic dance (1968); Piano Concerto (1973); Guitar Concerto (1976; rev. 1982); *Branches of Time* for 2 Pianos and Orch. (Santa Cruz, Calif., March 21, 1981); Violin Concerto (1986); also much chamber music, including 2 string quartets (1944, 1961); piano pieces; vocal works.

Barbaja, Domenico, successful Italian impresario; b. Milan, c.1775; d. Posilipo, near Naples, Oct. 19, 1841. Early in life he exhibited a talent for making money by concocting and selling food and sweets that satisfied popular tastes; he was reputed to be the inventor of whipped cream with coffee or chocolate, which became known as *barbajata,* or *granita di caffè.* In 1808 he obtained the lease of the gambling tables in Naples. On Oct. 7, 1809, he was appointed manager of all of the royal opera houses in Naples; so powerful did he become that he was nicknamed "Viceroy of Naples." Upon the advice of his mistress, the well-known singer Isabella Colbran, he entered the theatrical business, and in 1826 was appointed manager of La Scala in Milan; simultaneously he was impresario of San Carlo in Naples (1809–24) and 2 theaters in Vienna (1821–28). He continued the management of La Scala until 1832. A convivial character, he easily formed friendships with Rossini, Bellini, and Donizetti, and induced them to write operas for the theaters under his management. Emil Lucka wrote a novel, *Der Impresario* (Vienna, 1937), based on his life. **BIBL.:** G. Monaldi, *Impresari celebri del secolo XIX* (Milan, 1918).

Barbe, Helmut, German organist and composer; b. Halle, Dec. 28, 1927. He studied music theory in Berlin with Ernst Pepping and choral conducting with Gottfried Grote; was active as church organist and conductor in Berlin. In 1952 he became Kantor at St. Nikolai Church in Spandau; in 1955 was appointed member of the faculty of the Berlin Kirchenmusikschule. In 1973 he was named Landeskirchenmusikdirektor. In his own works he adopted a modified dodecaphony. He composed mostly sacred choral works and various organ pieces; also wrote a Violin Concerto (1966) and *Hovs Hallar* for Organ, 12 Solo Strings, and Percussion (1970). In his works he adopted a median modernistic technique with polytonal and atonal elements applied when necessary.

Barbeau, Marius, eminent French-Canadian anthropologist, ethnologist, and folklorist; b. Ste.-Marie-de-Beauce, Quebec, March 5, 1883; d. Ottawa, Feb. 27, 1969. As a Rhodes scholar he studied at Oriel College, Oxford; later took courses at the Sorbonne in Paris. In 1911 he was appointed anthropologist at the Museum Branch of the Geological Survey of Canada; was pensioned in 1948. His main study was devoted to the codification of folkloric materials of Canadian Indians and the French population of Quebec. He collected more than 6,000 melodies and 13,000 texts of French-Canadian folk songs and many thousands of Indian melodies, making use of phonograph recordings. From 1927 to 1930 he was in charge of folk-music festivals in Quebec. In 1956 he organized the Canadian Folk Music Soc. He publ. 30 books and 10 anthologies of songs in collaboration with other Canadian folklorists. Among his most important publications are "Chants populaires du Canada," *Journal of American Folklore* (with E. Massicotte; 1919); *Folksongs of French Canada* (with E. Sapir; New Brunswick, 1925); *Jongleur Songs of Old Quebec* (Toronto, 1962). For a bibliography of Barbeau's writings, almost 100 books and 600 articles, see Israel Katz, "Marius Barbeau, 1883–1969," *Journal of the Society for Ethnomusicology* (Jan. 1970).

Barber, Samuel, American composer of superlative gifts; b. West Chester, Pa., March 9, 1910; d. New York, Jan. 23, 1981. His mother was a good pianist; her sister was the famous opera contralto **Louise Homer.** Barber began taking piano lessons as a child with William Hatton Green; he also improvised, and composed a piano piece, entitled *Sadness.* At the age of 10 he attempted to write an opera, *The Rose Tree.* He played piano at school functions, and had an occasional job as organist in a local church. At the age of 14 he enrolled at the newly founded Curtis Inst. of Music in Philadelphia; there he studied piano with Isabelle Vengerova, composition with Rosario Scalero, and conducting with Fritz Reiner. He also took singing lessons with Emilio de Gogorza. So successful was he as a voice student that he ventured to appear in public as a mellow baritone. However, it was free composition that became his absorbing labor. At the time when most American composers exerted their ingenuity writing sophisticated music laced with unresolvable dissonances, Barber kept aloof from facile and fashionable modernism. He adopted an idiom, lyrical and romantic in nature, which had a distinct originality in its melodic and harmonic aspects. His *Overture to the School for Scandal*, after Sheridan (1933), attracted favorable attention. It was closely followed by *Music for a Scene from Shelley*, which had numerous performances. In 1935 Barber received a Pulitzer traveling scholarship and the American Prix de Rome. His *Symphony No. 1*, in 1 movement, which he composed in Rome, became the 1st American work to be presented at the Salzburg Festival of Contemporary Music (July 25, 1937). On Nov. 5, 1938, Toscanini conducted the NBC Sym. Orch. in Barber's *Essay for Orchestra No. 1* and *Adagio for Strings* (arranged from Barber's String Quartet); the *Adagio* was destined to become one of the most popular American works of serious music, and through some lurid aberration of circumstance, it also became a favorite selection at state funerals. It formed the background music at Roosevelt's commemorative service in 1945; the passionate serenity of its modal strains moved the family and friends of Princess Grace of Monaco to tears when it was played at her funeral on Sept. 18, 1982. From 1939 to 1942, Barber intermittently taught orchestration at the Curtis Inst. In the autumn of 1942 he joined the Army Air Force, which commissioned him to write a sym., his 2nd. The original score included an electronic instrument producing sound in imitation of radio signals; it was successfully performed by Koussevitzky with the Boston Sym. Orch. in 1944; but after the war Barber decided to eliminate such incidental intercalations; this demilitarized version was performed by the Philadelphia Orch. in 1949. Still dissatisfied with the resultant product, he discarded the work except for the 2nd movement, which he retitled as *Night Flight*, and had performed in Cleveland in 1964. Barber was discharged from the air force in 1945 and settled in Mount Kisco, N.Y., in a house (named "Capricorn") that he had purchased jointly with Gian Carlo Menotti in 1943. Barber was always devoted to the art of the theater. He wrote a ballet, *The Serpent Heart*, for Martha Graham (1946), which was later revised and produced by her group under the title *Cave of the Heart;* from it he drew an orch. suite, *Medea;* a further version of the music was *Medea's Meditation and Dance of Vengeance.* In his *Prayers of Kierkegaard* for Soprano, Chorus, and Orch. (1954), Barber essayed the style of modern oratorio. But it was not until 1957 that he wrote his 1st opera, *Vanessa*, with a romantic libretto by his lifelong friend Gian Carlo Menotti; it was produced by the Metropolitan Opera in N.Y. on Jan. 15, 1958, and earned Barber his 1st of 2 Pulitzer Prizes in music; a revised version was produced at the Spoleto Festival U.S.A. in Charleston, S.C., on May 27, 1978. A much more ambitious opera, commissioned by the Metropolitan Opera, was *Antony and Cleopatra*, in 3 acts, after Shakespeare, produced with a grand display of expectations at the opening of the new Metropolitan Opera House in N.Y. on Sept. 16, 1966. Unfortunately, the production was haunted by mechanical mishaps. A specially constructed revolving stage did not rotate properly, the acoustics were faulty, and the annoyed newspaper critics damned the music along with the staging. Barber attempted to recoup the work with a libretto revamped by Menotti, but the new version, performed at the Juilliard School of Music (1975), failed to justify his hopes. Disillusioned in his capacity to create a modern grand opera, Barber produced a light operatic sketch, *A Hand of Bridge*, to a libretto by Menotti (1959), but it passed without much notice. However, Barber was gloriously vindicated as an important composer by a succession of fine works of instrumental music; particularly notable was his Piano Con-

certo (1962), a striking work in an original modern idiom, spontaneously acclaimed in repeated performances in America and Europe, which won him his 2nd Pulitzer Prize. No less remarkable was his Piano Sonata, introduced by Vladimir Horowitz in 1949; in it Barber made ample use of modernistic resources, including incidental applications of 12-tone writing. Another example of Barber's brilliant use of pianistic resources was his witty piano suite *Excursions* (1945). Barber excelled in new American music primarily as a melodist; perhaps the circumstance that he studied singing as a youth had contributed to his sensitive handling of vocally shaped patterns. Although the harmonic structures of his music remained fundamentally tonal, he made free use of chromatic techniques, verging on atonality and polytonality, while his mastery of modern counterpoint enabled him to write canons and fugues in effective neo-Baroque sequences. His orchestration was opulent without being turgid; his treatment of solo instruments was unfailingly congenial to their nature even though requiring a virtuoso technique. Barber held 3 Guggenheim fellowships (1945, 1947, 1949). In 1959 Harvard Univ. conferred upon him an honorary degree of Doctor of Fine Arts.

WORKS: OPERAS: *Vanessa*, to a libretto by Menotti (Metropolitan Opera, N.Y., Jan. 15, 1958; rev. version, Spoleto Festival U.S.A., Charleston, S.C., May 27, 1978); *Antony and Cleopatra*, after Shakespeare (N.Y., Sept. 16, 1966; rev. version, Juilliard School of Music, N.Y., Feb. 6, 1975); *A Hand of Bridge*, 1-act opera, to a libretto by Menotti, for 4 Solo Voices and Chamber Orch. (1958; Festival of Two Worlds, Spoleto, Italy, June 17, 1959).

BALLETS: *The Serpent Heart* (perf. by Martha Graham and her dance group, N.Y., May 10, 1946; rev. and produced under the title *Cave of the Heart*, N.Y., Feb. 27, 1947).

ORCH.: *Overture to the School for Scandal*, after Sheridan (Philadelphia, Aug. 30, 1933); *Music for a Scene from Shelley* (N.Y., March 24, 1933); *Symphony No. 1*, in 1 movement (Rome, Dec. 13, 1936); *Adagio for Strings*, arranged from the slow movement of the String Quartet (N.Y., NBC Sym. Orch., Nov. 5, 1938, Toscanini conducting; his *Essay No. 1* was perf. at the same concert); *Essay No. 2* (N.Y. Phil., April 16, 1942, Bruno Walter conducting); *Commando March*, orig. for Military Band (symphonic version, Boston Sym., Oct. 29, 1943, Koussevitzky conducting); *Symphony No. 2* (Boston, March 3, 1944, Koussevitzky conducting; an antiseptic version, radically cleansed of instrumental irrelevancies, was perf. by the Philadelphia Orch., Ormandy conducting, Jan. 21, 1949; in another surgical operation, the 2nd movement was reworked, retitled *Night Flight*, and 1st perf. in Cleveland, Oct. 8, 1964); *Capricorn Concerto* for Flute, Oboe, Trumpet, and Strings (N.Y., Oct. 8, 1944); *Medea*, suite from the ballet *The Serpent Heart* (Philadelphia, Dec. 5, 1947); *Souvenirs*, ballet suite (orig. for Piano, 4-hands) for Orch. (Chicago, Nov. 13, 1953; stage production, N.Y., Nov. 15, 1955); *Medea's Meditation and Dance of Vengeance*, a rev. version of the symphonic suite *Medea* (N.Y., Feb. 2, 1956); *Toccata festiva* for Organ and Orch. (Philadelphia, Sept. 30, 1960); *Die Natali*, choral prelude for Christmas (Boston Sym. Orch., Lincoln Center, N.Y., Dec. 22, 1960); *Fadograph from a Yestern Scene*, after a line in James Joyce's *Finnegans Wake* (Pittsburgh, Sept. 10, 1971); *Essay No. 3* for Orch. (N.Y., Sept. 14, 1978); *Canzonetta* for Oboe and String Orch. (1980; incomplete; orchestrated by Charles Turner, and 1st perf. by the N.Y. Phil., Dec. 17, 1981).

CONCERTOS: Violin Concerto (Philadelphia, Feb. 7, 1941; Albert Spalding, soloist; Ormandy conducting); Cello Concerto (Boston Sym., April 5, 1946; Raya Garbuzova, soloist; Koussevitzky conducting); Piano Concerto (Boston Sym., Lincoln Center, N.Y., Sept. 24, 1962; John Browning, soloist; Erich Leinsdorf conducting).

VOCAL: *Dover Beach*, after a poem by Matthew Arnold, for Voice and String Quartet (1931; N.Y., March 5, 1933); *A Stopwatch and an Ordnance Map* for Male Chorus, Brass, and Timpani (Philadelphia, April 23, 1940); *Sure on This Shining Night*, to words by James Agee, for Voice and Orch. (1938); *Knoxville: Summer of 1915* for Voice and Orch., to a text of James Agee from his novel *A Death in the Family* (Boston Sym., April 9, 1948, Koussevitzky conducting); *Prayers of Kierkegaard* for Soprano, Chorus, and Orch. (Boston Sym., Dec. 3, 1954); *Andromache's Farewell* for Voice and Orch. (N.Y., April 4, 1963); *The Lovers* for Baritone, Chorus, and Orch., to words by Pablo Neruda (Philadelphia, Sept. 22, 1971).

CHAMBER: *Serenade* for String Quartet or String Orch. (Philadelphia, May 5, 1930); Cello Sonata (1932); String Quartet (1936; 2nd movement, *Adagio*, extracted from it and arranged for String Orch., was widely perf.); *Summer Music* for Woodwind Quintet (Detroit, March 20, 1956); *Canzone* for Flute and Piano (1962; arranged from the 2nd movement of the Piano Concerto); *Mutations from Bach* for Brass and Timpani (1968).

SONGS: *The Daisies*, to words by James Stephens (1927); *With Rue My Heart Is Laden*, to words by A.E. Housman (1928); 3 Songs to poems from *Chamber Music* by James Joyce (1936); *A Nun Takes the Veil*, to words by G.M. Hopkins (1937); *The Secrets of the Old*, to words by W.B. Yeats (1938); *The Queen's Face on the Summery Coin*, to words by Robert Horan (1942); *Monks and Raisins*, to words by J.G. Villa (1943); *Nuvoletta*, to words by James Joyce (1947); *Mélodies passagères*, 5 songs, to words by Rilke (1951); *Hermit Songs*, 10 songs after old Irish texts (Washington, D.C., Oct. 30, 1953; Leontyne Price, soloist); *Despite and Still*, 5 songs to words by Graves, Roethke, and Joyce (1969); *3 Songs* for Baritone and Piano (N.Y., April 30, 1974; Fischer-Dieskau, soloist).

CHORAL: *The Virgin Martyrs* (1935); *Let Down the Bars, O Death* (1936); *Reincarnation*, 3 songs after poems by Stephens, for Mixed Chorus a cappella (1940).

PIANO SOLO: *Excursions* (1944); Piano Sonata in E-flat minor (Havana, Cuba, Dec. 9, 1949; Horowitz, soloist; N.Y. perf., also by Horowitz, Jan. 23, 1950); *Souvenirs* for Piano, 4-hands, also for Orch. (1953); *Nocturne: Homage to John Field* (1959); *Ballade* (1977); also *Wonderous Love*, variations on a shape-note hymn, for Organ (1958).

BIBL.: N. Broder, *S. B.* (N.Y., 1954); A. Kozinn, "S. B.: The Last Interview and the Legacy," *High Fidelity* (June and July 1981); D. Hennessee, *S. B.: A Bio-Bibliography* (Westport, Conn., 1985); J. Kreiling, *The Songs of S. B.: A Study in Literary Taste and Text-Setting* (Ann Arbor, Mich., 1987).

Barbier, René (Auguste-Ernest), Belgian composer; b. Namur, July 12, 1890; d. Brussels, Dec. 24, 1981. He studied with Paul Gilson at the Brussels Cons. and with Sylvain Dupuis at the Liège Cons.; taught at the Liège Cons. (from 1920 to 1949) and at the Brussels Cons. (1949–55); concurrently served as director of the Cons. of Namur (1923–63). He received the Belgian Royal Academy Prize for his symphonic poem *Les Génies du sommeil* (1923).

WORKS: 2 operas: *Yvette* (1910) and *La Fête du vieux Tilleul* (1912); an operetta, *La Sultane de Paris*; 3 oratorios: *La Tour de Babel* (1932); *Le Chemin de la Croix* (The Way of the Cross), 14 commentaries for Narrator, Orch., and Organ (1952); *Lamentation de la 9ᵉ heure* (1961); a "pièce radiophonique," *La Mort de Prométhée* (1933); a ballet, *Les Pierres magiques* (1957); *Pièce symphonique* for Trumpet and Orch. (1918); 2 piano concertos (1922, 1934); *Les Éléments (Suite Platonicienne)* (1935); *Poème* for Cello and Orch. (1936); *Fantaisie concertante* for Violin and Orch. (1937); Cello Concerto (1938); *La Voix humaine* for Small Orch. (1940); *Poco adagio et Allegro brillante* for Clarinet and Orch. (1940); *Diptyque* for Orch., with Organ (1941); *La Musique de perdition*, symphonic poem (1947); *Petite suite* for Orch. (1955); *Introduction (Fanfare) et 3 Esquisses symphoniques* for Orch. (1956); *Pièce concertante* for Violin or Saxophone, and Orch. (1958); Guitar Concerto (1960); *Te Deum laudamus* for Chorus, Brass, and Organ (1962); *3 mouvements symphoniques* for String Orch. (1962); *Tableau symphonique* (1963); Horn Concerto (1964); Concertino for Woodwind Quartet or 4 Clarinets, and String Orch. (1964); Sinfonietta for Small Orch. (1966); *Introduction et Allegro symphonique* (1967); Concerto for Organ, Strings, and Percussion (1967); *Ouverture concertante* (1969); Concertino for 2 Guitars and

String Orch. (1971); Violin Sonata (1914); Piano Quintet (1915); Viola Sonata (1916); Piano Trio (1919); String Quartet (1939); Quartet for 4 Horns (1956); Quartet for 4 Saxophones (1961); *Divertissement* for 4 Clarinets (1962); *Petite suite* for Woodwind Quartet (1964); 2 *Petites suites* for 2 Guitars (1965, 1969); Trio for Flute, Cello, and Piano (1971).

Barbieri, Carlo Emanuele, Italian conductor and composer; b. Genoa, Oct. 22, 1822; d. Pest, Sept. 28, 1867. He was educated at the Naples Cons., where he studied voice with Crescenti and composition with Mercadante. In 1845 he embarked on a career as an opera conductor; eventually settled in Buda, where he conducted at the National Theater from 1862 until his death. He wrote 5 operas: *Cristoforo Colombo* (Berlin, 1848); *Nisida, la perla di Procida* (1851); *Carlo und Carlin* (1859); *Arabella* (Buda, 1862); and *Perdita, ein Wintermärchen* (Leipzig, 1865); church music, German and Italian songs.

Barbieri, Fedora, Italian mezzo-soprano; b. Trieste, June 4, 1920. She studied with local teachers; then moved to Milan, where her teacher was Giulia Tess. She made her professional debut at the Florence Opera in 1940; then filled engagements, in the midst of a raging war, in Germany, Belgium, and the Netherlands. After the end of hostilities she sang at La Scala in Milan, in Paris, in Vienna, and in London. She made her American debut in San Francisco, then sang in Chicago; from 1950 to 1953 and again in 1967 she appeared with the Metropolitan Opera in N.Y. Her best roles were Azucena in *Il Trovatore* and Amneris in *Aida*; she also sang the title role in *Carmen*.

Barbieri, Francisco Asenjo, Spanish composer; b. Madrid, Aug. 3, 1823; d. there, Feb. 19, 1894. He studied clarinet, voice, and composition at the Madrid Cons., then engaged in multifarious activities as a café pianist, music copyist, and choral conductor. He found his true vocation in writing zarzuelas, and composed 78 of them. The following, all produced in Madrid, were particularly successful: *Gloria y peluca* (March 9, 1850); *Jugar con fuego* (Oct. 6, 1851); *Los diamantes de la corona* (Sept. 15, 1854); *Pan y Toros* (Dec. 22, 1864); *El Barberillo de Lavapiés* (Dec. 18, 1874). Barbieri ed. a valuable collection, *Cancionero musical de los siglos XV y XVI*, and publ. a number of essays on Spanish music.

BIBL.: J. Subirá, *Manuscritos de B., existentes en la Biblioteca Nacional* (Madrid, 1936); G. Chase, "B. and the Spanish Zarzuela," *Music & Letters* (Jan. 1939); A. Martínez Olmedilla, *El maestro B. y su tiempo* (Madrid, 1941).

Barbieri-Nini, Marianna, Italian soprano; b. Florence, Feb. 18, 1818; d. there, Nov. 27, 1887. She studied with Luigi Barbieri, Pasta, and Vaccai; made her operatic debut in 1840 at La Scala in Milan in Donizetti's *Belisario*; unfortunately her peculiarly asymmetrical facial features and an ill-constructed bodily frame produced such a vociferous outburst of revulsion on the part of the notoriously unrestrained Italian opera audiences that she was advised to wear a mask and a bodice to conceal her repellent physique. However, she astutely selected the part of Lucrezia Borgia, a historically celebrated poisoner, in Donizetti's eponymous opera at her next appearance in Florence, and there her ugly countenance fitted the role to a high C. She was also very successful in other bloody roles, among them that of Lady Macbeth in Verdi's opera and of the sympathetic but murderous Gulnara in Verdi's *Il Corsaro*. Still, she had to retire at menopause.

Barbireau (or Barbirau, Barbarieu, Barbyrianus, Barberau, Barbacola), Jacques (Jacobus), Dutch composer; b. c.1420; d. Antwerp, Aug. 8, 1491. He was appointed maître de chapelle at Notre Dame Cathedral in Antwerp in 1448, and served there until his death. Barbireau was greatly esteemed by his contemporaries; his opinions were copiously cited by Tinctoris. He wrote exclusively for the church; composed a Mass for 5 Voices, *Virgo parens Christi*; *Missa Pascale* for 4 Voices; antiphons; Psalms; anthems. See B. Meier, ed., *J. B.: Opera omnia*, Corpus Mensurabilis Musicae, VII/1–2 (1954–57).

BIBL.: H. du Saar, *Het leven en de composities van Jacobus Barbireau* (Utrecht, 1946).

Barbirolli, Sir John (Giovanni Battista), eminent English conductor; b. London, Dec. 2, 1899, of Italian-French parentage; d. there, July 29, 1970. He studied cello; received a scholarship to the Trinity College of Music in 1910 and another to the Royal Academy of Music, graduating in 1916; he made his 1st appearance as a cellist at the age of 12, on Dec. 16, 1911, at the Queen's Hall. In 1916 he became a member of the Queen's Hall Orch. In 1918–19 he served in the British Army; afterward resumed his musical career. In 1923 he joined the International String Quartet and toured with it. In 1924 he organized a chamber orch. in Chelsea, which he conducted for several years; later was a conductor with the British National Opera Co. (1926–29). He gained recognition when on Dec. 12, 1927, he successfully substituted for Beecham at a concert of the London Sym. Orch. In 1928 he was a guest conductor at Covent Garden, and a regular conductor there from 1929 to 1933; in 1933 he was named conductor of the Scottish Orch., Glasgow, and the Leeds Sym. Orch. He made his American debut with the N.Y. Phil. on Nov. 5, 1936, and was engaged as its permanent conductor in 1937. However, he failed to impress the N.Y. critics, and in 1943 he returned to England, where he was named conductor of the Hallé Orch. of Manchester. In 1958 he was appointed its conductor-in-chief. Renewing his American career, he served as conductor of the Houston Sym. (1961–67), while continuing his tenancy of the Hallé Orch., from which he finally retired in 1968 with the title of Conductor Laureate for Life. He was knighted in 1949 and made a Companion of Honour in 1969. A commemorative postage stamp with his portrait was issued by the Post Office of Great Britain on Sept. 1, 1980. Barbirolli was distinguished primarily in the Romantic repertoire; his interpretations were marked by nobility, expressive power, and brilliance. He had a fine pragmatic sense of shaping the music according to its inward style, without projecting his own personality upon it. However, this very objectivity tempered his success with American audiences, accustomed to charismatic flamboyance in music-making. He had a special affinity for English music, and performed many works of Elgar, Delius, and Britten. He conducted the 1st performances of the 7th and 8th syms. by Vaughan Williams; also made transcriptions for string orch. and French horns of 5 pieces from the Fitzwilliam Virginal Book (perf. by him under the title *Elizabethan Suite* in Los Angeles, Dec. 4, 1941). He composed for his 2nd wife, the oboist Evelyn Rothwell, an Oboe Concerto on themes by Pergolesi.

BIBL.: C. Rigby, *J. B.* (Altrincham, 1948); M. Kennedy, *Hallé Orchestra* (Manchester, 1968; rev. ed., 1976); idem, *B., Conductor Laureate* (London, 1971); C. Reid, *J. B.* (London, 1971); H. Atkins and P. Cotes, *The B.s: A Musical Marriage* (London, 1983).

Barblan, Guglielmo, eminent Italian musicologist; b. Siena, May 27, 1906; d. Milan, March 24, 1978. He 1st studied jurisprudence; then entered the Rome Cons. as a cello student of Forino and Becker; also took courses in music theory at the Bolzano Cons. and attended lectures on musicology by Liuzzi in Rome and Sandberger in Munich. He served as a music critic for *La Provincia di Bolzano* (1932–50), and concurrently lectured on music history at the Bolzano Cons. (1932–49). In 1949 he became head librarian of the Milan Cons.; in 1965 was appointed prof. of music history there; also taught at the Univ. of Milan from 1961. Barblan's principal contribution as a music scholar was in the field of Italian music history. In addition to his books, he also ed. works by Bonporti and Cambini.

WRITINGS: *Un musicista trentino: F.A. Bonporti* (Florence, 1940); *Musiche e strumenti musicali dell'Africa orientale italiana* (Naples, 1941); *L'opera di Donizetti nell'età romantica* (Bergamo, 1948); ed. *Mozart in Italia: I viaggi e le lettere* (with A. Della Corte; Milan, 1956); *Guida al "Clavicembalo ben temperato" di J.S. Bach* (Milan, 1961); *Claudio Monteverdi nel*

quarto centenario della nascita (with C. Gallico and G. Pannain; Turin, 1967); ed. *Conservatorio di musica G. Verdi, Milano; Catalogo della biblioteca* (Florence, 1972).

Barblan, Otto, Swiss organist, conductor, teacher, and composer; b. Scanfs, March 22, 1860; d. Geneva, Dec. 19, 1943. He studied at the Stuttgart Cons. (1878–84); made his debut as an organist at Augsburg (1885); taught at Chur (1885–87); then became organist at the Cathedral of Geneva, prof. at the Cons., and conductor of the "Société de Chant Sacré" (1887). He wrote an *Ode patriotique* (1896); a *Festspiel* (Chur, May 28, 1899) commemorating the 400th anniversary of the battle of Calven, and containing the chorus *Terre des monts*, which has attained great popularity, placing it next to the national anthem as a patriotic song; *Post tenebras lux*, cantata for the Calvin jubilee (1909); String Quartet; Variations and Triple Fugue on B-A-C-H; Passion according to St. Luke (Geneva, April 9, 1919).

BIBL.: E. Perini, *O. B.* (Zürich, 1960).

Barbosa-Lima, Carlos, Brazilian guitarist; b. São Paulo, Dec. 17, 1944. He began to study the guitar when he was 7; made his debut in São Paulo at 12. His principal teachers were Isaias Savio in Brazil and Andrés Segovia in Spain. In 1967 he made his 1st tour of the U.S.; also gave concerts in South America, Europe, and Israel, with notable success. He commissioned works for guitar from Ginastera, Balada, and Mignone; also made effective transcriptions of works by Bach, Handel, and other classical composers. He combined his concert career with teaching; was a member of the faculty at the Manhattan School of Music.

Barbot, Joseph-Théodore-Désiré, French tenor; b. Toulouse, April 12, 1824; d. Paris, Jan. 1, 1897. He studied with Garcia at the Paris Cons.; was engaged to sing at the Paris Opéra in 1848; sang Faust at the premiere of Gounod's opera (March 19, 1859). In 1875 he became a prof. at the Paris Cons., succeeding Mme. Viardot.

Barbour, J(ames) Murray, American musicologist; b. Chambersburg, Pa., March 31, 1897; d. Homestead, Pa., Jan. 4, 1970. He studied with Otto Kinkeldey at Cornell Univ.; in 1932 received there the 1st doctorate in musicology awarded by an American univ., with the dissertation *Equal Temperament: Its History from Ramis (1482) to Rameau (1737)*; received a 2nd Ph.D. in music from the Univ. of Toronto in 1936. He taught English at Ithaca College (1932–39) before receiving an appointment as prof. of musicology at Michigan State College; retired in 1964. He publ. *Tuning and Temperament: A Historical Survey* (East Lansing, 1960); *Trumpets, Horns and Music* (East Lansing, 1964).

BIBL.: F. Kuttner, "J.M. B. (1897–1970)," *Journal of the American Musicological Society*, XXIII (1970).

Barce, Ramón, Spanish composer; b. Madrid, March 16, 1928. He studied languages at the Univ. of Madrid; in music he was largely autodidact. In 1958 he organized the group Nueva Música in Madrid; in 1964 he founded the Zaj group for action music; as a music critic, he supported modern tendencies in Spanish music. The titles of many of his works indicate his trend toward absolute music in abstract modern forms: *Estudio de sonoridades* for Piano (1962); *Parábola* for Wind Quintet (1963); *Objetos sonoros* for Chamber Orch. and Percussion (1964); *Coral hablado* (Spoken Chorus; 1965); *Las cuatro estaciones* for Orch. (1966); *Estudio de densidades* for Piano (1965); *Obertura fonética* for Wind Sextet (1968); also a theater piece, *Abgrund Hintergrund* (1964).

Barcewicz, Stanislaw, Polish violinist and conductor; b. Warsaw, April 16, 1858; d. there, Sept. 1, 1929. He studied at the Warsaw Inst. of Music and at the Moscow Cons., where he graduated with a gold medal for violin in 1876; he subsequently toured extensively in Europe. In 1886 he was engaged as a conductor at the Warsaw Opera; from 1886 to 1918 he also taught violin and viola at the Warsaw Inst. of Music.

Bardi, Giovanni de', Count of Vernio, Italian nobleman, patron of music and art, and composer; b. Florence, Feb. 5,

1534; d. Rome, Sept. 1612. He was the founder of the Florentine Camerata, a group of musicians who met at his home (1576–c.1582) to discuss the music of Greek antiquity; this led to the beginnings of opera. Count Bardi was descended from an old Guelph banking family; he was a philologist, mathematician, neo-Platonic philosopher, and lover of Dante. He was a member of the Crusca Academy, a literary group founded in 1583 whose ideas had great influence on the Camerata. Bardi is known to have been in Rome in 1567; he lent support to Vincenzo Galilei, a member of the Camerata. In 1580 Bardi married Lucrezia Salvati. The masques of 1589, commemorating the marriage of Grand Duke Ferdinand, were conceived largely by Bardi. In 1592 he left for Rome to become chamberlain at the court of Pope Clement VIII. Caccini was his secretary in 1592. Bardi's writings are: *Discorso sopra il giuoco del calzio fiorentino* (Florence, 1580); *Ristretto delle grandezze di Roma* (Rome, 1600); *Discorso mandato a Caccini sopra la musica antica* in Doni's *Lyra Barberina* (Florence, 1763). Among his compositions are a madrigal in 4 Voices, *Misere habitator* in Malvezzi's *Intermedi e concerti* (Venice, 1591); the madrigal *Lauro ohime lauro* in *Il lauro secco, lib.* I (Ferrara, 1582). Among contemporary documents which refer to him are Vincenzo Galilei's *Dialogo della musica antica e della moderna* (tr. in part in O. Strunk's *Source Readings in Music History*, N.Y., 1951; also included is a letter from Bardi's son to G.B. Doni commenting on Bardi's ideas).

BIBL.: G. Gasperini, *Intorno alle origini del melodramma* (Rome, 1902); H. Martin, "La Camerata du comte Bardi et la musique florentine du XVIᵉ siècle," *Revue de Musicologie* (Nov. 1932); N. Pirrotta, "Temperaments and Tendencies in the Florentine Camerata," *Musical Quarterly* (April 1954).

Bárdos, Lajos, Hungarian conductor and musicologist; b. Budapest, Oct. 1, 1899; d. there, Nov. 18, 1986. He studied at the Budapest Academy of Music as a violinist, then joined its faculty (1928–67). He was primarily active as a choral conductor and concurrently ed. Baroque music by Hungarian composers. He publ. essays and books, in Hungarian, on Liszt, Bartók, and Stravinsky.

Barenboim, Daniel, greatly talented Israeli pianist and conductor; b. Buenos Aires, Argentina, Nov. 15, 1942. He studied music with his parents; appeared in public as a child pianist in Buenos Aires at the age of 7; in 1952 the family settled in Israel. During the summers of 1954 and 1955 he was in Salzburg, where he studied piano with Edwin Fischer and took lessons in conducting with Igor Markevitch, and chamber music playing with Enrico Mainardi. From 1954 to 1956 he studied music theory with Nadia Boulanger in Paris; also enrolled at the Accademia di Santa Cecilia in Rome, where he became one of the youngest students to receive a diploma in 1956. He also studied conducting with Carlo Zecchi at the Accademia Musicale Chigiana in Siena. He gave piano recitals in Paris in 1955 and in London in 1956. On Jan. 20, 1957, he made his American debut at Carnegie Hall, N.Y., playing Prokofiev's 1st Piano Concerto with Leopold Stokowski conducting the Sym. of the Air. He gave his 1st U.S. solo recital in N.Y. on Jan. 17, 1958. He made his debut as a conductor in Haifa in 1957; in 1960 he played all 32 Beethoven sonatas in a series of concerts in Tel Aviv; he repeated this cycle in N.Y. As a pianist, he subordinated Romantic passion to Classical balance of form and thematic content. As a conductor he gave congenial performances of the masterpieces of Romantic music; became particularly engrossed in the music of Anton Bruckner, and was awarded the Bruckner Medal of the Bruckner Soc. of America. In 1967 he conducted the Israel Phil. on its tour of the U.S.; in 1968 he led the London Sym. Orch. at its appearance in N.Y.; he subsequently filled engagements with the Boston Sym., Chicago Sym., Philadelphia Orch., and N.Y. Phil. He made his 1st appearance as an opera conductor at the Edinburgh Festival in 1973. In 1975 he was named music director of the Orch. de Paris. On June 15, 1967, he married, in Jerusalem, the English cellist **Jacqueline DuPré**, who became converted to Judaism. They appeared in numerous

sonata programs until, tragically, she was stricken in 1972 with multiple sclerosis and had to abandon her career. In 1988 Barenboim was named artistic director of the new Bastille Opéra in Paris by the French Minister of Culture; however, following the presidential election in France, a new Minister of Culture was appointed and disagreements over artistic policy and remuneration led to Barenboim's abrupt dismissal (Jan. 1989). That same month he was appointed Solti's successor as music director of the Chicago Sym. Orch.

BIBL.: S. Elliott, "D. B.," *Ovation* (July 1989).

Barere, Simon, virtuoso Russian pianist; b. Odessa, Sept. 1, 1896; d. suddenly, while performing Grieg's Piano Concerto with the Philadelphia Orch. in Carnegie Hall, N.Y., April 2, 1951. He studied with Anna Essipoff at the St. Petersburg Cons. and, after her death, with Felix Blumenfeld. After graduation, he concertized in Germany, Sweden, and the U.S. He was praised for his extraordinary virtuosity, and was once described in the *New York Times* as "truly a giant of the keyboard."

Bargiel, Woldemar, German composer; b. Berlin, Oct. 3, 1828; d. there, Feb. 23, 1897. He was a half brother of **Clara Schumann.** As a boy he sang at the Berlin Cathedral and studied counterpoint with Dehn, and at the Leipzig Cons. (1846–50) with Hauptmann, Moscheles, Gade, and Rietz; became prof. at the Cologne Cons. in 1859. He was a teacher and conductor in Rotterdam (1865–75); in 1874 became prof. of composition at the Berlin Hochschule für Musik. He was greatly admired by Schumann and Brahms, and his works, in a Romantic vein, were frequently performed; almost all of his music was publ. during his lifetime. He wrote a Sym.; 3 overtures; String Octet; 4 string quartets; 3 piano trios; violin sonatas; numerous piano pieces and songs.

BIBL.: E. Rudorff, *Aus den Tagen der Romantik; Bildnis einer deutschen Familie* (Leipzig, 1938).

Bargielski, Zbigniew, Polish composer; b. Lomza, Jan. 21, 1937. He studied composition with Szeligowski at the State College of Music in Warsaw; musicology with Szabelski at the State College of Music in Katowice; completed his studies with Nadia Boulanger in Paris.

WORKS: *Danton, or Some Pictures from the History of the Great French Revolution,* surrealistic historical opera (1968–69); *Le Petit Prince* (1970); *Parades* for Orch. (1965); *Espace attrapé* for Orch. (1973); Percussion Concerto (1975); Violin Concerto (1975); *Ballad* for Winds and Percussion (1976); 3 *Sonnet-Capriccios* for Solo Clarinet (1976); *Impromptu* for Solo Percussion (1976); String Quartet (1976).

Barili, Alfredo, Italian-American pianist, composer, and pedagogue; b. Florence, Aug. 2, 1854; d. Atlanta, Ga., Nov. 17, 1935, in an accident when he took a walk and was struck by a bus. He was a scion of an illustrious musical family; his father, Ettore Barili, an excellent musician in his own right, was a half brother of the operatic diva **Adelina Patti.** Alfredo Barili was taken to America in his infancy and was taught piano by his father, making his public debut as a pianist in N.Y. on April 7, 1865. In 1868 the family relocated to Philadelphia, where he studied with Carl Wolfsohn, a German musician who claimed to be the 1st to perform all 32 piano sonatas of Beethoven in a series of concerts. In 1872 Barili enrolled at the Cologne Cons., studying piano with Friedrich Gernsheim and James Kwast, and composition with Ferdinand Hiller. Returning to the U.S. in 1880, he settled in Atlanta, taught for 6 years at the Atlanta Female Inst., and in 1886 founded his own "music academy," teaching piano at a fee of $1.50 per lesson. He maintained a cordial relationship with his famous aunt, Adelina Patti, and acted as her piano accompanist at a London concert in 1911. He also composed some perishable salon music in the approved manner of the time. His piano piece *Cradle Song* went into 26 eds.; also popular among his pupils were his *Danse caprice, Miniature Gavotte,* and *Spanish Serenade.*

BIBL.: N. Lee Orr, "A. B.: Atlanta Musician," *American Music* (Spring 1984).

Barilli, Bruno, Italian writer on music; b. Fano, Dec. 14, 1880; d. Rome, April 15, 1952. He studied in Parma and later in Munich; his collections of essays were publ. under the titles *Il sorcio nel violino* and *Il paese del melodramma*, in Milan (1926) and in Lanciano (1929), respectively. He wrote 2 operas, *Medusa* (1910; Bergamo, Sept. 11, 1938) and *Emiral* (Rome, March 11, 1924).
BIBL.: E. Falqui, ed., *Opere di B. B.* (Florence, 1963).

Barjansky, Alexander, Russian cellist; b. Odessa, Dec. 16, 1883; d. Brussels, Jan. 6, 1961. He left Russia before World War I and lived in Germany and Italy. He distinguished himself by giving performances of new works for cello, among them *Schelomo* by Ernest Bloch, which he played under Bloch's direction in Rome on Jan. 22, 1933; he also gave the premiere of the Cello Concerto by Delius on Jan. 31, 1921, in London. His wife publ. a book of recollections about him under the title *Portraits and Backgrounds* (London, 1940).

Bark, Jan (Helge Guttorm), Swedish composer; b. Härnösand, April 19, 1934. He was 1st a jazz trombonist; then studied at the Stockholm Musikhögskolan, taking courses in composition with Lars-Erik Larsson and Karl-Birger Blomdahl; was initiated into ultramodern music by György Ligeti in Stockholm; made an American trip in 1962 and worked with avant-garde groups at the Tape Music Center in San Francisco; in 1964 he traveled to the Far East to study oriental music. Returning to Sweden, he joined the radio and television center of the Swedish Broadcasting Service. He was co-founder with Folke Rabe of the Culture Quartet of 4 trombones, which explores the potentialities of modern trombone playing. Many of his pieces are of a theatrical, almost exhibitionistic, nature, often with a healthy radical tinge.
WORKS: Piano Sonata (1957); 2 string quartets (1959, 1962); *Metakronismer* for Orch. (1960; Oslo, March 4, 1961); 2 works for the Culture Quartet, composed in collaboration with Folke Rabe: *Bolos,* in an anarcho-Dadaistic manner (1962), and *Polonaise* (1965); *Lamento* for Percussion, Piano, and Double Basses (1962); *Boca Chica* for Chamber Ensemble (1962); *Pyknos* for Orch. (1962); *Eko* for News Broadcaster and 5 Tape Recorders (1962); *Missa Bassa* for Small Orch. with 7 Conductors, 6 of whom also sing (1964; Swedish Radio, April 1, 1967); *Nota* for "choreographic" Mixed Chorus (1964); *Ost-Funk* for 8 Jazz Musicians (1964); *Mansbot* for Male Chorus and 12 Guitars (1964); *Tredjedels Signeri* for 3 Hammond Organs (1967); *Bar,* electronic music (1967); *Light Music* for Chorus a cappella (1968); *Lyndon Bunk Johnson,* a "poster" work, composed collectively (1968); *Irk-Ork 1970* for Chamber Ensemble (1970); *Het Jacht von het vliegende Joachim* for Trombone, Cello, and Piano (1971); *Memoria in memoria* for Chamber Group (1974); *Utspel* for Band (1976); *Malumma* for Tuba and Band (1984); Concerto for Orch. (1985); various theater pieces, film music.

Barkauskas, Vytautas, outstanding Lithuanian composer; b. Kaunas, March 25, 1931. He studied music at the Vilnius College of Music while also studying mathematics at the Pedagogical Inst. there (1949–53); then took composition classes with Račiunas and orchestration with Balsis at the Lithuanian State Cons. (1953–59); in 1961 joined its faculty. He wrote several cantatas in the style of socialist realism; in his instrumental compositions he makes use of advanced cosmopolitan techniques, including serialism and aleatory improvisation.
WORKS: STAGE: *Conflict,* "choreographic scene" for 3 Performers (1965); *Legend about Love,* opera (Vilnius, March 29, 1975). ORCH.: *Tone Poem* for Piano and Orch. (1960); 5 syms. (1962, 1971, 1979, 1984, 1986); *Choreographic Miniatures* (1965); Concertino for 4 Chamber Groups (1966); *Expressivistic Structures* for Chamber Orch. (1967); *Paraphrase* for Chamber Orch. (1967); *3 Aspects* (1969); *Overture a priori* (1976); *Toccamento,* concerto for Chamber Orch. (1978); *The Sun,* symphonic picture (1983); Concerto piccolo for Chamber Orch. (1988). VOCAL: *Pathetic Thoughts* for Chorus (1962); *Word about Revolution,* cantata-poem for Narrator, Male Chorus, and Orch. (1967); *La vostra nominanza e color d'erba* for

Chamber Chorus and String Quintet (1971); *Prelude and Fugue* for Chorus (1974); *Salute Your Land,* oratorio-mystery for 4 Soloists, Female Chorus, and Orch. (1976); *Open Window,* 5 sketches for Mezzo-soprano and 5 Instruments (1978); *We Both,* cantata for Soprano, Bass, Chorus, and 5 Instruments (1986); *Hope,* oratorio (1988). CHAMBER: Piano Trio (1958); Partita for Solo Violin (1967); *Intimate Composition* for Oboe and 12 String Instruments (1968); *Contrast Music* for Flute, Cello, and Percussion (1969); *Pro memoria,* 3 movements for Flute, Bass Clarinet, Piano, and 5 Percussion Instruments (1970); *Monologue* for Solo Oboe (1970); 2 string quartets (1972, 1983); 3 sonatas for Violin and Piano: No. 1, *Sonata Subito* (1976); No. 2, *Dialogue* (1978); No. 3 (1984); Sonata for Double Bass and Piano (1987). PIANO: *Poetry,* cycle (1964); Variations for 2 Pianos (1967); *Sonate pathétique* (1969); 5 *Pictures of Vytukas* for Piano, 4-hands (1971); *Legend about Čiurlionis* (1972); *Elegy and Fantastical Toccata* (1972); *Prelude and Fugue* for 2 Pianos (1974). ORGAN: *Gloria Urbi* (1972); *Zodiac,* polyphonic cycle (1980); *The Rebirth of Hope* (1989).

Barkel, Charles, Swedish violinist and conductor; b. Stugun, Feb. 6, 1898; d. Stockholm, March 7, 1973. He studied at the Stockholm Cons. and the Copenhagen Cons.; then took lessons in Berlin with Carl Flesch; concurrently played in several Swedish orchs. In 1921 he joined the Stockholm Concert Soc. Orch. He founded his own string quartet in 1928; from 1942 to 1954 he was conductor of the Uppsala Concert Soc. Orch. From 1926 to 1965 he taught violin in Stockholm.

Barkin, Elaine R(adoff), American composer and writer on music; b. N.Y., Dec. 15, 1932. She studied with Karol Rathaus at Queens College of the City Univ. of N.Y. (B.A., 1954), with Irving Fine at Brandeis Univ. (M.F.A., 1956), and with Boris Blacher at the Berlin Hochschule für Musik (1957); subsequently taught at various colleges, finally joining the faculty of the Univ. of Calif. at Los Angeles. She was an ed. of the journal *Perspectives of New Music* (1963–85). In her early works she utilized serial techniques, later delving into what she described as "group interactive autonomous alternative music-making culture."
WORKS: String Quartet (1969); *Plus ça change* for String Orch. and Percussion (1971); *Prim Cycles* for Flute, Clarinet, Violin, and Cello (1972); *Inward and Outward Bound* for 13 Instruments (1975); *Ebb Tide* for 2 Vibraphones (1977); *De amore,* chamber mini-opera (1980); *Quilt Piece,* graphic score for 7 Instruments (1984); *Rhapsodies* for Flutes and Clarinet (1986); *[Be]coming Together Apart* for Violin and Marimba (1987); *Encore* for Javanese Gamelan Ensemble (1988).

Barlow, Fred, French composer; b. Mulhouse, Oct. 2, 1881; d. Boulogne, Seine, Jan. 3, 1951. He was of British parentage; moved to Paris, where he took composition lessons with Jean Huré and Charles Koechlin. Not a prolific composer, he wrote a comic opera, *Sylvie* (Paris, March 2, 1923), and a ballet, *La Grande Jatte* (Paris, July 12, 1950); another ballet, *Gladys,* was performed posthumously at Mulhouse on Jan. 7, 1956. Other works included some chamber music, piano pieces, and songs.

Barlow, Harold, American composer of popular songs, bandleader, and musical lexicographer; b. Boston, May 15, 1915. He studied violin at Boston Univ., and later played in various orchs.; also led a U.S. Army band. He compiled 2 valuable reference works, for which he designed an original method of indexing melodic themes by letters plus accidentals: *A Dictionary of Musical Themes* (N.Y., 1948) and *A Dictionary of Vocal Themes* (N.Y., 1950), both with S. Morgenstern.

Barlow, Howard, American conductor; b. Plain City, Ohio, May 1, 1892; d. Bethel, Conn., Jan. 31, 1972. He studied at the Univ. of Colorado and at Columbia Univ. He conducted the American National Orch., N.Y. (1923–25), and at the Neighborhood Playhouse (1925–27); was conductor of the CBS Sym. Orch. (1927–43), with which he presented numerous new works.

Barlow, Samuel (Latham Mitchill), American composer; b. N.Y., June 1, 1892; d. Wyndmoor, Pa., Sept. 19, 1982. He studied at the Groton School (1904–10) and at Harvard Univ. (1910–14); went to Paris, where he took piano lessons with Isidor Philipp; then traveled to Rome to study orchestration with Respighi. He served as a 1st lieutenant with the American Expeditionary Force in 1917; was decorated with the French Legion of Honor. He was active in various liberal causes; was a member of the Democratic Club Union in N.Y. and president of the Citizens Committee for Government Art Projects; also was moderator of the Forum for Democracy. In his compositions he endeavored to approach the taste of democratic audiences without sacrificing the inner meaning of the music. He presented his philosophical and artistic views in a book, *The Astonished Muse* (N.Y., 1961). His 1-act opera *Mon ami Pierrot* was the 1st by an American composer to be given at the Opéra-Comique in Paris (Jan. 11, 1935). He also wrote 2 more operas, *Eugénie* and *Amanda*. His symphonic concerto *Babar* (1935) employs magic lantern slides. He further wrote a Piano Concerto (Rochester, N.Y., Jan. 23, 1931, with himself as soloist); a symphonic suite, *Biedermeier Waltzes* (Rome, 1935); *Circus Overture* (1930); choruses; and piano pieces.

Barlow, Wayne (Brewster), American composer; b. Elyria, Ohio, Sept. 6, 1912. He studied with Bernard Rogers and Howard Hanson at the Eastman School of Music in Rochester, N.Y. (B.M., 1934; M.M., 1935; Ph.D., 1937); also took courses from Schoenberg at the Univ. of Southern Calif. in Los Angeles (1935). In 1937 he was appointed to the faculty of the Eastman School of Music; in 1968 became chairman of its composition dept. and director of its electronic music studio; retired in 1973 from the former post and continued to hold the latter until his retirement in 1978. He publ. *Foundations of Music* (N.Y., 1963).

Works: *De Profundis* for Orch. (1934); *False Faces,* ballet suite (1935); Sinfonietta No. 1 (1936); *Zion in Exile,* cantata (1937); *The Winter's Passed* for Oboe and Strings (Rochester, Oct. 18, 1938); *Songs from the Silence of Amor* for Soprano and Orch. (1939); *3 Moods for Dancing,* ballet (1940); *Lyrical Pieces* for Clarinet and Strings (1943); *The 23rd Psalm* for Chorus and Orch. (1944); *Nocturne* for 18 Instruments (1946); *Rondo Overture* (1947); Piano Sonata (1948); *Prelude, Air, and Variations* for Bassoon, Piano, and String Quartet (1949); Sinfonietta No. 2 (1950); Piano Quintet (1951); Mass in G (1953); *Tryptych* for String Quartet (1953); *Lento and Allegro* for Orch. (1955); *Night Song* for Orch. (1958); *Poems for Music* for Soprano and Orch. (1958); *Rota* for Chamber Ensemble (1959); *Missa Sancti Thomae* for Chorus and Organ (1959); *Intrada, Fugue, and Postlude* for Brass (1959); *Images* for Harp and Orch. (1961); *Sinfonia da camera* for Orch. (1962); *Vistas* for Orch. (1963); Trio for Oboe, Viola, and Piano (1964); *We All Believe in 1 God* for Chorus, Brass Quartet, and Organ (1965); *Study in Electronic Sound* for Prerecorded Tape (1965); *Dynamisms* for 2 Pianos (1967); *Wait for the Promise of the Father,* cantata (1968); *Elegy* for Viola and Piano (1968); *Duo* for Harp and Tape (1969); Concerto for Saxophone and Band (1970); *Moonflight* for Prerecorded Tape (1970); *Overture: Hampton Beach* (1971); *Soundscapes* for Tape and Orch. (1972); *Soundprints in Concrete* for Prerecorded Tape (1975); *Voices of Faith,* secular cantata (1976); *Vocalise and Canon* for Tuba and Piano (1976); *Out of the Cradle Endlessly Rocking* for Tenor, Chorus, Clarinet, Viola, Piano, and Tape (1978); *Divertissement* for Flute and Chamber Orch. (1980); *Frontiers* for Band (Brevard, N.C., Aug. 2, 1982); *Sonatine for 4* for Flute, Clarinet, Cello, and Harp (1984).

Bärmann, Heinrich (Joseph), renowned German clarinetist, father of **Karl Bärmann;** b. Potsdam, Feb. 14, 1784; d. Munich, June 11, 1847. He studied oboe at the School of Military Music in Potsdam, and as a youth served as bandmaster in the Prussian Life Guards; then studied clarinet with Beer and Tausch. He was in the Prussian army at Jena, and was captured by the French, but made his escape and traveled to Munich, where he obtained the post of a court musician. Weber became

his friend, and wrote a Clarinet Concertino and the 2 clarinet concertos for him; they appeared together at concerts in Prague and in Germany (1811–12); later Bärmann gave concerts in France, England, and Russia. He wrote a number of works for the clarinet, including concertos, fantasias, quintets, quartets, and sonatas; he also prepared teaching pieces and technical exercises for the clarinet, which are still in use in Germany. The Adagio from his Quintet No. 3, in E-flat major, op. 23, which he wrote in 1821, has been unaccountably attributed to Wagner, and so listed in numerous collections of clarinet pieces. It was republ. in 1971 by Breitkopf und Härtel under Bärmann's name.

Bibl.: P. Weston, *Clarinet Virtuosi of the Past* (London, 1971).

Bärmann, Karl, German clarinetist, son of **Heinrich (Joseph)** and father of **Karl Bärmann, Jr.;** b. Munich, Oct. 24, 1811; d. there, May 23, 1885. He was a pupil of his father, whom he accompanied on his tours; later succeeded him at the Munich court orch. He wrote a method for clarinet, with a supplement entitled *Materialien zur weiteren technischen Ausbildung.*

Bärmann, Karl, Jr., German-American pianist and music pedagogue, son of **Karl Bärmann;** b. Munich, July 9, 1839; d. Boston, Jan. 17, 1913. He studied piano with Wanner, Wahlmuth, and Liszt, and composition with Franz Lachner; was appointed a teacher at the Munich Cons., but emigrated to the U.S. in 1881. He settled in Boston.

Barnard, Charlotte (née **Arlington**), English songwriter; b. Louth, Dec. 23, 1830; d. Dover, Jan. 30, 1869. In 1866 she publ. under the pen name of **Claribel** the ballad *Come Back to Erin,* which attained great popularity. She also wrote poetry.

Barnby, Sir Joseph, English organist, conductor, and composer; b. York, Aug. 12, 1838; d. London, Jan. 28, 1896. He received his early training as a choirboy; then studied with Cipriani Potter at the Royal Academy of Music in London. In 1863 he was appointed organist at St. Andrew's Church in London, and soon presented sacred concerts there. In 1867 he founded Mr. Joseph Barnby's Choir. Subsequently he served as organist at St. Anne's, Soho (1871–76). In 1872 his own choir was merged with the Royal Albert Hall Choral Soc., which he led until his death. He also served as precentor at Eton College (1875–92), and was principal of the Guildhall School of Music from 1892 until his death. He was knighted in 1892. Barnby composed numerous pieces of sacred music, including *246 Hymn Tunes,* publ. in 1897.

Barnekow, Christian, Danish composer; b. St.-Sauveur, France, July 28, 1837; d. Copenhagen, March 20, 1913. He studied in Copenhagen; from 1871 to 1887 he directed the Soc. for Publication of Danish Music. He wrote numerous sacred choral works and also lieder in a folklike manner, as well as some estimable chamber music.

Barnes, Edward Shippen, American organist and composer; b. Seabright, N.J., Sept. 14, 1887; d. Idyllwild, Calif., Feb. 14, 1958. He was a student of Horatio Parker and David Stanley Smith at Yale Univ., and studied organ with Harry B. Jepson there. He was organist at St. Stephen's Episcopal Church in Philadelphia and later at the First Presbyterian Church in Santa Monica, Calif., retiring in 1954. He wrote 2 organ syms., much sacred music, and several books of organ arrangements for schools, among them *Bach for Beginners in Organ Playing.*

Barnes, Milton, Canadian conductor and composer; b. Toronto, Dec. 16, 1931. He studied composition with John Weinzweig; conducting with Victor Feldbrill, Boyd Neel, and Walter Susskind; and piano with Samuel Dolin at the Royal Cons. of Music of Toronto (1952–55). Then he pursued further training in conducting at the Accademia Musicale Chigiana in Siena, at the Berkshire Music Center at Tanglewood, and with Hans Swarowsky at the Vienna Academy of Music (graduated, 1961). He began his career as a jazz drummer and guitarist; during his student days, he composed many dramatic scores for productions at the Univ. of Toronto. He was music director and composer at the Crest Theatre (1961–63), and founder-conductor of the Toronto Repertory Orch. (1964–73); he also was conductor of the St. Catharines (Ontario) Sym. Orch. and Chorus (1964–73) and of the Niagara Falls (N.Y.) Phil. and Chorus (1965–73), and was composer and conductor-in-residence of the Toronto Dance Theatre (1968–73). An eclectic composer, he has utilized classical, jazz, and popular styles in several of his scores.

WORKS: STAGE AND/OR MULTI-MEDIA: *Amber Garden*, ballet suite (1972); *The Spiral Stairs* for 7 Instruments (1973); *The Dybbuk*, masque for Dancing Tenor and 6 Instruments (1977); film and television scores. ORCH.: *Invocations* (1962); 2 syms.: No. 1 (1964); No. 2 for String Orch. (1976); *Pinocchio*, symphonic poem (1966); Variations for Clarinet and Orch. (1968); *Classical Concerto* for Piano and Orch. (1973); *Shebetim*, tableau for String Orch. (1974); Concerto for Violin and Strings (1975); Chamber Concerto for Wind Quintet and Strings (1976); Viola Concerto (1977); Concerto No. 1 for Flute and String Orch. (1978); Serenade for String Quartet and String Orch. (1979); *Follies Overture* (1983); Double Concerto for 2 Guitars and String Orch. (1986; Toronto, Nov. 18, 1987). CHAMBER: *Burletta* for String Quartet (1957–58); Sonata for Flute and Piano (1965); Concerto Grosso for Flute, Clarinet, Violin, Cello, and 2 Pianos (1973); String Quartet No. 2, *Scenes from Jewish Life* (1978); *Annexus* for 5 Percussionists (1981); *Papageno Variations* for String Bass and Piano (1988); also solo vocal works; a cantata, *Thespis* (1956; rev. 1973); and choruses.

Barnet, Charlie (real name, **Charles Daly**), American jazz saxophonist and bandleader; b. N.Y., Oct. 26, 1913. He was the son of well-to-do parents who did not care for music, but he nonetheless organized a college band and engaged important soloists whom he could afford to pay; eventually he achieved a reputation as a swing-band leader and continued a notable career until swing itself became obsolete.

BIBL.: E. Edwards et al., *C. B. and His Orchestra* (Whittier, Calif., 1965; 2nd ed., rev., 1970); C. Garrod, *C. B. and His Orchestra* (Spotswood, N.J., 1973).

Barnett, Alice, American song composer; b. Lewiston, Ill., May 26, 1886; d. San Diego, Aug. 28, 1975. She studied piano with Felix Borowski and Rudolph Ganz in Chicago; then went to Berlin and took lessons with Hugo Kaun. Returning to the U.S. in 1917, she settled in San Diego. She wrote a number of agreeable songs in a romantic vein.

Barnett, Bonnie, American singer and composer; b. Chicago, May 2, 1947. She studied at the Univ. of Illinois (B.S., music ed., 1968) and with Kenneth Gaburo, Pauline Oliveros, and Robert Erickson at the Univ. of Calif., San Diego (M.A., 1972); then moved to San Francisco, where she developed the *TUNNEL HUM Project*, a series of participatory vocal events taking place in acoustically interesting environments. A conducive tonality is established by a group of instrumentalists (E-flat major is used often); the participating hummers then improvise on that tonality, following a written process score. Since 1981 Barnett has produced 29 *Hums* in a variety of contexts, including 2 satellite-linked live national radio broadcasts (1983; 1984), a Houston subterranean shopping mall (1986), and *Auto Hum*, a live radio broadcast for car-commuter participation throughout Southern California (1985). Her intent is to re-create the participatory pleasures of group vocalizations as a means of "tuning the world"; her *Global Hum*, part of the "Music and Peace" event sponsored by the World Phil. Orch. in Montreal, sent live singers in San Francisco worldwide through satellite broadcast. She was the recipient of a 1983 grant from National Public Radio and a 1984 N.E.A. grant. Since 1986 she has lived in Los Angeles, where she teaches privately and co-hosts the KPFK-radio program "Imaginary Landscape." She is currently developing a more elaborate *Global Hum* and, eventually, an *Intergalactic Hum*.

WRITINGS: "Aspects of Vocal Multiphonics," *Interface, Journal of New Music Research* (Amsterdam, 1977); "Live Radio Art," *Whole Earth Review* (Sausalito, Calif., Winter 1987).

Barnett, John, English composer, uncle of **John Francis Barnett**; b. Bedford, July 15, 1802; d. Leckhampton, April 17, 1890. He was the son of a German jeweler named Bernhard Beer, but Anglicized his name when he moved to England. He wrote operettas and various other pieces of light music before producing his 1st full-fledged opera, *The Mountain Sylph* (London, Aug. 25, 1834); this was followed by 2 more operas, *Fair Rosamond* (London, Feb. 28, 1837) and *Farinelli* (London, Feb. 8, 1839). In 1841 he settled in Cheltenham as a voice teacher, but about 1870 moved to a country residence, Cotteswold in Leckhampton, where he remained until his death. Among his works are a Sym., 3 string quartets, and songs numbering in the thousands. He also publ. 2 singing methods, *Systems and Singing Masters* (1842) and *School for the Voice* (1844).

Barnett, John (Manley), American conductor; b. N.Y., Sept. 3, 1917. He studied piano, violin, and trumpet; took courses in conducting with Leon Barzin in N.Y. and with Bruno Walter, Weingartner, Enesco, and Malko in Europe. From 1946 to 1956 he was associate conductor of the Los Angeles Phil., and from 1956 to 1958 its associate music director. In 1947 he organized the Phoenix (Ariz.) Sym. Orch., conducting it until 1949. He later served as music director of the Hollywood Bowl (1953–57) and of the Los Angeles Guild Opera Co. (1954–79). From 1958 to 1972 he was music director of the National Orch. Assoc. in N.Y.; from 1961 to 1971 he held the post of music director of the Phil. Sym. Orch. of Westchester, N.Y. From 1972 to 1978 he served as artistic consultant to the NEA. From 1979 to 1985 he was music director of the Puerto Rico Sym. Orch. in San Juan.

Barnett, John Francis, English composer, nephew of **John Barnett**; b. London, Oct. 16, 1837; d. there, Nov. 24, 1916. He studied piano in London and in Leipzig. In 1883 he was appointed to the staff of the Royal College of Music in London. He wrote a Sym. (1864), several playable symphonic overtures and singable cantatas, several of them inspired by literary works. Among his oratorios, *The Raising of Lazarus*, 1st performed in London on June 18, 1873, was much performed in churches. He publ. an engaging vol., *Musical Reminiscences and Impressions* (London, 1906).

Barolsky, Michael, Lithuanian-born German-Israeli composer; b. Vilnius, July 19, 1947. He studied piano, music theory, and ethnology; in 1965 took lessons in composition with Lutoslawski in Warsaw; in 1968 went to Moscow and studied privately with Denisov and Schnittke. From 1969 to 1971 he was music adviser at the Lithuanian Radio. In 1971 he emigrated to Germany. In 1972 he attended seminars with Ligeti, Kagel, and Stockhausen in Darmstadt; in 1974 went to Israel, and taught at the Pedagogic Inst. in Tel Aviv. In 1977 he settled in Cologne on a stipend of the Deutsche Akademie; also worked on electronic music with Humpert. In his compositions he devotes himself totally to the modern theater, astutely applying the full resources of electronic music.

WORKS: Violin Sonata (1964); String Trio (1964); Woodwind Quartet (1965); *Recitative and Melody* for Flute, Cello, and Piano (1966); Concertino for Violin, Trumpet, Trombone, Piano, and Percussion (1967); *Basso Ostinato* for Cello Solo (1967); *Telefonoballade*, cantata for Baritone, 6 Narrators, and Chamber Ensemble (1969); *Exodus* for Orch. (1970); *Scriptus*, after Kafka's letters, for Baritone, Mime, and Chamber Ensemble (1972); *Dakar* for Percussion, Piano, and Electronics (1972); *Photogenesis I, II, III*, and *IV*, respectively for Harpsichord, Brass Quintet, Bass Flute, and Solo Percussion (1973); *Melos* for Mezzo-soprano, Cello, Piano, Electric Organ, Percussion, and Synthesizer (1975); *Sublimatio* for Flute, Cello, 2 Pianos, Percussion, and Tape (1975); *Cries and Whispers* for Chamber Ensemble and Electronics (1975; Univ. of Chicago, Jan. 24, 1976); *Blue Eye, Brown Eye*, 1-act opera (Tel Aviv, July 29, 1976); *Apocalypse*, song cycle with Electronic Tape (1976); *Iris* for Flute, Oboe, Clarinet, Violin, Cello, and Piano

(1976); *Pranah* for Violin Solo and Electronic Tape (1976); *Sternengesang* for Chamber Orch. (1977); *The Book of Emanations* for Orch. (1978); *Ein Stück aus der Nacht* for Actor and Electronics (1978); *Tonus* for Quadraphonic Synthesizer (1979); *Cinderella* for Cello and Piano (1981); *Seelenkalender* for Mezzo-soprano and Piano (1982); *The Book of Changes* for Piano (1983); *Stück-Mund-Stück* for Trombone, Computer Sounds, and Video Tape (1983); *Piccolostück* for Piccolo and Computer Sounds (1983); *Rainbow Music* for 6 Recorders (Bonn, Feb. 12, 1984); *Trioirtrio* for Violin, Cello, and Piano (1984).

Baron, Ernst Gottlieb, German lutenist; b. Breslau, Feb. 17, 1696; d. Berlin, April 12, 1760. He studied lute playing with Kohott; later attended courses in philosophy and jurisprudence at the Univ. of Leipzig; then served as a court musician in various localities (1719–28); in 1728 he became court musician in Gotha, a post he held for 4 years; in 1737 he was appointed theorbist to Crown Prince Friedrich. He publ. a valuable manual, *Historisch-theoretische und praktische Untersuchung des Instruments der Laute* (1727), which was reprinted in English in 1976.

Baron, Maurice, French-American composer and conductor; b. Lille, Jan. 1, 1889; d. Oyster Bay, Long Island, N.Y., Sept. 5, 1964. He studied music in France; emigrated to America, where he became a theater conductor. He publ. several hundred pieces of light music under his own name and the whimsical noms de plume **Francis Delille** (i.e., "de Lille," a native of Lille) and **Morris Aborn** (anagram of Baron); also used the name of his wife, **Alice Tremblay.** Among his more ambitious works are *Ode to Democracy* for Narrator, Chorus, and Orch. (N.Y., Jan. 23, 1949).

Baron, Samuel, American flutist and conductor; b. N.Y., April 27, 1925. He studied at Brooklyn College and the Juilliard School of Music; his flute teachers were Georges Barrère and Arthur Lora; he also took lessons in conducting with Edgar Schenkman; then played flute in several orchs. In 1949 he helped to found the N.Y. Woodwind Quintet, with which he played for 20 years; in 1948 he organized the N.Y. Brass Ensemble. He was also active as a teacher, serving on the faculties of the Mannes and Yale schools of music; in 1966 he joined the faculty of the State Univ. of N.Y. at Stony Brook, and in 1977 joined the faculty at the Juilliard School. He publ. *Chamber Music for Winds* (N.Y., 1969).

Barraine, Elsa, French composer; b. Paris, Feb. 13, 1910. Her father was a cellist, her mother a singer. She studied at the Paris Cons. with Paul Dukas, Jean Gallon, and Caussade; received the 2nd Prix de Rome in 1928. She composed 3 syms. (1931, 1938, 1947) and a curiously realistic symphonic poem, *Pogromes* (Pogroms; referring to the Nazi persecutions of Jews; Paris, March 11, 1939). Other works include *Suite astrologique* for Orch. (1947); *Atmosphère* for Oboe and 10 Instruments, on Hindu rhythms (1967); *Musique rituelle* for Organ, Gongs, and Xylorimba (1968).

Barraqué, Jean, French composer of theosophic aspirations, proclaimed as an unfulfilled genius by enthusiasts of similar propensities; b. Paris, Jan. 17, 1928; d. there, Aug. 17, 1973. He took private composition lessons from Olivier Messiaen, a kindred spirit, but eschewed the latter's persistent Catholicism, let alone the Franciscan ornithophilia. Rather, Barraqué's grandiosity of musical ideals followed Scriabin's dreams of uniting all arts and all religions in an ultimate proclamation of universal faith. He had the advantage of using ultra-modern technical resources, particularly electronics, to create his world sym., which was to be in 13 connected parts. But as in Scriabin's *Mysterium*, the project remained in fragments. The work that first attracted attention was Barraqué's expansive Piano Sonata No. 1 (1950–52), cast in Lisztian dimensions and dialectic assumptions. This was followed by another significant work of philosophical intent, *Séquence* (1950–55), scored for Soprano, Piano, Harp, Violin, Cello, and Percussion. Of equal force were *Le Temps restitué* for Voice and Orch. (1957); *Au delà du hasard* for Voices, 4 Instrumental Groups, Vibraphone, and Clarinet (1958–59); *Chant après chant* for Voice, Percussion, and Piano (1966); Concerto for 6 Instrumental Groups, Vibraphone, and Clarinet (1968); and the majestic Piano Sonata No. 2 (1976). All these works were to constitute a preamble to his magnum opus, *Mort de Virgile,* inspired by a philosophical vol. of that title by Hermann Broch; the text refers to the Roman poet Virgil, traveling to the end of the universe. This work was to be composed for varying complexes of instruments, ranging from piano solo and string quartet to choral ensembles and to the ultimate climax, entitled *Discours,* scored for 11 voices and 130 instruments. In Barraqué's music, melodies and rhythms function as asymptotes converging on the verticals of harmony, with the tonal reference never totally absent. For further elucidation, a book by André Hodeir, *La Musique depuis Debussy,* is useful, if the reader detracts the extremities of the author's enthusiasm.

Barraud, Henry, French composer; b. Bordeaux, April 23, 1900. He studied music without a teacher while engaged in the family wine business in Bordeaux. In 1926 he entered the Paris Cons. and studied with Louis Aubert, but was expelled in 1927 for refusing to follow orthodox methods of composition; he also studied composition with Dukas and fugue with Caussade. In 1937 Barraud was appointed director of music for the International Exposition in Paris. He served in the French army during World War II; after the demobilization he lived in Marseilles. After the liberation of Paris in 1944 he was appointed music director of Radiodiffusion Française; he retired in 1965. In 1969 he received the Grand Prix National de la Musique. Barraud publ. books on Berlioz (Paris, 1955; 2nd ed., 1966); on the problems of modern music, *Pour comprendre les musiques d'aujourd'hui* (Paris, 1968); and on the analysis of selected operas, *Les Cinq Grands Opéras* (Paris, 1972).

Works: *Finale dans le mode rustique* (Paris, 1932); *Poème* for Orch. (1934); *Concerto da camera* for 30 Instruments (1936); *Le Mystère des Saints Innocents,* oratorio (1942–44); *Le Diable à la Kermesse,* ballet (1943; a symphonic suite from it was broadcast by Paris Radio, April 26, 1945); Piano Concerto (N.Y. Phil., Dec. 5, 1946); *Offrande à une ombre* (in memory of a brother killed by the Germans as a member of the Résistance; 1st U.S. perf., St. Louis, Jan. 10, 1947); *La Farce du Maître Pathelin* (Paris, June 24, 1948); *Symphonie de Numance* (Baden-Baden, Dec. 3, 1950); Concertino for Piano and 4 Winds (1953); *Numance,* opera (Paris, April 15, 1955); *Te Deum* for Chorus and 6 Instruments (1955); Sym. for String Orch. (1955); Sym. No. 3 (Boston, March 7, 1958); *Rapsodie cartésienne* for Orch. (1959); *Rapsodie dionysienne* for Orch. (1961); *Lavinia,* opera-buffa (Aix-en-Provence, July 20, 1961); Divertimento for Orch. (1962); Concerto for Flute and Strings (1963); *Symphonie concertante* for Trumpet and Orch. (1965); *3 études* for Orch.; *Une Saison en enfer,* symphonic suite after Rimbaud (1969).

Barrère, Georges, French flute virtuoso; b. Bordeaux, Oct. 31, 1876; d. Kingston, N.Y., June 14, 1944. He studied at the Paris Cons. (1889–95), graduating with 1st prize; was solo flutist at the Colonne Concerts and at the Paris Opéra (1897–1905). He went to America in 1905; played flute with the N.Y. Sym. Orch. (1905–28); taught at the Inst. of Musical Art, N.Y., and at the Juilliard School of Music. He was the founder of the Barrère Little Sym. (1914); composed a *Nocturne* for Flute; *Chanson d'automne* for Voice; also ed. works for flute.

Barret, Apollon (Marie-Rose), French oboist; b. Paris, c.1803; d. London, March 8, 1879. He studied at the Paris Cons.; played in the orchs. at opera houses; in 1874 went to London with the Italian Opera. Barret is the author of a standard manual, *Complete Method for the Oboe Comprising All the New Fingerings, New Tables of Shakes, Scales, Exercises.*

Barrett, Emma, black American jazz pianist, nicknamed "Sweet Emma, the Bell Gal"; b. New Orleans, March 25, 1898;

d. there, Jan. 28, 1983. Her entire career was connected with traditional jazz in New Orleans; beginning in 1961 she was associated with Preservation Hall there. She played with most of the leading bands, among them those headed by Oscar Celestin, William Ridgley, George McCullum, Sidney Desvigne, and Armand Piron; also formed her own bands. In 1967 she suffered a stroke which paralyzed her left side, but she continued to perform, playing the right-hand part and beating time vigorously. At most public functions she used a wheelchair. She played her last engagement on Jan. 18, 1983, only a few days before her death.

Barrett, "Syd" Roger, psychedelic English rock guitarist and lyricist; b. Cambridge, Jan. 6, 1946. He played guitar in a folk duo with his schoolmate Dave Gilmour (b. Cambridge, March 6, 1944); then teamed with Roger Waters (b. Great Bookham, Sept. 6, 1944), Nick Mason (b. Birmingham, Jan. 27, 1945), and Rick Wright (b. London, July 28, 1945) and played a rhythm-and-blues type of music, with Barrett playing the lead guitar, Wright handling the keyboard instruments, Waters on the string bass, and Mason on the drums. All of them did vocals. They adopted the collective name Pink Floyd, the origin of which is obscure, and plunged into the murky waters of contemporary alienation and lugubrious mysticism. Barrett's 1st single record, *Arnold Layne*, dealt with a perverted transvestite, so strange in its slimy contortions that even a London underground radio station refused to put it on the air. Barrett's next release, *See Emily Play*, became a hit, however; he then put out *The Piper at the Gates of Dawn*, released in America in 1967 under the name Pink Floyd, which became a top attraction. But Barrett began to fall apart psychologically, with bizarre behavior and drug abuse; paradoxically, it was just this eccentricity that exercised irresistible fascination to the similarly disoriented youth on both sides of the Atlantic. Barrett departed the group in 1969, but Pink Floyd continued to function, perpetuating Barrett's surrealist visions and cultivating outer-space fantasies, as exemplified by the album *The Dark Side of the Moon* (written by Roger Waters), which included the megasmash *Money*. Among their other successful albums were *Meddle*, with the extraordinary *Echoes*, and *Atom Heart Mother*, which featured a smattering of electronic sounds. In 1979 Pink Floyd produced a highly successful film, *The Wall*, dealing with lunacy.

Barrientos, Maria, Spanish coloratura soprano; b. Barcelona, March 10, 1884; d. Ciboure, France, Aug. 8, 1946. She studied at the Barcelona Cons. at age 6; made her operatic debut at the age of 15 as Inez in *L'Africaine* in Barcelona, on March 4, 1898, and while still very young made a successful tour of Europe. She made her American debut at the Metropolitan Opera House in N.Y. as Lucia on Jan. 31, 1916, and remained with it until 1920; then returned to Europe.

Barrière, Jean, French cellist and composer; b. c.1705; d. Paris, June 6, 1747. In 1730 he was appointed as a musician-in-ordinary at the Royal Academy of Music in Paris; then went to Rome, where he studied cello with Alborea; returned to Paris in 1739, and made a fine career as a virtuoso cellist at the Concert Spirituel. He publ. 6 books of cello sonatas (Paris, 1733–39).

Barrington, Daines, English lawyer and music amateur; b. London, 1727; d. there, March 14, 1800. He was the author of the famous account of Mozart as a child prodigy publ. in *Philosophical Transactions of the Royal Society* in 1770. He also publ. an interesting vol., *Experiments and Observations on the Singing of Birds* (London, 1773), and a description of the ancient Welsh crwth and pibcorn, also in *Philosophical Transactions of the Royal Society.*

Barrios Fernandez, Angel, Spanish composer; b. Granada, Jan. 4, 1882; d. Madrid, Nov. 27, 1964. Of a musical family (his father was a famous guitarist), he studied violin and played in bands as a child. He later studied theory with Conrado del Campo in Madrid and with Gédalge in Paris. At the same time, he perfected his guitar playing; formed a trio, Iberia,

and traveled in Europe playing Spanish popular music. He spent his declining years in Madrid. In collaboration with his teacher Conrado del Campo, he wrote a successful operetta, *El Avapiés* (Madrid, 1919), and several zarzuelas: *La Suerte, La Romería, Seguidilla gitana, Castigo de Dios, En Nombre del Rey,* and *Lola se va a los puertos;* also numerous overtures and other orch. pieces based on popular Spanish motifs.

Barron, Louis, American composer; b. Minneapolis, April 23, 1920. He studied at the Univ. of Minnesota. In 1947 he married **Bebe Barron** (née Charlotte Wind; b. Minneapolis, June 16, 1927), who studied political science and also took theory lessons with Riegger and Cowell in N.Y. (1947). In 1948 the couple founded an electro-acoustic music studio in N.Y., one of the 1st of its kind. They gained wide recognition with their electronic score for the film *Forbidden Planet* (1956). They were divorced in 1970 but continued to collaborate on various works. Among their electronic scores for films are *Bells of Atlantis* (1952), *Miramagic* (1954), *Forbidden Planet* (1956), *Jazz of Lights* (1956), *Bridges* (1959), *Crystal Growing* (1959), *The Computer Age* (1968), *More than Human* (1974), and *Cannabis* (1975).

Barroso Neto, Joaquim Antonio, Brazilian composer; b. Rio de Janeiro, Jan. 30, 1881; d. there, Sept. 1, 1941. He studied with Braga, Nepomuceno, and others; appeared as a pianist in public at an early age; his compositions, in a mildly Romantic manner, are mostly for piano. He enjoyed a fine reputation in Brazil as a teacher.
  Bibl.: T. Gomes, *B.N.* (Rio de Janeiro, 1939).

Barrows, John, American horn player; b. Glendale, Calif., Feb. 12, 1913; d. Madison, Wis., Jan. 11, 1974. His 1st instrument was the euphonium; he studied horn playing at the Eastman School of Music in Rochester, N.Y. (1930–32), theory and orchestration at San Diego State Teachers College (1933–34), and composition (with Donovan and Smith) and cello at Yale Univ. (1934–38). He played horn with the Minneapolis Sym. (1938–42), the N.Y. City Opera (1946–49), and N.Y. City Ballet orch. (1952–55), and in San Juan with the Casals Festival orch. (1958–61). Barrows was a member of the N.Y. Woodwind Quintet (1952–61); toured Europe with the Marlboro Festival Orch. He taught horn at Yale Univ. (1957–61), at N.Y. Univ. (1958–61), and at the Univ. of Wisconsin (1961–74). He composed 2 string quartets, a String Trio, and a Wind Quintet, and made arrangements for band.

Barry, Gerald, Irish composer; b. County Clare, April 28, 1952. He studied at Univ. College, Dublin (B.Mus., 1973; M.A., 1975); also studied composition with Peter Schat and organ with Piet Kee in Amsterdam, and with Stockhausen and Kagel at the Cologne Hochschule für Musik (1975–80), and received some guidance from Cerha in Vienna (1977). After a brief stint as a lecturer at Univ. College, Cork (1982–86), he concentrated on composing.
  Works: *Things That Gain by Being Painted* for Soprano, Speaker, Cello, and Piano (1977); *Ein Klavier Konzert* for Piano and Orch. (1978); *Décolletage* for Soprano and Actress (1979); _____ *Ensemble* (1979); *Ø* for 2 Pianos (1979); *Sleeping Beauty* for 2 Performers and Bass Drum (1980); *Unkrautgarten,* ballet (1980); *Sweet Cork* for Soprano, Bass, Recorder, Viol, and Harpsichord (1985); *Of Queens' Gardens* for Chamber Orch. (Dublin, Sept. 29, 1986); *Sweet Punishment* for Brass Quintet (1987); *Chevaux-de-frise* for Orch. (London, Aug. 15, 1988); Oboe Quartet (1988); *Diner* for Orch. (Belfast, Aug. 5, 1988).
  Bibl.: A. Jack, "Introducing G. B.," *Musical Times* (Aug. 1988).

Barry, Jerome, American baritone; b. Boston, Nov. 16, 1939. He studied voice and linguistics; in 1963 received his master's degree in languages from Tufts Univ., and acquired fluency in 8 European languages and in Hebrew. He studied voice privately with Pierre Bernac, Jennie Tourel, and Luigi Ricci; began his professional career in Italy; gave a great many concerts in Israel; returning to the U.S., he developed activities in many fields, as a lecturer and a singer; settled in Washington, D.C., where he organized the Washington Music Ensemble.

Barsanti, Francesco, Italian flutist, violist, and composer; b. Lucca, c.1690; d. London, 1772. He studied at the Univ. of Padua; served as a flutist and oboist in the Italian opera in London; then spent some time in Scotland, returning to London in 1743. He wrote 9 overtures; 12 violin concertos; 6 flute solos with Bass; 6 sonatas for 12 Violins with Bass; 6 antiphons in Palestrina style; numerous pieces for various instruments. He publ. *A Collection of Old Scots Tunes* (Edinburgh, 1742).
BIBL.: W. Bergmann, "F. B.," *Consort,* XVIII (1961).

Barshai, Rudolf (Borisovich), Russian conductor; b. Labinskaya, near Krasnodar, Sept. 28, 1924. He studied violin at the Moscow Cons. with Lev Zeitlin and viola with Borisovsky, graduating in 1948; also studied conducting with Ilya Musin in Leningrad; in 1955 he organized the Moscow Chamber Orch., which became extremely successful; many Soviet composers wrote works for it. In 1976 he emigrated to Israel, and led the Israel Chamber Orch. in Tel Aviv until 1981. He also appeared as a guest conductor in Europe, the U.S., and Japan. From 1982 to 1988 he was principal conductor and artistic adviser of the Bournemouth Sym. Orch.; also was music director of the Vancouver (B.C.) Sym. Orch. (1985–87) and principal guest conductor of the Orch. National de France in Paris (from 1987).

Barsova (real name, **Vladimirova**), **Valeria,** Russian soprano; b. Astrakhan, June 13, 1892; d. Sochi, Dec. 13, 1967. She studied voice with Umberto Mazetti at the Moscow Cons., graduating in 1919; from 1920 to 1948 she was on the staff of the Bolshoi Theater in Moscow. She distinguished herself mainly in the Russian repertoire, but also sang Violetta and Gilda. Her silvery coloratura enabled her to sing such demanding roles as Lakmé. From 1950 to 1953 she taught voice at the Moscow Cons. She gave solo recitals in Russia and abroad, including England and Germany.
BIBL.: G. Polyanovsky, *V.V. B.* (Moscow and Leningrad, 1941).

Barstow, Josephine (Clare), English soprano; b. Sheffield, Sept. 27, 1940. She studied at the Univ. of Birmingham; then joined Opera for All in 1964; later studied at the London Opera Centre; was a member of the Sadler's Wells Opera (1967–68); from 1968 sang with the Welsh National Opera; from 1969 made many appearances at Covent Garden. She made her Metropolitan Opera debut on March 28, 1977, as Musetta in *La Bohème;* in 1983 she sang the role of Gutrune in Wagner's *Ring* at Bayreuth. In 1985 she was made a Commander of the Order of the British Empire. She is a versatile singer whose repertoire ranges from traditional to contemporary roles. Among her best portrayals are Salome, Lady Macbeth, Violetta, Octavian, and Jenůfa. She also created roles in works by Tippett and Henze.

Bárta, Josef, Bohemian composer; b. Prague, c.1746; d. Vienna, June 13, 1787. After serving as an organist in Prague, he settled in Vienna; he composed his opera *La Diavolessa* for the Burgtheater (July 18, 1772); he wrote several other operas, as well as 13 syms., 6 string quartets, 6 keyboard sonatas, and other works.
BIBL.: J. Havlík, *Symfonie Antonína Laubeho a Josefa Bárty* (diss., Univ. of Prague, 1974).

Bárta, Lubor, Czech composer; b. Lubná, Aug. 8, 1928; d. Prague, Nov. 5, 1972. He studied with Řídký at the Prague Academy of Musical Arts (1948–52). His music presents an effective amalgam of modernistic procedures, influenced by Bartók in its rhythm, by Stravinsky in its meters, and by Hindemith in its neo-Classical harmony.
WORKS: 2 violin concertos (1952, 1970); 3 syms. (1955; *The Bitter Summer,* 1969; 1972); Concerto for Chamber Orch. (1956); Viola Concerto (1957); *Dramatic Suite* for Orch. (1958); Piano Concerto (1958–59); *From East Bohemia,* symphonic suite (1961); *Concertante Overture* (1964); *Ludi* for 8 Winds

and String Orch. (1964); *Musica Romantica* for Strings (1971); 2 cantatas: *Komsomol* (1951) and *Song of the New Age,* inspired by space flight (1962); 2 violin sonatas (1949, 1959); 2 wind quintets (Divertimento, 1949; 1969); 3 string quartets (1950, 1957, 1967); Piano Trio (1955); Trombone Sonatina (1956); Clarinet Sonata (1958); *Ballad and Burlesque* for Cello and Piano (1963); Concertino for Trombone and Piano (1964); Solo Guitar Sonata (1965); *4 Pieces* for Violin and Guitar (1966); Flute Sonata (1966); *Fragments* for Clarinet and Piano (1967); *Amoroso* for Horn and Piano (1970); Cello Sonata (1971); Variations for Piano (1948); 3 piano sonatas (1956, 1961, 1971); Harpsichord Sonata (1967); songs.

Bartalus, István, Hungarian musicologist; b. Bálványos-Váralja, Nov. 23, 1821; d. Budapest, Feb. 9, 1899. He received his musical training at the Kolozsvar Cons.; in 1851 went to Pest, where he was active as a teacher, pianist, musicologist, and journalist. He was one of the founders of Hungarian musicology; his ed. of *Magyar népdalok egyetemes gyüjteménye* (Universal Collection of Hungarian Folk Songs; 7 vols., Budapest, 1873–96) sustains validity even at the present time.

Bartay, Andreas, Hungarian composer, father of **Ede Bartay;** b. Széplak, April 7, 1799; d. Mainz, Oct. 4, 1854. He began his career as a civil servant. At the same time he was engaged in collecting Hungarian folk songs and became interested in music in general. In 1829 he became a director of the 1st Pest singing academy; in 1834 he publ. one of the earliest collections of Hungarian folk songs and also a Hungarian book on music theory, *Magyar Apollo* (1834). A militant patriot, he participated in the Hungarian struggle for independence of 1848; after its defeat he emigrated to France and eventually to Germany. He wrote 3 operas: *Aurelia,* oder *Das Weib am Konradstein* (Pest, Dec. 16, 1837), *Csel* (The Ruse; Pest, April 29, 1839), and *A magyarok Nápolyban* (The Hungarians in Naples; unperf.).

Bartay, Ede, Hungarian folk-song collector, son of **Andreas Bartay;** b. Pest, Oct. 6, 1825; d. Budapest, Aug. 31, 1901. He studied law and music and was for many years a practicing piano teacher. In 1876 he was appointed director of the National Cons. in Budapest, a post which he held until his death. In 1863 he founded the Hungarian Pension Fund for Musicians. Like his father, he was a Hungarian patriot. After the defeat of the Hungarian Revolution of 1848 he remained in Budapest, dedicating himself to collecting authentic Hungarian folk songs and dances. He also wrote a Sym.; an overture, *Pericles;* and many piano pieces.

Bartels, Wolfgang von, German composer; b. Hamburg, July 21, 1883; d. Munich, April 19, 1938. He studied with Beer-Walbrunn in Munich and with Gédalge in Paris; then became a music critic in Munich. His early works show impressionist influences; later he adopted an eclectic style.
WORKS: Melodramas: *The Little Dream,* after Galsworthy (Manchester, 1911); *Li-I-Lan* (Kassel, 1918); song cycles (*Li-Tai-Pe, Baltic Songs, Minnesänge*); Violin Concerto; Viola Concerto.

Barth, Hans, German-American pianist and composer; b. Leipzig, June 25, 1897; d. Jacksonville, Fla., Dec. 9, 1956. When a small child, he won a scholarship at the Leipzig Cons. and studied under Carl Reinecke; went to the U.S. in 1907, but made frequent trips to Germany. His meeting with Busoni inspired him to experiment with new scales; with the aid of George L. Weitz, he perfected a portable quarter-tone piano (1928), on which he played in Carnegie Hall (Feb. 3, 1930); composed a Piano Concerto for this instrument, with a string orch. also tuned in quarter-tones (played by him with Stokowski and the Philadelphia Orch., March 28, 1930). Other works using quarter-tones: Suite for Strings, Brass, and Kettledrums; Piano Quintet; also a Piano Concerto for normal tuning (1928) and 2 piano sonatas; operetta, *Miragia* (1938). He was the author of a piano manual, *Technic* (1935); various essays; etc.

Barth, Karl Heinrich, German pianist and teacher; b. Pillau, near Königsberg, July 12, 1847; d. Berlin, Dec. 23, 1922. He was a pupil of Hans von Bülow in Berlin; also studied with Bronsart and Tausig. He became a teacher at the Stern Cons., Berlin, in 1868; then at the Hochschule für Musik (1871); established, with De Ahna and Hausmann, the Barth Trio, which enjoyed considerable success.

Barth, Richard, German left-handed violin virtuoso; b. Grosswanzleben, June 5, 1850; d. Marburg, Dec. 25, 1923. He studied with Joachim in Hannover; attracted considerable attention because he was left-handed, using his left hand for bowing and his right hand for fingering. He was also a professional conductor; he led the Phil. concerts in Hamburg from 1894 to 1904. In 1908 he became director of the Hamburg Cons. He wrote chamber music in the manner of Brahms and was the author of a biography, *Johannes Brahms und seine Musik* (1904).
BIBL.: E. Deggeler-Engelke, *Zur Brahmsfolge: R. B. (1850–1923), Leben, Wirken und Werk* (Marburg, 1949).

Bartha, Dénes, Hungarian musicologist; b. Budapest, Oct. 2, 1908. He attended courses in musicology at the Univ. of Berlin with Blume, Sachs, Hornbostel, and Schering (1926–30); received his doctorate with the thesis *Benedictus Ducis und Appenzeller* (Wolfenbüttel, 1930). Returning to Budapest, he was a lecturer at the Franz Liszt Academy of Music and Privatdozent at the Univ. of Budapest. In 1964 he was a visiting prof. at Smith College; in 1966–67 he was on the faculty of Carnegie-Mellon Univ. in Pittsburgh, and from 1969 to 1978 was Andrew W. Mellon Prof. there. He also lectured at Harvard Univ. (1964–65) and Cornell Univ. (1965–66). He publ. *Das Musiklehrbuch einer ungarischen Klosterschule aus 1490* (Budapest, 1934); *Lehrbuch der Musikgeschichte* (Budapest, 1935); *Franz Liszt* (Leipzig, 1936); *Beethoven* (Budapest, 1939); *Die ungarische Musik* (with Kodály; Budapest, 1943); *Anthologie der Musikgeschichte* (Budapest, 1948); *J.S. Bach* (Budapest, 1956; 2nd ed., 1960); *Beethoven kilenc szimfóniája* (Budapest, 1956; 5th ed., rev., 1975); *Haydn als Opernkapellmeister* (with L. Somfai; Budapest-Mainz, 1960); ed. *J. Haydn: Gesammelte Briefe und Aufzeichnungen* (Kassel, 1965) and *Zénei Lexikon* (2nd ed., 3 vols., Budapest, 1965–66).

Barthe, Grat-Norbert, French composer; b. Bayonne, June 7, 1828; d. Asnières, Seine, Aug. 13, 1898. He was a pupil of Leborne at the Paris Cons.; won the Grand Prix de Rome (1854) with the cantata *Francesca da Rimini;* wrote the operas *Don Carlos* and *La Fiancée d'Abydos;* an oratorio, *Judith;* etc.

Barthélémon, François-Hippolyte, French violinist and composer; b. Bordeaux, July 27, 1741; d. London, July 20, 1808. His father was French and his mother Irish. He held posts as violinist in various theater orchs. in London; became acquainted with Haydn during Haydn's London visit in 1792. He was greatly praised as a violinist; Burney speaks of his tone as being "truly vocal." Barthélémon wrote mostly for the stage; among his operas, the most notable are *Pelopida* (London, May 24, 1766); *The Judgement of Paris* (London, Aug. 24, 1768); *Le Fleuve Scamandre* (Paris, Dec. 22, 1768); *The Maid of the Oaks* (The Oaks, near Epsom, June 1774); *Belphegor* (London, March 16, 1778). In addition, he wrote a Violin Concerto; 2 sets of duos for violins; several string quartets; catches and glees to English words (many of them publ.). He was married to Mary Young, a noted singer descended from Anthony Young; his daughter contributed a biographical ed. (London, 1827) of selections from Barthélémon's oratorio *Jefte in Masfa.*

Bartholomée, Pierre, Belgian conductor and composer; b. Brussels, Aug. 5, 1937. He studied with Louel, Souffrian, and Stekke at the Royal Cons. in Brussels (1952–57) and privately with Pousseur and Boulez. In 1962 he founded in Brussels an instrumental ensemble, Groupe Musiques Nouvelles, which he conducted until 1977. He also was prof. of analysis at the Royal Cons. in Brussels (from 1972). In 1977, he became music director of the Liège Orch.
WORKS: *Chanson* for Solo Cello (1964); *Cantate aux Alentours* for Voices, Instruments, and Live Electronics (1966); *La Ténèbre souveraine* for Soloists, Double Chorus, and Orch.

(1967); *Tombeau de Marin* for Violin, 2 Viole da Gamba, and Harpsichord (1967); *Premier alentour* for Flute and 2 Viole da Gamba (1967); *Catalogue* for 4 Harps (1968); *Deuxième alentour: "Cueillir"* for Mezzo-soprano, Piano, and Percussion (1969); *Harmonique* for Orch. (1970); *Fancy I* for Solo Harp and *Fancy II* for Instrumental Group (1974–75; can be played together under the title *Sonata quasi una fantasia*).

Bartlett, Ethel, English pianist; b. Epping Forest, June 6, 1896; d. Los Angeles, April 17, 1978. She studied with Matthay; specialized as a piano duet player with her husband, **Rae Robertson;** made annual tours in Europe and the U.S.

Bartlett, Homer Newton, American pianist, organist, and composer; b. Olive, N.Y., Dec. 28, 1845; d. Hoboken, N.J., April 3, 1920. He studied with Max Braun and Jacobsen; was organist at the Madison Avenue Baptist Church, N.Y., for 31 years. He was one of the founders of the American Guild of Organists. His publ. works include a cantata, *The Last Chieftain* (Boston, Jan. 29, 1891); a Sextet for Flute and Strings; quartets, anthems, carols, etc.; about 80 songs and piano pieces. The following are in MS: opera, *La Vallière;* unfinished Japanese opera, *Hinotito;* oratorio, *Samuel;* symphonic poem, *Apollo;* Violin Concerto; Cello Concerto; etc. His 1st opus number, a *Grand Polka de Concert,* was very popular.

Bartmuss, Richard, German organist and composer; b. Schleesen, Dec. 23, 1859; d. Dessau, Dec. 25, 1910. He studied with Grell and Löschhorn; in 1885 became court organist in Dessau. He wrote numerous organ works that enjoyed considerable popularity, among them 2 concertos, 4 sonatas, and 2 chorale-fantasias; also an oratorio, *Der Tag der Pfingsten;* a cantata, *Die Apostel in Philippi;* motets; and songs. His sacred work *Liturgische Vespern* represents a partial formulation of his attempt to modernize the Lutheran musical service.

Bartók, Béla, great Hungarian composer; b. Nagyszentmiklós, March 25, 1881; d. N.Y., Sept. 26, 1945. His father was a school headmaster; his mother was a proficient pianist, and he received his 1st piano lessons from her. He began playing the piano in public at the age of 11. In 1894 the family moved to Pressburg, where he took piano lessons with László Erkel, son of the famous Hungarian opera composer; he also studied harmony with Anton Hyrtl. In 1899 he enrolled at the Royal Academy of Music in Budapest, where he studied piano with István Thomán and composition with Hans Koessler; he graduated in 1903. His earliest compositions reveal the combined influence of Liszt, Brahms, and Richard Strauss; however, he soon became interested in exploring the resources of national folk music, which included not only Hungarian melo-rhythms but also elements of other ethnic strains in his native Transylvania, including Rumanian and Slovak. He formed a cultural friendship with Zoltán Kodály, and together they traveled through the land collecting folk songs, which they publ. in 1906. In 1907 Bartók succeeded István Thomán as prof. of piano at the Royal Academy of Music. His interest in folksong research led him to tour North Africa in 1913. In 1919 he served as a member of the musical directorate of the short-lived Hungarian Democratic Republic with Dohnányi and Kodály; was also deputy director of the Academy of Music. Although a brilliant pianist, he limited his concert programs mainly to his own compositions; he also gave concerts playing works for 2 pianos with his 2nd wife, Ditta Pásztory (d. Budapest, Nov. 21, 1982, at the age of 80). In his compositions he soon began to feel the fascination of tonal colors and impressionistic harmonies as cultivated by Debussy and other modern French composers. The basic texture of his music remained true to tonality, which he expanded to chromatic polymodal structures and unremittingly dissonant chordal combinations; in his piano works he exploited the extreme registers of the keyboard, often in the form of tone clusters to simulate pitchless drumbeats. He made use of strong asymmetrical rhythmic figures suggesting the modalities of Slavic folk music, a usage that imparted a somewhat acrid coloring to his music. The melodic line of his works sometimes veered toward atonality in its chromatic involutions; in some instances he employed melodic figures comprising the 12 different notes of the chromatic scale; however, he never adopted the integral techniques of the 12-tone method.

Bartók toured the U.S. as a pianist from Dec. 1927 to Feb. 1928; also gave concerts in the Soviet Union in 1929. He resigned his position at the Budapest Academy of Music in 1934, but continued his research work in ethnomusicology as a member of the Hungarian Academy of Sciences, where he was engaged in the preparation of the monumental Corpus Musicae Popularis Hungaricae. With the outbreak of World War II, Bartók decided to leave Europe; in the fall of 1940 he went to the U.S., where he remained until his death from polycythemia. In 1940 he received an honorary Ph.D. from Columbia Univ.; he also did folk-song research there as a visiting assistant in music (1941–42). His last completed score, the *Concerto for Orchestra*, commissioned by Koussevitzky, proved to be his most popular work. His 3rd Piano Concerto was virtually completed at the time of his death, except for the last 17 bars, which were arranged and orchestrated by his pupil Tibor Serly.

Throughout his life, and particularly during his last years in the U.S., Bartók experienced constant financial difficulties, and complained bitterly of his inability to support himself and his family. Actually, he was apt to exaggerate his pecuniary troubles, which were largely due to his uncompromising character. He arrived in America in favorable circumstances; his traveling expenses were paid by the American patroness Elizabeth Sprague Coolidge, who also engaged him to play at her festival at the Library of Congress for a generous fee. Bartók was offered the opportunity to give a summer course in composition at a midwestern college on advantageous terms, when he was still well enough to undertake such a task, but he proposed to teach piano instead, and the deal collapsed. Ironically, performances and recordings of his music increased enormously after his death, and the value of his estate reached a great sum of money. Posthumous honors were not lacking: Hungary issued a series of stamps with Bartók's image; a street in Budapest was named Bartók St.; the centenary of his birth (1981) was celebrated throughout the world by concerts and festivals devoted to his works. Forty-three years after his death, his remains were removed from the Ferncliff Cemetery in Hartsdale, N.Y., and taken to Budapest for a state funeral on July 7, 1988.

Far from being a cerebral purveyor of abstract musical designs, Bartók was an ardent student of folkways, seeking the roots of meters, rhythms, and modalities in the spontaneous songs and dances of the people. Indeed, he regarded his analytical studies of popular melodies as his most important contribution to music. Even during the last years of his life, already weakened by illness, he applied himself assiduously to the arrangement of Serbo-Croatian folk melodies of Yugoslavia from recordings placed in his possession. He was similarly interested in the natural musical expression of children; he firmly believed that children are capable of absorbing modalities and asymmetrical rhythmic structures with greater ease than adults trained in the rigid disciplines of established music schools. His remarkable collection of piano pieces entitled, significantly, *Mikrokosmos* was intended as a method to initiate beginners into the world of unfamiliar tonal and rhythmic combinations; in this he provided a parallel means of instruction to the Kodály method of schooling.

WORKS: STAGE: *A kékszakállú herceg vará* (Duke Bluebeard's Castle), opera in 1 act, op. 11 (1911; rev. 1912, 1918; Budapest, May 24, 1918, Egisto Tango conducting; U.S. premiere, N.Y. City Opera, Oct. 2, 1952); *A fából faragott királyfi* (The Wooden Prince), ballet in 1 act, op. 13 (1914–16; Budapest, May 12, 1917, Egisto Tango conducting; orch. suite, 1924; Budapest, Nov. 23, 1931; rev. 1932); *A czodálatos mandarin* (The Miraculous Mandarin), pantomime in 1 act, op. 19 (1918–19; Cologne, Nov. 27, 1926; orch. suite, 1924; rev. 1927; Budapest, Oct. 15, 1928, Ernst von Dohnányi conducting).

ORCH.: *Scherzo* (only scored movement of a projected sym.

in E-flat major, 1902; Budapest, Feb. 29, 1904); *Kossuth*, symphonic poem (1903; Budapest, Jan. 13, 1904); *Rhapsody* for Piano and Orch., op. 1 (1904; Paris, Aug. 1905; Bartók, soloist); Scherzo for Piano and Orch., op. 2 (1904; posthumous, Budapest, Sept. 28, 1961); Suite No. 1, op. 3 (1905; movements 1, 3–5 perf. in Vienna, Nov. 29, 1905; 1st complete perf., Budapest, March 1, 1909; rev. 1920); Suite No. 2 for Small Orch., op. 4 (1905–7; 1st perf. of 2nd movement, Scherzo, only; Berlin, Jan. 2, 1909; 1st complete perf., Budapest, Nov. 22, 1909; rev. 1920, 1943; transcribed for 2 Pianos, 1941); *2 Portraits*, op. 5 (No. 1, 1907–8; No. 2, 1911; No. 1, Budapest, Feb. 12, 1911; 1st complete perf., Budapest, April 20, 1916); Violin Concerto No. 1 (1907–8; score discovered in 1958; posthumous, Basel, May 30, 1958; Schneeberger, soloist; Paul Sacher conducting); *2 Pictures* (*Deux Images*), op. 10 (1910; Budapest, Feb. 25, 1913); *4 Pieces*, op. 12 (1912; orchestrated 1921; Budapest, Jan. 9, 1922); *Dance Suite* for Orch. (1923; Budapest, Nov. 19, 1923); 3 piano concertos: No. 1 (1926; Frankfurt, July 1, 1927; Bartók, soloist; Furtwängler conducting); No. 2 (1930–31; Frankfurt, Jan. 23, 1933; Bartók, soloist; Rosbaud conducting); No. 3 (1945; last 17 measures composed by Tibor Serly; posthumous, Philadelphia, Feb. 8, 1946; Sándor, soloist; Ormandy conducting); *Rhapsody* No. 1 for Violin and Orch. (1928; also versions for Violin or Cello, and Piano; Königsberg, Nov. 1, 1929; Szigeti, soloist; Scherchen conducting); *Rhapsody* No. 2 for Violin and Orch. (1928; also for Violin and Piano; Budapest, Nov. 25, 1929; Székely, soloist; E. Dohnányi conducting); *Music for Strings, Percussion, and Celesta*, one of Bartók's most often played works (1936; Basel, Jan. 21, 1937, Paul Sacher conducting); Violin Concerto No. 2 (1937–38; Amsterdam, March 23, 1939; Székely, soloist; Mengelberg conducting); *Divertimento* for String Orch. (1939; Basel, June 11, 1940); Concerto for 2 Pianos and Orch. (1940; orchestration of Sonata for 2 Pianos and Percussion; London, Nov. 14, 1942); Concerto for Orch. (commissioned by Koussevitzky, 1943; perf. under his direction, Boston, Dec. 1, 1944); Viola Concerto (1945; left unfinished in sketches; reconstructed and orchestrated by Tibor Serly, 1947–49; posthumous, Minneapolis, Dec. 2, 1949; Primrose, soloist; Dorati conducting; also arranged by Serly for Cello and Orch.); various orch. transcriptions of Rumanian and Hungarian folk and peasant dances, orig. for piano.

CHAMBER: 3 youthful, unnumbered violin sonatas: C minor, op. 5 (1895), A major, op. 17 (1897), and E minor (1903); Piano Quartet in C minor, op. 20 (1898); an unnumbered String Quartet in F major (1898); Duo for 2 Violins (1902); *Albumblatt* for Violin and Piano (1902); Piano Quintet (1904; Vienna, Nov. 21, 1904); 6 numbered string quartets: No. 1, op. 7 (1908; Budapest, March 19, 1910), No. 2, op. 17 (1915–17; Budapest, March 3, 1918), No. 3 (1927; London, Feb. 19, 1929), No. 4 (1928; Budapest, March 20, 1929), No. 5 (1934; Washington, D.C., April 8, 1935), No. 6 (1939; N.Y., Jan. 20, 1941); 2 numbered violin sonatas: No. 1 (1921; Vienna, Feb. 8, 1922), No. 2 (1922; London, Feb. 7, 1923); *Rhapsody* No. 1 for Violin and Piano (1928; Budapest, Nov. 22, 1929; Szigeti, violinist; Bartók, pianist; also versions for Cello and Piano, and Violin and Orch.); *Rhapsody* No. 2 for Violin and Piano (1928; Amsterdam, Nov. 19, 1928; rev. 1944; also a version for Violin and Orch.); *44 Duos* for 2 Violins (1931); Sonata for 2 Pianos and Percussion (1937; Basel, Jan. 16, 1938; Bartók and his wife, Ditta Bartók, soloists; also for Orch. as Concerto for 2 Pianos and Orch.); *Contrasts* for Violin, Clarinet, and Piano (1938; N.Y., Jan. 9, 1939); a ballet, *Caprichos*, based on the music of *Contrasts* (N.Y., Jan. 29, 1950); Sonata for Solo Violin (1944; N.Y., Nov. 26, 1944; Menuhin, soloist).

PIANO: *Rhapsody*, op. 1 (1904; Pressburg, Nov. 4, 1906; Bartók, soloist); *14 Bagatelles*, op. 6 (1908; Berlin, June 29, 1908); *10 Easy Pieces* (1908); *2 Elegies*, op. 8b (1908–9; Budapest, April 21, 1919; Bartók, soloist); *For Children* (orig. 85 easy pieces in 4 vols., 1908–9; rev., 1945, reducing the number to 79, divided into 2 vols.); *7 Sketches*, op. 9 (1908–10; rev. 1945); *4 Dirges* (1910); *3 Burlesques* (1908–11); *Allegro barbaro* (1911); *6 Rumanian Folk Dances* (1909–15); *Rumanian Christ-*

mas Carols, or *Colinde* (1915); Sonatina (1915); *Suite*, op. 14 (1916; Budapest, April 21, 1919; Bartók, soloist); *15 Hungarian Peasant Songs* (1914–18); *3 Études*, op. 18 (1918); *8 Improvisations on Hungarian Peasant Songs* (1920; Budapest, Feb. 27, 1921; Bartók, soloist); Sonata (1926; Budapest, Dec. 8, 1926; Bartók, soloist); *Out of Doors* (1926); *9 Little Pieces* (1926; Budapest, Dec. 8, 1926; Bartók, soloist); *3 Rondos on Folk Tunes* (No. 1, 1916; Nos. 2 and 3, 1927); *Petite Suite* (1936); *Mikrokosmos* (1926–39), 153 progressive pieces publ. in 6 vols., a unique attempt to write a piano method in a modern idiom with varying meters, modes, and dissonant counterpoint; *7 Pieces from Mikrokosmos* for 2 Pianos (c.1939); Suite for 2 Pianos (1941; transcription from Suite No. 2, for Small Orch., op. 4).

VOCAL: *20 Hungarian Folksongs* for Voice and Piano (1st 10 by Bartók, 2nd 10 by Kodály; 1906; rev., 1938); *8 Hungarian Folksongs* for Voice and Piano (1907–17); *3 Village Scenes* for Female Voices and Chamber Orch. (1926; N.Y., Feb. 1, 1927; this is a transcription of 3 of *5 Village Scenes* for Voice and Piano, 1924; Budapest, Dec. 8, 1926); *20 Hungarian Folksongs* for Voice and Piano (4 vols., 1929); *Cantata Profana* for Tenor, Baritone, Chorus, and Orch. (1930; BBC, London, May 25, 1934); *27 Choruses* for Women's or Children's Voices a cappella (1935); numerous settings of various folk songs.

WRITINGS: *Cântece poporale româneşti din comitatul Bihor (Ungaria)/Chansons populaires roumaines du département Bihar (Hongrie)* (Bucharest, 1913; rev. edition in Eng. as incorporated in B. Suchoff, ed., *Rumanian Folk Music*, The Hague, vols. I–III, 1967); *Erdélyi magyarság népdalok* (Transylvanian Folk Songs; Budapest, 1923; with Kodály); "Die Volksmusik der Rumänen von Maramureş," *Sammelbände für vergleichende Musikwissenschaft*, IV (Munich, 1923; in Eng. as incorporated in B. Suchoff, ed., *Rumanian Folk Music*, The Hague, vol. V, 1975); *A magyar népdal* (Budapest, 1924; in German as *Das ungarische Volkslied*, Berlin, 1925; in Eng. as *Hungarian Folk Music*, London, 1931; enl. edition, with valuable addenda, as *The Hungarian Folk Song*, ed. by B. Suchoff, Albany, N.Y., 1981); *Népzenénk és a szomszéd népek népzenéje* (Our Folk Music and the Folk Music of Neighboring Peoples; Budapest, 1934; in German as *Die Volksmusik der Magyaren und der benachbarten Völker*, Berlin, 1935; in French as "La Musique populaire des Hongrois et des peuples voisins," *Archivum Europae Centro Orientalis*, II; Budapest, 1936); *Die Melodien der rumänischen Colinde (Weihnachtslieder)* (Vienna, 1935; in Eng. in B. Suchoff, ed., *Rumanian Folk Music*, The Hague, vol. IV, 1975); *Miért és hogyan gyüjtsünk népzenét* (Why and How Do We Collect Folk Music?, Budapest, 1936; in French as *Pourquoi et comment recueille-t-on la musique populaire?*, Geneva, 1948); *Serbo-Croatian Folk Songs* (N.Y., 1951; with A. Lord; reprinted in B. Suchoff, ed., *Yugoslav Folk Music*, vol. I, Albany, N.Y., 1978); also articles in various musical magazines, among them "Hungarian Peasant Music," *Musical Quarterly* (July 1933).

The N.Y. Bartók Archive is publishing an ed. of Bartók's writings in English trs. in its Studies in Musicology series. The following vols., under the editorship of Benjamin Suchoff, have been publ.: *Rumanian Folk Music* (The Hague, vols. I–III, 1967; vols. IV–V, 1975); *Turkish Folk Music from Asia Minor* (Princeton, 1976); *Béla Bartók's Essays* (selected essays; London and N.Y., 1976); *Yugoslav Folk Music* (4 vols., Albany, N.Y., 1978); *The Hungarian Folk Song* (Albany, N.Y., 1981).

BIBL.: An extensive literature in many languages exists concerning various aspects of Bartók's life and music; in addition to the writings listed below, see the journal *Documenta Bartókiana* (Budapest, 1964–70; 1977–). *Musikblätter des Anbruch*, III/5 (Vienna, 1921); *Zenei Szemle*, VIII (Budapest, 1928); A. Révész, *Bartók Béla utja* (Budapest, 1936); D. Dille, *B. B.* (Antwerp, 1939); H. Pleasants and T. Serly, "B.'s Historic Contribution," *Modern Music*, XVII (1940); G. Abraham, "The B. of the Quartets," *Music & Letters* (Oct. 1945); M. Seiber, *The String Quartets of B. B.* (London, 1945); J. Demény, *B.* (Budapest, 1946); B. Kiss, *Bartók Béla müvészete* (Cluj, 1946); D. Dille, *B. B.* (Brussels, 1947); G. Láng, *B. élete és müvei* (Buda-

pest, 1947); J. Deményi, ed., *Bartók Béla levelei* (Budapest, 1948–71; 2nd ed., 1976; in German, 1960; 2nd ed., 1973; in Eng., 1971); J. Demény, *B. élete és müvei* (Budapest, 1948); A. Molnár, *B. müvészete* (Budapest, 1948); M. Babbitt, "The String Quartets of B.," *Musical Quarterly* (July 1949); "B. B., A Memorial Review," *Tempo*, 13–14 (1949–50); S. Moreux, *B. B., Sa vie, ses œuvres, son langage* (Paris, 1949; in German, Zürich, 1950; in Eng., London, 1953); C. Mason, "B. B. and Folksong," *Music Review*, XI (1950); B. Rondi, *B.* (Rome, 1950); *Új Zenei Szemle*, I/4 (Budapest, 1950); *Musik der Zeit*, III (Bonn, 1953); H. Stevens, *The Life and Music of B. B.* (a basic study in Eng.; N.Y., 1953; rev. ed., 1964); *Revue Musicale*, 244 (1955); P. Csobádi, *B.* (Budapest, 1955); E. Lendvai, *B. stilusa* (Budapest, 1955); F. Bónis, *B. élete képekben* (Budapest, 1956; 4th ed. for the Bartók centenary, 1980; in German, 1964; in French, 1964; in Eng. as *B. B.: His Life in Pictures*, 1964); B. Suchoff, *Guide to B.'s Mikrokosmos* (London, 1957; 3rd ed., N.Y., 1982); B. Szabolcsi, ed., *B., Sa vie et son œuvre* (Budapest, 1956; 2nd ed., 1968; in German, 1957; enl. ed., 1972); J. Szegö, *Bartók Béla a népdalkutató* (Bucharest, 1956); R. Traimer, *B. B.s Kompositionstechnik, dargestellt an seinen sechs Streichquartetten* (Regensburg, 1956); K. Kristóf, *Beszélgetések B. Bélaval* (Budapest, 1957); A. Fassett, *The Naked Face of Genius; B. B.'s American Years* (Boston, 1958; reprint as *B. B.; The American Years*, N.Y., 1970); R. Petzoldt, *B. B., Sein Leben in Bildern* (Leipzig, 1958); W. Reich, *B. B.; Eigene Schriften und Erinnerungen der Freunde* (Basel and Stuttgart, 1958); J. Ujfalussy, ed., *B. breviárium; Levelek, írások, dokumentumok* (Budapest, 1958; 2nd ed., rev., 1974); J. Uhde, *B. B.* (Berlin, 1959); J. Demény, ed., *Ausgewählte Briefe* (Budapest, 1960; in Eng., London, 1971); A. Forte, "B.'s 'Serial' Composition," *Musical Quarterly* (April 1960); L. Lesznai, *B. B.: Sein Leben, seine Werke* (Leipzig, 1961; in Eng. as *B.*, London, 1973); B. Szabolcsi, *B. B.: Leben und Werk* (Leipzig, 1961; 2nd ed., 1968); G. Kroó, *B. szinpadi müvei* (Budapest, 1962); V. Bator, *The B. B. Archives: History and Catalogue* (N.Y., 1963); P. Citron, *B.* (Paris, 1963); Z. Pálová-Vrbova, *B. B.: Život a dilo* (Prague, 1963); E. Lendvai, *B. dramaturgiája* (Budapest, 1964); W. Rudziński, *Warsztat kompozytorski Béli Bartóka* (Krakow, 1964); E. Helm, *B. B. in Selbstzeugnissen und Bilddokumenten* (Hamburg, 1965); J. Ujfalussy, *Bartók Béla* (Budapest, 1965; 3rd ed., 1976; in Eng., Boston, 1972; in Russian, 1971; in German, 1973); J. Kárpáti, *B. vonósnégyesei* (Budapest, 1967; rev. ed. as *B. kamarazenéje*, 1976; in Eng., 1975); A. Szöllösy, ed., *B. összegyüjtött irásai I* (Budapest, 1967); Sesja Bartókowska (Warsaw, 1967); J. Demény, *Bartók Béla a zongoramüvész* (Budapest, 1968; 2nd ed., 1973); H. Heinsheimer, *Best Regards to Aida* (includes material on B.'s American travels; N.Y., 1968); I. Martynov, *B. B.* (Moscow, 1968); I. Nestyev, *B. B.* (Moscow, 1969); J. Szegö, *Bartók Béla élete* (Budapest, 1969); F. Weselowski, ed., *Sesja Bartókowska* (Lodz, 1969); T. Zieliński, *B.* (Krakow, 1969; in German, Zürich, 1973); *B. B.: A Complete Catalogue of His Published Works* (London, 1970); V. Čižik, *B.s Briefe in die Slowakei* (Bratislava, 1971); E. Kraus, "Bibliographie und Diskographie: B. B.," *Musik und Bildung* (Oct. 1971); G. Kroó, *B. kalauz* (Budapest, 1971; in Eng., 1974; in German, 1974); T. Hundt, *B.'s Satztechnik in den Klavierwerken* (Regensburg, 1971); E. Lendvai, *B. költöi világa* (Budapest, 1971); idem, *B. B.: An Analysis of His Music* (London, 1971); *International Musicological Conference in Commemoration of B. B.: Budapest 1971*; P. Petersen, *Die Tonalität im Instrumentalschaffen von B. B.* (Hamburg, 1971); F. Bónis, *Bartók Béla élete képekben és dokumentumokban* (Budapest, 1972; in German, 1972; in Eng. as *B. B.: His Life in Pictures and Documents*, 1972); D. Dille, *Thematisches Verzeichnis der Jugendwerke B. B.s 1890–1904* (Budapest, 1974); H. Fladt, *Zur Problematik traditioneller Formtypen dargestellt an Sonatensätzen in den Streichquartetten B. B.s* (Munich, 1974); F. László, ed., *B.-dolgozatok* (Bucharest, 1974); J. McCabe, *B. Orchestral Music* (London, 1974); T. Crow, ed., *B. Studies* (Detroit, 1976); B. Suchoff, "B. in America," *Musical Times* (Feb. 1976); G. Perle, "The String Quartets of B. B.," in *A Musical Offering: Essays in Honor of Martin Bernstein*

(N.Y., 1977); E. Lendvai, *B. and Kodály* (4 vols., Budapest, 1978–80); F. Laszlo, *Bartók Béla: tanulmányok és tanúságok* (Bucharest, 1980); P. Autexier, ed., *B. B.: Musique de la vie* (Paris, 1981); B. Bartók, Jr., *Apám életének krónikája* (Budapest, 1981); idem, *Bartók Béla családi levelei* (Budapest, 1981); T. Tallián, *Bartók Béla* (Budapest, 1981); Y. Queffélec, *B. B.* (Paris, 1981); B. Bartók, Jr., *Bartók Béla mühelyében* (Budapest, 1982); H. Milne, *B.: His Life and Times* (Tunbridge Wells, 1982); S. Walsh, *B.'s Chamber Music* (London, 1982); E. Lendvai, *The Workshop of B. and Kodály* (Budapest, 1983); E. Antokoletz, *The Music of B. B.* (Berkeley, Los Angeles, and London, 1984); P. Griffiths, *B.* (London, 1984); D. Locke, "Numerical Aspects of B.'s String Quartets," *Musical Times* (June 1987); G. Ránki, ed., *B. and Kodály Revisited* (Budapest, 1987); E. Antokoletz, *B. B.: A Guide to Research* (N.Y., 1988); M. Gillies and A. Gombocz, "The 'Colinda' Fiasco: B. and Oxford University Press," *Music & Letters* (Oct. 1988); J. Platthy, *B.: A Critical Biography* (Santa Claus, Ind., 1988); D. Yeomans, *B. for Piano: A Survey of His Solo Literature* (Bloomington, Ind., 1988); M. Gillies, *B. in Britain* (Oxford, 1989); L. Somfai, "B. and the Paper Studies: The Case of String Quartet No. 4," *Hungarian Music Quarterly*, vol. 1, No. 1 (1989).

Bartoletti, Bruno, noted Italian conductor; b. Sesto Fiorentino, June 10, 1926. He studied flute at the Florence Cons.; then played flute at the Teatro Comunale in Florence, where in 1949 he became an assistant conductor; later conducted at the Maggio Musicale Fiorentino and the Royal Theater in Copenhagen. In 1956 he made his U.S. debut with the Lyric Opera of Chicago; in 1964 became its co-artistic director with Pino Donati, and sole artistic director in 1975; was also music director of the Rome Opera (1965–69); likewise was artistic director of the Teatro Comunale in Florence (from 1987). He made many guest appearances in Milan, Buenos Aires, San Francisco, and N.Y. In addition to his thorough knowledge of the Italian operatic repertoire, he also conducted French and Russian operas.

Bartolino da Padova (Magister **Frater Bartolinus** de Padua; **Frater carmelitus**), Italian composer; flourished in the 2nd half of the 14th century. He was a member of the Carmelite Order, active in Padua. Some 38 works have been attributed to him, consisting of ballads and madrigals in the style of Jacopo da Bologna. See J. Wolf, ed., *Der Squarcialupi-Codex Pal. 87 der Biblioteca Medicea Laurenziana zu Florenz* (Lippstadt, 1955); W. Marrocco, ed., *Italian Secular Music*, in Polyphonic Music of the Fourteenth Century, IX (1974). **BIBL.:** N. Goldine, "Fra B. d.P., Musicien de Court," *Acta Musicologica*, XXXIV (1962); P. Petrobelli, "Some Dates for B. d.P.," in *Studies in Music History: Essays for Oliver Strunk* (Princeton, N.J., 1968).

Bartolomeo degli Organi (Baccio Fiorentino), Italian organist and composer; b. Florence, Dec. 24, 1474; d. there, Dec. 12, 1539. At the age of 13 he became a singer at Ss. Annunziata in Florence; subsequently served as organist at several Florentine churches; also was a singer in the service of Lorenzo de' Medici, Duke of Urbino. In 1509 he was appointed principal organist at the Cathedral in Florence. Among his extant compositions are 10 Italian secular pieces and several instrumental works. See F. D'Accone, ed., *Music of the Florentine Renaissance*, in Corpus Mensurabilis Musicae, XXXII/2 (1967). **BIBL.:** F. D'Accone, "Alessandro Coppini and B. d.O.: Two Florentine Composers of the Renaissance," *Analecta Musicologica*, no. 4 (1967).

Bartolozzi, Bruno, Italian violinist and composer; b. Florence, June 8, 1911; d. Fiesole, Dec. 12, 1980. After studying violin at the Cherubini Cons. in Florence (1926–30), he was active as a violinist from 1941 to 1965 in the orch. of the Maggio Musicale Fiorentino; turned to composition quite late in life; took courses with Fragapane at the Cherubini Cons. (1946–49); in 1964 was appointed to its faculty. In his own music he followed the modified dodecaphonic techniques as promulgated by Dallapiccola, including triadic constructions. He wrote *New Sounds for Woodwind* (in Eng.; London, 1967; 2nd ed., rev., 1982), demonstrating the possibility of producing simultaneously several pitches on a single woodwind instrument. **WORKS: ORCH.:** Concerto for Orch. (1952; Rome, Jan. 18, 1956); Divertimento for Chamber Orch. (1953); 2 violin concertos: No. 1 for Violin, Strings, and Harpsichord (San Francisco, Dec. 2, 1957) and No. 2 (1979); *Concertazioni* for Bassoon, Strings, and Percussion (1963; Rome, March 6, 1965); *Memorie* for 3 Guitars and Orch. (1975; Florence, Oct. 7, 1977); *Risonanze* for 18 Instruments and Percussion (1978). **CHAMBER:** *Serenata* for Violin and Guitar (1952); *3 Pieces* for Guitar (1952); *Musica a 5* for Bassoon, Trumpet, Guitar, Violin, and Viola (1953); *Variazioni* for Solo Violin (1957); 2 string quartets (1960, 1979); *Concertazioni* for Solo Oboe, Viola, Guitar, Double Bass, and Percussion (1965); *Andamenti* for Solo Viola (1967); *Collage* for Solo Oboe (1968); *The Hollow Man* for Any Woodwind (1968); *Concertazioni a quattro* for Flute, Oboe, Clarinet, and Bassoon (1969); *Collage* for Solo Bassoon (1969); *Sinaulodia* for 4 Flutes (1969); *Cantilena* for Solo Flute (1970); *Musica per Piero* for 2 Violas (1971); *Auser* for Oboe and Guitar (1973); *Collage* for Solo Clarinet (1973); *Concertazioni* for Solo Clarinet, Horn, Trumpet, Trombone, Guitar, Viola, Cello, Double Bass, and Percussion (1973); *Repitu* for Flute, Viola, Guitar, and Percussion (1975); *Per Olga* for Solo Flute (1976); *The Solitary* for English Horn and Percussion (1976); *Adles* for Guitar (1977); *Atma* for 3 Groups of Solo Instruments (1978). **VOCAL:** *Sentimento del sogno* for Soprano and Orch. (1952); *Immagine*, after Rilke, for Soprano and 17 Instruments (1959); *Tres recuerdos del cielo* for Soprano and 10 Instruments (1967; Vienna Festival, Sept. 11, 1968).

Bartoš, František, Moravian ethnomusicologist; b. Mlatcová, March 16, 1837; d. there, June 11, 1906. He was educated at the Univ. of Vienna. He publ. 4 vols. of Moravian folk songs (1882–1901). His correspondence with Janáček was ed. by T. Straková (Gottwaldov, 1957).

Bartoš, František, Czech music critic, editor, and composer; b. Brněnec, June 13, 1905; d. Prague, May 21, 1973. He studied composition with Jirák and Křička at the Prague Cons. (1921–25), and later with J. B. Foerster (1925–28); wrote music criticism; was co-ed. of *Tempo* (1935–38; 1946–48); took part in the founding of the annual Prague Spring Festival; was chairman of the editorial committee that arranged for the publication of Dvořák's complete works. He brought out *Mozart in Letters* (Prague, 1937, 1956); *Smetana in Memories and Letters* (Prague, 1939; in Eng., 1955); *Gustav Mahler's Correspondence* (Prague, 1962). **WORKS:** Melodrama, *Jaro* (Spring; 1925); String Sextet (1926); 2 string quartets (1928, 1935); *Scherzo* for Wind Quintet (1932); *Rozhlasová hudba* (Radio Music) for Chamber Orch. (1936); *Škola žen* (The School for Women), after Molière, for Wind Quartet or Orch. (1936); Duo for Violin and Viola (1937); *Polka rusticana* for Wind Trio (1952); several song cycles.

Bartoš, Jan Zdeněk, Czech composer; b. Dvůr Králové nad Labem, June 4, 1908; d. Prague, June 1, 1981. He played the violin as a youth; then took composition lessons with Otakar Šín and with Jaroslav Křička at the Prague Cons., graduating in 1943. He earned his living playing in dance orchs.; from 1945 to 1956 he was a member of the Music Section of the Ministry of Education and Culture; in 1958 was appointed teacher of composition at the Prague Cons. In his music he followed the national traditions of the Czech school. **WORKS: STAGE:** Operas: *Rýparka* (Ripar's Wife; 1949); *Prokletý zámek* (The Accursed Castle; 1949); *Útok na nebe* (The Attack of Heaven; 1953–54); operetta, *Je libo ananas?* (Do You Like Pineapples?; 1956); 3 ballets: *Hanuman* (1941); *Mirella* (1956); *Král manéže* (King of the Manège; 1963). **ORCH.:** *Song of St. Matthias*, symphonic poem (1949); 7 syms: No. 1 (1949–52); No. 2, *da camera* (1956); No. 3, *Giocosa*, for Strings (1964–65); No. 4, *Concertante*, for Oboe d'Amore and String Orch. (1968); No. 5 for Wind Orch. (1973–74); No. 6 for Wind Quartet and String Orch. (1977); No. 7, *Brevis* (1978); *Intermezzo* (1961); *Concerto da camera* for Oboe and Strings (1963); 2 viola concertos (1963, 1970); *Fantasy* for Flute and Orch. (1964); *Inventions* for Bass Clarinet and String Orch. (1966); *Sonnets of Prague* for Narrator, Tenor, Harp, and String Orch. (1966); Concerto for Accordion and String Orch. (1966); Horn Concerto (1967); Concerto for Violin and String Orch. (1970); Concerto-Sym. for Violin and String Orch. (1973); *Fantasy* for Organ and String Orch. (1975); *Concerto per due Boemi* for Bass Clarinet, Piano, and String Orch. (1975); Concerto for Violin, Viola, and String Orch. (1976); *Music* for String Quartet and Orch. (1976); *Rhapsody* for Cello and String Orch. (1979).

CHAMBER: Cello Sonata (1938); 2 nonets (1939, 1974); 11 string quartets (1940, 1946, 1948, 1951, 1952, 1956, 1960, 1963, 1970, 1971, 1973); *Partita* for Solo Viola (1944); 3 wind quintets (1946–63); Quintet for Flute, Harp, Viola, Cello, and Guitar (1947); 17 divertimentos for various combinations of instruments (1956–79); Trio for Violin, Viola, and Harp (1961); Double-bass Sonata (1962); *Suite concertante* for Viola, Double Bass, and 9 Wind Instruments (1964); String Trio (1967); 4 piano trios (1968, 1969, 1971, 1979); Sextet for 2 Oboes, English Horn, 2 Bassoons, and Harp (1976); Trombone Sonata (1978); Trio for Viola, Clarinet, and Piano (1980); also 2 piano sonatas (1953, 1959); choruses; songs.

Bartoš, Josef, Czech writer on music; b. Vysoké Myto, March 4, 1887; d. Prague, Oct. 27, 1952. He studied with Stecker at the Prague Cons.; also with Hostinský and Nejedlý at the Univ. of Prague (1905–9); was active as a teacher and music critic. He publ. valuable monographs on Dvořák (1913), Fibich (1914; new ed., 1941), Foerster (1923), and Otakar Ostrčil (1936); also an important work on the National Opera of Prague (1938).

Barvík, Miroslav, Czech composer; b. Luzice, Sept. 14, 1919. He studied with Kaprál at the Brno Cons. and with Novák in Prague. In 1948 he was appointed director of the Prague Cons.; in 1966 he was named director of the state theater in Brno. In his works he followed the prescriptions of socialist realism, advocating immediate accessibility and clear national reference. In this manner he wrote his politico-patriotic cantatas *Song of the Fatherland* (1944) and *Thanks to the Soviet Union* (1946). His choral work *Hands Off Korea* was directed against the participation of U.S. forces or other non-Korean combatants in the conflict. He publ. 3 books: *Music of the Revolutionaries* (Prague, 1964), *Jak poslouchat hudbu* (Prague, 1961; 2nd ed., 1962), and *Hovory o hudbe* (Prague, 1961).

Barwahser, Hubert, German flutist and teacher; b. Herzogenrath, Sept. 28, 1906; d. Dalfsen, the Netherlands, April 29, 1985. He studied flute at the Cons. of Aachen; then joined the Hamburg Phil. as 1st flutist. In 1936 he became principal flutist of the Concertgebouw Orch. of Amsterdam, retiring in 1971.

Bary, Alfred (Erwin) von, tenor; b. Valletta, Malta, Jan. 18, 1873; d. Munich, Sept. 13, 1926. He studied medicine at Munich Univ. (M.D., 1898); later developed a dramatic tenor voice, and was engaged at the Dresden Court Opera (1903–15); then at the Court Opera in Munich; sang the roles of Parsifal, Siegmund, and Tristan at Bayreuth, for which he became known.

Baryphonus, Henricus (real name, **Heinrich Pipegrop**), German music theorist and composer; b. Wernigerode, Harz, Sept. 17, 1581; d. Quedlinburg, Saxe-Anhalt, Jan. 13, 1655. He studied at the Lateinschule in his native town; continued his education at the Univ. of Helmstedt. In 1605 he went to Quedlinburg, where he became cantor at St. Benedicti and a teacher at the Gymnasium; from 1606 was Subkonrector there. He wrote some 17 treatises on music, but only his *Pleiades musicae, quae in certas sectiones distributae praecipuas quaestiones musicas discutiunt* (Halberstadt, 1615) is extant, and only 2 of his compositions survive.

Barzin, Leon (Eugene), Belgian-American conductor; b. Brussels, Nov. 27, 1900. He was taken to the U.S. in 1902; became a naturalized citizen in 1924. His father played viola in the orch. of the Metropolitan Opera in N.Y.; his mother was a ballerina. He studied violin with his father and later in Belgium with Eugène Ysaÿe. In 1925 he was appointed 1st viola player of the N.Y. Phil., retaining his post until 1929, when he was engaged as assistant conductor of the American Orchestral Soc., which was reorganized in 1930 as the National Orchestral Assoc., with Barzin as principal conductor and music director; he continued in this capacity until 1958, and again from 1970 till 1976. He was also music director of the Ballet Soc. and the N.Y. City Ballet (1948–58); from 1958 until 1960 he conducted concerts of the Assoc. des Concerts Pasdeloup in Paris and was at the same time an instructor at the Schola Cantorum there. He received the Order of the Légion d'honneur in 1960. Barzin was particularly successful in training semi-professional and student orchs.; especially with the National Orchestral Assoc., he attained remarkable results.

Barzun, Jacques, eminent French-born American historian, educator, and author of books on music; b. Créteil, Seine, Nov. 30, 1907. He went to America in 1919; was educated at Columbia Univ. (A.B., 1927; Ph.D., 1932); became a lecturer in history there in 1927, and a full prof. in 1945; he became an American citizen in 1933. In 1955 he was made dean of the Columbia graduate faculties, then dean of faculties and provost in 1958; he also assumed the chair of Seth Low Prof. of History in 1960; he resigned these posts in 1967; continued to lecture there until 1975. He exercised considerable influence on American higher education by advocating broad reading in various fields rather than narrow specialization. His books concerned with music include *Darwin, Marx, Wagner; Critique of a Heritage* (Boston, 1941; rev. ed., 1958); *Berlioz and the Romantic Century* (the outstanding modern study of his life and works, based on exhaustive documentation; 2 vols., Boston, 1950; 3rd ed., rev., 1969); ed. *Pleasures of Music* (N.Y., 1951); ed. and tr. *Nouvelles lettres de Berlioz, 1830–1868; New Letters of Berlioz, 1830–1868* (N.Y., 1954); publ. a new tr. of Berlioz's *Evenings with the Orchestra* (N.Y., 1956; 2nd ed., 1973); also wrote a survey, *Music in American Life* (N.Y., 1956). He also publ. *Critical Questions on Music and Letters, Culture and Biography, 1940–1980* (N.Y., 1982).

BIBL.: D. Weiner and W. Keylor, eds., *From Parnassus: Essays in Honor of J. B.* (N.Y., 1976).

Bas, Giulio, Italian organist and music editor; b. Venice, April 21, 1874; d. Vobbia, near Genoa, July 27, 1929. He studied in Munich with Rheinberger and in Venice with Bossi; was organist in the churches of Venice and Rome; in 1915 became prof. of theory and history at the Milan Cons. He wrote several textbooks on music theory; was a dept. ed. of *Musica d'oggi*. Among his textbooks are *Metodo per l'accompagnamento del canto gregoriano* (Turin, 1920) and *Manuale di canto gregoriano* (Düsseldorf, 1910).

Baselt, Fritz (Friedrich Gustav Otto), composer; b. Öls, Silesia, May 26, 1863; d. Frankfurt, Nov. 11, 1931. He studied with Emil Kohler in Breslau and with Ludwig Bussler in Berlin; was a musician, music dealer, composer, teacher, and conductor in Breslau, Essen, and Nuremberg; after 1894 he settled in Frankfurt am Main, where he conducted the Philharmonischer Verein and the Frankfurt Sängervereinigung. He wrote many light operas: *Der Fürst von Sevilla* (Nuremberg, 1888); *Don Alvaro* (Ansbach, 1892); *Der Sohn des Peliden* (Kassel, 1893); *Die Annaliese* (Kassel, 1896); *Die Musketiere im Damenstift* (Kassel, 1896); *Die Circusfee* (Berlin, 1897); also 2 ballets: *Die Altweibermühle* (Frankfurt, 1906) and *Rokoko* (Frankfurt, 1907); some 100 male choruses; many instrumental pieces; songs.

Basevi, Abramo, Italian composer and writer on music; b. Livorno, Nov. 29, 1818; d. Florence, Nov. 25, 1885. He studied music with Pietro Romani, and also took courses in medicine at the Univ. of Pisa. He founded and ed. the periodical *Harmonia* (1856–59) and the journal *Boccherini* (1862–82). He publ. *Studio sulle opere di G. Verdi* (1859), *Studi sull'armonia* (1865), and *Compendio della storia della musica* (1866). His 2 operas, *Romilda ed Ezzelino* (Florence, Aug. 11, 1840) and *Enrico Odoardo* (Florence, 1847), were not successful.

Bashkirov, Dmitri, Russian pianist and pedagogue; b. Tbilisi, Nov. 1, 1931. He studied in Moscow with Alexander Goldenweiser. In 1955 he won 2nd prize in the Marguerite Long–Jacques Thibaud Competition in Paris; in 1970 he won the International Schumann Competition in Zwickau. In 1957 he became a member of the faculty of the Moscow Cons.; also taught at the Kiev Cons. from 1968. His repertoire is a comprehensive one, ranging from classical music to contemporary Soviet compositions.

Bashmakov, Leonid, Finnish composer of Russian extraction; b. Terijoki, April 4, 1927. He studied composition and conducting at the Sibelius Academy (1947–54). In 1960 he became a theater conductor in Tampere, and in 1979 he was appointed director of the Tampere Cons.

Works: Suite for Marimba and String Quartet (1951); *Fantastic Pictures* for Orch. (1953); 6 syms. (1963; 1965; Sinfonietta, 1971; 1977; 1979; 1982); Violin Concerto (1966); 2 violin sonatinas (1968–69); *Canzona I* for Chorus and Orch. (1969; Helsinki, Nov. 23, 1971); Octet for Piano, Winds, and Brass (1970); Sonata for Percussion (1970); *4 Bagatelles* for Flute and Percussion (1971); *Dialogues* for Organ and Percussion (1971); *Canzona II* for Soprano and Orch. (1971); Overture for Wind Orch. (1971); Divertimento for Oboe and Strings (1971); Sonata for Viola, Cello, and Piano (1971); String Quartet (1972); Fantasia for 3 Different Flutes, 1 Player (1972); Cello Concerto (1972); Flute Concerto (1973); Organ Concerto (1975); a ballet, *Tumma* (1976); *Conversazioni per 2* for Soprano and Violin Soloists, and Small Orch. (1978); Wind Quintet (1978); *Crescendo* for Wind Orch. (1980); music for plays and films.

Basie, Count (real name, **William**), topmost black American jazz pianist, exponent of the Big Band era of jazzification; b. Red Bank, N.J., Aug. 21, 1904; d. Hollywood, Fla., April 26, 1984. He received his early musical training from his mother, a professional pianist. After various peripeteias he became stranded in Kansas City in 1927, playing in a small band in a nightclub; it was there that he acquired the derisively nobiliary appellation Count. In 1936 he took his band to Chicago and then to N.Y. He attracted attention by his peculiar piano technique, emphasizing passages played by a single finger while directing his band with a glance, or a movement of the eyebrow. He met Fats Waller in Harlem and was fascinated by his discursive brilliance on the keys; he adopted Waller's manner but altered it in the direction of rich economy of means. He conducted big band engagements, but in 1950 decided to give up the large sound and formed an octet; however, in 1951 he organized a new big band, with which he made a highly successful tour of Europe; he played a command performance for the Queen of England during his British tour in 1957. In 1976 he suffered a heart attack, but after a period of recuperation, returned to an active career. In 1981 he received the Kennedy Center honors for achievement in the performing arts; at a White House reception that followed, President Ronald Reagan said that Count Basie had revolutionized jazz. In 1985 Reagan awarded him the Medal of Freedom (posth.). Among his greatest hits were *1 O'Clock Jump*, which became his theme song; *Jumpin' at the Woodside; Goin' to Chicago; Lester Leaps In; Broadway; April in Paris;* and *L'il Darlin'*. Roulette Records released a 2-record set, *The Count Basie Story* (1961), which includes a biographical booklet by Leonard Feather. With A. Murray, he prepared *Good Morning Blues: The Autobiography of C. B.* (N.Y., 1986). **Bibl.:** R. Horricks, *C. B. and His Orchestra* (N.Y., 1957; reprint, London, 1971); S. Dance, *The World of C. B.* (N.Y., 1980).

Basile, Andreana, famous Italian contralto and instrumentalist; b. Posilipo, c.1580; d. Rome, c.1640. She attracted the public by her extraordinary beauty and became known as "la bella Adriana." She often accompanied herself on the harp and guitar; in Naples she married Muzio Baroni, a Calabrian nobleman. In 1610 she was engaged by the court of Vincenzo Gonzaga, the Duke of Mantua; she remained a principal singer at his court until 1624, and was praised by Monteverdi for her musicianship. In 1633 she settled in Rome. Her daughter was Leonora Baroni, who became a famous singer in her own right.

Basili, Francesco, Italian composer and conductor; b. Loreto, Jan. 31, 1767; d. Rome, March 25, 1850. He studied with his father, Andrea Basili, and later with Giovanni Battista Borghi; then entered the Accademia di Santa Cecilia in Rome, where he took courses with Jannaconi. He served as conductor in various provincial Italian theaters; from 1827 to 1837 he was director of the Milan Cons. He wrote 13 operas, a number of dramatic oratorios, and many instrumental works, including a Piano Concerto and syms. In 1837 he became conductor at St. Peter's Cathedral in Rome.

Basilides, Mária, Hungarian contralto; b. Jolsva, Nov. 11, 1886; d. Budapest, Sept. 26, 1946. She was educated at the Royal Academy of Music in Budapest; in 1915 she became a member of the Budapest Opera, remaining on its roster until her death; she also made appearances with the Berlin State Opera, the Dresden State Opera, and the Bavarian State Opera of Munich. She championed the music of Bartók and Kodály as a soloist in recital and with sym. orchs. **Bibl.:** J. Molnár, *Basilides Mária* (Budapest, 1967).

Bašinskas, Justinas, Lithuanian composer and teacher; b. Mažoji Trakiškė, Jan. 22, 1923. He was a pupil at the Kaunas Music School (1945–50), then studied composition with Juzeliunas at the Lithuanian State Cons. in Vilnius (1950–55) and subsequently taught there. In 1983 he won the Lithuanian S.S.R. National prize and received the title of Merited Culture Worker. A prolific composer, he dedicated himself to optimistic themes, glorifying nature and extolling human friendship in his vocal music, while building tense tonal structures in his instrumental compositions.

Works: ballet: *The Accursed Monks* (1982). **orch.:** 8 syms.: No. 1 (1953); No. 2 (1960); No. 3 (1970); No. 4, *The Bells* (1973); No. 5, *Being* (1977); No. 6, *The Lamentations* (1979); No. 7, *In the Whirlpools* (1983); Chamber Sym. (1984); No. 8, *The Call of the Earth* (1986); *3 Symphonic Dances* (1967); Concerto for Flute, Strings, and Percussion (1971). **chamber:** Sonata for Violin and Piano (1979); String Quartet (1980); Sonata for Solo Viola (1983). **piano:** *Variations* (1951); Sonata (1952); Sonata for 4 Hands (1979). **vocal:** Oratorio, *Oak* (1957); 4 cantatas: *A Tale about Soldier's Bread* (1961); *Requiem* (1969); *Morning* (1974); *Mother's Hands* (1978). **song cycles for voice and piano:** *After the Storm* (1958); *The Animals in Winter* (1968); *The Autumn* (1969); *The Hour of the Eagle-Owl* (1985); choruses; solo songs; arrangements of Lithuanian folk songs.

Basiola, Mario, Italian baritone; b. Annico, July 12, 1892; d. there, Jan. 3, 1965. He studied in Rome; was engaged at the Metropolitan Opera in N.Y. (1925–32); at La Scala in Milan, and in Rome (1933–38); also sang at Covent Garden in London (1939) and in Australia (1949); then returned to Italy and was active there as a teacher.

Basner, Veniamin (Efimovich), Russian composer; b. Yaroslavl, Jan. 1, 1925. He studied violin at the Leningrad Cons. Upon graduation in 1949, he devoted himself to concert activities and composition. Among his works are *3 Musketeers*, ballet (1964); *The Polar Star*, musical comedy (1968); *The Southern Cross*, musical comedy (1970); *Spring Floods*, opera (1975); *Poem of the Besieged Leningrad*, symphonic poem (1957); Sym. No. 1 (1958); Violin Concerto (1966); *Eternal Fire* for Voices and Orch. (1971); 5 string quartets; *Goya*, monologue for Bass, English Horn, Bassoon, and Piano; film music.

Bassani (Bassano), Giovanni, Italian composer, singer, and violinist; b. c.1558; d. Venice, 1617. He was a singer at S. Marco in Venice in 1585; then served as singing teacher at the seminary there in 1595; in 1615 he was 1st violin soloist at the Chapel of the Basilica; remained there until his death. The following instrumental works by him are extant: *Fantasie a tre voci per cantar e sonar* (1585); *Il fiore dei capricci musicali a 4 voci* (1588); *Motetti, madrigali e canzioni francesi di diversi auttori . . . diminuiti per sonar con ogni sorti de stromenti* (1591; reprinted in 1602 in an arrangement for 1 voice with organ ad libitum; containing works of Clemens non Papa, Créquillon, Palestrina, and others; the term *diminuiti* refers to ornamentation of the original vocal compositions); 2 vols. of *Motetti per concerti ecclesiastici* for 5–12 Voices (1598–99); a vol. of *Canzonette* for 4 Voices (1587); etc.

Bassani (Bassano, Bassiani), Giovanni Battista, Italian composer, organist, and violinist; b. Padua, c.1647; d. Bergamo, Oct. 1, 1716. He studied with Legrenzi and Castrovillari in Venice; in 1667 he became a member of the funereally named Accademia della Morte in Ferrara, serving as organist and composer. On July 3, 1677, he became a member of the more cheerful Accademia Filarmonica in Bologna; also served as maestro di cappella and organist of the apocalyptic Confraternità del Finale in Modena (1677–80). In 1680 he became maestro di cappella to the Duke of Mirandola; in 1682 he was appointed principe of the Accademia Filarmonica; in 1683 and 1684 he was maestro di cappella of the Accademia della Morte. In 1687 he was named maestro di cappella of the Ferrara Cathedral, and in 1712 at S. Maria Maggiore in Bergamo; also taught at the music school of the Congregazione di Carità there. He is known to have written at least 9 operas, but these are lost; only a few arias from his opera *Gli amori alla moda* (Ferrara, 1688) have survived. Some 15 oratorios have been attributed to him, but these are also lost; however, the texts to 3 have survived. He also composed masses and other sacred works, secular vocal pieces, and instrumental works, all of which were publ. in his day.

BIBL.: F. Pasini, "Notes sur la vie de G.B. Bassani," *Sammelbände der Internationalen Musik-Gesellschaft,* VII (1906); R. Haselbach, *G.B. Bassani* (Kassel and Basel, 1955); W. Newman, *The Sonata in the Baroque Era* (Chapel Hill, 1959; 4th ed., rev., 1983).

Bassett, Leslie (Raymond), distinguished American composer; b. Hanford, Calif., Jan. 22, 1923. He studied piano; played the trombone in jazz combos; was a trombonist during his military service, playing in the 13th Armored Division Band. He then enrolled in Fresno (Calif.) State College (B.A., 1947); later studied composition with Ross Lee Finney at the Univ. of Michigan (M.M., 1949; D.M., 1956); also took private lessons with Arthur Honegger and Nadia Boulanger in Paris in 1950. In 1952 he was appointed to the faculty of the Univ. of Michigan; was made a prof. there in 1965 and became chairman of the composition dept. in 1970; in 1977 he became the Albert A. Stanley Distinguished Univ. Prof. of Music there. He held the American Prix de Rome in 1961–63, and received the National Inst. of Arts and Letters Award in 1964. In 1966 he received the Pulitzer Prize in music for his *Variations for Orchestra.* He held a Guggenheim fellowship in 1973–74 and again in 1980–81; in 1981 became a member of the American Academy and Inst. of Arts and Letters. In 1988 he held a Rockefeller Foundation grant for a stay at its Villa Serbelloni in Bellagio, Italy. In his music he pursues the ideal of structural logic within the judicial limits of the modern school of composition, with some serial elements discernible in his use of thematic rhythms and motivic periodicity.

WORKS: ORCH.: Suite in G (Fresno, Calif., Dec. 3, 1946); *5 Movements* (1961; Rome, July 5, 1962); *Variations for Orchestra* (Rome, July 6, 1963; received the Pulitzer Prize in 1966); *Colloquy* (Fresno, Calif., May 23, 1969); *Forces* (1972; Des Moines, Iowa, May 1, 1973); *Echoes from an Invisible World* (1974–75; Philadelphia, Feb. 27, 1976); Concerto for 2 Pianos and Orch. (1976; Midland, Mich., April 30, 1977); *Concerto*

lirico for Trombone and Orch. (1983; Toledo, Ohio, April 6, 1984); *From a Source Evolving* (1985; Midland, Mich., Nov. 1, 1986). **BAND AND WIND ENSEMBLES:** *Designs, Images, and Textures* (1964; Ithaca, N.Y., April 28, 1965); *Sounds, Shapes, and Symbols* (1977; Ann Arbor, Mich., March 17, 1978); *Concerto grosso* (1982; Ann Arbor, Mich., Feb. 4, 1983); *Colors and Contours* (1984). **CHAMBER:** 4 string quartets: No. 1 (1951); No. 2 (1957); No. 3 (1962); No. 4 (1978); Sonata for Horn and Piano (1952); Trio for Viola, Clarinet, and Piano (1953); Quintet for 2 Violins, Viola, Cello, and Double Bass (1954); Sonata for Viola and Piano (1956); *5 Pieces* for String Quartet (1957); Woodwind Quintet (1958); Sonata for Violin and Piano (1959); Quintet for 2 Violins, Viola, Cello, and Piano (1962); Nonet (1967); *Music* for Alto Saxophone and Piano (1968); Sextet for 2 Violins, 2 Violas, Cello, and Piano (1971); *Sounds Remembered* for Violin and Piano (1972); *Wind Music* for Wind Sextet (1975); Sextet for Flutes, Clarinets, and Strings (1979); Trio for Violin, Clarinet, and Piano (1980); *Concerto da camera* for Trumpet and Chamber Ensemble (1981); *Dialogues* for Oboe and Piano (1987); *Duo-Inventions* for 2 Cellos (1988); many choral works; songs; pieces for organ and for piano; electronic music.

Bassevi, Giacomo. See **Cervetto, Giacomo.**

Bassi, Amedeo (Vittorio), Italian tenor; b. Montespertoli, near Florence, July 20, 1874; d. Florence, Jan. 14, 1949. He studied with Pavese Negri in Florence, and made his operatic debut there in 1899. He subsequently toured South America (1902–7); sang at the Manhattan Opera House, N.Y. (1906–8) and at the Chicago Opera Co. (1910–16). His repertoire included more than 50 operas, mostly Italian. He created the role of Lionello in Mascagni's *Amica* (1905).

Bassi, Luigi, Italian baritone; b. Pesaro, Sept. 4, 1766; d. Dresden, Sept. 13, 1825. He studied with Pietro Morandi in Senigallia; made his debut in Pesaro at the age of 13; he then sang in Florence; in 1784 went to Prague, where he soon became greatly appreciated. Mozart wrote the part of Don Giovanni for him and heeded his advice in matters of detail. Bassi was in Vienna from 1806 until 1814, then briefly in Prague; in 1815 he joined an Italian opera company in Dresden.

Bastiaans, Johannes Gijsbertus, Dutch organist and composer; b. Wilp, Oct. 31, 1812; d. Haarlem, Feb. 16, 1875. He studied organ in Dessau with F. Rümpler and Schneider; then went to Leipzig, where he took organ lessons with C.F. Becker and composition with Mendelssohn. He subsequently occupied various posts as an organist: in Deventer (1838–40), then at Amsterdam's Zuiderkerk (1840–58); in 1858 he was appointed municipal organist at St. Bavo's in Haarlem. He composed mainly for organ and chorus; publ. several books of chorales. He was succeeded at St. Bavo's by his son, **Johann Bastiaans** (1854–85).

Bastianini, Ettore, Italian baritone; b. Siena, Sept. 24, 1922; d. Sirmione, Jan. 25, 1967. He made his debut as a bass in Ravenna in 1945; then sang baritone roles. He made his American debut as Germont in *La Traviata,* at the Metropolitan Opera in N.Y. on Dec. 5, 1953, remaining with the company until 1965; among his best roles were Rigoletto, Amonasro, Don Carlo, Escamillo, and Scarpia.

Bastin, Jules, Belgian bass; b. Pont, Aug. 18, 1933. He studied at the Brussels Cons.; in 1960 became a member of the Théâtre de la Monnaie in Brussels; also appeared in London, Chicago, N.Y., and Toronto. He is best known for his appearances in such French operas as *Le Prophète, Benvenuto Cellini, Pelléas et Mélisande,* and Massenet's *Cendrillon.* In 1979 he took part in the Paris premiere of the 3-act version of Berg's *Lulu.*

Baston, Josquin, Flemish composer of the mid-16th century. It is known that from May 1552 to Oct. 1553 he was at the Polish Court of Sigismund Augustus at Krakow. Motets and chansons by Baston appeared between 1542 and 1559 in various collections: Susato's *Het ierste musyck boexken* (Antwerp, 1551); Salbinger's *Concertus* (Augsburg, 1545); also in Louvain (publ. by Phalèse). His *Lament* has 2 middle voices singing the *Requiem aeternam* in canon 6 times while the other voices have fresh parts. See R. van Maldeghem, ed., *Trésor musical* (1865–93; vol. XII).

Bate, Jennifer (Lucy), English organist; b. London, Nov. 11, 1944. She received her Licentiate from the Royal Academy of Music in London (1959) and her B.A. from the Univ. of Bristol (1966). In 1976 she made her U.S. debut in Savannah, Ga., subsequently accumulating a vast repertoire of organ pieces comprising some 60 concertos and hundreds of solo works.

Bate, Philip, English music scholar; b. Glasgow, March 26, 1909. He studied clarinet in Aberdeen; then attended classes in general science at the Univ. of Aberdeen (B.Sc., 1932). In 1934 he joined the staff of the BBC in London, and subsequently held various positions there (until 1968). He gathered a valuable collection of wind instruments, which he donated to Oxford Univ. In 1946 he founded the Galpin Soc., serving as its 1st chairman; in 1977 became its president.

Writings: *The Oboe* (London, 1956; 3rd ed., 1975); *The Trumpet and Trombone* (London, 1966); *The Flute: A Study of Its History, Development and Construction* (London, 1969; 2nd ed., 1975).

Bate, Stanley (Richard), English composer; b. Plymouth, Dec. 12, 1911; d. (suicide) London, Oct. 19, 1959. He studied composition with Vaughan Williams and piano with Arthur Benjamin at the Royal College of Music in London (1931–35); then took courses with Nadia Boulanger in Paris and with Hindemith in Berlin. During World War II he was in Australia; in 1942 he went to the U.S.; in 1945 he was in Brazil; and in 1950 he returned to London. On Nov. 7, 1938, he married the Australian-born American composer **Peggy Glanville-Hicks** (divorced 1948). He wrote music in a finely structured cosmopolitan manner, making use of modern devices but observing the classical forms and shunning doctrinaire systems. He wrote several ballets, among them *Goyescas* (1937), *Perseus* (1938), and *Cap over Mill* (1938). He composed 4 syms.; of these, the 3rd (1940) was performed 14 years after its composition, at the Cheltenham Festival, July 14, 1954, with remarkable success. His 4th Sym. was given in London on Nov. 20, 1955. Other works are 3 piano concertos (he was the soloist in his 2nd Piano Concerto, which he performed with the N.Y. Phil., conducted by Sir Thomas Beecham, on Feb. 8, 1942), 2 sinfoniettas, 3 violin concertos, Viola Concerto, Cello Concerto, Harpsichord Concerto, 2 string quartets, Sonata for Recorder and Piano, Violin Sonata, Flute Sonata, Oboe Sonata, 9 piano sonatinas, and other piano pieces.

Bates, Joah, English organist; b. Halifax (baptized), March 8, 1741; d. London, June 8, 1799. He studied organ with Hartley in Rochdale and Wainwright in Manchester; then went to Eton and Cambridge for further education. In 1760 became a tutor of King's College in Cambridge; received his B.A. in 1764 and M.A. in 1767. He then went to London, where he organized the series known as Concerts of Antient Music (1776); also acted as conductor of the famous Handel Commemoration Festivals (1784–87; 1791).

Bates, Sarah (née **Harrop**), English singer; b. c.1755; d. London, 1811. She was born into a poor family; worked in a Halifax factory to support herself; finally she made her way to London and studied with **Joah Bates,** whom she married in 1780; she also took lessons with Antonio Sacchini. She made her formal debut at Covent Garden in *Judas Maccabaeus* on Feb. 14, 1777. She made regular appearances at her husband's Concerts of Antient Music series.

Bates, William, English composer who flourished in the 2nd half of the 18th century. He wrote popular English operas in the ballad-opera style. His most popular work was *Flora or Hob in the Well,* which he wrote and arranged in 1760 (Covent Garden, April 25, 1770), using 7 of John Hippisley's songs from the 1729 *Flora or Hob's Opera,* together with 8 new songs of his own and a new overture. Neither of his works is to be confused with Thomas Doggett's 1711 farce with songs, a fore-

runner of the true ballad opera, variously titled *The Country Wake or Hob* or *The Country Wake.* His other stage works are *The Jovial Crew* (1760; altered to *The Ladies Frolick* in 1770); *The Theatrical Candidates* (1775); *The Device, or The Marriage Officer* (1777); *Second Thought Is Best* (1778); also a grand opera, *Pharnaces* (London, Feb. 15, 1765).

Bateson, Thomas, English composer; b. Cheshire County; d. probably in Dublin, March 1630. He was organist at Chester Cathedral from 1599 to 1609. In 1609 he became vicar choral and organist of the Cathedral of the Holy Trinity in Dublin. He is said to have been the 1st music graduate of Trinity College, earning his Mus.B. in 1612 and his M.A. in 1622. As a composer, Bateson is especially noted for his madrigals, although they are regarded as inferior to those by Morley or Weelkes. In 1604 he publ. a collection of 29 madrigals for 3 to 6 voices; it included the madrigal *When Oriana walked to take the ayre,* orig. intended for publication in Morley's *Triumphs of Oriana.* A 2nd set of 30 madrigals was publ. in 1618. Both sets are reprinted in *The English Madrigal School* (vols. 21–22), ed. by E.H. Fellowes.

Bath, Hubert, English composer; b. Barnstaple, Nov. 6, 1883; d. Harefield, April 24, 1945. He studied at the Royal Academy of Music in London; conducted Thomas Quinlan's opera troupe on its world tour in 1913–14. Returning to England, he conducted classes in opera at the Guildhall School of Music in London. As a composer he showed natural flair for light operas, of which *Bubbles* (Belfast, Nov. 26, 1923) was quite successful. He also wrote a grand opera, *Trilby.* He furthermore composed a number of symphonic sketches, several of them on exotic subjects, such as *African Suite;* also 6 cantatas, more than 150 songs, and various pieces of chamber music.

Bathe, William, Irish writer on musical subjects; b. Dublin, April 2, 1564; d. Madrid, June 17, 1614. He studied at Oxford Univ.; instructed Queen Elizabeth in mnemonics and presented her with an Irish harp of his own design. In 1591 he went to Spain; then was in Flanders, where he entered the Jesuit order in 1596; was ordained in Padua in 1599; returned to Spain in 1601; held the post of spiritual director of the Irish College in Lisbon in 1604; eventually went to Madrid, where he remained until his death. His chief merit as a music theorist lay in fixing definite rules for the placing of accidentals and in changing the system of hexachordal modes to scales based on the octave. He was the author of one of the earliest theoretical works on music, *A Brief Introduction to the True Art of Musicke* (London, 1584); also publ. *A Brief Introduction to the Skill of Song* (London, c.1587).

Bibl.: J. Pulver, "W. B.," *Musical Times* (Oct. 1934); B. Rainbow, "B. and His Introduction to Music," ibid. (April 1982); P. Nixon, "W. B. and His Times," ibid. (Feb. 1983).

Bathori, Jane (Jeanne Marie), French mezzo-soprano; b. Paris, June 14, 1877; d. there, Jan. 21, 1970. She was educated at the Paris Cons. and made her operatic debut at Nantes in 1900. She subsequently devoted herself to the cultivation of modern vocal music by French composers; sang 1st performances of songs by Debussy, Ravel, Satie, and Milhaud. After 1926 she gave regular concerts in Argentina, and lived mostly in Buenos Aires. Returning to Paris, she was active mainly as a singing teacher. She publ. *Conseils sur le chant* (Paris, 1929) and *Sur l'interprétation des mélodies de Claude Debussy* (Paris, 1953).

Báthy, Anna, Hungarian soprano; b. Beregszász, June 13, 1901; d. Budapest, May 20, 1962. She studied voice at the Academy of Music in Budapest; made her operatic debut at the Municipal Theater there in 1928 as Elisabeth in *Tannhäuser;* in 1929 she joined the Budapest Opera, where she sang mostly in the Wagnerian repertoire.

Bibl.: V. Somogyi and I. Molnár, *Báthy Anna* (Budapest, 1969).

Batistin. See Stuck, Jean Baptist.

Bátiz (Campbell), Enrique, Mexican conductor; b. Mexico City, May 4, 1942. He commenced piano lessons at an early age and made his 1st public appearance when he was only 5; following studies at the Univ. of Mexico (degree, 1959) and Southern Methodist Univ. in Dallas (1960–62), he continued his musical training at the Juilliard School of Music in N.Y. (1963–65) and undertook postgraduate work at the Warsaw Cons. In 1969 he made his conducting debut in Mexico City, and in 1971 founded the Orquesta Sinfónia del Estado de México, which developed into one of Mexico's leading orchs. In 1983 he became artistic director of the Orquesta Filarmónica de la Ciudad de México; he also served (from 1984) as principal guest conductor of the Royal Phil. Orch. of London, which he conducted on a major tour of his homeland in 1988.

Batka, Richard, Czech music editor and critic; b. Prague, Dec. 14, 1868; d. Vienna, April 24, 1922. He was educated at the German Univ. in Prague; then went to Vienna, where he became active as a music critic. He publ. a number of valuable monographs on German composers, and historical essays, of which *Geschichte der Musik in Böhmen* (Prague, 1906) is of documentary importance. He also wrote *Allgemeine Geschichte der Musik* (3 vols., Stuttgart, 1909–15).

Bataille, Charles-Amable, French bass; b. Nantes, Sept. 30, 1822; d. Paris, May 2, 1872. He was originally a medical student; then turned to music and studied voice at the Paris Cons. He made his debut at the Opéra-Comique in *La Fille du régiment* (June 22, 1848); created several roles in operas by Thomas, Adam, Halévy, and Meyerbeer. A throat disorder ended his stage career; he retired in 1863. He was on the staff of the Paris Cons. from 1851. He publ. an extensive method of singing in 2 vols.: 1. *Nouvelles recherches sur la phonation* (1861); 2. *De la physiologie appliquée au mécanisme du chant* (1863).

Batten, Adrian, English organist and composer; b. Salisbury (baptized), March 1, 1591; d. London, 1637. He studied at Winchester with the Cathedral organist John Holmes; in 1614 went to London as vicar choral of Westminster Abbey. In 1626 he became vicar choral and organist at St. Paul's Cathedral. A prolific composer, he left 15 services and 47 anthems in MS. Some of his pieces are included in Boyce's *Cathedral Music.* A modern reprint of 1 of his services is included in *The Choir;* several anthems have been publ. by Novello. Batten also transcribed into organ score numerous sacred choral works, some of which have come down to us only through his transcriptions. His organ book is described in *Tudor Church Music* (1922, vol. II).
BIBL.: J.B. Clark, "A. B. and John Barnard: Colleagues and Collaborators," *Musica Disciplina* (1968); J.B. Clark and M. Bevan, "New Biographical Facts about A. B.," *Journal of the American Musicological Society* (Summer 1970).

Battishill, Jonathan, English organist and composer; b. London, May 1738; d. Islington, Dec. 10, 1801. He was a chorister at St. Paul's (1747); later apprenticed to William Savage; was deputy organist under Boyce at the Chapel Royal; then harpsichordist at Covent Garden and organist in several London parishes. He wrote an opera with Michael Arne, *Almena* (Drury Lane Theatre, Nov. 2, 1764); a pantomime, *The Rites of Hecate* (Drury Lane Theatre, Dec. 26, 1763); and many popular anthems, glees, and songs.
BIBL.: J.B. Trend, "J. B.," *Music & Letters* (July 1932).

Battistini, Gaudenzio, Italian composer, grandson of **Giacomo Battistini;** b. Novara, June 30, 1722; d. there, Feb. 25, 1800. He succeeded his father, Giuseppe Battistini, in 1747 as organist of the chapel of S. Gaudenzio in Novara, and served for more than 50 years until his death. He wrote numerous church works in a highly developed polyphonic style. A biographical sketch and examples of his music are found in Vito Fedeli, *Le cappelle musicali di Novara* in vol. III of *Istituzioni e monumenti dell'arte musicale italiana* (Milan, 1933).

Battistini, Giacomo, Italian organist and composer, grandfather of **Gaudenzio Battistini;** b. 1665; d. Novara, Feb. 5, 1719. He was maestro di cappella at the Novara Cathedral

(1694–1706); then at the church of S. Gaudenzio. He is reputed to have been the 1st to introduce the violoncello into instrumental accompaniment. He composed several masses, motets, and organ works; also contributed music to the 3rd act of the drama *Antemio in Roma* (1695; with A. Besozzi and D. Erba). See Vito Fedeli, *Le cappelle musicali di Novara* in vol. III of *Istituzioni e monumenti dell'arte musicale italiana* (Milan, 1933), containing musical illustrations from Battistini's works.

Battistini, Mattia, celebrated Italian baritone; b. Rome, Feb. 27, 1856; d. Colle Baccaro, near Rieti, Nov. 7, 1928. He 1st studied medicine at the Univ. of Rome; then began taking singing lessons; among his mentors were Persichini and Terziani. He made his debut at the Teatro Argentino in Rome on Dec. 11, 1878, as Alfonso XI in Donizetti's *La Favorita;* subsequently appeared at Covent Garden in London (1883), at the San Carlo Opera in Naples (1886), at Drury Lane in London (1887), and at La Scala in Milan (1888). He then embarked on a worldwide tour, and acquired great popularity in South America, Spain, and Russia; he continued his active career until the last months of his life. He was a master of bel canto, with a remarkably expressive high register; was particularly successful in the parts of Rigoletto, Figaro in Rossini's *Barber of Seville,* and Valentin in Gounod's *Faust.*
BIBL.: G. Fracassini, *M. B., profilo artistico* (Milan, 1915); F. Palmegiani, *M. B.* (Milan, 1948).

Battle, Kathleen, outstanding black American soprano; b. Portsmouth, Ohio, Aug. 13, 1948. She studied voice with Franklin Bens at the Univ. of Cincinnati College-Cons. of Music (B.Mus., 1970; M.Mus., 1971); then made her debut in 1972 in the Brahms *Requiem;* subsequently sang with the N.Y. Phil., the Cleveland Orch., the Los Angeles Phil., and other leading American orchs. She made her Metropolitan Opera debut in N.Y. as the Shepherd in *Tannhäuser* on Sept. 18, 1978; on June 17, 1985, she made her 1st appearance at London's Covent Garden as Zerbinetta. She was chosen by Karajan as his soloist for the New Year's Day Concert of the Vienna Phil. in 1987, which was telecast throughout the world. Excelling in the light, lyric soprano repertoire, she is particularly acclaimed for her portrayals of Sophie, Despina, Blonde, Zerlina, Nanetta, and Adina, as well as those already enumerated.

Batton, Désiré-Alexandre, French composer; b. Paris, Jan. 2, 1798; d. Versailles, Oct. 15, 1855. He was a pupil of Cherubini at the Paris Cons.; won the Prix de Rome in 1817 for his cantata, *La Mort d'Adonis.* In 1851 he was appointed inspector of the branch schools of the cons.; also taught singing there. His most successful opera was *La Marquise de Brinvilliers,* written in collaboration with Auber, Hérold, and others, and produced in Paris on Oct. 31, 1831; other operas were *La Fenêtre secrète* (Paris, Nov. 17, 1818); *Velleda* (1820); *Ethelvina* (1827); *Le Prisonnier d'état* (1828); *Le Camp du drap d'or* (1828); and *Le Remplaçant* (1837).

Battu, Pantaléon, French violinist; b. Paris, 1799; d. there, Jan. 17, 1870. He studied with R. Kreutzer at the Paris Cons.; was a member of the orch. of the Opéra and the court until his retirement in 1859. He wrote 3 violin concertos; 3 violin duos; etc.

Baud-Bovy, Samuel, Swiss musicologist; b. Geneva, Nov. 27, 1906; d. Nov. 2, 1986. He studied at the Univ. of Geneva and later with Pirro in Paris. He was an authority on Greek music; publ. *La Chanson populaire grecque du Dodécanèse* (Paris, 1936) and *Études sur la chanson cleftique* (Athens, 1958).

Baudiot, (Charles-) Nicolas, French cellist; b. Nancy, March 29, 1773; d. Paris, Sept. 26, 1849. He was a pupil of the elder Janson, whom he succeeded as cello prof. at the Paris Cons. (1795–1802; 1805–27); from 1816 was 1st cellist in the royal orch.; retired in 1832. With Levasseur and Baillot he wrote a cello method which for a time was used at the Paris Cons.; also *Instruction pour les compositeurs* (a guide to composers for cello); composed 2 cello concertos; 2 cello concertinos; a great variety of chamber music for cello.

Baudo, Serge (Paul), French conductor; b. Marseilles, July 16, 1927. He studied at the Paris Cons., conducting with Louis Fourestier and theory with Jean Gallon and Noël Gallon; received a premier prix as drummer (1948) and as conductor (1949). He was engaged as pianist and percussion player in the orch. of the Concerts Lamoureux; then toured as an opera conductor. In 1967 he was appointed music director and conductor of the Orch. de Paris; on Sept. 16, 1970, he made his Metropolitan Opera debut in N.Y. From 1969 to 1987 he was artistic director of the Orch. Philharmonique de Lyons. He is admired for his idiomatic performances of French music; he has also distinguished himself as an advocate of contemporary music.

Baudrier, Yves, French composer; b. Paris, Feb. 11, 1906; d. there, Nov. 9, 1988. He was self-taught in music. In 1936 he joined Messiaen, Jolivet, and Daniel-Lesur in La Jeune France, a group dedicated to purely French-style compositions, both modern and traditional. He composed a Trumpet Suite, a Sym., and a few other pieces, all in a specific French national style. His ideas were of some interest, but his music was forgettable.

Bauer, Harold, distinguished pianist; b. Kingston on Thames, near London, of an English mother and a German father, April 28, 1873; d. Miami, March 12, 1951. He studied violin with his father and Adolf Politzer; made his debut as a violinist in London; in 1892 he went to Paris and studied piano for a year with Paderewski; in 1893 made his 1st tour as a pianist in Russia; gave piano recitals throughout Europe; in 1900 made his U.S. debut with the Boston Sym. Orch.; appeared as soloist with other U.S. orchs., with eminent chamber music groups, and as a recitalist. He founded the Beethoven Assoc. in N.Y. (1918); was president of the Friends of Music in the Library of Congress, Washington, D.C. Among his writings are "Self-Portrait of the Artist as a Young Man," *Musical Quarterly* (April 1943), and *Harold Bauer, His Book* (N.Y., 1948). He ed. works by Schubert and Brahms, and Mussorgsky's *Pictures at an Exhibition*. A considerable corpus of his papers was acquired by the Music Division of the Library of Congress.

Bauer, Marion (Eugenie), American composer and writer; b. Walla Walla, Wash., Aug. 15, 1887; d. South Hadley, Mass., Aug. 9, 1955. Her parents were of French extraction; she received her early education from her father, who was an amateur musician. She then went to Paris, where she took piano lessons with Pugno, and theory with André Gédalge and Nadia Boulanger; also took some lessons with Jean Paul Ertel in Berlin. Returning to America, she continued her studies with Henry Holden Huss and others. She taught at N.Y. Univ. (1926–51); was associate prof. there (1930–51); was annual lecturer at the summer Chautauqua Inst. in 1928 and 1929; from 1933 through 1952 gave lecture recitals each summer; in 1940 joined the faculty at the Inst. of Musical Arts in N.Y.; taught at the Juilliard School of Music from 1940 to 1944. She was a member of the executive board of the League of Composers in N.Y., and had an active teaching career in music history and composition. Her music oscillates pleasurably between Germanic Romanticism and Gallic Impressionism. Prudently, she wrote mostly in small forms, and was at her best in her piano pieces; among them were *From New Hampshire Woods* (1921); *Indian Pipes* (1928); *Sun Splendor* (1926; later orchestrated and perf. by Stokowski with the N.Y. Phil., Oct. 25, 1947); *Dance Sonata* (1932). Her choral works include *3 Noëls* (1929); *A Garden Is a Lovesome Thing* (1938); *The Thinker* (1938); and *China* for Chorus, with Orch. (Worcester Festival, Oct. 12, 1945). She also wrote quite a few pieces of chamber music: String Quartet (1928); *Fantasia quasi una sonata* for Violin and Piano (1928); Suite for Oboe and Clarinet (1932); Viola Sonata (1936); *Pan,* choreographic sketch for 7 Instruments and Piano (1937); Concertino for Oboe, Clarinet, and String Quartet (1940); Sonatina for Oboe and Piano (1940); 2 trio sonatas for Flute, Cello,

and Piano (1944, 1951); and *American Youth Concerto* for Piano and Orch. (1943). She was a successful popularizer of music history. Her publications include *How Music Grew* (1925; with Ethel Peyser), which had several printings; *Music through the Ages* (1932; also with Peyser; rev. ed., 1967); *Twentieth Century Music* (1933, and still of use); and *How Opera Grew* (1955; once more with Peyser), which had, despite the clumsy title, several reprints.

Bauer-Theussl, Franz (Ferdinand), Austrian conductor; b. Zillingdorf, Sept. 25, 1928. He received his musical training in Frankfurt; also studied conducting with Clemens Krauss in Vienna. He then conducted opera in the Austrian resort of Baden, near Vienna (1950–52); subsequently conducted at Salzburg, at the Volksoper in Vienna (from 1957), and at the Netherlands Opera in Amsterdam (1960–64).

Bäuerle, Hermann, German music editor; b. Ebersberg, Oct. 24, 1869; d. Ulm, May 21, 1936. He studied theology and music in Tübingen; in 1895 took Holy Orders; in 1906 he became papal privy chamberlain. In 1921 he founded the Ulm Cons., of which he remained music director. He publ. several valuable papers on sacred music, among them *Der Vatikanische Choral in Reformnotation* (1907); *Liturgie,* a manual of the Roman Catholic liturgy (1908); and several school manuals on elementary music theory. His most important work, however, was the series Bibliothek Altklassischer Kirchenmusik in Moderner Notation, which he ed. beginning in 1903.

Bauermeister, Mathilde, German soprano; b. Hamburg, 1849; d. Herne Bay, Kent, England, Oct. 15, 1926. She studied at the Royal Academy of Music in London; gave recitals in Dublin in 1866; then joined the company of the Covent Garden Opera in London and sang there each season from 1887 to 1905. On Dec. 14, 1891, she made her 1st appearance at the Metropolitan Opera in N.Y., as Gertrude in *Roméo et Juliette;* she was on its roster again from 1893 to 1897 and from 1898 to 1906. Her repertoire was exceptionally large, numbering nearly 100 roles.

Bauld, Alison (Margaret), Australian composer; b. Sydney, May 7, 1944. After training at the National Inst. of Dramatic Art, she studied at the Univ. of Sydney (B.Mus., 1968), completing her education at the Univ. of York (Ph.D., 1974). She was music director of the Laban Centre for Dance at the Univ. of London (1975–78) and composer-in-residence at the New South Wales State Conservatorium in Sydney (1978).

WORKS: *On the Afternoon of the Pigsty* for Female Speaker, Piano, Alto Melodica, and Percussion (1971); *In a Dead Brown Land* for 2 Mime Actors, 2 Speakers, Soprano, Tenor, Chorus, and 5 Instruments (1971); *Humpty Dumpty* for Tenor, Flute, and Guitar (1972); *Pumpkin 2* for 4 Actors and 5 Instruments (London, June 21, 1973); *Egg* for Tenor, Flute, Cello, and Percussion (Snape, June 25, 1973); *Mad Moll* for Soprano (1973); *1 Pearl* for Soprano or Countertenor, and String Quartet (Southampton, Nov. 11, 1973); *Exiles* for 4 Actors, Tenor, Mezzo-soprano, Chorus, Flute, Alto Melodica, Percussion, and String Quartet (1974; Sydney, May 1975); *Concert for Pianist and Tape* (1st half for mime only, 2nd half for tape only; Sydney, Dec. 1974); *The Busker's Story* for Alto Saxophone, Bassoon, Trumpet, Violin, and Double Bass (Sydney, Sept. 25, 1978); *Richard III* for Voice and String Quartet (BBC, July 4, 1985); *Monday* for Flute (Sydney, Oct. 1, 1985); *Once upon a Time* for 5 Vocal Soloists and Small Chamber Orch. (BBC, Dec. 29, 1986); *Nell,* ballad opera (London, June 1, 1988).

BIBL.: A. Bauld, "Sounding a Personal Note," *Musical Times* (July 1988).

Bauldewijn (also **Bauldeweyn, Bauldoin, Baudoin,** etc.), **Noël,** Flemish composer; b. c.1480; d. Antwerp, 1530. He was magister cantorum at the church of St.-Rombaut in Mechelen (1509–13), then at Notre Dame Cathedral in Antwerp, a post he most likely kept until his death. He wrote masses, motets, and several secular works; for an exposition concerning conflicting attributions of his output, see E. Sparks, *The Music of N. B.* (N.Y., 1972).

Baumann, Hermann (Rudolf Konrad), noted German horn player and pedagogue; b. Hamburg, Aug. 1, 1934. He studied in Hamburg; then played 1st horn in Dortmund (1957–61) and with the Stuttgart Radio Sym. Orch. (1961–67); won the International Music Competition in Munich in 1964, and made tours in Germany and abroad. In 1969 he was appointed a prof. at the Staatliche Folkwang Hochschule in Essen, and, in 1980, at the Hochschule für Musik in Stuttgart.

Baumann, Max Georg, German composer; b. Kronach, Nov. 20, 1917. From 1939 to 1943 he studied composition and conducting at the Berlin Hochschule für Musik, where his teachers included Blacher and Distler; he became a lecturer there in 1946, and a prof. in 1953; was named director of its school music dept. in 1963; also made appearances as a conductor with the Berlin Collegium Musicum. He composed much sacred vocal music, including masses, motets, a cantata, and an oratorio; also a ballet, *Pelleas und Melisande* (1954).

Baumbach, Friedrich August, German composer and conductor; b. Gotha (baptized), Sept. 12, 1753; d. Leipzig, Nov. 30, 1813. He was active in various capacities as a singer, violinist, and conductor; conducted the Hamburg Opera (1777–89); then went to Leipzig. He wrote numerous pieces for different ensembles; also contributed musical articles to the *Kurzgefasstes Handwörterbuch über die schönen Künste* (Leipzig, 1794).

Baumfelder, Friedrich, German pianist and composer; b. Dresden, May 28, 1836; d. there, Aug. 8, 1916. He studied at the Leipzig Cons. with Moscheles, Wenzel, and Hauptmann; was conductor of the Schumann Singakademie at Dresden. He wrote a cantata, *Der Geiger zu Gmünd;* a collection of piano studies, *Tirocinium musicae;* and a great number of piano pieces in the salon style (totaling more than 300 opus numbers).

Baumgartner, Paul, Swiss pianist; b. Altstätten, July 21, 1903; d. Locarno, Oct. 19, 1976. He studied in St. Gall, Munich, and Cologne; was a piano teacher in Cologne (1927–35). In 1937 he became director of the piano dept. of the Basel Cons.; he continued to give concerts and play chamber music in Switzerland and elsewhere.

Baumgartner, Rudolf, Swiss violinist and conductor; b. Zürich, Sept. 14, 1917. He was educated at the Univ. of Zürich, and later went to Vienna and Paris for further study. He then began to appear as a violinist, both as a soloist and in chamber music ensembles. After World War II, he turned his energies to conducting. In 1956 he helped organize the Festival Strings at the Lucerne Music Festival, becoming its 1st music director. From 1960 to 1987 he was director of the Lucerne Cons.

Baumgartner, Wilhelm, Swiss pianist and composer; b. Rorschach, Nov. 15, 1820; d. Zürich, March 17, 1867. He attended the Gymnasium in Zürich and the Univ. of Zürich; studied piano and music theory with Alexander Müller. In 1842 he moved to St. Gall; in 1844 he went to Berlin, where he continued his musical studies with Taubert. In 1845 he returned to Switzerland, where he taught piano and conducted choruses. He became greatly honored in Switzerland when, in 1846, he wrote a patriotic male chorus in 4 parts, *O mein Heimatland,* which in time achieved the status of an unofficial national anthem. **BIBL.:** C. Widmer, *W. B., Ein Lebensbild* (Zürich, 1868); L. Gross, *W. B., Sein Leben und sein Schaffen* (diss., Univ. of Munich, 1930).

Bäumker, Wilhelm, German writer on music; b. Elberfeld, Oct. 25, 1842; d. Rurich, March 3, 1905. He studied theology and philology at Münster and Bonn; from 1892 was a priest at Rurich. His most important work is *Das katholische deutsche Kirchenlied in seinen Singweisen von den frühesten Zeiten bis gegen Ende des 17. Jahrhunderts* (4 vols., Freiburg, 1883–1911). Vol. II (1883) and vol. III (1891) appeared orig. as continuation of the work begun by K.S. Meister, who publ. vol. I in 1862; Bäumker revised this vol. in 1886; vol. IV (1911) was ed. by J. Gotzen from Bäumker's notes, and also contains supplements to the preceding vols. Other works by Bäumker are *Palestrina, Ein Beitrag* (1877); *Orlandus de Lassus, Ein historisches Bildniss* (1878); *Zur Geschichte der Tonkunst in Deutschland* (1881); *Der Todtentanz* (1881); *Niederländische geistliche Lieder nebst ihren Singweisen aus Handschriften des 15. Jahrhunderts* (1888); and *Ein deutsches geistliches Liederbuch,* melodies from the 15th century (Leipzig, 1896).

Baur, Jürg, German composer, pianist, and choral conductor; b. Düsseldorf, Nov. 11, 1918. He studied theory at the Cons. of Cologne with Philipp Jarnach, and musicology at the Univ. of Cologne with Fellerer. In 1946 he joined the faculty of the Düsseldorf Cons.; was its director from 1965 to 1976. In 1971 he succeeded Zimmermann as chairman of the composition dept. at the Hochschule für Musik in Cologne. The idiom of his works evolved from Lutheran neo-Classicism in the manner of Reger and Hindemith, later adopting Schoenberg's method of composition with 12 tones and eventually total serialism.
WORKS: Viola Concerto (1952); *Sinfonia montana* (1953); Concerto for Trautonium and String Quartet (1955); Concerto for Strings (1957); *Quintetto sereno* for 5 Wind Instruments (1958); *Concerto romano* for Oboe and Orch. (1960); Divertimento for Harpsichord and Percussion (1962); *Romeo and Juliet* for Orch. (1963); *Piccolo mondo* for Orch. (1963); *Dialogue* for Cello and Piano (1963); *Lo specchio* for Orch. (1966); *Pentagram* for Wind Quintet and Orch. (1966); *Abbreviations* for 13 String Instruments (1969); Piano Concerto (1970); also 3 string quartets; a song cycle to words by García Lorca; *Metamorphosen* for Piano Trio; and many choruses.

Bausch, Ludwig Christian August, celebrated German violin maker; b. Naumburg, Jan. 15, 1805; d. Leipzig, May 26, 1871. He established shops for making and repairing violins in Dresden (1826), Dessau (1828), Leipzig (1839), and Wiesbaden (1862). His son **Ludwig** (b. Dessau, Nov. 10, 1829; d. Leipzig, April 7, 1871) lived in N.Y. and later established his own violin shop in Leipzig. **Otto,** a younger son (b. Leipzig, Aug. 6, 1841; d. there, Dec. 30, 1875), inherited the business, which then passed to A. Paulus at Markneukirchen.

Bausznern, Waldemar von, German composer; b. Berlin, Nov. 29, 1866; d. Potsdam, Aug. 20, 1931. He studied music with Kiel and Bargiel in Berlin; subsequently was active mainly as a choral conductor; also taught at the Cons. of Cologne (1903–8), at the Hochschule für Musik in Weimar (1908–16), where he also served as director, and at the Hoch Cons. in Frankfurt, where he was a teacher and director (1916–23). He also taught at the Academy of Arts and the Academy for Church and School Music in Berlin. He was a prolific composer; wrote the operas *Dichter und Welt* (Weimar, 1897); *Dürer in Venedig* (Weimar, 1901); *Herbort und Hilde* (Mannheim, 1902); *Der Bundschuh* (Frankfurt, 1904); 8 syms., of which the 3rd and the 5th have choral finales; numerous sacred choral works; 4 string quartets; 2 piano quintets; 2 piano trios; 2 violin sonatas. He ed. the score of the opera *Der Barbier von Bagdad* by Peter Cornelius, and completed his unfinished opera *Gunlöd,* which was produced in this version in Cologne in 1906. His syms., academically Romantic in their high-flown idiom, still retain a spark of vitality, to judge by their infrequent performances in Germany.

Bautista, Julián, Spanish composer; b. Madrid, April 21, 1901; d. Buenos Aires, July 8, 1961. He studied violin with Julio Francés, piano with Pilar Fernández de la Mora, and composition with Conrado del Campo at the Madrid Cons.; then taught there during the Spanish Civil War. After Madrid fell, Bautista fled to Argentina, where he was on the faculty of the National Cons. of Buenos Aires. His music, delicately colored and rhythmically robust, invariably reflected Spanish folk melodies.
WORKS: *Juerga,* ballet (1921); *Colores,* 6 piano pieces (1922); Sonatina for String Trio (1924); *Obertura para una ópera*

grotesca for Orch. (1932); *Tres ciudades* for Voice and Orch. (1937); *4 poemas gallegos* for Voice, Flute, Oboe, Clarinet, Viola, Cello, and Harp (1946); *Sinfonia breve* (1956); Sym. No. 2 (1957); 3 string quartets; songs.

Bavicchi, John, American composer; b. Boston, April 25, 1922. He studied at the New England Cons. of Music in Boston with Carl McKinley and Francis Judd Cooke (B.M., 1952); then attended Harvard Univ. Graduate School, taking courses in theory with Archibald T. Davison, composition with Walter Piston, and musicology with Otto Gombosi (1953–56). He served in the U.S. Navy; saw action in Guadalcanal, Okinawa, and Japan (1943–45). Returning to Boston after the war, he devoted himself to teaching, composing, and conducting; led the Arlington-Belmont Chorale; lectured on music history at the Cambridge Center for Adult Education (1960–73). He also conducted the American Festival Ballet Co. (1962–65) and the Arlington Phil. (1968–82). His music is neo-Baroque, couched in Classical forms, while presenting a variegated texture of decidedly modernistic invention.

WORKS: ORCH.: *4 Songs* for Contralto and Orch. (1952); Concerto for Clarinet and String Orch. (1954); Suite No. 1 (1955); *A Concert Overture* (1957); *Fantasy* for Harp and Chamber Orch. (1959); Concertante for Oboe, Bassoon, and String Orch. (1961); *3 Psalms* for Soloists, Chorus, 2 Trumpets, and String Orch. (1963); *Caroline's Dance* (1974–75); *Mont Blanc,* overture (1976–77); *Music for Small Orch.* (1981); *Fusions* for Trombone and Orch. (1984–85); *There Is Sweet Music Here* for Soprano and Orch. (1985); *Pyramid* (1986); *Canto I* for String Orch. (1987). **CHAMBER:** 10 trios for a variety of instrumental combinations (1950–83); 2 sonatas for Cello and Piano (1953, 1956); 2 sonatas for Unaccompanied Clarinet (1956, 1959); Brass Quartet No. 1 (1956); *A Musical Sketch-book* for Flute, or for Flute, Oboe, Clarinet, Bassoon, and Piano (1960); String Quartet (1960); *Music* for Horn and Piano (1980); Concertino for Tuba and Brass Quartet (1984); Sonata for Flute and Piano (1986); *Triptych* for Multiple Horns (1987); also piano pieces, choral works, and songs.

Bax, Sir Arnold (Edward Trevor), outstanding English composer; b. London, Nov. 8, 1883; d. Cork, Ireland, Oct. 3, 1953. He entered the Royal Academy of Music in 1900; studied piano with Matthay and composition with Corder there; won the Academy's Gold Medal as a pianist in 1905, the year in which he completed his studies. After a visit to Dresden in 1905, he went to Ireland. Although not ethnically Irish, he became interested in ancient Irish folklore; wrote poetry and prose under the name of Dermot O'Byrne; also found inspiration in Celtic legends for his work as a composer. In 1910 he returned to England; that same year he visited Russia, and composed a series of piano pieces in a pseudo-Russian style: *May Night in the Ukraine, Gopak, In a Vodka Shop,* etc.; also wrote music to James M. Barrie's skit *The Truth about the Russian Dancers.* In 1931 he received the Gold Medal of the Royal Phil. Soc. of London; was awarded honorary degrees from Oxford Univ. in 1934 and Durham Univ. in 1935; was knighted at the Coronation of King George VI in 1937; was made Master of the King's Musick in 1941. He was an excellent pianist, but was reluctant to play in public; he never appeared as a conductor of his own works. Bax was an extremely prolific composer; his style is rooted in neo-Romanticism, but impressionistic elements are much in evidence in his instrumental compositions; his harmony is elaborate and rich in chromatic progressions; his contrapuntal fabric is free and emphasizes complete independence of component melodies. In his many settings of folk songs, he succeeded in adapting simple melodies to effective accompaniments in modern harmonies; in his adaptations of old English songs, he successfully re-created the archaic style of the epoch. He recorded the story of his life and travels in his candid autobiography, *Farewell, My Youth* (London, 1943).

WORKS: SYMS.: No. 1 (1921; London, Dec. 4, 1922); No. 2 (1924–25; Boston, Dec. 13, 1929); No. 3 (1929; London, March 14, 1930); No. 4 (1930; San Francisco, March 16, 1932); No.

5, dedicated to Sibelius (1931; London, Jan. 15, 1934); No. 6 (1934; London, Nov. 21, 1935); No. 7, dedicated to the American people (1939; N.Y., June 9, 1939).

BALLETS: *Between Dusk and Dawn* (1917); *The Truth about the Russian Dancers* (1920).

SYMPHONIC POEMS: *In the Faery Hills* (1909); *Christmas Eve on the Mountains* (1911–12); *Nympholept* (1912); *The Garden of Fand* (1913); *The Happy Forest* (1914; orchestrated 1921); *November Woods* (1917); *Tintagel* (1917); *Summer Music* (1920); *Mediterranean* (1920 version for Piano; orchestrated 1921).

OTHER ORCH.: 4 pieces: *Pensive Twilight, Dance in the Sun, From the Mountains of Home, Dance of Wild Irravel* (1912–13); *Scherzo sinfonico* (1913); *Romantic Overture* (1926); 2 *Northern Ballads* (1927, 1933); *Overture to a Picaresque Comedy* (1930); *The Tale the Pine Trees Knew* (1931); *Overture to Adventure* (1935–36); *Rogue's Comedy Overture* (1935–36); *London Pageant* (1937–38); *A Legend* (1944); *Coronation March* (1953).

INSTRUMENTAL WORKS WITH ORCH.: *Symphonic Variations* for Piano and Orch. (1917); *Phantasy* for Viola and Orch. (1920); Cello Concerto (1932); Violin Concerto (1937–38); Concertante for Piano, left-hand (1948–49).

VOCAL: *Fatherland* for Tenor, Chorus, and Orch. (1906–7); *Enchanted Summer* (from Shelley's *Prometheus Unbound*) for 2 Sopranos, Chorus, and Orch. (1910); *The Bard of the Dimbovitza,* 6 poems for Voice and Orch. (1914); *Mater Ora Filium,* motet (1921); *Of a Rose I Sing a Song* for Small Chorus, Harp, Cello, and Double Bass (1921); *Now Is the Time of Christymas* for Male Voices, Flute, and Piano (1921); *This Worlde's Joie,* motet (1922); *To the Name above Every Name* for Chorus and Orch. (1923); *The Boar's Head,* carol for Male Voices (1923); *St. Patrick's Breastplate* for Chorus and Orch. (1923); *Walsinghame* for Tenor, Chorus, and Orch. (1926); *I Sing of a Maiden* for 5-part Small Chorus (1928); *The Morning Watch* for Chorus and Orch. (1935–36); also many solo songs.

CHAMBER: 3 string quartets (1916; 1924–25; 1935–36); Piano Quintet (1915); Quintet for Strings and Harp (1919); Quintet for Oboe and Strings (1922); String Quintet (1930); Trio for Flute, Viola, and Harp (1916); *An Irish Elegy* for English Horn, Harp, and String Quartet (1916); Nonet for Flute, Oboe, Clarinet, Harp, and String Quintet (1930); Octet for Horn, Piano, and String Sextet (1934); Concerto for Flute, Oboe, Harp, and String Quartet (1934); Threnody and Scherzo for Bassoon, Harp, and String Sextet (1935–36); additional works include 3 violin sonatas (1910, 1915, 1927); 2 viola sonatas (1922; 2nd with Harp, known as the *Fantasy* sonata, 1924–25); Cello Sonata (1923); *Legend Sonata* for Cello and Piano (1943); also 6 piano sonatas: No. 1 (1897–98); No. 2 (1910); No. 3 (2 movements only; 1913); No. 4 (1919); No. 5 (1926); No. 6 (1932); Clarinet Sonata (1934); works for 2 pianos; etc.

BIBL.: E. Evans, "A. B.," *Musical Quarterly* (April 1923); R. Hull, *A Handbook on A. B.'s Symphonies* (London, 1932); A. Fleischmann, "A. B.," *Recorded Sound* (Jan./April 1968); R. Foreman, "Bibliography of Writings on A. B.," *Current Musicology* 10 (1970); idem, "The Musical Development of A. B.," *Music & Letters* (Jan. 1971); C. Scott-Sutherland, *A. B.* (London, 1973).

Bay, Emmanuel, Russian pianist; b. Simferopol, Crimea, Jan. 20, 1891; d. Jerusalem, Dec. 2, 1967. His father was cantor in the Lodz synagogue in Poland; in 1908 Bay enrolled at the St. Petersburg Cons., studying piano with Drosdov; graduated in 1913 with 1st prize. He subsequently took a master class in piano with Leopold Godowsky in Vienna. He became mainly known as an excellent accompanist; toured in that capacity with Efrem Zimbalist (1922–29) and with Jascha Heifetz (1931–51); also was accompanist to Mischa Elman, Nathan Milstein, Zino Francescatti, Joseph Szigeti, Gregor Piatigorsky, Jan Peerce, and Helen Traubel. He died of a heart attack on a trip to Israel.

Bayer, Josef, Austrian composer and conductor; b. Vienna, March 6, 1852; d. there, March 12, 1913. He studied at the

Vienna Cons. (1859–70) with Georg and Joseph Hellmesberger (violin), Dachs (piano), and Bruckner (theory). He wrote a great number of operettas and ballets which were quite popular, owing to his facility for melodic writing and piquant rhythms. He traveled a great deal through Europe as a conductor; visited N.Y. in 1881, and conducted there the 1st performance of his operetta *Chevalier von San Marco* on Feb. 4, 1881. Other operettas successfully produced in Vienna were *Menelaus* (1892), *Fräulein Hexe* (1898), and *Der Polizeichef* (1904). He also wrote 2 exotic comic operas: *Alien Fata*, on a Bosnian subject, and *Der Goldasoka*, on a Hindu theme. The list of his ballets includes the following, produced in Vienna: *Wiener Walzer* (1886); *Die Puppenfee* (1888); *Sonne und Erde* (1889); *Ein Tanzmärchen* (1890); *Rouge et Noir* (1892); *Die Donaunixe* (1892); *Eine Hochzeit in Bosnien* (1893; with Bosnian folk melodies); *Burschenliebe* (1894); *Rund um Wien* (1894); *Die Braut von Korea* (1896); *Die kleine Welt* (1904). Ballets produced at Berlin: *Deutsche Märsche* (1887); *Die Welt in Bild und Tanz* (1892); *Die Engelsjäger* (1896); *Columbia* (1893).

Bayle, François, French composer; b. Tamatave, Madagascar, April 27, 1932. He studied academic sciences and music in France; was a student in composition of Olivier Messiaen, and with Pierre Schaeffer, whose Groupe de Recherches Musicales he joined in 1966. His works are mostly montages, collages, and acoustical barrages, including: *Trois portraits d'un oiseau qui n'existe pas* (1962); *L'Archipel* (1963); *Pluriel* (1963); *Espaces inhabitables* (1967); *Trois rêves d'oiseau* (1972); *Vibrations composées* (1973); *Camera obscura* (1976); *Erosphère* (1978–80); *Les Couleurs de la nuit* (1982); *Son Vitesse-Lumière* (1980–83); *Aéroformes* (1982–84); *Motion-Emotion* (1985–86); *Aêr* (1987); *Théâtre d'ombres* (1989).

Bayoras, Feliksas, Lithuanian composer; b. Alitus, Oct. 7, 1934. He studied at the Lithuanian Cons. in Vilnius; in 1965 he was appointed music director of the Youth Theater there. He composed 3 syms. (1969, 1970, 1972); a Sym. for Strings (1970); *Green March* for Military Band (1968); some chamber music; and a number of piano pieces and songs, mostly inspired by Lithuanian subjects.

Bazelaire, Paul, French cellist and composer; b. Sedan, March 4, 1886; d. Paris, Dec. 11, 1958. He graduated from the Paris Cons. as a cellist at the age of 11, with the premier prix; after a concert career, became prof. of cello at the Paris Cons. (1918–56); founded a unique ensemble of 50 cellos.
  Works: *Suite française sur des chants populaires* for Orch.; symphonic poem, *Cléopâtre* (Paris, Jan. 23, 1908); *Suite grecque* for Small Orch. (1910); *Rapsodie dans le style russe* for Cello and Orch. (Paris, Feb. 2, 1941). He orchestrated Bach's 6 cello suites; publ. a teaching manual, *Pédagogie du violoncelle*.

Bazelon, Irwin (Allen), American composer; b. Evanston, Ill., June 4, 1922. He took piano lessons with Irving Harris and Magdalen Messmann; studied composition with Leon Stein. He received his B.A. from De Paul Univ. in Chicago in 1944 and his M.A. in 1945; then took composition lessons with Hindemith at Yale Univ., with Darius Milhaud at Mills College in Oakland, Calif. (1946–48), and with Ernest Bloch at the Univ. of Calif. in Berkeley (1947). In 1948 he settled in N.Y. and earned a living by writing commercial jingles; also contributed incidental music for Shakespeare plays produced at the American Shakespeare Theater in Stratford, Conn. In his compositions he makes use of quaquaversal techniques, ranging from rudimentary triadic progressions to complex dodecaphonic structures; rhythmically, he likes to inject jazz syncopation. He publ. *Knowing the Score: Notes on Film Music* in 1975.
  Works: Orch.: Syms.: No. 1 (1960; Kansas City, Nov. 29, 1963); No. 2, *Short Symphony* (Washington, D.C., Dec. 4, 1962); No. 3 for Brass, Percussion, Piano, and String Sextet (1963); No. 4 (1965; 1st movement perf. under the title *Dramatic Movement for Orchestra*, Seattle, Feb. 21, 1966); No. 5 (1966; Indianapolis, May 8, 1970); No. 6 (Kansas City, Nov. 17, 1970); No. 7, *Ballet for Orchestra* (1980); No. 8 for Strings

(1986); No. 8½ (1988). Other works include: *Suite* for Clarinet, Cello, and Piano (1947); *Ballet Suite* for Chamber Ensemble (1949); *Concert Overture* (1952; rev. 1960); *Adagio and Fugue* for String Orch. (1952); *Movimento da camera* for Flute, Bassoon, Horn, and Harpsichord (1954); *Chamber Symphony* for 7 Instruments (1957); *Suite* from *The Merry Wives of Windsor* (1958); *Overture to The Taming of the Shrew* (1960); *Ballet Centauri 17* for Orch. (1960); *Symphonie concertante* for Clarinet, Trumpet, Marimba, and Orch. (1963); Brass Quintet (1963); *Early American Suite* for Flute, Oboe, Clarinet, Bassoon, Horn, and Harpsichord or Piano (1965–75); *Excursion* for Orch. (Kansas City, March 5, 1966); *Churchill Downs* (Chamber Concerto No. 2; 1970); *Dramatic Fanfare* for Orch. (Cleveland, June 23, 1970); *Duo* for Viola and Piano (1970); *Concerto for 14 Players* (N.Y., May 16, 1971); *Propulsions*, concerto for 7 Percussionists (1974); Woodwind Quintet (N.Y., May 22, 1975); *A Quiet Piece for a Violent Time* for Chamber Orch. (New Orleans, Oct. 28, 1975); *Spirits of the Night* for Orch. (1976); *Concatenations* for Percussion Quartet and Viola (1976); *Double-Crossings* for Trumpet and Percussion (Boston, Dec. 5, 1976); *Triple Play* for 2 Trombones and Solo Percussion (1977); *Sound Dreams* for 6 Instruments (Boston, Nov. 13, 1977); *Cross-Currents* for Brass Quintet and Percussion (1978); *Imprints* for Piano (1978); *Junctures* for Orch. (1979); *De-Tonations* for Brass Quintet and Orch. (N.Y., April 3, 1979); *3 Men on a Dis-Course* for Clarinet, Cello, and Solo Percussion (1979; N.Y., April 9, 1980); *Partnership* for 5 Timpani and Marimba (N.Y., May 19, 1980); *Memories of a Winter Childhood* for an Instrumental Group (1981); *Spires* for Trumpet and Orch. (1981); *Tides* for Clarinet and Orch. (1982); *Re-Percussions* for 2 Pianos (1982); *Fusions* (Chamber Concerto No. 3; 1983; Washington, D.C., Oct. 22, 1984); Piano Concerto (1983–84); *Motivations*, concert piece for Trombone and Orch. (1985); *Legends and Love Letters*, 5 songs for Soprano and Chamber Orch. (after Hart Crane; 1987); *Fourscore +2* for Percussion Quartet and Orch. (1988); 2 string quartets; 3 piano sonatas; other chamber music.

Bazin, François-Emmanuel-Joseph, French composer; b. Marseilles, Sept. 4, 1816; d. Paris, July 2, 1878. He studied with Berton and Halévy at the Paris Cons.; was awarded the Prix de Rome in 1840; in 1844 was appointed to the faculty of the Paris Cons. He wrote 8 comic operas, none of which was retained in the repertoire, although *Le Voyage en Chine*, produced in 1865, was temporarily acclaimed. He also publ. a manual, *Cours d'harmonie théorique et pratique*, which was adopted at the Paris Cons.

Bázlik, Miroslav, Slovak composer and pianist; b. Partizánská Lupča, April 12, 1931. He studied piano at the Bratislava Cons., and became an accomplished concert pianist; then took a course in composition with Cikker at the Bratislava Academy of Musical Arts, graduating in 1961. His musical idiom evolved along modern Romantic lines; in his later compositions he resorts to serial techniques.
  Works: Opera, after Rolland, *Petr a Lucie* (1962–66; Bratislava, 1967); *Dvanást'* (The 12), oratorio after the poem of Alexander Blok (1967; Bratislava, Nov. 4, 1976); *Baroque Suite* for Small Orch. (1958); *5 Songs on Chinese Poetry* for Contralto, Flute, Piano, and Cello (1960); *Music for Violin and Orch.* (1961); *3 Pieces* for 14 Instruments (1964); *Music for Poetry* for Nonet, Harp, and Vibraphone (1966); *Bagatelles* for String Orch. or String Quartet (1972); *Pastorale* for Woodwinds and Harpsichord (1972); *Cantata without Words* for Mezzo-soprano, Madrigal Ensemble, and Chamber Orch. (1972); String Quartet (1974); Piano Sonata (1954); *Palette*, 5 bagatelles for Piano (1956).

Bazzini, Antonio, Italian violinist and composer; b. Brescia, March 11, 1818; d. Milan, Feb. 10, 1897. Encouraged by Paganini, before whom he played in 1836, Bazzini embarked upon a series of successful tours through Italy, France, Spain, Belgium, Poland, England, and Germany (1837–63); taught at the Milan Cons. from 1873, and in 1882 became its director.
  Works: *Turanda*, opera after Gozzi's *Turandot* (La Scala,

Milan, Jan. 13, 1867); *Francesca da Rimini*, symphonic poem (1890); symphonic overtures to Alfieri's *Saul* (1866) and to Shakespeare's *King Lear* (1868); numerous violin pieces, of which *Ronde des lutins* became extremely popular.

Beach, Mrs. H.H.A. (née **Amy Marcy Cheney**), American composer; b. Henniker, N.H., Sept. 5, 1867; d. N.Y., Dec. 27, 1944. She was descended of early New England colonists, and was a scion of a cultural family. She entered a private school in Boston; studied piano with Ernest Perabo and Carl Baermann; received instruction in harmony from Junius W. Hill. She made her debut as a pianist in Boston on Oct. 24, 1883, playing a concerto by Moscheles. On Dec. 3, 1885, at the age of 18, she married Dr. H.H.A. Beach, a Boston surgeon, a quarter of a century older than she was. The marriage was a happy one, and as a token of her loyalty to her husband, she used as her professional name Mrs. H.H.A. Beach. She began to compose modestly, mostly for piano, but soon embarked on an ambitious project, a Mass, which was performed by the Handel and Haydn Soc. in Boston on Feb. 18, 1892; she was the 1st woman to have a composition performed by that organization. On Oct. 30, 1896, her *Gaelic Symphony*, based on Irish folk tunes, was performed by the Boston Sym. with exceptional success. In 1897 she played her Violin Sonata with Franz Kneisel. On April 6, 1900, she appeared as the soloist with the Boston Sym. in the 1st performance of her Piano Concerto. She also wrote a great many songs in an endearing Romantic manner. Her husband died in 1910, and Mrs. Beach decided to go to Europe; she played her works in Berlin, Leipzig, and Hamburg, attracting considerable attention as the 1st of her sex and national origin to be able to compose music of a European quality of excellence. She returned to the U.S. in 1914 and lived in N.Y. Her music, unpretentious in its idiom and epigonic in its historical aspect, retained its importance as the work of a pioneer woman composer in America.
WORKS: Mass in E-flat (Boston, Feb. 18, 1892); *Gaelic Symphony* (Boston, Oct. 30, 1896); Piano Concerto (Boston, April 6, 1900). Cantatas: *The Minstrel and the King; Festival Jubilate; The Chambered Nautilus; Canticles of the Sun; Christ in the Universe; The Rose of Avontown, Sylvania; The Sea Fairies.* Chamber: Violin Sonata (1896); Piano Quintet (1908); String Quartet (1929); Piano Trio (1938). Piano: *Valse-Caprice; Ballad; 4 Sketches; Hermit Thrush at Morn; Nocturne; 5 Improvisations; Variations on Balkan Themes* for 2 Pianos. Her piano music was publ. in Women Composers, series X (N.Y., 1982).
BIBL.: P. Goetschius, *Mrs. H.H.A. B.* (Boston, 1906); B. Tuthill, "Mrs. H.H.A. B.," *Musical Quarterly* (July 1940); E. Merrill, *Mrs. H.H.A. B.: Her Life and Music* (diss., Univ. of Rochester, 1963); M. Eden, *Energy and Individuality in the Art of Anna Huntington, Sculptor, and A. B., Composer* (Metuchen, N.J., 1987).

Beach, John Parsons, American composer; b. Gloversville, N.Y., Oct. 11, 1877; d. Pasadena, Calif., Nov. 6, 1953. He studied piano at the New England Cons. in Boston; then went to Europe, where he took lessons with Gédalge in Paris and Malipiero in Venice. Returning to Boston, he took additional lessons with Loeffler. He held various teaching jobs; finally settled in Pasadena. His opera *Pippa's Holiday* was performed in Paris in 1915, and his ballet *Phantom Satyr* was given in Asolo, Italy, July 6, 1925; another ballet, *Mardi Gras*, was staged in New Orleans (Feb. 15, 1926). His orch. works include *New Orleans Street Cries* (Philadelphia, April 22, 1927, Stokowski conducting); *Asolani* (Minneapolis, Nov. 12, 1926); *Angelo's Letter* for Tenor and Chamber Orch. (N.Y., Feb. 27, 1929). He also composed *Naïve Landscapes* for Piano, Flute, Oboe, and Clarinet (1917); *Poem* for String Quartet (1920); *Concert* for Violin, Viola, Cello, Flute, Oboe, and Clarinet (1929); many songs.

Beard, John, renowned English tenor; b. c.1717; d. Hampton, Feb. 5, 1791. He studied with Bernard Gates at the Chapel Royal; while still a youth, he sang in Handel's *Esther* in London (1732). He left the Chapel Royal in 1734; on Nov. 9, 1734, he made his debut as Silvio in Handel's *Il Pastor fido* at Covent Garden; he subsequently appeared in about 10 operas, many oratorios, masques, and odes by Handel. In 1761 he became manager of Covent Garden, but continued to make appearances as a singer; he retired in 1767 owing to increasing deafness.

Beardslee, Bethany, American soprano; b. Lansing, Mich., Dec. 25, 1927. She studied at Michigan State Univ.; then received a scholarship to the Juilliard School of Music in N.Y., making her N.Y. debut in 1949. She soon became known as a specialist in modern music, evolving an extraordinary technique with a flutelike ability to sound impeccably precise intonation; she mastered the art of *Sprechstimme*, which enabled her to give fine renditions of such works as Schoenberg's *Pierrot Lunaire*; she also was a brilliant performer of vocal parts in scores by Alban Berg, Anton von Webern, and Stravinsky. In 1976 she joined the faculty of Westminster Choir College; in 1981–82 was a prof. of music at the Univ. of Texas in Austin. She married the composer **Godfrey Winham** in 1956.

Beattie, Herbert, American bass; b. Chicago, Aug. 23, 1926. He studied voice at the American Cons. of Music in Chicago; made his operatic debut with the N.Y. City Opera on Oct. 11, 1957, as Baron Douphol in *La Traviata;* also sang in Baltimore, San Francisco, Boston, and New Orleans. He taught voice at Hofstra Univ. (1959–82).

Beaulieu (real name, **Martin-Beaulieu**), **Marie-Désiré,** French composer and author; b. Paris, April 11, 1791; d. Niort, Dec. 21, 1863. He studied violin with Kreutzer, composition with Benincori and Abbé Roze; then studied with Méhul at the Paris Cons.; won the Prix de Rome in 1810; wrote the operas *Anacréon* and *Philadelphie;* the oratorios *L'Hymne du matin, L'Hymne de la nuit*, etc.; also other sacred music, as well as secular songs. He publ. the essays: *Du rythme, des effets qu'il produit et de leurs causes* (1852); *Mémoire sur ce qui reste de la musique de l'ancienne Grèce dans les premiers chants de l'Église* (1852); *Mémoire sur le caractère que doit avoir la musique de l'Église* (1858); *Mémoire sur l'origine de la musique* (1859). His main contribution to French musical culture was his organizing of annual music festivals in provincial towns; founded the Association Musicale de l'Ouest in 1835, and in 1860 the Société des Concerts de Chant Classique, to which he bequeathed 100,000 francs.

Beauvarlet-Charpentier, Jean-Jacques, famous French organist; b. Abbeville, June 28, 1734; d. Paris, May 6, 1794. His father was organist of the Hospice de la Charité in Lyons; his mother was the singer Marie Birol, who appeared on the stage under the name Marie Beauvarlet-Charpentier. He succeeded his father as organist in Lyons; from 1763 to 1771 he made appearances there at the Académie des Beaux Arts. He 1st played in Paris at a Concert Spirituel in 1759; in 1771 he was called to Paris as organist of the Royal Abbey of St. Victor; in 1772 he became organist at St. Paul, and also at St. Eloi des Orfèvres (from 1777) and Notre Dame (from 1783; with 3 other organists). He was also a composer, but his music attracted little notice. His son, **Jacques-Marie Beauvarlet-Charpentier** (b. Lyons, July 3, 1766; d. Paris, Sept. 7, 1834), was also an organist and composer.

Bécaud, Gilbert, French composer of popular songs; b. Toulon, Oct. 24, 1927. His real name was François Silly (sic; pronounced with the stress on the 2nd syllable, and so not necessarily silly). He studied at Toulon and Nice; began to write his chansons at 19. On Dec. 20, 1952, he made his debut as a chansonnier in Versailles, where he was featured as "Monsieur 100,000 Volts." With this electric sobriquet and a moderately winning smile he launched a highly lucrative career, singing his own songs with his own piano accompaniments; in 1953 he produced his 1st big hit, *Quand tu danses;* other successful songs were *Le Jour où la pluie viendra, Viens danser, Plein soleil,* and *L'Orange.* He was piano accompanist to Edith Piaf on her American tours. Apart from his popular songs, he tried his hand at serious music; composed a cantata, *L'Enfant à l'Étoile* (Paris, Jan. 7, 1962), and *Opéra d'Aran* (Paris, Oct. 22, 1962).

Becerra (-Schmidt), Gustavo, Chilean composer; b. Temuco, Aug. 26, 1925. He studied at the Santiago Cons. with Pedro Allende, and then with Domingo Santa Cruz; from 1953 to 1956 he traveled in Europe; from 1968 to 1970 he served as cultural attaché to the Chilean embassy in Bonn. In 1971 he received the Premio Nacional de Arte in music. His early works are set in the traditional manner of neo-Classical composition, but soon he adopted an extremely radical modern idiom, incorporating dodecaphonic and aleatory procedures and outlining a graphic system of notation, following the pictorial representation of musical sounds of the European avant-garde, but introducing some new elements, such as indication of relative loudness by increasing the size of the notes on a music staff with lines far apart. His works include the opera *La muerte de Don Rodrigo* (1958); 3 syms. (1955, 1958, 1960); the oratorios *La Araucana* (1965) and *Lord Cochrane de Chile* (1967); Violin Concerto (1950); Flute Concerto (1957); Piano Concerto (1958); 4 guitar concertos (1964–70); Concerto for Oboe, Clarinet, and Bassoon, with String Orch. (1970); 7 string quartets; Saxophone Quartet; 3 violin sonatas; Viola Sonata; 3 cello sonatas; Sonata for Double Bass and Piano; pieces for solo oboe and solo trombone; numerous choral works.

Becher, Alfred Julius, English composer and music critic, who became a martyr of the revolutionary movement in 1848; b. Manchester, April 27, 1803; d. Vienna (executed), Nov. 23, 1848. He studied in Germany; in 1841 went to Vienna; in 1848 he began issuing the revolutionary paper *Der Radikale,* and that same year was arrested for treason and shot. He publ. a monograph on Jenny Lind, in German (Vienna, 1846); he also wrote a Sym., some chamber music, and songs.

Bechet, Sidney (Joseph), famous black American jazz clarinetist and soprano saxophonist; b. New Orleans, May 14, 1897; d. Garches, France, May 14, 1959. He took up the clarinet when he was 6 years old; learned to play blues and rags in black honky-tonks in Storyville, the brothel district of New Orleans; after playing with many of the leading jazz musicians in New Orleans and on tour, he went to Chicago in 1917; settled in N.Y. in 1919. He made tours to London and Paris; then led his own band in N.Y.; later worked with Noble Sissle, Duke Ellington, Tommy Ladnier, and Zutty Singleton. During the 1940s he led his own jazz groups in N.Y.; in 1947 he settled in Paris. He was one of the most important jazz musicians of his era, highly acclaimed as the master of the soprano saxophone. He publ. an autobiography, *Treat It Gentle* (N.Y., 1960).
BIBL.: R. Mouly, *S. B.* (Paris, 1959); J. Chilton, *S. B.: The Wizard of Jazz* (Oxford, 1988).

Bechgaard, Julius, Danish composer; b. Copenhagen, Dec. 19, 1843; d. there, March 4, 1917. He studied at the Leipzig Cons. and with Gade in Copenhagen; lived in Germany, Italy, and Paris; then settled in Copenhagen. He wrote 2 operas: *Frode* (Copenhagen, May 11, 1893) and *Frau Inge* (Prague, 1894); many piano pieces and songs.

Bechi, Gino, Italian baritone; b. Florence, Oct. 16, 1913. He was educated at the Florence Cons.; then sang at the Rome Opera (1937) and at La Scala in Milan. He soon established himself as one of the leading Italian baritones of the day. After World War II, he appeared in many European music centers; also was well known in South America. He retired in 1965; then taught voice; also produced opera.

Bechler, Johann Christian, Moravian composer; b. island of Oesel, in the Baltic Sea, Jan. 7, 1784; d. Herrnhut, Saxony, April 15, 1857. He went to the U.S. in 1806 and became a prof. of theology at the seminary in Nazareth, Pa.; served as deacon, principal, and pastor in Philadelphia; returned to Europe in 1836 as a bishop, and was for some years active in Sarepta and Astrakhan, Russia. His works, which include anthems, hymns, and ariettas, are interesting more from a historical than a musical standpoint.

Bechstein, (Friedrich Wilhelm) Carl, German piano manufacturer; b. Gotha, June 1, 1826; d. Berlin, March 6, 1900. He worked in German factories; also in London; in 1853 set up a modest shop in Berlin; constructed his 1st grand piano in 1856; established branches in France, Russia, and England. After World War I, the London branch continued under the direction of C. Bechstein, grandson of the founder; after his death (1931), it became an independent British firm, Bechstein Piano Co., Ltd. The Bechstein piano possesses a particularly harmonious tone, capable of producing a mellifluous cantilena; for many years it was a favorite instrument of pianists of the Romantic school.
BIBL.: *B.-Chronik* (Berlin, 1926); Count du Moulin-Eckart, *Neue Briefe Hans von Bülow* (containing correspondence with Bechstein; Munich, 1927; Eng. tr., 1931); W. Huschke, "Zur Herkunft des Klavierbauers C. B.," *Genealogie* (1969), pp. 709–14.

Beck, Conrad, distinguished Swiss composer; b. Lohn, Schaffhausen, June 16, 1901; d. Basel, Oct. 31, 1989. He studied at the Zürich Cons. with Andreae, and in Paris with Ernst Lévy; lived in Paris and Berlin; settled in Basel in 1932 and became a radio conductor there. In 1939 he was appointed director of the music section of Radio Basel; resigned in 1966. A prolific composer, Beck adopted a neo-Classical style, rich in contrapuntal texture. Several of his works were featured at the festivals of the ISCM, among them the overture *Innominata* (Vienna, June 16, 1932) and Chamber Cantata (Warsaw, April 15, 1939). He wrote 7 syms. (1925–58; Sym. No. 7, *Aeneas-Silvius,* was 1st perf. in Zürich, Feb. 25, 1958); *Lyric Cantata* (Munich, May 22, 1931); Piano Concerto (1933); *Konzertmusik* for Oboe and String Orch. (Basel, April 30, 1933); Chamber Concerto for Cembalo and String Orch. (Basel, Nov. 27, 1942); Viola Concerto (1949); oratorio, *Der Tod zu Basel* (Basel, May 22, 1953); Concertino for Clarinet, Bassoon, and Orch. (1954); Christmas motet, *Es kommt ein Schiff geladen*; *Die Sonnenfinsternis,* cantata (Lucerne, Aug. 25, 1967); Clarinet Concerto (1968); *Fantasie* for Orch. (1969); *Sonata a quattro* for Violin, Flute, Oboe, and Bassoon (1970); Chamber Concerto (1970–71); Concerto for Wind Quintet and Orch. (1976); *Drei Aspekte* for Chamber Orch. (1976); *Cercles* for Orch. (1978–79); 4 string quartets; 2 violin sonatas; 2 cello sonatas; 2 string trios; piano music; choral works.
BIBL.: W. Schuh and D. Larese, *C. B.: Eine Lebensskizze: Der Komponist und sein Werk* (Amriswil, 1972).

Beck, Franz, German violinist and composer; b. Mannheim, Feb. 20, 1734; d. Bordeaux, Dec. 31, 1809. He studied violin with his father and also had some instruction from Johann Stamitz. About 1750 he went to Italy; in 1761 he settled in Bordeaux, where he conducted at the Grand Théâtre. In 1783 he visited Paris to hear the 1st performance of his *Stabat Mater.* His works include 24 syms.; several string quartets; piano sonatas; and church music; also operas including *La Belle Jardinière* (Bordeaux, Aug. 24, 1767); *Pandora,* melodrame (Paris, July 2, 1789); and *L'Île déserte* (not produced).
BIBL.: R. Sondheimer, "Die Sinfonien F. B.s," *Zeitschrift für Musikwissenschaft,* IV (1922).

Beck, Jean-Baptiste, Alsatian-American musicologist; b. Gebweiler, Aug. 14, 1881; d. Philadelphia, June 23, 1943. He studied organ; received his Ph.D. at Strasbourg Univ. with the dissertation *Die Melodien der Troubadours und Trouvères* (1908); later publ. a somewhat popularized ed. of it in French, *La Musique des troubadours* (Paris, 1910). Beck taught at the Univ. of Illinois from 1911 to 1914; then at Bryn Mawr College from 1914 to 1920. He settled in Philadelphia, where he taught at the Univ. of Pa., and from 1920 he taught at the Curtis Inst. In 1927 he initiated a project of publishing a Corpus Cantilenarum Medii Aevi, in 52 vols., but was able to bring out only 4 vols., under the subtitle *Les Chansonniers des troubadours et des trouvères* (all in French), containing phototype reproductions of medieval MSS, transcriptions in modern notation, and commentary: *Le Chansonnier cangé* (2 vols., Philadelphia, 1927); *Le Manuscrit du roi* (2 vols., Philadelphia, 1938). Among his other important writings is an essay, "Der Takt in den Musikaufzeichnungen des XII. und XIII. Jahrhunderts," *Riemann Festschrift* (1909). Beck was an outstanding scholar of medieval vocal music; his application of the modal rhythm of the polyphony of that time to the troubadour melodies was an important contribution to the problem of proper transcription into modern notation.

Beck, John Ness, American composer; b. Warren, Ohio, Nov. 11, 1930; d. Columbus, Ohio, June 25, 1987. He studied music at Ohio State Univ. and taught there for a while, later assuming the management of a retail music store in Columbus. He wrote mainly sacred choruses and also some educational piano pieces.

Beck, Karl, Austrian tenor; b. 1814; d. Vienna, March 3, 1879. He was the 1st to sing the role of Lohengrin (Weimar, Aug. 28, 1850).

Beck, Martha, American composer; b. Sodaville, Oreg., Jan. 19, 1900. She studied at the American Cons. in Chicago; eventually settled in Troy, N.Y., as a piano teacher. She publ. a number of piano pieces with exotic titles such as *Chinese Holiday* and *In Old Japan*. She also composed a *Prelude* for Orch., various choral pieces, and many didactic works for piano.

Beck, Sydney, American music librarian; b. N.Y., Sept. 2, 1906. He studied at the College of the City Univ. of N.Y., at N.Y. Univ., at the Inst. of Musical Art, and at the Mannes College of Music; during this period he took courses in violin and chamber music with Louis Svečenski, in composition with Wagenaar and Weisse, and in musicology with Sachs and Reese. In 1931 he became head of the Rare Book and Manuscript Collections of the N.Y. Public Library, holding this post until 1968. He also taught at the Mannes College of Music (1950–68). In 1968 he was appointed director of libraries at the New England Cons. of Music in Boston, retiring in 1976. He prepared eds. of works by F. Geminiani and J.M. Leclair.

Beck, Thomas Ludvigsen, Norwegian composer; b. Horten, Dec. 5, 1899; d. Olso, Sept. 9, 1963. He studied piano, organ, and composition at the Oslo Cons.; also took a course of music theory in Leipzig. From 1930 until his death he was active as an organist, choral conductor, and music teacher in Oslo; was a member of the board of the Soc. of Norwegian Composers (1938–46). He wrote many cantatas, among which are *Arnljot Gjelline* (1937), *Höifjell* (In the Mountains; 1945; Oslo, 1946), and *Heilag framtid* (Holy Future; Oslo, 1954); *Ballad on a Norwegian Folk Tune* for Orch. (Oslo, 1940); *3 Dances from Gudbrandsdal* for Orch. (Oslo, April 28, 1946); *Andante* for String Orch.; *Intrada* for Orch. or Piano; choruses; songs; film music.

Becker, Albert (Ernst Anton), German composer; b. Quedlinburg, June 13, 1834; d. Berlin, Jan. 10, 1899. He was a pupil of Dehn in Berlin (1853–56); was appointed teacher of composition at the Scharwenka Cons. (1881), and became the conductor of the Berlin Cathedral Choir (1891). His Sym. in G minor was awarded the prize of the Gesellschaft der Musikfreunde in Vienna (1861); he also wrote an opera, *Loreley* (1898), cantatas, and a number of sacred works.

Becker, Constantin Julius, German composer and author; b. Freiberg, Saxony, Feb. 3, 1811; d. Oberlössnitz, Feb. 26, 1859. He studied singing with Anacker and composition with Carl Becker; from 1837 to 1846, ed. the *Neue Zeitschrift für Musik*, in association with Schumann; in 1843, settled in Dresden; taught singing, composed, and wrote novels on musical subjects. In 1846 he went to Oberlössnitz, where he spent the remainder of his life. He wrote an opera, *Die Erstürmung von Belgrad* (Leipzig, May 21, 1848); a Sym.; various vocal works. However, he is best known for his manuals: *Männergesangschule* (1845), *Harmonielehre für Dilettanten* (1842), and *Kleine Harmonielehre* (1844). He also publ. the novel *Die Neuromantiker* (1840); tr. *Voyage musical* by Berlioz into German (1843).

Becker, Dietrich, German violinist, organist, and composer; b. Hamburg, 1623; d. there, 1679. He began his career as an organist in Ahrensburg, Holstein (1645); subsequently was active as a violinist in Hamburg. In 1658 he became violinist

at the court chapel in Celle. In 1662 he was appointed court violinist in Hamburg; was named director of the Court Orch. in 1667 and appointed director of music at the Hamburg Cathedral in 1674.

WORKS: *Musicalische Frühlings-Früchte* for 3 to 5 Instruments and Basso Continuo (Hamburg, 1668; 2nd ed., 1673); *Erster Theil . . . Sonaten und Suiten* for 2 Violins and Basso Continuo (Hamburg, 1674); *Trauer- und Begrabnüss-Musik* for Soprano, Alto, Tenor, Bass, Violin, Bassoon, 3 Viole da Braccio, and Basso Continuo (Glückstadt, 1678); *Ander Theil . . . Sonaten und Suiten* for 2 Violins and Basso Continuo (Hamburg, 1679); also sacred choral music and songs.

Becker, Frank, American composer; b. Paterson, N.J., March 29, 1944. He studied with Joseph Wood at the Oberlin Cons., and composition with Robert Palmer and jazz improvisation with Elston Husk. A Ford Foundation grant took him for 2 years to Wichita, Kans., where his works were widely performed; he subsequently went to Japan, becoming famous in avant-garde circles as a composer, performer (on synthesizer), and producer. Since his return to the U.S. in 1981, he has written more than a dozen film and television scores. Among his concert works are *Stonehenge* for Flute and Tape (a mixture of new-age, minimalist, and pseudo-Japanese styles) and *Philiapaideia* for Orch. (1973), which won the Prix Francis Salabert in 1975.

Becker, Günther (Hugo), German composer; b. Forbach, Baden, April 1, 1924. He studied conducting with G. Nestler at the Badische Hochschule für Musik in Karlsruhe (1946–49), composition with W. Fortner in Heidelberg and at the North-West German Academy of Music (1948–56), where he also studied choral conducting with K. Thomas (1953–55). He taught music at the Greek National School Anavryta in Athens (1956–58); also taught at the Goethe Inst. and the Dorpfeld Gymnasium there (1957–68). He then returned to Germany, where he founded the live electronic group Mega-Hertz (1969), and taught at the summer courses for new music in Darmstadt. He became a lecturer at the Musikhochschule Rheinland of the Robert Schumann Inst. in Düsseldorf (1973) and prof. of composition and live electronics at the Düsseldorf Hochschule für Musik (1974). Becker's works, at first influenced by his sojourn in Greece, eventually gave way to a unique and uncompromising style utilizing all the resources of contemporary compositional processes.

WORKS: *Nacht- und Traumgesänge* for Chorus and Orch. (1964; North German Radio, Hamburg, Feb. 16, 1965); *stabil-instabil* for Orch. (1965; West German Radio, Cologne, Oct. 28, 1966); *Correspondances I* for Clarinet and Chamber Orch. (Donaueschingen, Oct. 22, 1966); *Griechische Tanzsuite* for Plucked String Orch. (Saarbrücken, Aug. 29, 1967); *Caprices concertants* for Mandolin, Mandola, Guitar, Percussion, and Plucked String Orch. (1968; Hannover, May 18, 1969); *Transformationen* for Orch., Live Electronic Ensemble, and Tape (Warsaw, Sept. 24, 1970); *Attitude* for Orch. (1972–73; Bonn, June 4, 1973); *Konzert* for Electronic Modulated Oboe and Orch. (1973–74; Munich, April 5, 1974); *Ihre Bosheit wird die ganze Erde zu einer Wüste machen*, sacred concerto for Speaker, Alto, Chorus, Organ, Instrumental Ensemble, and Tape (1978; Düsseldorf, Feb. 14, 1979); *Magnum Mysterium—Zeugenaussagen zur Auferstehung*, scenic oratorio (1979–80; Düsseldorf, May 4, 1980); *Ariosi* for Oboe, English Horn, Clarinet, Bass Clarinet, Vibraphone, and Marimbaphone (1982); *Parenthesen* for String Sextet (1982); *Un poco giocoso* for Bass Tuba and Chamber Ensemble (1983; Witten, April 27, 1984); *Doppelte Ebenen* for Violin and Viola (1984–85); *Reverenz 1985* for 4 Instruments (1985).

Becker, Gustave Louis, American pianist and teacher; b. Richmond, Texas, May 22, 1861; d. Epsom, Surrey, England, Feb. 25, 1959. He made his public debut at the age of 11; studied in N.Y. with Sternberg and at the Hochschule für Musik, Berlin (1888–91). Returning to N.Y., he became Rafael Joseffy's assistant at the National Cons. He continued his teaching activities privately. On May 23, 1952, the 80th anniversary of his public appearance as a child prodigy, he gave a piano recital in Steinway Hall; on his 94th birthday, May 22, 1955, he played at a concert in N.Y. arranged by his friends. He wrote 2 suites for String Quartet; *Herald of Freedom* for Chorus (1925); many vocal and piano pieces, about 200 numbers in all. He publ. several pedagogic works: *Exercise for Accuracy; Superior Graded Course for the Piano; Musical Syllable System for Vocal Sight Reading;* and many magazine articles.

Becker, Heinz, German musicologist; b. Berlin, June 26, 1922. He studied at the Berlin Hochschule für Musik, taking courses in clarinet, piano, conducting, and composition; he then enrolled at Humboldt Univ. in Berlin; received his Ph.D. in 1951 with the dissertation *Zur Problematik und Technik der musikalischen Schlussgestaltung;* in 1956 he joined the musicological inst. of the Univ. of Hamburg as an assistant lecturer; he completed his Habilitation there with his *Studien zur Entwicklungsgeschichte der antiken und mittelalterlichen Rohrblattinstrumente* (1961; publ. in Hamburg, 1966). In 1966 he became a prof. of musicology at the Ruhr Univ. in Bochum, where he remained until his retirement in 1987. Apart from his professorial duties, he wrote music for the clarinet.
WRITINGS: *Der Fall Heine-Meyerbeer* (Berlin, 1958); *Geschichte der Instrumentation,* in the Das Musikwerk series, XXIV (1964); ed., *Giacomo Meyerbeer: Briefwechsel und Tagebücher* (Berlin, 1960–85); *Beiträge zur Geschichte der Musikkritik* (Regensburg, 1965); *Beiträge zur Geschichte der Oper* (Regensburg, 1969); *Das Lokalkolorit in der Oper des 19. Jahrhunderts* (Regensburg, 1976); *Giacomo Meyerbeer in Selbstzeugnissen und Bilddokumenten* (Reinbek, 1980); with G. Becker, *Giacomo Meyerbeer: Ein Leben in Briefen* (Wilhelmshaven, 1983).
BIBL.: J. Schläder and R. Quandt, eds., *H. B.: Festschrift zum 60. Geburtstag* (Laaber, 1982).

Becker, (Jean Otto Eric) Hugo, famous German cellist, son of **Jean Becker;** b. Strasbourg, Feb. 13, 1863; d. Geiselgasteig, July 30, 1941. He studied 1st with his father, later with Grützmacher, Kündinger, de Swert, and Piatti; was a cellist in the Frankfurt Opera orch. (1884–86) and a member of the Heermann quartet (1890–1906); taught at the Königliche Hochschule in Berlin (1909–29). He was not only one of the finest soloists, but also a remarkable ensemble player; was for many years a member of the Marteau-Dohnányi-Becker trio; also played with Ysaÿe and Busoni. Among his compositions are a Cello Concerto and smaller cello pieces. He publ. *Mechanik und Ästhetik des Violoncellspiels* (Vienna, 1929).

Becker, Jean, German violinist, father of **(Jean Otto Eric) Hugo Becker;** b. Mannheim, May 11, 1833; d. there, Oct. 10, 1884. He studied with his father; then with Vincenz Lachner and Hugo Hildebrandt; his principal teacher was Aloys Kettenus. He was concertmaster of the Mannheim Orch. from 1855 to 1865. In 1865 he settled in Florence, and established the renowned Florentine Quartet (dissolved in 1880). The remaining years of his life were spent touring with his children: **Jeanne,** pianist, pupil of Reinecke and Bargiel (b. Mannheim, June 9, 1859; d. there, April 6, 1893); **Hans,** violist (b. Strasbourg, May 12, 1860; d. Leipzig, May 1, 1917); and **Hugo Becker.**

Becker, John J(oseph), remarkable American composer; b. Henderson, Ky., Jan. 22, 1886; d. Wilmette, Ill., Jan. 21, 1961. He studied at the Cincinnati Cons.; then was at the Wisconsin Cons. in Milwaukee, where he was a pupil of Alexander von Fielitz, Carl Busch, and Wilhelm Middleschulte (Ph.D., 1923). From 1917 to 1927 he served as director of music at Notre Dame Univ.; was chairman of the fine arts dept. at the College of St. Thomas in St. Paul, Minn., from 1929 to 1935. He was subsequently Minnesota State Director for the Federal Music Project (1935–41) and prof. of music at Barat College of the Sacred Heart at Lake Forest, Ill. (1943–57); taught sporadically at the Chicago Musical College. His early works are characterized by romantic moods in a somewhat Germanic manner. About 1930 he was drawn into the circle of modern American

music; was on the editorial board of *New Music Quarterly,* founded by Cowell, and became associated with Charles Ives. He conducted modern American works with various groups in St. Paul. Striving to form a style that would be both modern and recognizably American, he wrote a number of pieces for various instrumental groups under the title *Soundpiece.* He also developed a type of dramatic work connecting theatrical action with music. Becker's music is marked by sparse sonorities of an incisive rhythmic character contrasted with dissonant conglomerates of massive harmonies.
WORKS: STAGE: *Dance Figure* for Singer, Dance Group, and Orch., on a poem by Ezra Pound (1932); *The Life of Man,* incidental music to the play by Leonid Andreyev (1932–43; unfinished); *Abongo: Dance Primitive* for 2 Solo Dancers, Dance Group, and Percussion (1933; N.Y., May 16, 1963); *A Marriage with Space,* "a drama in color, light, and sound" for Solo and Mass Recitation, Solo Dancer and Dance Group, and Large Orch., to a poem by Mark Turbyfill (1933–35); *Nostalgic Songs of Earth,* 3 dances for Solo Dancer and Piano (Northfield, Minn., Dec. 12, 1938); *Vigilante 1938* for Solo Dancer, Piano, and Percussion (Northfield, Minn., Dec. 12, 1938); *Rain Down Death,* incidental music for the play by Alfred Kreymborg (1939); *When the Willow Nods,* incidental music for the play by Kreymborg (1939); *Privilege and Privation,* "a playful affair with music," with libretto by Kreymborg (1940); *Antigone,* incidental music (1940); *Deirdre of the Sorrows,* lyric drama in 1 act, based on the play by John Synge (1945); *Faust,* monodrama (1951); *Madeleine et Judas,* incidental music for the play by Raymond Bruckberger (1958; radio perf., Paris, March 25, 1959). **ORCH.:** *The Cossacks,* 3 sketches (1912); 7 syms.: No. 1, *Étude primitive* (1912–15); No. 2, *Fantasia tragica* (1920); No. 3, *Symphonia brevis* (1929; 1st complete perf., Minneapolis, May 20, 1937, composer conducting); No. 4, *Dramatic Episodes* (1938; uses material from *A Marriage with Space*); No. 5, *Homage to Mozart* (1942); No. 6, *Symphony of Democracy,* with Narrator and Chorus (1942); No. 7, based on the *Sermon on the Mount,* with Narrator and Singing and Speaking Chorus (1953–54; unfinished); *Concerto Arabesque* for Piano and Orch. (1930; St. Paul, Minn., Dec. 7, 1931, composer conducting); *Concertino Pastorale,* "A Forest Rhapsodie" for 2 Flutes and Orch. (1933; Cincinnati, Jan. 13, 1976); Concerto for Horn and Small Orch. (1933; N.Y., Feb. 8, 1953); *Mockery,* scherzo for Piano and Dance or Chamber Orch. (1933; 1st concert perf., N.Y., March 17, 1974); Viola Concerto (1937); 2nd Piano Concerto, *Satirico* (1938; St. Paul, Minn., March 28, 1939); *Rain Down Death,* 1st orch. suite (1939); *When the Willow Nods,* 2nd orch. suite (1940; Albert Lea, Minn., Jan. 9, 1941); *Antigone,* symphonic dances (1940); *Victory March* (1942; last movement of 6th Sym.); *The Snow Goose: A Legend of World War II* (1944); Violin Concerto (1948). **VOCAL:** *Rouge Bouquet* for Male Chorus, with Trumpet and Piano (1917); *Out of the Cradle Endlessly Rocking,* cantata for Speaker, Soprano, Tenor, Chorus, and Orch. (1929; St. Cloud, Minn., July 19, 1931, composer conducting); *Missa Symphonica* for Male Chorus (1933); *Lincoln's Gettysburg Address* for Speaker, Chorus, and Orch. (1941); *Mass in Honor of the Sacred Heart* for Female Chorus (1944); *Moments from the Passion* for Solo Voice, Male and Female Voices, and Piano (1945); *Moments from the Liturgy* for Speaker, Women's Voices, Vocal Soloist, and Singing and Speaking Choruses (1948). **CHAMBER:** *An American Sonata* for Violin and Piano (South Bend, Ind., July 28, 1926, composer at the piano); 8 *Soundpieces:* No. 1 for Piano Quintet (1932; N.Y., Nov. 13, 1933), or for Piano and String Orch. (1935); No. 2, *Homage to Haydn* (String Quartet No. 1; 1936), also for String Orch. (1937); No. 3 (Sonata for Violin and Piano; 1936; St. Paul, Minn., April 1, 1940); No. 4 (String Quartet No. 2; 1937; Lake Forest, Ill., Oct. 19, 1947); No. 5 (Sonata for Piano; 1938; St. Paul, Minn., April 13, 1943, Ernst Krenek performing); No. 6 for Flute and Clarinet (1940; Chapel Hill, N.C., April 26, 1970); No. 7 for 2 Pianos (1949); No. 8 (String Quartet No. 3; 1959; unfinished). **ORGAN:** *Fantasia tragica* (1920); *Improvisation* (1960). **FILM:** Incidental music for *Julius Caesar,*

a film by David Bradley (1949). In 1934 he scored Ives's song *General William Booth's Entrance into Heaven* for Chamber Orch.

BIBL.: D. Gillespie, "J. B., Musical Crusader from Saint Paul," *Musical Quarterly* (April 1976); idem, "J. B.'s Correspondence with Ezra Pound," *Bulletin of Research in the Humanities* (Spring 1980).

Beckett, Wheeler, American conductor; b. San Francisco, March 7, 1898; d. Philadelphia, Jan. 25, 1986. He took a course in conducting in Basel, Switzerland (1928–30); then returned to the U.S., where he served as leader of various symphonic groups in San Francisco. In 1957 he organized a youth orch. in N.Y.; also traveled as a conductor in the Far East under the auspices of the State Dept. (1959–62). He composed some church music and solo songs.

Becking, Gustav (Wilhelm), German musicologist; b. Bremen, March 4, 1894; d. (in a street fight) Prague, May 8, 1945. He studied in Berlin with J. Wolf and in Leipzig with Riemann; received his doctorate for a paper on Beethoven (Leipzig, 1921); in 1922 he was appointed a lecturer at the Univ. of Erlangen; in 1929 he became a member of the faculty at the Univ. of Utrecht. In 1930 he became a prof. at the German Univ. in Prague. He publ. *Der Musikalische Rhythmus als Erkenntnisquelle* (Augsburg, 1928); also ed. the collected works of E.T.A. Hoffmann (2 vols., Leipzig, 1922–23).

Beckmann, Johann Friedrich Gottlieb, German composer and organist; b. Celle, Sept. 6, 1737; d. there, April 25, 1792. He was one of the finest players and improvisers on the organ of his time; was for many years active in Celle. He wrote an opera, *Lukas und Hännchen* (Braunschweig, 1768); 6 harpsichord concertos; 12 keyboard sonatas; miscellaneous piano pieces.

Beckwith, John, prominent Canadian composer, teacher, writer on music, and pianist; b. Victoria, British Columbia, March 9, 1927. He began piano lessons as a child with Ogreta McNeill and Gwendoline Harper; after attending Victoria College (1944–45), he settled in Toronto, studying piano privately with Alberto Guerrero (1945–50) and at the Univ. of Toronto (Mus.B., 1947). He also received private composition lessons from Nadia Boulanger in Paris (1950–52). He completed his education at the Univ. of Toronto (Mus.M., 1961). In 1950 he made his debut as a pianist in a lecture-recital in Toronto; he was also associate ed. of the *Canadian Music Journal* (1957–62), music reviewer for the Toronto *Star* (1959–62; 1963–65), and program annotator for the Toronto Sym. (1966–70). From 1952 to 1966 he taught theory at the Royal Cons. of Music of Toronto, and in 1952 joined the faculty at the Univ. of Toronto; in 1984 he was named Jean A. Chalmers Prof. of Canadian Music there, the 1st position of its kind created by a Canadian univ., and also founded and directed its Inst. for Canadian Music. He was area ed. for Canada for *The New Grove Dictionary of Music and Musicians* (1972–80) and general ed. of the Canadian Composers/Compositeurs Canadiens study series (from 1975); he also co-edited *The Modern Composer and His World* (with U. Kasemets; Toronto, 1961), *Contemporary Canadian Composers* (with K. MacMillan; Toronto, 1975), *Hello Out There!: Canada's New Music in the World, 1950–85* (with D. Cooper; Toronto, 1988), and *Musical Canada: Words and Music Honouring Helmut Kallmann* (with F. Hall; Toronto, 1988). In 1987 he was made a Member of the Order of Canada. His music is marked by pragmatic modernism, with ingenious application of urban folklore and structural collage.

WORKS: STAGE: *Night Blooming Cereus,* chamber opera (1953–58; radio premiere, Toronto, March 4, 1959; stage premiere, Toronto, April 5, 1960); *The Killdeer,* incidental music (1959); *The Shivaree,* opera (1965–66; 1978; Toronto, April 3, 1982). **ORCH.:** *Music for Dancing* for Small Orch. (1948; rev. 1959); *Montage* (1953); *Fall Scene and Fair Dance* for Violin, Clarinet, and String Orch. (1956); *Concerto Fantasy* for Piano and Orch. (1959); *Flower Variations and Wheels*

(1962); *Concertino for Horn and Orch.* (1963); *All the Bees and All the Keys* for Narrator and Orch. (1973); *A Concert of Myths* for Flute and Orch. (1984). **CHAMBER:** Quartet for Woodwinds (1951); *3 Studies* for String Trio (1951); *Circle, with Tangents* for Harpsichord and 13 Solo Strings (1967); *Taking a Stand* for 5 Players, 8 Brass Instruments, 14 Music Stands, and 1 Platform (1972); *Musical Chairs* for String Quintet (1973); Quartet for 2 Violins, Viola, and Cello (1977); *Case Study* for Any 5 Instruments (1980); *For Starters* for 11 Brass Instruments (1984). **COLLAGE:** *A Message to Winnipeg* for 4 Narrators, Clarinet, Violin, Piano, and Percussion (1960); *12 Letters to a Small Town* for 4 Narrators, Flute, Oboe, Guitar, and Piano or Harmonium (1961); *Wednesday's Child* for 3 Narrators, Soprano, Tenor, Flute, Viola, Piano, and Percussion (1962); *Canada Dash, Canada Dot* for Folksinger, 5 Narrators, Soprano, Contralto, Baritone, Bass, and Instruments (1965–67); *The Journals of Susanna Moodie* for 2 Keyboard Players and Percussion (1973); also many choruses, songs, and works for solo piano and solo organ.

Beckwith, John "Christmas," English organist; b. Norwich, Dec. 25, 1750; d. there, June 3, 1809. He studied at Oxford; became organist of St. Peter Mancroft (1794); was awarded the degrees Mus.B. and Mus.D., Oxon. (1803); became organist of Norwich Cathedral (1808). Beckwith's proficiency as an organist was coupled with fine musical scholarship. His collection of chants, *The First Verse of Every Psalm of David, with an Ancient or Modern Chant in Score, adapted as much as possible to the Sentiment of each Psalm* (London, 1808), includes a valuable preface, "A short history of chanting." He also publ. numerous pieces for chorus and organ.

Bečvařovský, Anton Felix (Antonín František), Bohemian organist; b. Mladá Boleslav, April 9, 1754; d. Berlin, May 15, 1823. He received his primary education in music at the Piarist College of Kosmonosy (1767–74); then had instruction in Prague with Kuchař; subsequently occupied various posts as organist: in Prague, in Braunschweig (1779–96), and finally in Berlin. He composed 5 keyboard concertos and several piano sonatas, as well as choral works.

Bedford, David (Vickerman), English composer, brother of **Steuart (John Rudolf) Bedford;** b. London, Aug. 4, 1937. He studied at the Royal Academy of Music in London with Lennox Berkeley (1958–61); then went to Italy, where he took lessons with Luigi Nono in Venice; also worked in the electronic music studios in Milan. Returning to England, he taught at Queen's College in London and played the organ in pop groups.

WORKS: *Concerto for 24 Instruments* (1960); *Piece II* for Electronic Instruments (1962); *+2, −2* for Orch. (1963); *Piece for Mo* for Percussion, Vibraphone, Accordion, and Strings (1963); *Music for Albion Moonlight* for Soprano and Chamber Ensemble (1964); *The Great Birds* for 30-part Chorus (1964); *Octet for 9* (1964); *A Dream of the 7 Lost Stars* for Chorus and Instruments (1965); *This One for You* for Chamber Orch. (1965); *Gastrula* for Orch. (1968); *The Tentacles of the Dark Nebula* for Tenor and Solo Strings (London, Sept. 22, 1969); *The Sword for Orion* for Flute, Clarinet, Violin, Cello, 4 Metronomes, and 32 Percussion Instruments (1970); *Holy Thursday with Squeakers* for Soprano and Instruments (1972); *When I Heard the Learn'd Astronomer* for Tenor and Wind Ensemble (1972); *Jack of Shadows* for Viola and Chamber Ensemble (1973); *Pancakes with Butter, Maple Syrup, and Bacon and the TV Weatherman* for Horn, 2 Trumpets, Trombone, and Tuba (1973); *A Horse, His Name Was Henry Fencewaver Walkins* for Guitar and Chamber Ensemble (1973); *12 Hours of Sunset* for Chorus and Orch. (1974); *Star's End* for 3 Rock Instruments and Orch. (1974); *Star's End* for Guitar and Orch. (London, Nov. 5, 1974); *The Rime of the Ancient Mariner,* children's opera (1975–76); *The Death of Baldur,* a school opera trilogy (1979); Sym. for 12 Musicians (1981); *SPNM Birthday Piece* for String Quartet (1983); Sym. No. 2 for Symphonic Wind Band (1985; Hertfordshire, April 7, 1986).

Bedford, Steuart (John Rudolf), English conductor, brother of **David (Vickerman) Bedford;** b. London, July 31, 1939.

also met important wealthy admirers, among them Count Ferdinand von Waldstein, who was to be immortalized by Beethoven's dedication to him of a piano sonata bearing his name. Beethoven continued to compose; some of his works of the period were written in homage to royalty, as a cantata on the death of the Emperor Joseph II and another on the accession of Emperor Leopold II; other pieces were designed for performance at aristocratic gatherings.

In 1790 an event of importance took place in Beethoven's life when Haydn was honored in Bonn by the Elector on his way to London; it is likely that Beethoven was introduced to him, and that Haydn encouraged him to come to Vienna to study with him. However that might be, Beethoven went to Vienna in Nov. 1792, and began his studies with Haydn. Not very prudently, Beethoven approached the notable teacher Johann Schenk to help him write the mandatory exercises prior to delivering them to Haydn for final appraisal. In the meantime, Haydn had to go to London again, and Beethoven's lessons with him were discontinued. Instead, Beethoven began a formal study of counterpoint with Johann Georg Albrechtsberger, a learned musician and knowledgeable pedagogue; these studies continued for about a year, until 1795. Furthermore, Beethoven took lessons in vocal composition with the illustrious Italian composer Salieri, who served as Imperial Kapellmeister at the Austrian court. Beethoven was fortunate to find a generous benefactor in Prince Karl Lichnowsky, who awarded him, beginning about 1800, an annual stipend of 600 florins; he was amply repaid for this bounty by entering the pantheon of music history through Beethoven's dedication to him of the *Sonate pathétique* and other works, as well as his 1st opus number, a set of 3 piano trios. Among other aristocrats of Vienna who were introduced into the gates of permanence through Beethoven's dedications was Prince Franz Joseph Lobkowitz, whose name adorns the title pages of the 6 String Quartets, op. 18; the *Eroica Symphony* (after Beethoven unsuccessfully tried to dedicate it to Napoleon); the Triple Concerto, op. 56; and (in conjunction with Prince Razumovsky) the 5th and 6th syms.—a glorious florilegium of great music. Prince Razumovsky, the Russian ambassador to Vienna, played an important role in Beethoven's life. From 1808 to 1816 he maintained in his residence a string quartet in which he himself played the 2nd violin (the leader was Beethoven's friend Schuppanzigh). It was to Razumovsky that Beethoven dedicated his 3 string quartets that became known as the Razumovsky quartets, in which Beethoven made use of authentic Russian folk themes. Razumovsky also shared with Lobkowitz the dedications of Beethoven's 5th and 6th syms. Another Russian patron was Prince Golitzyn, for whom Beethoven wrote his great string quartets opp. 127, 130, and 132.

Beethoven made his 1st public appearance in Vienna on March 29, 1795, as soloist in one of his piano concertos (probably the B-flat major Concerto, op. 19). In 1796 he played in Prague, Dresden, Leipzig, and Berlin. He also participated in "competitions," fashionable at the time, with other pianists, which were usually held in aristocratic salons. In 1799 he competed with Joseph Wölffl and in 1800 with Daniel Steibelt. On April 2, 1800, he presented a concert of his works in the Burgtheater in Vienna, at which his 1st Sym., in C major, and the Septet in E-flat major were performed for the 1st time. Other compositions at the threshold of the century were the Piano Sonata in C minor, op. 13, the *Pathétique;* the C-major Piano Concerto, op. 15; "sonata quasi una fantasia" for Piano in C-sharp minor, op. 27, celebrated under the nickname *Moonlight Sonata* (so described by a romantically inclined critic but not specifically accepted by Beethoven); the D-major Piano Sonata known as *Pastoral;* 8 violin sonatas; 3 piano trios; 5 string trios; 6 string quartets; several sets of variations; and a number of songs.

Fétis was the 1st to suggest the division of Beethoven's compositions into 3 stylistic periods. It was left to Wilhelm von Lenz to fully elucidate this view in his *Beethoven et ses trois styles* (2 vols., St. Petersburg, 1852). Despite this arbitrary chronological division, the work became firmly established in Beethoven literature. According to Lenz, the 1st period embraced Beethoven's works from his early years to the end of the 18th century, marked by a style closely related to the formal methods of Haydn. The 2nd period, covering the years 1801–14, was signaled by a more personal, quasi-Romantic mood, beginning with the *Moonlight Sonata;* the last period, extending from 1814 to Beethoven's death in 1827, comprised the most individual, the most unconventional, the most innovative works, such as his last string quartets and the 9th Sym., with its extraordinary choral finale.

Beethoven's early career in Vienna was marked by fine success; he was popular not only as a virtuoso pianist and a composer, but also as a social figure who was welcome in the aristocratic circles of Vienna; Beethoven's students included society ladies and even royal personages, such as Archduke Rudolf of Austria, to whom Beethoven dedicated the so-called Archduke Trio, op. 97. But Beethoven's progress was fatefully affected by a mysteriously growing deafness, which reached a crisis in 1802. On Oct. 8 and 10, 1802, he wrote a poignant document known as the "Heiligenstadt Testament," for it was drawn in the village of Heiligenstadt, where he resided at the time. The document, not discovered until after Beethoven's death, voiced his despair at the realization that the most important sense of his being, the sense of hearing, was inexorably failing. He implored his brothers, in case of his early death, to consult his physician, Dr. Schmidt, who knew the secret of his "lasting malady" contracted 6 years before he wrote the Testament, i.e., in 1796. The etiology of his illness leaves little doubt that the malady was the dreaded "lues," with symptoms including painful intestinal disturbances, enormous enlargement of the pancreas, cirrhosis of the liver, and, most ominously, the porous degeneration of the roof of the cranium, observable in the life mask of 1812 and clearly shown in the photograph of Beethoven's skull taken when his body was exhumed in 1863. However, the impairment of his hearing may have had an independent cause: an otosclerosis, resulting in the shriveling of the auditory nerves and concomitant dilation of the accompanying arteries. Externally, there were signs of tinnitus, a constant buzzing in the ears, about which Beethoven complained. His reverential biographer A.W. Thayer states plainly in a letter dated Oct. 29, 1880, that it was known to several friends of Beethoven that the cause of his combined ailments was syphilis. A full account of Beethoven's illness is found in Dr. Dieter Kerner's book *Krankheiten grosser Musiker* (Stuttgart, 1973; vol. 1, pp. 89–140).

To the end of his life Beethoven hoped to find a remedy for his deafness among the latest "scientific" medications. His *Konversationshefte* bear a pathetic testimony to these hopes; in one, dated 1819, he notes down the address of a Dr. Mayer, who treated deafness by "sulphur vapor" and a vibration machine. By tragic irony, Beethoven's deafness greatly contributed to the study of his personality, thanks to the existence of the "conversation books" in which his interlocutors wrote down their questions and Beethoven replied, a method of communication which became a rule in his life after 1818. Unfortunately, Beethoven's friend and amanuensis, Anton Schindler, altered or deleted many of these; it seems also likely that he destroyed Beethoven's correspondence with his doctors, as well as the recipes which apparently contained indications of treatment by mercury, the universal medication against venereal and other diseases at the time.

It is remarkable that under these conditions Beethoven was able to continue his creative work with his usual energy; there were few periods of interruption in the chronology of his list of works, and similarly there is no apparent influence of his moods of depression on the content of his music; tragic and joyful musical passages had equal shares in his inexhaustible flow of varied works. On April 5, 1803, Beethoven presented a concert of his compositions in Vienna at which he was soloist in his 3rd Piano Concerto; the program also contained performances of his 2nd Sym. and of the oratorio *Christus am Oelberge.* On May 24, 1803, he played in Vienna the piano part of his Violin Sonata, op. 47, known as the *Kreutzer Sonata,* although Kreutzer himself did not introduce it; in his place the violin part was taken over by the mulatto artist George Bridgetower. During the years 1803 and 1804 Beethoven composed his great Sym. No. 3, in E-flat major, op. 55, the *Eroica*. It has an interesting history. Beethoven's disciple Ferdinand Ries relates that Beethoven tore off the title page of the MS of the score orig. dedicated to Napoleon, after learning of his proclamation as Emperor of France in 1804, and supposedly exclaimed, "So he is a tyrant like all the others after all!" Ries reported this story shortly before his death, some 34 years after the composition of the *Eroica*, which throws great doubt on its credibility. Indeed, in a letter to the publishing firm of Breitkopf & Härtel, dated Aug. 26, 1804, long after Napoleon's proclamation of Empire, Beethoven still refers to the title of the work as "really Bonaparte." His own copy of the score shows that he crossed out the designation "Inttitulata Bonaparte," but allowed the words written in pencil, in German, "Geschrieben auf Bonaparte" to stand. In Oct. 1806, when the 1st ed. of the orch. parts was publ. in Vienna, the sym. received the title "Sinfonia eroica composta per festeggiare il sovvenire d'un grand' uomo" ("heroic symphony, composed to celebrate the memory of a great man"). But who was the great man whose memory was being celebrated in Beethoven's masterpiece? Napoleon was very much alive and was still leading his Grande Armée to new conquests, so the title would not apply. Yet, the famous funeral march in the score expressed a sense of loss and mourning. The mystery remains. There is evidence that Beethoven continued to have admiration for Napoleon. He once remarked that had he been a military man he could have matched Napoleon's greatness on the battlefield. Beethoven and Napoleon were close contemporaries; Napoleon was a little more than a year older than Beethoven.

In 1803 Emanuel Schikaneder, manager of the Theater an der Wien, asked Beethoven to compose an opera to a libretto he had prepared under the title *Vestas Feuer* (The Vestal Flame), but he soon lost interest in the project and instead began work on another opera, based on J.N. Bouilly's *Léonore, ou L'Amour conjugal*. The completed opera was named *Fidelio*, which was the heroine's assumed name in her successful efforts to save her imprisoned husband. The opera was given at the Theater an der Wien on Nov. 20, 1805, under difficult circumstances, a few days after the French army entered Vienna. There were only 3 performances before the opera was rescheduled for March 29 and April 10, 1806; after another long hiatus a greatly revised version of *Fidelio* was produced on May 23, 1814. Beethoven wrote 3 versions of the Overture for *Léonore;* for another performance, on May 26, 1814, he revised the Overture once more, and this time it was performed under the title *Fidelio Overture.*

An extraordinary profusion of creative masterpieces marked the years 1802–8 in Beethoven's life. During these years he brought out the 3 String Quartets, op. 59, dedicated to Count Razumovsky; the 4th, 5th, and 6th syms.; the Violin Concerto; the 4th Piano Concerto; the Triple Concerto; the *Coriolan* Overture; and a number of piano sonatas, including the D minor, op. 31; No. 2, the *Tempest;* the C major, op. 53, the *Waldstein;* and the F minor, op. 57, the *Appassionata.* On Dec. 22, 1808, his 5th and 6th syms. were heard for the 1st time at a concert in Vienna; the concert lasted some 4 hours. Still, financial difficulties beset Beethoven. The various annuities from patrons were uncertain, and the devaluation of the Austrian currency played havoc with his calculations. In Oct. 1808, King Jerome Bonaparte of Westphalia offered the composer the post of Kapellmeister of Kassel at a substantial salary, but Beethoven decided to remain in Vienna. Between 1809 and 1812, Beethoven wrote his 5th Piano Concerto; the String Quartet in E-flat major, op. 74; the incidental music to Goethe's drama *Egmont;* the 7th and 8th syms.; and his Piano Sonata in E-flat major, op. 81a, whimsically subtitled "Das Lebewohl, Abwesenheit und Wiedersehn," also known by its French subtitle, "Les Adieux, l'absence, et le retour." He also added a specific description to the work, "Sonate caractéristique." This explicit characterization was rare with Beethoven; he usually avoided

programmatic descriptions, preferring to have his music stand by itself. Even in his 6th Sym., the *Pastoral*, which bore specific subtitles for each movement and had the famous imitations of birds singing and the realistic portrayal of a storm, Beethoven decided to append a cautionary phrase: "More as an expression of one's feelings than a picture." He specifically denied that the famous introductory call in the 5th Sym. represented the knock of Fate at his door, but the symbolic association was too powerful to be removed from the legend; yet the characteristic iambic tetrameter was anticipated in several of Beethoven's works, among them the *Appassionata* and the 4th Piano Concerto. Czerny, who was close to Beethoven in Vienna, claimed that the theme was derived by Beethoven from the cry of the songbird Emberiza, or Emmerling, a species to which the common European goldfinch belongs, which Beethoven may have heard during his walks in the Vienna woods, a cry that is piercing enough to compensate for Beethoven's loss of aural acuity. However that may be, the 4-note motif became inexorably connected with the voice of doom for enemies and the exultation of the victor in battle. It was used as a victory call by the Allies in World War II; the circumstance that 3 short beats followed by one long beat spelled V for Victory in Morse code reinforced its effectiveness. The Germans could not very well jail people for whistling a Beethoven tune, so they took it over themselves as the 1st letter of the archaic German word "Viktoria," and trumpeted it blithely over their radios. Another famous nicknamed work by Beethoven was the *Emperor Concerto*, a label attached to the 5th Piano Concerto, op. 73. He wrote it in 1809, when Napoleon's star was still high in the European firmament, and some publicist decided that the martial strains of the music, with its sonorous fanfares, must have been a tribute to the Emperor of the French. Patriotic reasons seemed to underlie Beethoven's designation of his Piano Sonata, op. 106, as the *Hammerklavier Sonata*, that is, a work written for a hammer keyboard, or fortepiano, as distinct from harpsichord. But all of Beethoven's piano sonatas were for fortepiano; moreover, he assigned the title *Hammerklavier* to each of the 4 sonatas, namely opp. 101, 106, 109, and 110, using the old German word for fortepiano; by so doing, he desired to express his patriotic consciousness of being a German.

Like many professional musicians, Beethoven was occasionally called upon to write a work glorifying an important event or a famous personage. Pieces of this kind seldom achieve validity, and usually produce bombast. Such a work was Beethoven's *Wellingtons Sieg oder Die Schlacht bei Vittoria*, celebrating the British victory over Joseph Bonaparte, Napoleon's brother who temporarily sat on the Spanish throne. In 1814, Beethoven wrote a cantata entitled *Der glorreiche Augenblick*, intended to mark the "glorious moment" of the fall of his erstwhile idol, Napoleon.

Personal misfortunes, chronic ailments, and intermittent quarrels with friends and relatives preoccupied Beethoven's entire life. He ardently called for peace among men, but he never achieved peace with himself. Yet he could afford to disdain the attacks in the press; on the margin of a critical but justified review of his *Wellington's Victory*, he wrote, addressing the writer: "You wretched scoundrel! What I excrete [he used the vulgar German word *scheisse*] is better than anything you could ever think up!"

Beethoven was overly suspicious; he even accused the faithful Schindler of dishonestly mishandling the receipts from the sale of tickets at the 1st performance of the 9th Sym. He exaggerated his poverty; he possessed some shares and bonds which he kept in a secret drawer. He was untidy in personal habits; he often used preliminary drafts of his compositions to cover the soup and even the chamber pot, leaving telltale circles on the MS. He was strangely naive; he studiously examined the winning numbers of the Austrian government lottery, hoping to find a numerological clue to a fortune for himself. His handwriting was all but indecipherable. An earnest Beethoveniac spent time with a microscope trying to figure out what kind of soap Beethoven wanted his housekeeper to purchase for him; the scholar's efforts were crowned with triumphant success: the indecipherable word was *gelbe*—Beethoven wanted a piece of yellow soap. Q.E.D. The copying of his MSS presented difficulties; not only were the notes smudged, but sometimes Beethoven even failed to mark a crucial accidental. A copyist said that he would rather copy 20 pages of Rossini than a single page of Beethoven. On the other hand, Beethoven's sketchbooks, containing many alternative drafts, are extremely valuable, for they introduce a scholar into the inner sanctum of Beethoven's creative process.

Beethoven had many devoted friends and admirers in Vienna, but he spent most of his life in solitude. Carl Czerny reports in his diary that Beethoven once asked him to let him lodge in his house, but Czerny declined, explaining that his aged parents lived with him and he had no room for Beethoven. Deprived of the pleasures and comforts of family life, Beethoven sought to find a surrogate in his nephew Karl, son of Caspar Carl Beethoven, who died in 1815. Beethoven regarded his sister-in-law as an unfit mother; he went to court to gain sole guardianship over the boy; in his private letters, and even in his legal depositions, he poured torrents of vilification upon the woman, implying even that she was engaged in prostitution. In his letters to Karl he often signed himself as the true father of the boy. In 1826 Karl attempted suicide; it would be unfair to ascribe this act to Beethoven's stifling avuncular affection; Karl later went into the army and enjoyed a normal life.

Gallons of ink have been unnecessarily expended on the crucial question of Beethoven's relationship with women. That Beethoven dreamed of an ideal life companion is clear from his numerous utterances and candid letters to friends, in some of which he asked them to find a suitable bride for him. But there is no inkling that he kept company with any particular woman in Vienna. Beethoven lacked social graces; he could not dance; he was unable to carry on a light conversation about trivia; and behind it all there was the dreadful reality of his deafness. He could speak, but could not always understand when he was spoken to. With close friends he used an unwieldy ear trumpet; but such contrivances were obviously unsuitable in a social gathering. There were several objects of his secret passions, among his pupils or the society ladies to whom he dedicated his works. But somehow he never actually proposed marriage, and they usually married less hesitant suitors. It was inevitable that Beethoven should seek escape in fantasies. The greatest of these fantasies was the famous letter addressed to an "unsterbliche Geliebte," the "Immortal Beloved," couched in exuberant emotional tones characteristic of the sentimental romances of the time, and strangely reminiscent of Goethe's novel *The Sorrows of Young Werther*. The letter was never mailed; it was discovered in the secret compartment of Beethoven's writing desk after his death. The clues to the identity of the object of his passion were maddeningly few. He voiced his fervid anticipation of an impending meeting at some place indicated only by the initial letter "K."; he dated his letter as Monday, the 6th of July, without specifying the year. Eager Beethoveniacs readily established that the most likely year was 1812, when July 6 fell on a Monday. A complete inventory of ladies of Beethoven's acquaintance from 14 to 40 years of age was laid out, and the lengthy charade unfolded, lasting one and a half centuries. The most likely "Immortal Beloved" seemed to be Antoine Brentano, the wife of a merchant. But Beethoven was a frequent visitor at their house; his letters to her (sent by ordinary city post) and her replies expressed mutual devotion, but they could not be stylistically reconciled with the torrid protestation of undying love in the unmailed letter. And if indeed Frau Brentano was the "Immortal Beloved," why could not a tryst have been arranged in Vienna when her husband was away on business? There were other candidates; one researcher established, from consulting the town records of arrivals and departures, that Beethoven and a certain lady of his Vienna circle were in Prague on the same day, and that about 9 months later she bore a child who seemed to bear a remarkable resemblance to Beethoven. Another researcher, exploring the limits of the incredible, con-

cluded that Beethoven had sexual relations with his sister-in-law and that his execration of her stemmed from this relationship. It was asserted also that a certain musician conversant with the lowlife of Vienna supplied Beethoven with *filles de joie* for pay. The nadir of monstrous speculation was reached by a pseudo-Freudian investigator who advanced the notion that Beethoven nurtured incestuous desires toward his nephew and that his demands drove the boy to his suicide attempt.

The so-called 3rd style of Beethoven was assigned by biographers to the last 10 or 15 years of his life. It included the composition of his monumental 9th Sym., completed in 1824 and 1st performed in Vienna on May 7, 1824; the program also included excerpts from the *Missa Solemnis* and *Die Weihe des Hauses* (The Consecration of the House). It was reported that Caroline Unger, the contralto soloist in the *Missa Solemnis*, had to pull Beethoven by the sleeve at the end of the performance so that he would acknowledge the applause he could not hear. With the 9th Sym., Beethoven completed the evolution of the symphonic form as he envisioned it. Its choral finale was his manifesto addressed to the world at large, to the text from Schiller's ode *An die Freude* (To Joy). In it, Beethoven, through Schiller, appealed to all humanity to unite in universal love. Here a musical work, for the 1st time, served a political ideal. Beethoven's last string quartets, opp. 127, 130, 131, and 132, served as counterparts of his last sym. in their striking innovations, dramatic pauses, and novel instrumental tone colors.

In Dec. 1826, on his way back to Vienna from a visit in Gneixendorf, Beethoven was stricken with a fever that developed into a mortal pleurisy; dropsy and jaundice supervened to this condition; surgery to relieve the accumulated fluid in his organism was unsuccessful, and he died on the afternoon of March 26, 1827. It was widely reported that an electric storm struck Vienna as Beethoven lay dying; its occurrence was indeed confirmed by the contemporary records in the Vienna weather bureau, but the story that he raised his clenched fist aloft as a gesture of defiance to an overbearing Heaven must be relegated to fantasy; he was far too feeble either to clench his fist or to raise his arm. The funeral of Beethoven was held in all solemnity.

Beethoven was memorialized in festive observations of the centennial and bicentennial of his birth, and of the centennial and sesquicentennial of his death. The house where he was born in Bonn was declared a museum. Monuments were erected to him in many cities. Commemorative postage stamps bearing his image were issued not only in Germany and Austria, but in Russia and other countries. Streets were named after him in many cities of the civilized world, including even Los Angeles.

Beethoven's music marks a division between the Classical period of the 18th century, exemplified by the great names of Mozart and Haydn, and the new spirit of Romantic music that characterized the entire course of the 19th century. There are certain purely external factors that distinguish these 2 periods of musical evolution; one of them pertains to sartorial matters. Music before Beethoven was *Zopfmusik*, pigtail music. Haydn and Mozart are familiar to us by portraits in which their heads are crowned by elaborate wigs; Beethoven's hair was by contrast luxuriant in its unkempt splendor. The music of the 18th century possessed the magnitude of mass production. The accepted number of Haydn's syms., according to his own count, is 104, but even in his own catalogue Haydn allowed a duplication of one of his symphonic works. Mozart wrote about 40 syms. during his short lifetime. Haydn's syms. were constructed according to an easily defined formal structure; while Mozart's last syms. show greater depth of penetration, they do not depart from the Classical convention. Besides, both Haydn and Mozart wrote instrumental works variously entitled cassations, serenades, divertimentos, and suites, which were basically synonymous with syms. Beethoven's syms. were few in number and mutually different. The 1st and 2nd syms. may still be classified as *Zopfmusik*, but with the 3rd Sym. he entered a new world of music. No sym. written before had contained a clearly defined funeral march. Although the 5th Sym. had no designated program, it lent itself easily to programmatic interpretation. Wagner attached a bombastic label, "Apotheosis of the Dance," to Beethoven's 7th Sym. The 8th Sym. Beethoven called his "little sym.," and the 9th is usually known as the *Choral* sym. With the advent of Beethoven, the manufacture of syms. en masse had ceased; Schumann, Brahms, Tchaikovsky, and their contemporaries wrote but a few syms. each, and each had a distinctive physiognomy. Beethoven had forever destroyed *Zopfmusik*, and opened the floodgates of the Romantic era. His music was individual; it was emotionally charged; his Kreutzer Sonata served as a symbol for Tolstoy's celebrated moralistic tale of that name, in which the last movement of the sonata leads the woman pianist into the receptive arms of the concupiscent violinist. But technically the sonata is very difficult for amateurs to master, and Tolstoy's sinners were an ordinary couple in old Russia.

Similarly novel were Beethoven's string quartets; a musical abyss separated his last string quartets from his early essays in the same form. Trios, violin sonatas, cello sonatas, and the 32 great piano sonatas also represent evolutionary concepts. Yet Beethoven's melody and harmony did not diverge from the sacrosanct laws of euphony and tonality. The famous dissonant chord introducing the last movement of the 9th Sym. resolves naturally into the tonic, giving only a moment's pause to the ear. Beethoven's favorite device of pairing the melody in the high treble with triadic chords in close harmony in the deep bass was a peculiarity of his style but not necessarily an infringement of the Classical rules. Yet contemporary critics found some of these practices repugnant and described Beethoven as an eccentric bent on creating unconventional sonorities. Equally strange to the untutored ear were pregnant pauses and sudden modulations in his instrumental works. Beethoven was not a contrapuntist by taste or skill. With the exception of his monumental *Grosse Fuge*, composed as the finale of the String Quartet, op. 133, his fugal movements were usually free canonic imitations. There is only a single instance in Beethoven's music of the crab movement, a variation achieved by running the theme in reverse. But he was a master of instrumental variation, deriving extraordinary transformations through melodic and rhythmic alterations of a given theme. His op. 120, 33 variations for piano on a waltz theme by the Viennese publisher Diabelli, represents one of the greatest achievements in the art.

When Hans von Bülow was asked which was his favorite key signature, he replied that it was E-flat major, the tonality of the *Eroica*, for it had 3 flats: one for Bach, one for Beethoven, and one for Brahms. Beethoven became forever the 2nd B in popular music books.

The literature on Beethoven is immense. The basic catalogues are those by G. Kinsky and H. Halm, *Das Werk Beethovens. Thematisch-Bibliographisches Verzeichnis seiner sämtlichen vollendeten Kompositionen*, publ. in Munich and Duisburg in 1955, and by W. Hess, *Verzeichnis der Gesamtausgabe veröffentlichten Werke Ludwig van Beethovens*, publ. in Wiesbaden in 1957. Beethoven attached opus numbers to most of his works, and they are essential in a catalogue of his works.

Works: orch.: 9 syms.: No. 1, in C major, op. 21 (1800; Vienna, April 2, 1800); No. 2, in D major, op. 36 (1801–2; Vienna, April 5, 1803); No. 3, in E-flat major, op. 55, *Eroica* (1803–4; Vienna, April 7, 1805); No. 4, in B-flat major, op. 60 (1806; Vienna, March 5, 1807); No. 5, in C minor, op. 67 (sketches from 1803; 1807–8; Vienna, Dec. 22, 1808); No. 6, in F major, op. 68, *Pastoral* (sketches from 1803; 1808; Vienna, Dec. 22, 1808); No. 7, in A major, op. 92 (1811–12; Vienna, Dec. 8, 1813); No. 8, in F major, op. 93 (1812; Vienna, Feb. 27, 1814); No. 9, in D minor, op. 125, *Choral* (sketches from 1815–18; 1822–24; Vienna, May 7, 1824); also a fragment of a Sym. in C minor, Hess 298 from the Bonn period. Sketches for the 1st movement of a projected 10th Sym. were realized by Barry Cooper and performed under the auspices of the Royal Phil. Soc. in London on Oct. 18, 1988.—Incidental music: Overture to Collin's *Coriolan*, in C minor, op. 62 (1807; Vienna,

March 1807); *Egmont*, op. 84, to Goethe's drama (with overture; 1809–10; Vienna, June 15, 1810); *Die Ruinen von Athen* (The Ruins of Athens), op. 113, to Kotzebue's drama (with overture; 1811; Pest, Feb. 10, 1812); *König Stephan* (King Stephen), op. 117, to Kotzebue's drama (with overture; 1811; Pest, Feb. 10, 1812); Triumphal March in C major for Kuffner's *Tarpeja* (1813; March 26, 1813); music to Duncker's drama *Leonore Prohaska* (1815); Overture in C major, op. 124, to Meisl's drama *Die Weihe des Hauses* (The Consecration of the House; 1822; Vienna, Oct. 3, 1822).—Further overtures: 4 overtures written for the opera *Leonore*, later named *Fidelio*: *Leonore* No. 1, in C major, op. 138 (1806–7; Feb. 7, 1828); *Leonore* No. 2, op. 72a (1804–5; Vienna, Nov. 20, 1805); *Leonore* No. 3, op. 72b (1805–6; Vienna, March 29, 1806); *Fidelio*, op. 72c (1814; Vienna, May 26, 1814); *Namensfeier* (Name Day) in C major, op. 115 (1814–15; Vienna, Dec. 25, 1815).—Other works for Orch. or Wind Band: 12 Minuets, WoO 7 (1795); 12 German Dances (1795); 12 Contredanses (1802?); March "für die böhmische Landwehr" in F major (1809); March in F major (1810); Polonaise in D major, WoO 21 (1810); Écossaise in D major (1810); Écossaise in G major (1810); *Wellingtons Sieg oder Die Schlacht bei Vittoria* (Wellington's Victory or The Battle of Vittoria; also known as the *Battle* sym.), op. 91 (1813; Vienna, Dec. 8, 1813); March in D major (1816); *Gratulations-Menuet* in E-flat major, WoO 3 (1822; Nov. 3, 1822); March with Trio in C major (1822?).—Ballets: *Ritterballett* (Knight's Ballet; 1790–91; Bonn, March 6, 1791); *Die Geschöpfe des Prometheus* (The Creatures of Prometheus), op. 43 (overture, introduction, and 16 numbers; 1800–1801; Vienna, March 28, 1801).— Works for Solo Instruments and Orch.: Piano Concerto in E-flat major (1784); *Romance* in E minor for Piano, Flute, Bassoon, and Orch., Hess 13 (1786; only a fragment extant); Violin Concerto in C major (1790–92; only a portion of the 1st movement extant); Oboe Concerto in F major, Hess 12 (1792?–93?; not extant; only a few sketches survive); Rondo in B-flat major for Piano and Orch. (1793; solo part finished by Czerny); Piano Concerto No. 2, in B-flat major, op. 19 (probably begun during the Bonn period, perhaps as early as 1785; rev. 1794–95 and 1798; Vienna, March 29, 1795; when publ. in Leipzig in 1801, it was listed as "No. 2"); Piano Concerto No. 1, in C major, op. 15 (1795; rev. 1800; Vienna, Dec. 18, 1795; when publ. in Vienna in 1801, it was listed as "No. 1"); *Romance* in F major for Violin and Orch., op. 50 (1798?; Nov. 1798?); Piano Concerto No. 3, in C minor, op. 37 (1800?; Vienna, April 5, 1803); *Romance* in G major for Violin and Orch., op. 40 (1801?–2); Triple Concerto in C major for Piano, Violin, Cello, and Orch., op. 56 (1803–4; Vienna, May 1808); Piano Concerto No. 4, in G major, op. 58 (1805–6; Vienna, March 1807); Violin Concerto in D major, op. 61 (1806; Vienna, Dec. 23, 1806; cadenza for the 1st movement and 3 cadenzas for the finale; also arranged as a piano concerto in 1807); Fantasia in C minor for Piano, Chorus, and Orch., op. 80, *Choral Fantasy* (1808; Vienna, Dec. 22, 1808); Piano Concerto No. 5, in E-flat major, op. 73, *Emperor* (1809; Leipzig, 1810; 1st Vienna perf., Nov. 28, 1811); also 11 cadenzas for piano concertos nos. 1–4, and 2 for Mozart's Piano Concerto No. 20, in D minor, K. 466.

chamber: 3 Piano Quartets: E-flat major, D major, and C major (1785); Trio in G major for Piano, Flute, and Bassoon, WoO 37 (1786); Minuet in A-flat major for String Quartet, Hess 33 (1790); Piano Trio in E-flat major (1791); *Allegretto* in E-flat major for Piano Trio, Hess 48 (1790–92); Violin Sonata in A major, Hess 46 (1790–92; only a fragment is extant); *Allegro and Minuet* in G major for 2 Flutes (1792); Octet in E-flat major for 2 Oboes, 2 Clarinets, 2 Horns, and 2 Bassoons, op. 103 (1792–93); Variations in F major on Mozart's "Se vuol ballare" from *Le nozze di Figaro* for Piano and Violin (1792–93); *Rondino* in E-flat major for 2 Oboes, 2 Clarinets, 2 Horns, and 2 Bassoons (1793); Quintet in E-flat major for Oboe, 3 Horns, and Bassoon, Hess 19 (1793); *Rondo* in G major for Piano and Violin (1793–94); String Trio in E-flat major, op. 3 (1793; also arranged for Cello and Piano, op. 64); 3 Piano Trios: E-flat major, G major, and C minor, op. 1 (1794–95);

Trio in C major for 2 Oboes and English Horn, op. 87 (1795); String Quintet in E-flat major, op. 4 (1795; an arrangement of the Octet, op. 103); Variations in C major on Mozart's "La ci darem la mano" from *Don Giovanni* for 2 Oboes and English Horn (1795); Sextet in E-flat major for 2 Horns, 2 Violins, Viola, and Cello, op. 81b (1795); Sextet in E-flat major for 2 Clarinets, 2 Horns, and 2 Bassoons, op. 71 (1796); Sonatina in C minor for Piano and Mandolin (1796); *Adagio* in E-flat major for Piano and Mandolin (1796); Sonatina in C major for Piano and Mandolin (1796); *Andante and Variations* in D major for Piano and Mandolin (1796); 6 German Dances for Piano and Violin (1796); 2 Cello Sonatas: F major and G minor, op. 5 (1796); Variations in G major on Handel's "See the Conquering Hero Comes" from *Judas Maccabaeus* for Piano and Cello (1796); Variations in F major on Mozart's "Ein Mädchen oder Weibchen" from *Die Zauberflöte* for Piano and Cello, op. 66 (1796); Quintet in E-flat major for Piano, Oboe, Clarinet, Horn, and Bassoon, op. 16 (1796–97; also arranged for Piano and String Quartet); Duet in E-flat major for Viola and Cello (1796–97); Serenade in D major for String Trio, op. 8 (1796–97); Trio in B-flat major for Piano, Clarinet or Violin, and Cello, op. 11 (1797); 3 String Trios: G major, D major, and C minor, op. 9 (1797–98); 3 Violin Sonatas: D major, A major, and E-flat major, op. 12 (1797–98); March in B-flat major for 2 Clarinets, 2 Horns, and 2 Bassoons (1798); 6 String Quartets: F major, G major, D major, C minor, A major, and B-flat major, op. 18 (1798–1800); Septet in E-flat major for Clarinet, Horn, Bassoon, Violin, Viola, Cello, and Double Bass, op. 20 (1799–1800); Horn (or Cello) Sonata in F major, op. 17 (1800; Vienna, April 18, 1800); Violin Sonata in A minor, op. 23 (1800–1801); Violin Sonata in F major, op. 24, *Spring* (1800–1801); Variations in E-flat major on Mozart's "Bei Männern, welche Liebe fühlen" from *Die Zauberflöte* for Piano and Cello (1801); Serenade in D major for Flute, Violin, and Viola, op. 25 (1801); String Quintet in C major, op. 29 (1801); String Quartet in F major, Hess 34 (an arrangement of the Piano Sonata No. 9, in E major, op. 14, No. 1; 1801–2); 3 Violin Sonatas: A major, C minor, and G major, op. 30 (1801–2); 14 Variations in E-flat major for Piano, Violin, and Cello, op. 44 (sketches from 1792; 1802?); Violin Sonata in A major, op. 47, *Kreutzer* (1802–3; Vienna, May 24, 1803); Trio in E-flat major for Piano, Clarinet or Violin, and Cello, op. 38 (an arrangement of the Septet, op. 20; 1803); Variations in G major on Müller's "Ich bin der Schneider Kakadu" for Piano, Violin, and Cello, op. 121a (1803?; rev. 1816); Serenade in D major for Piano, and Flute or Violin, op. 41 (an arrangement of the Serenade in D major, op. 25; 1803); *Notturno* in D major for Piano and Viola, op. 42 (an arrangement of the Serenade in D major, op. 8; 1803); 3 String Quartets: F major, E minor, and C major, op. 59, *Razumovsky* (1805–6); Cello Sonata in A major, op. 69 (1807–8); 2 Piano Trios: D major and E-flat major, op. 70 (1808); String Quartet in E-flat major, op. 74, *Harp* (1809); String Quartet in F minor, op. 95, *Serioso* (1810); Piano Trio in B-flat major, op. 97, *Archduke* (1810–11); Violin Sonata in G major, op. 96 (1812); *Allegretto* in B-flat major for Piano Trio (1812); *3 equali* for 4 Trombones: D minor, D major, and B-flat major (1812); 2 Cello Sonatas: C major and D major, op. 102 (1815); String Quintet in C minor, op. 104 (an arrangement of the Piano Trio, op. 1, No. 3; 1817); Prelude in D minor for String Quintet, Hess 40 (1817?); Fugue in D major for String Quintet, op. 137 (1817); 6 National Airs with Variations for Piano, and Flute or Violin, op. 105 (1818?); 10 National Airs with Variations for Piano, and Flute or Violin, op. 107 (1818); Duet in A major for 2 Violins (1822); String Quartet in E-flat major, op. 127 (1824–25); String Quartet in A minor, op. 132 (1825); String Quartet in B-flat major, op. 130 (with the *Grosse Fuge* as the finale, 1825; *Rondo* finale, 1826); *Grosse Fuge* in B-flat major for String Quartet, op. 133 (1825); String Quartet in C-sharp minor, op. 131 (1825–26); String Quartet in F major, op. 135 (1826); String Quintet in C major, Hess 41 (1826; extant fragment in piano transcription only).

PIANO SONATAS: Three: in E-flat major, F minor, and D major, *Kurfürstensonaten* (1783); F major (1792); No. 1, in F minor,

op. 2, No. 1 (1793–95); No. 2, in A major, op. 2, No. 2 (1794–95); No. 3, in C major, op. 2, No. 3 (1794–95); No. 19, in G minor, op. 49, No. 1 (1797); No. 20, in G major, op. 49, No. 2 (1795–96); No. 4, in E-flat major, op. 7 (1796–97); No. 5, in C minor, op. 10, No. 1 (1795–97); No. 6, in F major, op. 10, No. 2 (1796–97); No. 7, in D major, op. 10, No. 3 (1797–98); C major, WoO 51 (fragment; 1797–98); No. 8, in C minor, op. 13, *Pathétique* (1798–99); No. 9, in E major, op. 14, No. 1 (1798); No. 10, in G major, op. 14, No. 2 (1799); No. 11, in B-flat major, op. 22 (1800); No. 12, in A-flat major, op. 26, *Funeral March* (1800–1801); No. 13, in E-flat major, op. 27, No. 1, "quasi una fantasia" (1800–1801); No. 14, in C-sharp minor, op. 27, No. 2, "quasi una fantasia," *Moonlight* (1801); No. 15, in D major, op. 28, *Pastoral* (1801); No. 16, in G major, op. 31, No. 1 (1801–2); No. 17, in D minor, op. 31, No. 2, *Tempest* (1801–2); No. 18, in E-flat major, op. 31, No. 3 (1801–2); No. 21, in C major, op. 53, *Waldstein* (1803–4); No. 22, in F major, op. 54 (1803–4); No. 23, in F minor, op. 57, *Appassionata* (1804–5); No. 24, in F-sharp major, op. 78 (1809); No. 25, in G major, op. 79 (1809); No. 26, in E-flat major, op. 81a, "Das Lebewohl, Abwesenheit und Wiedersehn"; also known by its French subtitle, "Les Adieux, l'absence, et le retour" (1809); No. 27, in E minor, op. 90 (1814); No. 28, in A major, op. 101 (1816); No. 29, in B-flat major, op. 106, *Hammerklavier* (1817–18); No. 30, in E major, op. 109 (1820); No. 31, in A-flat major, op. 110 (1821); No. 32, in C minor, op. 111 (1821–22).

VARIATIONS FOR PIANO: 9 Variations in C minor on a March by Dressler (1782); 24 Variations in D major on Righini's Arietta "Venni amore" (1790–91); 13 Variations in A major on the Arietta "Es war einmal ein alter Mann" from Dittersdorf's *Das rote Käppchen* (1792); 6 Variations in F major on a Swiss Song (1792?; also for Harp); 12 Variations on the "Menuet à la Viganò" from Haibel's *Le nozze disturbate* in C major (1795); 9 Variations in A major on the Aria "Quant' e più bello" from Paisiello's *La molinara* (1795); 6 Variations in G major on the Duet "Nel cor più non mi sento" from Paisiello's *La molinara* (1795); 8 Variations in C major on the Romance "Une Fièvre brûlante" from Grétry's *Richard Cœur de Lion* (1795?); 12 Variations in A major on a Russian Dance from Wranitzky's *Das Waldmädchen* (1796–97); 10 Variations in B-flat major on the Duet "La stessa, la stessissima" from Salieri's *Falstaff* (1799); 7 Variations in F major on the Quartet "Kind, willst du ruhig schlafen" from Winter's *Das unterbrochene Opferfest* (1799); 6 Variations in F major on the Trio "Tändeln und Scherzen" from Süssmayr's *Soliman II* (1799); 6 Variations in G major on an Original Theme (1800); 6 Variations in F major on an Original Theme, op. 34 (1802); 15 Variations and a Fugue in E-flat major on an Original Theme, op. 35, *Eroica* (1802); 7 Variations in C major on "God Save the King" (1803); 5 Variations in D major on "Rule Britannia" (1803); 32 Variations in C minor on an Original Theme (1806); 6 Variations in D major on an Original Theme, op. 76 (1809); 33 Variations in C major on a Waltz by Diabelli, op. 120 (1819; 1823).

OTHER WORKS FOR PIANO: Rondo in C major (1783); Rondo in A major (1783); 2 Preludes through All 12 Major Keys, op. 39 (1789; also for Organ); *Allemande* in A major (1793); *Rondo a capriccio* in G major, op. 129, "Rage over a Lost Penny" (1795); Fugue in C major, Hess 64 (1795); *Presto* in C minor (1795?); *Allegretto* in C minor (1796–97); *Allegretto* in C minor, Hess 69 (1796–97); Rondo in C major, op. 51, No. 1 (1796?–97?); Rondo in G major, op. 51, No. 2 (1798?); 7 Bagatelles: E-flat major, C major, F major, A major, C major, D major, and A-flat major, op. 33 (1801–2); Bagatelle "Lustig-Traurig" in C major, WoO 54 (1802); *Allegretto* in C major (1803); Andante in F major, "Andante favori" (1803); Prelude in F minor (1804); Minuet in E-flat major (1804); Fantasia in G minor/B-flat major, op. 77 (1809); Bagatelle "Für Elise" in A minor (1810); Polonaise in C major, op. 89 (1814); Bagatelle in B-flat major (1818); Concert Finale in C major, Hess 65 (1820–21); Allegretto in B minor (1821); 11 Bagatelles: G minor, C major, D major, A major, C minor, G major, C major,

C major, A minor, A major, and B-flat major, op. 119 (1820–22); 6 Bagatelles: G major, G minor, E-flat major, B minor, G major, and E-flat major, op. 126 (1823–24); Waltz in E-flat major (1824); *Allegretto quasi andante* in G minor (1825); Waltz in D major (1825); Écossaise in E-flat major (1825).—For Piano, 4-hands: 8 Variations in C major on a Theme by Count Waldstein (1792); Sonata in D major, op. 6 (1796–97); 6 Variations in D major on "Ich denke dein" (by Beethoven) (1799–1803); 3 Marches: C major, E-flat major, and D major, op. 45 (1803?); an arrangement of the *Grosse Fuge*, op. 133, as op. 134 (1826).

VOCAL: Operas: *Fidelio*, op. 72 (1st version, 1804–5; Theater an der Wien, Vienna, Nov. 20, 1805; 2nd version, 1805–6; Theater an der Wien, March 29, 1806; final version, 1814; Kärnthnertortheater, Vienna, May 23, 1814); also a fragment from the unfinished opera *Vestas Feuer* (The Vestal Flame), Hess 115 (1803); singspiels: "Germania," the finale of the pasticcio *Die gute Nachricht* (1814; Kärnthnertortheater, April 11, 1814), and "Es ist vollbracht," the finale of the pasticcio *Die Ehrenpforten* (1815; Kärnthnertortheater, July 15, 1815).—Choral works with Orch.: *Cantate auf den Tod Kaiser Joseph des Zweiten* (Cantata on the Death of the Emperor Joseph II; 1790); *Cantate auf die Erhebung Leopold des Zweiten zur Kaiserwürde* (Cantata on the Accession of Emperor Leopold II; 1790); oratorio, *Christus am Oelberge* (Christ on the Mount of Olives), op. 85 (1803; Vienna, April 5, 1803; rev. 1804 and 1811); Mass in C major, op. 86 (1807; Eisenstadt, Sept. 13, 1807; *Chor auf die verbündeten Fürsten "Ihr weisen Gründer"* (1814); cantata, *Der glorreiche Augenblick* (The Glorious Moment), op. 136 (1814; Vienna, Nov. 29, 1814); *Meeresstille und glückliche Fahrt* (Calm Seas and Prosperous Voyage), op. 112, after Goethe (1814–15; Vienna, Dec. 25, 1815; Mass in D major, op. 123, *Missa Solemnis* (1819–23; St. Petersburg, April 7, 1824); Opferlied, "Die Flamme lodert" (1822; 2nd version, op. 121b, 1823–24); Bundeslied, "In allen guten Stunden," op. 122, after Goethe (1823–24).—Additional choral works: Abschiedsgesang, "Die Stunde schlägt" (1814); Cantata campestre, "Un lieto brindisi" (1814); Gesang der Mönche, "Rasch tritt der Tod," from Schiller's *Wilhelm Tell* (1817); Hochzeitslied, "Auf Freunde, singt dem Gott der Ehen" (2 versions; 1819); Birthday Cantata for Prince Lobkowitz, "Es lebe unser theurer Fürst" (1823).—Works for Solo Voices and Orch.: Prüfung des Küssens "Meine weise Mutter spricht" for Bass (1790–92); "Mit Mädeln sich vertragen" from Goethe's *Claudine von Villa Bella* for Bass (1790?–92); *Primo amore*, scena and aria for Soprano (1790–92); 2 arias: "O welch' ein Leben" for Tenor and "Soll ein Schuh nicht drücken" for Soprano, for Umlauf's singspiel *Die schöne Schusterin* (1795–96); *Ah, perfido!*, scena and aria for Soprano from Metastasio's *Achille in Sciro*, op. 65 (1795–96); *No, non turbarti*, scena and aria for Soprano from Metastasio's *La tempesta* (1801–2); "Ne' giorni tuoi felici," duet for Soprano and Tenor from Metastasio's *Olimpiade* (1802–3); *Tremate, empi, tremate* for Soprano, Tenor, and Bass, op. 116 (1801–2; 1814); *Elegischer Gesang*: "Sanft wie du lebtest" for Soprano, Alto, Tenor, Bass, and String Quartet or Piano, op. 118 (1814).—Songs: More than 80, including the following: *O care selve* (1794); *Opferlied* (1794; rev. 1801–2); *Adelaide*, op. 46 (1794–95); 6 Songs, op. 48, after Gellert (1802); 8 Songs, op. 52 (1790–96); *An die Hoffnung*, op. 32 (1805); 6 Songs, op. 75 (1809); 4 Ariettas and a Duet for Soprano and Tenor, op. 82 (1809); 3 Songs, op. 83, after Goethe (1810); *Merkenstein*, op. 100 (1814–15); *An die Hoffnung*, op. 94 (1815); 6 Songs: *An die ferne Geliebte*, op. 98 (1815–16); *Der Mann von Wort*, op. 99 (1816); *Der Kuss*, op. 128 (1822); arrangements of English, Scottish, Irish, Welsh, Italian, and other folk songs for voice, piano, violin, and cello; numerous canons; etc.

BIBL.: COLLECTED EDITIONS, SOURCE MATERIAL: *L. v.B.'s Werke: Vollständige kritisch durchgesehene überall berechtigte Ausgabe*, the 1st major ed. of his works, was publ. by Breitkopf & Härtel (series 1–24, Leipzig, 1862–65; 25 [supplement], Leipzig, 1888). An extensive supplement was ed. by W. Hess, *L. v.B.: Sämtliche Werke: Supplemente zur Gesamtausgabe* (14

vols., Wiesbaden, 1959–71). A new critical ed., *L. v.B.: Werke; neue Ausgabe sämtlicher Werke* (Munich and Duisburg, 1961–), is being publ. by the Beethoven-Archiv of Bonn.

The standard thematic and bibliographic index of all of Beethoven's completed publ. works is to be found in G. Kinsky and H. Halm, *Das Werk B.s. Thematisch-Bibliographisches Verzeichnis seiner sämtlichen vollendeten Kompositionen* (Munich and Duisburg, 1955). An important supplement to this source is K. Dorfmüller, ed., *Beiträge zur B.-Bibliographie: Studien und Materialien zum Werkverzeichnis von Kinsky-Halm* (Munich, 1978). See also W. Hess, ed., *Verzeichnis der nicht in der Gesamtausgabe veröffentlichten Werke L. v.B.s* (Wiesbaden, 1957), which lists missing works in the old Leipzig edition.

Other sources include the following: The 1st valuable thematic catalogue, *Thematisches Verzeichniss sämmtlicher im Druck erschienen Werke von L. v.B.*, was publ. by Breitkopf & Härtel (Leipzig, 1851); it was thoroughly revised and enl. by G. Nottebohm and publ. as *Thematisches Verzeichniss der im Druck erschienenen Werke von L. v.B.* (Leipzig, 1868; new ed., together with *Bibliotheca Beethoveniana*, by E. Kastner, Leipzig, 1913; 2nd ed. by T. von Frimmel, Leipzig, 1925); A. Thayer, *Chronologisches Verzeichniss der Werke L. v.B.'s* (Berlin, 1865); G. Adler, *Verzeichniss der musikalischen Autographe von L. v.B. . . . im Besitze von A. Artaria in Wien* (Vienna, 1890); A. Artaria, *Verzeichnis von musikalischen Autographen . . . vornehmlich der reichen Bestände aus dem Nachlasse . . . L. v.B.'s . . .* (Vienna, 1893); A. Kalischer, "Die B.-Autographe der Königlichen Bibliothek zu Berlin," *Monatshefte für Musikgeschichte*, XXVII (1895) and XXVIII (1896); W. Haas, *Systematische Ordnung B.scher Melodien* (Leipzig, 1932); J. Schmidt-Görg, *Katalog der Handschriften des B.-Hauses und B.-Archivs Bonn* (Bonn, 1935); A. Tyson, *The Authentic English Editions of B.* (London, 1963); G. Biamonti, *Catalogo cronologico e tematico delle opere di B., comprese quelle inedite e gli abbozzi non utilizzati* (Turin, 1968); P. Willets, *B. and England: An Account of Sources in the British Museum* (London, 1970); D. MacArdle, *B. Abstracts* (Detroit, 1973); H. Goldschmidt, ed., *Zu B.: Aufsätze und Dokumente* (Berlin, 1984).

SKETCHES AND AUTOGRAPHS: G. Nottebohm, *Ein Skizzenbuch von B.* (Leipzig, 1865) and *Ein Skizzenbuch von B. aus dem Jahre 1803* (Leipzig, 1880). P. Mies republ. 2 of Nottebohm's eds. as *Zwei Skizzenbücher von B. aus den Jahren 1801 bis 1803* (Leipzig, 1924; Eng. tr. as *Two B. Sketchbooks*, London, 1979). W. Engelmann, ed., *B.s eigenhändiges Skizzenbuch zur 9. Symphonie* (facsimile; Leipzig, 1913); H. Mersmann, *B.s Skizzen* (Basel, 1924); P. Mies, *Die Bedeutung der Skizzen B.s zur Erkenntnis seines Stiles* (Leipzig, 1925; Eng. tr. as *B.'s Sketches* by D. Mackinnon, London, 1929); K. Mikulicz, *Ein Notierungsbuch von B. aus dem Besitze der Preussischen Staatsbibliothek zu Berlin* (transcription of the sketchbook of 1800–1801; Leipzig, 1927); J. Schmidt-Görg, *B.: Drei Skizzenbücher zur Missa Solemnis* (facsimile and transcription; Bonn, vol. I, *Ein Skizzenbuch aus den Jahren 1819/20* [1952]; vol. II, *Ein Skizzenbuch zum Credo* [1970]; and vol. III, *Ein Skizzenbuch zum Benedictus* [1970]); P. Mies, *Textkritische Untersuchungen bei B.* (Bonn, 1957); D. Weise, *B.: Ein Skizzenbuch zur Chorfantasie op. 80 und zu anderen Werken* (transcription; Bonn, 1957); H. Unverricht, *Die Eigenschriften und die Originalausgaben von Werken B.s in ihrer Bedeutung für die moderne Textkritik* (Kassel, 1960); D. Weise, *B.: Ein Skizzenbuch zur Pastoralsymphonie op. 68 und zu den Trios op. 70, 1 und 2* (transcription; Bonn, 1961); J. Schmidt-Görg, *B.: Ein Skizzenbuch zu den Diabelli-Variationen und zur Missa Solemnis, SV 154* (facsimile and transcription; 2 vols., Bonn, 1968 and 1972); H. Schmidt, "Verzeichnis der Skizzen B.s," *B.-Jahrbuch, 1965–68* (Bonn, 1969); J. Kerman, "B.'s Early Sketches," *Musical Quarterly* (Oct. 1970); idem, *L. v. B.: Autograph Miscellany from circa 1786 to 1799* (facsimile and transcription; London, 1970); L. Lockwood, "On B.'s Sketches and Autographs: Some Problems of Definition and Interpretation," *Acta Musicologica*, 42 (1970); A. Tyson and D. Johnson, "Reconstructing B.'s Sketchbooks," *Journal of the American Musicological Society*, 25 (1972); R. Wade, "B.'s Eroica Sketchbook," *Fontes Artis*

Musicae, XXIV (1977); D. Johnson, "B. Scholars and B.'s Sketches," *19th Century Music*, 2 (1978–79); B. Cooper, "Newly Identified Sketches for B.'s Tenth Symphony," *Music & Letters* (March 1985); D. Johnson, A. Tyson, and R. Winter, eds., *The B. Sketchbooks* (Berkeley, 1985); B. Cooper, "The Ink in B.'s 'Kafka' Sketch Miscellany," *Music & Letters* (Oct. 1987).

CONVERSATION BOOKS: G. Schünemann, ed., *L. v.B.s Konversationshefte* (not complete; 3 vols., Berlin, 1941–43); J.-G. Prod'homme, ed. and translator, *Les Cahiers de conversation, 1819–1827* (excerpts; Paris, 1946); D. MacArdle, *An Index to B.'s Conversation Books* (Detroit, 1962); K.-H. Köhler et al., eds., *L. v.B.s Konversationshefte* (a complete ed., with annotations; 6 vols. to date: Leipzig, vol. 1, 1972; vol. 2, 1976; vol. 4, 1968; vol. 5, 1970; vol. 6, 1974; vol. 7, 1978); D. Beck and G. Herre, "Einige Zweifel an der Überlieferung der Konversationshefte," *Internationaler B.-Kongress: Berlin 1977*; P. Stadlen, "Schindler's B. Forgeries," *Musical Times* (July 1977); D. Beck and G. Herre, "Anton Schindlers fingierte Eintragungen in den Konversationsheften," in H. Goldschmidt, ed., *Zu B.: Aufsätze und Annotationen* (Berlin, 1979).

CORRESPONDENCE, NOTEBOOKS, AND OTHER DOCUMENTS: L. Nohl, *Briefe B.s* (Stuttgart, 1865); idem, *Neue Briefe B.s* (Stuttgart, 1867); idem, *B.'s Brevier* (Leipzig, 1870; 2nd ed., 1901); idem, *Die B.-Feier und die Kunst der Gegenwart* (Vienna, 1871); A. Kalischer, ed., *B.s sämtliche Briefe* (5 vols., Berlin and Leipzig, 1906–8; partial Eng. tr. by J. Shedlock, 2 vols., London and N.Y., 1909; T. von Frimmel prepared a 2nd ed. of the German original, Berlin, 1908–11); F. Prelinger, ed., *L. v.B.s sämtliche Briefe und Aufzeichnungen* (5 vols., Vienna and Leipzig, 1907–11); E. Kastner, ed., *L. v.B.s sämtliche Briefe* (the standard German ed.; Leipzig, 1910; 2nd ed. prepared by J. Kapp, Leipzig, 1923); A. Leitzmann, ed., *B.s Persönlichkeit* (2 vols., Leipzig, 1914; 2nd ed. as *L. v.B., Berichte der Zeitgenossen*, 2 vols., Leipzig, 1921); M. Unger, *L. v.B. und seine Verleger, S. A. Steiner und Tobias Haslinger in Wien, Ad. Mart. Schlesinger in Berlin, ihr Verkehr und Briefwechsel* (Berlin and Vienna, 1921); idem, *B.s Handschrift* (Bonn, 1926); O. Sonneck, *B. Letters in America* (N.Y., 1927); G. Kinsky, *Die Handschriften zu B.s Egmont-Musik* (Vienna, 1933); A. Klarer, ed., *Briefe B.s und das Heiligenstädter Testament* (Zürich, 1944); H. Freiberger, *L. v.B., Ein Bekenntnis, mit Briefen und Zeitdokumenten* (Berlin, 1951); H. Müller von Asow, *Heiligenstädter Testament (Faksimile)* (Hamburg, 1952; several later eds.); E. Anderson, "The Text of B.'s Letters," *Music & Letters* (July 1953); D. Weise, ed., *B.: Entwurf einer Denkschrift an das Appellationsgericht in Wien vom 18. Februar 1820* (Bonn, 1953); D. MacArdle and L. Misch, eds. and translators, *New B. Letters* (annotated; Norman, Okla., 1957); J. Schmidt-Görg, *B. Dreizehn unbekannte Briefe an Josephine Gräfin Deym geb. v. Brunsvik* (facsimile; Bonn, 1957); E. Anderson, ed. and translator, *The Letters of B.* (the finest modern edition; 3 vols., London, 1961); D. von Busch-Weise, ed., "B.s Jugendtagebuch," *Studien zur Musikwissenschaft*, 25 (Graz, 1962); J. Schmidt-Görg, "Wasserzeichen in B.-Briefen," *B.-Jahrbuch* (Bonn, 1966); M. Braubach, ed., *Die Stammbücher B.s und der Babette Koch. Faksimile* (Bonn, 1970); K.-H. Köhler and G. Herre, eds., *L. v.B.: Neun ausgewählte Briefe an Anton Schindler* (facsimile and transcription; Leipzig, 1971); H. Goldschmidt, "B. in neuen Brunsvik-Briefen," *B.-Jahrbuch* (Bonn, 1977); S. Brandenburg, M. Staehelin et al., eds., *L. v.B.: Der Briefwechsel mit dem Verlag Schott* (Munich, 1985).

YEARBOOKS, HANDBOOKS, STUDIES: G. Nottebohm, *B.'s Studien* (Leipzig and Winterthur, 1873); T. von Frimmel, *Neue Beethoveniana* (Vienna, 1888; 2nd ed., 1890); idem, *B.-Studien* (2 vols., Munich and Leipzig, 1905–6); T. von Frimmel, ed., *B.-Jahrbuch* (2 vols., Munich and Leipzig, 1908–9); idem, *B.-Forschung, Lose Blätter* (10 issues, Vienna and Mödling, 1911–25); L. Schiedermair, ed., *Veröffentlichungen des B.-Hauses in Bonn* (10 vols., Bonn, 1920–34); A. Sandberger, ed., *Neues B.-Jahrbuch* (10 vols., Augsburg and Braunschweig, 1924–42); T. von Frimmel, *B.-Handbuch* (2 vols., Leipzig, 1926); P. Mies and J. Schmidt-Görg, eds., *B.-Jahrbuch* (this important series

began publication with the 1953–54 yearbook; Bonn, 1954–); P. Nettl, *B. Encyclopedia* (N.Y., 1956; 2nd ed. as *B. Handbook*, N.Y., 1967); L. Misch, *Neue B.-Studien* (Bonn, 1967); E. Schenk, ed., *B.-Studien* (Vienna, 1970); A. Tyson, ed., *B. Studies* (N.Y., 1973, and London, 1974); A. Tyson, ed., *B. Studies 2* (London, 1977); H. Goldschmidt, ed., *Zu B.: Aufsätze und Annotationen* (Berlin, 1979); R. Winter and B. Carr, *B., Performers, and Critics* (Detroit, 1980); A. Tyson, ed., *B. Studies 3* (London, 1982).

BIOGRAPHICAL: J. Schlosser, *L. v.B.* (Prague, 1828); F. Wegeler and F. Ries, *Biographische Notizen über L. v.B.* (Koblenz, 1838; Nachtrag by Wegeler, Koblenz, 1845; new ed. by A. Kalischer, Berlin and Leipzig, 1906); A. Schindler, *Biographie von L. v.B.* (Münster, 1840; new ed. by A. Kalischer, Berlin, 1909; Eng. tr. by I. Moscheles as *The Life of B.*, London, 1841, and Boston, n.d. [1841]. The 1860 German ed., publ. in Münster, was tr. and edited by D. MacArdle under the title *B. As I Knew Him*, London and Chapel Hill, N.C., 1966); W. von Lenz, *B.: Eine Kunststudie* (2 vols., Kassel, 1855; 2nd ed., Hamburg, 1860; new ed. by A. Kalischer, Berlin and Leipzig, 1908); A. Oulibicheff, *B., Ses critiques et ses glossateurs* (Leipzig and Paris, 1857); A. Marx, *L. v.B. Leben und Schaffen* (2 vols., Berlin, 1859; many subsequent eds.); A. Thayer, *L. v.B.s Leben* (still the standard and most extensive biography; publ. in a German tr. from the Eng. MS by H. Deiters, 3 vols., Berlin, 1866, 1872, and 1877. After the author's death, Deiters completed vols. IV and V from Thayer's material, but also died before their publication. He had also rev. and enl. vol. I, Leipzig, 1901. Deiters's MS was rev. and ed. by H. Riemann, vol. IV, Leipzig, 1907; vol. V, Leipzig, 1908. Vols. II and III were then rev. and enl. by Riemann and publ. in Leipzig, 1910–11. He completed his task by reediting vol. I, Leipzig, 1917. Thayer's original Eng. MS. was completed by H. Krehbiel and publ. as *The Life of L. v.B.*, 3 vols., N.Y., 1921. It was in turn rev. by E. Forbes and publ. as *Thayer's Life of B.*, 2 vols., Princeton, N.J., 1964; rev. ed., 1967); L. Nohl, *B.s Leben* (a major work based upon original sources; publ. in various eds. and formats, Vienna and Leipzig, 1864–77; new ed. by P. Sakolowski, 3 vols., Berlin, 1909–13, omits valuable material); G. von Breuning, *Aus dem Schwarzspanierhause . . .* (Vienna, 1874; rev. ed. by A. Kalischer, Berlin and Leipzig, 1907); L. Nohl, *Eine stille Liebe zu B.* (Leipzig, 1875; Eng. tr. as *An Unrequited Love*, London, 1876; 2nd German ed., Leipzig, 1902); idem, *B.: Nach den Schilderungen seiner Zeitgenossen* (Stuttgart, 1877; Eng. tr. as *B. as Depicted by His Contemporaries*, London, 1880); V. Wilder, *B., Sa vie et son œuvre* (Paris, 1883); W. von Wasielewski, *L. v.B.* (2 vols., Berlin, 1888; 2nd ed., 1895); T. von Frimmel, "B.," in Riemann's *Berühmte Meister* (Berlin, 1901; 6th ed., 1922); R. Rolland, *B.* (Paris, 1903); G. Fischer, *B., A Character Study* (N.Y., 1905); F. Kerst, *B. im eigenen Wort* (Berlin and Leipzig, 1904; Eng. tr. by H. Krehbiel as *B., The Man and the Artist, as Revealed in His Own Words*, N.Y., 1905); E. Walker, *B.* (London, 1905; 3rd ed., 1920); A. Kalischer, *B. und seine Zeitgenossen* (4 vols., Leipzig, n.d. [1908–10]); A. de Hevesy, *Petites amies de B.* (Paris, 1910); P. Bekker, *B.* (Berlin and Leipzig, 1911; Eng. tr. and adaptation by M. Bosman, London, 1925; new German ed., 1927); M. Belpaire, *B., Een kunsten levensbeeld* (Antwerp, 1911); V. d'Indy, *B.: Biographie critique* (Paris, 1911; Eng. tr. by T. Baker, Boston, 1913; 2nd French ed., 1927); F. Kerst, ed., *Die Erinnerungen an B.* (2 vols., Stuttgart, 1913; 2nd ed., 1925); W. Thomas-San-Galli, *L. v.B.* (Berlin, 1913; many subsequent eds.); A. Hensel, *B. Der Versuch einer musikphilosophischen Darstellung* (Berlin, 1918); La Mara, *B. und die Brunsviks* (Leipzig, 1920); G. Bilancioni, *La sordità di B.* (Rome, 1921); J.-G. Prod'homme, *La Jeunesse de B. . . .* (Paris, 1921; new ed., 1927); W. Schweisheimer, *B.s Leiden: Ihr Einfluss auf sein Leben und Schaffen* (Munich, 1922); T. von Frimmel, *B. im zeitgenössischen Bildnis* (Vienna, 1923); A. Albertini, *B., L'Uomo* (Turin, 1924; 4th ed., Milan, 1944); W. Krug, *B.s Vollendung* (Munich, 1924); M. Reinitz, *B. im Kampf mit dem Schicksal* (Vienna, 1924); S. Ley, *B.s Leben in authentischen Bildern und Texten* (Berlin, 1925; 2nd ed., 1970); L. Schiedermair, *Der junge B.* (Leipzig, 1925; 3rd ed., Wilhelmshaven, 1970); K. Kobald, *B.: Seine Beziehungen zu Wiens Kunst und Kultur, Gesellschaft und Landschaft* (Vienna, 1926; latest ed., 1953); O. Sonneck, ed., *B.: Impressions of Contemporaries* (N.Y., 1926); G. Adler, *B.s Charakter* (Regensburg, 1927); B. Bartels, *B.* (Hildesheim, 1927); L. Bertrán, *Anecdotario completo de B.* (Buenos Aires, 1927); A. de Hevesy, *B.: Vie intime* (Paris, 1926; Eng. tr. as *B. the Man*, London, 1927); S. Ley, *B. als Freund der Familie Wegeler-von Breuning* (Bonn, 1927); E. Newman, *The Unconscious B.: An Essay in Musical Psychology* (N.Y. and London, 1927; 2nd ed., 1969); A. Orel, *B.* (Vienna, 1927); J.-G. Prod'homme, *B. raconté par ceux qui l'ont vu* (Paris, 1927); idem, "B.'s Intellectual Education," *Musical Quarterly* (April 1927); A. Schmitz, *Das romantische B.bild* (Berlin and Bonn, 1927); W. Turner, *B., The Search for Reality* (London, 1927; 2nd ed., 1933); R. van Aerde, *Les Ancêtres flamands de B.* (Malines, 1927); E. Closson, *L'Élément flamand dans B.* (Brussels, 1928; Eng. tr., London, 1934; 2nd Brussels ed., 1946); R. Rolland, *B.: Les Grandes Époques créatrices* (5 vols. in 7; Paris, 1928–57; in 1 vol. as Édition définitive, Paris, 1966; Eng. tr. of 1st 2 vols. by E. Newman as *B. the Creator*, N.Y., 1929, and *Goethe and B.*, N.Y., 1931); R. Schauffler, *B., the Man Who Freed Music* (N.Y. and London, 1929); E. Herriot, *La Vie de B.* (Paris, 1929; Eng. tr. as *The Life of B.*, N.Y., 1935); A. Boschot, *B., La Musique et la vie* (Paris, 1931); R. Specht, *Bildnis B.s* (Hellerau, 1931; Eng. tr., London, 1933); E. Brümmer, *B., Im Spiegel der zeitgenössischen rheinischen Presse* (Würzburg, 1932); J. Heer, *Der Graf von Waldstein und sein Verhältnis zu B.* (Leipzig, 1933); E. Bücken, *L. v.B.* (Potsdam, 1934); F. Howes, *B.* (London, 1933); M. Scott, *B.* (London, 1934; rev. ed. by J. Westrup, 1974); C. Carpenter, *French Factors in B.'s Life* (N.Y., 1935); F. von Reinhöl, "Neues zu B.s Lehrjahr bei Haydn," *Neues B.-Jahrbuch* (1935); E. Buenzod, *Pouvoirs de B.* (Paris, 1936); W. Riezler, *B.* (Berlin and Zürich, 1936; 9th ed., 1966; Eng. tr., London, 1938); H. Schultz, *L. v.B., Sein Leben in Bildern* (Leipzig, 1936); H. Kesser, *B. der Europäer* (Zürich, 1937); A. Schmitz, ed., *B. und die Gegenwart: . . . Ludwig Schiedermair zum 60. Geburtstag* (Berlin and Bonn, 1937); H. von Hofmannsthal, *B.* (Vienna, 1938); R. Petzoldt, *L. v.B., Leben und Werk* (Leipzig, 1938); R. van Aerde, "À la recherche des ascendants de B.," *Revue Belge Archéologique*, 2 (1939); C. Brandt, *B., Su vida, su obra, y el sentido de su música* (Caracas, 1940); A. Orel, *Grillparzer und B.* (Vienna, 1941); H. Volkmann, *B. in seinen Beziehungen zu Dresden* (Dresden, 1942); J. Burk, *The Life and Works of B.* (N.Y., 1943); E. Corti, *B.-Anekdoten* (Berlin, 1943); W. Schweisheimer, "B.'s Physicians," *Musical Quarterly* (July 1945); S. Ley, *Aus B.s Erdentagen* (Bonn, 1948); A. Pryce-Jones, *B.* (London, 1948); D. MacArdle, "The Family v.B.," *Musical Quarterly* (Oct. 1949); R. Petzoldt, *L. v.B.: Sein Leben in Bildern* (Leipzig, 1952; 7th ed., 1968); B. Bartels, *B. und Bonn* (Dinkelsbühl, 1954); S. Ley, *B.: Sein Leben in Selbstzeugnissen, Briefen und Berichten* (Vienna, 1954; 2nd ed., 1970); E. and R. Sterba, *B. and His Nephew, A Psychoanalytical Study of Their Relationship* (N.Y., 1954); W. Forster, *B.s Krankheiten und ihre Beurteilung* (Wiesbaden, 1955); S. Ley, *Wahrheit, Zweifel und Irrtum in der Kunde von B.s Leben* (Wiesbaden, 1955); W. Hess, *B.* (Zürich, 1956; 2nd ed., 1976); D. MacArdle, "B. and George Thomson," *Music & Letters* (Jan. 1956); idem, "B. and the Bach Family," ibid. (Oct. 1957); idem, "B. and the Czernys," *Monthly Musical Record*, 88 (1958); idem, "The Brentano Family in Its Relations with B.," *Music Review*, XIX (1958); idem, "B. and Grillparzer," *Music & Letters* (Jan. 1959); R. Bory, *La Vie et l'œuvre de L. v.B.* (Paris, 1960; Eng. tr. as *L. v.B.: His Life and His Work in Pictures*, Zürich and N.Y., 1960); D. MacArdle, "B. and the Archduke Rudolph," *B.-Jahrbuch, 1959–60* (Bonn, 1962); idem, "B. and the Philharmonic Society of London," *Music Review*, XXI (1960); idem, "Anton Felix Schindler, Friend of B.," ibid., XXIV (1963); J. Schmidt-Görg, *B.: Die Geschichte seiner Familie* (Bonn, 1964); D. MacArdle, "B. and Ferdinand Ries," *Music & Letters* (Jan. 1965); idem, "B. and Schuppanzigh," *Music Review*, XXVI (1965); idem, "B. und Karl Holz," *Die Musikforschung*, XX

(1967); J. and B. Massin, *L. v.B.* (Paris, 1967); M. Solomon, "B. and Bonaparte," *Music Review*, XXIX (1968); G. Marek, *B.: Biography of a Genius* (N.Y., 1969); J. Schmidt-Görg and H. Schmidt, eds., *L. v.B.* (pictorial ed. with commentaries; Bonn, 1969; Eng. tr., N.Y., 1970); M. Cooper, *B.: The Last Decade, 1817–27* (with a medical appendix by E. Larkin; London, 1970; 2nd ed., rev., 1985); H.C. Robbins Landon, *B.: A Documentary Study* (N.Y. and London, 1970); A. Mann, "B.'s Contrapuntal Studies with Haydn," *Musical Quarterly* (Oct. 1970); M. Solomon, "B. and the Enlightenment," *Telos* (Spring 1970); J. Schmidt-Görg, ed., *Des Bonner Bäckermeisters Gottfried Fischer Aufzeichnung über B.s Jugend* (Bonn and Munich, 1971); F. Knight, *B. and the Age of Revolution* (London, 1973); R. Kramer, "Notes to B.'s Education," *Journal of the American Musicological Society*, 28 (1975); M. Solomon, "B.: The Nobility Pretense," *Musical Quarterly* (April 1975); idem, *B.* (a provocative study which offers a psychoanalytic profile of the composer; N.Y., 1977); idem, "Schubert and B.," *19th Century Music* (Nov. 1979); L. Finscher, *L. v.B.* (Darmstadt, 1983); R.M. James, *B.* (London, 1983); A. Orga, *B.* (Sydney, 1983); D. Matthews, *B.* (London, 1985); T. Volek and J. Macek, "B.'s Rehearsals at the Lobkowitz's," *Musical Times* (Feb. 1986); C. Dahlhaus, *L. v.B. und seine Zeit* (Laaber, 1987); G. Syer, "B. and William Gardiner," *Musical Times* (May 1987).

THE IMMORTAL BELOVED: La Mara, *B.s Unsterbliche Geliebte: Das Geheimnis der Gräfin Brunsvik und ihre Memoiren* (Leipzig, 1909); W. Thomas-San-Galli, *Die unsterbliche Geliebte B.s: Lösung eines vielumstrittenen Problems* (Halle, 1909); idem, *B. und die unsterbliche Geliebte: Amalie Sebald/Goethe/Therese Brunsvik und Anderes* (Munich, 1909); M. Unger, *Auf Spuren von B.s "Unsterblicher Geliebten"* (Langensalza, 1911); La Mara, *B. und die Brunsviks* (Leipzig, 1920); O. Sonneck, *The Riddle of the Immortal Beloved* (N.Y., 1927); K. Smolle, *B.s unsterbliche Geliebte* (Vienna, 1947); S. Kaznelson, *B.s ferne und unsterbliche Geliebte* (Zürich, 1954); M. Solomon, "New Light on B.'s Letter to an Unknown Woman," *Musical Quarterly* (Oct. 1972); H. Goldschmidt, *B.-Studien, 2: Um die unsterbliche Geliebte* (Leipzig, 1977); M. Solomon, "Antoine Brentano and B.," *Music & Letters* (April 1977); M.-E. Tellenbach, *B. und seine "Unsterbliche Geliebte" Josephine Brunswick* (Zürich, 1983); S. Brandenburg, *B.: Der Brief an die Unsterbliche Geliebte* (Bonn, 1986); M. Solomon, "Recherche de Josephine Deym," *B. Newsletter*, II/2 (1987); V. Beahrs, "The Immortal Beloved Riddle Reconsidered," *Musical Times* (Feb. 1988).

CRITICAL, ANALYTICAL: *GENERAL:* I. von Seyfried, ed., *L. v.B.'s Studien im Generalbass, Contrapunct, und in der Compositionslehre* (Vienna, 1832; Eng. tr. by H. Pierson, Leipzig, 1853; new German eds. by G. Nottebohm, Leipzig, 1873, and L. Köhler, Leipzig, 1880); W. von Lenz, *B. et ses trois styles* (2 vols. in 1, St. Petersburg, 1852; new ed. by M.D. Calvocoressi, Paris, 1909); H. Berlioz, *À travers chant: Études musicales, adorations, boutades, et critiques* (Paris, 1862); R. Wagner, *B.* (Leipzig, 1870; Eng. tr. by A. Parsons, N.Y., 1872; 3rd ed., 1883); G. Nottebohm, *Beethoveniana* (Leipzig and Winterthur, 1872; 2nd ed., 1925); L. Nohl, *B., Liszt, Wagner* (Vienna, 1874); E. Mandyczewski, ed., *Zweite Beethoveniana* (Leipzig, 1887; 2nd ed., 1925); T. de Wyzewa, *B. et Wagner* (Paris, 1898; 4th ed., 1914); D. Mason, *B. and His Forerunners* (N.Y., 1904; 2nd ed., 1930); H. Volkmann, *Neues über B.* (Berlin and Leipzig, 1904); F. Volbach, *B.* (Munich, 1905); R. Rolland, *B.* (tr. by B. Constance Hull, with brief analyses of the syms., sonatas, and quartets by A. Eaglefield Hull, N.Y., 1917; 6th ed., 1927); G. Becking, *Studien zu B.s Personalstil: Das Scherzothema* (Leipzig, 1921); H. Mersmann, *B., Die Synthese der Stile* (Berlin, n.d. [1922]); A. Schmitz, *B.s "zwei Prinzipe"* (Berlin and Bonn, 1923); F. Cassirer, *B. und die Gestalt: Ein Kommentar* (Stuttgart, 1925); A. Halm, *B.* (Berlin, 1926); J.W.N. Sullivan, *B.: His Spiritual Development* (London, 1927; 2nd ed., 1936); T. Veidl, *Der musikalische Humor bei B.* (Leipzig, 1929); H. Naumann, *Strukturkadenzen bei B.* (Meissen, 1931); A. Schering, *B. in neuer Deutung* (Leipzig, 1934); D. Tovey, *Essays in Musical Analysis* (7 vols., London, 1935–44); A Schering, *B. und* die Dichtung (Berlin, 1936); W. Broel, *Die Durchführungsgestaltung in B.s Sonatensätzen* (Braunschweig, 1937); A. Schering, *Zur Erkenntnis B.s; Neue Beiträge zur Deutung seiner Werke* (Würzburg, 1938); K. Storck and M. Wiemann, *Wege zu B.* (Regensburg, 1938); J. Boyer, *Le "Romantisme" de B.* (Paris, 1939); L. Schrade, *B. in France: The Growth of an Idea* (New Haven, 1942); D. Tovey, *B.* (London, 1944); K. von Fischer, *Die Beziehung von Form und Motiv in B.s Instrumentalwerken* (Strasbourg and Zürich, 1948; 2nd ed., 1977); L. Misch, *B.-Studien* (Berlin, 1950; Eng. tr. as *B. Studies*, Norman, Okla., 1953); K. Schönewolf, *B. in der Zeitenwende* (2 vols., Halle, 1953); L. Ronga, *Bach, Mozart, B.: Tre problemi critici* (Venice, 1956); S. Ley, *Aus B.s Erdentagen* (Siegburg, 1957); L. Misch, *Die Faktoren der Einheit in der Mehrsätzigkeit der Werke B.s* (Munich and Duisburg, 1958); P. Nettl, *B. und seine Zeit* (Hamburg, 1958); A. Tyson, "B.'s Heroic Phase," *Musical Times* (Feb. 1969); D. Arnold and N. Fortune, eds., *The B. Reader* (N.Y., 1971); M. Solomon, "B., Sonata, and Utopia," *Telos* (Fall 1971); T. Scherman and L. Biancolli, eds., *The B. Companion* (Garden City, N.Y., 1972); M. Solomon, "The Creative Periods of B.," *Music Review*, XXXIV (1973); H. Goldschmidt, *Die Erscheinung B.* (Leipzig, 1974); idem, *B.: Werkeinführungen* (Leipzig, 1975); I. Kolodin, *The Interior B.: A Biography of the Music* (N.Y., 1975); M. Solomon, "The Dreams of B.," *American Imago*, 32 (1975); A. Chan, *B. in the United States to 1865* (diss., Univ. of North Carolina, 1976); W. Drabkin, "Some Recent B. Research," *Musical Times* (Oct. 1981); G. Abraham, ed., "The Age of B., 1790–1830," vol. VIII of *The New Oxford History of Music* (London, 1982); J. Crabbe, *B.'s Empire of the Mind* (Newbury, 1982); D. Greene, *Temporal Processes in B.'s Music* (N.Y., 1982); W. Mellers, *B. and the Voice of God* (London, 1983); L. Lockwood and P. Benjamin, eds., *B. Essays: Studies in Honor of Elliot Forbes* (Cambridge, Mass., 1984); G. Pestelli, *The Age of Mozart and B.* (Cambridge, 1984); R. Wallace, *B.'s Critics: Aesthetic Dilemmas and Resolutions during the Composer's Lifetime* (Cambridge, 1986); M. Broyles, *B.: The Emergence and Evolution of B.'s Heroic Style* (N.Y., 1987); A. Comini, *The Changing Image of B.: A Study in Mythmaking* (N.Y., 1987); R. Kramer, "*Gradus ad Parnassum*: B., Schubert, and the Romance of Counterpoint," *19th Century Music* (Fall 1987); P. Badura-Skoda, "A tie is a tie is a tie: Reflections on B.'s pairs of tied notes," *Early Music* (Feb. 1988); C. Brown, "Perspectives on B.," *Musical Times* (Sept. 1988).

ORCH. MUSIC: G. Erlanger et al., *B.s Symphonien erläutert* (Frankfurt, 1896); G. Grove, *B.'s Nine Symphonies* (London, 1884; enl. ed. as *B. and His Nine Symphonies*, London, 1896; 3rd ed., 1898); A. Colombani, *Le nove sinfonie di B.* (Turin, 1897); J. Hartog, *L. v.B. en zijne negen symphonieën* (Amsterdam, 1904); J.-G. Prod'homme, *Les Symphonies de B.* (Paris, 1906; 5th ed., 1949); F. Weingartner, *Ratschläge für Aufführungen der Symphonien B.s* (Leipzig, 1906; 2nd ed., 1916; Eng. tr., N.Y., n.d. [1907]); M. Barroso, *La IX sinfonía de B.* (Madrid, 1912); H. Schenker, *B.s neunte Sinfonie* (Vienna and Leipzig, 1912; 2nd ed., 1969); E. Evans, Sr., *B.'s Nine Symphonies, fully described and analyzed* (2 vols., London, 1923–24); H. Schenker, *B.s Fünfte Sinfonie* (Vienna, n.d. [1925]; 2nd ed., Vienna, 1970); E. de la Guardia, *Las sinfonías de B.* (Buenos Aires, 1927); D. Berg, *B. and the Romantic Symphony* (N.Y., 1927); J. Braunstein, *B.s Leonore-Ouvertüren* (Leipzig, 1927); W. Hutschenruijter, *De symphonieën van B. geänalyseerd* (The Hague, 1928); K. Nef, *Die neun Sinfonien B.s* (Leipzig, 1928); O. Baensch, *Aufbau und Sinn des Chorfinales in B.s neunter Symphonie* (Berlin and Leipzig, 1930); H. Schenker, "B.s Dritte Sinfonie zum erstenmal in ihrem wahren Inhalt dargestellt," *Das Meisterwerk in der Musik*, 3 (Munich, 1930); J. Chantavoine, *Les Symphonies de B.* (Paris, 1932); E. Magni Dufflocq, *Le sinfonie di B.* (Milan, 1935); W. Osthoff, *L. v.B.: Klavierkonzert Nr. 3, C-moll op. 37* (Munich, 1965); A. Tyson, "The Textual Problems of B.'s Violin Concerto," *Musical Quarterly* (Oct. 1967); F. Kirby, "B.'s Pastoral Symphony as a *Sinfonia caracteristica*," *Musical Quarterly* (Oct. 1970); E. Forbes, ed., *Symphony no. 5 in C Minor: L. v.B.* (Norton Critical Score; N.Y.,

1971); P. Gossett, "B.'s Sixth Symphony: Sketches for the First Movement," *Journal of the American Musicological Society*, 27 (1974); A. Tyson, "The Problem of B.'s 'First' *Leonore* Overture," *Journal of the American Musicological Society*, 28 (1975); L. Treitler, "History, Criticism, and B.'s Ninth Symphony," *19th Century Music* (March 1980); R. Bockholdt, *L. v.B., VI Symphonie F-dur, op. 68, Pastorale* (Munich, 1981); A. Hopkins, *The Nine Symphonies of B.* (London, 1981); L. Lockwood, "B.'s Earliest Sketches for the *Eroica* Symphony," *Musical Quarterly* (Oct. 1981); B. Rivera, "Rhythmic Organization in B.'s Seventh Symphony," *19th Century Music* (Spring 1983); M. Tusa, "Die authentischen Quellen der 'Eroica,'" *Archiv für Musikwissenschaft*, XLII (1985); L. Della Croce, *L. v.B.: Le nove sinfonie e le altre opere per Orchestra* (Pordenone, 1986); M. Solomon, "B.'s Ninth Symphony: A Search for Order," *19th Century Music* (Summer 1986); C. Brown, "The Orchestra in B.'s Vienna," *Early Music* (Feb. 1988); B. Zander, "Did Karl get it wrong?: Further thoughts on B.'s tempo indications for the Ninth," *Musical America* (July 1989).

CHAMBER MUSIC: T. Helm, *B.s Streichquartette: Versuch einer technischen Analyse im Zusammenhang mit ihrem geistigen Gehalt* (Leipzig, 1885; 3rd ed., 1921); J. Matthews, *The Violin Music of B.* (London, 1902); H. Riemann, "B.s Streichquartette," *Musikführer* (Leipzig, 1901–7); idem, *B.s Streichquartette erläutert* (Berlin, 1910); S. Midgley, *Handbook to B.'s Sonatas for Violin and Pianoforte* (London, 1911); O. Rupertus, *Erläuterungen zu B.s Violinsonaten* (Cologne, 1915); H. Wedig, *B.s Streichquartett op. 18, 1 und seine erste Fassung* (Bonn, 1922); E. Albini, *B. e le sue cinque sonate per violoncello* (Turin, 1923); J. Wetzel, *B.s Violinsonaten, nebst den Romanzen und dem Konzert* (Berlin, 1924); J. de Marliave, *Les Quatuors de B.* (Paris, 1925; Eng. tr. by H. Andrews, London, 1928); M. Herwegh, *Technique d'interprétation sous forme d'essai d'analyse psychologique expérimental appliqué aux sonates pour piano et violon de B.* (Paris, 1926); W. Hadow, *B.'s Op. 18 Quartets* (London, 1926); H. Mersmann, *Die Kammermusik. Vol. II, B.* (Leipzig, 1930); W. Engelsmann, *B.s Kompositionspläne dargestellt in den Sonaten für Klavier und Violine* (Augsburg, 1931); S. Grew, "B.'s Grosse Fuge,'" *Musical Quarterly* (Oct. 1931); R. Giraldi, *Analisi formale ed estetica dei primi tempi Quartetti Op. 18* (Rome, 1933); S. Kjellstrom, *B.'s strakkvartetter, en orientering* (Stockholm, 1936); G. Abraham, *B.'s Second-Period Quartets* (London, 1942); D. Mason, *The Quartets of B.* (N.Y., 1947); D. Cooke, "The Unity of B.'s Late Quartets," *Music Review*, XXIV (1963); W. Kirkendale, "The 'Great Fugue' Op. 133: B.'s Art of Fugue,'" *Acta Musicologica*, XXXV (1963); I. Mahaim, *B.: Naissance et renaissance des derniers quatuors* (an original and informative investigation, including valuable biographical documentation on 19th-century performances of Beethoven's late quartets; 2 vols., Paris, 1964); J. Szigeti, *The Ten B. Sonatas for Piano and Violin* (Urbana, Ill., 1965); P. Radcliffe, *B.'s String Quartets* (London, 1965, and N.Y., 1968); J. Kerman, *The B. Quartets* (an important study; N.Y., 1967); H. Truscott, *B.'s Late String Quartets* (London, 1968); R. Stephan, "Zu B.s letzten Quartetten," *Die Musikforschung*, XXIII (1970); C. Wolff, ed., *The String Quartets of Haydn, Mozart, and B.: Studies of the Autograph Manuscripts* (a valuable investigation; Cambridge, Mass., 1980); M. Rostal, *B.: The Sonatas for Piano and Violin: Some Thoughts on Their Interpretation* (London, 1985); S. Brandenburg and H. Loos, eds., *Beiträge zu B.s Kammermusik: Symposon Bonn 1984* (Munich, 1987); O. Jander, "The 'Kreutzer' Sonata as Dialogue," *Early Music* (Feb. 1988).

PIANO MUSIC: E. von Elterlein, *B.s Klaviersonaten* (Leipzig, 1856; 5th ed., 1895; Eng. tr., London, 1898); A. Marx, *Anleitung zum Vortrag Beethovenscher Klavierwerke* (Berlin, 1863; 4th ed., 1912); C. Reinecke, *Die Beethovenschen Klaviersonaten* (Leipzig, 1873; many subsequent printings; Eng. tr., London, 1898); W. Nagel, *B. und seine Klaviersonaten* (2 vols., Langensalza, 1903–5; 2nd ed., 1923–24); R. Nesieht, *Das goldene Zeitalter der Klaviersonate* (Cologne, 1910); H. Schenker, ed., *Die letzten fünf Sonaten von B.: Kritische Ausgabe mit Einführung und Erläuterung* (4 vols., Vienna, 1913–21; new ed., abridged, 1971–72); H. Riemann, *L. v.B.s sämtliche Klavier-Solosonaten* (3 vols., Berlin, 1919–20); S. Leoni, *Le sonate per pianoforte di B.* (Turin, 1922); W. Behrend, *L. v.B.s klaversonater . . .* (Copenhagen, 1923; Eng. tr. as *L. v.B.'s Pianoforte Sonatas*, London, 1927); F. Volbach, *Erläuterungen zu den Klaviersonaten B.s* (3rd ed., Cologne, 1924); A. Milne, *B., The Pianoforte Sonatas* (London, 1925–28); I. Peters, *B.s Klaviermusik* (Berlin, 1925); J. Johnstone, *Notes on the Interpretation of 24 Famous Pianoforte Sonatas by B.* (London, 1927); D. Tovey, *A Companion to B.'s Pianoforte Sonatas (Bar-to-Bar Analysis)* (London, 1931); H. Westerby, *B. and His Piano Works* (London, 1931); A. Coviello, *Difficulties of B.'s Pianoforte Sonatas* (London, 1935); R. Kastner, *B.'s Pianoforte Sonatas; A Descriptive Commentary on the Sonatas in the Light of Schnabel's Interpretations* (London, 1935); H. Leichtentritt, *The Complete Pianoforte Sonatas of B.* (N.Y., 1936); J.-G. Prod'homme, *Les Sonates pour piano de B. (1782–1823)* (Paris, 1937; 2nd ed., 1950); E. Blom, *B.'s Pianoforte Sonatas Discussed* (London, 1938); E. Fischer, *L. v.B.s Klaviersonaten* (Wiesbaden, 1956; 2nd ed., 1966; Eng. tr., 1959); R. Rosenberg, *Die Klaviersonaten L. v.B.s* (Olten, 1957); J. Cockshoot, *The Fugue in B.'s Piano Music* (London, 1959); R. Réti, *Thematic Patterns in the Sonatas of B.* (London, 1965); W. Newman, *Performance Practices in B.'s Piano Music: An Introduction* (N.Y., 1971); A. Leicher-Olbrich, *Untersuchungen zu Originalausgaben Beethovenscher Klavierwerke* (Wiesbaden, 1976); G. Block, *The Genesis of B.'s Piano Concertos in C Major (Op. 15) and B-Flat Major (Op. 19): Chronology and Compositional Process* (diss., Harvard Univ., 1979); A. Münster, *Studien zu B.s Diabelli-Variationen* (Munich, 1982); B. Cooper, "B.'s Revisions to 'Für Elise,'" *Musical Times* (Oct. 1984); W. Meredith, "The Origins of B.'s op. 109," ibid. (Dec. 1985); idem, *The Sources for B.'s Piano Sonata in E Major, Opus 109* (diss., Univ. of North Carolina, 1985); G. Meyer, *Untersuchungen zur Sonatensatzform bei L. v.B.: Die Kopfsätze der Klaviersonaten Op. 79 und 110* (Munich, 1985); N. Marston, *B.'s Sketches for the Piano Sonata in E, Opus 109* (diss., Cambridge Univ., 1986); idem, "The Origins of B.'s op. 109: Further Thoughts," *Musical Times* (April 1986); B. Cooper, "B.'s Portfolio of Bagatelles," *Journal of the Royal Musical Association*, 112/2 (1987); W. Kinderman, *B.'s Diabelli Variations* (N.Y., 1987); E. McKay, *The Impact of the New Pianofortes on Classical Keyboard Style: Mozart, B. and Schubert* (West Hagley, West Midlands, 1987); J. Goldstein, *A B. Enigma: Performance Practice and the Piano Sonata, Opus 111* (N.Y., 1988); S. Rosenblum, "Two sets of unexplored metronome marks for B.'s piano sonatas," *Early Music* (Feb. 1988); R. Winter, "Performing B.'s Early Piano Concertos," ibid. (May 1988); N. Cook, "B.'s Unfinished Piano Concerto: A Case of Double Vision?," *Journal of the American Musicological Society* (Summer 1989); W. Newman, *B. on B.: Playing His Piano Music His Way* (N.Y. and London, 1989).

VOCAL AND CHORAL MUSIC: M. Bouchor, *La Messe en ré de B.* (Paris, 1886); M. Remy, *Missa solemnis* (Brussels, 1897); R. Sternfeld, *Zur Einführung in L. v.B.s Missa solemnis* (Berlin, 1900); H. de Curzon, *Les Lieder et airs détachés de B.* (Paris, 1905); W. Weber, *B.s Missa solemnis* (Leipzig, 1908); R. Hohenemser-Halensee, "B. als Bearbeiter schottischer und anderen Volksweisen," *Die Musik*, X (1910); M. Kufferath, *Fidelio de L. v.B.* (Paris, 1913); M. Chop, *L. v.B.: Missa solemnis geschichtlich und musikalisch analysiert* (Leipzig, 1921); H. Böttcher, *B.s Lieder* (Berlin, 1927); idem, *B. als Liederkomponist* (Augsburg, 1928); J. Schmidt, *Unbekannte Manuskripte zu B.s weltlichen und geistlichen Gesangmusik* (Leipzig, 1928); F. Lederer, *B.s Bearbeitung schottischer und anderer Volkslieder* (Bonn, 1934); A. Schering, *B. und die Dichtung* (Berlin, 1936); W. Hess, *B.s Oper Fidelio und ihre drei Fassungen* (Zürich, 1953); idem, *B.s Bühnenwerke* (Göttingen, 1962); M. Ruhnke, "Die Librettisten des *Fidelio*," *Opernstudien: Anna Amalie Abert zum 65. Geburtstag* (Tutzing, 1975); O. Zichenheiner, *Untersuchungen zur Credo-Fuge der Missa Solemnis von L. v.B.* (Munich, 1984); W. Hess, *Das Fidelio-Buch: B.s Oper Fidelio, ihre Geschichte und ihre drei Fassungen* (Winterthur, 1986).

MISCELLANEOUS: A. Orel, ed., *Ein Wiener B. Buch* (Vienna, 1921); *B.-Zentenarfeier internationaler musikhistorischer Kongress* (Vienna, 1927); G. Bosse, ed., *B.-Almanach der deutschen Musikbücherei* (Regensburg, 1927); J. Levien, *B. and the Royal Philharmonic Society* (London, 1927); *Musical Quarterly* (April 1927); *Music & Letters* (April 1927); *La Revue Musicale* (April 1927); A. Schmitz, ed., *B. und die Gegenwart* (Berlin and Bonn, 1937); L. Bachmann, *B. contra B.; Geschichte eines berühmten Rechtsfalles* (Munich, 1963); S. Kross and H. Schmidt, eds., *Colloquium Amicorum: Joseph Schmidt-Görg zum 70. Geburtstag* (Bonn, 1967); *Journal of the American Musicological Society* (Fall 1970); R. Klein, *Beethovenstätten in Österreich* (Vienna, 1970); H. Sittner, ed., *B.-Almanach 1970* (Vienna, 1970); *Musical Quarterly* (Oct. 1970; publ. separately as *The Creative World of B.*, ed. by P. Lang, N.Y., 1971); K. Smolle, *Wohnstätten L. v.B.s von 1792 bis zu seinem Tod* (Munich and Duisburg, 1970); H. Brockhaus and K. Niemann, eds., *Bericht über den internationalen B.-Kongress 10.–12. Dezember 1970 in Berlin* (Berlin, 1971); C. Dahlhaus et al., eds., *Bericht über den internationalen musikwissenschaftlichen Kongress Bonn 1970* (Kassel, 1971); E. Schenk, ed., *B.-Symposion Wien 1970* (Vienna, 1971); D. Kerner, *Krankheiten grosser Musiker* (Stuttgart, 1973; vol. I, pp. 89–140, attempts to prove that Beethoven was a victim of syphilis); F. Slezak, *B.s Wiener Originalverleger* (Vienna, 1987).

Beffara, Louis-François, French writer on music; b. Nonancourt, Eure, Aug. 23, 1751; d. Paris, Feb. 2, 1838. He was Commissaire de Police in Paris from 1792 to 1816; left his rare collection of books and MSS to the city of Paris. Practically all of these were burned during the Commune in 1871, but a few are preserved in the Opéra library and at the Bibliothèque Nationale. He wrote a *Dictionnaire de l'Académie royale de Musique* (7 vols.) and 7 vols. of rules and regulations of the Académie (Grand Opéra); also a *Dictionnaire alphabétique des acteurs*, etc. (3 vols.); *Tableau chronologique des représentations journalières*, etc. (from 1671); *Dictionnaire alphabétique des tragédies lyriques . . . non représentées à l'Académie*, etc. (5 vols.); and *Dramaturgie lyrique étrangère* (17 vols.).

Beglarian, Grant, American composer and pedagogue; b. Tiflis, Dec. 1, 1927. His family moved to Teheran, Persia; he emigrated to the U.S. in 1947; studied viola with Paul Doktor; then enrolled at the Univ. of Michigan, where he was a student of composition with Ross Lee Finney and musicology with Hans T. David, obtaining his doctorate in music in 1957. He was subsequently on the faculty of the Army School of Music in Munich. In 1969 he was appointed dean of the School of Performing Arts at the Univ. of Southern Calif. in Los Angeles; he left this post in 1982 to become president of the National Foundation for Advancement in the Arts in Miami. His compositions include: String Quartet (1948); Violin Sonata (1949); Symphony in 2 Movements (1950); Cello Sonata (1951); Divertimento for Orch. (1957); Sinfonia for Winds (1960); Woodwind Quintet (1966); Diversions for Viola, Cello, and Orch. (1972); Ballad for Cello (1978); Elegy for Cello (1979).

Béhague, Gerard (Henri), French-born American musicologist; b. Montpellier, Nov. 2, 1937. He studied piano and composition at the National School of Music at the Univ. of Brazil, and at the Brazilian Cons. of Music in Rio de Janeiro; subsequently took courses in musicology at the Inst. de Musicologie at the Univ. of Paris with Chailley; moving to the U.S., he continued his musicological studies with Gilbert Chase at Tulane Univ. (Ph.D., 1966). In 1974 he became a prof. of music at the Univ. of Texas in Austin. He made a specialty of American and Latin American music; in 1974 he became ed. of the periodical *Ethnomusicology*. He publ. *The Beginnings of Musical Nationalism in Brazil* (Detroit, 1971) and *Music in Latin America: An Introduction* (Englewood Cliffs, N.J., 1977); also ed. *Performance Practice: Ethnomusicological Perspectives* (Westport, Conn., 1984). He contributed a number of articles to *The New Grove Dictionary of Music and Musicians* (1980).

Beheim, Michel, German minnesinger; b. Sülzbach, near Weinsberg, Sept. 27, 1416; d. there (murdered), 1474. He was active as a soldier and singer in the service of various German, Danish, and Hungarian princes; was one of the earliest of the Meistersingers who still retained some of the characteristics of the minnesinger; finally settled in Sülzbach as village major or magistrate. He composed many songs; 11 are preserved at Heidelberg and Munich.

BIBL.: Alfred Kühn, *Rhythmik und Melodik M. B.s* (1907); C. Petzsch, "Text-Form-Korrespondenzen im mittelalterlichen Strophenlied. Zur Hofweise M. B.s," *Deutsches Vierteljahrsschrift für Literatur- und Geistesgeschichte* (1967); idem, "Frühlingsteien als Vertrags-form und seine Bedeutung im Bispel," *Deutsches Vierteljahrsschrift für Literaturwissenschaft und Geistesgeschichte* (March 1971).

Behm, Eduard, German composer; b. Stettin, April 8, 1862; d. Bad Harzburg, Feb. 6, 1946. He studied at the Leipzig Cons.; taught at the Erfurt Academy of Music; became director of the Scharwenka Cons. in Berlin (until 1901), and prof. in 1917. He was awarded the Mendelssohn prize for a Sym. and the Bösendorfer prize for a Piano Concerto. He wrote the operas *Der Schelm von Bergen* (Dresden, 1899), *Marienkind* (1902), and *Das Gelöbnis* (1914); a String Sextet, using the Stelzner Violotta; a Piano Trio; a Clarinet Quintet; 3 violin sonatas; a Violin Concerto; *Frühlingsidylle* for Violin and Orch.; male choruses, songs, etc. Behm wrote a short autobiography in *Musik in Pommern* (1932).

Behr, Franz, German composer; b. Lübtheen, Mecklenburg, July 22, 1837; d. Dresden, Feb. 15, 1898. He publ. many salon pieces for the piano, some under the pseudonyms of **Georges Bachmann, William Cooper, Charles Morley,** and **Francesco d'Orso.** His waltz *Les Sylphes* became very popular.

Behrend, (Gustav) Fritz, German composer; b. Berlin, March 3, 1889; d. there, Dec. 29, 1972. He studied composition with H. van Eycken, P. Rufer, and Humperdinck, and piano with Breithaupt (1907–11); after serving as a coach at the Braunschweig Hoftheater (1911–12), he taught at the Ochs-Eichelberg Cons. (1918–42) and the Klindworth-Scharwenka Cons. in Berlin (1942–49). His compositions did not meet with favor during the 3rd Reich, but later they achieved a modicum of recognition.

WORKS: STAGE: *König Renés Tochter* (1919); *Der schwangere Bauer* (1927); *Die lächerlichen Preziösen* (1928; Berlin, May 22, 1949); *Almansor* (1931); *Dornröschen* (1934); *Der Wunderdoktor* (1947); *Der fahrende Schüler im Paradies* (1949); *Der Spiegel* (1950); *Romantische Komödie* (1953). **ORCH.:** 7 syms.; *Rotkäppchensuite* (1912); *Lustspiel Overture* (1913); *Am Rhein* (1913); *Fantasie* for Piano and Orch. (1919); *Im Hochgebirge* (1920); *Penthesilea* (1926); *Lustspiel Overture* (1937). **CHAMBER:** 7 string quartets; 2 piano trios (1923, 1929); Violin Sonata (1925); Cello Sonata (1925); Wind Quintet (1951); also a String Trio, a Septet, an Octet, piano pieces, and over 100 songs.

Behrend, Jeanne, American pianist; b. Philadelphia, May 11, 1911; d. there, March 20, 1988. She studied piano with Josef Hofmann and composition with Rosario Scalero at the Curtis Inst. of Music in Philadelphia; subsequently devoted herself mainly to teaching. She also ed. songs of Stephen Foster and piano music of Gottschalk.

Behrend, Siegfried, German guitarist; b. Berlin, Nov. 19, 1933; d. Hausham, Sept. 20, 1990. His father, a guitar virtuoso, guided his early interest in that instrument. At the age of 16 he entered the Klindworth-Scharwenka Cons. in Berlin, where he studied piano, composition, and conducting; made his debut as a guitarist in Berlin in 1952; then toured Europe. He was particularly known for his performances of contemporary music, and commissioned many works for the guitar.

Behrend, William, Danish musicologist; b. Copenhagen, May 16, 1861; d. there, April 23, 1940. He studied law; held various government positions. At the same time he took courses in music theory; from 1917 taught music history at the Royal Danish Cons. He was one of the founders of the Wagner Soc. of Denmark. Under the influence of Niels Gade he turned to music criticism, and became critic of *Politiken*. Among his

writings are biographies of J.P.E. Hartmann (1895) and of Gade (1917). He contributed to the Danish *Illustreret Musikhistorie* (1905; vol. II, from Gluck to modern times); and to Salmonsen's *Konversationslexikon.*

Behrens, Hildegard, noted German soprano; b. Varel, Oldenburg, Feb. 9, 1937. Of an intellectual bent, she entered the Univ. of Freiburg in the faculty of jurisprudence, astoundingly graduating as a junior barrister. Making a sudden decision to exploit her natural vocal talents, she began to study voice with Ines Leuwen at the Freiburg Academy of Music. In 1971 she became a member of the Opera Studio of the Deutsche Oper am Rhein in Düsseldorf; in 1972 became a member of the Deutsche Oper; also made guest appearances with the Frankfurt Opera, Zürich Opera, Vienna State Opera, Salzburg Festival, Bavarian State Opera in Munich, and Paris Opéra. She was particularly impressive in dramatic roles in *Fidelio* and in modern operas such as Strauss's *Salome,* Berg's *Wozzeck,* and Janáček's *Kát'a Kabanová.* On Oct. 15, 1976, she made her American debut at the Metropolitan Opera, N.Y., as Giorgetta in *Il Tabarro;* in 1983 she appeared as Brünnhilde in the *Ring* cycle at Bayreuth, and in 1985 she made her N.Y. recital debut.

BIBL.: *Current Biography* (Jan. 1985).

Behrens, Jack, American composer; b. Lancaster, Pa., March 25, 1935. He studied composition at the Juilliard School of Music, N.Y., with Bergsma, Persichetti, and Mennin, graduating in 1959; then took courses at Harvard Univ. with Leon Kirchner and Roger Sessions, obtaining his Ph.D. in composition in 1973. He was subsequently on the faculty of the Univ. of Saskatchewan, Canada (1962–66), and of Calif. State College, Bakersfield (1970–76); in 1976 he was appointed chairman of the dept. of theory and composition at the Univ. of Western Ontario, London, Canada. In his music he adopts a sophisticated modern idiom without transgressing into the musically unfeasible.

WORKS: *Introspection* for Strings (1956); *Quarter-Tone Quartet* (1960); Concertino for Trombone and 8 Instruments (1961); Passacaglia for Piano (1963); *Declaration 1964* for Orch. (1964); *Pentad* for Vibraphone and Piano (1965); *The Lay of Thrym,* opera (Regina, Saskatchewan, April 13, 1968); *The Sound of Milo* for Orch. (1970); *Triple Concerto* for Clarinet, Violin, Piano, and Orch. (1971); *The Feast of Life* for Piano (1975); Fantasia on Francis Hopkinson's tune "My Days Have Been So Wondrous Free" for Orch. (Fresno, Calif., March 20, 1976).

Beiderbecke, Bix (real name, **Leon Bismarck Beiderbecke**), American jazz cornet player; b. Davenport, Iowa, March 10, 1903; d. N.Y., Aug. 6, 1931. His parents, German immigrants, were amateur musicians, and he began to play as a small child. As he grew he developed a flair for ragtime and jazz. He played cornet in various jazz groups in Chicago and St. Louis, and developed his distinctive style of rhythmic lyricism. In 1927 he joined the Paul Whiteman band. Although lacking a formal musical education, he wrote a number of beguilingly attractive piano pieces, of which one, *In a Mist,* shows a curious impressionistic coloring. Addicted to alcohol, he succumbed at the age of 28. His musical legacy was preserved in recordings, and soon a cult was formed around his name, which was greatly enhanced by the publication of Dorothy Baker's semi-fictional biography, *Young Man with a Horn* (N.Y., 1938). Two factual biographies were publ. in 1974: R. Berton, *Remembering Bix: A Memoir of the Jazz Age,* and R. Sudhalter and P. Evans, *Bix: Man and Legend.*

Beilschmidt, Curt, German composer; b. Magdeburg, March 20, 1886; d. Leipzig, March 7, 1962. He studied in Magdeburg with Fritz Kauffmann; then in Leipzig (1905–9) with Stephan Krehl (theory), Adolf Ruthardt (piano), and Hans Sitt (violin). He served in the German army in World War I; returned to Leipzig in 1923 and founded a choral-symphonic group, which he continued to lead until 1954; also taught at the Leipzig Hochschule für Musik (1946–56). His catalogue comprises

141 opus numbers, among them the dance opera *Das Abenteuer im Walde* (Leipzig, March 13, 1918); the opera buffa *Meister Innocenz, Der schlaue Amor* (Leipzig, July 6, 1921); the pastoral play *Der schlaue Amor* (Leipzig, 1921); the musical divertimento *Der Tugendwächter* (Halle, Oct. 14, 1927); and numerous works for orch. and chamber groups.

Beinum, Eduard van, eminent Dutch conductor; b. Arnhem, Sept. 3, 1900; d. Amsterdam, April 13, 1959. He studied violin with his brother, and piano with J.B. de Pauw; also took lessons in composition from Sem Dresden. He made his 1st appearance as a pianist with the Concertgebouw Orch. in Amsterdam in 1920; then devoted himself to choral conducting. In 1931 he was appointed associate conductor of the Concertgebouw Orch.; in 1945 he succeeded Mengelberg (who had been disfranchised for his collaboration with the Germans during their occupation of the Netherlands) as principal conductor of the orch. He was also a guest conductor of various European orchs.; he made his American debut with the Philadelphia Orch. on Jan. 8, 1954; in the autumn of 1954 toured the U.S. with the Concertgebouw. From 1957 until shortly before his death he was the principal guest conductor with the Los Angeles Phil. Beinum was regarded by most critics as an intellectual conductor whose chief concern was the projection of the music itself rather than the expression of his own musical personality. He was equally capable in Classical, Romantic, and modern works.
    Bibl.: W. Paap, *E. v.B. 25 Years Conductor of the Concertgebouw Orchestra* (Amsterdam, 1956).

Beissel, Johann Conrad, German-American composer of religious music; founder of the sect of Solitary Brethren of the Community of Sabbatarians; b. Eberbach on the Neckar, Palatinate, March 1, 1690; d. Ephrata, Pa., July 6, 1768. He migrated to America in 1720 for religious reasons. His 1st attempt to build up a "solitary" residence failed; but in 1732 he started the community at Ephrata, which became a flourishing religious and artistic center. Beissel, who styled himself Bruder Friedsam (Brother Peaceful), was a prolific writer of hymns in fanciful German, publ. in various collections, some printed by Benjamin Franklin, some by the community at Ephrata. He composed tunes for his hymns and harmonized them according to his own rules. His compositions were collected in beautifully illuminated MSS, many of which are preserved at the Library of Congress and the Library of the Historical Soc. of Pa. Beissel was not a trained musician, but had original ideas; his religious fanaticism inspired him to write some startling music; in several of his hymns he made use of an antiphonal type of vocal composition with excellent effect. He left a tract explaining his harmonic theory and his method of singing. Beissel's hymns are collected chiefly in *Zionistischer Weyrauchs Hügel* (1739), *Das Gesang der einsamen und verlassenen Turtel Taube, das ist der christlichen Kirche* (1747), and *Paradisisches Wunder Spiel* (2 independent publications, 1754 and 1766). Only texts were printed in these vols., but the 1754 issue was arranged so that the music could be inserted by hand. Beissel's life was 1st described in the *Chronicon Ephratense*, compiled by the brethren Lamech and Agrippa, publ. at Ephrata in a German ed. in 1786, and in an Eng. tr. by J.M. Hark at Lancaster in 1889.
    Bibl.: J.F. Sachse, *The German Sectarians of Pennsylvania* (Philadelphia, 1899–1900); idem, *The Music of the Ephrata Cloister* (Lancaster, 1903); *Church Music and Musical Life in Pennsylvania in the 18th Century* (Philadelphia, 1927); W.C. Klein, *J.C. B.: Mystic and Martinet* (Philadelphia, 1942); H.T. David, "Ephrata and Bethlehem in Pennsylvania: A Comparison," *Papers Read by Members of the American Musicological Society, 1941* (1946); T. Mann, *Doktor Faustus* (Stockholm, 1947; Eng. tr. by H.T. Lowe-Porter, N.Y., 1948); A. Briner, "Wahrheit und Dichtung um J.C. B.: Studie um eine Gestalt in Thomas Manns Dr. Faustus,'" *Schweizerische Musikzeitung* (Oct. 1958); L.G. Blakely, "J.C. B. and Music of the Ephrata Cloister," *Journal of Research in Music Education* (Summer 1967).

Bekker, (Max) Paul (Eugen), eminent German writer on music; b. Berlin, Sept. 11, 1882; d. N.Y., March 7, 1937. He studied violin with Rehfeld, piano with Sormann, and theory with Horwitz; began his career as a violinist with the Berlin Phil. He was music critic of *Berliner Neueste Nachrichten* (1906–9) and of *Berliner Allgemeine Zeitung* (1909–11); also served as chief music critic at *Frankfurter Zeitung* from 1911. Later he was Intendant of the Kassel Stadttheater (1925); then in Wiesbaden (1927). In 1933 he left Germany, being unable to cope with the inequities of the Nazi regime. He publ. biographies of Oskar Fried (1907) and Jacques Offenbach (1909); also *Das Musikdrama der Gegenwart* (1909); *Beethoven* (1911; in Eng., 1926); *Das deutsche Musikleben, Versuch einer soziologischen Musikbetrachtung* (1916); *Die Sinfonie von Beethoven bis Mahler* (1918; in Russian, 1926); *Franz Schreker* (1919); *Kunst und Revolution* (1919); *Die Weltgeltung der deutschen Musik* (1920); *Die Sinfonien G. Mahlers* (1921); *Richard Wagner* (1924; in Eng., 1931); *Von den Naturreichen des Klanges* (1924); *Musikgeschichte als Geschichte der musikalischen Formwandlungen* (1926; in French, 1929); *Das Operntheater* (1930); *Briefe an zeitgenössische Musiker* (1932); *Wandlungen der Oper* (Zürich, 1934; Eng. tr. by A. Mendel as *The Changing Opera*, N.Y., 1935); *The Story of the Orchestra* (N.Y., 1936).

Bekku, Sadao, Japanese composer; b. Tokyo, May 24, 1922. He studied theoretical physics at Tokyo Univ. (1943–50); then studied composition with Milhaud, Rivier, and Messiaen at the Paris Cons. (1951–54). Returning to Japan, he became engaged in pedagogy; was also a member of the Japanese section of the ISCM from 1955 (president, 1968–73). His works are set in neo-Classical forms; some of them make use of authentic Japanese modalities. He publ. a book, *The Occult in Music* (Tokyo, 1971).
    Works: 3 operas: *Le Dit les trois femmes* (The Story of 3 Women), opera buffa (1964; Rome, 1964); *Prince Arima* (1963–67; Tokyo, March 13, 1967); *Aoi–no–ue* (1979); *Deux prières* (2 Prayers) for Orch. (Tokyo, May 10, 1956); *Symphonietta* for String Orch. (Tokyo, Nov. 27, 1959); Sym. No. 1 (Tokyo, Jan. 18, 1962); Sym. No. 2 (1977); Violin Concerto (1969; Tokyo Radio, Nov. 13, 1969); Viola Concerto (Tokyo, March 3, 1972); Trio for Oboe, Clarinet, and Bassoon (1953); Flute Sonata (1954); 2 *Japanese Suites*: No. 1 for Wind Quintet (1955) and No. 2 for 12 Instruments and Percussion (1958); String Quartet No. 1 (1955); Piano Sonatina (1965); *Kaleidoscope*, suite for Piano (1966); Violin Sonata (1963–67); 3 *Paraphrases* for Piano (1968); Viola Sonata (1969; rearrangement of the Violin Sonata); *Sonatina in Classical Style* for Piano (1969); choruses.

Belafonte, Harry (Harold George, Jr.), American folksinger; b. N.Y., March 1, 1927, of a Jamaican mother and a Martiniquan father. As a youth he lived partly in N.Y., partly in Jamaica; worked as a janitor and a cart pusher in Manhattan. When his voice was discovered, he got singing jobs in Greenwich Village restaurants; acted the role of Joe in the film *Carmen Jones* (1954). From 1948 to 1957 he was married to the black child psychologist Frances Marguerite Byrd; his 2nd marriage was to Julie Robinson. His greatest success came as an interpreter of calypso songs, which he performed with great dramatic power. He made numerous tours abroad.

Belaiev (Belaieff), Mitrofan (Petrovich), renowned Russian music publisher; b. St. Petersburg, Feb. 22, 1836; d. there, Jan. 10, 1904. His father, a rich lumber dealer, gave him an excellent education. After his father's death in 1885, Belaiev decided to use part of the income from the business for a music publishing enterprise devoted exclusively to the publication of works by Russian composers (the printing was done in Leipzig); he also established concerts of Russian music in St. Petersburg (10 sym. concerts and 4 concerts of chamber music each season) and provided funds for prizes awarded for the best compositions. He placed Rimsky-Korsakov, Glazunov, and Liadov on the jury for these multifarious activities. The "Belaiev Editions" became a vital factor in the development of Russian national music. Although a conservative, Belaiev was generous toward representatives of the modern school, such as Scriabin; early in Scriabin's career, Belaiev provided the financial means for him to travel in Europe. The catalogue of Belaiev's publications includes the greatest names in Russian music: Mussorgsky, Rimsky-Korsakov, Borodin, Balakirev, Cui, Scriabin, Glière, Glazunov, Gretchaninov, Liadov, Liapunov, Taneyev, and Nicolas Tcherepnin, as well as many lesser and even obscure composers, such as Akimenko, Alferaky, Amani, Antipov, Artzibushev, Blumenfeld, Kalafati, Kopylov, Sokolov, Steinberg, Wihtol, Zolotarev, and others. The complete list of Belaiev's eds. is available in the *Verzeichnis der in Deutschland seit 1868 erschienenen Werke russischer Komponisten* (Leipzig, 1950).

BIBL.: M. Montague-Nathan, "B., Maecenas of Russian Music," *Musical Quarterly* (July 1918).

Belaiev, Victor, Russian writer on music; b. Uralsk, Feb. 6, 1888; d. Moscow, Feb. 16, 1968. He studied at the St. Petersburg Cons. (1908–14) with Liadov, Wihtol, and Glazunov. In 1923 he was a founder of the Soc. of Contemporary Music in Leningrad, which presented numerous works by Western modern composers. He wrote about 20 biographical brochures on contemporary composers; also ed. the correspondence between Scriabin and M.P. Belaiev (1922); wrote many valuable articles on folk music of Georgia, the Caucasus, and Central Asia.

Belcher, Supply, American hymn writer, dubbed "the Handel of Maine"; b. Stoughton, Mass., April 9, 1751; d. Farmington, Maine, June 9, 1836. He was a tavern keeper and original member (with Billings) of the Stoughton Musical Soc., the earliest American performing group that held regular meetings. He served in the Revolutionary War under George Washington; subsequently lived in Farmington, Maine. He publ., in 1794, a collection of hymns, *Harmony of Maine.*

Belcke, Friedrich August, German trombonist; b. Lucka, Altenburg, May 27, 1795; d. there, Dec. 10, 1874. He was a member of the Gewandhaus Orch. in Leipzig (1815) and a chamber musician in Berlin (1816–58); was the 1st concert virtuoso on the trombone, for which he wrote concertos and études.

Beliczay, Julius (Gyula) von, Hungarian composer; b. Komorn, Aug. 10, 1835; d. Budapest, April 30, 1893. He studied music in Pressburg with Joseph Kumlik; then moved to Vienna, where he had instruction in composition with Franz Krenn and Nottebohm; also took courses in engineering at the Vienna Technische Hochschule (1851–57). He remained in Vienna until 1871; in 1888 he was appointed prof. of music theory at the National Academy in Budapest. He wrote a Sym.; *Ave Maria* for Soprano, Chorus, and Orch.; a String Quartet; a *Serenade* for Strings; and a number of piano pieces and songs.

BIBL.: A. Jenetschek, *J. v.B.* (Carlsbad, 1889); I. Sonkoly, *Beliczay Gyula* (Budapest, 1943).

Belkin, Boris, Russian-born Israeli, later Belgian, violinist; b. Sverdlovsk, Jan. 26, 1948. He studied at the Moscow Cons. In 1972 he won 1st prize in the Soviet National Competition for violinists. In 1974 he left the Soviet Union and settled in Israel. He then played with several American orchs., including those of N.Y., Philadelphia, Boston, Cleveland, and Pittsburgh.

Bell, Donald (Munro), Canadian bass-baritone; b. South Burnaby, British Columbia, June 19, 1934. He studied at the Royal College of Music in London; made an impressive debut in a concert at Wigmore Hall in London in 1958; then sang at the Bayreuth Festivals (1958–60). In 1959 he made his American debut with the Philadelphia Orch. at Carnegie Hall in N.Y.; had guest engagements at the Glyndebourne Festival in 1963 and again in 1973–74. In 1963 he made a tour of Russia as a concert singer. He was a member of the Deutsche Oper am Rhein in Düsseldorf (1964–67).

Bell, Joshua, talented American violinist; b. Bloomington, Ind., Dec. 9, 1967. He 1st studied violin with Mimi Zweig; made his debut as a soloist with the Bloomington Sym.

Orch. in 1975 at the age of 7; subsequently studied with Josef Gingold at the Indiana Univ. School of Music; also took summer courses with Ivan Galamian and a master class with Henryk Szeryng. He won the grand prize in the 1st annual *Seventeen Magazine*/General Motors National Concerto Competition in Rochester, N.Y., which led to his appearance as a soloist with the Philadelphia Orch. under Riccardo Muti on Sept. 24, 1982; he was the youngest soloist ever to appear with it at a subscription concert. In 1985 he made his Carnegie Hall debut in N.Y. as soloist with the St. Louis Sym. Orch.

Bell, W(illiam) H(enry), English composer; b. St. Albans, Aug. 20, 1873; d. Gordon's Bay, Cape Province, South Africa, April 13, 1946. He studied at his hometown; won the Goss Scholarship for the Royal College of Music in London (1889); studied organ with Stegall, violin with Burnett, piano with Izard, and composition with Corder and Stanford. He taught harmony at his alma mater (1903–12); in 1912 was appointed director of the South African College of Music in Cape Town and then dean of the music faculty at the Univ. of South Africa (1919), retiring in 1936. He was extremely critical of himself as a composer, and destroyed many of his MSS. Among his surviving works are the operas *Hippolytus* (after Euripides; 1914) and *Isabeau* (1924). Other works include *Walt Whitman Symphony* (1899); Sym. No. 2 (1917–18); Sym. No. 3 (1918–19); *South African Symphony* (1927); Sym. in F minor (1932); *A Vision of Delight* (1906); *Arcadian Suite* (1908); symphonic poems: *Love among the Ruins* (1908), *The Shepherd* (1908), *La Fée des sources* (1912), and *Veldt Loneliness* (1921); Viola Concerto; Violin Sonata.

BIBL.: M. van Someren Godfrey, "The Symphonic Works of W.H. B.," *Musical Times* (May/June 1920); H. du Plessis, ed., *Letters from W.H. B.* (Cape Town and Johannesburg, 1973).

Bella, Johann Leopold (Ján Levoslav), Slovak composer; b. Lipto-Szentmiklós, Upper Hungary, Sept. 4, 1843; d. Bratislava, May 25, 1936. He studied theology in Banska Bystrica; then went to Vienna, where he studied composition with Sechter (1863–65). He was ordained a priest in 1866 and served as church music director at Kremnica (1869). In 1873 he received a scholarship to study in Germany and in Prague; in 1881 he relinquished his priesthood, and subsequently was organist at the Protestant church in Hermannstadt, Transylvania, and music director of the municipality there. He went to Vienna in 1921; in 1928 he returned to Bratislava. He wrote a great quantity of church music in the strict style; also composed an opera, *Wieland der Schmied* (Bratislava, April 28, 1926); a symphonic poem, *Schicksal und Ideal* (Prague, March 19, 1876); some chamber music; songs; piano pieces.

BIBL.: D. Orel, *J.L. B.* (Bratislava, 1924); J. Jindrá, "Ján Levoslav B.," *Der Auftakt*, XIV (1934); K. Hudek, *J.L. B.* (Prague, 1937); E. Zavárský, *Ján Levoslav B.: Život a dielo* (Bratislava, 1955).

Bellaigue, Camille, French music critic; b. Paris, May 24, 1858; d. there, Oct. 4, 1930. Orig. a law student, he took music courses at the Paris Cons. with Paladilhe and Marmontel; from 1885 was music critic for *La Revue des Deux Mondes;* also wrote for *Le Temps.* He bitterly opposed modern music and was particularly violent in his denunciation of Debussy, his classmate at the Paris Cons. His selected essays are publ. under the following titles: *L'Année musicale* (5 vols., 1886–91); *L'Année musicale et dramatique* (1893); *Psychologie musicale* (1894); *Portraits et silhouettes de musiciens* (1896; Eng., 1897; German, 1903); *Études musicales et nouvelles silhouettes de musiciens* (1898; Eng., 1899); *Impressions musicales et littéraires* (1900); *Études musicales* (2 vols.; 1903, 1907); *Mozart: Biographie critique* (1906); *Mendelssohn* (1907); *Les Époques de la musique* (2 vols., 1909); *Gounod* (1910); *Verdi* (1911); *Paroles et musique* (1925); etc.

BIBL.: L. Gillel, *C. B.* (Paris, 1931).

Bellamann, Henry, American author and pianist; b. Fulton, Mo., April 28, 1882; d. N.Y., June 16, 1945. He studied at the Univ. of Denver (1898–1900), and in London and Paris. He was dean of the School of Fine Arts, Chicora College for Women, Columbia, S.C. (1907–24); served as chairman of the examining board of the Juilliard School (1924–26) and of the Rockefeller Foundation (1927–28); was dean of the Curtis Inst. (1931–32). Among his writings on music are *A Music Teacher's Notebook* (1920); "Charles Ives, The Man and His Music," *Musical Quarterly* (Jan. 1933); etc. He was the author of a successful novel, *King's Row.*

Bellasio, Paolo, Italian organist and composer; b. Verona, May 20, 1554; d. Rome, July 10, 1594. He was active as an organist in Rome beginning in 1584; he later traveled to Verona, returning to Rome in 1592. He publ. 5 books of madrigals (1578) and *Villanelle alla Romana* (1595).
BIBL.: R. Casimiri, "P. B., musicista veronese 1554–1594: Nuovi documenti biografici," *Note d'Archivio per la Storia Musicale,* XIV (1937).

Bellère (or **Bellerus,** properly **Beellaerts**), **Jean,** music publisher; b. Liège, 1526; d. Antwerp, Oct. 15, 1595. He was a partner of Pierre Phalèse, *fils.* His son **Balthasar Bellère** transferred the business to Douai, and printed much music up to 1625. His catalogue of compositions, publ. from 1603 to 1605, was found by Coussemaker in the Douai library.
BIBL.: A. Goovaerts, *De muziekdrukkers Phalesius en Bellerus te Leuven* (Antwerp, 1882).

Bellermann, (Johann Gottfried) Heinrich, German music teacher and theorist, son of **Johann Friedrich Bellermann;** b. Berlin, March 10, 1832; d. Potsdam, April 10, 1903. He studied with Eduard Grell; from 1853 taught singing at Graues Kloster and in 1861 was appointed Royal Musikdirektor; in 1866 succeeded Marx as prof. of music at Berlin Univ. His book *Die Mensuralnoten und Taktzeichen des 15. und 16. Jahrhunderts* (Berlin, 1858; 4th enl. ed., Berlin, 1963) gives an excellent exposition of the theory of mensural music; his treatise *Der Kontrapunkt* (1862; 4th ed., 1901) revives the theories of J.J. Fux's *Gradus ad Parnassum.* Bellermann attempted to justify his adherence to Fux in a pamphlet, *Die Grösse der musikalischen Intervalle als Grundlage der Harmonie* (Berlin, 1873). He also contributed valuable articles to the *Allgemeine Musikalische Zeitung* (1868–74) and publ. a biography of Eduard Grell (1899).
BIBL.: O. Schneider, *H. B., Gedächtnisrede* (Berlin, 1903).

Bellermann, Johann Friedrich, German music scholar, father of **(Johann Gottfried) Heinrich Bellermann;** b. Erfurt, March 8, 1795; d. Berlin, Feb. 5, 1874. He dedicated himself mainly to the study of ancient Greek music; his chief work was *Die Tonleitern und Musiknoten der Griechen,* explanatory of the Greek system of notation (Berlin, 1847). He further wrote *Die alten Liederbücher der Portugiesen* (Berlin, 1840) and *Die Hymnen des Dionysios und Mesomedes* (Berlin, 1840), and ed. essays by authors of classical antiquity: *Anonymi scriptio de musica, Bacchii senioris introductio artis musicae* (Berlin, 1841); also ed. *Fragmentum graecae scriptionis de musica* (Berlin, 1840).
BIBL.: "F. B.; Seine Wirksamkeit auf dem Gebiet der Musik," reprint from the *Allgemeine Musikzeitung* (Leipzig, 1874, no. 9).

Belletti, Giovanni Battista, famous Italian baritone; b. Sarzana, Feb. 17, 1813; d. there, Dec. 27, 1890. He made his operatic debut in 1837 in Stockholm as Figaro in Rossini's *Il Barbiere di Siviglia;* made many appearances there with Jenny Lind; later toured with her in the U.S. He had his greatest successes in dramatic roles in Romantic operas.

Belleville-Oury, Caroline de. See **Oury, Anna Caroline.**

Bellezza, Vincenzo, Italian conductor; b. Bitonto, Bari, Feb. 17, 1888; d. Rome, Feb. 8, 1964. He studied piano with Alessandro Longo, composition with Nicola d'Arienzo, and conducting with Giuseppe Martucci at the Naples Cons. He made his conducting debut at the San Carlo Opera in Naples in 1908; then conducted throughout Italy; also had guest engagements at Covent Garden, London, from 1926 to 1930 and again in 1935–36; served as guest conductor at the Metropolitan Opera in N.Y. (1926–35). After his return to Italy he was on the staff of the Rome Opera House.

Bell'Haver, Vincenzo, Italian organist; b. Venice, c.1530; d. there, probably in Sept. 1587. He was a pupil of Andrea Gabrieli, and upon the latter's death, succeeded him as 1st organist of S. Marco on Oct. 30, 1586; he himself died a year later, and his position was taken over by Gioseffo Guami. Bell'Haver publ. several books of madrigals (1567–75), of which only Book II, containing works for 5 voices, is extant; single works survive in various collections.

Belli, Domenico, Italian composer; b. c.1590; d. (buried) May 5, 1627. He lived most of his life in Florence. On Sept. 19, 1619, he and his wife entered the service of the Medici court. As a composer, he was one of the earliest representatives of the new monodic style; Caccini praised his music. However, the claim that his short opera, *Il pianto d'Orfeo,* or *Orfeo Dolente* (Florence, 1616; reprinted Brussels, 1927, in Tirabassi's ed.), was the earliest opera ever written is questionable. Among his instrumental works is *Arie per sonarsi con il chitarrone* (Venice, 1616).
BIBL.: E. Schmitz, *Geschichte der weltlichen Solokantate* (Leipzig, 1914; 2nd ed., rev., 1955); A. Tirabassi, "The Oldest Opera: B.'s 'Orfeo Dolente,'" *Musical Quarterly* (Jan. 1929); M. Bukofzer, *Music in the Baroque Era* (N.Y., 1947).

Belli, Girolamo, Italian singer and composer; b. Argenta, near Ferrara, 1552; d. probably there, c.1620. He studied with L. Luzzaschi; was a singer at the Gonzaga court at Mantua. He publ. 3 books of madrigals *a 6* (1583, 1584, 1593); 9 books of madrigals *a 5* (1584; 1586; 9th ed., 1617); 2 books of canzonets *a 4* (1584, 1593); *Sacrae cantiones a 6* (1585), *a 8* (1589), and *a 10* (1594); 2 Magnificats (1610); *Salmi a 5;* some 5-part madrigals in the collection *De' floridi virtuosi d'Italia* (1586).

Belli, Giulio, Italian composer; b. Longiano, c.1560; d. probably in Imola, c.1621. He was a student of Cimello; joined the Franciscan order in 1579; held positions as maestro di cappella at Imola (1582), Carpi (1590), and Ferrara (1592–93). In 1594 he went to Venice, where he served at the church of the Cà Grande (1595), at Montagnana Cathedral (1596), and later at S. Marco (1615). His interim posts included service at the court of Duke Alfonso II d'Este and at the Accademia della Morte in Ferrara (1597), at the Osimo Cathedral in Ferrara (1599), at the Ravenna Cathedral (1600), and at Forlì (1603), S. Antonio, Padua (1606–08), the Imola Cathedral (1611–13), the Cà Grande in Venice (1615–21), and again at Imola (1621). He was a prolific composer; publications of his works appeared between 1584 and 1615, some being reissued several times, among them madrigals and canzonets (1584, 1593); Psalms and vespers (1596, 1604); masses (1586, 1595, 1599, 1608); *sacrae cantiones* (1600); motets (1605); *falsi bordoni* (1605, 1607); and *concerti ecclesiastici* (1613). Many of these works are provided with basso continuo.
BIBL.: A. Brigidi, *Cenni sulla vita e sulle opere di G. B. Longianese* (Modena, 1865).

Bellincioni, Gemma, Italian soprano; b. Monza, Aug. 18, 1864; d. Naples, April 23, 1950. She studied singing with her father; made her operatic debut in Naples at the age of 15. In 1884 she made a concert tour of Spain; in 1885 she sang in Rome, and in 1886 made her debut at La Scala, Milan. She married the once-famous Italian tenor **Roberto Stagno,** and the marriage proved fortunate; they sang together in opera and in concert all over Europe and in Buenos Aires, but somehow she was never invited to the U.S. On May 17, 1890, she sang Santuzza in the 1st performance of *Cavalleria rusticana,* with her husband in the role of her operatic ex-lover. On Nov. 17, 1898, she sang at the Teatro Lirico in Milan the title role in *Fedora* by Giordano at its premiere, with Caruso in the role of her Russian paramour. Her husband died in 1897, but she continued to appear in opera and gave concert tours. From 1911 to 1915 she conducted an opera studio in Berlin; then lived in Rome and Naples; in 1933 she became a prof. of singing at the Cons. of Naples. She publ. an autobiography, *Io ed il palcoscenico* (Milan, 1920).

BIBL.: B. Stagno-Bellincioni, *Roberto Stagno e G. B., intime* (Florence, 1943).

Bellini, Vincenzo, famous Italian opera composer and a master of operatic bel canto; b. Catania, Sicily, Nov. 3, 1801; d. Puteaux, near Paris, Sept. 23, 1835. He was a scion of a musical family; his grandfather was maestro di cappella to the Benedictines in Catania, and organist of the Sacro Collegio di Maria in Misterbianco; his father also served as maestro di cappella. Bellini received his 1st musical instruction from his father and grandfather, and soon revealed a fine gift of melody. The Duke and Duchess of San Martino e Montalbo took interest in him and in 1819 arranged to have him enter the Real Collegio di Musica di San Sebastiano in Naples, where he studied harmony and accompaniment with Giovanni Furno and counterpoint with Giacomo Tritto; Carlo Conti supervised him as a *maestrino* and tutor. He further studied the vocal arts with Girolamo Crescentini and composition with Nicola Zingarelli. Under their guidance he made a detailed study of the works of Pergolesi, Jommelli, Paisiello, and Cimarosa, as well as those of the German classics. While still in school he wrote several sinfonias, 2 masses, and the cantata *Ismene* (1824). His 1st opera, *Adelson e Salvini*, was given at the Collegio in 1825; it was followed by an important production on the stage of the Teatro San Carlo in Naples of his 2nd opera, *Bianca e Gernando* (1826), a score later revised as *Bianca e Fernando* (1828). In 1827 Bellini went to Milan, where he was commissioned by the impresario Barbaja to write an "opera seria" for the famous Teatro alla Scala; it was *Il Pirata*, which obtained fine success at its production in 1827; it was also given in Vienna in 1828. It was followed by another opera, *La Straniera*, produced at La Scala in 1829; also in 1829 Bellini had the opera *Zaira* produced in Parma. He was then commissioned to write a new opera for the Teatro La Fenice in Venice, on a Shakespearean libretto; it was *I Capuleti ed i Montecchi*; produced in 1830, it had a decisive success. Even more successful was his next opera, *La Sonnambula*, produced in Milan in 1831 with the celebrated prima donna Giuditta Pasta as Amina. Pasta also appeared in the title role of Bellini's most famous opera, *Norma*, produced at La Scala in Milan in 1831, which at its repeated productions established Bellini's reputation as a young master of the Italian operatic bel canto. His following opera, *Beatrice di Tenda*, produced in Venice in 1833, failed to sustain his series of successes. He then had an opportunity to go to London and Paris, and it was in Paris that he produced in 1835 his last opera, *I Puritani*, which fully justified the expectations of his admirers. Next to *Norma*, it proved to be one of the greatest masterpieces of Italian operatic art; its Paris production featured a superb cast, which included Grisi, Rubini, Tamburini, and Lablache. Bellini was on his way to fame and universal artistic recognition when he was stricken with a fatal affliction of amebiasis, and died 6 weeks before his 34th birthday. His remains were reverently removed to his native Catania in 1876.

Bellini's music represents the Italian operatic school at its most glorious melodiousness, truly reflected by the term "bel canto." In his writing, the words, the rhythm, the melody, the harmony, and the instrumental accompaniment unite in mutual perfection. The lyric flow and dramatic expressiveness of his music provide a natural medium for singers in the Italian language, with the result that his greatest masterpieces, *La Sonnambula* and *Norma*, remain in the active repertoire of opera houses of the entire world, repeatedly performed by touring Italian opera companies and by native forces everywhere.

For the libretti of his operas Bellini selected melodramatic subjects possessing a natural appeal to the public, with romantic female figures in the center of the action. In *Il Pirata*, the heroine loses her reason when her lover is condemned to death for killing her unloved husband; in *La Sonnambula*, the sleepwalker innocently wanders into the bedroom of a lord and is suspected of infidelity by her lover but is exonerated when she is observed again walking in her sleep; in *Norma* a Druid priestess sacrifices herself when she ascends a funeral pyre with her Roman lover as a penalty for her betrayal of her sacred duty; in *I Puritani*, set in the period of the civil war in Britain, the heroine goes mad when she believes she has been betrayed by her beloved, but regains her reason when he accounts for his essentially noble actions.

WORKS: OPERAS: *Adelson e Salvini*, dramma semiserio (1824–25; Real Collegio di Musica di San Sebastiano, Naples, between Feb. 10 and 15, 1825; 2nd version, 1826; not perf.); *Bianca e Gernando*, melodramma, (1825–26; Teatro San Carlo, Naples, May 30, 1826; rev. version as *Bianca e Fernando*, 1828; Teatro Carlo Felice, Genoa, April 7, 1828); *Il Pirata*, opera seria (1827; Teatro alla Scala, Milan, Oct. 27, 1827); *La Straniera*, opera seria (1828–29; Teatro alla Scala, Milan, Feb. 14, 1829); *Zaira*, opera seria (1829; Teatro Ducale, Parma, May 16, 1829); *I Capuleti ed i Montecchi*, tragedia lirica (1830; Teatro La Fenice, Venice, March 11, 1830); *La Sonnambula*, melodramma (1831; Teatro Carcano, Milan, March 6, 1831); *Norma*, opera seria (1831; Teatro alla Scala, Milan, Dec. 26, 1831); *Beatrice di Tenda*, opera seria (1833; Teatro La Fenice, Venice, March 16, 1833); *I Puritani*, melodramma serio (1834–35; 1st perf. as *I Puritani e i cavalieri* at the Théâtre-Italien, Paris, Jan. 24, 1835).

BIBL.: F. Gerardi, *Biografia di V. B.* (Rome, 1835); L. Scuderi, *Biografia di V. B.* (Catania, 1840); F. Cicconetti, *Vita di V. B.* (Prato, 1859); A. Pougin, *B.: Sa vie, ses œuvres* (Paris, 1868); A. Sciuto, *V. B.: Profilo biografico* (Catania, 1876); A. Tari, *V. B.: Reminiscenze* (Naples, 1876); F. Florimo, *B.: Memorie e lettere* (Florence, 1882); M. Scherillo, *V. B.: Note aneddotiche e critiche* (Ancona, 1882); G. Salvioli, *Lettere inedite di B.* (Milan, 1884); M. Scherillo, *Belliniana: Nuove note* (Milan, 1885); F. Florimo and M. Scherillo, eds., *Album—B.* (Naples, 1886); F. Florimo, ed., *Album B.—Premio B.* (Naples, 1887); A. Amore, *V. B.: Arte—Studi e ricerche* (Catania, 1892); idem, *V. B.: Vita—Studi e ricerche* (Catania, 1894); A. Cametti, *B. a Roma* (Rome, 1900); P. Voss, *V. B.* (Leipzig, 1901); A. Amore, *Belliniana (Errori e smentite)* (Catania, 1902); C. Reina, *V. B. (1801–35)* (Catania, 1902; 2nd ed. as *Il cigno catanese: B.—La vita e le opere*, Catania, 1935); W. Lloyd, *V. B.: A Memoir* (London, 1908); I. Pizzetti, *La musica di V. B.* (Milan, 1916); C. Gray, "V. B.," *Musical Times* (Jan. 1926); V. Ricca, *V. B.: Impressioni e ricordi, con documenti inediti* (Catania, 1932); L. Cambi, *B.* (Milan, 1934); N. Scaglione, *V. B. a Messina* (Messina, 1934); B. Condorelli, *Il Museo Belliniano: Catalogo storico-iconografico* (Catania, 1935); G. de Angelis, *V. B.: La vita, l'uomo, l'artista* (Brescia, 1935); A. Della Corte and G. Pannain, *V. B.: Il Carattere morale, i caratteri artistici* (Turin, 1935); G. Mezzatesta, *V. B. nella vita e nelle opere* (Palermo, 1935); F. Pastura, ed., *Le lettere di B. (1819–35)* (Catania, 1935); G. Policastro, *V. B. (1801–19)* (Catania, 1935); O. Tiby, *V. B.* (Rome, 1935); I. Pizzetti, ed., *V. B.: L'Uomo, le sue opere, la sua fama* (Milan, 1936); O. Tiby, *V. B.* (Turin, 1938); L. Cambi, ed., *V. B.: Epistolario* (Milan, 1943); P. Cavazzuti, *B. a Londra* (Florence, 1945); S. Pugliatti, *Chopin e B.* (Messina, 1952); F. Pastura, *B. secondo la storia* (the standard source on his life; Parma, 1959); F. Pastura, *V. B.* (Catania, 1959); F. Lippmann, "Quellenkundliche Anmerkungen zu einigen Opern V. B.s," *Analecta Musicologica*, 4 (Cologne and Graz, 1967); idem, "V. B. und die italienische opera seria seiner Zeit," *ibid.*, 6 (an exhaustive study of Bellini the composer; Cologne and Vienna, 1969); L. Orrey, *B.* (London and N.Y., 1969); H. Weinstock, *V. B.: His Life and His Operas* (the finest study in Eng.; N.Y., 1971); F. Lippmann, "Belliniana: Nuovi documenti," *Il melodramma italiano dell'ottocento: Studi e ricerche per Massimo Mila* (Turin, 1977); M. Adamo, *V. B.* (Turin, 1981); G. Tintori, *B.* (Milan, 1983); H.-K. Metzger and R. Riehn, eds., *V. B.* (1985); D. Danzuso, F. Gallo, and R. Monti, *Omaggio a B.* (Milan, 1986); C. Brauner, "Parody and Melodic Style in

B.'s *I Capuletti ed i Montecchi," Studies in the History of Music*, vol. 2 (N.Y., 1988).

Bellinzani, Paolo Benedetto, Italian composer; b. probably in Mantua, c.1690; d. Recanati, Feb. 25, 1757. He became maestro di cappella at the Udine Cathedral in 1715; received the benefice of S. Ermacora; subsequently was made a censor in Ferrara. He went to Pergola in 1718; in 1721 he resigned from his position in Udine, and in 1724 became maestro di cappella at the Pesaro Cathedral. He was subsequently maestro di cappella at the Urbino Cathedral (1730–34) and the Ferrara Cathedral (1734–35). From 1737 until his death he was maestro di cappella at the Recanati Cathedral. He composed both sacred and secular vocal works of excellent quality, and also wrote instrumental sonatas.

Bellman, Carl Michael, Swedish poet and composer; b. Stockholm, Feb. 4, 1740; d. there, Feb. 11, 1795. He publ. an important collection of songs to his own words; however, most of the music in it was taken from other sources, including publ. works by known composers. He also publ. lyric ballads expressive of folk life, *Fredmans epistlar* (1790) and *Fredmans sanger* (1791).
  BIBL.: H. Van Loon, *The Last of the Troubadours, C.M. B., His Life and His Music* (N.Y., 1939); P.B. Austin, *The Life and Songs of C.M. B.* (London, 1968); J. Massengale, "Did B. Write Music?," *Scandinavian Studies*, XLIV/3 (1972).

Bellmann, Karl Gottlieb, German organist; b. Muskau, Sept. 6, 1772; d. Schleswig, Dec. 26, 1861. He was an organist in Schleswig from 1813; composed the German national song *Schleswig-Holstein meerumschlungen*; a Christmas cantata; motets; etc.

Belloc-Giorgi, Teresa (née Maria Teresa Ottavia Faustina Trombetta), Italian mezzo-soprano of French descent; b. San Benigno Cavanese, near Turin, July 2, 1784; d. San Giorgio Cavanese, May 13, 1855. She made her debut in Turin in 1801; sang in Paris in 1803, and at La Scala, Milan, from 1804 to 1824; then toured through Italy; also appeared in Paris and London; retired in 1828. Her repertoire comprised roles in 80 operas, Rossini's being her favorites.
  BIBL.: C. Boggio, *La cantante T. B.* (Milan, 1895).

Bělohlávek, Jiří, Czech conductor; b. Prague, Feb. 24, 1946. He studied piano with his father; also took cello lessons at the Prague Cons., and attended the master classes in conducting held by Sergiu Celibidache. In 1970 he won 1st prize in the Czech national competition for young conductors. From 1970 to 1972 he was assistant conductor of the Czech Phil. Orch. He then was conductor of the Brno State Phil. Orch. (1972–77); also toured the U.S. with this ensemble. In 1977 he was appointed chief conductor of the Prague Sym. Orch., a position he held until 1985. He appeared widely in Europe and abroad as a guest conductor; frequently was conductor with the Czech Phil.; became its chief conductor in 1990.

Bely, Victor, Soviet composer; b. Berdichev, Jan. 14, 1904; d. Moscow, March 6, 1983. He studied composition at the Moscow Cons., then wrote some insignificant piano music and publ. a worthwhile collection of folk songs of the Ural region. He acquired particular notoriety as the organizer of the Procoll (Production Collective), with the purpose of initiating a system of composition *en masse;* from 1929 to 1932 he was also an active member of this so-called association of proletarian musicians. This kind of Communist extremism, however, proved unacceptable even from the official Soviet line, and Bely's organization was ingloriously dissolved. He eventually compromised by writing mass songs of social significance set to explosive revolutionary texts. A little monograph on him by one Yuri Korev was publ. in Moscow in 1962.

Belza, Igor. See Boelza, Igor.

Bemberg, Herman, French composer; b. Paris, March 29, 1859; d. Bern, Switzerland, July 21, 1931. He studied at the Paris Cons. with Dubois, Franck, and Massenet; won the Rossini prize in 1885. Among his works are a cantata for Soprano and Orch., *La Mort de Jeanne d'Arc* (1886); a short opera, *Le*

Baiser de Suzon (Paris, 1888); a grand opera, *Elaine* (Covent Garden, London, July 5, 1892; N.Y., Dec. 17, 1894). He also publ. numerous songs, of which *Chant hindou* became extremely popular.

Bembo, Antonia, Italian-born French composer; b. presumably in Venice, c.1670; place and date of death unknown. Between 1690 and 1695 she went to Paris; sang for Louis XIV, and received a pension from him, enabling her to devote herself to composition. Extant works (in the Paris Bibliothèque Nationale): *Produzioni armoniche,* collection of 40 pieces (motets, duets, soli for soprano, etc., with figured bass or instrumental accompaniment, set to sacred Latin, French, and Italian texts); *Te Deum* for 3 Voices and String Orch.; *Divertimento* for 5-voiced Chorus with String Orch.; *Te Deum,* with Large Orch.; *Exaudiat* for 3 Voices, 2 "symphonie" parts, and Basso Continuo; an opera, *L'Ercole Amante* (1707); *Les Sept Psaumes de David* for various vocal combinations with instrumental accompaniment.
  BIBL.: Y. Rokseth, "A. B., Composer to Louis XIV," *Musical Quarterly* (April 1937).

Ben-Haim, Paul, eminent German-born Israeli composer; b. Munich, July 5, 1897; d. Tel Aviv, Jan. 14, 1984. His original name was **Frankenburger;** he changed it to the Hebrew name Ben-Haim after the capture of Germany by the anti-Semitic Hitlerites. He played the violin as a child; then entered the Munich Academy of Arts (1915–20); in 1920 he became an assistant conductor at the Munich Opera, and from 1924 to 1931 conducted opera and a sym. orch. in Augsburg. He left Germany as soon as the country was taken over by the Nazis, and settled in Tel Aviv; there he engaged in a profound study of the folk music of the Middle East, and used it in many of his works, becoming a patriotic composer of his ancestral land. Still, he preserved his traditional learning of Baroque and Romantic European modalities, and continued to compose in the pragmatic forms of syms. and concertos; several of his scores are fermented by Hebrew melos. He received the Israel State Prize in 1957 for his work inspired by King David, *The Sweet Psalmist of Israel,* which was performed widely in Israel, and was conducted by Leonard Bernstein with the N.Y. Phil. in 1959. His *Kabbalai Shabbat* (Friday Evening Service) was performed in N.Y. in 1968 to mark the 20th anniversary of the founding of the State of Israel. Also popular was his Sonata in G for Violin Solo, which was frequently included in concert programs of Yehudi Menuhin.
  WORKS: Sym. No. 1 (Tel Aviv, June 5, 1941, composer conducting); Sym. No. 2 (Tel Aviv, Feb. 2, 1948); Piano Concerto (Tel Aviv, Feb. 1, 1950); Sonata for Violin Solo (1953); *The Sweet Psalmist of Israel* for Harpsichord, Harp, and Orch. (Tel Aviv, Oct. 18, 1956); *To the Chief Musician* for Orch. (1958); *Vision of a Prophet* for Tenor, Chorus, and Orch. (1959); *Capriccio* for Piano and Orch. (Tel Aviv, Sept. 25, 1960); *Dance and Invocation* for Orch. (Tel Aviv, Feb. 2, 1961); Violin Concerto (Tel Aviv, March 20, 1962); *3 Psalms for San Francisco* for Voices and Orch. (1963); *Myrtle Blossoms from Eden* for Soprano, Contralto, and Piano (1965); *The Eternal Theme* for Orch. (Tel Aviv, Feb. 12, 1966); *Hodaya Min Hamidban* (Thanksgiving from the Desert), oratorio (Kibbutz Yagour, Nov. 21, 1967); *Kabbalai Shabbat* (Friday Evening Service; 1968); Cello Concerto (Limburg, the Netherlands, Dec. 14, 1967); Sonata for String Instruments (1969).

Ben-Yohanan, Asher, Israeli composer; b. Kávala, Greece, May 22, 1929. He went to Palestine in 1935; studied composition privately with Ben-Haim in Tel Aviv; on a scholarship, studied with Copland in the U.S. at Tanglewood in Massachusetts (1966); worked with Nono in Venice (1966) and later at the Univ. of Cincinnati (1969–71); currently teaches at the Bar-Ilan Univ. in Ramat-Gan. His works use dodecaphony.
  WORKS: *Festive Overture* (1957); *2 Movements* for Orch. (1959); *Prelude and Toccata* for Piano (1960); String Quartet (1962–64); *Music* for Orch. (1967); *Chamber Music for 6* (1968); *Quartetto Concertato* for Piano, Clarinet, Trombone, and Cello (1969–70); *Mosaic,* after 5 poems by e.e. cummings,

for Soprano and 10 Players (1970–71); *Meditations on a Folk Song* for Flute, Clarinet, and Piano (1972); *Concertino* for String Orch. (1973); *Impressions* for Piano (1976); *Soliloquy* for Solo Violin (1977); *Variations* for Orch. (1980; rev. 1989); Woodwind Quintet (1985); *Delineation* for Cello (1986); *Divertimento* for Brass Trio (1988–89).

Beňačková, Gabriela, Czech soprano; b. Bratislava, March 25, 1947. She studied in Bratislava, won the Dvořák vocal competition (1969), then made her debut at the Prague National Theater (1970), where she sang regularly until 1981. She was awarded the National Prize (1976) and was given the titles of Artist of Merit (1979) and National Artist (1985) by the Czech government. She is particularly esteemed for her roles in operas by Smetana, Dvořák, and Janáček. In 1991 she made her Metropolitan Opera debut as Káťa Kabanová.

Benatzky, Ralph, Czech composer of light opera; b. Moravské-Budejovice, June 5, 1884; d. Zürich, Oct. 16, 1957. He studied in Prague with Veit and Klinger and in Munich with Mottl; then lived mostly in Vienna and Berlin. After the annexation of Austria by the Nazis in 1938, he went to America; after the war he settled in Switzerland. An exceptionally prolific composer, he wrote 92 stage works, about 250 motion picture scores, and perhaps 5,000 songs. His most successful operetta was *Im weissen Rössl* (Berlin, Nov. 8, 1930). His other operettas are *Der lachende Dreibund* (Berlin, Oct. 31, 1913); *Yuschi tanzt* (Vienna, April 3, 1920); *Adieu Mimi* (Vienna, June 9, 1926); *Casanova* (Berlin, Sept. 1, 1928); *Bezauberndes Fräulein* (1935); *Kleinstadtzauber* (1947); *Ein Liebestraum* (on Liszt's themes; 1951); *Don Juans Wiederkehr* (1953).

Benda, Franz (František), famous Bohemian violinist and important composer, brother of **Georg Anton (Jiří Antonín)** and father of **Friedrich (Wilhelm Heinrich)** and **Karl Hermann Heinrich Benda;** b. Alt-Benatek, Bohemia (baptized), Nov. 22, 1709; d. Neuendorf, near Potsdam, March 7, 1786. In 1718 he became a chorister at the Church of St. Nicolas in Prague; in 1720 he ran away to Dresden, where he sang at the Hofkapelle. In 1723 he returned to Prague. It was not until much later that he began a serious study of music, with Löbel, Koniček, and J.S. Graun at Ruppin. In 1733 he joined the orch. of the Crown Prince (afterward Friedrich II) as 1st violinist; in 1771 was named Konzertmeister. During his long years of service for Friedrich II he accompanied him at his flute concerts. Among his works are 17 violin concertos, 17 syms., numerous solo sonatas, and various pieces of chamber music. His autobiography was publ. in the *Neue Berliner Musikzeitung* in 1856.
    Bibl.: F. Berten, *F. B.* (Essen, 1928); F. Lorenz, *Die Musikerfamilie Benda. Vol. I. F. B. und seine Nachkommen* (Berlin, 1967); D. Lee, *F. B.: A Thematic Catalog of His Works* (N.Y., 1984).

Benda, Friedrich (Wilhelm Heinrich), German violinist, son of **Franz (František) Benda;** b. Potsdam, July 15, 1745; d. there, June 19, 1814. He studied violin with his father, and music theory with J.P. Kirnberger. From 1765 to 1810 he served as a royal chamber musician at Potsdam.
    Works: *Orpheus* (Berlin, Jan. 16, 1785; concert perf.); *Alceste* (Berlin, Jan. 15, 1786); *Das Blumenmädchen* (Berlin, July 16, 1806); 2 cantatas, *Pygmalion* and *Die Grazien;* 2 oratorios, *Die Jünger am Grabe des Auferstandenen* and *Das Lob des Höchsten;* 2 violin concertos; 2 flute concertos; numerous piano pieces; much chamber music.

Benda, Friedrich Ludwig, German violinist and composer, son of **Georg Anton (Jiří Antonín) Benda;** b. Gotha, Sept. 4, 1752; d. Königsberg, March 20, 1792. In 1775 he joined the orch. of the Seyler troupe in Gotha; after 1779 was employed as a violinist in theaters in Berlin and Hamburg. In 1782 he was engaged as violinist and Cammer-Compositeur to the Duke of Mecklenburg-Schwerin. In 1788 he settled in Königsberg. He composed the music for G.F. Grossmann's *Der Barbier von Sevilla* (Leipzig, May 7, 1776); also wrote cantatas and a number of instrumental works.

Bibl.: H. Güttler, *Königsberger Musikkultur im 18. Jahrhundert* (Kassel, 1925).

Benda, Georg Anton (Jiří Antonín), important Bohemian composer, brother of **Franz (František)** and father of **Friedrich Ludwig Benda;** b. Alt-Benatek (baptized), June 30, 1722; d. Köstritz, Nov. 6, 1795. He studied at the Jesuit college in Jicin (1739–42); then went to Prussia. In May 1750 he was appointed Kapellmeister to Duke Friedrich III of Saxe-Gotha. In 1765 he received a ducal stipend to go to Italy for half a year. In 1778 he went to Hamburg; also traveled to Vienna; finally settled in Köstritz. His works were distinguished for their dramatic use of rapidly alternating moods ("*Affekte*"), which became a characteristic trait of the North German school of composition and exercised considerable influence on the development of opera and ballad forms in Germany; his effective use of melodrama (spoken recitative accompanied by orch.) was an important innovation.
    Works: Operas: *Ariadne auf Naxos* (Gotha, Jan. 27, 1775); *Medea* (Leipzig, May 1, 1775); *Philon und Theone*, also known as *Almansor und Nadine* (Gotha, Sept. 20, 1779); the singspiels *Der Dorfjahrmarkt* (1775), *Romeo und Julia* (1776), and *Der Holzhauer* (1778); cantatas; piano concertos; syms.; sonatas; sacred music.
    Bibl.: R. Hodermann, *G.A. B.* (Coburg, 1895); F. Brückner, *G.A. B.* (Rostock, 1904); V. Helfert, *G. B. und J.J. Rousseau* (Munich, 1908); Z. Pilková, *Dramatická tvorba Jiřiho Bendy* (Prague, 1960); F. Lorenz, *Die Musikerfamilie B. II. G.A. B.* (Berlin, 1971).

Benda, Hans von, German conductor; b. Strasbourg, Nov. 22, 1888; d. Berlin, Aug. 13, 1972. He studied at the Stern Cons. in Berlin; also at the Univs. of Berlin and Munich. He was director of music of the Berlin Radio (1926–33); then Intendant of the Berlin Phil. Orch. (1934–39); after 1939 he organized the Berlin Chamber Orch., with which he toured throughout Europe, South America, and the Far East. From 1954 to 1958 he served as director of music of Radio Free Berlin.

Benda, Karl Hermann Heinrich, German violinist, son of **Franz (František) Benda;** b. Potsdam, May 2, 1748; d. Berlin, March 15, 1836. He studied with his father; entered the service of the Prussian court about 1766; in 1802 he was appointed Konzertmeister. He was the teacher of King Friedrich Wilhelm III. Of his works, only a Violin Sonata is extant.

Bendel, Franz, German pianist; b. Schönlinde, Bohemia, March 23, 1833; d. Berlin, July 3, 1874. He was a pupil of Proksch (Prague) and Liszt (Weimar); from 1862 taught at Kullak's Academy in Berlin.
    Works: Syms.; 4 masses; Piano Concerto; Piano Trio; salon pieces for Piano; Violin Sonata; nocturnes, romances, several books of songs; etc.

Bendeler, Johann Philipp, German organ theorist, father of **Salomon Bendler;** b. Riethnordhausen, near Erfurt (baptized), Nov. 20, 1654; d. Quedlinburg, Dec. 26, 1709. He went to Quedlinburg in 1681 as an instructor at the Gymnasium there; in 1687 added the duties of cantor, which post he held for the rest of his life. As an organ theorist he belongs, with Werckmeister, to the middle German group whose ideas were realized in the organs of Arp Schnitger. His most important work is *Organopoeia* (c.1690; reprinted in 1739 as *Orgelbaukunst;* facsimile ed., Amsterdam, 1972), a treatise on organ building. Other works are *Collegium Musicum de Compositione* (mentioned in Mattheson's *Ehrenpforte*); *Melopeia practica* (1686); and *Aerarium melopoeticum* (1688). In addition, he wrote 2 books on mathematics.
    Bibl.: C. Mahrenholz, *Die Berechnung der Orgelpfeifenmensuren* (Kassel, 1938).

Bender, Paul, esteemed German bass-baritone and bass; b. Driedorf, July 28, 1875; d. Munich, Nov. 25, 1947. He studied with Luise Reuss-Belce and Baptist Hoffmann; made his operatic debut as Sarastro in *The Magic Flute* in Breslau (1900). He subsequently joined the Munich Opera Co. and was a member from 1903 to 1933. He made his American debut at the Metropolitan Opera in N.Y. on Nov. 17, 1922, and remained on its roster until 1927. He included both serious and comic roles in his repertoire; was particularly effective in the bass parts in Wagner's operas. He created the role of Pope Pius V in Pfitzner's *Palestrina* (1917). In his concert recitals he performed a number of songs by Carl Loewe.

Bendinelli, Agostino, Italian composer and singer; b. Verona, c.1550; d. there, Nov. 23, 1598. He studied in Verona at the Scuola degli Accoliti; also took instruction from the maestro di cappella of the Cathedral, Gabriele Martinengo. He entered the priesthood and then was a singer in the Cathedral choir from 1580; also taught at the Scuola degli Accoliti. Between 1585 and 1594 he publ. 4 books of sacred vocal works.

Bendinelli, Agostino, Italian composer and teacher; b. Lucca, April 26, 1635; d. there, c.1703. He was active as canon of St. John Lateran in Rome; also served as superintendent of the monastery of S. Frediano in Lucca and as prior of S. Agostino in Piacenza and S. Leonardo in Lucca. His most famous pupil was G.M. Bononcini. His only extant publication is his *Psalmi vespertini ternis, quaternis, quinisque ad organum concinendi una cum litanis BVM,* op. 1 (Bologna, 1671).

Bendinelli, Cesare, Italian trumpeter; d. probably in Munich, 1617. He became a trumpeter in Vienna in 1567; was called to Munich in 1580 as chief trumpeter at the court, a post he held until his death. He prepared the earliest known trumpet method, *Tutta l'arte della trombetta* (publ. in Documenta Musicologica, 2nd series, V, 1975; Eng. tr., 1976).
    BIBL.: E.H. Tarr, "C. B.," *Brass Bulletin,* no. 17 (1977).

Bendix, Max, American conductor and composer; b. Detroit, March 28, 1866; d. Chicago, Dec. 6, 1945. He studied in Germany; was concertmaster of the Metropolitan Opera Orch. in N.Y. (1885), and the Thomas Orch. in N.Y. and Chicago (1886–96); later was an opera conductor in N.Y. He wrote a Violin Concerto; *Pavlova,* a valse-caprice for Orch.; also ballet scores for special productions.

Bendix, Otto, Danish pianist, teacher, and composer, brother of **Victor Emanuel Bendix;** b. Copenhagen, July 26, 1845; d. San Francisco, March 1, 1904. He was a pupil of Niels Gade; then studied with Kullak in Berlin and Liszt at Weimar; taught piano at the Copenhagen Cons., and was oboist in a theater orch.; went to the U.S. in 1880; settled in Boston as a piano teacher at the New England Cons.; in 1895 moved to San Francisco, where he established his own music school; gave successful concerts in Europe and America; publ. some piano pieces.

Bendix, Victor Emanuel, Danish pianist and conductor, brother of **Otto Bendix;** b. Copenhagen, May 17, 1851; d. there, Jan. 5, 1926. He studied at the Copenhagen Cons. with Gade and J.P.E. Hartmann; also took piano lessons with Liszt in Weimar. Returning to Copenhagen, he was appointed to the piano faculty of the Royal Academy of Music; in 1897 he organized the Copenhagen Phil. Concerts and conducted them for many years. He wrote 4 syms. in a Romantic vein, a Piano Concerto, and much choral music.

Bendl, Karl (Karel), Czech composer and conductor; b. Prague, April 16, 1838; d. there, Sept. 20, 1897. He studied at the Prague Organ School with Blažek, Pietsch, and Zvonař. In 1864–65 he was active as a conductor in Brussels, Amsterdam, and Paris. Returning to Prague in 1865, he conducted the male choral society Hlahol for 12 years; also was briefly deputy conductor at the Provisional Theater in Prague. He subsequently served as an organist at the church of St. Nicholas in Prague. He was an ardent supporter of Dvořák and Smetana in the cause of creating a national school of Czech music.
    WORKS: Operas: *Lejla* (1867; Prague, Jan. 4, 1868); *Břetislav* (1869; Prague, Sept. 18, 1870); *Starý ženich* (1871–74); *Die Wunderblume* (1876; Czech Radio, Prague, Aug. 30, 1940, in Czech); *Indická princezna,* operetta (1876–77; Prague, Aug. 26, 1877); *Černohorci* (1881; Prague, Oct. 11, 1881); *Karel*

Škréta (1883; Prague, Dec. 11, 1883); *Gina* (1884; not perf.); *Dítě Tabora* (1886–88; Prague, March 13, 1892); *Máti Míla* (1893–95; Prague, June 25, 1895); *Švanda dudák* (1895–96; Prague, April 29, 1907). Also, a ballet, *Česká svatba* (1894; Prague, Feb. 13, 1895); 2 masses; 2 cantatas; about 450 songs and choruses.
    BIBL.: E. Krasnohorska, *Z mládí Karla Bendla* (Prague, 1897; 2nd ed. as *Z mého mládí,* 1920); J. Polák, *Karel B.* (Prague, 1938).

Bendler, Salomon, famous German bass, son of **Johann Philipp Bendeler;** b. Quedlinburg, 1683; d. Braunschweig, 1724. He studied with his father; then sang throughout Germany and Italy; later made appearances in London (1712–17). Upon his return to Germany, he became a chamber singer at the court in Braunschweig, where he remained until his death.

Benedetti Michelangeli, Arturo. See **Michelangeli, Arturo Benedetti.**

Benedict, Sir Julius, German-English conductor and composer; b. Stuttgart, Nov. 27, 1804; d. London, June 5, 1885. He was the son of a Jewish banker; from his earliest childhood he showed a decisive musical talent. He took lessons with J.C.L. Abeille in Stuttgart; then had further instruction with Hummel at Weimar. Hummel introduced him to Weber, and he became Weber's private pupil. In 1823, Benedict was appointed conductor of the Kärnthnertortheater in Vienna; in 1825 he obtained a similar post at the Teatro San Carlo in Naples and also at the Fondo Theater there. He produced his 1st opera, *Giacinta ed Ernesto,* in Naples in 1827. His 2nd opera was *I Portoghesi in Goa,* produced in Naples on June 28, 1830. In 1834 Benedict went to Paris, and in 1835 he proceeded to London, where he remained for the rest of his life. In 1836 he became music director at the Opera Buffa at the Lyceum Theatre. He conducted opera at the Drury Lane Theatre from 1838 to 1848. His 1st opera in English, *The Gypsy's Warning,* was produced at Drury Lane under his direction on April 19, 1838. He also conducted at Covent Garden; led the Monday Popular Concerts; served as music director of the Norwich Festivals (1845–78); and conducted the Liverpool Phil. Soc. (1876–80). In recognition of his services, he was knighted in 1871. From 1850 to 1852 he accompanied Jenny Lind on her American tours. His reputation as a conductor and composer was considerable, in both Europe and America. Among his operas the most successful was *The Lily of Killarney,* which was produced at Covent Garden on Feb. 8, 1862; it was also staged in America and Australia. His other operas are *The Brides of Venice* (Drury Lane, April 22, 1844); *The Crusaders* (Drury Lane, Feb. 26, 1846); *The Lake of Glenaston* (1862); *The Bride of Song* (Covent Garden, Dec. 3, 1864). He also wrote the cantatas *Undine* (1860); *Richard Cœur-de-Lion* (1863); *The Legend of St. Cecilia* (1866); *Graziella* (1882); an oratorio, *St. Peter* (1870); a Sym.; 2 piano concertos; and other instrumental works. He publ. biographies of Mendelssohn (London, 1850) and Weber (London, 1881; 2nd ed., 1913); both contained information from his personal acquaintance with Mendelssohn and Weber.

Benedictus Appenzeller. See **Appenzeller, Benedictus.**

Benedito y Vives, Rafael, Spanish conductor; b. Valencia, Sept. 3, 1885; d. Madrid, Sept. 8, 1963. He studied at the Madrid Cons.; in 1917 he organized his own symphonic group, which he led at festivals and other public functions. He publ. several pedagogical pieces for aspiring young pianists.

Beneke, Tex (real name, **Gordon**), American jazz singer, tenor saxophonist, and bandleader; b. Fort Worth, Texas, Feb. 12, 1914. He worked with Ben Young (1935–37); then was a vocalist with the Glenn Miller orch. (1938–42); after serving in the U.S. Navy during World War II, he became leader of the Glenn Miller orch., which later toured as his own ensemble.

Benelli, Antonio Peregrino (Pellegrino), Italian tenor and composer; b. Forlì, Romagna, Sept. 5, 1771; d. Börnichau,

Saxony, Aug. 16, 1830. In 1790 he was 1st tenor at the Teatro San Carlo in Naples; held the same position in London in 1798, and in Dresden from 1801 to 1822, when his voice failed; then taught singing at the Royal Theater School in Berlin until 1829. His most valuable work is a vocal method, *Gesangslehre* (Dresden, 1819; orig. publ. in Italian as *Regole per il canto figurato*, 1814); he also wrote *Bemerkungen über die Stimme* in the *Allgemeine Musikalische Zeitung* (Leipzig, 1824); composed many vocal pieces and some piano pieces.

Benestad, Finn, distinguished Norwegian musicologist; b. Kristiansand, Oct. 30, 1929. He studied at the Univ. of Oslo (1948–53; M.A., 1953; Ph.D., 1961, with the diss. *Johannes Haarklou: Mannen og verket*, publ. in Oslo, 1961). After working as a music critic in Oslo, he served as prof. of musicology at the Univ. of Trondheim (1961–64) and at the Univ. of Oslo (from 1965); he was also a Fulbright scholar at the Univ. of Calif. at Los Angeles (1968–69). He publ. major studies on Norwegian composers of the 19th century.

WRITINGS: *Waldemar Thrane: an pionér i norsk musikkliv* (Oslo, 1961); *Musikkhistorisk oversikt* (Oslo, 1965; 3rd ed., 1976); ed. *Norsk musikk: Studier i Norge*, vol. VI (Oslo, 1968); with D. Schjelderup-Ebbe, *Edvard Grieg: Mennesket og kunstneren* (Oslo, 1980; Eng. tr. by W. Halverson and L. Sateren as *Edvard Grieg: The Man and the Artist*, Lincoln, Nebr., 1987).

Benet, John, English composer who flourished in the 15th century. He wrote mostly church music. The following works are extant: 2 motets, *Lux fulget ex Anglia* and *Tellus purpureum;* an isorhythmic motet, *Gaude pia Magdalena;* and several numbers from incomplete masses. Stylistically he belonged to the school of John Dunstable and Lionel Power. His *Sanctus* and *Agnus* are found in H. Wooldrige's *Early English Harmony* (2 vols., 1897 and 1913); *Gaude pia Magdalena* was ed. in *Early English Church Music*, VIII (1968); *Lux fulget ex Anglia* and *Tellus purpureum* in B. Trowell's *Music under the Plantagenets* (diss., Cambridge Univ., 1960).

Benevoli, Orazio, Italian composer; b. Rome, April 19, 1605; d. there, June 17, 1672. He was the son of a French baker who Italianized his name when he settled in Rome. He studied with Vincenzo Ugolini and sang in the boys' choir in the school "dei francesi" in Rome (1617–23); also had some instruction from Lorenzo Ratti. After completion of his study period he had successive posts as maestro di cappella; served at S. Maria in Trastevere (1624–30); at S. Spirito, Sassia (1630–38); and at S. Luigi dei Francesi (1638–44). In 1644 he went to Vienna, where he served at the Court until 1646; then returned to Rome as maestro di cappella at S. Maria Maggiore; was also admitted to the Vatican. His music shows influences of the Palestrina style, combined with polychoral techniques of the Venetians; some of his sacred works call for 12 separate choirs. A considerable controversy arose when some music historians attributed to Benevoli the composition of the *Missa salisburgensis*, containing 53 separate parts, which was cited as an example of Benevoli's extraordinary contrapuntal skill. Such a Mass was indeed commissioned by Salzburg in 1628, but it was not composed by Benevoli; whoever wrote it, its performance did not take place until about 1682. This Mass and a hymn in 56 voices were reprinted in Denkmäler der Tonkunst in Österreich; another Mass, which really was composed by Benevoli and was performed at the S. Maria sopra Minerva Church in Rome in 1650, is set for 12 choirs of 4 voices each.

BIBL.: A. Cametti, "La Scuola dei pueri cantus di San Luigi dei francesi in Roma e suoi principali allievi," *Rivista Musicale Italiana* (Oct. 1915); M. Bukofzer, *Music in the Baroque Era* (N.Y., 1947); L. Feininger, ed., *O. B.: Opera omnia* (Rome, 1966–); idem, "O. B. (1605–1672)," *1° congresso internazionale di musica sacra: Roma 1950;* E. Hintermaier, "The Missa Salisburgensis," *Musical Times* (Nov. 1975); idem, " 'Missa Salisburgensis': Neue Erkenntnisse über Entstehung, Actor und Zweckbestimmung," *Musicologica Austriaca*, I (1976).

Bengtsson, Gustaf Adolf Tiburtius (Tiburt), Swedish conductor and composer; b. Vadstena, March 29, 1886; d. there,

Oct. 5, 1965. He studied at the Stockholm Cons.; then in Berlin with Juon and in Leipzig with Riemann; returned to Sweden and settled in Karlstad as composer and teacher; from 1943 to 1949 was conductor of an orch. in Linköping.

WORKS: 3 syms. (1908, 1910, 1921); Violin Concerto; Cello Concerto; *Sinfonia concertante* for Violin, Viola, and Orch.; *Canone concertante* for Violin, Viola, and Chamber Orch. (1950); *Vettern*, symphonic poem (1950); String Quartet (1907); Piano Trio (1916); Violin Sonata; songs.

Bengtsson, (Lars) Ingmar (Olof), noted Swedish musicologist and editor; b. Stockholm, March 2, 1920; d. there, Dec. 3, 1989. He studied piano at the Stockholm Musikhögskolan and musicology at the univs. of Stockholm, Uppsala, and Basel; subsequently took his Ph.D. at the Univ. of Uppsala in 1955 with the dissertation *J.H. Roman och hans instrumentalmusik: Käll och stilkritiska studier* (publ. in Uppsala, 1955). Between 1942 and 1955 he made appearances as a pianist and harpsichordist; from 1943 to 1959 wrote music criticism for *Svenska Dagbladet* in Stockholm. In 1947 he joined the faculty of the musicological inst. at the Univ. of Uppsala as a lecturer; in 1961 he was named a prof. at the univ., where he remained until 1985. In 1961 he was elected president of the Swedish Soc. for Musicology; also ed. its journal. In 1962 he became ed. of *Studia Musicologica Upsaliensia: Nova Series*. He founded the Swedish Archives of the History of Music in 1965. He made a specialty of the musical developments in Sweden. He publ. the books *Bach och hans tid* (Stockholm, 1946); *Från visa till symfoni* (Stockholm, 1947; 5th ed., 1973); and *Handstilar och notpickturer i Kungl. musikaliska akademiens Romansamling* (Uppsala, 1955; with R. Danielsson). He also ed. *Modern nordisk musik* (Stockholm, 1957); *Något om det heroiska i 1800-talets dikt och ton* (Lund, 1984).

Benguerel, Xavier, Catalonian composer; b. Barcelona, Feb. 9, 1931. He was a pupil of Cristóbal Taltabull. His early works were influenced by French Impressionism; in 1958 he adopted the dodecaphonic techniques; then tilted toward extreme modernism, often in the manner of the New Polish School.

WORKS: Concerto for Piano and Strings (1955); *Contrasts* for Chamber Orch. (1959); *Cantata d'Amic i Amat* for Chamber Group, Contralto, and Chorus (1959); Concerto for 2 Flutes and Strings (1961); *Sinfonia continua* (Bilbao, Oct. 21, 1962); *Nocturno de los avisos* for Soprano, Chorus, and Orch. (1963); Violin Concerto (Barcelona, Oct. 9, 1965); *Sinfonia per a un Festival* (Barcelona, Oct. 30, 1966); *Sinfonia per a Petita Orquestra* (Hagen, Germany, April 24, 1967); *Paraules de Cada Dia* for Voice and Chamber Orch. (1967); *Sinfonia per a Gran Orquestra* (Barcelona, Oct. 2, 1968); *Test Sonata* for 17 Instruments and Percussion (1968); *Musica per a Oboe* for Oboe and Chamber Group (1968); *Dialogue orchestrale* (1969); *Musica riservata* for Strings (1969); *Joc* for 7 Instruments and Percussion (1969); *Consort Music* for Strings (1970); Organ Concerto (Baden-Baden, Sept. 17, 1971); Guitar Concerto (Kassel, Germany, Feb. 17, 1972); *Quasi una fantasia* for Cello and Chamber Orch. (Barcelona, Oct. 22, 1972); *Arbor*, cantata to words of Goethe, Dante, Shakespeare, Hitler, Mussolini, Martin Luther King, and Ché Guevara, for Soli, 4 Speakers, Chorus, and Orch. (Barcelona, Oct. 22, 1972); *Destructio* for Orch. (Madrid, March 23, 1973); *Capriccio stravagante* for Chamber Group (1974); *Thesis* for Chamber Group (1974); Concerto for Percussion and Orch. (1975); 2 violin sonatas (1953, 1959); String Quartet No. 1 (1954); *4 estructuras: I* for Violin (1957); *II* for Flute (1959); *III* for Cello (1964); *IV* for Piano (1966); *Successions* for Wind Quintet (1960); *Duo* for Clarinet and Piano (1963); *Musica* for 3 Percussionists (1967); *Crescendo* for Organ (1970); *Intento a dos* for Guitar and Percussion (1970); *Verses* for Guitar (1973); *El gran océano* for Soprano, Guitar, and Percussion (1975); *Vermelia* for 4 Guitars (1976).

Benincori, Angelo Maria, Italian composer; b. Brescia, March 28, 1779; d. Belleville, near Paris, Dec. 30, 1821. He studied in Parma with Rolla (violin) and counterpoint with Ghiretti; spent several years in Spain; in 1803 he settled in

Paris, where he was active mostly as a violin teacher. He brought out 3 unsuccessful operas, but performed a meritorious service in completing Isouard's opera *Aladin*.

Benjamin, Arthur, Australian composer and pianist; b. Sydney, Sept. 18, 1893; d. London, April 9, 1960. He received his musical training in Brisbane; then went to London, where he studied piano with Frederick Cliffe and composition with Charles Stanford at the Royal College of Music. After serving in the British army during World War I, he was a piano instructor at the Sydney Cons. in Australia (1919–21). Later he taught at the Royal College of Music in London; was engaged as conductor of the Vancouver Sym. Orch. in Canada (1941–46); eventually returned to London.

WORKS: 5 operas: *The Devil Take Her* (London, Dec. 1, 1931), *Prima Donna* (1933; London, Feb. 23, 1949), *A Tale of 2 Cities*, after Dickens (1949–50; BBC, London, April 17, 1953; prizewinner of Festival of Britain opera competition), *Mañana*, a television opera (1956), and *Tartuffe*, after Molière (1960; completed by A. Boustead; London, Nov. 30, 1964); *Orlando's Silver Wedding* (London, Festival of Britain, May 1951), ballet; Piano Concertino (1927); *Light Music*, suite (1928–33); Violin Concerto (1932); *Heritage*, ceremonial march (1935); *Romantic Fantasy* for Violin, Viola, and Orch. (London, March 24, 1938); *Overture to an Italian Comedy* (London, March 2, 1937); *Cotillon*, suite of 9 English dance tunes (1938); *2 Jamaican Pieces* (1938; includes the highly popular *Jamaican Rumba*; arranged also for 1 or 2 Pianos); *Prelude to Holiday* (Indianapolis, Jan. 17, 1941); Sonatina for Chamber Orch. (1940); Concerto for Oboe and Strings, transcribed from Cimarosa (1942); Sym. No. 1 (1944–45; Cheltenham Festival, June 30, 1948); Suite for Flute and Strings, transcribed from Scarlatti (1945); *Elegy, Waltz and Toccata*, concerto for Viola, and Orch. or Piano (1945); *From San Domingo* (1945); *Caribbean Dance* (1946); Ballade for Strings (1947); *Concerto quasi una fantasia* for Piano and Orch. (Sydney, Sept. 5, 1950, composer soloist); Harmonica Concerto (London, Aug. 15, 1953); *North American Square Dances* for 2 Pianos and Orch. (Pittsburgh, April 1, 1955); *3 Pieces* for Violin and Piano (1919); *3 Impressions* for Voice and String Quartet (1920); 2 string quartets: No. 1, *Pastorale Fantasia* (1924); No. 2 (1959); Violin Sonatina (1924); Suite for Piano (1927); Cello Sonatina (1938); *2 Jamaican Songs* for 2 Pianos (1949); *Le Tombeau de Ravel: Valse Caprice* for Clarinet or Viola, and Piano (1949); Divertimento for Wind Quintet (1960); songs and choral music.

Benjamin, George, gifted English composer and pianist; b. London, Jan. 31, 1960. He studied composition with Messiaen and Loriod in Paris (1976–78) and with A. Goehr at King's College, Cambridge (1978–82). His music is often intricate, exploiting the full range of timbral possibilities. His *Antara*, a complex synthesis of panpipe sonorities re-created in concerto form with IRCAM's famous 4X computer, was the subject of a 1987 documentary produced by the BBC. He teaches at the Royal College of Music in London.

WORKS: ORCH.: *Altitude* for Brass Band (1977); *Ringed by the Flat Horizon* (1979–80); *A Mind of Winter* for Soprano and Small Orch. (1981); *At 1st Flight* for Chamber Orch. (1982). **CHAMBER:** Violin Sonata (1976–77); Octet (1978); *Flight* for Flute (1979); Duo for Cello and Piano (1980); *Fanfare for Aquarius* for Ensemble (1983). **SOLO PIANO:** Sonata (1977–78); *Sortilèges* (1981); *Relativity Rag* (1984); *Fantasy on Iambic Pentameter* (1985).

Benjamin, William E(mmanuel), Canadian-born American composer; b. Montreal, Dec. 7, 1944. He attended McGill Univ. (1961–65), receiving his B.Mus.; studied composition with István Anhalt; also took piano lessons at the Conservatoire de Musique de la Province de Québec. In 1966 he enrolled at Princeton Univ., where his teachers were Milton Babbitt, Edward T. Cone, Peter Westergaard, and James K. Randall; received his M.F.A. in 1968. He taught at Wellesley College (1970–72), the Univ. of Michigan (1972–78), and the Univ. of British Columbia (from 1978). In his music he strives to fashion a rational multidimensional musical space, in which

dynamics, rhythm, and tonality are functional components in free serial arrangements. His works include *Mah Tovu* for Mixed Chorus a cappella (1965); *Variations* for 4 Players (1967); *At Sixes and Sevens*, a sextet (1968); Piano Concerto (1970–75); *2 Poems* for Contralto and Chamber Ensemble (1981); *Sequences* for Guitar (1982).

Bennard, George, American hymn composer; b. Youngstown, Ohio, Feb. 4, 1873; d. Reed City, Mich., Oct. 10, 1958. He served as a Salvation Army officer from 1892 to 1907; subsequently traveled as an evangelist in the U.S. and Canada. He wrote a number of sacred songs, among them *God Bless Our Boys, The Old Rugged Cross, Sweet Songs of Salvation.*

Bennet, John, English composer; b. probably in Lancashire, c.1570. In 1599 he publ. *Madrigalls to Foure Voyces*, containing 17 compositions. He contributed a well-known madrigal, *All creatures now are merry minded*, to *The Triumph of Oriana* (1601) and composed 6 songs for Ravenscroft's *A Briefe Discourse* (1614).

BIBL.: E.H. Fellowes, The English Madrigal School (1913–24; 2nd ed. rev. by T. Dart as The English Madrigalists, 1956); idem, *The English Madrigal Composers* (Oxford, 1921; 2nd ed., 1948).

Bennett, Joseph, English critic and writer on music; b. Berkeley, Gloucestershire, Nov. 29, 1831; d. Purton, June 12, 1911. After serving in various musical positions in London, he wrote music criticism for the *Sunday Times, Pall Mall Gazette,* and the *Graphic;* was annotator of the programs of the Phil. Soc. (1885–1903) and of the Saturday Popular Concerts; also wrote libretti for several English composers.

WRITINGS: *Letters from Bayreuth* (1877); *The Musical Year* (1883); *History of the Leeds Musical Festivals, 1858–1889* (1892; with F.R. Spark); *Story of Ten Hundred Concerts* (1887; an account of the origin and rise of the Saturday Popular Concerts, 1857–87); *Forty Years of Music* (1908).

Bennett, Richard Rodney, prolific and successful English composer; b. Broadstairs, Kent, March 29, 1936. He studied with Lennox Berkeley and Howard Ferguson at the Royal Academy of Music in London (1953–56); later took private lessons with Boulez in Paris (1957–58). Returning to London, he was engaged to teach at the Royal Academy of Music (1963–65); then went to the U.S. as a visiting prof. at the Peabody Cons. in Baltimore (1970–71). In 1977 he was made a Commander of the Order of the British Empire.

WORKS: STAGE: *The Ledge*, chamber opera (Sadler's Wells Theatre, London, Sept. 11, 1961); 3-act opera, *The Mines of Sulphur* (London, Feb. 24, 1965); comic opera, *Penny for a Song* (London, Oct. 31, 1967); children's opera, *All the King's Men* (Coventry, March 28, 1969); 3-act opera, *Victory*, after the novel by Conrad (Covent Garden, London, April 13, 1970); *Isadora*, ballet (Covent Garden, London, April 30, 1981).

ORCH.: Horn Concerto (1956); *Journal* (1960); *Calendar* for Chamber Ensemble (London, Nov. 24, 1960); *Suite française* for Chamber Orch. (1961); *London Pastoral* for Chamber Ensemble (1961); *Nocturnes* for Chamber Orch. (1962); *A Jazz Calendar* for 12 Instruments (1963–64; produced as a ballet, Covent Garden, 1968); *Aubade* (London, Sept. 1, 1964); *Soliloquy* for Voice and Jazz Ensemble (1966); *Epithalamion* for Chorus and Orch.; 2 syms.: No. 1 (London, Feb. 10, 1966); No. 2 (N.Y., Jan. 18, 1968); Piano Concerto (Birmingham, Sept. 19, 1968); Concerto for Oboe and String Orch. (Aldeburgh Festival, June 6, 1971); Concerto for Guitar and Chamber Ensemble (London, Nov. 18, 1970); Viola Concerto (N.Y., July 3, 1973); Concerto for Orch. (Denver, Feb. 25, 1974); Violin Concerto (Birmingham, March 25, 1976); *Zodiac* (Washington, D.C., March 30, 1976); *Serenade* (London, April 24, 1977); *Acteon* for Horn and Orch. (London, Aug. 12, 1977); *Music for Strings* (Cheltenham, July 7, 1978); Double-bass Concerto (London, Oct. 15, 1978); *Sonnets to Orpheus* for Cello and Orch. (Edinburgh, Sept. 3, 1979); Harpsichord Concerto (St. Louis, Dec. 4, 1980); *Anniversaries* (London, Sept. 9, 1982); *Memento* for Flute and Strings (1983); *Sinfonietta* (1984); *Mov-

ing into Aquarius (1984; London, Jan. 23, 1985); *Reflections on a Theme of William Walton* for 11 Solo Strings (London, May 20, 1985); *Dream Dancing* (London, May 28, 1986).

CHAMBER: 4 string quartets (1952, 1953, 1960, 1964); Sonatina for Solo Flute (1954); 4 improvisations for Solo Violin (1955); *Winter Music* for Flute and Piano (1960); Oboe Sonata (1961); Sonata for Solo Violin (1964); *Conversations* for 2 Flutes (1964); Trio for Flute, Oboe, and Clarinet (1965); Wind Quintet (1967–68); 5 impromptus for Solo Guitar (1968); *Commedia I* for 6 Players (1972); *Commedia II* for Flute, Cello, and Piano (1972–73); *Commedia III* for 10 Instruments (1972–73); *Commedia IV* for Brass Quintet (1972–73); *Scena II* for Solo Cello (1973); Oboe Quartet (1975); *Travel Notes*, No. 1 for String Quartet (1975); *Travel Notes*, No. 2 for Wind Quartet (1976); *Scena III* for Basset Horn (1977); Horn Sonata (1978); Violin Sonata (1978); *Metamorphoses* for String Octet (1980); *6 Tunes for the Instruction of Singing Birds* for Solo Flute (1981); Music for String Quartet (1981); Sonatina for Solo Clarinet (1981); *After Syrinx I* for Oboe and Piano (1982); Concerto for Wind Quintet (1983); *After Syrinx II* for Marimba (1984); *Lamento d'Arianna* for String Quartet (1986).

VOCAL: *The Approaches of Sleep* for 4 Voices and 10 Instruments (1959); *The Music That Her Echo Is*, cycle for Tenor and Piano (1967); *Jazz Pastoral* for Voice and Jazz Ensemble (1969); *Crazy Jane* for Soprano, Piano, Clarinet, and Cello (1968–69); *Sonnet Sequence* for Tenor and Instrumental Ensemble (1971); *The House of Sleep* for 6 Male Voices (1971); *Tenebrae* for Baritone and Piano (1971); *Devotions* for Chorus a cappella (1971); *Nightpiece* for Soprano and Tape (1972); *Times Whiter Series* for Countertenor and Lute (1974); *Spells* for Soprano, Chorus, and Orch. (Worcester, Aug. 28, 1975); *Letters to Lindbergh* for Female Voices and Piano Duet (1982); *Love Songs* for Tenor and Orch. (1984); *And Death Shall Have No Dominion* for Men's Chorus and Solo Horn (1986).

PIANO: Sonata (1954); 5 *Studies* (1962–64); *Capriccio* for Piano, 4-hands (1968); *Scena I* (1973); *4-piece Suite* for 2 Pianos (1974); *Kandinsky Variations* for 2 Pianos (1977); *Noctuary*, ballet score (1981); *Tango after Syrinx* (1985).

FILM MUSIC: *The Nanny* (1965); *Billion Dollar Brain* (1967); *Nicholas and Alexandra* (about the last Imperial Romanovs; 1971); *Murder on the Orient Express* (1974); *Equus* (1977).

BIBL.: C. Palmer and L. Foreman, "R.R. B.," *British Music Now*, ed. by L. Foreman (London, 1975); S. Bradshaw, "R.R. B.: The Last Decade," *Musical Times* (Sept. 1982).

Bennett, Robert Russell, American composer and expert arranger and orchestrator; b. Kansas City, June 15, 1894; d. N.Y., Aug. 17, 1981. He was a member of a musical family: his father played in the Kansas City Phil. and his mother was a piano teacher. He studied music theory with Carl Busch; in 1916 he moved to N.Y., where he earned a living copying music for G. Schirmer Co. He served in the U.S. Army in World War I; returning to civilian life, he began a career as orchestrator of musical comedy scores. Having earned enough money to travel, he went to Paris to study composition with Nadia Boulanger; in 1927 and 1928 he held a Guggenheim fellowship. He then undertook composition in earnest. Success haunted him. His music, which is distinguished by a facile flow of easily communicated melodies and rhythms in luscious harmonies and resplendent orchestration, found a receptive audience; he had no difficulties in having his works performed by top orchs. and celebrated conductors. However, his audience was limited to the U.S.; little of his music penetrated the cosmopolitan halls of Europe. He prospered mainly by his extraordinary expertise in arranging popular musical comedies in idiomatic instrumental colors. He provided arrangements for such successful shows as *Oklahoma!, Show Boat, South Pacific, The King and I, My Fair Lady,* and *The Sound of Music.* He received an Academy Award in 1955 for his scoring of the motion picture *Oklahoma!* He was also active as a conductor on the radio. His feats of organization and memory were extraordinary; he rarely had to revise his scoring, which he usually put down in calligraphic notation in the final copy. He publ.

a book on orchestration, *Instrumentally Speaking* (N.Y., 1975).

WORKS: Operas, *Maria Malibran* (N.Y., April 8, 1935) and *The Enchanted Kiss* (N.Y., Dec. 30, 1945); operetta, *Endymion* (1927). Orch.: *Charleston Rhapsody* (1926); *Paysage* (1928); *Sights and Sounds* (1929); March for 2 Pianos and Orch. (Los Angeles, July 18, 1930); *Abraham Lincoln Symphony* (Philadelphia, Oct. 24, 1931); *Adagio Eroico* (Philadelphia, April 25, 1935); Concerto Grosso for Band (Rochester, N.Y., Dec. 9, 1932); *Hollywood: Introduction and Scherzo* (NBC, Nov. 15, 1936); 8 *Études* for Orch. (CBS, July 17, 1938); Sym. in D "for the Dodgers" (N.Y., Aug. 3, 1941); Violin Concerto (NBC, Dec. 26, 1941); *The 4 Freedoms*, symphonic sketch after 4 paintings by Norman Rockwell (Los Angeles, Dec. 16, 1943); Sym. (1946); *A Dry Weather Legend* (Knoxville, 1947); Piano Concerto (1948); Violin Sonata (1927); *Toy Symphony* for 5 Woodwinds (1928); Organ Sonata (1929); *Water Music* for String Quartet (1937); *Hexapoda* for Violin and Piano (1940); 5 *Improvisations* for Trio (1946); *Sonatine* for Soprano and Harp (1947); 6 *Souvenirs* for 2 Flutes and Piano (1948); Concerto for Violin, Piano, and Orch. (Portland, Oreg., March 18, 1963); Concerto for Guitar and Orch. (1970); *Suite on Old American Dances* for Band (1949); *Symphonic Songs* for Band (1958); Concerto for Wind Quintet and Wind Orch. (1958); Sym. (1963).

Bennett, Tony (real name, **Anthony Dominick Benedetto**), American singer of popular music; b. Queens, N.Y., Aug. 3, 1926. He studied commercial art at the Manhattan School of Industrial Art; after military service, he took vocal lessons with Miriam Spier; subsequently appeared in nightclubs and on television as a leading singer of popular music until the advent of rock 'n' roll. He resumed his career successfully in 1962 with his recording of the song *I Left My Heart in San Francisco.*

Bennett, Sir William Sterndale, distinguished English pianist, conductor, and composer; b. Sheffield, April 13, 1816; d. London, Feb. 1, 1875. His father, Robert Bennett, an organist, died when he was a child, and he was then placed in the care of his grandfather, John Bennett, who was also a musician. At the age of 8 he was admitted to the choir of King's College Chapel, Cambridge, and at 10 he became a pupil at the Royal Academy of Music in London, where he studied theory with Charles Lucas and piano with William Henry Holmes, and played violin in the academy orch. under Cipriani Potter; he later studied music theory there with William Crotch. Soon he began to compose; he was 16 years old when he was the soloist in the 1st performance of his Piano Concerto No. 1 in Cambridge on Nov. 28, 1832. In 1836 he made an extensive visit to Leipzig, where he became a close friend of Mendelssohn and Schumann; also appeared as a pianist and conductor of his own works with the Gewandhaus Orch. there. He continued to compose industriously, and played his Piano Concerto No. 4 with the Gewandhaus Orch. in Leipzig on Jan. 17, 1839. He visited Germany again in 1841–42. From 1843 to 1856 he gave a series of chamber music concerts in London; in 1849 he founded the Bach Soc. From 1856 to 1866 he conducted the Phil. Soc. of London; concurrently he held the post of prof. of music at Cambridge Univ.; in 1866 he assumed the position of principal of the Royal Academy of Music. His reputation as a composer grew; Mendelssohn and Schumann were eloquent in praising his works. He amassed honors: in 1856 he received the honorary degree of D.Mus. from Cambridge Univ., which also conferred on him the degree of M.A. in 1867; he received the degree of D.C.L. from Oxford Univ. in 1870; in a culmination of these honors, he was knighted by Queen Victoria in 1871. The final honor was his burial in Westminster Abbey. His music seems to have been laid to posthumous immobility with his honored body; the great appreciation he enjoyed in Germany declined, and the desultory attempts to restore him to fame in England proved abortive; not a single work retained its erstwhile vitality. Yet at his best, Bennett could produce music not recognizably inferior to that of Schumann's lesser works. There is every reason and every chance for its natural resuscitation.

WORKS: Sym. No. 1, in E-flat major (London, June 16, 1832); Piano Concerto No. 1, in D minor, op. 1 (Cambridge, Nov. 28, 1832); Sym. No. 2, in D minor (1832–33); *The Tempest,* overture (1832); *Parisina,* overture, op. 3 (London, March 1835); Piano Concerto No. 2, in E-flat major, op. 4 (1833; London, May 24, 1834); Overture in D minor (1833); Sym. No. 4, in A major (1833–34; London, Jan. 5, 1835); *The Merry Wives of Windsor,* overture (1834); Piano Concerto No. 3, in C minor, op. 9 (1834; London, May 16, 1835; the original slow movement was rejected by the composer and replaced by a Romanza; the Adagio in G minor for Piano and Orch. was 1st perf. in Manchester on June 18, 1981); Sym. No. 5, in G minor (1835; London, Feb. 8, 1836); Piano Concerto No. 4, in F minor (London, July 1, 1836; rev. 1838; Leipzig, Jan. 17, 1839); *The Naiads,* overture, op. 15 (1836; London, Jan. 25, 1837); *The Wood Nymphs,* overture, op. 20 (1838; Leipzig, Jan. 24, 1839); *Caprice* in E major for Piano, op. 22 (London, May 25, 1838); Concert-Stück in A major for Piano and Orch. (1841–43; London, June 5, 1843); *Marie du Bois,* overture (1843; rev. 1844; London, June 25, 1845); *Paradise and the Peri,* fantasia-overture, op. 42 (London, July 14, 1862); Sym. No. 6, in G minor, op. 43 (London, June 27, 1864). Other works include *Zion,* an oratorio (1839); *The May Queen,* op. 39, a pastoral for Soprano, Alto, Tenor, Bass, Chorus, and Orch. (Leeds Festival, Sept. 8, 1858); *Ode for the Opening of the International Exhibition,* op. 40 (London, May 1, 1862); *Ode on the Installation of the Duke of Devonshire* (Cambridge, May 10, 1862); *The Woman of Samaria,* a cantata, op. 44 (Birmingham Festival, Aug. 28, 1867); also music to Sophocles' *Ajax* (1872?); String Quartet; Piano Sonata in A-flat major, op. 46, known as *The Maid of Orleans* (1873); numerous piano pieces; pedagogical works for piano; anthems; songs.

BIBL.: The *Musical Times* publ. a series of articles on S. B. in its issues of May–Aug. 1903; also an article by F. Corder in its issue of May 1916; see also J.R. Sterndale Bennett, *The Life of W. S. B.* (Cambridge, 1907); C. Stanford, "W. S. B., 1816–1875," *Musical Quarterly* (Oct. 1916); G. Spink, "Schumann and S. B.," *Musical Times* (June 1964); G. Bush, "S. B.: The Solo Piano Works," *Proceedings of the Royal Musical Association,* XCI (1964–65); idem, "S. B.: A Note on His Chamber and Piano Music," *Musical Times* (June 1972); N. Temperley, "S. B. and the Lied," ibid. (Nov.–Dec. 1975); A. Cope, "S. B.'s G minor Adagio," ibid. (June 1981); G. Bush, "S. B. and the Orchestra," ibid. (June 1986).

Bennewitz (Benevic), Antonín, Czech violinist and pedagogue; b. Přívaty, near Litomyše, March 1833; d. Doksy, near Litoměřice, May 29, 1926. He studied at the Prague Cons. (1846–52); in 1865 he was appointed a prof. of violin at the Prague Cons.; in 1882 he was named its director, a position he retained until 1901. Among his famous pupils were Ševčík, Suk, Halir, and Nedbal.

Benoist, André, French pianist; b. Paris, April 4, 1879; d. Monmouth Beach, N.J., June 19, 1953. He studied at the Paris Cons. with Pugno and Saint-Saëns; toured in Europe and America as accompanist to Casals, Heifetz, Albert Spalding, Tetrazzini, and other celebrated artists.

Benoist, François, French composer and organist; b. Nantes, Sept. 10, 1794; d. Paris, May 6, 1878. He studied at the Paris Cons. (1811–15) with Adam and Catel; won the Prix de Rome in 1815 with the cantata *Oenone;* returning from Italy in 1819, he was appointed to the staff of the Paris Cons., where he taught for 53 years; he was pensioned in 1872. He wrote mostly for the theater; among his operas are *Léonore et Félix,* produced at the Opéra-Comique in Paris on Nov. 27, 1821, and *L'Apparition* (Paris Opéra, June 16, 1848). He also wrote 4 ballets: *La Gipsy* (1839), *Le Diable amoureux* (1840), *Nisida, ou Les Amazones des Açores* (1848), and *Pâquerette* (1851). He publ. 12 books of organ pieces under the title *Bibliothèque de l'organiste.*

Benoit, Peter (Léopold Léonard), eminent Flemish composer; b. Harlebeke, Belgium, Aug. 17, 1834; d. Antwerp, March 8, 1901. He studied at the Brussels Cons. with Fétis (1851–55); while there he earned his living by conducting theater orchs. He also wrote music for Flemish plays; at the age of 22 he produced his 1st opera in Flemish, *Het dorp in't gebergte* (A Mountain Village), staged in Brussels on Dec. 14, 1856. With his cantata *Le Meurtre d'Abel* Benoit obtained the Belgian Prix de Rome (1857); however, he did not go to Italy, but traveled instead in Germany. As part of his duties he submitted a short *Cantate de Noël* to Fétis, who praised Benoit's music; he also wrote the essay *L'École de musique flamande et son avenir,* proclaiming his fervent faith in the future of a national Flemish school of composition, of which he was the most ardent supporter. His 1-act opera *Roi des Aulnes* was presented in Brussels (Dec. 2, 1859); the Théâtre-Lyrique of Paris tentatively accepted it; Benoit spent many months in Paris awaiting its production, which never took place; in the meantime he acted as 2nd conductor at the Bouffes-Parisiens. In 1863 he returned to Belgium, where he produced his 2nd Flemish opera, *Isa* (Brussels, Feb. 24, 1867). In 1867 he founded the Flemish Music School in Antwerp; he militated for many years to obtain official status for it. In 1898 it was finally granted, and the school became the Royal Flemish Cons.; Benoit remained its director to the end of his life. In Belgium Benoit is regarded as the originator of the Flemish musical tradition in both composition and education; but although he cultivated the Flemish idiom in most of his works, his musical style owes much to French and German influences. Apart from his successful early operas, he wrote the opera *Pompeja* (1895), which was not produced; Flemish oratorios: *Lucifer* (Brussels, Sept. 30, 1866; highly successful; considered his masterpiece); *De Schelde* (1868); *De Oorlog* (War; 1873); dramatic musical score, *Charlotte Corday* (1876); historical music drama, *De Pacificatie van Ghent* (1876); *Rubens Cantata* (1877; greatly acclaimed); children's oratorio, *De Waereld in* (In the World; 1878); cantatas: *Hucbald* (1880) and *De Genius des Vaderlands* (1880); oratorio, *De Rhijn* (1889); etc. Of his church music, the most important is his *Quadrilogie religieuse* (Antwerp, April 24, 1864), of which the component parts had been separately performed in 1860, 1862, and 1863; also *Drama Christi* (1871). Benoit wrote relatively little instrumental music; his symphonic poems for piano with orch. and for flute with orch. have been performed. He also composed many songs in French and in Flemish. In his propaganda for national Flemish music, Benoit contributed numerous papers and articles, among them *Considérations à propos d'un projet pour l'institution de festivals en Belgique* (1874); *Verhandeling over de nationale Toonkunde* (2 vols., Antwerp, 1877–79); *De Vlaamsche Muziekschool van Antwerpen* (1889; a history of the Flemish Music School); *De Oorsprong van het Cosmopolitisme in de Muziek* (1876). In 1880 he was elected a corresponding member of the Belgian Royal Academy; in 1882, a full member.

BIBL.: M.E. Belpaire, *Een vlaamsche meester; P. B.* (Belfort, 1901); C. Stoffels, *P. B. et le mouvement musical flamand* (Antwerp, 1901); T. Radoux, "Paroles prononcées à l'annonce de la mort de P. B.," *Bulletins Lettres et Beaux-Arts* (Brussels, 1901); J. Sabbe, *P. B.; Zijn leven, zijne werken, zijne beteekenis* (Ghent, 1902); L. Mortelmans, *P. B.* (Antwerp, 1911); H. Baggaert, *P. B., Een kampion der nationale gedachte* (Antwerp, 1919); H.P. Morgan-Browne, "P. B., né Pierre Benoit," *Music & Letters* (1929); J. Horemans, *P. B.* (Antwerp, 1934); A.M. Pols, *Het leven van P. B.* (Antwerp, 1934); C. van den Borren, *P. B.* (Brussels, 1942); R.R. Boschvogel, *P. B.* (Tiel, 1944); A. Corbet, *P. B., Leven, werk en beteekenis* (Antwerp, 1944); G.-M. Matthijs, *P. B.* (Brussels, 1944); F. van der Mueren, *P. B. in het huidig perspectief* (Antwerp, 1968); H. Willaert, *P. B., de levenswekker* (Brussels, 1984).

Benson, Joan, American keyboard player and teacher; b. St. Paul, Minn., Oct. 9, 1929. She studied at the Univ. of Illinois (B.Mus., M.Mus., 1951) and at Indiana Univ. (1953); then went to Europe, where she received additional instruction from Guido Agosti and others, returning to the U.S. in 1960. She pursued a successful career as a versatile keyboard artist, becoming especially well known as a clavichordist and fortepianist through numerous tours of the U.S., Europe, and the Far East. Her repertoire extends from Renaissance pieces to modern music.

Bent, Ian D(avid), English musicologist; b. Birmingham, Jan. 1, 1938. He studied at St. John's College, Cambridge (B.A., 1961; B.Mus., 1962); subsequently taught at King's College, London. He received his Ph.D. in 1969 from Cambridge Univ. with the dissertation. *The Early History of the English Chapel Royal, c.1066–1327.* In 1975 he became a prof. of music at the Univ. of Nottingham. In 1982–83 he was visiting prof. at Harvard Univ., and in 1986 joined the faculty of Columbia Univ. With his 1st wife, **Margaret Bent,** and B. Trowell, he edited the revised ed. of Dunstable's works in the Musica Britannica series. He was a senior consulting ed. of *The New Grove Dictionary of Music and Musicians* (1980). He ed. *Source Materials and the Interpretation of Music: A Memorial Volume to Thurston Dart* (London, 1981); also publ. *Music Analysis* (London and N.Y., 1987).

Bent, Margaret (Hilda), English musicologist; b. St. Albans, Dec. 23, 1940. She was an organ scholar at Girton College, Cambridge (B.A., 1962; B.Mus., 1963); also studied with Dart, receiving her Ph.D. in 1969 from Cambridge Univ. with the dissertation *The Old Hall Manuscript: A Palaeographical Study.* She taught at King's College (1965–75); also, concurrently, at Goldsmiths' College from 1972. In 1975 she joined the faculty of Brandeis Univ. at Waltham, Mass. She joined the faculty of Princeton Univ. in 1981; she also served as president of the American Musicological Soc. (1985–86). With A. Hughes, she ed. *The Old Hall Manuscript* in the Corpus Mensurabilis Musicae series, XLVI (1969–73); with her former husband, **Ian Bent,** and B. Trowell, she ed. the revised edition of Dunstable's works in the Musica Britannica series; also publ. a valuable study, *Dunstaple* (London, 1981).

Bentoiu, Pascal, Rumanian composer; b. Bucharest, April 22, 1927. He studied composition with Mihail Jora in Bucharest (1943–48); was head of the Folklore Inst. there (1953–56). He composed a comic opera, *Amorul doctor* (The Love Doctor; 1964; Bucharest, Dec. 23, 1966); a radio opera, *Jertfirea Iphgeniei* (The Immolation of Iphigenia; 1968); an opera, *Hamlet* (1969; Bucharest, Nov. 19, 1971); Piano Sonata (1947); *Concert Overture* (1948; rev. 1959); 6 string quartets (1953–82); 2 piano concertos (1954, 1960); *Suite Transylvania* for Orch. (1955); *Luceafărul* (The Morning Star), symphonic poem (1957); Violin Concerto (1958); *Bucharest Images,* 3 sym. movements (1959); Violin Sonata (1962); 7 syms. (1965–86).

Benton, Joseph. See **Bentonelli, Joseph.**

Benton, Rita, American musicologist and librarian; b. N.Y., June 28, 1918; d. Paris, March 23, 1980. She studied piano with James Friskin and music theory with Bernard Wagenaar at the Juilliard School of Music; then enrolled at the Univ. of Iowa; received her Ph.D. in musicology there in 1961. In 1967 she was appointed music librarian at the Univ. of Iowa and in 1975 became prof. of music there. In 1976 she became ed. of *Fontes Artis Musicae,* and held this position until her death. Her specialty was French music history, a subject on which she contributed numerous articles to American and French magazines. She compiled a valuable catalogue of works by Ignace Pleyel (N.Y., 1977).

Bentonelli, Joseph (Horace), American tenor; b. Sayre, Okla., Sept. 10, 1898; d. Oklahoma City, April 4, 1975. His real name was **Benton,** but following the frequent practice among American singers, he adopted an Italian-sounding name when he embarked on a singing career. He studied voice with Jean de Reszke in Paris and made his public debut with the de Reszke Ensemble in Nice in 1925. He returned to the U.S. in 1934; sang with the Chicago Opera; then for 3 seasons sang with the Metropolitan Opera in N.Y., where he made

his debut as Des Grieux in *Manon* (Jan. 10, 1936). He had an extensive opera repertoire, and sang all leading Italian tenor parts.

Bentzon, Jørgen, Danish composer, cousin of **Niels Viggo Bentzon;** b. Copenhagen, Feb. 14, 1897; d. Hørsholm, July 9, 1951. He studied composition with Carl Nielsen (1915–18). At the same time he took courses in jurisprudence; subsequently he was attached to the Ministry of Justice in Denmark, and served as clerk of records of the Danish Supreme Court. He also taught piano and theory at a People's School of Music in Copenhagen. As a composer he followed the Romantic trends current in Scandinavia; an influence of his teacher Carl Nielsen pervades his music.

WORKS: Opera, *Saturnalia* (Copenhagen, Dec. 15, 1944); *Dramatic Overture* (1923); *Variations on a Danish Folktune* for Piano, Strings, and Percussion (1928); 3 chamber concertos: No. 1, *Symphonic Trio,* for 3 instrumental groups of Violins, Horns, and Cellos (1928–29); No. 2, *Intermezzo Espressivo,* for Solo Oboe, Clarinet, Horn, Bassoon, Strings, and Percussion (1935); No. 3, for Clarinet and Chamber Orch. (1941); *Fotomontage,* overture (1934); *Variations* for Chamber Orch. (1935); *Cyklevise-Rhapsody* for Orch. (1936); *Sinfonia seria* for School Orch. (1937); *Sinfonia buffa* for School Orch. (1939); 2 syms.: No. 1, *Dickens-Symphonie* (1939–40); No. 2 (1946–47); Sinfonietta for String Orch. (1943); *Racconti 1–6,* each piece for from 3 to 5 Instruments (1935–50); 5 string quartets (1921–28); String Trio (1921); Sonatina for Flute, Clarinet, and Bassoon (1924); *Variazioni interrotti* for Clarinet, Bassoon, and String Trio (1925); *Duo* for Violin and Cello (1927); *Mikrofoni No. 1* for Baritone, Flute, and Piano Trio (1937–39); *Variations* for Piano (1921); Piano Sonata (1946); *En romersk Fortaelling* (A Roman Tale), cantata for Soloists, Chorus, and Piano (1937); songs; choruses.

Bentzon, Niels Viggo, eminent Danish composer; b. Copenhagen, Aug. 24, 1919. Something is weird in the state of Denmark. The king rides a bicycle, and the density of musical composers per square kilometer exceeds that of all other countries. Bentzon is an example. He writes music of all sorts, with preference given to instrumental compositions in neo-Classical forms. Beginning in 1960, his music shows an influx of ultra-modern techniques, including happenings, audiovisual scores, and graphic notation. The sheer quantity of his works precludes total enumeration lest it burst open the very limit of the present edition. A judiciously circumscribed presentation is therefore essential.

Bentzon is a descendant of **Johann Ernst Hartmann** (1726–93), an early German-born Danish composer. The musical tradition of the family continued through many generations (his cousin was the moderately prolific **Jørgen Bentzon**). He studied piano with his mother, then took classes in music theory with Knud Jeppesen. In 1950 he was appointed to the faculty of the Royal Danish Cons. in Copenhagen. In his early compositions he assimilated a neo-Classical idiom distinguished by compact contrapuntal writing and harmonic clarity without avoidance of justifiable dissonance, which integrates into a sui-generis serial technique, often derived from numerical progressions. In this bent he assayed the musical equivalent of such mathematical impossibilities as squaring the circle.

WORKS: STAGE: OPERAS: *Faust III,* after Goethe, Joyce, and Kafka (1961–62; Kiel, June 21, 1964); *Die Automaten,* based on motifs from *The Tales of Hoffmann* (1973; Kiel, May 1974); *The Bank Manager* (1974). **BALLETS:** *Metaphor* (Copenhagen, March 31, 1950); *The Courtesan* (Copenhagen, Dec. 19, 1953); *Døren* (The Door; Copenhagen, Nov. 14, 1962); *Jenny von Westphalen* (Århus, Sept. 9, 1965); *Duel* (Stockholm, Nov. 12, 1977). **ORCH.:** 18 numbered syms. (1942–88); 8 piano concertos (1947–82); 4 violin concertos (1951–76); 3 cello concertos (1956–82); 2 flute concertos (1963, 1976); 1 concerto each for Oboe (1952), 6 Percussion Players (1957), Accordion (1962), Clarinet (1970–71), Viola (1973), and Tuba (1975); numerous occasional pieces inspired by chance events: *Meet the Danes* for Small Ensemble (1964); *Suite for Foreigners* for Orch. (1964); Sinfonia for 6 Accordions (1965); *Eastern Gasworks No. 2* for Instruments (1969); *Formula*, in memory of Varèse, for Selected Instrumentation (1969); *Epitaph over Igor Stravinsky* for a Few Instruments (1971); *In an Atmosphere of Italian Futurism* for an Optional Ensemble (1979); also a surrealistic cantata, *Bonjour, Max Ernst*, for a Selected Group (1961), and the cantata *The Rusty Menagerie* (1972). **CHAMBER:** 5 wind quintets (1941–57); 11 string quartets (1940–76); 4 quartets for 4 Flutes (1974–77); *Bop Serenade* for Woodwind Quartet (1952); *Observations, Psycho-biological Suite* for Flute, Oboe, and Piano (1974); sonatas for 8 different solo wind instruments (1947–73); 7 violin sonatas (1940–73); 4 cello sonatas (1946–72); *Square Root of 3* for Violin and Piano (1944); *Margarine* for Double Bass and Piano (1977); *In the Zoo* for Solo Accordion (1967); *Variations on "The Volga Boatmen"* for Solo Cello (1974). **PIANO:** 15 numbered sonatas (1940–81); *Bones and Flesh* for 2 Pianos (1973); *Information and Scenery*, in optical notation (1967); *Vibrations* for Prepared Piano (1969, in 2 versions); *Micro-macro* (1973); Piece for 12 Pianos (1954); also 5 sets of 24 preludes and fugues (1964–79).

Benucci, Francesco, famous Italian bass; b. c.1745; d. Florence, April 5, 1824. He began his career in 1769; in 1783 he went to Vienna, where he created the roles of Figaro in *Le nozze di Figaro* (Vienna, May 1, 1786) and Guglielmo in *Così fan tutte* (Vienna, Jan. 26, 1790) by Mozart. He visited London in 1788–89; then lived again in Vienna. In 1795 he returned to Italy.

Benvenuti, Tommaso, Italian opera composer; b. Cavarzere (Venice), Feb. 4, 1838; d. Rome, Feb. 26, 1906. When he was 18 years old, his opera *Valenzia Candiano* was announced for performance in Mantua, but was taken off after a rehearsal. The following year, he succeeded in having his 2nd opera, *Adriana Lecouvreur*, produced in Milan (Nov. 26, 1857). Other productions followed: *Guglielmo Shakespeare* (Parma, Feb. 14, 1861); *La Stella di Toledo* (Milan, April 23, 1864); *Il Falconiere* (Venice, Feb. 16, 1878); *Beatrice di Suevia* (Venice, Feb. 20, 1890); opera buffa, *Le baruffe Chiozzotte* (Florence, Jan. 30, 1895). Although Benvenuti's operas are workmanlike and effective, they failed to hold the stage after initial successes.

Benzell, Mimi, American soprano; b. Bridgeport, Conn., April 6, 1922; d. Manhasset, Long Island, N.Y., Dec. 23, 1970. Her grandfather was a singer of Jewish folk songs in Russia before his emigration to America. She studied at the David Mannes Music School in N.Y.; appeared at the Metropolitan Opera on Jan. 5, 1945, in the role of the Queen of the Night in *The Magic Flute;* in the next 5 years she sang about 20 different roles with the Metropolitan, including Gilda in *Rigoletto* and Musetta in *La Bohème*. In 1949 she abandoned grand opera and became a popular singer in Broadway shows and in nightclubs.

Benzi, Roberto, French conductor; b. Marseilles, Dec. 12, 1937. He was educated at the Sorbonne in Paris; then appeared as a conductor with regional orchs. and opera houses of France. From 1973 to 1987 he was music director of the municipal orch. and opera at Bordeaux. He also was a guest conductor with the Philadelphia Orch. and with the Berlin Phil. In 1966 he married Jane Rhodes, a soprano.

Berardi, Angelo, Italian organist, theorist, and composer; b. S. Agata, Feltria, c.1630; d. Rome, April 9, 1694. He was a student of Mario Scacchi; served as maestro di cappella and organist at Tivoli (1673–79); was then at the Spoleto Cathedral (1681) and at the college of S. Angelo in Viterbo (1687). In 1693 he was a canon and maestro di cappella at S. Maria in Trastevere, Rome.
WRITINGS: *Ragionamenti musicali* (Bologna, 1681); *Documenti armonici* (Bologna, 1687); *Arcani musicale* (Bologna, 1690); *Il Perché musicale ovvero Staffetta armonica* (Bologna, 1693).
WORKS: *Missa pro defunctis* (1663); *Salmi concertati* (Bologna, 1668); *Concentus cum Missa* (Bologna, 1669); *Musiche diverse variemente concertate per camera* (Bologna, 1689); many canons.

Berat, Frédéric, French song composer; b. Rouen, 1800; d. Paris, Dec. 2, 1855. He was a friend of the poet Béranger, many of whose lyrics he set to music; wrote many popular romances and chansonettes: *A la frontière, Bibi, La Lisette de Béranger, Le Départ, Ma Normandie*, etc.

Berberian, Cathy, versatile American mezzo-soprano; b. Attleboro, Mass., July 4, 1925; d. Rome, March 6, 1983. She was of Armenian parentage; she studied singing, dancing, and the art of pantomime; took courses at Columbia Univ. and N.Y. Univ.; then went to Italy; attracted wide attention in 1958, when she performed the ultrasurrealist *Fontana Mix* by John Cage, which demanded a fantastic variety of sound effects. Her vocal range extended to 3 octaves, causing one bewildered music critic to remark that she could sing both Tristan and Isolde. Thanks to her uncanny ability to produce ultrahuman (and subhuman) tones, and her willingness to incorporate into her professional vocalization a variety of animal noises, guttural sounds, grunts and growls, squeals, squeaks and squawks, clicks and clucks, shrieks and screeches, hisses, hoots, and hollers, she instantly became the darling of inventive composers of the avant-garde, who eagerly dedicated to her their otherwise unperformable works. She married one of them, **Luciano Berio**, in 1950, but they were separated in 1966 and divorced in 1968. She could also intone classical music, and made a favorable impression with her recording of works by Monteverdi. Shortly before her death she sang her own version of the *Internationale* for an Italian television program commemorating the centennial of the death of Karl Marx (1983). She was an avant-garde composer in her own right; she wrote multimedia works, such as *Stripsody*, an arresting soliloquy of labial and laryngeal sounds, and an eponymously titled piano piece, *Morsicat(h)y*. She resented being regarded as a "circus freak," and insisted that her objective was merely to meet the challenge of the new art of her time.

Berbié, Jane, French mezzo-soprano; b. Villefranche-de-Lauragais, near Toulouse, May 6, 1934. She studied at the Toulouse Cons.; made her debut in 1958 at La Scala in Milan; in 1959 she became a member of the Paris Opéra. Her operatic roles include Despina, Marcellina, and Zerlina; she also gave solo recitals.

Berbiguier, Antoine (Benoit-) Tranquille, French flutist and composer; b. Caderousse, Vaucluse, Dec. 21, 1782; d. Pont-Levoy, near Blois, Jan. 28, 1838. He was a pupil of Wunderlich at the Paris Cons.; wrote many important works for flute, among them 15 books of flute duos; 2 books of duos for flute and violin; 10 concertos; 7 books of sonatas, with cello or viola; 8 sets of variations, with piano or orch.; 6 books of flute trios.

Berchem (or **Berghem**), **Jachet (de)** (also **Jaquet, Jacquet**), Flemish composer; b. Berchem, near Antwerp, c.1505; d. c.1565. He was in the service of the Duke of Ferrara from 1555. He has been confused with his contemporary Jachet de Mantua; also with Jachet Buus and Giaches de Wert. Berchem's 27 madrigals for 5 Voices appeared in 1546, and 24 madrigals for 4 Voices in 1555; 3 books containing settings of stanzas from *Orlando furioso* and dedicated to Duke Alfonso II of Ferrara were publ. in 1561. Modern reprints of Berchem's works are included in the following eds.: R. van Maldeghem, *Trésor musical* (1865–93), vols. XI and XX (chansons), vols. XXVII and XXVIII (madrigals); R. Eitner, *Publikationen älterer praktischer und theoretischer Musikwerke* (1873–1905), vols. IX and XI (chansons).
BIBL.: R. Eitner, "Jachet da Mantua und Jachet Berchem," *Monatshefte für Musikgeschichte* (1889); A. Einstein, *The Italian Madrigal* (Princeton, 1949).

Berens, (Johann) Hermann, German pianist and pedagogue; b. Hamburg, April 7, 1826; d. Stockholm, May 9, 1880. He studied with his father, Karl Berens of Hamburg; then had instruction with Reissiger in Dresden, and later with Czerny in Vienna. In 1847 he emigrated to Sweden; served as music director to the Hussar regiment in Örebro (1849–60); then was music director at Mindre Teatern, in Stockholm (from 1860). In 1861 he was appointed to the staff of the Stockholm Cons.; in 1868 was named prof. there. He wrote an operetta, *En sommarnattsdröm* (1856); the operas *Violetta* (1855), *Lully och Quinault* (1859), *En utflykt i det gröne* (1862), and *Riccardo* (1869), which sank without a trace. But his collection of piano studies, *Neueste Schule der Geläufigkeit*, modeled after Czerny's studies, remained popular with piano students and teachers for many years.

Berezovsky, Maximus (Sozontovich), Russian tenor and composer; b. Glukhov, Oct. 27, 1740; d. (suicide?) St. Petersburg, April 2, 1777. He studied at the Kiev Ecclesiastic Academy; then was chorister at the Court Chapel in St. Petersburg. He attracted attention by his lyric voice, and in 1765 was sent by the Russian government to Bologna for further study. He became a pupil of Padre Martini, and wrote an opera, *Demofoonte* (1773), which was produced in Bologna. Upon his return to Russia, he was unable to compete with Italian musicians who had acquired all the lucrative positions in the field of vocal teaching and opera; he became despondent and cut his throat. In addition to his opera, he left a *Credo* and 17 other sacred works; in these he made an attempt to follow the natural accents of the Russian text, which was an innovation at the time.
    Bibl.: N. Lebedev, *B. and Bortniansky as Church Music Composers* (St. Petersburg, 1882).

Berezowsky, Nicolai, talented Russian-born American composer; b. St. Petersburg, May 17, 1900; d. (suicide?) N.Y., Aug. 27, 1953. He studied piano, violin, and voice at the Imperial Chapel in St. Petersburg; graduated in 1916, and obtained work as a violinist in the orch. of the provincial opera theater in Saratov, on the Volga River; there he played until 1919, when he joined the orch. of the Bolshoi Theater in Moscow. He crossed the border to Poland in 1920, managed to obtain an American visa, and arrived in N.Y. in 1922. He was engaged as a violinist in the orch. of the Capital Theater; in 1923 he joined the N.Y. Phil., remaining there until 1929. At the same time he took violin lessons with Paul Kochanski and studied composition with Rubin Goldmark. In 1928 he became an American citizen. He began to compose in larger forms; his Clarinet Sextet was performed at a chamber music festival in Washington, D.C., on Oct. 7, 1926. In 1929 his orch. *Hebrew Suite* was conducted by Mengelberg with the N.Y. Phil. Soon Berezowsky obtained other opportunities; Koussevitzky let him conduct the Boston Sym. in performances of his 1st Sym. in 1931 and his 4th Sym. in 1943; Koussevitzky himself conducted Berezowsky's 2nd and 3rd Syms. The famous German violinist Carl Flesch played the solo part of Berezowsky's Violin Concerto with the Dresden Phil. in 1930; Primrose played his Viola Concerto in 1942; and Piatigorsky performed his *Concerto lirico* with Koussevitzky and the Boston Sym. Berezowsky continued to play violin and conduct. From 1932 to 1936 and from 1941 to 1946 he was violinist and assistant conductor with CBS, and from 1935 to 1940 was a member of the Coolidge String Quartet. He held a Guggenheim fellowship in 1948. His cantata *Gilgamesh* (1947) was favorably received, and his children's opera *Babar the Elephant* (1953) had numerous performances. His music possesses a Romantic quality, ingratiatingly Russian in color; in his later works he introduced fine impressionistic harmonies. He died of intestinal congestion apparently caused by a suicidal dose of powerful sedative drugs. His 1st wife (he was married twice) wrote a sweet little memoir, *Duet with Nicky*, describing his happier days.
    Works: Sinfonietta (NBC, N.Y., May 8, 1932; won a prize); Sym. No. 1 (Boston Sym., March 16, 1931, composer conducting); Sym. No. 2 (Boston Sym., Feb. 16, 1934); Sym. No. 3 (Rochester, N.Y., Jan. 21, 1937); Sym. No. 4 (Boston Sym. Orch., Oct. 22, 1943, composer conducting); *Hebrew Suite* for Orch. (1929); *Christmas Festival Overture* (N.Y., Dec. 23, 1943); *Soldiers on the Town* (N.Y., Nov. 25, 1943); Violin Concerto (Dresden, April 29, 1930; Carl Flesch, soloist; composer

conducting); *Concerto lirico* for Cello and Orch. (Boston, Feb. 22, 1935; Piatigorsky, soloist; Koussevitzky conducting); Viola Concerto (CBS Orch., N.Y., Oct. 11, 1941); Harp Concerto (Philadelphia, Jan. 26, 1945); *Passacaglia* for Theremin and Orch. (N.Y., Feb. 29, 1948); *Fantaisie* for 2 Pianos and Orch. (N.Y., Feb. 12, 1932); *Introduction and Waltz* for Orch. (N.Y., Oct. 15, 1939); *Theme and Variations*, a sextet for Strings, Clarinet, and Piano (Washington, D.C., Oct. 7, 1926); Cantata, *Gilgamesh* (N.Y., May 16, 1947); *Babar the Elephant*, children's opera (N.Y., Feb. 21, 1953); Sextet Concerto for String Orch. (1953); Duo for Clarinet and Viola (1931); Woodwind Quintet (1941).
    Bibl.: A. Berezowsky, *Duet with Nicky* (N.Y., 1943).

Berg, Adam, German music printer active at Munich between 1567 and 1599; d. Munich, 1610. He publ. the important collection *Patrocinium musices*, in 12 vols., printed between 1573 and 1598. Of these, 7 vols. are devoted to Orlandus Lassus.

Berg, Alban (Maria Johannes), greatly significant Austrian composer whose music combined classical clarity of design and highly original melodic and harmonic techniques that became historically associated with the New Viennese School; b. Vienna, Feb. 9, 1885; d. there, Dec. 24, 1935 (of an abscess that could have been cured by sulfa drugs overnight had such medication existed at his time). He played piano as a boy and composed songs without formal training. He worked as a clerk in a government office in Lower Austria; in 1904 he met Arnold Schoenberg, who became his teacher, mentor, and close friend; he remained Schoenberg's pupil for 6 years. A fellow classmate was Anton von Webern; together they initiated the radical movement known to history as the Second Vienna School of composition. In Nov. 1918 Schoenberg organized in Vienna the Soc. for Private Musical Performances (Verein für Musikalische Privataufführungen) with the purpose of performing works unacceptable to established musical society. So as to emphasize the independence of the new organization, music critics were excluded from attendance. The society was disbanded in 1922, having accomplished its purpose. In 1925 Berg joined the membership of the newly created ISCM, which continued in an open arena the promotion of fresh musical ideas.
    Berg's early works reflected the Romantic style of Wagner, Hugo Wolf, and Mahler; typical of this period were his 3 *Pieces for Orchestra* (1913–15). As early as 1917 Berg began work on his opera *Wozzeck* (after the romantic play by Büchner), which was to become his masterpiece. The score represents an ingenious synthesis of Classical forms and modern techniques; it is organized as a series of purely symphonic sections in traditional Baroque forms, among them a passacaglia with 21 variations, a dance suite, and a rhapsody, in a setting marked by dissonant counterpoint. Its 1st production at the Berlin State Opera, on Dec. 14, 1925, precipitated a storm of protests and press reviews of extreme violence; a similarly critical reception was accorded to *Wozzeck* in Prague on Nov. 11, 1926. Undismayed, Berg and his friends responded by publishing a brochure incorporating the most vehement of these reviews so as to shame and denounce the critics. Leopold Stokowski, ever eager to defy convention, gave the 1st American performance of *Wozzeck* in Philadelphia on March 19, 1931; it aroused a great deal of interest and was received with cultured equanimity. Thereafter, performances of *Wozzeck* multiplied in Europe (including Russia), and in due time it became recognized as the modern masterpiece that it is. The original MS was acquired from the composer by the Library of Congress in Washington, D.C. Shortly after the completion of *Wozzeck*, Berg wrote a *Lyric Suite* for String Quartet in 6 movements; it was 1st played in Vienna by the Kolisch Quartet on Jan. 8, 1927; in 1928 Berg arranged the 2nd, 3rd, and 4th movements for String Orch., which were performed in Berlin on Jan. 31, 1929. Rumors of a suppressed vocal part for the 6th movement of the suite, bespeaking Berg's secret affection for a married woman, Hanna Fuchs-Robettin, impelled Douglas M. Greene to institute a search for the original score; he discovered it

in 1976 and, with the help of the American scholar George Perle, decoded the vocal line in an annotated copy of the score that Berg's widow, understandably reluctant to perpetuate her husband's emotional aberrations, turned over to a Vienna library. The text proved to be Stefan Georg's rendition of Baudelaire's *De Profundis clamavi* from *Les Fleurs du mal.* Berg inserted in the score all kinds of semiotical and numerological clues to his affection in a sort of symbolical synthesis. The *Lyric Suite* with its vocal finale was performed for the 1st time at Abraham Goodman House, N.Y., by the Columbia String Quartet and Katherine Ciesinski, mezzo-soprano, on Nov. 1, 1979.

Berg's 2nd opera, *Lulu* (1928–35), to a libretto derived from 2 plays by Wedekind, was left unfinished at Berg's death; 2 acts and music from the *Symphonische Stücke aus der Oper Lulu* of 1934 were performed posthumously in Zürich on June 2, 1937. Again, Berg's widow intervened to forestall any attempt to have the work reconstituted by another musician. However, Berg's publishers, asserting their legal rights, commissioned the Viennese composer Friedrich Cerha to re-create the 3rd act from materials available in other authentic sources, or used by Berg elsewhere; the task required 12 years (1962–74) for its completion. After Berg's widow died (1976), several opera houses openly competed for the Cerha version of the work; the premiere of the complete opera, incorporating this version, was 1st presented at the Paris Opéra on Feb. 24, 1979; the 1st American performance followed in Santa Fe, N.Mex., on July 28, 1979. As in *Wozzeck*, so in *Lulu*, Berg organized the score in a series of classical forms; but while *Wozzeck* was written before Schoenberg's formulation of the method of composition in 12 tones related solely to one another, *Lulu* was set in full-fledged dodecaphonic techniques; even so, Berg allowed himself frequent divagations, contrary to the dodecaphonic code, into triadic tonal harmonies.

Berg's last completed work was a Violin Concerto commissioned by the American violinist Louis Krasner, who gave its 1st performance at the Festival of the ISCM in Barcelona, on April 19, 1936. The score bears the inscription "Dem Andenken eines Engels" ("To the memory of an angel"), the angel being the daughter of Alma Mahler and Walter Gropius who died of consumption at an early age. The work is couched in the 12-tone technique, with free and frequent interludes of passing tonality.

Works: operas: *Wozzeck*, after a play of Büchner, op. 7 (1917–22; Berlin, Dec. 14, 1925, E. Kleiber conducting; 1st U.S. perf., Philadelphia, March 19, 1931, Stokowski conducting; 1st British perf., London, Jan. 22, 1952, Kleiber conducting); *Lulu*, after Wedekind's plays *Erdgeist* and *Die Büchse der Pandora* (1928–35; Acts 1 and 2 complete, with Act 3 in short score; Acts 1 and 2, with music from the *Symphonische Stücke aus der Oper Lulu* [1934] to accompany the Act 3 death of Lulu, Zürich, June 2, 1937; 1st British perf., London, Oct. 1, 1962, L. Ludwig conducting; 1st U.S. perf., Santa Fe, N.Mex., Aug. 7, 1963, R. Craft conducting; 2nd version, with Act 3 realized by Friedrich Cerha, Paris, Feb. 24, 1979, Boulez conducting; 1st U.S. perf., Santa Fe, N.Mex., July 28, 1979, M. Tilson Thomas conducting; 1st British perf., London, Feb. 16, 1981, Sir Colin Davis conducting). **other works:** 70 lieder, including settings of Ibsen, Goethe, Rückert, Heine, Burns, and Rilke (1900–1905); 7 *frühe Lieder* for Voice and Piano (1905–8; rev. and orchestrated 1928; Vienna, Nov. 6, 1928); *Variations on an Original Theme* for Piano (Vienna, Nov. 6, 1928); Piano Sonata, op. 1 (1907–8; Vienna, April 24, 1911; rev. 1920); 4 *Lieder* for Medium Voice and Piano, op. 2 (1908–9; rev. 1920); String Quartet, op. 3 (1910; Vienna, April 24, 1911; rev. 1924); 5 *Orchesterlieder nach Ansichtskartentexten von Peter Altenberg*, op. 4 (1912; 2 numbers perf. in Vienna, March 31, 1913, Schoenberg conducting; 1st complete perf., Rome, Jan. 24, 1953, Horenstein conducting); 4 *Stücke* for Clarinet and Piano, op. 5 (1913; Vienna, Oct. 17, 1919); 3 *Stücke* for Orch., op. 6. (1913–15; rev. 1929; 1st complete perf., Oldenburg, April 14, 1930); 3 *Bruchstücke* from *Wozzeck* for Soprano and Orch., op. 7 (1923; Frankfurt, June 11, 1924,

Scherchen conducting); *Kammerkonzert* for Piano, Violin, and 13 Wind Instruments (the thematic material based on letternotes in the names of Schoen berg, Webern, and Berg; 1923–25; Berlin, March 27, 1927, Scherchen conducting; its *Adagio*, scored for Violin, Clarinet, and Piano, was arranged in 1934); *Lyrische Suite* for String Quartet (1925–26; Vienna, Jan. 8, 1927, Kolisch Quarter; movements 2–4 arranged for String Orch., 1928; Berlin, Jan. 31, 1929, Horenstein conducting; with newly discovered vocal finale, Abraham Goodman House, N.Y., Nov. 1, 1979, Columbia String Quartet; K. Ciesinski, mezzo-soprano); *Der Wein*, concert aria for Soprano and Orch., after Baudelaire (1929; Königsberg, June 4, 1930); *Symphonische Stücke aus der Oper Lulu* or *Lulu-Symphonie* (*Suite*), in 5 movements, with soprano soloist in no. 3, *Lied der Lulu* (Berlin, Nov. 30, 1934, Kleiber conducting); Concerto for Violin and Orch., *Dem Andenken eines Engels* (1935; Barcelona, April 19, 1936; L. Krasner, soloist; Scherchen conducting); also piano arrangements of Schreker's *Der ferne Klang* (1911) and Schoenberg's *Gurrelieder* (1912), and the last 2 movements of the String Quartet, op. 10, for Voice and Piano. He also made an arrangement for chamber ensemble of J. Strauss's waltz *Wine, Women, and Song.*

Writings: He contributed articles to many contemporary music journals; also wrote analyses for Schoenberg's *Gurrelieder, Kammersymphonie*, and *Pelléas und Mélisande.*

Bibl.: The International A. B. Soc. of the Graduate Center of the City Univ. of N.Y. issues a newsletter. See also the following: special issue of *Eine Wiener Musikzeitschrift* (Vienna, 1936); W. Reich, *A. B.: Mit B.s eigenen Schriftem und Beiträgen von Theodor Wiesengrund-Adorno und Ernst Krenek* (Vienna, 1937); R. Leibowitz, *Schoenberg et son école* (Paris, 1947; in Eng. as *Schoenberg and His School*, N.Y., 1949); H. Redlich, *A. B.: Versuch einer Würdigung* (Vienna, 1957; abridged Eng. tr. as *A. B.: The Man and His Music*, N.Y., 1957); W. Reich, ed., *A. B.: Bildnis im Wort. Selbstzeugnisse und Aussagen der Freunde* (Zürich, 1959); K. Vogelsang, *A. B.: Leben und Werk* (Berlin, 1959); W. Reich, *A. B.: Leben und Werk* (Zürich, 1963; in Eng. as *The Life and Work of A. B.*, London, 1965); G. Perle, "*Lulu*: The Formal Design," *Journal of the American Musicological Society*, XVII (1964); H. Berg, ed., *A. B.: Briefe an seine Frau* (Vienna, 1965; in Eng. as *A. B.: Letters to His Wife*, London, 1971); T. Adorno, *A. B., der Meister des Kleinsten Übergangs* (Vienna, 1968; rev. ed., 1978); G. Ploebsch, *A. B.s "Wozzeck"; Dramaturgie und Musikalischer Aufbau* (Strasbourg, 1968); K. Schweizer, *Die Sonatensatzform im Schaffen A. B.s* (Stuttgart, 1970); M. Carner, *A. B.: The Man and the Work* (London, 1975; 2nd ed., rev., 1983); E. Hilmar, *Wozzeck von A. B.* (Vienna, 1975); V. Scherleiss, *A. B.* (Hamburg, 1975); D. Jarman, *The Music of A. B.* (Berkeley, 1979); K. Monson, *A. B.* (Boston, 1979); F. Grasberger and R. Stephan, eds., *Die Werke von A. B.: Handschriftenkatalog* (Vienna, 1981); R. Klein, ed., *A. B. Symposion, Wien 1980: Tagungsbericht* (Vienna, 1981); G. Perle, *The Operas of A. B.* (2 vols., Berkeley, 1981 and 1985); J. Schmalfeldt, *B.'s Wozzeck: Harmonic Language and Dramatic Design* (London, 1983); E. Berg, *Der unverbesserliche Romantiker: A. B., 1885–1935* (Vienna, 1985); R. Hilmar, ed., *Katalog der Schriftstücke von der Hand A. B.s, der fremdschriftlichen und gedruckten Dokumente zur Lebensgeschichte und zu seinem Werk* (Vienna, 1985); P. Petersen, *A. B., Wozzeck: Eine semantische Analyse unter Einbeziehung der Skizzen und Dokumente aus dem Nachlass B.s* (Munich, 1985); J. Brand, C. Hailey, and D. Harris, eds., *The B.-Schönberg Correspondence* (N.Y., 1986); S. Rode, *A. B. und Karl Kraus: Zur geistigen Biographie des Komponisten der "Lulu"* (Frankfurt, 1988); D. Jarman, *A. B.: "Wozzeck"* (Cambridge, 1989); D. Gable and R. Morgan, eds., *A. B.: Historical and Analytical Perspectives* (Oxford, 1990).

Berg, Gunnar (Johnsen), Danish composer; b. St. Gall, Switzerland, to Danish parents, Jan. 11, 1909; d. Bern, Aug. 25, 1989. He studied composition with Jeppesen and piano with Hermann Koppel in Copenhagen (1935–48); went to Paris in 1948 to study with Honegger and stayed there until 1957;

returning to Copenhagen, he joined the avant-garde groups with the aim of liberating music from unnecessary academism. In his works he employs a sui generis serial technique in which each theme is a "cell" consisting of 5 to 10 notes, a model suggested to him by the experiments in cellular biology conducted by the bacteriologist Gaffky.

WORKS: *Hymnos* for String Orch. (1946); *Passacaglia* for Orch. (1948; Aarhus, Sept. 7, 1980); *Prosthesis* for Saxophone and Piano (1952); *Cosmogonie* for 2 Pianos (1952); ballet, *Mouture* (1953); *5 Études* for Double String Orch. (1955); *El triptico gallego* for Orch. (1957); *Pour piano et orchestre* (Danish Radio, Sept. 29, 1966); *Gaffky's*, piano cycle in 10 "assortments" (1959); *Pour violon et piano* (1960); 2 chamber cantatas: *Spring Thaw* (1961) and *Vision*, after Dylan Thomas (1962); *Frise* for Chamber Orch. and Piano (Copenhagen, May 17, 1961); *Pour clarinette et violon* (1962); *Pour quintette à vent* (1962); *Pour quatuor à cordes* (1966); *Uculang* for Piano and Orch. (1967; Danish Radio, April 15, 1969); *Random* for Cello and Percussion (1968); *Tronqué* for Xylophone, Cello, and Piano (1969); *Pour flûte, clarinet et violon* (1972); Flute Sonata (1972); *Pièce* for Trumpet, Violin, and Piano (1972); *Fresques I–III* for Solo Guitar (1976); *Mutationen* for Chamber Orch. (Danish Radio, Nov. 1, 1978); *Mouvement* for String Quartet (1978).

Berg, Josef, Czech composer; b. Brno, March 8, 1927; d. there, Feb. 26, 1971. He studied with Petrželka at the Brno Cons. (1946–50); was music ed. of Brno Radio (1950–53); wrote simple music for the Folk Art ensemble. Later he began using 12-tone techniques. His most original works are the satirical chamber operas, to his own texts: *The Return of Odysseus* (1962); *European Tourism* (1963); *Euphrides in Front of the Gates of Tymenas* (1964); *Breakfast at Slankenwald Castle* (1966). He also wrote 3 syms. (1950, 1952, 1955); Viola Sonata (1958); Fantasia for 2 Pianos (1958); Sextet for Piano, Harp, and String Quartet (1959); *Songs of the New Werther* for Bass-baritone and Piano (1962); Nonet for 2 Harps, Piano, Harpsichord, and Percussion (1962); *Sonata in Modo Classico* for Harpsichord and Piano (1963); *Organ Music on a Theme of Gilles Binchois* (1964); String Quartet (1966); 2 *Canti* for Baritone, Instrumental Ensemble, Organ, and Metronome (1966); *Ó Corino* for 4 Solo Voices and Classical Orch. (1967); *Oresteia* for Vocal Quartet, Narrator, and Instrumental Ensemble (1967).

Berg, (Carl) Natanael, Swedish composer; b. Stockholm, Feb. 9, 1879; d. there, Oct. 14, 1957. He first studied surgery; then entered the Stockholm Cons., where he studied singing; later he went abroad and took courses in composition in Germany. His works are couched in a characteristically Scandinavian Romantic manner.

WORKS: 5 operas, all produced in Stockholm: *Leila* (Feb. 29, 1912); *Engelbrekt* (Sept. 21, 1929); *Judith* (Feb. 22, 1936); *Brigitta* (Jan. 10, 1942); *Genoveva* (Oct. 25, 1947); 3 pantomime-ballets: *Älvorna* (1914); *Sensitiva* (1919); *Hertiginnans friare* (The Duchess's Suitors; 1920); 5 syms. with subtitles: No. 1, *Alles endet was entstehet* (1913); No. 2, *Årstiderna* (The Tides; 1916); No. 3, *Makter* (Power; 1917); No. 4, *Pezzo sinfonico* (1918; rev. 1939); No. 5, *Trilogia delle passioni* (1922); symphonic poems: *Traumgewalten* (1911; Feb. 3, 1917); *Varde ljus!* (1914); *Reverenza* (1949); Suite for Orch. (1930); oratorios: *Mannen och kvinnan* (Man and Woman; 1911); *Israels lovsång* (Israel's Hymns; 1915); *Das Hohelied* (1925); Violin Concerto (1918); Serenade for Violin and Orch. (1923); Piano Concerto (1931); Piano Quintet (1917); 2 string quartets (1917, 1919); songs.

Bergamo, Petar, Serbian composer; b. Split, Feb. 27, 1930. He studied composition at the Belgrade Academy of Music with Rajičič; in 1966 joined its faculty as assistant prof. His overture *Navigare necesse est* (Belgrade, Feb. 27, 1962) typifies his style and manner, with a reference to the necessity of navigating in finding one's way in the modern method of composition; his *Musica concertante* for Orch. (Belgrade, Feb. 18, 1963) points to a neo-Baroque formalism. He further wrote 2

syms. (1957, 1963); *Concerto abbreviato* for Clarinet Solo (1966); *Ritrovari per tre* for Piano Trio (1967); *I colori d'argento* for Flute, Harpsichord, and a Chamber Group (1968); a String Quartet (1958); a ballet, *Steps* (1970).

Berganza, Teresa, Spanish mezzo-soprano; b. Madrid, March 16, 1935. She studied at the Madrid Cons.; in 1957 she sang at the Florence May Festival. She made her American debut in Dallas in 1958; also sang at the Glyndebourne Festival and at Covent Garden in London. On Oct. 11, 1967, she made her Metropolitan Opera debut in N.Y. as Cherubino in *The Marriage of Figaro*; also gave recitals.

Berge, Sigurd, Norwegian composer; b. Vinstra, July 1, 1929. He studied composition with Thorleif Eken at the Oslo Cons. and with Finn Mortensen (1956–59); later took courses in electronic music in Stockholm, Copenhagen, and Utrecht. From 1959 he taught at the Sagene College of Education. His output ranges from traditional works to electronic pieces.

WORKS: *Dances from Gudbrandsdal* for Orch. (1955–56); Divertimento for Violin, Viola, and Cello (1956); *Episode* for Violin and Piano (1958); *Pezzo orchestrale* (1958); *Raga*, concerto-study in Indian music, for Oboe and Orch. (1959); *Sinus* for Strings and Percussion (1961); *Tamburo piccolo* for Strings and Percussion (1961); *Chroma* for Orch. (1963); *A* for Orch. (1964–65); *B* for Orch. (1965–66); *Flute Solo* (1966); *Oboe Solo* (1966); *Yang Guan* for Wind Quintet (1967); *Ballet* for 2 Dancers and Percussion (1967–68); *Gamma* for 7 Instruments (1970); *Epsilon* for Chamber Orch. (1970); *Delta* for Jazz Trio and Tape (1970); *Horn Call* for Solo Horn (1972); *Between Mirrors* for Violin and Chamber Orch. (1977); *Music* for Orch. (1978); *Gudbrand skalsspelet*, music drama (1980); *Wind*, ballet (1981); *Music for 4 Horns* (1984); over 25 electronic pieces.

Bergel, Erich, Rumanian conductor; b. Rosenau, June 1, 1930. He studied in Bucharest; in 1959 he was appointed conductor of the Cluj Phil., but was shortly afterward (May 9, 1959) arrested on suspicion of subversive activities. He was released from prison on Oct. 4, 1962, and was engaged as a trumpet player by the Cluj Phil.; in 1966 became its conductor. In 1971 he left Rumania and settled in West Germany. In 1975 he made his American debut as guest conductor with the Houston Sym. Orch.; from 1979 to 1981 he served as its principal guest conductor. He publ. a disquisition on Bach's *Art of the Fugue* (Bonn, 1979; 1st vol. only).

Berger, Andreas, German composer; b. Dolsenhaim, near Altenburg, Saxony, 1584; d. Ulm, Jan. 10, 1656. In 1606 he became a tenor at the court chapel in Stuttgart; from 1608 to 1612 was court composer there. From 1624 to 1634 he served as Kapellmeister to Count Ludwig Eberhard of Öttingen. He subsequently held posts as a public official in Augsburg, Leutkirch, and Ulm. He composed both sacred and secular vocal music.

Berger, Arthur (Victor), American composer and writer on music; b. N.Y., May 15, 1912. After preliminary study with Vincent Jones at N.Y. Univ., he moved to Boston. From 1934 to 1937 he studied at the Longy School of Music in Cambridge, Mass., and later attended the Harvard Graduate School, where he took courses in composition with Walter Piston, and academic musical subjects with Archibald T. Davidson and Hugo Leichtentritt. Subsequently he went to Paris to study composition with Nadia Boulanger. Returning to the U.S. in 1939, he entered Mills College in Oakland, Calif., to study composition with Darius Milhaud. In 1942–43 he was on the staff of Brooklyn College; in 1953 he was appointed prof. of music at Brandeis Univ. (retired in 1980); in 1973–74 he was visiting prof. of music at Harvard Univ.; in 1975–76 he was the recipient of a Guggenheim fellowship. His musical idiom reveals the influence of divergent schools of composition, including a sui generis serialism and the neo-Classical pragmatism of Stravinsky. His works, in whatever idiom, are characterized by a strong formal structure; the title of one of his most cogent scores, *Ideas of Order*, is a declaration of principles. Berger was also an able music critic; he covered concerts in N.Y. for the *New York Sun* (1943–46) and for the *New York Herald-Tribune* (1946–53). He also wrote a monograph on Aaron Copland (N.Y., 1953).

WORKS: 2 *Episodes* for Piano (1933); 3 *Songs of Yeats* for Voice, Flute, Clarinet, and Cello (1939); *Entertainment Piece* for 3 Dancers and "Modern-style Piano" (1940); Woodwind Quartet (1941); *Serenade Concertante* for Violin, Woodwind Quartet, and Chamber Orch. (1944; Rochester, N.Y., Oct. 24, 1945); 3 *Pieces* for Strings (N.Y., Jan. 26, 1946); *Duo No. 1* for Violin and Piano (1948); *Duo No. 2* for Violin and Piano (1950); *Duo No. 3* for Oboe and Clarinet (1952); *Ideas of Order* for Orch. (N.Y. Phil., April 11, 1953, Mitropoulos conducting); *Polyphony* for Orch. (Louisville, Ky., Nov. 17, 1956); *Chamber Music for 13 Players* (Los Angeles, April 4, 1960); String Quartet (1958); *Chamber Concerto* for Orch. (1959; N.Y., May 13, 1962; rev. 1978); *Septet* for Flute, Clarinet, Bassoon, Violin, Viola, Cello, and Piano (1966; Library of Congress, Washington, D.C., Nov. 25, 1966); *Trio* for Guitar, Violin, and Piano (1972); *Composition* for Piano, 4-hands (1976); 5 *Songs* for Tenor and Piano (1979); Piano Trio (1980); *Improvisation for A.C.* for Piano (1981); numerous other piano pieces.

BIBL.: J. Perkins, "A. B.; The Composer as Mannerist," *Perspectives of New Music* (Fall/Winter 1966); B. Northcott, "A. B.: An Introduction at 70," *Musical Times* (May 1982).

Berger, Erna, German soprano; b. Cossebaude, near Dresden, Oct. 19, 1900; d. Essen, June 14, 1990. She studied voice in Dresden with Melita Hirzel; made her operatic debut with the Dresden State Opera in 1925; sang there until 1930. On Nov. 21, 1949, she appeared at the Metropolitan Opera in N.Y. as Sophie in *Der Rosenkavalier;* remained on its roster until 1951; retired from the stage in 1955; returned to Germany and settled in Hamburg as a voice teacher. She gave her last solo recital in Munich on Feb. 15, 1968, at the age of 67. Her best operatic parts were Gilda in *Rigoletto* and Rosina in *Il Barbiere di Siviglia.* Her autobiography appeared as *Auf Flügeln des Gesanges* (Zürich, 1988).

BIBL.: K. Höcker, *E. B.: Die singende Botschafterin* (Berlin, 1961).

Berger, Francesco, English pianist and composer; b. London, June 10, 1834; d. there (at the age of 98), April 25, 1933. He studied harmony with Luigi Ricci in Trieste, piano with Karl Lickl in Vienna; later studied with Hauptmann and Plaidy at Leipzig; returned to London, where he was a prof. of piano at the Royal Academy of Music and at the Guildhall School of Music; made frequent concert tours through Great Britain and Ireland; was for some years director and, from 1884 to 1911, honorary secretary of the Phil. Soc. He composed an opera, *Il Lazzarone,* and a Mass; overtures and incidental music to Wilkie Collins's *The Frozen Deep* and *The Lighthouse;* many songs and piano pieces. He publ. *First Steps at the Pianoforte; Reminiscences, Impressions and Anecdotes; Musical Expressions, Phrases and Sentences;* and a *Musical Vocabulary in 4 Languages* (1922); in 1931 he publ. his memoirs, entitled (with reference to his age) 97.

Berger, Jean, German-born American choral conductor and composer; b. Hamm, Sept. 27, 1909. He studied music theory with Heinrich Besseler at the Univ. of Heidelberg (Ph.D., 1931), and also with Egon Wellesz at the Univ. of Vienna (1928–32). In 1931 he went to Paris, where he took lessons in composition with Louis Aubert; was also conductor of Les Compagnons de la Marjolaine, a mixed choral group specializing in his modern harmonizations of French folk tunes; in 1935 Berger acquired French citizenship. From 1939 to 1941 he was in Rio de Janeiro, where he was employed as French opera coach at the Municipal Theater. In 1941 he went to N.Y. He taught at Middlebury College in Vermont (1948–59), at the Univ. of Illinois, Urbana (1959–61), at the Univ. of Colorado (1961–68), and at other colleges. As a composer, he writes mostly for voice, in a melodious pragmatic idiom. In 1937 his work *Le Sang des autres* won 1st prize at the International Competition in Zürich. His compositions of the

American period include *Brazilian Psalm* for Chorus (1941); *Caribbean Concerto* for Mouth Harmonica and Orch., possibly the 1st of its kind, commissioned by Larry Adler and performed by him with the St. Louis Sym. Orch. on March 10, 1942; *Vision of Peace* for Chorus (1948); *Creole Overture* (1949); *Short Symphony* (1952); *Magnificat* for Soprano, Flute, Percussion, and Chorus (1960); *The Fiery Furnace,* dramatic cantata (1962); *A Song of Seasons* (1967); *The Pied Piper* for Vocal Groups and Orch. (1968); liturgical drama, *The Cherry Tree Carol* (1975).

Berger, Ludwig, German composer, pianist, and teacher; b. Berlin, April 18, 1777; d. there, Feb. 16, 1839. He studied flute and piano; went to Berlin in 1799; there he received instruction in harmony and counterpoint with Gürrlich. In 1804 he went to Russia, but fled in the face of Napoleon's invasion in 1812; in 1815 he returned to Berlin and was active mainly as a teacher; his students included Mendelssohn, Henselt, and Taubert. He wrote a Piano Concerto, 7 piano sonatas, songs, and numerous piano works.

BIBL.: L. Rellstab, *L. B.* (Berlin, 1846); D. Siebenkäs, *L. B.: Sein Leben und seine Werke unter besonderer Berücksichtigung seines Liedschaffens* (Berlin, 1963).

Berger, Roman, Slovak composer; b. Těšín, Aug. 9, 1930. He studied piano at the municipal music school in Katowice, Poland (1949–52); then established himself in Bratislava, where he took lessons in composition with Kafenda (1952–56); taught piano at the Bratislava Cons. (1956–65) and theory and composition at the Bratislava Academy of Musical Arts (1969–73). His style of composition follows the tenets of the modern Vienna School, formally well disciplined, melodically atonal, and harmonically complex.

WORKS: 3 piano sonatas (1960, 1965, 1975); Trio for Flute, Clarinet, and Bassoon (1962); *Ukolébavka* (Lullaby) for Mezzosoprano and Chamber Orch. (1962); Suite for Strings, Piano, and Percussion (1963); *Transformácie* for Orch. (1965); *Konvergenzioni I* for Violin and *II* for Viola; electronic pieces.

Berger, Rudolf, Czech baritone and tenor; b. Brünn, April 17, 1874; d. N.Y., Feb. 27, 1915. He began his career as a baritone with the Berlin Royal Opera (from 1898); then went to N.Y. and studied with Oscar Saenger; changed his voice to tenor; and returned to Germany. He made his American debut at the Metropolitan Opera in N.Y. on Feb. 5, 1914, as Siegmund in *Die Walküre;* was on its roster until his death. His repertoire consisted of 96 baritone and 18 tenor roles; he sang Jokanaan in *Salome* 79 times. He was married to the soprano **Marie Rappold.**

Berger, Theodor, Austrian composer; b. Traismauer, May 18, 1905. He studied in Vienna with Franz Schmidt; evolved under Schmidt's influence a strong Romantic idiom within the framework of Classical forms. His music acquired many important supporters in Austria and Germany, but rarely penetrates beyond Central Europe.

WORKS: *Malinconia* for String Orch. in 25 parts (1938); *Ballade* for Orch. (1941); *Rondo ostinato* for Wind Instruments and Percussion (1947); *Homerische Symphonie* (1948); *La Parola* for Orch. (based on the sequitone scale of alternating whole tones and semitones; 1955); *Sinfonia parabolica* (1956); *Sinfonia macchinale* (1956); *Symphonischer Triglyph,* on themes from Schubert's chamber music (1957); *Jahreszeiten* for Orch. (1958); *Frauenstimmen im Orchester* for Women's Chorus, Harps, and Strings (1959); Violin Concerto (1963); Divertimento for Men's Chorus, 7 Wind Instruments, and Percussion (1968).

Berger, Wilhelm (Reinhard), German composer; b. Boston (of German parents), Aug. 9, 1861; d. Jena, Jan. 15, 1911. He was taken to Germany as a child; studied at the Hochschule für Musik in Berlin (1878–81). From 1888 to 1903 he taught at the Klindworth-Scharwenka Cons. in Berlin; in 1903 was named a member of the Akademie der Künste in Berlin. He was a very prolific composer; wrote 105 opus numbers; his music, though lacking in originality, commanded respect for its technical skill.

Works: Sym. No. 1 (Boston, Nov. 4, 1899); Sym. No. 2; oratorio, *Euphorion;* Piano Quartet; numerous choral pieces; many songs.
Bibl.: E. Krause, *W. B.* (Leipzig, 1907); G. Ernest, *W. B.: Ein deutscher Meister* (Berlin, 1931).

Berger, Wilhelm Georg, Rumanian composer and musicologist; b. Rupea, Dec. 4, 1929. He studied at the Bucharest Cons. (1948–52); was a viola player in the Bucharest Phil. (1948–57). In 1968 he was elected Secretary of the Rumanian Composers' Union.
Works: stage: Oratorio, *Stefan Furtună* (1958). **orch.:** *Symphonic Variations* (1958); Concerto for String Orch. (1958); 17 syms.: No. 1, *Lyric* (1960); No. 2, *Epic* (1963); No. 3, *Dramatic* (1964); No. 4, *Tragic* (1965); No. 5, *Solemn Music* (1968); No. 6, *Harmony* (1969); No. 7, *Energetic* (1970); No. 8, *The Morning Star,* with Chorus (1971); No. 9, *Melodie* (1973–74); No. 10, with Solo Organ (1975); No. 11, *Sarmizegetusa* (1976); No. 12, *To the Star,* for String Orch. (1978); No. 13, *Sinfonia solemnis* (1980); No. 14 (1980–84); No. 15 (1984–86); No. 16 (1986); No. 17 (1986); 2 viola concertos (1960, 1962); *Rhapsodic Images* for Orch. (1964); Violin Concerto (1965; Brussels, Jan. 11, 1966; winner of the 1966 Queen Elisabeth of Belgium Composition Contest in the concerto category); Cello Concerto (1967); *Meditations,* cycle of variations for Chamber Orch. (1968); Variations for Wind Orch. (1968); Concerto for 2 Violas and Orch. (1968); *Concert Music* for Flute, Strings, and Percussion (1972); Concerto for Violin, Viola, and Orch. (1977); *Faust,* dramatic sym. (1981); *Horia,* symphonic poem (1985). **chamber:** Viola Sonata (1953); 15 string quartets (1954, 1956, 1957, 1959, 1961, 1965, 1966, 1966, 1967, 1967, 1967, 1967, 1979, 1980, 1983); Nonet (1957); Sonata for Solo Violin (1963); Quintet for 2 Violins, Viola, Cello, and Piano (1968); Concerto for Solo Organ (1981); *7 Serious Pieces* for String Quartet (1986); *7 Dramatic Pieces* for String Quartet (1986); songs.

Berggreen, Andreas Peter, Danish composer; b. Copenhagen, March 2, 1801; d. there, Nov. 8, 1880. He studied law and turned to music late in life; occupied various teaching posts in Copenhagen. His opera *Billedet og Busten* (The Portrait and the Bust) was produced in Copenhagen on April 9, 1832; he also wrote incidental music to plays. His most important contribution to music literature is the compilation of 11 vols. of folk songs, *Folke-sang og melodier, faedre landske og fremmede* (Copenhagen, 1842–55; 2nd ed., enl., 1861–71); he further publ. 14 vols. of songs for use in schools (1834–76) and ed. church anthems. Among his students was Niels Gade.
Bibl.: C. Skou, *A.P. B.* (Copenhagen, 1895).

Bergh, Arthur, American composer and conductor; b. St. Paul, Minn., March 24, 1882; d. aboard the S.S. *President Cleveland* en route to Honolulu, Feb. 11, 1962. He studied violin; played in the orch. of the Metropolitan Opera (1903–8); then conducted a series of municipal concerts in N.Y. (1911–14); later became associated with various recording companies. From 1941 Bergh lived in Hollywood as a librarian for motion picture companies. Among his works are 2 melodramas with Orch., *The Raven* and *The Pied Piper of Hamelin;* romantic opera, *Niorada;* symphonic chorale, *The Unnamed City;* 2 operettas: *In Arcady* and *The Goblin Fair;* about 100 songs; a number of violin pieces; etc.

Bergh, Rudolph, Danish composer; b. Copenhagen, Sept. 22, 1859; d. Davos, Switzerland, Dec. 7, 1924. He studied biology and music in Copenhagen and Berlin. He composed the choral works *Requiem für Werther* and *Geister der Windstille;* an oratorio, *The Mount of Holy Fire;* also about 150 songs; 50 piano pieces; chamber music; etc.

Berghem, Jachet de. See **Berchem, Jachet (de).**

Bergiron de Briou, Nicolas-Antoine, Seigneur du Fort Michon, French composer; b. Lyons, Dec. 12, 1690; d. there, before April 27, 1768. He studied classical literature and law at the Univ. of Paris; with J.P. Christin, he established in 1713 the Académie des Beaux-Arts in Lyons, and remained associated with it in various capacities until 1764. He composed a number of cantatas and motets; other works include divertissements and several operas.

Berglund, Joel (Ingemar), Swedish bass-baritone; b. Torsåker, June 4, 1903. He was educated at the Stockholm Cons.; made his debut there in 1928. He then appeared in Zürich, Vienna, and Buenos Aires; also sang in Chicago. He sang at Bayreuth in 1942; after World War II, he returned to America, appearing at the Metropolitan Opera in N.Y. (1946–49). He then was director of the Royal Opera in Stockholm (1949–56); he retired from the stage in 1970. He was regarded as one of the leading Wagnerian singers of his generation.

Berglund, Paavo (Allan Engelbert), Finnish conductor; b. Helsinki, April 14, 1929. He studied at the Sibelius Academy. In 1956 he became associate conductor of the Finnish Radio Sym. Orch. in Helsinki; in 1962 became its principal conductor. From 1972 to 1979 he served as music director of the Bournemouth Sym. Orch.; synchronously he conducted the Helsinki Phil. Orch. (1975–79). In 1981 he was appointed principal guest conductor of the Scottish National Orch. in Glasgow, which position he retained until 1985. In 1987 he became chief conductor of the Stockholm Phil. He was named an honorary Officer of the Order of the British Empire in 1977.

Bergman, Erik, distinguished Finnish composer, choral conductor, music critic, and pedagogue; b. Nykarleby, Nov. 24, 1911. He studied composition with Erik Furuhjelm at the Helsinki Cons. (1931–38); then with Heinz Tiessen at the Hochschule für Musik in Berlin, Joseph Marx in Vienna, and Wladimir Vogel in Switzerland. In 1963 he joined the staff of his Finnish alma mater (renamed the Sibelius Academy); retired in 1976. Bergman ranks among the most significant Finnish composers of his time. Stylistically, he cultivates varied techniques, ranging from medieval modality to dodecaphony. His predilection is for polyphonic vocal music.
Works: opera: *Det sjungande trädet* (The Singing Tree; 1986–88). **orch.:** *Suite* for Strings (1938); *Burla* (1948); *Tre aspetti d'una serie dodecafonica* (1957); *Aubade* (1958); *Simbolo* (1960); *Circulus* (1965); *Colori ed improvvisazioni* (1973); *Dualis* for Cello and Orch. (1978); *Birds in the Morning* for Flute and Orch. (1979); *Arctica* (Utrecht, Nov. 2, 1979); Piano Concerto (1980–81; Helsinki, Sept. 16, 1981); *Ananke* (1981–82; Helsinki, Oct. 6, 1982); Violin Concerto (1982; Mainz, May 11, 1984). **chamber:** Piano Trio (1937); *Dialogue* for Flute and Guitar (1977); String Quartet (Kuhmo, July 27, 1982); *Borealis* for 2 Pianos and Percussion (Washington, D.C., Nov. 19, 1983); *etwas rascher* for Saxophone Quartet (1985). **choral:** *Rubaiyat,* to the text by Omar Khayyám, for Baritone, Male Chorus, and Orch. (1953); *Adagio* for Baritone, Male Chorus, Flute, and Vibraphone (1957); *Svanbild* (Swan Picture) for Baritone, Vocal Quartet, and Male Chorus (1958); *Aton,* on the text "Hymn to the Sun" by the Pharaoh Akhenaten, for Baritone, Reciter, Chorus, and Orch. (1959); *4 Galgenlieder* for 3 Reciters and Speaking Chorus (1960); *Sela* for Baritone, Chorus, and Chamber Orch. (1962); *Fåglarna* (Birds) for Baritone, Male Chorus, 5 Solo Voices, Percussion, and Celesta (1962); *Springtime* for Baritone and Chorus (1966); *Snö* (Snow) for Baritone, Male Chorus, and Flute (1966); *Jesurun* for Baritone, Male Chorus, 2 Trumpets, 2 Trombones, and Percussion (1967); *Canticum fennicum* for Baritone, Solo Voices, 2 Solo Quartets, Male Chorus, and Orch. (1968); *Annonssidan* for Baritone, 3 Tenors, Reciters, and Male Chorus (1969); *Nox* for Baritone, Chorus, Flute, English Horn, and Percussion (1970); *Requiem for a Dead Poet* for Baritone, Chorus, Brass, Percussion, and Organ (1970); *Missa in honorem Sancti Henrici* for Soloists, Chorus, and Organ (1971); *Samothrake,* dramatic scene for Reciter, Chorus, Instrumental Ensemble, and Choreography (1971); *Hathor Suite* for Soprano, Baritone, Chorus, and Small Ensemble (1971). **vocal:** *Majnätter* (May Nights) for Soprano and Orch. (1946); *Ensamhetens sånger* (Songs of Solitude) for Voice and Orch. (1947); *Livets träd* (Tree of Life), chamber cantata for Soprano, Alto, Baritone, Horn, Clarinet, Percussion, Harp, and String Quartet (1947);

Bardo Thödol, after the Tibetan Book of the Dead, for Narrator, Mezzo-soprano, Baritone, Mixed Chorus, and Orch. (1974); *Loleila* for Girls' and Boys' Choruses, Soprano, Tenor, and Orch. (1974); *Noa* for Baritone, Chorus, and Orch. (1976).

BIBL.: J. Parsons, *E. B.: A Seventieth Birthday Tribute* (London, 1981).

Bergmann, Carl, German cellist and conductor; b. Ebersbach, Saxony, April 12, 1821; d. N.Y., Aug. 10, 1876. He was a pupil of Zimmerman in Zittau and of Hesse in Breslau; in consequence of his involvement in the revolutionary events of 1848–49, he left Germany and went to America. In 1850 he joined the traveling Germania Orch. as a cellist; later became its conductor; also led the Handel and Haydn Soc. of Boston (1852–54). In 1854 he went to N.Y. and became conductor of the German men's chorus Arion. On April 21, 1855, he made an impressive debut as a guest conductor of the N.Y. Phil., and was named its sole conductor for the 1855–56 season; from 1856 to 1866 he shared the conductorship with Theodore Eisfeld. In 1866 he became permanent conductor of the N.Y. Phil., a position he held until his death. He continued to perform as a cellist, taking part in the Mason-Thomas chamber music concerts; furthermore, he led a series of Sacred Concerts, in programs of both choral and orch. music. He was a progressive musician, and presented works of Berlioz, Liszt, and Wagner at the time when their music did not suit the tastes of the American public.

Bergmans, Paul (Jean Étienne Charles Marie), Belgian musicologist; b. Ghent, Feb. 23, 1868; d. there, Nov. 14, 1935. He studied at the Univ. of Ghent (Dr.Phil., 1887); in 1892 became assistant librarian there; in 1919, chief librarian and prof. He was a member of the Royal Academy of Belgium; publ. a number of very valuable studies and books, the most important of which are *P.J. Leblan, Carillonneur de la ville de Gand au XVIIIe siècle* (1884); *H. Waelput* (1886); *Variétés musicologiques* (3 vols.; 1891, 1901, 1920); *La Vie musicale gantoise au XVIIIe siècle* (1897); *Peter Philips* (1903); *Les Musiciens de Courtrai et du Courtraisis* (1912); *Notice sur Fl. van Duyse* (1919); *Corn. Verdonck* (1919); *Henri Vieuxtemps* (1920); *Le Baron Limnander de Nieuwenhove* (1920); *Quatorze lettres inédites du comp. Philippe de Monte* (1921); *Tielman Susato* (1923); *Notice sur le chevalier X. van Elewyck* (1925); *De l'histoire de la musique* (1927); *Les Origines belges de Beethoven* (1927); *Une Famille de musiciens belges du XVIIIe siècle: Les Loeillet* (Brussels, 1927; establishes for the 1st time accurate biographical data on members of the Loeillet family); *La Typographie musicale en Belgique au XVIe siècle* (1930). He also wrote an introduction to vol. I (1932; piano music, ed. by J. Watelet) of *Monumenta Musicae Belgicae.*

Bergner, Wilhelm, Latvian organist; b. Riga, Nov. 4, 1837; d. there, June 9, 1907. He was organist of the English church at Riga (1861) and at the Riga Cathedral (1868–1906); exercised great influence on the development of musical culture in Latvia.

Bergonzi, Carlo, Italian violin maker; b. Cremona, c. 1683; d. there, 1747. He began manufacturing violins about 1720, working independently of Stradivarius and other violin makers of his time. His son, **Michael Angelo Bergonzi,** continued the trade, as did his grandsons, **Carlo, Nicola,** and **Zosimo Bergonzi.**

Bergonzi, Carlo, noted Italian tenor; b. Polisene, near Parma, July 13, 1924. He studied voice in Parma with Grandini; made his operatic debut as a baritone in Lecce in 1948, singing Figaro in *Il Barbiere di Siviglia;* then established himself as a tenor; in 1951 sang the role of Andrea Chénier in Bari; in 1953 he appeared at La Scala in Milan with much success; from 1953 sang in London. He made his U.S. debut with the Chicago Lyric Opera in 1955; on Nov. 13, 1956, he made his 1st appearance at the Metropolitan Opera in N.Y. as Radames in *Aida,* and continued to be on its roster in subsequent seasons. He was particularly distinguished in the lyrico-dramatic roles in Italian operas.

Bergsma, William (Laurence), notable American composer; b. Oakland, Calif., April 1, 1921. His mother, a former opera singer, gave him piano lessons; he also practiced the violin. After the family moved to Redwood City, Bergsma entered Burlingame High School, where he had some music theory lessons. In 1937 he began to take lessons in composition with Howard Hanson, who was at that time teaching a course at the Univ. of Southern Calif. in Los Angeles. He composed a ballet, *Paul Bunyan,* and Hanson conducted a suite from it with the Rochester Civic Orch. in Rochester, N.Y., on April 29, 1939. Bergsma also took courses at Stanford Univ.; from 1940 to 1944 he attended the Eastman School of Music in Rochester, studying general composition with Hanson and orchestration with Bernard Rogers. He graduated in 1942, and received his M.M. degree in 1943. In 1944 Bergsma became an instructor in music at Drake Univ. in Des Moines. In 1946 and in 1951 he held Guggenheim fellowships. In 1946 he was appointed to the faculty of the Juilliard School of Music, N.Y., where he taught until 1963. From 1963 to 1971, Bergsma served as director of the School of Music of the Univ. of Washington in Seattle. In 1967 he was elected to membership in the National Inst. of Arts and Letters. During his teaching activities he continued to compose, receiving constant encouragement from an increasing number of performances of his works. His style of composition is that of classical Romanticism, having a strong formal structure without lapsing into modernistic formalism. The Romantic side of his music is reflected in his melodious lyricism. He never subscribed to fashionable theories of doctrinaire modernity.

WORKS: OPERAS: *The Wife of Martin Guerre* (N.Y., Feb. 15, 1956); *The Murder of Comrade Sharik* (1973; rev. 1978). **BALLETS:** *Paul Bunyan* (San Francisco, June 22, 1939); *Gold and the Señor Commandante* (Rochester, May 1, 1942).

ORCH.: Sym. for Chamber Orch. (Rochester, April 14, 1943); *Music on a Quiet Theme* (Rochester, April 22, 1943); Sym. No. 1 (1946–49; Radio Hilversum, April 18, 1950); *A Carol on Twelfth Night,* symphonic poem (1953); *Chameleon Variations* (1960); *In Celebration: Toccata for the 6th Day,* commissioned for the inaugural-week concert of the Juilliard Orch. during the week of dedication of Phil. Hall at Lincoln Center for the Performing Arts (N.Y., Sept. 28, 1962); *Documentary 1* (1963; suite from a film score); *Serenade, To Await the Moon* for Chamber Orch. (La Jolla, Calif., Aug. 22, 1965); Violin Concerto (Tacoma, Wash., May 18, 1966); *Documentary 2* (1967); Sym. No. 2, *Voyages* (Great Falls, Mont., May 11, 1976).

CHAMBER: *Concerto* for Wind Quintet (1958); *Fantastic Variations on a Theme from Tristan und Isolde* for Viola and Piano (Boston, March 2, 1961); Suite for Brass Quartet (1940); 5 string quartets (1942, 1944, 1953, 1970, 1982); *Showpiece* for Violin and Piano (1934); *Pieces for Renard* for Recorder and 2 Violas (1943); *Illegible Canons* for Clarinet and Piano (1969); *Changes for 7* for Wind Quintet, Percussion, and Piano (1971); *Clandestine Dialogues* for Cello and Percussion (1972); *Blatant Hypotheses* for Trombone and Piano (1977); Quintet for Flute and Strings (1979); *Masquerade* for Wind Quintet (1986); *A Lick and a Promise* for Saxophone and Chimes (1988).

VOCAL: *In a Glass of Water* (1945); *On the Beach at Night* (1946); *Confrontation,* from the *Book of Job,* for Chorus and 22 Instruments (Des Moines, Iowa, Nov. 29, 1963); *Wishes, Wonders, Portents, Charms* for Chorus and Instruments (N.Y., Feb. 12, 1975); *In Space* for Soprano and Instruments (Seattle, May 21, 1975); *I Told You So,* 4 songs for Voice and Percussion (1986). **PIANO:** *3 Fantasies* (1943); *Tangents* (1951); other piano works.

Berigan, Rowland Bernart ("Bunny"), American jazz trumpeter; b. Hilbert, Wis., Nov. 2, 1908; d. N.Y., June 2, 1942. He 1st took up violin, then turned to the trumpet; after playing in local bands, he went to N.Y., where he worked with Paul Whiteman, the Dorsey brothers, and Benny Goodman; from 1937 he led his own big band.

Berinbaum, Martin, American trumpet player; b. Philadelphia, June 14, 1942. He studied with James Stamp at the

Univ. of Southern Calif. in Los Angeles; then toured Europe and the Near East with the Roger Wagner Chorale; played 1st trumpet in the West Point Military Academy Band (1966–69); subsequently enrolled as a student of William Vachiano at the Juilliard School of Music in N.Y., graduating in 1970, and developed a career as a trumpet virtuoso.

Beringer, Oscar, German-born English pianist and pedagogue; b. Furtwangen, Baden, July 14, 1844; d. London, Feb. 21, 1922. His father, a political refugee, settled in London in 1849. Oscar Beringer received his rudimentary education at home; then enrolled in the Leipzig Cons., where he studied with Plaidy, Moscheles, and Reinecke (1864–66); he further studied in Berlin with Tausig; in 1869 became a prof. at Tausig's Schule des Höheren Klavierspiels; returned to London in 1871, and in 1873 established there an Academy for the Higher Development of Pianoforte Playing, organized on the model of Tausig's Berlin school. From 1885 he was also a prof. at the Royal Academy of Music. He was a pianist of great perfection of method; his book of technical exercises is valuable for students. Among his publ. compositions are a Piano Concerto; 2 piano sonatinas; various minor piano pieces; songs. He also publ. *Fifty Years' Experience of Pianoforte Teaching and Playing* (1907).

Berio, Luciano, noted Italian composer of extreme musico-scientific tendencies; b. Oneglia, Oct. 24, 1925. He studied music with his father, an organist, then entered the Milan Cons., where he took courses in composition with Ghedini and in conducting with Giulini. In 1951 he went to the U.S. and attended a seminar given by Luigi Dallapiccola at Tanglewood. In America he married an extraordinary singer named **Cathy Berberian,** who was willing and able to sing his most excruciating soprano parts; they were divorced in 1968, but magnanimously she continued to sing his music after their separation. Back in Italy, he joined the staff of the Italian Radio; founded the Studio di Fonologia Musicale for experimental work on acoustics; ed. the progressive magazine *Incontri Musicali*; later on he joined the Inst. de Recherche et de Coordination Acoustique/Musique (IRCAM) in Paris, working in close cooperation with its director, Pierre Boulez. From 1965 to 1972 he was on the faculty of the Juilliard School of Music in N.Y., and subsequently maintained a tenuous connection with America. In 1989 he was awarded Germany's Siemens Prize for his contributions to contemporary music. Perhaps the most unusual characteristic of his creative philosophy is his impartial eclecticism, by which he permits himself to use the widest variety of resources, from Croatian folk songs to *objets trouvés*. He is equally liberal in his use of graphic notation; some of his scores look like expressionist drawings. He is one of the few contemporary composers who can touch the nerve endings of sensitive listeners and music critics, one of whom described his *Sinfonia* with ultimate brevity: "It stinks." (The last traceable use of the word was applied by Hanslick in 1881 to Tchaikovsky's Violin Concerto.) But if *Sinfonia* stank, then so did, by implication, the ample quotes from Mahler, Ravel, and Richard Strauss used as *objets trouvés* in this work. Apart from pure (or impure, depending on perception) music, Berio uses in his works all the artifacts and artifices of popular pageants, including mimodrama, choreodrama, concrete noises, acrobats, clowns, jugglers, and organ grinders.

Works: *Concertino* for Clarinet, Vmolin, Harp, Celesta, and String Orch. (1949); *Opus No. Zoo* for Woodwind Quintet (1951); *2 Pezzi* for Violin and Piano (1951); *5 Variazioni* for Piano (1952); *Chamber Music*, to poems by James Joyce, for Voice, Clarinet, Cello, and Harp (1952); *Variazioni* for Chamber Orch. (1953); *Mimomusique*, ballet (1953); *Nones* for Orch. (1954); String Quartet (1955); *Allelujah I* for Orch. (1956); *Allelujah II* for 5 Instrumental Groups (1956–58); *Serenata* for Flute and 14 Instruments (1957); *Sequenze I* for Flute and 14 Instruments (1957); *Tempi concertati* for Chamber Orch. (1959); *Differences* for 5 Instruments and Stereophonic Tape (1959); *Circles*, to poems by e.e. cummings, for Voice, Harp, and Percussion (1960); *Quaderni* for Orch. (1960); *Se-*

quenze II for Harp (1963); *Traces* for Voices and Orch. (1964); *Sincronie* for String Quartet (1964); *Epifanie* for Female Voices, with Orch. (1959–63); *Chemins I* for Harp and Orch. (1965); *Chemins II* for Viola and 9 Instruments (1967); *Chemins II b* for Orch. (1969); *Chemins II c* for Orch. (1972); *Chemins III* for Viola, 9 Instruments, and Orch. (1968); *Chemins IV* for Oboe and Strings (1975); *Sequenze III* for Female Voice (1966); *Sequenze IV* for Piano (1966); *Sequenze V* for Trombone Solo (1966); *Sequenze VI* for Viola (1967); *Sequenze VII* for Oboe (1969); *Sequenze VIII* for Violin (1975–77); *Sequenze IX* for Percussion (1978–79); *Sequenze IX A* for Clarinet (1980); *Sequenze IX B* for Alto Saxophone (1981); *Sequenze X* for Trumpet (1984); multifarious agglutinations and sonoristic amalgamations for electronic instruments (*Mutazioni, Perspectives, Omaggio a Joyce, Momento*, etc.); *Sinfonia*, containing a movement based on remembered fragments of works by Mahler, Ravel, Richard Strauss, etc. (N.Y., Oct. 10, 1968); *Air* for Soprano and Orch. (1969); *Bewegung* for Orch. (1970; Glasgow, May 1, 1971); *Opera*, spectacle for Mixed Media (Santa Fe, N.Mex., Aug. 12, 1970; completely rev. 1976); *Memory* for Electronic Piano and Electronic Harpsichord (N.Y., March 12, 1971); *Prayer*, a speech sound event with Magnetic Tape Accompaniment (N.Y. April 5, 1971); *Recital* for Soprano and 17 Instruments (1971); *Amores* for 16 Vocal Soloists and 14 Instruments (1971–72); *Still* for Orch. (1973); Concerto for 2 Pianos and Orch. (1973); *Eindrücke* for Orch. (1973–74); *Linea* for 2 Pianos, Marimba, and Vibraphone (1974); *Points on the Curve to Find . . .* for Piano and 22 Instruments (1974); *Per la dolce memoria di quel giorno*, ballet (1974); *Après vidage* for Orch. (1974); *Coro* for 40 Voices and 40 Instruments (1974–76); *Il malato immaginario* for String Orch. (1975); Cello Concerto (1976); *Ritorno degli snovidenia* (Return of Dreams; "snovidenia" is a Russian word for "dream visions") for Cello and Orch. (Los Angeles, Jan. 25, 1979, composer conducting); *Entrata* for Orch. (San Francisco, Oct. 1, 1980); *Accordo* for 4 Wind Bands (1981); *Mille musiciens pour la paix* for 12 Wind Instruments (Lille, France, Nov. 22, 1981, composer conducting); *La vera storia*, opera to a highly diversified action, including Acrobats and featuring a Wordless Soprano (La Scala, Milan, March 9, 1982); *Entrata/Encore* for Orch. (Graz, Nov. 5, 1982); *Duo* for Baritone, 2 Violins, Chorus, and Orch. (1982); *Un Re in Ascolto*, opera in 2 acts (1979–83); *Voci* for Viola and Orch. (1984); *Formazioni* for Orch. (1985–87; Amsterdam, Jan. 15, 1987); *Festum* for Orch. (Dallas, Sept. 14, 1989).

BIBL.: M. Hicks, "Text, Music, and Meaning in B.'s *Sinfonia*, Third Movement," *Perspectives of New Music*, No. 20 (1981–82); *Contrechamps*, No. 1 (Paris, 1983; issue devoted to B.); D. Osmond-Smith, *Playing on Words: A Guide to L. B.'s "Sinfonia"* (London, 1985); L. Berio, *Two Interviews* (N.Y., 1985).

Bériot, Charles (-Auguste) de, celebrated Belgian violinist, pedagogue, and composer, father of **Charles-Wilfride de Bériot;** b. Louvain, Feb. 20, 1802; d. Brussels, April 8, 1870. A precocious virtuoso, he played in Paris in 1821, and later toured in England. The famous singer **Maria Malibran** was often a joint artist at his recitals; they became intimate in 1830, and were married in 1836, but she died as a result of a riding mishap a few months after their marriage. Bériot himself developed various ailments and had to retire from a concert career because of a paralysis of his left arm. He taught violin at the Brussels Cons. from 1843 to 1852. He wrote 10 violin concertos and 11 sets of variations for Violin, as well as numerous minor pieces of chamber music. His violin methods, *Premier guide des violonistes* and *Méthode de violon* (Paris, 1858), were popular pedagogical works.

BIBL.: E. Heron-Allen, "A Contribution towards an Accurate Biography of d.B. and Malibran," *De Fidiculis Opuscula*, no. VI (1894); A. Bachmann, *Les Grands Violonistes du passé* (Paris, 1913); A. van der Linden, "L'Exotisme dans la musique de C. d.B. (1802–1870) et d'Henri Vieuxtemps (1820–1881)," *Bulletin de la Classe des Beaux-Arts de l'Académie Royale de Belgique*, LII/10–11 (1970).

Bériot, Charles-Wilfride de, French pianist; b. Paris, Feb. 21, 1833; d. Sceaux du Gâtinais, Oct. 22, 1914. He was a natural son of **Charles (-Auguste) de Bériot** and **Maria Malibran,** born before their marriage (which took place in 1836). He studied piano with Thalberg, and later became a prof. of piano at the Paris Cons. He composed a symphonic poem, *Fernand Cortez;* 3 piano concertos; and a collection of pieces for violin and piano entitled *Opéras sans paroles.* With his father he compiled a *Méthode d'accompagnement pour piano et violon.*

Berkeley, Sir Lennox (Randall Francis), significant English composer, father of **Michael Berkeley;** b. Boar's Hill, near Oxford, May 12, 1903; d. London, Dec. 26, 1989. He studied French and philosophy at Merton College, Oxford (1922–26); then took lessons in composition with Nadia Boulanger in Paris (1927–32). Returning to London in 1935, he was on the staff of the music dept. of the BBC (1942–45); then was a prof. of composition at the Royal Academy of Music in London (1946–68). He was attracted from the beginning by the spirit of neo-Classical music, and his early works bear the imprint of the Paris manner as exemplified by the neo-Baroque formulas of Ravel and Stravinsky; but soon he formed an individual idiom which may be termed "modern English": broadly melodious, richly harmonious, and translucidly polyphonic. He was knighted in 1974.

WORKS: 4 operas: *Nelson* (1951; preview with Piano accompaniment, London, Feb. 14, 1953; 1st complete perf., London, Sept. 22, 1954; an orch. *Suite: Nelson* was drawn from it in 1955), *A Dinner Engagement* (Aldeburgh Festival, June 17, 1954), *Ruth* (London, Oct. 2, 1956), and *Castaway* (Aldeburgh Festival, June 3, 1967); ballet, *The Judgement of Paris* (1938); oratorio, *Jonah* (1935); Overture (Barcelona, April 23, 1936); *Domini est Terra* for Chorus and Orch. (1937; London, June 17, 1938); *Introduction and Allegro* for 2 Pianos and Orch. (1938); *Serenade* for String Orch. (1939); 4 syms.: No. 1 (1940; London, July 8, 1943); No. 2 (1956–58; Birmingham, Feb. 24, 1959; rev. 1976); No. 3, in 1 movement (1968–69; Cheltenham, July 9, 1969); No. 4 (1976–77; London, May 30, 1978); *Divertimento* for Orch. (1943); *Nocturne* for Orch. (1946); *4 Poems of St. Teresa* for Contralto and Strings (1947); *Stabat Mater* for 6 Solo Voices and 12 Instruments (1947); Concerto for Piano and Orch. (1947); 2-piano Concerto (1948); *Colonus' Praise* for Chorus and Orch. (1949); Sinfonietta (1950); *Gibbons Variations* for Tenor, Chorus, Strings, and Organ (1951); Flute Concerto (1952; London, July 29, 1953); Suite for Orch. (1953); Concerto for Piano and Double String Orch. (1958; London, Feb. 11, 1959); *An Overture* for Light Orch. (1959); *Suite: A Winter's Tale* for Orch. (1960); *5 Pieces* for Violin and Orch. (1961; London, July 3, 1962); Concerto for Violin and Chamber Orch. (1961); *Batter My Heart* for Soprano, Chorus, Organ, and Chamber Orch. (1962); *4 Ronsard Sonnets* (Set 2) for Tenor and Orch. (London, Aug. 9, 1963; version with Chamber Orch., Set 1, for 2 Tenors and Piano, 1952); *Partita* for Chamber Orch. (1965); *Signs in the Dark* for Chorus and Strings (1967); *Magnificat* for Chorus and Orch. (1968; London, July 8, 1968); *Windsor Variations* for Chamber Orch. (1969); *Dialogue* for Cello and Chamber Orch. (1970); *Sinfonia concertante* for Oboe and Chamber Orch. (London, Aug. 3, 1973); *Antiphon* for String Orch. (1973); *Voices of the Night* for Orch. (Birmingham, Aug. 22, 1973); Suite for Strings (1974); Guitar Concerto (London, July 4, 1974); 3 string quartets (1935, 1942, 1970); Violin Sonatina (1942); String Trio (1943); Viola Sonata (1945); *Introduction and Allegro* for Solo Violin (1946); *Theme and Variations* and *Elegy* and *Toccata,* all for Violin and Piano (all 1950); Trio for Violin, Horn, and Piano (1954); Sextet for Clarinet, Horn, and String Quartet (1955); Concerto for Flute, Violin, Cello, and Harpsichord or Piano (1955); Sonatina for Solo Guitar (1957); Oboe Sonatina (1962); *Diversions* for 8 Instruments (1964); *Nocturne* for Harp (1967); Quartet for Oboe and String Trio (1967); *Theme and Variations* for Solo Guitar (1970); *Introduction and Allegro* for Double Bass and Piano (1971); Duo for Cello and Piano

(1971); *In memoriam Igor Stravinsky* for String Quartet (1971); Quintet for Piano and Winds (1975); *Concert Studies* for Piano, sets 1 and 2 (1940, 1972); Sonata for Piano (1945); Sonatina for 2 Pianos (1959); Theme and Variations for 2 Pianos (1968); *3 Pieces* for Organ (1966–68); *Fantasia* for Organ (1976); numerous other pieces for piano; several songs, with piano, organ, harp, or guitar accompaniment; choruses.

Berkeley, Michael, English composer, son of **Sir Lennox (Randall Francis) Berkeley;** b. London, May 29, 1948. He was a chorister at Westminster Cathedral under the tutelage of George Malcolm; he also studied with his father at the Royal Academy of Music and then privately with Richard Rodney Bennett. He received the Guinness Prize for his *Meditations* for Orch. (1977); was associate composer to the Scottish Chamber Orch. (1979) and composer-in-residence at the London College of Music (1987–88). His anti-nuclear oratorio *Or Shall We Die?* (1982) brought him to international attention. His music is austere while still projecting a firm relationship to the English New Romantic movement.

WORKS: STAGE: *The Mayfly,* children's ballet (London, Sept. 30, 1984). **ORCH.:** Oboe Concerto (Burnham Market, Aug. 20, 1977); *Fantasia concertante* (London, March 5, 1978); *Primavera* (London, May 18, 1979); *Uprising,* sym. (Edinburgh, Dec. 18, 1980); *Flames* (Liverpool, Jan. 10, 1981); Cello Concerto (London, Feb. 20, 1983); Horn Concerto (Cheltenham, July 17, 1984); Organ Concerto (Cambridge, July 1987). **CHAMBER:** *Among the Lilies* for Brass Octet; String Trio (1978); Violin Sonata (1979); Chamber Sym. (London, Aug. 1, 1980); 2 string quartets (1981, 1984); Piano Trio (1982); *Music from Chaucer* for Brass Quintet (1983); Clarinet Quintet (1983); *Fierce Tears* for Oboe and Piano (1984); *For the Savage Messiah* for Piano Quartet and Bass (1985). **SOLO INSTRUMENTS:** *Strange Meeting* for Piano (1978); *Iberian Notebook* for Cello (1980); *Worry Beads* for Guitar (1981). **VOCAL:** *The Wild Winds* for Soprano and Small Orch. (London, Dec. 19, 1978); *Rain* for Tenor, Violin, and Cello (1979); *At the Round Earth's Imagin'd Corners* for Chorus (1980); *The Crocodile and Father William* for Chorus (1982); *Or Shall We Die?,* oratorio for Soprano, Baritone, Chorus, and Orch. (London, Feb. 6, 1983); *Songs of Awakening Love* for Soprano and Small Orch. (Cheltenham, July 15, 1986).

Berkenhead, John L., blind organist who was active in the U.S. toward the end of the 18th century. He arrived in America in 1795; was organist at Trinity Church in Newport from 1796 to 1804. His piece for Harpsichord, *Abolition of the Bastille,* was invariably featured at his concerts in Boston and other New England cities.

Berlijn, Anton (real name, **Aron Wolf**), Dutch composer; b. Amsterdam, May 2, 1817; d. there, Jan. 18, 1870. He studied with Friedrich Schneider in Berlin and with Spohr in Kassel; then went to Leipzig, where he took lessons with G.W. Fink; returning to Amsterdam in 1846, he became a conductor at the Royal Theater, but devoted himself mainly to composition. He wrote several operas, 2 of which were popular (*Die Bergknappen* and *Proserpina*); 7 ballets; an oratorio (*Moses auf Nebo*); and some instrumental music. He enjoyed a certain prestige in the Netherlands; a memorial vol., *Nachruf an den verstorbenden Komponist A.W. Berlijn,* compiled by P. Böhm, was publ. in Amsterdam shortly after Berlijn's death.

Berlin, Irving (real name, **Israel Balin**), fabulously popular Russian-born American composer of hundreds of songs that became the musical conscience of the U.S.; b. Mogilev, May 11, 1888; d. N.Y., Sept. 22, 1989, at the incredible age of 101. Fearing anti-Semitic pogroms, his Jewish parents took ship when he was 5 years old and landed in N.Y. His father made a scant living as a synagogue cantor, and Izzy, as he was called, earned pennies as a newsboy. He later got jobs as a busboy, in time graduating to the role of a singing waiter in Chinatown. He learned to improvise on the bar piano and, at the age of 19, wrote the lyrics of a song, *Marie from Sunny Italy.* Because of a printing error, his name on the song appeared as Berlin instead of Balin. He soon acquired the American vernacular and, throughout his career, never tried to experiment with sophisticated language, thus distancing himself from his younger contemporaries, such as Gershwin and Cole Porter. He was married in 1912, but his young bride died of typhoid fever, contracted during their honeymoon in Havana, Cuba. He wrote a lyric ballad in her memory, *When I Lost You,* which sold a million copies. He never learned to read or write music, and composed most of his songs in F-sharp major for the convenience of fingering the black keys of the scale. To modulate into other keys he had a special hand clutch built at the piano keyboard, so that his later songs acquired an air of technical variety. This piano is now installed at the Smithsonian Institution in Washington, D.C. His 1st biographer, Alexander Woollcott, referred to him as a "creative ignoramus," meaning it as a compliment. Victor Herbert specifically discouraged Irving Berlin from learning harmony for fear that he would lose his natural genius for melody, and also encouraged him to join the American Soc. of Composers, Authors, and Publishers (ASCAP) as a charter member, a position that became the source of his fantastically prosperous commercial success.

Berlin was drafted into the U.S. Army in 1917 but did not have to serve in military action. In the army he wrote a musical revue, *Yip, Yip, Yaphank,* which contained one of his most famous tunes, *God Bless America;* it was for some reason omitted in the original show, but returned to glory when songster Kate Smith performed it in 1938. The song, patriotic to the core, became an unofficial American anthem. In 1925, when Berlin was 37 years old, he met Ellin Mackay, the daughter of the millionaire head of the Postal Telegaph Cable Co., and proposed to her. She accepted, but her father threatened to disinherit her if she would consider marrying a Jewish immigrant. Money was not the object, for by that time Berlin was himself a contented millionaire. The yellow press of N.Y. devoted columns upon columns to the romance; the 2 eventually married in a civil ceremony at the Municipal Building. Ironically, it was the despised groom who helped his rich father-in-law during the financial debacle of the 1920s, for while stocks fell disastrously, Berlin's melodies rose in triumph all over America. The marriage proved to be happy, lasting 62 years, until Ellin's death in July of 1988. Berlin was reclusive in his last years of life; he avoided making a personal appearance when members of ASCAP gathered before his house to serenade him on his 100th birthday.

Berlin was extremely generous with his enormous earnings. According to sales records compiled in 1978, *God Bless America* brought in $673,939.46 in royalties, all of which was donated to the Boy and Girl Scouts of America. Another great song, *White Christmas,* which Berlin wrote for the motion picture *Holiday Inn,* became a sentimental hit among American troops stationed in tropical bases in the Pacific during World War II; 113,067,354 records of this song and 5,566,845 copies of sheet music for it were sold in America between 1942 and 1978. The homesick marines altered the 1st line from "I'm dreaming of a white Christmas" to "I'm dreaming of a white mistress," that particular commodity being scarce in the tropics. In 1954 Berlin received the Congressional Medal of Honor for his patriotic songs. His financial interests were taken care of by his publishing enterprise, Irving Berlin Music, Inc., founded in 1919, and also by ASCAP. According to some records, his income tax amounted to 91% of his total earnings. **Works: stage** (all perfs. in N.Y.): *Watch Your Step,* revue (Dec. 8, 1914); *Stop! Look! Listen!,* revue (1915); *The Century Girl,* revue (1916; with Victor Herbert); *Yip, Yip, Yaphank,* revue (Aug. 19, 1918); *Music Box Revue* (1921, 1922, 1923, 1924); *The Cocoanuts,* musical comedy (Dec. 8, 1925); *Ziegfeld Follies,* revue (1927); *Face the Music,* musical comedy (Feb. 17, 1932); *As Thousands Cheer,* revue (Sept. 30, 1933); *Louisiana Purchase,* musical comedy (May 28, 1940); *Me and My Melinda,* musical comedy (1942); *This Is the Army,* revue (July 4, 1942); *Annie Get Your Gun,* musical comedy (May 16, 1945); *Miss Liberty,* musical comedy (July 15, 1949); *Call Me Madam,* musical comedy (Oct. 12, 1950); *Mr. President,* musical play (Oct. 20, 1962). **FILM SCORES:** *The Cocoanuts*

(1929); *Puttin' On the Ritz* (1929); *Top Hat* (1935); *Follow the Fleet* (1936); *On the Avenue* (1937); *Carefree* (1938); *Alexander's Ragtime Band* (1938); *Second Fiddle* (1939); *Holiday Inn* (1942); *This Is the Army* (1943); *Blue Skies* (1946); *Easter Parade* (1948); *Annie Get Your Gun* (1950); *Call Me Madam* (1953); *White Christmas* (1954); *There's No Business Like Show Business* (1954). **SONGS:** *Marie from Sunny Italy* (1907; lyrics only); *Alexander's Ragtime Band* (1911); *Everybody's Doing It Now* (1911); *When I Lost You* (1911); *God Bless America* (1918; rev. version, 1938); *Always* (1925); *Remember* (1925); *The Song Is Ended but the Melody Lingers On* (1927); *Russian Lullaby* (1927); *Blue Skies* (1927); *White Christmas* (1942).

Bibl.: A. Woollcott, *The Story of I. B.* (N.Y., 1925); D. Jay, *The I. B. Songography* (New Rochelle, N.Y., 1969); M. Freedland, *I. B.* (N.Y., 1974); I. Whitcomb, *I. B. and Ragtime America* (N.Y., 1987).

Berlin, Johan Daniel, German-born Norwegian organist and composer; b. Memel, May 12, 1714; d. Trondheim, Nov. 4, 1787. He studied organ with his father; in 1730 proceeded to Copenhagen, where he continued his studies with Andreas Berg. In 1737 he became a city musician in Trondheim, a position he held until 1767; he was also organist at the city Cathedral from 1740 until his death. In addition to his various musical duties for the city, he collected musical instruments and wrote several treatises on music. He was a founding member of the Royal Norwegian Scientific Assoc. (1760). He composed some organ music, but few of his works are extant.

Bibl.: K. Michelesen, *J.D. B.* (diss., Univ. of Trondheim, 1971).

Berlinski, Herman, German-born American organist and composer; b. Leipzig, Aug. 18, 1910. He studied piano, theory, and conducting at the Leipzig Cons. (1927–32) and composition with Boulanger and piano with Cortot at the Paris École Normale de Musique (1934–38). In 1941 he settled in the U.S., and in 1947 became a naturalized citizen. He pursued training in organ with Joseph Yasser at the Jewish Theological Seminary of America in N.Y. (1953–60; Doctor of Sacred Music degree, 1960). From 1954 to 1963 he served as organist at N.Y.'s Temple Emanu-El; subsequently he served as minister of music of the Washington, D.C., Hebrew Congregation (1963–77). On Nov. 14, 1981, he appeared in his native city of Leipzig for the 1st time in 48 years as a recitalist at the new Gewandhaus. His extensive output reflects his dedication to liturgical musical expression.

Works: orch.: *Symphonic Visions* (1949); *Concerto da camera* (1952); Organ Concerto (1965); *Prayers for the Night* (1968). **CHAMBER:** *Chazoth,* suite for String Quartet and Ondes Martenot (1938); *Quadrille,* woodwind quartet (1952); String Quartet (1953); 11 sinfonias (1956–78). **VOCAL:** 3 oratorios: *Kiddush Ha-Shem* (1954–60); *Job* (1968–72; rev. 1984); *The Trumpets of Freedom* (Washington, D.C., Dec. 5, 1988); 4 cantatas: *The Earth Is the Lord's* (1966); *Sing to the Lord a New Song* (1978); *The Beadle of Prague* (1983); *The Days of Awe* (1965–85; Washington, D.C., Sept. 22, 1985); songs.

Bibl.: M. Kratzanstein, "The Organ Music of H. B.," *American Organist* (April 1989).

Berlinski, Jacques, Polish-born American composer; b. Radon, Dec. 13, 1913; d. Reseda, Calif., March 17, 1988. He emigrated to France in 1931 and studied theory with Nadia Boulanger. During World War II, he served in an artillery unit in the French army. In 1948 he received a prize in an American composition contest for his *Symphony of Glory,* dedicated to Winston Churchill. He settled in the U.S. and became a naturalized citizen in 1973. He wrote a choral sym. entitled *America, 1976* for the U.S. bicentennial (San Diego, May 6, 1976).

Berlioz, Gabriel Pierre, French composer (not related to Hector Berlioz); b. Paris, June 25, 1916. He studied in Paris with Roussel and d'Indy. He wrote a Viola Concerto (1935); *Francezaïc,* comic opera (1939); *Symphonie parisienne* (1942); *Jardin hanté,* ballet (1943); Piano Trio (1944); *Divertissement* for Violin, Cello, Piano, and String Orch. (1945); Concerto for Kettledrums and Orch. (1951; Paris, Jan. 25, 1953); Bassoon Concerto (1952); Sym. No. 2 (1953); pieces for tuba and piano, saxophone and piano, flute and piano, etc.

Berlioz, (Louis-) Hector, great French composer who exercised profound influence on the course of modern music in the direction of sonorous grandiosity, and propagated the Romantic ideal of program music, unifying it with literature; b. La Côte-Saint-André, Isère, Dec. 11, 1803; d. Paris, March 8, 1869. His father was a medical doctor who possessed musical inclinations; under his guidance Berlioz learned to play the flute, and later took up the guitar; however, he never became an experienced performer on any instrument. Following his father's desire that he study medicine, he went to Paris, where he entered the École de Médecine; at the same time he began taking private lessons in composition from Jean François Le Sueur. In 1824, he abandoned his medical studies to dedicate himself entirely to composition; his 1st important work was a *Messe solennelle,* which was performed at a Paris church on July 10, 1825; he then wrote an instrumental work entitled *La Révolution grecque,* inspired by the revolutionary uprising in Greece against the Ottoman domination. He was 22 years old when he entered the Paris Cons. as a pupil of his 1st music teacher, Le Sueur, in composition, and of Anton Reicha in counterpoint and fugue. In 1826, Berlioz wrote an opera, *Les Francs-juges,* which never came to a complete performance. In 1827 he submitted his cantata *La Mort d'Orphée* for the Prix de Rome, but it was rejected. On May 26, 1828, he presented a concert of his works at the Paris Cons., including the *Resurrexit* from the *Messe solennelle, La Révolution grecque,* and the overtures *Les Francs-juges* and *Waverley.* Also in 1828 he won the 2nd prize of the Prix de Rome with his cantata *Herminie.* In 1828–29 he wrote *Huit scènes de Faust,* after Goethe; this was the score that was eventually revised and produced as *La Damnation de Faust.* In 1829, he applied for the Prix de Rome once more with the score of *La Mort de Cléopâtre,* but no awards were given that year. He finally succeeded in winning the 1st Prix de Rome with *La Mort de Sardanapale;* it was performed in Paris on Oct. 30, 1830. In the meantime, Berlioz allowed himself to be passionately infatuated with the Irish actress Harriet Smithson after he attended her performance as Ophelia in Shakespeare's *Hamlet,* given by a British drama troupe in Paris on Sept. 11, 1827. He knew no English and Miss Smithson spoke no French; he made no effort to engage her attention personally; conveniently, he found a surrogate for his passion in the person of Camille Moke, a young pianist. Romantically absorbed in the ideal of love through music, Berlioz began to write his most ambitious and, as time and history proved, his most enduring work, which he titled *Symphonie fantastique;* it was to be an offering of adoration and devotion to Miss Smithson. Rather than follow the formal subdivisions of a sym., Berlioz decided to integrate the music through a recurring unifying theme, which he called an *idée fixe,* appearing in various guises through the movements of the *Symphonie fantastique.* To point out the personal nature of the work he subtitled it "Épisode de la vie d'un artiste." The artist of the title was Berlioz himself, so that in a way the sym. became a musical autobiography. The 5 divisions of the score are: I. *Reveries, Passions;* II. *A Ball;* III. *Scene in the Fields;* IV. *March to the Scaffold;* V. *Dream of a Witches' Sabbath.* Berlioz supplied a literary program to the music: a "young musician of morbid sensibilities" takes opium to find surcease from amorous madness. Berlioz himself, be it noted, never smoked opium, but this hallucinogenic substance was in vogue at the time, and was the subject of several mystic novels and pseudo-scientific essays. In the *Symphonie fantastique* the object of the hero's passion haunts him through the device of the *idée fixe;* she appears 1st as an entrancing, but unattainable, vision; as an enticing dancer at a ball; then as a deceptive pastoral image. He penetrates her disguise and kills her, a crime for which he is led to the gallows. At the end she reveals herself as a wicked witch at

a Sabbath orgy. The fantastic program design does not interfere, however, with an orderly organization of the score, and the wild fervor of the music is astutely subordinated to the symphonic form. The *idée fixe* itself serves merely as a recurring motif, not unlike similar musical reminiscences in Classical syms. Interestingly enough, in the *March to the Scaffold* Berlioz makes use of a section from his earlier score *Les Francs-juges,* and merely inserts into it a few bars of the *idée fixe* to justify the incorporation of unrelated musical material. No matter! *Symphonie fantastique* with or without Miss Smithson, with or without the *idée fixe,* emerges as a magnificent tapestry of sound; its unflagging popularity for a century and a half since its composition testifies to its evocative power. The work was 1st performed at the Paris Cons. on Dec. 5, 1830, with considerable success, although the Cons.'s director, the strict perfectionist Cherubini, who failed to attend the performance, spoke disdainfully of it from a cursory examination of the score. Nor did Miss Smithson herself grace the occasion by her physical presence. Incongruously, the publ. score of the *Symphonie fantastique* is dedicated to the stern Russian czar Nicholas I. That this apotheosis of passionate love should have been inscribed to one of Russia's most unpleasant czars is explained by the fact that Berlioz had been well received in Russia in 1847. Berlioz followed the *Symphonie fantastique* with a sequel entitled *Lélio, ou Le Retour à la vie,* purported to signalize the hero's renunciation of his morbid obsessions. Both works were performed at a single concert in Paris on Dec. 9, 1832, and this time La Smithson made her appearance. A most remarkable encounter followed between them; as if to prove the romantic notion of the potency of music as an aid to courtship, Berlioz and Smithson soon became emotionally involved, and they were married on Oct. 3, 1833. Alas, their marriage proved less enduring than the music that fostered their romance. Smithson broke a leg (on March 16, 1833) even before the marriage ceremony; and throughout their life together she was beset by debilitating illnesses. They had a son, who died young. Berlioz found for himself a more convenient woman companion, one Maria Recio, whom he married shortly after Smithson's death in 1854. Berlioz survived his 2nd wife, too; she died in 1862.

Whatever the peripeteias of his personal life, Berlioz never lost the lust for music. During his stay in Italy, following his reception of the Prix de Rome, he produced the overtures *Le Roi Lear* (1831) and *Rob Roy* (1831). His next important work was *Harold en Italie,* for the very unusual setting of a solo viola with orch.; it was commissioned by Paganini (although never performed by him), and was inspired by Lord Byron's poem *Childe Harold.* It was 1st performed in Paris on Nov. 23, 1834. Berlioz followed it with an opera, *Benvenuto Cellini* (1834–37), which had its 1st performance at the Paris Opéra on Sept. 10, 1838. It was not successful, and Berlioz revised the score; the new version had its 1st performance in Weimar in 1852, conducted by Liszt. About the same time, Berlioz became engaged in writing musical essays; from 1833 to 1863 he served as music critic for the *Journal des Débats;* in 1834 he began to write for the *Gazette Musicale.* In 1835 he entered a career as conductor. In 1837 he received a government commission to compose the *Grande messe des morts* (*Requiem*), for which he demanded a huge chorus. The work was 1st performed at a dress rehearsal in Paris on Dec. 4, 1837, with the public performance following the next day. On Dec. 16, 1838, Berlioz conducted a successful concert of his works in Paris; the legend has it that Paganini came forth after the concert and knelt in homage to Berlioz; if sources (including Berlioz himself) are to be trusted, Paganini subsequently gave Berlioz the sum of 20,000 francs. In 1839, Berlioz was named assistant librarian of the Paris Cons. and was awarded the Order of the Légion d'Honneur. On Nov. 24, 1839, Berlioz conducted, in Paris, the 1st performance of his dramatic sym. *Roméo et Juliette,* after Shakespeare; the work is regarded as one of the most moving lyrical invocations of Shakespeare's tragedy, rich in melodic invention and instrumental interplay. In 1840, Berlioz received another government commission to write a *Grande symphonie funèbre et triomphale*. This work gave Berlioz a clear imperative to build a sonorous edifice of what he imagined to be an architecture of sounds. The work was to commemorate the soldiers fallen in the fight for Algeria, and if contemporary reports can be taken literally, he conducted it with a drawn sword through the streets of Paris, accompanying the ashes of the military heroes to their interment in the Bastille column. The spirit of grandiosity took possession of Berlioz. At a concert after the Exhibition of Industrial Products in 1844 in Paris he conducted Beethoven's 5th Sym. with 36 double basses, Weber's *Freischütz Overture* with 24 French horns, and the *Prayer of Moses* from Rossini's opera with 25 harps. He boasted that his 1,022 performers achieved an ensemble worthy of the finest string quartet. For his grandiose *L'Impériale*, written to celebrate the distribution of prizes by Napoleon III at the Paris Exhibition of Industrial Products in 1855, Berlioz had 1,200 performers, augmented by huge choruses and a military band. As if anticipating the modus operandi of a century thence, Berlioz installed 5 subconductors and, to keep them in line, activated an "electric metronome" with his left hand while holding the conducting baton in his right. And it was probably at Berlioz's suggestion that Vuillaume constructed a monstrous Octo-bass, a double bass 10 feet high, for use in a huge orch.; it was, however, never actually employed. Such indulgences generated a chorus of derision on the part of classical musicians and skeptical music critics; caricatures represented Berlioz as a madman commanding a heterogeneous mass of instrumentalists and singers driven to distraction by the music. Berlioz deeply resented these attacks and bitterly complained to friends about the lack of a congenial artistic environment in Paris.

But whatever obloquy he suffered, he also found satisfaction in the pervading influence he had on his contemporaries, among them Wagner, Liszt, and the Russian school of composers. Indeed, his grandiosity had gradually attained true grandeur; he no longer needed huge ensembles to exercise the magic of his music. In 1844 he wrote the overture *Le Carnaval romain*, partially based on music from his unsuccessful opera *Benvenuto Cellini*. There followed the overture *La Tour de Nice* (later rev. under the title *Le Corsaire*). In 1845 he undertook the revision of his early score after Goethe, which now assumed the form of a dramatic legend entitled *La Damnation de Faust*. The score included the *Marche hongroise*, in which Berlioz took the liberty of conveying Goethe's Faust to Hungary. The march became extremely popular as a separate concert number. In 1847, Berlioz undertook a highly successful tour to Russia, and in the following year he traveled to England. In 1849 he composed his grand *Te Deum;* he conducted its 1st performance in Paris on April 28, 1855, at a dress rehearsal; it was given a public performance 2 days later, with excellent success. In 1852 he traveled to Weimar at the invitation of Liszt, who organized a festival of Berlioz's music. Between 1850 and 1854 he wrote the oratorio *L'Enfance du Christ;* he conducted it in Paris on Dec. 10, 1854. Although Berlioz was never able to achieve popular success with his operatic productions, he turned to composing stage music once more between 1856 and 1860. For the subject he selected the great epic of Virgil relating to the Trojan War; the title was to be *Les Troyens*. He encountered difficulties in producing this opera in its entirety, and in 1863 divided the score into 2 sections: *La Prise de Troie* and *Les Troyens à Carthage*. Only the 2nd part was produced in his lifetime; it received its premiere at the Théâtre-Lyrique in Paris on Nov. 4, 1863; the opera had 22 performances, and the financial returns made it possible for Berlioz to abandon his occupation as a newspaper music critic. His next operatic project was *Béatrice et Bénédict*, after Shakespeare's play *Much Ado about Nothing*. He conducted its 1st performance in Baden-Baden on Aug. 9, 1862. Despite frail health and a state of depression generated by his imaginary failure as composer and conductor in France, he achieved a series of successes abroad. He conducted *La Damnation de Faust* in Vienna in 1866, and he went to Russia during the 1867–68 season. There he had a most enthusiastic reception among Russian musicians, who welcomed him as a true prophet of the new era in music.

Posthumous recognition came slowly to Berlioz; long after his death some conservative critics still referred to his music as bizarre and willfully dissonant. No cult comparable to the ones around the names of Wagner and Liszt was formed to glorify Berlioz's legacy. Of his works only the overtures and the *Symphonie fantastique* became regular items on sym. programs. Performances of his operas were still rare events. Since Berlioz never wrote solo works for piano or any other instrument, concert recitals had no opportunity to include his name in the program. However, a whole literature was publ. about Berlioz in all European languages, securing his rightful place in music history.

WRITINGS: *Grand traité d'instrumentation et d'orchestration modernes* (Paris, 1843; numerous subsequent eds.; in Eng., 1948; eds. covering modern usages were publ. in German by Felix Weingartner, Leipzig, 1904, and Richard Strauss, Leipzig, 1905); *Le Chef d'orchestre, Théorie de son art* (Paris, 1855; in Eng. as *The Orchestral Conductor, Theory of His Art*, N.Y., 1902); *Voyage musical en Allemagne et en Italie, Études sur Beethoven, Gluck, et Weber. Mélanges et nouvelles* (2 vols., Paris, 1844); *Les Soirées de l'orchestre* (Paris, 1852; in Eng. as *Evenings in the Orchestra*, tr. by C. Roche, with introduction by Ernest Newman, N.Y., 1929; new Eng. tr. as *Evenings with the Orchestra* by J. Barzun, N.Y., 1956; 2nd ed., 1973); *Les Grotesques de la musique* (Paris, 1859); *À travers chants: Études musicales, adorations, boutades, et critiques* (Paris, 1862); *Les Musiciens et la musique* (a series of articles collected from the *Journal des Débats;* with introduction by A. Hallays, Paris, 1903); *Mémoires de Hector Berlioz* (Paris, 1870; 2nd ed. in 2 vols., Paris, 1878; in Eng., London, 1884; new tr. by R. and E. Holmes, with annotation by Ernest Newman, N.Y., 1932; another Eng. tr. by D. Cairns, N.Y., 1969; corrected ed., 1975). An incomplete ed. of literary works of Berlioz was publ. in German by Breitkopf & Härtel: *Literarische Werke* (10 vols. in 5, Leipzig, 1903–4) and *Gesammelte Schriften* (4 vols., Leipzig, 1864).

WORKS: OPERAS: *Estelle et Némorin* (1823; not perf.; score destroyed); *Les Francs-juges* (1826; not perf.; rev. 1829 and 1833; overture and 5 movements extant); *Benvenuto Cellini* (1834–37; Paris Opéra, Sept. 10, 1838; rev. 1852; Weimar, Nov. 17, 1852); *La Nonne sanglante* (1841–47; score unfinished); *Les Troyens* (1856–58; rev. 1859–60; divided into 2 parts, 1863: I, *La Prise de Troie* [1st perf. in German under Mottl, Karlsruhe, Dec. 6, 1890]; II, *Les Troyens à Carthage* [1st perf. under Deloffre, Théâtre-Lyrique, Paris, Nov. 4, 1863]; 1st perf. of both parts in French, with major cuts, Brussels, Dec. 26–27, 1906; 1st complete perf., *sans* cuts, alterations, etc., in Eng. under Alexander Gibson, Glasgow, May 3, 1969; in French, under Colin Davis, Royal Opera House, Covent Garden, London, Sept. 17, 1969); *Béatrice et Bénédict* (1860–62; Baden-Baden, Aug. 9, 1862).

SYMS.: *Symphonie fantastique: Épisode de la vie d'un artiste*, op. 14a (1830; Paris, Dec. 5, 1830; rev. 1831); *Harold en Italie* for Solo Viola and Orch., op. 16 (1834; Paris, Nov. 23, 1834); *Roméo et Juliette* for Solo Voices, Chorus, and Orch., op. 17 (1839; Paris, Nov. 24, 1839); *Grande symphonie funèbre et triomphale*, op. 15 (1840; Paris, July 28, 1840).

OTHER WORKS FOR ORCH.: *Waverley*, overture, op.1 (1827–28; Paris, May 26, 1828); *Rob Roy*, full title *Intrata di Rob Roy Macgregor*, overture (1831; Paris, April 14, 1833); *Le Roi Lear*, overture, op. 4 (1831; Paris, Dec. 22, 1833); *Rêverie et caprice*, romance for Violin and Orch., op. 8 (1841); *Le Carnaval romain*, overture, op. 9 (1844; Paris, Feb. 3, 1844); *La Tour de Nice*, overture (1844; Paris, Jan. 19, 1845; rev. 1851–52 as *Le Corsaire*, op. 21; Braunschweig, April 8, 1854); *Marche troyenne* (arranged from Act I of *Les Troyens;* 1864).

MAJOR CHORAL WORKS: *Mass* (1824; Saint-Roch, July 10, 1825; only Resurrexit extant); *La Révolution grecque*, scène héroïque (1825–26; Paris, May 26, 1828); *La Mort d'Orphée*, monologue et bacchanale (1827; 1st perf. under Cortot, Paris, Oct. 16, 1932); *Huit scènes de Faust* (1828–29; 1 movement only perf., Paris, Nov. 29, 1829); *La Mort de Sardanapale* (1830; Paris, Oct. 30, 1830); *Fantaisie sur la Tempête de Shakespeare* (1830; perf. as *Ouverture pour la Tempête de Shakespeare*, Paris, Nov. 7, 1830); *Le Retour à la vie*, op. 14b, monodrame lyrique (1831–32; Paris, Dec. 9, 1832; rev. 1854 as *Lélio, ou Le Retour à la vie*); *Grande messe des morts* (*Requiem*), op. 5 (1837; Paris, Dec. 4 [dress rehearsal], Dec. 5 [public perf.], 1837; rev. 1852 and 1867); *La Damnation de Faust*, légende dramatique, op. 24 (1845–46; Paris, Dec. 6, 1846); *Te Deum*, op. 22 (1849; Paris, April 28 [dress rehearsal], April 30 [public perf.], 1855); *L'Enfance du Christ*, trilogie sacrée, op. 25 (1850–54; Paris, Dec. 10, 1854).

FOR SOLO VOICE AND ORCH.: *Herminie*, scène lyrique (1828); *La Mort de Cléopâtre*, scène lyrique (1829). Also more than 40 songs, including 9 songs after Thomas Moore (1829; 3 orchestrated); *La Captive*, op. 12 (1832; orchestrated 1834 and 1848); *Les Nuits d'été*, 6 songs, op. 7 (1840–41; orchestrated 1843–56); *La Mort d'Ophélie* (1842; orchestrated 1848; publ. as *Tristia*, no. 2, 1849).

BIBL.: COLLECTED EDITIONS, SOURCE MATERIAL: The 1st major ed. of Berlioz's works (*Benvenuto Cellini*, *Les Troyens*, and several other scores excepted) was edited by C. Malherbe and F. Weingartner (20 vols., Leipzig, 1900–1907); see Supplement 5 in J. Barzun's *B. and the Romantic Century* (2 vols., Boston, 1950; 3rd ed., rev., 1969) for an extensive enumeration of its musical and other errors. A new critical ed. of all of the extant works, the *New B. Edition*, under the general editorship of Hugh Macdonald, began publication in Kassel in 1967. The definitive catalog is D. Holoman, *Catalogue of the Works of H. B.* (Kassel, 1987).

The standard bibliography is C. Hopkinson, *A Bibliography of the Musical and Literary Works of H. B. 1803–1869 …* (Edinburgh, 1951; 2nd ed. with additions and corrections by R. Macnutt, Tunbridge Wells, 1980). Another valuable source is M. Wright, *A Bibliography of Critical Writings on H. B.* (1967).

CORRESPONDENCE: D. Bernard, ed., *Correspondance inédite de B.* (Paris, 1879; Eng. tr. as *Life and Letters of B.*, I, 1882); *Lettres intimes* (preface by Charles Gounod; Paris, 1882; Eng. tr. as *Life and Letters of B.*, II, 1882); La Mara, ed., *Briefe von H. B. an die Fürstin Carolyne Sayn-Wittgenstein* (Leipzig, 1903); J. Tiersot, ed., *H. B.: Les Années romantiques* (1819–1842) (Paris, 1904), *H. B.: Le Musicien Errant* (1842–1852) (Paris, 1919), and *H. B.: Au Milieu du Chemin* (1852–1855) (Paris, 1930); G. Clarence, "Lettres inédites à B.," *La Revue Musicale*, 104 (1930); S. Ginsburg, "Correspondance russe inédite de B.," *La Revue Musicale*, 104 (1930); "Lettres inédites de B.," ibid., 154 (1935); J. Barzun, ed. and tr., *Nouvelles lettres de B., 1830–1868*; *New Letters of B., 1830–1868* (N. Y., 1954); P. Citron et al., eds., *Correspondance générale de H. B.* (the definitive ed.; Paris, vol. I, 1803–1832 [1972]; vol. II, 1832–1842 [1975]; vol. III, 1842–1850 [1978]; vol. IV, 1851–1855 [1983]; vol. V, 1855–1859 [1989]); R. Locke, "New Letters of B.," *19th Century Music*, 1 (1977).

BIOGRAPHICAL: W. Neumann, *B., Eine Biographie* (Kassel, 1855); E. de Mirecourt, *B.* (Paris, 1856); A. Jullien, *H. B.: La Vie et le combat; Les Œuvres* (Paris, 1882); J. Bennett, *B.* (London, 1883); E. Hippeau, *B. intime, d'après des documents nouveaux* (Paris, 1883; 2nd ed., 1889); A. Jullien, *H. B.: Sa vie et ses œuvres* (Paris, 1888); M. Brenet, *Deux pages de la vie de B.* (Paris, 1889); E. Hippeau, *B. et son temps* (Paris, 1890); L. Pohl, *H. B.: Leben und Werke* (Leipzig, 1900); A. Hahn et al., *H. B.: Sein Leben und seine Werke* (Leipzig, 1901); G. Allix, *Sur les éléments dont s'est formée la personnalité artistique de B.* (Grenoble, 1903); R. Louis, *H. B.* (Leipzig, 1904); J.-G. Prod'homme, *H. B.* (1803–1869): *Sa vie et ses œuvres* (Paris, 1904; 3rd ed., 1927); A. Boschot, *La Jeunesse d'un romantique; H. B., 1803–31* (Paris, 1906; rev. ed., 1946), *Un Romantique sous Louis-Philippe; H. B., 1831–42* (Paris, 1908; rev. ed., 1948), and *Le Crépuscule d'un romantique; H. B., 1842–69* (Paris, 1913; rev. ed., 1950); B. Schrader, *B.* (Leipzig, 1907); A. Coquard, *B.* (Paris, n.d.); P.-L. Robert, *Étude sur H. B.* (Rouen, 1914); J. Kapp, *B.: Eine Biographie* (Berlin and Leipzig,

1917; 7th ed., 1922); A. Boschot, *Une Vie romantique: H. B.* (Paris, 1919; numerous subsequent printings); P.-M. Masson, *B.* (Paris, 1923); E. Rey, *La Vie amoureuse de B.* (Paris, 1929); L. Constantin, *B.* (Paris, 1934); W. Turner, *B.: The Man and His Work* (London, 1934); T. Wotton, *H. B.* (London, 1935); J. Elliot, *B.* (London, 1938; 4th ed., rev., 1967); E. Lockspeiser, *B.* (London, 1939); G. de Pourtalès, *B. et l'Europe romantique* (Paris, 1939; rev. ed., 1949); P. Mouthier, *H. B.* (Dilbeck, 1944); J. Daniskas, *H. B.* (Stockholm, 1947; in Eng., 1949); F. Knuttel, *H. B.* (The Hague, 1948); J. Barzun, *B. and the Romantic Century* (2 vols., Boston, 1950; 3rd ed., rev., 1969); A. Ganz, *B. in London* (London, 1950); T. Tienot, *H. B.: Esquisse biographique* (Paris, 1951); H. Kühner, *H. B.: Charakter und Schöpfertum* (Olten, 1952); H. Barraud, *H. B.* (Paris, 1955; 2nd ed., 1966); H. Schonberg, *The Great Conductors* (N.Y., 1967; pp. 107–16); C. Ballif, *B.* (Paris, 1968); S. Demarquez, *H. B.: L'Homme et son œuvre* (Paris, 1969); J. Crabbe, *H. B.: Rational Romantic* (London, 1980); H. Macdonald, *B.* (London, 1982); R. Clarson-Leach, *B.: His Life and Times* (Tunbridge Wells, 1983); W. Dömling, *H. B. und seine Zeit* (Laaber, 1986); D. Cairns, *B., Volume One: The Making of an Artist* (London, 1989); D. Holoman, *B.* (Cambridge, Mass., 1989).

CRITICAL, ANALYTICAL: Important articles may be found in the *Berlioz Society Bulletin* and the *Bulletin de Liaison*; the latter is publ. by the Association Nationale Hector Berlioz in Paris (1964–). F. Liszt, "H. B. und seine Harold-Symphonie," *Sammlung Musikalische Vorträge*, 35–36 (1881; reprinted in vol. IV of Liszt's *Gesammelte Schriften*, L. Ramann, ed., Leipzig, 1882); A. Ernst, *L'Œuvre dramatique de H. B.* (Paris, 1884); R. Pohl, *H. B.: Studien und Erinnerungen* (Leipzig, 1884); J.-G. Prod'homme, *La Damnation de Faust* (Paris, 1896); E. Destranges, *Les Troyens de B.: Étude analytique* (Paris, 1897); J.-G. Prod'homme, *L'Enfance du Christ* (Paris, 1898); A. Hallays, "H. B., Critique musical," *Revue de Paris* (1903); J. Tiersot, *B. et la société de son temps* (Paris, 1904); idem, "Berlioziana," *Le Ménestrel* (Jan. 3, 1904–Dec. 1, 1906); P. Magnette, *Les Grandes Étapes dans l'œuvre de B., I: Symphonie fantastique* (1829–32) (Liège, 1908); E. Bernoulli, *H. B. als Ästhetiker der Klangfarben* (Zürich, 1909); A. Boschot, *Le Faust de B.* (Paris, 1910; rev. ed., 1946); M. Emmanuel, "B.," *Le Correspondant* (1920); P.-L. Robert, *B.: Les Troyens* (Rouen, 1920); C. Koechlin, "Le Cas B.," *Revue Musicale* (Feb. 1922); T. Mantovani, *La dannazione di Faust di Ettore B.* (Milan, 1923); J. Tiersot, *La Damnation de Faust de B.* (Paris, 1924); H. Harty, "B.," *Music & Letters* (Jan., April, and Dec. 1926); F. Bonavia, "B.," *Monthly Musical Record* (Aug. 1929); J. Elliot, "B.," *Musical Times* (July 1929); C. Grey, "Letter on B. in Reply to Feste," ibid. (July 1929); T. Wotton, "B. as Melodist," ibid. (Sept. 1929); idem, *B.: Four Works* (London, 1929); J. Tiersot, "B. of Fantastic Symphony," *Musical Quarterly* (July 1933); E. Lockspeiser, "B. and the French Romantics," *Music & Letters* (Jan. 1934); T. Wotton, "B. Funeral and Triumphal Symphony," *Musical Opinion* (July 1936); A. Boschot, *H. B., Critique musical* (Brussels, 1938); H. Bartenstein, *H. B.' Instrumentationskunst und ihre geschichtlichen Grundlagen* (Leipzig, 1939; rev. ed., 1974); F. Schlitzer, *Il Grande Requiem di Ettore B.* (Naples, 1939); E. Harazsti, "B., Liszt and Rákóczy," *Musical Quarterly* (April 1940); E. Meyerstein, "An Approach to B.," *Music Review*, IX (1948); R. Collet, "B.: Various Angles of Approach to His Work," *Score*, 10 (1954); R. Mendl, "B. and Shakespeare," *Chesterian*, XXIX and XXX (1955); G. Court, "B. and Byron and Harold in Italy," *Music Review*, XVII (1956); A. Dickinson, "B. and the Trojans," *Durham University Journal*, XX (1958); P. Friedheim, "Radical Harmonic Procedures in B.," *Music Review*, XXI (1960); J. Klein, "B. as a Musical Dramatist," *Chesterian*, XXXV (1960); C. Wallis, "B. and the Lyric Stage," *Musical Times* (June 1960); A. Court, *H. B.: The Role of Literature in His Life and Work* (diss., Univ. of London, 1961); G. Fraenkel, "B., the Princess and 'Les Troyens,' " *Music & Letters* (July 1963); A. Dickinson, "B.'s Rome Prize Works," *Music Review*, XXV (1964); G. Sandford, *The Overtures of H. B.: A Study in Musical Style* (diss., Univ. of Southern Calif., Los Angeles, 1964); J. Warrack, "B. and the 'Theatre of the

Mind,' " *Listener*, LXXII (1964); D. Cairns, "B.'s Epic Opera," ibid., LXXVI (1966); K. Lucas, *H. B. and the Dramatic Symphony* (diss., Univ. of Melbourne, 1966); E. Grabner, *B. and French Operatic Tradition* (diss., Univ. of York, 1967); R. Weirauch, *The Orchestrational Style of H. B.* (diss., Univ. of Cincinnati, 1968); D. Cairns, "B.: A Centenary Retrospect," *Musical Times* (March 1969); A. Dickinson, "B.'s Songs," *Musical Quarterly* (July 1969); H. Macdonald, *B. Orchestral Music* (a valuable study; London, 1969); H. Macdonald, "H. B. 1969: A Centenary Assessment," *Adam*, XXXIV (1969); J. Barzun, "B. a Hundred Years After," *Musical Quarterly* (Jan. 1970); E. Cone, *B.: Fantastic Symphony* (N.Y., 1971); N. Temperley, "The Symphonie fantastique and Its Program," *Musical Quarterly* (Oct. 1971); A. Dickinson, *The Music of B.* (London, 1972); H. Cohen, *B. and the Opera (1829–1849)* (diss., N.Y. Univ., 1973); B. Primmer, *The B. Style* (London, 1973); J. Rushton, "The Genesis of B.'s 'La Damnation de Faust,' " *Music & Letters* (April 1975); W. Dömling, *H. B.: Die symphonisch-dramatischen Werke* (Stuttgart, 1979); F. Piatier, *Benvenuto Cellini de B. ou Le Mythe de l'artiste* (Paris, 1979); J. Barzun, "The Meaning of Meaning in Music: B. Once More," *Musical Quarterly* (Jan. 1980); M. Clavaud, *H. B., Visages d'un masque* (Lyons, 1980); D. Holoman, *The Creative Process in the Autograph Musical Documents of H. B., ca. 1818–1845* (Ann Arbor, 1980); C. Berger, *Phantastik als Konstruktion: H. B.'s "Symphonie fantastique"* (Kassel, 1983); J. Langford, "The 'Damnation Symphonies' of B. as an Outgrowth of the French Operatic Tradition," *Musical Quarterly* (Winter 1983); J. Rushton, *The Musical Language of B.* (Cambridge, 1983); J. Langford, "Musical-Dramatic Parallels in the Operas of H. B.," *Studies in the History of Music*, vol. 2 (N.Y., 1988); K. Murphy, *H. B. and the Development of French Music Criticism* (Ann Arbor, 1988); P. Banks, "B.'s 'Marche au Supplice' and *Les Francs juges*— a re-examination," *Musical Times* (Jan. 1989).

Berman, Lazar (Naumovich), brilliant Soviet pianist; b. Leningrad, Feb. 26, 1930. He studied with Goldenweiser at the Moscow Cons., graduating in 1953. In 1956 he obtained the 5th prize at the Brussels International Contest under the sponsorship of Queen Elisabeth of Belgium, and in the same year obtained the 3rd prize at the Budapest Liszt contest. These were the modest beginnings of a brilliant career as a virtuoso pianist. In 1970 he made a highly successful tour of Italy; in 1976 he toured the U.S. with tremendous acclaim. In his repertoire he showed a distinct predilection for the Romantic period of piano music; among modern composers his favorites were Scriabin and Prokofiev. His titanic technique, astounding in the facility of bravura passages, did not preclude the excellence of his poetic evocation of lyric moods.

Bermudo, Juan, Spanish music theorist; b. Ecija, Seville, c.1510; d. Andalusia, after 1555. He 1st studied theology and devoted himself to preaching; later turned to music and studied at the Univ. of Alcalá de Henares. He spent 15 years as a Franciscan monk in Andalusia; in 1550 he entered the service of the Archbishop of Andalusia, where Cristóbal de Morales was choir director. The writings of Bermudo constitute an important source of information on Spanish instrumental music of the 16th century. His most comprehensive work is the *Declaración de instrumentos musicales* (Osuna, 1549 and 1555). It deals with theory, in which his authorities were Gaffurius, Glareanus, and Ornithoparchus; instruments, including problems of tuning, technique of performance, and repertoire; and critical evaluation of contemporary composers, showing familiarity with the works of Josquin Des Prez, Willaert, and Gombert. Bermudo also wrote *El Arte tripharia* (Osuna, 1550). Thirteen organ pieces by him are included in F. Pedrell, *Salterio Sacro-Hispano*.
    BIBL.: R. Stevenson, *J. B.* (The Hague, 1960).

Bernabei, Ercole, Italian composer, father of **Giuseppe Antonio Bernabei**; b. Caprarola, Papal States, 1622; d. Munich (buried), Dec. 6, 1687. He was a pupil of Orazio Benevoli, whom he succeeded in 1672 as chapel master at the Vatican; in 1674 he became court conductor in Munich. He wrote 5

operas, which were produced in Munich, and publ. a book of madrigals, *Concerto madrigalesco* (1669); also wrote masses, offertories, Psalms, and other sacred music.
    BIBL.: R. Casimiri, *E. B., Maestro di cappella musicale lateranse* (Rome, 1920); R. de Rensis, *E. B.* (Rome, 1920).

Bernabei, Giuseppe Antonio, Italian composer, son of **Ercole Bernabei;** b. Rome, 1649; d. Munich, March 9, 1732. He studied with his father, and served with him as a vice-Kapellmeister in Munich beginning in 1677; after his father's death in 1687, assumed his post as principal Kapellmeister. He wrote 15 operas and much sacred music.
    BIBL.: K. Forster, *G.A. B. als Kirchenkomponist* (Munich, 1933).

Bernac, Pierre, eminent French baritone; b. Paris, Jan. 12, 1899; d. Villeneuve-les-Avignon, Oct. 17, 1979. His real name was **Pierre Bertin,** which he changed in order to avoid confusion with another Pierre Bertin, an actor. He started on his career as a singer rather late in life, and was 1st engaged in finance as a member of his father's brokerage house in Paris. His musical tastes were decidedly in the domain of modern French songs; on May 2, 1926, he gave a recital in Paris with a program of songs by Francis Poulenc and Georges Auric; at other concerts he sang works by Debussy, Ravel, Honegger, and Milhaud. Eager to learn the art of German lieder, he went to Salzburg to study with Reinhold von Warlich. Returning to Paris, he devoted himself to concerts and teaching. He became a lifelong friend to Poulenc, who wrote many songs for him and acted as his piano accompanist in many of their tours through Europe and America. He also conducted master classes in the U.S. and was on the faculty of the American Cons. at Fontainebleau. He publ. a valuable manual, *The Interpretation of French Song* (N.Y., 1970; 2nd ed., 1976), and a monograph, *Francis Poulenc: The Man and His Songs* (N.Y., 1977).

Bernacchi, Antonio Maria, celebrated Italian castrato alto; b. Bologna (baptized), June 23, 1685; d. there, March 13, 1756. He studied voice with Pistocchi and G.A. Ricieri. In 1700 he was sopranist at the church of S. Petronio in Bologna; made his operatic debut in Genoa in 1703; between 1709 and 1735 had a number of engagements in Venice, and between 1712 and 1731 made several appearances in Bologna. He also sang in Munich (1720–27). In 1716–17 he sang in London, and in 1729 he was engaged by Handel as a substitute for Senesino for the London seasons of the Italian Opera; however, he failed to please British operagoers and returned to his native town of Bologna, where he opened a singing school. In his singing he cultivated the style of vocal embellishments in the manner of the French *roulades*. He composed some worthwhile pieces, among them *Grave et Fuga a 4; Kyrie a 5;* and *Justus ut palma a 5.*
    BIBL.: L. Frati, "A. B. e la sua scuola di canto," *Rivista Musicale Italiana* (Sept. 1922).

Bernard, Moritz (Matvey), Russian music publisher and composer; b. Mitau, 1794; d. St. Petersburg, May 9, 1871. He studied piano with John Field in Moscow, and later was active as a piano teacher; in 1822 he moved to St. Petersburg, where he purchased a music store of Dalmas, and began publishing music. Bernard's printing press publ. songs by Glinka and Dargomyzhsky, and piano pieces by Anton Rubinstein and other important Russian composers. In 1840 he began publishing a musical monthly, *Nouvelliste*, which continued publication until 1914, many years after his death. Bernard's son took charge of the music store until 1885, when the stock was purchased by Jurgenson. Bernard composed an opera, *Olga*, which was performed in St. Petersburg in 1845; also publ. a valuable collection, *Songs of the Russian People* (St. Petersburg, 1847); a collection of children's pieces, *L'Enfant-pianiste;* and some original piano pieces and songs, some of which were printed in the Soviet Union.

Bernard, Robert, Swiss-born composer, editor, and writer on music; b. Geneva, Oct. 10, 1900; d. Paris, May 2, 1971.

He studied in Geneva with G.T. Strong, Barblan, and Lauber. In 1926 he settled in Paris; in 1937 he became a lecturer at the Schola Cantorum and a music critic; from 1939 to 1951 he was ed. of *La Revue Musicale*. He publ. monographs on Franck, Aubert, Roussel, and other French composers.

WORKS: 3 operas: *Flen* (1918), *Le Chevalier au Barizel* (1919), and *Polyphème* (1929); Piano Concerto; Harp Concerto; Saxophone Quartet; Piano Trio; Trio for Oboe, Clarinet, and Trombone; a number of other piano pieces.

Bernardi, Bartolomeo, Italian violinist and composer; b. Bologna, c.1660; d. Copenhagen, May 23, 1732. He received an invitation from the Danish Court to serve as a violinist and composer, and began his work there on Jan. 1, 1703; after an absence of several years (1705–10), he returned to Copenhagen and was appointed director of court music. In Copenhagen he produced 2 operas, *Il Gige fortunato* (Aug. 26, 1703) and *Diana e la Fortuna* (Oct. 10, 1703); he also wrote an opera, *La Libussa*, for a production in Prague in 1703; the music of these operas is lost. His trio sonatas were publ. in Bologna (1692, 1696).

Bernardi, Francesco. See **Senesino, Francesco.**

Bernardi, Mario (Egidio), Canadian conductor; b. Kirkland Lake, Ontario, Aug. 20, 1930. He was sent to Italy when he was 6; studied piano, organ, and composition with Bruno Pasut at the Manzato Cons. in Treviso (1938–45), taking his examination in the latter year at the Venice Cons. He then took courses with Lubka Kolessa (piano) and Ettore Mazzoleni (conducting) at the Royal Cons. of Music of Toronto (1948–51), later studying conducting with Erich Leinsdorf at the Salzburg Mozarteum (1959). He commenced his career as a church organist and a concert pianist; he also worked as a coach and conductor with the Royal Cons. Opera School in Toronto (from 1953). In 1957 he made his 1st appearance as a conductor with the Canadian Opera Co., and in 1963 became assistant conductor at Sadler's Wells in London. In 1967 he made his U.S. debut conducting *La Bohème* at the San Francisco Opera. From 1969 to 1982 he served as the 1st music director of the new National Arts Centre Orch. in Ottawa; then was principal conductor of the CBC Vancouver Orch. (from 1983) and music director of the Calgary Phil. (from 1984). In 1972 he was made a Companion of the Order of Canada.

Bernardi, Stefano or **Steffano,** Italian music theorist and composer; b. Verona, c.1585; d. probably in Salzburg, 1636. He served as maestro di cappella at the church of the Santissima Madonna dei Monti in Rome; from 1611 to 1622 was music director at the Cathedral of Verona; became Kapellmeister at the Salzburg Cathedral in 1628; left Salzburg in 1634.

WORKS: 2 books of masses for 8 Voices, and 1 for 4 and 5 Voices; a book of madrigals for 3 Voices (Rome, 1611), and 2 for 5 Voices (Venice, 1611; Rome, 1612); 2 books of *madrigaletti*; Psalms and motets; also instrumental works (trio sonatas, etc.). Reprints of some of his sacred works are to be found in Denkmäler der Tonkunst in Österreich (vol. 69; formerly 36.i). He also wrote the manual *Porta musicale per la quale il principiante con facile brevità all'acquisto delle perfette regole del contrapunto vien introdotto* (Verona, 1615; 7 subsequent eds.).

BIBL.: F. Posch, *Steffano Bernardis weltliche Vokal- und Instrumental-Werke* (Munich, 1928).

Bernart de Ventadorn, troubadour poet and composer who flourished in the 2nd half of the 12th century. His vita states that he was born in the castle of Ventadorn in the province of Limousin, and later was in the service of the Duchess of Normandy, Eleanor of Aquitaine, and of Raimon V, Count of Toulouse. He is believed to have entered a monastery in Dordogne, where he lived until his death. Some 45 poems are attributed to him, and 18 survive with complete melodies.

BIBL.: S. Nichols and J. Galm, eds., *The Songs of B. d.V.* (Chapel Hill, N.C., 1962); M. Lazar, *B. d.V.—Chansons d'amour* (Paris, 1966).

Bernasconi, Andrea, Italian composer; b. probably in Marseilles, c.1706; d. Munich, Jan. 27?, 1784. It is known that he

was maestro di cappella at the Ospedale della Rieta in Venice during the season 1746–47. In 1753 he was in Munich, where he taught music to Princess Maria Anna Josepha (1754–55) and Princess Josepha Maria (1754–65); he also gave musical instruction to the Elector, Maximilian III Joseph. He was appointed Kapellmeister at the Munich court in 1755. He wrote a number of operas and pasticcios, some of which were produced in Munich; he also composed sacred music.

BIBL.: E.J. Weiss, *A. B. als Opernkomponist* (diss., Univ. of Munich, 1923).

Berneker, Constanz, German composer; b. Darkehmen, East Prussia, Oct. 30, 1844; d. Königsberg, June 9, 1906. He studied at the Institut für Kirchemusik and at the Akademie der Kunst in Berlin. In 1872 he was appointed director at the Königsberg Singakademie, and in 1873 was engaged as cathedral organist and teacher at the Königsberg Cons.; in 1885 he was named Royal Music Director; also was active as a music critic. He wrote a number of sacred and secular cantatas, and some instrumental music.

BIBL.: O. Laudien, *C. B.* (Berlin, 1909).

Berners, Lord (Sir Gerald Hugh Tyrwhitt-Wilson, Baronet), eccentric English composer, writer, and painter; b. Arley Park, Bridgnorth, Sept. 18, 1883; d. Farringdon House, Berkshire, April 19, 1950. He was mainly self-taught, although he received advice and encouragement from Stravinsky. He served as honorary attaché to the British diplomatic service in Constantinople (1909–11) and Rome (1911–19). Returning to England, he joined the literary smart set; he was on close terms with George Bernard Shaw, H.G. Wells, and Osbert Sitwell. He publ. half a dozen novels, including *The Girls of Radcliff Hall* (1937), *The Romance of a Nose* (1942), and *Far from the Madding War,* in which he portrays himself as Lord Fitzcricket. Berners affected bizarre social behavior; his humor and originality are reflected in his compositions, many of which reveal a subtle gift for parody. He wrote 2 autobiographical vols., *First Childhood* (London, 1934) and *A Distant Prospect* (London, 1945); also had successful exhibitions of his oil paintings in London (1931, 1936).

WORKS: OPERA: *Le Carrosse du Saint-Sacrement* (Paris, April 24, 1924). **BALLETS:** *The Triumph of Neptune* (London, Dec. 3, 1926); *Luna Park* (London, March 1930); *A Wedding Bouquet* (London, April 27, 1937); *Cupid and Psyche* (London, April 27, 1939); *Les Sirènes* (London, Nov. 12, 1946). **ORCH.:** 3 pieces: *Chinoiserie, Valse sentimentale,* and *Kasatchok* (1919); *Fantaisie espagnole* (1920); *Fugue* (1928). **PIANO:** 3 *Little Funeral Marches* (1914); *Le Poisson d'or* (1914); *Fragments psychologiques* (1915); *Valses bourgeoises* for Piano Duet (1915); also film scores, including *Nicholas Nickleby* (1947); songs, including *Lieder Album,* to texts by Heine (1913; "Du bist wie eine Blume" is set in accordance with the suggestion that the poem was not addressed to a lady but to a small white pig).

BIBL.: J. Holbrooke, *B.* (London, 1925); C. Lambert, *Music Ho!: A Study of Music in Decline* (London, 1934; 2nd ed., 1948); I. Stravinsky and R. Craft, *Memories and Commentaries* (N.Y., 1959); H. Bridgeman and E. Drury, *The British Eccentric* (N.Y., 1975); P. Dickinson, "Lord B., 1883–1950: A British avant-gardist at the time of World War I," *Musical Times* (Nov. 1983).

Bernet Kempers, Karel Philippus, Dutch writer on music; b. Nijkerk, Sept. 20, 1897; d. Amsterdam, Sept. 30, 1974. He studied in Munich with Sandberger; received his Dr.Phil. in 1926; in 1929 was appointed teacher of music history at the Royal Cons. in The Hague and was secretary of the Federation of Dutch Composers. In 1946 he was appointed a prof. at the Amsterdam Univ. Among his writings are *Jacobus Clemens non Papa und seine Motetten* (1928); *Italian Opera, Peri to Puccini* (1929; Eng. tr., 1947); *Muziekgeschiedenis* (Rotterdam, 1932; 4th ed., 1946); *Meesters der Muziek* (Rotterdam, 1939; 4th ed., 1948).

Bernhard, Christoph, German music theorist and composer; b. Kolberg, Jan. 1, 1628; d. Dresden, Nov. 14, 1692. He studied with Paul Siefert in Danzig and with Schütz in Dresden. The Elector sent him to study singing in Italy (1649); in 1655 he became 2nd Kapellmeister in Dresden, but was forced to resign through the disaffection of his Italian associates. He then went to Hamburg, where he served as a cantor (1664–74); was recalled by the Elector to Dresden and was appointed 1st Kapellmeister, as successor to Schütz. He enjoyed great respect as a composer, particularly for his mastery of counterpoint. He publ. *Geistliche Harmonien* (Dresden, 1665; new ed., Kassel, 1972) and *Prudentia prudentiana* (Hamburg, 1669); a treatise on composition and another on counterpoint are in MS. Three major treatises in tr., with annotation by W. Hilse, are publ. in "The Treatises of Christoph Bernhard," *Music Forum*, III (1973). Some of his cantatas were publ. by M. Seiffert in vol. VI of Denkmäler Deutscher Tonkunst.

BIBL.: J.M. Müller-Blattau, *Die Kompositionslehre Heinrich Schützens in der Fassung seines Schülers C. B.* (Leipzig, 1926; 2nd ed., 1963); H. Rauschning, *Musikgeschichte der Stadt Danzig* (1926).

Bernhard der Deutsche (known also as **Bernardo di Steffanino Murer**), celebrated German organist and the reputed inventor of organ pedals; b. in the early 15th century; d. 1459. He was an organist at San Marco in Venice.

Bernheimer, Martin, German-born American music critic; b. Munich, Sept. 28, 1936. He was taken to the U.S. as a child in 1940; studied music at Brown Univ. (B.A., 1958) and N.Y. Univ. (M.A., 1962); in the interim, took courses in music at the Munich Cons. (1958–59). Returning to the U.S., he was a member of the music faculty at N.Y. Univ. (1960–62); served as contributing critic for the *N.Y. Herald Tribune* (1959–62) and assistant music ed. of *Saturday Review* (1962–65). In 1965 he was appointed music ed. of the *Los Angeles Times*. As a critic, he possesses a natural facility and not infrequently a beguiling felicity of literary style; he espouses noble musical causes with crusading fervor, but he can be aggressively opinionated and ruthlessly devastating to composers, performers, or administrators whom he dislikes; as a polemicist he is a *rara avis* among contemporary critics, who seldom rise to the pitch of moral or musical indignation; Bernheimer also possesses a surprising knowledge of music in all its ramifications, which usually protects him from perilous pratfalls. In 1981 he received the Pulitzer Prize for distinguished classical music criticism.

Bernier, Nicolas, French composer; b. Mantes-la-Jolie, June 5 or 6, 1665; d. Paris, July 6, 1734. He held the post of organist at Chartres Cathedral (1694–98); in 1698 he was appointed maître de musique at St. Germain l'Auxerrois in Paris; then served at Sainte-Chapelle in Paris (1704–26). He publ. 8 books of "cantates profanes," of which *Les Nuits de Sceaux* is an important example of French secular cantatas. He also wrote a Te Deum. His *Principes de composition de M. Bernier* was tr. into Eng. by P. Nelson and publ. as *Nicolas Bernier: Principles of Composition* (Brooklyn, 1964).

Bernier, René, Belgian composer; b. Saint-Gilles, March 10, 1905; d. Brussels, Sept. 8, 1984. He took general music courses at the Brussels Cons. and also private lessons in composition with Paul Gilson. In 1925 he and 7 other students of Gilson formed the so-called Groupe des Synthétistes, whose aim was to combine Classical forms with modern techniques. Bernier wrote a number of stage works in this synthetic style, as well as a number of instrumental pieces for various combinations, often with humorous suggestions in the title, such as *Bassonnière* for Bassoon and Orch., *Hommage à Sax* for Saxophone and Orch., and *Sonate à deux* for Flute and Harp. He also composed some choruses on sacred texts and a number of songs.

Bernoulli, Eduard, Swiss music scholar; b. Basel, Nov. 6, 1867; d. Zürich, April 17, 1927. He studied at the Univ. of Leipzig, obtaining his doctorate in 1897 (diss., *Die Choralnotenschrift bei Hymnen und Sequenzen im späteren Mittelalter*); subsequently ed. several vols. of Denkmäler Deutscher Ton-

kunst. He publ. the valuable monographs *Berlioz als Ästhetiker der Klangfarben* (Zürich, 1909); *Aus Liederbüchern der Humanistenzeit* (1910); etc. From 1921 till his death, Bernoulli was a prof. at the Univ. of Zürich.

Berno von Reichenau, German music theorist; b. c.970; d. in the Cloister of Reichenau, June 7, 1048. In 1008 he was installed as Abbot of the Cloister of Reichenau; accompanied Emperor Henry II to Rome for coronation in 1014, and in 1027 attended the coronation in Rome of Emperor Conrad II. He wrote learned treatises on music, which can be found in J.P. Migne's *Patrologia cursus completus* (vol. 142) and in Gerbert's *Scriptores* (vol. 2). A monograph on his system of music was publ. by W. Brambach (Leipzig, 1881).

Bernstein, Elmer, talented American composer of film music; b. N.Y., April 4, 1922. He studied with Roger Sessions and Stefan Wolpe at the Juilliard School of Music in N.Y.; served in the U.S. Air Force during World War II; after the end of the war he settled in Hollywood and became a highly successful composer of background scores, particularly in dramatic films; of these the most effective were *The Man with the Golden Arm; The Ten Commandments; Desire under the Elms; The Magnificent Seven; To Kill a Mockingbird; Walk on the Wild Side; The Great Escape; The Carpetbaggers; Hawaii; Airplane!;* and *Ghostbusters.* He has also composed chamber music, the musical *How Now Dow Jones* (N.Y., Dec. 7, 1967), 3 orch. suites, and songs.

Bernstein, Lawrence F., American musicologist; b. N.Y., March 25, 1939. He studied at Hofstra Univ. (B.S., 1960) and with Reese at N.Y. Univ. (Ph.D., 1969, with the diss. *Cantus Firmus in the French Chanson for Two and Three Voices, 1500–1550*). He taught at the Univ. of Chicago (1965–70) and at the Univ. of Pa. (from 1970). He served as ed. in chief of the *Journal of the American Musicological Society* (1975–77).

Bernstein, Leonard, prodigiously gifted American conductor and composer, equally successful in writing symphonic music of profound content and strikingly effective Broadway shows, and, in the field of performance, an interpreter of magnetic powers, exercising a charismatic spell on audiences in America and the world; b. Lawrence, Mass., Aug. 25, 1918, of a family of Russian Jewish immigrants; d. N.Y., Oct. 14, 1990. His original name was Louis, but at the age of 16 he had it legally changed to Leonard to avoid confusion with another Louis Bernstein in the family. He studied piano in Boston with Helen Coates and Heinrich Gebhard. In 1935 he entered Harvard Univ., where he took courses in music theory with A. Tillman Merritt, counterpoint and fugue with Walter Piston, and orchestration with Edward Burlingame Hill; he graduated with honors in 1939. He then went to Philadelphia, where he studied piano with Isabelle Vengerova, conducting with Fritz Reiner, and orchestration with Randall Thompson at the Curtis Inst. of Music (diploma, 1941). During the summers of 1940 and 1941, he attended the Berkshire Music Center at Tanglewood, where he received help, instruction, and encouragement from his most important mentor in conducting, Serge Koussevitzky. In his free time, Bernstein did some ancillary work for music publishers under the name **Lenny Amber** (*Bernstein* is the German word for "amber"). He also conducted occasional concerts with local groups in Boston.

In 1943 he attained an important position as assistant conductor to Artur Rodzinski, music director of the N.Y. Phil. Bernstein's great chance to show his capacities came on Nov. 14, 1943, when he was called on short notice to conduct a particularly difficult program with the N.Y. Phil. He acquitted himself magnificently and was roundly praised in the press for his exemplary achievement. The occasion was the beginning of one of the most extraordinary careers in the annals of American music. In 1958 Bernstein became the 1st American-born music director of the N.Y. Phil.; that year he conducted concerts with it in South America, and in 1959 took the orch. on a grand tour of Russia and 16 other countries in Europe and the Near East; in 1960 he conducted it in Berlin, and in 1961 in Japan, Alaska, and Canada.

On July 9, 1967, he led a memorable concert with the Israel Phil. in Jerusalem, at the conclusion of Israel's victorious Six Day War, in a program of works by 2 great Jewish composers, Mendelssohn and Mahler. In 1953 he became the 1st American conductor to lead a regular performance (Cherubini's *Medea*) at La Scala in Milan. On May 6, 1964, he made his Metropolitan Opera debut in N.Y., conducting *Falstaff,* the work he also chose for his debut with the Vienna State Opera on March 14, 1966. By that time he was in such great demand as a conductor of opera and orchs. all over the world that he could afford the luxury of selecting occasions to suit his schedule. In 1969 he resigned his position as music director of the N.Y. Phil. in order to devote more time to composition and other projects; the orch. bestowed upon him the unprecedented title of "laureate conductor," enabling him to give special performances with it whenever he could afford the time. In the summer of 1976 he took the orch. on a Bicentennial tour of 11 European cities, giving 13 concerts during a period of 17 days.

Ebullient with communicative talents, Bernstein initiated in 1958 a televised series of "Young People's Concerts" with the N.Y. Phil. in which he served as an astute and self-confident commentator; these concerts became popular with audiences beyond the eponymous youth. He also arranged a series of educational music programs on television. His eagerness to impart his wide knowledge in various fields to willing audiences found its expression in the classes he conducted at Brandeis Univ. (1951–55), and, concurrently, in the summer sessions at the Berkshire Music Center at Tanglewood. In 1973 he was the prestigious Charles Eliot Norton Prof. in Poetry at Harvard Univ. and lectured at M.I.T.

He was the recipient of many honors: the Order of the Lion, Commander, of Finland (1965); that of Chevalier (1968), Officer (1978), and Commander (1985) of the French Légion d'honneur; that of Cavaliere, Order of Merit, of Italy (1969); the Austrian Honorary Distinction in Science and Art (1976); the Grand Honor Cross for Science and Art of Austria (1976); and the Grand Order of Merit of the Italian Republic (1988). In 1977 he was made a member of the Swedish Royal Academy of Music in Stockholm, in 1981 of the American Academy of Arts and Letters, in 1983 of the Vienna Phil., and in 1984 of the N.Y. Phil. In 1987 he was awarded the Gold Medal of the Royal Phil. Soc. of London. He was made president of the London Sym. Orch. in 1987 and laureate conductor of the Israel Phil. in 1988. His 70th birthday was the occasion for various tributes from around the world, highlighted by a major celebration at Tanglewood on Aug. 25–28, 1988.

An excellent pianist in his own right, Bernstein often appeared as a soloist in Classical or modern concerts, on occasion, conducting the orch. from the keyboard. An intellectual by nature, and a litterateur and modernistically inclined poet by aspiration, he took pride in publishing some excellent sonnets. He also took part in liberal causes, and was once dubbed by a columnist as a member of the "radical chic." His tremendous overflow of spiritual and purely animal energy impelled him to display certain histrionic mannerisms on the podium, which elicited on the part of some critics derisive comments about his "choreography."

Whatever judgment is ultimately to be rendered on Bernstein, he remains a phenomenon. History knows of a number of composers who were also excellent conductors, but few professional conductors who were also significant composers. Bernstein seemed unique in his protean power to be equally proficient as a symphonic and operatic conductor as well as a composer of complex musical works, and, last but not least, of original and enormously popular stage productions. In his *West Side Story* (1957) he created a significant social drama, abounding in memorable tunes. In his 2nd sym., *The Age of Anxiety* (1949; rev. 1965), he reflected the turbulence of modern life. As an interpreter and program maker, he showed a unique affinity with the music of Mahler, whose syms. he repeatedly performed in special cycles. Ever true to his Jewish heritage, Bernstein wrote a devout choral sym., *Kaddish* (1963;

rev. 1977). As a testimony to his ecumenical religious feelings, he produced a *Mass* (1971) on the Roman liturgy.

In 1989, Bernstein conducted celebratory performances of Beethoven's 9th Sym. on both sides of the Berlin Wall, the 1st at the Kaiser Wilhelm Memorial Church, a World War II memorial in West Berlin (Dec. 23, 1989), and the 2nd at the Schauspielhaus Theater in East Berlin (telecast to the world; Dec. 25, 1989); the orch. was made up of members from the Bavarian Radio Sym. Orch. in Munich, augmented by players from N.Y., London, Paris, Dresden, and Leningrad.

Bernstein's death (of progressive emphysema, complicated by a chronic pleurisy, eventuating in a fatal heart attack) shocked the music world and hundreds of his personal friends, particularly since he had been so amazingly active as a world-renowned conductor and as the composer of lasting works for the stage and concert hall until his final days.

WORKS: STAGE: *The Birds,* incidental music to Aristophanes' play (1938; Cambridge, Mass., April 21, 1939); *The Peace,* incidental music to Aristophanes' play (1940; Cambridge, Mass., May 23, 1941); *Fancy Free,* ballet (N.Y., April 18, 1944); *On the Town,* musical comedy (Boston, Dec. 13, 1944); *Facsimile,* ballet (N.Y., Oct. 24, 1946; 2nd version as *Parallel Lives,* Milwaukee, Oct. 19, 1986; 3rd version as *Dancing On,* Zagreb, March 31, 1988); *Peter Pan,* incidental music to J.M. Barrie's play (N.Y., April 24, 1950); *Trouble in Tahiti,* opera (1951; Waltham, Mass., June 12, 1952); *Wonderful Town,* musical comedy (New Haven, Conn., Jan. 19, 1953); *The Lark,* incidental music to J. Anouilh's play, adapted by L. Hellman (Boston, Oct. 28, 1955); *Salomé,* incidental music to O. Wilde's play (N.Y., Dec. 11, 1955; withdrawn); *Candide,* comic operetta (Boston, Oct. 29, 1956; rev. version, N.Y., Dec. 20, 1973; operatic version, N.Y., Oct. 13, 1982; rev., Glasgow, May 17, 1988); *West Side Story,* musical (Washington, D.C., Aug. 19, 1957); *The Firstborn,* incidental music to C. Fry's play (N.Y., April 29, 1958; withdrawn); *Mass,* theater piece for Singers, Players, and Dancers (Washington, D.C., Sept. 8, 1971; chamber version, Los Angeles, Dec. 26, 1972); *Dybbuk,* ballet (N.Y., May 16, 1974; retitled *Dybbuk Variations*); *By Bernstein,* musical cabaret (N.Y., Nov. 23, 1975; withdrawn); *1600 Pennsylvania Avenue,* musical (Philadelphia, Feb. 24, 1976); *A Quiet Place,* opera (Houston, June 17, 1983; withdrawn; rev. version, incorporating *Trouble in Tahiti,* Milan, June 19, 1984). **FILM SCORE:** *On the Waterfront* (1954). **ORCH.:** 3 syms.: No. 1, *Jeremiah,* for Mezzo-soprano and Orch. (1942; Pittsburgh, Jan. 28, 1944); No. 2, *The Age of Anxiety,* for Piano and Orch. (Boston, April 8, 1949; rev. version, N.Y., July 15, 1965); No. 3, *Kaddish,* for Speaker, Soprano, Chorus, Boys' Choir, and Orch. (Tel Aviv, Dec. 12, 1963; rev. version, Mainz, Aug. 25, 1977); *Suite from Fancy Free* (1944; Pittsburgh, Jan. 14, 1945; withdrawn); *3 Dance Variations from Fancy Free* (N.Y., Jan. 21, 1946); *3 Dance Episodes from On the Town* (1945; San Francisco, Feb. 13, 1946); *Facsimile,* choreographic essay (1946; Poughkeepsie, N.Y., March 5, 1947); *Prelude, Fugue, and Riffs* for Clarinet and Jazz Ensemble (1949; ABC-TV, Oct. 16, 1955); *Serenade* for Violin, Harp, Percussion, and Strings (Venice, Sept. 12, 1954); *Symphonic Suite from On the Waterfront* (Tanglewood, Aug. 11, 1955); *Symphonic Dances from West Side Story* (1960; N.Y., Feb. 13, 1961); *Fanfare* for the inauguration of President John F. Kennedy (Washington, D.C., Jan. 19, 1961); *Fanfare* for the 25th anniversary of N.Y.'s High School of Music and Art (N.Y., March 24, 1961); *2 Meditations from Mass* (Austin, Texas, Oct. 31, 1971); *Meditation III from Mass* (Jerusalem, May 21, 1972; withdrawn); *Dybbuk Variations* (Auckland, New Zealand, Aug. 16, 1974); *3 Meditations from Mass* for Cello and Orch. (Washington, D.C., Oct. 11, 1977); *Slava!,* "a political overture" for M. Rostropovich (Washington, D.C., Oct. 11, 1977); *CBS Music* (1977; CBS-TV, April 1, 1978; withdrawn); *Divertimento* (Boston, Sept. 25, 1980); *A Musical Toast,* in memory of A. Kostelanetz (N.Y., Oct. 11, 1980); *Halil,* nocturne for Flute and Orch. (Jerusalem, May 27, 1981). **CHAMBER:** Trio for Violin, Cello, and Piano (1937); Sonata for Violin and Piano (1940); *4 Studies* for 2 Clarinets, 2 Bassoons, and Piano (c.1940); Sonata for Clarinet and Piano (1941–42); *Brass Music*

(1948); *Red, White, and Blues* for Trumpet and Piano (1984). PIANO: Sonata (1938); *Scenes from the City of Sin* for Piano, 4-hands (1939); *7 Anniversaries* (1943); *4 Anniversaries* (1948); *5 Anniversaries* (1949–51); *Touches* (1981); *Moby Diptych* (1981); *13 Anniversaries* (1988); *For Nicky, in Ancient Friendship* for Nicolas Slonimsky's 95th birthday (Los Angeles, April 27, 1989). VOCAL: *Hashkiveinu* for Tenor, Chorus, and Organ (1945); *Yigdal* for Chorus and Piano (1950); *Harvard Choruses* (1957; withdrawn); *Chichester Psalms* for Boy Soloist, Chorus, and Orch. (N.Y., July 15, 1965); *Songfest* for 6 Singers and Orch. (Washington, D.C., Oct. 11, 1977); *Olympic Hymn* for Chorus and Orch. (Baden-Baden, Sept. 23, 1981; withdrawn); *Jubilee Games* for Baritone and Orch. (N.Y., Sept. 13, 1986; rev. version, incorporating *Opening Prayer*, retitled as *Benediction*, Tel Aviv, May 31, 1988); *Opening Prayer* for Baritone and Orch. (N.Y., Dec. 15, 1986; retitled as *Benediction* and incorporated in the rev. version of *Jubilee Games*, Tel Aviv, May 31, 1988); *Missa brevis* for Countertenor or Septet of Solo Voices, Chorus, and Percussion (Atlanta, April 21, 1988). SONGS FOR VOICE AND PIANO: *I Hate Music*, cycle of 5 children's songs for Soprano and Piano (1943); *Afterthought* (1945); *La Bonne Cuisine*, "4 recipes" (1947); *2 Love Songs*, after Rainer Maria Rilke (1949); *Silhouette*, for Jennie Tourel (1951); *On the Waterfront* (1954; withdrawn); *Get Hep!* (1955; withdrawn); *So Pretty* (1968); *An Album of Songs* (1974; withdrawn); *My New Friends* (1979); *Piccola Serenata*, vocalise for Karl Böhm's 85th birthday (1979); *Sean Song* (1986); *Song Album* (1988); *My 12-tone Melody*, for Irving Berlin's 100th birthday (1988); *Arias and Barcarolles*, song cycle for Mezzo-soprano, Baritone, and Piano Duet (1988; N.Y., Sept. 7, 1989).

WRITINGS: *The Joy of Music* (N.Y., 1959); *Leonard Bernstein's Young People's Concerts for Reading and Listening* (N.Y., 1961; rev. ed., 1970, as *Leonard Bernstein's Young People's Concerts*); *The Infinite Variety of Music* (N.Y., 1966); *The Unanswered Question: Six Talks at Harvard* (Cambridge, Mass., and London, 1976); *Findings* (N.Y., 1982).

BIBL.: J. Briggs, *L. B., The Man, His Work and His World* (Cleveland and N.Y., 1961); A. Holde, *L. B.* (Berlin, 1961); J. Gruen and K. Hyman, *The Private World of L. B.* (N.Y., 1968); P. Robinson, *B.* (N.Y., 1982); P. Gradenwitz, *L. B.: Eine Biographie* (Zürich, 1984; 2nd ed., 1990; Eng. tr., 1986); M. Freedland, *L. B.* (London, 1987); J. Peyser, *L. B.: A Biography* (N.Y., 1987); J. Gottlieb, ed., *L. B.: A Complete Catalog of His Works: Celebrating His 70th Birthday, August 25, 1988* (N.Y., 1988).

Bernstein, Martin, American musicologist; b. N.Y., Dec. 14, 1904. He was educated at N.Y. Univ. (graduated in 1925; B.Mus., 1927); played the double bass in the N.Y. Sym. Orch. (1925), the N.Y. Phil. Orch. (1926–28), and the Chautauqua Sym. Orch. (1929–36). He was for 48 years a member of the faculty of N.Y. Univ. (1924–72); then a prof. of music at Lehman College, City Univ. of N.Y. (1972–73). He publ. *Score Reading* (1932; 2nd ed., 1949) and the successful textbook *An Introduction to Music* (N.Y., 1937; 4th ed., 1972); contributed chapters on music to *An Intellectual and Cultural History of the Western World*, Harry Elmer Barnes, ed. (N.Y., 1937). A Festschrift, *A Musical Offering: Essays in Honor of M. B.*, ed. by E.H. Clinkscale and C. Brook, was publ. in 1977. A brother, **Artie Bernstein** (b. N.Y., Feb. 3, 1909; d. Los Angeles, Jan. 4, 1964), a classically trained cellist, became a leading jazz bassist in the 1930s and '40s, playing with many big bands, including Jimmy Dorsey's; from 1939 to 1941 he was part of the Benny Goodman Sextet; after World War II he became a studio musician.

Bernuth, Julius von, German conductor; b. Rees, Rhine Province, Aug. 8, 1830; d. Hamburg, Dec. 24, 1902. He was a practicing lawyer; studied music with Taubert and Dehn in Berlin, and at the Leipzig Cons., where he founded a chamber music society, Aufschwung (1857), and the Dilettanten-Orchester-Verein (1859); later became conductor of the Hamburg Phil. Orch.; in 1873 founded a cons. in Hamburg.

Béroff, Michel, French pianist; b. Épinal, Vosges, May 9, 1950. He studied piano with Yvonne Loriod at the Paris Cons., making his debut in Paris at 16; then toured as a concert pianist, often programming works of French avant-garde composers.

Berr (original name, **Beer**), **Friedrich,** German clarinetist and bassoonist; b. Mannheim, April 17, 1794; d. Paris, Sept. 24, 1838. He studied with Fétis and Reicha in Paris, and settled there in 1823; served as the 2nd clarinetist at the Théâtre-Italien; in 1828 became 1st clarinetist. In 1831 he was appointed to the faculty of the Paris Cons.; in 1836 he became director of the new School of Military Music. He was the author of a *Traité complet de la clarinette à 14 clefs* (1836); also composed many works for clarinet and bassoon, and some 500 pieces of military music.

Berry, "Chu" (Leon Brown), black American jazz tenor saxophonist; b. Wheeling, W.Va., Sept. 13, 1908; d. in an automobile accident in Conneaut, Ohio, Oct. 30, 1941. After attending West Virginia State College, he joined Sammy Stewart's big band in Chicago (1929). In 1930 he went to N.Y., where he worked with Benny Carter (1932), Spike Hughes (1933), Teddy Hill (1933–35), Fletcher Henderson (1935–36), and Cab Calloway (1936–37). He was one of the finest instrumentalists of the swing era.

BIBL.: J. Evensmo, *The Tenor Saxophone of C. B.* (Hosle, Norway, 1976).

Berry, Chuck, black American rock singer and guitarist; b. San Jose, Calif., Jan. 15, 1926. He was a carpenter's son; the family moved to Missouri when he was a child; he received his musical training as a chorister at the Antioch Baptist Church in St. Louis; learned to play a 6-stringed Spanish guitar, and improvised tunes in a then-current jazz manner. In 1955 he went to Chicago and sold his song *Maybelline* to a record company; it took off like a rocket, and reached No. 1 on the list in the 3 categories of rhythm-and-blues, country-and-western, and pop. This was followed by a brash bragging song with the lyrics "Roll over, Beethoven, tell Tchaikovsky the news; Roll over, Beethoven, dig these rhythm-and-blues." Moving into the big time, Berry opened in St. Louis the Chuck Berry Club Bandstand; it prospered, but he soon ran into trouble when a 14-year-old hatcheck girl employed in the club brought charges that he transported her across state lines for immoral purposes. He was found guilty and served 2 years in the federal penitentiary in Terre Haute, Ind. Jail failed to kill his spirit of happy-go-lucky insouciance, and he rebounded with the sexually oriented song *My Ding-a-Ling*, which made the coveted golden disk record. He became one of the most successful rock singers; when *Voyager 2* was launched into space on Aug. 20, 1977, it carried a sampler of terrestrial music on records, and next to Bach and Beethoven, the package included *Johnny B. Goode* by Chuck Berry.

BIBL.: H. De Witt, *C. B.: Rock 'n' Roll Music* (N.Y., 1981; 2nd ed., rev., 1985); K. Reese, *C. B.: Mr. Rock 'n' Roll* (N.Y., 1982).

Berry, Jan, Californian rock artist; b. Los Angeles, April 3, 1941. With a high-school friend, Dean Torrance (b. Los Angeles, March 10, 1940), he formed a duo named Jan and Dean and began recording songs specializing in doomsday topics, in which surfing, cars, and girls were somehow mixed with murky speculations about death, with such titles as *Dead Man's Curve*. In April 1966, Berry came very close to finality when in a wild speed drive in his car he struck a parked truck in Los Angeles and went into a coma, suffering from paralysis of his right side and impediment of speech and vision. Miraculously, he emerged from this condition and returned to work. Of his doubles with Torrance, the most successful was *Ride the Wild Surf*. They also issued the mock-sentimental song *The Little Old Lady from Pasadena*.

Berry, Wallace (Taft), American composer and music theorist; b. La Crosse, Wis., Jan. 10, 1928. He studied with Halsey Stevens at the Univ. of Southern Calif. (B.Mus., 1949; Ph.D., 1956) and with Nadia Boulanger at the Paris Cons. (1953–54); then taught at the Univ. of Southern Calif. (1956–57), the Univ. of Michigan (1957–77), and (from 1978) the Univ. of British Columbia, where he was also head of the music dept. (1978–84). He served as president of the Soc. for Music Theory (1982–85); also publ. *Form in Music* (Englewood Cliffs, N.J., 1966; 2nd ed., rev., 1985), *Eighteenth-Century Imitative Counterpoint: Music for Analysis* (with E. Chudacoff; N.Y., 1969), *Structural Functions in Music* (Englewood Cliffs, N.J., 1975; 2nd ed., 1987), and *Musical Structure and Performance* (New Haven, Conn., 1989).

WORKS: STAGE: *The Admirable Bashville*, chamber opera (1954). **ORCH.:** *4 Movements* for Chamber Orch. (1954); Piano Concerto (1964). **CHAMBER:** Clarinet Sonata (1950); Suite for String Trio (1950); Piano Quintet (1951); *Divertimento* for Harpsichord, Oboe, English Horn, and Cello (1952); 4 string quartets (1960, 1964, 1966, 1984); *Threnody* for Violin (1963–64); *Divertimento* for Wind Quintet, Piano, and Percussion (1964); Trio for Piano, Violin, and Cello (1970); *Anachronisms* for Violin and Piano (1973); Piano Sonata (1975). **VOCAL:** *Spoon River*, 6 songs for Soprano, Bass-baritone, and Orch. (1952); *Lover of the Moon Trembling Now at Twilight* for Soprano or Tenor, and Ensemble (1971); *Of the Changeless Night and the Stark Ranges of Nothing* for Mezzo-soprano, Cello, and Piano (1978–79); songs.

Berry, Walter, Austrian bass-baritone; b. Vienna, April 8, 1929. He 1st studied engineering; later decided to engage in a musical career, and enrolled at the Vienna Academy of Music. In 1950 he sang at the Vienna State Opera. On Oct. 2, 1966, he made his American debut at the Metropolitan Opera in N.Y. as Barak in *Die Frau ohne Schatten* by Richard Strauss. He distinguished himself in Wagnerian operas. He was married to **Christa Ludwig** in 1957, and appeared with her numerous times in corresponding roles (Carmen and Escamillo, Ortrud and Telramund, etc.); they were divorced in 1970, but continued to sing in tandem in the same operas.

Bersa, Blagoje, Croatian composer; b. Ragusa, Dec. 21, 1873; d. Zagreb, Jan. 1, 1934. He studied music in Vienna, where he remained until 1919. He wrote 2 operas, *Fire* and *The Cobbler of Delft*; the symphonic poems *Sunny Fields, Ghosts,* and *Hamlet*; a String Quartet; a Piano Trio; and songs. Bersa was for many years a prof. of composition at the Zagreb Cons., and influenced the development of the new generation of Croatian composers, several of whom were his pupils.

Bertali, Antonio, Italian violinist and composer; b. Verona, March 11, 1605; d. Vienna, April 17, 1669. He studied with Steffano Bernardi in Verona; in 1624 he went to Vienna, where he served as a court violinist; in 1649 he succeeded Giovanni Valentini as Imperial court Kapellmeister. He wrote about 11 operas and a number of secular cantatas and oratorios.

Bertalotti, Angelo Michele, Italian composer and teacher; b. Bologna, April 8, 1666; d. there, March 30, 1747. He studied in Bologna; then sang in the choirs of S. Luigi dei Francesi and S. Agostino in Rome (1687–90). In 1693 he became singing master at the Scuole Pie in Bologna; was a member of the choir of S. Petronio there from 1705 on. He publ. *Regole facilissime* (1706 and subsequent eds.); his *Solfeggi a canto e alto dati alle stampe per comodo delli putti delle Scuole pie* (1744; rev. ed., 1764) retains its value as a choral method.

Bertani, Lelio, Italian composer; b. Brescia, c.1550; d. there, c.1620. He was appointed maestro di cappella at the Brescia Cathedral in 1584 and remained there until c.1590; from 1598 to 1604 he held a similar post at the Padua Cathedral. His madrigals were greatly appreciated.

WORKS: *Il primo libro de madrigali* for 5 Voices (Brescia, 1584); *Il primo libro de madrigali* for 6 Voices (Venice, 1585); *Madrigali spirituali* for 3 Voices (Brescia, 1585).

Berté, Heinrich, Hungarian composer; b. Galgócz, May 8, 1857; d. Perchtoldsdorf, near Vienna, Aug. 23, 1924. He studied with Hellmesberger, Fuchs, and Bruckner in Vienna. He produced ballets: *Das Märchenbuch* (Prague, 1890), *Amor auf Reisen* (Vienna, 1895), *Der Karneval in Venedig* (Vienna, 1900), and *Automatenzauber* (Vienna, 1901); operettas: *Die Schnee-*

flocke (Prague, 1896), *Der neue Bürgermeister* (Vienna, 1904), *Die Millionenbraut* (Munich, 1905), *Der kleine Chevalier* (Dresden, 1907), *Der schöne Gardist* (Breslau, 1907), *Der Glücksnarr* (Vienna, 1909), *Kreolenblut* (Hamburg, 1911), *Der Märchenprinz* (Hannover, 1914), and *Das Dreimäderlhaus* (Vienna, Jan. 15, 1916). This last, based on Schubert melodies, was produced in English under the title *Blossom Time*, arranged by Romberg (N.Y., Sept. 21, 1921; very popular); also as *Lilac Time*, arranged by Clutsam (London, Dec. 22, 1922).

Berteau, Martin, famous French cellist; b. c.1700; d. Angers, Jan. 23, 1771. He studied the bass viol with Kozecz in Germany; then took up the cello, achieving mastery of its technique. He is regarded as the protagonist of the French school of cello playing. He also composed a number of effective pieces for cello.

Bertheaume, Isidore, French violinist; b. Paris, c.1752; d. St. Petersburg, March 20, 1802. A precocious musician, he joined the orch. of the Paris Opéra in 1767 and served there until 1769 and again from 1775 to 1781. He conducted the Concert Spirituel during the Revolution (1789–91); then left France and went to Germany; in 1801 emigrated to Russia, where he served as 1st violinist in the Imperial Orch. in St. Petersburg. He composed 2 syms. concertantes for 2 Violins; 6 sonatas for Clavecin, with Violin; violin concertos; and other works for violin.

Berti, Carlo, Italian composer and organist; b. probably in Florence, c.1555; d. Mantua, before Sept. 2, 1602. He became a novice in the Servite order at Ss. Annunziata in Florence (1577); was ordained at the convent of the order in 1580. In 1592 he became maestro di cappella at Ss. Annunziata, remaining there until 1598. He went to Mantua in 1601. Only 3 books of his sacred music are extant, all publ. in Venice (1592, 1593, 1596).

BIBL.: D. Nutter, *The Life and Works of C. B.* (diss., Rosary College, 1970).

Berti, Giovanni Pietro, Italian singer, organist, and composer; b. Venice, 1638. He was a tenor in the choir of S. Marco in Venice; was named 2nd organist there in 1624, and remained at that post until his death. His songs, particularly his strophic arias, are of considerable historical importance; 56 songs for solo voice and continuo are extant.

Bertin, Louise (-Angélique), French composer; b. Les Roches, near Paris, Feb. 15, 1805; d. Paris, April 26, 1877. She was a pupil of Fétis; composed the operas *Guy Mannering* (Les Roches, Aug. 25, 1825), *Le Loup-garou* (Paris, March 10, 1827), *Fausto* (Paris, March 7, 1831), and *La Esmeralda* (to a libretto adapted by Victor Hugo from his novel *Notre-Dame de Paris*; Paris, Nov. 14, 1836). She also wrote a number of instrumental works, of which 6 *Ballades* for Piano was publ.

Bertin de la Doué, Thomas, French composer; b. Paris, c.1680; d. there, 1745. He was maître de musique to the Princess of Orléans; then held the post of organist at the Théatins church in Paris; also served as violinist and keyboard musician with the Paris Opéra orch. (1714–34). As a composer, he was best known for his opera-ballet *Ajax* (Paris, April 30, 1716).

Bertini, (Benoît-) Auguste, French pianist, brother of **Henri (-Jérôme) Bertini**; b. Lyons, June 5, 1780; d. London, 1830. He took lessons with Clementi in London from 1793 to 1799; in 1806 he returned to Paris, where he publ. a didactic tract, *Stigmatographie, ou L'Art d'écrire avec des points, suivie de la mélographie, nouvel art de noter la musique* (Paris, 1812), in which he claimed to simplify musical notation. In London he publ., in 1830, another didactic pamphlet, extravagantly titled *New System for Learning and acquiring extraordinary facility on all musical instruments* (3rd ed., 1849).

Bertini, Domenico, Italian composer and pedagogue; b. Lucca, June 26, 1829; d. Florence, Sept. 7, 1890. He studied at the Lucca Music School; later with Michele Puccini; in 1857 was director of the music inst. and maestro di cappella at Massa Carrara; settled in Florence (1862) as a singing teacher and music critic; became director of the Cherubini Soc. He contributed to musical periodicals, including *Boccherini* of Florence and *La Scena* of Venice; also wrote a *Compendio de' principi di musica, secondo un nuovo sistema* (1866); composed 2 operas; masses and other sacred music; chamber music.

Bertini, Gary, Russian-born Israeli conductor and composer; b. Brichevo, May 1, 1927. He was taken to Palestine as a child and studied music in Tel Aviv; later went to Italy, where he studied at the Verdi Cons. in Milan; completed his musical education in Paris; graduated in conducting from the Paris Cons. in 1953. Returning to Israel, he was a frequent guest conductor with the Israel Phil. Orch.; also served as music director of the Jerusalem Sym. (1978–81); from 1981 to 1983 he was music adviser of the Detroit Sym. In 1983 he was appointed chief conductor of the Cologne Radio Sym. Orch. From 1987 to 1990 he was chief conductor of the Opera and Museumgesellschaft concerts in Frankfurt. He composed a Concerto for Horn, Strings, and Timpani (1952); a Solo Violin Sonata (1953); a ballet, *The Unfound Door* (1963); and incidental music to a number of plays.

Bertini, Giuseppe, Italian musicographer, son of **Salvatore Bertini;** b. Palermo, Jan. 20, 1759; d. there, March 15, 1852. He studied at the Scuole Pie degli Scolopi; later entered the priesthood without abandoning his work in musical lexicography. He compiled the *Dizionario storico-critico degli scrittori di musica* (Palermo, 1814–15), which is still of some value for its entries on obscure Italian musicians.

Bertini, Henri (-Jérôme), known as "Bertini le jeune," pianist and composer; b. London, Oct. 28, 1798; d. Meylau, near Grenoble, Oct. 1, 1876. When 6 months old, he was taken to Paris, where he was taught music by his father and his elder brother, **(Benoit-) Auguste Bertini;** at age 12, made a concert tour through the Netherlands and Germany; then studied in Paris and Great Britain; lived in Paris as a concert pianist from 1821 to 1859, when he retired to his estate at Meylau. He wrote valuable technical studies, some of which have been publ. in eds. by G. Buonamici and by Riemann; also arranged Bach's *48 Preludes and Fugues* for Piano, 4-hands; composed much chamber music, many piano pieces.

Bertini, Salvatore, Italian composer, father of **Giuseppe Bertini;** b. Palermo, 1721; d. there, Dec. 16, 1794. He studied in Palermo before entering the Jesuit College in Naples; subsequently took music courses with Fago and Leo at the Turchini Cons. In 1748 he was appointed substitute maestro di cappella at the Cappella Palatina in Palermo; was named maestro there in 1778. He composed mostly for the church.

Bertinotti (-Radicati), Teresa, Italian soprano; b. Savigliano, 1776; d. Bologna, Feb. 12, 1854. She studied with La Barbiera in Naples; married the singer Felice Radicati in 1801, and toured with him in a vocal duo, visiting Austria and Germany. She sang at the King's Theatre in London from 1810 to 1812; then was in Lisbon (1812–14). Upon her husband's death in 1820, she retired from the stage and devoted herself to teaching voice.

Bertoldo, Sperindio (Sper'in Dio), Italian organist and composer; b. Modena, c.1530; d. Padua, Aug. 13, 1570. He served as chief organist at the Cathedral of Padua. His surviving compositions include 2 books of madrigals in 5 Voices, publ. in Venice (book 1, 1561; book 2, 1562); the 1st book includes an *Echo a 6 voci* and a *Dialogo a 8 voci*. Several other madrigals are included in a collection by Cipriano and Annibale (Venice, 1561). Bertoldo's *Toccate, ricercari e canzoni francese . . . per sonar d'organo* (Venice, 1591) was publ. posth. Two ricercari for Organ are included in L. Torchi, *L'Arte musicale in Italia* (vol. III).

Bertolli, Francesca, Italian contralto; d. Bologna, Jan. 9, 1767. She sang in Bologna in 1728; then was engaged by Handel in 1729 for his Royal Academy of Music operatic perfor-

mances in London at the King's Theatre; in 1733 she left Handel's company to join his rival's establishment, the Opera of the Nobility; in 1736–37 she was again a member of Handel's company; she then returned to Italy, where she retired shortly afterward. She was noted for her performances of male roles in lieu of castrati.

Berton, Henri-Montan, French conductor and composer, son of **Pierre-Montan Berton;** b. Paris, Sept. 17, 1767; d. there, April 22, 1844. He was a pupil of Rey and Sacchini; in 1782 he joined the orch. of the Paris Opéra as a violinist; in 1795 he was appointed to the staff of the Paris Cons., and in 1818 succeeded Méhul as prof. of composition. From 1807 to 1809 he conducted at the Opéra-Bouffe; in 1809 became chorus master at the Paris Opéra; in 1815 he was elected a member of the French Academy. He wrote 47 operas, of which the most successful were *Montano et Stéphanie* (1799), *Le Délire* (1799), and *Aline, reine de Colconde* (1803); other works included several oratorios, 8 cantatas, and 4 ballets. He also publ. some theoretical works expressing his own views on musical values; they are curious in content but otherwise devoid of significance.

BIBL.: D. Raoul-Rochette, *Notice historique sur la vie et les ouvrages de M. B.* (Paris, 1846); H. Blanchard, *H.-M. B.* (Paris, 1839); M.S. Selden, "H. B. as Critic," *Journal of the American Musicological Society* (Summer 1971).

Berton, Pierre-Montan, French composer, father of **Henri-Montan Berton;** b. Maubert-Fontaines, Ardennes, Jan. 7, 1727; d. Paris, May 14, 1780. He studied organ and composition at the choir school of Senlis Cathedral; was a member of the chorus at the Paris Opéra; then became director of the Grand-Théâtre in Bordeaux. In 1755 he was appointed conductor of the Grand Opéra in Paris and was its general director from 1775 to 1778. In that capacity he supplemented the music of the operas of Lully, Rameau, and Gluck. He produced, in Paris, his operas *Érosine* (Aug. 29, 1766), *Théonis, ou Le Toucher* (Oct. 11, 1767), and *Adèle de Ponthieu* (Dec. 1, 1772). Additional works include a cantata, a motet, and songs.

Bertoni, Ferdinando Gioseffo, Italian organist and composer; b. Salò, near Venice, Aug. 15, 1725; d. Desenzano, Dec. 1, 1813. He studied with Padre Martini; in 1752 was appointed 1st organist of S. Marco in Venice; made 2 trips to London, where several of his operas were produced; on Jan. 21, 1785, he succeeded Galuppi as maestro di cappella at S. Marco; retired in 1808. From 1757 to 1797 he also served as choirmaster at the Cons. de' Mendicanti. He wrote about 50 operas; of these the following are important: *La Vedova accorta* (Venice, 1745), *Quinto Fabio* (Milan, Jan. 31, 1778), *Demofoonte* (London, Nov. 28, 1778), and *Nitteti* (Venice, Feb. 6, 1789). He also wrote a number of oratorios; harpsichord sonatas; chamber music.

BIBL.: I. Haas, *F. B.: Leben und Instrumentalwerk* (Vienna, 1958).

Bertouille, Gérard, Belgian composer; b. Tournai, May 26, 1898; d. Brussels, Dec. 12, 1981. He studied philosophy and jurisprudence and also took lessons in composition with Absil, Marsick, and Souris. He began to compose rather late in life but succeeded in creating a distinct style, pursuing a median path between a restrained Romantic idiom and distinct modernism. He wrote 4 syms. (1947, 1955, 1957, 1977), 2 violin concertos (1942, 1970), 2 piano concertos (1946, 1953), 2 trumpet concertos (1946, 1973), a Concertino for Clarinet and Strings (1970), 7 instrumental quartets (Nos. 1–3 and 5–7 for Strings, No. 4 for Flute and Strings), 5 violin sonatas, a Wind Quintet, a Concertino for 4 Clarinets (1977), and a number of songs.

Bertram, Theodor, German baritone; b. Stuttgart, Feb. 12, 1869; d. (suicide) Bayreuth, Nov. 24, 1907. He studied with his father, the baritone Heinrich Bertram; made his debut as the Hermit in *Der Freischütz* in Ulm in 1889; then sang at the Hamburg Opera (1891) and the Berlin Kroll Opera (1892); was a member of the Munich Court Opera (1893–99). He made his Metropolitan Opera debut in N.Y. on Jan. 6, 1900, as the Flying Dutchman, remaining on the roster for a year; he also sang at Covent Garden, London (1900, 1903, 1907), and at Bayreuth (1901–6). He was married to the soprano **Fanny Moran-Olden;** following her death, he became despondent and hanged himself.

Bertrand, Aline, notable French harpist; b. Paris, 1798; d. there, March 13, 1835. She studied at the Paris Cons. with Nadermann; then with Bochsa (1815); made her debut in 1820; then toured Europe, winning special acclaim upon her appearance in Vienna (1828). She publ. *Fantaisie sur la Romance de Joseph* (on themes of Méhul's opera) for Harp, and various other arrangements.

Bertrand, Antoine de, French composer; b. Fontanges (Cantal), c.1540; d. Toulouse, c.1581. He composed 7 books of 4-part chansons: *Les Amours de P. de Ronsard* (2 vols., 1576); *Sonets chrestiens* (2 vols., 1580); *Chansons* (3 vols., 1578). His music shows harmonic daring in the use of chromatic progressions. Vols. 4–7 of H. Expert's *Monuments de la musique française au temps de la Renaissance* are devoted to Bertrand's works.

Berutti, Arturo, Argentine opera composer; b. San Juan, March 27, 1862; d. Buenos Aires, Jan. 3, 1938. He was of Italian extraction, and naturalized the spelling of his last name as **Beruti.** He received his early training in music with his father; then went to Leipzig, where he became a student of Jadassohn. He subsequently lived in Italy, where he produced 3 of his operas: *La Vendetta* (Vercelli, May 21, 1892), *Evangelina* (Milan, Sept. 19, 1893), and *Taras Bulba* (Turin, March 9, 1895). Returning to Argentina in 1896, he produced the following operas in various theaters in Buenos Aires: *Pampa* (July 27, 1897), *Yupanki* (July 25, 1899), *Khrise* (June 21, 1902), *Horrida Nox* (the 1st opera by a native Argentine composer, written to a Spanish libretto, which was produced in Argentina; Buenos Aires, July 7, 1908), and *Los Heroes* (Aug. 23, 1919; his only opera produced at the Teatro Colón).

BIBL.: E.M. Navarro, *San Juan en la historia de la música* (San Juan, Argentina, 1964).

Berwald, Franz (Adolf), foremost Swedish composer of the 19th century, cousin of **Johan Fredrik Berwald;** b. Stockholm, July 23, 1796; d. there, April 3, 1868. His father, Christian Friedrich Berwald (1740–1825), was a German musician who studied with Franz Benda and settled in Stockholm in the 1770s as a member of the orch. of the Royal Chapel. Franz received training in violin from his father and cousin, and in composition from J.B.E. du Puy. He was a violinist and violist in the orch. of the Royal Chapel in Stockholm (1812–28); in 1819 he toured Finland with his brother, Christian August Berwald, and Russia. In 1829 he went to Berlin and in 1835 opened an orthopedic establishment, which soon flourished. In 1841 he went to Vienna, where he obtained short-lived success as a composer with his symphonic poems. He then returned to Stockholm and secured a foothold as a composer with his operettas and cantatas; on Dec. 2, 1843, his cousin conducted the premiere of his *Sinfonie sérieuse* (his only acknowledged sym. performed in his lifetime), but poor execution of the score did little to further his cause. In 1846 he returned to Vienna, where Jenny Lind sang in his stage cantata *Ein ländliches Verlobungfest in Schweden* at the Theater an der Wien; in 1847 he was elected an honorary member of the Salzburg Mozarteum. In 1849 he returned to his homeland in hopes of securing the position of either conductor of the Royal Opera in Stockholm or director of music in Uppsala. Hopes dashed, he became manager of a glassworks in Sandö, Ångermanland (1850–58) and part owner of a sawmill (1853), and briefly operated a brick factory. Berwald was shunned by the Swedish musical establishment (which he disdained), and his extraordinary gifts as a composer went almost totally unrecognized in his lifetime. Finally, in 1864, he was made a member of the Swedish Royal Academy of Music in Stockholm. In the last year of his life he was named to its composition chair, only to be unseated, however briefly, on a 2nd vote demanded by his enemies. Berwald's masterpiece is his *Sinfonie singulière* (1845), a singular work of notable distinction, which was not performed until 70 years after its composition. He also wrote 3 other fine syms. and a number of worthy chamber music pieces. His output reveals the influence of the German Romantic school in general, but with an unmistakably individual voice.

WORKS: OPERAS: *Estrella di Soria* (1841; Stockholm, April 9, 1862); *Drottningen av Golconda* (1864; Stockholm, April 3, 1968, for the 100th anniversary of Berwald's death); operettas. ORCH.: Sym. in A major (1820; Stockholm, March 3, 1821; discarded by Berwald; only fragments extant); *Sinfonie sérieuse* (No. 1) in G minor (1842; Stockholm, Dec. 2, 1843); *Sinfonie capricieuse* (No. 2) in D major (1842; perf. ed. by Ernst Ellberg, Stockholm, Jan. 9, 1914; critical ed. by Nils Castegren, 1968); *Sinfonie singulière* (No. 3) in C major (1845; Stockholm, Jan. 10, 1905); *Sinfonie* in E-flat major ("No. 4," or *Sinfonie naïve*, the latter title unauthorized; 1845; Stockholm, April 9, 1878); Violin Concerto (Stockholm, March 3, 1821); *Concertstück* for Bassoon and Orch. (1827); Piano Concerto (transcription for 2 pianos by Gustaf Heintze, Stockholm, Dec. 14, 1904; with orch., Stockholm, April 27, 1908); symphonic poems: *Elfenspiel* and *Erinnerung an die norwegischen Alpen* (Vienna, March 6, 1842); *Ernste und heitere Grillen* (Stockholm, May 19, 1842); *Bayaderen-Fest* (Stockholm, Dec. 6, 1842); *Wettlauf* (1842). CHAMBER: 2 piano quintets; 3 string quartets; 5 piano trios; Septet; vocal music.

BIBL.: A. Hillman, *F. B.* (Stockholm, 1920); R. Layton, *B.* (Stockholm, 1956; in Eng., London, 1959); I. Bengtsson, "*F. B. från vaggan till graven. En kronologisk tabell,*" *Musikrevy,* XXIII/6 (1968); S. Broman, "*F. B.'s stanträd,*" *Svensk tidskrift för musikforskning* (1968); I. Andersson, *F. B. II: Källhänvisningar och personregister Diskograki* (Stockholm, 1971); I. Bengtsson, N. Castegren, and E. Lömans, eds., *F. B.: Die Dokumente seines Lebens* (Kassel, 1979); A. Johnson, "*B. and the Queen of Golconda,*" *Musical Times* (Jan. 1982).

Berwald, Johan Fredrik (Johann Friedrich), Swedish violinist and composer, cousin of **Franz (Adolf) Berwald;** b. Stockholm, Dec. 4, 1787; d. there, Aug. 26, 1861. He was a member of a musical family of German nationality which settled in Sweden. A precocious musician, he played the violin in public at the age of 5; took lessons in composition with Abbé Vogler during the latter's stay in Sweden. At 16 he went to St. Petersburg and served as concertmaster in the Russian Imperial Court Orch. (1803–12). Returning to Sweden, he was appointed chamber musician to the King of Sweden, a post he held from 1815 until 1849; also conducted (from 1819) the Royal Orch. in Stockholm. He wrote his 1st sym. when he was 9 years old, but in his mature years he devoted himself mainly to theatrical productions. One of his light operas, *L'Héroïne de l'amour,* to a French libretto, was produced in St. Petersburg in 1811. In Stockholm he was also active as a teacher; among his pupils was his cousin Franz Berwald.

Berwald, William (Wilhelm), German-American composer; b. Schwerin, Dec. 26, 1864; d. Loma Linda, Calif., May 8, 1948. He studied with Rheinberger at the Munich Cons. (1882–87), and with Faiszt in Stuttgart (1887–88). After a series of engagements as orch. conductor in Germany and Russia, he settled in the U.S. (1892); from 1921 to 1924 he conducted the Syracuse Orch. Among his works are 3 cantatas: *7 Last Words of Christ, Crucifixion and Resurrection,* and *From Old Japan;* music drama, *Utopia* (1936); symphonic poem, *Eros and Psyche* (1943); numerous choruses and instrumental pieces and about 250 anthems. He received many prizes for his works, and continued to compose to the end of his life.

Besanzoni, Gabriella, Italian contralto; b. Rome, Sept. 20, 1888; d. there, June 6, 1962. She made her debut as a soprano in *Norma* in 1911; after 1915 she sang mezzo-soprano and contralto; was particularly successful as Carmen. She appeared at the Metropolitan Opera in N.Y. as Amneris in *Aida* on Nov. 19, 1919, but sang there only 1 season. She made her home principally in Rio de Janeiro; in 1938 she returned to Italy.

Besard, Jean-Baptiste, French lutenist and composer; b. Besançon, 1567; d. probably in Augsburg, 1625. He studied philosophy at the Univ. of Dôle; after his marriage in 1602, he went to Rome and studied with the lutenist Lorenzini. Later he lived in Germany, publishing at Cologne his *Thesaurus harmonicus* (1603), and at Augsburg his *Novus partus, sive Concertationes musicae duodena trium . . .* (1617) and *Isagoge in artem testudinariam* (1617). Some of the compositions in these works have been ed. by O. Chilesotti in *Biblioteca di rarità musicali*.
BIBL.: O. Chilesotti, *Di G.B. Besardo e del suo Thesaurus harmonicus* (Milan, 1886).

Besekirsky, Vasili. See **Bezekirsky, Vasili.**

Besler, Samuel, German composer; b. Brieg, Silesia, Dec. 15, 1574; d. Breslau, July 19, 1625. He was rector (from 1605) of the Gymnasium zum Heiligen Geist in Breslau; wrote a large number of sacred pieces, most of which are preserved at the library of St. Bernardinus in Breslau.

Besozzi, Alessandro, celebrated Italian oboist; b. Parma, July 22, 1702; d. Turin, July 26, 1793. He was a musician at the ducal chapel in Parma (1728–31); made concert tours with his brother, Girolamo (see 3 below); appeared with him in Paris in 1735; then lived in Turin. He publ. numerous trio sonatas for Flute, Violin, and Cello; 6 violin sonatas (with Basso Continuo); etc. Other members of the family who specialized in wind instruments were: (1) **Antonio,** oboist, nephew of Alessandro (b. Parma, 1714; d. Turin, 1781); (2) **Carlo,** oboist, son of Antonio (b. Naples, c.1738; d. Dresden, March 22, 1791); played in the Dresden orch. (1754); wrote several oboe concertos; (3) **Girolamo,** bassoonist, brother of Alessandro (b. Parma, April 17, 1704; d. Turin, 1778); (4) **Gaetano,** oboist, nephew of Alessandro (b. Parma, 1727; d. London, 1794); (5) **Girolamo,** oboist, son of Gaetano (b. Naples, c.1750; d. Paris, 1785); (6) **Henri,** flutist, son of Girolamo; played at the Opéra-Comique; (7) **Louis-Désiré,** son of Henri (b. Versailles, April 3, 1814; d. Paris, Nov. 11, 1879), a student of Le Sueur and Barbereau; he won the Prix de Rome in 1837, defeating Gounod.

Bessaraboff, Nicholas, Russian-American authority on musical instruments; b. Voronezh, Feb. 12, 1894; d. N.Y., Nov. 10, 1973. He was trained as a mechanical engineer and a draftsman, but he also played the French horn and became interested in the mechanics and acoustics of musical instruments. After the completion of his studies at the polytechnical inst. in St. Petersburg, he was sent in 1915 with a group of other Russian engineers to the U.S. in order to expedite the shipping of American military equipment for the Russian armed forces during World War I. He arrived in San Francisco in Dec. 1915, and remained in the U.S. after the Russian Revolution of 1917. He worked as a draftsman in Rochester, N.Y., at the same time doing extensive reading on the subject of musical instruments. In 1931 he moved to Boston, where he began working on cataloguing the collection of instruments in the Boston Museum of Fine Arts. In 1941 he publ. his magnum opus, *Ancient European Musical Instruments, An Organological Study of the Musical Instruments in the Leslie Lindsey Mason Collection at the Museum of Fine Arts, Boston.* In 1945 he officially changed his name to **Nicholas Bessaraboff Bodley,** adopting the maiden name of his American wife, Virginia Bodley.
BIBL.: D. Boyden, "N. B.'s *Ancient European Musical Instruments*," *Notes* (Sept. 1971).

Bessel, Vasili, Russian music publisher; b. St. Petersburg, April 25, 1842; d. Zürich, March 1, 1907. He was the founder (1869) of the music publishing firm of Bessel & Co. at St. Petersburg, which has publ. works by many distinguished Russian composers (Anton Rubinstein, Rimsky-Korsakov, Tchaikovsky, Mussorgsky); also 2 short-lived periodicals, *Musical Leaflet* (1872–77) and the *Russian Musical Review* (1885–89). Bessel wrote *Reminiscences of Tchaikovsky,* who was his fellow student at the St. Petersburg Cons. In 1920 the firm was transferred to Paris, where it continued under the direction of Bessel's sons, Vasili and Alexander.

Besseler, Heinrich, eminent German musicologist; b. Hörde, Dortmund, April 2, 1900; d. Leipzig, July 25, 1969. He studied mathematics and natural sciences; then turned to musicology; attended the courses of Gurlitt in Freiburg, of Adler in Vienna, and of Ludwig in Göttingen. He received his doctorate in Freiburg in 1923; then taught classes at the univs. at Heidelberg (1928–48), Jena (1948–56), and Leipzig (1956–65). In 1967 he received the honorary degree of Doctor of Humane Letters of the Univ. of Chicago. A Festschrift in his honor was publ. on his 60th birthday. He contributed valuable articles to various music journals, mostly on the musical problems of the Middle Ages and the Renaissance, but also on general subjects of musical esthetics; wrote several basic articles for *Die Musik in Geschichte und Gegenwart.* He also ed. the collected works of Dufay, Okeghem, and other musicians of their period.
WRITINGS: *Die Musik des Mittelalters und der Renaissance* (Potsdam, 1931); *Fünf echte Bildnisse J.S. Bachs* (Kassel, 1956); *Das musikalische Hören der Neuzeit* (Berlin, 1959; in the report of the transactions of the Saxon Academy of Sciences, vol. 104); *Die Besetzung der Chansons im 15. Jahrhundert* (Utrecht, 1952); *Singstil und Instrumentenstil in der europäischen Musik* (Bamberg, 1953); "Zur Chronologie der Konzerte J.S. Bachs," in the Festschrift for Max Schneider (Leipzig, 1955); "Das Renaissanceproblem in der Musik," in the Festschrift for Br. Stäblein (Kassel, 1967). He brought out (with Max Schneider) the excellent ed. *Musikgeschichte in Bildern* (begun serially in Leipzig, 1961; from 1968, his co-editor was W. Bachmann). A complete list of his writings (up to 1961) and eds. is found in the Festschrift in his honor (Leipzig, 1961).

Bessems, Antoine, Belgian violinist; b. Antwerp, April 6, 1809; d. there, Oct. 19, 1868. He was a pupil of Baillot at the Paris Cons. (1826); in 1829 was 1st violinist at the Théâtre-Italien, Paris; then made long concert tours; taught for a time in Paris; returned to Antwerp and, from 1847 to 1852, conducted the orch. of the Société Royale d'Harmonie. He composed a Violin Concerto; *12 grandes études* for Violin, with Piano; *12 grands duos de concert* for Violin, with Piano; many other violin pieces, masses, motets, Psalms, etc.

Best, W(illiam) T(homas), eminent English organist; b. Carlisle, Aug. 13, 1826; d. Liverpool, May 10, 1897. He studied organ in Liverpool; held various posts as a church organist in Liverpool and London. At his numerous concerts he introduced arrangements of symphonic works, thus enabling his audiences to hear classical works in a musicianly manner at a time when orch. concerts were scarce. His own works, popular in type, though classical in form, included sonatas, preludes, fugues, concert studies, etc. for organ. He publ. *Handel Album* (20 vols.); *Arrangements from the Scores of the Great Masters* (5 vols.); *Modern School for the Organ* (1853); *The Art of Organ Playing* (1870); etc.
BIBL.: O.A. Mansfield, "W.T. B.," *Musical Quarterly* (April 1918); J. Mewburn Levien, *Impressions of W.T. B.* (London, 1942).

Bethune, Thomas Greene (called **"Blind Tom"**), black American pianist and composer; b. Columbus, Ga., May 25, 1849; d. Hoboken, N.J., June 13, 1908. Born blind in slavery, he was purchased, along with his parents (Charity and Mingo Wiggins), by a Colonel Bethune in 1850. His master's wife was a music teacher who fostered his musical talent. At the age of 9 he was "leased" for 3 years to one Perry Oliver, who arranged concert appearances for him throughout the U.S., including a performance at the White House before President Buchanan. Colonel Bethune then took full charge of Tom's career, obtaining legal custody and a major part of his earnings. Bethune played in Europe and in America; his programs usually included Bach, Liszt, Chopin, Gottschalk, and his own compositions, mostly improvised character pieces in salon manner, arranged and supplied with appropriate titles by his managers, e.g., *Rainstorm* (1865); *Wellenlänge* (1882; publ. under the pseudonym **François Sexalise**); *Imitation of the Sewing Machine* (1889); *Battle of Manassas* (1894); etc. He also improvised on themes given by members of the audience.

BIBL.: J.M. Trotter, *Music and Some Highly Musical People* (Boston, 1885); G. Southall, "Blind Tom: A Misrepresented and Neglected Composer-Pianist," *Black Perspective in Music* (May 1975; the July 1976 issue of this journal reprints early testimonials by Charles Hallé, Ignaz Moscheles, and others, plus letters and articles, about Blind Tom).

Betti, Adolfo, Italian violinist; b. Bagni di Lucca, March 21, 1873; d. Lucca, Dec. 2, 1950. Of a musical family, he studied violin in Lucca; then with César Thomson in Liège (1892–96). In 1903 he became the 1st violinist of the famous Flonzaley Quartet and remained with it until it was disbanded in 1929; this group presented some 2,500 concerts in America and about 500 in Europe. In 1933 Betti was awarded the Coolidge Medal for eminent services to chamber music in America. He taught in N.Y. before returning to Italy. He publ. *La vita e l'arte di Francesco Geminiani* (Lucca, 1933); also ed. Schubert's string quartets.

Bettinelli, Bruno, Italian composer; b. Milan, June 4, 1913. He studied with Paribeni at the Milan Cons.; from 1941 to 1961 he was an instructor at his alma mater; in 1961 he became a member of the Accademia di Santa Cecilia in Rome. In his works he follows the structural forms of classical Italian music while adorning the harmonies with permissible discords; he also explored the resources of Gregorian chant.

WORKS: *Sinfonia da camera* (1939); *Concerto per orchestra* (1940); *Fantasia e Fuga su temi gregoriani* for String Orch. (1942); *Sinfonia drammatica* (1943); *Messa da requiem* for Chorus a cappella (1945); *Fantasia concertante* for String Quartet and Orch. (1950); *Concerto da camera* (1952); *Sinfonia breve* (1954); 2 piano concertos (1953, 1968); opera, *La Smorfia* (Como, Sept. 30, 1959); Concerto for 2 Pianos and Orch. (1962); opera, *Il pozzo e il pendolo* (The Pit and the Pendulum), after Poe (1958; Bergamo, Oct. 24, 1967); *Improvvisazione* for Violin and Piano (1968); opera, *Count Down* (Milan, March 26, 1970); *Variante per orchestra* (1970); 2 string quartets (1937, 1960); church music; vocal works.

Betts, Lorne, Canadian composer; b. Winnipeg, Aug. 2, 1918; d. Hamilton, Ontario, Aug. 5, 1985. He studied composition in Toronto, eventually settling in Hamilton, where he became active as a music teacher and a journalist. He wrote 2 operas, *Riders to the Sea* (1955) and *The Woodcarver's Wife* (1960); 2 syms. (1954, 1961); 2 piano concertos (1955, 1957); 3 *Saudades* for 11 Strings (1974); Concerto for Cello, Piano, and Orch. (1976); 3 string quartets (1950, 1951, 1970); Quartet for Flute, Clarinet, Bass Clarinet, and Celesta (1960); Violin Sonatina (1970); also songs.

Betz, Franz, German baritone; b. Mainz, March 19, 1835; d. Berlin, Aug. 11, 1900. He made his debut in Hannover in 1856 as the Herald in *Lohengrin;* then appeared at the Berlin Royal Opera on May 16, 1859, as Don Carlos in *Ernani;* was permanently engaged at the Berlin Royal Opera House until his retirement in 1897. He was best known for the roles of Hans Sachs at Munich and Wotan at Bayreuth.

Beurhaus, Friedrich, German music theorist; b. Immecke, near Meinerzhagen, 1536; d. Dortmund, Aug. 6, 1609. He was educated in Münster and Dortmund; received his M.A. in 1560 from the Univ. of Cologne; subsequently was cantor in several towns before taking up the post of cantor of the Reinoldi school in Dortmund in 1567; was named its rector in 1582. He publ. the important treatise *Musicae erotematum libri duo, ex optimis huius artis scriptoribus vera perspicuaque methodo descripto* (Dortmund, 1573; 2nd ed. as *Erotematum musicae libri duo,* 1580; 4th ed., 1591; facsimile ed., prepared by W. Thoene, in *Beiträge zur rheinischen Musikgeschichte,* Cologne, 1959).

BIBL.: W. Thoene, "F. B. und seine Musiktraktate," *Beiträge zur rheinischen Musikgeschichte* (Cologne, 1959).

Beurle, Jürgen, German composer; b. Ludwigsburg, Feb. 27, 1943. He studied philology and music in Stuttgart, Tübingen, and Utrecht; in 1967 he attended Stockhausen's lectures at the Darmstadt Summer School for New Music. He is a confirmed constructionist in his musical design.

WORKS: *Sinus* for Soprano, Baritone, Violin, Viola, and Percussion (1966); *Variable Realizations* for Indeterminate Performers (1967); *Statischdynamisch* for Orch. (1968); *Objets* for Chorus, Instruments, and Tape Recorder (1968); *Conditional* for Voice, Piano, and Tape Recorder (1969); *Madrigal* for Soprano, 2 Choruses, Percussion, and 5 Tape Recordings, with Audience participation (1969); *Differenz* for Indeterminate Performers grouped in 5 sections (1970).

Beversdorf, Thomas, American trombone player and composer; b. Yoakum, Texas, Aug. 8, 1924; d. Bloomington, Ind., Feb. 15, 1981. He studied trombone and baritone horn with his father, a band director; took courses in composition with Kent Kennan, Eric DeLamarter, and Anthony Donato at the Univ. of Texas (B.M., 1945) and with Bernard Rogers at the Eastman School of Music in Rochester, N.Y. (M.M., 1946); later attended a summer course in composition with Honegger and Copland at Tanglewood (1947); also had some lessons with Anis Fuleihan. He was trombone player with the Rochester Phil. (1945–46), the Houston Sym. (1946–48), and the Pittsburgh Sym. (1948–49); had special engagements as 1st trombonist with the Metropolitan Opera in N.Y., Ballets Russes de Monte Carlo, and Sadler's Wells Royal Ballet in London. He was an instructor at the Univ. of Houston (1946–48); in 1951 joined the faculty of Indiana Univ. in Bloomington as prof. of composition; in 1977 lectured at the Univ. of Guadalajara in Mexico.

WORKS: 2 operas: *The Hooligan* (1964-69) and *Metamorphosis,* after Kafka (1968); mystery play, *Vision of Christ* (Lewisburg, Pa., May 1, 1971). Orch.: *Essay on Mass Production* (1946); 4 syms.: No. 1 (1946); No. 2 (1950); No. 3 for Winds and Percussion (1954; Bloomington, May 9, 1954; version for Full Orch., 1958; Bloomington, Oct. 10, 1958); No. 4 (1958); *Mexican Portrait* (1948; rev. 1952); Concerto Grosso for Oboe and Chamber Orch. (Pittsburgh, April 28, 1950); 2-piano Concerto (1951; Bloomington, March 17, 1967); *New Frontiers* (Houston, March 31, 1953); *Danforth,* violin concerto (1959); ballet, *Threnody: The Funeral of Youth,* after Rupert Brooks (Bloomington, March 6, 1963; also known as Variations for Orch.); *Murals, Tapestries and Icons* for Symphonic Band, with Electric Bass and Electric Piano (1975); Concerto for Tuba and Wind Orch. (Bloomington, Feb. 11, 1976); horn sonata, *Christmas* (1945); 2 string quartets (1951, 1955); Sonata for Tuba and Piano (1956); Trumpet Sonata (1962); Violin Sonata (1964–65); Flute Sonata (1965–66); Cello Sonata (1967–69); *La Petite Exposition* for Solo Violin or Clarinet, and 11 Strings (Dallas, Feb. 28, 1976); Sonata for Violin and Harp (1976–77); *Corelliana Variations* for 2 Flutes and Cello (1980).

Bevignani, Enrico, Italian conductor and composer; b. Naples, Sept. 29, 1841; d. there, Aug. 29, 1903. He produced an opera, *Caterina Bloom,* in Naples in 1863; then received an appointment as theater conductor in London; also conducted at the Metropolitan Opera in N.Y. (1894); eventually returned to Naples.

Bevin, Elway, Welsh composer and organist; b. c.1554; d. Bristol (buried), Oct. 19, 1638. He may have been a pupil of Tallis; served as organist of the Bristol Cathedral in 1589 and Gentleman Extraordinary of the Chapel Royal in 1605. He publ. *A Briefe and Short Instruction in the Art of Musicke* (London, 1631); wrote songs; among them, *Hark, Jolly Shepherds* was popular; also composed an anthem, arranged in a canon of 20 voices.

Bewerunge, Henry, German cleric and music editor; b. Letmathe, Westphalia, Dec. 7, 1862; d. Maynooth, Ireland, Dec. 2, 1923. He was ordained a priest in 1885; took courses in church music in Regensburg; then settled in Ireland and taught at St. Patrick's College in Maynooth (1888–1914) and at the

Univ. of Dublin (1914–16). He publ. *Die Vatikanische Choralausgabe* (Düsseldorf, 1906; also in Eng. and French trs.). From 1891 to 1893 he ed. *Lyra ecclesiastica*.

Beyer, Frank Michael, German composer; b. Berlin, March 8, 1928. He received his earliest musical training from his father, a writer and amateur pianist; spent his childhood in Greece, returning to Berlin in 1938. He studied sacred music and organ; took composition lessons with Ernst Pepping (1952–55) at the Berlin Staatliche Hochschule für Musik; in 1960 he was appointed to the faculty of the Berlin Hochschule der Künste. He founded a concert series, "Musica Nova Sacra." As a composer, he applies the techniques of Bach's counterpoint to modern structures in the manner of Anton von Webern, with thematic materials based on secundal formations and the tritone; the rhythmic patterns of his music are greatly diversified; in dynamic coloration, he explores the finest gradations of sound, particularly in pianissimo.

WORKS: Concerto for Orch. (1957); 2 string quartets (1957, 1969); *Ode* for Orch. (1963); Flute Concerto (1964); Organ Concerto (1967); *Versi* for String Orch. (1968); *Maior Angelis*, cantata (1970); Wind Quintet (1972); *Rondo imaginaire* for Chamber Orch. (1973); *Griechenland* for 3 String Groups (1981; Berlin, June 22, 1982); *Notre-Dame-Musik* for Orch. (1983–84; Saarbrücken, Nov. 2, 1984); *Mysteriensonate* for Viola and Orch. (1986; Berlin, May 16, 1987); Concerto for Oboe and String Orch. (1986; Berlin, Oct. 7, 1987); *Geburt des Tanzes*, ballet (1987; Berlin, March 27, 1988); Sym. for 8 Players (Berlin, Feb. 6, 1989).

BIBL.: W. Burde, "Der Komponist F.M. B.," *Musica* (May/June 1975).

Beyer, Johanna Magdalena, German-American composer and musicologist; b. Leipzig, July 11, 1888; d. N.Y., Jan. 9, 1944. She studied piano and music theory in Germany. In 1924 she went to America and studied at the David Mannes School in N.Y.; received a teacher's certificate in 1928. She also took private lessons with Dane Rudhyar, Ruth Crawford, Charles Seeger, and Henry Cowell. She wrote music and several plays for various projects in N.Y. During Cowell's term in San Quentin prison (1937–41), Beyer acted as his secretary and took care of his scores. Her own compositional style is dissonant counterpoint. She composed much chamber music; among her more interesting works are 4 string quartets (1934, 1936, 1938, 1943), *Cyrnab* for Chamber Orch. (1937), *Reverence* for Wind Ensemble (1938), and *Music of the Spheres* for 3 Electrical Instruments or Strings (1938; from the unfinished opera *Status Quo*).

Bezdek, Jan, American pianist and composer; b. St. Louis, Aug. 29, 1896. She studied piano with Rudolf Ganz and composition with Felix Borowski in Chicago; subsequently she obtained her Ph.D. at the Eastman School of Music in Rochester, N.Y., in 1946. She publ. a number of successful teaching pieces for piano, among them *Bells, The Little Bird,* and *Marching.* Under the pseudonym **Julia Derleth,** she publ. easy pieces for piano.

Bezekirsky, Vasili, Russian violinist; b. Moscow, Jan. 26, 1835; d. there, Nov. 8, 1919. He studied violin in Moscow; in 1858 he went to Brussels, where he took violin lessons with Leonard and lessons in composition with Damcke. Returning to Moscow in 1860, he was concertmaster at the Bolshoi Theater (1861–91); from 1882 to 1902 he was prof. at the Moscow Phil. Inst. As a violin virtuoso, he was greatly regarded in Russia. Tchaikovsky wrote about him: "Although not a Czar of the first magnitude, Bezekirsky is brilliant enough on the dim horizon of present violin playing." Bezekirsky was also a composer; he wrote a Violin Concerto (Moscow, Feb. 26, 1873) and contributed cadenzas to the violin concertos of Beethoven and Brahms. He publ. a vol. of reminiscences, *From the Notebook of an Artist* (St. Petersburg, 1910).

Bhatkhande, Vishnu Narayan, eminent Indian musicologist; b. Bombay, Aug. 10, 1860; d. there, Sept. 19, 1936. He studied jurisprudence; concurrently investigated the systems of Indian ragas; while earning a living as a lawyer, he traveled throughout India to collect authentic ragas. In 1910 he abandoned his legal practice and dedicated himself exclusively to Indian folk music. His compilations of ragas are invaluable resources. He publ. *Hindusthāni sangit paddhati* (4 vols., Marathi, 1910–32), *Srimal-laksya sangitam* (Bombay, 1910), and *Kramik pustak mālikā* (6 vols., Marathi, 1919–37).

Bial, Rudolf, German violinist, composer, and conductor; b. Habelschwerdt, Silesia, Aug. 26, 1834; d. N.Y., Nov. 26, 1881. He was a member of the Breslau Orch.; then toured Africa and Australia with his brother Karl; settled in Berlin as conductor of the Kroll Orch. and of the Wallner Theater, where his numerous farces, operettas, etc. were performed; later conducted at the Italian opera in Berlin. In 1879 he settled in N.Y.

Bialas, Günter, German composer; b. Bielschowitz, Silesia, July 19, 1907. His father was the business manager of the local theater, and Bialas absorbed much music through personal connections with professional organizations. He pursued his formal studies at the Univ. of Breslau and at the Berlin Academy of Church and School Music. In 1940 he was appointed to teach music at the Univ. of Breslau; in 1950 he obtained a teaching post at the North-West German Academy of Music in Detmold, and in 1959 joined the faculty of the State Music School in Munich. In 1967 he received the music prize of the Bavarian Academy of Fine Arts, and in 1971 was awarded the Culture Prize of Upper Silesia. His idiom of composition is omnitonal; he uses dodecaphonic devices and folklike modalities with equal freedom; his music is pragmatic without being doctrinaire. He wrote 3 short operas: *Hero und Leander* (1966), *Die Geschichte von Aucassin und Nicolette* (1967–69), and *Der gestiefelte Kater* (1973–74); also several scores of incidental music for the theater. In his orch. works he adopts a Baroque manner à la moderne, exemplified by such works as *Kleine Konzertmusik* (1935); Viola Concerto (1940); Violin Concerto (1949); Cello Concerto (1962); *Musik* for 11 Strings (1969); *Der Weg nach Eisenstadt,* "Haydn-Fantasy" for Small Orch. (1980); *Marschfantasie* (1988). His choral music comprises both sacred and secular works; he also wrote 3 string quartets (1936, 1949, 1969); Viola Sonata (1946); Violin Sonata (1946); Flute Sonata (1946); *Moments musicaux* for Cello and Harp (1970); *Assonanzen* for 12 Cellos (1978); 9 *Bagatelles* for Wind Trio, String Trio, and Piano (1984); and 6 *Bagatelles* for Saxophone Quartet (1985–86).

Bianchi, Bianca (real name, **Bertha Schwarz**), German soprano; b. near Heidelberg, June 27, 1855; d. Salzburg, Feb. 1947. She studied in Heidelberg and Paris; made her debut as Barberina in *The Marriage of Figaro* at Karlsruhe (1873); sang in Vienna and London; in 1905 settled in Salzburg as a vocal teacher. She married her manager, Pollini, in 1897.

Bianchi, Francesco, Italian composer; b. Cremona, c.1752; d. (suicide) London, Nov. 27, 1810. He studied in Naples with Jommelli and Cafaro. He wrote nearly 80 operas, some quite pleasing, but ephemeral. His 1st opera *Giulio Sabino* (Cremona, 1772); it was followed by *Il Grand Cidde* (Florence, 1773). From 1775 to 1778 he was in Paris serving as maestro al cembalo at the Comédie-Italienne; there he produced his opera *La Réduction de Paris* (Sept. 30, 1775). In 1778 he went to Florence; in 1783 he became 2nd maestro at the Cathedral of Milan, a post he held until 1793; concurrently he worked in Venice from 1785 to 1791, and again from 1793 to 1797, when he served as 2nd organist at S. Marco. He subsequently was in Naples, where he produced his most significant opera, *La Vendetta de Nino* (Nov. 12, 1790). In 1794 he went to London, where he officiated as conductor at the King's Theatre (1795–1801); several of his operas were produced there under his supervision. Apart from his operas, he wrote instrumental music, and publ. a theoretical treatise, *Dell'attrazione armonica,* which was publ. in excerpts, in Eng., in the *Quarterly Musical Magazine and Review* (1820–21). Bianchi was also a successful teacher; among his English pupils was Henry Bishop.

Bianchi, Valentina, Russian soprano; b. Vilnius, 1839; d. Kurland, March 11, 1884. She studied at the Paris Cons.; made her debut as a soprano in Frankfurt (1855); sang at Schwerin (1855–61), St. Petersburg (1862–65), and Moscow (until 1867); retired in 1870. She married chief forester von Fabian in 1865. Her range was extraordinary, extending from low alto through high soprano notes.

Bianchini, Domenico, Italian lutenist and composer; b. c.1510; d. Venice, c.1576. He worked as a mosaicist at S. Marco in Venice (1540–76); as a composer, he publ. *Intabolatura de lauto . . . di recercari, motetti, madrigali, napolitane et balli, libro primo* (Venice, 1546).
BIBL.: R. de Morcourt, "Le Livre de tablature de luth de D. B. (1546)," *La Musique instrumentale de la Renaissance: CNRS Paris 1954.*

Bianco, Pietro Antonio, Italian singer and composer; b. Venice, c.1540; d. Graz (buried), Feb. 2, 1611. He was a canon at S. Salvatore in Venice; became a tenor at the Hofkapelle in Graz in 1578; was named Hofkapellmeister there in 1595. He composed both secular and religious vocal music.
BIBL.: H. Federhofer, "P. A. B. und seine Vorgänger A. Zweiller und P. Ragno an der Grazer Hofkapelle," *Kirchenmusikalisches Jahrbuch,* XXXVIII (1954).

Bibalo (Bibalitsch), Antonio (Gino), Italian-born Norwegian composer; b. Trieste, Jan. 18, 1922, of Slovak descent. He studied piano and composition at the Trieste Cons.; during the disruption caused by World War II, he earned his living as a nightclub pianist and a sanitation worker. He was in Australia briefly before going to England in 1953; studied advanced composition with Elisabeth Lutyens in London. In 1956 he went to Norway; became a naturalized citizen in 1968. He attracted the attention of the musical world with the production of his opera *The Smile at the Foot of the Ladder* (1958–62), after a short story by Henry Miller; the original libretto was in Italian as *Sorrisi ai piedi d'una scala,* but the production was in German under the name *Das Lächeln am Fusse der Leiter* at the Hamburg State Opera on April 6, 1965. His other works include a chamber opera, *Frøken Julie* (Miss Julie), after Strindberg (Århus, Denmark, Sept. 8, 1975); a ballet, *Pinocchio* (Hamburg, Jan. 17, 1969); a television ballet, *Nocturne for Apollo* (Norwegian Television, 1971); 2 piano concertos: No. 1 (1953; Oslo, Aug. 1, 1972); No. 2 (1971; Bergen, Norway, April 27, 1972); Piano Sonatina (1953); 2 chamber concertos: No. 1 for Piano and Strings (1954); No. 2 for Harpsichord, Violin, and Strings (1974); Fantasy for Violin and Orch. (1954; received 3rd prize at the Wieniawski Composer Competition, Warsaw, 1956); 4 *Balkan Dances* for Piano or Orch. (1956); 12 *Miniatures* for Piano (1956); *Concerto Allegorico* for Violin and Orch. (1957); 3 *Hommages* for Piano (1957); Toccata for Piano (1957); *Pitture Astratte* for Orch. (1958); *Elegia per un'era spaziale* (Elegy for a Space Age) for Soprano, Baritone, Chorus, and Instrumental Ensemble (1963); *Sinfonia notturna* (1968); *Overture,* after Goldoni's "Servant with 2 Masters" (1968); *Autumnale,* suite de concert for Piano, Flute, Vibraphone, and Double Bass (1968); 2 sonatinas for Wind Quintet (1971, 1972); String Quartet No. 1 (1973); 2 piano sonatas (1974, 1975); Suite for Orch. (1974); *Games* for Trombone and Flute (1975); *Gespenster,* opera, after Ibsen (1981); *Study in Blue* for Guitar (1983); *Racconto d'una Stagione Alta,* study for Cello and Piano (1985); *Musica* for Oboe, Strings, Percussion, and Harp (1986).

Biber, Heinrich (Ignaz Franz von), famous Bohemian violinist and composer; b. Wartenberg, Bohemia, Aug. 12, 1644; d. Salzburg, May 3, 1704. He was in the service of the Emperor Leopold I, who ennobled him on Dec. 5, 1690; he also served at other courts. In 1670 he was a member of the Kapelle at Salzburg; in 1679 he was appointed Vice-Kapellmeister there, and in 1684 became Kapellmeister. He was one of the founders of the German school of violin playing and was among the 1st to employ the "scordatura," a system of artificial mistuning to facilitate performance. He publ. a number of violin sonatas,

several of which were reprinted in David's *Hohe Schule* and in Denkmäler der Tonkunst in Österreich; composed 2 operas, *Chi la dura la vince* (Salzburg, 1687) and *L'ossequio de Salisburgo* (Salzburg, 1699), as well as several scores of sacred music, including a Requiem and numerous choruses. His only extant stage work is the opera *Chi la dura la vince.*
BIBL.: T. Russell, "The Violin 'Scordatura,' " *Musical Quarterly* (Jan. 1938); E. Schenk, "Ein *Singfundament* von H.I. B.," in H. Becker and R. Gerlach, *Speculum musicae artis. Festgabe für Heinrich Husman* (Munich, 1970); S. Dahms, "Neues zur Chronologie der Opern von B. und Moffat," *Österreichische Musikzeitschrift,* XXIX (1974).

Bibl, Andreas, Austrian organist, father of **Rudolf Bibl;** b. Vienna, April 8, 1807; d. there, April 30, 1878. He served for many years as organist at St. Stephen Cathedral in Vienna; was active as a teacher; among his pupils was his son.

Bibl, Rudolf, Austrian organist and composer; b. Vienna, Jan. 6, 1832; d. there, Aug. 2, 1902. He studied with his father, **Andreas Bibl;** occupied various posts as church organist in Vienna. He wrote 4 masses with orch. accompaniment; a Mass a cappella; 2 Requiems; much organ music; also a Violin Sonata and piano pieces. He publ. a valuable didactic vol., *Orgelschule.*

Bible, Frances, American mezzo-soprano; b. Sackets Harbor, N.Y., Jan. 26, 1927. She studied with Belle Julie Soudant and Queena Mario at the Juilliard School of Music in N.Y. (1939–47); made her debut as the Shepherd in *Tosca* at the N.Y. City Opera on Oct. 7, 1948, subsequently attaining a prominent place on its roster, singing principal roles there regularly until 1977. She was later a teacher (1979–82) and artist-in-residence (1982–83) at Rice Univ. in Houston. She was best known for her trouser roles.

Bie, Oskar, German music critic; b. Breslau, Feb. 9, 1864; d. Berlin, April 21, 1938. He studied music with Philipp Scharwenka in Berlin; devoted himself principally to musical journalism, and publ. a number of informative monographs. In the spring of 1914 he accompanied Koussevitzky on his concert tour of the Volga and reported his impressions in a privately publ. illustrated ed. in 1920. Among his publications are *Das Klavier und seine Meister* (Munich, 1898; in Eng. as *A History of the Pianoforte and Pianoforte Players,* London, 1899); *Intime Musik* (Berlin, 1904); *Tanzmusik* (Berlin, 1905); *Der Tanz* (Berlin, 1906, 1919, 1925); *Die moderne Musik und Richard Strauss* (Berlin, 1906; Leipzig, 1916, 1925); *Die Oper* (Berlin, 1913; many reprints); *Das Rätsel der Musik* (Leipzig, 1922); *Franz Schubert* (Berlin, 1925; in Eng. as *Schubert the Man,* N.Y., 1929); *Das Deutsche Lied* (Berlin, 1926); *Richard Wagner und Bayreuth* (Zürich, 1931).

Bielawa, Herbert, American composer; b. Chicago, Feb. 3, 1930, of Polish (paternal) and German (maternal) descent. He studied music at home; from 1954 to 1956 served in the U.S. Army in Germany, stationed in Frankfurt, where he also studied conducting with Bruno Vondenhoff. Returning to the U.S., he took courses in piano with Soulima Stravinsky at the Univ. of Illinois (B.M., 1954); enrolled at the Univ. of Southern Calif. in Los Angeles, and took courses in composition with Ingolf Dahl (1960–61), Halsey Stevens (1961–64), and Ellis Kohs (1961–63); also studied music for cinema with Miklós Rosza and David Raksin. In 1966 he was appointed to the faculty of San Francisco State Univ.; in 1967 established there the Electronic Music Studio. In his music he makes use of the entire field of practical resources, without prejudice.
WORKS: *Concert Piece* for Orch. (1953); *Essay* for String Orch. (1958); *A Bird in the Bush,* chamber opera (1962); *Abstractions* for String Orch. (1965); 4 *Legends* for Violins and Cellos (1967); *Divergents* for Orch. (1969); *A Dickinson Album* for Choir, Tape, Piano, and Guitar (1972); Quartet for Guitars (1978); electronic scores: *Additions* (1968); *Discoveries* (1972); *Laps, Caps* and *Overlaps* (1974); *Matrices* (1979); numerous organ pieces and choruses.

Bierdiajew, Walerian, Polish conductor; b. Grodno, March 7, 1885; d. Warsaw, Nov. 28, 1956. He studied composition with Max Reger and conducting with Arthur Nikisch at the Leipzig Cons.; began his conducting career in Dresden in 1906; in 1908 became regular conductor at the Maryinsky Opera Theater in St. Petersburg; then conducted in various Russian opera houses; from 1921 to 1925 he lived in Poland; from 1925 to 1930 was again engaged as a conductor in Russia and in the Ukraine. In 1930 he was appointed prof. of conducting at the Warsaw Cons.; from 1947 to 1949 was conductor of the Krakow Phil.; then taught at the Poznan Cons. (1949–54) and at the Warsaw Cons. (1954–56).

Bierey, Gottlob Benedikt, German conductor and composer; b. Dresden, July 25, 1772; d. Breslau, May 5, 1840. He was a pupil of Christian E. Weinlig at Dresden; then was director of a traveling opera troupe. He was appointed Kapellmeister at Breslau in 1808, succeeding Weber; retired in 1828. He composed 26 operas and operettas, 10 cantatas, masses, orch. and chamber music, etc.

Bigard, "Barney" (Alban Leon), black American jazz clarinetist; b. New Orleans, March 3, 1906; d. Culver City, Calif., June 27, 1980. He played in various local bands in New Orleans; in 1924 he went to Chicago, where he worked with King Oliver. In 1927 he joined Duke Ellington's band, with which he played until 1942. He later formed small bands of his own, working mostly in Los Angeles and N.Y.; he also played with Louis Armstrong's All Stars. He gradually acquired a reputation as one of the most ingenious jazz clarinet players; he also composed songs. As a sidekick for Duke Ellington, he co-authored *Mood Indigo,* which became one of the most famous meditation tunes in American popular music. His career is highlighted in his book *With Louis and the Duke: The Autobiography of a Jazz Clarinetist* (ed. by B. Martyn; N.Y. and London, 1985).

Biggs, E(dward George) Power, eminent English-born American concert organist; b. Westcliff, March 29, 1906; d. Boston, March 10, 1977. He studied at Hurstpierpoint College (1917–24); then entered the Royal Academy of Music in London, graduating in 1929. In 1930 he went to the U.S. and became a naturalized citizen in 1937. He made his N.Y. debut as an organist at the Wanamaker Auditorium in 1932. He was an organist in Newport, R.I. (1930–31); then moved to Cambridge, Mass., where he served as organist at Christ Church, and later became music director of the Harvard Church in Brookline. He toured Europe, and made a wide survey of old church organs in England, Iceland, Sweden, Norway, Denmark, Germany, the Netherlands, Austria, Italy, and Spain in search of the type of organ that Bach and Handel played. His repertoire consisted mostly of the Baroque masters, but he also commissioned works from American composers, among them Walter Piston, Roy Harris, Howard Hanson, and Quincy Porter; Benjamin Britten also wrote a work for him. Biggs became well known to American music lovers through his weekly broadcasts of organ recitals over the CBS network, which he gave from 1942 to 1958; he continued to give concerts until arthritis forced him to reduce his concert activities, but he was able to continue recording organ music, and he also ed. organ works for publication. Biggs refused to perform on electronic organs, which in his opinion vulgarized and distorted the classical organ sound. His own style of performance had a classical austerity inspired by the Baroque school of organ playing. **BIBL.:** B. Owen, *E.P. B.: Concert Organist* (Bloomington, Ind., 1987).

Bignami, Carlo, Italian violinist and composer; b. Cremona, Dec. 6, 1808; d. Voghera, Oct. 2, 1848. He studied violin with his father and elder brother. He played in theater orchs. in Cremona and Milan; in 1829 he was appointed director of the Teatro Sociale in Mantua; then was in Milan and Verona. Returning to Cremona in 1837 as director and 1st violinist of the orch., he made it one of the best in Lombardy. Paganini called him *"il primo violinista d'Italia,"* but he may have meant this phrase to express his low opinion of other Italian violinists

in comparison. Bignami wrote a number of violin pieces, including a Concerto, a *Capriccio, Studi per violino, Grande Adagio, Polacca,* fantasias, variations, etc.

Bigot, Eugène, French conductor; b. Rennes, Feb. 28, 1888; d. Paris, July 17, 1965. He studied violin and piano at the Rennes Cons., and later at the Paris Cons. In 1913 he was named chorus master at the Théâtre des Champs-Élysées; subsequently toured Europe with the Ballets Suédois; also conducted the Paris Cons. Orch. (1923–25); then served as music director at the Théâtre des Champs-Élysées (1925–27). In 1935 he became president and director of the Concerts Lamoureux, a post he held until 1950; also held the post of principal conductor of the Opéra-Comique (1936–47). In 1947 he became chief conductor of the Radio Orch. in Paris, a post he held until his death.

Bigot (de Morogues), Marie (née **Kiéné**), pianist; b. Colmar, Alsace, March 3, 1786; d. Paris, Sept. 16, 1820. After her marriage in 1804, she lived in Vienna, where she was known and esteemed by Haydn and Beethoven; in 1808 went to Paris, where she gave piano lessons from 1812 on; Mendelssohn was briefly her pupil in Paris at the age of 7.

Bijvanck, Henk, Dutch composer; b. Kudus, Java, Nov. 6, 1909; d. Heemstede, near Haarlem, Sept. 5, 1969. He studied composition with Franz Schmidt and piano with Andrassy in Vienna; was active as a pianist there; then taught piano at the Amsterdam Music Lyceum (1945–47). His works include: Piano Concerto (1943); *Liberation Symphony* (1944); *Lourdes Symphony* (1952); Sym. No. 2; chamber music; vocal works.

Bikel, Theodore, Austrian-born American singer and actor; b. Vienna, May 2, 1924. After the Anschluss in 1938, he fled with his family to Palestine; then made his way to London, where he studied at the Royal Academy of Dramatic Arts. He subsequently had a fine career as an actor on stage, screen, and television; concurrently established himself as a folksinger; in 1959 he scored a major Broadway success in the role of Georg von Trapp in the Rogers and Hammerstein musical *The Sound of Music.* He became an American citizen in 1961.

Bildstein, Hieronymus, important Austrian organist and composer; b. Bregenz, c.1580; d. c.1626. After studying music in Bregenz, he went to Konstanz, where he was active as court organist. He wrote 25 motets publ. as *Orpheus christianus seu Symphoniarum sacrarum prodromus, 5–8 vocum cum basso generali* (Regensburg, 1624); publ. in a modern ed. in Denkmäler der Tonkunst in Österreich, CXXII (1971) and CXXVI (1976). **BIBL.:** W. Pass, "H. B. und der Konstanzer Fürstbischof Jakob Fugger," *Ausstellungskatalog "Musik im Bodenseeraum um 1600"* (Bregenz, 1974).

Bilhon (Billhon, Billon), Jhan (Jean, Jan, Jehan, Joannes) de (du), French or Flemish composer who flourished from 1534 to 1556. His extant works include a Mass, a Magnificat, and other sacred works (publ. 1534–56).

Billings, William, pioneer American composer of hymns and anthems and popularizer of "fuging tunes"; b. Boston, Oct. 7, 1746; d. there, Sept. 26, 1800. A tanner's apprentice, he acquired the rudiments of music from treatises by Tans'ur; he compensated for his lack of education by a wealth of original ideas and a determination to put them into practice. His 1st musical collection, *The New England Psalm Singer* (Boston, 1770), contained what he described at a later date as "fuging pieces . . . more than twenty times as powerful as the old slow tunes." The technique of these pieces was canonic, with "each part striving for mastery and victory." His other publ. books were *The Singing Master's Assistant* (1778); *Music in Miniature* (1779); *The Psalm Singer's Amusement* (1781); *The Suffolk Harmony* (1786); and *The Continental Harmony* (1794). In one instance, he harmonized a tune, *Jargon,* entirely in dissonances; this was prefaced by a "Manifesto" to the Goddess of Discord. There was further a choral work, *Modern Music,* in which the proclaimed aim was expressed in the opening lines: "We are met for a concert of modern invention—To tickle the ear is our present intention." Several of his hymns became popular, particularly *Chester* and *The Rose of Sharon;* an interesting historical work was his *Lamentation over Boston,* written in Watertown while Boston was occupied by the British. However, he could not earn a living by his music; appeals made to provide him and his large family with funds bore little fruit, and Billings died in abject poverty. The combination of reverence and solemnity with humor makes the songs of Billings unique in the annals of American music, and aroused the curiosity of many modern American musicians; Henry Cowell wrote a series of "fuging tunes" for Orch. K. Kroeger and H. Nathan ed. *The Complete Works of William Billings* (4 vols., Charlottesville, Va., 1977–90).

BIBL.: O.G. Sonneck, *Early Concert Life in America* (Leipzig, 1907; reprinted 1949); E.H. Pierce, "The Rise and Fall of the Fugue Tune in America," *Musical Quarterly* (April 1930); P. Scholes, *The Puritans and Music in England and New England* (Oxford, 1934); C.E. Lindstrom, "W. B. and His Times," *Musical Quarterly* (Oct. 1939); J. Barbour, *The Church Music of W. B.* (East Lansing, 1960); D. McKay and R. Crawford, *W. B. of Boston* (Princeton, 1975); H. Nathan, *W. B., Data and Documents* (Detroit, 1976); K. Kroeger, "Word Painting in the Music of W. B.," *American Music* (Spring 1988).

Billington, Elizabeth (née **Weichsel**), famous English soprano; b. London, Dec. 27, 1765; d. near Venice, Aug. 25, 1818. Her mother, a singer, was a pupil of Johann Christian Bach; Elizabeth, too, had some lessons with him. She received her early musical training from her father, a German oboist. She also studied with James Billington, a double-bass player by profession, whom she married on Oct. 13, 1783. Her operatic debut took place in Dublin (1784), as Eurydice in Gluck's opera; she went to London, where she appeared as Rosetta in *Love in a Village* at Covent Garden on Feb. 13, 1786. Her success was immediate; she was reengaged at Covent Garden and also sang at the Concerts of Antient Music in London. Her career was briefly disrupted by the publication, in 1792, of anonymous *Memoirs* attacking her private life. This was immediately followed by an equally anonymous rebuttal, "written by a gentleman," defending her reputation. In 1794 she went to Italy, where she sang for the King of Naples. He made arrangements for her appearances at the San Carlo, where she performed in operas by Bianchi, Paisiello, Paer, and Himmel, all written specially for her. Her husband died in 1794; she remained in Italy for 2 more years; then lived in France, where she married M. Felissent. Returning to London in 1801, she sang alternately at Drury Lane and Covent Garden, with great acclaim, at 4,000 guineas a season. This period was the peak of her success. She retired in 1809, except for occasional performances. After a temporary separation from Felissent, she returned to him in 1817; they settled at their estate at St. Artien, near Venice.

Billroth, Theodor, eminent German surgeon and amateur musician; b. Bergen, on the island of Rügen, April 26, 1829; d. Abazzia, Feb. 6, 1894. He received a thorough musical education; was an intimate friend of Hanslick and Brahms; the musical soirees at his home in Vienna were famous. Almost all the chamber music of Brahms was played there (with Billroth as violist) before a public performance. He wrote the treatise *Wer ist musikalisch?* (1896, ed. by Hanslick). Billroth originated 2 crucial intestinal surgical operations, known in medical literature as Billroth I and Billroth II.

BIBL.: I. Fischer, *T. B. und seine Zeitgenossen* (1929); A. Frankel, *T. B.* (1931); O-G. Gottlieb, *B. und Brahms im Briefwechsel* (1935).

Bilse, Benjamin, German conductor; b. Liegnitz, Aug. 17, 1816; d. there, July 13, 1902. He was "Stadtmusikus" at Liegnitz (1843), and brought his orch. to a remarkable degree of perfection; then lived in Berlin (1868–84) and conducted at the Concerthaus; retired in 1894 with the title "Hofmusikus." He composed salon music.

Bilson, Malcolm, noted American pianist, fortepianist, and teacher; b. Los Angeles, Oct. 24, 1935. He studied at Bard College (B.A., 1957), the Vienna Academy of Music (1959), the Paris École Normale de Musique (1960), and the Univ. of Illinois (D.M.A., 1968); then championed the cause of performing works of the Classical era on original instruments or modern replicas. He toured widely in the U.S. and Europe, and was a founder of the Amadé Trio (1974). He joined the faculty at Cornell Univ. in 1968. He is particularly esteemed for insightful readings of the works of Haydn, Mozart, and Beethoven.

Bilt, Peter van der, Dutch bass-baritone; b. Jakarta, Aug. 30, 1936; d. Amsterdam, Sept. 25, 1983. He went to Amsterdam to study voice and made his operatic debut there in 1960; in 1963 he sang the part of Don Basilio in *Il Barbiere di Siviglia* at the San Francisco Opera, then returned to Europe. He made a successful career in both opera and concert performance.

Bimboni, Alberto, Italian-American pianist and composer; b. Florence, Aug. 24, 1882; d. N.Y., June 18, 1960. He studied in Florence; went to the U.S. in 1912 as an opera conductor. In 1930 he was appointed to the faculty of the Curtis Inst. in Philadelphia; taught opera classes at the Juilliard School of Music in N.Y. from 1933; appeared as a pianist in concerts with Ysaÿe, John McCormack, and other celebrated artists. He wrote the operas *Winona* (Portland, Oreg., Nov. 11, 1926), *Karin* (Minneapolis, 1928), *Il cancelleto d'oro* (N.Y., March 11, 1936), and *In the Name of Culture* (Rochester, N.Y., May 9, 1949); numerous songs (many of them publ.).

Binchois (Binch, Binche), Gilles (de), important Franco-Flemish composer; b. probably in Mons, Hainaut, c.1400; d. Soignies, near Mons, Sept. 20, 1460. His father was most likely Jean de Binch, counselor to 2 rulers of Hainaut. Binchois may have been in the service of William de la Pole, the Earl of Suffolk, in Paris in 1424; by the close of that decade he was in the service of the Burgundian court, where he advanced from 5th to 2nd chaplain, retaining the latter position until his death. He greatly distinguished himself as a composer of both sacred and secular works, many of which have been publ. since the 19th century; the most important modern eds. are those by W. Rehm in *Die Chansons von G. B. (1400–1460)* (Mainz, 1957) and A. Parris in *The Sacred Works of G. B.* (diss., Bryn Mawr College, 1965).

BIBL.: W. Rehm, *Das Chansonwerk von G. B.* (diss., Univ. of Freiburg, 1952); J. Kreps, *G. d. B., 1460–1960* (Louvain, 1960); J. Boucher, *The Religious Music of G. B.* (diss., Boston Univ., 1963); M. Schuler, "Neues zur Biographie von G. B.," *Archiv für Musikwissenschaft,* XXXIII (1976).

Binder, Abraham Wolfe, American composer and conductor; b. N.Y., Jan. 13, 1895; d. there, Oct. 10, 1966. He studied at Columbia Univ.; subsequently taught liturgical music at the Jewish Inst. of Religion, N.Y. He composed an opera, *A Goat in Chelm* (N.Y., March 20, 1960); a choral ballet, *Hora Vehodayah* (Praise and Dance); *The Legend of Ari* for Small Orch. (1963); and other symphonic works on Jewish themes.

Binder, Christlieb Siegmund, German organist and composer; b. Dresden (baptized), July 29, 1723; d. there, Jan. 1, 1789. He was organist at the court church in Dresden from 1753; wrote prolifically, in an "elegant style" akin to that of C.P.E. Bach.

WORKS: Sonatas for harpsichord solo, and for harpsichord in various combinations with violin and cello; 76 organ preludes; harpsichord concertos; quartets with harpsichord; and trio sonatas for 2 violins with basso continuo. Some of his compositions have been reprinted by O. Schmid in *Musik am sächsischen Hofe,* IV and VI (Leipzig, 1903–4).

BIBL.: H. Fleischer, *C.S. B.* (Regensburg, 1941).

Binder, Karl, Austrian composer; b. Vienna, Nov. 29, 1816; d. there, Nov. 5, 1860. He was a theater conductor by profession; composed mostly for the stage: a melodrama, *Der Wiener Schusterhut* (1840); an opera, *Die Drei Wittfrauen* (1841); a vaudeville comedy, *Purzel* (1843); overture and choruses to the drama *Elmar;* a parody on *Tannhäuser* (1857).

Binenbaum, Janco, Bulgarian-French composer; b. Adrianopol, Dec. 28, 1880; d. Chevreuse, Seine-et-Oise, France, Feb. 4, 1956. He studied in Munich with Rheinberger and others; was active as a piano teacher in Germany and France, eventually settling in Chevreuse, where he remained until his death. He wrote a considerable amount of symphonic and chamber music in an impressionistic vein, colored with Balkan rhythms, none of which was publ., and little ever performed. Nonetheless, Binenbaum found sincere admirers of his works, among whom M.D. Calvocoressi was the most vocal.

Binet, Jean, Swiss composer; b. Geneva, Oct. 17, 1893; d. Trélex, Feb. 24, 1960. He studied academic subjects at the Univ. of Geneva, and simultaneously obtained a diploma from the Inst. Jaques-Dalcroze; then took lessons in musicology and composition with Otto Barblan, William Montillet, and Templeton Strong. In 1919 he went to America, where he organized the 1st school of Dalcroze eurhythmics, and also took lessons with Ernest Bloch. In 1921 he was instrumental in founding, with Bloch, the Cleveland Cons. In 1923 he returned to Europe, and lived in Brussels, where he taught the Dalcroze method. In 1929 he went back to Switzerland, and settled in Trélex. Many of his works are based on Swiss national folk songs. Binet's musical idiom is determined by pragmatic considerations of performance and does not transcend the natural borders of traditional harmonies.

WORKS: Primarily interested in the musical theater, he wrote 6 operettas and radiophonic cantatas; ballets; *L'Île enchantée* (Zürich, 1947); *Le Printemps* (1950); *La Colline* for 5 Narrators and Orch. (1957); also several scores of incidental music for plays of Sophocles, Shakespeare, and contemporary writers. Other works include a number of sacred and secular choruses; songs with orch. accompaniment; String Quartet (1927); *Divertissement* for Violin and Orch. (1934); Sonatina for Flute and Piano (1942); *6 pièces* for Flute Solo (1947); *Petit concert* for Clarinet and String Orch. (1950); *Variations sur un chant de Noël* for Bassoon and Piano (1957); *3 Dialogues* for 2 Flutes (1957); educational pieces for piano; also harmonizations of popular melodies for chorus.

Bing, Sir Rudolf (Franz Joseph), Austrian-born English operatic impresario; b. Vienna, Jan. 9, 1902. He studied at the Univ. of Vienna; took singing lessons; then entered the managerial field in opera. After filling various positions with German agencies, he went to England in 1934; became a British subject in 1946. He was one of the most active organizers of the Edinburgh Festivals, and was their music director from 1947 to 1950. In 1950 he was appointed general manager of the Metropolitan Opera in N.Y., inaugurating one of the most eventful and, at times, turbulent periods in the history of the Metropolitan; his controversial dealings with prima donnas were legendary. He resigned in 1972; publ. an entertaining summary of his managerial experiences in a vol. entitled *5,000 Nights at the Opera* (N.Y., 1972) and in his memoir, *A Knight at the Opera* (N.Y., 1981). In 1971 Queen Elizabeth II of England conferred on him the title of Knight Commander of the Order of the British Empire.

Bingham, Seth (Daniels), American organist and composer; b. Bloomfield, N.J., April 16, 1882; d. N.Y., June 21, 1972. He studied with Horatio Parker; later in Paris with d'Indy, Widor (composition), and Guilmant (organ). Returning to America, he graduated from Yale Univ. (B.A., 1904); took his M.B. at Yale in 1908, and taught there until 1919; was an instructor and associate prof. at Columbia Univ. until 1954. His music is contrapuntal, occasionally chromatic, and, in later works, highly modal.

WORKS: *Wall Street Fantasy* (1912; perf. as *Symphonic Fantasy* by the N.Y. Phil., Feb. 6, 1916); *La Charelzenn,* opera (1917); *Tame Animal Tunes* for 18 Instruments (1918); *Memories of France,* orch. suite (1920); *Wilderness Stone* for Narrator, Soli, Chorus, and Orch. (1933); Concerto for Organ and Orch. (Rochester, Oct. 24, 1946); *Connecticut Suite* for Organ and

Strings (Hartford, March 26, 1954); Concerto for Brass, Snare Drum, and Organ (Minneapolis, July 12, 1954). Among his compositions for organ, the following have been frequently performed: *Suite* (1926); *Pioneer America* (1928); *Harmonies of Florence* (1929); *Carillon de Château-Thierry* (1936); *Pastoral Psalms* (1938); *12 Hymn-Preludes* (1942); *Variation Studies* (1950); *36 Hymn and Carol Canons* (1952).

Binički, Stanislav, Yugoslav composer and conductor; b. Jasika, near Kruševca, July 27, 1872; d. Belgrade, Feb. 15, 1942. He studied at the Univ. of Belgrade; later took courses in composition with Rheinberger in Munich. Returning to Belgrade, he helped organize the Serbian School of Music; was also active as an opera conductor. He composed a number of incidental pieces for the theater; also the opera *Na uranku* (Dawn; Belgrade, Jan. 2, 1904), as well as choruses and songs.

Binkerd, Gordon (Ware), American composer and teacher; b. Lynch, Nebr., May 22, 1916. He studied piano in South Dakota; composition with Bernard Rogers at the Eastman School of Music in Rochester, N.Y., and with Walter Piston at Harvard Univ.; from 1949 to 1971, was a member of the faculty of the Univ. of Illinois; received a Guggenheim fellowship in 1959.

WORKS: 4 syms.: No. 1 (Urbana, March 20, 1955); No. 2 (Urbana, April 13, 1957); No. 3 (N.Y., Jan. 6, 1961); No. 4 (St. Louis, Oct. 12, 1963; dismembered and reduced to a *Movement for Orchestra*); *A Part of Heaven,* 2 romances for Violin and Orch. (1972); 2 string quartets (1956, 1961); Trio for Clarinet, Viola, and Cello (1955); Cello Sonata (1952); Violin Sonata (1977); String Trio (1979); 4 piano sonatas (1955, 1981, 1982, 1983); various choral works; songs.

Binkley, Thomas (Eden), American lutenist, wind player, and music scholar; b. Cleveland, Dec. 26, 1931. He studied at the Univ. of Illinois (B.M., 1956), then pursued postgraduate studies at the Univ. of Munich (1957–58) and the Univ. of Illinois (1958–59). His principal mentors were Dragan Plamenac, Claude Palisca, John Ward, Thrasybulos Georgiades, and George Hunter. From 1960 to 1980 he was director of the Studio der frühen Musik in Munich; also taught and performed in the medieval program at the Schola Cantorum Basiliensis in Basel (1973–77). In 1979 he became prof. of music and director of the Early Music Inst. at the Indiana Univ. School of Music in Bloomington. As a performing musician, he made appearances in major music centers in America and Europe.

Binns, Malcolm, English pianist; b. Gedling, Nottingham, Jan. 29, 1936. He studied at the Royal College of Music in London. He made his debut in London in 1957; subsequently appeared with the leading English orchs. and gave recitals. He taught piano at the Royal College of Music from 1962 to 1969.

Biordi, Giovanni, Italian composer; b. Rome, 1691; d. there, March 11, 1748. He was maestro di cappella at Tivoli Cathedral (1714–16); in 1717 he became a chapel singer to the Pope. He was named maestro di cappella at the church of S. Giacomo degli Spagnuoli in Rome in 1722, and remained in this post until his death. He also was a voice teacher at the Papal College from 1724; was named secretary (1730) and then chamberlain (1737) of the Sistine Chapel. He composed many sacred works.

Birchall, Robert, English music publisher; b. London, 1760; d. there, Dec. 19, 1819. He was the 1st to publ. Beethoven's works in England; letters from Beethoven to Birchall are found in Nohl's collection. The firm, which later became Birchall, Lonsdale & Mills, had one of the 1st circulating music libraries ever established.

Birchard, Clarence C., American music publisher; b. Cambridge Springs, Pa., July 13, 1866; d. Carlisle, Mass., Feb. 27, 1946. He established his firm in Boston in 1901 and specialized in educational books for public schools; of these, a 10-book series, *A Singing School,* introduced lavish profusion of color in design and illustration; the firm also issued community songbooks, of which the most popular was *Twice 55 Community*

Songs (several million copies sold). The catalogue included scores by many American composers.

Bird, Arthur, American composer; b. Belmont, Mass., July 23, 1856; d. Berlin, Dec. 22, 1923. He studied in Berlin with Löschhorn; spent several months with Liszt at Weimar in 1885; returned to America briefly in 1886, and then lived in Berlin, identifying himself with conservative circles there. He was the Berlin correspondent for American music magazines; in his articles he violently attacked Richard Strauss and other modern composers. Among his own works is a Sym.; 2 *Decimettes* for Wind Instruments (won a Paderewski prize in 1901); a comic opera, *Daphne* (N.Y., Dec. 13, 1897); and many piano pieces.

BIBL.: W.L. Loring, "A. B., American Composer," *Musical Quarterly* (Jan. 1943).

Biriotti, León, Uruguayan conductor and composer; b. Montevideo, Dec. 1, 1929. He studied oboe, theory, and musicology; began to conduct experimentally without preliminary training; founded a string orch. in Montevideo; conducted the instrumental group Juventudes Musicales of Uruguay.

WORKS: 3 syms. (1964, 1965, 1968); *Suite* for Violin and Cello (1952); String Sextet (1957); Trio for Oboe, Clarinet, and Bassoon (1963); String Quartet (1965); Violin Sonata (1967); songs and piano pieces.

Biriukov, Yuri, Russian composer; b. Moscow, April 1, 1908; d. there, Nov. 1, 1976. He studied piano with Feinberg and composition with Miaskovsky at the Moscow Cons., graduating in 1936. Among his works are 2 operas, *Peasant Gentlewoman* (after Pushkin; 1947) and *Knight of the Golden Star* (1956); a ballet, *The Cosmonauts* (1962); a musical, *The Blue Express* (1971); a Sym. on Ingush themes (1968); 3 piano concertos (1941, 1945, 1970); 24 preludes and 4 toccatas for Piano; much music for the theater and the cinema.

Birkenstock, Johann Adam, German violinist and composer; b. Alsfeld, Feb. 19, 1687; d. Eisenach, Feb. 26, 1733. He studied in Kassel with Ruggiero Fedeli; then in Berlin with Volumier and in Bayreuth with Fiorelli; was employed in the Kassel Court Orch. (1709–30); in 1730 went to Eisenach, where he served as Kapellmeister. His sonatas for violin with basso continuo (Amsterdam, 1722) are included in several anthologies.

Birnbach, Heinrich, German pianist, music pedagogue, and composer, son of **Karl Joseph Birnbach**; b. Breslau, Jan. 8, 1793; d. Berlin, Aug. 24, 1879. He studied piano with his father; taught in Breslau from 1814 to 1821; settled in Berlin as a music teacher and founded a music inst. Among his pupils were Nicolai, Kücken, and Dehn. He composed 2 syms.; 2 overtures; concertos for oboe, clarinet, and guitar; piano concertos; a Piano Quintet; piano sonatas; piano duos; etc.; also publ. a treatise, *Der vollkommene Kapellmeister* (1845).

Birnbach, Karl Joseph, German composer, father of **Heinrich Birnbach**; b. Köpernick, Silesia, 1751; d. Warsaw, May 29, 1805. During the last years of his life he was conductor at the German Theater in Warsaw. A prolific composer, he wrote 2 operas, 10 syms., 16 piano concertos, 10 violin concertos, cantatas, masses, chamber music, piano pieces.

Birnie, Tessa (Daphne), New Zealand pianist and conductor; b. Ashburton, July 19, 1934. She studied piano with Paul Schramm in Wellington; then went to Europe and took lessons with Lefebure in Paris and K.U. Schnabel in Como; subsequently toured as a pianist in Australia and Asia; also played in the U.S. She organized the Sydney Camerata Orch. in 1963, appearing with it as both pianist and conductor; was founder-president of the Australian Soc. of Keyboard Music and founder of the journal *Key Vive Music*. In 1985 she was awarded the Medal of the Order of Australia.

Birtner, Herbert, German musicologist; b. Hamburg, June 16, 1900; d. in battle at Voronezh, Russia, Sept. 27, 1942. He 1st studied medicine; then took courses in musicology with Gurlitt and Kroyer; was an assistant lecturer at the Univ. of Leipzig (1924–28); a prof. at the Univ. of Marburg (1938–40). In 1940 he was drafted into the German army and was killed on the Russian front. He contributed important studies on the music of the Reformation; his publ. works include *Joachim à Burck als Motettenkomponist* (Leipzig, 1924) and *Studien zur niederländisch-humanistischen Musikanschauung* (Marburg, 1929).

Birtwistle, Sir Harrison (Paul), noted English composer; b. Accrington, Lancashire, July 15, 1934. He studied clarinet; won a scholarship in 1952 to the Royal Manchester College of Music, where he studied composition; also studied clarinet playing with Kell at the Royal Academy of Music in London. In 1966 he was visiting prof. at Princeton Univ.; in 1975 he became music director at the National Theatre, South Bank, London. In 1987 he received the Grawemeyer Award of the Univ. of Louisville. In 1988 he was knighted. In his compositions he departed completely from the folkloric trends popular in British modern music and adopted an abstract idiom, often with satirical overtones in his stage works.

WORKS: *Refrains and Choruses* for Wind Quintet (1957); *Monody for Corpus Christi* for Soprano Solo, Flute, Violin, and Horn (1959); *Précis* for Piano Solo (1959); *The World Is Discovered*, instrumental motet (1960; Festival of the ISCM, Copenhagen, June 2, 1964); *Chorales* for Orch. (1963); *Narration: The Description of the Passing of a Year* for a cappella Choir (1964); *3 Movements with Fanfares* for Chamber Orch. (1964); *Ring a Dumb Carillon* for Soprano, Clarinet, and Percussion (1965); *Verses* for Clarinet and Piano (1965); *Tragoedia* for Wind Quintet, Harp, and String Quartet (1965); *Carmen paschale* for Chorus and Organ (1965); *The Visions of Francesco Petrarca*, 7 sonnets for Baritone, Chamber Ensemble, and School Orch. (1966); *Punch and Judy*, chamber opera (1966–67; Aldeburgh Festival, June 8, 1968; rev. version, London, March 3, 1970); *Monodrama* for Speaker and Instrumental Ensemble (London, May 30, 1967); *Nomos* for 4 Amplified Wind Instruments and Orch. (London, Aug. 23, 1968); *Linoi* for Clarinet and Piano (1968); *Down by the Greenwood Side*, dramatic pastorale (1968; Brighton, May 8, 1969); *Medusa* for Chamber Orch. and Percussion (London, Oct. 22, 1969; rev. version, London, March 3, 1970); *4 Interludes* for Clarinet and Pre-recorded Tape (1970); *Verses and Ensembles* for 12 Players (London, Aug. 31, 1970); *Nenia on the Death of Orpheus* for Soprano and Instrumental Ensemble (1970); *The Triumph of Time* for Orch., after a painting of Breughel (1970; London, June 1, 1972); *Meridian* for Mezzo-soprano, Chorus, and an Instrumental Ensemble (1971); *Prologue to Agamemnon* by Aeschylus, for Tenor, Bassoon, Horn, 3 Trumpets, Trombone, Violin, and Double Bass (1971); *Chronometer* for 8-track Electronic Tapes (1971); *The Fields of Sorrow* for 2 Sopranos, Mixed Choir, and Instrumental Ensemble (1971); *An Imaginary Landscape* for Brass, Percussion, and 8 Double Basses (1971); *Epilogue: Full Fathom 5* for Tenor, Brass, and Percussion (1972); *La Plage*, 8 Arias of Remembrance for Soprano, 3 Clarinets, Piano, and Marimba (1972); *Tombeau*, in memory of Stravinsky (1972); *Grimethorpe Aria* for Brass Band (1973); *The Mask of Orpheus*, opera (1973–75; 1981–84; London, May 21, 1986); *Melancholia I* for Clarinet, Harp, and 2 String Orchs. (1976); *Silbury Air* for Woodwind Quartet, Trumpet, Horn, Trombone, String Quintet, Piano, Harp, and Percussion (1977); *Frames, Pulses and Interruptions*, ballet (1977); *Bow Down*, musical theater (London, July 4, 1977); *For O, for O the Hobby Horse Is Forgot* for 6 Percussion Players (1977); *Carmen Arcadiae Mechanicae Perpetuum* for Instrumental Ensemble (1977); . . . *agm* . . . for 16 Voices and 3 Instrumental Groups (1979); *Aventures des Mercures* for Instrumental Ensemble (1980); *On the Sheer Threshold of the Night*, madrigal (1980); *Yan, Tan, Tethera*, opera (1983–84; London, Aug. 5, 1986); *Earth Dances* for Orch. (1985–86); *Endless Parade* for Trumpet, Vibraphone, and Strings (1987).

BIBL.: M. Hall, *H. B.* (London, 1984); A. Clements, "B. counts sheep," *Musical Times* (Aug. 1986); M. Hall, "The Sanctity of the Context: B.'s Recent Music," ibid. (Jan. 1988).

Bischof, Rainer, Austrian composer; b. Vienna, June 20, 1947. He studied law, art history, and philosophy at the Univ. of Vienna (Ph.D., 1973). In his music he follows the tenets of the New Viennese School.

WORKS: Sonatine for Solo Clarinet (1969); Duo for Flute and Clarinet (1970); *Theme and 7 Variations* for Oboe and Cello (1970); Quartet for Flute, Oboe, Horn, and Bassoon (1971); *Deduction* for Strings (1973–74); *In Memoriam Memoriae*, song cycle for Mezzo-soprano, Speaker, Vibraphone, Celesta, Bass Clarinet, and Cello (1975–77); Flute Concerto (1978–79; Innsbruck, Jan. 22, 1981); Concerto for Violin, Cello, and Orch. (1979–80; Zürich, June 9, 1983); *Viola Tricolor*, 32 variations for Solo Viola (1982); *Music* for 6 Recorders (1982–83).

Bischoff, Hermann, German composer; b. Duisburg, Jan. 7, 1868; d. Berlin, Jan. 25, 1936. He was a pupil of Jadassohn at the Leipzig Cons.; lived for a time in Munich, where he was associated with Richard Strauss; then went to Berlin. He composed 2 syms.; the 1st Sym. had its world premiere in Essen, May 24, 1906; was given by the Boston Sym. under Karl Muck twice in 1 season (Jan. 4, 1908, and Feb. 29, 1908); attracted a great deal of attention at the time, but sank into oblivion later on. He also composed the symphonic poems *Pan* and *Gewittersegen*; publ. an essay, *Das deutsche Lied* (1905).

Bischoff, Marie. See **Brandt, Marianne.**

Bishop, Anna (née **Ann Riviere**), famous English soprano; b. London, Jan. 9, 1810; d. N.Y., March 18, 1884. She was of French descent. She studied at the Royal Academy of Music in London; in 1831 she married **Sir Henry Rowley Bishop.** She made her London debut on April 20, 1831. In 1839 she appeared in concerts with the French harpist Bochsa, with whom she apparently became intimate. In 1847 she went to America; she obtained a divorce in 1848 and married Martin Schultz. In 1866 she toured China and Australia; the ship she was on became grounded on a coral reef in the Marianas for 21 days, but despite this experience she completed her tour, eventually returning to N.Y. She retired in 1883.

Bishop, Sir Henry Rowley, noted English composer; b. London, Nov. 18, 1786; d. there, April 30, 1855. He was a pupil of Francesco Bianchi; attracted attention with his 1st opera, *The Circassian Bride* (Drury Lane, Feb. 23, 1809); from 1810 to 1824, was conductor at Covent Garden; in 1813, alternate conductor of the Phil.; in 1819, oratorio conductor at Covent Garden; in 1825, conductor at the Drury Lane Theatre; in 1830, music director at Vauxhall. He took the degree of B.Mus. at Oxford Univ. (1839); from 1840 was music director at Covent Garden, then prof. of music at Edinburgh (1841–43); was knighted in 1842; conducted the Concerts of Antient Music from 1840 to 1848; was then appointed (succeeding Dr. Crotch) prof. of music at Oxford, where he received the degree of D.Mus. in 1853. In 1831 he married **Anna Bishop,** but they were divorced in 1848. He was a remarkably prolific dramatic composer, having produced about 130 operas, farces, ballets, adaptations, etc. His operas are generally in the style of English ballad opera; some of the best are *Cortez, or The Conquest of Mexico* (1823); *The Fall of Algiers* (1825); *The Knight of Snowdoun* (after Walter Scott; 1811); *Native Land* (1824). His *Clari, or The Maid of Milan* (Covent Garden, May 3, 1823) contains the famous song *Home Sweet Home*, with text by the American John Howard Payne; it appears repeatedly throughout the opera. The tune, previously publ. by Bishop to other words, was thought to have been of Sicilian origin, but after much litigation was accepted as Bishop's original composition (the MS is owned by the Univ. of Rochester in N.Y.). A version of the melody was used by Donizetti in his opera *Anna Bolena*, giving rise to the erroneous belief that Donizetti was its composer. Bishop also wrote an oratorio, *The Fallen Angel* (1839); a cantata, *The 7th Day* (1834); many additions to revivals of older operas; etc.; his glees and other lyric vocal compositions are deservedly esteemed. Bishop also publ. vol. I of *Melodies of Various Na-*

tions; and 3 vols. of *National Melodies*, to which Moore wrote the poems.

BIBL.: F. Corder, "The Works of Sir H. B.," *Musical Quarterly* (Jan. 1918); R. Northcott, *The Life of Sir H.R. B.* (London, 1920).

Bishop-Kovacevich, Stephen, American pianist and conductor; b. Los Angeles (of Yugoslav parents), Oct. 17, 1940. He studied with Lev Schorr and in 1951 made his debut in San Francisco; after training from Dame Myra Hess in London (1959–61), he made his 1st appearance there in 1961. Subsequently he performed with major European and North American orchs., and toured extensively as a recitalist. In later years he was also active as a conductor; in 1988 he was named co-principal conductor and co-artistic director of the Orch. of St. John's in London. As a pianist, he has demonstrated notable command of a large repertoire, ranging from the standard classics to contemporary scores.

Bismillah Khan, Indian virtuoso on the shehnai; b. Dumraon, March 21, 1916. He studied instrumental and vocal music; earned great renown in India; appeared as soloist at the Commonwealth Arts Festival in London in 1965.

Bispham, David (Scull), American baritone; b. Philadelphia, Jan. 5, 1857; d. N.Y., Oct. 2, 1921. He 1st sang as an amateur in church choruses in Philadelphia; in 1886 went to Italy, where he studied with Vannuccini in Florence and Francesco Lamperti in Milan; later studied in London with Shakespeare and Randegger. He made his operatic debut as Longueville in Messager's *La Basoche* (English Opera House, London, Nov. 3, 1891), in which his comic acting ability, as well as his singing, won praise; made his 1st appearance in serious opera as Kurwenal in *Tristan und Isolde* (Drury Lane, June 25, 1892). He was particularly effective in the Wagnerian baritone roles; made his American debut with the Metropolitan Opera in N.Y. as Beckmesser (Nov. 18, 1896); was on the Metropolitan roster 1896–97, 1898–99, and 1900–1903. He was a strong advocate of opera in English; a Soc. of American Singers was organized under his guidance, presenting light operas in the English language. He publ. an autobiography, *A Quaker Singer's Recollections* (N.Y., 1920). A Bispham Memorial Medal Award was established by the Opera Soc. of America in 1921 for an opera in English by an American composer.

Bissell, Keith, Canadian composer; b. Meaford, Ontario, Feb. 12, 1912. He studied composition with Leo Smith at the Univ. of Toronto, graduating in 1942; took some instruction in Munich with Carl Orff (1960) and was instrumental in introducing the Orff method of elementary music education to Scarborough (borough of Toronto), where he was chief coordinator of music for public schools (1955–76). A great believer in the propagation of music among semi-professionals, he composed works specifically designed for amateur performance.

WORKS: Stage: *Rumpelstiltzkin* (1947); *His Majesty's Pie* (1966); *The Miraculous Turnip* (1980); *3 Pieces* for String Orch. (1960); *Little Suite* for Trumpet and Strings (1962); Concertino for Piano and Strings (1963); *5 Dances* for Small Orch. (1963); Divertimento for String Orch. (1964); *Canada 1967* for Orch. (1967); *A Bluebird in March* for Chorus, and Orch. or Piano (1967); *Christmas in Canada* for Narrator, Soli, Chorus, and Orch. (1967); *Passion According to St. Luke* for Soli, Chorus, Children's Chorus, and Orch. (Toronto, April 9, 1971); *Andante e Scherzo* for Small Orch. (1971); *Variations on a Canadian Folksong* for String Orch. (1972); *Theme, Variation and Epilogue* for Chorus, Solo Viola, and String Orch. (1975); *God's Grandeur* for Chorus and Orch. (1975); *Andante and Allegro* for Oboe and Strings (1976); *In Praise of Famous Men* for Soprano, Chorus, Organ, Brass Quintet, and String Orch. (Toronto, June 1, 1976); *Cantate Domino* for Female Chorus and Chamber Orch. (1977); Piano Sonata (1947); Violin Sonata (1948); Organ Sonata (1963); Serenade for Wind Quintet (1972); *Trio Suite* for Trumpet, Horn, and Trombone (1973); Suite for Bassoon, String Quartet, and Percussion (1977); Suite for Brass Quintet (1977); Suite for Winds (1978); choruses; songs.

Bitetti (Ravina), Ernesto (Guillermo), Argentine guitarist; b. Rosario, July 20, 1943. He studied guitar in Santa Fe; completed his education at the Univ. Nacional del Litoral (M. Mus., 1964). He made his debut in Rosario in 1958; then toured in the U.S., Europe, the Middle East, and the Orient. Several composers wrote guitar pieces especially for him.

Bitsch, Marcel, French composer; b. Paris, Dec. 29, 1921. He entered the Paris Cons. in 1939, studied composition with Busser, and won the 2nd Prix de Rome, 1943; 1st Prix de Rome, 1945. He has written *6 esquisses symphoniques* (1949); *Sinfonietta* (1950); cantata, *La Farce du contrebandier* (1946); *Divertissement* for Flute, Clarinet, Oboe, and Bassoon (1947); *3 Sonatinas* for Flute and Piano (1952); Concertino for Piano and Orch. (Paris, Nov. 28, 1954); etc.

Bitter, Carl Hermann, German writer on music; b. Schwedt-an-der-Oder, Feb. 27, 1813; d. Berlin, Sept. 12, 1885. He studied at the Univ. of Berlin and at Bonn Univ.; pursued a career in government; served in the finance dept.; in 1879 he was appointed Prussian Minister of Finance by Bismarck. He retired in 1882. He publ. a book on Bach in 2 vols. (Berlin, 1865; 2nd ed., 1880; abridged Eng. ed., 1873). Other books: *Mozarts Don Juan und Glucks Iphigenia in Taurus* (Berlin, 1866); *C.Ph.E. Bach und W.Fr. Bach und deren Brüder* (2 vols., Berlin, 1868); *Beiträge zur Geschichte des Oratoriums* (Berlin, 1872); *Die Reform der Oper durch Gluck und R. Wagner's Kunstwerke der Zukunft* (Braunschweig, 1884).

Bittner, Julius, Austrian composer; b. Vienna, April 9, 1874; d. there, Jan. 9, 1939. He 1st studied law; then music with Bruno Walter and Josef Labor; was a magistrate in Vienna until 1920. At the same time he composed industriously. He devoted most of his energy to opera and also wrote his own librettos; composed 2 syms., sacred choruses, and numerous songs for his wife, Emilie Bittner, a contralto. During his last years, he suffered from a crippling illness, necessitating the amputation of both legs.
WORKS: Operas: *Die rote Gret* (Frankfurt, Oct. 26, 1907); *Der Musikant* (Vienna, April 12, 1910); *Der Bergsee* (Vienna, Nov. 9, 1911; rev. 1938); *Der Abenteurer* (Cologne, Oct. 30, 1913); *Das höllisch Gold* (Darmstadt, Oct. 15, 1916); *Das Rosengärtlein* (Mannheim, March 18, 1923); *Mondnacht* (Berlin, Nov. 13, 1928); *Das Veilchen* (Vienna, Dec. 8, 1934); also operettas, ballets, and mimodramas.
BIBL.: R. Specht, *J. B.* (Munich, 1921); U. Bittner, *J. B.* (Vienna, 1969).

Bizet, Georges (baptismal names, **Alexandre-César-Léopold**), great French opera composer; b. Paris, Oct. 25, 1838; d. Bougival, June 3, 1875. His parents were both professional musicians: his father, a singing teacher and composer; his mother, an excellent pianist. Bizet's talent developed early in childhood; at the age of 9 he entered the Paris Cons., his teachers being Marmontel (piano), Benoist (organ), Zimmerman (harmony), and (for composition) Halévy, whose daughter, Geneviève, married Bizet in 1869. In 1852 he won a 1st prize for piano, in 1855 for organ and for fugue, and in 1857 the Grand Prix de Rome. Also in 1857 he shared (with Lecocq) a prize offered by Offenbach for a setting of a 1-act opera, *Le Docteur Miracle*; Bizet's setting was produced at the Bouffes-Parisiens on April 9, 1857. Instead of the prescribed Mass, he sent from Rome during his 1st year a 2-act Italian opera buffa, *Don Procopio* (not produced until March 10, 1906, when it was given in Monte Carlo in an incongruously ed. version); later he sent 2 movements of a sym., an overture (*La Chasse d'Ossian*), and a 1-act opera (*La Guzla de l'Émir*; accepted by the Paris Opéra-Comique, but withdrawn by Bizet prior to production). Returning to Paris, he produced a grand opera, *Les Pêcheurs de perles* (Théâtre-Lyrique, Sept. 30, 1863); but this work, like *La Jolie Fille de Perth* (Dec. 26, 1867), failed to win popular approval. A 1-act opera, *Djamileh* (Opéra-Comique, May 22, 1872), fared no better. Bizet's incidental music for Daudet's play *L'Arlésienne* (Oct. 1, 1872) was ignored by

the audiences and literary critics; it was not fully appreciated until its revival in 1885. But an orch. suite from *L'Arlésienne* brought out by Pasdeloup (Nov. 10, 1872) was acclaimed; a 2nd suite was made by Guiraud after Bizet's death. Bizet's next major work was his masterpiece, *Carmen* (based on a tale by Mérimée, text by Halévy and Meilhac), produced, after many difficulties with the management and the cast, at the Opéra-Comique (March 3, 1875). The reception of the public was not enthusiastic; several critics attacked the opera for its lurid subject, and the music for its supposed adoption of Wagner's methods. Bizet received a generous sum (25,000 francs) for the score from the publisher Choudens and won other honors (he was named a Chevalier of the Légion d'Honneur on the eve of the premiere of *Carmen*); although the attendance was not high, the opera was maintained in the repertoire. There were 37 performances before the end of the season; the original cast included Galli-Marie as Carmen, Lhérie as Don José, and Bouhy as Escamillo. Bizet was chagrined by the controversial reception of the opera, but it is a melodramatic invention to state (as some biographers have done) that the alleged failure of *Carmen* precipitated the composer's death (he died on the night of the 31st perf. of the opera). Soon *Carmen* became a triumphant success all over the world; it was staged in London (in Italian at Her Majesty's Theatre, June 22, 1878), St. Petersburg, Vienna, Brussels, Naples, Florence, Mainz, N.Y. (Academy of Music, Oct. 23, 1878), etc. The Metropolitan Opera produced *Carmen* 1st in Italian (Jan. 9, 1884), then in French, with Calvé as Carmen (Dec. 20, 1893). It should be pointed out that the famous *Habanera* is not Bizet's own, but a melody by the Spanish composer Yradier; Bizet inserted it in *Carmen* (with slight alterations), mistaking it for a folk song. Bizet also wrote an operetta, *La Prêtresse* (1854); the operas *Numa* (1871) and *Ivan le Terrible*, in 4 acts (Bordeaux, Oct. 12, 1951; the score was believed to have been destroyed by Bizet, but was discovered among the MSS bequeathed to the Paris Cons. by the 2nd husband of Bizet's widow); the cantatas *David* (1856) and *Clovis et Clothilde* (1857); *Vasco da Gama*, symphonic ode, with Chorus (1859); *Souvenirs de Rome*, symphonic suite in 3 movements (Paris, Feb. 28, 1869; publ. in 1880 as a 4-movement suite, *Roma*); orch. overture, *Patrie* (Paris, Feb. 15, 1874); *Jeux d'enfants*, suite for Piano, 4-hands; about 150 piano pieces of all kinds (Bizet was a brilliant pianist); etc. Bizet's 1st Sym., written at the age of 17, was discovered in the Bizet collection at the Paris Cons. in 1933, and was given its 1st performance anywhere by Felix Weingartner in Basel on Feb. 26, 1935; it rapidly became popular in the concert repertoire. Bizet also completed Halévy's biblical opera, *Noë* (1869).
BIBL.: E. Galabert, *G. B.* (Paris, 1877); C. Pigot, *B. et son œuvre* (1886; new ed., 1911); C. Bellaigue, *B.* (1891); P. Voss, *B.* (Leipzig, 1899); A. Weissmann, *B.* (Berlin, 1907); O. Séré, "*G. B.*," in *Musiciens français d'aujourd'hui* (Paris, 1911); H. Gauthier-Villars, *B.*; *Biographie critique* (Paris, 1911); R. Brancour, *La Vie et l'œuvre de B.* (Paris, 1913); P. Landormy, "*B.*," in *Les Maîtres de la musique* (1924); J. Rabe, *B.* (Stockholm, 1925); D.C. Parker, *B., His Life and Works* (London, 1926); E. Istel, *B. und Carmen* (Stuttgart, 1927); J. Tiersot, "*B.* and Spanish Music," *Musical Quarterly* (Oct. 1925); J.W. Klein, "Nietzsche and *B.*," ibid.; M. Delmas, *B.* (1930); R. Laparra, *B. et l'Espagne* (Paris, 1934); *B.* issue of the *Revue de Musicologie* (Nov. 1938); M. Cooper, *B.* (London, 1938); W. Dean, *G. B.: His Life and Work* (London, 1948; 3rd ed., 1975); M. Curtiss, "Unpublished Letters by *G. B.*," *Musical Quarterly* (July 1950); idem, *B. and His World* (N.Y., 1958); J. Roy, *B.* (Paris, 1983).

Bjelinski, Bruno, Croatian composer; b. Trieste, Nov. 1, 1909. He studied law at the Univ. of Zagreb and music at the Cons. there; in 1945 he joined the faculty of the Cons. His music is marked by romantic coloring, often related to literary subjects.
WORKS: *Simfonija Ljeta* (Summer Sym.; Zagreb, Oct. 15, 1956); Sym. No. 2, *In Memoriam Poetae*, with Children's Cho-

rus (1961); Sym. No. 3 (1964); Sym. No. 4 (1965); Sym. No. 5 (1969); Serenade for Trumpet, Piano, Strings, and Percussion (1957); *Mediterranean Sinfonietta* (Zagreb, Dec. 9, 1959); *Sinfonietta brasileira* (1961); operatic fairy tale, *Pčelica Maja* (Maya the Bee; 1952); *Sinfonietta concertante* (1967); Concertino for Horn and Orch. (1967); Clarinet Sonata (1966); several song cycles; piano pieces.

Bjerre, Jens, Danish organist and composer; b. Århus, Oct. 13, 1903; d. Copenhagen, Jan. 3, 1986. He took courses in piano and composition at the Copenhagen Cons.; in 1933 he became church organist there, continuing in this employ until 1972. His compositions are mostly for organ.

Bjoner, Ingrid, Norwegian soprano; b. Krakstad, Nov. 8, 1927. She studied at the Oslo Cons. and at the Hochschule für Musik in Frankfurt; made her opera debut as Donna Anna in Mozart's *Don Giovanni* at the Oslo Opera in 1957. She then sang at the Wuppertal Opera (1959–61). On Oct. 28, 1961, she made her American debut at the Metropolitan Opera in N.Y. as Elsa in *Lohengrin*. In 1985 she became active as an opera producer in Oslo. She distinguished herself as a Wagnerian singer at the Bayreuth Festivals.

Björlin, (Mats) Ulf (Stefan), Swedish conductor and composer; b. Stockholm, May 21, 1933. He studied conducting in Salzburg with Igor Markevitch and in Paris with Nadia Boulanger; from 1963 to 1968 he was director of the Royal Dramatic Theater in Stockholm. He has written music mainly for the theater.
    Works: *Pinocchio,* children's musical for Chamber Orch. (1966); *Ekon* for Orch. (1967); *Om fem år* (In 5 Years), after García Lorca, opera for Actors and Chamber Ensemble (Stockholm, Oct. 27, 1967); *Epitaph for Lars Görling* for Orch. (1967); *Aft vaemod* (Of Melancholy), choreographic oratorio (1970); opera, *Den stora teatern* (The Big Theater), opera, Feb. 25, 1972); short opera, *Balladen om Kasper Rosenröd,* opera (Vålberg-Karlstad, Nov. 15, 1972); *Mandala* for Orch. (Norrköping, May 9, 1974); *Kärlekin till Belisa,* radio opera (1981); Wind Quintet (1983); *Tillfälle gör Tiufven,* opera buffa (1983); *Den främmande kvinnan,* opera (1983–84).

Björling, Jussi (baptismal names, **Johan Jonatan**), eminent Swedish tenor; b. Stora Tuna, Feb. 5, 1911; d. Siarö, near Stockholm, Sept. 9, 1960. He studied singing with his father, a professional singer; made his 1st public appearance in 1916 as a member of the vocal Björling Male Quartet, which included his father, David Björling (1873–1926), and 2 other brothers, Johan Olof "Olle" (1909–65) and Karl Gustaf "Gösta" (1912–57), both of whom pursued careers as singers; another brother, Karl David "Kalle" (1917–75), was also a singer. The Björling Male Quartet gave concerts throughout Sweden (1916–19); made an extensive tour of the U.S. (1919–21); then continued to sing in Sweden until 1926. Jussi Björling had an excellent professional training with John Forsell at the Royal Academy of Music in Stockholm. He made his operatic debut as the Lamplighter in *Manon Lescaut* at the Royal Theater in Stockholm on July 21, 1930, and remained there until 1939; also sang as a guest artist with the Vienna State Opera and the Dresden State Opera, and at the Salzburg Festival. He made his professional U.S. debut in a concert broadcast from Carnegie Hall in N.Y. on Nov. 28, 1937, and his 1st appearance with the Metropolitan Opera as Rodolfo in *La Bohème* on Nov. 24, 1938; continued to sing there until 1941, when his career was interrupted by war. He resumed his appearances at the Metropolitan Opera in 1945 and sang there until 1954, and then again in 1956–57 and 1959. On March 15, 1960, he suffered a heart attack as he was preparing to sing the role of Rodolfo at the Royal Opera House, Covent Garden, London, but in spite of his great discomfort, went through with the performance. He appeared for the last time at a concert in Stockholm on Aug. 20, 1960. Björling was highly regarded for his fine vocal technique and his sense of style. He excelled in the Italian and French roles, and also essayed some Russian operas. He wrote an autobiography, *Med bagaget i strupen*

(Stockholm, 1945). The Jussi Björling Memorial Archive was founded in 1968 to perpetuate his memory.
    Bibl.: J. Porter and H. Henrysson, *A J. B. Discography* (a comprehensive discography with a biographical profile of his life; Indianapolis, 1982).

Björling, Sigurd, Swedish baritone; b. Stockholm, Nov. 2, 1907; d. Helsingborg, April 8, 1983. He studied at the Royal Cons. in Stockholm, made his debut in 1930 at the Royal Theater there; also had guest appearances at La Scala in Milan, Covent Garden in London, and in Paris. In 1951 he sang at the Bayreuth Festival; on Nov. 15, 1952, he made his Metropolitan Opera debut in N.Y. as Telramund in *Lohengrin;* then returned to Sweden. He was no relation to Jussi Björling.

Björnsson, Árni, Icelandic composer; b. Loni i Kelduhverfi, Dec. 23, 1905. He studied theory, composition, piano, and organ at the Reykjavík College of Music; later went to England, where he enrolled at the Royal Manchester College of Music; subsequently returned to Reykjavík, where he was appointed to the faculty of the College of Music. He composed orch. pieces and much choral music in a general Romantic vein.

Blacher, Boris, remarkable German composer; b. Newchwang, China (of half-German, quarter-Russian, and quarter-Jewish ancestry), Jan. 19 (Jan. 6 according to the Russian old-style calendar), 1903; d. Berlin, Jan. 30, 1975. His family moved to Irkutsk, Siberia, in 1914, remaining there until 1920. In 1922 Blacher went to Berlin; studied architecture, and then took a course in composition with F.E. Koch. From 1948 until 1970 he was prof. at the Hochschule für Musik in West Berlin, and from 1953 to 1970 served as its director. An exceptionally prolific composer, Blacher was equally adept in classical forms and in experimental procedures. He initiated a system of "variable meters," with time signatures following the arithmetical progression, alternatively increasing and decreasing, with permutations contributing to metrical variety. For the theater he developed a sui generis "abstract opera," incorporating an element of organized improvisation. In 1960 he was appointed director of the Seminar of Electronic Composition at the Technological Univ. in Berlin, and subsequently made ample use of electronic resources in his own compositions.
    Works: operas: *Habemeajaja* (1929; not extant); *Fürstin Tarakanowa* (1940; Wuppertal, Feb. 5, 1941); *Romeo und Julia,* after Shakespeare (1943; Berlin Radio, 1947); *Die Flut* (1946; Berlin Radio, Dec. 20, 1946); stage premiere, Dresden, March 4, 1947); *Die Nachtschwalbe* (The Night Swallow), "dramatic nocturne" (Leipzig, Feb. 22, 1948; aroused considerable commotion because of its subject, dealing with prostitutes and pimps); *Preussisches Märchen,* ballet-opera (1949; Berlin, Sept. 23, 1952); *Abstrakte Oper* No. 1 (text by Werner Egk, 1953; Frankfurt Radio, June 28, 1953; stage premiere, Mannheim, Oct. 17, 1953; rev. version, Berlin, Sept. 30, 1957); *Rosamunde Floris* (1960; Berlin, Sept. 21, 1960); *Zwischenfälle bei einer Notlandung* (Incidents at a Forced Landing), "reportage in 2 phases and 14 situations" for Singers, Instruments, and Electronic Devices (1965; Hamburg, Feb. 4, 1966); *200,000 Taler,* after Sholom Aleichem (1969; Berlin, Sept. 25, 1969); *Yvonne, Prinzessin von Burgund* (1972; Wuppertal, Sept. 15, 1973); *Das Geheimnis des entwendeten Briefes,* after *The Purloined Letter* by Edgar Allan Poe (1974; Berlin, Feb. 14, 1975).
    ballets: *Fest im Süden* (1935; Kassel, Feb. 4, 1935); *Harlekinade* (1939; Krefeld, Feb. 14, 1940); *Das Zauberbuch von Erzerum* (1941; Stuttgart, Oct. 17, 1942; rev. 1950 as *Der erste Ball;* Berlin, June 11, 1950); *Chiarina* (1946; Berlin, Jan. 22, 1950); *Hamlet* (1949; Munich, Nov. 19, 1950); *Lysistrata* (1950; Berlin, Sept. 30, 1951); *Der Mohr von Venedig,* after Shakespeare (1955; Vienna, Nov. 29, 1955); *Demeter* (1963; Schwetzingen, June 4, 1964); *Tristan* (1965; Berlin, Oct. 10, 1965); incidental music for *Romeo and Juliet* (1951); *Lulu,* after Wedekind (1952), Molière's *Georges Dandin* (1955), *War and Peace,* after Tolstoy (1955), *Robespierre,* after Romain Rolland (1963), *Henry IV,* after Shakespeare (1970).
    orch.: Concerto for 2 Trumpets and 2 String Orchs. (1931); *Kleine Marchmusik* (1932; Berlin, Nov. 22, 1932); *Capriccio*

(1933; Hamburg, May 14, 1935); Piano Concerto (1935; Stuttgart, Nov. 13, 1935); Divertimento for Wind Instruments (1936; Berlin, Feb. 24, 1937); *Geigenmusik* for Violin and Orch. (1936); *Concertante Musik* (1937; Berlin, Dec. 6, 1937); Sym. (1938; Berlin, Feb. 5, 1939); Concerto da camera for 2 Violins, Solo Cello, and String Orch. (1939); *Hamlet,* symphonic poem (1940; Berlin, Oct. 28, 1940); Concerto for String Orch. (1940; Hamburg, Oct. 18, 1942); Partita for String Orch. and Percussion (1945); 16 Variations on a Theme of Paganini (1947; Leipzig, Nov. 27, 1947); Concerto for Jazz Orch. (1947); Piano Concerto No. 1 (1947; Göttingen, March 20, 1948); Violin Concerto (1948; Munich, Nov. 17, 1950); Concerto for Clarinet, Bassoon, Horn, Trumpet, Harp, and Strings (1950; Berlin, June 14, 1950); *Dialog* for Flute, Violin, Piano, and Strings (1950); Piano Concerto No. 2 (1952; Berlin, Sept. 15, 1952); *Orchester-Ornament,* based on "variable meters" (1953; Venice Festival, Sept. 15, 1953); *Studie im Pianissimo* (1953; Louisville, Ky., Sept. 4, 1954); *Zwei Inventionen* (1954; Edinburgh Festival, Aug. 28, 1954); Viola Concerto (1954; Cologne, March 14, 1955); *Orchester-Fantasie* (1955; London, Oct. 12, 1956); *Hommage à Mozart* (1956; Berlin, Dec. 10, 1956); *Music for Cleveland* (1957; Cleveland, Nov. 21, 1957); *Musica giocosa* (1959; Saarbrücken, April 30, 1959); Variations on a Theme of Muzio Clementi for Piano and Orch. (1961; Berlin, Oct. 4, 1961); *Konzertstück* for Wind Quintet and Strings (1963; Donaueschingen, Oct. 19, 1963); Cello Concerto (1964; Cologne, March 19, 1965); *Virtuose Musik* for Solo Violin, 10 Wind Instruments, Percussion, and Harp (1966; Dartmouth College, Hanover, N.H., Aug. 19, 1967); arrangement of Bach's *Das musikalische Opfer* (1966); *Collage* (1968; Vienna, Oct. 5, 1969); Concerto for Trumpet and Strings (1970; Nuremberg, Feb. 11, 1971); Concerto for Clarinet and Chamber Orch. (1971; Schwetzingen, May 12, 1972); *Stars and Strings* for Jazz Ensemble and Strings (1972; Nuremberg, Jan. 12, 1973); *Poème* (1974; Vienna, Jan. 31, 1976); *Pentagram* for Strings (1974; Berlin, April 4, 1975).

CHAMBER: 5 string quartets: No. 1 (1930; Frankfurt, Dec. 6, 1939); No. 2 (1940; Venice, 1941); No. 3 (1944); No. 4 (1951; Berlin, Jan. 25, 1953); No. 5, *Variationen über einen divergierenden c-moll-Dreiklang* (1967; Berlin, March 8, 1968); Cello Sonata (1940); *Divertimento* for Trumpet, Trombone, and Piano (1948; Berlin, Jan. 23, 1948); *Divertimento* for 4 Woodwinds (1951; Munich, Sept. 28, 1951); Violin Sonata (1951; Berlin, Jan. 27, 1952); 2 *Poems* for Vibraphone, Double Bass, Percussion, and Piano (1957; N.Y., Nov. 14, 1958); *Perpetuum mobile* for Solo Violin (1963); Octet for Clarinet, Bassoon, Horn, and String Quintet (1965; Saarbrücken, Oct. 19, 1966); 4 *Ornamente* for Violin and Piano (1969; N.Y., Nov. 5, 1969); Piano Trio (1970); Sonata for 2 Cellos and 11 Instruments (1972; Berlin, Dec. 26, 1972); *Blues espagnola and Rumba philharmonica* for 12 Solo Cellos (1972; Tokyo, Oct. 28, 1973); Duo for Flute and Piano (1972); Quintet for Flute, Oboe, and String Trio (1973); *Tchaikovsky Variations* for Cello and Piano (1974).

VOCAL: *Jazz-Koloraturen* for Soprano, Saxophone, and Bassoon (1929); 5 *Sinnsprüche Omars des Zeltmachers* for Voice and Piano (1931); *Der Grossinquisitor,* oratorio, after Dostoyevsky (1942; Berlin, Oct. 14, 1947); 4 choruses to texts by Villon (1944); *Es taget vor dem Walde,* cantata (1946; Berlin, June 29, 1946); *Francesca da Rimini* for Soprano and Violin (1954); *Träume vom Tod und vom Leben,* cantata (1955; Wuppertal, June 5, 1955); 13 *Ways of Looking at a Blackbird,* to a text by Wallace Stevens, for Voice and Strings (1957; Vienna, Jan. 11, 1959); *Après-lude,* 4 lieder for Voice and Piano (1958); *Die Gesänge des Seeräubers O'Rourke und seiner Geliebten Sally Brown* for Soprano, Cabaret Singer, Baritone, Speaker, Chorus, and Orch. (1958; Vienna, Oct. 5, 1959); *Requiem* for Soprano, Baritone, Chorus, and Orch. (1958; Vienna, June 11, 1959); *Jüdische Chronik* for Soloists, Chorus, and Orch., a collective composition, with Dessau, K.A. Hartmann, Henze, and Wagner-Régeny (1961; Cologne, Jan. 14, 1966); 5 Negro spirituals for Voice and Instruments (1962; Vienna, March 9, 1963); *Parergon* to *Eugene Onegin* for Mezzo-soprano and Chamber

Ensemble (1966); Nursery Rhymes (1967); *For 7* for Soprano, Percussion, and Double Bass (1973).

PIANO: 2 sonatinas (1940, 1941); *3 pièces* (1943); *Ornamente, 7 Studies* (1950); Sonata (1951); 24 preludes (1974).

ELECTRONIC MUSIC: *Multiple Raumperspektiven* (1962); *Elektronische Studie über ein Posaunenglissando* (1962); *Persische elektronische Impulse* (1965); *Elektronisches Scherzo* (1965); *Musik für Osaka* (1969); *Ariadne,* duodrama for 2 Speakers and Electronics (1971).

BIBL.: F. Burt, "The Teaching and Ideas of B. B.," *Score* (1954, No. 9); H.H. Stuckenschmidt, *B. B.* (Berlin, 1973); Bote & Bock catalogue (Berlin, 1983).

Blachut, Beno, Czech tenor; b. Kovzit, June 14, 1913; d. Prague, Jan. 10, 1985. He studied at the Prague Cons. and made his career mostly in the Czech repertoire, in both opera and solo appearances. From 1941 he was a leading member of the Prague National Theater.

Black, Andrew, British baritone; b. Glasgow, Jan. 15, 1859; d. Sydney, Australia, Sept. 15, 1920. He studied singing in London with Randegger and Welch, then in Milan with Scafati; made his London debut at the Crystal Palace on July 30, 1887. In 1893 he was appointed prof. of singing at the Royal Manchester College of Music. In 1913 he settled in Australia.

Black, Frank, American conductor; b. Philadelphia, Nov. 28, 1894; d. Atlanta, Jan. 29, 1968. He studied piano with Raphael Joseffy in N.Y.; then devoted himself chiefly to conducting radio orchs.; in 1928 he organized the music dept. of NBC.

Black, Stanley, English pianist and conductor; b. London, June 14, 1913. He studied at the Matthay School of Music in London, and began his career as a jazz pianist and arranger; then was a conductor of the BBC Dance Orch. (1944–52); subsequently worked as a music director for films. In 1968–69 he was principal conductor of the BBC Northern Ireland Orch.; also appeared as a guest conductor with various orch. groups in England.

Blackburn, Bonnie, American musicologist; b. Albany, N.Y., July 15, 1939. She studied at Wellesley College (B.A., 1961) and the Univ. of Chicago (M.A., 1963; Ph.D., 1970). She was a visiting associate prof. at the Univ. of Chicago (1986) and also served as lecturer in the school of music at Northwestern Univ. (1987); later taught at the State Univ. of N.Y. at Buffalo (from 1989). In 1988–89 she held a Guggenheim fellowship. In 1971 she married **Edward Lowinsky,** with whom she ed. the vol. *Josquin des Prez: Proceedings of the International Josquin Festival-Conference* (London, 1976). She contributed articles to *The New Grove Dictionary of Music and Musicians* (1980) and ed. Johannis Lupi Opera Omnia (3 vols., 1980–) and *Music in the Culture of the Renaissance and Other Essays by Edward E. Lowinsky* (Chicago, 1989). She also publ. *Music for Treviso Cathedral in the Late Sixteenth Century: A Reconstruction of the Lost Manuscripts 29 and 30* (London, 1987).

Blackwood, Easley, American composer; b. Indianapolis, April 21, 1933. He studied piano in his hometown and appeared as a soloist with the Indianapolis Sym. Orch. at age 14; studied composition during summers at the Berkshire Music Center (1948–50), notably with Messiaen in 1949; then with Bernhard Heiden at Indiana Univ. and Hindemith at Yale (1949–51); received his M.A. from Yale in 1954; then went to Paris to study with Nadia Boulanger (1954–56). In 1958 he was appointed to the faculty of the Univ. of Chicago. His music is marked by impassioned Romantic éclat and is set in a highly evolved chromatic idiom. Blackwood is an accomplished pianist, particularly notable for his performances of modern works of transcendental difficulty, such as the Concord Sonata of Ives and the 2nd Piano Sonata of Boulez. He publ. *The Structure of Recognizable Diatonic Tunings* (Princeton, N.J., 1986).

WORKS: 5 syms.: No. 1 (1954–55; Boston, April 18, 1958; won the Koussevitzky Music Foundation prize); No. 2 (1960; Cleveland, Jan. 5, 1961; commissioned for the centenary of the music firm G. Schirmer); No. 3 for Small Orch. (1964; Chicago, March 7, 1965); No. 4 (1973); No. 5 (1978); Chamber

Sym. for 14 Wind Instruments (1955); Clarinet Concerto (Cincinnati, Nov. 20, 1964); *Symphonic Fantasy* (Louisville, Sept. 4, 1965); Concerto for Oboe and String Orch. (1966); Violin Concerto (Bath, England, June 18, 1967); Concerto for Flute and String Orch. (Hanover, N.H., July 28, 1968); Piano Concerto (1969–70; Highland Park, Ill., July 26, 1970); Viola Sonata (1953); 2 string quartets (1957, 1959); Concertino for 5 Instruments (1959); 2 violin sonatas (1960, 1973); Fantasy for Cello and Piano (1960); *Pastorale and Variations* for Wind Quintet (1961); Fantasy for Flute, Clarinet, and Piano (1965); *3 Short Fantasies* for Piano (1965); *Symphonic Episode* for Organ (1966); *Un Voyage à Cythère* for Soprano and 10 Players (1966); Piano Trio (1968); *12 Microtonal Études* for Synthesizer (1982).

Blades, Rubén, Panamanian singer and songwriter; b. Panama City, July 16, 1948. He was autodidact in music; studied law at the Univ. of Panama (graduated, 1974) and at Yale Univ. (M.A., 1985). His lyrics, highly charged with social and political significance and undergirded by salsa rhythms, secured his reputation as a musician of unusual gifts. Organizing his own band, Seis del Solar, he produced the successful album *Buscando América* (1984). He also wrote the score for and starred in the film *Crossover Dreams* (1986).
BIBL.: *Current Biography* (May 1986).

Blaes, Arnold Joseph, noted Belgian clarinetist; b. Brussels, Dec. 1, 1814; d. there, Jan. 11, 1892. He studied with Bachmann at the Brussels Cons., winning 1st prize there in 1834; traveled on concert tour in Europe; while in Russia, he married the soprano **Elisa Blaes** in 1843. He taught at the Brussels Cons. from 1844 to 1871; wrote an autobiography, *Souvenirs de ma vie artistique* (Brussels, 1888).
BIBL.: P. Weston, *Clarinet Virtuosi of the Past* (London, 1971).

Blaes, Elisa (née **Meerti**), Belgian soprano; b. Antwerp, Nov. 2, 1817; d. Brussels, Nov. 6, 1878. She 1st gained distinction in Leipzig as a soloist with Mendelssohn and the Gewandhaus Orch. (1839; 1841–42); sang with the Phil. Soc. of London in 1839. In 1843 she appeared in Russia, where she married the Belgian clarinetist **Arnold Joseph Blaes;** she often appeared in concerts with him. In her later years she taught voice in Belgium.

Blagrove, Henry Gamble, English violinist; b. Nottingham, Oct. 20, 1811; d. London, Dec. 15, 1872. He was extremely precocious in his development; at the age of 12 he was admitted to the Royal Academy of Music in London at its opening in 1823. From 1832 to 1834 he was in Germany and took lessons with Spohr in Kassel. He is credited with having established the 1st regular series of chamber music concerts in London in 1835.

Bláha, Ivo, Czech composer; b. Litomyšl, March 14, 1936. He studied with Řídký and Sommer at the Academy of Musical Arts in Prague, graduating in 1958; then joined the film-music dept. there.
WORKS: 3 string quartets (1957, 1966, 1983); Concerto for Orch. (1957); *3 Movements* for Violin and Piano (1961); Wind Quintet (1962); Concerto for Percussion and Orch. (1964); *Solitude*, sonata for Solo Violin (1965); *Music for Wind Quintet* (1965); *3 Toccata-Studies* for Piano (1967); Violin Concerto (1968); *Music to Pictures of a Friend* for Flute, Oboe, and Clarinet (1971); Cello Sonata (1972); *Oh, Love*, music to a poem of Jacques Prévert, for Narrator, Flute, Oboe, Clarinet, and Tape (1973); *2 Inventions* for Solo Flute (1974); *Variations on a Czech National Song* for 3 Flutes (1975); Duo for Bass Clarinet and Piano (1975); *Hymn* for Organ (1980); *Sonata transparenta* for Flute and Piano (1982).

Blahetka, Marie Léopoldine, Austrian pianist and composer; b. Guntramsdorf, near Vienna, Nov. 15, 1811; d. Boulogne, France, Jan. 12, 1887. She was a piano pupil of Kalkbrenner and Moscheles; also studied composition with Sechter. In 1840 she settled in Boulogne. She wrote a romantic opera, *Die Räuber und die Sänger*, which was produced in Vienna in 1830, and a considerable number of salon pieces for piano.

Blainville, Charles-Henri de, French cellist and music theorist; b. probably in or near Rouen, 1710; d. Paris, c.1770. His claim to musicological attention resides in his "discovery" of a 3rd "mode hellénique" (actually the Phrygian mode); in 1751 he wrote a sym. in which he made use of this mode. Rousseau, always eager to welcome a "historical" discovery, expressed his admiration for Blainville. Among Blainville's theoretical writings are *L'Harmonie théorico-pratique* (1746); *Essai sur un troisième mode*, expounding the supposed "mode hellénique"(1751); *L'Esprit de l'art musical* (1754); and *Histoire générale, critique et philologique de la musique* (1767). He composed 5 syms., publ. a book of sonatas "pour le dessus de viole avec la basse continue," and arranged Tartini's sonatas in the form of concerti grossi.

Blake, David (Leonard), English composer; b. London, Sept. 2, 1936. He studied music at Cambridge; then went to East Berlin, where he took lessons with Hanns Eisler. In 1964 he was appointed lecturer in music at York Univ. His early works were in a tonal idiom influenced by Bartók and Mahler, but later he began writing in the 12-tone system as promulgated by Schoenberg and Eisler. He then experimented in a wide variety of styles, including oriental scales and aleatory improvisation. While serving in the British army in the Far East, he learned Chinese.
WORKS: String Quartet No. 1 (1961–62); String Quartet No. 2 (1973); *It's a Small War,* musical for schools (1962); *3 Choruses* to poems by Robert Frost (1964); *Beata l'Alma* for Soprano and Piano (1966); Sym. for Chamber Orch. (1966); *Lumina*, cantata after Ezra Pound, for Soprano, Baritone, Chorus, and Orch. (1968–69); *Metamorphoses* for Orch. (1971); *Scenes* for Solo Cello (1972); Nonet (1971; London, June 21, 1971); *The Bones of Chuang Tzu* for Baritone and Chamber Orch. (1972; Glasgow, March 25, 1975); *In Praise of Krishna* for Soprano and 9 Players (1973; Leeds, March 7, 1973); *Toussaint*, opera in 3 acts (1974–76; London, Sept. 28, 1977; rev. version, London, Sept. 6, 1983); Violin Concerto No. 1 (1976; London, Aug. 19, 1976); *Sonata alla Marcia* for Chamber Orch. (1978; London, May 17, 1978); *From the Mattress Grave* for High Voice and 11 Players (1978; Durham, Feb. 3, 1979); *9 Poems of Heine* for High Voice and Piano (1978); *Cassation* for Wind Octet (1979; Sheffield, May 19, 1979); Clarinet Quintet (1980); *Capriccio* for 7 Players (1980); *The Spear* for Male Speaker, Mezzo-soprano, and 4 Players (1982); *Rise, Dove* for Baritone and Orch. (1982); String Quartet No. 3 (1982); Violin Concerto No. 2 (1983); *Scherzi ed Intermezzi* (Bedford, Nov. 17, 1984); *Seasonal Variants* for 7 Players (Norwich, Oct. 18, 1985); *The Plumber's Gift*, opera (London, May 25, 1989).

Blake, Eubie, black American jazz piano player, seeded buckdancer, vaudevillian, and composer of musicals, rags, études, waltzes, and a plethora of miscellaneous popular numbers; b. Baltimore, Feb. 7, 1883; d. N.Y., Feb. 12, 1983, 5 days after reaching his 100th birthday. Both his parents were former slaves. He was baptized **James Hubert Blake;** relatives and friends called him Hubie, which was abbreviated to Eubie. He grew up in an atmosphere of syncopated music and sentimental ballads played on music boxes, and had some piano lessons from a friendly church organist in Baltimore. At the age of 15 he got a regular job as a standard pianist in a "hook-shop" (a sporting house) run by Aggie Sheldon, a successful madam, which provided him with tips from both the inmates and their customers. He improvised rag music (his long fingers could stretch to 12 keys on the keyboard) and soon began to compose in earnest. In 1899 he wrote his *Charleston Rag,* which became a hit. In 1915 he joined a singer named Noble Sissle, and they appeared on the vaudeville circuit together, advertised as The Dixie Duo. They broke the tradition of blackface white comedians and devised an all-black musical, *Shuffle Along,* which opened in N.Y. on May 23, 1921, billed as "a musical mélange." The score included the song *I'm just wild about Harry,* which became a hit and was actually used as a campaign song for Harry Truman in 1948. Another hit song was *Memories of You,* which Blake wrote for the musical *Black* *birds of 1930.* Remarkably enough, he was moved by a purely scholarly interest in music and as late as 1949 took courses in the Schillinger System of Composition at N.Y. Univ. In 1969 he recorded the album *The 86 Years of Eubie Blake,* and in 1972 he formed his own record company. As his centennial approached there was a growing appreciation of his natural talent, and a Broadway musical billed simply *Eubie!* was produced with resounding success. In 1981 he received the Medal of Freedom from President Reagan. He made his last public appearance at the age of 99, at Lincoln Center in N.Y., on June 19, 1982.

BIBL.: A. Rose, *E. B.* (N.Y., 1979).

Blake, Ran, American composer; b. Springfield, Mass., April 20, 1935. He studied at Bard College (B.A., 1960) and at Columbia Univ. (1960–62), where he attended classes in improvisation with William Russo; later took lessons with Gunther Schuller, who inculcated him in "3rd stream" music (1960–67); also took straight jazz instruction at the Lenox School of Jazz. He composed mostly for piano, employing combined jazz-Baroque techniques and sonorities; his titles include *Aftermath, Chicken Monster, Crystal Trip, Glaciation, Interrogation at Logan Airport, Jim Crow, Klanwatch, Last Wave, Open City, Death Therapy, Deathwatch, East Wind, Field Cry, Police, Present Tense, Requiem for Mingus, Silver Fox, Sleep Secrets, Smoke after Smoke, Soul on Ice, Stoneciphering, Thursday, Touch of Evil, Turncoat, Vertigo,* and *Whirlpool;* also wrote many arrangements of original works for different ensembles, and improvisations on contemporary American songs. In 1967 he was appointed to the faculty of the New England Cons. in Boston.

Blake, Rockwell (Robert), gifted American tenor; b. Plattsburgh, N.Y., Jan. 10, 1951. He began his career by singing with various small opera companies, first attracting notice when he appeared as Lindoro with the Washington, D.C., Opera in 1976; then sang with the Hamburg State Opera (1977–79) and the Vienna State Opera (1978). On Sept. 23, 1979, he made his N.Y. City Opera debut as Count Ory, and on Feb. 2, 1981, his Metropolitan Opera debut in N.Y. as Lindoro. He sang at the Chicago Lyric Opera and at the Rossini Opera Festival in Pesaro in 1983, at the San Francisco Opera in 1984, at the Paris Opéra in 1985, at the Paris Opéra-Comique and the Bavarian State Opera in Munich in 1987, and in Montreal and at the Salzburg Festival in 1989. In 1990 he appeared in the leading tenor role in Pergolesi's *Annibal* in Turin. He also sang widely in concerts. Blessed with a remarkable coloratura, Blake won notable distinction as a true *tenore di grazia,* excelling in Mozart and Rossini.

BIBL.: S. Shirakawa, "R. B.: A Rare Breed of Tenor," *Ovation* (Dec. 1988).

Blakey, Art (Islamic name, **Abdullah Ibn Buhaina**), black American jazz drummer; b. Pittsburgh, Oct. 11, 1919; d. N.Y., Oct. 16, 1990. He 1st studied piano, then turned to drums. In 1939 he joined Fletcher Henderson's orch.; later played in Mary Lou Williams's orch. (1941), with Billy Eckstine's orch. (1944–47), and with Buddy De Franco's Quartet (1952–53). In 1954 he formed a group, the Jazz Messengers; they won a Grammy in 1984 for their album *New York Scene.* His hard-swing style was influential in the bop period of popular American music.

BIBL.: Z. Carno, "A. B.," *Jazz Review,* III/1 (1960); P. Danson, "A. B.," *Coda,* No. 173 (1980); *Current Biography* (Sept. 1988).

Blamont, François Colin de, French composer; b. Versailles, Nov. 22, 1690; d. there, Feb. 14, 1760. He was a pupil of Delalande; became superintendent of the King's music; wrote many court ballets, cantatas, and motets; publ. *Essai sur les goûts anciens et modernes de la musique française* (1754).

Blancafort (de Rosselló), Manuel, Spanish composer; b. Barcelona, Aug. 12, 1897; d. there, 1987. He studied in Barcelona with Lamote de Grignon. In his music he cultivates national Catalan subjects while adhering to the impressionistic

idiom set in neo-Classical forms. He wrote *Sardana sinfónica* for Orch. (1951); *Rapsódia catalana* for Cello and Orch. (1953); symphonic suite, *Evocaciones* (1969); and a number of piano pieces of a descriptive character (*Le Parc d'attractions, Chants intimes, Pastorale, Chemins,* etc.).

Blanchard, Esprit Joseph Antoine, French composer; b. Pernes, Comtat-Venaissin, Feb. 29, 1696; d. Versailles, April 19, 1770. He studied with Poitevin at the choir school of the St. Sauveur Cathedral in Aix-en-Provence. In 1717 he became maître de musique to the chapter of St. Victor in Marseilles; was then maître de chapelle at the Toulon, Besançon, and Amiens cathedrals. He succeeded Bernier as sous-maître at the Chapelle du Roi in Versailles in 1738; was maître de chapelle there from 1761 to 1765. He wrote mainly sacred choral music for performance at the churches where he was employed.

Blanco, Juan, Cuban composer; b. Havana, June 29, 1920. He studied composition with José Ardévol; after a period of writing in traditional forms, he devoted himself to experimentation, making use of electronic devices with purposive spatial arrangement. In this manner he constructed *Texturas* for Orch. and Tape (1964); 4 sets of *Contrapunto espacial* for different groups distributed through the area of performance (1965–70); *Vietnam,* soundlike composition (1968).

Bland, James A., black American song composer; b. Flushing, N.Y., Oct. 22, 1854; d. Philadelphia, May 5, 1911. He learned to play the banjo and joined a minstrel troupe, improvising songs in the manner of Negro spirituals. His most famous ballad, *Carry Me Back to Old Virginny,* was publ. in 1878; in 1940 it was designated the official song of the state of Virginia. From 1881 to 1901 Bland lived in England, enjoying excellent success as an entertainer, including a command performance for Queen Victoria, but he dissipated his savings and died in abject poverty.

Blangini, (Giuseppe Marco Maria) Felice, Italian composer; b. Turin, Nov. 18, 1781; d. Paris, Dec. 18, 1841. He was a choirboy at Turin Cathedral; in 1799 his family moved to Paris, where he gave concerts, wrote fashionable *romances,* and came into vogue as an opera composer when he completed Della-Maria's opera *La Fausse Duègne* (1802); he was also popular as a singing teacher. After producing an opera in Munich, he was appointed court Kapellmeister (1805); later was Generalmusikdirektor at Kassel (1809); upon his return to Paris in 1814, was made superintendent of the King's music, court composer, and prof. of singing at the Cons., positions which he held until 1830. See his autobiography, *Souvenirs de F. B.,* ed. by M. de Villemarest (Paris, 1834).

WORKS: 30 operas; 4 masses with Orch.; 170 nocturnes for 2 Voices; 174 *romances* for 1 Voice; etc.

Blank, Allan, American composer; b. N.Y., Dec. 27, 1925. He studied at the High School of Music and Art in N.Y.; subsequently at the Juilliard School of Music (1945–47), Washington Square College (B.A., 1948), the Univ. of Minnesota (M.A., 1950), and the Univ. of Iowa. He was a violinist in the Pittsburgh Sym. Orch. (1950–52); after teaching instrumental music in N.Y. high schools (1956–65), he taught at Western Illinois Univ. in Macomb (1966–68), Paterson (N.J.) State College (1968–70), Lehman College of the City Univ. of N.Y. (1970–77), and Virginia Commonwealth Univ. in Richmond (from 1978). He was also conductor (1984) and music director (1986–89) of the Richmond Community Orch.

WORKS: STAGE: *Aria da capo,* chamber opera (1958–60); *The Magic Bonbons,* opera (1980–83); *The Noise,* opera (1985–86); incidental music to *Othello* (1983) and *Measure for Measure* (1984). **ORCH.:** *Concert Piece* for Band (1960–63); *Music for Orchestra* (1964–67); *Some Thank-You Notes* for Jazz Band (1970); *6 Miniatures and a Fantasia* (1972); *Divertimento* for Tuba and Band (1979); *Kreutzer March* for Band (1981); Concertino for Bassoon and String Orch. (1984); Concertino for String Orch. (1987); *Overture for a Happy Occasion* (1987). **CHAMBER:** 2 string quartets (1958, 1981); Wind Quintet (1968–70); *Bicinium I* for Oboe and Bassoon, and

II for Clarinet and Bassoon (1974); Trio for Trumpet, Horn, and Trombone (1975); *An American Medley* for Brass Quintet, Flute, and Percussion (1976); *Music* for Tubas (1977); *4 Inventions* for Bassoon and Piano (1979); *Fantasy on Cantillation Motives* for Violin, Viola, and Cello (1983); 2 Studies for Brass Quintet (1984); Concertino for 5 Players (1984–86); *Bicinium III* for Clarinet and Bass Clarinet (1986); *Forked Paths*, suite of 11 miniatures for Trumpet (1988); songs.

Blankenburg, Quirin van (full name, **Quirinus Gerbrandszoon van Blankenburg**), Dutch organist; b. Gouda, 1654; d. The Hague, May 12, 1739. He studied organ with his father and served as a church organist in Rotterdam (1671–76) and in Gorinchem (1676–81). Later on he went to Leiden for further study in the univ. there; his next engagement was as organist at the Hoofkerk in The Hague (1687–1702); he was then employed at the Nieuwe Kerk. He publ. *Elementa musica* (The Hague, 1729); compiled *Clavicembel en Orgelboek der gereformeerde Psalmen en Kerkgezangen* (The Hague, 1732; 3rd ed., 1772); also a method for flute.

Blanter, Matvei (Isaakovich), Russian composer of popular songs; b. Pochep, Chernigov district, Feb. 10, 1903. He studied in Moscow with G. Conus; then devoted himself exclusively to the composition of light music. He wrote an operetta, *On the Banks of the Amur* (1939), and some incidental music. Of his songs, the most popular is *Katyusha* (famous during World War II), which combines the melodic inflection of the typical urban ballad with the basic traits of a Russian folk song. Blanter is regarded in Russia as a creator of the new Soviet song style.
    BIBL.: V. Zak, *M. B.* (Moscow, 1971).

Blanton, Jimmy (James), black American jazz string-bass player; b. Chattanooga, Tenn., Oct. 1918; d. Monrovia, Calif., July 30, 1942. He played the violin as a child; then began to play the string bass; in 1939 he joined Duke Ellington's orch., and continued as a member until his death.

Blaramberg, Pavel (Ivanovich), Russian composer; b. Orenburg, Sept. 26, 1841; d. Nice, March 28, 1907. His father was a geographer of French origin; his mother was Greek. At the age of 14 he went to St. Petersburg; later became a functionary of the Central Statistical Committee there. He was largely self-taught in music, apart from occasional advice from Balakirev and Rimsky-Korsakov. In 1878 he settled in Moscow as an instructor at the newly founded Phil. Inst. In 1898 he went to the Crimea, then to France.
    WORKS: Operas: *The Mummers* (1881); *Russalka* (Moscow, April 15, 1888); *Maria Tudor*, after Hugo (produced as *Mary of Burgundy* on account of the censor's objection to the original libretto; Moscow, Oct. 29, 1888); *Tushintsy* (Moscow, Feb. 5, 1895; his most successful opera; had several revivals); *The Waves* (1902). He also wrote a symphonic poem, *The Dying Gladiator* (1882); a Sym. (1886); songs.

Blatný, Josef, Czech organist and composer, father of **Pavel Blatný;** b. Brünn, March 19, 1891; d. there (Brno), July 18, 1980. He studied composition with Janáček in Brno; later served as his assistant; he then taught at the Brno Cons. (1928–56). He wrote several oratorios, some chamber music, piano pieces, and songs.

Blatný, Pavel, Czech composer and conductor, son of **Josef Blatný;** b. Brno, Sept. 14, 1931. He began his musical studies with his father; then studied piano and music theory at the Brno Cons. (1950–55) and musicology at the Univ. of Brno (1954–58); also took composition lessons with Bořkovec at the Prague Academy of Music (1955–59); attended summer courses of new music at Darmstadt (1965–69); in 1968 traveled to the U.S. and took lessons in jazz piano and composition at the Berklee College of Music. He became an exceedingly active musician in Czechoslovakia; wrote about 600 works, some of them paralleling the development of "3rd-stream music" initiated in the U.S. by Gunther Schuller, which constitutes a fusion of jazz and classical forms; played something like 2,000 piano recitals in programs of modern music; conducted a great

many concerts and participated in programs of the Czech Radio; in 1971 he was appointed chief of the music division of the television station in Brno; also taught at the Janáček Academy of Music and Dramatic Arts in Brno (from 1979). In his later compositions he turned to "serious" music, albeit with tonal manifestations.
    WORKS: STAGE: *Prohádky lesa (Studánka a Domeček)* (Forest Tales [The Well and Little House]), 2 television operas for children (1975); 3 cantatas, with Orch.: *Vrba* (The Willow Tree; 1980); *Štědrý den* (Christmas Eve; 1982); *Polednice* (The Midday Witch; 1982); also 3 musicals. **3RD-STREAM MUSIC:** *Per orchestra sintetica for Jazz and "Classic" Wind Orch.* (1960); *Concerto for Jazz Orch.* (1962–64); *Étude for Quarter-tone Trumpet* (1964); *Tre per S+H* for Jazz Septet (1964); *10'30"* for Sym. Orch. (1965); *D-E-F-G-A-H-C* for Jazz Orch. (1968); *4 Movements* for Big Band (1973); Concertino for Clarinet and Jazz Orch. (1974); *Uno pezzo per due Boemi* for Bass Clarinet and Piano (1981); *Music* for Piano and Orch. (1955); Concerto for Orch. (1956); *Zvony* (The Bells), symphonic movement (1981); *Hommage à Gustav Mahler* (1982). **CHAMBER:** Suite for Winds and Piano (1958); *Scene for Brasses* for Brass Quintet (1972); *2:3* for Wind Quintet (1975); *Due pezzi per quintetto d'ottoni* (1978); piano music.

Blatt, František Tadeáš, Bohemian clarinetist and composer; b. Prague, 1793; d. there, March 9, 1856. He studied clarinet with Václav Farník and composition with Dionys Weber at the Prague Cons. He was a member of the orch. at the Prague Opera; also taught at the Prague Cons. He publ. a method for clarinet (1828) and also composed a number of works for the clarinet; other works include duets, trios, and piano music.
    BIBL.: P. Weston, *Clarinet Virtuosi of the Past* (London, 1971).

Blaukopf, Kurt, Austrian musicologist; b. Czernowitz, Feb. 15, 1914. He studied music theory with Wolpe and conducting with Scherchen in Vienna (1932–37); then went to Jerusalem, where he took courses in music history with Gerson-Kiwi (1940–42); later served as ed. of the periodical *Phono* (1954–65). In 1962 he became a lecturer in music sociology at the Vienna Academy of Music; from 1965 was ed. of the periodical *HiFi Stereophonie* in Vienna. His writings include *Muziksoziologie* (Cologne, 1952; 2nd ed., 1972); *Grosse Dirigenten* (Teufen, 1953; Eng. tr., 1955); *Grosse Virtuosen* (Teufen, 1954; French tr., 1955); *Gustav Mahler, oder Zeitgenosse der Zukunft* (Vienna, 1969; Eng. tr., 1973); with H. Blaukopf, *Die Wiener Philharmoniker: Wesen, Werden, Wirken eines Grossen Orchesters* (Vienna, 1986). He ed. *Gustav Mahler: Sein Leben, sein Werk und seine Welt in zeitgenossischen Bildern und Texten* (Vienna, 1976; in Eng. as *Gustav Mahler: A Documentary Study*, N.Y., 1976); *Musik im Wandel der Gesellschaft: Grundzüge der Musiksoziologie* (Munich, 1982).
    BIBL.: I. Bontinck and O. Brusatti, eds., *Festschrift K. B.* (Vienna, 1975).

Blauvelt, Lillian Evans, American soprano; b. Brooklyn, N.Y., March 16, 1874; d. Chicago, Aug. 29, 1947. After studying violin for several years, she took vocal lessons in N.Y. and Paris; gave concerts in France, Belgium, and Russia; made her operatic debut at Brussels (1893); sang before Queen Victoria (1899); sang the coronation ode and received the coronation medal from King Edward VII (1902); appeared for several seasons at Covent Garden. She married the composer **Alexander Savine** in 1914; created the title role in his opera *Xenia* (Zürich, 1919).

Blavet, Michel, renowned French flutist and composer; b. Besançon (baptized), March 13, 1700; d. Paris, Oct. 28, 1768. He was self-taught as a musician, mastering both bassoon and flute; went to Paris in 1723 with Duke Charles-Eugène Lévis, and made his debut at the Concert Spirituel in 1726, remaining as its most celebrated artist for some 25 years. He was acknowledged as the foremost flute virtuoso of his time.
    WORKS: STAGE: *Floriane, ou La Grotte des spectacles*, comédie-ballet (Château de Berny, Aug. 25, 1752); *Les Jeux olympi-*

ques, ballet héroïque (Château de Berny, Aug. 25, 1753); *La Fête de Cythère*, opera (Château de Berny, Nov. 19, 1753). CHAMBER: 6 Sonates for 2 Flutes, op. 1 (Paris, 1728; ed. by H. Ruf, Mainz, 1967); [6] *Sonates mêlées de pièces* for Flute and Basso Continuo, op. 2 (Paris, 1732; ed. by W. Kolneder, Heidelberg, 1969); [6] Sonates for Flute and Basso Continuo, op. 3 (Paris, 1740); also a Flute Concerto (ed. in Florilegium Musicum, XI, Lorrach and Baden, 1956); also instrumental and vocal music in anthologies of his day.

BIBL.: M. François de Neuf-Château, "Éloge de M. B.," *Nécrologe des hommes célèbres* (Paris, 1770); L. de La Laurencie, "Deux imitateurs français des bouffons: B. et Dauvergne," *Année musicale*, II (1912); G. Migot, "Un grand musicien bisontin, M. B.," *Franche-Comté et Monts Jura*, XVII/197 (1935); C. Sachs, "Bach and B.," *Musical Quarterly* (Jan. 1944).

Blaze (called **Castil-Blaze**), **François-Henri-Joseph,** French writer on music, father of **Henri Blaze, Baron de Bury;** b. Cavaillon, Vaucluse, Dec. 1, 1784; d. Paris, Dec. 11, 1857. He studied with his father, a lawyer and amateur musician; went to Paris in 1799 as a law student; held various administrative posts in provincial towns in France. At the same time he studied music and compiled information on the opera in France. The fruit of this work was the publication in 2 vols. of his book *De l'opéra en France* (Paris, 1820; 1826). He became music critic of the influential Paris *Journal des Débats* in 1822, signing his articles "XXX." He resigned from this post in 1832 but continued to publish books on music, including valuable compilations of musical lexicography: *Dictionnaire de musique moderne* (2 vols., 1821; 2nd ed., 1825; 3rd ed., edited by J.H. Mees, with historical preface and a supplement on Netherlandish musicians, 1828, in 1 vol.); *Chapelle-musique des Rois de France* (1832); *La Danse et les ballets depuis Bacchus jusqu'à Mlle. Taglioni* (1832); *Mémorial du Grand Opéra* (from Cambert, 1669, down to the Restoration, 1847); "Le Piano; Histoire de son invention," *Revue de Paris* (1839–40); *Molière musicien* (1852); *Théâtres lyriques de Paris*, 2 vols., on the Grand Opéra (1855) and on the Italian opera (1856); *Sur l'opéra français; Vérités dures mais utiles* (1856); *L'Art des jeux lyriques* (1858); tr. into French many librettos of German and Italian operas; he himself wrote 3 operas; compiled a collection of *Chants de Provence;* some of his popular ballads attained considerable popularity.

Blaze, Henri, Baron de Bury, French music critic, son of **François-Henri-Joseph Blaze;** b. Avignon, May 17, 1813; d. Paris, March 15, 1888. He wrote many essays for the *Revue des Deux Mondes* and other periodicals; these essays were subsequently collected as *Musiciens contemporains* (1856); *Meyerbeer et son temps* (1865); *Musiciens du passé, du présent, etc.* (1880); *Goethe et Beethoven* (1882). His most valuable book is *La Vie de Rossini* (1854).

Blažek, Zdeněk, Czech composer; b. Žarošice, May 24, 1905; d. Prague, June 19, 1988. He studied in Brno and in Prague, then joined the faculty at the Brno Cons. in 1941 and was appointed its director in 1947, retiring in 1957. A prolific composer, he wrote an opera and much choral music, as well as instrumental pieces, among them 5 string quartets, a String Quintet, 4 so-called Romantic compositions for Violin and Piano, and a *Sonatina balladica.*

Blech, Harry, English violinist and conductor; b. London, March 2, 1910. He received his musical training at the Trinity College of Music in London and at the Royal Manchester College of Music; later was a violinist in the Hallé Orch. in Manchester (1929–30) and the BBC Sym. Orch. in London (1930–36); organized the Blech String Quartet in 1933 (disbanded in 1950). In 1942 he founded the London Wind Players, in 1946 the London Symphonic Players, and in 1949 the London Mozart Players; conducted numerous concerts with these ensembles, mostly in programs of Haydn and Mozart. In 1964 he was made an Officer of the Order of the British Empire and in 1984 a Commander of the Order of the British Empire.

Blech, Leo, eminent German conductor and composer; b. Aachen, April 21, 1871; d. Berlin, Aug. 25, 1958. As a young man he was engaged in a mercantile career; then studied briefly at the Hochschule für Musik in Berlin; returned to Aachen to conduct at the Municipal Theater (1893–99); also took summer courses in composition with Humperdinck (1893–96). He was subsequently engaged as opera conductor in Prague (1899–1906); then became conductor at the Berlin Royal Opera in 1906; was named Generalmusikdirektor in 1913. In 1923 he became conductor of the Deutsches Opernhaus in Berlin; in 1924 was with the Berlin Volksoper, and in 1925 with the Vienna Volksoper. In 1926 he returned to Berlin as a conductor with the Staatsoper, remaining there until 1937; then went to Riga as a conductor of the Riga Opera (1937–41). From 1941 to 1949 he conducted in Stockholm. In 1949 he returned to Berlin and served as Generalmusikdirektor of the Städtische Oper there, remaining at that post until 1953. He was considered a fine interpreter of the standard German and Italian repertoire, particularly in the works of Wagner and Verdi. His own music is in the Wagnerian tradition; his knowledge and understanding of instrumental and vocal resources enabled him to produce competent operas; however, after initial successes, they suffered total oblivion.

WORKS: Operas: *Aglaja* (1893), *Cherubina* (1894), *Das war ich,* an "opera-idyl" (Dresden, Oct. 6, 1902), *Alpenkönig und Menschenfeind* (Dresden, Oct. 1, 1903; rewritten and produced as *Rappelkopf* at the Berlin Opera, in 1917), *Aschenbrödel* (Prague, 1905), and *Versiegelt* (Hamburg, 1908; N.Y., 1912); *Die Strohwitwe,* operetta (Hamburg, 1920); 3 symphonic poems, *Die Nonne, Waldwanderung, Trost in der Natur; 10 Kleinigkeiten* for Piano, 4-hands; music for children; choruses; songs; piano pieces.

BIBL.: E. Rychnowsky, *L. B.* (Prague, 1905); idem, *L. B.,* in vol. III of Monographien Moderner Musiker (Leipzig, 1909); W. Jacob, *L. B.* (Hamburg, 1931).

Bledsoe, Jules, black American baritone and composer; b. Waco, Texas, Dec. 29, 1898; d. Los Angeles, July 14, 1943. He studied at the Chicago Musical College (B.A., 1919); then went to Europe, taking singing lessons in Paris and Rome. Returning to America, he distinguished himself as a fine performer in musical comedies and opera. He sang the central role in the premiere of Jerome Kern's *Show Boat* (1927), appeared in grand opera as Rigoletto and Boris, and sang the title role in Gruenberg's opera *Emperor Jones.* As a composer, he wrote an *African Suite* for Orch. and several songs in the manner of Negro spirituals.

Blegen, Judith, American soprano; b. Lexington, Ky., April 27, 1940. She studied violin as well as singing at the Curtis Inst. of Music in Philadelphia (1959–64). In 1963 she went to Italy, where she studied with Luigi Ricci; then sang at the Nuremberg Opera (1963–66). She made a successful appearance at the Santa Fe Opera on Aug. 1, 1969, in the role of Emily in Menotti's satirical opera *Help! Help! the Globolinks!,* written especially for her by the composer. She made her Metropolitan Opera debut on Jan. 19, 1970, in N.Y. as Papagena in *Die Zauberflöte,* and continued on in its repertoire in a variety of soprano parts. She also appeared at the Paris Opéra (1977) and at several other European opera houses.

Bleichmann, Yuli, Russian composer; b. St. Petersburg, Dec. 6, 1868; d. there, Jan. 8, 1910. He studied with Rimsky-Korsakov at the St. Petersburg Cons.; later with Jadassohn and Reinecke in Leipzig. Returning to St. Petersburg, he founded the Popular Sym. Concerts in 1893; also conducted the Phil. Sym. Concerts. He composed 2 operas, greatly influenced by Wagner: *St. Sebastian* and *The Dream-Princess* (Moscow, Oct. 23, 1900); also songs.

Blessinger, Karl, German musicologist; b. Ulm, Sept. 21, 1888; d. Pullach, near Munich, March 13, 1962. He studied in Heidelberg and Munich; was a theater conductor in Bremen and Bonn; was on the staff of the Akademie der Tonkunst in Munich (1920–45).

WRITINGS: *Ulmer Musikgeschichte im 17. Jahrhundert* (diss., Ulm, 1913); *Die musikalischen Probleme der Gegenwart*

(1920); *Die Überwindung der musikalischen Impotenz* (1920); *Grundzüge der musikalischen Formenlehre* (1926); *Melodielehre als Einführung in die Musiktheorie* (1930); *Mendelssohn, Meyerbeer, Mahler* (1938); *Judentum und Musik; Ein Beitrag zur Kultur- und Rassenpolitik* (Berlin, 1944; a "scientific" apologia for the anti-Semitic policy of the Nazi regime).

Blewitt, Jonathan, English composer; b. London, July 19, 1782; d. there, Sept. 4, 1853. He studied with his father, and with Battishill; was an organist at several churches; served as conductor at the Theatre Royal in Dublin. Returning to London (1825), he was appointed music director at Sadler's Wells Theatre. He composed many popular ballads; was the author of a treatise on singing, *The Vocal Assistant.*

Bleyer, Georg, German composer, poet, and court functionary; b. Tiefurt, near Weimar (baptized), Oct. 28, 1647; d. c.1694. He studied law and music in Jena (1664–66); was named chamber secretary at the court in Rudolstadt; was awarded the garland of poet laureate in 1672; then was active as a musician in Darmstadt at the court (1677–78). He composed sacred vocal music; also publ. a collection of dances for 4 and 5 instruments as *Lust-Music* (2 vols., Leipzig, 1670).
    BIBL.: C. Höfer, *G. B.: Ein thüringischer Tonsetzer und Dichter der Barockzeit* (*Zeitschrift des Vereins für thüringische Geschichte,* supplement XXIV, Jena, 1941).

Bleyer, Nicolaus, German violinist and composer; b. Stolzenau, Feb. 2, 1591; d. Lübeck, May 3, 1658. He studied with Brade (1614–17), and then joined the orch. of Count Ernst in Bückeburg; settled in Lübeck as town musician in 1621, remaining there until his death. About 1628 he publ. *Erster Theil neuer Paduanen, Galliarden, Balletten, Mascarden und Couranten.*

Bleyle, Karl, German composer; b. Feldkirch, Vorarlberg, May 7, 1880; d. Stuttgart, June 5, 1969. He studied with Wehrle (violin) and S. de Lange (composition) in Stuttgart and with Thuille (composition) in Munich. He was active as a teacher and a theater conductor in Graz, Weimar, and Munich; in 1923 he returned to Stuttgart.
    WORKS: 2 operas: *Hannele und Sannele* (Stuttgart, 1923) and *Der Teufelssteg* (Rostock, 1924); many works for Soli, Chorus, and Orch.: *An den Mistral, Lernt Lachen, Mignons Beisetzung, Heilige Sendung, Die Höllenfahrt Christi, Ein Harfenklang, Prometheus, Trilogie der Leidenschaft, Requiem,* etc.; orch. pieces: *Flagellantenzug, Gnomentanz, Siegesouvertüre, Reinecke Fuchs, Legende;* Sym.; Violin Concerto; String Quartet; Violin Sonata; songs; piano pieces; etc.

Blind Tom. See **Bethune, Thomas Greene.**

Bliss, Sir Arthur (Edward Drummond), significant English composer; b. London, Aug. 2, 1891; d. there, March 27, 1975. He studied at Pembroke College, Cambridge; then at the Royal College of Music in London, with Stanford, Vaughan Williams, and Holst. He served in the British Army during World War I; was wounded in 1916, and gassed in 1918. He resumed his musical studies after the Armistice; his earliest works, *Madam Noy* for Soprano and 6 Instruments (1918) and *Rout* for Soprano and Orch. (1919; Salzburg Festival, Aug. 7, 1922), were highly successful, and established Bliss as one of the most effective composers in the modern style. From 1923 to 1925 Bliss was in the U.S. as a teacher, living in California. Returning to London, he wrote the musical score for the film *Things to Come,* after H.G. Wells (1935). During World War II he was music director of the BBC (1942–44). He was knighted in 1950; in 1953 was appointed Master of the Queen's Musick as the successor to Sir Arnold Bax.
    WORKS: **OPERAS:** *The Olympians* (London, Sept. 29, 1949) and *Tobias and the Angel* (London, BBC television, May 19, 1960).
    BALLETS: *Checkmate* (Paris, June 15, 1937), *Miracle in the Gorbals* (London, Oct. 26, 1944), *Adam Zero* (London, April 8, 1946), and *The Lady of Shalott* (unofficially known also as *The Towers;* Berkeley, Calif., May 2, 1958).
    ORCH.: *Mêlée fantasque* (1921, rev. 1965); *A Colour Sym-*

phony (the title refers to 4 heraldic colors, 1 for each movement: purple, red, blue, and green; Gloucester, Sept. 7, 1922, under the composer's direction; rev. 1932); Concerto for 2 Pianos and Orch. (1924; orig. for Piano, Tenor, Strings, and Percussion, 1921); *Introduction and Allegro* (1926, rev. 1937); *Hymn to Apollo* (1926; rev. 1966); *Things to Come,* concert suite from music to the film (1934–35); *Music for Strings* (1935); *Conquest of the Air,* concert suite from music to the film (1937); Piano Concerto (commissioned by the British Council for the British Week at the N.Y. World's Fair, dedicated "to the people of the United States of America"; N.Y., June 10, 1939); *Theme and Cadenza* for Violin and Orch. (1946); Violin Concerto (London, May 11, 1955); *Meditations on a Theme of John Blow* (Birmingham, England, Dec. 13, 1955); *Edinburgh,* overture (1956); *Discourse* (Louisville, Ky., Oct. 23, 1957; recomposed 1965); Cello Concerto (1969–70; Aldeburgh Festival, June 24, 1970; Rostropovich, soloist); *Metamorphic Variations* (London, April 21, 1973, Stokowski conducting; orig. titled simply *Variations*); 2 *Contrasts* for String Orch. (1972; from movements 2 and 3 of Quartet No. 2).
    VOCAL: *Madame Noy* for Soprano and 6 Instruments (1918); *Rhapsody* for Wordless Mezzo-soprano and Tenor, Flute, English Horn, String Quartet, and Double Bass (1919; London, Oct. 6, 1920); *Rout* for Soprano and Orch. (1920); *The Women of Yueh,* cycle for Voice and Chamber Ensemble (1923–24); *Pastorale* for Mezzo-soprano, Chorus, Strings, Flute, and Drums (1928); *Serenade* for Baritone and Orch. (1929); *Morning Heroes,* sym. for Orator, Chorus, and Orch., dedicated to Bliss's brother, killed in action (Norwich, Oct. 22, 1930); *The Enchantress* for Contralto and Orch. (1951); *A Song of Welcome,* for the return of Queen Elizabeth II from her Australian journey, for Soprano, Baritone, Chorus, and Orch. (BBC, May 15, 1954; Joan Sutherland, soprano soloist); *Elegiac Sonnet* for Tenor, String Quartet, and Piano (1955); *The Beatitudes,* cantata (Coventry Festival, May 25, 1962); *Mary of Magdala,* cantata (Birmingham, Sept. 1, 1963); *A Knot of Riddles* for Baritone and 11 Instruments (1963); *The Golden Cantata* (1964); *The World Is Charged with the Grandeur of God,* chamber cantata for Chorus, 2 Flutes, 3 Trumpets, and 4 Trombones (1969); 2 *Ballads* for Female Chorus, and Orch. or Piano (1971); several song cycles, with piano; motets; anthems.
    CHAMBER: *Conversations* for Flute, Oboe, and String Trio (1920; a humorous work); Oboe Quintet (1927); Clarinet Quintet (1931); Viola Sonata (1933); 2 string quartets (1940, 1950; 2 earlier quartets are lost); *Flourish: Greeting to a City* for 2 Brass Choirs and Percussion (1961); *Belmont Variations* for Brass (1963).
    PIANO: Sonata (1952); *Triptych* (1971).
    BIBL.: L. Foreman, *A. B.: Catalogue of Complete Works* (Kent, England, 1980).

Bliss, Philip Paul, American hymn writer; b. in a log cabin in the woods of Clearfield County, Pa., July 9, 1838; d. in a train wreck near Ashtabula, Ohio, Dec. 29, 1876. He was an itinerant minstrel, traveling with a mechanical melodeon and an old horse. In 1864 he settled in Chicago, taught singing, and did some preaching. He publ. *Gospel Songs* (1874) and *Gospel Hymns* (1875), both highly successful.
    BIBL.: R.G. McCutchan, *Our Hymnody* (N.Y., 1937).

Bliss, P. Paul, American organist and music editor; b. Chicago, Nov. 25, 1872; d. Oswego, N.Y., Feb. 2, 1933. He studied in Philadelphia; then went to Paris, where he was a pupil of Guilmant (organ) and Massenet (composition). Returning to America, he was active as an organist in Oswego; served as music director with the John Church Co. (1904–10) and the Willis Music Co. (from 1911). He composed 3 operettas: *Feast of Little Lanterns, Feast of Red Corn,* and *In India;* cantatas: *Pan on a Summer Day, 3 Springs,* and *The Mound-Builders;* piano suite, *In October;* many songs and choruses; also compiled *Graded Course for Piano* (4 vols.).

Blitheman, John, English organist and composer; b. c.1525; d. London, May 23, 1591. He was from 1558 a Gentleman of the Chapel Royal; also held an annuity from Christ Church,

Oxford. John Bull is said to have been one of his pupils. He composed liturgical organ music and several vocal pieces. See D. Stevens, ed., *The Mulliner Book*, in the Musica Britannica series, 1 (1951; 2nd ed., rev., 1962).

Blitzstein, Marc, significant American composer; b. Philadelphia, March 2, 1905; d. Fort-de-France, Martinique, Jan. 22, 1964, from a brain injury sustained after a political altercation with a group of men in a bar. He studied piano and organ in Pennsylvania; composition with Scalero at the Curtis Inst. in Philadelphia; also took piano lessons with Siloti in N.Y. In 1926 he went to Europe, and took courses with Nadia Boulanger in Paris and Schoenberg in Berlin. Returning to America, he devoted himself chiefly to the cultivation of theatrical works of "social consciousness" of the type created in Germany by Bertolt Brecht and Kurt Weill; accordingly he wrote his stage works for performances in small theaters of the cabaret type. In 1940 he received a Guggenheim fellowship; during World War II he was stationed in England with the U.S. Armed Forces. His theater works include *Triple Sec*, opera-farce (Philadelphia, May 6, 1929); *Parabola and Circula*, 1-act opera-ballet (1929); *Cain*, ballet (1930); *The Harpies*, musical satire commissioned by the League of Composers (1931; 1st production, Manhattan School of Music, N.Y., May 25, 1953); *The Cradle Will Rock*, 1-act opera of "social significance" (N.Y., June 16, 1937, with the composer at the piano); *No for an Answer*, short opera (N.Y., Jan. 5, 1941); musical play, *I've Got the Tune* (CBS Radio, Oct. 24, 1937); *Idiots 1st*, opera based on Malamud (completed by Leonard Lehrman; Bloomington, Ind., March 14, 1976); also musical revues, 1 of which, *Regina*, to Lillian Hellman's play *The Little Foxes*, was expanded into a full-fledged opera (Boston, Oct. 11, 1949). Shortly before his death the Ford Foundation commissioned Blitzstein to write an opera on the subject of Sacco and Vanzetti, for production by the Metropolitan Opera House, but the work was never finished. Blitzstein further composed *Gods* for Mezzo-soprano and String Orch. (1926); oratorio, *The Condemned* (1930); *Airborne Symphony* (N.Y., March 23, 1946); *Cantatina* for Women's Voices and Percussion; *Jig-Saw*, ballet-suite (1927); *Romantic Piece* for Orch. (1930); Piano Concerto (1931); *Freedom Morning*, symphonic poem (London, Sept. 28, 1943); String Quartet; *Percussion Music* for Piano (1929); many other piano pieces. Blitzstein tr. Kurt Weill's *Threepenny Opera* into Eng. (1954), and his version scored great success.

BIBL.: H. Brant, "M. B.," *Modern Music* (July 1946); R. Dietz, *The Operatic M. B.* (diss., Univ. of Iowa, 1970); E. Gordon, *Mark the Music: The Life and Work of M. B.* (N.Y., 1989).

Bloch, André, French composer; b. Wissembourg, Alsace, Jan. 18, 1873; d. Viry-Chatillon, Essome, Aug. 7, 1960. He studied at the Paris Cons. with Guiraud and Massenet; received the Premier Grand Prix de Rome in 1893. He was conductor of the orch. of the American Cons. at Fontainebleau. His works include the operas *Maida* (1909), *Une Nuit de Noël* (1922), *Broceliande* (1925), and *Guignol* (1936); a ballet, *Feminaland* (1904); the symphonic poems *Kaa* (1933) and *L'Isba nostalgique* (1945); *Les Maisons de l'éternité* for Cello and Orch. (1930); and *Suite palestinienne* for Cello and Orch. (Paris, Nov. 14, 1948; his most successful instrumental work).

Bloch, Augustyn (Hippolit), Polish composer and organist; b. Grudziadz, Aug. 13, 1929. He studied composition with Szeligowski, and organ at the Warsaw State College of Music (1950–58); then was employed at the Polish State Radio as music ed. In his compositions he follows the neo-Romantic trend of modern Polish music.

WORKS: One-act opera-mystery, *Ayelet, Jephta's Daughter* (Warsaw, Sept. 22, 1968); children's opera-pantomime, *The Sleeping Princess* (Warsaw, Sept. 29, 1974); 5 ballets: *Voci* (Warsaw Television, 1967); *Oczekiwanie* (The Awaiting; Warsaw, May 8); *Byk* (The Bull; 1965; Holland Festival, Amsterdam, June 24, 1965); *Gilgamesh* (1968); *The Looking Glass* for Tape (1975); Concertino for Violin, String Orch., Piano, and Percussion (1958); *Meditations* for Soprano, Organ, and Percussion (1961); *Télégramme* for Children's Chorus, 2 Pianos, and Per-

cussion (1963); *Dialogues* for Violin and Orch. (1963); *Enfiando* for Orch. (1970); *Salmo gioioso* for Soprano and 5 Wind Instruments (1970); *Warsaw* for Narrator, Chorus, and Orch. (1974); *Wordsworth Songs* for Baritone and Chamber Ensemble (Warsaw, Sept. 23, 1976); *Clarinetto divertente* for Solo Clarinet (1976); Oratorio for Organ, Strings, and Percussion (1981–82); Music for Clarinet and String Quartet (1984–85); *Abide with Us, Lord* for Orch. (1986; Warsaw, Sept. 26, 1987); piano pieces; songs.

Bloch, Ernest, remarkable Swiss-born American composer of Jewish ancestry, father of **Suzanne Bloch;** b. Geneva, July 24, 1880; d. Portland, Oreg., July 15, 1959. He studied solfeggio with Jaques-Dalcroze and violin with Louis Rey in Geneva (1894–97); then went to Brussels, where he took violin lessons with Ysaÿe and composition with Rasse (1897–99); while a student, he wrote a string quartet and a "symphonie orientale," indicative of his natural attraction to non-European cultures and coloristic melos. In 1900 he went to Germany, where he studied music theory with Iwan Knorr at the Hoch Cons. in Frankfurt and took private lessons with Ludwig Thuille in Munich; there he began the composition of his 1st full-fledged sym., in C-sharp minor, with its 4 movements orig. bearing titles expressive of changing moods. He then spent a year in Paris, where he met Debussy; Bloch's 1st publ. work, *Historiettes au crépuscule* (1903), shows Debussy's influence. In 1904 he returned to Geneva, where he began the composition of his only opera, *Macbeth*, after Shakespeare; the project of another opera, *Jézabel*, on a biblical subject, never materialized beyond a few initial sketches. As a tribute to his homeland, he outlined the orch. work *Helvetia*, based on Swiss motifs, as early as 1900, but the full score was not completed until 1928. During the season 1909–10 Bloch conducted symphonic concerts in Lausanne and Neuchâtel. In 1916 he was offered an engagement as conductor on an American tour accompanying the dancer Maud Allan; he gladly accepted the opportunity to leave war-torn Europe, and expressed an almost childlike delight upon docking in the port of N.Y. at the sight of the Statue of Liberty. Maud Allan's tour was not successful, however, and Bloch returned to Geneva; in 1917 he received an offer to teach at the David Mannes School of Music in N.Y., and once more he sailed for America; he became an American citizen in 1924. This was also the period when Bloch began to express himself in music as an inheritor of Jewish culture; he explicitly articulated his racial consciousness in several verbal statements. His *Israel Symphony, Trois poèmes juifs,* and *Schelomo,* a "Hebrew rhapsody" for Cello and Orch., mark the height of Bloch's greatness as a Jewish composer; long after his death, *Schelomo* still retains its popularity at sym. concerts. In America, he found sincere admirers and formed a group of greatly talented students, among them Roger Sessions, Ernst Bacon, George Antheil, Douglas Moore, Bernard Rogers, Randall Thompson, Quincy Porter, Halsey Stevens, Herbert Elwell, Isadore Freed, Frederick Jacobi, and Leon Kirchner. From 1920 to 1925 he was director of the Inst. of Music in Cleveland, and from 1925 to 1930, director of the San Francisco Cons. When the magazine *Musical America* announced in 1927 a contest for a symphonic work, Bloch won 1st prize for his "epic rhapsody" entitled simply *America;* Bloch fondly hoped that the choral ending extolling America as the ideal of humanity would become a national hymn; the work was performed with a great outpouring of publicity in 5 cities, but as happens often with prizewinning works, it failed to strike the critics and the audiences as truly great, and in the end remained a mere by-product of Bloch's genius. From 1930 to 1939 Bloch lived mostly in Switzerland; then returned to the U.S. and taught classes at the Univ. of Calif., Berkeley (1940–52); finally retired and lived at his newly purchased house at Agate Beach, Oreg. In his harmonic idiom Bloch favored sonorities formed by the bitonal relationship of 2 major triads with the tonics standing at the distance of a tritone, but even the dissonances he employed were euphonious. In his last works of chamber music he experimented for the 1st time with thematic statements of 12 different notes, but he never adopted the strict Schoenbergian technique of deriving the entire contents of a composition from the basic tone row. In his early Piano Quintet, Bloch made expressive use of quarter-tones in the string parts. In his Jewish works, he emphasized the interval of the augmented second, without a literal imitation of Hebrew chants. Bloch contributed a number of informative annotations for the program books of the Boston Sym., N.Y. Phil., and other orchs.; also contributed articles to music journals, among them "Man and Music" in *Musical Quarterly* (Oct. 1933). An Ernest Bloch Soc. was formed in London in 1937 to promote performances of Bloch's music, with Albert Einstein as honorary president and with vice-presidents including Sir Thomas Beecham, Havelock Ellis, and Romain Rolland.

WORKS: OPERA: *Macbeth* (1904–9; Opéra-Comique, Paris, Nov. 30, 1910). **ORCH.:** *Poèmes d'automne,* songs for Mezzosoprano and Orch. (1906); Prelude and 2 Psalms (Nos. 114 and 137) for Soprano and Orch. (1912–14); *Vivre-aimer,* symphonic poem (1900; Geneva, June 23, 1901); Sym. in C-sharp minor (1901; 1st complete perf., Geneva, 1910; 1st American perf., N.Y. Phil., May 8, 1918, composer conducting); *Hiver-printemps,* symphonic poem (1904–5; Geneva, Jan. 27, 1906); *Israel,* sym. (1912–16; N.Y., May 3, 1917, composer conducting); *Trois poèmes juifs* (1913; Boston, March 23, 1917, composer conducting); *Schelomo,* Hebrew rhapsody for Cello and Orch. (1916; N.Y., May 3, 1917, composer conducting); Concerto Grosso No. 1 for Strings and Piano (1924–25; Cleveland, June 1, 1925, composer conducting); *America,* symphonic poem (1926; N.Y., Dec. 20, 1928; next day simultaneously in Chicago, Philadelphia, Boston, and San Francisco); *Helvetia,* symphonic poem (1928; Chicago, Feb. 18, 1932); *Voice in the Wilderness,* with Cello Obbligato (1936; Los Angeles, Jan. 21, 1937); *Evocations,* symphonic suite (1937; San Francisco, Feb. 11, 1938); Violin Concerto (1938; 1st perf. by Szigeti, Cleveland, Dec. 15, 1938); *Suite symphonique* (Philadelphia, Oct. 26, 1945); *Concerto symphonique* for Piano and Orch. (Edinburgh, Sept. 3, 1949); *Scherzo fantasque* for Piano and Orch. (Chicago, Dec. 2, 1950); *In Memoriam* (1952); *Suite hébraïque* for Viola and Orch. (Chicago, Jan. 1, 1953); *Sinfonia breve* (BBC, London, April 11, 1953); Concerto Grosso No. 2 for String Orch. (BBC, London, April 11, 1953); Sym. for Trombone Solo and Orch. (1953–54; Houston, April 4, 1956); Sym. in E-flat (1954–55; London, Feb. 15, 1956); *Proclamation* for Trumpet and Orch. (1955). **CHAMBER:** *Episodes* for Chamber Orch. (1926); Quintet for Piano and Strings, with use of quarter-tones (1923; N.Y., Nov. 11, 1923); 1st String Quartet (N.Y., Dec. 29, 1916); 2 Suites for String Quartet (1925); 3 Nocturnes for Piano Trio (1924); Suite for Viola and Piano (won the Coolidge prize, 1919); 1st Violin Sonata (1920); 2nd Violin Sonata, *Poème mystique* (1924); *Baal Shem* for Violin and Piano (1923); *Méditation hébraïque* and *From Jewish Life,* both for Cello and Piano (1925); Piano Sonata (1935); 2nd String Quartet (London, Oct. 9, 1946; received the N.Y. Music Critics Circle Award for chamber music, 1947); 3rd String Quartet (1951); 4th String Quartet (Lenox, Mass., June 28, 1954); 5th String Quartet (1956); 3 Suites for Cello Unaccompanied (1956); Piano Quintet No. 2 (1956; Dec. 6, 1959); *Suite modale* for Flute Solo and Strings (1957; Kentfield, Calif., April 11, 1965); 2 Suites for Unaccompanied Violin (1958); Suite for Unaccompanied Viola (1958; the last movement incomplete); 2 *Last Poems* for Flute and Chamber Orch.: *Funeral Music* and *Life Again?* (1958; anticipatory of death from terminal cancer). **PIANO:** *Poems of the Sea, In the Night, Nirvana, 5 Sketches in Sepia.* **VOCAL:** A modern Hebrew ritual, *Sacred Service* (1930–33; world premiere, Turin, Italy, Jan. 12, 1934); *Historiettes au crépuscule,* 4 songs for Mezzo-soprano and Piano (1903).

BIBL.: P. Rosenfeld, in *Musical Portraits* (N.Y., 1920); G.M. Gatti, "E. B.," *Musical Quarterly* (1921); R. Sessions, "E. B.," *Modern Music* (1927); R. Stackpole, "E. B.," ibid.; M.T. Chiesa, *Bibliografia delle opere musicali di E. B.* (Turin, 1931); idem, *E. B.* (Turin, 1933); D. Newlin, "The Later Works of E. B.," *Musical Quarterly* (Oct. 1947); H. Cowell, "Current Chronicle,"

ibid. (1954); D.Z. Kushner, "A Commentary on E. B.'s Symphonic Works," *Radford Review* (Summer 1967); W.M. Jones, "E. B.'s Five String Quartets," *Music Review* (May 1967); M. Griffel, "Bibliography of Writings on E. B.," *Current Musicology,* 6 (1968); D.Z. Kushner, "Catalogue of the Works of E. B.," *American Music Teacher* (Feb./March 1969); A.V. Knapp, "The Jewishness of B.: Subconscious or Conscious," *Proceedings of the Royal Music Association* (1970/71); D.Z. Kushner, *E. B. and His Music* (Glasgow, 1973); R. Strassburg, *E. B.: Voice in the Wilderness* (Los Angeles, 1977; contains a list of unpubl. works and of MSS in the Library of Congress in Washington, D.C., and in the Bloch Archive at the Univ. of Calif., Berkeley); S. Bloch, *E. B.: Creative Spirit,* a program sourcebook (by the composer's daughter, in collaboration with I. Heskes; N.Y., 1976); C. Wheeler, "E. B.'s Solo Piano Music," *American Music Teacher* (Nov./Dec. 1980); D. Sills, "B. Manuscripts at the University of California," *Notes* (Sept. 1985); idem, "B. Manuscripts at the Library of Congress," ibid. (June 1986); D. Kushner, *E. B.: A Guide to Research* (N.Y., 1988).

Bloch, Suzanne, Swiss-American lutenist and harpsichordist, daughter of **Ernest Bloch;** b. Geneva, Aug. 7, 1907. She went to the U.S. with her father; studied there with him and with Roger Sessions; then in Paris with Nadia Boulanger. She became interested in early polyphonic music and began to practice on old instruments to be able to perform music on the instruments for which it was written.

Block, Michel, Belgian pianist; b. Antwerp, June 12, 1937. He grew up in Mexico; made his debut as a soloist with the National Orch. in Mexico when he was 16; then went to N.Y., where he studied at the Juilliard School of Music. He made his N.Y. debut in 1959; then made a successful career as soloist with orchs. in the U.S. and Europe.

Blockx, Jan, significant Flemish composer; b. Antwerp, Jan. 25, 1851; d. Kapellenbos, near Antwerp, May 26, 1912. He studied organ with Callaerts and composition with Benoit. In 1885 he became a lecturer at the Flemish Music School; also was music director of the Cercle Artistique and other societies in Belgium. With Benoit, he is regarded as the strongest representative of the national Flemish school of composition; while the melodic and rhythmic materials in his music strongly reflect Flemish folk elements, the treatment, contrapuntal and harmonic, is opulent, approaching Wagnerian sonorities.

WORKS: Operas: *Jets vergeten* (Antwerp, Feb. 19, 1877); *Maître Martin* (Brussels, Nov. 30, 1892); *Herbergprinses* (Antwerp, Oct. 10, 1896; produced in French as *Princesse d'auberge,* N.Y., March 10, 1909); *Thyl Uylenspiegel* (Brussels, Jan. 12, 1900); *De bruid der zee* (Antwerp, Nov. 30, 1901); *De kapel* (Antwerp, Nov. 7, 1903); *Baldie* (Antwerp, Jan. 25, 1908; rev. and perf. under the title *Liefdelied;* Antwerp, Jan. 6, 1912); a ballet, *Milenka* (1887); *Rubens,* overture for Orch.; *Romance* for Violin and Orch.; several choral works with Orch., among them: *Vredezang; Het droom vant paradies; De klokke Roelandt; Op den stroom; Scheldezang.*

BIBL.: L. Solvay, *Notice sur J. B.* (1920); F. Blockx, *J. B.* (1943).

Blodek, Wilhelm (Vilém), Czech composer; b. Prague, Oct. 3, 1834; d. there, May 1, 1874. He studied with J.F. Kittl and A. Dreyschock; taught for 3 years in Poland; then returned to Prague, and became a prof. of flute at the Prague Cons. (1860–70). In 1870 he became insane and spent the rest of his life in an asylum. His opera in the Czech language, *V studni* (In the Well), was produced with excellent success in Prague (Nov. 17, 1867); it was also given in German under the title *Im Brunnen* (Leipzig, 1893). His 2nd opera, *Zitek,* remained unfinished at his death; it was completed by F.X. Vana, and produced in Prague at the centennial of Blodek's birth (Oct. 3, 1934). Blodek also wrote a Sym. in D minor (1859) and a Flute Concerto (1862).

BIBL.: R. Budiš, *V. B.* (Prague, 1964).

Blom, Eric (Walter), preeminent English writer on music; b. Bern, Switzerland, Aug. 20, 1888; d. London, April 11, 1959.

He was of Danish and British extraction on his father's side; his mother was Swiss. He was educated in England. He was the London music correspondent for the *Manchester Guardian* (1923–31); then was the music critic of the *Birmingham Post* (1931–46) and of *The Observer* in 1949; ed. *Music & Letters* from 1937 to 1950 and from 1954 to the time of his death; he was also the editor of the Master Musicians series. In 1946 he was elected a member of the music committee of the British Council; in 1948, became member of the Royal Musical Assoc. In 1955 he was made a Commander of the Order of the British Empire in recognition of his services to music and received the honorary degree of D.Litt. from Birmingham Univ. In his writings Blom combined an enlightened penetration of musical esthetics with a literary capacity for presenting his subjects and stating his point of view in a brilliant journalistic manner. In his critical opinions he never concealed his disdain for some composers of great fame and renown, such as Rachmaninoff. In 1946 he was entrusted with the preparation of a newly organized and greatly expanded ed. of *Grove's Dictionary of Music and Musicians*, which was brought out under his editorship in 1954, in 9 vols., and for which Blom himself wrote hundreds of articles and translated entries by foreign contributors. In his adamant determination to make this ed. a truly comprehensive work, he insisted on the inclusion of complete lists of works of important composers and exact dates of performance of operas and other major works. In 1946 Blom publ. his 1st lexicographical work, *Everyman's Dictionary of Music*, which was reissued in an amplified ed. by D. Cummings in 1988. His other books include *Stepchildren of Music* (1923); *The Romance of the Piano* (1927); *A General Index to Modern Musical Literature in the English Language* (1927; indexes periodicals for the years 1915–26); *The Limitations of Music* (1928); *Mozart* (1935); *Beethoven's Pianoforte Sonatas Discussed* (1938); *A Musical Postbag* (1941; collected essays); *Music in England* (1942; rev. 1947); *Some Great Composers* (1944); *Classics, Major and Minor, with Some Other Musical Ruminations* (London, 1958).

Blomberg, Erik, Swedish composer; b. Järnskog, May 6, 1922. He studied with Erland von Koch and Gunnar Bucht; later went to Uppsala, where he became a music teacher.
   Works: 7 syms.: No. 1, *4 dramatiska skisser* (1966); No. 2, *3 studier i melodik* (1968); No. 3, *Associationskedjor* (1971); No. 4 (1973); No. 5 (1974); No. 6 (1982); No. 7 (1984); *3 Orchestral Fragments* (1968); *Dialog* for Piano and Orch. (1969); *Debatt* for Wind Orch. (1970); *Vila i rörelse* for String Orch. (1970); *Vom Tod* for Soloists, Chorus, and Instruments (1970); *Die allerbeste Gabe* for Soloists, Chorus, and Orch. (1972); *Kompriment 1–20* for various instrumental formations (1971–78); 3 string quartets; *4 Miniatures* for String Trio (1966); 3 piano sonatas (1965, 1968, 1971); *Intoning* for Orch. (1981); *Uttoning* for Orch. (1981).

Blomdahl, Karl-Birger, significant Swedish composer; b. Växjö, Oct. 19, 1916; d. Kungsängen, near Stockholm, June 14, 1968. He studied composition with Hilding Rosenberg and conducting with Tor Mann in Stockholm; in 1946 he traveled in France and Italy on a state stipend; in 1954–55 he attended a seminar at Tanglewood on a grant of the American-Scandinavian Foundation. Returning to Sweden, he taught composition at the Stockholm Musikhögskolan (1960–64); in 1964 he was appointed music director at the Swedish Radio. He was an organizer (with Bäck, Carlid, Johanson, and Lidholm) of a "Monday Group" in Stockholm, dedicated to the propagation of an objective and abstract idiom as distinct from the prevalent type of Scandinavian romanticism. Blomdahl's early works are cast in a neo-Classical idiom, but he then turned to advanced techniques, including the application of electronic music. His 3rd Sym., subtitled *Facetter* (Facets), utilizes dodecaphonic techniques. In 1959 he brought out his opera *Aniara*, which made him internationally famous; it pictures a pessimistic future when the remnants of the inhabitants of the planet Earth, devastated by atomic wars and polluted by radiation, are forced to emigrate to saner worlds in the galaxy; the score

employs electronic sounds, and its thematic foundation is derived from a series of 12 different notes and 11 different intervals. At the time of his death, Blomdahl was working on an opera entitled *The Saga of the Great Computer*, incorporating electronic and concrete sounds, and synthetic speech.
   Works: Trio for Oboe, Clarinet, and Bassoon (1938); String Quartet No. 1 (1939); *Symphonic Dances* (Göteborg, Feb. 29, 1940); *Concert Overture* (Stockholm, Feb. 14, 1942); Suite for Cello and Piano (1944); Viola Concerto (Stockholm, Sept. 7, 1944); Sym. No. 1 (Stockholm, Jan. 26, 1945); Concerto Grosso (Stockholm, Oct. 2, 1945); *Vaknatten* (The Wakeful Night), theater music (1945); *3 Polyphonic Pieces* for Piano (1945); String Trio (1945); Suite for Cello and Piano (1945); *Little Suite* for Bassoon and Piano (1945); Concerto for Violin and String Orch. (Stockholm, Oct. 1, 1947); Sym. No. 2 (1947; Stockholm, Dec. 12, 1952); *Dance Suite No. 1* for Flute, Violin, Viola, Cello, and Percussion (1948); String Quartet No. 2 (1948); *Pastoral Suite* for String Orch. (1948); *Prelude and Allegro* for Strings (1949); Sym. No. 3, *Facetter* (Facets; 1950; Frankfurt Festival, June 24, 1951); *Dance Suite No. 2* for Clarinet, Cello, and Percussion (1951); *I speglarnas sal* (In the Hall of Mirrors), oratorio of 9 sonnets from Erik Lindegren's *The Man without a Road*, for Soli, Chorus, and Orch. (1951–52; Stockholm, May 29, 1953); Chamber Concerto for Piano, Woodwinds, and Percussion (Stockholm, Oct. 30, 1953); *Sisyfos*, choreographic suite for Orch. (Stockholm, Oct. 20, 1954; produced as a ballet, Stockholm, April 18, 1957); Trio for Clarinet, Cello, and Piano (1955); *Anabase* for Baritone, Narrator, Chorus, and Orch. (Stockholm, Dec. 14, 1956); *Minotaurus*, ballet (Stockholm, April 5, 1958); *Aniara*, futuristic opera with electronic sound, after Harry Martinson's novel about an interplanetary voyage; libretto by Erik Lindegren (1957–59; Stockholm, May 31, 1959; numerous perfs. in Europe); *Fioriture* for Orch. (Cologne, June 17, 1960); *Forma ferritonans* for Orch. (Oxelösund, June 17, 1961); *Spel för åtta* (Game for 8), ballet (Stockholm, June 8, 1962; also a choreographic suite for Orch., 1964); *Herr von Hancken*, comic opera (Stockholm, Sept. 2, 1965); *Altisonans*, electronic piece from natural sound sources (1966); . . . *resan i denna natt* (. . . the voyage in this night), cantata, after Lindegren, for Soprano and Orch. (Stockholm, Oct. 19, 1966).
   Bibl.: G. Bucht, ed., *"Facetter" av och om K.-B. B.* (Stockholm, 1970; contains a complete catalogue of works and dates of 1st perfs.); R.K. Inglefield, "K.-B. B.: A Portrait," *Musical Quarterly* (Jan. 1972).

Blomstedt, Herbert (Thorson), prominent American-born Swedish conductor; b. Springfield, Mass. (of Swedish parents), July 11, 1927. He took courses at the Stockholm Musikhögskolan and at the Univ. of Uppsala; after conducting lessons with Igor Markevitch in Paris, he continued his training with Jean Morel at the Juilliard School of Music in N.Y. and with Leonard Bernstein at the Berkshire Music Center in Tanglewood, where he won the Koussevitzky Prize in 1953. In 1954 he made his professional conducting debut with the Stockholm Phil., then was music director of the Norrköping Sym. Orch. (1954–61); he subsequently held the post of 1st conductor of the Oslo Phil. (1962–68) while being concurrently active as a conductor with the Danish Radio Sym. Orch. in Copenhagen, where he served as chief conductor from 1967 to 1977. From 1975 to 1985 he was chief conductor of the Dresden Staatskapelle, with which he toured Europe and the U.S. (1979, 1983). From 1977 to 1983 he was chief conductor of the Swedish Radio Sym. Orch. in Stockholm. In 1985 he became music director of the San Francisco Sym., leading it at its 75th-anniversary gala concert in 1986 and on a tour of Europe in 1987. He has appeared as a guest conductor with many of the principal orchs. of the world.
   Bibl.: M. Steinbrink, "The San Francisco Symphony and Maestro H. B.," *Ovation* (Feb. 1987).

Blon, Franz von, German composer; b. Berlin, July 16, 1861; d. Seilershof, Oct. 21, 1945. He studied in Berlin; was active as a conductor. He wrote the operettas *Die Amazone* (1903) and *Die tolle Prinzess* (1913), and much instrumental music of a light variety, particularly waltzes and marches.

Blondeau, Pierre-Auguste-Louis, French violist and composer; b. Paris, Aug. 15, 1784; d. there, 1865. He studied at the Paris Cons. with Baillot, Gossec, and Méhul; won the Prix de Rome in 1808 with his cantata, *Maria Stuart;* was violist in the Grand Opéra Orch. until 1842. He wrote an opera, *Alla fontana;* a ballet; 3 overtures; church music; chamber music; piano pieces; songs; also a number of theoretical works.

Bloomfield, Fannie. See Zeisler, Fannie Bloomfield.

Bloomfield, Theodore (Robert), American conductor; b. Cleveland, June 14, 1923. He studied piano at the Oberlin Cons. (Mus.B., 1944); then took courses in conducting at the Juilliard School in N.Y.; also studied piano with Claudio Arrau and conducting with Pierre Monteux. In 1946–47 he was apprentice conductor to George Szell at the Cleveland Orch.; then conducted the Cleveland Little Sym. and the Civic Opera Workshop (1947–52). He was subsequently music director of the Portland (Oreg.) Sym. (1955–59) and of the Rochester (N.Y.) Phil. (1959–63). He then settled in Germany; was 1st conductor of the Hamburg State Opera (1964–66) and Generalmusikdirektor of Frankfurt (1966–68). From 1975 to 1982 he was chief conductor of the West Berlin Sym. Orch. He has established a fine reputation for his programs of rarely performed works by early and contemporary composers.

Blount, Herman. See Sun Ra.

Blow, John, great English composer and organist; b. Newark-on-Trent, Nottinghamshire (baptized), Feb. 23, 1649 (1648, Julian calendar); d. Westminster (London), Oct. 1, 1708. In 1660–61 he was a chorister at the Chapel Royal, under Henry Cooke; he later studied organ with Christopher Gibbons. His progress was rapid, and on Dec. 3, 1668, he was appointed organist of Westminster Abbey. In 1679 he left this post and Purcell, who had been Blow's student, succeeded him. After Purcell's untimely death in 1695, Blow was reappointed, and remained at Westminster Abbey until his death; he was buried there, in the north aisle. He married Elizabeth Braddock in 1674; she died in 1683 in childbirth, leaving 5 children. Blow held the rank of Gentleman of the Chapel Royal from March 16, 1674; on July 23, 1674, he succeeded Humfrey as Master of the Children of the Chapel Royal; was Master of the Choristers at St. Paul's (1687–1703); in 1699 he was appointed Composer of the Chapel Royal. He held the honorary Lambeth degree of D.Mus., conferred on him in 1677 by the Dean of Canterbury. While still a young chorister of the Chapel Royal, Blow began to compose church music; in collaboration with Humfrey and William Turner, he wrote the *Club Anthem* ("I will always give thanks"); at the behest of Charles II, he made a 2-part setting of Herrick's poem "Goe, perjur'd man." He wrote many secular part-songs, among them an ode for New Year's Day 1681/82, "Great sir, the joy of all our hearts," an ode for St. Cecilia; 2 anthems for the coronation of James II; *Epicedium for Queen Mary* (1695); *Ode on the Death of Purcell* (1696). Blow's collection of 50 songs, *Amphion Anglicus,* was publ. in 1700. His best-known work is *Masque for the Entertainment of the King: Venus and Adonis,* written c.1685; this is his only complete score for the stage, but he contributed separate songs for numerous dramatic plays. Purcell regarded Blow as "one of the greatest masters in the world." Fourteen large works by Blow, anthems and harpsichord pieces, have been preserved; 11 anthems are printed in Boyce's *Cathedral Musick* (1760–78). Selected anthems are publ. in Musica Britannica, 7. The vocal score of his masque *Venus and Adonis* was publ. by G.E.P. Arkwright in the Old English Edition (No. 25; 1902); the complete score was publ. by the Éditions de l'Oiseau Lyre, as ed. by Anthony Lewis (Paris, 1939).

BIBL.: H.W. Shaw, "J. B., Doctor of Music," *Musical Times* (Oct.–Dec. 1937; also separately, London, 1943); idem, "B.'s Use of the Ground Bass," *Musical Quarterly* (Jan. 1938); idem, "J. B.'s Anthems," *Music & Letters* (Oct. 1938); H.L. Clarke, "J. B.: A Tercentenary Survey," *Musical Quarterly* (July 1949); W. Shaw, "The Autographs of J. B.," *Music Review,* XXV (1964); R. McGuinness, *English Court Odes 1660–1820* (Oxford, 1971); B. Wood, *J. B.'s Anthems with Orchestra* (diss., Cambridge Univ., 1977).

Blum, Robert (Karl Moritz), important Swiss composer; b. Zürich, Nov. 27, 1900. He studied at the Zürich Cons. with Andreae, Jarnach, and others; in 1923 he took some lessons with Busoni. Upon his return to Switzerland, he devoted himself to choral conducting and teaching. In 1943 he was appointed prof. at the Music Academy in Zürich. In his compositions he cultivates polyphonic music in the traditional style, enhanced by modern harmonies and occasionally dissonant contrapuntal lines.

WORKS: Opera, *Amarapura* (1924); oratorio, *Kindheit Jesu* (1933); many sacred choral works and Psalms for Voice and Orch.; 6 syms. (1924, 1926, 1927, 1959, 1965, 1969); *Passionskonzert* for Organ and String Orch. (1943); *Seldwyla-Symphonie* (1968); *4 Partite* for Orch. (1929, 1935, 1953, 1967); Concerto for Orch. (1955); *Overture on Swiss Themes* (1944); *Christ ist erstanden,* orch. variations (1962); *Lamentatio angelorum* for Chamber Orch. (1943); Viola Concerto (1951); Oboe Concerto (1960); Concerto for Wind Quintet (1962); Triple Concerto for Violin, Oboe, Trumpet, and Chamber Orch. (1963); Flute Quartet (1963); Sonata for Flute and Violin (1963); *Concertante symphonie* for Wind Quintet and Chamber Orch. (1964); *Divertimento* on a 12-tone row for 10 Instruments (1966); *Le Tombe di Ravenna* for 11 Woodwind Instruments (1968); Quartet for Clarinet and String Trio (1970); String Quartet (1970); numerous songs, organ pieces, and arrangements of early vocal compositions.

BIBL.: G. Fierz, *R. B.: Leben und Werk* (Zürich, 1967); *Festschrift zum 75. Geburtstag R. B.* (Baden, 1975).

Blume, (Ferdinand Anton) Clemens, German music scholar; b. Billerbeck, Jan. 31, 1862; d. Königstein, April 8, 1932. He studied theology; then taught it at the Catholic Univ. in Frankfurt. He was regarded as an authority on texts of medieval Latin hymns. His books include *Cursus Sanctus Benedicti* (liturgical hymns of the 6th to 9th centuries; 1908); *Guide to Chevalier's "Repertorium Hymnologicum"* (1911); *Analecta hymnica medii aevi* (his standard work; 1896–1922); vols. 1–48 co-ed. with C.M. Dreves; some vols. with H.M. Bannister). A selection from this valuable sourcebook of hymnological research was extracted as *Ein Jahrtausend lateinischer Hymnendichtung* (2 vols., 1909). Blume also publ. *Unsere liturgischen Lieder* (Pustet, 1932).

Blume, Friedrich, preeminent German musicologist and editor; b. Schlüchtern, Jan. 5, 1893; d. there, Nov. 22, 1975. He was the son of a Prussian government functionary; 1st studied medicine in Eisenach; in 1911 he went to the Univ. of Munich, where he began his musicological studies; then went to the univs. of Leipzig and Berlin. During World War I he was in the German army; was taken prisoner by the British and spent 3 years in a prison camp in England. In 1919 he resumed his studies at the Univ. of Leipzig, where he took his Ph.D. in 1921 with the dissertation *Studien zur Vorgeschichte der Orchestersuite im 15. und 16. Jahrhundert* (publ. in Leipzig, 1925); in 1923 he became a lecturer in music at the Univ. of Berlin; in 1925 he completed his Habilitation there with *Das monodische Prinzip in der protestantischen Kirchenmusik* (publ. in Leipzig, 1925); was made Privatdozent there that same year; also lectured in music history at the Berlin-Spandau School of Church Music from 1928 to 1934. In 1934 he joined the faculty of the Univ. of Kiel, where he was prof. from 1938 until his retirement in 1958; was then made prof. emeritus. He was an authority on Lutheran church music; his *Die evangelische Kirchenmusik* was publ. in Bücken's *Handbuch der Musikwissenschaft,* X (1931; 2nd ed., rev., as *Geschichte der evangelischen Kirchenmusik,* 1965; in Eng., as *Protestant Church Music: A History,* 1974). He prepared a collected edition of the works of M. Praetorius (21 vols., Berlin, 1928–41); was general ed. of *Das Chorwerk,* a valuable collection of early polyphonic music (1929–38); also ed. of *Das Erbe deutscher*

Musik (1935–43). In 1943 he was entrusted with the preparation of the monumental encyclopedia *Die Musik in Geschichte und Gegenwart* (14 vols., Kassel, 1949–68); following its publication, he undertook the further task of preparing an extensive Supplement, which contained numerous additional articles and corrections of ascertainable errors; its publication was continued after his death by his daughter, Ruth Blume. He also wrote *Wesen und Werden deutscher Musik* (Kassel, 1944); *Johann Sebastian Bach im Wandel der Geschichte* (Kassel, 1947; Eng. tr. as *Two Centuries of Bach,* 1950); *Goethe und die Musik* (Kassel, 1948); *Was ist Musik?* (Kassel, 1959); *Umrisse eines neuen Bach-Bildes* (Kassel, 1962). His life's work was a study in the practical application of his vast erudition and catholic interests in musicological scholarship.

BIBL.: A. Abert and W. Pfannkuch, eds., *Festschrift F. B. zum 70. Geburtstag* (Kassel, 1963); G. Feder, "F. B. zum 80. Geburtstag," and G. Henle, "Zum 80. Geburtstag von F. B.," in *Haydn Studien* (Jan. 1973).

Blumenfeld, Felix (Mikhailovich), Russian composer and conductor; b. Kovalevka, near Kherson, April 19, 1863; d. Moscow, Jan. 21, 1931. He studied piano in Elizavetgrad; then went to St. Petersburg, where he studied composition with Rimsky-Korsakov; upon graduation in 1885, he joined the staff of the Cons. and taught there until 1905, and again from 1911 to 1918; from 1895 to 1911 he was the conductor at the Imperial Opera in St. Petersburg; he was also a guest conductor in the Russian repertoire in Paris during the "Russian seasons" in 1908. He was a pianist of virtuoso caliber; was also active as an accompanist for Chaliapin and other famous singers. From 1918 to 1922 he was a prof. of piano at the Cons. of Kiev, and from 1922 to his death he taught at the Moscow Cons. Among his piano students was Vladimir Horowitz. As a composer, Blumenfeld excelled mainly in his piano pieces and songs, many publ. by Belaiev. He also wrote a sym., entitled *To the Beloved Dead;* a String Quartet; some other pieces.

Blumenfeld, Harold, American composer; b. Seattle, Oct. 15, 1923. He studied composition with Bernard Rogers at the Eastman School of Music in Rochester, N.Y. (1941–43); after military service in World War II, he took courses in composition with Paul Hindemith at Yale Univ. (B.M., 1949; M.M., 1950); also studied conducting with Robert Shaw and Leonard Bernstein and operatic stage direction with Boris Goldovsky at the Berkshire Music Center at Tanglewood. In 1951 he became an assistant prof. at Washington Univ. in St. Louis; was director of the Opera Studio there (1963–71). From 1964 to 1968 he also was artistic director of the Opera Theatre of St. Louis.

WORKS: 3 operas: *Amphitryon 4,* after Molière (1962; the *Miniature Overture* has become successful as an orch. piece), *Fritzi* (1979), and *4-Score: An Opera of Opposites,* after Johann Nestroy's *Haus der Temperamente* (1984); *Transformations* for Piano (1963); *Expansions* for Woodwind Quintet (1964); *Movement* for Brass (1965); *War Lament* for a cappella Chorus, with Guitar obbligato, after Siegfried Sassoon (1970); *Eroscapes* for Coloratura Soprano, String Trio, and Woodwind Quintet, after poems of Isabella Gardner (1971); *Song of Innocence* for Soloists, Large Chorus, Chamber Chorus, and Orch., after Blake (1973); *Starfires,* cantata (1975); *Circle of the Eye,* song cycle after poems of Tom McKeown (1975); *Rilke* for Voice and Guitar (1975); *La Vie antérieure,* "spatial" cantata after Baudelaire (1976); *Voyages,* cantata after Hart Crane (1977); *Silentium,* song cycle after poems of Osip Mandelstam (1979); *La Voix reconnue,* cantata after Verlaine (1979); *La Face cendrée,* cantata after Rimbaud (1981).

Blumental, Felicja, Polish-born Brazilian pianist; b. Warsaw, Dec. 28, 1918. She studied piano at the Warsaw Cons.; in 1945 she emigrated to Brazil and became a Brazilian citizen. Villa-Lobos dedicated his 5th Piano Concerto to her; she played this work many times under his direction. Penderecki wrote his *Partita* for Harpsichord and Orch. for her.

Blumer, Theodor, German conductor and composer; b. Dresden, March 24, 1881; d. Berlin, Sept. 21, 1964. He studied at the Dresden Cons.; was active as a pianist, and from 1925 to 1931 as a conductor on Dresden Radio. From 1931 to 1942 he conducted radio broadcasts in Leipzig, and in 1952 he moved to Berlin. He wrote several light operas, among them *Der Fünf-Uhr-Tee* (Dresden, 1911) and *Trau schau wem!;* 3 syms.; several overtures; a considerable amount of chamber music, including duo sonatas, trios, quartets, quintets, and sextets; a goodly amount of songs.

Blumner, Martin, German choral conductor and composer; b. Fürstenberg, Mecklenburg, Nov. 21, 1827; d. Berlin, Nov. 16, 1901. He studied philosophy and mathematics at Berlin Univ.; then music with Siegfried Dehn. In 1847 he became a member of the Berlin Singakademie; was appointed associate conductor (1853), then chief conductor (1876). He composed oratorios: *Abraham* (1860) and *Der Fall Jerusalems* (1874); cantatas: *Columbus* (1852); *In Zeit und Ewigkeit* (1885); *Festival Cantata* (1891); a Te Deum in 8 parts; motets; Psalms; etc.

BIBL.: E. Dryander, *Zum Gedächtnis M. B.* (Berlin, 1901).

Blüthner, Julius (Ferdinand), celebrated German piano maker; b. Falkenhain, near Merseburg, March 11, 1824; d. Leipzig, April 13, 1910. In 1853 he founded his establishment at Leipzig with 3 workmen; by 1897 it had grown to a sizable company, producing some 3,000 pianos yearly. Blüthner's specialty was the "Aliquotflügel," a grand piano with a sympathetic octave-string stretched over and parallel with each unison struck by the hammers. He was awarded many medals for his contributions to the advancement of piano construction. He was co-author, with H. Gretschel, of *Lehrbuch des Pianofortebaus in seiner Geschichte, Theorie und Technik* (Weimar, 1872; 4th ed., 1921).

Boatwright, Howard (Leake, Jr.), American violinist, conductor, and composer; b. Newport News, Va., March 16, 1918. His mother was a registered nurse, his father a dentist; both liked to paint and both were musical. Boatwright had some violin lessons as a child; then was sent to Norfolk, where he studied with a professional violinist, Israel Feldman; at the age of 17 he made a debut as soloist with the Richmond (Va.) Sym. Orch. From 1943 to 1945 he taught violin at the Univ. of Texas in Austin; then decided to acquire a more solid training in composition and enrolled in the class of Paul Hindemith at Yale Univ. (1945–48). Subsequently he taught there (1948–64); concurrently served as music director at St. Thomas' Church in New Haven, Conn. (1949–64). From 1964 to 1972 he was dean of the music school at Syracuse Univ.; then taught music theory there. He continued to give violin recitals, usually with his wife, the soprano **Helen Boatwright,** as joint artist. From 1950 to 1962 he was concertmaster of the New Haven Orch., and from 1957 to 1960 conducted the Yale Univ. Sym. He became greatly interested in the musical folklore of Eastern nations. In 1959 he went to India on grants from the Fulbright and Rockefeller foundations, and wrote 2 valuable monographs, *A Handbook of Staff Notation for Indian Music* and *Indian Classical Music and the Western Listener,* both publ. in Bombay in 1960. In his own works he successfully attempted to revive the modalities of early church music, using modern harmonies and linear counterpoint. His best works are of this type, mostly written for chorus.

WORKS: *Variations* for Chamber Orch. (1949); Sym. (1976); 2 string quartets (1947, 1975); *Serenade* for 2 String Instruments and 2 Wind Instruments (1952); Clarinet Quartet (1958); 12 pieces for Solo Violin (1977); Clarinet Sonata (1980); Mass in C (1958); *The Passion According to St. Matthew* for Chorus (1962); *Canticle of the Sun* for Chorus (1963); choral pieces and songs, including *6 Prayers of Kierkegaard* for Soprano and Piano (1978).

Boatwright, McHenry, black American baritone; b. Tennile, Ga., Feb. 29, 1928. He studied at the New England Cons. in Boston; made his concert debut in 1956; sang in London in 1962; was soloist with the N.Y. Phil., the Philadelphia Orch., and other orchs. in the U.S. He created the central role in

Gunther Schuller's opera *The Visitation* (Hamburg, Oct. 12, 1966).

Boccherini, (Ridolfo) Luigi, famous Italian composer and cellist; b. Lucca, Feb. 19, 1743; d. Madrid, May 28, 1805. He grew up in a musical environment and became a cello player. In 1757 he was engaged as a member of the orch. of the Court Theater in Vienna. From 1761 to 1763 he was in Lucca; after a year in Vienna he returned to Lucca and played cello at the theater orch. there. He then undertook a concert tour with the violinist Filippo Manfredi in 1766. Then he went to Paris, where he appeared at the Concert Spirituel in 1768. He became exceedingly popular as a performer, and his own compositions were publ. in Paris; his 1st publications were 6 string quartets and 2 books of string trios. In 1769 he received a flattering invitation to the Madrid court, and became chamber composer to the Infante Luis; after the latter's death he served as court composer to Friedrich Wilhelm II of Prussia; was appointed to the German court on Jan. 21, 1786. After the death of the King in 1797 he returned to Madrid. In 1800 he enjoyed the patronage of Napoleon's brother, Lucien Bonaparte, who served as French ambassador to Madrid. Despite his successes at various European courts, Boccherini lost his appeal to his patrons and to the public. He died in poverty; in a belated tribute to a native son, the authorities in Lucca had his remains transferred there and reinterred with great solemnity in 1927. Boccherini had profound admiration for Haydn; indeed, so close was Boccherini's style to Haydn's that this affinity gave rise to the saying, "Boccherini is the wife of Haydn." He was an exceptionally fecund composer, specializing almost exclusively in chamber music. A list of his works includes 26 chamber syms.; 2 octets; 16 sextets; 125 string quintets; 12 piano quintets; 24 quintets for Strings and Flute (or Oboe); 91 string quartets; 48 string trios; 21 violin sonatas; 6 cello sonatas; also 11 cello concertos. He further wrote much guitar music, a Christmas cantata, and some sacred works.

BIBL.: D.M. Cerù, *Cenni intorno alla vita e le opere di L. B.* (Lucca, 1864); H.M. Schletterer, *B.* (Leipzig, 1882); G. Malfatti, *L. B. nell'arte, nella vita e nelle opere* (Lucca, 1905); L. Parodi, *L. B.* (1930); A. Bonaventura, *B.* (Milan, 1931); G. de Rothschild, *L. B.* (Paris, 1962; London, 1965); Y. Gérard, *Thematic, Bibliographical and Critical Catalogue of the Works of L. B.* (London, 1969); P. Carmirelli, ed., *Le opere complete di L. B.* (Rome, 1970); M. Ophee, *L. B.'s Guitar Quintets: New Evidence* (Boston, 1981); L. della Croce, *Il divino B.: Vita, opere, epistolario* (Padua, 1988).

Bochsa, (Robert-) Nicolas-Charles, celebrated French harpist; b. Montmédy, Meuse, Aug. 9, 1789; d. Sydney, Australia, Jan. 6, 1856. He 1st studied music with his father; played in public at the age of 7; wrote a sym. when he was 9, and an opera, *Trajan,* at 15. He then studied with Franz Beck in Bordeaux, and later at the Paris Cons. with Méhul and Catel (1806). His harp teachers were Nadermann and Marin. Of an inventive nature, Bochsa developed novel technical devices for harp playing, transforming the harp into a virtuoso instrument. He was the court harpist to Napoleon, and to Louis XVIII. He wrote 7 operas for the Opéra-Comique (1813–16), several ballets, an oratorio, and a great number of works for the harp; also a method for harp. In 1817 he became involved in some forgeries, and fled to London to escape prison. He became very popular as a harp teacher in London society; organized a series of oratorio productions with Sir George Smart (1822). He was also the 1st prof. of harp at the Academy of Music in London, but in 1827 he lost his position when he committed bigamy. However, he obtained a position as conductor of the Italian Opera at the King's Theatre (1826–30). Another scandal marked Bochsa's crooked road to success and notoriety when he eloped with the soprano **Anna Bishop,** the wife of Henry Bishop, in Aug. 1839. He gave concerts with her in Europe, America, and Australia, where he died.

BIBL.: A. Pougin, "Un Musicien voleur, faussaire et bigame," *Le Ménestrel* (Jan. 19–March 9, 1907); J.B. Weidensaul, "B.: A Biographical Sketch," *American Harp Journal* (Fall 1970).

Bock, Jerry (Jerrold Lewis), American songwriter of popular music; b. New Haven, Conn., Nov. 23, 1928. He studied at the Univ. of Wisconsin; subsequently settled in N.Y. He gained wide recognition with his Broadway musicals *Mr. Wonderful* (1956), *The Body Beautiful* (1958), and *Fiorello!* (1959), the last based on the life of Fiorello LaGuardia. His greatest success was *Fiddler on the Roof* (1964), which was also made into a movie.

Bockelmann, Rudolf (August Louis Wilhelm), German bass-baritone; b. Bodenteich, April 2, 1892; d. Dresden, Oct. 9, 1958. He studied singing with Karl Scheidemantel and Oscar Lassner in Leipzig. In 1920 he made his operatic debut in Celle. He then sang at the Neues Theater (1921–26) and at the Stadttheater in Hamburg (1926–32); appeared at the Bayreuth Festival in 1928; in 1929 and from 1934 to 1938 he sang at Covent Garden, London; from 1930 to 1932 he was on the roster of the Chicago Opera Co. In 1932 he became a member of the Staatsoper in Berlin for the duration of the war. His crypto-Nazi inclinations precluded further engagements outside Germany. He was particularly noted for his congenial interpretations of villainous Wagnerian bass roles. His own notations on operatic techniques were publ. in the *Sammelbände der Robert-Schumann-Gesellschaft,* II/1966 (Leipzig, 1967).

Boda, John, American composer; b. Boycesville, Wis., Aug. 2, 1922. He studied at the Eastman School of Music in Rochester, N.Y.; in 1946 joined the faculty of Florida State Univ. at Tallahassee. His *Sinfonia* was 1st performed in Knoxville, Tenn., on Dec. 6, 1960.

Bodanzky, Artur, famous Austrian conductor; b. Vienna, Dec. 16, 1877; d. N.Y., Nov. 23, 1939. He studied at the Vienna Cons., and later with Zemlinsky. He began his career as a violinist in the Vienna Court Opera Orch. In 1900 he received his 1st appointment as a conductor, leading an operetta season in Budweis; in 1902 he became assistant to Mahler at the Vienna Court Opera; conducted in Berlin (1905) and in Prague (1906–9). In 1909 he was engaged as music director at Mannheim. In 1912 he arranged a memorial Mahler Festival, conducting a huge ensemble of 1,500 vocalists and instrumentalists. He conducted *Parsifal* at Covent Garden in London in 1914; his success there led to an invitation to conduct the German repertoire at the Metropolitan Opera in N.Y.; he opened his series with *Götterdämmerung* (Nov. 18, 1915). From 1916 to 1931 he was director of the Soc. of Friends of Music in N.Y.; from 1919 to 1922 he also conducted the New Sym. Orch. He made several practical arrangements of celebrated operas (*Oberon, Don Giovanni, Fidelio,* etc.), which he used for his productions with the Metropolitan Opera. His style of conducting was in the Mahler tradition, with emphasis on climactic effects and contrasts of light and shade.

Böddecker, Philipp Friedrich, German organist, bassoonist, and composer; b. Hagenau, Alsace (baptized), Aug. 5, 1607; d. Stuttgart, Oct. 8, 1683. He 1st studied in Stuttgart with J.U. Steigleder; from 1626 to 1629 served as organist and singing master in Buchsweiler, Alsace; was then organist and bassoonist at the courts in Darmstadt and Durlach. In 1638 he became organist at Frankfurt's Barfüsserkirche; in 1642 was appointed organist at the Strasbourg Cathedral; in 1648 received the post of organist and director of music at the Univ. of Strasbourg. In 1652 he settled in Stuttgart as organist at the collegiate church there. He publ. the treatise *Manuductio nova methodica-practica bassum generalem* (Stuttgart, 1701). He composed *Melos irenicum* for 6 Soloists, 4-part Chorus, and Instruments (Strasbourg, 1650); also 8 sacred concertos. His son, **Philipp Jakob Böddecker** (b. Frankfurt, 1642; d. Stuttgart, Feb. 1, 1707), was also an organist and composer; he succeeded his father as organist at the collegiate church in Stuttgart (from 1686).

Bode, Johann Joachim Christoph, German instrumentalist and composer; b. Barum, Jan. 12, 1730; d. Weimar, Dec. 13, 1793. He began his career as a bassoon player; also played cello in the Collegium Musicum in Helmstedt and oboe in Celle; in 1757 he went to Hamburg, where he was active as a teacher, writer, publisher, and translator; in 1778 he settled in Weimar as a diplomat. As a composer, he wrote several syms., a Cello Concerto, a Violin Concerto, a Bassoon Concerto, and songs.

BIBL.: E. Greeven, *J.J.C. B., Ein Hamburger Uebersetzer, Verleger und Drucker* (Weimar, 1938).

Bode, Rudolf, German acoustician and theorist of rhythmic gymnastics; b. Kiel, Feb. 3, 1881; d. Munich, Oct. 7, 1970. He studied physiology and philosophy at the Univ. of Leipzig, and music theory at the Leipzig Cons. After attending the Dalcroze Inst. of Eurhythmics in Hellerau, he formulated a system of "rhythmic gymnastics." In 1911 he founded a school in Munich with courses embodying his body theories, intended to achieve perfect physical and mental health. He publ. a number of books and essays on the subject: *Der Rhythmus und seine Bedeutung für die Erziehung* (Jena, 1920); *Ausdruckgymnastik* (Munich, 1922; in Eng. as *Expressions-Gymnastic*, N.Y., 1931); *Musik und Bewegung* (Kassel, 1930); *Energie und Rhythmus* (Berlin, 1939). He also wrote a manual of piano study as a rhythmic muscular action, *Rhythmus und Anschlag* (Munich, 1933).

Bodenschatz, Erhard, German theologian and music editor; b. Lichtenberg, 1576; d. Gross-Osterhausen, near Querfurt, 1636. He was a pupil of Calvisius in Pforta; then studied theology in Leipzig. In 1600 he became cantor in Schulpforta; in 1603 was pastor in Rehausen, and in 1608, in Gross-Osterhausen, where he remained until his death. He publ. several valuable collections of motets and hymns; particularly important is *Florilegium portense* in 2 parts: the 1st part orig. contained 89 motets (Leipzig, 1603; 2nd ed., with 120 motets, 1618) and the 2nd part (Leipzig, 1621) contained 150 motets, all by contemporary composers. There have been several reprints. He also publ. *Florilegium selectissimorum hymnorum* in 4 vols. (Leipzig, 1606). Bodenschatz's own compositions are not distinctive.

BIBL.: O. Riemer, *E. B. und sein Florilegium portense* (Leipzig, 1928).

Bodin, Lars-Gunnar, Swedish composer; b. Stockholm, July 15, 1935. He studied composition with Lennart Wenström (1956–60); attended the Darmstadt summer courses (1961); in 1972 he was composer-in-residence at Mills College in Oakland, Calif.; and in 1978 he became director of the electronic studio at the Stockholm Cons. In collaboration with the Swedish concrete poet and composer Bengt Emil Johnson, he produced a series of pieces described as "text-sound compositions."

WORKS: Dance: *Place of Plays* (1967); *. . . from one point to any other point* (1968); *Händelser och handlingar* (1971). Chamber: *Music for 4 Brass Instruments* (1960); *Arioso* for Clarinet, Trombone, Cello, Piano, and Percussion (1962); *Semikolon: Dag Knutson in memoriam* for Horn, Trombone, Electric Guitar, Piano, and Organ (1963); *Calendar Music* for Piano (1964). Live and Electronic: *My World—Is Your World* for Organ and Tape (1966); *Primary Structures* for Bassoon and Tape (1976); *Enbart för Kerstin* for Mezzo-soprano and Tape (1979); *Anima* for Soprano, Flute, and Tape (1984); *On Speaking Terms* for Trombone and Tape (1984); *Diskus* for Wind Quintet and Tape (1987). Electronic: *Winter Events* (1967); *Toccata* (1969); *Traces I* (1970) and *II* (1971); *Mémoires d'un temps avant la destruction* (1982); *For Jon II: Retrospective Episodes* (1986); also an intermedia piece, *Clouds* (1973–76); many text-sound compositions.

Bodky, Erwin, German-American music scholar; b. Ragnit, March 7, 1896; d. Lucerne, Switzerland, Dec. 6, 1958. He studied piano and theory in Berlin with Dohnányi and Juon; later attended classes of Richard Strauss and Busoni at the Meisterschule für Komposition (1920–22). He subsequently taught at the Scharwenka Cons. With the advent of the Nazi regime in 1933, Bodky went to Amsterdam, where he remained until 1938; then emigrated to the U.S., and taught at the Longy

School of Music in Cambridge, Mass. (1938–48); in 1949 was appointed a prof. at Brandeis Univ.

WRITINGS: *Der Vortag alter Klaviermusik* (Berlin, 1932); *Das Charakterstück* (Berlin, 1933); *The Interpretation of J.S. Bach's Keyboard Works* (Cambridge, Mass., 1960; also in German, Tutzing, 1970).

BIBL.: H. Slosbert et al., eds., *E. B.: A Memorial Tribute* (Waltham, Mass., 1965).

Bodley, Seóirse, Irish composer; b. Dublin, April 4, 1933. He studied at the Royal Irish Academy of Music and at Univ. College in Dublin (B.Mus., 1955). From 1957 to 1959 he took courses in composition with Johann Nepomuk David in Stuttgart. Returning to Dublin, he was appointed lecturer at Univ. College (D.Mus., 1960). He devoted himself to a thorough study of Gaelic folksinging; his own music reflects this preoccupation; but he also experimented with serial techniques and novel instrumental combinations. His works include 3 syms. (1958–59; 1980; 1981); 2 chamber syms. (1964, 1982); a Violin Sonata (1957); *Scintillae* for 2 Harps (1968); String Quartet (1969); choruses to English and Gaelic texts; and incidental music to the television documentary *James Joyce* (1981).

Body, Jack, New Zealand composer, teacher, and ethnomusicologist; b. Te Aroha, Oct. 7, 1944. He studied with Robin Maconie at the Univ. of Auckland, later traveling to Germany, where he studied with Mauricio Kagel and Gottfried Michael Koenig. In 1976–77 he taught at the Akademi Musik Indonesia in Java, and in 1980 joined the faculty of the Victoria Univ. at Wellington. Besides numerous works for conventional forces, he created tape and mixed-media works that imaginatively synthesize non-Western musical materials with contemporary compositional techniques; his *Melodies* for Orch. (1983) is made up of recompositions of Greek fiddle music, Japanese shakuhachi, and the music of an Indian street band. He is ed. of Wai-te-ata Music Editions and has exhibited work in experimental video and photography.

WORKS: *Musik Anak-Anak* (1978); *Fanfares* (1981); *5 Melodies* for Piano (1982); *Love Sonnets of Michelangelo* for Voices (1982); *Melodies* for Orch. (1983); *Jangkrik Genggong* (1986); also tape pieces.

Boeck, August de, Belgian composer; b. Merchtem, May 9, 1865; d. there, Oct. 9, 1937. He studied organ at the Brussels Cons.; subsequently was church organist in Brussels; later taught harmony at the Royal Flemish Cons. at Antwerp and at the Brussels Cons. In 1930 he returned to his native town. He wrote operas and incidental music for stage plays; *Rapsodie Dahoméenne* for Orch., on exotic African themes (1893); an orch. fantasy on Flemish folk songs (1923); many songs to French and Flemish texts. Much of his orch. music is infused with impressionistic colors.

BIBL.: F. Rasse, *A. D.B.* (Brussels, 1943).

Boehe, Ernst, German composer and conductor; b. Munich, Dec. 27, 1880; d. Ludwigshafen, Nov. 16, 1938. He studied with Rudolf Louis and Thuille in Munich; in 1907 was associate conductor, with Courvoisier, of the Munich Volkssymphoniekonzerte; from 1913 to 1920 was court conductor at Oldenburg; then conducted concerts in Ludwigshafen. His works are of a programmatic type, the orchestration emphasizing special sonorities of divided strings, massive wind instruments, and various percussive effects; his tone poems show a decisive Wagnerian influence, having a system of identification motifs. His most ambitious work was an orch. tetralogy on Homer's *Odyssey*, under the general title *Odysseus' Fahrten*, comprising *Odysseus' Ausfahrt und Schiffbruch* (Munich, Feb. 20, 1903; Philadelphia, Dec. 3, 1904), *Die Insel der Kirke, Die Klage der Nausikaa*, and *Odysseus' Heimkehr;* also the symphonic poem *Taormina* (Essen, 1906; Boston Sym., Nov. 29, 1907).

BIBL.: E. Istel, "E. B.," *Monographien moderner Musiker* (Leipzig, 1909).

Boëllmann, Léon, French composer; b. Ensisheim, Alsace, Sept. 25, 1862; d. Paris, Oct. 11, 1897. He studied organ with Gigout; later was an organ teacher in Paris. He left 68 publ.

works; his *Variations symphoniques* for Cello and Orch. became part of the repertoire of cello players. He wrote a sym., *Fantaisie dialoguée*, for Organ and Orch.; *Suite gothique* for Organ; Piano Quartet; Piano Trio; Cello Sonata; *Rapsodie carnavalesque* for Piano, 4-hands. He also publ. a collection of 100 pieces for organ under the title *Heures mystiques*.
BIBL.: P. Locard, *L. B.* (Strasbourg, 1901).

Boëly, Alexandre Pierre François, French organist and composer; b. Versailles, April 19, 1785; d. Paris, Dec. 27, 1858. His father, a court musician, gave him his 1st instruction in music. Boëly studied piano and organ; occupied various positions as a church organist in Paris. As a teacher, he exercised a profound influence; Franck and Saint-Saëns owed much to him in the development of their style of composition for organ.
BIBL.: A. Gastoué, "A Great French Organist: A. B. and His Works," *Musical Quarterly* (July 1944); N. Dufourcq, "Le 'Cas' B.," *L'Orgue* (April/June 1971).

Boelza, Igor, Russian music scholar and composer; b. Kielce, Poland, Feb. 8, 1904. He studied philology at the Univ. of Kiev; then taught at the Kiev Cons. (1929–41); then was on the staff of the Moscow Cons. (1942–49); was also a member of the board of the State Music Publishing House in Moscow (1941–48) and on the staff of the Inst. for the History of the Arts (1954–61); in 1961 he became a member of the Inst. for Slavonic Studies at the Academy of Sciences of the U.S.S.R. He contributed numerous informative articles dealing with the music of the Slavic countries to various publications; publ. *Handbook of Soviet Musicians* (London, 1943); *Czech Opera Classics* (Moscow, 1951); *History of Polish Musical Culture* (Moscow, 1954); and *History of Czech Musical Culture* (2 vols., Moscow, 1959–73).

Boepple, Paul, Swiss-American choral conductor and pedagogue; b. Basel, July 19, 1896; d. Brattleboro, Vt., Dec. 21, 1970. He took courses at the Dalcroze Inst. in Geneva, and adopted the Dalcroze system in his own method of teaching music; from 1918 to 1926 he was a member of the faculty of the Inst. In 1926 he emigrated to the U.S.; directed the Dalcroze School of Music in N.Y. (1926–32); then taught at the Chicago Musical College (1932–34) and at the Westminster Choir School in Princeton, N.J. (1935–38); subsequently he taught at Bennington College in Vermont. As a choral conductor, he gave numerous performances of modern works.

Boero, Felipe, Argentine opera composer; b. Buenos Aires, May 1, 1884; d. there, Aug. 9, 1958. He studied with Pablo Berutti; received a government prize for further study in Europe, and attended the classes of Vidal and Fauré at the Paris Cons. (1912–14). Returning to Buenos Aires, he became active as a teacher. Among his operas, the following were produced at the Teatro Colón: *Tucumán* (June 29, 1918); *Ariana y Dionisios* (Aug. 5, 1920), *Raquela* (June 25, 1923), *Las Bacantes* (Sept. 19, 1925), *El Matrero* (July 12, 1929), and *Siripo* (June 8, 1937).

Boesch, Christian, Austrian baritone; b. Vienna, July 27, 1941. He pursued his training at the Vienna Hochschule für Musik, and in 1966 made his operatic debut at the Bern Stadttheater. He became a member of the Vienna Volksoper in 1975, later scoring notable success at the Salzburg Festival in 1978 for his portrayal of Papageno, a role he also chose for his Metropolitan Opera debut in N.Y. on Feb. 17, 1979. He later sang Wozzeck and Masetto at the Metropolitan.

Boesch, Rainer, Swiss composer; b. Männedorf, Aug. 11, 1938. He studied in Zürich and Geneva; then took courses with Messiaen in Paris. After his return to Switzerland, he was active as a pianist. He composed a number of electronic and mixed-media works.

Boesmans, Philippe, Belgian composer; b. Tongeren, May 17, 1936. He studied composition with Froidebise and Pousseur, and piano at the Liège Cons. (1954–62). His music adheres to the abstract trends of cosmopolitan modernism, with structural formulas determining the contents.

WORKS: *Étude I* for Piano (1963); *Sonance I* for 2 Pianos (1964); *Sonance II* for 3 Pianos (1967); *Impromptu* for 23 Instruments (1965); *Corrélations* for Clarinet and 2 Instrumental Ensembles (Brussels, Sept. 16, 1967); *Explosives* for Harp and 10 Instrumentalists (1968); *Verticles* for Orch. (1969); *Blocage* for Voice, Chorus, and Chamber Ensemble (1970); *Upon La, Mi* for Voice, Amplified Horn, and Instrumental Ensemble (1970); *Fanfare* for 2 Pianos (1971); *Intervalles I* for Orch. (1972); *Intervalles II* for Orch. (1973); *Intervalles III* for Voice and Orch. (1974); *Sur Mi* for 2 Pianos, Electric Organ, Crotale, and Tam-Tam (1974); *Multiples* for 2 Pianos and Orch. (1974); *Element—Extensions* for Piano and Chamber Orch. (1976); *Doublures* for Harp, Piano, Percussion, and 4 Instrumental Groups (1977); *Conversions* for Orch. (1980); *La Passion de Gilles*, opera (Brussels, Oct. 18, 1983); *Ricercar sconvolto* for Organ (1983).

Boësset, Antoine (Sieur de Villedieu), French composer of ballets; b. Blois, 1586; d. Paris, Dec. 8, 1643. He was court musician to Louis XIII, and wrote many *Airs de cour* for court performances; an Eng. ed. of these works was publ. in 1629 under the title *French Court Aires;* a number of these were reprinted by H. Expert in *Chants de France et d'Italie.*

Boetius (or Boethius), Anicius Manlius Torquatus Severinus, Roman philosopher and mathematician; b. Rome, A.D. c.480; executed in 524 on suspicion of treason, by the Emperor Theodoric, whose counselor he had been for many years. Boetius wrote a treatise in 5 books, *De Institutione Musica*, which was the chief sourcebook for the theorizing monks of the Middle Ages; this treatise was publ. in Venice (1491, 1499), in Basel (1570), in Leipzig (1867), and in a German tr. by Oscar Paul (Leipzig, 1872); a French tr. by Fétis remains in MS. Whether the notation commonly called "Boetian" (using Latin indices to denote traditional Greek notation) is properly attributable to him has been questioned for about 3 centuries (cf. Meibom, *Antiquae musicae auctores septem;* p. 7 of introduction on Alypius). For a defense of its authenticity, see F. Celentano, "La Musica presso i Romani," *Rivista Musicale Italiana* (1913). In this connection see also H. Potizon, *Boèce, théoricien de la musique grecque* (Paris, 1961). L. Schrade wrote several essays on Boetius: "Das propädeutische Ethos in der Musikanschauung des Boetius," *Zeitschrift für Geschichte der Erziehung und des Unterrichts* (1930); "Die Stellung der Musik in der Philosophie des Boetius," *Archiv für Geschichte der Philosophie* (1932); and "Music in the Philosophy of Boetius," *Musical Quarterly* (April 1947).

Boettcher, Wilfried, German cellist and conductor; b. Bremen, Aug. 11, 1929. He studied cello with Arthur Troester in Hamburg and with Pierre Fournier in Paris; also took some lessons with Pablo Casals; was subsequently principal cellist of the Hannover Opera (1956–58); in 1958 he became a prof. of cello at the Vienna Academy of Music; in 1959 he founded a chamber group, Die Wiener Solisten, and toured with it abroad. In 1965 he became a prof. at the Hochschule für Musik in Hamburg; was also chief conductor of the Hamburg Sym. Orch. (1967–71), and had engagements as a guest conductor in Germany, England, and France. From 1986 he was principal guest conductor of the Northern Sinfonia of England at Newcastle upon Tyne.

Boetticher, Wolfgang, noted German musicologist; b. Bad Ems, Aug. 19, 1914. He studied musicology at the Univ. of Berlin with Schering, Schünemann, Blume, and others; received his Ph.D. there in 1939 with the dissertation *Robert Schumann: Einführung in Persönlichkeit und Werk* (publ. in Berlin, 1941); completed his Habilitation in musicology there in 1943 with his *Studien zur solistischen Lautenpraxis des 16. und 17. Jahrhunderts* (publ. in Berlin, 1943). In 1948 he joined the faculty of the Univ. of Göttingen; was prof. of musicology there from 1956 to 1959; from 1958 also taught at the Technical Univ. in Clausthal. He is an acknowledged authority on the music of the Renaissance and the 19th century; his writings on lute music, Orlando di Lasso, and Robert Schumann are valuable.

WRITINGS: *Robert Schumann in seinen Schriften und Briefen* (Berlin, 1942); *Orlando di Lasso und seine Zeit* (2 vols., Kassel and Basel, 1958); *Von Palestrina zu Bach* (Stuttgart, 1959; 2nd ed., enl., 1981); *Dokumente und Briefe um Orlando di Lasso* (Kassel, 1960); *Aus Orlando di Lassos Wirkungskreis, Neue archivalische Studien zur Münchener Musikgeschichte* (Kassel and Basel, 1963); *Neue Forschungsergebnisse im Gebiet der musikalischen Renaissance* (Göttingen, 1964); *Die Familienkassette Schumanns in Dresden: Unbekannte Briefe an Robert und Clara Schumann* (Leipzig, 1974); *Robert Schumanns Klavierwerke: Entstehung, Urtext, Gestalt: Untersuchungen anhand unveröffentlichter Skizzen und biographischer Dokumente* (Wilhelmshaven, 1976–).
BIBL.: H. Hüschen and D.-R. Moser, eds., *Convivium musicorum: Festschrift W. B. zum sechzigsten Geburtstag* (Berlin, 1974).

Bogatyrev, Anatoly (Vasilievich), Soviet composer; b. Vitebsk, Aug. 13, 1913. He studied composition with Zolotarev at the Belorussian Cons. in Minsk, graduating in 1937; was an instructor there from 1948. He wrote 2 patriotic operas: *In the Forests of Polesye* (Minsk, Aug. 28, 1939) and *Nadezhda Durova* (Minsk, Dec. 22, 1956); 2 syms. (1946, 1947); cantatas: *The Leningraders* (1942); *Belorussia* (1949); *Glory Be to Lenin* (1952); Cello Concerto (1962); Concerto for Double Bass and Orch. (1964).

Bogatyrev, Semyon(ovich), Russian musicologist and composer; b. Kharkov, Feb. 15, 1890; d. Moscow, Dec. 31, 1960. He studied law at the Univ. of Kharkov, graduating in 1912; then went to St. Petersburg, where he enrolled at the Cons. in the composition classes of Kalafati and Wihtol and the orchestration class of Maximilian Steinberg. Upon graduating, he joined the faculty of the Kharkov Cons. (1917–19); subsequently was a lecturer at the Kharkov Inst. of Music and Drama (1922–41). In 1943 he was appointed to the faculty of the Moscow Cons., and remained there until his death. He publ. the valuable manuals *Double Canon* (Moscow, 1947) and *Retrograde Counterpoint* (Moscow, 1960). Bogatyrev undertook in 1957 the reconstruction and completion of Tchaikovsky's unfinished Sym. in E-flat major, which was publ. as the 7th Sym. His own compositions include works for orch., as well as 2 string quartets and 2 piano sonatas. A memorial vol. containing his writings was publ. in Moscow in 1972.

Bogdanov-Berezovsky, Valerian (Mikhailovich), Soviet composer and musicologist; b. Starozhilovka, near St. Petersburg, July 17, 1903; d. Moscow, May 13, 1971. He studied with Maximilian Steinberg and Liapunov at the Leningrad Cons., graduating in 1927; taught there from 1945 to 1948, and was in charge of the artistic direction of the Leningrad Theater of Opera and Ballet from 1951 to 1962. He wrote operas: *The Frontier* (1941), *The Leningraders* (1943), and *Nastasia Filippovna,* after Dostoevsky's novel *The Idiot* (1964); several ballets, including *The Seagull,* after Chekhov (1959); 2 syms. (1933, 1953); Piano Concerto; Violin Concerto; some chamber music; choruses. He was known chiefly as a critic and historian of Russian music; wrote several monographs on Soviet composers and contributed numerous articles to Soviet journals.
BIBL.: I. Gusin, *V. B.-B.* (Leningrad, 1966).

Bogianckino, Massimo, Italian pianist, musicologist, and administrator; b. Rome, Nov. 10, 1922. He studied piano with Casella at the Accademia di Santa Cecilia in Rome and with Cortot at the École Normale de Musique in Paris; also took courses in musicology with Ronga at the Univ. of Rome and with P.M. Masson at the Sorbonne in Paris. He taught at the Carnegie Inst. in Pittsburgh (1948–51), at the Pesaro Cons. (1951–57), and at the Rome Cons. (1957–67). In 1967 he joined the faculty of the Univ. of Perugia. He served as artistic director of the Rome Opera (1963–68), the Spoleto Festival of Two Worlds (1968–71), La Scala in Milan (1972–74), and the Teatro Comunale in Florence (from 1975). From 1983 to 1985 he was director of the Paris Opéra; then was mayor of Florence. He wrote the vols. *L'arte clavicembalistica di Domenico Scarlatti* (Rome, 1956; in Eng. as *The Harpsichord Sonatas of Domenico Scarlatti,* Rome, 1968) and *Aspetti del teatro musicale in Italia e in Francia nell'età barocca* (Rome, 1968).

Boguslawski, Edward, Polish composer; b. Chorzów, Sept. 22, 1940. He studied composition with Szabelski in Katowice and with Haubenstock-Ramati in Vienna. In 1963 he joined the faculty of the State College of Music in Katowice. His music makes use of impressionistic techniques.
WORKS: *Intonazioni I* for 9 Instruments (1962); *Intonazioni II* for Orch. (1967); *Apocalypse* for Narrator, Chorus, and Instruments (1965); *Signals* for Orch. (1965–66); *Metamorphoses* for Oboe, Clarinet, 2 Violins, Viola, and Cello (1967); *Canti* for Soprano and Orch. (1967); Concerto for Oboe, Oboe d'Amore, English Horn, Musette, and Orch. (1967–68); *Versions* for 6 Instruments (1968); *Musica per Ensemble MW–2* for Flute, Cello, and 2 Pianos (1970); Trio for Flute, Oboe, and Guitar (1970); *Per Pianoforte* (1971); *Capriccioso-Notturno* for Orch. (1972); *Impromptu* for Flute, Viola, and Harp (1972); *L'Être* for Soprano, Flute, Cello, and 2 Pianos (1973); *Pro Varsovia* for Orch. (1973–74); *Musica notturna* for Musette and Piano (1974); *Evocations* for Baritone and Orch. (1974); *Divertimento* for Chamber Ensemble (1975); Concerto for Oboe, Soprano, and Orch. (1975–76); *Beelzebub's Sonata,* chamber opera (Wroclaw, Nov. 19, 1977); *Musica concertante* for Saxophone and Orch. (1980); Piano Concerto (1981); Sym. Concertante for Violin and Chamber Orch. (1982); *Polonia,* symphonic poem for Violin and Orch. (1984); *The Game of Dreams,* musical drama (1985); *Les Extrêmes se touchent* for Orch. (1986).

Boháč, Josef, Czech composer; b. Vienna, March 25, 1929. After a preliminary course of music studies in Vienna, he went to Brno, where he studied with Petrželka at the Janáček Academy of Music and Dramatic Art (1955–59); upon graduation he became active in the musical programming on Czech television; he was also secretary of the Union of Czech Composers (from 1979). His music follows the median line of Central European modernism, with occasional resort to serial methods.
WORKS: Chamber opera, after Chekhov, *Námluvy* (The Wooing; 1967; Ustí nad Laben, Dec. 15, 1972); television opera, *Oči* (The Eyes; 1973; Prague Television, Oct. 5, 1974); opera, *Goya* (1972–77; Ostrava, 1977); *Zlatá svatba* (Golden Wedding; 1981); Suite for String Quartet (1953); Cello Sonata (1954); *Rhapsody* for Orch. (1955); *Symphonic Overture* (1964); *Sinfonietta concertante* (1964–65; Prague, March 14, 1966); String Trio (1965); *Suita drammatica* for Strings and Timpani (1969–70; Prague, March 23, 1974); *My Lute Sounds,* monodrama cycle of 12 songs on love, sickness, and death, for Tenor and Nonet (1971); *Southern Rainbow,* suite for Orch. (1971); *Sonetti per Sonatori* for Flute, Bass Clarinet, Percussion, and Piano (1974; for the chamber group Sonatori di Praga); Piano Concerto (1974; Prague, March 29, 1976); Concerto for Orch. (1983); *Dramatic Variants* for Viola and Orch. (1983); *Sonata Giovane* for Piano (1983).

Böhm, Georg, German organist; b. Hohenkirchen, Thuringia, Sept. 2, 1661; d. Lüneburg, May 18, 1733. He studied at the Univ. of Jena; was in Hamburg in 1693; in 1698 he became organist at the Johanniskirche in Lüneburg. His organ preludes and harpsichord pieces are exemplars of keyboard works of his time; Bach himself was influenced by Böhm's style of writing. A complete ed. of Böhm's work was begun by Johannes Wolgast in 1927 in 2 vols.; a rev. ed. of both vols. was publ. in Wiesbaden in 1952 and 1963, respectively.
BIBL.: J. Wolgast, *G. B.* (Berlin, 1924).

Böhm, Joseph, violinist; b. Budapest, March 4, 1795; d. Vienna, March 28, 1876. He was a pupil of his father; at 8 years of age he made a concert tour to Poland and St. Petersburg, where he studied for some years under Pierre Rode. His 1st concert at Vienna (1815) was very successful; after a trip to Italy, he was appointed (1819) violin prof. at the Vienna Cons.; retired in 1848. He taught many distinguished pupils, including Joachim, Ernst, Auer, Rappoldi, and Hellmesberger (Sr.).

Böhm, Karl, Austrian conductor of great renown; b. Graz, Aug. 28, 1894; d. Salzburg, Aug. 14, 1981. He studied law before enrolling at the Graz Cons., where he took lessons in piano and theory; subsequently he studied music theory with Mandyczewski at the Vienna Cons. After service in the Austrian army during World War I he was appointed conductor at the Municipal Theater at Graz. He completed his studies of law, receiving a degree of Dr.Jur. in 1919. Although he never took formal lessons in conducting, he soon acquired sufficient technique to be engaged at the Bavarian State Opera in Munich (1921). He made rapid progress in his career; in 1927 he was appointed Generalmusikdirektor in Darmstadt; having already mastered a number of works by Mozart, Wagner, and Richard Strauss, he included in his repertoire modern operas by Krenek and Hindemith. In 1931 he conducted *Wozzeck* by Alban Berg, a performance which Berg himself warmly praised. From 1931 to 1933 Böhm held the post of Generalmusikdirektor of the Hamburg Opera; from 1934 to 1943 he was music director of the Dresden State Opera, where he gave the 1st performances of 2 operas by Richard Strauss: *Die Schweigsame Frau* (June 24, 1935) and *Daphne* (Oct. 15, 1938), which Strauss dedicated to him. During the last 2 years of the raging war, he was conductor at the Vienna State Opera. The rumors were rife of his at least passive adherence to the Nazis, although he categorically denied that he was ever a member of the party. After the war he was not allowed by the Allied authorities to give performances pending an investigation of his political past; he was cleared and resumed his career in 1947. In 1950 he went to Argentina, where he organized and conducted a German opera repertoire at the Teatro Colón in Buenos Aires; returning to Europe, he again served as principal conductor of the Vienna State Opera (1954–56). On Nov. 5, 1955, he conducted Beethoven's *Fidelio* at the opening in the reconstructed Vienna State Opera House. He made his 1st appearance in the U.S. with the Chicago Sym. Orch. on Feb. 9, 1956; on Oct. 31, 1957, he made his 1st appearance at the Metropolitan Opera in N.Y. with Mozart's *Don Giovanni.* He continued to conduct occasional performances at the Metropolitan until 1974. In 1961 he took the Berlin Phil. to the U.S., and in 1963–64 he made a tour in Japan with it. In 1975 he conducted an American tour with the Deutsche Oper of Berlin. In 1979 he took the Vienna State Opera to America for its 1st U.S. tour. He also conducted radio and television performances. Böhm received numerous honors and tokens of distinction, among them the Golden Mozart Memorial Medal from the International Mozarteum Foundation in Salzburg, the Brahms Medal from Hamburg, and the Bruckner Ring from the Vienna Sym. On his 70th birthday in 1964 a Böhm Day was celebrated in Vienna, and he was granted the rare honorary title of Generalmusikdirektor of Austria; his 80th birthday was observed in 1974 in Salzburg and Vienna, as well as his 85th in 1979. In 1977 Böhm was elected president of the London Sym. Orch. In the annals of the art of conducting, Böhm may well be regarded as a worthy successor of the glorious pleiad of German and Austrian conductors such as Karl Muck, Bruno Walter, and Wilhelm Furtwängler. He was admired for his impeccable rendition of classical opera scores, particularly those of Mozart, in which he scrupulously avoided any suggestion of improper romanticization; he was equally extolled for his productions of the operas of Wagner and Richard Strauss, and he earned additional respect for his audacious espousal of modern music. He publ. *Begegnung mit Richard Strauss* (Munich, 1964) and a personal memoir, *Ich erinnere mich ganz genau* (Zürich, 1968).

BIBL.: F. Endler, *K. B.: Ein Dirigentenleben* (Hamburg, 1981); H. Hoyer, *K. B. an der Wiener Staatsoper: Eine Dokumentation* (Vienna, 1981).

Böhm, Theobald, German flutist and inventor of the "Böhm flute"; b. Munich, April 9, 1794; d. there, Nov. 25, 1881. He was the son of a goldsmith and learned mechanics in his father's workshop; studied the flute, achieving a degree of virtuosity that made him one of the greatest flute players of his time; he was appointed court musician in 1818; gave concerts in Paris and London. His system of construction marks a new departure in the making of woodwind instruments. To render the flute acoustically perfect, he fixed the position and size of the holes so as to obtain, not convenience in fingering, but purity and fullness of tone; all holes are covered by keys, whereby prompt and accurate "speaking" is assured; and the bore is modified, rendering the tone much fuller and mellower. He publ. *Über den Flötenbau und die neuesten Verbesserungen desselben* (Mainz, 1847; ed. by K. Ventzke as *On the Construction of Flutes/Über den Flötenbau,* Baren, the Netherlands, 1982); *Die Flöte und das Flötenspiel* (Munich, 1871).

BIBL.: C. Welch, *History of the B. Flute* (London, 1883); V. Mahillon, *Étude sur le doigté de la flûte B.* (1885); R. Rockstro, *A Treatise on the Construction, the History and the Practice of the Flute* (London, 1890).

Böhme, Franz Magnus, German writer on music; b. Willerstedt, near Weimar, March 11, 1827; d. Dresden, Oct. 18, 1898. He was a pupil of Hauptmann and Rietz at Leipzig; taught at Dresden (1859–78) and at the Hoch Cons. in Frankfurt (1878–85); spent the remaining years of his life in Dresden.

WRITINGS: *Das Oratorium, Eine historische Studie* (Leipzig, 1861; rev. ed., Gütersloh, 1887, under the title *Geschichte des Oratoriums*); *Altdeutsches Liederbuch,* a collection of German folk songs of the 12th to 17th centuries (Leipzig, 1877; later eds., 1913 and 1925); *Aufgaben zum Studium der Harmonie* (Mainz, 1880); *Kursus in Harmonie* (Mainz, 1882); *Geschichte des Tanzes in Deutschland* (2 vols., Leipzig, 1886); *Volkstümliche Lieder der Deutschen im 18. und 19. Jahrhundert* (Leipzig, 1895); *Deutsches Kinderlied und Kinderspiel* (1897). He ed. Erk's *Deutscher Liederhort* (3 vols., 1893–94; new ed., 1925); also publ. several books of sacred songs and male choruses.

Böhme, Kurt (Gerhard), distinguished German bass; b. Dresden, May 5, 1908; d. Munich, Dec. 20, 1989. He was educated at the Dresden Cons.; made his debut at the Dresden State Opera in 1930 as Kaspar in *Der Freischütz;* remained as a member there until 1950. On Nov. 11, 1954, he made his American debut at the Metropolitan Opera in N.Y. as Pogner in *Die Meistersinger von Nürnberg;* also sang there during the season of 1956–57.

Bohnen, (Franz) Michael, German bass-baritone; b. Cologne, May 2, 1887; d. Berlin, April 26, 1965. He studied at the Cologne Cons.; sang at several opera houses in Germany, Spain, and Sweden; made his American debut at the Metropolitan Opera, N.Y., on March 1, 1923, and created the leading role in the 1st American performance of Krenek's opera *Jonny spielt auf* (Jan. 19, 1929); remained at the Metropolitan until 1932; then was on the roster of the Deutsches Opernhaus (1933–45); subsequently assumed its administration when it was renamed the Städtische Oper, serving there until 1947.

Böhner, (Johann) Ludwig, German composer; b. Töttelstedt, Gotha, Jan. 8, 1787; d. there, March 28, 1860. He studied with his father and with Johann Christian Kittel, a pupil of Bach. Having achieved considerable fame as a pianist and a composer, he failed to establish himself socially and economically, owing to his personal eccentricities. He wandered through Germany, often on foot, and worked irregularly as a theatrical conductor and a concert pianist. The claim he advanced, that other composers plagiarized him, is supported by the fact that Weber had unintentionally borrowed one of the themes in *Der Freischütz* from Böhner's Piano Concerto. Böhner's life and character are understood to have inspired the figure of the eccentric genius Kreisler in E.T.A. Hoffmann's *Kapellmeister Kreisler* as well as Schumann's *Kreisleriana.*

BIBL.: K.F. Bolt, *J.L. B. Leben und Werk* (Hildburghausen, 1940).

Bohnke, Emil, Polish-born German violist and composer; b. Zdunska Wola, Oct. 11, 1888; d. in an automobile accident in Pasewalk, Pomerania, May 11, 1928. He studied at the Leipzig Cons.; then was a violist in various chamber music groups. He wrote a Violin Concerto, a Piano Trio, a String Quartet, and several violin sonatas.

Boieldieu, François-Adrien, celebrated French opera composer; b. Rouen, Dec. 16, 1775; d. Jarcy, near Grosbois, Oct. 8, 1834. His father was a clerical functionary who at one time served as secretary to Archbishop Larochefoucauld; his mother owned a millinery shop; the parents were divorced in 1794. Boieldieu received his musical instruction from Charles Broche; he then was apprenticed to Broche as an assistant organist at the church of St. André in Rouen. When he was 17 his 1st opera, *La Fille coupable* (to his father's libretto), achieved a production in Rouen (Nov. 2, 1793). He composed patriotic pieces which were in demand during the revolutionary period. His *Chant populaire pour la Fête de la Raison* for Chorus and Orch. was presented at the Temple of Reason (former cathedral) in Rouen on Nov. 30, 1793. His 2nd opera, *Rosalie et Myrza,* was also staged in Rouen (Oct. 28, 1795). He was befriended by the composer Louis Jadin and the piano manufacturer Erard; he met Cherubini and Méhul; made a tour in Normandy with the tenor Garat. His songs, of a popular nature, were printed in Paris; also publ. were his piano sonatas; a complete ed. of these sonatas was reprinted by G. Favre in 2 albums (1944–45). A facile composer, Boieldieu produced one opera after another and had no difficulties in having them staged in Paris. Particularly successful was his opera *Le Calife de Bagdad* (Paris, Sept. 16, 1800), which appealed to the public because of its exotic subject and pseudo-oriental arias. On March 19, 1802, Boieldieu married the dancer Clotilde Mafleurai, but separated from her the following year. Opportunely, he received an invitation to go to Russia. His contract called for an attractive salary of 4,000 rubles annually, in return for writing operas for the Imperial theaters in St. Petersburg. He attended to his duties conscientiously, and produced operas every year. His salary was raised, but Boieldieu decided to leave Russia in 1811 and return to Paris. His estranged wife died in 1826, and Boieldieu married the singer Jenny Phillis. True to his custom, he resumed composing operas for the Paris theaters. In 1817 he was appointed prof. of composition at the Paris Cons.; he resigned in 1826. In 1821 he was named a Chevalier of the Legion of Honor. After a number of insignificant productions, he achieved his greatest success with his Romantic opera *La Dame blanche,* fashioned after Walter Scott's novels *The Monastery* and *Guy Mannering;* the dramatic subject and the effective musical setting corresponded precisely to the tastes of the public of the time. It was produced at the Opéra-Comique in Paris on Dec. 10, 1825, and became a perennial success in Paris and elsewhere; it was produced in London on Oct. 9, 1826, and in N.Y. on Aug. 24, 1827. In 1833 he received a grant of 6,000 francs from the French government and retired to his country house at Jarcy, where he died. During the last years of his life he became interested in painting; his pictures show a modest talent in landscape. He was also successful as a teacher; among his pupils were Fétis, Adam, and P.J.G. Zimmerman. Boieldieu composed about 40 operas, of which several were written in collaboration with Méhul, Berton, Hérold, Cherubini, Catel, Isouard, Kreutzer, and Auber; 9 of these operas are lost. Boieldieu's significance in the history of French opera is great, even though the nationalistic hopes of the French music critics and others that he would rival Rossini did not materialize; Boieldieu simply lacked the tremendous power of invention, both in dramatic and comic aspects, that made Rossini a magician of 19th-century opera. Boieldieu's natural son, **Adrien-Louis-Victor Boieldieu** (b. Paris, Nov. 3, 1815; d. Quincy, July 9, 1883), was also a composer; his mother was Thérèse Regnault, a singer. He wrote 10 operas, including *Marguerite,* which was sketched by his father but left incomplete, and *L'Aïeule.*
Works: operas: *La Fille coupable* (Rouen, Nov. 2, 1793); *Rosalie et Myrza* (Rouen, Oct. 28, 1795); *La Famille suisse* (Paris, Feb. 11, 1797); *Zoraine et Zulnare* (Paris, May 10, 1798);

La Dôt de Suzette (Paris, Sept. 5, 1798); *Beniowski* (Paris, June 8, 1800); *Le Calife de Bagdad* (Paris, Sept. 16, 1800); *Ma tante Aurore* (Paris, Jan. 13, 1803); *Aline, reine de Golconda* (St. Petersburg, March 17, 1804); *Abderkhan* (St. Petersburg, Aug. 7, 1804); *La Jeune Femme colère* (St. Petersburg, April 30, 1805); *Un Tour de soubrette* (St. Petersburg, April 28, 1806); *Télémaque dans l'isle de Calypso* (St. Petersburg, Dec. 28, 1806); *Les Voitures verseés* (St. Petersburg, April 16, 1808); *Rien de trop ou Les Deux Paravents* (St. Petersburg, Jan. 6, 1811); *Jean de Paris* (Paris, April 4, 1812); *Le Nouveau Seigneur de village* (Paris, June 29, 1813); *La Fête du village voisin* (Paris, March 5, 1816); *Le Petit Chaperon rouge* (Paris, June 30, 1818; highly successful); *La Dame blanche* (Paris, Dec. 10, 1825; his masterpiece; nearly 1,700 perfs. before 1914 in Paris alone). The following operas were products of collaboration: *La Prisonnière,* with Cherubini (1799); *Le Baiser et la quittance,* with Méhul, Kreutzer, and others (1803); *Bayard à Mézières,* with Cherubini, Catel, and Isouard (1803); *Les Béarnais, ou Henri IV en voyage,* with Kreutzer (1814); *Angéla, ou L'Atelier de Jean Cousin,* with Mme. Gail, a pupil of Fétis (1814); *Charles de France, ou Amour et gloire,* with Hérold (1816); *Blanche de Provence, ou La Cour des fées,* with Cherubini, Berton, and others (1821); *Les Trois Genres,* with Auber (1824); *La Marquise de Brinvilliers,* with Berton and others (1831). **instrumental:** Piano Concerto (1797); Harp Concerto (1800); Duo for Violin and Piano; 4 duos for Harp and Piano; 4 piano sonatas; numerous songs.
Bibl.: G. Héquet, *A. B., Sa vie et ses œuvres* (Paris, 1864); A. Pougin, *B., Sa vie et ses œuvres* (Paris, 1875); E. Neukomm, *Trois jours à Rouen, Souvenirs du centenaire de B.* (Paris, 1875); H. de Thannberg, *Le Centenaire de B., Anecdotes et souvenirs* (Paris, 1875); E. Duval, *B., Notes et fragments inédits* (1883); P.L. Robert, "Correspondance de B.," *Rivista Musicale Italiana,* XIX and XXII (also separately, Rouen, 1916); G. de Saint-Foix, "Les Premiers Pianistes parisiens: B.," *Revue Musicale* (Feb. 1926); G. Favre, "La Danseuse Clotilde Mafleurai, première femme d'A. B.," ibid. (Jan. 1940); idem, *B., Sa vie, son œuvre* (part I, Paris, 1944; part II, Paris, 1945; an exhaustive work on the subject).

Bois, Rob du, Dutch composer; b. Amsterdam, May 28, 1934. He had piano lessons as a child; then studied law; was mainly audodidact as a composer. His works are strongly contrapuntal in texture, following the classical Flemish tradition but applying ultramodern techniques, including serialism.
Works: Piano Concerto (1960; rev. 1968); *Cercle* for Piano, 9 Winds, and Percussion (1963); Concertino for School Orch. (1963); *Simultaneous* for Orch. (1965); *Breuker Concerto* for 2 Clarinets, 4 Saxophones, and 21 String Players (1968); *A Flower Given to My Daughter* for Orch. (1970); *Midas,* ballet (1970); *Le Concerto pour Hrisanide* for Piano and Orch. (1971; written for Rumanian virtuoso Alexandru Hrisanide); *Allegro* for Strings (1973); *3 pezzi* for Orch. (1973); Suite No. 1 for Orch. (1973); Violin Concerto (1975); *Vandaag is het morgen van gisteren* for Narrator, Soprano, Youth Choir, Orch., and Brass Band (1975); *Skarabee* for Orch. (1977); *Zodiak* for Various Instruments (1977); Concerto for 2 Violins and Orch. (1979); *Sinfonia da camera* for Wind Orch. (1980); *My Daughter's Flower* for Brass Band (1982); 7 pastorales: No. 1 for Oboe, Clarinet, and Harp (1960; rev. 1969); No. 2 for Recorder, Flute, and Guitar (1963; rev. 1969); No. 3 for Clarinet, Bongos, and Double Bass (1963; rev. 1969); No. 4 for Solo Guitar (1963); No. 5 for String Quartet (1964; rev. 1966); No. 6 for Piano (1964); No. 7 for Recorder (1964); *Music* for Solo Flute (1961); *Bewegingen* for Piccolo and Piano (1961); Trio for Flute, Oboe, and Clarinet (1961); *Rondeaux per deux* for Piano and Percussion (1962; 2nd series, for Piano, 4-hands, and Percussion, 1964); *Spiel und Zwischenspiel* for Recorder and Piano (1962); *3 Pieces* for Flute, Oboe, and Cello (1962); *Chants et contrepoints* for Wind Quintet (1962); *Une Façon de dire que les hommes de cent vingt ans ne chantent plus* for Soprano, Piano, and 4 Percussion Instruments (1963); *Espaces à remplir* for 11 Musicians (1963); Oboe Quartet (1964); *7 Bagatelles* for

Flute and Piano (1964); *Ad libitum* for Violin and Piano (1965); *Pour faire chanter la polonaise* for Flute, Soprano, and 3 Pianos (1965); *Pour 2 violons* (1966); *Words* for Mezzo-soprano, Flute, Cello, and Piano (1966); String Trio (1967); *Musica per quattro* for Horn, 2 Trumpets, and Trombone (1967); *Beat Music* for 2 Percussionists (1967); *Because Going Nowhere Takes a Long Time* for Medium Voice, Flute, and Piano (1967; version for Soprano, Clarinet, and Piano, 1969); *Rounds* for Clarinet and Piano (1967); *Ranta Music* for Percussionist (1968); *Music for a Sliding Trombone* (1968); *Musique d'atelier* for Clarinet, Trombone, Cello, and Piano (1968); *Enigma* for Flute, Bass Clarinet, Piano, and Percussion (1969); *Symposion* for Oboe, Violin, Viola, and Cello (1969); *Trio agitato* for Horn, Trombone, and Tuba (1969); *Réflexions sur le jour où Pérotin le Grand ressuscitera* for Wind Quintet (1969); *Polonaise* for a Pianist and a Percussionist (1971); *Fusion pour deux* for Bass Clarinet and Piano (1971); *The Dog Named Boo Has a Master Called Lobo* for Clarinet, Violin, and Piano (1972); *Because It Is* for 4 Clarinets (1973); *The 18th of June, Springtime, and Yet Already Summer* for 4 Saxophones (1974); *Melody* for Bass Clarinet and String Quartet (1974); *Inferno*, after Dante, for Soprano, 2 Violins, Cello, and Harpsichord (1974); *Eine Rede* for Soprano, Clarinet, Basset Horn, and Bass Clarinet (1974); *Forever Amber* for 2 Guitars (1985); *Das Liebesverbot* for 4 Wagner Tubas (1986); *Symphorine* for Flute (1987); Piano Sonatina (1960); *Voices* for Piano (1964); *Just Like a Little Sonata* for Piano (1964); *A Combination of Voices* for 2 Pianos (1968); *New Pieces* for Piano (1972); *Cadences* for Piano (1975); songs.

Boise, Otis Bardwell, American organist; b. Oberlin, Ohio, Aug. 13, 1844; d. Baltimore, Dec. 2, 1912. He studied with Moscheles and Richter in Leipzig and with Kullak in Berlin. Returning to America in 1865, he occupied various posts as an organist and a teacher; eventually settled in Baltimore, where he taught at the Peabody Cons. Among his pupils were Ernest Hutcheson, Howard Brockway, and Arthur Nevin. He publ. the textbooks *Harmony Made Practical* (N.Y., 1900) and *Music and Its Masters* (N.Y., 1902).

Boismortier, Joseph Bodin de, French composer; b. Thionville, Moselle, Dec. 23, 1689; d. Roissy-en-Brie, Oct. 28, 1755. He lived in Metz and Perpignan before settling in Paris in 1724. A prolific composer of instrumental music, he wrote more than 100 opus numbers; of these there are several for block flutes (i.e., recorders) and transverse flutes; 2 suites for clavecin; trio sonatas, among them one with the viola da gamba (1732; modern ed., Mainz, 1967); collections of pieces designed for amateurs (in the positive sense of this abused word), scored with a drone instrument, either the musette (a wind instrument) or the vielle (a string instrument), and publ. under such coaxing titles as "Gentillesses," or "Divertissements de campagne." He also wrote 3 ballet-operas: *Les Voyages de l'Amour* (1736), *Don Quichotte* (1743), and *Daphnis et Chloé* (1747); and a number of cantatas.
Bibl.: H. Tribout de Morembert, "B. d.B.; Notes sur un musicien lorrain," *Revue de Musicologie* (1967); M. Pincherle, "À propos de B.," *Journal Musical Français/Musica Disques* (Nov. 1968).

Boito, Arrigo (baptismal name, **Enrico**), important Italian poet and opera composer; b. Padua, Feb. 24, 1842; d. Milan, June 10, 1918. He studied at the Milan Cons. with Alberto Mazzucato and Ronchetti-Monteviti; his 2 cantatas, *Il 4 Giugno* (1860) and *Le Sorelle d'Italia* (1861), written in collaboration with Faccio, were performed at the Cons., and attracted a great deal of favorable attention; as a result, the Italian government granted the composers a gold medal and a stipend for foreign travel for 2 years. Boito spent most of his time in Paris, and also went to Poland to meet the family of his mother (who was Polish); he also visited Germany, Belgium, and England. He was strongly influenced by new French and German music; upon his return to Milan, he undertook the composition of his 1st and most significant large opera, *Mefistofele*, which contains elements of conventional Italian opera but also dra-

matic ideas stemming from Beethoven and Wagner. It was performed for the 1st time at La Scala (March 5, 1868). A controversy followed when a part of the audience objected to the unusual treatment of the subject and the music, and there were actual disorders at the conclusion of the performance. After the 2nd production, the opera was taken off the boards, and Boito undertook a revision to effect a compromise. In this new version, the opera had a successful run in Italian cities; it was also produced in Hamburg (1880), in London (in Italian, July 6, 1880), and in Boston (in Eng., Nov. 16, 1880). It was retained in the repertoire of the leading opera houses, but its success never matched that of Gounod's *Faust*. Boito never completed his 2nd opera, *Nerone*, on which he worked for more than half a century (from 1862 to 1916). The orch. score was revised by Toscanini and performed by him at La Scala on May 1, 1924. There are sketches for an earlier opera, *Ero e Leandro*, but not enough material to attempt a completion. Boito's gift as a poet is fully equal to that as a composer. He publ. a book of verses (Turin, 1877) under the anagrammatic pen name of **Tobia Gorrio;** he wrote his own librettos for his operas and made admirable trs. of Wagner's operas (*Tristan und Isolde; Rienzi*); wrote the librettos of *Otello* and *Falstaff* for Verdi (these librettos are regarded as his masterpieces); also for *Gioconda* by Ponchielli, *Amleto* by Faccio, etc. Boito also publ. novels. He held various honorary titles from the King of Italy; in 1892 he was appointed inspector-general of Italian conservatories; was made honorary D.Mus. by Cambridge Univ. and Oxford Univ.; in 1912 he was made a senator by the King of Italy. Boito's letters were ed. by R. de Rensis (Rome, 1932), who also ed. Boito's articles on music (Milan, 1931).
Bibl.: P.G. Molmenti, *Impressioni letterarie* (Milan, 1875); A. Boccardi, *A. B.* (Trieste, 1877); R. Giani, *Il Nerone di A. B.* (Turin, 1901); R. Barbiera, *A. B., inverso l'ideale* (Milan, 1905); M. Risolo, *Il primo Mefistofele di A. B.* (Naples, 1916); C. Trevor, "B.'s Nero," *Musical Times* (June 1916); A. Lualdi, "A. B., un' anima," *Rivista Musicale Italiana* (1919); A. Pompeati, *A. B.* (Florence, 1919); C. Ricci, *A. B.* (Milan, 1919); F. Torrefranca, "A. B.," *La Critica Musicale* (Nov./Dec. 1919); idem, "A. B.," *Musical Quarterly* (Oct. 1920); G.M. Gatti, "B.'s Nero," ibid. (Oct. 1924); V. Gui, *Il Nerone di A. B.* (Milan, 1924); A. Bonaventura, *A. B.; Mefistofele* (Milan, 1924); G. Cesari, "Note per una bibliografia delle opere di A. B.," *Rassegna di Coltura* (March 1924); R. de Rensis, *Franco Faccio e B., documento* (Milan, 1934); F. Ballo, *A. B.* (Turin, 1938); R. de Rensis, *A. B.; Aneddoti e bizzarrie poetiche e musicali* (Rome, 1942); P. Nardi, *Vita di A. B.* (Verona, 1942; 2nd ed., Milan, 1944); M. Vajro, *A. B.* (Brescia, 1955); C. Orselli, "A. B.: Un riesame," *Chigiana* (1968); G. Mariani, *A. B.* (Parma, 1973); G. Scarsi, *Rapporto poesia-musica in A. B.* (Rome, 1973).

Bok, Mary Louise Curtis, American patroness of music; b. Boston, Aug. 6, 1876; d. Philadelphia, Jan. 4, 1970. She inherited her fortune from Cyrus H.K. Curtis, founder of the Curtis Publishing Co. In 1924 she established in Philadelphia the Curtis Inst. of Music and endowed it initially with a gift of $12.5 million in memory of her mother. The school had a faculty of the most distinguished American and European musicians, and it provided tuition exclusively on a scholarship basis; many talented composers and performers were its students; among them were Leonard Bernstein, Samuel Barber, and Lukas Foss. Josef Hofmann was engaged to head the piano dept.; from 1926 to 1938 he served as director of the Curtis Inst. Mrs. Bok was 1st married to Edward W. Bok, in 1896; he died in 1930; in 1943 she married **Efrem Zimbalist,** who was director of the Curtis Inst. from 1941 until 1968. She purchased in England the famous Burrell Collection of Wagneriana and brought it to the U.S. In 1932 she received an honorary doctorate from the Univ. of Pa., and in 1934, an honorary doctorate from Williams College.

Bokemeyer, Heinrich, German music theorist and composer; b. Immensen, near Lehrte, Lower Saxony, March 1679; d.

Wolfenbüttel, Dec. 7, 1751. He attended the St. Martin's and St. Catherine's Church School in Braunschweig; in 1702 went to the Univ. of Helmstedt; he returned to Braunschweig in 1704 and served as cantor at St. Martin's; concurrently studied composition with Georg Oesterreich. In 1712 he became cantor in Husum; in 1717 he repaired to Wolfenbüttel; in 1720 he became cantor at the ducal palace there. He was a founding member of Mizler's Societät der Musikalischen Wissenschaften of Leipzig. Few of his compositions are extant, but several of his theoretical treatises survive. He collected a large music library. See H. Kümmerling, *Katalog der Sammlung Bokemeyer* (Kassel, 1970).

Bolcom, William (Elden), American pianist and composer; b. Seattle, May 26, 1938. He studied at the Univ. of Washington in Seattle with John Verrall (B.A., 1958); took a course in composition with Darius Milhaud at Mills College in Oakland, Calif. (M.A., 1961); attended classes in advanced composition with Leland Smith at Stanford Univ. (D.M.A., 1964); also studied at the Paris Cons. (2nd prize in composition, 1965). He received Guggenheim fellowships in 1964–65 and 1968–69. He taught at the Univ. of Washington in Seattle (1965–66), Queens College of the City Univ. of N.Y. (1966–68), and the N.Y. Univ. School of the Arts (1969–70). He joined the faculty of the school of music at the Univ. of Michigan in 1973; was made a full prof. in 1983. He was composer-in-residence of the Detroit Sym. Orch. (from 1987). In 1988 he won the Pulitzer Prize in Music for his *12 New Études* for Piano. After absorbing a variety of techniques *sine ira et studio*, he began to experiment widely and wildly in serial thematics, musical collage, sophisticated intentional plagiarism, and microtonal electronics. He was also active as a pianist, recording and giving recitals of ragtime piano; with his wife, the singer Joan Morris, he gave concerts of popular American songs from olden times. He publ., with Robert Kimbass, a book on the black American songwriting and musical comedy team of Noble Sissle and Eubie Blake, *Reminiscing with Sissle and Blake* (N.Y., 1973); also ed. the collected essays of George Rochberg, under the title *The Aesthetics of Survival: A Composer's View of 20th Century Music* (Ann Arbor, Mich., 1984).

WORKS: STAGE: *Dynamite Tonite,* an actors' opera (N.Y., Actors' Studio, Dec. 21, 1963); *Greatshot,* an actors' opera (1969); *Theatre of the Absurd* for Actor and Chamber Group (1970); *The Beggar's Opera,* an adaptation of John Gay's work, for Actors and Chamber Orch. (1978). **ORCH.:** Sym. (1957); Concertante for Violin, Flute, Oboe, and Orch. (1961); sym., *Oracles* (1964); *Concerto-Serenade* for Violin and String Orch. (1964); *Commedia* for "Almost" 18th-century Orch. (1971); *Summer Divertimento* for Chamber Orch. (1973); Piano Concerto (1976); *Humoresk* for Organ and Orch. (1979); *Symphony for Chamber Orchestra* (1979); *Ragomania* for Orch. (1982); Concerto for Violin and Orch. (1983); *Fantasia concertante* for Viola, Cello, and Orch. (1985); *Seattle Slew,* dance suite (1985–86); Sym. No. 4 (1986; St. Louis, March 13, 1987); *Spring Concertino* for Oboe and Chamber Orch. (1986–87). **CHAMBER:** 9 string quartets (1950–72); *Décalage* for Cello and Piano (1961); Octet for Flute, Clarinet, Bassoon, Violin, Viola, Cello, Contrabass, and Piano (1962); several works, each entitled *Session,* for various instrumental ensembles and mandatory drum play (1965, 1966, 1967); *Dream Music No. 2* for Harpsichord and Percussion (1966); Duets for Quintet of Flute, Clarinet, Violin, Cello, and Piano (1971); *Whisper Moon* for Alto Flute, Clarinet, Violin, Cello, and Piano (1971); Duo Fantasy for Violin and Piano (1973); Piano Quartet (1976); *Afternoon,* rag suite for Clarinet, Violin, and Piano (1979); Brass Quintet (1980); *Aubade* for Oboe and Piano (1982); *Capriccio* for Cello and Piano (1985); *5 Fold 5* for Woodwind Quintet and Piano (1987); many works for keyboard, including *Frescoes* for 2 Pianists, each doubling on a Harmonium and Harpsichord (Toronto, July 21, 1971); *3 Gospel Preludes* for Organ (3 books; 1979–81); *12 New Études* for Piano (1977–86); also songs, including *Songs of Innocence and of Experience,* after Blake (1956–81; also for Soloists, Chorus, and Orch., 1982).

Boldemann, Laci, Finnish-born Swedish composer; b. Helsinki, April 24, 1921; d. Munich, Aug. 18, 1969. He grew up in Germany; went to Sweden in 1939, but was forced to return to Germany for military service. His music is of a lyrical nature, showing the influence of Sibelius.

WORKS: Fairy-tale opera, *Svart är vitt, sa kejsaren* (Black Is White, Said the Emperor; Stockholm, Jan. 1, 1965); opera-musical, *Dårskapens timme* (Hour of Madness; Malmö, March 22, 1968); operatic scene, *Och så drömmer han om Per Jonathan* (And He Dreams of Per Jonathan; Stockholm, Nov. 29, 1969); *La Danza,* overture (1949–50); *Lieder der Vergänglichkeit,* cantata for Baritone and Strings (1951); *4 Epitaphs,* after Edgar Lee Masters, for Soprano and Strings (1952); Sinfonietta for Strings (1954); *Fantasia concertante* for Cello and Orch. (1954); Piano Concerto (1956); *Notturno* for Soprano and Orch. (1958); Violin Concerto (1959); Sym. (Munich, Jan. 13, 1964); *John Bauer,* oratorio (1967); Trumpet Concerto (Malmö, Feb. 11, 1969); *Med bleck och med trä,* little overture for Winds (1969); Violin Sonata (1950); *6 Small Pieces without Pedal* for Piano (1950); String Quartet (1950–57); *Canto elegiaco* for Cello and Piano (1962); about 50 songs.

Bolden, "Buddy" (Charles Joseph), black American jazz cornetist; b. New Orleans, Sept. 6, 1877; d. Jackson, La., Nov. 4, 1931. He was a pioneering figure in early jazz; was active mainly in New Orleans. His career was broken by a cerebral dysfunction; he was confined to a state hospital in Jackson in 1906, and lingered there for many years before succumbing.

Bolet, Jorge, brilliant Cuban-born American pianist; b. Havana, Nov. 15, 1914; d. Mountain View, Calif., Oct. 16, 1990. He went to the U.S. in 1926 and studied piano with David Saperton and conducting with Fritz Reiner at the Curtis Inst. in Philadelphia. In 1932 he took lessons with Leopold Godowsky and with Moriz Rosenthal; he also studied briefly with Rudolf Serkin. During World War II he was stationed in Japan; returning to the U.S., he took private lessons with Abram Chasins. Eventually he was appointed head of the piano dept. at the Curtis Inst. A virtuoso of maximal powers, he seemed a natural heir of his teachers Godowsky and Rosenthal.

Bolling, Claude, outstanding French jazz pianist, bandleader, composer, and arranger; b. Cannes, April 10, 1930. He began formal piano training at age 12, receiving thorough grounding in the classical repertoire while mastering the jazz idiom; later he studied harmony and composition with Maurice Duruflé in Paris, where he immersed himself in the jazz scene. He became a prominent figure in the crossover movement when he composed his Sonata for 2 Pianists (1970) for Jean-Bernard Pommier. His Suite for Flute and Jazz Piano Trio, written in 1975 for Jean-Pierre Rampal, became an internationally successful recording, attaining gold-record status in 1981. He also wrote *California Suite* (film score, 1976), Suite for Violin and Jazz Piano Trio (for Pinchas Zukerman; 1978), Suite for Chamber Orch. and Jazz Piano Trio (1983), and Suite for Cello and Jazz Piano Trio (for Yo-Yo Ma; 1984).

Bollius, Daniel, German organist and composer; b. Hechingen, c.1590; d. Mainz, c.1642. He studied at the Univ. of Dillingen; was court organist in Sigmaringen from 1613 to 1619; in 1626 was appointed organist to the elector of Mainz. His oratorio, *Representatio harmonica conceptionis et nativitatis S. Joannis Baptistae,* is historically significant as an early example of the Italian oratorio form in Germany.

Bologna, Jacopo da. See **Jacopo da Bologna.**

Bölsche, Franz, German music editor; b. Wegenstedt, near Magdeburg, Aug. 20, 1869; d. Bad Oeynhausen, Oct. 23, 1935. He studied with Bargiel and Spitta in Berlin; became a teacher of theory at the Cologne Cons. (1896–1931). He was an ed. for Denkmäler Deutscher Tonkunst, and wrote the successful manual *Übungen und Aufgaben zum Studium der Harmonielehre* (Leipzig, 1911; 18th ed., 1938). Also composed a Sym., 4 overtures (*Tragödie der Menschen, Judith, Hero und Leander, Othello*), etc.

Bolshakov, Nikolai, Russian tenor; b. Kharkov, Nov. 23, 1874; d. Leningrad, Jan. 20, 1958. He studied in St. Petersburg; made his debut there with the Kharkov Opera Co. in 1899; in 1902 he went to Milan, where he studied voice with A. Brogi; then sang with the Maryinsky Theater in St. Petersburg (1906–29); participated in the spectacles of Diaghilev's "Russian Seasons" in Paris and London (1911–13). Returning to Russia, he gave solo recitals; from 1923 to 1953 taught voice at the Leningrad Cons. He was noted for his interpretations of Faust and Don José.

Bolzoni, Giovanni, Italian composer and conductor; b. Parma, May 14, 1841; d. Turin, Feb. 21, 1919. He studied at the Parma Cons.; was active as a conductor in Perugia; served as director and prof. of composition at the Liceo Musicale in Turin (1887–1916); also conducted at the Teatro Regio there (1884–89). He composed several operas, the most successful were *Il matrimonio civile* (Parma, 1870), *La stella delle Alpi* (Savona, 1876), and *Jella* (Piacenza, 1881). A melodious minuet from one of his string quartets became a perennial favorite in numerous arrangements.

Bombardelli, Silvije, Croatian conductor and composer; b. Split, March 3, 1916. He studied violin in Belgrade; returning to Split in 1945, he organized an orch., and also conducted opera. In his music he applies modernistic procedures, including modified serial techniques. **Works:** Ballet, *Stranac* (The Stranger; Split, Jan. 25, 1956); *Plameni Vjetar* (The Flaming Wind) for Orch. and Speaking Chorus (Split, June 18, 1940); Sym. (Zagreb, Nov. 3, 1951); cantatas and choruses.

Bomtempo, João Domingos, Portuguese pianist; b. Lisbon, Dec. 28, 1775; d. there, Aug. 18, 1842. He studied in Paris; then went to London, where he stayed until 1811. Returning to Lisbon, he was active on the concert stage; in 1816 he went to London again; finally went back to Portugal in 1820. In 1822 he founded a phil. society in Lisbon; in 1833 became director of the Lisbon Cons. He wrote 6 syms., 4 piano concertos, 14 piano sextets, a Piano Quintet, and several piano sonatas; also an opera, *Alessandro in Efesso.* He publ. a piano method (London, 1816). **Bibl.:** M.A. de Lima Cruz, *D. B.* (Lisbon, 1937).

Bon, Maarten, Dutch pianist and composer; b. Amsterdam, Aug. 20, 1933. He graduated from the Muzieklyceum in Amsterdam in 1954; studied piano with T. Bruins and Spaanderman, and composition with Baaren; then gave recitals with his wife, the violinist Jeannelotte Hertzberger; in 1971 was appointed pianist with the Dutch Radio. His compositions are whimsical: *Caprichoso y Obstinato* for Solo Flute (1965); *Disturbing the Peace,* improvisation for 9 Players, more or less (1968–69); *Let's Go Out for a Drive (and Pollute the Air),* improvisation for Trombone, 3 Pianists, and Conductor (1970–74); *Free or Not* for 21 Wind Players (1972); *Sieben, jedenfalls sieben* for Chamber Ensemble (1976); *Display IV* for 6 Pianos and Piano Tuner (1980; rev. 1982); *Display V* for 12 Cellos (1983); *Solo* for Clarinet (1983–86).

Bon, Willem Frederik, Dutch composer and conductor; b. Amersfoort, June 15, 1940; d. Nijeholtpade, April 14, 1983. He studied clarinet, conducting, and composition at the Cons. of Amsterdam and The Hague, receiving a conducting diploma in 1971. In 1972 he became conductor of the Eindhoven Baroque Ensemble, and in 1973 he was named an assistant conductor of the Concertgebouw Orch. in Amsterdam. At the time of his death, he taught composition at the Groningen Cons. **Works: STAGE:** *Erik's wonderbaarlijke reis* (Erik's Miraculous Journey), instrumental opera for Children, Narrator, and Orch. (1979). **ORCH.:** *Dialogues and Monologues* for Piano and Orch. (1968); *Nocturnes* for String Orch. (1968); *Variations on a Theme of Sweelinck* for Chamber Orch. (1969); 2 syms.: No. 1, *Usher Symphony,* after Edgar Allan Poe's short story (1968–70; orig. intended as material for an opera); No. 2, *Les Prédictions* (1970); Concerto for String Orch. (1970); *Games* for 6 Wind Instruments, Piano, and String Orch. (1970); *To Catch a Heffalump* for Orch. and Tape (1971); *Circe,* prelude

(1972); *Passacaglia in Blue* for 12 Wind Instruments and Double Bass (1972); *Aforismen* for 15 Strings (1972); Concerto for Oboes (Oboe, Oboe d'Amore, and Heckelphone) and Strings (1974); Sym. for Strings (1982). **CHAMBER:** 2 wind quintets (1963–66; 1969); Cello Sonata (1966); *Sunphoneion I* for Flute, Vibraphone, and Piano (1968); *Sans paroles* for Clarinet, Bass Clarinet, and String Trio (1970); *Petite trilogie* for Solo Trumpet (1970); Sonata for Solo Bassoon (1970); *Riflessioni* for Flute and Harp (1971); *5 tours de passe-passe* for Flute and Piano (1971); *Allégorie* for Harp (1972); *3 Saturnien* for Piano Trio (1981). **PIANO SOLO:** *Miniatures* (1966). **VOCAL:** *3 poèmes de Verlaine* for Mezzo-soprano, Flute, Cello, and Piano (1967); *Missa brevis* for Mixed Chorus and 9 Wind Instruments (1969); *Jadis et naguère* for Mezzo-soprano, Clarinet, Violin, and Piano (1970); *1999, 4 Prophesies of Nostradamus* for Soprano and Orch. (1973); *Le Grand Age Millième,* 4 quatrains after Nostradamus, for a cappella Male Chorus (1974); *Les Quatre Saisons de Verlaine,* each for a different Vocal Soloist and Orch.: *Le Printemps* for Soprano, *L'Été* for Alto, *L'Automne* for Baritone, and *L'Hiver* for Tenor (1976–79); *Silence,* after Poe, for Mezzo-soprano, Wind Quintet, and Piano (1978); *Dag* (Hello), 4 songs for Mezzo-soprano and Percussion (1979). **BIBL.:** E. Vermeulen, "B.: Usher Symphony," *Sonorum Speculum,* No. 48 (Autumn 1971).

Bona, Giovanni, Italian cardinal; b. Mondovi, Oct. 12, 1609; d. Rome, Oct. 28, 1674. His tract *De divina psalmodia . . . tractatus historicus, symbolicus, asceticus* (Rome, 1653) contains valuable information on church music. A complete ed. of his works was publ. in Rome in 1747.

Bona (or **Buona**), **Valerio,** Italian composer; b. Brescia, c.1560; date of death unknown, but he was still living in 1619. He was a Franciscan monk; maestro di cappella at the cathedrals of Vercelli (1591) and Mondovi, and at the Church of S. Francesco in Milan (1596); musician at S. Francesco in Brescia (1611) and prefect at S. Fermo Maggiore in Verona (1614). He was a prolific composer, in polyphonic style, of sacred and secular vocal music (masses, litanies, Lamentations, motets, madrigals, etc.), many of which he wrote for 2 choirs. Also a theorist, he publ. *Regole del contrapunto, et compositione brevemente raccolte da diuersi auttori* (Casale, 1595); *Esempii delli passagi delle consonanze, et dissonanze* (Milan, 1596); etc.

Bonaventura, Anthony di, American pianist, brother of **Mario di Bonaventura;** b. Follansbee, W.Va., Nov. 12, 1930. A precocious talent, he played in public at the age of 13; then enrolled at the Curtis Inst. of Music in Philadelphia to study with Isabelle Vengerova. Upon graduation, he launched an ambitious career as a soloist with American and European orchs.; also played numerous recitals. He commissioned several composers of the avant-garde to write special works for him, among them Luciano Berio, Milko Kelemen, and Györgi Ligeti. In 1973 he was appointed to the piano faculty of Boston Univ.

Bonaventura, Arnaldo, Italian musicologist; b. Livorno, July 28, 1862; d. Florence, Oct. 7, 1952. He studied law, violin, and music theory, but made musicology his career. He was a prof. of music history and librarian at the Royal Inst. of Music until 1932; then became director of the Cons. and prof. of music history and esthetics. **WRITINGS:** *Manuale di storia della musica* (Livorno, 1898; 10th ed., 1920); *Elementi di estetica musicale* (Livorno, 1905; 3rd ed., 1926, as *Manuale di estetica musicale*); *Dante e la musica* (Livorno, 1904); *Storia degli stromenti musicali* (Livorno, 1908; many other eds.); *Niccolo Paganini* (1911; 3rd ed., 1925); *Saggio storico sul teatro musicale italiano* (Livorno, 1913); *Storia e letteratura del pianoforte* (Livorno, 1918); *Verdi* (Paris, 1923); *Bernardo Pasquini* (Ascoli Piceno, 1923); *Giacomo Puccini* (Livorno, 1925); *Manuale di cultura musicale* (1924); *"Mefistofele" di Boito* (Milan, 1924); *Storia del violino, dei violinisti e della musica per violino* (Milan, 1925); *L'opera italiana* (1928); *Domenico del Mela* (1928); *Luigi Boccherini* (1931); *Musicisti livornesi* (1931); *Rossini* (1934).

Bonaventura, Mario di, American conductor, educator, and music publisher, brother of **Anthony di Bonaventura;** b. Follansbee, W.Va., Feb. 20, 1924. He studied violin; won an award at the N.Y. Phil. in the Young Composers' Composition Competition in 1941; in 1947 went to Paris to study composition with Nadia Boulanger; also took a course in piano accompaniment at the Paris Cons. He subsequently studied conducting with Igor Markevitch at the Mozarteum in Salzburg and later in Paris; received a prize at the 1952 International Conducting Competition at Besançon; in 1953 was awarded the Lili Boulanger Memorial Prize in Composition. From 1954 to 1956 he served as staff pianist with the Pasdeloup Orch. in Paris; made jazz arrangements for the guitarist Django Reinhardt. Returning to the U.S., he conducted the Fort Lauderdale Sym. (1959–62); in 1962 was appointed to the faculty of Dartmouth College; in 1963 inaugurated there an auspicious series of summer festivals under the title "Congregation of the Arts" and commissioned a great number of special works from contemporary composers; altogether, 389 modern works were performed during 7 summers, which included 38 world premieres. In 1968 Bonaventura produced and directed the 4th International Anton von Webern Festival; also initiated programs for the furtherance of new music, which awarded 55 commissions to composers in 19 countries. As a conductor, he led orchs. on several European tours. In 1974 he was appointed vice-president and director of publications of G. Schirmer/Associated Music Publishers, N.Y.; in that capacity, too, he promoted publications of modern music; he resigned in 1979 and dedicated himself mainly to univ. teaching.

Bonavia, Ferruccio, Italian-British writer on music; b. Trieste, Feb. 20, 1877; d. London, Feb. 5, 1950. He studied violin in Trieste and Milan; in 1898 went to England; earned his living as a violinist; mastered the English language and became music critic of the *Manchester Guardian* and of the London *Daily Telegraph.* He publ. a monograph on Verdi (London, 1930; 2nd ed., 1947); miniature biographies of Mozart (1938) and Rossini (1941); and a fanciful book of imaginary conversations, *Musicians in Elysium* (1949). He was also a composer; he wrote a Violin Concerto, a String Octet, a String Quartet, and some songs.

Bonci, Alessandro, Italian lyric tenor; b. Cesena, Feb. 10, 1870; d. Viserba, Aug. 8, 1940. He studied with Carlo Pedrotti and Felice Coen in Pesaro; later took singing lessons with Della Sedie in Paris. He made his operatic debut in Parma on Jan. 20, 1896, as Fenton in *Falstaff;* then sang at La Scala, Milan, and later undertook a grand tour of Europe; also made appearances in South America and Australia. In 1906 he made his N.Y. debut at the new Manhattan Opera House, and remained on its roster for 3 seasons; on Nov. 22, 1907, he sang the role of the Duke in *Rigoletto* at his debut at the Metropolitan Opera, N.Y., and remained with it for 3 seasons. His voice was of great lyric charm; he was one of the few Italian artists to achieve distinction as a singer of German lieder.

Bond, Carrie (Minetta) Jacobs, American composer of sentimental songs; b. Janesville, Wis., Aug. 11, 1862; d. Glendale, Calif., Dec. 28, 1946. She was naturally gifted in music and painting, and improvised songs to her own words at the piano. She organized a music-selling agency and publ. her own songs under the imprint Carrie Jacobs Bond and Son. Although deficient in musical training, she succeeded in producing sweet melodies in lilting rhythms with simple accompaniment that became extremely popular in America. Her 1st song was *Is My Dolly Dead?* This was followed by her greatest hit, *A Perfect Day,* and a series of other successful songs: *I Love You Truly, God Remembers When the World Forgets, Life's Garden,* and many others. She publ. an autobiography, *The Roads of Melody* (1927), and an album of her poems with philosophical comments under the title *The End of the Road.*

Bond, Chapel, English organist and composer; b. Gloucester (baptized), Dec. 14, 1730; d. Coventry, Feb. 14, 1790. He studied with Martin Smith, the Cathedral organist; when he was 19 he became organist at St. Michael and All Angels in Coventry; from 1752 he also served as organist at Holy Trinity, retaining both posts until his death. He composed a number of effectively written instrumental pieces, including concerti grossi and concertos for trumpet and bassoon.

Bond, Victoria, American conductor and composer; b. Los Angeles, May 6, 1945. She was born into a family of professional musicians; studied composition with Ingolf Dahl at the Univ. of Southern Calif. (B.Mus., 1968) and with Sessions at the Juilliard School of Music in N.Y. (M.M., 1975; D.M.A., 1977), and conducting with Herbert von Karajan, Leonard Slatkin, Richard Dufallo, and Pierre Boulez. She has specialized in the unusual and has also actively championed works by women composers; among her American premieres are Joyce Barthelson's *The King's Breakfast,* Julia Smith's *The Shepherdess and the Chimneysweep,* and Margaret Garwood's *The Nightingale and the Rose.* In 1988 she was appointed music director of the Roanoke Sym. Orch. Among her own compositions is the opera *Gulliver,* based on *Gulliver's Travels* (1989).

Bondeville, Emmanuel (Pièrre Georges) de, French composer; b. Rouen, Oct. 29, 1898; d. Paris, Nov. 26, 1987. He studied organ and composition in Rouen and Paris; later was music director of the Eiffel Tower Radio Station (1935–49, when it closed) and head of the Paris Opéra (1952–70). He wrote 2 operas, both produced at the Opéra-Comique: *L'École des maris* (June 19, 1935) and *Madame Bovary* (June 1, 1951). He also composed a symphonic triptych after Rimbaud's *Les Illuminations* (Paris, Dec. 6, 1930); *Ophélie* (Paris, March, 29, 1933); and *Marine* (Paris, March 11, 1934). He further wrote several symphonic works, choruses, and chamber music. In 1959 he succeeded Florent Schmitt as a member of the Académie des Beaux-Arts.

Bondon, Jacques (Lauret Jules Désiré), French composer; b. Boulbon, Bouches-du-Rhône, Dec. 6, 1927. He studied violin and painting in Marseilles. In 1945 he went to Paris, where he took courses in composition with Koechlin, Milhaud, and Jean Rivier. After early experimentation with ultramodern techniques, he tergiversated to prudential modernism. He became associated with Martenot, and wrote a Concerto for Ondes Martenot and Orch. (1955); also composed music for films and for the radio.
WORKS: Orch.: *La Coupole* (1954); *Le Taillis ensorcelé* (1954); *Suite indienne* (1958); *Musique pour un autre monde* (1962); *Concert de printemps* for Trumpet, Strings, and Percussion (1957); *Concerto de Mars* for Guitar and Orch. (Paris, Nov. 20, 1966); *Mélousine au rocher,* radio opera (Luxembourg, Oct. 30, 1969); *Le Soleil multicolore* for Flute, Harp, and Viola (1970); *Giocoso* for Violin Solo and String Orch. (1970); *Lumières et formes animées* for String Orch. (Paris, Oct. 6, 1970); opera, *Ana et l'albatros* (Metz, Nov. 21, 1970); a science-fiction opera-ballet, *i. 330* (Nantes, May 20, 1975).
BIBL.: M.-J. Chauvin, "Entretien avec J. B.," *Courrier Musical de France* (Jan./April 1970).

Bonelli, Richard, American baritone; b. Port Byron, N.Y., Feb. 6, 1887; d. Los Angeles, June 7, 1980. His real name was **Bunn,** but he changed it to Bonelli when he began his career, since in his time it was difficult to succeed as a singer with an Anglo-Saxon name. He studied with Jean de Reszke in Europe; made his operatic debut as Valentine in *Faust* at the Brooklyn Academy of Music, N.Y., April 21, 1915; then sang at the Monte Carlo Opera, at La Scala in Milan, and in Paris. From 1925 to 1931 he was a member of the Chicago Opera Co.; he made his Metropolitan Opera debut as Germont in *La Traviata* on Dec. 1, 1932. He retired in 1945.

Bonfichi, Paolo, Italian organist and composer; b. Livraga, near Lodi, Oct. 6, 1769; d. Lodi, Dec. 29, 1840. He was self-taught as a keyboard performer; attended the Univ. of Parma, where he studied figured bass. He entered the order of Servi di Maria in 1787, but returned to music while in Rome as a student of counterpoint with Guglielmo. He then lived in a monastery in Poina (1796–1805); subsequently was in Milan;

in 1829 became maestro di cappella at the Santa Casa of Loreto, where he remained until 1839. He composed mainly music for the church, including oratorios and cantatas.

Bonhomme, Pierre, South Netherlands composer; b. c.1555; d. Liège, June 12, 1617. He was educated in Liège; received the tonsure in 1579; in 1594 was awarded a canonry at the collegiate church of Sainte-Croix in Liège, where he spent the rest of his life. He publ. *Melodiae sacrae* for 5 to 9 Voices (Frankfurt, 1603) and *Missae* for 6, 8, 10, and 12 Voices (Antwerp, 1616).

Boni, Guillaume, French composer who flourished in the 2nd half of the 16th century. He was maître de chapelle at the Cathedral in Toulouse. His sacred vocal works include motets and Psalms; he also composed secular sonnets after Ronsard.
    Bibl.: E. Droz, "G. B. de St. Flour en Auvergne, musicien de Ronsard," *Mélanges offerts à M. Abel Lefranc* (Paris, 1936).

Bonini, Severo, Italian composer, organist, and writer on music; b. Florence, Dec. 23, 1582; d. there, Dec. 5, 1663. He received the habit of the Vallombrosan Benedictines in 1595; professed in 1598; then studied theology and other subjects at the Univ. at Passignano; subsequently resided in an abbey in Florence. In 1611 he became organist at the abbey of S. Trinità; in 1613 assumed a similar position at S. Mercuriale in Forlì. In 1615 he was made camarlingo at the abbey of S. Michele in Forcole, Pistoia, and in 1619 at S. Mercuriale in Forlì. In 1623 he became curate at S. Martino in Strada, where he remained until 1637. In 1640 he was named organist and maestro di cappella at S. Trinità, posts he retained until his death. He wrote a valuable treatise on the beginnings of monody and opera, *Discorsi e regole sovra la musica et il contrappunto* (modern ed. and tr. by M. Bonino, Provo, Utah, 1978).
    Works: *Madrigali e canzonette spirituali* for Voice and Instruments (Florence, 1607); *Il primo libro delle canzonette affettuose in stile moderno* for 4 Voices (Florence, 1608; not extant); *Il primo libro de' motetti* for 3 Voices, Organ, and Instruments (Venice, 1609); *Il secondo libro de' madrigali e motetti* for 1 and 2 Voices and Instruments (Florence, 1609); *Lamento d'Arianna in stile recitativo* for 1 and 2 Voices (Venice, 1613); *Affetti spirituali* for 2 Voices (Venice, 1615); *Serena aleste, Motetti* for 1 to 3 Voices (Venice, 1615).
    Bibl.: M. Bonino, *Don S. B. (1582–1663): His "Discorsi e regole"* (diss., Univ. of Southern Calif., 1971).

Boninsegna, Celestina, Italian soprano; b. Reggio Emilia, Feb. 26, 1877; d. Milan, Feb. 14, 1947. Without the benefit of vocal training, she made her debut at the age of 15 at Reggio Emilia as Norina; then enrolled at the Pesaro Cons.; her official debut took place in Fano in 1896, when she appeared as Gilda; then sang in Milan, Rome, Genoa, and South America; also at Covent Garden, London (1904, 1905). On Dec. 21, 1906, she made her Metropolitan Opera debut as Aida, but remained on the roster for only that 1 season. Following her retirement, she taught voice; spent her last years in the Casa di Riposo in Milan.

Bónis, Ferenc, Hungarian musicologist; b. Miskolc, May 17, 1932. He was educated at the Budapest Academy of Music, studying composition with Szervánszky, Bartha, Kodály, and Szabolcsi (Ph.D., 1958, with the diss. *Mosónyi Mihály*). He was an ed. with Hungarian Radio (1950–52; 1957–70); became director of its programs in music for young audiences in 1970. From 1961 to 1973 he was engaged in musicological research at the Hungarian Academy of Sciences; was made a lecturer at the Budapest Academy of Music in 1972. He became ed. of *Magyar Zenetudomány* in 1959, and also of *Magyar Zenetörteneti Tanulmányok* in 1968.
    Writings: *Erkel Ferenc* (Budapest, 1953; 2nd ed., 1954); *Bartók élete képekben* (Budapest, 1956; 4th ed., for the Bartók centenary, 1980; in German, 1964; in French, 1964; in Eng. as *Béla Bartók: His Life in Pictures*, 1964); *Kadósa Pál* (Budapest, 1965); ed. *Tóth Aladár válogatott zenekritikai* (Budapest, 1968); *Bartók Béla élete képekben és documentumokban* (Buda-

pest, 1972; in German, 1972; in Eng. as *Béla Bartók: His Life in Pictures and Documents*, 1972).

Bonis, Mélanie (Mme. Albert Domange), French composer; b. Paris, Jan. 21, 1858; d. Sarcelles, Seine-et-Oise, March 18, 1937. She studied at the Paris Cons. with César Franck and Guiraud; wrote 22 chamber works (of which a Trio is still perf.); 150 piano pieces; 27 choruses; Fantasy for Piano and String Orch. About 200 of her works are publ.

Bonnet, Joseph (Élie Georges Marie), eminent French organist; b. Bordeaux, March 17, 1884; d. Ste. Luce-sur-Mer, Quebec, Aug. 2, 1944. He studied with his father, organist at Ste. Eulalie; at the age of 14 he was appointed regular organist at St. Nicholas, and soon after at St. Michel; entered the class of Guilmant at the Paris Cons. and graduated with 1st prize. In 1906 he won the post of organist at St. Eustache over many competitors. After extensive tours on the Continent and in England, he became organist of the Concerts du Conservatoire as successor to Guilmant (1911). He made his American debut in N.Y. (Jan. 30, 1917), followed by successful tours of the U.S. In 1940 he fled France and went to the U.S.; he finally settled in Quebec as a teacher at the Cons. He wrote many pieces for his instrument, and ed. for publication all the works played in his series of N.Y. concerts as *Historical Organ Recitals* (6 vols.); also publ. an anthology of early French organ music (N.Y., 1942).
    Bibl.: H.B. Gaul, "B., Bossi, Karg-Elert. Three Aperçus," *Musical Quarterly* (July 1918).

Bonno, Giuseppe, noted Austrian composer of Italian descent; b. Vienna, Jan. 29, 1711; d. there, April 15, 1788. His father, Lucrezio Bonno, was the imperial footman. Giuseppe Bonno began his musical studies with Johann Georg Reinhardt, the court organist. Charles VI sent Bonno to Naples in 1726 for further musical education; there he studied composition with Durante and Leo. His 1st opera, *Nigella e Nise*, was performed in Naples in 1732. In 1736 he returned to Vienna, where he brought out his 2nd opera, *L'amore insuperabile*. In 1737 he was made a court scholar in composition, and in 1739 was named court composer. In 1739 he brought out his oratorio *Eleazaro*, which proved highly successful. He subsequently joined Gluck and Dittersdorf as a Kapellmeister to Field Marshall Joseph Friedrich, Prince of Sachsen-Hildburghausen, in Schlosshof and Mannersdorf. In 1774 he succeeded Gassmann as Imperial Court Kapellmeister. Bonno was greatly esteemed as a teacher; Dittersdorf and Marianne di Martinez were among his pupils. He was a friend of the Mozart family, and recognized the budding genius of Mozart at an early date.
    Works: STAGE (all perf. at the Burgtheater in Vienna, unless otherwise stated): *Nigella e Nise*, pastorale (Naples, 1732); *L'amore insuperabile*, festa di camera (July 26, 1736); *Trajano*, festa di camera (Oct. 1, 1736); *La gara del genio con Giunone*, serenata (Laxenburg, May 13, 1737); *Alessandro Severo*, festa di camera (Oct. 1, 1737); *La generosità di Artaserse*, serenata (Nov. 4, 1737); a pastorale (Nov. 19, 1737); *La pace richiamata*, festa di camera (July 26, 1738); *La pietà di Numa*, festa di camera (Oct. 1, 1738); *La vera nobilità*, festa di camera (July 26, 1739); *Il natale di Numa Pompilio*, festa di camera (Oct. 1, 1739); *Il nume d'Atene*, festa di camera (Nov. 19, 1739); *La generosa Spartana*, serenata (Laxenburg, May 13, 1740); *Il natale di Giove*, azione teatrale (Favorita, Vienna, Oct. 1, 1740); *Il vero omaggio*, componimento drammatico (Schloss Schönbrunn, Vienna, March 13, 1743); *La danza*, cantata (April 1744); *Danae*, opera (1744; not extant); *Ezio*, opera (1749; not extant); *Il Re pastore*, dramma per musica (Schloss Schönbrunn, Vienna, Oct. 27, 1751); *L'Ero cinese*, opera (Schloss Schönbrunn, Vienna, May 13, 1752); *L'isola disabitata*, azione teatrale (Sept. 23, 1754); *Didone abbandonata*, opera (1752; not extant); *Colloquio amoroso fra Piramo e Tisbe* (1757); *Complimento*, for the Prince of Sachsen-Hildburghausen (1761; not extant); *L'Atenaide ovvero Gli affetti più generosi*, azione teatrale (1762); *Il sogno di Scipione* (1763); also, in collaboration with others, *Catone in Utica* (1742) and *L'Armida placata*

(Oct. 8, 1750). ORATORIOS (all perf. in Vienna): *Eleazaro* (1739); *San Paolo in Athene* (March 31, 1740); *Isacco figura del redentore* (March 18, 1759); *Il Giuseppe riconosciuto* (March 20, 1774). Also, masses and instrumental works.

BIBL.: E. Wellesz, "G. B.: Sein Leben und seine dramatischen Werke," *Sammelbände der Internationalen Musik-Gesellschaft*, XI (1909–10); A. Schienerl, *Die kirchlichen Kompositionen des G. B.* (diss., Univ. of Vienna, 1925); K. Breitner, *G. B. und sein Oratorienwerk* (diss., Univ. of Vienna, 1961).

Bononcini, Antonio Maria (not **Marco Antonio**, as he is often listed), Italian opera composer, son of **Giovannia Maria** and brother of **Giovanni Bononcini**; b. Modena, June 18, 1677; d. there, July 8, 1726. He studied with his father; his 1st success came with the production of his opera *Il trionfo di Camilla, regina dei Volsci* (Naples, Dec. 22, 1696). This opera was produced in many other theaters in Italy, sometimes under different titles, as *Amore per amore, La fede in cimento*, etc. It was presented in London (March 31, 1706) with great acclaim. In 1702 Bononcini was in Berlin; from 1704 to 1711 he was in Vienna, where he produced the operas *Teraspo* (Nov. 15, 1704), *Arminio* (July 26, 1706), *La conquista delle Spagne di Scipione Africano* (Oct. 1, 1707), *La presa di Tebe* (Oct. 1, 1708), and *Tigrane, re d'Armenia* (July 26, 1710). Returning to Italy, he produced the following operas in Milan: *Il Tiranno eroe* (Dec. 26, 1715), *Sesostri, re di Egitto* (Feb. 2, 1716), and *Griselda* (Dec. 26, 1718). In his native town of Modena, he directed his operas *L'enigma disciolto* (Oct. 15, 1716) and *Lucio Vero* (Nov. 5, 1716). His last opera, *Rosiclea in Dania*, was staged in Naples (Oct. 1, 1721). He wrote 19 operas in all, and 3 oratorios. His most famous opera, *Il trionfo di Camilla*, has often been erroneously attributed to his brother; several songs from it were publ. in London by Walsh.

BIBL.: L.F. Valdrighi, *I B. da Modena* (Modena, 1882).

Bononcini, Giovanni (not **Giovanni Battista,** despite the fact that this name appears on some of his compositions), Italian composer, son of **Giovanni Maria** and brother of **Antonio Maria Bononcini**; b. Modena, July 18, 1670; d. Vienna, July 9, 1747 (buried July 11). His 1st teacher was his father; he also studied with G.P. Colonna in Bologna, and took cello lessons from Giorgio. In 1687 he was a cellist in the chapel of S. Petronio in Bologna; in the same year he became maestro di cappella at S. Giovanni in Monte. He publ. his 1st work, *Trattenimenti da camera* for String Trio, in Bologna at the age of 15. This was followed in quick succession by a set of chamber concertos, "sinfonie" for small ensembles, masses, and instrumental duos (1685–91). In 1691 he went to Rome, where he produced his 1st opera, *Serse* (Jan. 25, 1694), and shortly afterward, another opera, *Tullo Ostilio* (Feb. 1694). In 1698 he went to Vienna as court composer; there he brought out his operas *La fede pubblica* (Jan. 6, 1699) and *Gli affetti più grandi vinti dal più giusto* (July 26, 1701). He spent 2 years (1702–4) at the court of Queen Sophie Charlotte in Berlin; at her palace in Charlottenburg he produced, in the summer of 1702, the opera *Polifemo;* here he also presented a new opera, *Gli amori di Cefalo e Procri* (Oct. 16, 1704). After the Queen's death (Feb. 1, 1705) the opera company was disbanded; Bononcini returned to Vienna and staged the following operas: *Endimione* (July 10, 1706), *Turno Aricino* (July 26, 1707), *Mario fuggitivo* (1708), *Abdolonimo* (Feb. 3, 1709), and *Muzio Scevola* (July 10, 1710). In 1711 Bononcini returned to Italy with his brother (who had also been in Vienna). In 1719 he was in Rome, where he produced the opera *Erminia*. In 1720 he received an invitation to join the Royal Academy of Music in London, of which Handel was director, and the Italian Opera Co. connected with it. A famous rivalry developed between the supporters of Handel, which included the King, and the group of noblemen (Marlborough, Queensberry, Rutland, and Sunderland) who favored Bononcini and other Italian composers. Indicative of the spirit of the time was the production at the King's Theatre of the opera *Muzio Scevola*, with the 1st act written by Amadei, the 2nd by Bononcini (he may have used material from his earlier setting of the same

subject), and the 3rd by Handel (April 15, 1721). By general agreement Handel won the verdict of popular approval; this episode may have inspired the well-known poem publ. at the time ("Some say, compar'd to Bononcini, That Mynheer Handel's but a ninny," etc.). Other operas brought out by Bononcini in London were *Astarto* (Nov. 19, 1720), *Crispo* (Jan. 10, 1722), *Farnace* (Nov. 27, 1723), *Calpurnia* (April 18, 1724), and *Astianatte* (May 6, 1727). He then suffered a series of setbacks: 1st the death of his chief supporter, Marlborough (1722), and then the revelation that a madrigal he had submitted to the Academy of Music was an arrangement of a work by Lotti, which put Bononcini's professional integrity in doubt. To this was added his strange association with one Count Ughi, a self-styled alchemist who claimed the invention of a philosopher's stone, and who induced Bononcini to invest his earnings in his scheme for making gold. After his London debacle, Bononcini went (in 1732) to Paris, where he was engaged as a cellist at the court of Louis XV. He was referred to in *Le Mercure de France* (Feb. 7, 1735) as the composer of 78 operas. In 1735 he was in Lisbon; in 1737, in Vienna, where he produced the oratorio *Ezechia* (April 4, 1737) and a Te Deum (1740). Reduced to poverty, he petitioned the young Empress Maria Theresa for a pension, which was granted in Oct. 1742, giving him a monthly stipend of 50 florins, received regularly until his death on July 9, 1747, at the age of 77. This date and the circumstances of his last years in Vienna were 1st made known in the valuable paper by Kurt Hueber, *Gli ultimi anni di Giovanni Bononcini, Notizie e documenti inediti*, publ. by the Academy of Sciences, Letters and Arts of Modena (Dec. 1954). Among Bononcini's works, other than operas, are 7 oratorios (including *Ezechia;* all on various biblical subjects), and instrumental works publ. in London by Walsh: several suites for Harpsichord; *Cantate e Duetti*, dedicated to George I (1721); Divertimenti for Harpsichord (1722); *Funeral Anthem for John, Duke of Marlborough* (1722); *12 Sonatas or Chamber Airs for 2 Violins and a Bass* (1732); etc.

BIBL.: K. Hueber, *Die Wiener Opern G. B.s von 1697 bis 1710* (diss., Univ. of Vienna, 1955); L. Lindgren, *A Bibliographic Scrutiny of Dramatic Works Set by G. and His Brother Antonio Maria Bononcini* (diss., Harvard Univ., 1972).

Bononcini, Giovanni Maria, Italian composer, father of **Giovanni** and **Antonio Maria Bononcini;** b. Montecorone, Sept. 23, 1642; d. Modena, Nov. 18, 1678. In 1671 he was awarded a ducal appointment as violinist at the Cathedral of Modena; also served as chamber musician to the Dowager Duchess Laura d'Este. He had 8 children, of whom the only 2 who survived infancy were Giovanni and Antonio Maria Bononcini. He publ. 11 sets of instrumental works: *I primi frutti del giardino musicale* (Venice, 1666); *Varii fiori* (Bologna, 1669); *Arie, correnti, sarabande, gighe e allemande* (Bologna, 1671); *Sonate* (Venice, 1672); *Ariette, correnti, gighe, allemande e sarabande* (Bologna, 1673); *Trattenimenti musicali* (Bologna, 1675); *Arie e correnti* (Bologna, 1678); also vocal works: *Cantate da camara* for Solo Voice and 2 Violins (Bologna, 1677); *Madrigali* for 5 Voices (Bologna, 1678). He further publ. a didactic manual, *Musico prattico* (Bologna, 1673; a German tr. was publ. in Stuttgart, 1701).

BIBL.: W. Klenz, *G.M. B. of Modena: A Chapter in Baroque Instrumental Music* (Durham, N.C., 1962).

Bononcini, Marco Antonio. See **Bononcini, Antonio Maria.**

Bonporti, Francesco Antonio, Italian composer; b. Trento (baptized), June 11, 1672; d. Padua, Dec. 19, 1748. He studied theology in Innsbruck and Rome; in 1695 returned to Trento; was ordained a priest and served as a cleric at the Cathedral of Trento. He publ. 3 sets of 10 trio sonatas each (Venice, 1696, 1698, and 1703); 10 sonatas for Violin and Bass (Venice, 1707); 10 "concerti a 4" and 5 "concertini" for Violin and Bass; 6 motets for Soprano, Violin, and Bass. He also wrote 2 sets of minuets (50 in each set), which are lost. Four of his "invenzioni" were mistaken for Bach's works and were included in the Bachgesellschaft ed. (XLV, part 1, p. 172). Henry Eccles publ. the 4th of these pieces as his own, incorporating it in his Violin Sonata No. 11.

BIBL.: G. Barblan, *Un Musicista trentino, F.A. B.* (Florence, 1940); C. Bouvet, "Un Groupe de compositions musicales de Bonporti publiées sous le nom de Bach," *Union Musicologique* (The Hague, 1921); G. Barblan, ed., *F.A. B. nel 3° centenario della nascita* (Trent, 1972); L. Feininger, *F.A. B.: Catalogus thematicus operum omnium* (Trent, 1975).

Bonsel, Adriaan, Dutch flutist and composer; b. Hilversum, Aug. 4, 1918. He studied at the Amsterdam Cons.; appeared as a flute soloist in recitals and with various orchs.

WORKS: Suite for Flute and String Orch. (1946); *Folkloristic Suite* for Orch. (1948); Clarinet Concerto (1950); 2 syms. (1956, 1957); Divertimento for Small Orch. (1957); *S.O.S.*, overture (1962); *Vrede-Oorlog-Vrede? (Peace-War-Peace?) Moto-perpetuo?* for Orch. (1975); *Minneliederen*, 6 love songs for Baritone, Chorus, and Small Orch. (1957); 2 wind quintets (1949, 1953); *Elegy* for Solo Viola (1961); *Concert Études* for Solo Flute (1963); *Musica* for Flute, Cello, and Piano (1971); *Anthriscus Sylvestris*, divertimento for 12 Flutes (1974); Octet for Winds (1975); *Intrada* for Horn, 2 Trumpets, 2 Trombones, and Tuba (1982).

Bontempi (real name, **Angelini**), **Giovanni Andrea,** Italian singer and composer; b. Perugia, c.1624; d. Torgiano, July 1, 1705. He was a castrato, and sang in the choir of S. Marco in Venice (1643–50). After studies with Mazzocchi, he was appointed joint Kapellmeister in Dresden, with Schütz and Vincenzo Albrici, in 1656. He assumed the name Bontempi after his patron, Cesare Bontempi. In 1680 he returned to Italy; sang at the Collegiata di S. Maria at Sapello, near Foligno, in 1682; was maestro di cappella there during the 1st half of 1686. He was one of the earliest composers of Italian operas and oratorios. His 1st opera, *Il Paride in musica*, to his own libretto, was produced in Dresden, on Nov. 3, 1662; it was the 1st Italian opera ever produced there. Two later operas, both produced in Dresden, were *Apollo e Dafne*, written in collaboration with Peranda and produced in Dresden on Sept. 3, 1671, and *Giove e Io* (also with Peranda), produced in Dresden on Jan. 16, 1673. He also composed an oratorio, *Martirio di San Emiliano*; publ. the treatises *Nova quatuor vocibus componendi methodus* (Dresden, 1660); *Tractus in quo demonstrantur occultae convenientiae sonorum systematis participati* (Bologna, 1690); *Historia musica, nella quale si ha piena cognitione della teorica e della pratica antica della musica harmonica secondo la dottrina de' Greci* (Perugia, 1695).

BIBL.: G.B. Rossi Scotti, *Di G.A. B. di Perugia* (1878); F. Briganti, *G.A. Angelini-B. (1624–1705), Musicista, letterato, architto: Perugia-Dresda* (Florence, 1956).

Bonynge, Richard (Alan), noted Australian conductor; b. Sydney, Sept. 29, 1930. He studied piano at the New South Wales Conservatorium of Music in Sydney and at the Royal College of Music in London, beginning his career as a pianist. After marrying the soprano **Joan Sutherland** in 1954, he devoted himself to helping her master the bel canto operatic repertoire. In 1962 he made his conducting debut in a concert with his wife in Rome; he then made his debut as an opera conductor with a performance of *Faust* in Vancouver (1963). He made his 1st appearance at London's Covent Garden in 1964, leading a performance of *I puritani*. On Dec. 12, 1966, he made his Metropolitan Opera debut in N.Y., conducting *Lucia di Lammermoor*, with his wife in the title role. In subsequent years he conducted concerts and operas throughout the world. He was music director of the Australian Opera in Sydney from 1976 to 1986, and in 1977 was made a Commander of the Order of the British Empire.

BIBL.: Q. Eaton, *Sutherland & B.: An Intimate Biography* (N.Y., 1987).

Bookspan, Martin, American music critic, administrator, and broadcaster; b. Boston, July 30, 1926. He was educated at the Boston Music School (violin and theory) and Harvard College (B.S. in German literature, 1947). He was executive director of the New England Opera Theater (1952–54); from 1956 to 1968 held various administrative positions with WQXR Radio in N.Y. In 1968 he was named coordinator for the sym. and concert activities of ASCAP. He was host and commentator for the Boston Sym. and Pops radio broadcasts (1957–68); from 1975 to 1988 he was host, commentator, and executive producer for the N.Y. Phil. radio broadcasts; from 1976 also commentator for the "Live from Lincoln Center" PBS telecasts. He has been a permanent member of the panel of critics for the "First Hearing" radio program; was a contributing ed. to *Stereo Review Magazine* (1958–76); also wrote for the *New York Times* (1963–65). He publ. *101 Masterpieces of Music and Their Composers* (N.Y., 1968); *Zubin: The Zubin Mehta Story* (N.Y., 1978); *André Previn: A Biography* (Garden City, N.Y., 1981).

Boone, "Blind" (John William), black American pianist and composer of popular music; b. Miami, Mo., May 17, 1864; d. Warrensburg, Mo., Oct. 4, 1927. He was educated at the Missouri School for the Blind, where he learned to play the piano; subsequently he traveled widely as a performer. His *Blind Boone's Southern Rag Medleys* Nos. 1 and 2 (1908–9) became quite popular; he also wrote waltzes, character pieces, and a number of songs. His *Marshfield Tornado* depicts a storm that hit the aforementioned Missouri town during the 1880s.

BIBL.: M. Fuell, *B. B.: His Early Life and His Achievements* (Kansas City, Mo., 1915); R. Darch, "B. B.: A Sensational Missouri Musician Forgotten," *Bulletin of the Missouri Historical Society,* XVII/3 (1961); M. Harrah, "The Incomparable B. B.," *Ragtimer* (July–Aug. 1969).

Boone, Charles, American composer of the avant-garde; b. Cleveland, June 21, 1939. He studied with Karl Schiske at the Vienna Academy of Music (1960–61); after returning to the U.S., he took private lessons with Ernst Krenek and Adolph Weiss in Los Angeles (1961–62); attended the Univ. of Southern Calif. (B.M., 1963) and San Francisco State College (M.A., 1968); served as chairman of the San Francisco Composers' Forum and coordinator of the Mills College Performing Group and Tape Music Center. His music creates a sonic environment on purely structural principles, employing serial matrices, coloristic contrasts, and spatial parameters of performing instruments, with resulting styles ranging from lyrical pointillism to static sonorism. Electronic resources make up part of his musical equipment.

WORKS: *Icarus* for Flute Solo (1964); *Song of Suchness* for Soprano, Flute, Piccolo, Viola, Piano, and Celesta (1964); *Parallels* for Violin and Piano (1964); *Oblique Formation* for Flute and Piano (1965); *Starfish* for Flute, E-flat Clarinet, Percussion, 2 Violins, and Piano (1966); *The Yellow Bird* for Orch. (1967); *Constant Comment* for Stereophonic Tape (1967); *Shadow* for Oboe Solo, Tape, and Orch. (1968); *The Edge of the Land* for Orch. (1968); *Not Now* for Clarinet Solo (1969); Quartet for Violin, Clarinet, Cello, and Piano (1970); *Zephyrus* for Oboe and Piano (1970); *Vermilion* for Oboe Solo (1970); *Chinese Texts* for Soprano and Orch. (1971); *2nd Landscape* for Chamber Orch. (1973); *Raspberries* for 3 Drummers (1974); *Linea Meridiana* for Chamber Ensemble (1975); *San Zeno/Verona* for Chamber Ensemble (1976); *Fields/Singing* for Soprano and Chamber Ensemble (1976); *Shunt* for 3 Drummers (1978); *String Piece* for String Orch. (1978); *Streaming for Solo Flute* (1979); *Winter's End* for Soprano, Countertenor, Viola da Gamba, and Harpsichord (1980); *The Watts Towers* for Solo Drummer (1981); *Trace* for Flute and 10 Players (1981); *Weft* for 6 Percussion (1982); *Drum Bug* for Mechanical Woodblocks (1983); *Solar 1* for Flute and Trumpet (1985); *Silence and Light* for String Quartet (1989–90); *Morphosis* for Percussion Quartet (1989–90).

Boone, Pat (Charles Eugene), American singer of popular music; b. Jacksonville, Fla., June 1, 1934. He studied at North Texas State Teachers College in Denton; continued his studies at Columbia Univ. (B.S., 1958). He 1st came to prominence as a singer of popular music on television in 1955; later became active as an evangelist. His daughter **Debby** (**Deborah Anni;** b. Hackensack, N.J., Sept. 22, 1956) is also a singer.

Booren, Jo van den, Dutch composer; b. Maastricht, March 14, 1935. He studied trumpet with Marinus Komst and composition with Kees van Baaren and Klaus Huber; was active as an orch. trumpet player. In his music he pursues the goal of sonorous structuralism; some of his works bear ostentatiously abstract titles.

WORKS: Trio for Oboe, Clarinet, and Bassoon (1960); Sonata for 3 Clarinets (1962); *Suite dionysienne* for English Horn and String Orch. (1963–64); *Estremi* for Oboe, Violin, Viola, and Cello (1967); *Spectra* for Wind Quintet (1967); *Capriccio* for Brass Orch. (1968); *Spiel I* for Oboe and Electronic Sound (1969); *Strofa I* for Solo Cello (1969); *Strofa II* for Solo Trumpet (1970); *Strofa III* for Solo Horn (1972); *Equilibrio* for Solo Flute (1970); *Ballade* for Solo Oboe (1971); *Intrada Festiva* for 4 Horns, 4 Trumpets, and 4 Trombones (1971); *Akirob* for Flute, Violin, and Viola (1972); *Potpourri 1973* for Brass Quintet (1973); *Sinfonia jubilata* for Orch. (Tilburg, Oct. 3, 1975); *Birds,* a "story" for 5 Flutes (1975); *Hymn* for Organ (1985); *Oblation* for Organ, 2 Trumpets, 2 Horns, and 2 Trombones (1985).

Boosey & Hawkes, British music publishers. **Thomas Boosey** was a London bookseller and a continental traveler since 1792. He was often asked to handle music, and in 1816 founded a music publishing house on Holles Street. On the Continent he met eminent musicians of the time; he visited Vienna and negotiated about publication with Beethoven (who mentions Boosey's name in one of his letters to the Royal Phil. Soc. in London). Boosey's main stock consisted of Italian and French operas; he owned copyrights of Bellini, Donizetti, and Verdi (until 1854); publ. inexpensive English eds. of standard European works. In the 1820s he put his son, **Thomas,** in charge of musical publications. In 1846 the firm of Boosey & Sons began publishing band music; in 1855 (in conjunction with the flutist R.S. Pratten) the manufacture of improved flutes was begun; in 1868 the firm acquired Henry Distin's factory for musical instruments, and supplied band instruments for the British and Colonial armies. It was this development that eventually brought about the merger of Boosey and Hawkes. **William Henry Hawkes** was a trumpeter-in-ordinary to Queen Victoria. He established in 1865 a workshop of band instruments and an ed. of concert music for orch. and became a strong competitor of Boosey & Sons from 1885 on. Economic pressure forced the amalgamation of the 2 firms in 1930, combining valuable eds. covering a whole century of music. A branch of Boosey & Sons had been established in N.Y. (1892), discontinued in 1900, and reestablished in 1906; after the merger, Boosey & Hawkes opened offices in N.Y., Chicago, and Los Angeles. In Canada, the business was inaugurated in 1913; a Paris branch, the Éditions Hawkes, was started in 1922; further affiliates were established in Australia (1933), India (1937), Argentina (1945), South Africa (1946), and Germany (1950). After World War II the factories for the manufacture of band instruments in London were greatly expanded; quantity production of wind instruments, harmonicas, and drums enabled the firm to extend the market to all parts of the world. For a few years after the war, Boosey & Hawkes leased Covent Garden. In 1927 the firm acquired the American rights of Enoch & Sons; in 1943 the catalogue of Adolph Fürstner, containing all the operas of Richard Strauss, was bought for certain territories; in 1947 the Koussevitzky catalogue (Édition Russe de Musique and Édition Gutheil) was purchased, including the major output of Stravinsky, Prokofiev, and Rachmaninoff. Other acquisitions include the copyrights of publications of Winthrop Rogers and Rudall Carte.

Borch, Gaston Louis Christopher, composer and conductor; b. Guines, France, March 8, 1871; d. Stockholm, Feb. 14, 1926. He studied in Paris with Massenet (composition) and Delsart (cello), then with Svendsen in Copenhagen; conducted various organizations in Norway (1896–99); went to the U.S. in 1899 as cellist with the Thomas Orch. in Chicago; then

played in the Pittsburgh Orch. (1903–6); conducted various orchs. in Switzerland, France, Belgium, the Netherlands, and Germany. He composed 3 symphonic poems: *Geneviève de Paris, Quo Vadis,* and *Frithjof;* made popular arrangements of standard classics for piano, violin, and cello. His 1-act opera, *Silvio* (written as a sequel to *Cavalleria rusticana*), was produced in Christiania in 1897. He publ. a *Practical Manual of Instrumentation* (Boston, 1918).

Borchard, Adolphe, French pianist and composer; b. Le Havre, June 30, 1882; d. Paris, Dec. 13, 1967. He studied at the Paris Cons. with Diémer and Lenepveu, where he won prizes for piano (1903) and composition (1905, 1907); toured extensively as a pianist, making his American debut in 1910; later settled in Paris as director of various musical activities sponsored by the French government. He composed *Es Kual Herria* (The Basque Country) for Piano and Orch. (Paris, 1922); *En marge de Shakespeare* for Orch. (1923); *L'Élan* for Orch. (1923); *Sept estampes amoureuses* for Orch. (1927); numerous songs.

Borck, Edmund von, talented German composer; b. Breslau, Feb. 22, 1906; killed in action near Nettuno, Italy, Feb. 16, 1944. He studied composition in Breslau (1920–26), and music history at the Univ. of Berlin; held several positions as opera conductor in Berlin and Frankfurt; then taught theory and composition in Berlin until drafted into the army in 1940. His progress as a composer was rapid; his early works indicated an original creative ability, and his death in combat was a great loss to German music. His style of composition is neo-Classical, with strong contrapuntal structure; the rather austere and reticent mode of expression assumes in Borck's music a colorful aspect through a variety of melodic and rhythmic devices, often in a rhapsodically romantic vein.

WORKS: Concerto for Alto Saxophone and Orch. (1932); Violin Sonata (1932); *Orchesterstücke* (1933); *Ländliche Kantate* (1934); Concerto for Orch. (1936); Sextet for Flute and Strings (1936); *Kleine Suite* for Unaccompanied Flute (1938); 2 *Fantasiestücke* for Orch. (1940); Piano Concerto (1941); *Orphika,* "an Apollonian transformation" for Orch. (1941); an opera, *Napoleon* (Gera, 1942).

BIBL.: K. Laux, "E. v.B.," in *Musik und Musiker der Gegenwart* (Essen, 1949).

Borde, Jean Benjamin de la. See **La Borde, Jean Benjamin de.**

Bordes, Charles (Marie Anne), French choral conductor; b. Roche-Corbon, near Vouvray-sur-Loire, May 12, 1863; d. Toulon, Nov. 8, 1909. He studied piano with Marmontel and composition with César Franck. In 1894, in association with Guilmant and Vincent d'Indy, he organized the Schola Cantorum in Paris, and in subsequent years organized chapters of it in Avignon and Montpellier. He made numerous tours with his choral group. In 1889 he was commissioned by the French government to make a study of Basque folk songs; he publ. 100 of these in *Archives de la tradition basque.* He also wrote several pieces based on Basque motifs, among them *Suite basque* for Flute and String Quartet (1888) and *Rapsodie basque* for Piano and Orch. (1890); also ed. several anthologies of early French music, publ. by the Schola Cantorum.

BIBL.: C. B., *In memoriam* (Paris, Schola Cantorum, 1909); P. Alibert, *C. B. à Maguelonne* (Paris, 1926); P. Dowd, *C. B. and the Schola Cantorum of Paris* (diss., Catholic Univ. of America, Washington, D.C., 1969).

Bordogni, Giulio Marco, Italian tenor and singing teacher; b. Gazzaniga, near Bergamo, Jan. 23, 1789; d. Paris, July 31, 1856. He was a pupil of Simon Mayr; made his operatic debut in 1808, at La Scala, Milan. From 1819 to 1833 he was engaged at the Théâtre-Italien in Paris; later devoted himself primarily to teaching; he joined the staff of the Paris Cons. in 1820. He publ. a collection of 36 vocalises, in 2 vols., which became a standard book of vocal exercises throughout Europe.

Bordoni, Faustina. See **Hasse, Faustina.**

Borel-Clerc (real name, **Clerc**), **Charles,** French composer of popular music; b. Pau, Sept. 22, 1879; d. Cannes, April 9,

1959. He studied music at 1st in Toulouse; at the age of 17 he went to Paris, where he studied the oboe at the Paris Cons. with Gillet, and composition with Lenepveu; then played oboe in various Paris orchs. He wrote numerous operettas, music revues, and a great number of songs; his greatest success came with *La Matchiche* (1903), a song that became world-famous. His other celebrated songs are *C'est jeune et ça n'sait pas; Madelon de la Victoire* (1918; a sequel to the war song *Madelon* by Camille Robert); many chansonettes for Maurice Chevalier and other artists.

Boretz, Benjamin (Aaron), American composer, editor, and music critic; b. N.Y., Oct. 3, 1934. He studied piano and cello, and received lessons in conducting from Julius Rudel and in harpsichord playing from Erwin Bodky; he also took courses at Brooklyn College (B.A., 1954), Brandeis Univ. (M.F.A., 1957), and Princeton Univ. (M.F.A., 1960; Ph.D., 1970). Among his composition mentors were Berger, Fine, Foss, Milhaud, and Sessions. He held many academic appointments, including N.Y. Univ. (1964–69), Columbia Univ. (1969–72), and Bard College (from 1973). He was music critic for the *Nation* (1962–70), and, with Berger, founded *Perspectives of New Music* (1961), serving as its ed. until 1984. With Edward T. Cone, he co-edited *Perspectives on Schoenberg and Stravinsky* (1968; 2nd ed., rev., 1972), *Perspectives on American Composers* (1971), *Perspectives on Contemporary Music Theory* (1972), and *Perspectives on Notation and Performance* (1976). His compositions include a Concerto Grosso for String Orch. (1956); a Violin Concerto (1956); a Divertimento for 5 Instruments (1957); a String Quartet (1958); *Group Variations I* (for Orch., 1967) and *II* (for Computer, 1971); *Liebeslied* for Piano (1974); "*. . . my chart shines high where the blue milk's upset . . .*" for Piano (1978); *Language, as a Music: 6 Marginal Pretexts for Composition* for Speaker, Piano, and Prerecorded Tape (1980); and *Soliloquy I* for Piano (1981). He also composed a series of works in sound score, the "notation" being in the form of sound on tape.

Borg, Kim, noted Finnish bass; b. Helsinki, Aug. 7, 1919. He 1st studied chemistry; then enrolled in the Sibelius Academy of Music; also took singing lessons in Sweden, Denmark, Austria, Italy, and America. He began his operatic career at Århus in 1951; made his Metropolitan Opera debut in N.Y. on Oct. 30, 1959, as Count Almaviva in *Le nozze di Figaro*, remaining on the company's roster until 1962. He was one of the few non-Russian artists to sing the title role of *Boris Godunov* at the Bolshoi Opera in Moscow. In 1972 he became a member of the faculty of the Royal Cons. of Music in Copenhagen. He furthermore distinguished himself as a composer; wrote 3 trios, a String Quartet, a Trombone Concerto, and a Double-bass Concerto; publ. a didactic manual, *ABC for the Finnish Singer.*

Borgatti, Giuseppe, Italian tenor, father of **Renata Borgatti;** b. Cento, March 17, 1871; d. Reno, Lago Maggiore, Oct. 18, 1950. He studied with Alessandro Busi in Bologna; made his operatic debut as Faust in Castelfranco Veneto in 1892; in 1896 sang the title role in *Andrea Chenier* at La Scala, Milan; also sang in Wagner's operas. He retired from the stage in 1914 owing to glaucoma; became totally blind in 1923. He publ. an autobiography, *La mia vita d'artista* (Bologna, 1927).

Borgatti, Renata, Italian pianist, daughter of **Giuseppe Borgatti;** b. Bologna, March 2, 1894; d. Rome, March 10, 1964. She pursued a fairly successful career mainly in recital, presenting programs of the complete works of Debussy. After the end of World War II, she lived in Rome.

Borge, Victor (real name, **Borge Rosenbaum**), variously talented Danish pianist and inborn humorist who, in his American avatar, carved for himself a unique niche as a provider of "comedy in music"; b. Copenhagen, Jan. 3, 1909, of Russian Jewish extraction (his father having left Russia to avoid being drafted into the imperial army). He entertained no ambition to become a 2nd Horowitz, but he developed a remarkable facility and prestidigital velocity on the keys. He escaped being

a wunderkind, however, and took some theory courses at the Copenhagen Cons. His next stop after Denmark was Berlin, where he became a pupil of a pupil of Liszt. Later he was a pupil of a pupil of Busoni. He never developed the necessary *Sitzfleisch* for a virtuoso career, but he was sufficiently adept at the piano to arrange for a concert tour in Sweden. In the meantime, the Nazis invaded Denmark and there was nothing for Borge to do but to go to the U.S., where he had connections through his American-born wife. He emigrated in 1940 and became a U.S. citizen in 1948. In America he changed his name to Victor Borge and inaugurated a Broadway show under the logo "Comedy in Music" (1953), giving a total of 849 performances—unprecedented in N.Y. annals for a 1-man show. As a diversion he also started a poultry farm on his rural estate, specializing in Rock Cornish hens. He mastered idiomatic English to such an extent that he could improvise jokes that invariably elicited chuckles. He also developed a sepulchral voice imitating bass singers and an ornithological coloratura à la Jenny Lind. Thus equipped, he made a career on television, continuing his solo appearances well into his 80s.

BIBL.: H. Temianka, "V. B. Zooms toward 80," *Musical America* (Jan. 1989).

Borghi, Adelaide, Italian mezzo-soprano; b. Bologna, Aug. 9, 1829; d. there, Sept. 28, 1901. Acting on the advice of Pasta, she trained herself for the stage; made her debut at Urbino (1846) in Mercadante's *Il Giuramento;* toured through Italy and in Vienna and Paris (1854–56); sang with the Grand Opéra in Paris (1856–59); appeared in London with great success (1860); then returned to Italy.

Borghi, Giovanni Battista, Italian composer; b. Camerino, Macerata, Aug. 25, 1738; d. Loreto, Feb. 25, 1796. He studied at the Cons. della Pietà dei Turchini in Naples (1757–59). From 1759 to 1778 he was maestro di cappella at the Macerata Cathedral; from 1778, at S. Casa of Loreto. He composed some 25 operas; *La morte di Semiramide* (Milan, Feb. 9, 1791) was moderately successful. He also wrote a number of oratorios and other sacred works.

Borgioli, Armando, Italian baritone; b. Florence, March 19, 1898; d. in an air raid on the Milan–Modena train near Codogno, Jan. 20, 1945. He made his debut as Amonasro at the Teatro Carcano in Milan in 1925; then sang at La Scala in Milan and Covent Garden in London. On Jan. 22, 1932, he made his Metropolitan Opera debut in N.Y., as Carlo in *La forza del destino;* continued on the company's roster until 1935. He was best known for his dramatic roles in Verdi's operas.

Borgioli, Dino, Italian tenor; b. Florence, Feb. 15, 1891; d. there, Sept. 12, 1960. He made his operatic debut at the Teatro Corso in Milan, in 1914; then sang leading parts in various Italian opera houses; also had guest engagements at Covent Garden, London. In 1924 he accompanied Nellie Melba on her farewell tour of Australia. On Dec. 31, 1934, he made his American debut at the Metropolitan Opera, N.Y., as Rodolfo in *La Bohème;* then returned to Italy, where he was active mainly as a voice teacher.

Borgström, Hjalmar, Norwegian critic and composer; b. Christiania, March 23, 1864; d. there (Oslo), July 5, 1925. He studied with Ursin, Svendsen, and Lindeman; also at Leipzig, Berlin, Paris, and London. In 1901 he returned to Christiania; was music critic of the *Aftenposten* from 1913.

WORKS: 2 operas, *Thora fra Rimol* and *Fiskeren;* 2 syms.; symphonic poems: *Hamlet; Jesus in Gethsemane; John Gabriel Borkman; Tanken; Reformation Cantata;* violin and piano concertos; chamber music; piano pieces; songs.

Bori, Lucrezia (real name, **Lucrecia Borja y Gonzalez de Riancho**), lyric soprano; b. Valencia, Dec. 24, 1887; d. N.Y., May 14, 1960. She studied with Melchior Vidal; made her debut in Rome on Oct. 31, 1908, as Micaëla; then sang in Milan, in Naples, and, in 1910, in Paris as Manon Lescaut, with the Metropolitan Opera Co., then on a European tour. In 1911 she sang at La Scala in Milan; made her debut at the Metropolitan Opera in N.Y. as Manon Lescaut on Nov.

11, 1912, and sang there until the end of the 1914–15 season. After a period of retirement occasioned by a vocal affliction, she reappeared in 1919 at Monte Carlo as Mimi, returning to the Metropolitan in 1921 in the same role. Thereafter she appeared in N.Y. with increasing success and popularity until the end of the 1935–36 season, when she retired from opera.

Borisov, Lilcho, Bulgarian composer; b. Sofia, Nov. 1, 1925. He studied composition with Ghedini and clarinet at the Verdi Cons. in Milan, graduating in 1952.
    WORKS: *Cosmic Scenes* for Wind Quartet (1958); Trio for Clarinet, Bassoon, and Piano (1958); Violin Sonata (1962); Clarinet Concerto (1966); *Scherzo* for Clarinet and Chamber Orch. (1966); 6 *Études* for 2 Clarinets (1966); *Sonatina concertante* for Violin and Chamber Orch.; Concerto for Violin and Chamber Orch. (1971); 5 *Pieces* for Violin and Piano (1973).

Borkh, Inge (real name, **Ingeborg Simon**), famous German soprano; b. Mannheim, May 26, 1917. She 1st appeared as a stage actress, then decided upon a singing career. She studied at the Milan Cons. and at the Mozarteum in Salzburg. She made her debut as Czipra in Johann Strauss's *Zigeunerbaron* at the Lucerne Opera in 1940; remained a member there until 1944; then sang at the Bern Opera until 1951. She made her American debut at the San Francisco Opera in 1953; on Jan. 24, 1958, she appeared at the Metropolitan Opera in N.Y. as Salome; she was on its roster also during the seasons of 1960–61 and 1970–71. She made her farewell operatic appearance at the Munich Festival in 1988.

Bořkovec, Pavel, Czech composer; b. Prague, June 10, 1894; d. there, July 22, 1972. He originally studied philosophy, and turned to composition rather late in life; took lessons with Jaroslav Křička and J.B. Foerster in 1919; from 1925 to 1927 attended master classes of Josef Suk at the Prague Cons. From 1946 to 1964, he was on the faculty of the Academy of Musical Arts in Prague. His early works were in the manner of Dvořák and Suk; later he experienced the influence of neo-Classicism and adopted the technique of dissonant counterpoint in the Baroque framework; also cultivated topical subjects from the world of sports, exemplified by his symphonic piece *The Start.*
    WORKS: 2 operas: *The Satyr*, after Goethe's poem (1937–38; Prague, Oct. 8, 1942), and *Paleček* (Tom Thumb; 1945–47; Czech Radio award, 1948; Prague, Dec. 17, 1958); ballet, *Krysař* (The Pied Piper; 1939; concert perf., Prague, Jan. 15, 1941; 1st stage perf., Oct. 8, 1942, along with *The Satyr*); *Stmívání* (Twilight), symphonic poem (1920); 3 syms. (1926–27; 1955; 1959); *The Start*, sym. allegro (1929; Prague, March 26, 1930); 2 piano concertos (1931; 1949–50); Violin Concerto (1933); *Partita* for Orch. (1936); Concerto Grosso for 2 Violins, Cello, Orch., and Piano (1941–42); 2 *Symphoniettas* (for Chamber Orch., 1944; 1963–68); Cello Concerto (1950–51); *Silentium Turbatum*, symphonic movement for Alto, Orch., and Electric Guitar (Prague, Feb. 28, 1965); Te Deum for Soli, Chorus, and Orch. (1968); Piano Quartet (1922); 5 string quartets (1924; 1928; 1940; 1947; 1961–62); Solo Viola Sonata (1931); Wind Quintet (1932); 2 violin sonatas (1934, 1956); Nonet (1941–42); Violin Sonatina (1942); *Intermezzo* for Horn and Piano (1965); Suite for Piano (1930); Partita for Piano (1935); 2 *Pieces* for Piano (1941–42); melodrama, *Jen jedenkrát* (Only Once; 1921); *Stadion* (The Stadium) for Voice, Wind Quintet, and Piano (1929); *Love Songs*, after Goethe and Villon, for Voice, and Piano or Small Orch. (1932); 5 *Songs*, to poems of Pasternak (1935); 6 *Madrigals about Time* for Chorus (1957).

Borkowski, Bohdan, Polish composer; b. Teczynek, near Krakow, Nov. 7, 1852; d. Warsaw, Nov. 6, 1901. He studied piano with Nowakowski and harmony with Moniuszko at the Warsaw Inst. of Music; then continued his studies with Saar in Vienna. Upon his return to Warsaw, he was active as a teacher of piano and composition. He was known mainly for his sacred music; he composed 3 masses and a number of choral works.

Bornefeld, Helmut, German organist and composer; b. Stuttgart-Untertürkheim, Dec. 14, 1906; d. Heidenheim, Feb. 11, 1990. He studied organ, piano, and composition at the Hochschule für Musik in Stuttgart; then was organist and choirmaster in Heidenheim. With Siegfried Reda, he organized the Heidenheim Arbeitstage für Neue Kirchenmusik in 1946, and remained actively engaged in its activities until 1960. His compositions include organ pieces and numerous choruses.
    WRITINGS: *Das Positiv* (Kassel, 1941); *Orgelbau und neue Orgelmusik* (Kassel, 1952); *Orgelspiegel* (Kassel, 1966).

Bornschein, Franz Carl, American composer; b. Baltimore, Feb. 10, 1879; d. there, June 8, 1948. He studied at the Peabody Cons. in Baltimore (1895–1902), and became a teacher of violin and conductor of the student orch. there in 1906.
    WORKS: *The Phantom Canoe*, Indian suite for Orch. (Baltimore, Nov. 24, 1916); *Onowa*, cantata (1916); *The Sea God's Daughter*, symphonic poem (Chicago, Feb. 10, 1924); *Old Louisiana*, symphonic poem (1930); *The Willow Plate*, operetta (1932); *Leif Ericson*, symphonic poem (Baltimore, Feb. 23, 1936); *Southern Nights*, symphonic poem (Washington, D.C., March 1, 1936); *Moon over Taos* for Flute, Percussion, and String Orch. (1939); some chamber music and vocal compositions.

Borodin, Alexander (Porfirievich), celebrated Russian composer; b. St. Petersburg, Nov. 12, 1833; d. there, Feb. 27, 1887. He was the illegitimate son of a Georgian prince, Gedianov; his mother was the wife of an army doctor. In accordance with customary procedure in such cases, the child was registered as the lawful son of one of Gedianov's serfs, Porfiry Borodin; hence, the patronymic, Alexander Porfirievich. He was given an excellent education; learned several foreign languages, and was taught to play the flute. He played 4-hand arrangements of Haydn's and Beethoven's syms. with his musical friend M. Shchiglev. At the age of 14 he tried his hand at composition; wrote a piece for flute and piano and a String Trio on themes from *Robert le Diable*. In 1850 he became a student of the Academy of Medicine in St. Petersburg, and developed a great interest in chemistry; he graduated in 1856 with honors, and joined the staff as assistant prof.; in 1858 received his doctorate in chemistry; contributed several important scientific papers to the bulletin of the Russian Academy of Sciences; traveled in Europe on a scientific mission (1859–62). Although mainly preoccupied with his scientific pursuits, Borodin continued to compose. In 1863 he married Catherine Protopopova, who was an accomplished pianist; she remained his faithful companion and musical partner; together they attended concerts and operas in Russia and abroad; his letters to her from Germany (1877), describing his visit to Liszt in Weimar, are of great interest. Of a decisive influence on Borodin's progress as a composer was his meeting with Balakirev in 1862; later he formed friendships with the critic Stasov, who named Borodin as one of the "mighty 5" (actually, Stasov used the expression "mighty heap"), with Mussorgsky and other musicians of the Russian national school. He adopted a style of composition in conformity with their new ideas; he particularly excelled in a type of Russian orientalism which had a great attraction for Russian musicians at the time. He never became a consummate craftsman, like Rimsky-Korsakov; although quite proficient in counterpoint, he avoided purely contrapuntal writing; his feeling for rhythm and orch. color was extraordinary, and his evocation of exotic scenes in his orch. works and in his opera *Prince Igor* is superb. Composition was a very slow process for Borodin; several of his works remained incomplete, and were ed. after his death by Rimsky-Korsakov and Glazunov.
    WORKS: OPERAS: *Prince Igor*, opera in 4 acts (begun in 1869, on the subject of the famous Russian medieval chronicle *Tale of Igor's Campaign*; completed posth. by Rimsky-Korsakov and Glazunov; 1st perf., St. Petersburg, Nov. 4, 1890; London, June 8, 1914, in Russian; N.Y., Dec. 30, 1915, in Italian); an opera-farce, *Bogatyry* (The Valiant Knights; anonymously produced in Moscow on Oct. 29, 1867; rediscovered in 1932, and produced in Moscow, Nov. 12, 1936, with a new libretto by Demian Biedny, to serve propaganda purposes in

an anti-religious campaign, but 2 days later banned by the Soviet government for its mockery of Russian nationalism); sketches for the 4th act of an opera, *Mlada* (never produced), each act of which was to have been written by a different composer. ORCH.: Sym. No. 1, in E-flat (1862–67; St. Petersburg, Jan. 16, 1869); Sym. No. 2, in B minor (1869–76; St. Petersburg, March 10, 1877); Sym. No. 3, in A minor (1886; unfinished; 2 movements orchestrated by Glazunov); symphonic sketch, *In the Steppes of Central Asia* (1880); *Polovtzian Dances* from *Prince Igor* (perf. as an orch. piece, St. Petersburg, March 11, 1879). CHAMBER: String Quartet No. 1, in A (1874–79); String Quartet No. 2, in D (1881); *Serenata alla Spagnola*, 3rd movement of a quartet on the name B-la-f, for their publisher Be-la-iev, by Borodin, Rimsky-Korsakov, Liadov, and Glazunov (1886); Scherzo for String Quartet in the collective set *Les Vendredis*. A String Trio (dated 1860) and a Piano Quintet were discovered in 1915. PIANO: *Polka, Requiem, Marche funèbre,* and *Mazurka* in the series of paraphrases on the theme of the *Chopsticks Waltz* (includes variations by Borodin, other members of the Russian school, and Liszt; 1880); *Petite suite,* comprising 7 pieces (*Au couvent, Intermezzo, Deux mazurkas, Rêverie, Sérénade, Nocturne;* 1885). VOCAL: *Sérénade de quatre galants à une dame* for a cappella Male Quartet (comical; n.d.); songs: *Sleeping Princess* (1867); *The Princess of the Sea, The Song of the Dark Forest, The False Note, My Songs Are Full of Venom* (1867–68); *The Sea* (1870); *From My Tears* (1873); *For the Shores of Your Distant Country* (1881); *Conceit* (1884); *Arabian Melody* (1885); *The Wondrous Garden* (1885).

BIBL.: V. Stasov, *A. B.* (St. Petersburg, 1882; French tr. by A. Habets, in 2 vols., Paris, 1893); R. Newmarch, *B. and Liszt* (London, 1895); E. Braudo, *B.* (Moscow, 1922); W. Kahl, "Die russischen Novatoren und B.," *Die Musik* (1923); G. Abraham, *B., the Composer and His Music* (London, 1927); 2 vols. of Borodin's letters, ed. by S. Dianin (Moscow, 1928, 1936); G. Abraham, "Prince Igor: An Experiment in Lyrical Opera," *Musical Quarterly* (Jan. 1931); M. Rinaldi, "B.," *Musica d'oggi* (1933); G. Khubov, *B.* (Moscow, 1933); N. Rimsky-Korsakov, *Memoirs of My Musical Life* (3rd to 5th eds.), with preface and notes by A. Rimsky-Korsakov; Moscow, 1932–35); Y. Kremlev, *B.* (Leningrad, 1934); G. Abraham, *Studies in Russian Music* (London, 1935); M.D. Calvocoressi and G. Abraham, *Masters of Russian Music* (London and N.Y., 1936); D. Brook, *Six Great Russian Composers* (London, 1946); M. Ilyin and E. Segal, *B.* (Moscow, 1953); S. Dianin, *B.* (Moscow, 1955; in Eng., 1963); W.B. Ober, "A. B., M.D. (1833–1887): Physician, Chemist, Composer," *New York State Journal of Medicine* (March 1967); L. Velluz, *Du laboratoire au Prince Igor, Pages sur Borodine* (Paris, 1971); M. Smirnov, *The Piano Works of Composers Comprising "The Five"* (Moscow, 1971); G. Golovinsky, *The Chamber Music of B.* (Moscow, 1972); E. Garden, "The 'Programme' of B.'s Second Quartet," *Musical Times* (Feb. 1987); R. Threlfall, "A B. MS in London," ibid.

Boroni, Antonio, Italian composer; b. Rome, 1738; d. there, Dec. 21, 1792. He studied with Martini in Bologna and with Abos and Lorenzo Fago at the Conservatorio Pietà dei Turchini in Naples (1757–58). He then devoted himself to writing operas; after composing works for Turin, Treviso, and Venice, he accompanied the Bustelli opera troupe to Prague (1767–68) and Dresden (1768–70). He served as Kapellmeister in Stuttgart (1770–77), then returned to Rome as maestro di cappella at St. Peter's (from 1778); he also held similar posts at S. Luigi de' Francesi and at S. Apollinare, the church of the Collegio Germanica (from c.1790).

WORKS: STAGE: *La Moda*, dramma giocoso (Turin, 1761; rev. Venice, 1769); *Demofoonte*, opera seria (Treviso, Carnival 1762); *L'amore in musica*, dramma giocoso (Venice, Oct. 15, 1763); *La Pupilla rapita*, dramma giocoso (Venice, 1763; in collaboration with S. Laurenti); *Sofonisba*, dramma per musica (Venice, Ascension 1764); *Siroe*, dramma per musica (Venice, 1764); *Le Villeggiatrici ridicole*, dramma comico (Venice, 1765); *La notte critica*, dramma giocoso (Venice, Carnival

1766); *Artaserse*, dramma per musica (Prague, Jan. 1767); *Didone*, dramma per musica (Prague, Carnival 1768); *Il carnevale*, dramma giocoso (Dresden, 1769); *Le Orfane svizzere*, dramma giocoso (Venice, 1770); *Le Contadine furlane*, dramma giocoso (Venice, Carnival 1771); *Le Déserteur*, opéra-comique (Stuttgart, 1774–75); *L'Amour fraternel*, opéra-comique (Stuttgart, 1774–75); *Zémire et Azor*, opéra-comique (Stuttgart, 1774–75); *L'isola disabitata*, intermezzo (Stuttgart, Dec. 31, 1775); *Enea nel Lazio*, dramma per musica (Rome, Carnival 1778); also a Sym. (1772) and other orch. works; much sacred music.

Borovsky, Alexander, Russian-American pianist; b. Mitau, March 18, 1889; d. Waban, Mass., April 27, 1968. He 1st studied with his mother (a pupil of Safonov), then with A. Essipova at the St. Petersburg Cons., winning the Rubinstein Prize in 1912. He taught master classes at the Moscow Cons. from 1915 to 1920; then went to Turkey, Germany, France, and England and gave a number of piano recitals; was a soloist with virtually all major European orchs.; he also made several successful tours in South America. In 1941 he settled in the U.S., and became a prof. at Boston Univ. (1956).

Borowski, Felix, English-American composer and critic; b. Burton, March 10, 1872; d. Chicago, Sept. 6, 1956. He studied violin with his father, a Polish émigré; took lessons with various teachers in London, and at the Cologne Cons.; then taught in Aberdeen, Scotland. His early *Russian Sonata* was praised by Grieg; this provided impetus to his progress as a composer. In 1897 he accepted a teaching engagement at the Chicago Musical College; was its president from 1916 to 1925. Subsequently he became active in musical journalism; in 1942 was appointed music ed. of the *Chicago Sun;* also served as program annotator for the Chicago Sym. Orch., beginning in 1908. For 5 years he taught musicology at Northwestern Univ. (1937–42). Among his many musical works, the violin piece entitled *Adoration* became widely popular. Borowski revised G.P. Upton's *The Standard Operas* in 1928, and *The Standard Concert Guide* in 1930.

WORKS: *Boudour*, ballet-pantomime (Chicago, Nov. 25, 1919); *Fernando del Nonsensico*, satiric opera (1935); Piano Concerto (Chicago, 1914); *Allegro de concert* for Organ and Orch. (Chicago, 1915); *Peintures* for Orch. (Chicago, Jan. 25, 1918); *Le Printemps passionné*, symphonic poem (Evanston, Ill., 1920); *Youth*, fantasy-overture (Evanston, Ill., May 30, 1923); *Ecce Homo*, symphonic poem (N.Y., Jan. 2, 1924); *Semiramis*, symphonic poem (Chicago, Nov. 13, 1925); 3 syms. (I, Chicago, 1933; II, Los Angeles, 1936; III, Chicago, 1939); *The Little Match Girl*, after Andersen, for Narrator and Orch. (1943); *Requiem for a Child* (1944); *The Mirror*, symphonic poem (Louisville, Ky., Nov. 27, 1954); 3 string quartets; many pieces for violin, organ, and piano; songs.

Børresen, (Aksel Ejnar) Hakon, Danish composer; b. Copenhagen, June 2, 1876; d. there, Oct. 6, 1954. He studied with Svendsen; was awarded the Ancker scholarship for composition in 1901. He was president of the Danish Composers Soc. from 1924 to 1949. His compositions include the operas *Den Kongelige Gaest* (Copenhagen, Nov. 15, 1919) and *Kaddara* (Copenhagen, March 16, 1921); a ballet, *Tycho Brahes Dröm* (Tycho Brahe's Dream; Copenhagen, March 1, 1924); 3 syms.; a Violin Concerto; chamber music; piano works; songs.

Borris, Siegfried, German music scholar, teacher, and composer; b. Berlin, Nov. 4, 1906; d. there, Aug. 23, 1987. He studied musicology with Arnold Schering at the Univ. of Berlin (Ph.D., 1933, with the diss. *Kirnbergers Leben und Werk*) and composition with Paul Hindemith (1927–29) at the Berlin Hochschule für Musik, where he later taught (1929–33, and again from 1945). He was also director of the Julius Stern Inst. (from 1967). Among his many publications are *Praktische Harmonielehre* (Berlin, 1938; 2nd ed., rev., 1972), *Der grosse Acker* (Berlin, 1946), *Beiträge zu einer neuen Musikkunde* (Berlin, 1947–48), and *Die grossen Orchester* (Düsseldorf, 1969). He composed in an accessible style highlighted by the use of folk music.

WORKS: STAGE AND/OR VOCAL: 2 radio operas: *Hans im Glück* (1947) and *Hirotas und Gerline* (1948); *Die Rübe*, Märchenoper (1953); *Frühlingsgesellen*, Liederspiel (1951); *Ruf des Lebens*, scenic cantata (1954); *Das letzte Spiel* (1955). **ORCH.:** *Suite* (1938); 5 syms. (1940–43); Piano Concerto (1962); Saxophone Concerto (1966); Horn Concerto (1967); *Evolution* for 19 Winds, 3 Double Basses, Harp, and Percussion (1972). **CHAMBER:** Wind Quintet (1938); 3 string quartets (1938, 1941, 1953); Wind Octet (1941); numerous other chamber works; works for keyboard; several sacred works, including *Missa "Dona nobis pacem"* (1953) and *Psalm CXXXV* for Solo Voices, Chorus, and Orch. (1963); also secular vocal works, including 14 sets of lieder.

Borroff, Edith, American musicologist and composer; b. N.Y., Aug. 2, 1925. She was educated at the Oberlin Cons., the American Cons. of Music in Chicago (B.Mus, 1946; M.M., 1948), and the Univ. of Michigan (Ph.D., 1958). She taught at Milwaukee-Downer College (1950–54), Hillsdale College in Michigan (1958–62), the Univ. of Wisconsin (1962–66), Eastern Michigan Univ. (1966–72), and the State Univ. of N.Y. at Binghamton (from 1973).

WRITINGS: *Elisabeth Jacquet de La Guerre* (1966); *The Music of the Baroque* (1970); *Music in Europe and the United States: A History* (1971; 2nd ed., 1989); ed. *Notations and Editions (A Book in Honor of Louise Cuyler)* (1974); with M. Irvin, *Music in Perspective* (1976); *Three American Composers* (1986).

WORKS: String Trio (1943); Variations for Cello and Piano (1944); Quintet for Clarinet and Strings (1948); Sonata for Cello and Piano (1949); *Sonatina giocoso* for Viola and Piano (1953; also for Violin and Piano, 1980); *Spring over Brooklyn*, musical (1954); Sonata for Horn and Piano (1955); *Variations and Theme* for Oboe and Piano (1956); *Voices in Exile*, 3 canons for Flute and Viola (1962); *IONS: 14 Pieces in the Form of a Sonnet* for Flute and Piano (1968); *The Sun and the Wind*, musical fable (1974–76); *Game Pieces*, suite for Woodwind Quintet (1980); Concerto for Marimba and Small Orch. (1981); Trio for Tenor Saxophone, Piano, and Percussion (1982); *The Elements*, sonata for Violin and Cello (1987); *Comic Miniatures*, suite for Violin and Piano (1988); *Mottoes*, suite for 8 Saxophones (1989); piano pieces; organ music; choral pieces; songs.

Bortkiewicz, Sergei (Eduardovich), Russian pianist and composer; b. Kharkov, Feb. 28, 1877; d. Vienna, Oct. 25, 1952. He was a pupil of Liadov at the St. Petersburg Cons. (1896–99); later studied with Jadassohn in Leipzig. He made his debut as a pianist in Munich, in 1902, and subsequently made concert tours of Germany, Australia, Hungary, France, and Russia. From 1904 to 1914, he lived in Berlin, and taught at the Klindworth-Scharwenka Cons.; then went back to Russia; was in Vienna from 1920 to 1929, in Berlin from 1929 to 1934, and again in Vienna after 1934. His compositions include an opera, *Acrobats*; 2 syms.; *Austrian Suite* and *Yugoslav Suite* for Orch.; 4 piano concertos; Violin Concerto; Cello Concerto; piano pieces; songs. He was the author of the book *Die seltsame Liebe Peter Tschaikowskys und der Nadezhda von Meck* (1938).

Bortniansky, Dimitri (Stepanovich), Russian composer; b. Glukhov, Ukraine, 1751; d. St. Petersburg, Oct. 10, 1825. He was a choirboy in the court chapel, where he attracted the attention of Galuppi, who was at the time conductor there; was sent to Italy, where he studied with Galuppi and with other Italian masters in Venice, Bologna, Rome, and Naples (1769–79). In Italy he produced his operas *Creonte* (Venice, Nov. 26, 1776; lost) and *Quinto Fabio* (Modena, Dec. 26, 1778). In 1779 he returned to St. Petersburg and became director of vocal music at the court chapel (1796); as a conductor of the chapel choir he introduced radical reforms for improvement of singing standards; composed for his choir a number of sacred works of high quality, among them a Mass according to the Greek Orthodox ritual; 35 sacred concerti in 4 parts; 10 Psalms in 8 parts; 10 concerti for Double Choir; etc. He also continued to compose for the stage; produced the comic operas, in French, *Le Faucon* (Gatchina, Oct. 22, 1786) and *Le Fils rival* (Pavlovsk,

Oct. 22, 1787). His sacred choral works are publ. in 10 vols., ed. by Tchaikovsky.

BIBL.: N. Findeisen, *History of Russian Music* (1929; vol. 2, pp. 260–76); B. Dobrohotov, *D. B.* (Moscow, 1950); A. Galkina, "About the Symphonism of B.," *Sovetskaya Muzyka* (Oct. 1973; in Russian).

Börtz, Daniel, Swedish composer; b. Osby, Hässleholm, Aug. 8, 1943. He studied composition privately with Hilding Rosenberg; then with Blomdahl and Lidholm at the Stockholm Musikhögskolan; later attended seminars in electronic music at Utrecht.

WORKS: Chamber opera, *Landskab med flod*, after Hesse (1972); 2 liturgical operas: *Muren—Vägen—Ordet* (1971–72) and *Den heliga Birgittas död och Mottagande i himmelen* (Lund, Oct. 7, 1973); *Bacchanterna*, opera (1988–90); *Intrada* for Orch. (1964); 5 *Preludes* for Flute (1964); *Il canto dei canti di Salomone* for Soprano and Instruments (1965); 4 *Monologhi: I* for Cello (1965–66), *II* for Bassoon (1966), *III* for Violin (1967), and *IV* for Piano and Tape (1970); 3 string quartets (1966; 1971; 1985–87); *In memoriam di . . .* for Orch. (Norrköping, May 29, 1969); *Voces* for 3 Voices, Tape, and Orch. (Stockholm, Sept. 19, 1968); *Josef K*, after Kafka, for Narrator, 8 Soli, Chorus, and Orch. (1969; Swedish Radio, Oct. 8, 1970); *Night Winds* for Vocal Quartet (1972); *Nightflies* for Mezzo-soprano and Chamber Ensemble (1973); 8 syms. (1973; 1974–75; 1975–76; 1976–77; 1980–81; 1981–83; 1984–86; 1987–88); Concerto Grosso (No. 1) for Orch. (1977–78) and No. 2 for Wind Orch. (1981); Violin Concerto (1985); Oboe Concerto (1986); *Parodos* for Orch. (1987).

Borup-Jørgensen, (Jens) Axel, Danish composer; b. Hjørring, Nov. 22, 1924. He grew up in Sweden; returned to Denmark after World War II and entered the Royal Cons. in Copenhagen, where he studied piano with Rachlew and orchestration with Schierbeck and Jersild (1946–51). His early compositions reflect the precise structural forms of Béla Bartók; later he experimented with the serial techniques of Anton von Webern.

WORKS: Concertino for Piano, Flute, Bassoon, and Strings (1948–49); *Fantasy* for Flute and String Orch. (1949); Clarinet Concerto (1949–50); 5 string quartets: No. 1 (1950); No. 2 (1951); No. 3 (1954–56); No. 4 (1960); No. 5, *Torso*, in the form of confrontations for 2 String Quartets, 1 of them prerecorded (1965); *Chamber Concerto* for Violin and Small Orch. (1951); Viola Sonata (1952–53); *Partita* for Solo Viola (1953–54); *Improvisations* for String Quartet (1955); *Music for Percussion and Viola* (1955–56); *Microorganisms* for String Quartet (1956); *Sommasvit* for String Orch. (1957); Sonatina for 2 Violins (1958); 7 *Preludes* for Piano (1958–59); *Winter Pieces* for Piano (1959); *Sonata breve* for Viola and Piano (1959–60); *Cretaufoni* for Orch. (1960–61); *Mobile*, after Calder, for Viola, Marimba, and Piano (1961); *Insulae* for String Orch. (1961–62); *Pocket Oratorium* for 16 Voices and Instruments (1963–64); *Nordic Summer Pastoral* for Small Orch. (1964); *Stykker* for Orch. (1963–65); *Vinterstykke* for String Quartet (1967); *Marin*, after Langston Hughes, for 24 Male Voices (1969); *Marin* for Orch. (1963–70; Danish Radio, April 16, 1970); *Tagebuch im Winter* for Flute, String Quartet, and Piano (1970–72); *Distichon* for Violin and Piano (1972–73); *Malinconia* for String Quartet (1972–74); *Recostruzioni* for Wind Quintet (1973–74); *Vinter-epigrammer* for Piano (1975); *Epigrammer* for Piano (1976); *Carambolage* for Piano, Electric Guitar, and Percussion (1976–77); *Musica Autumnalis* for Wind Instruments, Percussion, and Electric Organ (1977); *Favola* for Flute and Harp (1980); *Déjà vu* for Guitar and String Orch. (1983).

Borwick, Leonard, English pianist; b. Walthamstow, Feb. 26, 1868; d. Le Mans, France, Sept. 15, 1925. He studied with Clara Schumann in Frankfurt; made his debut there (1889), then in London (May 8, 1889), made a concert tour in America and Australia (1911); also played in Europe. His programs included classics and moderns; in the last years of his career he played much music of Debussy and Ravel; made a transcription for piano of Debussy's *L'Après-midi d'un faune*.

BIBL.: H. Plunket Greene, "L. B.," *Music & Letters* (1926).

Bory, Robert, Swiss writer on music; b. Geneva, April 1, 1891; d. Nyon, Oct. 9, 1960. He studied jurisprudence; at the same time took courses in composition with Jaques-Dal-croze and conducting with Gustave Doré; pursuing a legal career, he became a judge in Nyon in 1934. He publ. pictorial eds. on Mozart, Beethoven, Wagner, Liszt, and Chopin.

WRITINGS: *Une Retraite romantique en Suisse: Liszt et la Comtesse d'Agoult* (Geneva, 1923; 2nd ed., 1930); *La Vie de Franz Liszt par l'image* (Geneva, 1936); *Liszt et ses enfants, Blandine, Cosima et Daniel* (Paris, 1936); *Richard Wagner: Sein Leben und sein Werk in Bildern* (Frauenfeld, 1938); *La Vie et l'œuvre de Wolfgang-Amadeus Mozart par l'image* (Geneva, 1948; in Eng., 1948); *La Vie de Frédéric Chopin par l'image* (Geneva, 1951); *Le Séjour en Suisse de Wolfgang-Amadeus Mozart en 1766* (Lausanne, 1956); *La Vie et l'œuvre de Beethoven par l'image* (Zürich, 1960; in Eng., 1966).

Bos, Coenraad Valentyn, Dutch pianist and noted accompanist; b. Leiden, Dec. 7, 1875; d. Chappaqua, N.Y., Aug. 5, 1955. He was a pupil of Julius Röntgen at the Amsterdam Cons. (1892–95); later studied in Berlin. With 2 other countrymen, Jan van Veen (violin) and Jan van Lier (cello), he formed a trio in Berlin which enjoyed an enviable reputation during its active period (1896–1910). His masterly accompaniments on a tour with Ludwig Wüllner attracted more than ordinary attention, and made him one of the most celebrated accompanists both in Europe and in the U.S., where he eventually settled. He was the accompanist of Julia Culp, Frieda Hempel, Helen Traubel, Fritz Kreisler, Ernestine Schumann-Heink, Pablo Casals, Elena Gerhard, Jacques Thibaud, Geraldine Farrar, and many others. He taught at the Juilliard School of Music from 1934 to 1952; publ. (in collaboration with Ashley Pettis) a book, *The Well-Tempered Accompanist* (1949).

Bosch, Pieter Joseph van den, Netherlands organist; b. Hoboken, c.1736; d. Antwerp, Feb. 19, 1803. He became organist at the Antwerp Cathedral in 1765, remaining at this post until 1797. He composed a number of keyboard works.

Boschot, Adolphe, French music critic; b. Fontenay-sous-Bois, near Paris, May 4, 1871; d. Paris, June 1, 1955. He was music critic of *Echo de Paris* from 1910, of *Revue Bleue* from 1919; founded, with Théodore de Wyzewa, the Paris Mozart Soc.; was elected to the Institut de France in 1926, succeeding Widor as permanent secretary of the Académie des Beaux-Arts. His greatest work is an exhaustive biography of Berlioz in 3 vols.: *La Jeunesse d'un romantique, Hector Berlioz, 1803–31* (Paris, 1906); *Un Romantique sous Louis-Philippe, Hector Berlioz, 1831–42* (Paris, 1908); and *Crépuscule d'un romantique, Hector Berlioz, 1842–69* (Paris, 1913). For this work Boschot received a prize of the Académie. Other books are *Le Faust de Berlioz* (1910; new ed., 1945); *Carnet d'art* (1911); *Une Vie romantique, Hector Berlioz* (an abridgment of his 3-vol. work, 1919; 27th ed., 1951; also in Eng.; a definitive ed. appeared in Quebec in 1965); *Chez les musiciens* (3 vols., 1922–26); *Entretiens sur la beauté* (1927); *La Lumière de Mozart* (1928); *Le Mystère musical* (1929); *La Musique et la vie* (2 vols., 1931–33); *Théophile Gautier* (1933); *Mozart* (1935); *La Vie et les œuvres d'Alfred Bruneau* (1937); *Musiciens-Poètes* (1937); *Maîtres d'hier et de jadis* (1944); *Portraits de musiciens* (3 vols., 1946–50); *Souvenirs d'un autre siècle* (1947). Boschot tr. into French the librettos of several of Mozart's operas. He was also prominent as a poet; publ. the collections *Poèmes dialogués* (1901) and *Chez nos poètes* (1925).

Boscovich, Alexander Uriah, significant Israeli composer; b. Klausenburg, Transylvania, Aug. 16, 1907; d. Tel Aviv, Nov. 13, 1964. He studied in Budapest; later enrolled at the Vienna Academy of Music, where he studied piano with Victor Ebenstein and composition with Richard Stöhr; then went to Paris, where he took courses with Paul Dukas and Nadia Boulanger; also had a few lessons in piano with Alfred Cortot. From 1930 to 1938 he was engaged as conductor at the State Opera in Cluj; in 1938 he emigrated to Palestine; taught at the Tel Aviv Cons. (1945–64); wrote music criticism for the Israeli

paper *Haaretz.* In his music he incorporates quasi-oriental motifs in the framework of Western music; in several works he makes use of authentic Jewish folk songs, adorning them with modernistic harmonies. In this manner he wrote his most popular piece, *Chansons populaires juives* for Orch. (Haifa, March 15, 1938; orig. entitled *The Golden Chain*). Other works: Violin Concerto (1942); Oboe Concerto (1943); *Adonai Ro'i* (The Lord Is My Shepherd) for Alto Voice and Orch. (1946); *Semitic Suite* for Piano (1947; also for 2 Pianos, and for Orch.); *Piccola suite* for Flute, Snare Drum, and String Orch. (1956–57); *Psalm* for Violin and Piano (1957; contains thematic material from the Violin Concerto); *Cantico di ma'alot* (Song of Ascent) for Orch. (1960); *Bal Yisrael* (Daughter of Israel), cantata for Tenor, Chorus, and Orch. (1960–61); *With Joy and Gladness* for 2 Violins, with optional Drum and Triangle (1961); *Piece* for Oboe and Harpsichord (1961–62); *Lament* for Violin or Cello, and Piano (1962); *Concerto da camera* for Violin and Chamber Ensemble (1962); *Ornaments* for Flute and 4 Orch. Groups (1964).

Bose, Fritz, German musicologist; b. Messenthin, July 26, 1906; d. Berlin, Aug. 16, 1975. He studied at the Humboldt Univ. in Berlin, where his teachers included Abert and Schering (musicology), Hornbostel (ethnomusicology), and Sachs (organology); received his Ph.D. there in 1934 with the dissertation *Die Musik der Uitoto* (publ. in Berlin, 1934). He was a lecturer of the Univ. of Berlin from 1934 to 1945; in 1953 he was named director of the history dept. of the Institut für Musikforschung in Berlin, retiring in 1971; he also taught at the Technical Univ. of Berlin (1963–67). In 1966 he founded the Deutsche Gesellschaft für Musik des Orients, which he headed until 1972. He also served as ed. of the *Jahrbuch für musikalische Volks- und Völkerkunde* from 1963 until his death. He wrote the study *Musikalische Völkerkunde* (Freiburg and Zürich, 1953).

Bose, Hans-Jürgen von, German composer; b. Munich, Dec. 24, 1953. He took courses at the Hoch Cons. in Frankfurt (1969–72); then studied composition with Hans Ulrich Engelmann and piano with Klaus Billing at the Hochschule für Musik in Frankfurt. In 1986 he was elected to membership in the Akademie der Künste in Berlin.

WORKS: STAGE: Chamber opera, *Blutbund* (1974; Hamburg, June 8, 1977); chamber opera, *Das Diplom,* after Pirandello (1975; Ulm, Nov. 26, 1976); *Die Leiden des jungen Werthers* (1983–84; Schwetzingen, April 30, 1986); *Chimäre* (Aachen, June 11, 1986). Ballets: *Die Nacht aus Blei* (Berlin, Nov. 1, 1981); *Werther-Szenen* (1989). **ORCH.:** *Morphogenesis* (1975; Baden-Baden, Sept. 12, 1976); Sym. No. 1 (1976; Munich, March 10, 1978); *Music für ein Haus voll Zeit,* variations (1977); *3 Songs* for Tenor and Chamber Orch. (1977); *Travesties in a Sad Landscape,* variations for Chamber Orch. (1978); *Symphonic Fragment,* after Hölderlin, for Tenor, Baritone, Bass, Chorus, and Orch. (1980; Darmstadt, June 1, 1980); *Variations* for 15 Strings (1980; Frankfurt, March 29, 1981); *Idyllen* (1983; Berlin, April 23, 1983); *Symbolum* for Organ and Orch. (1985; Munich, May 27, 1988); Oboe Concerto (1986–87); *Zwei Studien* (1989). **CHAMBER:** 3 string quartets (1973; 1976–77; 1986–87); *5 Children's Rhymes* for Alto and 5 Instrumentalists (1974); *Threnos—Hommage à Bernd Alois Zimmermann,* a lament on his suicide, for Viola and Cello (1975); Solo Violin Sonata; *Variations* for Solo Cello (1978–79); *. . . vom Wege abkommen* for Solo Viola (1982); *Guarda el Canto,* 3 fragments after Bustos, for Soprano and String Quartet (1982); Wind Quintet (1986); *Karfreitags-Sonett* for Chorus (1986).

Bösendorfer, firm of piano makers at Vienna, specializing in concert grands. It was established by **Ignaz Bösendorfer** (b. Vienna, July 27, 1794; d. there, April 14, 1859) in 1828; later managed by his son **Ludwig** (b. Vienna, April 10, 1835; d. there, May 9, 1919). The firm, retaining its original name, was taken over by Carl Hutterstrasser (1863–1942). The Bösendorfer Saal (opened by Hans von Bülow in 1872, and used until 1913) was one of the finest chamber music concert halls in Europe.

Boskovsky, Willi, Austrian violinist and conductor; b. Vienna, June 16, 1909; d. Visp, Switzerland, April 21, 1991. He studied at the Vienna Academy of Music; in 1933 joined the Vienna Phil. and remained a member until 1970. In 1948 he organized the Wiener Oktet; in 1955 succeeded Clemens Krauss as conductor of the New Year's Day Concerts of the Vienna Phil. In 1969 he became principal conductor of the Johann Strauss Orch. of Vienna, orig. founded by Eduard Strauss in 1890; the ensemble was reorganized by the nephew of the older Eduard Strauss, and namesake of the original founder, who died in 1966. Boskovsky assumed the direction of the ensemble as successor to Eduard Strauss, Jr. He resigned as conductor of the New Year's Day Concerts of the Vienna Phil. in 1979. Boskovsky conducted his orch. holding the violin relaxedly in his left hand à la Johann Strauss, and directing his group in an ingratiatingly, authentically Viennese manner in flowing waltz time or rapid polka rhythm, with expressive Luftpausen to emphasize the syncopation.

Bosmans, Henriëtte (Hilda), Dutch pianist and composer; b. Amsterdam, Dec. 5, 1895; d. there, July 2, 1952. She studied piano with her mother at the Amsterdam Cons., and embarked on a career as a concert pianist. In 1927 she took lessons in composition with Willem Pijper. In her own music she cultivated an agreeable neo-Classical idiom, with coloristic éclat, suggesting the techniques and devices of French Impressionism; wrote many songs to texts by French poets. In her instrumental works she particularly favored the cello (her father was a well-known cellist, but he died when she was a year old).

WORKS: Cello Sonata (1919); 2 cello concertos (1922, 1924); *Poem* for Cello and Orch. (1926); Violin Sonata (1918); Piano Trio (1921); String Quartet (1928); Concertino for Piano and Orch. (1928; Geneva, April 6, 1929); *Konzertstück* for Flute and Orch. (1929); *Konzertstück* for Violin and Orch. (1934); *Doodenmarsch* (March of the Dead) for Narrator and Chamber Orch. (1946); piano pieces.

Bosquet, Émile, Belgian pianist; b. Brussels, Dec. 8, 1878; d. Uccle, near Brussels, July 18, 1958. He studied with Tinel and Busoni; taught at the Antwerp Cons. (1906–19) and in Brussels (from 1919); also made European tours. He publ. *La Musique de clavier* (Brussels, 1953).

Bosse, Gustave, German publisher; b. Vienenburg (Harz), Feb. 6, 1884; d. Regensburg, Aug. 27, 1943. He founded his firm in 1912 at Regensburg; publ. *Zeitschrift für Musik* (from 1929) and *Deutsche Musikbücherei* (a collection of music books).

Bosseur, Jean-Yves, French composer; b. Paris, Feb. 5, 1947. He studied privately with Stockhausen and Pousseur. His music is marked by experimentation without specific serial procedures. Among his works is a symphonic suite, *Un Arraché de partout,* for Brass, Hammond Organ, 2 Electric Guitars, Vibraphone, Xylorimba, Marimbaphone, and Percussion (Paris, March 22, 1968). He is also a prolific writer of articles on current music and musical life.

Bossi, (Marco) Enrico, Italian composer, father of **(Rinaldo) Renzo Bossi;** b. Salò, Brescia, April 25, 1861; d. at sea (en route from America to Europe), Feb. 20, 1925. Son and pupil of the organist **Pietro Bossi** of Morbegno (1834–96), he studied at the Liceo Rossini in Bologna (1871–73), and at Milan (1873–81) under Sangali (piano), Fumagalli (organ), Campanari (violin), Boniforti (counterpoint), and Ponchielli (composition). He subsequently was maestro di cappella and organist at Como Cathedral (1881–89); then prof. of organ and harmony in the Royal Cons. San Pietro at Naples (until 1896); prof. of advanced composition and organ at the Liceo Benedetto Marcello in Venice (1896–1902); and director of the Liceo Musicale at Bologna (1902–12). After a brief period of retirement from teaching, he was director of the Music School of the Accademia di Santa Cecilia in Rome (1916–23); toured Europe, England, and the U.S. as a pianist and organist. He also wrote *Metodo*

di studio per l'organo moderno (in collaboration with G. Tebaldini; Milan, 1893).

WORKS: Operas: *Paquita* (Milan, 1881); *Il Veggente* (Milan, 1890; rewritten and produced as *Il Viandante,* Mannheim, 1896); *L'Angelo della notte; Intermezzi Goldoniani* for String Orch.; *Concertstück* for Organ and Orch.; *Inno di Gloria* for Chorus and Organ; *Tota pulchra* for Chorus and Organ; *Missa pro Sponso et Sponsa* (Rome, 1896); *Il Cieco* for Solo, Chorus, and Orch. (1897); *Canticum Canticorum,* biblical cantata; *Il Paradiso Perduto* for Chorus and Orch. (Augsburg, 1903); *Surrexit pastor,* motet; *Giovanna d'Arco,* mystery play (Cologne, 1913); *Primavera classica* for 5-part Chorus a cappella; String Trio; Piano Trio; etc.

BIBL.: H.B. Gaul, "Bonnet, B., Karg-Elert, Three Aperçus," *Musical Quarterly* (July 1918); E. Dagnino, *M.E. B., Cenni biografici* (Rome, 1925); L. Orsini, *Fascicolo commemorativo* (Milan, 1926); G.C. Paribeni, L. Orsini, and E. Bontempelli, *M.E. B.: Il Compositore, l'organista, l'uomo* (Milan, 1934); F. Mompellio, *M.E. B.* (Milan, 1952; contains list of works).

Bossi, (Rinaldo) Renzo, Italian conductor and composer, son of **(Marco) Enrico Bossi;** b. Como, April 9, 1883; d. Milan, April 2, 1965. He studied in Venice and in Leipzig; took a course in conducting with Nikisch; conducted at various cities in Italy; in 1916 was appointed instructor at the Verdi Cons. in Milan.

WORKS: Operas: *Passa la ronda* (Milan, March 3, 1919), *Volpino il calderaio* (Milan, Nov. 13, 1925), and *La rosa rossa* (Parma, Jan. 9, 1940); ballet, *Il trillo del diavolo* (1948); Sym. in 5 movements; Violin Concerto; many minor pieces for various instruments.

BIBL.: His biographical data and a complete list of works are appended to F. Mompellio's monograph on Enrico Bossi (Milan, 1952). See also S. Pintacuda, *R. B.* (Milan, 1955).

Bostelmann, Otto, German-American composer; b. Hamburg, Aug. 22, 1907; d. Santa Barbara, Calif., March 16, 1981. He settled in the U.S. in 1926; studied with Wesley La Violette in Los Angeles; there in 1957 he organized the Bohemian Composers Group. His works comprise 3 syms.; 3 "crescendi" for Orch.; much chamber music.

Boswell, Connee (Connie), American jazz singer; b. New Orleans, Dec. 3, 1907; d. N.Y., Oct. 11, 1976. She was stricken with poliomyelitis and was forced to pursue her career in a wheelchair; with her sisters Helvetia and Martha, she formed the singing trio known as the Boswell Sisters, in which she also sometimes appeared as a saxophonist, trombonist, and pianist. The Boswell Sisters became well-known through their recordings with the Dorsey brothers.

Bote & Bock, German music publishing firm established in Berlin in 1838 by **Eduard Bote** (retired 1847) and **Gustav Bock** (b. 1813; d. 1863); the directorship was assumed after Gustav Bock's death by his brother **Eduard Bock** (d. 1871), followed by his son **Hugo Bock** (b. Berlin, July 25, 1848; d. there, March 12, 1932), who handled the affairs of the firm for over 60 years. He acquired for the firm a great number of operas and operettas, and also a number of instrumental works by celebrated 19th-century composers. In 1904 Hugo Bock purchased the catalogue of Lauterbach & Kuhn of Leipzig, including the works of Max Reger (from op. 66 on). His successor was his son **Gustav Bock** (b. Berlin, July 17, 1882; d. July 6, 1953), who headed the firm until 1938, and again from 1947. The headquarters of the firm remained in Berlin; in 1948 a branch was formed in Wiesbaden. Apart from its musical publications, the firm publ. the *Neue Berliner Musikzeitung* (1847–96). A centennial vol. was issued in 1938 as *Musikverlag Bote & Bock, Berlin, 1838–1938.*

Botstiber, Hugo, Austrian music scholar and writer; b. Vienna, April 21, 1875; d. Shrewsbury, England, Jan. 15, 1941. He was a pupil of R. Fuchs, Zemlinsky, H. Rietsch, and Guido Adler. In 1896 he became assistant librarian of the Vienna Cons.; in 1900, secretary of the Konzertverein there; in 1905, secretary of the Vienna Academy of Music. Until 1938 he was general secretary of the Vienna Konzerthaus-Gesellschaft; he was made a Knight of the Order of Franz Josef. He went to England in 1939. He ed. the *Musikbuch aus Österreich* (1904–11); also organ compositions by Pachelbel, piano works of the Vienna masters, and waltzes of Johann Strauss for Denkmäler der Tonkunst in Österreich; was the author of *Joseph Haydn und das Verlagshaus Artaria* (with Franz Artaria; Vienna, 1911); *Geschichte der Ouvertüre* (Leipzig, 1913); *Beethoven im Alltag* (Vienna, 1927); completed Pohl's biography of Haydn (vol. III, 1927; publ. a new ed. of Kretzschmar's *Führer durch den Konzertsaal* (1932). Of special interest to American musicians is his article "Musicalia in der New York Public Library" in the bulletin of the Société Internationale de Musique (Oct. 1903), calling international attention for the 1st time to the important music collection of the N.Y. Public Library.

Bott, Jean Joseph, German violinist and conductor; b. Kassel, March 9, 1826; d. N.Y., April 28, 1895. He received primary education from his father, a court musician, and later studied with Hauptmann and Spohr; subsequently served as assistant conductor to Spohr (1852–56); then served as court conductor at Meiningen (1857–65). He had trouble with excessive drinking, and in 1878 was forced to abandon his career after he appeared to be drunk while conducting Liszt's cantata *Die heilige Elisabeth*. In 1885 he went to N.Y. He wrote operas, overtures, and other music in a manner typical of Kapellmeister Musik, which had not even an infinitesimal value.

Bottée de Toulmon, Auguste, French writer on music; b. Paris, May 15, 1797; d. there, March 22, 1850. A lawyer by profession, he turned his attention to music, becoming a good amateur cellist; was the librarian of the Paris Cons. from 1831 to 1848.

WRITINGS: *L'Art musical depuis l'ère chrétienne jusqu'à nos jours* (Paris, 1836); *Observations sur les moyens de restaurer la musique religieuse dans les églises de Paris* (Paris, 1841); *Notice des manuscrits autographes de Cherubini* (Paris, 1843).

Bottenberg, Wolfgang, German-born Canadian composer; b. Frankfurt, May 9, 1930. He emigrated to Canada in 1958; studied music theory with R.A. Stangeland at the Univ. of Alberta, graduating in 1961; then with Scott Huston, J. Takács, and P. Cooper at the Univ. of Cincinnati, obtaining his M.Mus. (1962) and D.M.A. (1970). Returning to Canada, he taught music at the Acadia Univ. in Wolfville, Nova Scotia (1965–73), and at Concordia Univ. in Montreal. In his compositions he makes eclectic use of tonal, atonal, and serial resources.

WORKS: OPERA: *Inook* (1987). **ORCH.:** Passacaglia (1961; rev. 1971); *Sinfonietta* (1961; rev. 1969–70); Fantasia for Trumpet and Small Orch. (1966); *A Suite for Carols* (1963–67); *Ritual,* a satire-collage on commercial slogans and sounds, for Chorus and Small Orch. (1970); *Fantasia serena* (1973); Concerto for Organ and Small Orch. (1975). **CHAMBER:** Quartet for Flute, 2 Clarinets, and Bassoon (1960); Sonata for Flute and Clarinet (1960); Trio for Flute, Clarinet, and Bassoon (1963); Trio for Flute, Clarinet, and Piano (1964); Divertimento for 4 Flutes (1965); String Quartet (1968); *Variables* for Narrator, Wind Quartet, and String Quartet (1969); Octet (1972); *Fa So La Ti Do Re* for Soprano Saxophone and String Quartet (1972); *Tetralogue* for 2 Flutes, Clarinet, and Piano (1980); *5 for 5,* 5 Sketches for Woodwind Quintet (1984); *3 Sketches* for Piano (1987); *Canadian Madrigals* for Chorus (1988); also songs; piano pieces.

WRITINGS: *Building a Treble Viola da Gamba* (1980); *Florilegium Cantionum Mensuralium* (2 vols., 1982); *Reading Early Music from Original Notation* (1983).

Bottesini, Giovanni, Italian double-bass virtuoso, conductor, and composer; b. Crema, Dec. 22, 1821; d. Parma, July 7, 1889. He took lessons in double-bass playing with Rossi at the Milan Cons. (1835–39); played in various orchs.; in 1847 he visited the U.S.; and in 1848 he went to England, where he appeared as a cello soloist; made his independent concert debut in London on June 26, 1849. In 1853 he was once more in America; also was active as a conductor in Paris, in

Russia, and in Scandinavian countries. In 1871 he was invited by Verdi to conduct the world premiere of *Aida* in Cairo. He eventually retired to Parma as director of the cons. there. Bottesini was the 1st great virtuoso on the double bass, regarded as an unwieldy instrument, and thus became a legendary paragon for the few artists who essayed that instrument after him; thus Koussevitzky was often described as the Russian Bottesini during his early career as a double-bass player. Bottesini was the composer of a number of passable operas which had several performances in his lifetime.

WORKS: Operas: *Cristoforo Colombo* (Havana, 1847), *L'Assedio di Firenze* (Paris, Feb. 21, 1856), *Il Diavolo della notte* (Milan, Dec. 18, 1858), *Marion Delorme* (Palermo, Jan. 10, 1862), *Vinciguerra il bandito* (Monte Carlo, Feb. 22, 1870), *Alì Babà* (London, Jan. 18, 1871), *Ero e Leandro* (Turin, Jan. 11, 1879), and *La Regina di Nepal* (Turin, Dec. 26, 1880); oratorio, *The Garden of Olivet* (Norwich Festival, Oct. 12, 1887); overtures; string quartets; effective pieces for double bass, such as *Carnevale di Venezia* and *Tarantella*. He also wrote a valuable *Metodo complete per contrabasso,* in 2 parts, treating the double bass as an orch. and as a solo instrument (in Eng., adapted by F. Clayton, London, 1870).

BIBL.: C. Lesei, *G. B.* (Milan, 1886); A. Carniti, *In memoria di G. B.* (Crema, 1922).

Bottje, Will Gay, American flutist and composer; b. Grand Rapids, Mich., June 30, 1925. He studied composition with Vittorio Giannini at the Juilliard School of Music, N.Y. (1943–47); then went to Europe and took courses with Henk Badings in the Netherlands and with Nadia Boulanger in Paris (1952–53); worked at the electronic studios at the Univ. of Utrecht (1962–63) and in Stockholm (1973). His music is of a highly experimental nature, awash with corrosive dissonances in a manner influenced primarily by the developments cultivated in the avant-garde music laboratories in the Netherlands and in Sweden. His opera *Altgeld,* in mixed media, was produced at Southern Illinois Univ. in Carbondale, on March 6, 1968, while Bottje was the head of the electronic music laboratory there. Other works include 7 syms. (1950–70); and numerous pieces for quaquaversal instrumental combinations, with titles such as *Incognitos, Modules, Bandyings, Soundings, Mutations,* and *Fluctuations* (for 5 Clarinets).

Bottrigari, Ercole, Italian music theorist; b. Bologna (baptized), Aug. 24, 1531; d. San Alberto, near Bologna, Sept. 30, 1612. He was an illegitimate son of the nobleman Giovanni Battista Bottrigari; studied mathematics and music in the house of his father; learned to sing and play several instruments; his house teacher was Bartolomeo Spontone. In 1551 he married a rich lady. In his residence he met many celebrated poets of the day, including Tasso. Having acquired profound learning in several scientific and artistic disciplines, he devoted much of his energies to theoretical musical subjects; publ. numerous papers, many of a polemical nature.

WRITINGS: *Il Patricio ovvero De' tetracordi armonici di Aristosseno* (Bologna, 1593); *Il Desiderio ovvero De' concerti di vari stromenti musicali* (Venice, 1594, without Bottrigari's name, but under the pseudonym **Alemanno Benelli,** anagram of the name of his friend Annibale Melone; 2nd ed. with Bottrigari's name, Bologna, 1599; modern reprint of this ed., with introduction and annotations by Kathi Meyer, 1924; 3rd ed., Milan, 1601, under the name of Melone); *Il Melone, Discorso armonico* (Ferrara, 1602). He left trs. of Boetius and other writers in MS, preserved in the library of the Liceo Musicale in Bolonga.

BIBL.: *Notizie biografiche intorno agli studi ed alla vita del Cavaliere B.* (Bologna, 1842).

Boucher, Alexandre-Jean, famous French violinist; b. Paris, April 11, 1778; d. there, Dec. 29, 1861. A brilliant violin virtuoso, he styled himself "l'Alexandre des violons." Boucher began his career at the age of 6, playing with the Concert Spirituel in Paris; was soloist in the court of Charles IV of Spain (1787–1805); traveled extensively on the Continent and in England. He wrote 2 violin concertos.

BIBL.: G. Vallat, "B., Son temps," *Études d'histoire* (1890).

Boucourechliev, André, Bulgarian-French music critic; b. Sofia, July 28, 1925. He studied in Paris and settled there; in 1964 traveled in the U.S. He publ. a biography of Schumann (Paris, 1957; N.Y., 1959), a pictorial biography of Chopin (N.Y., 1962), and a biography of Beethoven (Paris, 1963); became a music critic; also composed music in an advanced idiom. For Beethoven's bicentennial he wrote *Ombres, Hommage à Beethoven* for String Orch. (Toulouse, June 8, 1970). An important work of his is the mobile *Archipel* series, comprising *Archipel I* for 2 Pianos and 54 Percussion, *II* for String Quartet, *III* for Piano and Percussion, *IV* for Piano, *V/A–E* for Instrumental Soli. He also composed *Signes* for Percussion, Flute, and Piano and *Grodek* for Soprano and 3 Percussion Groups. In 1987 he publ. *Stravinsky* (N.Y.).

Boudreau, Robert (Austin), American trumpeter and conductor; b. Bellingham, Mass., April 25, 1927. He studied trumpet with Georges Mager of the Boston Sym. and with William Vacchiano at the Juilliard School of Music in N.Y. He then taught music at Ithaca College (1951–52), Lehigh Univ. (1952–53), and Duquesne Univ. (1955–57). In 1957 he founded in Pittsburgh the American Wind Sym. Orch., specializing in contemporary music; it commissioned works from Henk Badings, Henry Brant, Paul Creston, Alan Hovhaness, Somers, Weinzweig, Penderecki, and Mayuzumi; the orch.'s performances take place aboard the *Point Counterpoint II*, a floating arts center that includes a theater and an art gallery.

Boughton, Rutland, English composer; b. Aylesbury, Jan. 23, 1878; d. London, Jan. 24, 1960. He studied at the Royal College of Music in London with Stanford and Walford Davies; without obtaining his diploma, he engaged in professional activity; was for a time a member of the orch. at Haymarket Theatre in London; taught at Midland Inst. in Birmingham (1905–11); also conducted a choral society there. He became a firm believer in the universality of arts on Wagnerian lines; formed a partnership with the poet Reginald Buckley; their book of essays, *The Music Drama of the Future*, expounding the neo-Wagnerian idea, was publ. in 1911. To carry out these plans, he organized stage festivals at Glastonbury, helped by his common-law wife, Christina Walshe. Boughton's opera, *The Immortal Hour*, was performed there on Aug. 26, 1914; his choral music drama, *The Birth of Arthur*, had a performance there in 1920; these productions were staged with piano instead of an orch. After an interruption during World War I, Boughton continued the Glastonbury festivals until 1926. In 1927 he settled in the country, in Gloucestershire. He continued to compose, however, and produced a number of stage works, as well as instrumental pieces, few of which have been performed. His ideas of universal art had in the meantime been transformed into concepts of socialist realism, with an emphasis on the paramount importance of folk music as against formal constructions. He publ. several pamphlets and essays: *The Death and Resurrection of the Music Festival* (1913); *The Glastonbury Festival Movement* (1922); *Bach, the Master* (1930); *Parsifal: A Study* (1920); *The Nature of Music* (1930); *The Reality of Music* (1934).
WORKS: STAGE: *The Birth of Arthur* (1909; Glastonbury, Aug. 16, 1920); *The Immortal Hour* (1913; Glastonbury, Aug. 26, 1914); *The Round Table* (Glastonbury, Aug. 14, 1916); *The Moon Maiden,* choral ballet for girls (Glastonbury, April 23, 1919); *Alkestis,* music drama (1922; Glastonbury, Aug. 26, 1922; Covent Garden, London, Jan. 11, 1924); *The Queen of Cornwall,* music drama after Thomas Hardy (Glastonbury, Aug. 21, 1924); *May Day,* ballet (1926); *The Ever Young,* music drama (1928; Bath, Sept. 9, 1935); *The Lily Maid,* opera (1934; Gloucester, Sept. 10, 1934); *Galahad,* music drama (1944); *Avalon,* music drama (1946). **ORCH.:** *The Skeleton in Armour,* symphonic poem with Chorus (1898); *The Invincible Armada,* symphonic poem (1901); *A Summer Night* (1902); *Oliver Cromwell,* sym. (1904); *Love and Spring* (1906); *Midnight* (1907); *Song of Liberty* for Chorus and Orch. (1911); *Bethlehem,* choral drama (1915; his most successful work); *Pioneers,* after Walt

Whitman, for Tenor, Chorus, and Orch. (1925); *Deirdre,* sym. (1927); Sym. in B minor (1937); Trumpet Concerto (1943). **CHAMBER:** Violin Sonata (1921); Quartet for Oboe and Strings (1930); String Trio (1944); Piano Trio (1948); Cello Sonata (1948); numerous choral works.
BIBL.: *The Self-Advertisement of R. B.* (anonymous pamphlet without date, c.1909); H. Antcliffe, "A British School of Music Drama: The Work of R. B.," *Musical Quarterly* (Jan. 1918); M. Hurd, *Immortal Hour: The Life and Period of R. B.* (London, 1962); idem, "The Glastonbury Festivals," *Musical Times* (Aug. 1984).

Boughton, William (Paul), English conductor; b. Birmingham, Dec. 18, 1948. He studied cello with Maurice Eisenberg in the U.S. and with Milos Sadlo at the Prague Academy of Music; after a brief career as a cellist with the Royal Phil., the London Sinfonietta, and several BBC orchs., he turned to conducting. In 1980 he founded the English String Orch. in Worcester, which made a major tour of Europe in 1986; he also was artistic director of the Malvern Festival (from 1984) and principal conductor of the Jyväskylä Sym. Orch. in Finland (from 1986). He appeared as guest conductor with many British orchs. His repertoire ranges from Haydn to Tippett.
BIBL.: O. Roca, "W. B.: Bringing Out the Best in British Music," *Ovation* (Oct. 1988).

Bouhy, Jacques (-Joseph André), Belgian-born French baritone; b. Pepinster, June 18, 1848; d. Paris, Jan. 29, 1929. He studied at the Liège Cons.; then entered the Paris Cons., where he studied piano, organ, and theory of composition, as well as singing. He made his debut as Méphistophélès in Gounod's *Faust* at the Paris Opéra on Aug. 2, 1871; on March 3, 1875, he sang Escamillo in the 1st performance of *Carmen* at the Opéra-Comique in Paris. He appeared at Covent Garden, London, on April 22, 1882; then sang at various opera houses in Europe, including that in St. Petersburg. In 1885 he went to N.Y. and served as director of the N.Y. Cons. (until 1889); was again in N.Y. from 1904 to 1907; then returned to Paris and settled there as a singing teacher.

Boulanger, Lili (Juliette Marie Olga), talented French composer, sister of **Nadia (Juliette) Boulanger;** b. Paris, Aug. 21, 1893; d. Mézy, Seine-et-Oise, March 15, 1918. She studied composition with Paul Vidal at the Paris Cons. (1909–13), and attracted considerable attention when she won the Grand Prix de Rome at graduation with her cantata *Faust et Hélène,* as the 1st woman to receive this distinction. Her early death at the age of 24 was lamented by French musicians as a great loss. Her talent, delicate and poetic, continued the tradition of French Romanticism on the borderline of Impressionism. Besides her prizewinning cantata she wrote 2 symphonic poems, *D'un soir triste* and *D'un matin de printemps;* her opera to Maeterlinck's play *La Princesse Maleine* remained incomplete. She also wrote several choral works with orch.: *Soir sur la plaine; Hymne au soleil; La Tempête; Les Sirènes; Sous bois; La Source; Pour les funérailles d'un soldat; 3 psaumes; Vieille prière bouddhique; Pie Jesu,* sacred chorus for Voice, Strings, Harp, and Organ; cycle of 13 songs to texts of Francis Jammes, *Clairières dans le ciel;* some flute pieces.
BIBL.: C. Mauclair, "La Vie et l'œuvre de L. B.," *Revue Musicale* (Aug. 1921); P. Landormy, "L. B.," *Musical Quarterly* (Oct. 1930); R. Dumesnil, *Portraits de musiciens français* (Paris, 1938); E. Lebeau, *L. B.* (Paris, 1968); L. Rosenstiel, *The Life and Works of L. B.* (1978).

Boulanger, Nadia (Juliette), illustrious French composition teacher, sister of **Lili (Juliette Marie Olga) Boulanger;** b. Paris, Sept. 16, 1887; d. there, Oct. 22, 1979. Both her father and grandfather were teachers at the Paris Cons.; her mother, Countess Myshetskaya, was a Russian and a professional singer; it is from her that Nadia Boulanger received her Russian diminutive (for Nadezhda) name, and it was from her that she had her 1st music lessons. She entered the Paris Cons., where she studied organ with Guilmant and Vierne, and composition with Gabriel Fauré; she graduated with prizes in organ and theory; in 1908 she received the 2nd Prix de Rome for her cantata *La Sirène;* she completed the composition of the opera by Raoul Pugno, *La Ville Morte,* left unfinished at his death; also composed cello music, piano pieces, and songs; realizing that she could not compare with her sister Lili in talent as a composer, she devoted herself to teaching, and it is in that profession, often regarded as ancillary and uncreative, that she found her finest vocation. She was assistant in a harmony class at the Paris Cons. (1909–24); was engaged as a teacher at the École Normale de Musique in Paris (1920–39); when the American Cons. was founded in 1921 at Fontainebleau, she joined its faculty as a teacher of composition and orchestration; she became its director in 1950. She also had a large class of private pupils from all parts of the world; many of them achieved fame in their own right; among Americans who went to Paris to study with her were Aaron Copland, Roy Harris, Walter Piston, Virgil Thomson, Elliott Carter, David Diamond, Elie Siegmeister, Irving Fine, Easley Blackwood, Arthur Berger, John Vincent, and Harold Shapero; others were Igor Markevitch, Jean Françaix, Lennox Berkeley, and Dinu Lipatti. Not all of her students were enthusiastic about her methods; some of them complained about the strict, and even restrictive, discipline she imposed on them; but all admired her insistence on perfection of form and accuracy of technique. Her tastes were far from the catholicity expected of teachers; she was a great admirer of Stravinsky, Debussy, and Ravel, but had little appreciation of Schoenberg and the modern Vienna School. She visited the U.S. several times; played the organ part in Aaron Copland's Organ Sym. (which she advised him to compose) with the N.Y. Sym. Orch., under the direction of Walter Damrosch (Jan. 11, 1925), and was the 1st woman to conduct regular subscription concerts of the Boston Sym. Orch. (1938) and of the N.Y. Phil. (Feb. 11, 1939). During World War II she stayed in America; taught classes at Radcliffe College, Wellesley College, and the Juilliard School of Music; returning to Paris in 1946, she took over a class in piano accompaniment at the Paris Cons.; continued her private teaching as long as her frail health permitted; her 90th birthday was celebrated in Sept. 1977, with sincere tributes from her many students in Europe and America.

Bibl.: A. Kendall, *The Tender Tyrant. N. B.: A Life Devoted to Music* (London, 1977); B. Mosaingeon, *Mademoiselle: Entretiens avec N. B.* (Luynes, 1980; Eng. tr., 1985); L. Rosenstiel, *N. B.: A Life in Music* (N.Y., 1982).

Boulez, Pierre, celebrated French composer and conductor; b. Montbrison, March 26, 1925. He studied composition with Olivier Messiaen at the Paris Cons., graduating in 1945; later took lessons with René Leibowitz, who initiated him into the procedures of serial music. In 1948 he became a theater conductor in Paris; made a tour of the U.S. with a French ballet troupe in 1952. In 1954 he organized in Paris a series of concerts called "Domaine Musical," devoted mainly to avant-garde music. In 1963 he delivered a course of lectures on music at Harvard Univ., and on May 1, 1964, made his American debut as conductor in N.Y. In 1958 he went to Germany, where he gave courses at the International Festivals for New Music in Darmstadt. It was in Germany that he gained experience as conductor of opera; he was one of the few Frenchmen to conduct Wagner's *Parsifal* in Germany; in 1976 he was engaged to conduct the *Ring* cycle in Bayreuth. The precision of his leadership and his knowledge of the score produced a profound impression on both the audience and the critics. He was engaged to conduct guest appearances with the Cleveland Orch., and in 1971 he was engaged as music director of the N.Y. Phil., a choice that surprised many and delighted many more. From the outset he asserted complete independence from public and managerial tastes, and proceeded to feature on his programs works by Schoenberg, Berg, Webern, Varèse, and other modernists who were reformers of music, giving a relatively small place to Romantic composers. This policy provoked the expected opposition on the part of many subscribers, but

the management decided not to oppose Boulez in his position as music director of the orch. The musicians themselves voiced their full appreciation of his remarkable qualities as a professional of high caliber, but they described him derisively as a "French correction," with reference to his extraordinary sense of rhythm, perfect pitch, and memory, but a signal lack of emotional participation in the music. In America, Boulez showed little interest in social amenities and made no effort to ingratiate himself with men and women of power. His departure in 1977 and the accession of the worldly Zubin Mehta as his successor were greeted with a sigh of relief, as an antidote to the stern regimen imposed by Boulez. While attending to his duties at the helm of the N.Y. Phil., he accepted outside obligations; from 1971 to 1975 he served as chief conductor of the London BBC Sym. Orch.; as a perfect Wagnerite he gave exemplary performances of Wagner's operas both in Germany and elsewhere. He established his residence in Paris, where he had founded, in 1974, the Inst. de Recherche & Coordination Acoustique/Musique, a futuristic establishment generously subsidized by the French government; in this post he could freely carry out his experimental programs of electronic techniques with the aid of digital synthesizers and a complex set of computers capable of acoustical feedback. In 1989 he was awarded the Praemium Imperiale prize of Japan for his various contributions to contemporary music. His own music is an embodiment of such futuristic techniques; it is fiendishly difficult to perform and even more difficult to describe in the familiar terms of dissonant counterpoint, free serialism, or indeterminism. He specifically disassociated himself from any particular modern school of music. He even publ. a pamphlet with the shocking title *Schoenberg est mort,* shortly after Schoenberg's actual physical death; he similarly distanced himself from other current trends.

Works: *Le Visage nuptial* for Soprano, Contralto Chorus, and Orch. (1946; rev. 1951; Cologne, Dec. 4, 1957, composer conducting); *Le Soleil des eaux,* cantata for Soprano, Men's Chorus, and Orch. (original music for radio play, 1948; rev. 1958 and 1965; Darmstadt, Sept. 9, 1958); *Livre pour quatuor* (1948–49; radically rev. as *Livre pour cordes,* 1968; Brighton, Dec. 8, 1968, composer conducting); *Polyphonie X* for 18 Solo Instruments (Donaueschingen, Oct. 6, 1951); *Le Marteau sans maître,* cantata for Contralto, Flute, Viola, Guitar, Vibraphone, and Percussion (1953–55; Baden-Baden, June 18, 1955); *Poésie pour pouvoir,* spatial work for 5-track Tape and 2 Orchs. (1958; Donaueschingen Festival, Oct. 19, 1958, under the direction of Boulez and Hans Rosbaud; *Pli selon pli, Portrait de Mallarmé* for Soprano and Orch. (Donaueschingen, Oct. 20, 1962); *Doubles* for Orch. (Paris, March 16, 1958; expanded as *Figures-Doubles-Prismes,* Strasbourg, Jan. 10, 1964); *Éclat* for Chamber Orch. (Los Angeles, March 26, 1965; rev. as *Éclats/Multiples;* London, Oct. 21, 1970); *Domaines,* for Solo Clarinet and 21 Instruments (Brussels, Dec. 20, 1968, composer conducting); *cummings ist der dichter* for 16 Voices and 24 Instruments (Stuttgart, Sept. 25, 1970); *. . . explosante-fixe . . .* for Vibraphone, Harp, Violin, Viola, Cello, Flute, Clarinet, Trumpet, and something called a Halaphone, run by a set of Computers (N.Y., Jan. 5, 1973; rev. 1973–74; La Rochelle, July 6, 1974); *Rituel in memoriam Bruno Maderna* (1974–75; London, April 2, 1975, composer conducting); *Messagesquisse* for 7 Cellos (1977); *Pour le docteur Kalmus* for Clarinet, Flute, Violin, Cello, and Piano (1977); *Notations* for Orch. (Paris, June 18, 1980); *Répons* for Chamber Orch. and 6 Solo Instruments, with Computer (Donaueschingen, Oct. 18, 1981; rev., London, Sept. 6, 1982); *Sonatine* for Flute and Piano (1946); Piano Sonata (1946); Sonata for 2 Pianos (Paris, April 29, 1950); *Structures I* for 2 Pianos (1951); *Structures II* for 2 Pianos (1956–61); Piano Sonata No. 2 (1948; Paris, April 29, 1950); Piano Sonata No. 3 (1957); music for the film *Symphonie mécanique* (1955); incidental music for Claudel's version of the *Oresteia* by Aeschylus (1955).

Writings: J.-J. Nattiez, ed., and M. Cooper, translator, *Orientations: Collected Writings* (London, 1986).

Bibl.: A. Goléa, *Rencontres avec P. B.* (Paris, 1958); V.M.

Ames, "What Is Music?," *Journal of Aesthetics and Art Criticism* (Winter 1967); S. Borris, "P. B.—Ein Komponistenporträt," *Musik im Unterricht*, B/LIV/5 (1968); J.P. Derrien, "P. B.," *Musique en Jeu* (1970); M. Fink, "P. B.: A Selective Bibliography," *Current Musicology*, 13 (1972); I. Stoianowa, "Pli selon pli, Portrait de Mallarmé," *Musique en Jeu* (June 1973); J. Peyser, *B., Composer, Conductor, Enigma* (N.Y., 1976); P. Griffiths, *B.* (N.Y., 1979); D. Jameux, *P. B.* (Paris, 1984); J. Hausler, ed., *Festschrift P. B.* (Vienna, 1985); T. Hirsbrunner, *P. B. und sein Werk* (Laaber, 1985); W. Glock, ed., *P. B.: A Symposium* (London, 1986); D. Stearns, "P. B.: The Evolution of a Revolutionary," *Ovation* (July 1986); P. Stacey, *B. and the Modern Concept* (Lincoln, Nebr., 1987); P. McCallum, "An Interview with P. B.," *Musical Times* (Jan. 1989).

Boulnois, Joseph, French composer; b. Paris, Jan. 28, 1884; killed in battle at Chalaines, Oct. 20, 1918. He studied piano and composition at the Paris Cons.; later became a church organist, and from 1909 was choir leader at the Opéra-Comique. He wrote an opera, *L'Anneau d'Isis*, a *Symphonie funèbre*, a Cello Sonata, and various pieces for organ, piano, and voice. His works remain mostly in MS. There has been a revival of interest in his music, which has resulted in some performances of his songs and choruses.

Boult, Sir Adrian (Cedric), eminent English conductor; b. Chester, April 8, 1889; d. London, Feb. 22, 1983. His mother, a professional writer on music, gave him piano lessons; at 12 he received some instruction in music from a science teacher, H.E. Piggott, at the Westminster School in London. At 19 he entered Christ Church, Oxford, and sang in the Oxford Bach Choir; then he studied with Hans Sitt at the Leipzig Cons. (1912–13), and also attended rehearsals and concerts of that city's Gewandhaus Orch. under Nikisch and sang in the Gewandhaus Choir. Upon his return to England, he took his D.Mus. at Oxford and joined the staff of London's Covent Garden in 1914. In 1916 he appeared as guest conductor with the Liverpool Phil. and in 1918 with the London Sym. Orch. During the autumn season of 1919, he was principal conductor of Diaghilev's Ballets Russes in London, and from 1919 to 1924 he was conductor of the British Sym. Orch., an ensemble made up of former soldiers in the British army. In 1919 he also became a teacher of conducting at the Royal College of Music in London, a post he retained until 1930. From 1924 to 1930 he was music director of the City of Birmingham Orch.; he also was music director of the Bach Choir from 1928 to 1931.

In 1930 he was appointed director of music for the BBC in London, and retained that important position until 1942. He was also charged with organizing the BBC Sym. Orch., which he conducted in its 1st concert on Oct. 22, 1930. He subsequently served as its chief conductor until 1950. Under his discerning guidance, it became one of the principal radio orchs. in the world. He led it on several tours abroad, including a notably successful one to Paris, Vienna, Zürich, and Budapest in 1936. During these years he also appeared as guest conductor with the Vienna Phil. (1933), the Boston Sym. Orch. (1935), the NBC Sym. Orch. in N.Y. (1938), the N.Y. Phil. (leading it in the premieres of Bax's 7th Sym. and Bliss's Piano Concerto at the 1939 World's Fair, June 9 and 10, respectively), the Chicago Sym. Orch. (1939), and the Concertgebouw Orch. of Amsterdam (1945). From 1942 to 1950 he was associate conductor of the Henry Wood Promenade Concerts in London. He was music director of the London Phil. from 1950 to 1957 and led it on a major tour of the Soviet Union in 1956. In 1959–60 he was again music director of the City of Birmingham Sym. Orch., and from 1962 to 1966 he once more taught conducting at the Royal College of Music. In 1937 he was knighted, and in 1969 was made a Companion of Honour. In 1944 he was awarded the Gold Medal of the Royal Phil. Soc. He was conductor at the coronations of King George VI in 1937 and Queen Elizabeth II in 1953.

Boult's style of conducting was devoid of glamorous self-assertion; his ideal was, rather, to serve the music with a minimum of display, and for this he was greatly respected by the musicians of the orchs. he conducted. Throughout his long and distinguished career he championed the cause of British music. He was particularly esteemed for his performances of the works of Vaughan Williams, whose *Pastoral Symphony* (Jan. 26, 1922), 4th Sym. (April 10, 1935), and 6th Sym. (April 21, 1948) received their premiere performances under his direction in London.

WRITINGS: *The Point of the Stick: A Handbook on the Technique of Conducting* (Oxford, 1920); *Thoughts on Conducting* (London, 1963); *My Own Trumpet*, an autobiography (London, 1973).

BIBL.: J. Moore, ed., *Music and Friends: Letters to A. B.* (London, 1979); H. Simeone and S. Mundy, eds., *Sir A. B., Companion of Honour: A Tribute* (Tunbridge Wells, 1980); M. Kennedy, *A. B.* (London, 1987).

Bour, Ernest, French conductor; b. Thionville, April 20, 1913. After musical studies at home, he entered the Univ. of Strasbourg, where he took courses in classical languages; later studied conducting with Fritz Munch and Hermann Scherchen. From 1935 to 1939 he was music director of Radio Strasbourg; from 1941 to 1947 and from 1950 to 1964 he was conductor of the Municipal Orch. there. From 1964 to 1979 he served as principal conductor of the Southwest German Radio Sym. Orch. of Baden-Baden. In that capacity he continued the tradition of his predecessor Hans Rosbaud in presenting modern music in his programs. He further conducted guest appearances with the Hamburg State Opera, the German Opera in West Berlin, the Berlin Phil. Orch., and the Concertgebouw Orch. of Amsterdam. In 1976 he was appointed principal conductor of the Radio Kamerorkest in Hilversum.

Bourdin, Roger, French baritone; b. Lavallois, June 14, 1900; d. Paris, Sept. 14, 1973. He studied at the Paris Cons.; made his operatic debut as Lescaut in *Manon* in 1922 at the Opéra-Comique; also sang at the Paris Opéra; made his Covent Garden debut in London in 1930 as Pelléas in Debussy's opera. He was married to the soprano Géori Boué.

Bourgault-Ducoudray, Louis-Albert, French composer; b. Nantes, Feb. 2, 1840; d. Paris, July 4, 1910. At the age of 18 he composed his 1st opera, *L'Atelier de Prague* (Nantes, 1858); was a pupil of Ambroise Thomas at the Paris Cons., taking the Grand Prix de Rome in 1862 with a cantata, *Louise de Mézières*. He founded an amateur choral society in Paris (1868); spent some time in research in Greece, after which he publ. *Souvenirs d'une mission musicale en Grèce*, 30 mélodies populaires de Grèce et de l'Orient, and *Études sur la musique ecclésiastique grecque* (1877). He was appointed prof. of music history at the Paris Cons. in 1878.

WORKS: 5 operas: *Thamara* (Paris Opéra, Dec. 28, 1891), *Michel Colomb* (Brussels, May 7, 1887), *Anne de Bretagne* (Nantes, Dec. 1892), *Myrdhin* (Nantes, March 28, 1912), and *L'Atelier de Prague* (Nantes, 1858). Orch.: *Le Carnaval d'Athènes* (from his *Danses grecques*, orig. for Piano, 4-hands); *Rapsodie cambodgienne*. Vocal: *François d'Amboise*, cantata (1866); *Stabat Mater* (1868); *La Conjuration des fleurs*; *Symphonie religieuse*; etc.; numerous songs, including *30 mélodies populaires de la Basse-Bretagne*, with French trs. (1885). He also wrote piano pieces.

BIBL.: M. Emmanuel, *Éloge funèbre de L.-A. B.-D.* (Paris, 1911; with complete catalogue of works); M. Poté, "B.-D.," *Bulletin de la Société Archéologique et Historique de Nantes* (1965).

Bourgeois, Loys (Louis), French composer; b. Paris, c.1510; d. there, c.1561. He was a follower of Calvin, with whom he lived (1545–52) in Geneva; then returned to France; was still living in 1561. He is renowned for having composed, or adapted, almost all the melodies the Calvinists sang to Marot's and Bèze's French versions of the Psalms. Clément Marot, poet in the service of Francis I as "valet de chambre," tr. (1533–39) 30 Psalms in metrical form, which found great favor with the court, who sang them to light melodies. However, the

Sorbonne soon condemned them, and in 1542 Marot had to flee to Geneva. The 1st ed. of Calvin's Genevan Psalter, containing Marot's 30 Psalms, his versifications of the Paternoster and Credo, 5 Psalms of Calvin, and his versions of the Song of Simeon and the Decalogue, was publ. at Geneva in 1542; 17 of the melodies, all but 3 of which were more or less altered, were adapted by Bourgeois from the earlier Strasbourg Psalter of Calvin (1539), and 22 new ones were added. After arriving at Geneva, Marot added 19 other Psalms and the Song of Simeon; these, together with the 30 previously publ., compose the so-called "Cinquante Pseaumes," which, with Marot's Décalogue, Ave, and Graces (all with music), were added in the 1543 ed. of the Psalter. By 1549, 17 of the melodies previously used were more or less altered by Bourgeois, and 8 others replaced; in 1551 he modified 4 and substituted 12 new tunes. Thus, several of the melodies are of later date than the Psalms. On Marot's death, in 1544, Théodore de Bèze undertook completing the Psalter. In 1551 he added 34 Psalms, in 1554 6 more, and in 1562 the remaining 60. Bourgeois composed, or adapted, the tunes to all except the last 40, these being set, supposedly, by Pierre Dubuisson, a singer. In 1557 Bourgeois left Geneva and severed his immediate contact with the work there, although he still continued his activity on the Psalter. Claude Goudimel publ. harmonized eds. of the Genevan Psalter after 1562, thereby creating the erroneous belief that he was the author of the melodies themselves. Bourgeois himself harmonized, and publ. (in 1547) 2 sets of Psalms in 4–6 parts, intended for private use only. His treatise *Le Droict Chemin de musique*, etc. (Geneva, 1550; Eng. tr. by B. Rainbow as *The Direct Road to Music*, Kilkenny, 1982) proposed a reform in the nomenclature of the tones to fit the solmisation syllables, which was generally adopted in France (see Fétis, *Biographie des musiciens*, vol. II, p. 42).

BIBL.: O. Douen, *Clément Marot et le Psaultier Huguenot* (2 vols., Paris, 1878–79); G.A. Crawford, "Clément Marot and the Huguenot Psalter," *Musical Times* (June/Nov. 1881); G.R. Woodward, "The Genevan Psalter of 1562," *Proceedings of the Music Association, Session 44* (London, 1918); Sir R.R. Terry, "Calvin's First Psalter," ibid., *Session 57* (Lecture; London, 1930); idem, *Calvin's First Psalter* (London, 1932; contains a facsimile and transcription into modern notation of the 1539 Strasbourg Psalter); W.S. Pratt, *The Music of the French Psalter of 1562* (N.Y., 1939); P.A. Gaillard, *L. B.: Sa vie, son œuvre comme pédagogue et compositeur* (Lausanne, 1948); P. Pidoux, "Loys B.' Anteil am Huguenotten-Psalter," *Jahrbuch für Liturgik und Hymnologie* (1970).

Bourgeois, Thomas-Louis (-Joseph), French singer and composer; b. Fontaine-L'Évêque, Oct. 24, 1676; d. Paris, 1750. He was maître de musique at the Strasbourg Cathedral (1703–6); sang with the Paris Opéra (1708–11); then was in the service of the Duke of Bourbon (1715–21). As a composer, he produced a number of fine cantatas, of which 19 are extant; he also wrote divertissements and ballets.

BIBL.: C. Lyon, "T.-L.-J. B.," *L'Éducation populaire* (1882).

Bourguignon, Francis de, Belgian composer; b. Brussels, May 29, 1890; d. there, April 11, 1961. He studied at the Brussels Cons. with Léon Dubois and Edgar Tinel (composition) and Arthur de Greef (piano); entered the Belgian army and was wounded in 1915; was evacuated to England. After the war he made a tour as a pianist with Nellie Melba in Australia; went on concert tours in Canada, South America, Asia, and Africa; circled the globe 6 times. In 1925 he returned to Brussels, and took a course in composition with Paul Gilson; with 7 other pupils of Gilson he formed the "Groupe des Synthétistes" with the proclaimed objective of promoting modern music. He taught at the Brussels Cons. from 1939 to 1955.

WORKS: Chamber opera, *Le Mauvais Pari* (1937); ballet, *La Mort d'Orphée* (1928); radio play, *Congo* (1936); oratorio, *La Nuit* (1945); symphonic poems: *Le Jazz vainqueur* (1929) and *Oiseaux de nuit* (Paris, June 28, 1937); symphonic suites: *Puzzle* (1938) and *Juventus* (1941); Piano Concertino (1927); *2 esquisses sud-américaines* for Orch. (1928); *Fête populaire,*

symphonic movement (1929); *Prelude and Dance* (1929); *Éloge de la folie* for Orch. (1934); Sym. (1934); *Fantasy on 2 Themes of Eugène Ysaïe* for Piano and Orch. (1938); Sinfonietta (1939); *Berceuse* (1940); Suite for Viola and Orch. (1940); *Recuerdos: 2 impressions sud-américaines* (1943); Concerto Grosso (1944); Violin Concerto (1947); Piano Concerto (1949); *Récitatif et Ronde* for Trumpet and Orch. (1951); Concertino for Piano and Chamber Orch. (1952); 2-piano Concerto (1953); *Ouverture martiale* (1960); String Trio; Piano Trio; 2 string quartets; Oboe Quintet; choral works; songs; several piano suites, including *Dans l'île de Pinang* (1925), *En Floride* (1927), and *2 danses* (1939).

BIBL.: A. Vandernoot, *F. d.B.* (Brussels, 1949).

Bournonville, Jacques de, French harpsichordist and composer; b. probably in Amiens, c.1675; d. Paris, c.1754. He was either the grandson or the great-grandson of **Jean de Bournonville.** He studied with Bernier; subsequently established himself as a harpsichord player. His motets for 1 and 2 voices with continuo were publ. in 1711.

Bournonville, Jean de, French composer, father of **Valentin de Bournonville;** b. Noyon, c.1585; d. Paris, May 27, 1632. In 1612 he was appointed director of music at the choir school of the collegiate church of St. Quentin; then was active in Amiens (1618–31). In 1631 he was named director of the choir school of the Sainte-Chapelle. He composed masses, Psalms, motets, and other church music.

Bournonville, Valentin de, French composer, son of **Jean de Bournonville;** b. probably in St. Quentin, c.1610; d. probably in Chartres, Dec. 1663. He studied with his father; became active as a musician in Amiens. In 1646 he became maître de musique at Notre Dame in Paris. In 1653 he was appointed choir director of the school in Chartres. In 1662 he returned to his former post at Notre Dame in Paris.

Bousquet, Georges, French conductor and music critic; b. Perpignan, March 12, 1818; d. St. Cloud, near Paris, June 15, 1854. He studied at the Paris Cons.; won the Prix de Rome (1838); conducted at the Opéra (1847) and at the Théâtre-Italien (1849–51); wrote music criticism for *Le Commerce, L'Illustration,* and the *Gazette Musicale.* He composed 3 operas, which were performed in Paris: *L'Hôtesse de Lyon* (Paris Cons., 1844); *Le Mousquetaire* (Opéra-Comique, 1844); *Tabarin* (Théâtre-Lyrique, 1852); also a cantata; church music; chamber music.

Bousset, Jean-Baptiste, French composer and singer; b. Dijon, 1662; d. Paris, Oct. 3, 1725. He was active as maître de musique at the chapel of the Louvre, the Académie Française, and the Académies des Sciences et des Inscriptions. He publ. 40 books of airs sérieux et à boire (Paris, 1690–1709), 2 books, both titled *Eglogue bachique* (Paris, 1693, 1695), and a book of cantatas (Paris, before 1710); his motets and an opera are lost. His son, **René Drouard de Bousset** (b. Paris, Dec. 11, 1703; d. there, May 19, 1760), was also a musician; he was active in Paris as an organist and composer.

Boutmy, Josse, Belgian organist and composer; b. Ghent, Feb. 1, 1697; d. Brussels, Nov. 27, 1779. He was a member of a musical family and received his training from his father, a church organist. In 1721 he went to Brussels, where he became a teacher of the clavecin; also was organist at the Royal Chapel (from 1744). He publ. 2 books of clavecin pieces (Brussels, 1738, 1750); partial reprints are in vol. V of Monumenta Musicae Belgicae (Antwerp, 1943), ed. by Suzanne Clercx, with a biographical essay in Flemish and French.

Boutry, Roger, French pianist, conductor, and composer; b. Paris, Feb. 27, 1932. He studied at the Paris Cons.; received 1st prize as a pianist at the age of 16; 1st prize as a conductor at 21; and the Premier Prix de Rome at 22. In 1963 he was awarded the Grand Prix Musical of the City of Paris. He embarked on a successful career as a pianist; toured in Europe, Russia, and Australia; as a conductor, he appeared with several orchs. in France; also conducted opera in Monte Carlo.

WORKS: Piano Concerto (1954); *Rapsodie* for Piano and Orch. (1956); *Ouverture-Tableau* for Orch. (1959); *Divertimento* for Saxophone and Orch. (1964); *Concerto-Fantaisie* for 2 Pianos and Orch. (Paris, Feb. 16, 1967); *Intermezzi* for Chamber Orch. (1970); Quartet for Trombones; Flute Concerto; 2 sextets; *Pastels et contours* for 5 Harps; also didactic pieces for various instruments.

Bouvet, Charles (René Clément), French musicologist; b. Paris, Jan. 3, 1858; d. there, May 24, 1935. He studied at the Paris Cons.; organized the Fondation J.S. Bach (1903–11); in 1924 he was appointed archivist of the Paris Opéra. He ed. works of Bonporti and Couperin; also publ. *Une Dynastie de musiciens français: Les Couperin . . .* (1919); *L'Opéra* (1924); and *Massenet* (1929).

Bouzignac, Guillaume, French composer who flourished in the early 17th century. Biographical data are lacking, but several specimens of his music are extant. It is known that he was a choirboy at Narbonne; in 1609 was the "maître des enfants" at the Grenoble Cathedral. His creative period comprises the years 1610–40; he wrote a number of effective motets in the popular French style, distinguished by dramatic expression, as well as religious works. H. Quittard publ. several of these pieces in his paper "Un Musicien oublié du XVIIᵉ siècle," *Bulletin de la Société Internationale de Musique* (Paris, 1905).

Bovet, Joseph, Swiss priest, teacher, conductor, and composer; b. Sâles, Gruyère, Oct. 7, 1879; d. Clarens, Feb. 10, 1951. He studied in Romont, Fribourg, and Einsiedeln, and at the Seckau Benedictine monastery; then became a priest and taught music at the Fribourg diocesan seminary. He was made conductor at the Fribourg Cathedral and conducted various choral groups; from 1909 to 1923 he was also conductor of the Fribourg sym. concerts. He wrote much church music for choral forces, music for plays, and part-songs.
BIBL.: *Hommage à l'abbé B.* (Fribourg, 1947); R. Loup, *L'abbé B.: Barde du pays* (Lausanne, 1952).

Bovy-Lysberg, Charles-Samuel, Swiss pianist and composer; b. Lysberg, near Geneva, Feb. 1, 1821; d. Geneva, Feb. 15, 1873. He went to Paris and was one of the few young pianists to study with Chopin (1835). Returning to Switzerland, he settled at Dardagny, near Geneva, in 1848; taught piano at the Geneva Cons., and gave recitals in the French cantons. His opera, *La Fille du carillonneur,* was produced in Geneva in 1854; he also wrote a romantically inspired piano sonata, *L'Absence;* but he became known chiefly by his effective salon pieces for piano (numbering about 130), among them *La Napolitaine, Le Réveil des oiseaux, Le Chant du rouet, Idylle, Les Ondines, Sur l'onde,* etc. His real name was **Bovy,** but he hyphenated it with Lysberg, the name of his birthplace.
BIBL.: P. Long, "C.-S. B.-L.," *Schweizerisches Jahrbuch für Musikwissenschaft,* III (1928).

Bovy, Vina, Belgian soprano; b. Ghent, May 22, 1900; d. there, May 16, 1983. She made her debut in her native city, then appeared as a guest artist in Brussels and in Paris. She had the extraordinary luck of being engaged by Toscanini at La Scala in Milan. On Dec. 24, 1936, she made her American debut as Violetta in *La Traviata* at the Metropolitan Opera in N.Y., remaining there for a single season and eventually returning to Belgium. A biography of her by J. Deleersnyder was publ. in Ghent in 1965.

Bowen, (Edwin) York, English composer and pianist; b. London, Feb. 22, 1884; d. Hampstead, Nov. 23, 1961. He studied at the Royal Academy of Music, where he won the Erard and Sterndale Bennett scholarships; his teachers were T. Matthay (piano) and F. Corder (composition). Upon graduation, he was appointed instructor in piano there. A prolific composer, Bowen wrote 3 syms.; 3 piano concertos; Violin Concerto; Viola Concerto; Rhapsody for Cello and Orch.; several symphonic poems (*The Lament of Tasso, Eventide,* etc.); orch. suites; many practical piano pieces in miniature forms. Bowen was the author of a manual, *Pedalling the Modern Pianoforte* (London, 1936).
BIBL.: M. Watson, *Y. B.: A Centenary Tribute* (London,

1984).

Bowers, Thomas J., esteemed black American tenor; b. Philadelphia, c.1823; d. there, Oct. 3, 1885. He studied organ with his brother, John C. Bowers, succeeding him as organist of Philadelphia's St. Thomas's African Episcopal Church (c.1838). After vocal training with Elizabeth Taylor Greenfield, he began a North American duo-recital tour with her with a performance at Philadephia's Sansom St. Hall (1854); critics hailed him as the "American Mario" and the "colored Mario."

Bowie, David, British rock musician, master of image manipulation; b. South London, Jan. 8, 1947. His real name was **David Jones,** which he changed to avoid confusion with a British singer, Davey Jones, of the American pop group The Monkees. After some inconclusive attempts to fuse with the latest British fashion in punk rock, he switched to something called "flower power," associated with extraterrestrial visions, which he embodied in his album *Space Oddity.* Dissatisfied with his directions, he opened the innovative Arts Lab, but was talked into returning to the punks. With the guitarist Mick Ronson and the drummer Woody Woodmansey, he put out a record, *The Man Who Sold the World,* with the cover showing him in drag; it gave the impetus to a subdivision of punk rock known as "glitter rock." The record was banned in the U.S. because the drag queen on the cover bore an uncanny resemblance to the movie star Lauren Bacall. Still carrying on his space obsession, Bowie released several "conceptual" albums, such as *Ziggy Stardust.* He also paid tribute to drug society in a number called *Rock-'n'-Roll Suicide.* His next avatar was in the "soul" sound of Philadelphia, exemplified by his hit song *Fame.* Then, all of a sudden, he decided to try his luck in the movies, and starred in the space fantasy *The Man Who Fell to Earth,* in which his somewhat introspective image and emaciated appearance fitted the hero's image. Always exploring new avenues, he took the role of the monstrously deformed *Elephant Man* on the legitimate stage (1980), depicting an actual case of a man afflicted by filariasis, a disease characterized by granulomatous lesions and resulting in gross expansion of the tissues of the face and scrotum. The play was a resounding success for Bowie, and for a time he moved away from rock to the stage; later returned to music as his primary focus.
BIBL.: P. Goddard, *D. B.: Out of the Cool* (N.Y., 1983); H. Edwards and T. Zanetta, *The D. B. Story* (N.Y., 1986); D. Thompson, *D. B.: Moonage Daydream* (London, 1987).

Bowie, Lester, American jazz trumpeter; b. Frederick, Md., Oct. 11, 1941. He began playing in St. Louis in the rhythm-and-blues bands of Albert King and Little Milton, then in 1965 moved to Chicago, where he helped found the Assoc. for the Advancement of Creative Musicians, an organization composed of young, avant-garde black jazz players. In 1969 he became a founding member of the Art Ensemble of Chicago; his performances, aside from those with the Ensemble, range from solo concerts to ones with his own bands, From the Root to the Source and Lester Bowie's Brass Fantasy. His most popular recordings include *Fast Last* (1974), *The 5th Power* (1978), and *All the Magic!* (1982). His *23 Facts in 2 Acts* for Musicians, Dancers, Chorus, and Actors was premiered at the Brooklyn Academy of Music on Nov. 11, 1989.

Bowles, Paul Frederic, American composer and novelist; b. Jamaica, N.Y., Dec. 30, 1910. As a callow youth he became fascinated with pictorial arts, belles lettres, and vocal projection of poetry. He took ship to Europe, making Paris his residence; dazzled by its intellectual resplendence, he exercised his penetrating mental powers to master the profundities of the French language, but could not come closer to literature than employment as a telephone operator in the offices of the Paris edition of the *N.Y. Herald Tribune.* Frustrated, he returned to N.Y., where he worked as a bookshop clerk. His hypnopomping talents as a composer then awakened. He impressed Aaron Copland by his early vocal pieces and was invited to study with him privately in Saratoga, N.Y. Paris was still his cynosure, however, and he set sail once more for the City of Light. There he established a connection with the fully Parisianized Virgil Thomson and took a course in counterpoint with the *nourrice* of a number of American musicians, Nadia Boulanger. In due course he became a habitué of the dadaist circles on the left bank of the Seine, presided over by the narcissistic grand vizier of iconoclastic illogic, Erik Satie. To this period belong Bowles's cantata, *Par le détroit* (1933), and the pseudo-Grecian *Scènes d'Anabase* scored for Voice, Oboe, and Piano (1932). In 1936 he returned to the U.S., where he wrote his 1st stage work, the ballet *Yankee Clipper*, which was duly performed by the American Ballet Caravan in Philadelphia on July 19, 1937. He further wrote a number of scores of incidental music for various theatrical productions, as well as a short opera, *The Wind Remains*, to a text by García Lorca, which was produced in N.Y. in 1943 with Leonard Bernstein conducting. The N.Y. scene failed to satisfy his psychological attraction to exotic lands, however, and he set his course for Tangier. A total change in his artistic orientation occurred in 1949 when he publ. the 1st of what would be many bone-chilling novels, short stories, and translations of native works about Morocco, *The Sheltering Sky*, which achieved an unexpected literary success and was even made into a motion picture. In 1988 Bowles became the subject of a solid biographical tome under the title *An Invisible Spectator*, by Christopher Sawyer-Lauçanno. Bowles also publ. an autobiography, entitled *Without Stopping* (1985). Another literary publication by Bowles was a slender booklet, *Points in Time* (1984), which he described as a "lyrical history." Among his other musical works are *A Picnic Cantata* for Women's Voices, 2 Pianos, and Percussion (N.Y., March 23, 1954), and *Yerma* (1959), to a libretto by García Lorca. Bowles was intermittently united in marriage to Jane Auer, who was quite an exciting novelist in her own right; she died in 1973.

Bowman, Euday (Louis), black American rag composer; b. Fort Worth, Tex., Nov. 9, 1887; d. N.Y., May 26, 1949. He was active as a pianist in "Hell's Half Acre," the former brothel district in Fort Worth. His most famous work was the *12th St. Rag* (1914), which attained the status of a classic among piano rags.

Bowman, James (Thomas), English countertenor; b. Oxford, Nov. 6, 1941. He was educated at New College, Oxford; made his operatic debut as Oberon in Britten's *A Midsummer Night's Dream* in London in 1967; subsequently sang with the Glyndebourne Festival, the Royal Opera House, Covent Garden, the English National Opera, London, and the Scottish Opera, Glasgow; also appeared with the Early Music Consort of London. He gained distinction as an interpreter of the castrato roles in Handel's operas; also sang non-castrato songs in oratorios.

Boxberg, Christian Ludwig, German composer; b. Sondershausen, April 24, 1670; d. Görlitz, Dec. 1, 1729. He studied at the Thomasschule in Leipzig; from 1692 to 1702 was organist in Grossenhain; also was active as a librettist, composer, and singer at the Leipzig Opera. In 1702 he became organist at Ss. Peter and Paul in Görlitz. He wrote librettos for the operas of N.A. Strungk. His own operas include *Orion* (Ansbach, 1697), *Die verschwiegene Treue* (Ansbach, 1698), *Sardanapolus* (Ansbach, 1698), and *Amyntas und Phyllis* (Leipzig, 1700). He also composed numerous cantatas.

BIBL.: H. Mersmann, *C.L. B. und seine Oper "Sardanapolus,"* *Ansbach, 1698* (diss., Univ. of Berlin, 1916).

Boyce, William, significant English organist and composer; b. London (baptized), Sept. 11, 1711; d. Kensington, Feb. 7, 1779. As a youth he was a chorister in St. Paul's Cathedral under Charles King; then studied organ with Maurice Greene, the cathedral organist. From 1734 to 1736 he was organist at the Earl of Oxford's Chapel; then was at St. Michael's, Cornhill, from 1736 to 1768. Concurrently he was named in 1736 composer to the Chapel Royal. In 1759 he was Master of the King's Musick. An increasing deafness forced him to abandon

active musical duties after 1769. His main task consisted in providing sacred works for performance; he also contributed incidental music to theatrical productions. He conducted the Festivals of the Three Choirs (Gloucester, Worcester, Hereford) in 1737, and served as Master of the Royal Band in 1755. His magnum opus was the compilation of the collection *Cathedral Music*, in 3 vols. (1760, 1768, and 1773; 2nd ed., 1788; later eds., 1844 and 1849). This collection comprises morning and evening services, anthems, and other church music by a number of British composers, namely Aldrich, Batten, Bevin, Blow, Bull, Byrd, Child, Clarke, Creyghton, Croft, Farrant, Gibbons, Goldwin, Henry VIII, Humfrey, Lawes, Locke, Morley, Mundy, Purcell, Rogers, Tallis, Turner, Tye, Weldon, and Wise. Of his own music, there are remarkable instrumental works: 12 overtures (London, 1770; reprinted in Musica Britannica, vol. XIII); 12 sonatas for 2 Violins and Bass (London, 1747); 8 syms. (London, 1760; modern ed. by M. Goberman, Vienna, 1964); 10 voluntaries for Organ or Harpsichord (London, 1779). Two overtures erroneously attributed to Boyce, and publ. in Lambert's ed. under the titles *The Power of Music* and *Pan and Syrinx*, were works by John Stanley, not by Boyce. His stage works include the following, all produced in London: *The Chaplet* (Dec. 2, 1749); *The Roman Father*, not extant (Feb. 24, 1750); *The Shepherd's Lottery* (Nov. 19, 1751); and *Harlequin's Invasion* (with M. Arne and T. Aylward, Dec. 31, 1759). Several of his vocal works were publ. in Lyra Britannica (1745–55); there were also 15 anthems (1780) and a collection of anthems (1750), which were republ. in Novello's ed. in 4 vols.; also, various songs were orig. publ. in the anthologies *The British Orpheus*, *The Vocal Musical Mask*, and others.

BIBL.: D.A. Dawe, "New Light on W. B.," *Musical Times* (Sept. 1968); J. Hawkins, "Memoirs of Dr. W. B." (introduction and notes by G. Beechey), *Musical Quarterly* (Jan. 1971); R. McGuinness, *English Court Odes 1660–1820* (Oxford, 1971).

Boyd, Anne (Elizabeth), Australian composer; b. Sydney, April 10, 1946. She studied flute at the New South Wales Cons. (1960–63) and composition at the Univ. of Sydney (1963–66); concluded studies at York Univ. in England (1969–72; Ph.D., 1972); then became a lecturer at Sussex Univ. (1975–77); served as head of the music dept. at the Univ. of Hong Kong (1980–88).

WORKS: *Air and Variations* for Flute and Piano (1960); Trio for Flute, Violin, and Piano (1962); *Infinity* for Piano (1964); *L'Altro* for Orch. (1964); *Exegesis No. 1* for 4 Flutes and 2 Piccolos (1964); *Synchrony No. 1*, trio for Oboe, Clarinet, and Bassoon (1964); *Chelidiones* for Solo Flute, Piccolo, and Tape (1965); *3 Piano Pieces* (1965); *The Fall of Icarus* for Flute, Clarinet, Cello, and Piano (1966); Trio for Oboe, Violin, and Cello (1966); *The Stairway*, ballet for 4 Instruments and Percussion (1968); 2 string quartets (*The 4th Generation*, 1968; 1973); *Games* for any number of Players (1969); *As Far as Crawls the Toad* for 5 Young Percussionists (1970); *Hidden in a White Cloud* for Wind Quintet, or for Flutes and Cellos (1970); *The Voice of the Phoenix* for Solo Piano, Guitar, and Harp (all amplified), 10 Percussionists, Orch. with Augmented Woodwinds, and an ad-lib VCS-3 Synthesizer (1971); *Greetings to Victor McMahon* for 12 Flutes (1971); *The Metamorphoses of the Solitary Female Phoenix* for Wind Quintet, Piano, and Percussion (1971); *The Rose Garden*, theater piece (1972); *Angklung* for Piano (1974); *The Little Mermaid*, children's opera (1978); *Angklung 2* for Violin (1980).

Boydell, Brian (Patrick), prominent Irish composer; b. Dublin, March 17, 1917. He took courses in music at the Evangelical Church Music Inst. of the Univ. of Heidelberg, with Hadley and Howells at the Royal College of Music in London (1938–39), at the Royal Irish Academy of Music in Dublin, and at the Univ. of Dublin (D.Mus., 1959); subsequently was a prof. of music there (1962–82). He was made a Commendatore della Repubblica Italiana for his services to Italian Renaissance music (1983) and a member of Aosdana for general contributions to the creative arts in Ireland. His music is distinguished by its assured command of traditional compositional techniques.

WORKS: ORCH.: Sym. for Strings (1945); *5 Joyce Songs* (1946); *In Memoriam Mahatma Gandhi* (1948); Violin Concerto (1953); *The Wooing of Etain*, 2 suites (1954); *Elegy and Capriccio* for Clarinet and Strings (1955); *Megalithic Ritual Dances* (1956); *Ceól Cas Corach* (Cas Corach's Music; 1958); *Richard's Riot* (1961); *Symphonic Inscapes* (1968); *Jubilee Music* (1976); *Partita Concertante* for Violin, Harp, and Orch. (1978); *A Wild Dance for Ceól Chumann na nóg* (1982). **CHAMBER:** Oboe Quintet (1940); String Trio (1944); Sonata for Cello and Piano (1945); 3 string quartets (1950, 1957, 1969); *A Pack of Fancies for a Travelling Harper* (1970); 5 *Mosaics* for Violin, and Piano or Harp (1972); *5 Blows for Brass Quintet* (1984); also many piano pieces. **VOCAL:** *An Easter Carol* for Chorus (1940); *Shatter Me, Music* for Chorus (1952); *The Deer's Cry* for Baritone and Orch. (1957); *Noël* for Chorus and Orch. (1960); *4 Yeats Poems* for Soprano and Orch. (1965); *Mouth Music* for Chorus (1974); *The Small Bell*, cantata (1980); *The Carlow Cantata or The Female Friend* (1985); songs.

Boyden, David Dodge, American musicologist; b. Westport, Conn., Dec. 10, 1910; d. Berkeley, Sept. 18, 1986. He studied at Harvard Univ. (M.A., 1938), then joined the faculty of the Univ. of Calif. at Berkeley, remaining there until 1975. He publ. a number of valuable treatises on music theory and history; to be noted are *A Manual of Counterpoint Based on Sixteenth-century Practice* (N.Y., 1944; 2nd ed., 1953), *The History and Literature of Music, 1750 to the Present* (1948), *An Introduction to Music* (N.Y., 1956; 2nd ed., 1970), and *The History of Violin Playing from Its Origins to 1761* (London, 1965).

Boy George (real name, **George Alan O'Dowd**), bizarre English rock singer; b. London, June 14, 1961. He became fascinated with the pop scene in childhood, his early streak of unconventional habits and dress leading to expulsion from school. He then hovered on the fringes of civilized society by immersing himself in gay, rock, and "new wave" scenes while holding down various odd jobs. His penchant for outlandish makeup and sartorial non-conformity found a natural outlet when he launched his singing career as Lieutenant Lash with the "new wave" outfit dubbed Bow Wow Wow. Although he could neither read nor write music, he established the interracial rock quartet known as Culture Club, gaining fame and lucre as the group's vocalist and songwriter. Their 1st album, *Kissing to Be Clever* (1982), became a hit on both sides of the Atlantic. In 1983 they made a successful tour of the U.S.; subsequent albums included *Color by Numbers* (1983) and *Waking Up with the House on Fire* (1984). In 1986 Boy George was arrested in London for drug possession.

BIBL.: *Current Biography* (Oct. 1985).

Boykan, Martin, American pianist and composer; b. N.Y., April 12, 1931. He studied composition with Walter Piston at Harvard Univ., and also with Hindemith at the Univ. of Zürich (1951–52) and at Yale Univ. (M.M., 1953). He taught at Brandeis Univ. (from 1957); he also held a Guggenheim fellowship (1984). In 1986 he was elected to membership in the American Academy and Inst. of Arts and Letters. As a pianist, he developed a remarkable technique entirely adequate for the most demanding contemporary compositions. As a composer, he writes mostly chamber music. His works include 4 string quartets (1949, 1967, 1974, 1984); Flute Sonata (1950); Duo for Violin and Piano (1951); Quintet for Flute, Piano, and Strings (1953); *Chamber Concerto* (1970).

Boyle, George Frederick, American pianist and composer; b. Sydney, Australia, June 29, 1886; d. Philadelphia, June 20, 1948. He received his early musical training from his parents; in 1905 went to Berlin, where he took piano lessons with Busoni. He began his career as an accompanist. In 1910 he settled in the U.S.; taught piano at the Peabody Cons. in Baltimore (1910–22), the Curtis Inst. in Philadelphia (1924–26), and the Inst. of Musical Art in N.Y. (1927–39). He wrote

Aubade for Orch. (St. Louis, March 5, 1916); Piano Concerto (Worcester Festival, Sept. 28, 1911); Cello Concerto (Washington, D.C., Feb. 7, 1918); 3 piano trios; Violin Sonata; Viola Sonata; Cello Sonata; about 100 piano pieces and 50 songs.

Boyvin, Jacques, French organist and composer; b. Paris, c.1649; d. Rouen, June 30, 1706. He studied in Paris; then was organist at the Hôpital des Quinze-Vingts (1663–74); from 1674 until his death he was organist at Notre Dame Cathedral in Rouen; also served at St. Herbland (1697–1702). He composed mainly for organ; his organ works were publ. in Paris in 2 books (1689–90 and 1700). See A. Guilmant and A. Pirro, eds., *J. B.: Œuvres complètes d'orgue* (Paris, 1905).

BIBL.: N. Pierront, "J. B.," *Études Normandes*, XXVI (1958).

Bozay, Attila, Hungarian composer; b. Balatonfüzfö, Aug. 11, 1939. He studied in Budapest, 1st at the Bartók Cons. (1954–57) and then at the Academy of Music with Ferenc Farkas (1957–62). In his music he makes use of modified serial techniques.

WORKS: Opera, *Küngisz királynö* (Queen Küngisz; 1968–69); Duo for 2 Violins (1958); *Episodes* for Bassoon and Piano (1959); String Trio (1960; rev. 1966); *Bagatelles* for Piano (1961); *Papírszeletek* (Slips of Paper), song cycle for Soprano, Clarinet, and Cello (1962); Wind Quintet (1962); *Ritornell* for Solo Violin (1963); *Kialtasok* (Outcries), song cycle for Tenor and Chamber Ensemble (1963); 2 string quartets (1964, 1971); Variations for Piano (1964); *Pezzo concertato* for Orch. (1965); *Trapéz és korlát* (Trapeze and Bars), cantata (1966); *Pezzo sinfonico* for Orch. (1967); *Intervals* for Piano (1969); *Formations* for Solo Cello (1969); *Sorozat* (Series) for Chamber Ensemble (1970); *Improvisations* for Solo Zither (1972); *Malom* (Mill) for Wind Instruments, Portable Organ, and Percussion (1973); *Pezzo concertato No. 2* for Zither and Orch. (1974–75); *Variazioni* for Orch. (1977); *Solo* for Recorder (1978); *Csongor és Tünde*, opera (1979–84; Budapest, Jan. 20, 1985).

Božič, Darijan, Slovenian composer; b. Slavonski Brod, April 29, 1933. He studied composition with Škerjanc and conducting with Švara at the Music Academy of Ljubljana; upon graduation, served as an opera conductor and artistic director of the Slovenian Phil. (1970–74). His music was at 1st influenced by jazz; later he adopted radical serial techniques.

WORKS: 4 operas: *Humoreske* (1958), *Spoštovanja vredna vlačuga* (1960), *Ares Eros* (1970), and *Lizistrata* (1975); a musical happening, *Jago*; a dramatic collage, *Polineikes* (1966); 2 ballets: *Baletska jednočinka* (1957) and *Gluha okna* (1967); Piano Concerto (1956); Saxophone Concerto (1958); Trombone Concerto (1960); Trumpet Concerto (1961); Sym. (1964–65); *Audiostructures* for Piano and Orch.; *Audiospectrum* for Orch. (1972); *Trije dnevni Ane Frank* (3 Days of Anne Frank) for 2 Narrators and Synthetic Sound (1963); *Gregora strniše* for Narrator and 7 Instruments (1965); *Kriki* (Cries) for Narrator, Brass Quintet, and Tape (1966); *Requiem* (to the Memory of a Murdered Soldier—My Father), sound collage for Narrator, Chorus, Instruments, and Concrete Sounds (1969); *Sonata in Cool I* for Flute and Piano (1961); *Sonata in Cool II* for Clarinet and Piano (1961); *Sonata in Cool III* for Flute, Bass Clarinet, and Harp (1965); *Pop-art-music* for String Quartet, Piccolo, and 2 Metronomes (1969); *Audiogemi I–IV* for String Quartet (1974).

Bozza, Eugène, French composer and conductor; b. Nice, April 4, 1905. He studied music at the Paris Cons.; received the Grand Prix de Rome in 1934. From 1939 to 1948 he was conductor of the Opéra-Comique in Paris; then moved to Valenciennes, where he was appointed director of the local cons.

WORKS: Opera, *Léonidas* (1947); lyric drama, *La Duchesse de Langeais* (Lille, 1967); ballets: *Fête romaine* (1942) and *Jeux de plage* (1946); Sym. (1948); Violin Concerto (1938); Cello Concerto (1947); *Luciolles* for 6 Clarinets; *Suite française* for 5 Woodwind Instruments; *3 Pieces* for 5 Trombones; and other compositions for unusual instrumental combinations.

Bradbury, William Batchelder, American music editor; b. York, Maine, Oct. 6, 1816; d. Montclair, N.J., Jan. 7, 1868.

He studied with Lowell Mason; then went to Germany, where he took courses with Hauptmann and Moscheles in Leipzig. Returning to America, he became active in various musical enterprises; from 1854 to 1867 he was in business as a maker of pianos. He ed. some 50 collections of songs and instrumental pieces; one of these collections, *Fresh Laurels for the Sabbath School* (1867), reached the circulation of 1.2 million copies; other collections were *Bradbury's Golden Shower of Sunday School Melodies; Bright Jewels for the Sunday School; Musical Gems for School and Home.* He wrote well-known hymn tunes: *He Leadeth Me; Saviour, Like a Shepherd Lead Me;* etc.

BIBL.: A. Wingard, *The Life and Works of W.B. B. (1816–1868)* (diss., Southern Baptist Theological Seminary, Louisville, Ky., 1973).

Brade, William, English-born German violinist and composer; b. 1560; d. Hamburg, Feb. 26, 1630. He settled in Germany about 1590; thereafter was a court musician in various localities, including Brandenburg, Copenhagen, Bückeburg, Hamburg, Güstrow, and Berlin. He composed a number of popular collections of dances.

WORKS: *Newe ausserlesene Paduanen, Galliarden, Canzonen, Allmand und Coranten . . . auff allen musicalischen Instrumenten lieblich zu gebrauchen* (Hamburg, 1609); *Newe ausserlesene Paduanen und Galliarden . . . auff allen musicalischen Instrumenten und insonderheit auff Fiolen lieblich zu gebrauchen* (Hamburg, 1614); *Newe ausserlesene liebliche Branden, Intraden, Mascharaden, Balletten, All'manden, Couranten, Volten, Aufzüge und frembde Tänze . . . insonderheit auff Fiolen zu gebrauchen* (Hamburg and Lübeck, 1617); *Melodieuses paduanes, chansons, galliardes* (Antwerp, 1619); *Newe lustige Volten, Couranten, Balletten, Paduanen, Galliarden, Masqueraden, auch allerley arth newer frantzösischer Täntze* (Berlin, 1621).

BIBL.: C. Huber, *The Life and Music of W. B.* (diss., Univ. of North Carolina, 1965).

Bradford, Alex, black American gospel singer and composer; b. Bessemer, Ala., Jan. 23, 1927; d. Newark, N.J., Feb. 15, 1978. He became a singer with the Protective Harmoneers, a children's gospel group, when he was 13; he also appeared on his own program on a local radio station. He later took courses at the Snow Hill (Ala.) Inst., where he worked as a student teacher and picked up the unearned title of "professor," which he used the rest of his life. After working with his own group, the Bradford Singers, he joined forces with Willie Webb and made the successful recording *Every Day and Every Hour* (1950); then organized the all-male Bradford Specials. Following the success of his own song *Too Close to Heaven,* which he recorded in 1953, he toured extensively. He also appeared in Langston Hughes's *Black Nativity* in 1962, and went on to Broadway, where he starred in *Don't Bother Me, I Can't Cope* (1972) and *Your Arms Too Short to Box with God* (1976).

Bradley, Gwendolyn, black American soprano; b. N.Y., Dec. 12, 1952. She received training at the North Carolina School of the Arts in Winston-Salem, N.C., the Curtis Inst. of Music in Philadelphia, and the Philadelphia Academy of Vocal Arts. In 1976 she made her operatic debut as Verdi's Nannetta at the Lake George (N.Y.) Opera, and on Feb. 20, 1981, she made her 1st appearance at the Metropolitan Opera in N.Y. as the Nightingale in *L'Enfant et les Sortilèges,* returning there to sing such roles as Blondchen, Gilda, and Offenbach's Olympia in subsequent years. She made her European debut at the Corfu (Greece) Festival in 1981, and later was guest artist with opera companies in Cleveland, Philadelphia, Amsterdam, Glyndebourne, Hamburg, Berlin, Monte Carlo, and Nice.

Bradshaw, Merrill (Kay), American composer and pedagogue; b. Lyman, Wyo., June 18, 1929. He received his academic education at Brigham Young Univ. in Salt Lake City and at the Univ. of Illinois; then began his musical studies; obtained an M.M. from Brigham Young Univ. in 1955 and a D.M.A. from the Univ. of Illinois in 1962. From 1957 he was

engaged in teaching at Brigham Young Univ. As a member of the Mormon Church, he contributed a great deal to the formulation of classical Mormon music.

WORKS: ORCH.: 5 syms.: No. 1 (1957); No. 2 (1962); No. 3 (1967); No. 4 (1968); No. 5 (1978; Auckland, New Zealand, July 4, 1979); Piano Concerto (1955); *Facets* (1965); *Feathers* (1968); *4 Mountain Sketches* (1974); *Nocturnes and Revels* (1974); *Lovers and Liars* (1976); Concerto for Viola and Orch., entitled *Homages* (Provo, Utah, July 14, 1979); Violin Concerto (Provo, March 5, 1981). **CHAMBER:** *Dialogue* for Flute and Horn (1956); String Quartet No. 1 (1957); String Quartet No. 2 (1969); Violin Sonata (1957); Suite for Viola (1967); Suite for Oboe and Piano (1966); Brass Quintet (1969); Nocturne for 2 Horns and Strings (1977). **VOCAL:** *The Restoration,* oratorio (Provo, March 23, 1974); *Love and Death, 4 Elizabethan Lyrics* for Viola, Soprano, and Strings (Provo, Sept. 10, 1982); a musical, *The Title of Liberty* (1975); a cappella choruses; hymns; Psalms; ballads. **PIANO:** *6 Bagatelles* (1958); *Moments* (1968); *20 Mosaics* (1972); *6 plus 4* for 10 Pianos (1976).

Bradsky, Wenzel Theodor, Bohemian composer; b. Rakovnik, Jan. 17, 1833; d. there, Aug. 10, 1881. He studied in Prague; then was a choir singer in Berlin; in 1874 he was given the title of court composer by Prince Georg of Prussia, whose drama *Iolanthe* he set to music. He wrote the operas *Roswitha* (Dessau, 1860); *Das Krokodil* (1862); *Jarmila* (Prague, 1879); *Der Rattenfänger von Hameln* (Berlin, 1881); also many choruses and solo songs.

Braein, Edvard Fliflet, Norwegian composer and conductor; b. Kristiansund, Aug. 23, 1924; d. Oslo, April 30, 1976. He was of a musical family; his grandfather was an organist and choirmaster, and his father, **Edvard Braein** (1887–1957), was a composer, organist, and conductor. E.F. Braein began his musical education at the Cons. in Oslo, graduating in 1943; then studied conducting with Odd Grüner-Hegge and composition with Bjarne Brustad; later took private lessons with Jean Rivier in Paris (1950–51). Upon returning to Oslo, he was active mainly as a choral conductor.

WORKS: STAGE: Opera, *Anne Pedersdotter* (Oslo, 1971); opera buffa, *Den stundesløse* (The Wastrel), based on the play by L. Holberg (Oslo, 1975); ballet, *The Little Matchstick Girl,* after the tale by Hans Christian Andersen (1976; unfinished). **ORCH.:** *Towards the Sea* for Chamber Orch. (1947); *Concert Overture* (1948); 3 syms. (1949–50; 1951–54; 1967); *Serenade* (1951–52); *Adagio* for Strings (1953); *Capriccio* for Piano and Orch. (1956–57); Divertimento for Flute and Orch. (1958); *Symphonic Prelude* (1959); *Largo* for Strings (1960–61); *Intrata* (1961); *Overture in Miniature* (1962); *Little Serenade* (1963); *Ritmico e melodico* (1971); *Til Arendal,* festival overture for the city of Arendal (1972); *Havljom* (Echo from the Sea; 1973). **CHAMBER:** Violin Sonata (1940); *The Merry Musicians* for Clarinet, Violin, Viola, and Cello (1947); Divertimento for Clarinet, Violin, Viola, and Cello (1962); String Trio (1964); *Humoresque* for Chamber Ensemble (1966).

Braga, (Antônio) Francisco, Brazilian composer; b. Rio de Janeiro, April 15, 1868; d. there, March 14, 1945. He played clarinet in military bands in Rio de Janeiro; at the age of 18 he composed an overture, which was played at the inauguration of the Soc. of Popular Concerts there. He then went to Paris, where he studied with Massenet; also traveled in Germany and Italy. Influenced mainly by Massenet and Mascagni, Braga wrote the opera *Jupira,* which was staged at Rio de Janeiro (March 20, 1899). From 1908 till 1933, he conducted sym. concerts in Rio. His symphonic works include the programmatic pieces *Insomnia, Cauchemar, Paysage,* etc. Braga was the teacher of many Brazilian composers and contributed much to the musical culture of his country.

BIBL.: T. Gomes, *F. B.* (Rio de Janeiro, 1937); *Exposição comemorativa do centenario do nascimento de F. B.* (Rio de Janeiro, 1968).

Braga, Gaetano, Italian cellist and composer; b. Giulianova, Abruzzi, June 9, 1829; d. Milan, Nov. 21, 1907. He studied at the Naples Cons. with C. Gaetano (1841–52); made tours as a cellist in Europe and America; lived mostly in Paris and London. His *Leggenda valacca,* known in English as *Angel's Serenade,* orig. written for voice with cello (or violin) obbligato, attained tremendous popularity and was arranged for various instrumental combinations. Braga wrote several operas: *Alina,* or *La spregiata* (1853), *Estella di San Germano* (Vienna, 1857), *Il ritratto* (Naples, 1858), *Margherita la mendicante* (Paris, 1859), *Mormile* (La Scala, Milan, 1862), *Ruy Blas* (1865), *Reginella* (Lecco, 1871), and *Caligola* (Lisbon, 1873); sacred choruses; and a valuable *Metodo di violoncello.*

BIBL.: V. Bindi, *G. B.: Da ricordi della sua vita* (Naples, 1927); A. de Angelis, "G. B.," *Rivista Musicale Italiana* (June 1929).

Braga-Santos, (José Manuel) Joly. See **Santos, (José Manuel) Joly Braga.**

Bragard, Roger, Belgian musicologist; b. Huy, Nov. 21, 1903; d. Brussels, Dec. 15, 1985. He studied philology at the Univ. of Liège; then went to Paris, where he studied musicology with Pirro and composition with Vincent d'Indy. Returning to Belgium, he taught music history at the Brussels Cons.; he publ. the valuable *Histoire de la musique belge* (3 vols.; 1946, 1949, 1956).

Braham (real name, **Abraham**), **John,** renowned English tenor; b. London, March 20, 1774; d. there, Feb. 17, 1856. He studied with Leoni in London, with Rauzzini in Bath, and with Isola in Genoa. He made his debut at Covent Garden (April 21, 1787); then appeared at Drury Lane in 1796, in the opera *Mahmoud* by Storace. He was subsequently engaged to sing at the Italian Opera House in London. In 1798 he undertook an extensive tour in Italy; also appeared in Hamburg. Returning to England in 1801, he was increasingly successful. Endowed with a powerful voice of 3 octaves in compass, he knew no difficulties in operatic roles. He was the original Huon in Weber's *Oberon* (1826). As a ballad writer, he was very popular; he wrote much of the music for the operatic roles which he sang; often he added portions to operas by other composers, as in *The Americans* (1811), with its famous song *The Death of Nelson;* contributed incidental music to 12 productions. In 1831 he entered upon a theatrical business venture; he acquired the Colosseum in Regent's Park; in 1836 he had the St. James's Theatre built, but failed to recoup his investment and lost much of his considerable fortune. He made an American tour from 1840 to 1842 despite the weakening of his voice with age; however, his dramatic appeal remained undiminished and he was able to impress the American public in concert appearances. He then returned to London; made his final appearance in 1852.

BIBL.: J. Mewburn Levien, *The Singing of J. B.* (London, 1945).

Brahms, Johannes, great German composer; b. Hamburg, May 7, 1833; d. Vienna, April 3, 1897. His father, who played the double bass in the orch. of the Phil. Soc. in Hamburg, taught Brahms the rudiments of music; later he began to study piano with Otto F.W. Cossel, and made his 1st public appearance as a pianist with a chamber music group at the age of 10. Impressed with his progress, Cossel sent Brahms to his own former teacher, the noted pedagogue Eduard Marxsen, who accepted him as a scholarship student, without charging a fee. Soon Brahms was on his own, and had to eke out his meager subsistence by playing piano in taverns, restaurants, and other establishments (but not in brothels, as insinuated by some popular biographers). On Sept. 21, 1848, at the age of 15, Brahms played a solo concert in Hamburg under an assumed name. In 1853 he met the Hungarian violinist Eduard Reményi, with whom he embarked on a successful concert tour. While in Hannover, Brahms formed a friendship with the famous violin virtuoso Joseph Joachim, who gave him an introduction to Liszt in Weimar. Of great significance was his meeting with Schumann in Düsseldorf. In his diary of the time, Schumann noted: "Johannes Brahms, a genius." He

reiterated his appraisal of Brahms in his famous article "Neue Bahnen" (New Paths), which appeared in the *Neue Zeitschrift für Musik* on Oct. 28, 1853; in a characteristic display of metaphor, he described young Brahms as having come into life as Minerva sprang in full armor from the brow of Jupiter. Late in 1853, Breitkopf & Härtel publ. his 2 piano sonatas and a set of 6 songs. Brahms also publ., under the pseudonym of G.W. Marks, a collection of 6 pieces for piano, 4-hands, under the title *Souvenir de la Russie* (Brahms never visited Russia). Schumann's death in 1856, after years of agonizing mental illness, deeply affected Brahms. He remained a devoted friend of Schumann's family; his correspondence with Schumann's widow Clara reveals a deep affection and spiritual intimacy, but the speculation about their friendship growing into a romance exists only in the fevered imaginations of psychologizing biographers. Objectively judged, the private life of Brahms was that of a middle-class bourgeois who worked systematically and diligently on his current tasks while maintaining a fairly active social life. He was always ready and willing to help young composers (his earnest efforts on behalf of Dvořák were notable). Brahms was entirely free of professional jealousy; his differences with Wagner were those of style. Wagner was an opera composer, whereas Brahms never wrote for the stage. True, some ardent admirers of Wagner (such as Hugo Wolf) found little of value in the music of Brahms, while admirers of Brahms (such as Hanslick) were sharp critics of Wagner, but Brahms held aloof from such partisan wranglings.

From 1857 to 1859 Brahms was employed in Detmold as court pianist, chamber musician, and choir director. In the meantime he began work on his 1st piano concerto. He played it on Jan. 22, 1859, in Hannover, with Joachim as conductor. Other important works of the period were the 2 serenades for orch. and the 1st string sextet. He expected to be named conductor of the Hamburg Phil. Soc., but the directoriat preferred to engage, in 1863, the singer Julius Stockhausen in that capacity. Instead, Brahms accepted the post of conductor of the Singakademie in Vienna, which he led from 1863 to 1864. In 1869 he decided to make Vienna his permanent home. As early as 1857 he began work on his choral masterpiece, *Ein deutsches Requiem;* he completed the score in 1868, and conducted its 1st performance in the Bremen Cathedral on April 10, 1868, although the 1st 3 movements had been given by Herbeck and the Vienna Phil. on Dec. 1, 1867. In May 1868 he added another movement to the work (the 5th, "Ihr habt nun Traurigkeit") in memory of his mother, who died in 1865; the 1st performance of the final version was given in Leipzig on Feb. 18, 1869. The title of the German Requiem had no nationalistic connotations; it simply stated that the text was in German rather than Latin. His other important vocal scores include *Rinaldo,* a cantata; the *Liebeslieder* waltzes for Vocal Quartet and Piano, 4-hands; the *Alto Rhapsody;* the *Schicksalslied;* and many songs. In 1869 he publ. 2 vols. of *Hungarian Dances* for Piano Duet; these were extremely successful. Among his chamber music works, the Piano Quintet in F minor; the String Sextet No. 2, in G major; the Trio for French Horn, Violin, and Piano; the 2 String Quartets, op. 51; and the String Quartet op. 67 are exemplary works of their kind. In 1872 Brahms was named artistic director of the concerts of Vienna's famed Gesellschaft der Musikfreunde; he held this post until 1875. During this time, he composed the *Variations on a Theme by Joseph Haydn,* op. 56a. The title was a misnomer; the theme occurs in a Feld-partita for Military Band by Haydn, but it was not Haydn's own; it was orig. known as the St. Anthony Chorale, and in pedantic scholarly eds. of Brahms it is called St. Anthony Variations. Otto Dessoff conducted the 1st performance of the work with the Vienna Phil. on Nov. 2, 1873.

For many years friends and admirers of Brahms urged him to write a sym. He clearly had a symphonic mind; his piano concertos were symphonic in outline and thematic development. As early as 1855 he began work on a full-fledged sym.; in 1862 he nearly completed the 1st movement of what was to be his 1st Sym. The famous horn solo in the finale of the

1st Sym. was jotted down by Brahms on a picture postcard to Clara Schumann dated Sept. 12, 1868, from his summer place in the Tyrol; in it Brahms said that he heard the tune played by a shepherd on an Alpine horn; and he set it to a rhymed quatrain of salutation. Yet Brahms was still unsure about his symphonic capacity. (A frivolous suggestion was made by an irresponsible psychomusicologist that it was when Brahms grew his famous luxuriant beard that he finally determined to complete his symphonic essay; such pogonological speculations illustrate the degree to which musical criticism can contribute to its own ridiculosity.) The great C-minor Sym., his 1st, was completed in 1876 and 1st performed at Karlsruhe on Nov. 4, 1876, conducted by Dessoff. Hans von Bülow, the German master of the telling phrase, called it "The 10th," thus placing Brahms on a direct line from Beethoven. It was also Hans von Bülow who cracked a bon mot that became a part of music history, in referring to the 3 B's of music, Bach, Beethoven, and Brahms. The original saying was not merely a vacuous alphabetical generalization; Bülow's phrase was deeper; in answering a question as to what was his favorite key, he said it was E-flat major, the key of Beethoven's *Eroica*, because it had 3 B's in its key signature (in German, B is specifically B-flat, but by extension may signify any flat)—1 for Bach, 1 for Beethoven, and 1 for Brahms. The witty phrase took wing, but its sophisticated connotation was lost at the hands of professional popularizers.

Brahms composed his 2nd Sym. in 1877; it was performed for the 1st time by the Vienna Phil. on Dec. 30, 1877, under the direction of Hans Richter, receiving a fine acclaim. Brahms led a 2nd performance of the work with the Gewandhaus Orch. in Leipzig on Jan. 10, 1878. Also in 1878 Brahms wrote his Violin Concerto; the score was dedicated to Joachim, who gave its premiere with the Gewandhaus Orch. on Jan. 1, 1879. Brahms then composed his 2nd Piano Concerto, in B-flat major, and was soloist in its 1st performance in Budapest, on Nov. 9, 1881. There followed the 3rd Sym., in F major, 1st performed by the Vienna Phil., under the direction of Hans Richter, on Dec. 2, 1883. The 4th Sym., in E minor, followed in quick succession; it had its 1st performance in Meiningen on Oct. 25, 1885. The symphonic cycle was completed in less than a decade; it has been conjectured, without foundation, that the tonalities of the 4 syms. of Brahms—C, D, F, and E—correspond to the fugal subject of Mozart's Jupiter Sym., and that some symbolic meaning was attached to it. All speculations aside, there is an inner symmetry uniting these works. The 4 syms. contain 4 movements each, with a slow movement and a scherzo-like Allegretto in the middle of the corpus. There are fewer departures from the formal scheme than in Beethoven, and there are no extraneous episodes interfering with the grand general line. Brahms wrote music pure in design and eloquent in sonorous projection; he was a true classicist, a quality that endeared him to the critics who were repelled by Wagnerian streams of sound, and by the same token alienated those who sought something more than mere geometry of thematic configurations from a musical composition.

The chamber music of Brahms possesses similar symphonic qualities; when Schoenberg undertook to make an orch. arrangement of the Piano Quartet of Brahms, all he had to do was to expand the sonorities and enhance instrumental tone colors already present in the original. The string quartets of Brahms are edifices of Gothic perfection; his 3 violin sonatas, his 2nd Piano Trio (the 1st was a student work and yet it had a fine quality of harmonious construction), all contribute to a permanent treasure of musical classicism. The piano writing of Brahms is severe in its contrapuntal texture, but pianists for a hundred years included his rhapsodies and intermezzos in their repertoire; and Brahms was able to impart sheer delight in his Hungarian rhapsodies and waltzes; they represented the Viennese side of his character, as contrasted with the profound Germanic quality of his syms. The song cycles of Brahms continued the evolution of the art of the lieder, a natural continuation of the song cycles of Schubert and Schumann.

Brahms was sociable and made friends easily; he traveled to Italy, and liked to spend his summers in the solitude of the Austrian Alps. But he was reluctant to appear as a center of attention; he declined to receive the honorary degree of Mus.D. from Cambridge Univ. in 1876, giving as a reason his fear of seasickness in crossing the English Channel. He was pleased to receive the Gold Medal of the Phil. Soc. of London in 1877. In 1879 the Univ. of Breslau proffered him an honorary degree of Doctor of Philosophy, citing him as "Artis musicae severioris in Germania nunc princeps." As a gesture of appreciation and gratitude he wrote an *Akademische Festouvertüre* for Breslau, and since there was no Channel to cross on the way, he accepted the invitation to conduct its premiere in Breslau on Jan. 4, 1881; its rousing finale using the German student song "Gaudeamus igitur" pleased the academic assembly. In 1887 he was presented with the Prussian Order "Pour le Mérite." In 1889 he received the freedom of his native city of Hamburg; also in 1889, Franz Joseph, the Emperor of Austria, made him a Commander of the Order of Leopold. With success and fame came a sense of self-sufficiency, which found its external expression in the corpulence of his appearance, familiar to all from photographs and drawings of Brahms conducting or playing the piano. Even during his Viennese period Brahms remained a sturdy Prussian; his ideal was to see Germany a dominant force in Europe philosophically and militarily. In his workroom he kept a bronze relief of Bismarck, the "Iron Chancellor," crowned with laurel. He was extremely meticulous in his working habits (his MSS were clean and legible), but he avoided wearing formal dress, preferring a loosely fitting flannel shirt and a detachable white collar, but no cravat. He liked to dine in simple restaurants, and he drank a great deal of beer. He was indifferent to hostile criticism; still, it is amazing to read the outpouring of invective against Brahms by George Bernard Shaw and by American critics; the usual accusations were of dullness and turgidity. When Sym. Hall was opened in Boston in 1900 with the lighted signs "Exit in Case of Fire," someone cracked that they should more appropriately announce "Exit in Case of Brahms." Yet, at the hands of successive German conductors Brahms became a standard symphonist in N.Y., Boston, Philadelphia, and Baltimore. From the perspective of a century, Brahms appears as the greatest master of counterpoint after Bach; one can learn polyphony from a studious analysis of the chamber music and piano works of Brahms; he excelled in variation forms; his piano variations on a theme of Paganini are exemplars of contrapuntal learning, and they are also among the most difficult piano works of the 19th century. Posterity gave him a full measure of recognition; Hamburg celebrated his sesquicentennial in 1983 with great pomp. Brahms had lived a good life, but died a bad death, stricken with cancer of the liver.

WORKS: ORCH.: 4 syms.: No. 1, in C minor, op. 68 (1855–76; Karlsruhe, Nov. 4, 1876, Dessoff conducting); No. 2, in D major, op. 73 (1877; Vienna, Dec. 30, 1877, Richter conducting); No. 3, in F major, op. 90 (1883; Vienna, Dec. 2, 1883, Richter conducting); No. 4, in E minor, op. 98 (1884–85; Meiningen, Oct. 17, 1885, Brahms conducting [private perf.]; public perf., Oct. 25, 1885, Bülow conducting).

OTHER WORKS FOR ORCH.: Piano Concerto No. 1, in D minor, op. 15 (1854–58; Hannover, Jan. 22, 1859; Brahms, soloist; Joachim conducting); Serenade No. 1, in D major, op. 11 (1st version, for small orch., 1857–58; Hamburg, March 28, 1859, Joachim conducting; 2nd version, for larger orch., 1859; Hannover, March 3, 1860, Joachim conducting); Serenade No. 2, in A major, op. 16 (1858–59; Hamburg, Feb. 10, 1860, composer conducting; rev. 1875); *Variations on a Theme by Joseph Haydn*, op. 56a (the theme, from the St. Anthony Chorale, is not by Haydn; 1873; Vienna, Nov. 2, 1873, Dessoff conducting); Violin Concerto in D major, op. 77 (1878; Leipzig, Jan. 1, 1879; Joachim, soloist; composer conducting); Piano Concerto No. 2, in B-flat major, op. 83 (1878–81; Budapest, Nov. 9, 1881; Brahms, soloist; Erkel conducting); *Akademische Festouvertüre*, op. 80 (1880; Breslau, Jan. 4, 1881, composer conducting); *Tragische Ouvertüre*, op. 81 (1880; Vienna, Dec. 26, 1880, Richter conducting; rev. 1881); Concerto in A minor for Violin and Cello, op. 102, the *Double* Concerto (1887; Cologne, Oct. 18, 1887; Joachim, violinist; Hausmann, cellist; Wüllner conducting); also 3 Hungarian Dances arranged for Orch. (1873): No. 1, in G minor; No. 3, in F major; No. 10, in F major.

CHAMBER: Piano Trio No. 1, in B major, op. 8 (1853–54; N.Y., Nov. 27, 1855; rev. 1889); Sextet No. 1, in B-flat major, for 2 Violins, 2 Violas, and 2 Cellos, op. 18 (1858–60; Hannover, Oct. 20, 1860); Piano Quartet No. 1, in G minor, op. 25 (1861; Hamburg, Nov. 16, 1861); Piano Quartet No. 2, in A major, op. 26 (1861–62; Vienna, Nov. 29, 1862); Piano Quintet in F minor, op. 34 (1861–64; Paris, March 24, 1868); Sextet No. 2, in G major, for 2 Violins, 2 Violas, and 2 Cellos, op. 36 (1864–65; Vienna, Feb. 3, 1867); Cello Sonata No. 1, in E minor, op. 38 (1862–65); Trio in E-flat major for Violin, Horn or Viola, and Piano, op. 40 (1865; Karlsruhe, Dec. 7, 1865); String Quartet No. 1, in C minor, op. 51 (1865?–73?; Vienna, Dec. 1, 1873); String Quartet No. 2, in A minor, op. 51 (1865?–73?; Vienna, Oct. 18, 1873); Piano Quartet No. 3, in C minor, op. 60 (1855–75; Ziegelhausen, Nov. 18, 1875); String Quartet No. 3, in B-flat major, op. 67 (1876; Berlin, Oct. 1876); Violin Sonata No. 1, in G major, op. 78 (1878–79; Vienna, Nov. 29, 1879); Piano Trio No. 2, in C major, op. 87 (1880–82; Frankfurt, Dec. 28, 1882); Quintet No. 1, in F major, for 2 Violins, 2 Violas, and Cello, op. 88 (1882; Frankfurt, Dec. 28, 1882); Cello Sonata No. 2, in F major, op. 99 (1886; Vienna, Nov. 24, 1886); Violin Sonata No. 2, in A major, op. 100 (1886; Vienna, Dec. 2, 1886); Piano Trio No. 3, in C minor, op. 101 (1886; Budapest, Dec. 20, 1886); Violin Sonata No. 3, in D minor, op. 108 (1886–88; Budapest, Dec. 22, 1888); Quintet No. 2, in G major, for 2 Violins, 2 Violas, and Cello, op. 111 (1890; Vienna, Nov. 11, 1890); Trio in A minor for Clarinet or Viola, Cello, and Piano, op. 114 (1891; Berlin, Dec. 1, 1891); Quintet in B minor for Clarinet and String Quartet, op. 115 (1891; Berlin, Dec. 1, 1891); 2 sonatas: No. 1, in F minor, and No. 2, in E-flat major, for Clarinet or Viola, and Piano, op. 120 (1894; Vienna, Jan. 7, 1895); also a Scherzo in C minor for Violin and Piano, a movement from the Sonata in A minor by Brahms, Schumann, and A. Dietrich. In 1924 a copy from the original score of a Trio in A major, presumably composed by Brahms when he was about 20 years old (see letter to R. Schumann, 1853), was discovered in Bonn; it was publ. in 1938.

SOLO PIANO: Scherzo in E-flat minor, op. 4 (1851; Vienna, March 17, 1867); Sonata No. 1, in C major, op. 1 (1852–53; Leipzig, Dec. 17, 1853); Sonata No. 2, in F-sharp minor, op. 2 (1852; Vienna, Feb. 2, 1882); Sonata No. 3, in F minor, op. 5 (1853; Vienna, Jan. 6, 1863); *Variations on a Theme by Schumann* in F-sharp minor, op. 9 (1854; Berlin, Dec. 1879); 4 Ballades, op. 10: D minor, D major, B minor, and B major (1854); Gavotte in A minor (1854); Gavotte in A major (1855); 2 Gigues: A minor and B minor (1855); 2 Sarabandes: A minor and B minor (1855; Vienna, Jan. 20, 1856); *Variations [13] on a Hungarian Song* in D major, op. 21 (1853; London, March 25, 1874); *Variations [11] on an Original Theme* in D major, op. 21 (1857; Copenhagen, March 1868); *Variations [25] and Fugue on a Theme by Handel* in B-flat major, op. 24 (1861; Hamburg, Dec. 7, 1861); *Variations [28] on a Theme by Paganini* in A minor, op. 35 (1862–63; Zürich, Nov. 25, 1865); 16 Waltzes, op. 39 (1865); 8 Piano Pieces, op. 76 (1871–78; Leipzig, Jan. 4, 1880); 2 Rhapsodies: B minor and G minor, op. 79 (1879; Krefeld, Jan. 20, 1880); *Fantasien [7]*, op. 116 (1892); 3 Intermezzos: E-flat major, B-flat minor, and C-sharp minor, op. 117 (1892); Piano Pieces [6], op. 118 (1892; London, Jan. 1894); Piano Pieces [4], op. 119 (1892; London, Jan. 1894); also 5 *Studien* for Piano (I, Study after Frédéric Chopin, in F minor, an arrangement of Chopin's Étude No. 2, op. 25; II, Rondo after Carl Maria von Weber, in C major, an arrangement of the finale of Weber's *Moto perpetuo*, op. 24; III and IV, Presto after J.S. Bach, in G minor (2 arrangements of the finale of BWV 1001); V, *Chaconne* by J.S. Bach, in D minor (an arrangement of the finale of BWV 1016); Theme and Variations in D minor (an arrangement of the slow movement of

the Sextet No. 1; 1860; Frankfurt, Oct. 31, 1865); Gavotte in A major (an arrangement from Gluck's *Paris ed Elena*; Vienna, Jan. 20, 1856; publ. 1871); 10 Hungarian Dances (an arrangement of nos. 1–10 from the original version for Piano, 4-hands; publ. 1872); 51 Exercises (publ. 1893); cadenzas to concertos by Bach (Harpsichord Concerto No. 1, in D minor, BWV 1052), Mozart (Piano Concertos Nos. 17, in G major, K. 453; 20, in D minor, K. 466; and 24, in C minor, K. 491), and Beethoven (Piano Concerto No. 4, in G major, op. 58).

PIANO, 4-HANDS: *Variations on a Theme by Schumann* in E-flat major, op. 23 (1861; Vienna, Jan. 12, 1864); 16 Waltzes, op. 39 (1865; Vienna, March 17, 1867); *Liebeslieder*, 18 waltzes, op. 52a (1874; an arrangement from the original version for 4 Voices and Piano, 4-hands); *Neue Liebeslieder*, 15 waltzes, op. 65a (1877; an arrangement from the original version for 4 Voices and Piano, 4-hands); Hungarian Dances (21 dances in 4 books; 1852–69).

2 PIANOS: Sonata in F minor, op. 34b (1864; Vienna, April 17, 1874); Variations on a Theme by Haydn, op. 56b (1873; Vienna, March 17, 1882); also arrangements of Joachim's *Demetrius* Overture and Overture to *Henry IV.*

ORGAN: Fugue in A-flat minor (1856); *O Traurigkeit, O Herzeleid,* chorale prelude and fugue in A minor (1856; Vienna, Dec. 2, 1882); 2 preludes and fugues: A minor and G minor (1856–57); 11 *Choralvorspiele*, op. 122 (1896).

VOCAL: CHORAL: Mass: *Kyrie* for 4-part Mixed Chorus and Keyboard, and *Sanctus, Benedictus,* and *Agnus Dei* for Mixed Chorus a cappella or with accompaniment (1856); *Geistliches Lied* for 4-part Chorus, and Organ or Piano, op. 30 (1856); *Ein deutsches Requiem* for Soprano, Baritone, Chorus, and Orch., op. 45 (1857–68; 1st 3 movements, under Herbeck, Vienna, Dec. 1, 1867; movements 1–4 and 6, under Brahms, Bremen, April 10, 1868; 1st complete perf., under Reinecke, Leipzig, Feb. 18, 1869); *Ave Maria* for Women's Voices, and Orch. or Organ, op. 12 (1858); *Begräbnisgesang* for Choir and Wind Instruments, op. 13 (1858; Hamburg, Dec. 2, 1859); *Marienlieder* for Mixed Chorus, op. 22 (Hamburg, Sept. 19, 1859); 4 Songs for Women's Voices, 2 Horns, and Harp, op. 17 (1859–60); *Der 13. Psalm* for Women's Voices, and Organ or Piano, with Strings ad libitum, op. 27 (1859; Hamburg, Sept. 19, 1864); 2 Motets for 5-part Chorus a cappella, op. 29 (1860; Vienna, April 17, 1864); 3 Sacred Choruses for Women's Voices a cappella, op. 37 (1859–63); 5 *Soldatenlieder* for 4-part Male Chorus a cappella, op. 41 (1861–62); 3 Songs for 6-part Mixed Chorus, with Piano ad libitum, op. 42 (1859–61); 12 Songs and Romances for Women's Voices, with Piano ad libitum, op. 44 (1859–63); *Rinaldo*, cantata for Tenor, Male Chorus, and Orch., op. 50, after Goethe (1863–68; Vienna, Feb. 28, 1869); *Rhapsodie* for Contralto, Male Chorus, and Orch., op. 53, after Goethe's *Harzreise im Winter* (1869; Jena, March 3, 1870); *Schicksalslied* for Chorus and Orch., op. 54 (1868–71; Karlsruhe, Oct. 18, 1871); Triumphlied for 8-part Chorus, Baritone, and Orch., op. 55 (1870–71; Karlsruhe, June 5, 1872); 7 Songs for 4- and 6-part a cappella Chorus, op. 62 (1874); *Nänie* for Chorus and Orch., op. 82, after Schiller (1880–81; Zürich, Dec. 6, 1881); 2 Motets for 4- and 6-part a cappella Chorus, op. 74 (1877; 2nd motet probably composed between 1860 and 1865; Vienna, Dec. 8, 1878); *Gesang der Parzen* for 6-part Chorus and Orch., op. 89, after Goethe's *Iphigenie auf Tauris* (1882; Basel, Dec. 10, 1882); 6 Songs and Romances for 4-part a cappella Chorus, op. 93a (1883–84; Krefeld, Jan. 27, 1885); *Tafellied* for 6-part Chorus and Piano, op. 93b (1884; Krefeld, Jan. 28, 1885); 5 Songs for 4- and 6-part a cappella Chorus, op. 104 (1888; Vienna, April 3, 1889); *Fest- und Gedenksprüche* for a Double a cappella Chorus, op. 109 (1886–88; Hamburg, Sept. 14, 1889); 3 Motets for 4- and 8-part a cappella Chorus, op. 110 (1889; Cologne, March 13, 1890); also 13 Canons for Women's Voices, op. 113 (1860–67); *Deutsche Volkslieder* (26 songs arranged for 4-part Chorus; 1854–73; publ. in 2 books, 1864 and 1926–27). **QUARTETS:** For Soprano, Alto, Tenor, Bass, and Piano: 3 Quartets, op. 31 (1859–63); *Liebeslieder*, 18 waltzes, with Piano, 4-hands, op. 52 (1868-69; Vienna, Jan. 5, 1870); 3 Quartets, op. 64 (1862–74); *Neue Liebeslieder*, 15 waltzes, with Piano, 4-hands, op. 65 (1874; Mannheim, May 8, 1875); 4 Quartets, op. 92 (1877–84); *Zigeunerlieder*, op. 103 (1887); 6 Quartets, op. 112 (1888–91); also *Liebeslieder*, Nos. 1, 2, 4–6, 8, 9, and 11 from op. 52 and No. 5 from op. 65, with Orch. (1870); *Kleine Hochzeitskantate* (1874). DUETS: With Piano Accompaniment: 3 Duets for Soprano and Alto, op. 20 (1858–60; Vienna, Jan. 29, 1878); 4 Duets for Alto and Baritone, op. 28 (1860–62; Vienna, Dec. 18, 1862); 4 Duets for Soprano and Alto, op. 61 (1874); 5 Duets for Soprano and Alto, op. 66 (1875; Vienna, Jan. 29, 1878); 4 Ballads and Romances, op. 75 (1877–78). SONGS: With Piano Accompaniment: 6 Songs, op. 7 (1851–52); 6 Songs, op. 3, for Tenor or Soprano (1852–53); 6 Songs, op. 6, for Soprano or Tenor (1852–53); 8 Songs and Romances, op. 14 (1858); 5 Poems, op. 19 (1858); Romances [15] from L. Tieck's "Magelone" (1861–68); Songs [9], op. 32 (1864); 7 Songs, op. 48 (1855–68); 4 Songs, op. 43 (1857–64); 5 Songs, op. 47 (1860–68); 4 Songs, op. 46 (1864–68); 5 Songs, op. 49 (1868); Songs [8], op. 57 (1871); Songs [8], op. 58 (1871); Songs [8], op. 59 (1871–73); Songs [9], op. 63 (1874); 4 Songs, op. 70 (1875–77); 9 Songs, op. 69 (1877); 5 Songs, op. 72 (1876–77); 5 Songs, op. 71 (1877); 6 Songs, op. 86 (1877–79); 6 Songs, op. 85 (1877–82); Romances and Songs [15] for 1 or 2 Female Voices, op. 84 (1881); 2 Songs for Alto, Viola, and Piano, op. 91 (1st song may have been begun as early as 1864, the 2nd in 1878; publ. 1884); 5 Songs, op. 94 (1884); 7 Songs, op. 95 (1884); 4 Songs, op. 96 (1884); 6 Songs, op. 97 (1884–85); 5 Songs, op. 105 (1886); 5 Songs, op. 106 (1886); 5 Songs, op. 107 (1886); *Vier ernste Gesänge* for Baritone, op. 121 (1896); also *Mondnacht* (1854); *Regenlied* (1872); 5 *Songs of Ophelia* for Soprano, with Piano ad libitum (1873); 14 *Volkskinderlieder*, arrangements for Voice and Piano (1858); 28 *Deutsche Volkslieder*, arrangements for Voice and Piano (1858; publ. 1926); arrangement of Schubert's *Memnon* for Voice and Orch. (1862); arrangement of Schubert's *An Schwager Kronos* for Voice and Orch. (1862); arrangement of Schubert's *Geheimes* for Voice, Horn, and Strings; 8 *Gypsy Songs*, an arrangement of op. 103, nos. 1–7 and 11, for Voice and Piano (1887); 49 *Deutsche Volkslieder*, arrangements for Voice and Piano (1894).

BIBL.: COLLECTED WORKS, SOURCE MATERIAL: H. Gál and E. Mandyczewski prepared the Gesellschaft der Musikfreunde ed.; it was publ. as *J. B.: Sämtliche Werke* (26 vols., Leipzig, 1926–28).

A thematic catalogue was prepared by N. Simrock, *Thematisches Verzeichniss sämmtlicher im Druck erschienenen Werke von J. B.* (Berlin, 1897; 3rd ed., 1909; Eng. tr. and augmented ed. by J. Braunstein as *Thematic Catalogue of the Collected Works of B.*, N.Y., 1956; rev. by M. McCorkle, N.Y., 1973). The standard thematic and bibliographic catalogue is found in M. McCorkle, *J. B. Thematisch-Bibliographisches Werkverzeichnis* (Munich, 1983).

Other sources include O. Keller, "J. B.-Literatur," *Die Musik*, XII/1 (1912–13); A. von Ehrmann, *J. B.: Thematisches Verzeichnis* (Leipzig, 1933); O. Deutsch, "The First Editions of B.," *Music Review*, XXI (1940); L. Koch, *B.-Bibliografia* (Budapest, 1943); G. Bozarth, E. Auman, and W. Parsons, *The Musical Manuscripts and Letters of J. B. in the Collections of the Music Division, Library of Congress* (Washington, D.C., 1983); M. McCorkle, "Filling the Gaps in B. Research," *Musical Times* (May 1983); R. Pascall, ed., *B.: Biographical, Documentary and Analytical Studies* (Cambridge, 1983); M. Musgrave, ed., *B. 2: Biographical, Documentary and Analytical Studies* (Cambridge, 1987); S. Antonicek and O. Biba, eds., *B.-Kongress, Wien 1983: Kongressbericht* (Tutzing, 1988).

CORRESPONDENCE: A major ed. of his correspondence was publ. by the Deutsche Brahmsgesellschaft as *J. B.: Briefwechsel* (16 vols., Berlin, 1906–22). See also B. Litzmann, ed., *Clara Schumann–J. B.: Briefe aus den Jahren 1853–1896* (2 vols., Leipzig, 1927; Eng. tr., n.d.); K. Geiringer, "J. B. im Briefwechsel mit Eusebius Mandyczewski," *Zeitschrift für Musikwissenschaft*, XV (1932–33); K. Stephenson, ed., *J. B.: Heimatbekenntnisse in Briefen an seine Hamburger Verwandten* (Hamburg,

1933); O.-G. Billroth, *Billroth und B. im Briefwechsel* (Vienna, 1935); K. Geiringer, "Wagner and B., with Unpublished Letters," *Musical Quarterly* (April 1936); F. Callomon, "Some Unpublished B. Correspondence," ibid. (Jan. 1943); R. Litterscheid, ed., *J. B. in seinen Schriften und Briefen* (Berlin, 1943); E. Müller von Asow, ed., *J. B. und Mathilde Wesendonck: Ein Briefwechsel* (Vienna, 1943); H. Barkan, ed., *J. B. and Theodore Billroth: Letters from a Musical Friendship* (Norman, Okla., 1957); A. Holde, "Suppressed Passages in the B.-Joachim Correspondence, Published for the First Time," *Musical Quarterly* (July 1959); K. Stephenson, *J. B. und Fritz Simrock, Weg einer Freundschaft: Briefe des Verlegers an den Komponisten* (Hamburg, 1961); K. Stephenson, *J. B. in seiner Familie: Der Briefwechsel* (Hamburg, 1973).

BIOGRAPHICAL: H. Deiters, "J. B. Eine Charakteristik," in *Sammlung musikalischer Vorträge* (Leipzig, 1880 and 1898); P. Spitta, "J. B.," *Zur Musik* (Berlin, 1892); H. Reimann, *J. B.* (Berlin, 1897; 6th ed., 1922); A. Dietrich, *Erinnerungen an J. B. in Briefen, besonders aus seiner Jugendzeit* (Leipzig, 1898; Eng. tr. by D. Hecht in *Recollections of J. B.*, London, 1899); J. Widmann, *J. B. in Erinnerungen* (Berlin 1898; 5th ed., 1947; Eng. tr. by D. Hecht in *Recollections of J. B.*, London, 1899); J. Widmann, *Sizilien und andere Gegenden Italiens: Reisen mit J. B.* (Frauenfeld, 1898; 3rd ed., 1912); W. Hübbe, *B. in Hamburg* (Hamburg, 1902); M. Kalbeck, *J. B.* (the most detailed biography; 8 vols., Berlin, 1904–14); H. Antcliffe, *B.* (London, 1905); J. Erb, *B.* (London, 1905); R. von der Leyen, *J. B. als Mensch und Freund* (Düsseldorf and Leipzig, 1905); F. May, *The Life of J. B.* (2 vols., London, 1905; 2nd ed., 1948; 3rd ed., rev., 1977); G. Henschel, *Personal Recollections of J. B.* (Boston, 1907); W. Pauli, *Moderne Geister: B.* (Berlin, 1907); H. Colles, *J. B.* (London, 1908; 2nd ed., 1920); R. von Perger, *B.* (Leipzig, 1908); J. Fuller Maitland, *B.* (London, 1911); W. Thomas-San-Galli, *J. B.* (Munich, 1912; 5th ed., 1922); L. Misch, *J. B.* (Bielefeld, 1913; 2nd ed., 1922); E. Lee, *B.: The Man and His Music* (London, 1915); W. Niemann, *J. B.* (Berlin, 1920; Eng. tr., N.Y., 1929); P. Landormy, *B.* (Paris, 1921; rev. ed., 1948); G. Ophüls, *Erinnerungen an J. B.* (Berlin, 1921); W. Nagel, *J. B.* (Stuttgart, 1923); J. Pulver, *J. B.* (London, 1926; new ed., 1933); J. Cooke, *J. B.* (Philadelphia, 1928); M. Komorn, *J. B. als Chordirigent in Wien und seine Nachfolger* (Vienna, 1928); R. Specht, *J. B.: Leben und Werk eines deutschen Meisters* (Hellerau, 1928; Eng. tr., 1930); W. Hutschenruyter, *B.* (The Hague, 1929); G. Ernest, *J. B.* (Berlin, 1930); P. Mies, *J. B.* (Leipzig, 1930); K. Geiringer, "B. als Musikhistoriker," *Die Musik*, XXV (1932–33); R. Schauffler, "B., Poet and Peasant," *Musical Quarterly* (Oct. 1932); G. Adler, "J. B.: Wirken, Wesen und Stellung," *Studien zur Musikwissenschaft*, XX (1933; Eng. tr. in *Musical Quarterly*, April 1933); A. von Ehrmann, *J. B.: Weg, Werk und Welt* (Leipzig, 1933); R. Fellinger, *Klänge um B.* (Berlin, 1933); K. Geiringer, "B. as a Reader and Collector," *Musical Quarterly* (April 1933); R. Hill, *B.* (London, 1933; 2nd ed., 1941); E. Hirschmann, *J. B. und die Frauen* (Vienna, 1933); L. Koch, *B. in Ungarn* (Budapest, 1933); M. Komorn, "B., Choral Conductor," *Musical Quarterly* (April 1933); J. Müller-Blattau, *J. B.* (Potsdam, 1933); W. Murdoch, *B.: With an Analytical Study of the Complete Pianoforte Works* (London, 1933); R. Schauffler, *The Unknown B.: His Life, Character and Works, Based on New Material* (N.Y., 1933); W. Schramm, *J. B. in Detmold* (Leipzig, 1933); K. Stephenson, *J. B.' Heimatbekenntnis* (Hamburg, 1933); S. Stojowski, "Recollections of B.," *Musical Quarterly* (April 1933); E. Blom, *J. B.* (N.Y., 1934); R. Hernried, *J. B.* (Leipzig, 1934); K. Geiringer, *J. B.: Leben und Schaffen eines deutschen Meisters* (Vienna, 1935; Eng. tr., London and N.Y., 1936; 3rd ed., rev. and enl., N.Y., 1981); K. Huschke, *J. B. als Pianist, Dirigent und Lehrer* (Karlsruhe, 1935); R. Lienau, *Erinnerungen an J. B.* (Berlin, 1935); K. Geiringer, "B.'s Family," *Musical Quarterly* (Jan. 1936); H.H. Stuckenschmidt, "J. B., 1833–1897," *Die grossen Deutschen* (Berlin, 1936); K. Geiringer, "B. and Chrysander," *Monthly Musical Record*, LXVII (1937); K. Huschke, *Frauen um B.* (Karlsruhe, 1937); A. Orel, *J. B.s Leben in Bildern* (Leipzig, 1937); R.

Gerber, *J. B.* (Potsdam, 1938); M. Goss and R. Schauffler, *B., the Master* (N.Y., 1943); K. Laux, *Der Einsame: J. B., Leben und Werk* (Graz, 1944); W. and P. Rehberg, *J. B.: Sein Leben und Werk* (Zürich, 1947; 2nd ed., 1963); J. Culshaw, *B.: An Outline of His Life and Music* (London, 1948); H. Eppstein, *B.* (Stockholm, 1948); P. Latham, *B.* (London, 1948; rev. ed. by J. Westrup, London, 1975); A. Orel, *J. B., Ein Meister und sein Weg* (Vienna, 1950); F. Grasberger, *J. B.: Variationen um sein Wesen* (contains a chronological and alphabetical list of his works; also new photographs; Vienna, 1952); L. Henning, *Die Freundschaft Clara Schumanns mit J. B.* (Zürich, 1952); A. Abell, *Talks with Great Composers* (N.Y., 1955); C. Rostand, *B.* (2 vols., Paris, 1954–55); L. Berger, *Vom Menschen J. B.* (Tübingen, 1959); F. Grasberger, "J. B. und Hugo Wolf," *Österreichische Muzikzeitschrift*, XV (1960); F. Müller-Blattau, *J. B.* (Königstein, 1960); H. Gál, *J. B.: Werk und Persönlichkeit* (particularly valuable for its critical survey of his music; Frankfurt, 1961; Eng. tr. as *J. B.: His Work and Personality*, N.Y., 1963); O. Goldhammer, "Liszt, B. und Reményi," *Studia musicologica Academiae scientiarum hungaricae*, V (1963); J. Laufer, *B.* (Paris, 1963); J. Bruyr, *B.* (Paris, 1965); W. Siegmund-Schultze, *J. B.* (Leipzig, 1966); F. Grasberger, "Das Jahr 1868," *Österreichische Musikzeitschrift*, XXIII (1968); Y. Tiénot, *B.: Son vrai visage* (Paris, 1968); K. Dale, *B.: A Biography with a Survey of Books, Editions & Recordings* (Hamden, Conn., and London, 1970); R. Heuberger, *Erinnerungen an J. B.: Tagebuchnotizen aus den Jahren 1875–97*, as ed. by K. Hofmann (Tutzing, 1971; 2nd ed., 1976); J. Clapham, "Dvorak's Relations with B. and Hanslick," *Musical Quarterly* (April 1971); J. Burnett, *B.: A Critical Study* (London, 1972); K. and I. Geiringer, "The B. Library in the Gesellschaft der Musikfreunde, Wien," *Notes* (Sept. 1973); J. Chissell, *B.* (London, 1977); K. Höcker, *J. B.: Begegnung mit dem Menschen* (Berlin, 1983); R. and K. Hofmann, *J. B.: Zeittafel zu Leben und Werk* (Tutzing, 1983); C. Schmidt, *J. B. und seine Zeit* (Laaber, 1983); P. Holmes, *B.: His Life and Times* (Southborough, 1984); R. Hughes, *Richard Heuberger's Erinnerungen an J. B.: The Life, Work, and Times of J. B. as Revealed by a Contemporary* (diss., Ball State Univ., 1987).

CRITICAL, ANALYTICAL: L. Köhler, *J. B. und seine Stellung in der Musikgeschichte* (Hannover, 1880); E. Krause, *J. B. in seinem Werken* (Hamburg, 1892); W. Nagel, *B. als Nachfolger Beethovens* (Leipzig, 1892); G. Ophüls, *B.-Texte* (Berlin, 1898; 3rd ed., 1923); R. Barth, *J. B. und seine Musik* (Hamburg, 1904); G. Jenner, *J. B. als Mensch, Lehrer und Kunstler: Studien und Erlebnisse* (Marburg, 1905; 2nd ed., 1930); W. Thomas-San-Galli, *J. B. Eine musikpsychologische Studie* (Strasbourg, 1905); J. Knorr and H. Riemann, *J. B. Symphonien und andere Orchesterwerke erläutert* (Berlin, 1908); E. Howard-Jones, "B. in His Pianoforte Music," *Proceedings of the Musical Association*, XXXVII (1910–11); M. Burkhardt, *J. B.: Ein Führer durch seine Werke* (Berlin, 1912); E. Evans, *Historical, Descriptive and Analytical Account of the Entire Works of J. B.* (London; vol. I, vocal works, 1912; vols. II and III, chamber and orch. works, 1933 and 1935; vol. IV, piano works, 1936); W. Hammermann, *J. B. als Liederkomponist* (diss., Univ. of Leipzig, 1912); G. Jenner, "Zur Entstehung des d-moll Klavierkonzerts von J. B.," *Die Musik*, XII/1 (1912–13); R. Specht, "Zur Brahmsschen Symphonik," ibid.; H. Wetzel, "Zur Harmonik bei B.," ibid.; W. Vetter, "Der erste Satz von B.' e-moll-Symphonie: Ein Beitrag zur Erkenntnis moderner Symphonik," ibid., XIII/3 (1913–14); W. Nagel, *Die Klaviersonaten von J. B.: Technisch-ästhetische Analysen* (Stuttgart, 1915); M. Kalbeck, *B. als Lyriker* (Vienna, 1921); M. Friedländer, *B.' Lieder* (Berlin and Leipzig, 1922; Eng. tr., London, 1928); A. Orel, "Skizzen zu J. B.' Haydn-Variationen," *Zeitschrift für Musikwissenschaft*, V (1922–23); F. Wunsiedler, *Liederschlüsse bei J. B.* (diss., Univ. of Erlangen, 1922); P. Mies, *Stilmomente und Ausdrucksstilformen im Brahmsschen Lied* (Leipzig, 1923); H. Schenker, "B.: Variationen und Fuge über ein Thema von Händel, op. 24," *Der Tonwille*, IV (1924); V. Urbantschitsch, *Die Sonatenform bei B.* (diss., Univ. of Vienna, 1925); V. Urbantschitsch, "Die Entwicklung der Sonatenform bei B.," *Stu-*

dien zur Musikwissenschaft, XIV (1927); J. Wetzel, "Eine neue Volksliedersammlung aus B.' Jugendzeit," *Zeitschrift für Musikwissenschaft*, X (1927–28); E. Tetzel, "Die Schumann-Variationen von B.," *Zeitschrift für Musik*, XCVI (1929); G. Knepler, *Die Form in den Instrumentalwerken J. B.* (diss., Univ. of Vienna, 1930); H. Meyer, *Linie und Form: Bach, Beethoven, B.* (Berlin, 1930); E. Markham Lee, *B.'s Orchestral Works* (London, 1931); D. Mason, "B.'s Third Symphony," *Musical Quarterly* (July 1931); H. Drinker, *The Chamber Music of B.* (Philadelphia, 1932); A. Schering, "B. und seine Stellung in der Musikgeschichte des 19. Jahrhunderts," *Jahrbuch Peters* (1932); A. Sturke, *Der Stil in J. B.' Werken* (diss., Univ of Würzburg, 1932); W. Blume, *B. in der Meininger Tradition* (Stuttgart, 1933); P. Browne, *B.: The Symphonies* (London, 1933); H. Colles, *The Chamber Music of B.* (London, 1933); D. Mason, *The Chamber Music of B.* (N.Y. and London, 1933; 2nd ed., 1950); R. Specht, "B. der Sinfoniker," *Die Musik*, XXV/2 (1933); E. Kurzweil, *Der Klaviersatz bei B.* (diss., Univ. of Vienna, 1934); G. Döhrn, *Die Volkslied-Bearbeitungen von J. B.* (diss., Univ. of Vienna, 1936); H. Düsterbehn, "Ein Beitrag zur Entstehung der FAE-Freundschafts-Sonate," *Zeitschrift für Musikwissenschaft*, CIII (1936); F. Brand, *Das Wesen der Kammermusik von B.* (diss., Univ. of Berlin, 1937); E. Bücken, "Ein neuaufgefundenes Jugendwerk von J. B.," *Die Musik*, XXX/1 (1937–38); F. Brand, "Das neue B.-Trio," ibid., XXXI/1 (1938–39); H. Feiertag, *Das orchestrale Klangbild in B.' Orchester-Werken* (diss., Univ. of Vienna, 1938); F. Kurzweil, *Die Harmonik als formbildendes Element bei J. B.* (diss., Univ. of Vienna, 1938); F. J. Harrison, *B. and His Four Symphonies* (London, 1939); R. Kratzer, *Die Kontrapunktik bei J. B. mit besonderer Berücksichtigung der grosskontrapunktischen Formen* (diss., Univ. of Vienna, 1939); R. Fellinger, "Ist das Klaviertrio in A-dur ein Jugendwerk von J. B.?," *Die Musik*, XXXIV (1941–42); H. Hautz, *Die Harmonik der Brahms'schen Soloklavierwerke* (diss., Univ. of Munich, 1942); J. Fry, "B.'s Conception of the Scherzo in Chamber Music," *Musical Times* (April 1943); E. Schenk, "Zur Inhaltsdeutung der Brahmsschen Worthersee-symphonie," *Festliche Jahresschrift des Musikvereins für Kärnten* (Klagenfurt, 1943); C. Mason, "B.'s Piano Sonatas," *Music Review*, V (1944); R. Gerber, "B. und das Volkslied," *Die Sammlung*, III (1948); R. Gerber, "Das Deutsche Requiem als Dokument Brahmsscher Frommigkeit," *Das Musikleben*, II (1949); W. Gieseler, *Die Harmonik bei J. B.* (diss., Univ. of Göttingen, 1949); B. Stäblein, "Die motivische Arbeit im Finale der ersten B.-Sinfonie," *Das Musikleben*, II (1949); W. Köser, *J. B. in seinen geistlichen Chorwerken a cappella* (diss., Univ. of Hamburg, 1950); A. Schoenberg, "B. the Progressive," in *Style and Idea* (N.Y., 1950); R. Hasse, *Studien zum Kontrapunktischen Klaviersatz von J. B.* (diss., Univ of Cologne, 1951); G. Jacob, "Schoenberg and B.'s Op. 25," *Music & Letters* (July 1951); W. Siegmund-Schultze, *Untersuchungen zum Brahmsstil und Brahmsbild* (Habilitationsschrift, Univ. of Halle, 1951); R. Tenschert, "Die Klangwelt von J. B.," *Osterreichische Musikzeitschrift*, VI (1951); W. Hill, "B." opus 51—A Diptych," *Music Review*, XXXIII (1952); S. Drinker, *B. and His Women's Choruses* (Merion, Pa., 1952); W. Morik, *J. B. und sein Verhältnis zum deutschen Volkslied* (diss., Univ. of Göttingen, 1953); G. Gärtner, "Das Terzmotiv, Keimzelle der 1. Sinfonie von J. B.," *Die Musikforschung*, VIII (1955); S. Kross, "B. und der Kanon," in *Festschrift Joseph Schmidt-Görg zum 60. Geburtstag* (Bonn, 1957); idem, *Die Chorwerke von J. B.* (diss., Univ. of Bonn, 1957; publ. in an enl. ed., Berlin, 1958; 2nd ed., 1963); O. Jonas, "Brahmsiana," *Die Musikforschung*, XI (1958); S. Kross, "Zur Frage der Brahmsschen Volksliedbearbeitung," ibid.; W. Siegmund-Schultze, "J. B." Orchesterwerke," in K. Schönewolf, ed., *Konzertbuch Orchestermusik* (vol. I, Berlin, 1958); K. Giebeler, *Die Lieder von J. B.* (diss., Univ. of Münster, 1959); I. Fellinger, *Über die Dynamik in der Musik von J. B.* (Berlin, 1961); H. Busch, "Die Orgelwerke von J. B.," *Ars organi*, XI (1963); A. Mitschka, *Der Sonatensatz in den Werken von J. B.* (Gütersloh, 1963); W. Newman, "A 'Basic Motive' in B.'s German Requiem," *Music Review*, XXIV (1963); H. Truscott, "B. and So-*

nata Style," ibid., XXV (1964); C. Dahlhaus, *B., Klavierkonzert Nr. 1 d-moll op. 15, Meisterwerke der Musik*, III (Munich, 1965); H. Hollander, "Gedanken zum strukturellen Aufbau des Brahmsschen Requiems," *Schweizerische Musikzeitung/Revue musical suisse*, CV (1965); W. Moritz, *J. B. und sein Verhältnis zum deutschen Volkslied* (Tutzing, 1965); J. Fairleigh, "Neo-Classicism in the Later Piano Works of B.," *Piano Quarterly* (Winter 1966–67); F. Kirby, "B. and the Piano Sonata," in *Paul A. Pisk: Essays in His Honor* (Austin, 1966); A. Brandes, *The Solo Piano Variations of J. B.* (diss., Boston Univ., 1967); W. Czesla, "Motivische Mutationen im Schaffen von J. B.," in S. Kross and H. Schmidt, eds., *Colloquium amicorum: Joseph Schmidt-Görg zum 70. Geburtstag* (Bonn, 1967); R. Rittenhouse, *Rhythmic Elements in the Symphonies of J. B.* (diss., Univ. of Iowa, 1967); J. Wetschky, *Die Kanontechnik in der Instrumentalmusik von J. B.* (Regensburg, 1967); W. Czesla, *Studien zum Finale in der Kammermusik von J. B.* (diss., Univ. of Bonn, 1968); S. Helms, *Die Melodienbildung in den Liedern von J. B. und ihr Verhältnis zu den Volksliedern und volkstümlichen Weisen* (Bamberg, 1968); J. Horton, *B. Orchestral Music* (London, 1968); R. Klein, "Die konstruktiven Grundlagen der B.-Symphonien," *Österreichische Musikzeitschrift*, XXIII (1968); K. Stahmer, *Musikalische Formung in soziologischem Bezug, dargestellt an der instrumentalen Kammermusik von J. B.* (diss., Univ. of Kiel, 1968); H.-W. Kulenkampf, "Warum ist B. berühmt? Provokation eines unzeitgemassen Themas," *Neue Zeitschrift für Musik* (Sept. 1969); K. Reinhardt, "Motivisch-Thematisches im *Deutschen Requiem* von B.," *Musik und Kirche*, XXXIX (1969); V. Gotwals, "B. and the Organ," *Music/ The A.G.O. Magazine*, IV/4 (1970); S. Helms, "J. B. und das deutsche Kirchenlied," *Der Kirchenmusiker*, XXI (1970); K. Blum, *Hundert Jahre "Ein deutsches Requiem" von J. B.* (Tutzing, 1971); M. Harrison, *The Lieder of B.* (N.Y., 1972); R. Pascall, *Formal Principles in the Music of B.* (diss., Oxford Univ., 1972); E. Sams, *B. Songs* (London, 1972); K. Stahmer, "Korrekturen am B. Bild," *Die Musikforschung* (April–June 1972); C. Floros, ed., *B.-Studien*, 1 (Hamburg, 1974); R. Pascall, "Some Special Uses of Sonata Form by B.," *Soundings*, IV (1974); C. Jacobsen, *Das Verhältnis von Sprache und Musik in ausgewählten Liedern von J. B.* (Hamburg, 1975); R. Jacobson, *The Music of J. B.* (London, 1977); A. Craig Bell, *The Lieder of B.* (Darley, Harrogate, 1979); J. Webster, "The C-sharp minor Version of B.'s op. 60," *Musical Times* (Feb. 1980); J. Dunsby, *Structural Ambiguity in B.* (Ann Arbor, 1981); R. Pascall, "B.'s First Symphony Slow Movement: The Initial Performing Version," *Musical Times* (Oct. 1981); V. Hancock, *B.'s Choral Compositions and His Library of Early Music* (Ann Arbor, 1983); F. Haas, "Die Erstfassung des langsamen Satzes der ersten Sinfonie von J. B.," *Die Musikforschung*, XXXVI (1983); H. Mayer, *Ein Denkmal für J. B.: Versuche über Musik und Literatur* (Frankfurt, 1983); M. Musgrave, "B. the Progressive: Another View," *Musical Times* (May 1983); R. Pascall, "B. and Schubert," ibid.; J. Finson, "Performing Practice in the Late Nineteenth Century, with Special Reference to the Music of J. B.," *Musical Quarterly* (Fall 1984); W. Frisch, *B. and the Principle of Developing Variation* (Berkeley, 1984); M. Musgrave, *The Music of B.* (London, 1985); J. Kraus, *J. B. als Klavierkomponist: Wege und Hinweise zu seiner Klaviermusik* (Wilhelmshaven, 1986); M. Rohn, *Die Coda bei J. B.* (Hamburg, 1986); R. Knapp, *B. and the Problem of the Symphony: Romantic Image, Generic Conception, and Compositional Challenge* (diss., Duke Univ., 1987); idem, "B.'s Revisions Revisited," *Musical Times* (Nov. 1988); G. Bozarth, ed., *B. Studies: Analytical and Historical Perspectives* (Oxford, 1990).

Brăiloiu, Constantin, Rumanian ethnomusicographer; b. Bucharest, Aug. 25, 1893; d. Geneva, Dec. 20, 1958. He studied in Austria and Switzerland; in 1928 founded the Archive of Folklore in Bucharest; also was a member of ethnomusicological organizations in Geneva and Paris.
WRITINGS: *Esquisse d'une méthode de folklore musical* (Paris, 1930); *La Musique populaire roumaine* (Paris, 1940); *Le Folklore musical* (Zürich, 1948); *Le Rythme aksak* (Paris, 1952); *La Rythmique enfantine* (Brussels, 1956); "Outline of a Method of Musical Folklore" (tr. by M. Mooney; ed. by A. Briegleb and M. Kahane), *Ethnomusicology* (Sept. 1970).
BIBL.: T. Alexandra, "C. B.," *Revista de etnografie şi foleor* (1968); special B. issue of *Cercetări de muzicologie*, II (1970); V. Cosma, *Muzicieni români* (Bucharest, 1970; pp. 75–79).

Brailowsky, Alexander, noted Russian-born French pianist; b. Kiev, Feb. 16, 1896; d. N.Y., April 25, 1976. After study with his father, a professional pianist, he was taken to Vienna in 1911 and was accepted by Leschetizky as a pupil; made his debut in Paris after World War I; presented a complete cycle of Chopin's works in Paris (1924), and repeated it there several times. He made a highly successful tour all over the world; made his American debut at Aeolian Hall in N.Y., Nov. 19, 1924; made a coast-to-coast tour of the U.S. in 1936; 1st gave the Chopin cycle in America during the 1937–38 season, in 6 recitals in N.Y.

Brain, Aubrey (Harold), English French-horn player, father of **Dennis Brain;** b. London, July 12, 1893; d. there, Sept. 20, 1955. He studied at the Royal College of Music in London; joined the London Sym. Orch.; then played in the BBC Sym. Orch.; retired in 1945. He was appointed prof. at the Royal Academy of Music in 1923, and held this position for 30 years. His father was also a horn player, as was his brother **Alfred** and his son Dennis.

Brain, Dennis, English French-horn virtuoso; b. London, May 17, 1921; d. in an automobile accident in Hatfield, Hertfordshire, Sept. 1, 1957. He studied with his father, **Aubrey (Harold) Brain;** served as 1st horn player in the Royal Phil., and later with the Philharmonia Orch. He rapidly acquired the reputation of a foremost performer on his instrument. Benjamin Britten's *Serenade* for Tenor, Horn, and Strings was written for Dennis Brain. He was killed when he drove at a high speed, at night, from Edinburgh to London, and hit a tree. His death caused a profound shock among English musicians.
BIBL.: S. Pettit, *D. B.: A Biography* (London, 1976).

Braithwaite, Nicholas (Paul Dallon), English conductor, son of **(Henry) Warwick Braithwaite;** b. London, Aug. 26, 1939. He was educated at the Royal Academy of Music in London; later went to Vienna, where he studied with Hans Swarowsky. He served as associate conductor of the Bournemouth Sym. Orch. (1967–70) and as associate principal conductor of the Sadler's Wells Opera (1970–74). From 1976 to 1980 he was music director of the Glyndebourne Touring Opera. In 1980 he was engaged as an assistant to Sir Georg Solti when the London Phil. Orch. made its tour of Japan and South Korea. In 1981 he became chief conductor of the Stora Theater Opera in Göteborg, Sweden. He also was principal conductor of the Manchester Camerata (from 1984) and chief conductor of the Adelaide (Australia) Sym. Orch. (from 1987).

Braithwaite, (Henry) Warwick, New Zealand conductor, father of **Nicholas (Paul Dallon) Braithwaite;** b. Dunedin, Jan. 9, 1896; d. London, Jan. 18, 1971. He studied at the Royal Academy of Music in London; won the Challen Gold Medal and the Battison Hayes Prize. He began his career as a conductor with the O'Mara Opera Co.; then conducted with the British National Opera Co. He was assistant music director of the BBC; then went to its Cardiff studio in Wales as music director; also conducted the Cardiff Musical Soc. (1924–31). He was a founder of the Welsh National Orch. From 1932 to 1940 he was a conductor at the Sadler's Wells Opera; then he led the Scottish Orch. in Glasgow (1940–46). Later he was a ballet conductor at the Royal Opera, Covent Garden, in London (1950–53); then conducted the National Orch. of New Zealand and served as artistic director of the National Opera of Australia (1954–55). From 1956 to 1960 he was music director of the Welsh National Opera; then was again a conductor at Sadler's Wells until 1968. He publ. *The Conductor's Art* (London, 1952).

Brambach, Caspar Joseph, German composer, brother of **Wilhelm Brambach;** b. Oberdollendorf, near Königswinter, July 14, 1833; d. there, June 19, 1902. He studied composition at the Cologne Cons.; then taught there (1858–61); later was active as a teacher and composer in Bonn (1861–69). He wrote many secular cantatas, among them *Trost in Tönen, Das Eleusische Fest, Die Macht des Gesanges, Prometheus,* and *Columbus* (awarded the $1,000 prize at the Milwaukee Festival; perf. there July 23, 1886); also an opera, *Ariadne;* concert overture, *Tasso;* Piano Concerto; Piano Sextet; String Sextet; 2 piano quartets; songs.

Brambach, Wilhelm, German musicologist, brother of **Caspar Joseph Brambach;** b. Bonn, Dec. 17, 1841; d. Karlsruhe, Feb. 26, 1932. He studied classical languages and musicology at the Univ. of Bonn; taught philology at the Univ. of Freiburg (1866–72); then was for 32 years librarian of the district library at Karlsruhe (1872–1904).

WRITINGS: *Das Tonsystem und die Tonarten des christlichen Abendlandes im Mittelalter* (Leipzig, 1881); *Die Musikliteratur des Mittelalters bis zur Blüte der Reichenauer Sängerschule* (Karlsruhe, 1883); *Hermanni Contracti musica* (Leipzig, 1884); *Die verloren geglaubte "Historia de Sancta Afra Martyri" und das "Salve regina" des Hermannus Contractus* (Karlsruhe, 1892); *Gregorianische-bibliographische Lösung der Streitfrage über die Ursprung des Gregorianischen Gesangs* (Leipzig, 1895; 2nd ed., 1901).

Brambilla, Marietta, Italian contralto, sister of **Teresa Brambilla;** b. Cassano d'Adda, June 6, 1807; d. Milan, Nov. 6, 1875. She was a member of a musical family; her 4 sisters were singers. She studied at the Milan Cons.; made her debut in London in 1827; then sang in Italy, Vienna, and Paris. She eventually settled in Milan as a teacher; publ. collections of vocalises.

Brambilla, Paolo, Italian composer; b. Milan, July 9, 1787; d. there, 1838. He wrote 4 operas, produced in Milan and Turin, and 6 ballets for La Scala. He was the father of **Marietta** and **Teresa Brambilla.**

Brambilla, Teresa, Italian soprano, sister of **Marietta Brambilla;** b. Cassano d'Adda, Oct. 23, 1813; d. Milan, July 15, 1895. She studied singing at the Milan Cons.; made her debut in 1831 in Milan and traveled through Europe, including Russia. Her appearances at La Scala were highly successful. After several seasons in Paris, she was engaged at the Teatro La Fenice in Venice, where she created the role of Gilda in *Rigoletto* (March 11, 1851).

Brancour, René, French music critic; b. Paris, May 17, 1862; d. there, Nov. 16, 1948. Educated at the Paris Cons., he became curator of its collection of musical instruments; in 1906 began a course of lectures on esthetics at the Sorbonne; also wrote newspaper criticism. A brilliant writer, he poured invective on the works of composers of the advanced school; his tastes were conservative, but he accepted French music of the Impressionist period. He wrote biographies of Félicien David (1911) and Méhul (1912) in the series Musiciens Célèbres; of Massenet (1923) and Offenbach (1929) in Les Maîtres de la Musique. Other books are *La Vie et l'œuvre de Georges Bizet* (1913); *Histoire des instruments de musique* (1921); *La Marseillaise et le chant du départ;* etc.

Brand, Max, Austrian-born American composer; b. Lemberg, April 26, 1896; d. Langenzersdorf, near Vienna, April 5, 1980. He studied with Franz Schreker at the Vienna Academy of Music. He made use of the 12-tone method of composition as early as 1927, but did not limit himself to it in his later works. His most spectacular work was the opera *Maschinist Hopkins,* to his own libretto, chosen as the best operatic work of the year by the Congress of German Composers, and 1st produced at Duisburg on April 13, 1929; it was later staged in 37 opera houses in Europe, including Russia; it marked the climactic point of the "machine era" in modern music between the 2 wars. Brand was also active in the field of experi-

mental musical films in the triple capacity of author, composer, and director. From 1933 to 1938 he remained in Vienna; then went to Brazil; in 1940 arrived in the U.S., becoming an American citizen in 1945. In 1975 he returned to Austria.

WORKS: *Nachtlied,* from Nietzsche's *Also sprach Zarathustra,* for Soprano and Orch. (1922); 3 songs to poems by Lao-Tse (Salzburg Festival, 1923); *Eine Nachtmusik* for Chamber Orch. (1923); String Trio (1923); *Die Wippe,* ballet (1925); *Tragœdietta,* ballet (1926); *5 Ballads,* a study in 12 tones (1927); *Maschinist Hopkins,* opera in 3 acts (1928); *The Chronicle,* scenic cantata for Narrator, Soli, Chorus, and Orch. (1938); *Piece for Flute and Piano,* in 12 tones (1940); *Kyrie Eleison,* study in 12 tones for Chorus (1940; perf. by Villa-Lobos, Rio de Janeiro, 1940); *The Gate,* scenic oratorio, with Narrator (N.Y., May 23, 1944); *The Wonderful 1-Hoss Shay,* symphonic rondo for Orch., after Oliver Wendell Holmes (Philadelphia, Jan. 20, 1950); *Night on the Bayous of Louisiana,* tone poem (1953); *Stormy Interlude,* opera in 1 act, libretto by the composer (1955). About 1958 Brand became absorbed in electronic music; wrote *The Astronauts, An Epic in Electronics* (1962); *Ilian 1 & 2* (1966); numerous pieces of music for modern plays.

BIBL.: C. Bennett, "Maschinist Hopkins: A father for Lulu?," *Musical Times* (Sept. 1986).

Brand, Oscar, Canadian folksinger and folklorist; b. Winnipeg, Feb. 7, 1920. He was taken to the U.S.; studied at Brooklyn College (B.A. in abnormal psychology, 1942); then served in the U.S. Army (1942–45). Following his discharge, he embarked upon a career as a folksinger; from 1945 was host of his own radio program in N.Y. He contributed informative articles on various aspects of folk music; his writings include *Bawdy Songs and Backroom Ballads* (1959), *Folk Songs for Fun* (1961), *The Ballad Mongers: Rise of the Modern Folksong* (1962), and *When I First Came to This Land* (1975).

Brandl, Johann Evangelist, German composer; b. Kloster Rohr, near Regensburg, Nov. 14, 1760; d. Karlsruhe, May 25, 1837. He studied in various religious schools and monasteries as a youth; then decided to devote himself to music, and became proficient as an organist and violinist; was attached to the court of the Archduke of Baden as music director.

WORKS: Operas: *Germania* (1800); *Triumph des Vaterherzens* (Karlsruhe, Jan. 15, 1811); *Omar der Gute* (Karlsruhe, Aug. 24, 1811); *Nanthild, das Mädchen von Valbella* (Karlsruhe, May 19, 1813); a "Grande Symphonie"; Bassoon Concerto; a number of string quartets and string quintets; many songs; oratorios; masses.

BIBL.: O. Danzer, *J.E. B.s Leben und Werke* (Leipzig, 1936); F. Leinert, *J.E. B. als Lieder- und Kammermusik Komponist* (Wolfenbüttel, 1937).

Brandt, Jobst vom (or **Jodocus de Brant**), German musician; b. Waldershof, near Marktredwitz, Oct. 28, 1517; d. Brand, near Marktredwitz, Jan. 22, 1570. In 1530 he enrolled at Heidelberg Univ.; in 1548 had become Captain of Waldsassen and Administrator of Liebenstein. He was one of the most important composers of the Senfl school; his music is distinguished by deep feeling and a skillful use of counterpoint.

WORKS: 45 *Psalmen und Kirchengesänge* (Eger, 1572–73); 55 vocal pieces in G. Forster's collection *Ein Auszug guter alter und neuer teutscher Liedlein* (III, Wittenberg, 1549; IV–V, 1556).

Brandt, Marianne (real name, **Marie Bischoff**), Austrian contralto; b. Vienna, Sept. 12, 1842; d. there, July 9, 1921. She studied voice in Vienna, and later with Pauline Viardot-Garcia in Baden-Baden (1869–70); she made her debut as Rachel in *La Juive* in Olmütz on Jan. 4, 1867; then sang in Hamburg and at the Berlin Opera (1868–82). In 1872 she appeared in London; made her American debut as Leonore at the Metropolitan Opera in N.Y. on Nov. 19, 1884, and remained on its staff until 1888; she also sang Italian roles in operas by Verdi and Meyerbeer. In 1890 she settled in Vienna as a singing teacher.

BIBL.: La Mara, *Musikalische Studienköpfe* (Leipzig, 1902).

Brandts-Buys, Jan, composer; b. Zutphen, the Netherlands, Sept. 12, 1868; d. Salzburg, Dec. 7, 1933. He was a pupil of M. Schwarz and A. Urspruch at the Raff Cons. in Frankfurt; lived for a time in Vienna; later settled in Salzburg. His 1st opera, *Das Veilchenfest* (Berlin, 1909), met with opposition; a 2nd opera, *Das Glockenspiel* (Dresden, 1913), was received more kindly; while a 3rd, *Die drei Schneider von Schönau* (Dresden, April 1, 1916), was quite successful. Subsequent operas were *Der Eroberer* (Dresden, 1918), *Micarême* (Vienna, 1919), *Der Mann im Mond* (Dresden, 1922), and *Traumland* (Dresden, 1927). He also wrote a ballet, *Machinalität* (Amsterdam, 1928); 2 piano concertos; a *Konzertstück* for Cello and Orch.; chamber music; piano pieces; songs.

Brandukov, Anatol (Andreievich), eminent Russian cellist; b. Moscow, Dec. 22, 1856; d. there, Feb. 16, 1930. He studied cello at the Moscow Cons. with Fitzenhagen (1868–77), and also attended Tchaikovsky's classes in harmony. In 1878 he undertook a concert tour of Europe; lived mostly in Paris until 1906. His artistry was appreciated by Tchaikovsky, who dedicated his *Pezzo capriccioso* for Cello and Orch. to him; he enjoyed the friendship of Saint-Saëns and Liszt. In 1906 he returned to Moscow, where he was prof. at the Phil. Inst.; from 1921 to 1930 he taught cello at the Moscow Cons. He composed a number of cello pieces and made transcriptions of works by Tchaikovsky, Rachmaninoff, and others.

BIBL.: L. Ginsburg, *A.A. B.* (Moscow, 1951).

Brannigan, Owen, English bass; b. Annitsford, March 10, 1908; d. there, May 10, 1973. He was educated at the Guildhall School of Music in London. He made his debut in 1943 as Sarastro at the Sadler's Wells Opera, becoming a member of the company (1944–49; 1952–58). He gained fame for creating several roles in the operas of Benjamin Britten. He also distinguished himself as a concert and oratorio singer.

Branscombe, Gena, Canadian-American educator, chorus leader, and composer; b. Picton, Ontario, Nov. 4, 1881; d. N.Y., July 26, 1977. She attended the Chicago Musical College, where she studied piano with Rudolph Ganz and composition with Felix Borowski; then went to Berlin, where she took a course with Engelbert Humperdinck. Returning to America, she took conducting lessons with Frank Damrosch and Albert Stoessel; became a U.S. citizen in 1910. In 1934 she organized the Branscombe Chorale, a women's ensemble that she conducted until 1954. She composed mostly choral works, often to her own texts; of these the most notable are *A Wind from the Sea*, after Longfellow (c.1924), *Pilgrims of Destiny* (1926), *The Phantom Caravan*, after Banning (c.1927), *Youth of the World* (c.1932), and *Coventry's Choir*, after Alvarez (c.1944). She also composed a symphonic suite, *Quebec* (1928), and some 150 songs. Amazingly energetic, she continued to be active until an improbable old age, and at the time of her death she was working on her autobiography.

Brant, Henry, American ultra-modern composer and pioneer of spatial music; b. Montreal (of American parents), Sept. 15, 1913. He learned the rudiments of music from his father; in 1929 the family moved to N.Y., where Brant studied elementary music theory with Leonard Mannes at the Inst. of Musical Art and also took private lessons in advanced composition with Wallingford Riegger and George Antheil. He further learned the elements of conducting from Fritz Mahler, nephew of Gustav Mahler. Having absorbed the totality of quaquaversal techniques of composition, he proceeded to teach others at various institutions of progressive musical learning. In 1982 he settled in Santa Barbara, Calif. An audacious explorer of sonic potentialities, he drew without prejudice upon resources ranging from kitchen utensils to tin cans in search of superior cacophony. He became a pioneer in the field of spatial music, in which the participating instruments were to be placed at specified points in space, on the stage, in the balcony, and in the aisles. In conducting his spatial music he developed an appropriate body language, turning at 90°, 135°, and 180° angles

to address his instrumentalists. He also gave cues by actually imitating the appearance of the entering instruments, miming the violin bow, a trombone valve, a piccolo, or a drum by the movement of his body or by facial movements. He also proposed to construct a concert hall with movable plywood partitions, changing configurations according to acoustical requirements, but this plan is relegated to a later century.

WORKS (a generous selection from a multitude of instrumental and vocal compositions): *Angels and Devils* for a Merry Murmuration of Innumerable Flutes (N.Y., Feb. 6, 1933); *Whoopee in D Major* (1938); *The Great American Goof,* ballet (N.Y., Jan. 11, 1940); Saxophone Concerto (1941; N.Y., May 12, 1945); *All Souls' Carnival* for Flute, Violin, Cello, Piano, and Accordion (1947); *Millennium No. 1* for Trumpets, Chimes, and Bells (1950); *Millennium No. 2* for Multiple Brass and Percussion (1954); *Millennium No. 3* for Brass and Percussion (1957); *Millennium No. 4* for Brass (1964); *From Bach's Menagerie* for Saxophone Quartet (1974); *Behold the Earth,* a Requiem cantata (1951); *Feuerwerk* for Speaker, Fireworks, and Instruments (1961); *Horizontals Extending* for 2 Chamber Orchs., Jazz Drummer, and 3 Karate Artists (1981). **NONDESCRIPT ENSEMBLES:** *5 & 10 Cent Store Music* for Violin, Piano, and Kitchen Hardware (1932); *Hommage aux frères Marx* for Solo Tin Whistle and Other Plebeian Contraptions (1938); *Kitchen Music* for Water Glasses, Bottles, and Assorted Junk, not omitting some perfectly awful offal (1946); *Machinations* for Flageolet, Double Ocarina, Ceramic Flute, Steel Harp, and What Have You (1970); *Solar Moth,* a pheromone to attract tonal insects (1979). **SPATIAL WORKS** (a cautious sampler): *Encephalograms* for Soprano and 7 Instruments (1955); *In Praise of Learning* for 16 Sopranos and 16 Percussionists (1958); *Mythical Beasts* for Soprano and 16 Instruments (1958); *Barricades* for Tenor and 9 Instruments (1961); *Verticals Ascending* for 2 Separate Instrumental Groups (1968); *6 Grand Pianos Bash Plus Friends* (1974); *American Weather* for Winds and Percussion (1976); *Cerberus* for Double Bass, Piccolo, Soprano, and Mouth Organ (1978); Piano Concerto for Piano, 16 Women's Voices, and Orch. (1978); *Revenge before Breakfast* for 2 Woodwinds, 2 Strings, 2 Percussion, and Piano (1982); *Meteor Farm* for Orch., Jazz Band, Gamelans, West African Drums, South Indian Singers, and 2 Western Sopranos (1982); Piano Concerto for 16 Women, Piano, and Orch. (1978); *Brant aan de Amstel,* water spectacle for Holland for 100 Flutes, 4 Jazz Drummers, 3 Choirs, 4 Street Organs, 4 Church Carillons, and 3 Bands (1984); *Knot-holes, Bent Nails & a Rusty Saw* for Anyone and Anybody Accompanied by Some Sonorous Garbage (1985); *Northern Lights over the Twin Cities* for 2 Choirs, Bagpipe Band, and 5 Pianos (1985); *An Era Any Time of Year* for a Walking Baritone Accompanied by Piano Strings Pizzicato and Other Things (1987); *Instant Sygyzy* for 2 String Quartets and Whatnot (1987); *Ghost Nets,* concerto for Double-bass Solo with 2 Chamber Seines Equipped with Imaginary Sinkers and Floats (1988); *Prisons of the Mind,* a "spatial sym." (Dallas, April 12, 1990).

Brant, Jan, Polish composer and theologian; b. probably in Poznan, 1554; d. Lwow, May 27, 1602. He entered the Jesuit order in 1571; was ordained in 1578; then studied theology in Rome. He returned to Poland in 1584, and subsequently held positions in a number of Polish convents. Some of his MSS were discovered in 1972 in the archives of the Univ. of Uppsala.

BIBL.: Z. Szweykowski, "J. B. (1554–1602) i jego nowo odkryta twórczość muzyczna," *Muzyka,* XVIII/2 (1973).

Branzell, Karin Maria, noted Swedish contralto; b. Stockholm, Sept. 24, 1891; d. Altadena, Calif., Dec. 14, 1974. She studied with Thekla Hofer in Stockholm, with Bachner in Berlin, and with Rosati in N.Y.; made her operatic debut in 1911. From 1912 to 1918 she was a member of the Stockholm Royal Opera; then sang with the Berlin State Opera (1919–23). She made her American debut as Fricka in *Die Walküre* with the Metropolitan Opera in N.Y. on Feb. 6, 1924, and remained on its roster for 20 seasons, retiring in 1944. Possessing a voice of exceptional range and power, she occasionally sang soprano roles. She was active as a voice teacher in N.Y.; in 1969 she moved to California.

Braslau, Sophie, American contralto; b. N.Y., Aug. 16, 1892; d. there, Dec. 22, 1935. She studied voice with Buzzi-Peccia; made her debut at the Metropolitan Opera in *Boris Godunov* (Nov. 26, 1914); was a member of the company until 1920; in 1931 toured Scandinavia and the Netherlands. A large collection of her programs, reviews, and biographical materials was given by the family to the Music Division of the N.Y. Public Library (1938).

Brassens, Georges, French chansonnier; b. Sète, Hérault, Oct. 22, 1921; d. there, Oct. 29, 1981. He began his career as a chansonnier, accompanying himself on the guitar in a repertoire of his own chansons, which he called "lyrisme plébéien"; indeed, his texts voice proletarian discontent, as revealed by such titles as *La Mauvaise Réputation, Le Pornographe,* and *Je suis un voyou* (I Am a Bum), calculated to shock the self-contented bourgeoisie. But the Establishment apparently did not recoil from these verbal blows, and in 1967 the Académie Française honored him with a poetry prize. Brassens also wrote a novel, *La Tour des miracles* (Paris, 1953).
BIBL.: J. Charpentreau, *G. B. et la poésie quotidienne de la chanson* (Paris, 1960); A. Larue, *B., ou La Mauvaise Herbe* (Paris, 1970); J. Sermonte, *G. B.* (Paris, 1988).

Brassin, Louis, French pianist; b. Aix-la-Chapelle, June 24, 1840; d. St. Petersburg, May 17, 1884. He was a pupil of Moscheles at the Leipzig Cons.; made concert tours with his brothers Leopold and Gerhard; taught at the Stern Cons. in Berlin (1866); at the Brussels Cons. (1869–79); then at the St. Petersburg Cons. He publ. the valuable *École moderne du piano;* composed 2 piano concertos, salon pieces for piano, and songs. His effective piano transcription of the Magic Fire music from *Die Walküre* is well known.

Brauer, Evald, Estonian flutist and composer; b. Väinjärve, July 26, 1904; d. Tallinn, Oct. 20, 1961. He studied flute at the Tallinn Cons., and then taught flute there (1935–40). He also publ. a textbook on flute playing in the Estonian language (1939). His compositions are set in an acceptable academic manner, with Estonian motifs lending an air of authenticity. In this ethnically colored idiom he wrote *Estonian Capriccio* for Orch. (1936); a symphonic poem, *Mahtra* (1958); overtures and choruses.

Braun, Carl, German bass; b. Meisenheim, Prussia, June 2, 1885; d. Hamburg, April 19, 1960. He studied with Hermann Gausche in Kreuznach and later with Eugen Robert Weiss. He sang at the Wiesbaden Opera (1906–11) and at the Vienna Court Opera (1911–12); then was engaged at the Berlin City Opera (1912–14). He also appeared at the Bayreuth Festivals (1906–31). On Feb. 8, 1913, he made his American debut at the Metropolitan Opera in N.Y., but was dismissed as an enemy alien in the spring of 1917 when the U.S. entered the war against Germany. In 1922–23 he made a South American tour; also sang in the U.S. in 1928 and 1931. In 1933 he was engaged as a stage director at the German Opera in Berlin, and in 1935–36 held similar posts at the Berlin Volksoper and at the Danzig Municipal Theater. In 1937 he retired from the stage and was thereafter active mainly as a concert agent in Hamburg.

Braun, Peter Michael, German composer; b. Wuppertal, Dec. 2, 1936. He studied in Dortmund; later took courses in Cologne with Frank Martin, Bernd Alois Zimmermann, and Herbert Eimert, and also in Detmold with Giselher Klebe. His musical style is governed by structural considerations; in his varied techniques he applies the resources of "organized sound" as formulated by Varèse, the theory of sets and devices of synthetic *musique concrète.* He wrote *Thesis-Medium* for Piano (1960); *Monophonie* for Electric Guitar (1961–67); *Wind Sextet* (1961); *Transfer* for Orch. (1968).

Braun, Wilhelm. See **Brown, William.**

Braunfels, Walter, German composer; b. Frankfurt am Main, Dec. 19, 1882; d. Cologne, March 19, 1954. He studied piano in Vienna with Leschetizky and composition in Munich with L. Thuille. He became active both as an educator and a composer. From 1913 to 1925 he lived near Munich; in 1925 he became a co-director of the Hochschule für Musik in Cologne. With the advent of the Nazi regime, he was compelled to abandon teaching; from 1933 to 1937 he was in Godesberg; from 1937 to 1945 in Überlingen. He excelled mainly as an opera composer; the following operas are notable: *Falada* (Essen, May 24, 1906); *Prinzessin Brambilla* (Stuttgart, March 25, 1909; rev. 1931); *Ulenspiegel* (Stuttgart, Nov. 9, 1913); *Die Vögel,* after Aristophanes (Munich, Dec. 4, 1920; his most successful opera); *Don Gil von den grünen Hosen* (Munich, Nov. 15, 1924); *Der gläserne Berg* (Krefeld, Dec. 4, 1928); *Galatea* (Cologne, Jan. 26, 1930); *Der Traum, Ein Leben* (1937); *Die heilige Johanna* (1942); also a mystery play, *Verkündigung,* after Paul Claudel (1936). He further wrote 2 piano concertos; Organ Concerto; *Revelation of St. John* for Tenor, Double Chorus, and Orch.; piano music and songs. He believed in the artistic and practical value of Wagnerian leading motifs; in his harmonies he was close to Richard Strauss, but he also applied impressionistic devices related to Debussy.

Bravničar, Matija, Slovene composer; b. Tolmin, Feb. 24, 1897; d. Ljubljana, Nov. 25, 1977. After service in the Austrian army (1915–18) he was a violinist at the opera theater in Ljubljana; meanwhile he studied composition at the Cons. there, graduating in 1932; was director of the Ljubljana Academy of Music (1945–49) and later taught composition there (1952–68); was president of the Soc. of Slovene Composers (1949–52) and of the Union of Yugoslavian Composers (1953–57). In his works, Bravničar cultivated a neo-Classical style, with thematic material strongly influenced by the melo-rhythmic inflections of Slovenian folk music.
WORKS: Opera buffa, *Pohujšanje v dolini Sentflorijanski* (Scandal in St. Florian's Valley; Ljubljana, May 11, 1930); opera, *Hlapec Jernij in njegova pravica* (Knight Jernej and His Justice; Ljubljana, Jan. 25, 1941); satirical revue, *Stoji, stoji Ljubljanca* (Ljubljana, Dec. 2, 1933); *Hymnus Slavicus* for Orch. (1931; Ljubljana, May 14, 1932); overture, *Kralj Matjaž* (King Mattias; 1932; Ljubljana, Nov. 14, 1932); *Slavik Dance Burlesques* for Orch. (1932); *Divertissements* for Piano and Strings (1933); *Belokranjska rapsodija* for Orch. (1938); *Simfonična antiteza* (Symphonic Antithesis; 1940; Ljubljana, Feb. 9, 1948); 3 syms.: No. 1 (1947; Ljubljana, Feb. 20, 1951); No. 2 (1951; Ljubljana, Oct. 27, 1952); No. 3 (1956); *Kurent,* symphonic poem (1950); *Plesne metamorfoze* for Orch. (1955); *Marcia-Rondo* for Orch. (1960); Violin Concerto (1961); Horn Concerto (1963); *Fantasia rapsodica* for Violin and Orch. (1967); *Simfonični plesi* (Symphonic Dances; 1969); *Elegie* for Horn and Piano (1929); 2 wind quintets (1930, 1968); Trio for Flute, Clarinet, and Bassoon (1930); *Dialog* for Cello and Piano (1965); Sonata for Solo Violin (1966); piano pieces.

Braxton, Anthony, black American jazz alto saxophonist, contrabass clarinetist, and composer; b. Chicago, June 4, 1945. After early studies in both jazz and classical music, he became a member of the Assoc. for the Advancement of Creative Musicians (1966) and in 1967 formed the Creative Construction Co. (with Leroy Jenkins and Leo Smith). He later went to N.Y., where he played in the improvisation ensemble Musica Elettronica Viva (1970) and with Chick Corea's free-jazz quartet, Circle (1970–71). Although his activities and influence have been principally in avant-garde jazz improvisation, his output in the 1970s included compositions for band and piano. His album *For Alto* (1968) was the 1st recording for unaccompanied saxophone.

Bream, Julian (Alexander), noted English guitarist and lutenist; b. London, July 15, 1933. He was educated at the Royal College of Music in London; made his debut at the age of 17. In 1960 he founded the Julian Bream Consort; also directed the Semley Festival of Music and Poetry from 1971. Through his numerous concerts and recordings he has helped to revive interest in Elizabethan lute music. He was named an Officer of the Order of the British Empire in 1964, and a Commander of the Order of the British Empire in 1985.

BIBL.: T. Palmer, *J. B.: A Life on the Road* (London, 1982).

Brecher, Gustav, German conductor and editor; b. Eichwald, near Teplitz, Bohemia, Feb. 5, 1879; d. (suicide) Ostend, May 1940. His family moved to Leipzig in 1889, and he studied there with Jadassohn. His 1st major work, the symphonic poem *Rosmersholm*, was introduced by Richard Strauss at a Liszt-Verein concert in Leipzig (1896); Brecher made his debut as a conductor there (1897); was a vocal coach and occasional conductor of operas in Leipzig (1898); conducted in Vienna (1901); served as 1st Kapellmeister in Olmütz (1902), Hamburg (1903), and Cologne (1911–16); then went to Frankfurt (1916–24) and Leipzig (1924–33). He committed suicide with his wife aboard a boat off the Belgian coast while attempting to flee from the advancing Nazi troops. His compositions include a symphonic fantasia, *Aus unserer Zeit.* He was the author of *Über die veristische Oper; Analysen zu Werken von Berlioz und Strauss;* and *Über Operntexte und Opernübersetzungen* (1911).

Brecknock, John, English tenor; b. Long Eaton, Nov. 29, 1937. He received his vocal training in Birmingham; then joined the chorus of the Sadler's Wells Opera; in 1967 he appeared in a minor role there, soon rising to prominence as one of its principal members; also sang at Covent Garden, London, the Scottish National Opera, and the Glyndebourne Festival. He made his American debut with the Metropolitan Opera in N.Y. on March 23, 1977, as Tamino in *Die Zauberflöte.* He was especially praised for his performances of the early 19th-century Italian operatic repertoire.

Bredemeyer, Reiner, German composer; b. Velez, Colombia, of German parents, Feb. 2, 1929. He studied composition with Karl Höller at the Akademie der Tonkunst in Munich (1949–53); then took courses with Wagner-Régeny at the Akademie der Künste in East Berlin (1955–57). In 1961 he was appointed conductor of the German Theater in East Berlin; in 1978 joined the faculty of the Akademie der Künste there. In his music he is an astute experimenter, but he adheres to the tenets of classical forms and avoids the extremes of modernism.

WORKS: STAGE: *Leben der Andrea,* short opera after Brecht's *Galileo* (1971); *Die Galoschenoper,* after *The Beggar's Opera* (1978); *Candide,* after Voltaire (1981–82; Halle, 1986). **ORCH.:** *Integration* (1961); *Variante* (1962); Violin Concerto (1963); *Komposition* for 56 Strings (1964); *Spiel* (1964); *Schlagstück 3* for Orch. and 3 Percussion Groups (1966); *Bagatellen für B.* for Piano and Orch. (1970); *Spiel zu 45* (1970); *Piano und . . . ,* piano concerto (1972); *Oktoberstück* (1973); Sym. (1974); *Anfangen—aufhören* (1974); Double Concerto for Harpsichord, Oboe, and Orch. (1974); *2 tempi* for Flute, Recorder, and Strings (1976); *Auftakte* for 3 Orch. Groups (1976); Concerto for Oboe and Strings (1977); *4 Pieces* (1979); *9 Bagatelles* for String Orch. (1984). **CHAMBER:** Quintet for Flute, Clarinet, Violin, Cello, and Double Bass (1956); Concertino for 12 (1957); Octet (1959); 2 quintets for Woodwinds (1959, 1969); *Schlagstück 1* for Solo Percussionist (1960); 3 string quartets (1961, 1968, 1983); String Quintet (1962); *5 Pieces* for Oboe and 3 Bassoons (1964); *Schlagstück 2* for Piano and Percussion (1965); *6 Serenades* for various instrumental combinations (1966–80); *Pointing* for 18 String Instruments (1966); Sonata for Violin, Viola, and Piano (1967); *Schlagquartett* for Piano, Double Bass, and 2 Percussionists (1967); *Schlagstück 5* for Piano and Percussion (1970); *Ab 14* for Piano and 13 String Instruments (1971); *(Cello)²* for Cello and Tape (1971); *8 Pieces* for String Trio (1971); *6 Solos* for Various Instruments (1973–80); *(Oboe)²* for Oboe and Tape (1975); *Grosses Duet* for 2 Instrumental Groups (1975); *Piano und . . .⁵* for Piano, Flute, Horn, Trombone, Cello, and Double Bass (1976); *Interludium* for Soprano Saxophone, Flute, Cello, Double Bass, and Percussion (1977); *Piano und . . .⁶* for Piano, 2 Cellos, Wind Instrument, and 3 Percussionists (1977); *5 Blechstücke* for 2 Trumpets and 2 Trombones (1979); *D für Paul Dessau* for 15 String

Instruments (1980); *Septet 80* for 2 Oboes, Cello, Double Bass, Percussion, Trombone, and Harpsichord (1980); *Septet 87* for 2 Guitars, Percussion, and String Quartet (1987). **VOCAL:** *Cantata* for Alto and Female Choir (1961); *Wostock* for Choir and Orch. (1961); *Karthago* for Chorus and Chamber Ensemble (1961); *Sätze und Sentenzen* for Chorus and Orch. (1963); *Canto* for Alto, Male Chorus, and 10 Instruments (1965); *Synchronisiert-Asynchron* for Soprano, Oboe, Bassoon, Cello, Piano, Percussion, and Tape (1975); *Zum 13. 7. (Für Schönberg),* commemorative dedication on the 25th anniversary of Schoenberg's death, for Female Voice, Clarinet, Saxophone, and Percussion (1976); *Cantata 2* for 16 Voices and 16 Instruments (1977); *Madrigal, Rezitativ und Arie* for Tenor and 8 Instruments (1979); *Das Alltägliche* for Soprano, Tenor, and Orch. (1980); *Die schöne Müllerin* for Baritone, String Quartet, and Horn Quartet, after Müller (1986; Berlin, Feb. 21, 1987); songs; piano pieces.

Brediceanu, Tiberiu, Rumanian composer; b. Lugoj, Transylvania, April 2, 1877; d. Bucharest, Dec. 19, 1968. He studied music mainly in Rumania; was a founding member of the Rumanian Opera and National Theater in Cluj (1919) and the Soc. of Rumanian Composers in Bucharest (1920); later became director of the Astra Cons. in Brasov (1934–40) and director-general of the Rumanian Opera (1941–44). He publ. valuable collections of Rumanian songs and dances, including 170 Rumanian folk melodies, 810 tunes of the Banat regions, and 1,000 songs of Transylvania.

WORKS: Operas: *Poemul muzical etnografic* (1905; rev. and retitled *Romania in port, joc si cintec,* 1929); and *La şezătoare* (1908); *Seara mare,* lyric scene (1924); *Învierea,* a pantomime (1932); *La seceriş* (1936); *4 Symphonic Dances* (1951); 2 suites for Violin and Piano (1951); piano pieces; songs.

Bree, Jean Bernard van (Johannes Bernardus van), Dutch violinist and composer; b. Amsterdam, Jan. 29, 1801; d. there, Feb. 14, 1857. He was a pupil of Bertelman; in 1820–21 he played in the orch. of the Théâtre Français in Amsterdam; in 1830 he became conductor of the Felix Meritis Soc.; in 1841 he founded the Cecilia Soc. in Amsterdam; later became director of the Music School of the Soc. for the Promotion of Music.

WORKS: Operas: *Sappho* (in Dutch; Amsterdam, March 22, 1834), *Le Bandit* (in French; Amsterdam, Dec. 22, 1835), and *Nimm dich in Acht* (in German; 1845); also 2 melodramas; several masses; cantatas; overtures; chamber music.

BIBL.: H. Beijermann, *J.B. v.B.* (1857).

Brehm, Alvin, American double-bass player, conductor, and composer; b. N.Y., Feb. 8, 1925. He studied with Fred Zimmerman (double bass) and V. Giannini (orchestration) at the Juilliard School of Music in N.Y. (1942–43); then with Riegger (composition) at Columbia Univ. (M.A., 1951). After making his debut as a double-bass player (1942), he performed with the Pittsburgh Sym. Orch. (1950–51), the Contemporary Chamber Ensemble (1969–73), the Group for Contemporary Music (1971–73), the Philomusica Chamber Music Soc. (1973–83), and the Chamber Music Soc. of Lincoln Center (1984–89). After making his debut as a conductor (1947), he was active in promoting contemporary music. He was founder-conductor of the Composer's Theatre Orch. (1967), and also taught at the State Univ. of N.Y. at Stony Brook (1968–75), the Manhattan School of Music (1969–75), and the State Univ. of N.Y. at Purchase (from 1982).

WORKS: ORCH.: *Hephaestus Overture* (1966); Concertino for Violin and Strings (1975); Piano Concerto (1977); Double-bass Concerto (1982); Tuba Concerto (1982). **CHAMBER:** Divertimento for Trumpet, Horn, and Trombone (1962); *Dialogues* for Bassoon and Percussion (1964); Divertimento for Woodwind Quintet (1965); Brass Quintet (1967); *Colloquy and Chorale* for Bassoon Quartet (1974); Cello Sonata (1974); *Quarks* for Flute, Bassoon, String Quartet, and Piano (1976); Sextet for Piano and Strings (1976); *A Pointe at His Pleasure* for Renaissance Instruments (1979); Sextet for Woodwind Quintet and Piano (1984); *Children's Games* for Flute, Clarinet, Violin, Viola, Cello, and Piano (1984–85).

Brehme, Hans, German composer; b. Potsdam, March 10, 1904; d. Stuttgart, Nov. 10, 1957. He studied piano in Berlin with Wilhelm Kempff; taught at Stuttgart and elsewhere. A highly diligent composer, he wrote music in many genres; the idiom of his compositions is fundamentally Classical, with a generous admixture of moderately modern harmonies. He wrote an opera, *Der Uhrmacher von Strassburg* (1941); operetta, *Versiegelten Bürgermeister* (1944); 2 syms.; 2 piano concertos; Flute Concerto; Sextet for Flute, Clarinet, Horn, Violin, Viola, and Cello; Clarinet Quintet; Saxophone Sonata; *Triptycon* for Orch., on a theme by Handel (highly successful); several works for Accordion.

Bréhy, Hercule, Belgian organist and composer; b. Brussels (baptized), Sept. 13, 1673; d. there (buried), Feb. 28, 1737. He was active as an organist in Brussels; from 1705 until his death he was singing master at Ste. Gudule. His works include masses, motets, and Lamentations.

Breil, Joseph Carl, American composer; b. Pittsburgh, June 29, 1870; d. Los Angeles, Jan. 23, 1926. He studied voice in Milan and Leipzig, and for a time sang in various opera companies. He was the composer of one of the earliest motion picture scores, *Queen Elizabeth* (Chicago, 1912); he also wrote the music for D.W. Griffith's film *The Birth of a Nation* (1915), as well as the words and music for the comic operas *Love Laughs at Locksmiths* (Portland, Maine, Oct. 27, 1910), *Prof. Tattle* (1913), and *The Seventh Chord* (1913). His serious opera, *The Legend,* was produced by the Metropolitan Opera in N.Y. on March 12, 1919. His opera *Asra* (after Heine) had a single performance, in Los Angeles (Nov. 24, 1925).

Breitengraser, Wilhelm, German composer; b. Nuremberg, c.1495; d. there (buried), Dec. 23, 1542. He studied at the Univ. of Leipzig; then was active as a teacher and musician in Nuremberg. His works include masses, Psalms, and hymns.

Bibl.: R. Wagner, "W. B.: Die Nürnberger Kirchen- und Schulmusik seiner Zeit," *Die Musikforschung,* II (1949).

Breithaupt, Rudolf (Maria), German pianist, pedagogue, and music scholar; b. Braunschweig, Aug. 11, 1873; d. Ballenstedt, April 2, 1945. He studied jurisprudence, philosophy, and musicology before he began taking piano lessons with Teichmüller at the Leipzig Cons.; then went to Berlin and was appointed piano teacher at the Stern Cons. there. He publ. valuable studies on piano playing: *Die natürliche Klaviertechnik* (Leipzig, 1905; in French, Paris, 1923); *Die Grundlagen der Klaviertechnik* (Leipzig, 1906; in French, 1908; in Eng., 1909; in Russian, 1929); *Praktische Studien* (1916–21). He also publ. *Musikalische Zeit und Streitfragen* (Berlin, 1906).

Breitkopf & Härtel, important German firm of book and music publishers. As an established printing firm in Leipzig, it was bought in 1745 by **Bernhard Christoph Breitkopf** (b. Klausthal Harz, March 2, 1695; d. Leipzig, March 23, 1777). His son, **Johann Gottlob Immanuel** (b. Nov. 23, 1719; d. Jan. 28, 1794), entered the business in 1745; it was his invention which made the basis for the firm's position in the publication of music. In 1756 he devised a font with much smaller division of the musical elements, and this greatly reduced the cost of printing chords (and hence piano music). The firm soon began to issue numerous piano reductions of popular operas for amateur consumption. The earliest music publications, such as the *Berlinische Oden und Lieder* (3 vols., 1756, 1759, 1763), were made by Johann Gottlob Immanuel Breitkopf himself, and bore the imprint "Leipzig, Druckts und Verlegts Johann Gottlob Immanuel Breitkopf"; from 1765 to 1777 the firm name appears as "Bernhard Christoph Breitkopf und Sohn"; from 1777 to 1787 (after Christoph's death) Johann's name again appears alone; his 2nd son, **Christoph Gottlob** (b. Leipzig, Sept. 22, 1750; d. there, April 4, 1800), joined the firm in 1787; from 1787 to 1795 publications were issued as "im Breitkopfischen Verlage" (or Buchhandlung, or Musikhandlung); in 1795 (the year after Immanuel's death) Christoph Gottlob Breitkopf took as his partner his close friend **Gottfried Christoph Härtel** (b. Schneeberg, Jan. 27, 1763; d. Cotta, near Leipzig, July 25, 1827); since 1795 the firm has been known as Breitkopf & Härtel, although no Breitkopf has been actively associated with the firm since Christoph Gottlob's death in 1800. Härtel's tremendous energy revitalized the firm. He added a piano factory; founded the important periodical *Allgemeine musikalische Zeitung* (1798; ed., J.F. Rochlitz); introduced pewter in place of the harder copper for engraving music; used Senefelder's new lithographic process for either title pages or music where suitable; issued so-called "complete" eds. of the works of Mozart, Haydn, Clementi, and Dussek. The firm also began the practice of issuing catalogues with thematic indexes and keeping stocks of scores. From 1827 to 1835 **Florenz Härtel** was head of the firm; **Hermann Härtel** (b. Leipzig, April 27, 1803; d. there, Aug. 4, 1875) and his brother, **Raimund Härtel** (b. Leipzig, June 9, 1810; d. there, Nov. 9, 1888), together dominated the book business of Leipzig (and thus all Germany) for many years; the sons of 2 sisters of Raimund and Hermann, **Wilhelm Volkmann** (b. Halle, June 12, 1837; d. Leipzig, Dec. 24, 1896) and **Dr. Oskar von Hase** (b. Jena, Sept. 15, 1846; d. Leipzig, Jan. 26, 1921), succeeded them. After Wilhelm Volkmann's death, his son, **Dr. Ludwig Volkmann** (1870–1947), headed the firm jointly with von Hase; von Hase's son **Hermann** (1880–1945) entered the firm in 1904 and was a co-partner from 1910 to 1914. Hermann von Hase publ. essays tracing the relation of J. Haydn, C.P.E. Bach, and J.A. Hiller to the firm; in 1915 he became a partner in the book business of K.F. Koehler. His brother **Dr. Hellmuth von Hase** (b. Jan. 30, 1891; d. Wiesbaden, Oct. 18, 1979) became director of the firm in 1919. The old house was destroyed during the air bombardment of Dec. 4, 1943; it was rebuilt after the war. In 1950 Dr. von Hase moved to Wiesbaden, where he established an independent business, reclaiming the rights for the firm in West Germany. Important enterprises of the firm throughout its existence were eds. of Bach, Beethoven, Berlioz, Brahms, Chopin, Gluck, Grétry, Handel, Haydn, Lassus, Liszt, Mendelssohn, Mozart, Palestrina, Schein, Schubert, Schumann, Schütz, Victoria, and Wagner. The German government supported the publication by Breitkopf & Härtel of the 2 series of Denkmäler Deutscher Tonkunst (1892–1931 and 1900–1931). Other publications of the firm are *Der Bär,* yearbook (since 1924); *Katalog des Archivs von Breitkopf und Härtel,* ed. by Dr. F.W. Hitzig (2 vols., 1925–26); *Allgemeine musikalische Zeitung* (weekly; 1798–1848 and 1863–65); *Monatshefte für Musikgeschichte* (1869–1905); *Mitteilungen des Hauses Breitkopf und Härtel* (1876–1940; resumed in 1950); *Vierteljahrsschrift für Musikwissenschaft* (1869–1906); *Zeitschrift der Internationalen Musikgesellschaft* (monthly; Oct. 1899–Sept. 1914); *Sammelbände der Internationalen Musikgesellschaft* (quarterly; 1899–1914); *Korrespondenzblatt des Evangelischen Kirchengesangvereins für Deutschland* (monthly; 1886–1922); *Zeitschrift für Musikwissenschaft* (monthly; 1919–35); *Archiv für Musikforschung* (1936–43).

Bibl.: B. Brook, ed., *The B. Thematic Catalogue . . . 1762–1787* (N.Y., 1966); R. Elvers, ed., *B. & H. 1719–1969. Ein historischer Überblick zum Jubiläum* (Wiesbaden, 1968); I. Hempel, ed., *Pasticcio auf das 250jahrige Bestehen des Verlages B. & H.* (Leipzig, 1968); O. von Hase, *B. & H. Gedenkschrift und Arbeitsbericht* (3 vols.: I, 1542–1827; II, 1828–1918; III, 1918–68; Wiesbaden, 1968); R. Elvers, "B. & H.s Verlagsarchiv," *Fontes Artis Musicae* (Jan.–Aug. 1970).

Brel, Jacques, Belgian-born French singer and songwriter; b. Brussels, April 8, 1929; d. Paris, Oct. 9, 1978. He rose to fame in France in the 1950s as a singer and writer of popular songs, which emphasized such themes as unrequited love, loneliness, death, and war. In 1967 he quit the concert stage and turned to the theater, as a producer, director, and actor. In 1968 the composer Mort Shuman brought Brel's songs to Broadway in his musical *Jacques Brel Is Alive and Well and Living in Paris.* The title proved ironic; stricken with cancer, Brel abandoned his career in 1974 and made his home in the Marquesas Islands; in 1977 he returned to Paris to record his final album, *Brel.*

BIBL.: J. Lorcey and J. Monserrat, *J. B.* (Paris, 1984); O. Todd, *J. B., Une Vie* (Paris, 1984).

Brelet, Gisèle, French musicologist and pianist; b. Fontenay-le-Comte, Vendée, March 6, 1915; d. Sèvres, June 21, 1973. She studied piano at the Nantes Cons. and at the Paris Cons.; also took courses in biology and philosophy at the Sorbonne (Ph.D., 1949). In 1950 she became director of the Bibliothèque Internationale de Musicologie. She wrote the important studies *Esthétique et création musicale* (Paris, 1947); *Le Temps musical* (Paris, 1949); and *L'Interprétation créatrice* (Paris, 1951).

Brema, Marie (real name, **Minny Fehrman**), English mezzo-soprano of German-American parentage; b. Liverpool, Feb. 28, 1856; d. Manchester, March 22, 1925. She studied singing with Georg Henschel; made her concert debut in London performing Schubert's *Ganymed* on Feb. 21, 1891, under the name of **Bremer** (her father being a native of Bremen). In 1894 she sang at the Bayreuth Festival, the 1st English singer to be so honored. On Nov. 27, 1895, she appeared as Brangäne in *Tristan und Isolde* at the Metropolitan Opera in N.Y., and remained on its roster through the 1895–96 season. Returning to England, she taught singing at the Royal Manchester College of Music.

Brémond, François, French horn player and pedagogue; b. Nîmes, Nov. 1, 1844; d. Houilles, near Paris, July 15, 1925. He studied at the Paris Cons. with J.-B. Mohr, winning a premier prix in 1869. From 1878 to 1888 he was principal horn of the Société des Concerts du Conservatoire in Paris; was also principal horn of the orch. at the Opéra-Comique. In 1891 he joined the faculty of the Paris Cons. He preferred to play the natural horn; in later years took up the valve horn as well.

Brendel, Alfred, eminent Austrian pianist; b. Wiesenberg, Moravia, Jan. 5, 1931. His principal teacher was Edwin Fischer; he also took some piano lessons with Paul Baumgartner, and later with Eduard Steuermann; he studied composition with Michl. He made his concert debut in Graz in 1948; then began a successful career in Europe. He played for the 1st time in America in 1963; also toured in South America, Japan, and Australia. He is particularly distinguished as an interpreter of the Vienna classics; but he also included in his active repertoire Schoenberg's difficult Piano Concerto. In May 1983 he presented in N.Y. a cycle of 7 concerts of the complete piano sonatas of Beethoven. In 1989 he received an honorary knighthood from Queen Elizabeth II of England. He publ. *Musical Thoughts and Afterthoughts* (London, 1976; 2nd ed., 1982).
BIBL.: P. Moor, "A. B.," *Musical America* (May 1988).

Brendel, (Karl) Franz, German writer on music; b. Stolberg, Nov. 26, 1811; d. Leipzig, Nov. 25, 1868. He was educated at the univs. of Leipzig and Berlin; studied piano with Wieck and through him entered the Schumann circle; ed. Schumann's periodical *Neue Zeitschrift für Musik* from 1845 until his death in 1868; also was co-editor, with R. Pohl, of the monthly *Anregungen für Kunst*. In 1846 he joined the faculty of the Leipzig Cons.; was also one of the founders, in 1861, of the Allgemeiner Deutscher Musikverein. In his articles he boldly championed the cause of the new German music, as symbolized by the works of Wagner and Liszt. He publ. a successful general music history, *Geschichte der Musik in Italien, Deutschland und Frankreich von den ersten christlichen Zeiten bis auf die Gegenwart* (1852; 7th ed., edited by Kienzl, 1888; new augmented ed., edited by R. Hövker, 1902, and reissued in 1906); also publ. a treatise commenting on "the music of the future," *Die Musik der Gegenwart und die Gesamtkunst der Zukunft* (1854), and other similar publications dealing with new developments in German music.

Brendel, Wolfgang, German baritone; b. Munich, Oct. 20, 1947. He joined the Bavarian State Opera in Munich in 1971, and became Kammersänger there in 1977. On Nov. 20, 1975, he made his Metropolitan Opera debut in N.Y. as Count Almaviva in *Le nozze di Figaro*; then appeared at the San Francisco Opera as Rodrigo in *Don Carlo* (1979), at Milan's La Scala as Count Almaviva (1981), at the Chicago Lyric Opera as Miller in *Luisa Miller* (1982), and at the Bayreuth Festival as Wolfram in *Tannhäuser* (1985). He made his debut at London's Covent Garden as Conte Di Luna in *Il Trovatore* on Oct. 12, 1985. He appeared in opera centers throughout Europe and the U.S.; his most noted roles include Rossini's Figaro, Papageno, Eugene Onegin, Amfortas, Silvio, and Pelléas.

Brendler, (Frans Fredric) Eduard, German-born Swedish flutist and composer; b. Dresden, Nov. 4, 1800; d. Stockholm, Aug. 16, 1831. He made his debut as a flutist in Stockholm when he was 10; later pursued a commercial career while continuing his interest in music. In 1823 he became a flutist in the Harmonisk Sällskap orch. His works include instrumental and choral pieces. His opera, *Ryno,* was completed by Prince Oscar in 1832 and was 1st performed at the Royal Opera in 1834. His early death was regretted by his admirers in Sweden.

Brenet, Michel (real name, **Antoinette Christine Marie Bobillier**), French musicologist; b. Lunéville, April 12, 1858; d. Paris, Nov. 4, 1918. After living in Strasbourg and Metz, she made her home in Paris from 1871.
WRITINGS: *Histoire de la symphonie à orchestre depuis ses origines jusqu'à Beethoven* (1882); *Grétry, Sa vie et ses œuvres* (1884); *Deux Pages de la vie de Berlioz* (1889); *Jean d'Okeghem* (1893); *La Musique dans les processions* (1896); *Sébastien de Brossard* (1896); *La Musique dans les couvents de femmes* (1898); *Claude Goudimel* (1898); *Notes sur l'histoire du luth en France* (1899); *Les Concerts en France sous l'ancien régime* (1900); *Additions inédites de Dom Jumilhac à son traité* (1902); *La Jeunesse de Rameau* (1903); *Palestrina* (1906; 3rd ed., 1910); *La Plus Ancienne Méthode française de musique* (1907); *Haydn* (1909; in Eng., 1926); *Les Musiciens de la Sainte-Chapelle: Documents inédits* (1910); *Musique et musiciens de la vieille France* (1911); *Handel* (1912); *La Musique militaire* (1917); *Dictionnaire pratique et historique de la musique* (posthumous; completed by A. Gastoué, Paris, 1926).
BIBL.: L. de La Laurencie, "M. B.," *Bulletin de la Société française de Cologne,* no. 4 (1919).

Brent, Charlotte, English soprano; b. c.1735; d. London, April 10, 1802. She studied with Arne; made her operatic debut in his *Eliza* at the Smock Alley Theatre in Dublin on Nov. 29, 1755; then sang at London's Drury Lane Theatre and at Covent Garden. She was noted for her performances of Polly in the *Beggar's Opera* and for corresponding roles in Handel's operas.

Brenta, Gaston, Belgian composer; b. Brussels, June 10, 1902; d. there, May 30, 1969. He studied music theory with Paul Gilson; in 1925, he and 7 other pupils of Gilson formed the Belgian "Groupe des Synthétistes," advocating a more modern approach to composition. From 1931 he was associated with the Belgian Radio; from 1953 to 1967 he was music director of the French Services there. His music follows the traditions of cosmopolitan romanticism, with exotic undertones.
WORKS: Opera, *Le Khâdi dupé* (Brussels, Dec. 16, 1929); 2 radio dramas, *Aucassin et Nicolette* (1934) and *Heracles* (1955); 3 full ballets: *Zo'har* (1928); *Florilège de Valses* (1940); *Candide* (1955); *Le Bal chez la Lorette* (1954), which forms a part of *Les Bals de Paris,* a large ballet consisting of passages contributed by several Belgian composers; oratorio, *La Passion de Notre-Seigneur* (1949). He also wrote *Variations sur un thème congolais* for Orch. (1926); *Nocturne* for Orch. (1934); *Arioso et Moto Perpetuo* for Orch. (1940); *War Music* for Orch. (1946); Sym. (1946); *In Memoriam Paul Gilson* for Orch. (1950); *Farandole burlesque* for Orch. (1951); 2 piano concertos (1952, 1968); Concertino for Trumpet, Strings, and Timpani (1958); *Saxiana,* concertino for Saxophone, Strings, Timpani, and Piano (1962); *Airs variés pour de belles écouteuses* for Bassoon and String Orch. (1963); *Pointes sèches de la Belle Époque* for Piano and String Orch. (1964); *Matinée d'été* for Orch. (1967); *Marche barbare* for Piano (1926); *Impromptu* for Piano (1926); *Étude de concert* for Piano (1931); String Quartet (1939); *Melopée* for Violin and Piano (1945); *Le Soldat fanfaron,* suite for Quintet (1952); Concertino for 5 Winds, Double Bass, Piano, and Percussion (1963); songs; choruses.

Brescianello, Giuseppe Antonio, Italian violinist and composer; b. probably in Florence, c.1690; d. Stuttgart, Oct. 4, 1758. He became a violinist at the Munich court in 1715; in 1716 he was made music director and master of the chamber music concerts at the Stuttgart court; was named chief Kapellmeister in 1717; in 1731 he was appointed Oberkapellmeister. He composed an opera, *La Tisbe* (1717–18); 2 cantatas; various instrumental pieces.
BIBL.: J. Mitchell, *The Works of G.A. B.* (diss., Univ. of North Carolina, 1962).

Bresgen, Cesar, German composer; b. Florence (of German parents), Oct. 16, 1913; d. Salzburg, April 7, 1988. He studied music in Germany, then moved to Salzburg. In his music he cultivated the spirit of pragmatic communication for educational purposes; he wrote a number of short operas suitable for school performances and also some instrumental music, including a Concerto for Guitar and Chamber Orch. (1962), a Wind Quintet (1964), and numerous choral pieces. He also publ. a valuable collection of Austrian folk songs.
BIBL.: D. Larese, *C. B.* (Amriswil, 1968); R. Luck, *Gespräche mit C. B.* (Vienna, 1975).

Bresnick, Martin, American composer; b. N.Y., Nov. 13, 1946. He studied with Arnold Franchetti at the Hartt College of Music in Hartford, Conn., and with Leland Smith and John Chowning at Stanford Univ. (M.A., 1968; D.M.A., 1972); received a Fulbright fellowship for study in Vienna (1969–70); there he took courses in composition with Gottfried von Einem and Friedrich Cerha. He taught at the San Francisco Cons. of Music (1971–72), Stanford Univ. (1972–75), and Yale Univ. School of Music. He received N.E.A. grants (1974, 1979), held the Rome Prize fellowship (1975–76), and won 1st prize in the Premio Ancona (1980) and International Sinfonia Musicale Competition (1982).
WORKS: Trio for 2 Trumpets and Percussion (1966); String Quartet (1968); *PCOMP,* a computer composition (Vienna, April 8, 1970); *Ocean of Storms* for Orch. (1970); *Wir weben, wir weben* for String Orch. (1978); *Just Time* for Woodwind Quintet (1985); *1* for Orch. (1986); *Lady Neil's Dumpe* for Synthesizer and Computer (1987); Trio for Violin, Cello, and Piano (1988); *Pontoosuc* for Orch. (1989); also music for films, including a computer score for the film *Pour* (Prague, March 5, 1970).

Bressler, Charles, American tenor; b. Kingston, Pa., April 1, 1926. After studies with Lucia Dunham, Sergius Kagen, and Marjorie Schloss at the Juilliard School of Music in N.Y. (graduated, 1950; postgraduate diploma, 1951), he became a founding member of the N.Y. Pro Musica, with which he toured widely. He also was a founding member of the N.Y. Chamber Soloists (from 1957). He taught at various schools, including N.Y.'s Mannes College of Music (from 1966) and Manhattan School of Music (from 1978). He was best known for his performances of early music.

Bressler-Gianoli, Clotilde, Italian contralto; b. Geneva (of Italian parents), June 3, 1875; d. there, May 12, 1912. She received her primary training at the Geneva Cons.; then enrolled at the Milan Cons., where she studied singing with Sangiovanni, Giocosa, and Ronconi. She made her operatic debut at the age of 19 in Geneva in *Samson et Dalila;* later sang at La Scala in Milan, at the Opéra-Comique in Paris, and with the San Carlo Co. at New Orleans. Her best roles were Carmen and Mignon.

Bretan, Nicolae, remarkable Rumanian composer; b. Năsăud, April 6, 1887; d. Cluj, Dec. 1, 1968. He studied at the Klausenburg Cons., composition and singing with Farkas and violin with Gyémánt (1906–8); then at the Vienna Academy of Music (1908–9) and at the Magyar Királyi Zeneakademia in Budapest (1909–12) with Siklos (theory) and Szerémi (violin). His primary career was that of an opera singer, performing baritone parts at the opera houses in Bratislava, Oradea, and Cluj between 1913 and 1944, also acting as a stage director. At the same time he surprisingly asserted himself as a composer of operas and lieder in an effective veristic manner, marked by a high degree of professional expertise and considerable originality.
WORKS: One-act operas: *Luceafărul* (The Evening Star; in Rumanian; tr. by the composer into Hungarian and German; Cluj, Feb. 2, 1921); *Golem* (in Hungarian; tr. by the composer into Rumanian and German; Cluj, Dec. 23, 1924); *Eroii de la Rovine* (in Rumanian; Cluj, Jan. 24, 1935); *Horia* (in Rumanian; also tr. into German by the composer; Cluj, Jan. 24, 1937); *Arald* (in Rumanian; 1939); *Requiem;* mystery play, *An Extraordinary Seder Evening* (in Hungarian; also tr. into Eng.); *Mein Liederland,* about 230 songs to Rumanian, Hungarian, and German words.

Bretón y Hernández, Tomás, Spanish composer; b. Salamanca, Dec. 29, 1850; d. Madrid, Dec. 2, 1923. As a youth he played in restaurants and theaters; graduated from the Madrid Cons. (1872); conducted at the Madrid Opera; in 1901 joined the faculty of the Madrid Cons. A fertile composer, he contributed greatly to the revival of the zarzuela. He was at his best in the 1-act comic type (*género chico*). Among his operas and zarzuelas (all produced in Madrid) are *Los amantes de Teruel* (1889); *Juan Garín* (1892); *La Dolores* (1895); *El Domingo de Ramos* (1896); *La Verbena de la Paloma* (1894); *Raquel* (to his own libretto; Jan. 20, 1900); *El caballo del señorito* (1901); *Farinelli* (1903); *Tabaré* (1913). He also wrote an oratorio, *Apocalipsia* (Madrid, 1882), and works for Orch.: *Escenas Andaluzas; Funeral March for Alfonso XII;* Violin Concerto; etc.
BIBL.: A. Salcedo, *T. B.: Su vida y sus obras* (1924).

Brett, Philip, English-born American musicologist; b. Edwinstowe, Oct. 17, 1937. He studied at King's College, Cambridge (B.A., 1958; Mus.B., 1961), and after a brief period at the Univ. of Calif. at Berkeley, completed his training at Cambridge (Ph.D., 1965). He joined the faculty at the Univ. of Calif. at Berkeley in 1966; became a naturalized U.S. citizen in 1979. With Thurston Dart, he prepared The English Madrigalists (1956; a rev. ed. of Fellowes's The English Madrigal School); he also was general ed. of the new critical edition of the works of Byrd. His book *Peter Grimes* (Cambridge, 1983) is highly respected.

Breuer, Hans (real name, **Johann Peter Joseph**), German tenor; b. Cologne, April 27, 1868; d. Vienna, Oct. 11, 1929. He studied voice at the Cologne Cons. (1890–92); made his operatic debut in 1896 as Mime at Bayreuth, and appeared regularly there until 1914. He also sang at the Vienna Hofoper from 1900 until his death. He made his Metropolitan Opera debut in N.Y. in *The Flying Dutchman* on Jan. 6, 1900.

Breval, Jean-Baptiste Sébastien, outstanding French cellist and composer; b. Paris, Nov. 6, 1753; d. Colligis, Aisne, March 18, 1823. He studied cello with Jean-Baptiste Cupis; made his debut in 1778 at a Concert Spirituel performing one of his own sonatas; subsequently was a member of its orch. (1781–91); then played in the orch. of the Théâtre Feydeau (1791–1800). He composed a great quantity of instrumental music, including syms., cello concertos, string quartets, trios, duos, and sonatas. He also wrote an opéra-comique, *Ines et Leonore, ou La Sœur jalouse,* performed in Versailles on Nov. 14, 1788.

Bréval, Lucienne (real name, **Berthe Agnes Lisette Schilling**), Swiss-born French soprano; b. Männedorf, Nov. 4, 1869; d. Paris, Aug. 15, 1935. She studied piano at the Lausanne Cons. and the Geneva Cons. and voice with Wartot at the Paris Cons., making her operatic debut at the Paris Opéra as Selika in *L'Africaine* on Jan. 20, 1892; she subsequently was a principal singer there for 25 years. In 1899 she sang at London's Covent Garden, and on Jan. 16, 1901, made her Metropolitan Opera debut in N.Y. as Chimène in *Le Cid,* remaining on the company's roster until 1902. She excelled in the French repertoire.

Brevik, Tor, Norwegian composer; b. Oslo, Jan. 22, 1932. He studied violin, viola, and music theory at the Cons. in Oslo, and in Sweden. He founded the Youth Chamber Orch.

in Oslo (1958); was active as a music critic. He wrote an opera, *Da kongen kom til Spilliputt* (1973); *Adagio and Fugue* for String Orch. (1958); *Overture* (1958); Serenade for Strings (1959); Chaconne for Orch. (1960); Concertino for Clarinets and Strings (1961); *Music* for Solo Violin (1963); *Canto elegiaco* for Orch. (1964); *Contrasts*, chamber ballet (1964); *Elegy* for Soprano, Viola, Double Bass, and Percussion (1964); Divertimento for Wind Quintet (1964); *Adagio religioso* for Solo Horn (1967); String Quartet (1967); Chamber Concerto for Strings (1967); *Music* for 4 Strings (1968); *Intrada* for Orch. (1969); *Romance* for Violin, and Orch. or Piano (1972); *Andante cantabile* for Violin and Strings (1975); *Fredens lys* (Light of Peace) for Soli, Chorus, and String Quartet or Orch. (1980); Viola Concerto (1982); choruses; songs.

Bréville, Pierre (-Onfroy de), French composer; b. Bar-le-Duc, Feb. 21, 1861; d. Paris, Sept. 24, 1949. He studied at the Paris Cons. with Théodore Dubois (1880–82) and later with César Franck. He was a prof. of counterpoint at the Schola Cantorum from 1898 to 1902; was active also as a music critic. He completed (with Vincent d'Indy and others) Franck's unfinished opera *Ghiselle;* in his own music he followed the traditions of French Romanticism. His opera, *Eros Vainqueur*, was produced in Brussels on March 7, 1910; he also wrote an overture to Maeterlinck's play *La Princesse Maleine*, and to his *Les Sept Princesses;* also composed the orch. suites *Nuit de décembre* and *Stamboul*, as well as numerous choral pieces.

Brewer, Sir (Alfred) Herbert, English organist and composer; b. Gloucester, June 21, 1865; d. there, March 1, 1928. He studied at the Royal College of Music with Parratt, Stanford, and Bridge; became organist of several churches, and director of musical societies. His compositions include many sacred cantatas (*Emmaus, The Holy Innocents, A Song of Eden*, etc.), which were performed at festivals in Gloucester, Worcester, Hereford, Cardiff, and Leeds; patriotic odes, such as *England, My England;* organ pieces; songs; etc. He was knighted in 1926.

Bibl.: A.H. Brewer, *Memories of Choirs and Cloisters* (London, 1931).

Brewster, W(illiam) Herbert, Sr., black American gospel songwriter; b. Somerville, Tenn., July 2, 1899; d. Memphis, Oct. 14, 1987. He had a fine baritone voice and served as an evangelist in a Baptist church in Memphis. He also acquired a reputation as a writer of religious songs. His chant *Surely God Is Able* was probably the 1st composition in gospel-singing usage to employ triple meter within the time signature of 12/8. Some of his moralistic songs, such as *How I Got Over*, sold over a million copies.

Brian, Havergal, English composer of extraordinary fecundity and longevity; b. Dresden, Staffordshire, Jan. 29, 1876; d. Shoreham-by-the-Sea, Sussex, Nov. 28, 1972. He studied violin, cello, and organ with local teachers; left school at 12 to earn his living and help his father, who was a potter's turner. At the same time he taught himself elementary music theory and also learned French and German without an instructor. From 1904 to 1949 he engaged in musical journalism. He attained a reputation in England as a harmless eccentric possessed by inordinate ambitions to become a composer; he attracted supporters among English musicians, who in turn were derided as gullible admirers of a patent amateur. But Brian continued to write music in large symphonic forms; some of his works were performed, mostly by non-professional organizations; amazingly enough, he increased his productivity with age; he wrote 22 syms. after reaching the age of 80, and 7 more after the age of 90. The total number of syms. at the time of his death was 32. Finally, English musicians, critics, conductors, and concert organizations became aware of the Brian phenomenon, and performances, mostly posthumous, followed. A Havergal Brian Soc. was formed in London, and there were a few timorous attempts to further the Brian cause outside of England. The slow acceptance of Brian's music was not due to his overindulgence in dissonance. Quite the contrary

is true; Brian was not an innovator; he followed the Germanic traditions of Richard Strauss and Mahler in the spirit of unbridled grandiosity, architectural formidability, and rhapsodically quaquaversal thematicism. Brian's modernism tended to be programmatic, as in the ominous whole-tone progressions in his opera *The Tigers*, illustrating the aerial attacks on London by zeppelins during World War I. Brian's readiness to lend his MSS to anyone showing interest in his music resulted in the loss of several of his works; a few of them were retrieved after years of search.

WORKS: OPERAS: *The Tigers*, to his own libretto (1916–19; orchestrated 1928–29; the score was regarded as lost, but was recovered in 1977, and a perf. was given by the BBC Radio, London, on May 3, 1983); *Deirdre of the Sorrows*, after Synge (1947; incomplete); *Turandot*, to a German libretto after Schiller (1950–51); *The Cenci*, after Shelley (1952); *Faust*, after Goethe (1955–56); *Agamemnon*, after Aeschylus, to an English libretto (1957). **32 SYMS.:** No. 1, *The Gothic*, for Vocal Soloists, Chorus, 4 Mixed Choirs, Children's Choir, 4 Brass Bands, and Very Large Orch. (1919–27; 1st perf. in London, June 24, 1961, by amateur forces; 1st professional perf., London, Oct. 30, 1966; broadcast to the U.S. by satellite, BBC-NPR, Washington, D.C., May 25, 1980); No. 2 (1930–31; Brighton, May 19, 1973); No. 3 (1931–32; private broadcast perf., BBC studios, London, Oct. 18, 1974); No. 4, *Das Siegeslied*, a setting of Psalm 68 in the Lutheran version, for Soprano, Double Mixed Chorus, and Orch., with a German text (1932–33; Manchester, July 3, 1967); No. 5, *Wine of Summer*, for Baritone and Orch., in 1 movement (1937; London, Dec. 11, 1969); No. 6, *Sinfonia tragica*, in 1 movement (1948; London, Sept. 21, 1966); No. 7 (1948; London, March 13, 1968); No. 8, in 1 movement (1949; London, Feb. 1, 1954); No. 9 (1951; London, March 22, 1958); No. 10, in 1 movement (1953–54; London, Nov. 3, 1958); No. 11 (1954; London, Nov. 5, 1959); No. 12, in 1 movement (1957; London, Nov. 5, 1959); No. 13, in 1 movement (1959; London, May 14, 1978); No. 14, in 1 movement (1959–60; London, May 10, 1970); No. 15, in 1 movement (1960; London, May 14, 1978); No. 16, in 1 movement (1960; private broadcast perf., BBC studios, London, June 18, 1975); No. 17, in 1 movement (1960–61; London, May 14, 1978); No. 18 (1961; London, Feb. 26, 1962); No. 19 (1961; Glasgow, Dec. 31, 1976); No. 20 (1962; London, Oct. 5, 1976); No. 21 (1963; London, May 10, 1970); No. 22, *Symphonia brevis* (1964–65; London, Aug. 15, 1971); No. 23 (1965; Univ. of Illinois, Urbana, Oct. 4, 1973); No. 24, in 1 movement (1965; private broadcast perf., BBC studios, London, June 18, 1975); No. 25 (1965–66; Glasgow, Dec. 31, 1976); No. 26 (1966; Stoke-on-Trent, May 13, 1976); No. 27 (1966; London, March 18, 1979); No. 28 (1967; London, Oct. 5, 1973); No. 29 (1967; Stoke-on-Trent, Nov. 17, 1976); No. 30 (1967; London, Sept. 24, 1976); No. 31, in 1 movement (1968; London, March 18, 1979); No. 32 (1968; London, Jan. 28, 1971).

OTHER WORKS FOR ORCH.: *Tragic Prelude* (1899–1900; lost); *Burlesque Variations on an Original Theme* (1903; lost; recovered in 1974; perf. by the City of Hull Youth Orch., March 13, 1980); *For Valour*, concert overture (1904; rev. 1906); *Hero and Leander*, symphonic poem (1904–5; London, Dec. 3, 1908); 5 *English Suites*: No. 1 (1904–6); No. 2, *Night Portraits* (1915; lost); No. 3 (1919–21; lost); No. 4, *Kindergarten* (1924); No. 5, *Rustic Scenes* (1953); *Fantastic Variations on an Old Rhyme* (1907; rev. 1912; lost); *Festal Dance* (1908); *In Memoriam*, tone poem (1910); 3 *Comedy Overtures*: No. 1, *Doctor Merryheart* (1911–12); No. 2, *The Tinker's Wedding* (1948); No. 3, *The Jolly Miller* (1962); Violin Concerto in C (1934–35; London, June 20, 1969); *Elegy*, symphonic poem (1954); Cello Concerto (1964; London, Feb. 5, 1971); Concerto for Orch. (1964; Leeds College of Music, April 12, 1975); *Legend: Ave Atque Vale* (1968).

VOCAL: *Requiem* for Baritone, Chorus, and Orch. (1897; lost); *Psalm 23* for Tenor, Chorus, and Orch. (1904; reconstructed 1945; Hove, March 10, 1973); *By the Waters of Babylon* for Baritone, Chorus, and Orch. (1905; rev. 1909; lost); *Carmilhan,* dramatic ballad for Soloists, Chorus, and Orch. (1906; lost); *Let God Arise* (*Psalm* 68) for Soloists, Chorus, and Orch. (1906–7; lost); *The Vision of Cleopatra*, tragic poem for Soloists, Chorus, Semi-chorus, and Orch. (1907; Stoke-on-Trent, July 7, 1907; lost); *Pilgrimage to Kevlaar*, ballad for Chorus and Orch. (1913–14; lost); *Prometheus Unbound*, lyric drama after Shelley, for Multiple Soloists, Double Chorus, Semi-chorus, and Orch. (1937–44; lost); choruses; songs.

CHAMBER: String Quartet (1903; lost); *Legend* for Violin and Piano (1919); *Adagio e dolente* for Cello and Piano (1947; fragment only extant).

PIANO: *3 Illuminations* (1916); *Double Fugue* (1924); *Prelude and Fugue* in C minor (1924); *Prelude and Fugue* in D major and D minor (1924); *John Dowland's Fancy*, prelude (1934).

BIBL.: R. Nettel, *Ordeal by Music: The Strange Experience of H. B.* (London, 1945); L. Foreman, ed., *H. B.: A Collection of Essays* (London, 1969); M. MacDonald, *H. B.: Perspective on the Music* (London, 1972); idem, *The Symphonies of H. B.*, vol. 1 (London, 1974), vol. 2 (London, 1978), and vol. 3 (London, 1983); R. Nettel, *H. B. and His Music* (London, 1976); L. Foreman, *H. B. and the Performance of His Orchestral Music: A History and a Sourcebook* (London, 1976); K. Eastaugh, *H. B.: The Making of a Composer* (London, 1976); P. Rapoport, *Opus Est* (London, 1979).

Briard, Étienne, French type-founder who flourished in Avignon in the early 16th century. In his engraving he employed round note heads instead of the ordinary angular ones, and separate notes instead of ligatures. Peignot holds that another printer, Granjon, used these methods prior to Briard (see his *Dictionnaire de la bibliologie*, supplement, p. 140). In any case, Briard's characters are much better formed and more easily read; Schmidt's *Ottaviano Petrucci* contains a facsimile of them. The *Liber primum missarum Carpentras* (works of Eleazar Genet, called "Il Carpentrasso"), printed with them at Avignon in 1532, is in the library of the Paris Cons.

BIBL.: K. Meyer, "Music Printing, 1473–1934," *Dolphin* (N.Y., 1935).

Briccetti, Thomas, American conductor and composer; b. Mt. Kisco, N.Y., Jan, 14, 1936. He attended the Eastman School of Music in Rochester, N.Y., and the Columbia Univ. School of Fine Arts; also studied privately with Samuel Barber and Peter Mennin. In 1958 he won the Prix de Rome; also held the Ford Foundation Composer's Fellowship (1960–61). In 1963 he helped to found the St. Petersburg (Fla.) Sym.; then served as associate conductor of the Indianapolis Sym. (1968–72). In 1970 he became music director of the Fort Wayne Phil. In 1975 he was appointed music director of the Omaha Sym. Orch. and the Nebraska Sinfonia; in 1978 he initiated in Peru, Nebr., the Festival of a Thousand Oaks. From 1988 he was artistic director of the Orch. Stabile in Bergamo, Italy, and also principal conductor of the Orch. Sinfonica in Umbria. Among his works are the opera *Eurydice*; a Sym.; a Violin Concerto; an overture, *The Fountain of Youth*; a symphonic poem, *Illusions;* a String Quartet; a Flute Sonata; and several choral pieces and songs.

Brice, Carol (Lovette Hawkins), black American contralto; b. Sedalia, N.C., April 16, 1918; d. Norman, Okla., Feb. 15, 1985. She 1st attracted attention when she sang in *The Hot Mikado* at the N.Y. World's Fair (1939); she was also chosen to sing at a concert for President Roosevelt's 3rd inauguration in 1941 and was the 1st black American to win the Naumburg Award (1943). Among her many stage roles were Addie in *Regina*, Maude in *Finian's Rainbow*, Maria in *Porgy and Bess*, Queenie in *Showboat*, and Harriet Tubman in *Gentlemen, Be Seated*. She was a member of the Vienna Volksoper (1967–71), then taught at the Univ. of Oklahoma (from 1974). With her husband, the baritone Thomas Carey, she founded the Cimarron Circuit Opera Co.

Brice, Fanny (real name, **Fannie Borach**), American comedienne and singer; b. N.Y., Oct. 29, 1891; d. Los Angeles, May 29, 1951. After singing in her parents' tavern, she toured the burlesque circuit; there she was discovered by Florenz Ziegfeld, who featured her in his *Follies of 1910*. Subsequently she appeared in other eds. of the Follies, and in Broadway musicals. Her most notable film role was her self-portrayal in *The Great Ziegfeld* (1936); in the *Ziegfeld Follies of 1934*, she also created the role of little Baby Snooks, a character she continued to portray on radio from 1938 until her death. Her 3rd husband was Billy Rose, the producer and songwriter (married, 1929; divorced, 1938). Her career was the subject of the 1964 Broadway musical *Funny Girl*, which was later made into a film starring Barbra Streisand (1968).

BIBL.: N. Katkov, *The Fabulous F.* (N.Y., 1951).

Bricken, Carl Ernest, American pianist and composer; b. Shelbyville, Ky., Dec. 28, 1898; d. Sweet Briar, Va., Jan. 25, 1971. He studied piano with Alfred Cortot in Paris. Returning to America, he taught piano in N.Y., in Chicago, and at the Univ. of Wisconsin in Madison. From 1944 to 1948 he was conductor of the Seattle Sym. Orch. His compositions include a Sym. (1935) and several pieces of competent and agreeable chamber music, as well as piano pieces. In 1964 he relinquished his musical career and devoted himself to painting.

Bricktop, Ada Beatrice. See **Smith, Ada Beatrice Queen Victoria Louise Virginia.**

Brico, Antonia, Dutch-born American pianist, teacher, and conductor; b. Rotterdam, June 26, 1902; d. Denver, Aug. 3, 1989. She moved to California in 1906 and took courses at the Univ. of Calif. at Berkeley, graduating in music in 1923; she then went to Berlin, where she had the good fortune of taking conducting lessons with no less a master than Karl Muck at the State Academy of Music. She also studied advanced piano with Sigismund Stojowski. She played piano recitals in Europe, but her main interest was in conducting. Overcoming the general skepticism about feminine conductorship, she raised funds to conduct a special concert with the Berlin Phil. on Jan. 10, 1930, which aroused some curiosity in music circles. She then received a conducting engagement in Finland, which gained her a commendation from Sibelius. She later became associated with Albert Schweitzer, visiting his hospital in South Africa and receiving from him some suggestions for performing the works of Bach. In 1974 she produced a film documentary entitled simply *Antonia*, in which she eloquently pleaded for the feminist cause in music and especially in conducting. On the strength of this film she obtained some engagements, among them an appearance at the Hollywood Bowl in a program of common favorites. That proved her undoing, for even the stout defenders of her cause had to sorrowfully admit that she had no gift for conducting. After this debacle she returned to Denver, where she maintained a studio as a piano teacher.

Bridge, Frank, distinguished English composer; b. Brighton, Feb. 26, 1879; d. Eastbourne, Jan. 10, 1941. He took violin lessons from his father; entered the Royal College of Music in 1899 and studied composition with Stanford, graduating in 1904; received an Arthur Sullivan Prize and the Gold Medal of the Rajah of Tagore for "the most generally deserving pupil." He specialized in viola playing; was a member of the Joachim String Quartet in 1906 and later of the English String Quartet. He also appeared as a conductor; was in charge of the New Sym. Orch. during Marie Brema's season (1910–11) at the Savoy Theatre in London; then conducted at Covent Garden during the seasons of Raymond Roze and Beecham; he also appeared as conductor at the Promenade Concerts. With a stipend from Elizabeth Sprague Coolidge, he toured the U.S. in 1923, conducting his own works with the orchs. of Rochester, Boston, Detroit, Cleveland, and N.Y.; he revisited the U.S. in 1934 and 1938. As a composer he received a belated recognition toward the end of his life, and posthumously; although he wrote a great deal of instrumental music, his name appeared but rarely in the programs of modern music festivals. Much of his music is generated by passionate emotionalism, soaring in the harmonic realms of euphonious dissonances, while most of his chamber music maintains a classical spirit of Baroque construction. Although he was greatly impressed by the works of the 2nd Vienna School, he never embraced serial methods of composition. Most remarkable of these advanced works was his 4th String Quartet, written in 1937. Benjamin Britten, who was an ardent student and admirer of Frank Bridge, wrote his *Variations on a Theme of Frank Bridge* based on the materials of his *Idyll* No. 2 for String Quartet.

WORKS: STAGE: *The Christmas Rose,* children's opera (1919–29; London, Dec. 8, 1932, composer conducting). **ORCH.:** *Symphonic Poem* (1904); *The Hag* (1904); *Isabella,* symphonic poem (London, Oct. 3, 1907); *Dance Rhapsody* (1908); incidental music for *The 2 Hunchbacks* (London, Nov. 17, 1910, composer conducting); *The Sea,* orch. suite (London, Sept. 24, 1912); *Dance Poem* (1913); London, March 16, 1914, composer conducting); *Summer,* symphonic poem (1914; London, March 13, 1916, composer conducting); *2 Poems* (London, Jan. 1, 1917); *Lament* for String Orch., in memory of the victims of the sinking of the *Lusitania* (London, Sept. 15, 1915); Suite for Strings (1908); incidental music for Frank Stayton's play *Threads* (London, Aug. 23, 1921); *Sir Roger de Coverley* for String Orch. (London, Oct. 21, 1922); *Enter Spring* for Orch. (1926; Norwich, Oct. 27, 1927, composer conducting); *There Is a Willow Grows Aslant a Brook* (1927; London, Aug. 20, 1927); *Oration* for Cello and Orch. (1930; London, Jan. 17, 1936); *Phantasm* for Piano and Orch. (1931; London, Jan. 10, 1934); *Rebus* (1940; London, Feb. 23, 1941). **CHAMBER:** Piano Trio No. 1 (London, Nov. 14, 1900); String Quartet No. 1 (London, March 14, 1901); String Quartet No. 2 (London, Dec. 4, 1901); Piano Quartet (London, Feb. 23, 1903); *Phantasie* for String Quartet (1905); *3 Idylls* for String Quartet (London, March 8, 1907); *Phantasie* for Piano Trio (1908); *Novellettes* for String Quartet (1910); *Phantasie* for Piano Quartet (1910); Viola Duos (1912); String Sextet (1912; London, June 18, 1913); Cello Sonata (1913–17; London, July 13, 1917); String Quartet (1915); 2 old English songs, *Sally in Our Alley* and *Cherry Ripe,* for String Quartet (1916); *Sir Roger de Coverley* for String Quartet (1922; also arranged for Orch.); String Quartet No. 3 (1926–27; Vienna, Sept. 17, 1927); *Rhapsody* for String Trio (1928); Piano Trio No. 2 (1928–29; London, Nov. 4, 1929); Violin Sonata (1932); String Quartet No. 4 (1937; Pittsfield, Mass., Sept. 13, 1938); Piano Sonata (1922–25); *4 Characteristic Pieces* for Piano (1914). **VOCAL:** *Romeo and Juliet: A Prayer* for Chorus and Orch. (1916); *Blow Out, You Bugles* for Tenor and Orch. (1918); *3 Tagore Songs* (1922–25); about 100 other songs and choruses.

BIBL.: P. Pirie, *F. B.* (London, 1971); A. Payne and L. Foreman, *F. B.* (London, 1976); P. Hindmarsh, *F. B.: A Thematic Catalogue* (London, 1983); A. Payne, *F. B.: Radical and Conservative* (London, 1984).

Bridge, Sir (John) Frederick, English organist, conductor, and composer, brother of **Joseph (Cox) Bridge;** b. Oldbury, near Birmingham, Dec. 5, 1844; d. London, March 18, 1924. At the age of 14 he was apprenticed to John Hopkins, organist of Rochester Cathedral; later studied under John Goss; was principal organist at Westminster Abbey (1882–1918); took the degree of D.Mus. at Oxford in 1874 with his oratorio *Mount Moriah;* then taught harmony and organ at various music schools, including the Royal College of Music (from 1883); was conductor of the Highbury Phil. Soc. (1878–86), the Madrigal Soc., and the Royal Choral Soc. (1896–1922); also served as chairman of Trinity College of Music. He was knighted in 1897. He publ. primers on counterpoint, canon, organ accompaniment, and other subjects; also *A Course of Harmony* (with Sawyer; 1899); *Samuel Pepys, Lover of Music* (1903); an autobiography, *A Westminster Pilgrim* (1918); *12 Good Musicians from John Bull to Henry Purcell* (1920); *The Old Cryes of London* (1921); *Shakespearean Music in the Plays and Early Operas* (1923); ed. selected motets of Orlando Gibbons (1907).

WORKS: Cantatas: *Boadicea* (1880); *Rock of Ages* (1885); *Callirrhoë* (1888); *The Lobster's Garden Party, or The Selfish Shellfish* (1904); dramatic oratorio, *The Repentance of Nineveh* (Worcester, 1890); concert overture, *Morte d'Arthur* (1896); choral ballades.

Bridge, Joseph (Cox), English organist and composer, brother of **Sir (John) Frederick Bridge;** b. Rochester, Aug. 16, 1853; d. St. Albans, March 29, 1929. He studied with his brother and with John Hopkins; from 1877 to 1925 was organist of Chester Cathedral; in 1879 he revived the Chester Triennial Music Festival and became its conductor until 1900; also founded (1883) and conducted for 20 years the Chester Musical Soc.; from 1908 was a prof. of music at Durham Univ.

WORKS: Oratorio, *Daniel* (1885); cantatas: *Rudel* (1891) and *Resurgam* (1897); *Evening Service,* with Orch. (1879); *Requiem Mass* (1900); operetta, *The Belle of the Area;* Sym. (1894); String Quartet; Cello Sonata; anthems, organ music, piano pieces, songs.

Bridgetower, George (Auguste Polgreen), mulatto violinist; b. Biala, Poland, Oct. 11, 1778; d. Peckham, Surrey, Feb. 28, 1860. His father was an Abyssinian; his mother, of Polish extraction. He studied with Giornovichi; as a youth he went to England and entered the service of the Prince of Wales. In 1791, at the age of 13, he played in the violin section of the Haydn-Salomon Concerts in London. On Oct. 4, 1807, he was elected to the membership of the Royal Soc. of Musicians in London. In 1811 he received his Bachelor of Music degree from Cambridge Univ. From about 1829 to 1843 he resided mostly in Paris and Rome, eventually returning to England, where he married and settled in Surrey. His name is historically important because of his association with Beethoven; it was Bridgetower who gave the 1st performance, from MS, of the *Kreutzer Sonata,* with Beethoven himself at the piano, in Vienna on May 24, 1803. Beethoven spelled his name in a German orthography as Brischdower.

Briegel, Wolfgang Carl, German organist and composer; b. Königsberg, May 1626; d. Darmstadt, Nov. 19, 1712. The received his musical training in Nuremberg; from 1645 to 1650 he was active in Schweinfurt; in 1650 was appointed cantor at the court of Gotha; in 1671 went to Darmstadt, where he served as court Kapellmeister until his death. He dedicated himself primarily to sacred choral composition, and publ. a number of collections for the Lutheran church service, among them *Evangelische Gespräch,* in 3 parts (1660, 1662, 1681); *Geistliche Arien,* in 2 parts (1660–61); *Evangelischer Blumengarten,* in 4 parts (1666–69); *Evangelischer Palmen-Zweig* (1685); *Evangelische Harpfen* (1685); *Apostolisch Chormusik* (1697); *Letzter Schwanengesang* (1709). He also wrote instrumental works in dance forms, for instruments and voices, under such inviting Baroque titles as *Musicalisches Tafelkonfekt* (1672); a singspiel, *Das triumphierende Siegesspiel der wahren Liebe;* and other theatrical music.

BIBL.: K.F. Hirschmann, *W.C. B.* (Giessen, 1936); E. Noack, *W.C. B.: Ein Barock-Komponist in seiner Zeit* (Berlin, 1963).

Brilioth, Helge, Swedish tenor; b. Vaxjo, May 7, 1931. He was educated at the Stockholm Musikhögskolan; then took courses at the Salzburg Mozarteum. Paradoxically, he began his career as a pianist and organist; then gave recitals as a baritone. After further vocal studies he made his debut as a tenor in 1965; then sang at Bayreuth and at Herbert von Karajan's Easter Festival at Salzburg; since 1970 he has appeared regularly at Covent Garden, London. He made his American debut at the Metropolitan Opera in N.Y. as Parsifal, on Nov. 14, 1970.

Brînduş, Nicolae, Rumanian musicologist and composer; b. Bucharest, April 16, 1935. He studied at the Bucharest Cons. with Zeno Vancea, Alfred Mendelsohn, Tudor Ciortea, and Anatol Vieru; from 1969 to 1981 he was an instructor there. In his music, he experiments with novel sonorities.

WORKS: *Balada lui Pintea Viteazul* (The Ballad of Pintea the Brave) for Tenor, Chorus, and Orch. (1964); *3 Pieces for Orchestra* (1964); *Music* for Chamber Orch. (1964); Concerto for Piano, Percussion, and Orch. (1964); *Strigoii* (The Ghosts), lyric poem for Soloists, 3 Choral-Instrumental Ensembles, and Tape (1966); *Mărturie* (The Witness), cantata for Mezzo-soprano, Chorus, 2 Orch. Groups, Percussion, Organ, and Piano

(1967); *Domnişoara Hus* (Miss Hus), cantata for 3 Basses and 3 Instrumental Groups (1968); *Phtora I,* symphonic cycle for any group of Instruments over a given minimum scoring (1968); *Inscripţie* (Inscription) for Small Orch. and Tape (1969); *Match* (*Phtora II*) for 2 Percussionists, and 4 Instruments or Instrumental Groups (1969); *Cantus firmus* (*Phtora III*) for Electric Organ or Piano, and any number of different Instruments (1970); *Idéophonie, Psaume XIII* (*Phtora IV*) for 2–5 Antiphonal Groups of 5 combined Instrumentalists and Voices (1970); *Soliloque* (*Phtora V*) for Tape and Small Ensemble (1971); *Antiphonie* for a minimum of 18 String Instruments (1971); *Vos vassales les symétries* for 4 Trombones, 4 Double Basses, 4 String Quartets, 4 Wind Instruments, and 4 Choral Groups (1971); *Vagues* for Piano, Percussion, Clarinet, Violin, Viola, and Cello (1972); *La ţigănci* (At the Gypsies), opera (1978–86); *Rhythmodia I–V* for Solo Percussion (1982); Concerto for 2 Pianos, Percussion, and Orch. (1983); *Sin-Euphonia,* electronic piece (1986).

Brinsmead, John, English piano maker; b. Weare Giffard, Devon, Oct. 13, 1814; d. London, Feb. 17, 1908. He founded his firm in London in 1835. In 1863 his sons, **Thomas** and **Edgar,** were admitted to partnership; in 1900 the firm was incorporated and assumed its permanent title, John Brinsmead & Sons, Ltd. In 1868 they patented an improvement in piano construction, "Perfect Check Repeater Action." In 1908, upon the death of John Brinsmead, the controlling interest was purchased by W. Savile, a director of J.B. Cramer & Co. The Brinsmead and Cramer pianos continued to be manufactured until 1967, when the firm was sold to Kemble & Co. **Edgar Brinsmead** (d. Nov. 28, 1907) wrote a *History of the Pianoforte* (1868; rev. and ed. 1879).

Bristow, George Frederick, patriotic American composer; b. Brooklyn, N.Y., Dec. 19, 1825; d. N.Y., Dec. 13, 1898. His father, **William Richard Bristow,** a professional English musician, went to America in 1824; he gave his son primary instruction in violin playing; Bristow's other teacher was the cellist W. Musgriff; he is also said to have taken violin lessons with Ole Bull. He began his career at the age of 13 by playing in the orch. of the Olympic Theater in N.Y.; in 1843 he joined the violin section of the newly formed N.Y. Phil., and remained with the orch. for 36 years; he also conducted the Harmonic Soc. from 1851 to 1863 and the Mendelssohn Soc. from 1867 to 1871. He began to compose with a determination to prove the possibility and the necessity of forming a national American school of composition; he orated at various public occasions defending his cause. He even withdrew from the N.Y. Phil. for several months in 1854 in protest against the neglect of American music in favor of foreigners. Actually, the N.Y. Phil. frequently placed his works on its programs. He was the concertmaster of the circus orch. when P.T. Barnum took Jenny Lind to America as a special attraction. He also played in the orch. at the N.Y. concerts led by the sensational French conductor Louis Antoine Jullien, and elicited from him a statement praising Bristow's String Quartet as a "truly classical work." Unfortunately, Bristow's own ostensibly American music sounded like a feeble imitation of German models. He merits his place in the annals of American music not for the originality of his own works but for his pioneering efforts to write music on American subjects.

WORKS: Opera, *Rip Van Winkle* (N.Y., Sept. 27, 1855); unfinished opera, *Columbus* (overture perf. by the N.Y. Phil., Nov. 17, 1866); oratorios: *Praise to God* (N.Y. Harmonic Soc., March 2, 1861) and *Daniel* (N.Y., Dec. 30, 1867); cantatas: *The Great Republic* (Brooklyn Phil. Soc., May 10, 1879) and *Niagara* for Soli, Chorus, and Orch. (Manuscript Soc., Carnegie Hall, N.Y., April 11, 1898); Sym. in D minor (Jullien's concert, N.Y. Phil., March 1, 1856); Sym. in F-sharp minor (N.Y. Phil., March 26, 1859); *Arcadian Symphony* (N.Y. Phil., Feb. 14, 1874); overture, *Jibbenainosay* (Harlem Phil., N.Y., March 6, 1889); 2 string quartets; organ pieces; piano pieces; songs.

WRITINGS: *New and Improved Method for Reed or Cabinet Organ* (N.Y., 1888).

BIBL.: D. Rogers, *Nineteenth-Century Music in New York City as Reflected in the Career of G.F. B.* (diss., Univ. of Michigan, 1967); B. Kauffman, *The Choral Works of G.F. B. (1825–1898) and William H. Fry (1815–1864)* (diss., Univ. of Illinois, 1975).

Britain, Radie, American composer; b. Silverton, near Amarillo, Texas, March 17, 1903. She studied piano at the American Cons. in Chicago (B.M., 1924); then went to Germany, where she studied music theory in Munich. She excels in writing for chorus; several of her choral compositions were awarded prizes by the National Federation of Music Clubs, the National League of American Penwomen, and other organizations dedicated to the appreciation of artistic works by American women.

WORKS: *A Heroic Poem* for Orch., inspired by Lindbergh's flight to Paris in 1927 (won a prize at the Hollywood Bowl Contest; Rochester, N.Y., March 3, 1932); *Light,* dedicated to Edison (received 1st prize in the National Contest for Women Composers in 1935; Chicago, Nov. 29, 1938); *Ubiquity,* music drama (1937); *Southern Symphony* (Chicago, March 4, 1940); Fantasy for Oboe and Orch. (1941); *Cactus Rhapsody* for Orch. (1945); *Happyland,* operetta (1946); *Carillon,* short opera (1952); *The Spider and the Butterfly,* children's operetta (1953); *Radiation* for Orch. (1955); *Cowboy Rhapsody* for Orch. (1956); *Minha Terra* for Orch. (1958); *Kuthara,* chamber opera (1960); *Cosmic Mist Symphony* (1962); *Chipmunks* for Woodwinds, Harp, and Percussion (1964); 2 string quartets; several song cycles, including *Translunar Cycle,* celebrating the lunar landing of 1969, and dedicated to the National Aeronautics and Space Administration; *Ode to NASA* for Brass Quintet (1981); *Soul of the Sea* for Cello and Piano (1984).

Britten, (Edward) Benjamin, Lord Britten of Aldeburgh, one of the most remarkable composers of England; b. Lowestoft, Suffolk, Nov. 22, 1913; d. Aldeburgh, Dec. 4, 1976. He grew up in moderately prosperous circumstances; his father was an orthodontist, his mother an amateur singer. He played the piano and improvised facile tunes; many years later he used these youthful inspirations in a symphonic work which he named *Simple Symphony.* In addition to piano, he began taking viola lessons with Audrey Alston. At the age of 13 he was accepted as a pupil in composition by Frank Bridge, whose influence was decisive on Britten's development as a composer. In 1930 he entered the Royal College of Music in London, where he studied piano with Arthur Benjamin and Harold Samuel, and composition with John Ireland. He progressed rapidly; even his earliest works showed a mature mastery of technique and a fine lyrical talent of expression. His *Fantasy Quartet* for Oboe and Strings was performed at the Festival of the ISCM in Florence on April 5, 1934. He became associated with the theater and the cinema and began composing background music for films. He was in the U.S. at the outbreak of World War II; returned to England in the spring of 1942; was exempted from military service as a conscientious objector. After the war he organized the English Opera Group (1947), and in 1948 founded the Aldeburgh Festival, in collaboration with Eric Crozier and the singer Peter Pears; this festival, devoted mainly to production of short operas by English composers, became an important cultural institution in England; many of Britten's own works were performed for the 1st time at the Aldeburgh Festivals, often under his own direction; he also had productions at the Glyndebourne Festival. In his operas he observed the economic necessity of reducing the orch. contingent to 12 performers, with the piano part serving as a modern version of the Baroque *ripieno.* This economy of means made it possible for small opera groups and univ. workshops to perform Britten's works; yet he succeeded in creating a rich spectrum of instrumental colors, in an idiom ranging from simple triadic progressions, often in parallel motions, to ultrachromatic dissonant harmonies; upon occasion he applied dodecaphonic procedures, with thematic materials based on 12 different notes; however, he never employed the formal design of the 12-tone method of composition. A sui generis dodecaphonic device is illustrated by the modulatory scheme in Britten's opera *The Turn of the Screw,* in which each successive scene begins in a different key, with the totality of tonics aggregating to a series of 12 different notes. A characteristic feature in Britten's operas is the inclusion of orch. interludes, which become independent symphonic poems in an impressionistic vein related to the dramatic action of the work. The cries of seagulls in Britten's most popular and musically most striking opera, *Peter Grimes,* create a fantastic quasi-surrealistic imagery. Britten was equally successful in treating tragic subjects, as in *Peter Grimes* and *Billy Budd;* comic subjects, exemplified by his *Albert Herring;* and mystical evocation, as in *The Turn of the Screw.* He was also successful in depicting patriotic subjects, as in *Gloriana,* composed for the coronation of Queen Elizabeth II. He possessed a flair for writing music for children, in which he managed to present a degree of sophistication and artistic simplicity without condescension. Britten was an adaptable composer who could perform a given task according to the specific requirements of the occasion. He composed a "realization" of Gay's *Beggar's Opera.* He also wrote modern "parables" for church performance, and produced a contemporary counterpart of the medieval English miracle play *Noye's Fludde.* Among his other works, perhaps the most remarkable is *War Requiem,* a profound tribute to the dead of many wars. In 1952 Britten was made a Companion of Honour; in 1965 he received the Order of Merit. In June 1976 he was created a life peer of Great Britain by Queen Elizabeth II, the 1st composer to be so honored. In collaboration with Imogen Holst, Britten wrote *The Story of Music* (London, 1958) and *The Wonderful World of Music* (Garden City, N.Y., 1968; rev. ed., 1970).

WORKS: OPERAS: *Paul Bunyan,* to a text by W.H. Auden (Columbia Univ., N.Y., May 5, 1941; rev. 1974; BBC, Feb. 1, 1976; Aldeburgh, June 14, 1976); *Peter Grimes,* after a poem by Crabbe, Britten's most popular opera (London, June 7, 1945; orig. commissioned by the Koussevitzky Foundation; Tanglewood, Aug. 6, 1946, Leonard Bernstein conducting); *The Rape of Lucretia,* to a text by Ronald Duncan, after Shakespeare (Glyndebourne, July 12, 1946; Chicago, June 1, 1947); *Albert Herring,* after Maupassant (Glyndebourne, June 20, 1947, composer conducting; Tanglewood, Aug. 8, 1949); *The Beggar's Opera,* a new realization of the ballad opera by John Gay (Cambridge, May 24, 1948, composer conducting); *The Little Sweep,* or *Let's Make an Opera,* "an entertainment for young people" to a text by Eric Crozier, with optional audience participation (Aldeburgh, June 14, 1949; St. Louis, March 22, 1950); *Billy Budd,* after Melville (1st version in 4 acts; Covent Garden, Dec. 1, 1951, composer conducting; NBC, N.Y., Oct. 19, 1952; rev. version in 2 acts, 1960; BBC, Nov. 13, 1960; Covent Garden, Jan. 6, 1964, Solti conducting; Chicago, Nov. 6, 1970); *Gloriana,* on the subject of Elizabeth and Essex (1st perf. during Coronation Week, June 8, 1953, at Covent Garden, conducted by Pritchard, in the disgruntled presence of Queen Elizabeth II, who was not amused by a stage presentation of her predecessor's amorous dallyings; Cincinnati, May 8, 1956); *The Turn of the Screw,* chamber opera after Henry James (Venice, Sept. 14, 1954, composer conducting; N.Y. College of Music, March 19, 1958; Noye's Fludde, 1-act children's opera (Aldeburgh, June 18, 1958; N.Y., March 16, 1959); *A Midsummer Night's Dream,* after Shakespeare (Aldeburgh, June 11, 1960, composer conducting; San Francisco, Oct. 10, 1961); *Curlew River,* church parable (Aldeburgh, June 12, 1964, composer conducting; N.Y. Caramoor Festival, June 26, 1966); *The Burning Fiery Furnace,* church parable (Aldeburgh, June 9, 1966, composer conducting; N.Y. Caramoor Festival, June 25, 1967); *The Prodigal Son,* church parable (Aldeburgh, June 10, 1968, composer conducting; Katonah, June 29, 1969); *Owen Wingrave,* after Henry James (May 16, 1971, composer conducting; simultaneous production by the BBC and the NET Opera Theater in N.Y.; stage premiere, Covent Garden, London, May 10, 1973; Santa Fe, Aug. 9, 1973); *Death in Venice,* after Thomas Mann (Aldeburgh, June 16, 1973; Metropolitan Opera, N.Y., Oct. 18, 1974); 2 realizations of operas by Purcell: *Dido*

and Aeneas (London, May 1, 1951, composer conducting) and *The Fairy Queen,* a shortened version for concert perf. (Aldeburgh, June 25, 1967); a ballet, *The Prince of the Pagodas* (Covent Garden, Jan. 1, 1957, composer conducting).

VOCAL: *A Hymn to the Virgin,* anthem for Mixed Voices (1930; Lowestoft, Jan. 5, 1931); *A Boy Was Born,* choral variations (1933; BBC, Feb. 23, 1934; rev. 1955); *Friday Afternoons* for Children's Voices (1935); *Te Deum in C* (1935; London, Jan. 27, 1936); *Our Hunting Fathers,* symphonic cycle for High Voice and Orch. (1936; Norwich, Sept. 25, 1936, composer conducting); *On This Island,* 5 songs, to texts by W.H. Auden (1937; BBC, London, Nov. 19, 1937); *4 Cabaret Songs,* to texts by W.H. Auden (1937–39); *Ballad of Heroes* for High Voice, Chorus, and Orch. (London, April 5, 1939); *Les Illuminations* for High Voice and Strings, to poems by Rimbaud (1939; London, Jan. 30, 1940); *7 Sonnets of Michelangelo* for Tenor and Piano (1940; London, Sept. 23, 1942); *Hymn to St. Cecilia* for 5-part Chorus (London, Nov. 22, 1942); *A Ceremony of Carols* for Treble Voices and Harp (Norwich, Dec. 5, 1942); *Rejoice in the Lamb* for Chorus, Soloists, and Organ (Northampton, Sept. 21, 1943); *Serenade* for Tenor, Horn, and Strings (London, Oct. 15, 1943); *Festival Te Deum* (1944; Swindon, April 24, 1945); *The Holy Sonnets of John Donne* for High Voice and Piano (London, Nov. 22, 1945); *Canticle I, "My Beloved Is Mine"* for High Voice and Piano (Aldeburgh, Nov. 1, 1947); *A Charm of Lullabies* for Mezzo-soprano and Piano (1947; The Hague, Jan. 3, 1948); *Saint Nicolas,* cantata (Aldeburgh, June 5, 1948); *Spring Symphony* for Soloists, Chorus, and Orch. (Amsterdam, July 9, 1949; Tanglewood, Aug. 13, 1949, Koussevitzky conducting); *5 Flower Songs* for Chorus (Dartington, South Devon, April 3, 1950); *Canticle II, Abraham and Isaac* (Nottingham, Jan. 21, 1952); *Choral Dances* from *Gloriana* (1953); *Winter Words* for High Voice and Piano, to poems by Thomas Hardy (Harewood House, Leeds, Oct. 8, 1953); *Canticle III, Still Falls the Rain,* for Tenor, Horn, and Piano, to a text by Edith Sitwell (London, Jan. 28, 1955); *Songs from the Chinese* for High Voice and Guitar (1957; Aldeburgh, June 17, 1958); *Nocturne* for Tenor, Obbligato Instruments, and Strings, to English poems (Leeds, Oct. 16, 1958); *6 Hölderlin Fragments* for Voice and Piano (Schloss Wolfsgarten, Nov. 20, 1958); *Cantata accademica* for Soloists, Chorus, and Orch. (1959; Basel, July 1, 1960); *Missa Brevis in D* for Boys' Voices and Organ (London, July 22, 1959); *War Requiem,* to the texts of the Latin Requiem Mass and 9 poems of Wilfred Owen, for Soloists, Chorus, and Orch. (Coventry, May 30, 1962, composer conducting; Tanglewood, July 27, 1963); *Cantata Misericordium* for Soloists, Small Chorus, and Orch., for the centenary of the International Red Cross (Geneva, Sept. 1, 1963); *Songs and Proverbs of William Blake* for Baritone and Piano (Aldeburgh, June 24, 1965); *Voices for Today,* anthem for Chorus, for the 20th anniversary of the United Nations (triple premiere, N.Y., Paris, and London, Oct. 24, 1965); *The Poet's Echo* for High Voice and Piano, to texts by Pushkin (Moscow, Dec. 2, 1965); *The Golden Vanity,* vaudeville for Boys' Voices and Piano (1966; Aldeburgh, June 3, 1967, with the Vienna Boys' Choir); *Children's Crusade,* ballad for Children's Voices and Orch., to a text by Brecht (1968; London, May 19, 1969); *Who Are These Children?,* song cycle for Tenor and Piano (1969; Edinburgh, May 4, 1971); *Canticle IV, Journey of the Magi,* to a text by T.S. Eliot, for Tenor, Counter-tenor, Baritone, and Piano (Aldeburgh, June 26, 1971); *Canticle V, The Death of St. Narcissus* for Tenor and Harp, to a text by T.S. Eliot (1974; Schloss Elmau, Bavaria, Jan. 15, 1975); *Sacred and Profane,* 8 medieval lyrics for Chorus (Aldeburgh, Sept. 14, 1975); *A Birthday Hansel* for Voice and Harp, to poems by Robert Burns (1975; Cardiff, March 19, 1976); *Phaedra,* cantata for Mezzo-soprano and Chamber Orch. (1975; Aldeburgh, June 16, 1976); *Welcome Ode* for Children's Chorus and Orch. (1976; Ipswich, July 11, 1977); *8 British Folksongs,* arranged for Voice and Orch.; *6 French Folksongs,* arranged for Voice and Orch.; 6 vols. of British folk-song arrangements, with Piano Accompaniment (1943–61); realizations of Purcell's *Orpheus Brittanicus,* with Peter Pears; *4 chansons françaises* for High Voice and Orch. (1928; 1st perf. in concert form at Aldeburgh, June 10, 1980).

ORCH.: Sinfonietta (1932; London, Jan. 31, 1933); *Simple Symphony* (1934; Norwich, March 6, 1934, composer conducting); *Soirées musicales*, suite from Rossini (1936); *Variations on a Theme of Frank Bridge* for String Orch. (Salzburg, Aug. 27, 1937); *Mont Juic*, suite of Catalan dances, with Lennox Berkeley (1937; BBC, Jan. 8, 1938); Piano Concerto (London, Aug. 18, 1938; rev. 1945; with an added 3rd movement, Cheltenham, July 2, 1946); Violin Concerto (1939; N.Y., March 28, 1940); *Young Apollo* for Piano, String Quartet, and Strings (1939; Toronto, Aug. 27, 1939); *Canadian Carnival* (1939; BBC, June 6, 1940); *Sinfonia da Requiem* (1940; N.Y., March 29, 1941); *An American Overture* (1942); *Diversions* for Piano, Left-hand, and Orch. (1940; rev. 1954; Philadelphia, Jan. 16, 1942; Paul Wittgenstein, left-hand pianist, soloist); *Matinées musicales*, suite from Rossini (1941); *Scottish Ballad* for 2 Pianos and Orch. (Cincinnati, Nov. 28, 1941); *Prelude and Fugue* for 18 Strings (London, June 23, 1943); *4 Sea Interludes*, from *Peter Grimes* (Cheltenham, June 13, 1945); *The Young Person's Guide to the Orchestra*, variations and fugue on a theme of Purcell (Liverpool, Oct. 15, 1946); Symphonic Suite from *Gloriana* (Birmingham, Sept. 23, 1954); *Pas de six* from *The Prince of the Pagodas* (Birmingham, Sept. 26, 1957); *Cello Symphony* (1963; Moscow, March 12, 1964; Rostropovich, soloist; composer conducting); *The Building of the House*, overture for the opening of the Maltings concert hall (Aldeburgh, June 2, 1967, composer conducting); *Suite on English Folk Tunes* (1974; Aldeburgh, June 13, 1975); *Lachrymae, Reflections on a Song of John Dowland* for Viola and String Orch. (1976; Recklinghausen, May 3, 1977).

CHAMBER: *Quartettino* for String Quartet (1930; London, May 23, 1983); *Phantasy in F minor* for String Quintet (1932; July 22, 1932); *Phantasy* for Oboe and String Trio (1932; Florence, April 5, 1934); Suite for Violin and Piano (1935; London, Jan. 27, 1936); *2 Insect Pieces* for Oboe and Piano (1935; Manchester, March 7, 1979); *3 Divertimenti* for String Quartet (1936; London, Feb. 25, 1936); *Temporal Variations* for Oboe and Piano (1936; London, Dec. 15, 1936); 3 string quartets: No. 1 (1941; Los Angeles, Sept. 21, 1941); No. 2 (1945; London, Nov. 21, 1945); No. 3 (1975; Aldeburgh, Dec. 19, 1976); *Lachrymae, Reflections on a Song of John Dowland* for Viola and Piano (1950; Aldeburgh; June 20, 1950); *6 Metamorphoses, after Ovid*, for Oboe Solo (1951; Thorpress, June 14, 1951); *Alpine Suite* for 3 Recorders (1955); Sonata in C for Cello and Piano (1961; Aldeburgh, July 7, 1961); *Nocturnal, after John Dowland*, for Guitar (1963; Aldeburgh, June 12, 1964); *3 Suites* for Solo Cello: No. 1 (1964; Aldeburgh, June 27, 1965); No. 2 (1967; Aldeburgh, June 17, 1968); No. 3 (1971; Aldeburgh, Dec. 21, 1974); String Quartet in D (1931; rev. 1974; Aldeburgh, June 7, 1975); *Gemini Variations* for Flute, Violin, and Piano, 4-hands (1965; Aldeburgh, June 19, 1965); Suite for Harp (1969; Aldeburgh, June 24, 1969).

PIANO: 5 waltzes (1923–25; rev. 1969); *Holiday Diary*, suite (1934); *Sonatina romantica* (1940; Aldeburgh, June 16, 1983).

BIBL.: A whole literature has arisen about Benjamin Britten. A voluminous compendium, *B. B.: A Commentary on His Works from a Group of Specialists*, was publ. under the editorship of D. Mitchell and H. Keller (London, 1953); other publications are E.W. White, *B. B.* (London, 1948; rev. ed., 1983); *Tribute to B. B. on His 50th Birthday*, a collection of articles (London, 1963); I. Holst, *B.* (London, 1966); M. Hurd, *B. B.* (London, 1966); P. Young, *B.* (London, 1966); P. Howard, *The Operas of B. B.* (N.Y., 1969); A. Kendall, *B. B.* (1973); D. Mitchell, *B. B., 1913–1976; A Pictorial Biography* (N.Y., 1978); D. Herbert, ed., *The Operas of B. B.* (London, 1979); P. Evans, *The Music of B. B.* (London, 1979); C. Headington, *B.* (London, 1981); A. Blyth, *Remembering B.* (London, 1981); R. Duncan, *Working with B.: A Personal Memoir* (Welcombe, Devon, 1981); A. Whittall, *The Music of B. and Tippett: Studies in Themes and Techniques* (Cambridge, 1982); P. Brett, *Peter Grimes* (Cambridge, 1983); C. Palmer, ed., *The B. Companion* (London, 1984); P. Alexander, "The Process of Composition of the Li-

bretto of B.'s 'Gloriana,'" *Music & Letters* (April 1986); B. Britten, *My Brother B.* (Bourne End, 1987); S. Corse, *Opera and the Uses of Language: Mozart, Verdi, and B.* (London and Toronto, 1987); J. Evans, P. Reed, and P. Wilson, eds., *A B. Source Book* (Aldeburgh, 1987); D. Mitchell, *B. B.: Death in Venice* (Cambridge, 1987); P. Reed, *The Incidental Music of B. B.: A Study and Catalogue of His Music for Film, Theatre and Radio* (diss., Univ. of East Anglia, 1988).

Brixi, Franz (František) Xaver, Bohemian composer of church music; b. Prague, Jan. 2, 1732; d. there, Oct. 14, 1771. He was a pupil of Segert in Prague; held several positions as a church organist; became Kapellmeister at St. Vitus's Cathedral in Prague on Jan. 1, 1759. He wrote a great number of sacred works: 105 masses; 263 offertories and anthems; 6 oratorios; 3 organ concertos; etc.

BIBL.: O. Kamper, *F.X. B.* (Prague, 1926); V. Novák, "Šimon a František B. . . . ," in *Zprávy Bertramky, jubilejní výtisk ke 40. výročí založení Mosartovy obce* (1967); idem, "Zur Katalogisierung von Werken der Familie B.," *Die Musikforschung* (July/Sept. 1969).

Brkanović, Ivan, Croation composer; b. Skaljari, Bocca of Kotor, Dec. 27, 1906; d. Zagreb, Feb. 20, 1987. He studied at Zagreb, then went to Paris, where he took a course at the Schola Cantorum. Returning to Zagreb, he was active as a pedagogue and music adviser of the Opera (1951–54). His compositions make emphatic use of folk themes of the Croatian countryside, embellished with some mildly modern devices. He wrote 2 operas, *Ekvinocij* (Equinox; 1945; Zagreb, Oct. 4, 1950) and *Zlato Zadra* (The Gold of Zadar; Zagreb, April 15, 1954); a ballet, *Heloti* (1959; Zagreb, March 17, 1963); and a rather opulent variety of instrumental pieces and songs.

Broadfoot, Eleanora. See **Cisneros, Eleanora de** (née **Broadfoot**).

Broadwood & Sons, oldest keyboard instrument manufacturer in existence; established in London in 1728 by the Swiss harpsichord maker **Burkhard Tschudi** or **Shudi** (b. Schwanden, Switzerland, March 13, 1702; d. London, Aug. 19, 1773). **John Broadwood** (b. Cockburnspath, Scotland, 1732; d. London, 1812), a Scottish cabinetmaker, was Shudi's son-in-law and successor; in 1773 he began to build square pianos modeled after Zumpe's instruments; in 1780 he marketed his own square pianos, which he patented in 1783; in these, he dispensed with the old clavichord arrangement of the wrest-plank and tuning-pins and transformed the harpsichord pedals into damper and piano pedals; another important invention came in 1788, when he divided the long bridge, which until then had been continuous. Broadwood's improvements were soon adopted by other manufacturers. In 1794 the range of the keyboard was extended to 6 octaves. John Broadwood's sons, **James Shudi Broadwood** (b. London, Dec. 20, 1772; d. there, Aug. 8, 1851) and **Thomas Broadwood,** were admitted to the firm in 1795 and 1807, respectively, and the business was then carried on under the name of John Broadwood & Sons. Beethoven received a Broadwood piano in 1817. **Henry John Tschudi Broadwood** (d. Feb. 8, 1911), great-grandson of the founder, patented the so-called "barless" grand piano; he became a director of John Broadwood & Sons, Ltd., established in 1901, with W.H. Leslie as chairman. In 1925 the firm moved to new quarters in New Bond Street. Members of the Broadwood family are still active in its affairs.

BIBL.: W. Dale, *Tschudi, the Harpsichord Maker* (London, 1913); D. Wainwright, *Broadwood, by Appointment: A History* (London, 1982).

Broche, Charles, French organist and composer; b. Rouen, Feb. 20, 1752; d. there, Sept. 30, 1803. He studied with Desmazures at the Rouen Cathedral; then served as church organist in Lyons (1771–72); later went to Bologna, where he studied with Padre Martini. He returned to Rouen in 1777 and succeeded Desmazures as cathedral organist there. Among his pupils was Boieldieu. He publ. 3 piano sonatas (1782) and wrote some organ pieces.

BIBL.: G. Favre, "Un Organiste de la Cathédrale de Rouen, C. B.," *Revue de Musicologie* (1937).

Brockway, Howard A., American composer and pianist; b. Brooklyn, Nov. 22, 1870; d. N.Y., Feb. 20, 1951. He studied in Berlin (1890–95); returning to the U.S., he settled in N.Y. as a teacher and concert pianist; from 1903 to 1910 taught at the Peabody Cons. in Baltimore.

WORKS: *Sylvan Suite* for Orch. (Boston, April 6, 1901); Sym. in D (Berlin, Feb. 23, 1895; Boston, April 6, 1907, Karl Muck conducting); *Moment musical* for Violin and Piano; many character pieces for Piano (*Moods, Dance of the Sylphs*, etc.). He ed. 2 vols. of Appalachian folk songs with Loraine Wyman, which were publ. as *Lonesome Tunes* (N.Y., 1916) and *20 Kentucky Mountain Songs* (Boston, 1920).

Brod, Max, significant Czech-born writer and composer; b. Prague, May 27, 1884; d. Tel Aviv, Dec. 20, 1968. In Prague he associated himself with Kafka and other writers of the New School, and himself publ. several psychological novels. He studied music at the German Univ. in Prague and became a music critic in various Czech and German publications. In 1939 he emigrated to Tel Aviv, where he continued his literary and musical activities. Among his compositions are *Requiem Hebraicum* (1943); *2 Israeli Peasant Dances* for Piano and Small Orch. (Tel Aviv, April 24, 1947); several piano suites and 14 song cycles. He wrote an autobiography, *Streitbares Leben* (Munich, 1960); a biography of Janáček (Prague, 1924); and a book on music in Israel (Tel Aviv, 1951).

Broder, Nathan, American musicologist and editor; b. N.Y., Dec. 1, 1905; d. there, Dec. 16, 1967. He studied at the College of the City of N.Y. In 1945 he became associate ed. of the *Musical Quarterly*, a position he held until his death; from 1946 to 1952 he was lecturer in music at Columbia Univ.; from 1959 to 1962, adjunct prof. of music there. In 1956 he received a Guggenheim fellowship grant; received a Ford Foundation grant for research in 1961. From 1963 until his death he was music ed. of W.W. Norton & Co.; also in 1963–64, president of the American Musicological Soc. He publ. a monograph on Samuel Barber (N.Y., 1954); ed. Mozart's piano sonatas and fantasies (Bryn Mawr, 1956); compiled *The Collector's Bach* (Philadelphia, 1958); was co-editor (with Paul Henry Lang) of *Contemporary Music in Europe* (N.Y., 1965).

Brodie, Paul (Zion), noted Canadian saxophonist and teacher; b. Montreal, April 10, 1934. He studied saxophone with Larry Teal at the Univ. of Michigan in Ann Arbor (M.Mus., 1958) and with Marcel Mule in Paris (1959), making his N.Y. recital debut in 1960 at Town Hall. He taught briefly at the Royal Cons. of Music of Toronto (1959–60), then became founder-director of the Brodie School of Music and Drama in Toronto (1961); he was also on the faculty of the Univ. of Toronto (1968–73). In 1969 he helped to found the World Saxophone Congress.

Brodsky, Adolf, famous Russian violinist; b. Taganrog, April 2, 1851; d. Manchester, England, Jan. 22, 1929. A precocious violinist, he made his public debut at the age of 9 in Odessa; he was then sent to Vienna, where he studied with Joseph Hellmesberger, Sr., and played the 2nd violin in his string quartet. From 1866 to 1868 he was a violinist in the Vienna Court Orch.; in 1873 he returned to Moscow, where he studied with Ferdinand Laub, whom he succeeded in 1875 as prof. at the Moscow Cons. In 1881 he made a European tour, and on Dec. 4, 1881, in Vienna, gave the world premiere of Tchaikovsky's Violin Concerto, which Tchaikovsky in gratitude dedicated to him, after it had been rejected by Leopold Auer as unplayable. He was praised for his virtuosity, but Tchaikovsky's Violin Concerto was damned as badly written for the violin; the review by Eduard Hanslick, which described the music as emitting a stench, became notorious for its grossness, and caused Tchaikovsky great pain. From 1883 to 1891 Brodsky taught violin at the Leipzig Cons., and also organized a string quartet there (with Hugo Becker, Hans Sitt, and Julius Klengel), which enjoyed an international reputation. In 1891 he went to America and served as concertmaster of the N.Y. Sym. Orch. (until 1894); in 1895 he went to England, where he became concertmaster of the Halle Orch. in Manchester (1895–96); also taught violin at the Royal Manchester College of Music; in 1896 he became its principal. In England he changed the spelling of his 1st name to **Adolph.** His wife publ. *Recollections of a Russian Home* (London, 1904).

Brodsky, Vera. See **Lawrence, Vera Brodsky.**

Broekman, David, Dutch-born American conductor and composer; b. Leiden, May 13, 1899; d. N.Y., April 1, 1958. He studied music with Van Anrooy in The Hague; went to the U.S. in 1924 as music ed. for M. Witmark & Sons; then went to Hollywood, where he wrote film scores and conducted pageants and various other shows. He contributed the sound track for several motion pictures, including *All Quiet on the Western Front* and *The Phantom of the Opera;* he further wrote 2 syms. (1934, 1947) and publ. an autobiography, *The Shoestring Symphony,* exhibiting a mandatory jaundiced view of Hollywood's life-style.

Brogi, Renato, Italian composer; b. Sesto Fiorentino, Feb. 25, 1873; d. San Domenico di Fiesole, Florence, Aug. 25, 1924. He studied music in Florence; then at the Milan Cons.; won the Steiner Prize in Vienna with his opera *La prima notte* (Florence, Nov. 25, 1898). He also composed the operas *L'Oblio* (Florence, Feb. 4, 1890) and *Isabella Orsini* (Florence, April 24, 1920); the operettas *Bacco in Toscana* and *Follie Veneziane* (both produced in Florence, 1923); Violin Concerto; String Quartet; Piano Trio; songs.

Brogue, Roslyn, American composer; b. Chicago, Feb. 16, 1919; d. Beverly, Mass., Aug. 1, 1981. She studied languages at the Univ. of Chicago and music at Radcliffe College (Ph.D., 1947). In 1944 she married her private student Ervin Henning. Her music follows dodecaphonic precepts.

WORKS: Trio for Oboe, Clarinet, and Bassoon (1946); *Suite for Small Orch.* (1947); *Suite for Recorders* (1949); Piano Quartet (1949); String Quartet (1951); Trio for Violin, Clarinet, and Piano (1953); many songs with varied instrumental accompaniments.

Broman, Natanael, Swedish pianist and composer; b. Kolsva, Dec. 11, 1887; d. Stockholm, Aug. 27, 1966. He studied in Stockholm and later in Berlin. From 1925 to 1951 he was in charge of the music division of Stockholm Radio. He was highly regarded as a pianist. In his compositions he follows the neo-Romantic trend with a strong undertow of Scandinavian melos. He composed a symphonic poem, *Fritiof och Ingeborg* (1912); some violin pieces; and a number of songs.

Broman, Sten, eminent Swedish composer, conductor, and music critic; b. Uppsala, March 25, 1902; d. Lund, Oct. 29, 1983. He studied at the German Music Academy in Prague, attending a master class in violin playing with Henri Marteau; subsequently studied musicology with Curt Sachs in Berlin. From 1929 to 1951 he played the viola in various Swedish string quartets; from 1946 to 1966 was conductor of the Phil. Soc. in Malmö. He was an influential music critic; served as chairman of the Swedish section of the ISCM from 1933 to 1962. In his idiom he followed a median line of Scandinavian Romanticism, but beginning about 1960 he adopted serial techniques and later experimented with electronic sound.

WORKS: *Choral Fantasia* for Orch. (1931); *Gothic Suite* for Strings (1932); a ballet, *Malmö Dances* (1952); 9 syms.: No. 1, *Sinfonia ritmica* (Malmö, March 20, 1962); No. 2 (Stockholm, Nov. 16, 1963); No. 3 (Malmö, April 27, 1965); No. 4 (1965; Detroit, Nov. 17, 1966); No. 5, with Soprano Solo (Stockholm, April 19, 1968); No. 6, with Taped Organ Sounds (Lund, Sweden, Oct. 13, 1970); No. 7, with Electronic Sound (Stockholm, May 5, 1972); No. 8 (Stockholm, April 5, 1975); No. 9 (Swedish Radio, June 15, 1977); *Sententia crevit* for Orch. and Concrete Sound Tape (Lund, June 13, 1968); *Musica Cathedralis* for Soprano, Bass, 3 Choruses, Tape, Orch., and 2 Organs (Lund, April 4, 1973); *Overture* for Orch. (1979); *Canon* for Piano (1929); 4 string quartets (1929, 1933, 1970, 1973);

Duo for Violin and Viola (1932); 3 suites for Viola and Piano (1935, 1937, 1942); Sextet for Strings, Percussion, and Piano (1963); Septet for Percussion, Celesta, and Piano (1968); Concerto for Brass (Malmö, Nov. 11, 1971); film music.

Bronarski, Ludwik (Ryszard Marian), Polish-Swiss musicologist; b. Lemberg, April 13, 1890; d. Fribourg, Nov. 9, 1975. He traveled to Vienna, where he studied musicology with Adler and Dietz at the Univ. (1909–13), later completing his training with Peter Wagner at the Univ. of Fribourg (Ph.D., 1919, with the diss. *Die Lieder der heiligen Hildegard*; publ. in Zürich, 1922); he subsequently received a law diploma (1926). He taught at the Fribourg Cons. (1946–67); with J. Turcyński, he ed. the Paderewski edition of Chopin's works (21 vols., Warsaw, 1949–63).

WRITINGS: *Harmonika Chopina* (Warsaw, 1935); *Études sur Chopin* (2 vols., Lausanne, 1944–46; 2nd ed., 1947–48); *Chopin et l'Italie* (Lausanne, 1946); *Szkice Chopinowskie* (Chopin Sketches; Krakow, 1961).

Bronfman, Yefim, Russian-born Israeli pianist; b. Tashkent, April 10, 1958. He began his training with his mother, a piano teacher; after the family emigrated to Israel in 1973, he took up formal study at the Rubin Academy of Music in Tel Aviv. In 1976 he appeared at the Marlboro (Vt.) Music Festival; then pursued additional training with Rudolf Serkin at the Curtis Inst. of Music in Philadelphia and at the Juilliard School in N.Y. As a soloist with the Israel Phil., he toured the U.S. (1976), Australia (1978), and South America (1979); also appeared as a soloist with major U.S. and European orchs.

Bronner, Georg, German organist and composer; b. Hamburg (baptized), Feb. 17, 1667; d. there (buried), March 8, 1720. In 1688 he became sacristan at the Heilig Geist hospital in Hamburg; in 1689 he also assumed the post of organist there, remaining in both positions until 1719. A number of his sacred works are extant.

Brons, Carel, Dutch composer; b. Groningen, Jan. 1, 1931; d. Hilversum, May 16, 1983. He studied piano with Luctor Ponse, organ with Cor Batenburg, and music theory with Johan Vetter (1949–55). He worked for Radio Holland (1954–72); after 1958 was music director of the Hilversum Radio. He adopted versatile idioms in his own compositions, making occasional use of serial methods.

WORKS: ORCH.: *Varianten* (1966; orchestration of organ work); *Epitaphium* (1967); *Music for Strings* (1969); *They Are Telling Us* for 2 Harps and Chamber Orch. (1976–78); *Symphonic Fantasy* for Organ and Orch. (1980). CHAMBER: *Balletto* for Wind Quintet (1961); *Dialogs I* for Oboe and Piano (1962); *Dialogs II* for Flute and Harp (1967); 3 string quartets (1962, 1969, 1977); *Serenata I* for Solo Flute (1963); *Serenata II* for Oboe, Clarinet, and Bassoon (1964); *Serenata III* for 4 Clarinets (1974); *Mutazione* for Wind Quintet (1964); *Monologue I* for Solo Oboe (1967); *Monologue II* for Solo Flute (1967); *Monologue III* for Solo Clarinet (1968); *Monologue IV* for Solo Bassoon (1968; rev. 1974); *Monologue V* for Solo Trumpet (1970); Concertino for Clarinet, Violin, and Piano (1977); *Gentle Vision* for Flute and Piano (1978); *Threnody* for Solo Flute (1978); *Ballade '81* for Saxophone Quartet (1981); *Springtime Music* for 11 Instruments (1982–83). VOCAL: *Vox mea,* cantata for Soprano, Chorus, Instrumental Soloists, and Orch. (1974–76). PIANO: *Imaginations I–III* (1966, 1966, 1974); *Telling a Story,* Nos. 1 and 2, for young Pianists (1970, 1978). ORGAN: *Invenzione* (1963); *Reflecties* (1965); *Varianten* (1965; orchestrated 1966); *Prismen* (1967); *Astrabikon* (1968); *Cyclus* (1969); *Litany* (1971); *Reflections* for 2 Organs (1975); *Suite* (1979); *Structures in Music* (1980).

Bronsart (von Schellendorf), Hans, German pianist and composer; b. Berlin, Feb. 11, 1830; d. Munich, Nov. 3, 1913. He studied piano with Kullak in Berlin and took lessons with Liszt in Weimar. In 1857 he undertook a concert tour through Germany, France, and Russia; from 1860 to 1867 he was active as a conductor in Leipzig, Dresden, and Berlin. He was the dedicatee and 1st performer of Liszt's 2nd Piano Concerto.

In his compositions he followed the Romantic trend in Schumann's tradition. His most successful was his youthful Piano Trio, his 1st opus number (1856); some of his piano pieces retained their popularity for a brief while. He also wrote a dramatic tone poem, *Manfred,* for Chorus and Orch., to his own text (Weimar, Dec. 1, 1901); 2 programmatic syms.; and choruses. In 1861 he married **Ingeborg Starck.**

Bronsart (von Schellendorf), Ingeborg (née **Starck**), German pianist and composer; b. St. Petersburg (of Swedish parents), Aug. 24, 1840; d. Munich, June 17, 1913. She studied piano with Liszt at Weimar; in 1861 she married **Hans Bronsart (von Schellendorf).** She composed 4 operas: *König Hjarne* (Berlin, Feb. 14, 1891), *Jery und Bätely* (Weimar, April 26, 1873), *Die Sühne* (Dessau, April 11, 1909), and *Die Göttin zu Sais;* also piano concertos, piano sonatas, salon pieces, violin pieces, cello pieces, and songs.

Bronskaya, Evgenya, Russian soprano; b. St. Petersburg, Feb. 1, 1882; d. there (Leningrad), Oct. 12, 1953. She 1st studied with her mother, E. de Hacke; then in Milan with Teresa Arkel; made her operatic debut in Tiflis in 1901; subsequently sang in Kiev (1902–3) and in Moscow (1904–5). From 1907 to 1910 she joined a traveling Italian opera troupe, and performed in Italy, France, and the U.S. (Boston, Chicago, and Philadelphia). Returning to Russia, she was a member of the Maryinsky Theater in St. Petersburg (1910–23); from 1923 to 1950 she taught voice at the Leningrad Cons. She was a brilliant coloratura soprano; was particularly impressive in the roles of Lucia, Gilda, and Violetta.

Brook, Barry S(helley), eminent American musicologist; b. N.Y., Nov. 1, 1918. He studied piano privately with Mabel Asnis, then entered the Manhattan School of Music, where he was a student of Louise Culver Strunsky in piano, of Hugh Ross in conducting, and of Roger Sessions in composition. He subsequently studied at the City College of the City Univ. of N.Y. (B.S., social sciences, 1939), then took courses in musicology with Paul Henry Lang at Columbia Univ. (M.A., 1942, with the diss. *Clément Janequin*). From 1942 to 1945 he was a member of the U.S. Air Corps. Selecting as his major subject French music history, he went to Paris, where he studied at the Sorbonne (Ph.D., 1959, with the diss. *La Symphonie française dans la seconde moitié du XVIIIᵉ siècle*). In 1967 he became a prof. of music and executive officer of the Ph.D. program at the Graduate School and Univ. Center of the City Univ. of N.Y., leaving these posts in 1989 to become director of the univ.'s Center for Music Research and Documentation. He also taught at the Inst. de Musicologie at the Univ. of Paris (1967–68), the Eastman School of Music in Rochester, N.Y. (1973), the Univ. of Adelaide (1974), the Juilliard School in N.Y. (from 1977), the Centre National de la Recherche Scientifique in Paris (1983), and the Univ. of Alabama (1987). He served as ed. in chief of RILM [Répertoire International de Littérature Musicale] *Abstracts of Music Literature* (from 1966), *The Symphony 1720–1840* (61 vols., N.Y., 1979–86), and *French Opera in the 17th and 18th Centuries* (75 vols., N.Y., 1984–); with F. Degrada and H. Hucke, he was general ed. of *Giovanni Battista Pergolesi Complete Works/Opere Complete* (18 vols., N.Y., 1986–). In 1954–55 he held a Ford Foundation fellowship, in 1958–59 a Fulbright Research scholarship, and in 1961–62 and 1966–67 Guggenheim fellowships. In 1965 he became the 1st American to receive the Dent Medal of the Royal Musical Assoc. of England, in 1972 he was made a Chevalier of the Order of Arts and Letters of France, in 1978 he was awarded the Smetana Medal of Czechoslovakia, and in 1989 he became the 1st non-Scandinavian musicologist to be elected to membership in the Royal Swedish Academy of Music. He has especially distinguished himself as an authority on 17th- and 18th-century music and on musical bibliography.

WRITINGS: *La Symphonie française dans la seconde moitié du XVIIIᵉ siècle* (3 vols., Paris, 1962); *The Breitkopf Thematic Catalogue, 1762–1787* (N.Y., 1966); ed. *Musicology and the Computer; Musicology 1960–2000: A Practical Program* (N.Y.,

1970); ed., with E. Downes and S. Van Solkema, *Perspectives in Musicology: The Inaugural Lectures of the Ph.D. Program in Music at the City University of New York* (N.Y., 1972; 2nd ed., rev., 1975); *Thematic Catalogues in Music: An Annotated Bibliography* (N.Y., 1972).

Brook, Peter (Stephen Paul), noted English opera producer; b. London, March 21, 1925. He was educated at Oxford Univ.; then worked briefly at London's Covent Garden in producing opera; from 1962 he was a co-director of the Royal Shakespeare Co.; from 1970 he spent much time in Paris with his Centre International de Créations Théâtrales, where he attempted to synthesize theatrical elements in a total media art. In 1981 he produced in Paris a modernistically compressed version of *Carmen*, which he also staged in N.Y. in 1983.
    BIBL.: J. Trewin, *P. B.* (London, 1971).

Brooks, Patricia, American soprano; b. N.Y., Nov. 7, 1937. She studied at the Manhattan School of Music in N.Y.; also took dance lessons with Martha Graham. She made her operatic debut as Marianne in *Der Rosenkavalier* at the N.Y. City Opera on Oct. 12, 1960; also sang with opera companies in San Francisco, Chicago, New Orleans, Philadelphia, Houston, and Santa Fe. She made her Covent Garden debut in London in 1969. She gave an excellent account of the standard soprano roles; was especially praised as Gilda in *Rigoletto* and Lucia in *Lucia di Lammermoor.*

Broome, William Edward, Canadian organist and composer; b. Manchester, England, 1868; d. Toronto, May 10, 1932. He studied piano and organ with Dr. Roland Rogers at Bangor Cathedral in Wales (1876–90); was church organist in Bangor (1883–90); went to Canada and became an organist in Montreal (1894–1905) and Toronto. He won prizes at Welsh National Festivals for his dramatic cantata *The Siege of Cardiff Castle* (1908) and other works; publ. much church music, including *Hymn of Trust.*

Broonzy, "Big Bill" (real name, **William Lee Conley**), black American blues singer; b. Scott, Miss., June 26, 1893; d. Chicago, Aug. 14, 1958. He 1st took up the fiddle; after making his way to Chicago in 1920, he learned to play the guitar and subsequently began his career as a blues singer. He was as popular in Europe as in the U.S., making tours in 1951, 1955, and 1957.

Broqua, Alfonso, Uruguayan composer; b. Montevideo, Sept. 11, 1876; d. Paris, Nov. 24, 1946. He studied with Vincent d'Indy at the Schola Cantorum in Paris, where he settled. His works are characterized by a fine feeling for exotic material, which he presents in the brilliant manner of French modern music.
    WORKS: Opera, *Cruz del Sur* (1918); *Thelen at Nagouëy,* Inca ballet (1934); *Isabelle,* romantic ballet (1936); *Tabaré,* poetic cycle for Soli, Women's Chorus, and Piano or Orch. (1908); *Poema de las Lomas,* triptych for Piano (1912); Piano Quintet; *3 cantos del Uruguay* for Voice, Flute, and 2 Guitars (1925); *Cantos de Parana* for Voice and Guitar (1929); *Evocaciones Criollas,* 7 pieces for Guitar (1929); *3 préludes Pampéens* for Piano (1938; also in orch. version).

Brosa, Antonio, Spanish violinist; b. Canonja, Tarragona, June 27, 1894; d. Barcelona, March 26, 1979. He studied in Barcelona and Brussels; then went to London, where he founded the Brosa String Quartet in 1925; made tours of Europe and the U.S. with it until 1938; then concentrated on a career as a soloist; lived in the U.S. during World War II; returned to Europe in 1946. He gave the world premiere of Benjamin Britten's Violin Concerto in N.Y. on March 28, 1940.

Broschi, Carlo. See Farinelli.

Broschi, Riccardo, Italian composer, brother of **Carlo Broschi;** b. Naples, c.1698; d. Madrid, 1756. He studied at the Cons. di Santa Maria di Loreto in Naples; brought out several operas in Naples, in which his brother sang. He later settled in Spain with his brother.

Brosig, Moritz, German church composer; b. Fuchswinkel, Upper Silesia, Oct. 15, 1815; d. Breslau, Jan. 24, 1887. He

studied with Franz Wolf, organist at the Cathedral at Breslau, and succeeded him in 1842. He wrote 4 grand and 3 short instrumental masses; 7 books of graduals and offertories; 20 books of organ pieces; *Orgelbuch; Choralbuch; Modulationstheorie* (1865); *Harmonielehre* (1874; 4th ed., 1899, as *Handbuch der Harmonielehre und Modulation,* ed. by Thiel); also *Über die alten Kirchenkompositionen und ihre Wiedereinführung* (1880). Leuckart publ. a selection of his works in 5 vols.

Brosmann (a Sancto Hieronymo), Damasus, Moravian composer; b. Fulnek, Sept. 7, 1731; d. Přibor, Sept. 16, 1798. He studied violin and cello with Weissgräber in Fulnek; then devoted himself to the Piarist calling, serving in various capacities in Moravian towns. He wrote mostly sacred music.
    BIBL.: Č. Gardavský, *D. B. à S.H.* (diss., Univ. of Brno, 1937).

Brossard, Sébastien de, French composer; b. Dompierre, Orne (baptized), Sept. 12, 1655; d. Meaux, Aug. 10, 1730. He studied theology at Caen (1670–76); was then in Paris (1678–87); in 1687 he went to Strasbourg; in 1689 became maître de chapelle at the Strasbourg Cathedral; in 1698 received a similar post at the Cathedral of Meaux; in 1709 he became canon there. His fame rests upon the authorship of what was erroneously regarded as the earliest dictionary of musical terms; it was in fact preceded by many publications: by the medieval compilation *De musica antica et moderna* (c.1100), the last section of which is a vocabulary of musical terms (to be found in Lafage's *Essais de dipthérographie musicale,* vol. I, pp. 404–7); by Joannes Tinctoris's *Terminorum musicae diffinitorium* (c.1475); and by Janowka's *Clavis ad thesaurum magnae artis musicae* (1701); Brossard had access to none of these, however. The title of Brossard's own vol. is *Dictionnaire de musique, contenant une explication des termes grecs, latins, italiens et français les plus usités dans la musique,* etc. (Paris, 1703; 2nd ed., 1705; there is an Amsterdam reprint, marked 6th ed., but this designation is erroneous; Eng. tr. by Grassineau, 1740). Brossard also wrote *Lettre à M. Demotz sur sa nouvelle méthode d'écrire le plain-chant et la musique* (1729); a considerable variety of church music, including *Canticum Eucharisticum* on the Peace of Ryswick (1697; new ed. by F.X. Mathias); motets; etc. He brought out several vols. of *Airs sérieux et à boire.* His library of MSS was acquired by Louis XV in 1724, and formed the nucleus of the music collection of the Bibliothèque Nationale.
    BIBL.: M. Brenet, *S. d.B.* (Paris, 1896); E. Lebeau, "L'Entrée de la collection musicale de S. d.B. à la Bibliothèque du Roi," *Revue de Musicologie* (Dec. 1950).

Brosses, Charles de, French magistrate and scholar; b. Dijon, Feb. 17, 1709; d. Paris, May 7, 1777. He 1st studied law, but later turned to science and literature, subjects on which he publ. several valuable dissertations; contributed the article "Musique" to the *Encyclopédie méthodique.* He was the 1st president of the parliament of Burgundy, and a member of the Académie des Belles-Lettres (1758).
    BIBL.: H. Mamet, *Le Président C. d.B., Sa vie et ses ouvrages* (Lille, 1874); Cunisset-Carnot, "La Querelle de Voltaire et du président C. d.B.," *Revue des Deux Mondes* (Feb. 15, 1888).

Bros y Bertomeu, Juan (Joaquín Pedro Domingo), Spanish composer; b. Tortosa (baptized), May 12, 1776; d. Oviedo, March 12, 1852. He studied with Queralt in Barcelona; served as assistant maestro de capilla there at the church of S. Maria del Mar and as organist of the chapel of S. Severo. From 1806 to 1823 he was maestro de capilla at the Cathedral of León; in 1824 was named maestro de capilla at the Cathedral of Oviedo. He wrote mostly church music.
    BIBL.: G. Bourligueux, "J. B. y B. (1776–1852), un maestro de capilla de la catedral de León: Semblanza biográfica," *Archivos Leoneses,* XXV/49 (1971).

Brott, Alexander, Canadian conductor, violinist, and composer, father of **Denis** and **Boris Brott;** b. Montreal, March 14, 1915. He studied piano, violin, and composition at the McGill Cons. in Montreal (1929–34); then composition with

Bernard Wagenaar, and conducting at Juilliard in N.Y. (1934–39). In 1939 he returned to Montreal; joined the faculty at McGill Univ.; then was engaged as concertmaster and assistant conductor of the Montreal Sym. Orch. (1945–58). In his music he follows the Romantic tradition, with impressionistic harmonies imparting an aura of modernity.

Works: Ballet, *Le Corriveau* (1966); for Orch.: *Oracle* (1938); *War and Peace* (1944); *Concordia* (1946); *From Sea to Sea*, suite (1947); Concerto for Violin and Chamber Orch. (Montreal, March 7, 1950); *Delightful Delusions* (1950); *Prelude to Oblivion* for Chamber Orch. (1951); *Fancy and Folly* (1953); *Scherzo* (1954); *Analogy in Anagram* (1955); *Israel* for Chorus and Orch. (1956); *Arabesque* for Cello and Chamber Orch. (1957); *The Vision of Dry Bones* for Baritone, Piano, and Strings (1958); *3 Astral Visions* for Strings (1959); *Spheres in Orbit* (1960); *Martlet's Muse* (1962); *Circle, Triangle, 4 Squares* for String Orch. (1963); *Profundium Praedictum* for Double Bass or Viola or Cello, and String Orch. (1964); *Centennial Celebration* for Narrator, Female Chorus, and Strings (1967); *Paraphrase in Polyphony*, variants based on a recently unearthed 10-bar canon written by Beethoven in 1825 (Montreal, Nov. 3, 1967); *The Young Prometheus*, 12 preludes and fugues based on Beethoven sketches (1969); *The Emperor's New Clothes* for Narrator and Orch. (Kingston, Ontario, Feb. 21, 1971); Quintet for Recorder and String Quartet (1940); String Quartet (1941); *Critic's Corner* for String Quartet and Percussion (1950); *5 Miniatures* for 8 Players (1950); *Vignettes en caricature* for Piano (1952); *Sept for 7* for Narrator, String Trio, Clarinet, Saxophone, and Piano (1955); *3 Acts for 4 Sinners* for Saxophone Quartet (1961); *Mutual Salvation Orgy* for Brass Quintet (1962); *World Sophisticate* for Soprano, Brass Quintet, and Percussion (1962); *Berceuse* for Saxophone Quartet (1962); *3 on a Spree* for Flute, Oboe, and Harp (1963); *Mini-Minus* for Clarinet, Bassoon, Trumpet, Trombone, Violin, Double Bass, and Percussion (1968); *Spasms for 6* for 6 Percussionists (1971); *Saties-Faction* for String Quartet (1972); choral works, with piano.

Brott, Boris, Canadian conductor, son of **Alexander** and brother of **Denis Brott;** b. Montreal, March 14, 1944. He was educated at McGill Univ. and at the Cons. in Montreal. He also had instruction in conducting at various times in various places with Pierre Monteux, Igor Markevitch, and Leonard Bernstein. From 1963 to 1965 he was assistant conductor of the Toronto Sym. Orch.; then conducted the Northern Sinfonia of England (1964–68). In 1969 he became music director of the Hamilton (Ontario) Phil.; he also was chief conductor of the BBC Welsh Sym. Orch. in Cardiff (1972–77) and the CBC Sym. Orch. in Winnipeg (1976–83).

Brott, Denis, Canadian cellist, son of **Alexander** and brother of **Boris Brott;** b. Montreal, Dec. 9, 1950. He studied with Walter Joachim at the Montreal Cons. (1959–67), with Zara Nelsova in Aspen (1963–68), with Janos Starker at Indiana Univ. (1968–71), and with Gregor Piatigorsky at the Univ. of Southern Calif. (1971–75); he then completed his training with Leonard Rose in N.Y., Maurice Gendron in Paris, and André Navarra in Siena. In 1967 he won 1st prize at the Merriweather Post Competition in Washington, D.C.; then placed 1st in the Montreal Sym. Orch. Concours that same year, which led to his debut with that orch. in the Dvořák Concerto (1967). He toured widely as a soloist in North America and Europe; from 1980 he was a member of the Orford String Quartet. He taught at the Univ. of North Carolina (1975–77) and at the Royal Cons. of Music of Toronto (from 1978).

Brouillon-Lacombe, Louis. See **Lacombe, Louis.**

Brounoff, Platon, Russian conductor and composer; b. Elizavetgrad, May 10, 1863; d. N.Y., July 11, 1924. He studied at the St. Petersburg Cons. (1890) with Rimsky-Korsakov. In 1891 he went to the U.S., where he was conductor of the Modern Sym. Orch., the Russian Choral Soc., and the People's Male Chorus in N.Y. He was the author of *Ten Commandments of Piano Practice* (publ. privately, 1910).

Works: Opera, *Ramona;* music dramas *Xilona* and *Titanic; Angel,* cantata for 2 Solo Voices, Chorus, and Orch.; *The Glory of God,* oratorio; *Russia,* festival overture (N.Y., 1897); orch. suites: *Flower Garden* (1897); *Russian Village; Palestine* (1908); piano pieces; collections of Russian and Jewish folk songs.

Brouwenstijn, Gré (van Swol), Dutch soprano; b. Den Helder, Aug. 26, 1915. She studied at the Amsterdam Music Lyceum, then made her operatic debut in *Die Zauberflöte* in Amsterdam (1940); she joined the Netherlands Opera there in 1946. She made her debut at London's Covent Garden as Aida in 1951, and continued to make regular appearances there until 1964; she also sang at the Bayreuth Festivals (1954–56), Buenos Aires's Teatro Colón (1958), and the Chicago Lyric Opera (1959); she made her farewell appearance in *Fidelio* in Amsterdam in 1971. She was best known for her Verdi and Wagner roles.

Brouwer, Leo, Cuban guitarist and composer; b. Havana, March 1, 1939. He studied in the U.S. with Persichetti and Stefan Wolpe at the Juilliard School of Music in N.Y. and with Isadore Freed at Hartt College in Hartford. Returning to Cuba, he occupied various administrative posts on Havana Radio; also traveled abroad as a concert guitar player. In his own compositions he cultivated the most advanced contemporary techniques, including stylized pop art and multimedia productions.

Works: *Sonograma* for Prepared Piano (1963); *2 conceptos del tiempo* for 10 Players (1965); *Conmutaciones* for Prepared Piano and 2 Percussionists (1966); *Tropos* for Orch. (1967); *Hexahedron* for 6 Players (1969); Flute Concerto (1972); numerous guitar pieces in Cuban guitar rhythms.

Brown, A(lfred) Peter, learned American musicologist; b. Chicago, April 30, 1943. He was educated at Northwestern Univ. in Evanston, Ill. (B.M.E., 1965; M.M., 1966; Ph.D., 1970, with the diss. *The Solo and Ensemble Keyboard Sonatas of Joseph Haydn: A Study of Structure and Style*); he later pursued postdoctoral work at N.Y. Univ. (1970), and held a Guggenheim fellowship (1978–79). He joined the faculty of Indiana Univ. in Bloomington in 1974, devoting much of his research to 18th-century music.

Writings: With J. Berkenstock and C. Brown, *Joseph Haydn in Literature: A Bibliography* (Munich, 1974); *Carlo d'Ordonez (1734–1786): A Thematic Catalog* (Detroit, 1978); *Performing Haydn's The Creation: Reconstructing the Earliest Renditions* (Bloomington, Ind., 1985); *Haydn's Keyboard Music: Sources and Style* (Bloomington, Ind., 1986); with R. Griscom, *The French Music Publisher Guera of Lyon: A Dated List* (Detroit, 1987).

Brown, Clifford ("Brownie"), black American jazz trumpeter; b. Wilmington, Del., Oct. 30, 1930; d. in an automobile accident on the Pennsylvania turnpike near Bedford, Pa., June 26, 1956. He studied at Delaware State College and Maryland State College; gained experience playing in college jazz bands; later joined Tadd Dameron's group; toured Europe in 1953 with Lionel Hampton's orch.; returning to the U.S., he worked with Art Blakey; subsequently formed the Brown-Roach Quintet with Max Roach. Brown was particularly successful as a master of improvisation.

Brown, David (Clifford), English musicologist; b. Gravesend, July 8, 1929. He studied at the Univ. of Sheffield (B.A., 1951; B.Mus., 1952); then was music librarian at the Univ. of London Library, Senate House (1959–62). In 1962 he was appointed a lecturer at the Univ. of Southampton. He was awarded a Ph.D. in 1971 by the Univ. of Southampton for his book *Thomas Weelkes: A Biographical and Critical Study* (London, 1969); also wrote *John Wilbye* (London, 1974); then specialized in Russian music; publ. *Mikhail Glinka* (London, 1974) and an extended 4-vol. biography of Tchaikovsky; its merits are marred by an easy acceptance of the untenable theory that Tchaikovsky committed suicide. He contributed articles on Russian music to *The New Grove Dictionary of Music and Musicians* (1980).

Brown, Earle (Appleton, Jr.), American composer of the avant-garde; b. Lunenburg, Mass., Dec. 26, 1926. He played trumpet in school bands; then enrolled in Northeastern Univ. in Boston to study engineering; played trumpet in the U.S. Army Air Force Band; also served as a substitute trumpet player with the San Antonio Sym. in Texas. Returning to Boston, he began to study the Schillinger system of composition; also took private lessons in music theory with Rosalyn Brogue Henning. He soon adopted the most advanced types of techniques in composition, experimenting in serial methods as well as in aleatory improvisation. He was fascinated by the parallelism existing in abstract expressionism in painting, mobile sculptures, and free musical forms; to draw these contiguities together he initiated the idea of open forms, using graphic notation with visual signs in musical terms. The titles of his works give clues to their contents: *Folio* (1952–53) is a group of 6 compositions in which the performer is free to vary the duration, pitch, and rhythm; *25 Pages* (1953) is to be played by any number of pianists up to 25, reading the actual pages in any desired order, and playing the notes upside down or right side up. Further development is represented by *Available Forms I* for 18 Instruments, consisting of musical "events" happening in accordance with guiding marginal arrows. Brown made much use of magnetic tape in his works, both in open and closed forms. Apart from his creative endeavors, he had numerous lecturing engagements in Europe and the U.S. He was composer-in-residence with the Rotterdam Phil. in the Netherlands in 1947, and guest prof. at the Basel Cons. in Switzerland in 1975; also served as visiting prof. at the Univ. of Southern Calif. in Los Angeles (1978), and at Yale Univ. (1980–81; 1986–87). He was composer-in-residence at the American Academy in Rome (1987), and from 1986 to 1989 served as president of the American Music Center. He professes no *parti pris* in his approach to techniques and idioms of composition, whether dissonantly contrapuntal or serenely triadic; rather, his music represents a mobile assembly of plastic elements, in open-ended or closed forms. As a result, his usages range from astute asceticism and constrained constructivism to soaring sonorism and lush lyricism, *sine ira et studio.*

WORKS: *Perspectives* for Piano (1952); *Music* for Violin, Cello, and Piano (1952); *Folio,* a set of 3 pieces, each playable by any number of instruments and bearing titles indicating the chronology of composition: *November 1952* (subtitled *Synergy*), *December 1952,* and *1953; 25 Pages* for any number of Pianos not exceeding 25 (1953); *Octet I* for 8 Spatially Directed Magnetic Tapes (1953); *Indices* for Chamber Orch. (1954); *Pentathis* for Flute, Bass Clarinet, Trumpet, Trombone, Harp, Piano, Violin, Viola, and Celesta (1957); *Hodograph* for Flute, Piano, Celesta, Bells, Vibraphone, and Marimba (1959); *Available Forms I* for 18 Musicians (Darmstadt, Sept. 8, 1961); *Light Music* for Electric Lights and variable numbers of Instruments (1961); *Available Forms II* for 98 Musicians and 2 Conductors (1962); *Times 5* for 5 Instruments and Tapes (1963); *From Here* for 20 Musicians and 4 Optional Choruses (1963); *Corroboree* for 3 Pianos (1964); String Quartet (1965); *9 Rarebits* for Harpsichord (1965); *Chef d'orchestre/Calder Piece* for a Mobile Solo struck by Pursuing Percussionists and colliding with Other Musicians in the process (1967; 1st American perf. at the Contemporary Music Festival in Valencia, Calif., March 9, 1980); *Event: Synergy II* for Chamber Groups (1967–68); *Syntagm* for 8 Instruments (1970); *New Piece Loops* for 18 Instruments (1971); *Time Spans* for Orch. (1972); *Sign Sounds* for Chamber Ensemble (1972); *Centering* for Violin and 10 Instruments (1973); *Cross Sections and Color Fields* for Orch. (1973–75); *Patchen* for Chorus and Orch., in memory of the American surrealist poet Kenneth Patchen (1979); *Windsor Jambs* for Mezzo-soprano and Chamber Orch. (1980); *Folio II* for any number of Instruments (1981); *Sounder Rounds* for Orch. (1982; Saarbrücken, May 12, 1983); *Tracer* for Flute, Oboe, Bassoon, Violin, Cello, Double Bass, and 4-track Tape (1984; Berlin, Feb. 8, 1985).

Brown, Eddy, American violinist; b. Chicago, July 15, 1895; d. Abano Terme, Italy, June 14, 1974. He was given his 1st lessons in violin playing by his father; then was taken to Europe, and studied in Budapest with Jenö Hubay. He won a violin competition at the age of 11 playing the Mendelssohn Concerto in Budapest. He then proceeded to London, and eventually to Russia, where he became a pupil of Leopold Auer. Returning to the U.S. in 1915, he made several transcontinental tours; was a soloist with the N.Y. Phil., the Chicago Sym. Orch., the Philadelphia Orch., and the Boston Sym. Orch. In 1922 he founded the Eddy Brown String Quartet; in 1932 he became president of the Chamber Music Soc. of America, which he organized. He became active in educational programs over the radio; was music director of the Mutual Broadcasting System (1930–37) and of station WQXR in N.Y. (1936–55). From 1956 to 1971 he was artistic coordinator of the Univ. of Cincinnati College-Cons. of Music.

Brown, Howard Mayer, American musicologist; b. Los Angeles, April 13, 1930. He studied composition with Walter Piston and musicology with Otto Gombosi at Harvard Univ. (B.A., 1951; M.A., 1954; Ph.D., 1959). He held a Guggenheim fellowship in Florence (1963–64); returning to the U.S., he was a member of the faculty at Wellesley College (1958–60); in 1960 was appointed to the staff of the Univ. of Chicago; in 1967 was named prof. there; in 1970 became chairman of the music dept. From 1972 to 1974 he taught at King's College, Univ. of London; then returned to the Univ. of Chicago. He publ. *Music in the French Secular Theater, 1400–1550* (Cambridge, Mass., 1963); *Instrumental Music Printed before 1600: A Bibliography* (Cambridge, Mass., 1965); *Music in the Renaissance* (Englewood Cliffs, N.J., 1976). In 1970 he was named ed. of the compendium *Italian Opera, 1640–1770: Major Unpublished Works in a Central Baroque and Early Classical Tradition* (N.Y., 1977– ; planned in 60 vols.).

Brown, Iona, English violinist and conductor; b. Salisbury, Wiltshire, Jan. 7, 1941. She studied violin as a child; in 1955 joined the National Youth Orch. of Great Britain, remaining its member for 5 years; she also studied with Hugh Maguire in London, Remy Principe in Rome, and Henryk Szeryng in Paris and Nice. From 1963 to 1966 she played in the Philharmonia Orch. of London; in 1964 she joined the Academy of St. Martin-in-the-Fields, and served as its director in 1974. In 1980 she was named music director of the Norwegian Chamber Orch. in Oslo, and in 1987 became music director of the Los Angeles Chamber Orch. She was made an Officer of the Order of the British Empire in 1986.

Brown, James, black American gospel-soul singer; b. near Augusta, Ga., May 3, 1928. He banged on keyboards, beat drums, and plucked the string bass; then formed a group which he called The Famous Flames. In 1956 he produced a triply emphatic song, *Please, Please, Please,* which made the top of the charts. Other big-time hits were *Try Me, Prisoner of Love, It's a Man's World, Out of Sight,* and *Papa's Got a Brand New Bag.* He then formed the James Brown Revue and produced stage shows. His songs acquired a political flavor, such as his militant proclamation *Black Is Beautiful, Say It Loud, I'm Black and I'm Proud.* He cultivated vocal sex motifs in such songs as *I Got Ants in My Pants, Hot Pants, Body Heat,* and *Sex Machine.* He also made an admonitory gesture to junkies in his song *King Heroin.* At the height of his fame as a soul singer he was called "Soul Brother Number One," "Godfather of Soul," and "King of Soul."

Brown, James Duff, British music bibliographer; b. Edinburgh, Nov. 6, 1862; d. London, Feb. 14, 1914. He was librarian of the Clerkenwell Library of London from 1888; co-author (with Stratton) of the valuable reference work *British Musical Biography: A Dictionary of Musical Artists, Authors and Composers Born in Great Britain and Its Colonies* (1897). He also publ. *Biographical Dictionary of Musicians* (1886); *Guide to the Formation of a Music Library* (1893); *Characteristic Songs and Dances of All Nations,* with historical notes and a bibliography (with Moffat, 1901); and *Subject Classification* (1908). His *Manual of Library Economy* was publ. in several eds. (3rd ed., London, 1920).

Brown, John, English writer; b. Rothbury, Northumberland, Nov. 5, 1715; d. (suicide) Newcastle upon Tyne, Sept. 23, 1766. He became vicar of Great Horkesley, Essex, in 1754, and of St. Nicholas's, Newcastle, in 1758. He is the author of *Dissertation on the Rise, Union, and Power, the Progressions, Separations and Corruptions of Poetry and Music, to which is prefixed The Cure of Saul, A Sacred Ode* (London, 1763). A revised ed. was publ. in 1764 as *The History of the Rise and Progress of Poetry, through Its Several Species* (in French, Paris, 1768; in German, Leipzig, 1769; in Italian, 1772).

Brown, Les(ter Raymond), American bandleader; b. Reinerton, Pa., March 14, 1912. He studied at the Ithaca Cons. of Music; subsequently (1932–35) enrolled in Duke Univ., where he led the Duke Blue Devils band. In 1938 he organized his own band, which became quite successful in its renditions of popular music on radio, in films, and on television. His Band of Renown became closely associated with the comedian Bob Hope, and it accompanied him on many tours abroad to entertain American troops through the years of war and peace.

Brown, Maurice J(ohn) E(dwin), noted English writer on music; b. London, Aug. 3, 1906; d. Marlborough, Sept. 27, 1975. He received his education at the Univ. of London (B.Sc., 1929; B.Mus., 1939); then pursued a career as a high-school and grammar-school teacher; concurrently he devoted himself to musical research, studying various aspects of the life and works of Schubert; his *Schubert: A Critical Biography* (London, 1958; in German, 1969) is a standard source; he was also an authority on Chopin. In addition to many articles for music periodicals, he wrote *Schubert's Variations* (London, 1954); *Chopin: An Index of His Work in Chronological Order* (London, 1960); *Essays on Schubert* (London, 1966); with O.E. Deutsch, *Schubert: Die Erinnerungen seiner Freunde* (Leipzig, 1966); *Schubert Songs* (London, 1967); *Schubert Symphonies* (London, 1970).

Brown, Merton (Luther), American composer; b. Berlin, Vt., May 5, 1913. He studied both piano and violin; moved to N.Y. in 1935 and took piano lessons with Anne Hull, and studied composition privately with Wallingford Riegger (1939–42) and with Carl Ruggles (1943–45). From 1949 to 1967 he lived in Rome; then returned to America, and settled in Boston. His music is set in dissonant counterpoint of great density without negating the lyrical flow of melody. **Works:** *Consort for 4 Voices,* scored for 2 Pianos (N.Y., April 21, 1947); Piano Sonata (1948); *Chorale* for Strings (1948); *Duo in 3 Movements* for Violin and Piano (1956); *Concerto breve per archi* (Naples, Italy, Jan. 23, 1960); *Metamorfosi per piano* (1965); *Dialogo* for Cello and Piano (1970); *Concertino* for String Orch. (1974); *Divertimento* for Piano, 4-hands (1975); *5 Pieces* for Clarinet and Piano (1976); *Psalm 13* (1976).

Brown, Nacio (Ignatio) Herb, American composer of popular songs; b. Deming, N.Mex., Feb. 22, 1896; d. San Francisco, Sept. 28, 1964. He was a clothier and later a real-estate agent; learned a little about music at the Musical Arts High School in Los Angeles, where he began producing songs that seemed to be blessed with a dollar sign. Among his greatest hits were *Singin' in the Rain* (1929), made famous by Judy Garland in her movie *Little Nellie Kelly* (1940), and *Temptation,* glorified by Bing Crosby in the screen musical *Going Hollywood* (1933).

Brown, Newel Kay, American composer and pedagogue; b. Salt Lake City, Feb. 29, 1932. He studied composition with Leroy Robertson at the Univ. of Utah (B.F.A., 1953; M.F.A., 1954) and with Howard Hanson, Wayne Barlow, and Barnard Rogers at the Eastman School of Music in Rochester, N.Y. (Ph.D., 1967). From 1961 to 1967 he taught at Centenary College for Women at Hackettstown, N.J.; from 1967 to 1970 he was on the faculty of Henderson State College, Arkadelphia, Ark.; in 1970 became prof. of composition at North Texas State Univ. in Denton. As a member of the Mormon Church,

he wrote a number of choral works which entered the permanent repertoire; of these, the Mormon children's choral work *I Hope They Call Me on a Mission* (1968) was tr. into 17 languages. **Works:** Saxophone Sonata (1968); *4 Pieces* for Flute and Clarinet (1968); Suite for 2 Trumpets (1968); Trombone Sonata (1969); Woodwind Quintet (1969); *Hopkins Set* for Baritone and Trombone (1971); *Postures* for Bass Trombone and Piano (1972); *Glaser Set* for Mezzo-soprano, Trumpet, Clarinet, and Piano (1974); *Anagrams* for Trumpet, Marimba, and Percussion (1977); *Windart I* for Tuba, Soprano, and Piano (1978); *Windart II* for Euphonium, 6 Clarinets, Vibraphone, and Percussion (1980); *4 Meditations* for Bass Voice, Alto Saxophone, and Percussion (1981); numerous sacred songs and choruses.

Brown, Ray(mond Matthews), remarkable black American jazz double-bass player; b. Pittsburgh, Oct. 13, 1926. After mastering the double bass, he went to N.Y., where he worked with a number of major jazz figures, including Charlie Parker, Bud Powell, and Dizzy Gillespie. He served as Ella Fitzgerald's music director from 1948 to 1951, during which period he was also her husband, and later became widely known through his association with Oscar Peterson. He then turned to the cello and found fame with that instrument; after leaving Peterson's trio in 1966, he pursued a career as a free-lance artist.

Brown, Rayner, American organist, teacher, and composer; b. Des Moines, Iowa, Feb. 23, 1912. He studied at the Univ. of Southern Calif. (B.Mus., 1938; M.Mus., 1947); his mentors included Ingolf Dahl, Hanns Eisler, and Lucien Cailliet. He was organist at Wilshire Presbyterian Church (1941–77) and a prof. of music at Biola Univ. in La Mirada, Calif. (1950–77). **Works:** orch.: 6 syms. (1952, 1957, 1958, 1980, 1982, 1982); 7 organ concertos (1959, 1966, 1980, 1980, 1982, 1983, 1986); Concerto for Clarinet and Wind Orch. (1979); Concerto for Bass Trombone and Wind Orch. (1981); Clarinet Concerto (1984); Concerto for Violin, Harp, and Orch. (1987). **chamber:** 3 sonatas for Flute and Piano (1944, 1959, 1985); Quartet for Violin, Viola, Cello, and Piano (1947); String Quartet (1953); Tuba Quartet (1980); Sym. for Flutes (1983); Sonata for Violin and Harp (1986).

Brown, Rosemary, British musical medium; b. London, July 27, 1917. She led a middle-class life as a housewife, and liked to improvise at the piano. Possessed of a certain type of musical mimicry, she began playing passages in the manner of her favorite compositions by Mozart, Beethoven, Schubert, Chopin, or Liszt; they usually consisted of short melodies invariably accompanied by broken triads and seventh-chords. Under the influence of popular literature dealing with communication with ghosts, she became convinced that the music she played was actually dictated to her by departed composers, and willingly recited stories about their human kindness to her (Chopin warned her to turn off the leaking faucet in the bathtub to prevent flooding). On an errand to a grocery store as a small child, she was approached by a tall, gray-haired gentleman who, observing that she carried a music book, introduced himself as Franz Liszt and volunteered to teach her piano without remuneration. She had similar happy encounters with other famous composers, and soon arranged to take dictation of posthumous works from them. She appeared on British television writing down notes under the dictation of Beethoven, but Beethoven's image failed to materialize on the screen, owing no doubt to some last-moment scruples on the part of the producers. She put out a couple of maudlin, maundering, meandering pamphlets dealing with her transcendental experiences, and a professional journalist publ. the story of her contacts with dead composers. Also transmitted were some postmortem essays by Tovey, well-known for his belief in spooks.

Brown, William, flute player and composer who settled in America in the middle of the 18th century. He gave a concert on the flute in Baltimore on Jan. 30, 1784; then went to Philadelphia, where he participated in numerous benefit concerts;

in 1785 he established a series of Subscription Concerts in N.Y. and Philadelphia (with Alexander Reinagle and Henri Capron). He composed 3 *Rondos for the Pianoforte or Harpsichord* (dedicated to Francis Hopkinson). He was probably a German; may be identical with Wilhelm Braun of Kassel.

BIBL.: J.D. Apell, *Galerie der vorzüglichsten Tonkünstler und merkwürdigen Musikdilettanten in Kassel* (1806); J.T. Howard, *Our American Music* (4th ed., N.Y., 1965); C. Engel, "Introducing Mr. B.," *Musical Quarterly* (Jan. 1944).

Browne, Jackson, American folk-rock musician and songwriter; b. Heidelberg, Germany, Oct. 9, 1948. He was taken to California as a child. He sang in hootenannies before joining The Nitty Gritty Dirt Band. He reached the big time in 1969 when he opened a show with Linda Ronstadt at the Troubadour Club in Hollywood. In 1971 he got together with the versatile guitarist David Lindley, with whom he produced *Doctor, My Eyes,* which became a smash hit. Another whammy was *Jamaica, Say You Will.* His record albums *Late for the Sky* and *The Pretender* made him a small fortune. Impassioned by the earnest desire to save the world from nuclear annihilation, he joined MUSE (Musicians United for Safe Energy) in 1979 and financed the fund- and consciousness-raising concert film *No Nukes.* He was briefly jailed in 1981 during a protest to obstruct the opening of the nuclear power plant at Diablo Canyon, Calif.

Browne, John Lewis, English-American organist and composer; b. London, May 18, 1864; d. Chicago, Oct. 23, 1933. He was a pupil of his father, William Browne, a noted organist; later studied with S.P. Warren (1884) and F. Archer (1887); settling in America, he was active as an organist in San Francisco, Atlanta, Philadelphia, and Chicago; during his career he gave more than 500 organ recitals. He designed an organ for Medinah Temple in Chicago, and inaugurated it with the 1st performance of Felix Borowski's *Allegro de Concert,* commissioned for the occasion.

WORKS: Opera, *La Corsicana* (received an honorable mention in the Sonzogno Competition in 1902; 1st perf. in Chicago, Jan. 4, 1923); ode, *The Granite Walls Rise Fair* (1911); *Missa Solemnis* (1913); many songs.

Browning, John, brilliant American pianist; b. Denver, May 22, 1933. His father was a professional violinist, his mother an accomplished pianist. Browning studied with her from childhood; played a Mozart piano concerto at the age of 10, and was accepted as a student by Rosina Lhévinne, who was giving a master course in Denver at the time. The family later moved to Los Angeles, where Browning became a private student of Lee Pattison. He soon moved to N.Y., where he entered the class of Lhévinne at the Juilliard School of Music; in 1954 he received the $2,000 Steinway Centennial Award. In 1955 he won the Leventritt Award. He made his N.Y. Phil. debut in 1956; then went to Belgium to compete for the International Piano Competition sponsored by Queen Elisabeth; he won 2nd prize, after Vladimir Ashkenazy, who received 1st prize. Returning to the U.S., he developed a nonstop career of uninterrupted successes. On Sept. 24, 1962, he gave the world premiere of Samuel Barber's Piano Concerto with the Boston Sym., conducted by Erich Leinsdorf at Lincoln Center for the Performing Arts in N.Y. The work became his honorific cachet; it was modern, it was difficult to play, but he performed it, according to his own calculations, more than 400 times in the 20 years following its premiere. He has also performed virtually the entire standard repertoire of piano concertos from Beethoven to Prokofiev, 43 concertos in all. In 1965 Browning was soloist with the Cleveland Orch. on a European tour under the auspices of the State Dept.; the itinerary included the Soviet Union; so successful was he there that he was reengaged for appearances in the U.S.S.R. in 1967 and in 1970. In 1971 he played in Japan.

Brownlee, John (Donald Mackensie), American baritone; b. Geelong, Australia, Jan. 7, 1900; d. N.Y., Jan. 3, 1969. He studied singing in Paris and made his operatic debut there

in 1926; on June 8, 1926, he sang in Covent Garden in London, at the farewell appearance of Melba. He was subsequently a member of the Paris Opéra (1926–33); then joined the Metropolitan Opera in N.Y., making his debut there in *Rigoletto* on Feb. 17, 1937; he sang his last performance there on Dec. 20, 1956. He held the title of director at the Manhattan School of Music from 1956 to 1958; in 1958 was appointed its president, and held this post until his death.

Brubeck, Dave (David Warren), prominent American jazz pianist, bandleader, and composer, brother of **Howard R(engstorff) Brubeck;** b. Concord, Calif., Dec. 6, 1920. He received classical piano training from his mother, and played in local jazz groups from age 13. He also studied music at the College of the Pacific in Stockton, Calif. (1941–42), and received instruction in composition from Milhaud at Mills College in Oakland, Calif., and from Schoenberg in Los Angeles. During military service in World War II, he led a band in Europe; he then founded his own octet and trio (1949). Subsequently, in 1951, he organized the Dave Brubeck Quartet, which acquired a reputation as one of the leading jazz groups of the era. His sons Darius (b. San Francisco, June 14, 1947), a keyboard player, Chris (b. Los Angeles, March 19, 1953), a bass-guitar and bass-trombone player, and Danny (b. Oakland, May 5, 1955), a drummer, often performed with him. His works include 2 ballets, *A Maiden in the Tower* (1956) and *Points on Jazz* (1961); a musical, *The Real Ambassador* (1962); several piano concertos; 2 oratorios: *The Light in the Wilderness* (1968) and *Beloved Son* (1978); 3 cantatas: *The Gates of Justice* (1969), *Truth Is Fallen* (1971), and *La fiesta de la posada* (1975); *Festival Mass to Hope* (1980); and piano pieces.

BIBL.: *Biography of D. B.* (N.Y., 1972); I. Storb, "D. B., Komponist und Pianist," *Jazzforschung,* XIII (1981).

Brubeck, Howard R(engstorff), American composer, brother of **Dave (David Warren) Brubeck;** b. Concord, Calif., July 11, 1916. After studying with Darius Milhaud and others, he devoted himself to teaching; was chairman of the music dept. at Palomar Junior College in San Marcos, Calif. (1953–78).

WORKS: *Elizabethan Suite* for Chamber Orch. and Women's Chorus (1944); *California Suite* for Orch. (1945); *Overture to the Devil's Disciple* (1954); 4 *Dialogues* for Jazz Combo and Orch. (San Diego, Aug. 1, 1956); *The Gardens of Versailles,* suite for Orch. (1960); Woodwind Quintet (1950); choruses; piano pieces; arrangements for jazz combo and orch. on Dave Brubeck's themes.

Bruce, (Frank) Neely, American pianist, conductor, music scholar, and composer; b. Memphis, Tenn., Jan. 21, 1944. He studied piano with Roy McAllister at the Univ. of Alabama (B.M., 1965); then was a pupil in piano (M.M., 1966) of Soulima Stravinsky and in composition (D.M.A., 1971) of Ben Johnston at the Univ. of Illinois. In 1974 he joined the faculty at Wesleyan Univ., where he also conducted the Wesleyan Singers. In 1977 he founded the American Music/Theatre Group, an ensemble devoted to the performance of American music from all eras.

WORKS: STAGE: *Pyramus and Thisbe,* chamber opera (1964–65); *The Trials of Psyche,* opera (1970–71); *Americana, or, A New Tale of the Genii,* opera (1978–83); incidental music to plays and films; dance scores. **ORCH.:** *Quodlibet on Christmas Tunes* for Chamber Orch. (1963); Concerto for Percussion and Orch. (1967); Concerto for Violin and Chamber Orch. (1974); *Atmo-Rag* for Chamber Orch. (1987); *Santa Ynez Waltz* for Chamber Orch. (1989); *Orion Rising* (1988–90). **SOLO PIANO:** *Variations on a Polonaise* (1969); 6 sonatas; *Introduction and Variations* (1978); *Furniture Music in the Form of 50 Rag Licks* (1980); 6 nocturnes; *Siagi Tamu Tango, or, Tango Rue Jardin* (1984); *Homage to Charlie* (1985). **ORGAN:** *Variations and Interludes* (1968); *Homage to Maurice* (1986). **HARPSICHORD:** *A Book of Pieces for the Harpsichord* (1968–85). **CHAMBER:** *A Feast of Fat Things,* cantata for Soprano and 7 Instruments (1977); *Perfumes and Meanings* for 16 Solo Voices (1980); *The Dream of the Other Dreamers* for 4 Singers and

2 SPX 90s (1987); 8 *Ghosts* for 4 Singers and 4 SPX 90s (1989). **SOLO SONGS IN SETS OR CYCLES:** *Chinese Love Poems* for Soprano and Piano (1961–80); *marriage—reflections on a theme in 9 poems* for Soprano, Flute, and Piano (1980; rev. 1985); *The Blades O'Bluegrass,* songbook in 3 parts for Various Soloists and Piano (1974–84); *Neighbors: A Song Cycle in the Form of 30 Pop/Rock Songs* for 2 Lead Singers, 4 Backup Singers, 2 Keyboards, Lead Guitar, Bass Guitar, and Traps (1984–88); *Paul Goodman Settings* (1989); also choral works, an oratorio, and solo songs.

Bruch, Max (Karl August), celebrated German composer; b. Cologne, Jan. 6, 1838; d. Friedenau, near Berlin, Oct. 2, 1920. His mother, a professional singer, was his 1st teacher. He afterward studied theory with Breidenstein in Bonn; in 1852 he won a scholarship of the Mozart Foundation in Frankfurt for 4 years, and became a pupil of Ferdinand Hiller, Reinecke, and Breuning. At the age of 14, he brought out a Sym. at Cologne, and at 20 produced his 1st stage work, *Scherz, List und Rache,* adapted from Goethe's singspiel (Cologne, Jan. 14, 1858). Between 1858 and 1861 he taught music in Cologne; also made prolonged visits to Berlin, Leipzig, Dresden, and Munich; in 1863 he was in Mannheim, where he produced his 1st full-fledged opera, *Die Loreley* (April 14, 1863), to the libretto by Geibel, orig. intended for Mendelssohn. About the same time he wrote an effective choral work, *Frithjof,* which was presented with great success in various German towns, and in Vienna. From 1865 to 1867 Bruch was music director of a concert organization in Koblenz; there he wrote his 1st Violin Concerto (in G minor), which became a great favorite among violinists; then was court Kapellmeister in Sonderhausen. In 1870 he went to Berlin; his last opera, *Hermione,* based on Shakespeare's *The Winter's Tale,* was produced at the Berlin Opera on March 21, 1872. In 1880 he accepted the post of conductor of the Liverpool Phil., and remained in England for 3 years; in 1883 he visited the U.S. and conducted his choral work *Arminius* in Boston. From 1883 to 1890 he was music director of an orch. society in Breslau; in 1891 he became a prof. of composition at the Hochschule für Musik in Berlin, retiring in 1910. Bruch was married to the singer **Clara Tuczek** (d. 1919). Cambridge Univ. conferred upon him the honorary degree of D.Mus. (1893); the French Academy elected him corresponding member; in 1918 the Univ. of Berlin gave him the honorary degree of Dr.Phil.

Bruch's music, although imitative in its essence and even in its melodic and harmonic procedures, has a great eclectic charm; he was a master of harmony, counterpoint, and instrumentation; he was equally adept at handling vocal masses. He contributed a great deal to the development of the secular oratorio, using soloists, chorus, and orch. In this genre he wrote *Odysseus, Arminius, Das Lied von der Glocke,* and *Achilleus;* also *Frithjof* for Baritone, Female Chorus, and Orch.; *Normannenzug* for Baritone, Male Chorus, and Orch.; and several other works for various vocal ensembles. Among his instrumental works, the so-called *Scottish Fantasy* for Violin and Orch. (1880) was extremely successful when Sarasate (to whom the work was dedicated) performed it all over Europe; but the most popular of all works by Bruch is his *Kol Nidrei,* a Hebrew melody for Cello and Orch., composed for the Jewish community of Liverpool in 1880; its success led to the erroneous assumption that Bruch himself was Jewish (he was, in fact, of a clerical Protestant family). His Concerto for 2 Pianos and Orch. was commissioned by the American duo-piano team Ottilie and Rose Sutro; when they performed it for the 1st time (Philadelphia Orch., Stokowski conducting, 1916), they drastically revised the original. In 1971 the authentic version was discovered in Berlin, and was given its 1st performance by Nathan Twining and Mer Berkofsky with the London Sym., Antal Dorati conducting, on May 6, 1974. **BIBL.:** F. Gysi, *M. B.* (Zürich, 1922); H. Pfitzner, *Meine Beziehungen zu M. B.; Persönliche Erinnerungen* (Munich, 1938); D. Kaemper, *M. B.-Studien. Zum 50. Todestag des Komponisten* (Cologne, 1970); J. Voois, "The Case of the Disappearing Dou-

ble Piano Concerto," *Symphony News* (June 1974); K. Fellerer, *M. B.* (Cologne, 1974).

Bruchollerie, Monique de la, French pianist; b. Paris, April 20, 1915; d. there, Dec. 15, 1972. She studied with Isidor Philipp; graduated from the Paris Cons. at the age of 13; toured widely as a concert pianist; also was active as a teacher. In 1964 she made a bold proposal to modernize the piano as a performing instrument by constructing a crescent-shaped keyboard to facilitate simultaneous playing in high treble and low bass. She further proposed to install electronic controls enabling the pianist to activate a whole chord by striking a single key.

Bruči, Rudolf, Serbian composer; b. Zagreb, March 30, 1917. He studied in Vienna with Uhl; returning to Serbia, he became a teacher and opera conductor in Novi Sad. In his works he employs polytonal and atonal devices, culminating in free dodecaphony. **WORKS:** *Maskal,* symphonic suite (1955); Concerto for Orch. (Belgrade, Nov. 25, 1959); *Čovek je vidik bez kraja,* cantata (Belgrade, Dec. 21, 1961); *Srbija,* cantata (Belgrade, May 24, 1962); *Sinfonia lesta* (received the Grand Prix at the Queen Elisabeth of Belgium Competition in Brussels, 1965); *Sinfonietta* for Strings (1965); *Salut au monde,* oratorio (1967).

Bruck (or **Brouck**), **Arnold von** (known also as **Arnold de Bruges** and **Arnoldo Flamengo**), Flemish composer; b. Bruges, c.1500; d. Linz, Feb. 6, 1554. He served as a choirboy in the chapel of Charles V; in 1527 he was named court Kapellmeister to Ferdinand I; retired on Dec. 31, 1545. Many of his motets, hymns, and German part-songs are preserved in MS collections of the 16th century; see also O. Wessely, ed., *A. v. B.: Sämtliche lateinschule Motetten,* Denkmäler der Tonkunst in Österreich, XCIX (1961). **BIBL.:** O. Wessely, *A. v.B.: Leben und Umwelt* (Habilitationsschrift, Univ. of Vienna, 1958).

Bruck, Charles, French conductor and pedagogue; b. Timișoara, Rumania, May 2, 1911. He studied at the Vienna Cons., then took courses with Perlemuter (piano) and Boulanger (composition) at the Paris École Normale de Musique; he also received instruction in conducting from Monteux (1934). After winning the conducting competition of the Orch. Symphonique de Paris (1936), he served as its assistant conductor; he later conducted at the Cannes and Deauville Casinos (1949–50), the Netherlands Opera in Amsterdam (1950–54), the Strasbourg Radio Sym. Orch. (1955–65), and the Orch. Philharmonique de l'ORTF in Paris (1965–70); subsequently he was director of Monteux's conducting school in Hancock, Maine.

Bruckner, (Josef) Anton, inspired Austrian composer; b. Ansfelden, Sept. 4, 1824; d. Vienna, Oct. 11, 1896. He studied music with his father, a village schoolmaster and church organist; also took music lessons at Hörsching with his cousin Johann Baptist Weiss. After his father's death in 1837, Bruckner enrolled as a chorister at St. Florian, where he attended classes in organ, piano, violin, and music theory. In 1840–41 he entered the special school for educational training in Linz, where he received instruction from J.N.A. Dürrnberger; he also studied music theory with Leopold Edler von Zenetti in Enns. While in his early youth, Bruckner held teaching positions in elementary public schools in Windhaag (1841–43) and Kronstorf (1843–45); later he occupied a responsible position as a schoolteacher at St. Florian (1845–55); also served as provisional organist there (1848–51). Despite his professional advance, he felt a lack of basic techniques in musical composition, and at the age of 31 went to Vienna to study harmony and counterpoint with the renowned pedagogue Simon Sechter. He continued his studies with him off and on until 1861. In 1856 he became cathedral organist in Linz, having successfully competed for this position against several applicants. Determined to acquire still more technical knowledge, he sought further instruction and began taking lessons in orchestration with Otto Kitzler, 1st cellist of the Linz municipal theater (1861–63). In the meantime he undertook an assiduous study of the Italian polyphonic school, and of masters of German polyphony, especially Bach. These tasks preoccupied him so completely that he did not engage in free composition until he was nearly 40 years old. Then he fell under the powerful influence of Wagner's music, an infatuation that diverted him from his study of classical polyphony. In 1865 he attended the premiere of *Tristan und Isolde* in Munich, and met Wagner. He also made the acquaintance of Liszt in Pest, and of Berlioz during his visit in Vienna. His adulation of Wagner was extreme; the dedication of his 3rd Sym. to Wagner reads: "To the eminent Excellency Richard Wagner the Unattainable, World-Famous, and Exalted Master of Poetry and Music, in Deepest Reverence Dedicated by Anton Bruckner." Strangely enough, in his own music Bruckner never embraced the tenets and practices of Wagner, but followed the sanctified tradition of Germanic polyphony. Whereas Wagner strove toward the ideal union of drama, text, and music in a new type of operatic production, Bruckner kept away from the musical theater, confining himself to symphonic and choral music. Even in his harmonic techniques, Bruckner seldom followed Wagner's chromatic style of writing, and he never tried to emulate the passionate rise and fall of Wagnerian "endless" melodies depicting the characters of his operatic creations. To Bruckner, music was an apotheosis of symmetry; his syms. were cathedrals of Gothic grandeur; he never hesitated to repeat a musical phrase several times in succession so as to establish the thematic foundation of a work. The personal differences between Wagner and Bruckner could not be more striking: Wagner was a man of the world who devoted his whole life to the promotion of his artistic and human affairs, while Bruckner was unsure of his abilities and desperately sought recognition. Devoid of social graces, being a person of humble peasant origin, Bruckner was unable to secure the position of respect and honor that he craved. A signal testimony to this lack of self-confidence was Bruckner's willingness to revise his works repeatedly, not always to their betterment, taking advice from conductors and ostensible well-wishers. He suffered from periodic attacks of depression; his entire life seems to have been a study of unhappiness, most particularly in his numerous attempts to find a woman who would become his life companion. In his desperation, he made halfhearted proposals in marriage to women of the people; the older he grew, the younger were the objects of his misguided affections; a notorious episode was his proposal of marriage to a chambermaid at a hotel in Berlin. Bruckner died a virgin.

A commanding trait of Bruckner's personality was his devout religiosity. To him the faith and the sacraments of the Roman Catholic Church were not mere rituals but profound psychological experiences. Following the practice of Haydn, he signed most of his works with the words *Omnia ad majorem Dei gloriam;* indeed, he must have felt that every piece of music he composed redounded to the greater glory of God. His original dedication of his Te Deum was actually inscribed "an dem lieben Gott." From reports of his friends and contemporaries, it appears that he regarded each happy event of his life as a gift of God, and each disaster as an act of divine wrath. His yearning for secular honors was none the less acute for that. He was tremendously gratified upon receiving an honorary doctorate from the Univ. of Vienna in 1891; he was the 1st musician to be so honored there. He unsuccessfully solicited similar degrees from the univs. of Cambridge, Philadelphia, and even Cincinnati. He eagerly sought approval in the public press. When Emperor Franz Josef presented him with a snuffbox as a sign of Imperial favor, it is said that Bruckner pathetically begged the Emperor to order Hanslick to stop attacking him. Indeed, Hanslick was the nemesis of the so-called New German School of composition exemplified by Wagner and Liszt, and to a lesser extent, also by Bruckner. Wagner could respond to Hanslick's hostility by caricaturing him in the role of Beckmesser (whom he had originally intended to name Hanslich), and Liszt, immensely successful as a virtuoso pianist, was largely immune to critical attacks. But Bruckner was highly vulnerable. It was not until the end of his unhappy

life that, thanks to a group of devoted friends among conductors, Bruckner finally achieved a full recognition of his greatness.

Bruckner himself was an inadequate conductor, but he was a master organist. In 1869 he appeared in organ recitals in France, and in 1871 he visited England, giving performances in the Royal Albert Hall and the Crystal Palace in London. He was also esteemed as a pedagogue. In 1868 he succeeded his own teacher Sechter as prof. of harmony, counterpoint, and organ at the Vienna Cons.; also in 1868 he was named provisional court organist, an appointment formally confirmed in 1878. Concurrently he taught piano, organ, and music theory at St. Anna College in Vienna (1870–74); in 1875 he was appointed lecturer in harmony and counterpoint at the Univ. of Vienna. In failing health, Bruckner retired from the Vienna Cons. in 1891 and a year later relinquished his post as court organist; in 1894 he resigned his lecturer's position at the Univ. of Vienna. The remaining years of his life he devoted to the composition of his 9th Sym., which, however, remained unfinished at his death.

Bruckner's syms. constitute a monumental achievement; they are characterized by a striking display of originality and a profound spiritual quality. His sacred works are similarly expressive of his latent genius. Bruckner is usually paired with Mahler, who was a generation younger, but whose music embodied qualities of grandeur akin to those that permeated the symphonic and choral works of Bruckner. Accordingly, Bruckner and Mahler societies sprouted in several countries, with the express purpose of elucidating, analyzing, and promoting their music.

The textual problems concerning Bruckner's works are numerous and complex. He made many revisions of his scores, and dejectedly acquiesced in alterations suggested by conductors who expressed interest in his music. As a result, conflicting versions of his syms. appeared in circulation. With the founding of the International Bruckner Soc., a movement was begun to publ. the original versions of his MSS, the majority of which he bequeathed to the Hofbibliothek in Vienna. A complete ed. of Bruckner's works, under the supervision of Robert Haas and Alfred Orel, began to appear in 1930; in 1945 Leopold Nowak was named its editor in chief. An excellent explication of the textual problems concerning Bruckner's works is found in Deryck Cook's article "The B. Problem Simplified," in the *Musical Times* (Jan.–Feb., April–May, and Aug. 1969). For a complete catalogue of his works, see R. Grasberger, ed., *Werkverzeichnis A. B.* (Tutzing, 1977).

WORKS: Bruckner rejected his 1st sym. as a student work; it is in F minor and is known as his *Schul-Symphonie* or *Studien-Symphonie* (Study Sym.; 1863; movements 1, 2, and 4 1st perf. under Moissl, Klosterneuburg, March 18, 1924; movement 3 1st perf. under Moissl, Klosterneuburg, Oct. 12, 1924). A 2nd early sym., in D minor, apparently held some interest for him, as he marked it No. 0, "Die Nullte" (1863–64; rev. 1869; movements 3 and 4 1st perf. under Moissl, Klosterneuburg, May 17, 1924; 1st complete perf. under Moissl, Klosterneuburg, Oct. 12, 1924). The following list of his 9 syms. is the standard canon: No. 1, in C minor (Version I, "Linz," 1865–66; 1st perf., with minor additions and alterations, under Bruckner, Linz, May 9, 1868; Version II, "Vienna," 1890–91, a thorough revision; 1st perf. under Richter, Vienna, Dec. 13, 1891); No. 2, in C minor (Version I, 1871–72; 1st perf., with minor revisions, under Bruckner, Vienna, Oct. 26, 1873; Version II, 1876–77, with cuts and alterations); No. 3, in D minor, the "Wagner" Sym. (Version I, 1873; 1st perf. in the Nowak ed. under Schönzeler, Adelaide, March 19, 1978; Version II, 1876–77, a thorough revision; 1st perf. under Bruckner, Vienna, Dec. 16, 1877; Version III, 1888–89, a thorough revision; 1st perf. under Richter, Vienna, Dec. 21, 1890; a 2nd Adagio [1876], unrelated to the other versions, was 1st perf. under C. Abbado, Vienna, May 24, 1980); No. 4, in E-flat major, the "Romantic" Sym. (Version I, 1874; 1st perf. in the Nowak ed. under K. Wöss, Linz, Sept. 20, 1975; Version II, 1877–78, with Finale of 1880, a thorough revision with a new Scherzo; 1st perf. under Richter, Vienna, Feb. 20, 1881; Version III,

1887–88, a major revision by Löwe, including a new Finale; 1st perf. under Richter, Vienna, Jan. 22, 1888); No. 5, in B-flat major (1875–76; minor revisions, 1876–78; 1st perf. in a recomposed version by F. Schalk, under his direction, Graz, April 8, 1894; 1st perf. in the Haas ed. under Hausegger, Munich, Oct. 20, 1935); No. 6, in A major (1879–81; Adagio and Scherzo under Jahn, Vienna, Feb. 11, 1883; with major cuts, under Mahler, Vienna, Feb. 26, 1899; 1st complete perf. under Pohlig, Stuttgart, March 14, 1901); No. 7, in E major (1881–83; 1st perf. under Nikisch, Leipzig, Dec. 30, 1884); No. 8, in C minor (Version I, 1884–87; 1st perf. in the Nowak ed. under Schönzeler, BBC, London, Sept. 2, 1973; Version II, 1889–90, a thorough revision; 1st perf. under Richter, Vienna, Dec. 18, 1892; 1st perf. in the Haas ed. [a composite version of I and II] under Furtwängler, Hamburg, July 5, 1939); No. 9, in D minor (movements 1–3, 1887–94; Finale [unfinished], 1894–96; 1st perf. in a recomposed version by Löwe, under his direction, Vienna, Feb. 11, 1903, with Bruckner's *Te Deum* substituted for the Finale; 1st perf. in the Haas ed. under Hausegger, Munich, April 2, 1932). Other major works are 3 masses: D minor (1864; Linz, Nov. 20, 1864; rev. 1876 and 1881); E minor (1866; Linz, Sept. 29, 1869; rev. 1869, 1876, and 1882); F minor (1867–68; Vienna, June 16, 1872; many revisions); String Quintet in F major (1878–79); *Te Deum* (1881; rev. 1883–84; 1st perf. with orch. under Richter, Vienna, Jan. 10, 1886); Psalm 150 (1892; Vienna, Nov. 13, 1892). Selected minor works are a Mass in C major (1842?); *Requiem* in D minor (1848–49; St. Florian, March 13, 1849); *Missa Solemnis* in B-flat minor (1854; St. Florian, Sept. 14, 1854); *Apollomarsch* for Military Band (1862; authenticity not established); March in D minor for Orch. (1862); 3 orch. pieces in E-flat major, E minor, and F major (1862); String Quartet in C minor (1862); Overture in G minor (1862–63; Klosterneuburg, Sept. 8, 1921); *Germanenzug* for Male Choir and Brass Instruments (1863); March in E-flat major for Military Band (1865); *Abendzauber* for Male Choir and 4 Horns (1878); *Intermezzo* for String Quintet (1879); *Helgoland* for Male Choir and Orch. (1893); other choral settings; motets; etc.

BIBL.: BIOGRAPHICAL: F. Brunner, *Dr. A. B.* (Linz, 1895); R. Louis, *A. B.* (Munich, 1905; 3rd ed., 1921); F. Gräflinger, *A. B.: Bausteine zu seiner Lebensgeschichte* (Munich, 1911; rev. ed., 1927); M. Morold, *A. B.* (Leipzig, 1912; 2nd ed., 1920); E. Decsey, *A. B., Versuch eines Lebens* (Berlin, 1920; 3rd ed., 1930); F. Gräflinger, *A. B.: Sein Leben und seine Werke* (Regensburg, 1921); A. Göllerich and M. Auer, *A. B.: Ein Lebens- und Schaffensbild* (4 vols., Regensburg, 1922–37; 2nd ed., 1938); K. Grunsky, *A. B.* (Stuttgart, 1922); H. Tessmer, *A. B.* (Regensburg, 1922); R. Wetz, *A. B.: Sein Leben und Schaffen* (Leipzig, 1923); J. Daninger, *A. B.* (Vienna, 1924); G. Gräner, *A. B.* (Leipzig, 1924); E. Kurth, *A. B.* (2 vols., Berlin, 1925); A. Orel, *A. B.: Ein Österreichischer Meister der Tonkunst* (Altötting, 1926); F. Gräflinger, *A. B.: Leben und Schaffen* (Berlin, 1927); M. Auer, *A. B.: Sein Leben und Werk* (Vienna, 1931; 6th ed., 1966); G. Engel, *The Life of A. B.* (N.Y., 1931); R. Haas, *A. B.* (Potsdam, 1934); A. Orel, *A. B., 1824–1896: Sein Leben in Bildern* (Leipzig, 1936); W. Paap, *A. B.: Zijn land, zijn leven en zijn kunst* (Bilthoven, 1936); W. Wiora, "A. B.," *Die grossen Deutschen* (Berlin, 1936; rev. ed., 1959); E. Schwanzara, *B.s Stamm- und Urheimat* (Berlin, 1937); K. Laux, *A. B.: Leben und Werk* (Leipzig, 1940; 2nd ed., 1947); L. van Vassenhove, *A. B.* (Neuchâtel, 1942); W. Wolff, *A. B.: Rustic Genius* (N.Y., 1942); A. Machabey, *La Vie et l'œuvre d'A. B.* (Paris, 1945); W. Reich, ed., *A. B.: Ein Bild seiner Persönlichkeit* (Basel, 1953); H. Redlich, *B. and Mahler* (London, 1955; rev. ed., 1963); P. Benary, *A. B.* (Leipzig, 1956); W. Abendroth, *B.: Eine Bildbiographie* (Munich, 1958); E. Doernberg, *The Life and Symphonies of A. B.* (London, 1960); L. Nowak, *A. B.: Musik und Leben* (Vienna, 1964); G. Wehle, *A. B. im Spiegel seiner Zeitgenossen* (Garmisch-Partenkirchen, 1964); J. Lassl, *Das kleine Brucknerbuch* (Salzburg, 1965; 2nd ed., 1972); H.-H. Schönzeler, *B.* (N.Y., 1970; rev. ed., 1978); J. Gallios, *B.* (Paris, 1971); L. Nowak, *A. B.: Musik und Leben* (Linz, 1973); H. Fischer, *A. B.: Sein Leben* (Salzburg, 1974); D. Watson, *B.*

(London, 1975); P. Langevin, *A. B., Apogée de la symphonie* (Lausanne, 1977); M. Wagner, *B.: Monographie* (Mainz, 1983); M. Hansen, *A. B.* (Leipzig, 1987).

CRITICAL, ANALYTICAL: A. Halm, *Die Symphonie A. B.s* (Munich, 1914; 2nd ed., 1923); A. Knapp, *A. B.: Zum Verständnis seiner Persönlichkeit und seiner Werke* (Düsseldorf, 1921); A. Orel, *Unbekannte Frühwerke A. B.s* (Vienna, 1921); E. Schwebsch, *A. B.: Ein Beitrag zur Erkenntnis von Entwicklungen in der Musik* (Stuttgart, 1921; 2nd ed., 1923); K. Kobald, ed., *In memoriam A. B.* (Vienna, 1924); O. Lang, *A. B.: Wesen und Bedeutung* (Munich, 1924; 3rd ed., 1947); K. Singer, *B.s Chormusik* (Stuttgart, 1924); A. Orel, *A. B.: Das Werk, der Künstler, die Zeit* (Vienna, 1925); R. Wickenhausen, *A. B.s Symphonien: Ihr Werden und Wesen* (Leipzig, 1926–27); M. Auer, *A. B. als Kirchenmusiker* (Regensburg, 1927); F. Munch, "La Musique religieuse d'A. B.," *Le Ménestrel* (Paris, 1928); H. Grunsky, *Das Formproblem in der A. B.s Symphonien* (Augsburg, 1929); F. Grüninger, *A. B.: Der metaphysische Kern seiner Persönlichkeit und Werke* (Augsburg, 1930); H. Grunsky, *Formenwelt und Sinngefüge in den B.-Symphonien* (2 vols., Augsburg, 1931); K. Grunsky, *Fragen der B.-Auffassung* (Stuttgart, 1936); A. Köberle, *Bach, Beethoven, B. als Symbolgestalten des Glaubens* (Berlin, 1936; 4th ed., 1941); F. Grüninger, *Der Ehrfürchtige: A. B.s Leben dem Volke erzählt* (Freiburg, 1937); O. Loerke, *A. B.: Ein Charakterbild* (Berlin, 1938; 3rd ed., 1943); A. Mecklenburg, "Hugo Wolf and A. B.," *Musical Quarterly* (July 1938); E. Wellesz, "A. B. and the Process of Musical Creation," ibid.; W. Abendroth, *Die Symphonien A. B.s: Einführungen* (Berlin, 1940; 2nd ed., 1942); F. Wohlfahrt, *A. B.s symphonisches Werk* (Leipzig, 1943); P. Raabe, *Wege zu B.* (Regensburg, 1944); D. Newlin, *B., Mahler, Schoenberg* (N.Y., 1947; rev. ed., 1978); L. Nowak, *Te Deum laudamus: Gedanken zur Musik A. B.s* (Vienna, 1947); E. Refardt, *Brahms, B., Wolf: Drei Wiener Meister des 19. Jahrhunderts* (Basel, 1949); F. Grüninger, *Der Meister von Sankt Florian—Wege zu A. B.* (Augsburg, 1950); E. Schenk, *Um B.s Persönlichkeit* (Vienna, 1951); G. Engel, *The Symphonies of A. B.* (N.Y., 1955); I. Krohn, *A. B.s Symphonien: Eine Untersuchung über Formenbau und Stimmungsgehalt* (3 vols., Helsinki, 1955–57); H. Raynor, "An Approach to A. B.," *Musical Times* (Feb. 1955); N. Tschulik, ed., *A. B. im Spiegel seiner Zeit* (Vienna, 1955); M. Dehnert, *A. B.: Versuch einer Deutung* (Leipzig, 1958); L. Nowak, "Symphonischer und kirchlicher Stil bei A. B.," in the *Festschrift* for Karl Gustav Fellerer (Regensburg, 1962); A. Orel, "B. und Wien," *Hans Albrecht in Memoriam* (Kassel, 1962); R. Simpson, *B. and the Symphony* (London, 1963); F. Grasberger, ed., *B.-Studien: Leopold Nowak zum 60. Geburtstag* (Vienna, 1964); H. Winterberger, *A. B. in seiner Zeit* (Linz, 1964); R. Simpson, *The Essence of B.: An Essay towards the Understanding of His Music* (London, 1967; Philadelphia, 1968); A. Howie, *The Sacred Music of A. B.* (diss., Univ. of Manchester, 1969); O. Wessely, ed., *B.-Studien* (Vienna, 1975); C. Floros, *Brahms und B.* (Wiesbaden, 1980); A. Howie, "Traditional and Novel Elements in B.'s Sacred Music," *Musical Quarterly* (Oct. 1981); P. Hawkshaw, "The Date of B.'s 'Nullified' Symphony in D Minor," *19th Century Music* (Spring 1983); W. Notter, *Schematismus und Evolution in der Sinfonik A. B.s* (Munich, 1983); T. Röder, *Auf dem Weg zur B.-Symphonie: Untersuchungen zu den ersten beiden Fassungen von A. B.s dritter Symphonie* (Wiesbaden, 1987); H.-H. Schönzeler, *Zu B.s IX Symphonie: Die Krakauer Skizzen/B.s 9th Symphony: The Crakow Sketches* (Vienna, 1987); C.-H. Mahling, ed., *A. B. Studien zu Werk und Wirkung. Walter Wiora zum 30. Dezember 1986* (Tutzing, 1988).

CORRESPONDENCE: F. Gräflinger, ed., *A. B., Gesammelte Briefe* (Regensburg, 1924); M. Auer, ed., *A. B., Gesammelte Briefe*, new series (Regensburg, 1924); A. Orel, *B.-Brevier; Briefe, Dokumente, Berichte* (Vienna, 1953).

PERIODICALS: The International Bruckner Soc. of Vienna publ. *B.-Blätter* from 1929 to 1937. The reconstituted Soc. has publ. *Mitteilungsblatt der Internationalen B.-Gesellschaft* since 1971. The Bruckner Soc. of America publ. *Chord and Discord* from 1932 to 1941; it resumed publication in 1947.

Brückner-Rüggeberg, Wilhelm, German conductor; b. Stuttgart, April 15, 1906; d. Hamburg, April 1, 1985. He received his musical education in Munich studying composition with Siegmund von Hausegger. He then served as conductor with the Hamburg State Opera (1936–71). He was esteemed for his performance of classical oratorios, as well as the regular opera repertoire.

Brudieu, Joan, French-Catalonian composer; b. in the diocese of Limoges, c.1520; d. Urgel, between April 22 and May 10, 1591. In 1539 he became choirmaster at the Urgel Cathedral, a post he held until 1577; then served as maestro de capilla and organist at Santa Maria del Mar in Barcelona (1578–79); subsequently resumed his Urgel post. His extant works include a 4-part Requiem Mass and Spanish madrigals.
  BIBL.: A. Mangeot, "The Madrigals of J. B.," *Score,* no. 7 (1952).

Brüggen, Frans, distinguished Dutch recorder player, flutist, and conductor; b. Amsterdam, Oct. 30, 1934. He studied the recorder with Kees Otten and flute at the Amsterdam Muzieklyceum; in addition, took courses in musicology at the Univ. of Amsterdam; then launched a major career as a virtuoso performer of music for the recorder; as a flute soloist, he was equally at home in performances of the Baroque masters and contemporary avant-garde composers; also gave informative lectures and illustrative performances of recorder music in Europe, and taught at the Royal Cons. in The Hague. In 1981 he founded the Orch. of the 18th Century, which he conducted with fine success on both sides of the Atlantic.

Brugnoli, Attilio, Italian composer; b. Rome, Sept. 7, 1880; d. Bolzano, July 10, 1937. He studied piano and composition at the Naples Cons. with Paolo Serrao (graduated in 1900); won the Rubinstein Prize in Paris (1905); taught at the conservatories of Parma (1907–21) and Florence (1921–37). His compositions include a Piano Concerto (1905); Violin Concerto (1908); piano suite, *Scene napolitane* (1909); several songs; piano pieces; also a pedagogic work, *Dinamica pianistica* (Milan, 1926).

Bruhns, Nicolaus, German violinist, organist, and composer; b. Schwabstedt, 1665; d. Husum, March 29, 1697. He studied organ and composition with Buxtehude in Lübeck; then traveled to Copenhagen, where he served as a church organist; in 1689 he moved to Husum, where he was appointed organist at the Cathedral there. He was reputed to be an inventive virtuoso who could play the violin while providing the basso continuo on organ pedals. He was a reputable composer; his 12 church cantatas were notable; he also wrote fugues and chorales for organ.
  BIBL.: H. Kölsch, *N. B.* (Kassel, 1958); M. Geck, *N. B.: Leben und Werk* (Cologne, 1968).

Brüll, Ignaz, Austrian pianist and composer; b. Prossnitz, Moravia, Nov. 7, 1846; d. Vienna, Sept. 17, 1907. He studied in Vienna with Epstein (piano) and Dessoff (composition); subsequently made extended recital tours; eventually settled in Vienna, where he was a prof. of piano at the Horak Inst. (1872–78). He was an intimate friend of Brahms, who greatly valued his advice.
  WORKS: Operas: *Die Bettler von Samarkand* (1864); *Das goldene Kreuz* (Berlin, Dec. 22, 1875; his most successful opera); *Der Landfriede* (Vienna, Oct. 4, 1877); *Bianca* (Dresden, Nov. 25, 1879); *Königin Marietta* (Munich, 1883); *Gloria* (Hamburg, 1886); *Das steinerne Herz* (Vienna, 1888); *Gringoire* (Munich, March 19, 1892); *Schach dem Könige* (Munich, 1893); *Der Husar* (Vienna, 1898; very successful); *Rübezahl* (unfinished); ballet, *Ein Märchen aus der Champagne* (1896); overture, *Im Walde;* 3 serenades and a Dance Suite for Orch.; 2 piano concertos; Violin Concerto; piano pieces; songs.
  BIBL.: H. Schwarz, *I. B. und sein Freundeskreis* (1922).

Brumby, Colin (James), Australian composer; b. Melbourne, June 18, 1933. He graduated from the Melbourne Univ. Cons. of Music in 1957; studied in London with Alexander Goehr

and John Carewe (1963). He lectured at the Brisbane Teacher's Training College (1959–64) and in 1964 became a senior lecturer at the Univ. of Queensland. His music is medium modern, with liberal application of avant-garde techniques.
  WORKS: *Aegean Suite* for Flute and Strings (1957); *Mediterranean Suite* for Strings (1958); *Partite* for Clarinet and Strings (1961); *Pantos* for Flute and Strings (1963); *Fibonacci Variations* for Orch. (1963); Wind Quintet (1964); *Antithesis* for Strings (1964); *Stabat Mater Speciosa,* a Christmas cantata (1965); Trio for Flute, Clarinet, and Horn (1965); *Doubles* for Wind Quartet (1965); *Diversion* for Horn and Orch. (1966); *Realisations* for Piano and Orch. (1966); *Antipodea* for Orch. (1966); *French Suite* for 6 Horns (1967); *Gilgamesh,* cantata for Narrator, Chorus, Brass, and Percussion (1967); String Quartet (1968); *3 Italian Songs* for High Voice and String Quartet (1968); *Charlie Bubbles' Book of Hours* for Soli, Chorus, Tape, and Orch. (1969); *5 Days Lost* for Narrator and Orch. (1969); *Bring Out Your Christmas Masks* for Narrator, Soli, Chorus, Tape, and Orch. (1969); *The 7 Deadly Sins,* opera (1970); Violin Concerto (1970); Concerto for Horn and Strings (1971); *A Ballade for St. Cecilia,* cantata (1971); *Celebrations and Lamentations* for Narrators, Soli, Chorus, and Orch. (1971); *Litanies of the Sun,* symphonic suite (1971); Viola Concertino (1972); *Ishtar's Mirror,* opera (1972); *This Is the Vine* for Soli, Chorus, and Orch. (1972; Melbourne, Feb. 24, 1973); *3 Baroque Angels,* cantata (1979); Quintet for Winds (1983); *Christmas Bells,* cantata (1984); *La Donna,* opera (1986); ballet music; songs; piano pieces.

Brumel, Antoine, celebrated French composer; b. 1460; d. after 1520. He served as a chorister at the Cathedral of Notre Dame in Chartres in 1483; in 1486 became a Master of the Innocents at St. Peter's in Geneva, where he remained until 1492. In 1497 he was Canon at Laon Cathedral. He was a singer at the ducal court in Chambéry in 1501; took up his duties at the court of Alfonso I, Duke of Ferrara, in Aug. 1506; remained in his service there until the chapel was disbanded in 1510. A number of his sacred works were publ. during his lifetime; other pieces are scattered in various anthologies. A complete ed. of his works was begun by A. Carapetyan in 1951 in Rome under the aegis of the American Inst. of Musicology. He composed masses, motets, Magnificats, and other sacred works. B. Hudson ed. the collection *A. Brumel: Opera omnia,* Corpus Mensurabilis Musicae, V/1–6 (1969–72).
  BIBL.: A. Pirro, "Dokumente über A. B., Louis van Pullaer und Crispin van Stappen," *Zeitschrift für Musikwissenschaft* (March 1929).

Brun, Fritz, Swiss composer and conductor; b. Lucerne, Aug. 18, 1878; d. Grosshöchstetten, Switzerland, Nov. 29, 1959. He studied in Lucerne (1892–95) and at Cologne (1896–1901); then lived in Berlin, London, and Dortmund; finally settled in Bern (1909), where he taught at the Cons. and conducted the Bern Sym. Orch. until 1943.
  WORKS: 10 syms. (1908–53); *Variations* for Piano and String Orch. (1944); Piano Concerto (1944); Cello Concerto; *Rhapsodie* for Orch. (1958); 4 string quartets (1898, 1921, 1943, 1949); Violin Sonata (1906); Cello Sonata (1953).
  BIBL.: *Kleine Festgabe für F. B.* (Bern, 1941).

Brün, Herbert, Israeli composer; b. Berlin, July 9, 1918. In 1936 he emigrated to Palestine; studied composition in Jerusalem with Stefan Wolpe; later took courses at Columbia Univ. in N.Y. He subsequently pursued research on the application of electroacoustic and electronic methods of sound production to composing in Paris, Cologne, and Munich; taught at the Univ. of Illinois (from 1963). In his music he explores the potentialities of computers as a catalytic factor for advanced techniques; the titles of his works often suggest paradoxical logic.
  WORKS: 3 string quartets (1953, 1957, 1961); *Mobile* for Orch. (1958); *Futility* for Electronic Sounds, and Voice on Tapes (1964); *Gestures for 11* for Chamber Ensemble (1964); *Sonoriferous Loops* for an Instrumental Ensemble and Tape (1964); a group of works for Varying Ensembles under the provocative title *Non sequitur* (1966); Trio for Trumpet, Trom-

bone, and Percussion (1966); *Mutatis mutandis* for "Interpreters" (1968); Nonet (1969). Also many electronic pieces, including *Piece of Prose* (1972), *Dust* (1976), *More Dust* (1977), and *I told you so* (1981); computer pieces.

Bruneau, (Louis-Charles-Bonaventure-) Alfred, French opera composer; b. Paris, March 3, 1857; d. there, June 15, 1934. In 1873 he entered the Paris Cons., where he was a pupil of Franchomme; won the 1st cello prize in 1876; later studied harmony with Savard and composition with Massenet; in 1881 he won the Prix de Rome with his cantata *Sainte-Geneviève.* He was a music critic for *Gil Blas* (1892–95); then for *Le Figaro* and *Le Matin;* in 1903–4 was 1st conductor at the Opéra-Comique; in 1900 he was made a member of the "Conseil Supérieur" at the Paris Cons., and in 1909 succeeded Reyer as inspector of music instruction. He made extensive tours of Russia, England, Spain, and the Netherlands, conducting his own works. He was made a Knight of the Légion d'honneur in 1895; received the title "Commandeur de St.-Charles" in 1907; became a member of the Académie des Beaux Arts in 1925. His role in the evolution of French opera is of great importance; he introduced realistic drama on the French musical stage, working along lines parallel with Zola in literature. He used Zola's subjects for his most spectacular opera, *L'Ouragan,* and also for the operas *Messidor* and *L'Enfant-Roi.* In accordance with this naturalistic trend, Bruneau made free use of harsh dissonance when it was justified by the dramatic action of the plot. He publ. *Musiques d'hier et de demain* (1900); *La Musique française* (1901); *Musiques de Russie et musiciens de France* (1903; German tr. by M. Graf in *Die Musik,* Berlin, 1904); *La Vie et les œuvres de Gabriel Fauré* (1925); *Massenet* (1934).

WORKS: Operas (most of them produced in Paris at the Opéra-Comique): *Kérim* (June 9, 1887), *Le Rêve* (June 18, 1891), *L'Attaque du Moulin* (Nov. 23, 1893), *Messidor* (Feb. 19, 1897), *L'Ouragan* (April 29, 1901), *Lazare* (1902), *L'Enfant-Roi* (March 3, 1905), *Naïs Micoulin* (Monte Carlo, Feb. 2, 1907), *La Faute de l'Abbé Mouret* (March 1, 1907), *Les Quatre Journées* (Dec. 25, 1916), *Le Roi Candaule* (Dec. 1, 1920), *Angelo, tyran de Padoue* (Jan. 16, 1928), and *Virginie* (Jan. 7, 1931); ballets: *L'Amoureuse Leçon* (Feb. 6, 1913) and *Les Bacchantes* (after Euripides; Oct. 30, 1912); overtures: *Ode héroïque* and *Léda;* symphonic poem, *La Belle au Bois dormant;* symphonic poem, with Chorus, *Penthésilée;* a Requiem; *Lieds de France* and *Chansons à danser* (both to poems by C. Mendès); *Les Chants de la vie* (to poems by H. Bataille, F. Gregh, etc.); *Le Navire* for Voice and Orch.; pieces for various combinations of string and wind Instruments.

BIBL.: A. Hervey, "A. B.," in *Living Masters of Music* (London, 1907); O. Séré in *Musiciens d'aujourd'hui* (Paris, 1911); J. Tiersot, *Un Demi-siècle de musique française* (1918); A. Boschot, *La Vie et les œuvres d'A. B.* (Paris, 1937).

Brunelli, Antonio, Italian music theorist and composer; b. Pisa, c.1575; d. there, c.1630. He was a pupil of G.M. Nanini; served as an organist at S. Miniato in Tuscany from 1604 to 1607; then went to Prato, where he served as maestro di cappella at the Cathedral. On April 12, 1612, he was appointed maestro di cappella of the Grand Duke of Tuscany. Between 1605 and 1621 he publ. motets, canzonelle, Psalms, madrigals, Requiems, and others sacred works; some of them were included in Donfried's *Promptuarium musicum* (1623). He publ. the theoretical treatises *Regole utilissime per li scolari che desiderano imparare a cantare* (Florence, 1606; one of the 1st publ. methods for voice); *Esercizi ad 1 e 2 voci* (Florence, 1607); and *Regole et dichiarazioni de alcuni contrappunti doppii* (Florence, 1610).

Brunetti, Domenico, Italian composer; b. Bologna, c.1580; d. there, April or May 1646. He was organist at the Church of S. Domenico (c.1609); then was maestro di cappella at the Bologna Cathedral (1618); with F. Bertacchi he founded the Accademia dei Filaschici (1633), which later was absorbed into the Accademia Filarmonica. His publications include *Euterpe* (Venice, 1606); *Varii Concentus unica, voce, duabus, tri-*

bus, quatuor vel pluribus cum gravi et acuto ad Organum (Venice, 1609); *Canticum Deiparae Virginis Octies iuxta singulos Rhytmorum Sacrorum* (Venice, 1621). Several of his compositions (motets, madrigals, etc.) were publ. in contemporary collections (1611–26) of A. Schadeo, G. Donfried, A.N. di Treviso, F. Sammaruco, Z. Zanetti, and G.P. Biandrà.

Brunetti, Gaetano, Italian violinist and composer; b. probably in Fano, 1744; d. Culminal de Oreja, near Madrid, Dec. 16, 1798. He studied with Nardini, and in about 1762 went to Madrid; in 1767 was appointed violinist in the Royal Chapel in Madrid; in 1788 became director of the Royal Chamber Orch., remaining in this post until his death. He composed many works for the Spanish court, and also for the Duke of Alba; Boccherini, who was in Madrid during the same years as Brunetti, was also favored by the court and the aristocracy, but there was apparently no rivalry between them, as commissions were plentiful. Brunetti's productivity was astounding; he wrote 28 syms., 6 overtures, numerous dances for orch.; 12 sextets, 70 minuets, 44 quartets, 30 trios; 64 sonatas for violin and basso continuo; 23 divertimenti for violin, viola, and cello; also an opera, *Jason,* produced in Madrid on Oct. 4, 1768. The Library of Congress in Washington has a large collection of Brunetti's MSS.

BIBL.: J. Subirá, *La música en la casa de Alba* (Madrid, 1927); A. Belgray, *G. B., An Exploratory Bio-bibliographical Study* (diss., Univ. of Michigan, 1970).

Bruni, Antonio Bartolomeo, Italian violinist and composer; b. Cuneo, Jan. 28, 1757; d. there, Aug. 5, 1821. He studied with Pugnani in Turin. In 1780 he went to Paris, and on May 15, 1780, appeared as a violinist at the Concert Spirituel; then served as a member of the orch. of the Comédie-Italienne (1781–89). He was subsequently director of the orch. of the Opéra-Comique (1799–1801); then at the Opéra-Italienne (1801–6). He wrote 22 operas, of which the most successful were *Célestine* (Paris, Oct. 15, 1787), *Claudine* (Paris, March 6, 1794), and *La Rencontre en voyage* (Paris, April 28, 1798). He also wrote music for the violin; publ. a violin method and a viola method (the latter reprinted in 1928).

BIBL.: G. Cesari, H. Closson, L. de La Laurencie, A. Della Corte, and C. Zino, *A.B. B., musicista cuneese* (Turin, 1931).

Brunold, Paul, French pianist, organist, and writer on music; b. Paris, Oct. 14, 1875; d. there, Sept. 14, 1948. He was a pupil of Marmontel (piano) and Lavignac (theory) at the Paris Cons.; later studied with Paderewski. In 1915 he became organist at St. Gervais, in Paris. With H. Expert, he ed. the *Anthologie des maîtres français du clavecin des XVIIe et XVIIIe siècles;* with A. Tessier, he brought out a complete edition of Chambonnières's works; he also ed. 2 vols. of works by Dieupart for the Lyre-Bird Press of Paris (6 *Suites pour clavecin* and *Airs et Chansons*). He publ. the book *Histoire du grand orgue de l'Église St. Gervais à Paris* (1934).

Brunswick, Mark, American composer; b. N.Y., Jan. 6, 1902; d. London, May 25, 1971. He studied theory of composition with Rubin Goldmark in N.Y. (1918–23); then took lessons with Ernest Bloch in Cleveland and with Nadia Boulanger in Paris (until 1929); later lived in Vienna. Returning to N.Y. in 1937, he taught at various schools; was a member of the music dept. of the College of the City of N.Y. from 1946 to 1967.

WORKS: 2 *Movements* for String Quartet (1925); *Lysistrata* for Mezzo-soprano, Women's Chorus, and Orch. (1930); Fantasia for Viola (1932); Sym. in B-flat (Minneapolis, March 7, 1947); Quartet for Violin, Viola, Cello, and Double Bass (1957); Septet for Wind Quintet, Viola, and Cello (1958); 5 madrigals for Chorus, Viola, Cello, and Double Bass (1958–66); also *Eros and Death,* a choral sym. to texts from Greek and Roman poetry (1932–54). He left an unfinished opera, *The Master Builder,* after Ibsen.

Bruscantini, Sesto, Italian baritone; b. Porto Civitanova, Dec. 10, 1919. He studied law; then went to Rome to study music with Luigi Ricci. He made his debut at La Scala in Milan in

1949, singing the bass role as Don Geronimo in Cimarosa's *Il matrimonio segreto.* He then sang at several festivals in Glyndebourne (1951–54); in 1952 he appeared at the Salzburg Festival. In 1961 he made his U.S. debut with the Chicago Lyric Opera. He was particularly renowned for his buffo roles. In 1953 he married the singer **Sena Jurinac.**

Brusilovsky, Evgeni, Russian composer; b. Rostov-on-the-Don, Nov. 12, 1905; d. Moscow, May 9, 1981. He studied composition with Maximilian Steinberg at the Leningrad Cons., graduating in 1931. In 1933 he was commissioned by the Leningrad Union of Composers to go to Kazakhstan, promote musical education there, and help native composers to write music based on their own ethnic sources. Brusilovsky settled in Alma-Ata, capital of Kazakhstan, and taught at the Alma-Ata Cons. of Music. He wrote a number of works making use of native motifs; particularly notable are his operas on folk subjects.
WORKS: Operas (all produced in Alma-Ata): *Kyz-Zhybek* (1934); *Zhalbyr* (1935; 2nd version, 1938; 3rd version, 1946); *Er-Targyn* (1937; 2nd version, 1954); *Ayman-Sholpan* (1938); *Altyn Styk* (1940); *Guard, Alga!* (1942); *Amangeldy* (1945); *Dudaray* (1953); *The Inheritors* (1963); a ballet, *Bayan-Slu* (1971); 8 syms. (1931, 1932, 1944, 1957, 1961, 1965, 1969, 1972); Piano Concerto (1948); Viola Concerto (1969); Trumpet Concerto (1967); 2 string quartets (1944, 1952); numerous choruses and songs; piano pieces; educational studies for various instruments.

Brusilow (real name, **Brusilovsky**), **Anshel,** American conductor; b. Philadelphia, Aug. 14, 1928, of Russian-Jewish parents. He studied violin at the Curtis Inst. of Music. Upon graduation, he served as concertmaster of the New Orleans Sym. Orch. (1954–55), associate concertmaster of the Cleveland Orch. (1955–59), and concertmaster of the Philadelphia Orch. (1959–66). He was also the founder of the Philadelphia Chamber Orch. (1961–65) and the Chamber Sym. of Philadelphia (1966–68). From 1970 to 1973 he was executive director and conductor of the Dallas Sym. In 1973 he joined the faculty of North Texas State Univ. in Denton, and in 1982 the faculty of Southern Methodist Univ. in Dallas.

Bruson, Renato, distinguished Italian baritone; b. Este, near Padua, Jan. 13, 1936. He studied at the Padua Cons.; made his debut with the opera in Spoleto in 1961 as Count Di Luna in Verdi's *Il Trovatore;* then sang with other Italian opera houses; on Feb. 1, 1969, he made his Metropolitan Opera debut in N.Y. as Enrico in Donizetti's *Lucia di Lammermoor;* sang at La Scala in Milan and the Edinburgh Festival in 1972; in 1976 appeared at Covent Garden. He is primarily noted for his congenial interpretation of lyrico-dramatic parts in the operas of Verdi and Donizetti.

Brusselmans, Michel, Belgian composer; b. Paris (of Belgian parents), Feb. 12, 1886; d. Brussels, Sept. 20, 1960. He studied with Huberti, Tinel, and Gilson at the Brussels Cons.; won the Agniez Prix in 1914 for his symphonic poem *Hélène de Sparte.* In 1922 he became ed. for the Paris music publisher Jamin, and spent most of his life in France. His music is Romantic in inspiration and programmatic in content.
WORKS: 3 ballets: *Les Néréides* (1911); *Kermesse flamande* (1912); *Les Sylphides* (on themes of Chopin); oratorio, *Jésus* (1936); *Psaume LVI* for Soprano, Chorus, and Orch. (1954); 3 syms. (1924; 1934; *Levantine,* 1956–57); *Ouverture fériale* (1908); *Scènes Breugheliennes* for Orch. (1911); *Télémaque a Gaulus* for Chamber Orch. (1923); *Esquisses flamandes* for Orch. (1927); *Légende du gapeau* for Horn, and Orch. or Piano (1930); *Rhapsodie flamande* for Orch. (1931); *Scènes provençales* for Orch. (1931); *Suite phrygienne* for Orch. (1932); *Suite d'après les Caprices de Paganini* for Orch. (1936); *Suite divertissement* for Orch. (1937); *Rhapsodie* for Horn and Orch. (1938); Organ Concerto (1938); *Ouverture héroïque* (1942); Sinfonietta (1954); Violin Sonata (1915); Cello Sonata (1916); *Prelude and Fugue* for 8 Winds (1923); *Visages de Paris* for Piano (1946); songs.

Brustad, Bjarne, Norwegian violinist, conductor, and composer; b. Christiania, March 4, 1895; d. there (Oslo), May 22, 1978. He studied at the Christiania Cons.; then took violin lessons with Carl Flesch in Berlin (1915–16). From 1919 to 1922 he was violinist in the Oslo Phil., and from 1929 to 1943 played 1st viola there. He also conducted orchs. in Oslo; in 1951 received a government life pension. His music is Romantic in its essence, and traditional in form.
WORKS: Opera, *Atlantis* (1945); 4 violin concertos (1922–61); Concertino for Viola and Chamber Orch. (1932); 9 syms. (1948, 1951, 1953, 1957, 1967, 1970, 1971, 1972, 1973); Clarinet Concerto (1970); 3 string quartets (1919, 1929, 1959); 3 sonatas for Solo Violin (1935, 1956, 1957); Trio for Clarinet, Violin, and Viola (1938); Trio for Clarinet, Violin, and Bassoon (1947); Violin Sonata (1950); *Divertimento* for Solo Flute (1958).

Bruynèl, Ton, Dutch composer of electronic music; b. Utrecht, Jan. 26, 1934. He studied piano at the Utrecht Cons.; then worked in the studio for electronic music at the Univ. of Utrecht; in 1957 organized a private electronic music studio. Most of his compositions involve instruments in combination with electronics, and some require theatrical visualizations.
WORKS: *Resonance I,* theater piece (ballet) in collaboration with Japanese-American sculptor Chinkichi Tajiri and American painter Sam Middleton (1960–62); *Reflexes* for Birma Drum (1961); *Resonance II,* theater piece in collaboration with the Dutch poet Gerrit Kouwenaar (1963); *Relief* for Organ and 4 Sound Tracks (1964); *Mobile* for 2 Sound Tracks (1965); *Milieu* for 2 Sound Tracks and Organ (1965–66); *Arc* for Organ and 4 Sound Tracks (1966–67); *Mekaniek* for Wind Quintet and 2 Sound Tracks (1967); *Decor,* ballet score (1967); *Signs* for Wind Quintet, 2 Sound Tracks, and Video Projection (1969); *Ingredients* for Piano and Sound Tracks (1970); *Intra I* for Bass Clarinet and Sound Track (1971); *Elegy* for Female Voice and 2 Sound Tracks (1972); *Looking Ears* for Bass Clarinet, Grand Piano, and Sound Tracks (1972); *Phases* for 4 Sound Tracks and Orch. (Utrecht, Jan. 10, 1975); *Soft Song* for Oboe and 2 Sound Tracks (1975); *Dialogue* for Bass Clarinet and Sound Tracks (1976); *Toccare* for Sound Tracks and Piano (1979); *John's Lullaby* for Chorus, Tape, and Orch. (1985).

Bruzdowicz, Joanna, Polish composer; b. Warsaw, May 17, 1943. She studied music theory with Sikorski at the Warsaw Cons. (M.A., 1966); then went to Paris, where she took lessons with Nadia Boulanger and Messiaen; worked there with the Groupe de Recherches Musicales. Eventually she went to live in Belgium.
WORKS: 3 operas: *The Penal Colony,* after Kafka (Tours, 1972), *Les Troyennes,* after Euripides (Saint-Denis, France, 1973), and *Bramy Raju* (The Gates of Paradise; Warsaw, 1987); ballet, *Le Petit Prince,* after Saint-Exupéry (Brussels, Dec. 10, 1976); *Sketches from the Harbor,* cycle for Mezzo-soprano, Flute, and Percussion (1967); *Esquisses* for Flute, Piano, Viola, and Cello (1969); *Jour d'ici et d'ailleurs* for Narrator, Chorus, and Instruments (1971); *Episode* for Piano and 13 Instruments (1973); *Epitaph* for Harpsichord and Tape (1973); *Esitanza* for Piano, 4-hands (1973); *Le Beau Danube bleu* for 2 Pianos and Tape (1973–74); Piano Concerto (1974); Sym. (1975); Violin Concerto (1975–76); *Dum Spiro Spero* for Flute and Tape (1981); 2 string quartets: No. 1, "La Vita" (1983); No. 2, with Speaker, "Cantus Aeternus" (1988); *Aurora Borealis* for Harp and Organ (1988); *En attendant Anaïs,* children's musical (Brussels, Feb. 11, 1988); much theater and film music.

Bryars, Gavin, English composer and teacher; b. Goole, Yorkshire, Jan. 16, 1943. He studied philosophy at Sheffield Univ. and composition with Cyril Ramsey and George Linstead, then began his career as a bassist, turning in 1966 to composition and quickly emerging as one of England's most influential experimental composers. His academic appointments have included Portsmouth College of Art, where he founded the Portsmouth Sinfonia (made up of amateurs), and Leicester Polytechnic (from 1970); he also ed. the *Experimental Music Catalogue* (1972–81) and is official biographer of the eccentric English composer, novelist, and painter Lord Berners. His compositions, indeterminate and replete with repetition, often utilize electronic means. His warmth and humor is evidenced in his *The Sinking of the Titanic* (1969), a multi-media, meditative collage work composed of excerpts from pieces the drowning orch. might have been playing. Other compositions include *Jesus' Blood Never Failed Me Yet* (1971), *Out of Laeski's Gazebo* (1977), *My 1st Homage* (1978), *The Vespertine Park* (1980), and *Effarene* (1984). He has collaborated with a number of well-known musicians, including Brian Eno, Steve Reich, and Cornelius Cardew; a number of his pieces have been choreographed by Lucinda Childs. In 1984, his opera *Medea*, in collaboration with Robert Wilson, was premiered at the Opéra de Lyon.

Brymer, Jack, distinguished English clarinetist; b. South Shields, Jan. 27, 1915. He studied at the Univ. of London; then served in the Royal Air Force in World War II. In 1947 he joined the Royal Phil. as principal clarinet; then held this position with the BBC Sym. Orch. (1963–71) and the London Sym. Orch. (1971–86). He was director of the London Wind Soloists; was prof. at the Royal Academy of Music, London (1950–59); also taught at Kneller Hall (1967–71) and the Guildhall School of Music (from 1982). In 1960 he was made an Officer of the Order of the British Empire. He wrote an autobiography under the title *From Where I Sit*, publ. in 1979. He also publ. *In the Orchestra* (1987).

Bryn-Julson, Phyllis (Mae), esteemed American soprano; b. Bowdon, N.Dak., Feb. 5, 1945. She studied piano, organ, violin, and voice at Concordia College, Moorehead, Minn.; then spent several summers at the Berkshire Music Center at Tanglewood and completed her studies at Syracuse Univ. On Oct. 28, 1966, she made her formal debut as soloist in Berg's *Lulu Suite* with the Boston Sym. Orch., and in 1976 made her operatic debut as Malinche in the U.S. premiere of Sessions's *Montezuma* in Boston. She often appears in recital with her husband, the organist Donald Sutherland. In addition to teaching at Kirkland-Hamilton College in Clinton, N.Y., and at the Univ. of Maryland, she conducted master classes on both sides of the Atlantic. She is particularly renowned as a concert singer, at ease with all periods and styles of music.

Bucchi, Valentino, Italian composer; b. Florence, Nov. 29, 1916; d. Rome, May 9, 1976. He studied composition with Frazzi and Dallapiccola, and music history with Torrefranca at the Univ. of Florence, graduating in 1944; subsequently held teaching posts at the Florence Cons. (1945–52 and 1954–57), the Venice Cons. (1952–54), and the Perugia Cons. (1957–58); was music director of the Accademia Filarmonica Romana (1958–60) and artistic director of the Teatro Comunale in Bologna (1963–65). In his works he continued the national Italian tradition of the musical theater, while in his techniques he attempted to modernize the polyphony of the Renaissance along the lines established by Malipiero. **WORKS:** Operas: *Il giuoco del barone* (Florence, Dec. 20, 1944), *Il Contrabasso*, after Chekhov (Florence, May 20, 1954), *Una notte in Paradiso* (Florence, May 11, 1960), and *Il coccodrillo* (Florence, May 9, 1970); ballets: *Racconto siciliano* (Rome, Jan. 17, 1956) and *Mirandolina* (Rome, March 12, 1957); also *Ballata del silenzio* (1951); *Concerto lirico* for Violin and Strings (1958); *Concerto grottesco* for Double Bass and String Orch. (1967); String Quartet (1956); Concerto for Clarinet Solo (1969); *Ison* for Cello Solo (1971); *Colloquio corale* for Narrator, Vocal Solo, Chorus, and Orch. (1971).

Bucci, Mark, American composer; b. N.Y., Feb. 26, 1924. He studied at St. John's Univ. in N.Y. (1941–42); after private training in composition from Tibor Serly (1942–45), he continued his studies with Frederick Jacobi and Vittorio Giannini at the Juilliard School of Music in N.Y. (B.S., 1951) and with Aaron Copland at the Berkshire Music Center at Tanglewood. In 1953–54 he held Guggenheim fellowships. He adopted a

pragmatic method of composition in a strong rhythmic style, in modern but tonal harmonies, particularly effective in his stage works. **WORKS: OPERAS:** *The Boor*, after Chekhov (N.Y., Dec. 29, 1949); *The Dress* (N.Y., Dec. 8, 1953); *Sweet Betsy from Pike* (N.Y., Dec. 8, 1953); *Tale for a Deaf Ear* (Tanglewood, Aug. 5, 1957); *The Hero* (N.Y., Sept. 24, 1965); *Midas* (1981). **MUSICALS:** *Caucasian Chalk Circle* (1948); *The 13 Clocks* (1953); *Our Miss Brooks* (1961); *2nd Coming* (1976); incidental music to *Cadenza* (1947), *Summer Afternoon* (1952), and *The Sorcerer's Apprentice* (1969); also film scores, a Flute Concerto, choral pieces, and songs.

Buchanan, Isobel, Scottish soprano; b. Glasgow, March 15, 1954. After training in Scotland, she made her operatic debut as Pamina with the Australian Opera in Sydney (1976); subsequently she appeared at the Glyndebourne Festival (1978), the Vienna State Opera (1978), and London's Covent Garden (1979). Among her most admired roles are Micaela, Adina, Zerlina, Donna Elvira, Susanna, and Fiordiligi.

Bucharoff (real name, **Buchhalter**), **Simon,** Russian-American pianist and composer; b. Berdichev, April 20, 1881; d. Chicago, Nov. 24, 1955. He settled in America as a youth; studied piano with Paolo Gallico in N.Y., and later with Julius Epstein and Emil Sauer in Vienna. He occupied various teaching posts; lived principally in Chicago and Hollywood. He publ. *The Modern Pianist's Textbook* (N.Y., 1931). **WORKS:** Operas: *A Lover's Knot* (Chicago Opera, Jan. 15, 1916); *Sakahra* (Frankfurt, Nov. 8, 1924; rev. 1953); *Jewel; Wastrel*; symphonic poems (*Reflections in the Water; Drunk; Doubt; Joy Sardonic*; etc.).

Buchbinder, Rudolf, Austrian pianist; b. Leitmeritz, Dec. 1, 1946. He studied with Bruno Seidlhofer at the Vienna Academy of Music; in 1965 he made a tour of North and South America; in 1966 he won a special prize awarded at the Van Cliburn Competition; then made a tour with the Vienna Phil., and also appeared as a soloist in Paris, Milan, Madrid, and London. In 1975 he made a tour of Japan and the U.S. with the Vienna Sym. Orch.; in addition, he taught piano at the Basel Academy of Music.

Bücher, Karl, German economist and writer on music; b. Kirchberg, near Wiesbaden, Feb. 16, 1847; d. Leipzig, Nov. 12, 1930. As a prof. of economics at Leipzig Univ. (1892–1916), he became interested in the correlation between social conditions among primitive peoples and music; he publ. a book, *Arbeit und Rhythmus* (1896), in which the origin of music is traced to natural rhythmic exertions during manual labor, with group singing in unison as a natural expedient for teamwork. The book aroused a great deal of controversy, and went through several printings; the 6th ed. was publ. in 1924. He also publ. his memoirs as *Lebenserinnerungen* (1919). **BIBL.:** L. Stratil-Sauer, *Volksliedhaftes unter B.s deutschen Arbeitsliedern* (Leipzig, 1931).

Buchla, Donald (Frederick), American electronic-instrument designer and builder, composer, and performer; b. Southgate, Calif., April 17, 1937. After studying physics at the Univ. of Calif. at Berkeley (B.A., 1961), he became active in the San Francisco Tape Music Center, where in 1966 he installed the first Buchla synthesizer. That same year he founded Buchla Associates in Berkeley for the manufacture of synthesizers. In addition to designing and manufacturing electronic instruments, he also installed electronic-music studios at the Royal Academy of Music in Stockholm and at IRCAM in Paris, among other institutions. In 1975 he became co-founder of the Electric Weasel Ensemble, a live electronic-music group, and in 1978 he became co-director of the Artists' Research Collective in Berkeley. He held a Guggenheim fellowship in 1978. **WORKS:** *Cicada Music* for some 2,500 Cicadas (1963); 5 *Video Mirrors* for Audience of 1 or More (1966); *Anagnorisis* for 1 Performer and Voice (1970); *Harmonic Pendulum* for Buchla Series 200 Synthesizer (1972); *Garden* for 3 Performers and Dancer (1975); *Keyboard Encounter* for 2 Pianos (1976);

Q for 14 Instruments (1979); *Silicon Cello* for Amplified Cello (1979); *Consensus Conduction* for Buchla Series 300 Synthesizer and Audience (1981); also an orchestration of D. Rosenboom's *How Much Better If Plymouth Rock Had Landed on the Pilgrims* for 2 Buchla Series 300 Synthesizers (1969).

Buchner, Hans, German organist; b. Ravensburg, Württemberg, Oct. 26, 1483; d. probably in Constance, mid-Feb. 1538. His father, an organist, gave Buchner his 1st instruction. He became organist at the Cathedral of Constance on June 19, 1506, and was given permanent employment in 1512. His magnum opus was a *Fundamentum,* a manual for composition and improvisation on the organ (1551).

Buchner, Philipp Friedrich, German organist; b. Wertheim, Sept. 11, 1614; d. Würzburg, March 23, 1669. He was a chorister in Frankfurt; then served as organist in the Barfüsserkirche there (1634–36); subsequently was engaged as Kapellmeister in Krakow (c.1637–47). In 1648 he was in Mainz. His *Concerti ecclesiastici* was publ. in 2 books (Venice, 1642, 1644); he also wrote instrumental music for violins, violas, and cembalo.

Bucht, Gunnar, Swedish composer, musicologist, and pedagogue; b. Stocksund, Aug. 5, 1927. He studied musicology at Uppsala Univ. (1947–53); concurrently took lessons in composition with Blomdahl (1947–51); received his Ph.D. at Uppsala in 1953; later studied composition in Germany with Orff (1954), in Italy with Petrassi (1954–55), and in Paris with Max Deutsch (1961–62). He taught at Stockholm Univ. (1965–69); was also employed in diplomatic service as cultural attaché at the Swedish Embassy in Bonn (1970–73). In 1975 he was appointed prof. of composition at the Musikhögskolan in Stockholm, where he became director in 1987. His music retains traditional forms while adopting diverse modern techniques.
WORKS: Opera, *Tronkrävarna* (The Pretenders), after Ibsen (1961–64; Stockholm, Sept. 10, 1966); opera-oratorio, *Jerikos murar* (The Walls of Jericho; 1966–67; reworked as an electronic piece, 1970); 8 syms.: No. 1 (1952; Swedish Radio, Dec. 6, 1953); No. 2 (1953); No. 3 (1954; Swedish Radio, April 17, 1955); No. 4 (1957–58; Stockholm, April 3, 1959); No. 5 (1960; Stockholm, Jan. 14, 1962); No. 6 (1961–62; Stockholm, Nov. 20, 1963); No. 7 (1970–71; Norrköping, March 26, 1972); No. 8 (1982–83; Stockholm, Sept. 13, 1984); *Introduction and Allegro* for String Orch. (1950); *Meditation* for Piano and Orch. (1950); Cello Concerto (1954); *Symphonic Fantasy* for Orch. (1955); Divertimento for Orch. (1955–56); *Dagen svalnar* (The Day Cools) for Soprano, and Orch. or Piano (1956); *Envar sin egen professor* for Tenor, Chorus, and Orch. (1957); *La fine della diaspora,* after Quasimodo's "Auschwitz," for Chorus and Orch. (1958; Stockholm, Oct. 4, 1963); *Couplets et Refrains* for Orch. (1960); *Dramma per musica* for Orch. (1963; symphonic intermezzo from 2nd act of his opera *Tronkrävarna*); *Strangaspel* for Strings (1965); *Eine lutherische Messe* for Soloists, Mixed and Children's Choruses, and Orch. (1972–73); *Winter Organ* for Orch. (1974); *Music for Lau* for Children's Chorus, Wind Orch., Percussion, Double Basses, and Tape (1974–75); Violin Concerto (1978; Stockholm, Nov. 5, 1980); *En Clairobscur* for Chamber Orch. (1980–81); *Tönend bewegte Formen* for Orch. (1987); *Theme and Variations* for Piano (1949); String Quintet (1949–50); 2 piano sonatas (1951, 1959); 2 string quartets (1951, 1959); 5 *Bagatelles* for String Quartet (1953); Sonata for Piano and Percussion (1955); *Hommage à Edith Södergran* for Mixed Chorus (1956); *Kattens öron* for Narrator, Saxophone, Double Bass, and Percussion (1959); *Hund skenar glad* (Dog Runs Happy), chamber cantata for Voice, Female Chorus, and 8 Instruments (1961); *Ein Wintermärchen* for Voice and Instrumental Ensemble (1962); 6 *arstidssånger* (Season Songs) for Voice and Piano (1965); *Symphonie pour la musique libérée* for Tape (1969); *Bald från mitt gulsippeänge* for Clarinet and Piano (1985; also for Harpsichord, 1988); *Unter vollem Einsatz* for Organ and 5 Percussion (1986–87).

Büchtger, Fritz, German composer; b. Munich, Feb. 14, 1903; d. Starnberg, Dec. 26, 1978. He studied organ, flute, voice, conducting, and music theory at the Music Academy of Mu-

nich; his instructors in composition were Beer-Walbrunn and Wolfgang von Waltershausen. He followed the contemporary trends of German music, but with the advent of the Nazis, when modernism became strictly *verboten,* he was compelled, as a certified Aryan, to write nationalistic and racially blatant stuff. In 1948 he swerved back to his original interests, formed a studio for new music in Munich, and began writing in a dodecaphonic idiom, adroitly applying it even to his religious compositions. He was also active internationally as chairman of the German section of "Jeunesses musicales."
WORKS: Oratorios: *Der weisse Reiter* (1948) and *Das gläserne Meer* (1953); *Himmelfahrt* (1957); *Die Verklärung* (1957); Christmas Oratorio (1959); *John the Baptist* (1962); Violin Concerto (1963); *Strukturen* for Nonet (1968); 4 string quartets (1948, 1957, 1958, 1969).
BIBL.: L. Wismeyer, *F. B.* (Regensburg, 1963).

Buck, Dudley, noted American organist, composer, and pedagogue; b. Hartford, Conn., March 10, 1839; d. West Orange, N.J., Oct. 6, 1909. He studied piano with W.J. Babcock; then traveled to Germany, where he took courses at the Leipzig Cons. with Plaidy and Moscheles (piano), Hauptmann (composition), and J. Rietz (instrumentation); later was in Paris (1861–62). Returning to the U.S., he served as church organist in Hartford, Chicago, Boston, and Brooklyn. He was one of the 1st American composers to achieve recognition for his church music.
WORKS: Comic opera, *Deseret, or A Saint's Affliction* (N.Y., Oct. 11, 1880); grand opera, *Serapis*; symphonic overture, *Marmion* (1880); cantata, *The Legend of Don Munio* (1874); *Canzonetta* and *Bolero* for Violin and Orch.; 2 grand sonatas for Organ; concert variations on *The Star Spangled Banner* for Organ; also several manuals for organ playing.
BIBL.: D. B.: *A Complete Bibliography* (N.Y., 1910).

Buck, Ole, Danish composer; b. Copenhagen, Feb. 1, 1945. Though largely self-taught, he began to compose energetically at an early age, adopting an elaborate serial idiom. Having reached an impasse on that primrose path, he experienced an epiphany upon contemplating Zen Buddhist paintings and reciting transcendental poetry, in which an act of sempiternal iteration becomes the guiding spirit of human art and music.
WORKS: *Kalligrafi* for Soprano and Orch. (1964); 2 sets of pieces, titled *White Flower Music:* No. 1 for 2 Flutes, 2 Clarinets, and Trumpet (1965) and No. 2 for Orch. (1973); *Envoi,* fragments for Orch. (1964–65); *Décor* for Chamber Orch. (1966; rev. for Orch., 1969); *Preludes I–IV* for Chamber Orch. (1966–67); *Signes* for Wind Quintet (1967); *Punctuations* for Orch. (1968); *Masques* for 6 Percussion Groups (1969); *Fairies* for Soprano and Orch. (1972); *Felix Luna,* ballet (1970–71; Copenhagen, Feb. 3, 1973); *Granulations* for Orch. (1971–72); *Kindergarten* for Flute, Oboe, Horn, and Violin (1972); *Christopher Columbus* for Chorus and Orch. (1973); *Pastorals* for Orch. (1975); choruses; songs; tape pieces.

Buck, Sir Percy Carter, English organist; b. London, March 25, 1871; d. there, Oct. 3, 1947. He studied at the Guildhall School and the Royal College of Music; subsequently served as church organist. From 1901 to 1927 he was music director at the Harrow School; was prof. of music at Trinity College in Dublin (1910–20) and at the Univ. of London (1925–37); also taught at the Royal College of Music in London. He was knighted in 1937. His works include an overture for Orch., *Cœur de Lion*; String Quartet; Piano Quintet; sonatas, piano pieces, etc. He was the author of *Ten Years of University Music in Oxford* (1894; with Mee and Woods); *Unfigured Harmony* (1911); *Organ Playing* (1912); *First Year at the Organ* (1912); *The Organ: A Complete Method for the Study of Technique and Style*; *Acoustics for Musicians* (1918); *The Scope of Music* (Oxford, 1924); *Psychology for Musicians* (London, 1944); also was ed. of the introductory vol. and vols. I and II of the 2nd edition of the *Oxford History of Music.*

Bücken, Ernst, eminent German musicologist; b. Aachen, May 2, 1884; d. Overath, near Cologne, July 28, 1949. He studied musicology at the Univ. of Munich with Sandberger and Kroyer; also took courses in composition with Courvoisier; received his Ph.D. there in 1912 with the dissertation *Anton Reicha; Sein Leben und seine Kompositionen* (publ. in Munich, 1912); completed his Habilitation at the Univ. of Cologne in 1920 with his *Der heroische Stil in der Oper* (publ. in Leipzig, 1924); was a prof. there from 1925 to 1945; then retired to Overath. His elucidation of musical styles remains an important achievement in his work as a musicologist; as such, he ed. the monumental Handbuch der Musikwissenschaft in 10 vols., which began publication in 1927; for this series he contributed *Musik des Rokokos und der Klassik* (1927), *Die Musik des 19. Jahrhunderts bis zur Moderne* (1929–31), and *Geist und Form im musikalischen Kunstwerk* (1929–32); he was also editor of the series Die Grossen Meister der Musik from 1932. His further writings include *Tagebuch der Gattin Mozarts* (Munich, 1915); *München als Musikstadt* (Leipzig, 1923); *Führer und Probleme der neuen Musik* (Cologne, 1924); *Musikalische Charakterköpfe* (Leipzig, 1924); ed. *Handbuch der Musikerziehung* (Wildpark-Potsdam, 1931); *Ludwig van Beethoven* (Wildpark-Potsdam, 1934); *Richard Wagner* (Wildpark-Potsdam, 1934; 2nd ed., 1943); *Deutsche Musikkunde* (Wildpark-Potsdam, 1935); *Musik aus deutscher Art* (Cologne, 1936); *Musik der Nationen* (Leipzig, 1937; 2nd ed., rev. as *Geschichte der Musik*, ed. by J. Völckers, 1951); ed. *Richard Wagner: Die Hauptschriften* (Leipzig, 1937); *Das deutsche Lied: Probleme und Gestalten* (Hamburg, 1939); *Robert Schumann* (Cologne, 1940); *Wörterbuch der Musik* (Leipzig, 1940); *Musik der Deutschen: Eine Kulturgeschichte der deutschen Musik* (Cologne, 1941); *Wolfgang Amadeus Mozart: Schöpferische Wandlungen* (Hamburg, 1942); *Richard Strauss* (Kevelaar, 1949). **BIBL.:** W. Kahl, "E. B.," *Die Musikforschung*, III (1950).

Buckley, Emerson, American conductor; b. N.Y., April 14, 1916; d. Miami, Nov. 17, 1989. He studied at Columbia Univ. (B.A., 1936), then made his conducting debut in N.Y. in 1936. After holding various posts with operatic and symphonic groups, he was music director of the Miami Opera Guild (1950–85). He became music director of the Fort Lauderdale Sym. Orch. in 1963 while continuing to direct in Miami, but he was principally known as a favorite conductor on tour with Pavarotti. With his silver hair and goatee he cut a striking figure and appeared in Pavarotti's film *Yes, Giorgio!* (1982); the film was unsuccessful, but Buckley's appearance produced an impression. He was also the conductor in a film documentary about Pavarotti, entitled *A Distant Harmony.*

Buckner, Milt(on), black American jazz pianist, organist, trombonist, and composer; b. St. Louis, July 10, 1915; d. Chicago, July 27, 1977. He played in Lionel Hampton's band, becoming known for his technique of "locked-hands" in parallel block chords. He was also known as the first jazz player to popularize the Hammond organ.

Buczek (Buczkowna), Barbara (Kazimiera Zofia), Polish composer; b. Krakow, Jan. 9, 1940. She pursued her training in her native city, beginning with piano lessons with Kazimierz Mirski and progressing on to study with Maria Bilińska-Riegerowa at the music school. She also took courses in piano (diploma, 1965) with Ludwik Stefanski and composition (diploma, 1974) with Boguslaw Schaeffer at the Academy of Music, where she later taught. **WORKS: ORCH.:** 2 *Impressions* (1970); *Anekumena*, concerto for 89 Instruments (1974; Warsaw, Sept. 25, 1975); *Assemblage* for Alto Flute and String Orch. (1975); Violin Concerto (1979; Turin, June 13, 1986); *Dikolon* (Salzburg, May 11, 1985); *Symfonia kameralna* (1988); Concerto for Cello, Choir, and Orch. (1989). **CHAMBER:** 2 string quartets: No. 1 (1968); No. 2, *Transgressio* (Vienna, Oct. 30, 1985); Wind Quintet (1969); Sextet for Violin, Flute, Soprano, Cello, and 2 Pianos (1974); *Duodecet* for 12 String Instruments (1976; Gdansk, Jan. 20, 1984); *Eidos I* for Violin (1977); *Eidos II* for Tuba (1977; also for Tuba and Piano, 1984); *Hipostaza*, quintet for Soprano, Flute, Vibraphone, Cello, and Saxophone (1978; Strasbourg and Rome, Oct. 8, 1984); *Eidos III* for Bassoon (1979); Motet for Baritone, Reciters, Instruments, and Tape (Basel, Nov. 29, 1984); "pri-

mus inter pares" for Horn and 6 Instruments (1985); also a Vocal Concerto for 12 Solo Voices (1969), and 2 didactic pieces: *8 Easy Preludes and 8 Diatonic Canons* for 2 Clarinets (1971) and *Unicoursal Figures* for Flute, Vibraphone, and Cello (1980).

Buczynski, Walter, Canadian composer and pianist; b. Toronto, Dec. 17, 1933. He studied music theory at the Cons. of Toronto; took lessons in composition in Paris with Darius Milhaud in the summer of 1956, and with Nadia Boulanger 1960 and 1962. He studied piano mainly in Warsaw, where he has ethnic roots. Returning to Canada in 1962, he was appointed teacher of piano and theory at the Royal Cons. of Music in Toronto; he then taught theory at the Univ. of Toronto (from 1970). His music is influenced by the modern Polish school of composition; the titles of his works are in the spirit of aggressive modernism. **WORKS:** Chamber opera, *From the Buczynski Book of the Living* (1972); *Naked at the Opera*, opera (1978); Piano Trio (1954); Suite for Wind Quintet (1955); Divertimento for Violin, Cello, Clarinet, and Bassoon (1957); *Mr. Rhinoceros and His Musicians* for Narrator, Soprano, and Baritone (Canadian Radio, Dec. 25, 1965); *Do Re Mi* for Soprano, Tenor, 2 Actors, and Instrumental Ensemble (Canadian Radio, Dec. 13, 1967); 2½ *Squares in a Circle* for Flute, Violin, Cello, and Strings (1967); 4 *Movements* for Piano and Strings (1969); *Zeroing In No. 1* for Speaking Voice, Prepared Piano, and Tape (1971); *Zeroing In No. 2 (Distraction and Then)* for Orch. Groups in the audience and on-stage Strings (1971); *Zeroing In No. 3* for String Quartet and Orch. (1973); *Zeroing In No. 4 (Innards and Outards)* for Soprano, Flute, Piano, and Orch. (1972); *Zeroing In No. 5 (Dictionary of Mannerisms)* for Piano (1972); *3 Against Many* for Flute, Clarinet, Bassoon, and Orch. (1973); 27 *Pieces for a 27-minute Show* for Piano (1973); Concerto for Violin, Cello, and Orch. (1975); *Olympics '76* for Brass Quintet (1976); *The Tales of Nanabozho* for Narrator and Wind Quintet (1976); Piano Concerto (1979); Piano Quintet (1984); *The August Collection*, 27 preludes (1987); *Litanies* for Accordion and Percussion (1988); songs; piano pieces for young people, for adults, and for diverse ages.

Budashkin, Nikolai, Russian composer; b. Lubakhovka, in Kaluga region, Aug. 6, 1910, of a peasant family; d. Moscow, Jan. 31, 1988. After working as a blacksmith, he went to Moscow and took a course with Miaskovsky at the Moscow Cons. He specialized in music for Russian popular instruments in symphonic combinations; he wrote 2 concertos for Domra and Orch. (1944, 1947); Concert Variations for Balalaika, with Orch., on a Russian folk song (1946); and works for ensembles consisting entirely of such instruments. His early *Festive Overture* (1937) achieved considerable success in Russia.

Budd, Harold, American composer of extreme avant-garde tendencies; b. Los Angeles, May 24, 1936. He studied composition and acoustics with Gerald Strang and Aurelio de la Vega at Calif. State Univ. at Northridge (B.A., 1963) and with Ingolf Dahl at the Univ. of Southern Calif. (M.Mus., 1966). From 1969 to 1976 he was on the faculty of the Calif. Inst. of the Arts. An exponent of optically impressive music, he judged the quality of a work by its appearance on paper, in the firm conviction that visual excellence is cosubstantial with audible merit. His compositions are mostly designed for mixed media; some of them are modular, capable of being choreographed one into another; some are mere verbalizations of the intended mode of performance, calculated to stultify, confuse, or exasperate the listening beholder. Perhaps the most arresting and bewildering of such misleading works in his catalogue is something called *Intermission Piece*, to be played at random with a "barely audible amplitude spectrum" during intermission, with the audience "physically or conceptually absent," so that the number of performances runs into thousands, including every time an intermission during a concert occurs any place in the world. **WORKS:** *Analogies from Rothko* for Orch. (1964); *The 6th This Year* for Orch. (1967); *September Music* (1967); *November* (1967; score displayed as a painting at the Museum of Contemporary Crafts in N.Y.); *Black Flowers*, a "quiet chamber ritual for 4 performers," to be staged in semidarkness on the threshold of visibility and audibility (1968); *Intermission Piece* (1968; 1st heard as musicians tuned their instruments and practiced various passages of the music scheduled to be played, during the intermission, at Hartford, Conn., Jan. 28, 1970); *1 Sound* for String Quartet glissando (1968); *Mangus Colorado* for Amplified Gongs (1969; Buffalo, Feb. 4, 1970); *Lovely Thing* for Piano, telling the player: "Select a chord—if in doubt call me (in lieu of performance) at 213-662-7819 for spiritual advice" (Memphis, Tenn., Oct. 23, 1969); *Lovely Thing* for Strings (1969); *California 99* (1969); *The Candy-Apple Revision* (1970); *Wonder's Edge* for Piano, Electric Guitar, and Electronics (San Francisco, Feb. 26, 1982).

Budden, Julian (Midforth), English musicologist; b. Holylake, Cheshire, April 9, 1924. He was educated at Queen's College, Oxford (B.A., 1948; M.A., 1951) and the Royal College of Music, London (B.Mus., 1955); from 1951 he worked for the BBC, serving as a producer for music programs (1955–70), chief producer for opera (1970–76), and music organizer for external services (1976–83). His studies of 19th-century Italian opera are important; especially valuable is *The Operas of Verdi* (3 vols., London, 1973–81). He also publ. the biography *Verdi* (London, 1985).

Buelow, George J(ohn), American musicologist; b. Chicago, March 31, 1929. He studied piano with Rudolph Ganz at the Chicago Musical College, where he received his M.B. (1950) and M.M. (1951) degrees; then studied musicology with Martin Bernstein, Sachs, and Reese at N.Y. Univ. (Ph.D., 1961, with the diss. *Johann David Heinichen, "Der General-bass in der Composition": A Critical Study with Annotated Translation of Selected Chapters*). In 1961 he joined the faculty of the Univ. of Calif. at Riverside; then was prof. of music at the Univ. of Kentucky at Louisville (1968–69) and Rutgers Univ. (1969–77). In 1977 he became prof. of musicology at Indiana Univ. in Bloomington. He is particularly noted for his studies of 17th- and 18th-century German music. He wrote *Thoroughbass Accompaniment according to Johann David Heinichen* (Berkeley, 1966; 2nd ed., rev., 1986), and *New Mattheson Studies* (with H. Marx; Cambridge, 1984).

Buffardin, Pierre-Gabriel, French flutist; b. Provence, c.1690; d. Paris, Jan. 13, 1768. He joined the Dresden Court Orch. in 1715; returned to France in 1750. He was highly regarded as a teacher; among his pupils were Johann Jacob Bach (brother of J.S. Bach) and J.J. Quantz.

Bughici, Dumitru, Rumanian composer; b. Iaşi, Nov. 14, 1921. After completing a course of elementary music at the Iaşi Cons., he went to Leningrad, where he studied at the Cons. with Salmanov and Schnitke (1950–55). Returning to Rumania, he was appointed to the faculty of the Bucharest Cons.

WORKS: ORCH.: 2 violin concertos (1955, 1977); *Poem concertant* for Cello and Orch. (1957); 2 sinfoniettas: *Simfonieta tinerţii* (1958) and *Simfonieta II*, "Cosmică" (1962); 9 *Simfonie* (1961–85; No. 7, "Simfonie lirico-dramatica—In Memoriam," for String Orch.); *Poemul bucuriei* (1962); *Bolero*, fantasy (1963); *Monumentul*, poem (1964); *Partita* (1965); *Dialoguri dramatice* for String Orch. and Flute (1967); *Sonata* for String Orch. (1969–70); *Melodie, Ritm, Culoare*, concerto for Orch. (1970); *Poem iubirii* (1971); *Symphonic Fantasia in Jazz Rhythm* (1973–74); Cello Concerto (1974); Trumpet Concerto (1975); *5 Images* for Chamber Orch. (1976); *Tablouri coregrafice* (1978); Sinfonie Concertanta No. 1 (1979–80) and No. 2 (1980–81); Jazz Concerto (1982–83). CHAMBER: *Scherzo* for Cello and Piano (1954); 5 string quartets (1954–79); *Divertimento* (Trio No. 1) for Violin, Cello, and Piano (1961); Violin Sonata (1963); *Mic (Small) divertissement* for Violin, Viola, Cello, Piano, Clarinet, and Percussion (1967); Sonata for Solo Violin (1968); *Fantasia Quartet* (1969); Trio No. 2 for Violin, Cello, and Piano (1977); *Fantasy* for Xylophone and Double Bass (1980); piano pieces.

Buhlig, Richard, American pianist; b. Chicago, Dec. 21, 1880; d. Los Angeles, Jan. 30, 1952. He studied in Chicago, and in Vienna with Leschetizky (1897–1900); made his debut in recital in Berlin (1901); then toured Europe and the U.S. (American debut with the Philadelphia Orch. in N.Y., Nov. 5, 1907). In 1918 he was appointed teacher of piano at the Inst. of Musical Arts in N.Y.; later returned to Europe; eventually settled in Los Angeles as a performer and teacher.

Bujarski, Zbigniew, Polish composer; b. Muszyna, Aug. 21, 1933. He studied composition with Wiechowicz and conducting with Wodiczko at the State College of Music in Krakow. His music is dense in its contrapuntal entanglements, without becoming viscous.

WORKS: *Burning Bushes*, cycle for Soprano, and Chamber Ensemble or Piano (1958); *Triptych* for String Orch. and Percussion (1959); *Synchrony I* for Soprano and Chamber Ensemble (1959), and *II* for Soprano, Chorus, and Orch. (1960); *Zones* for Chamber Ensemble (1961); *Kinoth* for Orch. (1963); *Chamber Composition* for Voice, Flute, Harp, Piano, and Percussion (1963); *Contraria* for Orch. (1965); *El Hombre* for Soprano, Mezzo-soprano, Baritone, Chorus, and Orch. (1969–73; Warsaw, Sept. 21, 1974); *Musica domestica* for 18 String Instruments (1977); Concerto for Strings (1979; Warsaw, Sept. 10, 1980); *Similis Greco*, symphonic cycle (1979–83); *Quartet on the Advent* (1984); *Quartet for the Resurrection* (1990).

Buketoff, Igor, American conductor; b. Hartford, Conn., May 29, 1915. He studied music at the Juilliard School in N.Y. (1939–42). In 1943 he began his conducting career; appeared as a guest conductor in America and in Europe; led the Young People's Concerts of the N.Y. Phil. (1948–53); then was director of the Fort Wayne (Ind.) Phil. (1948–66); also conducted the Iceland Sym. Orch. (1964–65); served as music director of the St. Paul Opera Assoc. (1968–74); was a visiting prof. at the Univ. of Houston (1977–79).

Bukofzer, Manfred F(ritz), eminent German-born American musicologist; b. Oldenburg, March 27, 1910; d. Oakland, Calif., Dec. 7, 1955. He studied at the Hoch Cons. in Frankfurt, and at the Univs. of Heidelberg, Berlin, and Basel (Ph.D., 1936); also took courses with Hindemith in Berlin. He lectured in Basel (1933–39); also at Oxford and Cambridge Univs. In 1939 he settled in the U.S.; became a naturalized citizen in 1945. He taught at Case Western Reserve Univ. in Cleveland (1940–41). In 1941 he became a member of the faculty of the Univ. of Calif. at Berkeley; a year before his untimely death he was appointed chairman of the music dept. His numerous publications are distinguished by originality of historical and musical ideas coupled with precision of factual exposition; having mastered the English language, he was able to write brilliantly in British and American publications; he was also greatly esteemed as a teacher.

WRITINGS: *Sumer Is Icumen In: A Revision* (Berkeley, 1944); *Music in the Baroque Era* (N.Y., 1947); *Studies in Medieval and Renaissance Music* (N.Y., 1950). He also edited the complete works of Dunstable (vol. VIII of Musica Britannica, 1953; 2nd ed., rev., 1970, by M. Bent, I. Bent, and B. Trowell).

BIBL.: D. Boyden, "In Memoriam: M.F. B.," *Musical Quarterly* (July 1956).

Bull, Edvard Hagerup. See Hagerup Bull, Edvard.

Bull, John, famous English organist and composer; b. probably in Old Radnor, Radnorshire, c.1562; d. Antwerp, March 12, 1628. He was a pupil of William Blitheman in the Chapel Royal; received his Mus.B. from Oxford in 1586. He was sworn in as a Gentleman of the Chapel Royal in Jan. 1586, becoming its organist in 1591. In 1596, on Queen Elizabeth's recommendation, he was appointed prof. of music at Gresham College, and on March 6, 1597, was elected 1st public lecturer there. He got into difficulties with Gresham College when he impregnated premaritally a maiden named Elizabeth Walter, and was forced to resign on Dec. 20, 1607; he hastened to take a marriage license 2 days later. In 1610 he entered the service of Prince Henry, but in 1613 was charged with adultery and had to flee England. In Sept. 1615 he became assistant organist at the Antwerp Cathedral in Belgium, and was named its principal organist on Dec. 29, 1617. In the Netherlands he became acquainted with the great Dutch organist and composer Sweelinck; both he and Bull exerted considerable influence on the development of contrapuntal keyboard music of the time. Bull also composed many canons and anthems. Various works previously attributed to him are now considered doubtful. For a modern edition of his keyboard works, see *J.B.: Keyboard Music in Musica Britannica,* XIV (ed. by T. Dart, F. Cameron, and J. Steele, 1960; 2nd edition, rev., 1967) and XIX (ed. by T. Dart, 1963; 2nd edition, rev., 1970).

BIBL.: H. Miller, "J. B.'s Organ Works," *Music & Letters* (Jan. 1947); W. Mellers, "J. B. and English Keyboard Music," *Musical Quarterly* (July and Oct. 1954); J. van der Meer, "The Keyboard Works in the Vienna B.-Manuscript," *Tijdschrift van de Vereniging voor Nederlandse muziekgeschiedenis,* XVIII/2 (1957); G. Dodd, "Coperario or B.?," *Chelys,* I (1969); W. Cunningham, *The Keyboard Music of J. B.* (Ann Arbor, 1984).

Bull, Ole (Bornemann), eccentric Norwegian violinist; b. Bergen, Feb. 5, 1810; d. Lyso, near Bergen, Aug. 17, 1880. He was extremely precocious, and played the violin experimentally even before acquiring the rudiments of music. At the age of 9 he played solos with the Bergen Harmonic Soc. His teachers were then Niels Eriksen and J.H. Poulsen; later he had regular instruction with M. Ludholm. Ignoring academic rules, he whittled the bridge almost to the level of the fingerboard, so as to be able to play full chords on all 4 strings. He was sent by his father to Christiania to study theology, but failed the entrance examinations; instead, he organized a theater orch., which he led with his violin. In 1829 he played in Copenhagen and Kassel. In 1831 he went to Paris, where he heard Paganini and became obsessed with the idea of imitating his mannerisms and equaling his success, a fantasy devoid of all imagined reality because of Bull's amateurish technique. However, he developed a personal type of playing that pleased the public, particularly in localities rarely visited by real artists. During the season 1836–37 he played 274 concerts in England and Ireland; in 1839 he visited the great German violinist and composer Spohr in Kassel, in the hope of receiving useful advice from him. In 1840 he played Beethoven's *Kreutzer Sonata* in London, with Liszt at the piano. On July 23, 1849, he announced the formation of a Norwegian Theater in Bergen, which was opened on Jan. 2, 1850. While he failed to impress serious musicians and critics in Europe, he achieved his dream of artistic success in America; he made 5 concert tours across the U.S., playing popular selections and his own compositions on American themes with such fetching titles as *Niagara, Solitude of the Prairies,* and *To the Memory of Washington,* interspersing them with his arrangements of Norwegian folk songs. He entertained a strong conviction that Norway should generate its own national art, but the practical applications of his musical patriotism were failures because of his lack of formal study and a concentration on tawdry effects; still, it may be argued that he at least prepared the ground for the emergence of true Norwegian music; indeed, it is on his recommendation that Grieg was sent to study at the Leipzig Cons. Characteristically, Ole Bull became attracted by the then-current ideas of communal socialism. In 1852 he purchased 11,144 acres in Pennsylvania for a Norwegian settlement, but his lack of business sense led his undertaking to disaster. The settlement, planned on strict socialist lines, was given the name Oleana, thus establishing a personal connection with the name of its unlucky founder. Oleana soon collapsed, but Ole Bull earned admiration in Norway as a great national figure. Many of his violin pieces, mostly sentimental or strident in nature, with such titles as *La preghiera d'una madre, Variazioni di bravura, Polacca guerriera,* etc., were publ., but they sank into predictable desuetude.

BIBL.: J. Lie, *O. B.s breve i utdreg* (Copenhagen, 1881); S.

Bull (his 2nd wife), *O. B.: A Memoir* (Boston, 1883; German ed., Stuttgart, 1886); O. Vik, *O. B.* (Bergen, 1890); C.A. Aarvig, *Den unge O. B.* (Copenhagen, 1935); A. Björndal, *O. B. og Norsk folkemusik* (Bergen, 1940); M.B. Smith, *The Life of O. B.* (Princeton, 1943); Z. Hopp, *Eventyret om O. B.* (Bergen, 1945); Ola Linge, *O. B.* (Oslo, 1953); I. Bull, *O. B. Returns to Pennsylvania* (N.Y., 1961).

Buller, John, English composer; b. London, Feb. 7, 1927. He studied music as a child, beginning formal composition lessons in 1959 with Anthony Milner in London. He served as composer-in-residence at the Univ. of Edinburgh (1975–76) and at Queens Univ. in Belfast (1985–86).

WORKS: *The Cave* for Flute, Clarinet, Trombone, Cello, and Tape (1970); *2 Night Pieces from Finnegans Wake* for Soprano, Flute, Clarinet, Piano, and Cello (1971); *Finnegans Floras* for 14 Voices, Hand Percussion, and Piano (1972); *Poor Jenny* for Flutes and Percussion (1973); *Le terrazze* for 14 Instruments and Tape (1974); *The Mime of Mick, Nick, and the Maggies* for Soprano, Tenor, Baritone, Chorus, Orch., and Speaker or Tape (1976; London, Feb. 6, 1978); *Proenca* for Mezzo-soprano, Electric Guitar, and Orch. (London, Aug. 6, 1977); *Sette spazi* for 2 Clarinets, Violin, Cello, and Piano (1978); *The Theatre of Memory* for Orch. (London, Sept. 7, 1981); *Kommos* for Solo Voices and Electronics (St. Bartholomew's Festival, June 21, 1982); *Towards Aquarius* for 15 Players and Tape (London, Nov. 1, 1983); *A la fontana del vergier* for Countertenor, 2 Tenors, and Baritone (1984); *Of 3 Shakespeare Sonnets* for Mezzo-soprano, Flute, Clarinet, Harp, 2 Violins, Viola, and Cello (London, June 12, 1985).

Bullock, Sir Ernest, English organist and educator; b. Wigan, Sept. 15, 1890; d. Aylesbury, May 24, 1979. He studied organ with Bairstow in Leeds; also took courses at the Univ. of Durham (B.Mus., 1908; D.Mus., 1914). After serving as suborganist at Manchester Cathedral (1912–15), he was organist and choirmaster at Exeter Cathedral (1919–27). In 1928 he was named organist and Master of the Choristers at Westminster Abbey, and as such participated in several coronations. He became Gardiner Prof. of Music at the Univ. of Glasgow in 1941. He was then director of the Royal College of Music in London from 1952 until his retirement in 1960. He was knighted by King George VI in 1951.

Bülow, Hans (Guido) von, celebrated German pianist and conductor of high attainment; b. Dresden, Jan. 8, 1830; d. Cairo, Feb. 12, 1894. At the age of 9 he began to study piano with Friedrich Wieck and theory with Max Eberwein; then went to Leipzig, where he studied law at the univ. and took a music course with Moritz Hauptmann; he also studied piano with Plaidy. From 1846 to 1848 he lived in Stuttgart, where he made his debut as a pianist. In 1849 he attended the Univ. of Berlin; there he joined radical social groups; shortly afterward he went to Zürich and met Wagner, who was there in exile. After a year in Switzerland, where he conducted theater music, Bülow proceeded to Weimar, where he began to study with Liszt. In 1853 he made a tour through Germany and Austria as a pianist. In 1855 he was appointed head of the piano dept. at the Stern Cons. in Berlin, retaining this post until 1864. He married Liszt's natural daughter, Cosima, in 1857. In 1864 he was called by Ludwig II to Munich as court pianist and conductor; the King, who was a great admirer of Wagner, summoned Wagner to Munich from exile. Hans von Bülow himself became Wagner's ardent champion; on June 10, 1865, he conducted at the Court Opera in Munich the 1st performance of *Tristan und Isolde,* and on June 21, 1868, he led the premiere of *Die Meistersinger von Nürnberg.* It was about this time that Wagner became intimate with Cosima; after her divorce she married Wagner, in 1870. Despite this betrayal, Bülow continued to conduct Wagner's music; his growing admiration for Brahms cannot be construed as his pique against Wagner. It was Bülow who dubbed Brahms "the 3rd B of music," the 1st being Bach, and the 2nd Beethoven. In fact, the context of this nomination was more complex than a mere alphabetical adumbration; according to reports, Bülow was asked to name his favorite key; he replied that it was E-flat major, the key signature of the *Eroica*, with the 3 B's (German colloquialism for flats) signifying Bach, Beethoven, and Brahms. Then he was asked why he did not instead nominate Bruckner for the 3rd B, and he is supposed to have replied that Bruckner was too much of a Wagnerian for him. Bülow was indeed renowned for his wit and his aptitude for alliterative punning; his writings are of elevated literary quality. In 1872 Bülow lived in Florence; then resumed his career as a pianist, winning triumphant successes in England and Russia; during his American tour in 1875–76 he gave 139 concerts; he revisited America in 1889 and 1890. An important chapter in his career was his conductorship in Meiningen (1880–85). In 1882 he married a Meiningen actress, Marie Schanzer. He was conductor of the Berlin Phil. from 1887 to 1893, when a lung ailment forced him to seek a cure in Egypt. He died shortly after his arrival in Cairo.

As a conductor, Hans von Bülow was an uncompromising disciplinarian; he insisted on perfection of detail, and he was also able to project considerable emotional power on the music. He was one of the 1st conductors to dispense with the use of the score. His memory was fabulous; it was said that he could memorize a piano concerto by just reading the score, sometimes while riding in a train. The mainstay of his repertoire was Classical and Romantic music, but he was also receptive toward composers of the new school. When Tchaikovsky, unable to secure a performance of his 1st Piano Concerto in Russia, offered the score to Bülow, he accepted it, and gave its world premiere as soloist with a pickup orch. in Boston, on Oct. 25, 1875; however, the music was too new and too strange to American ears of the time, and the critical reactions were ambiguous. Hans von Bülow encouraged the young Richard Strauss, and gave him his 1st position as conductor. Bülow was a composer himself, but his works belong to the category of "Kapellmeister Musik," competent, well structured, but devoid of originality. Among his compositions were a symphonic "mood picture," *Nirwana*; incidental music to Shakespeare's *Julius Caesar*; piano pieces and numerous songs. He made masterly transcriptions of the prelude to Wagner's *Meistersinger* and the entire opera *Tristan und Isolde*; also arranged for piano the overtures to *Le Corsaire* and *Benvenuto Cellini* by Berlioz. He annotated and edited Beethoven's piano sonatas; these eds. were widely used by piano teachers, even though criticism was voiced against his cavalier treatment of some passages and his occasional alterations of Beethoven's original to enhance the resonance. Hans von Bülow's writings were publ. by his widow, Marie von Bülow, under the title *Briefe und Schriften H. v.B.s* (8 vols., Leipzig, 1895–1908; vol. III, republ. separately in 1936, contains selected essays, while the other vols. contain letters); selected letters in Eng. tr. were publ. by C. Bache, *The Early Correspondence of H. v.B.* (London, 1896).

BIBL.: E. Zabel, *H. v.B.* (Hamburg, 1894); R. Sternfeld, *H. v.B.* (Leipzig, 1894); T. Pfeiffer, *Studien bei H. v.B.* (Berlin, 1894; 6th ed., 1909); J. Vianna da Motta, *Nachtrag zu den Pfeifferschen "Studien bei H. v.B."* (Leipzig, 1895); W. Altmann, *Chronik des Berliner philharmonischen Orchesters, 1882–1901; zugleich ein Beitrag zur Beurteilung H. v.B.s* (Berlin, 1902); H. Heimann, *H. v.B.: Sein Leben und sein Wirken* (Berlin, 1909); R. Du Moulin-Eckart, *H. v.B.* (1921); M. von Bülow, *H. v.B. in Leben und Wort* (1925); W. Damrosch, "H. v.B. and the 9th Symphony," *Musical Quarterly* (April 1927); L. Schemann, *H. v.B. im Lichte der Wahrheit* (Regensburg, 1935); W. Freitag, "An Annotated Biography of H. v.B. in the Harvard College Library," *Harvard Library Bulletin* (July 1967); H. Schonberg, *The Great Conductors* (N.Y., 1967; pp. 163–75); W. Stresemann, *The Berlin Philharmonic from B. to Karajan* (in German and Eng.; Berlin, 1979).

Bumbry, Grace (Melzia Ann), greatly talented black American mezzo-soprano; b. St. Louis, Jan. 4, 1937. She sang in church choirs as a child; in 1955 went to Northwestern Univ. to study voice with Lotte Lehmann, and continued lessons

with her at the Music Academy of the West in Santa Barbara, Calif. She made her professional debut in a concert in London in 1959; then made a spectacular operatic appearance as Amneris at the Paris Opéra in 1960. In a lucky strike, Wieland Wagner engaged her to sing Venus in *Tannhäuser* at the Bayreuth Festival on July 23, 1961; she was the 1st Afro-American to be featured in the role of a goddess. This event created immediate repercussions in liberal circles, and Grace Bumbry was invited by Jacqueline Kennedy to sing at the White House on Feb. 20, 1962. She then undertook a grand tour of concerts in the U.S.; in 1963 she performed the role of Venus again at the Chicago Lyric Opera, and also sang it at Lyons, France. On Oct. 7, 1965, she made her Metropolitan Opera debut in N.Y. as Princess Eboli in Verdi's *Don Carlos*. In 1966 she sang Carmen at the Salzburg Festival under the direction of Herbert von Karajan; she repeated this role at the Metropolitan with extraordinary success. The sensational element of her race was no longer the exclusive attraction; the public and the press judged her impartially as a great artist. In 1970 she sang Salome in the Strauss opera at Covent Garden in London, and she sang it again, in German, at the Metropolitan Opera on Sept. 19, 1973. She proved her ability to perform mezzo-soprano and high soprano roles with equal brilliance by singing both Aida and Amneris in Verdi's opera, and both Venus and Elisabeth in *Tannhäuser*. In 1963 she married the Polish tenor Erwin Jaeckel, who also became her business manager.

Bümler, Georg Heinrich, German singer and chamber musician; b. Berneck, near Bayreuth, Oct. 10, 1669; d. Ansbach, Aug. 26, 1745. He studied at the Lateinschule in Münchberg; became a chamber descantist at the court in Bayreuth; there he studied voice and keyboard playing with Ruggiero Fedeli. He subsequently pursued a career as a singer in Wolfenbüttel, Hamburg, Berlin, and Bayreuth. In 1698 he became chamber musician at the Ansbach court; in 1717 he was made Kapellmeister there.

Bunger, Richard Joseph, American pianist and composer; b. Allentown, Pa., June 1, 1942. He studied at Oberlin College Cons. (B.Mus., 1964) and the Univ. of Illinois (M.Mus., 1965). In 1973 he was appointed to the faculty of Calif. State College, Dominguez Hills. He became absorbed in the modern techniques of composition, particularly in the new resources of prepared piano; publ. an illustrated vol., *The Well-Prepared Piano* (1973), with a foreword by John Cage; also evolved a comprehensive notational system called "Musiglyph," which incorporates standard musical notation and musical graphics indicating special instrumental techniques. He is the inventor of the "Bungerack," a music holder for the piano, particularly convenient for scores of large size.

Bungert, (Friedrich) August, German composer; b. Mülheim, Ruhr, March 14, 1845; d. Leutesdorf, Oct. 26, 1915. He studied piano and composition at Cologne and Paris; lived mostly in Berlin. An ardent admirer of Wagner, Bungert devoted his life to the composition of a parallel work to Wagner's *Ring*, taking Homer's epics as the source of his librettos. The result of this effort was the creation of 2 operatic cycles: *The Iliad*, comprising *Achilleus* and *Klytemnestra*; and *The Odyssey*, a tetralogy. *The Iliad* was never completed for performance, but all 4 parts of *The Odyssey* were performed in Dresden: *Kirke* (Jan. 29, 1898); *Nausikaa* (March 20, 1901); *Odysseus' Heimkehr* (Dec. 12, 1896, prior to premieres of parts I and II); *Odysseus' Tod* (Oct. 30, 1903). There were also subsequent productions in other German cities, but everywhere Bungert's operas were received without enthusiasm, and the evident ambition to emulate Wagner without comparable talent proved his undoing. Among other works are the programmatic score *Zeppelins erste grosse Fahrt*; several symphonic overtures; *Symphonia Victrix*; *German Requiem*; many songs. His most successful work was a comic opera, *Die Studenten von Salamanka* (Leipzig, 1884); he also wrote a mystery play, *Warum? woher? wohin?* (1908); incidental music to Goethe's *Faust*; etc.

BIBL.: F.A. Geissler, "A. B.," *Die Musik* (Dec. 1907); M. Chop, *A. B., Ein deutscher Dichterkomponist* (Leipzig, 1916).

Bunin, Revol, Russian composer; b. Moscow, April 6, 1924; d. there, July 4, 1976. He was a student at the Moscow Cons., graduating in 1945 in the class of Shostakovich; in 1947 he became an assistant to Shostakovich at the Leningrad Cons. A prolific composer, he wrote an opera, *Masquerade*; 8 syms.; 2 string quartets; other chamber music; and film scores.

Bunin, Vladimir, Russian composer; b. Skopin, Riazan district, July 24, 1908; d. Moscow, March 23, 1970. He studied at the Moscow Cons. with A. Alexandrov, graduating in 1938. In his music, Bunin follows the traditions of Russian classicism. He wrote 2 syms. (1943, 1949); *Poem about Lenin* for Orch. (1969); Violin Concerto (1953); Piano Concerto (1965); many piano pieces and songs.

Buonamente, Giovanni Battista, Italian composer; b. c.1600; d. Assisi, Aug. 29, 1642. He was musicista da camera at the Austrian court in Vienna from 1626 to 1631; then served in a similar position at the Basilica of S. Francesco in Assisi, beginning in 1633. His importance rests on his sonatas for violin, some of which are the earliest examples of this form; he publ. 7 books of such works in Venice (1626–37); also wrote trio sonatas for 2 violins and bass.
BIBL.: P. Nettl, "G.B. B.," *Zeitschrift für Musikwissenschaft,* IX (1926–27).

Buonamici, Giuseppe, Italian pianist; b. Florence, Feb. 12, 1846; d. there, March 17, 1914. He 1st studied with his uncle, Giuseppe Ceccherini; then at the Munich Cons. with Hans von Bülow and Rheinberger (1868–70); in 1873 returned to Florence, where he was active as a teacher and choral conductor. He publ. a compilation of the technical figures found in Beethoven's piano music, in the form of daily studies; ed. the *Biblioteca del Pianista* and the complete Beethoven sonatas; also publ. piano pieces of his own.

Buononcini. See Bononcini.

Burada, Theodor, Rumanian violinist and folklorist; b. Iaşi, Oct. 3, 1839; d. there, Feb. 17, 1923. He studied in Rumania and at the Paris Cons. His significance lies in his pioneer work connected with Rumanian folklore and codifying folk melodies and popular ballads. He also wrote some violin music.

Burbure de Wesembeek, Léon-Philippe-Marie, Belgian music scholar; b. Dendermonde, Aug. 16, 1812; d. Antwerp, Dec. 8, 1889. A scion of an aristocratic family, he studied law at the Univ. of Ghent; he also received an excellent musical education at home with private teachers. In 1846 he settled at Antwerp, and became the keeper of Archives at the Cathedral. He made a profound study of materials on early music accessible to him, and publ. a number of valuable monographs dealing with the Renaissance music guilds of Antwerp, on lute makers, etc. He also composed some 200 works, including an opera, 25 orch. pieces, numerous choral works, etc.
WRITINGS: *Aperçu sur l'ancienne corporation des musiciens instrumentistes d'Anvers, dite de St. Job et de Ste. Marie-Madeleine* (Brussels, 1862); *Recherches sur les facteurs de clavecins et luthiers d'Anvers, depuis le XVIe jusqu'au XIXe siècle* (Brussels, 1869); *Notice sur Charles-Louis Hanssens* (Brussels, 1872); *Charles Luython (1550–1620), compositeur de musique de la Cour impériale* (Brussels, 1880); *Les Œuvres des anciens musiciens belges* (Brussels, 1882).
BIBL.: F.A. Gevaert, *Notice sur le Chevalier Léon de Burbure* (Brussels, 1893).

Burck (real name, **Moller**), **Joachim à,** German organist and composer; b. Burg, near Magdeburg, 1546; d. Mühlhausen, Thuringia, May 24, 1610. In 1563 he settled in Mühlhausen; became organist at the Protestant Church of St. Blasius in 1566.
WORKS: *Harmoniae sacrae* (5 books of motets; Nuremberg, 1566); *Die deutsche Passion* (Wittenberg, 1568); *Crepundia sacra* (4 books; Mühlhausen, 1578); several books of motets, odes, and German songs, reprinted in various collections.

BIBL.: A. Prüfer, *Untersuchungen über den ausserkirchlichen Kunstgesang in den evangelischen Schulen des 16. Jahrhundert* (Leipzig, 1890); R. Jordan, *Aus der Geschichte der Musik in Mühlhausen* (Mühlhausen, 1905).

Burette, Pierre-Jean, French writer on music; b. Paris, Nov. 21, 1665; d. there, May 19, 1747. A physician by profession, he had an interest in musical subjects; was the author of the valuable treatise *La Musique et la danse des anciens,* dealing mainly with the problems of Greek music. It was publ. in the *Mémoires de l'Académie des Inscriptions* (nos. 1–17).

Burganger, Judith, first-rank American pianist; b. Buffalo, N.Y., March 17, 1939. She studied at the Staatliche Hochschule für Musik in Stuttgart (diploma, 1961; M.M., 1965); subsequently won 1st prize in Munich's International Piano Competition. She performed with major U.S. orchs., including the Cleveland Orch. and the Chicago Sym. She has also been praised for her ensemble performances and for her recitals. She held teaching positions at the Cleveland Inst. of Music, Carnegie-Mellon Univ., and Florida Atlantic Univ. (from 1980).

Burge, David (Russell), American pianist, teacher, and composer; b. Evanston, Ill., March 25, 1930. He studied at Northwestern Univ. (B.M., 1951; M.M., 1952) and at the Eastman School of Music in Rochester, N.Y. (D.M.A., 1956); then studied piano with Pietro Scarpini in Florence, Italy, on a Fulbright scholarship (1956–57). He made annual concert tours of the U.S. from 1959; in 1962–75 he taught at the Univ. of Colorado, in 1965 becoming the conductor of the Boulder Phil., a position he held until 1972; in 1975 he joined the faculty of the Eastman School of Music. He gave premiere performances of many works by American composers. His own compositions include *Sources II* for Violin, Cello, and Piano (1966); *Sources III* for Clarinet and Percussion (1967); *Aeolian Music* for Flute, Clarinet, Piano, Violin, Cello, and Tape (1968); *That no one knew* for Violin and Orch. (1969); and a number of piano pieces.

Burgess, Anthony, celebrated British novelist, author of *A Clockwork Orange* and other imaginative novels, who began his career as a professional musician; b. Manchester, Feb. 25, 1917. He played piano in jazz combos in England, at the same time studying classical compositions without a tutor. Despite his great success as a novelist, he continued to write music, and developed a style of composition that, were it not for his literary fame, would have earned him a respectable niche among composers. His music is refreshingly rhythmical and entirely tonal, but not without quirky quartal harmonies and crypto-atonal melodic flights. He publ. *This Man and Music* (London, 1982).
WORKS: 3 syms. (1937; 1956, subtitled *Sinfoni Melayu,* and based on Malaysian themes; 1975); *Sinfonietta* for Jazz Combo (1941); symphonic poem, *Gibraltar* (1944); *Song of a Northern City* for Piano and Orch. (1947); *Partita* for String Orch. (1951); *Ludus Multitonalis* for Recorder Consort (1951); Concertino for Piano and Percussion (1951); *Cantata for Malay College* (1954); Concerto for Flute and Strings (1960); Passacaglia for Orch. (1961); Piano Concerto (1976); Cello Sonata (1944); 2 piano sonatas (1946, 1951); incidental music for various plays; songs.

Burghauser, Jarmil, Czech composer and conductor; b. Písek, Oct. 21, 1921. He studied composition with Křička and Jeremiáš (1933–40) and conducting with Talich and Dědeček at the Prague Cons. (1940–46); also took courses in musicology and psychology at the Charles Univ. in Prague (1945–48). From 1946 to 1953 he was conductor at the National Theater in Prague. He began to compose in a customary Central European style, but later developed a system described by him as "harmonic serialism." Several of his works appeared under the nom de plume **Michal Hájků.**
WORKS: STAGE: 4 operas: *Alladine and Palomide,* after Maeterlinck (1934; rewritten 1944), *Lakomec* (The Miser; 1949 Liberec, May 20, 1950), *Karolinka a lhář* (Caroline and the Liar; 1953; Olomouc, March 13, 1955), and an "anti-opera," *Most* (The Bridge; 1963–64; Prague, March 31, 1967); 3 ballets: *Honza a čert* (Honza and the Devil; 1954; Ostrava, Nov. 23,

1954; rev. 1960); *Sluha dvou pánů* (Servant of 2 Masters; 1957; Prague, May 9, 1958); *Tristram a Izalda* (1968–69). ORCH.: 3 syms.: No. 1 (1933; rev. 1974); No. 2 (1935; rev. 1979); No. 3 (1938; rev. 1950 and 1959); *Furiant* (1936; rev. 1970); *Spring Rondo* (1937); *Suite* for Chamber Orch. (1939; rev. 1977); Concerto for Wind Quintet and Strings (1942; Prague, Feb. 12, 1948); *Toccata* for Chamber Orch. (1947); *Symphonic Variations* (1952); *Sonata* (1954); *Symphonic Suite* (1957); *Sedm reliéfů* (7 Reliefs; 1962; Prague, Feb. 19, 1963); *Cesty* (The Paths), cycle of 8 movements for Strings, Percussion, Cimbalom, and Electric Guitar (1964; Prague, Feb. 21, 1965); *Barvy v čase* (Colors in Time; Wexford, Ireland, Oct. 25, 1967); *Strom života* (The Tree of Life; Graz, Austria, Oct. 22, 1969); *Ciaconna per il fine d'un tempo* for Piano and Orch. (1981–82). CHAMBER: 5 string quartets: No. 1 (1934; rev. 1953); No. 2 (1938; rev. 1953); No. 3 (1941); No. 4 (1944); No. 5 (1944–51); 4 wind quintets: No. 1 (1935; rev. 1945); No. 2 (1935); No. 3 (1939); No. 4 (1940); 2 trios for Flute, Viola, and Guitar (1939, 1962); Solo Guitar Sonata (1943); *Partita* for 2 Flutes (1945; rev. 1982); *Možnosti* (Possibilities) for Clarinet, Cimbalom, and Percussion (1965); *Deset skic* (10 Sketches) for Solo Flute (1965); *Patero zamyšlení* (5 Meditations) for Viola and Guitar (1966); *Pět barevných střepin* (5 Colored Splinters) for Solo Harp (1966); *Sarabande and Toccata* for Solo Guitar (1968); *Druhá suita* for 6 Clarinets (1970); *Neveselé vyprávění* (Cheerless Tale), sonata for Violin and Piano (1970); *Soumraky a svítání* (Dusks and Dawns) for Bass Clarinet and Piano (1971); *Stanze dell'ansieta e sperance*, 5 movements for Flute, Oboe, Harpsichord, Violin, Viola, and Cello (1971); *Plochy a čáry* (Surfaces and Lines) for Violin, Cello, and Guitar (1972); *Partita* for 2 Flutes, Guitar, and Cello (1976); Viola Sonata (1985). VOCAL: *Věčná oblaka* (The Eternal Clouds), small cantata for Soprano, Chorus, and Orch. (1942); *The Mystic Trumpeter*, after Whitman, cantata (1944); *Passion and Resurrection*, full-evening cantata (1937–46; Prague, May 26, 1946); *Zeme zamyslena* (The Pensive Country) for Narrator, Female Chorus, and Orch. (1966; Prague, March 24, 1968); *St. Luke Passion* for Soloists and Chorus a cappella (1977); choruses; songs. PIANO: Sonata (1938); *Šest malých leptů* (6 Little Etchings; 1970).
WORKS PUBL. UNDER THE NOM DE PLUME MICHAL HÁJKŮ: *Danse burlesque* for Orch. (1971); *Impressions indiennes* for Orch. (New Delhi, Nov. 1972); *Indiánská symfonie* for Orch. (1974); *Proprium de Nativitate* for Soloists, Chorus, Organ, and Orch. (1978); Sinfonia in F (1980); *Missa Brevis Pastoralis* for Soloists, Chorus, Organ, and Orch. (1980).
WRITINGS: *Orchestration of Antonín Dvořák's Symphonic Dances* (Prague, 1959); *Antonín Dvořák: Thematic Catalogue, Bibliography, and Survey of Life and Work* (Prague, 1960); *The Acoustical Fundamentals of Orchestration* (with A. Špelda, Prague, 1967; in German, 1971); *Modern Instrumentation* (begun by Jan Rychlík and completed by Burghauser, Prague, 1968).

Burghersh, Lord John Fane, 11th Earl of Westmorland, English politician, general, diplomat, and amateur musician; b. London, Feb. 3, 1784; d. Wansford, Northamptonshire, Oct. 16, 1859. He was educated at Harrow and at Trinity College, Cambridge (M.A., 1808), where he received training in music from Hague. He was active in several military campaigns during the Napoleonic wars, and served as aide-de-camp to the Duke of Wellington, his wife's uncle; he also was a member of Parliament for Lyme Regis (1806–16). In 1822 he was made privy councillor, in 1825 a major general, in 1838 a lieutenant general, and in 1854 a general; he was also the British envoy in Florence (1814–30), resident minister in Berlin (1841–51), and ambassador in Vienna (1851–55). Through his persistent efforts, the Royal Academy of Music was organized in London in 1822, and he ruled the institution with an iron hand for the rest of his life. His compositions were disdained in his day and are now mercifully forgotten.

Burgin, Richard, Polish-born American violinist and conductor; b. Warsaw, Oct. 11, 1892; d. Gulfport, Fla., April 29, 1981.

He studied violin with Auer at the St. Petersburg Cons.; played as a soloist with the Warsaw Phil. at the age of 11; in 1907 he made an American tour as a concert violinist. Abandoning a concert career, he served as concertmaster of the Helsinki Sym. Orch. (1912–15) and of the Christiania Phil. (1916–19). In 1920 he went to the U.S.; was appointed concertmaster of the Boston Sym., and in 1927 became its assistant conductor; he also conducted orchs. in various cities in New England, and was for many years active as instructor in conducting at the Berkshire Music Center, Tanglewood. In 1967 he went to Tallahassee, Fla., where he continued his activities as a conductor and violin teacher. He was greatly esteemed by orch. members for his pragmatic and reliable technique; however, he never aspired to major orch. posts. He was married to the violinist **Ruth Posselt.**

Burgmüller, Johann August Franz, German organist and conductor; b. Magdeburg, April 28, 1766; d. Düsseldorf, Aug. 21, 1824. He was of a clerical family; having received a good education, he became a teacher and then a traveling theatrical conductor; he founded a musical society in Düsseldorf, and enjoyed a considerable reputation among musicians as a scholar. His 2 sons, **Johann Friedrich Franz** and **Norbert,** were both musicians.

Burgmüller, Johann Friedrich Franz, German composer of piano music; b. Regensburg, Dec. 4, 1806; d. Beaulieu, near Paris, Feb. 13, 1874. He was the son of **Johann August Franz Burgmüller,** and brother of **Norbert;** having settled in Paris, he adopted a light style to satisfy the demands of Parisian music-lovers, and wrote numerous pieces of salon music for piano; he also publ. several albums of piano studies that have become standard works.

Burgmüller, Norbert, German composer, son of **Johann August Franz** and brother of **Johann Friedrich Franz Burgmüller;** b. Düsseldorf, Feb. 8, 1810; d. Aachen, May 7, 1836. He was extremely gifted, and composed music from early childhood. After study at home, he took lessons with Spohr; wrote many songs and a Sym. His 2nd Sym. remained incomplete at the time of his death at the age of 26; Schumann, who thought highly of him, orchestrated the 3rd movement, a scherzo; in this form, the sym. had many performances in Europe and America, and Norbert Burgmüller was mourned by musicians as another Schubert. The point of coincidence was that his unfinished sym. was in the same key as that of Schubert.
BIBL.: H. Eckert, *N. B.* (Augsburg, 1932).

Burgon, Geoffrey (Alan), significant English composer; b. Hambledon, July 16, 1941. He studied with Peter Wishart and Lennox Berkeley at the Guildhall School of Music in London; earned his living as a jazz trumpeter. As a composer, he became particularly successful in providing background music for television shows; he wrote the score for Evelyn Waugh's *Brideshead Revisited* and for Le Carré's thriller *Tinker, Tailor, Soldier, Spy.* His wide range of musical expression includes the English ecclesiastical tradition as well as medieval French music.
WORKS: BALLETS: *The Golden Fish* (1964); *Ophelia* (1964); *The Calm* (1974); *Persephone* (1979); *Chamber Dances* (London, April 15, 1982). THEATER MUSIC: *Epitaph for Sir Walter Raleigh* (1968); *Joan of Arc* (1970). ORCH.: Concerto for Strings (1963); 5 Pieces for Strings (1967); *Sanctus Variations* (London, Feb. 24, 1982); *Brideshead Variations* (London, March 21, 1982); *The World Again* (1982–83). VOCAL: Magnificat (1970); *The Golden Eternity* (1970); Requiem (1976); *The Fall of Lucifer* for Soloists, Chorus, and Orch. (1977); *Veni Spiritus* for Soprano, Baritone, Chorus, and Orch. (1979); *Orpheus,* dramatic oratorio (Wells Cathedral, July 17, 1982); *Hymn to St. Thomas of Hereford* (Hereford, Aug. 22, 1982); numerous settings for voice and piano, reflecting interest in mystical and devotional themes.

Burgstaller, Alois, German tenor; b. Holzkirchen, Sept. 21, 1871; d. Gmund, April 19, 1945. He was trained as a watch maker, and also sang; encouraged by Cosima Wagner, he made a serious study of singing, and performed the role of Siegfried at the Bayreuth Festival in 1896. He made his American debut at the Metropolitan Opera in N.Y. as Siegmund in *Die Walküre* on Feb. 12, 1903; remained on its roster until his final appearance, again as Siegmund, on Jan. 14, 1909. He also sang the title role in the 1st staged American performance of *Parsifal*, in N.Y., on Dec. 24, 1903, in violation of the German copyright; as a result, he was permanently banned from Bayreuth. In 1910 he returned to Germany.

Burian, Emil František, Czech composer; b. Pilsen, June 11, 1904; d. Prague, Aug. 9, 1959. He grew up in a musical family; his father, **Emil Burian** (1876–1926), was an operatic baritone; his uncle Karl Burian was a famous tenor. He studied with Foerster at the Prague Cons. From his 1st steps in composition, he adopted an extreme modernistic method—an eclectic fusion of jazz, Czech folk art, and French Impressionism; was also active as a film producer, dramatist, poet, jazz singer, actor, piano accompanist, and journalist. In 1927 he organized a "voice band" that sang according to prescribed rhythm but without a definite pitch; his presentation of the voice band at the Siena Festival of the ISCM (Sept. 12, 1928) aroused considerable interest, and achieved further notoriety through his association with his Dada theater in Prague (1933–41; 1945–49). During World War II Burian was put in a concentration camp by the Nazis, but he survived and returned to active life. He wrote monographs: *Polydynamika* (1926); *Modern Russian Music* (1926); *Jazz* (1928); *Almanack of the Burian Brothers* (1929); *Emil Burian* (1947); *Karel Burian* (1948).

Works: Fairy-tale opera, *Alladina and Palomid*, after Maeterlinck (1923); 1-act musical drama, *Before Sunrise* (Prague, 1925); opera buffa, *Mister Ipokras* (1925; Prague, 1926; reworked into the opera farce *I Beg Your Pardon*, Prague, 1956); jazz opera, *Bubu from Montparnasse* (1927); opera, *Maryša* (Brno, April 16, 1940; his most important work); operatic parody, *The Emperor's New Clothes* (1947); musical comedy, *Lovers from the Kiosk* (1935); singspiel, *Opera from the Pilgrimage* (Prague, Dec. 3, 1956); 4 ballets: *The Bassoon and the Flute* (1925; Prague, 1929); *Wooden Soldiers* (1926); *The Manège* (1927); *The Motorcoach* (1927; Prague, 1928); cantata, *May*, for Harp, 2 Pianos, Kettledrums, Solo Voice, and Chorus (1946); *Suita poetica* for Orch., in 5 separate movements (1925, 1947, 1950, 1951, 1953); *Cocktails*, song cycle for Voice and Jazz Orch. (1926); Suite for Oboe and String Orch. (1928); *Reminiscence*, symphonic suite (1929–36); sym., *Siréna* (1947; music used in film of the same title); Sym. No. 2, with Solo Piano (1948); Accordion Concerto (1949); *Overture to Socialism* (1950); Trio for Flute, Viola, and Cello (1924); *From Youth*, string sextet (1924); Duo for Violin and Cello (1925); *Requiem* for Voice Band and Jazz Band (1927); 8 string quartets (1927, 1929, 1940, 1947, 1947, 1948, 1949, 1951); Variations for Wind Quintet (1928); *Of Warm Nights*, suite for Violin and Piano (1928); *Passacaglia* for Violin and Viola (1929); *4 Pieces* for Wind Quintet (1929); Wind Quintet (1930); Suite for Cello and Piano (1935); *Children's Songs* for Voice and Nonet (1937); *Sonata romantica* for Violin and Piano (1938); *Lost Serenade* for Flute and Piano (1940); Duo for Violin and Piano (1946); Fantasie for Violin and Piano (1954); *American Suite* for 2 Pianos (1926); Piano Sonata (1927); *Echoes of Czech Dances* for Piano (1953); Piano Sonatina (1954); songs; film music.

Burk, John N(aglee), American writer on music; b. San José, Calif., Aug. 28, 1891; d. Boston, Sept. 6, 1967. He graduated from Harvard Univ. (A.B., 1916). In 1934 he succeeded Philip Hale as program annotator of the Boston Sym. Orch. He ed. Hale's Boston Sym. program notes (1935) and annotated *Letters of Richard Wagner*, from the Burrell Collection (N.Y., 1950). He was the author of the books *Clara Schumann, A Romantic Biography* (N.Y., 1940); *The Life and Works of Beethoven* (N.Y., 1943); *Mozart and His Music* (N.Y., 1959).

Burkhard, Paul, Swiss conductor and composer; b. Zürich, Dec. 21, 1911; d. Tösstal, Sept. 6, 1977. He studied at the Zürich Cons. From 1932 to 1934 he conducted at the Bern Stadttheater; he was engaged as a conductor at a Zürich theater (1939–45); then was conductor of the Beromünster Radio Orch. in Zürich (1945–57). As a composer he was successful mainly in light music; several of his operettas enjoyed considerable success in Switzerland; among them are *Hopsa* (1935; rev. 1957), *Dreimal Georges* (1936), *Der schwarze Hecht* (1939; revived under a new title, *Feuerwerk*, 1950), *Tic-Tac* (1942), *Casanova in der Schweiz* (1944), *Die kleine Niederdorfoper* (1954), and *Die Pariserin* (1957). He also wrote the fairy-tale operas *Die Schneekönigin* (1964) and *Bunbury* (1966); and the Christmas opera *Ein Stern geht auf aus Jaakob* (1970).

Burkhard, Willy, significant Swiss composer; b. Evillard sur Bienne (Leubringen bei Biel), April 17, 1900; d. Zürich, June 18, 1955. He studied with Teichmüller and Karg-Elert in Leipzig (1921), Courvoisier in Munich (1922–23), and Max d'Ollone in Paris (1923–24). Returning to Switzerland, he taught at the Bern Cons. (1928–33) and at the Zürich Cons. (1942–55). His music is neo-Classical in form and strongly polyphonic in structure; his astringent linear idiom is tempered by a strong sense of modal counterpoint.

Works: Opera, *Die Schwarze Spinne* (The Black Spider; 1947–48; Zürich, May 28, 1949; rev. 1954); oratorios: *Das Gesicht Jesajas* (The Vision of Isaiah; 1933–35; Basel, Feb. 18, 1936; his masterpiece); *Das Jahr* (The Year; 1940–41; Basel, Feb. 19, 1942); cantatas, with Strings or Orch.: *Biblische Kantate* (1923); *Till Ulenspiegel* (1929); *Vorfrühling* (1930); *Spruchkantate* (1933); *Genug ist nicht genug* (1938–39; Basel, June 11, 1940); *Lob der Musik* (1939); *Cantate Domino* (1940); *Heimatliche Kantate* (1940); *Psalmen-Kantate* (1952); several chamber and a cappella cantatas. Other vocal works include *Te Deum* for Chorus, Trumpet, Trombone, Kettledrum, and Organ (1931); *Das ewige Brausen* for Bass and Chamber Orch. (1936); *Psalm 93* for Chorus and Organ (1937); *Kreuzvolk der Schweiz* for Chorus and Organ (1941); *Magnificat* for Soprano and Strings (1942); *Cantique de notre terre* for Soli, Chorus, and Orch. (1943); *Mass* for Soprano, Bass, Chorus, and Orch. (1951; Zürich, June 28, 1951); *Psalm 148* for Chorus and Instruments (1954). Orch.: *Ulenspiegel Variations* (1932); *Fantasy* for Strings (1934); *Small Serenade* for Strings (1935); Concerto for Strings (1937); Toccata for Strings (1939); *Laupen-Suite* for Orch. (1940); Concertino for Cello and Strings (1940); Violin Concerto (1943; Zürich, Jan. 26, 1946); Sym. in 1 Movement (1944); Organ Concerto (1945); *Hymne* for Organ and Orch. (1945); *Concertante Suite* (1946); *Piccola sinfonia giocosa* for Small Orch. (1949); *Fantasia mattutina* (1949); Toccata for 4 Winds, Percussion, and Strings (1951; Zürich, Dec. 7, 1951); *Sonata da camera* for Strings and Percussion (1952); Viola Concerto (1953); Concertino for 2 Flutes, Harpsichord, and Strings (1954); String Trio (1926); String Quartet (1929); Fantasie for Organ (1931); Piano Trio (1936); Violin Sonatina (1936); Suite for 2 Violins (1937); Solo Viola Sonata (1939); Piano Sonata (1942); String Quartet in 1 Movement (1943); Serenade for 8 Instruments (1945); *Romance* for Horn and Piano (1945); Violin Sonata (1946); Cello Sonata (1952); *Serenade* for Flute and Clarinet (1953); *Choral-Triptychon* for Organ (1953); Suite for Solo Flute (1954–55); *6 Preludes* for Piano (1954–55).

Bibl.: E. Mohr, *W. B.: Leben und Werk* (Zürich, 1957); S. Burkhard and F. Indermühle, *W. B.* (17. April 1900–18. Juni 1955) *Werkverzeichnis* (Liebefeld, 1968); E. Schmidt, "'Ahnung einer neuen Weltordnung'—W. B.," in U. von Brück, ed., *Credo musicale. . . . Festgabe zum 80. Geburtstag des . . . Professor D. Dr. h.c. Rudolf Mauersberger* (Berlin, 1969).

Burkhardt, Max, German music analyst and composer; b. Löbau, Sept. 28, 1871; d. Berlin, Nov. 12, 1934. He studied at the Leipzig Cons.; received his Ph.D. with the dissertation *Beiträge zum Studium des deutschen Liedes* (1897); then was a choral conductor in Cologne; in 1906 settled in Berlin as a teacher and writer. He publ. several useful music guides: *Führer durch Richard Wagners Musikdramen* (Berlin, 1909; 3rd ed., 1913); *Führer durch die Konzertmusik* (Berlin, 1911; analyzes 1,500 works); *Johannes Brahms: Ein Führer durch seine Werke* (Berlin, 1912). He also wrote the operas *König Drosselbart* (Cologne, Jan. 1, 1904) and *Das Moselgretchen* (Schwerin, Jan. 21, 1912); choral works; and a series of *Lautenlieder* with lute accompaniment.

Burlas, Ladislav, Slovak composer; b. Trnava, April 3, 1927. He studied general musical subjects at Bratislava Univ. (1946–51) and composition with A. Moyzes at the Bratislava Cons. and at the Academy of Music there, graduating in 1955; then taught music theory at Comenius Univ. in Bratislava. He publ. monographs on J.L. Bella (Bratislava, 1953) and on A. Moyzes (Bratislava, 1956).
WORKS: *Symphonic Triptych* (1957); *Epitaph* for Orch. (1958); *Bagatelles* for String Orch. (1960); *Planctus* for String Orch. (1968); Concertino for Percussion and Winds (1971); *Wedding Songs* for Soloists, Chorus, and Orch. (1955); *The Miner's Cantata* (1955); *The Singing Heart,* string sextet (1960); Sonata for Solo Violin (1968); *Music* for String Quartet (1968–69); String Quartet No. 2, in memory of Prokofiev (1973); choruses; songs.

Burleigh, Cecil, American composer, violinist, and teacher; b. Wyoming, N.Y., April 17, 1885; d. Madison, Wis., July 28, 1980. In 1902 he went to Berlin, where he studied with Anton Witek (violin) and Hugo Leichtentritt (composition); returning to the U.S. in 1905, he studied with Felix Borowski and Émile Sauret at the Chicago Musical College. He subsequently taught at various colleges in Colorado, Iowa, and Montana (1909–19); was a concert violinist in N.Y. (1919–21); appeared in joint recitals with Rosa Ponselle, Louis Graveure, and Rudolph Ganz; in 1921, settled as a violin and composition teacher at the Univ. of Wisconsin. After retiring in 1955, he devoted himself mainly to painting.
WORKS: 3 violin concertos: No. 1 (1912); No. 2, *Indian* (1918; Cleveland, March 13, 1921); No. 3 (1927); a trilogy of syms. inspired by various books of the Bible (*Creation, Prophecy,* and *Revelation,* 1944; Univ. of Wisconsin, May 1, 1955); *Evangeline,* tone poem after Longfellow (1918); *Mountain Pictures* for Orch. (1918); 2 *Sketches from the Orient* for Concert Band (1927); *From the Muses* for Small Orch. (1944); 2 *Essays* for String Quartet (*Illusion* and *Transition,* 1945); 2 violin sonatas: *The Ascension* (1914) and *From the Life of St. Paul* (1926); descriptive violin and piano pieces (4 *Rocky Mountain Sketches, Up the Canyon,* 4 *Prairie Sketches,* 5 *Winter Evening Tales,* 6 *Nature Studies, The Avalanche, Elfin Lore,* etc.); songs.
BIBL.: J. Howard, *C. B.* (N.Y., 1929).

Burleigh, Henry Thacker, black American baritone and songwriter; b. Erie, Pa., Dec. 2, 1866; d. Stamford, Conn., Sept. 12, 1949. He studied at the National Cons. in N.Y. In 1894 he became baritone soloist at St. George's Church in N.Y.; retired in 1946 after 52 years of service. He gained wide popularity for his arrangements of *Heav'n, Heav'n; Deep River;* and *Go Down Moses.* On May 16, 1917, the National Assoc. for the Advancement of Colored People awarded him the Spingarn Medal for highest achievement by an American citizen of African descent during the year 1916.
WORKS: 6 *Plantation Melodies* for Violin and Piano (1901); *Southland Sketches* for Violin and Piano; *From the Southland* for Piano; *Jubilee Songs of the United States of America* (1916); *Old Songs Hymnal* (1929).
BIBL.: "In Retrospect . . . H.T. B. (1866–1949)," *Black Perspective in Music* (Sept. 1974).

Burmeister, Joachim, German musician; b. Lüneburg, March 5, 1564; d. Rostock, May 5, 1629. He received a master's degree from Rostock Univ.; publ. there the treatises *Hypomnematum Musicae Poeticae* (1599) and *Musicae Practicae sive artis canendi ratio* (1601); wrote several sacred songs, which were publ. in 1601.
BIBL.: M. Ruhnke, *J. B.* (Kassel, 1955); C. Palisca, "Ut oratoria musica: The Theoretical Basis of Musical Mannerism," *The Meaning of Mannerism* (Hanover, N.H., 1972).

Burmeister, Richard, German composer and pianist; b. Hamburg, Dec. 7, 1860; d. Berlin, Feb. 19, 1944. He studied with Liszt at Weimar, Rome, and Budapest, accompanying him on his travels; later taught at the Hamburg Cons., the Peabody Inst. in Baltimore, the Dresden Cons. (1903–6), and the Klindworth-Scharwenka Cons. in Berlin (1907–25). Burmeister also made extensive concert tours of Europe and the U.S. His works include the symphonic fantasy *Die Jagd nach dem Glück;* Piano Concerto; *The Sisters* (after Tennyson) for Alto, with Orch.; Romanza for Violin and Orch.; songs; piano pieces. He also rescored Chopin's F-minor Concerto, Liszt's *Mephisto Waltz* and 5th Rhapsody (with new orch. accompaniment), and Weber's *Konzertstück* for Piano and Orch.

Burney, Charles, celebrated English music historian; b. Shrewsbury, April 7, 1726; d. Chelsea, April 12, 1814. He was a pupil of Edmund Baker (organist of Chester Cathedral), of his eldest half brother, James Burney, and, from 1744 to 1747, of Arne in London. In 1749 he became organist of St. Dionis-Backchurch, and harpsichord player at the subscription concerts in the King's Arms, Cornhill; resigned these posts in 1751, and until 1760 was organist at King's Lynn, Norfolk, where he planned and began work on his *General History of Music.* He returned to London in 1760; received the degrees of B.Mus. and D.Mus. from Oxford Univ. in 1769. Having exhausted such material as was available in London for his *History of Music,* he visited France, Switzerland, and Italy in 1770 and Germany, the Netherlands, and Austria in 1772, consulting the libraries, attending the best concerts of sacred and secular music, and forming contacts with the leading musicians and scholars of the period (Gluck, Hasse, Metastasio, Voltaire et al.). The immediate result of these journeys was the publication of *The Present State of Music in France and Italy,* etc. (1771, in diary form) and *The Present State of Music in Germany, the Netherlands,* etc. (1773). His *General History of Music* appeared in 4 vols. (1776–89; new ed. by Frank Mercer in 2 vols. with "Critical and Historical Notes," London and N.Y., 1935), the 1st vol. concurrently with the complete work of his rival, Sir John Hawkins. From 1806 he received a government pension. Other publications: *La musica che si canta annualmente nelle funzioni della settimana santa nella Cappella Pontificia, composta de Palestrina, Allegri e Bai* (1771; a book of sacred works with Burney's preface); *An Account of the Musical Performances in Westminster Abbey . . . in Commemoration of Handel* (1785); *Memoirs of the Life and Writings of the Abate Metastasio* (3 vols., 1796); the articles on music for Rees's *Cyclopedia;* etc. He composed, for Drury Lane, music to the dramas *Alfred* (1745), *Robin Hood* and *Queen Mab* (1750), and *The Cunning Man* (1765; text and music adapted from *Le Devin du village* by Rousseau); also sonatas for piano and for violin; violin and harpsichord concertos; cantatas; flute duets; etc. Burney's daughter, Frances Burney (b. King's Lynn, Norfolk, June 13, 1752; d. London, Jan. 6, 1840), wrote the novel *Evelina* and *Memoirs of Dr. Burney* (3 vols., 1832), the latter a highly bowdlerized version; she destroyed much of the original MS, but fragments were discovered 120 years later; S. Klima, G. Bowers, and K. Grant ed. and annotated a new edition as *Memoirs of Dr. C. B., 1726–1769* (1988).
BIBL.: L.M. Isaacs, "A Friend of Dr. Johnson," *Musical Quarterly* (Oct. 1915); C. Ricci, B., *Casanova e Farinelli in Bologna* (Milan, 1920); C.H. Glover, *Dr. C. B.'s Continental Travels, 1770–72* (compiled from Burney's journals and other sources; London, 1927); P.A. Scholes, *The Great Dr. B.* (Oxford, 1948); R. Lonsdale, *Dr. C. B.: A Literary Biography* (London, 1965); G. Stefani, "Musica, chiesa, società negli scritti di C. B.," *Nuova Rivista Musicale Italiana* (Jan.–Feb. 1971); J.C. Kassler, "B.'s Sketch of a plan for a public music-school," *Musical Quarterly* (April 1972).

Burritt, Lloyd (Edmund), Canadian composer; b. Vancouver, British Columbia, June 7, 1940. He studied composition with J. Coulthard and electronic music with C. Hultberg at the Univ. of British Columbia (B.M., 1963; M.M., 1968); also studied with G. Jacob and H. Howells at the Royal College of

Music in London (1963–65) and with Schuller, Leinsdorf, Bernstein, and D. Hiatt at the Berkshire Music Center in Tanglewood (summers 1965, 1966).

Works: MUSIC THEATER AND MULTI-MEDIA: *Acid Mass* for Film, Tape, and Dancers (1969); *Electric Chair* for Actress, Alto Saxophone, and Tape (1971); *The Hobbit* for Actors, Singers, Dancers, Chorus, Flute, Horn, Percussion, and Piano (North Vancouver, Dec. 19, 1984; also concert version as *The Hobbit Suite*). ORCH.: Sym. (1964); *Assassinations* with Tape (Vancouver, Dec. 1, 1968); *Electric Tongue* with Tape (Vancouver, May 30, 1969); *New York* with Tape (1970); *Overdose* with Tape (Ottawa, Feb. 15, 1971); *Symphonic Overture* (1980). CHAMBER: Sonata for Violin and Piano (1963); *Icon* for Organ and Tape (1970); *Memo to RCCO* [Royal College of Canadian Organists] for Organ and Tape (1972). VOCAL: *3 Autumn Songs* for Mezzo-soprano and Orch. (1965; Vancouver, Feb. 27, 1968); *Once Again . . . Pop!* for Non-singing Chorus and Tape (1969); *Song for Marshall McLuhan* for Bass-baritone, Chorus, and Orch. (Vancouver, April 30, 1986); *Crystal Earth* for Soprano, Chorus, and Concert Band (1987; North Vancouver, Oct. 24, 1988).

Burrowes, Norma, Welsh soprano; b. Bangor, April 24, 1944. She studied at the Queen's Univ. in Belfast and the Royal Academy of Music in London; made her debut with the Glyndebourne Touring Opera in 1970; also in 1970 she sang at Covent Garden, London; in 1971 she joined the Sadler's Wells Opera; also appeared at the Bayreuth and Aix-en-Provence festivals; made her American debut at the Metropolitan Opera, N.Y., on Oct. 12, 1979.

Burrows, (James) Stuart, Welsh tenor; b. Pontypridd, Feb. 7, 1933. He was educated at Trinity College, Carmarthen, Wales. He made his debut in 1963 at the Welsh National Opera. In 1967 he sang at the San Francisco Opera; in 1970 appeared at the Vienna State Opera. On April 13, 1971, he made his Metropolitan Opera debut in N.Y. as Ottavio in *Don Giovanni*. He is regarded as one of the finest interpreters of Mozart roles.

Burt, Francis, English composer; b. London, April 28, 1926. He studied at the Royal Academy of Music in London with Howard Ferguson (1948–51) and at the Hochschule für Musik in Berlin with Boris Blacher (1951–54); was awarded the German Mendelssohn Scholarship; went for further study to Rome; in 1956 he received a stipend from the Fondation Européenne de la Culture; from 1957 lived mostly in Vienna.

Works: String Quartet (1953); *Iambics* for Orch. (1955); *Music* for 2 Pianos (1955); *The Skull*, cantata for Tenor and Orch. (1956); *Duo* for Clarinet and Piano (1956); *Bavarian Gentians* for Vocal Quartet and Piano (1957); *Espressione orchestrale* (1959); *Volpone*, opera after Ben Jonson (Stuttgart, June 2, 1960); *The Golem*, ballet (1962); *Fantasmagoria* for Orch. (1963); 1-act opera, *Barnstable, or Someone in the Attic* (Stuttgart, Nov. 30, 1969); *Und Gott der Herr sprach* for Mezzo-soprano, Baritone, Bass, Chorus, and Orch. (1983).

Burtius (also known as **Burci** or **Burzio**), **Nicolaus,** Italian theorist; b. Parma, c.1445; d. there, after 1518. He studied with J. Gallicus; received 1st clerical Orders in Parma in 1472; then studied ecclesiastical law in Bologna; in 1487 he publ. *Musices Opusculum,* which was one of the earliest printed books on music, containing mensural notes printed from woodblocks. In this work Burtius supports the Guidonian system, opposing the innovations introduced by Ramos de Pareja.

Burton, Frederick Russell, American writer on music; b. Jonesville, Mich., Feb. 23, 1861; d. Lake Hopatcong, N.J., Sept. 30, 1909. He was a graduate of Harvard Univ. (1882); then went to N.Y., where he was active as a music teacher. He made a study of Indian music and publ. *Songs of the Ojibway Indians* (1903; later expanded into *American Primitive Music,* publ. posth., 1909).

Burton, Stephen Douglas, American composer; b. Whittier, Calif., Feb. 24, 1943. He studied piano and theory at Oberlin Cons.; then went to Vienna, where he studied with Morris Browda at the Vienna Cons. (1957–60); subsequently enrolled

at the Mozarteum in Salzburg in classes of composition and conducting (1962–65); in 1963–64 he was music director of the Munich Kammerspiele; took private lessons with Hans Werner Henze (1962–66). In 1969 he held a Guggenheim fellowship. In 1974 he was appointed to the faculty of George Mason Univ. in Fairfax, Va. As a composer, Burton draws rapturously on the totality of modern resources, achieving impressive grandeur mitigated by beguiling dancing episodes, and producing audaciously euphonious sonorities unapologetically appealing to far-flung audiences.

Works: STAGE: *No Trifling with Love,* opera after Alfred de Musset (1970); *An American Triptych,* opera (1975); *The Duchess of Malfi,* opera (Wolf Trap, Va., Aug. 18, 1978); *Aimee,* opera (1983); *An American Triptych,* 3 1-act operas after Crane's *Maggie,* Hawthorne's *Dr. Heidegger's Experiment,* and Melville's *Benito Cereno* (Alexandria, Va., July 29, 1989); *Finisterre,* ballet (Newport, R.I., Aug. 21, 1977). ORCH.: Concerto da camera (1963); *Ode to a Nightingale,* after Keats, for Soprano, Flute, Harp, and String Orch. (Berlin, Oct. 9, 1963); Sym. No. 1 (Berlin, Jan. 31, 1968); *Stravinskiana* for Flute and Orch. (Chicago, Feb. 14, 1972); *Dithyramb* (Washington, D.C., Oct. 10, 1972); Sym. No. 2, surnamed *Ariel,* to words of Sylvia Plath's poems, for Mezzo-soprano, Baritone, and Orch. (Washington, D.C., Oct. 19, 1976); *Variations on a Theme of Mahler* for Chamber Orch. (Washington, D.C., Oct. 10, 1982); *The Pied Piper,* overture (Washington, D.C., Feb. 1, 1983); Violin Concerto (1983). CHAMBER: *Burlesque* for Clarinet, Piano, and String Quartet (1972); *Notturno* for Cello Solo (1972); *Partita* for Violin Solo (1973); String Quartet (1974); *Divertimento* for Woodwind Quintet (1975); *Rhapsody* for Alto Saxophone and Piano (1975); Piano Trio (1975); *3 Poems* for Flute Solo (1976); *Fantocciata* for Flute, Oboe, and Harpsichord (1976). VOCAL: *6 Hebrew Melodies,* after Byron (Washington, D.C., Oct. 28, 1973); *Songs of the Tulpehocken* for Tenor and Orch., to anonymous Pennsylvania German texts (Reading, Pa., Feb. 22, 1976); *6 Songs* for Voice and 13 Instruments (Washington, D.C., May 7, 1977); *I Have a Dream,* cantata for Narrator, Soprano, and Orch., after Martin Luther King, Jr. (Washington, D.C., May 17, 1987).

Bury, Edward, Polish composer and conductor; b. Gniezno, Sept. 18, 1919. He studied composition with Sikorski and conducting at the Warsaw Cons. (1937–44); from 1945 to 1954 he taught at the Krakow Cons. He publ. 2 books on conducting, *Podstawy techniki dyrygowania* (The Principles of Conducting Technique; Krakow, 1961) and *The Technique of Reading Scores* (Krakow, 1971).

Works: *Czech Fantasy* for Piano and Orch. (1948); *Little Suite* for Orch. (1950); *Triptych* for Orch. (1952); Violin Concerto (1954); *Concert Overture* (1954); *Suita giocosa* for Orch. (1956); *Maski* (The Masks), fantastic suite for Orch. (1957); 8 syms.: No. 1, *Symfonia wolności* (Freedom Sym.; 1960); No. 2 for 6 Concertante Instruments and Orch. (1962); No. 3, *Mówi Prezydent John F. Kennedy* (President Kennedy Speaks) for Male Speaker, Women's Speaking Chorus, Mixed Chorus, and Orch. (1964); No. 4, *De timpani a tutti,* for Solo Bass, Chorus, Tape, and Orch. (1966–67); No. 5, *Bohaterska* (Heroic; 1969); No. 6, *Pacem in terris,* to a text from the encyclical of Pope John XXIII, for Narrator, Church Bells, and Orch. (1972); No. 7 (1977); No. 8 (1980); *The Millennium Hymn* for Chorus and Orch. (1965); chamber music; piano pieces; choruses.

Busby, Thomas, English writer on music; b. Westminster, Dec. 1755; d. London, May 28, 1838. He was a chorister in London; then studied with Battishill (1769–74); served as church organist at St. Mary's, Newington, Surrey, and St. Mary Woolnoth, Lombard Street. He obtained the degree of B.Mus. from Cambridge Univ. in 1801. In collaboration with Arnold, he publ. *A Complete Dictionary of Music* (1801); he then publ. *A Grammar of Music* (1818) and *A General History of Music* (2 vols., compiled from Burney and Hawkins; London, 1819; reprinted 1968). In 1825 he brought out a set of 3 little vols. entitled *Concert Room and Orchestra Anecdotes of Music and Musicians, Ancient and Modern,* a compilation of some topical value, even though many of the stories are apocryphal. He also publ. *A Musical Manual, or Technical Directory* (1828). His anthology of sacred music, *The Divine Harmonist* (1788), is valuable. His own compositions (oratorios and odes) are imitative of Handel. A melodrama, *Tale of Mystery*, with Busby's music, was produced at Covent Garden (Nov. 13, 1807).

BIBL.: K.G.F. Spence, "The Learned Doctor B.," *Music & Letters* (April 1956).

Busch, Adolf (Georg Wilhelm), noted German violinist, brother of **Hermann** and **Fritz Busch;** b. Siegen, Westphalia, Aug. 8, 1891; d. Guilford, Vt., June 9, 1952. He studied at Cologne and Bonn; then served as concertmaster of the Vienna Konzertverein (1912–18); subsequently taught at the Hochschule für Musik in Berlin. In 1919 he organized the Busch Quartet and the Busch Trio (with his younger brother Hermann Busch, and his son-in-law **Rudolf Serkin**). The Busch Quartet gained renown with the appointment of Gösta Andreasson and Karl Doktor as members; Busch's brother Hermann became cellist in the Busch Trio in 1926 and in the Busch Quartet in 1930. Adolf Busch went to Basel in 1927; in 1939 he emigrated to America, and remained there until his death. In 1950 he organized the Marlboro School of Music in Vermont; Rudolf Serkin carried on his work after Busch's death.

Busch, Carl (Reinholdt), Danish-American conductor and composer; b. Bjerre, March 29, 1862; d. Kansas City, Mo., Dec. 19, 1943. He studied at the Royal Cons. in Copenhagen with Hartmann and Gade (1882–85), at the Brussels Cons. (1885), and with Godard in Paris (1886). In 1887 he went to Kansas City, where he was active as founder-conductor of the Sym. Orch. (1911–18); he also appeared as a guest conductor throughout the U.S. and Europe and was active as a teacher in Chicago, Salt Lake City, and South Bend, Ind. He received knighthoods from the kings of Denmark and Norway. A number of his compositions dealt with American subjects, most notably the American Indian.

WORKS: Sym. (1898); 6 suites for Orch. (1890–1928); 2 rhapsodies for Orch. (1897); 14 pieces for String Orch. (1897–1918); 4 symphonic poems (1898–1924); Cello Concerto (1919); 4 string trios (1893–1926); String Quartet (1897); Violin Sonata (1897); 44 string solos (1893–1926); 8 woodwind solos (1893–1940); 24 string études (1909); 26 pieces for Woodwind Ensemble (1930–43); 22 cantatas (1894–1929); numerous choral works; many songs; band music.

BIBL.: M. Barney, *Sir C. B.* (Kansas City, Mo., 1942); D. Lowe, *Sir C. B.: His Life and Work as a Teacher, Conductor, and Composer* (diss., Univ. of Missouri, 1972).

Busch, Fritz, eminent German conductor, brother of **Adolf (Georg Wilhelm)** and **Hermann Busch;** b. Siegen, Westphalia, March 13, 1890; d. London, Sept. 14, 1951. He studied at the Cologne Cons. with Steinbach, Boettcher, Uzielli, and Klauwell; was then conductor of the Deutsches Theater in Riga (1909–10); in 1912 he became music director of the city of Aachen, and then of the Stuttgart Opera in 1918. In 1922 he was named Generalmusikdirektor of the Dresden State Opera; during his tenure, he conducted many notable productions, including the world premieres of Strauss's *Intermezzo* and *Die Aegyptische Helena*. In 1933 he was dismissed from his Dresden post by the Nazi government; leaving Germany, he made many appearances as a conductor with the Danish Radio Sym. Orch. and the Stockholm Phil.; from 1934 to 1939 he served as music director of the Glyndebourne Festivals; from 1940 to 1945 he was active mainly in South America. On Nov. 26, 1945, he made his 1st appearance with the Metropolitan Opera in N.Y., conducting *Lohengrin;* he continued on its roster until 1949. He was equally distinguished as an operatic and symphonic conductor; he was renowned for his performances of Mozart's works. He wrote an autobiography, *Aus dem Leben eines Musikers* (Zürich, 1949; in Eng. as *Pages from a Musician's Life*, London, 1953). Recordings and publications are issued by the Brüder-Busch-Gesellschaft.

BIBL.: G. Busch, *F. B., Dirigent* (Frankfurt, 1970); B. Dopheide, *F. B.* (Tutzing, 1970).

Busch, Hermann, noted German cellist, brother of **Adolf (Georg Wilhelm)** and **Fritz Busch;** b. Siegen, Westphalia, June 24, 1897; d. Bryn Mawr, Pa., June 3, 1975. He studied at the Cologne Cons. and the Vienna Academy of Music; played cello in the Vienna Sym. Orch. (1923–27); in 1926 became a member of the Busch Trio; was also a member of the renowned Busch Quartet from 1930 until the death of his brother Adolf in 1952; during his last years of life he taught at the Marlboro School of Music in Vermont.

Busch, William, English pianist and composer; b. London, June 25, 1901; d. Woolacombe, Devon, Jan. 30, 1945. Of German origin, he received his education in America and England; then studied in Germany with Leonid Kruetzer (piano) and Hugo Leichtentritt (theory). He made his debut in London (Oct. 20, 1927). His music shows competent craftsmanship; among his works are: Piano Concerto (1939); Cello Concerto (1941); Piano Quartet (1939); pieces for piano solo.

Bush, Alan (Dudley), notable English composer; b. Dulwich, Dec. 22, 1900. He studied piano with Matthay and composition with Corder at the Royal Academy of Music in London; also took private piano lessons with Artur Schnabel and composition with John Ireland. In 1929 he went to Berlin and took courses in musicology and philosophy. Returning to England, he was on the staff of the Royal Academy of Music from 1925 to 1955. In 1935 he joined the Communist Party; in 1936 he organized in London the Workers' Music Assoc., remaining its president for 40 years. His early works contain some radical modernistic usages, but in accordance with his political views on art, he adopted the precepts of socialist realism, demanding a tonal idiom more easily appreciated by audiences. He made numerous trips to Russia and other countries of the Socialist bloc; several of his works had their 1st performance in East Germany. A *Tribute to Alan Bush* was publ. by the Workers' Music Assoc. on the occasion of his 50th birthday (1950). He publ. an autobiography, *In My Seventh Decade* (London, 1971); also *In My Eighth Decade and Other Essays* (London, 1980).

WORKS: He wrote several operas on historical subjects dealing with social revolt: *Wat Tyler* (awarded a prize at the Festival of Britain in 1951, but not perf. in England; its 1st production took place in concert form on the Berlin Radio, to a German libretto, on April 3, 1952); *The Men of Blackmoor* (Weimar, Nov. 18, 1956); *Guayana Johnny* (Leipzig, Dec. 11, 1966); *Joe Hill*, on the subject of the execution of the labor agitator Joe Hill in Salt Lake City on Nov. 19, 1915 (East Berlin, Sept. 29, 1970). Other works: Piano Concerto, with Baritone Solo and Male Chorus in the finale (1938); Sym. No. 1 (London, July 24, 1942, composer conducting); *Fantasia on Soviet Themes* for Orch. (London, July 27, 1945); *English Suite* for String Orch. (London, Feb. 9, 1946); *The Winter Journey*, cantata (Alnwick, Dec. 14, 1946); children's operetta, *The Press Gang* (Letchworth, March 7, 1947); *Piers Plowman's Day* for Orch. (Prague Radio, Oct. 16, 1947); Violin Concerto (London, July 16, 1948); Sym. No. 2, subtitled *Nottingham* (Nottingham, June 27, 1949); *Song of Friendship* for Bass Voice, Chorus, and Band (London, Nov. 6, 1949); *Defender of the Peace* for Orch. (Vienna Radio, May 24, 1952); cantata, *The Ballad of Freedom's Soldier* (1953); *Byron Symphony* for Chorus and Orch. (1960); *Time Remembered* for Chamber Orch. (1969); *Scherzo* for Wind Instruments and Percussion (1969); *Suite of 6* for String Quartet (1975).

BIBL.: R. Stevenson, ed., *Time Remembered—A. B.: An 80th Birthday Symposium* (Kidderminster, 1981).

Bush, Geoffrey, English organist, composer, and pedagogue; b. London, March 23, 1920. He studied at Balliol College, Oxford; received his B.M. degree in 1940 and D.M. in 1946; upon graduation, was active mainly as an organist, a teacher, and a music journalist. In 1952 he was appointed to the staff of the Univ. of London. He publ. *Musical Creation and the Listener* (London, 1954; rev. 1967) and *Left, Right and Centre* (London, 1984).

Works: Puppet opera, *The Spanish Rivals* (1948); *A Summer Serenade* for Chorus and Instruments (1949); Trio for Oboe, Bassoon, and Piano (1952); children's opera, *The Blind Beggar's Daughter* (1954); Sym. No. 1 (1954); 1-act opera, *If the Cap Fits* (1957); Sym. No. 2 (1957); Concerto for Light Orch. (1958); *Dialogue* for Oboe and Piano (1960); Concerto for Piano, Trumpet, and Strings (1962); Wind Quintet (1963); opera, *The Equation* (1968).

Bush, Kate, brilliant English pop vocalist, keyboardist, and songwriter; b. Catherine Bush (Plumstead), July 30, 1958. A precocious musician encouraged by a creative Irish family, she wrote over 200 songs by the age of 16. Endorsement by David Gilmour of the rock group Pink Floyd led to an unusual arrangement with the record label EMI, which supported her development for 2 years before any recordings were made. She studied mime with performance artist Lindsay Kemp, as well as dance and voice. Her 1st release, the number one hit *Wuthering Heights* (1978), was unusual for its complex narrative and wide vocal range. Her work combines various influences, including literature, dreams, and Irish folk music, in imaginative songs recorded with her brothers and friends. Among pop artists, she is remarkable for her originality, vocal strength, and physical beauty; she has become a musical force in Britain, winning a number of Best Female Singer and Artist awards. She has also recorded with Peter Gabriel. Among her 6 recorded albums, most notable are *Hounds of Love* (1985; based on Tennyson) and *The Sensual World* (1989; accompanied by Bulgarian voices). A collection of hits was released as *The Whole Story* (1987); the same songs were released as videos, many choreographed or directed by Bush.

Busnois, Antoine, greatly significant composer; b. probably in Busnes, France, c.1430; d. probably in Bruges, before Nov. 6, 1492. By 1460 he was active at the church of St. Martin in Tours, where he was a chori clerk and "heuriers" (clericos de choro et pannis); he received minor orders and was elevated to sub-deacon at the church of St. Venant there in 1465. He most likely was a priest by 1470, and subsequently held several minor benefices. He formally entered the service of Charles the Bold of Burgundy in 1467. After Charles's death in 1477, he entered the service of his daughter, Marie of Burgundy; following her marriage to Maximilian I of Austria that same year, he was active mainly in his household chapel until 1483. He spent his last years as rector cantoriae at the church of St. Sauveur in Bruges. Busnois was a master of imitative polyphony and varied contrapuntal techniques. Among his extant works are 7 chansons in early publications of Petrucci (1501–3); the masses *L'Homme armé, O crux lignum,* and *Regina coeli*; and some Magnificats, motets, and other chansons.

Bibl.: M. Bukofzer, "An Unknown Chansonnier of the 15th Century," *Musical Quarterly* (Jan. 1942); C. Brooks, *A. B. as a Composer of Chansons* (diss., N.Y. Univ., 1951); P. Higgins, *A. B. and Musical Culture in Late Fifteenth-Century France and Burgundy* (diss., Princeton Univ., 1986).

Busoni, Ferruccio (Dante Michelangiolo Benvenuto), greatly admired pianist and composer of Italian-German parentage; b. Empoli, near Florence, April 1, 1866; d. Berlin, July 27, 1924. His father played the clarinet; his mother, Anna Weiss, was an amateur pianist; Busoni grew up in an artistic atmosphere, and learned to play the piano as a child; at the age of 8 he played in public in Trieste. He gave a piano recital in Vienna when he was 10, and included in his program some of his own compositions. In 1877 the family moved to Graz, where Busoni took piano lessons with W. Mayer. He conducted his *Stabat Mater* in Graz at the age of 12. At 15 he was accepted as a member of the Accademia Filarmonica in Bologna; he performed there his oratorio *Il sabato del villaggio* in 1883. In 1886 he went to Leipzig; there he undertook a profound study of Bach's music. In 1889 he was appointed a prof. of piano at the Helsingfors Cons., where among his students was Sibelius (who was actually a few months older than his teacher). At that time Busoni married Gerda Sjostrand, whose father was a celebrated Swedish sculptor; they had 2 sons,

both of whom became well-known artists. In 1890 Busoni participated in the Rubinstein Competition in St. Petersburg, and won 1st prize with his *Konzertstück* for Piano and Orch. On the strength of this achievement he was engaged to teach piano at the Moscow Cons. (1890–91). He then accepted the post of prof. at the New England Cons. of Music in Boston (1891–94); however, he had enough leisure to make several tours, maintaining his principal residence in Berlin. During the season of 1912–13, he made a triumphant tour of Russia. In 1913 he was appointed director of the Liceo Musicale in Bologna. The outbreak of the war in 1914 forced him to move to neutral Switzerland; he stayed in Zürich until 1923; went to Paris, then returned to Berlin, remaining there until his death in 1924. In various cities, at various times, he taught piano in music schools; among his piano students were Brailowsky, Ganz, Petri, Mitropoulos, and Grainger. Busoni also taught composition; Weill, Jarnach, and Vogel were his pupils. He exercised great influence on Varèse, who was living in Berlin when Busoni was there; Varèse greatly prized Busoni's advanced theories of composition.

Busoni was a philosopher of music who tried to formulate a universe of related arts; he issued grandiloquent manifestos urging a return to classical ideals in modern forms; he sought to establish a unifying link between architecture and composition; in his eds. of Bach's works he included drawings illustrating the architectonic plan of Bach's fugues. He incorporated his innovations in his grandiose piano work *Fantasia contrappuntistica*, which opens with a prelude based on a Bach chorale, and closes with a set of variations on Bach's acronym, B-A-C-H (i.e., B-flat, A, C, B-natural). In his theoretical writings, Busoni proposed a system of 113 different heptatonic modes, and also suggested the possibility of writing music in exotic scales and subchromatic intervals; he expounded those ideas in his influential essay *Entwurf einer neuen Aesthetik der Tonkunst* (Trieste, 1907; Eng. tr. by T. Baker, N.Y., 1911). Busoni's other publications of significance were *Von der Einheit der Musik* (1923; in Italian, Florence, 1941; in Eng., London, 1957) and *Über die Möglichkeiten der Oper* (Leipzig, 1926). But despite Busoni's great innovations in his own compositions and his theoretical writing, the Busoni legend is kept alive, not through his music but mainly through his sovereign virtuosity as a pianist. In his performances he introduced a concept of piano sonority as an orch. medium; indeed, some listeners reported having heard simulations of trumpets and French horns sounded at Busoni's hands. The few extant recordings of his playing transmit a measure of the grandeur of his style, but they also betray a tendency, common to Busoni's era, toward a free treatment of the musical text, surprisingly so, since Busoni preached an absolute fidelity to the written notes. On concert programs Busoni's name appears most often as the author of magisterial and eloquent transcriptions of Bach's works. His gothic transfiguration for piano of Bach's *Chaconne* for Unaccompanied Violin became a perennial favorite of pianists all over the world.

Busoni was honored by many nations. In 1913 he received the order of Chevalier de la Légion d'honneur from the French government, a title bestowed on only 2 Italians before him: Rossini and Verdi. In 1949 an annual Concorso Busoni was established, with prizes given to contestants in piano playing. Another international award honoring the name of Busoni was announced by the Accademia di Santa Cecilia of Rome, with prizes given for the best contemporary compositions; at its opening session in 1950 the recipient was Stravinsky.

Works: operas: *Sigune, oder Das vergessene Dorf* (1889); *Die Brautwahl* (1908–11; Hamburg, April 13, 1912); *Arlecchino oder Die Fenster* (1916; Zürich, May 11, 1917, composer conducting); *Turandot*, after Gozzi (1917; Zürich, May 11, 1917, composer conducting); *Doktor Faust* (1916–24; unfinished; completed by Jarnach; Dresden, May 21, 1925).

orch.: *Symphonische Suite* (1883; Vienna, Nov. 25, 1883); *Konzertstück* for Piano and Orch. (1890; St. Petersburg, Aug. 27, 1890; won the Anton Rubinstein prize); *Konzert-Fantasie* for Piano and Orch. (1888–89; rev. as *Symphonisches Tonge-*

dicht; Boston, April 14, 1892); Suite No. 2 (1895; rev. 1903; Berlin, Dec. 1, 1904); Violin Concerto (1896–97; Berlin, Oct. 8, 1897); *Lustspielouvertüre* (1897; Berlin, Oct. 8, 1897; rev. 1904; Berlin, Jan. 11, 1907); Piano Concerto, with Male Chorus in the finale (1903–4; Berlin, Nov. 10, 1904; composer, soloist); *Turandot,* suite from incidental music (1904; Berlin, Oct. 21, 1905, composer conducting); *Berceuse élégiaque* (1909; adapted for Chamber Orch. from the original piano piece of 1907; conducted by Busoni at Mahler's last concert with the N.Y. Phil., Feb. 21, 1911); *Nocturne symphonique* (1912; Berlin, March 12, 1914); *Indianische Fantasie* for Piano and Orch. (1913; Berlin, March 12, 1914); *Die Brautwahl,* suite from the opera (1912; Berlin, Jan. 3, 1913); *Rondo arlecchinesco* (1915; Rome, March 5, 1916); *Indianisches Tagebuch,* book 1, subtitled *Gesang vom Reigen der Geister* (1915); *Concertino* for Clarinet and Orch. (1918; Zürich, Dec. 9, 1918); *Sarabande und Cortege,* 2 studies for *Doktor Faust* (1918–19; Zürich, March 31, 1919); *Divertimento* for Flute and Orch. (1920; Berlin, Jan. 13, 1921); *Tanzwalzer* (1920; Berlin, Jan. 13, 1921); *Romanza e scherzoso* for Piano and Orch. (1921; Basel, Dec. 10, 1921).

CHAMBER: String Quartet No. 1 (1880–81); *Serenata* for Cello and Piano (1882); *Kleine Suite* for Cello and Piano (1886); *Bagatelles* for Violin and Piano (1888); String Quartet No. 2 (1887; Leipzig, Jan. 28, 1888); Violin Sonata No. 1 (1890); *Kultaselle,* 10 variations on a Finnish folk song for Cello and Piano (1890); Violin Sonata No. 2 (Helsingfors, Sept. 30, 1898); *Elegie* for Clarinet and Piano (1920).

PIANO: 5 *Pieces* (1877); *3 morceaux* (1877); *Suite campestra* (1878); *Una festa di villaggio,* 6 pieces (1882); *3 pezzi nello stile antico* (1882); *Danze antiche* (1882); *Danza notturna* (1882); 24 Preludes (1879–81); 6 *Études* (1883); *Macchiette medioevali,* 6 pieces (1883); 2 *Klavierstücke* (1890); *Elegien,* 7 pieces, including the original version of *Berceuse élégiaque* (1907); *An die Jugend* (1908); *Fantasia nach J.S. Bach* (1909); *Fantasia contrappuntistica,* Busoni's Gothic masterpiece, based on Bach's *The Art of the Fugue* (1910; as *Grosse Fuge;* rev. 1912); 6 sonatinas (1910, 1912, 1916, 1917, 1919, 1920); *Indianisches Tagebuch,* book I (1915); 2 *Kontrapunktstudien nach J.S. Bach:* Fantasie and Fugue in A minor and Canonic Variations and Fugue (1917); Bach's Klavierübung, 1st ed. in 5 parts (1917–22), 2nd ed. in 10 parts (1925); *Toccata* (*Preludio, Fantasia, Ciacona*) (1921); 5 *kurze Stücke zur Pflege des polyphonischen Spiels* (1923); arrangements of keyboard works of Bach; a concert version of Schoenberg's piano piece, op. 11, No. 2. For 2 Pianos: *Improvisation* on Bach's chorale *Wie wohl ist mir* (1916); *Duettino concertante,* based on the finale of Mozart's 19th Piano Concerto (1919); a version of *Fantasia contrappuntistica* (1921; Berlin, Nov. 16, 1921).

VOCAL: Mass (1879); *Le quattro stagioni* for Male Chorus and Orch. (1882); *Il sabato del villaggio,* to a poem by Leopardi, for Soloists, Chorus, and Orch. (1883); 2 *Lieder,* to poems by Byron (1884); *Unter den Linden* for Soprano and Orch. (1893); *Zigeunerlied* and *Schlechter Trost* for Baritone and Orch., to Goethe's poems (1923); also cadenzas for Beethoven's 4th Piano Concerto and for 9 piano concertos of Mozart.

BIBL.: H. Leichtentritt, *F. B.* (Leipzig, 1916); idem, "F. B. as a Composer," *Musical Quarterly* (Jan. 1917); H. Pfitzner, *Futuristengefahr* (Munich, 1917; polemical assault on B.'s theories of new music); G. Selden-Goth, *F. B.* (Vienna, 1922); A. Cottlow, "My Years with B.," *Musical Observer* (June 1925); S. Nadel, *F. B.* (Leipzig, 1931); E.J. Dent, *F. B., A Biography* (London, 1933); G.M. Gatti, "The Stage Works of F. B.," *Musical Quarterly* (July 1934); A. Santelli, *B.* (Rome, 1939); G. Guerrini, *F. B., La vita, la figura, l'opera* (Florence, 1944); H.H. Stuckenschmidt, *F. B., Zeittafel eines Europaers* (Zürich, 1967; in Eng. as *F. B.: Chronicle of a European,* London, 1970); H. Meyer, *Die Klaviermusik F. B.s* (Zürich, 1969); H. Kosnick, *B., Gestaltung durch Gestalt* (Regensburg, 1971); J. Kindermann, *Thematisch-chronologisches Verzeichnis der musikalischen Werke von F. B.* (Regensburg, 1980); S. Sablich, *B.* (Turin, 1982); A. Beaumont, *B. the Composer* (London, 1985); L. Sitsky, *B. and the Piano: The Works, the Writings, and the Recordings*

(N.Y., 1986); A. Beaumont, ed. and translator, *F. B.: Selected Letters* (London, 1987); A. Riethmüller, *F. B.s Poetik* (Mainz and London, 1988).

Bussani, Dorothea, Austrian soprano; b. Vienna, 1763; d. after 1810. In 1786 she married the Italian bass **Francesco Bussani.** She created the roles of Cherubino in Mozart's *Le nozze di Figaro* (Vienna, May 1, 1786) and Despina in his *Così fan tutte* (Vienna, Jan. 26, 1790), opposite her husband's roles as Bartolo and Antonio. She made appearances in Italy with her husband between 1795 and 1805; subsequently appeared in Lisbon and London until she disappeared from the scene in 1810.

Bussani, Francesco, Italian bass; b. Rome, 1743; d. after 1807. He sang tenor roles; then turned to bass; was active from 1783 to 1794 in Vienna, where he married the Austrian soprano **Dorothea Bussani** in 1786. He created the roles of Bartolo and Antonio in Mozart's *Le nozze di Figaro* (Vienna, May 1, 1786); also created Don Alfonso in *Così fan tutte* (Vienna, Jan. 26, 1790). His wife appeared in both, as Cherubino and Despina. He returned to Italy with her in 1795 and continued to make appearances there until they went to Lisbon in 1807.

Busser, Henri-Paul, French composer, organist, and conductor; b. Toulouse, Jan. 16, 1872; d. Paris, Dec. 30, 1973, at the age of 101. After primary musical studies in his native town, he went to Paris, where he studied with Guiraud at the Paris Cons.; also took private lessons with Gounod, Widor, and César Franck. He won 2nd Premier Prix de Rome in 1893 with his cantata *Antigone.* A year before, he was appointed organist at St. Cloud; later served as choirmaster of the Opéra-Comique; in 1902, he was appointed conductor of the Grand Opéra, a post which he held for 37 years until his resignation in 1939; was reappointed after the war in 1946, and served his term until 1951. He also was for several years president of the Académie des Beaux Arts. He taught composition at the Paris Cons. from 1930 until 1948. During his long career as a conductor, he led several important productions, including the 3rd performance of Debussy's opera *Pelléas et Mélisande.* His centennial was grandly celebrated in January 1972 with performances of his works by the leading Paris orchs. and by an exhibition of his MSS at the Opéra. In 1958 he married the French opera singer **Yvonne Gall** (1885–1972). He completed and arranged for performance Bizet's unfinished opera *Ivan le Terrible;* publ. *Précis de composition* (Paris, 1943) and a vol. of memoirs, *De Pelléas aux Indes Galantes* (Paris, 1955).

WORKS: *Daphnis et Chloë,* a scenic pastorale (Opéra-Comique, Paris, Dec. 14, 1897, composer conducting); operas: *Colomba* (Nice, Feb. 4, 1921), *Les Noces corinthiennes* (Paris, May 10, 1922), *La Carosse du Saint Sacrement* (1936), *Diafoirus 60* (Lille, 1963), and *La Vénus d'Ille* (Lille, 1964); ballets: *La Ronde des saisons* (1905); *Le Vert Galant* (Paris, 1951); *Gayarni* (1963); *Le Sommeil de l'Enfant Jésus* for Violin and Orch.; *À la Villa Medicis,* symphonic suite for Orch.; *Minerva,* concert overture for Orch.; *Hercule au jardin des Hespérides,* symphonic poem; *Suite funambulesque* for Small Orch.; *À la lumière* (*Poème lyrique*); *Suite brève* for Small Orch.; *Messe de Noël* for 4 Voices, and Organ or Orch.; *Pièce de concert* for Harp and Orch.; *Appassionato* for Alto and Orch.; *Marche de Fête* for Orch.; *Hymne à la France* for Tenor and Orch.; *Impromptu* for Harp, with Orch.; several preludes and fugues for Organ on themes by Gounod, Massenet, A. Thomas, etc.

Bussler, Ludwig, German music theorist and pedagogue; b. Berlin, Nov. 26, 1838; d. there, Jan. 18, 1900. His father was the painter, author, and privy councillor Robert Bussler; his maternal grandfather was the famous tenor singer **Karl Bader.** He studied with Dehn, Grell, and Wieprecht; then taught theory at the Ganz School of Music in Berlin (1865) and at the Stern Cons. (from 1879); was also active as a conductor at various Berlin theaters. In 1883 he became the music critic for the *National-Zeitung.* His eminently practical writings are *Musikalische Elementarlehre* (1867; 3rd ed., 1882; Eng.

tr., N.Y., 1895; also in Russian); *Der strenge Satz* (1877); *Harmonische Übungen am Klavier* (1877; in Eng., N.Y., 1890); *Kontrapunkt und Fuge im freien Tonsatz* (1878); *Musikalische Formenlehre* (1878; Eng. ed., N.Y., 1883); *Praktische musikalische Kompositionslehre:* Part I, *Lehre vom Tonsatz* (1878), and Part II, *Freie Komposition* (1879); *Instrumentation und Orchestersatz* (1879); *Elementar-Melodik* (1879); *Geschichte der Musik,* 6 lectures (1882); *Modulationslehre* (1882); *Lexikon der musikalischen Harmonien* (1889).

Bussotti, Sylvano, Italian composer of the avant-garde; b. Florence, Oct. 1, 1931. He studied violin; at the age of 9 was enrolled in the Cherubini Cons. in Florence, where he studied theory with Roberto Lupi, and also took piano lessons with Luigi Dallapiccola, while continuing his basic violin studies. In 1956 he went to Paris, where he studied privately with Max Deutsch. He became active as a theatrical director; also exhibited his paintings at European galleries. From 1979 to 1981 he was artistic director of the Teatro La Fenice in Venice; he also taught at the Fiesole School of Music (from 1980). As a composer he adopted an extreme idiom, in which verbalization and pictorial illustrations are combined with aleatory discussions within the framework of multimedia productions. Many of his scores look like abstract expressionist paintings, with fragments of musical notation interspersed with occasional realistic representations of human or animal forms. From 1965 he devoted himself principally to creating works for the musical theater, which he described as BUSSOTTI-OPERABALLET.

WORKS: *Memoria* for Baritone, Chorus, and Orch. (1962); *Fragmentations* for Harp (1962); *La Passion selon Sade,* his crowning achievement, which makes use of theatrical effects, diagrams, drawings, surrealistic illustrations, etc., with thematic content evolving from a dodecaphonic nucleus, allowing great latitude for free interpolations, and set in an open-end form in which fragments of the music are recapitulated at will, until the players are mutually neutralized. The unifying element of the score is the recurrent motive D-Es-A-D-E, spelling the name De Sade, interwoven with that of B-A-C-H. The 1st production of *La Passion selon Sade* took place in Palermo on Sept. 5, 1965. His grand opera *Lorenzaccio,* in 23 scenes, employing a multitude of performers, which required 230 costumes, all designed by Bussotti himself, was produced at the opening of the Venice Festival of Contemporary Music on Sept. 7, 1972. Among Bussotti's other conceits is *5 Pieces for David Tudor* (1959), in which the dedicatee wears thick gloves to avoid hitting single and potentially melodious tones on the keyboard. Among his other works of various descriptions are 3 pieces for puppet theater: *Nottetempolunapark* (1954); *Arlechinbatocieria* (1955); *Tre mascare in gloria* (1956); *7 Fogli* for various instrumental combinations (1959); *Phrase à trois* for String Trio (1960); *Torso* for Voices, Speaker, and Instrumentalists (1960–63); *La Partition ne peut se faire que dans la violence* for Orch. (1962); *I semi di Gramsci* for Quartet and Orch. (1967); *Tableaux vivants* for 2 Pianos (1965); *Rara Requiem* to words in several languages (1969); *Opus Cygne* for Flute and Orch. (Baden-Baden, Oct. 20, 1979).

Bustabo, Guila, American violinist; b. Manitowoc, Wis., Feb. 25, 1917. She was a child prodigy; played at a benefit concert in Chicago at the age of 4; at age 10 was a soloist with the N.Y. Phil., performing a Wieniawski concerto (Nov. 2, 1929). She studied with Louis Persinger in N.Y. and with Enesco and Hubay in Europe. From 1964 to 1970, she was on the faculty of the Innsbruck Cons. in Austria.

Bustini, Alessandro, Italian composer; b. Rome, Dec. 24, 1876; d. there, June 23, 1970. He studied at the Accademia di Santa Cecilia in Rome with Sgambati (piano), Renzi (organ), and Falchi (composition), graduating in 1897. He was subsequently appointed to its faculty, and was its president from 1952 to 1964. His works, all written in the traditional Italian manner, include the opera *Maria Dulcis* (Rome, April 15, 1902); 2 syms. (1899, 1909); *Le Tentazioni,* a symphonic poem (1914);

Le Stagioni for Violin and Chamber Orch. (1934); 2 string quartets; songs; piano works.

Buswell, James Oliver IV, American violinist; b. Fort Wayne, Ind., Dec. 4, 1946. He was educated at Harvard College (B.A., 1970); studied violin with Ivan Galamian at the Juilliard School of Music; made his N.Y. recital debut in 1967. He was a visiting prof. at the Univ. of Arizona in Tucson (1972–73); in 1974 he joined the faculty of the Indiana Univ. School of Music in Bloomington. He left there in 1986 to join the faculty at the New England Cons. of Music in Boston.

Buths, Julius (Emil Martin), German pianist; b. Wiesbaden, May 7, 1851; d. Düsseldorf, March 12, 1920. He was a pupil of his father; later of Hiller in Cologne and Kiel in Berlin; conducted the "Cecilia" at Wiesbaden (1871–72); traveled to Milan and Paris (1873–74); conducted in Breslau (1875–79) and in Elberfeld (1879–90); from 1890 to 1908 was music director at Düsseldorf, and conducted several Rhine music festivals; in 1902 was appointed director of the Düsseldorf Cons. He wrote a Piano Concerto; Piano Quintet; String Quartet; Piano Suite; etc.

Butler (real name, **Whitwell**), **O'Brien,** Irish composer; b. Cahersiveen, c.1870; d. May 7, 1915 (lost on the *Lusitania*). He began his musical studies in Italy, then became a pupil of C.V. Stanford and W. Parratt at the Royal College of Music in London; later traveled extensively, and spent some time in India, where he wrote an opera, *Muirgheis,* the 1st opera to be written to a libretto in the Gaelic language; it was produced in Dublin, Dec. 7, 1903. Other compositions include a Sonata for Violin and Piano (on Irish themes) and songs.

Butt, Dame Clara (Ellen), English contralto; b. Southwick, Sussex, Feb. 1, 1872; d. North Stoke, Oxfordshire, July 13, 1936. She studied with J.H. Blower at the Royal College of Music in London; later took lessons with Bouhy in Paris and Etelka Gerster in Berlin; made her operatic debut as Ursula in Sullivan's *Golden Legend* (London, Dec. 7, 1892); then sang at the music festivals at Hanley and Bristol. She visited the U.S. in 1899 and 1913; in 1913–14 made a world tour with her husband, **R. Kennerley Rumford,** a noted baritone. Several composers wrote special works for her, among them Elgar's *Sea-Pictures* and H. Bedford's *Romeo and Juliet.* In 1920 she was made a Dame Commander of the Order of the British Empire.

BIBL.: W. Ponder, *C. B.* (London, 1928).

Butterley, Nigel (Henry), Australian composer; b. Sydney, May 13, 1935. He began piano lessons at the age of 4; studied at the New South Wales State Cons. with Noel Nickson and Raymond Hanson (1952–55); then in London with Priaulx Rainier (1962). From 1955 to 1972 he was music adviser to the Australian Broadcasting Commission.

WORKS: *Diversion* for Brass Quintet (1958); *Canticle of David* for Strings (1960); Oboe Sonatina (1960); *The Tell-Tale Heart,* after Poe, a ballet for 2 Pianos and Percussion (1961); *Laudes* (Praises) for Flute, Clarinet, Horn, Trumpet, Violin, Viola, Cello, and Piano (1963); 3 string quartets (1965, 1975, 1979); *Canticle of the Sun* for 3 amateur Instrumental Groups (1965); *The White-Throated Warbler* for Recorder and Harpsichord (1965); *In the Head the Fire,* a "radio tableau" for Narrator, Tenor, Baritone, Chorus, Winds, Piano, Organ, and Percussion (Italia Prize, 1966); *Interaction,* an "improvisation" for Painter and Orch. (1967; expanded into a television film); Variations for Wind Quintet, Piano, and Recorded Piano (Canberra, Sept. 30, 1967); *Meditations of Thomas Traherne* for Orch. and Recorder Ensemble (1968); *Carmina* for Voice and Wind Quintet (1968); Violin Concerto (1968–70); *Pentad* for 27 Wind Instruments (1969); *Refractions* for Wind Quintet and 28 String Instruments (1969); *Explorations* for Piano and Orch. (Sydney, May 2, 1970, in the presence of Queen Elizabeth II); *Voices* for Wind Quintet (1972); *1st Day Covers,* a "philharmonic philatelia" for Narrator and Orch. (1972); *Fire in the Heavens* for Orch. (1973); *The 4 Elements* for Orch. (1973); *Watershore,* after Walt Whitman, for 4 Narrators, Improvising Group, 3 Cellos, and Piano Roll (1977); Trio for Clarinet, Cello, and Piano (1979); Sym. (1980).

Butterworth, George (Sainton Kaye), talented English composer; b. London, July 12, 1885; d. in the battle of the Somme, near Pozières, Aug. 5, 1916. He learned to play the organ at school in Yorkshire, then studied with T. Dunhill at Eton (1899–1904) and at Trinity College, Oxford (1904–8). He then taught music at Radley and wrote music criticism for *The Times* of London; with C. Sharpe and Vaughan Williams, he became an ardent collector of folk songs, which were incorporated into several of his compositions. At the outbreak of World War I, he enlisted in the British army and was posthumously awarded the Military Cross for bravery. His death was greatly lamented. Before he left for France, he destroyed many MSS, including those of a Violin Sonata and a *Barcarolle* for Orch. that had been much praised.
WORKS: ORCH.: 2 *English Idylls* (Oxford, Feb. 8, 1912); *A Shropshire Lad,* rhapsody (originally called *The Cherry Tree,* prelude; Leeds, Oct. 2, 1913); *The Banks of Green Willow,* idyll (West Kirby, Feb. 27, 1914). VOCAL: *I fear thy kisses,* by Shelley (1909); 6 songs from *A Shropshire Lad,* by Housman (London, June 20, 1911); *Requiescat,* by Wilde (1911); *Bredon Hill,* by Housman (1912); *Love blows as the wind blows,* by Henley, for Baritone, and String Quartet or Piano or Orch. (1914). CHORAL: *On Christmas Night* (1902); *We get up in the morn* (1912); *In the Highlands,* by Stevenson (1912); *11 Folk Songs from Sussex* (1912); *Morris Dances* (with Sharpe; 1913).
BIBL.: S. Bayliss, "G. B., an appreciation," *Musical Mirror* (Aug. 1930); J. Rippin, "G. B. 1885–1916," *Musical Times* (Aug.–Sept. 1966); M. Barlow, "G. B.: The Early Years," *Journal of the British Music Society* (1983); I. Copley, *G. B. and His Music: A Centennial Tribute* (London, 1985).

Butting, Max, German composer; b. Berlin, Oct. 6, 1888; d. there, July 13, 1976. He studied organ in Berlin and composition in Munich. Returning to Berlin, he was a successful teacher, but in 1933 was deprived of his various positions for political reasons, being the former ed. of a socialist publication. He was able to return to his professional activities after the end of the war. In 1948 he was appointed a lecturer in the music division of the East Berlin Radio; in 1968 he received an honorary doctor's degree from Humboldt Univ. in East Berlin. His music is animated by polyphonic purposefulness and is marked by rhythmic vitality and lyric meditation. Since many of his works were destined for amateur performances, Butting shunned modernistic involvements; however, in his 9th and 10th syms. he applied dodecaphonic structures.
WORKS: Opera, *Plautus im Nonnenkloster* (Leipzig, Oct. 3, 1959); 10 syms. (1922–63); *Sinfonietta, with Banjo* (1929); Flute Concerto (1950); *Symphonic Variations* (1953); Sinfonietta, op. 100 (1960); Piano Concerto (1965); *Legende* for Orch. (1966); *Triptychon* for Orch. (1967); *Concert Overture* (1973); 10 string quartets (1914–71); String Quintet (1916); Quintet for Violin, Viola, Cello, Oboe, and Clarinet (1921); Wind Quintet (1925); Piano Trio (1947); String Trio (1952); numerous minor pieces of chamber music; a considerable number of piano pieces, choruses, and songs.
BIBL.: D. Brennecke, *Das Lebenswerk M. B.s* (Leipzig, 1973).

Buttstett, Johann Heinrich, German organist and composer; b. Bindersleben, near Erfurt, April 25, 1666; d. Erfurt, Dec. 1, 1727. He studied with Johann Pachelbel; was appointed organist at the Reglerkirche in Erfurt in 1684; in 1691 became organist at the Predigerkirche there, a post he held for 36 years, until his death. He publ. *Musicalische Clavier-Kunst und Vorraths-Kammer* for Harpsichord (Leipzig, 1713); also composed several masses and many chorale preludes for organ. His *Ut, mi, sol, re, fa, la, tota musica et harmonia aeterna* (Erfurt, 1716) is a polemical pamphlet directed against Mattheson.
BIBL.: E. Ziller, *J.H. B.* (diss., Univ. of Halle, 1934).

Buttykay, Akos, Hungarian pianist and composer; b. Halmi, July 22, 1871; d. Debrecen, Oct. 26, 1935. He studied at the Budapest Cons.; in 1894 went to Weimar for further courses in piano playing. He toured in Central Europe as a pianist; in 1907 settled in Budapest as a piano teacher at the Music Academy. He wrote several operettas which were modestly successful at their productions in Budapest: *The Flying Greek* (Budapest, Oct. 19, 1905); *Pompom* (1907); *Cinderella* (Budapest, Oct. 26, 1912); *A Love Storm* (Budapest, Feb. 6, 1920); 2 syms. (1900, 1902); *Magyar Suite* for Orch. (1900); *Magyar Rhapsody* for Orch. (1931); Violin Sonata (1908); *Capriccio* for Violin and Piano (1928); many songs.

Buus, Jacques (Jachet de or **van Paus; Jacobus Bohusius),** Flemish contrapuntist; b. c.1500; d. Vienna, late Aug. 1565. His 1st publications were 2 French songs, printed in Lyons in 1538. In 1541 he went to Italy and was engaged as assistant organist at S. Marco in Venice; in 1550 he settled in Vienna. He publ., in Venice, 2 books of instrumental *Canzoni francese* (1543, 1550); 2 books of *Ricercari* (1547, 1549); and 1 book of *Motetti* (1549); several of his madrigals were publ. in various collections of the period, and also reprinted in a number of anthologies.
BIBL.: G. Sutherland, "The Ricercari of J. B.," *Musical Quarterly* (Oct. 1945); W. Breitner, *Jacob Buus als Motettenkomponist* (Tutzing, 1977).

Buxtehude, Dietrich (Didericus), significant Danish-born German organist and composer; b. probably in Helsingborg, c.1637; d. Lübeck, May 9, 1707. His father, Johannes Buxtehude (1601–74), an organist of German extraction, was active in Holstein, which was under Danish rule. After receiving a thorough education, in all probability from his father, Dietrich became organist at St. Mary's in Helsingborg (1657 or 1658), and then at St. Mary's in Helsingør (1660). On April 11, 1668, he was appointed organist and Werkmeister in succession to the recently deceased Franz Tunder at St. Mary's in Lübeck, subject to the condition that he would abide by the custom of marrying the predecessor's unmarried daughter; he did so, marrying Anna Margaretha on Aug. 3, 1668. He continued the Abendmusiken, concerts consisting of organ music and concerted pieces for chorus and orch., held annually in Lübeck in late afternoon on 5 of the 6 Sundays immediately preceding Christmas. Mattheson and Handel visited Buxtehude on Aug. 17, 1703, with the ostensible purpose of being considered as his successor; but it is a valid surmise that the notorious marriage clause, which would have compelled the chosen one to marry Buxtehude's daughter, allegedly lacking in feminine charm, deterred them from further negotiations. In 1705 J.S. Bach made a pilgrimage allegedly to hear the Abendmusik, to study with Buxtehude, and possibly to investigate the impending opening; though details of Bach's trip are subject to speculation, there can be no doubt that Buxtehude exercised a profound influence on Bach, as both organist and composer. Buxtehude's daughter, 1 of 7, eventually married her father's successor, Johann Christian Schieferdecker, on Aug. 29, 1707. Buxtehude exerted a major influence on the organists who followed him by virtue of the significant role he played in the transitional period of music history from Froberger to the contrapuntal mastery of Bach. Though little of his music exists in MS, many composers were known to have made copies of his works for their own study. His major student was Nicolaus Bruhns. Buxtehude appears prominently in the painting *Domestic Music Scene* (1674) by Johannes Voorhout. For a detailed compilation of Buxtehude's works, see G. Karstädt, ed., *Thematisch-systematisches verzeichnis der musikalischen Werke von D. B.: B.-Werke-Verzeichnis* (Wiesbaden, 1974). Editions of his works include: P. Spitta, ed., *D. B.: Werke für Orgel* (1875–76; rev. and augmented, 1903–4, by M. Seiffert; supplement, 1939, by M. Seiffert); M. Seiffert, ed., *D. B.: Abendmusiken und Kirchenkantate,* in Denkmäler Deutscher Tonkunst, XIV (1903; 2nd ed., rev., 1957, by H.J. Moser); W. Gurlitt, ed., *D. B.: Werke* (Klecken and Hamburg, 1925–28); E. Bandert, ed., *D. B.: Klavervaerker* (Copenhagen, 1942); J. Hedar, ed., *D. B.: Orgelwerke* (Copenhagen, 1952); K. Beckmann, ed., *D. B.: Sämtliche Orgelwerke* (Wiesbaden, 1972); K. Snyder, general ed., *D. B.: The Collected Works* (18 vols., N.Y., 1987– ; includes rev. ed. of Gurlitt's vols.).

WORKS: The Buxtehude-Werke-Verzeichnis (BuxWV) number follows the work: VOCAL: *41 ARIAS: An filius non est Dei*, 6; *Att du, Jesu, will mig hôra*, 8; *Bedenke, Mensch, das Ende*, 9; *Das neugeborne Kindelein*, 13; *Dein edles Herz*, 14; *Du Lebensfürst, Herr Jesu Christ*, 22; *Entreisst euch, meine Sinnen*, 25; *Fallax mundus, ornat vultus*, 28; *Jesu, dulcis memoria*, 56; *Jesu, Komm, mein Trost und Lachen*, 58; *Jesu, meine Freud und Lust*, 59; *Jesulein, du Tausendschön*, 63; *Kommst du, Licht der Heiden*, 66; *Lauda Sion Salvatorem*, 68; *Mein Gemüt erfreuet sich*, 72; *Meine Seele, willtu ruhn*, 74; *Fried und Freudenreiche Hinfahrt*, 76; *Nun freut euch, ihr Frommen, mit mir*, 80; *O fröhliche Stunden, o fröhliche Zeit*, 85; *O fröhliche Stunden, o herrlich Zeit*, 86; *O Gottes Stadt*, 87; *O Jesu mi dulcissime*, 88; *O lux beata Trinitas*, 89; *O wie selig sind*, 90; *Pange lingua*, 91; *Salve, desiderium*, 93; *Schwinget euch himmelan*, 96; *Surrexit Christus hodie*, 99; *Was frag' ich nach der Welt*, 104; *Welt, packe dich*, 106; *Wenn ich, Herr Jesu, habe dich*, 107; *Wie schmeckt es so lieblich und wohl*, 108; *Wie soll ich dich empfangen*, 109; *Wie wird erneuet, wie wird erfreuet*, 110; *Auf, Saiten, auf!*, 115; *Auf! stimmet die Saiten*, 116; *Deh credete il vostro vanto*, 117; *Gestreuet mit Blumen*, 118; *Klinget für Freuden*, 119; *O fröhliche Stunden, o herrlicher Tag*, 120.

3 CANONS: *Canon duplex per Augmentationem*, 123; *Divertisons nous aujourd'hui*, 124; *Canon quadruplex*, 124a.

20 CANTATAS: *Alles, was ihr tut*, 4; *Drei schöne Dinge sind*, 19; *Eins bitte ich vom Herrn*, 24; *Frohlocket mit Händen*, 29; *Fürchtet euch nicht*, 30; *Gott fähret auf mit Jauchzen*, 33; *Gott hilf mir*, 34; *Herr, auf dich traue ich*, 35; *Herr, wenn ich nur dich habe*, 39; *Ich habe Lust abzuscheiden*, 46; *Ich habe Lust abzuschieden*, 47; *Ich halte es dafür*, 48; *Ich suchte des Nachts*, 50; *Ihr lieben Christen, freut euch nun*, 51; *Ist es recht*, 54; *Je höher du bist*, 55; *Membra Jesu nostri*, 75 (cycle of 7 cantatas); *Nichts soll uns scheiden*, 77; *O Gott, wir danken deiner Güt'*, 86; *Schlagt, Künstler, die Pauken*, 122.

16 CHORALE SETTINGS: *All solch dein Güt' wir preisen*, 3; *Befiehl dem Engel, dass er komm*, 10; *Du Frieden-Fürst, Herr Jesu Christ*, 20; *Du Frieden-Fürst, Herr Jesu Christ*, 21; *Erhalt uns, Herr, bei deinem Wort*, 27; *Gen Himmel zu dem Vater mein*, 32; *Herren vår Gud*, 40; *Herzlich lieb' hab ich dich, o Herr*, 41; *Herzlich tut mich verlangen*, 42; *In dulci jubilo*, 52; *Jesu, meine Freude*, 60; *Nimm von uns, Herr, du treuer Gott*, 78; *Nun lasst uns Gott dem Herren*, 81; *Wachet auf, ruft uns die Stimme*, 100; *Wär Gott nicht mit uns diese Zeit*, 102; *Walts Gott, mein Werk ich lasse*, 103.

6 CIACCONAS: *Herr, wenn ich nur dich hab'*, 38; *Jesu dulcis memoria*, 57; *Jesu, meines Lebens Leben*, 62; *Laudate pueri Dominum*, 69; *Liebster, meine Seele saget*, 70; *Quemadmodum desiderat cervus*, 92.

27 CONCERTOS: *Afferte Domino gloriam honorem*, 2; *Also hat Gott die Welt geliebet*, 5; *Aperite mihi portas justitiae*, 7; *Canite Jesu nostro*, 11; *Cantate Domino*, 12; *Der Herr ist mit mir*, 15; *Dixit Dominus*, 17; *Domine, salvum fac regem*, 18; *Ecce nunc benedicite Domino*, 23; *Fürwahr, er trug unsere Krankheit*, 31; *Herr, nun lässt du deinen Diener*, 37; *Ich bin die Auferstehung*, 44; *Ich bin eine Blume zu Saron*, 45; *Ich sprach in meinem Herzen*, 49; *In te, Domine, speravi*, 53; *Jubilate Domino*, 64; *Lauda anima mea Dominum*, 67; *Lobe den Herren, meine Seele*, 71; *Mein Herz ist bereit*, 73; *Nun danket alle Gott*, 79; *O clemens, o mitis*, 82; *O dulcis Jesu*, 83; *Salve Jesu*, 94; *Schaffe in mir, Gott*, 95; *Sicut Moses exaltavit serpentem*, 97; *Singet dem Herrn*, 98; *Benedicam Dominum*, 113.

4 DIALOGUES: *Herr, ich lasse dich nicht*, 36; *Jesu, meiner Freuden Meister*, 61; *Wo ist doch mein Freund geliehen?*, 111; *Wo soll ich fliehen hin?*, 112.

LITURGICAL: *Missa alla brevis*, 114.

2 PARODIES: *Erfreue dich, Erde!*, 26 (of 122); *Klinget mit Freuden*, 65 (of 119).

KEYBOARD: 12 canzoni, 166–176, 225; 9 chorale fantasias, 188, 194–196, 203–204, 210, 218, 223; 32 chorale preludes, 178, 180, 182–187, 189–193, 197–202, 206, 208–209, 211– 212, 214–215, 217, 219–222, 224; 6 chorale variations, 177, 179, 181, 205, 207, 213; 2 ciacconas, 159–160; Passacaglia, 161; Praeambulum, 158; 20 praeludia, 136–153, 162–163; 19 suites, 226–244; 5 toccatas, 155–157, 164–165; 6 variation sets, 145–150.

CHAMBER: 16 sonatas for Violin, Viola da Gamba, and Continuo, 252–265, 272–273 (252–258 publ. as op. 1, c.1694; 259–265 publ. as op. 2, 1696); 3 sonatas for 2 Violins, Viola da Gamba, and Continuo, 266, 269, 271; Sonata for Viola da Gamba, Violone, and Continuo, 267.

DOUBTFUL AND LOST WORKS: VOCAL: *Accedite gentes, accurite populi*, 1 (doubtful); *Die ist der Tag*, 16 (lost); *Heut triumphieret Gottes Sohn*, 43 (doubtful); *Wachet auf, ruft uns die Stimme*, 101 (doubtful).

KEYBOARD: 7 suites, "Die Natur oder Eigenschafft der Planeten," 251 (lost); Sonata for Viola da Gamba and Continuo, 268 (doubtful).

BIBL.: H. Jimmerthal, *B.* (Lübeck, 1877); C. Steihl, *Die Organisten an der Marienkirche und die Abendmusiken in Lübeck* (Leipzig, 1886); A. Pirro, *B.* (Paris, 1913; reprinted, 1966); S. Hagen, *D. B.* (Copenhagen, 1920); W. Stahl, *Franz Tunder und D. B.* (Leipzig, 1926); idem, *B.* (Kassel, 1937); C.-A. Moberg, *D. B.* (Helsingborg, 1946); J. Hedar, *D. B.s Orgelwerke* (Stockholm, 1951); F. Hutchins, *D. B.: The Man, His Music, His Era* (Paterson, N.J., 1955); H.J. Moser, *D. B.: Der Mann und sein Werk* (Berlin, 1957); S. Sørensen, *D. B.s vokale kirkenmusik* (Copenhagen, 1958); N. Friis, *D. B.* (Helsingør, 1960); M. Geck, *Die Vokalmusik D. B. und der frühe Pietismus* (Kassel, 1965); G. Karstadt, *Der Lübecker Kantatenband D. B.* (Lübeck, 1971); S. Sørenson, *Das B.bild im Wandel der Zeit* (Lübeck, 1972); H. Wettstein, *D. B. (1637–1707): Eine Bibliographie* (Freiburg, 1979); L. Archbold, *Style and Structure in the Praeludia of D. B.* (Ann Arbor, Mich., 1985); C. Defant, *Kammermusik und Stylus phantasticus. Studien zu D. B.s Triosonaten* (Frankfurt, 1985); K. Snyder, *D. B.* (N.Y., 1987).

Buzzolla, Antonio, Italian composer and conductor; b. Adria, March 2, 1815; d. Venice, March 20, 1871. He received his early education from his father, a professional theater conductor; then enrolled at the Naples Cons. as a student of Donizetti and Mercadante (1837–39). He was then active as a theater conductor in Italy, Germany, and France, returning to Venice in 1847. He wrote the operas *Ferramondo* (Venice, Dec. 3, 1836), *Mastino I della Scala* (Venice, May 31, 1841), *Gli Avventurieri* (Venice, May 14, 1842), *Amleto* (Venice, Feb. 24, 1848), and *Elisabetta di Valois* (Venice, Feb. 16, 1850). He also wrote an opera in Venetian dialect, *La Puta onorata*, which remained incomplete. In 1855 he was appointed maestro di cappella at S. Marco, for which he wrote much sacred music.

BIBL.: A. Casellati, "A. B.," *Musica d'Oggi* (July 1930).

Bychkov, Semyon, Russian-born American conductor; b. Leningrad, Nov. 30, 1952. He attended the Glinka Choir School in Leningrad as a youth; subsequently studied with Ilya Musin at the Leningrad Cons., graduating in 1974. In 1975 he emigrated to the U.S., where he received his Artist Diploma from the Mannes College of Music in N.Y. in 1976. From 1980 to 1985 he was music director of the Grand Rapids Sym. Orch.; was concurrently associate conductor of the Buffalo Phil. Orch., and in 1985 became its director. He also appeared as a guest conductor with the Minnesota Orch., National Sym. of Washington, D.C., Detroit Sym., Indianapolis Sym., and Vancouver (B.C.) Sym.; also conducted in England, Israel, and Japan. On July 4, 1983, he gave a special concert of the Grand Rapids Sym. Orch. to mark his naturalization as a U.S. citizen. In 1989 he became music director of the Orch. de Paris.

BIBL.: L. Marum, "S. B.," *Ovation* (Feb. 1986).

Bylsma, Anner, Dutch cellist; b. The Hague, Feb. 17, 1934. He studied cello with Carel Boomkamp at the Royal Cons. of Music in The Hague, receiving the Prix d'excellence in 1957; subsequently won the Pablo Casals Competition in Mexico City (1959). After serving as principal cellist of Amsterdam's Concertgebouw Orch. (1962–68), he devoted himself to an international career as a soloist and recitalist. He taught at his alma mater and at Amsterdam's Sweelinck Cons., and was the Erasmus Scholar at Harvard Univ. in 1982. His repertoire is comprehensive, ranging from the Baroque and early Classical periods (utilizing original instruments) to contemporary scores.

Byrd, Donald(son Toussaint L'Overture), inspired black American jazz trumpeter, flügelhornist, and teacher; b. Detroit, Dec. 9, 1932. He studied at Wayne State Univ. in Detroit (B.Mus., 1954) and at the Manhattan School of Music in N.Y. (M.A., in music ed.); then studied composition with Boulanger in Paris (1962–63). Following short stints with Art Blakey, Max Roach, Sonny Rollins, John Coltrane, and others, he teamed up with Pepper Adams (1958–61). Among his most notable recordings were *Byrd in Flight* (1960), *Electric Byrd* (1970), and *Black Byrd* (1972). In later years he served on the faculties of Rutgers Univ., the Hampton Inst., Howard Univ., and North Carolina Central Univ.

Byrd, Henry Roeland, American blues pianist; b. Bogalusa, La., Dec. 19, 1918; d. New Orleans, Jan. 30, 1980. He received rudimentary instruction in music from his mother; subsequently developed an individual style of playing which utilized blues, New Orleans, and Caribbean elements; such musicians as Fats Domino, Huey Smith, and Allen Toussaint made his style popular outside New Orleans. His "erudite" synthetic techniques earned for him the nickname "Prof. Longhair."

Byrd (or Byrde, Bird), William, great English composer; b. probably in Lincoln, 1543; d. Stondon Massey, Essex, July 4, 1623. There are indications that Byrd studied music with Tallis. On March 25, 1563, Byrd was appointed organist of Lincoln Cathedral; in 1568 he married Juliana Birley; in 1570 he was sworn in as a Gentleman of the Chapel Royal, while retaining his post at Lincoln Cathedral until 1572; he then assumed his duties, together with Tallis, as organist of the Chapel Royal. In 1575 Byrd and Tallis were granted a patent by Queen Elizabeth I for the exclusive privilege of printing music and selling music paper for a term of 21 years; however, the license proved unprofitable and they successfully petitioned the Queen in 1577 to give them an annuity in the form of a lease. In 1585, after the death of Tallis, the license passed wholly into Byrd's hands. The earliest publication of the printing press of Byrd and Tallis was the 1st set of *Cantiones sacrae* for 5 to 8 Voices (1575), printed for them by Vautrollier and dedicated to the Queen; works issued by Byrd alone under his exclusive license were *Psalmes, Sonets and Songs* (1588), *Songs of Sundrie Natures* (1589), and 2 further vols. of *Cantiones sacrae* (1589, 1591). Many of his keyboard pieces appeared in the MS collection *My Ladye Nevells Booke* (1591) and in Francis Tregian's *Fitzwilliam Virginal Book* (c.1612–19), among others. During the winter of 1592–93, he moved to Stondon Massey, Essex. He subsequently was involved in various litigations and disputes concerning the ownership of the property. Between 1592 and 1595 he publ. 3 masses, and between 1605 and 1607 he brought out 2 vols. of Gradualia. His last collection, *Psalmes, Songs and Sonnets*, was publ. in 1611. Byrd was unsurpassed in his time in compositional versatility. His masterly technique is revealed in his ecclesiastical works, instrumental music, madrigals, and solo songs.
Works (all publ. in London): *Cantiones, quae ab argumento sacrae vocantur* for 5 to 8 Voices (with Tallis, 1575); *Psalmes, Sonets and Songs* for 5 Voices (1588); *Liber primus sacrarum cantionum (Cantiones sacrae)* for 5 Voices (1589); *Songs of Sundrie Natures* for 3 to 6 Voices (1589); *Liber secundus sacrarum cantionum (Cantiones sacrae)* for 5 to 6 Voices (1591); *Mass* for 4 Voices (publ. without title page; c.1592); *Mass* for 3 Voices (publ. without title page; c.1593); *Mass* for 5 Voices (publ. without title page; c.1595); *Gradualia ac cantiones sacrae* for 3 to 5 Voices (1605); *Gradualia seu cantionum sacrarum, liber secundus* for 4 to 5 Voices (1607); *Psalmes, Songs and Sonnets . . .* for 3 to 6 Voices (1611). He also wrote a *Short Service* for 4 to 6 Voices; a *2nd Service* for 1 to 5 Voices; a

3rd Service for 5 Voices; a *Great Service* for 5 to 10 Voices; *1st Preces and Psalms 47, 54, and 100*; and *2nd Preces and Psalms 114, 55, 119, and 24*; several other works are incomplete. His keyboard music appeared in *My Ladye Nevells Booke* (1591), *The Fitzwilliam Virginal Book* (c.1612–19), *Parthenia* (c.1612–13), *Will Forster's Book* (1624), and other contemporary collections. Modern eds. of Byrd's works have been publ. in several series, including the Tudor Church Music and Musica Britannica series. E.H. Fellowes was a pioneer in the field; he brought out many of the works in his series on the English madrigalists, and also planned a complete ed. of the music, which was continued by T. Dart and others. Their efforts culminated in The Byrd Edition, ed. by P. Brett, which commenced appearing in 1971.
BIBL.: E.H. Fellowes, *The English Madrigal Composers* (Oxford, 1921; 2nd ed., 1948); idem, *W. B.: A Short Account of His Life and Work* (Oxford, 1923; 2nd ed., 1928); F. Howes, *W. B.* (London, 1928); E.H. Fellowes, *W. B.* (Oxford, 1936; 2nd ed., 1948); H. Andrews, *The Technique of B.'s Vocal Polyphony* (London, 1966); O. Neighbour, *The Consort and Keyboard Music of W. B.* (Berkeley, 1978); J. Kerman, *The Music of W. B.: vol. I, The Masses and Motets of W. B.* (London, 1981); R. Turbet, *W. B.: A Guide to Research* (N.Y., 1987).

Byrne, David, Scottish-born American musician; b. Dumbarton, May 14, 1952. He went to the U.S. in his tender years and entered the Rhode Island School of Design, where he developed his dominant conviction that dance, song, instrumental music, drama, and cinema were parts of a total art. As his own medium he selected modern dance music and vocal works, stretching in style from folk music to rock. He frequented the popular cabarets and dance halls of N.Y., where he absorbed the essence of urban folklore and the rhythmic ways of natural musicians. He joined the group Talking Heads, which made a specialty of exotic rhythms, especially Caribbean dance tunes, merengue, salsa, bomba, and cha-cha; from Colombia the Talking Heads took cambia; from Brazil, the classical samba. Much of the music that Byrne concocts of these elements is multilingual; one of his albums is titled *Speaking in Tongues*. Byrne also favors African sounds, such as that of the Nigerian juju. The titles of his own songs are fashionably nonsensical, e.g., *Stop Making Sense*, which seems to make plenty of sense to his public. He is an accomplished guitarist, and as a performer displays unbounded physical energy, allowing himself a free voice that ranges from a hiccup to a cry, while urging the accompanying chorus to intone such anarchistic declarations as "Don't Want to Be Part of Your World." The devotion that Byrne has for modern dance is exemplified by the remarkable score he wrote for *The Catherine Wheel*, choreographed by Twyla Tharp; it possesses the widely differing ingredients of new-wave rock and spiritual soul music, masculine and rough on the one hand and elegiac and devotional on the other. The resulting complex has also the additional element of African percussion. Taken as a whole, it represents a synthesis of urban beat and a largely unrelated Eastern rhythm. His 1989 album, *REI MOMO* (promoted in concert at the Brooklyn Academy of Music as part of the New Music America Festival), consists of songs that, backed by a 16-piece band, combine Latin and pop styles. There is a hypno-pompic quality in his inspiration as a composer, asymptotically lying in both reality and irreality, like a half-waking state.
BIBL.: K. Emerson, "D. B.: Thinking Man's Rock Star," *N.Y. Times Magazine* (May 5, 1985).

Byström, Oscar Fredrik Bernadotte, Swedish organist and composer; b. Stockholm, Oct. 13, 1821; d. there, July 22, 1909. After serving in the military, he became inspector of the cons. of the Royal Academy of Music in 1866; was named prof. there in 1872. In addition to the music he wrote for the church, he also composed an operetta, *Herman Vimpel*; a Sym. (1870–72; rev. 1895); and chamber music.

C

Caamaño, Roberto, Argentine composer, pedagogue, and pianist; b. Buenos Aires, July 7, 1923. He studied piano and composition at the Conservatorio Nacional de Música in Buenos Aires; toured as a pianist in Latin America, North America, and Europe (1944–61). He concentrated his activities in Buenos Aires, where he was on the faculties of the Universidad del Litoral (1949–52), the Conservatorio Nacional de Música (1956–74), and the Universidad Católica Argentina (from 1964); he also was artistic director of the Teatro Colón (1961–64). In 1969 he became a member of the Academia Nacional de Bellas Artes; in 1971 he received the Gran Premio of the Argentine Sociedad de Autores y Compositores. He publ. the valuable compendium *Historia del Teatro Colón* (2 vols., Buenos Aires, 1969) and *Apuntes para la formación del pianista profesional* (Buenos Aires, 1979).

WORKS: ORCH.: *Variaciones americanas* (1953–54; Buenos Aires, July 10, 1955); Bandoneón Concerto (Buenos Aires, Aug. 2, 1954); 2 piano concertos: No. 1 (1957; Washington, D.C., April 18, 1958); No. 2 (Buenos Aires, Aug. 9, 1971); *Tripartita* for Wind Orch. (1966); Harp Concerto (1973–74; Washington, D.C., May 1, 1974); Guitar Concerto (Buenos Aires, Nov. 30, 1974). **CHAMBER:** 2 string quartets (1945, 1947); Piano Quintet (1962); various piano pieces; choral works; solo songs.

BIBL.: N. Ceñal, "R. C. (1923)," *Revista del Instituto de Investigación Musicológica Carlos Vega*, No. 7 (Buenos Aires, 1986).

Caballé, Montserrat, celebrated Spanish soprano; b. Barcelona, April 12, 1933. She learned to sing at a convent which she attended as a child; at the age of 8 she was accepted at the Conservatorio del Liceo in Barcelona; her teachers there were Eugenie Kemini, Conchita Badia, and Napoleone Annovazzi. She graduated in 1953; then went to Italy, where she sang some minor roles. After a successful appearance as Mimi in *La Bohème* at the Basel Opera, she advanced rapidly, singing Tosca, Aida, Violetta, and other standard opera parts; she also proved her ability to master such modern and difficult parts as Salome, Elektra, and Marie in *Wozzeck*. She filled guest engagements at the Vienna State Opera, then made a grand tour through Germany. In 1964 she sang Manon in Mexico City. She made a triumphant American debut on April 20, 1965, when she was summoned to substitute for Marilyn Horne in the title role of Donizetti's *Lucrezia Borgia* in a concert performance at Carnegie Hall in N.Y.; the usually restrained N.Y. critics praised her without reservation for the beauty of her voice and expressiveness of her dramatic interpretation. There followed several other American appearances, all of which were highly successful. She made her debut at the Metropolitan Opera in N.Y. as Marguerite in *Faust* on Dec. 22, 1965; she continued her appearances with the Metropolitan Opera; among her most significant roles were Violetta, Mimi, Aida, Norma, Donna Anna, and other roles of the standard operatic repertoire. On Sept. 24, 1989, she created the role of Queen Isabella in Balada's *Cristóbal Colón* in Barcelona. In 1964 she married Bernabé Marti, a Spanish tenor. Subsequently they appeared together in joint recitals.

Cabanilles, Juan Bautista José, Spanish organist and composer; b. Algemesí, province of Valencia, Sept. 4, 1644; d. Valencia, April 29, 1712. He studied for the priesthood at Valencia and probably received his musical training at the Cathedral there; was appointed organist of the Valencia Cathedral May 15, 1665 (succeeding J. de la Torre), and retained that post until his death; was ordained a priest on Sept. 22, 1668. He was the greatest of the early Spanish composers for organ, and the most prolific. He composed chiefly "tientos," remarkable for the ingenious use of the variation form (on liturgical or popular themes). A complete ed. of his works, in 4 vols., has been edited by H. Anglès (Barcelona, 1927–52). The *Obras vocales* are edited by J. Climent (Valencia, 1971).

BIBL.: H. Anglès, "Orgelmusik der Schola Hispanica vom XV.–XVI. Jahrhundert," in *P. Wagner-Festschrift* (Leipzig, 1926); M. Bradshaw, "J. C.: The Toccatas and Tientos," *Musical Quarterly* (April 1973); A. Garcia Ferreras, *J.B. C.: Sein Leben und sein Werk* (Regensburg, 1973).

Cabezón (Cabeçon), Antonio de, great Spanish organist and composer; b. Castrillo de Matajudíos, near Burgos, 1510 (the exact date is unknown; see S. Kastner's letter to the ed. of *Music & Letters,* April 1955); d. Madrid, March 26, 1566. He became blind in infancy; went to Palencia about 1521 to study with the Cathedral organist García de Baeza and with Tomás Gómez. He was appointed organist to the court of the Emperor Charles V and Empress Isabella (1526); after her death, Cabezón entered the service of Prince Philip and accompanied him to Italy, Germany, the Netherlands (1548–51), and England (1554); he returned to Spain (1556) and remained court organist until his death. His keyboard style greatly influenced the development of organ composition on the Continent and the composers for the virginal in England; Pedrell called him "the Spanish Bach." The series Libro de Cifra Nueva (1557), which contains the earliest eds. of Cabezón's works, was reprinted by H. Anglès in *La música en la corte de Carlos V* (1944). His son and successor at the court of Philip II, **Hernando** (b. Madrid; baptized, Sept. 7, 1541; d. Valladolid, Oct. 1, 1602), publ. his instrumental works as *Obras de música para tecla, arpa y vihuela* (Madrid, 1578). This vol. contains exercises in 2 and 3 parts, arrangements of hymn tunes, 4-part "tientos," arrangements of motets in up to 6 parts by Josquin and other Franco-Flemish composers, and variations on tunes of the day (*El caballero,* etc.). See Cabezón's *Collected Works* (C. Jacobs, ed.; N.Y., 1967–76).

BIBL.: O. Kinkeldey, *Orgel und Klavier in der Musik des 16. Jahrhunderts* (Leipzig, 1910); W. Apel, "Early Spanish Music for Lute and Keyboard Instruments," *Musical Quarterly* (July 1934); S. Kastner, *A. d.C.* (Barcelona, 1952); T. Dart, "Cavazzoni and C.," *Music & Letters* (Jan. 1955); special issue of *Anuario Musical,* XXI (1966); G. Bourligueux, "A. d.C. Nota bibliográfia en su cuarto centenario," *Boletín de la Inst. Fernán González* (Jan.–June 1970); M. Kastner, *A. und Hernando d.C.: Ein Chronik* (Tutzing, 1977).

Caccini, Francesca (nicknamed **"La Cecchina"**), Italian composer, daughter of **Giulio Caccini;** b. Florence, Sept. 18, 1587; d. c.1640. She was probably the 1st woman composer of operas. Her opera-ballet *La liberazione di Ruggiero dall'isola d'Alcina* was produced at a palace near Florence on Feb. 2, 1625, and a book of songs from it was publ. in the same year. A modern reprint, ed. by D. Silbert, was publ. in Northampton, Mass. (1945). Caccini wrote further a *Ballo delle zingare* (Florence, Feb. 24, 1615) in which she acted as one of the gypsies. Her sacred opera *Il martirio di Sant'Agata* was produced in Florence, Feb. 10, 1622.

BIBL.: A. Bonaventura, "Il ritratto della Cecchina," *La cultura musicale* (1922); D. Silbert, "F. C. called 'La Cecchina,'" *Musical Quarterly* (Jan. 1946); C. Raney, "F. C.'s *Primo libro,*" *Music & Letters* (Oct. 1967).

Caccini, Giulio, Italian composer (called **Romano,** because he lived mostly in Rome); b. probably in Tivoli, Oct. 8, 1551; d. Florence (buried), Dec. 10, 1618. He was a pupil of Scipione delle Palla in singing and lute playing. His 1st compositions were madrigals in the traditional polyphonic style, but the new ideas generated in the discussions of the artists and literati of the "Camerata," in the houses of Bardi and Corsi at Florence,

inspired him to write vocal soli in recitative form (then termed "musica in stile rappresentativo"), which he sang with consummate skill to his own accompaniment on the theorbo. These 1st compositions in a dramatic idiom were followed by his settings of separate scenes written by Bardi, and finally by the opera *Il combattimento d'Apolline col serpente* (poem by Bardi); next was *Euridice* (1600; poem by Rinuccini) and *Il rapimento di Cefalo* (in collaboration with others; 1st perf., Oct. 9, 1600, at the Palazzo Vecchio in Florence). Then followed *Le nuove musiche,* a series of madrigals for solo voice, with bass (Florence, 1602; new eds., Venice, 1607 and 1615; a modern ed. of the 1602 publication, prepared by H. Wiley Hitchcock [Madison, Wis., 1970], includes an annotated Eng. tr. of Caccini's preface, realizations of the solo madrigals, airs, and the final section of *Il rapimento di Cefalo,* an introductory essay on Caccini, the music, the poetry, MSS, other eds., and a bibliography. A tr. of the preface is also available in O. Strunk, *Source Readings in Music History* [N.Y., 1950]). The song *Amarilli mia bella* from the 1st series became very popular. Caccini also publ. *Fuggilotio musicale* (Venice, 2nd ed., 1613; including madrigals, sonnets, arias, etc.). From 1565 Caccini lived in Florence as a singer at the Tuscan court. He was called, by abbate Angelo Grillo, "the father of a new style of music"; Bardi said of him that he had "attained the goal of perfect music." But his claim to priority in writing vocal music in the "stile rappresentativo" is not supported by known chronology. Caccini's opera *Il rapimento di Cefalo* was performed 3 days after Peri's path-breaking *Euridice;* the closeness in time of operatic productions by both Caccini and Peri is further emphasized by the fact that when Peri produced *Euridice* in Florence (1600), he used some of Caccini's songs in the score. Caccini later made his own setting of *Euridice* (1600), but it was not produced until Dec. 5, 1602. On the other hand, Caccini was undoubtedly the 1st to publish an operatic work, for his score of *Euridice* was printed early in 1601, before the publication of Peri's work of the same title.

BIBL.: A. Ehrichs, *G. C.* (Leipzig, 1908); R. Marchal, "G. C.," *La Revue Musicale* (June 1925); F. Ghisi, *Alle fonti della monodia* (Milan, 1940); L. Bianconi, "G. C. e il manierismo musicale," *Chigiana,* XXV/5 (1968); C. Morricone, "Considerazioni sul *Fuggilozio* de G. C.," *Rivista Italiana di Musicologia,* III (1968); H.W. Hitchcock, "Depriving C. of a Musical Pastime," *Journal of the American Musicological Society* (Spring 1972); idem, "A New Biographical Source for C.," ibid. (Spring 1973); T. Carter, "C.'s *Amarilli mia bella:* Some Questions (and a Few Answers)," *Journal of the Royal Musical Association,* 113/2 (1988).

Cacioppo, George (Emanuel), American composer of the avant-garde; b. Monroe, Mich., Sept. 24, 1927; d. Ann Arbor, Mich., April 4, 1984. He studied with Ross Lee Finney at the Univ. of Michigan (M.A., 1952) and with Leon Kirchner in Tanglewood; subsequently co-founded the ONCE Festival concerts in Ann Arbor (1960). His technique of composition is basically dodecaphonic; however, he allowed himself to deviate with all necessary caution from total serialism. He also experimented with "open end" forms of composition according to the fashionable aleatory principles. In that manner he produced *Piano Pieces* (1962–70) for any number of Pianos, with their realization on tape sounding synchronously or non-synchronously and lasting any practical (or impractical) length of time. Other works include *Time on Time in Miracles* for Soprano, 2 Horns, 2 Trombones, Cello, Piano, and Percussion (1964); *Holy Ghost Vacuum, or America Faints* for Electric Organ (Ann Arbor, March 29, 1966, composer at the manuals); and *Dream Concert* for Organ, Voice, and Percussion (1976).

Cadman, Charles Wakefield, American composer; b. Johnstown, Pa., Dec. 24, 1881; d. Los Angeles, Dec. 30, 1946. His great-grandfather was Samuel Wakefield, the inventor of the so-called Buckwheat Notation. Cadman studied organ with Leo Oehmler in Pittsburgh, and with Emil Paur. He was especially interested in American Indian music; gave lecture recitals with the Indian mezzo-soprano Tsianina Redfeather.

WORKS: STAGE: Opera, *Shanewis* (*The Robin Woman*), his most successful work (Metropolitan Opera, March 23, 1918); *The Sunset Trail*, operatic cantata (Denver, Dec. 5, 1922); *The Garden of Mystery* (N.Y., March 20, 1925); *A Witch of Salem* (Chicago, Dec. 8, 1926); radio play, *The Willow Tree* (NBC, Oct. 3, 1933). **ORCH.:** *Thunderbird Suite* (Los Angeles, Jan. 9, 1917); *Oriental Rhapsody* (1917); *Dark Dancers of the Mardi Gras* (1933); *Suite on American Folktunes* (1937); sym.: *Pennsylvania* (Los Angeles, March 7, 1940). Cantatas: *Father of Waters* (1928); *House of Joy; Indian Love Charm* for Children's Choir; *The Vision of Sir Launfal* for Male Voices, written for the Pittsburgh Prize Competition (1909). Also, Piano Sonata; violin pieces; about 180 songs, of which *At Dawning* acquired enormous popularity.

BIBL.: N. Fielder, *Complete Musical Works of C.W. C.* (Los Angeles, 1951; catalog); H. Perison, *C.W. C.: His Life and Works* (diss., Eastman School of Music, 1978).

Caduff, Sylvia, Swiss conductor; b. Chur, Jan. 7, 1937. She studied at the Lucerne Cons., receiving a piano diploma in 1961; then attended Karajan's conducting classes at the Berlin Cons.; continued conducting studies with Kubelik, Matačić, and Otterloo in Lucerne, Salzburg, and Hilversum (The Netherlands); made her debut with the Tonhalle Orch. of Zürich. She won 1st prize in the 1966 Dimitri Mitropoulos conducting competition in N.Y.; as a result, she was an assistant conductor under Bernstein with the N.Y. Phil. (1966–67); taught orch. conducting at the Bern Cons. (1972–77). In 1977 she became the 1st woman in Europe to be appointed a Generalmusikdirektor, when she took that position with the orch. of the city of Solingen, Germany. She left that position in 1985.

Cafaro (Caffaro), Pasquale, Italian composer; b. San Pietro, in Galatina, Lecce, Feb. 8, 1716; d. Naples, Oct. 23, 1787. He studied at the Naples Cons.; became 2nd master at the Naples Cons. della Pietà in 1759, and 1st master in 1771.

WORKS: OPERAS: *Ipermestra* (Naples, Dec. 18, 1751); *La disfatta di Dario* (Naples, Jan. 20, 1756); *L'incendio di Troia* (Naples, Jan. 20, 1757); *L'Olimpiade* (Naples, Jan. 12, 1769); *Antigono* (Naples, Aug. 13, 1770); 5 oratorios; cantatas; a *Stabat Mater.*

Caffarelli (real name, **Gaetano Majorano**), Italian castrato soprano (*musico*); b. Bitonto, April 12, 1710; d. Naples, Jan. 31, 1783. A poor peasant boy, endowed with a beautiful voice, he was discovered by a musician, Domenico Caffarelli, who taught him, and later sent him to Porpora at Naples. In gratitude to his patron, he assumed the name of Caffarelli. He studied for 5 years with Porpora, who predicted a brilliant career for him. Caffarelli became a master of pathetic song, and excelled in coloratura as well; read the most difficult music at sight, and was an accomplished harpsichord player. His debut at the Teatro Valle (Rome, 1724) in a female role was a triumph. From 1737 to 1745 he sang in London, then in Paris and Vienna. His last public appearance took place on May 30, 1754, in Naples. He was in Lisbon during the earthquake of 1755; he retired from the opera in 1756; upon his return to Naples, he bought the dukedom of Santo-Durato with the fortune he had amassed during his career, and assumed the title of duke.

Caffi, Francesco, Italian music scholar; b. Venice, June 14, 1778; d. Padua, Jan. 24, 1874. After a period of study in Venice, he produced an allegorical drama, *L'armonia richiamata,* which was performed at the opening of the Istituto Filarmonico there (Aug. 20, 1811). In 1827 he moved to Milan; in 1840 to Rovigo. His most important work was a *Storia della musica sacra nella gia Cappella Ducale di San Marco in Venezia dal 1318 al 1797* (2 vols., Venice, 1854–55; reprinted 1931). This was the 1st part of an ambitious project dealing with music in Venice; the 2nd part, *Storia della musica teatrale in Venezia durante la sua Repubblica,* was completed by Caffi shortly before his death, but remained in MS. He further publ. monographs on Bonaventura Furlanetto (1820); Zarlino (1836); Lotti; Benedetto Marcello (in Cicognia's *Venetiani iscritioni*); and Giam-

mateo Asola (Padua, 1862). Caffi's grandson, F.A. Salvagnini, wrote his biography (Rome, 1905).

Cage, John (Milton, Jr.), highly inventive American composer, writer, philosopher, and artist of ultramodern tendencies; b. Los Angeles, Sept. 5, 1912. So important did Cage's work eventually become in music history that even the *Encyclopaedia Britannica* described him as a "composer whose work and revolutionary ideas profoundly influenced mid–20th-century music." His father, John Milton Cage, Sr., was an inventor, his mother active as a clubwoman in California. He studied piano with Fannie Dillon and Richard Buhlig in Los Angeles and with Lazare Lévy in Paris; returning to the U.S., he studied composition in California with Adolph Weiss and Schoenberg, and with Henry Cowell in N.Y. On June 7, 1935, Cage married, in Los Angeles, Xenia Kashevaroff; they were divorced in 1945. In 1938–39 he was employed as a dance accompanist at the Cornish School in Seattle, where he also organized a percussion group. He developed Cowell's piano technique, making use of tone clusters and playing directly on the strings, and initiated a type of procedure to be called "prepared piano," which consists of placing on the piano strings a variety of objects, such as screws, copper coins, and rubber bands, which alter the tone color of individual keys. Eventually the term and procedure gained acceptance among avant-garde composers and was listed as a legitimate method in several music dictionaries. In 1949 Cage was awarded a Guggenheim fellowship and an award from the National Academy of Arts and Letters for having "extended the boundaries of music."

Cage taught for a season at the School of Design in Chicago (1941–42); he then moved to N.Y., where he began a fruitful association with the dancer Merce Cunningham, with whom he collaborated on a number of works that introduced radical innovations in musical and choreographic composition. He served as musical adviser to the Merce Cunningham Dance Co. until 1987. Another important association was his collaboration with the pianist David Tudor, who was able to reify Cage's exotic inspirations, works in which the performer shares the composer's creative role. In 1952, at Black Mountain College, he presented a theatrical event historically marked as the earliest musical Happening.

With the passing years Cage departed from the pragmatism of precise musical notation and definite ways of performance, electing instead to mark his creative intentions in graphic symbols and pictorial representations. He established the principle of indeterminacy in musical composition, producing works any 2 performances of which can never be identical. In the meantime, he became immersed in an earnest study of mushrooms, acquiring formidable expertise and winning a prize in Italy in competition with professional mycologists. He also became interested in chess, and played demonstration games with Marcel Duchamp, the famous painter turned chessmaster, on a chessboard designed by Lowell Cross to operate on aleatory principles with the aid of a computer and a system of laser rays. In his endeavor to achieve ultimate freedom in musical expression, he produced a piece entitled *4'33",* in 3 movements, during which no sounds are intentionally produced. It was performed in Woodstock, N.Y., on Aug. 29, 1952, by David Tudor, who sat at the piano playing nothing for the length of time stipulated in the title. This was followed by another "silent" piece, *0'00",* an idempotent "to be played in any way by anyone," presented for the 1st time in Tokyo, Oct. 24, 1962. Any sounds, noises, coughs, chuckles, groans, and growls produced by the listeners are automatically regarded as integral to the piece itself, so that the wisecrack about the impossibility of arriving at a fair judgment of a silent piece, since one cannot tell what music is not being played, is invalidated by the uniqueness of Cage's art.

Cage is a consummate showman, and his exhibitions invariably attract music-lovers and music-haters alike, expecting to be exhilarated or outraged, as the case may be. In many such public Happenings he departs from musical, unmusical, or even antimusical programs in favor of a free exercise of surrealist imagination, often instructing the audience to participate actively, as for instance going out into the street and bringing in garbage pails needed for percussion effects, with or without garbage. His music is publ. by C.F. Peters Corp. and has been recorded on many labels. In view of the indeterminacy of so many of Cage's works, the catalog publ. by Peters in 1969 can only serve as a list of titles and suggestions of contents. In order to eliminate the subjective element in composition, Cage resorts to a method of selecting the components of his pieces by dice throwing, suggested by the Confucian classic *I Ching*, an ancient Chinese oracle book; the result is a system of total serialism, in which all elements pertaining to acoustical pulses, pitch, noise, duration, relative loudness, tempi, combinatory superpositions, etc., are determined by previously drawn charts. His stage work *Europeras 1 & 2* (1987), which he wrote, designed, staged, and directed, is a sophisticated example, a collage comprised of excerpts from extant operas selected and manipulated by a computer software program, *IC* (short for *I Ching*), designed by Cage's assistant, Andrew Culver. The scheduled opening of *Europeras 1 & 2*, which was to take place on Nov. 15, 1987, was delayed and its location changed due to a fire, reportedly set by a vagrant in search of food, which devastated the Frankfurt Opera House just a few days before the opening.

Cage is also a brilliant writer, much influenced by the manner, grammar, syntax, and glorified illogic of Gertrude Stein. Among his works are *Silence* (1961), *A Year from Monday* (1967), *M* (1973), *Empty Words* (1979), and *X* (1983). He developed a style of poetry called "mesostic," which uses an anchoring string of letters down the center of the page that spell a name, a word, or even a line of text relating to the subject matter of the poem. Mesostic poems are composed by computer, the "source material" pulverized and later enhanced by Cage into a semi-coherent, highly evocative poetic text. He has also collaborated on a number of other projects, most recently *The First Meeting of the Satie Society*, with illustrations by Jasper Johns, Cy Twombly, Robert Rauschenberg, Sol LeWitt, Mell Daniel, Henry David Thoreau, and Cage himself, in preparation by the Limited Editions Club. Since Cage's works are multigenetic, his scores have been exhibited in galleries and museums; he returns annually to Crown Point Press in San Francisco to make etchings. A series of 52 paintings, the *New River Watercolors*, executed in 1987 at the Miles C. Horton Center at the Virginia Polytechnic Inst. and State Univ., has been shown at the Phillips Collection in Washington, D.C. (1990).

Cage was elected to the American Academy and Inst. of Arts and Letters in 1968 and to the American Academy of Arts and Sciences in 1978; he was inducted into the 50-member American Academy of Arts and Letters in 1989. In 1981 he received the Mayor's Award of Honor in N.Y. City. He was named Commander of the Order of Arts and Letters by the French Minister of Culture in 1982, and received an Honorary Doctorate of Performing Arts from the Calif. Inst. of the Arts in 1986. In 1988–89 Cage was Charles Eliot Norton Prof. of Poetry at Harvard Univ., for which he prepared a series of lengthy mesostic poems incorporating the writings of R. Buckminster Fuller, Henry David Thoreau, Marshall McLuhan, and others. In the summer of 1989 he was guest artist at the International Festivals in Leningrad and Moscow, at which he presented works characteristically entitled *Music for . . .* , which he conducted chironomically by pointing out instruments that were to enter. In late 1989 he traveled to Japan to receive the prestigious and lucrative Kyoto Prize.

Works: *1st Construction* (in metal) for 6 Percussion (1939); *Imaginary Landscape* No. 1 for 2 Variable-speed Phonograph Turntables, Frequency Recordings, Muted Piano, and Cymbal (1939); *2nd Construction* for 4 Percussion (1940); *3rd Construction* for 4 Percussion (1941); ballet, *Double Music* for 4 Percussion (with L. Harrison, 1941); *Credo in Us* for 4 Percussion (1942); *Imaginary Landscape* No. 2 for 5 Percussion (1942); *A Valentine Out of Season* for Prepared Piano (1944); *3 Dances* for Amplified Prepared Piano (1944–45); *The Seasons*

for Chamber Orch. (N.Y., May 13, 1947); *Sonata and Interludes* for Prepared Piano (1948); String Quartet (1950); Concerto for Prepared Piano and Chamber Orch. (1951); *16 Dances* for Flute, Trumpet, 4 Percussion, Violin, and Cello (1951); *Imaginary Landscape* No. 4 for 12 Radios, 24 Players, and Conductor (1951); *Music of Changes* for Piano (1951); *Water Music* for Pianist, Radio Receiver, and Drums (1952); *4'33''*, tacet piece for Piano (Woodstock, N.Y., Aug. 29, 1952); *Music for Piano 4–84* for 4, 5, 6 . . ., 84 Pianists (1953–56); *Winter Music* for 1, 2, 3, 4 . . ., 20 Pianists (1957); Concerto for Piano and Orch. (N.Y., May 15, 1958); *Fontana Mix* for 10 Transparencies permutated quaquaversally in 3 or more dimensions (1958); *Music for Amplified Toy Pianos* (Middletown, Conn., Feb. 25, 1960); *Cartridge Music* (Cologne, Oct. 6, 1960); *Theater Piece* for 1–8 Performers (1960); *Atlas eclipticalis* for Orch. (Montreal, Aug. 3, 1961); *0'00''*, "tacet piece to be played in any way by anyone" (Tokyo, Oct. 24, 1962); *Reunion* for Electronic Chessboard (Toronto, March 5, 1968); *HPSCHD* ("harpsichord minus the vowels and the r's"), a multimedia event, with Lejaren Hiller, realized for 7 Amplified Harpsichords, Tapes, Slides, and Films programmed by a Computer with 52 Projectors and 52-channel Tapes (Urbana, Ill., May 16, 1969); *Cheap Imitation* for Piano (1969; for Orch., 1972; for Violin, 1977); *32 études australes* for Piano (1970); *Lecture on the Weather* for 12 Vocalists reading excerpts from the writings of Thoreau, accompanied by electronically realized Wind, Rain, and Thunder (1975); *Child of Tree* for Amplified Cactus Plants (1975); *Renga* with *Apartment House 1776*, a bicentennial work for 2 Synchronized Orchs. and 4 Vocalists (Boston, Sept. 29, 1976); *Inlets* for Conch Shells and Tape (1977); *Freeman Études* for Violin (1977–80; rev. 1990); *Roaratorio, an Irish Circus on Finnegans Wake* for 8 Irish Musicians (1980); *Dance 4 Orchestras* for 4 Orchs. and 4 Conductors (1981; Aptos, Calif., Aug. 22, 1982); *30 Pieces* for 5 Orchs. (1981); *30 Pieces* for String Quartet (1983); *Music for . . .* for Variable Instruments (1984–); *Ryoanji* for 2 Violins, Flute, Oboe, Double Bass, Percussion, and Small Orch. (1984–85); *Europeras 1 & 2* (Frankfurt am Main, Dec. 12, 1987); *One Hundred and One* for Orch. (Boston, April 6, 1989).

WRITINGS: With K. Hoover, *Virgil Thomson: His Life and Music* (N.Y., 1959); *Silence* (Middletown, Conn., 1961); *A Year from Monday* (Middletown, 1967); *To Describe the Process of Composition Used in Not Wanting to Say Anything about Marcel* (Cincinnati, 1969); with A. Knowles, *Notations* (N.Y., 1969); *Writings '67–'72* (Middletown, 1973); *Writings through Finnegans Wake* (Tulsa, Okla., and N.Y., 1978); *Empty Words: Writings '73–'78* (Middletown, 1979); with D. Charles, *For the Birds* (Boston, 1981); with L. Long, *Mud Book* (N.Y., 1982; 2nd ed., 1988); *Themes and Variations* (N.Y., 1982); *X* (Middletown, 1983); *Cage: I–VI* (Boston, 1990).

BIBL.: S. Kubota, *Marcel Duchamp and J. C.* (N.Y., 1968); R. Kostelanetz, ed., *J. C.* (N.Y., 1970); E. Snyder, *J. C. and Music since World War II: A Study in Applied Aesthetics* (diss., Univ. of Wisconsin, 1970); M. Nyman, *Experimental Music: C. and Beyond* (N.Y., 1974); D. Charles, *Gloses sur J. C.* (Paris, 1978); H.-K. Metzger and R. Riehn, *J. C.* (Munich, 1978); P. Griffiths, *C.* (N.Y., 1981); P. Gena and J. Brent, eds., *A J. C. Reader: In Celebration of His 70th Birthday* (N.Y., 1982); R. Stevenson, "J. C. on His 70th Birthday: West Coast Background," *Inter-American Review*, V/1 (Fall 1982); T. DeLio, *Circumscribing the Open Universe: Essays on C., Feldman, Wolff, Ashley and Lucier* (Washington, D.C., 1984); D. Campana, *Form and Structure in the Music of J. C.* (diss., Northwestern Univ., 1985); T. Holmes, *Annotated Discography of the Music of J. C.* (Cherry Hill, N.J., 1986); R. Kostelanetz, ed., *Conversing with C.* (N.Y., 1987); J. Pritchett, *The Development of Chance Techniques in the Music of J. C., 1950–1956* (diss., N.Y. Univ., 1988).

Cagnoni, Antonio, Italian composer; b. Godiasco, near Voghera, Feb. 8, 1828; d. Bergamo, April 30, 1896. He studied at the Milan Cons. (1842–47), where 3 of his operas were produced: *Rosalia di San Miniato* (1845), *I due Savojardi* (1846), and his most successful work, *Don Bucefalo* (1847). From 1852 to 1873 he was maestro di cappella in the Cathedral of Vigevano; from 1873, in the Cathedral of Novarra; from 1887, in S. Maria Maggiore in Bergamo. From 1848 to 1874 he brought out 15 operas in various Italian theaters.

Cahier, Mme. Charles (née **Sara Jane Layton-Walker**), distinguished American contralto; b. Nashville, Jan. 8, 1870; d. Manhattan Beach, Calif., April 15, 1951. She studied in Paris with Jean de Reszke and in Vienna with Gustav Walter. She made her operatic debut in Nice (1904); married Charles Cahier on March 30, 1905. She was engaged at the Vienna Hofoper, and toured Europe and America for many years as a concert artist; later she taught at the Curtis Inst. of Music in Philadelphia. Her repertoire included Carmen, and Wagnerian contralto roles.

Cahn, Sammy, American song composer; b. N.Y., June 18, 1913. He played violin in variety shows and organized a dance band; in 1940 he went to Hollywood and wrote film scores. In 1955 he started a music publishing company. His tune *High Hopes* became J.F. Kennedy's campaign song in 1960. Among his film title songs were *Three Coins in the Fountain, Pocketful of Miracles,* and *Come Blow Your Horn.* He publ. *The Songwriter's Rhyming Dictionary* (N.Y., 1983).

Cailliet, Lucien, exceptionally apt French-born American orchestral arranger; b. Châlons-sur-Marne, May 22, 1891; d. Woodland Hills, Calif., Jan. 3, 1985. He studied at the Dijon Cons., graduating in 1913; then went to the U.S. in 1916, eventually settling in California and becoming a naturalized citizen in 1923. He made a clever arrangement for orch. of Mussorgsky's piano suite *Pictures at an Exhibition* (1937), which successfully stood comparison with Ravel's famous orch. version; on his own, he composed orch. suites, including *Memories of Stephen Foster* (1935), *Strains from Erin* (1936), and variations on the tune "Pop Goes the Weasel" (1938). He also wrote scores for several Hollywood movies. He was appreciated by his colleagues for an extraordinary readiness to produce scores at a maximum efficiency in a minimum amount of time.

Cairns, David (Adam), English music critic; b. Loughton, Essex, June 8, 1926. After study at Winchester and Trinity College, Oxford (1945–48), and Princeton Univ. (1950–51), he devoted himself mainly to music criticism, writing for the *Financial Times* of London (1962–67), the *New Statesman* (1967–70), and the *Sunday Times* of London (from 1973), where he served as chief music critic (from 1983). He was particularly noted for his work on Berlioz; he prepared a tr. of Berlioz's *Les Soirées de l'orchestre* (1963), tr. and ed. Berlioz's memoirs (1969; 2nd ed., 1977), and wrote the study *Berlioz, Vol. 1: The Making of an Artist* (1989). He also publ. a collection of his own journalistic writings, *Responses* (1973).

Caix d'Hervelois, Louis de, French viola da gamba player; b. Amiens, c.1680; d. Paris, 1760. He probably studied with Sainte-Colombe and Marin Marais; was active as a musician in the court of the Duc d'Orléans. His works include 5 vols. of *Pièces de viole* (1725–52) and 2 vols. of *Pièces pour la flûte* (1726, 1731). Some of these compositions have been ed. by Karl Schroeder; various arrangements of his viola da gamba pieces have been made for contemporary instruments.

Calabro, Louis, American composer and conductor; b. N.Y., Nov. 1, 1926. He studied with Persichetti at the Juilliard School of Music, graduating in 1952; in 1955 was appointed to the faculty at Bennington College, Vermont. In 1971 he founded the Sage City Sym. in North Bennington. He received Guggenheim fellowships in 1954 and 1959 and National Endowment of the Arts fellowships in 1973 and 1976.

Works: Concerto for String Orch. (1950); *Statement* for Orch. (1951); Piano Concerto (1953); 3 syms. (1956; for Strings, 1957; 1959–60); *10 Short Pieces* for Strings (1961); *Dadacantatadada* for Blues Singer and Orch. (1964); *Epitaphs* for Chorus and Orch. (1967); *Latitude 15.09° N (Longitude 108.5° E),* oratorio (1970); *Triple Concerto* for 3 Cellos and Orch. (1971); *The Young Pianist's Concertino* for Piano and Strings (1972); *Threnody* for String Orch. (1973); *Voyage,* Bicentennial work for Chorus and Orch. (1974–75); *Invention* for Symphonic Band (1975); *Lunarlied* for Chorus and Strings (1976); *Eos* for English Horn and Strings (1977); Trio for Clarinet, Cello, and Piano (1949); Piano Trio (1952); Violin Sonata (1953); 2 string quartets (1954, 1968); *Bodas de Sangre* for Piano, Violin, Clarinet, Cello, Timpani, and Guitar (1955); Solo Cello Sonata (1956); *Dynamogeny* for Viola and Piano (1958); *Co-Instances—Music without Order* for Piano, Cello, Violin, and Clarinet (1958); *Environments* for 12 Brasses and Solo Clarinet (1969); *Memoirs: Part 1* for Bassoon and Percussion (1973); *3 Pieces* for Solo Piccolo (1973); *Rare Birds* for Narrator and Flute (1976); *Kusehani* for 12 Players (1976); Piano Sonatina (1952); Piano Sonata (1954); *Diversities* for Piano (1966); *Piano Variations* (1968); songs.

Caland, Elisabeth, Dutch-German piano teacher and music editor; b. Rotterdam, Jan. 13, 1862; d. Berlin, Jan. 26, 1929. She studied piano with Deppe in Berlin. Her piano manuals, most of which have gone through several eds., include the authoritative exposition of Deppe's method, *Die Deppesche Lehre des Klavierspiels* (Stuttgart, 1897; in Eng. as *Artistic Piano-Playing,* 1903; also in French, Dutch, and Russian); *Technische Ratschläge für Klavierspieler* (Magdeburg, 1897; also in Eng. and Russian).

Calcaño, José Antonio, Venezuelan composer and musicologist; b. Caracas, March 23, 1900; d. there, Sept. 11, 1980. After studies at the Escuela Superior de Música in Caracas, he went to Bern, Switzerland, for further training. Returning to Venezuela, he was appointed to the faculty of the Univ. of Caracas and organized an indigenous Coro Creole there; later taught at the Escuela de Música Padre Sojo. His works include a ballet, *Mirando en Rusia,* a Sym., 2 string quartets, choruses; he also arranged classical music for various ensembles, and publ. several informative books, among them a historical survey of music in Caracas, *400 años de música caraqueña* (Caracas, 1967).

Caldara, Antonio, Italian cellist and composer; b. Venice, 1670; d. Vienna, Dec. 26, 1736. He likely was a pupil of Legrenzi; was maestro di cappella da chiesa e dal teatro to Ferdinando Carlo in Mantua (1699–1707); from 1709 to 1716 he served as maestro di cappella to Prince Ruspoli in Rome. Caldara was an extraordinarily prolific composer; he composed 90 operas and sacred dramas, 43 oratorios, about 30 masses, other church music, chamber music, etc. A selection of his church music is reprinted in Denkmäler der Tonkunst in Österreich, 26 (formerly 13.i; ed. by Mandyczewski); other vocal works (cantatas, madrigals, and canons) are in vol. 75 (formerly 39; ed. by Mandyczewski, with introduction and explanatory notes by Geiringer); *Dafne,* ed. by C. Schneider and R. John, is in vol. 91; further vocal works are reprinted in *Musique d'église des XVIIᵉ et XVIIIᵉ siècles* (ed. by Charles Pineau); a madrigal and 18 canons were ed. by Geiringer in *Das Chorwerk* (1933); 28 3-part instrumental canons from Caldara's *Divertimenti musicali* are in *Spielkanons* (Wolfenbüttel, 1928).

Bibl.: C. Gray, "A. C. (1670–1736)," *Musical Times* (March 1929); U. Kirkendele, *A. C.: Sein Leben und seine venezianische-römischen Oratorien* (Graz, 1966); R. Freeman, "La verità nella ripetizione," *Musical Times* (April 1968); M. Rinaldi, "Contributo alla futura biografia di A. C.," *Rivista Musicale Italiana* (Sept.–Oct. 1970); B. Pritchard, ed., *A. C.: Essays on His Life and Times* (London, 1987).

Caldicott, Alfred James, English conductor and composer; b. Worcester, Nov. 26, 1842; d. near Gloucester, Oct. 24, 1897. He received a B.M. degree at Cambridge (1878); was a prof. at the Royal College of Music in London (1883–92). His works include the cantatas *The Widow of Nain* (1881) and *A Rhine Legend* for Women's Voices (1883); 13 operettas; numerous glees, especially the popular *Humpty Dumpty* (1878).

Caldwell, Sarah, remarkable American conductor and operatic impresario; b. Maryville, Mo., March 6, 1924. She learned to play violin at home and appeared at local events as a child; then enrolled as a psychology student at the Univ. of Arkansas. She undertook serious violin study at the New England Cons. in Boston with Richard Burgin, concertmaster of the Boston Sym. Orch.; also studied viola with Georges Fourel. In 1947 she was engaged by Boris Goldovsky, head of the opera dept. at the New England Cons., as his assistant, which proved a valuable apprenticeship for her. In 1952 she was engaged as head of the Boston Univ. opera workshop. In 1958 she formed her own opera company in Boston, called the Opera Group; this was the beginning of an extraordinary career, in which she displayed her peculiar acumen in building up an operatic enterprise with scant musical and financial resources. In 1965 she changed the name of her enterprise to the Opera Co. of Boston, making use of a former vaudeville theater for her performances. In most of her productions she acts as producer, conductor, administrator, stage director, scenery designer, and publicity manager. Among her productions were *La Traviata* and *Falstaff* by Verdi, *Benvenuto Cellini* by Berlioz, *Don Quichotte* by Massenet, Bellini's *I Capuletti ed i Montecchi*, and several modern operas, among them Prokofiev's *War and Peace*, Schoenberg's *Moses und Aron*, Alban Berg's *Lulu*, Luigi Nono's *Intolleranza*, and *Montezuma* by Roger Sessions. She produced the American premieres in Boston of *The Ice Break* by Tippett and *The Soldiers* by Zimmermann. She was able to induce famous singers to lend their participation, among them Beverly Sills, Marilyn Horne, Tito Gobbi, Nicolai Gedda, and Placido Domingo. Because of her imposing corpulence (c.300 lbs.) she conducts performances sitting in a large armchair. Soberminded critics heap praise on Sarah Caldwell for her musicianship, physical and mental energy, imagination, and a sort of genius for opera productions. On Jan. 13, 1976, she became the 1st woman to conduct at the Metropolitan Opera in N.Y. (in a perf. of *La Traviata*).

Cale, John, English vocalist, composer, instrumentalist, and producer; b. Garnant, South Wales, Dec. 3, 1940. He was educated at Goldsmiths' College, London, and in N.Y. with Aaron Copland and La Monte Young. He was a founding member, with Lou Reed, of the N.Y. band Velvet Underground, whose album *White Light, White Heat* (1967) shows classical and avant-garde influences. His 1st solo album was *Vintage Violence* (1969); he subsequently collaborated with Terry Riley on *The Church of Anthrax* (1971) and *The Alchemy in Peril* (1972) and with Brian Eno on *June 1, 1974*. As a producer, he was a major influence on British punk.

Calegari, Antonio, Italian composer and music theorist; b. Padua, Feb. 17, 1757; d. there, July 22, 1828. He studied with Scalabrin and Betoni in Venice; was active as a composer there and in Padua. He was a conductor at the Teatro Nuovo in Padua (c.1790–96); spent the last years of his life, from 1801, as organist at the Church of San Antonio in Padua. He brought out 3 operas in Venice: *Le Sorelle rivali* (1784), *L'amor soldato* (1786), and *Il matrimonio scoperto* (1789); the authorship of all 3 is dubious, the last perhaps attributable to Luigi Caligari. Antonio Calegari publ. a curious treatise on composition, *Gioco pittagorico musicale* (Venice, 1801), which was republ. in Paris, during his residence there, as *L'Art de composer la musique sans en connaître les éléments* (1802). A harmonic system, *Sistema armonico* (1829), and a vocal method, *Modi generali del canto* (1836), were publ. posth.

Calkin, John Baptiste, English pianist, organist, and composer; b. London, March 16, 1827; d. there, April 15, 1905. He studied music with his father; then was active as an organist in several churches in London; also taught at the Guildhall School of Music. He wrote many sacred choruses and organ pieces.

Callaerts, Joseph, Belgian organist and composer; b. Antwerp, Aug. 22, 1838; d. there, March 3, 1901. He studied with Lemmens at the Brussels Cons.; was organist of the Jesuit College and later of the Antwerp Cathedral; from 1876 taught

organ at the Music School in Antwerp. He composed a comic opera, *Le Retour imprévu* (Antwerp, 1889); Sym. (1879); Piano Trio (1882); sacred music, organ pieces, piano pieces.

Callas, Maria, celebrated American soprano; b. N.Y., Dec. 3, 1923; d. Paris, Sept. 16, 1977. Her real name was **Maria Anna Sofia Cecilia Kalogeropoulos;** her father was a Greek immigrant. The family went back to Greece when she was 13; she studied voice at the Royal Academy of Music in Athens with the Spanish soprano Elvira de Hidalgo, and made her debut as Santuzza in the school production of *Cavalleria rusticana*, in Nov. 1938. Her 1st professional appearance was in a minor role in Suppé's *Boccaccio* at the Royal Opera in Athens when she was 16; her 1st major role, as Tosca, was there in July 1942. She went back to N.Y. in 1945; auditioned for the Metropolitan Opera Co. and was offered a contract, but decided to go to Italy, where she made her operatic debut in the title role of *La Gioconda* (Verona, Aug. 3, 1947). She was encouraged in her career by the famous conductor Tullio Serafin, who engaged her to sing Isolde and Aida at various Italian productions. In 1951 she became a member of La Scala in Milan. She was greatly handicapped by her absurdly excessive weight (210 lbs.); by a supreme effort of will she slimmed down to 135 pounds; with her classical Greek profile and penetrating eyes, she made a striking impression on the stage; in the tragic role of Medea in Cherubini's opera she mesmerized the audience by her dramatic representation of pity and terror. Some critics opined that she lacked a true bel canto quality in her voice and that her technique was defective in coloratura, but her power of interpretation was such that she was soon acknowledged to be one of the greatest dramatic singers of the century. Her personal life was as tempestuous as that of any prima donna of the bygone era. In 1949 she married the Italian industrialist Meneghini (d. Jan. 20, 1981), who became her manager, but they separated 10 years later. Her romance with the Greek shipping magnate Aristotle Onassis was a recurrent topic of sensational gossip. Given to outbursts of temper, she made newspaper headlines when she walked off the stage following some altercation, or failed to appear altogether at scheduled performances, but her eventual return to the stage was all the more eagerly welcomed by her legion of admirers. After leaving La Scala in 1958, she returned there from 1960 to 1962. From 1952 to 1959 she sang at Covent Garden in London, the Chicago Lyric Opera, and the Dallas Opera. Perhaps the peak of her success was her brilliant debut at the Metropolitan Opera in N.Y. as Norma on Oct. 29, 1956. Following a well-publicized disagreement with its management, she quit the company only to reach an uneasy accommodation with it to return as Violetta on Feb. 6, 1958; that same year she left the company again, returning only in 1965 to sing Tosca before abandoning the operatic stage altogether. In 1971 she gave a seminar on opera at the Juilliard School of Music, and her magic worked even in the novel capacity as instructor; her classes were enthusiastically received by the students. In 1974 she went on a concert tour with the tenor Giuseppe di Stefano; then she returned to Europe. She died suddenly of a heart attack in her Paris apartment. Her body was cremated; her ashes were scattered on the Aegean Sea. A radio commentator's characterization of Callas was that "If an orgasm could sing, it would sound like Maria Callas." Pleonastically speaking, she was an incarnation of carnality.

BIBL.: E. Gara and R. Hauert, *M. C.* (Geneva, 1957; in Eng., London, 1958); E. Callas, *My Daughter M. C.* (as told to L.G. Blochman; N.Y., 1960); G. Jellinek, *C.* (N.Y., 1960); M.T. Picchetti and M. Teglia, *El arte de M. C.* (Buenos Aires, 1969); S. Galatopoulos, *C.—La Divina: Art That Conceals Art* (London, 1963; 3rd ed., rev. and augmented, 1976, as *C.: Prima donna assoluta*); J. Ardoin, *The C. Legacy* (N.Y., 1977); P.-J. Remy, *C.: Une vie* (Paris, 1978); A. Stassinopoulos, *M. C.: The Woman behind the Legend* (N.Y., 1981); G.B. Meneghini (with Renzo Allegri), *My Wife M. C.* (N.Y., 1982); D. Lowe, ed., *C., as They Saw Her* (N.Y., 1986); N. Stancioff, *M.: C. Remembered* (N.Y., 1987).

Callaway, Paul (Smith), American organist and conductor; b. Atlanta, Ill., Aug. 16, 1909. He attended Westminster College in Fulton, Mo. (1927–29); studied organ with Tertius Noble in N.Y. (1930–35), with Leo Sowerby in Chicago, and with Marcel Dupré in Paris. He served as organist and choirmaster at St. Thomas's Chapel in N.Y. (1930–35); then at St. Mark's Chapel in Grand Rapids, Mich.; in 1939 he began his 38-year regime as principal organist and music director of the Washington, D.C., National Cathedral, with an interruption during his service in the U.S. Army (1942–46). In 1941 he founded the Cathedral Choral Soc.; in 1962 was one of the founders of the College of Church Musicians at the Washington Cathedral, leading it until 1969. He was also music director of the Opera Soc. of Washington (1956–67) and directed the Lake George, N.Y., Opera Festival (1967–77); appeared as guest conductor of the National Sym. Orch. in Washington; conducted the notable 1st performances at the Library of Congress of Menotti's work *The Unicorn, the Gorgon, and the Manticore* (1956) and of Dallapiccola's *5 canti* (1956). Owing to his close affiliation with the Anglican Church, he was engaged to conduct the Cathedral Choir at Westminster Abbey in London during the celebration of the 900th anniversary of the Abbey (1966). On Nov. 30, 1977, he was made an honorary Member of the Order of the British Empire in ceremonies at the British Embassy in Washington. After becoming organist and choirmaster emeritus of the Washington Cathedral in 1977, he served on the faculty of the Univ. of Illinois at Carbondale, periodically returning to Washington to conduct the Cathedral Choral Soc.

Callcott, John Wall, English organist and composer; b. London, Nov. 20, 1766; d. Bristol, May 15, 1821. Early in life he developed a particular talent for composing glees and catches; won 3 prize medals at a contest of the Catch Club of London (1785) for his catch *O Beauteous Fair;* a canon, *Blessed Is He;* and a glee, *Dull Repining Sons of Care.* He received his Mus.Bac. and Mus.Doc. from Oxford (1785, 1800); was a co-founder of the Glee Club (1787). During Haydn's visit to London in 1791, Callcott took a few lessons with him and wrote a sym. in imitation of his style. His mind gave way from overwork on a projected biographical dictionary of musicians, and he was institutionalized just before he reached the quirky letter Q. He recovered; but not sufficiently to continue his work, and was released in 1812. In addition to numerous glees, catches, and canons, he wrote *A Musical Grammar* (London, 1806), a standard elementary textbook that went through numerous eds. in England and America. A 3-vol. collection of glees, catches, and canons, with a biographical memoir, was publ. posthumously by his son-in-law, William Horsley (London, 1824).

Calleja, Gómez Rafael, Spanish composer; b. Burgos, Dec. 23, 1874; d. Madrid, Feb. 7, 1938. He studied at the Madrid Cons.; subsequently conducted in Spain, Portugal, and South America. He composed about 300 revues and musical comedies, including *El Príncipe Carnaval* and *El mozo crúo;* publ. collections of folk songs from Santander, Galicia, and Asturias.

Calligaris, Sergio, Argentine-born Italian pianist, teacher, and composer; b. Rosario, Jan. 22, 1941. He commenced piano lessons with Domingo Scarafia; in 1964 he became a student of Arthur Loesser at the Cleveland Inst. of Music (artist's diploma, 1966), where he also taught, and then completed his training with Guido Agosti at the Accademia di Santa Cecilia in Rome. In 1969 he became a teacher of piano at Calif. State Univ. in Los Angeles; in 1973 he founded the American Academy of the Arts in Europe in Verona, serving as its 1st artistic director. In 1974 he became a naturalized Italian citizen and began teaching at the Cons. of San Pietro a Majello in Naples; from 1977 he taught at the Alfredo Casella Cons. in L'Aquila. His playing is distinguished by a Romantic élan and virtuoso technique. As a composer, he effectively utilizes Romantic and post-Romantic styles in a thoroughly contemporary idiom.

Works: orch.: Concerto for String Orch. (1989). **chamber:** Sonata for Cello and Piano (1978); *Suite da Requiem No. 1* for Violin, Horn, and Piano (1984) and *No.* 2 for 2 Pianos, 4 Timpani ad libitum, and Chorus ad libitum (1985). **piano:** *Il quaderno pianistico di Renzo* (1978); *24 studi* (1978–80); *Scene coreografiche* for Piano Duet or 2 Pianos (1979); *Passacaglia* for 3 Pianos, after Bach (1983); *BHS,* divertimento on music by Bach, Handel, and Scarlatti for 2 Pianos and Female Voices ad libitum (1984–85); *Vivaldiana,* divertimento on themes by Vivaldi for 2 Pianos (1986); *Due danze concertanti* for 2 Pianos (1986); other chamber works; vocal settings; choral works.

Callinet, François, French organ manufacturer; b. Ladoix, Bourgogne, Oct. 1, 1754; d. Rouffach, Alsace, May 21, 1820. He was apprenticed to K. Riepp in Dijon, and later worked with Joseph Rabiny, with whom he became associated in organ building in 1786. His 2 sons, **Joseph** and **Claude-Ignace,** and the latter's son **Louis-François** carried on the family trade; **Louis Callinet,** a nephew of the founder of the firm, joined Daublaine & Co., and continued organ manufacture.

Callinet, Louis, French organ manufacturer; b. Weiler Ladoix, Bourgogne, April 19, 1786; d. Paris, Aug. 1, 1845. He was a nephew of **François Callinet.** He entered into partnership with Daublaine, who attended to the commercial interests of the firm known as Daublaine & Callinet, but broke with him and destroyed all the instruments that he had built.

Calloway, Cab(ell), noted black American jazz singer and bandleader; b. Rochester, N.Y., Dec. 25, 1907. After making his way to Chicago, he began his career as a singer and dancer; in 1928–29 he led the Alabamians, and in 1929 took over the leadership of the Missourians, with which he established himself in N.Y. (1930); he subsequently led various other groups. He was a proponent of scat singing, characterized by nonsense syllabification and rapid glossolalia with the melodic line largely submerged under an asymmetric inundation of rhythmic heterophony. He compiled *Hepster's Dictionary,* listing jazz terms (1938), and publ. an informal autobiography, *Of Minnie the Moocher and Me* (N.Y., 1976).

Calvé (real name, **Calvet de Roquer**), **(Rosa-Noémie) Emma,** famous French soprano; b. Décazeville, Aveyron, Aug. 15, 1858; d. Millau, Jan. 6, 1942. She studied voice with Puget in Paris and with Marchesi and Laborde; made her operatic debut as Marguerite in Gounod's *Faust* at the Théâtre de la Monnaie in Brussels, on Sept. 23, 1881; then sang at the Opéra-Comique in Paris 3 years later. She sang at La Scala in 1887. In 1892 she appeared at Covent Garden in London. She made her American debut at the Metropolitan Opera House on Nov. 29, 1893, and remained on its staff until 1904; her greatest role was that of Carmen. Subsequently she made sporadic, but successful, appearances in Europe and America; after 1910 she sang mainly in recitals. Calvé's biography was publ. in 1902 (A. Gallus, *Emma Calvé, Her Artistic Life*), and so great was the aura of her successes that her life was made the subject of a novel by Gustav Kobbé, *Signora, A Child of the Opera House* (N.Y., 1903). She publ. an autobiography, in Eng., *My Life* (N.Y., 1922); toward the end of her life she publ. an additional vol. of memoirs, *Sous tous les ciels j'ai chanté* (Paris, 1940). Forty of her letters, along with an extended biographical sketch, appear in A. Lebois, "Hommages à Emma Calvé (1858–1942)," *Annales, Faculté des Lettres de Toulouse* (Sept. 1967).

Calvisius, Sethus (real name, **Seth Kallwitz**), German music theorist; b. Feb. 21, 1556; d. Leipzig, Nov. 24, 1615. He supported himself while studying in the Gymnasia of Frankenhausen and Magdeburg, and the Univs. at Helmstadt and Leipzig. In Leipzig he became music director at the Paulinerkirche (1581); from 1582 to 1592 he was cantor at Schulpforta, then cantor of the Thomasschule at Leipzig, and in 1594 became music director at the Thomaskirche and Nicolaikirche there. Calvisius was not only a musician, but a scholar of high attainments. His writings are valuable sources: *Melopoeia seu melodiae condendae ratio* (1582; 2nd ed., 1592); *Compendium musicae practicae pro incipientibus* (1594; 3rd ed. as *Musicae artis praecepta nova et facillima,* 1612); *Harmoniae cantionum ecclesiasticarum a M. Luthero et aliis viris piis Germaniae composi-*

tarum 4 voc. (1596); *Exercitationes musicae duae* (1600); *Auserlesene teutsche Lieder* (1603); *Exercitatio musicae tertia* (1611); *Biciniorum libri duo* (1612).

BIBL.: K. Benndorf, "S. C. als Musiktheoretiker," *Vierteljahrsschrift für Musikwissenschaft* (1894); G. Pietzch, "S. C. und Joh. Kepler," *Die Musikpflege* I/8 (1930).

Calvocoressi, Michel Dimitri, eminent Greek writer on music; b. Marseilles, Oct. 2, 1877; d. London, Feb. 1, 1944. He studied music in Paris, but was mostly an autodidact; also pursued the social sciences. In 1914 he settled in London. He wrote music criticism and correspondences for French and other journals. He mastered the Russian language and became an ardent propagandist of Russian music; made excellent trs. into English and French of Russian and German songs. Among his books are *La Musique russe* (Paris, 1907); *The Principles and Methods of Musical Criticism* (London, 1923; rev. 1933); *Musical Taste and How to Form It* (London, 1925); *Musicians' Gallery: Music and Ballet in Paris and London* (London, 1933); also monographs on Liszt (Paris, 1906), Mussorgsky (Paris, 1908), Glinka (Paris, 1911), Schumann (Paris, 1912), Debussy (London, 1941); a new extensive biography of Mussorgsky was posth. publ. (London, 1946). With G. Abraham, he publ. the valuable *Masters of Russian Music* (London, 1936).

Calzabigi, Ranieri (Simone Francesco Maria) di, Italian poet and music theorist; b. Livorno, Dec. 23, 1714; d. Naples, July 1795. In 1750 he went to Paris, then proceeded to Brussels in 1760; from 1761 until 1772 he remained in Vienna, and was in Pisa by 1775. He engaged in polemics regarding the relative merits of French and Italian operas; lent energetic support to Gluck in his ideas of operatic reform. He wrote for Gluck the libretti of *Orfeo, Alceste,* and *Paride ed Elena.* He publ. *Dissertazione su le poesie drammatiche del Sig. Abate Pietro Metastasio* (1755), a controversial work concerning Metastasio and Hasse.

BIBL.: H. Welti, "Gluck und C.," *Vierteljahrsschrift für Musikwissenschaft* (1891); G. Lazzeri, *La vita e l'opera letteraria di R. C.* (1907); J.-G. Prod'homme, "Deux collaborateurs italiens de Gluck," *Rivista Musicale Italiana* (1916); R. Haas, *Gluck in Durazzo* (1924); H. Hammelmann and M. Rose, "New Light on C. and Gluck," *Musical Times* (June 1969).

Camarata, Salvador (a.k.a. **"Tutti"**), American composer and conductor of popular music; b. Glen Ridge, N.J., May 11, 1913. He studied composition at the Juilliard School of Music, N.Y., with Wagenaar and Jan Meyerowitz; earned his living by playing trumpet in dance bands around N.Y.; then was music director for the Walt Disney Co., in Hollywood. He wrote a number of catchy tunes, among them *Hollywood Pastime* and *Moonlight Masquerade.*

Cambert, Robert, French opera composer; b. Paris, c.1628; d. London, 1677. He was a pupil of Chambonnières. His 1st venture on the lyric stage was *La Pastorale,* written with the librettist Perrin and successfully produced at the Château d'Issy in 1659; it was followed by *Ariane, ou Le Mariage de Bacchus* (rehearsed in 1661) and *Adonis* (1662; not perf.; MS lost). In 1669 Perrin received letters patent for establishing the Académie Royale de Musique (the national operatic theater, now the Grand Opéra); he brought out, in collaboration with Cambert, the opera *Pomone* (1671); another opera, *Les Peines et les plaisirs de l'amour,* was written, and produced in Paris in March 1671, before Lully secured the patent. In 1673, after Lully secured the patent in violation of the agreement with Molière, Cambert went to London.

BIBL.: A. Pougin, *Les Vrais Créateurs de l'opéra français, Perrin et C.* (Paris, 1881).

Cambini, Giuseppe Maria (Gioacchino), Italian composer; b. Livorno, Feb. 13, 1746; d. Bicêtre, Dec. 29, 1825. He was a prolific composer of instrumental works, writing over 60 syms. within a few years; also 149 string quartets; ballets, operas, and oratorios. He died in an almshouse.

BIBL.: D.L. Trimpert, *Die "Quatuors concertants" von G. C.* (Tutzing, 1967); H. Bol, "Een rivaal van Mozart te Parijs, G.G. C. (1746–1825)," *Mens en Melodie* (March 1968).

Cambreling, Sylvain, French conductor; b. Amiens, July 2, 1948. He received his musical training at the Paris Cons.; in 1975 he became assistant conductor of the Orch. de Lyon; also conducted opera in Lyon; beginning with the 1979–80 season he appeared regularly as a conductor at the Paris Opéra. In 1981 he became joint music director (with John Pritchard) of the Théâtre Royal de la Monnaie in Brussels. He also conducted at the Glyndebourne Festival, the Frankfurt Opera, La Scala in Milan, in the U.S., and in Canada. On Jan. 9, 1986, he made his Metropolitan Opera debut in N.Y. conducting *Roméo et Juliette.*

Camden, Archie (Archibald Leslie), English bassoon virtuoso; b. Newark-upon-Trent, March 9, 1888; d. Wheathampstead, Feb. 16, 1979. He studied at the Royal Manchester College of Music. In 1906 he joined the Hallé Orch. of Manchester, where he played 1st bassoon from 1914 to 1933; during the same period he taught bassoon at the Royal Manchester College of Music. In 1933 he joined the BBC Sym. Orch.; then played with the Royal Phil. (1946–47); finally was a member of the London Mozart Players (1954–71). He did much to establish the bassoon as a solo instrument; his performances of works by Vivaldi, Mozart, and Weber were outstanding. His autobiography was publ. as *Blow by Blow* (London, 1982).

Cameron, (George) Basil, English conductor; b. Reading, Aug. 18, 1884; d. Leominster, June 26, 1975. He studied music in York with Tertius Noble; then at the Berlin Hochschule für Musik (1902–6); also took a course in composition with Max Bruch. Returning to England, he sought to obtain a conducting position by Germanizing his name as **Basil Hindenberg,** seeing that German conductors dominated the field in England, but changed it back to his real name when England went to war with Germany in 1914. He served in the British army and was wounded in action in 1918. He conducted the Hastings Municipal Orch. (1923–30); then was guest conductor of the San Francisco Sym. Orch.; from 1932 to 1938 he was conductor of the Seattle Sym. Orch.; during his tenure he played many new works by modern composers. He belonged to the category of "objective" conductors; was more interested in the music itself than in his individual communication, an attitude that in the end hampered his American success. He filled in a few engagements in Europe and eventually returned to London, where he was made a Commander of the Order of the British Empire in 1957.

Cametti, Alberto, Italian musicologist; b. Rome, May 5, 1871; d. there, June 1, 1935. He studied at the Accademia di Santa Cecilia in Rome; was a member of the commission appointed by Pope Pius X to investigate the condition of church music. In April 1914 he publ. a thematic catalog of works by Orazio Michi.

WRITINGS: *Cenni biografici di G.P. da Palestrina* (1894); *Documenti inediti su Luigi Rossi* (1912); *Dove fu sepolto il Palestrina?* (1929); *Bibliografia delle opere di Costanzo Festa* (1931); biographical studies of Felice Anerio (1915), Giacomo Carissimi (1917), G.B. Costanzi (1924), Leonardo Vinci (1924), Ruggiero Giovanelli (1925).

Camidge, Matthew, English organist; b. York, May 25, 1764; d. there, Oct. 23, 1844. He was the son of John Camidge, Sr., whom he succeeded at the York Minster on Nov. 11, 1799, and at St. Michael-le-Belfry on July 2, 1801. He publ. *Cathedral Music; 24 Original Psalm- and Hymn-tunes;* piano sonatas and marches; etc.

Campagnoli, Bartolommeo, renowned Italian violinist; b. Cento di Ferrara, Sept. 10, 1751; d. Neustrelitz, Germany, Nov. 6, 1827. He studied in Bologna with Dall'Ocha and in Florence with Nardini; for several years gave concerts in Italy; became music director to the Duke of Kurland in Dresden (1779–97); then was concertmaster at the Gewandhaus in Leipzig (1797–1818). He made several successful concert tours while in his service; from 1797 to 1818 was active as a violinist in Leipzig. He composed 41 *Capricci per l'alto viola* (rev. by E. Kreuz and A. Consolini as *Caprices pour le viola,* 1922); a

Violin Concerto; études for violin; chamber music. He was the author of several pedagogic manuals for the violin, including *Nouvelle méthode de la mécanique progressive du jeu de violon* (1791; in Eng., 1856), and *Metodo per violino* (1797; his chief work; publ. and reprinted in all European languages).

BIBL.: G. Atti, *Biografia di B. C.* (Bologna, 1892).

Campana, Fabio, Italian singing teacher and composer; b. Livorno, Jan. 14, 1819; d. London, Feb. 2, 1882. He studied in Bologna; produced the operas *Caterina di Guisa* (Livorno, 1838); *Giulio d'Este* (Livorno, 1841); *Vannina d'Ornano* (Florence, 1842); *Luisa di Francia* (Rome, 1844); then went to London, where he settled as a singing teacher. His opera *Almina* was staged in London at Her Majesty's Theatre (April 26, 1860); another opera, *Esmeralda,* was produced in St. Petersburg (Dec. 20, 1869); Patti sang the title role in its productions in western Europe. Campana also wrote hundreds of songs.

Campanari, Giuseppe, Italian baritone, brother of **Leandro Campanari;** b. Venice, Nov. 17, 1855; d. Milan, May 31, 1927. He began his career as a cellist; played in the orch. of La Scala, and started to study singing; went to the U.S. in 1884, and played cello in the Boston Sym. Orch. until 1893, when he joined Hinrich's Opera Co. in N.Y. as a baritone; made his debut (June 15, 1893) as Tonio in *Pagliacci;* after several years at the Metropolitan Opera he devoted himself to concert work and teaching.

Campanari, Leandro, Italian violinist and conductor, brother of **Giuseppe Campanari;** b. Rovigo, Oct. 20, 1857; d. San Francisco, April 22, 1939. He studied in Padua; attended the Milan Cons., graduating in 1877; after a tour of Europe, he went to the U.S. in 1881 and settled in Boston, where he organized the Campanari String Quartet. He became a proficient conductor and was in charge of the Grand Orch. Concerts at La Scala in Milan from 1897 till 1905. In Feb. 1907 he was engaged to complete the season of the Philadelphia Orch. after the sudden illness of the regular conductor, Fritz Scheel. Campanari failed to impress the orch. or the audience, and was not reengaged.

Campanella, Michele, Italian pianist; b. Naples, June 5, 1947. He was educated at the Cons. in Naples, winning the Casella Competition while still a student there in 1966; taught at the Milan Cons. (1969–73), and subsequently made tours as soloist with the leading orchs. of Europe and the U.S.

Campanini, Cleofonte, eminent Italian-American operatic conductor, brother of **Italo Campanini;** b. Parma, Sept. 1, 1860; d. Chicago, Dec. 19, 1919. He studied violin at the Parma Cons. and later at the Cons. of Milan; made his conducting debut with *Carmen* at Parma (1882); conducted the 1st American performance of *Otello* at the N.Y. Academy of Music (April 16, 1888) while his brother, Italo, was impresario. Between 1888 and 1906, he conducted in Italy, in England, and in South America. A larger field opened to him in 1906, when Hammerstein engaged him for the new Manhattan Opera House in N.Y. Differences with Hammerstein led him to resign in 1909. In the following year he was engaged as principal conductor of the newly formed Chicago Opera Co.; in 1913 he was appointed general director, which post he held until his death. Among opera conductors he occupied a place in the 1st rank; he seemed to be equally at home in all styles of music. He introduced many new operas in the U.S., among them Massenet's *Hérodiade,* Debussy's *Pelléas et Mélisande,* Charpentier's *Louise,* Wolf-Ferrari's *Il segreto di Susanna,* etc. On May 15, 1887, he married, in Florence, **Eva Tetrazzini** (sister of **Luisa Tetrazzini**).

Campanini, Italo, famous Italian tenor, brother of **Cleofonte Campanini;** b. Parma, June 30, 1845; d. Corcagno, near Parma, Nov. 22, 1896. In his early years he was an apprentice in his father's blacksmith shop; joined Garibaldi's army and was wounded in the Italian struggle for unification. Subsequently, he studied with Griffini and Lamperti; appeared at Bologna in *Lohengrin* (Nov. 1, 1871), which started him on the road to fame. He made his London debut as Gennaro in *Lucrezia Borgia* (May 4, 1872), and his American debut, also as Gennaro, at the N.Y. Academy of Music (Oct. 1, 1873). He appeared in *Faust* at the opening of the Metropolitan Opera (Oct. 22, 1883); was on its roster until 1894; was briefly active as an impresario; brought over his brother Cleofonte Campanini to conduct the American premiere of Verdi's *Otello* at the N.Y. Academy of Music (April 16, 1888).

Campbell, Aline. Pen name of **Merle Montgomery.**

Campbell, Glen (Travis), American singer of country music and guitarist; b. Delight, Ark., April 22, 1938. He began his career as a singer and guitarist; worked as a studio musician on the West Coast; subsequently went to Nashville, Tenn., where he launched a solo career in country music. He gained much success in 1967 with his performances of *Gentle on My Mind* and *By the Time I Get to Phoenix.* His other hits included *Wichita Lineman, Houston,* and *Southern Nights.*

Campbell-Tipton, Louis, American composer; b. Chicago, Nov. 21, 1877; d. Paris, May 1, 1921. He studied at Leipzig (1896–99) with Carl Reinecke and Gustav Schreck; returned to Chicago and was an instructor of theory at the Chicago Musical College; then lived in Paris. He wrote chiefly for piano (*Sonata Heroic, Sea Lyrics, The 4 Seasons,* Suite, Serenade, etc.); *Suite pastorale* for Piano and Violin; also a number of very effective songs.

Campbell-Watson, Frank, American music editor; b. N.Y., Jan. 22, 1898, d. there, Feb. 27, 1980. He studied at the Leipzig Cons. with Max Reger. Returning to the U.S., he held positions as ed. with various publishing firms. He made transcriptions for string orch. of Bach, Reger, Mendelssohn, and Albéniz. He was also the author of *University Course of Music Study* (1923) and *Modern Elementary Harmony* (1930); ed. *International Library of Music* (piano, 14 vols.; vocal, 12 vols.; violin, 14 vols.); *La mejor música del mundo* (in Spanish, also in Portuguese; for piano, 14 vols.).

Campenhout, François van, Belgian tenor and composer, author of the Belgian national anthem; b. Brussels, Feb. 5, 1779; d. there, April 24, 1848. Beginning as violinist in the Théâtre de la Monnaie, he studied singing under Plantade, and became a fine tenor, appearing in Belgium, the Netherlands, and France. He wrote 6 operas, 9 cantatas, etc. He is, however, chiefly remembered as the composer of *La Brabançonne,* which was written during the revolution of 1830, and eventually became the national anthem of Belgium.

Campion, François, French instrumentalist, theorbist, and composer of English descent; b. Rouen, c.1686; d. Paris, Jan. or Feb. 1748. He was a theorbist and guitarist at the Académie Royale de Musique in Paris (1703–19); was also active as a lutenist. Among his works, all publ. in Paris, were *Nouvelles découvertes . . . contenant plusieurs suites de pièces sur 8 manières d'accorder* for Guitar, op. 1 (1705); *Avantures pastorales meslées de vers,* op. 3 (1719; 54 airs); and *Second recueil d'airs,* op. 5 (1734).

WRITINGS (all publ. in Paris): *Traité d'accompagnement et de composition selon la règle des octaves de musique,* op. 2 (1716); *Lettres du Sieur Campion à un philosophe disciple de la règle de l'octave* (1729); *Addition au traité de l'accompagnement et de composition par la règle de l'octave,* op. 4 (1730); *Lettre de Monsieur l'abbé Carbasus à Monsieur D+++, auteur du Temple du Goust, sur la mode des instruments de musique* (1739).

Campion (Campian), Thomas, English physician, poet, composer, and dramatist; b. London, Feb. 12, 1567; d. there, March 1, 1620. He studied at Cambridge from 1581 to 1584, residing at Peterhouse; entered Gray's Inn on April 27, 1586. He received his M.D. degree from the Univ. of Caen in France on Feb. 10, 1605. He was first called a "Doctor of Physick" in an English publication in Barnabe Barnes's *Four Books of Offices* in 1606; earlier evidence of his having studied medical science is an oblique reference of Philip Rosseter in 1601, speaking of Campion's poetry and music as "the superfluous blossoms of his deeper studies." Campion was primarily a lyric poet; his music was to enhance the beauty of the poetry by supplying unobtrusive and simple harmonies; in this he differed from such contemporaries as John Dowland, who contrived elaborate lute accompaniments.

Works: 3 songs (1596); *A Booke of Ayres, Set Foorth to Be Sung to the Lute Orpherian, and Base Violl* (1601; consists of 2 separate books, one by Campion and one by Rosseter; Campion wrote both the words and the music for his half of the work); *First and Second Books of Airs* (1613?); *Third and Fourth Books of Airs* (1617?); songs for masques at the marriages of Sir James Hay (1607), Princess Elizabeth (1613), and Robert, Earl of Somerset (1613); songs for a masque at Caversham House (1613); *Songs of Mourning* (for Prince Henry; 1613; words by Campion, music by John Coperario); *A New Way for Making Foure Parts in Counterpoint* (1618; also in Playford's *Introduction to the Skill of Musick*, 1655 and following years). Campion also publ. *Poemata*, a vol. of Latin epigrams and elegiacs (1595; reprinted 1619), *Observations on the Art of English Poesie* (1602; condemns "the vulgar and unartificial custom of riming"), etc. The 4 books of airs and the songs from Rosseter's *Booke of Ayres* are reprinted in E.H. Fellowes, *English School of Lutenist Song-Writers*.

Bibl.: M. Kastendieck, *England's Musical Poet, T. C.* (Oxford, 1938); W.R. Davis, ed., *The Works of T. C.; Complete Songs, Masques, and Treatises* (Garden City, N.Y., 1967); S.J. London, "T. C., M.D. (1567–1620)," *New York State Journal of Medicine* (Dec. 1967); J.T. Irwin, "T. C. and the Musical Emblem," *Studies in English Literature, 1500–1900* (Winter 1970); E. Lowbury, T. Salter, and A. Young, *T. C.: Poet, Composer, Physician* (N.Y., 1970); W. Davis, *T. C.* (Boston, 1987); M. Pilkington, *C., Dowland and the Lutenist Songwriters* (London, 1989).

Campioni, Carlo Antonio, French-born Italian composer; b. Lunéville, Nov. 16, 1720; d. Florence, April 12, 1788. He went to Florence in 1763, and was active there as a composer of church music and maestro di cappella to the ducal court at the Cathedral of S. Maria del Fiore, and in the oratory of S. Giovanni Battista. He also publ. instrumental works, among them 6 sonatas for 2 violins, which were fraudulently issued in Amsterdam as the works of Haydn, and were reprinted still under Haydn's name in Mainz in 1953. The very fact that these pieces could pass as Haydn's for 2 centuries obliquely testifies to Campioni as a highly competent composer.

Campo (y Zabaleta), Conrado del, Spanish violinist and composer; b. Madrid, Oct. 28, 1879; d. there, March 17, 1953. He studied at the Madrid Cons.; in 1915 became a prof. of composition there. Most of his operas were produced at the Madrid Opera House.

Works: Operas: *El final de Don Alvaro* (1910); *Paolo e Francesca* (1911); *La tragedia del beso* (1911); *El Avapiés* (Madrid, March 8, 1919); *La Dama desconocida; La culpa; Leonor Teller; Romeo y Julieta; Dies irae; La Malquerida; Fantochines* (1922); *La flor del agua; El arbol de los ojos* (1930); *Lola, la piconera* (1949); *El pájaro de dos colores* (1951); symphonic poems: *La divina comedia; Granada; Airinos;* oriental fantasy, *Kasida; Evocación medieval* for Chorus and Orch.; 12 string quartets, of which the *Caprichos románticos* (1908) became popular.

Bibl.: T. Borrás, *C. d.C.* (Madrid, 1954).

Campora, Giuseppe, Italian tenor; b. Tortona, Sept. 30, 1923. He studied voice in Genoa and Milan; made his debut in Bari in 1949; in 1951 he joined La Scala, Milan; also sang with other Italian opera houses. He made his Metropolitan Opera debut in N.Y. as Cavaradossi on Feb. 5, 1955.

Campos-Parsi, Héctor, Puerto Rican composer; b. Ponce, Oct. 1, 1922. He studied in Ponce, then at the Univ. of Puerto Rico in Río Piedras (1938–44). After taking courses at the New England Cons. of Music in Boston (1947–50) and with Copland and Messiaen at the Berkshire Music Center in Tanglewood (1949, 1950), he studied with Boulanger in Fontaine-

bleau (1951–53). Returning to Puerto Rico in 1955, he was active as a composer, poet, journalist, music critic, television commentator, and concert manager.

Works: ORCH.: *Divertimento de Sur* for Flute, Clarinet, and Strings (1953); *Oda a Cabo Rojo* (1959); *Rapsodia elegíaca* for Strings (1960); *Kollagia* for Orch., Percussion, and Tape (1963); *Dúo trágico* for Piano and Orch. (1964); *Tissú* for Accordion and Small Orch. (1984); *Tureyareito* (1984). BALLETS: *Incidente* (1949); *Melos* (1951); *Juan Bobo y las fiestas* (1957); *Urayoán* (1958); *Areyto boriken* (1974); *De Diego* (1974). CHAMBER: Serenata for String Trio (1949); Violin Sonata (1949); *Música* for 3 Violins (1949); String Quartet (1950); *El secreto* for Flute, Oboe, 2 Clarinets, Cello, and Piano (1957); *Petroglifos* for Piano Trio (1966); *Arawak* for Cello and Tape (1970); *Fanfare for an American Festival* for 3 Trumpets, 2 Trombones, and Percussion (1982); *Tiempo sereno* for Strings (1983); piano pieces; also choruses; songs.

Bibl.: F. Caso, *H. C.-P. in the History of Twentieth-Century Music in Puerto Rico* (diss., Indiana Univ., 1972).

Campra, André, important French composer; b. Aix, Provence, Dec. 4, 1660; d. Versailles, June 29, 1744. He studied with Guillaume Poitevin; then embraced an ecclesiastical vocation; was made chaplain at Aix on May 27, 1681; served as maître de musique at St. Étienne in Toulouse from 1683 to 1694, and at Notre Dame from 1694 to 1700; then was active at the Paris Opéra. In 1723 he received a court appointment as sous-maître with Bernier and Gervais. His operas had numerous performances in Paris.

Works (all 1st perf. in Paris unless otherwise given): *L'Europe galante,* opéra-ballet (Oct. 24, 1697); *Le Carnaval de Venise,* ballet (Jan. 20, 1699; Act 3 includes the Italian opera *Orfeo nell'inferni*); *Hésione,* tragédie lyrique (Dec. 20, 1700); *Aréthuse, ou La Vengeance de l'Amour,* tragédie lyrique (July 14, 1701); *Tancrède,* tragédie lyrique (Nov. 7, 1702); *Les Muses,* opéra-ballet (Oct. 28, 1703); *Iphigénie en Tauride,* tragédie lyrique based on the unfinished work of Desmarets (May 6, 1704); *Télémaque,* extracts from operas by Campra et al. (Nov. 11, 1704); *Alcine,* tragédie lyrique (Jan 15, 1705); *Hippodamie,* tragédie lyrique (March 6, 1708); *Les Fêtes vénitiennes,* opéra-ballet (June 17, 1710); *Idomenée,* tragédie lyrique (Jan. 12, 1712); *Les Amours de Vénus et de Mars,* ballet (Sept. 6, 1712); *Téléphe,* tragédie lyrique (Nov. 28, 1713); *Camille, reine des volsques,* tragédie lyrique (Nov. 9, 1717); *Ballet représenté à Lion devant M. le marquis d'Harlincourt,* ballet (Lyons, May 17, 1718; not extant); *Les Âges,* opéra-ballet (Oct. 9, 1718); *Achille et Deidamie,* tragédie lyrique (Feb. 24, 1735); several divertissements (most of them not extant); 3 books of *Cantates françoises* (1708, 1714, 1728); 5 books of motets (1695–1720); Mass (1700); 2 books of Psalms (1737–38).

Bibl.: A. Pougin, *A. C.* (Paris, 1861); L. de La Laurencie, "Notes sur la jeunesse d'A. C.," *Sammelbände der Internationalen Musik-Gesellschaft,* X/2 (1909); idem, "A. C., musicien profane," *L'Année Musicale* (1913); idem, *L'École française de violon de Lulli à Viotti* (1922–24); M. Barthélemy, *A. C.* (Paris, 1957); C. Castle, *The Grand Motets of A. C.* (diss., Univ. of Michigan, 1962); J. Anthony, *The Opera-Ballet of A. C.: A Study of the First Period French Opera-Ballet* (diss., Univ. of Southern Calif., 1964); A. Baker, *The Church Music of A. C.* (diss., Univ. of Toronto, 1978).

Camps, Pompeyo, Argentine composer; b. Paraná, Oct. 27, 1924. After playing piano in bands in his native town, he settled in Buenos Aires in 1947; studied with Jaime Pahissa and adopted Pahissa's "intertonal system" of convertible counterpoint. In 1964 he modified this technique by incorporating serial procedures. He is also active as a music critic.

Works: Piano Sonata (1954); 2 string quartets (1957, 1974); *La pendiente,* opera in 1 act (1959); *Fantasia* for String Orch. (1961); *The Ballad of Reading Gaol* (1964) for Men's Choir, Narrator, and Orch.; *Sinfónia para un poeta* for Baritone and Orch. (obtained 1st municipal prize of Buenos Aires in 1967); *Tríptico arcáico* for Flute, Viola, Cello, and Guitar (1961); *Danzas* for Percussion (1966); *Reflejos* for 13 Brasses and Percussion (1968); *Ciudad sin tregua* for String Quartet (1974); songs; piano pieces.

Camussi, Ezio, Italian composer; b. Florence, Jan. 16, 1877; d. Milan, Aug. 11, 1956. He studied in Rome with Falchi and Sgambati; later with Massenet in Paris and at the Liceo Musicale in Bologna.

WORKS: Operas: *La Dubarry* (Milan, Nov. 7, 1912); *I fuochi di San Giovanni* (Milan, March 27, 1920); *Il donzello, Scampolo* (Trieste, Feb. 22, 1925); *Il volto della Virgine* (Bari, Jan. 23, 1937); *La principessa lontana, I Romanzeschi, Intermezzi giocosi* for Puppet Theater; for Orch.: *Balletto sinfonico, Pantomima romantica, Suita romanesca, Intermezzi Goldoniani, Fantasticherie* for Small Orch.; *Festival Miniature Overture; Scene medioevali* for Violin and Orch.; songs.

Canal, Marguerite, French composer; b. Toulouse, Jan. 29, 1890; d. there, Jan. 27, 1978. She studied at the Paris Cons. with Paul Vidal; in 1920 won the Grand Prix de Rome for her symphonic scene *Don Juan.* In 1919 she was appointed to the faculty of the Paris Cons. Her works include a Violin Sonata (1922); *Spleen* for Cello and Chamber Ensemble (1926); several piano pieces; about 100 songs.

Caniglia, Maria, noted Italian soprano; b. Naples, May 5, 1905; d. Rome, April 16, 1979. She made her debut in Turin in 1930; from 1930 to 1951 she sang at La Scala, where she attained prominence. On Nov. 24, 1938, she made her Metropolitan Opera debut in N.Y. as Aida, but remained on its staff for only 1 season (1938–39). At the outbreak of World War II she returned to Italy. She was married to the Italian composer **Pino Donati.** Among her finest roles were Tosca, Aida, Leonora in *La forza del destino,* and Adriana Lecouvreur.

Canino, Bruno, Italian pianist, harpsichordist, teacher, and composer; b. Naples, Dec. 30, 1935. He studied with Calace and Bettinelli at the Milan Cons., then toured widely in Europe, the U.S., and Japan. He was a member of the Trio di Milano, and also made many duo piano appearances with Antonio Ballista. From 1961 he taught at the Milan Cons. He was especially known as a proponent of contemporary music; he also wrote some orch. pieces and chamber music in a fairly advanced style.

Cannabich, (Johann) Christian (Innocenz Bonaventura), German composer, violinist, and conductor; b. Mannheim (baptized), Dec. 28, 1731; d. Frankfurt, Jan. 20, 1798. He studied with Johann Stamitz in Mannheim; became a violinist in the Mannheim Orch. (1746); was sent by the Elector to Rome, where he studied with Jommelli (1750–53); he returned to Mannheim and, after Stamitz's death (1757), became 1st violinist of the orch.; in 1774 was director of the instrumental music; in 1778 he moved to Munich. Cannabich is usually credited with bringing the Mannheim Orch. to a degree of perfection theretofore never attained, particularly in the carefully graduated crescendo and diminuendo. He was also a prolific composer.

WORKS: Some 100 syms.; 3 violin concertos; 60 various pieces of chamber music; a singspiel, *Azakia* (Mannheim, 1778); melodrama, *Elektra* (Mannheim, 1781); 40 ballets.

BIBL.: H. Hofer, *C. C.: Biographie und vergleichende Analyse seiner Sinfonien* (diss., Univ. of Munich, 1921); R. Kloiber, *Die dramatischen Ballette von C. C.* (diss., Univ. of Munich, 1928).

Cannon, (Jack) Philip, English composer; b. Paris, Dec. 21, 1929, of English-French parentage. He was educated in England; studied composition with Imogen Holst; then at the Royal College of Music in London with Gordon Jacob. He subsequently took lessons with Hindemith. After graduation from the Royal College, he was appointed lecturer on music at the Univ. of Sydney in Australia; in 1960 he joined the staff of the Royal College of Music in London. His style of composition is neo-Romantic, but adheres to Classical forms, preserving a clear sense of tonality.

WORKS: *Morvoren,* opera on a Cornish legend (London, July 15, 1964); 2 Rhapsodies for Piano (1943); String Quartet No.

1 (1944); String Trio (1945); *In the Time of the Breaking of Nations,* after Thomas Hardy, for Voice and Piano Quintet (1945); Fantasia for String Quartet (1946); Sextet for Flute, Oboe, and String Quartet (1946); Sinfonietta for Chamber Orch. (1947); *Symphonic Study: Spring* for Orch. (1949); *Songs to Delight* for Women's Chorus and Strings (1950); *Galop Parisien* for 2 Pianos (1950); Sinfonietta for Strings (1952); *5 Chansons de Femme* for Soprano and Harp (1952); *L'Enfant s'amuse,* suite for Piano (1954); *Sonatine champêtre* for Piano (1959); Sonata for 2 Pianos (1960); *Son of Science,* cantata for the Machine Age, for Boys' Voices, Chorus, Tenor, Piano, Percussion, and Strings (Aylesbury, Dec. 2, 1961); *Fanfare to Youth* for 8 Trumpets (1963); String Quartet No. 2 (1964); *Kai-kaus* (*A Persian Suite*) for Chamber Group (1965); *Lacrimae mundi* for Piano Trio (1974); *Son of Man* for Chorus and Orch. (Liverpool, June 26, 1975); *Lord of Light,* oratorio (1980).

Cantelli, Guido, brilliant Italian conductor; b. Novara, April 27, 1920; d. in an airplane crash in Orly, near Paris, Nov. 24, 1956. A gifted child, he was given a place in his father's military band when he was a small boy; appeared as organist at the local church from age 10, and made his debut as a pianist at age 14. He pursued formal studies with Pedrollo and Ghedini at the Milan Cons. He then was conductor of Novara's Teatro Coccia in 1941, but was compelled to give up his post and join the Italian army in 1943. When he refused to support the Fascist cause, he was sent to the Nazi-run Stettin labor camp (1943–44); after being transferred to Bolzano, he escaped to Milan, but was captured and sentenced to death. He was saved by the liberation of his homeland in 1944. After World War II, he conducted at Milan's La Scala; Toscanini heard his performances and was sufficiently impressed to invite him as guest conductor with the NBC Sym. Orch. in N.Y. He made his American debut on Jan. 15, 1949, and subsequently conducted there regularly. Cantelli was one of the most gifted conductors of his generation. A perfectionist, he conducted both rehearsals and concert and operatic performances from memory. He was able to draw the most virtuosic playing from his musicians without losing sight of the intrinsic worth of each score. A few days before his death he was appointed artistic director of La Scala.

BIBL.: L. Lewis, *G. C.: Portrait of a Maestro* (London, 1981).

Cantelo, April (Rosemary), English soprano; b. Purbrook, April 2, 1928. She studied piano and voice at the Royal College of Music in London; was subsequently a member of the New English Singers and the Deller Consort; also appeared in opera with the Glyndebourne Opera and the English Opera Group; she also gave solo recitals.

Canteloube (de Malaret), (Marie-) Joseph, French pianist, composer, and writer on music; b. Annonay, near Tournon, Oct. 21, 1879; d. Grigny, Seine-et-Oise, Nov. 4, 1957. His name was simply Canteloube, but he added "de Malaret" after the name of his ancestral estate. He studied piano in Paris with Amélie Doetzer, a pupil of Chopin, and composition with d'Indy at the Schola Cantorum. He became an ardent collector of French folk songs and arranged and publ. many of them for voice with instrumental accompaniment. His *Chants d'Auvergne* (4 sets for Voice, with Piano or Orch., 1923–30) are frequently heard. Among his other albums, *Anthologie des chants populaires français* (4 sets, 1939–44) is a comprehensive collection of regional folk songs. He also publ. a biography of Vincent d'Indy (Paris, 1949).

WORKS: 2 operas: *Le Mas* (1910–13; Paris Opéra, April 3, 1929) and *Vercingetorix* (1930–32; Paris Opéra, June 26, 1933); symphonic poem, *Vers la princesse lointaine* (1910–11); 3 symphonic sketches: *Lauriers* (Paris, Feb. 22, 1931); *Pièces françaises* for Piano and Orch. (1935); *Poème* for Violin and Orch. (1937); *Rustiques* for Oboe, Clarinet, and Bassoon (1946).

Cantor, Eddie (real name, **Isidore Itzkowitz**), American singer and actor; b. N.Y., Jan. 31, 1892; d. Los Angeles, Oct. 10, 1964. He worked in vaudeville before attracting notice for his performance in the *Ziegfeld Follies of 1917*; he subsequently starred in the *Ziegfeld Follies* of 1918, 1919, 1923, and 1927, and also in *Kid Boots* (1923) and *Whoopee* (1928). After settling in Hollywood in 1929, he appeared in a variety of films and in his own radio program. He became phenomenally popular as a song stylist; among his most famous renditions were *Alabamy Bound, Dinah, If You Knew Susie,* and *Makin' Whoopee*. With the help of a professional journalist, he authored 3 autobiographical books: *My Life in Your Hands* (1928), *Take My Life* (1957), and *The Way I See It* (1959).

Capdevielle, Pierre, French composer and pianist; b. Paris, Feb. 1, 1906; d. Bordeaux, July 9, 1969. He studied at the Paris Cons. with Gédalge and Vidal, and privately with d'Indy; composed an opera, *Les Amants captifs* (1947–50); the orch. works *Incantation pour la mort d'un jeune spartiate* (1931), *Ouverture pour le pédant joué* (1943), and *Cantate de la France retrouvée* (1946); *Fille de l'homme,* lyric tragedy (Paris Radio, Nov. 9, 1967); 3 syms. (1936; 1942; Chamber Sym., 1953); *Épaves retrouvées,* 4 symphonic tableaux (1955); *Concerto del Dispetto* for Piano and Orch. (1959); Sonata Concertante for Trombone and Piano (1963); *Sonatine pastorale* for Flute and Piano; String Quartet; etc.

Cape, Safford, American-Belgian choral conductor; b. Denver, June 28, 1906; d. Brussels, March 26, 1973. He studied in Europe, principally in Brussels, with Charles Van den Borren, whose daughter he married. In 1933 he established in Brussels a music society, Pro Musica Antiqua, with which he gave numerous performances of choral and instrumental works by medieval and Renaissance composers.

Capecchi, Renato, Italian baritone; b. Cairo, Egypt, Nov. 6, 1923. He studied violin; then went to Milan to study voice. In 1950 he joined La Scala, Milan; on Nov. 24, 1951, he made his Metropolitan Opera debut in N.Y. as Germont *père* in *La Traviata,* remaining on its roster for several subsequent seasons. He also sang at Covent Garden, London, and at many of the major European festivals.

Capell, Richard, English writer on music; b. Northampton, March 23, 1885; d. London, June 21, 1954. He studied cello in London and at the Lille Cons.; was music critic for the London *Daily Mail* (1911–33); then joined the *Daily Telegraph*; during World War II was its war correspondent in the French, Greek, and Italian campaigns. From 1928 to 1933 he was an ed. of the *Monthly Musical Record*; from 1950 to 1954 he edited *Music & Letters*. In 1946 he was made an Officer of the Order of the British Empire. He publ. *Schubert's Songs* (London, 1928), a biography of Gustav Holst (London, 1928), and *Opera* (London, 1930).

Capet, Lucien, distinguished French violinist and teacher; b. Paris, Jan. 8, 1873; d. there, Dec. 18, 1928. He studied at the Paris Cons.; from 1896 to 1899 was concertmaster of the Lamoureux Orch.; from 1899 to 1903 taught violin at the Cons. of Ste. Cécile in Bordeaux. In 1904 he founded the celebrated Capet Quartet, and played 1st violin in it until 1921, specializing particularly in the later Beethoven quartets. In 1924 he was appointed director of the Inst. de Violon in Paris. He composed *Le Rouet,* symphonic poem; *Prélude religieux* for Orch.; *Devant la mer* for Voice and Orch.; *Poème* for Violin and Orch.; 5 string quartets; 2 violin sonatas; 6 violin études. He publ. *La Technique supérieure de l'archet* (Paris, 1916); *Les 17 Quatuors de Beethoven;* also a philosophical work, *Espérances*.

Caplet, André, French composer; b. Le Havre, Nov. 23, 1878; d. Paris, April 22, 1925. He studied violin in Le Havre, and played in theater orchs. there and in Paris; entered the Paris Cons. (1896), where he studied with Leroux and Lenepveu; in 1901 received the Grand Prix de Rome for his cantata *Myrrha.* His *Marche solennelle* for the centennial of the Villa Medicis was performed in Rome (April 18, 1903). He was active in France as a choral and operatic conductor; conducted the 1st performance of Debussy's *Le Martyre de St. Sébastien* (Paris, May 22, 1911); also conducted opera in the U.S. with the

Boston Opera Co. (1910–14) and in London at Covent Garden (1912). He served in the French army during World War I; later continued his musical activities. Caplet's music is unequivocally impressionistic, with a lavish use of whole-tone scales and parallel chord formations; he combined this impressionism with neo-archaic usages and mystic programmatic ideas. He was a close friend of Debussy; recent discoveries show that he collaborated with Debussy on several of his orch. works and even completed sections left unfinished by Debussy. His correspondence with Debussy was publ. in Monaco in 1957.

WORKS: Oratorio, *Miroir de Jésus* (Paris, May 1, 1924); *Prières* for Voice and Chamber Orch.; *The Masque of the Red Death,* after Poe, for Harp and Orch. (Paris, March 7, 1909; later arranged for Harp and String Quartet and retitled *Conte fantastique;* perf. Paris, Dec. 18, 1923); *Épiphanie* for Cello and Orch. (Paris, Dec. 29, 1923); Double Wind Quintet (Paris, March 9, 1901); *Messe des petits de St. Eustache* (Paris, June 13, 1922); Sonata for Voice, Cello, and Piano; Septet for Strings and 3 Female Voices; *Suite persane* for Woodwind Instruments; piano duets; piano pieces; minor choral works and songs. He left unfinished a *Sonata da chiesa* for Violin and Organ (1924) and *Hommage à Ste. Cathérine de Sienna* for Organ and Orch.

BIBL.: M. Brillant, Roland-Manuel, and A. Hoerée, "A. C., musicien mystique," *La Revue Musicale* (July 1925); R. Dumesnil, *Portraits de musiciens français* (Paris, 1938); *A. C.* (Paris, 1976).

Capocci, Gaetano, Italian organist, composer, and teacher; b. Rome, Oct. 16, 1811; d. there, Jan. 11, 1898. He studied music with Valentino Fioravanti and organ with Sante Pascoli; at the same time he took courses in theology. In 1830 he was appointed organist and music director at the Church of S. Maria in Rome; was then organist at S. Maria Maggiore (from 1839) and at S. Giovanni in Laterano (from 1855). He had numerous students, among them Margherita of Savoy, the future Queen of Italy. His chief merit as a composer was a successful revival of the Classical oratorio. He wrote the oratorios *Il Battista* (Rome, March 31, 1833) and *Assalonne* (Rome, Dec. 8, 1842); numerous sacred choruses and organ pieces.

Capoianu, Dumitru, Rumanian composer; b. Bucharest, Oct. 19, 1929. He studied at the Bucharest Cons. (1941–53) with Jora, Mendelsohn, Vancea, Andricu, and Rogalski; from 1969 to 1973 he was manager of the Georges Enesco Phil. Orch.

WORKS: 2 suites for Orch. (1953, 1954); *Divertissement* for String Orch. and 2 Clarinets (1956); Violin Concerto (1957); *Cosmos 60,* ballet scene (1960); 5 *Songs of Transylvania* for Female Chorus, Oboe, and Strings (1961); *Cinematographic Variations* for Orch. (1965); *Steel,* ballet (1965); *Curtea domnească* (The Princely Courtyard), a "spectacle" of sound and light (1969); *Moto perpetuo* for Solo Violin or Group of Violins, and Orch. (1972); *Chemări '77* for Orch. (1977); *Muzică de ambianță* for Orch. (1980); *Fațete,* symphonic jazz suite (1984); *Valses ignobles et sentimentales du tout* . . . for Mezzo-soprano and String Orch. (1986); 2 musicals: *Dragostea prințesei* (1982) and *Cenușăreasa* (1984); choral works; Wind Quintet (1950); Viola Sonata (1952); 2 string quartets (1954, 1959); Trio for Violin, Viola, and Cello (1968); film music.

Capoul, (Joseph-Amédée-) Victor, brilliant French tenor; b. Toulouse, Feb. 27, 1839; d. Pujaudran-du-Gers, Feb. 18, 1924. He studied voice at the Paris Cons.; made his debut at the Opéra-Comique on Aug. 26, 1861; then sang opera in London and N.Y. In 1897 he was appointed manager of the Grand Opéra in Paris.

BIBL.: A. de Lassus, *V. C.,* in *La Revue Musicale* (May 1906).

Cappuccilli, Piero, Italian baritone; b. Trieste, Nov. 9, 1929. He studied voice privately; then made his debut at the Teatro Nuovo in Milan (1957). On March 26, 1960, he made his Metropolitan Opera debut in N.Y. as Germont *père* in *La Traviata.* In 1964 he joined La Scala Opera, Milan, achieving distinction in the roles in Verdi's operas. .

Caprioli, Alberto, Italian composer and conductor; b. Bologna, Nov. 16, 1956. He studied composition with Franco Margola (1973–79) and Camillo Togni (1980–83; diploma, 1983) and conducting with Piero Guarino (1977–78) at the Padua Cons. and with Tito Gotti at the Bologna Cons. (1976–79; diploma, 1979); he also attended conducting courses given by Kondrashin in Hilversum (1978) and by Suitner (1979–83) and Cerha (1982–83; diploma, 1983) at the Vienna Academy of Music. He later pursued composition training with Boguslaw Schaeffer at the Salzburg Mozarteum (1986–88).

WORKS: *Frammenti* for Piano (1975–84); *Fantasia zu "Canto notturno"* for Chamber Orch. (1976); *Abendlied* for Soprano and Orch. (after Hölderlin; 1977; Parma, May 15, 1978, composer conducting); *Omnia qui magni dispexit lumina mundi* for Bassoon and String Orch. (1979); *Variazioni su un tema di Schumann* for Orch. (1982); *Sonata in memoriam Alban Berg* for Piano (1982); *Sonetti di Shakespeare* for Child Reciter and 10 Instruments (Salzburg, Oct. 4, 1983); Trio for Piano, Violin, and Cello (Salzburg, Sept. 28, 1984); *del celeste confine,* fragment for String Quartet (1985; Krakow, April 7, 1987); *Dialogue* for Double Bass and 2 String Quartets (Undine, Oct. 2, 1986); *Per lo dolce silentio de la notte* for Piano and Computer or Tape (Salzburg, May 25, 1987); *Symphoniae I e II* for Violin (Salzburg, May 5, 1988); *Due Notturni d'oblio* for 10 Players (Stuttgart, Sept. 10, 1988).

Capron, Henri, prominent American cellist and composer of French origin. He was a pupil of Gaviniés in Paris (1768); 1st appeared in Philadelphia in 1785; became active as manager (with Reinagle, William Brown, and Juhan) of subscription concerts in Philadelphia and N.Y.; played in the Old American Co. orch. in N.Y., where he lived from 1788 to 1792; in 1794 he settled permanently in Philadelphia and later was principal of a French boarding school. He wrote *New Contredances;* some songs.

BIBL.: O. Sonneck, *Early Concert Life in America* (N.Y., 1907).

Capuana, Franco, Italian conductor; b. Fano, Sept. 29, 1894; d. while conducting Rossini's *Mosè* at the Teatro San Carlo, Naples, Dec. 10, 1969. He studied composition at the Naples Cons.; began his career as an opera conductor in 1915; from 1930 to 1937 was music director of the Teatro San Carlo in Naples; from 1937 was conductor at La Scala in Milan, then its music director (1949–52). He specialized in Italian verismo operas, but also excelled in presenting the operas of Wagner, Strauss, and several modern composers.

Caracciolo, Franco, Italian conductor; b. Bari, March 29, 1920. He studied composition and piano at the Cons. in San Pietro a Majella in Naples and conducting with Molinari at the Accademia di Santa Cecilia in Rome. In 1949 he went to Naples as conductor of the Alessandro Scarlatti Orch. In 1964 he settled in Milan as principal conductor of RAI (Radiotelevisione Italiana), retiring in 1987. In his programs, Caracciolo revived many of the forgotten orch. works of Italian composers; also conducted contemporary works.

Carafa (de Colobrano), Michele (Enrico-Francesco-Vincenzo-Aloisio-Paolo), prolific Italian composer of operas; b. Naples, Nov. 17, 1787; d. Paris, July 26, 1872. He was a son of Prince Colobrano, Duke of Alvito; began to study music at an early age. Though he became an officer in the army of Naples, and fought in Napoleon's Russian campaign, he devoted his leisure time to music, and after Waterloo adopted it as a profession. In 1827 he settled in Paris; succeeded Le Sueur as a member of the Academy (1837); in 1840 was appointed a prof. of composition at the Paris Cons.

WORKS: OPERAS: *Gabriella di Vergy* (Naples, July 3, 1816); *Ifigenia in Tauride* (Naples, June 19, 1817); *Berenice in Siria* (Naples, July 29, 1818); *Elisabetta in Derbyshire* (Venice, Dec. 26, 1818); the following operas were produced at the Opéra-Comique in Paris: *Jeanne d'Arc* (March 10, 1821); *Le Solitaire* (Aug. 17, 1822); *Le Valet de chambre* (Sept. 16, 1823); *L'Auberge*

supposée (April 26, 1824); *Sangarido* (May 19, 1827); *Masaniello* (Dec. 27, 1827; on the same subject as Auber's *La Muette de Portici,* staged at the Paris Opéra 2 months later; yet Carafa's *Masaniello* held the stage in competition with Auber's famous opera for 136 nights); *La Violette* (Oct. 7, 1828); *Jenny* (Sept. 26, 1829); *Le Livre de l'ermite* (Aug. 11, 1831); *La Prison d'Edimbourg* (July 20, 1833); *Une Journée de la Fronde* (Nov. 7, 1833); *La Grande Duchesse* (Nov. 16, 1835); *Thérèse* (Sept. 26, 1838). He also composed ballets, cantatas, and much church music.

Carapetyan, Armen, American musicologist and editor of Armenian descent; b. Esfahan, Persia, Oct. 11, 1908. He studied at the American College in Tehran (diploma, 1927); after receiving training in violin and composition in Paris and N.Y., he continued composition studies with Malipiero; then took courses in musicology at Harvard Univ. (M.A., 1940; Ph.D., 1945, with the diss. *The "Musica nova" of Adriano Willaert, with Reference to the Humanistic Society of Sixteenth-Century Venice*). In 1945 he became founder-director of the American Inst. of Musicology with headquarters in Rome and Cambridge, Mass.; he served as general ed. of Corpus Mensurabilis Musicae, Corpus Scriptorum de Musica, and Musicological Studies and Documents, and was ed. of the journal *Musica Disciplina* (from 1946). He contributed numerous important articles on the music of the Middle Ages and the Renaissance to U.S. and European journals.

Cardew, Cornelius, English composer of extreme avant-garde tendencies; b. Winchcombe, Gloucester, May 7, 1936; d. in a road accident, London, Dec. 13, 1981. He sang in the chorus at Canterbury Cathedral until puberty; then studied composition with Howard Ferguson at the Royal Academy of Music in London (1953–57); in 1957 he went to Cologne and worked at the electronic studio there as an assistant to Karlheinz Stockhausen (1958–60). Returning to England, he organized concerts of experimental music; from 1963 to 1965 he was in Italy, where he had some private lessons with Goffredo Petrassi in Rome. In 1967 he was appointed to the faculty of the Royal Academy of Music in London. In 1969, together with Michael Parsons and Howard Skempton, he organized the Scratch Orch., a heterogeneous group for performances of new music, militantly latitudinarian and disestablishmentarian. Under the influence of the teachings of Mao Zedong, Cardew renounced his modernistic past as a bourgeois deviation detrimental to pure Marxism, and subsequently attacked his former associate, Stockhausen, in a book ominously entitled *Stockhausen Serves Imperialism* (London, 1974). He also repudiated his own magnum opus, *The Great Learning,* which was orig. performed at the 1968 Cheltenham Festival, scored for a non-singing chorus to the words of Ezra Pound's tr. of Confucius, a chorus which was admonished to bang on tapped stones, to whistle and shriek, but never to stoop to vocalizing. In the revised version of the work he appended to the title the slogan "Apply Marxism–Leninism–Mao Zedong Thought in a living way to the problems of the present." This version was first performed by the Scratch Orch. in the Promenade Concert in London on Aug. 24, 1972. His other works include *Volo Solo* for Any Handy Musical Instrument (1965); *3 Winter Potatoes* for Piano and various assorted Concrete Sounds, as well as for Newspapers, Balloons, Noise, and People Working (Focus Opera Groups, London, March 11, 1968). He also publ. several pamphlets containing some confusing confutations of Confucius. In addition, he compiled a seminal manual, *Scratch Music* (London, 1970).

Cardoso, Manuel, distinguished Portuguese composer; b. Fronteira, near Portalegre (baptized), Dec. 11, 1566; d. Lisbon, Nov. 24, 1650. After studies with Manuel Mendes and Cosme Delgado at the Évora Cathedral choir school, he was made a member of the Carmelite order (1588) and took his vows (1589) at Lisbon's Convento do Carmo, where he was active as an organist and choirmaster. He wrote much sacred music, most of which perished in the devastating Lisbon earthquake and fire of 1755. His extant works, all publ. in Lisbon, include

Cantica BVM for 4 to 5 Voices (1613), *Missae* for 4 to 6 Voices, lib. 1 (1625), *Missae* for 4 to 6 Voices, lib. 2 (1636), *Missae de BVM* for 4 to 6 Voices, lib. 3 (1636), and *Livro de varios motetes officio da semana santa e outras cousas* for 4 Voices (1648), all of which have been ed. in Portugaliae Musica, series A, V–VI, XIII, XX, XXII, XXVI (1962–74).

BIBL.: M. de Sampayo Ribeiro, *Frei M. C.: Contribuição para o estudo da sua vida e da sua obra*, Achegas para a História da Música em Portugal, VI (Lisbon, 1961).

Cardus, Sir Neville (John Frederick), English writer on music and cricket; b. Manchester, April 3, 1888; d. London, Feb. 28, 1975. He studied singing, then turned to journalism; wrote essays on numerous subjects, but primarily on cricket and music. In 1917 he joined the staff of the *Manchester Guardian*; became its chief music critic (1927–39); from 1939 to 1947 he was in Australia, writing on cricket and music for the *Sydney Morning Herald*. Returning to London, he became music critic for the *Manchester Guardian* in 1951. He received the Wagner Medal of the City of Bayreuth in 1963; was knighted in 1967. His literary style is quasi-Shavian in its colloquial manner and stubborn persuasion.

WRITINGS: *Autobiography* (1947); *Second Innings: More Autobiography* (1950); *Sir Thomas Beecham: A Memoir* (1961); *Gustav Mahler: His Mind and His Music* (1965); *The Delights of Music: A Critic's Choice* (1966); *Full Score* (1970).

BIBL.: R. Daniels, ed., *Conversations with C.* (London, 1976); C. Brookes, *His Own Man: The Life of N. C.* (London, 1985); A. Lamb, "C. Reaches His Century," *Musical Times* (April 1988).

Carestini, Giovanni, greatly renowned Italian castrato alto; b. Filottrano, near Ancona, c.1705; d. probably there, c.1760. He studied in Milan, then made his operatic debut in a female role in A. Scarlatti's *Griselda* in Rome (1721), where he continued to sing until 1723. He is known to have appeared in Venice (until 1726), Parma and Genoa (1726), Rome (1727–30), Milan (1727–32), Naples (1728–29), where he found a rival in Bernacchi, and again in Venice (1729, 1731); he also served as chamber virtuoso to the Duke of Parma. From 1731 to 1741 he was in the service of the Elector of Bavaria in Munich, but he remained active in other music centers. He made his London debut in the pasticcio *Semiramide riconosciuta* (Oct. 30, 1733); there Handel chose him to create the leading male roles in his *Arianna in Creta* (Jan. 26, 1734), *Il Parnasso in festa* (March 13, 1734), *Ariodante* (Jan. 8, 1735), and *Alcina* (April 16, 1735), as well as the completely revised role of Mirtillo in *Il Pastor fido* (May 18, 1734). After appearances in Venice (1735) and Naples and Bologna (1736), he sang once again in London (1739–40). On Dec. 26, 1740, he sang in the inaugural performance at Turin's Teatro Regio of Feo's *Arsace*; he also sang in Reggio (1741), in Milan (1742–44), where he created the principal roles in Gluck's *Demofoonte* (Jan. 6, 1743) and *Sofonisba* (Jan. 13, 1744), in Padua (1743), and in Venice (1743–45). He entered the service of the Elector of Saxony in Dresden in 1747. After serving Frederick the Great in Berlin (1750–54), he went to St. Petersburg, where he won the approbation of the Empress Elizabeth.

Carewe, John (Maurice Foxall), English conductor; b. Derby, Jan. 24, 1933. After studies with W. Goehr, Deutsch, and Boulez at the Guildhall School of Music in London, and with Messiaen at the Paris Cons., he organized the New Music Ensemble (1958). He was also on the staff of Morley College (1958–66) and was principal conductor of the BBC Welsh Sym. Orch. in Cardiff (1966–71); he subsequently was music director of the Brighton Phil. Soc. (1974–87) and principal conductor of the Fires of London (1980–84).

Carey, Henry, English composer; b. probably in Yorkshire, c.1687; d. (suicide) London, Oct. 5, 1743. He was a natural son of Henry Savile, Lord Eland; studied music with Linnert, Roseingrave, and Geminiani; settled c.1710 in London, where he was active as a poet, librettist, playwright, and composer; wrote 6 ballad-operas, of which *The Contrivances* (Drury Lane,

London, June 20, 1729) achieved the greatest success. He wrote the words of the popular song *Sally in Our Alley* and composed a musical setting for it, but his setting was replaced in 1790 by the tune *What Though I Am a Country Lass*, which has since been traditionally sung to Carey's original poem; also popular was his intermezzo with singing, *Nancy, or The Parting Lovers* (1739). He publ. a collection of 100 ballads, *The Musical Century* (2 vols., 1737 and 1740); also 6 *Cantatas* (1732) and 3 *Burlesque Cantatas* (1741). Carey's claim to the authorship of *God Save the King* was put forth by his son, George Savile Carey (1743–1807), more than 50 years after his father's death, without any supporting evidence; many anthologies still list Carey's name as the author of the British national anthem. For a complete account of this misattribution of the tune, see P.A. Scholes, *God Save the Queen!* (London, 1954). See also W. Cummings, *"God Save the King," The Origin and History of the Music and Words* (London, 1902); O.G. Sonneck, *Report on the Star-Spangled Banner* (1909); F.S. Boas and J.E. Borland, *The National Anthem* (London, 1916); J.A. Fuller Maitland, "Facts and Fictions about *God Save the King*," *Musical Quarterly* (Oct. 1916); E.A. Maginty, "*America*: The Origin of Its Melody," ibid. (July 1934).

Caridis, Miltiades, Greek conductor; b. Gdansk, Poland, May 9, 1923. He attended the Cons. in Athens and the Academy of Music in Vienna, where he studied conducting with Hans Swarowsky, Herbert von Karajan, and Hermann Scherchen. He conducted opera at Bregenz (1947–48), Graz (1945–59), and Cologne (1959–62). From 1960 to 1967 he was principal conductor of the Phil. Hungarica Orch. in Marl, West Germany; from 1964 to 1967 toured the U.S. with his ensemble; in 1969 was appointed conductor of the Oslo Phil. Orch. From 1975 to 1981 he was Generalmusikdirektor of the Duisburg Sym. From 1981 to 1985 he was chief conductor of the Niederösterreichisches Tonkünstler Orch. in Vienna.

Carissimi, Giacomo, Italian composer; b. Marino, near Rome (baptized), April 18, 1605; d. Rome, Jan. 12, 1674. From 1625 to 1627 he was organist at the Cathedral of Tivoli; from 1628 to his death, maestro di cappella in the Church of S. Apollinare in Rome; he also served as maestro di cappella of the Collegio Germanico in Rome. A prolific and original composer, he broke with the Palestrina tradition, devoting himself to perfecting the monodic style, as is evidenced by his highly developed recitative and more pleasing and varied instrumental accompaniments. His MSS were dispersed at the sale of the library of the Collegio Germanico, and many are lost, but a few printed works are still extant. There were publ. the 4 oratorios *Jephte* (his masterpiece), *Judicium Salomonis, Jonas, Balthazar*; 2 collections of motets *a* 2, 3, and 4 (Rome, 1664, 1667); masses *a* 5 and 9 (Cologne, 1663, 1667); *Arie de camera* (1667); and separate pieces in several collections. The finest collection of his works is that made by Aldrich at Christ-Church College, Oxford. Carissimi also wrote a treatise, publ. only in German: *Ars cantandi, etc.* (Augsburg; 2nd ed., 1692; 3rd ed., 1696; another ed., 1718). The complete works are being publ. by the Istituto Italiano per la Storia della Musica (1951–). C. Sartori has compiled *Carissimi, Catalogo delle opere attribuite* (Milan, 1975).

BIBL.: M. Brenet, "Les Oratorios de C.," *Rivista Musicale Italiana* (1897); A. Schering, *Geschichte des Oratoriums* (Leipzig, 1911); A. Cametti, "Primo contributo per una biografia di G. C.," *Rivista Musicale Italiana*, XXIV/3 (1917); F.B. Pratella, "G. C. ed i suoi oratori," ibid., XXIX/1 (1920); J. Loschelder, "Nuovi contributi a una biografia di G. C.," *Archiv für Musikwissenschaft* (1940); G. Massenkeil, "Die Wiederholungsfiguren in den Oratorien G. C.," ibid. (Jan. 1956); E. Rosend, "Four Oratorios by G. C.," *Amor Artis Bulletin* (Feb. 1967); L. Bianci, *C. . . . e l'oratorio musicale* (Rome, 1969); A. Jones, *The Motets of C.* (diss., Oxford Univ., 1979); G. Dixon, *C.* (London, 1985).

Carl, William Crane, American organist; b. Bloomfield, N.J., March 2, 1865; d. N.Y., Dec. 8, 1936. He 1st studied in N.Y.;

in 1890 went to Paris, where he studied with Guilmant; returning to America, he was engaged as organist of the Old First Presbyterian Church in N.Y., a post which he held until his death. He made 7 tours to the Pacific coast and 1 to Alaska; was also active as a choral conductor in N.Y.; was a founder and served on the Council of the American Guild of Organists. He publ. *Masterpieces for the Organ; 30 Postludes for the Organ; 2 vols.* of *Novelties for the Organ; Master Studies for the Organ.*

Carlid, Göte, Swedish composer; b. Högbo, Dec. 26, 1920; d. Stockholm, June 30, 1953. He was a philosophy student at the Univ. of Uppsala; then served as a municipal librarian in Enköping (1946–48) and Sollentuna (1948–50). As a composer, he was largely autodidact, but from the outset he adopted a modern idiom, making use of impressionistic and expressionistic techniques. His last works before his early death show a learned approach to the problems of new music.
    Works: *Notturno* for String Orch. (1945); *Small Pieces* for Piano (1947); Piano Sonata (1948); *Quartetto elegiaco* for String Quartet (1948); *3 Songs* for Female Voice, Flute, Clarinet, and Cello (1946–49); *A Little Tea Music* for Flute, 2 Clarinets, and Cello (1949); *Mass* for Strings (1949); *Monologues* for Piano (1944–50); *Triad* for Saxophone and Piano (1950); *Hymnes à la beauté* for Chorus and Orch., to poems by Baudelaire (ISCM Festival, Salzburg, 1952); *The Music Bus* for Soli, Children's Chorus, and Instruments (1952).

Carlos, Wendy (née **Walter**), American organist, composer, and electronics virtuoso; b. Pawtucket, R.I., Nov. 14, 1939. He played piano as a child; then studied music and physics at Brown Univ. and at Columbia Univ., where he took courses with Vladimir Ussachevsky. At the same time he began working with the electronic engineer Robert Moog in perfecting the Moog Synthesizer. The result of their experiments with versified tone-colors was a record album under the title *Switched-on Bach*, which became unexpectedly successful, especially among the wide-eyed, susceptible American youth, selling some million copies. This was followed in 1969 by *The Well-Tempered Synthesizer*, engineered entirely by Carlos. Then, at the age of 32, he suddenly became aware of his sexual duality, a woman's psyche imprisoned in a man's body. To remedy this sundering nature, he underwent a transsexual operation with his penis being everted to create a fairly respectable and conceivably receptive vagina; on St. Valentine's Day, Feb. 14, 1979, he officially changed his 1st name from Walter to Wendy. She/he described his sexual tergiversation in a candid interview in *Playboy* (May 1979), illustrated with photographs "before and after."
    Works: Opera: *Noah* (1964–65); *Timesteps* for Synthesizer (1970); *Sonic Seasons* for Synthesizer and Tape (1971); *Pompous Circumstances* for Synthesizer or Orch. (1974–75); *Variations on Dies irae* for Orch. (1980); film scores: *A Clockwork Orange* (1971); *The Shining* (1978–80); *TRON* (1981–82); some chamber music and other pieces.

Carlson, Claudine, French-American mezzo-soprano; b. Mulhouse, Feb. 26, 1937. She studied in California and at the Manhattan School of Music in N.Y. with Jennie Tourel and Esther Andreas; then engaged on a successful career as a concert singer. In 1977 she made her debut at the Metropolitan Opera in N.Y. in Debussy's *Pelléas et Mélisande*. Gifted with a voice of fine quality, she gained renown in the French repertoire.

Carlstedt, Jan, Swedish composer; b. Orsa, June 15, 1926. He studied composition with Lars-Erik Larsson at the Stockholm Musikhögskolan (1948–52), and later in England (1952–53) and Italy (1954–55). Returning to Stockholm, he became active in furthering the cause of modern music; was a founder of the Contemporary Music Assoc. in Stockholm (1960).
    Works: 5 string quartets (1951–52; 1966; 1967; 1972; 1977); 2 syms.: No. 1 (1952–54; rev. 1960; Stockholm, Oct. 4, 1961); No. 2, in memory of Martin Luther King, Jr. (1968; N.Y., Dec. 20, 1970); String Trio (1955–56); Sonata for String Orch. (1956); Sonata for 2 Violins (1956); *12 Miniatures* for

Violin, Clarinet, and Cello (1958); 8 Duets for 2 Violins (1958); Sinfonietta for Wind Quintet (1959); Sonata for Solo Violin (1959); *Ballata* for Solo Cello (1960); Divertimento for Oboe and String Trio (1962); Wind Quintet (1962); *Pentastomos* for Wind Quintet (1972–73); *Metamorfoser* for Flute, Oboe, Violin, and Cello (1974); *Intrada* for Orch. (1985); *Metamorphosi* for Strings (1986).

Carlyle, Joan (Hildred), English soprano; b. Wirral, April 6, 1931. She studied in London, making her operatic debut as Frasquita at London's Covent Garden in 1955. She continued to sing there regularly until 1969 in such roles as Mimi, Nedda, Sophie, Arabella, Pamina, Desdemona, Britten's Titania, and Tippett's Jenifer; she also appeared at the Edinburgh Festival, the Glyndebourne Festival, the Vienna State Opera, the Bavarian State Opera in Munich, and the Teatro Colón in Buenos Aires.

Carmichael, Hoagy (Hoagland Howard), American pianist and composer of popular music; b. Bloomington, Ind., Nov. 22, 1899; d. Rancho Mirage, Calif., Dec. 27, 1981. His ambition as a youth was to become a lawyer, and in fact, he graduated from the Indiana Univ. Law School, and played the piano only for relaxation. In 1929 he went to Hollywood but failed to obtain work as a musician. Working on his own, he organized a swing band and composed songs for it. Although unable to write music professionally, he revealed a natural gift for melody, and soon made a success with such songs as *Riverboat Shuffle* and *Washboard Blues*. He made a hit with his song *Stardust*, which became the foundation of his fame and fortune. Among his other popular tunes were *Georgia on My Mind* (brought to the height of its popularity by Ray Charles); *Ivy; I Get Along without You Very Well; Heart and Soul;* and *In the Cool, Cool, Cool of the Evening*, which won the Academy Award as the best movie song for 1951. He was also active as an actor in films and on television. He publ. *The Stardust Road* (N.Y., 1946) and *Sometimes I Wonder: The Story of Hoagy Carmichael* (with S. Longstreet; N.Y., 1965). For an edition of his works, see R. Schiff, ed., *The Star Dust Melodies* (Melville, N.Y., 1983).
    Bibl.: A. Wilder, *American Popular Song: The Great Innovators, 1900–1950* (N.Y., 1972); J. Hasse, *The Works of H. C.* (Cincinnati, 1983).

Carmirelli, Pina, Italian violinist; b. Varzi, Jan. 23, 1914. She studied at the Cons. in Milan, graduating in 1930, and at the Accademia di Santa Cecilia in Rome. She began her concert career in 1937; in 1949 she founded the Boccherini Quintet, and in 1954 the Carmirelli Quartet, with which she toured throughout Europe. In 1941 she joined the faculty of the Rome Cons.; she also ed. works by Boccherini and Vivaldi. From 1975 to 1986 she was concertmaster of I Musici.

Carner, Mosco, Austrian-born English musical journalist; b. Vienna, Nov. 15, 1904; d. Cornwall, Aug. 3, 1985. He studied musicology with Guido Adler, receiving his Ph.D. from the Univ. of Vienna in 1928; then was active as an opera conductor until 1933, when the advent of the Nazi regime forced him to emigrate. He settled in London and rapidly acquired commendable fluency in the English language. He wrote biographical studies on Dvořák (London, 1941), Puccini (London, 1958; 2nd ed., rev., 1974), and Alban Berg (London, 1975; 2nd ed., rev., 1983), as well as studies on modern harmony (1942) and on the songs of Hugo Wolf (1982).

Carneyro, Claudio, Portuguese composer; b. Oporto, Jan. 27, 1895; d. there, Oct. 18, 1963. He studied composition with Lucien Lambert at the Oporto Cons. and later in Paris with Widor (1919–22) and Paul Dukas (1934); taught composition at the Oporto Cons. (1922–58); was its director from 1955 to 1958. In his music, he made ample use of authentic Portuguese motives, adorning them by sonorous impressionistic harmonies.
    Works: Piano Quartet (1914); *Pregões romarias e processões* for Orch. (1928); *Memento* for String Orch. (1933); *Cantarejo e dancara* for Orch. (1938); *Pavana e gelharda* for String Orch.

(1939); *Catavento* for Piano and Chamber Orch. (1942); *Portugalesas* for Orch. (1949); *Khroma* for Viola and Orch. (1954); *Roda dos degredados* for Violin and Orch. (1960); *Bailadeiras* for Orch. (1962); *Gradualis* for Orch. (1962); Piano Quartet (1914); *Partita* for String Trio (1928–35); Violin Sonata (1929); String Quartet (1947); *Poemas em prosa* for Piano (1930–31); choruses; songs.

Carnicer (y Batlle), Ramón, Spanish conductor, teacher, and composer; b. Tárrega, near Lérida, Oct. 24, 1789; d. Madrid, March 17, 1855. He studied in Barcelona with Francisco Queralt and Carlos Baguer; from 1818 to 1820 conducted the Coliseo Theater orch. in Barcelona; from 1828 to 1830 was conductor of the Royal Opera in Madrid; from 1830 to 1854 was a prof. of composition at the Madrid Cons. One of the creators of Spanish national opera (the zarzuela), he composed 10 operas, wrote much church music, many syms., Spanish songs, etc.; also *Dulce Patria*, the national hymn of Chile.

Carol-Bérard, French composer and theorist; b. Marseilles, April 5, 1881; d. Paris, Dec. 13, 1942. He studied with Albéniz in Barcelona; then settled in Paris. His music, impressionistic with an oriental flavor, remains largely unpubl. He evolved a theory of "chromophonie" (color in movement) and wrote several papers on the subject in *La Revue Musicale* and other publications. He also wrote poetry under the pseudonym **Olivier Realtor.**

Works: *Symphonie dansée; Symphonie des forces mécaniques* (in 3 movements: *Navire perdu; Gare nocturne; L'Aéroplane sur la ville,* utilizing phonograph records of noises); *L'Oiseau des îles,* lyric piece in 2 acts (to his own words); 3 piano suites: *Égypte, D'une existence antérieure,* and *Extrême-Asie;* humorous piano pieces: *Les Heures civiles et militaires* and *L'Élégie à jouer dans une cave;* a number of songs to poems of Verlaine and Mallarmé.

Carolan, Turlough, Irish song composer; b. near Nobber, County Meath, 1670; d. near Kilronan, March 25, 1738. He was an itinerant harper, and improvised Irish verses and tunes; these were publ. in various 18th-century collections of Irish music; the number of his original tunes is about 220. He is also known under the name **O'Carolan.**
Bibl.: D. O'Sullivan, *C.: The Life, Times and Music of an Irish Harper* (London, 1958).

Caron, Philippe, famous Burgundian composer who flourished in the 15th century. He was a pupil of Binchois or Dufay. O.J. Gombosi, in his monograph *Jacob Obrecht, eine stilkritische Studie* (Leipzig, 1925), groups Caron with composers of the Cambrai school interested in continuing Dufay's style; this work also contains a reprint of a 3-part chanson, *Vive Carloys,* MSS of which are in libraries at Rome and Florence. Other extant works include 4 masses *a* 4 in the Papal Chapel and a MS of 3- and 4-part chansons at Paris. Petrucci publ. a 5-part chanson, *Hélas que pourra deuenir,* in his *Odhecaton* (1501). The Inst. of Medieval Music (Brooklyn, N.Y.) issued the complete works from 1971 to 1976.

Caron, Rose (Lucille) (née **Meuniez**), French soprano; b. Monerville, Nov. 17, 1857; d. Paris, April 9, 1930. She entered the Paris Cons. in 1880, leaving in 1882 to study with Marie Sasse in Brussels, where her debut was made as Alice in *Robert le Diable* (1883). She sang for 2 years at the Paris Opéra, and again in Brussels, creating Lorance (in *Jocelyn*), Richilde, and Salammbô (1890); in 1890 she returned to the Paris Opéra, where she sang Sieglinde (1893) and Desdemona (1894) in the 1st performances of *Die Walküre* and *Otello* in France; in 1898 she sang Fidelio at the Opéra-Comique. From 1900 she appeared almost exclusively on the concert stage; in 1902 she was appointed a prof. of singing at the Paris Cons.
Bibl.: H. de Curzon, *Croquis d'artistes* (Paris, 1898).

Carpani, Giuseppe (Antonio), Italian writer on music; b. Villalbese, Jan. 28, 1752; d. Vienna, Jan. 22, 1825. He studied and practiced law in Milan, later abandoning it for a literary career and writing on music. He was ed. of the *Gazzetta di Milano* (1792–96); the French invasion forced him to go to Venice and then to Vienna. A great admirer of Haydn, he publ. a monograph, *Le Haydine ovvero Lettere su la vita e le opere del celebre Giuseppe Haydn* (Milan, 1812; enl. ed., Padua, 1823). Stendhal printed a major part of this book as his own work, in French, under the pseudonym of Bombet (Paris, 1814); Carpani protested against this act of plagiarism in his pamphlet *Lettere dell'Autore delle Haydine* (Vienna, 1815), but Stendhal ignored the protest and republ. his book in 1817, this time under the signature Stendhal. Carpani also wrote a monograph on Rossini, *Le Rossiniane* (Padua, 1824).
Bibl.: H. Jacobs, ed., *Literatur, Musik, und Gesellschaft in Italien und Österreich in der Epoche Napoleons und der Restauration: Studien zu G. C. (1751–1825)* (2 vols., Frankfurt am Main, 1988).

Carpenter, John Alden, American composer; b. Park Ridge, Chicago, Feb. 28, 1876; d. Chicago, April 26, 1951. He received his B.A. degree from Harvard Univ. in 1897; also studied music there with John K. Paine; entered his father's shipping supply business, and from 1909 to 1936 was vice-president of the firm. During his earlier years in business he continued his musical studies in Rome (1906) and with Bernard Ziehn in Chicago (1908–12); was made a Knight of the French Legion of Honor (1921); received an honorary M.A. from Harvard Univ. (1922) and an honorary Mus.Doc. from the Univ. of Wisconsin (1933). After his retirement from business in 1936, he devoted himself entirely to composing; in 1947 was awarded the Gold Medal of the National Inst. of Arts and Letters. From his musical contacts abroad he absorbed mildly modernistic and impressionistic techniques and applied them to his music based on American urban subjects, adding the resources of jazz rhythms. His 1st work in this American idiom was a "jazz pantomime," *Krazy Kat,* after a well-known cartoon series (1921); he then wrote a large-scale musical panorama, *Skyscrapers* (1926), performed as a ballet and an orch. suite in America and abroad, attracting much critical comment as the 1st symphonic work descriptive of modern American civilization; as such, the score has historical significance.

Works: Ballets: *The Birthday of the Infanta* (Chicago Opera, Dec. 23, 1919); *Krazy Kat* (Chicago, Dec. 23, 1921); *Skyscrapers* (Metropolitan Opera, N.Y., Feb. 19, 1926; Munich, 1928); orch. suite, *Adventures in a Perambulator* (Chicago, March 19, 1915); Concertino for Piano and Orch. (Chicago, March 10, 1916; rev. 1947); Sym. No. 1, "Sermons in Stones" (Norfolk, Conn., June 5, 1917; rev. for the 50th anniversary of the Chicago Sym. and perf. there, Oct. 24, 1940); *A Pilgrim Vision* for Orch. (Philadelphia, Nov. 23, 1920); *Patterns* for Piano and Orch. (Boston, Oct. 21, 1932); *Sea-Drift,* symphonic poem after Whitman (Chicago, Nov. 30, 1933; rev. 1944); *Danza* for Orch. (1937); Violin Concerto (1936; Chicago, Nov. 18, 1937); Sym. No. 2 (N.Y., Oct. 22, 1942); symphonic poem, *The Anxious Bugler* (N.Y., Nov. 17, 1943); *The 7 Ages,* orch. suite (N.Y., Nov. 29, 1945); *Carmel Concerto* for Piano and Orch. (1948); *Song of David* for Cello, Women's Voices, and Orch. (1951); Violin Sonata (1911); String Quartet (Elizabeth Coolidge Festival, Washington, D.C., 1927); Piano Quintet (1934); *Improving Songs for Anxious Children* (1904); *Gitanjali,* song cycle to poems by Tagore (1913; also arranged for Voice and Orch.); *Water Colors,* 4 Chinese songs with Chamber Orch. (1918); many other songs and piano pieces.
Bibl.: O. Downes, "J.A. C., American Craftsman," and F. Borowski, "J.A. C.," both in *Musical Quarterly* (Oct. 1930); T. Pierson, *The Life and Music of J.A. C.* (diss., Univ. of Rochester, 1952).

Carpenter, Karen, American pop singer; b. New Haven, Conn., March 2, 1950; d. Downey, Calif., Feb. 4, 1983. She formed a pop-jazz group, playing drums, with her brother Richard on keyboards; they soon changed to vocals; she sang contralto. They became enormously popular, with record albums selling into the millions; she preferred soft, sentimental songs and rock singles, such as *We've Only Just Begun, Rainy Days and Mondays,* and *Close to You,* winning 2 Grammy awards in 1970. Their album *The Carpenters* won another Grammy award in 1971. Obsessed with thinning out her already fragile frame, she became a victim of anorexia nervosa and died of heart failure.

Carpentras (**Il Carpentrasso** in Italian; real name, **Elzéar Genet**), composer and priest; b. Carpentras (Vaucluse), c.1470; d. Avignon, June 14, 1548. In 1508 he was the leading singer in, and from 1513 to 1521 maestro di cappella of, the Pontifical Chapel in Rome; in 1521 he was sent to Avignon on negotiations connected with the Holy See; in 1524 he made his last visit to Rome; in 1526 he went to France, where he became dean of St. Agricole. Four vols. of his works (masses, 1532; Lamentations, 1532; hymns, 1533; Magnificats, 1537), printed at Avignon by Jean de Channey, are of great interest for being the 1st works to introduce Briard's new types, with round instead of diamond-shaped and square notes, and without ligatures; a complete copy is in the Vienna Staatsbibliothek, an incomplete one in the Paris Cons. library. His works, though severe and dignified in style, were highly esteemed by his contemporaries. A few motets are printed in Petrucci's *Motetti della Corona* (vol. I, 1514; vol. III, 1519); other works in various contemporary collections, including the ed. by A. Seay in Corpus Mensurabilis Musicae, LVIII (1972–73).
BIBL.: H. Quittard, "E. G. de C.," *Tribune de St. Gervais*, 7–9 (1899); C. Requin, "E. G., dit il Carpentrasso," in *Mémoires de l'Académie de Vaucluse* (1918); J. Tiersot, "E. G., dit C. et la chanson 'a lombre d'ung buissonet,'" *Bulletin de la Société Française de Musicologie*, 3 (1918); C. Miller, "Jerome Cardan on Gombert, Phinot, and C.," *Musical Quarterly* (July 1972).

Carpitella, Diego, Italian ethnomusicologist; b. Reggio di Calabria, June 12, 1924. After receiving an arts degree from Rome Univ. in 1947, he made an extensive collection of documents and field recordings of the music of central and southern Italy; 2 of his recordings were released in collaboration with Alan Lomax in 1957. He publ. studies on the musics of Tunisia, Brazil, Uruguay, and Argentina, popular and jazz music, and general issues of ethnomusicology. He taught at the Univs. of Trent, Chieti, and Rome (from 1975); organized Italy's 1st ethnomusicology congress in 1974. His writings include *Musica popolare e musica di consumo* (1955), *La musica nei rituali sardi dell'argia* (1967), and *Musica e tradizione orale* (1973).

Carr, Benjamin, English-American composer and publisher; b. London, Sept. 12, 1768; d. Philadelphia, May 24, 1831. He studied music with Samuel Arnold, Samuel Wesley, and Charles Wesley; established himself as a composer in London. He went to America in 1793; settled in Philadelphia and established Carr's Musical Repository, one of the most important early American music stores and music publishing houses; the following year (1794) he opened branches in N.Y. and Baltimore. He was co-founder in 1820 of the Musical Fund Soc. in Philadelphia. A versatile musician, he was proficient as a singer, pianist, and organist, and was an influential figure in early American musical life.
WORKS: *Philander and Silvia,* pastoral piece (London, Oct. 16, 1792); *The Archers, or Mountaineers of Switzerland,* ballad opera (N.Y., April 18, 1796); *Dead March for Washington* (1799); numerous songs and ballads. The N.Y. Public Library owns the only known copy of Carr's *Federal Overture* (Philadelphia, 1794), a medley of popular airs, including the 1st printing of *Yankee Doodle.*
BIBL.: W.H. Richards, *C. Genealogy* (1931); V. Redway, "The C.s, American Music Publishers," *Musical Quarterly* (Jan. 1932); J. Mates, *The American Musical Stage before 1800* (1962); C. Sprenkle, *The Life and Works of B. C.* (diss., Peabody Cons. of Music, 1970).

Carraud, Michel-Gaston, French music critic and composer; b. Le Mee-sur-Seine, near Paris, July 20, 1864; d. Paris, June 15, 1920. He studied with Massenet at the Paris Cons.; received the Premier Prix de Rome for his cantata *Cléopâtre* (1890). He abandoned composition after 1905 and was mainly active as a music critic; publ. *La Vie, l'œuvre et la mort d'Albéric Magnard* (Paris, 1921).

Carré, Albert, French opera impresario, nephew of the librettist Michael Carré; b. Strasbourg, June 22, 1852; d. Paris, Dec. 12, 1938. He assumed the directorship of the theater at Nancy in 1884, and from 1885 to 1890 headed the Cercle at Aix-les-Bains. From 1898 to 1912 he was director of the Opéra-Comique, succeeding Carvalho.

Carreño, Inocente, Venezuelan composer; b. Porlamar, Dec. 28, 1919. He studied French horn, clarinet, piano, and theory in Caracas; graduated in composition in 1946; subsequently became engaged in pedagogical work; also played the horn in the Caracas Sym. Orch. and conducted choruses. His works include a symphonic poem, *El Pozo* (1946); *Suite Breve* for String Orch. (1947); *Margariteña,* suite for Orch. (1954); Concerto for Horn and Strings (1958); *Sinfonieta satírica* for 11 Instruments (1965); *Dialogo* for Flute and Chamber Orch. (1965); chamber music and choruses.

Carreño, (Maria) Teresa, famous Venezuelan pianist; b. Caracas, Dec. 22, 1853; d. N.Y., June 12, 1917. As a child she studied with her father, an excellent pianist; driven from home by a revolution, the family in 1862 settled in N.Y., where she studied with Gottschalk. At the age of 8 she gave a public recital in N.Y. (Nov. 25, 1862). She began her career in 1866, after studying with G. Mathias in Paris and A. Rubinstein. She lived mainly in Paris from 1866 to 1870; then in England. She developed a singing voice and made an unexpected appearance in opera in Edinburgh as the Queen in *Les Huguenots* (May 24, 1872), in a cast that included Tietjens, Brignoli, and Mario; was again in the U.S. early in 1876, when she studied singing in Boston. For the Bolivar centenary celebration in Caracas (Oct. 29, 1885), she appeared as singer, pianist, and composer of the festival hymn, written at the request of the Venezuelan government; hence the frequent but erroneous attribution to Carreño of the national hymn of Venezuela, *Gloria al bravo pueblo* (the music of which was actually composed in 1811 by J. Landaeta, and officially adopted as the Venezuelan national anthem on May 25, 1881). In Caracas she once again demonstrated her versatility, when for the last 3 weeks of the season she conducted the opera company managed by her husband, the baritone **Giovanni Tagliapietra**. After these musical experiments she resumed her career as a pianist; made her German debut in Berlin, Nov. 18, 1889; in 1907 toured Australia. Her last appearance with an orch. was with the N.Y. Phil. (Dec. 8, 1916); her last recital was in Havana (March 21, 1917). She impressed her audiences by the impetuous élan of her playing, and was described as "the Valkyrie of the piano." She was married 4 times: to the violinist **Émile Sauret** (June 1873), to the baritone Giovanni Tagliapietra (1876), to **Eugène d'Albert** (1892–95), and to Arturo Tagliapietra, a younger brother of Giovanni (June 30, 1902). Early in her career, she wrote a number of compositions, some of which were publ.: a String Quartet; *Petite danse tsigane* for Orch.; 39 concert pieces for piano; a waltz, *Mi Teresita,* which enjoyed considerable popularity; and other small pieces. She was one of the 1st pianists to play MacDowell's compositions in public; MacDowell took lessons from her in N.Y. She was greatly venerated in Venezuela; her mortal remains were solemnly transferred from N.Y., where she died, and reburied in Caracas, on Feb. 15, 1938.
BIBL.: M. Milinowski, *T. C.* (New Haven, 1940); A. Marquez Rodriguez, *Esbozo biográfico de T. C.* (Caracas, 1953).

Carreras, José (Maria), prominent Spanish tenor; b. Barcelona, Dec. 5, 1946. He was a pupil of Jaime Francesco Puig at the Barcelona Cons. In 1970 he sang Gennaro opposite Caballé's portrayal of Lucrezia Borgia in Barcelona, and in 1971 made his Italian debut as Rodolfo in Parma, as well as his 1st appearance in London, in a concert performance of *Maria Stuarda* as Leicester. On March 15, 1972, he made his N.Y. City Opera debut as Pinkerton; he continued to sing there until 1975. He made his Metropolitan Opera debut in N.Y. as Cavaradossi on Nov. 18, 1974; later that year he made his 1st appearance at London's Covent Garden, and in 1975 at Milan's La Scala. In 1987 he was stricken with acute lympho-cytic leukemia; after exhaustive medical treatment, he ap-peared at a special Barcelona outdoor concert in 1988 that drew an audience of 150,000 admirers; that same year he founded the José Carreras Leukemia Foundation. In 1989 he sang in recital in Seattle and N.Y. and also returned to the operatic stage, singing the role of Jason in Cherubini's *Medea* in Mérida, Spain. On Sept. 24, 1989, he created the role of Christopher Columbus in Balada's *Cristóbal Colón* in Barce-lona. Among his other fine roles are Alfredo, Edgardo, Nemo-rino, Don José, Andrea Chénier, the Duke of Mantua, and Don Carlos.

BIBL.: J. Pérez Senz, *J. C. El placer de cantar: Un retrato autobiográfico* (Barcelona, 1988); N. Malitz, "J. C.'s Courageous Comeback," *Ovation* (Aug. 1989).

Carrillo (-Trujillo), Julián (Antonio), Mexican composer; b. Ahualulco, San Luis Potosí, Jan. 28, 1875; d. Mexico City, Sept. 9, 1965. He was of Indian extraction; lived mostly in Mexico City, where he studied violin with Pedro Manzano and composition with Melesio Morales. He graduated from the National Cons. in 1899 and received a government stipend for study abroad as a winner of the President Díaz Prize. He took courses at the Leipzig Cons. with Hans Becker (violin), Jadassohn (theory), and Hans Sitt (orchestration); played violin in the Gewandhaus Orch. under Nikisch. From 1902 to 1904 he studied at the Ghent Cons., winning 1st prize as violinist. He returned to Mexico in 1905 and made numerous appear-ances as a violinist; also conducted concerts; was appointed general inspector of music, and director of the National Cons. (1913–14 and again 1920–24). He visited the U.S. many times, and conducted his works in N.Y. and elsewhere. During his years in Leipzig he wrote a Sym., which he conducted there in 1902; at the same time he began experimenting with frac-tional tones; developed a theory which he named *Sonido 13,* symbolically indicating divisions beyond the 12 notes of the chromatic scale. He further devised a special number notation for quarter-tones, eighth-tones, and sixteenth-tones, and con-structed special instruments for performance of his music in these intervals, such as a harpzither with 97 strings to the octave; he also publ. several books dealing with music of frac-tional tones, and ed. a monthly magazine, *El Sonido 13,* in 1924–25.

WORKS: OPERAS: *Ossian* (1903); *Matilda* (1909); *Zultil* (1922). **ORCH.:** Sym. No. 1 (1901); Sym. No. 2 (1905); Sym. No. 3 (1948); 3 syms. for fractional tones (1926); Triple Con-certo for Violin, Flute, Cello, and Orch. (1918); Concertino for Violin, Guitar, Cello, Piccolo, and Harp in fractional tones, with Orch. in normal tuning (1926; Philadelphia, March 4, 1927); *Horizontes* for Violin, Cello, and Harp in fractional tones, and Orch. (1947; Pittsburgh, Nov. 30, 1951); Concertino, subti-tled *Metamorfoseador Carrillo,* for Piano in third-tones, and Orch. (1950; Brussels, Nov. 9, 1958); Concerto for Cello in quarter- and eighth-tones, and Orch. (1954; Brussels, Nov. 9, 1958); *Balbuceos* for Piano in sixteenth-tones, and Chamber Orch. (Houston, March 18, 1960); 2 concertos for Violin in quarter-tones, and Orch. (1963, 1964). **CHAMBER:** String Sextet (1902); Piano Quintet (1918); 4 atonal quartets (1928–48); *Preludio a Cristóbal Colón* for Soprano, with 5 Instruments in fractional tones (Mexico City, Feb. 15, 1925); Sonata in Quarter-Tones for Guitar (1925); also sonatas for string instru-ments in quarter-tones, with piano; *Mass for Pope John XXIII* for Chorus a cappella (1962).

WRITINGS: *Julián Carrillo, Su vida y su obra* (Mexico, 1945); *Leyes de metamórfosis musicales* (Mexico, 1949); several man-uals of music theory.

BIBL.: A. Pike, "The Discoveries and Theories of J. C., 1875–1965," *Inter-American Music Bulletin,* IV (1966).

Carrodus (real name, **Carruthers**), **John (Tiplady),** English violinist; b. Keighley, Yorkshire, Jan. 20, 1836; d. London, July 12, 1895. He studied with his father, a local musician of considerable attainments; played in public as a child; then commenced serious study with Molique in London and in

Stuttgart, where he joined the Court Orch., of which Molique was 1st violinist. Upon his return to England, Carrodus occu-pied various positions in theatrical orchs.; was appointed violin instructor at the National Training School (1876); toured in South Africa in 1880. He publ. several pieces for the violin.

BIBL.: A. Carrodus, *J.T. C., Violinist: A Life Story* (London, 1897).

Carron (real name, **Cox**), Arthur, English tenor; b. Swindon, Dec. 12, 1900; d. there, May 10, 1967. He joined the Old Vic Theatre in 1929; also sang at the Sadler's Wells Opera and at Covent Garden; in 1936 he went to the U.S., where he won the Metropolitan Opera Auditions of the Air, and made his debut with the Metropolitan on May 29, 1936, as Canio in *Pagliacci;* he was chosen to sing the role of Nolan in the world premiere of Walter Damrosch's *The Man without a Coun-try* on May 12, 1937; remained on the roster of the Metropolitan Opera until 1946; then returned to England, where he sang at Covent Garden until 1951.

Carruthers, John. See **Carrodus, John.**

Carse, Adam (von Ahn), English composer and writer on music; b. Newcastle upon Tyne, May 19, 1878; d. Great Missen-den, Buckinghamshire, Nov. 2, 1958. He studied with F. Corder and Burnett at the Royal Academy of Music in London; from 1909 to 1922 taught music at Winchester College; taught har-mony and composition at the Royal Academy of Music (1923–40). He assembled a collection of about 350 wind instruments, which he presented in 1947 to the Horniman Museum in London; publ. a catalog of this collection in 1951.

WORKS: Symphonic poems: *The Death of Tintagiles* (Lon-don, 1902) and *In a Balcony* (London, Aug. 26, 1905); Sym. in C minor (London, July 3, 1906); Sym. in G minor (London, Nov. 19, 1908; rev. 1909); orch. suites: *The Merry Milkmaids* (1922) and *The Nursery* (1928); *Judas Iscariot's Paradise,* bal-lade for Baritone Solo, Chorus, and Orch. (1922); 2 sketches for String Orch. (1923); *Barbara Allen* for String Orch.; *Norwe-gian Fantasia* for Violin and Orch.; *The Lay of the Brown Rosary,* dramatic cantata; numerous choruses; chamber music; piano pieces; songs.

WRITINGS: *Summary of the Elements of Music; Practical Hints on Orchestration; Harmony Exercises* (2 vols., 1923); *The History of Orchestration* (1925); *Orchestral Conducting* (1929); *Musical Wind Instruments* (London, 1939); *The Or-chestra in the 18th Century* (Cambridge, 1940; 2nd ed., 1950); *The Orchestra from Beethoven to Berlioz* (Cambridge, 1948); *The Orchestra* (London, 1948); *18th Century Symphonies* (Lon-don, 1951); *The Life of Jullien* (Cambridge, 1951).

Cartan, Jean, talented French composer; b. Nancy, Dec. 1, 1906; d. Bligny, March 26, 1932. His father was the famous mathematician Elie Cartan. Jean Cartan studied music with Marcel Samuel Rousseau; then with Paul Dukas at the Paris Cons. His works, composed within the brief period of 6 years, showed extraordinary promise, and his death at the age of 25 was mourned as a great loss to French music. He left a cantata, *Pater Noster;* 2 string quartets; a Sonatina for Flute and Clarinet (Oxford, July 25, 1931); piano pieces and several cycles of songs.

BIBL.: A. Roussel, "J. C.," *La Revue Musicale* (May 1932).

Carte, Richard D'Oyly, English impresario; b. London, May 3, 1844; d. there, April 3, 1901. He studied at Univ. College in London; wrote an opera, *Dr. Ambrosias,* and songs; later turned to music management; he represented, among others, Gounod, Adelina Patti, and the tenor Mario. He then became interested in light opera and introduced in England Lecocq's *Giroflé-Girofla,* Offenbach's *La Périchole,* and other popular French operettas. His greatest achievement was the launching of comic operas by Gilbert and Sullivan; he commissioned and produced at the Royalty Theatre their *Trial by Jury* (1875) and then formed a syndicate to stage other productions of works by Gilbert and Sullivan at the London Opéra-Comique Theatre. Dissension within the syndicate induced him to build the Savoy Theatre (1881), which subsequently became celebrated as the home of Gilbert and Sullivan productions, with Carte himself as the leading "Savoyard." He successfully operated the Savoy Theatre until his death; the enterprise was continued by his wife (Helen Lenoir) until her death in 1913; thereafter by his sons, and finally by his granddaughter; it was disbanded in 1982. In 1887 Carte attempted to establish serious English opera through the building of a special theater (now known as the Palace Theatre), and the production in 1891 of Sullivan's grand opera *Ivanhoe*, followed by commissions to other English composers to write operas. D'Oyly Carte introduced many improvements in theatrical management, including the replacement of gaslight by electric illumination.

Bibl.: F. Cellier and C. Bridgeman, *Gilbert, Sullivan and d'O. C.* (London, 1914).

Carter, Benny (Bennett Lester), outstanding black American jazz instrumentalist, bandleader, arranger, and composer; b. N.Y., Aug. 8, 1907. He was mainly autodidact as a musician; after learning to play the piano as a child, he took up the trumpet and the alto saxophone. He worked with various bands (1923–28) before gaining wide recognition as a leading arranger. He led his own band (1932–34), then went to London, where he was an arranger for the BBC dance orch. (1936–38); concurrently he was active as an instrumentalist, a bandleader, and a recording artist. Upon his return to the U.S. in 1938, he led his own orch. in N.Y. (until 1940); he then organized a big band and settled in Los Angeles (1942). After 1946, he devoted himself mainly to composing and arranging scores for films and television, and also worked as an arranger for major jazz singers. He made occasional appearances as an instrumentalist in later years, including tours abroad, and also made a number of recordings. He also assumed a new role as a teacher, giving lectures at various univs. and colleges. One of the outstanding jazz alto saxophonists of his day, Carter also shone as a trumpeter, trombonist, clarinetist, and pianist. In 1974 he was awarded an honorary doctorate from Princeton Univ.

Bibl.: J. Evensmo et al., *The Alto Saxophone, Trumpet, and Clarinet of B. C., 1927–1946* (Hosle, Norway, 1982); M. Berger et al., *B. C.: A Life in American Music* (Metuchen, N.J., 1982).

Carter, Betty (née **Lillie Mae Jones**), black American jazz singer; b. Flint, Mich., May 16, 1930. She studied piano at the Detroit Cons.; began singing in local jazz clubs, on the same bill with such celebrated jazz artists as Charlie Parker, Miles Davis, and Dizzy Gillespie; then joined Lionel Hampton's band (1948–51). She gained widespread acclaim at the Newport Jazz Festivals at Carnegie Hall in 1977 and 1978. She soon rose to the loftiest plateau on the jazz firmament; her voice was remarkable for its operatic qualities and resourceful adaptation to quaquaversal situations.

Carter, Elliott (Cook, Jr.), outstanding American composer; b. N.Y., Dec. 11, 1908. After graduating from the Horace Mann High School in 1926, Carter entered Harvard Univ., majoring in literature and languages; at the same time studied piano at the Longy School of Music in Cambridge, Mass. In 1930 he devoted himself exclusively to music, taking up harmony and counterpoint with Walter Piston, and orchestration with Edward Burlingame Hill; also attended in 1932 a course given at Harvard Univ. by Gustav Holst. He obtained his M.A. in 1932, and then went to Paris, where he studied with Nadia Boulanger at the École Normale de Musique, receiving there a *licence de contrepoint*; in the interim he learned mathematics, Latin, and Greek. In 1935 he returned to America; was music director of the Ballet Caravan (1937–39); gave courses in music and also in mathematics, physics, and classical Greek at St. John's College in Annapolis, Md. (1939–41); then taught at the Peabody Cons. in Baltimore (1946–48). He was appointed to the faculty of Columbia Univ. (1948–50) and also taught at Yale Univ. from 1958 to 1962. In 1962 he was the American delegate at the East-West Encounter in Tokyo; in 1963 was composer-in-residence at the American Academy in Rome, and in 1964 held a similar post in West Berlin. In 1967–68 he was a professor-at-large at Cornell Univ. He held Guggenheim

fellowships in 1945 and 1950, and the American Prix de Rome in 1953. In 1965 he received the Creative Arts Award from Brandeis Univ. In 1953 he received 1st prize in the Concours International de Composition pour Quatuor à Cordes in Liège for his 1st String Quartet; in 1960 he received the Pulitzer Prize for his 2nd String Quartet, which also received the N.Y. Music Critics Circle Award and was further elected as the most important work of the year by the International Rostrum of Composers. He again won the Pulitzer, for his 3rd String Quartet, in 1973. In 1985 he was awarded the National Medal of Arts by President Reagan. His reputation as one of the most important American composers grew with every new work he produced; Stravinsky was quoted as saying that Carter's Double Concerto was the 1st true American masterpiece. The evolution of Carter's style of composition is marked by his constant preoccupation with taxonomic considerations. His early works are set in a neo-Classical style. He later absorbed the Schoenbergian method of composition with 12 tones; finally he developed a system of serial organization in which all parameters, including intervals, metric divisions, rhythm, counterpoint, harmony, and instrumental timbres, become parts of the total conception of each individual work. In this connection he introduced the term "metric modulation," in which secondary rhythms in a polyrhythmic section assume dominance expressed in constantly changing meters, often in such unusual time signatures as 10/16, 21/8, etc. Furthermore, he assigns to each participating instrument in a polyphonic work a special interval, a distinctive rhythmic figure, and a selective register, so that the individuality of each part is clearly outlined, a distribution which is often reinforced by placing the players at a specified distance from one another.

Works: *Tom and Lily,* comic opera in 1 act (1934); Flute Sonata (1934); *Tarantella* for Male Chorus and Orch. (1936); ballet, *The Ball Room Guide* (1937); *The Bridge,* oratorio (1937); *Madrigal Book* for Mixed Voices (1937); Concerto for English Horn (1937); ballet, *Pocahontas* (N.Y., May 24, 1939); *Heart Not So Heavy as Mine* for a cappella Chorus (1939); Suite for Quartet of Alto Saxophones (1939); *The Defense of Corinth,* after Rabelais, for Speaker, Men's Chorus, and Piano, 4-hands (Cambridge, Mass., March 12, 1942); Adagio for Viola and Piano (1943); Sym. No. 1 (Rochester, N.Y., April 27, 1944); *The Harmony of Morning* for Female Chorus and Small Orch. (N.Y., Feb. 25, 1945); *Canonic Suite* for 4 Clarinets (1945); *Warble for Lilac Time,* after Walt Whitman, for Soprano and Instruments (Yaddo, Sept. 14, 1946); Piano Sonata (1946); *The Minotaur,* ballet (N.Y., March 26, 1947); *Holiday Overture* for Orch. (Baltimore, Jan. 7, 1948); Woodwind Quintet (N.Y., Feb. 27, 1949); 8 pieces for 4 Timpani (1949; Nos. 3 and 6 composed and added in 1966); Cello Sonata (N.Y., Feb. 27, 1950); String Quartet (1951); 8 Études and a Fantasy, for Flute, Oboe, Clarinet, and Bassoon (N.Y., Oct. 28, 1952); Sonata for Flute, Oboe, Cello, and Harpsichord (N.Y., Nov. 19, 1953); Variations for Orch. (Louisville, April 21, 1956); 2nd String Quartet (1959); Double Concerto for Harpsichord and Piano with 2 Chamber Orchs. (N.Y., Sept. 6, 1961); Piano Concerto (Boston, Jan. 6, 1967); Concerto for Orch. (N.Y. Phil., Feb. 5, 1970); String Quartet No. 3 (1971); Brass Quintet (1974); Duo for Violin and Piano (1974); *A Mirror on Which to Dwell* for Soprano and 9 Players, to a cycle of 6 poems by Elizabeth Bishop (N.Y., Feb. 24, 1976); *A Symphony of 3 Orchestras* (N.Y., Feb. 17, 1977); *Syringa,* cantata for Soprano and Small Ensemble (N.Y., Dec. 10, 1978); *Night Fantasies* for Piano (1980); *In Sleep, in Thunder,* song cycle for Tenor and 14 Players, to poems by Robert Lowell (1981); *Triple Duo* for Paired Instruments: Flute/Clarinet; Violin/Cello; Piano/Percussion (1982; London, April 23, 1983); *Changes* for Guitar Solo (1983); *Penthode* for 5 Instrumental Quartets (1984–85; London, July 26, 1985); String Quartet No. 4 (1986); *A Celebration of Some 100 × 150 Notes* for Orch. (1987); Oboe Concerto (1987; Zürich, June 17, 1988); *Remembrance* for Orch. (1988); *Enchanted Preludes* for Flute and Cello (1988); Violin Concerto (1990).

Bibl.: A. Skulsky, "E. C.," *American Composers Alliance Bulletin* (Summer 1953); R.F. Goldman, "The Music of

E. C.," *Musical Quarterly* (April 1957); E. Stone and K. Stone, eds., *The Writings of E. C. An American Composer Looks at Modern Music* (N.Y., 1977); D. Schiff, *The Music of E. C.* (N.Y., 1982); idem, "E. C.," *Ovation* (Dec. 1983); C. Rosen, *The Musical Languages of E. C.* (Washington, D.C., 1984); R. Dreier, "E. C.," *Musical America* (Nov. 1988).

Carter, John, American jazz instrumentalist; b. Fort Worth, Texas, Sept. 24, 1929; d. Los Angeles, March 31, 1991. He played in jazz and blues groups throughout the Southwest in the 1940s and 1950s, then formed a quartet with Bobby Bradford (1965); he also played with Ornette Coleman, conducting an orch. performance of Coleman's music in 1965. His albums include *A Suite of Early American Folk Pieces for Solo Clarinet* (1979), *Clarinet Summit* (1984), and *Dance of the Love Ghosts.*

Carter, Maybelle ("Mother"), American folk and country music singer; b. Nickelsville, Va., May 10, 1909; d. Nashville, Tenn., Oct. 23, 1978. With other members of her family, she formed the famous singing group known as the Carter Family in 1927; through recordings and radio broadcasts, they led the way to the widespread popularity of mountain folk and country music; among their greatest successes were their versions of *Wildwood Flower, It Takes a Worried Man to Sing a Worried Song, Will the Circle Be Unbroken, Wabash Cannonball,* and *Amazing Grace.* In later years she appeared as a soloist on the "Grand Ole Opry" radio program in Nashville, where she displayed her talents as a guitarist, autoharpist, and songwriter. She also made appearances with her son-in-law, the singer **Johnny Cash.**

Carter, Ron(ald Levin), black American jazz double bass player; b. Ferndale, Mich., May 4, 1937. He took up the cello at 10 and the double bass at 17; then studied formally at the Eastman School of Music in Rochester, N.Y. (B.Mus., 1959), where he played in its Philharmonia Orch., and at the Manhattan School of Music in N.Y. (M.Mus., 1961). After playing in the Chico Hamilton quintet, he did stints with Cannonball Adderley, Thelonious Monk, and others; he then was a member of Miles Davis's quintet (1963–68). In subsequent years he worked with the N.Y. Jazz Quartet and led his own quartet. He publ. a method book for his instrument, *Building a Jazz Bass Line* (1966; 2nd ed., 1970).

Carterette, Edward (Calvin), respected American psychologist and acoustician; b. Mount Tabor, N.C., July 10, 1921. He studied mathematics at the Univ. of Chicago and psychology at Harvard Univ. and Indiana Univ. in Bloomington (Ph.D., 1957). After conducting research at MIT, Indiana Univ., and the Univ. of Calif. at Berkeley, he joined the faculty of the Univ. of Calif. at Los Angeles as prof. of experimental psychology (1968). He is noted for his studies in psychoacoustics and music cognition; he was associate ed. of the journal *Music Perception* (from 1982), and his books and numerous publ. articles include studies on perception of non-Western instruments, as well as the psychoacoustics of rhythm and musical memory.

Cartier, Jean-Baptiste, French violinist and composer; b. Avignon, May 28, 1765; d. Paris, 1841. He was a pupil of Viotti; was a violinist at the Grand Opéra (1791–1821); from 1804 to 1815 he was a member of the Imperial Orch. under Paisiello; then of the Royal Orch. (1815–30). He composed 2 operas; 2 syms.; sonatas, variations, duets, and études for violin; publ. a manual, *L'Art du violon* (Paris, 1798, 1801, 1803; reprinted, N.Y., 1973), containing selections from eminent French, Italian, and German masters of the 17th and 18th centuries.

Carulli, Ferdinando, Italian guitar player and composer; b. Naples, Feb. 20, 1770; d. Paris, Feb. 17, 1841. He went to Paris in 1808 and prospered there as a guitar teacher. He is generally regarded as the 1st guitarist to use his instrument for artistic performances; he publ. a method, *L'Harmonie appliquée à la guitarre* (Paris, 1825). His works number nearly 400 items, including concertos, quartets, trios, duos, fantasias, variations, and solos of all descriptions. In 1830 he composed a piece of program music for guitar entitled *Les Trois Jours,* descriptive of the days of the July 1830 revolution.

Caruso, Enrico (Errico), celebrated Italian tenor; b. Naples, Feb. 27, 1873; d. there, Aug. 2, 1921. He was the 18th child of a worker's family, his father being a machinist. All 17 children born before him died in infancy; 2 born after him survived. He sang Neapolitan ballads by ear; as a youth he applied for a part in *Mignon* at the Teatro Fondo in Naples, but was unable to follow the orch. at the rehearsal and had to be replaced by another singer. His 1st serious study was with Guglielmo Vergine (1891–94); he continued with Vincenzo Lombardi. His operatic debut took place at the Teatro Nuovo in Naples on Nov. 16, 1894, in *L'Amico Francesco,* by an amateur composer, Mario Morelli. In 1895 he appeared at the Teatro Fondo in *La Traviata, La Favorita,* and *Rigoletto;* during the following few seasons he added *Aida, Faust, Carmen, La Bohème,* and *Tosca* to his repertoire. The decisive turn in his career came when he was chosen to appear as leading tenor in the 1st performance of Giordano's *Fedora* (Teatro Lirico, Milan, Nov. 17, 1898), in which he made a great impression. Several important engagements followed. In 1899 and 1900 he sang in St. Petersburg and Moscow; between 1899 and 1903 he appeared in 4 summer seasons in Buenos Aires. The culmination of these successes was the coveted opportunity to sing at La Scala; he sang there in *La Bohème* (Dec. 26, 1900), and in the 1st performance of Mascagni's *Le Maschere* (Jan. 17, 1901). At the Teatro Lirico in Milan he took part in the 1st performances of Franchetti's *Germania* (March 11, 1902) and Cilea's *Adriana Lecouvreur* (Nov. 6, 1902). In the spring season of 1902 he appeared (with Melba) in Monte Carlo, and was reengaged there for 3 more seasons. He made his London debut as the Duke in *Rigoletto* (Covent Garden, May 14, 1902) and was immediately successful with the British public and press. He gave 25 performances in London until July 28, 1902, appearing with Melba, Nordica, and Calvé. In the season of 1902–3, Caruso sang in Rome and Lisbon; during the summer of 1903 he was in South America. Finally, on Nov. 23, 1903, he made his American debut at the Metropolitan Opera, in *Rigoletto.* After that memorable occasion, Caruso was connected with the Metropolitan to the end of his life. He traveled with various American opera companies from coast to coast; he happened to be performing in San Francisco when the 1906 earthquake nearly destroyed the city. He achieved his most spectacular successes in America, attended by enormous publicity. In 1907 Caruso sang in Germany (Leipzig, Hamburg, Berlin) and in Vienna; he was acclaimed there as enthusiastically as in the Anglo-Saxon and Latin countries. A complete list of his appearances is given in the appendix of his biography by Pierre Key and Bruno Zirato (Boston, 1922). Caruso's fees soared from $2 as a boy in Italy in 1891 to the fabulous sum of $15,000 for a single performance in Mexico City in 1920. He made recordings in the U.S. as early as 1902; his annual income from this source alone netted him $115,000 at the peak of his career. He excelled in realistic Italian operas; his Cavaradossi in *Tosca* and Canio in *Pagliacci* became models which every singer emulated. He sang several French operas; the German repertoire remained completely alien to him; his only appearances in Wagnerian roles were 3 performances of *Lohengrin* in Buenos Aires (1901). His voice possessed such natural warmth and great strength in the middle register that as a youth he was believed to be a baritone. The sustained quality of his bel canto was exceptional and enabled him to give superb interpretations of lyrical parts. For dramatic effect, he often resorted to the "coup de glotte" (which became known as the "Caruso sob"); here the singing gave way to intermittent vocalization without tonal precision. While Caruso was criticized for such usages from the musical standpoint, his characterizations on the stage were overwhelmingly impressive. Although of robust health, he abused it by unceasing activity. He was stricken with a throat hemorrhage during a performance at the Brooklyn Academy of Music (Dec. 11, 1920), but was able to sing in N.Y. one last time, on Dec. 24, 1920.

Several surgical operations were performed in an effort to arrest a pleurisy; Caruso was taken to Italy, but succumbed to the illness after several months of remission. He was known as a convivial person and a lover of fine food (a brand of macaroni was named after him). He possessed a gift for caricature; a collection of his drawings was publ. in N.Y. in 1922 (2nd ed., 1951). His private life was turbulent; his liaison (never legalized) with Ada Giachetti, by whom he had 2 sons, was painfully resolved by court proceedings in 1912, creating much disagreeable publicity; there were also suits brought against him by 2 American women. In 1906 the celebrated "monkey-house case" (in which Caruso was accused of improper behavior toward a lady while viewing the animals in Central Park) threatened for a while his continued success in America. On Aug. 20, 1918, he married Dorothy Park Benjamin of N.Y., over the strong opposition of her father, a rich industrialist. Caruso received numerous decorations from European governments, among them the Order of Commendatore of the Crown of Italy; the Légion d'honneur; and the Order of the Crown Eagle of Prussia. A fictional film biography, *The Great Caruso*, was made of his life in 1950.

BIBL.: E. Caruso, *How to Sing* (London, 1913; German tr. by A. Spanuth, *Wie man singen soll*, Berlin, 1914); J. Wagenmann, *E. C. und das Problem der Stimmbildung* (Altenburg, 1911); M. Flint, *C. and His Art* (N.Y., 1917); P. Key and B. Zirato, *E. C.* (Boston, 1922); E. Ledtner, *Erinnerungen an C.* (1922); S. Fucito and B. Beyer, *C. and the Art of Singing* (N.Y., 1922); P. Marafioti, *C.'s Method of Voice Production* (N.Y., 1922; new ed., 1981); D. Caruso and Mrs. T. Goddard, *Wings of Song: The Story of C.* (1928); C. Armin, *E. C.s Stimme und ihr Verhältnis zum Stauprinzip* (1929); N. Daspuro, *E. C.* (Milan, 1938); E. Gara, *C., Storia di un Emigrante* (Milan, 1947); D. Caruso, *E. C., His Life and Death* (N.Y., 1945); T. Ybarra, *C.: The Man of Naples and the Voice of Gold* (N.Y., 1953); F. Robinson, *C.: His Life in Pictures* (N.Y., 1957); J. Freestone and H. Drummond, *E. C.: His Recorded Legacy* (London, 1960); J. Bolig, *The Recordings of E. C.* (Dover, Del., 1973); H. Greenfield, *C.* (N.Y., 1983); M. Scott, *The Great C.: A Biography* (N.Y., 1988).

Carvalho, Caroline (née **Caroline-Marie Félix-Miolan**), French soprano; b. Puys, Seine-Inférieure, Dec. 31, 1827; d. near Dieppe, July 10, 1895. She entered the Paris Cons. at 12; studied under Duprez; made her operatic debut on Dec. 14, 1849, in *Lucia di Lammermoor* at the Opéra-Comique, where she was engaged from 1849 to 1855; from 1856 to 1867 she sang at the Théâtre-Lyrique, where she created the soprano parts in Gounod's *Faust, Roméo et Juliette*, and *Mireille*, and in Clapisson's *La Fanchonette*; from 1868 to 1885 she sang at the Paris Opéra and at the Opéra-Comique; also appeared in London, Berlin, Brussels, St. Petersburg, etc.; retired in 1885. In 1853 she married **Léon Carvalho**.

BIBL.: E. Accoyer-Spoll, *Mme. C.* (Paris, 1885).

Carvalho, Eleazar de, brilliant Brazilian conductor and composer; b. Iguatú (Ceará), July 28, 1912. His father was of Dutch extraction and his mother was part Indian. He studied in Fortaleza at the Apprentice Seaman's School; later joined the National Naval Corps in Rio de Janeiro and played tuba in the band. In 1941 he became assistant conductor of the Brazilian Sym. Orch. in Rio de Janeiro. In 1946 he went to the U.S. to study conducting with Koussevitzky at the Berkshire Music Center, and Koussevitzky invited him to conduct a pair of concerts with the Boston Sym. Orch. Carvalho demonstrated extraordinary ability and musicianship by leading all rehearsals and the concerts without score in a difficult program; his sense of perfect pitch is exceptional. He subsequently conducted a number of guest engagements with orchs. in America and in Europe. From 1963 to 1968 he was conductor of the St. Louis Sym. Orch.; during his tenure he introduced many modern works into his programs, much to the discomfiture of the financial backers of the orch.; still, he lasted a few seasons in St. Louis. From 1969 to 1973 he was conductor of the Hofstra Univ. Orch. in Hempstead, N.Y., which offered him a more

liberal esthetic climate; then returned to Brazil, where he became artistic director of the São Paulo State Sym. Orch. He married **Jocy de Oliveira.**

WORKS: 2 operas on Brazilian subjects: *Descuberta do Brasil* (Rio de Janeiro, June 19, 1939) and *Tiradentes* (Rio de Janeiro, Sept. 7, 1941, dealing with the exploits of a revolutionary dentist during the war of liberation); *Sinfonia branca* (1943); symphonic poems: *A Traicao* (1941); *Batalha Naval de Riachuelo* (1943); *Guararapes* (1945); 3 overtures; 2 trios; 2 string quartets; Violin Sonata; songs.

Carvalho, João de Sousa, eminent Portuguese pedagogue and composer; b. Estremoz, Feb. 22, 1745; d. Alentejo, 1798. He studied at the Colégio dos Santos Reis in Vila Viçosa and with Cotumacci at the Conservatorio di S. Onofrio in Naples; he then settled in Lisbon, where he became a member of the Brotherhood of St. Cecilia and prof. of counterpoint (1767), mestre (1769–73), and mestre de capela (1773–98) at the Seminário Patriarcal. He was the most gifted Portuguese composer of his day, excelling in both sacred and secular vocal music. In 1778 he became music teacher to the royal family.

WORKS: OPERAS (all 1st perf. in Lisbon unless otherwise noted): *La Nitteti* (Rome, Carnival 1766; not extant); *L'amore industrioso* (1769); *L'Eumene* (June 6, 1773); *L'Angelica* (July 25, 1778); *Perseo* (July 5, 1779); *Testoride argonauta* (July 5, 1780); *Seleuco rè di Siria* (July 5, 1781); *Everardo II rè di Lituania* (July 5, 1782); *Penelope nella partenza da Sparta* (Dec. 17, 1782); *Tomiri amazzone guerríera* (Dec. 17, 1783); *L'Endimione* (July 25, 1783); *Adrasto rè degli Argivi* (July 5, 1784); *Nettuno ed Eglé* (April 25?, 1785); *Alcione* (July 25, 1787); *Numa Pompilio II rè dei romani* (June 24, 1789); also sacred vocal pieces.

Carvalho (real name, **Carvaille**), **Léon,** distinguished French baritone and opera manager; b. Port-Louis, near Paris, Jan. 18, 1825; d. Paris, Dec. 29, 1897. He studied at the Paris Cons.; began his career as a singer; in 1853 married the French soprano **Caroline Carvalho.** From 1856 to 1868 he was director of the Théâtre-Lyrique; from 1869 to 1875 was chief producer at the Paris Opéra; concurrently was manager of the Théâtre du Vaudeville (1872–74); then acted as stage manager at the Opéra; from 1876 to 1887 was director of the Opéra-Comique, succeeding du Locle. After the fire at the Opéra-Comique in 1887, in which 131 persons perished, he was arrested and sentenced to 6 months' imprisonment, but was acquitted on appeal, and reinstated in 1891. He had the reputation of an enlightened administrator, encouraging young artists and young composers.

Carver, Robert, Scottish composer; b. 1487; d. after 1546. He was a Monk of Scone Abbey; developed a melismatic style of composition; wrote masses on the medieval song "L'Homme armé" and many motets, 1 of them in 19 independent parts. He is regarded as an equal of Dunstable in melodic and rhythmic excellence. Vol. 1 of his collected works was publ. by the American Inst. of Musicology, ed. by Denis Stevens, in 1959.

Cary, Annie Louise, celebrated American contralto; b. Wayne, Maine, Oct. 22, 1841; d. Norwalk, Conn., April 3, 1921. She studied in Boston and Milan; made her operatic debut in Copenhagen as Azucena; studied under Mme. Viardot-García at Baden-Baden; was engaged at Hamburg, Stockholm, Brussels, London, and St. Petersburg. Returning to the U.S., she continued her operatic career in N.Y. theaters; was the 1st American woman to sing a Wagnerian role in the U.S. (Ortrud in *Lohengrin*, 1877). She married C.M. Raymond in 1882, and retired at the height of her powers. She appeared in concert or oratorio in all leading cities of America.

Casabona, Francisco, Brazilian composer and pedagogue; b. São Paulo, Oct. 16, 1894. He studied in Brazil and in Italy; attended classes of Alessandro Longo (piano), Camillo de Nardis (theory), and Giovanni Barbieri (composition) at the Cons. of Naples. Returning to Brazil, he became a prof. at the São Paulo Cons. In his music, Casabona follows an Italianate expressive style, excelling equally in vocal and instrumental works.

WORKS: Comic operas: *Godiamo la Vita* (Rome, 1917) and *Principessa dell'Atelier* (Naples, 1918); symphonic poems: *Nero* (1915); *Crepúsculo Sertanejo* (1926); *Noite de São João* (1934); Sinfonia No. 1 (1937); Sinfonia No. 2 (1940); *La Fable d'Einstein* for Orch. (1946); *Maracatú*, Afro-Brazilian dance (1964); Violin Sonata; piano pieces in the Brazilian idiom; choruses and songs.

Casadesus, François Louis, French conductor and composer, brother of **Henri** and **Marius Casadesus;** b. Paris, Dec. 2, 1870; d. Suresnes, near Paris, June 27, 1954. He studied at the Paris Cons.; conducted the Opéra and the Opéra-Comique on tour in France (1890–92); in 1895 conducted the Opéra on a European tour; was the founder and director (1918–22) of the American Cons. at Fontainebleau; later was active as a radio conductor; wrote music criticism. A collection of valedictory articles was publ. in honor of his 80th birthday (Paris, 1950).

WORKS: Operas: *Cachaprès* (Brussels, 1914); *La Chanson de Paris* (1924); *Bertran de Born* (Monte Carlo, 1925); *Messie d'Amour* (Monte Carlo, 1928); *Symphonie scandinave; Au beau jardin de France* for Orch.; Sym. in E major; smaller compositions for orch.; numerous songs.

Casadesus, Gaby (née **Gabrielle L'Hôte**), French pianist and teacher; b. Marseilles, Aug. 9, 1901. She studied with Louis Diémer and Marguerite Long at the Paris Cons., where she won the premier prix in 1917; she then toured widely as a soloist, and later in duo concerts with her husband, **Robert Casadesus.** She devoted much time to pedagogy, serving on the faculties of the Salzburg Mozarteum, the Paris Schola Cantorum, and the American Cons. in Fontainebleau. In 1975 she helped organize the Robert Casadesus International Piano Competition in Cleveland.

Casadesus, Henri, French violinist, brother of **François** and **Marius Casadesus;** b. Paris, Sept. 30, 1879; d. there, May 31, 1947. He studied with Lavignac and Laforge in Paris; from 1910 to 1917 was a member of the Capet Quartet; was a founder and director of the Société Nouvelle des Instruments Anciens, in which he played the viola d'amore; subsequently toured in the U.S. Rare and ancient instruments collected by Casadesus are in the museum of the Boston Sym. Orch.

Casadesus, Jean (Claude Michel), French pianist, son of **Robert** and **Gaby Casadesus;** b. Paris, July 7, 1927; d. in an automobile accident, near Renfrew, Ontario, Canada, Jan. 20, 1972. He studied piano with his parents; at the outbreak of World War II, he went to the U.S.; studied at Princeton Univ.; won the contest for young soloists held by the Philadelphia Orch. in 1946; appeared as soloist with the N.Y. Phil. and with major European orchs.; made tours of the U.S. and Canada.

Casadesus, Jean-Claude, French conductor, nephew of **Robert** and **Gaby Casadesus;** b. Paris, Dec. 7, 1935. He studied at the Paris Cons.; in 1959 he received 1st prize as a percussion player there; he was then engaged as timpanist of the Concerts Colonne and of the Domaine Musical; also studied conducting with Dervaux at the École Normale de Musique and with Boulez in Basel. In 1969 he became resident conductor of the Paris Opéra and of the Opéra-Comique. In 1971 he became assistant conductor to Dervaux with the Orch. Philharmonique des Pays de la Loire in Angers. In 1976 he founded the Lille Phil. Orch.; also appeared as a guest conductor with the BBC Sym., Leningrad Phil., Scottish National Orch., Covent Garden, English National Opera, and other orchs. and opera houses in Europe. He was made an officer of the National Order of Merit for his services to French culture.

Casadesus, Marius, French violinist, brother of **Henri** and **François Casadesus;** b. Paris, Oct. 24, 1892; d. Suresnes (Paris), Oct. 13, 1981. He studied at the Paris Cons., graduating in 1914 with 1st prize in violin; subsequently toured in Europe and America; gave numerous sonata recitals with his nephew,

the pianist **Robert Casadesus.** He was a founding member of the Société Nouvelle des Instruments Anciens (1920–40), organized with the purpose of reviving old string instruments, such as the Quinton and Diskantgambe. He wrote a number of pieces for the violin, some choral music, and songs, but his most notorious contribution to violin literature was the so-called Adelaide Concerto, supposedly composed by Mozart when he was 10 years old and dedicated to the oldest daughter of Louis XV, Adelaide (hence the nickname). It was performed in Paris on Dec. 24, 1931, with considerable publicity, but skepticism arose when Casadesus failed to produce either the MS or a contemporary copy of it. In 1977, in the course of a litigation for his copyright as the arranger of the "Adelaide Concerto," Casadesus admitted that the piece was entirely his own work.

Casadesus, Robert, eminent French pianist and composer; b. Paris, April 7, 1899; d. there, Sept. 19, 1972. A scion of a remarkable musical family, he absorbed music at home from his earliest childhood. His uncles were **Henri, Marius,** and **François Casadesus;** another uncle, **Marcel Louis Lucien** (1882–1917), was a cellist, and his aunt Rose was a pianist. He received his formal musical education studying piano with Diémer and composition with Leroux at the Paris Cons. In 1922 he embarked on a wide-ranging tour as a concert pianist; after the outbreak of World War II he went to the U.S.; taught classes at various schools. After the war he taught at the American Cons. at Fontainebleau. He was a prolific composer; wrote 7 syms., of which the last was performed in N.Y. on Nov. 8, 1972. He appeared with his wife, **Gaby Casadesus,** in his Concerto for 2 Pianos and Orch. with the N.Y. Phil. on Nov. 25, 1950. He also wrote a Concerto for 3 Pianos and String Orch., which he performed for the 1st time with his wife and his son **Jean** in N.Y., July 24, 1965. As a pianist, Casadesus was distinguished for his Gallic sense of balance and fine gradation of tonal dynamics.

BIBL.: S. Stookes, *The Art of R. C.* (London, 1960); E. Feder, "R. C.: Composer, Performer, Pedagogue," *Ovation* (Aug. 1983).

Casals, Pablo (Pau Carlos Salvador Defilló), great Spanish cellist; b. Vendrell, Catalonia, Dec. 29, 1876; d. San Juan, Puerto Rico, Oct. 22, 1973. He was the 2nd child of a progeny orig. numbering 11, 7 of whom died at birth. Legend has it that Pablo Casals barely escaped the same fate when the umbilical cord became entangled around his neck and nearly choked him to death; another legend (supported by Casals himself) is that he was conceived when Brahms began his B-flat Major Quartet, of which Casals owned the original MS, and that he was born when Brahms completed its composition. This legend is rendered moot by the fact that the quartet in question was completed and performed before Casals was born. But even the ascertainable facts of the life of Casals make it a glorious legend. His father, the parish organist and choirmaster in Vendrell, gave Casals instruction in piano, violin, and organ. When Casals was 11 he 1st heard the cello performed by a group of traveling musicians, and decided to study the instrument. In 1888 his mother took him to Barcelona, where he enrolled in the Escuela Municipal de Música. There he studied cello with José García, music theory with José Rodoreda, and piano with Joaquín Malats and Francisco Costa Llobera. His progress as a cellist was nothing short of prodigious, and he was able to give a solo recital in Barcelona at the age of 14, on Feb. 23, 1891; he graduated with honors in 1893. Albéniz, who heard him play in a café trio, gave him a letter of introduction to Count Morphy, the private secretary to María Cristina, the Queen Regent, in Madrid. Casals was asked to play at informal concerts in the palace, and was granted a royal stipend for study in composition with Tomás Bretón. In 1893 he entered the Cons. de Música y Declamación in Madrid, where he attended chamber music classes of Jesús de Monasterio. He also played in the newly organized Quartet Soc. there (1894–95). In 1895 he went to Paris and, deprived of his stipend from Spain, earned a living by playing the 2nd cello in the theater orch. of the Folies Marigny. He decided to return to Spain, where he received, in 1896, an appointment to the faculty of the Escuela Municipal de Música in Barcelona; he was also principal cellist in the orch. of the Gran Teatro del Liceo. In 1897 he appeared as soloist with the Madrid Sym. Orch., and was awarded the Order of Carlos III from the Queen. His career as a cello virtuoso was now assured. In 1899 he played at the Crystal Palace in London, and was later given the honor of playing for Queen Victoria at her summer residence at Cowes, Isle of Wight. On Nov. 12, 1899, he appeared as a soloist at a prestigious Lamoureux Concert in Paris, and played with Lamoureux again on Dec. 17, 1899, obtaining exceptional success with both the public and the press. He toured Spain and the Netherlands with the pianist Harold Bauer (1900–1901); then made his 1st tour of the U.S. (1901–2). In 1903 he made a grand tour of South America. On Jan. 15, 1904, he was invited to play at the White House for President Theodore Roosevelt. In 1906 he became associated with the talented young Portuguese cellist Guilhermina Suggia, who studied with him and began to appear in concerts as Mme. P. Casals-Suggia, although they were not legally married. Their liaison was dissolved in 1912; in 1914 Casals married the American socialite and singer Susan Metcalfe; they became separated in 1928, but were not divorced until 1957. Continuing his brilliant career, Casals organized, in Paris, a concert trio with the pianist Cortot and the violinist Thibaud; they played concerts together until 1937. Casals also became interested in conducting, and in 1919 he organized, in Barcelona, the Orquesta Pau Casals and led its 1st concert on Oct. 13, 1920. With the outbreak of the Spanish Civil War in 1936, the Orquesta Pau Casals ceased its activities. Casals was an ardent supporter of the Spanish Republican government, and after its defeat vowed never to return to Spain until democracy was restored there. He settled in the French village of Prades, on the Spanish frontier; between 1939 and 1942 he made sporadic appearances as a cellist in the unoccupied zone of southern France and in Switzerland. So fierce was his opposition to the Franco regime in Spain that he even declined to appear in countries that recognized the totalitarian Spanish government, making an exception when he took part in a concert of chamber music in the White House on Nov. 13, 1961, at the invitation of President Kennedy, whom he admired. In June 1950 he resumed his career as conductor and cellist at the Prades Festival, organized in commemoration of the bicentennial of the death of Bach; he continued leading the Prades Festivals until 1966. He made his permanent residence in 1956, when he settled in San Juan, Puerto Rico (his mother was born there when the island was still under Spanish rule). In 1957 an annual Festival Casals was inaugurated there. During all these years he developed energetic activities as a pedagogue, leading master classes in Switzerland; Italy; Berkeley, Calif.; and Marlboro, Vt.; some of these sessions were televised. Casals was also a composer; perhaps his most effective work is *La sardana*, for an ensemble of cellos, which he composed in 1926. His oratorio *El pessebre* (The Manger) was performed for the first time in Acapulco, Mexico, on Dec. 17, 1960; in subsequent years he conducted numerous performances of the score. One of his last compositions was the *Himno a las Naciones Unidas* (Hymn of the United Nations); he conducted its 1st performance in a special concert at the United Nations on Oct. 24, 1971, 2 months before his 95th birthday. On Aug. 3, 1957, at the age of 80, Casals married his young pupil Marta Montañez; following his death, she married the pianist Eugene Istomin, on Feb. 15, 1975. Casals did not live to see the liberation of Spain from the Franco dictatorship, but he was posth. honored by the Spanish government of King Juan Carlos I, which issued in 1976 a commemorative postage stamp in honor of his 100th birthday. **BIBL.:** L. Littlehales, *P. C.* (N.Y., 1929; rev. ed., 1948); A. Conte, *La Légende de P. C.* (Perpignan, 1950); J. Corredor, *Conversations with C.* (an Eng. tr. of the 1954 French ed. by A. Mangeot; London, 1956); A. Seiler, *C.* (with many photographs by P. Moeschlin; Olten, 1956); P. and A. Kahn, *Joys and Sorrows: Reflections by P. C. as Told to Albert E. Kahn* (N.Y., 1970; French tr., Paris, 1970; Japanese tr., Tokyo, 1973); H. Kirk, *P. C. A Biography* (N.Y., 1974); D. Blum, *C. and the Art of Interpretation* (London, 1977); J. Lloyd Webber, ed., *Song of the Birds: Sayings, Stories, and Impressions of P. C.* (London, 1985).

Casamorata, Luigi Fernando, Italian composer and music editor; b. Würzburg, May 15, 1807; d. Florence, Sept. 24, 1881. He studied law and music in Florence; became co-ed. of the Florentine *Gazzetta Musicale* from its start (1842) and was the founder of the Istituto Musicale in Florence (1860); publ. its history, *Origine, storia e ordinamento dell'Istituto musicale fiorentino;* also publ. *Manuale di armonia* (1876). His ballets and operas were unsuccessful, and he turned to instrumental and choral works, of which he wrote many.

Casanova, André, French composer; b. Paris, Oct. 12, 1919. He studied law as well as music; took lessons with René Leibowitz and others in Paris. His music is cast in a neo-Classical framework, with some atonal deviations.

WORKS: Sym. No. 1 (1949); Sym. No. 2 for Chamber Orch. (1952; Nice, Feb. 20, 1971); *Ballade* for Clarinet and Chamber Orch. (1954–55); Capriccio for Oboe and Chamber Orch. (1960); *Anamorphoses* for Orch. (Strasbourg, June 21, 1963); Violin Concerto (1963); *La Clé d'argent,* lyric drama (1965); Trumpet Concerto (1966); *Le Bonheur dans le crime,* opera (1969); *Notturno,* ballet (Paris, June 20, 1972); Sym. No. 3, *Dithyrambe* (Paris, Feb. 13, 1973); *Récitatifs* for Orch. (Nice, Feb. 2, 1974).

Casanovas, Narciso, Spanish composer; b. Sabadell, near Barcelona, Feb. 17, 1747; d. Montserrat, April 1, 1799. He was a member of the famous Catalan school of Montserrat; was ordained a priest in 1763; served as organist at the Montserrat monastery. He wrote 5 motets, 13 Psalms, several litanies, and many works for organ. His Sonata in F (in Haydn's style) is reprinted in J. Nin's *17 sonates et pièces anciennes d'auteurs espagnols* (Paris, 1929).

Casavola, Franco, Italian composer; b. Modugno, July 13, 1891; d. Bari, July 7, 1955. He studied in Rome with Respighi; abandoned his academic pursuits, joined the futurist movement, and composed music glorifying the mechanical age; also wrote futurist poetry. Among his works in this genre is a ballet, *Fantasia meccanica,* and *La danza dell'elica* for Flute, Clarinet, Violin, Percussion, Wind Machine, and Blasting Machine. At a later period he changed his ideas and veered toward musical realism with Romantic overtones. His operas *Il gobbo del califfo* (Rome, May 4, 1929), *Astuzie d'amore* (Bari, Jan. 28, 1936), and *Salammbô* (1948) have been produced with some success; he also wrote 2 ballets, *L'alba di Don Giovanni* (1932) and *Il castello nel bosco* (1931).

Casazza, Elvira, Italian mezzo-soprano; b. Ferrara, Nov. 15, 1887; d. Milan, Jan. 24, 1965. She studied in Ferrara and Milan; made her debut in Varese in 1909; then sang at La Scala in Milan (1915–42); also sang at Covent Garden, London (1926, 1931). After her retirement, she taught voice in Pesaro and Rome.

Casella, Alfredo, outstanding Italian composer; b. Turin, July 25, 1883; d. Rome, March 5, 1947. He began to play the piano at the age of 4 and received his early instruction from his mother; in 1896 he went to Paris, and studied with Diémer and Fauré at the Paris Cons.; won 1st prize in piano in 1899. He made concert tours as pianist in Europe, including Russia; appeared as guest conductor with European orchs.; in 1912 conducted the Concerts Populaires at the Trocadéro; taught piano classes at the Paris Cons. from 1912 to 1915; returned to Rome and was appointed a prof. of piano at the Accademia di Santa Cecilia, as successor to Sgambati. In 1917 he founded the Società Nazionale di Musica (later the Società Italiana di Musica Moderna; since 1923 the Corporazione delle Musiche Nuove, Italian section of the ISCM). On Oct. 28, 1921, Casella made his American debut with the Philadelphia Orch. in the triple capacity of composer, conductor, and piano soloist; he also appeared as a guest conductor in Chicago, Detroit, Cincinnati, Cleveland, and Los Angeles; was conductor of the Boston Pops from 1927 to 1929, introducing a number of modern works, but failing to please the public. In 1928 he was awarded the 1st prize of $3,000 given by the Musical Fund Soc. in Philadelphia; in 1934 won the Coolidge Prize. In 1938 he returned to Italy, where he remained until his death. Apart from his activities as pianist, conductor, and composer, he was a prolific writer on music, and contributed numerous articles to various publications in Italy, France, Russia, Germany, and America; he possessed an enlightened cosmopolitan mind, which enabled him to penetrate the musical cultures of various nations; at the same time he steadfastly proclaimed his adherence to the ideals of Italian art. In his music he applied modernistic techniques to the old forms; his style may be termed neo-Classical, but in his early years he cultivated extreme modernism.

WORKS: OPERAS: *La donna serpente* (Rome, March 17, 1932); *La favola d'Orfeo* (Venice, Sept. 6, 1932); *Il deserto tentato,* mystery in 1 act (Florence, May 6, 1937). BALLETS: *Il convento veneziano* (1912; La Scala, Feb. 7, 1925); *La Giara,* "choreographic comedy" after Pirandello (Paris, Nov. 19, 1924; his most successful work); *La camera dei disegni,* for children (Rome, 1940); *La rosa del sogno* (Rome, 1943). ORCH.: Sym. No. 1, in B minor (1905); Sym. No. 2, in C minor (1908–9); Sym. No. 3, op. 63 (Chicago, March 27, 1941); Suite in C (1909); *Italia,* rhapsody based on folk themes (Paris, April 23, 1910); *Le Couvent sur l'eau,* symphonic suite based on the ballet *Il convento veneziano* (Paris, April 23, 1914); *Notte di Maggio* for Voice and Orch. (Paris, March 29, 1914); *Elegia eroica* (Rome, Jan. 21, 1917); *Pagine di guerra* (1916); *Pupazzetti,* 5 pieces for Puppets (1918); *Partita* for Piano and Orch. (N.Y., Oct. 29, 1925); *Scarlattiana,* on themes by Scarlatti, for Piano and Orch. (N.Y., Jan. 22, 1927); *Concerto romano* for Organ and Orch. (N.Y., March 11, 1927); Violin Concerto in A minor (Moscow, Oct. 8, 1928); *Introduzione, Aria e Toccata* (Rome, April 5, 1933); Concerto for Trio and Orch. (Berlin, Nov. 17, 1933); Concerto (Amsterdam, 1937); *Paganiniana,* on themes by Paganini (Vienna, 1942). VOCAL: *L'Adieu à la vie,* cycle of 4 Hindu lyrics after Tagore's *Gitanjali* (1915; also for Voice and Orch., 1926); *4 favole romanesche* (1923); *Ninna nanna popolare genovese* (1934); *3 canti sacri* for Baritone and Orch. (1943); *Missa solemnis pro pace* (1944). CHAMBER: *Barcarola e scherzo* for Flute and Piano (1904); 2 cello sonatas (1907, 1927); *Siciliana e burlesca* for Flute and Piano (1914; 2nd version for Piano Trio, 1917); 5 *pezzi* for String Quartet (1920); Concerto for String Quartet (1923–24; also arranged for String Orch.); *Serenata* for Clarinet, Bassoon, Trumpet, Violin, and Cello (1927); *Sinfonia* for Clarinet, Trumpet, Cello, and Piano (1932); Piano Trio (1933). PIANO: Many pieces, including 2 series of stylistic imitations, *À la manière de . . . :* Wagner, Fauré, Brahms, Debussy, Strauss, Franck (1911), and (in collaboration with Ravel) Borodin, d'Indy, Chabrier, Ravel (1913); *Sonatina* (1916); *A notte alta* (1917; also for Piano and Orch., 1921); *11 pezzi infantili* (1920); *2 ricercari sul nome Bach* (1932); 3 pieces for Pianola (1918). Casella orchestrated Balakirev's *Islamey;* ed. Beethoven's sonatas and piano works of Albéniz; arranged Mahler's 7th Sym. for piano, 4-hands.

WRITINGS: *L'evoluzione della musica* (publ. in Italian, French, and Eng. in parallel columns; 1919); *Igor Stravinsky* (1926; new ed., 1951); *"21 + 26"* (1931); *Il pianoforte* (1938); *I segreti della Giara* (1941; tr. into Eng. as *Music in My Time: The Memoirs of Alfredo Casella;* 1955); *La tecnica dell'orchestra contemporanea* (completed by V. Mortari; 1950).

BIBL.: L. Cortese, *A. C.* (Genoa, 1935); G. Gatti, *Musicisti moderni d'Italia e di fuori* (Bologna, 1925); idem, "In Memory of A. C.," *Musical Quarterly* (July 1947); a special number of *Rassegna Musicale* in honor of C.'s 60th birthday (May–June 1943); F. d'Amico & G. Gatti, eds., *A. C.* (Milan, 1958).

Cash, Johnny, American popular singer of partly Indian descent (one-quarter Cherokee); b. in a railroad shack near Kingsland, Ark., Feb. 26, 1932. He worked as a water boy in a farmer's family; sang Baptist hymns in church; at the age of 17 won $5 at a local amateur talent contest. In 1950 he enlisted in the U.S. Air Force; served in Germany, returning to the U.S. in 1954. He learned to play the guitar while in the service; in 1955 began a series of appearances on the radio and various country circuits specializing in country-western music, and soon began to compose his own songs, both lyrics and tunes. He could never learn to read the notes, a fact of no importance in his professional life. The subjects of his songs include the miseries of common folks as well as prison life. His most popular songs are *Folsom Prison Blues* (inspired by his imprisonment overnight in El Paso on the charge of smuggling tranquilizer tablets from Mexico) and *I Walk the Line.* He publ. *Man in Black* (Grand Rapids, Mich., 1975). In 1967 he married the well-known country-music singer **June Carter Cash** (b. Maces Spring, Va., June 23, 1929). His daughter by an earlier marriage, **Rosanne Cash** (b. Memphis, Tenn., May 24, 1955), is also a country-music singer.

BIBL.: C. Wren, *Winners Got Scars Too: The Life and Legends of J. C.* (N.Y., 1971); J. Smith, *The J. C. Discography* (Westport, Conn., 1985).

Casimiri, Raffaele Casimiro, Italian musicologist; b. Gualdo Tadino, Nov. 3, 1880; d. Rome, April 15, 1943. He studied in Padua; dedicated himself to musical journalism; also conducted church choirs in the provinces. He founded the ecclesiastical magazines *Psalterium* (1907) and *Sacri Concentus;* also *Note d'Archivio* (1924). His specialty was polyphonic music of the time of Palestrina, whose collected works he ed. (1939–42). He contributed numerous articles to Italian publications; some of his findings on Palestrina have been disputed; his ingenious hoax, which he unveiled in *Note d'Archivio* of March 1924, claiming a discovery of a notebook of Palestrina establishing the date of Palestrina's birth, was deliberately contrived to confute his learned colleagues; he exposed it in a series of scurrilous letters. He also composed 2 oratorios, several masses, motets, and offertories.

BIBL.: E. Dagnino, "R. C.," *Rassegna Musicale* (April 1943).

Casini, Giovanni Maria, Italian organist and composer; b. Florence, Dec. 16, 1652; d. there, Feb. 25, 1719. He studied composition in Florence, and later in Rome with Matteo Simonelli and Bernardo Pasquini (organ). He became a priest and served as organist at the Cathedral of Florence from 1703; retired in 1711 owing to ill health. As a keyboard composer, Casini represents the late Baroque style. As a theorist, he was a follower of Nicolo Vicentino and Giovanni Battista Doni in their studies of the music of Greek antiquity.

WORKS: *Canzonette spirituali* (Florence, 1703); a collection of motets for 4 Voices, op. 1 (Rome, 1706); *Responsori per la Settimana Santa,* op. 2 (Florence, 1706); *Pensieri per l'organo,* op. 3 (Florence, 1714); several oratorios.

Casken, John (Arthur), English composer; b. Barnsley, July 15, 1949. He studied music theory with John Joubert and Peter Dickinson at the Univ. of Birmingham (1967–71). Upon graduation he received a Polish government scholarship, and in 1971 went to Warsaw, where he took courses with Andrzej Dobrowolski at the Warsaw Cons. Upon his return to England he joined the music dept. at Birmingham Univ. (1973–79); then taught at Huddersfield Polytechnic (1979–81) and in 1981 became a lecturer of music at Durham Univ. As a composer, Casken was influenced by the developments of modern Polish music, and adopted a system of graphic music notation characteristic of modern techniques of composition in Poland and elsewhere. The influence of Lutoslawski is an important factor in Casken's music.

WORKS: *Kagura,* for 13 Wind Instruments, based on a medieval Japanese court ritual (1972); *Music for the Crabbing Sun* for Flute, Oboe, Cello, and Harpsichord (1974); *Music for a Tawny-Gold Day* for Viola, Alto Saxophone, Bass Clarinet, and Piano (1976); *Arenaria* for Flute, Harp, Piano, Percussion, and 9 String Instruments (1976); *Tableaux des trois âges* for an Instrumental Ensemble (1977); *Ia Orana, Gauguin* for Soprano and Piano (1978); *Firewhirl* for Voice and Piano (1978); Piano Concerto (1981; Manchester, Jan. 24, 1982); String Quartet (1981–82); *Erin* for Double Bass and Small Orch. (1982–83); *Orion over Farne* for Orch. (1984); *Salamandra, Fire-Haunt* for 2 Pianos (1986); *Golem*, chamber opera (1988).

Cassadó (Moreau), Gaspar, distinguished Spanish cellist, son of **Joaquín Cassadó (Valls);** b. Barcelona, Sept. 30, 1897; d. Madrid, Dec. 24, 1966. He studied cello with Casals; toured Europe; made his debut in N.Y. on Dec. 10, 1936; made another U.S. tour in 1949. He composed a Cello Sonata, a Cello Concerto, and other pieces for his instrument. His *Catalonian Rhapsody* for Orch. was performed by the N.Y. Phil. on Nov. 8, 1928. Cassadó also made arrangements for cello and orch. of a Mozart horn concerto and Weber's Clarinet Concerto.

Cassadó (Valls), Joaquín, Spanish organist and composer, father of **Gaspar Cassadó (Moreau);** b. Mataró, near Barcelona, Sept. 30, 1867; d. Barcelona, March 25, 1926. He served as a choir director and organist at several churches in Barcelona; wrote a comic opera, *El monjo negro* (Barcelona, Jan. 24, 1920); *Hispania* for Piano and Orch.; church music.

Cassel, (John) Walter, American baritone and teacher; b. Council Bluffs, Iowa, May 15, 1910. He studied voice with Harry Cooper in Council Bluffs, where he also received training in trumpet and piano; after attending Creighton Univ. in Omaha, he pursued vocal studies with Frank La Forge in N.Y. In 1938 he began singing on radio shows, and on Dec. 12, 1942, made his Metropolitan Opera debut in N.Y. as Brétigny in *Manon*, remaining on its roster until 1945, and then again from 1954 to 1970 and in 1973–74. On March 21, 1948, he made his 1st appearance at the N.Y. City Opera as Escamillo, singing there regularly until 1954, and then intermittently until 1969. He taught at Indiana Univ. in Bloomington (from 1974). He proved equally at home in both serious and light roles, but he was best known for his roles in operas by Wagner and R. Strauss. He sang the role of Horace Tabor in the 1st performance of Douglas Moore's *The Ballad of Baby Doe* (1956).

Cassilly, Richard, American tenor; b. Washington, D.C., Dec. 14, 1927. He studied at the Peabody Cons. in Baltimore; after singing Michele in Menotti's *The Saint of Bleecker Street* in N.Y. (1955), he made his N.Y. City Opera debut as Vakula in Tchaikovsky's *The Golden Slippers* (Oct. 13, 1955); was on its roster until 1959, and again from 1960 to 1963 and from 1964 to 1966. He made his European debut in Sutermeister's *Raskolnikoff* in Geneva (1965) and that same year sang at the Hamburg State Opera, where he appeared regularly (1966–77). He was concurrently a member of London's Covent Garden (1968–78) and also sang in major European opera centers. He made his Metropolitan Opera debut in N.Y. as Radames on Jan. 20, 1973. He resumed his association with the Metropolitan Opera in 1978, and subsequently appeared in such roles as Tannhäuser, Don José, Tristan, Samson, Otello, Jimmy Mahoney in *Mahagonny*, and Captain Vere in *Billy Budd*.

Cassiodorus, Magnus Aurelius, Roman historian, statesman, and monk; b. Scyllacium (Squillace), Bruttii, c.485; d. Vivarese, Calabria, c.580. He was a contemporary of Boetius; held various civil offices under Theodoric and Athalaric until c.540, when he retired. He founded the monasteries of Castellum and Vivarium; at the latter he wrote his *De artibus ac disciplinis liberalium litterarum;* the section treating of music, *Institutiones musicae,* a valuable source, is printed in Gerbert's *Scriptores,* vol. I; a partial reproduction is to be found in Strunk's *Source Readings in Music History* (N.Y., 1950).
BIBL.: A. Franz, *A. C.* (1872); G. Wille, *Musica Romana* (Amsterdam, 1967).

Cassirer, Fritz, German conductor and writer on music; b. Breslau, March 29, 1871; d. Berlin, Nov. 26, 1926. He first studied philosophy (1889–92); then turned to music; was an orch. and operatic conductor in many German towns; also in London (1905–7).
WRITINGS: *Edgar,* a poem (1894); "Beethovens Briefe," *Die*

Musik (1909); *Helldunkle Weltgeschichte* (1920; pseudonym: Friedrich Leopold); *Beethoven und die Gestalt* (1925).

Cassuto, Alvaro (Leon), Portuguese conductor and composer; b. Oporto, Nov. 17, 1938. He studied violin and piano as a small child; then took courses in composition with Artur Santos and Lopes Graça. During the season 1960–61 he attended classes in new music in Darmstadt, Germany, with Ligeti, Messiaen, and Stockhausen, and at the same time had instruction in conducting with Herbert von Karajan. He further studied conducting with Pedro de Freitas Branco in Lisbon and Franco Ferrara in Hilversum, the Netherlands. He served as an assistant conductor of the Gulbenkian Orch. in Lisbon (1965–68) and with the Little Orch. in N.Y. (1968–70). In 1970 he was appointed permanent conductor of the National Radio Orch. of Lisbon, and in 1975 was elected its music director. In 1974 he was appointed a lecturer in music and conductor of the Sym. Orch. of the Univ. of Calif. at Irvine, remaining there until 1979. From 1979 to 1985 he was music director of the Rhode Island Phil. in Providence, and from 1981 to 1987 the music director of the National Orchestral Assoc. in N.Y. He also was guest conductor of numerous orchs. in Europe, South America, and the U.S. In 1969 he received the Koussevitzky Prize in Tanglewood. A progressive-minded and scholarly musician, he amassed a large repertoire of both classical and modern works, displaying a confident expertise. He is also a composer of several orch. works in a modern idiom, as well as of chamber pieces.
WORKS: *Sinfonia breve No. 1* (Lisbon, Aug. 29, 1959); *Sinfonia breve No. 2* (1960); Variations for Orch. (1961); *Permutations* for 2 Orchs. (1962); String Sextet (1962); Concertino for Piano and Orch. (1965); *Cro (mo-no)fonia* for 20 String Instruments (1967); *Canticum in Tenebris* for Soloists, Chorus, and Orch. (1968); *Evocations* for Orch. (1969); *Circle* for Orch. (1971); *In the Name of Peace,* 1-act opera (1971); *Song of Loneliness* for 12 Players (1972); *To Love and Peace,* symphonic poem (1973); *Homage to My People,* suite for Band on Portuguese folk songs (1977); *Return to the Future* for Orch. (1985); *The 4 Seasons* for Piano and Orch. (1986).

Castagna, Bruna, Italian mezzo-soprano; b. Bari, Oct. 15, 1905; d. Pinamar, Argentina, July 10, 1983. She learned to play the piano; then went to Milan to study voice with Tina Scognamiglio; made her debut at Mantua in 1925; then traveled to South America, where she sang for 3 seasons at the Teatro Colón in Buenos Aires and in the provinces (1927–30). Returning to Italy, she sang at La Scala in Milan; then made guest appearances in the U.S. in Chicago, St. Louis, and San Francisco. On March 2, 1936, she successfully performed at the Metropolitan Opera House in N.Y. as Amneris in *Il Trovatore;* there followed a far-flung tour, in Australia, Brazil, Egypt, Rumania, and Spain. Eventually she made her home in Argentina. Her most applauded role was Carmen.

Castaldi, Alfonso, Italian-born Rumanian composer; b. Maddalone, April 23, 1874; d. Bucharest, Aug. 6, 1942. He studied at the Cons. in Naples with Francisco Cilea and Umberto Giordano; taught at the Bucharest Cons. (1904–40), and was greatly esteemed as a pedagogue. He wrote several operas in an Italianate style; the symphonic poems *Thalassa* (1906) and *Marsyas* (1907); a Sym. (1920); 3 string quartets; other chamber music; numerous choruses.
BIBL.: Z. Vancea, *Creatia muzicală romaneâscă sec. XIX–XX* (Bucharest, 1968).

Castaldo, Joseph, American composer; b. N.Y., Dec. 23, 1927. He studied in N.Y. and was active as a clarinetist; he then joined classes in composition at the Accademia di Santa Cecilia in Rome (1947). Returning to the U.S., he had special courses with Giannini at the Manhattan School of Music in N.Y. and with Persichetti at the Philadelphia Cons. (B.M., M.M.), where he subsequently was appointed chairman of composition and theory (1960); when it merged with the Philadelphia Musical Academy in 1966, he assumed the presidency; he continued in this capacity (until 1983) when it became the Philadelphia

College of Performing Arts (1976). Among his works are *Lacrimosa I* (1976) and *II* (1977) for Strings; a Cello Concerto (1984); *Theoria* for Wind Ensemble, Piano, and Percussion (1971; rev. 1972); a cantata, *Flight* (1960); 2 string quartets; *Dichotomy* for Woodwind Quintet; and choruses.

Castan, Comte Armand de. See **Castelmary.**

Castel, Louis-Bertrand, French acoustician; b. Montpellier, Nov. 11, 1688; d. Paris, Jan. 9, 1757. He became interested in Newton's observation on the correspondence, in proportionate breadth, of the 7 prismatic rays with the string-lengths required for the scale *re, mi, fa, sol, la, si, do;* acting upon this observation, he attempted the construction of a "clavecin oculaire," to produce color-harmonies for the eye as the ordinary harpsichord produces tone-harmonies for the ear. His theory is explained in an essay, *Nouvelles expériences d'optique et d'acoustique* (1735; Eng. tr., London, 1757).

Castelmary (real name, **Comte Armand de Castan**), French bass; b. Toulouse, Aug. 16, 1834; d. N.Y., Feb. 10, 1897, on the stage of the Metropolitan Opera House, just after the 1st act of *Martha.* He made his operatic debut at the Paris Opéra (1863); remained there till 1870; then sang in London and N.Y.; made his debut at the Metropolitan on Nov. 29, 1893, as Vulcan in *Philemon;* was particularly successful as Méphistophélès in *Faust.*

Castelnuovo-Tedesco, Mario, greatly significant Italian-born American composer; b. Florence, April 3, 1895; d. Los Angeles, March 16, 1968. He studied at the Cherubini Inst. with del Valle (piano) and Pizzetti (composition); he began to compose at an early age; his 1st organized composition, *Cielo di settembre* for Piano, revealed impressionistic tendencies. He wrote a patriotic song, *Fuori i barbari,* during World War I. He attained considerable eminence in Italy between the 2 wars, and his music was often heard at European festivals. Political events forced him to leave Italy; in 1939 he settled in the U.S. In 1946 he became a naturalized citizen. He became active as a composer for films in Hollywood, but continued to write large amounts of orch. and chamber music. His style is remarkably fluent and adaptable to the various moods evoked in his music, often reaching rhapsodic eloquence.

WORKS: OPERAS: *La mandragola* (libretto by the composer, after Machiavelli; Venice, May 4, 1926; won the National Prize); *The Princess and the Pea,* after Andersen, overture with Narrator (1943); *Bacco in Toscana,* dithyramb for Voices and Orch. (Milan, May 8, 1931); *Aucassin et Nicolette,* puppet show with Voices and Instruments (1938; Florence, June 2, 1952); *All's Well That Ends Well,* after Shakespeare (1959); *Saul,* biblical opera (1960); *Il Mercante di Venezia,* after Shakespeare (Florence, May 25, 1961); *The Importance of Being Earnest,* after Oscar Wilde, chamber opera (1962); *The Song of Songs,* scenic oratorio (Hollywood, Aug. 7, 1963); *Tobias and the Angel,* scenic oratorio (1965). **BIBLICAL ORATORIOS:** *Ruth* (1949) and *Jonah* (1951). **ORCH.:** *Cipressi* (Boston, Oct. 25, 1940; orig. for Piano, 1920); Piano Concerto No. 1 (Rome, Dec. 9, 1928); Piano Concerto No. 2 (N.Y. Phil., Nov. 2, 1939, composer soloist); 3 violin concertos: *Concerto italiano* (Rome, Jan. 31, 1926); *The Prophets* (N.Y., April 12, 1933); 3rd Violin Concerto (1939); Cello Concerto (N.Y. Phil., Jan. 31, 1935; Piatigorsky, soloist; Toscanini conducting); *Variazioni sinfoniche* for Violin and Orch. (Rome, 1930); overtures to Shakespeare's plays: *The Taming of the Shrew* (1930); *Twelfth Night* (1933); *The Merchant of Venice* (1933); *Julius Caesar* (1934); *A Midsummer Night's Dream* (1940); *Coriolanus* (1947); etc.; *Poem* for Violin and Orch. (1942); *The Birthday of the Infanta* (1942; New Orleans, Jan. 28, 1947); *Indian Songs and Dances,* suite (Los Angeles, Jan. 7, 1943); *An American Rhapsody* (1943); Serenade for Guitar and Orch. (1943); *Octoroon Ball,* ballet suite (1947); *Noah's Ark,* movement for Narrator and Orch., from *Genesis,* a suite; other movements by Schoenberg, Stravinsky, Toch, Milhaud, Tansman, and N. Shilkret, who commissioned the work (Portland, Oreg., Dec. 15, 1947). **CHAMBER:** *Signorine: 2 profili* for Violin and Piano (1918); *Ritmi* for Violin and

Piano (1920); *Capitan Fracassa* for Violin and Piano (1920); *Notturno adriatico* for Violin and Piano (1922); *I nottambuli* for Cello and Piano (1927); Cello Sonata (1928); 1st Piano Trio (1928); 1st String Quartet (1929); *Sonata quasi una fantasia* for Violin and Piano (1929); *The Lark* for Violin and Piano (1930); 1st Piano Quintet (1932); 2nd Piano Trio (1932); Toccata for Cello and Piano (1935); *Capriccio diabolico* for Guitar (1935; later arranged as a guitar concerto); Concertino for Harp and 7 Instruments (1937); *Ballade* for Violin and Piano (1940); Divertimento for 2 Flutes (1943); Sonata for Violin and Viola (1945); Clarinet Sonata (1945); Sonatina for Bassoon and Piano (1946); 2nd String Quartet (1948); Quintet for Guitar and Strings (1950); Sonata for Viola and Cello (1950); Fantasia for Guitar and Piano (1950); *Concerto da camera* for Oboe and Strings (1950); Sonata for Violin and Cello (1950); 2nd Piano Quintet (1951). **PIANO:** *English Suite* (1909); *Questo fu il carro della morte* (1913); *Il raggio verde* (1916); *Alghe* (1919); *I naviganti* (1919); *La sirenetta e il pesce turchino* (1920); *Cantico* (1920); *Vitalba e Biancospino* (1921); *Epigrafe* (1922); *Alt-Wien,* Viennese rhapsody (1923); *Piedigrotta* (1924); *Le stagioni* (1924); *Le danze del Re David* (1925); *3 poemi campestri* (1926); *3 corali su melodie ebraiche* (1926); Sonata (1928); *Crinoline* (1929); *Candide,* 6 pieces (1944); *6 canoni* (1950). **SONGS:** *Le Roy Loys* (1914); *Ninna-Nanna* (1914; very popular); *Fuori i barbari,* a patriotic song (1915); *Stelle cadenti* (1915); *Coplas* (1915); *Briciole* (1916); *3 fioretti di Santo Francesco* (1919; also with Orch.); *Girotondo de golosi* (1920); *Étoile filante* (1920); *L'infinito* (1921); *Sera* (1921); *2 preghiere per i bimbi d'Italia* (1923); *1830,* after Alfred de Musset (1924); *Scherzi,* 2 series (1924–25); music to 33 Shakespeare songs (1921–25); *Indian Serenade* (1925); *Cadix* (1926); *3 Sonnets from the Portuguese,* after E.B. Browning (1926); *Laura di Nostra Donna* (1935); *Un sonetto di Dante* (1939); *Recuerdo* (1940); *Le Rossignol* (1942); *The Daffodils* (1940). **CHORAL:** 2 madrigals a cappella (1915); *Lecho dodi,* synagogue chant for Tenor, Men's Voices, and Organ (1936); *Sacred Synagogue Service* (1943); *Liberty, Mother of Exiles* (1944). Numerous pieces for guitar, including: *Les Guitares bien temperées,* 24 preludes and fugues for 2 Guitars (1962); 2 guitar concertos (1939, 1953); Concerto for 2 Guitars and Orch. (1962); 3rd String Quartet (1964); Sonatina for Flute and Guitar (1965); Sonata for Cello and Harp (1966).

BIBL.: G. Rossi-Daria, "M. C.-T.," *Chesterian* (Jan.–Feb. 1926); R. von Weber, "M. C.-T.," in D. Ewen, ed., *The Book of Modern Composers* (N.Y., 1942; 3rd ed., 1961); N. Rossi, *Complete Catalogue of Works by M. C.-T.* (N.Y., 1977); B. Scalin, *Operas by M. C.-T.* (diss., Northwestern Univ., 1980).

Castéra, René d'Avezac, French composer; b. Dax, Landes, April 3, 1873; d. Angoume, Landes, Oct. 8, 1955. He studied at the Paris Schola Cantorum with d'Indy and Guilmant. In 1902 he founded the Édition Mutuelle for the publication of works by French composers. He wrote an opera, some symphonic pieces, a Piano Trio, Violin Sonata, songs, and character pieces for piano.

Castiglioni, Niccolò, Italian pianist and composer of avant-garde tendencies; b. Milan, July 17, 1932. He studied composition with Ghedini, Desderi, and Margola at the Verdi Cons. in Milan, and piano with Gulda at the Mozarteum in Salzburg; also took composition lessons with Blacher. He began his career as a pianist; in 1966 emigrated to the U.S.; was composer-in-residence at the Center of Creative and Performing Arts at the State Univ. of N.Y. in Buffalo (1966–67); then was on the faculty of the Univ. of Michigan (1967) and Univ. of Washington at Seattle (1968–69); in 1970 he was appointed instructor at the Univ. of Calif. in San Diego. In his music he follows a pragmatically modernistic line of composition, making use of any and all mannerisms of the neo-Classical, neo-Romantic, and experimental resources while preserving a necessary minimum of communicable sound production.

WORKS: Opera, *Uomini e no* (1955); radio opera, *Attraverso lo specchio* (Through the Looking Glass), after Lewis Carroll (1961; Italian Radio, Oct. 1, 1961); chamber opera, *Jabber-*

wocky, after Lewis Carroll (1962); 1-act opera, *Sweet,* for Baritone, Piano, Bells, and Winds (Rome, 1968); opera-triptych, *3 Mystery Plays* (Rome, Oct. 2, 1968; material made up of *Silence, Chordination,* and *The Rise and Rebellion of Lucifer and Aria*); *Concertino per la notte di Natale* for Strings and Woodwinds (1952); Sym. No. 1 for Soprano and Orch., to a text by Nietzsche (Venice, Sept. 15, 1956); Sym. No. 2 (1956–57; Italian Radio, Nov. 23, 1957); *Canti* for Orch. (1956); *Ouverture in tre tempi* (1957); *Elegia* for 19 Instruments and Soprano (1957); *Impromptus* for Orch. (1957–58); *Inizio di movimento* for Piano (1958); *Movimento continuato* for Piano and 11 Instruments (1958–59); *Sequenze* for Orch. (1959); *Tropi* for 6 Players (1959); *Aprèslude* for Orch. (1959); *Cangianti* for Piano (1959); *Eine kleine Weihnachtsmusik* (A Little Christmas Music) for Chamber Orch. (1959–60); *Disegni* for Chamber Orch. (1960); *Gymel* for Flute and Piano (1960); *Rondels* for Orch. (1960–61); *Décors* for Orch. (1962); *Consonante* for Flute and Chamber Orch. (1962); *Synchromie* for Orch. (1963); Concerto for Orch. (1963); *A Solemn Music I,* after Milton, for Soprano and Chamber Orch. (1963); *Gyro* for Chorus and 9 Instruments (1963); *Caractères* for Orch. (1964); *A Solemn Music II,* a rev. version of *I* (1964–65); *Figure,* a mobile for Voice and Orch. (1965); *Alef* for Solo Oboe (1965); *Anthem,* composition in 5 strophes for Chorus and Orch. (1966); *Ode* for 2 Pianos, Wind Instruments, and Percussion (1966); *Canzoni* for Soprano and Orch. (Naples, Oct. 18, 1966); *Carmina* for Chamber Ensemble (1967); *Sinfonia guerriere et amorose* for Organ (1967); *Granulation* for 2 Flutes and 2 Clarinets (1967); *Masques* for 12 Instruments, a bouillabaisse of polytonally arranged fragments of dimly remembered tunes by other composers (1967); *The New Melusine* for String Quartet (1969); *La Chant du signe,* concerto for Flute and Orch. (1969); *Sinfonia in Do,* after Ben Jonson, Dante, Shakespeare, and Keats, for Chorus and Orch. (1968–69; Rome, May 21, 1971); *Sinfonia con giardino* for Orch. (1978); *Couplets* for Harpsichord and Orch. (1979); *Le favole di Esopo,* oratorio for Chorus and Orch. (1980); Concerto for 3 Pianos and Orch. (1983); *Geistliches Lied* for Soprano and Orch. (1983).

Castil-Blaze. See Blaze, François-Henri-Joseph.

Castilla, Alberto, Colombian composer; b. Bogotá, April 9, 1883; d. Ibague, June 10, 1937. He studied engineering; was at one time connected with the government of Colombia. In 1898 he settled in Tolima, where he founded a music school. He wrote a number of songs, some of which achieved popularity. In 1954 the Colombian government issued a postage stamp in his honor.

Castillon (de Saint-Victor), (Marie) Alexis, French composer; b. Chartres, Dec. 13, 1838; d. Paris, March 5, 1873. He pursued a military career before turning to music. He studied with Victor Massé, and later took lessons with César Franck; was one of the founders of the Société Nationale de Musique. He composed mainly for chamber music groups; also wrote a Sym., 2 overtures, a Mass, and other religious music; his Piano Concerto was accepted for performance by Saint-Saëns, but was utterly unsuccessful.

Castleman, Charles (Martin), American violinist; b. Quincy, Mass., May 22, 1941. A *wunderkind* since his cradle, he appeared as a soloist with Arthur Fiedler and the Boston Pops Orch. at the age of 7; when he grew up he entered the Curtis Inst. of Music in Philadelphia as a student of Ivan Galamian; also received sporadic counsel from Josef Gingold, Henryk Szeryng, and David Oistrakh. In 1970 he founded the Quartet Program in Troy, N.Y., with the aim of promoting professional chamber groups. He played in the New String Trio of N.Y. (1972–75); then in the Raphael Trio, with which he made tours abroad. In 1975 he joined the violin faculty at the Eastman School of Music in Rochester, N.Y. He commissioned and gave the world premiere of David Amram's Violin Concerto in St. Louis in 1981.

Caston, Saul (real name, **Solomon Cohen**), American trumpet player and conductor; b. N.Y., Aug. 22, 1901; d. Winston-Salem, N.C., July 28, 1970. He studied at the Curtis Inst. in Philadelphia with Abram Chasins (piano), Scalero (composition), and Reiner (conducting); played trumpet in the Philadelphia Orch. (1918–45); taught trumpet at the Curtis Inst. (1924–42); was associate conductor of the Philadelphia Orch. (1936–45), conductor of the Reading Sym. Orch. (1941–44); in 1944 was appointed conductor of the Denver Sym. Orch., retiring in 1964.

Castro, Jean (Juan) de, composer; b. probably in Liège, c.1540; d. c.1611. From 1582 to 1584 he was assistant choirmaster in Vienna; later (1593–96), in Cleve, near Cologne. **Works:** *Missae à 3* (Cologne, 1599); *Sacrae cantiones,* 5–8 parts (1571), 3 parts (1593, 1596), and 5–8 parts (1588); *Tricinia sacra* (1574); *Bicinia sacra* (1594); *Chansons, Odes et Sonnets par P. Ronsard à 4–8 voix* (1576); *Cantiones sacra* (1591; reprinted in Denkmäler Rheinischer Musik, 16, 1972); *Chansons, Stances, Sonnets et Épigrammes à 2 voix* (Antwerp, 1592); *Quintines, Sextines, Sonnets à 5 voix* (1594). Many of these works are of interest because of the exact rhythmical arrangement of the verses.

Castro, José María, Argentine composer and conductor, brother of **Juan José** and **Washington Castro;** b. Avellaneda, near Buenos Aires, Dec. 15, 1892; d. Buenos Aires, Aug. 2, 1964. He studied in Buenos Aires; then went to Paris, and like his brother Juan José, took a course with Vincent d'Indy. Returning to Argentina in 1930, he became conductor of the Orquesta Filharmónica in Buenos Aires; from 1933 to 1953 also led the Banda Municipal de la Ciudad de Buenos Aires. **Works:** 3 ballets: *Georgia* (1937; Buenos Aires, June 2, 1939; composer conducting), *El sueño de la botella* (1948), and *Falarka* (1951); a monodrama, *La otra voz* (1953); *Concerto grosso* (1932; Buenos Aires, June 11, 1933); *Obertura para una ópera cómica* (1934); Piano Concerto (Buenos Aires, Nov. 17, 1941; rev. 1955); Concerto for Orch. (1944); Concerto for Cello and 17 Instruments (1945); *Tres pastorales* for Orch. (1945); *Preludio y Toccata* for String Quartet and String Orch. (1949); *Tema coral con variaciones* for Orch. (1952); Concerto for Violin and 18 Instruments (1953); *Diez improvisaciones breves* for Chamber Orch. or Piano (1957); *Preludio, Tema con variaciones y Final* for Orch. (1959); *Sinfonía de Buenos Aires* (1963); *El libro de los sonetos* for Voice and Orch. (1947); *Cinco líricas* for Voice and Orch. (1958); 13 sonnets, *Con la patria adentro,* for Tenor and Orch. (1964); Violin Sonata (1918); Sonata for Cello and Violin (1933); Sonata for 2 Cellos (1938); 3 string quartets (1943, 1947, 1956); *Sonata poética* for Violin and Piano (1957); 6 piano sonatas (1919; 1924; 1927; 1931; *Sonata de primavera,* 1939; *Sonata dramática,* 1944); piano pieces.
Bibl.: N. Ceñal, "J.M. C. (1892–1964)," *Revista del Instituto de Investigación Musicológica Carlos Vega,* No. 7 (Buenos Aires, 1986).

Castro, Juan José, eminent Argentine composer and conductor, brother of **José María** and **Washington Castro;** b. Avellaneda, near Buenos Aires, March 7, 1895; d. Buenos Aires, Sept. 3, 1968. After study in Buenos Aires he went to Paris, where he took a course in composition with Vincent d'Indy. Returning to Argentina in 1929, he organized in Buenos Aires the Orquesta de Nacimiento, which he conducted; in 1930 he conducted the ballet season at the Teatro Colón; conducted opera there from 1933; also became the music director of the Asociación del Profesorado Orquestal and Asociación Sinfónica, with which he gave 1st local performances of a number of modern works. In 1934 he received a Guggenheim Foundation grant. From 1947 to 1951 he conducted in Cuba and Uruguay; from 1952 to 1953 he was principal conductor of the Victorian Sym. Orch. in Melbourne, Australia; in 1955 he returned to Argentina; from 1956 to 1960 he was conductor of the Orquesta Sinfónica Nacional in Buenos Aires; from 1959 to 1964 was director of the Cons. of San Juan, Puerto Rico. He was proficient in all genres of composition, but his works were rarely performed outside South America, and he himself conducted most of his symphonic compositions.

WORKS: His most signal success on the international scene was the prize he received at the contest for the best opera at La Scala in Milan, for *Proserpina e lo straniero* (in the original Spanish, *Proserpina y el extranjero*), of which he conducted the 1st perf. at La Scala in Milan on March 17, 1952; his other operas were *La Zapatera prodigiosa*, after García Lorca (Montevideo, Dec. 23, 1949); *Bodas de sangre*, also after Lorca (Buenos Aires, Aug. 9, 1956); *Cosecha negra* (1961). Ballets: *Mekhano* (Buenos Aires, July 17, 1937) and *Offenbachiana* (Buenos Aires, May 25, 1940); 5 syms.: No. 1 (1931); *Sinfonía biblica* for Orch. and Chorus (1932); *Sinfonía Argentina* (Buenos Aires, Nov. 29, 1936); *Sinfonía de los campos* (Buenos Aires, Oct. 29, 1939); No. 5 (1956); *Dans le jardin des morts* (Buenos Aires, Oct. 5, 1924); *A una madre* (Buenos Aires, Oct. 27, 1925); *La Chellah*, symphonic poem based on an Arabian theme (Buenos Aires, Sept. 10, 1927); *Allegro, Lento y Vivace* (1931); *Anunciación, Entrada a Jerusalem, Golgotha* (Buenos Aires, Nov. 15, 1932); *Corales criollos* No. 3, symphonic poem (1953; won 1st prize at the Caracas Music Festival, 1954); *Epitafio en ritmos y sonidos* for Chorus and Orch. (1961); *Negro* for Soprano and Orch. (1961); *Suite introspectiva* (1961; Los Angeles, June 8, 1962); Violin Concerto (1962); Violin Sonata (1914); Cello Sonata (1916); String Quartet (1942); Piano Concerto (1941); 2 piano sonatas (1917, 1939); *Corales criollos* No. 1 and No. 2 for Piano (1947); songs.
BIBL.: R. Arizaga, *J.J. C.* (Buenos Aires, 1963).

Castro, Ricardo, Mexican composer and pianist; b. Durango, Feb. 7, 1864; d. Mexico City, Nov. 27, 1907. He studied with Melesio Morales in Mexico; in 1883 he appeared as pianist at the New Orleans Cotton Exposition. In 1902 he went to Europe and presented concerts of his works in Paris; he was soloist in his own piano concerto in Antwerp (Dec. 28, 1904). Returning to Mexico, he produced an opera, *La leyenda de Rudel* (Nov. 8, 1906). He composed 3 more operas (*Atzimba, Satán vencido,* and *La Rousalka*), 2 syms. (1883, 1887), and a number of piano pieces.

Castro, Washington, Argentine conductor and composer, brother of **José María** and **Juan José Castro;** b. Buenos Aires, July 13, 1909. He studied cello; from 1947 devoted himself mainly to conducting and teaching.
WORKS: *Sinfonía primaveral* (1956); Piano Concerto (1960); *Sinfonía breve* for Strings (1960); Concerto for Orch. (1963); *Rhapsody* for Cello and Orch. (1963); *3 Pieces* for Orch. (1970); 3 string quartets (1945, 1950, 1965); piano pieces; songs.

Castrucci, Pietro, Italian violinist; b. Rome, 1679; d. Dublin, Feb. 29, 1752. He was a pupil of Corelli; came to London (1715) as leader of Handel's opera orch. He was a fine player on the "violetta marina," a stringed instrument invented by himself, and resembling the viola d'amore in tone. In *Orlando,* Handel wrote an air accompanied on 2 "violette marine" "per gli Signori Castrucci" (Pietro, and Prospero, his brother). Castrucci publ. violin concertos and 2 books of violin sonatas.

Catalani, Alfredo, greatly talented Italian composer; b. Lucca, June 19, 1854; d. Milan, Aug. 7, 1893. He studied music with his father, a church organist; in 1872 studied with Fortunato Magi and Bazzini at the Istituto Musicale Pacini in Lucca; then went to Paris, where he attended classes of Bazin (composition) and Marmontel (piano). He returned to Italy in 1873; in 1886 became the successor of Ponchielli as prof. of composition at the Milan Cons. It was in Milan that he became acquainted with Boito, who encouraged him in his composition; he also met young Toscanini, who became a champion of his music. Catalani was determined to create a Wagnerian counterpart in the field of Italian opera, and he selected for his libretti fantastic subjects suitable for dramatic action. After several unsuccessful productions he finally achieved his ideal in his last opera, *La Wally;* he died of tuberculosis the year after its production.
WORKS: His operas include *La Falce* (Milan, July 19, 1875); *Elda* (Turin, Jan. 31, 1880; rev. as *Loreley,* Turin, Feb. 16, 1890); *Dejanice* (Milan, March 17, 1883); *Edmea* (Milan, Feb. 27, 1886); *La Wally* (Milan, Jan. 20, 1892); he further com-

posed *Sinfonia a piena orchestra* (1872); *Il Mattino,* romantic sym. (1874); *Ero e Leandro,* symphonic poem (Milan, May 9, 1885); a number of piano pieces and songs.
BIBL.: D. Pardini, *A. C.* (Lucca, 1935); J. Klein, "A. C.," *Musical Quarterly* (July 1937); A. Bonaccorsi, *A. C.* (Turin, 1942); C. Gatti, *A. C.* (Milan, 1953); J. Klein, "Toscanini and C.—A Unique Friendship," *Music & Letters* (July 1967).

Catalani, Angelica, Italian soprano; b. Sinigaglia, May 10, 1780; d. Paris, June 12, 1849. She was taught at the convent of S. Lucia di Gubbio in Rome; made her operatic debut at the Teatro La Fenice in Venice (1795); then sang at La Pergola in Florence (1799), and at La Scala in Milan (1801). In 1801, while engaged at the Italian Opera in Lisbon, she married Paul Valabrègue, an attaché of the French embassy; subsequently gave highly successful concerts in Paris and London. From 1814 to 1817 she undertook, without signal success, the management of the Théâtre des Italiens in Paris while continuing her singing career, appearing in major European cities and at provincial festivals until 1828, when she retired to her country home near Florence. She won great acclaim for her commanding stage presence, wide vocal range, and mastery of the bravura singing style.

Catel, Charles-Simon, French composer and pedagogue; b. l'Aigle, Orne, June 10, 1773; d. Paris, Nov. 29, 1830. He studied in Paris with Gossec and Gobert at the École Royale de Chant; served as accompanist and teacher there (1787); was accompanist at the Opéra and assistant conductor (to Gossec) of the band of the Garde Nationale (1790). In 1795, on the establishment of the Cons., he was appointed prof. of harmony, and was commissioned to write a *Traité d'harmonie* (publ. 1802; a standard work at the Cons. for 20 years thereafter). In 1810, with Gossec, Méhul, and Cherubini, he was made an inspector of the Cons., resigning in 1816; was named a member of the Académie des Beaux-Arts in 1817. As a composer, Catel was at his best in his operas, written in a conventional but attractive style of French stage music of the time.
WORKS: Operas (perf. at the Paris Opéra and the Opéra-Comique): *Sémiramis* (May 4, 1802); *L'Auberge de Bagnères* (April 23, 1807); *Les Artistes par occasion* (Jan. 22, 1807); *Les Bayadères* (Paris Opéra, Aug. 8, 1810); his most successful work); *Les Aubergistes de qualité* (June 11, 1812); *Bayard à Mézières* (Feb. 12, 1814); *Le Premier en date* (Nov. 3, 1814); *Wallace, ou Le Ménestrel écossais* (March 24, 1817); *Zirphile et Fleur de Myrte, ou Cent ans en jour* (June 29, 1818); *L'Officier enlevé* (May 4, 1819); also several syms. and chamber works.
BIBL.: J. Carlez, *C.: Étude biographique et critique* (Caen, 1895); F. Hellouin and J. Picard, *Un Musicien oublié: C.* (Paris, 1910); S. Suskin, *The Music of C.-S. C. for the Paris Opéra* (diss., Yale Univ., 1972).

Catelani, Angelo, Italian music historian; b. Guastalla, March 30, 1811; d. San Martino di Mugnano, Sept. 5, 1866. He studied piano with Asioli and harmony with M. Fusco; also at the Naples Cons. (1831) and privately with Donizetti and Crescentini; conducted at Messina (1835–36) and at Correggio (1837); was appointed maestro di cappella at the Cathedral of Modena (1837–39); was maestro di cappella at the court of Modena (1846). He composed 3 operas, of which 1 was successfully produced; then turned to writing on music.
WRITINGS: *Epistolario di autori celebri in musica* (1852–54); *Bibliografia di due stampe ignote di Ottaviano Petrucci da Fossombrone* (1858); *Della vita e delle opere di Orazio Vecchi* (1858); *Della vita e delle opere di Claudio Merulo da Correggio* (1860); *Delle opere di Alessandro Stradella* (1866).

Catlett, Sidney ("Big Sid"), black American jazz drummer; b. Evansville, Ind., Jan. 17, 1910; d. Chicago, March 25, 1951. After the family moved to Chicago, he took up drums; played with local musicians; then joined the bands of Fletcher Henderson (1936), Don Redman (1936–38), Louis Armstrong (1938–42), and others; led his own quartet from 1944 to 1947; then appeared with Armstrong's All Stars (1947–49); played at Carnegie Hall in N.Y. in 1950.

Catoire, Georgi Lvovitch, Russian composer of French descent; b. Moscow, April 27, 1861; d. there, May 21, 1926. While a student of mathematics at the Univ. of Berlin, he took lessons in piano with Klindworth and in composition with Rüfer; later studied with Liadov in St. Petersburg; lived in Moscow and devoted himself to composing; also taught composition at the Moscow Cons. He publ. a manual on harmony (2 vols., 1924, 1925).

WORKS: Sym. in C minor; symphonic poem, *Mtsyri;* Piano Concerto; cantata, *Rusalka;* 3 poems of Tiutchev for Female Voices, with Piano; String Trio; String Quartet; String Quintet; 4 preludes for Piano; violin sonata, *Poème;* Piano Quartet; Piano Quintet; many songs.

BIBL.: V. Belayev, *G. C.* (Moscow, 1926).

Catunda, Eunice, Brazilian pianist and composer; b. Rio de Janeiro, March 14, 1915. She studied piano and harmony; took special courses in modern music and orchestration with Guarnieri and H.J. Koellreuter; in 1948 she went to Europe and took a course in conducting with Scherchen. In 1946 she joined the modernistic group Musica Viva; in 1973 she was appointed a lecturer at the Univ. of Brasilia. Her compositions include a Piano Concerto (1955); *Hommage à Schönberg* for a Chamber Ensemble (1949); *Seresta* for 4 Saxophones (1958); several piano pieces; and songs.

Caturla, Alejandro García, Cuban composer; b. Remedios, March 7, 1906; assassinated there, Nov. 12, 1940. He studied with Pedro Sanjuán in Havana; then with Nadia Boulanger in Paris (1928); was founder (1932) and conductor of the Orquesta de Conciertos de Caibarién (chamber orch.) in Cuba; served as district judge in Remedios. His works have been performed in Cuba, Europe, and the U.S. In Caturla's music, primitive Afro-Cuban rhythms and themes are treated with modern techniques and a free utilization of dissonance.

WORKS: Suite of 3 Cuban dances: *Danza del tambor, Motivos de danzas, Danza Lucumí* (Havana, 1928); *Bembé* for 14 Instruments (Paris, 1929); *Dos poemas Afro-Cubanos* for Voice and Piano (Paris, 1929; also arranged for Voice and Orch.); *Yambo-O,* Afro-Cuban oratorio (Havana, Oct. 25, 1931); *Rumba* for Orch. (1931); *Primera suite cubana* for Piano and 8 Wind Instruments (1930); *Manita en el Suelo,* "mitologia bufa Afro-Cubana" for Narrator, Marionettes, and Chamber Orch., to the text of Alejo Carpentier (1934).

BIBL.: A. Carpentier, *Música en Cuba* (Havana, 1946); O. Mayer-Serra, *Música y músicos de Latino-América* (Mexico, 1947); A. Salazar, "La obra musical de A. C.," *Revista Cubana* (Jan. 1938); N. Slonimsky, "C. of Cuba," *Modern Music* (Jan. 1940); R. Nodal Consuegra, "La figure de A. G. C. en la musica cubana," *Exilo* (Summer 1971).

Cauchie, Maurice, French musicologist; b. Paris, Oct. 8, 1882; d. there, March 21, 1963. He was 1st a physicist and chemist; after 1917 devoted himself exclusively to music; specialized in the study of French music of the 16th and 17th centuries. He ed. *Deux chansons à 5 voix de Clément Janequin* (1925); *Quinze chansons françaises du XVI³ siècle à 4 et 5 voix* (1926); *Trente chansons de Clément Janequin* (1928); the collected works of Clément Janequin; wrote *La Pratique de la musique* (1948); numerous essays in French magazines on Ockeghem, Attaignant, Janequin, Cléreau, Costeley, Boesset, Couperin, Gluck, Beethoven, etc.; compiled a thematic index of the works of François Couperin (1949).

Caudella, Edoardo, Rumanian violinist and composer of Italian origin; b. Iaşi, June 3, 1841; d. there, April 15, 1924. He studied in Berlin and in Paris, where he took violin lessons with Vieuxtemps. Returning to Rumania, he taught at the Cons. of Iaşi. He wrote 2 violin concertos; 4 operas: *Olteanca* (Iaşi, March 8, 1880), *Hatmanul Baltag* (Bucharest, March 1, 1884), *Fata razesului* (Bucharest, March 2, 1893), *Petru Raresch* (Bucharest, Nov. 14, 1900).

Caurroy, Eustache du. See **Du Caurroy, François-Eustache.**

Caussade, Georges, French composer and pedagogue; b. Port-Louis, Mauritius, Nov. 20, 1873; d. Chanteloupe-les-Vignes, Yvelines, Aug. 5, 1936. He received 1st prizes in harmony (1891) and counterpoint and fugue (1896) at the Paris Cons.; beginning in 1905 he taught counterpoint there. His textbook *Technique de l'harmonie* (1931) became a standard work in France. He was married to **Simone Plé-Caussade,** a significant composer in her own right. Among his many students were M. Duruflé, E. Barraine, H. Barraud, D. Lesur, and J. Rivier.

Cavaccio, Giovanni, Italian composer; b. Bergamo, 1556; d. there, Aug. 11, 1626. He was maestro di cappella at the Cathedral of Bergamo (1581–98) and at S. Maria Maggiore in Bergamo (1604–26). Among his publ. works are collections of madrigals (1583, 1591, 1599); Psalms (1585); a Requiem (Milan, 1611); and a collection of keyboard pieces, *Sudori musicali* (Venice, 1626). Music by Cavaccio was included in a publication of Psalms dedicated to Palestrina (1592), and pieces by him were printed in Bonometti's *Parnassus musicus.* A *Canzon francese per organo* and a toccata are reprinted in L. Torchi, *L'arte musicale in Italia* (vol. III).

Cavaillé-Coll, Aristide, celebrated French organ builder; b. Montpellier, Feb. 4, 1811; d. Paris, Oct. 13, 1899. His father, Dominique Hyacinthe (1771–1862), was also an organ builder. Aristide went to Paris in 1833; built the organ at St.-Denis, and thereafter many famous organs in Paris (St.-Sulpice, Madeleine, etc.), the French provinces, Belgium, the Netherlands, and elsewhere. He invented the system of separate wind chests with different pressures for the low, medium, and high tones; also the "flûtes octaviantes." He publ. *Études expérimentales sur les tuyaux d'orgues* (report for the Académie des Sciences, 1849) and *Projet d'orgue monumental pour la Basilique de Saint-Pierre de Rome* (1875).

BIBL.: A. Peschard, *Notice biographique sur A. C.-C. et les orgues électriques* (Paris, 1899); C. and E. Cavaillé-Coll, *A. C.-C.: Ses origines, sa vie, ses œuvres* (Paris, 1928); M. Vanmackelberg, "L'Esthétique d'A. C.-C.," *L'Orgue* (July–Sept. 1968).

Cavalieri, Catarina (real name, **Franziska Cavalier**), Austrian soprano of Italian descent; b. Wahring, near Vienna, Feb. 19, 1760; d. Vienna, June 30, 1801. She studied with Salieri; made her operatic debut as Sandrina in Anfossi's *La finta giardiniera* at the Italian Opera in Vienna on April 29, 1775; she subsequently sang with notable success at the German Opera there. Salieri, with whom she maintained a liaison, composed several operas for her. Mozart, too, composed the roles of Constanze in *Die Entführung aus dem Serail* (July 16, 1782) and Mme. Silberklang in *Der Schauspieldirektor* (Feb. 7, 1786) for her, as well as the extra aria "Mi tradì" (K. 540c) in *Don Giovanni,* for the 1st Vienna performance in 1788. In a letter of May 21, 1785, Mozart described her as "a singer of whom Germany might well be proud." She retired from the stage in 1793.

Cavalieri, Emilio del, Italian composer; b. c.1550; d. Rome, March 11, 1602. He was a nobleman who served as Inspector-General of Art and Artists at the Tuscan court in Florence (1588). He was one of the "inventors" and most ardent champions of the monodic style, or "stile recitativo," which combines melody with accompanying harmonies. His chief work, *La rappresentazione di anima e di corpo* (publ. by A. Guidotti, Rome, 1600, with explanatory preface; reprints: L. Guidiccioni-Nicastro, Livorno, 1911; Munich, 1921), once regarded as the 1st oratorio, is really a morality play set to music; other dramatic works (*Il satiro,* 1590; *Disperazione di Filene,* 1590; *Giuoco della cieca,* 1595) exemplify in similar manner the beginnings of modern opera form. In all of Cavalieri's music there is a *basso continuato* with thoroughbass figuring; the melodies are also crudely figured. A facsimile ed. of the libretto for *La rappresentazione* was publ. by D. Alaleona (Rome, 1912); a facsimile ed. of the orch. score is to be found in Mantica's *Collezione di prime fioriture del melodramma italiano* (Rome, 1912).

BIBL.: D. Alaleona, "Su E. C.," *Nuova Musica* (Florence, 1905); H. Prunières, "Une lettre inédite d'E. de C.," *Revue*

Musicale (1923); U. Rolandi, "E. de C.," *Rivista Musicale Italiana* (1929); B. Becherini, "La musica nelle Sacre Rappresentazioni fiorentini," ibid. (1951); T. Antonicek, "E. de'C. und seine *Rappresentazione di anima e di corpo*," *Österreichische Musikzeitschrift* (Aug. 1969).

Cavalieri, Lina (Natalina), famous Italian soprano; b. Viterbo, Dec. 25, 1874; d. in an air raid on Florence, Feb. 8, 1944. As a young woman of striking beauty, she became the cynosure of the Paris boulevardiers via her appearances in cafés (1893) and at the Folies-Bergère (1894). During a trip to Russia in 1900, she married Prince Alexander Bariatinsky, who persuaded her to take up an operatic career. After studying in Paris, she made a premature debut as Nedda at the Teatro São Carlo in Lisbon (1900); at her 2nd appearance, the audience's disapproval brought the performance to a halt. She and the Prince then parted company, but she continued her vocal studies with Maddalena Mariani-Masi in Milan, returning successfully to the stage as Mimi at the Teatro San Carlo in Naples (1900); she then sang in St. Petersburg and Warsaw (1901). In 1905 she was chosen to create the role of L'Ensoleillad in Massenet's *Chérubin* in Monte Carlo, and on Dec. 5, 1906, she made her Metropolitan Opera debut in N.Y. as Fedora, winning subsequent praise for her dramatic portrayals there of Tosca and Mimi. In 1907, after divorcing her husband, she contracted a lucrative marriage with the American millionaire Winthrop Chandler, but left him in a week, precipitating a sensational scandal that caused the Metropolitan to break her contract; she made her farewell appearance there in a concert on March 8, 1908. She sang at London's Covent Garden (1908), N.Y.'s Manhattan Opera House (1908), the London Opera House (1911), and the Chicago Grand Opera (1913–14; 1921–22). She married the tenor **Lucien Muratore** in 1913, but abandoned him in 1919; she then married Paolo D'Arvanni, making her home at her Villa Cappucina near Florence. Among her other fine roles were Adriana Lecouvreur, Manon Lescaut, and Salomé in *Hérodiade*. She publ. an autobiography, *La mie veritá* (1936). She was the subject of an Italian film under the telling title *La Donna più bella dello mondo* (1957), starring Gina Lollobrigida.

Cavalli (Caletti), Pier Francesco, historically significant Italian opera composer; b. Crema, Feb. 14, 1602; d. Venice, Jan. 14, 1676. His father, Giovanni Battista Caletti (known also as Bruni), was maestro di cappella at the Cathedral in Crema; he gave him his 1st instruction in music; as a youth he sang under his father's direction in the choir of the Cathedral. The Venetian nobleman Federico Cavalli, who was also mayor of Crema, took him to Venice for further musical training; and as it was a custom, he adopted his sponsor's surname. In December 1616 he entered the choir of S. Marco in Venice, beginning an association there which continued for the rest of his life; he sang there under Monteverdi; also served as an organist at Ss. Giovanni e Paolo (1620–30). In 1638, he turned his attention to the new art form of opera, and helped to organize an opera company at the Teatro San Cassiano. His 1st opera, *Le nozze di Teti e di Peleo*, was performed there on Jan. 24, 1639; 9 more were to follow within the next decade. In 1639 he successfully competed against 3 others for the post of 2nd organist at S. Marco. In 1660 Cardinal Mazarin invited him to Paris, where he presented a restructured version of his opera *Serse* for the marriage festivities of Louis XIV and Maria Theresa. He also composed the opera *Ercole amante* while there, which was given at the Tuileries on Feb. 7, 1662. He returned to Venice in 1662; on Jan. 11, 1665, he was officially appointed 1st organist at S. Marco; on Nov. 20, 1668, he became maestro di cappella there. After Monteverdi, Cavalli stands as one of the most important Venetian composers of opera in the mid-17th century. In recent years several of his operas have been revived; Raymond Leppard ed. *L'Ormindo* (London, 1969) and *Calisto* (London, 1975); Jane Glover ed. *L'Eritrea* (London, 1977). Cavalli also composed much sacred music; several works are available in modern eds.

Works: Operas: *Le nozze di Teti e di Peleo* (Venice, Jan.

24, 1639); *Gli amori d'Apollo e di Dafne* (Venice, 1640); *Didone* (Venice, 1641); *Amore innamorato* (Venice, Jan. 1, 1642; music not extant); *La virtù de' strali d'Amore* (Venice, 1642); *Egisto* (Venice, 1643); *L'Ormindo* (Venice, 1644); *Doriclea* (Venice, 1645); *Titone* (Venice, 1645; music not extant); *Giasone* (Venice, Jan. 5, 1649); *Euripo* (Venice, 1649; music not extant); *Orimonte* (Venice, Feb. 20, 1650); *Oristeo* (Venice, 1651); *Rosinda* (Venice, 1651); *Calisto* (Venice, 1651); *L'Eritrea* (Venice, 1652); *Veremonda l'amazzone di Aragona* (Naples, Dec. 21, 1652); *L'Orione* (Milan, June 1653); *Ciro* (orig. composed by Francesco Provenzale; prologue and arias added by Cavalli for Venice, Jan. 30, 1654); *Serse* (Venice, Jan. 12, 1655); *Statira principessa di Persia* (Venice, Jan. 18, 1656); *Erismena* (Venice, 1656); *Artemisia* (Venice, Jan. 10, 1657); *Hipermestra* (Florence, June 12, 1658); *Antioco* (Venice, Jan. 21, 1659; music not extant); *Elena* (Venice, Dec. 26, 1659); *Ercole amante* (Paris, Feb. 7, 1662); *Scipione Affricano* (Venice, Feb. 9, 1664); *Mutio Scevola* (Venice, Jan. 26, 1665); *Pompeo Magno* (Venice, Feb. 20, 1666); *Eliogabalo* (composed in 1668; not perf.); *Coriolano* (Piacenza, May 27, 1669; music not extant); *Massenzio* (composed in 1673; not perf.; music not extant). The following operas have been ascribed to Cavalli but are now considered doubtful: *Narciso et Ecco immortalati; Deidamia; Il Romolo e 'l Remo; La prosperità infelice di Giulio Cesare dittatore; Torilda; Bradamante; Armidoro; Helena rapita da Theseo;* also *La pazzia in trono, overo Caligola delirante,* which is a spoken drama with some music. None of the music is extant for any of these works.

Bibl.: H. Kretschmar, "Die Venetianische Oper und die Werke C.s und Cestis," *Vierteljahrsschrift für Musikwissenschaft,* VIII (1892); E. Wellesz, "C. und der Stil der venezianischen Oper von 1640–1660," *Studien zur Musikwissenschaft,* I (1913); T. Wiel, "F. C. e la sua musica scenica," *Nuovo archivio veneto,* XXVIII (1914); H. Prunières, *C. et l'opéra venetien au dix-septième siècle* (Paris, 1931); U. Rolandi, "Le opere teatrali di F. C.," *Accademia musicale chigiana; La scuola veneziana* (1941); B. Hjelmborg, "Une Partition de C. Quelques remarques complémentaires aux recherches C.ennes," *Acta Musicologica,* XVI–XVII (1944–45); F. Bussi, *La Messa concertata et la musique sacrée de P.F. C.* (Paris, 1960); H. Powers, "Il Serse trasformato," *Musical Quarterly* (Oct. 1961 and Jan. 1962); B. Hjelmborg, "Aspects of the Aria in the Early Operas of C.," in *Natalica musicologica: Knud Jeppesen, septuagenario collegis oblata* (Copenhagen, 1962); D. Arnold, "F. C.: Some Recently Discovered Documents," *Music and Letters* (Jan. 1965); F. Bussi, "La produzione sacra di C. e i suoi rapporti con quella di Monteverdi," *Rivista Italiana di Musicologica,* II/2 (1967); G. Crain, "F. C. and the Venetian Opera," *Opera* (June 1967); R. Leppard, "C.'s Operas," *Proceedings of the Royal Musical Association,* XCIII (1967); H. Powers, "L'Erismena travestita," in *Studies in Music History* (Princeton, N.J., 1968); D. Swale, "C.: The *Erismena* of 1655," in *Miscellanea Musicologica, Adelaide Studies in Musicology,* III (1968); A. Hicks, "C. and *La Calisto,*" *Musical Times* (May 1970); E. Rosand, *Aria in the Early Operas of F. C.* (diss., N.Y. Univ., 1971); J. Glover, "C. and Rosinda," *Musical Times* (Feb. 1973); L. Bianconi, *F. C. und die Verbreitung der venezianischen Oper in Italien* (diss., Univ. of Heidelberg, 1974); E. Rosand, "L'Ormindo travestito in Erismena," *Journal of the American Musicological Society,* XXVIII (1975); J. Glover, "Aria and Closed Form in the Operas of F. C.," *Consort,* XXXII (1976); H. Powers, "Il Mutio tramutato: Sources and Libretto," in M. Muraro, ed., *Venezia e il melodramma nel seicento* (Florence, 1976); E. Rosand, "Aria as Drama in the Early Operas of F. C.," ibid.; idem, "Comic Contrast and Dramatic Unity: Observations on the Form and Function of Aria in the Operas of F. C.," *Music Review,* XXXVII (1976); J. Glover, *C.* (N.Y., 1978); M. Turnbull, "Ercole and Hercule: Les Goûts désunis?," *Musical Times* (May 1980); J. Glover, "C. and L'Eritrea," ibid. (Feb. 1982).

Cavallo, Enrica, Italian pianist; b. Milan, May 19, 1921. She was educated at the Verdi Cons. in Milan. She married the

Italian violinist **Franco Gulli**; in 1947 they formed the noted Gulli-Cavallo Duo; in subsequent years they toured all over the world; in addition, she taught at the Verdi Cons. In 1973 she was appointed to the faculty of the Indiana Univ. School of Music.

Cavazzoni, Girolamo, Italian organist and composer; b. Urbino, c.1520; d. Venice, c.1577. He was a son of **Marco Antonio Cavazzoni** and godson of Cardinal Pietro Bembo. He was organist at S. Barbara in Mantua until 1577; supervised the building of the organ there in 1565–66. His *Intavolatura cioè Ricercari, Canzoni, Hinni, Magnificati* (Venice, 1542) contains the 1st examples of the polyphonic ricercare of the 16th century. His organ ricercari, though related to the motet, differ from it in their extension of the individual sections by means of more numerous entries of the subject and more definite cadences between sections. The 2 canzonas from the same work mark the beginnings of an independent canzona literature for the keyboard. Reprints of Cavazzoni's works are found in L. Torchi, *L'arte musicale in Italia* (vol. III); Tagliapietra, *Antologia di musica* (vol. I); Davison and Apel, *Historical Anthology of Music*; and Schering, *Geschichte der Musik in Beispielen*. O. Mischiati ed. his organ works (2 vols., Mainz, 1959 and 1961).

BIBL.: C. Sartori, "Precisazioni bibliografiche sulle opere di G. C.," *Rivista Musicale Italiana* (1940).

Cavazzoni (also called **da Bologna** and **d'Urbino**), **Marco Antonio,** Italian composer and singer, father of **Girolamo Cavazzoni**; b. Bologna, c.1490; d. c.1570 (the date appearing on his will is April 3, 1569). He went to Urbino about 1510 and became acquainted with Cardinal Pietro Bembo; then became a musician in the private chapel of Pope Leo X (1515). In Venice (1517) he was employed by Francesco Cornaro, nephew of the Queen of Cyprus. Back in Rome (1520) he was again in the employ of Pope Leo X. From 1522 to 1524 and from 1528 to 1531 he was in Venice, and in 1536–37 was organist at Chioggia. From 1545 to 1559 he was a singer at S. Marco (Venice), where Adriaen Willaert was maestro di cappella. As a youth Cavazzoni wrote a Mass, *Domini Marci Antonii,* so named because he derived its theme from the solmization syllables of his Christian names. His most important work is a collection of keyboard pieces, *Recerchari, motetti, canzoni, Libro I* (Venice, 1523). The ricercari are toccata-like rather than contrapuntal, and the motets and canzonas are instrumental transcriptions of vocal pieces. Modern reprints (with biographical notes) are found in Benvenuti's *I classici musicali italiani* (Milan, 1941) and in K. Jeppesen, *Die italienische Orgelmusik am Anfang des Cinquecento* (Copenhagen, 1943).

BIBL.: T. Dart, "C. and Cabezón" (suggesting that Marco Antonio may have been a brother of Cabezón, the latter being a possible Spanish form of Cavazzoni's name), *Music & Letters* (Feb. 1955); a rebuttal to this by Jeppesen appears in *Journal of the American Musicological Society* (Summer 1955), together with a final postscript by Dart.

Cavos, Catterino, Italian-Russian composer; b. Venice, Oct. 30, 1775; d. St. Petersburg, May 10, 1840. He studied with Francesco Bianchi; his 1st work was a patriotic hymn for the Republican Guard, performed at the Teatro La Fenice (Sept. 13, 1797); he then produced a cantata, *L'Eroe* (1798). That same year he received an invitation to go to Russia as conductor at the Imperial Opera in St. Petersburg. He was already on his way to Russia when his ballet *Il sotterraneo* was presented in Venice (Nov. 16, 1799). He remained in St. Petersburg for the rest of his life. His Russian debut as a composer was in a collaborative opera, *Rusalka* (adapted from *Das Donauweibchen* by F. Kauer; Nov. 7, 1803). This was followed by the operas *The Invisible Prince* (May 17, 1805), *The Post of Love* (1806), *Ilya the Bogatyr* (Jan. 12, 1807), *3 Hunchback Brothers* (1808), *The Cossack Poet* (May 27, 1812), and several ballets. His most significant work was *Ivan Susanin,* which he conducted at the Imperial Theater on Oct. 30, 1815. The subject of this opera was used 20 years later by Glinka in his opera

A Life for the Tsar; the boldness of Cavos in selecting a libretto from Russian history provided the necessary stimulus for Glinka and other Russian composers. (Cavos conducted the premiere of Glinka's opera.) His subsequent operas were also based on Russian themes: *Dobrynia Nikitich* (1818) and *The Firebird* (1822). Cavos was a notable voice teacher; among his pupils were several Russian singers who later became famous.

BIBL.: R. Aloys Mooser, "Un musicista veneziano in Russia: C. C.," *Nuova Rivista Musicale Italiana* (Jan.–Feb. 1969).

Cazden, Norman, American pianist, musicologist, and composer; b. N.Y., Sept. 23, 1914; d. Bangor, Maine, Aug. 18, 1980. He studied piano with Ernest Hutcheson and composition with Bernard Wagenaar at the Juilliard Graduate School (teacher's diploma, 1932); he later studied composition with Piston and Copland and took courses in musicology at Harvard Univ. (Ph.D., 1948, with the diss. *Musical Consonance and Dissonance*). He subsequently taught at the Univ. of Maine in Orono (1969–80). He wrote *A Book of Nonsense Songs* (N.Y., 1961), and with H. Haufrecht and N. Studer, *Folk Songs of the Catskills* (Albany, 1982). His compositions reflect some interesting technical ideas in a general format of acceptable modernity.

WORKS: STAGE: *The Lonely Ones,* ballet (1944); *Dingle Hill,* dramatic cantata (1958); incidental music to *The Merry Wives of Windsor* (1962) and *The Tempest* (1963). ORCH.: *Preamble* (1938); *On the Death of a Spanish Child* (1939); *6 Definitions* (1930–39); *3 Dances* (1940); *Stony Hollow* (1944); Sym. (1948); *3 Ballads* (1949); *Songs from the Catskills* for Band (1950); *Woodland Valley Sketches* (1960); *Adventure* (1963); Chamber Concerto for Clarinet and Strings (1965); Viola Concerto (1972). CHAMBER: String Quartet (1936); Concerto for 10 Instruments (1937); 3 chamber sonatas for Clarinet and Viola (1938); Quartet for Clarinet and String Trio (1939); String Quintet (1941); Horn Sonata (1941); Flute Sonata (1941); Suite for Violin and Piano (1943); Suite for 2 Trumpets, Horn, Baritone Horn, Trombone, and Tuba (1954); Quintet for Oboe and String Quartet (1960); 2 *Elizabethan Suites* for 2 Trumpets, Horn, Trombone, and Tuba (1964) and for String Quartet (1965); Wind Quintet (1966); Piano Trio (1969); Bassoon Sonata (1971); English Horn Sonata (1974); Tuba Sonata (1974); also choral works and folk-music arrangements.

Cebotari (real name, **Cebutaru**), **Maria,** Moldavian soprano; b. Kishinev, Bessarabia, Feb. 23, 1910; d. Vienna, June 9, 1949. She sang in a church choir; from 1924 to 1929 studied at the Kishinev Cons.; then went to Berlin, where she took voice lessons with Oskar Daniel at the Hochschule für Musik. In 1929 she sang with a Russian émigré opera troupe in Bucharest and in Paris. In 1931 she made an auspicious debut as Mimi in *La Bohème* at the Dresden State Opera; also appeared at the Salzburg Festival. In 1936 she joined the Berlin State Opera; in 1946 became a member of the Vienna State Opera. She also filled guest engagements in other European opera houses. She had a large repertoire which included the standard soprano roles, among them Violetta, Madama Butterfly, Pamina, and Manon; she also gave brilliant performances in modern operas; Richard Strauss greatly prized her abilities, and entrusted to her the role of Aminta in the premiere of his opera *Die schweigsame Frau.* Thanks to her cosmopolitan background, she sang the part of Tatiana in Russian in Tchaikovsky's opera *Eugene Onegin* and the part of Antonida in Glinka's *A Life for the Tsar.* She also appeared in sound films. She was married to the Russian nobleman Count Alexander Virubov; she divorced him in 1938 and married the film actor Gustav Diessl.

BIBL.: A. Mingotti, *M. C., Das Leben einer Sängerin* (Salzburg, 1950).

Ceccato, Aldo, Italian conductor; b. Milan, Feb. 18, 1934. He studied at the Verdi Cons. in Milan (1948–55), with Albert Wolff and Willem van Otterloo in the Netherlands (1958), and at the Berlin Hochschule für Musik (1959–62). In 1960 he served as assistant to Sergiu Celibidache at the Accademia

Musicale Chigiana in Siena. In 1964 he won 1st prize in the RAI conducting competition, and in 1969 he made his U.S. debut at the Chicago Lyric Opera and his 1st appearance at London's Covent Garden. He was music director of the Detroit Sym. Orch. (1973–77) and Generalmusikdirektor of the Hamburg State Phil. (1975–83); he then served as chief conductor of the Hannover Radio Orch. (from 1985) and the Bergen Sym. Orch. (from 1985). His father-in-law was **Victor de Sabata.**

Ceely, Robert (Paige), American composer; b. Torrington, Conn., Jan. 17, 1930. He studied at the New England Cons. of Music (B.Mus., 1954), with Milhaud and Kirchner at Mills College (M.A., 1955), with Sessions at the Berkshire Music Center at Tanglewood (1955), and with Sessions, Babbitt, and Cone (analysis) and Strunk (musicology) at Princeton Univ. (1957–59); he later attended summer courses in contemporary music in Darmstadt (1962, 1964), and seminars in electronic music and digital sound synthesis in the U.S. He taught at the U.S. Naval School of Music (1955–57), Robert College in Istanbul (1961–63), the New England Cons. of Music (from 1967), Emmanuel College (1969–73), and Northeastern Univ. (1984–85). He publ. *Electronic Music Resource Book* (1983).
    Works: String Trio (1953); *Composition for 10 Instruments* (1963); *Stratti* for Magnetic Tape (1963); *Elegia* for Magnetic Tape (1964); *Vonce* for Magnetic Tape (1967); *Logs* for 2 Double Basses (1968); *Kyros*, theatrical documentary for Viola, Optics, and Tape (1969); *Beyond the Ghost Spectrum*, ballet (1969); *Mitsyn 1971* for Magnetic Tape (1971); *Slide Music* for Trombone Quartet (1974); *La Fleur, les fleurs* for Magnetic Tape (1975); *Rituals for 40 Flutes* (1978); *Flee, Floret, Florens* for 15 Solo Voices (1979); *Piano Piece* (1980); *Bottom Dogs* for 4 Double Basses (1981); *Totems* for Oboe and Tape (1982); *Dialogues* for Solo Flute (1983); *Infractions* for Magnetic Tape (1985); *Minute Rag* for Piano (in honor of Gunther Schuller's 60th birthday; 1985); *Pitch Dark* for Jazz Ensemble (1985).

Cehanovsky, George, Russian baritone, b. St. Petersburg, April 14, 1892; d. Yorktown Heights, N.Y., March 25, 1986. He was a member of the Russian navy in World War I; after the war he studied singing with his mother, who was a professional singer. He made his professional debut as Valentin in *Faust* in Petrograd in 1921. In 1923 he emigrated to the U.S., and in 1926 entered the membership of the Metropolitan Opera in N.Y., with which he remained until 1966. He filled 78 different roles during his long career; however, most were secondary roles, and thus he never reached the rank of celebrity. In 1956 he married the German soprano **Elisabeth Rethberg.**

Čelanský, Ludvík Vítězslav, Czech conductor and composer; b. Vienna, July 17, 1870; d. Prague, Oct. 27, 1931. He studied at the Prague Cons.; then conducted theater orchs. in Pilsen and Zagreb. Returning to Prague, he made the Czech Phil. into an independent organization (1901), and conducted it for the 1st season and again in 1918–19; he also conducted opera and concerts abroad.
    Works: Opera, *Camille* (Prague, Oct. 23, 1897); symphonic trilogy, *Adam, Noë, Moïse* (1915–19); church music; songs.
    Bibl.: A valedictory brochure, ed. by V. Balthasar, was publ. in honor of his 50th birthday (Prague, 1920).

Celibidache, Sergiu, transcendently endowed Rumanian conductor; b. Roman, June 28, 1912. He studied at the Berlin Hochschule für Musik, where his teachers included Kurt Thomas, Heinz Thiessen, Fritz Stein, and Heinz Gmeindl; he also took courses in musicology with Schering and Schünemann at the Univ. of Berlin. In 1945 he was appointed conductor of the Berlin Phil. as successor to Furtwängler; he continued in that capacity until Furtwängler formally resumed his position in 1952. After engagements as a guest conductor throughout Europe, he was chief conductor of the Swedish Radio Sym. Orch. in Stockholm (1964–71), the Stuttgart Radio Sym. Orch. (1971–77), and the Orch. National de France in Paris (1973–75). In 1979 he became Generalmusikdirektor of the Munich Phil. He also went to the U.S. and became engaged as conduc-

tor of the student orch. at the Curtis Inst. of Music in Philadelphia (1983–84). So remarkable was his progress in training this student group that he was engaged to make a formal U.S. debut as a conductor with it at Carnegie Hall in N.Y. on Feb. 27, 1984, at which he astonished the audience and the critics with his mastery of a diversified program of works by Rossini, Wagner, Debussy, and Prokofiev. In 1989 he took the Munich Phil. on an 11-city tour of the U.S., winning extraordinary acclaim. A cosmopolitan existentialist, he lectured on musical phenomenology at the Univ. of Mainz; he also composed in his leisure time, producing 4 syms., a Piano Concerto, and a variety of minor pieces.

Celis, Frits, Belgian conductor and composer; b. Antwerp, April 11, 1929. He studied composition at the Flemish Cons. in Antwerp, and harp at the Brussels Cons.; then attended the summer conducting course at the Mozarteum in Salzburg (1949–51) and similar courses at the Hochschule für Musik in Cologne (1953–54). He then became conductor of the Théâtre de la Monnaie in Brussels (1954–59) and also conducted in Czechoslovakia, the Netherlands, France, and Spain. In 1960 he was appointed to the faculty of the Flemish Cons. of Antwerp. His compositions are all written in a *laissez-faire* manner sparingly seasoned with atonality.
    Works: *Music* for Strings (1951); Violin Sonata (1951); String Trio (1958); *De Geestelijke bruiloft* for Voice, and Piano or Chamber Orch. (1958); Cello Sonata (1963); *Élégie* for Orch. (Antwerp, Dec. 8, 1967); *3 Symphonic Movements* (1969); *Intrada and Toccata* for Oboe and Piano (1972); *Episodes* for Viola and Harpsichord (1973); *Variazioni* for Chamber Orch. (1974); 3 syms.: No. 1 (1979); No. 2 (1986); No. 3, *Incanti* (1987); *Cantilena* for Orch. (1980); *Preludio e Narrazione* for Soprano and Orch. (1983); *Incantations* for Clarinet Choir (1987); choruses; songs.

Celletti, Rodolfo, Italian music critic; b. Rome, June 13, 1917. He obtained a law degree from the Univ. of Rome; then devoted himself to music criticism, writing for various newspapers in Milan. He also ed. the valuable reference work *Le grandi voci: Dizionario critico-biografico dei cantanti* (Rome, 1964).

Cellier, Alfred, English conductor and composer; b. London (of French parents), Dec. 1, 1844; d. there, Dec. 28, 1891. He was a chorister at St. James' Chapel Royal; studied music with Thomas Helmore; in 1866 was conductor, at Belfast, of the Ulster Hall concerts and the Phil.; from 1871 to 1875 conducted at the Prince's Theatre in Manchester; from 1877 to 1879 at the London Opéra-Comique, and (with Sullivan) at the Promenade Concerts in Covent Garden. He then spent some years in America and Australia, returning to London in 1887.
    Works: Light operas: *Charity Begins at Home* (London, 1870); *The Foster Brothers* (London, June 17, 1873); *The Sultan of Mocha* (Manchester, Nov. 16, 1874); *The Tower of London* (Manchester, Oct. 4, 1875); *Nell Gwynne* (Manchester, Oct. 16, 1876); *Dora's Dream* (London, Nov. 17, 1877); *The Spectre Knight* (London, Feb. 9, 1878); *Bella Donna, or The Little Beauty and the Great Beast* (Manchester, April 27, 1878); *After All* (London, Dec. 16, 1878); *In the Sulks* (London, Feb. 21, 1880); *The Masque of Pandora*, after Longfellow (Boston, Jan. 10, 1881); *The Carp* (London, Feb. 11, 1886); *Dorothy* (London, Sept. 25, 1886); *Mrs. Jarramie's Genie* (London, Feb. 14, 1888); *Doris* (London, April 20, 1889); *The Mountebanks* (London, Jan. 4, 1892); also a setting of Gray's *Elegy*, written for the Leeds Festival (Oct. 10, 1883); a symphonic suite; many popular songs.

Čeremuga, Josef, Czech composer; b. Ostrava-Kunčice, June 14, 1930. He studied composition with Řídký and Dobiáš and quarter-tone music with A. Hába at the Prague Academy of Music (1950–53); after completing his postgraduate studies there (1953–56), he joined the faculty, serving in a variety of capacities. His works reflect the modern Czech and Russian styles, with broad neo-Romantic melos sharpened by euphonious dissonances.

Works: opera: *Juraj Čup* (1958–60; Prague, April 27, 1963). **ballet:** *Princezna se zlatou hvězdou na čele* (The Princess with a Golden Star on Her Forehead; 1980–82). **orch.:** 3 syms. (1952; 1966–67; 1975); 2 violin concertos (1955; 1970–80); 3 *Symphonic Frescoes* (1958–59); Piano Concerto (1962; Teplice, Jan. 21, 1963); *Hommage aux étudiants*, overture (1964); *Concerto da camera* for Wind Quintet and Strings (1970–71); *Festive Overture* (1977); *Prague Symfonietta* (1977); *3 Silesian Dances* (1977–80); Concerto for Piano, Trumpet, and Orch. (1982). **chamber:** 3 string quartets (1956, 1961, 1973); Piano Trio (1959–60); Sonata for Cello and Piano (1957); Sonata for Viola and Piano (1961); *4 Pictures* for Clarinet and Accordion (1961); 2 wind quintets (1964, 1967); Quintet for Flute, Oboe, Violin, Viola, and Cello (1975); *Faun's Moods* for Flute, Guitar, and Marimba (1980); *Dialogue* for Cello and Piano (1982); songs.

Cererols, Joan, Catalan composer; b. Martorell, Sept. 9, 1618; d. Montserrat, Aug. 28, 1676. In 1636 he entered the Monastery of Montserrat; studied organ and violin there. He wrote a great number of sacred vocal works. The Monastery of Montserrat publ., in its series Música Instrumental, his Psalms and Vespers (vol. I, 1930), masses (vol. II, 1931), and villancicos (vol. III, 1932), ed. by Dom David Pujol.

Cerha, Friedrich, Austrian composer of the avant-garde; b. Vienna, Feb. 17, 1926. He studied violin with Vasa Prihoda and composition with Alfred Uhl at the Vienna Academy of Music (1946–51); also studied musicology and philosophy at the Univ. of Vienna (Ph.D., 1950). Upon graduation, he became active in the modernistic movement as a violinist, conductor, and composer. In 1958 he organized (with Kurt Schwertsik) the Vienna concert ensemble Die Reihe, devoted to new music. In 1960 he became director of the electronic-music studio and a lecturer at the Vienna Academy, becoming a prof. in 1969. He was commissioned by the publisher of Alban Berg to re-create the 3rd act of *Lulu* (1962–74); it was 1st performed at the Paris Opéra on Feb. 24, 1979. His own music pursues the aim of "atomization of thematic materials" as a means toward total integration of infinitesimal compositional quantities, with minimal variations of successive temporal units.

Works: 2 *éclats en reflexion* for Violin and Piano (1956); *Formation et solution* for Violin and Piano (1956–57); *Espressioni fondamentali* for Orch. (1956–57; Berlin, Nov. 17, 1960); *Relazioni fragili* for Harpsichord and Chamber Orch. (1957; Vienna, May 16, 1960); *Enjambements* for 6 Players (1959; Paris, March 7, 1962); *Fasce* for Orch. (1959; fair-copied in 3 stages, 1967–68, 1972–73, and 1975; Graz, Oct. 8, 1975); *Intersecazioni I* (1959–61) and *II* (1959–73; Graz, Oct. 16, 1973) for Violin and Orch.; *Mouvements I–III* for Chamber Orch. (1960); *Spiegel I–VII* for Orch., some movements with Tape (1960–61; fair-copied 1961–71; 1st complete perf. of the entire 80-minute score, Graz, ISCM Festival, Oct. 9, 1972); *Exercises* for Baritone, Narrator, and Chamber Ensemble (1962–67); *Elegie* for Piano (1963); *Phantasme 63* for Organ (3 Players) and Chamber Orch. (1963); *Symphonien* for Winds and Timpani (1964); *Catalogue des objets trouvés* for Chamber Orch. (1968–69; West Berlin, Oct. 1, 1970); *Verzeichnis* for chorus a cappella (1969); *Langegger Nachtmusik I* and *II* for Orch. (1969, 1970); *Curriculum* for 12 Winds (1972); Sym. (1975); *Double Concerto* for Violin, Cello, and Orch. (1975); opera, *Baal*, after Brecht (1973–81; Salzburg, Aug. 7, 1981); Double Concerto for Flute, Bassoon, and Orch. (1982; Graz, Oct. 7, 1983); *Requiem für Hollensteiner* for Speaker, Baritone, Chorus, and Orch. (1983); *Keintate I* (1983) and *II* (1985) for Voice and Chamber Ensemble; Flute Concerto (1986); *Der Rattenfänger*, stage piece (1987); *An die Herrscher der Welt*, cantata (1988).

Černohorsky, Bohuslav. See **Czernohorsky, Bohuslav.**

Černý, Ladislav, Czech violist; b. Pilsen, April 13, 1891; d. Dobříš, July 13, 1975. He studied viola at the Prague Cons.; then played viola at the opera in Ljubljana (1916–21); returning to Prague, he organized the Zik Quartet, known as the Prague

Quartet from 1929; was a member until his death; taught at the Prague Cons. (1940–46); from 1946 to 1973 was a prof. at the Prague Music Academy. Hindemith dedicated his Sonata for Solo Viola to him.

Cerone, Domenico Pietro, Italian tenor and music theorist; b. Bergamo, 1566; d. Naples, 1625. In 1592 he went to Spain and became a singer in the court choir; later was appointed teacher of plainsong to the clergy of the church of the Annunciation at Naples; from 1610 until his death, sang in the Royal Chapel Choir there. He publ. the manual *Regole per il canto fermo* (Naples, 1609) and *El Melopeo y Maestro, tractado de música teórica y práctica* (Naples, 1613). This treatise, written in Spanish, numbers 1,160 pages, containing a compendium of early music theory; it is divided into 22 books and 849 chapters; its pedantic exposition and inordinate length were the main target of Eximeno's satirical novel *Don Lazarillo Vizcardi*; Book XII is publ. in Eng. in O. Strunk's *Source Readings in Music History* (N.Y., 1950).

Bibl.: F. Pedrell, *P. Antonio Eximeno* (1920); G. Pannain, *L'oratorio dei Filippini* (1934); R. Hannas, "C., Philosopher and Teacher," *Musical Quarterly* (Oct. 1935), and "C.'s Approach to the Teaching of Counterpoint," *Papers of the American Musicological Society* (1937); A. Howell, "Symposium on Seventeenth-century Music Theory," *Journal of Music Theory* (1972).

Cerreto, Scipione, Italian composer, lutenist, and theorist; b. Naples, 1551; d. there, c.1632. He publ. 2 theoretical works containing valuable information on the music and musical instruments of his time: *Della prattica musica vocale e strumentale* (Naples, 1601) and *Arbore musicale* (Naples, 1608); a 3rd work, *Dialogo harmonico*, remained unpubl. (2 forms, 1628 and 1631).

Certon, Pierre, significant French composer; b. c.1510; d. Paris, Feb. 22, 1572. He was made matins clerk at Notre Dame in Paris (1529), then clerk (1532) and master of the choristers (1536) at the Sainte-Chapelle. He was "compositeur de musique de la chapelle du Roy" from c.1570 and also held a canonry at Notre Dame in Melun.

Works: masses: *Missae tres . . .* for 4 Voices (Paris, 1558); others in contemporary collections. **motets:** *Recens modulorum editio . . . 24 motettorum, liber secundus* (Paris, 1542); others in contemporary collections. **psalms, chansons, and spirituelles:** *Trente et un pseaumes* for 4 Voices (Paris, 1546); *Premiere livre de [13] psalmes . . . reduitz en tabulature de leut par Maistre G. Morlaye* (Paris, 1554); *Cinquante pseaulmes de David* for 4 Voices (Paris, 1555); *Les Meslanges*: 15 chansons spirituelles for 4, 5, and 6 Voices (Paris, 1570). **chansons:** *Premier livre de [16] chansons* for 4 Voices (Paris, 1552); *Les Meslanges*: 84 chansons (Paris, 1570); others in contemporary collections. For modern editions of his works, see F. Lesure and R. de Morcourt, eds., *Psaumes de P. C. réduits pour chant et luth par G. Morley* (Paris, 1957); A. Seay, ed., *P. C.: Zehn Chansons zu 4 Stimmen*, Das Chorwerk, LXXXII (1961); A. Agnel, ed., *Chansons de P. C.*, Cahiers de polyphonie (Paris, 1965); H. Expert and A. Agnel, eds., *P. C.: Chansons polyphoniques publiées par P. Attaingnant*, Maîtres Anciens de la Musique Française, I–III (Paris, 1967–68).

Bibl.: P. Pidoux, "Les Psaumes d'Antoine de Mornable, Guillaume Morlaye et P. C.," *Annales Musicologiques*, V (1957); S. Van Solkema, *The Liturgical Music of P. C.* (diss., Univ. of Michigan, 1962).

Cervantes (Kawanag), Ignacio, Cuban pianist and composer; b. Havana, July 31, 1847; d. there, April 29, 1905. He studied with Gottschalk (1859–61) and at the Paris Cons. (1866–68), with Alkan and Marmontel; in 1870 returned to Cuba; in 1898 went to Mexico; also visited the U.S. He was one of the pioneers of native Cuban music; in his *Danzas cubanas* for Piano he employs Cuban rhythms in an effective salon manner; he also wrote 3 operas, *El submarino Peral* (1889), *Los Saltimbanquis* (1899), and *Maledetto* (1895; unfinished), and some orch. pieces.

BIBL.: E. Sánchez de Fuentes, *I. C. K.* (Havana, 1936); A. Carpentier, *La música en Cuba* (Mexico, 1946).

Červený, Wenzel Franz (Václav František), Bohemian inventor of brass instruments; b. Dubeč, Sept. 27, 1819; d. Königgrätz, Jan. 19, 1896. He was a good performer on most brass instruments when he was only 12 years old; learned his trade with Bauer, a musical instrument maker in Prague; worked at various times in Brünn, Bratislava, Vienna, and Budapest; in 1842 established his own shop at Königgrätz. He invented the following instruments: Cornon (1844), Contrabass (1845), Phonikon (1848), Baroxiton (1853), Contrafagotto in metal (1856), Althorn obbligato (1859), Turnerhorn, Jägerhorn, army trombones (1867), and Primhorn (1873). After the success of the Primhorn, he created the complete Waldhorn quartet, which he considered his greatest achievement. Then followed the Subcontrabass and the Subcontrafagotto, and finally an entire family of improved cornets ("Kaiserkornette") and the "Triumph" cornet. His "roller" cylinder-mechanism is an invention of the greatest importance. He also improved the Euphonion, the Russian Signal-horns, the Screw-drum, and the church kettledrum. His instruments took 1st prizes at exhibitions in Europe and America.

Cervetti, Sergio, Uruguayan composer; b. Dolores, Nov. 9, 1940. He studied in Uruguay; then went to the U.S. and attended classes of Ernst Krenek and Stefan Grove at the Peabody Cons. (1963–67). In 1970, he was appointed a teacher at the N.Y. Univ. School of the Arts.
WORKS: String Trio (1963); Piano Sonata (1964); 5 *Sequences* for Flute, Horn, Cello, Electric Guitar, Piano, and Percussion (1966); *Orbitas* for Orch. (1967); *El Carro de Heno* for Small Chorus and Orch. (1967); *Zinctum* for String Quartet (Washington, D.C., June 24, 1968); *Dies tenebrarum* for Electric Organ, 3 Percussionists, Male Chorus, and Strings (1968); *Pulsar* for Brass Sextet (1969); *Prisons No. 1* for Singers, Dancers, Pantomime, 2 Trombones, Electric Organ, Electric Guitar, Double Bass, and Percussion (1969); *Prisons No. 2* for Speaking Chorus, Orch., and Tape (1970–71); *Peripetia* for 20–100 Singers and Instrumentalists (1970); *Cocktail Party* for Amplified Instruments and any number of Invitations (Malmö, Nov. 9, 1970); *Plexus* for Small Orch. (Washington, D.C., May 18, 1971); *4 fragmentos de Pablo Neruda* for Soprano, Oboe, Guitar, Cello, and Percussion (1970); *Graffiti* for Speaking Chorus, Orch., and Tape (1971); *. . . de la tierra . . .* for Ensemble (1972); *Raga 1, 2, and 3* for Trombone and Tape (1973); Trumpet Concerto (1977); *Music for Rachel* for Chamber Ensemble (1979); *Wind Devil* for Electronics (1983); *Night Trippers* for Electronics (1986).

Cervetto (real name, **Bassevi**), **Giacomo,** Italian cellist; b. c.1682; d. London, Jan. 14, 1783. In 1728 he settled in London, where he was a player and then manager of the Drury Lane Theatre; wrote some chamber music. He lived to be 100 years old. His son, **James Cervetto** (b. London, 1747; d. there, Feb. 5, 1837), was a cellist, too, and also lived to a very old age. He composed several cello pieces.

Cesana, Otto, American composer; b. Brescia, Italy, July 7, 1899; d. N.Y., Dec. 9, 1980. He came to the U.S. as a young man, and studied music with Julius Gold in California. He specialized in writing film music without, however, relinquishing his more ambitious pursuits. He wrote 6 syms. and 6 concertos: 1 for Clarinet, 1 for Trumpet, 1 for Trombone, 1 for Piano, 1 for 2 Pianos, and 1 for 3 Pianos; also composed a ballet, *Ali Baba and the 40 Thieves,* and a jazzy piece entitled *Swing Septet* (Indianapolis, Jan. 23, 1942). He was the author of several manuals, among them *Course in Modern Harmony* (1939), *Course in Counterpoint* (1940), and *Voicing the Modern Dance Orchestra* (1946).

Cesari, Gaetano, Italian musicologist; b. Cremona, June 24, 1870; d. Sale Marasino, Oct. 21, 1934. He was a pupil of Mottl, Sandberger, and Kroyer at the Univ. of Munich. Returning to Italy, he was employed as a teacher, music critic, and librarian. He publ. several valuable essays on Italian music,

among them "Musica e musicisti alla corte Sforzesca," publ. in *Rivista Musicale Italiana* (1922); a monograph, *Amilcare Ponchielli nell' arte del suo tempo* (Cremona, 1934); and, in collaboration with A. Luzio, the important source book *Giuseppe Verdi: I copialettere pubblicati e illustrati* (Leipzig, 1913; Eng. tr. in an abridged ed. by C. Osborne as *Letters of Giuseppe Verdi,* 1971).

Cesi, Beniamino, Italian pianist and pedagogue; b. Naples, Nov. 6, 1845; d. there, Jan. 19, 1907. He studied music with his father; then was a pupil of the celebrated pianist Thalberg; after a European tour he was a piano instructor at the Royal Collegio in Naples (1866–85) and at the St. Petersburg Cons. (1885–91). In 1895 he returned to the Cons. of Naples, where he taught until his death. His 2 sons, **Napoleone** and **Sigismondo,** were both pianists, whom he trained for a concert career; among other pupils were Martucci, Cilea, and A. Longo. He publ. a valuable *Metodo per pianoforte,* and also wrote an opera, *Vittor Pisani.*
BIBL.: A. Longo, "B. C.," *L'Arte Pianistica* (Jan. 1914).

Cesti, Antonio (baptismal name, **Pietro**), renowned Italian composer; b. Arezzo (baptized), Aug. 5, 1623; d. Florence, Oct. 14, 1669. Although earlier reference works give his name as Marc' Antonio Cesti, this rendering is incorrect; he adopted the name Antonio when he joined the Franciscan order. He was a choirboy in Arezzo before joining the Franciscan order in Volterra in 1637; he served his novitiate at S. Croce in Florence and then was assigned to the Arezzo monastery. He is reported to have received his musical training from Abbatini in Rome and Città di Castello (1637–40) and from Carissimi in Rome (1640–45). While in Volterra, he was accorded the patronage of the Medici family. His 1st opera, *Orontea* (Venice, Jan. 20, 1649), was highly successful. He was active at the court of Archduke Ferdinand Karl in Innsbruck from 1652 to 1657; then was a tenor in the Papal Choir in Rome (1659–60). After being released from his vows, he quit the Papal Choir with the intention of returning to his court duties in Innsbruck. In spite of a threat of excommunication, he went to Innsbruck until the death of the Archduke in 1665 led to the removal of its musical entourage to Vienna in 1666. He was made "Capelan d'honore und intendenta delle musiche theatrali" at the Vienna court in 1666, and in 1668 returned to Italy and served as maestro di cappella at the Tuscan court in Florence during the last years of his life. Cesti was one of the most important composers of secular vocal music of his time.
WORKS: OPERAS: *Orontea* (Venice, Jan. 20, 1649); *Alessandro vincitor di se stesso* (Venice, 1651); *Il Cesare amante* (Venice, 1651); *La Cleopatra* (Innsbruck, 1654); *L'Argia* (Innsbruck, 1655); *La Dori* (Innsbruck, 1657); *La magnanimità d'Alessandro* (Innsbruck, 1662); *Il Tito* (Venice, Feb. 13, 1666); *Nettunno e Flora festeggianti* (Vienna, July 12, 1666); *Le disgrazie d'Amore* (Vienna, Feb. 19, 1667); *La Semirami* (Vienna, July 9, 1667); *Il pomo d'oro* (Vienna, July 13–14, 1668); also several doubtful works. He also wrote over 60 secular cantatas and some sacred vocal music. See D. Burrows, ed., *A. C.: The Italian Cantata,* I, Wellesley Edition, V (1963).
BIBL.: H. Kretzschmar, "Die venetianische Oper und die Werke Cavallis und C.s," *Vierteljahrsschrift für Musikwissenschaft,* VIII (1892); F. Coradini, "Padre A. C. (5 agosto 1623–14 ottobre 1669): Nuove notizie biografiche," *Revista Musicale Italiana,* XXX (1923); P. Nettl, "Ein verschollenes Tournierballet von M.A. C.," *Zeitschrift für Musikwissenschaft,* VIII (1925–26); F. Schlitzer, *Intorno alla "Dori" di A. C.* (Florence, 1957); idem, *"L'Orontea" di A. C.: Storia e bibliografia* (Florence, 1960); D. Burrows, *The Cantatas of A. C.* (diss., Brandeis Univ., 1961); A. Peters, *A. C.'s Solo Cantatas for Bass Voice* (diss., Univ. of Iowa, 1968); T. Antonicek, "A. C. alla corte di Vienna," *Nuova Rivista Musicale Italiana,* IV (1970); C. Schmidt, *The Operas of A. C.* (diss., Harvard Univ., 1973); idem, "A. C.'s Il pomo d'oro: A Reexamination of a Famous Hapsburg Court Spectacle," *Journal of the American Musicological Society,* XXIX (1976).

Cezar, Corneliu, Rumanian composer; b. Bucharest, Dec. 22, 1937. He studied composition at the Bucharest Cons. with T. Ciortea, M. Jora, A. Mendelsohn, and A. Vieru. After graduating, he was active mainly as a piano teacher.

WORKS: STAGE: *Galileo Galilei,* opera (1962; Bucharest, Dec. 16, 1964); *Pinocchio,* theater piece (1983). **ORCH.:** *Cronika* for Orch. and Tape (1968); *Alpha Lirae* (1984). **CHAMBER:** Piano Sonata (1959); Quartet for Flute, Violin, Viola, and Bassoon (1959); *Taaroa* for Narrator, 2 Prepared Pianos, Carillon on Tape, and Clarinet (1968); various tape pieces, including *AUM* (1970), *Rota* (1978), and *Ziua fără sfîrşiṭ* (1978).

Chabrier, (Alexis-) Emmanuel, famous French composer; b. Ambert, Puy de Dôme, Jan. 18, 1841; d. Paris, Sept. 13, 1894. He studied law in Paris (1858–61); also studied composition with Semet and Hignard, piano with Edouard Wolff, and violin with Hammer. He served in the government from 1861; at the same time cultivated his musical tastes; with Duparc, Vincent d'Indy, and others he formed a private group of music lovers, and was an enthusiastic admirer of Wagner. He began to compose in earnest, and produced 2 light operas: *L'Étoile* (Paris, Nov. 28, 1877) and *Une Éducation manquée* (Paris, May 1, 1879). In 1879 he went to Germany with Duparc to hear Wagner's operas; returning to Paris, he publ. some piano pieces; then traveled to Spain; the fruit of this journey was his most famous work, the rhapsody *España* (Paris, Nov. 4, 1883), which produced a sensation when performed by Lamoureux in 1884. Another work of Spanish inspiration was the *Habanera* for Piano (1885). In the meantime he served as chorus master for Lamoureux; this experience developed his knowledge of vocal writing; he wrote a brief cantata for mezzo-soprano and women's chorus, *La Sulamite* (March 15, 1885), and his operas *Gwendoline* (Brussels, April 10, 1886), *Le Roi malgré lui* (Opéra-Comique, Paris, May 18, 1887), and *Briséis* (concert perf., Paris, Jan. 31, 1897; stage perf., Royal Opera, Berlin, Jan. 14, 1899). In his operas Chabrier attempted a grand style; his idiom oscillated between passionate Wagnerianism and a more conventional type of French stage music; although these operas enjoyed a *succès d'estime,* they never became popular, and Chabrier's place in music history is secured exclusively by his *España,* and piano pieces such as *Bourrée fantasque* (1891; orchestrated by Felix Mottl); his *Joyeuse Marche* for Orch. (orig. entitled *Marche française,* 1888) is also popular. Other works are *Ode à la musique* for Voices and Orch. (1890); *10 pièces pittoresques* for Piano (1880; 4 of them orchestrated and perf. as *Suite pastorale*); *3 valses romantiques* for 2 Pianos (1883); songs.

BIBL.: O. Séré, *Musiciens français d'aujourd'hui* (Paris, 1911); R. Martineau, *E. C.* (Paris, 1911); G. Servières, *E. C.* (Paris, 1912); A. Cortot, "L'Œuvre pianistique de E. C.," *La Revue Musicale* (Oct. 1926); J. Desaymard, *C. d'après ses lettres* (Paris, 1934); J.-G. Prod'homme, "C. in His Letters," *Musical Quarterly* (Oct. 1935); F. Poulenc, *E. C.* (Paris, 1961); R. Myers, *E. C. and His Circle* (London, 1969); F. Robert, *E. C. L'Homme et son œuvre* (Paris, 1970); R. Delage and F. Durif, "E. C. en Espagne," *Revue de Musicologie,* LVI/2 (1970); R. Delage, *C.* (Geneva, 1982).

Chadabe, Joel, American composer; b. N.Y., Dec. 12, 1938. He studied with Will Mason at the Univ. of North Carolina at Chapel Hill (B.A., 1959) and Elliott Carter at Yale Univ. (M.M., 1962), then taught at the State Univ. of N.Y. at Albany (from 1965), served as consultant to Bennington (Vt.) College (from 1971), and was president of Intelligent Computer Music Systems, Inc. (from 1986). In 1964 he held a Ford Foundation fellowship, later receiving grants from the N.E.A. (1976) and the Rockefeller Foundation (1977). In 1985 he was given the N.Y. Foundation for the Arts Award. From 1978 to 1987 he was president of Composer's Forum, Inc. His compositions reflect interest in synthesizers and make use of electronic and computer technologies.

WORKS: *Prelude to Naples* for 4 Instruments (1965); *Street Scene* for English Horn, Tape, and Projections (1967); *Ideas*

of Movement at Bolton Landing for Electronic Sounds on Tape (1971); *Shadows and Lines* for Electronic Sounds on Tape (1972); *Flowers* for Stringed Instrument and Electronic Sounds on Tape (1975); *Settings for Spirituals* for Singer and Computer-generated Accompaniment (1977); *Solo* for Computer or Synthesizer (1978; rev. 1981); *Scenes from Stevens* for Computer or Synthesizer (1979); *Rhythms* for Computer or Synthesizer and Percussion (1980); *Variation* for Piano (1983); *The Long Ago and Far Away Tango* for Piano (1984); *Bar Music* for Computer or Synthesizer (1985); *Several Views of an Elusive Lady* for Soprano and Electronic Sounds on Tape (1985); *After Some Songs* for Computer or Synthesizer and Solo Instruments (1987).

Chadwick, George W(hitefield), eminent American composer; b. Lowell, Mass., Nov. 13, 1854; d. Boston, April 4, 1931. He first studied music with Eugene Thayer in Boston; then became head of the music dept. at Olivet College in Michigan (1876); in 1877–78 studied at the Leipzig Cons. with Reinecke and Jadassohn; his graduation piece was an overture to *Rip Van Winkle,* which he conducted with the Leipzig Cons. Orch. on June 20, 1879; then studied organ and composition at Munich under Rheinberger; in 1880 returned to Boston as organist of the South Congregational Church; in 1882 became a teacher of harmony and composition at the New England Cons.; in 1897 succeeded Faelten as director. He received the honorary degree of M.A. from Yale, and an honorary LL.D. from Tufts College in 1905; received the Gold Medal of the Academy of Arts and Letters in 1928; for several seasons was conductor of the Worcester Music Festival; also head of music festivals in Springfield and Worcester, Mass.; was a member of the Boston Academy of Arts and Letters. Chadwick was one of the leading American composers; usually regarded as a pillar of the "Boston Classicists," he was actually an ardent romanticist; his musical style was formed under the influence of the German programmatic school; his harmonies are Wagnerian, his orchestration full and lush.

WORKS: STAGE: Comic operas: *The Quiet Lodging* (privately perf., Boston, 1892) and *Tabasco* (Boston, Jan. 29, 1894); *Judith,* lyric drama (Worcester Festival, Sept. 26, 1901); *The Padrone,* opera (1915); *Love's Sacrifice,* pastoral operetta (1916; Chicago, Feb. 1, 1923); incidental music to *Everywoman* (N.Y. and London, 1911). **ORCH.:** 3 syms.: No. 1, in C (Boston, Feb. 23, 1882); No. 2, in B-flat (Boston, Dec. 11, 1886); No. 3, in F (Boston, Oct. 20, 1894); overtures: *Rip Van Winkle, Thalia, The Miller's Daughter, Melpomene* (Boston, Dec. 24, 1887; also arranged for Piano, 1888), *Adonais* (Boston, Feb. 3, 1900), *Euterpe* (Boston, April 23, 1904), and *Anniversary Overture* (Norfolk Festival, 1922); Serenade in F for String Orch.; *A Pastoral Prelude* (Boston, 1894); Sinfonietta in D (Boston, Nov. 21, 1904); symphonic poems: *Cleopatra* (Worcester Festival, 1905) and *Angel of Death* (N.Y., 1919); *Symphonic Sketches,* suite (*Jubilee, Noël, Hobgoblin,* and *A Vagrom Ballad;* 1895–1904; Boston, Feb. 7, 1908); Theme, Variations, and Fugue for Organ and Orch. (Boston, 1908); *Suite symphonique* (Philadelphia, 1911; 1st prize of the National Federation of Music Clubs); *Aphrodite,* symphonic fantasy (Norfolk Festival, 1912); *Tam O'Shanter,* symphonic ballad (Norfolk Festival, 1915). **CHORAL:** *Dedication Ode* (1886) for Soli, Chorus, and Orch.; *Lovely Rosabelle,* ballad for Solo, Chorus, and Orch. (Boston, 1889); *The Pilgrims* for Chorus and Orch. (Boston, 1891); *Ode for the Opening of the Chicago World's Fair* for Chorus, with Piano or Orch. (1892); *Phoenix Expirans* for Soli, Chorus, and Orch. (Springfield Festival, 1892); *The Lily Nymph,* cantata (1893); *Lochinvar* for Baritone and Orch. (Springfield Festival, 1897); *Noël,* Christmas pastoral for Soli, Chorus, and Orch. (Norfolk Festival, 1908); *Aghadoe,* ballad for Alto and Orch.; numerous sacred works: *Ecce jam noctis* (Yale, 1897); *The Beatitudes; Jubilate;* etc.; many choruses for men's, women's, and mixed voices; also school choruses. **CHAMBER:** 5 string quartets (I, in G minor; II, in C; III, in D; IV, in E minor; V, in D minor); Piano Quintet (1888); violin and cello pieces;

etc. He composed about 100 songs with piano, organ, or orch. (*Allah, Ballad of the Trees and Masters, The Danza, Before the Dawn,* etc.). ORGAN: *10 Canonic Studies for Organ* (1885); *Progressive Pedal Studies for Organ* (1890); miscellaneous pieces (*Requiem, Suite in Variation Form,* etc.); also numerous piano pieces.

WRITINGS: *Harmony, a Course of Study* (Boston, 1897; rev. ed., 1922); *Key to the Textbook on Harmony* (Boston, 1902); co-ed., *A Book of Choruses for High Schools and Choral Societies* (N.Y., 1923).

BIBL.: C. Engel, "G.W. C.," *Musical Quarterly* (July 1924); A.L. Langley, "C. and the New England Conservatory," ibid. (Jan. 1935).

Chaikovsky. See **Tchaikovsky.**

Chailley, Jacques, eminent French musicologist; b. Paris, March 24, 1910. He studied composition with Boulanger, Delvincourt, and Busser; musicology with Pirro, Rokseth, and Smijers; conducting with Mengelberg and Monteux; also took courses in the history of medieval French literature at the Sorbonne (1932–36; received his Ph.D. there in 1952 with 2 dissertations: *L'École musicale de Saint-Martial de Limoges jusqu'à la fin du XIe siècle* [publ. in Paris, 1960] and *Chansons de Gautier du Coinci* [publ. as *Les Chansons à la Vierge de Gautier de Coinci* in *Monuments de la musique ancienne,* XV, 1959]). He was general secretary (1937–47), vice-principal (1947–51), and prof. of the choral class (1951–53) at the Paris Cons.; in 1952 he became director of the Inst. of Musicology at the Univ. of Paris; also taught at the Lycée La Fontaine (1951–69); from 1962 to 1981 he was director of the Schola Cantorum. He has written authoritatively on many subjects, including medieval music, the music of ancient Greece, musical history, and the music of Bach, Mozart, Wagner, and others. He also wrote 2 operas, a ballet, orch. works, etc.

WRITINGS: *Petite Histoire de la chanson populaire française* (Paris, 1942); *Théorie de la musique* (with H. Challan; Paris, 1949); *Histoire musicale du Moyen Âge* (Paris, 1950; 2nd ed., 1969); *Les Notations musicales nouvelles* (Paris, 1950); *La Musique médiévale* (Paris, 1951); *Traité historique d'analyse musicale* (Paris, 1951); *Formation et transformations du langage musical* (Paris, 1954); *Chronologie musicale: I, années 300 à 1599* (Paris, 1955); ed. *Précis de musicologie* (Paris, 1958; 2nd ed., rev., 1984); *40,000 ans de musique: L'Homme à la découverte de sa musique* (Paris, 1961; Eng. tr. as *40,000 Years of Music: Man in Search of Music,* N.Y., 1964); *Les Passions de J.S. Bach* (Paris, 1963; 2nd ed., rev., 1984); *Tristan et Isolde de Wagner* (Paris, 1963; 2nd ed., 1972); ed. *Alia musica* (Paris, 1965); *Cours d'histoire de la musique* (Paris, 1967–); *Expliquer l'harmonie?* (Lausanne, 1967); *La Musique et le signe* (Lausanne, 1967); *"La Flûte enchantée," opéra maçonnique: Essai d'explication du livret et de la musique* (Paris, 1968; Eng. tr. as *The Magic Flute, Masonic Opera,* N.Y., 1971; London, 1972); *"L'Art de la fugue" de J.S. Bach. Étude critique des sources* (Paris; I, 1971, II, 1972); *Le "Carnaval" de Schumann* (Paris, 1971); *Les Chorals d'orgue de Bach* (Paris, 1974); *La Musique* (Tours, 1975); *Le Voyage d'hiver de Schubert* (Paris, 1975); *Solfège-déchiffrage pour les jeunes pianistes* (Paris, 1975).

Chailly, Luciano, prominent Italian music administrator, teacher, and composer, father of **Riccardo Chailly;** b. Ferrara, Jan. 19, 1920. He studied violin in Ferrara (diploma, 1941) and pursued academic training at the Univ. of Bologna (B.A., 1943); after composition studies with R. Bossi at the Milan Cons. (diploma, 1945), he studied with Hindemith in Salzburg (1948). He was director of music programming for the RAI (1950–67), and artistic director of Milan's La Scala (1968–71), Turin's Teatro Regio (1972), Milan's Angelicum (1973–75), and Verona's Arena (1975–76). He was again associated with La Scala (from 1977) and was artistic director of the Genoa Opera (1983–85); he also taught at the Milan Cons. (1968–83). His music is composed in a communicative neo-Classical idiom, with some dodecaphonic incrustations and electronic effects.

WORKS: OPERAS: *Ferrovia soprelevata* (Bergamo, Oct. 1,

1955); *Una domanda di matrimonio* (Milan, May 22, 1957); *Il canto del cigno* (Bologna, Nov. 16, 1957); *La riva delle Sirti* (Monte Carlo, March 1, 1959); *Procedura penale* (Como, Sept. 30, 1959); *Il mantello* (Florence, May 11, 1960); *Era proibito* (Milan, March 5, 1963); *Vassiliev* (Genoa, 1967); *Markheim* (Spoleto, 1967); *L'Idiota* (Rome, Feb. 14, 1970); *Sogno (ma forse no)* (Trieste, 1975); *Il libro dei reclami* (Vienna, 1975); *La Cantatrice calva* (Vienna, Nov. 5, 1985). BALLETS: *Fantasmi al Grand-Hotel* (Milan, 1960); *Il cappio* (Naples, 1962); *L'urlo* (Palermo, 1967); *Shee* (Melbourne, 1967); *Anna Frank* (Verona, 1981); *Es-Ballet* (1983). INSTRUMENTAL: *Toccata* for Orch. (1948); *12 Sonate tritematiche* (for various instrumentations; 1951–61); *Sequenze dell'artide* for Orch. (1961); *Piccole serenate* for Strings (1967); *Contrappunti a quattro dimensioni* for Orch. (1973); *Newton-Variazioni* for Chamber Orch. (1979); *Es-Konzert* for Orch. (1980); *Psicosi* for Instruments and Percussion (1980); *Es-Kammerkonzert* for Small Instrumental Group (1983); chamber works; piano pieces; also choral works; songs; music for television.

Chailly, Riccardo, noted Italian conductor, son of **Luciano Chailly;** b. Milan, Feb. 20, 1953. He studied composition with his father, and then with Bruno Bettinelli at the Milan Cons.; he also studied conducting with Piero Guarino in Perugia, Franco Caracciolo in Milan, and Franco Ferrara in Siena. He was assistant conductor of the sym. concerts at Milan's La Scala (1972–74); his international career began with his U.S. debut at the Chicago Lyric Opera conducting *Madama Butterfly* (1974); he subsequently was a guest conductor at the San Francisco Opera, Milan's La Scala, London's Covent Garden, and the Vienna State Opera. He made his Metropolitan Opera debut in N.Y. with *Les Contes d'Hoffmann* on March 8, 1982. From 1982 to 1989 he was chief conductor of the (West) Berlin Radio Sym. Orch., which he led on its 1st tour of North America in 1985; he also was principal guest conductor of the London Phil. (1982–85) and artistic director of the Teatro Comunale in Bologna (1986–89). In 1988 he became chief conductor of the Concertgebouw Orch. of Amsterdam, which was renamed the Royal Concertgebouw Orch. that same year by Queen Beatrix in honor of the 100th anniversary of its founding. Chailly is one of the leading conductors of his generation, and has won praise for his performances in both the opera pit and the concert hall.

Chaix, Charles, French organist, teacher, and composer; b. Paris, March 26, 1885; d. Thônex, near Geneva, Feb. 16, 1973. He studied music at the École Niedermeyer in Paris; in 1904 he went to Geneva, where he studied with Otto Barblan at the Geneva Cons., graduating in 1908. He subsequently joined its staff (1910–14); served in the French army during World War I, returning to Geneva after the Armistice. He combined his pedagogical activities with service as a church organist; also conducted advanced classes in counterpoint at the Cons. of Lyons in France. He retired from teaching in 1961. His works include 2 syms. (1914, 1928); a Piano Quintet (1941); String Quartet (1948); also choral works. He publ. a treatise on harmony, *Éléments d'écriture musicale* (Geneva, 1935).

Chajes, Julius, Polish-American pianist and composer; b. Lemberg, Dec. 21, 1910; d. Royal Oak, Mich., Feb. 24, 1985. He studied piano and composition in Vienna; in 1937 he emigrated to the U.S. and became director of music at the Jewish Community Center in Detroit, for which most of his later compositions were written. He wrote several cantatas on biblical subjects, many of which were performed in Vienna.

Chalabala, Zdeněk, noted Czech conductor; b. Uherské Hradiště, April 18, 1899; d. Prague, March 4, 1962. He studied composition with Vítězslav Novák in Prague, then took courses in violin, conducting, and composition at the Brno Cons., where his principal teachers were Leoš Janáček and František Neumann. He was conductor of the Slovak Phil. (1924–25), the National Theater in Brno (1925–29), and the Prague National Theater (1936–45), and chief conductor of the Ostrava Opera (1945–49), the Brno National Theater (1949–52), and the Slovak National Theater in Bratislava (1952–53). In 1953 he returned to the Prague National Theater as chief conductor, a post he held with distinction until his death.

Chaliapin, Feodor (Ivanovich), celebrated Russian bass; b. Kazan, Feb. 13, 1873; d. Paris, April 12, 1938. He was of humble origin; at the age of 10 he was apprenticed to a cobbler; at 14 he got a job singing in a chorus in a traveling opera company; his companion was the famous writer Maxim Gorky, who also sang in a chorus; together they made their way through the Russian provinces, often forced to walk the railroad tracks when they could not afford the fare. Chaliapin's wanderings brought him to Tiflis, in the Caucasus, where he was introduced to the singing teacher Dimitri Usatov (1847–1913), who immediately recognized Chaliapin's extraordinary gifts and taught him free of charge, helping him besides with board and lodgings. In 1894 Chaliapin received employment in a summer opera company in St. Petersburg, and shortly afterward he was accepted at the Imperial Opera during the regular season. In 1896 he sang in Moscow with a private opera company and produced a great impression by his dramatic interpretation of the bass parts in Russian operas. He also gave numerous solo concerts, which were sold out almost immediately; young music-lovers were willing to stand in line all night long to obtain tickets. Chaliapin's 1st engagement outside Russia was in 1901, at La Scala in Milan, where he sang the role of Mefistofele in Boito's opera; he returned to La Scala in 1904 and again in 1908. On Nov. 20, 1907, he made his American debut at the Metropolitan Opera as Mefistofele; then sang Méphistophélès in Gounod's *Faust* on Jan. 6, 1908; sang Leporello in Mozart's *Don Giovanni* on Jan. 23, 1908. He did not return to America until 1921, when he sang one of his greatest roles, that of the Czar Boris in *Boris Godunov* (Dec. 9, 1921); he continued to appear at the Metropolitan between 1921 and 1929. He sang in Russian opera roles at Covent Garden in London in 1913; returned to Russia in 1914, and remained there during World War I and the Revolution. He was given the rank of People's Artist by the Soviet government, but this title was withdrawn after Chaliapin emigrated in 1922 to Paris, where he remained until his death, except for appearances in England and America. The critical attitude toward Chaliapin in Russia on account of his emigration changed when he was recognized as a great Russian artist who elevated the art of Russian opera to the summit of expressive perfection; numerous articles dealing with Chaliapin's life and career were publ. in the Russian language. He was indeed one of the greatest singing actors of all time; he dominated every scene in which he appeared, and to the last he never failed in his ability to move audiences, even though his vocal powers declined considerably during his last years. He was especially famed for his interpretation of the role of Boris Godunov in Mussorgsky's opera; both dramatically and vocally he created an imperishable image. He was equally great as Méphistophélès in *Faust* and in the buffo roles of Don Basilio in *The Barber of Seville* and Leporello in *Don Giovanni*. He also played the title role in a film version of *Don Quixote*. His last American recital took place in N.Y. on March 3, 1935. He wrote *Pages from My Life* (N.Y., 1926) and *Man and Mask* (N.Y., 1932).
BIBL.: M. Yankovsky, *C.* (Leningrad, 1972); V. Drankov, *The Character of C.'s Talent* (Leningrad, 1973); V. Borovsky, *C.: A Critical Biography* (N.Y., 1988).

Chamberlain, Houston Stewart, English-born German writer on music; b. Portsmouth, Sept. 9, 1855; d. Bayreuth, Jan. 9, 1927. He studied in Versailles and at Cheltenham College, Gloucester, then went to Stettin (1870), where he took up the cause of German culture and civilization. He lived in Dresden (1885–89), where he wrote for German, English, and French journals, and in Vienna (1889–1908), where he married Wagner's daughter, Eva (1908); settled in Bayreuth, and became a naturalized German citizen. He was one of the most ardent apostles of Wagner's art and also the chief protagonist of Wagner's ideas of German supremacy, which he presented in a simplified and vulgar manner, combined with pseudoscien-

tific speculation and heavy doses of anti-Semitism. As early as 1923 he was attracted to Hitler, but he did not live to see the establishment of the 3rd Reich. His books on Wagner are of value as a reflection of the time, even though the biographical sections are incomplete and out of focus. He also wrote an autobiography, *Lebenswege meines Denkens* (1919).
WRITINGS: *Das Drama Richard Wagners* (Leipzig, 1892; 6th ed., 1921; Eng. tr., 1915); *Richard Wagner, echte Briefe an F. Praeger* (Bayreuth, 1894; 2nd ed., 1908); *Richard Wagner* (Munich, 1896; 9th ed., 1936; Eng. tr., 1897); *Die ersten 20 Jahre der Bayreuther Bühnenfestspiele* (Bayreuth, 1896); *Parsifalmärchen* (Munich, 1900; 3rd ed., 1916); *Die Grundlagen des 19. Jahrhunderts* (Munich, 1899–1901; 10th ed., 1914; Eng. tr., 1910).
BIBL.: L. von Schroeder, *H.S. C.* (1918); A. Chamberlain (his 1st wife, 1878–1908), *Meine Erinnerungen an H.S. C.* (1923).

Chambers, Stephen A(lexander). See **Hakim, Talib Rasul.**

Chambonnières, Jacques Champion (called **Champion de Chambonnières**), French clavecinist and composer; b. c.1601; d. Paris, April 1672. He was 1st chamber musician to Louis XIV until 1662, and the teacher of the elder Couperins, d'Anglebert, Lebègue, Hardelle, and others. Considered the founder of the French clavecin school, he was famed throughout Europe and his style strongly influenced that of contemporary German composers, among them Froberger. Two books of his clavecin pieces were printed (Paris, 1670; reprint of *Les Pièces de clavessin* in the series Monuments of Music . . . in Facsimile, Paris, 1967). Chambonnières's complete works were publ. by Brunold & Tessier (Paris, 1925; reprinted with Eng. tr. and new preface, 1961).
BIBL.: H. Quittard, "C.," *Revue Internationale de Musique,* 12 (1898); idem, "Un Claveciniste français du XVIIᵉ siècle: J. C. de C.," *Tribune de St. Gervais* (1901); B. Huys, "J. C. de C., humanist, klavicinist en komponist," *Vlaams Muziektijdschrift* (Oct. 1972); G.B. Sharp, "Gaultier and C. Two French Tercentenaries," *Musical Times* (Dec. 1972).

Chaminade, Cécile (Louise Stéphanie), French composer and pianist; b. Paris, Aug. 8, 1857; d. Monte Carlo, April 13, 1944. She was a pupil of Lecouppey, Savard, and Marsick; later studied composition with Benjamin Godard. She became successful as a concert pianist; wrote a great number of agreeable piano pieces, in the salon style, which acquired enormous popularity in France, England, and America; her more serious works were much less successful. She made her American debut playing the piano part of her *Concertstück* with the Philadelphia Orch. (Nov. 7, 1908); also wrote a lyric sym., *Les Amazones* (Antwerp, 1888); 2 orch. suites; 2 piano trios; more than 200 piano pieces in a Romantic style, including *Étude symphonique, Valse-Caprice, Les Sylvains, La Lisonjera, Arabesque, Impromptu, 6 Airs de ballet,* etc.; numerous songs.

Champagne (Desparois dit Champagne), Claude (Adonaï), Canadian composer; b. Montreal, May 27, 1891; d. there, Dec. 21, 1965. He studied violin, piano, and composition in Montreal; then went to Paris, where he took courses in composition with Gédalge, Koechlin, and Laparra (1921–29). Returning to Canada, he joined the staff of McGill Univ. in Montreal (1932–41). From 1942 to 1962 he served as associate coordinator at the Cons. of Quebec. In his music he follows the modern French tradition.
WORKS: *Hercule et Omphale,* symphonic poem (1918; Paris, March 31, 1926); *Prélude et Filigrane* for Piano (1918); *Suite canadienne* for Chorus and Orch. (Paris, Oct. 20, 1928); *Habanera* for Violin and Piano (1929); *Danse villageoise* for Violin and Piano (1929; also orchestrated); *Quadrilha brasileira* for Piano (1942); *Images du Canada français* for Chorus and Orch. (1943; Montreal, March 9, 1947); *Évocation* for Small Orch. (1943); *Gaspésia* for Orch. (1944; rev. as *Symphonie gaspésienne,* 1945); Piano Concerto (1948; Montreal, May 30, 1950); String Quartet (1951); *Paysanna* for Small Orch. (1953); *Suite*

miniature for Flute, Cello, and Harpsichord (1958; rev. as *Concertino grosso* for String Orch., 1963); *Altitude* for Chorus and Orch., with Ondes Martenot (Toronto, April 22, 1960); organ pieces; songs.

Champein, Stanislas, French composer; b. Marseilles, Nov. 19, 1753; d. Paris, Sept. 19, 1830. He studied under Peccico and Chavet in Paris; at 13 he became maître de musique at the Collegiate Church at Pignon, for which he wrote a Magnificat, a Mass, and Psalms; in 1776 he went to Paris, where some sacred works and 2 operettas made his name known. Up to 1792 he produced 30 works for the stage, the best of which were the operas *La Mélomanie* (1781), *Les Dettes* (1787), and *Le Nouveau Don Quichotte* (1789). From 1793 to 1804 he filled a government position; continued to compose for the stage, but without success; spent the last years of his life in poverty; a pension, arranged for him through the efforts of Boieldieu and Scribe, came only 18 months before his death. Though Champein was one of the best-known stage composers of his time, his works are wholly forgotten.

Champion, Jacques. See **Chambonnières, Jacques Champion.**

Chanler, Theodore Ward, American composer; b. Newport, R.I., April 29, 1902; d. Boston, July 27, 1961. He studied in Boston with Hans Ebell (piano) and with Arthur Shepherd (composition); then at the Cleveland Inst. of Music with Ernest Bloch; later went to England, where he took courses at Oxford Univ. (1923–25); also studied with Nadia Boulanger in Paris. He returned to America in 1933. His music, mostly in smaller forms, is distinguished by a lyrical quality; his songs are particularly expressive; he employed the modern idiom of polytonal texture without overloading the harmonic possibilities; the melody is free, but usually within tonal bounds.

WORKS: 2 song cycles, *Epitaphs* (1937); *Pas de Trois*, ballet; *Ann Gregory* for Chorus; *Joyful Mystery*, fugue for 2 Pianos; *The Children*, song cycle; Violin Sonata (1927); 5 *Short Colloquies*, piano suite (1936); *The Pot of Fat*, chamber opera (Cambridge, Mass., May 8, 1955).

Chanot, François, French violin maker; b. Mirecourt, March 25, 1788; d. Rochefort (Charente-Maritime), Nov. 12, 1825. He was the son of an instrument maker; became a naval engineer, was retired on half-pay, and during his forced inactivity constructed a violin on the principle that the vibratory power would be increased by preserving the longitudinal wood fibers intact as far as possible. Thus his violin had no bouts, but slight incurvations like a guitar; the sound holes were almost straight, and the belly nearly flat; the strings were attached to the edge of the belly, instead of to a tailpiece. The violin was submitted to the Academy, whose report after testing it rated it equally with those of Stradivari and Guarneri; despite this evaluation, Chanot's violin never became popular. His brother, a *luthier* at Paris, manufactured a number of them, but gave it up when a few years had demonstrated their unpractical character.

Chantavoine, Jean (François Henri), French writer on music; b. Paris, May 17, 1877; d. Mussy-sur-Seine, July 16, 1952. He studied history of music with Friedländer in Berlin (1898, 1901–2); he was music critic of *Revue Hebdomadaire* (from 1903 to 1920) and *Excelsior* (1911–21); from 1921 to 1923 lived in Wiesbaden as a member of the International Commission for the Rhine Province; in 1923 was appointed General Secretary of the Paris Cons., a post he held until 1937.

WRITINGS: He ed. the biographical series Les Maîtres de la Musique, to which he contributed the monographs on Beethoven (1906) and Liszt (1910; 5th ed., 1950); publ. *Musiciens et poètes* (Paris, 1912; contains an account of Liszt's early opera *Don Sanche*, the score of which was found by Chantavoine); *De Couperin à Debussy* (1921); *Les Symphonies de Beethoven* (1932); *Petit guide de l'auditeur de musique* (Paris, 1947); *Mozart dans Mozart* (1948).

Chapin, Harry, American singer and songwriter; b. N.Y., Dec. 7, 1942; d. in an automobile accident, Long Island, N.Y.,

July 16, 1981. With a blend of folk song and rock, he established himself as a popular balladeer of his own "story songs" which chronicled the misery of the poor. He was a dedicated social activist, and devoted much of his time and talents to radical causes. In 1979 he was appointed to the Presidential Council on World Hunger by President Carter. His most popular ballads included *Cat's in the Cradle*, *Sniper*, *I Still Remember You*, *You're the Only Song*, *All My Life's a Circle*, and particularly *Taxi*.

Chapin, Schuyler G(arrison), American music administrator; b. N.Y., Feb. 13, 1923. After working for NBC (1941–51), Tex and Jinx McCary Enterprises (1951–53), and Columbia Artists Management (1953–59), he was head of the Masterworks Division of Columbia Records (1959–63); he later was associated with N.Y.'s Lincoln Center for the Performing Arts, and, from 1969 to 1971, was executive producer for Amberson Enterprises. He then was general manager of N.Y.'s Metropolitan Opera (1972–75). From 1976 to 1987 he served as dean of Columbia Univ.'s School of the Arts. He publ. his memoirs as *Musical Chairs: A Life in the Arts* (1977).

Chapí (y Lorente), Ruperto, Spanish composer; b. Villena, near Alicante, March 27, 1851; d. Madrid, March 25, 1909. He studied at the Cons. of Madrid; received a stipend from the Spanish Academy for further study in Rome (1874); wrote some operas (*La hija de Jefte*, *La hija de Garcilaso*, etc.), but discovered that his talent found more suitable expression in the lighter zarzuela, in which form his 1st success was won with *La Tempestad* (Tivoli, March 11, 1882); his work is noted for elegance, grace, and exquisite orchestration; of one of his zarzuelas (*La revoltosa*, Apolo, Nov. 25, 1897), Saint-Saëns remarked that Bizet would have been proud to sign his name to the score. His last zarzuela, *Margarita la Tornera* (Madrid, Feb. 24, 1909), was produced shortly before his death. Chapí wrote 155 zarzuelas and 6 operas. In 1893 he founded the Sociedad de Autores, Compositores y Editores de Música.

BIBL.: A. Salcedo, *R. C., Su vida y sus obras* (Madrid, 1929); J. Aguilar Gómez, *R. C. y su obra lirica* (Alicante, 1973).

Chappell & Co., London music publishers, concert agents, and piano manufacturers, founded in 1810 by Samuel Chappell, J.B. Cramer (the pianist), and F.T. Latour. Cramer retired in 1819, Latour in 1826, and S. Chappell died in 1834, when his son **William** (1809–88) became the head of the firm. In 1840 he established the Musical Antiquarian Soc., for which he ed. Dowland's songs; he also ed. and publ. *A Collection of National English Airs* (2 vols., 1838–39), later enl. as *Popular Music of the Olden Time* (2 vols., 1855–59; rev. by H.E. Wooldridge and publ. in 2 vols., 1893); he left an unfinished *History of Music* (vol. I, London, 1874). His brothers, **Thomas Patey** (1819–1902) and **S. Arthur** (1834–1904), were respectively the founder and manager of the Monday and Saturday Popular Concerts. In 1897 the partnership became a limited company, and Thomas was succeeded by his son, **T. Stanley** (d. 1933), as board chairman; later, William Boosey became managing director. In 1929 the firm was acquired by **Louis Dreyfus.** The American branch, under the direction of **Max Dreyfus,** brother of Louis, publ. the songs and musical comedies of Richard Rodgers, Jerome Kern, Cole Porter, Harold Arlen, and other popular composers.

Chapuis, Auguste (Paul Jean-Baptiste), French composer; b. Dampierre-sur-Salon, Haute-Saône, April 20, 1858; d. Paris, Dec. 6, 1933. He studied at the Paris Cons. with Dubois, Massenet, and César Franck, winning 1st prize for organ playing. He was active as a church organist in Paris; in 1894 was appointed prof. of harmony at the Paris Cons.; retired from there in 1923. He wrote several operas which were produced without much success: *Enguerrande* (1892); *Tancrède* (1898); *Les Demoiselles de Saint-Cyr* (1921); also several oratorios and dramatic cantatas; numerous choruses; several pieces of chamber music. He publ. a harmony manual, *Traité d'harmonie théorique et pratique*.

Charles, Ernest, American songwriter; b. Minneapolis, Nov. 21, 1895; d. Beverly Hills, Calif., April 16, 1984. He began his career as a singer in Broadway revues and in vaudeville; also wrote songs in an appetizing semi-classical genre, suitable for recitals. His 1st commercial success came in 1932 when the popular baritone John Charles Thomas sang his song *Clouds* in a N.Y. recital. Encouraged, Charles put out something like 50 solo songs, many of which made the top listing among recitalists: *Let My Song Fill Your Heart; My Lady Walks in Loneliness; When I Have Sung My Songs; If You Only Knew; Sweet Song of Long Ago; Oh, Lovely World.*

BIBL.: L. Wolz, "The Songs of E. C.," *NATS Bulletin* (March/April 1983).

Charles, Ray (full name, **Ray Charles Robinson**), outstanding black American rhythm-and-blues and soul singer, pianist, arranger, and songwriter; b. Albany, Ga., Sept. 23, 1930. Born to impoverished parents, he was stricken with glaucoma and became totally blind at the age of 6; nevertheless, he began playing the piano and was sent to the St. Augustine (Fla.) School for the Deaf and Blind, where he received instruction in composition and learned to compose in Braille; he also learned to play the trumpet, alto saxophone, clarinet, and organ. He quit school when he was 15 and formed his own combo; he settled in Seattle, where he acquired a popular following. Shortening his name to Ray Charles to avoid confusion with the boxer Sugar Ray Robinson, he scored his 1st hit recording with *Baby Let Me Hold Your Hand* (1951). It was followed by *I've Got a Woman* (1955), *Hallelujah, I Love Her So* (1956), *The Right Time* (1959), *What'd I Say* (1959), *Hit the Road Jack* (1961), *1 Mint Julep* (1961), and *I Can't Stop Loving You* (1962); among his notable albums were *The Genius of Charles* (1960) and *Modern Sounds in Country and Western Music* (1962). He also toured widely and frequently performed on radio and television. Having been a drug addict most of his mature years, he had several scrapes with the law before undergoing curative treatment in 1965. With D. Ritz, he publ. a chronicle of his life in *Brother Ray: Ray Charles' Own Story* (N.Y., 1978).

BIBL.: D. Rader, "R. C. Sees the Beauty," *Parade* (Aug. 7, 1988).

Charpentier, Gustave, famous French opera composer; b. Dieuze, Lorraine, June 25, 1860; d. Paris, Feb. 18, 1956. He studied at the Paris Cons. (1881–87), where he was a pupil of Massart (violin), Pessard (harmony), and Massenet (composition). He received the Grand Prix de Rome in 1887 with the cantata *Didon.* Charpentier evinced great interest in social problems of the working classes, and in 1900 formed the society L'Œuvre de Mimi Pinson, devoted to the welfare of the poor, which he reorganized during World War I as an auxiliary Red Cross society. He owes his fame to 1 amazingly successful opera, *Louise,* a "roman musical" to his own libretto (his mistress at the time was also named Louise, and like the heroine of his opera, was employed in a dressmaking shop), which was produced at the Opéra-Comique in Paris on Feb. 2, 1900. The score is written in the spirit of naturalism and includes such realistic touches as the street cries of Paris vendors. Its success was immediate, and it entered the repertoire of opera houses all over the world; its 1st American production, at the Metropolitan Opera in N.Y., took place on Jan. 15, 1921. Encouraged by this success, Charpentier wrote a sequel under the title *Julien* (June 4, 1913), but it failed to arouse interest comparable to that of *Louise.*

BIBL.: O. Séré, "G. C.," *Musiciens français d'aujourd'hui* (Paris, 1911); A. Homonet, *Louise* (Paris, 1922); M. Delmas, *G. C. et le lyrisme français* (Paris, 1931); K. Hoover, "G. C.," *Musical Quarterly* (July 1939).

Charpentier, Jacques, French composer and organist; b. Paris, Oct. 18, 1933. He studied piano with Maria Cerati-Boutillier; lived in Calcutta (1953–54), where he made a study of Indian music; prepared a valuable thesis, *Introduction à l'étude de la musique de l'Inde.* Upon his return to Paris he studied composition with Tony Aubin and musical analysis with Mes-

siaen at the Paris Cons. In 1954 he was appointed organist at the church of St.-Benoit-d'Issy; in 1966 was named chief inspector of music of the French Ministry of Cultural Affairs, and in 1975 was made Inspector General of the Secretariat of State for Culture; he traveled to Brazil and the U.S.S.R.; in 1974 was named official organist of the Church of St. Nicolas du Chardonnet in Paris. Several of his works are based on Hindu melorhythms.

WORKS: Violin Concerto (1953); *4 psaumes de Toukaram* for Soprano and Orch. (1957); 4 syms.: No. 1, *Symphonie brève,* for String Orch. (1958); No. 2, *Sinfonia sacra,* for String Orch. (1965); No. 3, *Shiva Nataraja* (Shiva—the King of the Dance; 1968; Paris, March 2, 1969); No. 4, *Brasil,* in homage to Villa-Lobos (1973); Concerto for Ondes Martenot and Orch. (1959); Concertino, *Alla francese,* for Ondes Martenot, Strings, and Percussion (1959–60); *Tantum ergo* for 4 Voices and Orch. (1962); Octuple Concerto for 8 Winds and Strings (1963); *La Croisade des pastoureaux,* oratorio (1964); *Prélude pour la Genèse* for String Orch. (1967); *Récitatif* for Violin and Orch. (1968); 7 concertos: No. 1 for Organ and Strings (1969); No. 2 for Guitar and Strings (1970); No. 3 for Harpsichord and Strings (1971); No. 4 for Piano and Strings (1971); No. 5 for Saxophone and Strings (1975); No. 6 for Oboe and Strings (1975); No. 7 for Trumpet and Strings (1975); *Béatris,* opera (Aix-en-Provence, July 23, 1971); *Musiques pour un Zodiaque,* oratorio (1971); 2 string quartets (1955, 1956); Piano Quintet (1955); Quartet for Ondes Martenot (1958); *Suite karnatique* for Solo Ondes Martenot (1958); *Prelude and Allegro* for Bass Saxophone and Piano (1959); *Lalita* for Ondes Martenot and Percussion (1961); *Pour Diane* for Horn and Piano (1962); *Pour Syrinx* for Flute and Piano (1962); *Mouvement* for Flute, Cello, and Harp (1965); *Gavambodi 2* for Saxophone and Piano (1966); *Pour le Kama Soutra* for Percussion Ensemble (1969); *Pour une Apsara* for 2 Harps (1970); *Esquisses* for Flute and Piano (1972); *Tu dors mais mon cœur veille* for Solo Violin (1974); *Une Voix pour une autre* for 2 Female Voices, Flute, Clarinet, and Percussion (1974); *Prélude* for Harpsichord (1975); *Toccata* for Piano (1954); *Etudes karnatiques* for Piano, in 4 cycles (1957–61); *Messe* for Organ (1964); *Répons* for Organ (1968).

Charpentier, Marc-Antoine, significant French composer; b. Paris, c.1645–50; d. there, Feb. 24, 1704. He studied with Carissimi in Italy. After returning to Paris, he became active as a composer to Molière's acting troupe; he was also in the service of Marie de Lorraine, the Duchess of Guise, later serving as her haute-contre, and finally as her maître de musique until her death (1688); likewise he was in the service of the grand Dauphin. Louis XIV granted him a pension (1683); he subsequently served as music teacher to Philippe, Duke of Chartres, was maître de musique to the Jesuit church of St. Louis, and finally held that post at Sainte-Chapelle (1698–1704). Charpentier was one of the leading French composers of his era, distinguishing himself in both sacred and secular works. His extensive output of sacred music includes 11 masses, 10 Magnificats, 4 Te Deums, 37 antiphons, 19 hymns, 84 Psalms, and over 200 motets, many of which are akin to oratorios; he also composed sacred instrumental works. He wrote some 30 works for the stage, including the tragédies lyriques *David et Jonathas* (1688) and *Médée* (1693), cantatas, overtures, ballet airs, pastorals, incidental pieces, airs sérieux, airs à boire, etc.; he also composed secular instrumental pieces, including dances for strings. H. Hitchcock has prepared *Les Œuvres de Marc-Antoine Charpentier: Catalogue raisonné* (Paris, 1982).

BIBL.: H. Hitchcock, *The Latin Oratorios of M.-A. C.* (diss. Univ. of Michigan, 1954); C. Barber, *The Liturgical Music of M.-A. C. (1634–1704): The Masses, Motets, Leçons de Ténèbres* (diss., Harvard Univ., 1955); D. Loskant, *Untersuchungen über die Oratorien M.-A. C.s* (diss., Univ. of Mainz, 1957); J. Dunn, *The "Grands motets" of M.-A. C. (1634–1704)* (diss., Iowa State Univ., 1962); J. Burke, *M.-A. C. (c.1634–1704): Sources of Style in the Liturgical Works* (diss., Oxford Univ., 1985); A. Parmley,

The Secular Stage Works of M.-A. C. (diss., Univ. of London, 1985); H. Hitchcock, *M.-A. C.* (Oxford, 1990).

Charpentier, Raymond (Louis Marie), French composer and music critic; b. Chartres, Aug. 14, 1880; d. Paris, Dec. 27, 1960. He studied composition with André Gédalge; from 1921 to 1943 he was music director of the Comédie Française; then was active on the French radio (1944–50). Beginning in 1908, he wrote music criticism for various journals. As a composer, he wrote some 20 scores of incidental music for the plays produced at the Comédie Française and a comic opera, *Gérard et Isabelle* (Paris, 1912); also several symphonic overtures; 2 string quartets; Wind Quartet; Viola Sonata; piano pieces; songs to texts by Ronsard and Baudelaire.

Charteris, Richard, Australian musicologist; b. Chatham Islands, New Zealand, June 24, 1948. He studied at Victoria Univ. in Wellington (B.A., 1970), the Univ. of Canterbury (M.A., 1972), and the Univ. of London (Ph.D., 1976, with the diss. *John Coprario (Cooper) c. 1575–1626: A Study and Complete Critical Edition of His Instrumental Music*). He was Rothmans Research Fellow in the music dept. at the Univ. of Sydney (1976–78) and served as chief investigator of the Australian Research Grants Scheme (1981–86) and its successor, the Australian Research Council (from 1986). His scholarly interests include English and Italian music of the 16th and 17th centuries.

WRITINGS: *John Coprario: A Thematic Catalogue of His Music with a Biographical Introduction* (N.Y., 1977); *A Catalogue of the Printed Books on Music, Printed Music and Music Manuscripts in Archbishop Marsh's Library, Dublin* (Kilkenny, 1982); *Alfonso Ferrabosco the Elder (1543–1588): A Thematic Catalogue of His Music with a Biographical Calendar* (N.Y., 1984); ed., *Altro Polo: Essays on Italian Music in the Cinquecento* (Sydney, 1990).

Chase, Gilbert, eminent American musicologist; b. Havana, Cuba (of American parents), Sept. 4, 1906. He studied at Columbia Univ. and at the Univ. of North Carolina at Chapel Hill; also studied piano. From 1929 to 1935 he lived in Paris and was active as a music correspondent for British and American music periodicals. In 1935 he returned to the U.S.; during 1940–43 he was consultant on Spanish and Latin American music at the Library of Congress in Washington; simultaneously was active in an advisory capacity to musical radio programs. From 1951 to 1953 he was cultural attaché at the American Embassy in Lima, and from 1953 to 1955 served in the same capacity in Buenos Aires. He then became director of the School of Music at the Univ. of Oklahoma (1955–57); from 1958 to 1960 was cultural attaché in Belgium; from 1960 to 1966 he was a prof. of music and director of Latin American studies at Tulane Univ. in New Orleans; in 1965 he became ed. of the *Yearbook of Inter-American Musical Research*. In 1963 he organized the 1st Inter-American Conference on Musicology in Washington. In 1955 the Univ. of Miami bestowed upon him the title of Honorary Doctor of Letters. He also taught at the State Univ. of N.Y. in Buffalo (1973–74) and at the Univ. of Texas in Austin from 1975.

WRITINGS: *The Music of Spain* (N.Y., 1941; 2nd ed., 1959; in Spanish, Buenos Aires, 1943); *A Guide to the Music of Latin America* (Washington, D.C., 1962); *America's Music: From the Pilgrims to the Present* (N.Y., 1955; 3rd ed., rev., 1983; also tr. into German, French, Portuguese, and Spanish); *Introducción a la musica americana contemporánea* (Buenos Aires, 1958); *The American Composer Speaks: A Historical Anthology, 1770 to 1965* (Baton Rouge, 1966); *Two Lectures in the Form of a Pair: 1, Music, Culture and History; 2, Structuralism and Music* (Brooklyn, 1973); *Roger Reynolds: Profile of a Composer* (N.Y., 1982).

Chasins, Abram, greatly talented American pianist, composer, writer, and educator; b. N.Y., Aug. 17, 1903; d. there, June 21, 1987. He studied piano with Ernest Hutcheson and Rubin Goldmark; he was also a protégé of Josef Hofmann. At Hofmann's recommendation, he was appointed at age 23 to the faculty of the Curtis Inst. of Music in Philadelphia. On Jan. 18, 1929, he appeared as soloist in his own piano concerto with the Philadelphia Orch., with Ossip Grabrilowitsch conducting, and was again soloist in his 2nd piano concerto on March 3, 1933, with the Philadelphia Orch., under the direction of Leopold Stokowski. An adroit stylist in composition, he wrote a set of 24 preludes for piano and made virtuoso arrangements for 2 pianos of excerpts from *Carmen*. His 3 *Chinese Pieces* for Piano Solo became quite popular; an orch. version of one, entitled *Flirtation in a Chinese Garden*, was conducted by Toscanini with the N.Y. Phil. on April 8, 1931; this was the 1st work by an American composer selected for performance by Toscanini. In 1941 Chasins began a series of classical music radio broadcasts on WQXR in N.Y. From 1972 to 1977 he was on the faculty of the Univ. of Southern Calif. in Los Angeles. He publ. several books, among them *Speaking of Pianists* (N.Y., 1957; 3rd ed., rev., 1981), *The Van Cliburn Legend* (N.Y., 1959), *The Appreciation of Music* (N.Y., 1966), *Music at the Crossroads* (N.Y., 1972), and *Leopold Stokowski: A Profile* (N.Y., 1979).

Chatman, Stephen (George), American composer; b. Faribault, Minn., Feb. 28, 1950. He was a pupil of Walter Aschaffenburg and Joseph Wood at the Oberlin Cons. (B.M., 1972) and of Ross Lee Finney, Leslie Bassett, William Bolcom, and Eugene Kurtz at the Univ. of Michigan in Ann Arbor (M.M., 1973). After working with Karlheinz Stockhausen at the Cologne Hochschule für Musik on a Fulbright scholarship (1974), he completed his education at the Univ. of Michigan in Ann Arbor (D.M.A., 1977). In 1976 he joined the faculty of the Univ. of British Columbia in Vancouver.

WORKS: ORCH.: *2 Followers of Lien* (1973); *Occasions* (1975–77); *Grouse Mountain Lullaby* (1978); *They All Replied* (1978); *Crimson Dream* (1982–83); *Mirage* (1987). CHAMBER: *Music for Timpani with Alto Flute, Trombone, and Piano* (1971); *O lo velo* for Alto Saxophone and Percussion (1973); *Quiet Exchange* for Alto Saxophone or Clarinet, and Percussion (1976); *5 Scenes* for Flute and Guitar (1978); *Variations on "Home on the Range"* for String Quartet or Saxophone Quartet (1979); *Fleeting Thoughts* (1980); *Screams and Whispers* for Saxophone Quartet (1981); *Fanfare* for 3 Trumpets and 3 Trombones (1982). CHORAL: *Whisper, Baby* for Chorus, Piano, and Percussion (1975); *And There Will Be Signs* (1977); *Moonset* for Chorus, 5 Percussion, and Organ (1979); *You Have Ravished My Heart* (1981); *Elizabethan Spring* (1983); also songs.

Chaun, František, Czech composer and painter; b. Kaplice, Jan. 26, 1921; d. Prague, Dec. 31, 1981. A pharmacist by profession and a painter by avocation, he studied music privately with Jindřich Feld and Klement Slavický in Prague (1954–61). Stylistically and ideologically he modeled his works after those of Stravinsky, with both the parody and classical formality in a curiously synthetic design.

WORKS: ORCH.: *Fantasy* (1960); Sinfonietta Concertante for Bassoon, Strings, and Piano (1963); Kafka Trilogy (Prague, Nov. 26, 1968); *Ghiribizzo* for Piano and Orch. (1969); *Sinfonietta buffa* (1970); *Hommage à Dubuffet*, double concerto for Violin, Cello, Strings, 2 Oboes, and 2 Horns (1970; Prague, March 4, 1971); *Pět obrázků* (5 Pictures; 1971; Prague, March 24, 1974); *Obrázek* (Little Picture; 1980; Prague, March 27, 1981); choral and chamber works; piano pieces.

Chausson, (Amédée-) Ernest, distinguished French composer; b. Paris, Jan. 20, 1855; d. Limay, near Mantes, June 10, 1899 (in a bicycle accident). He studied with Massenet at the Paris Cons.; then took private lessons with César Franck, and began to compose. The influence of Wagner as well as that of Franck determined the harmonic and melodic elements in Chausson's music; but despite these derivations, he succeeded in establishing an individual style, tense in its chromaticism and somewhat flamboyant in its melodic expansion. The French character of his music is unmistakable in the elegance and clarity of its structural plan. He was active in musical society in Paris and was secretary of the Société Nationale de Musique. He composed relatively little music; possessing private means, he was not compelled to seek employment as a professional musician.

WORKS: OPERAS: *Les Caprices de Marianne* (1882–84); *Hélène* (1883–84); *Le Roi Arthus* (Brussels, Nov. 30, 1903); incidental music to *The Tempest* (1888) and *La Légende de Sainte Cécile* (Paris, Jan. 25, 1892); *Viviane,* symphonic poem (1882; rev. 1887); *Solitude dans les bois* (1886); Sym. in B-flat major (Paris, April 18, 1898); *Poème* for Violin and Orch. (Paris, April 4, 1897); *Poème de l'amour et de la mer* for Voice and Orch. (1882–92; rev. 1893); *Chanson perpétuelle* for Voice and Orch. (1898); *Hymne védique* for Chorus and Orch. (1886); *Chant nuptial* for Women's Voices and Piano (1887); Piano Trio; Piano Quartet; String Quartet (unfinished); songs: *Chansons de Miarka,* to words by Jean Richepin; *Serres chaudes,* to words by Maeterlinck; 2 *poèmes,* to words by Verlaine; etc.

BIBL.: O. Séré, *Musiciens français d'aujourd'hui* (Paris, 1911); Special issue of *La Revue Musicale* (Dec. 1925); H. Oulmont, *Musique de l'amour: E. C. et la "bande à Franck"* . . . (1935); J. Barricelli and L. Weinstein, *E. C.* (Norman, Okla., 1955); J. Gallois, *E. C.: L'Homme et son œuvre* (Paris, 1967); L. Davies, *César Franck and His Circle* (Boston, 1970); R.S. Grover, *E. C.: The Man and His Music* (London, 1980).

Chauvet, Charles-Alexis, French organist and composer; b. Marines (Seine-et-Oise), July 7, 1837; d. Argentan (Orne), Jan. 28, 1871. He studied organ and composition at the Paris Cons.; in 1869 he was appointed chief organist at the Trinité in Paris. He publ. numerous organ works and piano pieces adaptable for teachers, students, and performers.

Chavarri, Eduardo Lopez, Spanish conductor, teacher, writer on music, and composer; b. Valencia, Jan. 31, 1871; d. there, Oct. 28, 1970. He was a pupil of F. Pedrell; taught and conducted at the Valencia Cons.; founded a chamber orch. there. His compositions include *Acuarelas valencianas* for String Orch.; *Rapsodía valenciana* for Piano and Orch.; *Concerto español* for Piano and String Orch.; *Leyenda* for Chorus and Orch.; *Quarteto hispano;* quartets for 4 Violins; *Andaluza* for Cello and Piano; *Leyenda del Castillo Moro* for Piano; piano pieces; songs. He publ. a music history (2 vols.; 3rd ed., 1929); *Música popular española* (1927; 2nd ed., 1940); *Chopin* (Valencia, 1950); *Folklore musical español* (Madrid, 1955).

Chávez (y Ramírez), Carlos (Antonio de Padua), distinguished Mexican composer and conductor; b. Calzada de Tacube, near Mexico City, June 13, 1899; d. Mexico City, Aug. 2, 1978. He studied piano as a child with Pedro Luis Ogazón; studied harmony with Juan B. Fuentes and Manuel Ponce. He began to compose very early in life; wrote a Sym. at the age of 16; made effective piano arrangements of popular Mexican songs and also wrote many piano pieces of his own. His 1st important work was a ballet on an Aztec subject, *El fuego nuevo,* which he wrote in 1921, commissioned by the Secretariat of Public Education of Mexico. Historical and national Mexican subject matter remained the primary source of inspiration in many works of Chávez, but he rarely resorted to literal quotations from authentic folk melodies in his works; rather, he sublimated and distilled the melorhythmic Mexican elements, resulting in a sui generis style of composition. In 1922–23 he traveled in France, Austria, and Germany, and became acquainted with the modern developments in composition. The influence of this period of his evolution as a composer is reflected in the abstract titles of his piano works, such as *Aspectos, Energía, Unidad.* Returning to Mexico, he organized and conducted a series of concerts of new music, giving the 1st Mexican performances of works by Stravinsky, Schoenberg, Satie, Milhaud, and Varèse. From 1926 to 1928 he lived in N.Y. In the summer of 1928 he organized the Orquesta Sinfónica de Mexico, of which he remained the principal conductor until 1949. Works of modern music occupied an important part in the program of this orch., including 82 1st performances of works by Mexican composers, many of them commissioned by Chávez; Silvestre Revueltas was among those encouraged by Chávez to compose. During his tenure as conductor Chávez engaged a number of famous foreign musicians as guest con-

ductors, as well as numerous soloists. In 1948 the orch. was renamed Orquesta Sinfónica Nacional; it remains a permanent institution. Chávez served as director of the Conservatorio Nacional de Música from 1928 to 1933 and again in 1934; he was general director of the Instituto Nacional de Bellas Artes from 1946 to 1952. Beginning in 1936 Chávez conducted a great number of concerts with major American orchs., and also conducted concerts in Europe and South America. Culturally, Chávez maintained a close connection with progressive artists and authors of Mexico, particularly the painter Diego Rivera; his *Sinfonía proletaria* for Chorus and Orch. reflects his political commitment. In 1958–59 Chávez was Charles Eliot Norton Lecturer at Harvard Univ.; these lectures were publ. in book form under the title *Musical Thought* (Cambridge, 1960); Chávez also publ. a book of essays, *Toward a New Music* (N.Y., 1937). A detailed catalog of his works in 3 languages, Spanish, Eng., and French, was publ. in Mexico City in 1971.

WORKS: OPERA: *Panfilo and Lauretta,* 1st produced in Eng. (1953; N.Y., May 9, 1957; then rev. and produced in a Spanish version as *El Amor propiciado,* Mexico City, Oct. 28, 1959; still later retitled *The Visitors*).

BALLETS: *El fuego nuevo* (1921; Mexico City, Nov. 4, 1928), *Los cuatro soles* (1925; Mexico City, July 22, 1930), *Caballos de Vapor* (1926; 1st produced in Eng. under the title *HP,* i.e., *Horsepower,* Philadelphia, March 31, 1932), *Antígona* (Mexico City, Sept. 20, 1940; orig. conceived as incidental music for Sophocles' *Antigone,* 1932), *La hija de Cólquide* (Daughter of Colchis; 1943; presented by Martha Graham under the title *Dark Meadow,* N.Y., Jan. 23, 1946), and *Pirámide* (1968).

ORCH.: *Sinfonía* (1915); *Cantos de Méjico* for Mexican Orch. (1933); *Sinfonía de Antígona,* Sym. No. 1, derived from his incidental music for *Antigone* (Mexico City, Dec. 15, 1933); *Obertura republicana* (Mexico City, Oct. 18, 1935); *Sinfonía India,* Sym. No. 2 (1935; broadcast, N.Y., Jan. 23, 1936); Concerto for 4 Horns (1937; Washington, D.C., April 11, 1937; rev. 1964); Piano Concerto (1938–40; N.Y. Phil., Jan. 1, 1942); *Cuatro nocturnos* for Soprano, Contralto, and Orch. (1939); *Toccata* (1947); Violin Concerto (1948; Mexico City, Feb. 29, 1952); Sym. No. 3 (1951; Caracas, Dec. 11, 1954); *Sinfonía romántica,* Sym. No. 4 (1952; Louisville, Feb. 11, 1953); Sym. No. 5, for Strings (Los Angeles, Dec. 1, 1953); Sym. No. 6 (1961; N.Y., May 7, 1964); *Soli No. 3* for Bassoon, Trumpet, Viola, Timpani, and Orch. (1965; Baden-Baden, Nov. 24, 1965); Sym. No. 7 (1960– ; unfinished); *Resonancias* (Mexico City, Sept. 18, 1964); *Elatio* (Mexico City, July 15, 1967); *Discovery* (Aptos, Calif., Aug. 24, 1969); *Clio,* symphonic ode (Houston, March 23, 1970); *Initium* (1972; Akron, Ohio, Oct. 9, 1973); *Mañanas Mexicanas* (1974; orig. for Piano, 1967); *Sonante* for String Orch. (1974); Trombone Concerto (1975–76; Washington, D.C., May 9, 1978).

CHORAL: *Tierra mojada* for Chorus, Oboe, and English Horn (Mexico City, Sept. 6, 1932); *El Sol* for Chorus and Orch. (Mexico City, July 17, 1934); *Sinfonía proletaria* (*Llamadas*) for Chorus and Orch. (Mexico City, Sept. 29, 1934); *La paloma azul* for Chorus and Chamber Orch. (1940); *Prometheus Bound,* cantata (1956; Aptos, Calif., Aug. 27, 1972).

CHAMBER: Piano and String Sextet (1919); 3 string quartets (1921, 1932, 1944); *3 Pieces* for Guitar (1923); Violin Sonatina (1924); Cello Sonatina (1924); *Energía* for 9 Instruments (1925; Paris, June 11, 1931); Sonata for 4 Horns (1929); 3 of 4 pieces under the generic title *Soli* (No. 1 for Oboe, Clarinet, Trumpet, and Bassoon, 1933; No. 2 for Wind Quintet, 1961; No. 4 for Brass Trio, 1966); *3 Espirales* for Violin and Piano (1934); *Xochipilli Macuilxochitl* for 4 Wind Instruments and 6 Percussionists (N.Y., May 16, 1940); *Toccata* for 6 Percussionists (1942; Mexico City, Oct. 31, 1947); 2 of 3 instrumental pieces, under the generic title *Invention* (No. 2 for String Trio, 1965; No. 3 for Harp, 1967), introducing an inductive method of thematic illation in which each musical phrase is the logical consequent of the one immediately preceding it; *Upingos* for Solo Oboe (1957); *Fuga HAG,C* for Violin, Viola, Cello, and Double Bass (1964); *Tambuco* for 6 Percussionists (1964); Variations for Violin and Piano (1969).

PIANO: 6 sonatas (*Sonata fantasía*, 1917; 1919; 1928; 1941; 1960; 1961); *Berceuse* (1918); *7 Madrigals* (1921–22); *Polígonos* (1923); *Aspectos I* and *II* (1923); Sonatina (1924); *Blues* (1928); *Fox* (1928); *Paisaje* (1930); *Unidad* (1930); *10 Preludes* (1937); *Fugas* (1942); *4 Études* (1949); *Left Hand Inversions of 5 Chopin Études* (1950); *Invention* No. 1 (1958); *Estudio a Rubinstein*, in minor seconds (1974); *5 caprichos* (1975–76).

VOICE AND PIANO: *3 exágonos* (1923); *Inutil epigrama* (1923); *Otros 3 exágonos* (1924); *3 poemas* (1938); *La casada infiel* (1941).

BIBL.: H. Weinstock, "C. C.," *Musical Quarterly* (Oct. 1936); R. Morillo, *C. C., vida y obra* (Buenos Aires, 1960); R. Halffter, compiler, *C. C., Catalogo completo de sus obras* (Mexico City, 1971); R. Parker, *C. C., Mexico's Modern-Orpheus* (Boston, 1983); idem, "Copland and C.: Brothers-in-Arms," *American Music* (Winter 1987).

Chaynes, Charles, French composer; b. Toulouse, July 11, 1925. He studied violin at the Cons. of Toulouse; later took courses in harmony and counterpoint with Jean and Noël Gallon, and composition with Milhaud and Rivier at the Paris Cons. He received the Premier Grand Prix de Rome in 1951 and stayed at the Villa Medicis in Rome to compose; returned to France in 1955; in 1964 was appointed program director on the French Radio. In his music he makes use of "chromatic totality," which extends into free dodecaphony and aleatory usages.

WORKS: Concerto No. 1 for String Orch. (1953); dramatic overture, *Ode pour une mort tragique* (1954); Sym. (1955); Trumpet Concerto (1958); Violin Concerto (1958; Paris, March 14, 1961); *4 illustrations pour la flûte de jade* for Solo Flute, Strings, Harp, and Percussion (1960); Concerto for Piano and Chamber Orch. (1961); Concerto No. 2 for Orch. (1961); *3 études linéaires* for 13 Instruments and Percussion (1963); *Commentaires concertants* for Violin and Orch. (1964); *Expressions contrastées* for Orch., Piano, and Percussion (Strasbourg Festival, June 23, 1966); Concerto for Organ, Strings, and Percussion (1966); *Transmutations* for Orch. (1971); *Peintures noires* for Orch. (1975); Flute Sonatina (1951); Violin Sonata (1952); *Serenade* for Wind Quintet (1954); *Quadretti italiani* for Violin and Piano (1957); *Réflexes* for Violin and Piano (1963); *Concordances* for Piano and Percussion (1967); *Irradiations* for Violin, Cello, and Harpsichord (1968); *Interférences* for Cello and Piano (1972); *Tarquinia*, 3 fresques for Ondes Martenot, Piano, and Percussion (1973); *Joutes* for Organ and Harpsichord (1975); *Valeurs transposées* for 14 Instruments (1979); *Capriccio* for Piano (1954); *Substances convergentes* for Piano (1964); *M'zab*, suite for Piano (1972); *Par ces chemins du cœur*, suite for Soprano and Orch. (1953); chamber cantata, *Joie aux âmes* (1962); *Alternances* for Alto and Piano (1965); *4 poèmes de Sappho* for Soprano and String Trio (1968).

Checker, Chubby (real name, **Ernest Evans**), black American rock-and-roll singer and dancer; b. Philadelphia, Oct. 3, 1941. Adopting the name Chubby Checker as a takeoff on Fats Domino, he 1st attracted a following with his recording of *The Class* (1959). Fame, however brief, was achieved with his recording of Hank Ballard's *The Twist* (1960); he then toured the U.S. to exploit the new dance craze. With the invasion of the Beatles in 1964 his career was aborted; in later years his performances were relegated to the U.S. nostalgia circuit.

Cheek, John (Taylor), American bass-baritone; b. Greenville, S.C., Aug. 17, 1948. He received a B.Mus. degree from the North Carolina School of Arts; then studied in Siena with Gino Bechi at the Accademia Musicale Chigiana, where he received the Diploma of Merit; he subsequently served in the U.S. Army. He made his professional debut in 1975. On Oct. 11, 1977, he made his Metropolitan Opera debut in N.Y. in the role of the physician in *Pelléas et Mélisande*; he later sang Pimen in *Boris Godunov*, Ferrando in *Il Trovatore*, Wurm in *Luisa Miller*, Klingsor in *Parsifal*, and also Panthée in *Les Troyens* at the opening-night celebration of the Metropolitan's

centenary season in 1983–84. In 1987 he won the North Carolina Arts Prize.

Chélard, Hippolyte-André(-Jean)-Baptiste, French composer; b. Paris, Feb. 1, 1789; d. Weimar, Feb. 12, 1861. He studied with Fétis and Gossec at the Paris Cons.; won the Grand Prix de Rome in 1811; in Rome he studied with Baini, and then took lessons in Naples with Paisiello. Returning to Paris, he produced the opera *Macbeth* (libretto by Rouget de Lisle) on June 29, 1827, with meager success. He was much more fortunate in Germany as an opera composer; in Munich he produced a German version of *Macbeth*; a new opera, *Mitternacht* (June 19, 1831); and a German version of his French opera *La Table et le logement*, under the title *Der Student* (Feb. 19, 1832). These were followed by the opera *Die Hermannsschlacht* (Munich, Sept. 12, 1835). From 1840 to 1852 he was court conductor at Weimar, where he brought out 2 comic operas, *Der Scheibentoni* (1842) and *Die Seekadetten* (1844). He also wrote a symphonic poem in 8 movements entitled *La Symphonéide* (1848).

Chelleri (real name, **Keller**), **Fortunato,** Italian composer; b. Parma, May 1690; d. Kassel, Dec. 11, 1757. He studied music with his uncle, F.M. Bassani, who was maestro di cappella at Piacenza Cathedral. His 1st opera, *Griselda* (Piacenza, 1707), was followed by 18 more, written for various Italian stages. He settled in Kassel in 1725 as court music director, and remained there until his death, except for brief journeys to London (1726) and Stockholm (1731). Besides his operas, he wrote 8 oratorios, including *Dio sul Sinai* (1731); overtures; church music; etc. He publ. a vol. of cantatas, and arias (London, 1726) and a collection of "Lessons" for harpsichord (London, 1750), containing 2 piano sonatas (really suites).

Chemin-Petit, Hans (Helmuth), German composer; b. Potsdam, June 24, 1902; d. Berlin, April 12, 1981. His family was of remote French origin; both his father and grandfather were professional musicians. He studied cello in Berlin with Hugo Becker and composition with Paul Juon; subsequently was mostly active as a cello teacher; was on the staff of the Berlin Hochschule für Musik and later at the Akademie der Künste; in 1968 was appointed director of its music dept. As a composer, he followed the median line of neo-Classicism.

WORKS: Chamber operas: *Der gefangene Vogel* (1927), *Lady Monika* (1930), *König Nicolo* (1962), *Die Komödiantin* (1968), and *Die Rivalinnen* (1970); 2 syms. (1932, 1949); Cello Concerto (1932); Concerto for Orch. (1944); Concerto for Organ, Strings, and Kettledrums (1963); *Music* for Orch. (1968); Sym. Cantata (1967); 2 sonatas for Recorder (1958, 1960); several cantatas; church music; piano pieces. He publ. a collection of choral arrangements of German folk songs (Berlin, 1949).

Chenoweth, Wilbur, American pianist and composer; b. Tecumseh, Nebr., June 4, 1899; d. Los Angeles, March 23, 1980. He studied piano with Sigismund Stojowski and Alexander Lambert in N.Y. and composition with Pietro Yon. In 1938 he moved to Los Angeles. He wrote some effective piano pieces, such as his *Concert Waltz*, and a lot of singable solo songs.

Cherbuliez, Antoine-Élisée, Swiss musicologist; b. Mulhouse, Alsace, Aug. 22, 1888; d. Zürich, Oct. 15, 1964. He studied science at the Univ. of Strasbourg and took private organ lessons with Albert Schweitzer. He studied music with his grandfather Adolphe Koekkert in Geneva, and took courses at the Zürich Cons. From 1913 until 1916 he studied privately with Max Reger in Jena. He served for a time as an organist; in 1923 was appointed instructor in musicology at the Univ. of Zürich. He wrote some chamber music and choruses, but devoted his energies mainly to writing. He publ. *Gedankliche Grundlagen der Musikbetrachtung* (Zürich, 1924); *Zum problem der religiösen Musik* (Basel, 1924); *Die Anwendung der Sievers'schen Theorien auf die musikalische Interpretation* (Zürich, 1925); *Peter Cornelius* (Zürich, 1925); *Die Schweiz in der deutschen Musikgeschichte* (Zürich, 1926); *Geschichte der Musikpedagogik in der Schweiz* (Bern, 1943); biographies of Bach, Handel, Haydn, Chopin, Grieg, Verdi, and Tchaikovsky;

monographs on Mozart, Beethoven, and Brahms; many articles for musical journals.

Chéreau, Patrice, prominent French theater, film, and opera producer; b. Lézigne, Maine-et-Loire, Nov. 2, 1944. He was a leading theater producer from 1964, serving as co-director of the Théâtre National Populaire (1979–81) and director of the Théâtre des Amandiers in Nanterre (from 1982). As an opera producer, he caused a major stir with his deconstructionist version of the centennial mounting of the *Ring* cycle at the Bayreuth Festival (1976–80); he also produced the premiere staging of the 3-act version of *Lulu* in Paris (1979).

Cherepnin. See **Tcherepnin.**

Cherkassky, Shura (Alexander Isaakovich), remarkable Russian-born American pianist; b. Odessa, Oct. 7, 1911. He began his piano training with his mother; while still a child, he was taken by his family to the U.S., where he continued his studies with Josef Hofmann at the Curtis Inst. of Music in Philadelphia. After making his debut in Baltimore at the age of 11, he appeared as a soloist with Walter Damrosch and the N.Y. Sym. Orch. and performed at the White House (1923); he made his 1st tour abroad in 1928 with visits to Australia and South Africa. Following a major tour of Europe in 1946, he pursued extensive tours to most of the major music centers in the world. In 1976 he went to Russia for a series of acclaimed concerts, and returned there in 1977 and 1987. He gave many recitals at N.Y.'s 92nd Street Y, which honored him in 1986 with the establishment of the Shura Cherkassky Recital Award to be given annually to a gifted young pianist. A typical product of the Russian school of pianists, Cherkassky excels in Romantic music. Thus it was a surprise when on Nov. 14, 1989, at the age of 78, he presented with great success at N.Y.'s Carnegie Hall a diversified program containing a sonata by Alban Berg and Stockhausen's *Klavierstück IX*, along with works by Handel, Weber, and Chopin.

Cherney, Brian, Canadian composer; b. Peterborough, Ontario, Sept. 4, 1942. He studied composition with Weinzweig and Dolin, and piano at the Univ. of Toronto (B.M., 1964; M.M., 1967; Ph.D., 1974); had short periods of study at Columbia Univ. and at the international summer courses for new music in Darmstadt; taught at the Univ. of Victoria (1971–72) and since 1972 at McGill Univ. in Montreal. His music is determined by structural factors, and is largely atonal; visually it is drawn in graphic notation.

WORKS: ORCH.: 2 sets of *Variations* (1962, 1967); *2 Songs* for Soprano and Chamber Orch. (1963); Violin Concerto (1964); *6 Miniatures* for Oboe and Strings (1968); *Mobile IV* for Soprano and Chamber Ensemble (1970); *7 Images* for 22 Players (1971); Chamber Concerto for Viola and 10 Players (1975); *Into the Distant Stillness . . .* for Chamber Orch. (1984). CHAMBER: Violin Sonata (1961); *3 Pieces* for String Quartet (1961); Suite for Solo Oboe (1962); Quintet for Saxophone and String Quartet (1962); *Interlude and Variations* for Wind Quintet (1965); *Suite* for Viola and Piano (1965); Wind Quintet (1965); 2 string quartets (1966, 1970); *Mobile II* for Solo Cello (1968); *Kontakion (Quiet Music for 11 Players;* 1969); *Mobile IIIa* for Oboe (1970); *Notturno* for Flute, Oboe, Clarinet, Bassoon, Horn, and Piano (1974); *Tangents I* for Solo Cello, Tape, Piano, Double Bass and Piano (1975); *Tangents II* for Oboe (1976); String Trio (1976); *In the Stillness between . . .* for Large Wind Ensemble and Percussion (1982); *Gan Eden* for Violin and Piano (1983). PIANO: *Fantasy* (1966); Sonata (1966); *Interludes, Shapes and Patterns* (1968); *6 Miniatures* (1968); *Jest* (1968); *In the Stillness of the 7th Autumn* (1983). ORGAN: *Gothic Scenes and Interludes* (1983–84).

Cherry, Don(ald), black American jazz cornetist, trumpeter, and pianist; b. Oklahoma City, Nov. 18, 1936. He studied trumpet and harmony while attending high school in Los Angeles; began his career in 1951, appearing with Red Mitchell, Dexter Gordon, and other jazz musicians; he then went to N.Y., where he worked and recorded with Ornette Coleman; after 1963 he toured extensively in Europe, and also in Africa.

A proponent of "free" jazz, he adopted instruments of other folk cultures in his performances.

Cherubini, (Maria) Luigi (Carlo Zenobio Salvatore), famous Italian composer and teacher; b. Florence, Sept. 14, 1760; d. Paris, March 15, 1842. He first studied music with his father, the maestro al cembalo at the Teatro della Pergola in Florence, and then composition with Bartolomeo Felici and his son Alessandro and with Bizarri and Castrucci. In 1778 he received a grant from the Grand Duke Leopold of Tuscany, which enabled him to continue his studies with Sarti in Milan. By this time he had composed a number of works for the church and also several stage intermezzi. While studying with Sarti, he wrote arias for his teacher's operas as well as exercises in the early contrapuntal style. His 1st operatic success came with *Armida abbandonata* (Florence, Jan. 25, 1782). In the autumn of 1784 he set out for London, where he was commissioned to write an opera for the King's Theatre. *La finta principessa* was given there on April 2, 1785, followed by *Il Giulio Sabino* (March 30, 1786), which brought him public acceptance and the admiration of the Prince of Wales. He made his 1st visit to Paris in the summer of 1785; there he was introduced to Marie Antoinette by the court musician Giovanni Battista Viotti; in the spring of 1786 he made Paris his home. He made 1 last visit to Italy to oversee the production of his opera *Ifigenia in Aulide* (Turin, Jan. 12, 1788). His 1st opera for Paris, *Démophon* (Paris Opéra, Dec. 2, 1788), was a failure, due largely to J.F. Marmontel's inept libretto and Cherubini's less than total command of French prosody. In 1789, Leonard, a member of the Queen's household, assisted by Viotti, obtained a license to establish an Italian opera company at the Tuileries (Théâtre de Monsieur); Cherubini became its music director and conductor. After the company moved to a new theater in the rue Feydeau, he produced his opera *Lodoïska* (July 18, 1791), with notable success; with this score, he effectively developed a new dramatic style, destined to have profound impact on the course of French opera. The increased breadth and force of its ensemble numbers, its novel and rich orchestral combinations, and its generally heightened dramatic effect inspired other composers to follow his lead, particularly Méhul and Le Sueur. With the French Revolution in full swing, the Italian Opera was disbanded (1792). Cherubini then went to Normandy, but returned to Paris in 1793 to become an inspector at the new Inst. National de Musique (later the Cons.). His opera *Médée* (March 13, 1797), noteworthy for its startling characterization of Medea and for the mastery of its orchestration, proved a major step in his development as a dramatic composer. With *Les Deux Journées, ou Le Porteur d'eau* (Jan. 16, 1800), he scored his greatest triumph with the public as a composer for the theater; the opera was soon performed throughout Europe to much acclaim.

In 1805 Cherubini received an invitation to visit Vienna, where he was honored at the court. He also met the foremost musicians of the day, including Haydn and Beethoven. He composed the opera *Faniska*, which was successfully premiered at the Kärnthnertortheater on Feb. 25, 1806. After Napoleon captured Vienna, Cherubini was extended royal favor by the French emperor, who expressed his desire that Cherubini return to Paris. When Cherubini's opera *Pimmalione* (Nov. 30, 1809) failed to please the Parisians, Cherubini retired to the château of the Prince of Chimay, occupying himself with botanizing and painting. At the request to compose a Mass for the church of Chimay, he produced the celebrated 3-part Mass in F major. He subsequently devoted much time to composing sacred music. In 1815 he was commissioned by the Phil. Soc. of London to compose a sym., a cantata, and an overture; he visited London that summer for their performances. In 1816 he was appointed co-superintendent (with Le Sueur) of the Royal Chapel, and in 1822 became director of the Paris Cons., a position he held until a month before his death. In 1814 he was made a member of the Inst. and a Chevalier of the Légion d'honneur, and in 1841 he was made a Commander of the Légion d'honneur, the 1st musician to be so honored. He was accorded a state funeral, during which ceremony his Requiem in D minor (1836) was performed.

Cherubini was an important figure in the transitional period from the Classical to the Romantic eras in music. His influence on the development of French opera was of great historical significance. Although his operas have not found a permanent place in the repertoire, several have been revived in modern times. His Sym. in D major is still performed by enterprising conductors. He also played a predominant role in music education in France during his long directorship of the Paris Cons. His influence extended beyond the borders of his adoptive homeland through his valuable treatise Cours de contrepoint et de fugue (written with Halévy; Paris, 1835; Eng. tr., 1837).

As the all-powerful director of the Paris Cons., Cherubini established an authoritarian regimen; in most of his instruction of the faculty he pursued the Italian type of composition. He rejected any novel deviations from strict form, harmony, counterpoint, or orchestration; he regarded Beethoven's 9th Sym. as an aberration of a great composer's mind. He rejected descriptive music and demonstratively refused to attend rehearsals or performances of the Symphonie fantastique by Berlioz, who was then a student at the Paris Cons. But his insistence on the letter of the musical law was nonetheless a positive factor; the treatise on counterpoint ed. by him remained for many years a fundamental study of the art of composition.

WORKS: A. Bottée de Toulmon prepared a Notice des manuscrits autographes de la musique composée par feu M.-L.-C.-Z.-S. C. (Paris, 1843; reprint, London, 1967); it contains the composer's own catalog of works. A modern catalog is included in A. Damerini, ed., L. C. nel II centenario della nascita (Florence, 1962). STAGE (only wholly extant works listed): Il giuocatore, intermezzo (1775); untitled intermezzo (dei Serviti, Florence, Feb. 16, 1778); Armida abbandonata, opera (Teatro alla Pergola, Florence, Jan. 25, 1782); Mesenzio re d'Eturia, opera (Teatro alla Pergola, Florence, Sept. 6, 1782); Il Quinto Fabio, opera (Torre Argentina, Rome, Jan. 1783); Lo sposo di tre e marito di nessuna, opera (San Samuele, Venice, Nov. 1783); Olimpiade, opera (c.1783); Il Giulio Sabino, opera (King's Theatre, London, March 30, 1786); Ifigenia in Aulide, opera (Teatro Regio, Turin, Jan. 12, 1788); Démophon, opera (Opéra, Paris, Dec. 2, 1788); La Molinarella, parody (Tuileries, Paris, Oct. 31, 1789); Lodoïska, heroic comedy (Feydeau, Paris, July 18, 1791); Eliza, ou Le Voyage aux glaciers du Mont St.-Bernard, opera (Feydeau, Paris, Feb. 23, 1794); Médée, opera (Feydeau, Paris, March 13, 1797); L'Hôtellerie portugaise, comic opera (Feydeau, Paris, July 25, 1798); La Punition, opera (Feydeau, Paris, Feb. 23, 1799); La Prisonnière, pasticcio (with Boieldieu; Montansier, Paris, Sept. 12, 1799); Les Deux Journées, ou Le Porteur d'eau, opera (Feydeau, Paris, Jan. 16, 1800; in Eng. as The Water Carrier and in German as Der Wasserträger); Epicure, opera (with Méhul; Favart, Paris, March 14, 1800); Anacréon, ou L'Amour fugitif, opéra-ballet (Opéra, Paris, Oct. 4, 1803); Achille à Scyros, ballet-pantomime (pasticcio, but most of the music by Cherubini; Opéra, Paris, Dec. 18, 1804); Faniska, opera (Kärnthnertortheater, Vienna, Feb. 25, 1806); Pimmalione, opera (Tuileries, Paris, Nov. 30, 1809); Le Crescendo, opera (Opéra-Comique, Paris, Sept. 30, 1810); Les Abencérages, ou L'Étendard de Grenade, opera (Opéra, Paris, April 6, 1813); Bayard à Mézières, comic pasticcio (with Boieldieu, Catel, and Nicolo; Opéra-Comique, Paris, Feb. 12, 1814); Blanche de Provence, ou La Cour de fées, pasticcio (with Berton, Boieldieu, Kreutzer, and Paër; Tuileries, Paris, May 1, 1821); La Marquise de Brinvilliers, pasticcio (with 8 other composers; overture by Cherubini; Opéra-Comique, Paris, Oct. 31, 1831); Ali-Baba, ou Les Quarante Voleurs, opera (Opéra, Paris, July 22, 1833). OTHER VOCAL MUSIC: 15 masses (4 not extant), including the Requiem Mass in C minor (1816; St. Denis, Jan. 21, 1817), Mass in A major (Rheims, May 29, 1825; for the coronation of Charles X), and Requiem Mass in D minor (1836; Paris, March 23, 1838; composed by Cherubini for his own funeral); 14 cantatas (4 not extant); motets, Kyries, Credos, etc.; other vocal works and sets of solfeggi. ORCH.: Sym. in D major (1815); Overture in G major (1815); marches; dances.

CHAMBER: 6 string quartets (1814, 1829, 1834, 1835, 1835, 1837); String Quintet in E minor (1837). KEYBOARD: 6 sonatas for Harpsichord (1780); Fantasia in C major for Piano (1810).

BIBL.: I. Arnold, L. C.: Seine kurze Biographie und ästhetische Darstellung seiner Werke (Erfurt, 1810); C. Place, Essai sur la composition musicale: Biographie et analyse phrénologique de C. (Paris, 1842); L. Picchianti, Notizie sulla vita e sulle opere di L. C. (Milan, 1843); D. Denne-Baron, Mémoires historiques d'un musicien: C., sa vie, ses travaux, leur influence sur l'art (Paris, 1862); B. Gamucci, Intorno alla vita ed alle opere di L. C. (Florence, 1869); E. Bellasis, C.: Memorials Illustrative of His Life (London, 1874; 3rd ed., rev., 1912); F. Crowest, C. (London, 1890); M. Wittmann, C. (Leipzig, 1895); R. Hohenemser, L. C.: Sein Leben und seine Werke (Leipzig, 1913); M. Quatrelles-L'Épine, C. (1760–1842): Notes et documents inédits (Lille, 1913); L. Schemann, C. (Stuttgart, 1925); P. Espil, Les Voyages de C. ou l'enfance de Mozart (Bayonne, 1946); G. Confalonieri, Prigionia di un artista: Il romanzo di L. C. (2 vols., Milan, 1948); M. Selden, The French Operas of L. C. (diss., Yale Univ., 1951); F. Schlitzer, Ricerche su C. (Siena, 1954); A. Damerini, ed., L. C. nel II centenario della nascita (Florence, 1962); C. Reynolds, C. (Ilfracombe, 1963); B. Deane, C. (London, 1965); M. White, The Motets of C. (diss., Univ. of Michigan, 1968); C. Parker, A Bibliography and Thematic Index of L. C.'s Instrumental Music (diss., Kent State Univ., 1972); G. Confalonieri, C. (Turin, 1978).

Cheslock, Louis, American composer; b. London, Sept. 9, 1898; d. Baltimore, July 19, 1981. He was brought to the U.S. as a child; studied violin with Van Hulsteyn and Gittelson, and composition with Strube at the Peabody Cons., in Baltimore; in 1916 became violin instructor there; then taught theory and composition. He served as a violinist in the Baltimore Sym. Orch. (1916–37), and also appeared as guest conductor. His music is of a neo-Romantic vein, with occasional incursions into modernity. He publ. Introductory Study on Violin Vibrato (Baltimore, 1931); ed. H.L. Mencken on Music (N.Y., 1961).

WORKS: Opera, The Jewel Merchants (Baltimore, Feb. 26, 1940); Sym. (1932); tone poems for Orch.: Cathedral at Sundown, 'Neath Washington Monument, and At the Railway Station (Chicago, April 29, 1923); ballet, Cinderella (Baltimore, May 11, 1946; enl. and rev. 1958); oratorio, The Congo (Akron, Ohio, Oct. 30, 1942); Violin Concerto (Baltimore, Feb. 25, 1926); Horn Concerto (1936); The Legend of Sleepy Hollow for Orch. (1936; Baltimore, May 2, 1978); Rhapsody in Red and White (An American Divertissement) for Orch. (1941); Set of 6 for Small Orch. (1946); piano pieces.

Chevalier, Maurice, popular French chansonnier; b. Paris, Sept. 12, 1888; d. there, Jan. 1, 1972. He began his career as a singer in Parisian cafés and music halls; then acted in films. In 1929 he went to Hollywood, and soon established himself as one of the foremost musical comedy stars, speaking and singing in English with an ingratiating French accent, affecting a debonair mien, carrying a cane, and wearing a straw hat. His early films included The Innocents of Paris (1929), Love Me Tonight (1932), and The Merry Widow (1934). He remained in France during the German occupation and gave shows for French prisoners of war in Germany. This activity led to accusations of collaboration with the enemy, but Chevalier was able to explain his conduct as a desire to maintain the public spirit among Frenchmen, and he was exonerated. His later films included Gigi (1958), Can-Can (1960), and Fanny (1961). A special Academy Award was presented to him in 1958 in appreciation of his contributions to popular entertainment.

BIBL.: C. Kirgener, M. C.: Itinéraire d'un inconnu célèbre (Paris, 1988).

Chevé, Émile-Joseph-Maurice, French music theorist; b. Douarnenez, Finistère, May 31, 1804; d. Fontenay-le-Comte, Aug. 26, 1864. A physician of great merit, he became a zealous advocate of Pierre Galin's method of musical instruction, explained in Galin's Exposition d'une nouvelle méthode pour l'en-

seignement de la musique (1818; 3rd ed., 1831), which attained considerable popularity; married **Nanine Paris** (d. 1868) and collaborated with her in a *Méthode élémentaire de musique vocale* (Paris, 1844; 2nd ed., 1863), in the preface to which he "exposes" and attacks the "defective" methods of the Cons. He and his wife also publ. *Méthode élémentaire d'harmonie* (Paris, 1846); and Mme. Chevé wrote *Nouvelle Théorie des accords, servant de base à l'harmonie* (Paris, 1844). He publ. a long series of essays and articles by which he vainly sought to draw out the profs. of the Cons. Acrimonious polemics raged for years, and numerous pamphlets were issued in Paris by adherents and foes of the Chevé method.

BIBL.: A. Pagés, *La Méthode musicale Galin-Paris-C.* (Paris, 1860); A.L. Montandon, *École Galin-Paris-C.; Problème musical, historique, pédagogique, prophétique* (Paris, 1861); O. Comettant, *Les Musiciens, les philosophes et les gaîtés de la musique en chiffres* (Paris, 1870).

Chevillard, (Paul Alexandre) Camille, French composer and conductor; b. Paris, Oct. 14, 1859; d. Chatou, Seine-et-Oise, May 30, 1923. He studied piano with Georges Mathias; was chiefly self-taught in composition. In 1897 he became assistant conductor of the Lamoureux Concerts in Paris; in 1899 succeeded Lamoureux as conductor after having married his daughter; from 1914 was conductor at the Grand Opéra.

WORKS: Orch. (all 1st perf. in Paris): *Ballade symphonique* (Feb. 23, 1890); *Le Chêne et le roseau* (March 8, 1891); *Fantaisie symphonique* (Oct. 21, 1894); also *Étude chromatique* for Piano; Piano Quintet, Piano Quartet, Piano Trio; String Quartet; Violin Sonata; Cello Sonata; songs with Orch., *L'Attente* and *Chemins d'amour*.

BIBL.: R. Rolland, *Musiciens d'aujourd'hui* (1908); O. Séré, "C. C.," in *Musiciens français d'aujourd'hui* (Paris, 1911); R. Dumesnil, *Portraits des musiciens français* (Paris, 1938); H. Schonberg, *The Great Conductors* (N.Y., 1967).

Chevreuille, Raymond, Belgian composer; b. Brussels, Nov. 17, 1901; d. Montignies-le-Tilleul, May 9, 1976. He took a course in harmony at the Brussels Cons., but was largely self-taught in composition. From 1936 to 1959 he was employed as a sound engineer at the Belgian Radio. His style of composition embodies distinct elements of French impressionism, with its searing melodies and rich harmonies within a framework of emancipated tonality, often verging on polytonal syncretism.

WORKS: Chamber opera, *Atta Troll* (1952); 4 ballets: *Jean et les Argayons* (1934); *Cendrillon* (1946); *La Bal chez la portière* (1954); *Spéléomagie,* miniature ballet for TV (1959); 2 symphonic radio plays: *D'un diable de briquet* (1950; Prix Italia, 1950) and *L'Élixir du révérend père Gaucher* (1951); 9 syms.: No. 1 (1939); No. 2, *Symphonie des souvenirs,* with Soloists and Chorus optional (Brussels, Nov. 23, 1945); No. 3 (Brussels, June 25, 1952); No. 4, *Short Symphony* (1952); No. 5, *Symphonie printanière* (1954); No. 6 (1957); Sym. for Chamber Orch. (1958); No. 7 (1964); No. 8 (1970); *Petite suite* for Orch. (1931); 3 piano concertos (1937, 1952, 1968); *Mouvements symphoniques* (1938); 2 cello concertos (1940, 1965); 3 violin concertos (1941, 1953, 1965); *Burlesque* for Cello and Orch. (1941); Concerto for Oboe, Clarinet, Bassoon, and Orch. (1943); Double Concerto for Piano, Saxophone or Viola, and Orch. (1946); *Divertissement* for Orch. (1946; extract from the ballet *Cendrillon*); Concerto for Orch. (1947); *Divertissement* for Chamber Orch. (1948); *Barbe-Bleue* (Bluebeard) *for Orch.* (1949); *Horn Concerto* (Brussels, July 12, 1950); *Trumpet Concerto* (1954); *Récréation de midi* for String Orch. (1955); *Mouvements,* suite for Brass (1956); *Carnaval à Ostende,* symphonic suite (1959); *Presto Giocoso* for Orch. (1961); Concerto Grosso for 2 Trumpets and Orch. (1961); Concerto for Flute and Chamber Orch. (1961); *Bruegel, peintre des humbles,* symphonic suite (1963); Concerto for Clarinet, String Orch., and Percussion (1968); 2 *Airs* for Orch. (1971); 6 string quartets (1930, 1934, 1934, 1939, 1943, 1945); Piano Trio (1936); String Trio (1937); Piano Quartet (1938); Cello Sonata (1941); *Divertissement* for Wind Quintet (1942); *Musiques lilliputiennes* for 4 Flutes (1942); Quartet for 4 Cellos (1942); Piano Sonatina (1943); Suite for

Piano (1943); Variations for Violin and Piano (1946); *Récit et Air gai* for Clarinet and Piano (1950); 5 Bagatelles for String Quartet (1952); Serenade for Wind Quintet (1958); Viola Sonatina (1959); *Récitatif et Marche* for Double Bass and Piano (1961); Wind Quartet (1964); Trio for Flute, Viola, and Double Bass or Piano (1961); Clarinet Quintet (1968); *Prelude, Scherzando et Marche* for Horn and Piano (1968); Clarinet Sonatina (1970); several cantatas: *Le Fléau* (1930); *Le Cantique de soleil* (1941); *L'Éléphant et le papillon* (1941); *La Dispute des orgues* (Brussels, Jan. 10, 1942); *Évasions* (1942); *Saisons* (1943); *Prière pour les condamnés à mort* for Narrator and Orch. (Brussels, Oct. 14, 1945); *Assonances* for Narrator and Chamber Orch. (1962); *Rhapsody* for Female Voice and Chamber Orch. (1969).

Chiara, Maria, Italian soprano; b. Oderzo, near Venice, Nov. 24, 1939. She studied with Antonio Cassinelli, who later became her husband, and with Maria Carbone. In 1965 she made her operatic debut in Venice as Desdemona. She subsequently appeared with the Bavarian State Opera in Munich and with the Vienna State Opera (1970); her debut at London's Covent Garden came in 1973 as Liù. In 1977 she made her U.S. debut as Manon Lescaut at the Chicago Lyric Opera; her Metropolitan Opera debut in N.Y. followed on Dec. 16, 1977, as Violetta. Among her most noted roles are Anna Bolena, Maria Stuarda, Amelia Boccanegra, and Elisabeth de Valois.

Chiari, Giuseppe, Italian composer; b. Florence, Sept. 26, 1926. He studied piano; organized the group Musica e Segno in association with Sylvano Bussotti; participated in the Fluxus festival in Wiesbaden (1962), and in avant-garde manifestations in N.Y. (1964) and at the Centre de Musique in Paris (1965). Eventually he returned to Florence, where he owned a clothing store. In his productions he follows the most latitudinarian and disestablishmentarian trends of metadadaistic fragmentationarianism, both in tonal and verbal structures. He publ. *Musica senza contrappunto,* a varitype anthology of disjected observations (Rome, 1969). In it he launched the slogan "Musica gestuale," which deals with audiovisual and tactile events, volitional as well as aleatory. His works include: *Intervalli* for Piano (1956); *Per arco* for Cello (1962); *Teatrino* for Actor-Pianist, Rubber Dolls, Alarm Clocks, and Handsaw (1963); *Don't Trade Here* for Action Theater (1965).

Chickering, Jonas, American piano maker; b. New Ipswich, N.H., April 5, 1798; d. Boston, Dec. 8, 1853. In 1818 he was apprenticed to John Osborn, a Boston piano maker; in 1823, he founded (with James Stewart) the firm of Stewart & Chickering, from 1829 known as Chickering & Mackay (John Mackay, d. 1841), later as Chickering & Sons. Jonas Chickering pioneered in the development of the upright piano, and the full metal plate for square and grand pianos. His son and successor, **Col. Thomas E. Chickering** (b. Boston, Oct. 22, 1824; d. there, Feb. 14, 1871), was named a Chevalier of the Legion of Honor, in addition to taking the 1st prize for pianofortes at the Paris Exposition of 1867. His 3 sons and their successors carried on the factory, which was famous for quality and high rate of production, until 1908, when it became part of the American Piano Co., and the factory was moved from Boston to East Rochester, N.Y. Later the firm became a subsidiary of the Aeolian American Corp.

BIBL.: R. Parker, *A Tribute to the Life and Character of J. C.* (Boston, 1854); *The Commemoration of the Founding of the House of C.* (Boston, 1904).

Chihara, Paul, American composer of Japanese descent; b. Seattle, July 9, 1938. After the outbreak of World War II, his family was relocated, with many other Japanese-Americans, to Minadoka, Idaho. He studied piano as a child; took courses in English literature at the Univ. of Washington (B.A., 1960) and at Cornell Univ. (M.A., 1961); then went to Europe, where he studied composition with Nadia Boulanger in Paris (1962–63) and with Ernst Pepping in West Berlin (1965–66); in the interim he obtained his A.M.D. at Cornell Univ. (1965). From 1966 till 1974 he was on the music faculty of the Univ. of Calif., Los Angeles; traveled to Japan for research in 1967.

In his music he utilizes advanced forms of serial techniques, occasionally extending them to aleatory procedures. In his choral compositions he follows the time-honored polyphonic methods of the Renaissance.

WORKS: Viola Concerto (1963); String Quartet (1965); *Tree Music* for 3 Violas and 3 Trombones (1966); *Branches* for 2 Bassoons and Percussion (1966); *Magnificat* for Treble Voices (1966); *The 90th Psalm,* choral cantata (1966); Nocturne for 24 Solo Voices (1966); *Redwood* for Viola and Percussion (1967); *Willow, Willow* for Bass Flute, Tuba, and Percussion (1968); *Rain Music,* tape collage using brewery noises, commissioned by Rainier Breweries in Seattle (1968); *Forest Music* for Orch. (1968; Los Angeles, May 2, 1971); *Driftwood* for Violin, 2 Violas, and Cello (1969); *Logs XVI* for Amplified String Bass and Magnetic Tape (1970); *Ceremony I* for Oboe, 2 Cellos, Double Bass, and Percussion (1971); *Ceremony II* for Flute, 2 Cellos, and Percussion (1972); *Ceremony III* for Small Orch. (1973); *Ceremony IV* for Orch. (1974); *Ceremony V, Symphony in Celebration* (1973–75; Houston, Sept. 8, 1975); *Grass,* concerto for Double Bass and Orch. (1971; Oberlin [Ohio] Cons., April 14, 1972); *Wild Song* for Cello and Orch. (1972); *Missa Carminum* for Chorus a cappella (Los Angeles, Jan. 15, 1976); Saxophone Concerto (Boston, Jan. 30, 1981); Sym. No. 2 (Los Angeles, March 20, 1982); *Sequoia* for String Quartet and Tape (1984).

Child, William, English organist and composer of sacred music; b. Bristol, 1606; d. Windsor, March 23, 1697. He was a boy chorister at Bristol Cathedral under Elway Bevin; studied at Oxford (B.Mus., 1631; Mus. Doc., 1663); in 1632 was in Windsor as organist at St. George's Chapel (succeeding J. Mundy) and then in London at the Chapel Royal; from 1643 to 1660 he apparently lived in retirement, devoting himself to composition; in 1660 he was appointed chanter at the Chapel Royal, and a member of the King's private band.

WORKS: He publ. Psalms (1639; later eds., 1650 and 1656), services, anthems, compositions in "Court Ayres," canons, catches, etc. (included in collections of Arnold Boyce, Hilton, Playford, and others); also instrumental works. Numerous services, anthems (including *O Lord, grant the King a long life*), a motet (*O bone Jesu*), and chants exist in MS.

BIBL.: F. Hudson and W.R. Large, "W. C.: A New Investigation of Sources," *Music Review* (Nov. 1970).

Childs, Barney (Sanford), American composer; b. Spokane, Wash., Feb. 13, 1926. He studied intermittently with Leonard Ratner, Carlos Chávez, Aaron Copland, and Elliott Carter; obtained a B.A. degree in English from the Univ. of Nevada (1949), an M.A. from Oxford Univ. as a Rhodes Scholar (1955), and a Ph.D. in literature from Stanford Univ. (1959). He taught English at the Univ. of Arizona (1956–65); then served as dean of Deep Springs College in California (1965–69). From 1969 to 1971 he taught music theory at Wisconsin College-Cons. in Milwaukee; in 1971 joined the faculty at Johnston College of the Univ. of Redlands in California; became a prof. there in 1973. Not overly concerned with public tastes and current fashions of cosmopolitan styles, he cultivates indeterminate structures. He ed., with Elliott Schwarz, *Contemporary Composers on Contemporary Music* (N.Y., 1967).

WORKS: 2 syms. (1954, 1956); 8 string quartets (1951–74); 5 wind quintets (1951–69); 2 violin sonatas (1950, 1956); Sonata for Clarinet (1951); *Concerto da camera* for Trumpet and Woodwinds (1951); Trio for Flute, Oboe, and Clarinet (1952); Quartet for Clarinet and Strings (1953); Sonata for Bassoon and Piano (1953); *4 Involutions* for English Horn (1955); *5 Considerations* for French Horn (1955); *7 Epigrams* for Soprano and Clarinet (1955); Concerto for English Horn, Strings, Harp, and Percussion (1955); Quartet for Bassoons (1958); Sonata for Oboe (1958); Brass Trio (1959); Flute Sonata (1960); Sonata for Trombone (1961); 6 pieces under the generic title *Interbalances* for various groups (1941–64); *Take 5* for 5 Instruments (1962); *Stances* for Flute and Silence (1963); Quartet for Flute, Oboe, Double Bass, and Percussion (1964); *6 Events* for Band (1965); *Music* for Piano and Strings (1965); *Jack's New Bag*

for 10 Players (1966); *The Golden Bubble* for Double Bass Sarrusophone and Percussion (1967); *Operation Flabby Sleep* for Any Instruments (1968); *Music* for 6 Tubas (1969); *Keet Seel* for Chorus a cappella (1970); Concerto for Clarinet and Orch. (1970); *Supposes: Imago Mundi* for Band (1970); *37 Songs* for Piano (1971); *When Lilacs Last in the Dooryard Bloom'd . . .* for Soloists, Chorus, and Band (1971); Trio for Clarinet, Cello, and Piano (1972); *Of Place, as Altered* for 5 Clarinets (1972); *Supposes: Cloud Busters* for Tuba (1972); *Of Place, as Particular* for Soprano and Tape (1973); *A Music; That It Might Be . . .* for 2 Clarinets (1973); *Concert Piece for Tuba and Band* (1973); Quintet for Winds, Harp, and Percussion (1974); *The Golden Shore* for Band (1974); *Lanterns and Candlelight* for Marimba and Soprano (1975); *Bowling Again with the Champs* for 6 Improvisers and Tape (1976); *A Question of Summer* for Tuba and Harp (1976); *4 Pieces for 6 Winds* for Wind Quintet and Saxophone (1977); *Couriers of the Crimson Dawn* for Any Instruments (1977); *Quartet/ Fantasy* for 4 Tubas (1977); *The Big New Improved Everybody Play Summer Music Clinic 12 Clarinet Fun Piece* (1977); *A Cello Piece* (1978); *September with Band* for Band (1978); *Featuring: "Mighty" Joe Nowhere und die Greater Wairopi All*Stars* for 7 Equal Instruments (1978); *Overture to Measuring a Meridian* for Wind Sextet and Percussion (1978); *As Endless Autumn* for High School Chorus, Horn, and Oboe (1978); *7 Quiet Studies* for Percussion (1978); *6 Gamut Studies* for Marimba (1978); *A Clarinet Piece* for Clarinet (1978); *Since Then* for Piano (1979); *The Word from Department R* for Clarinet and Alto Saxophone (1979); *Mosaic on a Theme of Balakirev* for Alto Saxophone (1979); *A Continuance, in 7 Parts* for Band (1979); *Heaven to Clear When Day Did Close* for Piano (1980); *Sky Visit* for Cello (1980); *Clay Music* for 4 Players on special handmade clay instruments (1980); *!BANANA FLANNEL-BOARD!—the Historic 1st Album* for 3 Readers and Tape Delay (1980); *Orrery for Band* (1980); *Sleep, and Then Going On* for Clarinet and 2 Cymbals (1980); *13 Classic Studies for the Contrabass* (1981); *The Edge of the World* for Bass Clarinet and Organ (1981); *Real Music* for 2 Clarinets (1981); *81 Licks for Trombone* (1983); *Pastorale* for Bass Clarinet and Tape (1983); *Sunshine Lunchh, & Like Matters* for Bass Clarinet, Baritone, Percussion, and Electronic Music Machine (1984; "Lunchh" is the emphatically designated rendering by the composer); Horn Octet (1984); *Instant Winners* for E-flat Clarinet (1986); *A Box of Views* for Wind Quintet and Piano (1988); Concerto for Timpani and Orch. (1989).

Chilesotti, Oscar, Italian music historiographer; b. Basano, July 12, 1848; d. there, June 23, 1916. He was a graduate in law of Padua Univ.; was also a good flutist and cellist; self-taught in harmony. He lived in Milan, where he wrote regularly for the *Gazzetta Musicale.*

WRITINGS: *Biblioteca di rarità musicali* (9 vols., Milan, 1883), containing transcriptions from little-known works of the early 17th century, and (vol. IV) *Arianna* by Benedetto Marcello; *I nostri Maestri del passato* (Milan, 1882), biographical notes on the greatest Italian musicians, from Palestrina to Bellini; *Di G.B. Besardo e del suo "Thesaurus Harmonicus"* (Milan, 1886; French ed., 1901); *Sulla lettera critica di B. Marcello contra A. Lotti* (Bassano, 1885); *Sulla melodia popolare del cinquecento* (Milan, 1889); *Lautenspieler des 16. Jahrhunderts* (Leipzig, 1891); *L'evoluzione nella musica, appunti sulla teoria di H. Spencer* (Turin, 1911); etc.

BIBL.: V. Fedeli, "Il Dr. O. C.," *Rivista Musicale Italiana,* XXIII/3–4 (1916).

Chilingirian, Levon, Cypriot violinist; b. Nicosia, May 28, 1948. After studies in Nicosia, he pursued formal training at the Royal College of Music in London and with M. Parikian. With the pianist Clifford Benson, he won 1st prize in the BBC Beethoven Competition in 1969 and in the Munich International Competition in 1971; they toured widely in recital from 1970. In 1971 he organized the Chilingirian String Quartet, which acquired a fine reputation.

Chiriac, Mircea, Rumanian composer; b. Bucharest, May 19, 1919. He studied harmony with Otescu and Jora at the Bucharest Cons. (1936–45); in 1966 he was appointed to its faculty.
Works: ballets: *Iancu Jianu* (1959–63; Bucharest, Feb. 7, 1964); *Vapăia* (1973–74; Bucharest, Feb. 17, 1974). **orch.:** *Nocturne* (1945); 2 rhapsodies (1951, 1955); *Festival Overture* (1953); *Poem* for Violin and Orch. (1954); *Bucureştiul de altă dată* (1957); *Sinfonietta* (1965); Concerto for String Orch. (1966); *Simfonie de cameră* (1969); *Prelude, Intermezzo, and Toccata,* symphonic triptych (1971); *Divertissement* for String Orch. (1971); *Terra Daciae,* 3 poems for Tenor and Orch. (1977); Variations for Piano and Orch. (1978); *Ars poetica,* 5 poems for Tenor and Orch. (1980); *Thalassa,* symphonic poem (1982). **chamber:** 4 string quartets (1945; 1972; 1980; 1984–85); Trio for Piano, Violin, and Cello (1975); Sonata for Clarinet and Piano (1981); Quintet for Flute, Oboe, Clarinet, Horn, and Bassoon (1982); songs.

Chisholm, Erik, Scottish composer and conductor; b. Glasgow, Jan. 4, 1904; d. Rondebosch, South Africa, June 7, 1965. He 1st studied music in Glasgow; then in London and in Edinburgh with Donald Tovey (composition) and Puishnov (piano); received his Mus.Bac. in 1931, and his Mus.Doc. from Edinburgh Univ. in 1934. He was conductor of the Glasgow Grand Opera Soc. from 1930 to 1939; in 1940 joined the Carl Rosa Opera Co. as conductor; in 1943 toured with the Anglo-Polish Ballet; later went to the Far East; organized the Singapore Sym. Orch. in 1945, and conducted 50 concerts in Malaya; in 1946 was appointed prof. of music and director of the South African College of Music at Cape Town Univ.; also conducted operas in South Africa. His book, *The Operas of Leoš Janáček,* was publ. posth. (N.Y., 1971). Chisholm's style of composition is marked by considerable complexity; elements of oriental scale formations are notable.
Works: operas: *The Feast of Samhain* (1941); *The Inland Woman* (Cape Town, Oct. 21, 1953); *Dark Sonnet,* after O'Neill's drama *Before Breakfast* (Cape Town, Oct. 20, 1952); *Simoon,* after Strindberg (1953); *Dark Sonnet* and *Simoon* were later combined with a 3rd short opera, *Black Roses* (libretto by the composer), to form a trilogy entitled *Murder in 3 Keys* (N.Y., July 6, 1954). **ballets:** *The Pied Piper of Hamelin* (1937); *The Forsaken Mermaid* (1940); *The Earth Shapers* (1941); *The Hoodie* (1947). **orch.:** *Straloch Suite* (1933); Sym. No. 1 (1938); Sym. No. 2 (1939); *The Adventures of Babar,* with Narrator (1940); *Piobaireachd Concerto* for Piano and Orch. (1940); *Pictures from Dante* (1948); *Hindustani Concerto* for Piano and Orch. (Cape Town, Nov. 22, 1949); Violin Concerto (Cape Town Festival, March 18, 1952); Concerto for Orch. (Cape Town, March 29, 1952). **chamber:** Double Trio for Clarinet, Bassoon, Trumpet, Violin, Cello, and Double Bass. Also choral works, songs, piano pieces.

Chladni, Ernest (Florens Friedrich), eminent German acoustician; b. Wittenberg, Nov. 30, 1756; d. Breslau, April 3, 1827. At first a student and prof. of law at Wittenberg and Leipzig, he turned to physics, and made highly important researches in the domain of acoustics. He discovered the "Tonfiguren" (tone-figures; i.e., the regular patterns assumed by dry sand on a glass plate set in vibration by a bow); invented the Euphonium (glass-rod harmonica) and Clavicylinder (steelrod keyboard harmonica). To introduce his ideas and inventions, he made long journeys and delivered many scientific lectures. His earlier publications, *Entdeckungen über die Theorie des Klanges* (1787), *Über die Longitudinal-schwingungen der Saiten und Stäbe,* and a series of minor articles in various periodicals, were followed by the important works *Die Akustik* (1802; 2nd ed., 1830; French tr., 1809); *Neue Beiträge zur Akustik* (1817); *Beiträge zur praktischen Akustik* (1821); *Kurze Übersicht der Schall- und Klanglehre* (1827).
Bibl.: W. Bernhardt, *Dr. E. C., der Akustiker* (Wittenberg, 1856).

Chlubna, Osvald, Czech composer; b. Brünn, June 22, 1893; d. there (Brno), Oct. 30, 1971. He studied composition with

Janáček in Brno (1914–15) and later at the Brno branch of the Master School of the Prague Cons. (1923–24); taught in Brno at the Cons. (1919–35) and at the Janáček Academy of Music (1953–59). His music is marked by rhapsodic élan; many of his works reflect national events. In 1948 he completed Janáček's unfinished symphonic poem, *Dunaj* (The Danube; 1923–28).
Works: 8 operas: *Pomsta Catullova* (Catullus's Revenge; 1917; Brno, Nov. 30, 1921); *Aladina and Palomid,* after Maeterlinck (1921–22; Brno, Jan. 31, 1925); *Nura* (1930; Brno, May 20, 1932); *Freje pana z Heslova* (The Love Affairs of the Squire of Heslov; 1939–40; Brno, Jan. 28, 1949); *Jiří of Kunštát and Poděbrady* (1941–42); *Kolébka* (The Cradle; 1952; Brno, 1953); *Eupyros* (1962); *Rytíř Jan z Linhartic* (Knight Jan von Linhartic; 1967); scenic mystery play, *V den počátku* (The Day of Beginning; 1935; Brno, Jan. 24, 1936); 7 cantatas: *České vzkříšení* (The Czech Resurrection; 1943); *My Land Is Beautiful* (1955); *In the Name of Life* (1959); *The Eternal Vigils of Life and Death* (1964); *Only Once,* chamber cantata (1967); *Leonydas,* chamber cantata (1968); *The Death of Caesar,* chamber cantata (1968); 7 symphonic poems: *Distance and Dreams* (1916); *Before I Grow Silent* (1918); *2 Fairy Tales* (1920); *A Song of Longing* (1922); *From Hills, Mountains and Forests* (1934); *Nature and Man* (a trilogy including the separate works *Spring, Summer Serenade,* and *Carnival of Autumn,* 1949–53); *This Is My Land* (a cycle including the separate works *The Fountains of Brno, The Abyss of Macocha, Pernštejn Castle, Moravian Slovakia,* and *Brno Portals and Frescoes,* 1956–62); *Sinfonietta* (1924); 3 syms.: No. 1, *Symphony of Life and Love* (1927); No. 2, *Brno Symphony* (1946); No. 3 (1960); Piano Concerto (1937); Cello Concerto (1938); Violin Concerto (1950); 5 string quartets (1925, 1928, 1933, 1963, 1969); Sonata for Violin and Cello (1925); Violin Sonata (1948); Cello Sonata (1948); choruses; songs.
Bibl.: M. Černohorská, *O. C.* (Brno, 1963).

Chmura, Gabriel, Polish-born Israeli conductor; b. Wroclaw, May 7, 1946. His family emigrated in 1955 to Israel, where he studied piano, theory, and composition at the Tel Aviv Academy of Music; he then studied conducting with Dervaux in Paris (1968), Ferrara in Siena (1969), and Swarowsky in Vienna (1969–71). He won the Gold Medal at the Cantelli Competition in Milan and 1st prize at the Karajan Competition in Berlin in 1971; he subsequently served as Karajan's assistant until 1973. He was Generalmusikdirektor in Aachen (1974–82) and of the Bochum Sym. Orch. (from 1982), and appeared throughout Europe as a guest conductor, making his North American debut with the N.Y. Phil. in 1980. From 1987 to 1990 he was principal conductor and music director of the National Arts Centre Orch. in Ottawa.

Chomiński, Józef Michal, eminent Polish musicologist; b. Ostrów, near Przemyśl, Aug. 24, 1906. He took courses in musicology with Chybiński and in ethnography with Adam Fischer at the Univ. of Lwow (1926–31; M.A., 1931; Ph.D., 1936); he completed his Habilitation in 1949 at the Univ. of Poznan. He taught at the Poznan music school (1945–48) and the Univ. of Warsaw (1947–76), and also served as chairman of the music division in the art inst. of the Polish Academy of Sciences (1951–68). He ed. *Muzyka* (1956–71) and the Monumenta Musicae in Polonia series (1964–71).
Writings: *Preludia Chopina* (Krakow, 1950); ed. with Z. Lissa, *Muzyka polskiego Odrodzenia* (Music of the Polish Renaissance; Warsaw, 1953; 4th ed., 1958); ed. with K. Wilkowska-Chomińska, *Formy muzyczne* (Krakow; vol. I, *Male formy instrumentalne* [Small Instrumental Forms], 1954; 2nd ed., augmented, 1983; vol. II, *Wielkie formy instrumentalne* [Large Instrumental Forms], 1956; vol. III, *Piesn* [Song], 1974; vol. IV, *Opera i drama* [Opera and Drama], 1976; vol. V, *Wielkie formy wokalne* [Large Vocal Forms], 1984); ed. with Z. Lissa, *Kultura muzyczna Polski ludowej 1944–1955* (Musical Culture of the People's Republic of Poland 1944–1955; Krakow, 1957); ed., *Historia muzyki powszechnij* (A General History of Music;

Krakow, 1957–64); *Historia harmonii i kontrapunktu* (3 vols., Krakow, 1958, 1962, 1988); *Sonaty Chopina* (Krakow, 1960); ed., *Z życia i twórczości Karola Szymanowskiego* (Life and Works of Karol Szymanowski; Krakow, 1960); ed., *Słownik muzyków polskich* (A Dictionary of Polish Music; Krakow, 1964–67); *Muzyka Polski ludowej* (Music in the People's Republic of Poland; Warsaw, 1968); *Studia nad twórczością Karola Szymanowskiego* (Krakow, 1969); *Chopin* (Krakow, 1978).

Chookasian, Lili, American contralto; b. Chicago, Aug. 1, 1921. She studied with Phillip Manuel, then made her concert debut as soloist in Mahler's 3rd Sym. with Bruno Walter and the Chicago Sym. Orch. (1957). Her operatic debut followed as Adalgisa at the Arkansas Opera Theater in Little Rock (1959), and, after additional training with Rosa Ponselle, she made her Metropolitan Opera debut in N.Y. as La Cieca in *La Gioconda* (March 9, 1962). She made her 1st European appearance at the Bayreuth Festival in 1963 and in subsequent years sang widely in both opera and concert performances, appearing often in contemporary works.

Chop, Max (pen name, **Monsieur Charles**), German writer on music and composer; b. Greuzen, Thuringia, May 17, 1862; d. Berlin, Dec. 20, 1929. A law student turned musician, he publ. several books of songs and ballades, 3 piano concertos, a Piano Trio, and 2 orch. suites; he lived from 1885 to 1888 in Berlin as a writer of musical feuilletons; then, until 1902, in Neu-Ruppin as music critic and ed. of the *Märkische Zeitung;* in 1902 he was again in Berlin; from 1920 until his death, was ed. in chief of *Die Signale*. An ardent admirer of August Bungert, he publ. his detailed biography (Berlin, 1915) and analyses of his music dramas; was (from 1911) the ed. of *Der Bund*, the official organ of the Bungert Association. He publ. *Zeitgenössische Tondichter* (2 vols., 1888–90, each containing 12 sketches); analyses of Liszt's symphonic poems, Wagner's music dramas, etc.; a sketch of August Bungert in vol. III of *Monographien moderner Musiker* (1903); *Vademecum für den Konzertsaal* (1904, et seq.); biographies of Delius (1907) and Reznĭček (1920); *Führer durch die Musikgeschichte* (Berlin, 1912).

Chopin, Frédéric (-François) (Fryderyk Franciszek), greatly renowned Polish composer, incomparable genius of the piano who created a unique romantic style of keyboard music; b. Zelazowa Wola, near Warsaw, in all probability on March 1, 1810, the date given by Chopin himself in his letter of acceptance of membership in the Polish Literary Soc. in Paris in 1833 (but in his certificate of baptism the date of birth is given as Feb. 22, 1810); d. Paris, Oct. 17, 1849. His father, Nicolas Chopin, was a native of Marainville, France, who went to Warsaw as a teacher of French; his mother, Tekla Justyna Krzyzanowska, was Polish. Chopin's talent was manifested in early childhood; at the age of 8 he played in public a piano concerto by Gyrowetz, and he had already begun to compose polonaises, mazurkas, and waltzes. He received his primary musical instruction from the Bohemian pianist Adalbert Żywny, who resided in Warsaw at the time. A much more important teacher was Joseph Elsner, director of the Warsaw School of Music, who gave him a thorough instruction in music theory and form. Chopin was 15 years old when his Rondo for Piano was publ. in Warsaw as op. 1. In the summer of 1829 he set out for Vienna, where he gave highly successful concerts on Aug. 11 and Aug. 18, 1829. While in Vienna he made arrangements to have his variations on Mozart's aria *Là ci darem la mano*, for Piano and Orch., publ. by Haslinger as op. 2. It was this work that attracted the attention of Schumann, who saluted Chopin in his famous article publ. in the *Allgemeine Musikalische Zeitung* of Dec. 7, 1831, in which Schumann's alter ego, Eusebius, is represented as exclaiming, "Hats off, gentlemen! A genius!" The common assumption in many biographies that Schumann "launched" Chopin on his career is deceptive; actually Schumann was some months younger than Chopin, and was referred to editorially merely as a student of Prof. Wieck. Returning to Warsaw, Chopin gave the 1st public performance of his Piano Concerto in F

minor, op. 21, on March 17, 1830. On Oct. 11, 1830, he was soloist in his Piano Concerto in E minor, op. 11. A confusion resulted in the usual listing of the E-minor Concerto as 1st, and the F-minor Concerto as his 2nd; chronologically, the composition of the F-minor Concerto preceded the E-minor. He spent the winter of 1830–31 in Vienna. The Polish rebellion against Russian domination, which ended in defeat, determined Chopin's further course of action, and he proceeded to Paris, visiting Linz, Salzburg, Dresden, and Stuttgart on the way. He arrived in Paris in Sept. 1831, and was introduced to Rossini, Cherubini, and Paër. He also met Bellini, Meyerbeer, Berlioz, Victor Hugo, and Heinrich Heine; he became particularly friendly with Liszt. Paris was then the center of Polish emigration, and Chopin maintained his contacts with the Polish circle there. He presented his 1st Paris concert on Feb. 26, 1832. He also taught the piano. The Paris critics found an apt Shakespearean epithet for him, calling him "the Ariel of the piano." In 1834 he went with F. Hiller to Germany, where he met Mendelssohn and Clara and Robert Schumann. In July 1837 he went with C. Pleyel to London. In 1836 he met the famous novelist Aurore Dupin (Mme. Dudevant), who publ. her works under the affected masculine English name George Sand. They became intimate, even though quite incompatible in character and interests. Sand was involved in social affairs and held radical views; Chopin was a poet confined within his inner world; it has been said that she was the masculine and he the feminine partner in their companionship. In the winter of 1838–39 Chopin accompanied Sand to the island of Majorca, where she attended to him with total devotion; yet she portrayed him in her novel *Lucrézia Floriani* as a weakling. Indeed, she was quite overt in her reference to him as a lover; in a personal letter dated 1838 she said that she had difficulty in inducing him to submit to a sensual embrace, and implied that she lived as an immaculate virgin most of the time they were together. They parted in 1847; by that time he was quite ill with tuberculosis; a daguerreotype taken of him represents a prematurely aged man with facial features showing sickness and exhaustion, with locks of black hair partly covering his forehead. Yet he continued his concert career. He undertook a tour as pianist in England and Scotland in 1848; he gave his last concert in Paris on Feb. 16, 1848. *La Revue et Gazette Musicale* of Feb. 20, 1848, gives a precious account of the occasion: "The finest flower of feminine aristocracy in the most elegant attire filled the Salle Pleyel," the paper reported, "to catch this musical sylph on the wing." Chopin played his last concert in London, a benefit for Polish émigrés, on Nov. 16, 1848. He died the following year; Mozart's Requiem was performed at Chopin's funeral at the Madeleine, with Habeneck conducting the orch. and chorus of the Paris Cons. and Pauline Viardot and Lablache singing the solo parts. He was buried at Père Lachaise between the graves of Cherubini and Bellini; however, at his own request, his heart was sent to Warsaw for entombment in his homeland.

Chopin represents the full liberation of the piano from traditional orch. and choral influences, the authoritative assumption of its role as a solo instrument. Not seeking "orchestral" sonorities, he may have paled as a virtuoso beside the titanic Liszt, but the poesy of his pianism, its fervor of expression, the pervading melancholy in his nocturnes and ballades, and the bounding exultation of his scherzos and études were never equaled. And, from a purely technical standpoint, Chopin's figurations and bold modulatory transitions seem to presage the elaborate transtonal developments of modern music.

WORKS: SOLO PIANO: *Albumleaf* (*Moderato*) in E major (1843); *Allegro de concert* in A major, op. 46 (1832–41); *Andante spianato* in G major, op. 22 (1834); *Andantino* in G minor (1838); 4 ballades: G minor, op. 23 (1831–35); F major/A minor, op. 38 (1836–39); A-flat major, op. 47 (1840–41); F minor, op. 52 (1842); *Barcarolle* in F-sharp major, op. 60 (1845–46); *Berceuse* in D-flat major, op. 57 (1843–44); *Introduction* in C major and *Bolero* in A minor/A major, op. 19 (1833); *Canon* in F minor (1839?); *Cantabile* in B-flat major (1834); *3 Écossaises*, in D major, G major, and D-flat major, op. 72, no. 3

(1826); 24 études: 4, in F major, F minor, A-flat major, and E-flat major, op. 10, nos. 8–11 (1829); 2, in G-flat major and E-flat minor, op. 10, nos. 5–6 (1830); 2, in C major and A minor, op. 10, nos. 1–2 (1830); C minor, op. 10, no. 12 (1830); C major, op. 10, no. 7 (1832); E major, op. 10, no. 3 (1832); C-sharp minor, op. 10, no. 4 (1832); 6, in A minor, E minor, G-sharp minor, D-flat major, G-flat major, and B minor, op. 25, nos. 4–6 and 8–10 (1832–34); A minor, op. 25, no. 11 (1834); F minor, op. 25, no. 2 (1836); C-sharp minor, op. 25, no. 7 (1836); 2, in F major and C minor, op. 25, nos. 3 and 12 (1836); A-flat major, op. 25, no. 1 (1836); *Fantaisie* in F minor/A-flat major, op. 49 (1841); *Fantaisie-impromptu* in C-sharp minor, op. 66 (1835); *Fugue* in A minor (1841–42); *Funeral March* in C minor, op. 72, no. 2 (1827); 3 impromptus: A-flat major, op. 29 (1837); F-sharp minor, op. 36 (1839); G-flat major, op. 51 (1842); *Introduction and Variations on the German air Der Schweizerbub* in E major (1826); *Introduction* in C major and *Rondo* in E-flat major, op. 16 (1832); *Introduction and Variations on Hérold's "Je vends des scapulaires" from Ludovic* in B-flat major, op. 12 (1833); *Largo* in E-flat major (1837?); 56 mazurkas: D major (1820?; not extant); A-flat major (1825; earlier version of op. 7, no. 4); A minor (1825; earlier version of op. 17, no. 4); 2, in G major and B-flat major (1826); A minor, op. 68, no. 2 (1827); F major, op. 68, no. 3 (1829); C major, op. 68, no. 1 (1829); D major (1829); A minor (1829; earlier version of op. 7, no. 2); 4, in F-sharp minor, C-sharp minor, E major, and E-flat minor, op. 6 (1830); 5, in B-flat major, A minor, F minor, A-flat major, and C major, op. 7 (1831); B-flat major (1832); 4, in B-flat major, E minor, A-flat major, and A minor, op. 17 (1832–33); C major (1833); A-flat major (1834); 4, in G minor, C major, A-flat major, and B-flat minor, op. 24 (1834–35); 2, in G major and C major, op. 67, nos. 1 and 3 (1835); 4, in C minor, B minor, D-flat major, and C-sharp minor, op. 30 (1836–37); 4, in G-sharp minor, D major, C major, and B minor, op. 33 (1837–38); E minor, op. 41, no. 2 (1838); 3, in C-sharp minor, B major, and A-flat major, op. 41, nos. 1, 3, and 4 (1839–40); A minor (1840); A minor (1840); 3, in G major, A-flat major, and C-sharp minor, op. 50 (1842); 3, in B major, C major, and C minor, op. 56 (1843); 3, in A minor, A-flat major, and F-sharp minor, op. 59 (1845); 3, in B major, F minor, and C-sharp minor, op. 63 (1846); A minor, op. 67, no. 4 (1846); G minor, op. 67, no. 2 (1849); F minor, op. 68, no. 4 (1849); *Military March* (1817; not extant); 21 nocturnes: E minor, op. 72, no. 1 (1827); C-sharp minor (1830); 3, in B-flat major, E-flat major, and B major, op. 9 (1830–31); 2, in F major and F-sharp major, op. 15, nos. 1–2 (1830–31); G minor, op. 15, no. 3 (1833); C-sharp minor, op. 27, no. 1 (1835); D-flat major, op. 27, no. 2 (1835); 2, in B major and A-flat major, op. 32 (1836–37); C minor (1837); G minor, op. 37, no. 1 (1838); G major, op. 37, no. 2 (1839); 2, in C minor and F-sharp minor, op. 48 (1841); 2, in F minor and E-flat major, op. 55 (1843); 2, in B major and E major, op. 62 (1846); 15 polonaises: G minor (1817); B-flat major (1817); A-flat major (1821); G-sharp minor (1822); D minor, op. 71, no. 1 (1825?); B-flat minor, *Adieu* (1826); B-flat major, op. 71, no. 2 (1828); F minor, op. 71, no. 3 (1828); G-flat major (1829); 2, in C-sharp minor and E-flat minor, op. 26 (1834–35); A major, op. 40, no. 1 (1838); C minor, op. 40, no. 2 (1839); F-sharp minor, op. 44 (1840–41); A-flat major, op. 53 (1842); *Polonaise-fantaisie* in A-flat major, op. 61 (1845–46); 26 preludes: A-flat major (1834); 24, op. 28 (1836–39); C-sharp minor, op. 45 (1841); rondos: C minor, op. 1 (1825); F major, op. 5, "à la Mazur" (1826); C major (1828; earlier version of the Rondo in C major for 2 Pianos, op. 73); 4 scherzos: B minor, op. 20 (1831–32); B-flat minor, op. 31 (1837); C-sharp minor, op. 39 (1839); E major, op. 54 (1842); 3 sonatas: C minor, op. 4 (1828); B-flat minor, op. 35, *Funeral March* (1839; 3rd movement is a *Funeral March* in B-flat minor, composed in 1837); B minor, op. 58 (1844); *Sostenuto* in E-flat major (1840); *Tarantelle* in A-flat major, op. 43 (1841); *3 nouvelles études*, for Moscheles's *Methode* (1839); Variation No. 6, in E major, from the *Hexameron* (*Variations on the March from Bellini's I Puritani*) (1837; other

variations by Liszt, Thalberg, Pixis, Herz, and Czerny); Variations in A major, *Souvenir de Paganini* (1829); 19 valses: A-flat major (1827); E-flat major (1827); B minor, op. 69, no. 2 (1829); D-flat major, op. 70, no. 3 (1829); E major (1829); E minor (1830); E-flat major, op. 18 (1831); A minor, op. 34, no. 2 (1831); G-flat major, op. 70, no. 1 (1833); A-flat major, op. 34, no. 1 (1835); A-flat major, op. 69, no. 1, *L'Adieu* (1835); F major, op. 34, no. 3 (1838); A-flat major, op. 42 (1840); F minor, op. 70, no. 2 (1841); A minor (1843?); 3, in D-flat major (*Minute*), C-sharp minor, and A-flat major, op. 64 (1846–47); *Galopp* in A-flat major (1846); B major (1848). **PIANO, 4-HANDS:** *Introduction, Theme, and Variations* in D major (1826). **2 PIANOS:** Rondo in C major, op. 73 (1828; later version of Rondo in C major for Solo Piano).

PIANO AND ORCH.: *Variations on Mozart's "Là ci darem la mano" from Don Giovanni* in B-flat major, op. 2 (1827); *Fantasia on Polish Airs* in A major, op. 13 (1828); *Krakowiak*, rondo in F major, op. 14 (1828); Piano Concerto No. 2, in F minor, op. 21 (1829–30; Warsaw, March 17, 1830, composer soloist; although listed as "No. 2," it was his 1st concerto in order of composition); Piano Concerto No. 1, in E minor, op. 11 (1830; Warsaw, Oct. 11, 1830, composer soloist; although listed as "No. 1," it was his 2nd concerto in order of composition); *Grand Polonaise* in E-flat major, op. 22 (1830–31).

CHAMBER: Piano Trio in G minor, op. 8 (1828–29); *Introduction and Polonaise* for Cello and Piano, in C major, op. 3 (1829–30); *Grand Duo on Themes from Meyerbeer's "Robert le diable"* for Cello and Piano, in E major (1832); Cello Sonata in G minor, op. 65 (1845–46).

SONGS: 17, op. 74 (to Polish texts; 1829–47).

BIBL.: COLLECTED EDITIONS, SOURCE MATERIAL: A number of so-called complete eds. of Chopin's works have been issued since the 19th century. The complete ed. begun by Paderewski and publ. by the Chopin Inst. of Warsaw and Polskie Wydawnictwo Muzyczne of Krakow (26 vols., 1937–66) is extensively annotated but is unreliable in parts since the editors did not always have access to important sources. In 1967 a new "National Edition" was begun under the editorship of J. Ekier. Breitkopf & Härtel publ. a *Thematisches Verzeichniss der im Druck erschienenen Kompositionen von Friedrich C.* (Leipzig, 1852; 2nd ed., rev., 1888). Another thematic catalog was prepared by F. Listy and H. Opieński (Warsaw, 1937). The most valuable is M.J.E. Brown, *C.: An Index of His Works in Chronological Order* (London, 1960; 2nd ed., rev., 1972). Other sources include the following: B. Sydow, *Bibliografia F.F. C.a* (Warsaw, 1949; supplement, 1954); K. Michalowski, *Bibliografia chopinowska/A C. Bibliography 1849–1969* (Krakow, 1970); A. Hedley, *Catalogues des manuscrits de F. C.* (Krakow, 1971); K. Kobylańska, *F. C., Thematisch-bibliographisches Werkverzeichnis* (Munich, 1979); D. Pistone, ed., *Sur les traces de F. C.* (Paris, 1984).

CORRESPONDENCE: M. Karlowicz, ed., *Nie wydane dotychczas pamiatki po C.ie* (New Unpubl. Souvenirs of C.; Warsaw, 1904; French tr., 1904); B. Scharlitt, ed., *Friedrich C.s gesammelte Briefe* (Leipzig, 1911); H. Opieński, ed., *C.; Collected Letters* (tr. from the original Polish and French, with a preface and editorial notes by E. Voynich; N.Y., 1931); B. Sydow, ed., *Korespondencja Fryderyka C.a* (2 vols., Warsaw, 1955; French tr., 1953–60); A. Hedley, ed., *Selected Correspondence of Fryderyk C.* (London, 1962); Z. Lissa, "C.s Briefe an Delfine Potocka," *Die Musikforschung*, XV (1962); J. Smoter, *Spór o "listy" C.a do Delfiny Potockiej* (The Controversy over C.'s "Letters" to Delfina Potocka; Krakow, 1967); M. Gliński, ed., *C.: Listy do Delfiny* (C.: Letters to Delfina; N.Y., 1972); K. Kobylańska, ed., *Korespondencja Fryderyka C.a z rodziny* (C.'s Correspondence with His Family; Warsaw, 1972).

In addition to the writings listed below, consult *Rocznik chopinowski/Annales C.* and *C. Jahrbuch* for important articles on his life and works.

BIOGRAPHICAL: G. Sand, *Un Hiver à Majorque* (Paris, 1842; 5th ed., 1929); idem, *Histoire de ma vie* (Paris, 1854; 7th ed., 1928); M. Karasowski, *Friedrich C.: Sein Leben, seine Werke und Briefe* (2 vols., Dresden, 1877; 4th ed., 1914; Eng. tr.,

London, 1879; 3rd ed., 1938); F. Niecks, *Frederick C. as a Man and Musician* (2 vols., London, 1888; German tr., Leipzig, 1890; 3rd Eng. ed., 1902); C. Willeby, *F.F. C.: A Biography* (London, 1892); J. Huneker, *C.: The Man and His Music* (N.Y., 1900; new ed., 1925); J. Hadden, *C.* (London, 1903; 2nd ed., rev., 1935); F. Hoesick, *C.* (Warsaw, 1904; rev., enl. ed. as *C.: Zycie i twórczość* [C.: Life and Work], 3 vols., 1910–11; further rev., 4 vols., Krakow, 1962–68); H. Leichtentritt, *C.* (Berlin, 1905); E. Ganche, *F. C.: Sa vie et ses œuvres* (Paris, 1909; Eng. tr., 1922; 7th French ed., 1949); B. Scharlitt, *C.* (Leipzig, 1919); Z. Jachimecki, *Fryderyk C.* (Krakow, 1926; French tr., 1930; 2nd Polish ed., 1949); G. de Pourtalès, *C. ou Le Poète* (Paris, 1927; Eng. tr. as *Frederick C.: A Man of Solitude*, 1927; 2nd ed. as *Polonaise: The Life of C.*, 1933; 10th French ed., 1963); E. Vuillermoz, *La Vie amoureuse de C.* (Paris, 1927; 2nd ed., rev., 1960); L. Binental, *C.* (Paris, 1934); W. Murdoch, *C. and His Life* (London, 1934); B. Ferra, *C. and George Sand in Majorca* (Palma de Mallorca, 1936); A. Hedley, *C.* (London, 1947; 3rd ed., rev., 1974); A.-E. Cherbuliez, *F. C., Leben und Werk* (Zürich, 1948); M. Gliński, "Kiedy urodzil się C.?," *Ruch Muzyczny*, 19 (1948; an attempt to prove that C. was born on March 1, 1809); N. Slonimsky, "C.iana, Some Materials for a Biography," *Musical Quarterly* (Oct. 1948); B. Sydow, "O date urodzenia Fr. C.a," *Ruch Muzyczny*, 10 (1948; the author argues in favor of acceptance of C.'s birth date as March 1, 1810, and publishes, for the 1st time, a facsimile of C.'s letter to the Polish Literary Soc. of Paris, giving this date); W. Rehberg, *C., Sein Leben und seine Werke* (Zürich, 1949); H. Weinstock, *C.: The Man and His Music* (N.Y., 1949; 2nd ed., 1959); K. Wierzyński, *The Life and Death of C.* (N.Y., 1949; in Polish, 1953; 2nd Eng. ed., 1972); R. Bory, *La Vie de F. C. par l'image* (Geneva, 1951); A. Cœuroy, *C.* (Paris, 1951); F. Zagiba, *C. und Wien* (Vienna, 1951); M. Idzikowski and B. Sydow, eds., *Portret Fryderyka C.a* (45 plates and annotations to C.'s portraits; Krakow, 1952; French tr., 1953; 2nd Polish ed., enl., 1963); J. Iwaszkiewicz, *C.* (Krakow, 1955; German tr., 1958; 2nd ed., 1964; French tr., 1966; 3rd Polish ed., 1965); K. Kobylańska, *C. w kraju: Dokumenty i pamiątki* (C. in His Homeland: Documents and Souvenirs), a lavish folio (Krakow, 1955; Eng. tr., 1955); E. Long, *A History of the Therapy of Tuberculosis and the Case of Frederic C.* (Lawrence, Kans., 1956); C. Bourniquel, *C.* (Paris, 1957; Eng. tr., 1960); J. Rousselot, *La Vie passionnée de F. C.* (Paris, 1957); A. Czartkowski and Z. Jezewska, *Fryderyk C.* (Warsaw, 1958; 5th ed., 1975); M. Godeau, *Le Voyage à Majorque de George Sand et F. C.* (Paris, 1959); I. Belza, *Fryderyk F. C.* (Moscow, 1960; Polish tr., 1969); A. Boucourechliev, *C.: A Pictorial Biography* (London, 1963); M. Gliński, *C. the Unknown* (Windsor, Ontario, 1963); J. Grenier, *C.* (Paris, 1964); V. Seroff, *Frederic C.* (N.Y., 1964); M. Mirska and W. Hordyński, *C. na obczyźnie: Dokumenty i pamiątki* (C. Abroad: Documents and Souvenirs; Krakow, 1965); A. Harasowski, *The Skein of Legends around C.* (Glasgow, 1967); A. Murgia, *The Life and Times of C.* (London, 1967); Smoter, *Spór o "listy" C.a do Delfiny Potockiej* (Warsaw, 1967); L. Ripoll, *The Majorcan Episode of C. and George Sand 1838–1839* (Palma de Mallorca, 1969); W. Duleba, *C.* (Krakow, 1975); A. Orga, *C.: His Life and Times* (Tunbridge Wells, 1976); A. Zamoyski, *C.: A New Biography* (Garden City, N.Y., 1979); J. Chomiński, *Fryderyk C.* (in German; London, 1980); A. Orga, *C.* (Sydney, 1983); G. Belotti, *C.* (Turin, 1984); J. Bruzzone, *F. C., ou, Le Chant d'un exilé* (Gourdon, 1984); A. Karenberg, *F. C. (1810–1849) als Mensch, Patient und Künstler* (Bergisch Gladbach, 1986); W. Atwood, *Fryderyk C.: Pianist from Warsaw* (N.Y., 1987); G. Ladaique, *Les Ancêtres paternels de F.F. C.* (2 vols., Paris, 1987). CRITICAL, ANALYTICAL: F. Liszt, *F. C.* (Paris, 1845; Eng. tr., London, 1877; German tr., Leipzig, 1880); J. Kleczyński, *C. w cenniejszych swoich utworach* (Warsaw, 1886; Eng. tr. as *C.'s Greatest Works: How They Should Be Understood*, London, 1896; 2nd ed., 1898); G. Jonson, *A Handbook to C.'s Works* (London, 1905; 2nd ed., rev., 1908); R. Koczalski, *C.-Zyklus: Vier Klavier-vorträge* (Leipzig, 1909); E. Kelley, *C. the Composer* (N.Y., 1913); J. Dunn, *Ornamentation in the Works of Frederick*

C. (London, 1921; 2nd ed., 1930); H. Leichtentritt, *Analyse der C.schen Klavierwerke* (2 vols., Berlin, 1921 and 1922); E. Ganche, *Dans le souvenir de F. C.* (Paris, 1925); H. Windakiewiczowa, *Die Urtypen C.'scher Melodik in der polnischen Volksmusik* (Krakow, 1926); S. Barbag, *Über die Lieder von F. C.* (Lwow, 1927); E. Ganche, *Voyages avec F. C.* (Paris, 1934); J. Porte, *C.: The Composer and His Music: An Analytical Critique of Famous Traditions and Interpretations* (London, 1935); R. Koczalski, *F. C.: Betrachtungen, Skizzen, Analysen* (Cologne, 1936); M. Ottich, *Die Bedeutung des Ornaments im Schaffen Friedrich C.s* (Berlin, 1937); G. Abraham, *C.'s Musical Style* (London, 1939; 4th ed., rev., 1960); L. Bronarski, *Études sur C.* (2 vols., Lausanne, 1944 and 1946); idem, *C. et l'Italie* (Lausanne, 1946); A. Gide, *Notes sur C.* (Paris, 1948; Eng. tr., 1949); A. Cortot, *Aspects de C.* (Paris, 1949; Eng. tr. as *In Search of C.*, London, 1951); B. von Pozniak, *C.: Praktische Anweisungen für das Studium der C.-Werke* (Halle, 1949); J. Holcman, *The Legacy of C.* (N.Y., 1954); J. Chomiński, *Sonaty C.a* (C.'s Sonatas; Krakow, 1960); Z. Lissa, ed., *The Book of the First International Musicological Congress Devoted to the Works of F. C., Warsaw 16–22 February 1960* (Warsaw, 1963); A. Walker, ed., *F. C.: Profiles of the Man and the Musician* (London, 1966; 2nd ed. as *The C. Companion*, 1973); F. McGinnis, *C.: Aspects of Melodic Style* (diss., Indiana Univ., 1968); Z. Lissa, ed., *Studia nad twórczócia Fryderyka C.a* (Krakow, 1970); D. Branson, *John Field and C.* (London, 1972); J. Holland, *C.'s Teaching and His Students* (diss., Univ. of North Carolina, 1973); D. Zebrowski, ed., *Studies in C.* (Warsaw, 1973); J. Samson, *The Music of C.* (London, 1985); S. Guignard, *F. C.s Walzer: Eine text- und stilkritische Studie* (Baden-Baden, 1986); K. Kirk, *The Golden Ratio in C.'s Preludes, Opus 28* (diss., Univ. of Cincinnati, 1986); J. Samson, "An Unknown C. Autograph," *Musical Times* (July 1986); J.-J. Eigeldinger, *C.: Pianist and Teacher as Seen by His Pupils* (Cambridge, 1987); J. Samson, ed., *C. Studies* (Cambridge, 1988).

Chorley, Henry F(othergill), English writer on music; b. Blackley Hurst, Lancashire, Dec. 15, 1808; d. London, Feb. 16, 1872. He was at various times active as a dramatist, translator, art critic, poet, novelist, and journalist; from 1831 to 1868 was music critic of the London *Athenaeum*. During his extensive travels he heard all the best music of the day and met many musical celebrities; a partisan of Mendelssohn and Spohr, he was intolerant toward new musical ideas and attacked Chopin, Schumann, and particularly Wagner, with extraordinary violence. **WRITINGS:** *Music and Manners in France and Germany* (3 vols., London, 1841); *Modern German Music* (2 vols., 1854); *Thirty Years' Musical Recollections* (2 vols., 1862; abridged American ed., N.Y., 1926); an interesting *Autobiography, Memoirs and Letters* (2 vols., 1873; ed. by H.G. Hewlett); *National Music of the World* (1880; ed. by Hewlett; 3rd ed., 1911); *Handel Studies* (1859); a novel, *A Prodigy: A Tale of Music* (3 vols., 1866).

Choron, Alexandre (Étienne), French music editor and theorist; b. Caen, Oct. 21, 1771; d. Paris, June 28, 1834. A student of languages, and passionately fond of music, he took interest in music theory and through it in mathematics, which he studied till the age of 25; then, by several years' serious application to the Italian and German theorists, he acquired a thorough knowledge of the theory and practice of music. Becoming (1805) a partner in a music publishing firm, he devoted his entire fortune to editing and publishing classic and theoretical works and compositions, meanwhile contributing new works of his own. In 1811 he became a corresponding member of the Académie Française; he was entrusted with the reorganization of the maîtrises (training schools for church choirs), and was appointed conductor of religious festivals. In 1816, as director of the Académie Royale de Musique, he reopened the Cons. (closed in 1815) as the École Royale de Chant et de Déclamation. Losing his directorship (1817) because he favored new works by unknown composers, he established, with a very moderate subsidy, the Institution de Musique Classique et Religieuse, for which he labored indefatigably until the July Revolution (1830).

WRITINGS: *Principes d'accompagnement des écoles d'Italie* (1804); *Principes de composition des écoles d'Italie* (3 vols., 1808; 2nd ed., 6 vols., 1816); *Dictionnaire historique des musiciens* (2 vols., 1810–11; with Fayolle); *Méthode élémentaire de musique et de plainchant* (1811); rev. and enl. Francœur's *Traité général des voix et des instruments d'orchestre* (1813); trs. of Albrechtsberger's *Gründliche Anweisung zur Komposition* and *Generalbassschule* (1814, 1815; new ed., 1830; Eng. tr. by A. Merrick, 1835) and of Azopardi's *Musico prattico* (1816); *Méthode concertante de musique à plusieurs parties* (written for his Cons., 1818; new ed., 1833); *Méthode de plainchant* (1818); *Manuel complet de musique vocale et instrumentale, ou Encyclopédie musicale* (1836–39; 6 vols. letterpress and 5 vols. plates; with La Fage).

BIBL.: L.E. Gautier, *Éloge de C.* (Caen, 1845); H. Réty, *Notice historique sur C. et son école* (Paris, 1873); J. Carlez, *C., Sa vie et ses travaux* (Caen, 1880); G. Vauthier, *C. sous l'Empire* (Poitiers, 1909).

Chorzempa, Daniel (Walter), American organist, harpsichordist, pianist, and composer; b. Minneapolis, Dec. 7, 1944. He was educated at the Univ. of Minnesota (Ph.D., 1971, with a diss. on Reubke); then went to Germany and enrolled at the Hochschule für Musik in Cologne; became a member of the Studio für Elektronische Musik in Cologne in 1970, and composed works for the medium. He subsequently began a career as an organist, and made several wide-ranging tours giving solo recitals.

Chotzinoff, Samuel, Russian-American pianist and music critic; b. Vitebsk, July 4, 1889; d. N.Y., Feb. 9, 1964. He was taken to America as a child; studied piano with Oscar Shack and music theory with Daniel Gregory Mason at Columbia Univ., graduating in 1912. He subsequently became an expert accompanist; toured with Zimbalist and Heifetz. He served as music critic of the *N.Y. World* (1925–30) and the *N.Y. Post* (1934–41). He then occupied various teaching and administrative positions; was for several years music director of NBC. He wrote a novel on Beethoven's life, entitled *Eroica*; a book of reminiscences, *A Lost Paradise* (1955); and a monograph, *Toscanini, an Intimate Portrait* (N.Y., 1956). His autobiographical *Days at the Morn* and *A Little Night Music* were publ. posth. in 1964.

Chouquet, (Adolphe-) Gustave, French writer on music; b. Le Havre, April 16, 1819; d. Paris, Jan. 30, 1886. He lived in America as a music teacher from 1840 to 1856; in 1860 went to Paris. He twice won the Prix Bordin: in 1864 for a history of music from the 14th to the 18th century, and in 1868 for *Histoire de la musique dramatique en France depuis ses origines jusqu'à nos jours* (publ. 1873). From 1871, he was custodian of the collection of instruments in the Cons.; in 1875 he publ. a catalog of them (2nd ed., 1884; supplemented by L. Pillaut, 1894, 1899, 1903).

Chou Wen-chung, remarkable Chinese-born American composer; b. Chefoo, June 29, 1923 (corresponding to May 16, 1923, according to the lunar calendar in the Chinese Year of the Bear). He studied civil engineering at the National Univ. in Chungking (1941–45), then went to the U.S. on a scholarship to study architecture. Turning his attention to music, he studied composition with Slonimsky in Boston (1946–49), Luening at Columbia Univ. (M.A., 1954), and Varèse in N.Y. (1949–54); he also held 2 Guggenheim fellowships (1957, 1959). In 1958 he became a naturalized U.S. citizen. He was composer-in-residence at the Univ. of Illinois in Urbana (1958), and on the faculties of Brooklyn College (1961–62), Hunter College (1963–64), and Columbia Univ. (from 1964). In 1982 he became an elected member of the Inst. of the American Academy and Inst. of Arts and Letters. His music combines Chinese elements of structure and scale formation with free dissonant counterpoint related to Varèse's theory of "organized sound."

WORKS: ORCH.: *Landscapes* (1949; San Francisco, Nov. 19, 1953); *All in the Spring Wind* (1952–53); *And the Fallen Petals*

(1954; Louisville, Feb. 9, 1955); *In the Mode of Chang* for Chamber Orch. (1956; N.Y., Feb. 2, 1957); *Metaphors* for Winds (1960–61); *Riding the Wind* for Winds (1964); *Pien*, chamber concerto for Piano, Percussion, and Winds (1966). **CHAMBER:** Suite for Harp and Wind Quintet (1950); *2 Miniatures from the T'ang Dynasty* for 10 Instruments (1957); *To a Wayfarer* for Clarinet, Harp, Percussion, and Strings (1958); *Soliloquy of a Bhiksuni* for Trumpet, Brass, and Percussion (1958); *Yü Ko* for 9 Instruments (1965); *Ceremonial* for 3 Trumpets and 3 Trombones (1968); also choral and piano works; film scores.

Chowning, John, American composer; b. Salem, N.J., Aug. 22, 1934. He studied at Wittenberg Univ. in Springfield, Ohio (B.M., 1959), with Nadia Boulanger in Paris (1959–62), and at Stanford Univ. (Ph.D., 1966), where he later joined the faculty and served as director of both its Computer Music and Acoustics Group (1966–74) and its Center for Computer Research in Music and Acoustics (from 1975). A leading figure in computer-music circles, he utilized frequency modulation in his development of "Chowning FM." His works for computer-generated quadraphonic sound include *Sabelithe* (1972), *Turenas* (1972), *Stria* (1977), and *Phōnē* (1981).

BIBL.: C. Roads, "J. C. on Composition," *Composers and the Computer* (Los Altos, Calif., 1985).

Christensen, Dieter, German ethnomusicologist; b. Berlin, April 17, 1932. He studied with Reinhard and Dräger at the Free Univ. of Berlin (Ph.D., 1957, with a diss. on the music of New Guinea), then became curator and director of the ethnomusicology department of the Folk Museum of Berlin (1958–71) and prof. of music and director of the Center for Studies in Ethnomusicology at Columbia Univ. His research has focused upon the musics of Oceania, Mexico, and West Africa, and the methodology and history of ethnomusicology. He publ. *Kurdish Folk Music from Western Iran* (1965), "On the Preservation of Arab Music," *II. Internationaler Kongress für arabische Musik* (1969), "Musical Style and Social Context in Kurdish Songs," *Asian Music* (1975), as well as a series of pamphlets (with Gerd Kock) on Micronesian dance.

Christian, Charlie, black American guitarist and blues singer; b. Bonham, Texas, July 29, 1916; d. N.Y., March 2, 1942. His parents and his 4 brothers were musicians; as a child he played in the family band; at maturity he began playing electric guitar; from 1939 to 1941 he played in Benny Goodman's Sextet; later played with Dizzy Gillespie and Thelonious Monk. He was stricken with a paralyzing ailment and died at the age of 25.

Christiansen, Fredrik Melius, Norwegian-American choral conductor, father of **Olaf Christiansen;** b. Eidsvold, April 1, 1871; d. Northfield, Minn., June 1, 1955. He emigrated to the U.S. in 1888; studied at the Northwestern Cons. of Music; then went to Germany, where he took courses at the Leipzig Cons. (1897–99). Returning to America, he served as director of the School of Music at St. Olaf's College in Northfield, Minn.; he organized the important St. Olaf's Lutheran Choir there. He publ. several useful choral collections: *St. Olaf Choir Series* (6 vols., 1920); *Young Men's Choral Assembly for Schools* (1936); ed. *50 Famous Hymns for Women's Voices* (1914); and publ. *Practical Modulation* (1916).

BIBL.: L. Bergmann, *Music Master of the Middle West* (Minneapolis, 1944).

Christiansen, Olaf, American choral conductor of Norwegian descent, son of **Fredrik Melius Christiansen;** b. Minneapolis, Aug. 12, 1901; d. Northfield, Minn., April 12, 1984. He was trained by his father, and upon his death in 1955 succeeded him as director of the St. Olaf Lutheran Choir in Northfield, remaining at this post until his own retirement in 1968. He was also co-founder of the Christiansen Choral School, which had a very large attendance among choral conductors.

Christie, William (Lincoln), esteemed American harpsichordist, conductor, and teacher; b. Buffalo, Dec. 19, 1944. He learned to play the piano and organ before studying harpsichord with Igor Kipnis at the Berkshire Music Center, Tanglewood; took courses in music and art history at Harvard Univ. (B.A., 1966); then studied harpsichord with Ralph Kirkpatrick, organ with Charles Krigbaum, and musicology with Claude Palisca and Nicholas Temperley at Yale Univ. (M.Mus., 1970). After a brief teaching assignment at Dartmouth College (1970–71), he went to France and became a member of the Five Centuries Ensemble (1971–75) and the Concerto Vocale (from 1972); he also made appearances as a recitalist. In 1978 he founded Les Arts Florissants, a vocal and instrumental ensemble that won distinction for performances of the French and Italian Baroque repertoire. He taught at the Sommer Akademie für alte Musik in Innsbruck (1977–83) and in 1982 became the 1st American prof. at the Paris Cons.

Christoff, Boris (Kirilov), celebrated Bulgarian bass; b. Plovdiv, May 18, 1914. He sang in the Gusla Choir in Sofia, where he was heard by King Boris, who made it possible for him to go to Rome to study with Stracciari; he later studied in Salzburg with Muratti. He made his debut in a concert in Rome in 1946; that same year he made his opera debut there at the Teatro Argentina as Colline in *La Bohème*. He made his 1st appearance at La Scala in Milan in 1947, at Covent Garden in London in 1949, and his U.S. debut as Boris Godunov with the San Francisco Opera on Sept. 25, 1956. During his distinguished career, he appeared with many leading opera houses, singing most of the principal bass roles in the operas of Verdi, as well as such roles as Gurnemanz, Ivan Susanin, Hagen, Rocco, Konchak, and King Mark. He was most renowned for his dramatic portrayal of Boris Godunov, which recalled the interpretation of Chaliapin. His brother-in-law was **Tito Gobbi.**
    BIBL.: F. Barker, *Voice of the Opera: B. C.* (London, 1951); G. Lauri-Volpi, *Voci parallele: B. C.* (Milan, 1955); monograph by O. Deikowa (in Bulgarian; Sofia, 1966); A. Bozhdov, *B. Khristov* (Sofia, 1985).

Christoff, Dimiter, Bulgarian composer; b. Sofia, Oct. 2, 1933. He studied composition with M. Goleminov at the Bulgarian State Cons. in Sofia (1951–56), where he later taught (from 1970). He was also vice-president of the Bulgarian Composers Union (1972–85) and general secretary of the International Music Council of UNESCO (1975–79).
    WORKS: OPERAS: *Game* (1978); *The Golden Fish Line*, chamber opera (1984). ORCH.: 2 piano concertos: No. 1 (1954); No. 2 with Wind Orch. (1983); Sinfonietta for Strings (1956); *Poem* (1957); 3 syms. (1958, 1964, 1969); *Overture* (1961); *Symphonic Episodes* (1962); Violin Concerto (1966); *Chamber Suite* for Flute, Piccolo, and Chamber Orch. (1966); Cello Concerto (1969); *Concert Miniatures* (1970); *Overture with Fanfares* (1974); *Quasi una fantasia-gioco* (1981); *Game* for Cello and Orch. (1983); *Perpetui mobili in pianissimi* (1987). CHAMBER: *Suite* for Wind Quintet (1953); 2 *Dances* for Trumpet and Piano (1960); Solo Cello Sonata (1965); Concerto for 3 Small Drums and 5 Instruments (1967); String Quartet (1970); Quartet for Flute, Viola, Harp, and Harpsichord (1973). PIANO: 4 sonatas (1962, 1974, 1974, 1974); choruses; songs.

Christopher, Cyril (Stanley), English organist and composer; b. Oldbury, Worcestershire, June 23, 1897; d. Sutton Coldfield, March 31, 1979. He studied organ with Alfred Hollins; held numerous posts as a church organist and a choral conductor; also taught music theory at the Birmingham School of Music. He wrote mainly for chorus; among his instrumental works are Fantasy-Trio for Clarinet, Violin, and Piano (1939); Trio for Oboe, Bassoon, and Piano (1954); Oboe Sonata (1956); Serenade for Wind Instruments, Cello, and Double Bass (1967); 2 short symphonic poems, *Midsummer Night* and *The Lone Shore*.

Christoskov, Peter, Bulgarian composer and violinist; b. Sofia, March 8, 1917. He studied violin at the Bulgarian State Cons. in Sofia, graduating in 1936; then went to Berlin, where he continued his violin studies; returning to Bulgaria, he was appointed head of the instrumental dept. of the Bulgarian State Cons. In his works he often applies the asymmetrical rhythms

of Bulgarian folk songs, using dissonant harmonies for coloristic effects.
    WORKS: *Moto Perpetuo* for String Orch. (1956); 2 violin concertos (1958, 1961); Concerto for Orch. (1964); *Children's Album* for Violin and Chamber Orch. (1966); Aria and Toccata for Violin and Orch. (1967); *Concerto-Improvisation* for Cello and Orch. (1970); Piano Concerto (1972); *Symphonic Sketches* (1973); *Concerto-Poem* for Cello and Orch. (1973).

Christou, Jani, remarkable Greek composer; b. Heliopolis, Egypt, Jan. 8, 1926, to Greek parents; d. in an automobile accident, with his wife, near Athens, on his 44th birthday, Jan. 8, 1970. He studied at Victoria College in Alexandria; then took courses in philosophy under Wittgenstein at King's College in Cambridge, England (M.A., 1948); concurrently studied composition with Hans Redlich in Letchworth (1945–48); then enrolled in the summer courses of the Accademia Musicale Chigiana in Siena (1949–50); during the same period he attended Karl Jung's lectures on psychology in Zürich. Christou returned to Alexandria in 1951; then lived on his family estate on the island of Chios. He evolved a system of composition embracing the totality of human and metaphysical expression, forming a "philosophical structure" for which he designed a surrealistic graphic notation involving a "psychoid factor," symbolized by the Greek letter psi; aleatory practices are indicated by the drawing of a card; a sudden stop, by a dagger, etc. His score *Enantiodromia (Opposed Pathways)* for Orch. (1965; rev. 1968; 1st perf. in Oakland, Calif., Feb. 18, 1969), in such a graphic notation, is reproduced in the avant-garde publication *Source*, 6 (1969). His notation also includes poetry, choreographic acting, special lighting, film, and projection meant to envelop the listener on all sides. At his death he left sketches for a set of 130 multimedia compositions of a category he called *Anaparastasis* ("proto-performances, meant to revive primeval rituals as adapted to modern culture").
    WORKS: *Phoenix Music* for Orch. (1948–49); Sym. No. 1 (1950; London, April 29, 1951); *Latin Mass* for Chorus, Brass, and Percussion (1953; posthumous, Athens, Sept. 26, 1971); *David's Psalms* for Baritone, Chorus, and Orch. (1953); 6 *Songs* for Voice and Piano, to poems by T.S. Eliot (1955; orchestrated 1957); Sym. No. 2 for Chorus and Orch. (1954–58; uses an adapted version of the Latin Mass as its finale); *Gilgamesh*, oratorio (1958); *Patterns and Permutations* for Orch. (1960; Athens, March 11, 1963); Sym. No. 3 (1959–62); Toccata for Piano and Orch. (1962); *The 12 Keys* for Mezzo-soprano and Chamber Ensemble (1962); *The Breakdown*, opera (1964); *Tongues of Fire*, Pentecost oratorio (1964; English Bach Festival, Oxford, June 27, 1964); *Enantiodromia (Opposed Pathways)* for Orch. (1965; rev. 1968; Oakland, Calif., Feb. 18, 1969); *Mysterion*, oratorio for Soli, 3 Choirs, Actors, Orch., and Tape, to ancient Egyptian myths (1965–66); *Praxis for 12* for 11 Strings and Pianist-Percussionist-Conductor (1966; Athens, April 18, 1966; an alternate version exists, titled simply *Praxis*, for 44 Strings and Pianist-Percussionist-Conductor); *Oresteia*, unfinished "super-opera," after Aeschylus (1967–70). Performable works from the cycle *Anaparastasis* are: *The Strychnine Lady* for Female Viola Player, 2 groups of Massed Strings, Brass, Percussion, Tapes, Metal Sheet, Sound-producing Objects and Toys, Red Cloth, and 5 Actors (Athens, April 3, 1967); *Anaparastasis I (Astron)* for Baritone and Instrumental Ensemble (Munich, Nov. 12, 1968); *Anaparastasis III (The Pianist)* for Actor, Variable Instrumental Ensemble, and 3 Stereo Tapes (Munich, Nov. 13, 1969); *Epicycle* for Variable Instrumental Ensemble that may take a chiliad or a hebdomad, a nanosecond or a quindecillion of non-zero moments to perform (concise version, Athens, Dec. 15, 1968; extended version, Athens, Dec. 20, 1968); stage music for *The Persians* (1965), *The Frogs* (1966), and *Oedipus Rex* (1969).
    BIBL.: J. Papaioannou, *J. C. and the Metaphysics of Music* (London, 1970).

Christov, Dobri, noted Bulgarian composer; b. Varna, Dec. 14, 1875; d. Sofia, Jan. 23, 1941. He was first a schoolteacher;

then a pupil of Dvořák at Prague; spent the greater part of his career as director and teacher of composition of the Sofia Cons. He composed orch. suites based on folk tunes; an overture, *Jvailo;* the ballad *Zar Samuil;* 50 Bulgarian choral songs; he also ed. Bulgarian folk songs.

Christy, Edwin Pearce, American minstrel show promoter and performer; b. Philadelphia, Nov. 28, 1815; d. (suicide) N.Y., May 21, 1862. In 1842 he founded the Christy Minstrels, which played a decisive role in the formation of a typical American variety show, consisting of songs, comic skits, and short plays and parodies. He opened his enterprise in Buffalo; in 1846 he introduced his troupe in N.Y. and played there for 8 years, then went to San Francisco; retired from performing in 1855. It was Christy who had Stephen Foster write his most famous "Ethiopian" songs for him; as was common in his time, Christy appropriated the authorship of these songs, but was decent enough to give Foster credit when the songs became greatly popular. Christy became mentally deranged and ended his life by jumping out of a window.

Chrysander, (Karl Franz) Friedrich, eminent German musicologist and editor; b. Lübtheen, Mecklenburg, July 8, 1826; d. Bergedorf, near Hamburg, Sept. 3, 1901. He began his career as a private tutor; in 1855 he received his Ph.D. from Rostock Univ. His major undertaking was a biography of Handel, but it remained incomplete, bringing the account only to 1740 (3 vols., 1858–67; reprint, 1966). With Gottfried Gervinus, the literary historian, he organized the Deutsche Händelgesellschaft in 1856 for the purpose of publishing a complete ed. of Handel's works. After the 1st vol. was issued in 1858, disagreements among the members caused Chrysander and Gervinus to carry the task alone. King George of Hannover granted them, in 1860, an annual subvention of 1,000 thaler, which they continued to receive until the annexation of Hannover by Prussia in 1866; in 1870, Prussia renewed the subvention from Hannover; after the death of Gervinus in 1871, Chrysander continued the task alone. The resulting publication, *Georg Friedrich Händels Werke: Ausgabe der Drutschen Händelgesellschaft* (100 vols., Leipzig and Bergedorf bei Hamburg, 1858–94; 6 supplementary vols., 1888–1902), was a monumental achievement, but it was superseded by the new critical edition ed. by M. Schneider and R. Steglich (Kassel, 1955–). Chrysander also served as ed. of the *Allgemeine Musikalische Zeitung* (1868–71 and 1875–82), to which he contributed many articles. He ed. an important collection of essays in the *Jahrbuch für Musikalische Wissenschaft* in 1863, and again in 1867. In 1885 he helped to found (with Philipp Spitta and Guido Adler) the *Vierteljahrsschrift für Musikwissenschaft,* and contributed to it until 1894. His other writings include *Über die Molltonart in den Volksgesängen* (Schwerin, 1853), *Über das Oratorium* (Schwerin, 1853), and *Händels biblische Oratorien in geschichtlicher Betrachtung* (Hamburg, 1897; 4th ed., 1922). **BIBL.:** B. Baselt, "Beiträge zur C.-Forschung," *Händel-Jahrbuch* (1969/70); W. Schardig, *F. C.: Leben und Werk* (Hamburg, 1986).

Chrysanthos of Madytos, learned Greek cleric and music theorist; b. Madytos, Turkey (hence, known as "of Madytos"), c.1770; d. Bursa, Turkey, 1846. He was bishop of the Greek Orthodox Church in Constantinople, and taught at the music school of the Patriarchate there from 1815 to 1821. He subsequently served as bishop in Durazzo, in Smyrna, and finally in Bursa, where he died. He undertook the reform of the post-Byzantine music notation by reducing the number of neumes and interval indexes; also revived the division of scales into the ancient Greek modes—diatonic, chromatic, and enharmonic. He publ. 2 manuals in the Greek language: *Introduction into the Theory and Practice of Church Music* (Paris, 1821) and *Great Music Instruction* (Trieste, 1832).

Chueca, Federico, Spanish composer of zarzuelas; b. Madrid, May 5, 1846; d. there, June 20, 1908. He was a medical student; organized a band at the Univ. of Madrid; also conducted theater orchs. He began to compose for the stage in collaboration with Valverde, who helped him to harmonize and orchestrate his melodies. Thanks to his prodigious facility, he wrote a great number of zarzuelas, of which *La gran via,* produced in Madrid (July 2, 1886), became his greatest success, obtaining nearly 1,000 performances in Madrid alone; it has also been performed many times in Latin America and the U.S. The march from his zarzuela *Cadiz* served for a time as the Spanish national anthem; dances from his *El año pasado por agua* and *Locuras madrileñas* also enjoyed great popularity. Chueca is regarded as one of the creators of the "género chico" (light genre) of Spanish stage music. **BIBL.:** M. Zurita, *Historia del género chico* (Madrid, 1920); J. Delito y Piñuela, *Origen y apogeo del género chico* (Madrid, 1949).

Chung, Kyung-Wha, brilliant Korean violinist, sister of **Myung-Wha** and **Myung-Whun Chung;** b. Seoul, March 26, 1948. She began to study the violin as a small child; made her orch. debut in Seoul at the age of 9, playing the Mendelssohn Concerto; in 1961 she went to the U.S., where she studied with Ivan Galamian at the Juilliard School of Music in N.Y. In 1967 she shared 1st prize with Pinchas Zukerman in the Leventritt Competition. In 1968 she appeared as soloist with the N.Y. Phil.; made her European debut in 1970 with the London Sym. Orch. She then embarked upon a wide-flung concert tour in Europe and Asia. She gave numerous trio concerts with her sister and brother, and also appeared as a soloist with her brother acting as conductor.

Chung, Myung-Wha, Korean-born American cellist, sister of **Kyung-Wha** and **Myung-Whun Chung;** b. Seoul, March 19, 1944. She studied cello in Seoul; made her orch. debut there in 1957; in 1961 she went to the U.S., where she studied with Rose at the Juilliard School of Music in N.Y.; then attended a master class given by Gregor Piatigorsky at the Univ. of Southern Calif. in Los Angeles. She made her U.S. debut in San Francisco (1967) and her European debut in Spoleto (1969); she won 1st prize in the Geneva Competition (1971), the same year she became a naturalized U.S. citizen. She appeared as soloist with orchs. in Europe and America; also played trio concerts with her sister and brother.

Chung, Myung-Whun, Korean-born American pianist and conductor, brother of **Myung-Wha** and **Kyung-Wha Chung;** b. Seoul, Jan. 22, 1953. He played piano as a child, making his debut as soloist with the Seoul Phil. when he was 7; he then went to the U.S., where he studied with Nadia Reisenberg (piano) and Carl Bamberger (conducting) at the Mannes College of Music in N.Y., and at the Juilliard School (diplomas in piano and conducting, 1974); he received additional tutelage in conducting there from Sixten Ehrling (1975–78). He made his conducting debut in Seoul (1971), subsequently winning 2nd prize in piano at the Tchaikovsky Competition in Moscow (1974). He became a naturalized U.S. citizen in 1973. He pursued a dual career as a pianist and conductor; he gave trio concerts with his sisters; was assistant conductor of the Los Angeles Phil. (1978–81), and chief conductor of the Saarland Radio Sym. Orch. in Saarbrücken (1984–90). On Feb. 21, 1986, he made his Metropolitan Opera debut in N.Y. conducting *Simon Boccanegra.* In 1989 he became music director-designate and in 1990 was confirmed in the most prestigious position, as music director of the new Bastille Opera in Paris. This appointment, considering his relative youth and his absence from the customary engagements at European musical centers, created a sensation among impresarios and the press.

Chusid, Martin, American musicologist; b. N.Y., Aug. 19, 1925. He studied at the Univ. of Calif. at Berkeley (B.A., 1950; M.A., 1955; Ph.D., 1961, with the diss. *The Chamber Music of Schubert*); taught at the Univ. of Southern Calif. in Los Angeles (1959–63) and at N.Y. Univ. (1963–68), where he also served as chairman of the music dept. (1967–70), associate dean of the graduate school of arts and sciences (1970–72), and director of the American Inst. for Verdi Studies (from 1976). He edited the Norton Critical Score ed. of Schubert's *Unfinished Symphony* (N.Y., 1968; 2nd ed., 1971), and was a contributor to the new critical ed. of Verdi's complete works; he also edited *A Catalog of Verdi's Operas* (Hackensack, N.J., 1974) and, with W. Weaver, *The Verdi Companion* (N.Y., 1979).

Chybiński, Adolf (Eustachy), eminent Polish musicologist; b. Krakow, April 29, 1880; d. Poznan, Oct. 31, 1952. After attending the Univ. of Krakow, he pursued musicological studies with Sandberger and Kroyer at the Univ. of Munich (Ph.D., 1908, with the diss. *Beiträge zur Geschichte des Taktschlagens;* publ. in Krakow, 1912); he also studied composition privately with Thuille in Munich (1905–7) and completed his Habilitation at the Univ. of Lemberg in 1912 with his *Teoria mensuralna w polskiej literaturze muzycznej pierwszej polowy XVI wieku* (Mensural Theory in Polish Music Literature of the 1st Half of the 16th Century; publ. in Krakow, 1912). He joined the faculty of the Univ. of Lemberg (later Lwow) in 1912, and was prof. of theory at the Lemberg (later Lwow) Cons. from 1916. In 1945 he became director of the musicological inst. at the Univ. of Poznan, a position he retained until his death. Chybiński particularly distinguished himself as an authority on Polish music history. He ed. several Polish music journals and prepared a number of early Polish compositions for publication, including works by G.G. Gorczycki, Jan of Lublin, and M. Zieleński. His autobiography, *W czasach Straussa i Tetmajera* (In the Time of Strauss and Tetmajer), was publ. posth. (Krakow, 1959). On his 50th birthday he was honored with a Festschrift (Krakow, 1930), and again on his 70th birthday (Krakow, 1950).
WRITINGS: "Tabulatura organowa Jana z Lublina" (The Organ Tablature of Jan of Lublin), *Kwartalnik muzyczny,* I (1911–13); "Przyczynki bio- i bibliograficzne do dawnej muzyki polskiej" (Bio- and Bibliographical Contributions to Early Polish Music), *Przegląd muzyczny,* II, nos. 1, 4, and 5 (1926) and V, nos. 2 and 11 (1929); "Z dziejow muzyki polskiej do 1800 roku" (The History of Polish Music to 1800), *Muzyka,* IV/7–9 (1927); *Grzegorz Gerwazy Gorczycki. Cz. I: Zycie, dzialalność, dziela* (A Study of His Life and Music; Poznan, 1928); "Stosunki muzyczne Polski z Francją w XVI stuleciu" (Musical Relations between Poland and France in the 16th Century), *Przegląd muzyczny,* IV, nos. 3 and 4 (1928; also publ. separately, Poznan, 1928); *Mieczyslaw Karlowicz* (Warsaw, 1939; 2nd ed., augmented, 1949); *Slownik muzykow dawnej Polski do roku 1800* (A Dictionary of Early Polish Musicians to 1800; Krakow, 1949).

Ciamaga, Gustav, Canadian composer; b. London, Ontario, April 10, 1930. He studied music theory with Weinzweig and Beckwith at the Univ. of Toronto (1953–56); studied composition and musicology with Arthur Berger, Harold Shapero, and Irving Fine at Brandeis Univ.; in 1963 he was appointed to the music faculty at the Univ. of Toronto, where he is director of its electronic music studio. His electronic scores include: *Ottawa 1967* (1966); *Curtain Raiser* (1969); *1-Part Invention* (1965); 8 *2-Part Inventions* (1965–70); *Ragamuffin Nos. 1 and 2* (1967); he wrote several scores of computer music, among them *Canon for Stravinsky* (1972); for voice, instruments, and tape he composed *Solipsism while Dying* (1972).

Ciccolini, Aldo, Italian pianist; b. Naples, Aug. 15, 1925. He studied with Paolo Denza at the Naples Cons.; in 1949 he was the winner of the Long-Thibaud prize in Paris. He toured in France, Spain, and South America; on Nov. 2, 1950, he made his American debut with Tchaikovsky's Concerto No. 1 (N.Y. Phil.). He has since appeared with several major orchs. in the U.S., and has also continued his concerts in Europe. In 1971 he was appointed prof. at the Paris Cons. Ciccolini possesses a virtuoso technique combined with a lyrical sense of phrasing.

Ciconia, Jean (Johannes), Walloon music theorist and composer; b. Liège, c.1335; d. Padua, between Dec. 11 and Dec. 24, 1411. Little is known about his life; he was in Italy from 1358 to 1367; was in Liège from 1372 until 1401. In 1402 he went to Padua, where he was a canon. He wrote the treatise *De proportionibus musicae.* Ciconia's significance lies in his

early use of musical devices that did not become current until much later; he applied the technique of French isorhythmic style as well as canonic imitation. For his works, see M. Bent and A. Hallmark, eds., *The Works of Johannes Ciconia* in Polyphonic Music of the Fourteenth Century, XXIV (1984).
BIBL.: S. Clercx, *Johannes C. de Leodio* (Amsterdam, 1953); idem, "Question de Chronologie," *Revue Belge de Musicologie* (1955); idem, *Johannes C.: Un Musicien liégeois et son temps* (Brussels, 1960).

Ciesinski, Katherine, American mezzo-soprano, sister of **Kristine Ciesinski;** b. Newark, Del., Oct. 13, 1950. She studied at Temple Univ. (B.M., 1972; M.M., 1973) and at the Curtis Inst. of Music in Philadelphia (opera diploma, 1976); she won 1st prize in the Geneva International Competition (1976) and Grand Prize in the Paris International Competition (1977). She made her concert debut with the Philadelphia Orch. (1974) and her operatic debut as Leonora in *La Favorita* with the Opera Co. of Philadelphia (1975). She sang Erika in Barber's *Vanessa* at the Spoleto Festival U.S.A. (1978), then gained wide recognition as Countess Geschwitz in the 1st U.S. production of the 3-act version of Berg's *Lulu* at the Santa Fe Opera (1979). In 1988 she sang in the premiere performance of Argento's *The Aspern Papers* in Dallas. As a concert artist, she appeared with leading orchs. in both North America and Europe; she also gave duo recitals with her sister. Among her prominent roles are Ottavia in *L'Incoronazione di Poppea,* Laura in *La Gioconda,* Eboli in *Don Carlos,* Dalila in *Samson et Dalila,* Charlotte in *Werther,* Octavian in *Der Rosenkavalier,* and the Composer in *Ariadne auf Naxos.*

Ciesinski, Kristine, American soprano, sister of **Katherine Ciesinski;** b. Wilmington, Del., July 5, 1952. She studied at Temple Univ. (1970–71), the Univ. of Delaware (1971–72), and Boston Univ. (1973–74; B.A., 1974); in 1977 she won the Gold Medal in the Geneva International Competition and 1st prize in the Salzburg International Competition. She made her N.Y. concert debut as a soloist in Handel's *Messiah* (1977) and her European operatic debut as Baroness Freimann in Lortzing's *Der Wildschütz* at the Salzburg Landestheater (1979), where she remained on its roster until 1981. She was subsequently a member of the Bremen State Opera (1985–88). She made guest appearances with the Cincinnati Opera, Milwaukee's Florentine Opera (1983, 1987), the Cleveland Opera (1985), Glasgow's Scottish National Opera (1985), Toronto's Canadian Opera Co. (1986), Leeds's Opera North (1986), the Augsburg Opera (1986), Cardiff's Welsh National Opera (1986), and in Mexico City (1987). She also sang extensively in concerts, often appearing with her sister. Her finest roles include Iphigénie, Medea, Beethoven's Leonora, Cassandra, La Wally, Eva, Elisabeth in *Tannhäuser,* Chrysothemis, Ariadne, Salome, and Tosca. She married **Norman Bailey** in 1985.

Cifra, Antonio, Italian composer; b. probably near Terracina, 1584; d. Loreto, Oct. 2, 1629. He was a choirboy in the church of S. Luigi dei Francesi in Rome; from 1594 to 1596, was a pupil of G.B. Nanino; also studied with Palestrina; in 1609, was maestro di cappella at the Collegio Germanico in Rome; from 1609 to 1622 and from 1626, was maestro di cappella at Santa Casa di Loreto; from 1623 to 1626, was maestro di cappella at S. Giovanni in Laterano, Rome. A prolific composer, he is considered one of the best of the Roman school; he publ. (between 1600 and 1629) 14 books of motets; 3 of Psalms; 5 of masses; 10 sets of *concerti ecclesiastici* (over 200 numbers); many more motets and Psalms (in 2–12 parts); antiphons; litanies; madrigals; ricercari; *Scherzi ed arie a 1, 2, 3 e 4 voci, per cantar del clavicembalo;* etc.
BIBL.: Article by A. Cametti, in *Rivista Musicale Italianas,* XXI (1915).

Cigna, Gina (real name, **Ginetta Sens**), French soprano; b. Paris, March 6, 1900. She studied at the Paris Cons.; made her operatic debut at La Scala in Milan in 1927; returned every season from 1929 to 1943; sang at the Metropolitan Opera in N.Y. in 1937 (debut as Aida, Feb. 6, 1937). After a few more performances in N.Y., she returned to Europe, and settled in Milan as a voice teacher. She abandoned her singing career after World War II, following an auto accident. From 1953 to 1957 she taught at the Royal Cons. in Toronto.

Cikker, Ján, eminent Slovak composer; b. Banská Bystrica, July 29, 1911; d. Bratislava, Dec. 21, 1989. He studied composition at the Prague Cons. with Jaroslav Křička and Vítězslav Novák; took a course in conducting with Felix Weingartner in Vienna. From 1938 to 1951 he was a prof. of theory at the Bratislava Cons.; then was a prof. of composition at the Bratislava School of Musical Arts (1951–76). He was awarded state prizes in 1955, 1963, and 1975; was made a National Artist in 1966; also received the Herder Prize of the Univ. of Vienna in 1966. An exceptionally prolific composer, Cikker was distinguished particularly in his works for the musical theater.

WORKS: Operas: *Juro Jánošík* (1950–53; Bratislava, Nov. 10, 1954); *Beg Bajazid* (Prince Bajazid; Bratislava, Feb. 16, 1957); *Mr. Scrooge,* after Dickens's *A Christmas Carol* (1958–59; German version as *Abend, Nacht und Morgen,* Kassel, Oct. 5, 1963); *Vzkriesenie* (Resurrection), after Tolstoy's novel (1961; Prague, May 18, 1962); *Hra o láske a smrti* (A Play about Love and Death), after Romain Rolland (1967; Munich, Aug. 1, 1969); *Coriolanus,* after Shakespeare (1972; Prague, March 21, 1974); *Zo života hmyzu* (From the Life of Insects; 1986); Sym. in C (1930); *Epitaph,* symphonic poem (1931); *Symphonic Prologue* (1934); *Capriccio* for Orch. (1936); *Spring Symphony* (1937); Sinfonietta (1940; instrumentation of his Piano Sonatina); cantata, *Cantus Filiorum* (1940); symphonic trilogy, *About Life: Léto* (Summer; 1941), *Vojak a matka* (The Soldier and the Mother; 1943), and *Ráno* (Morning; 1944–46); Piano Concertino (1942); *Slovak Suite* for Orch. (1942); *The Bucolic Poem,* ballet music (1944); *Spomienky* (Recollections) for 5 Wind Instruments and String Orch. (1947); *Dupák,* folk dance for Chamber Orch. (1950); *Dramatic Fantasia* for Orch. (1957); *Orchestrálne štúdie k činohre* (Orchestral Studies on a Drama; 1965); *Hommage à Beethoven* for Orch. (1970); *Variations on a Slovak Folk Song* for Orch. (1971; also for Piano); *Epitaph* (*Over an Old Trench*), symphonic poem (1973); *Symphony 1945* (1974–75; Bratislava, May 22, 1975); *Oda na radost* (Ode to Joy), cantata for Soloists, Chorus, and Orch. (1982); 2 string quartets (1935); Piano Sonatina (1933); 3 Études (*Tatra Mountain Streams*) for Piano (1954); *What Children Told Me* for Piano (1957); film music. **BIBL.:** J. Šamko, *J. C.* (Bratislava, 1955).

Cilèa, Francesco, Italian composer; b. Palmi, Calabria, July 23, 1866; d. Varazze, Nov. 20, 1950. He studied at the Naples Cons. (1881–89) with Cesi (piano) and Serrao (composition); taught piano there (1894–96); then harmony at the Istituto Musicale in Florence (1896–1904); was head of the Palermo Cons. (1913–16); director of the Cons. di San Pietro a Majella in Naples (1916–35). He was a member of the Reale Accademia Musicale in Florence (1898) and a knight of the Order of the Crown of Italy (1893). **WORKS:** Operas: *Gina* (Naples, Feb. 9, 1889); *La Tilda* (Florence, April 7, 1892); *L'Arlesiana,* after Daudet (Milan, Nov. 27, 1897; rev., Milan, Oct. 22, 1898); *Adriana Lecouvreur,* after Scribe (Milan, Nov. 6, 1902); his most famous opera); *Gloria* (La Scala, Milan, April 15, 1907); *Il matrimonio selvaggio* (1909); *Poema sinfonico* for Solo, Chorus, and Orch. (Genoa, July 12, 1913); Piano Trio (1886); Cello Sonata (1888); Variations for Violin and Piano (1931); piano pieces; songs. **BIBL.:** E. Moschino, *Sulle opere di F. C.* (Milan, 1932); C.P. Gaianus, *F. C. e la sua nuova ora* (Bologna, 1939); T. d'Amico, *F. C.* (Milan, 1960).

Cillario, Carlo Felice, Italian conductor; b. San Rafael, Argentina, Feb. 7, 1915. He began his musical training in Buenos Aires, then studied violin and composition at the Bologna Cons. After making appearances as a violinist, he received instruction in conducting from Enesco; he then went to Russia, where he continued his training at the Odessa Cons. He made his conducting debut at the Odessa Opera (1942), and after World War II embarked on a far-flung career as an operatic and

sym. conductor, making guest appearances in most of the leading music centers of Europe, North America, and South America. He was music director of the Australian Opera in Sydney (1969–71), and served as its principal guest conductor and music consultant from 1987.

Cima, Giovanni Paolo, Italian organist and composer; b. Milan, c.1570; d. during the 1st half of the 17th century. In 1609 he was organist at S. Celso in Milan. Publications of his works, including *Concerti ecclesiastici* and motets, appeared between 1599 and 1626. His *Partito de Ricercari e Canzoni alla francese* (Milan, 1606) is a keyboard collection with an appendix containing rules for tuning keyboard instruments. The *canzoni alla francese* of this collection are specially written for keyboard, and the ricercari are highly developed in their use of imitation. A modern reprint of *Ricercare per organo* is contained in L. Torchi's *L'arte musicale in Italia* (vol. III).

Cimadoro, Giovanni Battista, Italian composer; b. Venice, 1761; d. Bath, England, Feb. 27, 1805. After early successes in Italy, where he produced an opera, *Pimmaglione* (Pygmalion; Venice, Jan. 26, 1790), he settled in London; several arias from the opera were publ. in London, and acquired considerable popularity. While in England, he used a shortened form of his name, **Cimador.**

Cimara, Pietro, Italian conductor; b. Rome, Nov. 10, 1887; d. Milan, Oct. 1, 1967. He was educated at the Accademia di Santa Cecilia in Rome; made his debut as a conductor in 1916 in Rome. In 1933 he began conducting at the Metropolitan Opera; remained at this post for 26 years. He composed many songs, which were publ. in Italy and America.

Cimarosa, Domenico, famous Italian composer; b. Aversa, near Naples, Dec. 17, 1749; d. Venice, Jan. 11, 1801. He was the son of a stonemason. After his father's death, his mother placed him in the monastery school of the church of S. Severo dei Padri Conventuali in Naples, where he began his musical training with Father Polcano, the monastery organist. He then enrolled at the Cons. di S. Maria di Loreto (1761), where he studied voice, violin, and keyboard playing with Fenaroli, P.A. Gallo, and Carcais. Following his graduation in 1771, he studied voice with the castrato Giuseppe Aprile. His 1st opera, *Le stravaganze del conte,* was staged in Naples in 1772. From 1776 he composed operas at a prolific rate, producing about 65 works for the major Italian opera centers as well as those abroad. In 1779 he was named supernumerary organist of the Royal Chapel in Naples; in 1785 he became its 2nd organist. He also served for a time as maestro of the Ospedaletto, a cons. for girls in Venice. In 1787 he was given the post of maestro di cappella to the court of Catherine the Great in St. Petersburg. During his Russian sojourn, he wrote 3 operas and various other works for the court and the nobility. However, the court cut back on its funding of music and Cimarosa's contract was allowed to lapse in 1791. He proceeded to Vienna, where Emperor Leopold II appointed him Kapellmeister. He then composed his masterpiece, *Il matrimonio segreto,* which was premiered with great acclaim at the Burgtheater on Feb. 7, 1792. The Emperor was so taken by the opera that he ordered that it be repeated that evening, undoubtedly the most elaborate encore in operatic annals. The opera's fame spread throughout Europe, and Cimarosa returned to Italy in 1793 as one of the most celebrated musicians of the age. In 1796 he was appointed 1st organist of the Royal Chapel in Naples. In 1799 he welcomed the republican movement in Naples by composing a patriotic hymn for the burning of the royal flag; however, the monarchy was restored later that year and Cimarosa's efforts miscarried. In consequence of this, he was arrested in Dec. 1799 and sent to prison for 4 months. He was released only after the intervention of several prominent individuals. He then went to Venice, where he died while working on his opera *Artemisia.* It was rumored abroad that he had been poisoned by order of Queen Caroline of Naples; the rumor was so persistent, and popular feelings so pronounced, that the Pope's personal physician, Piccioli, was sent to Venice to make an examination; according to his sworn statement (April 5, 1801), Cimarosa died of a gangrenous abdominal tumor.

Cimarosa was an outstanding composer of Italian opera buffa in his day. His melodic inventiveness, command of form, superb vocal writing, and masterly orchestration were unexcelled until Rossini arrived upon the scene. **WORKS: OPERAS:** *Le stravaganze del conte* (Naples, Carnival 1772); *La finta parigina* (Naples, Carnival 1773); *I sdegni per amore* (Naples, Jan. 1776); *I matrimoni in ballo* (Naples, Carnival 1776); *La Frascatana nobile* or *La finta frascatana* (Naples, 1776); *I tre amanti* (Rome, Carnival 1777); *Il Fanatico per gli antichi romani* (Naples, 1777); *L'armida immaginaria* (Naples, 1777); *Gli amanti comici, o sia La famiglia in scompiglio* (Naples, 1778?); *Il ritorno di Don Calandrino* (Rome, Carnival 1778); *Le stravaganze d'amore* (Naples, 1778); *Il matrimonio per raggiro* or *La Donna bizzarra* (Rome, 1778–79?); *L'Italiana in Londra* (Rome, Carnival 1779); *L'infedeltà fedele* (Naples, 1779); *Le Donne rivali* (Rome, Carnival 1780); *Cajo Mario* (Rome, Carnival 1780); *I finti nobili* (Naples, Carnival 1780); *Il Falegname* (Naples, 1780); *Il capriccio drammatico* (Turin, 1781?); *Il Pittor parigino* (Rome, Carnival 1781); *Alessandro nell'Indie* (Rome, Carnival 1781); *L'Amante combattuto dalle donne di Punto* (Naples, 1781); *Giunio Bruto* (Verona, 1781); *Giannina e Bernardone* (Venice, 1781); *Il convito* (Venice, Carnival 1782); *L'amor costante* (Rome, Carnival 1782); *L'Eroe cinese* (Naples, 1782); *La Ballerina amante* (Naples, 1782); *La Circe* (Milan, Carnival 1783); *I due baroni di Rocca Azzurra* (Rome, Carnival 1783); *La Villana riconosciuta* (Naples, 1783); *Oreste* (Naples, 1783); *Chi dell'altrui si veste presto si spoglia* (Naples, 1783); *I matrimoni impensati* or *La bella greca* (Rome, Carnival 1784); *L'apparenza inganna, o sia La villeggiatura* (Naples, 1784); *La vanità delusa* or *Il mercato di Malmantile* (Florence, 1784); *L'Olimpiade* (Vicenza, 1784); *I due supposti conti, ossia Lo sposo senza moglie* (Milan, 1784); *Artaserse* (Turin, 1784); *Il Marito disperato* or *Il Marito geloso* (Naples, 1785); *La Donna sempre al suo peggior s'appiglia* (Naples, 1785); *Il Credulo* (Naples, Carnival 1786); *Le trame deluse* (Naples, 1786); *L'Impresario in angustie* (Naples, 1786); *Volodimiro* (Turin, Carnival 1787); *Il Fanatico burlato* (Naples, 1787); *La felicità inaspettata* (St. Petersburg, March 1788); *La Vergine del sole* (St. Petersburg, 1788?); *La Cleopatra* (St. Petersburg, Oct. 8, 1789); *Il matrimonio segreto* (Vienna, Feb. 7, 1792); *Amor rende sagace* (Vienna, April 1, 1793); *I traci amanti* (Naples, June 19, 1793); *Le astuzie femminili* (Naples, Aug. 26, 1794); *Penelope* (Naples, Carnival 1795); *Le nozze in garbuglio* (Messina, 1795); *L'impegno superato* (Naples, 1795); *La finta ammalata* (Lisbon, 1796); *I Nemici generosi* (Rome, Carnival 1796); *Gli Orazi ed i Curiazi* (Venice, Carnival 1797); *Achille all'assedio di Troja* (Rome, Carnival 1797); *L'imprudente fortunato* (Rome, Carnival 1797); *Artemisia regina di Caria* (Naples, 1797); *L'apprensivo raggirato* (Naples, 1798); *Il secreto* (Turin, 1798); *Artemisia* (Venice, Carnival 1801; left unfinished); some 30 other stage works have been attributed to Cimarosa, but many are doubtful. **ORATORIOS:** *Giuditta* (Venice, 1782?); *Absalom* (Venice, 1782); *Il sacrificio d'Abramo* (Naples, 1786); *Il trionfo delle fede* (Naples, May 1794); *Il martirio* (Naples, 1795); *S. Filippo Neri che risuscita Paolo Massimi* (Rome, 1797). He also composed many masses and other sacred works, secular cantatas, a Harpsichord Concerto, a Concerto for 2 Flutes, chamber music, and keyboard music. **BIBL.:** M. Trevisan, *Nel primo centenario di D. C.* (Venice, 1900); A. Delle Corte, *L'opera comica italiana nel 1700* (Bari, 1923); R. Vitale, *D. C., La vita e le opere* (Aversa, 1929); G. Biamonti, *Il matrimonio segreto di D. C.* (Rome, 1930); M. Tibaldi-Chiesa, *C. e il suo tempo* (Milan, 1939); F. Schlitzer, *Goethe e C.* (Siena, 1950); R.-A. Mooser, *Annales de la musique et des musiciens en Russie au XVIIIᵉ siècle*, vol. II (Geneva, 1951); J. Johnson, *D. C. (1749–1801)* (diss., Univ. College, Cardiff, 1976).

Cinti-Damoreau, Laure (née **Laure Cinthie Montalant**), noted French soprano; b. Paris, Feb. 6, 1801; d. Chantilly, Feb. 25, 1863. She studied with Plantade, Bordogni, and Cata-

lani at the Paris Cons.; after Italianizing her middle name to Cinti, she made her operatic debut in *Una cosa rara* at the Théâtre-Italien on Jan. 8, 1816; she sang there until 1818, and then at the Théâtre-Louvois (1819–22). After appearing at the King's Theatre in London (1822–23), she became a prominent member of the Paris Opéra (1825–35), where she created leading roles in Rossini's *Le Siège de Corinthe* (1826), *Moïse et Pharaon* (1827), *Le Comte Ory* (1828), and *Guillaume Tell* (1829); she also created the role of Isabelle in Meyerbeer's *Robert le diable* (1831) and subsequently sang at the Opéra-Comique (1836–41), creating leading roles in works by Auber, including *Le Domino noir* (1837). She also made concert tours of Europe and toured the U.S. with the violinist Artôt in 1843–44, making her last concert appearance in 1848. She taught at the Paris Cons. (1833–56) and also publ. *Méthode de chant* (1849). In 1827 she married the **tenor V.C. Damoreau** (1793–1863).
BIBL.: A. de Rovray, "L. C.-D.," *Le Moniteur Universel* (March–June 1865).

Ciortea, Tudor, Rumanian composer; b. Brasov, Dec. 11, 1903; d. Bucharest, Oct. 13, 1982. He studied composition with Nadia Boulanger and Paul Dukas in Paris; then taught at the Bucharest Cons. (1941–71). His music reflects influence from the French school of composition while retaining the formal outlines of classical music. Among his works are 2 string quartets (1952, 1954), a Clarinet Sonata (1962), a Trumpet Sonata (1964), a Brass Quintet (1970), and numerous piano pieces and songs.

Cipra, Milo, Croatian composer; b. Vares, Oct. 13, 1906; d. Zagreb, July 9, 1985. He studied at the Zagreb Academy of Music, graduating in 1933, and was on the faculty (from 1941). He steadily followed the national type of composition, making use of thematic elements typical of song patterns of Croatia while sustaining the formal elements of universal classicism. He composed 5 string quartets and other chamber music as well as 2 syms. and a number of songs.

Cirino, Giulio, Italian bass; b. Rome, Feb. 15, 1880; d. there, Feb. 26, 1970. He made his opera debut in Rome in 1903; subsequently sang at La Scala in Milan; was on the roster of the Teatro Colón in Buenos Aires from 1909 to 1923; retired from the stage in 1935. He was particularly successful in buffo roles, in the Italian repertoire; but he also sang in Wagner's operas.

Cisneros, Eleanora de (née **Broadfoot**), American mezzo-soprano; b. N.Y., Nov. 1, 1878; d. there, Feb. 3, 1934. She studied singing in N.Y. with Mme. Murio-Celli and later in Paris with Jean de Reszke. In 1901 she married Count Francesco de Cisneros of Havana, Cuba, and appeared professionally under this name. She enjoyed a brilliant career; first appeared with the Metropolitan Opera Co. on tour in Chicago on Nov. 24, 1899, as Rossweisse in *Die Walküre;* then made her N.Y. Metropolitan Opera debut in the same role on Jan. 5, 1900; sang in Italy between 1902 and 1914, and annually in London from 1903 to 1908. Between 1906 and 1911 she was the principal mezzo-soprano at the Manhattan Opera, and later was a member of the Chicago Opera. In 1915 she toured Australia; then lived in Paris until 1929, when she returned to N.Y.

Citkowitz, Israel, Polish-American composer; b. Skierniewice, Poland, Feb. 6, 1909; d. London, May 4, 1974. He was taken to the U.S. as a child; studied with Copland and Sessions in N.Y., and with Nadia Boulanger in Paris. He taught at the Dalcroze School of Music in N.Y. from 1939; in 1969 moved to London. He composed mainly for voice; his songs and choral works possess considerable expressive power.

Ciuciura, Leoncjusz, Polish composer; b. Grodzisk Mazowiecki, July 22, 1930. He studied with Szeligowski at the State College of Music in Warsaw. All of his works are essays in combinatorial permutation with optional instrumental or vocal additions, subtractions, multiplications, or divisions.
WORKS: *Canti al fresco* for 9 Female Voices and Instrumen-

tal Ensemble (1961); *Concertino de camera* for Chamber Orch. (1961); *Ornament* for Flute, Bassoon, Clarinet, and Strings (1962); *Penetrations* for 4 Orch. Groups, 4 Conductors, and Composer (1963); *Spirale I per uno* for Baritone and 36 Percussion Instruments (1964) and *Spirale II per uno e più* for Optional Instrumental Ensemble (1964); *Emergenza* for 3 Orch. Groups, 3 Conductors, and Composer (1964); *Incidenti* for Optional Voices and Instrumental Ensemble (1964); *Per 5* for a group which would include any combination of Flute, Oboe, Horn, Bassoon, and Trumpet (1972); *Creatoria I* and *II* for Optional Solo Voice or Instrument or Groups of Instruments or Voices (1975); *Music* for Solo Flute and 8 Instruments (1976).

Čiurlionis, Mikolajus Karstantinas, Lithuanian composer; b. Varena, Oct. 4, 1875; d. Pustelnik, near Warsaw, April 10, 1911. He studied composition with Noskowski, and at the Leipzig Cons. with Carl Reinecke and Jadassohn. From 1902 till 1909 he was active in Warsaw as a choral conductor. His music reflects the Germanic Romantic tendencies, but he also developed interesting theories of so-called "tonal ground formations," anticipating the serial methods of Schoenberg and Hauer. Čiurlionis was also a remarkable painter in an abstract expressionist manner; many of his paintings carry musical titles, such as *Prelude and Fugue, Spring Sonata*, etc. His musical works include the symphonic poems *In the Forest* (1901) and *The Ocean* (1907); cantata, *De profundis* (1899); String Quartet; numerous piano pieces and songs.

BIBL.: V. Čiurlionyté-Karužiene et al., *M.K. Č. Bibliografia* (Vilnius, 1970); J. Čiurlionyté, *Atsiminimai apie M.K. Č.* (Vilnius, 1970); V. Landsbergis, *Spring Sonata. The Creative Activity of M.K. Č.* (Leningrad, 1971).

Civil, Alan, noted English horn-player; b. Northampton, June 13, 1929; d. London, March 19, 1989. He studied with Aubrey Brain in London and with Willy von Stemm in Hamburg. He was principal horn of the Royal Phil. (1952–55), and later co-principal horn, with Dennis Brain, of the Philharmonia Orch. (1955–57); after Brain's tragic death, was principal horn (1957–66); from 1966 to 1988 he was principal horn of the BBC Sym. Orch. In 1966 he became a prof. of horn at the Royal College of Music in London. In 1979 he became president of the British Horn Soc. He was made a member of the Order of the British Empire in 1985.

Claflin, (Alan) Avery, American composer; b. Keene, N.H., June 21, 1898; d. Greenwich, Conn., Jan. 9, 1979. He studied law and banking, and pursued a business career; also took music courses at Harvard Univ. He attracted attention as a composer by his amusing choral work, a fiscal madrigal entitled *Lament for April 15* (1955), to the text of an Internal Revenue tax form. Among his other compositions are the operas *Hester Prynne* (after *The Scarlet Letter* of Hawthorne), of which Scene II of Act II was performed at Hartford on Dec. 15, 1934; *The Fall of Usher* (not performed); *La Grande Bretèche*, after Balzac's story (NBC Radio, Feb. 3, 1957); *Uncle Tom's Cabin* (1961–64); 2 syms.; *Teen Scenes* for Strings (1955); *Pop Concert Concerto* for Piano and Orch. (1958); Piano Trio; other chamber music.

Clapham, John, English musicologist; b. Letchworth, July 31, 1908. He studied cello with Douglas Cameron, and took courses in harmony and counterpoint at the Royal Academy of Music in London; then studied at the Univ. of London (B.Mus., 1934; D.Mus., 1946). He was a lecturer at the Univ. College of Wales in Aberystwyth (1946–62); then was senior lecturer (1962–69) and lecturer (1969–73) at the Univ. of Edinburgh. He distinguished himself in studies of Czech music.

WRITINGS: *Antonín Dvořák: Musician and Craftsman* (London, 1966); *Smetana* (London, 1972); *Dvořák* (Newton Abbot, 1979).

Clapp, Philip Greeley, American composer and pedagogue; b. Boston, Aug. 4, 1888; d. Iowa City, April 9, 1954. He studied piano with his aunt Mary Greeley James (1895–99) and violin with Jacques Hoffman in Boston (1895–1905); also took lessons in music theory with John Marshall (1905). He then entered Harvard Univ., studying music theory and composition with Spalding, Converse, and Edward Burlingame Hill; received his B.A. (1908), M.A. (1909), and Ph.D. (1911). He also studied composition and conducting in Stuttgart with Max von Schillings (1909–10). He became a teaching fellow at Harvard (1911–12); was music director at Dartmouth College (1915–18); in 1919 he was appointed director of the music dept. at the Univ. of Iowa, and remained at that post for the rest of his life. Clapp was a prolific composer and a competent teacher; he was also a brilliant pianist, but did not dedicate himself to a concert career; he also appeared as conductor of his own works and was in charge of the univ. orch. at Iowa City. His music is conceived in an expansive Romantic idiom much influenced by the modern German style of composition, and yet introducing some advanced melodic and harmonic patterns, such as building harmonies in fourths.

WORKS: ORCH.: 12 syms.: No. 1, in E major (1910; Waterloo, Iowa, April 27, 1933, composer conducting); No. 2, in E minor (Boston, April 10, 1914, composer conducting); No. 3, in E-flat major (Boston, April 6, 1917, composer conducting); No. 4, in A major (1919; rev. 1941); No. 5, in D major (1926; rev. 1941; Iowa City, July 26, 1944, composer conducting); No. 6, in B major, *Golden Gate* (1926; San Jose, Calif., June 5, 1951); No. 7, in A major (Boston, March 22, 1931, composer conducting); No. 8, in C major (1930; rev. 1941; N.Y., Feb. 7, 1952); No. 9, in E-flat minor, *The Pioneers* (1931; Iowa City, July 16, 1939); No. 10, in F major, *Heroic* (1935; Iowa City, May 23, 1951, composer conducting); No. 11, in C major (1942; rev. 1950); No. 12, in B-flat major (1944); *Norge*, symphonic poem, with Piano obbligato (Cambridge, Mass., April 29, 1909; his most popular work); *Song of Youth*, symphonic poem (1910); *Dramatic Poem with Solo Trombone* (Cambridge, Mass., April 24, 1912, composer conducting); *Summer*, prelude (St. Louis, Jan. 16, 1914); *Overture to a Comedy* (1933; Cleveland, Dec. 28, 1940); *A Highly Academic Diversion on 7 Notes* for Chamber Orch. (Iowa City, Feb. 17, 1933, composer conducting); *Fantasy on an Old Plain Chant* for Cello and Orch. (Iowa City, Jan. 17, 1940); Concerto for 2 Pianos and Orch. (Iowa City, Dec. 20, 1945). **CHAMBER:** Violin Sonata (1909); String Quartet (1909); Suite for Brass Sextet (1938); Concerto Suite for 4 Trombones (1939); *Prelude and Finale* for Woodwind Quintet (1939). Numerous choral works, among them *A Chant of Darkness* for Chorus and Orch., to the text by Helen Keller (1919; rev. 1933; Iowa City, April 16, 1935, composer conducting); also 2 operas, *The Taming of the Shrew*, after Shakespeare (1948), and *The Flaming Brand*, libretto by the composer on the exploit of John Brown (1949–53). All his MSS are in the Music Library of the Univ. of Iowa.

BIBL.: D. Holcomb, *P.G. C.* (Iowa City, 1972).

Clapton, Eric (Patrick), English virtuoso on the electric guitar; b. Ripley, Surrey, March 30, 1945. He played guitar as a youth; at 18 he joined the Metropolis Blues Quartet, a group which later changed its name to The Yardbirds. Clapton played with it for a few months, but was turned off by its rank commercialism, and in 1965 joined John Mayall's Bluesbreakers; in another year he organized a group named simply Cream, which turned the rock world upside down by introducing prolonged improvisational jams. When in the course of human events Cream soured, Clapton organized a "supergroup," Blind Faith, with Ginger Baker, Stevie Winwood, and Rick Grech, but like so many men of little faith, Blind Faith soon gave up the ghost. Only Clapton's spiritual hymn *In the Presence of the Lord* maintained the flame. In 1970, Clapton formed Derek and the Dominoes, which received a certified Gold Award in 1971 with its album *Layla*. The group disbanded after a year or so of feverish activity. Depressed by these recurrent failures, Clapton went into crooning, fully aware that he was no Mick Jagger. His songs expressed his pessimism, as in *E.C. Was Here, There's One in Every Crowd*, and *No Reason to Cry*. In 1979, after a long period of doldrums, he hit the jackpot with *Lay Down Sally*. He also paid a debt to the middle-class fascination with coke with the promotional tunes *Tulsa Time* and *Cocaine*. In 1980 he finally found his niche with the album *Just One Night*; subsequent successful albums include *Another Ticket* (1981), *Money and Cigarettes* (1983), and *August* (1986).

Clari, Giovanni Carlo Maria, Italian composer; b. Pisa, Sept. 27, 1677; d. there, May 16, 1754. He studied with his father and with Francesco Alessi in Pisa; then under Colonna at Bologna, where his opera *Il Savio delirante* was produced in 1695; from 1703 to 1724 he was in Pistoia as maestro di cappella of the Cathedral; then went to Pisa. His best-known work is a collection of madrigals for 2 and 3 voices (1720; reprinted by Carli, Paris, 1825); he also wrote masses, Psalms, a Requiem, and other sacred music.

BIBL.: E. Saville, "Liturgical Music of G. C.: An Annotated Index," *Fontes Artis Musicae,* XV/1 (1968).

Claribel. See **Barnard, Charlotte.**

Clark, Edward, English conductor; b. Newcastle upon Tyne, May 10, 1888; d. London, April 29, 1962. He studied in Paris, in Vienna, and in Berlin with Schoenberg. He led the orch. for Diaghilev's London seasons (1924–26); was with the BBC (1927–36); in 1940 he founded the North Eastern Regional Orch. in Newcastle. In 1947 he was elected president of the International Soc. for Contemporary Music. He was married to the composer **Elizabeth Lutyens.**

Clark, Frederick Scotson, English clergyman, organist, and composer; b. London, Nov. 16, 1840; d. there, July 5, 1883. He studied with Sergent in Paris and with E.J. Hopkins; also studied at the Royal Academy of Music in London with Bennett, Goss, Engel, Pettit, and Pinsuti; received his religious education at Cambridge and Oxford; was organist of Exeter College, Oxford; took further music lessons in Leipzig and Stuttgart; returned in 1873 to London, where he founded the London Organ School; he was the representative English organist at the Paris Exposition of 1878. His organ compositions (15 marches, 48 voluntaries, 6 communions; offertories, improvisations, impromptus, etc.) are his best works; he composed over 100 piano pieces; sacred vocal music, songs, etc.; he also played and composed for the harmonium.

Clark, Melville, American instrument maker, uncle of **Melville Antone Clark;** b. Oneida County, N.Y., 1850; d. Chicago, Nov. 5, 1918. In 1875 he established himself as an organ builder in Oakland, Calif.; moved to Chicago in 1880; in 1894 he also opened a piano factory, after he had become interested in pneumatic actions; his experiments leading to practical results which convinced him of the possibilities of the player piano, he sold his organ factory, and, in 1900, organized the Melville Clark Piano Co., of which he was president. In 1901 he patented and marketed the 88-note roll, utilizing the full compass of the piano, and thus gave the impetus to the phenomenal player-piano industry which later developed. In 1911 he patented a recording mechanism which aimed to reproduce the actual performance of great pianists. He also held many other important patents.

Clark, Melville Antone, American harpist and harp manufacturer, nephew of **Melville Clark;** b. Syracuse, N.Y., Sept. 12, 1883; d. there, Dec. 11, 1953. He received his 1st instruction on the harp from his father; was a pupil of Van Veachton Rogers (1896–99) and of John Aptommas in London (1908). While on a tour of Great Britain in 1908 he acquired a small Irish harp, formerly the property of the poet Thomas Moore; by the application of acoustic principles he improved the model and succeeded in producing a small, portable harp (39 inches high) of considerable tone volume; founded the Clark Harp Manufacturing Co. at Syracuse, which turned out the 1st small Irish harps in 1913; on a tour of the U.S. with John McCormack (1913–14) the inventor demonstrated the possibilities of the new instrument; took out 14 patents on improvements for the portable harp, and developed a new method of pedaling the concert harp; played about 4,000 recitals in the U.S., Canada, and England; was co-founder of the Syracuse Sym. Orch.; treasurer of the National Assoc. of Harpists; president of the Clark Music Co. (1910).

WRITINGS: *How to Play the Harp, Romance of the Harp, Singing Strings.*

Clark, Roy (Linwood), American country-music singer and instrumentalist; b. Meherrin, Va., April 15, 1933. As a teenager he learned to play the banjo, guitar, and fiddle; later took up piano, trumpet, trombone, drums, and singing; at the age of 21 he formed his own band. In 1969 he became co-host (with Buck Owens) of the *Hee Haw* country-music television program; its jejune quality was relieved somewhat by Clark's natural gifts as a singer and instrumentalist. In addition to his many recordings, he toured the U.S. and Canada. In 1976 he made a successful tour of the Soviet Union.

Clarke, Henry Leland, American musicologist and composer; b. Dover, N.H., March 9, 1907. He studied piano and violin; then took courses at Harvard Univ. (M.A., 1929; Ph.D., 1947). In 1929 he went to Paris, where he took composition lessons with Nadia Boulanger at the École Normale de Musique. Upon returning to the U.S., he occupied himself mainly with teaching; was on the faculty of Westminster Choir College (1938–42), the Univ. of Calif., Los Angeles (1947–58), and the Univ. of Washington, Seattle (1958–77). As a composer, Clarke applies a number of interesting innovations, e.g., "Intervalescent Counterpoint" (with interval values constantly changing from one voice to another), "Lipophony" (with certain notes systematically omitted), "Word Tones" (whenever a word recurs, it is assigned to the same pitch), and "Rotating Triskaidecaphony" (a 12-tone series returning to note 1 for the 13th note, with the next row starting and ending on note 2, etc.).

WORKS: *Danza de la muerte,* a choreography for Oboe and Piano (1937); *Monograph* for Orch. (1952); chamber opera, *The Loafer and the Loaf* (1951; Los Angeles, May 1, 1956); *Nocturne* for Viola and Piano (1955); *Saraband for the Golden Goose* for Orch. (1957); *Points West* for Wind and Percussion (1960); *Encounter* for Viola and Orch. (1961); *Lysistrata,* opera (1968–72; Marlboro, Vt., Nov. 9, 1984); *A Game That 2 Can Play* for Flute and Clarinet (1966); *Concatenata* for French Horn and Woodwind Quartet (1969); *Danza de la vida,* choreography for Oboe and Piano (1975); *These Are the Times That Try Men's Souls* for Chorus, to the text of Thomas Paine (1976); *The Young Dead Soldiers* for Chorus, to words by Archibald MacLeish (1977); *Give and Take* for 2 Keyboards (1977); *Drastic Measures* for Trombone (1982); *The Sun Shines Also Today* for Chorus, after Ralph Waldo Emerson (1983); *The Earth Mourns* for Chorus, after Isaiah (1984); also numerous piano pieces; various songs; organ music; 3 string quartets (1928, 1956, 1958).

Clarke, Hugh Archibald, Scottish-American organist; b. near Toronto, Canada, Aug. 15, 1839; d. Philadelphia, Dec. 16, 1927. He was a pupil of his father, **James Paton Clarke;** was organist in several churches in Philadelphia; in 1875 was elected prof. of the science of music at the Univ. of Pa.; retired in 1925.

WORKS: Music to Euripides' *Iphigenia in Tauris;* oratorio, *Jerusalem* (1891); piano music; songs.

WRITINGS: A treatise on harmony and one on counterpoint; textbooks for organ; a book of fiction, *The Scratch Club* (1888); *Music and the Comrade Arts* (1900); *Highways and Byways of Music* (1901).

Clarke, (James) Hamilton (Smee), English organist; b. Birmingham, Jan. 25, 1840; d. Banstead, July 9, 1912. He was apprenticed to a land surveyor (1855–61); then turned to music, and in 1866 became organist to Queen's College, Oxford. In 1872 he succeeded Sullivan as organist of St. Peter's in South Kensington; was conductor of the D'Oyly Carte company on tour (1878); and also at the Lyceum Theatre, writing music for dramas given by Henry Irving. In 1893, he became 1st conductor of the Carl Rosa Co.

WORKS: He publ. about 400 works, including music to *Hamlet, The Merchant of Venice,* and *King Lear;* sacred cantata, *Praise;* 8-part anthem, *The Lord is my light;* 2 syms.; 6 overtures; organ music.

Clarke, James Paton, Scottish-American organist, father of **Hugh Archibald Clarke;** b. 1808; d. Toronto, Aug. 27, 1877. In 1829 he was the leader of psalmody in St. George's Church in Glasgow; in 1834 became organist of St. Mary's Episcopal Chapel, succeeding Thomas Macfarlane; he emigrated to Canada in 1835 and became a farmer; went to Toronto about 1845. In 1846 he took his Mus.Bac. degree at King's College with the 8-part anthem *Arise, O Lord God, forget not the poor.*
BIBL.: H. Kallmann, "J.P. C.—Canada's Mus. Bac.," *Cahiers Canadiens de Musique* (Spring–Summer 1970).

Clarke, Jeremiah, English composer and organist; b. London, c.1673; d. there (suicide), Dec. 1, 1707. He was a chorister in the Chapel Royal; in 1700 was made Gentleman Extraordinary of the Chapel Royal; in 1704 was appointed joint organist (with Croft) there. A hopeless love affair caused Clarke to take his own life. He composed (with others) the stage works *The World in the Moon* (1697) and *The Island Princess* (1699); wrote incidental music to several plays; was the 1st composer to set Dryden's *Alexander's Feast* to music (for St. Cecilia's Day, Nov. 22, 1697); also wrote a cantata, an ode, anthems, songs, etc. He was the real author of the famous *Trumpet Voluntary,* erroneously ascribed to Purcell, and popularized by Sir Henry Wood's orch. arrangement.
BIBL.: C. Cudworth, "Some New Facts about the Trumpet Voluntary," *Musical Times* (Sept. 1953); T. Taylor, "J. C.'s Trumpet Tunes: Another View of Origins," *Musical Quarterly* (July 1970); R. McGuinness, *English Court Odes 1660–1820* (Oxford, 1971); T. Taylor, *Thematic Catalog of the Works of J. C.* (Detroit, 1977).

Clarke (Clarke-Whitfield), John, English organist and composer; b. Gloucester, Dec. 13, 1770; d. Holmer, near Hereford, Feb. 22, 1836. He studied organ at Oxford with Philip Hayes; received his B.Mus. degree in 1793; was church organist at Ludlow, Armagh, and Dublin; in 1799 he became organist at Trinity and St. John's College in Cambridge; from 1820 to 1833 he was organist at the Hereford Cathedral. He was stricken with paralysis; was forced to resign his post, and was an invalid for the rest of his life.
WORKS: 2 oratorios: *The Crucifixion* and *The Resurrection* (Hereford, 1822); 4 vols. of cathedral services and anthems (1805); 12 glees (1805); 12 songs; *Selection of Single and Double Chants;* etc.

Clarke, Kenny ("Klook"), black American jazz drummer; b. Pittsburgh, Jan. 9, 1914; d. Montreuil-sous-Bois, Paris, Jan. 26, 1985. While in school, he played piano, trombone, drums, and vibes. In 1935 he joined the band of Roy Eldridge, then played with Teddy Wilson's group; later appeared with Charlie Parker and Dizzy Gillespie. He was a founding member of the Modern Jazz Quartet in 1952, and played with it until 1955. Moving to Europe, he formed the Clarke-Boland Big Band with the Belgian pianist-arranger Francy Boland in Paris in 1960; it disbanded in 1973; he then worked with a small group in Europe, making occasional visits to the U.S.

Clarke, Rebecca (Thacher), English-born American composer and violist; b. Harrow, Aug. 27, 1886; d. N.Y., Oct. 13, 1979. She studied violin with Hans Wessely at the Royal Academy of Music (1902–4) and composition with C. Stanford at the Royal College of Music (1904–10) in London; she then switched to the viola, taking a few private lessons from L. Tertis and becoming the 1st female member of Henry Wood's Queen Hall Orch. (1912). In 1928 she formed the English Ensemble, with which she played until 1929. She married **James Friskin** in 1944; she then lived in N.Y. Her music, comprising entirely chamber works, was quite advanced, being on the fringe of atonality in outline, but remaining firmly rooted in English Impressionism. For some of her compositions, she used the name **Anthony Trent.**
WORKS: String Quartet (1924); *3 Irish Country Songs* for Voice and Violin (1926); *Prelude, Allegro, and Pastorale* for Clarinet and Viola (1941; ISCM Festival, Berkeley, Calif., Aug. 6, 1942); *Combined Carols* for String Quartet and Strings

(1941). **WITH PIANO:** Sonata for Violin (1909); *Morpheus* for Viola (1917); Sonata for Viola (1919); Piano Trio (1921); *Epilogue* for Cello (1921); *Rhapsody* for Cello (1923); *Midsummer Moon* for Violin (1924); *Passacaglia on an Old English Tune* for Viola (1941); over 60 songs.
BIBL.: M. Ponder, "R. C.," *Journal of the British Music Society* (1983); C. MacDonald, "R. C.'s Chamber Music," *Tempo* (March 1987).

Clarke, Robert Coningsby, English organist and composer; b. Old Charlton, Kent, March 17, 1879; d. Walmer, Kent, Jan. 2, 1934. He studied with John Frederick Bridge at Westminster Abbey; then served as church organist at Oxford. He wrote a number of popular ballads and piano pieces.

Clarus, Max, German conductor and composer; b. Mühlberg, March 31, 1852; d. Braunschweig, Dec. 6, 1916. He studied with his father, who was a municipal music director, and with Löschhorn in Berlin. He became a theatrical conductor, traveling in Germany, Austria, and Hungary; composed mostly for the stage and for chorus.
WORKS: Operas (all 1st perf. in Braunschweig): *Des Königs-Rekrut* (1889); *Ilse* (1895); the fairy operas *Der Wunschpeter* (1910) and *Der Zwerg Nase* (1912); several ballets; *Die Wacht vor Samoa* for Baritone Solo, Male Chorus, and Orch.; numerous a cappella choruses.

Claudin le Jeune. See Le Jeune, Claudin.

Claussen, Julia (née **Ohlson**), Swedish mezzo-soprano; b. Stockholm, June 11, 1879; d. there, May 1, 1941. She studied at the Royal Academy of Music in Stockholm (1897–1902); then in Berlin with Friedrich. She made her debut as Leonora in *La Favorite* at the Stockholm Opera (Jan. 19, 1903); was engaged there from 1903 until 1912; made her debut at Covent Garden in London in 1914; was a member of the Chicago Opera Co. (1912–17). She made her 1st appearance at the Metropolitan Opera in N.Y. as Dalila on Nov. 23, 1917, and remained in the company until 1929; in 1934 she returned to Stockholm as a teacher at the Cons. After her death a memorial fund for vocal scholarships was established in Stockholm.

Clay, Frédéric (Emes), English composer; b. Paris, Aug. 3, 1838; d. Great Marlow, near London, Nov. 24, 1889. He studied with Molique at Paris and with Hauptmann in Leipzig.
WORKS: His early operettas, *The Pirate's Isle* (1859) and *Out of Sight* (1860), were performed privately in London; his 1st operetta to be produced at Covent Garden was *Court and Cottage* (1862); other light dramatic works subsequently performed at Covent Garden included *Constance* (1865); *Ages Ago* (1869); *The Gentleman in Black* (1870); *Happy Arcadia* (1872); *Cattarina* (1874); *Princess Toto* (1876); *Don Quixote* (1876). He also composed 2 cantatas, *The Knights of the Cross* (1866) and *Lalla Rookh* (1877; including the well-known aria *I'll sing thee songs of Araby*).
BIBL.: A. Jacobs, "Cradled among the Reeds: Two Victorian Operettas," *Musical Times* (May 1988).

Clayton, Buck (Wilbur Dorsey), black American jazz trumpeter; b. Parsons, Kans., Nov. 12, 1911. His father taught him to play the trumpet; he became a member of Count Basie's band (1936–43). After serving in the U.S. Army (1943–46), he resumed his career; also made arrangements for Basie, Benny Goodman, and other bandleaders; toured Europe (1949–50; 1953); later appeared at jazz festivals. With N. Elliott, he publ. *Buck Clayton's Jazz World* (N.Y., 1987).

Clemencic, René, Austrian recorder player, harpsichordist, conductor, and composer; b. Vienna, Feb. 27, 1928. He took courses in musicology at the Sorbonne in Paris, the Collège de France, and the Univ. of Vienna (Ph.D., 1956), then studied recorder, harpsichord, and theory with H. Staeps, harpsichord with E. Harich-Schneider, and early music with J. Mertin in Vienna; he also received recorder training from J. Collette in Nijmegen and from L. Hoffer v. Wintersfeld and W. Nitschke in Berlin. In 1958 he founded the Musica Antiqua in Vienna, which became the Ensemble Musica Antiqua in 1959; with this group he gave performances of music from the Middle Ages to the Baroque, utilizing authentic instruments. In 1969 he founded the Clemencic Consort, and led it in a vast repertoire, extending from the medieval period to the avant-garde. He also taught at the Vienna Academy of Music and authored 2 books, *Old Musical Instruments* (London, 1968; also in German) and *Carmina Burana, Kommentar zur Gesamtausgabe der Melodien* (Munich, 1979). Among his compositions for recorder are *Fantasia dodekafonica* (1964), *Maraviglia I* and *II* (1968), *Bicinia nova* for 2 Recorders or Piccolo Flutes (1969), *Chronos I* for Recorder, Violin, and Tape (1971) and *II* for 4 Recorders (1975); he has also composed a number of works for other instruments in a variety of combinations, including *Realitäten* for Voice and Chamber Ensemble (1979), *Estasi* for 6 Percussionists (1988), *Passatempo* for Brass and Wind Quintet (1989), and *Musica instrumentalis* for Chamber Ensemble (1989).

Clemens, Hans, German tenor; b. Bicken-Gelsenkirchen, July 27, 1890; d. Montrose, Colo., Aug. 25, 1958. After successful appearances in Germany and at Covent Garden in London, he came to the U.S.; made his N.Y. debut at the Metropolitan Opera House in *The Flying Dutchman* (Nov. 1, 1930); appeared also in other Wagnerian roles; was particularly effective as David in *Die Meistersinger*, a role which he sang more than 100 times. In 1938 he settled in Los Angeles as a vocal teacher.

Clemens non Papa (real name, **Jacob Clement**), eminent Franco-Flemish composer; b. probably in Ieper, c.1510; d. Dixmuiden, near Ieper, 1555 or 1556. He was first called "non Papa" in 1545 when he entered into business transactions with the Antwerp publisher Susato. It was formerly believed that "non Papa" meant "not the Pope," to distinguish him from Pope Clement VII, but it was also suggested that it was intended to differentiate him from the poet Jacobus Papa, who also resided in Ieper. The real meaning of the designation has been lost. Nothing is known of his early years. His earliest extant work, the chanson "Le departir est sans department," was publ. in 1536. In the records of St. Donaas in Bruges, he is mentioned as presbyter in 1544; that same year he was nominated succentor "per modum probae." He served as succentor at Bruges Cathedral in 1544–45 and was active with the Marian Brotherhood in 's-Hertogenbosch in 1550. He was a prolific composer of sacred music, producing 15 masses (2 mass fragments are also extant), over 230 motets, 2 Magnificat cycles, and 159 3-voice souterliedekens and lofzangen (the 1st polyphonic settings of the 150 Psalms in Dutch; publ. by Susato in Antwerp, 1556–57). His secular works include 89 chansons (10 are doubtful), 8 Dutch songs, and several other pieces. K. Bernet Kempers ed. *Clemens non Papa: Opera omnia* in Corpus Mensurabilis Musicae, IV/1–21 (1951–76). **BIBL.:** K. Bernet Kempers, "Zur Biographie C. n. P.s," *Zeitschrift für Musikwissenschaft*, IX (1926–27); idem, "Die 'Souterliedekens' des Jacobus C. n. P.," *Tijdschrift van de Vereniging voor Nederlandse muziekgeschiedenis*, XII/4 and XIII/2 (1929); idem, *Jacobus C. n. P. und seine Motetten* (Augsburg, 1929); idem, "Jacobus C. n. P.'s Chansons in Their Chronological Order," *Musica Disciplina*, XV (1961); idem, "Bibliography of the Sacred Works of Jacobus C. n. P.: A Classified List, with a Notice on His Life," ibid., XVIII (1964).

Clément, Edmond (Frédéric-Jean), esteemed French tenor; b. Paris, March 28, 1867; d. Nice, Feb. 24, 1928. He was a pupil of Warot at the Paris Cons. in 1887; took 1st prize in 1889; his debut was at the Opéra-Comique, Nov. 29, 1889, as Vincent in Gounod's *Mireille*. His success was instantaneous, and he remained there until 1910 with frequent leave for extended tours; sang in the principal theaters of France, Belgium, Spain, Portugal, England, and Denmark; on Dec. 6, 1909, he made his debut at the Metropolitan Opera in N.Y. in one of his finest roles, Massenet's Des Grieux; from 1911 to 1913, sang with the Boston Opera Co. His voice was a light tenor of very agreeable quality, with a range of 2 octaves. He created the chief tenor parts in the following operas (all at the Opéra-Comique): Bruneau's *L'Attaque du Moulin* (1893);

Saint-Saëns's *Phryné* (1893); Cui's *Le Flibustier* (1894); Godard's *La Vivandière* (1895); Dubois's *Xavière* (1895); Hahn's *L'Île du rêve* (1898); Erlanger's *Le Juif polonais* (1900); Saint-Saëns's *Hélène* (1904); Dupont's *La Cabrera* (1905); Vidal's *La Reine Fiammette* (1908).

Clément, (Jacques) Félix (Alfred), French organist, choirmaster, and writer on music; b. Paris, Jan. 13, 1822; d. there, Jan. 23, 1885. He devoted himself especially to historical studies; filled several positions as an organist and teacher, and finally became organist and choirmaster at the Church of the Sorbonne. In 1849 the government chose him to direct sacred music at the Ste.-Chapelle du Palais; during his tenure there he brought out a number of works of 13th-century music; they were publ. in full score as *Chants de la Sainte-Chapelle* (1849; 3rd ed., 1855). He was active in establishing the Institution for Church Music. **WRITINGS:** *Méthode complète du plain-chant* (1854, 1872); *Histoire générale de la musique religieuse* (1860); *Les Musiciens célèbres depuis le XVIᵉ siècle* (1868; 4th ed., 1887); *Dictionnaire lyrique, ou Histoire des opéras* (1869, 4 supplements to 1881; new augmented ed. by A. Pougin, 1897 and 1904, as *Dictionnaire des opéras*); *Méthode d'orgue, d'harmonie et d'accompagnement* (1874; 2nd ed., 1894); *Histoire de la musique depuis les temps anciens jusqu'à nos jours* (1885); etc.

Clement, Franz, Austrian violinist and composer; b. Vienna, Nov. 17, 1780; d. there, Nov. 3, 1842. He learned to play the violin as a child, and at the age of 10 went to London, where he appeared as a soloist at concerts directed by Salomon and Haydn. Returning to Vienna, he continued his successful career; was conductor at the Theater an der Wien (1802–11); made a tour in Germany and Russia (1813–18); participated in the concerts of the famous singer Angelica Catalani. He was greatly esteemed as a violinist and musician by his contemporaries; Beethoven wrote his Violin Concerto for him, and Clement gave its 1st performance in Vienna (Dec. 23, 1806). He wrote 6 concertos and 25 concertinos for violin, as well as numerous technical studies. **BIBL.:** R. Haas, "The Viennese Violinist F. C.," *Musical Quarterly* (Jan. 1948).

Clement, Jacob. See **Clemens non Papa.**

Clementi, Aldo, Italian composer of avant-garde tendencies; b. Catania, May 25, 1925. He took piano lessons as a child in Catania and later was a piano pupil of Pietro Scarpini in Siena; subsequently studied composition with Alfredo Sangiorgi, a pupil of Schoenberg, in Catania (1945–52) and with Petrassi in Rome (1952–54); then attended summer courses in new music at Darmstadt (1955–62). After an initial period of writing music in a neo-Baroque manner, he adopted serial techniques, employing rhythmic indeterminacy and dense, clustered sonics. **WORKS:** *3 piccoli pezzi* for Flute, Oboe, and Clarinet (1955); Sonata for Trumpet, Guitar, and Piano (1955); *2 studi* for Trumpet, Violin, and Piano (1956); *Concertino in forma di Variazioni* for 9 Instruments (1956); *3 studi* for Chamber Orch. (1956–57; Darmstadt, July 27, 1957); *Composizione No. 1* for Piano (1957); *Episodi* for Orch. (1958); *Ideogrammi No. 1* for 16 Instruments and *No. 2* for Flute and 17 Instruments (both 1959); *Triplum* for Flute, Oboe, and Clarinet (1960); *7 Scene* for Chamber Orch. (1961); *Informel 1* for 12 Percussion and Keyboard Instruments (1961), 2 for 15 Players (1962), and 3 for Orch. (1961–63; Palermo, Oct. 2, 1963); *Collage 1*, a 1-act "musical action" for the stage, for Chamber Ensemble and Visuals (1961), 2 for Tape (1962), and 3, *Dies irae*, for Tape (1966–67); *Intavolatura* for Harpsichord (1963); *Variante A* for Chorus and Orch. (1964; Rome, April 6, 1974) and *B* for Orch. (Venice Festival, Sept. 12, 1964); *Reticolo: 11* for 11 Instruments (1966); *Silben* for Female Voice, Clarinet, Violin, and 2 Pianos (1966); Concerto for Wind Orch. and 2 Pianos (1967; Venice Festival, Sept. 12, 1970); *Reticolo: 4* for String Quartet (1968); *B.A.C.H.* for Piano (1970); Concerto for Piano and 7 Instruments (1970; Venice Festival, Sept. 10, 1972);

Reticolo: 12 for 12 Strings (1970); *Silbenmerz* (1971); *Replica* for Harpsichord (1972); *Manualiter* for Organ (1973); *Blitz*, "musical action" for Chamber Ensemble (1973); *Sinfonia da camera* (Milan, April 22, 1974); Concerto for Piano, 24 Instruments, and Carillons (1975); *Reticolo: 3* for 3 Guitars (1975); *Clessidra* for 11 Instruments (1976); *Collage Jesu meine Freude,* azione mimo-visiva for 8 Strings, 8 Winds, and Tape (1979); *AEB* for 17 Instruments (1983); *Finale* for 4 Sopranos and Orch. (1984); *O Du Selige* for Orch. (1985); Concerto for Piano and 11 Instruments (1986).

Clementi, Muzio (baptized **Mutius Philippus Vincentius Franciscus Xaverius**), celebrated Italian pianist and composer; b. Rome, Jan. 23, 1752; d. Evesham, Worcestershire, England, March 10, 1832. He began to study music as a child with Antonio Buroni, and at the age of 7 commenced studies with the organist Cordicelli. He later studied voice with Giuseppe Santarelli. By Jan. 1766 he was organist of the parish San Lorenzo in Damaso. About this time Peter Beckford, cousin of the English novelist William Beckford, visited Rome; he was struck by Clementi's youthful talent and, with the permission of Clementi's father, took the boy to England. For the next 7 years Clementi lived, performed, and studied at his patron's estate of Stepleton Iwerne in Dorset. During the winter of 1774–75, Clementi settled in London, making his 1st appearance as a harpsichordist in a benefit concert on April 3, 1775. For the next several years he appears to have spent most of his time as harpsichordist at the King's Theatre, where he conducted operatic performances. In 1779 his 6 sonatas, op. 2, were publ., which brought him his 1st public success, both in England and on the Continent. In 1780 he embarked on a tour of the Continent, giving a series of piano concerts in Paris; in 1781 he continued his tour with appearances in Strasbourg, Munich, and Vienna. It was during his stay in Vienna that the famous piano contest with Mozart took place at court before Emperor Joseph II on Dec. 24, 1781. In 1786 several of his syms. were performed in London, only to be eclipsed by the great syms. of Haydn. In 1790 he retired from public performances as a pianist, but he continued to conduct orch. concerts from the keyboard. After 1796 he appears to have withdrawn from all public performances, devoting himself to teaching, collecting large fees. He lost part of his fortune through the bankruptcy of Longman and Broderip in 1798; however, with John Longman, he formed a partnership on the ruins of the old company and became highly successful as a music publisher and piano manufacturer; his business acumen was keen, and he remained most successful with subsequent partners during the next 3 decades. From 1802 to 1810 he traveled extensively on the Continent, pursuing business interests, teaching, composing, and giving private concerts. While in Vienna in 1807, he met Beethoven and arranged to become his major English publisher. He returned to England in 1810, and in 1813 helped organize the Phil. Soc. of London, with which he appeared as a conductor. In 1816–17 he conducted his syms. in Paris, followed by engagements in Frankfurt in 1817–18. He again visited Paris in 1821, and was in Munich in 1821–22. In Jan. 1822 he conducted his works with the Gewandhaus Orch. in Leipzig. Returning to England, he made several more conducting appearances with the Phil. Soc. until 1824; however, his syms. were soon dropped from the repertoire as Beethoven's masterpieces eclipsed his own efforts. In 1830 he retired from his mercantile ventures, and eventually made his home at Evesham, Worcestershire. As a teacher, Clementi had many distinguished pupils, including Johann Baptist Cramer, John Field, Karl Zeuner, Alexander Klengel, Friedrich Kalkbrenner, and Ludwig Berger.

WORKS: The *Oeuvres complettes de M. C.* was publ. by Breitkopf and Härtel (13 vols., Leipzig, 1803–19; facsimile reprint, 15 vols., N.Y., 1973); however, it is not complete. A. Tyson prepared a *Thematic Catalogue of the Works of M. C.* (Tutzing, 1967). Clementi composed a number of syms., but many of them have not survived. MSS are now housed at the Library of Congress in Washington, D.C., and the British Library in London. Autographs of 4 syms. survive, but they are not complete. Alfredo Casella reconstructed 2 of the syms., 1 in C major (listing it as No. 1) and 1 in D major (listing it as No. 2). He conducted his version of the C major in Turin on Dec. 13, 1935, and the D major in Rome on Jan. 5, 1936. He publ. them in Milan in 1938. Another D-major sym., now listed as No. 4, survives in the form of a 1st movement in autograph, and sketches for the remaining movements. There is also a G-major sym., known as the *Great National Symphony,* which survives in autograph movements and fragments. Two early syms., one in B-flat major and the other in D major, op. 18 (1787), have been ed. by Renato Fasano (Milan, 1959–61). His other works include over 100 keyboard sonatas (about half with violin, cello, or flute), 6 duets for 4 hands, 2 duos for 2 keyboard instruments, fugues, preludes, and exercises, etc. With the exception of the op. 36 sonatinas and several of the sonatas, Clementi's works have been generally neglected; however, in recent years, the publication of new eds. of some of his works, as well as the issuing of recordings, has brought renewed interest in his output. Also of interest is the didactic *Introduction to the Art of Playing on the Pianoforte,* op. 42 (London, 1801; reprint, N.Y., 1973), which includes 50 lessons for the beginner. His major didactic work, the *Gradus ad Parnassum* (3 vols., Leipzig, 1817–26), contains 100 compositions that attest to his greatness as a teacher of piano.

BIBL.: The Clementi-Archiv of the Netherlands issues the *Blätter aus dem C.-Archiv.* See also G. Froio, *M. C., La sua vita, le sue opere e sua influenza sul progresso dell'arte* (Milan, 1876); J. Shedlock, *The Pianoforte Sonata: Its Origin and Development* (London, 1895); M. Unger, *M. C.s Leben* (Langensalza, 1914); G. Paribeni, *M. C. nella vita e nell'arte* (Milan, 1921); A. Stauch, *M. C.s Klavier-Sonaten im Verhältnis zu den Sonaten von Haydn, Mozart und Beethoven* (diss., Univ. of Cologne, 1930); E. di Laura, *L'estetica nell'arte didattica di M. C.* (Rome, 1934); J. Kohn, *The Manuscript Sonatas by M. C. at the Library of Congress: A Comparative Edition with Commentary* (diss., Univ. of Iowa, 1967); L. Plantinga, *C.: His Life and Music* (London, 1977); M. Stoelzel, *Die Anfänge vierhändiger Klaviermusik: Studien zur Satztypik in den Sonaten M. C.s* (Frankfurt, 1984).

Clemm, John (Johann Gottlob), German-American organ builder; b. Dresden, 1690; d. Bethlehem, Pa., May 5, 1762. Clemm reputedly learned organ making from A. Silbermann, probably while serving the Moravian Church settlement at Herrnhut, Saxony. He came to America with a group of Schwenkfelders in 1735, became a Separatist, and settled in Philadelphia in 1736. His 1st known organ was installed at Trinity Church in N.Y., in 1741. Subsequently, he assisted the Swedish-American organ builder Hesselius in Philadelphia. He reunited with the Moravians and moved to Bethlehem, Pa. (1756–58). There he continued his work with his assistant, David Tannenberg, until his death. His descendants were important music dealers and publishers in Philadelphia up to 1879. His son, **John Clemm, Jr.,** was the 1st organist at N.Y.'s Trinity Church.

BIBL.: A. Messiter, *History of the Choir and Music of Trinity Church* (N.Y., 1907); D. McCorkle, "The Moravian Contribution to American Music," *Music Library Association Notes* (Sept. 1956).

Cleonides, Greek writer on music who flourished in the 1st half of the 2nd century A.D. His treatise *Eisagoge harmonike (Introductio harmonica),* based on the theories of Aristoxenos, was for a long time ascribed to the mathematician Euclid, because it had been publ. under Euclid's name by Pena (Paris, 1557) and Meibom (Amsterdam, 1652), although it had been printed with the real author's name by Valla (Venice, 1497). A new critical ed. was publ. by K. von Jan in *Musici Scriptores Graeci.* There is a French tr. by Ruelle (1896); for an Eng. tr., see Strunk's *Source Readings in Music History* (N.Y., 1950).

Clérambault, Louis Nicolas, French composer and organist; b. Paris, Dec. 19, 1676; d. there, Oct. 26, 1749. He studied with André Raison; was organist at various Paris churches. He was a successful composer of theatrical pieces for the court: *Le Soleil vainqueur* (Paris, Oct. 21, 1721); *Le Départ du roi* (1745); etc. He also wrote a number of solo cantatas, in which genre he excelled; composed much organ music; some of his organ works are republ. in Guilmant's *Archives des maîtres de l'orgue*. His son, **César François Nicolas Clérambault** (1700–1760), was also an organist and composer.

Clercx, Suzanne, Belgian musicologist; b. Houdeng-Aimeries, June 7, 1910; d. Liège, Sept. 27, 1985. She studied at the Univ. of Liège; took courses in musicology with Charles van den Borren; obtained her Ph.D. in 1939 with the dissertation *Essai sur l'évolution de la musique instrumentale dans les Pays-Bas au XVIII siècle;* was then a librarian at the Royal Cons. in Brussels (1941–49); in 1945 was appointed lecturer at the Univ. of Liège; became a prof. in 1966 at the Univ., where she was active until 1975; in 1980 she was granted the title of prof. emeritus.
    WRITINGS: *Henri-Jacques de Croes* (Brussels, 1940); *Grétry, 1741–1813* (Brussels, 1944); *Le Baroque et la musique* (Brussels, 1948); *Pierre van Maldère* (Brussels, 1948); *Johannes Ciconia: Un Musicien liégeois et son temps* (Brussels, 1960).

Cléreau, Pierre, 16th-century French composer. Virtually nothing is known about his life, except that he was a chorister in Toul as a youth. However, many of his sacred works and 3-part chansons have been preserved. The following are extant: 4 masses (Paris, 1554); *Missa pro mortuis* (Paris, 1554); *Missa* (Paris, 1557); 2 books of odes to Ronsard's words (Paris, 1566; several reprints); *Cantiques spirituels* (Paris, 1567).
    BIBL.: G. Thibault and L. Perceau, *Bibliographie des chansons de Ronsard mises en musique au XVIe siècle* (Paris, 1941).

Clérice, Justin, Argentine-born French composer; b. Buenos Aires, Oct. 16, 1863; d. Toulouse, Sept. 9, 1908. He left Argentina as a young boy and spent most of his life in Paris, studying at the Paris Cons. with Delibes and Pessard (1882). He wrote many comic operas, most of which were performed in Paris: *Figarella* (June 3, 1889); *Le 3e Hussards* (March 14, 1894); *Pavie* (Jan. 28, 1897); *L'Ordre de l'empereur* (March 3, 1902); etc. His most successful comic opera, *Le Meunier d'Alcala*, was 1st performed in Portuguese (Lisbon, April 11, 1887); he also wrote an operetta, *Phrynette* (1895); a pantomime, *Léda* (1896); a ballet-opera, *Au temps jadis* (Monte Carlo, 1905).

Cleva, Fausto (Angelo), Italian-born American conductor; b. Trieste, May 17, 1902; d. Athens (collapsed while conducting a performance at the odeum of Herodes Atticus), Aug. 6, 1971. He studied in Milan; began his conducting career as a youth; in 1920 emigrated to the U.S.; became an American citizen in 1931. He was chorus master of the Metropolitan Opera (1935–42); then was conductor of the San Francisco Opera Co. (1942–44 and 1949–55); again with the Metropolitan (1951 until his death).

Cleve, Halfdan, Norwegian composer and pianist; b. Kongsberg, Oct. 5, 1879; d. Oslo, April 6, 1951. He studied with his father, an organist, and with Winter-Hjelm in Christiania; continued his studies in Berlin with O. Raif and with the Scharwenka brothers (1899–1903). He made his debut as a pianist in Berlin (1902); returned to Christiania in 1910, and settled as a pianist and teacher.
    WORKS: 5 piano concertos (1902, 1904, 1906, 1910, 1916); Piano Quintet; Violin Sonata; Ballade for Cello and Piano; many piano pieces and songs.

Cleveland, James, black American gospel singer and composer; b. Chicago, Dec. 5, 1931; d. Los Angeles, Feb. 9, 1991. He was reared in a gospel milieu in which he was encouraged to develop his natural talent for music by the pianist Roberta Martin. He was a pianist and singer with the group known as the Caravans and then formed his own Gospel Chimes in 1959; he also became a licensed minister of the Church of God in Christ. His song *Grace Is Sufficient* (1948) became a gospel standard, and his album *Peace Be Still* (1963) added further to his renown. In 1970 he founded the Corner-

stone Institutional Baptist Church, for which he also served as pastor.
    BIBL.: *Current Biography* (Aug. 1985).

Cliburn, Van (Harvey Lavan, Jr.), brilliant American pianist; b. Shreveport, La., July 12, 1934. His mother, Rildia Bee Cliburn, was a pupil of Arthur Friedheim; she was his only teacher until 1951, when he entered the Juilliard School of Music in N.Y. as a student of Rosina Lhévinne, graduating in 1954. He was 4 when he made his 1st appearance in public in Shreveport; after winning the Texas State Prize in 1947, he appeared as a soloist with the Houston Sym. Orch. In 1948 he won the National Music Festival Award, in 1952 the Dealy Award and the Kosciuszko Foundation Chopin prize, in 1953 the Juilliard School of Music concerto competition, and in 1954 the Roeder Award and the Leventritt competition in N.Y.; that same year he appeared as a soloist with the N.Y. Phil. In 1958 he captured 1st prize at the Tchaikovsky Competition in Moscow, the 1st American to achieve this feat; upon his return to N.Y., he received a hero's welcome in a ticker-tape parade. In subsequent years he toured extensively, appearing as a soloist with leading orchs. and as a recitalist. In 1978 he withdrew from public performances, but appeared again in 1987 as a recitalist in a concert for President Reagan and Soviet General Secretary Gorbachev at the White House in Washington, D.C. In 1989 he appeared as soloist in the Liszt and Tchaikovsky 1st piano concertos with the Philadelphia Orch.; that same year he accepted Gorbachev's invitation to perform in Moscow, and on Sept. 8 was the soloist with Eduardo Mata and the Dallas Sym. Orch. in the gala opening of the Morton H. Meyerson Sym. Center. Van Cliburn's playing combines a superlative technique with a genuine Romantic sentiment, particularly effective in the music of Tchaikovsky and Rachmaninoff. The Van Cliburn International Piano Competition was organized in 1962 and is held quadrennially in Fort Worth, Texas, the home of the Van Cliburn Foundation.
    BIBL.: A. Chasins, *The V. C. Legend* (N.Y., 1959); S. Isacoff, "The Rise and Fall and Rise of V. C.," *Ovation* (Sept. 1989).

Clicquot, French family of organ builders, of whom the earliest was **Robert Clicquot,** builder of the organ in the Versailles Chapel for Louis XIV (1711), and organs in the cathedrals of Rouen (1689) and St.-Quentin (1703). His sons **Jean-Baptiste** (b. Rheims, Nov. 3, 1678; d. Paris, March 16, 1746) and **Louis-Alexandre** (b. c.1680; d. Paris, Jan. 25, 1760) were his helpers. The most renowned of the family was **François-Henri Clicquot** (b. 1732; d. Paris, May 24, 1790), who constructed the great organ of Versailles Cathedral (installed Oct. 31, 1761) and the organ of St. Sulpice, with 5 manuals, 66 stops, and a 32-foot pedal (1781).
    BIBL.: F. Raugel, *Les Grandes Orgues des églises de Paris* (Paris, 1927); N. Dufourcq, *Les C.* (Paris, 1942); J. Villard, *F.-H. C., facteur d'orgues du roi* (Poitiers, 1975).

Cliffe, Frederic, English organist and composer; b. Bradford, Yorkshire, May 2, 1857; d. London, Nov. 19, 1931. He studied with his father, and showed such a precocious musical talent that at the age of 11 he performed his duties as organist at Wyke Parish Church; then was organist of the Bradford Festival Choral Soc. (1873–76); at the same time he continued his studies with Arthur Sullivan, Prout, Stainer, and Franklin Taylor as a scholarship student. In 1883 he joined the staff of the Royal College of Music in London, a post which he kept until his death.
    WORKS: Sym. No. 1 (London, April 20, 1889); Sym. No. 2 (Leeds, 1892); tone poem, *Cloud and Sunshine* (1890); Violin Concerto (1896); *Ode to the North-East Wind* for Chorus and Orch. (1905); church music.

Cline, Patsy (née **Virginia Patterson Hensley**), American country-music singer; b. Winchester, Va., Sept. 8, 1932; d. in an airplane crash, Camden, Tenn., March 5, 1963. She became an accomplished singer of country music; in 1957 she won national recognition on Arthur Godfrey's "Talent Scouts" television program with her rendition of *Walkin' after*

Midnight; among her hits were *Heartaches* and *Sweet Dreams of You*. In 1973 she was elected to the Country Music Hall of Fame. She was at the peak of her popularity when she met her untimely death.

Clokey, Joseph Waddell, American organist, teacher, and composer; b. New Albany, Ind., Aug. 28, 1890; d. Covina, Calif., Sept. 14, 1960. He studied at Miami Univ. (B.A., 1912) and at the Cincinnati Cons. of Music (graduated 1915); from 1915 to 1926 taught music theory at Miami Univ.; from 1926 to 1939 taught organ at Pomona College in Claremont, Calif.; from 1939 to 1946 was dean of the School of Fine Arts at Miami Univ.; retired and lived in Claremont. He wrote much music for schools. He publ. the manuals *Plainsong* (Boston, 1934) and *In Every Corner Sing: An Outline of Church Music for the Layman* (N.Y., 1945).

Works: Short operas: *The Pied Piper of Hamelin* (Miami Univ., May 14, 1920); *The Nightingale*, after Andersen (Miami Univ., Dec. 12, 1925); *Our American Cousin* (Claremont, March 2, 1931); sacred cantatas: *The Vision; When the Christ Child Came; For He Is Risen; We Beheld His Glory; Adoramus Te; Christ Is Born*; organ pieces; songs.

Clooney, Rosemary, American singer of popular music; b. Maysville, Ky., May 23, 1928. She sang on a Cincinnati radio station when she was 13, later touring as a soloist with Tony Pastor's Orch. (1945–49). She acquired popular success with her recording of *Come on-a My House* (1951), subsequently pursuing a lively career as a singer in nightclubs and on recordings, radio, and television. A long-standing dependence on drugs resulted in a mental collapse in 1968; however, she was able to resume her career in 1976. She publ. an autobiography, *This for Remembrance* (1977).

Closson, Ernest, Belgian writer on music; b. St. Josse ten Noode, near Brussels, Dec. 12, 1870; d. Brussels, Dec. 21, 1950. He was self-taught in music; occupied various posts as an archivist; was assistant curator for the collection of musical instruments at the Cons. of Brussels (1896–1924) and chief curator from 1924 to 1935; taught at the Brussels Cons. (1912–35) and the Cons. of Mons (1917); retired in 1935. From 1920 to 1940 he was music critic of *L'Indépendance Belge*. In some of his writings he used the pen name **Paul Antoine.**

Writings: *Siegfried de Wagner* (1891); *Edvard Grieg* (1892); *La Musique et les arts plastiques* (1897); *Chansons populaires des provinces belges* (1905; anthology); *20 Noëls français anciens* (1911); *Le Manuscrit dit des basses-danses de la Bibliothèque de Bourgogne* (1912); *Notes sur la chanson populaire en Belgique* (1913); *Esthétique musicale* (1921); *L'Élément flamand dans Beethoven* (1928; 2nd ed., 1946; in Eng., London, 1936).

Clough-Leighter, Henry, American music editor and composer; b. Washington, D.C., May 13, 1874; d. Wollaston, Mass., Sept. 15, 1956. He began to play piano as a child; then studied organ with G. Walter; held various positions as church organist. In 1901 he settled in Boston; was associate ed. with Oliver Ditson & Co. (1901–8) and with the Boston Music Co. (1908–21); then from 1921 to 1956, was ed. in chief with E.C. Schirmer, Inc., of Boston. He composed several cantatas and a number of other choral works; ed. numerous music collections.

Cluer, John, English publisher and engraver of music; d. London, 1728. He claimed to be the inventor of engraving on tin plates. He set up his shop in London about 1715. He engraved and publ. Handel's operas *Giulio Cesare* (1724), *Tamerlano, Scipione*, and others; also Handel's *Suites de pièces de clavecin* (1720) and an octavo collection of operatic arias.

Bibl.: F. Kidson, *British Music Publishers, Printers and Engravers* (London, 1900); C. Humphries and W. Smith, *Music Publishing in the British Isles* (London, 1954; 2nd ed., 1970).

Clutsam, George H(oward), Australian pianist and composer; b. Sydney, Sept. 26, 1866; d. London, Nov. 17, 1951. As a young pianist, he made tours of Australia, India, China, and Japan; settled in London in 1889 and became a professional accompanist; gave concerts with Melba (1893). From 1908 until 1918 he was a music critic of the *Observer* in London; at the same time wrote music for the stage.

Works: Operas: *The Queen's Jester* (1905); *A Summer Night* (London, July 23, 1910); *After a Thousand Years* (1912); *König Harlekin* (Berlin, 1912); several musical comedies: *Gabrielle, Lavender, The Little Duchess* (Glasgow, Dec. 15, 1922). His greatest popular success was the production of *Lilac Time*, an arrangement of Heinrich Berté's operetta *Das Dreimäderlhaus*, based on Schubert's melodies; Clutsam's version in Eng. was first staged in London on Dec. 22, 1922, and had many revivals. Another theatrical medley, arranged from Chopin's melodies, was Clutsam's musical comedy *The Damask Rose* (London, June 17, 1929).

Cluytens, André, noted Belgian-born French conductor; b. Antwerp, March 26, 1905; d. Neuilly, near Paris, June 3, 1967. He studied piano at the Antwerp Cons. His father, conductor at the Théâtre Royal in Antwerp, engaged him as his assistant (1921); later he conducted opera there (1927–32). He then settled in France, and became a French citizen in 1932. He served as music director at the Toulouse Opera (1932–35); in 1935 was appointed opera conductor in Lyons. In 1944 he conducted at the Paris Opéra; in 1947 he was appointed music director of the Opéra-Comique in Paris. In 1949 he was named conductor of the Société des Concerts du Conservatoire de Paris, and in 1955 he became the 1st French conductor to appear at the Bayreuth Festival. On Nov. 4, 1956, he made his U.S. debut in Washington, D.C., as guest conductor of the Vienna Phil. during its 1st American tour. In 1960 he became chief conductor of the Orch. National de Belgique in Brussels, a post he held until his death. Cluytens was highly regarded as a fine interpreter of French music.

Bibl.: B. Gavoty, *A. C.* (Geneva, 1955).

Cluzeau-Mortet, Luis, Uruguayan composer; b. Montevideo, Nov. 16, 1889; d. there, Sept. 28, 1957. He studied piano and theory with his maternal grandfather, who was the 1st Uruguayan to receive a prize at the Paris Cons. Cluzeau-Mortet played piano and the viola in radio bands in Montevideo and composed industriously. His music is marked by Romantic influences, with occasional excursions into cautious modernism. All of his orch. works were first performed by the radio orch. SODRE, in Montevideo, of which he was a member.

Works: *Llanuras* (Oct. 14, 1944); *Rancherío* (Aug. 2, 1947); *Artigas* (Aug. 13, 1955); *Sinfonía del Este* (unfinished; a movement, *La laguna negra*, was played on Aug. 16, 1958, as a posthumous act of homage); *Fantasía concerto* for Piano and Chamber Orch.; *4 ritmos criollos* for String Quartet; *Bagatelas criollas* for 4 Flutes; songs and piano pieces.

Coates, Albert, eminent English conductor; b. St. Petersburg, Russia (of an English father and a mother of Russian descent), April 23, 1882; d. Milnerton, near Cape Town, South Africa, Dec. 11, 1953. He went to England for his general education; enrolled in the science classes of Liverpool Univ., and studied organ with an elder brother who was living there at the time. In 1902 he entered the Leipzig Cons., studying cello with Klengel, piano with Robert Teichmüller, and conducting with Artur Nikisch; served his apprenticeship there and made his debut as conductor in Offenbach's *Les Contes d'Hoffmann* at the Leipzig Opera. In 1905 he was appointed (on Nikisch's recommendation) chief conductor of the opera house at Elberfeld; from 1907 to 1909 he was a joint conductor at the Dresden Opera (with Schuch); then at Mannheim (1909–10, with Bodanzky). In 1911 he received the appointment at the Imperial Opera of St. Petersburg, and conducted many Russian operas. From 1913 he conducted in England, specializing in Wagner and the Russian repertoire; was a proponent of Scriabin's music. In 1920 he made his American debut as guest conductor of the N.Y. Sym. Orch.; during 1923–25 he led conducting classes at the Eastman School of Music in Rochester, N.Y.; also conducted the Rochester Phil. and appeared as guest conductor with other American orchs. Subsequent engagements included a season at the Berlin State Opera (1931) and concerts with the Vienna Phil. (1935). In 1946 he settled in South Africa, where he conducted the Johannesburg Sym. Orch. and taught at the Univ. of South Africa at Cape Town. Coates was a prolific composer, but his operas and other works had few performances. He was, however, one of the most outstanding, if unheralded, conductors of his generation; he excelled in the Romantic operatic and symphonic repertoire, conducting particularly memorable performances of Russian music and Wagner's music dramas.

BIBL.: M. Stroff, "A. C.," *Le Grand Baton* (March 1980).

Coates, Edith (Mary), English mezzo-soprano; b. Lincoln, May 31, 1908; d. Worthing, Jan. 7, 1983. She studied at Trinity College of Music in London; later took lessons with Clive Carey and Dino Borgioli; in 1924 she joined the Old Vic Theatre; sang major roles there from 1931; she appeared at Covent Garden in 1937; was on its roster from 1947 to 1963. She sang the leading roles in the world premieres of Britten's *Peter Grimes* (1945) and *Gloriana* (1953), and in *The Olympians* by Arthur Bliss (1949). In 1977 she was named an Officer of the Order of the British Empire.

Coates, Eric, English composer and viola player; b. Hucknall, Nottinghamshire, Aug. 27, 1886; d. Chichester, Dec. 21, 1957. He took instruction at the Royal Academy of Music in London with Tertis (viola) and Corder (composition). He was a member of the Hambourg String Quartet, with which he made a tour of South Africa (1908); was 1st violist in the Queen's Hall Orch. in London (1912–19). In 1946 he visited the U.S., conducting radio performances of his works; in 1948 toured in South America. He gives a detailed account of his career in his autobiography *Suite in Four Movements* (London, 1953). As a composer, Coates specialized in semi-classical works for orch. His valse serenade *Sleepy Lagoon* (1930) attained enormous popularity all over the world, and was publ. in numerous arrangements. His *London Suite* (1933) was equally successful; its *Knightsbridge* movement became one of the most frequently played marches in England and elsewhere. He further wrote an orch. suite, *4 Centuries* (1941), tracing typical historical forms and styles in 4 sections (*Fugue, Pavane, Valse,* and *Jazz*); *3 Elizabeths* for Orch.; a great number of songs and instrumental pieces.

BIBL.: G. Self, *In Town Tonight: A Centenary Study of the Life and Music of E. C.* (London, 1986).

Coates, Gloria, American composer; b. Wausau, Wis., Oct. 10, 1938. She studied with Helen Gunderson and Kenneth Klaus at Louisiana State Univ., with Alexander Tcherepnin at the Salzburg Mozarteum, and at Columbia Univ. with Otto Luening and Jack Beeson; also took courses in theater arts, developed a singing voice, and began a quaquaversal career as an actress, stage director, librettist, singer, impresario, and teacher. In 1971 she concentrated on composition; experimented with multiphonic techniques and gave demonstrations of her variegated prowesses at European festivals. In 1971 she organized in Munich a German-American Contemporary Music Series, which she supervised until 1983. In 1975 she inaugurated for the Univ. of Wisconsin a series of International Programs in Music; was also active as moderator and commentator for German radio programs in Cologne and Bremen. She traveled to Russia, India, China, and all over Europe, giving performances in her various capacities. Her own music is compact and dense, replete with euphonious dissonances in the framework of involute counterpoint. In 1978 she gained wide recognition when her *Music on Open Strings* was performed at the Warsaw Autumn Festival; in 1979 she became the 1st non-socialist composer to have a commissioned work performed at the East Berlin Festival.

WORKS: ORCH.: *Point Counterpoint* for School Orch. (1972–73; Munich, Feb. 3, 1973); *Music on Open Strings* for String Orch. (1973–74; Warsaw, Sept. 20, 1978); *Planets: 3 Movements for Orchestra* (1974; Hannover, Feb. 2, 1975; also for Chamber Orch. as *Planets, Nonett,* or *Halley's Comet,* Rome, March 23, 1980); *Sinfonietta della notte* (1974–80; Lund, July 4, 1982); *The Elements* for Orch. and Chorus (1974–75); *Fonte*

di Rimini: Sinfonia brevis for Orch. and Chorus (1976–84; Nuremberg Radio, Aug. 22, 1984); *Vita* or *Anima della terra* for Soli, Chorus, and Orch. (1976–84; Nuremberg Radio, Aug. 22, 1984); *Symphony Nocturne* for String Orch. (1976–84; Heidelberg, June 24, 1988); *Transitions* for Chamber Orch. (1984–85; Munich, June 23, 1985); *3 Mystical Songs* for Chorus and Orch. (1985–86); *Music in Microtones* (1986; Boston, Nov. 6, 1987); *Resistances* (1986–87); *Missed* for School Orch. (Erding, Sept. 26, 1987); *Music in Abstract Lines* (1988–89; N.Y., Nov. 16, 1989). **CHAMBER:** *Glissando Quartet* (1962); *Passacaglia Fugue* for String Quartet (1964); 4 string quartets: No. 1, *Protestation Quartet* (1965–66); No. 2, *Mobile* (1972); No. 3 (1976); No. 4 (1977); Trio for 3 Flutes (1967); *5 Pieces* for 4 Wind Players (1967–75); *Spring Morning at Grobholzes* for 3 Flutes and Tape (1975); *6 Movements* for String Quartet (1978); *Breaking Through* for Alto Recorder (1988); *Snowflakes* for Flute, Viola, and Harp (1989); *Voices of Women in Wartime* for Voice and Chamber Ensemble (Munich, May 6, 1989); also numerous other vocal and chamber works; choruses.

Coates, John, English tenor; b. Girlington, Yorkshire, June 29, 1865; d. Northwood, Middlesex, Aug. 16, 1941. He studied with his uncle, J.G. Walton, at Bradford; sang as a small boy at a Bradford church; began serious study in 1893, and took lessons with William Shakespeare in London. He sang baritone parts in Gilbert & Sullivan operettas, making his debut at the Savoy Theatre in *Utopia Limited* (1894); toured in the U.S. with a Gilbert & Sullivan company. He made his debut in grand opera as Faust at Covent Garden (1901); also sang Lohengrin in Cologne and other German cities with considerable success; later sang nearly all the Wagner parts in English with the Moody-Manners Co., with the Carl Rosa Co., and with Beecham (1910); from 1911 to 1913 he toured with Quinlan's opera company in Australia and South Africa. He served in the British army during World War I; in 1919, returned to London, devoting himself chiefly to teaching; also gave recitals of songs by English composers.

Cobbett, Walter Willson, English patron of music; b. London, July 11, 1847; d. there, Jan. 22, 1937. He was a businessman and amateur violinist. An ardent enthusiast, he traveled widely in Europe and met contemporary composers. He was particularly active in promoting the cause of British chamber music, and arranged a series of Cobbett Competitions; also commissioned special works and established a Cobbett Medal for services to chamber music; the recipients included Thomas Dunhill (1924), Mrs. E.S. Coolidge (1925), and A.J. Clements (1926). Among composers who received the Cobbett commissions and awards were Frank Bridge, York Bowen, John Ireland, Vaughan Williams, and Herbert Howells. Cobbett ed. the extremely valuable *Cobbett's Cyclopedic Survey of Chamber Music* (2 vols., London; vol. I, 1929; vol. II, 1930; a supplement to vol. I. was publ. in London in 1957; to vol. II, in 1963).

Cocchi, Gioacchino, Italian composer; b. probably in Naples, c.1720; d. probably in Venice, after 1788. He may have studied with Giovanni Veneziano at the Conservatorio di S. Maria di Loreto in Naples; he began his career as a composer for the theater with the opera *Adelaide* (Rome, Carnival 1743), subsequently bringing out many operas for Rome and Naples, winning his most popular success with *La Maestra* (Naples, 1747). He was in Venice by 1750, where he served as choir director at the Ospedale degli Incurabili until 1757; he then went to London as composer and music director of the Haymarket Theatre until 1762; he returned to Venice c.1772. He excelled in opera buffa; among such works, in addition to those given above, were *L'Elisa* (Naples, 1744), *L'Irene* (Naples, 1745), *I due fratelli beffati* (Naples, 1746), *La Serva bacchettona* (Naples, 1749), *La mascherata* (Venice, Dec. 27, 1750), *Il Tutore* (Rome, 1752), and *Il Pazzo glorioso* (Venice, 1753). He also composed a significant number of other stage works, oratorios, serenatas, cantatas, vocal chamber pieces, and instrumental music.

Coccia, Carlo, Italian composer; b. Naples, April 14, 1782; d. Novara, April 13, 1873. He was 9 when he began musical training with Pietro Casella; he then studied singing with Saverio Valente and counterpoint with Fedele Fenaroli at the Conservatorio S. Maria di Loreto in Naples, and with Paisiello. He served as maestro accompagnatore al pianoforte in the private musical establishment of Joseph Bonaparte, King of Naples (1806–8); he also began his career as a composer, becoming best known for his operas semiseria and scoring his greatest success with *Clotilde* (Venice, June 8, 1815). In 1820 he went to Lisbon as maestro concertatore at the Teatro San Carlos, and in 1824 went to London as conductor at the King's Theatre; he also taught at the Royal Academy of Music. He returned to Italy in 1827 and scored a fine success with his opera *Caterina di Guise* (Milan, Feb. 14, 1833); he was made inspector of music and director of singing at the Accademia Filarmonica in Turin in 1836, and then settled in Novara as maestro di cappella at S. Gaudenzio (1840). He wrote 38 operas, which, in addition to those listed above, included *La verità nella bugia* (Venice, 1809), *Maria Stuart, regina di Scozia* (London, June 7, 1827, excerpts only), *Enrico di Monfort* (Milan, Nov. 12, 1831), and *Giovanna II regina di Napoli* (Milan, March 12, 1840). He also wrote various other secular vocal works, including cantatas and songs, and much sacred music.

BIBL.: "Biographische Notizen und Verzeichniss der Compositionen des Herrn. C.," *Allgemeine Musikalische Zeitung,* XXXV (1833); G. Carotti, *Biografia di C. C.* (Turin, 1873).

Cochereau, Pierre, French organist; b. St. Mandé, near Paris, July, 9, 1924; d. Lyons, March 6, 1984. He studied organ at the Paris Cons. with Marcel Dupré and composition with Maurice Duruflé. He served as organist at St. Roch in Paris (1942–54); in 1955 was engaged as organist at Notre Dame; was also director of the Le Mans Cons. (1950–56), the Nice Cons. (1961–79), and the Lyons Cons. (1979–84). He made successful tours as an organist in Europe, the U.S., and the Far East. He composed a Sym. (1957), 2 concertos for Organ, and other pieces; like many other organists, he was proficient in effective improvisation.

Cochlaeus (real name, **Johannes Dobnek**), German music theorist; b. Wendelstein, near Nuremberg, Jan. 10, 1479; d. Breslau, Jan. 10, 1552. He studied philosophy at the Univ. of Cologne (B.A., 1505; M.A., 1507); in 1509 became a prof. there. In 1510 he taught history and geography in Nuremberg. From 1515 he traveled in Italy; obtained the degree of doctor of theology in Ferrara (1517); then was ordained a priest in Rome; subsequently held various ecclesiastical posts in Germany; during the last 7 years of his life he was at the Breslau Cathedral. Cochlaeus opposed Luther at the councils of Worms and Augsburg. He publ. numerous theological papers; was also the author of the treatise *Musica* (Cologne, 1507; enl. ed., under the title *Tetrachordum musices,* Nuremberg, 1511, and 6 later eds.; Eng. tr. by C. Miller in Musicological Studies and Documents, XXIII, 1970).

BIBL.: M. Spahn, *J. C.* (Berlin, 1898).

Cochran, William, American tenor; b. Columbus, Ohio, June 23, 1943. He studied at Wesleyan Univ. and with Martial Singher at the Curtis Inst. of Music in Philadelphia, making his Metropolitan Opera debut in N.Y. as Vogelsang in *Die Meistersinger von Nürnberg* on Dec. 21, 1968. In 1970 he joined the Frankfurt Opera, where he subsequently sang principal roles in both standard and contemporary operas.

Cocker, Joe, English vocalist in the American rhythm-and-blues style; b. Sheffield, May 20, 1944. He beat the drums, and began to croon as a boy. In 1963 he was lead vocalist of a group called The Avengers. His 1st success came with a blues version of the Beatles' song *With a Little Help from My Friends.* In 1969 he formed The Grease Band, with which he toured the U.S. The measure of his success can be gauged by the release of a record exclamatorily titled *Joe Cocker!* With his big vocal hit *She Came In through the Bathroom Window* he ascended to the top of the best-sellers. To emphasize his British allegiance in the world of psychedelic delirium tremens, he joined a group which annexed a line from Noël Coward,

Mad Dogs and Englishmen. He excited the hordes of acid heads at the Woodstock Festival in 1969 with his epileptic twitches and facial contortions. Periodically, he freaked out and vanished into the starry vacuum, but invariably returned after a few months in outer mental space.

Cocks & Co., London firm of music publishers, founded in 1823 by **Robert Cocks;** his sons, **Arthur Lincoln Cocks** and **Stroud Lincoln Cocks,** became partners in 1868. Upon the death of the original founder in 1887, **Robert Macfarlane Cocks** became the proprietor and carried on the business until 1898, when he retired and transferred the house to Augener and Co. The catalog of publications comprised 16,000 numbers.

Cockshott, Gerald Wilfred, English composer; b. Bristol, Nov. 14, 1915; d. London, Feb. 3, 1979. He specialized in English literature; was head of the English dept. at Whittinghame College, Brighton (1948–64), and at Ifield Grammar School, Crawley, Sussex (1965–78). He studied composition privately with Vaughan Williams; became active primarily as a writer on musical subjects. His music is transparently tonal and is impressed with melorhythms of English folk songs, but its simplicity is of a sophisticated nature.

WORKS: 2 1-act operas: *Apollo and Persephone* (N.Y., Feb. 22, 1956) and *A Faun in the Forest* (Westport, Conn., Aug. 9, 1959); Sym. in B minor (1949); *Serenade* for Flute and Strings (1952); *3 Pieces on Appalachian Folk Tunes* for Cello and Piano (1962); songs; carols; choruses; numerous arrangements of American, English, French-Canadian, Danish, and Dutch songs.

Coclico, Adrianus Petit, Flemish musician and theorist; b. in Flanders, c.1500; d. Copenhagen, 1563 (of the plague). He was a disciple of Josquin; held a teaching post at the Univ. of Wittenberg (1545); then was in Frankfurt an der Oder (1546), in Königsberg (1547), and in Nuremberg (1550). In 1555 he was in Wismar; was compelled to leave Germany when a charge of bigamy was made against him; he settled in Copenhagen in 1556 as organist and singer at the court chapel. He was the author of the important tracts *Compendium musices* (1552; reproduced in facsimile [Kassel, 1955] in the series Documenta Musicologica, ed. by M. Bukofzer; Eng. tr. by A. Seay in Translations Series 5 [Colorado Springs, 1973]) and *Musica reservata* (1552).

BIBL.: M. Van Crevel, *A. P. C.* (The Hague, 1940).

Coelho, Ruy, eminent Portuguese composer; b. Alcáçer do Sal, March 3, 1891; d. Lisbon, May 5, 1986. After preliminary studies in Lisbon, he went to Berlin, where he took lessons in composition with Engelbert Humperdinck, Max Bruch, and Schoenberg (1910–13); he subsequently took a course in counterpoint with Paul Vidal in Paris, eventually returning to Portugal, where he devoted himself mainly to the composition of operas. Several of his operas had successful productions at the Lisbon Opera, including *Inês de Castro* (Jan. 15, 1927), *Belkiss* (June 9, 1928), *Don João IV* (Dec. 1, 1940), *Rosas de todo o ano* (May 30, 1940), *A rosa de papel* (Dec. 18, 1947), *Auto da barca do Inferno* (Jan. 15, 1950), and *O vestido de novia* (Jan. 4, 1959). He further composed *Oratorio da paz* (peace oratorio, 1967), *5 Sinfonias camoneanas* (1912, 1917, 1943, 1951, 1957), 2 piano concertos (1909, 1948), a considerable number of chamber music pieces, and songs. He was greatly esteemed in Portugal but virtually none of his compositions ever reached audiences elsewhere.

Coenen, Franz, Dutch violinist, brother of **Willem Coenen;** b. Rotterdam, Dec. 26, 1826; d. Leyden, Jan. 24, 1904. He was a pupil of his father, an organist; then of Vieuxtemps and Molique. After tours as a violinist with Henri Herz, and in South America with E. Lübeck, he settled in Amsterdam; until 1895 he was director at the Cons.

Coenen, Johannes (Meinardus), Dutch bassoonist and conductor; b. The Hague, Jan. 28, 1824; d. Amsterdam, Jan. 9, 1899. He was a pupil of Lübeck at the Hague Cons.; from 1857 was conductor of the Felix Meritis orch.; in 1865, was conductor at the Grand Dutch Theater in Amsterdam; then at the Palais d'Industrie. The Palais Orch., which he founded, became world-famous. He retired in 1896.

Coenen, Willem, Dutch pianist, brother of **Franz Coenen;** b. Rotterdam, Nov. 17, 1837; d. Lugano, March 18, 1918. He traveled in South America and the West Indies; taught, gave concerts, and composed in London (1862–1909); then retired and lived near Lugano. He wrote an oratorio, *Lazarus* (1878); publ. piano music and songs; many cantatas, masses, etc., remain in MS.

Coerne, Louis (Adolphe), American composer; b. Newark, N.J., Feb. 27, 1870; d. Boston, Sept. 11, 1922. He studied violin with Kneisel in Boston and composition at Harvard Univ. with J.K. Paine (1888–90); then went to Germany, where he took courses with Rheinberger in Munich. Returning to America, he became the 1st recipient of the degree of Ph.D. in music given by an American univ., with the dissertation *The Evolution of Modern Orchestration* (1905; publ. in N.Y., 1908) at Harvard.

WORKS: Opera, *Zenobia* (1902; Bremen, Dec. 1, 1905); *Hiawatha*, symphonic poem (1893); *Romantic Concerto* for Violin and Orch.; *Beloved America*, patriotic hymn for Male Chorus and Orch.; many part-songs; *Swedish Sonata* for Violin and Piano; 3 piano trios in canon.

Coertse, Mimi, South African soprano; b. Durban, June 12, 1932. She studied in Johannesburg and Vienna; made her debut with the Vienna State Opera on tour in Naples in 1955; then sang in Basel and at the Teatro San Carlo in Naples; in 1957 she became a member of the Vienna State Opera; also appeared in London, Cologne, Rome, Brussels, and other major European music centers.

Coeuroy, André (real name, **Jean Belime**), distinguished French music critic; b. Dijon, Feb. 24, 1891; d. Chaumont, Haute-Marne, Nov. 8, 1976. He went to Germany to study with Max Reger, returning to Paris in time to be drafted into the army during World War I. He was taken prisoner and, thanks to his knowledge of the German language, was allowed to organize concerts and give lectures on Wagner in the camps of prisoners of war, which were culturally liberal during that relatively decent conflict. Returning to Paris after the Armistice, he devoted himself mainly to music criticism. He publ., in Paris, a number of books of some historical value dealing with modern music, phonography, and jazz.

Cogan, Philip, Irish organist, teacher, and composer; b. Cork, 1748; d. Dublin, Feb. 3, 1833. He was a chorister at Cork; in 1772 went to Dublin, where he occupied various posts as a church organist. He acquired great renown as a teacher and performer; Michael Kelly and Thomas Moore were his pupils. Cogan wrote numerous pieces for the harpsichord and the piano, 2 piano concertos, and 2 comic operas: *The Ruling Passion* (Dublin, Feb. 24, 1778) and *The Contract* (Dublin, May 14, 1782; revived under the title *The Double Stratagem*, 1784). In some of his piano works he incorporated Irish rhythms, and is therefore regarded as a pioneer composer of instrumental music in Ireland.

Cohan, George M(ichael), celebrated American composer of popular songs; b. Providence, R.I., July 3, 1878 (Cohan, himself, believed that he was born on July 4, but the discovery of his birth certificate proves July 3 to be correct); d. N.Y., Nov. 5, 1942. He was a vaudeville performer and had a natural talent for writing verses and simple melodies in the ballad style. His greatest song, *Over There* (1917), became sweepingly popular during World War I. A congressional medal was given to him for this song. The film *Yankee Doodle Dandy* (1942) and the Broadway musical *George M!* (1968) were both based on his life. He publ. an autobiography, *Twenty Years on Broadway and the Years It Took to Get There* (N.Y., 1924); on July 3, 1978, the U.S. Postal Service issued a commemorative stamp in honor of the 100th anniversary of his birth.

BIBL.: W. Morehouse, *G.M. C., Prince of the American Theater* (Philadelphia, 1943); J. McCabe, *G.M. C.: The Man Who Owned Broadway* (N.Y., 1973).

Cohen, Harriet, distinguished English pianist; b. London, Dec. 2, 1895; d. there, Nov. 13, 1967. She studied piano with her parents; then took an advanced course in piano playing with Matthay; made her 1st public appearance as a solo pianist at the age of 13. She then engaged in a successful career in England, both as a soloist with major orchs. and in chamber music concerts. She made a specialty of early keyboard music, but also played many contemporary compositions; Vaughan Williams, Arnold Bax, and other English composers wrote special works for her. In 1938 she was made a Commander of the Order of the British Empire in appreciation of her services. She publ. a book on piano playing, *Music's Handmaid* (London, 1936; 2nd ed., 1950). Her memoirs, *A Bundle of Time*, were publ. posthumously (London, 1969).

Cohen, Isidore, American violinist; b. N.Y., Dec. 16, 1922. He studied violin with Ivan Galamian at the Juilliard School of Music in N.Y.; from 1958 to 1966 was a member of the Juilliard Quartet; in 1968 he joined the Beaux Arts Trio, and subsequently toured widely.

Cohen, Joel (Israel), American lutenist and conductor; b. Providence, R.I., May 23, 1942. He took courses in composition and musicology at Brown Univ. (B.A., 1963) and Harvard Univ. (M.A., 1965), then studied theory and composition with Boulanger in Paris (1965–67). In 1968 he became conductor of the Boston Camerata, which he led in works from the medieval, Renaissance, and Baroque eras.

Cohen, Jules-Émile-David, French composer; b. Marseilles, Nov. 2, 1835; d. Paris, Jan. 13, 1901. He studied at the Paris Cons., piano with Marmontel, organ with Benoist, and composition with Halévy, and carried 1st prizes in each of these courses. He then served as an instructor of choral singing at the Paris Cons.; in 1877 was engaged as chorus master at the Grand Opéra. He produced several operas, none too successful, among them *Les Bleuets* (Paris, Oct. 23, 1867) and *Dea* (Paris, April 30, 1870); he also wrote 3 cantatas; several masses; symphonic and chamber music; some 200 songs and 200 piano pieces.

Cohen, Leonard, Canadian balladeer; b. Montreal, Sept. 21, 1934. One of the few Jews who made it as a pop singer, he went into such highbrow stuff as writing poetry and publishing sentimental novels. At the same time, he strummed his guitar and sang such maudlin romances as *Suzanne* and such alienation tunes as *Stranger Song*, such heart-impinging implorations as *Hey, That's No Way to Say Goodbye*, and such beseeching tunes as *Sisters of Mercy*. He sang at the Newport Folk Festival in 1967 and teamed with Judy Collins in his American tour. Like Bob Dylan and other troubled songsters, Cohen periodically withdrew from public view to meditate about his alienation. His *Songs of Love and Hate* exemplified such psychological quaquaversality. He returned to the world at large and released an album symbolic of his healing graft, *New Skin for the Old Ceremony.*

Cohn, Al(vin Gilbert), American jazz tenor saxophonist and composer; b. N.Y., Nov. 24, 1925; d. East Stroudsburg, Pa., Feb. 15, 1988. He studied clarinet and piano; later took up the tenor saxophone, then played with several bands, including those of Buddy Rich (1947), Woody Herman (1948–49), and Artie Shaw (1949). He devoted much of his time to composing music for radio and television.

Cohn, Arthur, versatile American composer, conductor, lexicographer, and publishing executive; b. Philadelphia, Nov. 6, 1910. He studied violin and later took a course in composition at the Juilliard School of Music in N.Y. with Rubin Goldmark. Returning to Philadelphia, he was appointed director of the Edwin A. Fleisher Collection at the Free Library (1934–52). From 1942 to 1965 he conducted the Sym. Club of Philadelphia; also the Germantown Sym. Orch. (1949–55), the Philadelphia Little Sym. (1952–56); and in 1958 was appointed conductor of the Haddonfield, N.J., Sym. Orch. From 1956 to 1966 he was head of symphonic and foreign music at Mills Music Co., and from 1966 to 1972 held a similar position with MCA Music. In 1972 he was appointed Director of Serious Music at Carl

Fischer. He publ. *The Collector's Twentieth-Century Music in the Western Hemisphere* (N.Y., 1961); *Twentieth-Century Music in Western Europe* (N.Y., 1965); *Musical Quizzical* (77 puzzles; N.Y., 1970); *Recorded Classical Music: A Critical Guide to Compositions and Performances* (N.Y., 1981); *The Encyclopedia of Chamber Music* (N.Y., 1990).

WORKS: 6 string quartets (1928–45); *5 Nature Studies* (1932); *Retrospections* for String Orch. (Philadelphia, April 3, 1935); *Music for Brass Instruments* (1935); Suite for Viola and Orch. (1937); *Machine Music* for 2 Pianos (1937); 4 Preludes for String Orch. (N.Y., May 26, 1937); *4 Symphonic Documents* (1939); *Music for Ancient Instruments* (1939); Quintuple Concerto for 5 Ancient Instruments, with Modern Orch. (1940); Concerto for Flute and Orch. (1941); Variations for Clarinet, Saxophone, and String Orch. (1945); *Music for Bassoon*, unaccompanied (1947); *Kaddish* for Orch. (1964). Perhaps the most remarkable of his works is *Quotations in Percussion* for 103 Instruments for 6 Players (1958).

Cohn, Heinrich. See **Conried, Heinrich.**

Cohn, James (Myron), American musicologist, inventor, and composer; b. Newark, N.J., Feb. 12, 1928. He studied with Wayne Barlow at the Eastman School of Music, with Roy Harris at Cornell Univ., and with Bernard Wagenaar at the Juilliard School of Music (B.S., 1949; M.S., 1950). Besides his compositions, he has several patents for devices that can be applied to keyboards or fingerboards to control pitch, intonation, loudness, vibrato, and tremolo.

WORKS: Opera: *The Fall of the City* (Athens, Ohio, July 8, 1955). Orch.: Sym. No. 1 (1947); Sym. No. 2 (Brussels, Dec. 11, 1953); Sym. No. 3 (Detroit, Dec. 17, 1959); Sym. No. 4 (Florence, Italy, Oct. 1, 1960); Sym. No. 5 (1959); Sym. No. 6 (1965); Sym. No. 7 (1967); Sym. No. 8 (1978); Sinfonietta (1946); Variations on *The Wayfaring Stranger* (Detroit, Oct. 4, 1962); several overtures; Concerto for Concertina and Strings (1966); Concerto for Clarinet and String Orch. (1986); 3 string quartets; Wind Quintet; many piano and choral works.

Colasse, Pascal, French composer; b. Rheims, Jan. 22, 1649; d. Versailles, July 17, 1709. He was a pupil of Lully, who entrusted him with writing out the parts of his operas from the figured bass and melody. Later Colasse was accused of appropriating scores thrown aside by his master as incomplete. In 1683 he was appointed Master of the Music; in 1696, royal chamber musician. He was a favorite of Louis XIV, and obtained the privilege of producing operas at Lille, but the theater burned down; his opera *Polyxène et Pyrrhus* (1706) failed, and his mind became disordered. Of 10 operas, *Les Noces de Thétys et Pélée* (1689) was his best. He also composed songs, sacred and secular.

Colbran, Isabella (Isabel Angela), famous Spanish soprano; b. Madrid, Feb. 2, 1785; d. Bologna, Oct. 7, 1845. She studied with Pareja in Madrid, then with Marinelli and Crescentini in Naples; made her debut in a concert in Paris in 1801. After her successful appearances in Bologna (1807) and La Scala in Milan (1808), the impresario Barbaja engaged her for Naples in 1811; she became his mistress, only to desert him for Rossini, whom she married on March 16, 1822 (they were legally separated in 1837). She created the leading soprano roles in several of Rossini's operas, beginning with *Elisabetta, Regina d'Inghilterra* (1815) and concluding with *Semiramide* (1823); with her voice in decline, she retired from the stage in 1824. During the early years of the 19th century she was acclaimed as the leading dramatic coloratura soprano.

Colding-Jørgensen, Henrik, Danish composer; b. Riisskov, March 21, 1944. He studied composition with Holmboe at the Royal Cons. in Copenhagen, graduating in 1966; taught organ in Copenhagen (1967–70) and music theory at the Odense Cons. (1969–75). In 1975 he became active as a church organist and choirmaster in Copenhagen.

WORKS: ORCH.: Sym. No. 1 (1965); *At elske musikken* (To Love Music; 1975; Copenhagen, May 6, 1976); *Ballade* for Tuba and Chamber Orch. (1979); *Le Alpi nel Cuore* (1988).

CHAMBER:Divertimento for 8 Instruments (1964); String Quartet No. 1 (1965); *Sinusrhapsodie* for 2 Cellos (1968); *Avnstrup Suite* for Recorder, Violin, and Guitar (1969); *Mourn* for Guitar (1969); *Suite à deux* for Flute and Clarinet (1971); *Cello* for Cello (1972); *Solo Grande* for Percussion (1972); *Balancer* for Violin and Percussion (1974); *Puer natus* for 5 Tubas (1976); *Boast* for Tuba (1980); *Toccata, Aria e Minuetto* for Oboe (1986). VOCAL: *Lapidary Landscapes* for Mezzo-soprano, Bass-baritone, Oboe, English Horn, Viola, Cello, and Percussion (1965); *På din taerskel* (At Your Doorstep) for Contralto and Orch. (1966); *Enfance III* for Contralto, Horn, and Harp (1967) and *IV* for Contralto and Piano (1968); *Barbare* for 6 Soloists, Choir, and Orch. (1967; Copenhagen Radio, Jan. 21, 1972; *Altid noget andet* (Always Something Else) for Tenor and Viola d'Amore (1973); *Ava Maria* for Contralto (1974); *Fra først af* (From the Beginning) for Mixed Chorus, Trumpet, Trombone, and Organ (1975); *Victoria through the Wood* for Alto and Orch. (1975); *Det er mig der vaelter* (It Is I Who Am Overturned) for Soprano, Mezzo-soprano, and Organ (1980); 2 songs by Keats for Soprano and Guitar (1988). ORGAN: *Logbogsblade* (Logbook Sheets; 1969); *Magnus* (1972).

Cole, Bob (Robert Allen), black American lyricist and composer; b. Athens, Ga., July 1, 1863; d. (suicide) Catskill, N.Y., Aug. 2, 1911. After graduating from Atlanta Univ., he settled in N.Y., where he worked with Billy Johnson. Among their most popular coon songs was *La Hoola Boola* (1897); they also put together the 1st all-black musical comedy, *A Trip to Coontown* (April 4, 1898). He later worked with J. Rosamond Johnson and James Weldon Johnson, their collaboration resulting in several hit songs, including *The Shoofly Regiment* (Aug. 6, 1907) and *The Red Moon* (May 3, 1909); they also wrote songs for white Broadway musicals.

Cole, Nat "King" (real name, **Nathaniel Adams Coles**), black American pianist and singer; b. Montgomery, Ala., March 17, 1917; d. Santa Monica, Calif., Feb. 15, 1965. He worked as a jazz pianist in Los Angeles nightclubs; in 1939 formed the original King Cole Trio (piano, guitar, bass); then turned to singing. He was the 1st black artist to acquire a sponsor on a radio program; also had a brief series on television. He created a distinct style of velvet vocalization and satin softness in the rendition of intimate, brooding, sentimental songs. His appeal was universal; his tours in South America, Europe, the Middle East, and the Orient attracted great multitudes of admirers who knew him by his recordings. The sole exception was his native state; at his concert in Birmingham, Ala., on April 10, 1956, he was attacked by 6 white men and suffered a minor back injury.

BIBL.: M. Cole and L. Robinson, *N. K. C.: An Intimate Biography* (N.Y., 1971).

Cole, Rossetter Gleason, American composer, organist, and teacher; b. Clyde, Mich., Feb. 5, 1866; d. Lake Bluff, Ill., May 18, 1952. He studied music with C.B. Cady; in 1890 went to Germany, where he studied composition with Max Bruch in Berlin, and organ with Middleschulte. Returning to America in 1892, he occupied various posts as a teacher and organist in Wisconsin, Iowa, and Illinois; lived mostly in Chicago.

WORKS: *The Maypole Lovers*, opera (1931; a suite from it was perf. in Chicago, Jan. 9, 1936); *Hiawatha's Wooing* for Narrator and Orch. (1904); *King Robert of Sicily* for Narrator and Orch. (1906); *Ballade* for Cello and Orch. (Minneapolis, 1909); *Symphonic Prelude* (Chicago, March 11, 1915); *Pioneer Overture* (composed for the centenary of the state of Illinois; Chicago, March 14, 1919); *Heroic Piece* for Organ and Orch. (Chicago, Feb. 11, 1924); cantatas: *The Passing of Summer* (1902); *The Broken Troth* (1917); *The Rock of Liberty* (1920); Violin Sonata; several organ pieces; piano pieces (*From a Lover's Notebook, In Springtime, Sunset in the Hills,* etc.); songs (*Lilacs, Love's Invocation,* etc.).

Cole, Ulric, American composer and pianist; b. N.Y., Sept. 9, 1905. She studied with Goetschius and Rubin Goldmark (composition) and Josef Lhévinne (piano). She wrote 2 piano concertos; a Piano Quintet; 2 violin sonatas; and many piano pieces. She was the soloist in the premiere of her Divertimento for Piano and String Orch. with the Cincinnati Sym. (March 31, 1939).

Cole, William Randolph "Cozy," black American jazz drummer; b. East Orange, N.J., Oct. 17, 1906; d. Columbus, Ohio, Jan. 29, 1981. After taking up the drums while young, he began his career in 1928; he played with Jelly Roll Morton, Stuff Smith, and others before joining Cab Calloway's band in 1938; then appeared on radio; he played on Broadway in 1943 in the musical *Carmen Jones*, displaying his expertise in the number *Beat Out Dat Rhythm on a Drum*; also appeared in the 1945 production of *The Seven Lively Arts* with Benny Goodman's Quintet. He later played with Louis Armstrong; then formed his own band, which toured Africa in 1962; was also a member of the Jonah Jones Quintet (1969–76); then was artist-in-residence at Capital Univ. in Columbus, Ohio.

Coleman, Cy (real name, **Seymour Kaufman**), American composer of popular music; b. N.Y., June 14, 1929. He studied at the N.Y. College of Music, and began his career as a composer for radio and television. With the lyricist Joseph A. McCarthy, he composed the songs *I'm Gonna Laugh You Out of My Life* and *Why Try to Change Me Now?* To the words of Carolyn Leigh he wrote the song *Witchcraft;* as propelled through the pharynx and larynx of Frank Sinatra it became a hit. He also wrote the musical *Wildcat* (1960), best remembered for the song *Hey, Look Me Over; Little Me* followed in 1962. He achieved further success with *Sweet Charity*, composed in 1966, to the lyrics of Dorothy Fields. He also used her lyrics for *Seesaw* (1973). Among his later works were *I Love My Wife* (1977), *On the Twentieth Century* (1978), *Barnum* (1980), and *City of Angels* (1989).

Coleman, Ornette, innovative black American jazz alto saxophonist and composer; b. Fort Worth, Texas, March 9, 1930. He was largely autodidact; served his apprenticeship playing in carnival and "rhythm and blues" bands. His own studies of harmony and theory led him to develop a distinctive style in which the improvisational melodic line is independent of the pre-assigned harmonic scheme. He also writes concert music in a respectable modernistic idiom; among his works are *Forms and Sounds* for Woodwind Quintet (1965), *Skies of America* for Orch. (1972), and *Sex Spy* (1977).
    BIBL.: D. Wild and M. Cuscuna, *O. C. 1958–1979: A Discography* (Ann Arbor, 1980); C. Sheridan, "O. C.," *Jazz Journal International*, XXXIII/11 (1980) and XXXIV/1 (1981).

Coleridge-Taylor, Samuel, esteemed English composer of African descent (his father was a native of Sierra Leone; his mother English); b. London, Aug. 15, 1875; d. Croydon, Sept. 1, 1912. He studied violin at the Royal College of Music (1890); won a composition scholarship (1893); studied under Stanford until 1896. In 1903 he founded at Croydon an amateur string orch. which was very successful; later he added professional woodwind and brass; was appointed a violin teacher at the Royal Academy of Music (1898); became a prof. of composition at Trinity College in London (1903) and at the Guildhall School (1910); was conductor of the London Handel Soc. (1904–12); lived as a composer and teacher in Croydon. He made 3 concert tours of the U.S., in 1904, 1906, and 1910, conducting his own works. From the very beginning his compositions showed an individuality that rapidly won them recognition, and his short career was watched with interest.
    WORKS: STAGE: 3-act opera, *Thelma* (1909); operettas: *Dream Lovers* and *The Gitanos* (1898). **ORCH.:** Ballade for Violin and Orch.; Sym. in A minor (London, 1896); *Legend* for Violin and Orch.; Ballade in A minor (Gloucester Festival, 1898); *African Suite;* Romance for Violin and Orch.; *Solemn Prelude* (Worcester, 1899); *Scenes from an Everyday Romance,* suite (London, 1900); *Idyll* (Gloucester Festival, 1901); *Toussaint l'Ouverture,* concert overture (London, Oct. 26, 1901); *Hemo Dance; Ethiopa Saluting the Colours,* concert march; *4 Novelletten* for String Orch.; *Symphonic Variations on an African Air* (London, June 14, 1906, composer conducting); *Bam-*

boula, rhapsodic dance (Norfolk [Conn.] Festival, 1910); Violin Concerto in G minor (Norfolk Festival, 1911); *Petite suite de concert;* incidental music to Phillips's *Herod* (1900), *Ulysses* (1902), *Nero* (1906), *Faust* (1908). **CHAMBER:** Piano Quintet; Nonet for Piano, Strings, and Woodwind (1894); *Fantasiestücke* for String Quartet (1895); Clarinet Quintet; String Quartet; Violin Sonata. **VOCAL:** for Soli, Chorus, and Orch.: the successful trilogy *The Song of Hiawatha,* including *Hiawatha's Wedding Feast* (London, 1898), *The Death of Minnehaha* (North Staffordshire, 1899), and *Hiawatha's Departure* (London, 1900); the entire trilogy was 1st performed in Washington, D.C. (Nov. 16, 1904, composer conducting); *The Blind Girl of Castel Cuille* (Leeds, 1901); *Meg Blane* (Sheffield, 1902); *The Atonement* (Hereford, 1903); *Kubla Khan* (London, 1906); *Endymion's Dream,* (Brighton, Feb. 3, 1910); *A Tale of Old Japan* (London, 1911); *Zara's Earrings,* rhapsody for Voice and Orch.; *Land of the Sun,* part-song; *In Memoriam,* 3 rhapsodies for Voice and Piano; *The Soul's Expression,* 4 songs for Contralto and Orch.; *Sea Drift,* rhapsody for Chorus; services, anthems, solo songs. **PIANO:** *Silhouettes; Cameos; Scènes de ballet;* etc.
    BIBL.: W. Sayers, *S. C.-T., His Life and Letters* (1915); Mrs. S. Coleridge-Taylor, *S. C.-T., A Memory Sketch* (1942); W. Tortolano, *S. C.-T.: Anglo-Black Composer, 1875–1912* (Metuchen, N.J., 1977); A. Coleridge-Taylor, *The Heritage of S. C.-T.* (London, 1979); J. Green, "A Note on C.-T.'s Origins," *Musical Times* (Aug. 1985); S. Butterworth, "C.-T.: New Facts for Old Fiction," ibid. (April 1989).

Coletti, Filippo, noted Italian baritone; b. Anagni, May 11, 1811; d. there, June 13, 1894. He studied with Alessandro Busti in Naples; made his debut there at the Teatro del Fondo in Rossini's *Il Turco in Italia* in 1834; subsequently established himself as a distinguished interpreter of roles in operas by Bellini, Donizetti, and Verdi.

Colgrass, Michael (Charles), American composer; b. Chicago, April 22, 1932. He studied at the Univ. of Illinois (Mus.B., 1956); attended classes at the Berkshire Music Center, Tanglewood (1952–54). His principal teachers were Darius Milhaud, Lukas Foss, Wallingford Riegger, and Ben Weber. A percussion player by profession, he was employed in various ensembles in N.Y. In his own music, percussion plays a significant melo-rhythmic role. He also studied theater arts, including special techniques of the Commedia dell'Arte of the Piccolo Teatro of Milan and physical training for actors at the Polish Theater Laboratory; wrote drama and poetry. He received Guggenheim fellowship awards in 1964 and 1968; won the Pulitzer Prize in 1978.
    WORKS: *Chamber Music* for 4 Drums and String Quartet (1954); Percussion Quintet (1955); Divertimento for 8 Drums, Piano, and Strings (1960); Rhapsody for Clarinet, Violin, and Piano (1962); *Light Spirit* for Flute, Viola, Guitar, and Percussion (1963); *Sea Shadow* for Orch. (1966); *As Quiet as . . .* for Orch. (1966); *New People,* song cycle for Mezzo-soprano, Viola, and Piano (1969); *The Earth's a Baked Apple* for Chorus and Orch. (1969); *Letter from Mozart,* collage for Piano and Orch. (N.Y., Dec. 3, 1976); *Best Wishes, U.S.A.* for Black Chorus, White Chorus, Jazz Band, Folk Instruments, 4 Vocalists, and Orch. (1976); *Concertmasters,* concerto for 3 Violins and Orch. (1976); *Déjà vu,* concerto for 4 Percussionists and Orch. (1978; received the Pulitzer Prize); Piano Concerto (Miami, Fla., June 25, 1982); *Chaconne* for Viola and Orch. (Toronto, Sept. 27, 1984); *Winds of Nagual—A Musical Fable* for Wind Ensemble, on the writings of Carlos Castaneda (Boston, Feb. 14, 1985).

Collaer, Paul, Belgian pianist and writer on music; b. Boom, June 8, 1891; d. Brussels, Dec. 10, 1989. He studied science at the Univ. of Brussels; then became interested in music; organized concerts; from 1937 to 1953 was director of the Brussels Radio and promoted performances of modern music.
    WRITINGS: *Stravinsky* (1930); *J.S. Bach* (1936); *Signification de la musique* (1943); *Darius Milhaud* (1947); *La Musique moderne* (1955; amplified ed., 1963, as *A History of Modern*

Music); with A. Van der Linden, *Atlas historique* (Paris, 1960); *Ozeanien* (Leipzig, 1965); *Amerika; Eskimo und indianische Bevölkerung* (Leipzig, 1967); *La Musique populaire traditionelle en Belgique* (Brussels, 1974); *Musique traditionelle Sicilienne* (2 vols., 1981).

Collard, family of piano makers in London. M. Clementi, in partnership with John Longman, bought out the music publishers Longman & Broderip in 1798. Longman left to establish his own enterprise, and Clementi entered into a new partnership with Banger, F.A. Hyde, F.W. Collard, and Davis; after several changes, the firm was known as Clementi, Collard & Collard (1823); following Clementi's death in 1832, it was known as Collard & Collard. While Clementi undoubtedly played an important part in the success of the business, it was Collard's patented inventions that gave the pianos their distinctive character, and established the firm's reputation in that field. The firm was taken over by Chappell Piano Co. in 1929.

Collard, Jean-Philippe, French pianist; b. Mareuil-sur-Aÿ, Jan. 27, 1948. He began piano studies as a child; then studied at the Paris Cons. with Pierre Sancan, graduating at age 16 with a 1st prize; subsequently won several honors, including 3rd prize in the Marguerite Long–Jacques Thibaud Competition; appeared as soloist with the leading European orchs. and in recitals. He made his American debut in 1973 with the San Francisco Sym. Orch.; then made a number of coast-to-coast tours of the U.S.; in 1983 appeared as soloist with the Indianapolis Sym. Orch. at Carnegie Hall in N.Y.

Colles, H(enry) C(ope), eminent English music scholar; b. Bridgnorth, Shropshire, April 20, 1879; d. London, March 4, 1943. He studied at the Royal College of Music in London with Parry (music history), Walter Alcock (organ), and Walford Davies (theory). Subsequently he received a scholarship at Worcester College, Oxford, to study organ; then entered Oxford Univ., obtaining his B.A. (1902), Mus.Bac. (1903), and M.A. (1907); also received an honorary Mus.Doc. (1932). In 1905 he became music critic of the *Academy;* from 1905 to 1943 he was music critic of the *Times;* in 1919 was appointed teacher of music history and criticism at the Royal College of Music; was also music director of Cheltenham Ladies' College. He was the editor of the 3rd and 4th eds. of *Grove's Dictionary of Music and Musicians* (1927–29 and 1939–40); also edited, vol. VII of *The Oxford History of Music* (1934).

WRITINGS: *Brahms* (1908; in German, 1913); *The Growth of Music: A Study in Music History for Schools* (3 vols., 1912–16; 3rd ed., by E. Blom, 1956); *Voice and Verse, a Study in English Song* (1928); *The Chamber Music of Brahms* (1933); *English Church Music* (1933); *The Royal College of Music; A Jubilee Record, 1883–1933* (1933); *On Learning Music* (1940); *Walford Davies* (1942); *Essays and Lectures* (1945).

Collet, Henri, French music critic and composer; b. Paris, Nov. 5, 1885; d. there, Nov. 23, 1951. He was a pupil of J. Thibaut and Barès in Paris; then studied Spanish literature with Menéndez Pidal in Madrid, continuing his music studies under Olmeda. He coined the title Les Six Français for a group of young French composers comprising G. Auric, L. Durey, A. Honegger, D. Milhaud, F. Poulenc, and G. Tailleferre.

WORKS: *El Escorial,* symphonic poem; *Danses castillanes* for Orch.; *Gitanerías* for Orch.; *La cueva di Salamanca,* orch. intermezzo; *Impressions* (*Vers Burgos*) for String Quartet; *Rhapsodie castillane* for Viola and Orch.; *Romería castellana* for Woodwinds; Piano Quintet; String Quartet; *Trio castillan; Sonata castillane* for Violin and Piano; many songs (based on texts by F. James and on Spanish folk themes).

WRITINGS: *Un tratado de Canto de órgano (siglo XVI°) MS. en la Biblioteca Nacional de Paris* (Madrid, 1913); *Le Mysticisme musical espagnol au XVIᵉ siècle* (Paris, 1913); a biography of Victoria, in *Maîtres de la musique* (Paris, 1914); *Albéniz et Granados* (1926); *Samson et Dalila* (guide to Saint-Saëns's opera; 1926); *L'Essor de la musique espagnole au XXᵉ siècle* (1929); also historical essays in *Bulletin Hispanique* and *L'Année Musicale.*

Collette, Buddy (William Marcell), black American jazz flutist and composer; b. Los Angeles, Calif., Aug. 6, 1921. He studied composition with Ernest Kanitz. He played flute with the Henry Mancini, Quincy Jones, and Benny Carter bands; appeared at the San Remo Festival in Italy in 1962. He favors the West Coast jazz style in an eloquently cool technique; his song *Blue Sands* has become a jazz standard.

Collier, Marie, Australian soprano; b. Ballarat, April 16, 1926; d. London, Dec. 7, 1971 (in an accidental fall from a window). She studied in Melbourne; then continued her musical training in Milan. In 1956 she sang in London. On March 17, 1967, she made her Metropolitan Opera debut in N.Y., creating the role of Christine Mannon in the opera *Mourning Becomes Electra* by Marvin David Levy. She was highly regarded for her performances of contemporary music.

Collier, Ronald, Canadian composer; b. Coleman, Alberta, July 3, 1930. He played trombone in a school band in Vancouver (1943–49); studied composition privately with Gordon Delamont in Toronto (1951); later studied with Hall Overton in N.Y. He was a trombonist in several orchs., including the Toronto Sym.; then formed his own jazz group, and was the 1st jazz composer to receive a Canada Council grant (1965); in 1971 became composer-in-residence at Humber College in Toronto.

WORKS: Pieces for jazz orch., including a ballet, *Aurora Borealis* (1967); music for a television drama, *Silent Night, Lonely Night* (1965); *Cambodian Suite* (1959); *The City,* with Narrator-Singer (1960); *Requiem for JFK* (1964); *Bonjour Canada Opening* (1967); *The Carnival,* with Narrator-Singer and Solo Flugelhorn (1969); *Celebration,* with Solo Piano (in collaboration with Duke Ellington, 1972); *Humber Suite* (1973); chamber pieces for jazz ensemble: *Invention Nos. 1* and *2* (1955); *Opus for Quintet* (1956); *Stratford Adventure* (1956); *Jazz Ballet* (1960); *2 Shades of Blue* (1962); *Impressions* (1963); *Hear Me Talkin' to Ya,* with Narrator and Singer (1964); *Walkin' Out* (1965); *Lyric for Trumpet* for Trumpet and Concert Band (1970); *Waterfront, Night Thoughts* for Flute and Piano (1965).

Collin (Colin) de Blamont, François, prominent French composer; b. Versailles, Nov. 22, 1690; d. there, Feb. 14, 1760. He commenced his musical training with his father, Nicolas Colin, who served as ordinaire de la musique du roi, then entered the service of the Duchess of Maine when he was 17, becoming a pupil of Lalande. In 1719 he was made surintendant de la musique de la chambre, and, upon Lalande's death, was named his successor as a maître de musique de la chambre (1726); he received Letters of Nobility (1750) and was made Chevalier of the Order of St. Michel (1751). With Fuzelier, he created the ballet héroïque with their *Festes grecques et romaines* (1723). He publ. the polemical book *Essaie sur les goûts anciens et modernes de la musique françoise relativement aux paroles d'opéra* (Paris, 1754), which was aimed primarily at Rousseau.

WORKS: STAGE: *Les Festes grecques et romaines,* ballet héroïque (Paris, July 13, 1723; in collaboration with Fuzelier); *Le Retour des dieux sur la terre,* divertissement (for the marriage of Louis XV, 1725); *La Caprice d'Erato ou Les Caractères de la Musique,* divertissement (1730); *Endymion,* pastorale héroïque (Paris, May 17, 1731); *Les Caractères de l'amour,* ballet héroïque (1736); *Les Fêtes de Thétis,* ballet héroïque (Versailles, Jan. 14, 1750); several secular cantatas; numerous "airs sérieux et à boire"; a vol. of motets, which includes a *Te Deum* (Paris, 1732).

BIBL.: J. Vasseur, "Notice sur C.d.B.," *Mémoires de la Société des Sciences Morales de Seine-et-Oise,* XIII (1883); C. Massip, *F. C.d.B.: Musicien du roi* (diss., Paris Cons., 1971).

Collingwood, Lawrance (Arthur), English composer and conductor; b. London, March 14, 1887; d. Killin, Perthshire, Dec. 19, 1982. He studied at the Guildhall School of Music in London and later at Exeter College, Oxford (1907–11). In 1912 he went to Russia and took courses at the St. Petersburg Cons. with Glazunov, Wihtol, Steinberg, and Tcherepnin; in

1918 he returned to England and became active as a conductor; was principal conductor (1931–41) and music director (1941–47) at Sadler's Wells in London. In 1948 he was made a Commander of the Order of the British Empire.

WORKS: Operas: *Macbeth* (London, April 12, 1934) and *The Death of Tintagiles* (concert perf., London, April 16, 1950); Piano Concerto; Piano Quartet; 2 piano sonatas.

BIBL.: C.H. Glover, "L. C.," *Musical Quarterly* (April 1926).

Collins, Anthony (Vincent Benedictus), English conductor; b. Hastings, Sept. 3, 1893; d. Los Angeles, Dec. 11, 1963. He studied violin at the Royal College of Music in London, and composition there with Holst; was then a violist in the London Sym. Orch. and in the orch. of the Royal Opera House, Covent Garden; from 1936 he pursued a career as conductor, appearing with the Carl Rosa Opera Co., the Sadler's Wells Opera, and the London Sym. Orch. In 1939 he settled in the U.S., making his home in California as a conductor and composer for motion pictures. He also wrote 2 syms., 2 violin concertos, 4 operas, and other works.

Collins, Judy (Marjorie), American singer of folk and popular music; b. Seattle, Wash., May 1, 1939. She studied piano with Antonia Brico in hopes of a concert career, but deterred by the odds against success, she turned to folk music. After attending MacMurray College in Jacksonville, Ill., and the Univ. of Colorado in Denver, she began her career as a singer in 1959, accompanying herself on the guitar; she obtained a prestigious engagement at Carnegie Hall in N.Y. in 1965. She subsequently toured in Japan and other exotic lands. Her repertoire presents a wide spectrum from the traditional Anglo-American folk ballad to hard, loud rock.

Collins, Phil(ip), English rock singer and songwriter; b. London, Jan. 30, 1951. He took up the drums as a young boy; in 1970 he became drummer for the rock group Genesis and later rose to prominence as its lead singer. He also pursued a successful solo career, his song *Against All Odds* (1984) winning a Grammy Award. His hit album *No Jacket Required* (1985), which included the smash single *1 More Night*, catapulted him into rock stardom and captured for him several Grammy Awards in 1986.

BIBL.: *Current Biography* (Nov. 1986); *1987 Britannica Book of the Year.*

Collum, Herbert, German organist, harpsichordist, conductor, and composer; b. Leipzig, July 18, 1914. He studied organ with Straube and Ramin at the Hochschule für Musik in Leipzig; also piano with Adolf Martienssen and composition with J.N. David. In 1934 he became organist of the Kreuzkirche in Dresden; founded the Collum Concerts (1935) and the Collum Choir (1946) of Dresden. He was a distinguished interpreter of the music of Bach, both as organist and as harpsichordist; also composed concertos for harpsichord and many vocal works.

Colobrano, Michele Enrico Carafa de. See **Carafa, Michele.**

Colombo, Pierre, Swiss conductor; b. La Tour-de-Peilz, May 22, 1914. He studied flute and theory at the Ribaupierre Inst.; conducting with Scherchen and H. Münch at the Basel Cons. and also with Clemens Krauss. He was conductor of the Lausanne Bach Choir (1947–63); from 1955 he served as program director of the radio service in Geneva. As a conductor, he was particularly known for his adequate performances of modern music.

Colonna, Giovanni Paolo, eminent Italian composer of church music; b. Bologna, June 16, 1637; d. there, Nov. 28, 1695. He studied organ with Filipucci in Bologna; composition in Rome with Carissimi, Benevoli, and Abbatini. In 1659 he became organist at San Petronio in Bologna; was appointed maestro di cappella in 1674. He was several times elected president of the Accademia Filarmonica. He wrote much sacred music, including *Motetti* for 2 and 3 Voices (1681); 3 books

of *Salmi brevi* for 8 Voices and Organ (1681, 1686, 1694); *Motetti sacri a voce sola con due violini e bassetto di viola* (1681); *Litanie con le quattro antifone della B. Vergine* for 8 Voices (1682); *Messe piene* for 8 Voices, with Organ (1684); *Messa, salmi e responsori per li defonti* for 8 Voices (1685); *Compieta con le tre sequenze dell'anno* for 8 Voices (1687); *Sacre lamentazioni della settimana santa* for Solo Voice (1689); *Messa e salmi concertati* for 3 and 5 Voices with Instruments (1691); *Psalmi ad vesperas* for 3–5 Voices (1694).

BIBL.: L. Frati, "Per la storia della musica in Bologna nel secolo XVII," *Rivista Musicale Italiana,* XXXII (1925); A. Schnoebelen, *The Concerted Mass at San Petronio in Bologna: ca. 1660–1730* (diss., Univ. of Illinois, 1966).

Colonne, Édouard (real name, **Judas**), French conductor and violinist; b. Bordeaux, July 23, 1838; d. Paris, March 28, 1910. He studied at the Paris Cons. under Girard and Sauzay (violin) and with Elwart and Ambroise Thomas (composition). In 1873 he founded the Concerts Nationaux (which later became famous as the Concerts du Châtelet; then Concerts Colonne), at which he brought out the larger works of Berlioz, and many new orch. scores by contemporary German and French composers. In 1878 he conducted the official Exposition concerts; was conductor at the Grand Opéra from 1891 to 1893; appeared frequently as a visiting conductor in London; also in Russia and Portugal, and with the N.Y. Phil. (1905).

BIBL.: H. Schonberg, *The Great Conductors* (N.Y., 1967).

Coltellini, Celeste, Italian mezzo-soprano; b. Livorno, Nov. 26, 1760; d. Capodimonte, near Naples, July 28, 1828. She studied with G.B. Mancini and G. Manzuoli; then sang at La Scala in Milan (1780); in 1781 she became a member of the Teatro dei Fiorentini in Naples. She was well known for her interpretations of roles in operas by Mozart, Paisiello, and Cimarosa.

Coltrane, John (William), remarkable black American jazz musician, a virtuoso on the tenor saxophone; b. Hamlet, N.C., Sept. 23, 1926; d. Huntington, Long Island, N.Y., July 17, 1967. He studied at the Ornstein School of Music in Philadelphia; played in the bands of Dizzy Gillespie, Johnny Hodges, Miles Davis, and Thelonious Monk. He enhanced the resources of his style by studying ancestral African and kindred Asian music, absorbing the fascinating modalities of these ancient cultures. Coltrane was a master musician, whose theory and practice stimulated the creation of sophisticated jazz performance. Although a controversial figure, he was duly recognized as a major contributor to the avant-garde jazz movement of his era.

BIBL.: C. Simpkins, *C.: A Biography* (N.Y., 1975); J. Thomas, *Chasin' the Trane: The Music and Mystique of J. C.* (N.Y., 1975); B. Cole, *J. C.* (N.Y., 1976); B. Priestly, *J. C.* (London, 1987).

Colvig, William, American instrument maker and performer; b. Medford, Oreg., March 13, 1917. He was born into a musical family; he studied piano from the age of 6 and played in bands and orchs. during his formal studies at the Univ. of Calif. at Berkeley and the College of the Pacific in Stockton. In 1967 he initiated an association with the composer Lou Harrison, for whom he has built many instruments, including psalteries, harps, flutes, monochords, and several complete gamelans; he performed on these instruments in many of Harrison's compositions, as well as on traditional instruments in concerts and lectures. His instruments have been used by the San Francisco Sym. and San Francisco Opera Co., among others; he built the gamelans housed at the Univ. of Calif. at Berkeley and at Mills College in Oakland.

Combarieu, Jules (-Léon-Jean), eminent French music historian; b. Cahors, Lot, Feb. 4, 1859; d. Paris, July 7, 1916. He studied at the Sorbonne; later in Berlin with Spitta; received the degree of docteur ès lettres; was a prof. of music history at the Collège de France (1904–10).

WRITINGS: *Études de philologie musicale:* 1. *Théorie du* *rhythme dans la composition moderne d'après la doctrine antique* (1896); 2. *Essai sur l'archéologie musicale au XIXe siècle et le problème de l'origine des neumes* (1896); 3. *Fragments de l'Énéide en musique d'après un manuscrit inédit* (1898); *Éléments de grammaire musicale historique* (1906); *La Musique: Ses lois, son évolution* (1907; numerous eds.; in Eng., 1910); *Histoire de la musique des origines au début du XXe siècle* (3 vols., Paris, 1913–19; 9th ed. of vol. I, 1953; 6th ed. of vol. II, 1946; 3rd ed. of vol. III, 1947; rev. 1955).

Combe, Édouard, Swiss conductor and composer; b. Aigle, Sept. 23, 1866; d. Lausanne, Nov. 19, 1942. He studied in Paris; served as musical secretary to the conductor Lamoureux; was for a season a conductor in Cairo (1895–96). In 1896 he was appointed to the staff of the Geneva Cons.; from 1902 to 1914 he taught music history in Lausanne. He contributed numerous articles on music to the *Gazette Musicale de la Suisse Romande* and other music journals. He composed a symphonic poem, *Les Alpes;* several overtures and marches.

Combs, Gilbert Raynolds, American organist; b. Philadelphia, Jan. 5, 1863; d. there, June 14, 1934. His father, a distinguished organist, was his 1st teacher. He orig. studied medicine but made such progress in music that he decided to become a professional musician. He studied violin and cello as well as organ; in 1885 founded his own cons. in Philadelphia. He publ. a number of piano pieces; also wrote a *Dramatic Symphony;* compiled the manuals *The Science of Piano Playing* and *Introductory Steps to the Science of Piano Playing.*

Comden, Betty, American musician, lyricist, and dramatist; b. N.Y., May 3, 1915. She received her B.S. degree from N.Y. Univ. in 1938; then sang, danced, and acted with "The Revuers"; worked in this group with the musician and playwright Adolph Green; their 1st venture as co-authors was *On the Town* (1944; music by Leonard Bernstein); subsequent successes included *Billion Dollar Baby, Two on the Aisle,* and *Bells Are Ringing.* She also authored successful screenplays; received Tony awards for her contributions to *Applause* (1970) and *On the 20th Century* (1978).

Comes, Juan Bautista, Spanish composer; b. Valencia, c.1582; d. there, Jan. 5, 1643. He studied with Juan Perez; was a choirboy at the Valencia Cathedral from 1594 to 1596; in 1605 became choirmaster at the Cathedral of Lérida; then was vice-maestro of the Patriarca in Valencia (1608–13); became maestro of the Cathedral there (1613); in 1618 was called by Philip III to Madrid, serving as vice-maestro of the Royal Chapel; from 1628 was again in Valencia; served as maestro of the Cathedral there from 1632 to 1638. He left over 200 works, sacred (masses, Psalms, litanies, etc.) and secular (villancicos, tonadas), most of them in MS, preserved at the Escorial. Two vols. of selected numbers were publ. in Madrid in 1888.
Bibl.: M. Palau, *La obra del músico Valenciano J.B. C.* (Valencia, 1943); J. Climent, *J.B. C. y su tiempo* (Madrid, 1977).

Comettant, (Jean-Pierre-) Oscar, French music critic and composer; b. Bordeaux, April 18, 1819; d. Montvilliers, near Le Havre, Jan. 24, 1898. He entered the Paris Cons. in 1839 and studied with Elwart and Carafa; developed considerable proficiency as a composer of semipopular songs and marches; also publ. piano transcriptions of famous operas, variations, and fantasias. From 1852 to 1855 he lived in America, where he continued to write salon music. Returning to France, he became the music *feuilletoniste* for *Le Siècle,* and a contributor to various music journals; founded (with his wife, a singer) a musical inst. (1871).
Writings: *Histoire d'un inventeur au 19e siècle: Adolphe Sax, ses ouvrages et ses luttes* (1860); *Portefeuille d'un musicien; Musique et musiciens* (1862); *La Musique, les musiciens et les instruments de musique chez les différents peuples du monde* (1869); *Les Musiciens, les philosophes et les gaîtés de la musique en chiffres* (1870); *Francis Planté* (1874); *Les Compositeurs illustres de notre siècle* (1883); *La Norvège musicale à Paris* (1889); *Histoire de cent mille pianos et d'une salle de concert: Histoire de la Maison Pleyel, Wolff et Cie.* (1890); *La Musique de la Garde Républicaine en Amérique* (1894); etc.

Comissiona, Sergiu, prominent Rumanian-born American conductor; b. Bucharest, June 16, 1928. He studied conducting with Silvestri and Lindenberg, making his conducting debut at the age of 17 in Sibiu in a performance of Gounod's *Faust.* He became a violinist in the Bucharest Radio Quartet (1946), and then in the Rumanian State Ensemble (1947), where he was subsequently assistant conductor (1948–50) and music director (1950–55). From 1955 to 1959 he was principal conductor of the Rumanian State Opera in Bucharest. Being Jewish, he was moved to emigrate to Israel, where he was music director of the Haifa Sym. Orch. (1960–66) and founder-director of the Ramat Gan Chamber Orch. (1960–67). In 1963 he appeared in North America as conductor of the Israel Chamber Orch., and, in 1965, as guest conductor of the Philadelphia Orch. He then was music director of the Göteborg Sym. Orch. (1966–77), music adviser of the Northern Ireland Orch. in Belfast (1967–68), and music director of the Baltimore Sym. Orch. (1969–84). On July 4, 1976, he became a naturalized U.S. citizen. He was music director of the Chautauqua (N.Y.) Festival Orch. (1976–80), music adviser of the Temple Univ. Festival in Ambler (1977–80) and of the American Sym. Orch. in N.Y. (1977–82), and chief conductor of the Radio Phil. Orch. in Hilversum (from 1982), and was associated in various capacities with the Houston Sym. Orch. (1980–88). In 1987–88 he was also music director of the N.Y. City Opera, and from 1990 was chief conductor of the Helsinki Phil.
Bibl.: B. Paolucci, "S. C.," *Musical America* (March 1987).

Commer, Franz, German music historian; b. Cologne, Jan. 23, 1813; d. Berlin, Aug. 17, 1887. He was a pupil of Leibl and Josef Klein at Cologne; in 1828, became organist of the Carmelite Church and chorister at the Cathedral. In 1832 he went to Berlin to study with A.W. Bach (organ) and A.B. Marx and Rungenhagen (composition). Commissioned to arrange the library of the Royal Inst. for Church Music, he pursued historical research, and ed. important collections of early music. He was the founder (1844), with Küster and Kullak, of the Berlin Tonkünstlerverein; wrote incidental music to Aristophanes' *The Frogs* and Sophocles' *Electra;* he also wrote masses, cantatas, and choruses.

Como, Perry (Pierino), American singer of popular music; b. Canonsburg, Pa., May 18, 1912. After a stint as a barber, he joined the Freddie Carlone Orch. as a singer; then sang with the Ted Weems Orch. (1937–43); subsequently he became one of the most successful popular vocalists through his numerous radio and television appearances. His recordings included such favorites as *I Think of You, It's Impossible,* and *Shadow of Your Smile.*

Compère, Loyset (Louis), important French composer; b. Hainaut, c.1450; d. St. Quentin, Aug. 16, 1518. He was a chorister in St. Quentin; then a singer in the chapel of the Duke of Milan (1474–75); then was singer in the service of Charles VIII of France; was subsequently canon of St. Quentin. He was greatly esteemed by his contemporaries. Not many of his works are extant; they include masses, motets, a Magnificat, and chansons; these have been ed. by L. Finscher in Corpus Mensurabilis Musicae.
Bibl.: O. Gombosi, "Ghizeghem und C.; Zur Stilgeschichte der burgundischen Chanson," in *Adler-Festschrift* (Vienna, 1930); J. Delporte, "L'École polyphonique franco-flamande; L. C.," *Revue Liturgique et Musicale* (July–Aug. 1932); L. Finscher, *L. C. (c.1450–1518); Life and Works* (Rome, 1964).

Concone, (Paolo) Giuseppe (Gioacchino), Italian singing teacher and composer; b. Turin, Sept. 12, 1801; d. there, June 1, 1861. From 1837 until 1848 he lived in Paris, where he became a popular singing teacher. His collection of solfeggi in 5 vols. (*50 Lezioni, 30 Esercizi, 25 Lezioni, 15 Vocalizzi,* and *40 Lezioni per Basso*) became a standard work for singing teachers, showing no signs of obsolescence and continuing much in use all over the world. He also wrote an opera, *Un episodio del San Michele* (Turin, June 8, 1836).

Condon, Eddie (Albert Edwin), American jazz banjo player, guitarist, and bandleader; b. Goodland, Ind., Nov. 16, 1905; d. N.Y., Aug. 4, 1973. He first learned to play the ukelele; then took up the banjo and the guitar. He worked with Bix Beiderbecke, Louis Armstrong, Fats Waller, and Red Nichols. After settling permanently in N.Y., he led his own band and gave a series of jazz concerts in Town Hall. He operated his own club (1945–67); led his own band on tours to England (1957) and the Far East (1964); also appeared at the major jazz festivals in the U.S.

WRITINGS: With T. Sugrue, *We Called It Music: A Generation of Jazz* (N.Y., 1947; new ed. by G. Giddins, 1988); ed. with R. Gehman, *E. C.'s Treasury of Jazz* (N.Y., 1956); with H. O'Neal, *The E. C. Scrapbook of Jazz* (N.Y., 1973).

BIBL.: B. Esposito, "Remembering E. C.," *Jazz Journal,* XXVI/10 (1973); B. White, *The E. C. "Town Hall Broadcasts" 1944–5: A Discography* (Oakland, Calif., 1980); W. Kenney, III, "Jazz and the Concert Halls: The E. C. Concerts, 1942–48," *American Music,* I/2 (1983).

Cone, Edward T(oner), American composer, pianist, teacher, and writer on music; b. Greensboro, N.C., May 4, 1917. He studied composition with Roger Sessions at Princeton Univ. (B.A., 1939; M.F.A., 1942); also took piano lessons with Jeffrey Stoll, Karl Ulrich Schnabel, and Eduard Steuermann. After military service in World War II, he joined the faculty of Princeton Univ. in 1946; was made an associate prof. in 1952 and a full prof. in 1960, retiring in 1985. He received a Guggenheim fellowship in 1947. In addition to composing and teaching, he gave piano recitals. He was also active as a writer; was ed. of the periodical *Perspectives of New Music* (1966–72).

WRITINGS: *Musical Form and Musical Performance* (N.Y., 1968); *The Composer's Voice* (Berkeley, 1974); co-ed. (with B. Boretz) *Perspectives on Schoenberg and Stravinsky* (Princeton, 1968), *Perspectives on American Composers* (N.Y., 1971), and *Perspectives on Notation and Performance* (N.Y., 1975); ed. *Roger Sessions on Music* (Princeton, 1979); P. Morgan, ed., *Music: A View from Delft: Selected Essays* (Chicago, 1989).

WORKS: ORCH.: Sym. (1953); *Elegy* (1953); *Nocturne and Rondo* for Piano and Orch. (1955–57); Violin Concerto (1959); *Music for Strings* (1964); *Variations for Orchestra* (1967–68); *Cadenzas* for Violin, Oboe, and String Orch. (1979). **CHAMBER:** 2 string quartets (1939–49); 2 violin sonatas (1940, 1948); *Rhapsody* for Viola and Piano (1947); Piano Trio (1951); Piano Quintet (1960); *Funereal Stanzas* for Wind Quintet (1965); String Sextet (1966); Capriccio for String Quartet (1981); Piano Quartet (1983). **VOCAL:** *Scarabs* for Soprano and String Quartet (1948); *Philomela* for Soprano and Chamber Ensemble (1954–70); *Around the Year* for Madrigal Group and String Quartet (1956); songs. **PIANO:** *Fantasy* (1950); *Prelude, Passacaglia and Fugue* (1957); *Fantasy* for 2 Pianos (1965).

Confalonieri, Giulio, Italian music critic; b. Milan, May 23, 1896; d. there, June 29, 1972. He studied at the Univ. of Milan and the Cons. of Bologna; lived for some years in London; returned to Milan, where he settled as a teacher and music critic. He wrote an opera, *Rosaspina* (Bergamo, 1939); edited works by Cimarosa and Cherubini; publ. a comprehensive biography of Cherubini under the title *Prigionia di un artista: Il romanzo di Luigi Cherubini* (2 vols., Milan, 1948).

Conforti (Conforto), Giovanni Luca, Italian theorist; b. Mileto (Calabria), c.1560; date and place of death unknown. He entered the Papal Choir in 1580 and remained there until Oct. 31, 1585, when he returned to Mileto; was chorister at the Papal Chapel again from Nov. 4, 1591. According to Baini, he was the 1st of his period to restore the "trillo."

WRITINGS: *Breve et facile maniera d'essercitarsi ad ogni scolaro . . . a far passaggi . . .* (Rome, 1593; facsimile ed., with tr., edited by J. Wolf, Berlin, 1922) and *Passaggi sopra tutti li salmi . . .* (Venice, 1607; contains a set of vocal ornamentations to be used in the singing of the Psalms employed on Sundays and holidays throughout the year).

Confrey, Zez (Edward Elezear), American pianist and composer of light music, especially of a style known as "novelty piano"; b. Peru, Ill., April 3, 1895; d. Lakewood, N.J., Nov. 22, 1971. He studied at the Chicago Musical College and privately with Jessie Dunn and Frank Denhart. He appeared as piano soloist, along with George Gershwin, at Paul Whiteman's concert "Experiment in Modern Music" (1924), at which Gershwin's *Rhapsody in Blue* was premiered.

WORKS: *Kitten on the Keys* (1921; his most popular piece); *Stumbling* (1922); *Dizzy Fingers, Valse Mirage,* and *3 Little Oddities* (1923); *Concert Etude* (1922); *Buffoon* (1930); *Grandfather's Clock* (1933); *Oriental Fantasy* (1935); *Ultra Ultra* (1935); *Rhythm Venture* (1936); *Della Robbia* (1938); *Champagne;* etc.

Conley, Eugene, American tenor; b. Lynn, Mass., March 12, 1908; d. Denton, Texas, Dec. 18, 1981. He studied voice with Harriet Barrows and Ettore Verna; began his career as a radio singer in 1939, when NBC put him on the air in a program entitled "NBC Presents Eugene Conley." He made his operatic debut at the Brooklyn Academy of Music as the Duke in *Rigoletto;* then sang with the San Carlo Opera Co. in N.Y., the Chicago Opera Co., and the Cincinnati Summer Opera. In 1942 he joined the Army Air Corps. In 1949 he became the 1st American opera singer to open the season at La Scala, Milan; he later appeared in the Opéra-Comique in Paris, the Covent Garden Opera in London, and the Royal Opera of Stockholm. On Jan. 25, 1950, he made his 1st appearance at the Metropolitan Opera in N.Y., in the title role of Gounod's *Faust.* He remained on its roster until 1956. In 1960 he was appointed artist-in-residence at North Texas State Univ. in Denton, retiring in 1978.

Conlon, James, American conductor; b. N.Y., March 18, 1950. He graduated from the Juilliard School of Music in N.Y., and conducted the Juilliard Orch. He was the youngest conductor ever invited to lead a subscription concert of the N.Y. Phil., in 1974. He then appeared with virtually every major orch. in the U.S.; made his Metropolitan Opera debut in N.Y. in 1976. In 1979 he became music director of the Cincinnati May Festival; from 1983 to 1991 he was chief conductor of the Rotterdam Phil. and from 1989 of the Cologne Opera. He also served as Generalmusikdirektor of the city of Cologne and as chief conductor of the Gürzenich Orch. there (from 1991).

Conniff, Ray, American conductor, arranger, and composer of popular music; b. Attleboro, Mass., Nov. 6, 1916. He studied at the Juilliard School of Music in N.Y.; played trombone in various bands and arranged music for Artie Shaw and Harry James; also conducted his own groups.

Connolly, Justin (Riveagh), English composer; b. London, Aug. 11, 1933. He studied composition with Peter Racine Fricker at the Royal College of Music in London; held a Harkness Fellowship at Yale Univ. (1963–65); was then instructor in music theory there (1965–66). Returning to London, he joined the faculty of his alma mater. As a composer he followed the structural techniques of the avant-garde; in this direction he was influenced by new American trends, such as the theory of combinatoriality of Milton Babbitt and the practice of metrical modulation of Elliott Carter; he also made use of electronic sound. His works are often arranged in sets unified by a generic title and a numerical rubric; in this he also paid tribute to the mathematical concepts of sets and matrixes.

WORKS: *The Marriage of Heaven and Hell* for Soloists, Chorus, and Orch., after Blake; *Antiphones* for 36 Players; *Cinquepaces* for Brass Quintet; *Poems of Wallace Stevens:* No. I for Soprano and 7 Players (1967); No. II for Soprano, Clarinet, and Piano (1970); *Rebus* for Orch. (1970); *Anima* for Viola and Orch. (1974); *Diaphony* for Organ and Orch. (1977); various chamber music pieces as *Triads* (i.e., trios) and *Tesserae; Regeneration* for Chorus and Brass (1977); *Sentences* for Chorus, Brass, and Organ (1979); *Chimaera* for Dancer, Alto, Baritone, Chorus, Piano, Percussion, and Cello (1979; rev. 1981);

Obbligati V for Violin, Viola, Cello, and Strings (1981); *Fourfold from the Garden Forking Path* for 2 Pianos (1983); *Annead, Night Thoughts* for Piano (1983).

Conradi, August, German organist, conductor, and composer; b. Berlin, June 27, 1821; d. there, May 26, 1873. He was a pupil of Rungenhagen (composition); organist of the "Invalidenhaus" in 1843; went in 1846 to Vienna, and brought out a Sym. with marked success; was for years an intimate friend of Liszt at Weimar; then conducted in Stettin, Berlin, Düsseldorf, Cologne, and (from 1856) again in Berlin.
Works: Operas (all 1st perf. in Berlin): *Rübezahl* (1847); *Musa, der letzte Maurenfürst* (1855); *Die Braut des Flussgottes* (1850); *Die Sixtinische Madonna* (1864); *Knecht Ruprecht* (1865); *So sind die Frauen; Im Weinberge des Herrn* (1867); *Das schönste Mädchen im Städtchen* (1868); also vaudevilles, farces, 5 syms., overtures, string quartets, etc. He arranged many popular potpourris.

Conried (real name, **Cohn**), **Heinrich,** Austrian-American operatic impresario; b. Bielitz, Sept. 13, 1848; d. Meran, Tirol, April 27, 1909. He started as an actor in Vienna; in 1877 he managed the Bremen Municipal Theater; went to the U.S. in 1878 and took over the management of the Germania Theater in N.Y.; then was in charge of various theatrical enterprises; from 1892 was director of the Irving Place Theater in N.Y., which he brought to a high degree of efficiency. From 1903 till 1908 he was the manager of the Metropolitan Opera and was instrumental in engaging numerous celebrated artists, including Caruso. During his 1st season he gave the 1st American production of *Parsifal*, despite the heated controversy regarding the rights of Wagner's heirs; his decision to produce the opera *Salomé* by Richard Strauss in 1907 also aroused a storm of protests. Conried resigned in 1908 because of dissension within the management of the Metropolitan, and retired in Europe. He was decorated by several European governments; received an honorary M.A. from Harvard Univ.
Bibl.: M. Moses, *H. C.* (N.Y., 1916).

Consoli, Marc-Antonio, Italian-born American composer; b. Catania, May 19, 1941. He studied with Rieti at the N.Y. College of Music (B.M., 1966), with Krenek at the Peabody Cons. of Music in Baltimore (M.M., 1967), and with Goehr at the Yale Univ. School of Music (M.M., 1971; D.M.A., 1977); he also took courses with Schuller and Crumb at the Berkshire Music Center in Tanglewood, with Donatoni at the Accademia Musicale Chigiana in Siena, and at the Warsaw Cons. He became a naturalized U.S. citizen in 1967. He was founder-director of the Musica Oggi Ensemble (1978–80) and served as a church music director and organist (from 1988). He was also ed. of the Hargail Music Press (1978–84) and ed. and publisher of Rinaldo Music Press (from 1983). His honors include Guggenheim fellowships (1971, 1979), N.E.A. grants (1979, 1981, 1985), and an award from the American Academy and Inst. of Arts and Letters (1975).
Works: **ballets:** *Naked Masks: 3 Frescoes from a Dream* (N.Y., Dec. 13, 1980); *The Last Unicorn* (1981; N.Y., Feb. 24, 1989). **orch.:** *Profiles* (1973); *Music for Chambers* (1974; Hilversum, Sept. 13, 1975); *Odefonia* (1976; N.Y., May 23, 1978); *Afterimages* (1982; N.Y., June 2, 1983); *Musiculi: Le quattro stagioni* (1985–86); Cello Concerto (N.Y., May 9, 1988). **chamber:** *Brazilian Fantasy* for Clarinet and Piano (1965); *Interactions I* for 6 Instruments (1970), *II* for Flute and Harp (1971), *III* for Violin, Cello, and Piano (1971), *IV* for 5 Players (1971), and *V* for Flute and String Quartet (1972); *Sciuri novi* for Flute (1974); *Sciuri novi II* for Bass and Tape (1975); String Quartet (1983); *Sans parole I* for Cello (1983); *Reflections* for 5 Players (1986); *Sans parole II* for Violin (1988); also piano pieces. **vocal:** *Equinox I* (1967) and *II* (1968) for Soprano and Chamber Group; *Isonic* for Soprano and Chamber Group (1970); *Canti trinacriani* for Baritone, Tape, and Orch. (1975; Royan, March 21, 1976); *Tre canzoni* for Soprano or Mezzo-soprano, Flute, and Cello (1976); *Vuci siculani* for Mezzo-soprano and Chamber Group (1979); *Greek Lyrics* for Soprano,

Chorus, and Orch. (N.Y., June 5, 1988); also choruses and solo songs.

Constant, Franz, Belgian composer and pianist; b. Montignies-le-Tilleul, Nov. 17, 1910. He studied music at the Charleroi Academy of Music and at the Brussels Cons. with M. Maas, L. Jongen, Bourguignon, and Absil; in Paris, studied with Tomasi. He became a concert pianist and formed a successful duo with his wife, Jeanne Pellaerts. In 1947 he was appointed to the faculty of the Brussels Cons. As a composer, he pursues the ideal of blending the modalities of the classical Belgian School with coloristic harmonies.
Works: **orch.:** Rhapsodie for Violin and Orch. (1962); Saxophone Concerto (1963); Trumpet Concerto (1965); Sinfonietta for Flute, Oboe, and String Orch. (1968); Fantasia for Saxophone and Orch. (1969); Concertino for Flute and String Orch. (1970); Violin Concerto (1971); Rhapsodie (1973); *Expressions* for Violin, Piano, and Strings (1973); Clarinet Concertino (1975); Concerto for Brass and Wind Orch. (1987). **chamber:** *Allegro* for Trumpet and Piano (1959); *4 séquences* for 4 Saxophones (1962); *Impressions* for 4 Clarinets (1964); Flute Sonata (1967); *Évocation* for Flute and Piano (1969); *Suo tempore* for Violin and Piano (1969); *Dialogue* for Clarinet and Piano (1970); *Sonatine picturale* for Clarinet and Piano (1970); *Couleur provençale* for Horn and Piano (1970); *Pour la guitare I* and *II* (1971); *5 Miniatures* for Violin, Flute, and Piano (1971); Piano Quartet (1971); *Divertissement* for Bassoon and Piano (1972); *Rythme et expression* for Violin, Saxophone, Piano, and Percussion (1972); *Musique à deux* for Flute and Guitar (1973); String Quartet (1985); *Épisodes* for Alto Saxophone and Piano (1985); *Impromptu* for Alto Saxophone and Piano (1987); many piano pieces. **vocal:** *Jeanne de Naples*, cantata for Soprano, Narrator, Children's Voices, Speaking and Singing Choruses, and Orch. (1972); *Histoires du dimanche* for Children's Chorus, and Piano or Ensemble of 11 Instruments (1973); songs.

Constant, Marius, Rumanian-born French composer and conductor; b. Bucharest, Feb. 7, 1925. He graduated from the Bucharest Cons. in 1944; then went to Paris, where he studied conducting with Fournet and composition with Messiaen, Nadia Boulanger, and Honegger (1945–49); he was director of the Ballets de Paris of Roland Petit (1956–66); was founder, president, and music director of Ars Nova (1963–71), a Parisian ensemble for new music; in 1967 he was a guest lecturer at Stanford Univ.; in 1970 gave lectures in Hilversum, the Netherlands. His early compositions are impressionistic; later he adopted serial and aleatory procedures, particularly in multimedia productions.
Works: Improvised opera, *La Serrure* (The Lock; 1969); other operas: *Le Souper* for Baritone and Vocal Orch. (1969) and *La Tragédie de Carmen* (Paris, Nov. 5, 1981); ballets: *Joueur de flûte* (The Flute Player; 1952); *Haut-Voltage* (1956); *Cyrano de Bergerac* (1960); *Éloge de la folie*, with Soprano (1966); *Paradise Lost* (1967); *Candide* (1970; Hamburg, Jan. 24, 1971; material reworked for a concert piece with Solo Harpsichord, 1971); *Le Jeu de Sainte Agnes*, "ecclesiastical action" on a 14th-century MS, for 6 Singers, 5 Actors, Dancer, Hammond Organ, Electric Guitar, Trombone, and Percussion (Besançon, Sept. 6, 1974); *Chants de Maldoror* for Narrator, Dancer-Conductor, 23 Improvising Instrumental Soloists, and 10 Cellos (1962); Piano Concerto (1954); *24 préludes* for Orch. (1957); Concerto for Tuba and String Orch. (1958); *Concert Music* for Saxophone and 11 Instruments (1960); *Turner*, 3 essays for Orch. (1961); *Chaconne et marche militaire* for Orch. (1967); *5 chants et une vocalise* for Dramatic Soprano and Orch. (1968); *Winds* for 13 Winds and Double Bass (1968); *Traits*, based on the 1930s game of surrealist poets, "exquisite corpse," for 6 to 25 Musicians (1969); *Equal* for 5 Percussionists (1969); *14 Stations* for 92 Percussion Instruments (1 Player) and 6 Instrumentalists (1969–70); *Candide* for Amplified Harpsichord and Orch. (1971); *Strings* for Strings (1972); *Faciale Anno 1973* for 24 Violins and Orch. (Paris, July 19, 1973); *Piano Personnage* for Piano and Chamber Ensemble (Paris,

Jan. 15, 1974); *For Clarinet* for Solo Clarinet (1974); Sym. for Winds (Montreal, March 17, 1978); *Alleluias* for Trumpet and Organ (1980); *D'une élégie slave* for Solo Guitar (1981); *103 regards dans l'eau* for Violin and Orch. (1981); *Précis de décomposition* for Clarinet, Bassoon, Horn, String Quartet, and Tape (1982).

Constantinescu, Dan, Rumanian composer; b. Bucharest, June 10, 1931. He studied with Martian Negrea, Theodor Rogalski, and Mihail Jora at the Bucharest Cons.; later joined its staff as instructor in music theory. His works are written in a compact neo-Classical idiom, with occasional melodic excursions into atonality. He wrote *Divertissement in a Classical Style* for String Orch. (1954); *Toma Alimos,* ballad for Orch. (1955); Partita for Orch. (1957); Concerto for Piano and String Orch. (1963); Chamber Sym. (1968); *Sinfonia Concertante* for Orch. (1970); Concerto for 2 Pianos and Orch. (1972); Trio for Violin, Clarinet, and Piano (1964); Cello Sonata (1964); Clarinet Sonata (1965); Variations for Piano and String Trio (1966); String Quartet (1967); songs.

Constantinescu, Paul, eminent Rumanian composer; b. Ploesti, July 13, 1909; d. Bucharest, Dec. 20, 1963. He studied composition at the Bucharest Cons. with Castaldi, Cuclin, and Jora; then went to Vienna, where he took courses with Schmidt and Joseph Marx. He was 1st engaged as a violinist in Ploesti (1927–34); then taught at the academy for religious music in Bucharest (1937–41). In 1941 he was appointed a prof. at the Bucharest Cons., and retained this post until his death. **WORKS:** 2 operas: *O noapte furtunoasă* (Bucharest, Oct. 25, 1935; rev. 1950; Bucharest, May 19, 1951) and *Pană Lesnea Rusalim* (Bucharest, 1956; enjoyed excellent success); 5 ballets: *Nunta în Carpați* (1938); *Spune, povesteste, spune* (1947); *Pe malul Dunării* (1947); *Tîrg pe muntele Găina* (1953); *Înfrățire* (1959); 2 Byzantine oratorios: *Patimile și Învierea Domnului* (1946; rev. 1948) and *Nașterea Domnului* (1947); Violin Sonatina (1933); *Burlesque* for Piano and Orch. (1937); Sinfonietta (1937); Sym. (1944; rev. 1955); Concerto for String Quartet (1947); Piano Concerto (1952); *Rapsodie olteneascǎ* for Orch. (1956); Violin Concerto (1957); Harp Concerto (1960); *Sinfonia Ploieșteană* (1961); Concerto for Violin, Cello, Piano, and Orch. (Bucharest, Dec. 28, 1963); piano pieces; songs and choruses. **BIBL.:** V. Tomescu, *P. C.* (Bucharest, 1967).

Conti, Carlo, Italian composer and pedagogue; b. Arpino, Oct. 14, 1796; d. Naples, July 10, 1868. He studied at the Naples Cons. with Zingarelli and J.S. Mayr; taught there from 1819 to 1821; rejoined its faculty as a teacher of counterpoint from 1846 to 1858; in 1862 became its assistant director. An industrious composer, he wrote 11 operas and much church music. Rossini called him "the best Italian contrapuntist of the day." His distinction lies principally in his excellence as a teacher; among his famous pupils was Bellini.

Conti, Francesco Bartolomeo, Italian composer; b. Florence, Jan. 20, 1681; d. Vienna, July 20, 1732. He was assistant court theorbist (1701–8), principal theorbist (1708–26), and court composer (from 1713); wrote about 30 stage works to Italian and German texts, including *Clotilda* (1706) and *Don Chisciotte in Sierra Morena* (1719); also 11 oratorios, many secular cantatas, and songs. **BIBL.:** H. Williams, *F.B. C.: His Life and Operas* (diss., Columbia Univ., 1964); C. and E. Fruchtman, "Instrumental Scoring in the Chamber Cantatas of F. C.," in J.W. Pruett, *Studies in Musicology* (Chapel Hill, N.C., 1969).

Conti, Gioacchino, celebrated Italian castrato soprano, known as "Gizziello" and "Egizziello," after his teacher; b. Arpino, Feb. 28, 1714; d. Rome, Oct. 25, 1761. He began study at the age of 8 with Domenico Gizzi in Naples, making his debut in Vinci's *Artaserse* in Rome (Feb. 4, 1730), where he scored a triumph. He subsequently sang in various Italian music centers, and also appeared in Vienna. Handel then called him to London, where he made his debut in *Ariodante* at Covent Garden (May 5, 1736; he had no time to learn the title role,

however, and was compelled to sing Italian arias); he then created the roles of Meleager in *Atalanta* (May 12, 1736), Sigismondo in *Arminio* (Jan. 12, 1737), Anastasio in *Giustino* (Feb. 16, 1737), and Alessandro in *Berenice* (May 18, 1737), all of which were composed for him by Handel. Returning to Italy, he sang in Rome (1738, 1741), Padua (1739), and Florence (1742); after a sojourn in Lisbon (from 1743), he returned to Italy and sang in Naples (1747–50), Lucca (1749), and Padua (1751). He appeared at the court theater of Lisbon (1752–55) before retiring in Italy. Conti possessed a brilliant voice with a compass of 2 octaves.

Conti-Guglia (originally **Contiguglia**), **Richard** and **John,** brilliant American duo-pianists; b. identical twins, N.Y., April 13, 1937. They began taking twin piano lessons in earliest childhood, and grew in parallel congruence; they played in a duo recital in public when they were 6 years of age; continued to develop in close consanguinity; they composed music for 2 pianos and transcribed solo works for their concerts. When they were 12, Percy Grainger invited them to play during one of his recitals; he subsequently befriended them and gave them valuable advice; later they took piano lessons with Jean Wilder and with Bruce Simonds at Yale Univ.; upon graduation, they received a Ditson Fellowship, which enabled them to study with Dame Myra Hess in London. They made their professional debut in London in 1962, playing piano 4-hands; in 1964 they made a major European tour. In addition to the standard literature for duo-pianos, they performed piano transcriptions for 2 pianos and for piano 4-hands of obscure works by forgotten composers. In 1971 they gave an all-Liszt concert in London, which included his piano transcription of his symphonic poems *Mazeppa* and *Orpheus,* and of his arrangements of excerpts from Bellini's *Norma* and *La Sonnambula* and Mozart's *Don Giovanni.* In 1972 they played Liszt's transcriptions of Beethoven's 9th Sym. in London, arousing considerable curiosity, and repeated this exhibition in N.Y. in 1974. They gave the 1st performance of Liszt's *Grosses Konzertstück über Mendelssohn's "Lieder ohne Worte"* for 2 Pianos, composed in 1834, in Utrecht on Oct. 19, 1986. They further played duo-piano works by Bartók and Grainger. For better professional identification of their gemination, they split their original fetal name, Contiguglia, into 2 fungible parts, Conti-Guglia.

Contilli, Gino, Italian composer; b. Rome, April 19, 1907; d. Genoa, April 4, 1978. He studied at the Accademia di Santa Cecilia in Rome with Respighi. After 1942 he taught composition at the Liceo Musicale in Messina. **WORKS:** *Saul,* opera (1941); 2 concertos for Orch. (1936, 1942); *Sinfonia italiana* (1938); Violin Sonata (1947); *La notte,* lyric suite for Voice and Small Ensemble (1950); *In Lunam,* cantata (1957; Italian Radio, Nov. 20, 1964); *Espressioni sinfoniche* for Orch. (Venice, Sept. 21, 1960); *Offerta musicale* for Soprano and 5 Instruments (1959); *Immagini sonore* for Soprano and 11 Instruments (1964); *Preludi* for Orch. (1966).

Conus, Georgi (Eduardovich), Russian composer and theorist, brother of **Julius Conus;** b. Moscow, Sept. 30, 1862; d. there, Aug. 29, 1933. He studied at the Moscow Cons. with Taneyev and Arensky; from 1891 to 1899 he taught there; from 1902, was a prof. at the music school of the Phil. Soc. He developed an original theory of metric analysis and publ. a brief outline of it; also wrote several symphonic works, piano pieces, and songs.

Conus, Julius, Russian violinist and composer, brother of **Georgi (Eduardovich)** and father of **Sergei Conus;** b. Moscow, Feb. 1, 1869; d. Malenki, Ivanov District, Jan. 3, 1942. He studied at the Moscow Cons.; later taught violin there. He was a friend of Tchaikovsky and was greatly esteemed in Moscow musical circles. His Violin Concerto, 1st performed by him in Moscow in 1898, has retained its popularity in Russia.

Conus, Sergei, Russian-American pianist and composer, son of **Julius Conus;** b. Moscow, Oct. 18, 1902. He studied music with his father, with his uncle, Leo Conus, and with Oskar Riesemann. In 1920 he went to Paris, where he studied piano with Cortot and Isidor Philipp; then lived in Serbia, Bulgaria, and Poland. He was again in France from 1937 to 1949, and in Morocco from 1949 to 1959; in 1959 settled in America; taught piano at the Boston Cons. His compositions are mostly for piano (24 preludes, many miniatures, a concerto); he also wrote a Sym. His style is characteristically Russian, closely resembling that of Rachmaninoff.

Converse, Charles (Crozat), American composer; b. Warren, Mass., Oct. 7, 1832; d. Englewood, N.J., Oct. 18, 1918. He studied at the Leipzig Cons. with Richter, Hauptmann, and Plaidy (1855–59). Upon his return to America he was a practicing lawyer in Erie, Pa.; then lived in Highwood, N.J. He wrote a number of patriotic overtures and cantatas, among them *American Concert Overture* on *Hail, Columbia* (1869); *God for Us*, an American hymn (1887); also vocal quartets, music for strings, 2 syms., 2 oratorios, etc. His hymn *What a Friend We Have in Jesus* is widely sung. In his writings he used the pen name **Karl Redan.** A man of many interests, he wrote articles on philosophical and philological subjects; proposed the use of the genderless pronoun of the 3rd person, "thon," which has been included in several dictionaries.

Converse, Frederick Shepherd, distinguished American composer; b. Newton, Mass., Jan. 5, 1871; d. Westwood, Mass., June 8, 1940. He graduated from Harvard Univ. (1893); studied music in Boston with Carl Baermann and Chadwick (1894–96); then in Munich at the Royal Academy of Music with Rheinberger, graduating in 1898. Returning to Boston, he taught harmony at the New England Cons. of Music (1900–1902; 1920–36; dean, 1931–37); was an instructor of composition at Harvard Univ. (1901–7). He was vice-president of the Boston Opera Co. (1911–14); received a Mus.Doc. from Boston Univ. (1933); became a member of the American Academy of Arts and Letters (1937). His early works reflect the influence of academic German training; later he began to apply more advanced harmonies; in his *Flivver 10 Million*, written to glorify the 10 millionth Ford car, he adopted a frankly modern idiom, modeled after Honegger's *Pacific 231*. He sketched some material for a 5th Sym. in 1937, but did not complete it. He had renumbered his syms. in 1936, calling his previously unnumbered Sym. No. 1 and upping Nos. 1, 2, and 3 by one, giving the title of Sym. No. 5 to the undeveloped sketches for that work. But his Syms. Nos. 2, 3, and 4 were premiered, respectively, as Nos. 1, 2, and 3.

WORKS: OPERAS: *The Pipe of Desire* (Boston Opera, Jan. 31, 1906; 1st American opera to be produced by the Metropolitan Opera Co., March 18, 1910; won the David Bispham medal); *The Sacrifice* (Boston, March 3, 1911); *Sinbad the Sailor* (1913; not perf.); *The Immigrants* (1914; not perf.). **ORATORIOS:** *Job*, dramatic poem for Soli, Chorus, and Orch. (Worcester Festival, Oct. 2, 1907); *Hagar in the Desert*, dramatic narrative for Low Voice and Orch. (Hamburg, 1908). **CANTATAS:** *The Peace Pipe* (1914); *The Answer of the Stars* (1919); *The Flight of the Eagle* (1930). **OTHER VOCAL WORKS:** *La Belle Dame sans merci*, ballade for Baritone with Orch. (1902); Psalm, *I Will Praise Thee, O Lord* (1924).

ORCH.: Syms.: in D minor, not numbered (Munich, July 14, 1898); No. 1 (Boston, Jan. 30, 1920); No. 2 (Boston, April 21, 1922); No. 3 (1936); No. 6 (Indianapolis, Nov. 29, 1940); concert overture, *Youth; Festival of Pan* (Boston, Dec. 21, 1900); *Endymion's Narrative* (1901; Boston, April 9, 1903); *Night and Day*, 2 poems for Piano and Orch. (Boston, Jan. 21, 1905); overture, *Euphrosyne* (Boston, 1903); orch. fantasy, *The Mystic Trumpeter* (Philadelphia, March 3, 1905); symphonic poem, *Ormazd* (St. Louis, Jan. 26, 1912); symphonic poem, *Ave atque Vale* (St. Louis, Jan. 26, 1917); Fantasia for Piano and Orch. (1922); *Song of the Sea* (Boston, April 18, 1924); *Elegiac Poem* (Cleveland, Dec. 2, 1926); fantasy, *Flivver 10 Million* (Boston, April 15, 1927); *California*, festival scenes (Boston, April 6, 1928); symphonic suite, *American Sketches* (Boston, Feb. 8, 1935).

CHAMBER: 3 string quartets; Violin Sonata; Cello Sonata; Piano Trio; also Violin Concerto, with Piano Accompaniment

(1902); *Valzer poetici* for Piano, 4-hands; *Scarecrow Sketches* (excerpts from the photo-music-drama *Puritan Passions*, commissioned by the Film Guild of N.Y., 1923; orig. for Piano; orchestrated, Boston, Dec. 18, 1923); piano pieces and songs.

BIBL.: R. Severence, *The Life and Works of F.S. C.* (diss., Boston Univ., 1932); R. Garofalo, *The Life and Works of F.S. C. (1871–1940)* (diss., Catholic Univ. of America, Washington, D.C., 1969).

Conyngham, Barry, Australian composer; b. Sydney, Aug. 27, 1944. He studied jurisprudence; in 1966 entered the New South Wales Cons.; also took private lessons with Meale, and later with Sculthorpe at the Univ. of Sydney. In 1970 he traveled to Japan and had instruction in advanced techniques with Toru Takemitsu. Returning to Australia, he became a lecturer in Perth at the Univ. of Western Australia; then went to the U.S. to study electronic music at the Univ. of Calif. in San Diego and at Princeton Univ.; eventually received an appointment to teach at Melbourne Univ.

WORKS: Opera, *Ned* (1975–78); *The Apology of Bony Anderson* (1978); *Jazz Ballet* for Saxophone, Double Bass, Drums, Flute, and Piano (1964); Cello Sonata (1965); Piano Sonata (1966–67); *Dialogue* for String Trio (1967); *Lyric Dialogues* for 5 Flutes, Oboe, and Cello (1967); *Crisis: Thoughts in a City* for 2 String Orchs. and Percussion (1968); *Prisms* for 6 Violins (1968); *3* for 2 Percussion Groups and String Quartet (1969); *5 Windows* for Orch. (1969); *Ice Carving* for Amplified Violin and 4 String Orchs. (1970); *Water . . . Footsteps . . . Time* for Solo Piano, Harp, Electric Guitar, Tam-tam, and Orch. (1970–71); *Ends* for Piano (1970); theater piece, *Edward John Eyre*, for Female Voice, Actors, Wind Quintet, and String Orch. (1971); *5* for Wind Quintet (1970–71); *6* for 6 Percussionists and Orch. (1971); *Voss* for Female Voice, Chorus, Piano, and Orch. (1972); *Snowflake* for Electric Piano, interchangeable with Harpsichord and Celesta (1973); *Without Gesture* for Percussion and Orch. (1973); *Mirror Images* for 4 Actors, Saxophone, Cello, Double Bass, and Percussion (1975); Percussion Concerto (1977); *Sky* for Strings (1977); *Shadows of Noh*, double-bass concerto (1978); *Mirages* for Orch. (1979); String Quartet (1979); *Horizons*, concerto for Orch. (1981); *Southern Cross*, double concerto for Violin, Piano, and Orch. (1981); *Basho* for Soprano and Instruments, after verses by Matsuo Basho (London, Oct. 13, 1981).

Cooder, Ry(land Peter), American guitarist, singer, and songwriter; b. Los Angeles, March 15, 1947. He played guitar as a youth, then formed the Rising Sons with Taj Mahal and played on recordings by Captain Beefheart, Phil Ochs, and Randy Newman. His own debut came in 1970 with *Ry Cooder*, a collection of songs about the Great Depression by Woody Guthrie, Leadbelly, and Sleepy John Estes. His 1st commercial success was *Paradise and Lunch* (1974); interest in unusual tunings (Bahamian, Hawaiian) resulted in his particularly interesting *Chicken Skin Music* (1976). Cooder's masterful bottleneck guitar playing and inimitable singing style garnered a loyal cult following; later albums included *The Slide Area* (1982) and *Get Rhythm* (1987), with songs by Johnny Cash, Chuck Berry, and Bob Dylan. He also composed atmospheric scores for films, including Wim Wenders's extraordinary *Paris, Texas* (1984).

Cook, Will Marion, black American conductor and composer; b. Washington, D.C., Jan. 27, 1869; d. N.Y., July 19, 1944. He entered the Oberlin (Ohio) Cons. to study violin when he was 13, continuing his studies with Joachim in Germany and at the National Cons. in N.Y. He had a brief career as a concert violinist before devoting himself to composition for the black musical theater in N.Y.; he was director and composer for the Bert Williams–George Walker productions (1900–1908) and founded his own "syncopated" sym. orch. (1918), with which he toured extensively. In his later years he was active mainly as a conductor and teacher in N.Y.

WORKS: *Clorindy*, or *The Origin of the Cakewalk* (1898); *Jes' Lak White Fo'ks* (1899); *The Cannibal* (1901); *The Southerners* (1904); *The Traitor* (1913); *Darkeydom* (1915); *Swing*

Along (1929; in collaboration with W. Vodery); also choral works, songs.

Bibl.: M. Carter, *W.M. C.: Afro-American Violinist, Composer and Conductor* (diss., Univ. of Illinois).

Cooke, Arnold, English composer; b. Gomersal, Yorkshire, Nov. 4, 1906. He studied at Cambridge (Mus.B., 1929; Mus.D., 1948); also with Hindemith at the Berlin Hochschule für Musik to 1932; taught at the Royal Manchester College of Music (1933–38); was a prof. at the Trinity College of Music in London from 1947.

Works: Piano Concerto (1943); Concerto for String Orch. (1947); Sym. No. 1 (1949); Clarinet Concerto (1955); Oboe Sonata (1957); Violin Concerto (1958); Clarinet Sonata (1959); Suite for 3 Clarinets (1959); *Jabez and the Devil,* ballet (1961); Clarinet Quintet (1962); Sym. No. 2 (1963); *Variations on a Theme of Dufay* for Orch. (1966); Sym. No. 3 (1967); Piano Quintet (1970); Suite for Recorder, Strings, and Percussion (1972); 2 organ sonatas (1971, 1980); Cello Concerto (1972–73); Sym. No. 4 (1974); Sym. No. 5 (1978–79); Concerto No. 2 for Clarinet and Orch. (1981–82); other chamber works, including 2 cello sonatas (1941, 1979–80) and 5 string quartets (1933, 1945, 1967, 1976, 1978).

Cooke, Benjamin, English organist and composer; b. London, 1734; d. there, Sept. 14, 1793. He studied with Pepusch, whom he succeeded in 1752 as conductor at the Academy of Ancient Music; in 1757 he became choirmaster (after Gates), in 1758 lay vicar, and in 1762 organist, of Westminster Abbey; received a Mus.Doc. from Cambridge (1775) and from Oxford (1782); became organist of St. Martin-in-the-Fields in 1782; in 1789 he resigned the Academy conductorship in favor of Arnold. His best works are in the form of glees, canons, and catches, for which he took several Catch Club prizes (*Collection of 20 Glees, Catches, and Canons for 3–6 Voices in Score,* London, 1775; *9 Glees and 2 Duets,* 1795). He also wrote odes, instrumental concertos, church music, pieces for organ and harpsichord, etc., and added choruses and accompaniments to Pergolesi's *Stabat Mater* (1759) and Galliard's *Morning Hymn* (1772) for the Academy of Ancient Music. His son **Robert** (b. Westminster, 1768; d. Aug. 13, 1814) became organist of St. Martin-in-the-Fields after his father's death in 1793, and on the death of Arnold, in 1802, was appointed organist and choirmaster of Westminster Abbey; ended his life by drowning himself in the Thames. He publ. a collection of glees in 1805.

Cooke, Deryck (Victor), English musicologist; b. Leicester, Sept. 14, 1919; d. London, Oct. 26, 1976. He studied piano privately and composition at Cambridge Univ. with Patrick Hadley and Robin Orr, earning his B.A. in 1940, M.A. in 1943, and Mus.B. in 1947. From 1947 to 1959 he was a member of the music staff of the BBC (rejoined in 1965); after 1959, he devoted most of his time to writing on music and broadcasting. He attracted considerable attention by his scholarly and congenial arrangement of Mahler's unfinished 10th Sym., which he completed using authentic fragments from Mahler's sketch; this version was approved by Alma Mahler, the composer's widow. It was first performed at a BBC Henry Wood Promenade Concert at the Albert Hall in London, on Aug. 13, 1964. Cooke publ. *The Language of Music* (London, 1959); *I Saw the World End: A Study of Wagner's Ring* (London, 1979); *Gustav Mahler: An Introduction to His Music* (N.Y., 1980); *Variations: Essays on Romantic Music* (London, 1982).

Cooke, James Francis, American writer on music and composer; b. Bay City, Mich., Nov. 14, 1875; d. Philadelphia, March 3, 1960. He was educated in Brooklyn and studied music with R.H. Woodman and W.H. Hall; went to Germany in 1900, and continued his studies with Meyer-Olbersleben and H. Ritter. As ed. of the *Etude* (1908–49), he brought it to a high degree of popularity by promoting special features (columns dealing with performance and technique; simple arrangements of classics; etc.). He composed a number of successful piano pieces (*White Orchids, Moon Mist, Ballet Mignon, Sea Gardens, Italian Lake Suite*), and songs.

Writings: *A Standard History of Music* (Philadelphia, 1910); *Great Pianists on Piano Playing* (4th ed., 1914); *Mastering the Scales and Arpeggios* (1913); *Musical Playlets for Children* (1917); *Great Singers on the Art of Singing* (1921); *Great Men and Famous Musicians* (1925); *Young Folks' Picture-History of Music* (1925); *Light, More Light* (1925); *Johannes Brahms* (1928); *Claude Debussy* (1928); *Musical Travelogues* (1934); *How to Memorize Music* (1947); many non-musical works, including plays and poems.

Cooke, Sam (real name, **Samuel Cook**), black American balladeer; b. Chicago, Jan. 22, 1931; shot to death in Los Angeles, Dec. 11, 1964. He sang in a lyric tenor voice, avoiding the shouts and the screams that often covered up vocal incompetence among so many pop singers; rather, his songs recalled the Negro spirituals and the texts reflected religious sentiments, or else the throes of unrequited love. Among his big hits were *You Send Me, Chain Gang, Twistin' the Night Away,* and *Cupid.* He also sang gospel hymns such as *Nearer to Thee, Touch the Hem of His Garment, Wonderful, God Is So Wonderful,* and *Jesus, Wash Away My Troubles.* He was shot by a jealous girlfriend.

Cooke, Thomas (Simpson) "Tom," Irish tenor, instrumentalist, composer, and singing teacher; b. Dublin, 1782; d. London, Feb. 26, 1848. He studied with his father; while still a youth, served as concertmaster of the orch. at the Crow Street Theatre in Dublin. From 1806 to 1812 he ran a music shop; also filled tenor parts at Drury Lane in London; in 1815 he became conductor and later music director there (1821–35). In 1846 he joined the ensemble of the Concerts of Antient Music as concertmaster. His versatility as an instrumentalist was displayed when, at one of his benefit concerts at Drury Lane, he performed alternately on the violin, flute, clarinet, bassoon, horn, cello, double bass, and piano. He also was esteemed as a singing teacher (Sims Reeves was his pupil); wrote 2 vocal treatises, *Singing Exemplified in a Series of Solfeggi* and *Singing in Parts* (London, 1942). He composed over 50 pieces of incidental music for Drury Lane.

Cooley, "Spade" (Donnell Clyde), American country fiddler, once renowned as the "King of Western Swing"; b. in a stone cellar under a shack near Saddle Paddle Creek, Okla., Dec. 17, 1910; d. Oakland, Calif., Nov. 23, 1969, while on a furlough from the Calif. State Medical Facility at Bakersfield, the minimum-security state prison where he was confined from 1961 for the murder of his wife, Ella Mae. Cooley was one-quarter Cherokee Indian; he joined the cowboy star Roy Rogers in Hollywood in his act, and acquired the nickname "Spade" after a spectacular poker game during which he filled several successive flushes in spades. He replenished his financial resources from these winnings and went into the real estate business. He was author of the song *Shame, Shame on You.*

Coolidge, Elizabeth (Penn) Sprague, American music patron; b. Chicago, Oct. 30, 1864; d. Cambridge, Mass., Nov. 4, 1953. In 1918 she established at Pittsfield, Mass., the Berkshire Festivals of Chamber Music, which were held annually under her auspices; later was the sponsor of the Elizabeth Sprague Coolidge Foundation in the Library of Congress, created in 1925 for the purpose of producing concerts and music festivals, awarding prizes, etc., under the administration of the Music Division of the Library. Numerous modern composers, including Loeffler, Schoenberg, Malipiero, Bartók, Casella, Stravinsky, Prokofiev, Piston, and Hanson, have written works commissioned for it. The auditorium of the Library of Congress was likewise a gift of Mrs. Coolidge. In 1932 she founded the Elizabeth Sprague Coolidge Medal "for eminent services to chamber music," awarded annually (until 1949) to 1 or more persons; its recipients included Adolfo Betti, Walter W. Cobbett, Carl Engel, and E.T. Rice. She also initiated performances of modern and classical chamber music throughout the U.S. and Europe. Her sponsorship of the appearances of artists in the U.S. and abroad (the Pro Arte, Coolidge, Roth quartets, etc.) was an important factor in the musical life of the U.S. In recognition of her many cultural contributions she was made honorary M.A. (Yale Univ., Smith College, Mills College), L.D. (Mt. Holyoke College), Mus.Doc. (Pomona College), and LL.D. (Univ. of Calif.). She received the Cobbett Medal and various foreign decorations.

Cools, Eugène, French composer; b. Paris, March 27, 1877; d. there, Aug. 5, 1936. He studied at the Paris Cons. with Gédalge, Fauré, and Widor; won the Prix Cressent for his Sym. (1906); was assistant of Gédalge at the Cons. (1907–23); taught at the École Normale de Musique (1919); was music critic for *Le Monde Musical;* in 1928 he was appointed ed. in chief for Max Eschig, a Paris music publisher.

Works: 2 operas: *Le Jugement de Midas* (1922) and *Kymris;* opera buffa, *Beaumarchais,* on themes by Rossini; operettas: *Magda, Les Violettes de la Malmaison,* and *Ravioli;* symphonic poem, *La Mort de Chénier; Hamlet,* symphonic suite; *2 pièces russes* for Orch. (most of these pieces are also available in piano arrangements); Piano Quintet; String Quartet; Violin Sonata; Flute Sonata; about 80 songs; many piano pieces.

Cooper, Emil (Albertovich), Russian conductor of English descent; b. Kherson, Dec. 20, 1877; d. N.Y., Nov. 16, 1960. He studied at the Odessa Cons., then went to Vienna, where he took lessons in violin with Joseph Hellmesberger, Jr.; later studied in Moscow with Taneyev. At the age of 22 he began to conduct at the Kiev Opera. In 1909 he conducted the Russian Ballet and Opera with the Diaghilev troupe in Paris. He then conducted in Moscow; in 1923 he went abroad; in 1929 he conducted the Chicago Civic Opera; from 1944 to 1950 was on the staff of the Metropolitan Opera Co.; then became music director of the Montreal Opera Guild; subsequently lived in N.Y.

Cooper, Kenneth, highly talented American harpsichordist, conductor, and musicologist; b. N.Y., May 31, 1941. He studied harpsichord playing with Sylvia Marlowe at the Mannes College of Music in N.Y.; also took harpsichord lessons with Fernando Valenti; then entered Columbia Univ. (B.A., 1962; M.A., 1964; Ph.D. in musicology, 1971). He subsequently developed an energetic schedule of teaching; was an instructor of music at Barnard College (1967–71), lecturing on all academic music subjects; an adjunct assistant prof. at Brooklyn College (1971–73); in 1975 was appointed prof. of harpsichord at the Mannes College of Music. A man of latitudinarian and panoramic faculties, Kenneth Cooper encompasses a 360° range of activities, specializing in playing piano and harpsichord, improvisation, authentication of performing usages of the Baroque, translation from musically important languages (Italian, German), and last but not least, revivification of ragtime. He has publ. a number of scholarly articles dealing with the Baroque period; directed stage performances of neglected operas by Handel; and given concerts of Bach's music at midnight. He has further commissioned works for harpsichord to composers of the avant-garde; played recitals in England and at the Salzburg Festival; traveled as a concert artist in Russia, Rumania, and Greece under the auspices of the U.S. Dept. of State; made frequent appearances with his wife, the soprano Josephine Mongiardo, whom he married in 1969.

Cooper, Martin (Du Pré), English music critic; b. Winchester, Jan. 17, 1910; d. Richmond, Surrey, March 15, 1986. He was educated at Hertford College, Oxford (B.A., 1931), and then took a course with Egon Wellesz in Vienna (1932–34). Returning to London, he was active as a music critic; publ. articles in the *Daily Herald* and *Daily Telegraph.* He was also ed. of the *Musical Times* (1953–56). Among his books are biographies of Gluck (London, 1935), Bizet (London, 1938), and Beethoven (London, 1970); he further wrote a vol. on Russian opera (London, 1951) and ed. vol. X of *The New Oxford History of Music* (London, 1974), for which he wrote the section on stage works from 1890 to 1918.

Cooper, Paul, American composer and teacher; b. Victoria, Ill., May 19, 1926. He studied at the Univ. of Southern Calif. under Ernest Kanitz (M.A., 1953; D.M.A., 1956); was a private

student of Nadia Boulanger in Paris (1953–54). Upon return to the U.S., he held the posts of prof. of music at the Univ. of Michigan (1955–67) and composer-in-residence at the Univ. of Cincinnati (1968–74) and at Rice Univ. in Houston (1974). He held 2 Guggenheim fellowships (1965, 1972). He also served as visiting prof. at the Royal Academy of Music in Stockholm (1985) and at the Royal Cons. of Music in Copenhagen (1988). He publ. *Perspectives in Music Theory* (1973; 2nd ed., 1981).

Works: dramatic: *Mysterion* for Soprano, Narrator, Chamber Orch., and Optional Dancers (1988). **orch.:** Sinfonia for Strings (1952); 6 syms. (*Concertant* for Solo Woodwind, Brass, String Quartet, Percussion, and Strings, 1966; *Antiphons* for Oboe and Symphonic Winds, 1971; *Lamentations* for Strings, 1971; *Landscape* for Flute, Trumpet, Viola, and Orch., 1973–75; *Sym. in 2 Movements,* 1982–83; *In Memoriam,* 1987); Overture (1953); Concerto for Orch. (1966); Violin Concerto (1967); *A Shenandoah* (for the centennial of Charles Ives, 1974). **chamber:** 6 string quartets (1952; 1954; 1959; 1964; *Umbrae,* 1973; 1977); *Canonic Variations* for Wind Quintet (1960); Viola Sonata (1961); Concerto for Harpsichord and Organ (1962); Violin Sonata (1962); Cello Sonata (1962); Sonata for Flutes and Piano (1963); Double-bass Sonata (1964); *Concert for 2* for Cello and Piano (1965); *Concert for 4* for Flute, Oboe, Harpsichord, and Double Bass (1965); *Concert for 5* for Wind Quintet (1965); *Epitaphs* for Alto Flute, Harp, and Double Bass (1969); *Soliloquies* for Violin and Piano (1970); *Chimera,* piano quartet (1972); *Variants II* for Viola and Piano (1972); *Aegina Music* for Violin, Cello, and Piano (1973). **piano:** Sonata (1963); *Partimento* (1967); *Cycles* (1969). **organ:** Concerto for Antiphonal Organs (1954); Toccata (1959); *Variants I* (1971). **choral:** *Missa Brevis* (1954); *Chorales of Nativity* (1954); *4 Madrigals* (1956); *Genesis II* (1969); *Credo* for Double Chorus and Orch. (1970); *?* for Boys' Chorus (1972); *Cantigas* for Double Chorus and Orch. (1972).

Coover, James B(urrell), American music librarian and pedagogue; b. Jacksonville, Ill., June 3, 1925. He was educated at the Univ. of Northern Colorado (B.A., 1949; M.A., 1950) and the Univ. of Denver (M.A., 1953). He was associated with the Bibliographical Center for Research in Denver (1951–53), serving as its assistant director (1952–53), then was director of the George Sherman Dickinson Music Library at Vassar College (1953–67). Subsequently he was prof. of music and director of the music library at the State Univ. of N.Y. at Buffalo (from 1976). He also served as president (1959–60) and as executive board member (1987–90) of the Music Library Assoc.

Writings: *Music Lexicography* (Denver, 1952; 3rd ed., rev. and enl., 1971); with R. Colvig, *Medieval and Renaissance Music on Long-Playing Records* (Detroit, 1964; 2nd ed., 1973); *Provisional Checklist of Priced Antiquarian Catalogues Containing Musical Materials* (Buffalo, 1981); *Musical Instrument Collections* (Detroit, 1981; rev. ed., 1987, as *Antiquarians' Catalogues of Musical Interest*); *Music Publishing, Copyright and Piracy in Victorian England, 1881–1906* (London, 1985); ed., with C. Bradley, *Richard S. Hill: Tributes from Friends* (1987); *Music at Auction: Puttick & Simpson (of London), 1794–1971* (1988).

Cope, David (Howell), eclectic American writer, composer, and teacher; b. San Francisco, May 17, 1941. He was educated at Arizona State Univ. and the Univ. of Southern Calif. in Los Angeles; then served on the faculties of Miami Univ. of Ohio and at the Univ. of Calif., Santa Cruz. He is well known for his didactic books on contemporary composition, which include *New Directions in Music* (Dubuque, 1971; 5th ed., rev., 1989), *New Music Composition* (N.Y., 1977), and *Computer Analysis of Musical Style* (N.Y., 1990). Among his compositions are *Threshold and Visions* for Orch. (1977), *Experiments in Musical Intelligence* (1988), and *Cradle Falling,* opera for Soprano and Orch. (1989).

Coperari, Giovanni. See **Coprario, Giovanni.**

Copland, Aaron, greatly distinguished and exceptionally gifted American composer; b. N.Y., Nov. 14, 1900; d. North

Tarrytown, N.Y., Dec. 2, 1990. He was educated at the Boys' High School in Brooklyn; began to study piano with Victor Wittgenstein and Clarence Adler as a young child. In 1917 he took lessons in harmony and counterpoint with Rubin Goldmark in N.Y., and soon began to compose. His first publ. piece, *The Cat and the Mouse* for Piano (1920), subtitled *Scherzo humoristique*, shows the influence of Debussy. In 1920 he entered the American Cons. in Fontainebleau, near Paris, where he studied composition and orchestration with Nadia Boulanger. Returning to America in 1924, he lived mostly in N.Y.; became active in many musical activities, not only as a composer but also as a lecturer, pianist, and organizer in various musical societies. He attracted the attention of Serge Koussevitzky, who gave the 1st performance of his early score *Music for the Theater* with the Boston Sym. Orch. in 1925; then engaged Copland as soloist in his Concerto for Piano and Orch. in 1927; the work produced a considerable sensation because of the jazz elements incorporated in the score, and there was some subterranean grumbling among the staid subscribers to the Boston Sym. concerts. Koussevitzky remained Copland's steadfast supporter throughout his tenure as conductor of the Boston Sym., and later as the founder of the Koussevitzky Music Foundation. In the meantime, Walter Damrosch conducted in N.Y. Copland's Sym. for Organ and Orch., with Nadia Boulanger as soloist. Other orchs. and their conductors also performed his music, which gained increasing recognition. Particularly popular were Copland's works based on folk motifs; of these the most remarkable are *El Salón México* (1933–36) and the American ballets *Billy the Kid* (1938), *Rodeo* (1942), and *Appalachian Spring* (1944). A place apart is occupied by Copland's *Lincoln Portrait* for Narrator and Orch. (1942), with the texts arranged by the composer from speeches and letters of Abraham Lincoln; this work has had a great many performances, with the role of the narrator performed by such notables as Adlai Stevenson and Eleanor Roosevelt. His patriotic *Fanfare for the Common Man* (1942) achieved tremendous popularity and continued to be played on various occasions for decades; Copland incorporated it *in toto* into the score of his 3rd Sym. He was for many years a member of the board of directors of the League of Composers in N.Y.; with Roger Sessions he organized the Copland-Sessions Concerts (1928–31), and was also a founder of the Yaddo Festivals (1932) and of the American Composers' Alliance (1937); was also a participant in such organizations as the Koussevitzky Music Foundation, the Composers Forum, the Cos Cob Press, etc. He was head of the composition dept. at the Berkshire Music Center at Tanglewood from 1940 to 1965, and from 1957 to 1965 was chairman of the faculty. He lectured extensively and gave courses at The New School for Social Research in N.Y. and at Harvard Univ. (1935 and 1944); was the Charles Eliot Norton Lecturer at Harvard in 1951–52. He was the recipient of many awards: Guggenheim fellowship (1925–27); RCA Victor award of $5,000 for his *Dance Symphony*; Pulitzer Prize and N.Y. Music Critics' Circle Award for *Appalachian Spring* (1945); N.Y. Music Critics' Circle Award for the 3rd Sym. (1947); Oscar award for the film score *The Heiress* from the Academy of Motion Picture Arts and Sciences (1950); Gold Medal for Music from the American Academy of Arts and Letters (1956); Presidential Medal of Freedom (1964); Howland Memorial Prize of Yale Univ. (1970); was also decorated with a Commander's Cross of the Order of Merit in West Germany; was elected to honorary membership of the Accademia di Santa Cecilia in Rome. He held numerous honorary doctor's degrees: Princeton Univ. (1956); Brandeis Univ. (1957); Wesleyan Univ. (1958); Temple Univ. (1959); Harvard Univ. (1961); Rutgers Univ. (1967); Ohio State Univ. (1970); N.Y. Univ. (1970); Columbia Univ. (1971); also York Univ. in England (1971). About 1955 Copland developed a successful career as a conductor, and led major sym. orchs. in Europe, the U.S., South America, and Mexico; he also traveled to Russia under the auspices of the State Dept. In 1982 the Aaron Copland School of Music was created at Queens College of the City Univ. of N.Y. In 1983 he made his last appearance as a

conductor in N.Y. His 85th birthday was widely celebrated; Copland attended a special concert given in his honor by Zubin Mehta and the N.Y. Phil., which was televised live by PBS. He was awarded the National Medal of Arts (1986). As a composer, Copland made use of a broad variety of idioms and techniques, tempering dissonant textures by a strong sense of tonality. He enlivened his musical textures by ingenious applications of syncopation and polyrhythmic combinations; but in such works as Piano Variations he adopted an austere method of musical constructivism. He used a modified 12-tone technique in his Piano Quartet (1950) and an integral dodecaphonic idiom in the score of *Connotations* (1962).

WORKS: STAGE: *Grohg*, ballet (1922–25; not perf.; material incorporated into *Dance Symphony*); *Hear Ye! Hear Ye!*, ballet (Chicago, Nov. 30, 1934); *The 2nd Hurricane*, play-opera for high school (1936; N.Y., April 21, 1937); *Billy the Kid*, ballet (Chicago, Oct. 16, 1938); *From Sorcery to Science*, music for a puppet show (N.Y., May 12, 1939); *Rodeo*, ballet (N.Y., Oct. 16, 1942); *Appalachian Spring*, ballet (Washington, D.C., Oct. 30, 1944); *The Tender Land*, opera (N.Y., April 1, 1954); *Dance Panels*, ballet (1959; rev. 1962; Munich, Dec. 3, 1963; arranged for Piano, 1965).

FILM MUSIC: *The City* (1939); *Of Mice and Men* (1939); *Our Town* (1940); *North Star* (1943); *The Cummington Story* (1945); *The Red Pony* (1948); *The Heiress* (1948; received an Academy Award, 1949); *Something Wild* (1961).

INCIDENTAL MUSIC TO PLAYS: *Miracle at Verdun* (1931); *The 5 Kings* (1939); *Quiet City* (1939).

ORCH.: *Music for the Theater* (Boston, Nov. 20, 1925); Sym. for Organ and Orch. (N.Y., Jan. 11, 1925; rev. version without organ, designated as Sym. No. 1, 1928; also as *Prelude* for Chamber Orch., 1934); Concerto for Piano and Orch. (1926; Boston, Jan. 28, 1927); *Symphonic Ode* (1927–29; composed for the 50th anniversary of the Boston Sym. Orch.; Boston, Feb. 19, 1932; rev. 1955 for the 75th anniversary of the Boston Sym. Orch. and rededicated to the memory of Koussevitzky; Boston, Feb. 3, 1956); *A Dance Symphony* (1930; based on the ballet *Grohg*; received the RCA Victor Competition prize; Philadelphia, April 15, 1931); *Short Symphony* (Sym. No. 2) (1932–33; Mexico City, Nov. 23, 1934); *Statements* (1932–35; 1st complete perf., N.Y., Jan. 7, 1942); *El Salón Mexico* (1933–36; Mexico City, Aug. 27, 1937); *Music for Radio* (*Prairie Journal*), subtitled *Saga of the Prairie* (CBS, N.Y., July 25, 1937); *An Outdoor Overture* (N.Y., Dec. 16, 1938; arranged for Band, 1941); *John Henry* for Chamber Orch. (CBS, N.Y., March 5, 1940; rev. 1952); *Our Town*, suite from the film (CBS, N.Y., June 9, 1940); *Quiet City*, suite from the film, for English Horn, Trumpet, and Strings (1939; N.Y., Jan. 28, 1941); *Billy the Kid*, suite from the ballet (NBC, N.Y., Nov. 9, 1940); *Lincoln Portrait* for Speaker and Orch. (Cincinnati, May 14, 1942); *Rodeo*, 4 dance episodes from the ballet (1942; Boston, May 28, 1943); *Music for Movies* for Chamber Orch. (from the films *The City*, *Of Mice and Men*, and *Our Town*; 1942; N.Y., Feb. 17, 1943); *Fanfare for the Common Man* for Brass and Percussion (1942; Cincinnati, March 12, 1943); *Letter from Home* (N.Y. broadcast, Oct. 17, 1944; rev. 1962); *Variations on a Theme by Eugene Goossens* (with 9 other composers; 1944; Cincinnati, March 23, 1945); *Appalachian Spring*, suite from the ballet (N.Y., Oct. 4, 1945); *Danzón Cubano* (orig. for 2 Pianos, 1942; orch. version, 1944; Baltimore, Feb. 17, 1946); Sym. No. 3 (1944–46; Boston, Oct. 18, 1946); Concerto for Clarinet, Strings, Harp, and Piano (1947–48; N.Y., Nov. 6, 1950); *The Red Pony*, suite from the film (Houston, Nov. 1, 1948); *Preamble for a Solemn Occasion* for Speaker and Orch. (N.Y., Dec. 10, 1949; arranged for Organ, 1953; arranged for Band, 1973); Orch. Variations (orch. version of the Piano Variations; 1930; 1957; Louisville, March 5, 1958); *Connotations* (composed entirely in the 12-tone technique; commissioned for the opening of Phil. Hall, Lincoln Center, N.Y., Sept. 23, 1962); *Music for a Great City* (symphonic suite descriptive of life in N.Y. City; London, May 26, 1964); *Emblems* for Band (1964); *Down a Country Lane* for School Orch. (London, Nov. 20, 1964); *Inscape* (commissioned by the N.Y. Phil. and 1st perf. by that orch. at the Univ. of Michigan,

Ann Arbor, Sept. 13, 1967); *Inaugural Fanfare* (Grand Rapids, Mich., June 1969; rev. 1975); *3 Latin American Sketches: Estribillo, Paisaje mexicano, Danza de Jalisco* (N.Y., June 7, 1972); *Proclamation* (1982; orchestrated by P. Ramey, 1985; N.Y., Nov. 14, 1985).

VOCAL: Choral: *4 Motets* (1921); *The House on the Hill* for Women's Voices (1925); *An Immorality* for Soprano, Women's Voices, and Piano (1925); *What Do We Plant?* for Women's Voices and Piano (1935); *Lark* for Bass and Mixed Chorus (1938); *Las agachadas* for Mixed Chorus (1942); *Song of the Guerrillas* for Baritone, Men's Voices, and Piano (1943); *The Younger Generation* for Mixed Chorus and Piano (1943); *In the Beginning* for Mezzo-soprano and Mixed Chorus (commissioned for the Harvard Symposium; Cambridge, Mass., May 2, 1947); *Canticle of Freedom* (1955; rev. 1965). Songs: *Melancholy* (1917); *Spurned Love* (1917); *After Antwerp* (1917); *Night* (1918); *A Summer Vacation* (1918); *My Heart Is in the East* (1918); *Simone* (1919); *Music I Heard* (1920); *Old Poem* (1920); *Pastorale* (1921); *As It Fell upon a Day* (1923); *Poet's Song* (1927); *Vocalise* (1928); *12 Poems of Emily Dickinson* (1949–50); *Old American Songs* for Voice and Orch. (arrangements in 2 sets, 1950 and 1952); *Dirge in Woods* (1954).

CHAMBER: *Capriccio* for Violin and Piano; *Poem* for Cello and Piano; *Lament* for Cello and Piano; *Preludes* for Violin and Piano; String Quartet (unfinished); Piano Trio (unfinished); *Rondino* for String Quartet (1923; N.Y., Oct. 18, 1984); *Nocturne* for Violin and Piano (1926); *Ukelele Serenade* for Violin and Piano (1926); *Lento molto* for String Quartet (1928); *Vitebsk, Study on a Jewish Theme* for Piano Trio (1928; N.Y., Feb. 16, 1929); *Elegies* for Violin and Viola (1932); Sextet for Clarinet, Piano, and String Quartet (arranged from *Short Symphony*; 1932–33; 1937; N.Y., Feb. 26, 1939); Sonata for Violin and Piano (1942–43); Quartet for Piano and Strings (Washington, D.C., Oct. 29, 1950); *Nonet* for 3 Violins, 3 Violas, and 3 Cellos (1960; Washington, D.C., March 2, 1961); Duo for Flute and Piano (1971); *Threnody I: Igor Stravinsky, In Memoriam* for Flute and String Trio (1971); *Vocalise* for Flute and Piano (arrangement of *Vocalise;* 1928; 1972); *Threnody II: Beatrice Cunningham, In Memoriam* for G-Flute and String Trio (1973).

PIANO: *Moment musical* (1917); *Danse caractéristique* for Piano Duet or Orch. (1918); *Waltz Caprice* (1918); *Sonnets, 1–3* (1918–20); *Moods (3 esquisses): Amertume, pensif, jazzy* and *Petit portrait*, a supplement (1920–21); Piano Sonata in G major (1920–21); *Scherzo humoristique: Le Chat et la souris* (1920); *Passacaglia* (1921–22); *Sentimental Melody* (1926); *Piano Variations* (1930; orch. version, 1957); *Sunday Afternoon Music (The Young Pioneers)* (1935); Piano Sonata (1939–41; Buenos Aires, Oct. 21, 1941, composer pianist); *4 Piano Blues* (1926–48); *Piano Fantasy* (1952–57); *Down a Country Lane* (1962); *Rodeo* (arrangement from the ballet; 1962); *Danza de Jalisco* for 2 Pianos (1963; orch. version, 1972); *Dance Panels* (arrangement from the ballet; 1965); *In Evening Air* (excerpt arranged from the film score *The Cummington Story;* 1969); *Night Thoughts (Homage to Ives)* (1972); *Midsummer Nocturne* (1977); *Midday Thoughts* (1982); *Proclamation* (1982).

WRITINGS: *What to Listen for in Music* (N.Y., 1939; 2nd ed., 1957; tr. into German, Italian, Spanish, Dutch, Arabic, and Chinese); *Our New Music* (N.Y., 1941; 2nd ed., rev. and enl. as *The New Music, 1900–1960,* N.Y., 1968); *Music and Imagination,* a collection of lectures delivered at Harvard in 1951–52 (Cambridge, Mass., 1952); *Copland on Music* (N.Y., 1960); an autobiography, *Copland* (with V. Perlis; 2 vols., N.Y., 1984, 1989).

BIBL.: P. Rosenfeld, *An Hour with American Music* (Philadelphia, 1929); T. Chanler, "A. C.," in H. Cowell, ed., *American Composers on American Music* (Stanford, 1933); A. Berger, "The Music of A. C.," *Musical Quarterly* (Oct. 1945); idem, *A. C.* (N.Y., 1953); J. Smith, *A. C.: His Work and Contribution to American Music* (N.Y., 1955); R. Goldman, "A. C.," *Musical Quarterly* (Jan. 1961); E. Cone, "Conversation with A. C.," *Perspectives of New Music* (Spring/Summer 1968); C. Peare, *A. C. His Life* (N.Y., 1969); D. Hamilton, "A. C.: A Discography

of the Composer's Performances," *Perspectives of New Music* (Fall/Winter 1970); special issue of *Tempo,* devoted to C. on the occasion of his 70th birthday (Winter 1970/71); B. Northcott, "Notes on C.," *Musical Times* (Nov. 1980); Q. Hilliard, *A Theoretical Analysis of the Symphonies of A. C.* (diss., Univ. of Florida, 1984); N. Butterworth, *The Music of A. C.* (N.Y., 1985); P. Ramey, "A. C.: Genial Patriarch of American Music," *Ovation* (Nov. 1985); J. Skowronski, *A. C.: A Bio-Bibliography* (Westport, Conn., 1985); R. Parker, "C. and Chávez: Brothers-in-Arms," *American Music* (Winter 1987).

Coppens, Claude A(lbert), Belgian pianist, teacher, and composer; b. Schaerbeek, Dec. 23, 1936. He studied at the Brussels Cons. (1944–52), then with Jacques Février and Marguerite Long in Paris, completing his education at the Univ. of Brussels (doctorate in law, 1960). He was active as a teacher at the conservatories in Brussels, Antwerp, and Ghent.

WORKS: *Symetries A* for 9 Instruments (1960–61); Piano Sonata (1964); *Due sinfonie per tre gruppi* (1965–66); *Concerting Variations* for Violin and 9 Instruments (1970); *Gedichtje van St. Niklaas,* cantata for Boy's Chorus and Small Orch. (1970–71); *The Horn of Plenty,* musical play (1978); Saxophone Quartet (1979–80); Sonata for Flute and Cello (1981–82); *Skiai* for Trombone and Percussion (1982); *XIII Pages for XIII Clarinets: Portrait of the Artist as a Young-Old Man* for Clarinet Orch. (1982–83); *. . . un coup de dés jamais n'abolira le hasard . . .* for Marimba and Clarinet Orch. (1984; also for Harpsichord and String Orch.); *Logoganic Patterns* for Double Percussion (1984).

Coppet, Edward J. de, American patron of art and founder of the Flonzaley Quartet; b. N.Y., May 28, 1855; d. there, April 30, 1916. A man of wealth and refined artistic tastes, he engaged various artists for private quartet performances at his residence. When he realized that constant practice was indispensable for the attainment of a perfect ensemble, he commissioned A. Pochon, in 1902, to find 4 men of the highest artistic standing who were willing to devote all their time to quartet playing. In the summer of the following year Adolfo Betti, Alfred Pochon, Ugo Ara, and Ivan d'Archambeau (1st violin, 2nd violin, viola, and cello, respectively) began to practice at Flonzaley, de Coppet's summer residence near Lausanne, Switzerland; in the spring of 1904 they made their 1st European tour, arousing admiration by the perfection of their ensemble; on Dec. 5, 1905, they gave their 1st public concert in America (Carnegie Chamber Music Hall, N.Y.), with overwhelming success. They then appeared regularly in America and Europe. After de Coppet's death, his son, **André,** continued the original policy until 1929, when the quartet disbanded.

BIBL.: D.G. Mason, "E.J. de C.," *Musical Quarterly* (Oct. 1916); E.T. Rice, "The de C. Music Room in New York and Switzerland," ibid. (Oct. 1937).

Coppola, Piero, Italian conductor and composer; b. Milan, Oct. 11, 1888; d. Lausanne, March 13, 1971. He studied at the Milan Cons., graduating in 1909; in 1913 he filled engagements as a conductor at La Scala; in 1914 was in London; in 1921 settled in Paris, where he was active as music director of the recording company "His Master's Voice" (1923–34); eventually settled in Switzerland. He wrote 3 operas, *Sirmione, Nikita* (1914), and *La Sposa di Corinto* (1918); a Sym. (Paris, Nov. 13, 1924, composer conducting); a symphonic sketch, *La Ronde sous la cloche* (1924); and various other pieces.

BIBL.: W. Holmes, "Episodes in the Life and Times of an Artist: The Story of P. C.," *Le Grand Baton* (Sept.–Dec. 1973).

Coppola, Pietro Antonio (Pierantonio), Italian composer; b. Castrogiovanni, Sicily, Dec. 11, 1793; d. Catania, Nov. 13, 1877. For a short time he studied at the Naples Cons.; then began to compose operas, which obtained sufficient success to enable his friends and admirers to present him as a rival to Rossini. From the time he was 19, he produced one opera after another, but without much success until he composed *La Pazza per amore* (Rome, Feb. 14, 1835). This was his 5th opera and it became popular all over Europe (presented in

Paris under the title *Eva*). From 1839 to 1843, and again from 1850 till 1871, he was conductor of the Lisbon Royal Opera. His other operas were: *Gli Illinesi* (Turin, Dec. 26, 1835); *Enrichietta di Baienfeld* (Vienna, June 29, 1836); *La bella Celeste degli Spadari* (Milan, June 14, 1837); *Giovanna prima di Napoli* (Lisbon, Oct. 11, 1840); *Il Folletto* (Rome, June 18, 1843). He also wrote church music, notably a *Salve Regina* which was highly regarded.

BIBL.: U. Coppola, *P.A. C.* (Catania, 1898).

Coprario or **Coperario, Giovanni** (real name, **John Cooper**), famous English lutenist, viola da gambist, and composer; b. c.1575; d. London, 1626. He went to Italy about 1600; upon his return to England, he adopted the Italianized name Giovanni Coprario. With the patronage of Sir Robert Cecil and Edward Seymour, Earl of Hertford, he gained renown in his homeland as an instrumentalist and composer. According to tradition, he was the music teacher of James I's children; he also was the teacher of Henry and William Lawes. His works are patterned closely on Italian models. He wrote a fine series of fantasias for viols, many with organ; music for 2 masques; anthems; songs (*Funeral Teares for the Death of Right Honorable the Earle of Devonshire*, London, 1606, and *Songs of Mourning: Bewailing the Untimely Death of Prince Henry*, London, 1613). See R. Charteris, *John Coprario (Cooper) c. 1575–1626: A Study and Complete Critical Edition of His Instrumental Music* (diss., Univ. of Canterbury, New Zealand, 1976). He wrote the treatise *Rules How to Compose* (c.1610; facsimile ed. by M. Bukofzer, Los Angeles, 1951).

BIBL.: J. Pulver, "Giovanni Coperario alias John Cooper," *Monthly Musical Record* (April 1927); G. Dodd, "Coperario or Bull?" and "The Coperario-Lupo Five-part Books at Washington," *Chelys*, I (1969); R. Charteris, *John C.: A Thematic Catalogue of His Music with a Biographical Introduction* (N.Y., 1977).

Coquard, Arthur (-Joseph), French composer and music critic; b. Paris, May 26, 1846; d. Noirmoutier, Vendée, Aug. 20, 1910. He took private lessons with César Franck (1862–66); was music critic for *Le Monde* and *Écho de Paris*. He publ. *De la musique en France depuis Rameau* (Paris, 1892), which received a prize from the Académie des Beaux-Arts.

WORKS: Operas: *L'Épée du roi* (Angers, 1884); *Le Mari d'un jour* (Paris, 1886); *L'Oiseau bleu* (Paris, 1894); *La Jacquerie* (Paris, 1895); *Jahel* (Lyons, 1900); *La Troupe Jolicœur* (Paris, May 30, 1902); oratorio, *Jeanne d'Arc*.

BIBL.: N. Dufourcq, *Autour de C., Franck et d'Indy* (Paris, 1952).

Corboz, Michel (-Jules), Swiss conductor; b. Marsens, Feb. 14, 1934. He was educated at the École Normale in Fribourg; then became a director of church music in Lausanne, where he organized the Ensemble Vocal et Instrumental de Lausanne, with which he has given numerous performances of Baroque vocal and orch. music.

Corder, Frederick, English composer and teacher, father of **Paul Corder;** b. London, Jan. 26, 1852; d. there, Aug. 21, 1932. He was a pupil at the Royal Academy of Music in London (1873–75); in 1875 won the Mendelssohn Scholarship; studied with Ferdinand Hiller at Cologne (1875–78); was conductor of the Brighton Aquarium Concerts from 1880 to 1882, and greatly improved their quality; from 1886, was a prof. of composition at the Royal Academy of Music and, from 1889, also curator. In 1905 he founded the Soc. of British Composers. He was remarkably successful as a teacher, many prominent British composers having been his pupils; a zealous apostle of Wagner, he and his wife made the first Eng. tr. of *The Ring of the Nibelung, Die Meistersinger,* and *Parsifal.*

WORKS: Operas: *Morte d'Arthur* (1877); *Nordisa* (Liverpool, Jan. 26, 1887); *Ossian* (1905); operettas: *Philomel* (1880); *A Storm in a Teacup* (1880); *The Nabob's Pickle* (1883); *The Noble Savage* (1885); cantatas: *The Cyclops* (1881); *The Bridal of Triermain* (1886); *The Blind Girl of Castel-Cuillé* (1888); *The Sword of Argantyr* (1889). Orch.: *Evening on the Sea Shore,* idyll (1876); *Im Schwarzwald,* suite (1876); *Ossian,* overture

(1882); *Nocturne* (1882); *Prospero,* overture (1885); *Roumanian Suite* (1887); *Pippa Passes,* orch. poem (1897); *A Fairy Tale* (1913); incidental music to *The Tempest* (1886), *The Termagant* (1898), *The Black Tulip* (1899); *Dreamland,* ode for Chorus and Orch. (1883); *Roumanian Dances* for Violin and Piano (1883); *The Minstrel's Curse,* ballad for declamation, with Orch. (1888); *True Thomas,* musical recitation (1895); *The Witch's Song* (1904); *Elegy* for 24 Violins (1908); *Empire Pageant Masque* (1910); *The Angels,* biblical scene for 6 Choirs (1911); *Sing unto God,* 50-part motet (1912).

WRITINGS: *Exercises in Harmony and Musical Composition* (1891); *The Orchestra and How to Write for It* (1895; 2nd ed., 1902); *Modern Composition* (1909); *Musical Encyclopaedia* (1915); *History of the Royal Academy of Music* (1922).

BIBL.: *Musical Times* (Nov. 1913).

Corder, Paul, English composer, son of **Frederick Corder;** b. London, Dec. 14, 1879; d. there, Aug. 6, 1942. He entered the Royal Academy of Music in London in 1895, studying piano with Oscar Beringer and Tobias Matthay, and composition with his father; was appointed a prof. of harmony and composition there in 1907.

WORKS: 2 operas: *Grettir the Strong* and *Rapunzel* (1917); *The Moon Slave,* terpsichorean fantasy; *Cyrano de Bergerac,* overture; *Dross,* music drama without words; op. 8, *Morar,* a "Gaelic fantasy"; *The Dryad,* ballet; *Prelude and Fugue; Sea-Songs;* 2 *Choral Songs; Heroic Elegy;* many piano works (*Transmutations,* 9 *Preludes, Passacaglia,* etc.); songs.

Cordero, Roque, Panamanian composer; b. Panama, Aug. 16, 1917. He first studied in Panama; then came to the U.S. (1943); studied with Krenek in Minneapolis and with Stanley Chapple (conducting) at the Berkshire Music Center at Tanglewood. He was a prof. at the National Inst. of Music in Panama from 1950 to 1966, and its director from 1953 to 1964; taught at Indiana Univ. in Bloomington (1966–69) and at Illinois State Univ. from 1972; was also active as a conductor.

WORKS: *Capriccio interiorano* for Band (1939); Piano Concerto (1944); Sym. No. 1 (1947); 8 *Miniatures* for Orch. (1948); *Rapsodia campesina* for Orch. (1949); Quintet for Flute, Clarinet, Violin, Cello, and Piano (1949); Sym. No. 2 (1956); 5 *mensajes breves* for Orch. (1959); 4 string quartets (1960, 1968, 1973, 1983); Cello Sonata (1962); Violin Concerto (1962); Sym. No. 3 (1965); *Sonata breve* for Piano (1966); *Circunvoluciones y moviles* for 57 Players (1967); *Permutaciones* 7 for 7 Instrumentalists (1967); *Paz, Paix, Peace* for 4 Trios and Harp (1969); *Variations and Theme for 5* for Woodwind Quartet and Horn (1975); *Music for 5 Brass* (1980); *Petite Mobiles* for Bassoon and Trios (1983).

Cordon, Norman, American baritone; b. Washington, N.C., Jan. 20, 1904; d. Chapel Hill, N.C., March 1, 1964. He attended the Fishburne Military School; later studied at the Univ. of North Carolina and at the Nashville Cons. of Music; was a voice student of Gaetano de Lucas and Hadley Outland; in 1933 made his debut as Scarpia at the Civic Opera in Chicago, of which he was a member until 1936; from 1936 to 1946 he was a member of the Metropolitan Opera in N.Y.; he also appeared with the San Francisco Opera, the Cincinnati Summer Opera, and on Broadway.

Corea, "Chick" (Armando Anthony), American jazz pianist and composer; b. Chelsea, Mass., June 12, 1941. He began his career as a sideman with Mongo Santamaria, Willie Bobo, Blue Mitchell, and Herbie Mann; also worked with Miles Davis. After leading a group known as The Circle (1970–71), he worked with Stan Getz. His popularity grew as he turned to rock music, playing with a group known as Return to Forever.

Corelli, Arcangelo, famous Italian violinist and composer; b. Fusignano, near Imola, Feb. 17, 1653; d. Rome, Jan. 8, 1713. His violin teacher was G. Benvenuti in Bologna; he learned counterpoint with Matteo Simonelli. Little is known of his early life; about 1671 he went to Rome, where he was a violinist at the French Church (1675); in the beginning of 1679, he played in the orch. of the Teatro Capranica; Rome remained his chief residence to the end of his life, except for visits to Modena (1689–90) and Naples (1702). There is no substance to the story that in 1672 he went to Paris and was driven out by the intrigues of Lully; biographers mention also his stay at the court of the Elector of Bavaria in Munich about 1680, but there is no documentary evidence of this stay. Equally unfounded is the story that while he was in Naples, a mediocre violinist, Giuseppe Valentini, won the favor of the Roman public so that Corelli returned to Rome a broken man and died shortly afterward. Quite contrary to these fanciful legends, Corelli enjoyed respect, security, and fame. In Rome he had a powerful protector in Cardinal Benedetto Pamphili; later he lived in the palace of Cardinal Pietro Ottoboni, conducting weekly concerts which were attended by the elite of Roman society. One of Corelli's admirers was Queen Christina of Sweden, who lived in Rome at the time. Among his pupils were Baptiste Anet, Geminiani, Locatelli, and Giovanni Somis. Corelli was famous as a virtuoso on the violin and may be regarded as the founder of modern violin technique; he systematized the art of proper bowing, and was one of the 1st to use double stops and chords on the violin. His role in music history is very great despite the fact that he wrote but few works; only 6 opus numbers can be definitely attributed to him. His greatest achievement was the creation of the concerto grosso. Handel, who as a young man met Corelli in Rome, was undoubtedly influenced by Corelli's instrumental writing. Corelli was buried in the Pantheon in Rome.

WORKS: 12 sonate a 3, 2 violini e violone o arcileuto col basso per l'organo, op. 1 (Rome, 1681; dedicated to Queen Christina of Sweden); 12 sonate da camera a 3, 2 violini e violone o cembalo, op. 2 (Rome, 1685); 12 sonate a 3, 2 violini e violone o arcileuto, col basso per l'organo, op. 3 (Rome, 1689); 12 sonate a 3, op. 4 (Rome, 1694; in Amsterdam as Balleti da camera); 12 sonate a violino e violone o cembalo, op. 5 (Rome, 1700; later arranged by Geminiani as Concerti grossi; the 12th sonata of op. 5 is La Follia, the celebrated set of variations for Violin); Concerti grossi con 2 violini e violoncello di concertino obbligati, e 2 altri violini, viola, e basso di concerto grosso ad arbitrio che si potranno raddoppiare, op. 6 (Amsterdam, 1714). All these were variously reprinted at the time; an important ed. is by Pepusch (London, opp. 1–4 and 6); Joachim and Chrysander issued the "complete works" in 1888–91 (London; opp. 1–6); a new critical ed. has been started at the Musikwissenschaftliches Institut der Universität Basel (1976–   ).

BIBL.: C. Piancastelli, In onore di C. (Bologna, 1914); F. Arnold, "A C. Forgery" (about a forged Antwerp ed. of 1693), Proceedings of the Musical Association (1921); A. Cametti, "C. à Saint-Louis des Français à Rome," Revue Musicale (Jan. 1922); F. Vatielli, "Il C. e i maestri bolognesi del suo tempo," Arte e Vita Musicale a Bologna (1927); A. Toni, "A. C., cenni biografici," Bolletino Bibliografico Musicale (1927); M. Pincherle, C. (Paris, 1933; rev. ed., 1954; Eng. tr., N.Y., 1956); C. Sartori, "Le 44 edizioni italiane delle sei opere di C.," Rivista Musicale Italiana (Jan.–March 1953); M. Rinaldi, A. C. (Milan, 1953); D. Boyden, "The C. 'Solo' Sonatas and Their Ornamental Additions . . . ," Musica Antiqua, III (Bydgoszcz, 1972); D. Libby, "Interrelationships in C.," Journal of the American Musicological Society (Summer 1973).

Corelli, Franco (Dario), outstanding Italian tenor; b. Ancona, April 8, 1921. He studied naval engineering at the Univ. of Bologna; in 1947 entered the Pesaro Cons. to study voice; dissatisfied with the academic training, he left the Cons. and proceeded to learn the repertoire by listening to recordings of great singers. He made his operatic debut at the Spoleto Festival in 1952 as Don José in Carmen; then sang at the Rome Opera in 1953 and at La Scala, Milan, in 1954; he appeared at London's Covent Garden in 1957. On Jan. 27, 1961, he made his Metropolitan Opera debut in N.Y. as Manrico in Il Trovatore; from that time he appeared with most of the major opera houses of the world. Among his finest roles were Radames, Ernani, and Don Alvaro.

Corena, Fernando, Swiss bass; b. Geneva, Dec. 22, 1916; d. Lugano, Nov. 26, 1984. He studied in Geneva and with Enrico Romani in Milan; after making his operatic debut in 1937, he sang with the radio and municipal theater in Zürich. He 1st gained wide notice as Varlaam in Boris Godunov in Trieste in 1947, and subsequently was invited to sing with major opera houses in Europe and the U.S.; he made his Metropolitan Opera debut in N.Y. as Leporello in Don Giovanni (Feb. 6, 1954). He 1st appeared at London's Covent Garden on May 16, 1960, as Dr. Bartolo in Il Barbiere di Siviglia. He was particularly known for his buffo roles. Among his other roles were Don Pasquale, Dulcamare in L'elisir d'amore, Alfonso in Così fan tutte, Osmin in Die Entführung aus dem Serail, and Gianni Schicchi.

Coria, Miguel Angel, Spanish composer; b. Madrid, Oct. 24, 1937. He studied at the Cons. of Madrid, and later took a course in electronic music in Utrecht, the Netherlands. Returning to Spain, he organized the ultramodern studio Alea, promoting aleatory and electronic music.

WORKS: Imágenes for Flute, Oboe, Vibraphone, Violin, and Viola (1963); Vértices for Small Ensemble (1964); Volúmenes for Small Ensemble (1967); Joyce's Portrait for Chamber Orch. (1968); several pieces for Small Ensemble under the generic name Lúdica.

Corigliano, John, American violinist, father of **John (Paul) Corigliano;** b. N.Y., Aug. 28, 1901; d. Norfolk, Conn., Sept. 1, 1975. He studied with Leopold Auer in N.Y.; gave violin recitals; in 1935 he was appointed assistant concertmaster of the N.Y. Phil., and in 1943 concertmaster; he resigned his position in 1966; subsequently served as concertmaster of the San Antonio Sym.

Corigliano, John (Paul), American composer, son of **John Corigliano;** b. N.Y., Feb. 16, 1938. He studied at Columbia Univ. with Otto Luening (B.A., 1959), with Vittorio Giannini at the Manhattan School of Music, and privately with Paul Creston. He was subsequently employed at the radio stations WBAI and WQXR in N.Y. and as assistant director for CBS-TV (1961–72). He held a Guggenheim fellowship in 1968–69. In 1971 he joined the faculty of the Manhattan School of Music, and from 1973 taught at Lehman College. From 1987 to 1990 he was composer-in-residence of the Chicago Sym. Orch. His style of composition shows a fine capacity for lyrical expression, and an incisive sense of rhythm, in the generic tradition of Béla Bartók and Prokofiev. Despite the dissonant freedom of his polyphonic writing, his music retains a firm tonal anchorage.

WORKS: THEATER: The Naked Carmen, mixed-media opera (1970); A Figaro for Antonio, grand opera buffa (1986); incidental music for plays; film scores. **ORCH.:** Elegy (1965; San Francisco, June 1, 1966); Tournaments Overture (1966; Louisville, Jan. 11, 1980); Piano Concerto (San Antonio, April 7, 1968); Gazebo Dances for Band (1973; Evansville, Ind., May 6, 1973; also for Orch., 1974; Woodbury, N.J., Feb. 20, 1981); Aria for Oboe and Strings (1975; 4th movement of the Oboe Concerto, 1975); Oboe Concerto (N.Y., Nov. 9, 1975); Voyage for String Orch. (1976; Rockland County, N.Y., April 22, 1977; also for Flute and String Orch., London, Nov. 26, 1983, and for Flute and String Quintet, 1988); Clarinet Concerto (N.Y., Dec. 6, 1977); Pied Piper Fantasy, concerto for Flute and Orch. (1981; Los Angeles, Feb. 4, 1982); Promenade Overture (Boston, July 10, 1981); 3 Hallucinations (1981; Syracuse, N.Y., Jan. 22, 1982); Summer Fanfare (Miami, June 21, 1982); Fantasia on an Ostinato (N.Y., Sept. 18, 1986); Campagne di Ravello (Chicago, Oct. 9, 1987); Sym. No. 1 (1989; Chicago, March 15, 1990). **CHAMBER:** Kaleidoscope for 2 Pianos (1959; Spoleto, June 28, 1961); Sonata for Violin and Piano (1963; Spoleto, July 10, 1964); Scherzo for Oboe and Percussion (1975). **VOCAL:** Fern Hill for Mezzo-soprano, Chorus, and Orch. (1961; Washington, D.C., Dec. 11, 1965; also for String Orch., N.Y., Dec. 19, 1961); What I Expected Was . . . for Chorus, Brass, and Percussion (Tanglewood, Aug. 16, 1962); Poem in October for

Tenor and 8 Instruments (N.Y., Oct. 25, 1970; also for Tenor and Orch., Washington, D.C., April 24, 1976); *Creations* for Narrator and Orch. (1972; rev. 1984; Milwaukee, Oct. 3, 1984); *Poem on His Birthday* for Baritone, Chorus, and Orch. (Washington, D.C., April 24, 1976; also for Baritone, Chorus, and Piano); the 3 preceding works constitute *A Dylan Thomas Trilogy*, choral sym. for Chorus, Soloists, and Orch. (1st complete perf., Washington, D.C., April 24, 1976); also choruses; solo piano works; songs.

Cornelis, Evert, Dutch conductor; b. Amsterdam, Dec. 5, 1884; d. Bilthoven, Nov. 23, 1931. He was a pupil of de Pauw at the Amsterdam Cons.; in 1904, won the organ prize. He was conductor at the Amsterdam Opera (1908); assistant conductor of the Concertgebouw Orch. (1910–19); from 1922 conductor of the orch. at Utrecht and later choral director at Rotterdam; conductor of the Netherlands Bach Soc. (1927). He toured Europe, the Dutch East Indies, Australia, etc., as a guest conductor. He pioneered extensively for modern music.
    BIBL.: C. Cornelius, *P. C.* (1925).

Cornelius, Peter, important German composer and writer; b. Mainz, Dec. 24, 1824; d. there, Oct. 26, 1874. A nephew of the painter Peter von Cornelius, he at first became an actor, but after an unsuccessful debut, changed his mind; he studied theory with Dehn at Berlin (1845–52) and then joined Liszt's following in Weimar as a champion of Wagner, contributing frequent articles to the *Neue Zeitschrift für Musik*. His masterpiece, the opera *Der Barbier von Bagdad*, was produced at Weimar (Dec. 15, 1858) under the direction of Liszt, who resigned his position there because of hostile demonstrations while he was conducting the opera. In 1861 Cornelius went to Wagner at Vienna, and followed him to Munich (1865), where he was appointed reader to King Ludwig II, and prof. of harmony and rhetoric at the Royal Music School. A 2nd opera, *Der Cid*, was produced at Weimar on May 21, 1865; a 3rd, *Gunlöd* (from the Edda), remained unfinished (completed by Lassen and produced at Weimar, May 6, 1891). *Der Barbier von Bagdad* was revived at Karlsruhe on Feb. 1, 1884, in a drastically altered version by F. Mottl. Cornelius publ. *Lieder-Cyclus* (op. 3); duets for Soprano and Baritone (op. 6); *Weihnachtslieder* (op. 8); *Trauerchöre* for Male Chorus (op. 9). A vol. of *Lyrische Poesien* was issued in 1861. A complete ed. of Cornelius's works was issued by Breitkopf & Härtel (1905–6).
    BIBL.: A Sandberger, *Leben und Werke des Dichtermusikers P. C.* (Leipzig, 1887); E. Istel, *P. C.* (Leipzig, 1904); E. Sulger-Gebing, *P. C. als Mensch und Dichter* (Munich, 1908); M. Hasse, *Der Dichtermusiker P. C.* (2 vols., Leipzig, 1923); C. Cornelius, *P. C., der Wort-und Tondichter* (2 vols., Regensburg, 1925); E. Istel, "*P. C.,*" *Musical Quarterly* (July 1934); P. Egert, *P. C.* (Berlin, 1940).

Cornelius, Peter (real name, **Lauritz Peter Corneliys Petersen**), esteemed Danish tenor; b. Labjerggaard, Jan. 4, 1865; d. Snekkersten, near Copenhagen, Dec. 30, 1934. He studied with Nyrop in Copenhagen, making his operatic debut there in the baritone role of Escamillo (1892). After further appearances as a baritone, he then studied with Lieban, Revilliers, and Spiro in Berlin and made his tenor debut as the Steersman in *Der fliegende Holländer* in Copenhagen (1899), where he was subsequently a principal member of the Royal Danish Theater until 1922. He also sang at the Bayreuth Festival in 1906 and at London's Covent Garden (1907–14); made guest appearances in Paris, Stockholm, and Oslo. Although he returned briefly to the stage in 1927, his later years were devoted mainly to teaching. He was particularly known for his Wagnerian roles, which included Tannhäuser, Siegfried, Lohengrin, Siegmund, and Tristan.

Corner, Philip (Lionel), American composer, performer, and teacher; b. N.Y., April 10, 1933. He studied with Mark Brunswick at the City College of N.Y. (B.A., 1955), then pursued training in musical philosophy with Messiaen at the Paris Cons. (2nd prix, 1957), composition with Otto Luening and

Henry Cowell at Columbia Univ. (M.A., 1959), and piano with Dorothy Taubman (1961–75). While serving in the U.S. Army in South Korea (1959–60), he became immersed in Asian music; upon his discharge, he was active with various avant-garde groups in N.Y., and taught at Rutgers Univ. (from 1972). One of the earliest minimalists, he has extended his compositional horizon to include Western and non-Western forms of expression, carefully recorded in his own graphic notation. He publ. *I Can Walk through the World as Music* (1980).
    WORKS: ORCH.: *This Is It . . . This Time* (1959). **INSTRUMENTAL:** *Sang-teh* (1959); *Air Effect* (1961); *Certain Distilling Processes* (1962); *Pond* (1968); *OM Emerging* (1970); *OM series* (1970–74); *Elementals* (1976). **GAMELAN** (works in open score): *Gamelan* (1975); *Gamelan II* (1975); *Gamelan IX* (1975); *The Barcelona Cathedral* (1978); *Gamelan P. C.* (1979); *Gamelan LY* for Gamelan Ensemble, Erhu, and Clarinet (1979); *Gamelan IRIS* for Gamelan Ensemble and Flute (1980); *Gamelan CONCERT!O* for Gamelan Ensemble, Harpsichord, and Electric Guitar (1980); theater pieces; electronic works; piano music.

Coronaro, Gellio (Benvenuto), Italian pianist and composer; b. Vicenza, Nov. 30, 1863; d. Milan, July 26, 1916. He was 8 years old when he made his debut as a pianist; at 13, was theater conductor at Marosteca, and chorus master at 15; in 1882 he entered the Liceo Rossini at Bologna, where his teachers were Busi, Parisini, and Mancinelli; he graduated in 1883, winning the 1st prize with a 1-act opera, *Jolanda*, which was produced at the Milan Cons. (1883). Other works: 1-act dramatic sketch, *Festa a Marina* (took 1st Sonzogno Prize in 1892); operetta, *Minestrone napoletano* (Messina, 1893); operas: *Claudia* (Milan, 1895); *Turiddu* (Vicenza, Nov. 30, 1905); *Bertoldo* (Milan, 1910); he also wrote 2 masses, a String Quartet, songs, piano pieces, etc.

Correa de Arauxo, Francisco, important Spanish organist; b. Seville, c.1576; d. Segovia, Oct. 31, 1654. He held the post of organist at the Church of San Salvador in Seville (1599–1636), at the Cathedral of Jaen (1636–40), and at Segovia (from 1640 until his death). His *Facultad orgánica* (orig. publ. in Alcalá de Henares, 1626) contains 70 pieces for organ in tablature (most of them his own compositions), reproduced in the series Monumentos de la Música Española, ed. by S. Kastner (Madrid, 1950).
    BIBL.: C. Jacobs, *F. C.d.A.* (The Hague, 1973); J. Ayarra Jarne, *F. C.d.A., organista sevillano del siglo XVII* (Seville, 1986).

Correa de Azevedo, Luis Heitor, Brazilian musicologist; b. Rio de Janeiro, Dec. 13, 1905. He studied at the Instituto Nacional de Música in Rio de Janeiro; in 1932 was appointed librarian there; in 1939 became prof. of national folklore; in 1943 organized the Centro de Pesquisas Folklóricas at the Escuela Nacional de Música. He publ. numerous valuable studies on Brazilian music: *Escala, ritmo e melodia na música dos Indios brasileiros* (Rio de Janeiro, 1938); *Relação das operas de autores brasileiros* (Rio de Janeiro, 1938); *A música brasileira e seus fundamentos* (Washington, D.C., 1948); *Música e músicos do Brasil* (Rio de Janeiro, 1950); *150 años de música no Brasil* (Rio de Janeiro, 1956); *La Musique en Amérique latine* (Paris, 1957); several informative articles in Brazilian, French, and American magazines. From 1947 to 1965 he was in charge of the music division of UNESCO in Paris.

Corrette, Michel, French organist, composer, and writer on music; b. Rouen, 1709; d. Paris, Jan. 22, 1795. He was the son of the organist Gaspard Corrette. He was active in Paris as an organist in several churches and also in the service of several patrons of music. He was a prolific composer, producing concertos for harpsichord, organ, flute, and hurdy-gurdy, sonatas, organ works, and a large output of sacred music. He also prepared 17 methods on performing practice, 6 of which are lost.
    BIBL.: H. Eliza, *The Organ Masses, Hymns, and Magnificats of Gaspard and M. C.* (diss., Indiana Univ., 1967).

Corri, Domenico, Italian composer; b. Rome, Oct. 4, 1744; d. London, May 22, 1825. He was a pupil of Porpora in Naples;

in 1771 went to Edinburgh as an opera conductor. His attempt to organize his own opera company and a publishing firm there was a failure, and he sought better fortune in London (1790). There he engaged in various enterprises as a publisher, composer, and impresario. His opera, *The Travelers, or Music's Fascination,* was given at Drury Lane on Jan. 22, 1806, with little success. He publ. 4 music manuals in Eng.: *A Complete Musical Grammar* (1787); *A Musical Dictionary* (1798); *The Art of Fingering* (1799); and *The Singer's Preceptor* (1810). His daughter, **Sophia Giustina Corri Dussek** (b. Edinburgh, May 1, 1775; d. after 1828), a talented pianist and singer, married Dussek; his sons, **Montague Corri** (1784–1849) and **Haydn Corri** (1785–1860), were also musicians.

BIBL.: P. Revitt, "D. C.'s 'New System' for Reading Thorough-Bass," *Journal of the American Musicological Society* (Spring 1968).

Corselli (real name, **Courcelle**), **Francesco,** Italian composer; b. Piacenza, c.1702; d. Madrid, April 3, 1778. He became an accomplished tenor, violinist, and harpsichordist; he then went to Parma, where he was made maestro di cappella at the Steccata Church (1727), a position that extended to include the period of rule by the Duke of Parma (1727–33). He was then called to Madrid (1734), where he was appointed suffragan royal maestro de capilla and music teacher to the royal children. In 1737 he was named coadjutor of the royal chapel, serving as its titular maestro from 1738; he also was rector of the choir school.

WORKS: OPERAS (all 1st perf. in Madrid unless otherwise given): *Venere placata* (Venice, 1731); *Nino* (Venice, Carnival 1732); *La Cautela en la amistad y el robo de las Sabinas* (1735); *Alessandro nelle Indie* (May 9, 1738); *Farnace* (Nov. 4, 1739); *Achille in Sciro* (Dec. 8, 1744); *La clemenca de Tito* (Carnival 1747; Act 1 by Corselli, Act 2 by F. Corradini, and Act 3 by G.B. Mele); *El Polifemo* (Carnival 1748; Act 1 by Corselli, Act 2 by Corradini, and Act 3 by Mele); also much sacred music.

BIBL.: N. Solar-Quintes, "El compositor Francisco Courcelle: Nueva documentación para su biografia," *Anuario musical,* VI (1951).

Corsi (Corso), Giuseppe (called **Celano** after his birthplace), Italian composer; b. Celano, May 1630; d. Dec. 1690. He studied with Carissimi; served as maestro di cappella at S. Maria Maggiore in Rome (1659–61); at the Lateran Palace chapel (1661–65); at S. Casa di Loreto (1668–75); then returned to Rome, but because of his dissemination of books placed on the Church Index, was persecuted and forced to leave (1678); from 1681 to 1688 he was at the court of the Duke of Parma. Among his pupils were Jacopo Perti (at Parma) and Petronio Franceschini. He publ. *Motetti a 2, 3 e 4 voci* (Rome, 1667), *Miserere a 5,* and *Motetti a 9;* various other works in MS. Several of his works appeared in collections of the time. He is mentioned in Giuseppe Pitoni's *Guida armonica.*

Corsi, Jacopo, Italian nobleman and patron of art; b. Florence, July 17, 1560; d. there, Dec. 29, 1602. In his palace, as in Bardi's, were held the memorable meetings of the "Camerata" in which Peri, Caccini, Emilio del Cavaliere, Galilei, the poet Rinuccini, and others took part, leading to the creation of the earliest operas. Corsi was a good musician, a skillful player on the harpsichord, and a composer; he wrote the concluding 2 numbers of the 1st opera by Peri, *Dafne,* which was performed at his home in 1598; these settings are preserved in the library of the Brussels Cons.; they were publ. in Solerti's *Albori del Melodramma* (Milan, 1905).

BIBL.: W. Porter, "Peri and C.'s *Dafne:* Some New Discoveries and Observations," *Journal of the American Musicological Society,* XVIII (1965).

Corso, Giuseppe. See **Corsi, Giuseppe.**

Corte, Andrea della. See **Della Corte, Andrea.**

Corteccia, Francesco Bernardo (baptized **Pier Francesco**), Italian composer and organist; b. Florence, July 27, 1502; d. there, June 27, 1571. He studied music with Bernardo Pi-

sano; was a choirboy at S. Giovanni Battista in Florence; later prepared for the priesthood, and was chaplain at S. Giovanni from 1527 to 1531; in 1531–32 was organist at S. Lorenzo, then at S. Giovanni (1535–39); was maestro di cappella there and at the Florence Cathedral from 1540 until his death. He wrote musical intermezzi for various stage works, including *Il furto* by Francesco d'Ambra (1544); wedding music (for Duke Cosimo the Great); 9 pieces *a* 4, 6, and 8 (Venice, 1539); 3 books of madrigals (1544, 1547, 1547); *Responsoria et lectiones* (1570); 32 hymns *a* 4; *Canticorum liber primus* (1571); many others. Modern eds. of his works include *Francesco Corteccia: Hinnario secondo l'uso della chiesa romana e fiorentina,* ed. by G. Haydon (Cincinnati, 1958 and 1960); A.C. Minor and B. Mitchell, eds., *A Renaissance Entertainment: Festivities for the Marriage of Cosimo I, Duke of Florence, in 1539* (Columbia, Mo., 1968); *Francesco Corteccia: Eleven Works to Latin Texts,* ed. by A. McKinley in Recent Researches in the Music of the Renaissance, XXVI (1969).

Cortés, Ramiro, American composer of Mexican extraction; b. Dallas, Nov. 25, 1933; d. Salt Lake City, July 2, 1984. He studied with Henry Cowell in N.Y. and at the Univ. of Southern Calif. with Halsey Stevens and Ingolf Dahl. From 1956 to 1958 he was in Rome on a Fulbright fellowship; there he studied with Petrassi. Returning to America in 1958, he had sessions with Roger Sessions at Princeton Univ. He taught at the Univ. of Calif. in Los Angeles (1966–67), the Univ. of Southern Calif. in Los Angeles (1967–72), and the Univ. of Utah (1972–84).

WORKS: *Elegy* for Flute and Piano (1952); Divertimento for Flute, Clarinet, and Bassoon (1953); Piano Quintet (1953); Piano Sonata (1954; awarded Steinway Centennial prize); *Sinfonia sacra* for Orch. (1954; received George Gershwin Memorial Award; N.Y. Phil., April 9, 1955; rev. 1959); *Night Music* for Chamber Orch. (1954; received 1st prize of Broadcast Music Incorporated Awards); *Yerma,* symphonic portrait after a play by García Lorca (1955); *Xochitl* for Orch. (1955; Hollywood, April 22, 1956); Chamber Concerto for Cello Solo and 12 Wind Instruments (1958; 1st prize of BMI Awards); Sym. (1953–58); *Sinfonia breve* (1955–58); String Quartet (1958); Piano Trio (1959); *Prometheus,* opera in 1 act (1960); *The Eternal Return* for Orch. (1963; rev. 1965); Violin Concerto (1965); Wind Quintet (1967–68); *Homage to Jackson Pollock* for Solo Viola (1968); *Charenton,* suite for Chamber Orch. (1968–71); *Movements in Variation* for Orch. (1972); *Bridges* for Wind Ensemble (1982); choruses; songs.

Cortese, Luigi, Italian pianist and composer; b. Genoa, Nov. 19, 1899; d. there, June 10, 1976. He studied music with Mario Ferrari in Genoa, with Casella in Rome, and with Gédalge in Paris. From 1951 to 1964 he served as director of the Istituto Musicale in Genoa. He was a prolific composer, and was also active as a music critic. He publ. the monographs *Alfredo Casella* (Genoa, 1935), *Il Bolero di Ravel* (1944), and *Chopin* (1949).

WORKS: STAGE: 3 operas: *Prometeo* (1941–47; Bergamo, Sept. 22, 1951), *La notte veneziana* (1953–55; Turin Radio, 1955), and *Le notte bianche* (1970); oratorio, *David* (1938; Genoa, Feb. 20, 1941). ORCH.: *Prelude and Fugue* (1940); *Canto notturno* (1940); *4 odes de Ronsard* for Voice and Orch. (1948–57; Naples, Aug. 4, 1961); Sym. (1953–56); Violin Concerto (1961); *Fantasia* (1964); *Sinfonia Sacra,* subtitled *Inclina, Domine, aurem tuam,* for Chorus and Orch. (1967; Turin, April 24, 1969); 3 *Salmi* for Soprano and Orch. (1975). CHAMBER: Violin Sonatina (1935); *Salmo VIII* for Female Voice, Flute, and Piano (1943); Horn Sonata (1955); Cello Sonata (1960); *Improvviso* for Viola and Piano (1966); *Invenzione* for 2 Flutes (1973); numerous piano pieces and songs.

Cortesi, Francesco, Italian composer; b. Florence, Sept. 11, 1826; d. there, Jan. 3, 1904. He studied at Bologna under Rossini and others; became a conductor and a composer of many light stage works; settled in Florence about 1880 as a singing master and was appointed head of the vocal dept. in the government music school. Many celebrated singers were his pupils.

Works: Operas: *Il Trovatore* (Trieste, 1852; in Florence as *La Schiava*); *Almina* (Rome, 1859); *La Dama a servire* (Ancona, 1859); *La colpa del cuore* (Florence, 1870); *Mariulizza* (Florence, 1874); *L'Amico di casa* (Florence, 1881).

Cortis, Antonio, Spanish tenor; b. on a ship between Oran and Altea, Aug. 12, 1891; d. Valencia, April 2, 1952. He went to Madrid, where he sang in the children's chorus (1901–5) and the adult chorus (from 1911) at the Teatro Real; he was soon singing operatic roles in Barcelona and Valencia. During the 1910s and 1920s, he made appearances in South America and Italy, and was a member of the Chicago Opera (1924–32) and the San Francisco Opera (1925–26). In 1931 he sang at London's Covent Garden, and from 1935 pursued his career in Spain; he made his farewell appearance as Cavaradossi in Saragossa (1951). Held in high esteem in his homeland, he became known as the Spanish Caruso. Among his most prominent roles were Radames, Canio, Don José, Edgardo, and Andrea Chénier.

Cortolezis, Fritz, German composer and conductor; b. Passau, Feb. 21, 1878; d. Bad Aibling, Bavaria, March 13, 1934. He studied in Munich with H. Bussmeyer (piano) and with L. Thuille (composition) from 1899 to 1902; was répétiteur at the opera in Schwerin (1903), chorus master at the National Theater in Berlin (1904), 1st conductor in Regensburg (1905) and in Nuremberg (1906); upon Mottl's recommendation he was appointed conductor of the Court Opera in Munich; was engaged by Beecham in 1911 for the Wagner and Strauss performances in London; in 1912 was 1st conductor at the Kurfürstenoper in Berlin, then in Karlsruhe (1913–24) and at the Breslau Opera (1925–28).

Works: Operas: *Rosemarie* (Bremen, 1919); *Das verfemte Lachen* (Rostock, Jan. 28, 1924); *Der verlorene Gulden* (Breslau, March 1, 1928).

Cortot, Alfred (Denis), famous French pianist; b. Nyon, Switzerland (of a French father and a Swiss mother), Sept. 26, 1877; d. Lausanne, June 15, 1962. He was a pupil at the Paris Cons., and studied with Decambes, Rouquou, and Diémer; he won the 1st prize for piano in 1896; the same year he made his debut in Paris, playing Beethoven's C-minor Concerto at one of the Colonne concerts, and won signal success; he went to Bayreuth (1898) and studied Wagner's works with J. Kniese, and acted as répétiteur at the festivals from 1898 to 1901. Returning to Paris, he began a most active propaganda for the works of Wagner; on May 17, 1902, he conducted the French premiere of *Götterdämmerung* at the Théâtre du Château d'Eau, and in the same year established the Association des Concerts A. Cortot, which he directed for 2 years, educating the public to an appreciation of Wagner; in 1904 he became conductor of the orch. concerts of the Société Nationale and of the Concerts Populaires at Lille (till 1908). In 1905, together with Jacques Thibaud (violin) and Pablo Casals (cello), he formed a trio, which soon gained a great European reputation. He founded, with A. Mangeot, the École Normale de Musique (1919), and became its director, also giving a summer course in piano interpretation there annually; gave many lecture recitals and appeared as a guest conductor with various orchs.

Writings: *Principes rationnels de la technique pianistique* (French and Eng., Paris, 1928; American ed., Boston, 1930); *La Musique française de piano* (vol. I, 1930; Eng. tr., London, 1932; vol. II, 1932); *Cours d'interprétation* (vol. I, Paris, 1934; Eng. tr., London, 1937); *Aspects de Chopin* (Paris, 1949; Eng. tr., *In Search of Chopin*, London, 1951).

Bibl.: B. Gavoty, *A. C.* (Paris, 1977).

Cosma, Viorel, Rumanian musicologist; b. Timişoara, March 30, 1923. He studied composition with Mihail Jora, Ion Dumitrescu, Paul Constantinescu, Theodor Rogalski; musicology with Zeno Vancea. He was active as a choral conductor; joined the faculty at the Bucharest Cons. in 1951; then devoted himself mainly to music criticism; publ. several valuable monographs on Rumanian musicians (Ciprian Porumbescu, Ion Ivanovici, and others). He compiled a uniquely useful biographical dictionary of Rumanian composers and musicologists, *Muzicieni Români* (Bucharest, 1965; rev. and augmented ed., 1970); he also edited *Interpreti romani lexicon*, a dictionary of performing Rumanian musicians (Bucharest, 1977).

Cossa, Dominic, American baritone and teacher; b. Jessup, Pa., May 13, 1935. He studied with Anthony Marlowe and Robert Weede; made his debut at the N.Y. City Opera in 1961; then made appearances in Europe; in 1967 he sang at the San Francisco Opera; made his Metropolitan Opera debut in N.Y. on Jan. 30, 1970, as Silvio in *Pagliacci*, remaining on its roster until 1976. Among his best roles were Germont, Zurga, Rigoletto, and Dr. Malatesta.

Cossetto, Emil, Croatian composer; b. Trieste, Oct. 12, 1918. He studied in Zagreb. His compositions, based mostly on patriotic themes, include *Borbena kantata* (Cantata of the Struggle; 1947), inspired by the wartime resistance in Yugoslavia; *Zagreb kantata* (Zagreb, May 7, 1950); *Konjanik,* a "cavalcade" for Men's Voices and Orch. (Zagreb, Dec. 9, 1957); numerous choruses.

Cossmann, Bernhard, German cellist; b. Dessau, May 17, 1822; d. Frankfurt, May 7, 1910. He was a pupil of Espenhahn and Drechsler; also of Theodor Müller and Kummer (in Dresden); was a member of the Italian Opera Orch. in Paris (1840); London (1841); Opéra-Comique, Paris (till 1846); was a member of the Gewandhaus Orch. in Leipzig (1847–48), as solo cellist, also studying composition under Hauptmann; at Weimar with Liszt (in 1850); was a prof. at the Moscow Cons. (1866–70); lived at Baden-Baden (1870–78); thereafter, was a prof. of cello at the Frankfurt Cons.

Cossotto, Fiorenza, Italian contralto; b. Crescentino, Vercelli, near Turin, April 22, 1935. She studied at the Turin Cons.; sang at La Scala in Milan as a student; made her formal debut there as Sister Mathilde in *Les Dialogues des Carmélites* (Jan. 26, 1957); also sang at the Vienna State Opera, at Covent Garden in London, in Paris, in South America, and in Russia. She made her American debut in 1964 at the Lyric Opera in Chicago; was soloist in Verdi's *Requiem* in N.Y. with the orch. of the Teatro alla Scala during its American visit in 1967. On Feb. 6, 1968, she sang Amneris at her Metropolitan Opera debut in N.Y. Among her most successful roles was that of Santuzza in *Cavalleria rusticana*. She is married to the Italian bass Ivo Vinco.

Cossutta, Carlo, Italian tenor; b. Trieste, May 8, 1932. He was taken to Argentina while young; received his musical training there. He sang at the Teatro Colón in Buenos Aires in 1958; in 1964 appeared at Covent Garden, London. On Feb. 17, 1973, he made his Metropolitan Opera debut in N.Y. as Pollione in *Norma*. He also sang with the Chicago Lyric Opera, the Paris Opéra, and the Vienna State Opera. He distinguished himself in dramatic roles.

Costa, Don, American conductor and film composer; b. Boston, June 10, 1925; d. N.Y., Jan. 19, 1983. He moved to California early in his career and became active as a composer for films and television, as well as a conductor of theater music. His movie scores included *Rough Night in Jericho, Madigan,* and *The Impossible Years*. He also put out, with his 10-year-old daughter, Nikka, an album, *Out Here on My Own*, which sold into the millions of copies.

Costa, Mary, American soprano; b. Knoxville, Tenn., April 5, 1932. She received her primary musical training in Los Angeles; sang at the Hollywood Bowl and with the San Francisco Opera. On Jan. 6, 1964, she made her debut at the Metropolitan Opera in N.Y. as Violetta in *La Traviata;* in 1970 she sang opera at the Bolshoi Theater in Moscow. She also made many concert appearances. In 1972 she starred in the film *The Great Waltz*. In 1978 she founded the Knoxville (Tenn.) Opera Co. In 1979 the Mary Costa Scholarship was established at the Univ. of Tennessee.

Costa, Sir Michael (Andrew Agnus) (Michele Andrea Agniello), eminent Italian-born conductor of Spanish descent; b. Naples, Feb. 4, 1806; d. Hove, England, April 29, 1884. He studied with his maternal grandfather, **Giacomo Tritto;** with his father, Pasquale Costa (a composer of church music); and with Giovanni Furno. He then studied at the Naples Cons. with Crescentini (singing) and Zingarelli (composition). His operas *Il sospetto funesto* (Naples, 1826), *Il delitto punito* (1827), *Il carcere d'Ildegonda* (Naples, 1828), and *Malvina* (Naples, 1829) were well received; when Zingarelli was commissioned to write a Psalm (*Super Flumina Babilonis*) for the Music Festival at Birmingham, England, he sent Costa to conduct it. When Costa arrived in Birmingham, the directors of the Festival refused to accept him as a conductor owing to his extreme youth, but offered to pay him a similar fee for performance as tenor in Zingarelli's Psalm and in other works. He was compelled to accept, but his debut as a singer was disastrous. Despite this setback, he decided to remain in England, a decision in which he was encouraged by Clementi, who was impressed by Costa's scoring of a Bellini aria. In 1830 Costa was engaged as maestro al cembalo at the King's Theatre in London; in 1832 he became music director; and in 1833, director and conductor. During this time he produced 3 of his ballets, *Kenilworth* (1831), *Une Heure à Naples* (1832), and *Sir Huon* (1833, for Taglioni). In 1846 he became conductor of the Phil. and of the Royal Italian Opera; from 1848 to 1882 he conducted the Sacred Harmonic Soc. From 1849 he was the regular conductor of the Birmingham Festivals; from 1847 to 1880, of the Handel Festivals. He was knighted in 1869; was appointed "director of the music, composer, and conductor" at Her Majesty's Opera, Haymarket, in 1871, serving till 1881. He produced 2 operas in London: *Malek Adel* (May 18, 1837; a revision of *Malvina*) and *Don Carlos* (June 20, 1844).

BIBL.: H. Schonberg, *The Great Conductors* (N.Y., 1967).

Costeley, Guillaume, French organist and composer; b. c.1531; d. Évreux, Jan. 28, 1606. Theories that he was an Irishman named Costello who settled in France, or that he was of Scottish extraction, have been discarded. He was court organist to Charles IX of France. In 1570 he became the 1st annually elected "prince" or "maître" of a society organized in honor of St. Cecilia, which, beginning in 1575, awarded a prize each year for a polyphonic composition. Costeley excelled as a composer of polyphonic chansons; his *Musique,* a book of such works for 4–6 voices, appeared in 1570. Modern eds. of some of those for 4 voices are in H. Expert, Maîtres Musiciens de la Renaissance Française (vols. III, XVIII, XIX, 1896–1904); an example for 5 voices is in Cauchie's *Quinze chansons.*

BIBL.: M. Cauchie, "Documents pour servir à une biographie de G. C.," *Revue de Musicologie* (May 1926); I. Godt, *G. C., Life and Works* (diss., N.Y. Univ., 1969).

Costello, Elvis (real name, **Declan McManus**), English rocker and songwriter; b. London, Aug. 25, 1954. He spent his childhood in Liverpool, the city of the Beatles. When he was quite young he managed to get a contract with a company called Stiff Records. His songs were permeated with the feeling of doom, personal as well as universal. A typical title was *Waiting for the End of the World.* Among his 1st hits were *Less than Zero, Watching the Detectives,* and a love ballad, *Alison,* all on his album *My Aim Is True.* His next album, *This Year's Model,* increased his popularity.

Cotapos (Baeza), Acario, Chilean composer; b. Valdivia, April 30, 1889; d. Santiago, Nov. 22, 1969. He studied music in Santiago; in 1916 went to N.Y., where he took lessons with 10 teachers, among them Ernest Bloch. He lived in France until 1934; then went to Spain to work in defense of the Loyalists during the Spanish Civil War; in 1939 he returned to Chile. An experimenter by nature, he adopted an advanced quasi-serial technique of monothematic mottoes of 8 or more notes. He wrote a music drama, *Voces de gesta* (1933); several symphonic preludes; String Quartet; *Sonata fantasia* for Piano (1924); songs; piano pieces.

Čotek, Pavel, Czech composer; b. Fryšava, March 12, 1922. He studied at the Prague Cons. and the Janáček Academy in Brno; then was active as a choirmaster and music critic.

WORKS: *Concertino grosso* for Oboe, Clarinet, Horn, and Strings (1964); *Symphonic Etudes* (1965); Concerto for 2 Solo Percussionists and Orch. (Olomouc, Oct. 22, 1968); *Responsoria* for Organ and Orch. (1969); *3 Romantic Compositions* for Horn and Piano (1954); *Dance Suite* for Wind Quintet (1955); Suite for Violin and Piano (1958); *3 Compositions* for Flute and Piano (1962); Violin Sonata (1962); *Portrait of a Bird,* melodrama for 2 Narrators, Flute, Viola, Bass Clarinet, Celesta, and Harp (1963); *Chamber Music* for String Quartet and Percussion (1963); *5 Short Movements* for Clarinet and Piano (1964–69); *Wind Music* for Piccolo, Trumpet, Bass Trumpet, Bass Trombone, and Piano (1970); *Agoge* for Viola and Piano (1973); choruses; songs.

Cotogni, Antonio, Italian baritone; b. Rome, Aug. 1, 1831; d. there, Oct. 15, 1918. He studied voice with Achille Faldi; made his operatic debut in Rome in 1852 in the role of Belcore in *L'elisir d'amore;* subsequently sang at La Scala in Milan (1860), at Covent Garden in London (1867), and at other European opera houses. He had an enormous repertoire of Italian and French operas. He retired in 1898 and devoted the rest of his life to teaching. Among celebrated singers who were his pupils were Jean de Reszke, Battistini, Lauri-Volpi, Gigli, and Stabile.

Cotrubaş, Ileana, outstanding Rumanian soprano; b. Galaţi, June 9, 1939. After studies at the Scolă Specială de Muzică (1952–57) and with Eugenia Elinescu and Constantin Stroescu at the Bucharest Cons. (1957–63), she made her operatic debut as Yniod in *Pelléas et Mélisande* in Bucharest (1964). She took 1st prize in both the 's-Hertogenbosch (1965) and Munich Radio (1966) competitions, and then completed her studies at the Vienna Academy of Music (1967). She appeared at the Salzburg Festival in 1967, then was a member of the Frankfurt Opera (1968–71). In 1969 she appeared as Mélisande at the Glyndebourne Festival and as Pamina at the Vienna State Opera, where she subsequently appeared regularly; she was made an Austrian Kammersängerin in 1981. In 1973 she made her U.S. debut as Mimi at the Chicago Lyric Opera; she then sang in Paris (1974) and at Milan's La Scala (1975). On March 23, 1977, she made her Metropolitan Opera debut in N.Y. in the role of Mimi. Among her other notable roles are Amina, Susanna, Norina, Adina, Violetta, Gilda, Marguerite, Elisabetta, Antonia, and Micaela.

Cotton, John (or **Johannis Cottonis;** also **Joannes Musica, Johannes filius Dei,** and **Johannes of Afflighem**), early music theorist (11th to 12th century); probable author of the treatise *Epistola ad Fulgentium* (printed by Gerbert in *Scriptores,* vol. II), a valuable work on music describing the modal system of the time and a phase of the development of organum. Six MS copies are preserved: 1 each in Leipzig, Paris, Antwerp, and the Vatican Library, and 2 in Vienna. Various theories have been advanced concerning its authorship. In the copies at Antwerp and Paris the author is referred to as Cotton or Cottonius, while 2 others give the author's name as Joannes Musica. In an anonymous work, *De script. eccles.,* quoted by Gerbert, there is a reference to a certain Joannes, an erudite English musician; the dedication of this vol., "Domino et patri sua venerabili Anglorum antistiti Fulgentio," adds further strength to the contention that the author of the *Epistola* was English. However, J. Smits van Waesberghe identifies him with the Flemish theorist Johannes of Afflighem, author of the treatise *De Musica cum tonario* (reprinted Rome, 1950). Other sources suggest that Cotton is also one Johannes filius Dei.

BIBL.: L. Ellinwood, "J. C. or John of Afflighem?," *Notes* (Sept. 1951); J. Smits van Waesberghe's reply in *Musica Disciplina,* VI (1952); E. Flindell, "Johannis Cottonis, Corrigenda et Addenda," ibid., XXIII (1969).

Cottrau, Teodoro, Italian composer of Neapolitan ballads; b. Naples, Nov. 27, 1827; d. there, March 30, 1879. His father,

Guglielmo Louis Cottrau (b. Paris, Aug. 9, 1797; d. Naples, Oct. 31, 1847), was also a composer of Neapolitan canzonettas (some of them used by Liszt in his piano work *Venezia e Napoli*), as was his brother **Giulio Cottrau** (b. Naples, Oct. 29, 1831; d. Rome, Oct. 25, 1916). Teodoro Cottrau was the composer of the perennial favorite *Santa Lucia* (1850).

Coulthard, Jean, Canadian pianist and composer; b. Vancouver, Feb. 10, 1908. She studied piano with her mother; went to London to study composition with Vaughan Williams (1929–30); had lessons at various times and at various places with Arthur Benjamin (1939), Milhaud (1942), Bartók (1944), Wagenaar (1945, 1949), Nadia Boulanger (1955), and Gordon Jacob (1965–66). In 1947 she joined the staff of the newly created dept. of music at the Univ. of British Columbia; retired in 1973. In her music she rarely strays from conventional usages, but it is not devoid of occasional modernistic whimsicalities.

WORKS: *Canadian Fantasy* for Orch. (1939); *Excursion*, ballet (1940); *Ballade (A Winter's Tale)* for String Orch. (1940); *Song to the Sea*, overture (1942); *Music on a Quiet Song* for Flute and Strings (1946); Sym. No. 1 (1950–51); *Nightwind*, song cycle for Mezzo-soprano, and Orch. or Piano (1951); *Rider on the Sands* for Orch. (1953); *A Prayer for Elizabeth* for Strings (1953); *Music for St. Cecilia* for Strings, Organ, and Tape (1954; rev. 1969); Violin Concerto (1955–59); *The Devil's Fanfare: 4 Bizarre Dances*, ballet for Violin, Piano, and 3 Dancers (1958–60); Fantasie for Piano, Violin, and Chamber Orch. (1960–61); *Musenade* for String Orch. (1961); *The Bird of Dawning Singeth All Night Long* for Violin, 9 Strings, and Harp (1962); Piano Concerto (1963; rev. 1967); *Endymion* for Orch. (1964); *Symphonic Ode* for Cello and Orch. (1965); *This Land*, choral sym., with Tape (1966–67); *Pastorale Cantata* for Narrator, Chorus, Brass Quintet, and Organ (1967); 2 *Visionary Songs* for Soprano, Flute, and Strings (1970); *Kalamalka (Lake of Many Colors)* for Orch. (1974); *Canadian Mosaic* for Orch. (1974); Sym. No. 3 (1975); *Burlesca* for Piano and Orch. (1977); *Symphonic Ode* for Violin and Chamber Orch. (1977); Piano Quintet (1932); 2 violin sonatinas (1945); Cello Sonata (1947); Oboe Sonata (1947); Piano Sonata (1947–48); 3 *Shakespearean Sonnets* for Soprano and String Quintet (1948); 2 string quartets (1948; 1953, rev. 1969); 2 violin sonatas: *Duo Sonata* (1952) and *Correspondence* (1964); Piano Quartet (1957); *Sonata Rhapsody* for Viola and Piano (1962); Divertimento for Wind Quintet and Piano (1968); *The Pines of Emily Carr* for Narrator, Contralto, String Quintet, Piano, and Timpani (1969); 12 *Essays on a Cantabile Theme*, string octet (1972); *The Birds of Lansdowne* for Violin, Cello, Piano, and Bird Songs on Tape (1972); 4 *Prophetic Songs* for Contralto, Flute, Cello, and Piano (1975); piano pieces; songs.

Couperin, renowned family of French musicians. Its musical prominence dates from the 3 sons of **Charles Couperin,** merchant and organist of Chaume, in the dept. of Brie (now part of the dept. of Seine et Marne), and his wife, Marie Andry. The eldest of these, **Louis,** established the family in Paris, where it remained until the extinction of the male line in 1826. He was also the 1st of his name to hold the post of organist at St.-Gervais in Paris. He was followed in this position by his youngest brother, **Charles; François le Grand,** son of Charles, and the family's most illustrious representative; **Nicolas,** son of **François** (called **Sieur de Crouilly**); **Armand-Louis,** son of Nicolas; and by the 2 sons of Armand-Louis, **Pierre-Louis** and **Gervais-François.** The following articles, arranged alphabetically, give the individual histories of the members of the Couperin family:

Couperin, Armand-Louis, organist and composer, son of **Nicolas Couperin;** b. Paris, Feb. 25, 1727; d. there, Feb. 2, 1789. His virtuosity on the organ was extraordinary; in 1748, he succeeded his father as organist at St.-Gervais; was also organist to the King (1770–89), and held appointments at St.-Barthélemy, Ste.-Marguerite, Ste.-Chapelle, St.-Jean-en-Grève, etc. He was one of the 4 organists of Notre-Dame. He died a violent death, having been knocked down by a runaway horse. His compositions include sonatas, a trio, motets, and

other church music. His wife, **Elisabeth-Antoinette** (née **Blanchet;** b. Paris, Jan. 14, 1729), was also a remarkable organist and clavecinist, still playing in public at the age of 81 (in 1810). She was the daughter of Blanchet, the famous clavecin maker, and sister-in-law to **Pascal Joseph Taskin,** the court instrument keeper under Louis XV. D. Fuller ed. *A.-L. Couperin: Selected Works for Keyboard* (Madison, Wis., 1975).

Couperin, Charles, organist; b. Chaumes (baptized), April 9, 1638; d. Paris, between Jan. 15 and Feb. 26, 1679. He succeeded his brother **Louis** as organist at St.-Gervais in 1661. He married Marie Guérin (Feb. 20, 1662), and is principally remembered as being the father of the celebrated **François le Grand.**

BIBL.: C. Bouvet, "Quelques précisions biographiques sur C. Louis Couperin," *Revue de Musicologie* (Paris, 1930).

Couperin, François, Sieur de Crouilly, organist and teacher; b. Chaumes, c.1631; d. Paris, after 1708. He was a pupil of Chambonnières in harmony and clavecin playing; was active as a music teacher and organist. His daughter, **Marguerite Louise** (b. Paris, 1676; d. Versailles, May 30, 1728), was a well-known singer and harpsichordist. She was a fellow member of the Chambre du Roi with her cousin **François le Grand,** who wrote for her the verset *Qui dat nivem* and other pieces.

Couperin, François (surnamed **le Grand** for his superiority in organ playing), the most illustrious member of a distinguished family, and one of the greatest of early French composers, son of **Charles Couperin;** b. Paris, Nov. 10, 1668; d. there, Sept. 11, 1733. He studied with his father; later was a pupil of Jacques-Denis Thomelin, organist of the King's chapel; in 1685 he became organist of St.-Gervais, which post he held until his death; on Dec. 26, 1693, after a successful competition, he succeeded Thomelin as organist of the Chapelle Royale, receiving the title of "organiste du roi"; in 1701 he was appointed "claveciniste de la chambre du roi, et organiste de sa chapelle," and in 1717 he received the title "Ordinaire de la musique de la chambre du roi"; also was made a chevalier of the Order of Latran; he was music master to the Dauphin and other members of the royal family, and ranked high in the favor of Louis XIV, for whom he composed the *Concerts royaux,* which, during 1714–15, were played in Sunday concerts in the royal apartments. He married Marie-Anne Ansault (April 26, 1689), by whom he had 2 daughters: **Marie-Madeleine** (b. Paris, March 9, 1690; d. Montbuisson, April 16, 1742), who became organist of the Abbey of Montbuisson, and **Marguerite-Antoinette** (b. Paris, Sept. 19, 1705; d. there, 1778), who was a talented clavecin player; from 1731 to 1733, she substituted for her father as clavecinist to the King, being the 1st woman to hold this position (cf. C. Bouvet, "Les Deux d'Anglebert et Marguerite-Antoinette Couperin," *Revue de Musicologie,* 1928); there were also 2 sons, **Nicolas-Louis** (b. July 24, 1707), who died young, and **François-Laurent** (b. c.1708). Famed as an organist, Couperin also acquired a high reputation for his remarkable ability as a performer on the clavecin.

WORKS: His compositions may be conveniently divided into 3 categories: those written for the church, those for the King, and those for the general public. More than half of his creative life was taken up with the religious compositions of the 1st 2 periods. These include *Pièces d'orgue consistantes en deux Messes* (1690, a total of 42 pieces), formerly attributed to his uncle François, and, indeed, publ. under the latter's name in vol. 5 of *Archives des maîtres de l'orgue,* ed. by Guilmant, but now established, through the researches of A. Tessier and P. Brunold, as the early work of Couperin le Grand; motets; *Elévations; Leçons de ténèbres;* etc. Couperin's last and most prolific period was concerned exclusively with instrumental works, and in this field he achieved his greatest and most enduring distinction. In 1713, 1716, 1722, and 1730, he publ. the 4 vols. of his *Pièces de clavecin,* consisting of about 230 pieces or 27 "Ordres" or Suites, each suite being a series of dance forms, programmatic in title and content (*La Majes-*

tueuse, La Nanette, Les Petits Moulins à vent, Le Carillon de Cythère, Les Barricades mystérieuses, Les Tic-Toc-Choc ou Les Maillotins, etc.). In 1716 he publ. an expository work pertaining to the execution of his clavecin pieces, L'Art de toucher le clavecin, which attained wide celebrity, and which influenced the keyboard style of Couperin's great contemporary, J.S. Bach. Couperin also introduced the trio sonata to France, his 1st works in this form being an imitation of Corelli. Later, in 1726, he publ. 4 sonatas, Les Nations, described as "Sonades" or "Suites de symphonies en trio," 3 of which are partial reworkings of earlier pieces. They are composed alternately in the strict primitive form, sonata de chiesa, and the more flexible composite of dance forms, sonata de camera. The 3rd of the series, L'Impériale, perhaps represents his most mature and inspired style. Living at a time during which the rivalry between French and Italian music reached its climax, Couperin sought to adapt the new Italian forms to his own personal, and essentially French, style. In his Les Goûts réunis (1724), a series of concerted pieces with strings very similar in form and spirit to the Pièces de clavecin, one finds titles such as Sicilienne and Ritratto dell' amore. In the following year he publ. an Apothéose de Lully, in which the rivals Lully and Corelli are made to unite for the furtherance of art. Couperin's style of composition was based on the basso continuo, the most important voices usually being the uppermost, carrying the melody, and the bass. Nevertheless, his music sometimes attains considerable complexity (on occasion requiring as many as 3 harpsichordists for its proper execution). His melodic invention, particularly in his use of the rondeau, was virtually inexhaustible, his themes swift and expressive. An outstanding feature was his inventive mode of ornamentation, in the "gallant style" of the period. In 1933 the Lyrebird Press in Paris publ. a "complete" ed. of Couperin's works, in 12 vols., under the chief editorship of Maurice Cauchie, assisted by P. Brunold, A. Gastoué, A. Tessier, and A. Schaeffner. The contents are as follows: vol. I, Didactic works: Règle pour l'accompagnement and L'Art de toucher le clavecin; vols. II–V, the 4 books of Pièces de clavecin; vol. VI, Pièces d'orgue consistantes en deux Messes; vols. VII–X, chamber music, including Concerts royaux, Les Goûts réunis ou Nouveaux Concerts à l'usage de toutes les sortes d'instruments de musique, Les Nations, Le Parnasse ou l'Apothéose de Corelli, Apothéose de Lully, Pièces de violes avec la basse chiffrée, and Sonades inédites; vols. XI and XII, secular vocal music and religious music I and II. More recent eds. are in the Le Pupitre series, vols. 8 (Leçons de ténèbres; 1968), 21–24 (Pièces de clavecin, books 1–4; 1969–72), 45 (9 motets; 1972), and 51 (Pièces de violes; 1974); also separate eds. of Pièces de clavecin, edited by M. Cauchie (1968–72) and by K. Gilbert (1969–72).

BIBL.: H. Quittard, Les Couperin (Paris, 1913); C. Bouvet, Une Dynastie de musiciens français: Les Couperin . . . (Paris, 1919); L. de La Laurencie, L'École française de violon de Lully à Viotti (1922–24); J. Llongueras, C. o la Gracia (1925); A. Tessier, C. (Paris, 1926); J. Tiersot, Les Couperin (Paris, 1926); idem, "Two Centuries of a French Musical Family—The Couperins," Musical Quarterly (July 1926); P. Brunold, Le Grand Orgue de St.-Gervais à Paris (Paris, 1934); M. Riemann, Untersuchungen zur Formgeschichte der französischen Klavier-Suite . . . (1940; reprinted Regensburg, 1968); P. Brunold, F. C. (Eng. tr., Monaco, 1949); M. Cauchie, Thematic Index of the Works of C. (Monaco, 1949); W. Mellers, F. C. and the French Classical Tradition (London, 1950; 2nd ed., rev., 1986); M. Antoine, "Autour de F. C.," Revue de Musicologie (Dec. 1952); P. Citron, C. (Paris, 1956); Mélanges F. C. Publiés à l'occasion du tricentenaire de sa naissance (Paris, 1968); V. Schwarz, "F. C. und seine Zeit. Zum 300. Geburtstag des Meisters," Österreichische Musikzeitschrift (Nov. 1968); T. Dart, "On C.'s Harpsichord Music," Musical Times (June 1969); N. Dufourcq, "F. C., Musicien de la terre, de la ville, de l'église, de la cour," XVIIᵉ siècle, 82 (1969); F. Neumann, "C. and the Downbeat Doctrine for Appoggiaturas," Acta Musicologica (Jan.–June 1969); M. Pincherle, "F. C. et la conciliation des 'goûts' français et italien," Chigiana, XXV/5 (1968); N. Dufourcq, "Les Bari-cades mistérieuses de F. C.," Recherches sur la Musique Française, XIII (1973); D. Tunley, C. (London, 1982).

Couperin, Gervais-François, organist and composer, 2nd son of **Armand-Louis Couperin;** b. Paris, May 22, 1759; d. there, March 11, 1826. He succeeded his brother, **Pierre-Louis,** as organist at St.-Gervais in 1789, also taking over his other appointments. He composed sonatas, variations, etc. He was the last of the Couperins to serve as organist at St.-Gervais, although his daughter, **Céleste** (b. 1793; d. Belleville, Feb. 14, 1860), played there at the time of her father's death. She was a teacher of singing and piano at Beauvais for about 10 years.

BIBL.: C. Bouvet, "La Fin d'une dynastie d'artistes: G.-F. C. et sa fille," Revue de Musicologie (1926).

Couperin, Louis, organist, violinist, violist, and composer; b. Chaumes, c.1626; d. Paris, Aug. 29, 1661. He went to Paris with Chambonnières, whose pupil he was; in 1653 became organist of St.-Gervais, a post in which he was succeeded, without interruption, by other members and descendants of the Couperin family until 1826; from 1656, he was a violinist and violist in the orchs. of the court ballets, and musician of the Chambre du Roi. He composed Pièces de clavecin, Carillons for Organ, violin pieces, etc. He was one of the earliest of French composers for the harpsichord in the new harmonic style employing the basso continuo, possibly being preceded only by his teacher, Chambonnières. The Lyrebird Press in Paris publ. a "complete" edition of his works, ed. by P. Brunold. His Pièces de clavecin is publ. as vol. 18 of Le Pupitre (1970).

BIBL.: A. Pirro, "L. C.," Revue de Musicologie (1930).

Couperin, Nicolas, organist, son of **François, Sieur de Crouilly;** b. Paris, Dec. 20, 1680; d. there, July 25, 1748. In 1733 he succeeded his cousin **François le Grand** as organist at St.-Gervais.

Couperin, Pierre-Louis, organist and composer, known as **M. Couperin l'aîné** or **Couperin fils,** son of **Armand-Louis Couperin;** b. Paris, March 14, 1755; d. there, Oct. 10, 1789. He was organist to the King, later at Notre-Dame, St.-Jean, St.-Merry, and St.-Gervais (succeeded his father early in 1789; died 8 months later). Some of his compositions were publ. in contemporary collections; others are in MS.

Cour, Niels la, Danish composer; b. Copenhagen, Nov. 14, 1944. He studied music theory and history at the Royal Danish Cons. of Music in Copenhagen, graduating in 1969; subsequently taught at the Funen Academy of Music in Odense (1969–77).

WORKS: Imago for Flute, Clarinet, Violin, Viola, Cello, and Piano (1967); 6 string quartets: No. 1, Das innere Licht (The Inner Light; 1968); No. 2, Mild und leise (Mild and Gentle; 1969); No. 3, Communio (1971); No. 4, Quatuor classique (1972); No. 5 (1977); No. 6 (1977); 5 Stilleben (Still Lifes) for Viola and Piano (1969); Mythos for String Orch. (1969; Copenhagen, Oct. 29, 1971); Archetypon for Organ (1970); Imago for Orch. (1971); Vinger (Wings) for Female Chorus a cappella (1973); 2 wind quintets (1972–73, 1975); Symphonic Fragments (1974); De profundis for Organ (1974); 3 Intermezzi for Organ (1974); Divertimento for Orch. (1976); 5 Motets for Chorus a cappella (1977).

Couraud, Marcel, French conductor; b. Limoges, Oct. 20, 1912; d. Loches, Sept. 14, 1986. He studied organ with André Marchal in Paris, then enrolled in music theory courses at the École Normale de Musique there; also took lessons in composition with Nadia Boulanger and in conducting with Charles Munch. In 1945 he formed the Marcel Couraud Vocal Ensemble, which he conducted until 1954; in 1967 he was appointed artistic director of the ORTF choirs in Paris.

Courboin, Charles (Marie), Belgian-American organist; b. Antwerp, April 2, 1884; d. N.Y., April 13, 1973. He studied at the Cons. of Brussels with J. Blockx and A. Mailly; in 1904 emigrated to the U.S.; made several transcontinental tours of the U.S. and Canada, and 2 European tours; in 1919 he played the organ in the 1st performance of Widor's 6th Symphony (dedicated to Courboin) with the Philadelphia Orch. under Stokowski. He designed 144 important organs in the U.S., among them Wanamaker's in N.Y.

Courtois, Jean, Franco-Flemish composer of the 1st half of the 16th century. He was maître de chapelle at Cambrai Cathedral in 1540, when a 4-part motet of his, *Venite populi terrae,* was performed before Charles V of Spain. Many of his motets, Psalms, and songs appeared in publications of the period (printed at Paris, Lyons, Antwerp, Nuremberg, etc.); H. Expert reprinted some of his songs in Les Maîtres Musiciens de la Renaissance Française. Masses, motets, and songs in MS are in the Munich State Library and the library at Cambrai.

Courvoisier, Karl, Swiss violinist and teacher; b. Basel, Nov. 12, 1846; d. Liverpool, Jan. 31, 1908. He studied with David and Röntgen at Leipzig Cons. (1867–69), and Joachim in Berlin (1869–70). In 1885 he settled in Liverpool as a teacher. He publ. *Die Violintechnik* (1878; Eng. tr. by H.E. Krehbiel, *The Techniques of Violin Playing;* 2nd ed., N.Y., 1896); *École de la vélocité* for violin; and *Méthode de violon* (text in German, Eng., and French; London, 1892).

Courvoisier, Walter, Swiss composer; b. Riehen, near Basel, Feb. 7, 1875; d. Locarno, Dec. 27, 1931. He first studied medicine (M.D., 1900), later music with Thuille in Munich (whose son-in-law he became); taught composition at the Academy of Music in Munich (1910–30).

WORKS: Operas: *Lanzelot und Elaine* (Munich, Nov. 3, 1917) and *Die Krähen* (Munich, April 19, 1921); oratorio, *Totenfeier;* chamber music; piano pieces; about 150 songs.

Coussemaker, (Charles-) Edmond (-Henri) de, French music scholar; b. Bailleul, Nord, April 19, 1805; d. Bourbourg, Jan. 10, 1876. He studied music as a child. His main profession was the law; while studying law at the Univ. of Paris, he took private lessons with Pellegrini in singing and Anton Reicha in harmony. He continued his studies with Lefebvre in Douai, after becoming a practicing lawyer. At this time (1831–35) he found leisure to compose music of the most varied description, all of which, with the exception of a few *romances* and 2 sets of songs, is unpubl., and apparently lost. His interest in history and archaeology led him to the study of the authentic documents of music; he was also influenced by the scholarly articles in *La Gazette et Revue Musicale* (then ed. by Fétis). During successive terms as judge in Hazebrouck, Dunkirk, and Lille, he continued to accumulate knowledge of musical documentation; he assembled a vast library; 1,075 items in his library are listed in the *Catalogue des livres, manuscrits et instruments de musique du feu M. Charles Coussemaker* (Brussels, 1877; issued for an auction).

WRITINGS: *Mémoire sur Hucbald* (1841); *Notice sur les collections musicales de la bibliothèque de Cambrai . . .* (1843); *Histoire de l'harmonie au moyen-âge* (1852); *Trois chants historiques* (1854); *Chants populaires des Flamands de France* (1856); *Drames liturgiques du moyen-âge* (1860); *Les Harmonistes des XIIe et XIIIe siècles* (1865); *Scriptorum de musica medii ævi nova series* (4 vols., 1864–76; new ed., Graz, 1908); *L'Art harmonique aux XIIe et XIIIe siècles* (1865); *Œuvres complètes d'Adam de la Halle* (1872); etc.

BIBL.: A. Desplanque, *Étude sur les travaux d'historie et d'archéologie de M. E. d.C.* (Paris, 1870); R. Debevere, "E. d.C. (1805–1876), Een belangrijk frans-vlaming," *Ons Erfdeel,* XII/2 (1968).

Coverly, Robert, Portuguese composer of light music; b. Oporto, Sept. 6, 1864; d. there, Sept. 19, 1944. He studied in London and N.Y.; composed a great number of effective marches and songs, of which *The Passing Regiment,* a military march for band, achieved great popularity.

Coward, Sir Henry, English choral conductor; b. Liverpool, Nov. 26, 1849; d. Sheffield, June 10, 1944. He was apprenticed to be a cutler but attended classes of solfeggio. He organized a choral group at Sheffield and became its conductor. After a period of hard study, he obtained the B.Mus. degree at Oxford (1889), and later D.Mus. (1894). He organized spectacular choral festivals in Sheffield, in which thousands of choristers participated; gave concerts with his chorus in Germany (1906); in 1908 he presented 16 concerts in Canada with members of the Sheffield Choral Union, headed by him. There followed in 1911 a world tour, which included the U.S., Canada, Australia, and South Africa. Coward was the leader of choral groups at Leeds and Glasgow; acted as a judge at competition festivals. He was knighted in 1926. He composed several cantatas and other choral works; ed. a collection of Methodist hymns (1901); publ. *Choral Technique and Interpretation* (1914) and *Reminiscences* (1919).

BIBL.: J.A. Rodgers, *Dr. H. C., The Pioneer Chorus-master* (London, 1911).

Coward, Sir Noel, English playwright and author of musical comedies; b. Teddington, Middlesex, Dec. 16, 1899; d. Port Maria, Jamaica, March 25, 1973. At the age of 11, he appeared on the stage, and was associated with the theater ever after, in the triple capacity of actor, playwright, and producer. Having had no formal education in music, he dictated his songs to a musical amanuensis. Among the musical comedies for which he wrote both words and music are *This Year of Grace* (N.Y., Nov. 7, 1928); *Bitter Sweet* (London, July 18, 1929); *Conversation Piece* (London, Feb. 16, 1934); *Pacific 1860* (London, Dec. 19, 1946); *Ace of Clubs* (London, July 7, 1950); *After the Ball,* to Wilde's *Lady Windermere's Fan* (London, June 10, 1954); 51 songs from his musical plays are publ. in the *Noel Coward Song Book* (N.Y., 1953) with the author's introduction. He also publ. an autobiography, *Present Indicative* (London, 1937); 2nd vol., *Future Indefinite* (London, 1954). He was knighted in 1970.

BIBL.: C. Lesley (N. C.'s valet-companion), *Remembered Laughter* (N.Y., 1976); G. Payn and S. Morley, eds., *The N. C. Diaries* (London, 1982).

Cowell, Henry (Dixon), remarkable, innovative American composer; b. Menlo Park, Calif., March 11, 1897; d. Shady, N.Y., Dec. 10, 1965. His father, of Irish birth, was a member of a clergyman's family in Kildare; his mother was an American of progressive persuasion. Cowell studied violin with Henry Holmes in San Francisco; after the earthquake of 1906, his mother took him to N.Y., where they were compelled to seek support from the Soc. for the Improvement of the Condition of the Poor; they returned to Menlo Park, where Cowell was able to save enough money, earned from menial jobs, to buy a piano. He began to experiment with the keyboard by striking the keys with fists and forearms; he named such chords "tone clusters" and at the age of 13 composed a piece called *Adventures in Harmony,* containing such chords. Later he began experimenting in altering the sound of the piano by placing various objects on the strings, and also by playing directly under the lid of the piano *pizzicato* and *glissando.* He first exhibited these startling innovations on March 5, 1914, at the San Francisco Musical Soc. at the St. Francis Hotel, much to the consternation of its members, no doubt. The tone clusters per se were not new; they were used for special sound effects by composers in the 18th century to imitate thunder or cannon fire. The Russian composer Vladimir Rebikov applied them in his piano piece *Hymn to Inca,* and Charles Ives used them in his *Concord Sonata* to be sounded by covering a set of white or black keys with a wooden board. However, Cowell had a priority by systematizing tone clusters as harmonic amplifications of tonal chords, and he devised logical notation for them. The tone clusters eventually acquired legitimacy in the works of many European and American composers. Cowell also extended the sonorities of tone clusters to instrumental combinations and applied them in several of his symphonic works. In the meantime Cowell began taking lessons in composition with E.G. Strickland and Wallace Sabin at the Univ. of Calif. in Berkeley, and later with Frank Damrosch at the Inst. of Musical Art in N.Y., and, privately, with Charles Seeger (1914–16). After brief service in the U.S. Army in 1918, where he was employed first as a cook and later as arranger for the U.S. Army Band, he became engaged professionally to give a series of lectures on new music, illustrated by his playing his own works on the piano. In 1928 he went to Russia, where he attracted considerable attention as the 1st American composer to visit there; some of his pieces were publ. in a Russian ed., the 1st such publications by an American. Upon return to the U.S., he was appointed lecturer on music at The New School in N.Y.

In 1931 he received a Guggenheim fellowship grant, and went to Berlin to study ethnomusicology with Erich von Hornbostel. This was the beginning of his serious study of ethnic musical materials. He had already experimented with some Indian and Chinese devices in some of his works; in his *Ensemble* for Strings (1924) he included Indian thundersticks; the piece naturally aroused considerable curiosity. In 1931 he formed a collaboration with the Russian electrical engineer Leon Theremin, then visiting the U.S.; with his aid he constructed an ingenious instrument which he called the Rhythmicon; it made possible the simultaneous production of 16 different rhythms on 16 different pitch levels of the harmonic series. He demonstrated the Rhythmicon at a lecture-concert in San Francisco on May 15, 1932. He also composed an extensive work entitled *Rhythmicana*, but it did not receive a performance until Dec. 3, 1971, at Stanford Univ., using advanced electronic techniques. In 1927 Cowell founded the *New Music Quarterly* for publication of ultramodern music, mainly by American composers.

Cowell's career was brutally interrupted in 1936, when he was arrested in California on charges of homosexuality (then a heinous offense in California) involving the impairment of the morals of a minor. Lulled by the deceptive promises of a wily district attorney of a brief confinement in a sanatorium, Cowell pleaded guilty to a limited offense, but he was vengefully given a maximum sentence of imprisonment, up to 15 years. Incarcerated at San Quentin, he was assigned to work in a jute mill, but indomitably continued to write music in prison. Thanks to interventions in his behalf by a number of eminent musicians, he was paroled in 1940 to Percy Grainger as a guarantor of his good conduct; he obtained a full pardon on Dec. 9, 1942, from the governor of California, Earl Warren, after it was discovered that the evidence against him was largely contrived. On Sept. 27, 1941, he married Sidney Robertson, a noted ethnomusicologist. He was then able to resume his full activities as ed. and instructor; he held teaching positions at The New School for Social Research in N.Y. (1940–62), the Univ. of Southern Calif., Mills College, and the Peabody Cons. of Music in Baltimore (1951–56); was also appointed adjunct prof. at summer classes at Columbia Univ. (1951–65). In 1951 Cowell was elected a member of the National Academy of Arts and Letters; received an honorary Mus.D. from Wilmington College (1953) and from Monmouth (Ill.) College (1963). In 1956–57 he undertook a world tour with his wife through the Near East, India, and Japan, collecting rich prime materials for his compositions, which by now had acquired a decisive turn toward the use of ethnomusicological melodic and rhythmic materials, without abandoning, however, the experimental devices which were the signposts of most of his works. In addition to his symphonic and chamber music, Cowell publ. in 1930 an important book, *New Musical Resources*. He also ed. a symposium, *American Composers on American Music*; in collaboration with his wife he wrote the basic biography of Charles Ives (1955).

WORKS: STAGE: Unfinished opera, *O'Higgins of Chile* (1949); a pageant, *The Building of Bamba* (Halcyon, near Pismo Beach, Calif., Aug. 18, 1917).

16 HYMN AND FUGUING TUNES (based on fuguing tunes of William Billings): No. 1 for Band (1943); No. 2 for String Orch. (1944); No. 3 for Orch. (1944); No. 4 for 3 Instruments (1944); No. 5 for String Orch. (1945; version for Orch. incorporated into Sym. No. 10); No. 6 for Piano (1946); No. 7 for Viola and Piano (1946); No. 8 for String Quartet or String Orch. (1947–48); No. 9 for Cello and Piano (1950); No. 10 for Oboe and Strings (1955); No. 11, became *7 Rites of Music* for Male Chorus and Orch. (1956); No. 12 for 3 Horns (1957);

No. 13 for Trombone and Piano (1960); No. 14 for Organ (1961); No. 15A, a duet for the anniversary of his marriage (Sept. 27, 1961); No. 15B for 2 Violins or Any Combination (2 versions, 1 with a more extended ground bass); No. 16 for Violin and Piano (1965; N.Y., Oct. 6, 1966; also for Violin and Orch.).

20 SYMS.: No. 1 (1916–17); No. 2, *Anthropos* (Mankind; 1938); No. 3, *Gaelic Symphony* (1942); No. 4, *Short Symphony* (1946; Boston, Oct. 24, 1947); No. 5 (1948; Washington, D.C., Jan. 5, 1949); No. 6 (1950–55; Houston, Nov. 14, 1955); No. 7 (1952; Baltimore, Nov. 25, 1952); No. 8, *Choral*, for Chorus and Orch. (1952; Wilmington, Ohio, March 1, 1953); No. 9 (1953; Green Bay, Wis., March 14, 1954); No. 10 for Chamber Orch. (1953; U.S. premiere, N.Y., Feb. 24, 1957); No. 11, *The 7 Rituals of Music* (1953; Louisville, May 29, 1954); No. 12 (1955–56; Houston, March 28, 1960); No. 13, *Madras Symphony,* for Small Orch. and 3 Indian Instruments (1957–58; Madras, India, March 3, 1959); No. 14 (1960–61; Washington, D.C., April 27, 1961); No. 15, *Thesis* (1961; Bowling Green, Ky., Oct. 7, 1961); No. 16, *Icelandic Symphony* (1962; Reykjavík, March 21, 1963); No. 17 (1962–63; 1st movement perf. as *Lancaster Overture,* Lancaster, Pa., 1963); No. 18 (1964); No. 19 (1965; Nashville, Tenn., Oct. 18, 1965); No. 20 (1965).

OTHER WORKS FOR ORCH.: *Vestiges* (1914–20); *Some Music* (1915); *Some More Music* (1915–16); *Communication* (1920); Sinfonietta for Small Orch. (1924–28; Boston, Nov. 23, 1931, Slonimsky conducting); *Irish Suite* for Solo String, Percussion, and Piano (1928; Boston, March 11, 1929, Slonimsky conducting; a scoring of the piano pieces *The Banshee, Leprechaun,* and *Fairy Bells* with Chamber Orch. accompaniment); Piano Concerto (1929; Havana, Dec. 28, 1930; 1st complete U.S. perf., Omaha, Oct. 12, 1978); *Polyphonica* for 12 Instruments (1930); *Synchrony* (1930; Paris, June 6, 1931, Slonimsky conducting); *Reel No. 1* and *No. 2* (1930, 1932); *2 Appositions* for String Orch. (1931); *Rhythmicana,* Concerto for Rhythmicon and Orch. (1931; Palo Alto, Calif., Dec. 3, 1971); 3 pieces for Chamber Orch.: *Competitive Sport, Steel and Stone,* and *Heroic Dance* (all 1931); *4 Continuations* for String Orch. (1933); *Old American Country Set* (1937; Indianapolis, Feb. 28, 1940); *Celtic Set* (Selinsgrove, Pa., May 6, 1938); *American Melting Pot* (1939); *Symphonic Set* (1939; orchestration of *Toccanta*); *Shoonthree* (*Sleep Music*) (1939; also for Band); *Pastoral & Fiddler's Delight* (1940; N.Y., July 26, 1949, Stokowski conducting); *Ancient Desert Drone* (1940); *Tales of Our Countryside* for Piano and Orch. (1940; Atlantic City, May 11, 1941; composer soloist; Stokowski conducting; based on piano pieces written 1922–30); *Vox Humana* (1940); *Little Concerto* for Piano, and Orch. or Band (1942; also known as *Concerto piccolo*); Suite for Piano and String Orch. (1943); *American Pipers* (1943); *United Music* (1944); *Big Sing* (1945); *Festival Overture* for 2 Orchs. (1946); *Saturday Night at the Firehouse* (1948); *Aria* for Violin and String Orch. (1952); *Rondo* (1953); *Ballad* for Strings (1955); *Variations* (1956); *Persian Set* for 12 Instruments (1956–57); *Music 1957* (1957); *Ongaku* (1957; Louisville, March 26, 1958); *Antiphony* for 2 Orchs. (1958; Kansas City, Mo., Nov. 14, 1959); Percussion Concerto (1958; Kansas City, Jan. 7, 1961); *Mela and Fair* (New Delhi, India, Dec. 11, 1959); *Characters* (1959); *Chiaroscuro* (1960; Guatemala City, Oct. 13, 1961); *Variations on Thirds* for 2 Solo Violas and Strings (1960); *Concerto brevis* for Accordion and Orch. (1960); Harmonica Concerto (1960); *Air and Scherzo* for Saxophone and Small Orch. (1961); *Duo concertante* for Flute, Harp, and Orch. (1961; Springfield, Ohio, Oct. 21, 1961); 2 koto concertos: No. 1 (1963; Philadelphia, Dec. 18, 1964) and No. 2 (Hanover, N.H., May 8, 1965); *Concerto grosso* for 5 Instruments and Orch. (1963; Miami Beach, Jan. 12, 1964); Harp Concerto (1965); *Carol* (1965; new orchestration of slow movement of Koto Concerto No. 1).

OTHER WORKS FOR BAND: *A Curse and a Blessing* (1938); *Shoonthree* (1940; also for Orch.); *Celtic Set* (1943; orig. for Orch., 1938); *Animal Magic* (1944); *Grandma's Rumba* (1945); *Fantasie* (West Point, N.Y., May 30, 1952); *Singing Band* (1953).

OTHER WORKS FOR VOICE: *The Thistle Flower* for Women's Voices a cappella (1928); *Vocalise* for Voice, Flute, and Piano (1937); *Chrysanthemums* for Soprano, 2 Saxophones, and 4 Strings (1937); *Toccanta* for Soprano, Flute, Cello, and Piano (1938); *The Coming of Light* for Chorus a cappella (1939); *Fire and Ice*, after Frost's poem, for 4 Male Soloists, and Orch. or Band (1942); Sonatina for Baritone, Violin, and Piano (1942); *American Muse* for Soprano, Alto, and Piano (1943); *To America* for Chorus a cappella (1947); *The Commission*, cantata for 4 Soloists and Orch. (1954); . . . *if He Please* for Mixed and either Boys' or Women's Choruses, and Orch. (1954); Septet for 5 Voices without words, Clarinet, and Piano (1955–56); *A Thanksgiving Psalm from the Dead Sea Scrolls* for Male Chorus and Orch. (1956; orig. *Hymn and Fuguing Tune* No. 11); *Edson Hymns and Fuguing Tunes* for Chorus and Orch. (1960); *The Creator* for Chorus and Orch. (1963); *Ultima Actio* for Chorus a cappella (1965).

OTHER CHAMBER WORKS: *Quartet Romantic* for 2 Flutes, Violin, and Viola (1915–17); 5 string quartets: No. 1, *Pedantic* (1915–16); No. 2, *Movement* for String Quartet (1928); No. 3, *Mosaic* (1935); No. 4, *United* (1936); No. 5 (1956; rev. 1962); also the unnumbered *Quartet Euphometric* (1916–19); other pieces; also unnumbered *Ensemble* for 2 Violins, Viola, 2 Cellos, and 3 Thundersticks (1924; version for String Orch. without Thundersticks, 1959); 7 *Paragraphs* for String Trio (1925); Suite for Violin and Piano (1927); *Exultation* for 10 Strings (1928); Suite for Wind Quintet (1930); 3 works for Percussion: *Pulse, Return,* and *Ostinato Pianissimo* (1930–34); 6 *Casual Developments* for Clarinet and Piano (1935); *Soundform for Dance* for Flute, Clarinet, Bassoon, and Percussion (1936); *Sarabande* for Oboe, Clarinet, and Percussion (1937); *Trickster Coyote* for Flute and Percussion (1941); *Action in Brass* for 5 Brasses (1943); Violin Sonata (1945; rev. 1947); Saxophone Quartet (1946); *Tall Tale* for Brass Sextet (1947); *Set for 2* for Violin and Piano (1948); 4 *Declamations and Return* for Cello and Piano (1949); *Set of 5* for Violin, Piano, and Percussion (1951); *Set* for Harpsichord, Flute, Oboe, and Cello (1953); *Set of 2* for Harp and Violin (1955); *Homage to Iran* for Violin and Piano (1957); *Iridescent Rondo* for Solo Accordion (1959); *Air and Scherzo* for Saxophone and Piano (1961); Quartet for Flute, Oboe, Cello, and Harp (1962); *Gravely and Vigorously*, in memory of John F. Kennedy, for Solo Cello (1963; orig. the *Hymn and Fuguing Tune* No. 17); 26 *Simultaneous Mosaics* for Violin, Cello, Clarinet, Piano, and Percussion (N.Y., Dec. 1, 1964); Piano Trio (1965); *Cleistogamy* (self-pollinating flowerlets), a collection of pieces written between 1941 and 1963.

PIANO: *The Tides of Manaunaun* (1912); *Advertisements* (1914; rev. 1959); *Dynamic Motion* (1914); 6 *Ings: Floating-Fleeting-Wafting-Seething-Frisking-Scooting* (1916); *It Isn't It* (1922); *The Snows of Fujiyama* (1922); *Aeolian Harp* (1923); *Piece for Piano with Strings* (Paris, 1924); *The Banshee* (1925); *Lilt of the Reel* (1925); *Sinister Resonance* (1925); *Tiger* (1927); 2 *Woofs* (1930); *Hilarious Curtain Opener and Ritournelle* (1937); hundreds of other pieces with similar fanciful titles; also some organ pieces.

WRITINGS: *New Musical Resources* (N.Y., 1930); ed., *American Composers on American Music: A Symposium* (Stanford, Calif., 1933; reprinted, N.Y., 1962); *Charles Ives and His Music* (N.Y., 1955; in collaboration with his wife, Sidney Cowell).

BIBL.: N. Slonimsky, "H. C.," in *American Composers on American Music: A Symposium* (Stanford, Calif., 1933; reprinted, N.Y., 1962); M. Goss, *Modern Music-Makers* (N.Y., 1952); H. Weisgall, "The Music of H. C.," *Musical Quarterly* (Oct. 1959); O. Daniel, "H. C.," *Stereo Review* (Dec. 1974); R. Mead, *H. C.'s New Music, 1925–1936* (N.Y., 1981); M. Manion, *Writings about H. C.: An Annotated Bibliography* (N.Y., 1982); W. Lichtenwanger, *The Music of H. C.: A Descriptive Catalog* (Brooklyn, 1986).

Cowen, Sir Frederic (Hymen), English conductor and composer; b. Kingston, Jamaica, Jan. 29, 1852; d. London, Oct. 6, 1935. His evident talent for music caused his parents to

take him to England to study at the age of 4. He was a pupil of Benedict and Goss in London; studied at the Leipzig Cons. under Hauptmann, Moscheles, Reinecke, Richter, and Plaidy (1865–66); in Berlin under Kiel (1867–68); was conductor of the Phil. Soc. of London (1888–92), succeeding Sullivan, and again from 1900 to 1907; was music director of the Melbourne Centennial Exhibition (1888–89); conductor of the Liverpool Phil. from 1896 to 1913; Sir Charles Hallé's successor as conductor of the Manchester Concerts (1896–99); conducted the Scottish Orch. in Glasgow (1900–1910) and the Handel Triennial Festival (Crystal Palace, 1903–12). He received the degree of Mus.D. from Edinburgh Univ. (1910); was knighted in 1911. He publ. his memoirs as *My Art and My Friends* (London, 1913), and an amusing glossary of musical terms, *Music as She Is Wrote* (London, 1915); also books on Haydn, Mozart, Mendelssohn, and Rossini.

WORKS: 4 operas: *Pauline* (London, Nov. 22, 1876); *Thorgrim* (London, April 22, 1890); *Signa* (Milan, Nov. 12, 1893); *Harold, or The Norman Conquest* (London, June 8, 1895); oratorios: *The Deluge* (1878); *St. Ursula* (1881); *Ruth* (1887); *The Veil* (Cardiff Festival, Sept. 20, 1910; his most successful work); cantatas. Orch.: 6 syms.: No. 1, in C minor (1869); No. 2, in F minor (1872); No. 3, in C minor, *Scandinavian* (1880); No. 4, in B-flat minor, *Welsh* (1884); No. 5, in F (1887); No. 6, in E, *Idyllic* (1897); 3 suites: *The Language of Flowers, In the Olden Time, In Fairyland;* Sinfonietta; Piano Concerto; 4 overtures; *Of Life and Love,* fantasy. Chamber: 2 piano trios; 2 string quartets; piano pieces; over 250 songs; etc.

BIBL.: J. Potts, "Sir F.H. C. (1852–1935)," *Musical Times,* XCIV (1953).

Cowie, Edward, English composer and conductor; b. Birmingham, Aug. 17, 1943. He studied with Fricker at Morley College (1961) and privately with A. Goehr (1964–68), then attended the Univs. of Southampton (1970–71) and Leeds (1971–73); he also worked with Lutoslawski in Poland (1971). He was on the faculties of the Univs. of Lancaster (1973), Kassel (1979), and Wollongong in Australia (1983); from 1983 to 1986 he was composer-in-residence of the Royal Liverpool Phil. In 1988 he founded the Australian Composers' Ensemble, and in 1989 became artistic director of the Australian Sinfonietta. An artist of wide-ranging attainments, he studied not only music but also painting and ornithology; often his compositions portrayed his pictorial visions of birds, not by literal imitation but rather through inner kinship. His intellectual inspirations were Leonardo da Vinci and Goethe in their universal thinking and practice. Eschewing musicological pedantry, he used techniques ranging from static triadic tonality to serialistic atonality, from abstract tonal formations to concrete references to external objects.

WORKS: STAGE: *Commedia,* opera (1976–78); *Kate Kelly's Roadshow,* music theater piece for Mezzo-soprano and Ensemble (1982). **ORCH.:** Concerto for Clarinet and Tape (1969); *Leviathan,* symphonic poem (1975); Clarinet Concerto No. 2 (1975); Piano Concerto (1976–77); *L'Or de la trompette d'été* for 18 Strings (1977); Concerto for Orch. (1979–80); *Leonardo* for Chamber Orch. (1980–81); syms.: No. 1, *The American* (1980–81; Liverpool, Feb. 1, 1984); No. 2, *The Australian* (1982); *Choral Symphony: Symphonies of Rain, Sea, and Speed* for Baritone, Chorus, and Orch. (1981–82); Harpsichord Concerto (1981–82); *Atlas,* suite (Liverpool, May 13, 1986). **CHAMBER:** 4 string quartets (1973, 1977, 1983, 1983); *Kelly Passacaglia* for String Quartet (1980); *Harlequin* for Harp (1980); *Commedia Lazzis* for Guitar (1980); *Kelly-Nolan-Kelly* for Clarinet (1980); also choruses; piano pieces.

Cox, Jean, American tenor; b. Gadsen, Ala., Jan. 16, 1922. He studied at the Univ. of Alabama, and at the New England Cons. in Boston. He sang with the New England Opera Theater; then went to Europe; made his debut with the Kiel Stadttheater in 1954; in succeeding years he appeared with many of the major European and American opera houses; also sang at Bayreuth. He made his Metropolitan Opera debut in N.Y. on April 2, 1976, as Walther in *Die Meistersinger von Nürnberg.*

Crabbé, Armand (Charles), Belgian baritone; b. Brussels, April 23, 1883; d. there, July 24, 1947. He studied with Désiré Demest at the Brussels Cons. (1902–4); made his debut at the Théâtre de la Monnaie in Brussels as the Night Watchman in *Die Meistersinger* in 1904; there he also created the role of the Friar in Massenet's *Jongleur de Nôtre-Dame* (also sung by him for the 1st time at Covent Garden, N.Y., Boston, etc.). In 1907 he joined Hammerstein's Manhattan Opera in N.Y.; then was with the Chicago Grand Opera (1910–14); returning to Europe, he settled in Brussels as a voice teacher. He wrote an opera, *Les Noces d'or* (in collaboration with Auguste Maurage).

Craft, Robert (Lawson), American conductor and brilliant writer on music; b. Kingston, N.Y., Oct. 20, 1923. He studied at the Juilliard School of Music (B.A., 1946) and the Berkshire Music Center; took courses in conducting with Monteux. During World War II he was in the U.S. Army Medical Corps. In 1947 he conducted the N.Y. Brass and Woodwind Ensemble. He was conductor of the Evenings-on-the-Roof and the Monday Evening Concerts in Los Angeles (1950–68). A decisive turn in his career was his encounter with Stravinsky in 1948, whom he greatly impressed by his precise knowledge of Stravinsky's music; gradually he became Stravinsky's closest associate. He was also instrumental in persuading Stravinsky to adopt the 12-tone method of composition, a momentous turn in Stravinsky's creative path. He collaborated with Stravinsky on 6 vols. of a catechumenical and discursive nature: *Conversations with Igor Stravinsky* (N.Y., 1959); *Memories and Commentaries* (N.Y., 1960); *Expositions and Developments* (N.Y., 1962); *Dialogues and a Diary* (N.Y., 1963); *Themes and Episodes* (N.Y., 1967); *Retrospections and Conclusions* (N.Y., 1969). Resentful of frequent referral to him as a musical Boswell, Craft insists that his collaboration with Stravinsky was more akin to that between the Goncourt brothers, both acting and reacting to an emerging topic of discussion, with Stravinsky evoking his ancient memories in his careful English, or fluent French, spiced with unrestrained discourtesies toward professional colleagues on the American scene, and Craft reifying the material with an analeptic bulimia of quaquaversal literary, psychological, physiological, and culinary references in a flow of finely ordered dialogue. His other publications include *Prejudices in Disguise* (N.Y., 1974); *Stravinsky in Photographs and Documents* (with Vera Stravinsky; London, 1976; N.Y., 1978); *Current Convictions: Views and Reviews* (N.Y., 1977); *Present Perspectives* (N.Y., 1984). He also tr. and ed. *Stravinsky, Selected Correspondence* (2 vols., N.Y., 1982, 1984).
    BIBL.: J. Peyser, "Stravinsky-C., Inc.," *American Scholar*, LII (1983).

Cramer, Johann Baptist, famous German pianist and pedagogue, son of **Wilhelm Cramer**; b. Mannheim, Feb. 24, 1771; d. London, April 16, 1858. He was taken to London as an infant, and throughout his life regarded it as his home. He received a fine musical education, first from his father, then from Clementi (1783–84) and C.F. Abel (1785). He began to travel as a concert pianist in 1788; visited Vienna, where he met Beethoven (1799–1800); in later years (1835–45) spent considerable time as a teacher in Munich and Paris, finally returning to London. His greatest work is his piano method, *Grosse Praktische Pianoforte Schule* (1815) in 5 parts, the last of which, *84 Studies* (op. 50; later rev. and publ. as op. 81, including *16 nouvelles études*) is famous in piano pedagogy. Hans von Bülow made a selection of 50 studies from this collection, later revised and annotated in collections of 52 and 60; Henselt issued a different selection, with accompaniment of a 2nd piano; other eds. of Cramer's studies are by Coccius, Riemann, Pauer, Lack, and Lickl; *100 Progressive Etudes* is also well known. Apart from his pedagogic collections, Cramer wrote 9 piano concertos, over 50 piano sonatas, 2 piano quartets, 2 piano quintets, and numerous piano pieces of the salon type; but all these are quite forgotten, while his piano studies, with those of Czerny, maintained their value for more than a century. He first entered the music publishing business in 1805, as

head of the firm Cramer & Keys; was in partnership with Samuel Chappell (1810–19). In 1824, together with R. Addison and T.F. Beale, Cramer established a music publishing house (now J.B. Cramer & Co., Ltd.), of which he was director until 1842; in 1844 Addison retired and was succeeded by W. Chappell, the firm then becoming Cramer, Beale & Chappell; after Cramer's death in 1858, and Chappell's retirement in 1861, G. Wood became Beale's partner; about 1862 the firm began to devote much attention to the manufacture of pianos; on Beale's death in 1863, Wood became sole director, continuing it successfully until his death in 1893, although devoting more consideration to piano manufacture than to music publishing. His 2 nephews succeeded him. In 1897 the firm became a limited company.
    BIBL.: J. Pembaur, *Die 84 Etüden von J.B. C.*; *Anleitung zu gründlichem Studieren und Analysieren derselben* (Leipzig, 1901); T. Schlesinger, *J.B. C. und seine Klavier-Sonaten* (Munich, 1928); A. Hyatt King, "Mozart and C.," in *Mozart in Retrospect: Studies in Criticism and Bibliography* (London, 1955; 3rd ed., 1970); P. Ganz, "J.B. C. and His Celebrated Etudes," *Clavier* (Feb. 1967); H. Goldschmidt, "Beethovens Anweisungen zum Spiel der C.-Etüden," in H.A. Brockhaus and K. Niemann, *Bericht über den Int. Beethoven-Kongress 10.–12. Dezember 1970* (Berlin, 1971).

Cramer, Wilhelm, German violinist and composer, father of **Johann Baptist Cramer**; b. Mannheim (baptized), June 2, 1746; d. London, Oct. 5, 1799. He received his musical training from his father, **Jacob Cramer** (1705–70), who was a violinist in the Mannheim Orch., and also studied with Johann Stamitz and Cannabich; from 1752 to 1769 he was a member of the Mannheim Orch.; then went to Paris. In 1772 he went to London, where he became a successful violinist and conductor. He was concertmaster of the orch. of the Anacreontic Soc. during its most prestigious years (1773–91); was chamber musician to the King. He wrote 11 violin concertos, 6 string quartets, 6 violin sonatas, and other string music.

Cranz, August, German music publishing firm in Hamburg, founded 1813 by **August Heinrich Cranz** (1789–1870). His son **Alwin** (b. Hamburg, 1834; d. Vevey, April 10, 1923), who succeeded him in 1857, bought the firm of C.A. Spina of Vienna in 1876, and in 1886 the firm of C.A. Böhme of Hamburg. Alwin's son, **Oskar** (pen name, **Anton Toska**; d. Boston, Aug. 24, 1929), entered as a partner in 1896. In 1897 the firm removed to Leipzig. Branches were established in Vienna (1876), Brussels (1883), and London (1896). After World War II its permanent headquarters were in Wiesbaden.

Cras, Jean Émile Paul, French composer; b. Brest, May 22, 1879; d. there, Sept. 14, 1932. He was an officer in the French navy, reaching the rank of vice-admiral; he grew up in a musical atmosphere and when still a child began to compose; took lessons with Henri Duparc. Under the influence of Duparc's style, Cras composed a number of miniatures in an impressionistic vein; he was at his best in lyrical songs and instrumental pieces.
    WORKS: Opera, *Polyphème* (Paris, Opéra-Comique, Dec. 28, 1922; won the Prize of the City of Paris); *Journal de Bord*, symphonic suite (1927); *Légende* for Cello and Orch. (1929); Piano Concerto (1931); Voice and Orch.: *L'Offrande lyrique* (1920); *Fontaines* (1923); *3 Noëls* (1929); many pieces of chamber music; a number of songs.
    BIBL.: R. Dumesnil, "J. C.," *Portraits de musiciens français* (Paris, 1938).

Crass, Franz, German bass-baritone; b. Wipperfurth, Feb. 9, 1928. He studied in Cologne; made his debut at Krefeld in 1954; gained prominence as a member of the Vienna State Opera; also appeared at the German Opera in West Berlin, La Scala in Milan, and the Bayreuth Festival. He is generally recognized as one of the foremost interpreters of bass roles in the operas of Mozart and Wagner.

Crawford, Robert (McArthur), Canadian-American baritone, conductor, and composer; b. Dawson, Yukon Territory,

July 27, 1899; d. N.Y., March 12, 1961. He studied at Princeton Univ., and also took courses at the Juilliard Graduate School and at the American Cons. at Fontainebleau, France. Returning to the U.S., he held various posts as a choral teacher and conductor; composed several orch. suites and songs, of which the most popular is *The U.S. Air Force* ("Off we go . . .").

Crawford, Ruth Porter, remarkable American composer; b. East Liverpool, Ohio, July 3, 1901; d. Chevy Chase, Md., Nov. 18, 1953. She studied composition with **Charles Seeger,** whom she later married; her principal piano teacher was Heniot Lévy. She dedicated herself to teaching and to collecting American folk songs; when still very young, she taught at the School of Musical Arts in Jacksonville, Fla. (1918–21); then gave courses at the American Cons. in Chicago (1925–29) and at the Elmhurst College of Music in Illinois (1926–29). In 1930 she received a Guggenheim fellowship. She became known mainly as a compiler of American folk songs; publ. *American Folk Songs for Children* (1948), *Animal Folk Songs for Children* (1950), and *American Folk Songs for Christmas* (1953). Her own compositions, astonishingly bold in their experimental aperçus and insights, often anticipated many techniques of the future avant-garde; while rarely performed during her lifetime, they had a remarkable revival in subsequent decades.
Works: Violin Sonata (1926); Suite for Piano and Woodwind Quintet (1927; rev. 1929; Cambridge, Mass., Dec. 14, 1975); 4 *Diaphonic Suites* for Various Instruments (1930); 3 *Songs* for Alto, Oboe, Percussion, Piano, and Optional Orch., to words by Carl Sandburg (*Rat Riddles; Prayers of Steel; In Tall Grass;* Berlin, March 10, 1932); String Quartet (1931; N.Y., Nov. 13, 1933); *Risselty Rosselty* for Small Orch. (1939); Suite for Wind Quintet (1952); several sets of piano pieces; 2 *Ricercari* for Voice and Piano (*Sacco, Vanzetti; Chinaman, Laundryman;* 1932).
Bibl.: C. Seeger, "R. C.," in H. Cowell, *American Composers on American Music* (Stanford, Calif., 1933); M. Gaume, *R. C. Seeger: Her Life and Works* (diss., Indiana Univ., 1973); D. Nicholls, "R. C. Seeger: An Introduction," *Musical Times* (July 1983); M. Gaume, *R. C. Seeger: Memoirs, Memories, Music* (Metuchen, N.J., 1986); R. Wilding-White, "Remembering R. C. Seeger: An Interview with Charles and Peggy Seeger," *American Music* (Winter 1988).

Creatore, Giuseppe, Italian-American conductor and impresario; b. Naples, June 21, 1871; d. N.Y., Aug. 15, 1952. He studied at the Naples Cons. with Nicola d'Arienzo and Camillo de Nardis. In 1900 he came to the U.S., organized his own band, and toured from coast to coast and in Canada. In 1906 he returned to Italy, where he established a band which he brought to America for a tour. He then settled in N.Y. and was active as impresario of various opera companies, which, however, were not successful; conducted band concerts during summer seasons in various U.S. cities.

Crécquillon (Créquillon), Thomas, Franco-Flemish composer; b. between c.1480 and c.1500; d. probably in Béthune, 1557. It is known that he was maître de chapelle at Béthune in 1540; was court musician to Charles V of Spain; later was canon at Namur, Termonde, and Béthune. His works, which rank with the best of that period, consist of 12 masses in 4, 5, and 6 Voices; 116 motets; *cantiones;* and 192 French chansons in 4, 5, and 6 parts. Reprints appear in Commer's *Collectio operum musicorum Batavorum saeculi XVI* and Maldeghem's *Trésor musical.* An edition of his works was publ. by N. Bridgman and B. Hudson, eds., *Thomas Crécquillon: Opera omnia,* in Corpus Mensurabilis Musicae, LXIII/1 (1974–   ).

Crescentini, Girolamo, one of the last and finest of the Italian castrato mezzo-sopranos; b. Urbania, near Urbino, Feb. 2, 1762; d. Naples, April 24, 1846. He studied singing with Gibelli at Bologna; began his career in Padua in 1782 and then sang in Rome in 1783; subsequent successes in other European capitals earned him the surname of "Orfeo Italiano." He sang at Livorno, Padua, Venice, Turin, London (1786), Milan, and Naples (1788–89). Napoleon, having heard him in 1805, deco-

rated him with the Iron Crown, and engaged him to teach singing to his family from 1806 to 1812; Crescentini then retired from the stage and left Paris, on account of vocal disorders induced by the climate; in 1816 he became a prof. of singing in the Royal Cons. in Naples. Cimarosa wrote his *Orazi e Curiazi* for him. Crescentini publ. several collections of *Ariette* (Vienna, 1797) and a *Treatise on Vocalization in France and Italy,* with vocal exercises (Paris, 1811).

Creser, William, English organist and composer; b. York, Sept. 9, 1844; d. London, March 13, 1933. He was taught by his father, in whose choir (at St. John's Church) he sang; studied later with G.A. Macfarren (organ and composition); as early as 1856 he occasionally acted as Barnby's substitute at Holgate Road Church; was appointed organist at Holy Trinity in Micklegate in 1859, and later succeeded Barnby; then filled various other positions; was organist at the Chapel Royal, St. James' (1891–1902); from 1902, examiner of Trinity College of Music, in which capacity he made frequent visits to musical institutions throughout the British colonies; received a Mus.Bac. (1869) and a Mus.Doc. (1880) from Oxford. His wife (née Amelia Clarke) was a well-known mezzo-soprano.
Works: Oratorio, *Micaiah;* cantatas: *Eudora* (Leeds, 1882); *The Sacrifice of Freia* (Leeds, 1889); *The Golden Legend; Tegner's Drapa;* Mass; 2 Psalms; *Old English Suite* for Orch.; String Quartet; Piano Trio; Violin Sonata; organ music.

Crespin, Régine, outstanding French soprano, later mezzo-soprano; b. Marseilles, Feb. 23, 1927. She studied pharmacology; then began taking voice lessons with Suzanne Cesbron-Viseur and Georges Jouatte in Paris. She made her debut in Mulhouse as Elsa in 1950 and then sang at the Paris Opéra. She acquired a European reputation as one of the best Wagnerian singers; she sang Kundry in *Parsifal* at the Bayreuth Festivals (1958–60); appeared also at La Scala in Milan, at Covent Garden in London, and on Nov. 19, 1962, made her debut with the Metropolitan Opera in N.Y. in the role of the Marschallin in *Der Rosenkavalier;* she remained with the Metropolitan until her farewell appearance as Mme. De Croissy in *Dialogues of the Carmelites* on April 16, 1987. She sang the parts of Elsa in *Lohengrin,* Sieglinde in *Die Walküre,* and Amelia in *Un ballo in maschera;* also appeared as a concert singer. Her sonorous, somewhat somber voice suited dramatic parts excellently.

Creston, Paul (real name, **Giuseppe Guttoveggio**), American composer; b. N.Y., Oct. 10, 1906; d. San Diego, Aug. 24, 1985. He studied piano and organ and began composing haphazardly as a child; he waited until he was 26 to write down some dance tunes for piano. To make a living, he took jobs as a theater organist in silent movies and also held teaching positions at various colleges in N.Y. In 1976 he moved to San Diego. Exceptionally prolific, he wrote more than 100 major works, including 6 syms., 15 concertos, and 35 other ensemble works. His harmonic and rhythmic idiom reached a high degree of complexity in some of his instrumental works; of considerable theoretical importance are his 2 books, *Principles of Rhythm* (N.Y., 1964) and *Creative Harmony* (N.Y., 1970). In his articles he militated against illogical binary meters and proposed such time signatures as 6/12 or 3/9; he used some of these metrical designations in his own compositions.
Works: 6 syms.: No. 1 (N.Y., Feb. 22, 1941); No. 2 (N.Y., Feb. 15, 1945); No. 3 (Worcester Festival, Oct. 27, 1950); No. 4 (Washington, D.C., Jan. 30, 1952); No. 5 (Washington, D.C., April 4, 1956); No. 6 for Organ and Orch. (Washington, D.C., June 28, 1982); Saxophone Concerto (1941; N.Y., Jan. 27, 1944); *Fantasy* for Trombone and Orch. (Los Angeles, Feb. 12, 1948); 2 violin concertos (1956, 1960); *Sadhana* for Cello and Chamber Orch., inspired by the philosophy of the Indian poet Rabindranath Tagore (Los Angeles, Oct. 3, 1981); chamber music; choral works.
Bibl.: H. Cowell, "P. C.," *Musical Quarterly* (Oct. 1948).

Crews, Lucile, American composer; b. Pueblo, Colo., Aug. 23, 1888; d. San Diego, Calif., Nov. 3, 1972. She studied at the New England Cons. of Music; later went to Europe, where she took private lessons with Nadia Boulanger in Paris and Hugo Kaun in Berlin. She wrote a symphonic poem, *To an Unknown Soldier* (1926); a miniature opera, *Ariadne and Dionysus* (1935); a "grand opera," *800 Rubles* (1926); *Suite* for Strings and Woodwinds; Viola Sonata; piano pieces; songs.

Crimi, Giulio, Italian tenor; b. Paterno, May 10, 1885; d. Rome, Oct. 29, 1939. He made his debut in Palermo in 1910; then sang at Covent Garden in London (1914). On Dec. 14, 1918, he sang at the Metropolitan Opera in N.Y. in the world premieres of Puccini's *Gianni Schicchi* (as Rinuccio) and *Il Tabarro* (as Luigi); continued to sing there until 1921; also made appearances in Chicago (1916–18; 1922–24); then sang in Milan and Rome. After his retirement, he taught voice; one of his most famous pupils was Tito Gobbi.

Crist, Bainbridge, American composer; b. Lawrenceburg, Ind., Feb. 13, 1883; d. Barnstable, Mass., Feb. 7, 1969. He studied piano and flute; later law at George Washington Univ. (LL.B.); was a lawyer in Boston for 6 years (until 1912), continuing his music as an avocation. He went to Europe to complete his musical training (theory with P. Juon in Berlin and C. Landi in London, and singing with William Shakespeare); he taught singing in Boston (1915–21) and Washington, D.C. (1922–23); returned to Europe (1923) and spent 4 years in Florence, Paris, Lucerne, and Berlin; then settled in Washington, D.C. He is author of *The Art of Setting Words to Music* (N.Y., 1944).

WORKS: STAGE: *Le Pied de la momie,* choreographic drama (1915; Bournmouth Festival, England, 1925); *Pregiwa's Marriage,* Javanese ballet in 1 scene (1920); *The Sorceress,* choreographic drama (1926). **ORCH.:** *Egyptian Impressions,* suite (Boston Pops, June 22, 1915); *Abhisarika* for Violin and Orch. (1921); *Intermezzo* (1921); *Chinese Dance* (1922); *Arabian Dance* (1922); *Nautch Dance* (1922); *Dreams* (1924); *Yearning* (1924); *Nocturne* (1924); *An Old Portrait* (1924); *La Nuit revécue* (1933; N.Y., March 8, 1936); *Vienna 1913* (1933); *Frivolité* (1934); *Hymn to Nefertiti* (1936); *Fête espagnole* (1937); *American Epic 1620,* tone poem (Washington, D.C., Feb. 28, 1943). **VOICE AND ORCH.:** *A Bag of Whistles* (1915); *The Parting,* poem (1916); *Rhymes* (1917); *O Come Hither!* (1918); *Drolleries* (1920); *Colored Stars,* suite of 4 songs (1921); *Remember* (1930); *The Way That Lovers Use* (1931); *Noontime* (1931); *Evening* (1931); *By a Silent Shore* (1932). Choral works for Mixed, Male, and Female Voices. Also piano pieces; songs.

BIBL.: J.T. Howard, *B. C.* (N.Y., 1929).

Cristoforeanu, Florica, Rumanian soprano; b. Rîmnicu-Sărat, Aug. 16, 1887; d. Rio de Janeiro, March 1, 1960. She studied at the Milan Cons. with Filippi and Bodrilla; made her debut in Capodistria in 1908 as Lucia; then sang operetta in Bucharest; from 1927 to 1932 she appeared at La Scala, Milan. She also sang in Rome and South America; retired in 1940. In addition to her classical roles, she was known for her performances of works by contemporary Italian composers.

Cristofori, Bartolomeo, celebrated Italian instrument maker; b. Padua, May 4, 1655; d. Florence, Jan. 27, 1731. He was the inventor of the 1st practical piano as opposed to the clavichord (which also employs a type of hammer action), although 2-keyed instruments called "Piano e Forte" are known to have existed in Modena in 1598, and a 4-octave keyboard instrument shaped like a dulcimer, with small hammers and no dampers, dating from 1610, is yet in existence. He was a leading maker of clavicembali in Padua; about 1690 went to Florence, where he was instrument maker to Ferdinando de' Medici; on the latter's death in 1713, he was made custodian of the court collection of instruments by Cosimo III. According to an article by Maffei (publ. 1711, *Giornale dei Letterati d'Italia*), Cristofori had up to that year made 3 "gravecembali col piano e forte," these having, instead of the usual jacks plucking the strings with quills, a row of little hammers striking the strings from below. The principle of this hammer action was adopted, in

the main, by Gottfried Silbermann, the Streichers, and Broadwood (hence called the "English action"). Following the designation by its inventor, the new instrument was named pianoforte. A piano of Cristofori's make is in the possession of the Metropolitan Museum of Art in N.Y.

BIBL.: F. Casaglia, *Per le onoranze a B. C.* (1876).

Crivelli, Giovanni Battista, Italian composer; b. Scandiano, Modena, date unknown; d. Modena, March 1652. He was organist at the Reggio Emilia Cathedral (1614–19); then served as director at the Accademia dello Spirito Santo in Ferrara (1626); subsequently was organist at the electoral court in Munich. He became maestro di cappella at the Milan Cathedral (1638–42) and at S. Maria Maggiore in Bergamo (1642–48). He publ. *Motetti concertati* (1626; 3rd ed., 1635) and *Madrigali concertati* (1626; 2nd ed., 1633).

Croce, Giovanni, eminent Italian composer, known as "Il Chiozzotto" after his birthplace; b. Chioggia, c.1557; d. Venice, May 15, 1609. He went at an early age to Venice, where he was a pupil of Zarlino, who placed him in the choir of S. Marco. After taking holy orders, he was active at the church of S. Maria Formosa; he then returned to S. Marco, teaching singing at its seminary (from 1593) and serving as vice-maestro and, later, maestro di cappella (from 1603). He was one of the leading Venetian composers of sacred music and madrigals. Among his sacred works, all publ. in Venice, were *Motetti* for 8 Voices (1594); *Messe* for 5 Voices (1596; ed. in Antiquae Musicae Italicae, Monumenta Venta, I, 1964), *Vespertina omnium solemnitatum* for 8 Voices (1597), and *Sacrae cantiones* for 5 Voices (1601). His secular works included *Il primo libro de madrigali* for 6 Voices (1590), *Il secondo libro de madrigali* for 5 Voices (1592), and *Triaca musicale . . . nella quale vi sono diversi caprici* for 4 to 7 Voices (1595; this vol. of caprices in Venetian dialect includes the contest between the cuckoo and the nightingale as judged by the parrot; ed. in *Capolavori polifonici del secolo XVI,* III, Rome, 1943).

BIBL.: F. Haberl, "G. C.: Eine bio-bibliographische Skizze," *Kirchenmusikalisches Jahrbuch,* III (1888); D. Arnold, "G. C. and the Concertato Style," *Musical Quarterly* (Jan. 1953); idem, "C. and the English Madrigal," *Music & Letters,* XXXV (1954); J. Kerman, *The Elizabethan Madrigal* (N.Y., 1962).

Croce, Jim, talented American songwriter and singer; b. Philadelphia, Jan. 10, 1942; d. (in an airplane crash) Natchitoches, La., Sept. 20, 1973. After he graduated from Villanova Univ., where he was a disc jockey for a folk-music program, his musical career suffered from a lack of compensatory recognition; to make ends meet, he worked at a variety of menial tasks, including selling ads, digging ditches, teaching summer courses at a Philadelphia ghetto school, and driving a truck. His 1st album, recorded with his wife, Ingrid, was a flop; he subsequently paired with the guitarist Maury Muehleisen (1949–73), with whom he recorded *You Don't Mess Around with Jim* (1972), which became an instant hit. Their next album, *Life and Times* (1973), also met with success; a single recorded that same year, *Bad, Bad Leroy Brown,* rocketed to the top of the charts. Just as fame had arrived for the duo, their lives were ended in an airplane crash following a concert at Northwestern State Univ. of La. in Natchitoches (pronounced Na-ki-tish), La. Two other songs, *I've Got a Name* and *Time in a Bottle,* brought further posthumous fame.

Crocker, Richard L(incoln), American musicologist; b. Roxbury, Mass., Feb. 17, 1927. He studied with Schrade at Yale Univ. (B.A., 1950; Ph.D., 1957, with the diss. *The Repertoire of Proses at St. Martial de Limoges*), later conducting research in England and France on a Guggenheim fellowship (1969–70). He taught at his alma mater (1955–63), then joined the faculty of the Univ. of Calif. at Berkeley (from 1963). He publ. *A History of Musical Style* (N.Y., 1966), *Listening to Music* (with A. Basart; N.Y., 1971), and *The Early Medieval Sequence* (Berkeley and Los Angeles, 1977); he also ed., with D. Hiley, vol. II: *The Early Middle Ages to 1300* in *The New Oxford History of Music* (Oxford, 1990).

Croes, Henri-Jacques de, Belgian violinist and composer; b. Antwerp, Sept. 19, 1705; d. Brussels, Aug. 16, 1786. He was violinist at the church of St.-Jacques in Antwerp (1723); in 1729, became music director to the Prince of Thurn and Taxis, at Brussels, Frankfurt, and Regensburg. He went to Brussels in 1744 as 1st violinist in the chapel of Charles of Lorraine; from 1746 to 1755 was maître de chapelle to Charles of Lorraine.
WORKS: Masses, motets, anthems, and other church music; also syms., sonatas, etc.
BIBL.: S. Clercx, *H.-J. d.C., compositeur et Maître de Musique du Prince Charles de Lorraine* (Brussels, 1940).

Croft (or Crofts), William, English organist and composer; b. Nether Ettington, Warwickshire (baptized), Dec. 30, 1678; d. Bath, Aug. 14, 1727 (buried in Westminster Abbey). He was a chorister in the Chapel Royal, under Dr. Blow; became a Gentleman of the Chapel Royal in 1700, and (with J. Clarke) joint organist in 1704; he succeeded Blow as organist of Westminster Abbey, Master of the Children, and Composer of the Chapel Royal (1708).
WORKS: *Musica sacra,* numerous anthems *a* 2–8, and a burial service in score (1724; the 1st English work of church music engraved in score on plates); *Musicus apparatus academicus* (2 odes written for his degree of Mus.Doc., received from Oxford, 1713); overtures and act tunes for several plays; violin sonatas; flute sonatas; etc. Modern editions include H. Ferguson and C. Hogwood, eds., *William Croft: Complete Harpsichord Works* (London, 1974); R. Platt, ed., *William Croft: Complete Organ Works* (London, 1976–77).
BIBL.: F.G.E., "Dr. W. C.," *Musical Times* (Sept. 1900); A. R. Carpenter, "W. C.'s Church Music," ibid. (March 1971).

Crooks, Richard (Alexander), American tenor; b. Trenton, N.J., June 26, 1900; d. Portola Valley, Calif., Sept. 29, 1972. He studied voice with Sydney H. Bourne and also took lessons with Frank La Forge; was a boy soprano soloist in N.Y. churches, later tenor soloist; made his debut with the N.Y. Sym. Orch. under Damrosch in 1922; gave concerts in London, Vienna, Munich, Berlin, and the U.S. (1925–27); made his American debut as Cavaradossi with the Philadelphia Grand Opera Co. (Nov. 27, 1930); made his debut at the Metropolitan Opera as Des Grieux (Feb. 25, 1933); toured Australia (1936–39); gave concerts from coast to coast in the U.S. and Canada; appeared in recitals, as an orch. soloist, and in festivals.

Crosby, Bing (actually, **Harry Lillis**), popular American singer; b. Tacoma, Wash., May 2, 1901; d. while playing golf at La Moraleja golf course outside Madrid, Oct. 14, 1977. He was a drummer in school bands; intermittently attended classes in law at Gonzaga Univ. in Spokane, Wash.; when he became famous, the school gave him an honorary degree of doctor of music. In 1926 he went to Los Angeles, where he filled engagements as a singer. He made his mark on the radio, and his success grew apace; he used his limited vocal resources to advantage by a cunning projection of deep thoracic undertones. He never deviated from his style of singing—unpretentious, sometimes mock-sentimental, and invariably communicative; he became a glorified crooner. Apart from his appearances in concert and with bands, he also made movies; his series with Bob Hope, beginning with *Road to Morocco,* made in 1942, with their invariable girl companion Dorothy Lamour, became classics of the American cinema. He continued his appearances until the last months of his life. The origin of his nickname is in dispute; it was derived either from the popular comic strip "The Bingville Bugle," or from his habit of popping a wooden gun in school, shouting, "Bing! Bing!" In 1953 he publ. his autobiography under the title *Call Me Lucky.* His brother **Bob Crosby** (b. Spokane, Wash., Aug. 25, 1913) was a jazz singer and a bandleader; Bing Crosby's 4 sons from his 1st marriage are also crooners.
BIBL.: T. Crosby, *The Story of B. C.* (N.Y., 1937; 2nd ed., 1946); B. Ulanov, *The Incredible C.* (N.Y., 1947); C. Thompson,

B. (N.Y., 1976); G. Crosby, *Going My Own Way,* an anti-paternal account of life with a famous father by a disrespectful son (N.Y., 1983); K. Crosby, *My Life with B.* (Wheeling, Ill., 1983).

Crosby, John (O'Hea), American opera conductor and impresario; b. N.Y., July 12, 1926. He studied violin and piano with his mother. Upon graduating from high school in 1944, he was drafted into the U.S. Army, serving in the infantry as a corporal; he played various instruments in the dance band of his regiment; after the end of the war he played trombone and double bass in dance orchs. He then entered Yale Univ., where he studied composition with Hindemith, receiving his B.A. in music in 1950. In 1951 he took courses in conducting at Columbia Univ. with Rudolph Thomas; later he attended conducting seminars in Maine under Pierre Monteux. From 1951 to 1956 he worked as an accompanist, coach, and conductor at the N.Y. City Opera. In 1956 Crosby persuaded his father, an affluent lawyer, to give him enough money to build an outdoor opera house in Santa Fe, N.Mex. He inaugurated the Santa Fe Festival in the summer of 1957, producing a season of classical and modern operas. The theater burned down in 1967, but Crosby collected enough money to build a new fireproof building for his enterprise, which eventually became known as the Santa Fe Opera. Crosby was able to persuade Stravinsky to conduct a performance of his opera *The Rake's Progress;* Hindemith was engaged to conduct his own opera *Neues vom Tage.* Weather has been an uncertain factor through the Santa Fe seasons, and once or twice a cloudburst forced the postponement of a performance. In 1975 Crosby took over the presidency of Opera America, a cartel coordinating 43 opera companies; from 1976 to 1986 he was president of the Manhattan School of Music.
BIBL.: W. Sargeant, "A Miracle in the Desert," *New Yorker* (Aug. 1, 1975).

Cross, Joan, English soprano; b. London, Sept. 7, 1900. She was educated at Trinity College, London. In 1931 she joined Sadler's Wells Opera; also appeared at Covent Garden. Subsequently she helped to found the English Opera Group in London, devoted to performances of new works; sang in several 1st performances of Benjamin Britten's operas. In 1948 she founded the Opera School (now the National School of Opera), serving as one of its teachers for many years. In 1955 she began to produce opera at Sadler's Wells and Covent Garden.

Cross, Lowell (Merlin), American composer and electro-musicologist; b. Kingsville, Texas, June 24, 1938. He studied mathematics and music at Texas Technological Univ., graduating in 1963; then entered the Univ. of Toronto in Canada, obtaining his M.A. in musicology in 1968; attended classes of Marshall McLuhan in environmental technology there; took a course in electronic music with Myron Schaeffer and Gustav Ciamaga. He was director of and a teacher at the Mills Tape Music Center (1968–69), and from 1968 to 1969 he served as resident programmer for Experiments in Art and Technology at Expo '70 in Osaka, Japan, and guest consultant in electronic music at the National Inst. of Design in Ahmedabad, India; in 1971 he was engaged as artist-in-residence at the Univ. of Iowa's Center for New Performing Arts. Eschewing any preliminary serial experimentation, Cross espoused a cybernetic totality of audiovisual, electronic, and theatrical arts. The notation of Cross's audiovisual compositions consists of color photographs of television images resulting from the programmed manipulation of sound-producing mechanisms in the acoustical space (see his technical paper *Audio/Video/Laser,* publ. in *Source,* Sacramento, Calif., No. 8, 1970). He compiled a valuable manual, *A Bibliography of Electronic Music* (Toronto, 1967). As a pioneer in astromusicology, he created the selenogeodesic score *Lunar Laser Beam* (broadcast as a salutatory message on Nicolas Slonimsky's 77th birthday, April 27, 1971, purportedly via Leningrad, the subject's birthplace; the Sea of Tranquillity on the moon; and the Ciudad de Nuestra Señora Reina de Los Angeles in California). As director of the Video/Laser Laboratory at the Univ. of Iowa, Cross was responsible for the production of Scriabin's *Prometheus* by the Iowa Univ. Orch., conducted by James Dixon, with color projections coordinated with the "color organ" (*luce*) as prescribed in the score (Iowa City, Sept. 24, 1975).

WORKS: 4 *Random Studies* for Tape (1961); *0.8 Century* for Tape (1962); *Eclectic Music* for Flute and Piano (1964); *Antiphonies* for Tape (1964); *After Long Silence* for Soprano and Tape (1964); *3 Etudes* for Tape (1965); *Video I* and *II* for Variable Media, including Tape, Audio System, Oscilloscope, and Television (1965–68); *Musica Instrumentalis* for Acoustical Stereophonic Instruments, Monochrome and Polychrome Television (1965–68); *Video III* for Television and Phase-derived Audio System (1968); *Reunion* for Electronic Chessboard (constructed by Cross and 1st demonstrated in Toronto, March 5, 1968, the main opponents in the chess game being John Cage and the painter Marcel Duchamp, who won readily); *Electro-Acustica* for Instruments, Laser Deflection System, Television, and Phase-derived Audio System (1970–71); *Video/Laser I–IV* for Laser Deflection System (1969–80).

Cross, Ronald, American instrumentalist, composer, and musicologist; b. Fort Worth, Texas, Feb. 18, 1929. He studied at Guilmant Organ School in N.Y., at Centenary College of Louisiana, and at N.Y. Univ. (Ph.D., 1962). In 1955 he received a Fulbright fellowship to travel in Italy. In 1958 he was appointed to the faculty of Notre Dame College of Staten Island. In 1968 he joined the faculty of Wagner College in N.Y.; became chairman of the music dept. and director of the Collegium Musicum. He wrote a number of choral pieces; also chamber music; ed. the collected works of Matthaeus Pipelare.

Crosse, Gordon, English composer; b. Bury, Lancashire, Dec. 1, 1937. He studied at Oxford Univ., where he took courses in music history with Egon Wellesz; did postgraduate work in medieval music. In 1962 he went to Rome, where he attended the classes of Goffredo Petrassi at the Accademia di Santa Cecilia. Returning to England, he taught at Birmingham Univ. (extramurally); from 1969 to 1976 he was a fellow in the music dept. of Essex Univ. His absorption in the studies of early music, in combination with an engrossment in modern techniques, determines the character of his compositions.

WORKS: *Concerto da camera* for Violin and Orch. (Violin Concerto No. 1, 1962; London, Feb. 18, 1968); *For the Unfallen* for Tenor, Horn, and Strings (1963; Liverpool, Sept. 17, 1968); *Meet My Folks*, a multi-child presentation for Voices, Instruments, and Adults (1964); Syms. for Chamber Orch. (Birmingham, Feb. 13, 1965); *Sinfonia concertante* for Orch. (Cheltenham, July 15, 1965; withdrawn and rev. as Sym. No. 1, 1976); *Changes*, nocturnal cycle for Soprano, Baritone, Chorus, and Orch. (1965); *Purgatory*, opera after Yeats (Cheltenham, July 7, 1966); *Ceremony* for Cello and Orch. (London, Aug. 4, 1966); *The Grace of Todd*, 1-act opera (Aldeburgh, June 7, 1967); *The Demon of Adachigahara* for Speaker, Adolescent Chorus, Mime, and Instruments (1968); Concerto for Chamber Orch. (Budapest, July 3, 1968); Violin Concerto No. 2 (Oxford, Jan. 29, 1970); *The History of the Flood* for Children's Voices and Harp (London, Dec. 6, 1970); *Some Marches on a Ground* for Orch. (1970); *Memories of Morning: Night*, monodrama for Soprano and Orch. (London, Dec. 8, 1971); *Wheel of the World*, "entertainment" based on Chaucer's *Canterbury Tales*, for Actors, Children's Chorus, Mixed Chorus, and Orch. (Aldeburgh Festival, June 5, 1972); *Ariadne* for Solo Oboe and 12 Players (Cheltenham Festival, July 11, 1972); *The Story of Vasco*, opera (London, March 13, 1974); *Celebration* for Chorus (London, Sept. 16, 1974); *Holly from the Bongs*, opera (Manchester, Dec. 9, 1974); *Potter Thompson*, children's opera (London, Jan. 9, 1975); Sym. No. 2 (London, May 27, 1975); *Epiphany Variations: Double Variations for Orchestra* (N.Y., March 18, 1976); *Playground* for Orch. (1977; Manchester, March 2, 1978); *Wildboy* for Clarinet and Ensemble (1977; version for Full Orch., 1980); *Dreamsongs* for Chamber Orch. (1978); Cello Concerto (1979); String Quartet (1980); *Young Apollo*, ballet (1984); *Array* for Trumpet and Strings (London, Aug.

9, 1986); *Quiet* for Wind Band (1987); sacred and secular choruses.

BIBL.: A. Burn, "G. C. at 50," *Musical Times* (Dec. 1987).

Crossley, Ada (Jessica), Australian mezzo-soprano; b. Tarraville, Gippsland, March 3, 1874; d. London, Oct. 17, 1929. She was a pupil of Fanny Simonson (voice) in Melbourne; having sung in several churches, she made her concert debut with the Melbourne Phil. Soc. in 1892; went to London in 1894, studied with Santley, and later with Mme. Marchesi in Paris; made her London debut at the Queen's Hall on May 18, 1895; her success was so emphatic that she sang by command 5 times before Queen Victoria within the next 2 years; appeared as a soloist at all important English festivals; her tour of Australia in 1904 was a succession of triumphs; also made successful tours of the U.S. and South Africa.

Crossley, Paul (Christopher Richard), English pianist; b. Dewsbury, Yorkshire, May 17, 1944. He attended Oxford Univ. as an organ scholar at Mansfield College there; also studied piano with Fanny Waterman in Leeds. In 1967 he received a scholarship from the French government to continue his studies with Messiaen and Yvonne Loriod. In 1968 he made his 1st major tour, garnering praise in England and on the Continent as an interpreter of the Romantic repertoire. In 1988 he was named joint artistic director of the London Sinfonietta.

Crossley-Holland, Peter, English ethnomusicologist and composer; b. London, Jan. 28, 1916. He studied physiology at St. John's College, Oxford (B.A., 1936; M.A., 1941); then took courses in composition with Ireland, Seiber, and Julius Harrison at the Royal College of Music in London (B.Mus., 1943); subsequently pursued postgraduate work in Indian music at the London School of Oriental and African Studies. From 1943 to 1945 he was regional director of the British Arts Council; from 1948 to 1963 was engaged in the music division of the BBC; then became assistant director of the Inst. of Comparative Music Studies and Documentation in Berlin. In 1969 he joined the faculty at the Univ. of Calif. in Los Angeles; became a prof. there in 1972; retired in 1984. In 1965 he became ed. of the *Journal of the International Folk Music Council*. As an ethnomusicologist, he has concentrated mostly on Celtic, Tibetan, and native American music. He ed. *Music in Wales* (London, 1948) and *Artistic Values in Traditional Music* (Berlin, 1966); also publ. *Music: A Report on Musical Life in England* (London, 1949). He composed songs; also pieces for chorus and for recorders.

Crotch, William, eminent English organist, teacher, and composer; b. Norwich, July 5, 1775; d. Taunton, Dec. 29, 1847. His extraordinary precocity may be measured by the well-authenticated statement (Burney's paper, "Account of an Infant Musician," in the *Philosophical Transactions* of 1779) that when 2 and a half years old he played on a small organ built by his father, a master carpenter. In 1779, he was brought to London, and played in public. At the age of 11 he became assistant to Dr. Randall, organist of Trinity and King's colleges at Cambridge; at 14, he composed an oratorio, *The Captivity of Judah* (Cambridge, June 4, 1789); he then studied for the ministry (1788–90); returning to music, he was organist of Christ Church, Oxford; graduated from Oxford with a Mus.Bac. in 1794; received a Mus.Doc. in 1799. In 1797 he succeeded Hayes as prof. of music at Oxford and as organist of St. John's College. Crotch lectured in the Music School (1800–1804), and in the Royal Institution in London (1804, 1805, 1807, and again from 1820); was principal of the new Royal Academy of Music from 1822 to 1832.

WORKS: 2 oratorios: *Palestine* (London, April 21, 1812) and *The Captivity of Judah* (Oxford, June 10, 1834; a different work from his juvenile oratorio of the same name); 10 anthems (1798); 3 organ concertos; piano sonatas; an ode, *Mona on Snowdown calls*; a glee, *Nymph, with thee*; a motet, *Methinks I hear the full celestial choir* (these last 3 were very popular); other odes; other glees, fugues; he also wrote *Elements of Musical Composition* (London, 1812; reprint, 1833; 2nd ed., 1856);

Practical Thorough-bass; etc. A complete list of his compositions appeared in *Musical News* (April 17 and 24, 1897).

BIBL.: J. Rennert, *W. C.* (London, 1975).

Crouch, Frederick Nicholls, English conductor and composer; b. London, July 31, 1808; d. Portland, Maine, Aug. 18, 1896. He studied with Bochsa (cello), and entered the Royal Academy of Music in London in 1822 (teachers: Crotch, Attwood, Howes, Lindley, and Crivelli). At the age of 9 he was a cellist in the Royal Coburg Theater; played in Queen Adelaide's private band till 1832; was a teacher and singer in Plymouth, and cellist in various theaters. He went to N.Y. in 1849; was in Philadelphia in 1856 as conductor of Mrs. Rush's Saturday Concerts; served in the Union Army, and settled in Baltimore as a singing teacher. Cora Pearl, the famous Parisian courtesan of the 2nd Empire, was his daughter. He composed 2 operas; many collections of songs, some original (including the well-known *Kathleen Mavourneen*).

Crozier, Catharine, esteemed American organist; b. Hobart, Okla., Jan. 18, 1914. She studied organ at the Eastman School of Music, where she received a master's degree in music; then taught organ there (1938–53); became head of the organ dept. in 1953. She was prof. of organ at Eastman (from 1938) and at Rollins College, Winter Park, Fla. (1955–69). She was married to the organist and musicologist **Harold Gleason,** who had been her teacher.

Crüger, Johann, noted German composer; b. Grossbreesen, near Guben, April 9, 1598; d. Berlin, Feb. 23, 1662. A student of divinity at Wittenberg in 1620, he had received thorough musical training at Regensburg under Paulus Homberger. He then traveled in Austria and Hungary; spent some time in Bohemia and Saxony before settling in Berlin, where he was cantor at the Nicolaikirche from 1622 until his death. His fame rests on the composition of many fine chorales (*Jesu, meine Freude; Jesu, meine Zuversicht; Nun danket alle Gott;* etc.), which were orig. publ. in the collection *Praxis pietatis melica* (Berlin, 1644; reprinted in 45 eds. before 1736). In addition, he publ. the following collections: *Neues vollkömmliches Gesangbuch Augsburgischer Konfession . . .* (1640); *Geistliche Kirchenmelodeyen . . .* (1649); *Dr. M. Luthers wie auch andrer gottseliger christlicher Leute Geistliche Lieder und Psalmen* (1657); *Psalmodia sacra . . .* (1658); the valuable theoretical works *Synopsis musica* (1630; enl. 1634), *Praecepta musicae figuralis* (1625), and *Quaestiones musicae practicae* (1650).

BIBL.: E. Langbecker, *J. C.s Choral-Melodien* (Berlin, 1835); E. Fischer-Krückeberg, "J. C. als Musiktheoretiker," *Zeitschrift für Musikwissenschaft,* XII; idem, "J. C.s Choralbearbeitungen," ibid., XIV; idem, "J. C. und das Kirchenlied des 17. Jahrhundert," *Monatsschrift für Gottesdienst und kirchliche Kunst,* XXXIV, 2; O. Brodde, *J. C., Sein Weg und sein Werk* (Leipzig, 1936); J. Hoffmeister, *Der Kantor zu St. Nicolai: Beschreibung des Lebens von J. C.* (Berlin, 1964).

Crumb, George (Henry Jr.), distinguished and innovative American composer; b. Charleston, W.Va., Oct. 24, 1929. He was brought up in a musical environment; his father played the clarinet and his mother was a cellist; he studied music at home; began composing while in school, and had some of his pieces performed by the Charleston Sym. Orch. He then took courses in composition at Mason College in Charleston (B.M., 1950); later enrolled at the Univ. of Illinois (M.M., 1952) and continued his studies in composition with Ross Lee Finney at the Univ. of Michigan (D.M.A., 1959); in 1955 he received a Fulbright fellowship for travel to Germany, where he studied with Boris Blacher at the Berlin Hochschule für Musik. He further received grants from the Rockefeller (1964), Koussevitzky (1965), and Coolidge (1970) foundations; in 1967 held a Guggenheim fellowship, and also was given the National Inst. of Arts and Letters Award. In 1968 he was awarded the Pulitzer Prize in music for his *Echoes of Time and the River.* Parallel to working on his compositions, he was active as a music teacher. From 1959 to 1964 he taught piano and occasional classes in composition at the Univ. of Colorado at Boulder; in 1965 he joined the music dept. of the Univ. of

Pa.; in 1983 he was named Annenberg Prof. of the Humanities there. In his music, Crumb is a universalist. Nothing in the realm of sound is alien to him; no method of composition is unsuited to his artistic purposes; accordingly, his music can sing as sweetly as the proverbial nightingale, and it can be as rough, rude, and crude as a primitive man of the mountains. The vocal parts especially demand extraordinary skills of lungs, lips, tongue, and larynx to produce such sound effects as percussive tongue clicks, explosive shrieks, hissing, whistling, whispering, and sudden shouting of verbal irrelevancies, interspersed with portentous syllabification, disparate phonemes, and rhetorical logorrhea. In startling contrast, Crumb injects into his sonorous kaleidoscope citations from popular works, such as the middle section of Chopin's *Fantaisie-Impromptu,* Ravel's *Bolero,* or some other "objet trouvé," a procedure first introduced facetiously by Erik Satie. In his instrumentation, Crumb is no less unconventional. Among the unusual effects in his scores is instructing the percussion player to immerse the loudly sounding gong into a tub of water, having an electric guitar played with glass rods over the frets, or telling wind instrumentalists to blow soundlessly through their tubes. Spatial distribution also plays a role: instrumentalists and singers are assigned their reciprocal locations on the podium or in the hall. All this is, of course, but an illustrative décor; the music is of the essence. Like most composers who began their work around the middle of the 20th century, Crumb adopted the Schoenbergian idiom, seasoned with pointillistic devices. After these preliminaries, he wrote his unmistakably individual *Madrigals,* to words by the martyred poet Federico García Lorca, scored for voice and instrumental groups. There followed the most extraordinary work, *Ancient Voices of Children,* performed for the 1st time at a chamber music festival in Washington, D.C., on Oct. 31, 1970; the text is again by Lorca; a female singer intones into the space under the lid of an amplified grand piano; a boy's voice responds in anguish; the accompaniment is supplied by an orch. group and an assortment of exotic percussion instruments, such as Tibetan prayer stones, Japanese temple bells, a musical saw, and a toy piano. A remarkable group of 4 pieces, entitled *Makrokosmos,* calls for unusual effects; in one of these, the pianist is ordered to shout at specified points of time. Crumb's most grandiose creation is *Star-Child,* representing, in his imaginative scheme, a progression from tenebrous despair to the exaltation of luminous joy. The score calls for a huge orch., which includes 2 children's choruses and 8 percussion players performing on all kinds of utensils, such as pot lids, and also iron chains and metal sheets, as well as ordinary drums; it had its 1st performance under the direction of Pierre Boulez with the N.Y. Phil. on May 5, 1977.

WORKS: Sonata for Solo Cello (1955); *Variazioni* for Orch. (1959; Cincinnati, May 8, 1965); 5 *Pieces for Piano* (1962); *Night Music I* for Soprano, Piano or Celesta, and Percussion, to verses by Federico García Lorca (1963; Paris, Jan. 30, 1964); 4 *Nocturnes (Night Music II)* for Violin and Piano (1963; Buffalo, N.Y., Feb. 3, 1965); *Madrigals, Book I* for Soprano, Contrabass, and Vibraphone, to a text by García Lorca (1965; Philadelphia, Feb. 18, 1966); *Madrigals, Book II* for Soprano, Flute, and Percussion, to a text by García Lorca (1965; Washington, D.C., March 11, 1966); 11 *Echoes of Autumn, 1965 (Echoes I)* for Violin, Alto Flute, Clarinet, and Piano (Brunswick, Maine, Aug. 10, 1966); *Echoes of Time and the River (Echoes II: 4 Processionals for Orchestra)* (Chicago, May 26, 1967); *Songs, Drones, and Refrains of Death* for Baritone, Electric Guitar, Electric Contrabass, Amplified Piano (and Amplified Harpsichord), and 2 Percussionists, to a text by García Lorca (1968; Iowa City, Iowa, March 29, 1969); *Madrigals, Book III* for Soprano, Harp, and 1 Percussion Player, to a text by García Lorca (1969; Seattle, March 6, 1970); *Madrigals, Book IV* for Soprano, Flute, Harp, Contrabass, and 1 Percussion Player, to a text by García Lorca (1969; Seattle, March 6, 1970); *Night of the 4 Moons* for Alto, Alto Flute, Banjo, Electric Cello, and 1 Percussion Player, to a text by García Lorca (Washington, Pa., Nov. 6, 1969); *Black Angels (13 Images from the Dark Land: Images*

I) for Electric String Quartet (Ann Arbor, Mich., Oct. 23, 1970); *Ancient Voices of Children* for Soprano, Boy Soprano, Oboe, Mandolin, Harp, Electric Piano (and Toy Piano), and 3 Percussion Players, to a text by García Lorca (Washington, D.C., Oct. 31, 1970); *Lux aeterna for 5 Masked Players* for Soprano, Bass Flute (and Soprano Recorder), Sitar, and 2 Percussion Players (1971; Richmond, Va., Jan. 16, 1972); *Vox balaenae* (Voice of the Whale) *for 3 Masked Players* for Electric Flute, Electric Cello, and Amplified Piano (1971; Washington, D.C., March 17, 1972); *Makrokosmos, Volume I (12 Fantasy-Pieces after the Zodiac for Amplified Piano)* (1972; Colorado Springs, Feb. 8, 1973); *Makrokosmos, Volume II (12 Fantasy-Pieces after the Zodiac for Amplified Piano)* (1973; N.Y., Nov. 12, 1974); *Music for a Summer Evening (Makrokosmos III)* for 2 Amplified Pianos and 2 Percussion Players (Swarthmore, Pa., March 30, 1974); *Dream Sequence (Images II)* for Violin, Cello, Piano, 1 Percussion Player, and 2 Offstage Musicians playing Glass Harmonica (1976); *Star-Child*, a parable for Soprano, Antiphonal Children's Voices, Male Speaking Choir, Bell Ringers, and Large Orch., demanding the coordinating abilities of 4 conductors (N.Y., May 5, 1977, under the general direction of Pierre Boulez); *Celestial Mechanics (Makrokosmos IV)*, cosmic dances for Amplified Piano, 4-hands (N.Y., Nov. 18, 1979); *Apparition*, elegiac songs and vocalises for Soprano and Amplified Piano, to a text by Walt Whitman (1979; N.Y., Jan. 13, 1981); *A Little Suite for Christmas, A.D. 1979* for Piano (Washington, D.C., Dec. 14, 1980); *Gnomic Variations* for Piano (1981); *Pastoral Drone* for Organ (1982); *Processional* for Piano (1983); *A Haunted Landscape* for Orch. (N.Y., June 7, 1984); *An Idyll for the Misbegotten* for Amplified Flute and 3 Percussionists (1985; Toronto, Nov. 16, 1986); *Federico's Little Songs* for Children for Soprano, Flute, and Percussion, after García Lorca (1986; Philadelphia, June 12, 1988); *Zeitgeist* for 2 Amplified Pianos (1987; Duisburg, Jan. 17, 1988).

Bibl.: D. Cope, *G. C.: A Biography* (N.Y., 1984; with annotated list of works compiled by D. Gillespie); D. Gillespie, ed., *G. C.: Profile of a Composer* (N.Y., 1986).

Crusell, Bernhard Henrik, noted Finnish clarinetist and composer; b. Uusikaupunki, near Turku, Oct. 15, 1775; d. Stockholm, July 28, 1838. He took clarinet lessons from a member of the military band at Sveaborg Castle; then moved to Stockholm in 1791; there he had a chance to study with Abbé Vogler. While improving his general knowledge of music, Crusell continued to play the clarinet; in 1798 he went to Berlin to study with Franz Tausch. In 1803 he went to Paris, where he studied composition with Berton and Gossec. In his instrumental music Crusell followed the tradition of Gluck; his vocal works reveal Nordic traits. In Sweden he acted as translator of opera librettos for Stockholm productions. The Swedish Academy awarded him its gold medal shortly before his death.

Works: orch.: 3 clarinet concertos (1811, 1818, 1828); *Concertante* for Horn, Bassoon, Clarinet, and Orch. (1816); *Introduction et air suédois* for Clarinet and Orch. (1830); *Concertino* for Bassoon and Orch. Chamber: 3 quartets for Clarinet and Strings (1811, 1817, 1823); 3 clarinet duos (1821); *Divertimento* for Oboe and Strings (1823). Vocal: 37 songs for 4-part Chorus; *Den lilla slavinnan* (The Little Slave Girl; Stockholm, Feb. 18, 1824).

Cruz, Celia, highly skilled Cuban singer of popular music; b. Havana, Oct. 21, 1924. She began singing on Cuban radio in the late 1940s, then studied at the Cons. of Music (1947–50). In 1950 she became lead singer with the popular band La Sonora Matancera, with which she toured and recorded extensively until 1965. She settled in the U.S. in 1960, and in 1966 joined the Tito Puente Orch. In 1973 she sang at Carnegie Hall in the role of Gracia Divina in Larry Harlow's *Hommy—A Latin Opera*, and in 1974 she won a gold record for the album *Celia and Johnny*, recorded with the Johnny Pacheco Orch. Her later albums include *Celia-Ray-Adalberto-Tremendo Trio!* (1983), *De Nuevo* (1985), and *The Winners* (1987). On Oct. 23, 1982, she was honored at a special reunion

concert event at Madison Square Garden in N.Y. She became known as the "Queen of Salsa" for her extraordinary improvisational skills, which she applied to such hit songs as *La Danza del Cocoye, Yerbero Moderno,* and *Burundanga* (gold record, 1957).

Cruz, Ivo, Portuguese conductor and composer; b. Corumbá, Brazil, May 19, 1901; d. Lisbon, Sept. 8, 1985. He was taken to Portugal, where he studied law at Lisbon Univ. (1919–24); he then went to Munich, where he took courses in composition and conducting. Returning to Portugal in 1931, he founded in 1937 the Lisbon Phil., which he conducted until 1971. He cultivated native subjects in his works, as demonstrated in his 3 syms.: *Coimbra* (1945), *Lisboa* (1946), and *Sinfonia de Amadis* (1952). He also wrote ballet music and several song cycles. His music lacked distinction, however, and had few performances except those promoted by himself.

Cruz-Romo, Gilda, Mexican soprano; b. Guadalajara, Feb. 12, 1940. She studied at the Cons. of Mexico; made her debut there in 1962. On May 8, 1970, she appeared at the Metropolitan Opera in N.Y. as Maddalena in *Andrea Chénier*; continued to sing there in subsequent seasons; also sang in Chicago, Houston, Dallas, etc. In Europe, she appeared in London, Milan, Moscow, Paris, and Vienna.

Crzellitzer, Franz, German-born Israeli composer; b. Berlin-Charlottenburg, Nov. 1, 1905; d. Tel Aviv, Jan. 27, 1979. In 1934 he settled in Tel Aviv.

Works: *Charaktermarsch* for Orch. (1939); 2 unnumbered syms. (1940–41; 1968–70); a ballet pantomime, *Pied Piper of Hamelin* (1944–46); *Improvisation* for Orch. (1951); 3 *Suites* for String Orch. (1952; 1968–74; 1974); 2 *Symphonic Fantasies* for Orch. (1958, 1959); *Fantasy* for Violin and Orch. (1960); *Fantasy* for Cello and Orch. (1962); 2-piano Concerto (1966); Trumpet Concerto (1967); Viola Concerto (1967); *Capriccio* for Piano and Chamber Orch. (1970); Concertino for Clarinet and String Orch. (1971); *Concert Piece* for Trombone and Orch. (1971); Sinfonietta (1972); *Concert Piece* for Horn, Clarinet, and Strings (1972); *Die Wüste* (The Desert), passacaglia for Orch. (1974); Concertino for Bassoon and Strings (1975); Concertino for Flute and Strings (1975); Concertino for Violin and Strings (1976); *Concert Piece* for Organ and Orch. (1976); *Concert Piece* for Orch. (1977); 2 violin sonatas (1948); Piano Quintet (1949); 2 string quartets (1954, 1963); Oboe Quartet (1955); Wind Quintet (1966); 2 piano trios (1968, 1971); Cello Sonata (1971); Flute Sonata (1972); Trio for Horn, Violin, and Piano (1973); Viola Sonata (1974); Brass Quintet (1975); 5 *Preludes* for Piano (1947); 7 *Preludes* for Piano (1968–69); *Theme and Variations* for Piano (1973); *Toccata and 2 Etudes* for Piano (1976); *Passacaglia* for Organ (1972).

Csiky, Boldizsár, Rumanian composer; b. Tîrgu-Mureş, Oct. 3, 1937. He studied at the Tîrgu-Mureş Music College (1953–55) and with Demian, Toduţă, and Jodál at the Cons. in Cluj (1956–61); taught at Tîrgu-Mureş from 1961 to 1968. In his music he applies dissonant sonorism, striving for coloristic effects.

Works: Chamber opera, *Görög Ilona* (1966); *Octombrie*, cantata (1960); *Purtătorii de Făclii*, cantata (1961); Overture (1960); Sinfonia (1960); *Cîntec de Vitejie* for Chamber Orch. (1971); *Recitativo, Adagio and Fugue* for Flute and Piano (1958); 2 piano sonatas (1960, 1964); 4 pieces for Piano (1978); choruses; songs.

Ctesibius, Greek physicist and inventor of the hydraulis. He flourished between 246 and 221 B.C., and is known in literature as Ctesibius of Alexandria. The weight of evidence collected by H.G. Farmer tends to demonstrate that the 1st hydraulis was indeed constructed by Ctesibius.

Bibl.: P. Tannery, "Athénée sur C. et l'hydraulis," *Revue des Études Grecques* (1896); H. Farmer, *The Organ of the Ancients* (London, 1931).

Cuclin, Dimitrie, prolific Rumanian composer; b. Galati, April 5, 1885; d. Bucharest, Feb. 7, 1978. He studied with Castaldi in Bucharest; in 1907 went to Paris, where he took courses with Vincent d'Indy at the Schola Cantorum. Returning to Rumania, he taught violin at the Bucharest Cons. (1918–22). From 1924 to 1930 he was in America as violin teacher at the Brooklyn College of Music; in 1930 he returned to Rumania, devoting himself mainly to teaching and composition; he continued to write symphonic and other music well into his 90s.

WORKS: 20 syms.: No. 1 (1910); No. 2, *Triumph of the People's Union* (1938); No. 3 (1942); No. 4 (1944); No. 5, with Soloists and Chorus (1947); No. 6 (1948); No. 7 (1948); No. 8 (1948); No. 9 (1949); No. 10, with Chorus (1949); No. 11 (1950); No. 12, with Soloists and Chorus (1951); No. 13 (1951); No. 14 (1952); No. 15 (1954); No. 16, *Triumph of Peace* (1959); No. 17 (1965); No. 18 (1967); No. 19 (1971); No. 20 (1972); 5 operas: *Soria* (1911), *Trian si dochia* (1921), *Agamemnon* (1922), *Bellérophon* (1924), and *Meleagridele;* Violin Concerto (1920); Piano Concerto (1939); *Rumanian Dances* for Orch. (1961); Clarinet Concerto (1968); 3 string quartets (1914, 1948, 1949) and numerous other chamber works; piano pieces; sacred choruses; songs.

Cudworth, Charles (Cyril Leonard), English librarian and musicologist; b. Cambridge, Oct. 30, 1908; d. there, Dec. 26, 1977. He served at the Music Division of the Library of Cambridge Univ. from 1943; from 1946 to 1973 was curator of the Pendlebury Library of Music there; in 1965 was elected a Fellow of the Univ. College at Cambridge; in 1968 was a visiting prof. at the Univ. of Southern Calif., Los Angeles. His specialty was the music of the 18th century. He publ. *Thematic Index of English Eighteenth Century Overtures and Symphonies* (London, 1953) and *Handel* (London, 1972); contributed numerous valuable articles to British and American music journals.

BIBL.: C. Hogwood and R. Luckett, eds., *Music in Eighteenth-century England: Essays in Memory of C. C.* (Cambridge, 1983).

Cuénod, Hugues (-Adhémar), Swiss tenor; b. Corseaux-sur-Vevey, June 26, 1902. He studied voice in Lausanne, Basel, Geneva, and Vienna. After a long sojourn in Paris, where he made his stage debut in *Jonny spielt auf* (1928), he toured the U.S. (1937–39); during the war he taught at the Geneva Cons. (1940–46); then resumed his career as an opera singer; he appeared at La Scala in Milan in 1951, and at Covent Garden in London in 1954. On March 12, 1987, he made his belated Metropolitan Opera debut in N.Y. as the Emperor in *Turandot,* just 3 months before his 85th birthday.

Cugat, Xavier, Spanish-American bandleader; b. Barcelona, Jan. 1, 1900; d. there, Oct. 27, 1990. As a youth he went to Cuba, then to the U.S.; studied violin with Franz Kneisel; played at concerts with Caruso; became a caricaturist for the *Los Angeles Times.* In 1928 he organized a dance orch.; led a combo, with his niece, the actress Margo, as a dancer. In 1933 he was engaged as bandleader of the Hotel Astoria in N.Y.; played engagements at hotels and nightclubs, achieving popularity by his astute arrangements of Latin American dances; invented a congat (a crossbreed of bongos and a conga). He was married to the singers **Carmen Castillo** (1929–45), **Lorraine Allen** (1946–50), **Abbe Lane** (1952–63), and **Charo.** He publ. an autobiography, *The Rumba Is My Life* (N.Y., 1949).

Cugley, Ian (Robert), Australian composer; b. Melbourne, June 22, 1945. He studied with Peter Sculthorpe and Peter Maxwell Davies at the Univ. of Sydney (1963–66); in 1967 was appointed to the faculty of the Univ. of Tasmania; also was percussionist in the Tasmanian Sym. Orch.; organized a contemporary music ensemble, Spectrum. His music represents a curious polarization of techniques, in which starkly primitive melorhythms enter a tangential relationship with total serialism.

WORKS: Variations for Flute, Oboe, and Horn (1963); *Adagio* for 4 Horns or String Quartet (1964); *Pan, the Lake* for Flute, Horn, Cello, Strings, and Percussion, including 8 Indonesian Kulintang Gongs (1965); Prelude for Orch. (1965); Sonata for Flute, Viola, and Guitar or Harp (1966); *Canticle of All Created*

Things for Chorus, Harp, and Percussion (1966); *Canticle II (In Cenerem Reverteris)* for Soli, Chorus, and Orch. (1967); *5 Variants* for String Orch. (1968); *3 Pieces* for Chamber Orch. (1968); *The 6 Days of Creation,* cantata (1969); *Chamber Symphony* for 11 Wind Instruments (1971); *Aquarelles* for Piano (1972); *Sonata Movement* for Violin and Piano (1972); Violin Concerto (1973); numerous works for school orchs.; 3 electronic studies (1967–72); sacred music.

Cui, César (Antonovich), Russian composer; b. Vilnius, Jan. 18, 1835; d. Petrograd, March 26, 1918. He was the son of a soldier in Napoleon's army who remained in Russia, married a Lithuanian noblewoman, and settled as a teacher of French in Vilnius. Cui learned musical notation by copying Chopin's mazurkas and various Italian operas; then tried his hand at composition on his own. In 1849 he took lessons with Moniuszko in Vilnius. In 1850 he went to St. Petersburg, where he entered the Engineering School in 1851 and later the Academy of Military Engineering (1855). After graduation in 1857 he became a topographer and later an expert in fortification. He participated in the Russo-Turkish War of 1877; in 1878 he became a prof. at the Engineering School and was tutor in military fortification to Czar Nicholas II. In 1856 Cui met Balakirev, who helped him master the technique of composition. In 1858 he married Malvina Bamberg; for her he wrote a scherzo on the theme *BABEG* (for the letters in her name) and *CC* (his own initials). In 1864 he began writing music criticism in the St. Petersburg *Vedomosti* and later in other newspapers, continuing as music critic until 1900. Cui's musical tastes were conditioned by his early admiration for Schumann; he opposed Wagner, against whom he wrote vitriolic articles; he attacked Strauss and Reger with even greater violence. He was an ardent propagandist of Glinka and the Russian national school, but was somewhat critical toward Tchaikovsky. He publ. the 1st comprehensive book on Russian music, *Musique en Russie* (Paris, 1880). Cui was grouped with Rimsky-Korsakov, Mussorgsky, Borodin, and Balakirev as one of the "Moguchaya Kuchka" (Mighty 5); the adjective in his case, however, is not very appropriate, for his music lacks grandeur; he was at his best in delicate miniatures, e.g., *Orientale,* from the suite *Kaleidoscope,* op. 50. A vol. of his *Selected Articles* (1864–1917) was publ. in Leningrad in 1953.

WORKS: 6 operas premiered in St. Petersburg: *The Mandarin's Son* (1859; Dec. 19, 1878); *The Prisoner of the Caucasus* (1857–59; rev. 1881; Feb. 16, 1883); *William Ratcliff* (Feb. 26, 1869); *Angelo* (Feb. 13, 1876); *The Saracen* (Nov. 14, 1899); *The Captain's Daughter* (1907–9; Feb. 27, 1911). Other operas: *Le Flibustier* (Opéra-Comique, Paris, Jan. 22, 1894); *Mam'zelle Fifi* (Moscow, Nov. 17, 1903); *Matteo Falcone* (Moscow, Dec. 27, 1907). *A Feast in Time of Plague,* written orig. as a dramatic cantata, was produced as a 1-act opera (Moscow, Nov. 24, 1901). Children's operas: *The Snow Giant* (Yalta, May 28, 1906); *Little Red Ridinghood; Puss in Boots* (Tiflis, Jan. 12, 1916); *Little Ivan the Fool.* Orch.: *Tarantella* (1859); *Marche solennelle* (1881); *Suite miniature* (1882); *Suite concertante* for Violin, and Orch. or Piano (1884); *2 morceaux* for Cello, and Orch. or Piano (1886); Suite No. 2 (1887); Suite No. 4, *À Argenteau* (1887); Suite No. 3, *In modo populari* (1890); 3 Scherzos (op. 82; 1910). Chamber: 3 string quartets (c.1890, 1907, 1913); *5 Little Duets* for Flute and Violin; violin pieces: *2 Miniatures;* Violin Sonata; *Petite Suite; 12 Miniatures* (op. 20); *Kaleidoscope,* 24 numbers; *6 Bagatelles* (op. 51); many songs; piano pieces; choruses. Cui contributed a number to a set of variations on "Chopsticks" (with Borodin, Liadov, and Rimsky-Korsakov). From 1914 to 1916 Cui completed Mussorgsky's opera *The Fair at Sorotchinsk.*

BIBL.: L. Mercy-Argenteau, *C. C., Esquisse critique* (Paris, 1888); N. Findeisen, *"C.A. C.," Russian Musical Gazette* (1894); A. Koptyayev, "C. C. as a Composer for the Pianoforte," ibid. (1895); P. Weimarn, *C. C. as a Songwriter* (St. Petersburg, 1896); *Musical Festival in Honor of C.A. C.* (St. Petersburg, 1910); G. Abraham, *Studies in Russian Music* (N.Y. and London, 1935); M. Calvocoressi and G. Abraham, *Masters of Rus-*

sian Music (N.Y., 1936); E. Guglielmi, "C. C. e l'Ottocento musicale russo," *Chigiane*, XXV/5 (1968); M. Smirnov, *The Piano Works of Composers Comprising "The Five"* (Moscow, 1971).

Culp, Julia, Dutch contralto; b. Groningen, Oct. 6, 1880; d. Amsterdam, Oct. 13, 1970. She first studied violin as a child; then became a voice pupil of Cornelia van Zanten at the Amsterdam Cons. (1897), and later of Etelka Gerster in Berlin; made her formal debut in Magdeburg in 1901; her tours of Germany, Austria, the Netherlands, France, Spain, and Russia were highly successful from an artistic standpoint, establishing her as one of the finest singers of German lieder. Her American debut took place in N.Y. on Jan. 10, 1913; for many years, she visited the U.S. every season.

Culshaw, John (Royds), English recording producer; b. London, May 28, 1924; d. there, April 27, 1980. He studied music while serving in the British army. From 1954 to 1967 he was manager and chief producer with the Decca Record Co.; from 1967 to 1975 he held the same post with the BBC. He was awarded the rank of Officer of the Order of the British Empire in 1966. He made a mark in the recording industry by introducing the stereo-reproduction process, which created a 3-dimensional effect. His principal achievement was the stereophonic recording of the entire *Ring of the Nibelung,* issued by the Decca Record Co. under the direction of Sir Georg Solti. Culshaw related the background of this undertaking in his books *Ring Resounding* (London, 1967) and *Reflections on Wagner's Ring* (London, 1976). His other publications are *Sergei Rachmaninov* (London, 1949) and *A Century of Music* (London, 1952). He also publ. an autobiography, *Odyssey of a Recording Pioneer: Putting the Record Straight* (N.Y., 1981).

Culver, (David) Andrew, inventive American-Canadian composer, instrument maker, and performer; b. Morristown, N.J., Aug. 30, 1953. He studied composition with John Rea and Bengt Hambraeus, electronic music with Alcides Lanza, and sound recording with Wieslaw Woczcyk at McGill Univ. in Montreal (B.M., 1977; M.M., 1980); subsequently he was a founding member of SONDE, a Canadian music design and performance ensemble. He pioneered the musical application of R. Buckminster Fuller's tensegrity structural principle, devising richly resonant music sculptures that vibrate synergistically. His output takes 4 forms: stage performances by music sculpture ensemble, interactive music sculpture installations, computer-displayed text and electroacoustic music projections, and scores for traditional instruments. Solo stage works include *Viti* (1981) and *Music with Tensegrity Sound Source #5* (1983), which he has performed in Europe, Canada, and the U.S.; his *Hard Lake Frozen Moon* (1989), for 2 performers active in an elaborate stage environment built up of 19 sound sources, was commissioned by Toronto's New Music Concerts and the Laidlaw Foundation. *Quasicrystals . . .* (1989), developed with pianist Thomas Moore at the Yellow Springs Inst. for Contemporary Studies and the Arts, is a work for 2 performers on separate and complex itineraries within a field of 21 amplified, hanging music sculptures. Chance-composed lighting is an essential, determining element of these and other works. He has also created public installations of interactive music sculptures, including those at the Staten Island Children's Museum (1983) and the Children's Museum of Manhattan (1989–91). Since 1984, he has worked with the composer John Cage, developing computer programs toward the realization of Cage's musical and poetic processes. His programs *ic* and *tic,* computer simulations of the I Ching coin-tossing oracle, were used in all aspects of the composition and direction of Cage's *Europeras 1 & 2* (1987).

Culwick, James C., English organist and composer; b. West Bromwich, Staffordshire, April 28, 1845; d. Dublin, Oct. 5, 1907. He was a pupil of T. Bedsmore; was assistant organist at Lichfield Cathedral and organist at various churches until 1881, when he was appointed to the Chapel Royal at Dublin, where he remained till his death; also was a prof. of piano

and theory at Alexandra College, and conductor of the Harmonic Soc. and Orpheus; received a Mus.Doc. (*honoris causa*) from Dublin Univ. in 1893. He wrote a dramatic cantata, *The Legend of Stauffenberg* (1890); piano pieces (suite, ballade, sonatina, etc.); several anthems and church services.

WRITINGS: *Rudiments of Music* (1880; 2nd ed., 1882); *The Study of Music and Its Place in General Education* (1882); *The Works of Sir R. Stewart* (1902).

Cumberworth, Starling, American composer; b. Remson Corners, Ohio, July 25, 1915; d. Cleveland, Aug. 8, 1985. He studied at the Cleveland Inst. of Music with Herbert Elwell and Arthur Shepherd; then at Yale Univ. with Quincy Porter and Paul Hindemith (M.M., 1948) and at the Eastman School of Music in Rochester, N.Y., with Bernard Rogers and Howard Hanson (Ph.D., 1956). In 1956 he joined the staff of the Cleveland Music School Settlement, remaining there until 1971. Among his works are an opera, *Home Burial* (1955); 2 string quartets; Suite for Oboe and Piano; Suite for Flute and Piano; Violin Sonata; Trio for Violin, Clarinet, and Piano.

Cummings, W(illiam) H(ayman), English tenor and music antiquarian; b. Sidbury, Devonshire, Aug. 22, 1831; d. London, June 6, 1915. He was a chorister in London at St. Paul's and at the Temple Church; organist of Waltham Abbey (1847); tenor in the Temple, Westminster Abbey, and Chapel Royal; a prof. of singing at the Royal Academy of Music (1879–96); from 1882 to 1888, conductor of the Sacred Harmonic Soc.; precentor of St. Anne's, Soho (1886–98); principal of the Guildhall School of Music (1896–1910). He received an honorary degree of Mus.D. from Trinity College in Dublin (1900). He was a cultivated singer and a learned antiquarian; was instrumental in founding the Purcell Soc., and edited its 1st publications; was the author of a biography of Purcell (London, 1882; 2nd ed., 1911); also publ. *Primer of the Rudiments of Music* (1877) and *Biographical Dictionary of Musicians* (1892). His library of 4,500 vols. contained many rare autographs. He composed a cantata, *The Fairy Ring* (1873); sacred music; glees; part-songs; etc.; adapted the tune of the 2nd no. of Mendelssohn's *Festgesang* to the hymn *Hark the Herald Angels Sing,* publishing in 1856 his version, which became universally popular.

Cundell, Edric, English composer and conductor; b. London, Jan. 29, 1893; d. Ashwell, Hertfordshire, March 19, 1961. He was first a horn player, then a pianist; taught at Trinity College (1914). In 1935, he founded the Edric Cundell Chamber Orch.; in 1938, he was made director of the Guildhall School of Music in London; retired in 1959; in 1949 was made a Commander of the Order of the British Empire.

WORKS: Sym.; symphonic poems: *Serbia* (1919) and *The Tragedy of Deirdre* (1922); sonnet, *Our Dead,* for Tenor and Orch. (1922); Piano Concerto; Piano Quartet, String Sextet, String Quartet, Rhapsody for Viola and Piano; piano pieces; songs.

Cunningham, Arthur, black American composer; b. Piermont, N.Y., Nov. 11, 1928. He commenced piano studies at the age of 6 and was composing for his own jazz group when he was 12; he later received formal training at Fisk Univ. (B.A., 1951), Columbia Univ. Teachers College (M.A., 1957), and the Juilliard School of Music. In addition to composing, he was active as a teacher and conductor. His output runs the gamut of styles and techniques, ranging from serious to rock.

WORKS: *Adagio* for Oboe and Strings (1954); *Night Lights* for Orch. (1955); *Lights across the Hudson,* tone poem (1956); *The Beauty Part,* musical (1963); *Dialogues* for Piano and Chamber Orch. (1966); *Ballet* for String Quartet and Jazz Quartet (1968); *His Natural Grace,* rock opera (1969); *Harlem Suite,* ballet (1971); Double-bass Concerto (1971); *The Prince* for Baritone and Orch. (1973); *Rooster Rhapsody* for Narrator and Orch. (1975); *Crispus Attucks* for Band (1976); *Night Bird* for Voice, Jazz Quintet, and Orch. (1978); also chamber pieces, piano pieces, choral partsongs and suites, and songs.

Curci, Giuseppe, Italian composer; b. Barletta, June 15, 1808; d. there, Aug. 5, 1877. He studied in Naples with Zingarelli and Crescentini; became a singing teacher; composed several operas, including *Il Proscritto* (Turin, 1837) and *Don Desiderio* (Venice, 1837); traveled in Germany and Austria; taught voice in Paris (1848–56), where his opera *Il Baccelliere* was produced; then returned to his native town. He publ. a manual, *Il bel canto.*

Curran, Alvin, American composer; b. Providence, R.I., Dec. 13, 1938. He studied piano and trombone in his youth, later receiving training in composition from Ron Nelson at Brown Univ. (B.A., 1960) and from Elliott Carter and Mel Powell at Yale Univ. (M.Mus., 1963). He went to Rome (1965), where he founded the Musica Elettronica Viva ensemble for the performance of live electronic music with Richard Teitelbaum and Frederic Rzewski; the ensemble later evolved to include all manner of avant-garde performance practices. His compositions range from tape works to experimental pieces using the natural environment.
WORKS: *Music for Every Occasion,* 50 monodic pieces for Any Use (1967–77); *Songs and Views from the Magnetic Garden* for Voice, Flugelhorn, Synthesizer, and Tape (1973–75); *Light Flowers, Dark Flowers* for Piano, Ocarina, Synthesizer, and Tape (1974–77); *The Works* for Voice, Piano, Synthesizer, and Tape (1977–80); *The Crossing* for 4 Sopranos, Chorus, 7 Instruments, and Tape (1978); *Maritime Rites,* environmental concerts for Choruses in Rowboats, Ship, and Foghorns (1981); *Natural History* for Tape (1984); *Maritime Rites Satellite Music,* 10 radio concerts for the Sounds of the Eastern U.S. Seaboard and Soloists (1984–85); *Electric Rags I* for Piano and Computer-controlled Synthesizers (1985); *Crystal Psalms* for 6 Choruses, Percussion, Instrumental Ensembles, Accordions, Shofars, and Tape (1988); *Vsto for Giacinto* for String Quartet (1989); *Electric Rags II* for Saxophone Quartet and Computer Electronics (1989).

Curry, Arthur Mansfield, American composer and pedagogue; b. Chelsea, Mass., Jan. 27, 1866; d. Atlanta, Dec. 30, 1953. He studied with Franz Kneisel (violin) and Edward MacDowell (composition); taught at the New England Cons. of Music in Boston (1915–39).
WORKS: Orch. overture, *Blomidon* (Worcester, Mass., 1902); symphonic poem, *Atala,* after Chateaubriand (Boston, April 21, 1911); *The Winning of Amarac,* Celtic legend for Narrator, Women's Chorus, and Orch. (Boston, 1934); choruses; piano pieces and many songs.

Curschmann, Karl Friedrich, German singer and composer; b. Berlin, June 21, 1805; d. Langfuhr, near Danzig, Aug. 24, 1841. Orig. a law student, he devoted himself to music, studying with Hauptmann and Spohr at Kassel, where his 1-act opera *Abdul und Erinnieh* was produced (Oct. 29, 1828). His songs possess a fine poetic quality; a collection of 83 lieder and 9 duets and trios was publ. posth. in 2 vols. (Berlin, 1871). He was also a noted singer and gave concerts in Germany and Italy.
BIBL.: G. Meissner, *K.F. C.* (Bautzen, 1899); D. Curschman-Undenheim, *Das Geschlecht C.* (Oppenheim am Rhein, 1937).

Curti, Franz, German composer; b. Kassel, Nov. 16, 1854; d. Dresden, Feb. 6, 1898. He studied medicine; became a dentist by profession; at the same time took music courses in Dresden with Kretschmer and Schulz-Beuthen. He wrote several operas: *Hertha* (Altenburg, 1887); *Reinhardt von Ufenau* (Altenburg, 1889); *Erlöst* (Mannheim, 1894); melodrama, *Schneefried* (Mannheim, 1895); 1-act Japanese fairy opera, *Lili-Tsee* (Mannheim, 1896); *Das Rösli vom Säntis* (Zürich, 1898); also a cantata, *Die Gletscherjungfrau;* music to *Die letzten Menschen,* by W.E. Kirchbach; songs.

Curtin, Phyllis (née **Smith**), American soprano; b. Clarksburg, W.Va., Dec. 3, 1922. She studied with Olga Avierino in Boston; sang with the New England Opera Co.; was a member of the N.Y. City Opera; made successful appearances at the Teatro Colón in Buenos Aires (1959) and at the Vienna State Opera (1960–61). She made her debut with the Metropolitan Opera Co. on Nov. 4, 1961. Among her most successful roles is Salome; she also sang leading parts in 1st performances of several American operas. She was married to Phillip Curtin in 1946; divorced and married Eugene Cook in 1956. She taught master classes at the Berkshire Music Center in Tanglewood; then was head of the voice dept. at Yale Univ., and later dean of the School of Fine Arts at Boston Univ.

Curtis, Alan (Stanley), American musicologist, harpsichordist, fortepianist, and conductor; b. Mason, Mich., Nov. 17, 1934. He studied at Michigan State Univ. (B.Mus., 1955) and the Univ. of Illinois (M.Mus., 1956; Ph.D., 1963); also studied the harpsichord with Gustav Leonhardt in Amsterdam (1957–59). He joined the faculty of the Univ. of Calif. at Berkeley in 1960; became a full prof. there in 1970. He wrote *Sweelinck's Keyboard Music: A Study of English Elements in 17th-century Dutch Composition* (London and Leiden, 1969); he also ed. *Pièces de clavecin* by L. Couperin (1970) and by Balbastre (1980), and Monteverdi's *L'incoronazione di Poppea* (1989).

Curtis, Natalie, American writer on folk music; b. N.Y., April 26, 1875; d. Paris, Oct. 23, 1921. She studied with Arthur Friedheim, with Busoni in Berlin, Alfred Giraudet in Paris, and Julius Kniese at the "Wagner-Schule" in Bayreuth; returning to the U.S., she became an ardent investigator of songs, legends, and customs of the North American Indians. She was married to Paul Burlin of N.Y. (July 25, 1917).
WRITINGS: *Songs of Ancient America* (1905); *The Indian's Book* (1907; 2nd ed., rev., 1923; contains over 200 songs of 18 different tribes); *A Child's Garden of Verse: Negro Folk Songs* (4 vols., 1918–19); *Songs and Tales from the Dark Continent* (1920).

Curtiss, Mina (née **Kirstein**), American writer; b. Boston, Oct. 13, 1896; d. Bridgeport, Conn., Nov. 1, 1985. She was educated at Smith College (M.A., 1918); was an associate prof. of English literature there (1920–34). Apart from her literary publications, she contributed articles to the *Musical Quarterly;* wrote *Bizet and His World* (N.Y., 1958). In 1977 she publ. a memoir, *Other People's Letters.*

Curtis-Smith, Curtis O(tto) B(ismarck), American composer, pianist, and teacher; b. Walla Walla, Wash., Sept. 9, 1941. He studied piano with David Burge at Whitman (Wash.) College (1960–62) and Gui Mombaerts at Northwestern Univ. (B.M., 1964; M.M., 1965) and with Kenneth Gaburo (1966) and Bruno Maderna (1972) at the Berkshire Music Center in Tanglewood. He taught at Western Michigan Univ. in Kalamazoo (from 1968), making concurrent appearances as a recitalist and soloist with various orchs. Among his honors are the Koussevitzky Prize (1972), the Gold Medal of the Concorso Internazionale di Musica e Danza G.B. Viotti (1975), N.E.A. grants (1975, 1980), the Prix du Francis Salabert (1976), annual ASCAP awards (from 1977), a Guggenheim fellowship (1978–79), an American Academy and Inst. of Arts and Letters award (1978), and Michigan Council for the Arts grants (1981, 1984). In 1972 he developed the technique of "piano bowing" in which a fishing line is drawn across the strings of the instrument to produce continuous single and clustered pitches; his *Rhapsodies* and *Unisonics* employ this technique.
WORKS: ORCH.: *Winter Pieces* for Chamber Orch. (1974); *(Bells) Belle de Jour* for Piano and Orch. (1974–75); *The Great American Symphony (GAS!)* (1981); *Songs and Cantillations* for Guitar and Orch. (1983); *Chaconne à son goût* (1984); *". . . Float Wild Birds, Sleeping"* (1988; Kalamazoo, Mich., Jan. 20, 1989). **CHAMBER:** Flute Sonata (1963); 3 string quartets (1964, 1965, 1980); *Xanthie/Fanfare for the Dark* for 9 Instrumental Groups (1972); *Music for Handbells* for 10 Players (1976–77); *Tonalities* for Clarinet and Percussion (1978); *Plays and Rimes* for Brass Quintet (1979); *The Great American Guitar Solo (GAGS!)* (1982); *Ragmala (A Garland of Ragas)* for Guitar and String Quartet (1983); *Sardonic Sketches* for Woodwind Quintet (1986). **PIANO:** *Pianacaglia* (1967); *Trajectories* (1967–68); *Piece du jour* (1971); *Rhapsodies* (1973); *Tristana Varia-*

tions (1975–76); *Unisonics* for Alto Saxophone and Piano (1976); *For Gatsby* (Steinway #81281) (1982). VOCAL: *All Day I Hear* for Chorus (1965); *"Till Thousands Thee. LPS.": A Secular Alleluia without . . .* for 6 Sopranos, 2 Trumpets, 4 Percussionists, Celesta, and Water Glasses (1969); *Comedie* for 2 Sopranos and Chamber Orch. (1972); *Invocation: Alap (Raga Kedar)* for Chorus (1982); solo songs; also organ pieces; compositions for tape.

Curwen, John, English music theorist, father of **John Spencer Curwen;** b. Heckmondwike, Yorkshire, Nov. 14, 1816; d. Manchester, May 26, 1880. He was a Congregational minister; studied at Wymondley College and Univ. College in London; in 1844 was pastor at Plaistow, Essex. Becoming interested in Miss S.A. Glover's "Tonic Sol-Fa" system of teaching, he labored to improve it; established the Tonic Sol-Fa Assoc. and the *Tonic Sol-Fa Reporter* in 1853, and the Tonic Sol-Fa College in 1869, having resigned his pastorate in 1867 to devote himself entirely to propagating the system. His numerous publications relate chiefly to Tonic Sol-Fa (issued by Novello). In 1863 Curwen founded the firm of John Curwen & Sons, publishers of works for school use, choral music, etc., also of the periodicals *Musical News and Herald* (weekly) and *Sackbut* (monthly; discontinued in 1934). In 1923 the business merged with F. & B. Goodwin.

BIBL.: J.S. Curwen, *Memorials of J. C.* (London, 1882).

Curwen, John Spencer, English music theorist, son of **John Curwen;** b. Plaistow, Sept. 30, 1847; d. London, Aug. 6, 1916. He was a pupil of his father and G. Oakey, and later of G.A. Macfarren, Sullivan, and Prout at the Royal Academy of Music. Like his father, he was an active promoter of the Tonic Sol-Fa system; became president of the Tonic Sol-Fa College in 1880; was a frequent contributor to the *Tonic Sol-Fa Reporter* and its continuation, the *Musical Herald.* He publ. *Studies in Worship Music* (1880) and a 2nd series in 1885; *Memorials of John Curwen* (London, 1882); *Musical Notes in Paris* (1882); etc.

Curzon, Sir Clifford (Michael), eminent English pianist; b. London, May 18, 1907; d. there, Sept. 1, 1982. His father was an antique dealer; both he and his wife were music-lovers and they encouraged their son's studies, first in violin playing and then as a pianist. In 1919 he enrolled at the Royal Academy of Music in London, where he studied piano with Charles Reddie and Katharine Goodson; he won 2 scholarships and the Macfarren Gold Medal. At the age of 16, he made a prestigious appearance as soloist at the Queen's Hall in London. He was only 19 when he was given a post as a teacher at the Royal Academy of Music, but he decided to continue his studies and went to Berlin (1928), where he was tutored by Artur Schnabel, and then to Paris (1930), where he took courses with Wanda Landowska in harpsichord and with Nadia Boulanger in general music culture. On Feb. 26, 1939, he made an auspicious American debut in N.Y., and in subsequent years made regular concert tours in the U.S. One of his last American appearances took place on May 2, 1978, when he played the Mozart C-minor Concerto with the Philadelphia Orch. Curzon was a scholarly virtuoso who applied his formidable technique with a careful regard for the music. He was particularly praised for his congenial interpretations of works by Romantic composers, especially Schubert, Schumann, and Brahms. In 1958 he was made a Commander of the Order of the British Empire. He received the degree of D.Mus. *honoris causa* from Leeds Univ. in 1970. He was knighted by Queen Elizabeth II in 1977. In 1980 he received the Gold Medal of the Royal Phil. Soc. in London.

Curzon, (Emmanuel-) Henri (-Parent) de, French music critic and writer; b. Le Havre, July 6, 1861; d. Paris, Feb. 25, 1942. He was keeper of the government archives at Paris from 1892 until 1926; then became librarian of the Opéra-Comique; was music critic of the *Gazette de France* (1889–1918); contributed to the *Guide Musical, Bulletin de la Société de l'Histoire du Théâtre,* etc.

WRITINGS: *Les Dernières Années de Piccini à Paris* (1890); *La Légende de Sigurd dans l'Edda; L'Opéra d'E. Reyer* (1890); *Musiciens du temps passé* (1893); *Croquis d'artistes* (1898); *Les Lieder de Schubert* (1899); *État sommaire des pièces et documents concernant la musique* (1899); *Guide de l'amateur d'ouvrages sur la musique* (1901); *Felipe Pedrell et "Les Pyrénées"* (1902); *Les Lieder de Beethoven* (1905); *Essai de bibliographie mozartienne* (1906); *Grétry, biographie critique* (1907); *L'Évolution lyrique au théâtre* (1908); *Meyerbeer, Biographie critique* (1910); *Documents inédits sur le "Faust" de Gounod* (with A. Soubies; 1912); *Mozart, Biographie critique* (1914); *Rossini* (1920); *L'Œuvre de R. Wagner à Paris et ses interprètes* (1920); *A. Thomas* (1921); *J.B. Fauré* (1923); *E. Reyer* (1924); *Jean Elleviou* (1930); *Cosima Wagner et Bayreuth* (1930); *Berlioz, L'Homme et le musicien* (1932).

Cusins, Sir William (George), English organist, pianist, conductor, pedagogue, and composer; b. London, Oct. 14, 1833; d. Remouchamps, Ardennes, Aug. 31, 1893. He was a pupil of Fétis at the Brussels Cons. (1844), and of Bennett, Potter, Lucas, and Sainton at the Royal Academy of Music in London (1847). He took the King's Scholarship in 1847 and 1849; in the latter year he was appointed organist of the Queen's private chapel, and became a violinist in the Italian Opera orch. In 1851 he became prof. at the Royal Academy of Music; succeeded Bennett (1867–83) as conductor of the Phil. Soc., and also became conductor of the Royal Band in 1870; served as Master of the Queen's Musick from 1870 until his death; also succeeded Bennett as examining prof. at Queen's College (1875); was a prof. at Trinity College and a prof. of piano at the Guildhall School of Music (1885). He was knighted in 1892.

WORKS: *Royal Wedding Serenata* (1863); 2 concert overtures: *Les Travailleurs de la mer* (1869) and *Love's Labour's Lost* (1875); oratorio, *Gideon* (Gloucester Festival, 1871); Piano Concerto; Septet for Winds and Double Bass; piano pieces; songs.

Custer, Arthur, American composer; b. Manchester, Conn., April 21, 1923. He studied composition with Paul Pisk at the Univ. of Redlands, Calif., and with Philip Bezanson at the Univ. of Iowa; after graduation, he took a course of studies in composition with Nadia Boulanger. Subsequently he held numerous teaching jobs, including posts at Kansas Wesleyan Univ. in Salina (1952–55) and the Univ. of Omaha (1955–58). In 1970 he was appointed director of the Arts in the Education Project of the Rhode Island Council on the Arts; resigned from this post in 1973, but continued as composer-in-residence there until 1975.

WORKS: Sextet for Woodwinds and Piano (1959); *Colloquy* for String Quartet (1961); *Sinfonia de Madrid* (Madrid, April 28, 1962); *Cycle* for a Heterogeneous Ensemble (1963); Concertino for 2nd Violin and Strings, in reality his String Quartet No. 2 (1964); *2 Movements* for Wind Quintet (1964); *Permutations* for Violin, Clarinet, and Cello (1967); Concerto for Brass Quintet (1968); *Rhapsodality Brass!* for Orch. (1969); *Interface I* for String Quartet and 2 Recording Engineers, being (minus affectation) his String Quartet No. 3 (1969) and a thing entitled *Rhapsodality Brown!* for Orch. (1969); *Parabolas* for Trombone and Percussion (1969); *Parabolas* for Viola and Piano (1969); *Doubles* for Violin and Chamber Orch. (1972; rev. 1975); *Eyepiece* for Oboe and Tape (1974); *Sweet 16* for Clarinet and Piano (1976); *Interface II* for Ensemble, Slide Projectors, and Audience (1976).

Cutler, Henry Stephen, American organist and composer; b. Boston, Oct. 13, 1824; d. there, Dec. 5, 1902. He studied in Germany; returning to the U.S., he held posts as a church organist in Boston, N.Y., and Philadelphia. His anthem *The Son of God Goes Forth to War* is well known.

Cuvillier, Charles (Louis Paul), French composer of light opera; b. Paris, April 24, 1877; d. there, Feb. 14, 1955. He studied privately with Fauré and Messager, and with Massenet at the Paris Cons.; then became interested in the theater;

his 1st operetta, *Avant-hier matin*, was produced at the Théâtre des Capucines in Paris (Oct. 20, 1905); at the same theater, Cuvillier produced *Son petit frère* (April 10, 1907); *Algar* (1909); *Les Muscadines* (1910); and *Sapho* (1912). His most successful operetta, *La Reine s'amuse*, was first staged in Marseilles (Dec. 31, 1912); was revised and produced in Paris as *La Reine joyeuse* (Nov. 8, 1918) and in London as *The Naughty Princess* (1920). His other operettas were *La Fausse Ingénue* (Paris, 1918); *Bob et moi* (1924); *Boufard et ses filles* (Paris, 1929); etc. Cuvillier was also music director at the Odéon in Paris. The waltz from *La Reine joyeuse* has retained its popularity in numerous arrangements.

Cuyler, Louise (Elvira), American musicologist; b. Omaha, March 14, 1908. She studied at the Eastman School of Music in Rochester, N.Y. (B.M., 1929; Ph.D., 1948), and at the Univ. of Michigan (M.M., 1933), where she was a member of the staff from 1929 to 1975, with wartime leave (1942–45) for service with the American Red Cross in the Pacific. In 1975 she went to Smith College as Neilson Distinguished Prof. She contributed a number of informative papers to various scholarly publications, among them "Mozart's Quartets Dedicated to Haydn" in the memorial vol. for Curt Sachs (N.Y., 1965) and "Music in Biographies of Emperor Maximilian" in the Festschrift for Gustave Reese (N.Y., 1966); also ed. Isaac's *Choralis Constantinus*, Part III (Ann Arbor, Mich., 1950), and *Five Polyphonic Masses of Heinrich Isaac* (Ann Arbor, 1956). She publ. *The Emperor Maximilian I and Music* (London, 1973) and *The Symphony* (N.Y., 1973).

BIBL.: E. Borroff, ed., *Notations and Editions: A Book in Honor of L. C.* (Dubuque, Iowa, 1974).

Cuzzoni, Francesca, celebrated Italian soprano; b. Parma, c.1700; d. Bologna, 1770. She studied with Lanzi; sang in Parma, Bologna, Genoa, and Venice (1716–18); was engaged at the Italian opera in London, making her debut as Teofane in Handel's opera *Ottone* (Jan. 12, 1723). She made a profound impression on London opera lovers, and was particularly distinguished in lyric roles; but later her notorious rivalry with Faustina Bordoni nearly ruined her career. Following some appearances in Venice, she returned to London (1734); after several seasons she went to the Netherlands, where she became impoverished and was imprisoned for debt. Eventually, she returned to Bologna, where she subsisted by making buttons.

Czekanowska, Anna, Polish ethnomusicologist; b. Lwow, June 25, 1929. She studied with Chybiński at the Univ. of Poznan (1947–52) and with Chomiński at the Univ. of Warsaw (Ph.D., 1958; Habilitation, 1968). In 1969 she joined the ethnomusicology faculty at the Univ. of Warsaw and in 1975 became director of the Inst. of Musicology. Her research has focused on Slavonic music; among her publications are *Ethnografia muzyczna: Metodologia i metodyka* (Musical Ethnography: Methodology and Methods; 1971) and "Principles of Construction of Ancient Slavic Songs," *Narodno stvaraštvo* (1972).

Czernohorsky (Černohorský), Bohuslav, Bohemian composer; b. Nimburg, Feb. 16, 1684; d. Graz, July 1, 1742. He studied at Prague Univ. A Minorite monk, he was organist at Assisi from 1710 to 1715 (Tartini was one of his pupils) and choirmaster at S. Antonio in Padua from 1715 to 1720. Returning to Bohemia, he was Kapellmeister at the Teinkirche in Prague, and (1735) at St. Jacob's (Gluck was among his pupils); he was again organist in Padua from 1731 to 1741. Many of his MSS were lost at the burning of the Minorite monastery (1754). An offertory *a* 4 and several organ fugues and preludes were publ. by O. Schmid in *Orgelwerke altböhmischer Meister*; 5 organ fugues have been ed. by K. Pietsch; a *Regina Coeli* for Soprano, Organ, and Cello obbligato, and a motet, *Quem lapidaverunt*, are also extant; *Composizioni per organo* constitute vol. 3 of *Musica antiqua Bohemica* (Prague, 1968). The contrapuntal skill of Czernohorsky's fugal writing is remarkable; Kretzschmar described him as "the Bach of Bohemia"; Czech writers refer to him as "the father of Bohemian music" despite the fact that Czernohorsky never made thematic use of native rhythms or melodies.

BIBL.: O. Schmid, *Die böhmische Altmeisterschule C.s* (1900); A. Hnilička, *Porträte* (1922); Z. Culka, "Varhanní skladby Bohuslava Matěje Černohorského?," *Hudební Věda*, V/4 (1968).

Czerny, Carl, celebrated Austrian pianist, composer, and pedagogue; b. Vienna, Feb. 20, 1791; d. there, July 15, 1857. He was of Czech extraction (*czerny* means "black" in Czech), and his 1st language was Czech. He received his early training from his father, Wenzel Czerny, a stern disciplinarian who never let his son play with other children and insisted on concentrated work. Czerny had the privilege of studying for 3 years with Beethoven, and their association in subsequent years became a close one. Czerny also received advice as a pianist from Hummel and Clementi. He made trips to Leipzig (1836); visited Paris and London (1837) and Italy (1846); with these exceptions, he remained all his life in Vienna. His self-imposed daily schedule for work was a model of diligence; he denied himself any participation in the social life of Vienna and seldom attended opera or concerts. Very early in life he demonstrated great ability as a patient piano teacher; Beethoven entrusted to him the musical education of his favorite nephew. When Czerny himself became a renowned pedagogue, many future piano virtuosos flocked to him for lessons, among them Liszt (whom he taught without a fee), Thalberg, Theodore Kullak, Döhler, Jaëll, and Anna Belleville-Oury. Despite the heavy teaching schedule, Czerny found time to compose a fantastic amount of piano music, 861 opus numbers in all, each containing many individual items; these included not only piano studies and exercises, for which he became celebrated, but also sonatas, concertos, string quartets, masses, and hymns. In addition, he made numerous piano arrangements of classical syms., including all of Beethoven's, and wrote fantasies for piano on the themes from famous operas of the time. So dedicated was he to his chosen work that he renounced all thoughts of marriage (but a secret confession of his Platonic adoration of an unnamed female person was found among his MSS); in this wistful deprivation, Czerny's fate paralleled Beethoven's. For a century there has been a fashion among musical sophisticates to deprecate Czerny as a pathetic purveyor of manufactured musical goods; his contemporary John Field, the originator of the genre of piano nocturnes, described Czerny as a "Tintenfass"—an inkpot. A quip was circulated that Czerny hated children, and that he publ. his voluminous books of piano exercises to inflict pain on young pianists. Of late, however, there has been a change of heart toward Czerny as a worthy composer in his own right. Stravinsky expressed his admiration for Czerny, and modern composers have written, with a half-concealed smile, pieces "à la manière de Czerny." Czerny was unexpectedly revealed to be a musician of imaginative fancy and engaging pedantic humor, as for instance in his Brobdingnagian arrangement of Rossini's Overture to *William Tell* for 16 pianists playing 4-hands on 8 pianos; pieces for 3 pianists playing 6-hands on a single keyboard; etc. Obsessed by an idea of compassing all musical knowledge at once, he publ. an *Umriss der ganzen Musikgeschichte* (Mainz, 1851), and also a vol. in English entitled *Letters to a Young Lady on the Art of Playing the Pianoforte from the Earliest Rudiments to the Highest State of Cultivation* (the young lady in the title was never identified). Of his studies the most famous are *Schule der Geläufigkeit*, op. 299, and *Schule der Fingerfertigkeit*, op. 740; others are *Die Schule des Legato und Staccato*, op. 335; *40 tägliche Studien*, op. 337; *Schule der Verzierungen*, op. 355; *Schule des Virtuosen*, op. 365; *Schule der linken Hand*, op. 399; etc. His Sonata, op. 7, was popular; among his piano transcriptions to be mentioned is *Fantaisie et Variations brillantes* on an aria from Persiani's opera *Ines de Castro*. Czerny's autobiography, *Erinnerungen aus meinem Leben*, was ed. by W. Kolneder (Baden-Baden, 1968; publ. in part in Eng. in the *Musical Quarterly*, July 1956).

BIBL.: W. Malloch, "C. C.'s Metronome Marks for Haydn and Mozart Symphonies," *Early Music* (Feb. 1988).

Czerwenka, Oskar, Austrian bass; b. Vöcklabruck, near Linz, July 5, 1924. He made his debut in Graz in 1947; in 1951 he joined the Vienna State Opera; from 1953 he sang at Salzburg. He made his Metropolitan Opera debut in N.Y. on Dec. 26, 1959, but continued to pursue his career in Europe, principally in Vienna. He was best known for his buffo roles.

Czibulka, Alphons, Hungarian bandmaster and composer; b. Szepes-Várallya, May 14, 1842; d. Vienna, Oct. 27, 1894. Orig. a pianist, he became Kapellmeister at the Karltheater in Vienna in 1865; was bandmaster of the 17th Regiment, and later of the 25th Regiment at Prague; finally settled in Vienna, where he brought out the operetta *Pfingsten in Florenz* (Dec. 20, 1884). Other stage works are *Der Glücksritter* (1887); *Gil Blas* (Hamburg, 1889); *Der Bajazzo* (Vienna, 1892); *Signor Annibale* (1893).

Cziffra, György, noted Hungarian-born pianist; b. Budapest, Sept. 5, 1921. He studied with Dohnányi at the Budapest Academy of Music; his education was interrupted by World War II, when he served in the Hungarian army; after the war he continued his studies at the Budapest Academy of Music with Ferenczi, but was once more distracted from music when he was arrested in 1950 for his rebellious political views. He was released from jail in 1953, but was again endangered by the abortive Hungarian revolt in 1956. Convinced that he could have no peace under Communist rule, he went to Paris, where he made successful appearances as a concert pianist; eventually he became a French citizen. He was best known for his interpretations of the works of the Romantic repertoire; especially brilliant were his renditions of the music of Liszt.

Czukay, Holger, German new-wave composer; b. Danzig, March 24, 1938. A musical iconoclast, Czukay fell through the cracks of both jazz and classical instruction until he studied with Karlheinz Stockhausen (1962); he subsequently went to Switzerland, where he encountered rock music through the guitarist Michael Karoli, with whom he formed the pioneer new-wave group Can (1968–78). Can followed the early Stockhausen esthetic, utilizing "found" music from shortwave radio as well as techniques of tape splicing and collage of ethnic music. Czukay anticipated trends in alternative pop music not apparent to most people until well into the 1980s; the ethnic-based constructions in his *Forgery* series of the 1970s were acknowledged by David Byrne and Brian Eno as an influence in their collaboration, *My Life in the Bush of Ghosts.*

Czyż , Henryk, Polish conductor and composer; b. Grudziadz, June 16, 1923. He studied law at Torun Univ.; then went to the Poznan Academy of Music, where he studied conducting with Bierdiajew and composition with Szeligowski. In 1952 he was appointed conductor at the Poznan Opera; from 1953 to 1956 he conducted the Polish Radio and Television Sym. Orch. in Katowice. He was subsequently chief conductor of the Lodz Phil. (1957–60); from 1964 to 1968 he conducted the Krakow Phil.; from 1971 to 1974 served as Generalmusikdirektor of the Düsseldorf Sym. Orch.; from 1972 to 1980 again assumed the post of chief conductor of the Lodz Phil. He made his American debut with the Minnesota Orch. in 1973. In 1980 he became a prof. at the Warsaw Academy of Music. His works include *Etude for Orchestra* (1949); *Symphonic Variations* (1952); the musical *Bialowlosa* (1960); and the comic opera *Kynolog w rosterce* (1964).

D

Da-Oz, Ram (real name, **Avraham Daus**), German-born Israeli composer; b. Berlin, Oct. 17, 1929. He went to Palestine as a child in 1934; studied oboe and piano at the Cons. in Tel Aviv, and composition with André Hajdu at the Music Academy there; he lost his eyesight during the Israeli war for independence in 1948.

WORKS: *Von Trauer und Trost* for Orch. (1960); Concerto for Violin and String Orch. (1961); *Dmuyoth umassechot* (Changing Phantoms), movements for Chamber Ensemble (1967); *Improvisation on a Song* for 10 Instruments (1968); *Quartet* for Narrator and Small Orch. (1970); *Rhapsody on a Jewish Yemenite Song* for Piano and Strings (1971); *3 Romances* for Violin and Small Orch. (1975); *Introduction and Passacaglia* for Orch. (1981); 4 string quartets (1955–70); Violin Sonata (1960); String Trio (1961); *Suite* for Harpsichord, Flute, Oboe, and Cello (1963); Piano Trio (1963); *Dialogue* for 2 Clarinets (1965); *Illumination* for Solo Violin (1966); *4 Miniatures* for Recorders and Piano (1975); Divertimento for Brass Quartet (1977); songs. For piano solo: 2 sonatas (1955; *Movimenti quasi una sonata*, 1963); *5 Contrasts* (1958); *Capriccio* (1960); *8 Little Pictures* (1962); *Aspects* (1969); *Bells* (1973); *Mood Ring* (1976); *Pictures in Procession* (1979); *RuTaNoWa* (1980).

D'Accone, Frank A(nthony), American musicologist; b. Somerville, Mass., June 13, 1931. He studied with Geiringer and Read at Boston Univ. (B.Mus., 1952; M.Mus., 1953), then with Pirrotta, Merritt, and Piston at Harvard Univ. (M.A., 1955; Ph.D., 1960). He taught first at the State Univ. of N.Y. at Buffalo (1960–68); also was a visiting prof. of music at the Univ. of Calif. at Los Angeles (1965–66), to which he returned in a permanent capacity in 1968. He is ed. of the *Music of the Florentine Renaissance* in the Corpus Mensurabilis Musicae series, XXXII (1966–); he also publ. *Alessandro Scarlatti's "Gli equivoci nel sambiante": The History of a Baroque Opera* (N.Y., 1985).

Dachs, Joseph, Austrian pianist and pedagogue; b. Regensburg, Sept. 30, 1825; d. Vienna, June 6, 1896. He studied in Vienna with Czerny and Sechter; in 1861 was appointed prof. of piano at the Vienna Cons.; he had numerous distinguished pupils, among them Vladimir de Pachmann, Laura Rappoldi, and Isabelle Vengerova. He also gave concerts which were well received in Vienna.

Dadelsen, Georg von, distinguished German musicologist; b. Dresden, Nov. 7, 1918. He studied musicology at the Univ. of Kiel, at Humboldt Univ. in Berlin, and at the Free Univ. of Berlin (Ph.D., 1951, with the diss. *Alter Stil und alte Techniken in der Musik des 19. Jahrhunderts*); completed his Habilitation at the Univ. of Tübingen in 1958 with his *Beiträge zur Chronologie der Werke J.S. Bachs* (publ. in Trossingen, 1958). He was an assistant lecturer at the Univ. of Tübingen (1952–58); was then prof. of musicology at the Univ. of Hamburg (1960–71); from 1971, held the same title at the Univ. of Tübingen. He is particularly noted for his valuable contribution to the study of Bach's music.

WRITINGS: *Bemerkungen zur Handschrift J.S. Bachs, seiner Familie und seines Kreises* (Trossingen, 1957); *Editionsrichtlinien musikalischer Denkmäler und Gesamtausgaben* (Kassel, 1967); A. Feil and T. Kohlhase, eds., *Über Bach und anderes: Aufsätze und Vortrage, 1957–1982* (Laaber, 1983).

Daffner, Hugo, German composer and musicologist; b. Munich, June 2, 1882; d. in the concentration camp in Dachau, Oct. 9, 1936. He studied composition with Thuille and musicology with Sandberger and Kroyer at the Royal Academy in Munich (Ph.D., 1904, with the diss. *Die Entwicklung des Klavierkonzerts bis Mozarts;* publ. in Leipzig, 1908); subsequently took private lessons with Max Reger. He conducted at the Munich opera house from 1904 to 1906; was active as a music critic in Königsberg and Dresden; decided to study medicine, and obtained the degree of M.D. in 1920; in 1924 he went to live in Berlin as a practicing physician. He became a victim of the Nazi program of extermination of Jews.

WORKS: 3 operas: *Macbeth, Truffaldino, Der eingebildete Kranke* (after Molière); 2 syms.; 2 string quartets; 2 piano trios; 2 piano quintets; various other pieces.

Dahl, Ingolf, distinguished Swedish-born American composer, conductor, and teacher; b. Hamburg (of Swedish parents), June 9, 1912; d. Frutigen, near Bern, Switzerland, Aug. 6, 1970. He studied composition with Jarnach at the Cons. of Cologne (1930–32) and musicology at the Univ. of Zürich (1932–36), where he received instruction in conducting from Andreae. He went to the U.S. in 1938; settled in California, where he became active as a conductor and composer; was appointed an assistant prof. at the Univ. of Southern Calif. (1945); received 2 Guggenheim fellowships (1952 and 1960). He taught at the Berkshire Music Center, Tanglewood, in the summers of 1952–55. As a composer, he adhered to an advanced polyphonic style in free dissonant counterpoint.

WORKS: *Andante and Arioso* for Flute, Clarinet, Oboe, Horn, and Bassoon (1942); *Music for Brass Instruments* (1944); *Concerto a tre* for Clarinet, Violin, and Cello (1946); Duo for Cello and Piano (1946); Divertimento for Viola and Piano (1948); Concerto for Saxophone and Wind Orch. (1949); *Symphony concertante* for 2 Clarinets and Orch. (1953); *Sonata seria* for Piano (1953); *The Tower of Saint Barbara,* symphonic legend (Louisville, Jan. 29, 1955); Piano Quartet (1957); *Sonata Pastorale* for Piano (1960); *Serenade* for 4 Flutes (1960); *Sinfonietta* for Concert Band (1961); Piano Trio (1962); *Aria sinfonica* (Los Angeles, April 15, 1965); *Elegy Concerto* for Violin and Small Orch. (1963; completed by Donal Michalsky, 1971); *Duo concertante* for Flute and Percussion (1966); *Sonata da camera* for Clarinet and Piano (1970); *Intervals* for String Orch. (1970).

BIBL.: J. Berdahl, *I. D.: His Life and Works* (diss., Univ. of Miami, 1975).

Dahl, Viking, Swedish composer; b. Osby, Oct. 8, 1895; d. Stockholm, Jan. 1, 1945. He studied at the Malmö and Stockholm Conservatories; later in Paris and London with Vidal, Viñes, and Ravel; studied dancing with Isadora Duncan.

WORKS: Ballets: *Oriental Suite* (Stockholm, 1919) and *Maison des fous* (Paris, 1920); *Pastorale* for Oboe and Orch.; chamber music; many songs.

Dahlhaus, Carl, eminent German musicologist and editor; b. Hannover, June 10, 1928; d. Berlin, March 13, 1989. He studied musicology at the Univ. of Göttingen with Gerber; also at the Univ. of Freiburg with Gurlitt; received his Ph.D. from the Univ. of Göttingen in 1953 with the diss. *Studien zu den Messen Josquins des Prés.* He was a dramatic adviser for the Deutsches Theater in Göttingen from 1950 to 1958; from 1960 to 1962, was an ed. of the *Stuttgarter Zeitung;* then joined the Inst. für Musikalische Landesforschung of the Univ. of Kiel; completed his Habilitation there in 1966 with his *Untersuchungen über die Entstehung der harmonischen Tonalität* (publ. in Kassel, 1968). In 1966–67 he was a research fellow at the Univ. of Saarbrücken; in 1967 he became prof. of music history at the Technical Univ. of Berlin. He was the ed. in chief of the complete edition of Wagner's works, which began publication in 1970; was also an ed. of the Supplement to the 12th edition of the *Riemann Musik-Lexikon* (2 vols., Mainz, 1972, 1975); with Hans Eggebrecht, of the *Brockhaus-Riemann Musik-Lexikon* (2 vols., Wiesbaden and Mainz, 1978–79); and of *Pipers*

Enzyklopädie des Musiktheaters (from 1986); in addition, was co-ed. of the *Neue Zeitschrift für Musik* (1972–74), *Melos/NZ für Musik* (1975–78), *Musik und Bildung* (1978–80), and *Musica* (from 1981). He was one of the foremost musicologists of the 2nd half of the 20th century. A scholar of great erudition, he wrote authoritatively and prolifically on a vast range of subjects, extending from the era of Josquin to the present day.

WRITINGS: *Musikästhetik* (Cologne, 1967; Eng. tr. as *Esthetics of Music,* 1982); *Studien zur Trivialmusik des 19. Jahrhunderts* (Regensburg, 1967); *Analyse und Werturteil* (Mainz, 1970; Eng. tr., 1983, as *Analysis and Value Judgment*); *Das Drama Richard Wagners als musikalisches Kunstwerk* (Regensburg, 1970); *Richard Wagners Musikdramen* (Velber, 1971; Eng. tr. as *Richard Wagner's Music Dramas,* 1979); *Richard Wagner: Werk und Wirkung* (Regensburg, 1971); *Wagners Konzeption des musikalischen Dramas* (Regensburg, 1971); *Zwischen Romantik und Moderne: Vier Studien zur Musikgeschichte des späteren 19. Jahrhunderts* (Munich, 1974; Eng. tr., 1980, as *Between Romanticism and Modernism: Four Studies in the Music of the Later Nineteenth Century*); *Grundlagen der Musikgeschichte* (Cologne, 1977; Eng. tr., 1983, as *Foundations of Music History*); *Schönberg und andere: Gesammelte Aufsätze zur neuen Musik* (Mainz, 1978; Eng. tr., 1988, as *Schoenberg and the New Music*); with R. Katz, *Contemplating Music: Source Readings in the Aesthetics of Music* (N.Y., 1987); *Ludwig van Beethoven und seine Zeit* (Laaber, 1987; 2nd ed., 1988); *Klassische und romantische Musikästhetik* (Laaber, 1988).

BIBL.: H. Danuser et al., eds., *Das musikalische Kunstwerk: Geschichte, Ästhetik, Theorie: Festschrift C. D. zum 60. Geburtstag* (Laaber, 1988).

Dahms, Walter, German music critic; b. Berlin, June 9, 1887; d. Lisbon, Oct. 5, 1973. He studied with Adolf Schultze in Berlin (1907–10), then engaged in music criticism; also composed some minor piano pieces and songs. About 1935 he went to Lisbon, where he changed his name to Gualtério Armando, and continued to publ. books on music in the German language, but for some unfathomable reason he persistently denied his identity. The reasons for his leaving Germany are obscure; he was not a Jew (in fact, he wrote some anti-Semitic articles, directed against Schoenberg and others, as early as 1910), and presumably had nothing to fear from the Nazi government, unless he regarded it as unduly liberal. A clue to his true identity was the synonymity of his first names in German (Walter) and in Portuguese (Gualtério).

WRITINGS: *Schubert* (Berlin, 1912); *Schumann* (1916); *Mendelssohn* (1919); *Die Offenbarung der Musik: Eine Apotheose Friedrich Nietzsches* (Munich, 1921); *Musik des Südens* (1923); *Paganini* (Berlin, 1960); *Liszt* (Berlin, 1961); *Wagner* (Berlin, 1962).

Dalayrac, Nicolas(-Marie), French composer; b. Muret, Haute-Garonne, June 8 (baptized, June 13), 1753; d. Paris, Nov. 26, 1809. (He signed his name d'Alayrac, but dropped the nobiliary particle after the Revolution.) His early schooling was in Toulouse; returning to Muret in 1767, he studied law and played violin in a local band. He then entered the service of the Count d'Artois in his Guard of Honor, and at the same time took lessons in harmony with François Langlé at Versailles; he also received some help from Grétry. In 1781 he wrote 6 string quartets; his 1st theater work was a 1-act comedy, *L'Eclipse totale* (Paris, March 7, 1782). From then on, he devoted most of his energies to the theater. He wrote over 56 operas; during the Revolution he composed patriotic songs for special occasions. He also enjoyed Napoleon's favors later on. During his lifetime, and for some 3 decades after his death, many of his operas were popular not only in France but also in Germany, Italy, and Russia; then they gradually disappeared from the active repertoire, but there were several revivals even in the 20th century. Dalayrac's natural facility enabled him to write successfully in all operatic genres. The list of his operas produced in Paris (mostly at the Opéra-Comique) in-

cludes the following: *Le Petit Souper, ou L'Abbé qui veut parvenir* (1781); *Le Chevalier à la mode* (1781); *Nina* (May 15, 1786; one of his most successful operas); *Sargines* (May 14, 1788); *Les Deux Petits Savoyards* (Jan. 14, 1789); *Raoul, Sire de Créqui* (Oct. 31, 1789); *La Soirée orageuse* (May 29, 1790); *Camille* (March 19, 1791); *Philippe et Georgette* (Dec. 28, 1791); *Ambroise* (Jan. 12, 1793); *Adèle et Dorsan* (April 27, 1795); *Marianne* (July 7, 1796); *La Maison isolée* (May 11, 1797); *Gulnare* (Dec. 30, 1797); *Alexis* (Jan. 24, 1798); *Adolphe et Clara* (Feb. 10, 1799); *Maison à vendre* (Oct. 23, 1800; many revivals); *Léhéman* (Dec. 12, 1801); *L'Antichambre* (Feb. 26, 1802); *La Jeune Prude* (Jan. 14, 1804); *Une Heure de mariage* (March 20, 1804); *Gulistan* (Sept. 30, 1805); *Deux mots* (June 9, 1806); *Koulouf* (Dec. 18, 1806); *Le Poète et le musicien* (Paris, May 30, 1811).
Bibl.: R. de Pixérécourt, *Vie de D.* (Paris, 1810); A. Fourgeaud, *Les Violons de D.* (Paris, 1856); W. Kloppenburg, "N. D.," *Mens en melodie*, IX (1954).

Dalberg, Johann Friedrich Hugo, German pianist, composer, and writer on music; b. Aschaffenburg, May 17, 1760; d. there, July 26, 1812. He studied theology; became a canon in Trier; was also counsellor to the Elector of Trier at Coblenz. He traveled in Italy (1775) and England (1798); gave private concerts as a pianist. Although he was not a professional musician, his compositions and particularly his writings reveal considerable musical culture. He publ. many vocal works; set to music Schiller's *Ode an die Freude* (1799); also wrote songs to Eng. and French texts.
Writings: *Blicke eines Tonkünstlers in die Musik der Geister* (Mannheim, 1787); *Vom Erfinden und Bilden* (Frankfurt, 1791); *Untersuchungen über den Ursprung der Harmonie* (Erfurt, 1800); *Die Äolsharfe, Ein allegorischer Traum* (Erfurt, 1801); etc.; tr. Jones's *The Musical Modes of the Hindus* (1802).

D'Albert, Eugène. See Albert, Eugène d'.

Dalcroze, Emile Jaques. See Jaques-Dalcroze, Emile.

Dale, Benjamin (James), English composer; b. Crouch Hill, July 17, 1885; d. London, July 30, 1943. He studied at the Royal Academy of Music with F. Corder; was organist at St. Stephen's Ealing; then taught composition at the Royal Academy of Music.
Works: Overture, *The Tempest* (1902); Piano Sonata in D minor (1905); suites for Piano and Viola (1907); *Before the Paling of the Stars* for Chorus and Orch. (1912); *Songs of Praise* for Chorus and Orch. (1923); *The Flowing Tide* for Orch. (1924; 1943); *Rosa mystica* and *Cradle Song* for Mixed Chorus; 2 songs (after Shakespeare) for Voice, with Viola obbligato; Sextet for Violas; Violin Sonata; piano pieces; songs; etc.

Dale, Clamma, black American soprano; b. Chester, Pa., July 4, 1948. She began to study piano as a child; later studied clarinet and singing; at 14 she began to study voice at Philadelphia's Settlement Music School; subsequently enrolled at the Juilliard School of Music in N.Y. (B.Mus., 1970; M.S., 1975); her teachers were Hans Heinz, Alice Howland, and Cornelius Reed. She made her debut with the N.Y. City Opera as Antonia in *Les Contes d'Hoffmann* in 1975; her other roles were Nedda in *Pagliacci*, Musetta in *La Bohème*, Countess Almaviva in *Le nozze di Figaro*, Pamina in *Die Zauberflöte*, and Bess in *Porgy and Bess*.

D'Alembert, Jean le Rond. See Alembert, Jean le Rond d'.

Dal Farra, Ricardo, Argentine composer and electroacoustic music performer; b. Buenos Aires, Nov. 19, 1957. He is prof. of electroacoustic composition at the Conservatorio Municipal de Música, co-director of the Electronic Music Laboratory of the Sociedad Argentina de Educación Musical (ISME), and director of the radio program "Musica Electroacustica y por Computadora" on LS1 Radio Municipal de Buenos Aires. His compositions, processed live during performance, involve sophisticated computer programming and the most modern techniques for producing and manipulating synthesized sound.

Among these are 2 tape pieces, *Estudio sobre ritmo y espacio* (1982) and *Karma* (1986), *Ancestros* for Aerophones and Electroacoustic Processors (1986), several works for Guitar and Electroacoustic Processors, including *Integrados* (1986), *Double* (1986), and *Clones* (1986), and *G* (*I. Gravitacional* and *II. Inercial*) for MIDI Guitar and a DX7 Digital Synthesizer (1987).

Dalhart, Vernon (real name, **Marion Try Slaughter**), American country-music singer; b. on a ranch near Jefferson, Texas, April 6, 1883; d. Bridgeport, Conn., Sept. 14, 1948. He studied at the Dallas Cons. of Music; then went to N.Y., where he sang in opera and operetta; he also became a successful recording artist, mostly of popular music. In 1924 he recorded *The Wreck of the Old '97* and *The Prisoner's Song*; with these recordings the commercial country-music industry was vigorously launched; he remained a leading figure in country music until the Great Depression, when the success of Jimmie Rodgers, the Carter Family, and others obscured his pioneering efforts.

D'Alheim, Marie. See Olénine d'Alheim, Marie.

Dalis, Irene, American mezzo-soprano, teacher, and operatic administrator; b. San Jose, Calif., Oct. 8, 1925. She studied at San Jose State Univ. (A.B., 1946; M.S., 1957) and at Columbia Univ. Teachers College (M.A., 1947); received vocal training from Edyth Walker (1947–50) and Paul Althouse (1950–51) in N.Y., and from Otto Müller (1952) in Milan. In 1953 she made her operatic debut as Eboli in *Don Carlo* at the Oldenburg Landestheater; sang with the Städtische Oper in Berlin (1955–60). On March 16, 1957, she made her Metropolitan Opera debut in N.Y. as Eboli, and continued to sing there regularly until 1977. She also made guest appearances at Covent Garden in London, the Chicago Lyric Opera, and the Bayreuth Festivals. In 1976 she became a prof. of music at San Jose State Univ.; became director of its opera workshop; it served as the nucleus for the fully professional Opera San Jose, with Dalis as executive director (1984–88) and as artistic director (from 1988).

Dall'Abaco, Evaristo Felice. See Abaco, Evaristo Felice dall'.

Dall'Abaco, Joseph. See Abaco, Joseph Marie Clément dall'.

Dallapiccola, Luigi, distinguished Italian composer and pedagogue; b. Pisino, Istria, Feb. 3, 1904; d. Florence, Feb. 19, 1975. He took piano lessons at an early age; went to school at the Pisino Gymnasium (1914–21), except in 1917–18, when his family was politically exiled in Graz; studied piano and harmony in nearby Trieste (1919–21); in 1922 moved to Florence, where he took courses at the Cherubini Cons., studying piano with Ernesto Consolo (graduated 1924) and composition with Vito Frazzi (graduated 1931); was active in the Italian section of the ISCM from the early 1930s. In 1934 Dallapiccola was appointed to the faculty of the Cherubini Cons., where he stayed until 1967. As a composer, Dallapiccola became interested from the very first in the melodic application of atonal writing; in 1939 he adopted the dodecaphonic method of Schoenberg with considerable innovations of his own (for example, the use of mutually exclusive triads in thematic structure and harmonic progressions). He particularly excelled in his handling of vocal lines in a difficult modern idiom. He visited London in 1946 and traveled on the Continent; taught several courses in American colleges: Berkshire Music Center, Tanglewood, Mass. (1951); Queens College, N.Y. (1956, 1959); the Univ. of Calif., Berkeley (1962); Dartmouth College (summer, 1969); Aspen Music School (1969); and Marlboro (1969). A collection of his essays was publ. under the title *Appunti incontri meditazioni* (Milan, 1970).
Works: stage: *Volo di notte* (Night Flight), 1-act opera after the St. Exupéry novel *Vol de nuit* (1937–39; Florence, May 18, 1940); *Il Prigioniero* (The Prisoner), 1-act opera with a prologue, after Villiers de l'Isle and Charles de Coster (1944–48; rev. for Reduced Orch., Turin Radio, Dec. 4, 1949; stage premiere, Florence, May 20, 1950); *Ulisse*, 2-act opera with

prologue, after Homer's *Odyssey* (1959–68; premiere, as *Odysseus*, Berlin, Sept. 29, 1968, to a German libretto; in Italian, Milan, 1969); *Marsia*, ballet in 1 act (1942–43; Venice Music Festival, Sept. 9, 1948). **INSTRUMENTAL:** *Partita* for Orch., with Soprano in the last movement (1930–32; Florence, Jan. 22, 1933); *Musica* for 3 Pianos (1935); *Piccolo Concerto per Muriel Couvreaux* for Piano and Chamber Orch. (1939–41; Rome, May 1, 1941); *Sonatina canonica*, after Paganini's *Caprices*, for Piano (1942–43); *Ciaccona, Intermezzo e Adagio* for Solo Cello (1945); *Due studi* for Violin and Piano (1946–47); *Due pezzi* for Orch. (1947; arrangement and elaboration of the *Due studi*); *Tartiniana*, divertimento on themes from Tartini sonatas, for Violin and Chamber Orch. (1951; Bern, March 4, 1952); *Quaderno musicale di Annalibera* for Piano (1952, rev. 1953; transcribed for organ by Rudy Shackelford, 1970); *Variazioni per orchestra* (1953–54; Louisville, Ky., Oct. 2, 1954; orch. version of the *Quaderno musicale di Annalibera*); *Piccola musica notturna* for Orch. (Hannover, June 7, 1954; arranged for 8 Instruments, 1961); *Tartiniana seconda* for Violin and Piano (1955–56; chamber orch. version made with an added movement, 1956; chamber orch. version, Turin Radio, March 15, 1957); *Dialoghi* for Cello and Orch. (1959–60; Venice, Sept. 17, 1960); *3 Questions with 2 Answers* for Orch. (1962; based on material from *Ulisse*; New Haven, Conn., Feb. 5, 1963). **VOCAL:** *Due canzoni di Grado* for Mezzo-soprano, Small Female Chorus, and Small Orch. (1927); *Dalla mia terra*, song cycle for Mezzo-soprano, Chorus, and Orch. (1928); *Due laudi di Fra Jacopone da Todi* for Soprano, Baritone, Chorus, and Orch. (1929); *La Canzone del Quarnaro* for Tenor, Male Chorus, and Orch. (1930); *Due liriche del Kalewala* for Tenor, Baritone, Chamber Chorus, and 4 Percussion Instruments (1930); *3 studi* for Soprano and Chamber Orch. (1932; also based on the Kalevala epos); *Estate* for Male Chorus a cappella (1932); *Rhapsody* for Voice and Chamber Orch. (1934); *Divertimento in quattro esercizi* for Soprano, Flute, Oboe, Clarinet, Viola, and Cello (1934); *Cori di Michelangelo* in 3 sets: I for Chorus a cappella (1933), II for Female Chorus and 17 Instruments (1935), and III for Chorus and Orch. (1936); *3 laudi* for Soprano and Chamber Orch. (1936–37); *Canti di prigionia* (Songs of Captivity) for Chorus, 2 Pianos, 2 Harps, and Percussion (1938–41; 1st complete perf., Rome, Dec. 11, 1941); *Liriche greche* in 3 sets: I, *Cinque frammenti di Saffo* for Voice and 15 Instruments (1942); II, *Due liriche di Anacreonte* for Soprano, 2 Clarinets, Viola, and Piano (1945); III, *Sex carmina Alcaei*, for Soprano and 11 Instruments (1943); *Roncesvals* for Voice and Piano (1946); *Quattro liriche di Antonio Machado* for Soprano and Piano (1948; version with Chamber Orch., 1964); *3 poemi* for Soprano and Chamber Ensemble (1949); *Job*, biblical drama for 5 Singers, Narrator, Chorus, Speaking Chorus, and Orch. (1949–50; Rome, Oct. 30, 1950); *Goethe-Lieder* for Female Voice and 3 Clarinets (1953); *Canti di liberazione* (Songs of Liberation) for Chorus and Orch. (1951–55; Cologne, Oct. 28, 1955); *An Mathilde*, cantata for Female Voice and Orch. (1955); *5 canti* for Baritone and 8 Instruments (1956); *Concerto per la notte di Natale dell'anno 1956* (Christmas Concerto for the Year 1956) for Soprano and Chamber Orch. (Tokyo, Oct. 11, 1957); *Requiescant* for Mixed Chorus, Children's Chorus, and Orch. (1957–58; Hamburg Radio, Nov. 17, 1959); *Preghiere* (Prayers) for Baritone and Chamber Orch. (Berkeley, Calif., Nov. 10, 1962); *Parole di San Paolo* for Medium Voice and Chamber Ensemble (Washington, D.C., Oct. 10, 1969); *Sicut umbra . . .* for Mezzo-soprano and 4 Instrumental Groups (1969–70; Washington, Oct. 30, 1970); *Tempus destruendi/ Tempus aedificandi* for Chorus a cappella (1970–71); *Commiato* for Soprano and Chamber Ensemble (Murau, Austria, Oct. 15, 1972). A complete catalog of his works is publ. in the March 1976 issue of *Tempo* (No. 115). **BIBL.:** G. Gatti, "L. D.," *Monthly Musical Record* (Feb. 1937); D. de Paoli, "An Italian Musician: L. D.," *Chesterian* (July 1938); "Nota bio-bibliografica," *Rassegna Musicale* (1950); H. Nathan, "The Twelve-Tone Compositions of L. D.," *Musical Quarterly* (April 1958); B. Zanolini, *L. D.: La conquista di un linguaggio* (Padua, 1974); special issue of *Revue Musicale Suisse*

(July/Aug. 1973); D. Kamper, *Gefangenschaft und Freiheit: Leben und Werk des Komponisten L. D.* (Cologne, 1984).

Dallapozza, Adolf, Italian-born Austrian tenor; b. Bolzano, March 14, 1940. His parents settled in Austria when he was 5 months old. He received his musical education at the Vienna Cons.; then joined the Chorus of the Volksoper; in 1962 made his debut as soloist in the role of Ernesto in Donizetti's *Don Pasquale*. In 1967 he became a member of the Vienna State Opera; also sang with the Bavarian State Opera in Munich and made appearances in Milan, Basel, Hamburg, Zürich, and Buenos Aires. In 1976 the President of Austria made him a Kammersänger. He is highly regarded for his versatility, being equally competent in opera, oratorio, and operetta.

Dalla Rizza, Gilda, Italian soprano; b. Verona, Oct. 2, 1892; d. Milan, July 4, 1975. She received her musical training in Bologna; made her debut there as Charlotte in *Werther* in 1912; in 1915 she sang at La Scala in Milan; Puccini so admired her singing that he created the role of Magda in *La Rondine* for her (Monte Carlo, March 27, 1917). She sang in Rome (1919), at London's Covent Garden (1920), and again at La Scala (1923–39); then taught voice at the Venice Cons. (1939–55). Her students included Anna Moffo and Gianna d'Angelo. She was married to the tenor Agostino Capuzzo (1889–1963). Her most famous role was Violetta.

Dalla Viola, Alfonso, Italian instrumentalist and composer; b. Ferrara, c.1508; d. there, c.1573. He was in the service of the Este family in Ferrara from 1528. He acquired a fine reputation as an instrumentalist and composer; he was also maestro di cappella at Ferrara Cathedral (c.1563–72). Among his extant works are the vols. *Primo libro di madrigali* for 4 Voices (Ferrara, 1539) and *Il secondo libro di madrigali* for 4 Voices (Ferrara, 1540).

Dalla Viola, Francesco, Italian composer; b. Ferrara, date unknown; d. there, March 1568. He sang at Ferrara Cathedral (c.1522–26); a teacher of Ercole II, he also found a patron in the latter's brother, Cardinal Ippolito II; he was given a benefice by Ercole II in 1553; served as maestro di cappella at the Ferrara court (from 1559). He publ. *Il primo libro di madrigali* for 4 Voices (Venice, 1550); several of his sacred works are also extant.

Dal Monte, Toti (real name, **Antonietta Meneghelli**), outstanding Italian soprano; b. Mogliano, near Treviso, June 27, 1893; d. Pieve di Soligo, Treviso, Jan. 26, 1975. She studied piano at the Venice Cons., then singing with Barbara Marchisio. She made her operatic debut at La Scala in Milan as Biancafiore in Zandonai's *Francesca da Rimini* in 1916, and then sang throughout Italy. After a brilliant appearance as Gilda at La Scala in 1922, she pursued a notably acclaimed career in Europe, singing in Paris, Vienna, London, and Berlin with extraordinary success. On Dec. 5, 1924, she made her Metropolitan Opera debut in N.Y. as Lucia, remaining on its roster for 1 season; she also sang at the Chicago Civic Opera (1924–28) and at London's Covent Garden (1926). She continued to sing in opera until World War II, after which she made her farewell performance at the Verona Arena in 1949; thereafter she taught voice. She publ. an autobiography, *Una voce nel mondo* (Milan, 1962). Her other remarkable roles included Madama Butterfly, Mimi, and Stravinsky's Nightingale.

Dalmorès, Charles (real name, **Henry Alphonse Binn**), French tenor; b. Nancy, Jan. 1, 1871; d. Los Angeles, Dec. 6, 1939. After taking 1st prizes at the local Cons. for solfeggio and horn at 17, he received from the city of Nancy a stipend for study at the Paris Cons., where he took 1st prize for horn at 19; played in the Colonne Orch. (2 years) and the Lamoureux Orch. (2 years); at 23, became a prof. of horn playing at the Lyons Cons. His vocal teacher was Dauphin; his stage debut as a tenor took place on Oct. 6, 1899, at Rouen; later he sang at the Théâtre de la Monnaie in Brussels (1900–1906) and at London's Covent Garden (1904–5; 1909–11). On Dec. 7, 1906, he made his debut as Faust at the Manhattan Opera

House in N.Y., then was with the Chicago Opera Co. (1910–18). His repertoire was large, and included Wagnerian as well as French operas; in Chicago he sang Tristan and the title role in the 1st performance of *Parsifal* to be presented there.

d'Alvimare, (Martin-)Pierre. See **Dalvimare, (Martin-)Pierre.**

Dalvimare (real name, **d'Alvimare**), **(Martin-)Pierre,** French harpist and composer; b. Dreux, Eure-et-Loire, Sept. 18, 1772; d. Paris, June 13, 1839. In 1800 he was harpist at the Paris Opéra; became harpist to Napoleon in 1806; harp teacher to the Empress Josephine (1807); retired to his estate at Dreux in 1812. He wrote several sonatas for harp and violin; duets for 2 harps, for harp and piano, and for harp and horn; fantasies, variations, etc.

Damase, Jean-Michel, French composer and pianist; b. Bordeaux, Jan. 27, 1928. He studied with Delvincourt at the Paris Cons.; received the Grand Prix de Rome in 1947; made his U.S. debut April 20, 1954, in N.Y. as a pianist-composer.

WORKS: Operas: *Colombe* (Bordeaux, May 5, 1961) and *Eurydice* (Bordeaux Festival, May 26, 1972). Ballets: *Le Saut du Tremplin* (Paris, 1944); *La Croqueuse de diamants* (Paris, 1950); *Interludes* for Orch. (Nice, 1948); Rhapsody for Oboe and String Orch. (Paris Radio, 1948); Piano Concerto (Cannes, 1950); Violin Concerto (Paris, Dec. 22, 1956); 2nd Piano Concerto (Paris, Feb. 6, 1963). Chamber: Quintet for Violin, Viola, Cello, Flute, and Harp (1947); Trio for Flute, Harp, and Cello (1949); piano pieces and songs.

Dambois, Maurice, Belgian cellist and teacher; b. Liège, March 30, 1889; d. there, Nov. 12, 1969. He studied at the Liège Cons. (1899–1905) and won many prizes (piano, harmony, chamber music, fugue, cello); made his debut at 12 with Saint-Saëns's A-minor Concerto; toured Germany (1905), England (1906–8), France, Portugal, and the Netherlands; was appointed director of the Académie de Musique at Liège (1910), and prof. of cello at the Brussels Cons. (1912). After the outbreak of World War I (1914), he went to England (until 1916); went to the U.S. in 1917 with Ysaÿe; made his American debut in N.Y., April 21, 1917, followed by successful tours. In 1926 he settled in Brussels, and resumed his post as prof. of cello at the Cons., retaining it for 30 years.

Damcke, Berthold, German conductor and composer; b. Hannover, Feb. 6, 1812; d. Paris, Feb. 15, 1875. He was a pupil of Alexander Schmitt and F. Ries at Frankfurt; in 1837, became conductor of the Potsdam Phil. Soc., and of the Choral Union for operatic music (grand concerts, 1839–40); was active in St. Petersburg (1845), Brussels (1855), and Paris (1859). He was a friend and devoted admirer of Berlioz. He rev. and ed., with F. Pelletan, Gluck's 2 *Iphigénies*; composed oratorios, part-songs, and piano pieces.

BIBL.: *B. D., Etude biographique et musicale* (Paris, 1895).

Damerini, Adelmo, Italian musicologist; b. Carmignano, near Florence, Dec. 11, 1880; d. there, Oct. 12, 1976. He studied with Edgardo Binelli and Giannotto Bastianelli. He held teaching positions at the American Methodist Inst. in Rome, at the Palermo Cons. (1922), and at the Cons. Boito in Parma; from 1933 till 1962, was a prof. at the Cons. of Florence. He publ. *Origine e svolgimento della sinfonia* (Pistoia, 1919); *Le sinfonie di Beethoven* (Rome, 1921); *Lorenzo Perosi* (Rome, 1924; 2nd ed., rev., 1953); *Classicismo e romanticismo nella musica* (Florence, 1942); *Il R. Conservatorio di musica "Luigi Cherubini" di Firenze* (Florence, 1942); *L'Istituto Giovanni Pacini di Lucca* (Florence, 1942); *Boezio: Pensieri sulla musica* (Florence, 1955); *Profilo delle grandi epoche musicale* (Milan, 1955); *Guglielmo de Machaut e l' "Ars nova" italiana* (Florence, 1960); with G. Roncaglia, *Volti musicali di Falstaff* (Siena, 1961); *Luigi Cherubini nel II centenario della nascita* (Florence, 1962).

Dameron, "Tadd" (Tadley Ewing), black American jazz pianist, bandleader, arranger, and composer; b. Cleveland, Feb. 21, 1917; d. N.Y., March 8, 1965. He was inspired to follow a career as a jazz musician by his brother Caesar, a saxophone player; he subsequently played piano with Freddie Webster, Zack White, and Blanche Calloway; also became an accomplished arranger, working in Chicago and N.Y. His career was plagued by his addiction to narcotics, as a result of which he served time in the federal prison in Lexington, Ky. (1958–60).

Damone, Vic, American singer of popular music; b. N.Y., June 12, 1928. He 1st came to prominence on the radio; subsequently became a successful nightclub singer; also appeared on television. He made several film appearances as an actor, but concentrated mainly on his vocal career.

Damoreau, Laure Cinti-. See **Cinti-Damoreau, Laure.**

Da Motta, José Vianna. See **Vianna da Motta, José.**

Damrosch, Frank (Heino), German-American conductor and teacher, son of **Leopold** and brother of **Walter (Johannes) Damrosch;** b. Breslau, June 22, 1859; d. N.Y., Oct. 22, 1937. He studied piano and composition in his youth; in 1871 he went with his family to N.Y., then went to Denver, where he conducted the Chorus Club (1882–85) and was supervisor of music in the public schools (1884–85). Returning to N.Y., he was chorus master and assistant conductor at the Metropolitan Opera (1885–91). After studying composition with Moszkowski in Berlin (1891), he returned to N.Y. and organized the People's Singing Classes in 1892, which he conducted as the People's Choral Union (1894–1909). In 1893 he founded the Musical Art Soc., a professional chorus devoted to a cappella choral works, which he led until 1920; he also conducted the Oratorio Soc. (1898–1912). From 1898 to 1912 he conducted a series of sym. concerts for young people that were continued by his brother Walter; he also served as supervisor of music in N.Y. public schools (1897–1905). In 1905 he established the splendidly equipped Inst. of Musical Art, which, in 1926, became affiliated with the Juilliard School of Music; he retained his position as dean until his retirement in 1933. He received the degree of D.Mus. (*honoris causa*) from Yale Univ. in 1904. He publ. *Popular Method of Sight-Singing* (N.Y., 1894), *Some Essentials in the Teaching of Music* (N.Y., 1916), and *Institute of Musical Art, 1905–1926* (N.Y., 1936).

BIBL.: L. and R. Stebbins, *F. D.* (1945); G. Martin, *The D. Dynasty: America's First Family of Music* (N.Y., 1983).

Damrosch, Leopold, eminent German-American conductor and violinist, father of **Frank (Heino)** and **Walter (Johannes) Damrosch;** b. Posen, Oct. 22, 1832; d. N.Y., Feb. 15, 1885. He took the degree of M.D. at Berlin Univ. in 1854, but then, against his parents' wishes, embraced the career of a musician, studying with Ries, Dehn, and Böhmer. He appeared at 1st as a solo violinist in several German cities, later as a conductor at minor theaters, and in 1857 procured, through Liszt, the position of solo violinist in the Weimar Court Orch. While there, he was intimate with Liszt and many of his most distinguished pupils, and won Wagner's lifelong friendship; in Weimar, too, he married the singer **Helene von Heimburg** (b. Oldenburg, 1835; d. N.Y., Nov. 21, 1904). From 1858 to 1860 Damrosch was conductor of the Breslau Phil. Concerts; gave up the post to make tours with Bülow and Tausig; organized the Breslau Orch. Soc. in 1862. Besides this, he founded quartet *soirées*, and a choral society; conducted the Soc. for Classical Music, and a theater orch. (for 2 years); frequently appeared as a solo violinist. In 1871 he was called to N.Y. to conduct the Arion Soc., and made his debut, in April 1871, as conductor, composer, and violinist. In N.Y. his remarkable capacity as an organizer found free scope; besides bringing the Arion to the highest pitch of efficiency and prosperity, he was conductor of the N.Y. Phil. (1876–77); he founded the Sym. Soc. in 1878, the latter's concerts succeeding those of the Thomas Orch. at Steinway Hall. In 1880 Columbia College conferred on him the honorary degree of D.Mus.; in 1881 he conducted the 1st major music festival held in N.Y., with an orch. of 250 and a chorus of 1,200; in 1883 he made a highly successful Western tour with his orch.; in 1884–85 he organized the German Opera Co., and, together with Anton Seidl, conducted a season of German opera at the Metropolitan Opera, presenting Wagner's *Ring des Nibelungen*, *Tristan und Isolde*, and *Die Meistersinger von Nürnberg* for the 1st time in the U.S. He also tried his hand at composing, producing a large output of music of little lasting value.

BIBL.: E. Rice, "Personal Recollections of L. D.," *Musical Quarterly* (July 1942); G. Martin, *The D. Dynasty: America's First Family of Music* (N.Y., 1983).

Damrosch, Walter (Johannes), famous German-American conductor, composer, and educator, son of **Leopold** and brother of **Frank (Heino) Damrosch;** b. Breslau, Jan. 30, 1862; d. N.Y., Dec. 22, 1950. He studied harmony with his father, also with Rischbieter and Draeseke in Dresden; piano with von Inten, Boekelmann, and Max Pinner in the U.S.; and conducting with his father and with Hans von Bülow. He succeeded his father as conductor of the N.Y. Oratorio Soc. (1885–98) and of the N.Y. Sym. Soc. (1885–98); was assistant conductor of German opera at the Metropolitan Opera (1885–91); organized the Damrosch Opera Co. (1894), which he directed for 5 seasons, giving German opera (chiefly Wagner) in the principal cities of the U.S.; among the artists whom he 1st brought to the U.S. were Klafsky, Gadski, and Ternina. On March 3, 1886, he presented *Parsifal* in N.Y., in concert form for the 1st time in America; from 1900 to 1902 he conducted Wagner's operas at the Metropolitan; then was conductor of the N.Y. Phil. Soc. (1902–3); in 1903 the N.Y. Sym. Soc. was reorganized with Damrosch as its regular conductor, a post he held until it was merged with the N.Y. Phil. in 1928; he organized at the request of General Pershing the American Expeditionary Force bands and founded schools for bandmasters in Chaumont, France (1918); conducted a concert by the N.Y. Sym. Soc. Orch. in the 1st chain broadcast over the network of the newly organized NBC (Nov. 15, 1926); was appointed musical adviser to NBC (1927, retired 1947); was conductor of the NBC Sym. Orch. in a weekly series of music appreciation hours for the schools and colleges of the U.S. and Canada (1928–42). He conducted many famous works for the 1st time in the U.S. (Brahms' 3rd and 4th syms.; Tchaikovsky's 4th and 6th syms.; etc.). He received degrees of D.Mus. (*honoris causa*) from Columbia Univ. (1914), Princeton Univ. (1929), Brown Univ. (1932), Dartmouth College (1933), and N.Y. Univ. (1935); was awarded the David Bispham medal (1929) and the gold medal of the National Inst. of Arts and Letters (1938). He publ. an autobiography, *My Musical Life* (N.Y., 1923; 2nd ed., 1930); was co-ed., with Gartlan and Gehrkens, of the Universal School Music Series.

WORKS: Operas: *The Scarlet Letter* (Damrosch Opera Co., Boston, Feb. 10, 1896); *Cyrano de Bergerac* (Metropolitan Opera, N.Y., Feb. 27, 1913; rev. 1939); *The Man without a Country* (Metropolitan Opera, May 12, 1937); *The Opera Cloak*, 1-act opera (N.Y. Opera Co., Nov. 3, 1942); comic opera, *The Dove of Peace* (Philadelphia, Oct. 15, 1912). Other works: *Manila Te Deum* (N.Y., 1898); *An Abraham Lincoln Song* (N.Y., 1936); incidental music to Euripides' *Iphigenia in Aulis* and *Medea* (Berkeley, Calif., 1915), and to Sophocles' *Electra* (N.Y., 1917); Violin Sonata; *At Fox Meadow* (1899); *Dunkirk*, a setting of R. Nathan's poem, for Baritone, Solo, Male Chorus, and Chamber Orch. (NBC broadcast, May 2, 1943); many songs, including *Death and General Putnam* (1936), *Danny Deever*, etc.

BIBL.: W. Henderson, "W. D.," *Musical Quarterly* (Jan. 1932); G. Damrosch Finletter, *From the Top of the Stairs* (Boston, 1946); G. Martin, *The D. Dynasty: America's First Family of Music* (N.Y., 1983).

Dan, Ikuma, Japanese composer; b. Tokyo, April 7, 1924. He studied at the Tokyo Music Academy with K. Shimofusa and S. Moroi; taught at the Tokyo Music School (1947–50); has been active as a film music director and composer and, since 1967, has presented pop music concerts on television.

WORKS: 5 operas: *Yûzuru* (The Twilight Crane; 1950–51; Tokyo, Jan. 30, 1952; rev. 1956); *Kikimimi-zukin* (The Listening Cap; 1954–55; Tokyo, March 18, 1955); *Yang Kwei-fei* (1957–58; Tokyo, Dec. 11, 1958); *Chanchiki* (Cling-Clang; 1961–63); *Hikarigoke* (1972; Osaka, April 27, 1972); *Symphonic Poem* (1948); 5 syms. (1949–50; 1955–56; 1959–60; 1964–65; 1965); *Sinfonia burlesca* (1953; Tokyo, Jan. 26, 1959); dance suite for Orch., *The Silken Road* (1953–54; Tokyo, June 23, 1955); *Journey through Arabia*, symphonic suite (1958); *Olympic Games Overture* (1964); *Festival Overture* (1965); *Japanese Poem* No. 1 for Orch. (Tokyo, Sept. 25, 1967); *Hymn to the Sai-kai* for Chorus and Orch. (1969); *A Letter from Japan* No. 2 for Orch. (1969); *Rainbow Tower* for Orch. (1970); String Trio (1947); Piano Sonata (1947); String Quartet (1948); Divertimento for 2 Pianos (1949); *Futari Shizuka*, dance drama for Flute, Percussion, and String Ensemble (1961); Concerto Grosso for Harpsichord and String Ensemble (1965); choruses.

Dana, William Henry, American music pedagogue and composer; b. Warren, Ohio, June 10, 1846; d. there, Feb. 18, 1916. He studied at Kullak's Academy of Music in Berlin and at the Royal Academy of Music in London (1881). He was a founder of the American Music Teachers' National Assoc. He publ. several manuals: *Practical Thorough-bass* (1873), *Orchestration* (1875), *Instrumentation for Military Bands* (1876), *Practical Harmony* (1884). He also composed a *De profundis* for Soli, Chorus, and Orch.; motets, songs, piano pieces.

Danbé, Jules, French violinist, conductor, and composer; b. Caen, Nov. 16, 1840; d. Vichy, Nov. 10, 1905. He was a pupil at the Paris Cons.; was 2nd conductor of the Cons. concerts till 1892; conductor at the Opéra-Comique (1877–98); from 1899 until his death, was conductor at the Théâtre Lyrique.

Danckert, Werner, German musicologist; b. Erfurt, June 22, 1900; d. Krefeld, March 5, 1970. He studied natural science and mathematics at the Univ. of Jena, then musicology at the Univ. of Leipzig with Riemann and Abert, at the Univ. of Erlangen with Becking, and at the Leipzig Cons. with Schering. He received his Ph.D. in 1924 at the Univ. of Erlangen with the dissertation *Geschichte der Gigue* (publ. in Leipzig, 1924); he completed his Habilitation at the Univ. of Jena in 1926 with his *Personale Typen des Melodiestils* (publ. in an enl. ed. as *Ursymbole melodischer Gestaltung* in Kassel, 1932). He was Becking's assistant at the Univ. of Erlangen (1924–25); then taught piano at the Weimar Academy of Music (1929–32) and was a music critic in Erfurt (1932–37). He became a lecturer at the Univ. of Berlin in 1937, prof. in 1939, and head of the musicology dept. in 1943; then was in Graz (1943–45). He was briefly a prof. at the Univ. of Rostock in 1950, but returned to West Germany that same year; then lived in Krefeld.

WRITINGS: *Beiträge zur Bachkritik* (Kassel, 1934); *Das europäische Volkslied* (Berlin, 1939; 2nd ed., 1970); *Grundriss der Volksliedkunde* (Berlin, 1939); *Claude Debussy* (Berlin, 1950); *Goethe: Der mythische Urgrund seiner Weltenschau* (Berlin, 1951); *Offenes und geschlossenes Leben: Zwei Daseinsaspekte in Goethes Weltenschau* (Bonn, 1963); *Unehrliche Leute: Die verfemten Berufe* (Bern and Munich, 1964); *Das Volkslied im Abendland* (Bern and Munich, 1966); *Tonreich and Symbolzahl in Hochkulturen und in der Primitivenwelt* (Bonn, 1966); *Symbol, Metaphor, Allegorie im Lied der Völker* (Bonn, 1977).

Danckerts, Ghiselin, Flemish composer and music theorist; b. Tholen, Zeeland, c.1510; d. after Aug. 1565. He entered the Papal Chapel in Rome as a chorister in 1538; was pensioned in 1565. Although collections of his works were publ., they are lost; however, single works are extant. His ingenuity in counterpoint is demonstrated in the so-called Chessboard Canon for 4 voices with alternating black and white notes. His treatise (c.1551) pronouncing judgment on the theoretical dispute between Vincentino and Lusitano on the nature of ancient modes subsequently appeared in 2 versions (c.1555–56 and 1559–60).

Dancla, Arnaud Phillipe, French cellist and composer, brother of **(Jean Baptiste) Charles** and **(Jean Pierre) Léopold Dancla;** b. Bagnères-de-Bigorre, Jan. 1, 1819; d. there,

Feb. 1, 1862. He studied cello with Norblin at the Paris Cons. (premier prix, 1841) and was a cellist in the orch. of the Société des Concerts du Conservatoire (1847–61); he was also in the orch. of the Opéra-Comique. He was the author of a method for cello; he also composed études, duos, and melodies for his instrument.

Dancla, (Jean Baptiste) Charles, French violinist, teacher, and composer, brother of **Arnaud Phillipe** and **(Jean Pierre) Léopold Dancla;** b. Bagnères-de-Bigorre, Dec. 19, 1817; d. Tunis, Nov. 9, 1907. He studied violin with Dussert in Bagnères-de-Bigorre, then entered the Paris Cons. (1828), where he studied violin with Guérin and Baillot (premier prix, 1833), counterpoint and fugue with Halévy, and composition with Berton (graduated, 1840). He joined the orch. of the Société des Concerts du Conservatoire in 1834, serving as its principal violinist (1841–63). He also taught at the Paris Cons. (from 1855), where he was prof. of violin (1860–92). His quartet soirées were famous. Besides 4 syms., he composed some 130 works for violin, 14 string quartets, and 4 piano trios.

WRITINGS: Méthode élémentaire et progressive pour le violon; École du mécanisme; L'École de la mélodie; École de l'expression; and (with Panseron) L'Art de moduler sur le violon; also books of essays, Les Compositeurs chefs d'orchestre (1873) and Miscellanées musicales (1876).

BIBL.: C. D., Notes et souvenirs (Paris, 1893; 2nd ed., 1898).

Dancla, (Jean Pierre) Léopold, French violinist and composer, brother of **Arnaud Phillipe** and **(Jean Baptiste) Charles Dancla;** b. Bagnères-de-Bigorre, June 1, 1822; d. Paris, April 29, 1895. He studied violin with Dussert in Bagnères-de-Bigorre, then entered the Paris Cons., where he studied cornet with Meifred (premier prix, 1838) and violin with Baillot (premier prix, 1842). He became a violinist in the orch. of the Société des Concerts du Conservatoire (1846); he also joined the orchs. of the Paris Opéra (1853) and the Théâtre-Italien (1858). He wrote much chamber music, works for violin, and vocal pieces.

Danco, Suzanne, Belgian soprano; b. Brussels, Jan. 22, 1911. She studied at the Brussels Cons.; in 1936 won the International Bel Canto Prize at Venice; in 1948 was engaged as soloist at the Edinburgh Festival; also sang in Milan; in 1950 made her American debut. She has gained a fine reputation in Europe and America for her musicianly performances in opera (ranging from Mozart to Alban Berg) and in concert recitals (notably in Debussy's songs).

Dandara, Liviu, Rumanian composer; b. Miorcani, near Botoşani, Dec. 3, 1933. He studied with Paul Constantinescu, Ion Dumitrescu, and Tudor Ciortea at the Bucharest Cons. (1953–59).

WORKS: 3 cantatas: 1907 (1957); Construcţii (1969); Cetire pentru Cenotaful lui Decebal (1976); Sinfonietta lirica (1958); Ouverture solennelle (1959); Suite for Orch. (1962); Divertissement for Orch. (1964); Expresii umane for Orch. (1968); Spaţii, stereophonic music for 32 Instruments and Amplifiers (1971); Piano Concerto (1972); 3 Slow Movements for Clarinet and Piano (1963); Ipostaze for Wind Quartet (1966); Sonata for Solo Clarinet (1966); Dialoguri cu axa timpului for Flute, Violin, Piano, and Percussion (1968); Pentaedre per la "Musica Nova," quintet for Clarinet, Violin, Viola, Cello, and Piano (1969; "Musica Nova" is a Rumanian ensemble); Bamba! for Wind Instruments, or Voices and Percussion (1971); Trei stări despre linişte for Violin and Piano (1980); Miniatures for Piano (1959); Piano Sonatina (1961); Toccata for Piano (1965); Sonata brevis for Piano (1966); Quadriforium for Piano and Tape (1970; variable timing); Timpul suspendat for Tape (1971); Imnurile verii, 3 madrigals for Double Chorus, Xylophone, and Vibraphone (1967); songs; film music.

Dandelot, Georges (Edouard), French composer; b. Paris, Dec. 2, 1895; d. St.-Georges de Didonne, Charente-Maritime, Aug. 17, 1975. He studied with Widor at the Paris Cons.; later took lessons with Dukas and Roussel. He was in the French army during World War I, and received the Croix de Guerre for valor. In 1919 he became an instructor at the École Normale de Musique in Paris; in 1942, was appointed a prof. at the Paris Cons. Dandelot composed an oratorio, Pax (1st prize at the International Exposition in Paris, 1937); 2 operas: Midas (1947) and L'Ennemi (1948); ballets: Le Souper de famine (1943); Le Jardin merveilleux (1944); Pierrot et la rose (1948); Sym. (1941); Piano Concerto (Paris, Jan. 7, 1934); Concerto romantique for Violin and Orch. (1944); chamber music; songs.

Dandrieu, Jean François, French organist and composer; b. Paris, 1682; d. there, Jan. 17, 1738. He was organist at Saint-Merry, Paris, in 1704; in 1721, became organist at the Royal Chapel. He publ. Livre de sonates en trio (1705); Livre de sonates for Solo Violin (1710); Principes de l'accompagnement du clavecin (1718); Pièces de clavecin (3 albums, 1724); organ pieces, airs. His importance lies in his works for clavecin, written in a style closely resembling Couperin's.

BIBL.: P. Brunold, D. (Paris, 1954).

Daneau, Nicolas, Belgian composer; b. Binche, June 17, 1866; d. Brussels, July 12, 1944. He studied at the Ghent Cons. with Adolphe Samuel, graduating in 1892; won the 2nd Prix de Rome in 1895. He was director of the Cons. of Tournai (1896–1919), and of the Cons. of Mons (1919–31). His daughter, **Suzanne Daneau** (b. Tournai, Aug. 17, 1901; d. there, Nov. 29, 1971), was his pupil. She wrote orch. works, chamber music, and piano pieces, mostly based on native folk songs.

WORKS: Linario, lyric drama (Tournai, 1906); Myrtis, opera-idyll (Tournai, 1910); Le Sphynx, opera; La Brute, lyric drama. For Orch.: Villes d'Italie; Adima et Hevah; Arles; Mardi-Gras; Petite suite. Chamber music: Suite for Violin and Piano; String Quartet; Piano Quintet.

BIBL.: L. Beatrice, D.; Histoire d'une famille d'artistes (Brussels, 1944).

Danhauser, Adolphe-Léopold, French composer and teacher; b. Paris, Feb. 26, 1835; d. there, June 9, 1896. He studied at the Paris Cons. with Halévy and Reber; won 1st prize in harmony (1857); 1st prize in fugue (1859); 2nd Prix de Rome (1862); was chief inspector of instruction in singing in the communal schools in Paris and prof. of solfeggio at the Cons. He wrote Théorie de la musique; publ. Soirées orphéoniques, a collection of 3-part choruses for equal voices. He composed Le Proscrit, a musical drama with choruses, which was produced (1866) in a religious institution at Auteuil; a 3-act opera, Maures et Castillans (not perf.). His Solfège des solfèges (3 vols.; tr. into Eng. and Spanish) was used throughout the U.S. and South America.

Daniel-Lesur. See **Lesur, Daniel.**

Daniel, Minna (née **Lederman**), legendary American editor and writer on music; b. N.Y., March 3, 1898. She studied music and dance professionally before taking a degree at Barnard College (1917) and beginning her career as a journalist. In 1923 she joined the newly formed League of Composers, and in 1924 helped launch its Review, which in 1925 became Modern Music, the 1st American journal to serve as a forum for contemporary composers. During her tenure as its sole ed. (1924–46), she encouraged a generation of American composer-critics, publishing essays and reviews by such musical activists as Thomson, Cage, Carter, Blitzstein, and Bowles; she also publ. articles by Berg, Schoenberg, and Bartók. The journal attained an international reputation. In 1975 she established Archives of Modern Music at the Library of Congress, and in 1983 she publ. the informative chronicle The Life and Death of a Small Magazine. She also ed. Stravinsky in the Theatre (N.Y., 1949; 3rd ed., 1975). In 1989 she commenced writing From Then to Now, an overview vol. of reflections about the period of American musical and dance culture spanning the mid-1920s to the present.

Daniel, Oliver, American music administrator and writer on music; b. De Pere, Wis., Nov. 24, 1911; d. Scarsdale, N.Y., Dec. 30, 1990. He attended St. Norbert College in West De Pere (1925–29), then studied piano in Europe and at the New England Cons. of Music in Boston. He was active as a pianist and as a piano teacher until becoming music director of the educational division of CBS radio in 1942; he was head of the concert-music division of BMI (1954–77) and was associated with the International Music Council of UNESCO (from 1958). With Leopold Stokowski, he founded the Contemporary Music Soc. in 1952; later was active with various other organizations, including the American Music Center, the Charles Ives Soc., and the American Composers Orch. He wrote a column for the *Saturday Review* (1957–68); also contributed to other journals. He ed. various collections of works by early American composers and publ. the study *Leopold Stokowski: A Counterpoint of View* (1982).

Daniel, Salvador (real name, **Francisco Daniel;** also known as **Salvador-Daniel**), French composer and political revolutionary; b. Bourges, Feb. 17, 1831; killed during the Paris Commune, May 23, 1871. For a brief time he was director of the Paris Cons. under the Commune. He taught music in an Arab school in Algiers; studied native folk songs of North Africa; wrote a valuable book, *La Musique arabe* (Algiers, 1863, publ. in Eng. as *The Music and Musical Instruments of the Arabs,* London, 1915).

Daniélou, Alain, French musicologist; b. Paris, Oct. 4, 1907. He devoted himself mainly to the study of Asian music; lived mostly in India; lectured at the Univ. of Benares (1949–54); was director of research in Madras (1954–56) and at the Inst. of Indology in Pondicherry (1956–59). In 1959 he was appointed instructor at the École Française d'Extrême Orient in Paris. In 1963 he assumed the post of director of the International Inst. for Comparative Studies.
WRITINGS: *Introduction to the Study of Musical Scales* (London, 1943); *Northern Indian Music* (2 vols., Calcutta, 1949, 1953; 2nd ed., rev., as *The Ragas of Northern Indian Music,* 1968); *La Musique du Cambodge et du Laos* (Pondicherry, 1957); *Traité de musicologie comparée* (Paris, 1959); *Purānas: Textes des Purānas sur la théorie musicale* (Pondicherry, 1959); *Bharata, Muni, Le Gitālamkāra* (Pondicherry, 1960); *Inde* (Paris, 1966); *Sémantique musicale* (Paris, 1967); *La Situation de la musique et des musiciens dans les pays d'orient* (Florence, 1971; Eng. tr., 1971).

Daniels, Barbara, American soprano; b. Newark, Ohio, May 7, 1946. She studied at Ohio State Univ. (B.Mus., 1969) and the Univ. of Cincinnati College–Cons. of Music (M.A., 1971). In 1973 she made her operatic debut as Susanna in *Le nozze di Figaro* at the West Palm Beach (Fla.) Opera; then was a member of the Innsbruck Landestheater (1974–76), Kassel Staatstheater (1976–78), and Cologne Opera (1978–82). In 1978 she appeared as Rosalinde at London's Covent Garden, and on Sept. 30, 1983, she made her Metropolitan Opera debut in N.Y. as Musetta, also making guest appearances at the Vienna State Opera, the Chicago Lyric Opera, the Paris Opéra, and the Bavarian State Opera in Munich. Among her other roles are Violetta, Alice Ford, Massenet's Manon, and Micaela.

Daniels, Charlie, American country-music violinist; b. Wilmington, N.C., Oct. 28, 1936. He played in a group known as the Jaguar band; then joined the country-music ensembles of Earl Scruggs and Marty Robbins; in 1971 he founded his own Charlie Daniels Band, which won a Grammy award in 1980 and became one of the most popular country-and-western groups before the public.

Daniels, Mabel Wheeler, American composer; b. Swampscott, Mass., Nov. 27, 1878; d. Boston, March 10, 1971. She studied at Radcliffe College (B.A., magna cum laude, 1900) and with Chadwick in Boston; then with Thuille in Munich; was director of the Radcliffe Glee Club (1911–13); head of music at Simmons College in Boston from 1913 to 1918; received an honorary M.A. from Tufts College in 1933; an honorary D.Mus. from Boston Univ. in 1939. As a composer, she excelled in vocal writing; her instrumental pieces are cautiously modernistic. She wrote a lively book, *An American Girl in Munich* (Boston, 1905).
WORKS: Operetta, *The Court of Hearts* (Cambridge, Mass.,

Jan. 2, 1901; she sang the part of Jack of Hearts); operatic sketch, *Alice in Wonderland Continued* (Brookline, Mass., May 20, 1904). Vocal works with Orch.: *The Desolate City* (1913); *Peace with a Sword* (Boston, 1917); *Songs of Elfland* (St. Louis, Feb. 2, 1924); *The Holy Star* (1928); *Exultate Deo* (Boston, May 31, 1929); *Song of Jael,* cantata for Dramatic Soprano, Mixed Voices, and Orch. (Worcester Festival, Oct. 5, 1940); *A Psalm of Praise* (Cambridge, Mass., Dec. 3, 1954); choral cycle for Women's Voices, *In Springtime* (1910); 3-part women's choruses, with Piano and 2 Violins: *Eastern Song* and *The Voice of My Beloved* (prize of the National Federation of Music Clubs, 1911); sacred choruses a cappella (*The Christ Child, Salve festa dies,* etc.); duets; part-songs. Orch.: *Deep Forest,* prelude for Small Orch. (N.Y., June 3, 1931; rescored for Full Orch., 1934; Boston, April 16, 1937); *Pirates' Island* (Harrisburg, Pa., Feb. 19, 1935). Chamber: *Pastoral Ode* for Flute and Strings (1940); *3 Observations* for Oboe, Clarinet, and Bassoon (1943); *Digressions,* ballet for Strings (Boston, 1947).

Danjou, Jean-Louis-Félix, French music teacher; b. Paris, June 21, 1812; d. Montpellier, March 4, 1866. He studied organ with François Benoist at the Paris Cons.; then played organ at various churches from 1830; was organist at Notre Dame from 1840 till 1847. With his essay *De l'état de l'avenir du chant ecclésiastique* (1844), he became the pioneer in the movement for reforming plainchant; and his journal *Revue de la Musique Religieuse, Populaire et Classique* (1845–49) showed profound erudition gained by assiduous historical research. He was the discoverer (1847) of the celebrated "Antiphonary of Montpellier." He labored to promote organ building in France; made a special study of organ manufacture in Germany and the Netherlands; entered into partnership with the organ builders Daublaine & Callinet of Paris, but lost his entire capital, gave up music, and in 1849 became a political journalist in Marseilles and Montpellier.

Dankevich, Konstantin, eminent Ukrainian composer; b. Odessa, Dec. 24, 1905; d. Kiev, Feb. 26, 1984. He studied with Zolotarev at the Odessa Cons., graduating in 1929. In 1942 he was artistic director of the Red Army Ensemble of Songs and Dance in Tbilisi. From 1944 to 1953 he was a prof. of composition at the Odessa Cons.; in 1953 he was appointed to the faculty of the Kiev Cons. In his works he successfully presents the motifs of Ukrainian and Russian folk songs. He 1st attracted attention with his opera *Bogdan Khmelnitsky* (Kiev, Jan. 29, 1951), on a subject from Ukrainian history; the opera was attacked for its libretto and its unsuitable music, and Dankevich revised the score, after which it gained favorable notices in Russia. He also wrote the opera *Nazar Stodolya* (Kharkov, May 28, 1960). His most popular score is *Lileya,* a ballet, produced in 1939. Other works include 2 syms. (1937, 1945), several overtures, and patriotic choruses, including *Poem of the Ukraine* (1960) and the ideological cantata to his own words, *The Dawn of Communism Has Risen over Us* (1961). A monograph on him was publ. in Ukrainian in Kiev (1959).

Danks, H(art) P(ease), American song composer; b. New Haven, Conn., April 6, 1834; d. Philadelphia, Nov. 20, 1903. He studied at Saratoga Springs with L.E. Whiting; in 1851 moved to Chicago, where he became a photographer, and also sang bass in church. In 1864 he settled in N.Y. and developed energetic activity as a prolific composer of sacred hymns and popular songs; publ. a total of about 1,300 separate numbers; also compiled books of church anthems; wrote 2 operettas: *Pauline, or the Belle of Saratoga* (1872) and *Conquered by Kindness* (1881). Of his sacred songs, the most popular was *Not Ashamed of Christ* (1873); in the light genre, his greatest successes were the songs *Don't be angry with me, darling* (1870) and *Silver threads among the gold* (1872).

Dankworth, John (Philip William), English alto saxophonist, clarinetist, bandleader, and composer-arranger; b. London, Sept. 20, 1927. He studied at the Royal Academy of Music (1944–46); then played alto saxophone and clarinet in jazz groups; formed his own septet in 1950, then his own jazz orch. in 1953. After his marriage to the singer **Cleo Laine** in 1958, he toured with her, appearing as a guest conductor in England and the U.S. His compositions include *Improvisations* (1959; composed with Mátyás Seiber); *Escapade* (1967); *Tom Sawyer's Saturday* for Narrator and Orch. (1967); String Quintet (1971); Piano Concerto (1972). In 1974 he was made a Commander of the Order of the British Empire.

BIBL.: G. Collier, *Cleo and J.* (London, 1976).

Dannreuther, Edward (George), pianist and music scholar, brother of **Gustav Dannreuther;** b. Strasbourg, Nov. 4, 1844; d. London, Feb. 12, 1905. He went with his parents in 1849 to Cincinnati, where he was taught by F.L. Ritter; then studied at the Leipzig Cons. with Richter, Moscheles, and Hauptmann (1859–63). On April 11, 1863, he made his debut in London, playing Chopin's Concerto in F minor. He introduced into England the piano concertos of Liszt, Grieg, and Tchaikovsky. In 1872 he founded the London Wagner Soc., and conducted its concerts in 1873–74; was an active promoter of the Wagner Festival (1877); was appointed a prof. at the Royal Academy of Music in 1895. An indefatigable champion of the new composers, he was equally active on behalf of the older masters; the chamber music concerts that he gave at his home (1874–93) were famous. Dannreuther visited the U.S. several times.

WRITINGS: "Richard Wagner and the Reform of the Opera," *Monthly Musical Record* (separately, London, 1873; 2nd ed., rev., 1904); *Richard Wagner, His Tendencies and Theories* (London, 1873); *Musical Ornamentation* (2 vols., London, 1893–95); *The Romantic Period,* vol. VI of the *Oxford History of Music* (London, 1905; 3rd ed., 1931).

Dannreuther, Gustav, American violinist, brother of **Edward (George) Dannreuther;** b. Cincinnati, July 21, 1853; d. N.Y., Dec. 19, 1923. He studied at the Hochschule für Musik, Berlin, under de Ahna and Joachim (violin) and Heitel (theory); then lived in London; in 1877 he joined the Mendelssohn Quintette Club of Boston, traveling through the U.S., Canada, and Newfoundland. From 1882 to 1884 he was director of the Buffalo Phil. Soc. (a chamber music organization). In 1884 he founded the Beethoven String Quartet of N.Y. (renamed the Dannreuther Quartet in 1894). From 1907 he taught violin at Vassar College.

Danon, Oskar, Yugoslav conductor; b. Sarajevo, Feb. 7, 1913. He was educated at the Prague Cons. and the Univ. of Prague (Ph.D., 1938). In 1940 he became a conductor at the Belgrade Opera; was its director (1945–60). He also conducted throughout Europe, both opera and sym. concerts.

Danzi, Franz (Ignaz), German composer and teacher; b. Schwetzingen, June 15, 1763; d. Karlsruhe, April 13, 1826. He received primary instruction in music from his father, Innocenz Danzi, a cellist; later took theory lessons with Abbé Vogler. In 1783 he joined the Court Orch. in Munich; then (1807–12) served as Kapellmeister at Stuttgart, where he was the teacher of Carl Maria von Weber. He was an excellent singing teacher, and wrote vocal exercises of practical value.

WORKS: *Cleopatra,* duodrama (Mannheim, Jan. 30, 1780); *Azakia,* comedy (Mannheim, June 6, 1780); *Die Mitternachtsstunde,* singspiel (Munich, April 1788); *Der Sylphe,* singspiel (Munich, 1788); *Der Triumph der Treue,* melodrama (Munich, Feb. 1789; not extant); *Der Quasi-Mann,* comedy (Munich, Aug. 1789; not extant); *Deucalion et Pirrha,* opera (c.1795); *Der Kuss,* comedy (Munich, June 27, 1799); *El Bondocani,* singspiel (Munich, 1802; not extant); *Iphigenie in Aulis,* grand opera (Munich, Jan. 27, 1807); *Dido,* melodrama (Stuttgart, 1811; not extant); *Camilla und Eugen oder Der Gartenschlüssel,* comedy (Stuttgart, March 15, 1812); *Rübezahl,* singspiel (Karlsruhe, April 19, 1813); *Malvina,* singspiel (Karlsruhe, Dec. 20, 1814); *Turandot,* singspiel (Karlsruhe, Feb. 9, 1817); *Die Probe,* opera (Karlsruhe, Oct. 1817); *L'Abbe de Attaignant oder Die Theaterprobe,* opera (Karlsruhe, Sept. 14, 1820); oratorios; cantatas; masses; the 128th Psalm for Chorus and Orch.; syms.; quintets; quartets; concertos; sonatas.

BIBL.: E. Reipschläger, *Schubaur, D. und Poissl als Opernkomponisten* (diss., Univ. of Rostock, 1911); M. Herre, *F. D.* (diss., Univ. of Munich, 1924).

Da Ponte, Lorenzo (real name, **Emanuele Conegliano**), famous Italian librettist; b. Ceneda, near Venice, March 10, 1749; d. N.Y., Aug. 17, 1838. He was of a Jewish family; was converted to Christianity at the age of 14, and assumed the name of his patron, Lorenzo da Ponte, Bishop of Ceneda. He then studied at the Ceneda Seminary and at the Portogruaro Seminary, where he taught from 1770 to 1773; in 1774 obtained a post as prof. of rhetoric at Treviso, but was dismissed in 1776 for his beliefs concerning natural laws. He then went to Venice, where he led an adventurous life, and was banished in 1779 for adultery; subsequently lived in Austria and in Dresden; in 1782 he settled in Vienna and became official poet to the Imperial Theater; met Mozart and became his friend and librettist of his most famous operas, *Le nozze di Figaro, Don Giovanni,* and *Così fan tutte.* From 1792 to 1798 he was in London; traveled in Europe; then went to N.Y. in 1805. After disastrous business ventures, with intervals of teaching, he became interested in various operatic enterprises. In his last years he was a teacher of Italian at Columbia College. He publ. *Memorie* (4 vols., N.Y., 1823–27; Eng. tr., London, 1929, and Philadelphia, 1929).

BIBL.: A. Marchesan, *Della vita e delle opere di L. d.P.* (Treviso, 1900); J. Russo, *L. d.P., Poet and Adventurer* (N.Y., 1922); A. Fitzlyon, *The Libertine Librettist* (London, 1955); S. Hodges, *L. d.P.: The Life and Times of Mozart's Librettist* (London, 1985); A. Steptoe, *The Mozart–D.P. Operas: The Cultural and Musical Background to Le nozze di Figaro, Don Giovanni, and Così fan tutte* (Oxford, 1988).

Daquin, Louis-Claude, French organist and composer; b. Paris, July 4, 1694; d. there, June 15, 1772. He was a pupil of Marchand; at 6 played on the clavecin before Louis XIV; at 12 became organist at St.-Antoine, where his playing attracted crowds of curious listeners. From 1727 until his death he was organist at St.-Paul, having won the position in competition with Rameau. He publ. a book of *Pièces de clavecin* (Paris, 1735; contains the celebrated piece *Le Coucou*; 1st complete modern ed. by C. Hogwood, London, 1983); a collection of *Noëls pour l'orgue ou le clavecin* (reprinted by Guilmant in *Archives des Maîtres de l'Orgue*), and a cantata, *La Rose.*

D'Aranyi, Jelly. See **Aranyi, Jelly.**

D'Archambeau, Iwan. See **Archambeau, Iwan.**

Darclée, Hariclea (real name, **Haricly Hartulary**), Rumanian soprano; b. Brăila, June 10, 1860; d. Bucharest, Jan. 10, 1939. She studied in Bucharest and Paris; made her debut as Marguerite at the Paris Opéra in 1888; then sang at La Scala in Milan, creating La Wally in 1892; also sang in Rome, N.Y., St. Petersburg, Moscow, and in South America. She retired in 1918. She was particularly distinguished for her Italian repertoire; she created the role of Tosca; also was known for her performances of roles in Wagner's operas.

Darcy, Robert, French-born Belgian cellist and composer; b. Paris, Nov. 10, 1910; d. Schaerbeek, near Brussels, June 6, 1967. He obtained the Premier Prix in cello at the Lyons Cons. (1928); studied composition with Francis Bousquet and Paul Vidal; played the cello in orchs. in Paris and Brussels. Mobilized in 1939, he was taken prisoner of war in June 1940; while in captivity, he organized a prisoners' orch.; returned to Belgium, becoming a naturalized citizen in 1949. His style is rooted in neo-Classicism, with an admixture of atonal elements.

WORKS: *Scherzo* for Orch. (1923); *Rêverie* for Orch. (1931); *7 Sketches* for Small Orch. (1933); Suite for Wind Orch. (1935); Suite for String Orch. (1936); Concerto for 4 Cellos and Wind Orch. (1936); *Piece* for 2 Cellos and Orch. (1937); Fantasie for Cello and Orch. (1937); *3 Marines* for Orch. (1939); Concerto for 4 Saxophones and Orch. (1939); *Danses mosanes* for Orch. (1943); Trumpet Concerto (1948); Piano Concerto (1951); Sym. (1953); Concerto for Orch. (1965); 3 quartets for 4 Cellos (1935–37); 3 string quartets (1936–50); *Caprice for Wind Quintet* (1936); *Sextet for Winds* (1937); *6 Pieces for 4 Cellos* (1937); Trio for Oboe, Clarinet, and Bassoon (1938); Quartet for 4 Saxophones (1938); Bassoon Sonata (1948); *Piece for Wind Quintet* (1962); songs.

Dargomyzhsky, Alexander (Sergeievich), outstanding Russian composer; b. in Tula province, Feb. 14, 1813; d. St. Petersburg, Jan. 17, 1869. From 1817 he lived in St. Petersburg; studied piano with Schoberlechner and Danilevsky, and violin with Vorontsov. At 20 he was a brilliant pianist; from 1827 to 1843 he held a government position, but then devoted himself exclusively to music, studying assiduously for 8 years; visited Germany, Brussels, and Paris in 1845; at Moscow (Dec. 17, 1847) produced an opera, *Esmeralda* (after Victor Hugo's *Notre-Dame de Paris*), with great success (excerpts publ. in piano score, Moscow, 1948). From 1845 to 1855 he publ. over 100 minor works (vocal romances, ballads, airs, and duos; waltzes, fantasies, etc.); on May 16, 1856, he brought out his best opera, *Rusalka*, at St. Petersburg (vocal score, with indications of instruments, publ. at Moscow, 1937); in 1867, an opera-ballet, *The Triumph of Bacchus* (written in 1845; perf. in Moscow, Jan. 23, 1867); a posthumous opera, *Kamennyi gost* (*The Stone Guest*, after Pushkin's poem of the same title), was scored by Rimsky-Korsakov and produced at St. Petersburg on Feb. 28, 1872; of *Rogdana*, a fantasy-opera, only a few scenes were sketched. At first a follower of Rossini and Auber, Dargomyzhsky gradually became convinced that dramatic realism with nationalistic connotations was the destiny of Russian music; he applied this realistic method in treating the recitative in his opera *The Stone Guest* and in his songs (several of these to satirical words). His orch. works (*Finnish Fantasia, Cossack Dance, Baba-Yaga,* etc.) enjoyed wide popularity. In 1867 he was elected president of the Russian Music Soc. **BIBL.:** N. Findeisen, *A.S. D.: His Life and Work* (Moscow, 1902); S. Fried, *A.S. D.* (St. Petersburg, 1913); A. Drozdov, *A.S. D.* (Moscow, 1929); M. Pekelis, *A. D. and His Circle* (2 vols., Moscow, 1966, 1973).

Darin, Bobby (real name, **Walden Robert Cassatto**), American pop crooner; b. N.Y., May 14, 1936; d. Los Angeles, Dec. 20, 1973. He slogged drums, banged on the piano keys, and ripped the guitar strings as a child. He changed his name to avoid the ethnic curse and began to compose music in the rhythm-and-blues manner. His songs were marked by kinetic vitality, exemplified in such tunes as *Splish Splash* (1958) and *Queen of the Hop* (1959). In a more romantic mood he wrote *Dream Lover* (1959). In 1959 he brought out a pop version of *Mack the Knife* from Kurt Weill's *Die Dreigroschenoper*, and captured a Grammy Award. **BIBL.:** A. DiOrio, *Borrowed Time* (N.Y., 1985).

Darke, Harold (Edwin), English organist and composer; b. London, Oct. 29, 1888; d. Cambridge, Nov. 28, 1976. He studied organ with Parratt and composition with Stanford at the Royal College of Music in London; from 1916 to 1966 he served as organist at St. Michael's Church, Cornhill, London. He wrote several cantatas and other sacred music, as well as organ pieces and songs.

Darnton, (Philip) Christian, English composer and writer; b. near Leeds, Oct. 30, 1905; d. Hove, April 14, 1981. He took piano lessons at the age of 4 and began to compose at 9; then studied piano with Craxton and composition with Benjamin Dale, Charles Wood, and Rootham at Cambridge; went to Berlin in 1928 and took some lessons in composition with Butting. In 1952 he decided to abandon composition and to devote himself to the writing of philosophical essays and poetry. His works include an opera, *Fantasy Fair*, 3 syms., 2 piano concertos, a *Suite concertante* for Violin and Chamber Orch. (1938), 5 *Orchestral Pieces* (Warsaw, April 14, 1939), a cantata, *Jet Pilot* (1950), and a Concerto for Orch. (1970–73). He publ. a book, *You and Music* (Harmondsworth, 1939). **BIBL.:** A. Rawsthorne, "C. D.," *Monthly Musical Record* (Jan. 1939).

Darré, Jeanne-Marie, French pianist; b. Givet, July 30, 1905. She studied with Marguerite Long and Isidor Philipp in Paris; after numerous concerts in France and elsewhere in Europe, she made her U.S. debut in N.Y. (1962); then made a successful series of tours in the U.S., appearing with major American orchs. In 1958 she became a teacher at the Paris Cons. A virtuoso in a grand manner, she produced a sensation by playing several piano concertos on a single night.

Darrell, R(obert) D(onaldson), American writer on music; b. Newton, Mass., Dec. 13, 1903; d. Kingston, N.Y., May 1, 1988. He studied at Harvard Univ. and the New England Cons. of Music in Boston; upon graduation, he devoted himself mainly to publishing descriptive catalogs of recordings. He publ. the valuable compilations *The Gramophone Shop Encyclopedia of Recorded Music* (1936) and *Schirmer's Guide to Books on Music and Musicians* (annotated bibliography of books in Eng. available in print; N.Y., 1951); also *Good Listening* (N.Y., 1953).

Dart, (Robert) Thurston, eminent English musicologist; b. London, Sept. 3, 1921; d. there, March 6, 1971. He studied keyboard instruments at the Royal College of Music in London (1938–39); also took courses in mathematics at Univ. College, Exeter (B.Sc., 1942). In 1947 he became an assistant lecturer in music at Cambridge Univ., then a full lecturer in 1952, and finally a prof. of music in 1962. In 1964 he was named King Edward Prof. of Music at King's College of the Univ. of London. As a performing musician, he made numerous appearances on the harpsichord; also appeared as organist and performer on Baroque keyboard instruments. He served as ed. of the *Galpin Society Journal* (1947–54) and secretary of the documentary ed. Musica Britannica (1950–65). His magnum opus was *The Interpretation of Music* (London, 1954; 5th ed., 1984; also in German, under the title *Practica musica*, Bern, 1959, and in Swedish, Stockholm, 1964). He also ed. works by Morley, Purcell, John Bull, and others. **BIBL.:** I. Bent, ed., *Source Materials and the Interpretation of Music: A Memorial Volume to T. D.* (London, 1981).

Darvas, Gábor, Hungarian composer; b. Szatmárnémeti, Jan. 18, 1911; d. Budapest, Feb. 18, 1985. He studied at the Liszt Academy of Music in Budapest with Kodály; subsequently traveled to South America as assistant conductor to Erich Kleiber. He returned to Hungary in 1948; was ed. in chief of Editio Musica Budapest (1955–57) and artistic director of Hungaroton Records (1957–59). Among his compositions are *Sectio aurea* (Golden Section) for 3 Percussion Groups and Orch. (1964), *Der Turm* for Soloists, Chorus, Percussion, 2 Pianos, and String Orch. (1967), *Gyermekzene* (Children's Music) for Soprano and 12 Performers, 11 of whom play on child-sized instruments (1969), *Passion Music* for Voices and Tape (1974–78), and *Poèmes électroniques* for Tape (1982–83).

Dārziņš, Emils, Latvian composer and writer on music; b. Lunpiebama, Nov. 3, 1875; d. (run over by a train) Riga, Aug. 31, 1910. From 1898 to 1901 he was a pupil in composition of Rimsky-Korsakov at the St. Petersburg Cons. Returning to Latvia, he became active as a choral conductor and music critic while continuing to compose. He excelled particularly in vocal music; among his choral works, *Broken Pines* and *In the Faraway Land of Dreams* are best known. His style is marked by a fine mastery of old-fashioned Germanic Romanticism, reflected through Slavic harmonic and melodic folkways. Among his symphonic pieces, only his *Melancholy Waltz* survives.

Daser (Dasser, Dasserus), Ludwig, German composer; b. Munich, c.1525; d. Stuttgart, March 27, 1589. He preceded Orlando di Lasso as Kapellmeister at Munich to Duke Albert V of Bavaria; held that post until 1559. He publ. a Passion *a* 4 (1578), plus motets in the *Orgeltabulaturbuch* of J. Paix.

Dashow, James (Hilyer), American composer; b. Chicago, Nov. 7, 1944. After studies with Babbitt, Cone, Kim, and Randall at Princeton Univ. (B.A., 1966), with Berger, Boykan, and Shifrin at Brandeis Univ. (M.F.A., 1969), and with Petrassi at the Accademia di Santa Cecilia in Rome (diploma, 1971), he founded the Forum Players (1971–75), a contemporary chamber music group. He also served as director of the Studio di Musica Elettronica Sciadoni in Rome (from 1975). From 1982 he taught computer music at the Centro di Sonologia Computazionale at the Univ. of Padua; also was guest lecturer in various European and U.S. cities. In 1969 he held a Fulbright fellowship; later accolades included grants from the N.E.A. (1976, 1981) and the Rockefeller Foundation (1982), an award from the American Academy and Inst. of Arts and Letters (1984), and a Guggenheim fellowship (1989).

Works: *Songs of Despair* for Soprano and 11 Instruments (1968–69); *Transformations* for Dance and Electronics (1969); *Astrazioni Pomeridiane* for Orch. (1970–71); *BURST!* for Soprano and Electronics (1971); *Maximus* for Soprano, 3 Wind Players, Piano, and Percussion (1972–73); *At Delphi* for Soprano and Electronics (1975); *Whispers out of Time* for Electronics (1975–76); *Effetti collaterali* for Clarinet and Computer-generated Electronics (1976); *Il piccolo principe*, opera (1981–82); *Songs from a Spiral Tree* for Mezzo-soprano, Flute, and Harp (1984–86); *Oro, argento, and legno* for Flute and Computer (1987); *Archimede*, theater piece (1988); *Disclosures* for Cello and Computer (1988–89).

Dasser, Ludwig. See **Daser, Ludwig.**

Daublaine et Callinet, firm of Paris organ builders; founded in 1838 as Daublaine et Cie. Daublaine was the business partner, Callinet the practical mechanician, and Danjou (the initiator of the business) an intelligent and progressive theorist. After a quarrel in 1843, Callinet demolished the new work partly finished for the organ of St.-Sulpice, dissolved the partnership, and entered Cavaillé's workshops. The firm name became Ducroquet et Cie. in 1845; in 1855 it was succeeded by a limited company, later by Merklin, Schütze et Cie. from Brussels; subsequently Merklin continued the business alone until his death in 1905. As a manufacturer of instruments, the firm no longer exists.

Daugherty, Michael, American composer; b. Cedar Rapids, Iowa, April 28, 1954. He studied with Charles Wuorinen at the Manhattan School of Music (M.A., 1976), and with Jacob Druckman, Earle Brown, Roger Reynolds, Bernard Rands, and Gil Evans at Yale Univ. (M.M.A., 1982; D.M.A., 1986); then traveled to Hamburg, where he studied with György Ligeti at the Hochschule für Musik (1982–84). He also studied at IR-CAM on a Fulbright fellowship (1978–80). He received an NEA Composition Fellowship in 1980; subsequently joined the faculty at Oberlin College Cons. of Music (from 1986), becoming director of its Summer Electronic Music Workshop.

Works: ORCH.: *5 Seasons* (1980); *Mxyzptlk* for 2 Flute Soloists and Chamber Orch. (1988; Cleveland, Feb. 6, 1989); *Oh Lois!* (St. Paul, Minn., April 4, 1989); *Lex* (1990). CHAMBER ENSEMBLE: *Future Music, Part I* (1984); *Future Funk* (1985); *Piano Plus* (1985); *Re: Percussion* (1986); *Blue Like an Orange* (1987); *SNAP!* (1987); *Bounce I* (1988); *Lex* (1989); also synthesizer/computer pieces.

Dauney, William, Scottish music historian; b. Aberdeen, Oct. 27, 1800; d. Georgetown, British Guiana, July 28, 1843. He studied at Dulwich College in London and at the Univ. of Edinburgh; was admitted to the Scottish bar in 1823, then settled in British Guiana (c.1839), where he became solicitor-general. In the Advocates' Library at Edinburgh he discovered what is now known as the "Skene MS," a collection of 114 English and Scottish dances, ballads, and songs (written in tablature between 1614 and 1620), containing the oldest known (and probably original) versions of *John Anderson My Jo, The Flowers of the Forest*, etc. Dauney transcribed these into modern notation, and publ. them in 1838 as *Ancient Scottish Melodies from a MS. of the Reign of King James VI*, together with *An Introductory Enquiry Illustrative of the History of Music of Scotland*.

Dauprat, Louis-François, celebrated French horn player and composer; b. Paris, May 24, 1781; d. there, July 16, 1868.

He studied with Kenn at the Paris Cons.; joined the band of the Garde Nationale, and in 1799 the band of the Garde des Consuls, with which he passed through the Egyptian campaign. From 1801 to 1805 he studied theory at the Cons. under Catel and Gossec, and studied again with Reicha from 1811 to 1814; from 1806 to 1808 was 1st horn at the Bordeaux Theater; succeeded Kenn in the Opéra orch. in Paris, and Duvernoy (as *cor solo*), retiring in 1831. He was chamber musician to Napoleon (1811) and Louis XVIII (1816); in 1816 he was appointed prof. of horn in the Cons., resigning in 1842.

Dauriac, Lionel (-Alexandre), French psychologist and writer on music; b. Brest, Finisterre, Nov. 19, 1847; d. Paris, May 26, 1923. He graduated from the École Normale Supérieure of Brest in 1867; received the degree of *docteur ès lettres* from the Univ. of Paris in 1878 (with the diss. *Des Notions de matière et de force dans les sciences de la nature* and *De Heraclito Ephesio*); held teaching positions in philosophy at Brest, Toulouse, and Montpellier; was a lecturer at the Sorbonne on musical psychology (1896–1903); a laureate of the Academy of Moral and Political Sciences (awarded the Prix Gegner, 1916); 1st president of the Paris section of the International Music Soc.; from 1907, its honorary president. Besides many works dealing with philosophy, he publ. the following concerning music: *Introduction à la psychologie du musicien* (Paris, 1891); *La Psychologie dans l'opéra français* (Paris, 1897); *Essai sur l'esprit musical* (Paris, 1904); *Rossini, biographie critique* (Paris, 1906); *Le Musicien-poète Richard Wagner* (Paris, 1908); *Meyerbeer* (Paris, 1913).

Daussoigne-Méhul, Louis-Joseph, French composer; b. Givet, Ardennes, June 10, 1790; d. Liège, March 10, 1875. He was the nephew and foster son of **Etienne-Nicolas Méhul;** studied under him and Catel at the Cons.; took the Grand Prix de Rome in 1809; after writing 4 operas, which were rejected, he at length produced his 1-act *Aspasie* at the Grand Opéra (1820) with moderate success. He did still better with *Valentine de Milan*, a 3-act opera left unfinished by his foster father which he completed. In 1827 he accepted the directorship of the Liège Cons., which he retained, with great benefit to the school, until 1862. Daussoigne-Méhul was an associate of the Royal Academy, Brussels. He brought out a cantata with full orch. in 1828, and a choral sym., *Une Journée de la Révolution*, in 1834.

Dauvergne, Antoine, French composer, violinist, and conductor; b. Moulins, Oct. 3, 1713; d. Lyons, Feb. 11, 1797. He received his 1st instruction from his father, then went for further study to Paris, where he was appointed a violinist in the chambre du roi (1739) and in the orch. of the Opéra (1744). In 1755 he was appointed composer to the court and in 1762 became conductor and one of the directors of the Concerts Spirituels; he was one of the directors of the Opéra (1769–76; 1780–82; 1785–90) before retiring to Lyons. He introduced into France the forms of the Italian intermezzo, substituting spoken dialogue for the recitative, and thus was the originator of a style that soon became typical of French dramatic composition. He composed 18 stage works, the 1st being *Les Troqueurs* (Paris, July 30, 1753), which is regarded as the 1st opéra-comique; also 2 books of syms. (1751), 12 sonatas for Violin and Basso Continuo (1739), 6 sonatas for 2 Violins and Basso Continuo (c.1739), choral music, etc.

Davaux, Jean-Baptiste, prominent French composer; b. La Côte–St. André, July 19, 1742; d. Paris, Feb. 2, 1822. He studied music with his parents, then settled in Paris, where he made a name for himself as a violinist and composer. Although he continued to be active as a composer in subsequent years, he found employment in the Ministry of War; upon retiring, he was made a member of the Légion d'honneur (1814). Davaux was highly regarded as a composer of orch. and chamber music. In his *Trois simphonies à grand orchestre*, op. 11 (1784), he included his chronomètre, thus anticipating Maelzel's invention.

Works: OPERAS: *Théodore, ou Le Bonheur inattendu*, comic opera (Fontainebleau, March 4, 1785; not extant); *Cécilia, ou Les Trois Tuteurs*, comic opera (Paris, Dec. 14, 1786). ORCH.: 8 syms. concertantes (c.1772–85) *Sinfonie concertante mêlée d'airs patriotiques* (1794); *Simphonie concertante* (1800); 4 violin concertos (1769–71); 3 simphonies for Strings (1784). CHAMBER: 6 quatuors concertants for String Quartet (1779); 6 quatuors d'airs connus for String Quartet (1780); 6 duos for 2 Violins (1788); 4 quartetti for String Quartet (London, 1790); 6 trios for 2 Violins and Viola (c.1792); 3 quatuors concertants for 2 Violins, Cello, and Bass (c.1800); 4 Quintettos for 2 Violins, 2 Violas, and Cello.

Davenport, Francis William, English composer; b. Wilderslowe, near Derby, April 9, 1847; d. Scarborough, April 1, 1925. He studied law at Oxford, but preferred music, and became the pupil (later son-in-law) of G.A. Macfarren. In 1879, he became a prof. at the Royal Academy of Music, and in 1882 at the Guildhall School of Music.
WORKS: 2 syms.; overture, *12th Night;* 6 pieces for Piano and Cello; *Pictures on a Journey,* a series of piano pieces; part-songs and songs.

Davico, Vincenzo, Italian composer; b. Monaco, Jan. 14, 1889; d. Rome, Dec. 8, 1969. He studied in Turin, and later in Leipzig with Max Reger; graduated from the Leipzig Cons. in 1911; then he settled in Rome.
WORKS: Operas: *La dogaressa* (Monte Carlo, Feb. 26, 1920) and *La Principessa prigioniera* (Bergamo, Sept. 29, 1940); ballets: *L'agonia della rosa* (Paris, May 2, 1927) and *Narciso* (San Remo, Feb. 19, 1935); oratorio, *La Tentation de Saint Antoine* (Monte Carlo, Dec. 15, 1921); *Requiem per la morte d'un povero* (1950); for Orch.: *La Principessa lontana* (after Rostand's *Princesse lointaine;* won the Augusteo prize, 1911); *Poema erotico* (won the Augusteo prize, 1913); *Polifemo,* symphonic poem (Turin, 1920); *Impressioni dal mio diario di viaggio* (1949); piano pieces and numerous songs.
BIBL.: G. Franchi, *V. D.* (1924); R. Petit, *Les Mélodies de V. D.* (Nice, 1925).

David, Félicien (-César), French composer; b. Cadenet, Vaucluse, April 13, 1810; d. St.-Germain-en-Laye, Aug. 29, 1876. After the death of his parents, he was sent to be a chorister at the cathedral of St. Sauveur in Aix-en-Provence. He entered the Paris Cons. in 1830, where he studied with F. Fétis (fugue) and F. Benoist (organ); he also studied privately with H. Reber. In 1831 he joined the St. Simonians, a messianic socialistic cult patterned after the ideas of Claude-Henri de Rouvroy, Count of St.-Simon (1760–1825). After its forced disbanding in 1832, he made a pilgrimage to Egypt and the Near East, where he absorbed the flavor of the Orient. Returning to Paris in 1836, he produced a number of works based upon his travels, many with titles reflecting oriental exoticism. His 1st success came in 1844 with the symphonic ode *Le Désert* for Soloists, Male Chorus, and Orch. After visiting Mendelssohn and Meyerbeer in Germany in 1845, he turned his attention to opera; he achieved little success, with the exception of his *Lalla-Roukh* (1862), which retained its popularity for many years. Although he received many awards, including the rank of Officier de la Légion d'Honneur (1862) and membership into the Académie des Beaux Arts (succeeding Berlioz, 1869), his music virtually disappeared; occasional revivals are fostered by those with an interest in the exoticism of the period.
WORKS (all 1st perf. in Paris): STAGE: *Le Jugement dernier, ou La Fin du monde,* incidental music (1849). OPERAS: *La Perle du Brésil* (Nov. 22, 1851); *Le Fermier de Franconville* (1857); *Herculanum* (March 4, 1859); *Lalla-Roukh* (May 12, 1862); *La Captive* (1860–64); *Le Saphir* (based on Shakespeare's *All's Well That Ends Well;* March 8, 1865). ORCH. WITH CHORUS: *Le Désert,* symphonic ode (Dec. 8, 1844); *Moïse au Sinai,* oratorio (March 24, 1846); *Christophe Colomb,* symphonic ode (March 7, 1847); *L'Eden,* oratorio (Aug. 25, 1848); full score lost. ORCH.: 4 syms. (1837, 1838, 1846, 1849). CHAMBER: 2 nonets (1839, lost; 1839); *Les Quatre Saisons,* 24 miniature string quintets (1845–46); String Quartet (1868); 3 piano trios (1857); many piano works; choruses; songs.

BIBL.: S. St.-Etienne, *Biographie de F. D.* (Marseilles, 1845); A. Azevedo, *F. D.* (Paris, 1863); R. Brancour, *F. D.* (Paris, 1911); M. Achter, *F. D., Ambroise Thomas and French Opéra Lyrique* (diss., Univ. of Michigan, 1972); P. Gradenwitz, "F.D.(1810–1876) and French Romantic Orientalism," *Musical Quarterly* (Oct. 1976); R. Locke, *Music and the St. Simonians: The Involvement of F. D. and Other Musicians in a Utopian Socialist Movement* (diss., Univ. of Chicago, 1980); D. Hagan, *F. D. 1810–1876: A Composer and a Cause* (Syracuse, N.Y., 1985).

David, Ferdinand, noted German violinist, pedagogue, and composer; b. Hamburg, Jan. 19, 1810; d. near Klosters, Switzerland, July 18, 1873. In 1823–24 he studied with Spohr and Hauptmann at Kassel; played in the Gewandhaus Orch. in Leipzig, 1825; from 1826 to 1829 was a member of the Königstadt Theater in Berlin. In 1829 he became the 1st violinist in the private string quartet of the wealthy amateur Baron von Liphardt of Russia, whose daughter he married. He remained in Russia until 1835, giving concerts in Riga, Moscow, and St. Petersburg with great acclaim. In 1836 he was appointed 1st violinist of the Gewandhaus Orch., of which Mendelssohn was the conductor. They became warm friends; Mendelssohn had a great regard for him, and consulted him while writing his Violin Concerto; it was David who gave its 1st performance (Leipzig, March 13, 1845). When the Leipzig Cons. was established in 1843, David became one of its most important teachers; his class was regarded as the finishing school of the most talented violinists in Europe; among his pupils were Joachim and Wilhelmj. He publ. many valuable eds. of violin works by classical composers, notably *Die hohe Schule des Violinspiels,* containing French and Italian masterpieces of the 17th and 18th centuries. His pedagogical activities did not interfere with his concert career; he played in England in 1839 and 1841 with excellent success and was compared with Spohr as a virtuoso; also made occasional appearances on the Continent.
WORKS: 5 violin concertos; many other pieces for violin; an opera, *Hans Wacht* (Leipzig, 1852); 2 syms.; string quartets and other chamber music. His violin pieces, *Bunte Reihe,* were transcribed for piano by Liszt.
BIBL.: J. Eckardt, *F. D. und die Familie Mendelssohn-Bartholdy* (Leipzig, 1888); A. Bachmann, "F. D.," in *Les Grands Violinistes du passé* (Paris, 1913); B. Schwarz, *Great Masters of the Violin* (N.Y., 1983).

David, Giacomo, Italian tenor, father of **Giovanni David;** b. Presezzo, near Bergamo, 1750; d. Bergamo, Dec. 31, 1830. He studied in Naples; made his debut in 1773 in Milan; then made many appearances at La Scala in Milan (1782–83; 1799–1800; 1802–3; 1806–8); also sang in concert in London (1791); was a featured singer at the 1st performances given at the Teatro Nuovo in Trieste (1801) and at the Teatro Carcano in Milan (1803).

David, Giovanni, Italian tenor, son of **Giacomo David;** b. Naples, Sept. 15, 1790; d. St. Petersburg, 1864. He studied with his father; made his debut in 1808 in Siena; created the role of Narciso in Rossini's *Il Turco in Italia* at La Scala in Milan on Aug. 14, 1814; also created other roles in Rossini operas; sang in London in 1818 and 1831; quit the stage in 1839 and later became manager of the St. Petersburg Opera.

Dávid, Gyula, Hungarian composer; b. Budapest, May 6, 1913; d. there, March 14, 1977. He studied with Kodály at the Academy of Music in Budapest; won the Erkel Prize in 1952 and 1955 and the Kossuth Prize in 1957. His music is marked by a fashionable modernism, while retaining the traditional virtues of euphonious tonality.
WORKS: 4 syms. (1947, 1957, 1960, 1970); Viola Concerto (1950); Sinfonietta (1960); *Felhötlenég* (Cloudless Skies), cantata (1964); Violin Concerto (1966); *Égö szavakkal* (With Flaming Words), cantata (1969); Horn Concerto (1971); 5 wind quintets (1949, 1955, 1964, 1967, 1968); Flute Sonata (1955); Piano Sonata (1955); 2 string quartets (1962, 1974); *Miniatures*

for Brass Sextet (1968); Violin Sonata (1968); Viola Sonatina (1969); Sonata for Violin Solo (1971); Piano Trio (1972); incidental music; songs and motets.

BIBL.: J. Breuer, *D. G.* (Budapest, 1966).

David, Hal, American lyricist, brother of **Mack David;** b. N.Y., May 25, 1921. He studied journalism at N.Y. Univ.; then became collaborator with Bacharach and other composers of popular songs. His lyrics for *Raindrops Keep Falling on My Head* (1969) won an Academy Award. The lyrics he wrote for Bacharach include *Here Am I, Magic Moments, My Little Red Book, Love Can Break a Heart, Send Me No Flowers, The Story of My Life, What's New, Pussycat?,* and *Wives and Lovers.* They wrote the popular Broadway musical *Promises, Promises* (1968). He also contributed lyrics to several films, among them *Lost Horizon, Butch Cassidy and the Sundance Kid,* and *Moonraker.* From 1980 to 1986 he served as president of ASCAP.

David, Hans T(heodor), German-American musicologist; b. Speyer, Palatinate, July 8, 1902; d. Ann Arbor, Mich., Oct. 30, 1967. He studied at the Univs. of Tübingen and Göttingen; received the degree of Dr.Phil. from the Univ. of Berlin (1928). In 1936 he emigrated to the U.S.; occupied various positions as a researcher and librarian; headed the dept. of musicology at Southern Methodist Univ. in Dallas (1945–50); in 1950 was appointed to the faculty of the Univ. of Michigan. He publ. *Bach's Musical Offering, History, Interpretation and Analysis* (N.Y., 1945); ed., with A. Mendel, *The Bach Reader* (N.Y., 1945; 2nd ed., rev., 1966); was co-author, with A.G. Rau, of *A Catalogue of Music of American Moravians, 1742–1842, from the Archives of the Moravian Church at Bethlehem, Pa.* (Bethlehem, Pa., 1938).

David, Johann Nepomuk, outstanding Austrian composer and teacher, father of **Thomas Christian David;** b. Eferding, Nov. 30, 1895; d. Stuttgart, Dec. 22, 1977. He studied with Joseph Marx at the Vienna Academy of Music (1921–22), and after serving as a schoolteacher, organist, and choirmaster in Wels (1924–34), he joined the faculty of the Leipzig Landeskonservatorium (later the Hochschule für Musik) in 1934, becoming its director in 1942. He was subsequently director at the Salzburg Mozarteum (1945–48). In 1948 he was appointed prof. of composition at the Musikhochschule in Stuttgart, serving until 1963. His mastery of counterpoint is revealed in all of his works, which are polyphonic in structure.

WRITINGS: *Die Jupitersymphonie* (Göttingen, 1953); *Die zweistimmigen Inventionen von Johann Sebastian Bach* (Göttingen, 1957); *Die dreistimmigen Inventionen von Johann Sebastian Bach* (Göttingen, 1959); *Das wohltemperierte Klavier: Versuch einer Synopsis* (Göttingen, 1962); *Der musikalische Satz im Spiegel der Zeit* (Graz, 1963).

WORKS: ORCH.: Concerto Grosso for Chamber Orch. (1923); Flute Concerto (1934); 2 partitas (1935, 1939); 8 numbered syms.: No. 1 in A minor (1936); No. 2 (1938); No. 3 (1940); No. 4 (1945); No. 5 (1951; Stuttgart, May 3, 1952); No. 6 (1954; Vienna, June 22, 1955); No. 7 (1956; Stuttgart, Oct. 10, 1957); No. 8 (1964–65; Stuttgart, Nov. 20, 1965); *Kume, kum, geselle min,* divertimento on old folk songs (1938); *Variationen über ein Thema von Johann Sebastian Bach* (1942); *Symphonische Variationen über ein Thema von Heinrich Schütz* (1942); 3 concertos for Strings: No. 1 (1950); No. 2 (1951); No. 3 (1974; Berlin, Feb. 20, 1975); 2 violin concertos: No. 1 (1952; Stuttgart, April 25, 1954); No. 2 (1957; Munich, April 22, 1958); *Deutsche Tänze* for Strings (1953; Wiesbaden, July 7, 1954); *Sinfonia preclassica super nomen H-A-S-E* (1953; St. Veit, Carinthia, Oct. 16, 1954); *Sinfonia breve* (1955; Baden-Baden, March 4, 1956); *Melancholia* for Viola and Chamber Orch. (1958; Lucerne, Aug. 31, 1961); *Magische Quadrate* (1959; Recklinghausen, March 23, 1960); *Sinfonia per archi* (1959; Linz, Nov. 30, 1960); *Spiegelkabinett,* waltz (Dresden, Nov. 20, 1960); Organ Concerto (1965; Cologne, Nov. 28, 1966); *Variationen über ein Thema von Josquin des Prés* for Flute, Horn, and Strings (1966; Munich, April 17, 1969); Concerto for Violin, Cello, and Small Orch. (1969); Chaconne (1972). **SACRED CHORAL:** *Stabat Mater* for 6-part a cappella

Chorus (1927); *Deutsche Messe* for Mixed a cappella Chorus (1952; Leipzig, Feb. 19, 1953); *Missa choralis (de Angelis) ad quattuor voces inaequales* (1953; Linz, Jan. 17, 1954); *Requiem chorale* for Soloists, Chorus, and Orch. (1956; Vienna, June 11, 1957); *Ezzolied,* oratorio for Soloists, Chorus, and Orch. (1957; Berlin, May 17, 1960); *O, wir armen Sünder,* cantata for Alto, Chorus, and Organ (1966); *Mass* (1968); *Komm, Heiliger Geist,* cantata for 2 Choruses and Orch. (1972; Linz, March 26, 1974); also motets. **CHAMBER:** String Trio (1935); *Duo concertante* for Violin and Cello (1937); Sonata for Flute, Viola, and Guitar (1940); Trio for Flute, Violin, and Viola (1942); solo sonatas for Flute (1942), Violin (1943), Viola (1943), Cello (1944), and Lute (1944); Sonata for Flute and Viola (1943); Sonata for 2 Violins (1945); 4 string trios (1945, 1945, 1948, 1948); Sonata for Clarinet and Piano (1948); Sonata for 3 Cellos (1962); Sonata No. 2 for Solo Violin (1963); Trio for Flute, Violin, and Cello (1974). **ORGAN:** *Ricercare* (1925); *Chaconne* (1927); 2 *Hymnen* (1928); *Passamezzo and Fugue* (1928); *Toccata and Fugue* (1928); *Fantasia super "L'homme armé"* (1929); *Preambel und Fuge* (1930); *Das Choralwerk* (21 vols., 1932–73); 2 *Fantasias and Fugue* (1935); *Ricercare* (1937); *Introitus, Chorale and Fugue on a Theme of Bruckner* for Organ and 9 Wind Instruments (1939); *Chaconne and Fugue* (1962); *Toccata and Fugue* (1962); *Partita über B-A-C-H* (1964); *12 Orgelfugen durch alle Tonarten* (1968); *Partita* (1970); *Partita* for Violin and Organ (1975).

BIBL.: R. Klein, *J.N. D.* (Vienna, 1964); H. Bertram, *Material—Struktur—Form: Studien zur musikalischen Ordnung bei J.N. D.* (Wiesbaden, 1965); H.H. Stuckenschmidt, *J.N. D.* (Wiesbaden, 1965); G. Sievers, ed., *Ex Deo nascimur: Festschrift zum 75. Geburtstag von J.N. D.* (Wiesbaden, 1970).

David, José, French composer, son of **Léon David;** b. Sables-d'Olonne, Jan. 6, 1913. He entered the Paris Cons. in 1933; studied with Fauchet, Jacques de la Presle, and Henri Busser; also took organ lessons with Marcel Dupré and music history with Maurice Emmanuel. He was mobilized in 1939 and served in the artillery regiment of the French army during World War II. After the Armistice, he returned to Paris. He collaborated with N. Obouhov in *Traité d'harmonie tonale et atonale* (Paris, 1947).

WORKS: *Impressions de Vendée* for Piano (1944; also for Orch.); *La Ballade de Florentin Prunier* for Voice, Violin, Cello, and Piano (1947); *Symphonie* for Ondes Martenot and Orch. (1948); ballet, *Jacquet le Prioux* (1950); Violin Sonata (1955); *Laudate dominum* for 3 Male Voices and Organ (1960); 2 *Poems* for Voice and Piano (1973).

David, Karl Heinrich, Swiss composer; b. St. Gall, Dec. 30, 1884; d. Nervi, Italy, May 17, 1951. He studied in Cologne and Munich; taught at the Basel Cons. (1910–14); then at Cologne and Berlin (1914–17); in 1918, returned to Switzerland. He was the ed. of the *Schweizer Musikzeitung* in Zürich (1928–41).

WORKS: Operas: *Aschenputtel* (Basel, Oct. 21, 1921); *Der Sizilianer* (Zürich, Oct. 22, 1924); *Jugendfestspiel* (Zürich, June 8, 1924); *Traumwandel* (Zürich, Jan. 29, 1928); *Weekend,* comic opera (1933). Other works: Piano Concerto (1929); *Ballet* for Orch. (1931); *Pezzo sinfonico* (1945); Concerto for Saxophone and String Orch. (1947); *Symphonie de la côte d'argent* (1948); *Mascarade,* overture (1950); *Andante and Rondo* for Violin and Chamber Orch.; 2 Pieces for Piano and 9 Woodwinds; Viola Suite; Piano Trio; Quartet for Saxophone, Violin, Cello, and Piano (1946); Duet for Horn and Piano (1951); *Das hohe Lied Salomonis* for Soprano, Tenor, Female Chorus, and Orch.; songs.

David, Léon, French tenor, father of **José David;** b. Sables-d'Olonne, Dec. 18, 1867; d. there, Oct. 27, 1962. He studied singing at the Cons. of Nantes and later at the Paris Cons.; made his debut at the Opéra-Comique in Paris in 1892; appeared subsequently in Brussels, Monte Carlo, Marseilles, Bordeaux, Cairo, Lisbon, Bucharest, etc. He was a prof. of singing at the Paris Cons. from 1924 to 1938.

David, Mack, American lyricist and composer, brother of **Hal David;** b. N.Y., July 5, 1912. He studied at Cornell Univ. and at St. John's Univ. Law School. Turning to writing for Broadway and for films, he collaborated with Count Basie, Burt Bacharach, Ernest Gold, Elmer Bernstein, David Raksin, Henry Mancini, and other composers. Among his best-known songs are *Bibbidi, Bobbidi, Boo* (1948); *Cat Ballou* (1965); *The Hanging Tree* (1959); *It's a Mad, Mad, Mad, Mad World* (1963); *My Own True Love* (1954). David won a spectacular lawsuit for copyright infringement of his song *Sunflower* (1948), which he claimed was plagiarized by Jerry Herman for the latter's sensationally popular song *Hello, Dolly* (1964). The sum paid in an out-of-court settlement to David was in excess of half a million dollars.

David, Samuel, French composer; b. Paris, Nov. 12, 1836; d. there, Oct. 3, 1895. He studied at the Paris Cons. with Halévy; won the Grand Prix de Rome (1858) for his cantata *Jephté,* and another prize for a work for male chorus and orch., *Le Génie de la terre,* performed by a chorus of 6,000 singers (1859); was a prof. at the Collège de Sainte-Barbe (1861) and a music director in Paris synagogues (1872). He wrote several operas, 4 syms., choruses, and songs.

David, Thomas Christian, prolific Austrian composer, son of **Johann Nepomuk David;** b. Wels, Dec. 22, 1925. He was a choirboy at Leipzig's Thomaskirche and studied with his father at the Leipzig Hochschule für Musik. He taught flute at the Salzburg Mozarteum (1945–48), then went to Vienna, where he taught composition at the Academy of Music (from 1957), later serving as prof. of harmony at the Hochschule für Musik (from 1973) and director of the Austrian Composers Soc. (from 1986). He also taught at the Univ. of Teheran and was director of the Iranian Television Orch. (1967–73). He made various appearances as a flutist, harpsichordist, pianist, choral director, and conductor and received several awards for his compositions, which are noted for their innovative, modernistic uses of contrapuntal devices.
WORKS: OPERAS: *Atossa* (1968); *Der Weg nach Emmaus* (Alpach, Aug. 28, 1982); *Als Oedipus kam* (in prep.). **ORCH.:** Concerto No. 1 for Strings (1961; Munich, Sept. 20, 1962); Concerto for 12 Strings (1964); Sym. No. 1 (1965); Concerto (1967); Concerto No. 2 for Strings (1971; Teheran, Jan. 10, 1973); Concerto No. 3 for Strings (1974; Linz, Nov. 30, 1975); Concerto grosso (1978; Prague, Feb. 21, 1982). **CONCERTOS WITH ORCH.:** Piano (1960); Clarinet (1961); 5 Brass Instruments and Strings (1962); Violin (1962; Munich, May 26, 1965); Violin and Strings (Teheran, Sept. 3, 1970); Oboe (1975; Hagen, March 18, 1976); Organ (1976; Vienna, Dec. 11, 1981); Bass (1979; Hagen, Oct. 16, 1980); Flute (1982; Vienna, March 3, 1983); Cello (1983; Vienna, March 20, 1987); Sinfonia Concertante for Violin, Clarinet, and Piano with Wind Orch. (1986). **CHAMBER:** 5 string quartets (1952, 1953, 1954, 1965, 1967); Concerto for 9 Instruments (1961; Vienna, Feb. 28, 1962); Quintet for Clarinet and String Quartet (1963); 3 Intermezzi for Violin and Piano (1964); 2 wind quintets (1966, 1979); Sonata for Cello and Piano (1970); 3 canzonas for Flute, Cello, and Piano (1977); *Tricinium* for Flute, English Horn or Viola, and Cello (1977); Quartet for Oboe and String Trio (1979); Sonata for Clarinet and Violin (1980); Trio for Violin, Viola, and Cello (1984); Toccata for 9 Flutes (1985); Trio for Violin, Cello, and Piano (1985); Quintet for 2 Flutes, Violin, Cello, and Piano (1987); many works for solo instruments. **VOCAL:** 10 madrigals (1950–82); *Wer ist es,* motet (1960); *Missa in honorem Mariae* (1965); *Das Lied des Menschen,* oratorio (1975; Gumersbach, May 1978); *Die Vogel,* cantata for Soprano, Flute, Clarinet, and Piano (1981); 15 songs (1963–86).

Davidenko, Alexander, Russian composer; b. Odessa, April 13, 1899; d. Moscow, May 1, 1934. He organized, with Bely, the Procoll (Production Collective of Composers) in Russia in 1925; wrote workers' songs. His most important work is the opera *1905* (written in 1929–33, with Boris Shekhter); another opera, *Down the Cliff,* was left incomplete.

BIBL.: M. Koval, "At the Side of A. D.," *Sovietskaya Muzyka* (Feb. 1967); N. Martynov, ed., *A. D.* (Leningrad, 1968).

Davidov, Carl, outstanding Russian cellist; b. Goldingen, Latvia, March 15, 1838; d. Moscow, Feb. 26, 1889. He studied cello in Moscow with Heinrich Schmidt and in St. Petersburg with K. Schuberth; in 1859 went to Leipzig, where he studied composition with Hauptmann. In 1860, at the age of 22, he was appointed an instructor at the Leipzig Cons; also played in the Gewandhaus Orch. In 1862 he returned to Russia; from 1862 till 1887 was a prof. at the St. Petersburg Cons., and acting director from 1876 to 1887. He made several European tours, during which he played recitals with Anton Rubinstein, Saint-Saëns, and Liszt. Davidov was also a reputable composer; he wrote 4 cello concertos; a fantasy on Russian songs for Cello and Orch.; a symphonic poem, *The Gifts of the Terek River;* String Quartet; String Sextet; Piano Quintet; songs. He also publ. a cello method (Leipzig, 1888; Russian ed., supervised by L. Ginsburg, Moscow, 1947).
BIBL.: V. Hutor, *C. D. und seine Art das Violoncell zu behandeln* (Moscow, 1899); S. Ginsburg, *C. D.* (Moscow, 1950).

Davidov, Stepan Ivanovich, Russian composer; b. 1777; d. St. Petersburg, May 22, 1825. He studied with Giuseppe Sarti in St. Petersburg and was subsequently active as a singing teacher, répétiteur, and composer at the Drama School there. After serving as music director to Count Sheremetev, he was a singing teacher at the Moscow Drama School. He was one of the leading Russian composers of music for the stage in his day.
WORKS: STAGE: OPERAS: *Lesta, the Dnepr Water Nymph* (St. Petersburg, Nov. 6, 1805); *Rusalka* (St. Petersburg, 1807); also numbers for Kauer's *Das Donauweibchen,* given in Russian as *Rusalka* (St. Petersburg, Nov. 7, 1803). **BALLETS:** *Virtue Crowned* (St. Petersburg, Oct. 7, 1801); *Thank Offering* (St. Petersburg, 1802); *The Victory Celebration* (1814); several comical divertissements; incidental music; sacred works.

Davidovich, Bella, esteemed Russian-born American pianist and pedagogue, mother of **Dmitry Sitkovetsky;** b. Baku, July 16, 1928. Her maternal grandfather was concertmaster of the Baku opera orch. and her mother was a pianist. She began formal piano training when she was 6; at age 9 she appeared as soloist in the Beethoven 1st Piano Concerto in Baku. In 1939 she was sent to Moscow to pursue her studies with Konstantin Igumnov, with whom she subsequently also studied at the Moscow Cons. (1946–48), where she completed her training with Yakov Flier (1948–54). In 1949 she captured joint 1st prize at the Chopin Competition in Warsaw, which launched her upon a highly successful career in Russia and Eastern Europe; she was a soloist each season with the Leningrad Phil. (1950–78) and also taught at the Moscow Cons. (1962–78). In 1967 she made her 1st appearance outside Russia, playing in Amsterdam; in 1971 she made a tour of Italy. Following the defection of her son to the West in 1977, she was refused permission to perform there by the Soviet government. In 1978 she emigrated to the U.S., becoming a naturalized U.S. citizen in 1984. In 1979 she made an acclaimed debut in a recital at N.Y.'s Carnegie Hall. In 1982 she joined the faculty of the Juilliard School in N.Y. but continued to pursue an international career. In 1988 she and her son returned to Russia, being the first émigrés to be invited to perform there by Goskontsert since the Gorbachev era of reform was launched.
BIBL.: *Current Biography* (May 1989).

Davidovsky, Mario, Argentine composer; b. Buenos Aires, March 4, 1934. He studied composition and theory with Guillermo Graetzer in Buenos Aires and also took courses with Teodor Fuchs, Erwin Leuchter, and Ernesto Epstein. He continued his training with Milton Babbitt at the Berkshire Music Center, Tanglewood (summer 1958). He worked at the Columbia-Princeton Electronic Music Center (from 1960) and taught at the Univ. of Michigan (1964), the Di Tella Inst. of Buenos Aires (1965), the Manhattan School of Music in N.Y. (1968–69), Yale Univ. (1969–70), City College of the City Univ.

of N.Y. (1968–80), and Columbia Univ. (from 1981), where he served as director of the Columbia-Princeton Electronic Music Center. He held 2 Guggenheim fellowships (1960, 1971) and in 1971 received the Pulitzer Prize in Music for his *Synchronisms No. 6* for Piano and Electronics. In 1982 he was elected a member of the Inst. of the American Academy and Inst. of Arts and Letters. His method of composition tends toward mathematical parameters; his series of 8 compositions entitled *Synchronisms* derives from the numerical coordinates of acoustical elements; electronic sound is integral to most of his work.

WORKS: Concertino for Percussion and Strings (1954); *Suite sinfonica para "El payaso"* (1955); *Serie sinfonica* (1959); *Contrastes* No. 1 for Strings and Electronics (1960); *Pianos* for Orch. (1961); *Transientes* for Orch. (1972); *Consorts* for Sym. Band (1980); Divertimento for Cello and Orch. (1984); 4 string quartets (1954, 1958, 1976, 1980); Quintet for Clarinet and Strings (1955); *3 Pieces* for Woodwind Quintet (1956); *Noneto* for 9 Instruments (1956); Trio for Clarinet, Trumpet, and Viola (1962); *Inflexions* for Chamber Ensemble (1965); *Junctures* for Flute, Clarinet, and Violin (1966); *Music* for Violin (1968); *Chacona* for Violin, Cello, and Piano (1971); *Pennplay* for 16 Players (1978); String Trio (1982); *Capriccio* for 2 Pianos (1985); 8 pieces entitled *Synchronisms*: No. 1 for Flute and Electronics (1963); No. 2 for Flute, Clarinet, Violin, Cello, and Electronics (1964); No. 3 for Cello and Electronics (1965); No. 4 for Male Voices or Mixed Chorus and Electronics (1967); No. 5 for Percussion Ensemble and Electronics (1969); No. 6 for Piano and Electronics (1970); No. 7 for Orch. and Electronics (1973); No. 8 for Woodwind Quintet and Electronics (1974); *Scenes from Shir-ha-shirim* for Soprano, 2 Tenors, Baritone, and Chamber Orch. (1975); *Romancero* for Soprano, Flute, Clarinet, Violin, and Cello (1983); 3 studies for Tape (1961, 1962, 1965).

Davidson, Lyle, American composer; b. Randolph, Vt., Feb. 25, 1938. He studied at the Univ. of Vermont (1956–58); then entered the New England Cons. (B.M., 1962; M.M., 1964); subsequently attended Brandeis Univ. and Boston Univ. From 1971 to 1973 he was a lecturer in music at the Mass. Inst. of Technology; in 1977–78 was a visiting lecturer in music at Harvard Univ. He became active promoting the cause of avant-garde music in Boston; composed for the theater, dance, and films. His own works are marked by concision, brevity, and immediacy of aural receptivity; in other words, he composes for the people, albeit in highly modernized techniques. The titles of his pieces, most of them brief, are indicative of their intent: *Crystals* for Piano; *Blocks* for Flute, Clarinet, Violin, and Piano; *Phrase* for 2 Trumpets; *Detours* for any 3 String Instruments; *March Detours* for Viola, Cello, and Electronic Tape; *And a Certain Gurgling Melodiousness* for Double Bass; and *Furies of Complexity* for Various Small Groups. For electronic works he is apt to dip into high math, e.g., *Fibonacci Rehearsed.* He was a consultant of Project Zero and Aphasia Research. He also wrote a paper on the etiology of brain damage among composers.

Davidson, Tina, American composer; b. Stockholm (of American parents), Dec. 30, 1952. She studied piano at the State Univ. of N.Y. at Oneonta (1962–70) and at the School of Music in Tel Aviv (1971), and composition with Brant, Fine, and Nowak at Bennington (Vt.) College (1972–76). In 1978 she became associate director of RELACHE, a Philadelphia-based ensemble for the performance of contemporary music. Her music is replete with colorful sonoric effects and extra-musical influences.

WORKS: *Recollections of Darkness,* string trio (1975); *Complex* for Wind Orch. (1977); *Man-Faced-Scarab* for Soprano, Flute, Clarinet, and Oboe (1978); *Witches' Hammer* for Voice and Percussion (1979); *Dancers* for Orch. (Philadelphia, May 25, 1980); Piano Concerto (1981; Philadelphia, Feb. 28, 1981); *Unicorn/Tapestry* for Voice, Cello, and Tape (1982); *Wait for the End of Dreaming* for 2 Baritone Saxophones and Double Bass (1983–85); *Day of Rage* for Piano (1984); *Blood Memory:*

A Long Quiet after the Call for Cello and Orch. (1985; Bennington, Vt., June 1, 1986); *Never Love a Wild Thing* for Variable Ensemble (1986); *Star Myths* for Piano or Variable Ensemble (1987).

Davies, Ben(jamin) Grey, Welsh tenor; b. Pontardawe, near Swansea, South Wales, Jan. 6, 1858; d. Bath, England, March 28, 1943. He studied at the Royal Academy of Music in London under Randegger, Sr., winning the bronze, silver, and gold medals for best declamatory English singing. His debut was in Birmingham, Oct. 11, 1881, in *The Bohemian Girl.* He created the title role in Sullivan's *Ivanhoe* (London, Jan. 31, 1891). In 1892 he made his debut at London's Covent Garden as Faust. He made his 1st appearance in the U.S. at the Chicago World's Fair in 1893; was mainly active as a concert and oratorio singer from 1894; sang regularly at the Handel Festivals until 1926.

Davies, Dennis Russell, American conductor; b. Toledo, Ohio, April 16, 1944. He studied piano with Lonny Epstein and Sascha Gorodnitzki and conducting with Jean Morel and Jorge Mester at the Juilliard School of Music in N.Y. (B.Mus., 1966; M.S., 1968; D.M.A., 1972), where he also taught (1968–71) and was co-founder (with Luciano Berio) of the Juilliard Ensemble (1968–74). He was music director of the Norwalk (Conn.) Sym. Orch. (1968–73), the St. Paul (Minn.) Chamber Orch. (1972–80), the Cabrillo (Calif.) Music Festival (from 1974), and the American Composers Orch. in N.Y. (from 1977). In 1978 he made his 1st appearance at the Bayreuth Festival, conducting *Der fliegende Holländer.* He was Generalmusikdirektor of the Württemberg State Theater in Stuttgart (1980–87), principal conductor and director of Classical music programming at the Saratoga (N.Y.) Performing Arts Center (1985–88), and Generalmusikdirektor of Bonn (from 1987). In 1990 he also assumed the posts of music director of the Brooklyn Academy of Music and principal conductor of the Brooklyn Phil. In 1987 he received the Alice M. Ditson conductor's award. Davies has acquired a notable reputation as a champion of contemporary music. He has conducted numerous premieres in the U.S. and Europe.

BIBL.: N. Malitz, "D.R. D.," *Ovation* (Aug. 1987).

Davies, Fanny, English pianist; b. Guernsey, June 27, 1861; d. London, Sept. 1, 1934. She studied at the Leipzig Cons. with Reinecke and Paul (piano) and Jadassohn (theory) in 1882–83, and at the Hoch Cons. in Frankfurt with Clara Schumann (1883–85); also was a pupil of Scholz in fugue and composition. Her London debut took place at the Crystal Palace, Oct. 17, 1885; then she made successful tours in England, Germany, France, and Italy.

Davies, Hugh (Seymour), English composer and instrument inventor; b. Exmouth, April 23, 1943. He was a pupil of Rubbra at Oxford Univ. (1961–64) and subsequently an assistant to Stockhausen as well as a member of his electronic music group (1964–66); then was director of the electronic music studio at Goldsmiths' College in London (from 1967). In addition to works for traditional instruments, he wrote music utilizing instruments of his own invention, tape, and electronics.

WORKS: *Contact* for Piano (1963); *Vom ertrunkenen Mädchen* for Soprano, Flute, Clarinet, and Piano (1964); Quintet for Electronics (1967–68); *Interfaces* for Tape and Electronics (1967–68); *Kangaroo* for Organ (1968); *Beautiful Seaweeds* for Players, Dancers, and Slides (1972–73); Wind Trio (1973–75); *The Musical Educator* for Speaker, Players, Dancers, and Slides (1974); *Natural Images* for Tape (1976); *Melodic Gestures* for Flute, Violin, Cello, and Piano (1978); *Ex una voce* for Tenor and Synthesizer (1979). **FOR SPECIALLY CONSTRUCTED INSTRUMENTS:** *Shozyg I, II, I + II* (1968); *Spring Song* (1970); *Gentle Springs* (1973); *Music for Bowed Diaphragms* (1973); *My Spring Collection* (1975); *Salad* (1977); *The Search for the Music of the Spheres* (1978); *At Home* (1978).

Davies, (Albert) Meredith, English organist, conductor, and music educator; b. Birkenhead, July 30, 1922. He studied at the Royal College of Music in London and was an organ scholar at Keble College, Oxford, later becoming organist at St. Albans Cathedral (1947) and at Hereford Cathedral (1949). He then pursued conducting studies with Previtali at the Accademia di Santa Cecilia in Rome (1954, 1956). He was organist at New College, Oxford (1956–60), associate conductor (1957–59) and deputy music director (1959–60) of the City of Birmingham Sym. Orch., and director of the City of Birmingham Choir (1957–64). He was music director of the English Opera Group in London (1963–65) and of the Vancouver (B.C.) Sym. Orch. (1964–71), and also chief conductor of the BBC Training Orch. in London (1969–72). From 1979 to 1988 he was principal of Trinity College of Music in London. In 1982 he was made a Commander of the Order of the British Empire.

Davies, Sir Peter Maxwell, remarkable English composer and conductor; b. Manchester, Sept. 8, 1934. He went to Leigh Grammar School and then to the Royal Manchester College of Music and Manchester Univ. In 1957 he won a scholarship from the Italian government and proceeded to Rome, where he studied with Goffredo Petrassi; his orch. work *Prolation* (named after the medieval metrical division) received the Olivetti Prize in 1958 and was performed at the Festival of the ISCM in Rome on June 10, 1959. Returning to England, he served as director of music at Cirencester Grammar School (1959–62); it was there that he introduced for the 1st time his neo-Socratic method of schooling, encouraging his students to exercise their curiosity. In 1962 he went to the U.S. on a Harkness fellowship and took a fruitful succession of sessions with Sessions at Princeton Univ. In 1965 he joined the UNESCO Conference on Music in Education and traveled around the world on a lecture tour. In 1966–67 he served as composer-in-residence at the Univ. of Adelaide in Australia. In 1967 he organized with Harrison Birtwistle in London an ensemble called the Pierrot Players; in 1970 they decided to rename it The Fires of London, with programs of provocative modernistic works. In 1970 Davies made his home in the Orkney Islands; in 1977 he organized there the annual St. Magnus Festival, which gave its presentations at the Norse Cathedral of St. Magnus; there he also staged many of his own compositions, inspired by medieval chants. Despite the remoteness of the Orkney Islands from musical centers, the festival attracted attention. In 1979 Davies was awarded an honorary doctorate of music at Edinburgh Univ.; he was also appointed successor to Sir William Glock as director of music at Dartington Summer School and was named Composer of the Year by the Composers' Guild of Great Britain. He was commissioned to write a sym. for the Boston Sym. Orch. on the occasion of its centennial in 1981. In 1985 he was named composer-in-residence and associate conductor of the Scottish Chamber Orch. in Glasgow, with which he toured. In 1987 he was knighted. In his works Davies combines seemingly incongruous elements, which include reverential evocations of medieval hymnody, surrealistic depictions of historical personages, and hedonistic musical theatrics. His most arresting work in this synthetic manner is a set of *8 Songs for a Mad King,* a fantastic suite of heterogeneously arranged pieces representing the etiology of the madness of King George III; at the other end of the spectrum is *Vesalii Icones,* inspired by the anatomical drawings of Christ's Passion and Resurrection by the Renaissance artist Vesalius. Davies is a fervent political activist, a participant in the movement combating the spread of nuclear weapons, and a staunch defender of the planetary environment against industrial pollution.

WORKS: STAGE: *Nocturnal Dances,* ballet (London, May 31, 1970); *Blind Man's Buff,* masque for High Voice, Mime, and Chamber Orch. (London, May 29, 1972); *Taverner,* opera to a libretto by Davies, descriptive of the life of the English composer Taverner (1962–70; London, July 12, 1972); *The Martyrdom of Saint Magnus,* chamber opera in 9 scenes (Kirkwall, Orkney, June 18, 1977); *The 2 Fiddlers,* opera for young people (Kirkwall, Orkney, June 16, 1978); *Le Jongleur de Notre Dame,* masque (Kirkwall, Orkney, June 18, 1978); *Salome,* ballet (Copenhagen, Nov. 10, 1978; concert suite drawn from the score,

London, March 6, 1979); *The Lighthouse,* chamber opera (1979; Edinburgh, Sept. 2, 1980); *Cinderella,* pantomime for Child Actors (Kirkwall, Orkney, June 21, 1980); *The Rainbow,* theatrical work for children (Kirkwall, Orkney, June 20, 1981); *The No. 11 Bus* for Soloists, Dancers, Mime, and Ensemble (1984); *Resurrection,* opera (1987).

ORCH.: *Antechrist* for Chamber Ensemble (London, May 30, 1967); *Stedman Caters* for Chamber Ensemble (London, May 30, 1968); *Worldes Blis* (London, Aug. 28, 1968); *Vesalii Icones* for Dancer, Solo Cello, and Instruments, in 14 movements, after 14 anatomical drawings by Andreas Vesalius depicting Christ's Passion and Resurrection (London, Dec. 9, 1969); *Ave Maris Stella* for Chamber Ensemble (Bath, May 27, 1975); Sym. No. 1 (1976; London, Feb. 2, 1978); Sym. No. 2, commissioned by the Boston Sym. Orch. for its centennial (1980; Boston, Feb. 26, 1981); *Image, Reflection, Shadow* (Lucerne Festival, Switzerland, Aug. 22, 1981); *Sinfonia concertante* for Chamber Orch. (1982; Aug. 12, 1983); *Sinfonietta accademica* (Edinburgh, Oct. 6, 1983); Sym. No. 3 (1984; Manchester, Feb. 19, 1985); Violin Concerto (1986); Oboe Concerto: *Strathclyde Concerto No. 1* (Glasgow, April 29, 1988); Trumpet Concerto (1988); Sym. No. 4 (London, Sept. 10, 1989).

CHAMBER: Sonata for Trumpet and Piano (1955); *Alma redemptoris mater* for Flute, Oboe, 2 Clarinets, Horn, and Bassoon (1957); *St. Michael* for 17 Wind Instruments (London, July 13, 1959); *Hymnos* for Clarinet and Piano (1967); *Canon in Memoriam Igor Stravinsky* for Flute, Clarinet, Harp, and String Quartet (London, June 17, 1972); *All Sons of Adam* for Flute, Clarinet, Marimba, Celesta, Guitar, Viola, and Cello (London, Feb. 20, 1974); *Little Quartet* for String Quartet (1980); *A Welcome to Orkney* for Flute, Oboe, Clarinet, Bassoon, Horn, 2 String Quartets, and Double Bass (Kirkwall, Orkney, June 20, 1980); Brass Quintet (1981; N.Y., March 19, 1982); *Birthday Music for John* for Viola, Flute, and Cello (London, Jan. 25, 1983).

VOCAL: *O magnum mysterium,* 4 carols for Chorus a cappella (Cirencester, Dec. 8, 1960); *Leopardi Fragments* for Soprano, Contralto, and Instruments (1962); *Veni sancte spiritus* for Solo Soprano, Contralto, and Bass, plus Chorus and Chamber Ensemble (Cheltenham Festival, July 10, 1964); *The Shepherd's Calendar* for Chorus and Instruments (Sydney, Australia, May 20, 1965); *Revelation and Fall* for Soprano and 16 Instruments (London, Feb. 26, 1968, composer conducting); *8 Songs for a Mad King* for Male Voice and Instruments, his most important and popular work (London, April 22, 1969, composer conducting); *From Stone to Thorn* for Mezzo-soprano and Instrumental Ensemble (Oxford, June 30, 1971, composer conducting); *Hymn to Saint Magnus* for Mezzo-soprano obbligato and Instrumental Ensemble (London, Oct. 13, 1972, composer conducting); *Notre Dame des Fleurs* for Soprano, Mezzo-soprano, Countertenor, and Instruments, to an obscene French text by the composer (London, March 17, 1973); *Dark Angels* for Mezzo-soprano and Guitar (1974); *Miss Donnithorne's Maggot* for Mezzo-soprano and Instruments (Adelaide Festival, March 9, 1974, composer conducting); *Fiddlers at the Wedding* for Mezzo-soprano and Instruments (Paris, May 3, 1974); *The Blind Fiddler,* song cycle for Soprano and Instrumental Ensemble (Edinburgh, Feb. 16, 1976, composer conducting); *Anakreontika* for Mezzo-soprano and Instrumental Ensemble (London, Sept. 17, 1976, composer conducting); *Westerlings* for Chorus a cappella (London, Oct. 15, 1977); *Solstice of Light* for Tenor Solo, Chorus, and Organ (St. Magnus Festival, Kirkwall, Orkney, June 18, 1979); *Black Pentecost,* cantata for Mezzo-soprano, Baritone, and Orch., decrying industrial air pollution (1979; London, May 11, 1982); *The Yellow Cake Revue* for Singers and Piano, to texts by the composer inveighing against the ominous threat of uranium mining in the Orkney Islands (Kirkwall, Orkney, June 21, 1980, composer conducting); *Into the Labyrinth,* cantata (Kirkwall, Orkney, June 22, 1983); *The Peat-Cutters,* cantata (Edinburgh, Aug. 18, 1985); *Winterfold* for Mezzo-soprano and Ensemble (1986).

SOLO INSTRUMENTS: Organ Fantasia from *O magnum mysterium* (Cirencester, Dec. 8, 1960); *The Door of the Sun* for

Viola (1975); *Farewell to Stromness* (a town in the Orkney Islands), piano interlude from *The Yellow Cake Revue* (St. Magnus Festival, Kirkwall, Orkney, June 21, 1980, composer conducting); Piano Sonata (1981); Organ Sonata (1982); *Sea Eagle* for Horn (1982).

FOR YOUNG PERFORMERS: 5 *Klee Pictures* for School Orch. (1959; rev. 1976); 3 *Studies for Percussion* for 11 Percussionists (1975); *Kirkwall Shopping Songs* for Children's Voices, Recorders, Percussion, and Piano, to words by the composer (1979); *Songs of Hoy* for Children's Voices and Instruments, to a text by the composer (1981); 7 *Songs Home* for Unaccompanied Children's Voices, to texts by Davies (1981).

BIBL.: J. Arnold, compiler, *P.M. D.: The Complete Catalogue of Printed Works* (London, 1981); P. Griffiths, *P.M. D.* (London, 1982); S. Pruslin, "P.M. D.'s Symphony No. 4," *Musical Times* (Sept. 1989).

Davies, Ryland, Welsh tenor; b. Cwm, Ebbw Vale, Feb. 9, 1943. He studied at the Royal Manchester College of Music; made his debut as Almaviva in 1964 with the Welsh National Opera; then sang in Glasgow, Glyndebourne, and London (1969). He sang in San Francisco in 1970; made his Metropolitan Opera debut in N.Y. on Oct. 15, 1975, as Ferrando in *Così fan tutte.* In 1966 he married **Anne Howells.**

Davies, Tudor, Welsh tenor; b. Cymmer, Nov. 12, 1892; d. London, April 2, 1958. He studied in Cardiff and at the Royal Academy of Music in London; then appeared at the Old Vic; joined the British National Opera Co. in 1922; created the title role in *Hugh the Drover* by Vaughan Williams (London, July 14, 1924); in 1928 he sang in the U.S. with the Civic Opera in Philadelphia; then was a principal singer with the Old Vic and the Sadler's Wells Opera (1931–41); was a member of the Carl Rosa Opera Co. (1941–46); also appeared in concerts.

Davies, Sir (Henry) Walford, eminent Welsh organist, educator, and composer; b. Oswestry, Sept. 6, 1869; d. Wrington, Somerset, March 11, 1941. He was a pupil of Walter Parratt at St. George's Chapel in Windsor, where he served as his assistant (1885–90); then studied with Parry and Stanford at the Royal College of Music in London, where he subsequently taught (1895–1903). He was conductor of the Bach Choir (1903–7); held positions as organist at Christ Church, Hampstead (1891–98), at the Temple Church (1898–1918), and at St. George's Chapel (1927–32); was a prof. of music at the Univ. of Wales (1919–26). Between 1924 and 1934 he led the novel broadcasting series "Music Lessons in Schools." He was knighted in 1922; was appointed Master of the King's Musick in 1934. He publ. *The Musical Outlook in Wales* (London, 1926); *The Pursuit of Music* (London, 1935); *Music and Worship* (with Harvey Grace, London, 1935). As a composer, Davies is remembered for his *Solemn Melody* for Organ and Strings (1908) and his march for the Royal Air Force (1917); he also wrote a Sym. (1911), *Conversations* for Piano and Orch. (London, Oct. 14, 1914), overtures, choral music, chamber music, songs, and many pieces for school performance.

WORKS: Choruses: *The Temple* (1902); *Lift Up Your Hearts* (1906); 5 *Sayings of Jesus* (1911); *Heaven's Gate* (1916); *Men and Angels* (1925); *Christ in the Universe* (1929); several orch. overtures: *Dedication Overture* (1893); *Festal Overture* (1910); many works for school performance, including *A Children's Symphony* (1927) and *London Calling the Schools* for Piano, Orch., and Radio Announcer (1932); *Conversations* for Piano and Orch. (London, Oct. 14, 1914); 2 violin sonatas (1894, 1896); *Peter Pan* for String Quartet (1909); numerous part-songs.

BIBL.: H.C. Colles, *W. D., A Biography* (London, 1942).

Davis, Andrew (Frank), esteemed English conductor; b. Ashbridge, Hertfordshire, Feb. 2, 1944. He studied piano at the Royal Academy of Music in London, and after taking organ lessons with Peter Hurford and Piet Kee, was an organ scholar at King's College, Cambridge (1963–67). He then received instruction in conducting from Franco Ferrara at the Accade-

mia di Santa Cecilia in Rome. Following a successful guest conducting engagement with the BBC Sym. Orch. in London in 1970, he served as assistant conductor of the BBC Scottish Sym. Orch. in Glasgow until 1973, making his debut as an opera conductor that same year at the Glyndebourne Festival. He was associate conductor of the New Philharmonia Orch. in London (1973–75) and principal guest conductor of the Royal Liverpool Phil. (1974–76). In 1974 he made his North American debut as a guest conductor with the Detroit Sym. Orch. He then was music director of the Toronto Sym. (1975–88), which, under his guidance, acquired a fine international reputation via major tours of North America, Europe, the People's Republic of China, and Japan. In 1982 he inaugurated the orch.'s new home, the Roy Thomson Hall in Toronto, in a gala concert. After completing his tenure, he served as the orch.'s conductor laureate from 1988 to 1990. In 1988 he was named chief conductor of the BBC Sym. Orch. in London and music director of the Glyndebourne Festival. His vast repertoire encompasses works from virtually every era, all of which display his wide sympathies, command of technique, and musical integrity.

Davis, Anthony, black American composer and pianist; b. Paterson, N.J., Feb. 20, 1951. He studied at Yale Univ. (B.A., 1975), proving himself to be an extremely facile jazz pianist; was co-founder of Advent (1973), a free jazz ensemble that included trombonist George Lewis, and then played in trumpeter Leo Smith's New Delta Ahkri band (1974–77). He also played in N.Y. with violinist Leroy Jenkins (1977–79) and with flutist James Newton, both active proponents of the Assoc. for the Advancement of Creative Musicians. His compositions, while strictly notated, are improvisational in tone. His opera X, based on the life of Malcolm X, was produced in Philadelphia (1985) and at N.Y.'s Lincoln Center (1989). Among his many recordings are *Of Blues and Dreams* (1978), *Hidden Voices* (with J. Newton; 1979), and *Under the Double Moon* (with J. Hoggard; 1982).

BIBL.: R. Palmer, "A. D.'s New Musical Language," *Rolling Stone*, no. 316 (May 1, 1980); F. Davis, "A. D.," *Down Beat*, XLIX/1 (1982).

Davis, Sir Colin (Rex), eminent English conductor; b. Weybridge, Sept. 25, 1927. He studied the clarinet at the Royal College of Music in London, and played in the band of the Household Cavalry while serving in the army. He began his conducting career with the semi-professional Chelsea Opera Group; in 1958 he conducted a performance of *Die Entführung aus dem Serail* at London; from 1961 to 1965 served as music director of Sadler's Wells. He made his U.S. debut as a guest conductor with the Minneapolis Sym. Orch. on Dec. 30, 1960; subsequently had engagements with the N.Y. Phil., the Philadelphia Orch., and the Los Angeles Phil. From 1972 to 1983 he served as principal guest conductor of the Boston Sym. Orch. On Jan. 20, 1967, he made his Metropolitan Opera debut in N.Y., conducting *Peter Grimes.* From 1967 to 1971 he was chief conductor of the BBC Sym. Orch. in London. In 1965 he conducted at the Royal Opera at Covent Garden; he succeeded Solti as its music director in 1971. Among his notable achievements was the production at Covent Garden of the entire cycle of *Der Ring des Nibelungen* in 1974–76; in 1977 he became the 1st British conductor to appear at the Bayreuth Festival, conducting *Tannhäuser.* He conducted the Royal Opera during its tours in South Korea and Japan in 1979, and in the U.S. in 1984. In 1983 he was appointed chief conductor of the Bavarian Radio Sym. Orch. in Munich, which he led on a tour of North America in 1986. In 1986 he stepped down as music director at Covent Garden to devote himself fully to his duties in Munich and to pursue far-flung engagements as a guest conductor with the major orchs. and opera houses of the world. He was made a Commander of the Order of the British Empire in 1965, and was knighted in 1980.

BIBL.: A. Blyth, *C. D.* (London, 1972); N. Wheen, "C. D.," *Ovation* (April 1986).

Davis, Eddie "Lockjaw," black American jazz tenor saxophonist; b. N.Y., March 2, 1921; d. Culver City, Calif., Nov. 3, 1986. He taught himself to play the tenor saxophone; began his career as a musician in Harlem; later worked with Cootie Williams, Andy Kirk, Louis Armstrong, and Count Basie; subsequently led his own combos.

Davis, Ivan, American pianist; b. Electra, Texas, Feb. 4, 1932. He studied piano with Silvio Scionti at North Texas State Univ. in Denton and later at the Accademia di Santa Cecilia in Rome with Carlo Zecchi. He also took private lessons with Vladimir Horowitz, beginning in 1961. He obtained 1st prizes at the Busoni Competition in Bolzano (1958), the Casella Competition at Naples (1958), and the Franz Liszt Competition in N.Y. (1960). He appeared as a soloist with the N.Y. Phil., Boston Sym., Philadelphia Orch., Chicago Sym., London Sym., Concertgebouw Orch. in Amsterdam, etc. In addition to serving on the faculty of the Univ. of Miami in Coral Gables (from 1966), he was a visiting prof. at the Indiana Univ. School of Music in Bloomington (1971–72) and gave master classes in various locales throughout the U.S.

Davis, John David, English composer and teacher; b. Birmingham, Oct. 22, 1867; d. Estoril, Portugal, Nov. 20, 1942. He studied music at Frankfurt and Brussels; returned to England in 1889; taught in various schools in Birmingham; in 1905, was appointed prof. of composition at the Guildhall School of Music in London. He wrote an opera on a Russian subject, *The Zaporoges*, which was produced in Birmingham on May 7, 1895; also a concert overture, *Germania*; 2 string quartets; 2 violin sonatas; piano pieces and songs.

Davis, (Morris) Mac, American singer and songwriter of country and rock music; b. Lubbock, Texas, Jan. 21, 1942. He took up the guitar as a teenager; then attended Emory Univ. in Atlanta and organized his own rock group; also took a few courses at Georgia State College. He gained commercial success when a number of his songs were sung by Bobby Goldsboro, Kenny Rogers, and Glen Campbell; he also wrote songs for Elvis Presley. At the perihelion of his luminary career, he made lucrative tours and television appearances. Among his most popular songs are *In the Ghetto, Don't Cry Daddy, I Believe in Music,* and *Stop and Smell the Roses.*

Davis, Miles (Dewey, III), famous black American jazz trumpeter and bandleader; b. Alton, Ill., May 25, 1926. He learned to play trumpet while attending elementary school in East St. Louis, Ill., then continued his studies in high school, where he played in the band; even before his graduation he made professional appearances. In 1944 he went to N.Y. and entered the Juilliard School of Music; he also frequented the jazz spots in the city. After deciding upon a full-time career as a jazz musician, he quit Juilliard in 1945 and commenced working with Charlie Parker, Coleman Hawkins, Benny Carter, and Billy Eckstine. His bebop style was modified in 1948, when a band he led included such an untypical jazz instrument as the horn (played by Gunther Schuller), and was exemplified by such numbers as *Boplicity.* He introduced a "cool" manner of playing as contrasted with the frantic "hot" bebop. His arranger was Gil Evans; he had John Coltrane on the saxophone and Philly Joe Jones on the drums. In his own numbers he introduced the lyrical and quiet "modal" type of setting, favoring the Lydian scale with its enervating tritone base, and he found suitable harmonies for it. By 1958 he abandoned standard pop practices and plunged into the mystical depths of exotic jazz in such far-out numbers as *Nefertiti* and *Sorcerer.* He then annexed electronics, forming a "fusion style" with hard rock. To emphasize his departure from his native territory, he affected pseudo-African vestments at his public appearances. He began to use hallucinogenic drugs, and had some close encounters with unfeeling law enforcers. As he prospered from megamillion sales of recordings, he became the target of extortionists eager to muscle in on the action; some inartistic malefactors peppered his snazzy Ferrari car with machinegun bullets; he suffered a hip injury that required the implanta-

tion of an artificial bone. After a hiatus from 1975 to 1981, he returned to center stage with his album *The Man with the Horn* (1981). In 1982 he made an extensive tour of Europe. Always searching for new avenues of expression, he adapted the songs of such rock artists as Michael Jackson and Cyndi Lauper for use in his concerts. In 1986 he collaborated on a recording project with Prince. He also tried his skill at painting and appeared on television as an actor. In 1981 he married the actress Cicely Tyson, but they divorced in 1988. With Q. Troupe, he publ. *Miles: The Autobiography* (N.Y., 1989).

BIBL.: M. James, *M. D.* (London, 1961); L. Feather, *From Satchmo to M.* (N.Y., 1972); B. Cole, *M. D.: A Musical Biography* (N.Y., 1974); I. Carr, *M. D.: A Critical Biography* (London, 1982; U.S. ed., 1982, as *M. D.: A Biography*); J. Chambers, *Milestones I: The Music and Times of M. D. to 1960* (Toronto, 1984) and *Milestones II: The Music and Times of M. D. since 1960* (Toronto, 1985).

Davis, Sammy, Jr., popular black American singer; b. N.Y., Dec. 8, 1925; d. Beverly Hills, May 16, 1990. His father, Sammy Davis, Sr., was a vaudeville dancer; his mother, a chorus girl. He was taken on tour with them as a child; at the age of 8 he obtained a role in a film musical; very soon he became enormously successful as an all-around entertainer; sang in the Broadway musicals *Mr. Wonderful* (1956) and *Golden Boy* (1964); also made numerous appearances on television and in nightclubs. His autobiography, *Yes, I Can,* was publ. in 1965.

Davison, A(rchibald) T(hompson), eminent American music educator; b. Boston, Oct. 11, 1883; d. Brant Rock (near Marshfield), Mass., Feb. 6, 1961. He studied at Harvard Univ. (B.A., 1906; M.A., 1907; Ph.D., 1908, with the diss. *The Harmonic Contributions of Claude Debussy*); took lessons in organ with Widor in Paris (1908–9). Returning to America, he was organist and choirmaster at Harvard Univ. (1910–40); conducted the Harvard Glee Club (1912–33) and the Radcliffe Choral Soc. (1913–28); he began teaching at Harvard in 1917 as assistant prof.; subsequently he was associate prof. (1920–29), prof. of choral music (1929–40), and the James Edward Ditson Prof. of Music (1940–54). He held numerous honorary degrees, including those of D.Mus. at Williams College and Oxford Univ.; Fellow of the Royal College of Music, London; Litt.D. from Washington Univ. (1953); and L.H.D. from Temple Univ. (1955). He wrote 2 comic operas, the musical comedy *The Girl and the Chauffeur* (Boston, April 16, 1906), the *Tragic Overture,* and the symphonic poem *Hero and Leander.* His greatest achievement was as an educator and popularizer of musical subjects: his lectures on music appreciation were broadcast and enjoyed considerable success among radio listeners. He was associate ed., with T. Surette, of a multivolume collection of vocal and instrumental pieces, the Concord Series of Educational Music, for which he made numerous arrangements.

WRITINGS: *Music Education in America* (N.Y., 1926); *Protestant Church Music in America* (Boston, 1920; enl. ed., 1933); *Choral Conducting* (1940); *The Technique of Choral Composition* (Cambridge, Mass., 1946); ed., with W. Apel, *Historical Anthology of Music* (Cambridge, 2 vols., 1946, 1950; rev. ed., 1950); *Bach and Handel: The Consummation of the Baroque in Music* (Cambridge, 1951); *Church Music: Illusion and Reality* (Cambridge, 1952). A dedicatory vol., *Essays on Music in Honor of A.T. Davison by His Associates,* was publ. at Cambridge in 1957.

Davison, J(ames) W(illiam), renowned English music critic; b. London, Oct. 5, 1813; d. Margate, March 24, 1885. He was founder and ed. of the *Musical Examiner* (1842–44) and ed. of the *Musical World* (1844–85); a contributor to the *Saturday Review, Pall Mall Gazette,* and *Graphic;* and was the influential critic of the *Times* (1846–78). In 1859 he married his pupil **Arabella Goddard.** He wrote the analytical program books for the Popular Concerts and the Hallé recitals; composed a few songs, several piano pieces, and a dramatic overture (for Piano Duet) to *Fortunatus,* a fairy tale. His memoirs were publ. by H. Davison as *From Mendelssohn to Wagner* (1912).

BIBL.: C. Reid, *The Music Monster: A Biography of J.W. D., Music Critic of the Times of London, 1846–78, with Excerpts from His Critical Writings* (London, 1984).

Davison, William (Edward) "Wild Bill," American jazz cornetist and bandleader; b. Defiance, Ohio, Jan. 5, 1906; d. Santa Barbara, Calif., Nov. 14, 1989. He 1st took up the mandolin, banjo, and guitar; then turned to the mellophone and cornet; after working with local bands, he played in Chicago (1927–32) and Milwaukee (1933–41); was also active as a bandleader. He served in the U.S. Army during World War II; then resumed his career, playing with Eddie Condon. He was a major figure in Chicago jazz circles.

Davy, Gloria, black American soprano; b. N.Y., March 29, 1931. She attended the Juilliard School of Music; then toured widely in the production of *Porgy and Bess* in 1953. In 1957 she made her European operatic debut in Nice. She sang at the Metropolitan Opera in N.Y. for the 1st time on Feb. 12, 1958, as Aida; then appeared at the Vienna State Opera (1959) and Covent Garden (1960). She was particularly noted for her fine performances of contemporary music.

Davy, John, English song composer and violinist; b. Upton-Helions, near Exeter, Dec. 23, 1763; d. London, Feb. 22, 1824. He studied at Exeter, and then settled in London, where he played the violin at Covent Garden. He wrote the music to a number of plays: *A Pennyworth of Wit* (London, April 18, 1796); *Alfred the Great*, a "grand historical ballet" (London, June 4, 1798); etc. *The Bay of Biscay, O!*, one of the songs from his incidental music to a play, *Spanish Dollars*, was extremely popular. He also composed an opera, *The Caffres, or Buried Alive* (Covent Garden, London, June 2, 1802).

Dawson, Ted, Canadian composer and teacher; b. Victoria, British Columbia, April 28, 1951. After training in violin, piano, and composition at the Victoria School of Music, he studied composition with Brian Cherney and Rudolf Komorous at the Univ. of Victoria (B.Mus., 1972); concurrently played viola in the Victoria Sym. Orch. He then pursued graduate studies in electronic music and composition with Gustav Ciamaga at the Univ. of Toronto (1972); he was also a student of Bengt Hambraeus and Alcides Lanza at McGill Univ. in Montreal (M.M.A., 1974) and took courses in music and visual arts at the Univ. of Toronto (1984), where he obtained his honors specialist certificate in music (1987). He taught at Concordia Univ. (1974–78) and Vanier College (1978–80) in Montreal, and then was assistant prof. of composition and music education at Queen's Univ. in Kingston, Ontario (from 1987).

WORKS: *Pentad* for String Quartet (1971); *Concerto grosso I* for Quadraphonic Tape, or Amplified Viola, Amplified Bassoon, Trombone, Percussion, and Stereo Tape (1973–74); *Concerto grosso II* for 5 Instrumental Soloists and Orch. (1973); *Chameleon* for Amplified Flute (1974–75); *The Land of Nurr* for Electronics (1975); *The Clouds of Magellan* for 3 Slide Projectors, Computerized Dissolver, Synchronization Tape, and Quadraphonic Audiotape (1976–77); *Binaries in Lyrae* for 4 Dancers, 2 Amplified Percussion Ensembles, Amplified Piano, and Lights (1977–78); *Megatherium* for 2 Amplified Pianos, Synthesizer, and Audiotape (1977–78); *Binaries* for 4 Optional Dancers, 2 Amplified Percussion, and Amplified Piano (1980); *Joint Actions* for Female Dancers and Double Bass (1980–81); *Traces in Glass* for Flute, Piano, and Percussion (1986); *5 Songs from the Late T'ang* for Baritone and Orch. (1987–88; also for Voice, Piano, and Percussion); *Portraits in a Landscape* for Tape (1988).

Dawson, William Levi, black American composer; b. Anniston, Ala., Sept. 26, 1898; d. Tuskegee, Ala., May 2, 1990. He ran away from home at 13 to enter the Tuskegee Inst.; later played trombone on the Redpath Chautauqua Circuit; graduated from the Tuskegee Inst. in 1921; studied with Carl Busch in Kansas City and at the American Cons. in Chicago (M.A., 1927). He played 1st trombone in the Chicago Civic Orch. (1926–30); then conducted the Tuskegee Choir. Among

his works is a Negro folk sym. in 3 movements (Philadelphia Orch., Stokowski conducting, Nov. 16, 1934).

Day, Charles Russell, English writer on music; b. Horstead, Norwich, 1860; d. Paardeberg, South Africa, Feb. 18, 1900. He was a soldier in the British army from 1880; served in India and later in South Africa, where he was killed in battle. His chief work was *Music and Musical Instruments of Southern India and the Deccan* (London, 1891).

De Ahna, Heinrich Karl Hermann, Austrian violinist; b. Vienna, June 22, 1835; d. Berlin, Nov. 1, 1892. He studied in Vienna with Mayseder and at the Prague Cons. with Mildner; made his debut as a violinist at the age of 12, playing in Vienna, London, etc. He settled in 1862 in Berlin as a member of the Royal Orch., becoming its concertmaster in 1868.

Deák, Csaba, Hungarian-born Swedish composer; b. Budapest, April 16, 1932. He studied clarinet and composition at the Béla Bartók Cons. in Budapest (1949–55) and composition with Ferenc Farkas at the Budapest Academy of Music (1955–56); he subsequently went to Sweden, where he took composition lessons with Hilding Rosenberg. He also studied composition, clarinet, and conducting at the Ingesund School of Music in Arvika; he received his music teacher's certification from the Stockholm Musikhögskolan (1969). He taught at the Swedish State School of the Dance in Stockholm (from 1969) and at the Univ. of Göteborg (1971–74).

WORKS: *Fäderna* (The Fathers), chamber opera (Stockholm, Oct. 16, 1968); *Lucie's Ascent into Heaven*, an "astrophonic minimelodrama" (1973); *Bye-bye, Earth, A Play about Death* (1976–77); *Etude on Spring*, electronic ballet (1970); theater music; *Jubilemus Salvatori*, chamber cantata (1958); *Eden* for Sym. Band (1978); *The Piper's Wedding* for Wind Quintet and Sym. Band (1979); *Vivax* for Orch. (1982); *5 Short Pieces* for Sym. Band (1983); *Farina Pagus* for Sym. Band (1983); 2 string quartets (1959, 1967); *Duo Suite* for Flute and Clarinet (1960); *Air* for Violin and Piano (1961); *121* for Winds, Percussion, and Double Bass (1969); Trio for Flute, Cello, and Piano (1971); *Andante och Rondo* for Wind Quintet (1973); *Verbunk* for Brass Sextet (1976); *Hungarian Dances* for Wind Quintet (1977); Octet for Wind Quintet and String Trio (1977); *Herykon* for Brass Quintet (1981); *Mässallians* for Trumpet, Trombone, Brass Ensemble, and Percussion (1985); Saxophone Quartet (1986); also choral works; songs.

De Amicis, Anna Lucia, famous Italian soprano; b. Naples, c.1733; d. there, 1816. She studied with her father and began her career singing with her family in comic opera productions in Pisa and Florence (1754), Bologna (1755), Paris (1758), Brussels (1759), and Dublin (1762). In 1762 she appeared for the 1st time in London at the King's Theatre, where she made her debut in serious opera in J.C. Bach's *Orione* (Feb. 19, 1763); subsequently sang in Milan (1764–65), Venice (1764), Innsbruck (1765), and Naples (1766), then again in Venice (1768–69; 1770–71) and Naples (1769–70; 1771–72). Mozart attended her performances in the latter cities and chose her to sing in the premiere of his *Lucio Silla* (Milan, Dec. 26, 1772). After further engagements in Naples (1773–76), Turin (1776–79), and Bologna (1778), she settled in Naples, where she continued to sing in private performances during the next decade, before retiring. She was generally considered one of the greatest singers of her time, winning acclaim for her astounding vocal as well as dramatic gifts.

Dean, Stafford (Roderick), English bass; b. Kingswood, Surrey, June 20, 1937. He studied at the Royal College of Music; later took lessons with Howell Glynne and Otakar Kraus; then sang with Opera for All in London; subsequently made appearances at Glyndebourne (1964), Sadler's Wells (1964), and Covent Garden (1969). He made his Metropolitan Opera debut in N.Y. on Feb. 6, 1976, as Figaro.

Dean, Winton (Basil), English writer on music; b. Birkenhead, March 18, 1916. He pursued studies in the liberal arts at Kings College, Cambridge (B.A., 1938; M.A., 1941); took private music lessons with Philip Radcliffe; then devoted himself to musicological research; publ. several valuable biographical essays on Handel, Bizet, and others.

WRITINGS: *Bizet* (London, 1948; 2nd ed., rev., 1965, as *Georges Bizet: His Life and Work;* 3rd ed., 1976); *Carmen* (London, 1949); *Franck* (London, 1950); *Introduction to the Music of Bizet* (London, 1950); *Handel's Dramatic Oratorios and Masques* (London, 1959); *Handel and the Opera Seria* (Berkeley, 1969); with J. Knapp, *Handel's Operas 1704–1726* (Oxford, 1987); *Essays on Opera* (Oxford, 1990).

BIBL.: N. Fortune, ed., *Music and Theatre: Essays in Honour of W. D.* (Cambridge, 1987).

De Angelis, Nazzareno, noted Italian bass; b. Aquila, Nov. 17, 1881; d. Rome, Dec. 14, 1962. As a boy he sang in the Sistine and Justine chapel choirs in Rome; made his operatic debut in Aquila in 1903; then appeared with major Italian opera houses; in America, he was on the roster of the Manhattan Opera House in N.Y. (1909–10); then of the Chicago Opera (1910–11; 1915–20); later made appearances with the Rome Opera (until 1938); also gave song recitals. He was regarded as one of the most cultured bass singers of the Italian school of opera; and he was equally appreciated in Wagnerian roles.

Debain, Alexandre-François, French inventor of the harmonium; b. Paris, 1809; d. there, Dec. 3, 1877. He established a factory of pianos and organs in Paris (1834), and after long experimentation with free reeds patented his harmonium in 1840. He also invented the antiphonel and the harmonichorde, and improved the accordion.

De Boeck, Auguste, Belgian composer; b. Merchtem, near Brussels, May 9, 1865; d. there, Oct. 9, 1937. He studied composition with Paul Gilson; taught organ (1893–1902) and harmony (1920–30) at the Brussels Cons. and was director of the Cons. at Mechelen (1920–30); also taught organ at the Antwerp Cons. (1909–21).

WORKS: 5 operas: *Théroigne de Méricourt* (1901); *Winternachtsdroom* (*Le Songe d'une nuit d'hiver;* 1903); *De Rijndevergen* (*Les Gnomes du Rhin;* 1906); *Reinaert le Renard* (1909); *Francesca* (*La Route d'Emeraude;* 1921); 3 ballets: *Assepoes* (*Cendrillon;* 1895); *De Nachtvlinder* (*La Phalène;* 1896); *La Tentation du poète* (1929); *Rhapsodie dahoméenne* for Orch. (1893); Sym. (1896); *Fantaisie sur deux airs flamande* for Orch. (1923); Violin Concerto (1925); various pieces for piano; songs; etc.

Debussy, (Achille-)Claude, great French composer whose music created new poetry of mutating tonalities and became a perfect counterpart of new painting in France; b. St.-Germain-en-Laye, Aug. 22, 1862; d. Paris, March 25, 1918. Mme. Mauté de Fleurville, the mother-in-law of the poet Verlaine, prepared him for the Paris Cons.; he was admitted at the age of 10 and studied piano with Marmontel (2nd prize, 1877) and solfège with Lavignac (3rd medal, 1874; 2nd, 1875; 1st, 1876). He further took courses in harmony with Emile Durand (1877–80) and practiced score reading under Bazille. In 1880 Marmontel recommended him to Mme. Nadezhda von Meck, Tchaikovsky's patroness. She summoned him to Interlaken, and they subsequently visited Rome, Naples, and Fiesole. During the summers of 1881 and 1882, Debussy stayed with Mme. von Meck's family in Moscow, where he became acquainted with the syms. of Tchaikovsky; however, he failed to appreciate Tchaikovsky's music and became more interested in the idiosyncratic compositions of Mussorgsky. Back in France, he became friendly with Mme. Vasnier, wife of a Paris architect and an amateur singer.

Debussy made his earliest professional appearance as a composer in Paris on May 12, 1882, at a concert given by the violinist Maurice Thieberg. In Dec. 1880 he enrolled in the composition class of Guiraud at the Paris Cons. with the ambition of winning the Grand Prix de Rome; after completing his courses, he won the 2nd Prix de Rome in 1883. Finally, on June 27, 1884, he succeeded in obtaining the Grand Prix de Rome with his cantata *L'Enfant prodigue,* written in a poetic but conservative manner reflecting the trends of French roman-

ticism. During his stay in Rome he wrote a choral work, *Zuleima* (1885–86), after Heine's *Almanzor,* and began work on another cantata, *Diane au bois.* Neither of these 2 incunabulae was preserved. His choral suite with orch., *Printemps* (1887), failed to win formal recognition. He then set to work on another cantata, *La Damoiselle élue* (1887–89), which gained immediate favor among French musicians.

In 1888 Debussy visited Bayreuth, where he heard *Parsifal* and *Die Meistersinger von Nürnberg* for the 1st time, but Wagner's grandiloquence never gained his full devotion. What thoroughly engaged his interest was the oriental music that he heard at the Paris World Exposition in 1889. He was fascinated by the asymmetric rhythms of the thematic content and the new instrumental colors achieved by native players; he also found an inner valence between these oriental modalities and the verses of certain French impressionist poets, including Mallarmé, Verlaine, Baudelaire, and Pierre Louÿs. The combined impressions of exotic music and symbolist French verses were rendered in Debussy's vocal works, such as *Cinq poèmes de Baudelaire* (1887–89), *Ariettes oubliées* (1888), *Trois mélodies* (1891), and *Fêtes galantes* (1892). He also wrote *Proses lyriques* (1892–93) to his own texts. For the piano, he composed *Suite bergamasque* (1890–1905), which includes the famous *Clair de lune.* In 1892 he began work on his instrumental *Prelude à l'après-midi d'un faune,* after Mallarmé, which comprises the quintessence of tonal painting with its free modal sequences under a subtle umbrage of oscillating instrumentation. The work was 1st heard in Paris on Dec. 22, 1894; a program book cautioned the audience that the text contained sensuous elements that might be distracting to young females. It was about that time that Debussy attended a performance of Maeterlinck's drama *Pelléas et Mélisande,* which inspired him to begin work on an opera on that subject. In 1893 there followed *Trois chansons de Bilitis,* after prose poems by Louÿs, marked by exceptional sensuality of the text in a musical context of free modality; a later work, *Les Chansons de Bilitis* for 2 harps, 2 flutes, and celesta, was heard in Paris in 1901 as incidental music to accompany recited and mimed neo-Grecian poetry of Louÿs. Between 1892 and 1899 Debussy worked on 3 *Nocturnes* for orch.: *Nuages, Fêtes,* and *Sirènes.*

As the 20th century dawned, Debussy found himself in a tangle of domestic relationships. A tempestuous liaison with Gabrielle Dupont (known as Gaby Lhéry) led to a break, which so distressed Gaby that she took poison. She survived, but Debussy sought more stable attachments; on Oct. 19, 1899, he married Rosalie Texier, with whom he made his 1st attempt to form a legitimate union. But he soon discovered that like Gaby before her, Rosalie failed to satisfy his expectations, and he began to look elsewhere for a true union of souls. This he found in the person of Emma Bardac, the wife of a banker. He bluntly informed Rosalie of his dissatisfaction with their marriage. Like Gaby 7 years before, Rosalie, plunged into despair by Debussy's selfish decision, attempted suicide; she shot herself in the chest but missed her suffering heart. Debussy, now 42 years old, divorced Rosalie on Aug. 2, 1905. Bardac and her husband were divorced on May 4, 1905; Debussy married her on Jan. 20, 1908. They had a daughter, Claude-Emma (known as "Chouchou"), born Oct. 15, 1905; she was the inspiration for Debussy's charming piano suite, *Children's Corner* (the title was in English, for Chouchou had an English governess). She survived her father by barely a year, dying of diphtheria on July 14, 1919.

With his opera *Pelléas et Mélisande,* Debussy assumed a leading place among French composers. It was premiered at the Opéra-Comique in Paris on April 30, 1902, after many difficulties, including the open opposition of Maeterlinck, who objected to having the role of Mélisande sung by the American soprano Mary Garden, whose accent jarred Maeterlinck's sensibilities; he wanted his mistress, Georgette Leblanc, to be the 1st Mélisande. The production of the opera aroused a violent controversy among French musicians and littérateurs. The press was vicious in the extreme: "Rhythm, melody, tonality, these are 3 things unknown to Monsieur Debussy," wrote the doyen of the Paris music critics, Arthur Pougin. "What a pretty series of false relations! What adorable progressions of triads in parallel motion and fifths and octaves which result from it! What a collection of dissonances, sevenths and ninths, ascending with energy! . . . No, decidedly I will never agree with these anarchists of music!" Camille Bellaigue, who was Debussy's classmate at the Paris Cons., conceded that *Pelléas et Mélisande* "makes little noise," but, he remarked, "it is a nasty little noise." The English and American reports were no less vituperative, pejorative, and deprecatory. "Debussy disowns melody and despises harmony with all its resources," opined the critic of the *Monthly Musical Record* of London. Echoing such judgments, the *Musical Courier* of N.Y. compared Debussy's "disharmony" with the sensation of "an involuntary start when the dentist touches the nerve of a sensitive tooth." And the American writer James Gibbons Huneker exceeded all limits of permissible literary mores by attacking Debussy's physical appearance. "I met Debussy at the Café Riche the other night," he wrote in the N.Y. *Sun*, "and was struck by the unique ugliness of the man. . . . [H]e looks more like a Bohemian, a Croat, a Hun, than a Gaul." These utterances were followed by a suggestion that Debussy's music was fit for a procession of head-hunters of Borneo, carrying home "their ghastly spoils of war."

Debussy's next important work was *La Mer*, which he completed during a sojourn in England in 1905. It was 1st performed in Paris, on Oct. 15, 1905. Like his String Quartet, it was conceived monothematically; a single musical idea permeated the entire work despite a great variety of instrumentation. It consists of 3 symphonic sketches: *De l'aube à midi sur la mer* (From Sunrise to Moon); *Jeux de vagues* (Play of the Waves); and *Dialogue du vent et de la mer* (Dialogue of Wind and the Sea). *La Mer* was attacked by critics with even greater displeasure than *Pelléas et Mélisande*. The American critic Louis Elson went so far as to suggest that the original title was actually *Le Mal de mer*, and that the last movement represented a violent seizure of vomiting. To summarize the judgment on Debussy, a vol. entitled *Le Cas Debussy* was publ. in Paris in 1910. It contained a final assessment of Debussy as a "déformateur musical," suffering from a modern nervous disease that affects one's power of discernment.

Meanwhile, Debussy continued to work. To be mentioned is the remarkable orch. triptych, *Images* (1906–12), comprising *Gigues*, *Ibéria*, and *Rondes de printemps*. In 1908 he conducted a concert of his works in London; he also accepted engagements as conductor in Vienna (1910), Turin (1911), Moscow and St. Petersburg (1913), and Rome, Amsterdam, and The Hague (1914). Among other works of the period are the piano suites, *Douze préludes* (2 books, 1909–10; 1910–13) and *Douze études* (2 books, 1915). *En blanc et noir*, for 2 pianos, dates from 1915. On May 15, 1913, Diaghilev produced Debussy's ballet *Jeux* in Paris. On May 5, 1917, Debussy played the piano part of his Violin Sonata at its premiere in Paris with violinist Gaston Poulet. But his projected tour of the U.S. with the violinist Arthur Hartmann had to be abandoned when it was discovered that Debussy had irreversible cancer of the colon. Surgery was performed in Dec. 1915, but there was little hope of recovery. The protracted 1st World War depressed him; his hatred of the Germans became intense as the military threat to Paris increased. He wrote the lyrics and the accompaniment to a song, *Noël des enfants*, in which he begged Santa Claus not to bring presents to German children whose parents were destroying the French children's Christmas. To underline his national sentiments, he emphatically signed his last works "musicien français." Debussy died on the evening of March 25, 1918, as the great German gun, "Big Bertha," made the last attempt to subdue the city of Paris by long-distance (76 miles) bombardment.

Debussy emphatically rejected the term "impressionism" as applied to his music. But it cannot alter the essential truth that like Mallarmé in poetry, he created a style peculiarly sensitive to musical mezzotint, a palette of half-lit delicate colors. He systematically applied the oriental pentatonic scale for ex-

otic evocations, as well as the whole-tone scale (which he did not invent, however; earlier samples of its use are found in works by Glinka and Liszt). His piece for piano solo, *Voiles*, is written in a whole-tone scale, while its middle section is set entirely in the pentatonic scale. In his music Debussy emancipated discords; he also revived the archaic practice of consecutive perfect intervals (particularly fifths and fourths). In his formal constructions, the themes are shortened and rhythmically sharpened, while in the instrumental treatment the role of individual solo passages is enhanced and the dynamic range made more subtle.

WORKS: CHORAL, DRAMATIC, AND LITERARY: *Hymnis*, cantata (1880; unfinished); *Daniel*, cantata for 3 Voices (1880–84); *Printemps* for Women's Chorus and Orch. (1882; publ. as *Salut printemps*, 1928); *Le Gladiateur*, cantata (June 22, 1883); *Invocation* for 4 Male Voices and Orch. (1883; publ. 1957); *L'Enfant prodigue*, cantata for Soprano, Tenor, Baritone, Chorus, and Orch. (Paris, June 27, 1884; reorchestrated 1905 and 1908); *Printemps* for Chorus (1884); *Diane au bois*, cantata (1884–86; unfinished); *La Damoiselle élue*, cantata for Soprano, Mezzo-soprano, Women's Chorus, and Orch. (1887–89; Paris, April 7, 1893); *Axel*, music for a scene to Villiers de l'Isle Adam's drama (1889); *Rodrigue et Chimène*, opera (1890–92; unfinished); *Pelléas et Mélisande*, opera (1893–95; 1901–2; Opéra-Comique, Paris, April 30, 1902, Messager conducting); *F.E.A. (Frères en art)*, play written with René Peter (1896–1900; unfinished); *Esther et la maison des fous*, text for a dramatic work (1900); *Le Diable dans le beffroi*, opera after Poe's *The Devil in the Belfry* (1902–3; unfinished; only notes for the libretto and sketch for Scene I extant); *Trois chansons de Charles d'Orléans* for Unaccompanied Chorus (2 pieces composed in 1898 incorporated into score of 1908; Paris, April 9, 1909, composer conducting); *Masques et Bergamasques*, scenario for a ballet (1910); *La Chute de la maison Usher*, opera after Poe's *The Fall of the House of Usher* (1908–18; unfinished; only sketches and final version of the libretto and incomplete vocal score extant); *Le Martyre de Saint-Sébastien*, incidental music to the mystery play by Gabriele d'Annunzio for Soprano, 2 Contraltos, Chorus, and Orch. (Paris, May 22, 1911); *Jeux*, ballet (1912; Paris, May 15, 1913, Monteux conducting); *Khamma*, ballet (1912; Paris, Nov. 15, 1924, Pierné conducting); *Ode à la France*, cantata for Solo, Chorus, and Orch. (1916; completed from the sketches by Marius-François Gaillard; piano score, 1928; orch. score, 1954).

ORCH.: *Intermezzo*, after Heine's *Intermezzo* (1882); *Suite d'orchestre* (1883–84); *Printemps*, symphonic suite for Orch. and Chorus (1887; full score destroyed in a fire; later reduction for voices and piano, 5-hands, by Durand, 1904; definitive version reorchestrated by Henri Busser, 1913; Paris, April 18, 1913, Rhené-Baton conducting); *Fantaisie* for Piano and Orch. (1889; London, Nov. 20, 1919, Coates conducting); *Prélude à l'après-midi d'un faune* (1892–94; Paris, Dec. 22, 1894, Doret conducting); *Nocturnes: Nuages; Fêtes; Sirènes* (the latter with wordless women's chorus) (1892–99; *Nuages* and *Fêtes*, Paris, Dec. 9, 1900, Chevillard conducting; 1st complete perf., Paris, Oct. 27, 1901, Chevillard conducting); *Danse sacrée* and *Danse profane* for Harp and Strings (1903; Paris, Nov. 6, 1904); *La Mer*, 3 symphonic sketches: 1, *De l'aube à midi sur la mer*; 2, *Jeux de vagues*; 3, *Dialogue du vent et de la mer* (1903–5; Paris, Oct. 15, 1905, Chevillard conducting); *King Lear*, incidental music to Shakespeare's play: *Fanfare* and *Sommeil de Lear* (1904; Paris, Oct. 30, 1926, Wolff conducting; also notes in MS for 6 other pieces); *Images: Gigues* (1909–12); *Ibéria* (1906–8); *Rondes de printemps* (1908–9) (orchestration of *Gigues* completed by Caplet; *Gigues*, Paris, Jan. 26, 1913, Pierné conducting; *Ibéria*, Paris, Feb. 20, 1910, Pierné conducting; *Rondes de printemps*, Paris, March 2, 1910, composer conducting).

CHAMBER: Trio in G major for Piano, Violin, and Cello (1880); *Intermezzo* for Cello and Piano (1882); *Scherzo* for Cello and Piano (1882); String Quartet (Paris, Dec. 29, 1893); *Chansons de Bilitis*, incidental music for the poems of Louÿs for 2 Flutes, 2 Harps, and Celesta (1900; Paris, Feb. 7, 1901); *Rapsodie* for Saxophone and Piano (1903–5; unfinished; piano accompaniment orchestrated by Roger-Ducasse; Paris, May 14, 1919, Caplet conducting); *Première rapsodie* for Clarinet and Piano (1909–10; Paris, Jan. 16, 1911; orchestrated by the composer, 1910); *Petite pièce* for Clarinet and Piano (1910); *Syrinx* for Unaccompanied Flute (Paris, Dec. 1, 1913); Sonata for Cello and Piano (1915; 1st confirmed perf., London, March 4, 1916); Sonata for Flute, Viola, and Harp (1915; Paris, Dec. 10, 1916 [private perf.]); Sonata for Piano and Violin (1916–17; Paris, May 5, 1917, composer pianist, Poulet violinist).

SOLO PIANO: *Danse bohémienne* (1880); *Deux arabesques* (1880); *Rêverie; Ballade; Danse* (orch. by Ravel); *Valse romantique; Nocturnes* (1890); *Suite bergamasque: Prélude; Menuet; Clair de lune; Passepied* (1890–1905); *Mazurka* (1891); *Pour le piano: Prelude; Sarabande* (orchestrated by Ravel); *Toccata* (1896–1901; Paris, Jan. 11, 1902, Viñes pianist); *Estampes: Pagodes; Soirée dans Grenade; Jardins sous la pluie* (1903; 1st complete perf., Paris, Jan. 9, 1904, Viñes pianist); *D'un cahier d'esquisses* (1903; Paris, April 20, 1910, Ravel pianist); *Masques* (1904) and *L'Isle joyeuse* (1904; orchestrated by B. Molinari; Paris, Feb. 18, 1905, Viñes pianist); *Images,* 1st series: *Reflets dans l'eau; Hommage à Rameau; Mouvement* (1905; Paris, March 3, 1906, Viñes pianist); *Children's Corner: Doctor Gradus ad Parnassum; Jimbo's Lullaby; Serenade for the Doll; Snow Is Dancing; The Little Shepherd; Golliwog's Cake-walk* (1906–8; Paris, Dec. 18, 1908, Harold Bauer, pianist; orchestrated by Caplet); *Images,* 2nd series: *Cloches à travers les feuilles; Et la lune descend sur le temple qui fut; Poissons d'or* (1907–8; Paris, Feb. 21, 1908, Viñes pianist); *Le Petit Nègre* (1909); *Hommage à Haydn* (1909; Paris, March 11, 1911); *Douze préludes,* Book I: *Danseuses de Delphes* (Paris, May 25, 1910, composer pianist); *Voiles* (Paris, May 25, 1910, composer pianist); *Le Vent dans la plaine; Les Sons et les parfums tournent dans l'air du soir; Les Collines d'Anacapri* (Paris, Dec. 26, 1909, Viñes pianist); *Des Pas sur la neige; Ce qu'a vu le Vent d'Ouest; La Fille aux cheveux de lin; La Sérénade interrompue* (Paris, Jan. 14, 1911, Viñes pianist); *La Cathédrale engloutie* (Paris, May 25, 1910, composer pianist); *La Danse de Puck; Minstrels* (1909–10); *La Plus que lente* (1910; orchestrated by the composer, 1912); *Douze préludes,* Book II: *Brouillards; Feuilles mortes; La Puerta del Vino; Les Fées sont d'exquises danseuses; Bruyères; General Lavine—eccentric; La Terrasse des audiences du clair de lune; Ondine; Hommage à S. Pickwick, Esq., P.P.M.P.C.; Canope; Les Tierces alternées; Feux d'artifice* (1910–13); *La Boîte à joujoux,* children's ballet (1913; Paris, Dec. 10, 1919, Inghelbrecht conducting); *Berceuse héroïque pour rendre hommage à S.M. le Roi Albert I de Belgique et à ses soldats* (1914; orchestrated by the composer, 1914; Paris, Oct. 26, 1915, Chevillard conducting); *Douze études,* Book I: *Pour les cinq doigts; Pour les tierces; Pour les quartes; Pour les sixtes; Pour les octaves; Pour les huit doigts* (1915); *Douze études,* Book II: *Pour les degrés chromatiques; Pour les agréments; Pour les notes répétées; Pour les sonorités opposées; Pour les arpèges; Pour les accords* (1915; both books perf. Dec. 14, 1916, Walter Morse Rummel pianist).

PIANO DUET: *Symphonie en si* (1 movement, 1880; intended for orch.; Paris, Jan. 27, 1937); *Triomphe de Bacchus* (1882; intended as an orch. interlude; orchestrated by Gaillard, 1927); *Petite suite: En bateau; Cortège; Menuet; Ballet* (1889); *Marche écossaise sur un thème populaire* (The Earl of Ross March; 1891; orchestrated by the composer, Paris, Oct. 22, 1913, Inghelbrecht conducting); *Six epigraphes antiques: Pour invoquer Pan, dieu du vent d'été; Pour un tombeau sans nom; Pour que la nuit soit propice; Pour la danseuse aux crotales; Pour l'Egyptienne; Pour remercier la pluie au matin* (1900–1914; also for piano solo; orchestrated by Ansermet).

2 PIANOS: *Lindaraja* (1901; Paris, Oct. 28, 1926); *En blanc et noir* (3 pieces; 1915; Paris, Dec. 21, 1916, composer and Roger-Ducasse pianists).

SONGS (author of text precedes date of composition): *Ballade à la lune* (Alfred de Musset; 1876?); *Beau soir* (Paul Bourget; 1876?); *Fleur des eaux* (Maurice Bouchor; 1876?); *Nuit d'étoiles* (Théodore de Banville; 1876?); *Fleur des blés* (André Girod;

1877); *Mandoline* (Paul Verlaine); *La Belle au bois dormant* (Vincent Hypsa); *Voici que le printemps* (Bourget); *Paysage sentimental* (Bourget; all composed 1880–83); *L'Archet* (Charles Cros); *Séguedille* (J.L. Vauthier); *Les Roses; Chanson espagnole* (for 2 voices); *Rondel chinois;* 3 songs on poems by Gourget: *Regret; Romance d'Ariel; Musique;* 6 songs on poems by Banville: *Caprice; Aimons-nous; O floraison divine des lilas; Souhait; Sérénade; Fête galante;* 3 songs on poems by Leconte de Lisle: *La Fille aux cheveux de lin; Jane; Eclogue* (for soprano and tenor); *Il dort encore* (from Banville's *Hymnis*); *Coquetterie posthume* (Théophile Gautier); *Flots, palmes, sables* (Armand Renaud; all composed 1880–84); *Zéphyr* (Banville; 1881); *En sourdine* (Verlaine; 1st version, 1882); *Rondeau* (Musset; 1882); *Pantomime* (Verlaine); *Clair de lune* (Verlaine); *Pierrot* (Banville); *Apparition* (Stéphane Mallarmé; all composed 1882–84); *Cinq poèmes de Baudelaire: Le Balcon; Harmonie du soir; Le Jet d'eau* (piano accompaniment orchestrated by the composer); *Recueillement; La Mort des amants* (all composed 1887–89); *Ariettes oubliées* (Verlaine): *C'est l'extase . . . ; Il pleure dans mon coeur . . . ; L'ombre des arbres . . . ; Chevaux de bois; Green; Spleen* (all composed 1888); *Deux romances* (Bourget): *Romances; Les Cloches* (1891); *Les Angélus* (G. le Roy; 1891); *Dans le jardin* (Paul Gravolet; 1891); *Trois mélodies* (Verlaine): *La mer est plus belle . . . ; Le Son du cor s'afflige . . . ; L'Echelonnement des haies* (1891); *Fêtes galantes* (Verlaine), 1st series: *En sourdine; Fantoches; Clair de lune* (1892); *Proses lyriques* (composer): *De rêve; De grève; De fleurs; De soir* (1892–93); *Trois chansons de Bilitis* (Pierre Louÿs): *La Flûte de Pan; La Chevelure; Le Tombeau des Naïades* (1897); *Fêtes galantes* (Verlaine), 2nd series: *Les Ingénus; Le Faune; Colloque sentimental* (1904); *Trois chansons de France: Rondel: Le temps a laissé son manteau . . .* (Charles d'Orléans); *La Grotte* (Tristan Lhermite; identical to *Auprès de cette grotte sombre,* below); *Rondel: Pour ce que plaisance est morte . . .* (Charles d'Orléans; all composed 1904); *Le Promenoir des deux amants* (Lhermite): *Auprès de cette grotte sombre . . . ; Crois mon conseil . . . ; Je tremble en voyant ton visage* (1910); *Trois ballades de François Villon* (orchestrated by the composer): *Ballade de Villon à s'amye; Ballade que feit Villon à la requeste de sa mère pour prier Nostre-Dame; Ballade des femmes de Paris* (1910); *Trois poèmes de Stéphane Mallarmé: Soupir; Placet futile; Eventail* (1913); *Noël des enfants qui n'ont plus de maison* (composer; 1915).

WRITINGS: Debussy contributed numerous critical articles to *La Revue Blanche, Gil Blas, Musica, La Revue S. I. M.* et al. A selection of these, some abridged, appeared as *Monsieur Croche, antidilettante* (Paris, 1921; 2nd ed., 1926; Eng. tr. as *Monsieur Croche the Dilettante-Hater,* London, 1927; 2nd ed., 1962; new ed. by F. Lesure as *Monsieur Croche et autres écrits,* Paris, 1971; Eng. tr. as *D. on Music: The Critical Writings of the Great French Composer C. D.,* N.Y., 1977).

BIBL.: SOURCE MATERIAL: A periodical, *Cahiers D.,* began publication in 1974 (issued by the Centre de Documentation C. D. in St.-Germain-en-Laye, France). F. Lesure has prepared a *Catalogue de l'oeuvre de C. D.* (Geneva, 1977). The *Oeuvres complètes* began publication in 1986. Other sources include the following: A. Martin, *C. D.: Chronologie de sa vie et de ses oeuvres* (Paris, 1942); A. Gauthier, *D.: Documents iconographiques* (Geneva, 1952); *Catalogue de la collection Walter Straram: Manuscrits de C. D.* (Rambouillet, 1961); F. Lesure, *C. D., Catalogue de l'Exposition* (Paris, 1962); C. Abravanel, *C. D.: A Bibliography* (Detroit, 1974); F. Lesure, *Iconographie musicale: D.* (Geneva, 1974); M. Rolf, "Orchestral Manuscripts of C. D.: 1892–1905," *Musical Quarterly* (Fall 1984); J. Briscoe, *C. D.: A Guide to Research* (N.Y., 1990).

CORRESPONDENCE: J. Duran, ed., *Lettres de C. D. à son éditeur* (Paris, 1927); *Correspondance de C. D. et P.-J. Toulet* (Paris, 1929); J. André-Messager, ed., *La Jeunesse de Pelléas: Lettres de C. D. à André Messager* (Paris, 1938); C. D.: *Lettres à deux amis: 78 lettres inédites à Robert Godet et G. Jean-Aubry* (Paris, 1942); H. Borgeaud, ed., *Correspondance de C. D. et Pierre Louÿs* (Paris, 1945); E. Lockspeiser, ed., *Lettres inédites de C. D. à André Caplet* (Monaco, 1957); P. Vallery-Radot, ed.,

Lettres de C. D. à sa femme Emma (Paris, 1957); F. Lesure, ed., "C. D.: Textes et documents inédits," *Revue de Musicologie*, XLVIII (1962); idem, "Lettres inédites de C. D. à Pierre Louÿs," ibid., LVII (1971).

BIOGRAPHICAL: L. Liebich, *C.-A. D.* (London, 1908); L. Laloy, *C. D.* (Paris, 1909; 2nd ed., augmented, 1944); G. Jean-Aubry, "C. D.," *Musical Quarterly* (Oct. 1918); idem, "Some Recollections of D.," *Musical Times* (May 1918); J.-G. Prod'homme, "C.-A. D.," *Musical Quarterly* (Oct. 1918); E. Vuillermoz, *C. D.* (Paris, 1920); R. Jardillier, *C. D.* (Dijon, 1922); A. Suarès, *D.* (Paris, 1922; 2nd ed., augmented, 1936); R. Paoli, *D.* (Florence, 1924; 2nd ed., 1947); F. Shera, *D. and Ravel* (London, 1925); F. Gysi, *C. D.* (Zürich, 1926); R. van Santen, *D.* (The Hague, 1926; 2nd ed., 1947); C. Koechlin, *D.* (Paris, 1930); R. Peter, *C. D.* (Paris, 1931; 2nd ed., augmented, 1944); L. Vallas, *C. D. et son temps* (Paris, 1932; 2nd ed., 1958; Eng. tr., 1973); E. Decsey, *C. D.* (Graz, 1936); E. Lockspeiser, *D.* (London, 1936; 5th ed., rev., 1980); idem, "Mussorgsky and D.," *Musical Quarterly* (Oct. 1937); O. Thompson, *D., Man and Artist* (N.Y., 1937); H. Strobel, *C. D.* (Zürich, 1940; 3rd ed., rev., 1948); L. Vallas, *A.-C. D.* (Paris, 1944); R. Paoli, *D.* (Florence, 1947; 2nd ed., 1951); G. Ferchault, *C. D., musicien français* (Paris, 1948); H. Harvey, *C. of France: The Story of D.* (N.Y., 1948); R. Malipiero, *D.* (Brescia, 1948); J. van Ackere, *C. D.* (Antwerp, 1949); R. Myers, *D.* (London, 1949); W. Danckert, *C. D.* (Berlin, 1950); G. and D.-E. Inghelbrecht, *C. D.* (Paris, 1953); V. Seroff, *D., Musician of France* (N.Y., 1956); E. Vuillermoz, *C. D.* (Geneva, 1957); M. Dietschy, "The Family and Childhood of D.," *Musical Quarterly* (July 1960); J. Barraqué, *D.* (Paris, 1962; Eng. tr., 1972); E. Lockspeiser, *D.: His Life and Mind* (2 vols., London, 1962 and 1965; rev. ed., Cambridge, 1978); Y. Tiénot and O. d'Estrade-Guerra, *D.: L'Homme, son oeuvre, son milieu* (Paris, 1962); A. Goléa, *D.* (Paris, 1965); P. Young, *D.* (London, 1966); G. Gourdet, *D.* (Paris, 1970); R. Nichols, *D.* (London, 1973); C. Goubault, *C. D.* (Paris, 1986).

CRITICAL, ANALYTICAL: L. Gilman, *D.'s "Pelléas et Mélisande"* (N.Y., 1907); F. Santoliquido, *Il Dopo-Wagner, C. D. e Richard Strauss* (Rome, 1909); C. Caillard and J. de Bérys, *Le Cas D.* (Paris, 1910); G. Setaccioli, *D. è un innovatore?* (Rome, 1910); D. Chennevière, *C. D. et son oeuvre* (Paris, 1913); C. Paglia, *Strauss, D., e compagnia bella* (Bologna, 1913); A. Lualdi, "C. D. La sua Arte e la sua Parabola," *Rivista Musicale Italiana*, XXV/2 (1918); E. Newman, "The Development of D.," *Musical Times* (May and Aug. 1918); G. Gatti, "The Piano Works of C. D.," *Musical Quarterly* (July 1921); A. Cortot, "La Musique de piano de D.," *La Revue Musicale*, I (1920; Eng. tr. as *The Piano Music of D.*, London, 1922); J. Palache, "D. as Critic," *Musical Quarterly* (July 1924); M. Emmanuel, *Pelléas et Mélisande* (Paris, 1926); L. Vallas, *Les Idées de C. D., musicien français* (Paris, 1927; Eng. tr. as *The Theories of C. D.*, London, 1929); M. Dumesnil, *How to Play and Teach D.* (N.Y., 1932); A. Liess, *C. D. Das Werk in Zeitbild* (2 vols., Strasbourg, 1936); H. Kölsch, *Der Impressionismus bei D.* (Düsseldorf, 1937); E. Lockspeiser, "D.'s Unpublished Songs," *Radio Times* (Sept. 23, 1938); A. Liess, *C. D. und das deutsche Musikschaffen* (Würzburg, 1939); A. Jakobik, *Die assoziative Harmonik in den Klavier-Werken C. D.s* (Würzburg, 1940); G. Schaeffner, *C. D. und das Poetische* (Bern, 1943); A. Gauthier, *Sous l'influence de Neptune: Dialogues avec D.* (Paris, 1945); J. d'Almendra, *Les Modes grégoriens dans l'oeuvre de C. D.* (Paris, 1948); E. Decsey, *D.s Werke* (Graz, 1949); V. Jankélévitch, *D. et le mystère* (Neuchâtel, 1949; 2nd ed., 1962); E. Robert Schmitz, *The Piano Works of C. D.* (N.Y., 1950; 2nd ed., 1966); J. van Ackere, *Pelléas et Mélisande* (Brussels, 1952); A. Golea, *Pelléas et Mélisande, analyse poetique et musicale* (Paris, 1952); A. Schaeffner, "D. et ses rapports avec la musique russe," in P. Souvtchinsky, ed., *Musique russe* (Vol. I, Paris, 1953); H. Busser, *De Pelléas aux Index galantes* (Paris, 1955); O. d'Estrade-Guerra, "Les Manuscrits de Pelléas et Mélisande," *La Revue Musicale*, no. 235 (1957); M. Long, *Au piano avec C. D.* (Paris, 1960; Eng. tr., 1972); M. Dietschy, *La Passion de C. D.* (Neuchâtel, 1962); E. Lockspeiser, *D. et Edgar Poe* (Monaco, 1962); "Souvenir et présence de D.," *La Revue Belge de Musicologie*,

XVI (1962); E. Lockspeiser, "D.'s Concept of the Dream," *Proceedings of the Royal Musical Association*, LXXXIX (1962–63); F. Lesure, "C. D. after His Century," *Musical Quarterly* (July 1963); "C. D. 1862–1962: Livre d'or," *La Revue Musicale*, no. 258 (1964); S. Jarocinski, *D., a impresjonizm i synmbolizm* (Krakow, 1966; French tr., 1971; in Eng. as *D.: Impressionism and Symbolism*, London, 1976); P. Ruschenburg, *Stilkritische Untersuchungen zu den Liedern C. D.s* (diss., Univ. of Hamburg, 1966); E. Hardeck, *Untersuchungen zu den Klavierliedern C. D.s* (Regensburg, 1967); R. Park, *The Later Style of C. D.* (diss., Univ. of Michigan, 1967); V. Jankélévitch, *La Vie et la mort dans la musique de D.* (Neuchâtel, 1968); F. Dawes, *D. Piano Music* (London, 1969); W. Austin, ed., *D.: Prelude to "The Afternoon of a Faun"* (Norton Critical Score ed., containing background, criticism, and analysis; N.Y., 1970); D. Cox, *D.'s Orchestral Music* (London, 1974); C. Zenck, *Versuch über die wahre Art D. zu analysieren* (Munich, 1974); A. Whittall, "Tonality and the Whole-tone Scale in the Music of D.," *Music Review*, XXXVI (1975); V. Jankélévitch, *D. et le mystère de l'instant* (Paris, 1976); A. Wenk, *D. and the Poets* (Berkeley and Los Angeles, 1976); R. Holloway, *D. and Wagner* (London, 1979); R. Orledge, "D.'s Piano Music: Some Second Thoughts and Sources of Inspiration," *Musical Times* (Jan. 1981); M. Cobb, ed., *The Poetic D.: A Collection of His Song Texts and Selected Letters* (annotated; Boston, 1982); E. Lang-Becker, *D. Nocturnes* (Munich, 1982); R. Orledge, *D. and the Theatre* (Cambridge, 1982); R. Howat, *D. in Proportion: A Musical Analysis* (Cambridge, 1983); J. Trilling, *Untersuchungen zur Rezeption C. D.s in der zeitgenössischen Musikkritik* (Tutzing, 1983); A. Wenk, *C. D. and Twentieth-Century Music* (Boston, 1983); D. Grayson, "The Libretto of D.'s 'Pelléas et Mélisande,'" *Music & Letters* (March 1985); R. Orledge, "D. et 'La Girl' anglaise': The Legend of 'Khamma,'" *Musical Times* (March 1986); idem, "The Genesis of D.'s 'Jeux,'" ibid. (Feb. 1987); H. Ferguson, "D.'s Emendations to 'Pelléas,'" ibid. (Aug. 1988); R. Nicols and R. Smith, *C. D.: Pelléas et Mélisande* (Cambridge, 1989).

Decadt, Jan, Belgian composer; b. Ypres, June 21, 1914. He studied with Joseph Ryelandt at the Ghent Cons., and later with Jean Absil in Brussels. He was director of the music school in Harelbeke from 1945, and in 1957 was appointed prof. of fugue at the Antwerp Cons.; from 1971 taught composition at the Ghent Cons. His musical style is marked by strong polyphonic structures with impressionistic coloration.

WORKS: *Variations on "Sir Halewijn"* for Orch. (1943); *Ballada op een boom* (Ballade on a Tree) for Soprano, Flute, Oboe, and String Trio (1945); *Habanera* for Orch. (1947); Piano Concerto (1953); Sym. No. 1 (1958); *Constant Permeke*, cantata (1963); *Monographie musicale d'un grand peintre* for Orch. (Johannesburg, Nov. 17, 1964); *Concerto Overture* for Flute, Oboe, and String Orch. (1964); Suite for Trumpet and Chamber Orch. (1967); *Petite planète* for Narrator, Soprano, Flute, Viola, and Cello (1967); *Concertante Fantasia* for Oboe and Piano (1970); *Introduction and Capriccio* for Clarinet and Piano (1972); Saxophone Concerto (1973); Quartet for Saxophones (1974); *Wens-album* for Flute and Clarinet (1976); *Kleine fanfare* for Brass Band (1981); *Naar Wiegeland* for Voice and Piano (1986).

Decaux, Abel, French organist and composer; b. Auffay, 1869; d. Paris, March 19, 1943. He studied organ with Widor and Guilmant and composition with Massenet at the Paris Cons. He served as organist at the church of Sacré-Cœur in Montmartre; then was prof. of organ at the Paris Schola Cantorum; from 1923 to 1937 he taught organ at the Eastman School of Music in Rochester, N.Y. Decaux composed very little; but he attracted posthumous attention by the discovery, and performance, of his group of piano pieces under the title *Clairs de lune* (the plural being of the essence): *Minuit passe, La Ruelle, Le Cimétière,* and *La Mer,* written between 1900 and 1907 and publ. in 1913, seem to represent early examples of piano writing usually associated with Debussy and Ravel; the similarity of styles is indeed striking, which indicates that Impressionism was "in the air," and in the ears, of impressionable French musicians early in the new century.

Dechevrens, Antoine, Swiss musicologist; b. Chêne-Bourg, near Geneva, Nov. 3, 1840; d. Geneva, Jan. 17, 1912. He entered the Jesuit order in 1861; was a prof. of theology and philosophy at the Univ. of Angers; devoted himself to the study of Gregorian chant and of neume notation. He publ. *Du rythme dans l'hymnographie latine* (1895); *Études de science musicale* (3 vols., Paris, 1898); *Composition musicale et composition littéraire* (Paris, 1910).

Decker, Franz-Paul, German conductor; b. Cologne, June 23, 1923. He was educated at the Cologne Hochschule für Musik and the Univ. of Cologne. He was chief conductor of the Rotterdam Phil. (1962–68). In 1967 he became music director of the Montreal Sym. Orch., a post he held until 1975. He then was principal guest conductor and music adviser of the Calgary (Alberta) Phil. (1975–77). In 1981–82 he was artistic adviser of the Winnipeg Sym. Orch., and then was principal guest conductor of the New Zealand Sym. Orch. in Wellington (1984–85; 1986–88). In 1986 he became music director of the Barcelona Sym. Orch.

Decoust, Michel, French composer; b. Paris, Nov. 19, 1936. He studied at the Paris Cons. with Olivier Messiaen and others; received the Premier 2nd Grand Prix de Rome (1963). His works include *Mouvement* for Strings and Percussion (1964); *Études* for Flutes and Cellos (1966); *Polymorphée* for Orch. (Royan, April 1, 1967); *Instants-Stabiles* for Chamber Ensemble (1967); *Actions* for Voice and Piano, with Audience Participation (Angers, April 18, 1972); *T' Ai* for Double Bass, Electric Guitar, Percussion, Harpsichord, and Voice (Paris, Jan. 25, 1972); *Et, ée* for Chorus and Orch. (Paris, July 23, 1973).

Decreus, Camille, French pianist; b. Paris, Sept. 23, 1876; d. Fontainebleau, Sept. 26, 1939. He studied piano with Pugno at the Paris Cons.; had a successful career as a pianist; made tours in England and Germany; after several concerts as assisting artist and accompanist in the U.S., he settled in Washington, D.C., as a private teacher in the family of Senator W. Clark; then returned to France. In 1924 he was appointed director of the American Cons. at Fontainebleau, a post which he held until his death.

Decsényi, János, Hungarian composer; b. Budapest, March 24, 1927. He studied in Budapest with Rezsö Sugár at the Cons. (1948–52) and with Endre Szervánszky at the Academy of Music (1952–56). From 1951 he was active with the Hungarian Radio, becoming head of its dept. of serious music and director of its electronic music studio. In 1986 he was made a Merited Artist by the Hungarian government.

Works: STAGE: *Képtelen történet* (An Absurd Story), ballet (1962); *Az orr* (The Nose), pantomime (1979). **ORCH.:** *Csontváry-képek* (Csontváry Pictures; 1967); *Melodiae hominis* for Chamber Orch. (1969); *Gondolatok—nappal, éjszaka* (Thoughts—by Day, by Night; 1971); *Kommentárok Marcus Aureliushoz* (Commentaries on Marcus Aurelius) for 16 Solo Strings (1973); *Double* for Chamber Orch. (1974); Variations for Piano and Orch. (1976); *Concerto grosso* for Chamber Orch. (1978); *A tücsökszót ki érti meg?* (Who Understands the Speech of Crickets?) for Chamber Orch. and Tape (1983); Cello Concerto (1984); *A harmadik* (The 3rd One) for 15 Solo Strings (1985); Sym. (1986). **CHAMBER:** String Quartet (1978). **VOCAL:** *Szerelem* (Love) for Soprano and Orch. (1957); *Sírfelirat Aquincumból* (Epitaph from Aquincum) for Soprano, Electric Organ, and 16 Solo Strings (1979); *Weöres Sándor tizenkettedik szimfóniája* (The 12th Symphony of Sándor Weöres) for Soprano and Percussion (1980). **ELECTRONIC:** *Kövek* (Stones; 1987); *Prospero szigete* (Prospero's Island; 1989). Other works include choral music, songs, incidental music for theater, film, and radio, and pedagogical pieces.

Decsey, Ernst (Heinrich Franz), German-born Austrian writer on music; b. Hamburg, April 13, 1870; d. Vienna, March 12, 1941. He studied law in Vienna (doctorate in law, 1894); then studied composition with Bruckner and Robert Fuchs at the Vienna Cons.; was active as a music critic in Graz and in Vienna. He was the author of a major biography of Hugo Wolf (4 vols., Berlin, 1903–6; abridged 1-vol. ed., 1921). He also wrote *Anton Bruckner* (Berlin, 1920); *Johann Strauss* (Berlin, 1922; 2nd ed., 1947); *Franz Lehár* (Vienna, 1924); *Franz Schubert* (Vienna, 1924); *Maria Jeritza* (Vienna, 1931); *Claude Debussy* (2 vols., Graz, 1936); and *Debussys Werke* (Graz and Vienna, 1948).

Dedler, Rochus, Austrian composer; b. Oberammergau, Jan. 15, 1779; d. Vienna, Oct. 15, 1822. He wrote the music of the Passion play at Oberammergau.

Deering (or **Dering**), **Richard,** English organist and composer; b. Kent, c.1580; d. London (buried, March 22), 1630. He was educated in Italy; returned to England as a well-known musician and practiced in London; in 1610, took the degree of B.Mus. at Oxford; in 1617, became organist at the convent of English nuns at Brussels; in 1625, was appointed organist to Queen Henrietta Maria.

Works: *Cantiones sacrae sex vocum cum basso continuo ad organum* (Antwerp, 1597); *Cantiones sacrae quinque vocum* (1617); *Cantica sacra ad melodium madrigalium elaborata senis vocibus* (Antwerp, 1618); *Cantiones sacrae quinque vocum* (1619); 2 books of *Canzonette*, one for 3 Voices and one for 4 (1620; author's name given as Richardo Diringo Inglese); *Cantica sacra ad duos et tres voces, composita cum basso continuo ad organum* (London, 1662).

BIBL.: P. Platt, "D.'s Life and Training," *Music & Letters* (Jan. 1952); E. Brennecke, "The Country Cryes of R. D.," *Musical Quarterly* (July 1956).

DeFabritiis, Oliviero (Carlo), Italian conductor; b. Rome, June 13, 1902; d. there, Aug. 12, 1982. He studied with Setaccioli and Refice; made his conducting debut at the Teatro Adriano in Rome in 1920; subsequently was a conductor at the Rome Opera (1934–61). He made numerous guest appearances with the major European opera houses; also conducted in the U.S.

Defauw, Désiré, Belgian conductor; b. Ghent, Sept. 5, 1885; d. Gary, Ind., July 25, 1960. He was a pupil of Johan Smit (violin); from 1914 to 1918, led his own quartet, the Allied Quartet of London. He was prof. of conducting at the Brussels Cons. and conductor of its concerts (from 1926); he also conducted his own concert series in Brussels and was founder-conductor of the Orch. National de Belgique there in 1937. In 1940 he went to Canada, where he was music director of the Montreal Sym. Orch. (1941–53); he was also music director of the Chicago Sym. Orch. (1943–47) and then of the Gary (Ind.) Sym. Orch. (1950–58).

BIBL.: M. Herzberg, *D. D.* (Brussels, 1937).

De Fesch (also **Defesch, du Feche, de Feghe, de Veg**), **Willem,** prominent Dutch violinist and composer; b. Alkmaar, 1687; d. London, c.1757. He married the daughter of the violinist Karel Rosier, vice-Kapellmeister at the court of the Elector of Cologne in Bonn, in 1711; he most likely studied with Rosier. He was active in Amsterdam (1710–25), and, after serving as Kapelmeester of Antwerp Cathedral (1725–31), he settled in London, where he pursued a career as a violinist and composer until about 1750. He was an accomplished composer, following in the pathway marked out by Vivaldi, Corelli, and Handel. His 2 sets of sonatas, opp. 8a and 8b, are particularly notable.

Works (all publ. in London unless otherwise given): **VOCAL:** *Canzonette ed arie* for Soprano, Basso Continuo, and Violin or Flute (1739); *XX canzonette* for Soprano, Basso Continuo, and Violin, Flute, or Mandolin (c.1745); *VI English Songs* for Voice, Violins, Flutes, and Harpsichord (c.1748); *6 New English Songs* for Voice, Violin, Flute, and Harpsichord (1749); *Mr. Defesch's Songs Sung at Marybon-Gardens* (1753); various other songs publ. separately; also 3 oratorios (all lost) and a cantata. **INSTRUMENTAL:** *VI duetti* for 2 Violins, op. 1a (Amsterdam, 1716; 2nd ed., Paris, 1738); *VI concerti* for 4 Violins, Viola, Cello, and Organ, op. 2a (Amsterdam, 1716–17); *VI concerts:* 4 for 4 Violins, Viola, and Basso Continuo and 2 for Oboe, 2

Violins, Cello, and Basso Continuo, op. 3a (Amsterdam, 1716–17); *XII sonate:* 6 for Violin, Violone, and Harpsichord and 6 for 2 Cellos, op. 4 (Amsterdam, 1725); *VI concerti:* 4 for 2 Flutes, 2 Violins, Viola, and Organ and 2 for 4 Violins, Viola, Cello, and Organ, op. 5 (Amsterdam, c.1725–31); *VI sonate* for Violin or Flute and Organ, op. 6 (Brussels, 1725–31); *X sonate* a tre for 2 Flutes or Violins and Cello or Basso Continuo, op. 7 (Amsterdam, 1733); *XII Sonatas:* 6 for Violin and Basso Continuo and 6 for 2 Cellos, op. 8a (1733; nos. 1–6 ed. in Hortus Musicus, CXXVII–CXXVIII, 1958; nos 7–12 ed. in Moeck's Kammermusik, XIX–XX, Celle, 1940); *6 Sonatas* for Cello and Harpsichord, op. 8b (1736); *Sonatas* for 2 Cellos, Bassoons, or Viols, op. 1b (Paris, 1738); *VI Sonatas* for 2 Flutes, op. 9 (1739); *VIII Concertos in 7 Parts:* 6 for 2 Violins, Viola, and Cello, with 2 others for Violin, 1 for Flute with all the other Instruments, and 1 for 2 Flutes, 2 Violins, Viola, Cello, and Harpsichord, op. 10 (1741); *Musical Amuzements* (1744; also as *30 Duets* for 2 Flutes, op. 11, 1747); *12 Sonatas* for 2 Flutes or Violin and Cello or Harpsichord, op. 12 (1748); *VI Sonatas* for Cello and Harpsichord, op. 13 (c.1750).

BIBL.: F. van den Bremt, *W. d. F. (1687–1757?), Nederlands componist en virtuoos: Leven en werk* (Louvain and Brussels, 1949); H. O'Douwes, "De cellocomposities van W. d. F.," *Mens en Melodie,* XIV (1959); I. Cholij, "D.'s 'Tempest' Songs," *Musical Times* (June 1986).

Deffés, Pierre-Louis, French composer; b. Toulouse, July 25, 1819; d. there, June 10, 1900. He was a pupil of Halévy at the Paris Cons., taking the Grand Prix de Rome in 1847 for the cantata *L'Ange et Tobie.*

Defossez, René, Belgian composer and conductor; b. Spa, Oct. 4, 1905; d. Brussels, May 20, 1988. He was 1st trained in music by his father, and then with Rasse at the Liège Cons., receiving the Belgian Prix de Rome in 1935 for his opera *Le Vieux Soudard.* He subsequently devoted himself to conducting; was conductor at the Théâtre Royal de la Monnaie in Brussels (1936–59). From 1946 to 1971 he also was prof. of conducting at the Brussels Cons. In 1969 he was elected a member of the Royal Belgian Academy.

WORKS: STAGE: OPERAS: *La Conversion de St. Hubert* (1933); *Le Subterfuge improvisé* (1938); *L'Amour est roi* (1946). **BALLETS:** *Floriante* (1942); *Le Sens du divin* (1947); *Le Rêve de l'astronome* (1950); *Les Jeux de France* (1959); *Le Pêcheur et son âme* (1965); *Le Regard* (1970; Charleroi, March 27, 1971); *Lieges libertés,* historical fresco (1981); *Images sous-marines* for Orch. (1930); *Symphonie wallonne* (1935); Trombone Concerto (1948); Violin Concerto (1951); Piano Concerto (1956); *Sinfonietta de printemps* (1975); 2 string quartets (1934, 1950); Ballad for Clarinet and Piano (1942); Wind Trio (1946); 4 *églogues* for 4 Flutes and 2 Percussionists; *Petit quatuor* for Violin, Piano, Saxophone, and Percussion (1973); numerous educational piano pieces and children's songs.

De Franco, "Buddy" (Boniface Ferdinand Leonardo), American jazz clarinetist; b. Camden, N.J., Feb. 17, 1923. He took up the clarinet at the age of 12; worked with many leading jazz musicians, including Gene Krupa (1941–42), Charlie Barnet (1943–44), Tommy Dorsey (1944–46), and Count Basie (1950); then organized his own big band (1951) and quartet (1952), appearing with the latter for many years with much success. He led the Glenn Miller Orch. from 1966 to 1974; then resumed touring on his own.

DeGaetani, Jan(ice), remarkable American mezzo-soprano; b. Massillon, Ohio, July 10, 1933; d. Rochester, N.Y., Sept. 15, 1989. Her father was a lawyer who encouraged her musical talents. She married the conductor Thomas DeGaetani, and assumed her conjugal name in her career. However, the marriage was not successful, and they were soon divorced. She subsequently married Philip West, an oboist. She studied at the Juilliard School of Music in N.Y. with Sergius Kagan. Upon graduation, she joined the Contemporary Chamber Ensemble, with which she developed a peculiar technique essential for performance of ultramodern vocal works. Since that sort of thing was commercially unrewarding, she uncomplain-

ingly took menial jobs, including baby-sitting and waiting on tables in restaurants. She devoted her free time to a detailed study of the solo part in Schoenberg's *Pierrot lunaire,* which became one of her finest interpretations. She mastered the most challenging techniques of new vocal music, including fractional intervals and even tongue-clicking required in some new works. DeGaetani also mastered foreign languages so as to be able to perform a wide European repertoire. She became a faithful interpreter of the most demanding works by modern composers, among them Boulez, George Crumb, Jacob Druckman, Peter Maxwell Davies, György Ligeti, Elliott Carter, and Mario Davidovsky. She also developed a fine repertoire of Renaissance songs, and soon became a unique phenomenon as a lieder artist, excelling in an analytical capacity to express the most minute vocal modulations of the melodic line while parsing the words with exquisite intellectual penetration of their meaning, so that even experienced critics found themselves at a loss of superlatives to describe her artistry. From 1973 she taught at the Eastman School of Music in Rochester, N.Y. With N. and R. Lloyd, she publ. the useful vol. *The Complete Sightsinger* (1980). She died of irreversible leukemia.

Degen, Helmut, German composer; b. Aglasterhausen, near Heidelberg, Jan. 14, 1911. He studied piano, composition, and conducting at the Hochschule für Musik in Cologne; then took courses at the Univ. of Bonn with Schiedermair and Schrade; taught at the Cons. of Duisburg, then in Trossingen. His music is couched in a well-defined, neo-Classical idiom, with strong points of reference to Baroque forms. He also publ. a *Handbuch der Formenlehre* (Regensburg, 1957).

WORKS: 3 syms. (1945, 1947, 1948); *Symphonisches Spiel I* (1956), *II* for Violin, Cello, Piano, and Orch. (1957), and *III* (1960); Piano Concerto (1940); Organ Concerto (1943); Concertino for 2 Clarinets and Orch. (1944); Cello Concerto (1945); Concerto for Harpsichord and 6 Instruments (1945); *Triptychon* (1952); 2 string quartets (1941, 1950); Piano Trio (1943); Trio for Flute, Viola, and Clarinet (1950); Saxophone Sonata (1950); Nonet for Wind Instruments and Strings (1951); 4 piano sonatas; numerous concert studies; choruses.

Degeyter, Pierre, French wood-carver and author of the famous workers' song *Internationale* (1888); b. Ghent, Oct. 8, 1848; d. St. Denis, near Paris, Sept. 27, 1932. The authorship of the song was contested by Pierre's brother, Adolphe, a blacksmith (b. 1858; d. Lille, Feb. 15, 1917), but after 18 years of litigation, the Paris Appellate Court decided in favor of Pierre.

Degner, Erich Wolf, German composer; b. Hohenstein-Ernstthal, April 8, 1858; d. Berka, near Weimar, Nov. 18, 1908. He studied at the grand-ducal school of music at Weimar, and later at Würzburg; taught at Regensburg and Gotha; in 1885 became director of the music school at Pettau, Styria; in 1888, instructor at the grand-ducal music school at Weimar; in 1891, director of the music school of the Styrian Music Soc. at Graz; in 1902 was again in Weimar as director of the music school.

WORKS: Sym. for Organ and Orch.; *Maria und die Mutter* for Soli, Chorus, and Orch.; pieces for piano; songs. He publ. *Anleitung und Beispiele zum Bilden von Kadenzen* (1902).

BIBL.: R. Mojsisowicz, *E.W. D.* (1909).

Degrada, Francesco, esteemed Italian musicologist; b. Milan, May 23, 1940. He studied piano, composition, and conducting at the Milan Cons., obtaining a simultaneous arts degree from the Univ. of Milan (1964). He joined the music history faculty of the Univ. of Milan in 1964; also taught at the Milan Cons. (1966–73) and gave lectures at various European and U.S. univs., including N.Y. Univ. (1986). His interest in Baroque music led him to organize the chamber group Complesso Barocco di Milan in 1967, with which he was associated as director and harpsichordist until 1976.

WRITINGS: *Al gran sole carico d'amore. Per un nuovo teatro musicale* (Milan, 1974; 2nd ed., 1977); *Sylvano Bussotti e il suo teatro* (Milan, 1976); *Antonio Vivaldi da Venezia all'Europa* (Milan, 1977); *Il palazzo incantata. Studi sulla tradizione del* *melodramma dal Barocco al Romanticismo* (2 vols., Florence, 1979); *Vivaldi veneziano europea* (Florence, 1980); ed. *Studi Pergolesiani/Pergolesi Studies* (2 vols., N.Y., 1986, 1988); *Andrea Gabrieli e il suo tempo* (Florence, 1988).

De Grassi, Alex, American composer and guitarist; b. Yokosuka, Japan, Feb. 13, 1953. He began playing guitar at the age of 13, inspired by folk-blues guitarists John Renbourn and Burt Jansch. He is a cousin of New Age guitarist-entrepreneur William Ackerman (Ackerman was adopted by de Grassi's uncle). De Grassi's 1st recording (1978) was one of the 1st releases on Ackerman's Windham Hill label, and can thus be considered one of the earliest New Age recordings. De Grassi's guitar music shares stylistic traits with that of his cousin, although it is somewhat brighter and more syncopated. He is a "crossover" artist who has received awards in both folk and jazz categories. His highly successful *Altiplano* (1987) was his 1st release on a label other than Windham Hill; it shows a considerably freer style and wider range of jazz and ethnic influences. De Grassi has toured North America and Europe, performing at venues including N.Y.'s Carnegie Hall, Davies Sym. Hall in San Francisco, and the Kennedy Center in Washington, D.C.
WORKS: *Turning: Turning Back* for Guitar (1978); *Slow Circle* for Guitar (1979); *Clockwork* for Guitar and Other Instruments (1981); *Southern Exposure* for Guitar (1983); *Altiplano* for Guitar and Other Instruments (1987).

Degtiarev, Stepan (Anikievich), Ukrainian composer; b. Borisovka, Kursk District, 1766; d. Kursk, May 5, 1813. He was a serf bonded to the Sheremetev family. Trained as a chorister, he became musical director of Sheremetev's domestic and theatrical ensembles, including the opera troupe at the summer theater-palace at Ostankino, near Moscow. In 1805 he publ. a Russian tr. of F. Manfredini's *Regole armoniche*. In addition to at least 76 Orthodox choral concerti and various liturgies and cantatas, he composed a dramatic patriotic oratoria, *Minin i Pozharskii, ili Osvobozhdenie Moskvy* (Minin and Pozharskii, or the Freeing of Moscow; 1811).
BIBL.: C. Hughes, *The Origins of the First Russian Patriotic Oratorio: S.A. D.'s "Minin i Pozharskii" (1811)* (diss., Univ. of North Carolina, 1984); E. Levashev, *Istorii russkoi muzyki, 1800–1825* (Moscow, 1986); H. Smither, *A History of the Oratorio* (vol. 3, Chapel Hill, 1987).

De Guide, Richard, Belgian composer; b. Basècles, March 1, 1909; d. Brussels, Jan. 12, 1962. He studied with Paul Gilson and Jean Absil; worked for the Inst. National de Radiodiffusion (1938–45); was director of the music academy of Woluwé-St.-Pierre in Brussels (1946–61); also taught at the Liège Cons. (1950–53) and at the Mons Cons. (1961). He wrote a monograph, *Jean Absil, vie et œuvre* (Tournai, 1965).
WORKS: *Mouvements symphoniques* (1938); *Illustration pour un Jeu de l'Oie* for Voice, and Piano or Orch. (1939–41); *Concerto for 11* for Winds and Percussion (1940); 3 syms.: No. 1 (1943); No. 2, with Organ (1951); No. 3 for Strings, Harp, and Timpani (1957); *Vincti non devicti*, symphonic poem (1948); piano concerto, *Le Téméraire* (1952); *Le Tombeau de Montaigne*, symphonic suite (1955); ballet, *Les Danaïdes* (1956); *Hommage à Hindemith* for Chamber Orch. (1958); *Humoresque* for Piano (1927); *Préludes* for Organ (1942); Duo for 2 Trumpets (1944); Duo for 2 Violins (1945); *Speciosa miracula*, sextet for Wind Quintet and Piano (1948); *Préludes and Toccata* for Piano (1949); *2 nômes* for Flute (1951); Suite *"Les caractères du trombone"* for Trombone and Piano (1958); *4 symptômes* for Piano, left-hand (1960).

Dehn, Siegfried (Wilhelm), famous German music theorist and teacher; b. Altona, Feb. 24, 1799; d. Berlin, April 12, 1858. He was a law student at Leipzig from 1819 to 1825; also studied harmony and cello playing. He studied theory assiduously with Bernhard Klein in Berlin; at Meyerbeer's insistence he was appointed librarian of the music dept. of the Royal Library in 1842. From 1842 to 1848 he was also ed. of the *Caecilia;* then was a prof. at the Royal Academy of Arts

(1849–58). Dehn was a profound theorist, and very successful as a teacher of theory, numbering among his pupils Anton Rubinstein and Glinka.
WRITINGS: *Theoretisch-praktische Harmonielehre* (Berlin, 1840; 2nd ed., Leipzig, 1860; his most important work); *Analyse dreier Fugen aus J.S. Bachs Wohltemperiertem Clavier und einer Vokaldoppelfuge G.M. Buononcinis* (Leipzig, 1858); *Lehre vom Kontrapunkt, dem Kanon und der Fuge* (Berlin, 1859; 2nd ed., 1883).

Deis, Carl, American organist, music editor, and composer; b. N.Y., March 7, 1883; d. there, July 24, 1960. He studied piano at home from early childhood under the guidance of his father, who was a trombone player; then was a pupil at the National Cons. of Music and the N.Y. College of Music. In 1906 he became a choral conductor and voice teacher at various private schools in N.Y.; was engaged as organist at the Soc. for Ethical Culture (1919–33). In 1917 he was appointed music ed. of G. Schirmer, Inc.; retired in 1953. He wrote several attractive songs, among them *New Year's Day, The Flight of the Moon, Come Down to Kew, The Drums, Were I a Star.*

Deiters, Hermann (Clemens Otto), German writer on music; b. Bonn, June 27, 1833; d. Koblenz, May 11, 1907. He studied jurisprudence in Bonn, where he took the degrees of Dr.Jur. (1854) and Dr.Phil. (1858). He taught in the gymnasia at Bonn (1858) and Düren (1869); was director of gymnasia at Konitz (1874), Posen (1878), and Bonn (1883); "Provincial-Schulrath" at Koblenz (1885–93); assistant in the Ministry of Public Worship at Berlin (1890); he retired in 1903, living thereafter in Koblenz. Deiters wrote many articles for journals. His greatest achievement was his masterly tr. into German of Thayer's *Life of Beethoven*, with critical comments by Deiters (3 vols., Berlin, 1866–77; 2nd ed., with 2 additional vols. ed. by Riemann, Leipzig, 1907–8; vols. I, II, and III re-ed. by Riemann, Leipzig, 1910–17).

Dejoncker, Theodore, Belgian composer; b. Brussels, April 11, 1894; d. Asse, July 10, 1964. He studied with Gilson; in 1925, founded, with 7 other composers, the progressive Groupe des Synthétistes.
WORKS: *Sinfonia la classica* (1939); *Symphonie burlesque; Symphonie romantique;* overture, *Brutus; Prologue symphonique; Portrait de Bernard Shaw* for Orch.; String Quartet; Saxophone Quartet; String Trio (1960).

De Jong, Conrad J(ohn), American composer; b. Hull, Iowa, Jan. 13, 1934. He studied trumpet at North Texas State Univ. in Denton, majoring in music education; received his B.M.Ed. in 1954; later studied composition with Bernhard Heiden at Indiana Univ. in Bloomington, obtaining his M.M. in 1959; subsequently took lessons with Ton de Leeuw in Amsterdam (1969). He was appointed to the music faculty of the Univ. of Wisconsin in River Falls in 1959.
WORKS: *Unicycle* for Harpsichord or Piano (1960); *3 Studies* for Brass Septet (1960); *Music for 2 Tubas* (1961); *Essay* for Brass Quintet (1963); String Trio (1964); *Fun and Games* for Any Instrument with Piano (1966; rev. 1970); *Aanraking (Contact)* for Trombone (1969); *Hist Whist* for Soprano, Flute, Viola, and Percussion (1969); *Grab Bag* for Tuba Ensemble (1970); *Resound*, trio for Flute, Guitar, and Percussionist or Half-Track Stereo Tape with Tape Delay System and 35mm Slide Projection (1974); *3 Short Variation Fanfares* for Brass Quintet (1980).

De Jong, Marinus. See **Jong, Marinus de.**

De Koven, (Henry Louis) Reginald, American composer; b. Middletown, Conn., April 3, 1859; d. Chicago, Jan. 16, 1920. He was educated in Europe from 1870, taking his degree at St. John's College, Oxford, in 1879. Before this he studied piano under W. Speidel at Stuttgart, and after graduation studied there another year under Lebert (piano) and Pruckner (harmony). After a 6-month course in Frankfurt under Hauff (composition), he studied singing with Vannucini at Florence, and operatic composition under Genée in Vienna and Delibes in Paris. In 1902 he organized the Phil. Orch. at Washington,

D.C., which he conducted for 3 seasons. He was music critic for the *Chicago Evening Post* (1889–90), *Harper's Weekly* (1895–97), *N.Y. World* (1898–1900; 1907–12), and later for the *N.Y. Herald.*

Works: Operettas: *The Begum* (Philadelphia, Nov. 7, 1887); *Don Quixote* (Boston, Nov. 18, 1889); *Robin Hood* (his best-known work; Chicago, June 9, 1890; as *Maid Marian*, London, Jan. 5, 1891; the celebrated song *O Promise Me* was introduced into the score shortly after its 1st perf.; it was originally publ. as a separate song in 1889); *The Fencing Master* (Boston, 1892); *The Knickerbockers* (Boston, 1893); *The Algerian* (Philadelphia, 1893); *Rob Roy* (Detroit, 1894); *The Tzigane* (N.Y., 1895); *The Mandarin* (Cleveland, 1896); *The Paris Doll* (Hartford, Conn., 1897); *The Highwayman* (New Haven, 1897); and the following, all of which had their premieres in N.Y.: *The 3 Dragoons* (1899); *Red Feather* (1903); *Happyland* (1905); *Student King* (1906); *The Golden Butterfly* (1907); *The Beauty Spot* (1909); *The Wedding Trip* (1911); *Her Little Highness* (1913). A grand opera, *The Canterbury Pilgrims,* was produced at the Metropolitan Opera, N.Y., March 8, 1917; another grand opera, *Rip van Winkle,* was performed by the Chicago Grand Opera (Jan. 2, 1920). In addition, he wrote some 400 songs and a Piano Sonata.

Bibl.: A. de Koven, *A Musician and His Wife* (N.Y., 1926).

Dela, Maurice (real name, **Albert Phaneuf**), Canadian composer and organist; b. Montreal, Sept. 9, 1919; d. there, April 28, 1978. He studied composition with Champagne at the Montreal Cons. and orchestration with Leo Sowerby in Chicago. He subsequently became a church organist in the province of Quebec, a composer and arranger for the CBC (1951–65), and a teacher in Montreal. His music is pragmatic in style and idiom, tending toward Baroque consistency but energized by an injection of euphonious dissonance.

Works: Orch.: Ballade for Piano and Orch. (1945); Piano Concerto (1946); *Ronde* for Soprano, and Small Orch. or Piano (1949); *Le Chat, la belette et le petit lapin* for Narrator and Orch. (1950; rev. 1965); *Les Fleurs de Glais* for Narrator and Orch. (1951); *Scherzo* (1952); *Adagio* for String Orch. (1956); Piano Concertino (1962); *2 esquisses* (1962); *Projection* (1966); 2 syms. (1968, 1972); *3 Dances* (1971); *Triptyque* (1973); *Suite 437* for Band (1977); *Petite suite maritime* for Wind Instruments (1946); Suite for Flute, Cello, and Piano (1953–54); 2 string quartets (1960, 1963); *Divertissement* for Brass Quintet (1962); *Miniatures* for 3 Recorders (1968); *Hommage* for Piano (1950); *2 Impromptus* for Piano (1964); songs; arrangements of folk songs of Quebec province.

Delaborde, Elie (Miriam) (né **Elie Miriam**), eccentric French pianist, pedagogue, and composer; b. Paris, Feb. 8, 1839; d. there, Dec. 9, 1913. Though no official documents exist to authenticate the claim, evidence is substantial that he was the natural son of **Charles-Valentin Alkan,** his teacher, and Lina Eraîm Miriam, a lady of means. He also studied with Moscheles and Henselt, and subsequently made successful tours of England, Germany, and Russia. During the Franco-Prussian War in 1870, he fled with 121 parrots and cockatoos (later also kept 2 apes, named Isidore and Sara, in his apartment) to London, where he introduced some of his father's works for piano with pédalier. In 1873 he was appointed prof. of piano at the Paris Cons.; his students included Olga Samaroff. He was reputed to have had an affair with Bizet's wife, which was substantiated by the announcement of their marriage shortly following Bizet's death. Indeed, he was a close friend of Bizet, having been his swimming companion in the Seine when Bizet caught his fatal illness. He wrote an opéra-comique, *La Reine dort;* an overture, *Attila;* a Piano Quintet; 12 Preludes, Études, and Fantaisies for Piano; and a number of songs.

Bibl.: R. Smith, *Alkan: The Enigma* (London, 1976).

Delacôte, Jacques, French conductor; b. Remiremont, Vosges, Aug. 16, 1942. He studied conducting with Hans Swarowsky at the Vienna Academy of Music; in 1971 he won the Mitropoulos Competition in N.Y.; in 1972 he appeared as a conductor with the N.Y. Phil.; subsequently conducted at the Hamburg State Opera, the Düsseldorf Opera, the Paris Opéra, and Covent Garden in London. As a sym. conductor, he had engagements with the London Sym., the Cleveland Orch., and the San Francisco Sym. Naturally, he is especially praised for his congenial performances of French operas.

Delage, Maurice (Charles), French composer; b. Paris, Nov. 13, 1879; d. there, Sept. 19, 1961. He took lessons with Ravel. Subsequently he made voyages to the Orient, and was greatly impressed with Japanese art. His music reveals oriental traits in subject matter as well as in melodic progressions. An ardent follower of Debussy's principles, Delage wrote music in a highly subtilized manner with distinctive instrumental colors. After 1920 he lived mostly in Paris.

Works: Symphonic poem, *Conte par la mer* (1908); several songs, with Small Orch.; *4 poèmes hindous* (1921); *Roses d'Octobre* (1922); *7 Haï-Kaï* (1923); *3 chants de la jungle* (1935); *2 fables de La Fontaine* (1949); *In Morte* (1951); String Quartet (1948).

Delalande (also **de La Lande, Lalande,** etc.), **Michel-Richard,** noted French organist, harpsichordist, and composer; b. Paris, Dec. 15, 1657; d. Versailles, June 18, 1726. He was the 15th child of a Paris tailor. He joined the choir of the royal church of St.-Germain-l'Auxerrois about 1666 and sang there until his voice broke at age 15; became a distinguished organist and harpsichordist, giving instruction on the latter to 2 of the daughters of Louis XIV by his mistress Mme. de Montespan. He was also active as a church organist in Paris. In 1683 he became 1 of the 4 sous-maîtres of the Royal Chapel; he was in sole charge from 1714 until 1723, when Louis XV restored the other 3 positions; he then was joined by Campra, Bernier, and Gervais. In 1685 he was named compositeur de la musique de la chambre, a title he solely held from 1709 to 1718. He also was surintendant de la musique de la chambre from 1689 to 1719. He was made a Chevalier of the Order of St. Michel by Louis XV in 1722. Delalande's grand motets are outstanding, being notable for their mastery of the Versailles style. He is also distinguished by his music for the stage. He deftly used music from his ballets and divertissements in his *Sinfonies pour les soupers du Roi,* which were played at the dinners of Louis XIV and Louis XV.

Works: OPERA BALLET: *Les Éléments* (Tuileries Palace, Paris, Dec. 31, 1721; major portion by Destouches; ed. by d'Indy, 1883). BALLETS, PASTORALES, AND DIVERTISSEMENTS: *La Sérénade* (Fontainebleau, 1682); *L'Amour berger* (Paris, 1683); *Les Fontaines de Versailles* (Versailles, April 5, 1683); *Epithalame* (Versailles, June 25, 1685; music not extant); *Le Ballet de la jeunesse* (Versailles, Jan. 28, 1686); *Le Palais de Flore* (Versailles, Jan. 5, 1689); *Ballet de M. de La Lande* (Versailles, Aug. 25, 1691); *Adonis* (1696); *L'Amour, fléchy par la constance* (Fontainebleau, 1697); *La Noce de village* (Sceaux, Feb. 21, 1700); *L'Hymen champestre* (Marly, 1700); *Ode à la louange du Roy* (Sceaux, Oct. 24, 1704; music not extant); *Ballet de la paix* (Marly, July 1713); *L'Inconnu* (Paris, Feb. 1720); *Les Folies de Cardenio* (Paris, Dec. 30, 1720); etc. His grand motets number more than 70; Philidor prepared a manuscript copy of 27 motets (1689–90), Hue publ. 40 motets (Paris, 1729–33), and the so-called Cauvin manuscript of the mid-18th century contains 41 motets. A number of these have appeared in modern eds. His instrumental works include *Sinfonies pour les soupers du Roi* (Suite No. 1 ed. by R. Desormière, Paris, 1947; Suite No. 4 ed. by Clerisse, Paris, 1954; 2 Caprices ed. by Paillard, Paris, 1965); *Symphonies des Noëls* (more than 20 in all; Nos. 1–4 ed. by A. Cellier, Paris, 1937); 18 suites, etc.

Bibl.: J. Richards, *The "Grand Motet" of the Late Baroque in France as Exemplified by M.-R. d.L.* (diss., Univ. of Southern Calif., 1950); J. Anthony, "La Structure musicale des récits de M.-R. d.L.," *Le Grand Motet français* (1663–1792): *CNRS Paris 1984.*

De Lamarter, Eric, American organist, conductor, music critic, teacher, and composer; b. Lansing, Mich., Feb. 18, 1880;

d. Orlando, Fla., May 17, 1953. He studied organ with Fairclough in St. Paul, Middleschulte in Chicago, and Guilmant and Widor in Paris (1901–2), then held several organ positions in Chicago, notably with the 4th Presbyterian Church (1914–36). He was music critic for the *Chicago Inter-Ocean* (1901–14), the *Chicago Record-Herald* (1905–8), and the *Chicago Tribune* (1909–10); he also taught at Olivet College (1904–5), Chicago Musical College (1909–10), Univ. of Missouri, Ohio State Univ., and the Univ. of Texas. He was assistant conductor of the Chicago Sym. Orch. and conductor of the Chicago Civic Orch. (1918–36).

WORKS: ORCH.: 4 syms.: No. 1 (Chicago, Jan. 23, 1914); No. 2 (Philadelphia, June 5, 1925); No. 3 (1931; Chicago, Feb. 16, 1933); No. 4 (1932); *The Faun*, overture (Chicago, Nov. 18, 1913); *Serenade* (1915); *Masquerade*, overture (1916); *Fable of the Hapless Folktune* (Chicago, April 6, 1917); *The Betrothal*, incidental music (N.Y., Nov. 19, 1918); 2 organ concertos: No. 1 (Chicago, April 2, 1920); No. 2 (Chicago, Feb. 24, 1922); *Weaver of Tales* for Organ and Chamber Orch. (1926); *The Black Orchid*, suite taken from *The Dance of Life*, ballet (Chicago, Feb. 27, 1931); *Serenade near Taos* (N.Y., Jan. 11, 1938); *The Giddy Puritan*, overture (original title, *They, Too, Went t'Town*, 1921; NBC, June 6, 1938); *Huckleberry Finn*, overture (1948); *Ol' Kaintuck*, overture (1948); *Cluny*, dialogue for Viola and Orch. (1949); chamber music; organ works; songs.

Delamont, Gordon (Arthur), Canadian composer; b. Moose Jaw, Saskatchewan, Oct. 27, 1918; d. Toronto, Jan. 16, 1981. He studied trumpet and played in his father's band in Vancouver; played in dance orchs. and led his own dance band (1945–49). His works are all in the jazz idiom. For jazz orch., he wrote *Allegro and Blues* (1962), *Ontario Suite* (1965), *Centum* (1966), *Song and Dance* (1967), and *Collage No. 3* (1967). He also wrote *Portrait of Charles Mingus* for Octet (1963), 3 *Entertainments* for Saxophone Quartet (1969), *Moderato and Blues* for Brass Quintet (1972), and *Conversation* for Flugelhorn and Alto Saxophone (1977). He publ. *Modern Arranging Techniques* (N.Y., 1965), *Modern Harmonic Techniques* (2 vols., N.Y., 1965), *Modern Contrapuntal Techniques* (N.Y., 1969), *Modern 12-Tone Techniques* (N.Y., 1973), and *Modern Melodic Techniques* (N.Y., 1976).

De Lancie, John (Sherwood), prominent American oboe virtuoso and teacher; b. Berkeley, Calif., July 26, 1921. His father was an electrical engineer and an amateur clarinet player; his brother played the violin. In 1935 he won an audition for the Philadelphia Orch., and was also accepted to study oboe in the class of Marcel Tabuteau at the Curtis Inst. of Music. He was engaged as oboist with the Pittsburgh Sym. Orch. (1940–42). In 1942 he was drafted into the U.S. Army as a member of the U.S. Army Band; in 1943 the band was sent to Algiers, to Eisenhower's headquarters; he was subsequently employed by the Office of Strategic Services (now the CIA). After the war de Lancie joined the Philadelphia Orch. in 1946, serving as its principal oboe (1954–74). In 1977 he was appointed director of the Curtis Inst., succeeding Rudolf Serkin. He retired from this position in 1985. He rapidly advanced to the position of one of the greatest virtuosos on his instrument. An interesting episode in his career concerns his meeting with Richard Strauss, during which he asked Strauss why he would not compose a concerto for oboe, in view of the fact that there are so many beautiful oboe solos in many of his works. This suggestion bore fruit, but he was not the 1st to play it; the 1st performance was given by Marcel Saillet on Feb. 26, 1946, in Zürich. He did, however, commission and give 1st performances of a number of works, including Jean Françaix's *L'Horloge de Flore* and Benjamin Lee's Oboe Concerto.

Delaney, Robert (Mills), American composer; b. Baltimore, July 24, 1903; d. Santa Barbara, Calif., Sept. 21, 1956. He studied music in the U.S., later in Italy, then in Paris (1922–27) with Capet (violin) and Nadia Boulanger and Arthur Honegger (composition). He won the Guggenheim fellowship in 1929; in 1933 he received a Pulitzer Traveling Fellowship for his music to Stephen Vincent Benét's *John Brown's Body*. He then occupied various teaching posts; settled in Santa Barbara.

WORKS: *Don Quixote Symphony* (1927); *John Brown's Song*, choral sym. (1931); *Night* for Chorus, String Orch., and Piano, after William Blake (1934); *Work 22*, overture (1939); Symph. No. 1 (1942); *Western Star* for Chorus and Orch. (1944); 3 string quartets.

Delannoy, Marcel, French composer; b. La Ferté-Alais, July 9, 1898; d. Nantes, Sept. 14, 1962. He served in the French army in World War I; then took lessons with Gédalge and Honegger. After a few years of instruction, he produced an effective stage work, *Poirier de Misère* (Paris, Feb. 21, 1927), which obtained excellent success. Other works are the ballet-cantata *Le Fou de la dame* (concert perf., Paris, Nov. 9, 1928; stage perf., Geneva, April 6, 1929; *Cinderella*, ballet (Chicago, Aug. 30, 1931; rev. as *La Pantoufle de vair*, Paris, May 14, 1935); Sym. (Paris, March 15, 1934); *Ginevra*, comic opera (Paris, July 25, 1942); *Arlequin radiophile*, chamber opera (Paris, April 1, 1946); *Puck*, fairy opera after Shakespeare (Strasbourg, Jan. 29, 1949); *Concerto de mai* for Piano and Orch. (Paris, May 4, 1950); *Travesti*, ballet (Enghien-les-Bains, June 4, 1952); ballet, *Les Noces fantastiques* (Paris, Feb. 9, 1955); Sym. for Strings and Celesta (1952–54); *Le Moulin de la galette*, symphonic poem (1958).

De Lara (real name, **Cohen**), **Isidore,** English composer; b. London, Aug. 9, 1858; d. Paris, Sept. 2, 1935. He began to study the piano at the age of 10 with H. Aguilar; also studied singing with Lamperti and composition with Mazzucato at the Milan Cons. He then went to Paris to study with Lalo; returning to London, he wrote 1 opera after another, and easily secured performances.

WORKS: Operas: *The Light of Asia* (1892); *Amy Robsart* (London, July 20, 1893); *Moina* (Monte Carlo, March 14, 1897); *Messalina* (Monte Carlo, March 21, 1899; his most successful work); *Sanga* (Nice, Feb. 21, 1906); *Solea* (Cologne, Dec. 12, 1907); *Les Trois Masques* (Marseilles, Feb. 24, 1912); *Naïl* (Paris, April 22, 1912); *Les Trois Mousquetaires* (Cannes, March 3, 1921).

DeLay, Dorothy, greatly respected American violin pedagogue; b. Medicine Lodge, Kans., March 31, 1917. Her father was a cellist and her mother a pianist; she attended Oberlin College (1933–34) before pursuing violin studies with Michael Press at Michigan State Univ. (B.A., 1937) and Louis Persinger and Raphael Bronstein at the Juilliard Graduate School of Music in N.Y. (diploma, 1941). She established herself as one of the foremost violin teachers in the world; after working as an assistant to Ivan Galamian, she taught at the Juilliard School of Music (from 1947), Sarah Lawrence College (1948–87), the Meadowmount School of Music in Westport, N.Y. (1948–70), the Aspen Music School (from 1971), the Univ. of Cincinnati College–Cons. of Music (from 1974), the Philadelphia College of the Performing Arts (1977–83), and the New England Cons. of Music in Boston (1978–87); she also conducted master classes all over the world. Among her most celebrated pupils were Itzhak Perlman, Shlomo Mintz, and Cho-Liang Lin.

BIBL.: B. Sand, "D. D.: Teaching Genius," *Musical America* (May 1988).

Delcroix, Léon Charles, Belgian composer; b. Brussels, Sept. 15, 1880; d. there, Nov. 14, 1938. He studied piano with J. Wieniawski, organ with A. Mailly, and composition with Théophile Ysaÿe in Brussels and Vincent d'Indy in Paris. He conducted theater orchs. in Belgium (1909–27); then devoted his entire time to composition. He wrote a biography of J. Wieniawski (Brussels, 1908).

WORKS: Stage: *Ce n'était qu'un rêve* (1 act); *La Bacchante* , ballet (Ghent, 1912); *Le Petit Poucet*, opera (Brussels, Oct. 9, 1913). Orch.: Sym. (won the award of the Belgian Academy); *Le Roi Harald, Çunacépa, Soir d'été à Lerici, Le Val harmonieux; Rapsodie languedocienne; Marche cortège; Sérénade* for Clarinet, Piano, and Orch.; *Elégie et Poème* for Violin and Orch.; many chamber music works (quartets, quintets, sonatas, etc.);

piano works; church music (*Pie Jesu, Resurrexi, Ecce panis*); songs.

Delden, Lex van, prominent Dutch composer; b. Amsterdam, Sept. 10, 1919; d. there, July 1, 1988. He studied medicine at the Univ. of Amsterdam; then turned to music; wrote criticism in Dutch newspapers. In composition, he was entirely autodidact; his extensive output was basically tonal.

WORKS: 3 oratorios: *De Vogel Vrijheid* (The Bird of Freedom; 1955); *Anthropolis* (1962); *Icarus*, radiophonic oratorio, with Tape (1963). Orch.: 8 syms.: No. 1, *De stroom, Mei 1940* (The Torrent, May 1940) for Soprano, Chorus, 8 Instruments, and Percussion (1952; alternate version with orch. scoring, 1954; describes the destruction of Rotterdam at the beginning of World War II); No. 2, *Sinfonia giocosa* (1953); No. 3, *Facetten* (Facets; 1955); No. 4 (1957); No. 5 (1959); No. 6 (1963); No. 7, *Sinfonia concertante*, for 11 Winds (1964); No. 8 for String Orch. (1964); *Allegretto* for Orch. (1949); *Introduction and Allegro*, small concerto for Violin, Piano, and Orch. (1951); Harp Concerto (1951); *In memoriam* (1953); Trio for String Orch. (1954); *Tij en Ontij* (Time and Tide), ballet music (1956); Trumpet Concerto (1956); 2-oboe Concerto (1959); Piano Concerto (1960); *Piccolo Concerto* for 12 Winds and Percussion (1960); Concerto for 2 String Orchs. (1961); *Piccola musica concertata* for 3 Trombones and String Orch. (1963); Flute Concerto (1965); Concerto for Violin, Viola, Double Bass, and Orch. (1965); Concerto for 2 Soprano Saxophones and Orch. (1967); *Musica sinfonica* (1967); Concerto for Percussion, Celesta, and String Orch. (1968); Organ Concerto (1973); *Rubáiyát* for Soprano, Tenor, Chorus, 2 Pianos, and Percussion (1947); *Het spoorboekje* (The Railway Timetable) for Men's Chorus (1952; a setting of a number of sections from the regulations of Dutch railways); *Canto della guerra* for Chorus and Orch. (1967); *Adonias' Dood* (Adonias's Death) for Men's Chorus and Band (1986); songs. Chamber: Suite for Violin and Piano (1939); *Ballet* for Flute, Viola, Bassoon, and Guitar (1946); Piano Sonata (1949); *Introduction and Dance* (*Judith*) for Flute, Clarinet, Violin, Viola, Cello, and Piano (1950); Duo for Flute and Harp (1950); *Small Suite* for 12 Harps (1951; in collaboration with Marius Flothuis); Saxophone Sonatina (1952); 3 string quartets (1954, 1965, 1979); 4 Pieces for Piano (1954); *Impromptu* for Harp (1955); *Sonatina eroica* for Piano (1956); Quartet for Flute, Violin, Viola, and Cello (1957); Solo Cello Sonata (1958); *Intrada and Dance* for 6 Harps (1961); Concertino for 2 Harps (1962); Violin Sonata (1964); Fantasia for Harp and 8 Winds (1965); *Musica notturna a 5* for 4 Cellos and Harp (1967); 2 piano trios (1969, 1988); Quartet for Flute, Oboe, Violin, and Cello (1970); *Sestetto* for 6 Strings (1971); *Quintetto* for Brass Quintet (1981); *Sestetto per Gemelli* for Flute, Oboe, Violin, Viola, Cello, and Piano (1983); *Tomba* for 4 Saxophones (1985).

Deldevez, Edouard(-Marie-Ernest), French conductor and composer; b. Paris, May 31, 1817; d. there, Nov. 6, 1897. He studied violin with Habeneck and music theory with Halévy and Berton at the Paris Cons. He was assistant conductor (1859–73) and then principal conductor (1873–77) at the Paris Opéra; also was assistant conductor (1860–72) and then principal conductor (1872–85) of the Société des Concerts du Conservatoire. He taught orch. playing at the Paris Cons. (1874–85).

WORKS: Ballets: *Eucharis* (1844); *Paquita* (1846); *Vert-Vert* (1851; with Tolbecque); operas: *Samson* and *Le Violon enchanté*; 3 syms.; chamber music; sacred choruses and songs.

WRITINGS: *Curiosités musicales* (1873); *La Notation de la musique classique comparée à la notation de la musique moderne, et de l'exécution des petites notes en général*; *L'Art du chef d'orchestre* (1878); *La Société des Concerts de 1860 à 1885* (1887); *De l'exécution d'ensemble* (1888); *Le Passé à propos du présent* (1892), a continuation of his personal recollections publ. in 1890 as *Mes mémoires*.

BIBL.: C. Malherbe, "Notice sur D.," *Revue Internationale de Musique* (1899).

de Leone, Francesco (Bartolomeo), American conductor, pedagogue, and composer; b. Ravenna, Ohio (of Italian parents), July 28, 1887; d. Akron, Ohio, Dec. 10, 1948. He studied at Dana's Musical Inst., Warren, Ohio (1901–3), and at the Royal Cons. of Naples (1903–10); returned to the U.S. and established his home in Akron, where he founded the de Leone School of Music, and organized and directed the music dept. of the Univ. of Akron; also conducted the Akron Sym. Orch. He wrote the operas *Alglala* (Akron, May 23, 1924); *A Millionaire Caprice* (in Italian; Naples, July 26, 1910); *Cave Man Stuff*, operetta; *Princess Ting-Ah-Ling*, operetta; the sacred musical dramas *Ruth, The Prodigal Son, The Golden Calf*, and *David*; *The Triumph of Joseph*, oratorio; orch.: *6 Italian Dances, Italian Rhapsody, Gibraltar Suite*; over 400 songs; piano pieces.

Delgadillo, Luis (Abraham), Nicaraguan composer; b. Managua, Aug. 26, 1887; d. there, Dec. 20, 1961. He studied at the Milan Cons.; returning to Nicaragua, he became a band conductor and opened a music school, which later became a cons. His music is permeated with native rhythm and melos; virtually all of his output is descriptive of some aspect of Latin American culture and history.

WORKS: Orch.: *Sinfonia indigena* (1921); *Sinfonia mexicana* (1924); *Teotihuacan* (1925); *Sinfonia incaica* (1926; Caracas, May 20, 1927); *Sinfonia serrana* (1928); 12 short syms., all composed in one year (1953) and couched in different styles, from classical to modernistic; overtures in the styles of Debussy and Schoenberg (*Obertura Debussyana* and *Obertura Schoenbergiana*, 1955); 7 string quartets; church music; piano pieces.

Delibes, (Clément-Philibert-)Léo, famous French composer; b. St.-Germain-du-Val, Sarthe, Feb. 21, 1836; d. Paris, Jan. 16, 1891. He received his early musical training with his mother and an uncle; then enrolled in the Paris Cons. in 1847 as a student of Tariot; won a premier prix in solfège in 1850; also studied organ with Benoist and composition with Adam. In 1853 he became organist of St. Pierre de Chaillot and accompanist at the Théâtre-Lyrique. In 1856 his 1st work for the stage, *Deux sous de charbon*, a 1-act operetta, humorously designated an "asphyxie lyrique," was produced at the Folies-Nouvelles. His 2nd work, the opérette bouffe *Deux vieilles gardes*, won considerable acclaim at its premiere at the Bouffes-Parisiens on Aug. 8, 1856. Several more operettas were to follow, as well as his 1st substantial work for the stage, *Le Jardinier et son seigneur*, given at the Théâtre-Lyrique on May 1, 1863. In 1864 he became chorus master of the Paris Opéra. With Louis Minkus, he collaborated on the ballet score *La Source*, which was heard for the 1st time at the Paris Opéra, on Nov. 12, 1866. It was with his next ballet, *Coppélia, ou La Fille aux yeux d'émail*, that Delibes achieved lasting fame after its premiere at the Paris Opéra on May 25, 1870. Another ballet, *Sylvia, ou La Nymphe de Diane* (Paris Opéra, June 14, 1876), was equally successful. He then wrote a grand opera, *Jean de Nivelle* (Opéra-Comique, March 8, 1880), which was moderately successful; it was followed by his triumphant masterpiece, the opera *Lakmé* (Opéra-Comique, April 14, 1883), in which he created a most effective lyric evocation of India; the "Bell Song" from *Lakmé* became a perennial favorite in recitals. In 1881 he was appointed prof. of composition at the Paris Cons.; in 1884, was elected a member of the Inst. His last opera, *Kassya*, was completed but not orchestrated at the time of his death; Massenet orchestrated the score, and it was premiered at the Opéra-Comique on March 24, 1893. Delibes was a master of melodious elegance and harmonious charm; his music possessed an autonomous flow in colorful timbres, and a finality of excellence that seemed effortless while subtly revealing a mastery of the Romantic technique of composition.

WORKS: STAGE (all 1st perf. at the Bouffes-Parisiens in Paris unless otherwise given): *Deux sous de charbon, ou Le Suicide de Bigorneau* (asphyxie lyrique; Folies-Nouvelles, Feb. 9, 1856); *Deux vieilles gardes* (opérette bouffe; Aug. 8, 1856); *Six demoiselles à marier* (opérette bouffe; Nov. 12, 1856); *Maître Griffard* (opéra-comique; Théâtre-Lyrique, Oct. 3, 1857);

La Fille du golfe (opéra-comique; publ. 1859); *L'Omelette à la Follembuche* (opérette bouffe; June 8, 1859); *Monsieur de Bonne-Etoile* (opéra-comique; Feb. 4, 1860); *Les Musiciens de l'orchestre* (opérette bouffe; Jan. 25, 1861; in collaboration with Offenbach, Hignard, and Erlanger); *Les Eaux d'Ems* (comédie; 1861); *Mon ami Pierrot* (operette; 1862); *Le Jardinier et son seigneur* (opéra-comique; Théâtre-Lyrique, May 1, 1863); *La Tradition* (prologue en vers; Jan. 5, 1864); *Grande nouvelle* (opérette; publ. 1864); *Le Serpent à plumes* (farce; Dec. 16, 1864); *Le Bœuf Apis* (opéra bouffe; April 25, 1865); *La Source, ou Naïla* (ballet; Opéra, Nov. 12, 1866; in collaboration with Louis Minkus); *Valse, ou Pas de fleurs* (divertissement; Opéra, Nov. 12, 1867; for Adam's *Le Corsaire*); *Malbrough s'en va-t-en guerre*, Act 4 (opérette bouffe; Athénée, Dec. 13, 1867; Act 1 by Bizet, 2 by E. Jonas, and 3 by Legouix); *L'Écossais de Chatou* (opérette; Jan. 16, 1869); *La Cour du roi Pétaud* (opéra bouffe; Variétés, April 24, 1869); *Coppélia, ou La Fille aux yeux d'émail* (ballet; Opéra, May 25, 1870); *Le Roi l'a dit* (opéra-comique; Opéra-Comique, May 24, 1873); *Sylvia, ou La Nymphe de Diane* (ballet; Opéra, June 14, 1876); *Jean de Nivelle* (opéra; Opéra-Comique, March 8, 1880); *Le Roi s'amuse, six airs de danse dans le style ancien* (incidental music to Hugo's play; Comédie-Française, Nov. 22, 1882); *Lakmé* (opera; Opéra-Comique, April 14, 1883); *Kassya* (drame lyrique; Opéra-Comique, March 24, 1893; orchestrated by Massenet); also sketches for *Le Roi des montagnes* (opéra-comique); 2 works not extant: *Le Don Juan suisse* (opéra bouffe) and *La Princesse Ravigote* (opéra bouffe). He also wrote *Alger* (1865), a cantata, a number of choral works, songs, duets, pieces for organ and piano, etc.

Bibl.: E. Guiraud, *Notice sur la vie et les œuvres de L. D.* (Paris, 1892); H. de Curzon, *L. D.* (Paris, 1926); A. Coquis, *L. D.: Sa vie et son œuvre (1836–1891)* (Paris, 1957); W. Studwell, ed., *Adolphe Adam and L. D.: A Guide to Research* (N.Y., 1987).

DeLio, Thomas, American composer and music theorist; b. N.Y., Jan. 7, 1951. He studied composition at the New England Cons. of Music in Boston (B.M., 1972) and at Brown Univ., where he worked in an interdisciplinary program involving music, mathematics, and visual art (Ph.D., 1979, with the diss. *Structural Pluralism*). He taught at Clark Univ. (1977), the New England Cons. (1977–80), and the Univ. of Maryland (from 1980). He was co-founder and co-ed. of the journal *Sonus* (1980–85); his articles have appeared in various other art and music journals. His research focuses on open structures and mathematical concepts in composition. As a composer, he has created live electronic sound installations and computer-aided compositions; among his works are *Text* for Piano (1985), *Against the silence . . .* for Percussion and Tape (1985), and *contrecoup . . .* for Chamber Ensemble (1989). He publ. *Circumscribing the Open Universe* (Lanham, Md., 1983), and ed. *Contiguous Lines: Issues and Ideas in the Music of the '60s and '70s* (Lanham, Md., 1985).

Delius, Frederick (baptized, **Fritz Theodor Albert**), significant English composer of German parentage; b. Bradford, Jan. 29, 1862; d. Grez-sur-Loing, France, June 10, 1934. His father was a successful merchant, owner of a wool company; he naturally hoped to have his son follow a career in industry, but did not object to his study of art and music. Delius learned to play the piano and violin. At the age of 22 he went to Solano, Fla., to work on an orange plantation owned by his father; a musical souvenir of his sojourn there was his symphonic suite *Florida*. There he met an American organist, Thomas F. Ward, who gave him a thorough instruction in music theory; this study, which lasted 6 months, gave Delius a foundation for his further progress in music. In 1885 he went to Danville, Va., as a teacher. In 1886 he enrolled at the Leipzig Cons., where he took courses in harmony and counterpoint with Reinecke, Sitt, and Jadassohn. It was there that he met Grieg, becoming his friend and admirer. Indeed Grieg's music found a deep resonance in his own compositions. An even more powerful influence was Wagner, whose princi-

ples of continuous melodic line and thematic development Delius adopted in his own works. Euphonious serenity reigns on the symphonic surface of his music, diversified by occasional resolvable dissonances. In some works he made congenial use of English folk motifs, often in elaborate variation forms. Particularly successful are his evocative symphonic sketches *On Hearing the 1st Cuckoo in Spring, North Country Sketches, Brigg Fair, A Song of the High Hills*, etc. His orch. nocturne *Paris: The Song of a Great City* is a tribute to a city in which he spent many years of his life. Much more ambitious in scope is his choral work *A Mass of Life*, in which he draws on passages from Nietzsche's *Also sprach Zarathustra*.

Delius settled in Paris in 1888; in 1897 he moved to Grez-sur-Loing, near Paris, where he remained for the rest of his life, except for a few short trips abroad. In 1903 he married the painter Jelka Rosen. His music began to win recognition in England and Germany; he became a favorite composer of Sir Thomas Beecham, who gave numerous performances of his music in London. But these successes came too late for Delius; a syphilitic infection which he had contracted early in life eventually grew into an incurable illness accompanied by paralysis and blindness; as Beecham phrased it, "Delius had suffered a heavy blow in the defection of his favorite goddess, Aphrodite Pandemos, who had returned his devotions with an affliction which was to break out many years later." Still eager to compose, he engaged as his amanuensis the English musician Eric Fenby, who wrote down music at the dictation of Delius, including complete orch. scores. In 1929, Beecham organized a Delius Festival in London (6 concerts; Oct. 12 to Nov. 1, 1929), and the composer was brought from France to hear it. In the same year Delius was made Companion of Honour by King George V and an Hon.Mus.D. by Oxford. A motion picture was made by the British filmmaker Ken Russell on the life and works of Delius. However, he remains a solitary figure in modern music. Affectionately appreciated in England, in America, and to some extent in Germany, his works are rarely performed elsewhere.

Works: stage: *Zanoni*, incidental music after Bulwer Lytton (1888; unfinished); *Irmelin*, opera (1890–92; Oxford, May 4, 1953); *The Magic Foundation*, lyric drama (1893–95; BBC, London, Nov. 20, 1977); *Koanga*, lyric drama (1895–97; Elberfeld, March 30, 1904); *Folkeraadet*, incidental music to G. Heiberg's drama (Christiania, Oct. 18, 1897); *A Village Romeo and Juliet*, lyric drama (1899–1901; Berlin, Feb. 21, 1907); *Margot la Rouge*, lyric drama (1902; concert perf. BBC, London, Feb. 21, 1982; stage perf., St. Louis, June 8, 1983); *Fennimore and Gerda*, opera (1908–10; Frankfurt am Main, Oct. 21, 1919); *Hassan, or The Golden Journey to Samarkand*, incidental music to J. Flecker's drama (1920–23; Darmstadt, June 1, 1923; full version, London, Sept. 20, 1923).

orch.: *Florida*, suite (1887; private perf., Leipzig, 1888; rev. 1889; public perf., London, April 1, 1937); *Hiawatha*, tone poem (1888; unfinished; excerpt, Norwegian Television, Oslo, Jan. 13, 1984); *Suite* for Violin and Orch. (1888; BBC, London, Feb. 28, 1984); *Rhapsodic Variations* (1888; unfinished); *Idylle de Printemps* (1889); *Suite d'orchestre* (1889); *3 Small Tone Poems: Summer Evening, Winter Night [Sleigh Ride]*, and *Spring Morning* (1889–90; Westminster, Nov. 18, 1946); *Légendes* for Piano and Orch. (1890; unfinished); *Petite suite d'orchestre for Small Orch.* (1890; Stratford-upon-Avon, May 13, 1978); *Paa vidderne* (On the Heights), symphonic poem after Ibsen (1890–91; Christiania, Oct. 10, 1891); *Légende* for Violin and Orch. (1895?; London, May 30, 1899); *Over the Hills and Far Away*, fantasy overture (1895–97; Elberfeld, Nov. 13,1897); *Appalachia: American Rhapsody* (1896; London, Dec. 10, 1986; rev. as *Appalachia: Variations on an Old Slave Song* for Baritone, Chorus, and Orch.; 1902–3; Elberfeld, Oct. 15, 1904); Piano Concerto in C minor (1st version in 3 movements, 1897; Elberfeld, Oct. 24, 1904; 2nd version in 1 movement, 1906; London, Oct. 22, 1907); *La Ronde se déroule*, symphonic poem after H. Rode (London, May 30, 1899; rev. 1901, as *Lebenstanz* [Life's Dance]; Düsseldorf, Jan. 21, 1904; 2nd rev., 1912; Berlin, Nov. 15, 1912); *Paris: A Nocturne* (The Song of a Great City) (1899; Elberfeld, Dec. 14, 1901); *Brigg Fair: An English Rhapsody* (Basel, 1907); *In a Summer Garden*, rhapsody (London, Dec. 11, 1908; rev., Boston, April 19, 1912); *A Dance Rhapsody*, No. 1 (1908; Hereford, Sept. 8, 1909); 2 *Pieces* for Small Orch: *On Hearing the 1st Cuckoo in Spring* (1912) and *Summer Night on the River* (1911; Leipzig, Oct. 23, 1913); *North Country Sketches* (1913–14; London, May 10, 1915); *Air and Dance* for Strings (private perf., London, 1915; public perf., London, Oct. 16, 1929); *Double Concerto for Violin, Cello, and Orch.* (1915–16; London, Feb. 21, 1920); *Violin Concerto* (1916; London, Jan. 30, 1919); *A Dance Rhapsody*, No. 2 (1916; London, Oct. 20, 1923); *Eventyr* (Once upon a Time), ballad after Asbjørnsen (1917; London, Jan. 11, 1919); *A Song before Sunrise* for Small Orch. (1918; London, Sept. 19, 1923); *Poem of Life and Love* (1918); *Cello Concerto* (1920–21; Frankfurt am Main, Jan. 30, 1921); *A Song of Summer* (1929–30; London, Sept. 7, 1931); *Caprice and Elegy* for Cello and Chamber Orch. (1930); *Irmelin Prelude* (1931; London, Sept. 23, 1935); *Fantastic Dance* (1931; London, Jan. 12, 1934).

VOCAL: *6 German Partsongs* for Chorus (1885–87); *Paa vidderne* (On the Heights) for Reciter and Orch., after Ibsen (1888; Norwegian Television, Oslo, May 17, 1983); *Sakuntala* for Tenor and Orch. (1889); *Twilight Fancies* for Voice and Piano (1889; orchestrated 1908; Liverpool, March 21, 1908); *The Bird's Story* for Voice and Piano (1889; orchestrated 1908; Liverpool, March 21, 1908); *Maud*, 5 songs for Tenor and Orch., after Tennyson (1891); *2 Songs* for Voice and Orch. or Piano (1897; 5 songs, London, March 30, 1899; 2 songs, Paris, March 16, 1901); *Mitternachtslied Zarathustras* for Baritone, Men's Chorus, and Orch., after Nietzsche (1898; London, May 30, 1899); *The Violet* for Voice and Piano (1900; orchestrated 1908; Liverpool, March 21, 1908); *Summer Landscape* for Voice and Piano (1902; orchestrated 1903); *Appalachia: Variations on an Old Slave Song* for Baritone, Chorus, and Orch. (1902–3; Elberfeld, Oct. 15, 1904; rev. of *Appalachia: American Rhapsody* for Orch., 1896; London, Dec. 10, 1986); *Sea Drift* for Baritone, Chorus, and Orch., after Whitman (1903–4; Essen, May 24, 1906); *A Mass of Life* for Soprano, Alto, Tenor, Baritone, Chorus, and Orch., after Nietzsche's *Also sprach Zarathustra* (1904–5; partial perf., Munich, June 4, 1908; complete perf., London, June 7, 1909); *Songs of Sunset* for Mezzo-soprano, Baritone, Chorus, and Orch., after E. Dowson (1906–7; London, June 16, 1911); *On Craig Ddu* for Chorus (1907; Blackpool, 1910); *Wanderer's Song* for Men's Chorus (1908); *Midsummer Song* for Chorus (1908); *La Lune blanche* for Voice and Orch. or Piano, after Verlaine (1910); *An Arabesque* for Baritone, Chorus, and Orch. (1911; Newport, Monmouthshire, May 28, 1920); *The Song of the High Hills* for Wordless Chorus and Orch. (1911–12; London, Feb. 26, 1920); *2 Songs for Children* (1913); *I-Brasîl* for Voice and Orch. or Piano (1913; Westminster, Nov. 21, 1946); *Requiem* for Soprano, Baritone, Chorus, and Orch. (1913–14; London, March 23, 1922); *To Be Sung of a Summer Night on the Water*, 2 songs for Wordless Chorus (1917; London, June 28, 1921); *The splendour falls on castle walls* for Chorus, after Tennyson (1923; London, June 17, 1924); *A Late Lark* for Tenor and Orch. (1924, 1929; London, Oct. 12, 1929); *Cynara* for Baritone and Orch. (1907, 1929; London, Oct. 18, 1929); *Songs of Farewell* for Chorus and Orch., after Whitman (1920?, 1930; London, March 21, 1932); *Idyll: Once I passed through a populous city* for Soprano, Baritone, and Orch., after Whitman (1932; London, Oct. 3, 1933; based on *Margot la Rouge*). **SOLO SONGS:** *Over the Mountains High* (1885); *Zwei braune Augen* (1885); *Der Fichtenbaum* (1886); *5 Songs from the Norwegian: Slumber Song, The Nightingale, Summer Eve, Longing,* and *Sunset* (1888); *Hochgebirgsleben* (1888); *O schneller, mein Ross* (1888); *Chanson de Fortunio* (1889); *7 Songs from the Norwegian: Cradle Song, The Homeward Journey, Evening Voices, Sweet Venevil, Minstrel, Love Concealed,* and *The Bird's Story* (1889–90; Nos. 3 and 7 orchestrated); *Skogen gir susende, langsom besked* (1890–91); *4 Songs*, after Heine: *Mit deinen blauen Augen, Ein schöner Stern, Hör' ich das Liedchen klingen,* and *Aus deinen Augen*

(1890–91); *3 Songs*, after Shelley: *Indian Love Song, Love's Philosophy,* and *To the Queen of My Heart* (1891); *Lyse Naetter* (1891); *Jeg havde en nyskaare Seljefløjte* (1892–93); *Nuages* (1893); *2 Songs*, after Verlaine: *Il pleure dans mon coeur* and *Le ciel est, par-dessus le toit* (1895; also orchestrated); *The page sat in the lofty tower* (1895?); *7 Danish Songs: Summer Nights, Through Long, Long Years, Wine Roses, Let Springtime Come, Irmelin Rose, In the Seraglio Garden,* and *Silken Shoes* (1896–97; also orchestrated); *Traum Rosen* (1898?); *Im Glück wir lachend gingen* (1898?); *4 Songs*, after Nietzsche: *Nach neuen Meeren, Der Wanderer, Der Einsame,* and *Der Wanderer und sein Schatten* (1898); *The Violet* (1900; also orchestrated); *Autumn* (1900); *Black Roses* (1901); *Jeg hører i Natten* (1901); *Summer Landscape* (1902; also orchestrated); *The nightingale has a lyre of gold* (1910); *La Lune blanche*, after Verlaine (1910; also orchestrated); *Chanson d'automne*, after Verlaine (1911); *I-Brasîl* (1913; also orchestrated); *4 Old English Lyrics: It was a lover and his lass, So white, so soft is she, Spring, the sweet spring,* and *To Daffodile* (1915–16); *Avant que tu ne t'en ailles*, after Verlaine (1919, 1932).

CHAMBER: 2 string quartets: No. 1 (1888; unfinished); No. 2 (original version in 3 movements, London, Nov. 17, 1916; rev. version in 4 movements, London, Feb. 1, 1919); *Romance* for Violin and Piano (1889); *Violin Sonata in B major* (1892; private perf., Paris, 1893); *Violin Sonata No. 1* (1905, 1914; Manchester, Feb. 24, 1915); *Violin Sonata No. 2* (1923; London, Oct. 7, 1924); *Violin Sonata No. 3* (London, Nov. 6, 1930); *Romance* for Cello and Piano (1896; Helsinki, June 22, 1976); *Cello Sonata* (1916; London, Oct. 31, 1918); *Dance* for Harpsichord (1919).

PIANO: *Zum Carnival Polka* (1885); *Pensées mélodieuses* (1885); *Valse* and *Rêverie* (1889–90; unfinished); *Badinage* (1895?); *5 Pieces* (1922–23); *3 Preludes* (1923; London, Sept. 4, 1924).

BIBL.: P. Heseltine, *F. D.* (London, 1923; 2nd ed., rev., 1952); R. Hull, *F. D.* (London, 1928); E. Blom, "D. and America," *Musical Quarterly* (July 1929); C. Delius, *F. D., Memories of My Brother* (London, 1935); E. Fenby, *D. as I Knew Him* (London, 1936; 3rd ed., 1966); A. Hutchings, *D., A Critical Biography* (London, 1948); T. Beecham, *F. D.* (London, 1959; 2nd ed., rev., 1975); G. Jahoda, *The Road to Samarkand: F. D. and His Music* (N.Y., 1969); E. Fenby, *D.* (London, 1971); W. Randel, "F. D. in America," *Virginia Magazine of History & Biography* (July 1971); L. Carley and R. Threlfall, *D. and America* (London, 1972); A. Jefferson, *D.* (London, 1972); R. Lowe, *F. D., 1862–1934; A Catalogue of the Music Archives of the D. Trust, London* (London, 1974); L. Carley, *D.: The Paris Years* (London, 1975); C. Palmer, *D.: Portrait of a Cosmopolitan* (London, 1976); C. Redwood, ed., *A D. Companion* (London, 1976); L. Carley and R. Threlfall, *D.: A Life in Pictures* (London, 1977); R. Threlfall, *A Catalogue of the Compositions of F. D.* (London, 1977); D. Redwood, *Flecker and D.: The Making of "Hassan"* (London, 1978); L. Carley, *D.: A Life in Pictures:* vol. I, *1862–1908* (London, 1983; Cambridge, Mass., 1984) and vol. II, *1909–1934* (Aldershot, 1988); *D. 1862–1934* (50th anniversary brochure by the D. Trust, London, 1984); R. Threlfall, *F. D.: A Supplementary Catalogue* (London, 1986).

Della Casa, Lisa, noted Swiss soprano; b. Burgdorf, Feb. 2, 1919. She commenced vocal studies with Margarete Haeser in Zürich when she was 15; made her operatic debut as Cio-Cio-San in Solothurn-Biel (1941), then was a member of the Zürich Stadttheater (1943–50). She made her 1st appearance at the Salzburg Festival as Zdenka in 1947, then appeared as the Countess in *Le nozze di Figaro* at the Glyndebourne Festival in 1951. That same year she sang Sophie and Arabella, her most celebrated portrayal, in Munich. She subsequently was a leading member of the Vienna State Opera (1952–74). She made her Metropolitan Opera debut in N.Y. as Mozart's Countess on Nov. 20, 1953, and continued to sing there with distinction until 1968; she was chosen to sing the role of the Marschallin at the opening of the new Salzburg Festspielhaus

(1960). She was held in great esteem for her remarkable portrayals of roles in operas by Mozart and Richard Strauss.

BIBL.: D. Debeljević, *Ein Leben mit L. d. C.* (1975).

Della Ciaia, Azzolino Bernardino, Italian organist, organ builder, and composer; b. Siena, March 21, 1671; d. Pisa, Jan. 15, 1755. He constructed a large organ with 4 manuals and 100 stops for the St. Stephen Church in Pisa. He publ. *Salmi concertati* for 4 Voices, with Instruments (Bologna, 1700); *Cantate da camera* (Lucca, 1701); *Sonate per cembalo* (Rome, 1727). Much of his church music is extant in MS. He is regarded by some as an Italian originator of the sonata form; his instrumental music, however, is more interesting for its florid ornamentation than for strict formal development.

BIBL.: F. Torrefranca, "L'impressionismo ritmico e le sonate del D. C.," *Rivista dei Amici della Musica in Milano* (1913); F. Baggiani, *L'organo di A.B. D. C.* (Pisa, 1974).

Della Corte, Andrea, eminent Italian musicologist; b. Naples, April 5, 1883; d. Turin, March 12, 1968. He was self-taught in music; devoted himself mainly to musical biography and analysis. He taught music history at the Turin Cons. (1926–53) and at the Univ. of Turin (1939–53). From 1919 till 1967 he was music critic of *La Stampa.* He also ed. song textbooks for Italian Schools.

WRITINGS: *Paisiello* (Turin, 1922); *Saggi di critica musicale* (Turin, 1922); *L'opera comica italiana del 1700* (2 vols., Bari, 1923); *Piccola antologia settecentesca, XXIV pezzi inediti o rari* (Milan, 1925); *Disegno storico dell'arte musicale* (Turin, 5th ed., 1950); with G. Gatti, *Dizionario di musica* (1926; 6th ed., 1959); *Antologia della storia della musica* (2 vols., Turin, 1927–29; 4th ed., 1945); *Niccolò Piccinni* (Bari, 1928); *Scelta di musiche per lo studio della storia* (Milan, 3rd ed., 1949); *La vita musicale di Goethe* (Turin, 1932); with G. Pannain, *Storia della musica* (Turin, 1936; 4th ed., 1964); with G. Pannain, *Vincenzo Bellini* (Turin, 1936); *Ritratto di Franco Alfano* (Turin, 1936); *Pergolesi* (Turin, 1936); *Un Italiano all'estero: Antonio Salieri* (Turin, 1937); *Tre secoli di opera italiana* (Turin, 1938); *Verdi* (Turin, 1939); *Toscanini* (Vicenza, 1946; in French, Lausanne, 1949); *Satire e grotteschi di musiche e di musicisti d'ogni tempo* (Turin, 1947); *Le sei più belle opere di Verdi: Rigoletto, Il Trovatore, La Traviata, Aida, Otello, Falstaff* (Milan, 1947); *Gluck* (Florence, 1948); *Baldassare Galuppi* (Siena, 1949); *Arrigo Serato* (Siena, 1949); *L'interpretazione musicale e gli interpreti* (Turin, 1951).

Della Maria, (Pierre-Antoine-)Dominique, French opera composer; b. Marseilles, June 14, 1769; d. Paris, March 9, 1800. Son of an Italian mandolinist, he was remarkably precocious; played the mandolin and cello at an early age, and at 18 produced a grand opera at Marseilles. He then studied composition in Italy (for a time with Paisiello) and produced in Naples a successful opera, *Il maestro di cappella* (1792). He went to Paris in 1796; obtaining a libretto (*Le Prisonnier*) from Duval, he set it to music in 8 days, brought it out at the Opéra-Comique (Jan. 29, 1798), and was at once famous. Before his death he finished 6 more operas, 4 of which were produced during his lifetime; a posthumous opera, *La Fausse Duègne* (completed by Blangini), was produced at Paris in 1802; several church compositions.

Della Valle, Pietro, Italian man of letters and composer, known as "Il Pellegrino"; b. Rome, April 11, 1586; d. there, April 21, 1652. He studied harpsichord with Stefano Tavolaccio, Quinzio Solini, and Paolo Quagliati; counterpoint, continuo playing, and theorbo with Solini; and viola da gamba with Marco Fraticelli. After extended travel abroad (1614–26), he returned to Rome, becoming a significant figure in the cultural life of the city, and publ. an account of his adventures as *Viaggi descritti in 54 lettere famigliari* (4 vols., Rome, 1650–58). Almost all of his music is lost, but his valuable *Della musica dell'età nostra che non è punto inferiore, anzi è migliore di quella dell'età* (Jan. 16, 1640) may be found in A. Gori, *G.B. Doni: Trattati di musica,* II (Florence, 1763).

BIBL.: V. Losito, *P. d. V.* (Varese, 1928); A. Ziino, "P. d. V.

e la 'musica erudita': Nuovi documenti," *Analecta Musicologica,* no. 4 (1967).

Deller, Alfred (George), English countertenor; b. Margate, May 31, 1912; d. Bologna, July 16, 1979. He studied voice with his father; began singing as a boy soprano, later developing the alto range. He sang in the choirs of the Canterbury Cathedral (1940–47) and at St. Paul's in London. In 1950 he formed his own vocal and instrumental ensemble, the Deller Consort, acting as conductor and soloist in a repertoire of old English music. This unique enterprise led to a modest revival of English madrigals of the Renaissance. In 1963 he founded the Stour Music Festival in Kent. Britten wrote the part of Oberon in his *A Midsummer Night's Dream* for Deller. In 1970 Deller was named a Commander of the Order of the British Empire.

BIBL.: M. and M. Hardwick, *A. D.: A Singularity of Voice* (London, 1968; 2nd ed., rev., 1982).

Delle Sedie, Enrico, Italian baritone and singing teacher; b. Livorno, June 17, 1822; d. La Garennes-Colombes, near Paris, Nov. 28, 1907. His teachers were Galeffi, Persanola, and Domeniconi. After imprisonment as a revolutionist (1848), he resumed the study of singing and made his debut in San Casciano (1851) in Verdi's *Nabucco.* Until 1861 he sang in the principal Italian cities; appeared in London in 1861; was then engaged at the Théâtre-Italien, Paris, and was prof. of singing in the Cons. (1867–71); was regarded as one of the best singing teachers in Paris. His basic manuals, *Arte e fisiologia del canto* (Milan, 1876; in French as *L'Art lyrique,* Paris, 1876) and *L'estetica del canto e dell'arte melodrammatica* (Milan, 1886), were publ. in N.Y. in Eng. as *Vocal Art* (3 parts) and *Esthetics of the Art of Singing, and of the Melodrama* (4 vols.). A condensation (by the author) of both manuals was publ. in 1 vol. as *A Complete Method of Singing* (N.Y., 1894).

Dellinger, Rudolf, German composer and conductor; b. Graslitz, Bohemia, July 8, 1857; d. Dresden, Sept. 24, 1910. He was a pupil at the Prague Cons.; played clarinet in the city orch. at Brünn; became 2nd conductor there in 1880; in 1883, occupied the same post at the Carl Schulze Theater in Hamburg; from 1893 till his death, was conductor at the Residenz-Theater in Dresden. He produced the operettas *Don Caesar* (Hamburg, March 28, 1885; highly popular), *Lorraine* (Hamburg, 1886), *Capitän Fracassa* (Hamburg, 1889), *Saint-Cyr* (Hamburg, 1891), *Die Chansonnette* (Dresden, 1894; Prague, 1895, as *Die Sängerin*), *Jadwiga* (Dresden, 1901), and *Der letzte Jonas* (1910).

Dello Joio, Norman, able American composer of pleasurable music; b. N.Y., Jan. 24, 1913, of an Italian-American family whose original surname was Ioio. His father, his grandfather, and his great-grandfather were church organists. Dello Joio acquired skill as an organist and pianist at home; at the age of 12 he occasionally substituted for his father on his job at the Church of Our Lady of Mount Carmel in Manhattan. He took additional organ lessons from his well-known godfather, **Pietro Yon,** and studied piano with Gaston Déthier at the Inst. of Musical Art (1933–38); in the meantime he played jazz piano in various groups in N.Y. From 1939 to 1941 he studied composition with Bernard Wagenaar at the Juilliard School of Music; in 1941 he enrolled in the summer class of composition led by Hindemith at the Berkshire Music Center in Tanglewood; he continued to attend Hindemith's courses at Yale Univ. from 1941 to 1943. During this period he wrote several works of considerable validity, among them a piano trio, a ballet entitled *The Duke of Sacramento,* a Magnificat, a piano sonata, and other pieces. He taught composition at Sarah Lawrence College (1945–50); held 2 consecutive Guggenheim fellowships (1944, 1945); and composed music with utmost facility and ingratiating felicity. His *Concert Music* was played by the Pittsburgh Sym., conducted by Fritz Reiner, on Jan. 4, 1946, and his *Ricercari* for Piano and Orch. was introduced by the N.Y. Phil. on Dec. 19, 1946, with George Szell conducting, and the piano part played by Dello Joio himself. There followed a number of major works in a distinctive Joioan manner, some of them deeply rooted in medieval ecclesiasticism, profoundly liturgical, and yet overtly modern in their neo-modal moderately dissonant counterpoint. He also exhibited a flair for writing on topical American themes, ranging from impressions of the Cloisters in N.Y. to rhythmic modalities of Little Italy. On May 9, 1950, at Sarah Lawrence College, where he taught, he produced his 1st opera, *The Triumph of St. Joan;* he later used its thematic material in a sym. in 3 movements, *The Triumph of St. Joan,* originally titled *Seraphic Dialogue.* He then wrote another opera on the subject of St. Joan, to his own libretto, *The Trial of Rouen,* 1st performed on television, by the NBC Opera Theater, April 8, 1956; still another version of the St. Joan theme was an opera in which Dello Joio returned to the original title, *The Triumph of St. Joan,* but composed the music anew; it had its production at the N.Y. City Opera on April 16, 1959. In 1957 Dello Joio received the Pulitzer Prize for his *Meditations on Ecclesiastes,* scored for string orch.; it was 1st performed in Washington, on Dec. 17, 1957, but the material was used previously for a ballet, *There Is a Time.* In 1961 he produced an opera, *Blood Moon,* brought out by the San Francisco Opera, to a scenario dealing with the life and times of an adventurous actress, Adah Menken, who exercised her charms in New Orleans at the time of the Civil War. Returning to liturgical themes, Dello Joio composed three masses, in 1968, 1975, and 1976. He continued his activities as a teacher; from 1956 to 1972 he was on the faculty of the Mannes College of Music in N.Y.; from 1972 to 1979 he taught at Boston Univ. In 1964 he traveled to Rumania, Bulgaria, and the Soviet Union under the auspices of the Cultural Program of the State Dept. He held honorary doctorates in music from Lawrence College in Wisconsin (1959), Colby College in Maine (1963), and the Univ. of Cincinnati (1969). On Feb. 16, 1958, he was the subject of a CBS television documentary titled "Profile of a Composer." He received the N.Y. Music Critics' Award twice, in 1947 and 1959.

WORKS: STAGE: Operas on the subject of St. Joan: *The Triumph of St. Joan* (Bronxville, N.Y., May 9, 1950); *The Trial at Rouen* (NBC-TV Opera Theater, April 8, 1956); *The Triumph of St. Joan,* a new version of the St. Joan theme, bearing the title of the original work (N.Y. City Opera, April 16, 1959; received a N.Y. Music Critics' Circle Award). Other operas: *The Ruby* (Bloomington, Ind., May 13, 1955); *Blood Moon* (San Francisco, Sept. 18, 1961).

DANCE: *The Duke of Sacramento* (1942); *Diversion of Angels,* dance by Martha Graham (New London, Conn., Aug. 13, 1948); *Seraphic Dialogue,* choreographed by Martha Graham (Louisville, Ky., Dec. 5, 1951; material taken from *The Triumph of St. Joan Symphony*).

ORCH.: Sinfonietta (1940); Concerto for 2 Pianos and Orch. (1941); *Magnificat* (1942); *To a Lone Sentry* for Chamber Orch. (1943); *On Stage* (Cleveland, Nov. 23, 1945); *Concert Music* (Pittsburgh, Jan. 4, 1946); *Ricercari* for Piano and Orch. (N.Y., Dec. 19, 1946); Harp Concerto (N.Y., Oct. 20, 1947); *Variations, Chaconne and Finale* (originally titled *3 Symphonic Dances;* Pittsburgh, Jan. 30, 1948); *Concertato* for Clarinet and Orch. (Chautauqua, May 22, 1949); *Serenade* (Cleveland, Oct. 20, 1949); *New York Profiles* (La Jolla, Calif., Aug. 21, 1949); *The Triumph of St. Joan Symphony* (Louisville, Dec. 5, 1951); *Epigraph* (Denver, Jan. 29, 1952); *Meditations on Ecclesiastes* for String Orch. (Washington, D.C., Dec. 17, 1957; received the Pulitzer Prize); *Air Power,* suite (1957); *Anthony and Cleopatra* for Chamber Group (1960); *Fantasy and Variations* for Piano and Orch. (Cincinnati, March 9, 1962); *Variants on a Medieval Tune* (Duke Univ., May 8, 1963); *From Every Horizon* for Band (1964); *Antiphonal Fantasy on a Theme of Vincenzo Albrici,* dedicated to the memory of Hindemith (1966); *5 Images* (1967); *Homage to Haydn* (Little Rock, Ark., June 3, 1969); *Songs of Abélard* for Band (1969; earlier version titled *A Time of Snow*); *Satiric Dances for a Comedy by Aristophanes* for Band (Concord, Mass., July 17, 1975); *Colonial Variants* (Philadelphia, May 27, 1976); *Ballabili* (1981); *East Hampton Sketches* for Strings (1983); *Variants on a Bach Chorale* (1985).

CHAMBER: Quartet for Bassoons (1937); Sextet for 3 Recorders, Violin, Viola, and Cello (1941); *Fantasia on a Gregorian Theme* for Violin and Piano (1943); Trio for Flute, Cello, and Piano (N.Y., March 1, 1944); *Duo concertante* for Cello and Piano (1945); *Variations and Capriccio* for Violin and Piano (1948); *Colloquies* for Violin and Piano (1964); *Developing Flutist* for Flute and Piano (1972); 3 Essays for Clarinet and Piano (1974); *Lyric Fantasies* for Viola, String Quartet, and Double Bass (1973); String Quartet (1974); Trumpet Sonata (1979).

PIANO: 3 sonatas (1933, 1943, 1948); *Aria and Toccata* for 2 Pianos (1952); *Family Album* for Piano, 4-hands (1962); *Capriccio on the Interval of a Second* (1969); *Lyric Pieces for the Young* (1971); *Diversions* (1975); *Concert Variations* (1980); *Short Intervallic Etudes* (1986).

VOCAL: 3 masses: Mass for Chorus, Brass, and Organ (1968); Mass in Honor of the Blessed Virgin Mary (Washington, Dec. 8, 1975); Mass in Honor of the Eucharist for Chorus, Brass, Strings, and Organ (1976); *The Mystic Trumpeter,* cantata after Walt Whitman (1943); *The Assassination* for Low Voice and Piano (1947); *Song of Affirmation,* symphonic cantata (1952); *Song of the Open Road* for Chorus, Trumpet, and Piano, after Walt Whitman (1952); *The Lamentation of Saul* for Baritone and Orch. (1954); *As of a Dream* for Narrator, Chorus, and Orch., after Walt Whitman (Midland, Mich., May 18, 1979); *Love Songs at Parting* (Indianapolis, Nov. 7, 1982); *Nativity* for Soloists, Chorus, and Orch. (1987).

BIBL.: T. Bumgardner, *N. D. J.* (Boston, 1986).

Dell'Orefice, Giuseppe, Italian composer; b. Fara, Abruzzio Chietino, Aug. 22, 1848; d. Naples, Jan. 3, 1889. He was a pupil of Fenaroli and Miceli at the Naples Cons.; from 1878, was conductor at the San Carlo Theater in Naples; wrote the ballet *I fantasmi notturni* (Naples, 1872) and the operas *Romilda de' Bardi* (Naples, 1874), *Egmont* (Naples, 1878), *Il segreto della Duchesa* (Naples, 1879), and *L'oasi* (Vicenza, 1886); also songs and piano pieces.

Delmar, Dezso, Hungarian-American composer; b. Timișoara, July 14, 1891; d. Contra Costa Co., Calif., Oct. 20, 1985. He studied piano with Béla Bartók and theory with Kodály at the Royal Academy of Music in Budapest, graduating in 1913; concurrently took courses in jurisprudence, obtaining a law degree. He served in the Austro-Hungarian army in World War I; after demobilization, devoted himself entirely to music. He went to the U.S. in 1922; lived in N.Y. until 1929, then moved to Los Angeles; in 1946 settled in Sacramento as a teacher of piano and theory. His works include a Sym. (1949); *Hungarian Sketches* for Orch. (1947); 3 string quartets, String Trio, Violin Sonata, etc.; choral music; many piano pieces and songs. His works reflect the melorhythmic modalities of Hungarian folk music.

Del Mar, Norman (René), English conductor, teacher, and writer on music; b. London, July 31, 1919. He studied composition with R.O. Morris and Vaughan Williams at the Royal College of Music in London; also played the violin and the horn in the student orch. He then took lessons in conducting with Constant Lambert. During World War II he played in the Royal Air Force bands and visited the U.S. with the Royal Air Force Sym. in 1944. That same year he organized the Chelsea Sym. Orch. in London; in 1948 he conducted the Sadler's Wells Ballet during its tour in Germany. He was principal conductor of the English Opera Group from 1949 to 1955; was conductor and prof. at the Guildhall School of Music (1953–60); then conducted the BBC Scottish Sym. (1960–65), the Göteborg (Sweden) Sym. (1969–73), and the Chamber Orch. of the Royal Academy of Music (1973–77). In 1972 he was appointed instructor in conducting at the Royal College of Music. In 1975 he was made a Commander of the Order of the British Empire. From 1982 to 1985 he was principal guest conductor of the Bournemouth Sinfonietta; then was artistic director of the Århus Sym. Orch. (1985–88). He publ. several valuable books: *Paul Hindemith* (London, 1957); *Richard Strauss, A Critical Commentary of His Life and Works* (3 vols., London, 1962, 1968, 1972); *Modern Music and the Conductor* (London, 1960); *Anatomy of the Orchestra* (London, 1981); *A Companion to the Orchestra* (London, 1987).

Delmas, Jean-François, famous French bass-baritone; b. Lyons, April 14, 1861; d. St. Alban de Monthel, Sept. 29, 1933. He was a pupil of Bussine and Obin at the Paris Cons., where he won 1st prize for singing in 1886; made his debut at the Opéra in 1886, as St.-Bris in *Les Huguenots;* then was a regular member of the Opéra, idolized by the public, and unexcelled as an interpreter of Wagner, in whose works he created the principal bass parts in several French premieres; he created also the chief roles in Massenet's *Le Mage* (1891) and *Thaïs* (1894), Leroux's *Astarté* (1901), Saint-Saëns's *Les Barbares* (1901), Erlanger's *Le Fils de l'étoile* (1904), etc.; besides an enormous French repertoire, he also sang in the operas of Gluck, Mozart, and Weber.

Delmas, Marc-Jean-Baptiste, talented French composer; b. St. Quentin, March 28, 1885; d. Paris, Nov. 30, 1931. He was a pupil of Vidal and Leroux; won the Prix de Rossini (1911), the Grand Prix de Rome (1919), the Chartier Prix for chamber music, the Prix Cressent, and other awards for various compositions. He also wrote the books *G. Bizet* (Paris, 1930) and *G. Charpentier et le lyrisme française* (1931).

Works: operas: *Jean de Calais* (1907); *Laïs* (1909); *Stéfano* (1910); *Cyrce* (1920; perf. 1927); *Iriam* (1921); *Anne-Marie* (1922); *Le Giaour* (1925). **orch.:** *Les Deux Routes* (1913); *Au pays wallon* (1914); *Le Poète et la fée* (1920); *Le Bateau ivre* (1923); *Penthésilée* (1922); *Rapsodie ariégeoise* for Cello and Orch.; chamber music; piano pieces.

Del Monaco, Mario, powerful Italian tenor; b. Florence, July 27, 1915; d. Mestre, near Venice, Oct. 16, 1982. His father was a government functionary, but his mother loved music and actually sang. Del Monaco haunted provincial opera theaters, determined to be a singer; indeed, he was allowed to sing a minor part in a theater at Mondolfo, near Pesaro, when he was only 13. Rather than take regular voice lessons, he listened to operatic recordings; at 19 he entered the Rossini Cons. in Pesaro, but left it after an unhappy semester of academic vocal training with unimaginative teachers. In 1935 he won a prize in a singing contest in Rome. In 1939 he made his operatic debut as Turriddu in Pesaro. On Jan. 1, 1941, he made his Milan debut as Pinkerton in *Madama Butterfly,* but had to serve time out in the Italian army during the war. After the war's end, he developed a busy career singing opera in a number of Italian theaters, including La Scala of Milan. In 1946 he sang at the Teatro Colón in Buenos Aires, and also in Rio de Janeiro and Mexico City. On Sept. 26, 1950, he sang the role of Radames in *Aida* at the San Francisco Opera; on Nov. 27, 1950, he made his Metropolitan Opera debut in N.Y. as Des Grieux in *Manon Lescaut;* he continued to sing at the Metropolitan until 1958 in virtually every famous tenor part, as Don José in *Carmen,* Manrico in *Il Trovatore,* Cavaradossi in *Tosca,* Canio in *Pagliacci,* etc. On Nov. 16, 1954, he scored considerable success in the role of Andrea Chénier. He sang 102 times at the Metropolitan and appeared in its tours 38 times. Numerically, the maximum of his appearances in the same role was as Otello, which he sang at various opera theaters 427 times. In 1973 he deemed it prudent to retire, and he spent the rest of his life in a villa near Venice, devoting his leisure to his favorite avocations, sculpture and painting. Unlike most Italian tenors, who tend to grow corpulent with success, Del Monaco managed to preserve his lean, slender figure, which ensured his mobility on the stage and enabled him to honor the Italian operatic tradition of scurrying to the footlights at the approach of the high C. So energetic was he at climactic scenes that he nearly broke the wrist of Risë Stevens when he threw her down in the last act of *Carmen.* Del Monaco was buried in his Otello costume, while the funeral hymns were intoned in his own voice on a phonograph record.

Delna (real name, **Ledan**), **Marie,** French contralto; b. Meudon, near Paris, April 3, 1875; d. Paris, July 23, 1932. She made her debut at the Opéra-Comique, June 9, 1892, as Dido in Berlioz's *Les Troyens;* sang there for 6 years with great success; from 1898 to 1901 was at the Paris Opéra; then again at the Opéra-Comique until in 1903 she married a Belgian, A.H. de Saone, and retired temporarily from the stage; her reappearance at the Opéra-Comique in 1908 was acclaimed with great applause; after that she was a prime favorite. On March 5, 1910, she sang Orfeo (in Gluck's opera) at the Metropolitan Opera in N.Y. and later Marcelline in Bruneau's *L'Attaque du moulin* at the New Theater, making a deep impression; then returned to Paris, where she continued to sing at the Opéra-Comique until her retirement in 1922.

Delogu, Gaetano, Italian conductor; b. Messina, April 14, 1934. He studied violin as a child, but began his university education as a law student. He then decided upon a musical career; studied conducting with Franco Ferrara. In 1964 he won 1st prize at the Florence Young Conductors' Competition. In 1968 he won 1st prize in the Mitropoulos Competition in N.Y. He then embarked upon an international career, conducting many of the major orchs. of Europe and the U.S. He was conductor at the Teatro Massimo in Palermo (1975–78) and from 1979 to 1986 he was music director of the Denver Sym. Orch.

Del Tredici, David (Walter), remarkable American composer; b. Cloverdale, Calif., March 16, 1937. He studied piano, and made his debut as a soloist with the San Francisco Sym. at the age of 16; then enrolled at the Univ. of Calif. in Berkeley, studying composition with Seymour Shifrin, Andrew Imbrie, and Arnold Elston (B.A., 1959). He undertook additional studies at Princeton Univ., where his teachers were Earl Kim and Roger Sessions (M.F.A., 1963). He also continued his pianistic practice, taking private lessons with Robert Helps in N.Y. During the summers of 1964 and 1965 he served as pianist at the Berkshire Music Center in Tanglewood. In 1966 he received a Guggenheim fellowship award; in 1966–67 he was resident composer at the Marlboro Festival in Vermont. From 1966 to 1972 he was assistant prof. of music at Harvard Univ.; in 1973 he joined the music faculty at Boston Univ. In 1984 he began teaching at City College and Graduate School of the City Univ. of N.Y. While thus retained by pedagogy, he composed avidly. Fascinated by the creation of new literary forms and the novel language of James Joyce, he wrote the work *I Hear an Army,* based on a Joyce poem, scored for soprano and string quartet, which was performed at Tanglewood on Aug. 12, 1964, and immediately caught the fancy of the cloistered but influential cognoscenti, literati, and illuminati; another significant Joyce poem set by Del Tredici was *Night Conjure-Verse* for Soprano, Mezzo-soprano, Woodwind Septet, and String Quartet, which he conducted in San Francisco on March 5, 1966. Yet another work inspired by the verbal music of James Joyce was *Syzygy* for Soprano, Horn, Bells, Drums, and Chamber Orch., performed in N.Y. on July 6, 1968. For these works, he plied a modified dodecaphonic course in a polyrhythmic context, gravid with meaningful pauses without fear of triadic encounters. But Del Tredici achieved rare fame with a series of brilliant tone pictures after *Alice in Wonderland* by Lewis Carroll, in which he projected, in utter defiance of all modernistic conventions, overt tonal proclamations, fanfares, and pretty tunes that were almost embarrassingly attractive, becoming melodiouser and harmoniouser with each consequent tone portrait of Alice. And in a couple of the *Alice* pieces he disarmingly attached a personal signature, the vocal countdown of 13, his last name Tredici, in Italian. In 1980 he received the Pulitzer Prize in Music for his score *In Memory of a Summer Day.* In 1984 he was elected a member of the Inst. of the American Academy and Inst. of Arts and Letters. From 1988 to 1990 he was composer-in-residence of the N.Y. Phil.

Works: *4 Songs* for Voice and Piano, after James Joyce (1958–60; Berkeley, Calif., March 1, 1961); *Soliloquy* for Piano (1958); String Trio (1959; Berkeley, Calif., March 1, 1961); *2 Songs,* after Joyce (1959; rev. 1978; Washington, D.C., Feb. 11, 1983); *Fantasy Pieces* for Piano (1959–60); *Scherzo* for

Piano, 4-hands (1960); *I Hear an Army* for Soprano and String Quartet, after Joyce (1963–64; Tanglewood, Aug. 12, 1964); *Night Conjure-Verse* for Soprano, Mezzo-soprano or Contralto, and Chamber Ensemble, after Joyce (1965; San Francisco, March 5, 1966); *Syzygy* for Soprano, Horn, and Chamber Ensemble, after Joyce (1966; N.Y., July 6, 1968); *The Last Gospel* for Soprano, Chorus, Rock Group, and Orch. (1967; San Francisco, June 15, 1968; rev. 1984); *Pop-pourri* for Amplified Soprano, Contralto or Mezzo-soprano ad libitum, Chorus, Rock Group, and Orch. (La Jolla, Calif., July 28, 1968; rev. 1973); *An Alice Symphony*, after Lewis Carroll (1, *Speak Gently/Speak Roughly*; 2, *The Lobster Quadrille*; 3, *'Tis the Voice of the Sluggard*; 4, *Who Stole the Tarts?*; 5, *Dream Conclusion*; 2, London, Nov. 14, 1969; 1, 4, and 5 as *Illustrated Alice*, San Francisco, Aug. 8, 1976; 2, 3, and 5 as *In Wonderland*, Aspen, Colo., July 29, 1975); *Adventures Underground*, after Carroll (1971; Buffalo, N.Y., April 13, 1975; rev. 1977); *Vintage Alice: Fantascene on A Mad Tea Party* for Amplified Soprano, Folk Group, and Orch., after Carroll (Saratoga, Calif., Aug. 5, 1972); *Final Alice* for Amplified Soprano, Folk Group, and Orch., after Carroll (Chicago, Oct. 7, 1976); *Child Alice* for Amplified Soprano and Orch., after Carroll (1977–81; 1, *In Memory of a Summer Day*, St. Louis, Feb. 23, 1980; 2, *Quaint Events*, Buffalo, Nov. 19, 1981, *Happy Voices*, San Francisco, Sept. 16, 1980, and *All in the Golden Afternoon*, Philadelphia, May 8, 1981); *March to Tonality* for Orch. (1983–85; Chicago, June 13, 1985); *Haddock's Eyes* for Soprano and Chamber Ensemble (1985–86; N.Y., May 2, 1986); *Steps* for Orch. (1990).

De Luca, Giuseppe, Italian baritone; b. Rome, Dec. 25, 1876; d. N.Y., Aug. 26, 1950. He studied music with Vinceslao Persichini at the Accademia di Santa Cecilia in Rome; made his 1st professional appearance in Piacenza (Nov. 6, 1897) as Valentine in *Faust;* then sang in various cities of Italy; from 1902, was chiefly in Milan at the Teatro Lirico, and from 1903 at La Scala; he created the principal baritone role in the world premieres of *Adriana Lecouvreur* and *Madama Butterfly.* He made his American debut at the Metropolitan Opera in N.Y. as Figaro in *Il barbiere di Siviglia* on Nov. 25, 1915, with excellent success, immediately establishing himself as a favorite; on Jan. 28, 1916, he sang the part of Paquiro in the world premiere of *Goyescas* by Granados, at the Metropolitan, of which he was a member until 1935; after a sojourn in Italy, he returned to the U.S. in 1940, and made a few more appearances at the Metropolitan, his vocal powers undiminished by age; he made his farewell appearance in a concert in N.Y. in 1947. He sang almost exclusively the Italian repertoire; his interpretations were distinguished by fidelity to the dramatic import of his roles; he was praised by the critics for his finely graduated dynamic range and his mastery of *bel canto.*

De Lucia, Fernando, famous Italian tenor; b. Naples, Oct. 11, 1860; d. there, Feb. 21, 1925. He made his debut in Naples on March 9, 1885, as Faust; then appeared in London at Drury Lane (1887); on Oct. 31, 1891, he created in Rome the role of Fritz in Mascagni's *L'Amico Fritz;* on Jan. 10, 1894, he made his American debut at the Metropolitan Opera in N.Y., again as Fritz in Mascagni's opera; then returned to Europe. He retired from the stage in 1917; sang for the last time in public at Caruso's funeral (1921). De Lucia was one of the finest representatives of the *bel canto* era; he was especially praised for his authentic interpretations of Italian operatic roles, excelling in operas by Rossini, Bellini, and Verdi.

Delune, Louis, Belgian composer; b. Charleroi, March 15, 1876; d. Paris, Jan. 5, 1940. He studied with Tinel at the Brussels Cons.; won the Belgian Prix de Rome with his cantata *La Mort du roi Reynaud* (1905); then traveled as accompanist for César Thomson. He lived many years in Paris, and wrote most of his works there; composed *Symphonie chevaleresque;* the opera *Tania;* a ballet, *Le Fruit défendu;* Piano Concerto; violin pieces; etc.

Delvaux, Albert, Belgian composer; b. Louvain, May 31, 1913. He studied 1st at the Cons. in Louvain and completed his studies with Joseph Leroy at the Liège Cons. He won a 3rd prize (1957, for *Esquisses*) and a 1st prize (1961, for *Sinfonia burlesca*) in the Queen Elisabeth International Composition Competition in Brussels.

WORKS: ORCH.: *Héro et Léandre* for Soloists, Chorus, and Orch. (1941); *5 Pieces* for String Orch. (1942); *Scherzo* (1942); *Symphonic Poem* (1943); *Symphonic Suite* (1948); Symphonic Variations (1948); *Sinfonietta* (1952); Concerto for Cello and Chamber Orch. (1957); *Concerto da camera* for Chamber Orch. (1957); *Sinfonia burlesca* (1960); *5 Bagatelles* for Chamber Orch. (1960); *Miniatures* (1960); 2 violin concertos (1961, 1974); *Sinfonia concertante* for Violin, Viola, and Strings (1963); *Mouvement symphonique* (1966); Concerto for Flute, Oboe, Clarinet, Bassoon, and Chamber Orch. (1967); *Sinfonia* (1969); Concerto for Violin, Cello, and Strings (1970); *Introduction et Allegro* for Strings (1971); *Divertimento* for Strings (1981); Concerto for Viola and Chamber Orch. (1984); *Sinfonia in Sol* (1986); *Capriccio* (1988). **CHAMBER:** 2 string trios (1939, 1961); Sonata for Flute, Oboe, Clarinet, and Bassoon (1940); 4 string quartets (1943, 1945, 1955, 1961); Trio for Oboe, Clarinet, and Bassoon (1948); Oboe Sonatina (1956); *5 Impromptus* for Flute, Oboe, Clarinet, and Piano (1959); Violin Sonata (1962); *Sonata a 4* for 4 Clarinets, or Flute, Oboe, Clarinet, and Bassoon (1964); *Walliser Suite* for Wind Quintet (1966); *Cassazione* for Violin, Oboe, Clarinet, and Cello (1966); *Andante e Scherzando* for Violin and Piano (1972); Saxophone Quartet (1982); Duo for Clarinets (1987); also choruses and songs.

Delvincourt, Claude, outstanding French composer; b. Paris, Jan. 12, 1888; d. in an automobile accident in Orbetello, province of Grosseto, Italy, April 5, 1954. He studied with Boëllmann, Busser, Caussade, and Widor at the Paris Cons.; in 1913 received the Prix de Rome for his cantata *Faust et Hélène* (sharing the prize with Lili Boulanger). He was in the French army in World War I, and on Dec. 31, 1915, suffered a crippling wound. He recovered in a few years, and devoted himself energetically to musical education and composition. In 1931 he became director of the Cons. of Versailles; in 1941 he was appointed director of the Paris Cons. His music is distinguished by strong dramatic and lyric quality; he was most successful in his stage works.

WORKS: *Offrande à Siva,* choreographic poem (Frankfurt, July 3, 1927); *La Femme à barbe,* musical farce (Versailles, June 2, 1938); *Lucifer,* mystery play (Paris Opéra, Dec. 8, 1948); 2 orch. suites from the film score *La Croisière jaune: Pamir* (Paris, Dec. 8, 1935) and *Films d'Asie* (Paris, Jan. 16, 1937). He also wrote *Ce monde de rosée* for Voice and Orch. (Paris, March 25, 1935); some chamber music (Trio for Oboe, Clarinet, and Bassoon; Violin Sonata; etc.); piano pieces. **BIBL.:** W.L. Landowski, *L'Œuvre de C. D.* (Paris, 1947).

Delz, Christoph, Swiss-born German composer and pianist; b. Basel, Jan. 3, 1950. He began studies in performance and counterpoint early, completing a concert pianist diploma before finishing school. He then studied with Stockhausen (composition), Aloys Kontarsky (piano), and Volker Wangenheim (conducting) in Cologne at the Musikhochschule (1974–81). His compositions involve musical collage, theatrical gestures, eclectically combined styles, and revolutionary agendas, and have been performed at ISCM World Music Days in Cologne, Paris, Donaueschingen, Venice, and London. In 1983 he received the Music Prize of the City of Cologne.

WORKS: Piano Quartet (1975–76; Bonn, Nov. 25, 1977); *Kölner Messe* for Tape and Chorus (1977–81; Cologne, Nov. 4, 1983); *Im Dschungel, Ehrung für Rousseau den Zöllner* for Large Orch. (1981–82; Donaueschingen, Oct. 16, 1983); String Quartet (1982; Witten, April 28, 1985); *Arbeitslieder* for Soli, Chorus, Piano, and Wind Quintet (1983–84; Venice, Nov. 23, 1985); Piano Concerto (1984–85; London, Feb. 22, 1986).

De Main, John (Lee), American conductor; b. Youngstown, Ohio, Jan. 11, 1944. He studied piano with Adele Marcus at the Juilliard School of Music in N.Y. (B.M., 1966) and conducting there with Jorge Mester (M.S., 1968). He served as associate conductor of the St. Paul Chamber Orch. (1972–74); from 1974 to 1976 was music director of the Texas Opera Theater; in 1979 he assumed the post of music director of the Houston Grand Opera, and from 1983 concurrently conducted the opera company in Omaha.

Demantius, (Johannes) Christoph, German composer; b. Reichenberg, Dec. 15, 1567; d. Freiberg, Saxony, April 20, 1643. He became cantor at Zittau in 1597; was at Freiberg from 1604 to 1643; as a prolific composer of sacred and secular music, he ranks with Hassler, M. and H. Prätorius, and Eccard. He wrote *Deutsche Passion, nach dem Evangelisten S. Iohanne* (1631; ed. and publ. by F. Blume, 1934); *Triades precum vespertinarum* (1602); etc. He was the author of an instruction book, *Isagoge artis musicae* (Nuremberg, 1605; 10th ed., 1671).

DeMarinis, Paul, American composer; b. Cleveland, Oct. 6, 1948. He was educated at Antioch (Ohio) College (B.A., 1971) and Mills College in Oakland, Calif., where he studied with Robert Ashley (M.F.A., 1973) and subsequently taught composition and computer art (1973–78). He also taught at Wesleyan Univ. (1979–81) and San Francisco State Univ. (1987–89), and was a sound designer for Atari video games (1982–84). As a performer, he has appeared solo and in collaboration with such artists as Ashley and David Tudor in venues including the Kitchen (N.Y.), Festival d'Automne (Paris), and New Music America (1980, 1981, 1982, 1985). He is best known for his performance works, computer/sound installations, and interactive electronic inventions. His computer audio-graphics systems have been installed at the Museum of Contemporary Art in Chicago and at the Wadsworth Athenaeum; he has also created permanent audio installations at the Exploratorium in San Francisco and at the Boston Children's Museum. Much of his recent work, such as *Kokole* (1985) and *I Want You* (1986), involves computer-processed speech. Among his installations are *Pygmy Gamelan* (Paris, N.Y., Los Angeles, 1976–80), *Music Room/Faultless Jamming* (San Francisco, Boston, 1982–), and *Laser Disk* (Eindhoven, Netherlands, 1989).

Demarquez, Suzanne, French composer; b. Paris, July 5, 1899; d. there, Oct. 23, 1965. She studied at the Paris Cons.; composed chamber music, including a sprightly *Sonatine* for Flute and Piano (1953). She publ. *André Jolivet* (Paris, 1958); *Manuel de Falla* (Paris, 1963; in Eng., Philadelphia, 1968); *Hector Berlioz* (Paris, 1969).

Demény, Desiderius, Hungarian composer; b. Budapest, Jan. 29, 1871; d. there, Nov. 9, 1937. He was a pupil of V. Herzfeld and S. von Bacho; was ordained as a priest at Gran in 1893; became court chaplain (1897); on 3 different occasions he won the Géza Zichy Prize (with *Ungarische Tanzsuite, Festouvertüre,* and *Rhapsodie*); in 1902 he founded *Zeneközlöny,* an important Hungarian music journal.
Works: 8 masses; *Hungarian Suite* for Mixed Chorus; *Scherzo* for Male Chorus; *2 Bilder aus Algier; Serenata sinfonica;* operetta, *Der sieghafte Tod;* several melodramas; many other choral and vocal works, including about 100 songs (most to German texts).

Demessieux, Jeanne, French organist; b. Montpellier, Feb. 14, 1921; d. Paris, Nov. 11, 1968. At the age of 12 she played organ at the church of St.-Esprit; she studied at the Paris Cons. with Tagliaferro, Jean and Noël Gallon, and Dupré; won premiers prix in harmony (1937), piano (1938), and fugue and counterpoint (1940). She gave her 1st public recital in Paris in 1946; then toured widely in Europe; made her 1st highly successful visit to the U.S. in 1953. In 1952 she became a prof. at the Liège Cons.; also served as organist at the Madeleine from 1962. She possessed a phenomenal technique and was regarded as one of the most brilliant improvisers on the organ.

Demian, Wilhelm, Rumanian composer and conductor; b. Brasov, June 22, 1910. He studied music in his hometown (1925–28); then in Vienna (1929–33); from 1935 to 1940 conducted the Phil. in Cluj; after 1949 was conductor of the Hungarian State Opera there. His music is marked by a distinct

neo-classical idiom in the manner of the modern German school. Among his works are an opera, *Capcana* (1964); Sym. (1947); Piano Concertino (1953); Violin Concerto (1956); *Liberté,* cantata (1957); Oboe Concerto (1963); musical, *Attention! On tourne!* (1972).

De Mol, Pierre, Belgian composer; b. Brussels, Nov. 7, 1825; d. Alost, July 2, 1899. He was a pupil at the Brussels Cons.; took the Grand Prix de Rome (1855); was 1st cellist at the Besançon Theater and a teacher at the Cons.; later was director of the Cons. at Alost.
Works: 3 cantatas: *Les Chrétiens Martyrs; Le Dernier Jour d'Herculaneum; La Fête de Belsazar;* oratorio, *St. Cecilia;* Mass; 12 string quartets; opera, *Quentin Metsys.*

Demougeot, (Jeanne Marguerite) Marcelle (Decorne), remarkable French soprano; b. Dijon, June 18, 1871; d. Paris, Nov. 24, 1931. She studied in Dijon and Paris; made her operatic debut at the Paris Opéra in 1902 as Donna Elvira in *Don Giovanni;* continued to sing there until 1925. She was one of the foremost French Wagnerian sopranos of her time, noted for her fine renditions as Brünnhilde, Elisabeth, Kundry, and Venus.

Dempster, Stuart (Ross), American trombonist and composer; b. Berkeley, Calif., July 7, 1936. He studied at San Francisco State College (B.A. in perf., 1958; M.A. in composition, 1967) and also had private trombone instruction from A.B. Moore, Orlando Giosi, and John Klock. He taught at the San Francisco Cons. of Music (1961–66) and at California State College at Hayward (1963–66); in 1968 he joined the faculty of the Univ. of Washington in Seattle. He received a Fulbright-Hays Award as a senior scholar in Australia (1973) and a Guggenheim fellowship (1981). His interests also include non-Western instruments, especially the Australian didjeridu. He publ. the study *The Modern Trombone: A Definition of Its Idioms* (Berkeley, Calif., 1979).
Works: 5 pieces for Brass Quintet (1957–59); Sonata for Bass Trombone and Piano (1961); *Adagio and Canonic Variations* for Brass Quintet (1962); *Chamber Music 12* for Voice and Trombones (1964); *The Road Not Taken* for Voice, Chorus, and Orch. (1967); *10 Grand Hosery,* mixed media ballet (1971–72); *Life Begins at 40,* concert series and musical gallery show (1976); *Didjeridervish* for Didjeridu (1981; in collaboration with Bill Fontana); *Hornfinder* for Trombone and Audience (1982); *Aix en Providence* for Multiple Trombones (1983); *JDBBBDJ* for Didjeridu and Audience (1983); *Sound Massage Parlor* for Didjeridu, Garden Hoses, Shell, and Audience (1986); *SWAMI* (State of Washington as a Musical Instrument), performance piece for the state of Washington centennial (1987–89).

Demus, Jörg (Wolfgang), noted Austrian pianist; b. St. Polten, Dec. 2, 1928. At the age of 11 he entered the Vienna Academy of Music; also took lessons in conducting with Swarowsky and Krips and in composition with Joseph Marx; continued his piano studies with Gieseking at the Saarbrücken Cons.; then worked with Kempff, Benedetti Michelangeli, Edwin Fischer, and Yves Nat. He made his debut as a concert pianist at the age of 14 in Vienna; made his London debut in 1950; then toured South America (1951). In 1956 he won the Busoni prize of the International Competition for Pianists. Apart from his solo recitals, he distinguished himself as a lieder accompanist to Dietrich Fischer-Dieskau and other prominent singers. Demus assembled a large collection of historic keyboard instruments; publ. a book of essays, *Abenteuer der Interpretation,* and, with Paul Badura-Skoda, an analysis of Beethoven's piano sonatas. In 1977 he was awarded the Beethoven Ring and in 1979 the Mozart Medal of Vienna.

Demuth (real name, **Pokorný**), **Leopold,** esteemed Austrian baritone; b. Brünn, Nov. 2, 1861; d. while giving a concert in Czernowitz, March 4, 1910. He studied with Joseph Gänsbacher in Vienna; made his debut in 1889 in Halle as Hans Heiling; sang in Leipzig (1891–95) and Hamburg (1895–97); then joined the Vienna Court Opera, remaining on its roster until his death; he also sang at Bayreuth (1899), where he gained recognition as a fine Wagnerian singer.

Demuth, Norman, English composer and writer on music; b. London, July 15, 1898; d. Chichester, April 21, 1968. He studied with Parratt and Dunhill at the Royal College of Music in London; played organ in London churches. Later he became a choral conductor; in 1930, became a prof. of composition at the Royal Academy of Music. His works are influenced mainly by French music; in later years he became better known as the author of many books and unorthodox essays on music.
WORKS: 5 syms. (2 of which are entitled *Symphonic Study*); *Threnody* for Strings (1942); *Overture for a Joyful Occasion* (1946); Violin Concerto (1937); Saxophone Concerto (1938); Piano Concerto (1943); Piano Concerto for the Left Hand (1947); 3 violin sonatas; Cello Sonata; Flute Sonata; many piano pieces.
WRITINGS (all publ. in London except the last): *The Gramophone and How to Use It* (1945); *Albert Roussel* (1947); *Ravel*, in the Master Musicians Series (1947); *An Anthology of Musical Criticism* (1948); *César Franck* (1949); *Paul Dukas* (1949); *The Symphony: Its History and Development* (1950); *Gounod* (1950); *Vincent d'Indy* (1951); *A Course in Musical Composition* (1951); *Musical Trends in the 20th Century* (1952); *Musical Forms and Textures* (1953); *French Piano Music: A Survey with Notes on Its Performance* (1959); *French Opera: Its Development to the Revolution* (Sussex, 1963).

Dencke, Jeremiah, American Moravian minister, organist, and composer; b. Langenbilau, Silesia, Oct. 2, 1725; d. Bethlehem, Pa., May 28, 1795. In 1748 he became organist at Herrnhut, the center of the European Moravians; came to America (1761) and served the Moravian settlements in Pennsylvania in various capacities. During the Revolutionary War he was warden of the Bethlehem congregation. Dencke was apparently the 1st individual to compose vocal concerted church music in the Moravian settlements in Pennsylvania, and possibly the 1st to write such music in colonial America. He was an able composer. The earliest work he is known to have composed in America is a simple anthem for chorus, strings, and figured bass, written for a *Liebesmahl* ("love feast," a service of spiritual devotion and earthly fraternalism, composed of hymn singing and a light meal of a roll and beverage) on Aug. 29, 1765. His finest works are 3 sets of sacred songs for soprano, strings, and organ, composed in 1767–68. The 1st, written for the annual festival of the "choir" of small girls, is included in the 1st vol. of the series Music of the Moravians in America, issued by the N.Y. Public Library in 1938. The other sets of solos were written for Christmas services. Dencke's compositions are listed in A.G. Rau and H.T. David, *A Catalogue of Music by American Moravians, 1742–1842, from the Archives of the Moravian Church at Bethlehem, Pa.* (Bethlehem, Pa., 1938).
BIBL.: H.T. David, "Musical Life in the Pennsylvania Settlements of the *Unitas Fratrum,*" *Transactions of the Moravian Historical Society* (1942; reprinted as Moravian Music Foundation Publication No. 6, Winston-Salem, N.C., 1959); "Recent Discoveries in the Foundation Archives," *Moravian Music Foundation Bulletin* (Spring–Summer 1974).

Denéréaz, Alexandre, Swiss composer and musicologist; b. Lausanne, July 31, 1875; d. there, July 25, 1947. He studied at the Lausanne Cons. with Blanchet and at the Dresden Cons. with Draeseke and Döring; in 1896 was appointed a prof. at the Lausanne Cons.; also taught musicology at Lausanne Univ.; publ. an original theory of harmony. He was the author, in collaboration with C. Bourguès, of *La Musique et la vie intérieure: Histoire psychologique de l'art musical* (appendix entitled *L'Arbre généalogique de l'art musical;* 1919).
WORKS: 3 syms.; many symphonic poems; cantatas; Concerto Grosso for Orch. and Organ; string quartets; organ works; a male chorus; music to René Morax's *La Dîme.*

Dengremont, Maurice, Brazilian violinist; b. Rio de Janeiro, March 19, 1866, of French parents; d. Buenos Aires, Sept.

1893. As a child prodigy, he attracted general notice in Europe in 1877, but his early death did not allow him to develop his gifts.

Denis, Didier, French composer; b. Paris, Nov. 5, 1947. He studied at the Paris Cons. with Henri Challan, Marcel Bitsch, Olivier Messiaen, and Jean Rivier, graduating in 1968.
WORKS: Trio for Flute, Clarinet, and Bassoon (1966); *Sagesse, Force, Beauté, l'Amour* for Coloratura Soprano, 12 Instruments, and 6 Percussion Instruments (1967); *Cinq fois je t'aime* for Speaker, Soprano, and Orch. (1968); *Fugue indoue* for 2 groups of Percussion Instruments (1968); *Chants de Tse Yeh* for Piano and 12 Instruments (1969); *Puzzle* for Voice, Spanish Guitar, and Percussion (1970).

Denisov, Edison, remarkable, innovative Russian composer; b. Tomsk, April 6, 1929. He was named after Thomas Alva Edison by his father, an electrical engineer; another aspect in so naming him was that the surname Denisov is anagrammatic with Edison, leaving out the last letter. He studied mathematics at the Univ. of Moscow, graduating in 1951, and composition at the Moscow Cons. with Shebalin (1951–56). In 1959 he was appointed to the faculty of the Cons. An astute explorer of tonal possibilities, Denisov writes instrumental works of an empirical genre; typical of these is *Crescendo e diminuendo* for Harpsichord and 12 String Instruments, composed in 1965, with the score written partly in graphic notation. The titles of his pieces reveal a lyric character of subtle nuances, often marked by impressionistic colors: *Aquarelle, Silhouettes, Peinture, La Vie en rouge, Signes en blanc, Nuages noires.*
WORKS: STAGE: Opera, *Soldier Ivan* (1959); *L'Écume des jours,* lyric drama (1981); *Confession,* ballet after Alfred de Musset (1984). ORCH.: Sym. in C (1955); *Sinfonietta on Tadzhik Themes* (1957); *Peinture* (Graz, Oct. 30, 1970); Cello Concerto (Leipzig, Sept. 25, 1973); Flute Concerto (Dresden, May 22, 1976); Violin Concerto (Milan, July 18, 1978); Piano Concerto (Leipzig, Sept. 5, 1978); *Partita* for Violin and Orch. (Moscow, March 23, 1981); Concerto for Bassoon, Cello, and Orch. (1982; Venice, Sept. 24, 1984); *Tod ist ein langer Schlaf,* variations on a theme by Haydn, for Cello and Orch. (Moscow, May 30, 1982); Chamber Sym. (Paris, March 7, 1983); *Epitaphe* for Chamber Orch. (Reggio Emilia, Italy, Sept. 11, 1983); *Colin et Chloé,* suite from the opera *L'Écume des jours* (Moscow, Oct. 17, 1983). CHAMBER: Sonata for 2 Violins (1958); *Musique* for 11 Wind Instruments and Timpani (Leningrad, Nov. 15, 1965); String Quartet No. 2 (1961); Violin Sonata (1963); *Crescendo e diminuendo* for Harpsichord and 12 String Instruments (Zagreb, May 14, 1967); *Ode in Memory of Ché Guevara* for Clarinet, Piano, and Percussion (Moscow, Jan. 22, 1968); *Musique romantique* for Oboe, Harp, and String Trio (Zagreb, May 16, 1969); *3 Pieces* for Cello and Piano (1969); String Trio (1969); *D-S-C-H,* a monogram for Shostakovich (1969); Wind Quintet (1969); *Silhouettes* for Flute, 2 Pianos, and Percussion (1969); *Chant des oiseaux* for Prepared Piano and Tape (1969); Sonata for Alto Saxophone and Piano (1970); Piano Trio (1971); Cello Sonata (1971); *Solo per flauto* (1971); *Solo per oboe* (1971); *Canon in Memory of Igor Stravinsky* for Flute, Clarinet, and Harp (1971); Sonata for Clarinet Solo (1972); *3 Pieces* for Harpsichord and Percussion (1972); *2 Pieces* for Alto Saxophone and Piano (1974); *Choral varié* for Trombone and Piano (1975); *Aquarelle* for 24 String Instruments (1975); *4 Pieces* for Flute and Piano (1977); *Concerto piccolo* for 4 Saxophones and 6 Percussionists (Bordeaux, April 28, 1979); Sonata for Flute and Guitar (1977); Sonata for Solo Violin (1978); Concerto for Guitar Solo (1981); Trio for Oboe, Cello, and Harpsichord (1981); Sonata for Bassoon Solo (1982); Sonata for Violin and Organ (1982); *Musique de chambre* for Viola, Harpsichord, and Strings (1982); 5 études for Bassoon Solo (1983); Sonata for Flute and Harp (1983); *Es ist genug,* variations for Viola and Piano on a theme of Bach (1984); *Diane dans le vent d'automne* for Viola, Vibraphone, Piano, and Double Bass (1984). VOCAL: *Canti di Catulli* for Bass and 3 Trombones (1962); *Soleil des Incas* for Soprano and Instrumental Ensemble, to poems by Gabriela Mistral (Leningrad,

Nov. 30, 1964); *Chansons italiennes* for Soprano, Flute, Horn, Violin, and Harpsichord (1966); *Pleurs* for Soprano, Piano, and Percussion, on texts from Russian folk songs (1966); *5 Geschichten vom Herrn Keuner* for Tenor and 7 Instruments, to Brecht's poems (1968); *Automne,* 13 poems to surrealist vocables by Khlebnikov (1969); 2 songs for Soprano and Piano, to poems by Bunin (1970); *Chant d'automne* for Soprano and Orch., to poems by Baudelaire (Zagreb, May 16, 1971); *La Vie en rouge* for Voice, Flute, Clarinet, Violin, Cello, and Piano (1973); *Requiem* for Soprano, Tenor, Chorus, and Orch. (Hamburg, Oct. 30, 1980); *Colin et Chloé,* suite from the opera *L'Ecume des jours,* for Soloists, Chorus, and Orch. (1981); *Lumière et ombres* for Bass and Piano, to poems by Vladimir Soloviev (1982); *Ton image charmante* for Voice and Orch., to words by Pushkin (1982); *Venue du printemps* for Chorus a cappella (1984). PIANO: *Variations* (1961); *3 Pieces* for Piano, 4-hands (1967); *Signes en blanc* (1974); also *Feuilles mortes* for Harpsichord. ORCHESTRATIONS: Mussorgsky: *Nursery Songs, Sunless,* and *Songs and Dances of Death;* Mossolov: *Advertisements,* arranged for Voice and Orch.; also several Schubert dances.

Dennée, Charles (Frederick), American pianist and pedagogue; b. Oswego, N.Y., Sept. 1, 1863; d. Boston, April 29, 1946. At the New England Cons. of Music in Boston he studied piano with A.D. Turner and composition with S.A. Emery; also studied piano with Hans von Bülow during von Bülow's last visit to the U.S. (1889–90); in 1883 he was appointed a teacher of piano at the New England Cons. of Music; an accident to his right wrist caused his retirement in 1897, after he had played almost 1,100 recitals; subsequent devotion to teaching was fruitful, for many of his pupils held prominent positions on the faculties of various conservatories and music colleges. He was among the 1st to give illustrated lecture-recitals in the U.S. A selection of his essays was publ. as *Musical Journeys* (Brookline, Mass., 1938). Some of his teaching pieces achieved steady popularity with piano students; he also publ. a manual, *Progressive Technique.*

Denny, William D(ouglas), American composer and pedagogue; b. Seattle, July 2, 1910; d. Berkeley, Calif., Sept. 2, 1980. He studied at the Univ. of Calif., Berkeley (A.B., 1931; M.A., 1933); after graduation he went to Paris, where he took lessons with Paul Dukas at the École Normale de Musique. He returned to the U.S. in 1935, and taught at Vassar and Harvard. In 1945 he was appointed to the faculty of his alma mater in Berkeley, where he remained until his retirement in 1978. His compositions are marked by a strong contrapuntal texture, with the fugal element much in evidence.
WORKS: ORCH.: Concertino (1937; San Francisco, April 25, 1939, composer conducting); Sym. No. 1 (CBS Radio, May 1939); Sinfonietta for Strings (NBC Radio, 1940); Suite for Chamber Orch. (1940); Overture for Strings (1945; San Francisco, May 2, 1946); *Praeludium* (1946; San Francisco, Feb. 5, 1947, composer conducting); Sym. No. 2 (1949; San Francisco, March 22, 1951, composer conducting); Sym. No. 3 (1955–57; San Francisco, Jan. 16, 1963, composer conducting). **CHAMBER:** 3 string quartets (1938, 1952, 1955); Viola Sonata (1943–44); Trio for Strings (1965); Partita for Organ (1958); Toccata, Aria, and Fugue for Organ (1966). **CHORAL:** Cantata, *Most Glorious Lord of Life* (1943); 3 motets (1946–47).

Densmore, Frances, American ethnomusicologist; b. Red Wing, Minn., May 21, 1867; d. there, June 5, 1957. She studied at the Oberlin (Ohio) Cons. (hon. M.A., 1924); then took courses with Leopold Godowsky (piano) and J.K. Paine (counterpoint); began study of Indian music in 1893 at the World's Fair in Chicago, continuing privately until 1907, when she began systematic research for the Bureau of American Ethnology (Smithsonian Inst.), including an exhaustive study of the Cheyenne, Arapaho, Maidu, Santo Domingo Pueblo, and New Mexican Indian tribes. She lectured extensively on Indian music, and publ. a number of books and articles on the subject. A Frances Densmore ethnological library has been established at Macalester College in St. Paul, Minn.

WRITINGS: *Chippewa Music,* a collection of Indian songs in 2 vols. (1910–13); *Poems from Sioux and Chippewa Songs* (words only; 1917); *Tetom Sioux Music* (1918); *Indian Action Songs* (1921); *Northern Ute Music* (1922); *Mandan and Hidatfa Music* (1923); *The American Indians and Their Music* (1926; 2nd ed., 1936); *The Music of the Tule Indians of Panama* (1926); *Some Results of the Study of American Indian Music* (reprinted from the *Journal of the Washington Academy of Sciences,* XVIII/14; 1928); *Pawnee Music* (1929); *Papago Music* (1929); *What Intervals Do Indians Sing?* (reprinted from the *American Anthropologist,* April/June, 1929); *Yaman and Yaqui Music* (U.S. Bureau of American Ethnology, Bulletin 110; 1932); *Menominee Music* (ibid., Bulletin 102; 1932); *Cheyenne and Arapaho Music* (Southwest Museum, 1936); *Alabama Music* (Texas Folk-Lore Soc., 1937); *Music of Santo Domingo Pueblo, New Mexico* (Southwest Museum, 1938); *Nootka and Quileute Music* (Washington, D.C., 1939); *Music of the Indians of British Columbia* (Washington, 1943); *Choctaw Music* (1943); *Seminole Music* (1956).

Dent, Edward J(oseph), eminent English musicologist, teacher, and critic; b. Ribston, Yorkshire, July 16, 1876; d. London, Aug. 22, 1957. He studied music with C.H. Lloyd at Eton College; then went to Cambridge to continue his studies with Charles Wood and Stanford (Mus.B., 1899; M.A., 1905); he was elected a Fellow of King's College there in 1902, and subsequently taught music history, harmony, counterpoint, and composition until 1918. He was also active in promoting operatic productions in England by preparing translations of libretti for performances at Cambridge, particularly of the operas of Mozart. From 1918 he wrote music criticism in London; in 1919 he became one of the founders of the British Music Soc., which remained active until 1933. The ISCM came into being in 1922 largely through his efforts, and he served as its president until 1938 and again in 1945; he also was president of the Société Internationale de Musicologie from 1931 until 1949. In 1926 he was appointed prof. of music at Cambridge, a position he held until 1941. He was made an honorary Mus.D. at Oxford (1932), Harvard (1936), and Cambridge (1947) Univs. After his death, the Royal Musical Assoc. created, in 1961, the Dent Medal, which is given annually to those selected for their important contributions to musicology. A scholar of the widest interests, he contributed numerous articles to music journals, encyclopedias, dictionaries, and symposia.

WRITINGS: *Alessandro Scarlatti* (London, 1905; 2nd ed., rev. by F. Walker, 1960); *Mozart's Operas: A Critical Study* (London, 1913; 3rd ed., rev., 1955); *Terpander, or Music and the Future* (London, 1926); *Foundations of English Opera: A Study of Musical Drama in England during the Seventeenth Century* (Cambridge, 1928); *Ferruccio Busoni* (London, 1933; 2nd ed., 1966); *Handel* (London, 1934); *Opera* (Harmondsworth, 1940; 5th ed., rev., 1949); *Notes on Fugue for Beginners* (Cambridge, 1941); *A Theatre for Everybody: The Story of the Old Vic and Sadler's Wells* (London, 1945; 2nd ed., rev., 1946); *The Rise of Romantic Opera* (ed. by W. Dean; Cambridge, 1976); *Selected Essays* (ed. by H. Taylor; Cambridge, 1979).
BIBL.: L. Haward, "E.J. D.: Bibliography," *Music Review,* VII (1946; publ. separately, Cambridge, 1956); W. Dean, "E. J. D.: A Centenary Tribute," *Music & Letters* (Oct. 1976); P. Radcliffe, *E.J. D.: A Centenary Memoir* (Rickmansworth, 1976).

Denver, John (real name, **Henry John Deutschendorf, Jr.**), popular American singer and songwriter; b. Roswell, N.Mex., Dec. 31, 1942. He played guitar as a youngster; for a time attended Texas Technical Univ. in Lubbock; then made his way to N.Y., where he played in the Mitchell Trio and wrote the popular song *Leaving on a Jet Plane* (1967). In 1968 he launched a solo career, appearing in concerts all over the U.S.; also made television appearances and recordings. His successful songs included *Rocky Mountain High, Take Me Home,* and *Country Roads.* He appeared in the movie *Oh, God!*

Denza, Luigi, Italian composer; b. Castellammare di Stabia, Feb. 24, 1846; d. London, Jan. 26, 1922. He studied with Serrao and Mercadante at the Naples Cons. Besides the opera

Wallenstein (Naples, May 13, 1876), which was not especially successful, he wrote about 600 songs (some in Neapolitan dialect), many of which won great popularity. In 1879 he settled in London; was appointed prof. of singing at the Royal Academy of Music (1898); was made a Chevalier of the order of the Crown of Italy. His most famous song is *Funiculi-Funicula*, which was used (under the mistaken impression that it was a folk song) by Richard Strauss in *Aus Italien*.

Denzler, Robert, Swiss conductor and composer; b. Zürich, March 19, 1892; d. there, Aug. 25, 1972. He studied with Volkmar Andreae in Zürich; held posts as conductor at the Zürich Opera (1915–27), at the Berlin Städtische Oper (1927–32), and again in Zürich (1934–47), where he conducted the world premieres of Berg's *Lulu* (1937) and Hindemith's *Mathis der Maler* (1938). He wrote a Piano Concerto, several instrumental suites, and songs.

De Peyer, Gervase (Alan), English clarinetist, conductor, and teacher; b. London, April 11, 1926. He studied with Frederick Thurston at the Royal College of Music in London and with Louis Cahuzac in Paris (1949). He then pursued an international career as a clarinet virtuoso; served as 1st clarinetist of the London Sym. Orch. (1955–72), was founder-conductor of the Melos Sinfonia, and associate conductor of the Haydn Orch. in London. He taught at the Royal Academy of Music in London (from 1959) and performed with the Chamber Music Soc. of Lincoln Center in N.Y. (1969–89). He gave master classes all over the globe and also commissioned a number of works for clarinet.

Deppe, Ludwig, famous German piano pedagogue; b. Alverdissen, Lippe, Nov. 7, 1828; d. Bad Pyramont, Sept. 5, 1890. He was a pupil of Marxsen at Hamburg in 1849; later of Lobe at Leipzig. He settled in Hamburg in 1857 as a music teacher, and founded a singing society, which he conducted till 1868. He went to Berlin in 1874, and from 1886 to 1888 was court conductor; also conducted the Silesian Musical Festivals established by Count Hochberg in 1876. He wrote a sym. and 2 overtures, *Zriny* and *Don Carlos*.
BIBL.: A. Fay, "D. as Teacher," *Music Study in Germany* (1897); H. Klose, *D.sche Lehre des Klavierspiels* (Hamburg, 1886); E. Caland, *Die D.sche Lehre des Klavierspiels* (Stuttgart, 1897; 5th ed., 1921; in Eng. as *Artistic Piano Playing*, 1903).

DePreist, James (Anderson), greatly talented black American conductor, nephew of **Marian Anderson;** b. Philadelphia, Nov. 21, 1936. He studied at the Univ. of Pa. (B.S., 1958; M.A., 1961) and with Vincent Persichetti at the Philadelphia Cons. of Music (1959–61). He conducted the Contemporary Music Guild in Philadelphia (1959–62); then was a music specialist for the U.S. State Dept. During a tour of the Far East in 1962, he was stricken with poliomyelitis, but persevered in his career; conducted in Bangkok (1963–64). In 1964 he won 1st prize in the Mitropoulos conducting competition in N.Y., then was assistant conductor of the N.Y. Phil. (1965–66). He was principal guest conductor of the Sym. of the New World in N.Y. (1968–70). In 1969 he made his European debut with the Rotterdam Phil. After serving as associate conductor (1971–75) and principal guest conductor (1975–76) of the National Sym. Orch. in Washington, D.C., he was music director of L'Orchestre Symphonique de Québec (1976–83). He was music director of the Oregon Sym. Orch. in Portland (from 1980), and principal conductor designate (1990–91) and principal conductor (from 1991) of the Malmö Sym. Orch. DePreist has won critical accolades for his impeccable performances of an extensive orch. repertoire. He has also publ. 2 vols. of poetry, *This Precipice Garden* (1987) and *The Distant Siren* (1989).

Déré, Jean, French composer; b. Niort, June 23, 1886; d. Sainte Suzanne, Mayenne, Dec. 6, 1970. He studied at the Paris Cons. with Caussade, Diémer, and Widor; won the 2nd Prix de Rome (1919). Among his works are the symphonic poem *Krischna*; incidental music for Marlowe's *Faustus; 3 esquisses* for Piano and Orch.; chamber music; piano pieces; songs.

De Rensis, Raffaello, Italian music critic; b. Casacalenda, Campobasso, Feb. 17, 1879; d. Rome, Nov. 3, 1970. He founded the weekly magazine *Musica* in 1908; wrote music criticism in daily newspapers. He publ. *Il cantore del popolo, B. Gigli* (Rome, 1934); *F. Faccio e Verdi* (Milan, 1934); *Ottorino Respighi* (Turin, 1935); *E. Wolf-Ferrari* (Milan, 1937); *A. Boito* (Florence, 1942); *U. Giordano e R. Leoncavallo* (Siena, 1949); *F. Cilèa* (Palmi, 1950); *Musica vista* (Milan, 1960).

De Reszke, Edouard, famous Polish bass, brother of **Jean (Jan Mieczislaw)** and **Josephine de Reszke;** b. Warsaw, Dec. 22, 1853; d. Garnek, May 25, 1917. He studied with Ciaffei in Warsaw; also was trained by his brother, Jean, and by Steller and Coletti. He then went to Italy, where he continued his study with various teachers. His professional debut was at the Théâtre des Italiens in Paris, when he sang Amonasro in *Aida* under Verdi's direction (April 22, 1876). He continued to make appearances in Paris for 2 seasons, and later sang at La Scala in Milan. From 1880 to 1884 he sang in London with extraordinary success. He made his American debut in Chicago as the King in *Lohengrin* (Nov. 9, 1891); then as Frère Laurent in *Roméo et Juliette* at the Metropolitan Opera in N.Y. (Dec. 14, 1891); his brother Jean made his N.Y. debut as Roméo at the same performance. Edouard's greatest role was that of Méphisthophélès in *Faust;* he sang this part at its 500th performance at the Paris Opéra (his brother Jean sang the title role), on Nov. 4, 1887; he made a special final appearance at a Metropolitan gala on April 27, 1903, in the last act of *Faust*. He then retired, and died in extreme poverty as a result of the depredations brought on by World War I.
BIBL.: H. Klein, "E. d.R.: The Career of a Famous Basso," *Musical Times* (July 1917).

De Reszke, Jean (Jan Mieczislaw), celebrated Polish tenor, brother of **Edouard** and **Josephine de Reszke;** b. Warsaw, Jan. 14, 1850; d. Nice, April 3, 1925. His mother gave him his 1st singing lessons; he then studied with Ciaffei and Cotogni. He sang at the Warsaw Cathedral as a boy; then went to Paris, where he studied with Sbriglia. He was 1st trained as a baritone, and made his debut in Venice (1874) as Alfonso in *La Favorita* under the name of Giovanni di Reschi. He continued singing in Italy and France in baritone parts; his 1st appearance as a tenor took place in Madrid on Nov. 9, 1879, in *Robert le Diable*. He created the title role of Massenet's *Le Cid* at the Paris Opéra (Nov. 30, 1885) and became a favorite tenor there. He appeared at Drury Lane in London as Radames on June 13, 1887 (having previously sung there as a baritone in 1874). He then sang at Covent Garden (until 1900). On Nov. 9, 1891, he made his American debut in Chicago as Lohengrin; he made his Metropolitan Opera debut in N.Y. on Dec. 14, 1891, as Roméo; he remained with the Metropolitan for 11 seasons. In order to sing Wagnerian roles, he learned German, and made a sensationally successful appearance as Tristan (N.Y., Nov. 27, 1895). His last appearance at the Metropolitan was as Tristan on April 29, 1901, in Act 2 during a postseason gala performance. The secret of his success rested not so much on the power of his voice (some baritone quality remained in his singing to the end) as on his controlled interpretation, musical culture, and fine dynamic balance. When he retired from the stage in 1902, settling in Paris as a voice teacher, he was able to transmit his method to many of his students, several of whom later became famous on the opera stage.
BIBL.: C. Leiser, *J. d.R. and the Great Days of Opera* (London, 1933); P. Hurst, *J. d.R.: 40 Years of Opera, 1874–1914* (London, 1958).

De Reszke, Josephine, Polish soprano, sister of **Jean (Jan Mieczislaw)** and **Edouard de Reszke;** b. Warsaw, June 4, 1855; d. there, Feb. 22, 1891. She studied at the St. Petersburg Cons.; 1st appeared in public under the name of Giuseppina di Reschi at Venice in 1874; sang Marguerite in Gounod's *Faust* (Aug. 1, 1874), with her brother Jean as Valentin; then was engaged at the Paris Opéra, where she made her debut as Ophelia in *Hamlet* by Ambroise Thomas (Paris, June 21, 1875); later sang in Madrid and Lisbon; appeared as Aida at Covent Garden in London on April 18, 1881. She retired from the stage upon her marriage in 1885 and settled in Poland.

Dering, Richard. See **Deering, Richard.**

Dérivis, Henri Etienne, French bass, father of **Prosper Dérivis**; b. Albi, Aug. 2, 1780; d. Livry, Feb. 1, 1856. He made his debut at the Paris Opéra as Sarastro in the French version of *Die Zauberflöte* under the title of *Les Mystères d'Isis* in 1803; during the next 25 years he was a principal singer there, creating roles in works by Spontini (*La Vestale, Fernand Cortez,* and *Olympie*), Cherubini (*Les Abencérages*), Rossini (*Le Siège de Corinthe*), and others.

Dérivis, Prosper, distinguished French bass, son of **Henri Etienne Dérivis**; b. Paris, Oct. 28, 1808; d. there, Feb. 11, 1880. He studied with Pellegrini and Nourrit in Paris; made his debut at the Paris Opéra in 1831; subsequently created roles there in operas by Berlioz (*Benvenuto Cellini*), Meyerbeer (*Les Huguenots*), Donizetti (*Les Martyrs*), etc.; appeared at La Scala in Milan (1842–43), singing in the premieres of Verdi's *Nabucco* and *I Lombardi*; also sang in the 1st performance of Donizetti's *Linda di Chamounix* in Vienna in 1842; retired from the stage in 1857; then taught voice in Paris.

Dermota, Anton, Austrian tenor; b. Kropa (now in Yugoslavia), June 4, 1910; d. Vienna, June 22, 1989. He studied at the State Academy in Ljubljana and at the Vienna Academy of Music. In 1936 he became a member of the Vienna State Opera; also sang at the Salzburg Festival. After retirement, he joined the faculty of the Vienna Academy of Music (1966).

Dernesch, Helga, Austrian soprano; b. Vienna, Feb. 3, 1939. She was educated at the Vienna Cons.; made her operatic debut at the Bern Stadttheater in 1961; then sang in Wiesbaden and Cologne; subsequently appeared at the Bayreuth Festivals; in 1969 Herbert von Karajan chose her for his Salzburg Easter Festival; in 1970 she made her debut at Covent Garden, London; also sang with the Hamburg State Opera, the Berlin Städtische Oper, and the Vienna State Opera. She sang many Wagnerian dramatic roles and those of Richard Strauss; from 1979 she turned her attention to mezzo-soprano parts. On Oct. 14, 1985, she made her Metropolitan Opera debut in N.Y. as Mussorgsky's Marfa. She married **Werner Krenn.**

De Rogatis, Pascual, Argentine composer; b. Teora, Italy, May 17, 1880; d. Buenos Aires, April 2, 1980, a few weeks before his 100th birthday. He was taken to Buenos Aires as a child; studied piano and composition with Alberto Williams and violin with Pietro Melani and Rafael Albertini. He subsequently established himself in Buenos Aires as a violin teacher and composer. His music followed the Italian tradition, but he often selected local subjects from history and folklore for his dramatic works. Among his works are an opera, *La novia del hereje* or *La Inquisición en Lima* (c.1924; Buenos Aires, June 13, 1935), *Suite árabe* for Orch. (1902; Buenos Aires, Oct. 10, 1904), several symphonic poems, including *Marko y el hada* (1905) and *Zupay* (1910), and the *Oratorio laico* for Soprano, Tenor, Chorus, and Orch. (1910; Buenos Aires, May 5, 1928).

BIBL.: C. Munoz, "P. d.R. (1880–1980)," *Revista del Instituto de Investigación Musicológica Vega,* No. 7 (Buenos Aires, 1986).

De Rose, Peter, American composer of popular music; b. N.Y., March 10, 1900; d. there, April 24, 1953. After a desultory musical education, he formed a radio team, The Sweethearts of the Air, with May Singhi Breen, whom he married. He gained fame with a piano piece entitled *Deep Purple*; it was introduced in an orch. version by Paul Whiteman (N.Y., May 10, 1934) and subsequently converted into a saccharine ballad with lachrymose lyrics which became a commercial hit. Other lucrative songs by De Rose are *The Lamp Is Low* (derived

from a malformed fragmentation of Ravel's *Pavane*) and *As Years Go By*, a sentimentalized misinterpretation of Brahms's *Hungarian Dance No. 4.*

Dervaux, Pierre, noted French conductor; b. Juvisy-sur-Orge, Jan. 3, 1917. He entered the Paris Cons. at the age of 9, studying piano and composition. In 1934 he became timpanist of the Pasdeloup Orch. in Paris; made his debut as conductor with that orch. in 1945. In 1948 he became chief conductor of the Opéra-Comique. In 1956 he was appointed chief conductor of the Paris Opéra. He served as music director of the Orchestre Symphonique de Québec (1968–71), chief conductor of the Orchestre Philharmonique des Pays de la Loire (1971–78), and music director in Nice (1979–82). His performances of the French repertoire are noted for their authentic color and technical brilliance.

De Sabata, Victor (Vittorio), outstanding Italian conductor and composer; b. Trieste, April 10, 1892; d. Santa Margherita Ligure, Dec. 11, 1967. He studied with Michele Saladino and Giacomo Orefice at the Milan Cons. (1901–11). An extremely versatile musician, he could play piano with considerable élan, and also took lessons on cello, clarinet, oboe, and bassoon. He was encouraged in his career as conductor by Toscanini; at the same time he began to compose operas; his 1st production was *Il Macigno*, 1st performed at La Scala in Milan on March 30, 1917. His symphonic poem *Juventus* (1919) was conducted at La Scala by Toscanini. De Sabata's style of composition involved Romantic Italian formulas, with lyric and dramatic episodes receiving an equal share of his attention. In the meantime he filled engagements as an opera and sym. conductor in Italy. In 1927 he conducted concerts in N.Y. and Cincinnati, in 1936 he conducted at the Vienna State Opera, in 1939 he was a guest conductor with the Berlin Phil., and in 1946 he conducted in Switzerland. On April 21, 1946, he was invited to conduct a sym. concert in London, the 1st conductor from an "enemy country" to conduct in England after World War II. He conducted the Chicago Sym. Orch. in Oct. 1949; in March 1950 he conducted 14 concerts at Carnegie Hall with the N.Y. Phil.; the following Aug. he was guest conductor with the Boston Sym. Orch. In April 1951 he conducted 6 concerts with the N.Y. Phil. in Carnegie Hall. He became popular with American audiences, and in 1952 was engaged to conduct in N.Y., Philadelphia, Washington, Baltimore, St. Louis, and Detroit. In 1953 he conducted in Philadelphia, Los Angeles, San Francisco, and Santa Barbara, Calif. On Feb. 18, 1957, he conducted at the funeral of Toscanini; this was his last appearance on the podium. He was the father-in-law of **Aldo Ceccato.**

WORKS: Operas: *Il Macigno* (*The Rock*; La Scala, Milan, March 30, 1917; 2nd version, *Driada*, Turin, Nov. 12, 1935); *Lisistrata* (1920); theater music for Max Reinhardt's production of *The Merchant of Venice* (*Il mercante di Venezia*; Venice, July 18, 1934); ballet, *Le mille e una notte* (La Scala, Milan, Jan. 20, 1931); symphonic poems, *Juventus* (1919); *La notte di Platon* (1924); *Gethsemani* (1925).

BIBL.: R. Mucci, *V. d.S.* (Lanciano, 1937); T. Celli, *L'arte di V. d.S.* (Turin, 1978).

Desarzens, Victor, Swiss conductor; b. Château d'Oex, Oct. 27, 1908; d. Lausanne, Feb. 13, 1986. He received his musical education at the Lausanne Cons.; studied conducting with Franz von Hoesslin. He played violin in the Orch. de la Suisse Romande in Geneva; also led a series of chamber music concerts there and later served as conductor of the Lausanne Chamber Orch. In 1945 he was appointed music director of the Musikkollegium of Winterthur, a post he held until his retirement in 1976.

Deschamps-Jehin, (Marie-)Blanche, outstanding French contralto; b. Lyons, Sept. 18, 1857; d. Paris, June 1923. She studied at the Cons. in Lyons; later at the Paris Cons.; made her debut in Brussels in *Giroflé-Girofla* in 1874; then sang at the Théâtre Royal de la Monnaie in Brussels (1879–85); during her tenure there, she created the role of Hérodiade in

Massenet's opera (1881); then sang in Paris at the Opéra-Comique (1885–91) and the Opéra (1891–1902), and at Covent Garden in London (1891); in later years she appeared at the Monte Carlo Opera and then mainly in concerts. She was married to **Léon Jehin.**

Desderi, Ettore, Italian composer; b. Asti, Dec. 10, 1892; d. Florence, Nov. 23, 1974. He studied with Luigi Perrachio at the Turin Cons. and then with Franco Alfano in Bologna. From 1933 to 1941 he was director of the Liceo Musicale in Alessandria; from 1941 to 1951, a teacher of composition at the Milan Cons. From 1951 to 1963 he was director of the Cons. of Bologna. He publ. *La musica contemporanea* (Turin, 1930) and numerous articles in Italian and German journals.

Works: *Intermezzi all' Antigone* for Orch. (1924); *Job*, biblical cantata (1927); *Sinfonia davidica* for Soli, Chorus, and Orch. (1929); Violin Sonata; Cello Sonata; many choral works.

Bibl.: A. Bonacorsi, "E. D.," *Il Pianoforte* (July 1926); M. Rinaldi, *E. D.* (Tivoli, 1943); *A E. D. nel suo 70 compleanno* (Bologna, 1963).

De Segurola, Andrés, Spanish bass; b. Valencia, March 27, 1874; d. Barcelona, Jan. 22, 1953. He studied with Pietro Farvaro; sang at the Teatro Liceo in Barcelona; made his American debut at the Metropolitan Opera as the king in *Aida* (March 3, 1902). After further appearances in Europe, he returned to the Metropolitan for the 1909–20 seasons. For 20 years (1931–51) he taught voice in Hollywood; then returned to Spain.

Deshevov, Vladimir, Russian composer; b. St. Petersburg, Feb. 11, 1889; d. there (Leningrad), Oct. 27, 1955. He studied with Steinberg and Liadov at the St. Petersburg Cons. Many of his themes are drawn from folk sources. Among his works are the revolutionary operas *The Red Hurricane* (Leningrad, Oct. 29, 1924), *Ice and Steel*, based on the Kronstadt rebellion of 1921 (Leningrad, May 17, 1930), and *The Hungry Steppe*, about socialist distribution of land in Uzbekistan.

Deslandres, Adolphe-Edouard-Marie, French organist and composer; b. Batignolles, Monceaux, Jan. 22, 1840; d. Paris, July 30, 1911. He was a pupil of Leborne and Benoist at the Paris Cons.; in 1862, was appointed organist at Ste.-Marie. He wrote the operas *Dimanche et lundi* (1872), *Le Chevalier Bijou* (1875), and *Fridolin* (1876); *Ode à l'harmonie*; *La Banque brisée*; a patriotic dirge, *Les Sept Paroles*; many sacred choruses.

Des Marais, Paul (Emile), American composer; b. Menominee, Mich., June 23, 1920. He studied with Leo Sowerby in Chicago (1937–41), Nadia Boulanger in Cambridge, Mass. (1941–42), and Paris (1949), and Walter Piston at Harvard Univ. (B.A., 1949; M.A., 1953). He received the Lili Boulanger prize (1947–48), the Boott prize in composition from Harvard (1949), and a John Knowles Paine Traveling Fellowship (1949–51). After teaching at Harvard (1953–56), he was on the faculty of the Univ. of Calif. at Los Angeles (from 1956), where he received the Inst. of Creative Arts Award (1964–65); he later held the Phoebe Ketchum Thorne award (1970–73). He publ. the study *Harmony* (1962) and contributed articles to *Perspectives of New Music*. His early music was oriented toward neoclassicism, with pandiatonic excrescences in harmonic structures. He later moved to a free combination of serial and nonserial elements, functioning on broad tonal planes.

Works: stage: *Epiphanies*, chamber opera (1968); *Orpheus*, theater piece for Narrator and Instruments (1987); incidental music to Dryden's *A Secular Masque* (1976), Shakespeare's *A Midsummer Night's Dream* (1976), Sophocles' *Oedipus* (1978), G.B. Shaw's *St. Joan* (1980), Dryden's *Marriage à la Mode* (1981), Shakespeare's *As You Like It* (1983), and G. Etherege's *The Man of Mode* (1984). **dance:** *Triplum* for Organ and Percussion (1981); *Touch* for 2 Pianos (1984). **chamber:** 2 piano sonatas (1947, 1952); *Theme and Changes* for Harpsichord (1953); *Capriccio* for 2 Pianos and Percussion (1962); *2 Movements* for 2 Pianos and Percussion (1972; rev. and enl. as *3 Movements*, 1975); *Baroque Isles: The Voyage Out* for 2 Keyboard Percussionists (1986). **choral:** *Polychoric*

Mass for Unaccompanied Voices (1949); *Motet* for Mixed Voices, Cellos, and Double Basses (1959); *Psalm 121* for Chorus Unaccompanied (1959); *Organum 1–6* for Chorus, Organ, and Percussion (1972; rev. and enl. 1980); *Brief Mass* for Chorus, Organ, and Percussion (1973); *Seasons of the Mind* for Chorus, Piano 4-hands, and Celesta (1980–81). **vocal:** *Le Cimetière marin* for Voice, Keyboards, and Percussion (1971); also solo songs.

Desmarets, Henri, important French composer; b. Paris, Feb. 1661; d. Lunéville, Sept. 7, 1741. He was a boy soprano in the Paris royal chapel, subsequently becoming one of the most highly regarded musicians of his day. Many of his works were performed at the court of Louis XIV. He served as maître de chapelle at the Jesuit College of Louis-le-Grand. His personal life was stormy; after the death of his wife, he became involved with one of his students; when the girl's father objected, the lovers fled to Brussels in 1699. In 1701 he was made maître de musique de la chambre to Philip V in Madrid, and in 1707 became surintendant de la musique to Leopold I, Duke of Lorraine, in Lunéville. Having been sentenced to death in absentia for personal indiscretions, he was unable to return to France until he was pardoned by the regent in 1720. For the most part, he spent his remaining years in Lunéville.

Works: operas (all 1st perf. in Paris): *Didon* (Sept. 11, 1693); *Circé* (Oct. 1, 1694); *Venus et Adonis* (March 7, 1697); *Théagène et Cariclée* (Feb. 3, 1695); *Iphigénie en Tauride* (May 6, 1704); *Renaud, ou La Suite d'Armide* (March 5, 1722). **ballets:** *Les Amours de Momus* (May 25, 1695) and *Les Fêtes galantes* (May 10, 1698).

Bibl.: M. Brenet, "D., un compositeur oublié du 17ᵉ siècle," *Le Ménestrel*, 39–40 (1883); M. Antoine, *Henry D.* (Paris, 1965).

Desmond, Paul (real name, **Paul Emile Breitenfeld**), American jazz alto saxophonist; b. San Francisco, Nov. 25, 1924; d. N.Y., May 30, 1977. He picked up his professional name from a telephone book at random. He gained the rudiments of music from his father, who played the organ for silent movies; Desmond played the clarinet in the school orch.; then at San Francisco State Univ.; eventually concentrated on the alto saxophone. He made rapid strides toward recognition and modest fame when he joined the Dave Brubeck Quartet (1951), and continued with it until it was disbanded in 1967. He wrote some pieces for the Brubeck Quartet, of which *Take Five*, a jazz composition in 5/4 meter, was adopted as their signature song and became popular.

Desormière, Roger, brilliant French conductor; b. Vichy, Sept. 13, 1898; d. Paris, Oct. 25, 1963. He studied at the Paris Cons.; conducted the Swedish Ballet in Paris (1924–25) and the Ballets Russes (1925–29), and later at La Scala, at Covent Garden, and in Monte Carlo; was at the Opéra-Comique (1937–46); at the Paris Opéra (1945–46); conducted the BBC in London (1946–47). In 1950 he was stricken with aphasia and other disorders, and was soon compelled to give up his career.

Bibl.: D. Mayer and P. Souvchinsky, *R. D. et son temps* (Monaco, 1966).

Des Prez, Josquin, great Franco-Flemish composer; b. probably in Hainaut, c.1440; d. Condé-sur-Escaut, near Valenciennes, Aug. 27, 1521. His surname was variously spelled: *Després, Desprez, Deprés, Depret, Deprez, Desprets, Dupré,* and by the Italians *Del Prato* (Latinized as *a Prato, a Pratis, Pratensis*), etc.; while Josquin (contracted from the Flemish Jossekin, "little Joseph") appears as *Jossé, Jossien, Jusquin, Giosquin, Josquinus, Jacobo, Jodocus, Jodoculus,* etc. His epitaph reads *Jossé de Prés.* However, in the motet *Illibata Dei Virgo Nutrix* (contained in vol. 9 of the Josquin ed.), of which the text is quite likely of Josquin's authorship, his name appears as an acrostic, thus: *I, O, S, Q, V, I, N, D[es], P, R, E, Z;* this seems to leave little doubt as to its correct spelling. Few details of Josquin's early life are known. He may have been a boy chorister of the Collegiate Church at St.-Quentin, later becoming canon and choirmaster there; possibly was a pupil of Ockeghem, whom he greatly admired (after Ockeghem's death, in 1497, he wrote *La Déploration de Johan Okeghem*); from 1459 to 1472 he sang at the Milan Cathedral; by July 1474, was at the Court of Duke Galeazzo Maria Sforza, Milan, as chorister; after the Duke's assassination he entered the service of the Duke's brother, Cardinal Ascanio Sforza; from 1486 to 1494, was a singer in the papal choir under the Popes Innocent VIII and Alexander VI; he was also active, for various periods, in Florence, where he met the famous theorist Pietro Aron; in Modena; and in Ferrara (where Isaac was also) as maestro di cappella in 1503–4. Later Josquin returned to Burgundy, settling in Condé-sur-Escaut (1504), where he became provost of Notre Dame. As a composer, he was considered by contemporary musicians and theorists to be the greatest of his period, and he had a strong influence on all those who came into contact with his music or with him personally, as a teacher; Adriaan Petit Coclicus, who may have been one of Josquin's pupils, publ. a method in 1552 entitled *Compendium musices*, based on Josquin's teaching. He described Josquin as "princeps musicorum." His works were sung everywhere, and universally admired; in them he achieves a complete union between word and tone, thereby fusing the intricate Netherlandish contrapuntal devices into expressive and beautiful art forms. Two contrasting styles are present in his compositions: some are intricately contrapuntal, displaying the technical ingenuity characteristic of the Netherlands style; others, probably as a result of Italian influence, are homophonic.

WORKS: Masses (In Petrucci's Lib. I, Venice, 1502): *L'Omme armé; La sol fa re mi; Gaudeamus; Fortunata desperata; L'Omme armé, sexti toni.* (Ibid., II, 1505): *Ave Maris stella; Hercules, dux Ferrarae; Malheur me bat; Lami Baudichon; Una musque de Buscaya; Dung aultre amor.* (Ibid., III, 1514): *Mater patris; Faysans regrets; Ad fugam; Di dadi; De Beata Virgine; Sine nomine.* Petrucci's vols. contain all but 1 of the extant masses. (In Graphäus's *Missae III*): *Pange lingua; Da pacem; Sub tuum praesidium.* Some of these are scattered in other collections, and fragments are found in still others. Motets were publ. by Petrucci (8 in the *Odhecaton*, 1501; others in his books of motets); by Peutinger (*Liber selectarum cantionum*, 1520); and by others of the period. French chansons were publ. by T. Susato (1545), P. Attaignant (1549), and Du Chemin (1553). A complete ed. of Josquin's works was issued (1921–69; 55 vols.) by the Vereeniging voor Nederlandsche Muziekgeschiedenis under the general editorship of A. Smijers, M. Amlonowycz, and W. Elders. The New Josquin Edition, under general ed. W. Elders, was launched in 1988. The International Josquin Festival Conference was held in N.Y. from June 21 to 25, 1971; reports appeared in *Journal of the American Musicological Society* (Fall 1971), *Die Musikforschung* (Oct.–Dec. 1971), and *Current Musicology*, 14 (1972); papers presented at the conference were publ. ed. by E. Lowinsky (London, 1976).

BIBL.: F. de Ménil, *Les Grands Musiciens du Nord: J. de Prés* (Paris, 1897); A. Schering, *Die niederländische Orgelmesse im Zeitalter des J.* (Leipzig, 1912); A. Gastoué, "J. des Prés, ses précurseurs et ses émules," *La Tribune de St. Gervais* (1921); T. Werner, "Anmerkungen zur Kunst J.s und zur Gesamt-Ausgabe seiner Werke," *Zeitschrift für Musikwissenschaft*, VII (1924); O. Ursprung, "J. D. P.; Eine Charakterzeichnung," *Bulletin of the Union Musicologique*, VI/1 (1926); A. Smijers, in *Proceedings of the Musical Association, Session 53* (London, 1926–27); E. Lowinsky, *Secret Chromatic Art in the Netherlands Motet* (N.Y., 1946); C. van den Borren, *Geschiedenis van de muziek in de Nederlanden* (Antwerp, 1948); M. Antonowitsch, *Die Motette "Benedicta Es" von J. D. P.* (Utrecht, 1951); C. Sartori, article in *Annales Musicologiques* (1956; discusses birth date); H. Osthoff, *J. Desprez* (2 vols., Tutzing, 1962, 1965); W. Elders, *Studien zur Symbolik in der Musik der alten Niederländer* (Bilthoven, 1968); idem, "Das Symbol in der Musik von J. d. P.," *Acta Musicologica* (July–Dec. 1969); A. Ghislanzoni, *J. D. P. (Joducus Pratensis)* (Frosinone, 1976); S. Charles, *J. des Pres.: A Guide to Research* (N.Y. and London, 1983); J.-P. Ouvrard, *J. Desprez et ses*

con *temporains: De l'écrit au sonore, guide pratique d'interprétation* (Arles, 1986); R. Sherr, "*Illibata Dei Virgo Nutrix* and J.'s Roman Style," *Journal of the American Musicological Society* (Fall 1988); W. Elders, "The Performance of Cantus Firmi in J.'s Masses Based on Secular Monophonic Song," *Early Music* (Aug. 1989).

Dessau, Bernhard, German violinist and composer; b. Hamburg, March 1, 1861; d. Berlin, April 28, 1923. He studied violin with Joachim and Wieniawski; held various posts as concertmaster in Germany and the Netherlands; in 1906 was appointed a prof. at the Berlin Cons. He was a prolific composer; his Violin Concerto "im alten Stil" was widely known.

Dessau, Paul, German composer; b. Hamburg, Dec. 19, 1894; d. East Berlin, June 27, 1979. He learned to play the violin at an early age and gave a concert when he was 11 years old. In 1910 he enrolled at the Klindworth-Scharwenka Cons. in Berlin, where he studied violin with Florian Zajic and composition with Eduard Behm and Max Loewengard. In 1913 he worked as répétiteur at the Hamburg City Theater; in 1914 he was drafted into the German army. After the Armistice in 1918 he became engaged as a composer and conductor in various chamber groups in Hamburg; then served as coach and conductor at the Cologne Opera (1919–23) and in Mainz (1924). In 1925 he was appointed second conductor at the Städtische Oper in Berlin, holding this position until 1933; with the usurpation of power by the Nazis, he left Germany; lived in various European cities, and also visited Palestine. In 1939 he emigrated to America; lived for some time in N.Y., and in 1944 went to Hollywood, where he worked on the background scores for 14 films as a composer or orchestrator. He returned to Berlin in 1948 and took an active part in German musical life, aligning himself with the political, social, and artistic developments in the German Democratic Republic; he became closely associated with Bertolt Brecht and composed music for several of his plays. Dessau's operas, choral works, songs, and instrumental music are imbued with the progressive ideals of socialist realism; while he believed in the imperative of music for the masses, he made use of modern techniques, including occasional applications of Schoenberg's method of composition with 12 tones.

WORKS: STAGE: Opera, *Lanzelot und Sanderein* (Hamburg, 1918); 2 children's operas: *Das Eisenbahnspiel* (1931) and *Tadel der Unzuverlässigkeit* (1931); opera, *Die Verurteilung des Lukullus*, after Brecht (Berlin, March 17, 1951; original title, *Das Verhör des Lukullus*; new version, 1968); *Geschäftsbericht*, "minimal" opera of 600 seconds' duration (Leipzig, April 29, 1967); stage music for Brecht's plays: *Furcht und Elend des Dritten Reiches* (1938; originally entitled 99%); *Mutter Courage und ihre Kinder* (1946); *Der gute Mensch von Sezuan* (1947); *Herr Puntila und sein Knecht Matti* (1949); *Mann ist Mann* (1951); *Der kaukasische Kreidekreis* (1954); also music to Brecht's productions of classical drama: *Faust*, after Goethe (1949); *Don Juan*, after Molière (1953); *Coriolan*, after Shakespeare (1964).

ORCH.: Sym. No. 1 (1926); Sym. No. 2 (derived from *Hommage à Bartók;* 1962); *Sozialistische Festouvertüre* (originally, *Symphonischer Marsch;* 1953; rev. 1963); *In memoriam Bertolt Brecht* (1957); *Bach-Variationen* (on themes of J.S. Bach and C.P.E. Bach, 1963); *Divertimento* for Chamber Orch. (1964); *Meer der Stürme*, symphonic poem (East Berlin, Oct. 14, 1967); *Lenin*, with a choral finale (1970).

CHAMBER: 5 string quartets (1932, 1943, 1946, 1948, 1955); Suite for Saxophone and Piano (1935); 5 *Tanzstücke* for Mandolin, Guitar, and Accordion (1951); *Jewish Dance* for Violin and Piano (1940); *Quattuordrama 1965* for 4 Cellos, 2 Pianos, and 2 Percussionists (1965).

PIANO: Sonata (1914); 12 etudes (1932); *10 Kinderstücke* (1934); *Zwölfton Versuche* (1937); *Guernica* (1938); *11 Jüdische Volktänze* (1946); *Sonatine* (1955); *4 kleine Klavierstücke* (1955); *3 Intermezzi* (1955).

VOCAL: *Symphonische Kantate* (1917); scenic oratorio, *Haggada* (1936); *Deutsches Miserere* (1944–47); *5. März 1953, 21*

Uhr 50 (day and hour of Stalin's death; composed in 1954); *Hymne auf den Beginn einer neuen Geschichte der Menschheit* (1959); *Appell der Arbeiterklasse* (1961); *Requiem für Lumumba* (1963); *Armeebefehl No. 13* for Speaker, Chorus, and 9 Instruments (1967); several funerary odes: *Grabschrift für Gorki* (1947); *Grabschrift für Rosa Luxemburg* (1948); *Grabschrift für Karl Liebknecht* (1948); *Grabschrift für Lenin* (1951); numerous a cappella choruses to biblical texts; also a setting of the Communist manifesto, *Proletarier aller Länder, vereinigt euch* (1948); a number of mass songs to politically inspired texts.

WRITINGS: *Musikarbeit in der Schule* (Berlin, 1968); *Aus Gesprächen* (Leipzig, 1975); other writings ed. by F. Hennenberg as *Notizen und Noten* (Leipzig, 1974).

BIBL.: F. Hennenberg, *D.-Brecht, Musikalische Arbeiten* (Berlin, 1963); idem, *P. D.* (Leipzig, 1965; contains list of works).

Dessauer, Josef, composer; b. Prague, May 28, 1798; d. Mödling, near Vienna, July 8, 1876. He studied piano with Tomaschek and composition with Dionys Weber in Prague. He wrote several operas: *Lidwina* (Prague, 1836); *Ein Besuch in Saint-Cyr* (Dresden, May 6, 1838; his best work); *Paquita* (Vienna, 1851); *Domingo* (1860); and *Oberon* (not perf.); also overtures, string quartets, piano pieces, etc.

BIBL.: O. Sestl, *J. D. (1798–1876): Ein Liedermeister des Wiener Biedermeier* (diss., Univ. of Innsbruck, 1951).

Dessoff, Margarethe, Austrian choral conductor; b. Vienna, June 11, 1874; d. Locarno, Switzerland, Nov. 19, 1944. She was educated at the Frankfurt Cons.; taught there from 1912 to 1917. She organized a madrigal singing group, and traveled with it in Germany (1916–21). In 1922 she settled in America, where she presented interesting programs of choral music (gave the 1st complete perf. in N.Y. of Vecchi's *L'Amfiparnaso*, 1933). In 1936 she went to Switzerland, where she remained until her death. The leadership of the Dessoff Choir, which she established in N.Y., was taken over in 1936 by Paul Boepple.

Dessoff, (Felix) Otto, eminent German conductor; b. Leipzig, Jan. 14, 1835; d. Frankfurt am Main, Oct. 28, 1892. He studied at the Leipzig Cons. with Moscheles, Hauptmann, and Rietz; then was a theater conductor in various German cities (1854–60). From 1860 to 1875 he was a conductor of the Vienna Court Opera; also conducted the Vienna Phil., and taught at the Vienna Cons. From 1875 to 1881 he occupied similar posts at Karlsruhe; in 1881 he became conductor in Frankfurt. He was greatly esteemed by his many celebrated friends for his musicianship; his correspondence with Brahms was publ. by the Brahms Soc. He also wrote chamber music (Piano Quintet; Piano Quartet; etc.).

Destinn (real name, **Kittl**), **Emmy,** famous Czech soprano; b. Prague, Feb. 26, 1878; d. České Budějovice, Jan. 28, 1930. She 1st studied the violin; her vocal abilities were revealed later by Mme. Loewe-Destinn, whose 2nd name she adopted as a token of appreciation. She made her debut as Santuzza at the Kroll Opera in Berlin (July 19, 1898) and was engaged at the Berlin Royal Opera as a regular member until 1908. She then specialized in Wagnerian operas, and became a protégée of Cosima Wagner in Bayreuth; because of her ability to cope with difficult singing parts, Richard Strauss selected her for the title role in the Berlin and Paris premieres of his *Salome.* She made her London debut at Covent Garden on May 2, 1904, as Donna Anna; her success in England was spontaneous and unmistakable, and she continued to sing opera in England until the outbreak of World War I. She made her American debut in *Aida* with the Metropolitan Opera in N.Y., Toscanini conducting, on Nov. 16, 1908, and remained with the company until 1914. She returned to America to sing *Aida* at the Metropolitan (Dec. 8, 1919); retired from the opera stage in 1926 but continued to make concert appearances until shortly before her death. For a few years following World War I, she used her Czech name, Ema Destinnová, but dropped it later on. Her voice was a pure soprano of great power; she was a versatile

singer; her repertoire included some 80 parts. A film biography of her life, *The Divine Emma,* was produced in Czechoslovakia in 1982.

BIBL.: L. Brieger-Wasservogel, *E. D. und Maria Laiba* (1908); A. Rektorys, *Ema D.ová* (Prague, 1936); M. Martínková, *Život Emy D.ová* (Pilzen, 1946); V. Holzknecht and B. Trita, *E. D.ová ve slovech a obrazech* (D. in Words and Pictures; Prague, 1972); M. Pospíšil, *Veliké srdce: Život a umění Emy Destinové* (A Great Heart: The Life and Art of D.; Prague, 1974; with discography).

Destouches, André-Cardinal, French composer; b. Paris (baptized), April 6, 1672; d. there, Feb. 7, 1749. After attending a Jesuit school in Paris, he went as a boy to Siam with his teacher, the missionary Gui Tachard (1686). He returned to France in 1688; served in the Royal Musketeers (1692–94), and later took lessons from André Campra, contributing 3 airs to Campra's opera-ballet *L'Europe galante* (1697). After this initiation, Destouches produced his 1st independent work, *Issé,* a "heroic pastorale" in 3 acts (Fontainebleau, Oct. 7, 1697); its popularity was parodied in several productions of a similar pastoral nature (*Les Amours de Vincennes* by P.F. Dominique, 1719; *Les Oracles* by J.A. Romagnesi, 1741). Among his other operas, the following were produced in Paris: *Amadis de Grèce* (March 22, 1699), *Omphale* (Nov. 10, 1701), and *Callirhoé* (Dec. 27, 1712). With Delalande, he wrote the ballet *Les Eléments,* which was produced at the Tuileries Palace in Paris on Dec. 22, 1721. In 1713 Louis XIV appointed him inspector general of the Académie Royale de Musique; in 1728 he became its director, retiring in 1730. A revival of *Omphale* in 1752 evoked Baron Grimm's famous *Lettre sur Omphale,* inaugurating the so-called "Guerre des Bouffons" between the proponents of the French school, as exemplified by Destouches, and Italian opera buffa.

BIBL.: K. Dulle, *A.C. D.* (Leipzig, 1908); A. Tessier, "Correspondance d'A.C. D. et du Prince Antoine 1er de Monaco," *Revue Musicale* (Dec. 1926–May 1927); D.R.B. Kimball, "The Amadis Operas of D. and Handel," *Music & Letters* (Oct. 1968).

Destouches, Franz (Seraph) von, German conductor and composer; b. Munich, Jan. 21, 1772; d. there, Dec. 10, 1844. He was a pupil of Haydn in Vienna in 1787; was appointed music director at Erlangen (1797); then was 2nd concertmaster at the Weimar theater (1799), later becoming 1st concertmaster and director of music (1804–8); in 1810, was a prof. of theory at Landshut Univ.; then a conductor at Hamburg (1826–42); retired to Munich in 1842.

WORKS: *Die Thomasnacht,* opera (Munich, Aug. 31, 1792); *Das Missverständniss,* operetta (Weimar, April 27, 1805); comic opera, *Der Teufel und der Schneider* (1843; not perf.); incidental music: to Schiller's version of Gozzi's *Turandot* (1802); to Schiller's *Die Braut von Messina* (1803), *Die Jungfrau von Orleans* (1803), and *Wilhelm Tell* (1804); to Kotzebue's *Die Hussiten vor Naumburg* (1804); and to Zacharias Werner's play *Wanda, Königin der Sarmaten* (1808); also a Piano Concerto; piano sonatas; fantasias; variations for piano; Piano Trio; Clarinet Concerto; Mass; oratorio, *Die Anbetung am Grabe Christi.*

BIBL.: E. von Destouches, *F. v.D.* (Munich, 1904).

Destranges, Louis (Augustin Etienne Rouillé), French music critic; b. Nantes, March 29, 1863; d. there, May 31, 1915. He publ.: *L'Œuvre théatrale de Meyerbeer* (1893); *L'Evolution musicale chez Verdi* (1895); *Les Femmes dans l'œuvre de Richard Wagner* (1899); *Consonances et dissonances* (1906).

Deswert, Jules. See **Swert, Jules de.**

Déthier, Edouard, Belgian violinist and teacher, brother of **Gaston-Marie Déthier;** b. Liège, April 25, 1886; d. N.Y., Feb. 19, 1962. He studied at the Liège Cons. (1895–1901); then at the Brussels Cons. (1901–2); subsequently taught there (1902–4). He settled in the U.S. in 1906, appearing with the principal orchs.; taught at the Inst. of Musical Art and at the Juilliard Graduate School.

Déthier, Gaston-Marie, Belgian organist and teacher, brother of **Edouard Déthier;** b. Liège, April 18, 1875; d. N.Y.,

May 26, 1958. He studied at the Liège Cons. and later with Guilmant in Paris; went to the U.S. in 1894; was organist at St. Francis Xavier's, N.Y.; taught at the Inst. of Musical Art.

Detoni, Dubravko, Croatian pianist and composer; b. Križevci, Feb. 22, 1937. He graduated in piano from the Zagreb Academy of Music in 1960; studied with Alfred Cortot in Siena (1960–61); then took lessons in composition with Šulek at the Zagreb Academy, graduating in 1965; had advanced studies with Bacewicz and Lutoslawski at the experimental studio of the Polish Radio in Warsaw (1966–67) and with Stockhausen and Ligeti in Darmstadt. He was the founder and artistic leader of ACEZANTEZ, the Ensemble of the Center for New Tendencies in Zagreb. His music rejects all established formulas and seeks new conceptions in sound through serial, aleatory, and musical-theater resources.

Works: *Passacaglia* for 2 Pianos and Strings (1962); *Musica a cinque* for Orch. (1962); *Preobrazbe* (Transfigurations) for Orch. (1963; Zagreb, June 7, 1965); *Dramatski prolog* for Orch. (1965); *Stravaganze* for Wind Quintet (1966); *Likovi i plohe* (Forms and Surfaces) for Chamber Orch. (1967; Graz, Austria, Sept. 26, 1968); *Phonomorphia 1* for Electronic and Concrete Sounds (1967), 2 for Piano and Tape (1968), and 3 for Voices, Instrumental Ensemble, and Tape (1969); *Grafika I* for Organ (1968), *II* for Chamber Ensemble (1968), *III* for Vocal Ensemble, 6 Flutes, Ondes Martenot, Organ, and Piano (1969), *IV* for ad libitum Chamber Ensemble (1971), and *V*, instrumental "theater" for Chamber Ensemble (1972; Graz, Oct. 14, 1973); *Assonanze No. 1* for Cello and Piano (1968); *Assonanze No. 2* for Cello and Orch. (1971); *Elucubrations* for Piano and Orch. (1969; Zagreb, Jan. 7, 1970); *Forte-Piano, Arpa, Crescendo* for 2 Pianos and Percussion (1969); *Notturni* for 4 Vocal Groups, 4 Instrumental Ensembles, Organ, and Tape (1970); *Einflüsse* for 2 Cellos and Orch. (1971); *Monos 1–3*, cycle for variable orchestration (1970–72); *Music, or Tract about the Superfluous* for Narrating Actor, Organ, Piano, Percussion, Clarinet, and Orch. (1973); *10 Beginnings* for String Quartet (1973); *Dokument 75* for Chamber Ensemble (1975); *Fragment 75* for Chamber Ensemble (Graz, Oct. 11, 1975).

Dett, R(obert) Nathaniel, distinguished black American composer, conductor, and anthologist; b. Drummondville, Quebec, Canada, Oct. 11, 1882; d. Battle Creek, Mich., Oct. 2, 1943. He came from a musical family; both his parents were amateur pianists and singers. In 1893 the family moved to Niagara Falls, N.Y.; Dett studied piano with local teachers. He earned his living by playing at various clubs and hotels; then enrolled at the Oberlin (Ohio) Cons., where he studied piano with Howard Handel Carter and theory of composition with Arthur E. Heacox and George Carl Hastings, obtaining his B.Mus. in 1908. He also conducted a school choir; eventually, choral conducting became his principal profession. He taught at Lane College in Jackson, Tenn. (1908–11), the Lincoln Inst. in Jefferson, Mo. (1911–13), the Hampton Inst. in Virginia (1913–32), and Bennett College in Greensboro, N.C. (1937–42). Concerned about his lack of technical knowledge in music, he continued taking courses. He took lessons with Karl Gehrkens at Oberlin in 1913; attended classes at Columbia Univ., the American Cons. of Music in Chicago, Northwestern Univ., the Univ. of Pa., and, during the academic year 1919–20, Harvard Univ., where he studied composition with Arthur Foote. In the summer of 1929, he went to France to study with Nadia Boulanger at the American Cons. in Fontainebleau; during 1931–32, he attended the Eastman School of Music in Rochester, N.Y., obtaining his M.Mus. in 1932. In the meantime, he developed the artistic skills of the Hampton Choir, which toured in Europe in 1930 with excellent success, receiving encomiums in England, France, Belgium, the Netherlands, Germany, and Switzerland. He also periodically led his choir on the radio; in 1943 he became a musical adviser for the USO, and worked with the WAC (Women's Army Corps) on service duty at Battle Creek, where he died. His dominating interest was in cultivating Negro music, arranging Negro spirituals, and publishing collections of Negro folk songs. All of

his works were inspired by black melos and rhythms; some of his piano pieces in Negro idiom became quite popular, among them the suite *Magnolia* (1912); *In the Bottoms* (1913), which contained the rousing *Juba Dance*; and *Enchantment* (1922). He also wrote a number of choral pieces, mostly on biblical themes, such as his oratorios *The Chariot Jubilee* (1921) and *The Ordering of Moses* (Cincinnati, May 7, 1937). His choruses *Listen to the lambs*, *I'll never turn back no more*, and *Don't be weary, traveler*, became standard pieces of the choral repertoire. He publ. the anthologies *Religious Folk Songs of the Negro* (1926) and *The Dett Collection of Negro Spirituals* (4 vols., 1936). His piano compositions were publ. in 1973 in Evanston, Ill., with introductory articles by D.-R. de Lerma and V. McBrier.

Bibl.: M. Stanley, "R.N. D. of Hampton Institute," *Musical America* (July 1918); V. McBrier, *R.N. D.: His Life and Works: 1882–1943* (Washington, D.C., 1977); J. Spencer, "R.N. D.'s Views on the Preservation of Black Music," *Black Perspective in Music*, X (1982).

Deutekom, Cristina (real name, **Stientje Engel**), Dutch soprano; b. Amsterdam, Aug. 28, 1932. She was educated at the Amsterdam Cons.; sang with the Netherlands Opera; also appeared in Munich, Hamburg, Vienna, London, and Milan. She made her American debut at the Metropolitan Opera in N.Y. as the Queen of the Night in *Die Zauberflöte*, on Sept. 28, 1967; also appeared in concerts. She was acknowledged as one of the finest coloratura sopranos of her generation.

Deutsch, Diana, significant English-born American music psychologist; b. London, Feb. 15, 1938. She studied music theory and composition in London; received a 1st-class honors B.A. in psychology from Oxford (1959) and a Ph.D. in psychology from the Univ. of Calif. at San Diego (1970), where she became a research psychologist at its Center for Human Information Processing. In 1989 she obtained professorial status there. She has contributed highly creative research in psychoacoustics and the psychology of music. Her work has included extensive study of auditory illusions and paradoxes; she also created a model of the process of analyzing musical shape that has received widespread attention. She ed. the text *The Psychology of Music* (N.Y., 1982), and in 1983 founded the journal *Music Perception*, of which she is ed. Important articles authored by her include "An Auditory Illusion," *Nature*, 1251 (1974), "Internal Representation of Pitch Sequences in Tonal Music," *Psychological Review*, lxxxviii (1981), and "Pitch Class and Perceived Height: Some Paradoxes and Their Implications," *Explorations in Music, the Arts and Ideas*, ed. by Narmour and Solie (N.Y., 1988).

Deutsch, Max, Austrian-born French composer, conductor, and pedagogue; b. Vienna, Nov. 17, 1892; d. Paris, Nov. 22, 1982. He studied composition privately with Schoenberg; also took courses at the Univ. of Vienna. He began his career by conducting operetta in Vienna; in 1923 he went to Berlin, where he organized his own orch. group concentrating mainly on modern music, emulating Schoenberg's Soc. for Private Performances of Vienna. In 1925 he settled in Paris, where he founded a Jewish theatrical ensemble, Der Jiddische Spiegel; also conducted concerts of modern music. From 1933 to 1935 he was in Madrid, where he was in charge of a film enterprise; in 1939 he went to France; served in the Foreign Legion until 1945; then returned to Paris, where he devoted himself to teaching, using Schoenberg's method. In 1960 he founded the Grands Concerts de la Sorbonne. In his compositions, he pursued novel ideas; he was the 1st to write a complete film sym., in 5 movements, for the production of the German motion picture *Der Schutz* (1923); he furthermore composed 2 syms. and a choral sym., *Prière pour nous autres mortels*, after the text of Charles Peguy.

Deutsch, Otto Erich, eminent Austrian musicologist; b. Vienna, Sept. 5, 1883; d. there, Nov. 23, 1967. He studied literature and the history of art at the univs. of Vienna and Graz; was the art critic of Vienna's *Die Zeit* (1908–9); then served as an assistant at the Kunsthistorisches Institut of the Univ.

of Vienna (1909–12); later was a bookseller, and then music librarian of the important collection of Anthony van Hoboken in Vienna (1926–35). In 1939 he emigrated to England and settled in Cambridge; in 1947 he became a British subject, but returned to Vienna in 1951. A scholar of impeccable credentials, he was considered one of the foremost authorities on Handel, Mozart, and Schubert; his documentary biographies of these composers constitute primary sources; he was also responsible for initiating the critical edition of Mozart's letters, which he ed. with W. Bauer and J. Eibl as *Mozart: Briefe und Aufzeichnungen* (7 vols., Kassel, 1962–75).

WRITINGS: *Schubert-Brevier* (Berlin, 1905); *Beethovens Beziehungen zu Graz* (Graz, 1907); *Franz Schubert: Die Dokumente seines Lebens und Schaffens* (in collaboration, 1st with L. Scheibler, then with W. Kahl and G. Kinsky), which was planned as a comprehensive work in 3 vols. containing all known documents, pictures, and other materials pertaining to Schubert, arranged in chronological order, with a thematic catalog, but of which only 2 vols. were publ.: vol. III, *Sein Leben in Bildern* (Munich, 1913), and vol. II, part 1, *Die Dokumente seines Lebens* (Munich, 1914; Eng. tr. by E. Blom, titled *Schubert: A Documentary Biography*, London, 1946; American ed., titled *The Schubert Reader: A Life of Franz Schubert in Letters and Documents*, N.Y., a 2nd German ed., enl., publ. in the *Neue Ausgabe sämtlicher Werke* of Schubert, in 1964); *Franz Schuberts Briefe und Schriften* (Munich, 1919; in Eng., London, 1928; 4th German ed., Vienna, 1954); *Die historischen Bildnisse Franz Schuberts in getreuen Nachbildungen* (Vienna, 1922); *Die Originalausgaben von Schuberts Goethe-Liedern* (Vienna, 1926); *Franz Schubert: Tagebuch: Faksimile der Originalhandschrift* (Vienna, 1928); *Mozart und die Wiener Logen* (Vienna, 1932); *Leopold Mozarts Briefe an seine Tochter* (with B. Paumgartner; Salzburg, 1936); *Das Freihaustheater auf der Wieden 1787–1801* (Vienna, 1937); *Wolfgang Amadé Mozart: Verzeichnis aller meiner Werke. Faksimile der Handschrift mit dem Beiheft "Mozarts Werkverzeichnis 1784–1791"* (Vienna, 1938; in Eng., 1956); *Schubert: Thematic Catalogue of All His Works in Chronological Order* (with D. Wakeling; London, 1951; in German as *Franz Schubert: Thematisches Verzeichnis seiner Werke*, publ. in the *Neue Ausgabe sämtlicher Werke* of Schubert in a rev. ed., 1978); *Handel: A Documentary Biography* (N.Y., 1954; London, 1955); *Franz Schubert: Die Erinnerungen seiner Freunde* (Leipzig, 1957; in Eng., 1958); *Mozart: Die Dokumente seines Lebens* (Kassel, 1961; in Eng. as *Mozart: A Documentary Biography*, Palo Alto, Calif., 1965; 2nd ed., 1966; supplement, 1978); *Mozart und seine Welt in zeitgenössischen Bildern* (completed by M. Zenger, Kassel, 1961); also numerous articles on Mozart, Haydn, Beethoven, and others contributed to German, Eng., and American music publications.

BIBL.: *O.E. D. zum 75. Geburtstag* (Vienna, 1958); W. Gerstenberg, J. LaRue, and W. Rehm, eds., *Festschrift O.E. D.* (Kassel, 1963); J. Stone, "More on the Mozart Puzzles," *Musical Times* (July 1988).

Devčić, Natko, Croatian composer; b. Glina, June 30, 1914. He studied piano and composition at the Zagreb Academy of Music, graduating in 1939; he studied with Joseph Marx in Vienna (1949–50) and Jean Rivier in Paris (1953); attended courses led by Boulez at Darmstadt (summer 1965) and researched the potentialities of electronic sound with Davidovsky at the Columbia-Princeton Electronic Studio in N.Y. (1966–67). His early works are based on folklore resources; later on, he experimented with advanced techniques.

WORKS: Opera, *Labinska vještica* (The Witch of Labin; Zagreb, Dec. 25, 1957); ballet, *Dia . . .* (Zagreb, May 20, 1971); *Scherzo* for Orch. (1936); *Nocturne* for Orch. (1941; rev. 1956); *Istarska suite* (Istrian Suite) for Orch. (Zagreb, Dec. 8, 1948); Sym. (1953); *Balada* for Piano and Orch. (1953); Concertino for Violin and Chamber Orch. (1958); *Prolog* for Winds and Percussion (1965); *Fibula* for 2 Orchs. (Zagreb, May 12, 1967); Concerto for Voice, Ondes Martenot, and Chamber Ensemble (Graz, Oct. 23, 1969); *Panta rei* (All Things Change, a motto

of Heraclitus) for Piano and Orch. (1973); *Entre nous* for Orch. (Zagreb, March 26, 1975); *Kantata o bezimenima* (Cantata about a Nameless One) for Chamber Chorus and 12 Instruments (1959); *Ševa* (The Lark), cantata (Zagreb, March 30, 1960); *Igra riječi* (Play of Words) for 2 Narrators, Chorus, Instrumental Ensemble, and Tape (Zagreb, May 9, 1969); *8 Minutes* for Piano and Chamber Ensemble (1965); *Odrazi* (Reflections) for Chamber Ensemble (1965); *Micro-tune* for Viola and Piano (1971); *Sonata-Fantasy* for Piano (1940); *Koraci* (Steps), 5 movements for Piano (1962); *Micro-suite* for Piano (1965); *Structures transparentes* and *Structures volantes* for Solo Harp (1966, 1971); *Columbia 68* for Tape (1968).

Devienne, François, versatile French musician; b. Joinville, Haute-Marne, Jan. 31, 1759; d. in the insane asylum at Charenton, Sept. 5, 1803. A flutist and bassoonist, member of the band of the Gardes Suisses, bassoonist at the Théâtre de Monsieur (1789–1801), and a prof. at the Paris Cons. (from 1795), he was an extraordinarily prolific composer of peculiar importance from the impulse which he gave to perfecting the technique of wind instruments.

WORKS: 12 operas; many concerted pieces for various wind instruments, with orch.; overtures; concertos, quartets, trios, sonatas, etc., for flute, piano, and other instruments; *12 suites d'harmonies à 8 et 12 parties*; numerous romances, chansons, etc.; also a valuable *Méthode de flûte* (Paris, 1795), which went through several eds.

BIBL.: W. Montgomery, *The Life and Works of F. D., 1759–1803* (diss., Catholic Univ. of America, 1975).

De Vito, Gioconda, Italian violinist; b. Martina Franca (Lecce), July 26, 1907. She studied at the Liceo Musicale in Pesaro, graduating in 1921; then performed throughout Europe. She taught at the Bari Cons., retiring in 1961.

Devlin, Michael (Coles), American bass-baritone; b. Chicago, Nov. 27, 1942. He studied at Louisiana State Univ. (Mus.B., 1965) and received vocal training from Norman Treigle and Daniel Ferro in N.Y. In 1963 he made his operatic debut as Spalanzani in *Les Contes d'Hoffmann* in New Orleans, and in 1966 he made his 1st appearance at the N.Y. City Opera as the Hermit in the U.S. premiere of Ginastera's *Don Rodrigo*, continuing on its roster until 1978. In 1974 he made his British debut at the Glyndebourne Festival as Mozart's Almaviva; he 1st sang at London's Covent Garden in 1975, then appeared at the Holland Festival, the Frankfurt Opera, and the Bavarian State Opera in Munich in 1977. On Nov. 12, 1978, he made his Metropolitan Opera debut in N.Y. as Escamillo, and subsequently returned there regularly; he also sang with opera companies in San Francisco (1979), Hamburg and Paris (1980), Miami and Monte Carlo (1981), Dallas (1983), Chicago (1984), and Los Angeles (1986).

De Vocht, Lodewijk, Belgian conductor and composer; b. Antwerp, Sept. 21, 1887; d. 's Gravenzel, near Antwerp, March 27, 1977. He studied with Gilson and Mortelmans at the Royal Flemish Cons. in Antwerp; played the violin in the orch. of the Société des Concerts Nouveaux (from 1903) and became its conductor in 1921; conducted the choir of the Antwerp Cathedral (1912–50); for more than half a century led the Chorale Caecilia that he had founded (1915–68); also the Assoc. des Concerts of the Antwerp Cons. (1935–53); taught music at the Royal Flemish Cons. (1921–53). His compositions are in a Romantic style.

WORKS: 3 syms. (No. 1, with Chorus, 1932); Violin Concerto (Antwerp, May 20, 1944); Cello Concerto (1955); Concerto for Recorder and Orch. (1957); *Primavera*, pastoral poem for Soprano, Tenor, Chorus, and Orch. (1963–65); *Scaldis aeterna*, cantata (1966); several symphonic poems, among them *Sortilèges des bois*; Wind Trio (1955); *Tylliederen*, 7 ballads for Baritone, and Guitar or Piano (1968); *Suite champêtre* for Guitar (1971–73); many choruses; 2 piano sonatas; preludes and fugues for organ.

DeVoto, Mark (Bernard), American composer, writer on music, pianist, and conductor; b. Cambridge, Mass., Jan. 11, 1940.

His father was the American novelist, journalist, historian, and critic Bernard (Augustine) DeVoto. He studied at the Longy School of Music (1946–56), then with Thompson, Piston, Pirrotta, and Ward at Harvard Univ. (B.A., 1961), with Foss at the Berkshire Music Center in Tanglewood (summer 1959), and with Sessions, Kim, Babbitt, and Cone at Princeton Univ. (M.F.A., 1963; Ph.D., 1967, with the diss. *Alban Berg's Picture-Postcard Songs*). He taught at Reed College (1964–68), the Univ. of New Hampshire (1968–81), and Tufts Univ. (from 1981). He was founding ed. of the International Alban Berg Soc. *Newsletter* (1968–75); also rev. and augmented Piston's *Harmony* (4th ed., 1978; 5th ed., 1987).

WORKS: ORCH.: 4 piano concertos: No. 1 (1956); No. 2 (1965–66); No. 3, *The Distinguished Thing* (1968); No. 4 with Sym. Wind Ensemble, Women's Voices, and Viola obbligato (1983); *Night Songs and Distant Dances* (1962); *3 Little Pieces* (1964). **CHAMBER:** 2 *Etudes* for Piano, left hand (1970); Quartet for Flute, Clarinet, Guitar, and Harp (1987); *Lux benigna* for Euphonium, Violin, Organ, and Piano (1988). **VOCAL:** *Fever-Dream Vocalise* for Soprano, Flute, Cello, Piano, and Percussion (1968); *Ornieres* for Soprano, Piano, Organ, and Percussion Ensemble (1974); *The Caucasian Chalk Circle* for Voices and 9 Instruments (1979–80); *H* for Reciter and Flute Choir (1981); *Psalm 98* for Chorus, 2 Trumpets, and 2 Trombones (1983); also arrangements for band.

Devreese, Frédéric, Belgian conductor and composer, son of **Godefroid Devreese;** b. Amsterdam, June 2, 1929. He studied 1st at the Mechelen Cons.; then took courses in composition from Poot and conducting from Defossez at the Brussels Cons.; subsequently studied with Pizzetti at the Accademia di Santa Cecilia in Rome (1952–55). Returning to Belgium, he became associated with Flemish Television as program director.

WORKS: An opera that won the 1964 Prix Italia, *Willem van Saeftinghe* (Brussels TV, Sept. 28, 1964; 1st stage perf., Antwerp, Nov. 21, 1964); TV opera, *De vreemde ruiter* (1966); 2 ballets: *Mascarade* (1955; Aix-les-Bains, France, 1956) and *L'Amour de Don Juan* (1973). **ORCH.:** 4 piano concertos (1949; 1952; 1955–56; 1983); Violin Concerto (1951); Sym. (1953); *Mouvement lent* for String Orch. (1953); *Recitativo et Allegro* for Trumpet and Orch. (1959); *Mouvement vif* for String Orch. (1963); *Evocation*, suite (1967); Divertimento for String Orch. (1970); *Prelude* (1981); Suite for Brass Band (1985); *L'Oeuvre au noir*, suite (1988). **CHAMBER:** *Complainte* for Cello or Oboe, and Piano (1951); Quintet for Flute, Clarinet, Bassoon, Piano, and Percussion (1957); *Ensorbeelden*, suite for Brass Quintet (1972); Suite No. 2 for Brass Quintet (1981); 5 *Divertimenti* for 4 Saxophones (1985); piano pieces; choruses.

Devreese, Godefroid, Belgian conductor and composer, father of **Frédéric Devreese;** b. Kortrijk, Jan. 22, 1893; d. Brussels, June 4, 1972. He studied at the Brussels Cons. with Ysaÿe and César Thomson (violin) and Rasse and Gilson (composition); was a conductor of the Antwerp Opera (1919–20); a violinist with the Concertgebouw Orch. in Amsterdam (1925–30); director of the Mechelin Cons. (1930–59), concurrently giving courses at the Brussels Cons. (1944–59).

WORKS: Ballet, *Tombelène* (1927); *Poème héroïque* for Orch. (1923); *Symphonic Variations on a Popular Scottish Theme* (1923); Concertino for Cello and Chamber Orch. (1926); *In memoriam* for Orch. (1928); 2 violin concertos (1936, 1970); Piano Concerto (1938); 4 syms.: No. 1, *Gothique* (1944); No. 2, *Goethe*, with Chorus (1952); No. 3, *Sinfonietta* (1962); No. 4 (1965–66); Rhapsodie for Clarinet and Orch. (1948); *Allegro* for Trumpet and Orch. (1950); Suite for Orch. (1953); Sinfonietta for String Orch. (1962); 6 *Variations on a Popular Theme* for String Orch. (1963); *Capriccio* for Violin and String Orch. (1963); *Stabat mater* for Soprano, Chorus, and Orch. (1965); *Te Deum* for Chorus and Orch. (1967; posth., Brussels, March 30, 1973); Violin Sonata (1924); Cello Sonata (1926); String Quartet (1937); Piano Trio (1950); *Scherzo de concert* for Piano (1921); *Danse lente* for Piano (1924); 7 piano sonatinas (1944–45); Piano Sonata (1945); songs.

Devrient, Eduard (Philipp), German baritone, librettist, and writer on music; b. Berlin, Aug. 11, 1801; d. Karlsruhe, Oct. 4, 1877. He studied singing and thorough-bass with Zelter in Berlin; gave his 1st public performance there in 1819; then joined the Royal Opera, but after the loss of his voice (1834) went over to the spoken drama, without losing his interest in music. He sang the role of Christ in the famous performance of Bach's *St. Matthew Passion* under Mendelssohn on March 11, 1829; was chief producer and actor at the Dresden Court Theater (1844–46) and director at the Karlsruhe Court Theater (1852–70); he was the author of the text to Marschner's *Hans Heiling*, and also created the title role (1833). His chief work is *Geschichte der deutschen Schauspielkunst* (5 vols., 1848–74); his works concerning music are *Briefe aus Paris* (1840; about Cherubini) and *Meine Erinnerungen an Felix Mendelssohn-Bartholdy und seine Briefe an mich* (Leipzig, 1869). Within weeks after publication of the latter, Wagner issued a polemical pamphlet entitled *Herr Eduard Devrient und sein Styl* (Munich, 1869) under the pseudonym Wilhelm Drach, violently attacking Devrient for his literary style. Devrient's book was publ. in Eng. (London, 1869; 3rd ed., 1891).
BIBL.: J. Bab, *Die D.s* (Berlin, 1932).

Devroye, Théodore-Joseph, Belgian music scholar; b. Villers-la-Ville, Brabant, Aug. 19, 1804; d. Liège, July 19, 1873. He trained for the priesthood at the seminaries in Mechelen and Liège; was ordained in Münster in 1828. He was active at the church of St. Christophe in Liège (1830–35), then was canon at Liège Cathedral and precentor for the Liège diocese. He advocated the restoration of churches, the building of organs, and the revitalization of church music; he also promoted the reform of plainsong melodies in Catholic liturgy.
WRITINGS (all publ. in Liège unless otherwise given): *Traité de plainchant à l'usage des séminaires* (1831; 2nd ed., 1839); *Vesperale romanum sive Antiphonale romanum abreviatum cum Psalterio* (1842; 3rd ed., 1860); *Manuale cantorum ad laudes et parvas horas, juxta Breviarum romanum, cum psalmis capitulis et orationibus* (1849); *Processionale romanum continens responsoria, hymnos, antiphonas psalmos in processionibus dicenda additis laudibus vespertinis de SS. Sacramento de S. Cruce de Beata M.V. et suppleneto ex pontificali romano* (1849); *Graduale romanum juxta missale et officia nomvissme auctoritate Apostolica pro universali ecclesia approbata* (1851; 3rd ed., 1869); *Manuale cantorum officia propria Sanctorum ecclesiae cathedralis civitatis et diocesis Leodiensis* (1858); *Concours de musiques religieuses* (Brussels, 1867); *Sur la peinture chrétienne* (Antwerp, 1871).
BIBL.: J. Helbig, "Le chanoine D.," *Bulletin de l'Institut Archéologique Liègeois*, XIV (1878).

Deyo, Felix, American composer and pianist, 2nd cousin of **Ruth Lynda Deyo;** b. Poughkeepsie, N.Y., April 21, 1888; d. Baldwin, N.Y., June 21, 1959. He studied piano with his mother, **Mary Forster Deyo** (1857–1947); then at the Brooklyn Cons. of Music; after graduation, he taught there (1911–39). In 1939 he became director of the Baldwin (Long Island) Cons. of Music; wrote 3 syms.: *A Lyric Symphony* (Babylon, Long Island, Dec. 8, 1949); *An Ancient Symphony; A Primeval Symphony;* also 2 piano sonatas, a Violin Sonata, and numerous piano pieces of a programmatic nature (*Flight of the Dodo Bird*, etc.). His wife, **Asta Nygren Deyo** (1898–1953), was a piano teacher.

Deyo, Ruth Lynda, American pianist, 2nd cousin of **Felix Deyo;** b. Poughkeepsie, N.Y., April 20, 1884; d. Cairo, March 4, 1960. She studied piano with William Mason and Teresa Carreño; composition with MacDowell; made her debut at the age of 9 at the World's Columbian Exposition in Chicago (1893); made her concert debut in Berlin (March 23, 1904); subsequently played with major orchs. in the U.S. and in Europe; appeared in recitals with Kreisler and Casals. In 1925 she settled in Egypt and devoted herself mainly to composition. In 1930 she completed the full score of a large opera on Egyptian themes, *The Diadem of Stars* (libretto by her husband,

Charles Dalton; unperf.). The Prelude to this opera was perf. by Stokowski with the Philadelphia Orch. (April 4, 1931).

Dezède, Nicolas, composer; b. c.1742; d. Paris, Sept. 11, 1792. He is believed to have been of noble birth. After initial training in the fundamentals of music and the harp, he settled in Paris and studied composition; subsequently launched a successful career as a composer for the theater, scoring a major triumph with his opéra-comique *Blaise et Babet, ou La Suite des trois fermiers* (Versailles, April 4, 1783) and finding a patron in Duke Maximilian of Zweibrücken in 1785. Dezède's liaison with Mme. Belcour of the Comédie-Française resulted in a daughter, Florine (b. c.1766; d. c.1792), who wrote the comedy *Lucette et Lucas, ou La Paysanne curieuse* (Paris, 1781). Mozart used the air "Lison dormait dans un bocage" from Dezède's opéra-comique *Julie* as the theme for his 9 variations for piano, K. 264. Dezède is believed to have composed the air "Ah, vous dirais-je, Maman?," celebrated in English as "Twinkle, Twinkle, Little Star" and used by Mozart for his variations, K. 265.

WORKS: STAGE (all 1st perf. in Paris unless otherwise noted): *Julie* (opéra-comique; Sept. 28, 1772); *L'erreur d'un moment, ou La Suite de Julie* (opéra-comique; June 14, 1773); *Le Stratagème découvert* (comédie; Oct. 4, 1773); *Les Trois Fermiers* (comédie; May 24, 1777); *Fatmé, ou Le Langage des fleurs* (comédie-ballet; Fontainebleau, Oct. 30, 1777); *Zulima ou L'Art et la nature, ou La Nature et l'art* (opéra-comique; May 9, 1778); *Le Porteur de chaise* (opéra-comique; Dec. 10, 1778); rev. as *Jerôme et Champagne*, Jan. 11, 1781); *Cécile* (opéra-comique; Versailles, Feb. 24, 1780); *A trompeur, trompeur et demi, ou Les Torts du sentiment* (opéra-comique; May 3, 1780; also known as *Fin contre fin*); *Blaise et Babet, ou La Suite des trois fermiers* (opéra-comique; Versailles, April 4, 1783); *Péronne sauvée* (opéra; May 27, 1783); *Alexis et Justine* (opéra-comique; Versailles, Jan. 14, 1785); *Alcindor* (opéra-féerie; April 17, 1787); *Auguste et Théodore, ou Les Deux Pages* (opéra-comique; March 6, 1789); *Les Trois Noces* (pièce champêtre; Feb. 23, 1790); *Ferdinand, ou La Suite des Deux Pages* (comédie; June 19, 1790); *Adéle et Didier* (opéra-comique; Nov. 5, 1790); *Paulin et Clairette, ou Les Deux Espiègles* (prose comédie; Jan. 5, 1792); *Mélite* (opéra-comique; March 19, 1792); *La Fête de la cinquantaine* (opéra; Jan. 9, 1796).

BIBL.: A. Pougin, "D.," *Revue et Gazette Musicale de Paris*, XXIX (1862; also publ. separately, Paris, 1862).

D'Haene, Rafaël, Belgian composer; b. Gullegem, Sept. 29, 1943. He studied piano with E. del Pueyo in Brussels, and composition with H. Dutilleux in Paris (Licence de Composition, 1968) and V. Legley at the Chapelle Musicale Reine Elisabeth. In 1970 he became prof. of counterpoint and fugue at the Brussels Cons. and prof. of musical analysis at the Chapelle Musicale Reine Elisabeth.

WORKS: *9 Stukken* for Piano (1967–68); *Werk uit Roemenië*, lieder cycle for Baritone (1969); *Miroir des vanités* for Chorus (1970); String Quartet (1971); *Klage der Ariadne*, cantata for Soli, Chorus, and Orch. (1971–72); *5 Orchestral Lieder* (1972); *Praeludia* for Orch. (1974); *Impressions*, lieder cycle for Mezzo-soprano (1980); *Canzone* for Piano (1983); *Lettres persanes* for Orch. (1986); *Sonette an Orpheus*, 3 lieder for Soprano and Orch. (1987).

D'Hoedt, Henri-Georges, Belgian composer; b. Ghent, June 28, 1885; d. Brussels, May 14, 1936. He was a student of Emile Mathieu and Leo Moeremans; became director of the Cons. at Louvain in 1924, serving until his death. He was one of the 1st Belgian composers to depart from late-19th-century Romanticism and come under the influence of French Impressionism.

WORKS: Opera, *Klaas au Pays de Cocagne* (*Klaas in t'Luilekerkland*; Antwerp, 1926); satirical symphonic study, *Les Brèves Chroniques de la vie bourgeoise* (1934); *Narcisse* for Orch.; *L'Ile de Cythère* for Chorus and Orch.; *La Vocation de Siddartha*, symphonic trilogy; *Dionysos*, symphonic poem; *Poème pantagruélique* for Orch.; chamber music.

Diabelli, Anton, Austrian composer and publisher; b. Mattsee, near Salzburg, Sept. 5, 1781; d. Vienna, April 8, 1858. He was a choirboy in the monastery at Michaelbeurn, and at Salzburg Cathedral; studied for the priesthood at the Munich Latin School, but continued his musical work, submitting his compositions to Michael Haydn, who encouraged him. On the secularization of the Bavarian monasteries, Diabelli, who had already entered that at Raichenhaslach, embraced the career of a musician, went to Vienna (where Joseph Haydn received him kindly), taught piano and guitar for a living, and in 1818 became a partner of Cappi, the music publisher, assuming control of the firm (Diabelli & Co.) in 1824. He publ. much of Schubert's music, but underpaid the composer, and complained that he wrote too much. In 1852 he sold his firm to C.A. Spina. A facile composer, Diabelli produced an opera, *Adam in der Klemme* (Vienna, 1809; 1 perf.), masses, cantatas, chamber music, etc., which were consigned to oblivion; his sonatinas are still used for beginners. His name was immortalized through Beethoven's set of 33 variations (op. 120) on a waltz theme by Diabelli.

BIBL.: A. Weinmann, *Verlagsverzeichnis A. D. & Co., 1824 bis 1840* (Vienna, 1985).

Diaghilev, Sergei (Pavlovich), famous Russian impresario; b. Gruzino, Novgorod district, March 31, 1872; d. Venice, Aug. 19, 1929. He was associated with progressive artistic organizations in St. Petersburg, but his main field of activity was in western Europe. He established the Ballets Russes in Paris; he commissioned Stravinsky to write the ballets *The Firebird*, *Petrouchka*, and *Le Sacre du printemps*; also commissioned Prokofiev, Milhaud, Poulenc, Auric, and other composers of the younger generation. Ravel and Manuel de Falla also wrote works for him. The great importance of Diaghilev's choreographic ideas lies in the complete abandonment of the classical tradition; in this respect he was the true originator of the modern dance.

BIBL.: D. issue of *La Revue Musicale* (Dec. 1930); *The Russian Ballet* (London, 1931); C. Beaumont, *S. D.* (London, 1933); A. Haskell, *D., His Artistic and Private Life* (London, 1935); V. Kamenev, *Russian Ballet through Russian Eyes* (London, 1936); S. Lifar, *S. D.: His Life, His Work, His Legend* (London, 1940); C. Beaumont, *The D. Ballet in London, A Personal Record* (London, 1940); S. Grigoriev, *The D. Ballet* (London, 1953); R. Buehle, *In Search of D.* (N.Y., 1956); B. Kochno, *D. and the Ballets Russes* (N.Y., 1970); R. Buckle, *D.* (N.Y., 1979).

Diamond, David (Leo), highly significant and fantastically prolific American composer; b. Rochester, N.Y., July 9, 1915. His parents were of eastern European extraction; his father was a cabinetmaker and his mother a dressmaker for the Yiddish theater. To make ends meet, he worked behind the food counter at a N.Y. drugstore. He studied composition with Bernard Rogers at the Eastman School of Music in his hometown (1930–34); then took courses privately with Roger Sessions in N.Y. Seeking a wider application of his growing talents, he went to Paris in 1937, where he took courses with the fabulous French *nourrice* of a generation of composers, Nadia Boulanger, and where he became associated with the most important musicians and writers of the time. While in France and elsewhere in Europe, he exercised his exceptional linguistic capacity, acquiring fluency in French, Italian, and even Russian by cultivating international acquaintances. Returning to N.Y., he devoted his time exclusively to composition; various grants and awards enabled him to obtain relative financial security. He held the Juilliard Publication Award, 3 Guggenheim fellowships, an American Academy in Rome award, the Paderewski Prize, and a grant from the National Academy of Arts and Letters. He was also lucky in having his music conducted by Hanson, Monteux, Koussevitzky, and Mitropoulos. Other conductors who eventually led his works were Charles Munch, Eugene Ormandy, and Leonard Bernstein.

As a composer, Diamond soon succeeded in establishing an original and recognizable style of harmonic and contrapuntal writing with the sense of tonality clearly present; the element of pitch, often inspired by natural folklike patterns, is very strong in all of his music. In his later works he adopted a modified dodecaphonic method, while keeping free of doctrinaire serialism. His instrumental and vocal writing is invariably idiomatic, which makes his music welcome to performers and audiences alike. Some of his works, like *Rounds* for String Orch., acquired a flattering popularity in concert performances; this score won the N.Y. Music Critics' Circle Award in 1944. His strongest power lies in symphonic and chamber music, but he also shows a marked ability for vocal writing, as exemplified by his choral works. In 1989 he was invited to the Soviet Union, where his music was performed to considerable acclaim. He also taught; in 1973 he was appointed to the faculty of the Juilliard School in N.Y. In 1985 he received the William Schuman Award of Columbia Univ.

WORKS: ORCH.: 9 syms.: No. 1 (N.Y., Dec. 21, 1941); No. 2 (Boston, Oct. 13, 1944); No. 3 (1945; Boston, Nov. 3, 1950); No. 4 (Boston, Jan. 23, 1948); No. 5 (1947–64; N.Y., April 28, 1966); No. 6 (Boston, March 8, 1957); No. 7 (N.Y., Jan. 26, 1962); No. 8 (N.Y., Oct. 26, 1961, prior to Sym. No. 7); No. 9 (N.Y., Nov. 17, 1985); *To Music*, choral sym. for Soloists, Chorus, and Orch. (1967); 3 violin concertos: No. 1 (N.Y., March 24, 1937); No. 2 (Vancouver, Feb. 29, 1948); No. 3 (N.Y., April 1, 1976); *Hommage à Satie* (1934); *Threnody* (1935); *Psalm* for Orch. (Rochester, N.Y., Dec. 10, 1936); 1st suite from the ballet *Tom* (1936); *Variations on an Original Theme* (1937; Rochester, N.Y., April 23, 1940); *Elegy in Memory of Maurice Ravel* for Brass, Harp, and Percussion (Rochester, N.Y., April 28, 1938); *Heroic Piece* (Zürich, July 29, 1938); Cello Concerto (1938; Rochester, N.Y., April 30, 1942); *Concert Piece* (N.Y., May 16, 1940); Concerto for Chamber Orch. (Yaddo, N.Y., Sept. 7, 1940, composer conducting); *Rounds* for String Orch. (Minneapolis, Nov. 24, 1944; his most successful work); *Romeo and Juliet* (N.Y., Oct. 20, 1947); *The Enormous Room*, after e.e. cummings (Cincinnati, Nov. 19, 1949); *Timon of Athens*, after Shakespeare (Louisville, 1949); Piano Concerto (1949; N.Y., April 28, 1966); *Ahavah* for Narrator and Orch. (Washington, D.C., Nov. 17, 1954); *Diaphony* for Brass, 2 Pianos, Timpani, and Organ (N.Y., Feb. 22, 1956); *Sinfonia concertante* (Rochester, N.Y., March 7, 1957); *World of Paul Klee*, orch. suite (Portland, Oreg., Feb. 15, 1958); *Music for Chamber Orch.* (1969); *A Buoyant Music*, overture No. 2 (1970). **CHAMBER:** Partita for Oboe, Bassoon, and Piano (1935); Concerto for String Quartet (1937); String Trio (1937); Quintet for Flute, String Trio, and Piano (1937); Piano Quartet (1938); Cello Sonata (1938); 10 string quartets (1940, 1943, 1946, 1951, 1960, 1962, 1963, 1964, 1966–68, 1966); Violin Sonata (1945); *Canticle for Perpetual Motion* for Violin and Piano (1947); Chaconne for Violin and Piano (1947); Quintet for Clarinet, 2 Violas, and 2 Cellos (1951); Piano Trio (1951); Nonet for 3 Violins, 3 Violas, and 3 Cellos (1962); Piano Quintet (1972); Violin Sonata No. 2 (1981). **VOCAL:** *This Is the Garden*, Chorus a cappella (1935); *3 Madrigals*, after James Joyce, for Chorus a cappella (1937); *Young Joseph*, after Thomas Mann, for Women's Chorus and String Orch. (1944); *L'Âme de Claude Debussy*, extracts from Debussy's letters to Jacques Durand (1949); *The Midnight Meditation*, cycle of 4 songs (1950); *This Sacred Ground* for Chorus, Male Voice, and Orch. (Buffalo, Nov. 17, 1963); *A Secular Cantata*, to texts from James Agee's *Permit Me Voyage* (N.Y., Feb. 5, 1977). **PIANO:** Sonatina (1935); Concerto for 2 Pianos (1941); *Album for the Young* (1946); Sonata (1947).

BIBL.: V. Kimberling, *D. D.: A Bio-bibliography* (Metuchen, N.J., 1987).

Diamond, Neil (Leslie), enormously popular American singer and songwriter; b. N.Y., Jan. 24, 1941. After a brief interlude as a medical student in N.Y., he plunged into the nightclubs of N.Y., singing his own songs with subtly sexual undertones and overtones, *Solitary Man*, *I Got the Feelin'*, *Kentucky Woman*, *I'm a Believer*, and *I Am, I Said*. His recording albums, such as *Hot August Night*, *Jonathan Livingston Seagull*, *Beautiful Noise*, etc., hit the populace with inexplicable impact;

soon he rose to a high plateau in the world of commercial music; his concerts began to attract mobs of plebs in quest of easy thrills, and the wave of success never abated as he, still unmellowed, reached his middle age. He composed the scores for the films *Jonathan Livingston Seagull* (1973) and *The Jazz Singer* (1980).

BIBL.: A. Grossman, B. Truman, and R. Yamanaka, *D.: A Biography* (Chicago, 1987).

Dianda, Hilda, Argentine composer; b. Córdoba, April 13, 1925. She studied in Europe with Scherchen and Malipiero; from 1958 to 1962 worked at Radiodiffusion Française in Paris. Upon returning to Argentina, she devoted herself to composition and organization of concerts of ultramodern music.

WORKS: 3 string quartets (1947, 1960, 1962); Concertante for Cello and Chamber Orch. (1952); Trio for Flute, Oboe, and Bassoon (1953); Wind Quintet (1957); *Díptico* for 16 Instruments (1962); *Núcleos* for String Orch., 2 Pianos, and Percussion (1964); works for various ensembles under the generic titles *Resonancias* and *Ludus* (1964–69).

Dianin, Sergei, Russian writer on music; b. St. Petersburg, Dec. 26, 1888; d. Davidovo, Vladimir district, Oct. 26, 1968. A son of Borodin's assistant in chemistry, he became a mathematician by profession; having access to Borodin's archives, he publ. 4 vols. of Borodin's letters (Moscow, 1928, 1936, 1949, 1950) and a biography, *Borodin, Life, Materials, Documents* (Moscow, 1955; 2nd ed., 1960; in Eng., London, 1963).

Dianov, Anton, Russian composer; b. Moscow, Feb. 19, 1882; d. there, March 25, 1939. He was a pupil of the Moscow Cons., graduating in 1912; in 1920 became director of the Music School in Moscow. He wrote effective piano pieces, music for violin and piano (*Lyrische Fragmente*), and many songs.

Diaz (de la Peña), Eugène(-Emile), French composer, son of the celebrated painter; b. Paris, Feb. 27, 1837; d. Coleville, Sept. 12, 1901. He was a pupil at the Paris Cons., studying with Halévy and Reber; produced the comic opera *Le Roi Candaule* (Paris, 1865) and won the government prize for the opera *La Coupe du roi de Thulé* (Paris, Jan. 10, 1873), which, however, proved a complete failure.

Díaz, Justino, noted Puerto Rican bass; b. San Juan, Jan. 29, 1940. He studied at the Univ. of Puerto Rico (1958–59) and at the New England Cons. of Music in Boston (1959–62); he also received training from Frederick Jagel. In 1957 he made his operatic debut as Ben in Menotti's *The Telephone* in San German, Puerto Rico, and in 1961 appeared with the New England Opera Theater in Boston. After winning the Metropolitan Opera Auditions of the Air, he made his debut with the company in N.Y. as Monterone on Oct. 23, 1963; was chosen to create the role of Antony in Barber's *Antony and Cleopatra* at the opening of the new Metropolitan Opera house at Lincoln Center on Sept. 16, 1966. He made guest appearances in Salzburg, Hamburg, Vienna, Munich, Milan, and other European music centers. On Sept. 10, 1971, he appeared in the premiere of Ginastera's *Beatrix Cenci*, which inaugurated the opera house at the Kennedy Center in Washington, D.C. On March 4, 1973, he made his N.Y. City Opera debut as Francesco in the same opera. In 1976 he made his 1st appearance at London's Covent Garden as Escamillo.

Dibdin, Charles, English composer; b. Dibdin, near Southampton (baptized, March 4), 1745; d. London, July 25, 1814. From 1756 to 1759 he was a chorister at Winchester Cathedral; took lessons there from Kent and Fussell, but was chiefly self-taught in composition; at 15 went to London; was engaged at Covent Garden as a singing actor, and soon began to write for the stage. His 1st piece, *The Shepherd's Artifice*, was produced at his benefit performance, at Covent Garden, on May 21, 1764. He was engaged at Birmingham from 1763 to 1765, and at Covent Garden again till 1768, when he went over to Drury Lane. Falling out with Garrick, he went to France in 1776 to avoid imprisonment for debt, remaining there until 1778, when he was appointed composer to Covent Garden, having up to that time brought out 8 operas. From 1782 to

1784, he was manager of the newly erected Royal Circus (later the Surrey Theatre). After the failure of certain theatrical enterprises, and a projected journey to India, he commenced a series of monodramatic "table-entertainments," of which song was a principal feature, and which were extremely popular from 1789 to 1805; in these Dibdin appeared as author, composer, narrator, singer, and accompanist. He then built and managed a small theater of his own, which opened in 1796; he retired in 1805 on a pension, which was withdrawn for a time, but subsequently restored. Dibdin also composed numerous sea songs which were very popular at the time. He publ. *The Musical Tour of Mr. Dibdin* (1788), *History of the Stage* (5 vols., 1795), *The Professional Life of Mr. Dibdin* (4 vols., 1803), and various novels. His grandson, **Henry Edward Dibdin** (b. London, Sept. 8, 1813; d. Edinburgh, May 6, 1866), was an organist, harpist, and teacher who compiled the collection *The Standard Psalm Tune Book* (1851).

BIBL.: E. Dibdin, *A. C. D. Bibliography* (Liverpool, 1937); E. Holmes, *C. D.* (diss., Univ. of Southampton, 1974).

di Bonaventura, Anthony. See **Bonaventura, Anthony di.**

di Bonaventura, Mario. See **Bonaventura, Mario di.**

Di Capua, Eduardo, Italian composer of Neapolitan ballads; b. Naples, 1864; d. there, 1917. He earned his living by playing in small theaters and cafés in and around Naples, and later in the cinemas; also gave piano lessons. His most famous song was *O sole mio* (1898); its popularity was immense, and never abated. Other celebrated songs were *Maria Marì* (1899); *Torna maggio* (1900); *Canzona bella*; etc. Di Capua sold these songs to publishers outright, and so did not benefit by their popularity. He died in extreme poverty.

Dichter, Misha, talented American pianist; b. Shanghai (of Polish-Jewish refugees), Sept. 27, 1945. He was reared in Los Angeles; at the age of 15 he won a contest of the Music Educators National Conference, Western Division. While attending the Univ. of Calif. at Los Angeles, he enrolled in a master class conducted by Rosina Lhévinne; later joined her class at the Juilliard School of Music in N.Y. In 1966 he entered the International Tchaikovsky Competition in Moscow and won 2nd prize, scoring popular acclaim among Russian audiences. Returning to the U.S., he made his Boston Sym. Orch. debut as soloist at the Tanglewood Festival in 1966; numerous appearances with major American and European orchs. followed; he also gave recitals. His wife, **Cipa** (b. Rio de Janeiro, May 20, 1944), is a fine pianist in her own right; they frequently appear together in duo recitals. Dichter's natural predilections lie in the Romantic repertoire; his playing possesses a high emotional appeal; but he also can render full justice to Classical masterpieces, as demonstrated by his appropriate rendition of Mozart's concertos.

Dick, Marcel, Hungarian-American violist and composer; b. Miskolcz, Aug. 28, 1898. He came from a musical family; the famous Hungarian violinist **Eduard Reményi** was his great-uncle. Dick studied violin with Joseph Bloch and composition with Kodály. He was 1st violist in the Vienna Sym. Orch. (1924–27), and was also a member of the Kolisch Quartet and of the Rosé Quartet. In 1934 he went to the U.S.; was 1st violist of the Cleveland Orch. (1943–49); in 1948, was appointed head of the dept. of theory of the Cleveland Inst. of Music; he retired in 1973. He wrote a Sym. (Cleveland, Dec. 14, 1950) and a Sym. for 2 String Orchs. (1964); also some chamber music and songs.

Dickens, "Little Jimmy" (James), American country-western singer, guitarist, and songwriter; b. Bolt, W.Va., Dec. 19, 1920. He began his career as a performer on WILS radio in Beckley, W.Va., when he was 17, being dubbed "Jimmy the Kid"; then sang on radio stations in Indianapolis, Cincinnati, and Saginaw, Mich. In 1948 he became a member of the "Grand Ole Opry" in Nashville. As a recording artist, he gathered a following with such comic numbers as *Take an Old Cold Tater* (1949), *A-sleepin' at the Foot of the Bed* (1949), *Bessie the*

Heifer (1950), and *I'm Little but I'm Loud* (1950). In 1983 he was elected to the Country Music Hall of Fame.

Dickenson, Vic(tor), black American jazz trombonist and bandleader; b. Xenia, Ohio, Aug. 6, 1906; d. N.Y., Nov. 16, 1984. He learned to handle the trombone; played with Blanche Calloway (1933–36), Benny Carter (1939), Count Basie (1940–41), and Sidney Bechet (1941). In 1949 he formed his own band, and appeared at the major U.S. jazz festivals. He later appeared with Bobby Hackett, Red Allen, and Wild Bill Davison; led his own trio from 1979.

Dickie, Murray, Scottish tenor; b. Bishopton, April 3, 1924. He received his musical training in Glasgow and London. He sang in London at Covent Garden and in Milan at La Scala; eventually became a member of the Vienna State Opera. On Oct. 18, 1962, he made his debut at the Metropolitan Opera in N.Y. as David in *Die Meistersinger von Nürnberg.*

Dickinson, Clarence, American composer; b. Lafayette, Ind., May 7, 1873; d. N.Y., Aug. 2, 1969. He studied music with Weidig in Chicago; then went to Germany, where he took courses with Riemann; further had piano lessons with Moszkowski; he moved to Paris, where he became a pupil of Guilmant in organ playing and with Pierné in composition. Returning to America in 1909, he settled in N.Y. as a church organist; from 1912 to 1945 he served as director of sacred music at the Union Theological Seminary; also made lecture tours in the U.S., Canada, France, England, and Spain. He composed the operas *The Medicine Man* and *Priscilla;* numerous organ pieces and songs; ed. the collections *Historical Recitals for Organ* (50 numbers), *Book of 80 Amens,* and *Book of 40 Antiphons.* He also publ. *Excursions in Musical History* (1917); *Troubadour Songs* (1920); *Technique and Art of Organ Playing* (1921).

Dickinson, George Sherman, American music educator; b. St. Paul, Minn., Feb. 9, 1888; d. Chapel Hill, N.C., Nov. 6, 1964. He studied at Oberlin College (B.A., 1909); at the Oberlin Cons. of Music (Mus.Bac., 1910); and at Harvard Univ. (M.A., 1912); also studied with Kaun and Juon in Berlin (1913–14). He taught at the Oberlin Cons. from 1914 to 1916, and was a member of the faculty of Vassar College from 1922 to 1953. He wrote *The Growth and Use of Harmony* (vol. 4 of *Fundamentals of Musical Art;* N.Y., 1927); *Classification of Musical Compositions* (Poughkeepsie, 1938); *The Pattern of Music* (Poughkeepsie, 1939); *Music as a Literature: An Outline* (Poughkeepsie, 1953); *The Study of Music as a Liberal Art* (Poughkeepsie, 1953); *The Study of the History of Music in the Liberal Arts College* (N.Y., 1953); *A Handbook of Style in Music* (N.Y., 1965).

Dickinson, Peter, English composer; b. Lytham St. Annes, Lancashire, Nov. 15, 1934. Of a musical family, he studied piano and began to compose early in life. He entered Cambridge Univ.; after obtaining his M.A. degree in music there, he went to the U.S. on a Rotary Foundation fellowship, and studied with Bernard Wagenaar at the Juilliard School of Music in N.Y. (1958–60). Returning to England, he became a lecturer at the College of St. Mark and St. John in London (1962–66); then at the Univ. of Birmingham (1966–70). From 1974 to 1985 he was a prof. at Keele Univ. In his music he combines the esoteric techniques of serialism with pragmatic considerations for performance.

WORKS: *Jesus Christ Is Risen Today* for Chorus (1955); *4 Auden Songs* for Voice and Piano (1956; rev. 1977); *Variations for Piano* (1957); *String Quartet* (1958; rev. 1974); *Monologue for String Orch.* (1959); *A Dylan Thomas Song Cycle* for Baritone and Piano (1959); *Vitalitas,* ballet (1959); *Violin Sonata* (1961); *4 Duos* for Oboe or Flute and Cello (1962; rev. 1978); Trio for Flute, Oboe, and Harpsichord (1962; rev. 1978); *Carillon* for Organ (1964); *The Judas Tree,* musical drama for Speakers, Tenor, Chorus, and Orch. (London, May 27, 1965); *Outcry* for Contralto, Chorus, and Orch. (Leamington, May 10, 1969); *5 Diversions* for Orch. (Leamington, Nov. 23, 1969); *Transformations: Homage to Satie* for Orch. (Cheltenham, July

3, 1970); Organ Concerto (Gloucester Cathedral, Aug. 22, 1971); Concerto for Strings, Percussion, and Electronic Organ (Birmingham, Jan. 22, 1971); String Quartet No. 2 with Tape or Piano (1975); Piano Concerto (1978–84; Cheltenham, July 22, 1984); *London Rags* for 2 Trumpets, Horn, Trombone, and Tuba (1986); Violin Concerto (1986; Leeds, Jan. 31, 1987).

BIBL.: R. Norrington, "P. D.," *Musical Times* (Feb. 1965).

Diddley, Bo (real name, **Ellas Bates McDaniel**), black American rock-and-roll singer and guitarist; b. Magnolia, Miss., Dec. 30, 1928. He was taken to Chicago in early childhood, where he learned to play the violin and guitar. In 1955 he first attracted attention with his recordings of *Bo Diddley* and *I'm a Man*; later that year he appeared on Ed Sullivan's television show and at N.Y.'s Carnegie Hall. His pelvic gyrations and so-called Bo Diddley beat influenced the 1st generation of rock-and-roll musicians, including Elvis Presley. In 1959 he scored great success with his recording of *Say Man*. In 1963 he performed in England and in 1972 at the Montreux Jazz Festival. Later tours included Europe (1986) and Japan (1988).

BIBL.: *Current Biography* (June 1989).

Diderot, Denis, illustrious French man of letters and philosopher; b. Langres, Oct. 5, 1713; d. Paris, July 30, 1784. In his work *Mémoirs sur différents sujets de mathématiques* (The Hague, 1748) are the essays "Des principes d'acoustique" and "Projet d'un nouvel orgue," the latter being an impracticable idea for a new kind of barrel organ. For his writings on music, see B. Durand-Sendrail, ed., *D. D.: Écrits sur la musique* (Paris, 1987).

Di Domenica, Robert, American composer and flutist; b. N.Y., March 4, 1927. He graduated in music education from N.Y. Univ. in 1951; studied composition privately with Wallingford Riegger; also took flute lessons with Harold Bennett (1949–55). He performed as a flutist with various orch. groups. He taught flute privately in N.Y.; in 1969 he was appointed to the faculty of the New England Cons. of Music in Boston; was an associate dean (1973–76) and dean (1976–78); subsequently taught theory and composition there. In 1972 he held a Guggenheim fellowship.

WORKS: Opera, *The Balcony* (1972); Flute Sonata (1957); Sextet for Piano, Flute, Oboe, Clarinet, Horn, and Bassoon (1957); Quartet for Violin, Flute, Horn, and Piano (1959); Quartet for Flute, Violin, Viola, and Cello (1960); *The First Kiss of Love* for Soprano and Piano (1960); String Quartet (1960); Sym. (1961; Boston, Nov. 15, 1972); *Variations on a Tonal Theme* for Flute (1961); Concerto for Violin and Chamber Orch. (1962; N.Y., April 15, 1965); 2 piano concertos (1963, 1982); Concerto for Wind Quintet, Strings, and Timpani (1964); Quintet for Clarinet and String Quartet (1965); Trio for Flute, Bassoon, and Piano (1966); Violin Sonata (1966); *Saeculum aureum* for Flute, Piano, and Tape (1967); *Music* for Flute and String Orch. (1967); Saxophone Sonata (1968); *Songs from 12th Night* for Tenor, Flute, Viola da Gamba, and Harpsichord (1976); *Black Poems* for Baritone, Piano, and Tape (1976); *Variations on a Theme by Gunther Schuller* for 13 Instruments (1983; Boston, Dec. 11, 1984); *Dream Journeys* for Orch. (1984; Plymouth, Mass., Oct. 5, 1985); *The Scarlet Letter*, opera (1986); also other chamber works and piano pieces.

Didur, Adamo, famous Polish bass; b. Wola Sekowa, near Sanok, Galicia, Dec. 24, 1874; d. Katowice, Jan. 7, 1946. He studied with Wysocki in Lemberg and Emmerich in Milan, where he made his debut in a concert in 1894; later that year he made his operatic debut as Méphistophélès in Rio de Janeiro. He sang at the Warsaw Opera (1899–1903), Milan's La Scala (1903–6), London's Covent Garden (1905), and Buenos Aires's Teatro Colón (1905–8). On Nov. 4, 1907, he made an auspicious N.Y. debut as Alvise at the Manhattan Opera; his Metropolitan Opera debut followed as Ramfis on Nov. 16, 1908, and he remained on its roster as one of its leading artists until 1932. He then returned to Poland; his appointment as director of the Warsaw Opera in 1939 was aborted by the outbreak of World War II. He later settled in Katowice as a voice teacher, founding an opera company (1945) and becoming director of the Cons. His portrayals of Leporello and Boris Godunov were particularly memorable.

Didymus, Chalcenterus (Of the Brazen Guts), Greek scholar and grammarian of Alexandria who flourished from c.80 to 10 B.C. He earned the nickname of Chalcenterus for his large output of books, which is said to have numbered about 3,500 vols. He wrote a tract on music, now known only by an epitome of Porphyry's, and some quotations by Ptolemy. In his system the octave of the diatonic genus is formed by 2 precisely similar tetrachords, and in all 3 species of tetrachord (diatonic, chromatic, enharmonic) the ratio for the interval of the major third is 4:5. He also recognized the difference between the major and minor whole tone; this difference $(9/8:10/9 = 81:80)$ is, therefore, rightly termed the "comma of Didymus." Salinas and Doni have written on his musical system.

Diemer, Emma Lou, American composer, keyboard player, and teacher; b. Kansas City, Mo., Nov. 24, 1927. She was a pupil of Donovan and Hindemith at Yale Univ. (B.M., 1949; M.M., 1950), of Toch and Sessions at the Berkshire Music Center in Tanglewood (summers 1954, 1955), and of Rogers, Hanson, and Craighead at the Eastman School of Music in Rochester, N.Y. (Ph.D., 1960). She was composer-in-residence for the Ford Foundation Young Composers Project in Arlington, Va. (1959–61), and also on the faculties of the Univ. of Maryland (1965–70) and the Univ. of Calif. at Santa Barbara (from 1971).

WORKS: ORCH.: 4 syms. (1953; 1955; *On American Indian Themes*, 1959; *Symphonie antique*, 1961); Piano Concerto (1953); Concerto for Harpsichord and Chamber Orch. (1958); *Pavane* for String Orch. (1959); *Youth Overture* (1959); *Festival Overture* (1961); Flute Concerto (1963); *Fairfax Festival Overture* (1967); *Concert Piece* for Organ and Orch. (1977); Trumpet Concerto (1983; rev. as a violin concerto, 1983); *Suite of Homages* (1985); Serenade for String Orch. (1988). BAND: *Brass Menagerie*, suite (1960); *La Rag* (1981). CHAMBER: Woodwind Quintet No. 1 (1960); Sextet for Piano and Woodwind Quintet (1962); Toccata for Flute Chorus (1968); *Music* for Woodwind Quartet (1972); Trio for Flute, Oboe, Harpsichord, and Tape (1973); *Pianoharpsichordorgan* for 1 or 3 Performers (1974); *Movement* for Flute, Oboe, Clarinet, and Piano (1976); *Quadralogue* for Flute Quartet (1978); *Summer of 82* for Cello and Piano (1982); String Quartet No. 1 (1987); also piano pieces; organ music; choral works; songs; electronic scores.

Diémer, Louis (-Joseph), distinguished French pianist; b. Paris, Feb. 14, 1843; d. there, Dec. 21, 1919. He was a pupil of Marmontel at the Paris Cons., where he took 1st piano prize in 1856; also of Ambroise Thomas and Bazin for composition, taking 1st harmony prize, 2d organ prize, and 1st prize for fugue. He played with great success at the Alard, Pasdeloup, and Paris Cons. concerts; succeeded Marmontel (1887) as prof. of piano at the Cons. The immense success of his series of historical recitals, in 1889, made him resolve to specialize in early music, and led to his establishing the Société des Anciens Instruments. Widor, Saint-Saëns, Lalo, and others wrote pieces for him which he played at the Colonne and Lamoureux concerts. He ed. a number of early French keyboard pieces; his collection *Clavecinistes français* was publ. posth. in 1928.

Diepenbrock, Alphons (Johannes Maria), eminent Dutch composer; b. Amsterdam, Sept. 2, 1862; d. there, April 5, 1921. He learned to play violin and piano in his childhood. In 1880 he entered the Univ. of Amsterdam, where he studied classical philology; received his Ph.D. in 1888; taught academic subjects at the grammar school at 's-Hertogenbosch (1888–94); then abandoned his pedagogical activities and devoted himself primarily to music; studied works of the Flemish School of the Renaissance, and later perused the scores of Berlioz, Wagner, and Debussy. Despite this belated study, he succeeded in developing a rather striking individual style of composition, in which Wagnerian elements curiously intertwine with impressionistic modalities. However, he had difficulty in putting the results into definite shape, and he left more than 100 incomplete MSS at his death. His Catholic upbringing led him to concentrate mainly on the composition of sacred choral music; he wrote no syms., concertos, or instrumental sonatas.

WORKS: *Stabat Mater* for Men's Chorus; *Missa in die festo* for Tenor, Male Chorus, and Organ (1890–91); *Les Elfes* for Soprano, Baritone, Women's Chorus, and Orch. (1896); *Te Deum* for Soloists, Double Chorus, and Orch. (1897); 2 *Hymnen an die Nacht*, after Novalis, 1 each for Soprano and Contralto, with Orch. (1899); *Vondel's vaart naar Agrippine* (Vondel's Journey to Agrippina) for Baritone and Orch. (1902–3); *Im grossen Schweigen*, after Nietzsche, for Baritone and Orch. (Amsterdam, May 20, 1906); *Hymne aan Rembrandt* for Soprano, Women's Chorus, and Orch. (1906); incidental music to Verhagen's mythical comedy *Marsyas of De betooverde bron* (Marsyas or The Enchanted Well; 1909–10); *Die Nacht*, after Hölderlin, for Mezzo-soprano and Orch. (1910–11); *Lydische Nacht* for Baritone and Orch. (1913); incidental music to Aristophanes' *The Birds* (1917; a concert overture from this music is fairly popular); incidental music to Goethe's *Faust* (1918); incidental music to Sophocles' *Electra* (1920); numerous choruses and songs. A collection of Diepenbrock's writings, *Verzamelde geschriften*, ed. by E. Reeser, was publ. in Utrecht (1950); a catalog of his works was issued in Amsterdam in 1962. E. Reeser brought out his *Brieven en documenten* (Letters and Documents; 2 vols., Amsterdam, 1962–67); he also wrote "Some Melodic Patterns in the Music of Alphons Diepenbrock," *Composers' Voice*, 3 (1976/1).

Dieren, Bernard van, important Dutch composer and writer; b. Rotterdam, Dec. 27, 1887; d. London, April 24, 1936. After studying in Germany and the Netherlands, he settled in 1909 in London as music correspondent of the *Nieuwe Rotterdamsche Courant*; later devoted his time exclusively to composing. His works show radical tendencies. He wrote a book on the modern sculptor Jacob Epstein (1920) and a collection of essays, *Down among the Dead Men* (London, 1935).

WORKS: 6 *Sketches* for Piano (1911); 4 string quartets (1912, 1917, 1919, 1923); Sym. for Soli, Chorus, and Orch., on Chinese texts (1914); *Diaphony* for Baritone and Chamber Orch., on 3 Shakespearean sonnets; *Overture to an Ideal Comedy* (1916); *Les Propous des Beuveurs*, introit for Orch. (after Rabelais; London, 1921); *Sonata tyroica* for Violin and Piano (1927); many songs (also with string quartet and chamber orch.).

BIBL.: E. Davis, "B. v.D.," *Musical Quarterly* (April 1938); G. Grouse, "B. v.D.—Three Early Songs in Relation to His Subsequent Development," *Music Review* (May 1968); A. Chisolm, *B. v.D.: An Introduction* (London, 1984).

Diet, Edmond-Marie, French composer; b. Paris, Sept. 25, 1854; d. there, Oct. 30, 1924. He was a pupil of César Franck and Guiraud; produced the operas *Stratonice* (1887), *Le Cousin Placide* (1887), *Fleur de vertu* (1894), *La Revanche d'Iris* (1905); also ballets and pantomimes: *Scientia* (1889); *La Grève; Masque rose; M. Ruy-Blas* (1894); *La Belle et la bête* (1895); *L'Araignée d'or* (1896); *Rêve de Noël* (1896); *Watteau* (1900; with Pujet); 3-act operetta, *Gentil Crampon* (Paris, 1897); songs; church music.

Diether, Jack, Canadian-American musicologist; b. Vancouver, British Columbia, Feb. 26, 1919; d. N.Y., Jan. 22, 1987. He was educated at the Univ. of British Columbia; served in the Canadian army and air force during World War II. In 1955 he settled in the U.S.; was employed at the Pickwick Bookshop in Hollywood and at G. Schirmer's music store in N.Y. In the meantime he wrote for music journals, concentrating on the clarification of obscure periods in the lives and works of Bruckner and Mahler; contributed valuable articles to the journal of the Bruckner Soc. of America, *Chord and Discord*, of which he became the ed. in 1969; wrote annotations for orch. programs and for phonograph records. From 1975 to 1987 he was music critic of N.Y.'s *The Westsider*.

Dietrich, Albert (Hermann), German conductor and composer; b. Forsthaus Golk, near Meissen, Aug. 28, 1829; d. Berlin, Nov. 19, 1908. He was a pupil of J. Otto in Dresden (1842–47) and of Moscheles and Rietz at Leipzig (1847–51); studied with Schumann (was one of Schumann's best pupils) at Düsseldorf (1851–54). From 1855 to 1861 he was a concert conductor, and from 1859 municipal music director, at Bonn; from 1861, at Oldenburg; he retired in 1890 and lived in Berlin; was made Royal Prof. in 1899. He wrote *Erinnerungen an Johannes Brahms in Briefen, besonders aus seiner Jugendzeit* (Leipzig, 1898; in Eng., 1899).

WORKS: Operas: *Robin Hood* (Frankfurt am Main, 1879); *Das Sonntagskind* (Bremen, 1886); incidental music; orch. works, chamber music, including the 1st movement of the *F-A-E* Sonata for Violin (other movements by Brahms and Schumann); songs.

Dietrich or **Dieterich, Sixtus,** important German composer; b. Augsburg, c.1493; d. St. Gallen, Switzerland, Oct. 21, 1548. He was a chorister in Constance (1504–8), then studied in Freiburg. After returning to Constance (1517), he became informator choralium at the Cathedral chapter; was made altar prebend and then became a priest (1522), remaining there after the Catholic clergy left as a result of the Reformation (1527). He was also a guest lecturer at the Univ. of Wittenberg (1540–41). He was a significant composer of early Protestant sacred music.

WORKS: *Epicedion Thomae Sporeri* (Strasbourg, 1534); *Magnificat octo tonorum . . . liber primus* (Strasbourg, 1535); *Novum ac insigne opus musicum 36 antiphonarum* (Wittenberg, 1541; ed. by W. Buszin, Kassel and St. Louis, 1964); *Novum opus musicum tres tomos* [122] *sacrorum hymnorum* (Wittenberg, 1545; ed. by H. Zenck and W. Gurlitt in Das Erbe Deutscher Musik, 1st series, XXIII, 1942–60); *Laudate Dominum* for 4 Voices (Augsburg, 1547); various other works were publ. in contemporary collections.

BIBL.: H. Zenck, *S. D.: Ein Beitrag zur Musik und Musikanschauung im Zeitalter der Reformation* (Leipzig, 1928); A. Grauer, *The Vocal Style of S. D. and Johann Eccard and Their Contributions to Lutheran Church Music* (diss., Univ. of Rochester, 1960).

Dietsch, (Pierre-)Louis(-Philippe), French conductor and composer; b. Dijon, March 17, 1808; d. Paris, Feb. 20, 1865. He studied at Choron's Institution Royale de Musique Classique et Religieuse in Paris, then with A. Reicha (counterpoint) and M.-P. Chenie (double bass) at the Paris Cons., winning a premier prix for the latter (1830). He played double bass in the orchs. of the Théâtre-Italien and the Paris Opéra; was also maître de chapelle at St. Eustache (1830–39) and at the Madeleine (from 1849), as well as chorus master at the Opéra (from 1840). With Paul Foucher and Henri Révoil as librettists, he wrote the opera *Le Vaisseau fantôme* (Opéra, Nov. 9, 1842), a subject also treated by Wagner in his opera *Der fliegende Holländer*. Dietsch's opera received only 11 hearings and then was totally forgotten. He became conductor of the Paris Opéra in 1860, where he led the 3 notorious performances of the Paris version of Wagner's *Tannhäuser* in 1861; after an argument with Verdi, he resigned his post in 1863. He also wrote many masses and other sacred works.

BIBL.: B. Millington, " 'The Flying Dutchman,' 'Le Vaisseau fantôme,' and Other Nautical Yarns," *Musical Times* (March 1986).

Dietz, Howard, American lyricist; b. N.Y., Sept. 9, 1896; d. there, July 30, 1983. He began writing lyrics for popular songs in 1918; wrote texts for Jerome Kern, Gershwin, and Vernon Duke; also collaborated in writing lyrics with Arthur Schwartz. In 1919 he joined the Goldwyn Pictures Corp. as publicity director; when the firm merged into Metro-Goldwyn-Mayer in 1924 he remained with it, becoming its vice-president in 1940. He devised its pseudo-Latin logo, Ars Gratia Artis (the correct word sequence would be Ars Artis Gratia). In 1974 he publ. an autobiography, *Dancing in the Dark*. Of his hobbies, to be noted is the invention of the 2-handed bridge game which was named after him. He also painted and translated librettos. As a publicity man for Metro-Goldwyn-Mayer, he popularized, and possibly made up, Greta Garbo's line "I want to be alone," which became famous.

Dietz, Max, Austrian musicologist; b. Vienna, April 9, 1857; d. there, Aug. 5, 1928. Having obtained his degree (Ph.D.) from the Univ. of Vienna, he spent some time in France in research work, the results of which he publ. in his *Geschichte des musikalischen Dramas in Frankreich während der Revolution bis zum Direktorium* (1885), a most valuable contribution to the history of opera; in 1886 he established himself as docent of musicology at the Univ. of Vienna; ed. several masses, a *Stabat Mater* and Requiem by Emperor Leopold I (1891), and *Recitativo e Duetto fra l'anima e Gesù Cristo* by A. de Liguori (1895).

Dieupart, Charles François, French violinist, harpsichordist, and composer; b. c.1670; d. London, c.1740. He went to London in 1700; was maestro al cembalo, for several years, of Handel's operas; died almost destitute. He publ. *6 Suites de clavecin . . . composées et mises en concert pour un violon et une flûte, avec basse de viole et un archiluth.* Bach copied 2 of Dieupart's clavecin suites, and used various themes in his own *English Suites.* The Lyrebird Press of Paris publ. 2 vols. of Dieupart's works, ed. by P. Brunold (1934; vol. I, *6 suites pour clavecin;* vol. II, *Airs et Chansons*).

Di Giuseppe, Enrico, American tenor; b. Philadelphia, Oct. 14, 1932. He was a pupil of Richard Bonelli at the Curtis Inst. of Music in Philadelphia and of Hans Heinz at the Juilliard School of Music in N.Y. In 1959 he made his operatic debut as Massenet's Des Grieux in New Orleans; then toured with the Metropolitan Opera National Co. On March 18, 1965, he made his 1st appearance at the N.Y. City Opera as Michele in Menotti's *The Saint of Bleecker Street;* he then sang there regularly from 1967 to 1981. He made his Metropolitan Opera debut in N.Y. as Turiddu on June 20, 1970, where he later sang many Italian and French roles. Among his finest portrayals were Mozart's Ferrando and Almaviva, Bellini's Pollione, Verdi's Alfredo, Massenet's Werther, and Puccini's Pinkerton in *Madama Butterfly.*

Dijk, Jan van, Dutch pianist and composer; b. Oostzaan, June 4, 1918. He studied composition with Willem Pijper in Rotterdam (1936–46); gave piano recitals; taught at the Brabant Cons. in Tilburg from its founding in 1955, and at the Royal Cons. in The Hague from 1961. A prolific composer, he wrote hundreds of works, not counting orchestrations of piano pieces by classical composers. He also produced music in the 31-tone system devised by the Dutch physicist Adriaan Fokker. **WORKS: OPERAS:** *Flying Dutchman* (1953) and *Protesilaus and Laodamia* (1968). **ORCH.:** Dance Suite for Orch. and Jazz Combo (1961); Concertino for Flute, Piano, Percussion, and Strings (1938); 3 sinfoniettas (1940, 1952, 1956); *Cassatio* for Strings and Piano obbligato (1943); 4 syms. (1944, 1947, 1948, 1951); *Capriccio* for Viola and Orch. (1946); 4 piano concertinos (1948–49, 1953, 1966, 1966); Concertino for 2 Pianos and String or Wind Orch. (1949); *Suite pastorale* for Oboe, English Horn, and Small Orch. (1953); 3 *Suites da Sonar* (1954, 1955, 1958); *Cortège en Rondeau* (1955); Saxophone Concertino (1956); Toccata for String Orch. (1957); Concertino for Recorder and Chamber Orch. (1958); Serenade for Winds, Percussion, and Piano (1959); 4 *Bagatelles* (1960); Concertino for Accordion and String Orch. (1960); *17 Projections* (1962); Double-bass Concerto (1962); *Salon symphonique* (1963); Concerto for Piano, 4-hands, and Small Orch. (1963); *Contrasts* for Orch. and Jazz Combo (1964); *Décorations et décompositions* (1964); *Duetto accompagnato* for Saxophone, Trombone, and String Orch. (1964); 2 serenades for Small Orch. (1966, 1970); *Jardin public,* divertimento for Flute and Orch. (1967); Triple Concerto for Flute, Recorder, Harpsichord, and Orch. (1968); *Makedonski,* suite for Chamber Orch. (1969); 2 *Résumés* for Piano and Small Orch. (1970); *Touch after Finish* for Trumpet, Organ, Piano, and Strings (1971); *Fantaisie* for Double Bass and Orch. (1972); *About* (1973); *Kleine Concertante* for 2 Flutes and Chamber Orch. (1974); *Affiche pour la*

réouverture du magasin (1974); *Accomplishement* for Small Orch. (1975); *Sinfonia e Fughetta* (1976); *Parties sur l'amitié* (1977). **VOCAL:** *Jaergetijde* for Chorus and Orch. (1944); *Het masker van den Rooden Dood* (The Mask of the Red Death), after Edgar Allan Poe, for Narrator and Chamber Orch. (1952); *Zwartbaard* for Male Chorus and Orch. (1953); *De Kommandeur* for Soloists, Narrator, Boys' Chorus, and String Quartet or String Orch. (1958); *Heer en Knecht,* cantata (1963); *Coornhert,* cantata (1964); *Quodlibet* for Chorus and Orch. (1967); *Pros romaious,* cantata (1968); *Ars vivendi* for Chorus and Orch. (1977); *Onbedvidende polka en twee wiegeliedjes* for Chorus and Orch. (1985); *Nijmegen, Nijmegen* for Chorus and Orch. (1985). **CHAMBER:** 5 string quartets (1940, 1941, 1942, 1965, 1974); Divertimento for Clarinet, Viola, and Cello (1941); Septet (1949–50); Piano Trio (1950); Divertimento for 2 Violins and Cello (1951); Duo for Cello and Piano (1953); Cello Sonatina (1953); Violin Sonatina (1953); Saxophone Sonata (1953); Sonatina for Violin and Piano (1954); Serenade for Trumpet and Horn (1955); Suite for 2 Flutes and Piano (1957); 2 sonatas for Solo Flute (1961, 1966); *Musica sacra I* for 2 Violins, Viola, and Organ (1966), *II* for Flute, Cello, and Piano (1968), and *III* for Clarinet, Violin, and Piano (1975); *Musique à trois* for Flute, Recorder, and Harpsichord (1967); Solo Violin Sonata (1968); *Quintetto* for Mandolin, Bass Clarinet, Percussion, Organ, and Piano (1969); *4 Caprices* for Accordion (1969); *Pet* for Flute, Saxophone, Trumpet, Violin, and Double Bass (1973); *Concertino à 3* for Flute, Violin and Viola (1975). **PIANO:** Sonata (1942); 18 sonatinas (1944–74); *Rondino* (1955); Sonatina for 4-hands (1956); 2 *Kantieks* (1964, 1976); *Couple* (1969); *Something for 2 Piano Players* (1969); *Partita piccola* (1970); *Alba Communis* (1973); 3 *Inventions* (1976). **31-TONE PIECES:** 7 *Pieces* for Organ (1948); *Musica per organo trentunisono I* for 31-tone Organ (1950–51) and *II,* 7 pieces for 31-tone Organ (1957); Concertino for Trombone, Violin, and Cello (1961).

Diller, Angela, American pianist and pedagogue; b. Brooklyn, Aug. 1, 1877; d. Stamford, Conn., April 30, 1968. She studied music at Columbia Univ. with Edward MacDowell and Percy Goetschius; also with Johannes Schreyer in Dresden; from 1899 to 1916 was head of the theory dept. of the Music School Settlement in N.Y.; from 1916 to 1921, was an administrator at the David Mannes School; then director of the Diller-Quaile School of Music in N.Y.; was on the faculty of the Univ. of Southern Calif. (1932), Mills College (1935), and the New England Cons. (1936–37); was co-founder, with Margarethe Dessoff, of the Adesdi Chorus and A Cappella Singers of N.Y.; ed., with E. Quaile, K. Stearns Page, and Harold Bauer, many educational music works. In 1953 she received a Guggenheim fellowship award. She publ. *First Theory Book* (1921); *Keyboard Harmony Course* (4 books, 1936, 1937, 1943, 1949), and *The Splendor of Music* (1957).

Dilling, Mildred, noted American harpist and teacher; b. Marion, Ind., Feb. 23, 1894; d. N.Y., Dec. 30, 1982. She studied with Louise Schellschmidt-Koehne and later, in Paris, with Henriette Renié. After her concert debut in Paris, she played in N.Y. (1913) with the Madrigal Singers of the MacDowell Chorus; appeared in joint recitals in Europe with the de Reszkes and Yvette Guilbert, and in the U.S. with Alma Gluck and Frances Alda; toured the U.S. and Great Britain many times; also made concert tours in South America, the Middle East, and the Orient. She had 7 engagements to play at the White House. She had numerous private pupils who became well-known harp players; her most famous student was the comedian Harpo Marx. She cultivated calluses on her fingers to achieve sonority. She was the owner of a large collection of harps which she acquired in different parts of the world. She publ. *Old Tunes for New Harpists* (1934) and *30 Little Classics for the Harp* (1938). **BIBL.:** E. Kahn, Jr., "The Harp Lady," *New Yorker* (Feb. 3, 1940).

Dillon, Fannie Charles, American pianist and composer; b. Denver, March 16, 1881; d. Altadena, Calif., Feb. 21, 1947.

She studied at Claremont College in Pomona, Calif., and in Berlin (1900–6) with Godowsky and Hugo Kaun; later in N.Y. with Rubin Goldmark; she made her debut as a pianist in 1908; taught at Pomona College (1910–13), and from 1918 in Los Angeles high schools. Her orch. works included *Celebration of Victory* (1918), *The Cloud* (1918), *The Alps* (1920), and *Chinese Symphonic Suite* (1936); she also wrote piano pieces, including the popular *Birds at Dawn* (1917).

Dillon, Henri, French composer; b. Angers, Oct. 9, 1912; d. in Indochina, in combat, July 9, 1954. He studied at the Military School in St.-Cyr; was in the army during World War II. He was largely self-taught in music, and adopted a classical style of composition, derived mainly from the melodic patterns of French folk songs.

WORKS: Cello Concerto (1949); Violin Concerto (1949); Viola Concerto (1952); Concerto for 2 Trumpets and Orch. (1953); *Arlequin*, divertimento for String Orch. (1949); *Cassation* for 12 Wind Instruments (1953); Sonata for Saxophone and Piano (1949); Violin Sonata (1952); Concerto for 2 Pianos (Paris, Dec. 15, 1952); Piano Sonata (1953); various works for piano.

Dima, Gheorghe, Rumanian composer; b. Brasov, Oct. 10, 1847; d. Cluj, June 4, 1925. He was a pupil of Giehne in Karlsruhe, of Uffmann in Vienna, of Thieriot in Graz, and of Richter, Jadassohn, and Reinecke at the Leipzig Cons.; directed musical societies and church choirs in Sibiu and Brasov; also taught music in those cities.

WORKS: *La Mère d'Etienne le Grand*, oratorio; *Voilà la hora qui tourne* for Mixed Chorus and Orch.; *Salvum fac regem* for Voices and Orch.; etc.

Dimas de Melo Pimenta, Emanuel, Brazilian composer, architect, designer, and urban planner; b. São Paulo, June 3, 1957. He studied at the Braz Cubas Univ. in São Paulo (degree in architecture and urbanism, 1985); in 1986 settled in Lisbon, where he began and quickly aborted his postgraduate studies in art history at the Universidade Nova; also studied Zen techniques of composition, gagaku, ragas, and occidental music with Hans Joachim Koellreutter, and learned to play alto and soprano flutes. His compositions, in particular the tape works, represent an eclectic incorporation of unusual source materials and utilization of novel compositional methods. His career has spanned the arts to include graphic and urban design, photography, and creative writing; he publ. a highly creative theoretical treatise, *Tapas: Architecture and the Unconscious* (São Paulo, 1985). Exhibits of his graphic scores have been shown at the São Paulo Cultural Centre (1984) and the Calouste Gulbenkian Foundation in Lisbon (1987).

WORKS: ACOUSTIC: *Spheres* for Large Ensemble (1981); *Cantos* for Ensemble (1982); *Quartet 1* for Bass Clarinet, Tenor Saxophone, Clarinet, and Flute (1984) and 2 for Piano, Flute, Clarinet, and Cello (1984); *Concert for 2 Musicians and 1 Piano* (1985). ELECTROACOUSTIC: *Spheres III* for Ensemble and Tape (1981–82); *O vazio deita as unhas de fora e morde no veu estendido a beira da imagem* for Chorus, Percussion, Keyboards, and Tape (1982); *Frankenstern*, minimal opera for 20 TV Sets, Videos, Soprano, 2 Mezzo-sopranos, Baritone, Piano, and Tape (São Paulo, Dec. 12, 1984); *20 TV Sets and a Priest* for 20 TV Sets and Tape (1984); *A Bao a Qu* for Ensemble, Synthesizers, Video Score, and Tape (1985); *Concert for Only 1 Cricket*, with Brazilian forest sounds (1986); *Factory* for 2 Tenors and Tape, based on a fragment from Mozart's *Don Giovanni* (1986–87). MAGNETIC TAPE: *Emiedrico* (1981); *La Mer* (1984; also an acoustic version, 1985; won the 1985 Brazilian Assoc. of Art Critics prize); *Airports*, environmental piece using white noise (1984); *Spaces* (1984); *Short Waves 1985*, utilizing radio emissions (1985), and *SBb(r)* (1986), both for the Merce Cunningham Dance Co.; *On Bartók*, based on the 1st movement of Bartók's *Music for Strings, Percussion, and Celesta* (1986); *Stones*, using indigenous Brazilian instruments (1988). DIGITAL TAPE: *Music from 144 Voices* (1987); *Webern Variation*, based on Webern's *3 Works for Orchestra* (1987); *Sun*, using the structure of the sound waves from the sun (1987); *Plan*, using

sound particles of medieval instruments from 8th- to 11th-century Islamic music from Andalusia, structured on patterns 1st used by Palestrina (1987); *Twilight*, based on gagaku music (1987); *wHALLtz*, using 32 loudspeakers from 3 structural fragments of the *King's Waltz* by Johann Strauss (1987); *Crossing Over* (1988); *Beethoven Quartet*, based on a fragment from Beethoven's Quartet, op. 130 (1988); *Strange Loopings*, following Kurt Gödel's theorem (1988); *Musak*, "kitsch music" for supermarkets, elevators, shopping centers, postal centers, etc. (1988); *Constellations* for 4 or 20 Computer-controlled Marimbas (2 versions; 1989); *Dipak*, based on an ancient North Indian evening raga, in 3 parts (1989); *Finnegans* for Voice and Computer (1989); *Music for Nothing*, "constructed from a graphical complex drawn from the frontiers of chaos" (1989); *Gravity Sound Waves* and *Gravitational Sounds*, based on Michel Hénon's attractor (both 1990).

Dimitrova, Ghena, Bulgarian soprano; b. Beglj, May 6, 1941. She studied with Christo Brumbarov at the Sofia State Cons.; then sang with the Sofia Opera. After winning 1st prize in the Sofia Competition in 1970, she scored a major success as Amelia in *Un ballo in maschera* in Parma (1972); subsequently held engagements in France, Spain, South America, Moscow, Vienna, and Rome. In 1983 she made her London debut in a concert performance of *La Gioconda;* later that year she appeared as Turandot at Milan's La Scala. In 1984 she sang at N.Y.'s Carnegie Hall and at the Salzburg Festival; later operatic roles included Turandot at London's Covent Garden (1985) and Leonora in *Il Trovatore* at the San Francisco Opera (1986). On Dec. 14, 1987, she made her Metropolitan Opera debut in N.Y. as Turandot. Other notable roles include Leonora in *La forza del destino*, Santuzza, and Tosca.

Dimov, Bojidar, Bulgarian composer; b. Lom, Jan. 31, 1935. He studied composition with Veselin Stoyanov in Sofia and with Karl Schiske in Vienna. In 1968 he settled in Cologne, where he founded a group for promotion of new music, called Trial and Error. His own compositions follow the experimental method symbolized by the name of this group, striving to obtain a pragmatic modern style and technique.

WORKS: *Incantations I–III* for Soprano and Chamber Orch. (1963–69); *Komposition I* for Piano (1963), *II* for String Quartet (1964), and *III* for Orch. (1967–68); *Continuum*, subtitled *Trauerminuten für Dana Kosanova*, for Chamber Orch., commemorating a 15-year-old Czech girl student killed in the course of the Soviet invasion of Czechoslovakia in 1968 (Graz, Oct. 25, 1969); *Raumspiel* for Piano and Chamber Orch., a work of spatial music (1969); *Symphonies* for Voice and Chamber Orch. (1970); *Dual* for 7 Instruments (1971).

Dimov, Ivan, Bulgarian composer; b. Kazanlak, Dec. 13, 1927. He studied composition with Goleminov at the Bulgarian State Cons. in Sofia, graduating in 1953; then took courses in advanced composition at the Moscow Cons.

WORKS: 2 operas: *They Have Stolen the Council* (1966) and *The Emigrant* (1973); ballet, *Laughter of Africa* (1966); *Pieces* for Oboe and Piano (1955); *Kardjalii*, dance drama for Orch. (1959); Violin Concertino (1961); *Dramatic Poem* for Orch. (1964); String Quartet in 2 parts (1971); *Miniatures* for Piano (1973); choruses; songs.

D'Indy, Vincent. See Indy, Vincent d'.

Dinerstein, Norman (Myron), American music educator and composer; b. Springfield, Mass., Sept. 18, 1937; d. Cincinnati, Dec. 23, 1982. He studied at Boston Univ. (B.M., 1960), the Hartt College of Music in Hartford, Conn. (M.M., 1963), and Princeton Univ. (Ph.D., 1974); also took courses at the Berlin Hochschule für Musik (1962–63), at the Berkshire Music Center in Tanglewood (1962, 1963), and in Darmstadt (1964). He was then on the faculties of Princeton Univ. (1965–66), the New England Cons. of Music in Boston (1968–69; 1970–71), Hartt College (1971–76), and the Univ. of Cincinnati College–Cons. of Music (1976–81), where he was dean until his death.

Works: *Cassation* for Orch. (1963); *Schir ha Schirim* for Chorus and Orch. (1963); *Intermezzo* for Orch. (1964); *Contrasto* for Orch. (1968); *The Answered Question* for Wind Ensemble (1972); *Songs of Remembrance* for Soprano and Strings (1976–79); *Golden Bells* for Chorus and Orch. (1980–82; completed by M. Schelle); several choral pieces; *4 Movements* for 3 Woodwind Instruments (1961); *Terzetto* for Brass Trio (1961); Serenade for Oboe, Clarinet, Harp, Violin, and Cello (1963); *Pezzi piccoli* for Flute and Viola (1966); *Tubajubalee* for Tuba Ensemble (1978); also song cycles; piano pieces.

Dinicu, Grigoraş, Rumanian violinist and composer of light music; b. Bucharest, April 3, 1889; d. there, March 28, 1949. He was of a family of musicians; in 1902, studied violin with Carl Flesch, who taught at the Bucharest Cons. At his graduation in 1906, Dinicu played a violin piece of his own based on popular Rumanian rhythms, *Hora staccato*; Jascha Heifetz made a virtuoso arrangement of it in 1932. Subsequently Dinicu played in hotels, restaurants, nightclubs, and cafés in Bucharest and in western Europe. Apart from *Hora staccato*, he composed numerous other pieces of light music in the gypsy and Rumanian manner.

Dippel, (Johann) Andreas, German-American tenor and operatic impresario; b. Kassel, Nov. 30, 1866; d. Los Angeles, May 12, 1932. He studied with Nina Zottmayr in Kassel, Julius Hey in Berlin, Alberto Leoni in Milan, and Johannes Ress in Vienna. In 1887 he made his operatic debut as Lionel in *Martha* in Bremen, where he sang until 1892; he also appeared at the Bayreuth Festival in 1889. On Nov. 26, 1890, he made his Metropolitan Opera debut in N.Y. as Asrael, returning on its roster from 1898 to 1902 and from 1903 to 1910; he also sang in Breslau (1892–93), at the Vienna Court Opera (1893), and at London's Covent Garden (1897–1900). With Gatti-Casazza, he shared administrative duties at the Metropolitan Opera (1908–10), then was manager of the Chicago Grand Opera (1910–13). After managing his own light opera company, he settled in Los Angeles as a vocal coach. His repertoire included almost 150 roles; he was particularly successful in operas by Wagner.

Diruta, Girolamo, celebrated Italian organist, teacher, and music theorist; b. Deruta, near Perugia, c.1554; d. after 1610. He was a pupil of Zarlino, Costanzo Porta, and Claudio Merulo, the last of whom mentions the fact with pride in the preface of Diruta's *Il Transilvano.* In 1574 Diruta was in the Franciscan monastery at Correggio; then was church organist in Venice (1582–93); was at the Cathedral of Chioggia (1593–1603); and at Agobbio (Gubbio) Cathedral (1609–10). His *Il Transilvano* is a valuable treatise on organ playing, the 1st work to treat the organ and its playing technique as distinct and separate from the clavier. It is in 2 parts, in dialogue form: *Dialogo sopra il vero modo di sonar organi e istromenti da penna* (Venice, 1593; further eds., 1597, 1609, 1612, 1625) and *Dialogo diviso in quattro libri . . . il vero modo e la vera regola d'intavolare ciascun canto* (Venice, 1609; 2nd ed., 1622). Dannreuther, in his *Musical Ornamentation,* gives a thorough analysis of Diruta's system of ornamentation. Vol. III of L. Torchi's *L'arte musicale in Italia* contains a Ricercare and 2 toccatas for organ by Diruta.
Bibl.: F. Briganti, "Il primo libro dei Contrapunti di G. D.," *Perugia,* VI (Sept. 23, 1950).

Di Stefano, Giuseppe, noted Italian tenor; b. Motta S. Anastasia, near Catania, July 24, 1921. He studied with Luigi Montesanto in Milan; then was conscripted into the Italian army in the infantry, and was taken prisoner during World War II; he escaped and went to Switzerland. Returning to Italy after the war, he made his operatic debut in Reggio Emilia in 1946; then sang in Rome and at La Scala in Milan. On Feb. 25, 1948, he made his debut as the Duke of Mantua in *Rigoletto* at the Metropolitan Opera in N.Y.; he was on its roster until 1952, and again in 1955–56 and 1964–65. On Oct. 8, 1950, he sang the role of Rodolfo in *La Bohème* at the San Francisco Opera. He also appeared as a guest artist with the Chicago

Lyric Opera during the season 1965–66; his other engagements were at La Scala, the Vienna State Opera, the Berlin State Opera, Covent Garden in London, the Paris Opéra, and the Teatro Colón in Buenos Aires. In 1973–74 he made a much-publicized concert tour with Maria Callas. His opera roles were limited almost exclusively to the Italian repertoire, but he also sang Faust in Gounod's opera, Don José in *Carmen,* and Des Grieux in *Manon.*

Distler, Hugo, important German composer; b. Nuremberg, June 24, 1908; d. (suicide) Berlin, Nov. 1, 1942. He studied at the Leipzig Cons. with Grabner, Ramin, and Martienssen. In 1931 he became a church organist at Lübeck; joined the faculty of the Cons. there (1933–37); also was a teacher at the School for Church Music in Spandau (1933–37); taught at the Stuttgart Hochschule für Musik (1937–40); from 1940 he was in Berlin. His early training and his connection with church music determined his style as a composer; his music is marked by a strong sense of polyphony. He wrote a Concerto for Harpsichord and String Orch. (1935–36); 3 secular cantatas: *An die Natur* (1933); *Das Lied von der Glocke* (1933–34); *Lied am Herde* (1940). His oratorio *Die Weltalter* (1942) remained unfinished. He also publ. *Funktionelle Harmonielehre* (Kassel and Basel, 1941).
Bibl.: L. Palmer, *H. D. and His Church Music* (St. Louis, 1967); U. Herrmann, *H. D.—Rufer und Mahner* (Berlin, 1972).

Ditson, Oliver, American music publisher, founder of the firm of **Oliver Ditson & Co.;** b. Boston, Oct. 20, 1811; d. there, Dec. 21, 1888. He established himself as a music seller and publisher in Boston in 1835; became a partner of G.H. Parker, his employer, under the firm name of Parker & Ditson; carried on the business in his own name (1842–57); when J.C. Haynes joined the firm, Ditson changed its name to O. Ditson & Co. His eldest son, **Charles,** took charge of the N.Y. branch (Ch. H. Ditson & Co.) in 1867, the business being continued until his death. A Philadelphia branch, opened in 1875 by J. Edward Ditson as J. E. D. & Co., was in existence until 1910. A branch for the importation and sale of instruments, etc., was established at Boston in 1860 as John C. Haynes & Co. On Oliver Ditson's death, the firm of Oliver Ditson & Co. was reorganized as a corporation, with J.C. Haynes as president (d. May 3, 1907); from 1907 until his death, on May 14, 1929, Charles H. Ditson managed the business; he was succeeded by H.H. Porter. In 1931 Theo. Presser Co., of Philadelphia, took over the management of the firm; its catalog embraced about 52,000 titles; it publ. the *Musical Record* (a monthly periodical) from 1878 to 1903, the *Musician* from 1896 to 1918, and several library series. The music house Lyon & Healy was founded by Oliver Ditson in Chicago in 1864 as a western branch.
Bibl.: W. Fisher, *Notes on Music in Old Boston* (Boston, 1918); idem, *One Hundred and Fifty Years of Music Publishing in the U.S.* (Boston, 1933).

Dittersdorf, Karl Ditters von (original name, **Karl Ditters**), eminent Austrian composer and violinist; b. Vienna, Nov. 2, 1739; d. Schloss Rothlhotta, Neuhof, Bohemia, Oct. 24, 1799. He played violin as a child; then studied with König and Ziegler; the Prince of Sachsen-Hildburghausen made it possible for him to take private violin lessons with Trani and to study composition with Bonno; he played in the Prince's orch. from 1751 to 1761. In 1761 he went to Vienna, where he was engaged as a member of the Court Theater Orch. (until 1764). He was befriended by Gluck, who took him along on his Italian journey, where he had an occasion to appear in public as a violinist. In 1765 he assumed the post of Kapellmeister to the Bishop of Grosswardein in Hungary, where he remained until 1769. His career as a composer began in earnest at this time; he wrote an oratorio, *Isacco, figura del redentore;* several cantatas; and many pieces of orch. and chamber music. In 1770 he became Kapellmeister to the Prince-Bishop of Breslau, Count von Schaffgotsch, at Johannisberg in Silesia. There he wrote mostly for the stage, bringing out 12 works between 1771 and 1776. However, he wrote his most important dramatic works in Vienna and for the ducal theater in Oels. He gained fame with his 1st singspiel, *Doctor und Apotheker*, produced in Vienna on July 11, 1786; it was followed by other successful stage works, *Betrug durch Aberglauben*, *Die Liebe im Narrenhause*, *Das rote Käppchen*, and *Hieronymus Knicker*. He received several honors during his lifetime; in 1770 the Pope bestowed upon him the Order of the Golden Spur; in 1773 he was ennobled by the Emperor as von Dittersdorf. Upon the death of the Prince-Bishop in 1795, he was granted a small pension, and found himself in straitened circumstances until a friend, Baron von Stillfried, took him into his castle, Rothlhotta, where he remained until his death. Dittersdorf was an important figure in the Viennese Classical school of composition, although he lacked the genius of Haydn and Mozart. He was able to fuse the common folk-song elements of the period with brilliant ensembles characteristic of opera buffa. His singspiels reveal a jovial humor, melodic charm, and rhythmic vitality. His syms. and concertos are also of interest as characteristic specimens of the period.

WORKS: STAGE: *Il viaggiatore americano in Joannesberg*, farce (Johannisberg, May 1, 1771; not extant); *L'amore disprezzato (Pancratio; Amore in musica)*, operetta buffa (Johannisberg, 1771); *Il finto pazzo per amore*, operetta giocosa (Johannisberg, June 3, 1772); *Il tutore e la pupilla*, dramma giocoso (Johannisberg, May 1, 1773); *Lo sposo burlato*, operetta giocosa (Johannisberg, 1773 or 1775; another version as *Der gefoppte Bräutigam*); *Il tribunale di Giove*, serenade with prologue (Johannisberg, 1774); *Il maniscalco*, operetta giocosa (Johannisberg, May 1, 1775); *La contadina fedele*, opera giocosa (Johannisberg, 1776); *La moda ossia Gli scompigli domestici*, dramma giocoso (Johannisberg, June 3, 1776); *L'Arcifanfano, re de' matti*, opera giocosa (Johannisberg, 1776); *Il barone di Rocca Antica*, operetta giocosa (Johannisberg, 1776; not extant); *I visionari* (Johannisberg, 1776; not extant); *Doctor und Apotheker (Der Apotheker und der Doctor)*, singspiel (Vienna, July 11, 1786); *Betrug durch Aberglauben oder Die Schatzgräber (Der glückliche Betrug; Die dienstbaren Geister)*, singspiel (Vienna, Oct. 3, 1786); *Democrito corretto*, opera giocosa (Vienna, Jan. 24, 1787; performed under various titles); *Die Liebe im Narrenhause*, singspiel (Vienna, April 12, 1787); *Das rote Käppchen oder Hilft's nicht so schadt's nicht (Die rote Kappe; Das Rotkäppchen)*, comic operetta (Vienna, 1788); *Im Dunkeln ist nicht gut munkeln oder Irrung über Irrung (25,000 Gulden)*, comic opera (Vienna, Feb. 1789); *Hieronymus Knicker (Lucius Knicker; Chrisostomus Knicker; Hokus Pokus oder Die Lebensessenz)*, singspiel (Vienna, July 7, 1789); *Die Hochzeit des Figaro*, singspiel (Brünn, 1789?; music not extant); *Der Schiffspatron oder Der neue Gutsherr*, singspiel (Vienna, 1789); *Hokus-Pokus oder Der Gaukelspiel*, comic opera (Vienna, 1790); *Der Teufel ein Hydraulikus*, comedy (Gratz, 1790); *Der Fürst und sein Volk*, pasticcio (Leipzig, March 5?, 1791; music not extant; in collaboration with F. Piterlin and F. Bertoni); *Das Gespenst mit der Trommel (Geisterbanner)*, singspiel (Oels, Aug. 16, 1794); *Don Quixote der Zweyte (Don Chisciotto)*, singspiel (Oels, Feb. 4, 1795); *Gott Mars und der Hauptmann von Bärenzahn (Gott Mars oder Der eiserne Mann)*, singspiel (Oels, May 30, 1795); *Der Durchmarsch*, an arrangement of J. Paneck's *Die christliche Judenbraut*, singspiel (Oels, Aug. 29, 1795); *Der Schach von Schiras*, singspiel (Oels, Sept. 15, 1795); *Die befreyten Gwelfen (Die Guelfen)*, prologue (Oels, Oct. 29, 1795); *Ugolino*, serious singspiel (Oels, June 11, 1796); *Die lustigen Weiber von Windsor*, singspiel (Oels, June 25, 1796); *Der schöne Herbsttag*, dialogue (Oels, Oct. 29, 1796); *Der Ternengewinnst oder Der gedemütigte Stolz (Terno secco)*, singspiel (Oels, Feb. 11, 1797); *Der Mädchenmark*, singspiel (Oels, April 18, 1797); *Die Opera buffa*, comic opera (Vienna, 1798); *Don Coribaldi ossia L'usurpata prepotenza*, drama (Dresden, 1798?); *Ein Stück mit kleinen Liedern*, opera based on *Frau Sybilla trinkt keinen Wein* and *Das Reich der Toten*; comic opera version based on *Amore in musica* (Grosswardein, 1767?; not extant); etc.

OTHER VOCAL: *Isacco, figura del redentore*, oratorio (Grosswardein, 1766); *Il Davide nella Valle di Terebintho (Davidde penitente)*, oratorio (Johannisberg, 1771); *L'Esther ossia La Liberatrice del popolo giudaico nella Persia*, oratorio (Vienna, Dec. 19, 1773); *Giobbe (Hiob)*, oratorio (Vienna, April 8–9, 1786); also several cantatas, both sacred and secular; masses; offertories; graduals; motets; etc.

ORCH.: A great number of syms. have been attributed to Dittersdorf, with over 100 being most likely by him. Most famous are the 12 syms. on Ovid's *Metamorphoses*; only Nos. 1–6 are extant, although Nos. 7–12 have survived in arrangements for Piano, 4-hands, by Dittersdorf. He also composed many concertos, including 18 for violin, 3 for 2 violins, 1 for cello, 5 for viola, 4 for oboe, 5 for harpsichord, and 1 for flute.

CHAMBER: 15 divertimentos, including *Il combattimento dell'umane passioni*; 4 string serenades (with 2 horns); numerous string quartets; many sonatas for 4-hands; preludes; etc.

WRITINGS: "Briefe über Behandlung italienischer Texte bei der Composition," *Allgemeine musikalische Zeitung* (Leipzig, 1799); an autobiography publ. as *K. v. D.s Lebensbeschreibung, Seinem Sohne in die Feder diktiert* (Leipzig, 1801; Eng. tr., London, 1896; new ed. by N. Miller, Munich, 1967).

BIBL.: C. Krebs, *D.iana* (Berlin, 1900); K. Holl, *Carl D. v. D.s Opern für das wiederhergestellte Johannisberger Theater* (diss., Univ. of Bonn, 1913); H. Kralik, *Carl D. v. D.s Symphonien und Konzerte* (diss., Univ. of Vienna, 1913); L. Riedinger, "K. v. D. als Opernkomponist," *Studien zur Musikwissenschaft*, II (1914); G. Rigler, "Die Kammermusik D.," *Studien zur Musikwissenschaft*, XIV (1927); F. Souper, "The Music of D.," *Music and Letters*, XI (1930); M. Grave, *D.'s First-movement Form as a Measure of His Symphonic Development* (diss., N.Y. Univ., 1977).

Dittrich, Paul-Heinz, German composer; b. Gornsdorf, Erzgebirge, Dec. 4, 1930. He studied composition with Fidelio-Finke and choral conducting with Günther Ramin at the Leipzig Hochschule für Musik (1951–56). Later he took a seminar in advanced composition with Rudolf Wagner-Régeny at the Academy of Arts in East Berlin (1958–60). He was a choral director in Weimar (1956–58) and taught counterpoint and harmony at the Hanns Eisler Hochschule für Musik in East Berlin (1963–76). In 1980 he visited America. In his music, Dittrich reveals himself as an astute creator of modern forms and technical idioms, while carefully observing and preserving the pragmatic elements of instrumental and vocal components. He obtained numerous awards for his compositions, among them a prize of the ISCM (1975) and a UNESCO prize (1976).

WORKS: Violin Sonata (1956); String Quartet (1959); *Pentaculum* for Wind Quintet (1960); Sextet for Wind Instruments, Percussion, and Guitar (1960); *Orchestermusik* (1960); *Golgotha*, oratorio for Soloists, Chorus, and Orch. (1967); *Musik for Piano and 4 Speakers* (1969); *Stabiles and Mobiles* for Orch. and Vocal Ensemble (1969); *Les Fleurs de Baudelaire* for 3 Sopranos and Instruments (1969); *Kammermusik I* for 4 Woodwinds, Piano, and Tape (1970); *Begegnung* for 9 Instruments (1970); *Schlagzeilen* for 2 Pianos, 2 Percussionists, and Tape (1971); String Quartet with Electronic Instruments (1971); *Memento vitae* for Baritone Solo, 12 Voices, 4 Choral Groups, and 9 Percussions, to words by Brecht (1971); *Die anonyme Stimme* for Oboe, Trombone, and Tape (1972); *Vokalblätter* for Soprano Solo and 12 Voices, to words by James Joyce, Brecht, and Goethe (1972–73); *Areae sonantes* for Instrumental and Vocal Groups (1972–73); Concerto for Oboe and Chamber Orch. (1973–74); *Collage* for Oboe, Cello, Piano, and Electronic Sounds (1973); *Rondo à la Rossini* for Cello and Double Bass (1974); *Kammermusik II* for Oboe, Cello, Piano, and Tape (1974); *Kammermusik III* for Wind Quintet and Baritone (1974); Concerto for Cello and Orch. (1974–75); *Aktion-Reaktion* for Oboe, Tape, and Synthesizer (1975); *Cantus I* for Orch. (1975); *Illuminations* for Orch. (1976); *Concerts avec plusieurs instruments No. 1* for Harpsichord and 7 Instruments (1976–77); *Kammermusik IV* for Soprano, Piano, Flute, Clarinet, Violin, Cello, Guitar, Percussion, and Synthesizer (1977); *Kammermusik V* for Wind Quintet and Electronic Sounds (1977); *Cantus II* for Soprano, Cello, Orch., and Tape, to words by Eluard (1977); *Concerts avec plusieurs instruments No. 2* for

Viola, Cello, and 2 Orch. Groups (1978); *Concerts avec plusieurs instruments No. 3* for Flute, Oboe, Orch., and Synthesizer (1978); Double Concerto for Flute, Oboe, and Orch. (1979).

Divitis (de Ryche, le Riche), Antonius (Antoine), celebrated Flemish composer; b. Louvain, c.1475; d. after 1526. He was a singer and choirmaster at St. Donatien in Bruges (Brugge) from 1501 to 1504; in 1504–5, was choirmaster at St. Rombaut in Malines; then was in the service of Philippe le Beau in Brussels; was a chapel singer to Louis XII from 1506 to 1515.

Works: Motets and chansons are scattered in collections, e.g., *Motetti de la corona* (1514), and others printed by Rhaw, Attaignant, etc. At Cambrai is a mass in MS; at Munich, 2 credos and a Salve Regina *a* 5; at Rome, *Quem dicunt homines* for 4 Voices.

Bibl.: G. van Doorslaer, "A. D.," *Tijdschrift der Vereeniging voor Nederlandsche Muziekgeschiedenis*, XIII, 1 (1929); W. Nugent, *The Life·and Works of A. D.* (diss., North Texas State Univ., 1970).

Dixon, (Charles) Dean, black American conductor; b. N.Y., Jan. 10, 1915; d. Zug, near Zürich, Nov. 3, 1976. He showed a musical talent as a child and began to take violin lessons. At the age of 17 he organized at his high school in the Bronx a group that he was pleased to call the Dean Dixon Sym. Soc. He studied violin at the Juilliard School of Music (1932–36); on a conducting fellowship he took lessons with Albert Stoessel at the Juilliard Graduate School (1936–39); also enrolled in academic classes at Columbia Univ. Teachers College, receiving an M.A. in 1939. On May 7, 1938, he made his professional conducting debut at N.Y.'s Town Hall; that same year he founded the N.Y. Chamber Orch. Eleanor Roosevelt became interested in his career, and helped him to obtain some conducting engagements, including an appearance with the N.Y. Phil. at the Lewisohn Stadium on Aug. 10, 1941, making him the 1st of his race to conduct this orch. In 1944 Dixon organized the American Youth Orch., which had a limited success. In 1949 he went to Europe in the hopes of securing wider opportunities. These hopes were fully realized; he was engaged as music director of the Göteborg Sym. Orch. (1953–60) and the Hessian Radio Orch. in Frankfurt (1961–70); he served as music director of the Sydney (Australia) Sym. (1964–67). Returning briefly to the U.S. in 1970, he was guest conductor for a series of N.Y. Phil. summer concerts in Central Park, then went back to Europe and settled in Switzerland in 1974. His career was cut short when he underwent open-heart surgery in 1975.

Dixon, James, American conductor; b. Estherville, Iowa, April 26, 1928. He studied at the Univ. of Iowa (B.M., 1952; M.M., 1956); was conductor of the U.S. 7th Army Sym. Orch. in Germany (1951–54); the Univ. of Iowa Sym. Orch. in Iowa City (1954–59); the New England Cons. Sym. Orch. in Boston (1959–61). In 1962 he returned to the Univ. of Iowa Sym. Orch. as conductor; from 1965, served as conductor of the Tri-City Sym. Orch. in Davenport, Iowa, and Rock Island, Ill. In addition, he was associate conductor of the Minneapolis Sym. Orch. (1961–62). He was the recipient of the Gustav Mahler Medal in 1963. As an interpreter, he follows the style of Mitropoulos, under whose influence he began his career, combining precision of rhythmic flow with expressive shaping of melodic phrases.

Dizi, François-Joseph, famous French harpist; b. Namur, Jan. 14, 1780; d. Paris, Nov. 1847. He set out for London when only 16; lost his harp on the way but went on without it, and introduced himself to Érard, who gave him a harp and obtained pupils for him. Besides winning fame as a concert player and as a harpist at the principal theaters, he invented the "perpendicular harp" (which was unsuccessful), and composed sonatas, romances, variations, studies, etc., for harp; also publ. *Ecole de Harpe, Being a Complete Treatise on the Harp* (London, 1827). In 1830 he went to Paris, and established a harp factory with Pleyel, which did not do well. There he was appointed harp teacher to the royal princesses.

Dlabacž, Gottfried Johann (actually, **Bohumír Jan Dlabač**), Bohemian music scholar; b. Cerhenice, near Český Brod, July 17, 1758; d. Prague, Feb. 4, 1820. He was librarian and choirmaster of the Premonstratensian monastery in Prague; publ. a valuable reference work, *Allgemeines historisches Künstlerlexikon für Böhmen . . .* (3 vols., 1815–18), and contributed articles to Riegger's *Materialien zur alten und neuen Statistik von Böhmen.*

Dlugoszewski, Lucia, American composer; b. Detroit, June 16, 1931. She studied piano, and concurrently attended classes in physics at Wayne State Univ. (1946–49). Fascinated with the mathematical aspects of music, she began to study with Edgar Varèse, whose works illuminated this scientific relationship for her. Accordingly, in her own works she emphasizes the sonorific element of music; inspired by the example of Varèse's *Ionisation,* she invented or perfected a number of percussion instruments; 1 of her inventions is the timbre piano, in which she makes use of bows and plectra on the piano strings.

Works: Many dance scores, including *Openings of the Eye* (1958); *8 Clear Places* (1958–60); *Geography of Noon* (1964); *Dazzle on a Knife's Edge* (1966); *Agathlon Algebra* (1968). Other works: *50 Transparencies* "for everyday sounds" (1951); *Arithmetic Progressions* for Orch. (1954); *Instants in Form and Movements* for Timbre Piano and Chamber Orch. (1957); *Delicate Accidents in Space* for Rattle Quintet (1959); *Archaic Aggregates* for Timbre Piano, Ladder Harps, Tangent Rattles, Unsheltered Rattles, and Gongs (1961); *4 Attention Spans* for Orch. (1964); *Strange Tenderness of Naked Leaping* for Orch. (Santa Fe, N.Mex., Nov. 13, 1977); *Wilderness Elegant Tilt,* concerto for 11 Instruments (1981–84); *Duende amor* for Orch. (1983–84); *Quidditas String Quartet* (1984).

Doane, William H(oward), American hymn writer; b. Preston, Conn., Feb. 3, 1832; d. South Orange, N.J., Dec. 24, 1915. He served as a clerk and later entered the manufacturing business. He composed more than 2,000 gospel songs and a Christmas cantata, *Santa Claus.* His hymn *Pass Me Not* was popular.

Bibl.: R. McCutchan, *Our Hymnody* (N.Y., 1937).

Döbber, Johannes, German composer; b. Berlin, March 28, 1866; d. there, Jan. 26, 1921. He was a pupil, in the Stern Cons. in Berlin, of R. Radecke, L. Bussler (composition), and C. Agghazy (piano). He taught the 1st piano class in the Kullak Cons. in Berlin; became Kapellmeister at Darmstadt; then was at Coburg-Gotha as tutor in music to Princess Beatrice; was a teacher and music critic of the *Volkszeitung* in Berlin (1908).

Works: Operas: *Die Strassensängerin* (Gotha, 1890); *Der Schmied von Gretna-Green* (Berlin, 1893); *Dolcetta* (Brandenburg, 1894); *Die Rose von Genzano* (Gotha, 1895); *Die Grille* (Leipzig, 1897); *Die drei Rosen* (Coburg, 1902); *Der Zauberlehrling* (Braunschweig, 1907); *Die Franzosenzeit* (Berlin, 1913); song-play, *Fahrende Musikanten* (Magdeburg, 1917); operettas: *Die Millionenbraut* (Magdeburg, 1913) and *Des Kaisers Rock* (Berlin, 1915); Sym.; piano pieces; over 60 songs; quartets, duets, etc.

Dobbs, Mattiwilda, black American soprano and teacher; b. Atlanta, July 11, 1925. She was educated at Spelman College in Atlanta (B.A., 1946) and at Columbia Univ. (M.A., 1948); pursued vocal training with Lotte Leonard in N.Y. (1946–50) and Pierre Bernac in Paris (1950–52). In 1948 she won the Marian Anderson scholarship contest and made her debut as a concert artist; in 1951 she won 1st prize in singing in the Geneva Competition. After appearing in opera and recitals in Holland (1952), she sang at Milan's La Scala, the Glyndebourne Festival, and London's Covent Garden (1953). In 1955 she appeared at the San Francisco Opera; on Nov. 9, 1956, she made her Metropolitan Opera debut in N.Y. as Gilda. In 1957 she made her 1st appearance at the Royal Swedish Opera in Stockholm; also sang at the Hamburg State Opera (1961–63; 1967). In addition to her operatic and concert engagements in the U.S. and Europe, she also toured in Australia, New Zealand, and Israel. She was a visiting prof. at the Univ. of Texas in Austin (1973–74); then was a prof. at the Univ. of Illinois (1975–76), the Univ. of Georgia (1976–77), and Howard Univ. in Washington, D.C. (from 1977).

Dobiáš, Václav, Czech composer; b. Radčice, near Semily, Sept. 22, 1909; d. Prague, May 18, 1978. He studied violin and composition at the Prague Cons., where he also took courses in microtonal music with Alois Hába, and wrote a *Lento* for 3 Harps (1940) and a Violin Concerto (1941) making use of quarter-tones. After 1945 he became involved in the political problems of musical education; in conformity with the ideology of the Communist Party, he began to write music for the masses in the manner of socialist realism; in 1958 he was elected to the Central Committee of the Communist Party and was a member of the National Assembly from 1960 to 1969.

WORKS: Chamber Sym. (1939); 2 numbered syms. (1943, 1956–57); Sinfonietta (1946–47; rev. 1962); Sonata for Piano, Wind Quintet, Strings, and Timpani (1947); *The Grand Procession,* symphonic poem (1948); cantatas: *Stalingrad* (1945); *The Order No. 368* (1946); and *Build Up Your Country and Strengthen Peace,* also known as *Czech Polka* (1947–50); *Praho Jediná* (Only Prague), a song cycle with Orch. (1960–61); a plethora of mass choruses; 4 string quartets (1931, 1936, 1938, 1942); Violin Sonata (1936); Cello Sonata (1939); *Říkadla* (Rhymes) for 9 Instruments (1938); *Pastoral Wind Quintet* (1943); *4 Nocturnes* for Cello and Piano (1944); *Quartettino* for String Quartet (1944); *Dance Fantasy* for 9 Instruments (1948); 2 piano sonatas (1931, 1940); a fistful of playable piano pieces and a scattering of songs.

BIBL.: J. Štilec, *V. D.* (Prague, 1985).

Dobos, Kálmán, Hungarian composer; b. Szolnok, July 22, 1931. He became nearly blind at the age of 14, but pursued studies of music at the Academy of Music in Budapest, graduating in 1957; later he worked on the Hungarian State Radio. He composed a Cello Sonata (1956); Sym. (1957); Piano Sonata (1957); *Adagio and Fugue* for String Quartet (1959); 2 *Movements* for Piano Trio (1960); *Musica da camera* for Violin and Piano (1962); String Trio (1963); *Villanások* (Flashes) for Soprano and Piano Trio (1963); *3 Hungarian Dances* for Orch. (1964); *Meditation* for Piano (1964); *Sound Phenomena* for Orch. (1968); *Manifestations* for String Quartet, Piano, and Percussion (1969); *Belsö mozdulatok* (Inner Movements) for Clarinet, Piano, and Percussion (1970); *Ringató* (Rocking) for Piano (1972); *Vetületek* (Projections) for Orch. (1973); *Összefüggések* (Connections) for Cello, Piano, and Percussion (1985); sacred music; choruses; songs; incidental music.

Dobronić, Antun, Croatian composer; b. Jelsa, island of Hvar, April 2, 1878; d. Zagreb, Dec. 12, 1955. He studied music with Novák in Prague; then returned to Yugoslavia; in 1921 was appointed a prof. at the Cons. of Zagreb. He wrote many stage works, among them the operas *Ragusean Diptych; The Man of God; Mara; Dubrovnički triptihon* (1925); *Udovica Rozlinka* (1934); *Rkac* (1938); *Goran* (1944); ballet, *The Giant Horse;* 8 syms.; symphonic poems: *Au long de l'Adriatique* (1948) and *Les Noces* (1949); chamber music in the national style, including a Piano Quintet, subtitled *Bosnian Rhapsody;* 5 string quartets; choruses and songs.

Dobrowen, Issay (Alexandrovich) (real name, **Ishok Israelevich Barabeichik**), distinguished Russian conductor; b. Nizhny-Novgorod, Feb. 27, 1891; d. Oslo, Dec. 9, 1953. His orphaned mother was adopted by Israil Dobrovel; Issay Dobrowen changed his legal name, Dobrovel, to Dobrowein, and later to Dobrowen. He studied at the Nizhny-Novgorod Cons. as a small child (1896–1900); then entered the Moscow Cons. and studied with Igumnov (piano) and Taneyev (composition); went to Vienna for additional study with Leopold Godowsky (piano). Returning to Moscow, he became conductor of the Moscow Opera; in 1922 he led the Dresden State Opera in the German premiere of Mussorgsky's opera *Boris Godunov;*

in 1924 he conducted opera in Berlin; during the season 1927–28 he conducted opera in Sofia, Bulgaria. In 1931 he made his American debut conducting the San Francisco Sym. Orch.; was guest conductor with the Minneapolis Sym. Orch., Philadelphia Orch., and the N.Y. Phil. He was a regular conductor of the Budapest Opera from 1936 to 1939; at the outbreak of World War II he went to Sweden, where he won his greatest successes, as conductor of both opera and sym., at the Stockholm Opera and the Phil. of Göteborg. From 1948 he conducted at La Scala in Milan. On frequent occasions Dobrowen acted as stage director as well as conductor in German, Italian, and Swedish opera houses. He was a prolific composer; wrote several piano concertos and pieces for piano solo, in a Romantic vein; also an orch. fairy tale, *1,001 Nights* (Moscow, May 27, 1922).

Dobrowolski, Andrzej, Polish composer; b. Lwow, Sept. 9, 1921; d. Graz, Aug. 8, 1990. He studied organ, clarinet, and singing at the Warsaw Cons., then composition with A. Malawski and theory with S. Lobaczewska at the Krakow State College of Music (1947–51). He taught at the Warsaw State College of Music (1954–75), then was a prof. of composition at the Graz Hochschule für Musik (from 1976), serving as head of its faculty of composition, theory, and conducting (from 1980). His music is a paradigm of modern structuralism and textural abstraction.

WORKS: *Symphonic Variations* (1949); *Overture* (1950); Bassoon Concerto (1953); Sym. No. 1 (1955); *Music for Strings and 4 Groups of Wind Instruments* (1964); *Music for Strings, 2 Groups of Wind Instruments, and 2 Loudspeakers* (1967); *Music for Orch.* (1968); *Amar,* music for Orch. No. 2 (1970); *Music for Orch. No. 3* (1972–73); *A-La,* music for Orch. No. 4 (1974); *Passacaglia,* music for Orch. No. 5 (1978–79); *Music for Orch. No. 6* (1981–82); *Music for Chamber Orch.* (1982–83); *Music for Orch. and Oboe* (1984–85); *Flütchen* for Chamber Ensemble and Reciter (1986); Trio for Oboe, Clarinet, and Bassoon (1956); Studies for Oboe, Trumpet, Bassoon, and Double Bass (1959); *Passacaglia from 40 to 5,* electronic music (1959); *Music for Tape No. 1* (1962); *Music for Tape and Oboe* (1965); *Krabogapa* for 4 Instruments (1969); *Music for Magnetic Tape and Double Bass* (1977); *Music for 3 Accordions, Mouth Harmonicas, and Percussion* (1977); *Music for Magnetic Tape and Clarinet* (1980); *Musik für Grazer Bläserkreis* for 8 Trumpets, 8 Horns, 8 Trombones, and Percussion (1984).

Dobrzynski, Ignacy Felix, Polish pianist and composer; b. Romanov, Volhynia, Feb. 15, 1807; d. Warsaw, Oct. 10, 1867. The son of composer **Ignacy Dobrzynski** (b. Warsaw, Feb. 2, 1779; d. there, Aug. 16, 1841), he was taught by his father; then, being a fellow pupil and close friend of Chopin, by Chopin's teacher Elsner; on subsequent pianistic tours to Leipzig, Dresden, and Berlin (1845–47), he had great success. For a time he directed opera in Warsaw, where he finally settled. He wrote an opera, *Monbar or The Filibuster* (1838; Warsaw, Jan. 10, 1863); *Symphonie caractéristique;* String Sextet; 2 string quintets; 3 string quartets; Piano Trio; Violin Sonata; a nocturne for Violin and Piano, *Les Larmes;* mazurkas for piano; songs. His son **Bronislaw Dobrzynski** publ. a monograph on him (Warsaw, 1893).

Doche, Joseph-Denis, French organist, conductor, and composer; b. Paris, Aug. 22, 1766; d. Soissons, July 20, 1825. He was a chorister at the Cathedral of Meaux; then was organist at Coutances in Normandy. He played string instruments in a theater orch. in Paris from 1794 till 1810; then became a conductor, retiring in 1823. He wrote numerous successful vaudevilles; also operas: *Point de bruit, ou Le Contrat simulé* (Paris, Oct. 25, 1802); *Les Deux Sentinelles* (Paris, Sept. 27, 1803).

Dodds, Johnny (John M.), black American jazz clarinetist and alto saxophonist, brother of **Warren "Baby" Dodds;** b. New Orleans, April 12, 1892; d. Chicago, Aug. 8, 1940. He began playing the clarinet when he was 17; although he had lessons with Lorenzo Tio, Jr., he was mainly autodidact. After playing in Kid Ory's band in New Orleans (1912–17; 1919) and in Fate Marable's riverboat band (1917–19), he settled in Chicago; was a member of King Oliver's band and recorded in the mid-1920s with Louis Armstrong's Hot Five and Hot Seven combos. He led his own band in the 1930s, then joined his brother's quartet in 1940. He was a leading exponent of the New Orleans style.

BIBL.: G. Lambert, *J. D.* (N.Y., 1962).

Dodds, Warren "Baby," black American jazz drummer, brother of **Johnny (John M.) Dodds;** b. New Orleans, Dec. 24, 1898; d. Chicago, Feb. 14, 1959. He was the youngest of 6 children, hence his nickname. He studied drums with Dave Perkins, Walter Brundy, and Louis Cottrell, Sr., and, after performing with local jazz musicians, he joined Fate Marable's riverboat band in 1918. He settled in Chicago in 1921, where he played and recorded with King Oliver; he then worked with Louis Armstrong and Jelly Roll Morton and later played with his brother in several combos. He appeared with Jimmie Noone (1941), Bunk Johnson (1944–45), and Art Hodes (1946–47). In 1949–50 he suffered several strokes, and thereafter made infrequent appearances until his retirement in 1957. He was the foremost drummer in the New Orleans style of his era.

BIBL.: L. Gara, *The B. D. Story* (Los Angeles, 1959).

Dodge, Charles (Malcolm), American composer and teacher; b. Ames, Iowa, June 5, 1942. He studied composition with Richard Hervig and Philip Bezanson at the Univ. of Iowa (B.A., 1964), Darius Milhaud at the Aspen Music School (summer 1961), and Gunther Schuller at the Berkshire Music Center in Tanglewood (summer 1964), where he also attended seminars given by Arthur Berger and Lukas Foss. He then studied composition with Chou Wen-chung and Otto Luening, electronic music with Vladimir Ussachevsky, and music theory with William J. Mitchell at Columbia Univ. (M.A., 1966; D.M.A., 1970). He was a teacher at Columbia Univ. (1967–69; 1970–77) and Princeton Univ. (1969–70); was associate prof. (1977–80) and prof. (from 1980) of music at Brooklyn College of the City Univ. of N.Y. He was president of the American Composers Alliance (1971–75) and the American Music Center (1979–82). In 1972 and 1975 he held Guggenheim fellowships. With T. Jerse, he publ. *Computer Music: Synthesis, Composition, and Performance* (N.Y., 1985).

WORKS: *Composition in 5 Parts* for Cello and Piano (1964); *Solos and Combinations* for Flute, Clarinet, and Oboe (1964); *Folia* for Chamber Orch. (1965); *Rota* for Orch. (1966); *Changes* for Computer Synthesis (1970); *Earth's Magnetic Field* for Computer Synthesis (1970); *Speech Songs* for Computer-Synthesized Voice (1972); *Extensions* for Trumpet and Computer Synthesis (1973); *The Story of Our Lives* for Computer-Synthesized Voice (1974; also for Videotape, 1975); *In Celebration* for Computer-Synthesized Voice (1975); *Palinode* for Orch. and Computer Synthesis (1976); *Cascando,* radio play by Samuel Beckett (1978); *Any Resemblance Is Purely Coincidental* for Piano and Computer-Synthesized "Caruso Voice" (1980); *Han motte henne i parken,* radio play by Richard Kostelanetz (1981); *He Met Her in the Park,* radio play by Richard Kostelanetz (1982); *Distribution, Redistribution* for Violin, Cello, and Piano (1983); *Mingo's Song* for Computer-Synthesized Voice (1983); *The Waves* for Soprano and Computer Synthesis (1984); *Profile* for Computer Synthesis (1984); *Roundelay* for Chorus and Computer Synthesis (1985); *A Postcard from the Volcano* for Soprano and Computer Synthesis (1986); *Song without Words* for Computer Synthesis (1986); *A Fractal for Wiley* for Computer Synthesis (1987); *Viola Elegy* for Viola and Computer Synthesis (1987); *Clarinet Elegy* for Bass Clarinet and Computer Synthesis (1988); *Wedding Music* for Violin and Computer Synthesis (1988); *Allemande* for Computer Synthesis (1988); *The Voice of Binky* for Computer Synthesis (1989).

Dodgson, Stephen (Cuthbert Vivian), English composer; b. London, March 17, 1924. He studied with R.O. Morris at the Royal College of Music in London, where he subsequently taught (1965–82). He was also active as a broadcaster.

WORKS: Opera, *Margaret Catchpole* (1979); 2 concertos for Guitar and Chamber Orch. (1959, 1972); Bassoon Concerto (1969); Clarinet Concerto (1983); Trombone Concerto (1986); *Magnificat* for Soloists and Orch. (1975); *Sir John,* cantata for Chorus and Horn Trio (1980); 2 string trios (1951, 1964); Suite for Wind Quintet (1965); Quintet for Piano and String Quartet (1966); 2 piano trios (1967, 1973); *Cadilly,* entertainment for 4 Singers and Wind Quintet (1968); *Epigrams from a Garden* for Contralto and Clarinet Choir (1977); String Quartet (1986); 3 piano sonatas (1959, 1975, 1983); numerous solo works for guitar, harpsichord, lute, etc.; songs.

Doebler, Curt, German composer of sacred music; b. Kottbus, Jan. 15, 1896; d. Berlin, June 19, 1970. He studied organ with A. Dreyer. From 1919 to 1932 he was organist and choral leader at the Catholic church in Charlottenburg; after occupying various positions as an organist and a teacher elsewhere, he returned to Charlottenburg (1950). In his music Doebler attempts to establish a modern style based on Palestrina's polyphony. His numerous choruses a cappella enjoy considerable renown in Germany.

Doenhoff, Albert von, American pianist and composer; b. Louisville, Ky., March 16, 1880; d. N.Y., Oct. 3, 1940. He studied at the Cincinnati College of Music and then in N.Y. with Rafael Joseffy; made his professional debut in N.Y. on March 8, 1905; subsequently developed a successful career as a concert pianist. He publ. many pieces for piano (*Arabesque, Revery,* etc.); also pedagogical material (*Three Modern Etudes for the Virtuoso; Six Special Studies Adapted to Small Hands;* etc.).

Doflein, Erich, German musicologist; b. Munich, Aug. 7, 1900; d. Kirchzarten, Oct. 29, 1977. He studied with Weismann, Auerbach, and Praetorius, and later with Kaminski; was a music instructor in Freiburg im Breisgau (1924–41); taught in Breslau (1941–44); was a prisoner of war in Russia (1944–46). After his return to Germany, he taught at the Musikhochschule in Freiburg im Breisgau (1947–65); he prepared modern eds. of 6 sonatas by Boismortier (2 books, 1960); concertos by F. Durante (1966); etc. A Festschrift was publ. in Mainz in 1972 in his honor.

Döhler, Theodor (von), Austrian pianist and composer; b. Naples, April 20, 1814; d. Florence, Feb. 21, 1856. He was a pupil of Julius Benedict at Naples and of Czerny (piano) and Sechter (composition) at Vienna. In 1831 he became pianist to the Duke of Lucca; lived for a time in Naples; made brilliant pianistic tours from 1836 to 1846 in Germany, Italy, France, the Netherlands, and England; in 1843 went to Copenhagen, thence to Russia, and in 1846 to Paris; settled in Florence in 1848. In 1846 the Duke, his patron, ennobled him, and he married a Russian countess. He wrote an opera, *Tancreda,* which was performed posthumously in Florence in 1880; many piano pieces; nocturnes; tarantellas; *12 études de concert; 50 études de salon;* variations, fantasias, and transcriptions.

Dohnányi, Christoph von, eminent German conductor of Hungarian descent, grandson of **Ernst (Ernö) von Dohnányi;** b. Berlin, Sept. 8, 1929. He began to study the piano as a child; his musical training was interrupted by World War II. His father, Hans von Dohnányi, a jurist, and his uncle, Dietrich Bonhoeffer, the Protestant theologian and author, were executed by the Nazis for their involvement in the July 20, 1944, attempt on Hitler's life. After the war, he studied jurisprudence at the Univ. of Munich; in 1948 he enrolled at the Hochschule für Musik in Munich, and won the Richard Strauss Prize for composition and conducting. Making his way to the U.S., he continued his studies with his grandfather at Florida State Univ. at Tallahassee; also attended sessions at the Berkshire Music Center at Tanglewood. Returning to Germany, he received a job as a coach and conductor at the Frankfurt Opera (1952–57). Progressing rapidly, he served as Generalmusikdirektor in Lübeck (1957–63) and Kassel (1963–66), chief conductor of the Cologne Radio Sym. Orch. (1964–70), and director of the Frankfurt Opera (1968–77). From 1977 to 1984 he was Staatsopernintendant of the Hamburg State Opera. In 1984 he assumed the position of music director of the Cleveland Orch., having been appointed music director–designate in 1982, succeeding Lorin Maazel. In the meantime, he had engagements as guest conductor of the Vienna State Opera, Covent Garden in London, La Scala in Milan, the Metropolitan Opera in N.Y., the Berlin Phil., the Vienna Phil., and the Concertgebouw Orch. in Amsterdam. Both as sym. and opera conductor, Dohnányi proved himself a master technician and a versatile musician capable of congenial interpretation of all types of music, from Baroque to the avant-garde. He is regarded as a leading exponent of the works of the modern Vienna School, excelling in fine performances of the works of Schoenberg, Berg, and Webern. He is married to **Anja Silja.**

Dohnányi, Ernst (Ernö) von, eminent Hungarian pianist, composer, conductor, and pedagogue, grandfather of **Christoph von Dohnányi;** b. Pressburg, July 27, 1877; d. N.Y., Feb. 9, 1960. He began his musical studies with his father, an amateur cellist; then studied piano and music theory with Károly Forstner. In 1894 he entered the Royal Academy of Music in Budapest, where he took courses in piano with István Thomán and in composition with Hans Koessler. In 1896 he received the Hungarian Millennium Prize, established to commemorate the thousand years of existence of Hungary, for his sym. He graduated from the Academy of Music in 1897, and then went to Berlin for additional piano studies with Eugen d'Albert. He made his debut in a recital in Berlin on Oct. 1, 1897; on Oct. 24, 1898, he played Beethoven's 4th Piano Concerto in London; then followed a series of successful concerts in the U.S. Returning to Europe, he served as prof. of piano at the Hochschule für Musik in Berlin (1908–15). He then returned to Budapest, where he taught piano at the Royal Academy of Music; served briefly as its director in 1919, when he was appointed chief conductor of the Budapest Phil. Orch. In 1928 he became head of the piano composition classes at the Academy of Music; in 1934 he became its director. In 1931 he assumed the post of music director of the Hungarian Radio. As Hungary became embroiled in war and partisan politics which invaded even the arts, Dohnányi resigned his directorship in 1941, and in 1944 he also resigned his post as chief conductor of the Budapest Phil. Personal tragedy also made it impossible for him to continue his work as a musician and teacher: both of his sons lost their lives; one of them, the German jurist Hans von Dohnányi, was executed for his role in the abortive attempt on Hitler's life; the other son was killed in combat. Late in 1944, he moved to Austria. At the war's end rumors were rife that Dohnányi used his influence with the Nazi overlords in Budapest to undermine the position of Bartók and other liberals, and that he acquiesced in anti-Semitic measures. But in 1945 the Allied occupation authorities exonerated him of all blame; even some prominent Jewish-Hungarian musicians testified in his favor. In 1947–48 he made a tour of England as a pianist; determined to emigrate to America, he accepted the position of piano teacher at Tucumán, Argentina; in Sept. 1949 he reached the U.S., where he became composer-in-residence at Florida State Univ. in Tallahassee.

Dohnányi was a true virtuoso of the keyboard, and was greatly esteemed as a teacher; among his pupils were Georg Solti, Geza Anda, and Bálint Vázsonyi. His music represented the terminal flowering of European Romanticism, marked by passionate eloquence of expression while keeping within the framework of Classical forms. Brahms praised his early efforts. In retrospect, Dohnányi appears as a noble epigone of the past era, but pianists, particularly Hungarian pianists, often put his brilliant compositions on their programs. His most popular work with an orch. is *Variations on a Nursery Song;* also frequently played is his Orch. Suite in F-sharp minor. Dohnányi himself presented his philosophy of life in a poignant pamphlet under the title *Message to Posterity* (Jacksonville, Fla., 1960).

WORKS: STAGE: *Der Schleier der Pierrette* (Pierrette's Veil), op. 18, pantomime (1908–9; Dresden, Jan. 22, 1910); *Tante Simona,* op. 20, comic opera (1911–12; Dresden, Jan. 20, 1913); *A vajda tornya* (The Tower of the Voivod), op. 30, opera (1915–22; Budapest, March 19, 1922); *Der Tenor,* op. 34, comic opera (1920–27; Budapest, Feb. 9, 1929).

ORCH.: Sym. in F major (not numbered) and *Zrinyi,* overture (1896; Budapest, June 3, 1897); Piano Concerto No. 1 in E minor, op. 5 (1897–98; Budapest, Jan. 11, 1899); Sym. No. 1 in D minor, op. 9 (1900–1901; Manchester, Jan. 30, 1902); *Konzertstück* for Cello and Orch., op. 12 (1903–4; Budapest, March 7, 1906); Suite in F-sharp minor, op. 19 (1908–9; Budapest, Feb. 21, 1910); *Variationen über ein Kinderlied* (Variations on a Nursery Song), for Piano and Orch., op. 25 (1913; Berlin, Feb. 17, 1914, Dohnányi, soloist); Violin Concerto No. 1 in D minor, op. 27 (1914–15, Copenhagen, March 5, 1919); *Unnepi nyitány* (Festival Overture), op. 31 (1923); *Ruralia hungarica,* 5 pieces for Orch., op. 32b (1924; Budapest, Nov. 17, 1924, Dohnányi, conductor); *Szimfonikus percek* (Symphonic Minutes), op. 36 (1933); *Suite en valse,* op. 39 (1942–43); Sym. No. 2 in E major, op. 40 (1943–44; London, Nov. 23, 1948; rev. 1953–56; Minneapolis, March 15, 1957); Piano Concerto No. 2 in B minor, op. 42 (1946–47; Sheffield, England, Dec. 3, 1947); Violin Concerto No. 2, op. 43 (scored for Orch. without Violins; 1949–50; San Antonio, Jan. 26, 1952); Concertino for Harp and Chamber Orch., op. 45 (1952); *American Rhapsody,* op. 47 (1953; Athens, Ohio, Feb. 21, 1954, Dohnányi, conductor).

VOCAL: *Magyar hiszekegy* (Hungarian Credo) for Tenor, Choir, and Orch. (1920); *Missa in Dedicatione Ecclesiae* (Mass of Szeged) for Soloist, Chorus, Organ, and Orch., op. 35 (1930); consecration of the Cathedral of Szeged, Oct. 25, 1930); *Cantus vitae,* symphonic cantata, op. 38 (1939–41); *Stabat Mater* for 3 Soloists, Children's Chorus, and Orch., op. 46 (1952–53; Wichita Falls, Texas, Jan. 16, 1956); also songs, including 6 Poems, op. 14 (1905–6); *Im Lebenslenz,* op. 16 (1906–7); 3 Songs, with Orch., op. 22 (1912); Hungarian Folk Songs (1922).

CHAMBER: Piano Quintet No. 1, op. 1 (1895); String Quartet No. 1, op. 7 (1899); Sonata for Cello and Piano, op. 8 (1899); *Serenade* for String Trio, op. 10 (1902); String Quartet No. 2, op. 15 (1906); Sonata for Violin and Piano, op. 21 (1912); Piano Quintet No. 2, op. 26 (1914); *Ruralia hungarica,* 3 pieces for Violin and Piano, op. 32c (1924); *Ruralia hungarica,* 1 piece for Cello or Violin and Piano, op. 32d (1924); String Quartet No. 3, op. 33 (1926); Sextet for Piano, Clarinet, Horn, and String Trio, op. 37 (1935); *Aria,* for Flute and Piano (1958); *Passacaglia* for Flute, op. 48 (1959).

PIANO: 4 Pieces, op. 2: *Scherzo* in C-sharp minor, *Intermezzo* in A minor, *Intermezzo* in F minor, *Capriccio* in B minor (1896–97); *Waltz* in F-sharp minor, for 4 hands, op. 3 (1897); Variations and Fugue on a Theme of E(mma) G(ruber), op. 4 (1897); Gavotte and Musette in B-flat major (1898); Passacaglia in E-flat minor, op. 6 (1899); 4 Rhapsodies, in G minor, F-sharp minor, C major, E-flat minor, op. 11 (1902–3); *Winterreigen,* 10 bagatelles: *Widmung, Marsch der lustigen Brüder, An Ada, Freund Viktor's Mazurka, Sphärenmusik, Valse aimable, Um Mitternacht, Tolle Gesellschaft, Morgengrauen, Postludium,* op. 13 (1905); *Humoresken in Form einer Suite:* March, Toccata, Pavane with Variations, Pastorale, Introduction, and Fugue, op. 17 (1907); 3 Pieces: *Aria, Valse impromptu, Capriccio,* op. 23 (1912); Fugue, for left hand or 2 hands (1913); *Suite im alten Stil:* Prelude, Allemande, Courante, Sarabande, Menuet, Gigue, op. 24 (1913); 6 Concert Etudes, op. 28 (1916); Variations on a Hungarian Folk Song, op. 29 (1917); Pastorale, Hungarian Christmas Song (1920); *Ruralia hungarica,* 7 pieces, op. 32a (1923); Essential Finger Exercises (1929); *Suite en valse* for 2 pianos, op. 39a (1945); 6 Pieces: Impromptu, Scherzino, Canzonetta, Cascade, Ländler, Cloches, op. 41 (1945); 12 Short Studies for the Advanced Pianist (1950); 3 Singular Pieces: *Burletta, Nocturne* (Cats on the Roof), *Perpetuum mobile,* op. 44 (1951); Daily Finger Exercises (3 vols., 1960).

BIBL.: V. Papp, *D. Ernö* (Budapest, 1927); M. Reuth, *The*

Tallahassee Years of E. v.D. (diss., Florida State Univ., 1962); L. Podhradszky, "The Works of Ernö D.," *Studia musicologica Academiae scientiarum hungaricae*, VI (1964); B. Vázsonyi, *D. Ernö* (Budapest, 1971).

Doire, René, French composer and conductor; b. Evreux, June 13, 1879; d. Paris, July 9, 1959. He studied in Rouen and later in Paris, with Widor and d'Indy; then was engaged as a bandleader in the casinos of various French spas. He composed a 1-act opera, *Morituri* (1903); a cycle of songs, *Reflets de jeunesse,* for Voice and Piano, or Orch. (1902); *Vision d'Espagne* for Violin and Orch. (1916); Violin Sonata (1918); *Dramatico* for Piano and Orch. (1923); songs.

Dokshitcher, Timofei, Russian trumpet virtuoso; b. Nezhin, Dec. 13, 1921. He studied trumpet with Tabakov in Moscow, and conducting at the Moscow Cons., graduating in 1957. In 1945 he became a member of the Bolshoi Theater orch. in Moscow. He enjoys a reputation as one of the finest artists on his instrument.

Doktor, Paul (Karl), distinguished Austrian-born American violist and pedagogue; b. Vienna, March 28, 1919; d. N.Y., June 21, 1989. He studied with his father, Karl Doktor, violinist of the renowned Busch Quartet; graduated as a violinist at the Academy of Music in Vienna in 1938, but subsequently changed to viola, and in 1942 received the 1st prize at the International Competition in Geneva. He left Vienna in 1938; from 1939 to 1947 was solo violist of the Lucerne Orch.; emigrated to the U.S. in 1947; in 1948 he made his U.S. debut at the Library of Congress in Washington, D.C.; in 1952 he became a naturalized U.S. citizen. In 1953 he was appointed to the faculty of the Mannes College of Music in N.Y.; taught at the Philadelphia Musical Academy from 1970 and the Juilliard School from 1971. He commissioned several composers to write works for his instrument, including Walter Piston and Quincy Porter; he also prepared various transcriptions for viola and ed. a number of viola pieces by other composers.

Dolega-Kamiénski. See **Kamiénski, Lucian.**

Doles, Johann Friedrich, German composer; b. Steinbach, April 23, 1715; d. Leipzig, Feb. 8, 1797. He studied theology in Leipzig; then became a pupil of Bach (1740–44), who recommended him for the post of cantor in Salzwedel; he became, instead, cantor in Freiberg, Saxony, in 1744. In 1743–44 he conducted a series of concerts in Leipzig which proved to be the precursor to the famous concerts of the Gewandhaus Orch. In 1756 he became cantor at the St. Thomas School in Leipzig; was also director of the St. Thomas Church until 1789, when he resigned. He wrote a great number of sacred works.

Bibl.: H. Banning, *J.F. D.: Leben und Werke* (Leipzig, 1939).

Doležálek, Jan Emanuel, Czech musician; b. Chotěboř, May 22, 1780; d. Vienna, July 6, 1858. He studied music in Vienna with Beethoven's teacher, Albrechtsberger, and through him came to know Beethoven himself. It is owing chiefly to this association that Doležálek's name is known in music history. He arranged a number of Czech songs, and publ. a collection of them.

Dolin, Samuel (Joseph), Canadian composer; b. Montreal, Aug. 22, 1917. He studied piano in Montreal and Toronto; later took lessons in composition with Weinzweig and Krenek. In 1945 he was appointed to the faculty of the Royal Cons.; was active in various musical organizations; he organized the Electronic Music Studio of the Royal Cons. in 1966, and also served as president of the Canadian League of Composers (1969–73).

Works: Opera, *Casino* (*Greed;* 1966–67); *Drakkar,* "an entertainment" for Narrator, Mezzo-soprano, 2 Baritones, 2 Dancers, Chamber Ensemble, 2 Synthesizers, and Amplifiers (1972; Toronto, Feb. 17, 1973); *Hero of Our Time* for Baritone, Male Chorus, Dancers, and Orch. Ensemble (1985); Sinfonietta (1950; the *Scherzo* movement is often played as a separate piece); Serenade for Strings (1951); 3 syms. (1956, 1957, 1976);

Isometric Variables (*Bassooneries in Free Variations*) for Bassoon and Strings (1957); Sonata for String Orch. (1962); Fantasy for Piano and Chamber Orch. (1967); Piano Concerto (1974); Concerto for Accordion and Orch. (1984); Violin Sonatina (1954); Violin Sonata (1960); *Portrait* for String Quartet (1961); *Barcarolle* for Violin and Piano (1962); Concerto Grosso (*Georgian Bay*) for Percussion, Accordion, and Tape (1970); Sonata for Solo Accordion (1970); *Marchbankantata* for Baritone, Chorus, Piano, and Synthesizer (1971); Mass for 6 Voices, Congregation, and Organ (1972); 3 sonatas: for Solo Violin, Solo Flute, and Solo Cello, each with Tape (all 1973); *Ricercar* for Guitar (1974); *Adikia* for 1 to 5 Accordions in any combination, and Tape (1975); Sonata for Cello and Piano (1978); Quintet for Brass (1981); *Psalmody* for Oboe (1982); 4 *Miniatures* for Piano (1943); 3 Preludes for Piano (1949); Piano Sonata (1950); *Little Toccata* for Piano (1959); Piano Sonatina (1959); Variation for 2 Pianos (1967); *If* for Piano (1972); choruses; songs.

Dolmetsch, (Eugène) Arnold, eminent French-born English music scholar and instrumentalist, father of **Carl Frederick Dolmetsch;** b. Le Mans, Sarthe, Feb. 24, 1858; d. Haslemere, Surrey, Feb. 28, 1940. His father and maternal grandfather maintained an organ and piano workshop in Le Mans in which he was apprenticed in the construction and repair of instruments. He received piano lessons at age 4, then took violin lessons from an itinerant violinist, and later from his uncle. After his father's death in 1874, he carried on the family business. In 1878, however, he eloped to Nancy with Marie Morel, a widow 10 years his senior; following the birth of their daughter, they proceeded to London, where they were married (May 28, 1878). In 1879 he went to Brussels to study violin with Vieuxtemps; he then came under the influence of Gevaert at the Brussels Cons., where he studied harmony and counterpoint with Kufferath and piano with de Greef (1881–83); also learned to play the viola d'amore. Upon his return to London, he took courses in violin with Henry Holmes, in harmony and counterpoint with Frederick Bridge, and in composition with Parry at the Royal College of Music (1883–85). From 1885 to 1889 he was an assistant violin teacher at Dulwich College; he also spent much time researching and copying early MSS in the Royal College of Music library, and later in the British Library. He began collecting old books on early music, and proceeded to collect and restore viols; he also taught his wife, daughter, and selected pupils to play the instruments, and presented concerts of Elizabethan music. Expanding his activities still more widely, he set about restoring a variety of keyboard instruments, and later learned to build the instruments himself. At the invitation of Bridge, he performed the music of Byrd, Bull, Purcell, Locke, Lawes, Jenkins, and Simpson at Bridge's lecture at Gresham College on Nov. 21, 1890; this was the 1st time the music of these early composers had been played on original instruments in modern times. On April 27, 1891, he gave a notable "Concert of Ancient Music of the XVI and XVII Centuries" in London, playing works on the viols, lute, and harpsichord, assisted by 2 vocal soloists. He worked industriously to establish himself as an authority on early music and instruments, a distinguished performer, and a skilled craftsman; his cause was championed by George Bernard Shaw. Dolmetsch and his wife separated in 1893 and were divorced in 1899. From 1895 he lived with his divorced sister-in-law, Elodie, a fine keyboard player; in 1899 they were married. Dolmetsch, his wife, and Mabel Johnston, a player on the viola da gamba and the violone, made their U.S. debut in N.Y. on Jan. 6, 1903. Dolmetsch and his 2nd wife were divorced later that year, at which time he married Johnston; with Kathleen Salmon, his pupil and a harpsichordist, they made an extensive U.S. tour in 1904–5. He was hired by Chickering & Sons of Boston in 1905 to oversee the manufacture of early keyboard instruments, viols, and lutes. From 1906 to 1911 he lived in Cambridge, Mass.; he also continued to give concerts. In 1911 he began working at the Gaveau factory in Fontenay-sous-Bois, near Paris. In 1914 he returned to En-

gland and settled in Haslemere in 1917, where he maintained a workshop and built the 1st modern recorder (1918). In 1925 he organized the Haslemere Festivals, where he and his family presented annual concerts. In 1927 the Dolmetsch Foundation was organized by his pupils and friends with the goal of furthering his work. Its journal, *The Consort*, began publication in 1929. Dolmetsch was awarded the cross of the Légion d'honneur of France (1938) and an honorary doctorate in music from the Univ. of Durham (1939). He prepared eds. of early music, including *Select English Songs and Dialogues of the 16th and 17th Centuries* (2 vols., London, 1898, 1912), *English Tunes of the 16th and 17th Centuries for Treble Recorder in F and Pieces for 2, 3 and 4 Recorders* (Haslemere, 1930), *Select French Songs from the 12th to the 18th Centuries* (London, 1938), and *The Dolmetsch Collection of English Consorts* (ed. by P. Grainger; N.Y., 1944). He also contributed articles to journals and publ. the book *The Interpretation of the Music of the XVII and XVIII Centuries* (London, 1915; 2nd ed., 1946). U. Supper ed. *A Catalogue of the Dolmetsch Library* (Haslemere, 1967).
BIBL.: R. Donington, *The Work and Ideas of A. D.* (Haslemere, 1932); P. Grainger, "A. D., Musical Confucius," *Musical Quarterly* (April 1933); W. McNaught, "A. D. and His Work," *Musical Times* (April 1940); N. Ferguson, "The Development of the D. Movement," *Hinrichsen's Musical Year Book* (1947); M. Dolmetsch, *Personal Recollections of A. D.* (London, 1958); E. Herrin, "A. D.," *The Consort* (July 1958); M. Campbell, *D.: The Man and His Work* (London and Seattle, 1975).

Dolmetsch, Carl Frederick, French recorder player, son of **(Eugène) Arnold Dolmetsch;** b. Fontenay-sous-Bois, near Paris, Aug. 23, 1911. He received thorough training in instrumentation from his father; eventually succeeded him as a leader of the Haslemere Festival. He devoted himself mainly to the publication of music for the recorder; publ. a survey, *Recorder and German Flute during the 17th and 18th Centuries* (London, 1957), and *An Introduction to the Recorder in Modern British Music* (London, 1960). He also publishes the annual bulletin *The Consort*.

Dolphy, Eric (Allan), black American jazz alto saxophonist, bass clarinetist, and flutist; b. Los Angeles, June 20, 1928; d. Berlin, June 29, 1964. He took up the clarinet in early childhood, later studying music at Los Angeles City College. After working with local groups, including Chico Hamilton's quintet (1958–59), he went to N.Y., where he performed with Charles Mingus's Quartet (1959–60). He co-led a quintet with Booker Little (1961), then worked with John Coltrane, John Lewis, and again with Mingus. He was a master at improvisation, excelling in both jazz and "3rd-stream" genres. His repertoire included several avant-garde works, including Varèse's *Density 21.5* for solo flute.
BIBL.: V. Simosko and B. Tepperman, *E. D.: A Musical Biography and Discography* (Washington, D.C., 1974); R. Horricks, *The Importance of Being E. D.* (Tunbridge Wells, 1989).

Dolukhanova, Zara, Russian mezzo-soprano of Armenian extraction; b. Moscow, March 5, 1918. She studied with private teachers; joined the Moscow Radio staff in 1944; was awarded the Lenin Prize in 1966. A lyric singer, she excelled in the Romantic Russian repertoire. In 1959 she made her 1st American tour, enjoying great acclaim; she toured America again in 1970.

Domange, Mme. Albert. See **Bonis, Mélanie.**

Domaniewski, Boleslaus, Polish pianist; b. Gronowek, July 16, 1857; d. Warsaw, Sept. 11, 1925. He studied at the St. Petersburg Cons.; from 1890 to 1900 taught at the Krakow Cons.; in 1902 he became director of the Warsaw Music School. His piano method, *Vademecum pour le pianiste* (Leipzig, 1897), enjoyed considerable popularity.

Domanínská (real name, **Klobásková**), **Libuše,** Czech soprano; b. Brno, July 4, 1924. She studied in Brno, where she made her operatic debut as Blaženka in Smetana's *Tajemství* (1945); in 1955 she joined the Prague National Theater, and

from 1958 to 1968 was also a member of the Vienna State Opera. She won praise for her performances in Czech operas, especially those by Janáček.

Domanský, Hanuš, Slovak composer; b. Nový Hrozenkov, March 1, 1944. He studied composition with Jan Duchaň at the Brno Cons. and with D. Kardoš at the Bratislava Academy of Musical Arts; later was active with the Czech Radio in Bratislava. His music combines the Czech tradition of Janáček with techniques of Stravinsky and Berg. His Sym. (1980) received the Slovak Composers Award in 1983.
WORKS: ORCH.: Concerto piccolo (1970); Sym. (1980); Piano Concerto (1984). **CHAMBER:** *Music* for Trumpet, Flute, and Bass Clarinet (1966); Piano Sonata (1967); String Quartet (1968); *Musica giocosa* for Violin and Piano (1971); *Dianoia* for Solo Violin (1976); A Fragment of a Sonata for Piano (1977); Bagatelles for Piano (1978); *Dithyrambs* for Piano (1980). **VOCAL:** *About Winter*, cantata for Narrator, Children's Choir, and Orch. (1968); *Fiat lux*, oratorio for Narrator, Soprano, Chorus, and Orch. (1970); *Disobedient Chants* for Children's Choir (1971); *Klapancie* (Versifying) for Chorus and Percussion (1972); *Recruit Songs* for Men's Chorus (1978); also songs.

Domarkas, Ionas, Lithuanian composer; b. Lengiru, May 23, 1934. He studied at the Lithuanian Cons. in Vilna, and was subsequently active in radio broadcasting and teaching. Among his works are *Symphonic Dances* for Orch. (1969); a Violin Sonata (1972); and several pieces for clarinet, oboe, and bassoon, as well as for piano.

Domgraf-Fassbänder, Willi, German baritone, father of **Brigitte Fassbänder;** b. Aachen, Feb. 9, 1897; d. Nuremberg, Feb. 13, 1978. He first studied in Aachen, where he made his operatic debut (1922), then with Jacques Stückgold and Paul Bruns in Berlin and with Giuseppe Borgatti in Milan. He sang in Berlin, Düsseldorf, and Stuttgart, and was a leading member of the Berlin State Opera from 1928 until the end of World War II; he also appeared at the Glyndebourne Festivals (1934–35; 1937). After the war, he sang in Hannover, Vienna, Munich, and Nuremberg, serving as chief producer at the latter opera house (1953–62). He also taught at the Nuremberg Cons. (from 1954). Among his finest roles were Figaro, Papageno, and Guglielmo.

Domingo, Plácido, famous Spanish tenor; b. Madrid, Jan. 21, 1941. His parents were zarzuela singers; after a tour of Mexico, they settled there and gave performances with their own company. Plácido joined his parents in Mexico at the age of 7 and began appearing with them in various productions while still a child; he also studied piano with Manuel Barajas in Mexico City and voice with Carlo Morelli at the National Cons. there (1955–57). He made his operatic debut in the tenor role of Borsa in *Rigoletto* with the National Opera in Mexico City in 1959. His 1st major role was as Alfredo in *La Traviata* in Monterrey in 1961; that same year he made his U.S. debut as Arturo in *Lucia di Lammermoor* with the Dallas Civic Opera; then was a member of the Hebrew National Opera in Tel Aviv (1962–64). He made his 1st appearance with the N.Y. City Opera as Pinkerton in *Madama Butterfly* on Oct. 17, 1965. On Aug. 9, 1966, he made his Metropolitan Opera debut as Turiddu in a concert performance of *Cavalleria rusticana* at N.Y.'s Lewisohn Stadium; his formal debut on the stage of the Metropolitan followed on Sept. 28, 1968, when he essayed the role of Maurice de Saxe in *Adriana Lecouvreur*, establishing himself as one of its principal members. He also sang regularly at the Vienna State Opera (from 1967), Milan's La Scala (from 1969), and London's Covent Garden (from 1971). His travels took him to all the major operatic centers of the world, and he also sang for recordings, films, and television. He also pursued conducting. He made his formal debut as an opera conductor with *La Traviata* at the N.Y. City Opera on Oct. 7, 1973, and on Oct. 25, 1984, he appeared at the Metropolitan Opera, conducting *La Bohème*. He commissioned Menotti's opera *Goya* and sang the title role at its premiere in Washington, D.C., on Nov. 15, 1986. In 1987 he had the honor of singing Otello at the 100th anniversary performances at La Scala. On New Year's Eve 1988 he appeared as a soloist with Zubin Mehta and the N.Y. Phil in a gala concert televised live to millions, during which he also conducted the orch. in the overture to *Die Fledermaus*. One of the best-known lyric tenors of his era, Domingo has gained international renown for his portrayals of such roles as Cavaradossi, Des Grieux, Radames, Don Carlo, Otello, Don José, Hoffmann, Canio, and Samson. He publ. an autobiography, *Plácido Domingo: My First Forty Years* (N.Y., 1983).

BIBL.: D. Snowman, *The World of P. D.* (London, 1985).

Domingues, Oralia, Mexican contralto; b. San Luis Potosí, Oct. 15, 1928. She studied at the National Cons. in Mexico City, subsequently making her operatic debut at the Mexico City Opera (1950). She commenced her European career in 1953 with appearances at Milan's La Scala, the Vienna State Opera, and the Paris Opéra; made her debut at London's Covent Garden as Sosostris in Tippett's *A Midsummer Marriage* (1955).

Dominiceti, Cesare, Italian composer; b. Desenzano, July 12, 1821; d. Sesto di Monza, June 20, 1888. He studied in Milan, where all his operas were brought out; lived for a long time in Bolivia; made a fortune there. In 1881 he was appointed prof. of composition at the Milan Cons. He wrote the operas *Due mogli in una* (June 30, 1853), *La maschera* (March 2, 1854), *Morovico* (Dec. 4, 1873), *Il lago delle fate* (May 18, 1878), and *L'Erreditiera* (Feb. 14, 1881).

Domino, "Fats" (Antoine, Jr.), black American singer, pianist, and bandleader; b. New Orleans, Feb. 26, 1928. Although he sustained a severe hand injury as a youth, he pursued his career as a pianist; gained fame during the early years of the rock-'n'-roll era by mixing blues elements with straight rock; he was successful in nightclubs and movies as a purveyor of popular, jazz, and blues genres.

Donalda (real name, **Lightstone**), **Pauline,** Canadian soprano; b. Montreal, March 5, 1882; d. there, Oct. 22, 1970. She received her 1st musical training at Royal Victoria College in Montreal, and then was a private pupil of Duvernoy in Paris; made her debut as Massenet's Manon in Nice, Dec. 30, 1904; the next year she appeared at the Théâtre Royal de la Monnaie in Brussels and at Covent Garden; in 1906–7, at the Manhattan Opera House in N.Y.; then chiefly at the Opéra-Comique. From the time of her retirement, in 1922, to 1937, she had a singing school in Paris; in 1937, returned to Montreal. In 1938 she presented her valuable music library (MSS, autographs, and music) to McGill Univ. In 1942 she founded the Opera Guild in Montreal, serving as its president until it ceased operations in 1969. In 1967 she was made an Officer of the Order of Canada. Her stage name was taken in honor of Sir Donald Smith (later Lord Strathcona), who endowed the Royal Victoria College and was her patron.

BIBL.: C. Brotman, *P. D.* (1975).

Donath, Helen (born **Helen Erwin**), American soprano; b. Corpus Christi, Texas, July 10, 1940. She was educated at Del Mar College. She then settled in West Germany; made her debut at the Cologne Opera in 1960; sang with fine success in Hannover, Frankfurt, and Munich; also appeared at Bayreuth, being one of the few American singers to gain such distinction. In America, she sang at the San Francisco Opera. She was a favorite singer at Herbert von Karajan's annual Easter Festival in Salzburg.

Donati or **Donato, Baldassare,** famous Italian composer; b. Venice, c.1527; d. there, c.June 1603. He became a chorister at San Marco in Venice in 1550, where he also became a singing teacher to the choirboys in 1562; was director of the cappella piccola there from 1564 until it was disbanded by Zarlino when he became maestro di cappella in 1565. Donati then resumed his place as a chorister at San Marco; was appointed maestro of the singers at the Scuola Grande di San Rocco in 1577, but again resumed his place at San Marco in 1578. He was made maestro di canto to the Seminario Gregoriano di San Marco in 1580, and in 1588 was named vice-maestro

di cappella at San Marco, succeeding Zarlino as its maestro di cappella in 1590. He was a particularly notable composer of secular works in a lighter vein.

WORKS (all publ. in Venice): *Le napollitane et alcuni madrigali* for 4 Voices (1550); *Il primo libro di madrigali* for 5 to 6 Voices *con 3 dialoghi* for 7 Voices (1553); *Il secondo libro de madrigali* for 4 Voices (1558); *Il primo libro de motetti* for 5 to 6 and 8 Voices (1599); various other works in contemporary collections.

Donati, Ignazio, Italian composer; b. Casalmaggiore, near Parma, c.1575; d. Milan, Jan. 21, 1638. He served as maestro di cappella at Urbino Cathedral (1596–98; 1612–15), Pesaro (1600), Fano (1601–5), the Accademia dello Spirito Santa in Ferrara (1616), Casalmaggiore (1618–23), Novara Cathedral (1623–29), Lodi Cathedral (1629–30), and Milan Cathedral (1631–38).

WORKS (all publ. in Venice): *Sacri concentus* for 1 to 5 Voices and Organ (1612); *Motetti* for 5 Voices, *in concerto con due sorti di letanie della beata vergine et nel fine alcuni canoni* (1616); *Concerti ecclesiastici* for 2 to 5 Voices and Basso Continuo (organ), op. 4 (1618); *Concerti ecclesiastici* for 1 to 4 Voices and Basso Continuo (organ), op. 5 (1618); *Motetti concertati* for 5 to 6 Voices, *con dialoghi, salmi e letanie della beata vergine* and Basso Continuo (organ), op. 6 (1618); *Il primo libro de motetti* for Voice and Basso Continuo, op. 7 (1619; 2nd ed., 1634); *Messe* for 4 to 6 Voices, *parte da cappella e da concerto* and Basso Continuo (organ) (1622); *Salmi boscarecci concertati* for 6 Voices and 6 Voices ad libitum . . . *con una messa* . . . and Basso Continuo (organ), op. 9 (1623); *Madre de quatordeci figli . . . il secondo libro de motetti, in concerto . . . fatti sopra il basso generale Perfecta sunt in te* for 5 Voices (1629); *Le fanfalughe* for 2 to 5 Voices (1630); *Il secondo libro delle messe da cappella* for 4 to 5 Voices, op. 12 (1633); *Li vecchiarelli et perregrini concerti* for 2 to 4 Voices, *con una messa* for 3 to 4 Voices *concertata*, op. 13 (1636); *Il secondo libro de motetti* for Voice and Basso Continuo, op. 14 (1636); various other works in contemporary collections.

BIBL.: H. McElrath, *A Study of the Motets of I. D. (ca. 1575–1638)* (diss., Univ. of Rochester, 1967).

Donati, Pino, Italian opera director, administrator, and composer; b. Verona, May 9, 1907; d. Rome, Feb. 24, 1975. He studied violin; then took composition lessons with Paribeni. He served as artistic coordinator of the Chicago Lyric Opera from 1958. He wrote 2 operas: *Corradino lo Svevo* (Verona, April 4, 1931) and *Lancillotto del lago* (Bergamo, Oct. 2, 1938); also chamber music. His wife was **Maria Caniglia.**

Donato, Anthony, American violinist, conductor, teacher, and composer; b. Prague, Nebr., March 8, 1909. He studied at the Eastman School of Music in Rochester, N.Y., with Hanson, Rogers, and Royce; obtained the degrees of M.Mus. (1937) and Ph.D. (1947). He was a violin teacher at Drake Univ. (1931–37); Iowa State Teachers College (1937–39); the Univ. of Texas (1939–46); Northwestern Univ. (1947–77). He publ. *Preparing Music Manuscript* (Englewood Cliffs, N.J., 1963).

WORKS: 2 syms. (1944, 1945); opera, *The Walker through Walls* (Evanston, Ill., Feb. 26, 1965, composer conducting); *March of the Hungry Mountains* for Chorus and Orch. (1949); *Solitude in the City* for Narrator and Instruments (1954); *Centennial Ode* for Orch., commissioned by the Nebraska State Centennial (Omaha, Dec. 11, 1967); *Improvisation* for Orch. (Kansas City, May 3, 1969); 4 string quartets (1941, 1947, 1951, 1975; the *Andante* from String Quartet No. 1 is also arranged for String Orch.); 2 violin sonatas (1938, 1949); *Pastorale and Dance* for 4 Clarinets (1947); Sonatina for 3 Trumpets (1949); Sonata for Horn and Piano (1950); Piano Trio (1959); Sonata for Clarinet and Piano (1966); *Discourse* for Flute and Piano (1969); many choral works and piano teaching pieces.

Donatoni, Franco, Italian composer; b. Verona, June 9, 1927. He studied with Desderi in Milan, Liviabella in Bologna, and Pizzetti at the Accademia di Santa Cecilia in Rome, graduating in 1953. He was then an instructor at the Cons. of Bologna, the Verdi Cons. in Milan, the Verdi Cons. in Turin, and, from 1970, at the Accademia Musicale Chigiana in Siena. In his music he adopts a system of serial techniques.

WORKS: String Quartet (1950); Viola Sonata (1952); Concerto for Bassoon and Strings (1952); Concertino for Strings, Brass, and Percussion (1952); *Sinfonia* for Strings (1953); Overture (1953); *Divertimento I* for Violin and Orch. (1954); 5 *Pieces* for 2 Pianos (1954); *La Lampara*, ballet (1956); *Quartetto II* for String Quartet (1958); *Serenata* for Soprano and 16 Instruments, to words by Dylan Thomas (1959); *Strophes* for Orch. (Radio Rome, Jan. 30, 1960); *Movimento* for Harpsichord, Piano, and 9 Instruments (1959); *Sezioni* (*Sections*) for Orch. (1960; Hamburg Radio, May 14, 1962); *Quartetto III* for 4-track Tape (1961); *Puppenspiel I*, study for stage music, for Orch. (Palermo, Oct. 8, 1962); *Per orchestra* (1962; Warsaw Autumn Festival, Sept. 24, 1963); *Quartetto IV* for String Quartet (1963; an aleatory work); *Asar* for 10 String Instruments (1964); *Black and White* for 37 String Instruments (1964); *Divertimento II* for String Orch. (1965); *Puppenspiel II* for Flute and Orch. (Valdagno, Sept. 17, 1966); *Souvenir*, subtitled *Kammersymphonie*, for 15 Instruments (Venice Festival, Sept. 12, 1967); *Etwas ruhiger im Ausdruck* for Flute, Clarinet, Violin, Cello, and Piano (1968; the title is taken from an expression mark in bar 8 of the 2nd of Schoenberg's 5 *Piano Pieces*, op. 23); *Black and White No. 2*, exercises for 10 fingers for Keyboard Instrument (1968); *Orts* (*Souvenir No. 2*) for 14 Instruments with Optional Lecturer (1969); *Solo* for 10 String Instruments (1969); *Doubles II* for Orch. (Rome, June 13, 1970; as a ballet, Venice, Jan. 15, 1971); *Lied* for 13 Instruments (1972); *Voci* for Orch. (1972–73; Rome, Feb. 3, 1974); *Lumen* for 6 Instruments (1975); *Diario 1976* for 4 Trombones and 4 Trumpets (1976); *Ash* for 8 Instruments; 4 works under the generic title *Estratto* (Extract): No. 1 for Piano (1969); No. 2 for Harp, Harpsichord, and Piano (1970); No. 3 for Piano and 8 Wind Instruments (1975); No. 4 for 8 Instruments (1975); *Sinfonia op. 63 "A. Webern"* for Orch. (1981); *In cauda* for Chorus and Orch. (1983); *Atem*, theater piece (1984); *Ecco* for Chamber Orch. (1986).

Donaudy, Stefano, composer; b. Palermo (of a French father and an Italian mother), Feb. 21, 1879; d. Naples, May 30, 1925. He was a pupil at the Palermo Cons. of G. Zuelli from 1896 to 1900; wrote the operas *Folchetto* (Palermo, 1892); *Scampagnata* (Palermo, 1898); *Theodor Körner* (Hamburg, Nov. 27, 1902); *Sperduti nel buio* (Palermo, April 27, 1907); *Ramuntcho* (Milan, March 19, 1921); *La Fiamminga* (Naples, April 25, 1922); symphonic poem, *Le Rêve de Polysende; 12 airs de style ancien* for Voice and Piano; and numerous piano pieces.

Dönch, Karl, German bass-baritone; b. Hagen, Jan. 8, 1915. He studied at the Dresden Cons., then made his operatic debut in Görlitz (1936). He sang in Reichenberg, Bonn, and Salzburg, later becoming a member of the Vienna State Opera (from 1947) and making regular appearances at the Salzburg Festivals (from 1951). He was a guest artist at the Berlin Städtische Oper, the Deutsche Oper am Rhein in Düsseldorf, Milan's La Scala, and the Teatro Colón in Buenos Aires. On Jan. 27, 1959, he made his Metropolitan Opera debut in N.Y. as Beckmesser; was on its roster from 1962 to 1965 and again from 1966 to 1969. In addition to the standard Austro-German repertoire, he sang in several contemporary works, including Liebermann's *Penelope* (1954) and Frank Martin's *Tempest* (1956).

Donfrid, Johannes, German music editor; b. Veringenstadt, 1585; d. Rottenburg, Aug. 4, 1650. He was rector of a school, and cantor at St. Martin's Church in Rottenburg. His most important publication is the *Promptuarium musicum* (3 vols., Strasbourg, 1622–27), containing sacred works by various composers; he also publ. a collection of songs, *Viridarium Musico-Marianum* (Strasbourg, 1627); and *Corolla musica*, including 37 masses (Strasbourg, 1628).

Doni, Antonio Francesco or **Antonfrancesco,** Italian writer; b. Florence, May 16, 1513; d. Monselice, near Padua, Sept. 1574. For several years he was a member of the Servite fraternity in Florence; after leaving it in 1539, he led a wandering life as a lay priest. He publ., besides various non-musical treatises, a *Dialogo della musica* (Venice, 1544; includes a list of 17 composers living in Venice at the time, with works of each) and *La libraria* (2 vols., Venice, 1550–51), containing a description of all publ. and unpubl. musical books in Italian known to him at the time, as well as a list of the music academies then in existence and details of their foundation.

BIBL.: A. Einstein, "The 'Dialogo della Musica' of Messer A.F. D.," *Music & Letters,* XV (1934); J. Haar, "The *Libraria* of A. D.," *Musica Disciplina,* XXIV (1970).

Doni, Giovanni Battista, Italian music theorist; b. 1594; d. Florence, Dec. 1, 1647. He studied literature and philosophy at Bologna and Rome; from 1613 to 1618 he was a law student at Bourges, France, and took his degree at Pisa. In 1621 he accompanied Cardinal Corsini to Paris, where he zealously pursued his literary and antiquarian studies; went to Rome in 1622, at the invitation of Cardinal Barberini, who was passionately fond of music, and with whom he traveled. In the intervals of his profound study of ancient music, he found time to construct the "Lira Barberina," or "Amphichord," a species of double lyre which he dedicated to Pope Urban VIII. Recalled to Florence in 1640 by deaths in his family, he settled there, married the next year, and accepted a professorship of elocution offered him by the Grand Duke. His criticism and discussions of the earliest operas are very valuable, and were publ. for the 1st time by A. Solerti in *Origini del melodramma. Testimonianze dei contemporanei* (Turin, 1903).

WRITINGS: *Compendio del trattato de' generi e de' modi della musica* (Rome, 1635); *Annotazioni* on the above (Rome, 1640); *De praestantia musicae veteris libri tres* (Florence, 1647).

BIBL.: A. Blandini, *Commentarium de vita et scriptis G.B. D.* (Florence, 1755); F. Vatielli, *La lira barberina di G.B. D.* (Pesaro, 1909).

Donington, Robert, distinguished English musicologist; b. Leeds, May 4, 1907; d. Firle, Sussex, Jan. 20, 1990. He studied at Queen's College, Oxford (B.A., 1930; B. Litt., 1946); also took a course in composition with Egon Wellesz at Oxford; became associated with Arnold Dolmetsch in his workshop in Haslemere and studied the technique of old instruments; contributed to the revival of Elizabethan instruments and music. He was a member of the English Consort of Viols (1935–39); then played with the London Consort (1950–60); in 1956 he founded the Donington Consort, and led it until 1961. He lectured extensively in the U.S. He was made a Commander of the Order of the British Empire in 1979.

WRITINGS: *The Work and Ideas of Arnold Dolmetsch* (Haslemere, 1932); *A Practical Method for the Recorder* (with Edgar Hunt; 2 vols., London, 1935); *The Instruments of Music* (London, 1949; 4th ed., rev., 1982, as *Music and Its Instruments*); *Music for Fun* (London, 1960); *Tempo and Rhythm in Bach's Organ Music* (London, 1960); *The Interpretation of Early Music* (N.Y., 1963; 3rd ed., rev., 1974; corrected ed., 1989); *Wagner's "Ring" and Its Symbols* (London, 1963; 3rd ed., rev. and enl., 1974); *A Performer's Guide to Baroque Music* (London, 1973); *String-playing in Baroque Music* (London, 1977); *The Opera* (London, 1978); *The Rise of Opera* (London, 1981); *Baroque Music: Style and Performance: A Handbook* (London, 1982).

Donizetti (real name, **Ciummei**), **Alfredo,** composer; b. Smyrna, Sept. 2, 1867; d. Rosario, Argentina, Feb. 4, 1921. He studied (1883–89) at the Milan Cons. under Ponchielli and Dominiceti; then settled in Argentina. He wrote the operas *Nama* (Milan, 1890) and *Dopo l'Ave Maria* (Milan, 1896); also piano pieces and songs.

Donizetti, (Domenico) Gaetano (Maria), famous Italian composer, brother of **Giuseppe Donizetti;** b. Bergamo, Nov. 29, 1797; d. there, April 1, 1848. His father was from a poor family of artisans who obtained the position of caretaker in the local pawnshop. At the age of 9, Gaetano entered the Lezioni Caritatevoli di Musica, a charity institution which served as the training school for the choristers of S. Maria Maggiore; he studied singing and harpsichord there; later studied harmony and counterpoint with J.S. Mayr. With the encouragement and assistance of Mayr, he enrolled in the Liceo Filarmonico Comunale in Bologna in 1815, where he studied counterpoint with Pilotti; later studied counterpoint and fugue with Padre Mattei. His 1st opera, *Il Pigmalione* (1816), appears never to have been performed in his lifetime. He composed 2 more operas in quick succession, but they were not performed. Leaving the Liceo in 1817, he was determined to have an opera produced. His next work, *Enrico di Borgogna*, was performed in Venice in 1818, but it evoked little interest. He finally achieved popular success with his opera buffa *Il Falegname di Livonia, o Pietro il grande, czar delle Russie* (Venice, Dec. 26, 1819). In Dec. 1820 he was exempted from military service when a woman of means paid the sum necessary to secure his uninterrupted work at composition. His opera seria *Zoraide de Granata* (Rome, Jan. 28, 1822) proved a major success. During the next 9 years, Donizetti composed 25 operas, none of which remain in the active repertoire today; however, the great success of his *L'Ajo nell'imbarazzo* (Rome, Feb. 4, 1824) brought him renown at the time. In 1825–26 he served as musical director of the Teatro Carolino in Palermo. From 1829 to 1838 he was musical director of the royal theaters in Naples. With *Anna Bolena* (Milan, Dec. 26, 1830), Donizetti established himself as a master of the Italian operatic theater. Composed for Pasta and Rubini, the opera was an overwhelming success. Within a few years it was produced in several major Italian theaters, and was also heard in London, Paris, Dresden, and other cities. His next enduring work was the charming comic opera *L'elisir d'amore* (Milan, May 12, 1832). The tragic *Lucrezia Borgia* (Milan, Dec. 26, 1833), although not entirely successful at its premiere, soon found acceptance and made the rounds of the major opera houses. In 1834 Donizetti was appointed prof. of counterpoint and composition at the Conservatorio di San Pietro a Majella in Naples. His *Maria Stuarda* (Oct. 18, 1834) was given its 1st performance as *Buondelmonte* in Naples after the Queen objected to details in the libretto. He then went to Paris, where his *Marino Faliero* had a successful premiere at the Théâtre-Italien on March 12, 1835. Returning to Italy, he produced his tragic masterpiece *Lucia di Lammermoor* (Naples, Sept. 26, 1835). Upon the death of Zingarelli in 1837, Donizetti was named director pro tempore of the Conservatorio in Naples. On July 30, 1837, he suffered a grievous loss when his wife died following the 3rd stillbirth of a child, after 9 years of marriage. On Oct. 29, 1837, *Roberto Devereux* garnered acclaim at its 1st performance in Naples. In 1838 Donizetti resigned his positions at the Conservatorio when his post as director was not made a permanent appointment. When the censor's veto prevented the production of *Poliuto* due to its sacred subject (it was written for Nourrit after Corneille's *Polyeucte*), he decided to return to Paris. He produced the highly successful *La Fille du régiment* there on Feb. 11, 1840. It was followed by *Les Martyrs* (April 10, 1840), a revision of the censored *Poliuto*, which proved successful. His *La Favorite* (Dec. 2, 1840) made little impression at its 1st performance, but it soon became one of his most popular operas. He spent 1841–42 in Italy, and then went to Vienna. His *Linda di Chamounix* received an enthusiastic reception at its premiere there on May 19, 1842. The Emperor appointed Donizetti Maestro di Cappella e di Camera e Compositore di Corte. In 1843 he once more went to Paris, where he brought out his great comic masterpiece *Don Pasquale*. With such famous singers as Grisi, Mario, Tamburini, and Lablache in the cast, its premiere on Jan. 3, 1843, was a triumph. He then returned to Vienna, where he conducted the successful premiere of *Maria di Rohan* on June 5, 1843. Back again in Paris, he produced *Dom Sébastien* (Nov. 11, 1843). The audience approved the work enthusiastically, but the critics were not pleased. Considering the opera to be his masterpiece, Donizetti had to wait until the Vienna premiere (in German) of 1845 before the work was universally acclaimed. The last opera produced in his lifetime was *Caterina Cornaro* (Naples, Jan.

12, 1844). By this time Donizetti began to age quickly; in 1845 his mental and physical condition progressively deteriorated as the ravages of syphilis reduced him to the state of an insane invalid; in 1846 he was placed in a mental clinic at Ivry, just outside Paris; in 1847 he was released into the care of his nephew, and was taken to his birthplace to await his end. Donizetti was a prolific composer of operas whose fecundity of production was not always equaled by his inspiration or craftsmanship. Many of his operas are hampered by the poor librettos he was forced to use on so many occasions. Nevertheless, his genius is reflected in many of his operas. Indeed, his finest works serve as the major link in the development of Italian opera between the period of Rossini and that of Verdi. Such operas as *Anna Bolena*, *L'elisir d'amore*, *Lucia di Lammermoor*, *Roberto Devereux*, *La Favorite*, *La Fille du régiment*, and *Don Pasquale* continue to hold a place in the repertoire.

WORKS: OPERAS: *Il Pigmalione* (scena drammatica, 1816; 1st perf. at the Teatro Donizetti, Bergamo, Oct. 13, 1960); *L'ira d'Achille* (1817; not perf.); *L'Olimpiade* (1817; not perf.); *Enrico di Borgogna* (opera semiseria, 1818; Teatro San Luca, Venice, Nov. 14, 1818); *Una follia (di Carnevale)* (farsa, 1818; Teatro San Luca, Venice, Dec. 15, 1818); *Piccioli Virtuosi ambulanti* (also known as *Piccoli Virtuosi di musica ambulanti*) (opera buffa, 1819; Bergamo, 1819); *Il Falegname di Livonia, o Pietro il grande, czar delle Russie* (opera buffa, 1819; Teatro San Samuele, Venice, Dec. 26, 1819); *Le nozze in villa* (opera buffa, 1820; Teatro Vecchio, Mantua, 1820 or 1821); *Zoraide di Granata* (opera seria, 1822; Teatro Argentina, Rome, Jan. 28, 1822); *La Zingara* (opera seria, 1822; Teatro Nuovo, Naples, May 12, 1822); *La lettera anonima* (farsa, 1822; Teatro del Fondo, Naples, June 29, 1822); *Chiara e Serafina, o I Pirati* (opera semiseria, 1822; Teatro alla Scala, Milan, Oct. 26, 1822); *Alfredo il grande* (opera seria, 1823; Teatro San Carlo, Naples, July 2, 1823); *Il Fortunato inganno* (opera buffa, 1823; Teatro Nuovo, Naples, Sept. 3, 1823); *L'Ajo nell'imbarazzo, o Don Gregorio* (opera buffa, 1823–24; Teatro Valle, Rome, Feb. 4, 1824); *Emilia di Liverpool* (also known as *Emilia* or *L'eremitaggio di Liverpool*) (opera semiseria, 1824; Teatro Nuovo, Naples, July 28, 1824); *Alahor di Granata* (opera seria, 1825; Teatro Carolino, Palermo, Jan. 7, 1826); *Il castello degli invalidi* (farsa, 1825–26?; 1st perf. may have taken place at the Teatro Carolino, Palermo, 1826); *Elvida* (opera seria, 1826; Teatro San Carlo, Naples, July 6, 1826); *Gabriella di Vergy* (opera seria, 1826; Teatro San Carlo, Naples, Nov. 22, 1869; 2nd version, 1838?; Whitla Hall, Belfast, Nov. 7, 1978); *La bella prigioniera* (farsa, 1826; not perf.); *Olivo e Pasquale* (opera buffa, 1826; Teatro Valle, Rome, Jan. 7, 1827); *Otto Mesi in due ore, ossia Gli Esiliati in Siberia* (opera romantica, 1827; Teatro Nuovo, Naples, May 13, 1827); *Il Borgomastro di Saardam* (opera buffa, 1827; Teatro Nuovo, Naples, Aug. 19, 1827); *Le convenienze ed inconvenienze teatrali* (farsa, 1827; Teatro Nuovo, Naples, Nov. 21, 1827); *L'Esule di Roma, ossia Il Proscritto* (also known as *Settimio il proscritto*) (opera seria, 1827; Teatro San Carlo, Naples, Jan. 1, 1828); *Alina, regina di Golconda* (also known as *La Regina di Golconda*) (opera buffa, 1828; Teatro Carlo Felice, Genoa, May 12, 1828); *Gianni di Calais* (opera semiseria, 1828; Teatro del Fondo, Naples, Aug. 2, 1828); *Il Giovedì grasso, o Il nuovo Pourceaugnac* (farsa, 1828; Teatro del Fondo, Naples, 1828); *Il Paria* (opera seria, 1828; Teatro San Carlo, Naples, Jan. 12, 1829); *Elisabetta al castello di Kenilworth* (also known as *Il castello di Kenilworth*) (opera seria, 1829; Teatro San Carlo, Naples, July 6, 1829); *I Pazzi per progetto* (farsa, 1830; Teatro del Fondo, Naples, Feb. 7, 1830); *Il diluvio universale* (azione tragico-sacra, 1830; Teatro San Carlo, Naples, Feb. 28, 1830); *Imelda de' Lambertazzi* (opera seria, 1830; Teatro San Carlo, Naples, Aug. 23, 1830); *Anna Bolena* (opera seria, 1830; Teatro Carcano, Milan, Dec. 26, 1830); *Francesca di Foix* (opera semiseria, 1831; Teatro San Carlo, Naples, May 30, 1831); *La Romanziera e l'uomo nero* (opera buffa, 1831; Teatro del Fondo, Naples, June 18, 1831); *Gianni di Parigi* (opera comica, 1831; Teatro alla Scala, Milan, Sept. 10, 1839); *Fausta* (opera seria, 1831; Teatro San Carlo, Naples, Jan. 12,

1832); *Ugo, conte di Parigi* (opera seria, 1832; Teatro alla Scala, Milan, March 13, 1832); *L'elisir d'amore* (opera comica, 1832; Teatro della Canobbiana, Milan, May 12, 1832); *Sancia di Castiglia* (opera seria, 1832; Teatro San Carlo, Naples, Nov. 4, 1832); *Il Furioso all'isola di San Domingo* (opera semiseria, 1832; Teatro Valle, Rome, Jan. 2, 1833); *Parisina* (opera seria, 1833; Teatro della Pergola, Florence, March 17, 1833); *Torquato Tasso* (also known as *Sordello il trovatore* or *Sordello*) (opera seria, 1833; Teatro Valle, Rome, Sept. 9, 1833); *Lucrezia Borgia* (opera seria, 1833; Teatro alla Scala, Milan, Dec. 26, 1833); *Rosmonda d'Inghilterra* (opera seria, 1834; Teatro della Pergola, Florence, Feb. 27, 1834); *Maria Stuarda* (opera seria, 1834; 1st perf. as *Buondelmonte* at the Teatro San Carlo, Naples, Oct. 18, 1834; 1st perf. as *Maria Stuarda* at the Teatro alla Scala, Milan, Dec. 30, 1835); *Gemma di Vergy* (opera seria, 1834; Teatro alla Scala, Milan, Dec. 26, 1834); *Adelaide* (opera comica, 1834?; not completed); *Marino* (or *Marin*) *Faliero* (opera seria, 1835; Théâtre-Italien, Paris, March 12, 1835); *Lucia di Lammermoor* (opera seria, 1835; Teatro San Carlo, Naples, Sept. 26, 1835); *Belisario* (opera seria, 1835–36; Teatro La Fenice, Venice, Feb. 4, 1836); *Il campanello* (*di notte* or *dello speziale*) (farsa, 1836; Teatro Nuovo, Naples, June 1, 1836); *Betly* (or *Bettly*), *ossia La Capanna svizzera* (opera giocosa, 1836; Teatro San Carlo, Naples, Aug. 24, 1836); *L'assedio di Calais* (opera seria, 1836; Teatro San Carlo, Naples, Nov. 19, 1836); *Pia de' Tolomei* (opera seria, 1836–37; Teatro Apollo, Venice, Feb. 18, 1837); *Roberto Devereux, ossia Il Conte di Essex* (opera seria, 1837; Teatro San Carlo, Naples, Oct. 29, 1837); *Maria di Rudenz* (opera seria, 1837; Teatro La Fenice, Venice, Jan. 30, 1838); *Poliuto* (opera seria, 1839; 1st perf. as *Les Martyrs* at the Opéra, Paris, April 10, 1840; 1st perf. as *Poliuto* at the Teatro San Carlo, Naples, Nov. 30, 1848); *L'Ange de Nisida* (incomplete opera; transformed into *La Favorite* [1840]); *Le Duc d'Albe* (1839 and later; not completed; finished by Matteo Salvi and tr. into Italian by Angelo Zanardini as *Il Duca d'Alba*, Teatro Apollo, Rome, March 22, 1882); *La Fille du régiment* (opéra-comique, 1839–40; Opéra-Comique, Paris, Feb. 11, 1840); *Les Martyrs* (grand opera, 1840; rev. version of *Poliuto* [1839]; Opéra, Paris, April 10, 1840); *La Favorite* (grand opera, 1840; rev. version of *L'Ange de Nisida* [1839]; Opéra, Paris, Dec. 2, 1840); *Adelia, o La Figlia dell'arciere* (opera seria, 1840–41; Teatro Apollo, Rome, Feb. 11, 1841); *Rita, ou Le Mari battu* (also known as *Deux hommes et une femme*) (opéra-comique, 1841; Opéra-Comique, Paris, May 7, 1860); *Maria Padilla* (opera seria, 1841; Teatro alla Scala, Milan, Dec. 26, 1841); *Linda di Chamounix* (opera semiseria, 1842; Kärnthnertortheater, Vienna, May 19, 1842); *Don Pasquale* (opera buffa, 1842; Théâtre-Italien, Paris, Jan. 3, 1843); *Maria di Rohan* (opera seria, 1843; Kärnthnertortheater, Vienna, June 5, 1843); *Dom Sébastien, roi de Portugal* (grand opera, 1843; Opéra, Paris, Nov. 11, 1843); *Caterina Cornaro* (opera seria, 1842–43; Teatro San Carlo, Naples, Jan. 12, 1844). His other vocal music includes 28 cantatas, several masses, vespers, Psalms, motets, many songs, ariettas, duets, and canzonets. His instrumental music includes many sinfonias, marches, 19 string quartets, and quintets.

BIBL.: The Donizetti Soc. of London issues an annual journal and a quarterly newsletter. See also F. Regli, *G. D. e le sue opere* (Turin, 1850); F. Cicconetti, *Vita di G. D.* (Rome, 1864); A. Bellotti, *D. e i suoi contemporanei* (Bergamo, 1866); F. Alborghetti and M. Galli, *G. D. e G. Simone Mayr, Notizie e documenti* (Bergamo, 1875); B. Zendrini, *D. e Simone Mayr* (Bergamo, 1875); F. Marchetti and A. Parisotti, eds., *Lettere inedite di G. D.* (Rome, 1892); A. Gabrielli, "La casa di D. a Napoli," *Fanfulla della Domenica*, 53 (1893); G. Roberti, "D.ana," *Rivista Musicale Italiana*, II (1895); E. Verzino, *Contributo ad una biografia di G. D.* (Bergamo, 1896); P. Bettòli, ed., *G. D. Numero Unico nel Primo Centenario della sua nascita, 1797–1897* (Bergamo, n.d.); A. Calzado, *D. e l'opera italiana in Spagna* (Paris, 1897); C. Malherbe, *Centenaire de G. D., Catalogue bibliographique de la Section Française à l'exposition de Bergame* (Paris, 1897); I. Valetta, *D.* (Rome, 1897); E. Verzino, *Le opere di G. D.: Contributo alla loro storia* (Bergamo and

Milan, 1897); A. Gabrielli, *G. D.* (Rome and Turin, 1904); A. Cametti, *D. a Roma* (Milan, Turin, and Rome, 1907); N. Bennati, *Quattro lettere inedite di G. D. e una lettera di Giacomo Meyerbeer* (Ferrara, 1908); C. Caversazzi, *G. D.: La casa dove nacque, La famiglia, L'inizio della malattia* (Bergamo, 1924); G. Donati-Pettèni, *L'Istituto musicale G. D. La Cappella musicale di Santa Maria Maggiore. Il Museo D.ano* (Bergamo, 1928); idem, *Studi e documenti D.ani* (Bergamo, 1929); idem, *D.* (Milan, 1930; 3rd ed., 1940); G. Morazzoni, *Lettere inedite* (Milan, 1930); G. Zavadini, *Museo D.ano di Bergamo: Catalogo generale* (Bergamo, 1936); G. Gavazzeni, *D.: Vita e musiche* (Milan, 1937); A. Geddo, *D.* (Bergamo, 1938); G. Monaldi, *G. D.* (Turin, 1938); A. Geddo, "D. e la sua casa natale," *Rivista di Bergamo*, 19 (1940); G. Zavadini, *G. D.: Vicende della sua vita artistica* (Bergamo, 1941); G. Pinetti, *Le opere di D. nei teatri di Bergamo* (Bergamo, 1942); G. Barblan, *L'opera di D. nell'età romantica* (Bergamo, 1948); M. Daub-Mohr, "Ein Meister der italischen Oper: Zum 100. Todestag von D.," *Neue Musikzeitschrift* (July 1948); J. Klein, "G. D., 1797–1848: A Centennial Tribute," *Musical Opinion* (1948); A. and G. Rizzi, *G. D. nel primo centenario della morte* (Bergamo, n.d.); F. Schlitzer, "Curiosità epistolari inedite nella vita teatrale di G. D.," *Rivista Musicale Italiana* (July–Dec. 1948); G. Zavadini, *D.: Vita—Musiche—Epistolario* (Bergamo, 1948); C. Fumagalli, "Memoria riguardante la riesumazione delle ossa di G. D. avvenuto in Santa Maria Maggiore le sera del 26 luglio 1951," *Bergomum* (Oct.–Dec. 1951); F. Walker, "D., Verdi and Mme. Appiani," *Music & Letters* (Jan. 1951); L. Bossi, *D.* (Brescia, 1956); A. Geddo, *D. (L'uomo—le musiche)* (Bergamo, 1956); F. Walker, "The Librettist of 'Don Pasquale,'" *Monthly Musical Record* (Nov.–Dec. 1958); G. Barblan and F. Walker, "Contributo all'epistolario di G. D.: Lettere inedite o sparse," *Studi D.ani*, I (1962); H. Weinstock, *D. and the World of Opera in Italy, Paris, and Vienna in the First Half of the Nineteenth Century* (N.Y., 1963); W. Ashbrook, *D.* (London, 1965); G. Barblan, "Lettura di un'opera dimenticata: *Pia de' Tolomei* di D. (1836)," *Chigiana*, XXIV/4 (1967); P. Rattalino, "Il processo compositivo nel *Don Pasquale* di D.," *Nuova Rivista Musicale Italiana* (Jan.–April 1970); V. Sacchiero et al., *Il Museo D.ano di Bergamo* (Bergamo, 1970); J. Freeman, "D. in Palermo and *Alahor in Granata*," *Journal of the American Musicological Society* (Summer 1972); F. Speranze, ed., *Studi D.ani*, II (1972); J. Allitt, *D. and the Tradition of Romantic Love: A Collection of Essays on a Theme* (London, 1975); F. Lippmann, "Verdi und D.," *Opernstudien: Anna Amalie Abert zum 65. Geburtstag* (Tutzing, 1975); W. Ashbrook, *D. and His Operas* (Cambridge, 1982); G. Barblan and B. Zanolini, *G. D.: Vita e opera di un musicista romantico* (Bergamo, 1983); W. Crutchfield, "A D. Discovery," *Musical Times* (Sept. 1984); P. Gossett, *Anna Bolena and the Artistic Maturity of G. D.* (Oxford, 1985); G. Tomlinson, "Opera and *Drame*: Hugo, D. and Verdi," *Studies in the History of Music* (Vol. 2, N.Y., 1988).

Donizetti, Giuseppe, Italian bandmaster and composer, brother of **(Domenico) Gaetano (Maria) Donizetti;** b. Bergamo, Nov. 9, 1788; d. Constantinople, Feb. 10, 1856. In 1832 he was summoned by the sultan of Turkey to take charge of Turkish military bands. He accepted, and successfully accomplished the task of introducing Western instruments and modernizing the repertoire. The sultan richly rewarded him with honors and money, and Donizetti remained in Constantinople to the end of his life.

Donner, Henrik Otto, Finnish composer; b. Tampere, Nov. 16, 1939. He studied composition at the Sibelius Academy in Helsinki with Nils-Eric Fougstedt and Joonas Kokkonen; then attended seminars in electronic music in Bilthoven, the Netherlands; also took private lessons with Ligeti. For some years he earned his living as a jazz trumpeter in Helsinki; staged "happenings," with free improvisation on preprogrammed themes.

WORKS: *3 Pieces* for Flute and Piano (1962); *Cantata profana* (1962); *Ideogramme I* for Flute, Clarinet, Trombone, Percussion, and 12 Radios (1962); *Ideogramme II,* employing 20 Musicians, a Tape Recording, and renting a Promenade Room (1963); *For Emmy* 2 for 3 Female Voices and an Amplified Chamber Ensemble (1963); *Kinetique* for Jazz Band and Chamber Ensemble (1964); *Moonspring, or Aufforderung zum . . . or Symphony 1,* subtitled "Hommage à Ives," for Strings, Guitar, Harp, and Hammond Organ (1964); 6 *Bagatelles* for String Quartet (1965); *Gilbert,* a musical (1965); *To Whom It May Concern* for Orch., with Jazz Drums (1966); *XC* for Soprano, Chorus, and Chamber Orch., on a text by Ezra Pound (1969); String Quartet No. 1, with Baritone Solo, on a text of Lenin (1970); *In the Afternoon* for Viola (1971); *Notte* for Guitar (1971); *Etyd för sommarvind (Etude for Summer Wind)* for Male Chorus (1971); music for films.

Donohoe, Peter (Howard), talented English pianist; b. Manchester, June 18, 1953. He studied at Chetham's School of Music in Manchester; made his debut at the age of 12 playing Beethoven's 3rd Piano Concerto at Manchester's Free Trade Hall; then enrolled in the Royal Manchester College of Music; took lessons in Paris with Yvonne Loriod. International recognition followed in 1982, when he became joint 2nd-prize winner in the International Tchaikovsky Competition in Moscow. He subsequently made several world tours, performing in Japan, Canada, the U.S., Australia, and throughout Europe; he was particularly popular in Russia. His repertoire includes the entire range of Classical and Romantic works, but he also cultivates modern piano music, delivering such transcendentally difficult pieces as Liszt's opera transcriptions and Stravinsky's *Petrouchka.* He also became active as a conductor; was artistic director of the Northern Chamber Orch. (from 1984) and was founder-conductor of the Manchester Sinfonietta (from 1986).

Donostia, José Antonio de (real name, **José Gonzalo Zulaica y Arregui**), Spanish organist, musicologist, and composer; b. San Sebastián, Jan. 10, 1886; d. Lecároz, Navarre, Aug. 30, 1956. He studied with Echazarra at the Lecároz Franciscan College, Esquerrá in Barcelona, Gaviola in San Sebastián, and Cools and Roussel in Paris. He worked in Toulouse (1936), Paris (1939–40), and Bayonne (1941–43) as an organist and choirmaster, then became head of the folklore dept. of Barcelona's Spanish Inst. of Musicology (1943), where he brought out monographs and eds. of Basque folk song.
Works: STAGE AND VOCAL: *Les Trois Miracles de Ste. Cécile* for Chorus and Orch. (1920); *La Vie profonde de St. François d'Assise* for Chorus and Orch. (1926); *Le Noël de Greecio* for Chorus and Orch. (1936); *Poema de la Pasión* for 2 Sopranos, Chorus, and English Horn (1937); *La Quête héroïque de Graal* for 4 Ondes Martenot and Piano (1938); *Missa pro defunctis* for Chorus and Organ (1945). CHAMBER: String Quartet (1906); *3 piezas* for Cello and Piano (1906); *Página romántica* for Violin and Piano (1941); piano pieces; organ music.
Writings: *La música popular vasca* (Bilbao, 1918); *Euskel eres-sorta* (Bilbao, 1922); *Essai d'une bibliographie musicale populaire basque* (Bayonne, 1932); *Música y músicos en el pais vasco* (San Sebastian, 1951); *El "Moto proprio" y la canción popular religiosa* (San Sebastian, 1954); *Euskal-erriko otoitzak* (San Sebastian, 1956).
Bibl.: J. de Riezu, *J.A. d.D.* (Pamplona, 1956).

Donovan (born **Donovan Leitch**), Scottish folksinger and songwriter; b. Glasgow, May 10, 1943. He belonged to the generation of "flower children" who hid their troubled psyches behind the curtain of strewn petals and clouds of incense. His song *Season of the Witch* was typical of the hallucinatory aspect of his personality, as was *Mellow Yellow,* which made reference to the popular if ineffective practice of smoking dried banana skins as a means to a natural high. His 2-record album *A Gift from a Flower to a Garden* (1968) was a terrific hit, both in the U.K. and in the U.S. Other popular songs were *Hurdy Gurdy Man* and *Lalena.* He composed the score for the film *Brother Sun, Sister Moon* (Zeffirelli, 1972); he also appeared at an Amnesty International benefit show in London (1982).

Donovan, Richard Frank, American organist, conductor, teacher, and composer; b. New Haven, Conn., Nov. 29, 1891; d. Middletown, Conn., Aug. 22, 1970. He studied music at Yale Univ. and at the Inst. of Musical Art in N.Y. (M.B., 1922); also took lessons in organ playing with Widor in Paris. Returning to America, he served as organist in several N.Y. churches; from 1923 to 1928 he was on the faculty of Smith College; in 1928 he was appointed to the School of Music at Yale Univ.; was a prof. of theory there from 1947 to 1960. He conducted the New Haven Sym. Orch. from 1936 till 1951; was also organist and choirmaster of Christ Church in New Haven. As a composer, he adopted a modern polyphonic style in his choral works, while his instrumental scores often reveal impressionistic traits.
Works: ORCH.: *Smoke and Steel,* symphonic poem (1932); Sym. for Chamber Orch. (1936); *New England Chronicle,* overture (1947); *Passacaglia on Vermont Folk Tunes* (1949); Sym. in D (1956); *Epos* (1963). CHAMBER: *Wood-Notes* for Flute, Harp, and Strings (1925); Sextet for Wind Instruments and Piano (1932); Piano Trio No. 1 (1937); Serenade for Oboe, Violin, Viola, and Cello (1939); *Terzetto* for 2 Violins and Viola (1950); Woodwind Quartet (1953); *Soundings* for Trumpet, Bassoon, and Percussion (1953); *Music for 6* (1961); Piano Trio No. 2 (1963). CHORAL: *Fantasy on American Folk Ballads* for Men's Voices and Piano (1940); *Mass for Unison Voices* with Organ, 3 Trumpets, and Timpani (1955); *Forever, O Lord* for Chorus a cappella (1965). For Keyboard: 2 suites for piano; numerous organ works.
Bibl.: A. Frankenstein, "R. D.," *American Composers Alliance Bulletin* (1956).

Dont, Jakob, Austrian violinist, teacher, and composer; b. Vienna, March 2, 1815; d. there, Nov. 17, 1888. He was the son of the cellist **Joseph Valentin Dont** (b. Georgenthal, Bohemia, April 15, 1776; d. Vienna, Dec. 14, 1833); was a pupil of Böhm and Hellmesberger (Sr.) at the Vienna Cons.; joined the orch. of the Hofburgtheater in 1831, and the court orch. in 1834. He taught in the Akademie der Tonkunst and the Seminary at St. Anna; Leopold Auer was his pupil. From 1873 he was a prof. at the Vienna Cons. His book of violin studies, *Gradus ad Parnassum,* is widely known; he publ. altogether some 50 works.

Dooley, William (Edward), American baritone; b. Modesto, Calif., Sept. 9, 1932. He studied at the Eastman School of Music in Rochester, N.Y., then with Lucy Lee Call and in Munich with Viktoria Prestel and Hedwig Fichtmüller; made his operatic debut as Rodrigo in *Don Carlos* in Heidelberg in 1957. On Feb. 15, 1964, he made his debut at the Metropolitan Opera in N.Y. in the title role of Tchaikovsky's *Eugene Onegin.* He also made successful appearances as a concert singer, both in the U.S. and in Europe.

Door, Anton, noted Austrian pianist and pedagogue; b. Vienna, June 20, 1833; d. there, Nov. 7, 1919. He was a pupil of Czerny (piano) and Sechter (composition) in Vienna. He gave successful concerts in Germany; after a tour in Sweden (1856–57), he went to Russia; taught at the Moscow Cons. (1864). In 1869 he returned to Vienna and was prof. of the advanced piano class at the Cons. (1869–1901).

Doorslaer, Georges van, Belgian music scholar; b. Mechelen, Sept. 27, 1864; d. there, Jan. 16, 1940. He studied medicine; music was his avocation. In association with Charles van den Borren, he began a detailed study of old Belgian music; became particularly interested in the history of the carillon. He wrote numerous articles on Philippe de Monte, and ed. his works with van den Borren (31 vols., Bruges, 1927–39; reprint 1965).
Writings: *La vie et les oeuvres de Philippe de Monte* (Brussels, 1921); *Le Carillon de la Tour de Saint-Rombaut à Malines* (Mechelen, 1926).
Bibl.: P. Verheyden, "In Memoriam Dr. G. v.D., 1864–1940," *Bulletin du Cercle Archéologique de Malines,* XLV (1940; with list of writings).

Dopper, Cornelis, eminent Dutch composer and conductor; b. Stadskanaal, near Groningen, Feb. 7, 1870; d. Amsterdam,

Sept. 18, 1939. He studied at the Leipzig Cons.; returning to the Netherlands, he became assistant conductor of the Concertgebouw Orch. in Amsterdam (1908), and was associated with that orch. until 1931. He also traveled as an opera conductor in America (1906–8).

Works: 4 operas: *Het blinde meisje von Castel Cuille* (1892); *Het Eerekruis* (Amsterdam, 1894); *Fritjof* (1895); *Willem Ratcliff* (1896–1901); ballet, *Meidevorn*, with Soli and Chorus; 8 syms.: No. 1, *Diana*, ballet sym. (1896); No. 2 (1903; finished after the 3rd); No. 3, *Rembrandt* (1892; later rewritten); No. 4, *Symphonietta* (1906); No. 5, *Symphonia epica*, with Chorus and Soli (1914); No. 6, *Amsterdam* (1912); No. 7, *Zuiderzee*; No. 8; *Paris*, symphonic rhapsody; 5 suites; Divertimento; *Ciaconna gotica*, symphonic variations (his best-known work; Amsterdam, Oct. 24, 1920, composer conducting); Concertino for Trumpet and 3 Kettledrums; Cello Concerto; 2 overtures; String Quartet; violin sonatas; Cello Sonata; Scherzo for Woodwinds and Piano; many choral works; songs; piano pieces.

Doppler, Árpád, Austrian pianist and composer, son of **Karl (Károly) Doppler;** b. Pest, June 5, 1857; d. Stuttgart, Aug. 13, 1927. He went to Stuttgart as a young man and studied there; was engaged to teach in N.Y. and spent 3 years there (1880–83); later returned to Stuttgart and taught at the Cons. He publ. a number of salon pieces for piano; also wrote 2 operas, *Halixula* (Caligula; Stuttgart, 1891) and *Much Ado about Nothing.*

Doppler, (Albert) Franz (Ferenc), Austrian flutist, composer, and conductor, brother of **Karl (Károly) Doppler;** b. Lemberg, Oct. 16, 1821; d. Baden, near Vienna, July 27, 1883. He studied music with his father; played 1st flute in the Pest Opera Orch.; in 1858 settled in Vienna as ballet conductor at the court opera; taught flute at the Vienna Cons. from 1865. His 1st opera, *Benjowsky,* was well received in Pest (Sept. 29, 1847) and had several revivals under the title *Afanasia;* the following operas were also produced in Pest: *Ilka* (Dec. 29, 1849); *Wanda* (Dec. 20, 1850); *A két huszár* (March 12, 1853); his last opera, *Judith,* was produced in Vienna (Dec. 30, 1870). He also wrote 15 ballets, various orch. works, choral music, etc.

Doppler, Karl (Károly), Austrian flutist, composer, and conductor, brother of **(Albert) Franz (Ferenc) Doppler;** b. Lemberg, Sept. 18, 1825; d. Stuttgart, March 10, 1900. Like his father and his brother, he became an excellent flute player; gave concerts in all the major cities of Europe. He was then appointed as court Kapellmeister in Stuttgart, and held this position for 33 years (1865–98). He wrote an opera, *A gránátos tábor* (The Grenadier Camp; Pest, 1853), and pieces for the flute.

Doran, Matt (Higgins), American composer; b. Covington, Ky., Sept. 1, 1921. He studied at the Univ. of Southern Calif. with Ernst Toch; also took courses in composition with Hanns Eisler and Gail Kubik in Los Angeles, and orchestration with Cailliet. His works include 10 operas, including *The Committee* (Corpus Christi, May 25, 1955) and *The Marriage Counselor* (Los Angeles, March 12, 1977); 4 syms. (1946, 1959, 1977, 1979); Double Concerto for Flute, Guitar, and Strings (Los Angeles, May 21, 1976); Flute Concerto (1953); Horn Concerto (1954); Woodwind Quintet; Trio for Flute, Clarinet, and Piano; many songs and piano pieces.

Dorati, Antal, distinguished Hungarian-born American conductor and composer; b. Budapest, April 9, 1906; d. Gerzensee, near Bern, Nov. 13, 1988. He studied with Leo Weiner, both privately and at the Franz Liszt Academy of Music in Budapest, where he also received instruction in composition from Kodály (1920–24). He was on the staff of the Budapest Opera (1924–28); after conducting at the Dresden State Opera (1928–29), he was Generalmusikdirektor in Münster (1929–32). In 1933 he went to France, where he conducted the Ballets Russes de Monte Carlo, which he took on a tour of Australia (1938). He made his U.S. debut as guest conductor with the National Sym. Orch. in Washington, D.C., in 1937. In 1940 he settled

in the U.S., becoming a naturalized citizen in 1947. He began his American career as music director of the American Ballet Theatre in N.Y. (1941–44); after serving as conductor of the Dallas Sym. Orch. (1945–49), he was music director of the Minneapolis Sym. Orch. (1949–60). From 1963 to 1966 he was chief conductor of the BBC Sym. Orch. in London; then of the Stockholm Phil. (1966–70). He was music director of the National Sym. Orch. in Washington, D.C. (1970–77), and of the Detroit Sym. Orch. (1977–81); was also principal conductor of the Royal Phil. in London (1975–79). He made numerous guest conducting appearances in Europe and North America, earning a well-deserved reputation as an orch. builder. His prolific recording output made him one of the best-known conductors of his time. His recordings of the Haydn syms. and operas were particularly commendable. In 1984 he was made an honorary Knight Commander of the Order of the British Empire. In 1969 he married **Ilse von Alpenheim,** who often appeared as a soloist under his direction. His autobiography was publ. as *Notes of Seven Decades* (London, 1979).

Works: *Divertimento* for Orch.; ballet, *Graduation Ball,* arranged from the waltzes of Johann Strauss; dramatic cantata, *The Way of the Cross* (Minneapolis, April 19, 1957); Sym. No. 1 (Minneapolis, March 18, 1960); 7 *Pieces* for Orch. (1961; perf. as a ballet, *Maddalena*); Piano Concerto (1974; Washington, D.C., Oct. 28, 1975); Cello Concerto (Louisville, Oct. 1, 1976); Sym. No. 2, *Querela pacis* (Detroit, April 24, 1986); chamber music.

Doret, Gustave, Swiss composer and conductor; b. Aigle, Sept. 20, 1866; d. Lausanne, April 19, 1943. He received his 1st instruction at Lausanne; studied violin with Joachim in Berlin (1885–87); then entered the Paris Cons. as a pupil of Marsick (violin) and Dubois and Massenet (composition); was conductor of the Concerts d'Harcourt and of the Société Nationale de Musique in Paris (1893–95); at the Opéra-Comique (1907–9); also appeared as a visiting conductor in Rome, London, and Amsterdam. In his music Doret cultivated the spirit of Swiss folk songs; his vocal writing is distinguished by its natural flow of melody. He publ. *Musique et musiciens* (1915); *Lettres à ma nièce sur la musique en Suisse* (1919); *Pour notre indépendance musicale* (1920); *Temps et contretemps* (1942).

Works: operas: *Maedeli* (1901); *Les Armaillis* (Paris, Oct. 23, 1906; enl. version, Paris, May 5, 1930); *Le Nain du Hasli* (Geneva, Feb. 6, 1908); dramatic legend, *Loÿs* (Vevey, 1912); *La Tisseuse d'Orties* (Paris, 1926); *Voix de la Patrie,* cantata (1891); oratorio, *Les Sept Paroles du Christ* (1895); *La Fête des vignerons* (1905); incidental music to Shakespeare's *Julius Caesar* and to plays by René Morax: *Henriette, Aliénor, La Nuit des quatre-temps, Wilhelm Tell, Davel* (all produced at Mézières); String Quartet; Piano Quintet; about 150 songs.

Bibl.: J. Dupérier, *G. D.* (Paris, 1932).

Dörffel, Alfred, German music editor; b. Waldenburg, Jan. 24, 1821; d. Leipzig, Jan. 22, 1905. He went to Leipzig at the age of 14, and studied with G.W. Fink and K.G. Müller. Mendelssohn and Schumann became interested in his musical education; in 1845 Schumann recommended him as an arranger to Breitkopf & Härtel. In 1861 he opened a circulating library in Leipzig; it was later purchased by C.F. Peters and became the nucleus of the *Musikbibliothek Peters* at Leipzig in 1894. The fame of the *Edition Peters* is in large measure due to Dörffel's careful editorship. He publ. a catalog of his library (1861; with supplement, 1890); a German tr. of Berlioz's *Traité d'instrumentation* (Leipzig, 1863, authorized by Berlioz himself; 4th ed., 1888) and *Le Chef d'orchestre* (Leipzig, 1864); *Führer durch die musikalische Welt* (Leipzig, 1868); *Geschichte der Gewandhausconcerte zu Leipzig 1781–1881* (Leipzig, 1884; a very valuable compilation, with commentary, of programs given by the Gewandhaus Orch. for 100 seasons); thematic catalogs of Bach's instrumental works (Leipzig, 1867; 2nd ed., 1882) and of Schumann's complete works (Leipzig, 1871).

Dorfmann, Ania, Russian-American pianist and teacher; b. Odessa, July 9, 1899; d. N.Y., April 21, 1984. As a very young child in Russia she teamed up with Jascha Heifetz in duo recitals; then was accepted at the age of 12 at the Paris Cons., where her teacher was Isidor Philipp. She returned to Russia just before the Revolution, but was able to leave again in 1920; she toured in Europe as a concert pianist; in 1936 she emigrated to America; gave her 1st American recital in N.Y. on Nov. 27, 1936; on Dec. 2, 1939, she appeared as a soloist with Toscanini and the NBC Sym. Orch. She then devoted herself mainly to teaching; was on the faculty of the Juilliard School of Music in N.Y.

Doria, Clara. See **Rogers, Clara Kathleen** (née **Barnett**).

Dorian, Frederick (real name, **Friedrich Deutsch**), eminent Austrian-born American music scholar and commentator; b. Vienna, July 1, 1902; d. Pittsburgh, Jan. 24, 1991. He studied musicology with Guido Adler at the Univ. of Vienna (Dr.Phil., 1925); also took piano lessons with Eduard Steuermann and studied composition privately with Anton von Webern. He was also closely associated with Schoenberg; Dorian's family apartment housed the headquarters of the famous Soc. for Private Musical Performances, organized by Schoenberg, Alban Berg, and Webern. He also took courses in conducting, achieving a high degree of professionalism. He served as music critic of the *Berliner Morgenpost* (1930–33); with the advent of the Nazi regime to power in Germany, he emigrated to the U.S., becoming an American citizen in 1941. From 1936 to 1954 he was a member of the Carnegie-Mellon Univ. in Pittsburgh (formerly named Carnegie Inst. of Technology); there he organized an opera dept., and conducted its inaugural performance; from 1971 to 1975 he served as Andrew Mellon Lecturer there. From 1975 to 1977 he was visiting lecturer on music history at the Curtis Inst. in Philadelphia. In 1978 he gave lectures on musicology at the Hebrew Univ. in Jerusalem. He also served, beginning in 1945, as program annotator for the Pittsburgh Sym. program magazine. **WRITINGS:** *Hausmusik alter Meister* (3 vols., Berlin, 1933); *The History of Music in Performance* (N.Y., 1942; 2nd ed., 1966); *The Musical Workshop* (N.Y., 1947); *Commitment to Culture* (Pittsburgh, 1964).

Doring, Ernest Nicholas, American specialist in violins; b. N.Y., May 29, 1877; d. Fort Worth, Texas, July 9, 1955. He studied violin in Chicago; in 1894 he joined the violin maker John Friedrich of N.Y. and remained with the firm until 1927. In 1933 he moved back to Chicago; was manager of the rare violin dept. of the Wurlitzer Co. In 1938 he began publishing the magazine *Violins and Violinists.* He wrote *How Many Strads?* (Chicago, 1945) and *The Guadagnini Family of Violin Makers* (Chicago, 1949).

Döring, (Carl) Heinrich, German piano pedagogue; b. Dresden, July 4, 1834; d. there, March 26, 1916. He was a pupil at the Leipzig Cons. (1852–55) and studied with Hauptmann, Lobe, Plaidy, and Richter; in 1858 joined the staff of the Dresden Cons. He publ. the piano collection *Die Grundpfeiler des Klavierspiels* in 3 parts: *Praktische Studien und Übungsstücke für das polyphone Klavierspiel; Technische Hülfs- und Bildungsmittel; Rückblicke auf die Geschichte der Erfindung des Hammerklaviers im 18. Jahrhundert* (Dresden, 1898).

Dorn, Alexander (Julius Paul), German pianist, conductor, and composer, son of **Heinrich (Ludwig Egmont) Dorn;** b. Riga, June 8, 1833; d. Berlin, Nov. 27, 1901. He studied with his father; traveled as a pianist and choral conductor; was in Egypt (1855–65); then settled in Berlin, where he taught piano at the Hochschule für Musik. He wrote more than 400 compositions, including masses and operettas; also a number of salon pieces for piano.

Dorn, Heinrich (Ludwig Egmont), noted German conductor, pedagogue, and composer, father of **Alexander (Julius Paul) Dorn;** b. Königsberg, Nov. 14, 1800; d. Berlin, Jan. 10, 1892. He was a law student at Königsberg in 1823, but studied music diligently, continuing in Berlin under L. Berger (piano), Zelter, and B. Klein. After teaching in Frankfurt, he became Kapellmeister of the Königsberg Theater in 1828; in

1829 he became music director of the Leipzig Theater; in 1830 Schumann became his pupil. In 1832 he went to the Hamburg Theater; was concurrently music director at St. Peter's Cathedral in Riga. Wagner conducted the premiere of his opera *Der Schöffe von Paris* in Riga in 1838; after Wagner lost his post at the Riga Theater in 1839, Dorn was named his successor; the 2 subsequently became bitter enemies. Dorn next went to Cologne, where he served as Kapellmeister at the theater and of the concerts of the Singverein and Musikalischen Gesellschaft (1843–44); then was conductor of the Lower Rhenish Music Festivals (1844–47). In 1845 he founded the Rheinische Musikschule, which became the Cologne Cons. under Hiller's directorship in 1850. For his services to music in Cologne, he was accorded the title of Royal Musikdirektor in 1847. In 1849 he succeeded Nicolai as court Kapellmeister of the Royal Opera in Berlin. In 1854 he anticipated Wagner by bringing out his opera *Die Nibelungen;* although initially successful, it was eventually supplanted by Wagner's masterful *Ring* cycle. Dorn was pensioned with the title of Royal Prof. in 1869. He subsequently busied himself with teaching and writing music criticism. He publ. an autobiography, *Aus meinem Leben* (7 vols., Berlin, 1870–86; includes various essays).
WORKS: OPERAS: *Die Rolandsknappen* (Berlin, 1826); *Der Zauberer und das Ungethüm* (Berlin, 1827); *Die Bettlerin* (Königsberg, 1827); *Abu Kara* (Leipzig, 1831); *Das Schwärmermädchen* (Leipzig, 1832); *Der Schöffe von Paris* (Riga, Sept. 27, 1838); *Das Banner von England* (Riga, 1841); *Die Musiker von Aix-la-Chapelle* (1848); *Artaxerxes* (Berlin, 1850); *Die Nibelungen* (Berlin, March 27, 1854); *Ein Tag in Russland* (Berlin, 1856); *Der Botenläufer von Pirna* (Mannheim, March 15, 1865); *Gewitter bei Sonnenschein* (Dresden, 1865); also a ballet, *Amors Macht* (Leipzig, 1830); orch. music; choral pieces; songs; piano music.
BIBL.: A. Rauh, *H. D. als Opernkomponist* (diss., Univ. of Munich, 1939); R. Sietz, "H. D.," *Jahrbuch des Kölner Geschichtsvereins,* XXIX–XXX (1954–55).

Dorsey, Jimmy (James), popular American jazz clarinetist, saxophonist, and dance-band leader, brother of **Tommy (Thomas) Dorsey;** b. Shenandoah, Pa., Feb. 29, 1904; d. N.Y., June 12, 1957. He took up the slide trumpet and cornet when he was 7, and then turned to reed instruments when he was 11; led several groups with his brother before working as a freelance musician in N.Y. (1925–34), becoming well known through his recordings. He then was co-leader of the Dorsey Brothers Orch. (1934–35); after an argument with his brother, he took sole charge, later rejoining him in the new Dorsey Brothers Orch. (1954–56). He appeared in several films, including the fictionalized *The Fabulous Dorseys* (1947).
BIBL.: E. Edwards et al., *J. D. and His Orchestra: A Complete Discography* (Whittier, Calif., 1966); H. Sandford, *Tommy and J.: The D. Years* (New Rochelle, N.Y., 1972); C. Garrod, *J. D. and His Orchestra* (Zephyrhills, Fla., 1980).

Dorsey, Thomas A(ndrew) "Georgia Tom," black American pianist, blues singer, and gospel songwriter; b. Villa Rica, Ga., 1899. His father was a revivalist preacher; he went to Atlanta in his youth, where he first encountered blues pianists. He later took courses at the Chicago College of Composition and Arranging, and then launched his career as a pianist, arranger, and composer, organizing his own Wildcats Jazz Band, and making recordings with Ma Rainey as "Georgia Tom." After founding the National Convention of Gospel Choirs and Choruses (with Sallie Martin) and the Thomas A. Dorsey Gospel Songs Music Publishing Co. (1931), he devoted himself entirely to gospel music; wrote the gospel standard *Precious Lord, Take My Hand* (1932).

Dorsey, Tommy (Thomas), popular American jazz trombonist and dance-band leader, brother of **Jimmy (James) Dorsey;** b. Shenandoah, Pa., Nov. 19, 1905; d. Greenwich, Conn., Nov. 26, 1956. He studied trumpet with his father before turning to the trombone; led several groups with his brother and then was active in dance bands, pit orchs., and other groups in

N.Y. He was co-leader of the Dorsey Brothers Orch. (1934–35); following an argument with his brother, he set out on his own as a dance-band leader, becoming a leading figure in the big-band era; his brother rejoined him in the new Dorsey Brothers Orch. (1953–56). He appeared in the fictionalized film *The Fabulous Dorseys* (1947). As an instrumentalist, he developed a virtuoso technique highlighted by his remarkable legato playing.

BIBL.: H. Sandford, *T. and Jimmy: The D. Years* (New Rochelle, N.Y., 1972); C. Garrod, *T. D. and His Orchestra* (Zephyrhills, Fla., 1980–82; rev. ed., 1988).

Dostal, Nico, Austrian composer of light music; b. Korneuburg, Nov. 25, 1895; d. Salzburg, Oct. 27, 1981. He was brought up in a musical family; his uncle, **Hermann Dostal** (1874–1930), was a composer of celebrated military marches. Dostal studied in Linz and Vienna; specialized in arrangements of popular music, and began to compose on his own much later in life. Eventually he went to Salzburg to live. His autobiography was publ. as *Ans Ende deiner Träume kommst du nie: Berichte, Bekenntnisse, Betrachtungen* (Innsbruck, 1982).

WORKS: Numerous successful operettas: *Clivia* (Berlin, 1933); *Die Vielgeliebte* (Berlin, 1934); *Prinzessin Nofretete* (Cologne, 1935); *Extrablätter* (Bremen, 1937); *Monika* (Stuttgart, 1937); *Die Flucht ins Glück* (Stuttgart, 1940); *Manina* (Berlin, 1942); *Zirkusblut* (Bielefeld, 1951); *Dr. Eisenbart* (Nuremberg, 1952); *Rhapsodie der Liebe* (Nuremberg, 1963).

Dotzauer, (Justus Johann) Friedrich, famous German cellist; b. Häselrieth, near Hildburghausen, Jan. 20, 1783; d. Dresden, March 6, 1860. He studied piano and violin with Heuschkel and Gleichmann, cello with Hessner, and composition with Rüttinger in Hildburghausen; made his debut as a cellist at a court concert (1798) and then completed his cello studies with Kriegck in Meiningen (1799). He was a member of the Meiningen Court Orch. (1801–5) and the Leipzig Gewandhaus Orch. (1805–11) before joining the Dresden Court Orch. (1811), where he served as 1st cellist (1821–50). He prepared several valuable teaching manuals; wrote an opera, *Graziosa* (Dresden, 1841), syms., overtures, cello concertos and other works for cello, sonatas, masses, etc., but these works are conventional and undistinguished. Among his pupils were Carl Schuberth, Friedrich Kummer, and his own son, Karl Ludwig (Louis) Dotzauer (b. Dresden, Dec. 7, 1811; d. Kassel, July 1, 1897), who was cellist in the Kassel Court Orch. (1830–97).

Doubrava, Jaroslav, Czech composer; b. Chrudim, April 25, 1909; d. Prague, Oct. 2, 1960. He studied privately with Otakar Jeremiáš (1931–37); was active mainly in the musical theater. He wrote the operas *A Midsummer Night's Dream*, after Shakespeare (1942–49; completed by Jiří Jaroch, 1966; Opava, Dec. 21, 1969), and *Lazy John* (1952); *Balada o lásce* (*Ballad of Love*; 1959–60; completed by Jan Hanuš; Prague, June 21, 1962); 3 ballets: *The Tale of the Pea* (1935); *King Lavra* (1951); *Don Quixote* (1954–55); 3 syms.: No. 1, with Chorus (1938–40); No. 2, *Stalingrad* (1943–44); No. 3 (1956–58); oratorio, *The Message* (1939–40); *Ballad about a Beautiful Death* for Women's Chorus and Orch. (1941); symphonic marches: *Partisan March* and *Festive March* (1945); *Autumn Pastorale* (1960; fragment of his unfinished 4th Sym., arranged by Otmar Mácha); Piano Sonatina (1937); 2 violin sonatas (1942, 1958); Sonata for Solo Violin (1942); Piano Sonata (1948–49); piano pieces for children; song cycles.

Dougherty, Celius (Hudson), American pianist and composer; b. Glenwood, Minn., May 27, 1902; d. Effort, Pa., Dec. 22, 1986. He studied piano and composition at the Univ. of Minnesota with Donald Ferguson, and later at the Juilliard School with Rubin Goldmark (composition) and Josef Lhévinne (piano). He became a highly successful accompanist and toured with many celebrated singers. He publ. a number of songs, some of which became popular in recitals (*Weathers*, *Song for Autumn*, *5 American Sea-Chanties*). He also wrote an opera, *Many Moons*, based on a story of James Thurber, which was 1st performed at Vassar College on Dec. 6, 1962.

Douglas, Barry, Irish pianist; b. Belfast, April 23, 1960. He studied clarinet, cello, and organ, and also received piano lessons from Felicitas Lewinter; he then attended the Belfast School of Music, winning a scholarship to continue his training with John Barstow at the Royal College of Music in London, and with Maria Curcio. In 1981 he made his London debut, subsequently winning the Silver Medal at the Arthur Rubinstein Competition in Israel (1983), the Bronze Medal at the Van Cliburn Competition in Fort Worth, Texas (1985), and the Gold Medal at the Tchaikovsky Competition in Moscow (1986). In 1988 he made his N.Y. recital debut at Carnegie Hall. During the 1988–89 season, he toured in the U.S., concluding his engagements with an appearance as soloist with the St. Louis Sym. Orch. at N.Y.'s Lincoln Center.

BIBL.: K. Tompkins, "B. D.," *Musical America* (Sept. 1988).

Douglas, Clive (Martin), Australian conductor and composer; b. Rushworth, Victoria, July 27, 1903; d. Melbourne, April 29, 1977. He studied at the Melbourne Univ. Cons. (Mus.B., 1934) and later at Melbourne Univ. (D.Mus., 1958); was attached to the Australian Broadcasting Commission as a resident staff conductor in various cities (1936–66); taught at the Melbourne Cons. (1953–66). His music draws on indigenous Australian subjects and melorhythmic patterns; some abstractions suggesting serial techniques are found in his chamber music.

WORKS: 4 operas: *The Scarlet Letter*, after Hawthorne (1927–28); *Ashmadai* (1935); *Kaditcha* (1937–38); opera-trilogy, *Eleanor* (1940–43); 3 syms. (*Jubilee*, 1951; *Namatjira*, 1956; 1963); symphonic poems: *Carwoola* (1939) and *Sturt 1829* (1952); *Symphonic Fantasy* (1938); *Festival of Perth*, sinfonietta (1961); *Symphonic Variations* (1961); *Divertimento No. 2* for 2 Pianos and Chamber Orch. (1962); *3 Frescoes* for Orch. (1969); *Pastoral* for Orch. (1970); *Discourse* for Strings (1971); *The Hound of Heaven* for Baritone, Chorus, and Orch. (1932–33); *Terra australis* for Narrator, Soprano, Chorus, and Orch. (1959); 2 string quartets (1933, 1935); *Divertimento No. 1* for Wind Quintet (1962–63).

Dounias, Minos, Greek violinist, musicologist, and music critic; b. Cetate, Rumania, Sept. 26, 1900; d. Athens, Oct. 20, 1962. He studied at Robert College in Constantinople, where he received instruction in violin, and with A. Moser and G. Kulenkampff at the Berlin Hochschule für Musik (1921–26); then studied musicology with A. Abert and A. Schering at the Univ. of Berlin (Ph.D., 1932, with the diss. *Die Violinkonzerte Giuseppe Tartinis*; publ. in Wolfenbüttel, 1935; 2nd ed., 1966). He settled in Athens in 1936, where he taught at Pierce College, wrote music criticism, and made appearances as a violinist. He was particularly active in the promotion of early music.

Dounis, Demetrius Constantine, Greek-American violinist and teacher; b. Athens, Dec. 7, 1886; d. Los Angeles, Aug. 13, 1954. He studied violin with Ondriček in Vienna and simultaneously enrolled as a medical student at the Univ. of Vienna; made several tours as a violinist in Europe, including Russia; after World War I he was appointed prof. at the Salonika Cons. He then lived in England and eventually settled in America; established his N.Y. studio in 1939; went to Los Angeles in 1954. He originated the technique of the "brush stroke," in which the bow is handled naturally and effortlessly. He wrote numerous manuals.

BIBL.: V. Leland, *D. Principles of Violin Playing* (London, 1949); C. Costantakos, *D.C. D.: His Method in Teaching the Violin* (N.Y., 1988).

Dourlen, Victor(-Charles-Paul), French pedagogue and composer; b. Dunkerque, Nov. 3, 1780; d. Batignolles, near Paris, Jan. 8, 1864. He studied with Gossec and F.A. Boieldieu at the Paris Cons. (1799–1805), sharing the Prix de Rome in 1805 for his cantata *Cupidon pleurant Psyché*. He subsequently taught there (1812–42). Of his 9 operas, 8 were produced at the Opéra-Comique: *Philoclès* (Oct. 4, 1806); *Linnée, ou La*

Mine de Suéde (Sept. 10, 1808); *La Dupe de son art* (Sept. 9, 1809); *Cagliostro, ou Les Illuminés* (with A. Reicha; Nov. 27, 1810); *Plus heureux que sage* (May 25, 1816); *Le Frère Philippe* (Jan. 20, 1818); *Marini, ou Le Muet de Venise* (June 12, 1819); *La Vente après décès* (Théâtre du Gymnase-Dramatique; Aug. 1, 1821); *Le Petit Souper* (Feb. 22, 1822). He also wrote a Piano Concerto, chamber music, and songs. He publ. 3 harmony textbooks based upon the methods of C.S. Catel.

Dowland, John, great English composer and famous lutenist, father of **Robert Dowland;** b. probably in London, 1563; d. there (buried), Feb. 20, 1626. In 1580 he went to Paris in the service of Sir Henry Cobham; by 1584 he was back in England, where he eventually married; on July 8, 1588, he was admitted to his Mus.B. from Christ Church, Oxford; in 1592 he played before the Queen. Unsuccessful in his effort to secure a position as one of the Queen's musicians, he set out in 1594 for Germany, where he received the patronage of the Duke of Braunschweig in Wolfenbüttel and the Landgrave of Hesse in Kassel; he then went to Italy and visited Venice, Padua, Genoa, Ferrara, and Florence; in Florence he played before Ferdinando I, the Grand Duke of Tuscany; he then made his way home, returning to England in 1595. In 1598 he was appointed lutenist to King Christian IV of Denmark, remaining in his service until 1606; he then returned to England, where he became lutenist to Lord Howard de Walden. In 1612 he became one of the lutenists to King Charles I. Dowland was a foremost representative of the English school of lutenist-composers. He was also noted for his songs, in which he made use of novel chromatic developments; he treated the accompanying parts as separate entities, thereby obtaining harmonic effects quite advanced for his time.

WORKS: *The 1st Booke of Songes or Ayres of fowre partes with Tableture for the Lute . . .* (London, 1597); *The 2nd Booke of Songs or Ayres, of 2. 4. and 5. parts; With Tableture for the Lute or Orpherian . . .* (London, 1600); *The 3rd and Last Booke of Songs or Aires . . .* (London, 1603); *Lachrimae, or 7 Teares Figvred in Seaven Passionate Pauans, . . . set forth for the Lute, Viols, or Violons, in fiue parts* (London, 1604); songs in *A Mvsicall Banquet* (London, 1612) and *A Pilgrimes Solace. Wherein is contained Musicall Harmonie of 3. 4. and 5. parts, to be sung and plaid with the Lute and Viols* (London, 1612). **WRITINGS:** He tr. into Eng. *The Micrologus* of Ornithoparcus (Andreas Vogelsang) (London, 1609; modern ed. in Eng. and Latin, ed. by G. Reese and S. Ledbetter, N.Y., 1973); also with his son Robert, the *Necessarie Observations Belonging to the Lute, and Lvte playing, by John Baptisto Besardo* [Jean-Baptiste Besard] *of Visconti: with choise varietie of Lvte-lessons . . .* (includes compositions by John Dowland; London, 1610). **EDITIONS:** These include E. Fellowes's eds. of *The 1st Book of Songs* (London, 1920; rev. ed., 1965, by T. Dart), *The 2nd Book of Songs* (London, 1922; rev. ed., 1969, by T. Dart), *The 3rd and Last Book of Songs* (London, 1923; rev. ed., 1970, by T. Dart), *A Pilgrimes Solace* (London, 1924; rev. ed., 1969, by T. Dart), and *7 Hymn Tunes . . . Lamentatio Henrici Noel* (London, 1934); P. Warlock, *Lachrimae or 7 Tears . . . Transcribed from the original edition of 1605* (without tablature; London, 1927); T. Dart and N. Fortune, eds., *Ayres for 4 Voices,* in *Musica Britannica* (vol. 6, London, 1953; 2nd ed., rev., 1963); D. Poulton and B. Lam, eds., *The Collected Lute Music of J. D.* (London, 1974). **BIBL.:** E. Fellowes, *The English Madrigal Composers* (London, 1921; 2nd ed., 1948); P. Warlock, *The English Ayre* (London, 1926); D. Poulton, "D.'s Songs and Their Instrumental Settings," *The Monthly Musical Record,* LXXXI (1951); C. Hill, "J. D.: Some New Facts and a Quatercentenary Tribute," *Musical Times* (Nov. 1963); P. Brown, "Influences on the Early Lute Songs of J. D.," *Musicology,* 3 (1968–69); V. Reed, "Doleful D.," *English Language Notes* (Sept. 1968); D. Poulton, *J. D.: His Life and Works* (Berkeley and Los Angeles, 1972; 2nd ed., rev., 1982); M. Pilkington, *Campion, D. and the Lutenist Songwriters* (London, 1989).

Dowland, Robert, English lutenist and composer, son of **John Dowland;** b. London, 1591; d. there, Nov. 28, 1641. He remained in London after his father went abroad; in 1626, succeeded his father as lutenist to Charles I. He ed. the anthologies *Varietie of Lute Lessons* (London, 1610) and *A Musicall Banquett,* a collection of English, French, Spanish, and Italian airs (reprinted in *The English Lute Songs,* vol. 20).

Downes, Edward (Thomas), English conductor; b. Aston (Birmingham), June 17, 1924. He studied at the Univ. of Birmingham (1941–44), taking a B.A. in music, and at the Royal College of Music in London (1944–46), studying horn, theory, and composition. In 1948 he was awarded the Carnegie Scholarship, which he used for taking a course in conducting with Hermann Scherchen. His 1st professional post as conductor was with the Carl Rosa Opera (1950); from 1952 to 1969 he was a staff conductor at the Covent Garden Opera in London, with which he conducted numerous works, including the complete *Ring of the Nibelung* cycle; in 1969 he left the Covent Garden staff as a regular member in order to devote himself to sym. conducting, but continued to fill in occasional opera engagements. From 1972 to 1976 he was music director of the Australian Opera; in 1980 became chief conductor of the BBC Northern Sym. Orch. in Manchester, retaining that post when it became the BBC Phil. in 1983. He conducted the world premiere of Richard Rodney Bennett's opera *Victory* (April 13, 1970). He also conducted the world premieres of Havergal Brian's 14th and 21st syms. with the London Sym. Orch. on May 10, 1970. In 1986 he was made a Commander of the Order of the British Empire.

Downes, Edward O(lin) D(avenport), American music critic and lecturer, son of **(Edwin) Olin Downes;** b. Boston, Aug. 12, 1911. He studied at Columbia Univ. (1929–30), the Univ. of Paris (1932–33), the Univ. of Munich (1934–36, 1938), and Harvard Univ. (Ph.D., 1958). Under the tutelage of his father, he entered the career of a music critic; wrote for the *N.Y. Post* (1935–38), the *Boston Transcript* (1939–41), and the *N.Y. Times* (1955–58); was program annotator for the N.Y. Phil. (from 1960); from 1958 acted as quizmaster for the Metropolitan Opera broadcasts. He was a lecturer in music at Wellesley College (1948–49), Harvard Univ. (1949–50), the Univ. of Minnesota (1950–55), and Queens College (1966–83). **WRITINGS:** *Verdi, The Man in His Letters* (N.Y., 1942); *Adventures in Symphonic Music* (N.Y., 1943); *The New York Philharmonic Guide to the Symphony* (N.Y.,1976; 2nd ed., 1981, as *Guide to Symphonic Music*).

Downes, (Edwin) Olin, eminent American music critic, father of **Edward O(lin) D(avenport) Downes;** b. Evanston, Ill., Jan. 27, 1886; d. N.Y., Aug. 22, 1955. He studied piano with L. Kelterborn and Carl Baermann; harmony with Homer Norris, Clifford Heilman, and J.P. Marshall; then devoted himself mainly to musical journalism. From 1906 to 1924 he was music critic of the *Boston Post;* in 1924 was appointed music critic of the *N.Y. Times;* held this post until his death. He was awarded the Order of Commander of the White Rose, Finland (1937); an hon. Mus.Doc., Cincinnati Cons. of Music (1939). **WRITINGS:** *The Lure of Music* (N.Y., 1918); *Symphonic Broadcasts* (N.Y., 1931); *Symphonic Masterpieces* (N.Y., 1935); *Sibelius the Symphonist* (N.Y., 1956). He ed. *Select Songs of Russian Composers* (N.Y., 1922); compiled and annotated *Ten Operatic Masterpieces, from Mozart to Prokofiev* (N.Y., 1952). A selection from his writings was publ. in 1957 under the title *Olin Downes on Music,* ed. by his widow, Irene Downes.

Downes, Ralph (William), English organist, organ designer, and teacher; b. Derby, Aug. 16, 1904. He studied at the Royal College of Music in London (1922–25); then was an organ scholar at Keble College, Oxford. Making his way to the U.S., he was music director and organist at Princeton Univ. (1928–36); he then returned to London, where he became organist of Brompton Oratory; in 1948 he became resident organist of the London Phil. Orch. He was appointed a prof. at the Royal College of Music in 1954. He designed many notable organs, including the instrument for London's Royal Festival Hall. He publ. the vol. *Baroque Tricks: Adventures with the Organ Builders* (Oxford, 1983). In 1969 he was made a Commander of the Order of the British Empire.

Downey, John (Wilham), American composer; b. Chicago, Oct. 5, 1927. He studied with Leon Stein at De Paul Univ. in Chicago (B.M., 1949) and with Alexander Tcherepnin, Krenek, and Rieti at the Chicago Musical College (M.M., 1951); went to Paris and took private lessons with Nadia Boulanger, Milhaud, and Honegger (1952); returning to the U.S., he was appointed in 1964 to the music faculty of the Univ. of Wisconsin in Milwaukee.

WORKS: ORCH.: *La Joie de la paix* (1956); *Chant to Michelangelo* (1958); Concerto for Harp and Chamber Orch. (1964); *Jingalodeon* (1968); *Prospectations III–II–I* for 3 Orchs. (1970); *Symphonic Modules 5* (1972); Double Bass Concerto (1985). CHAMBER/VOCAL: String Trio (1953); Violin Sonata (1954); Wind Octet (1954); 2 string quartets (1964, 1975); *Eartheatrics* for 8 Percussionists (1967); *Tabu* for Tuba (1967); *Ambivalences I* for Any Chamber Combination (1972); *What If?*, after e.e. cummings, for Chorus, Brass Octet, Timpani, and 3 Gongs (1973); *A Dolphin* for High Voice, Flute, Viola, Piano, and Percussion (1974); *Crescendo* for Percussion (1977); *High Clouds and Soft Rain* for 24 Flutes (1977); Piano Trio (1984); *Recombinance* for Double Bass and Piano (1985). PIANO: 2 sonatas (1949, 1951); *Adagio lyrico* for 2 Pianos (1953); *Eastlake Terrace* (1959); *Edges* (1960); *Pyramids* (1961); *Ambivalences II* (1973); also choruses; songs.

Doyen, Albert, French composer and choral conductor; b. Vendresse, Ardennes, April 3, 1882; d. Paris, Oct. 22, 1935. He studied composition with Widor at the Paris Cons. In 1917 he established the choral society Fêtes du Peuple. Among his works are a Sym., an ode in memory of Zola, String Quartet, Piano Trio, Violin Sonata, and numerous choral compositions.

D'Oyly Carte, Richard. See **Carte, Richard D'Oyly.**

Dozier, Lamont, black American songwriter; b. Detroit, June 16, 1941. He sang in a church choir directed by his grandmother and as a youth joined the Motown organization dedicated to the promotion of "soul" music as urbanized in the Motown sound, the name being a reference to Motor Town, that is, Detroit. He teamed with Brian Holland (b. Detroit, Feb. 15, 1941) and Eddie Holland (b. Detroit, Oct. 30, 1939), and together they created the great Motown hits *Heat Wave, Nowhere to Run, Mickey's Monkey, How Sweet It Is (to Be Loved by You), Reach Out, I'll Be There, Where Did Our Love Go, Baby Love, Stop! In the Name of Love, I Hear a Symphony, My World Is Empty without You, Heaven Must Have Sent You,* etcetera, ad infinitum.

Draeseke, Felix (August Bernhard), significant German composer; b. Coburg, Oct. 7, 1835; d. Dresden, Feb. 26, 1913. He entered the Leipzig Cons. at the age of 17, where he studied composition with Julius Rietz; his advanced proclivities met with opposition there, so he continued his studies privately with Rietz. In 1857 he met Liszt and in 1861 Wagner, and thereafter was an ardent champion of the New German School of composition. In 1862 he went to Switzerland and was active as a piano teacher; in 1876 he returned to Germany and in 1884 joined the faculty of the Dresden Cons. Although regarded as a radical composer by many, he did not accept the modern tendencies in music of the early years of the 20th century, which he attacked in his pamphlet *Die Konfusion in der Musik* (1906), directed chiefly against Richard Strauss. He was a prolific composer, but his works are virtually unknown outside Germany. A Draeseke Soc., formed in Germany in 1931, issued sporadic bulletins.

WRITINGS: *Answeisung zum kunstgerechten Modulieren* (Freienwalde, 1876); *Die Beseitigung des Tritonus* (Leipzig, 1880); *Die Lehre von der Harmonia in lustige Reimlein gebracht* (Leipzig, 1883; 2nd ed., augmented, 1887); *Der gebundene Stil: Lehrbuch für Kontrapunkt und Fuge* (Hannover, 1902).

WORKS: OPERAS: *König Sigurd* (1853–57; fragment perf., Meiningen, 1867); *Herrat (Dietrich von Bern)* (1877–79; Dresden, March 10, 1892); *Gudrun* (Hannover, Jan. 11, 1884); *Bertrand de Born* (1892–94); *Fischer und Kalif* (1894–95; Prague, April 15, 1905); *Merlin* (1903–5; Gotha, May 10, 1913); a choral trilogy, *Mysterium: Christus* (1895–99; Dresden and Berlin, 1912); Sym. in G Major (1868–72); Sym. in F Major (1870–76); *Symphonia tragica* (1885–86); *Symphonia comica* (1912); 3 symphonic poems (1859–1903); Violin Concerto (1881); Piano Concerto (1885–86); 3 string quartets (1879–80; 1886; 1895); Quintet for Piano, Violin, Viola, Cello, and Horn (1888); sacred and secular choruses; songs.

BIBL.: H. Platzbecker, *F. D.* (Leipzig, 1909); O. zur Nedden, *F. D.s Opern und Oratorien* (diss., Univ. of Marburg, 1925); E. Röder, *F. D.* (2 vols., Dresden, 1930, Berlin, 1935); A. Krueck, *The Symphonies of F. D.* (diss., Univ. of Zürich, 1967).

Draga, Gheorghe, Rumanian composer; b. Bîrsa-Aldeşti, April 26, 1935. He studied with Vancea, Vieru, and Ion Dumitrescu at the Bucharest Cons. (1957–63); in 1963 became ed. of the periodical *Muzica.*

WORKS: Piano Sonata (1962); Clarinet Sonata (1963); *Se construieşte lumea noastră,* cantata (1963); Sym. (1965); *Cantata festiva* (1967); *Concert Music* for Orch. (1968); String Quartet (1968); *Eterofonii* for Strings, Brass, and Percussion (1969); *Concert Overture* (1969); *Prelude* for Orch. (1971); *Sarmizegetusa,* symphonic poem (1983).

Dräger, Hans-Heinz, German-born American musicologist; b. Stralsund, Dec. 6, 1909; d. Austin, Texas, Nov. 9, 1968. He studied musicology with Blume, Schering, Hornbostel, Schünemann, and Sachs at the Univ. of Berlin (Ph.D., 1937, with the diss. *Die Entwicklung des Streichbogens und seine Anwendung in Europa;* publ. in Kassel, 1937), completing his Habilitation at the Univ. of Kiel in 1946 with his *Prinzip einer Systematik der Musikinstrumente* (publ. in Kassel, 1948). While in Berlin he was active with the State Inst. for German Music Research (1937–38) and at the State Museum of Musical Instruments (1938–39); also was lecturer in organology at the Hochschule für Musik (1939). He was prof. of musicology at the Univs. of Greifswald (1947–49) and Rostock (1948–49), at Humboldt Univ. in East Berlin (1949–53), and at the Free Univ. in West Berlin (1953–61). In 1955 he was a visiting prof. at Stanford Univ. He settled in the U.S. in 1961 and became a U.S. citizen in 1966; he was on the musicology faculty at the Univ. of Austin (1961–66).

BIBL.: H.-B. Dietz, "In Memoriam H.-H. D. (1909–68)," *Die Musikforschung,* XXII (1969).

Draghi, Antonio, noted Italian-born Austrian composer; b. Rimini, c.1634; d. Vienna, Jan. 16, 1700. He received musical training in his homeland and was active as a bass singer in Venice by 1657. He settled in Vienna in 1658, where he was assistant Kapellmeister (1668–69) and then Kapellmeister (1669–82) to the dowager empress Eleonora. He was appointed director of dramatic music at the Imperial court in 1673 and then its Kapellmeister in 1682. Draghi was a leading representative of the Venetian school of composition at Vienna's Imperial court, being a prolific composer of operas, oratorios, and other dramatic works. From 1666 to 1700 he composed over 100 operas, prologues, and intermezzi, some 13 oratorios, 29 Sepolcri, vocal chamber works, and other sacred works. Much of his music is not extant.

BIBL.: M. Neuhaus, "A. D.," *Studien zur Musikwissenschaft,* I (1913); R. Schnitzler, *The Sacred-Dramatic Music of A. D.* (diss., Univ. of North Carolina, 1971); N. Hiltl, *Die Oper am Hofe Kaiser Leopolds I. mit besonderer Berücksichtigung der Tätigkeit von Minato und D.* (diss., Univ. of Vienna, 1974); H. Seifert, *Neues zu A. D.s weltlichen Werken* (Vienna, 1978).

Draghi, Giovanni Battista, Italian composer; b. c.1640; d. London, 1708. He was organist to the Queen from 1673; also music teacher to the princesses Mary and Anne. He wrote the music to Dryden's ode *From Harmony, from Heavenly Harmony* for the *Song for St. Cecilia's Day* (1687) and (with

Locke) to Shadwell's *Psyche* (1675) and d'Urfey's *The Wonders in the Sun, or The Kingdom of Birds* (1706); also many songs, and instructive harpsichord lessons.

BIBL.: E. Brennecke, "Dryden's Odes and D.'s Music," *Proceedings of the Modern Language Association,* XLIX (1934).

Drăgoi, Sabin V(asile), eminent Rumanian composer and folklorist; b. Selişte, June 18, 1894; d. Bucharest, Dec. 31, 1968. He studied with Novák and Ostrčil in Prague (1920–22); from 1924 to 1942 taught at the Timişoara Cons.; then was a prof. at the Cluj Cons. (1943–45); was director of the Folklore Inst. of Bucharest (1950–64) and a prof. of folklore at the Bucharest Cons. (1950–52).

WORKS: operas: *Năpasta* (Disaster; 1927; Bucharest, May 30, 1928; rev. 1958; Bucharest, Dec. 23, 1961); *Constantin Brâncoveanu* (1929); *Kir Ianulea* (1937; Cluj, Dec. 22, 1939); *Horia* (1945); *Păcală* (1956; Brasov, May 6, 1962); oratorio, *Povestea bradului* (1952); 3 cantatas: *Slăvită lumină* (1937); *Mai multă lumină* (1951); *Cununa* (1959); *3 Symphonic Tableaus* (1922); *Divertissement rustic* for Orch. (1928); *Divertissement sacru* for Chamber Orch. (1933); Piano Concerto (1941); Concertino for Tarogato and Orch. (1953); *7 Popular Dances* for Orch. (1960); *Suită tătară* for Small Orch. (1961); *Suită lipovană* for Small Orch. (1962); Violin Sonata (1949); String Quartet (1952); *Dixtour* for Winds, Strings, and Piano (1955); *50 Colinde* for Piano (1957); *10 Miniatures* for Piano (1960); *12 Miniatures* for Piano (1968); songs; film music.

BIBL.: N. Rădulescu, *S.V. D.* (Bucharest, 1971).

Dragon, Carmen, American conductor, composer, and arranger; b. Antioch, Calif., July 28, 1914; d. Santa Monica, Calif., March 28, 1984. He learned to play piano, double bass, accordion, trumpet, and trombone. He studied music at San Jose State College; then went to San Francisco, where he played the piano in a nightclub. His next move was to Hollywood, where he effloresced as an arranger for movie stars who could not read music. He conducted background music for radio shows. In a higher elevation, he composed a patriotic band piece, *I'm an American.* His concerts supplied pleasurable fare for contented music-lovers. His son **Daryl Dragon** (b. Los Angeles, Aug. 27, 1942) became one-half of the popular music team Captain and Tennille.

Dragonetti, Domenico (Carlo Maria), noted Italian double-bassist; b. Venice, April 7, 1763; d. London, April 16, 1846. The "Paganini of the contra-basso" was self-taught, excepting a few lessons from Berini, bassist at San Marco, whom he succeeded in 1782; he had already played in the orchs. of the Opera Buffa and Opera Seria for 5 years, and composed concertos with double-bass parts impracticable for anyone but himself. He appeared at London in 1794; with the cellist Lindley, his close friend for 52 years, he played at the Antient Concerts and the Phil. As late as 1845, his virtuosity still unimpaired, he led the double basses, at the unveiling of the Beethoven monument in Bonn, in the C minor Sym. To the British Museum he left a remarkable collection of scores, engravings, and old instruments; to San Marco, his favorite cello (a Gasparo da Salò).

BIBL.: F. Caffi, *Vita di D. D.* (Venice, 1846); R. Slatford, "D. D.," *Proceedings of the Royal Musical Association,* XCVII (1970–71).

Drake, Earl R(oss), American violinist and composer; b. Aurora, Ill., Nov. 26, 1865; d. Chicago, May 6, 1916. He studied violin in Chicago, and later with Joachim in Berlin. He was head of the violin dept. at the Gottschalk Lyric School in Chicago (1893–97); organized his own school of music in Chicago in 1900.

WORKS: *The Blind Girl of Castel-Cuille,* opera and ballet (Chicago, Feb. 19, 1914); *The Mite and the Mighty,* light opera (Chicago, 1915); *Dramatic Prologue* for Orch.; *Ballet* for Orch.; *Gypsy Scenes* for Violin and Orch.; pieces for violin and piano (*Polish Dance, Mazurka, An Alpine Farewell,* etc.).

Drangosch, Ernesto, Argentine pianist, teacher, and composer; b. Buenos Aires, Jan. 22, 1882; d. there, June 26, 1925.

He studied in Buenos Aires with Alberto Williams and Aguìrre, and in Berlin with Max Bruch, Humperdinck, and Ansorge; later toured Europe and America as a pianist; returned to Buenos Aires (1905), and founded his own cons.

Dranishnikov, Vladimir, Russian conductor and composer; b. St. Petersburg, June 10, 1893; d. Kiev, Feb. 6, 1939. He studied at the St. Petersburg Cons. with Essipova (piano); Steinberg, Liadov, and Wihtol (composition); and Nikolai Tcherepnin (conducting). He was employed as a rehearsal pianist at the St. Petersburg Imperial Opera (1914–18); in 1918, became conductor there, earning great esteem for his professional skill in both the classical and the modern repertoire; he conducted the 1st Soviet performance of Alban Berg's *Wozzeck,* and of numerous Soviet operas; in 1930 he was appointed conductor of the Kiev Opera. He also wrote symphonic works and choruses.

Drdla, Franz, Bohemian composer and violinist; b. Saar, Moravia, Nov. 28, 1868; d. Badgastein, Sept. 3, 1944. After 2 years at the Prague Cons., he studied at the Vienna Cons. under Hellmesberger, Jr. (violin), and Krenn and Bruckner (composition), winning 1st prize for violin and the medal of the Gesellschaft der Musikfreunde; was a violinist in the orch. of the Vienna Court Opera (1890–93); then was concertmaster of the orch. of the Theater an der Wien (1894–99). He then made successful tours of Europe; in 1923–25, lived in the U.S.; then in Vienna and Prague. His pieces for violin and piano won enormous popularity, especially *Souvenir, Vision,* and the 1st Serenade in A (dedicated to, and played by, Jan Kubelik); he also composed 2 operettas, *Das goldene Netz* (Leipzig, 1916) and *Die Ladenkomtesse* (Brünn, 1917).

Drechsler, Joseph, Bohemian-born Austrian composer; b. Wällisch-Birken, Bohemia, May 26, 1782; d. Vienna, Feb. 27, 1852. He was a pupil of the organist Grotius at Florenbach; was assistant Kapellmeister (1812) at the Vienna Court Opera, then conductor in the theaters at Baden (near Vienna) and Pressburg; returning to Vienna, he became organist of the Servite church; in 1816 precentor at St. Ann's; in 1823 Kapellmeister at the Univ. church and the Hofpfarrkirche; from 1824 to 1830 he was also Kapellmeister at the Leopoldstadt Theater.

WORKS: 6 operas, including *Die Feldmühle* (singspiel; Vienna, Sept. 29, 1812) and *Pauline* (opera; Vienna, Feb. 23, 1821); about 30 operettas, vaudevilles, and pantomimes; a Requiem, 16 masses, 3 cantatas, offertories, etc.; string quartets, organ fugues, piano sonatas, other piano music, songs, etc.; a method for organ, and a treatise on harmony.

BIBL.: C. Preiss, *J. D.* (Graz, 1910).

Drechsler, Karl, German cellist and teacher; b. Kamenz, May 27, 1800; d. Dresden, Dec. 1, 1873. He studied in Dresden with F. Dotzauer (1824–26) and was a cellist in the Dessau Court Orch. (1820–71). Among his distinguished pupils were B. Cossmann, F. Grützmacher, A. Lindner, and C. Schröder.

Dreier, Per, Norwegian conductor; b. Trondheim, Dec. 25, 1929. He studied conducting with Paul van Kempen and Willem van Otterloo at the Royal Cons. of Music in The Hague. He made his debut with the Trondheim Sym. Orch. in 1953. He then was a conductor at the Württemberg State Theater at Stuttgart (1953–57) and chief conductor and artistic director of the Århus Sym. Orch. (1957–73); also served as chief conductor of the Jutland Opera (1957–71). He has done much to promote contemporary Norwegian music.

Drejsl, Radim, Czech composer; b. Dobruska, April 29, 1923; d. (suicide) Prague, April 20, 1953. He studied piano at the Prague Cons. and composition with Bořkovec at the Prague Academy of Musical Arts (1946–50); was music director of the Vít Nejedlý Army Artistic Ensemble from 1949 until his death.

WORKS: 2 piano suites (1945, 1946); 2 piano sonatas (1946, 1947); Flute Sonatina (1947); Bassoon Sonatina (1948); *Spring* for Wind Quintet (1948); Sym. for Strings (1948); Piano Concerto (1948–49); *Dožínková Suite* (Harvest Home Suite) for Oboe or English Horn, and Piano (1949–50); military marches; choruses; songs.

Dresden, Sem, notable Dutch composer and pedagogue; b. Amsterdam, April 20, 1881; d. The Hague, July 30, 1957. He studied first in Amsterdam with Zweers; then went to Berlin, where he took a course in composition with Hans Pfitzner (1903–5). Returning to the Netherlands, he was active as a choral conductor; from 1919 to 1924 taught composition at the Amsterdam Cons.; then became its director (1924–37); subsequently was director of The Hague Cons. (1937–49, with a break during World War II). From 1914 till 1926 he led the Motet and Madrigal Soc. in Amsterdam. As a composer, Dresden was influenced primarily by German neo-Romanticism, but his harmonic idiom reveals some impressionistic usages; in many of his works there is a distinctive strain of Dutch melodic rhythms.

Works: Opera, *François Villon* (1956–57, piano score only; orchestrated by Jan Mul, Amsterdam, June 15, 1958); operetta, *Toto* (1945); oratorios: *Saint Antoine* (1953) and *St. Joris* (1955); *Carnival Cantata* for Soprano, Male Chorus, and Orch. (1954); *Chorus tragicus* for Chorus, 5 Trumpets, 2 Bugles, and Percussion (1927); *4 Vocalises* for Mezzo-soprano and 7 Instruments (1935); *O Kerstnacht* for Chorus and Strings (1939); *Chorus symphonicus* for Soprano, Tenor, Chorus, and Orch. (1943–44; rev. 1955); *Psalm 99* for Chorus, Organ, and 4 Trombones (1950); *Psalm 84* for Soprano, Tenor, Chorus, and Orch. (1954); *De wijnen van Bourgondië* (The Wines of Burgundy) for Chorus and Orch. (1954); *Catena musicale* for Soprano, Solo Woodwind Quartet, Solo String Trio, and Orch. (1956); *Rembrandt's "Saul and David"* for Soprano and Orch. (1956). Orch.: Theme and Variations (Amsterdam, March 29, 1914); 2 violin concertos (1936, 1942); *Symphonietta* for Clarinet and Orch. (1938); Oboe Concerto (1939); Piano Concerto (1942–46); Flute Concerto (1949); *Dansflitsen* (Dance Flashes) for Orch. (The Hague, Oct. 20, 1951); Organ Concerto (1952–53). Chamber: 3 sextets (1910, 1913, 1920); 2 piano trios (1902, 1942); Violin Sonata (1905); Trio for 2 Oboes and English Horn (1912); 2 cello sonatas (1916, 1942); Sonata for Flute and Harp (1918); String Quartet (1924); Solo Violin Sonata (1943); Suite for Solo Cello (1943–47); piano pieces; organ pieces; choruses; songs.

Bibl.: J. Wouters, "S. D.," *Sonorum Speculum*, 25 (Winter 1965).

Dresel, Otto, German pianist and composer; b. Geisenheim, Dec. 20, 1826; d. Beverly, Mass., July 26, 1890. He was a pupil of Hiller at Cologne, and of Mendelssohn at Leipzig. He went to N.Y. as a concert pianist and teacher in 1848; revisited Germany, but in 1852 settled in Boston, where he was very influential in introducing German music to the American public. He publ. a few songs and piano pieces.

Dresher, Paul (Joseph), American composer and performer; b. Los Angeles, Jan. 8, 1951. He studied music at the Univ. of Calif. at Berkeley (B.A., 1977) and composition with Robert Erickson, Roger Reynolds, and Pauline Oliveros at the Univ. of Calif. at San Diego (M.A., 1979); also received training in Ghanaian drumming, Javanese and Balinese gamelan, and North Indian classical music. In 1984 he founded the Paul Dresher Ensemble. His awards include an N.E.A. grant (1979), the Goddard Lieberson fellowship of the American Academy and Inst. of Arts and Letters (1982), and a Fulbright fellowship (1984). In addition to orch. and chamber works, he has written experimental operatic and theater pieces (many in collaboration with theater director George Coates), as well as various electroacoustic taped scores for use in theater, dance, video, radio, and film. As a composer, his intent has been to integrate the more traditional formal aspects of music with what he terms a "pre-maximalist" vocabulary.

Works: Guitar Quartet (1975); *Z* for Soprano, 6 Percussion, and Tape (1978); *Liquid and Stellar Music*, live perf. solo piece (1981); *The Way of How*, music theater (1981); *Dark Blue Circumstance*, live perf. solo piece for Electric Guitar and Electronics (1982); *Casa Vecchia* for String Quartet (1982); *Are Are*, music theater (1983); *Seehear*, music theater (1984); *re:*

act:ion for Orch. (1984); *Was Are/Will Be*, staged concert piece (1985); *Freesound* (1985–88); *Slow Fire*, music theater/opera (1985–88); *Figaro Gets a Divorce*, theater score (1986); *The Tempest*, theater score (1987); *Shelflife*, live perf. dance piece (1987); *Rhythmia*, tape piece for Dance (1987); *Loose the Thread*, dance piece for Violin, Piano, and Percussion (1988); *Power Failure*, music theater/opera (1988–89); *Pioneers*, music theater/opera (1989–90; Spoleto Festival, May 26, 1990).

Dressel, Erwin, German composer; b. Berlin, June 10, 1909; d. there, Dec. 17, 1972. He studied with Wilhelm Klatte and Paul Juon in Berlin; then was active as a conductor and arranger.

Works: Operas: *Der arme Columbus* (Kassel, Feb. 19, 1928); *Der Kuchentanz* (Kassel, May 18, 1929); *Der Rosenbusch der Maria* (Leipzig, June 23, 1930); *Die Zwillingsesel* (Dresden, April 29, 1932); *Jery und Bätely* (Berlin, 1932); *Die Laune der Verliebten* (Hamburg and Leipzig, 1949); *Der Bär* (Bern, 1963); 4 syms. (1927, 1929, 1932, 1948); Concerto for Oboe, Clarinet, Bassoon, and Orch. (1951); Clarinet Concerto (1961); *Cassation* for Orch. (1961); Viola Concerto (1969); 2 string quartets; String Trio; choral music; songs; piano pieces.

Dresser (real name, **Dreiser**), **(John) Paul (, Jr.),** American composer of popular songs, brother of the great American novelist Theodore Dreiser; b. Terre Haute, Ind., April 22, 1858; d. N.Y., Jan. 30, 1906. He learned to play guitar and piano in his youth and began touring with a traveling show when he was 16; subsequently played with the Billy Rose Minstrels and became a successful composer of sentimental ballads. Among his most popular songs were *On the Banks of the Wabash* (1897) and *My Gal Sal* (1905). His brother wrote the screenplay for the film *My Gal Sal* (1942), a so-called biography of Dresser, and also ed. *The Songs of Paul Dresser* (N.Y., 1927).

Bibl.: A. Markle, "Some Light on P. D.," *Terre Haute Tribune and Terre Haute Star* (April 14, 1940).

Dressler, Gallus, important German composer and music theorist; b. Nebra, Thuringia, Oct. 16, 1533; d. Zerbst, Anhalt, c.1584. He entered the Jena Academy (later Univ.) in 1557; the following year he was made Kantor at the Magdeburg grammar school. In 1570 he received his master's degree at the Univ. of Wittenberg, then went to Zerbst as a deacon (1575). He is of historical significance for his contributions to the development of the German-language motet and to modal theory.

Works: *Aliquot psalmi latini et germanici* for 4 to 6 Voices (1560); *Zehen deutscher Psalmen* for 4 to 5 Voices (Jena, 1562); *XVII cantiones sacrae* for 4 to 5 Voices (Wittenberg, 1565; ed. in Publikationen älterer praktischer und theoretischer Musikwerke, XXIV, 1903); *Epitaphium piissimae et honestissimae matronae Magdalenae conjugis . . . Christophori Petzelii* (Wittenberg, 1566); *XVIII cantiones* for 4 or more Voices (Magdeburg, 1567); *XVII cantiones sacrae* for 4 to 5 Voices (Wittenberg, 1568); *Das schöne Gebet, Herr Jesu Christ* for 4 Voices (Magdeburg, 1569); *XIX cantiones* for 4 to 5 Voices (Magdeburg, 1569); *XC cantiones* for 4 or more Voices (Magdeburg, 1570); *XVI Geseng* for 4 or more Voices (Magdeburg, 1570); *Opus sacrarum cantionum, nunc denou recognitum, et multo quam antea correctius* for 4 or more Voices (Nuremberg, 1570); *Magnificat octo tonorum* for 4 Voices (Magdeburg, 1571); *Ausserlesene teutsche Lieder* for 4 to 5 Voices and Instruments (Nuremberg, 1575).

Writings: *Practica modorum explicatio* (Jena, 1561); *Praecepta musicae poeticae* (MS, 1563; ed. by B. Engelke in *Geschichtsblätter für Stadt und Land Magdeburg*, XLIX–1, 1914–15); *Musicae practicae elementa in usum scholae Magdeburgensis edita* (Magdeburg, 1571; 4th ed., 1601).

Bibl.: B. Engelke, "Einige Bemerkungen zu D.s 'Praecepta musicae poeticae,'" *Geschichtsblätter für Stadt und Land Magdeburg*, XLIX–1 (1914–15); W. Luther, *G. D.: Ein Beitrag zur Geschichte des Schulkantorats im 16. Jahrhundert* (Kassel, 1941).

Dreves, Guido Maria, German music historian; b. Hamburg, Oct. 27, 1854; d. Mitwitz, near Kronach, June 1, 1909. He entered the Jesuit order; lived in Vienna and Würzburg. For distinguished service to the cause of hymnology and medieval music, the Univ. of Munich made him a Ph.D. (*honoris causa*).

WRITINGS: Co-ed., with C. Blume and H. Bannister, *Analecta hymnica medii aevi* (55 vols., 1886–1922); *Cantiones bohemicae* (1886); *Die Hymnen des Johannes von Jenstein* (1886); *Aurelius Ambrosius, der Vater des Kirchengesanges* (1893); *Psalteria rhythmica* (1901); *Die Kirche der Lateiner in ihren Liedern* (1908).

Drew, James (Mulcro), American composer, pianist, and conductor; b. St. Paul, Minn., Feb. 9, 1929. He studied at the N.Y. School of Music (1954–56); also had private sessions with Edgar Varèse (1956) and Wallingford Riegger (1956–59); continued his studies at Tulane Univ. (M.A., 1964). He taught at Northwestern Univ. (1965–67), Yale Univ. (1967–73), Louisiana State Univ. (1973–76), Calif. State Univ. in Fullerton (1976–77), and the Univ. of Calif. in Los Angeles (1977–78). In 1972–73 he held a Guggenheim fellowship. He developed a sui generis program of performance arts in which he acted interchangeably as composer, conductor, pianist, conferencier, and entertainer. In 1980 he was appointed director of music and experimental theater at the Contemporary Arts Center in New Orleans. In 1984 he became director of the MMT Theater; also was founder of the Ensemble Drew (from 1985) and associate composer-director of the Rainero Production Group in Amsterdam (from 1987). Drew's style of composition is built on flexible techniques, both polythematic and monothematic, often deriving from varying elements of instrumental Klangfarbe; sometimes literal repetition of whole sections is used for emphasis. The stylistic sources of his music can be found in the works of Scriabin and Varèse. A professional pianist, he often appears as a soloist in programs of contemporary music, including jazz. A polymath in his vocations and avocations, Drew drew the Downbeat International Jazz Critics Award in the New Star category in 1961.

WORKS: *Passacaglia* for Orch. (1957); *Indigo Suite* for Piano, Double Bass, and Percussion (1959); *Divisiones* for 6 Percussionists (1962); Piano Trio (1962); *Polifonica I* for Flute, Clarinet, Oboe, String Quartet, and Piano (1963); *The Lute in the Attic* for Voice, Flute, Clarinet, Cello, and 3 Gongs (1963); *Contrappunto* for Orch. (1965); *Polifonica II* for Flute and Percussion (1966); Sym. No. 1 for Chamber Orch. (1968); *Symphonies* for Orch., Chorus, and 3 Conductors (1969); *October Lights* for Orch. (New Haven, Oct. 18, 1969); Concerto for Violino Grande and Orch. (1970); *Metal Concerto* for Percussion (N.Y., Feb. 2, 1971); Sym. No. 2 for Chorus and Orch. (Norfolk, Va., Aug. 20, 1971); *Almost Stationary* for Piano Trio (1971); *Gothic Lights* for Brass Ensemble (1972); Concerto for Percussion (N.Y., March 21, 1973); *Tango* for Cello Solo (1973); *West Indian Lights* for Orch. (Tanglewood, Aug. 9, 1973); *Epitaphium pour Stravinsky* for 3 Trombones, Horn, Tuba, and Piano (Atlanta, Feb. 14, 1974); *Crucifixus Domini Christi*, dramatic stage work (Baton Rouge, Jan. 30, 1975); *The Fading of the Visible World*, oratorio (1975); *Suspense Opera* for Voices and Chamber Ensemble (1975); *Metal Assemblage* for Wind Orch. (1976); Sym. No. 3 (1977); Violin Concerto (1977); String Quartet No. 2 (1977); *Dr. Cincinnati*, dramatic entertainment for Actors, Dancers, Singers, Instrumentalists, and Magnetic Tape Segments (1977); *The Orangethorpe Aria* for Soprano, Piano Trio, and Clarinet (1978); *Trio for the Fiery Messengers* for Piano Trio (1979); Sonata for Violin and Piano (1979); Sonata for Cello and Piano (1980); *St. Mark Triple Concerto* for Violin, Cello, Piano, and Brass/ Winds (1981); *5 O'Clock Ladies*, dramatic stage work (1981); *Himself, the Devil*, dramatic stage work (1982); *Whisper*, dramatic video work (1982); Sonata for Solo Viola (1983); *Open/ Closed Forms* for Chamber Ensemble (1983); *Trinity* for Soprano and Chamber Ensemble (1983); *American Elegy* for Brass Quintet (1983); *Courtyard Music* for Chamber Orch. and specially designed instruments called Kinisones (1983); *Faustus, an Epilogue* for 2 Pianos, Viola, and Chamber Ensemble (1984); *Becket: The Final Moments*, automated drama (1984); *One Last Dance*, theater and/or video piece (1984); *Chartres Street Processional* for Brass (1986); *"Live" from the Black Eagle*, stage piece (1987–88); String Quartet No. 3 (1989); *Surprise Operas* for Singers and Chamber Ensemble (1989).

Dreyer, Johann Melchior, German organist and composer; b. Röttingen, Württemberg, June 24, 1747; d. Ellwangen, March 22, 1824. He studied in Ellwangen, where he became a church organist; wrote chiefly church music. Among his publ. works are *18 Missae breves* (1790–1802); *24 Hymni brevissimi ad vesperas* (1791); *Te Deum* (1800); organ music.

BIBL.: E. Bonitz, "J.M. D.," *Kirchenmusikalisches Jahrbuch*, XLV (1961).

Dreyfus, George (Georg), German-born Australian bassoonist, conductor, and composer; b. Wuppertal, July 22, 1928. He studied clarinet and bassoon at the Melbourne Conservatorium, then completed his training at the Vienna Academy of Music (1955–56). He played in various Australian orchs., including the Melbourne Sym. Orch. (1953–64); in 1958 he founded the New Music Ensemble in Melbourne, which became the George Dreyfus Chamber Orch. in 1970. In 1976 he held the Prix de Rome of the German Academy in Rome, and in 1983 was artist-in-residence at the Tianjin Cons. of Music in China. He publ. an autobiography entitled *The Last Frivolous Book* (Sydney, 1984).

WORKS: OPERAS: *Garni Sands* (1965–66; Sydney, July 12, 1972); *The Takeover*, school opera (1969); *The Gilt-Edged Kid* (1970; Melbourne, April 11, 1976); *The Lamentable Reign of Charles the Last*, a "pantopera" (1975; Adelaide, March 23, 1976). MUSICALS: *Smash Hit!* (1980); *The Sentimental Bloke* (Melbourne, Dec. 17, 1985). ORCH.: *Music for Music Camp* (1967); 2 syms. (1967, 1976); *Jingles*, 5 pieces (1968; a potpourri of styles from Mahler, Stravinsky, rock and roll, ballads, and the Tijuana Brass); *Song of the Maypole*, cantata for Children's Choruses and Orch. (1968); *Reflections in a Glass-House*, an image of Capt. James Cook, for Narrator, Children's Chorus, and Orch. (1969); *The Illusionist*, mime-drama for Solo Dancer and Orch. (1972); *Mo* for Baritone, String Orch., and Continuo (1972); *. . . and more Jingles*, 5 further pieces (1972); *Hallelujah for Handel* for Brass Band and Orch. (1976); *Terrigal* for Choir and Orch. (1977); *Symphonie concertante* for Bassoon, Violin, Viola, Cello, and String Orch. (1978); *Grand Ridge Road*, suite for Small Orch. (1980); *Celebration*, cantata for Women's Voices, Piano, and Orch. (1981); *Folk Music with Large Orch.* (1982); *German Teddy*, sym. for Mandolin Orch. (1984; Wuppertal, April 27, 1986); *The Box Hill Gloria*, cantata for Choir, Children's Choir, Pop Singer, Concert Band, Brass Band, Pipe Band, and String Orch. (1986); also many chamber works.

Dreyschock, Alexander, brilliant Bohemian pianist, teacher, and composer, brother of **Raimund Dreyschock;** b. Zack, Oct. 15, 1818; d. Venice, April 1, 1869. A student of Tomaschek, he acquired a virtuoso technique and was regarded as a worthy rival of Liszt in technical dexterity. At 8 he was able to play in public; toured North Germany (1838); spent 2 years in Russia (1840–42); visited Brussels, Paris, and London, then the Netherlands and Austria. In 1862 he was called to St. Petersburg as a prof. at the newly founded Cons. In 1868 he went to Italy. His astounding facility in playing octaves, double sixths, and thirds, and performing solos with the left hand alone cast a glamour about his performance.

WORKS: Opera, *Florette, oder Die erste Liebe Heinrichs des IV.*; Overture for Orch.; Rondo for Orch.; String Quartet; 140 piano pieces of the salon type.

Dreyschock, Felix, German pianist, son of **Raimund Dreyschock;** b. Leipzig, Dec. 27, 1860; d. Berlin, Aug. 1, 1906. He studied under Grabau, Ehrlich, Taubert, and Kiel; gave successful concerts, and was a prof. at the Stern Cons. in Berlin. His piano pieces are well written and effective; he also publ. a Violin Sonata and songs.

Dreyschock, Raimund, Bohemian violinist, brother of **Alexander** and father of **Felix Dreyschock;** b. Zack, Aug. 20,

1824; d. Leipzig, Feb. 6, 1869. He was a pupil of Pixis in Prague; was concertmaster at the Gewandhaus concerts (1850–69) and a violin teacher in the Cons. at Leipzig. His wife, **Elizabeth** (née **Nose,** b. Cologne, 1832; d. there, July, 1911), was a contralto singer who founded and managed a vocal academy in Berlin.

Drieberg, Friedrich von, German music historian and composer; b. Charlottenburg, Dec. 10, 1780; d. there, May 21, 1856. He served in the Prussian army until 1804, when he went to Paris to study composition with Spontini; also traveled to Vienna. He produced 2 operas, *Don Cocagno* (Berlin, 1812) and *Der Sänger und der Schneider* (Berlin, Nov. 23, 1814), but became known mainly through his speculative publications concerning Greek music, promulgating theories and conclusions that were utterly unfounded. However, they were publ. and seriously discussed, if only in refutation. These are *Die mathematische Intervallenlehre der Griechen* (1818); *Aufschlüsse über die Musik der Griechen* (1819); *Die praktische Musik der Griechen* (1821); *Die pneumatischen Erfindungen der Griechen* (1822); *Wörterbuch der griech. Musik* (1835); *Die griechische Musik, auf ihre Grundgesetze zurückgeführt* (1841); *Die Kunst der musikalischen Composition . . . nach griechischen Grundsätzen bearbeitet* (1858).

Driessler, Johannes, German composer; b. Friedrichsthal, near Saarbrücken, Jan. 26, 1921. He studied organ and theory with Karl Rahner at the Cons. of Saarbrücken. By the age of 13 he was filling a regular position as church organist. In 1946 he was engaged as an instructor at the Northwest German Music Academy in Detmold; in 1960 became its director. He devoted himself mainly to choral composition, in which he attained such an outstanding practical craft that his works entered the active repertoire of both sacred and secular institutions in Germany.
Works: Choral: *Sinfonia sacra* (1948); *Dein Reich komme* (1949); *Cantica nova* (1950); *Triptychon* (1950); secular oratorio, *Gaudia mundana* (1951); *De profundis* (1952); oratorio, *Der Lebendige* (1956); oratorio, *Der grosse Lobgesang* (1959); 2 *Concerti sacri* (1961); lyric opera, *Claudia amata* (1952); 3 syms.: No. 1, *Dum spiro spero* (1964); No. 2, *Dum ludo laudo* (1966); No. 3, *Amo dum vivo* (1969); works for chamber ensembles and numerous teaching pieces.

Drigo, Riccardo, Italian composer and conductor; b. Padua, June 30, 1846; d. there, Oct. 1, 1930. He studied music in Padua and Venice; conducted opera in Venice and Milan. In 1879 he was engaged to conduct the Italian opera in St. Petersburg; in 1886 became permanent ballet conductor of the Imperial Theater there; conducted 1st performances of Tchaikovsky's ballets *The Sleeping Beauty* and *The Nutcracker.* After Tchaikovsky's death, Drigo ed. the score of the ballet *Swan Lake* and orchestrated a number of Tchaikovsky's piano pieces. Drigo's own ballets, melodious and easy to listen to, also enjoyed excellent success in Russia. Particularly popular was his ballet *Les Millions d'Arlequin* (Harlequin's Millions), which includes the famous *Serenade* for a soulful cello solo and the ingratiating *Valse bluette.* Drigo conducted the 1st performance of this ballet in St. Petersburg on Feb. 10, 1900. From 1914 to 1916 he was in Italy; from 1916 to 1920 he was again in St. Petersburg, finally returning to Italy.
Bibl.: S. Travaglia, *R. D., L'uomo e l'artista* (Padua, 1929).

Dring, Madeleine, English violinist, pianist, singer, and composer; b. Hornsey, Sept. 7, 1923; d. London, March 26, 1977. She studied violin at the Junior Dept. of the Royal College of Music in London, and also acquired professional skill as a pianist, singer, and actress. She took courses in composition at the Royal College of Music with Hubert Howells and Vaughan Williams; developed a knack for writing attractively brief pieces. She also wrote a short opera called *Cupboard Love,* several trios, a suite for Harmonica and Piano, and incidental-music scores for radio and television.

Drinker, Henry S(andwith, Jr.), American music scholar and translator; b. Philadelphia, Sept. 15, 1880; d. Merion, Pa.,

March 9, 1965. He was a lawyer by profession, but devoted much time to musical pursuits. He founded the Accademia dei Dilettanti di Musica in his home in 1930, which gave performances of choral music ranging from the 17th to the 20th centuries until it was disbanded in 1960. He also founded the Drinker Library of Choral Music, which he later donated to the Free Library of Philadelphia. He tr. the texts of 212 cantatas by Bach, as well as the *St. Matthew Passion,* the *St. John Passion,* the *Christmas Oratorio,* the *Easter Oratorio,* and the *Magnificat;* also all of Mozart's choral music, all of Schumann's songs, all of the solo songs of Schubert and Wolf, and the complete vocal works of Brahms. His wife, **Sophie (Lewis)** (née **Hutchinson**) **Drinker** (b. Philadelphia, Aug. 24, 1888; d. Chestnut Hill, Pa., Sept. 6, 1967) was a champion of women in music; she publ. *Music and Women* (1948) and *Brahms and His Women's Choruses* (1952).
Writings: *The Chamber Music of Johannes Brahms* (Philadelphia, 1932); *Bach's Use of Slurs in Recitativo Secco* (Merion, Pa., 1946); *Drinker Library of Choral Music: Catalogue* (Philadelphia, 1957); *Accademia dei Dilettanti di Musica, 1930–1960* (Merion, Pa., 1960).

Drobisch, Moritz Wilhelm, German scholar; b. Leipzig, Aug. 16, 1802; d. there, Sept. 30, 1896. In 1826 he became a prof. extraordinary of mathematics, and in 1842 a prof. ordinary of philosophy, at Leipzig Univ. Besides various works on mathematics and philosophy, he wrote several valuable essays on musical subjects.
Writings: *Über die mathematische Bestimmung der mus. Intervalle* (1846); *Über mus. Tonbestimmung und Temperatur* (1852); *Nachträge zur Theorie der mus. Tonverhältnisse* (1855); *Über reine Stimmung und Temperatur der Töne* (1877).

Drouet, Louis François-Philippe, famous French flutist and composer; b. Amsterdam, April 14, 1792; d. Bern, Sept. 30, 1873. He studied composition at the Paris Cons.; at the age of 16, was appointed solo flutist to King Louis of the Netherlands, and at 19 became solo flutist to Napoleon; after Napoleon's defeat, he played the flute with fine impartiality for King Louis XVIII. In 1817 he went to London, and subsequently made concert tours across Europe. In 1840 he was appointed Kapellmeister at Coburg; in 1854 he visited America for a few months; then lived in Gotha and Frankfurt before going to Switzerland. He composed mainly for the flute; among his works are 10 flute concertos; 2 fantasias for flute and piano; 3 trios for 3 flutes; numerous sonatas and variations for flute and assorted instruments.

Drozdov, Anatol, Russian pianist, pedagogue, and writer on music; b. Saratov, Nov. 4, 1883; d. Moscow, Sept. 10, 1950. He studied piano at the St. Petersburg Cons., graduating in 1909; then engaged in teaching; was a prof. of piano at the conservatories of Ekaterinoder (1911–16), Saratov (1918–20), and Moscow (1920–24). He publ. a number of articles in Russian music journals; also composed 2 piano sonatas, other piano pieces, and chamber music. His brother, **Vladimir Drozdov** (b. Saratov, June 6, 1882; d. N.Y., March 10, 1960), was a pianist and composer.

Drozdowski, Jan, Polish pianist and teacher; b. Krakow, Feb. 2, 1857; d. there, Jan. 21, 1918. He studied at the Vienna Cons. with Dachs and Epstein; also took lessons with Bruckner. In 1889 he was appointed prof. of piano at the Krakow Cons. and retained that post till his death. He publ. a piano method, *Systematic School of Pianoforte Technique* (Polish ed., 1887; German ed., Munich, 1889, under the pseudonym Jan Jordan).

Druckman, Jacob (Raphael), outstanding American composer; b. Philadelphia, June 26, 1928. After taking courses in solfège, harmony, and counterpoint with Longy and L. Gesensway in Philadelphia, he studied composition with Copland at the Berkshire Music Center in Tanglewood (summers 1949, 1950), with Mennin, Persichetti, and Wagenaar at the Juilliard School of Music in N.Y. (B.S., 1954; M.S., 1956), and with Aubin at the École Normale de Musique in Paris on a Fulbright fellowship (1954–55). He taught at the Juilliard School of Music in N.Y. (1957–72) and at Bard College (1961–67); was an associate at the Columbia-Princeton Electronic Music Center (1967) and director of the electronic music studio at Yale Univ. (1971–72). After serving as associate prof. of composition at Brooklyn College of the City Univ. of N.Y. (1972–76), he was chairman of the composition dept. and director of the electronic music studio at Yale Univ. (from 1976). From 1982 to 1986 he was composer-in-residence of the N.Y. Phil. He held Guggenheim fellowships in 1957 and 1968. In 1972 he won the Pulitzer Prize in Music for his *Windows* for Orch., and in 1978 was elected a member of the Inst. of the American Academy and Inst. of Arts and Letters. In his music he happily combines the strict elements of polyphonic structure, harking back to Palestrina, with modern techniques of dissonant counterpoint, while refusing to adhere to any doctrinaire system of composition. In his orchestrations he makes use of a plethora of percussion instruments, including primitive drums; electronic sonorities have also had increasing importance in his works.

WORKS: ORCH.: *Music for the Dance* (1949); Concerto for Strings (1951); *Volpone Overture* (1953); Concerto for Violin and Small Orch. (1956); *Odds and Evens: A Game* for Children's Orch. (1966); *Windows* (Chicago, March 16, 1972); *Lamia* for Soprano and Orch. (Albany, N.Y., April 20, 1974; rev. version, N.Y., Oct. 17, 1975); *Mirage* (St. Louis, March 4, 1976); *Chiaroscuro* (Cleveland, March 14, 1977); Viola Concerto (N.Y., Nov. 2, 1978); *Aureole* (N.Y., June 6, 1979); *Prism* (Baltimore, May 21, 1980); *Athanor* (N.Y., May 8, 1986); *In Memoriam Vincent Persichetti* for Winds, Brass, and Percussion (N.Y., Dec. 6, 1987); *Brangle* (Chicago, March 28, 1989). **BALLETS:** *Suite* (1953) and *Performance* (1956). **INSTRUMENTAL:** 3 string quartets (1948, 1966, 1981); Divertimento for Clarinet, Horn, Harp, Violin, Viola, and Cello (1950); *Spell*, ballet for 2 Pianos (1951); *Interlude*, ballet for Flute, Clarinet, and Timpani (1953); *Animus I* for Trombone and Tape (1966); *Animus II* for Soprano or Mezzo-soprano, 2 Percussion, and Tape (1968); *Incenters* for 13 Instruments (1968; also for Trumpet, Horn, Trombone, and Orch., Minneapolis, Nov. 23, 1973); *Animus III* for Clarinet and Tape (1969); *Synapse* for Tape (1971); *Delizie contente che l'alme beate* for Woodwind Quintet and Tape (1973); *Other Voices* for Brass Quintet (1976); *Animus IV* for Tenor, Violin, Trombone, Piano or Electric Piano, Electric Organ, Percussion, and Tape (1977); *Bō* for Bass Clarinet, 3 Women's Voices, Harp, and Marimba (1979); *Tromba marina* for 4 Double Basses (1981); also much vocal music.

Drury, Stephen, American pianist; b. Spokane, Wash., April 13, 1955. His mother taught him piano; he then went to Harvard Univ., where he worked at the Electronic Music Studio. In 1977 he continued his piano studies in N.Y., with William Masselos; then returned to Harvard and organized an Experimental Music Festival, during which he gave a complete performance of Satie's piano piece *Vexations*, repeated 840 times. He also played the piano sonatas of Ives and piano pieces by John Cage. While preoccupied with avant-garde music, he took occasional lessons in classical piano playing with Claudio Arrau in N.Y. On the musical far-out frontier, he became a member of a conceptual team called Beaux Eaux Duo.

Drysdale, (George John) Learmont, Scottish composer; b. Edinburgh, Oct. 3, 1866; d. there, June 18, 1909. He was a pupil at the Royal Academy of Music in London, and winner of the Lucas prize for composition (1890). He composed the orch. overtures *Tam O'Shanter* (1890; awarded a prize by the Glasgow Soc. of Musicians) and *Herondean* (1893); also 2 operas, *The Red Spider* (1898) and *Fionn and Tera* (1909); some choral works.

Drzewiecki, Zbigniew, distinguished Polish pianist and pedagogue; b. Warsaw, April 8, 1890; d. there, April 11, 1971. After preliminary training in Warsaw, he studied with C. Prohaska at the Vienna Academy of Music (1909–11) and privately with Maria Prentner (1911–15). He was assistant to Leschetizky, and later had a few private lessons with Paderewski

(1928). In 1916 he made his debut as a soloist with the Warsaw Phil.; he taught at the Warsaw Academy of Music (1916–44; 1945–68) and at the Lvov Cons. (1930–40); in 1945 he founded the Krakow Cons., where he was rector (1945–50) and teacher (until 1968). His fame as a pedagogue reached beyond his homeland, for his students included Roger Woodward from Australia and Fou Ts'ong from China. He was active in ISCM activities in Poland and served as a jurist for the Chopin Piano Competition, in which 1st prizes were captured by his students Halina Czerny-Stefanska (1949) and Adam Harasiweicz (1955).

BIBL.: S. Kisielewski, *Z. D.* (Krakow, 1973).

Dubensky, Arcady, Russian-American violinist and composer; b. Viatka, Oct. 15, 1890; d. Tenafly, N.J., Oct. 14, 1966. He studied violin at the Moscow Cons. with Jan Hřimaly and composition with Ilyinsky, graduating in 1909; was a violinist at the Moscow Opera (1910–19); played in hotels and restaurants in Constantinople (1920); settled in the U.S. in 1921; was a member of the N.Y. Sym. Orch., and then of the N.Y. Phil. Orch., retiring in 1953. His music is conservative in its idiom; however, an impression of originality is created by his adroit use of unusual combinations (such as a quartet for double basses, a fugue for 18 violins, a suite for 9 flutes).

WORKS: *Romance with Double Bass,* comic opera (N.Y., Oct. 31, 1936); *Russian Bells,* symphonic poem (N.Y., Dec. 29, 1927); Prelude and Fugue (1932; Boston, April 12, 1943); *Tom Sawyer,* overture (for Mark Twain's centennial, Philadelphia, Nov. 29, 1935); *Political Suite* for Orch. (*Russian Monarchy, Nazi and Fascist, Communist;* N.Y. radio broadcast, Sept. 17, 1936); *Fantasy on a Negro Theme* for Tuba and Orch. (1938); *Stephen Foster,* symphonic suite (Indianapolis, Jan. 31, 1941); *Trumpet Overture* for 18 Toy Trumpets and 2 Bass Drums (N.Y., Dec. 10, 1949); *Trombone Concerto* (1953); *Gossips* for Strings (Philadelphia, Nov. 24, 1928); Fugue for 18 Violins (his most successful work; Philadelphia, April 1, 1932); Prelude and Fugue for 4 Bassoons (N.Y., Feb. 16, 1947); Suite for 9 Flutes, including a Piccolo and Basset Horn (N.Y., Jan. 26, 1936); other chamber works for various combinations of instruments.

Dubois, Léon, Belgian conductor and composer; b. Brussels, Jan. 9, 1859; d. Boitsfort, Nov. 19, 1935. He won the Prix de Rome at the Brussels Cons. in 1885; conducted opera at the Théâtre de la Monnaie in Brussels (1890–97); was director of the Louvain Music School (1899–1912); then director of the Brussels Cons. (1912–26). He wrote the operas *Son Excellence ma femme* (1884), *La Revanche de Sganarelle* (1886), *Édénie* (Antwerp, March 7, 1912), and *Vers la gloire* (Brussels, March 28, 1919); a ballet, *Smylis* (Brussels, 1891); the mimodrama *La Mort* (Brussels, 1894); chamber music.

Dubois, Pierre-Max, French composer; b. Graulhet, Tarn, March 1, 1930. He studied at the Cons. in Tours, obtaining a prize in piano at the age of 15; later studied composition with Darius Milhaud at the Paris Cons. His works include *Impressions foraines* for Orch. (1949); *Divertissement* for Saxophone and Orch. (1952); *Sérénades* for Bassoon and Orch. (1953); *Capriccio* for Violin and Orch. (1954); *Concertstück* for Saxophone and Piano (1955); Violin Concerto (Strasbourg, June 20, 1957); Cello Concerto (1958); Concerto for Saxophone and String Orch. (1959); Sym. No. 1, subtitled *Drame pour Epidaure* (1960); *Le Docteur OX,* ballet-bouffe, after Jules Verne (Lyons, Feb. 23, 1964); Quartet for 4 French Horns (1961); Quartet for 4 Flutes (1961); Quartet for 4 Trombones (1961); *Concerto italien* for 2 Pianos and Orch. (1962); Concerto for Violin, Piano, and Orch. (Besançon, Sept. 15, 1963); Quartet for 4 Clarinets (1962); Sym. No. 2 (*Symphonie-Sérénade*) for Strings (1964); *Musique pour un Western* for Orch. (1964); *Cover Girls,* a choreographic spectacle (1965); *Concerto ironico* for Bassoon and Orch. (1968); Concertino for 4 Saxophones and Orch. (1969); *Beaujency concerto* for Clarinet and Orch. (1969); *Sinfonia militaire* (1969).

Dubois, (François-Clément) Théodore, eminent French organist and composer; b. Rosnay, Marne, Aug. 24, 1837; d.

Paris, June 11, 1924. He entered the Paris Cons. in 1853, working under Marmontel (piano), Benoist (organ), and Bazin and Ambroise Thomas (composition); he graduated in 1861; was the recipient of the Grand Prix de Rome with the cantata *Atala*, after having taken 1st prizes in all depts. Returning to Paris, he was maître de chapelle at Sainte-Clotilde until 1869 and at the Madeleine until 1877, and then succeeded Saint-Saëns there as organist. In 1871 he was made prof. of harmony at the Paris Cons., succeeding Elwart; in 1891 became prof. of composition; in 1894 was elected to the chair in the Academy left vacant by Gounod's death; in 1896 he succeeded Ambroise Thomas as director of the Paris Cons.; retired in 1905. Dubois publ. a practical manual, *Traité de contrepoint et de fugue* (1901), which was a standard work at the Paris Cons.

WORKS: Comic operas: *La Guzla de l'émir* (Paris, April 30, 1873) and *Le Pain bis, ou La Lilloise* (Opéra-Comique, Feb. 26, 1879); *Aben Hamet* (produced in Italian, Théâtre du Châtelet, Dec. 16, 1884); "idylle dramatique," *Xavière* (Opéra-Comique, Nov. 26, 1895); ballet, *La Farandole* (Paris Opéra, Dec. 14, 1883); 2 oratorios: *Les Sept Paroles du Christ* (1867) and *Le Paradis perdu* (1878; won the City of Paris prize); several cantatas (*L'Enlèvement de Proserpine, Hylas, Bergerette, Les Vivants et les morts, Délivrance*); masses and other church music; many orch. works: 3 syms.; *Marche héroïque de Jeanne d'Arc; Fantaisie triomphale* for Organ and Orch.; *Hymne nuptiale; Méditation-Prière* for Strings, Oboe, Harp, and Organ; *Concerto-Capriccio* for Piano; 2nd Piano Concerto; Violin Concerto; 2 symphonic poems: *Notre Dame de la Mer* and *Adonis; Symphonie française* (1908); *Fantasietta* (1917); piano pieces (*Chœur et danse des lutins; 6 poèmes sylvestres*); pieces for organ and for harmonium; a cappella choruses; etc.

BIBL.: M. Widor, *Notice sur la vie et les travaux de T. D.* (Paris, 1924).

Dubrovay, László, Hungarian composer; b. Budapest, March 23, 1943. He studied at the Bartók Cons. and the Academy of Music in Budapest (graduated 1966), his principal mentors being István Szelényi, Ferenc Szabó, and Imre Vincze; then continued his training in West Germany on a scholarship from the Deutscher Akademischer Austauschdienst, receiving instruction in composition from Stockhausen and in electronic music from Hans-Ulrich Rumpert (1972–74). Returning to Budapest, he taught music theory at the Academy of Music (from 1976); was awarded the Erkel Prize (1985). In some of his works he utilizes electronic and computer resources.

WORKS: ORCH.: *Verificazione* (1970); *Succession* (1974); Concerto for 11 Strings (1979); Concerto for Flute and 45 Strings (1981); Concerto for Trumpet and 15 Strings (1981); Concerto for Piano, Orch., and Synthesizer (1982); Piano Concerto (1984); *Variations on an Oscillating Line* (1987). **CHAMBER:** *Sei duo* for Violin and Percussion (1969); 2 brass quintets (1971, 1980); 2 wind quintets (1972, 1983); *Magic Squares* for Violin and Cimbalom (1975); *Matuziáda* Nos. 1 to 5 for 4 Flutes (1976); *Geometrum II*: String Quartet No. 2 (1976); *Numberplay No. 1* for 20 Players (1976); *Interferences* No. 1 for 2 Cimbaloms (1976); *Music* for 2 Cimbaloms (1977); Brass Septet for 3 Trumpets, Horn, 2 Trombones, and Tuba (1980); String Quartet No. 3 (1983); Octet for Clarinet, Bassoon, Horn, and String Quartet (1985–87); also works for solo instruments, choruses, live electronics, computer, and tape.

Dubuque, Alexander, Russian pianist, composer, and teacher; b. Moscow, March 3, 1812; d. there, Jan. 8, 1898. He was a pupil of John Field, about whom he publ. a vol. of memoirs; was a prof. at the Moscow Cons. (1866–72). He wrote piano pieces, songs, and a work on piano technique (1866).

Du Cange, Charles Du Fresne, Sieur, eminent French scholar; b. Amiens, Dec. 18, 1610; d. Paris, Oct. 23, 1688. He belonged to the famed group of 17th-century French writers who established the precepts of modern linguistic criticism; he is important to musicology because he included definitions of Latin musical terms in his lexicographies. The most valuable of his many works are the *Glossarium ad scriptores mediae*

et infimae latinitatis (3 vols., Paris, 1678) and the *Glossarium ad scriptores mediae et infimae graecitatis* (Lyons, 1688).

BIBL.: H. Hardouin, *Essai sur la vie et sur les ouvrages de D. C.* (Amiens, 1849); L. Feugère, "Étude sur la vie et les ouvrages de D. C.," *Journal de l'Instruction Publique* (Paris, 1852).

Du Caurroy, François-Eustache, Sieur de St.-Frémin, French composer; b. Beauvais (baptized), Feb. 4, 1549; d. Paris, Aug. 7, 1609. He was a member of the French nobility; his father was "procureur du roi." He entered the Royal Chapel as a singer in 1569; in 1575 received a prize for a chanson, *Beaux yeux*; in 1578 he was "sous-maître"; in 1599 became superintendent of "la musique du roi." Influenced by Le Jeune, he began to compose "musique mesurée"; advanced in the favor of the court, receiving honors and awards; held the ecclesiastical titles of canon at the Ste. Chapelle of Dijon, Ste. Croix of Orleans, and other provincial posts. His greatest work was the collection *Meslanges de la musique,* containing Psalms, "chansons mesurées," noëls, in 4, 5, and 6 Voices (Paris, 1610; some specimens reprinted in Expert's *Maîtres musiciens,* vol. XIII). Other works: *Preces ecclesiasticae* for 4 to 7 Voices (Paris, 1609); instrumental *Fantaisies* for 3 and 6 parts (Paris, 1610; several publ. separately by Expert); *Missa pro defunctis* for 5 Voices (Paris, 1636).

BIBL.: M. Luillier, *Note sur quelques artistes-musiciens dans la Brie* (1870); N. Dufourcq, "A propos d'E. D. C.," *Revue de Musicologie* (Dec. 1950); F. Lesure, "La Carrière et les fonctions de D. C.," ibid. (1952).

Ducis (Duch), Benedictus, distinguished composer; b. probably near Constance, c.1490; d. Schalckstetten, near Ulm, 1544. He may or may not be identical with **Benedictus de Opitiis,** who was organist at the Antwerp Cathedral (1514–16) and at the Chapel Royal in London (1516–22). It is known for a certainty that Benedictus Ducis was in Vienna c.1515; he probably studied there; in 1532 he applied for a pastorate at Ulm (under the name Benedict Duch), but failed to obtain it. In 1533 he succeeded in receiving a pastorate at Stubersheim, near Geislingen; in 1535 he became pastor at Schalckstetten. Benedictus Ducis has been confused by many writers with Benedictus Appenzeller; the long list of Ducis's works given by Fétis is spurious; Barclay Squire, in "Who was Benedictus?," *Sammelbände der Internationalen Musik-Gesellschaft* (Jan. 1912), brought conclusive evidence that a considerable number of these works must be attributed to Benedictus Appenzeller. Two works by Ducis were publ. in facsimile by M. Nijhoff (The Hague, 1925); 10 sacred motets are reprinted in Denkmäler Deutscher Tonkunst, vol. XXXIV (ed. by J. Wolf).

BIBL.: F. Spitta, "B. D.," *Monatsschrift für Gottesdienst und kirchliche Kunst* (Jan.–March 1913); C. Van den Borren, "B. de Opitiis," *Musica sacra* (Sept. 1927); D. Bartha, *B. D. und Appenzeller* (Wolfenbüttel, 1930).

Duckles, Vincent H(arris), American musicologist; b. Boston, Sept. 21, 1913; d. Berkeley, Calif., July 1, 1985. He began his studies at the Univ. of Calif., Berkeley (A.B., 1936); after studies at Columbia Univ. (M.A. in music education, 1937; Ed.D., 1941), he pursued training once more at the Univ. of Calif., Berkeley (B.L.S., 1949; Ph.D. in musicology, 1953, with the diss. *John Gamble's Commonplace Book*); also held Fulbright senior research scholarships at Cambridge Univ. (1950–51) and at the Univ. of Göttingen (1957–58), and a grant-in-aid from the American Council of Learned Societies for research in Europe (1964–65). He was a music librarian (1949–57), associate prof. (1957–60), and prof. (1960–81) at the Univ. of Calif., Berkeley. He specialized in 17th-century English song literature, music bibliography, and the history of musical scholarship. He publ. the valuable source *Music Reference and Research Materials: An Annotated Bibliography* (N.Y., 1964; 4th ed., rev., 1988 by M. Keller).

BIBL.: P. Elliott and M. Roosa, "V. D. (1913–1985): A Bibliography of His Publications," *Notes* (Dec. 1987).

Duckworth, William (Ervin), American composer, teacher, and writer on music; b. Morganton, N.C., Jan. 13, 1943. He studied with Martin Mailman (composition) at East Carolina Univ. (B.M., 1965) and with Ben Johnston (composition), Robert Gray (trombone), and Charles Leonhard (education) at the Univ. of Illinois (M.S., 1966; D.M.Ed., 1972, with the diss. *Expanding Notational Parameters in the Music of John Cage*). He was founder-director of the Assoc. of Independent Composers and Performers (1969–72) and president of the Media Press (1969–72); in 1973 he joined the music faculty at Bucknell Univ. With E. Brown, he publ. *Theoretical Foundations of Music* (1978); also publ. *A Creative Approach to Music Fundamentals* (1981; 3rd ed., 1988) and ed., with R. Fleming, *John Cage at Seventy-Five* (1989).

WORKS: *Gambit* for Solo Percussion and Tape (1967); *Pitch City* for Any 4 Wind Players (1969); *When in Eternal Lines to Time Thou Grow'st* for Orch. (1970; Philadelphia, June 22, 1974); *A Mass for These Forgotten Times* for Chorus (1973); *7 Shades of Blue* for Flute, Clarinet, Violin, Cello, and Piano (1974); *A Summer Madrigal* for Flute, Violin, Piano, 2 Percussion, and Rock Singer (1976); *Music in 7 Regions* for Amplified Piano (1979); *Songs of the Pale Horseman* for Chorus and Electronics (Los Angeles, Nov. 30, 1984); *31 Days* for Any Solo Woodwind (1986); *Music in the Combat Zone* for Soprano and Chamber Ensemble (Philadelphia, Nov. 1, 1986); *12 Words* for Solo Instrument or Voice and 4 Similar Instruments (1989; N.Y., March 24, 1990).

Ducloux, Walter, Swiss-born American conductor; b. Kriens, April 17, 1913. He studied at the Univ. of Munich (Ph.D., 1935) and at the Academy of Music in Vienna (1935–37); was assistant to Toscanini at the Lucerne Festival (1938–39). After service in the U.S. Army, he became active as a sym. and opera conductor; he was music director for opera of CBS-TV and of the Voice of America (1950). He became director of opera at the Univ. of Southern Calif. in Los Angeles (1953), then prof. of music and drama at the Univ. of Texas (1968). From 1973 to 1975 he was conductor of the Austin (Texas) Sym. Orch. and from 1986 the Lyric Opera.

Dudarova, Veronika, Russian conductor; b. Baku, Dec. 5, 1916. She studied piano in Leningrad and took a course in conducting at the Moscow Cons. with Leo Ginsburg, graduating in 1947; in the same year became associate conductor of the Moscow State Orch. She is one of the foremost women conductors of the Soviet Union.

Dufallo, Richard (John), American conductor; b. East Chicago, Ind., Jan. 30, 1933. He played clarinet as a youngster; then enrolled at the American Cons. of Music in Chicago. He subsequently studied composition with Lukas Foss at the Univ. of Calif., Los Angeles; in 1957 he joined the Improvisation Chamber Ensemble organized by Foss, and showed an exceptional talent for controlled improvisation in the ultramodern manner. He then joined Foss as his associate conductor with the Buffalo Phil. (1962–67); also served on the faculty of the State Univ. of N.Y. at Buffalo (1963–67), where he directed its Center of Creative and Performing Arts. He attended a conducting seminar with William Steinberg in N.Y. (1965); Pierre Boulez gave him additional instruction in Basel (1969). In 1967 he went to Japan and other Asian countries as assistant tour conductor with the N.Y. Phil. In 1971 he made his European conducting debut in Paris. He served as conductor of the "Mini-Met," an adjunct to the Metropolitan Opera in N.Y. (1972–74), and was director of the series of new music sponsored by the Juilliard School of Music in N.Y. (1972–79). From 1970 to 1985 he was artistic director of the Aspen Music Festival's Conference on Contemporary Music. From 1980 to 1982 he also served as artistic adviser of Het Gelders Orkest in Arnhem, the Netherlands. In 1984–85 he was acting director of the Aspen Inst. Italia in Rome. He appeared as a guest conductor with many orchs. in the U.S. and Europe, securing a reputation as an advocate of contemporary music. He publ. the book *Trackings: Composers Speak with Richard Dufallo* (N.Y. and Oxford, 1989).

Dufay, Guillaume, great French composer; b. probably in or near Cambrai, c.1400; d. there, Nov. 27, 1474. His last name is pronounced "du-fah-ee," in 3 syllables, as indicated by the way he set his name to music in *Ave regina caelorum*. He was a choirboy at Cambrai Cathedral, where he came under the influence of Nicolas Malin, its *magister puerorum*, and his successor, Richard Loqueville. Although there is no evidence that he formally studied with these men, he undoubtedly learned his craft while working under them and other musicians. He remained in Cambrai until at least 1418; shortly thereafter, he entered the service of the Malatesta family in Pesaro, and in 1426 returned to Cambrai. Dufay was in Rome as a singer in the papal choir (Dec. 1428–Aug. 1433), during which period he consolidated his reputation as one of the most significant musicians of his day. His motet *Ecclesie militantis* may have been composed for the consecration of Pope Eugene IV in 1431. He found a patron in Niccolò III, Marquis of Ferrara, in 1433, and made a visit to his court in May 1437; he also found a patron in Louis, Duke of Savoy. On Feb. 8, 1434, he served as maître de chapelle for the marriage of Louis and Anne of Cyprus at the Savoy court. After a visit to Cambrai in Aug. 1434, he returned to Savoy. He was again a singer in the papal choir (June 1435–June 1437), which was maintained at this time in Florence until 1436, and then in Bologna. It was about this time that he received a degree in canon law from the Univ. of Turin. In 1436 he was made canon of Cambrai Cathedral. After again serving the Savoy court (1437–39), he returned to Cambrai in 1440 to assume his duties as canon. In 1446 he was also made canon of Ste. Waudru in Mons. In 1450 he returned to Italy; he visited Turin from May to July of that year and then was subsequently active in Savoy from 1451 to 1458, serving once more as maître de chappelle at the court (May 1, 1455–May 1, 1456). In 1458 he returned to Cambrai, where he lived and worked in comfort for the rest of his life. He was held in the highest esteem in his lifetime by the church authorities and his fellow musicians; Compère described him as "the moon of all music, and the light of all singers." He was the foremost representative of the Burgundian school of composition. He proved himself a master of both sacred and secular music, producing masses, motets, and chansons of extraordinary beauty and distinction. His contributions to the development of faux-bourdon and the cyclic mass are particularly noteworthy. A list of his works, including MS sources and approximate dates of composition, is found in C. Hamm's *A Chronology of the Works of Guillaume Dufay Based on a Study of Mensural Practice* (Princeton, N.J., 1964). The *Opera omnia*, ed. by G. de Van and H. Besseler in the Corpus Mensurabilis Musicae series, i/1–6 (1947–49; 1951–66), also contains valuable commentary. A compilation of the papers read at the Dufay Quincentennial Conference held at Brooklyn College on Dec. 6–7, 1974, was ed. by A. Atlas and publ. in 1976.

BIBL.: C. van den Borren, *G. D.: Son importance dans l'évolution de la musique au XVe siècle* (Brussels, 1925); H. Besseler, "Neue Dokumente zum Leben und Schaffen D.s," *Archiv für Musikwissenschaft,* IX (1952); R. Bockholdt, *Die frühen Messenkompositionen von G. D.* (Tutzing, 1960); S. Brown, *The Motets of Ciconia, Dunstable, and D.* (diss., Indiana Univ., 1962); C. Hamm, *A Chronology of the Works of G. D. Based on a Study of Mensural Practice* (Princeton, N.J., 1964); W. Nitschke, *Studien zu den Cantus-Firmus-Messen G. D.s* (Berlin, 1968); A. Atlas, ed., *Papers Read at the D. Quincentenary Conference, Brooklyn College, December 6–7, 1974* (Brooklyn, 1976); D. Fallows, *D.* (London, 1982; rev. ed., 1987).

Dufourcq, Norbert, distinguished French music historian and organist; b. St. Jean-de-Braye, Loiret, Sept. 21, 1904; d. Paris, Dec. 19, 1990. He was educated at the Sorbonne, where he studied history and geography; then at the École Nationale des Chartes (1924–28), graduating as an archivist-palaeographer; also studied piano and music history with Gastoué (1913–20), organ with André Marchal (1920–40), and harmony, counterpoint, and fugue with Marie-Rose Hublé. He took his Ph.D. at the Univ. of Paris in 1935 with the dissertation *Esquisse d'une histoire de l'orgue en France: XIIIe–XVIIIe siècles* (publ. in Paris, 1935). He was a teacher of history at the Collège Stanislas in Paris (1935–46); also prof. of music history and musicology at the Paris Cons. (1941–76). In addition to other teaching positions, he also appeared as an organist. He ed. performing and scholarly eds. of works for the organ and harpsichord of 17th- and 18th-century French composers.

WRITINGS: *Documents inédits pour servir à l'histoire de l'orgue* (Paris, 1935); *Les Clicquot, facteurs d'orgues du Roy* (Paris, 1942); *Jean-Sébastien Bach: génie allemand, génie latin?* (Paris, 1947; 2nd ed., 1949); *Jean-Sébastien Bach, le maître de l'orgue* (Paris, 1948; 2nd ed., 1973); *L'Orgue* (Paris, 1948; 5th ed., 1976); *César Franck* (Paris, 1949); *La Musique française* (Paris, 1949; 2nd ed., augmented, 1970); *Le Clavecin* (Paris, 1949; 2nd ed., 1967); *Autour de Coquard, César Franck et Vincent d'Indy* (Paris, 1952); *Nicolas Lebègue* (Paris, 1954); *Jean-Baptiste Boesset, surintendant de la Musique du Roi* (Paris, 1963); *Le livre de l'orgue français, 1589–1789* (Paris, 1969–   ); *Les Grandes Dates de l'histoire de la musique* (with M. Benoit and B. Gagnepain; Paris, 1969; 2nd ed., 1975).

Dufranne, Hector (Robert), Belgian bass-baritone; b. Mons, Oct. 25, 1870; d. Paris, May 3, 1951. He studied in Brussels, making his operatic debut there at the Théâtre Royal de la Monnaie as Valentine in *Faust* (Sept. 9, 1896); then went to Paris as a member of the Opéra-Comique (1899–1909) and the Opéra (from 1909). He also sang at the Manhattan Opera in N.Y. (1908–10), the Chicago Grand Opera (1910–22), and London's Covent Garden (1914); he retired from the stage in 1939. He created roles in several French operas, including Golaud in Debussy's *Pelléas et Mélisande* (1902).

Dugan, Franjo, Croatian composer and organist; b. Krapinica, Sept. 11, 1874; d. Zagreb, Dec. 12, 1948. He studied music with Max Bruch in Berlin, and also attended classes in mathematics. He settled in Zagreb as a church organist; taught at the Zagreb Cons.; publ. manuals on orchestration and musical form; composed many organ pieces.

Dugazon, Louise (Rosalie), famous French mezzo-soprano; b. Berlin, June 18, 1755; d. Paris, Sept. 22, 1821. She was brought up in the atmosphere of the theater; her father, F.J. Lefèbvre, was a French dancer at the Berlin Royal Opera and the Paris Opéra; she herself began her career as a ballet dancer; encouraged mainly by Grétry, who thought highly of her talent, she studied with Favart. She made her debut in Paris in Grétry's opera *Sylvain* (June 19, 1774); in 1776 she married an actor who used the professional name Dugazon; although they were soon separated, she adopted this name for her professional appearances. She sang mostly at the Opéra-Comique; created some 60 new roles; her last public appearance was at the Paris Opéra on Feb. 29, 1804. She was greatly admired by her contemporaries, and her name became a designation of certain types of operatic parts ("jeune Dugazon"; i.e., an ingenue). Her son Gustave (1782–1826) was a composer.
BIBL.: H. and A. Leroux, *La D.* (Paris, 1926).

Duggan, Joseph Francis, Irish pianist and composer; b. Dublin, July 10, 1817; d. London, 1900. He was engaged at the Italian Opera in N.Y.; taught in Philadelphia, Baltimore, and Washington; then lived in London; became a prof. of singing in the Guildhall School of Music. He wrote 2 successful operas, *Pierre* (London, 1853) and *Leonie* (London, 1854); 2 syms.; 6 string quartets; numerous piano pieces; also publ. *The Singing Master's Assistant*.

Duhamel, Antoine, French composer, son of the famous writer Georges Duhamel; b. Valmondois, near Paris, July 30, 1925. He studied with René Leibowitz and from the very 1st began to compose in the dodecaphonic technique; has written a quintet for piano and wind instruments; also publ. a book, *L'Opéra depuis Wagner* (Liège, 1950).

Duiffoprugcar (real name, **Tieffenbrucker**), **Gaspar,** German-born French viol maker; b. Tieffenbruck, Bavaria, 1514; d. Lyons, Dec. 16, 1571. He was long reputed to be the 1st maker of violins; but Vidal, in his *Les Instruments à archet,* states that all the so-called Duiffoprugcar violins are spurious,

having been made by Vuillaume, who in 1827 conceived the idea of making violins after the pattern of a viola da gamba by Duiffoprugcar. Apparently, the latter learned his trade in Italy, the usual spellings of his name showing it to be Italianized rather than gallicized; he settled in Lyons in 1553, and was naturalized in 1558.
BIBL.: H. Coutagne, *G. D. et les luthiers lyonnais du XVIᵉ siècle* (Paris, 1893).

Dukas, Paul, famous French composer and teacher; b. Paris, Oct. 1, 1865; d. there, May 17, 1935. From 1882 to 1888 he was a student at the Paris Cons., studying under G. Mathias (piano), Théodore Dubois (harmony), and E. Guiraud (composition); won 1st prize for counterpoint and fugue in 1886, and the 2nd Prix de Rome with a cantata, *Velléda* (1888); began writing music reviews in 1892; was music critic of the *Revue Hebdomadaire* and *Gazette des Beaux-Arts*; also a contributor to the *Chronique des Arts, Revue Musicale,* etc.; in 1906, was made a Chevalier of the Légion d'honneur; from 1910 to 1913, and again from 1928 to 1935, was prof. of the orch. class at the Cons.; in 1918, was elected Debussy's successor as a member of the *Conseil de l'enseignement supérieur* there; also taught at the École Normale de Musique; assisted in the revising and editing of Rameau's complete works for Durand of Paris. Although he was not a prolific composer, he wrote a masterpiece of modern music in his orch. *L'Apprenti sorcier*; his opera *Ariane et Barbe-Bleue* is one of the finest French operas in the impressionist style. Among his other notable works are the Sym. in C major and the ballet *La Péri*. Shortly before his death he destroyed several MSS of his unfinished compositions.

WORKS: 3 overtures: *King Lear* (1883); *Götz von Berlichingen* (1884); *Polyeucte* (1891); Sym. in C (Paris, Jan. 3, 1897); *L'Apprenti sorcier* (Paris, May 18, 1897; his most famous work); opera, *Ariane et Barbe-Bleue* (Paris, May 10, 1907); ballet, *La Péri* (Paris, April 22, 1912); *Villanelle* for Horn and Piano (1906); Piano: Sonata in E-flat minor; *Variations, Interlude et Finale,* on a theme by Rameau; *Prélude élégiaque*. Together with Saint-Saëns, he completed Guiraud's opera *Frédégonde*.
BIBL.: G. Samazeuilh, *P. D.* (Paris, 1913; 2nd ed., 1936); V. d'Indy, *Emmanuel Chabrier et P. D.* (Paris, 1920); G. Samazeuilh, *P. D., musicien français* (Paris, 1936); D. issue of the *Revue Musicale* (May–June 1936); G. Favre, *P. D.: Sa vie, son œuvre* (Paris, 1948); idem, *L'Œuvre de P. D.* (Paris, 1969); idem, ed., *Correspondance de P. D.* (Paris, 1971).

Duke, John (Woods), American pianist, pedagogue, and composer; b. Cumberland, Md., July 30, 1899; d. Northampton, Mass., Oct. 26, 1984. He studied piano with Harold Randolph and composition with Gustav Strube at the Peabody Cons. in Baltimore (1915–18), then studied piano with Franklin Cannon and composition with Howard Brockway and Bernard Wagenaar in N.Y.; later received instruction in piano from Artur Schnabel in Berlin and in composition from Nadia Boulanger in Paris (1929). He was assistant prof. (1923–38) and prof. (1938–67) of music at Smith College in Northampton, Mass., becoming prof. emeritus at his retirement. He composed over 200 songs, some of which are outstanding contributions to the genre.
WORKS: OPERAS: *Captain Lovelock* (Hudson Falls, N.Y., Aug. 18, 1953) and *The Sire de Maledroit* (Schroon Lake, N.Y., Aug. 15, 1958); operetta, *The Yankee Pedlar* (Schroon Lake, N.Y., Aug. 17, 1962); Concerto for Piano and Strings (1938); *Carnival Overture* (1940); Suite for Solo Viola (1933); *Fantasy* for Violin and Piano (1936); String Trio (1937); 2 string quartets (1941, 1967); Piano Trio (1943); choral works; more than 200 songs, including major cycles to poems of Emily Brontë and Emily Dickinson.

Duke, Vernon. See **Dukelsky, Vladimir.**

Dukelsky, Vladimir (pen name as composer of light music: **Vernon Duke**), versatile Russian-born American composer of both "serious" and popular music; b. Oct. 10, 1903, in the railroad station of the Russian village of Parfianovka (during his mother's trip to Pskov); d. Santa Monica, Calif., Jan. 16, 1969. He was a pupil at the Kiev Cons. of Glière and Dombrovsky; left Russia in 1920 and went to Turkey, going to the U.S. shortly afterward; later lived in Paris and London; settled in N.Y. in 1929 (naturalized, 1936); was a lieutenant in the Coast Guard (1939–44); went back to France (1947–48); but then returned to the U.S. to live in N.Y. and Hollywood. He began to compose at a very early age; was introduced to Diaghilev, who commissioned him to write a ballet, *Zéphyr et Flore,* the production of which put Dukelsky among the successful group of ballet composers. Another important meeting was with Koussevitzky, who championed his music in Paris and in Boston. In the U.S. Dukelsky began writing popular music; many of his songs, such as *April in Paris,* have enjoyed great popularity. At George Gershwin's suggestion, he adopted the name Vernon Duke for popular music works; in 1955 he dropped his full name altogether, and signed both his serious and light compositions Vernon Duke. He publ. an amusing autobiography, *Passport to Paris* (Boston, 1955), and the polemical book *Listen Here! A Critical Essay on Music Depreciation* (N.Y., 1963). See Igor Stravinsky, "A Cure for V.D.," in the unperiodical magazine *Listen* (Sept. 1964), a curiously undignified polemical incursion.

WORKS: STAGE: *Zéphyr et Flore* (Paris, Jan. 31, 1925); *Demoiselle paysanne,* opera (1928); *Le Bal des blanchisseuses,* ballet (Paris, Dec. 19, 1946); *Souvenir de Monte Carlo,* ballet (1949–56). ORCH.: Piano Concerto (1924; not orchestrated); 3 syms.: No. 1 (Paris, June 14, 1928); No. 2 (Boston, April 25, 1930); No. 3 (Brussels Radio, Oct. 10, 1947); *Ballade* for Piano and Small Orch. (1931); *Dédicaces* for Soprano, Piano, and Orch. (Boston, Dec. 16, 1938); Violin Concerto (Boston, March 19, 1943); Cello Concerto (Boston, Jan. 4, 1946); *Ode to the Milky Way* (N.Y., Nov. 18, 1946). CHORAL: *Dushenka,* duet for Women's Voices and Chamber Orch. (1927); *Epitaph* (on the death of Diaghilev) for Soprano Solo, Chorus, and Orch. (Boston, April 15, 1932); *The End of St. Petersburg,* oratorio (N.Y., Jan. 12, 1938); *Moulin-Rouge* for Mixed Chorus (1941). CHAMBER: Trio (Variations) for Flute, Bassoon, and Piano (1930); Etude for Bassoon and Piano (1932); *Capriccio mexicano* for Violin and Piano (1933); *3 Pieces* for Woodwind (1939); Violin Sonata (1949); String Quartet (1956). SONGS: *The Musical Zoo,* 20 songs to Ogden Nash's lyrics (1946); *A Shropshire Lad,* song cycle (1949). PIANO: Sonata (1927); *Surrealist Suite* (1944); *Souvenir de Venise* (1948); *Serenade to San Francisco* (1956). He wrote songs for the musical comedies *The Show Is On, Garrick Gaieties, Walk a Little Faster, Three's a Crowd, Americana, Ziegfeld Follies, Cabin in the Sky,* etc.; added 2 ballets and several songs to *Goldwyn Follies,* an unfinished film score by George Gershwin (1937).

Dulcken, Ferdinand Quentin, German pianist and composer, son of **Luise** (née **David**) **Dulcken** and nephew of **Ferdinand David;** b. London, June 1, 1837; d. Astoria, N.Y., Dec. 10, 1901. He was a pupil of Moscheles and Gade at the Leipzig Cons.; also received encouragement from Mendelssohn. He subsequently taught at the Warsaw Cons., and also at Moscow and St. Petersburg; made many concert tours in Europe as a pianist with Wieniawski, Vieuxtemps, and others. In 1876 he emigrated to America and gave concerts with Reményi; settled in N.Y. as a teacher and composer. He publ. nearly 400 piano pieces of the salon type and also some vocal works.

Dulcken, Luise (née **David**), German pianist, sister of **Ferdinand David** and mother of **Ferdinand Quentin Dulcken;** b. Hamburg, March 29, 1811; d. London, April 12, 1850. She was taught by C.F.G. Schwencke and Wilhelm Grund; played in public (in Germany) when 11 years of age. She married in 1828, and went to London, where she met with brilliant success as a pianist and teacher. Queen Victoria was one of her many pupils.

Dulichius (Dulich, Deulich, Deilich), Philipp (Philippus), esteemed German composer; b. Chemnitz, Dec. 18, 1562; d. Stettin, March 24, 1631. He studied at the Univ. of Leipzig (1579); became cantor at the Stettin ducal Gymnasium (1587)

and at the Marienkirche and director of music at the Pomeranian court; deputized as cantor at Danzig's Marienkirche in 1604–5, and then returned to his positions in Stettin. He retired in 1630. He was highly regarded as a composer of sacred music, and was called the "Pomeranian Lassus." His works, all publ. in Stettin, include *Cantiones compositae* for 5 to 6 Voices (1589), *6 cantiones sacrae concinnatae* for 5 Voices (1593), *Fasciculus novus continens dicta insigniora ex evangeliis . . . desumta* for 5 Voices (1598), *Ego flos campi: Hymenaeus solemnibus nuptiarum . . . Guilhelmi Simonis . . . ac . . . Elisabetham* for 7 Voices (1605), *Dictum psalmi XXX . . . cui usitata melodia cum textu germanico inserta est* (1611), and *Primus tomus centuriae harmonias sacras laudibus sanctissimae triados consecratas continentis* for 6 Voices (1630).

BIBL.: R. Schwartz, "Philippus D.," *Monatsschrifte für Gottesdienst und Kirchliche Kunst* (1896).

Du Locle, Camille Théophile Germain du Commun, French librettist; b. Orange, Vacluse, July 16, 1832; d. Capri, Oct. 9, 1903. He was secretary of the Opéra under Perrin's direction; later, director of the Opéra-Comique. He commissioned Bizet to compose *Carmen;* was also instrumental in the preparation of the libretto for Verdi's opera *Aida.*

Dülon, Friedrich Ludwig, blind German flutist and composer; b. Oranienburg, near Potsdam, Aug. 14, 1769; d. Würzburg, July 7, 1826. He was taught by his father (flute) and Angerstein (theory); in 1783 his concert travels began, and extended all over Europe. In 1793–94 he was chamber musician at the St. Petersburg court (gave his 1st concert in St. Petersburg on March 30, 1793); settled (1823) in Würzburg. He wrote an autobiography: *Dülons des blinden Flötenspielers Leben und Meinungen, von ihm selbst bearbeitet* (Zürich, 2 vols., 1807–8, ed. by Wieland).

Dumesnil, Maurice, French-American pianist; b. Angoulême, Charente, April 20, 1886; d. Highland Park, Mich., Aug. 26, 1974. He studied at the Paris Cons. with Isidor Philipp, graduating in 1905. He received personal coaching from Debussy in playing Debussy's piano works, and was subsequently considered an authority on the subject. He publ. *How to Play and Teach Debussy* (1933) and *Claude Debussy, Master of Dreams* (1940). Apart from his principal occupation as a piano teacher, he was also active as a conductor in Mexico (1916–20); eventually settled in N.Y.

Dumesnil, René (Alphonse Adolphe), French writer; b. Rouen, June 19, 1879; d. Paris, Dec. 24, 1967. He studied literature at the Sorbonne in Paris; was active as a literary critic. Besides his publications dealing with literature, he wrote a number of books on music.

WRITINGS: *Le Rythme musical* (1921; 2nd ed., 1949); *Le Monde des musiciens* (1924); *Le Don Juan de Mozart* (1927; 2nd ed., 1955); *Musiciens romantiques* (1928); *Richard Wagner* (1929); *La Musique contemporaine en France* (1930; 2nd ed., 1949); *Le Livre du disque* (with P. Hemardinquer; 1931); *Histoire illustrée de la musique* (1934); *Portraits de musiciens français* (1938); *La Musique romantique française* (1944); *La Musique en France entre les deux guerres* (Geneva, 1946); *L'Envers de la musique* (Paris, 1949); *Histoire illustrée du théâtre lyrique* (Paris, 1953); received the Grand Prix for musical literature); *Richard Wagner* (Paris, 1954; a much larger work than his 1st Wagner book of 1929); *L'Opéra* (Paris, 1964); *Mozart présent dans ses œuvres lyriques* (Brussels, 1965).

BIBL.: G. van der Kemp, *Notice sur la vie et les travaux de R. D.* (Paris, 1970).

Dumitrescu, Gheorghe, Rumanian composer, brother of **Ion Dumitrescu;** b. Oteșani, Dec. 28, 1914. He studied with Cuclin, Perlea, and Jora at the Bucharest Cons. (1935–41); was active as a violinist, conductor, and composer at the National Theater in Bucharest (1935–46), and was composer-counselor for the Armatei artistic ensemble (1947–57). In 1951 he was appointed a prof. at the Bucharest Cons. His music is marked by a vivacious quality typical of the operetta style.

WORKS: STAGE: *Tarsița și Rosiorul,* operetta (1949; Bucharest, Dec. 12, 1950); *Ion Vodă cel Cumplit*, opera (1955; Bucharest, April 12, 1956); *Decebal*, musical tragedy (1957); *Răscoala*, popular music drama (Bucharest, Nov. 20, 1959); *Fata cu garoafe*, opera (Bucharest, May 6, 1961); *Meşterul Manole*, opera-legend (1970; Bucharest, Oct. 4, 1971); *Geniu pustiu*, opera (1973); *Vlad Tepeş*, musical drama (1974); *Orfeu*, lyric tragedy (1976–77); *Luceafărul*, ballet-opera (concert perf., Bucharest, Dec. 29, 1981); *Marea iubire*, opera (concert perf., Dec. 13, 1982); *Ivan Turbincă*, opera (1983); *Prometheu*, lyric tragedy (1985); *Mihai Viteazul*, music drama (1986). ORATORIOS: *Tudor Vladimirescu* (1950); *Griviţa* (1963); *Zori le de aur* (1964); *Din lumea cor dor, în cea fără dor* (1966); *Pămînt dezrobit* (1968); *Soarele neatîrnării* (1976); *Marea trecere* (1979); *Memento mori* (1984); many cantatas. ORCH.: 4 syms.: No. 1 (1945); No. 2, with Chorus (1962); No. 3 (1965); No. 4 (1970); *Poemul psaltic* (1939); *Poemul rustic* (1939); *Poemul amurgului* (1941); *Poemul vesel* (1941); *Poemul trist* (1941); 4 suites: no. 1, *Pitorească* (1942); No. 2 (1943); No. 3, *A primăverii* (1944); No. 4, *Cîmpeneasca* (1963); *Uvertură eroică* (1943); Cello Concerto (1947). CHAMBER: 2 piano sonatas (1938, 1939); Viola Sonata (1939); Violin Sonata (1939); Piano Quintet (1940); piano pieces; songs.

Dumitrescu, Ion, Rumanian composer, brother of **Gheorghe Dumitrescu**; b. Oteşani, June 2, 1913. He studied conducting with Perlea and composition with Cuclin at the Bucharest Cons. (1934–41); was a composer and conductor at the National Theater in Bucharest (1940–47); taught at the Bucharest Cons. from 1944. He writes in classical forms with undertones of Rumanian folk music.
WORKS: 3 suites for Orch. (1938, 1940, 1944); *2 Pieces* for Orch. (1940); *Poeme* for Cello and Orch. (1940); Sym. No. 1 (1948); *Symphonic Prelude* (1952); Concerto for String Orch. (1956); Suite from the film *Muntele Retezat* (1956); *Sinfonietta* (1955–57); Piano Sonata (1938); *Suite în stil vechi* for Viola and Piano (1939); Piano Sonatina (1940); *2 Pieces* for Piano (1942); String Quartet No. 1 (1949; transcribed for String Orch., 1961); film music; songs.

Du Mont or **Dumont** (real name, **de Thier**), **Henri** or **Henry,** eminent Belgian-born French organist, harpsichordist, and composer; b. Villers-L'Evêque, near Liège, 1610; d. Paris, May 8, 1684. He entered the choir school of Maastricht Cathedral in 1621, and after serving as its organist (1630–32), studied with Léonard de Hodemont in Liège. In 1638 he settled in Paris, where he was organist at St. Paul's Church (1643–84); he also served as organist and harpsichordist to the Duke of Anjou, brother of the King (c.1652–60), and harpsichordist to Queen Marie-Thérèse (1660). In 1663 he was made sous-maître of the royal chapel, sharing his duties with Gobert, and later with Expilly and Robert. After Gobert and Expilly retired in 1669, Du Mont and Robert shared the title of compositeur de musique de la Chapelle Royale (1672–83). Du Mont was also maître de la musique de la Reine from 1673 to 1681. He was a significant composer of sacred music; his *Cinq messes en plain-chant* (Paris, 1669) were widely esteemed. Among his other works, all publ. in Paris, were *Meslanges à 2–5* and Basso Continuo . . . *livre second* (1657; 21 chansons, 19 preludes, 12 motets, 2 Psalm paraphrases, 2 allemandes, and 1 pavan), and *Airs à 4, basso continuo, et quelques-uns à 3 en forme de motets à la fin du livre, sur la paraphrase de quelques pseaumes et cantiques de Messire Anthoine Godeau* (1663; 30 Psalm paraphrases for 4 Voices, 10 airs for 3 Voices, and 3 motets for 2 Voices).
BIBL.: L.-H. Collard, "Quelques documents sur H. D. M.," *Recherches sur la Musique Française Classique*, XV (1975).

Dunayevsky, Isaak, Russian composer; b. Lokhvitza, near Poltava, Jan. 30, 1900; d. Moscow, July 25, 1955. He studied piano as a child; then entered the Kharkov Cons. and studied violin with Joseph Achron. He devoted himself mainly to popular music; some songs from his operettas and film scores have become famous. At one time he experimented with jazz

rhythms. He received many honors from the Soviet government; in 1941 he won the 1st Stalin Prize for his music to the film *The Circus*.
BIBL.: L. Danilevich, *I. D.* (Moscow, 1947); A. Chernov, *I. D.* (Moscow, 1961).

Dunbar, W. Rudolph, black flutist, conductor, teacher, and writer; b. Nabaclis, British Guiana, April 5, 1907; d. London, June 10, 1988. He was clarinetist in the British Guiana Militia Band (1916–19), then went to the U.S., where he studied clarinet, piano, and composition at the Inst. of Musical Art in N.Y. (graduated, 1924). He pursued further training in Paris with Louis Cahuzac, Philippe Gaubert, and Paul Vidal and in Vienna with Felix Weingartner. In 1931 he settled in London, becoming the 1st black musician to conduct a band on the BBC (1934) and the London Phil. (April 26, 1942). While working as a newspaper correspondent with the Allies in France, he appeared as conductor with the Pasdeloup Orch. in Paris (Nov. 18, 1944); in 1945 he conducted the Berlin Phil. He subsequently devoted himself mainly to the cause of racial justice and wrote extensively on international affairs. In 1964 he became the 1st black musician to conduct in the Soviet Union.
BIBL.: "In Retrospect: W. R. D.," *Black Perspective in Music*, IX (1981).

Duncan, William Edmondstoune, English composer and writer on music; b. Sale, Cheshire, April 22, 1866; d. there, June 26, 1920. He studied at the Royal College of Music with Parry and Stanford; then acted as music critic and correspondent for British and American music magazines. He wrote an opera, *Perseus* (1892); a setting of Milton's sonnet *To a Nightingale* for Soprano and Orch. (1895); etc. He also publ. several books on music: *Schubert* (1905; 2nd ed., 1934); *The Story of Minstrelsy* (1907); *A History of Music* (1908); *The Story of the Carol* (1911); *Encyclopedia of Musical Terms* (1914); *Ultra-Modernism in Music* (1917).

Dunham, Henry Morton, American organist, teacher, and composer; b. Brockton, Mass., July 29, 1853; d. Brookline, Mass., May 4, 1929. He studied at the New England Cons. of Music in Boston; was an organist at various churches in and around Boston; taught at the New England Cons. (1876–1929). His works include 3 organ sonatas, marches, preludes, fugues, passacaglias, and other organ music; also numerous arrangements. He publ.: *Organ School* (in 4 books); *A System of Technique for Piano; The Choir Manual; Hymn Music*. His autobiography, *The Life of a Musician, Woven into a Strand of History of the New England Conservatory of Music*, was publ. posth. (N.Y., 1931).

Dunhill, Thomas (Frederick), English composer, teacher, and writer on music; b. London, Feb. 1, 1877; d. Scunthorpe, Lincolnshire, March 13, 1946. He entered the Royal College of Music in London in 1893, and studied with Franklin Taylor (piano) and Stanford (theory); in 1905 was appointed a prof. there; in 1907 he founded the Concerts of British Chamber-Music, which he oversaw until 1916. He publ.: *Chamber Music* (a treatise for students, 1912); *Mozart's String Quartets* (2 vols., 1927); *Sullivan's Comic Operas* (1928); *Sir Edward Elgar* (1938).
WORKS: Operas: *The Enchanted Garden* (London, 1928); *Tantivy Towers* (London, Jan. 16, 1931); *Happy Families* (Guildford, Nov. 1, 1933); ballet, *Gallimaufry* (Hamburg, Dec. 11, 1937); *Phantasy* for String Quartet; Piano Quintet; Quintet for Violin, Cello, Clarinet, Horn, and Piano; Quintet for Horn and String Quartet; Piano Quartet; Viola Sonata; 2 violin sonatas; *The Wind among the Reeds*, song cycle for Tenor and Orch.; violin pieces; compositions for cello.

Duni, Egidio (Romualdo), noted Italian composer; b. Matera, Feb. 9, 1709; d. Paris, June 11, 1775. Nothing definitive is known about his musical training. He may have studied at the Loreto Cons. in Naples. His 1st opera, *Nerone*, was successfully premiered in Rome on May 21, 1735. He visited London in 1737; produced his opera *Demofoonte* at the King's Theatre there on May 24, 1737. Making his way to Holland, he studied at the Univ. of Leiden (1738). He returned to Italy in 1739; was appointed maestro di cappella of S. Nicola di Bari in Naples in 1743, and took up the same post at the court of the Duke of Parma about 1748, where he also served as music teacher to the Duke's daughter. His opéra-comique *Le Peintre amoureux de son modèle* was premiered in his presence in Paris on July 26, 1757. Following its success, he settled in Paris. From 1761 to 1768 he was music director of the Comédie-Italienne, where he brought out such successful works as *Mazet* (1761), *Les Deux Chasseurs et la laitière* (1763), *L'École de la jeunesse* (1765), *La Clochette* (1766), and *Les Moissonneurs* (1768). Duni was a significant contributor to the opéra-comique genre; by fusing Italian and French strains in his work, he was instrumental in developing the comédie mêlée d'ariettes.

BIBL.: A. Pougin, "D. et les commencements de l'opéra-comique," *Le Ménestrel*, XLVI (1879–80).

Dunkley, Ferdinand (Luis), English-American organist and composer; b. London, July 16, 1869; d. Waldwick, N.J., Jan. 5, 1956. At the Royal Academy of Music in London he was a pupil of Parry, Bridge, Martin, Gladstone, Sharpe, and Barnett; then was organist of St. Jude's, London (1885–87) and of St. Aubyn's, London (1888–93). In 1893 he was engaged as music director at St. Agnes' School in Albany, N.Y.; was organist at Temple Sinai, New Orleans (1924–34); in 1934 was appointed a prof. at Loyola Univ., New Orleans. He made his last public appearance on his 82nd birthday, when he gave an organ recital.

WORKS: *The Wreck of the Hesperus*, ballade for Soli, Chorus, and Orch.; choral works: *Praise the Lord* (1919); *Green Branches* (1919); *God is my strong salvation* (1921); *Street Cries* (1924); *Blessed is the man* (1937); etc.

Dunlop, Isobel, Scottish violinist and composer; b. Edinburgh, March 4, 1901; d. there, May 12, 1975. She studied with Tovey and Dyson; gave concerts presenting her own works.

Dunn, James Philip, American organist, teacher, and composer; b. N.Y., Jan. 10, 1884; d. Jersey City, N.J., July 24, 1936. He studied at the College of the City of N.Y. (B.A., 1903); then at Columbia Univ. with MacDowell, and subsequently with Cornelius Rybner. He was then active as a teacher and church organist in N.Y. and elsewhere. As a composer, he attracted attention by his symphonic poem descriptive of Lindbergh's transatlantic flight, *We* (N.Y., Aug. 27, 1927). He also wrote an *Overture on Negro Themes* (N.Y., July 22, 1922), some chamber music, and organ pieces.

BIBL.: J. Howard, *J.P. D.* (N.Y., 1925).

Dunn, John, English violinist and composer; b. Hull, Feb. 16, 1866; d. Harrogate, Dec. 18, 1940. He received his 1st instruction from his brother, who was conductor of the Hull Theatre Orch.; then was a pupil at the Leipzig Cons. of Schradieck (violin) and Jadassohn (theory); toured England and Germany. He wrote a Violin Concerto and a spate of short violin pieces; publ. *Manual of Violin Playing* (London, 1898).

Dunn, John Petri, Scottish pianist and writer on music; b. Edinburgh, Oct. 26, 1878; d. there, Feb. 4, 1931. He studied in London with Matthay; toured Europe as accompanist of Jan Kubelik in 1904; later was a prof. at the Stuttgart and Kiel Conservatories; in 1914, returned to Great Britain; was a prof. of music at the Univ. of Edinburgh from 1920 until his death.

WRITINGS: *Ornamentation in the Works of Chopin* (London, 1921); *A Student's Guide for Orchestration* (London, 1928); *The Basis of Pianoforte Playing* (London, 1933).

Dunn, Mignon, American mezzo-soprano; b. Memphis, Tenn., June 17, 1931. She attended Southwestern Univ. in Memphis and the Univ. of Lausanne; at 17 she was awarded a Metropolitan Opera scholarship and pursued vocal training in N.Y. with Karin Branzell and Beverley Johnson. In 1955 she made her operatic debut as Carmen in New Orleans, and

then appeared as Maddalena in Chicago later that year; on March 28, 1956, she made her N.Y. City Opera debut as the 4th Lady in Walton's *Troilus and Cressida*, remaining on its roster until 1957; sang there again in 1972 and 1975. On Oct. 29, 1958, she made her Metropolitan Opera debut in N.Y. as the Nurse in *Boris Godunov*; in subsequent seasons she appeared in more than 50 roles there, including Amneris, Azucena, Fricka, Herodias, Marina, and Ortrud. She also made guest appearances in San Francisco, London, Paris, Berlin, Hamburg, Milan, and Vienna. In 1972 she married the Austrian conductor Kurt Klippstatter.

Dunn, Thomas (Burt), American conductor; b. Aberdeen, S.Dak., Dec. 21, 1925. He studied at the Peabody Cons. of Music, Johns Hopkins and Harvard Univs., and the Amsterdam Cons.; his teachers included Virgil Fox and E. Power Biggs (organ) and Robert Shaw (choral conducting) in the U.S., and Gustav Leonhardt (harpsichord) and Anton van der Horst (conducting) in the Netherlands. He began his career as a church music director in Baltimore and Philadelphia; in 1959 he was appointed director of the Cantata Singers in N.Y.; also organized the Festival Orch. there, and led it from 1959 until 1969. From 1967 to 1986 he was music director of the Handel and Haydn Soc. of Boston.

Dunstable or **Dunstaple, John,** great English composer; b. c.1390; d. London, Dec. 24, 1453. Almost nothing is known about his life with any certainty. He may have been the John Dunstaple who was in the service of the Duke of Bedford; if he was the same man, he may have accompanied his patron to France. He appears to have been well versed in astronomy and mathematics. The J. Dunstaple buried in the church of St. Stephen, Walbrook (destroyed in the Great Fire of 1666), was undoubtedly the composer. The Old Hall Manuscript and other MSS reveal the existence of a highly developed art in England in the early 15th century, antedating the full flowering of the Burgundian school of Dufay, Binchois, and other masters. Dunstable's style appears to be a direct outgrowth of the English school. He was the most important figure in English music in his time. His works were widely known on the Continent as well as in his homeland. Most of his known compositions are preserved in manuscripts on the Continent, although discoveries have recently been made in England. Some works formerly attributed to him are now known to be by Power, Benet, Binchois, and others. Other works remain doubtful. The styles of Dunstable and Power are so comparable that it has not always been possible to separate their works. Undoubtedly, some of Dunstable's works are in anonymous collections and await verification. M. Bukofzer ed. *John Dunstable: Complete Works* in Musica Britannica, VIII (London, 1953; 2nd ed., rev., 1970 by M. and I. Bent and B. Trowell); the rev. ed. includes 73 works, several of which are now considered doubtful.

BIBL.: C. Stainer, "D. and the Various Settings of *O Rosa Bella*," *Sammelbände der Internationalen Musik-Gesellschaft*, II (1900–1901); C. van den Borren, "The Genius of D.," *Proceedings of the Musical Association*, XLVII (1920–21); M. Bukofzer, "Über Leben und Werke von J. D.," *Acta Musicologica*, VIII (1936); idem, "J. D. and the Music of His Time," *Proceedings of the Musical Association*, LXV (1938–39); idem, "J. D.: A Quincentenary Report," *Musical Quarterly* (Jan. 1954); R. Greene, "J. D.: A Quincentenary Supplement," ibid. (July 1954); E. Kovarik, "A Newly Discovered D. Fragment," *Journal of the American Musicological Society*, XXI (1968); M. and I. Bent, "Dufay, D., Plummer—A New Source," ibid., XXII (1969); M. Bent, *Dunstaple* (London, 1981); A. Wathey, "D. in France," *Music & Letters* (Jan. 1986).

Duparc (actually, **Fouques-Duparc**), **(Marie-Eugène) Henri,** notable French composer of songs; b. Paris, Jan. 21, 1848; d. Mont-de-Marsan, Feb. 12, 1933. He studied with César Franck, who regarded him as his most talented pupil. Duparc suffered from a nervous affliction, which forced him to abandon his composition and seek rest in Switzerland. He destroyed the MS of his Cello Sonata, and several symphonic suites; of his instrumental works only a few MSS have survived, including the symphonic poems *Aux étoiles* (perf. in Paris, April 11, 1874) and *Lénore* (1875) and a suite of 6 piano pieces, *Feuilles volantes*. His songs, to words by Baudelaire and other French poets, are distinguished by exquisitely phrased melodies arranged in fluid modal harmonies; among the best are: *Invitation au voyage, Extase, Soupir, Sérénade, Chanson triste, La Vague et la cloche, Phidilé, Elégie, Testament, Lamento,* and *La Vie antérieure.*

BIBL.: G. Ferchault, *H. D.* (Paris, 1944); S. Northcote, *The Songs of H. D.* (London, 1949); N. Van Der Elst, *H. D.: L'Homme et son œuvre* (diss., Univ. of Paris; Lille, 1972; contains a complete catalog of works, correspondence, and bibliography).

Dupin, Paul, French composer; b. Roubaix, Aug. 14, 1865; d. Paris, March 6, 1949. He worked in a factory; then was a menial clerk, but turned to music against all odds; took some lessons with Emile Durand, and then proceeded to compose with fanatic compulsion; somehow he managed to have more than 200 works actually publ. Of these, the most original are about 500 canons for 3–12 voices, and 40 string quartets titled *Poèmes*; he wrote much other chamber music; some pretty piano pieces with fanciful titles, such as *Esquisse fuguées* and *Dentelles*; he even wrote a grand opera, *Marcelle,* which he later hopefully renamed *Lyszelle* for exotic effect. He was much admired in Paris for his determination to succeed, but his works were rarely performed.

BIBL.: R. Rolland, "P. D.," *Bulletin Français de la S.I.M.* (Dec. 15, 1908); C. Koechlin, "D.," *Revue Musicale* (Jan. 1923); P. Ladmirault, *Les Chœurs en canon de P. D.: Notice biographique et analytique* (Paris, 1925).

Dupont, Gabriel, French composer; b. Caen, March 1, 1878; d. Vésinet, Aug. 2, 1914. He was a pupil of his father, the organist at the Cathedral; later, of Gédalge; then of Massenet and Widor at the Paris Cons.; won the 2nd Prix de Rome in 1901. In a contest conducted in 1903 by Sonzogno, the publishing house in Milan, his opera *La Cabrera* was selected, along with 2 others, to be performed and judged by the public (237 works were submitted); it was produced at Milan on May 17, 1904, with great success, thereby winning for Dupont the prize of 50,000 lire. He wrote other operas: *La Glu* (Nice, Jan. 24, 1910); *La Farce du cuvier* (Brussels, March 21, 1912); *Antar* (1913; Paris Opéra, March 14, 1921); also *Les Heures dolentes* for Orch., 4 pieces from a suite of 14 compositions for Piano (1903–5); *Poèmes d'automne* for Piano; symphonic poems: *Hymne à Aphrodite* and *Le Chant de la destinée; Poème* for Piano Quintet; many other piano pieces; songs.

BIBL.: M. Léna, "G. D.," *Souvenirs,*" and H. Collet, "Antar," *Le Ménestrel* (March 18, 1921); E. Vuillermoz, "Antar de G. D. à l'Opéra," *Revue Musicale* (April 1921); M. Dumesnil, "G. D., Musician of Normandy," *Musical Quarterly* (Oct. 1944).

Dupont, Pierre, French songwriter; b. Rochetaillée, near Lyons, April 23, 1821; d. St. Etienne, July 25, 1870. The son of a laborer, and himself uneducated, he attracted attention by his political and rustic ditties. He wrote the words, and then sang the airs to Reyer, who put them into shape. His political songs (*Le Pain, Le Chant des ouvriers,* etc.) created such disturbances that he was banished in 1851, but in 1852 he was pardoned. His song *Les Bœufs* enjoyed some popularity.

Duport, Jean-Louis, famous French cellist, brother of **Jean-Pierre Duport;** b. Paris, Oct. 4, 1749; d. there, Sept. 7, 1819. He made his public debut at a Concert Spirituel (1768); joined his brother in Berlin at the outbreak of the Revolution; returning in 1806, he became musician to Charles IV, the ex-king of Spain, at Marseilles; in 1812, returned to Paris; taught at the Paris Cons. (1813–15). He wrote 6 cello concertos, sonatas, duos, airs variées, 9 nocturnes (for harp and cello), etc. His *Essai sur le doigté du violoncelle et la conduite de l'archet, avec une suite d'exercices* was for decades a standard textbook, and practically laid the foundations of modern cello virtuosity.

Duport, Jean-Pierre, eminent French cellist, brother of **Jean-Louis Duport;** b. Paris, Nov. 27, 1741; d. Berlin, Dec. 31, 1818. He studied with Berteau; made his debut at a Concert Spirituel in Paris (1761), where he subsequently gave concerts regularly; was also in the service of the Prince of Conti. In 1773 he settled in Berlin as 1st cellist in the orch. of the Royal Chapel, continuing to play there until 1811; was also director of the court concerts (1787–1806). In addition to his brother, he taught Prince Friedrich Wilhelm II. He composed a number of works for his instrument, including a concerto and many sonatas. Beethoven composed his 2 cello sonatas, op. 5, for Duport; Beethoven played these works with him during his visit to the Berlin court in 1796.

Duprato, Jules-Laurent, French composer; b. Nimes, Aug. 20, 1827; d. Paris, May 20, 1892. He studied with Leborne at the Paris Cons.; in 1848, won the Prix de Rome. He composed operettas, cantatas, songs, etc.; also recitatives for Hérold's *L'Illusion* and Balfe's *The Bohemian Girl.*

BIBL.: F. Clauzel, *J. D.* (1896).

DuPré, Jacqueline, renowned English cellist; b. Oxford, Jan. 26, 1945; d. London, Oct. 19, 1987. She entered the London Cello School at the age of 5; while still a child, she began studies with her principal mentor, William Pleeth, making her 1st public appearance on British television when she was 12. She was awarded a gold medal upon graduation from the Guildhall School of Music in London (1960); also studied with Casals in Zermatt, Switzerland, with Tortelier at Dartington Hall and in Paris, and with Rostropovich in Moscow. After winning the Queen's Prize (1960), she made her formal debut in a recital at London's Wigmore Hall on March 1, 1961. She made her North American debut at N.Y.'s Carnegie Hall as soloist in Elgar's Cello Concerto with Dorati and the BBC Sym. Orch. on May 14, 1965, an appearance that electrified the audience and elicited rapturous critical reviews. On June 15, 1967, she married in Jerusalem the pianist and conductor **Daniel Barenboim,** with whom she subsequently performed. In 1973 she was diagnosed as having multiple sclerosis, at which time she abandoned her career. She later gave master classes as her health permitted. In 1976 she was made an Officer of the Order of the British Empire, and in 1979 was awarded an honorary doctorate in music by the Univ. of London. The Jacqueline DuPré Research Fund was founded to assist in the fight against multiple sclerosis. Her life was the subject of a Broadway play, *Duet for One* (1981).

BIBL.: W. Wordsworth, ed., *J. d.P.: Impressions* (N.Y., 1983; 2nd ed., 1989); C. Easton, *J. d.P.: A Biography* (London, 1989).

Dupré, Marcel, celebrated French organist, pedagogue, and composer; b. Rouen, May 3, 1886; d. Meudon, near Paris, May 30, 1971. He was a pupil of his father, Albert Dupré, also an organist; studied organ with Guilmant in 1898; he then entered the Paris Cons. (1902–14) and studied with Vierne, Diémer, and Widor, winning 1st prizes for organ (1907) and for fugue (1909); in 1914 he won the Grand Prix de Rome for the cantata *Psyché.* He was interim organist at Notre-Dame in 1916; in 1920 he gave at the Paris Cons. a cycle of 10 recitals of Bach's complete organ works, playing from memory; that same year he became assistant organist under Widor at St. Sulpice. On Nov. 18, 1921, he made his U.S. debut in N.Y., followed by a transcontinental tour, performing 94 recitals in 85 American cities; a 2nd U.S. tour in 1923 included 110 concerts; he made his 10th tour of the U.S. in 1948. In 1939 he gave 40 concerts in Australia on his world tour. He had, meanwhile, been appointed prof. of organ at the Paris Cons. in 1926; in 1934 he succeeded Widor as organist at St. Sulpice; continued there until his death at the age of 85; became general director of the American Cons. in Fontainebleau in 1947 and was appointed director of the Paris Cons., in succession to Delvincourt, in 1954 (until 1956). Dupré wrote his 1st work, the oratorio *La Vision de Jacob,* at the age of 14; it was performed on his 15th birthday at his father's house in Rouen, in a domestic production assisted by a local choral society. Most of his organ works are products of original improvisations. Thus *Symphonie-Passion,* 1st improvised at the Wanamaker organ in Philadelphia (Dec. 8, 1921), was written down much later

and performed in its final version at Westminster Cathedral in London (Oct. 9, 1924). Similarly, *Le Chemin de la Croix* was improvised in Brussels (Feb. 13, 1931) and performed in a definitive version in Paris the following year (March 18, 1932). Among precomposed works there are syms. for Organ: No. 1 (Glasgow, Jan. 3, 1929) and No. 2 (1946); Concerto for Organ and Orch. (Groningen, Netherlands, April 27, 1938, composer soloist); *Psalm XVIII* (1949); 76 chorales and several a cappella choruses; also numerous "verset-préludes." He is the author of *Traité d'improvisation à l'orgue* (1925), *Méthode d'orgue* (Paris, 1927), and *Manuel d'accompagnement du plain-chant gregorien* (Paris, 1937); R. Kneeream ed. and tr. his autobiography as *Recollections* (Melville, N.Y., 1975).
BIBL.: R. Delestre, *L'Œuvre de M. D.* (Paris, 1952); M. Murray, *M. D.: The Work of a Master* (Boston, 1985).

Duprez, Gilbert(-Louis), French tenor and pedagogue; b. Paris, Dec. 6, 1806; d. there, Sept. 23, 1896. He began his training in Paris at Choron's Inst. de Musique Classique et Religieuse, then continued his studies with Rogat at the Cons. He made his operatic debut as Count Almaviva at Paris's Odéon (1825); dissatisfied with his performance, he pursued further vocal training in Italy, where he became notably successful in Italian roles (1829–35); Donizetti chose him to create the role of Edgardo in *Lucia di Lammermoor* (Naples, 1835). Returning to France, he was a principal member of the Paris Opéra (1837–49), where he created a number of roles, including Berlioz's Benvenuto Cellini (1838), Donizetti's Polyeucte in *Les Martyrs* (1840), and Fernando in *La Favorite* (1840); retired from the stage in 1855. He taught at the Paris Cons. (1842–50) and founded his own vocal school (1853). His most famous pupil was Emma Albani. He wrote several operas and other works. He also publ. the methods *L'Art du chant* (Paris, 1845) and *La Mélodie, études complémentaires vocales et dramatiques de l'Art du chant* (Paris, 1846); he also publ. *Souvenirs d'un chanteur* (Paris, 1880) and *Récréations de mon grand âge* (Paris, 1888). His wife, **Alexandrine** (née **Duperron**) (b. Nantes, 1808; d. Brussels, Feb. 27, 1872), and his daughter, **Caroline** (b. Florence, April 10, 1832; d. Pau, April 17, 1875), were also singers.
BIBL.: A. Elwart, *D., Sa vie artistique* (Paris, 1838).

Dupuis, Albert, outstanding Belgian composer; b. Verviers, March 1, 1877; d. Brussels, Sept. 19, 1967. He studied piano, violin, and flute at the Music Academy in Verviers; later entered the classes of Vincent d'Indy at the newly created Schola Cantorum in Paris (1897); returned to Belgium in 1899 and later won the Belgian Prix de Rome with his cantata *La Chanson d'Halewyn* (Brussels, Nov. 25, 1903); arranged and perf. as a 3-act opera, Antwerp, Feb. 14, 1914). He became director of the Verviers Cons. in 1907, retiring in 1947. His other operas include *Bilitis* (Verviers, 1899); *Jean Michel* (1901–2; Brussels, Jan. 4, 1903); *Martille* (1904; Brussels, March 3, 1905); *Fidélaine* (Liège, March 10, 1910); *Le Château de la Grande Bretèche* (Nice, March 28, 1913); *La Passion* (Monte Carlo, April 2, 1916; over 150 perfs. in Europe); *La Captivité de Babylone* (biblical drama); *La Barrière* (Verviers, 1920); *La Délivrance* (Verviers, Dec. 19, 1918); *Le Sacrifice* (Antwerp, 1921); *La Victoire* (Brussels, March 28, 1923); *Ce n'était qu'un rêve* (Antwerp, 1935); *Hassan,* oriental fairy tale (Brussels, 1938); *Un Drame sous Philippe II* (Brussels, Jan. 18, 1938); oratorios: *Les Cloches nuptiales* (1899); *Œdipe à Colone; Psalm 118;* ballets: *Rêve d'enfant,* after Schumann (1951); *Au temps jadis* (1952); *Evocations d'Espagne* (1954); cantatas: *Vers le progrès, Pour la paix, La Gileppe,* and a *Cantata jubilaire* for Belgian independence; 2 syms. (1904, 1922–23); *Fantaisie rhapsodique* for Violin and Orch. (1906); *Poème oriental* for Cello and Orch. (1924); *Hermann et Dorothée,* overture; Cello Concerto (1926); *Epitaphe* for Orch. (1929); *Aria* for Viola and Orch. (1933); Piano Concerto (1940); *Caprice rhapsodique* for Orch. (1941); Violin Concerto (1944); *Caprice* for Flute and Orch.; *Solo de concours* for Horn and Orch. and for Trombone and Orch.; *Valse joyeuse* for Orch.; *La Navarraise* for Orch.; 2 concertinos for Timpani and Orch.; Violin Sonata (1904); String

Quartet; 2 piano trios; Piano Quartet; *Scherzo* for Solo Horn; Variations for Solo Horn; *5 pièces paradoxales* for Piano; many other works for piano; choruses; songs; etc.
BIBL.: J. Dor, *A. D.* (Liège, 1935); R. Michel, *Un grand musicien belge méconnu: A. D.* (Verviers, 1967).

Dupuis, Sylvain, Belgian conductor and composer; b. Liège, Oct. 9, 1856; d. Bruges, Sept. 28, 1931. He was a pupil at the Liège Cons., winning the Prix de Rome in 1881; became a teacher of counterpoint there; was conductor of the singing society La Légia; established in 1888 the Nouveaux Concerts Symphoniques; was appointed 1st conductor at the Théâtre Royal de la Monnaie in Brussels in 1900, and conductor of the Concerts Populaires; from 1911 until 1926, was director of the Cons. at Liège.
WORKS: 2 operas: *Coûr d'Oignon* and *Moïna;* 3 cantatas: *La Cloche de Roland, Camoëns,* and *Le Chant de la Création;* a symphonic poem, *Macbeth;* Concertino for Oboe and Orch.; 2 suites for Orch.; pieces for violin; choruses.

Durand, Emile, French composer and teacher; b. St.-Brieuc, Feb. 16, 1830; d. Neuilly, May 6, 1903. In 1850, while still a student at the Paris Cons., he was appointed teacher of an elementary singing class; in 1871 he became prof. of harmony there. He publ. *Traité d'harmonie* and *Traité de composition musicale;* also wrote several light operas.

Durand, Marie-Auguste, French organist and music publisher; b. Paris, July 18, 1830; d. there, May 31, 1909. He studied organ with Benoist; in 1849, was organist at St. Ambroise; then at Ste.-Geneviève, St.-Roch, and (1862–74) St. Vincent de Paul. He also occupied himself with music criticism and composition (his Chaconne and *Valse* for piano were especially popular). In 1870 he entered into partnership with Schönewerk (acquiring Flaxland's music publishing business), the firm then being known as Durand & Schönewerk; when his son, **Jacques** (b. Paris, Feb. 22, 1865; d. Bel-Ebat, Aug. 22, 1928), replaced Schönewerk in 1891, the title became Durand & Fils. The house is now known as Durand & Cie.; it has made a specialty of publishing works of the outstanding French composers, and also brought out French eds. of Wagner, as well as several eds. of early masters, including a complete critical ed. of Rameau. Jacques Durand publ. the following works: *Cours professionel à l'usage des employés du commerce de musique* (2 vols., 1923); *Quelques souvenirs d'un éditeur de musique* (2 vols., 1924–25); *Lettres de Cl. Debussy à son éditeur* (Paris, 1927).

Durante, Francesco, celebrated Italian composer and pedagogue; b. Frattamaggiore, March 31, 1684; d. Naples, Sept. 30, 1755. His uncle, Don Angelo Durante, was a priest and composer. Francesco most likely received his early training at home from his uncle; then continued his studies with him at the Conservatorio S. Onofrio a Capuana in Naples (1702–5) and with the violinist Gaetano Francone there; he may have subsequently studied with Pasquini and Pitoni in Rome. He taught at the Conservatorio S. Onofrio a Capuana (1710–11) and was maestro of the Congregatione and Accademia di Santa Cecilia in Rome (1718). Little else is known about him until he was appointed primo maestro of the Conservatorio Poveri di Gesù Cristo in Naples in 1728, which position he held until 1739. In 1742 he became primo maestro there of the Conservatorio S. Maria di Loreto, and also of the Conservatorio S. Onofrio a Capuana in 1745; he retained both positions until his death. With his fellow Neapolitans Porpora, Leo, Feo, and Vinci, Durante ranks among the most important composers of his era. Although the former were renowned as composers of opera, Durante was a particularly significant composer of sacred music, his output being notable for its resourcefulness of styles and practices as well as for originality. He was greatly renowned as a teacher; among his pupils were Pergolesi, Abos, Anfossi, Traetta, Sacchini, Piccini, and Paisiello.
WORKS: SACRED DRAMAS: *Prodigii della divina misericordia verso i devoti del gloriosa S. Antonio di Padova* (scherzo drammatico; Naples, June 13, 1705; music not extant); *La cerva*

assetata ovvero L'anima nelle fiamme della gloria (Naples, Feb. 18, 1719; not extant); *Abigaile* (Rome, Nov. 22, 1736; music not extant); *S. Antonio di Padova* (Venice, 1754); 5 choruses for *Flavio Valente*, a tragedy by Duke Annibale Marchese (publ. in *Tragedie cristiane*, Naples, 1729); other sacred music: 19 masses; 3 Mass cycles, including *Missa in Palestrina* (1739; ed. by V. Dufaut, Paris, 1921); 3 Requiem masses, including one in G minor (1738; ed. in *Periodico di musica sacra*, Rome, 1880); Mass movements; 30 Psalms; 14 motets, including *Nascere, nascere dive puellule* (ed. by R. Ewerhart in *Cantico sacro geistliche Solokantaten*, II, Cologne, 1954); antiphons; hymns; sequences; cantatas; arias; duets; terzettos; *XII duetti* (madrigali; canzoni) *da camera*, based on recitatives from solo cantatas of A. Scarlatti (ed. by M. Ivanoff-Boretsky, Moscow, 1931); etc. **INSTRUMENTAL:** 8 *concerti per quartetto* (Nos. 1, 2, and 4 ed. by E. Doflein, Mainz, 1966); Harpsichord Concerto (c.1750; ed. by F. Degrada, Milan, 1968); 6 *sonate per cembalo divisi in studii e divertimenti* (Naples, c.1732; ed. by B. Paumgartner, Kassel, 1949); 7 harpsichord sonatas; other keyboard works; pedagogical pieces.

BIBL.: V. de Rubertis, *Dos Bajetes de F. D., erroneamente interpretados por Fétis y de Nardis* (Buenos Aires, 1947); A. Lualdi, "Musiche sconosciute del fondatore della scuola musicale di Napoli: F. D.," *Rivista Musicale Italiana*, LI (1949); U. Prota-Giurleo, "F. D.," *Riscatto: Giornale Provinciale di Frattamaggiore*, III/5 (1952) and IV/1–4 (1953); J. Auerbach, *Die Messen des F. D.* (diss., Univ. of Munich, 1954); A. Lualdi, "F. D. da Frattamaggiore," *Tutti vivi* (Milan, 1955); F. Degrada, "Appunti critici sui concerti di F. D.," *Chigiana*, XXIV (1967); G. Brungardt, *Some Selected Motets of F. D.* (diss., Univ. of Illinois, 1967).

Durante, Jimmy (James Francis), American comedian, singer, and honky-tonk pianist; b. N.Y., Feb. 10, 1893; d. Santa Monica, Calif., Jan. 29, 1980. He began playing piano in N.Y. bars when he was 17; then was active as a vaudeville performer, teaming up with singer Eddie Jackson and actor Lou Clayton to perform at their own Club Durant and on Broadway. Durante became highly successful on the radio and appeared in many films; also had his own television show (1950–56). Dubbed the "great Schnozzola" in honor of his protruding proboscis, he was one of the most beloved entertainers of his day. His 62-year career was ended by a stroke.

BIBL.: G. Fowler, *Schnozzola* (N.Y., 1951).

Durey, Louis (Edmond), French composer; b. Paris, May 27, 1888; d. St. Tropez, July 3, 1979. He studied with Léon Saint-Requier (1910–14); was a member of Les Six. Durey wrote music fashionable during a wave of anti-Romanticism, proclaiming the need of constructive simplicity in modern dress, with abundant use of titillating discords. Although he was the oldest of Les Six, he wrote the least music. Durey's esthetic code was radically altered in 1936 when he joined the French Communist Party. During the German occupation of France, he was active in the Resistance, for which he wrote anti-Fascist songs. In 1948 he was elected vice-president of the Assoc. Française des Musiciens Progressives; in 1950 he became the music critic of the Paris Communist newspaper *L'Humanité*. In 1961 he received the Grand Prix de la Musique Française.

WORKS: *Le Navire* for Voice and Orch. (1916); *Judith*, monodrama (1918); *Le Bestiaire* for Voice and 12 Instruments (1919); *Le Printemps au fond de la mer* for Voice and Wind Instruments (1920); *L'Occasion*, lyric drama after Mérimée (1928); *Fantaisie concertante* for Cello and Orch. (1947); 3 *poèmes de Paul Eluard* for Voice and Orch. (1952); *Trio-Serenade* for Violin, Viola, and Cello (1955); overture, *Ile-de-France* (1955); Concertino for Piano, 16 Wind Instruments, Double Bass, and Timpani (1956); 10 *chœurs de métiers* for Chorus, 2 Flutes, Clarinet, Violin, Celesta, and Piano (1957); 3 *Polyphonies vocales et intrumentales* for Vocal Quartet and 8 Instruments (1963); *Mouvement symphonique* (1964); *Les Soirées de Valfère* for Wind Instruments (1964); *Cantate de la rose et de l'amour* for Soprano and Strings (1965); Sinfonietta (1966);

4 *octophonies* for 8 String Instruments (1966); *Dilection* for Strings (1969); *Obsession* for Wind Instruments, Harp, Double Bass, and Percussion (1970); political cantatas, *Paix aux hommes par millions* (1949); *La Longue Marche* (1949); 3 string quartets; numerous solo songs; piano pieces.

BIBL.: F. Robert, *L. D., L'Aîné des Six* (Paris, 1968).

Durham, Eddie, black American jazz trombonist, guitarist, composer, and arranger; b. San Marcos, Texas, Aug. 19, 1906; d. N.Y., March 6, 1987. He received initial training from his brother, later attending the Chicago Cons. He performed with his siblings in the Durham Brothers Orch., and in the orchs. of Bennie Moten (1929–33), Jimmie Lunceford (1935–37), and Count Basie (from 1937); also performed with the Harlem Blues and Jazz Band (from 1977). Throughout his career he composed and arranged for various leading jazz musicians; with Buster Smith, he wrote the standard *One O'Clock Jump* for Basie. He was also a pioneering figure in the development of the electric guitar.

Durkó, Zsolt, Hungarian composer; b. Szeged, April 10, 1934. He studied composition at the Academy of Music at Budapest with Ferenc Farkas (1955–60) and at the Accademia di Santa Cecilia in Rome with Petrassi (1961–63). Many of his works have scientific connotations, at least in their titles; but some are rooted in Hungarian melorhythmic patterns.

WORKS: **OPERA:** *Moses* (1972–77; Budapest, May 15, 1977). **ORCH.:** *Episodi sul tema B-A-C-H* (1962–63); *Organismi* for Violin and Orch. (1964); *Una rapsodia ungherese* for 2 Clarinets and Orch. (1964–65); *Fioriture* (1966–67); *Altamira* (1967–68); *Cantilene* for Piano and Orch. (1968); *Refrains* for Violin and Chamber Orch. (1978); *Quattro dialoghi* for 2 Percussion Soloists and Orch. (1979); Piano Concerto (1980). **CHAMBER:** 11 *pezzi per quartetto d'archi* (1962); *Improvvisazioni* for Wind Quintet (1965); 2 string quartets (1966, 1969); *Symbols* for Horn and Piano (1968–69); *Quartetto d'ottoni* for 2 Trumpets, Trombone, and Tuba or Trombone (1970); *Iconography* No. 1 for 2 Cellos or Bass Viols, and Piano or Harpsichord (1970); *Serenata* for 4 Harps (1973); *Movements* for Tuba and Piano (1980); Octet for Winds (London, Oct. 11, 1988). **VOCAL:** *Dartmouth Concerto* for Voice and Chamber Orch. (1966–67); Cantata No. 1 for Baritone, Choir, and Orch. (1971); Cantata No. 2 for Choir and Orch. (1972); *Burial Prayer*, oratorio for Tenor, Baritone, Choir, and Orch. (1967–72); *Széchenyi Oratorio* (1981–82); *Ilmarinen* for Choir (Zagreb, Feb. 20, 1989); also various works for chamber ensemble; organ and piano pieces.

Durlet, Emmanuel, Belgian pianist and composer; b. Antwerp, Oct. 11, 1893; d. there, Feb. 7, 1977. He studied piano with Frans Lenaerts; took a course in Vienna with Leopold Godowsky (1912–14). Returning to Belgium, he developed a brilliant career as a pianist; gave a cycle of all 32 sonatas by Beethoven. He held the post of prof. of advanced piano playing at the Cons. of Antwerp (1920–59). Among his works are a Piano Concerto, a Violin Concerto, a Violin Sonata, and numerous teaching pieces for piano in a Romantic vein, as well as songs.

Durme, Jef van. See **Van Durme, Jef.**

Dürr, Alfred, distinguished German musicologist and editor; b. Charlottenburg, March 3, 1918. He studied musicology at the Univ. of Göttingen, receiving his Ph.D. there in 1950 with the dissertation *Studien über die frühen Kantaten Johann Sebastian Bachs* (publ. in Leipzig, 1951). In 1951 he joined the Johann-Sebastian-Bach-Inst. in Göttingen as a research assistant; from 1962 to 1981 he was its director. From 1953 he ed. (with W. Neumann) the *Bach-Jahrbuch*; also ed. works for the Bach *Neue Ausgabe sämtlicher Werke*. His books include *Johann Sebastian Bach, Weihnachtsoratorium* (Munich, 1967) and *Die Kantaten von Johann Sebastian Bach* (Kassel and Munich, 1971; 5th ed., rev., 1985).

BIBL.: W. Rehm, ed., *Bachiana et alia musicologica: Festschrift A. D. zum 65. Geburtstag am 3. März 1983* (Kassel and N.Y., 1983).

Dürrner, Ruprecht Johannes Julius, German conductor and composer; b. Ansbach, Bavaria, July 15, 1810; d. Edinburgh, June 10, 1859. He was a pupil of Friedrich Schneider at Dessau; from 1831 to 1842, was a cantor at Ansbach, then studied under Mendelssohn and Hauptmann at Leipzig, and settled in Edinburgh as a conductor and vocal teacher. His choruses and quartets for male voices won great favor.

Duruflé, Maurice, noted French organist, teacher, and composer; b. Louviers, Eure, Jan. 11, 1902; d. Paris, June 16, 1986. He studied piano and organ with local teachers; in 1919 went to Paris, where he studied organ with Tournemire, Guilmant, and Louis Vierne. In 1920 he enrolled at the Paris Cons., where he took courses in organ with Gigout (1st prize, 1922), harmony with Jean Gallon (1st prize, 1924), fugue with Caussade (1st prize, 1924), and composition with Paul Dukas (1928). In 1930 he was appointed organist of the church of St. Etienne-du-Mont in Paris. In 1943 he became a prof. at the Paris Cons., remaining on its staff until 1969. He composed a number of sacred works and organ pieces. His best-known compositions are a Requiem (1947) and a Mass (1967).

Dushkin, Samuel, Polish-American violinist; b. Suwalki, Dec. 13, 1891; d. N.Y., June 24, 1976. He was taken to America as a child and was adopted by the composer Blair Fairchild, who gave him primary musical education. He studied violin with Leopold Auer in N.Y. and later took several lessons with Fritz Kreisler. He made his European debut as a violinist in 1918, and subsequently toured widely in Europe and America. In 1928 he became associated with Stravinsky and helped him in solving the technical problems in the violin part of his Violin Concerto, and was the soloist in the 1st performance of this work in Berlin on Oct. 23, 1931, with Stravinsky conducting. He also gave the 1st performance of Stravinsky's *Duo concertant* for Violin and Piano, with Stravinsky playing the piano part (Berlin, Oct. 28, 1932). He recounted the details of his collaboration with Stravinsky in his article "Working with Stravinsky," publ. in the Merle Armitage collection *Stravinsky* (N.Y., 1936).

Dussek or **Dušek (Dusík), Franz (František Xaver),** Bohemian pianist and composer; b. Chotěborky, Dec. 8, 1731; d. Prague, Feb. 12, 1799. He studied in Prague with F. Habermann and in Vienna with Wagenseil. He settled in Prague in 1763, as a teacher and performer; was a close friend of Mozart. He wrote several keyboard sonatas and concertos, syms., quartets, and trios.
Bibl.: V. Sýkora, *František Xaver Dušek: Život a dilo* (Life and Works; Prague, 1958; contains a thematic catalog of his works).

Dussek (Dussík, Dusík), Johann Ladislaus (Ludwig) (Jan Ladislav), outstanding Bohemian pianist and composer; b. Tschaslau, Feb. 12, 1760; d. St.-Germain-en-Laye, March 20, 1812. He studied piano at age 5 and organ at age 9; then became a chorister at the Iglau Minorite church and a pupil at the Jesuit Gymnasium. After further studies at the Kuttenberg Jesuit Gymnasium, he continued his studies at Prague's New City Gymnasium (1776–77) and at the Univ. of Prague (1778). He found a patron in Count Männer, with whose assistance he was able to go to Malines in 1779, where he became active as a piano teacher; he made his public debut there as a pianist on Dec. 16, 1779, and then set out on a highly successful tour, visiting Bergen op Zoom, Amsterdam, and The Hague. He then went to Hamburg, where he gave a concert on July 12, 1782; he also met C.P.E. Bach, with whom he may have studied. In 1783 he played at the St. Petersburg court; after spending about a year in the service of Prince Karl Radziwill as Kapellmeister in Lithuania, he made a major tour of Germany in 1784, winning notable acclaim in Berlin, Mainz, Kassel, and Frankfurt as a piano and glass harmonica virtuoso. In 1786 he went to Paris, where he performed at the court for Marie Antoinette; except for a brief trip to Milan and Bohemia, he remained in Paris until the outbreak of the French Revolution in 1789 compelled him to flee to London. On June 1, 1789, he made his London debut at the Hanover Square Rooms. He soon became successful as a pianist and teacher

in the British capital; appeared regularly at Salomon's concerts and was an active participant in these concerts during Haydn's 2 visits. In 1792 Dussek married the singer, pianist, and harpist Sophia Corri. With his father-in-law, Domenico Corri, he became active as a music publisher. Both men were ill suited for such a venture, however, and Dussek's love for the good life further contributed to the failure of the business. Dussek fled to Hamburg in 1799, leaving his father-in-law to serve a jail sentence for debt. Dussek apparently never saw his wife or daughter again. He seems to have spent about 2 years in Hamburg, where he was active as a performer and teacher. In 1802 he played in his birthplace, and then in Prague; from 1804 to 1806 he served as Kapellmeister to Prince Louis Ferdinand of Prussia. After the latter's death at the battle of Saalfeld (Oct. 10, 1806), Dussek composed a piano sonata in his memory, the *Elégie harmonique sur la mort du Prince Louis Ferdinand de Prusse,* op. 61. He then was briefly in the service of Prince Isenburg. In 1807 he settled in Paris, where he served Prince Talleyrand, gave concerts, and taught. His health began to fail due to excessive drinking, and he was compelled to abandon his career. Dussek was a remarkable composer for the piano, proving himself a master craftsman capable of producing the most brilliant works for the instrument. In his later works he presaged the development of the Romantic school, anticipating such composers as Chopin, Mendelssohn, Schumann, and even Brahms. As a celebrated virtuoso of the keyboard, he shares with Clementi the honor of having introduced the "singing touch." He publ. *Instructions on the Art of Playing the Piano Forte or Harpsichord* (London, 1796; numerous later eds.; in French as *Methode pour le piano forte,* Paris, 1799; in German as *Pianoforte-Schule,* Leipzig, 1802).
Works: *The Captive of Spilberg,* musical drama (London, Nov. 14, 1798); incidental music to Sheridan's melodrama *Pizarro* (London, Jan. 19, 1799); *Auszug aus einer Oster-Cantate* (1786); Mass (1807); 15 piano concertos (1 not extant; 4 arranged for Harp); Concerto for 2 Pianos and Orch.; Harp Concerto (not extant); 34 piano sonatas (several arranged for other instruments); 9 sonatas for Piano, 4-hands (several arranged for other instruments); 68 sonatas for Piano and Violin (several arranged for Piano and Flute); 16 sonatas for Piano, Violin, and Cello (6 not extant); 2 sonatas for Piano, Flute, and Double Bass; many solo piano pieces, including *The Sufferings of the Queen of France* (1793); Piano Quartet; Piano Quintet; 3 string quartets; numerous other chamber works, including the Sonata for Piano, Violin, Cello, and Percussion entitled *The Naval Battle and Total Defeat of the Dutch by Admiral Duncan* (London, Oct. 11, 1797). A complete ed. of his works was publ. by Breitkopf und Härtel (12 vols., Leipzig, 1813–17; reprint, 6 vols., N.Y., 1976). A number of his works have appeared in modern eds. in the Musiqua Antiqua Bohemica series. See also H. Craw, ed., *J.L. D.: Selected Piano Works* (Madison, Wis., 1977).
Bibl.: F. Schiffer, *J.L. D.: Seine Sonaten und seine Konzerte* (Leipzig, 1914); H. Craw, *A Biography and Thematic Catalog of the Works of J.L. D. (1760–1812)* (diss., Univ. of Southern Calif., 1964).

Dutilleux, Henri, talented French composer; b. Angers, Jan. 22, 1916. He studied at the Paris Cons. with H. Busser and with Jean and Noël Gallon; won the 1st Grand Prix de Rome in 1938; was director of singing at the Paris Opéra in 1942; subsequently was active on the Paris radio (1943–63). In 1961 he was a prof. at the École Normale de Musique and in 1970 at the Paris Cons. He has developed a modernistic style which incorporates many procedures of Impressionism. His instrumental works have had numerous performances in France, England, and America; his most impressive work is his Sym. No. 1 (Paris, June 7, 1951). Other works: *Les Hauts de Hurle-Vent,* symphonic suite; *Symphonie de danses; Salmacis,* ballet; *Sarabande* for Orch. (1941); Sonatine for Flute and Piano (1943); *La Giole* for Voice and Orch. (1944); *La Princesse d'E-lide,* incidental music to Molière's play (1946); Piano Sonata (1946–48); *Monsieur de Pourceaugnac,* incidental music to Mo-

lière's play (1948); *Le Loup*, ballet (Paris, March 18, 1953); Sym. No. 2 (Boston, Dec. 11, 1959); *5 métaboles* for Orch. (Cleveland, Jan. 14, 1965); *Tout un monde lointain* for Cello and Orch. (Aix-en-Provence, July 25, 1970); *Timbres, espace, mouvement* for Orch. (Washington, D.C., Jan. 10, 1978); *Summer's End*, ballet (1981); *3 strophes sur le nom de SACHER* for Cello (1981); Violin Concerto (Paris, Nov. 5, 1985); chamber music; piano pieces; film music and songs.
BIBL.: R. Jacobs, *H. D.* (Paris, 1974); P. Mari, *H. D.* (Paris, 1974); D. Humbert, *H. D.: L'Œuvre et le style musical* (Paris and Geneva, 1985).

Dutoit, Charles (Edouard), outstanding Swiss conductor; b. Lausanne, Oct. 7, 1936. His father was Swiss-French; his mother was part German, part English, and, in her remote ancestry, part Brazilian. He learned to play the violin, viola, piano, and drums; studied conducting by watching Ansermet's rehearsals with the Orch. de la Suisse Romande. He studied music theory at the Lausanne Cons. and at the Geneva Cons.; then took courses at the Accademia Musicale in Siena and at the Cons. Benedetto Marcello in Venice; also attended a summer seminar at the Berkshire Music Center in Tanglewood. Returning to Switzerland, he joined the Lausanne Chamber Orch. as a viola player. He made his conducting debut with the Bern Sym. Orch. in 1963; was engaged as music director there (1967–77). From 1964 to 1971 he was artistic director of the Zürich Radio Orch. For several years he was artistic director of the National Orch. in Mexico City. In 1975 he was appointed conductor of the Göteborg Sym. Orch. in Sweden. In 1977 he was engaged as music director of the Montreal Sym. Orch.; he found the work congenial, since it was centered on French culture; he greatly expanded the orch.'s repertoire; conducted Haydn syms., much music of Mozart and Beethoven, and especially French music, beginning with Berlioz and including Debussy and Ravel. He also promoted new Canadian music. In 1983 he was appointed principal guest conductor of the Minnesota Orch. in Minneapolis, and was artistic director and principal conductor of the Philadelphia Orch. summer seasons (1990–91). On Dec. 21, 1987, he made his Metropolitan Opera debut in N.Y., conducting *Les Contes d'Hoffmann*. In 1990 he was named chief conductor of the Orch. National de France in Paris. He was married 3 times; his 2nd wife was the pianist **Martha Argerich.**
BIBL.: G. Nicholson, *C.D., le maître de l'orchestre* (Lausanne, 1986).

Duval, Denise, French soprano; b. Paris, Oct. 23, 1921. She studied at the Paris Cons.; sang with the Bordeaux Opera and the Folies-Bergère in Paris. In 1947 she joined the Paris Opéra; also sang at the Opéra-Comique; then toured in the U.S., Italy, and England; upon her retirement in 1965, she became a voice teacher. She was best known for her roles in French operas.

Duvernoy, Charles, French clarinetist, teacher, and composer, father of **Henri-Louis-Charles Duvernoy;** b. Montbéliard, 1776; d. Paris, Feb. 28, 1845. He went to Paris in 1810, and was 1st clarinet at the Théâtre de Monsieur and the Feydeau, retiring in 1824. Till 1802 he was also a prof. at the Cons. He wrote several clarinet sonatas and clarinet duets.

Duvernoy, Frédéric Nicolas, outstanding French horn player and teacher; b. Montbéliard, Oct. 16, 1765; d. Paris, July 19, 1838. He was self-taught; having settled in Paris, he became a member of the orch. of the Comédie-Italienne (1788); also appeared at the Concert Spirituel. He was made 2nd horn in the orch. of the Opéra-Comique (1790); joined the orch. of the Opéra (1796), serving as its principal horn (1799–1817), and also served as 1st horn in the Imperial Chapel under Napoleon, and, later, under Louis XVIII and Charles X. He was on the faculty of the Cons. (1795–1816); became a Chevalier of the Légion d'honneur (1815). He developed the cor mixte technique of horn playing, specializing in the middle register; wrote a *Methode pour le cor* (1802). He also composed horn concertos and chamber music.

Duvernoy, Henri-Louis-Charles, French composer and teacher, son of **Charles Duvernoy;** b. Paris, Nov. 16, 1820; d. there, Jan. 1906. He was a pupil of Halévy and Zimmerman at the Paris Cons.; in 1848, was appointed a prof. there. He publ. (with Kuhn) *Nouveaux choix de psaumes et de cantiques* (1848); *Solfège des chanteurs* (1855); *Solfège à changements de clefs* (1857); and *Solfège artistique* (1860); also some 100 light piano pieces.

Duvernoy, Victor-Alphonse, French pianist and composer; b. Paris, Aug. 30, 1842; d. there, March 7, 1907. He was a pupil of Bazin and Marmontel at the Paris Cons., taking the 1st prize for piano (1855). In 1869 he founded, together with Léonard, Stiehle, Trombetta, and Jacquard, a series of chamber music concerts; he devoted his time otherwise to composing and teaching, and held a professorship at the Cons. For some 11 years, he was music critic of the *République Française;* he was made a Chevalier of the Legion of Honor, and was an officer of public instruction. As a dramatic composer, he produced the opera *Sardanapale* (concert perf., Paris, 1882), the "scène lyrique" *Cléopâtre*, and the opera *Hellé* (Paris, 1896). His symphonic poem *La Tempête* won the City of Paris prize in 1880; he also wrote a ballet, *Bacchus* (1902); an overture, *Hernani;* much piano music.

Duvosel, Lieven, Belgian composer; b. Ghent, Dec. 14, 1877; d. Sint-Martens-Latem, April 20, 1956. He studied in Antwerp and Paris; lived in Berlin (where Nikisch and R. Strauss performed his works), later in The Hague and Haarlem. His most representative work is the symphonic cycle in 5 parts *Leie:* 1. *De Morgen;* 2. *De Leie;* 3. *De Liefde aan de Leie;* 4. *Kerstnacht* (Christmas); 5. *Het Leieland.* Other compositions: 3 syms.; the symphonic poem *Den Avond* (Evening); *Wereldwee* (World's Grief); many cantatas; male and mixed choruses; songs.
BIBL.: F. van Durme, *L. D.* (Antwerp, 1943); E. Collumbien, *Lijst der werken van D.* (Ghent, 1950).

Dux, Claire, German-American soprano; b. Witkowicz, Poland, Aug. 2, 1885; d. Chicago, Oct. 8, 1967. She studied voice with Teresa Arkel in Berlin; made her operatic debut in Cologne in 1906; 1911–18, was a member of the Berlin Royal Opera (made her debut in *La Bohème* with Caruso); 1912–14, sang at Covent Garden in London; 1918–21, was a member of the Royal Opera in Stockholm; went to the U.S. in 1921 and joined the Chicago Civic Opera Co.; toured the U.S.; then retired in 1932.

Dvarionas, Balis, Lithuanian composer, conductor, and teacher; b. Leipaia, June 19, 1904; d. Vilnius, Aug. 23, 1972. He studied at the Leipzig Cons. with Teichmüller (piano) and Karg-Elert (composition). In 1926 he went to Kaunas and taught piano there, until 1940; in 1947 he became a prof. at the Lithuanian Cons. in Vilna; also conducted the Lithuanian Phil. there (1940–41; 1958–61). Among his works are: Sym. (1947); Violin Concerto (1948; received a State Prize); 2 piano concertos (1958, 1962); opera, *Dalia* (1959); many choral works. He wrote the music for the national anthem of the Lithuanian Soviet Socialist Republic (1950).
BIBL.: Y. Gandrimas, *B. D.* (Moscow, 1960).

Dvořáček, Jiří, prominent Czech composer and pedagogue; b. Vamberk, June 8, 1928. He studied organ at the Prague Cons. (1943–47) and composition with Řídký and Dobiáš at the Prague Academy of Music (1949–53), where he subsequently taught (from 1953). In 1983 he was made an Artist of Merit by the Czech government, and in 1987 was named president of the Union of Czech Composers and Concert Artists. His works represent a median course of Central European modernism.
WORKS: OPERA: *Ostrov Afrodity* (Aphrodite's Island; 1967; Dresden, Feb. 13, 1971). **ORCH.:** 2 syms. (1953, 1985); *Symphonic Suite* (1958); *Overture* (1958); *Concertante Suite* (1962); *Ex post*, symphonic movement for Piano and Orch. (1963); *Quattro episodi*, symfonietta (1971); *Žija a zpívám* (I Am Living and Singing), cantata for Soloists, Choir, Reciter, Children's Choir, and Orch. (1978); *Giubilo* (1983). **CHAMBER:** *Invention*

for Trombone and Piano or Small Orch. (1961); *Music* for Harp (1970); *Due per duo*, 2 rondos for Horn and Piano (1970); Brass Quintet (1973); Sonata for Trumpet and Piano (1977); Organ Sonata (1979); Accordion Sonata (1979); *Tema con Variazioni per trombone e pianoforte* (1980); *Prague Transformations* for Wind Quintet (1981); *Partita* for Oboe and Bassoon (1986); *Partita piccola* for Violin, Guitar, and Harmonica (1987); also choral music; songs.

Dvořák, Antonín (Leopold), famous Czech composer; b. Mühlhausen, Sept. 8, 1841; d. Prague, May 1, 1904. His father ran a village inn and butcher shop and intended Antonín to learn his trade. However, when he showed his musical inclinations, his father let him study piano and violin with a local musician. He also received financial help from an uncle. Later, Dvořák went to Prague, where he studied with the director of a church music school, Karel Pitsch, and his successor, Josef Krejčí. He also began to compose so assiduously that in a short time he completed 2 syms., 2 operas, and some chamber music. His 1st public appearance as a composer took place in Prague on March 9, 1873, with a perf. of his cantata *The Heirs of the White Mountain* (*Hymnus*). An important event in his career occurred in Prague on March 29, 1874, when Smetana conducted his Sym. in E-flat major, op. 10. Dvořák then entered several of his works in a competition for the Austrian State Prize, adjudicated by a distinguished committee that included Herbeck, Hanslick, and Brahms. He won the prize in 1875 and twice in 1877. Brahms, in particular, appreciated Dvořák's talent and recommended him to Simrock for publication of his *Moravian Duets* and the highly popular *Slavonic Dances*. His *Stabat Mater* (Prague, Dec. 23, 1880) and Sym. in D major, op. 60 (Prague, March 25, 1881), followed in close succession, securing for him a leading position among Czech composers.

At the invitation of the Phil. Soc. of London, Dvořák visited England in 1884 and conducted several of his works; then he was commissioned to compose a new sym. for the Phil. Soc.; this was his Sym. in D minor, op. 70, which he conducted in London on April 22, 1885. His cantata *The Spectre's Bride*, composed for the Birmingham Festival, was accorded an excellent reception when he conducted the English performance there on Aug. 27, 1885. On his 3rd visit to England, he conducted the premiere of his oratorio *St. Ludmila*, at the Leeds Festival on Oct. 15, 1886. In 1890 he appeared as a conductor of his own works in Russia. On Feb. 2, 1890, he conducted in Prague the 1st performance of his Sym. in G major, op. 88, which became one of his most popular works. In 1891 Dvořák was appointed prof. of composition at the Prague Cons.; he then received honorary degrees from the Charles Univ. in Prague (Ph.D.) and Cambridge Univ. (D.Mus.). There followed his brilliant *Carnival Overture* of 1891.

In 1892 Dvořák accepted the position of director of the National Cons. of Music of America in N.Y. He composed his *Te Deum* for his 1st U.S. appearance as a conductor (N.Y., Oct. 21, 1892); he also conducted a concert of his music at the 1892 World Columbian Exposition in Chicago. It was in the U.S. that he composed his most celebrated work, the Sym. in E minor, op. 95, *From the New World*, which received its premiere performance on Dec. 15, 1893, with Anton Seidl conducting the N.Y. Phil. The melodies seemed to reflect actual Negro and Indian music, but Dvořák insisted upon their absolute originality. The sym. is essentially a Czech work from the old world; nevertheless, by appearing as a proponent of the use of Negro-influenced themes in symphonic music, Dvořák had a significant impact on American musical nationalism. He discussed the idea in an article, "Music in America" (*Harper's New Monthly Magazine*, Feb. 1895), stating that although Americans had accomplished marvels in most fields of endeavor, in music they were decidedly backward and were content to produce poor imitations of European music; the way to greatness, he suggested, was in the development of a national style based on the melodies of Negroes and Indians. His proposal was greeted with enthusiasm by one segment of America's

musical world and roundly rejected by those fearing musical miscegenation. The controversy raged for more than 2 decades. Dvořák also composed his great Cello Concerto during his American sojourn, and conducted its 1st performance in London on March 19, 1896. Resigning his N.Y. position in 1895, he returned home to resume his duties at the Prague Cons.; he became its director in 1901. During the last years of his life, Dvořák devoted much of his creative efforts to opera; *Rusalka* (1900) remains best known outside Czechoslovakia. He made his last appearance as a conductor on April 4, 1900, leading a concert of the Czech Phil. in Prague. Dvořák was made a member of the Austrian House of Lords in 1901, the 1st Czech musician to be so honored. Czechs celebrated his 60th birthday with special performances of his music in Prague.

Dvořák's musical style was eclectic. His earliest works reflect the influence of Beethoven and Schubert, then Wagner, culminating in the Classicism of Brahms. After mastering his art, he proved himself to be a composer of great versatility and fecundity. A diligent and meticulous craftsman, he brought to his finest works a seemingly inexhaustible and spontaneous melodic invention, rhythmic variety, judicious employment of national folk tunes, and contrapuntal and harmonic skill. His last 5 syms., the Cello Concerto, *Stabat Mater*, his *Slavonic Dances*, the *Carnival Overture*, and many of his chamber works have become staples of the repertoire.

WORKS (the B. numbers are those established by J. Burghauser in *A. D.: Thematic Catalogue, Bibliography, and Survey of Life and Work* [Prague, 1960]): **OPERAS:** *Alfred*, B.16 (1870; Czech Theater, Olomouc, Dec. 10, 1938); *Kraál a uhlíř* (King and Charcoal Burner), B.21 (1st version, 1871; National Theater, Prague, May 28, 1929; 2nd version, 1874, with music recomposed, op. 14, B.42; Provisional Theater, Prague, Nov. 24, 1874; rev. 1887 and listed as B.151; National Theater, Prague, June 15, 1887); *Tvrdé palice* (The Stubborn Lovers), op. 17, B.46 (1874; New Czech Theater, Prague, Oct. 2, 1881); *Vanda*, op. 25, B.55 (1875; Provisional Theater, Prague, April 17, 1876; rev. 1879 and 1883); *Šelma sedlák* (The Cunning Peasant), op. 37, B.67 (1877; Provisional Theater, Prague, Jan. 27, 1878); *Dmitrij*, op. 64, B.127 (1881–82; New Czech Theater, Prague, Oct. 8, 1882; rev. 1883, 1885, and 1894–95; the latter is listed as B.186; National Theater, Prague, Nov. 7, 1894); *Jakobín* (The Jacobin), op. 84, B.159 (1887–88; National Theater, Prague, Feb. 12, 1889; rev. 1897 and listed as B.200; National Theater, Prague, June 19, 1898); *Čert a Káča* (The Devil and Kate), op. 112, B.201 (1898–99; National Theater, Prague, Nov. 23, 1899); *Rusalka*, op. 114, B.203 (1900; National Theater, Prague, March 31, 1901); *Armida*, op. 115, B.206 (1902–3; National Theater, Prague, March 25, 1904). Also the overture *Domov můj* (My Home), B.125a, and the incidental music to F. Šamberk's drama *Josef Kajetán Tyl*, op. 62, B.125 (1881–82; Provisional Theater, Prague, Feb. 3, 1882).

ORCH.: Syms.: No. 1 in C minor, *Zlonické zvony* (The Bells of Zlonice), B.9 (1865; score lost until 1923; Brno, Oct. 4, 1936); No. 2 in B-flat major, op. 4, B.12 (1865; rev. 1887; Prague, March 11, 1888); No. 3 in E-flat major, op. 10, B.34 (1873; Prague, March 29, 1874, Smetana conducting; No. 4 in D minor, op. 13, B.41 (1874; scherzo only perf. in Prague, May 25, 1874, Smetana conducting; 1st complete perf. in Prague, April 6, 1892, composer conducting); No. 5 (old No. 3, op. 24) in F major, op. 76, B.54 (1875; Prague, March 25, 1879; rev. 1887); No. 6 (old No. 1, op. 58) in D major, op. 60, B.112 (1880; Prague, March 25, 1881); No. 7 (old No. 2) in D minor, op. 70, B.141 (1884–85; London, April 22, 1885, composer conducting; rev. 1885); No. 8 (old No. 4) in G major, op. 88, B.163 (1889; Prague, Feb. 2, 1890, composer conducting); No. 9 (old No. 5) in E minor, *Z nového světa* (From the New World), op. 95, B.178 (1893; N.Y., Dec. 15 [public rehearsal], Dec. 16 [official premiere], 1893, Anton Seidl conducting); Cello Concerto in A major, B.10 (1865; left unorchestrated; unidiomatic ed. by G. Raphael, 1929; later ed. by J. Burghauser, 1977); Piano Concerto in G minor, op. 33, B.63 (1876; Prague, March 24, 1878; rev. 1883); Violin Concerto in A minor, op. 53, B.96 and 108 (1879–80; rev. 1882; Prague, Oct. 14, 1883); Cello Concerto in B minor, op. 104, B.191 (1894–95; rev. 1895; London, March 19, 1896, Leo Stern soloist, composer conducting). OVERTURES: *Tragic Overture (Dramatic Overture)*, B.16a (1870; overture from the opera *Alfred*); Concert Overture in F major, B.21a (1871; overture from the 1st version of the opera *Král a uhlíř*; Prague, April 14, 1872, Smetana conducting); *Romeo and Juliet*, B.35 (not extant); *Husitská* (Hussite), op. 67, B.132 (Prague, Nov. 18, 1883); Triple Overture or *Příroda, Život a láska* (Nature, Life, and Love), op. 91, Nos. 1–3 (1891–92; Prague, April 28, 1892, composer conducting; later listed as *V přírodě* [In Nature's Realm], op. 91, B.168, *Karneval* [Carnival], op. 92, B.169, and *Othello*, op. 93, B.174). SYMPHONIC POEMS: *Vodník* (The Watersprite), op. 107, B.195 (London, Nov. 14, 1896, Henry J. Wood conducting); *Polednice* (The Noonday Witch), op. 108, B.196 (London, Nov. 21, 1896, Wood conducting); *Zlatý kolovrat* (The Golden Spinning Wheel), op. 109, B.197 (London, Oct. 26, 1896, Hans Richter conducting); *Holoubek* (The Wild Dove), op. 110, B.198 (1896; Brünn, March 20, 1898, Leoš Janáček conducting); *Píseň bohatýrská* (Heroic Song), op. 111, B.199 (1897; Vienna, Dec. 4, 1898, Gustav Mahler conducting); other works include Romance in F minor for Violin and Orch., op. 11, B.39 (1873–79; a transcription of the andante con moto of the String Quartet in F minor, op. 9, B.37); Symphonic Poem or Rhapsody in A minor, op. 14, B.44 (1874); Nocturne in B major for String Orch., op. 40, B.47 (1875?; from the String Quartet in E minor, B.19, and the String Quintet in G major, B.49; rev. 1882–83); Serenade in E major for Strings, op. 22, B.52 (1875; Prague, Dec. 10, 1876); Symphonic Variations on a theme from the male chorus *Já jsem huslař* (I Am a Fiddler), op. 78 (old 28), B.70 (Prague, Dec. 2, 1877); Serenade in D minor for Wind Instruments, op. 44, B.77 (Prague, Nov. 17, 1878); *3 Slavonic Rhapsodies*, op. 45, B.86 (Nos. 1 and 2, Prague, Nov. 17, 1878, composer conducting; No. 3, 1878); *8 Slavonic Dances*, op. 46, B.83 (1878); *Czech Suite* in D major, op. 39, B.93 (Prague, May 16, 1879); *Mazurek* for Violin and Orch., op. 49, B.90 (1879); *10 Legendy* (Legends), op. 59, B.122 (1881; orchestrated from a piano duet version); *Scherzo capriccioso*, op. 66, B.131 (Prague, May 16, 1883); *8 Slavonic Dances*, op. 72, B.147 (1886–87); Rondo in G minor for Cello and Orch., op. 94, B.181 (1893); *Klid* (Silent Woods) for Cello and Orch., op. 68/5, B.182 (1893); Suite in A major, op. 98b, B.190 (1895–96).

CHORAL: Mass in B-flat major, B.2 (1857–59; not extant); *Dědicové bílé hory* (The Heirs of the White Mountain) or *Hymnus* for Mixed Chorus and Orch., op. 30, B.27 (1872; Prague, March 9, 1873; rev. 1880 and listed as B.102; rev. 1884 and perf. in London, May 13, 1885, composer conducting; *Stabat Mater* for Soprano, Alto, Tenor, Bass, Chorus, and Orch., op. 58, B.71 (1876–77; Prague, Dec. 23, 1880); *149th Psalm*, op. 79, B.91 (1st version for male voice chorus and orch., 1879; Prague, March 16, 1879; 2nd version for mixed chorus and orch., 1887, and listed as B.154; Boston, Feb. 27, 1890); *Svatební košile* (The Spectre's Bride), cantata for Soprano, Tenor, Bass, Chorus, and Orch., op. 69, B.135 (1884; Pilsen, March 28, 1885, composer conducting; *St. Ludmila*, oratorio for Soprano, Alto, Tenor, Bass, Chorus, and Orch., op. 71, B.144 (1885–86; Leeds Festival, Oct. 15, 1886, composer conducting; with added recitative, 1901, and listed as B.205; this version 1st perf. as *Svatá Ludmila* in Prague, Oct. 30, 1901); Mass in D major for Soprano, Alto, Tenor, Bass (or Semi-Chorus), Chorus, and Organ, op. 86, B.153 (1st perf. privately, Luzany, Sept. 11, 1887; rev. version for orch., 1892, and listed as B.175; London, March 11, 1893); Requiem Mass for Soprano, Alto, Tenor, Bass, Chorus, and Orch., op. 89, B.165 (1890; Birmingham Festival, Oct. 9, 1891, composer conducting); *Te Deum* for Soprano, Bass, Chorus, and Orch., op. 103, B.176 (N.Y., Oct. 21, 1892, composer conducting); *Americký prapor* (The American Flag), cantata for Alto, Tenor, Bass, Chorus, and Orch., op. 102, B.177 (1892–93; N.Y., May 4, 1895); *Slavnostní zpěv* (Festival Song) or *Ode* for Mixed Chorus and Orch., op. 113, B.202 (1st perf. privately, Prague, May 29, 1900).

CHAMBER: *STRING QUARTETS:* A major, op. 2, B.8 (1862; rev. 1887); B-flat major, B.17 (1869–70); D major, B.18 (1869–70); E minor, B.19 (1870); F minor, op. 9, B.37 (1873; original version not extant; publ. version by G. Raphael, 1929); A minor, op. 12, B.40 (1873, unfinished; completed by J. Burghauser and publ. in the complete ed. of Dvořák's works in 1979); A minor, op. 16, B.45 (1874); E major, op. 80 (originally op. 27), B.57 (1876; rev. 1888); D minor, op. 34, B.75 (1877; rev. 1879); E-flat major, op. 51, B.92 (1878–79); C major, op. 61, B.121 (1881); F major, *The American*, op. 96, B.179 (1893); G major, op. 106, B.192 (1895); A-flat major, op. 105, B.193 (1895). *STRING QUINTETS:* A minor for 2 Violins, 2 Violas, and Cello, op. 1, B.7 (1861; rev. 1887); G major for 2 Violins, Viola, Cello, and Double Bass, op. 77 (originally op. 18), B.49 (1875; rev. 1888); E-flat major for 2 Violins, 2 Violas, and Cello, *The American*, op. 97, B.180 (1893); also a Sextet in A major for 2 Violins, 2 Violas, and 2 Cellos, op. 48, B.80 (1878). *PIANO TRIOS:* Op. 13/1, B.25 (1871–72; not extant); op. 13/2, B.26 (1871–72; not extant); B-flat major, op. 21, B.51 (1875); G minor, op. 26, B.56 (1876); F minor, op. 65, B.130 (1883); *Dumkas* (Dumky) Trio, op. 90, B.166 (1890–91). *PIANO QUINTETS:* A major, op. 5, B.28 (1872); A major, op. 81, B.155 (1887). *PIANO QUARTETS:* D major, op. 23, B.53 (1875); E-flat major, op. 87, B.162 (1889). Also Sonata in F minor for Cello and Piano, B.20 (1870–71; not extant); Sonata in A minor for Violin and Piano, B.33 (1873; not extant); Sonata in F major for Violin and Piano, op. 57, B.106 (1880); also many solo keyboard pieces, duets, etc. Numerous songs, including *Cypřiše* (Cypresses), B.11 (18 songs, 1865); *Biblické písné* (Biblical Songs), op. 99, B.185 (10 songs, 1894); also the *Moravské dvojzpěvy* (Moravian Duets), 3 sets: for Soprano or Contralto and Tenor, op. 20, B.50 (1875); for Soprano and Contralto, op. 32, B.60 and 62 (1876), and for Soprano and Contralto, op. 38, B.69 (1877).

BIBL.: O. Šourek inaugurated a complete ed. of D.'s works, which commenced publ. in Prague in 1955. The standard thematic catalog was compiled by J. Burghauser as *A. D.: Thematic Catalogue, Bibliography, and Survey of Life and Work* (in Czech, German, and Eng.; Prague, 1960). See also the following: J. Zubatý, *A. D.: Eine biographische Skizze* (Leipzig, 1886; Eng. tr. by W. Hadow in Studies in Modern Music, 2nd series, London, 1895; 2nd ed., 1904); J. Bartoš, *A. D.* (Prague, 1913); O. Šourek, *Život a dílo A.a D.a* (The Life and Work of A. D.; 4 vols., Prague, 1916–33; Vols. I–II, 3rd ed., 1955–56; Vols. III–IV, 2nd ed., 1957–58; in German as *D.: Leben und Werk*, 1 vol., abridged by P. Stefan, Vienna, 1935; in Eng. tr. by Y. Vance as *A. D.*, N.Y., 1941); idem, *D.'s Werke: Ein vollständiges Verzeichnis in chronologischer, thematischer und systematischer Anordnung* (Berlin, 1917; rev. Czech ed., Prague, 1960); idem, *D.ovy symfonie* (Prague, 1922; 3rd ed., 1948; abridged ed. in German in *A. D. Werkanalysen I, Orchesterwerke*, Prague, 1954, and in Eng. in *The Orchestral Works of A. D.*, Prague, 1956); K. Hoffmeister, *A. D.* (Prague, 1924; Eng. tr. by R. Newmarch, London, 1928); O. Šourek, *A. D.* (Prague, 1929; 4th ed., 1947; Eng. tr. as *A. D.: His Life and Work*, Prague, 1952); idem, *D.ve vzpomínkach a dopisech* (Prague, 1938; 9th ed., 1951; in Eng. as *D.: Letters and Reminiscences*, Prague, 1954); H. Sirp, *A. D.* (Potsdam, 1939); O. Šourek, *D.ovy skladby komorní* (Prague, 1943; 2nd ed., 1949; abridged ed. in German in *A. D. Werkanalysen II, Kammermusik*, Prague, 1954, and in Eng. in *The Chamber Music of A. D.*, Prague, 1956); idem, *D.ovy skladby orchestralní* (2 vols., Prague, 1944 and 1946; abridged ed. in German in *A. D. Werkanalysen I, Orchesterwerke*, Prague, 1954, and in Eng. in *The Orchestral Works of A. D.*, Prague, 1956); A. Robertson, *D.* (London, 1945; 2nd ed., 1964); H. Kull, *D.s Kammermusik* (Bern, 1948); H. Boese, *Zwei Urmusikanten: Smetana, D.* (Zürich, 1955); A. Hořejš, *A. D.: The Composer's Life and Work in Pictures* (Prague, 1955); R. Smetana, *A. D.: O místo a význam skladatelského díla v českém hudebním vyvoji* (A. D.: The Place and Meaning of D.'s Compositions in the Development of Czech Music; Prague, 1956); J. Clapham, "D., and the Philharmonic Society," *Music & Letters*, XXXIX (1958); idem, "The Evolution of D.'s Symphony 'From the New World,'" *Musical Quarterly*, XLIV (1958); idem, "The Operas of A. D.," *Proceedings of the Royal Musical Association*, LXXXIV (1958); A. Sychra, *Estetika D.ovy symfonické tvorby* (The Esthetics of D.'s Symphonic Work; Prague, 1959; in German as *A. D.: Zur Ästhetik seines sinfonischen Schaffens*, Leipzig, 1973); J. Clapham, "The National Origins of D.'s Art," *Proceedings of the Royal Musical Association*, LXXXIX (1963); idem, "D.'s Visit to Russia," *Musical Quarterly*, LI (1965); A. Hetschko, *A. D.* (Leipzig, 1965); M. Aborn, *The Influence on American Musical Culture of D.'s Sojourn in America* (Ann Arbor, 1966); J. Burghauser, *A. D.* (Prague, 1966; in German and Eng., 1967); J. Clapham, *A. D.: Musician and Craftsman* (London and N.Y., 1966); idem, "D. and the American Indian," *Musical Times*, CVII (1966); E. Herzog, *A. D. v obrazech* (A. D. in Pictures; Prague, 1966); J. Clapham, "D.'s Musical Directorship in New York," *Music & Letters*, XLVIII (1967); G. Hughes, *D.: His Life and Music* (N.Y., 1967); J. Berkovec, *A. D.* (Prague, 1969); J. Clapham, "D.'s Relations with Brahms and Hanslick," *Musical Quarterly*, LVII (1971); K. Honolka, *A. D. in Selbstzeugnissen und Bilddokumenten* (Reinbek, 1974); D. Beveridge, "Sophisticated Primitivism: The Significance of Pentatonicism in D.'s American Quartet," *Current Musicology*, no. 24 (1977); J. Clapham, "D.'s Aufstieg zum Komponisten," *Die Musikforschung*, XXX (1977); idem, "Indian Influence in D.'s American Chamber Music," *Colloquium Musica Cameralis Brno 1971* (Brno, 1978); idem, "D.'s Musical Directorship in New York: A Postscript," *Music & Letters*, LIX (1978); R. Layton, *D. Symphonies and Concertos* (London, 1978); J. Clapham, *D.* (London and N.Y., 1979); idem, "D.'s Cello Concerto in B minor: A Masterpiece in the Making," *Music Review*, XL/3 (1979); N. Butterworth, *D.: His Life and Times* (Tunbridge Wells, 1980); H.-H. Schönzeler, *D.* (London, 1984); J. Vysloužil, "D. and Janáček: Their Time and Work," *Bericht zum Colloquium Brno 1984* (Brno, 1985); J. Clapham, "D.'s Ordeal during the American Depression," *Musical Times* (Nov. 1989); D. Vaughan, "D.: Getting to the Truth," *Musical America* (Nov. 1989).

Dvořáková, Ludmila, Czech soprano; b. Kolin, July 11, 1923. She made her professional debut at Ostrava in 1949; also sang in Bratislava, Prague, and Vienna (1956). She then appeared in Berlin (1960) and Bayreuth (1965). On Jan. 12, 1966, she made her Metropolitan Opera debut in N.Y. as Leonore in *Fidelio*. In addition to the German repertoire, she sang many roles in Verdi's operas.

Dvorský, Peter, Czech tenor; b. Partizánske, Sept. 25, 1951. He graduated from the Bratislava Cons. in 1973, making his operatic debut in *Eugene Onegin* at the Slovak National Theater in Bratislava. After winning 5th prize at the Tchaikovsky Competition in Moscow (1974) and 1st prize at the Geneva Competition (1975), he sang in Bratislava, Prague, Budapest, Moscow, Vienna, Milan, and London. On Nov. 15, 1977, he made his Metropolitan Opera debut in N.Y. as Alfredo. In 1986 he was made an Austrian Kammersänger. He won particular praise for his performances in operas by Smetana, Dvořák, and Janáček; also sang in operas by Verdi and Puccini with distinction.

Dwight, John Sullivan, American music critic and editor; b. Boston, May 13, 1813; d. there, Sept. 5, 1893. He graduated from Harvard in 1832, and was one of the founders and most active members of the Harvard Musical Assoc. After studying for the ministry, in 1840 he took charge of the Unitarian Church at Northampton, Mass. His literary and socialistic proclivities, however, gained the mastery; he gave up his pastorate, and entered the ill-starred Brook Farm Community as a teacher of German music and the classics. Returning to Boston in 1848, after the failure of the socialistic experiment, he devoted himself to literature, founded *Dwight's Music Journal* in 1852, and remained its ed. in chief until its discontinuance in 1881. A prominent feature in this periodical was the valuable historical essays of A.W. Thayer. The entire journal is available in reprint (N.Y., 1968). Dwight also publ. *Translations of Select Minor Poems from the German of Goethe and Schiller, with Notes.*

BIBL.: G. Cooke, *J.S. D., Brook-Farmer, Editor, and Critic of Music* (Boston, 1898); E. Waters, "J.S. D., First American Critic of Music," *Musical Quarterly* (Jan. 1935).

Dyer-Bennet, Richard, English-born American ballad singer; b. Leicester, Oct. 6, 1913. He emigrated to the U.S. in 1925; became a naturalized citizen in 1935. He studied voice with Cornelius Reid, and guitar with José Rey De La Torre. He made his concert debut in N.Y. in 1944; also sang in nightclubs. In 1970 he joined the State Univ. of N.Y. at Stony Brook as an instructor in the theater arts dept. He acquired popularity mainly as a singer of English and American ballads, but he was also praised for his performance of Schubert song cycles, especially *Die schöne Müllerin* in his own tr., under the title "The Lovely Milleress."

Dyer, Louise (Mrs. Louise B.M. Hanson), Australian patroness of music and publisher; b. Melbourne, July 16, 1890; d. Monaco, Nov. 9, 1962. She established in Monaco an important publishing enterprise, L'Oiseau-Lyre (The Lyre-Bird Press), financing it entirely out of her own resources. The Lyre-Bird Press has issued a great number of unpubl. or obscure works of medieval and Renaissance French music.

Dykema, Peter (William), American music pedagogue; b. Grand Rapids, Mich., Nov. 25, 1873; d. Hastings-on-Hudson, N.Y., May 13, 1951. He studied law at the Univ. of Michigan (B.S., 1895; M.L., 1896); then took lessons in singing and in music theory at the Inst. of Musical Art in N.Y. (1911–12); later supplemented his musical education in Germany; returning to America, he held numerous teaching positions in high schools in Illinois and Indiana; from 1913 to 1924 was on the faculty of the Univ. of Wisconsin; from 1924 to 1939 was a prof. of music education at Teacher's College, Columbia Univ. He publ. a number of music handbooks for schools, among them *Twice 55 Community Songs* (6 vols., 1919–27); *School Music Handbook* (1931; rev. ed., by H. Cundiff, Boston, 1955); *Singing Youth* (1935); *Golden Key Orchestral Series* (1937); *Modern Band Training Series* (with N. Church, 1938); *The Teaching and Administration of High School Music* (with K. Gehrkens, Boston, 1941).

BIBL.: H. Eisenkramer, *P.W. D.: His Life and Contribution to Music Education* (diss., Univ. of Michigan, 1963).

Dykes, John Bacchus, English composer of hymn tunes; b. Kingston-upon-Hull, March 10, 1823; d. Ticehurst, Sussex, Jan. 22, 1876. He was educated at Cambridge, and was ordained a minor canon and precentor at Durham Cathedral in 1849; in 1862 became vicar of St. Oswald, Durham. He composed numerous anthems and part-songs.

BIBL.: J. Fowler, *Life and Letters of J.B. D.* (London, 1897).

Dylan, Bob (real name, **Robert Allen Zimmerman**), American folksinger and songwriter; b. Duluth, Minn., May 24, 1941. He adopted the name Dylan out of admiration for the poet Dylan Thomas. Possessed by wanderlust, he rode freight trains across the country; played guitar and crooned in the coffeehouses of N.Y. He also improvised songs to his own lyrics. His nasalized country-type semi-Western style and his self-haunted soft guitar-strumming captured the imagination not only of untutored adolescents but also of certified cognoscenti in search of convincing authenticity. In 1966 he broke his neck in a motorcycle accident, which forced him to interrupt his charismatic career for 2 years. In 1970 he was awarded an honorary doctorate from Princeton Univ., the 1st such honor given to a popular singer innocent of all academic training. A group of militants in the Students for a Democratic Soc. adopted the name "Weathermen" after a line from Dylan's song *Subterranean Homesick Blues*, "You don't need a weatherman to know which way the wind blows." The Weathermen claimed credit for several bombings in N.Y. City during 1969 and 1970.

BIBL.: D. Kramer, *B. D.* (N.Y., 1967); A. Scaduto, *B. D.* (N.Y., 1972); J. Cott, *D.* (Garden City, N.Y., 1984).

Dyson, Sir George, English organist and composer; b. Halifax, Yorkshire, May 28, 1883; d. Winchester, Sept. 28, 1964. He studied at the Royal College of Music in London; was its director from 1937 to 1952. He was knighted in 1941. His works include a Sym. (1937); Violin Concerto (1943); an oratorio, *Quo Vadis?* (1949); Suite for Small Orch.; *3 Rhapsodies* for String Quartet; piano pieces; numerous pedagogic pieces and songs. His cantata *The Canterbury Pilgrims,* to words modernized from Chaucer's *Canterbury Tales,* is his best-known work; the overture to it was extracted in 1946, and performed separately under the title *At the Tabard Inn.* He further composed numerous sacred choruses; publ. the books *The New Music* (1924), *The Progress of Music* (1932), and a candid autobiography, *Fiddling While Rome Burns: A Musician's Apology* (London, 1954).

BIBL.: C. Palmer, *G. D.: A Centenary Appreciation* (Borough Green, 1984).

Dzegelenok, Alexander (Mikhailovich), Russian composer; b. Moscow, Aug. 24, 1891; d. there, Jan. 31, 1969. He studied at the Phil. Inst. in Moscow with Koreshchenko. He composed an orch. suite, *Egypt;* also *Hiawatha* for Voice and Instruments; piano pieces and songs.

Dzerzhinsky, Ivan (Ivanovich), Russian composer; b. Tambov, April 9, 1909; d. Leningrad, Jan. 18, 1978. He studied with Asafiev at the Leningrad Cons. (1932–34). As a composer he espoused the doctrine of socialist realism. Possessing a facile gift of flowing melodiousness, he made a mark in Soviet music by his 1st opera, *Quiet Flows the Don,* to a libretto from the novel by the Soviet writer Sholokhov; in it he made use of peasant folk-song elements, emphasizing mass choruses. It was produced in Leningrad on Oct. 22, 1935, and became immediately successful when Stalin attended a performance in Moscow and personally congratulated the composer on his ability to create music in a characteristically Soviet style. He followed it with a sequel, *Virgin Soil Upturned,* which was produced in Moscow on October 23, 1937. His subsequent operas were *The Storm* (after Ostrovsky, 1940); *The Blood of the People* (Leningrad, Jan. 21, 1942); *The Blizzard* (after Pushkin, 1946); *Nadezhda Svetlova* (Orenburg, Sept. 8, 1943); and *A Man's Destiny* (Moscow, Sept. 30, 1961). He further wrote 3 piano concertos (1932, 1934, 1945); numerous piano pieces; songs.

BIBL.: O. Tompakova, *Essays on the Life and Work of I. D.* (Leningrad, 1964).

E

Eames, Emma (Hayden), famous American soprano; b. Shanghai, China, Aug. 13, 1865; d. N.Y., June 13, 1952. Her mother, who was her 1st teacher, took her to America as a child; she then studied with Clara Munger in Boston and with Marchesi in Paris. She made her operatic debut at the Paris Grand Opéra on March 13, 1889, as Juliette in Gounod's *Roméo et Juliette*. On April 7, 1891, she made her 1st appearance at London's Covent Garden as Marguerite, and continued to sing there until 1901. On Nov. 9, 1891, she made her U.S. debut as Elsa in *Lohengrin* in Chicago. On Dec. 14, 1891, she made her debut at the Metropolitan Opera House in N.Y., again in the role of Juliette. She remained with the Metropolitan until 1909, appearing as Marguerite in *Faust*, Desdemona in *Otello*, Elisabeth in *Tannhäuser*, Aida, Tosca, and Donna Anna in *Don Giovanni*. She received the Jubilee Medal from Queen Victoria, and was decorated by the French Academy with the order of Les Palmes Académiques. Her emotional life was turbulent; she married the painter Julian Story in 1891, but they were separated in the midst of a widely publicized scandal; in 1911 she married the baritone **Emilio de Gogorza,** but left him too. She publ. an autobiography, *Some Memories and Reflections* (N.Y., 1927).

Eames, Henry Purmort, American pianist and music educator; b. Chicago, Sept. 12, 1872; d. Claremont, Calif., Nov. 25, 1950. After completing preliminary music education in the U.S., he went to Europe, where he took piano lessons with Clara Schumann and Paderewski; after a career as a concert pianist, he devoted himself to teaching; was on the faculty at the Univ. of Nebraska (1898–1908), and eventually at the American Cons. in Chicago (1923–28). He then settled in California, where he taught at Scripps College, Claremont. He was also a composer; wrote for chorus, voice, and piano.

Earhart, Will, American music educator; b. Franklin, Ohio, April 1, 1871; d. Los Angeles, April 23, 1960. From 1900 to 1912 he was a school supervisor in various localities in Ohio and Indiana; in 1912 he went to Pittsburgh, where he was director of music in the public schools (1912–40); was also founder and head of public school music at the Univ. of Pittsburgh (1913) and a lecturer on music education at the Carnegie Inst. of Technology. He publ. a number of books on musical education, among them *Music in the Public Schools* (1914); *Music in Secondary Schools* (with O. McConathy; 1917); *Music to the Listening Ear* (1932); *The Meaning and Teaching of Music* (1935); and *Elements of Music Theory* (with C.N. Boyd; 2 vols., 1938); ed. *Art Songs for High Schools* (1910); *The School Credit Piano Course* (with others; 1918).

BIBL.: F. McKernan, *W. E.: His Life and Contributions to Music Education* (diss., Univ. of Southern Calif., Los Angeles, 1956); C. Buttelman, ed., *W. E.: Teacher, Philosopher, Humanitarian* (Washington, D.C., 1962).

Easdale, Brian, English composer; b. Manchester, Aug. 10, 1909. He studied at the Royal College of Music in London (1925–33). He became interested in theatrical music; wrote 3 operas, *Rapunzel* (1927), *The Corn King* (1935), and *The Sleeping Children* (1951); incidental music to Shakespeare's plays; also several film scores, of which the most successful was *The Red Shoes* (1948). Other works include a Piano Concerto (1938) and several orch. pieces of a descriptive nature

(*Dead March; The Phoenix; Bengal River;* etc.); also a *Cavatina* for Brass Ensemble (1961).

East (Easte, Este), Thomas, English music printer and publisher of Elizabethan madrigals; b. London, c.1535; d. there, Jan. 1608. He received his license as a printer in 1565; his 1st musical publication was Byrd's collection *Psalmes, Sonets and Songs of Sadnes and Pietie* (1588); he was also the assignee of Byrd's patent for printing music paper and musical compositions. In 1592 he brought out *The Whole Booke of Psalmes, with their wonted tunes as they are sung in Churches, composed in 4 parts,* containing harmonizations by Allison, Blancks, Cavendish, Cobbold, Dowland, Farmer, Farnaby, Hooper, Johnson, and Kirbye (republ. 1594 and 1604; reprinted in score by the Musical Antiquarian Soc., 1844). This collection is of historical significance, for it was the 1st to be printed in score rather than in separate part-books; also for the 1st time, the tunes were designated by specific names, such as "Kentish" and "Cheshire." Other works printed by East are Yonge's *Musica Transalpina* (1588 and 1597); Byrd's *Songs of Sundrie Natures* (1589); Watson's *Madrigals* (1590); Byrd's *Cantiones Sacrae* (2 books, 1589, 1591); Morley's *Canzonets* (1593); Mundy's *Songs and Psalmes* (1594); Kirbye's *Madrigals* (1596); Wilbye's *Madrigals* (1598); Dowland's *Ayres* (1600); Bateson's *Madrigals* (1603); Michael East's *Madrigals* (1604); Pilkington's *Songs or Ayres* (1605); Byrd's *Gradualia* (1605); Youll's *Canzonets* (1607). East's presumed son Michael East (c.1580–1648) was a composer; his set of madrigals was publ. by Thomas East in 1604. He served as organist at Lichfield Cathedral; received the degree of B.Mus. at Cambridge (1606); he publ. 6 sets of vocal pieces (madrigals, anthems, etc.) and a set of instrumental works (1638).—**Bibl.:** F. Kidson, *British Music Publishers* (London, 1900); E. Fellowes, *The English Madrigal Composers* (London, 1921; 2nd ed., 1948).

Eastman, George, prominent American industrialist and philanthropist; b. Waterville, N.Y., July 12, 1854; d. (suicide) Rochester, N.Y., March 14, 1932. He perfected a process for making dry plates for photocopy (1880) and in 1884 founded the Eastman Dry Plate and Film Co., which in 1892 became the Eastman Kodak Co., subsequently one of the leading companies of its kind in the world. A munificent philanthropist, he gave away more than $75 million to various scientific, educational, and cultural organizations. He founded the Eastman School of Music of the Univ. of Rochester (1921), and also endowed the Eastman Theatre. He took his own life after learning that he had cancer.—**Bibl.:** C. Ackerman, *G. E.* (1930).

Easton, Florence (Gertrude), English soprano; b. South Bank, Yorkshire, Oct. 25, 1882; d. N.Y., Aug. 13, 1955. She studied with Agnes Larkcom at the Royal Academy of Music in London and with Elliott Haslam in Paris; in 1903 she made her operatic debut as the Shepherd in *Tannhäuser* with the Moody-Manners Co. in Newcastle upon Tyne; toured the U.S. with Savage's opera company in 1904–5 and 1906–7. She was a member of the Berlin Royal Opera (1907–13) and the Hamburg Opera (1912–16); after singing with the Chicago Grand Opera (1915–17), she made her Metropolitan Opera debut in N.Y. as Santuzza on Dec. 7, 1917, remaining on its roster until 1929; she created the role of Lauretta in *Gianni Schicchi* there in 1918. In 1927 and 1932 she sang at London's Covent Garden and in 1934 appeared at Sadler's Wells Opera in London. She then returned to the Metropolitan Opera in 1936 as Brünnhilde in *Die Walküre* before retiring from the stage. Her 1st husband was **Francis Maclennan.**

Eaton, John (Charles), American composer; b. Bryn Mawr, Pa., March 30, 1935. He received his A.B. and M.F.A. degrees from Princeton Univ., where he studied composition with Milton Babbitt, Edward Cone, and Roger Sessions (1953–59); subsequently won 3 American Prix de Rome awards and 2 Guggenheim grants. From 1971 he was prof. of music at the Indiana Univ. School of Music in Bloomington. He lectured at the Salzburg Center in American Studies (1976) and was composer-in-residence at the American Academy in Rome (1975–76). In his works he avails himself of all resources of modern music, including serial techniques, microtones, and electronic media. In several of his scores he makes use of the Syn-Ket (a portable electronic synthesizer built by the Roman sound engineer Ketoff). He publ. *Involvement with Music: New Music since 1950* (1976).—**Works:** Operas: *Ma Barker* (1957); *Heracles* (1964; Turin, Oct. 10, 1968); *Myshkin,* after Dostoevsky's novel *The Idiot* (1971; Bloomington, Ind., April 23, 1973); *The Lion and Androcles,* for children (1973; Indianapolis, May 1, 1974); *Danton and Robespierre* (Bloomington, April 21, 1978); *The Cry of Clytaemnestra* (1979; Bloomington, March 1, 1980); *The Tempest,* after Shakespeare (1983–85; Santa Fe, July 27, 1985); *The Rev. Jim Jones* (1989). Other works: *Song Cycle on Holy Sonnets of John Donne* for Voice and Piano (1956); Piano Variations (1957); String Quartet (1958); *Tertullian Overture* (1958); *Adagio and Allegro* for Flute, Oboe, and Strings (1960); *Concert Piece* for Clarinet and Piano (1960); *Concert Music* for Solo Clarinet (1961); *Songs for R.P.B.* for Voice, Piano, and Synthesizer (1964); *Microtonal Fantasy* for 2 Pianos (1965); *Concert Piece* for Syn-Ket (1966); *Thoughts on Rilke* for Soprano, 2 Syn-Kets, and Syn-Mill (1966); *Concert Piece* for Syn-Ket and Orch. (1966; Berkshire Music Festival, Tanglewood, Mass., Aug. 9, 1967); *Soliloquy* for Electronic Sound Synthesizer (1967); *Vibrations* for 2 Oboes, 2 Clarinets, and Flute (1967); Duet for Syn-Ket and Moog Synthesizer (1968); *Blind Man's Cry* for Soprano and Orch. of Electronic Synthesizers (1968); Mass for Soprano, Clarinet, 3 Syn-Kets, Moog Synthesizer, and Syn-Mill (1970); *Sonority Movement* for Flute and 9 Harps (1971); *In Memoriam Mario Cristini,* piano trio (1971); *Ajax* for Baritone and Orch., after Sophocles (1972); *Guillen Songs* for Voice and Piano (1974); Duo for Mixed Chorus (1977); *A Greek Vision* for Soprano, Flute, and Electronics (Chicago, Dec. 7, 1981); Sym. No. 2 (1980–81); *Burlesca* for Tuba and Piano (1981); *Remembering Rome,* sinfonietta for Strings (Bloomington, March 1, 1987).—**Bibl.:** R. Morgan, "J. E. and 'The Tempest,'" *Musical Times* (July 1985).

Ebel, Arnold, German composer, organist, and choral conductor; b. Heide, Holstein, Aug. 15, 1883; d. Berlin, March 4, 1963. He studied at Berlin Univ.; also took private lessons with Max Bruch; from 1909 was active in Berlin as an organist, choral conductor, and teacher; served as president of the German Composers' Assoc. (1920–33, and again from 1949). He wrote numerous piano pieces and songs; also a *Sinfonietta giocosa* for Orch.

Eben, Petr, Czech composer; b. Žamberk, Jan. 22, 1929. He studied piano with František Rauch; was a composition student of Bořkovec at the Prague Academy of Music (1948–52). He became a teacher of music history at the Charles Univ. in Prague in 1955, and also taught composition at the Royal Northern College of Music in Manchester (1977–78). In his works he follows the traditions of Central European Classicism, with modern techniques adding zest to old forms.—**Works:** *Kletby a dobrořečení* (Curses and Blessings), ballet (1983); 2 organ concertos: No. 1, *Symphonia gregoriana* (1954); No. 2 (1982); Piano Concerto (1961); *Vox clamantis,* symphonic movement for 3 Trumpets and Orch. (1969); *Night Hours,* concertant sym. (1975); *Hořká hlína* (Bitter Earth), cantata for Baritone, Chorus, and Organ (1959); *Apologia Socratus,* oratorio for Contralto, Baritone, Chorus, Children's Chorus, and Orch. (1967); *Procta Karlu IV* (Homage to Charles IV), cantata for Male Chorus and Orch. (1978); Sonata for Oboe and Piano (1950); *Balladica Suite* for Cello and Piano (1955); *Sonatina semplice* for Violin or Flute, and Piano (1955); *Duetti per due trombe* (1956); *Ordo modalis* for Oboe and Harp (1964); Wind Quintet (1965); *Fantasia vespertina* for Trumpet and Piano (1967); Brass Quintet (1969); *Music* for Oboe, Bassoon, and Piano (1970); *Windows* for Trumpet and Organ (1976); *Sonata per flauto a marimbaphono* "Wood and Wind" (1978);

String Quartet (1981); *Fantasia* for Viola and Organ (1982); choral works; songs; piano pieces; organ music.

Eberhardt, Siegfried, German violin pedagogue, son of the violinist and pedagogue Goby Eberhardt (1851–1926); b. Frankfurt am Main, March 19, 1883; d. Zwickau, June 29, 1960. He studied violin with Dessau at the Stern Cons. in Berlin, and then with Serato; was a teacher of violin at the Stern Cons. (1908–35); then lived in Halle and Lübeck; in 1945, founded the Hochschule für Theater und Musik in Halle and the Zwickau Academy.
  WRITINGS: *Der beseelte Violinton* (with C. Flesch; 1910; also in Eng.); *Absolute Treffsicherheit auf der Violine* (1911; 22 eds.; also in Eng., French, and Swedish); *Virtuose Violin-Technik* (1921); *Paganinis Geigenhaltung* (1921); *Die Lehre der organischen Geigenhaltung* (1922); *Der Körper in Form und Hemmung* (1926); *Wiederaufstieg oder Untergang der Kunst der Geigen* (1956).
  BIBL.: K. Schröter, *Flesch-E., Naturwidrige oder natürliche Violintechnik?* (1924).

Eberl, Anton (Franz Josef), Austrian pianist and composer; b. Vienna, June 13, 1765; d. there, March 11, 1807. On Feb. 27, 1787, he produced in Vienna the singspiel *La Marchande des modes*; there followed several other stage works, including *Die Zigeuner* (Vienna, 1793). His syms. and piano music were praised by Mozart and Gluck. He made a concert tour with Mozart's widow in 1795; lived in St. Petersburg from 1796 to 1799; revisited Russia in 1801; gave concerts there on Dec. 8, 15, and 28, 1801, presenting the 1st performances in Russia of Haydn's *The Creation;* returned to Vienna early in 1802; traveled through Germany in 1806. Besides 4 more stage works, he wrote 2 cantatas, syms., piano concertos, much chamber music, many piano works (especially sonatas), songs, etc.
  BIBL.: F. Ewens, *A. E.: Ein Beitrag zur Musikgeschichte in Wien um 1800* (Dresden, 1927; with thematic catalog); R. Haas, "A. E.," *Mozart-Jahrbuch 1951* (Salzburg, 1953); A. White, *The Piano Works of A. E.* (1765–1807) (diss., Univ. of Wisconsin, 1971).

Eberlin (Eberle), Johann Ernst, German composer; b. Jettingen, Bavaria, March 27, 1702; d. Salzburg, June 19, 1762. He settled in Salzburg, where he studied at the Benedictine Univ. (1721–23); was 4th organist (1726–29) and principal organist and choirmaster (1729–49) at the Cathedral, then was court and cathedral Kapellmeister (1749–62). Anton Adlgasser was his pupil and son-in-law. Among his compositions are a pastoral play, *Daphne* (1758), 61 school plays, intermezzos, 3 syms., much keyboard music (especially for organ), and much sacred music, including 21 oratorios and about 70 masses.
  BIBL.: R. Haas, "E.s Schuldramen und Oratorien," *Studien zur Musikwissenschaft,* VIII (1921); A. Layer, "J.E. E.," *Lebensbilder aus dem Bayerischen Schwaben,* VI (Munich, 1958); R. Pauly, "J.E. E.'s Motets for Lent," *Journal of the American Musicological Society,* XV (1962); M. Cuvay-Schneider, *Die Instrumentalwerke J.E. E.s* (diss., Univ. of Salzburg, 1975).

Ebert, (Anton) Carl, noted German opera producer and administrator; b. Berlin, Feb. 20, 1887; d. Santa Monica, Calif., May 14, 1980. He studied acting with Max Reinhardt; then appeared in theaters in Berlin and Frankfurt. In 1927 he became general administrator of the State Theater in Darmstadt and began to produce operas there. He then held a similar post at the Berlin City Opera (1931–33); he left Germany when the Nazis came to power. Ebert was one of the founders of the famous Glyndebourne Festival (1934), serving as its artistic director until 1939; in 1936 he organized the Turkish National School for Opera and Drama in Ankara, serving as its director until 1947; then was again artistic director at Glyndebourne (1947–59); was also a prof. and head of the opera dept. at the Univ. of Southern Calif., Los Angeles (1948–54). He subsequently was administrator of the Berlin Städtische Oper (1956–61). As a producer, he gave much importance to the fusion of the music with the dramatic action on stage.

Eberwein, (Franz) Carl (Adalbert), German violinist and composer, brother of **Traugott (Maximilian) Eberwein;** b. Weimar, Nov. 10, 1786; d. there, March 2, 1868. He was a member of a musical family; after a study of general subjects at the Weimar Hochschule für Musik he received an appointment as a court musician at the age of 16. He then studied with Zelter in Berlin; returning to Weimar, he held the posts of chamber musician (1810–18), music director of the Weimar cathedral church (1818–26), and conductor of the Weimar Opera (1826–49). He was a friend of Goethe, who often mentions him, and for whom he composed some songs.
  WORKS: 3 singspiels: *Die Heerschau; Der Graf zu Gleichen; Der Teppichhändler;* several cantatas written for various state occasions; some chamber music; a great number of songs with piano accompaniment.
  BIBL.: W. Bode, *Goethes Schauspieler und Musiker* (1912, with autobiographical sketch of Eberwein); H. Moser, *Goethe und die Musik* (Leipzig, 1949).

Eberwein, Traugott (Maximilian), German violinist and composer, brother of **(Franz) Carl (Adalbert) Eberwein;** b. Weimar, Oct. 27, 1775; d. Rudolstadt, Dec. 2, 1831. He played the violin in the Weimar Court Orch. as a very young man; like his brother, he was a protégé of Goethe; wrote 2 singspiels, *Claudine von Villa Bella* (1815) and *Der Jahrmarkt von Plundersweilen* (1818), to texts by Goethe; he further composed church music and instrumental concertos.

Eccard, Johannes, eminent German composer; b. Mühlhausen, 1553; d. Berlin, 1611. He studied at the Mühlhausen Lateinschule; was a chorister at the Weimar court Kapelle (1567–71) and the Bavarian Hofkapelle in Munich (1571–73), where he studied with Lassus. He was in the service of Jakob Frugger in Augsburg (1577–78), then became a member of the Hofkapelle of Margrave Georg Friedrich of Brandenburg-Ansbach in Königsberg; subsequently was Kapellmeister to the Elector of Berlin (1608). He was one of the most significant Protestant composers of chorale motets of his day.
  WORKS (all publ. in Mühlhausen unless otherwise given): *20 neue christliche Gesäng Ludovici Helmboldi . . . artlich und lieblich zu singen, und auff allerley Instrumenten der Musik zu spielen* for 4 Voices (1574); *Neue deutsche Lieder* for 4 to 5 Voices, *gantz lieblich zu singen, und auff allerley musicalischen Instrumenten zu gebrauchen* (1578); *Neue Lieder* for 4 to 5 Voices, *ganz lieblich zu singen und auff allerley Instrumenten zu gebrauchen* (Königsberg, 1589); *20 odae sacrae Ludovici Helmboldi I. Harmonicis numeris pro scansione versuum, ornatae et compositae* for 4 Voices (1596); *Der erste Teil geistlicher Lieder auff den Choral oder gemeine Kirchenmelodey durchauss gerichtet* for 5 Voices (Königsberg, 1597); *Der ander Teil geistlicher Lieder auf den Choral oder gemeine Kirchenmelodey durchauss gerichtet* for 5 Voices (Königsberg, 1597); also publications with Joachim à Burck.
  BIBL.: A. Grauer, *The Vocal Style of Sixt Dietrich and Johann E. and Their Contributions to Lutheran Church Music* (diss., Univ. of Rochester, 1960).

(1) Eccles (Eagles), Solomon, English virginalist, violist, and teacher; b. c.1617; d. London, Jan. 2, 1682. He was born into a musical family. He was active as a musician and teacher until becoming a Quaker about 1660; he then publicly burned his music and instruments and thereafter preached against the evils of music. He wrote a tract entitled *A Musick-lector* (1667).
(2) Eccles (Eagles), Solomon, English bass violinist and composer; b. between 1640 and 1650; d. Guildford (buried), Dec. 1, 1710. He was a member of the King's Private Musick from Aug. 31, 1685, to Aug. 6, 1710. He composed music for a number of plays.
(3) Eccles (Eagles), Henry, English musician, father of **(5) John Eccles;** b. between 1640 and 1650; d. London (buried), March 31, 1711. He became a member of the King's Private Musick on July 17, 1689.
(4) Eccles, Henry, English violinist and composer; b. between

1675 and 1685; d. between 1735 and 1745. He is 1st mentioned in a concert notice in London in 1705, and later was in the service of the Duke d'Aumont, the French ambassador to London; subsequently he served the Duke in Paris. He publ. under his own name 12 violin sonatas in Paris in 1720; 18 movements were adapted from Valentini's *Allettamenti per camera*, op. 8, and 1 movement from Bonporti's *Invenzioni*, op. 10; he also brought out there several more violin sonatas and 2 flute sonatas in 1723.

(5) Eccles, John, English composer, son of **(3) Henry Eccles (Eagles);** b. probably in London, c.1668; d. Hampton Wick, Jan. 12, 1735. He became a composer for the United Companies at the Drury Lane Theatre in 1693; was also a musician-in-ordinary without pay in the King's band. In 1695 he was made music director of the theater company at Lincoln's Inn Fields. He composed numerous songs and other music for plays presented there until his retirement in 1706. He was made 1 of the King's 24 musicians-in-ordinary in 1696; was named Master of Musick in 1700. Eccles excelled as a composer of songs for the theater. He composed several important masques and other dramatic works, and also numerous court odes.
      WORKS: Masques and other dramatic pieces (all perf. in London): *Macbeth*, after Shakespeare (Dorset Garden, 1694); *The Rape of Europa* (1694?); *The Loves of Mars and Venus*, after Motteux (perf. in Ravenscroft's *The Anatomist*, Lincoln's Inn Fields, Nov. 1696; with G. Finger); *A Musical Entertainment: Joy to the Youthful Pair* (perf. in Ravenscroft's *The Italian Husband*, Lincoln's Inn Fields, Nov. 1697); *Ixion*, after Ravenscroft (perf. in Ravenscroft's *The Italian Husband*, Lincoln's Inn Fields, Nov. 1697); *Europe's Revels for the Peace*, written for the Peace of Ryswick, after Motteux (Lincoln's Inn Fields, Nov. 1697); *Hercules*, after Motteux (perf. in Motteux's *The Novelty*, Lincoln's Inn Fields, June 1698); *Rinaldo and Armida*, after J. Dennis (Lincoln's Inn Fields, Nov. 1698); *Acis and Galatea*, after Motteux (perf. in Motteux's *The Mad Lover*, Lincoln's Inn Fields, Dec.[?] 1700); *The Judgment of Paris, or The Prize of Music*, after Congreve (Dorset Garden, March 1701); *The British Enchanters, or No Magick Like Love*, an adaptation of Lully's *Amadis* (Haymarket, Feb. 1706; with W. Corbett; only 2 songs extant); *Semele*, after Congreve (1707; not perf.). He composed incidental music to more than 60 plays, including Dryden's *Troilus and Cressida, or Truth Found Too Late* (1694?), Dryden's *Aureng-Zebe* (1694), and Congreve's *The Way of the World* (Lincoln's Inn Fields, March 1700). His odes number about 400, but many have been lost. He also publ. *Theatre Musick, Being a Collection of the Newest Aires for Violin* (London, 1698), *A Collection of Lessons and Aires for the Harpsichord or Spinnett Composed by Mr. J. Eccles, Mr. D. Purcell and Others* (London, 1702), *A Sett of Airs Made for the Queen's Coronation* (London, 1702), and *A Collection of Songs for One, Two and Three Voices* (London, 1704).
      BIBL.: J. Jeffreys, *The E. Family* (Enfield, 1951); S. Lincoln, *John E.: The Last of a Tradition* (diss., Oxford Univ., 1963).

Echaniz, José, Cuban pianist and conductor; b. Havana, June 4, 1905; d. Pittsford, N.Y., Dec. 30, 1969. He studied piano in Havana; appeared as a soloist with major American orchs., receiving praise for his brilliant interpretations. In 1944 he joined the staff of the Eastman School of Music in Rochester, N.Y. He also served as conductor of the Grand Rapids Sym. Orch.

Eckard (Eckardt, Eckart), Johann Gottfried, German pianist and composer; b. Augsburg, Jan. 21, 1735; d. Paris, July 24, 1809. He was a copper engraver by profession and learned music in his spare time. In 1758 he was taken to Paris by the piano manufacturer J.A. Stein, and remained there. He acquired a great facility as a pianist, and gave successful concerts in Paris. In the preface to his album of 6 sonatas he states that his task was to compose music suitable for any keyboard instrument, but the indications of dynamics in the MS show that he had mainly the then-novel piano in view. Mozart admired Eckard's works, and there are traits in Mozart's keyboard music of the Paris period that may be traced to Eckard's usages. A complete ed. of Eckard's works for piano, ed. by E. Reeser and annotated by J. Ligtelijn, has been publ. (Amsterdam, 1956).
      BIBL.: E. Reeser, "J.G. E., 1735–1809," *Tijdschrift van de Vereniging voor Nederlandse muziekgeschiedenis*, XVII/2 (1949); idem, *Ein Augsburger Musiker in Paris: J.G. E. (1735–1809)* (Augsburg, 1984).

Eckardt, Hans, distinguished German musicologist; b. Magdeburg, Oct. 9, 1905; d. Berlin, Feb. 26, 1969. He studied philology in Leipzig, Berlin, Paris, and Heidelberg (1925–29); musicology with Sachs, Hornbostel, and Schünemann (1925–32). From 1932 to 1935 he taught at the Imperial Univ. in Fukuoka, Japan; from 1938 to 1945 he was in Kyoto as director of the Japanese-German Research Inst. of Cultural History. In 1948 he settled in Heidelberg; in 1958 he joined the faculty at the Free Univ. in Berlin. He was an authority on Japanese music; contributed articles to *Die Musik in Geschichte und Gegenwart;* wrote several papers in Japanese for *Monumenta Nipponica.*

Eckelt, Johann Valentin, German organist; b. Werningshausen, near Erfurt, May (baptized, May 8) 1673; d. Sondershausen, Dec. 18, 1732. From 1696 he was organist at Wernigerode; from 1703, at Sondershausen. He composed a Passion, cantatas, and organ works. His valuable library was acquired by E.L. Gerber, who utilized it in the compilation of his dictionary.
      BIBL.: E. Jacobs, "Der Orgelspieler und Musikgelehrte J.V. E., 1673–1732," *Vierteljahrsschrift für Musik-Wissenschaft*, IX (1893).

Eckerberg, (Axel) Sixten (Lennart), Swedish conductor, pianist, and composer; b. Hjältevad, Ingatorp, Sept. 5, 1909. He studied at the Stockholm Cons. (1927–32); received a Jenny Lind stipend to study conducting with Weingartner in Basel (1932–34); also was a piano pupil of Emil Sauer in Vienna and of Isidor Philipp in Paris. From 1937 to 1969 he was chief conductor of the Swedish Radio Orch. in Göteborg. He publ. an autobiography, *Musiken och mitt lif* (Stockholm, 1970).
      WORKS: 3 syms. (1941, 1944, 1965); *Sommarmusik* for Orch. (1941); *Sub luna*, symphonic poem (1942); 3 piano concertos (1943, 1949, 1971); *Visione* for Orch. (1961); Piano Concertino (1962); *Triologi* for Voice, Flute, and Percussion (1969); *La danza della vita* for Orch. (1970); Nocturne for Alto and Orch. (1970–71); *Promenade Suite* for Winds and Percussion (1971); *Sagan om asarna* for Orch. (1971); Serenade for Orch. (1972); *Skogssuset* for Orch. (1973); *Ånger*, musical after Maupassant (1972; Radio Sweden, July 22, 1975); Cello Concerto (1974); chamber music; piano pieces.

Eckert, Karl (Anton Florian), German composer and conductor; b. Potsdam, Dec. 7, 1820; d. Berlin, Oct. 14, 1879. At the age of 6 he was considered a prodigy; the poet F. Förster became interested in him and sent him to the best teachers; he studied piano with Rechenberg and Greulich, violin with Botticher and Ries, and composition with Rungenhagen in Berlin. At the age of 10 he wrote an opera, *Das Fischermädchen;* at 13, an oratorio, *Ruth.* After completing his training with Mendelssohn in Leipzig, he began his career as a conductor at the Berlin Royal Opera; his opera *Das Käthchen von Nürnberg* was premiered there in 1837. With the outbreak of revolution in 1848, he went to the Netherlands and Belgium; he then conducted at the Théâtre-Italien in Paris (1851–53), and also toured the U.S. as an accompanist to Henriette Sontag (1852). He was conductor of the Vienna Court Opera (1853–60) and of the Vienna Phil. (1854–60); after serving as conductor of the Stuttgart Court Opera (1860–67), he was called to Berlin in 1869 to succeed Heinrich Dorn as conductor of the Royal Opera. Unlike Dorn, Eckert was a friend and champion of Wagner. Although he composed several ambitious works, his music met with little success; his songs, however, proved popular; of these, the *Swiss Echo Song* is best known.
      WORKS: OPERAS: *Das Fischermädchen* (1830); *Das Käthchen von Nürnberg* (Berlin, 1837); *Der Laborant im Riesengebirge*

(1838); *Scharlatan* (Königsberg and Berlin, 1840); *Wilhelm von Oranien* (Berlin, 1846); oratorios; Cello Concerto; songs.

Eckert, Rinde, American avant-garde vocalist, librettist, and composer; b. Mankato, Minn., Sept. 20, 1951. He studied at the Univ. of Iowa (B.M., 1973) and Yale Univ. (M.M., 1975), then was on the faculty of the Cornish Inst. (1980–82) and resident stage director of the Cornish Opera Theater. Since 1980 he has worked primarily with the composer Paul Dresher, and is principal performer and collaborator on their American opera trilogy (*Slow Fire* [1985–88], *Power Failure* [1989], and *Pioneers*). He was also principal performer and collaborator on the *How Trilogy* with George Coates Performance Works (*The Way of How* [1981], *are are* [1983], and *Seehear* [1984]; music by Dresher). Other works with Dresher include *Was Are/Will Be* (1983–85), *Shelf Life* (1987, with choreographer Margaret Jenkins), and *Secret House* (1990, with the Oberlin Dance Collective). His intense vocal style indicates both classical and rock training; his libretti are complex explorations, drenched with verbal paradox, of the pressure and instability of contemporary life. Among his own musical compositions are a radio opera, *Shoot the Moving Things* (1987), *Shorebirds Atlantic* for Voice, Harmonica, and Tape (1987), and *Dry Land Divine* for Voice, Accordion, Harmonica, and Electronics (1988).

Eckhard, Jacob, German-American organist and composer; b. Eschwege, Hesse, Nov. 24, 1757; d. Charleston, S.C., Nov. 10, 1833. He went to the U.S. in 1776 and settled in Richmond, Va. In 1786 he was organist of St. John's Lutheran Church in Charleston; in 1809 received the post of organist at St. Michael's Episcopal Church. He publ. a hymn book (Boston, 1816); wrote 2 patriotic naval songs, *The Pillar of Glory* and *Rise, Columbia, Brave and Free.*

BIBL.: G. Williams, "J. E. and His Choirmaster's Book," *Journal of the American Musicological Society* (Spring 1954).

Eckhardt-Gramatté, S(ophie)-C(armen) "Sonia," Russian-born Canadian violinist, pianist, teacher, and composer; b. Moscow, Jan. 6, 1899; d. in a traffic accident in Stuttgart, Dec. 2, 1974. Her mother, a former pupil of Anton and Nikolai Rubinstein, gave her piano lessons in Paris (1906–8). She then studied violin with Alfred Brun and Guillaume Rémy, piano with S. Chenée, and chamber music with d'Indy and Chevillard at the Paris Cons. (1909–13); while still a student, she gave concerts in Paris, Geneva, and Berlin, appearing as both a violinist and a pianist; she later received additional violin training from Huberman. In 1920 she married the painter Walter Gramatté; they lived in Barcelona (1924–26), but spent most of their time in Germany, where she toured as a duo pianist with Edwin Fischer in 1925. Her husband died in 1929. During the 1929–30 season, she toured the U.S., settling again in Germany in 1934, where she married the art critic Ferdinand Eckhardt; she assumed the name Eckhardt-Gramatté in 1939. She took additional courses in composition from Max Trapp at Berlin's Preussische Akademie (from 1936). The couple went to Vienna in 1939 and to Winnipeg in 1953. In 1958 she became a naturalized Canadian citizen. Her works are marked by an impressive craftsmanship.

WORKS: 3 piano concertos (1925, 1946, 1967); 2 syms. (1939; *Manitoba,* 1969–70); *Capriccio concertante* for Orch. (1940); Concertino for String Orch. (1947); *Markantes Stück* for 2 Pianos and Orch. (1946–50); Triple Concerto for Trumpet, Clarinet, Bassoon, Strings, and Timpani (1949); Bassoon Concerto (1950); 2 violin concertos (1951, 1952); Concerto for Orch. (1953–54); *Symphony-Concerto* for Piano and Orch. (1966–67); 4 suites for Violin (1922–68); 6 piano suites (1923–52); Concerto for Violin (1925); *10 Caprices* for Violin (1924–34); 6 *Caprices* for Piano (1934–36); 3 string quartets (1938; 1943; 1962–64); 2 duos for 2 Violins (1944); Duo for Viola and Cello (1944); Duo for 2 Cellos (1944); Wind Quartet (1946); 2 string trios (1947); *Ruck-Ruck Sonata* for Clarinet and Piano (1947; rev. 1962); Wind Trio (1947); 2 violin sonatas (1950, 1951); *Duo concertante* for Flute and Violin (1956); *Duo concertante* for Cello and Piano (1959); Wind Quintet (1962–63);

Nonet (1966); Piano Trio (1967); Woodwind Trio (1967); Concertino for Viola da Gamba and Harpsichord (1971); *Fanfare for 8 Brasses* (1971).

BIBL.: L. Watson, "S.C. E.-G.," *The Canadian Music Educator* (Fall 1975); F. Eckhardt, *Music from Within: A Biography of the Composer S.C. E.-G.* (Manitoba, 1985).

Eckstein, Pavel, Czech musicologist; b. Opava, April 27, 1911. He studied jurisprudence at Charles Univ. in Prague, graduating in 1935; received his musical education there. During the German occupation (1941–45) he was in a concentration camp in Lodz, Poland, but survived and returned to Prague, where he became active as an organizer of music festivals, an ed., and a writer on music. Among his books are *Czechoslovak Opera* (Prague, 1964) and *The Czechoslovak Contemporary Opera—Die tschechoslowakische zeitgenössische Oper* (Prague, 1967).

Eckstine, Billy (William Clarence), black American jazz singer and bandleader; b. Pittsburgh, July 8, 1914. He worked in nightclubs as a crooner; formed a band of his own in 1944, proselytizing for bebop, in association with such bop figures as Dizzy Gillespie and Miles Davis; later became successful as a balladeer of "cool" jazz.

Écorcheville, Jules (Armand Joseph), French writer on music; b. Paris, July 17, 1872; d. in a battle in Perthes-lès-Hurlus, Feb. 19, 1915. He was a pupil of Franck (1887–90); then studied literature and art history at the Sorbonne (bachelier ès lettres, 1891; licencié ès lettres, 1894; Ph.D., 1906, with the diss. *Vingt suites d'orchestre du XVIIe siècle français;* publ. in Paris and Berlin, 1906; supplementary diss., 1906, *De Lulli à Rameau, 1690–1730: L'Esthétique musicale;* publ. in Paris, 1906); he also studied musicology with Riemann at the Univ. of Leipzig (1905). He was active as a writer on history and esthetics of music; he was ed. of the *Mercure musical et bulletin français de la S.I.M.* (and its successors) from 1907; ed. *Actes d'État-civil de musiciens insinués au Chatelet de Paris (1539–1650)* (Paris, 1907); also prepared a *Catalogue du fonds de musique ancienne de la Bibliothèque Nationale* (some 10,000 items projected in 10 vols., of which only 8 were publ.).

BIBL.: L. Laloy, L. de la Laurencie, and E. Vuillermoz, *Le Tombeau de J. É.: Suivi de lettres inédites* (Paris, 1916).

Eda-Pierre, Christiane, French soprano; b. Fort-de-France, Martinique, March 24, 1932. She studied at the Paris Cons.; made her operatic debut in 1962 at the Paris Opéra in the title role of Donizetti's *Lucia di Lammermoor;* subsequently appeared as a guest artist with the Deutsche Oper in Berlin, the Hamburg State Opera, and the Chicago Lyric Opera. On April 3, 1980, she made her Metropolitan Opera debut in N.Y. as Constanze in Mozart's *Die Entführung aus dem Serail.* An outstanding coloratura soprano, she possesses a large operatic repertoire.

Eddy, (Hiram) Clarence, distinguished American organist; b. Greenfield, Mass., June 23, 1851; d. Winnetka, Ill., Jan. 10, 1937. He studied with Dudley Buck in N.Y.; in 1871 he went to Berlin to study piano with Löschhorn. He made frequent tours in America and Europe; appeared at the Vienna Exposition of 1873; at the Philadelphia Centennial in 1876; gave a series of 100 organ recitals in Chicago (1879) with completely different programs; appeared at the Chicago Columbian Exposition in 1893, etc. He wrote many pieces for organ; publ. *The Church and Concert Organist* (2 vols., 1882–85); *The Organ in Church* (1887); *A Method for Pipe Organ* (1917).

Eddy, Nelson, popular American baritone; b. Providence, R.I., June 29, 1901; d. Miami Beach, March 6, 1967. He studied voice with W. Vilonat in N.Y.; then in Dresden and Paris; was for 4 years a member of the Philadelphia Opera Co.; then sang on the radio with sensational success; also was a singing actor in 8 films with Jeannette MacDonald, including *Maytime* (1937), *Sweethearts* (1939), and *I Married an Angel* (1942).

BIBL.: E. Knowles, *Films of Jeannette MacDonald and N. E.* (1975).

Edelmann, Jean-Frédéric (Johann Friedrich), famous Alsatian harpsichordist, pianist, composer, and teacher; b. Strasbourg, May 5, 1749; d. (executed by guillotine) Paris, July 17, 1794. He studied law at the Univ. of Strasbourg (matriculated, 1770). He went to Paris about 1774, where he gained distinction as a performer, teacher, and composer. His students included Jean-Louis Adam and Méhul. His life took a tempestuous and ultimately tragic turn after he joined the Jacobin cause. Returning to Strasbourg in 1789, he was appointed administrator of the Lower Rhine. However, he soon fell out with his former friend Philippe-Frédéric Dietrich, the mayor of Strasbourg. Edelmann assisted in bringing about his arrest, trial, and execution in 1793. After further Jacobin intrigues, Edelmann himself became a victim of the Reign of Terror and was executed by guillotine. Through his teaching and compositions, Edelmann helped to make the piano a fashionable instrument in Paris. Many of his keyboard works were publ. in his lifetime. Ironically, his lyric drama *Arianne dans l'isle de Naxos* (1782) was dedicated to Joseph Ignace Guillotin.

Works: Stage: *La Bergère des Alpes,* scène lyrique (Paris, July 20, 1781); *Ariane dans l'isle de Naxos,* drame lyrique (Opéra, Paris, Sept. 24, 1782); *Diane et l'amour,* opéra-ballet (Paris, 1802); ballet, *Feu* (Opéra, Paris, Sept. 24, 1782). He also wrote an oratorio, *Esther* (Concert Spirituel, Paris, April 8, 1781; not extant). His instrumental works include *Six sonates pour le clavecin* and Violin ad libitum, op. 1 (Paris, 1775); *Six sonates pour le clavecin* and Violin ad libitum, op. 2 (Paris, 1776); *2 divertissements pour le clavecin* and Violin ad libitum, op. 3 (Paris, 1776); *Sinfonie pour le clavecin,* accompanied by 2 Violins, 2 Horns, and Cello ad libitum, op. 4 (Paris, 1776); *4 sonates* for Clavecin with Violin ad libitum, op. 5 (Paris, 1777); *3 sonates* for Clavecin with Violin ad libitum, op. 6 (Paris, 1778); *2 sonates* for Clavecin with Violin ad libitum, op. 7 (Paris, 1779); *3 sonates* for Clavecin with Violin ad libitum, op. 8 (Paris, 1779; No. 2 composed by Edelmann's sister); *4 quatuor* for Clavecin, 2 Violins, and Viola, op. 9 (Paris, 1781); *4 sonates* for Clavecin with Violin ad libitum, op. 10 (Paris, 1782); Concerto for Clavecin, 2 Violins, 2 Oboes, and Bass ad libitum, op. 12 (Paris, 1782); *4 sonates en quatuor* for Clavecin, accompanied by 2 Violins with Bass ad libitum, op. 13 (Paris, 1784); *3 concerts* for Clavecin, 2 Violins, and Viola, op. 14 (Paris, 1785); *4 divertissements* for Clavecin, 2 Violins, and Viola, op. 15 (Paris, 1786); *Airs pour clavecin ou le forte piano,* op. 16 (Paris, 1788). See R. Benton, "The Instrumental Music of Jean-Frédérich Edelmann: A Thematic Catalogue and List of Early Editions," *Fontes Artis Musicae,* XI/2 (1964).

BIBL.: M. Vogeleis, *Quellen und Bausteine zu einer Geschichte der Musik und des Theaters im Elsass 500–1800* (Strasbourg, 1911); G. de Saint-Foix, "Les Premiers Pianistes parisiens III: J.-F. E.," *La Revue Musicale,* V (1924); W. Newman, *The Sonata in the Classic Era* (Chapel Hill, 1963; 3rd ed., rev., 1983); R. Benton, "J.-F. E., A Musical Victim of the French Revolution," *Musical Quarterly* (April 1964).

Edelmann, Otto (Karl), noted Austrian bass-baritone; b. Brünn am Gebirge, near Vienna, Feb. 5, 1917. He studied with Lierhammer and Graarud at the Vienna Academy of Music, making his operatic debut as Mozart's Figaro in Gera in 1937; he then sang in Nuremberg (1938–40). After military service during World War II, he resumed his career as a leading member of the Vienna State Opera from 1947. He also sang at the Bayreuth Festival, the Salzburg Festival, La Scala in Milan, the Hamburg State Opera, the Edinburgh Festival, and other major operatic centers. On Nov. 11, 1954, he made his Metropolitan Opera debut in N.Y. as Hans Sachs in *Die Meistersinger von Nürnberg,* a role in which he particularly excelled; he continued to sing there regularly until 1970. His most famous role was that of Baron Ochs in *Der Rosenkavalier.*

BIBL.: S.-M. Schlinke, *O. E.: Ein Meistersinger aus Wien* (Vienna, 1987).

Edelmann, Sergei, remarkable Russian-born pianist; b. Lwow, July 22, 1960. He trained with his father, the head of the piano dept. at the Lwow Cons., then made his public debut at the age of 10 as soloist in Beethoven's 1st Piano Concerto with the Lwow Phil. After emigrating to the U.S. in 1979, he continued his studies with Firkušný at the Juilliard School in N.Y., and with Claude Frank at the Aspen School of Music. Blessed with an extraordinary virtuoso technique, he is esteemed for his performances of the Romantic repertoire.

Eder, Helmut, Austrian composer; b. Linz, Dec. 26, 1916. He studied at the Linz Cons. and took courses in composition with Hindemith in Salzburg (1947, 1950), Orff in Munich (1953–54), and J.N. David in Stuttgart (1954). He joined the faculty of the Linz Cons. in 1950; with Hans Paluj, he organized its electronic music studio in 1959, where he led a series of avant-garde concerts (1966–69). He also taught at the Salzburg Mozarteum (from 1967).

WORKS: OPERAS: *Ödipus* (1958); *Der Kardinal* (1962); *Die weisse Frau* (1968); *Konjugationen 3,* for television (1969); *Der Aufstand* (1975); *Georges Dandin oder Der betrogene Ehemann* (1978–79). **BALLETS:** *Moderner Traum* (1957); *Anamorphose* (1963); *Die Irrfahrten des Odysseus* (1964–65). **ORCH.:** 5 syms.: No. 1 (1950); No. 2 (1962); No. 3 for String Orch. (1959); No. 4, *Choral Symphony* (1973–75); No. 5, *Organ Symphony* (1979–80); *Musik* for 2 Trumpets and String Orch. (1955); *Concerto semiserio* for 2 Pianos and Orch. (1960); 2 violin concertos (1963, 1964); Concerto for Bassoon and Chamber Orch. (1968); *Pastorale* for Strings (1974); *Jubilato* for Chamber Orch. (1976); Double Concerto for Cello, Double Bass, and Orch. (1977–78); *Concerto A. B.* for Chamber Orch. (1982; also for Orch., 1983); *Haffner Concerto* for Flute and Orch. (1984); *Pièce de concert* for String Orch. (1984); much chamber music, including a String Quartet (1948), Piano Trio (1971), *Szene* for 6 Horns (1977), and a Quartet for Flute and String Trio (1983); piano pieces; organ music; choral works.

BIBL.: G. Gruber and G. Kraus, *H. E.* (Vienna, 1988).

Edlund, Lars, Swedish teacher, composer, and conductor; b. Karlstad, Nov. 6, 1922. He was educated at the Ingesund Music School and at the Stockholm Musikhögskolan (1942–47), then did further study at the Basel Schola Cantorum. He served as a church organist from 1948 to 1960, then was appointed to the Stockholm Musikhögskolan to teach aural musicianship, the subject of his internationally known *Modus novus: Lärobok i fritonal melodiläsning* (The New Way: A Textbook in Atonal Melody Reading; 1963) and *Modus vetus: Gehörstudier i dur/moll-tonalitet* (The Old Way: Ear Training in Major/Minor Tonalities; 1967). The former, which includes examples by Webern, Blomdahl, Stravinsky, and others, is in wide use in teaching atonal sight-singing. As a composer, he has written numerous choral works with various accompaniments, as well as works for instruments, particularly harpsichord.

Edmunds (St. Edmunds), John (Charles Sterling), American music scholar and composer; b. San Francisco, June 10, 1913; d. Berkeley, Dec. 9, 1986. He studied with Scalero at the Curtis Inst. of Music in Philadelphia and with Walter Piston at Harvard Univ. (M.A., 1941). As a recipient of several grants and fellowships, he was enabled to go to Europe for further study. Returning to the U.S., he held various lectureships. He wrote numerous vocal pieces, but his most important contribution is his astute eds. of Elizabethan songs and realizations of the basso continuo of classical Italian songs; he also compiled a 12-vol. anthology of songs and solo cantatas by 17th-century English composers.

Edson, Lewis, American composer; b. Bridgewater, Mass., Jan. 22, 1748; d. Woodstock, N.Y., 1820. Originally a blacksmith by trade, he became very active as a music teacher. He went to N.Y. in 1776; moved to Woodstock in 1817. He compiled (with Thomas Seymour) *The New York Collection of Sacred Music;* composed the hymn tunes *Bridgewater, Lenox, Greenfield,* and others.

Edwards, Clara, American singer, pianist, and song composer; b. Mankato, Minn., April 18, 1887; d. N.Y., Jan. 17,

1974. She studied voice in Vienna; returned to America in 1914 and became active as a singer and pianist. She wrote a number of songs to her own words, among them *By the Bend of the River* and *Into the Night;* also composed music for children's plays and animated cartoons.

Edwards, Julian, English-born American composer; b. Manchester, Dec. 11, 1855; d. Yonkers, N.Y., Sept. 5, 1910. He was a pupil in Edinburgh of Sir H. Oakeley, and in London of G. Macfarren; conducted the Royal English Opera Co. (1877) and the English Opera at Covent Garden (1883); went to the U.S. in 1888, settling in Yonkers and devoting himself to composition. Some of his comic operas achieved more than average success, among them *Victoria* (Sheffield, March 6, 1883); *Jupiter* (N.Y., April 14, 1892); *Friend Fritz* (N.Y., Jan. 26, 1893); *King Rene's Daughter,* lyric drama (N.Y., Nov. 22, 1893); *Madeleine* (N.Y., July 31, 1894); *The Goddess of Truth* (N.Y., Feb. 26, 1896); *Brian Boru,* romantic Irish opera (N.Y., Oct. 19, 1896); *The Wedding Day* (N.Y., April 8, 1897); *The Patriot* (1907; N.Y., Nov. 23, 1908; revived, July 24, 1975, at the Newport, R.I., Music Festival; the libretto deals with an attempted assassination of George Washington).

Edwards, Richard, English poet, dramatist, and composer; b. Somerset, 1524; d. London, Oct. 31, 1566. He studied at Oxford (M.A., 1547); was (from 1561) master of the children of the Chapel Royal. With these choirboys he presented in 1564 his musical play *Damon and Pithias.* Edwards is believed to be the composer of the madrigal *In going to my naked bed,* written about 20 years before the madrigal became popular in England (this piece is reprinted by Fellowes in The English Madrigal School, 36).

Edwards, Ross, Australian composer; b. Sydney, Dec. 23, 1943. He studied at the New South Wales State Cons. (1959–62); privately with Richard Meale (1963) and Peter Sculthorpe (1965); at the Univ. of Adelaide with visiting composers Peter Maxwell Davies and Sándor Veress (1966–69). In 1976 he joined the faculty of the New South Wales Conservatorium in Sydney.
    Works: *Chamber Symphony* (1962); Piano Sonata (1962); Wind Quintet No. 1 (1963); Trio for Flute, Harp, and Viola (1965); *Music* for Flute and Tape (1965); Wind Quintet No. 2 (1965); Sextet for Flute, Clarinet, Horn, Harp, Viola, and Cello (1966); Sonata for Wind Quintet, Violin, Viola, Cello, and Harp (1967); 3 string quartets (1968, 1969, 1972); Etude for Orch. (1969; Sydney, April 3, 1971); *Monos I* for Cello (1970), *II* for Piano (1970), *III* for Violin (1971); *Choros* for Piano and Orch. (1971); *Kan-Touk* for Female Voice, Harp, 2 Pianos, 2 Percussion Instruments, and Tape (1973); *Antiphon* for Chorus, 3 Trumpets, 3 Trombones, Organ, and Tam-tams (1973); *Mountain Village in a Clearing Mist* for Orch. (1973); *Laikan I* (1979) and *II* (1981) for 6 Players.

Eeden, Jean-Baptiste van den, Belgian composer; b. Ghent, Dec. 26, 1842; d. Mons, April 4, 1917. He was a pupil in the conservatories at Ghent and Brussels, winning at the latter the 1st prize for composition (1869) with the cantata *Faust's laatste nacht.* In 1878, he was appointed director of the Mons Cons., succeeding Huberti.
    Works: OPERAS: *Numance* (Antwerp, Feb. 2, 1897) and *Rhena* (Brussels, Feb. 15, 1912); oratorios: *Brutus; Jacqueline de Bavière; Jacob van Artevelde; Le Jugement dernier;* dramatic scene for 3 Voices, *Judith;* 2 cantatas: *Het Woud* and *De Wind;* symphonic poem, *La Lutte au XVIᵉ siècle; Marche des esclaves;* etc.; also choruses and songs.
    Bibl.: P. Bergmans, "Notice sur J. v.d.E.," in the annual publication of the Académie Royale (Brussels, 1924; contains a complete catalog of works); M. Delsaux, *J. v.d.E. et son œuvre* (Mons, 1925).

Effinger, Cecil, American composer; b. Colorado Springs, July 22, 1914; d. Boulder, Colo., Dec. 22, 1990. He took courses in mathematics at Colorado College (B.A., 1935); then studied harmony and counterpoint with Frederick Boothroyd in Colorado Springs (1934–36). He then studied composition with

B. Wagenaar in N.Y. (1938) and Boulanger in Fontainebleau (1939), where he was awarded the Stoval composition prize. He was oboist in the Colorado Springs Sym. Orch. (1932–41) and the Denver Sym. Orch. (1937–41); taught at Colorado College (1936–41) and the Colorado School for the Blind (1939–41). During World War II, he conducted the 506th Army Band (1942–45); then taught at the American Univ. in Biarritz, France (1945–46). After teaching at Colorado College (1946–48), he was music ed. of the *Denver Post* (1947–48); then was head of the composition dept. (1948–81) and composer-in-residence (1981–84) at the Univ. of Colorado in Boulder. In 1954 he patented a practical music typewriter as the "Musicwriter." In his music he maintained a median modern style, making use of polytonal and atonal procedures, without abandoning the basic sense of tonality.
    Works: OPERAS: *Pandora's Box,* children's opera (1961); *Cyrano de Bergerac* (Boulder, July 21, 1965); *The Gentleman Desperado,* music theater (1976); incidental music. ORCH.: 5 syms. (1946–58); Concerto Grosso (1940); *Western Overture* (1942); Concertino for Organ and Small Orch. (1945); Piano Concerto (1946); Trio Concertante for Trumpet, Trombone, Horn, and Chamber Orch. (1964; also for 2 Pianos, 1968); Violin Concerto (1972); *Toccata* for Chamber Orch. (1980); *Landscape II* (1984). CHAMBER: 6 string quartets (1943, 1944, 1948, 1963, 1985; No. 2, n.d., unfinished); Viola Sonata (1944); 3 piano sonatas (1946, 1949, 1968); Piano Trio (1973); *Intrada* for Brass Quintet (1982); Flute Sonata (1985). ORATORIOS: *The Invisible Fire* for Soloists, Chorus, and Orch. (1957); *Paul of Tarsus* for Chorus, Strings, and Organ (1968). CANTATAS: *Cantata for Easter* for Chorus and Organ (1971); *Cantata Opus 111: From Ancient Prophets* for Chorus, Wind, Cello, and Double Bass (1983); other vocal works.

Egenolff, Christian, German music publisher; b. Hadamar, July 26, 1502; d. Frankfurt am Main, Feb. 9, 1555. He publ. 2 collections of 4-part songs, *Gassenhawerlin* and *Reutterliedlin* (1535; facsimile ed. publ. by Moser, Augsburg, 1927), which are of decided value.

Egge, Klaus, prominent Norwegian composer; b. Gransherad, Telemark, July 19, 1906; d. Oslo, March 7, 1979. He studied piano with Nils Larsen and composition with Fartein Valen; after a brief period of further instruction at the Hochschule für Musik in Berlin, he became engaged in organizational work in Norway; was president of the Soc. of Norwegian Composers from 1945 to 1972. In 1949 he received the State Salary of Art (a government life pension for outstanding artistic achievement). His style of composition is conditioned by Scandinavian modalities, within a framework of euphonious and resonantly modernistic harmonies. He liked to sign his scores with the notes E-g-g-e of his name, a motto which also served him occasionally as a basic theme.
    Works: 3 piano concertos: No. 1 (Oslo, Nov. 14, 1938); No. 2 (Oslo, Dec. 9, 1946); No. 3 (Bergen, April 25, 1974); *Sveinung Vreim* for Soli, Chorus, and Orch. (Oslo, Dec. 1, 1941); *Fjell-Norig* (Mountainous Norway) for Voice and Orch. (Oslo, Oct. 1, 1945); *Noreg-songer* (The Norway Song) for Chorus and Orch. (Oslo, May 2, 1952); 5 syms.: No. 1, *Lagnadstonar* (Sounds of Destiny; Oslo, Oct. 4, 1945); No. 2, *Sinfonia giocosa* (Oslo, Dec. 9, 1949); No. 3, *Louisville Symphony* (Louisville, Ky., March 4, 1959); No. 4, *Sinfonia seriale sopra B.A.C.H—E.G.G.E* (Detroit, March 28, 1968); No. 5, *Sinfonia dolce quasi passacaglia* (Oslo, Sept. 27, 1969); *Elskhugskvaede* (Love Song) for Voice and Strings (1942); *Draumar i stjernesno* (Starsnow Dreams), 3 songs for Soprano and Orch. (1943); *Fanitullen* (Devil's Dance), ballet (Oslo, 1950); *Tårn over Oslo,* overture (1950); Violin Concerto (Oslo, Nov. 5, 1953); Cello Concerto (Oslo, Sept. 9, 1966); Violin Sonata (1932); 2 piano sonatas: No. 1, *Draumkvede* (Dream Vision; 1933), and No. 2, *Patética* (1955); String Quartet (1933; rev. 1963); 3 Fantasies for Piano in the rhythms of the Norwegian dances Halling, Springar, and Gangar (1939); 2 wind quintets (1939, 1976); Piano Trio (1941); *Duo concertante* for Violin and Viola (1950); Sonatina for Harp (1974); choruses and songs.

Eggebrecht, Hans Heinrich, eminent German musicologist and editor; b. Dresden, Jan. 5, 1919. He attended the Gymnasium in Schleusingen, of which his father was superintendent; was drafted into the army during World War II, and was severely wounded; then studied music education in Berlin and Weimar; he received his teacher's certificate in 1948. He subsequently studied musicology with H.J. Moser, R. Münnich, and M. Schneider; received his Ph.D. in 1949 from the Univ. of Jena with the dissertation *Melchior Vulpius.* He was assistant lecturer under W. Vetter in music history at the Univ. of Berlin from 1949 to 1951; then did lexicographical work in Freiburg and taught musicology at the Univ. there (1953–55); he completed his Habilitation there in 1955 with his *Studien zur musikalischen Terminologie* (publ. in Mainz, 1955; 2nd ed., 1968). He was Privatdozent at Erlangen Univ. (1955–56) and taught musicology at the Univ. of Heidelberg (1956–57). In 1961 he succeeded W. Gurlitt as prof. of musicology at the Univ. of Freiburg. In 1964 he became ed. of the *Archiv für Musikwissenschaft.* One of his major musicological contributions was his publication of the vol. on musical terms and historical subjects (*Sachteil*) for the 12th ed. of the *Riemann Musik-Lexikon* (Mainz, 1967), in which he settles many debatable points of musical terminology. Equally important has been his editorship of the *Handwörterbuch der musikalischen Terminologie* since 1972. He also was an ed. of the *Brockhaus-Riemann Musik-Lexikon* with Carl Dahlhaus (2 vols., Wiesbaden and Mainz, 1978–79; supplement, 1989) and of *Meyers Taschenlexikon Musik* (3 vols., Mannheim, 1984).

WRITINGS: *Heinrich Schütz: Musicus poeticus* (Göttingen, 1959); *Ordnung und Ausdruck im Werk von Heinrich Schütz* (Kassel, 1961); *Die Orgelbewegung* (Stuttgart, 1967); *Schütz und Gottesdienst* (Stuttgart, 1969); *Versuch über die Wiener Klassik: Die Tanzszene in Mozarts Don Giovanni* (Wiesbaden, 1972); *Zur Geschichte der Beethoven-Rezeption: Beethoven 1970* (Wiesbaden, 1972); *Die Musik Gustav Mahlers* (Munich, 1982); *Die mittelalterliche Lehre von der Mehrstimmigkeit* (Darmstadt, 1984).

BIBL.: W. Breig, R. Brinkmann, and E. Budde, eds., *Analysen: Beiträge zu einer Problemgeschichte des Komponierens. Festschrift für H.H. E. zum 65. Geburtstag* (Stuttgart, 1984).

Eggen, Arne, Norwegian organist and composer, brother of **Erik Eggen;** b. Trondheim, Aug. 28, 1881; d. Baerum, near Oslo, Oct. 26, 1955. He studied in Christiania and in Leipzig; toured Norway and Sweden giving organ recitals; from 1927 to 1945 was president of the Soc. of Norwegian Composers. In 1934 he received the Norwegian State Salary of Art (a government life pension).

WORKS: 2 operas: *Olav Liljekrans,* after Ibsen (1931–40; Oslo, 1940), and *Cymbeline,* after Shakespeare (1943–48; Oslo, Dec. 7, 1951); Sym. (Christiania, March 4, 1920); *King Olav,* oratorio (Oslo, March 30, 1933); Chaconne for Organ (1917); 2 violin sonatas; Piano Trio; many songs and choral works.

Eggen, Erik, Norwegian composer and musicologist, brother of **Arne Eggen;** b. Trondheim, Nov. 17, 1877; d. Ringsaker, June 7, 1957. He was a schoolteacher in southern Norway (1898–1939); was ed. of *Norsk Toneblad* (1910–17); concurrently devoted himself to the study of folk music; composed *Norsk rapsodi* for Orch., a cantata, and choral works, mostly in a folk-song vein; publ. a monograph on Grieg (1911).

Egghard, Julius (pen name of **Count Hardegen**), Austrian pianist; b. Vienna, April 24, 1834; d. there, March 23, 1867. He was a pupil of Czerny and became a concert pianist; wrote a number of piano pieces in salon style, which were extremely popular.

Egidi, Arthur, German organist and composer; b. Berlin, Aug. 9, 1859; d. there, June 3, 1943. He studied in Berlin; taught at Hoch's Cons. in Frankfurt (1885–92); then was organist and choral conductor in Berlin. He composed mostly for the organ.

Egk (real name, **Mayer**), **Werner,** significant German composer; b. Auchsesheim, near Donauwörth, May 17, 1901; d.

Inning, near Munich, July 10, 1983. Rumor had it that he took the name Egk as a self-complimentary acronym for "ein grosser (or even ein genialer) Komponist." Egk himself rejected this frivolous suspicion, offering instead an even more fantastic explanation that Egk was a partial acronym of the name of his wife Elisabeth Karl, with the middle guttural added "for euphony." He studied piano with Anna Hirzel-Langenhan and composition with Carl Orff in Munich, where he made his permanent home. Primarily interested in theater music, he wrote several scores for a Munich puppet theater; was also active on the radio; then wrote ballet music to his own scenarios and a number of successful operas. He was also active as opera conductor and music pedagogue. He conducted at the Berlin State Opera from 1938 to 1941, and was head of the German Union of Composers from 1941 to 1945. He was commissioned to write music for the Berlin Olympiad in 1936, for which he received a Gold Medal. He also received a special commission of 10,000 marks from the Nazi Ministry of Propaganda. The apparent favor that Egk enjoyed during the Nazi reign made it necessary for him to stand trial before the Allied Committee for the de-Nazification proceedings in 1947; it absolved him of political taint. From 1950 to 1953 he was director of the Berlin Hochschule für Musik. As a composer, Egk continued the tradition of Wagner and Richard Strauss, without excluding, however, the use of acidulous harmonies, based on the atonal extension of tonality. The rhythmic investiture of his works is often inventive and bold. He publ. a vol. of essays under the title *Musik, Wort, Bild* (Munich, 1960).

WORKS: Piano Trio (1922); Passacaglia for Strings (1923); String Quartet (1924); String Quintet (1924); radio opera, *Columbus* (1932; Bavarian Radio, Munich, July 13, 1933; 1st stage perf., Frankfurt, Jan. 13, 1942); *Die Zaubergeige,* opera in 3 acts (Frankfurt, May 19, 1935; rev. Stuttgart, May 2, 1954); *Fürchtlosigkeit und Wohlwollen* (Baden-Baden, April 3, 1936); *Olympische Festmusik* for Orch. (Berlin Olympiad, Aug. 1, 1936); cantatas: *Natur-Liebe-Tod* and *Mein Vaterland* (both perf. at Göttingen, June 26, 1937); *Peer Gynt,* opera (Berlin, Nov. 24, 1938, composer conducting; highly successful despite the inevitable comparisons with Grieg); *Joan von Zarissa,* ballet (Berlin, Jan. 20, 1940); *La Tentation de Saint Antoine* for Contralto and String Quartet (Baden-Baden, May 18, 1947); Piano Sonata (1947); *Abraxas,* ballet (Baden-Baden Radio, Dec. 7, 1947; stage perf., June 6, 1948, in Munich); *Circe,* opera after Calderón (1945; Berlin, Dec. 18, 1948, composer conducting; rev. as *17 Tage und 4 Minuten,* Stuttgart, June 2, 1966); 2 sonatas for Orch. (1948, 1969); *Französische Suite,* after Rameau, for Orch. (Munich, Jan. 28, 1950); *Ein Sommertag,* ballet (Berlin, June 11, 1950); *Allegria,* suite for Orch. (Baden-Baden radio, April 25, 1952); *Die chinesische Nachtigall,* ballet after Andersen (Munich, May 6, 1953); *Chanson et Romance* for Coloratura Soprano and Chamber Orch. (Aix-en-Provence, July 19, 1953); *Irische Legende,* opera after Yeats (Salzburg, Aug. 17, 1955; rev. 1970); *Der Revisor,* opera after Gogol (Schwetzingen, May 9, 1957); *Variations on a Caribbean Theme* for Orch. (1959; Baden-Baden, Jan. 18, 1960); *Die Verlobung in San Domingo,* opera (Munich, Nov. 27, 1963); *Casanova in London,* ballet (Munich, Nov. 23, 1969); *Moria* for Orch. (Nuremberg, Jan. 12, 1973); *Spiegelzeit* for Orch. (1979); *Ouvertüre* (1979–80).

BIBL.: B. Kohl and E. Nölle, eds., *W. E.: Das Bühnenwerk* (Munich, 1971); E. Krause, *W. E.: Oper und Ballet* (Wilhelmshaven, 1971).

Egli, Johann Heinrich, Swiss composer; b. Seegräben, near Zürich, March 4, 1742; d. Zürich, Dec. 19, 1810. He studied voice, violin, piano, and composition; diligently perused theoretical works by Kirnberger and C.P.E. Bach. He composed mainly sacred choruses; publ. several song collections, among them *Lieder der Weisheit und Tugend* (Zürich, 1790); also publ. arrangements of Swiss folk songs, *Schweizerlieder* (Zürich, 1787).

Egmond, Max von, Dutch bass-baritone; b. Semarang (Java), Feb. 1, 1936. He received his musical training in the Netherlands; gained experience by entering voice competitions in Brussels and Munich. His career was enhanced by appearances in concerts and oratorios. He sang widely in Europe, and also had engagements in America.

Egorov, Youri, talented Russian pianist; b. Kazan, May 28, 1954; d. Amsterdam, April 15, 1988. He was a precocious child who learned to play piano at home; at the age of 17 he won a prize at the Long-Thibaud competition in Paris, and at 20 received 3rd prize at the Tchaikovsky Competition in Moscow. In 1978 he made his N.Y. debut, followed by solo performances with various American orchs. He settled in the Netherlands, where his career was cut tragically short by AIDS.

Ehlers, Alice (Pauly), Austrian-born American harpsichordist; b. Vienna, April 16, 1887; d. Los Angeles, March 1, 1981. She studied piano with Leschetizky in Vienna; during World War I she took lessons in harpsichord playing with Wanda Landowska in Berlin. In 1936 she emigrated to the U.S. From 1941 to 1967 she taught harpsichord at the Univ. of Southern Calif. in Los Angeles; she also gave courses at the Juilliard School of Music in N.Y. and the Univ. of Calif. in Berkeley. She continued to appear in concert as a harpsichordist and gave occasional performances even as a nonagenarian.

Ehlert, Louis, German composer, conductor, and writer on music; b. Königsberg, Jan. 13, 1825; d. Wiesbaden, Jan. 4, 1884. In 1845 he entered the Leipzig Cons., where he studied with Mendelssohn and Schumann; then took music courses in Vienna and Berlin, where he lived from 1850 to 1863. He visited Italy; conducted the Società Cherubini in 1869; from 1869 to 1871 taught piano at Tausig's school for advanced pianists; then was active in Meiningen and Wiesbaden mainly as a piano teacher. He wrote a great many piano pieces; also *Frühlingssinfonie* and *Requiem für ein Kind.* His collection of essays, *Aus der Tonwelt* (Berlin, 1877), was publ. also in Eng. under the title *From the Tone World* (N.Y., 1885); he also wrote an entertaining vol., *Briefe über Musik an eine Freundin* (Berlin, 1859), which was issued in an Eng. tr. as *Letters on Music, to a Lady* (Boston, 1870).

Ehmann, Wilhelm, German musicologist; b. Freistatt, Dec. 5, 1904; d. Freiburg, April 16, 1989. He studied musicology at the Univs. of Freiburg and Leipzig; received his Ph.D. in 1934 with the dissertation *Adam von Fulda als Vertreter der ersten deutschen Komponisten-Generation* (Berlin, 1936) from the Univ. of Freiburg; completed his Habilitation there with his *Der Thibaut-Behaghel-Kreis* in 1937. From 1934 to 1940 he was on the faculty of the Univ. of Freiburg; from 1940 to 1945 he taught at the Univ. of Innsbruck. In 1948 he founded and became director of the church-music school in Westphalia (later named the Hochschule für Kirchenmusik); he retired in 1972. He also taught at the Univ. of Münster (1948–54).
Writings: *Die Chorführung* (2 vols., Kassel, 1949; 3rd ed., 1956; vol. II, in Eng., Minneapolis, 1936); *Tibilustrium: Das geistliche Blasen, Formen und Reformen* (Kassel, 1950); *Erziehung zur Kirchenmusik* (Gütersloh, 1951); *Erbe und Auftrag musikalischer Erneuerung: Entromantisierung der Singbewegung* (Kassel, 1951); *J.S. Bach in unserem Leben* (Wolfenbüttel, 1952); *Das Chorwesen in der Kulturkrise* (Regensburg, 1953); *Kirchenmusik, Vermächtnis und Aufgabe* (Darmstadt, 1958); *Alte Musik in der neuen Welt* (Darmstadt, 1961); *Der Bläserchor: Besinnung und Aufgabe* (Kassel, 1969).

Ehrenberg, Carl (Emil Theodor), German conductor and composer; b. Dresden, April 6, 1878; d. Munich, Feb. 26, 1962. He studied with Draeseke at the Dresden Cons. (1894–98); from 1898 on was engaged as a conductor in Germany; from 1909 to 1914 conducted concerts in Lausanne, Switzerland; from 1915 to 1918 was an opera conductor in Augsburg; then conducted at the Berlin State Opera (1922–24). Subsequently he devoted himself mainly to teaching; was a prof. at the Cologne Hochschule für Musik (1924–35) and at the Akademie der Tonkunst in Munich (1935–45).
Works: 2 operas: *Und selig sind* (1904) and *Anneliese* (after a tale by Hans Christian Andersen, 1922); several overtures;

2 syms.; Sinfonietta; Cello Concerto; 4 string quartets; Piano Trio; Wind Quartet; String Trio; Violin Sonata; many choruses; songs; piano pieces.
Bibl.: A. Würz, "Komponist, Dirigent, Musikerzieher: Zu C. E.s 75. Geburtstag," *Zeitschrift für Musik,* CXIII (1953).

Ehrlich, Abel, German-born Israeli composer; b. Cranz, Sept. 3, 1915. He studied music in Germany; then studied at the Music Academy of Zagreb (1934–38). He went to Palestine in 1939 and studied composition with Solomon Rosowsky at the Jerusalem Academy of Music (1939–44); attended the summer courses in new music led by Stockhausen, Nono, and others at Darmstadt (1959, 1961, 1963, 1967). In Israel he taught in various schools. Until 1955 he based his music on Middle Eastern themes and folklore; since then he has developed a personal amalgam of traditional Jewish cantillation and modern serialism.
Works: 6 string quartets (1947, 1947, 1952, 1962, 1967, 1969); *Bashrav* for Violin (1953); *A Game of Chess* for Winds, Percussion, Piano, and Double Bass (1957); *The Towers and the Shadows* for Narrator, Singers, and Instruments (1960); *Testimony* for 2 Flutes (1961); *The Writing of Hezekiah* for Soprano, Violin, Oboe, and Bassoon (1962); 4 wind quintets (1966–70); *Radiations* for Piano (1967); *And Though Thou Set Thy Nest among the Stars* for Orch. (1969); *Music for Solo Cello* (1970); *Evolution* for Orch. (1970); *The Answer* for Tenor, Flute, and Saxophone (1970); *Deliver Them That Are Drawn unto Death* for String Orch. (1970); Trio for Violins (1970); *Improvisations with a Game in Hell* for String Trio (1970); Trio for Horn, Cello, and Percussion (1970); *Immanuel Haromi,* musical spectacle (1971); *The Unicorn* for 12 Singers, 3 Percussionists, and 3 Oboes (1971); *7 Minutes* for Strings (1971); *Seeing . . .* for Singer, Violin, and Cello (1971); Divertimento for Oboe, Clarinet, 2 Horns, and Strings (1971); *Job 7, 11–16* for Baritone, Chorus, and Orch. (1971); *Ne subito . . .* for Chorus and Orch. (1971); *Comedy* for Orch. (1971); Trio for Violin, Flute, and Bassoon (1971); *arpmusic* for Baritone, Mime, 8 Instruments, and Electro-acoustics, a tribute to the surrealist sculptor Hans Arp (1971); Trio for Horn, Violin, and Piano (1972); Piano Sonata (1973); Music for Violin, Cello, and 2 Tape Recorders (1974); *Carolus-Music* for Instrumental Ensemble (1975); *Diario* for Flute (1975); *A Vision of God* for 8 Groups, each consisting of Soprano, Alto, Violin, and Viola (1975); *Personal Boxes* for Soprano and Instruments (1976); *Many Wonders* for Soprano and Wind Quintet (1977); *Sonnets,* after Shakespeare, for Soprano, Baritone, Chorus, Oboe, Violin, and Viola (1977); *Dead Souls,* opera buffa after Gogol (1978); *Let Us Proclaim,* oratorio for Soloists, Chorus, and Orch. (1982); *Ice Plants* for Organ (1985); *Giordano Bruno,* semi-oratorio (1986); *Because You Are My Kinsman* for Soprano, Cello, and Piano (1989).

Ehrlich, (Karl) Heinrich (Alfred), Austrian pianist and writer on music; b. Vienna, Oct. 5, 1822; d. Berlin, Dec. 30, 1899. He was a pupil of Henselt and Thalberg (piano), and of Sechter (composition). For several years he lived at Hannover as court pianist. He was a piano teacher at the Stern Cons. in Berlin from 1864 to 1872 and again from 1886 to 1898. He was also music critic of the *Berliner Tageblatt.*

Ehrling, (Evert) Sixten, noted Swedish conductor; b. Malmö, April 3, 1918. He studied piano, organ, composition, and conducting at the Royal Academy of Music's Cons. in Stockholm. After a brief career as a concert pianist he joined the staff of the Royal Opera in Stockholm as a rehearsal pianist, and made his conducting debut there in 1940. He then took conducting lessons with Karl Böhm in Dresden (1941) and, after the end of World War II, with Albert Wolff in Paris. In 1942 he was appointed conductor in Göteborg; in 1944 he became a conductor at the Royal Opera in Stockholm, where he served as chief conductor from 1953 to 1960. From 1963 to 1973 he was music director of the Detroit Sym. Orch.; then headed the orch. conducting class at the Juilliard School of Music, N.Y. In 1978 he became music adviser and principal guest conductor of the Denver Sym. Orch., and from 1979 to 1985, principal guest conductor; he was also artistic adviser to the San Antonio Sym. Orch. (1985–88). He excels in the repertoire of Romantic music, and particularly in his authentic interpretation of works by Scandinavian composers.

Eibenschütz, José, German conductor; b. Frankfurt am Main, Jan. 8, 1872; d. Sülzhayn, Harz, Nov. 27, 1952. He studied at the Hoch Cons. in Frankfurt; in 1894 was appointed orch. conductor in Åbo, Finland; there he remained until 1905; subsequent positions as conductor were at Görlitz (1905–8) and with the Verein Hamburgischer Musikfreunde (1908–20), the Oslo Phil. (1921–27), and North German Radio in Hamburg (1928–33). From 1938 to 1946 he conducted in Scandinavia and in Russia; he returned to Germany in 1946.

Eichberg, Julius, German violinist and composer; b. Düsseldorf, June 13, 1824; d. Boston, Jan. 19, 1893. His 1st teachers were J. Fröhlich (at Würzburg) and J. Rietz (at Düsseldorf); he then (1843–45) attended the Brussels Cons., studying under Fétis, Meerts, and Bériot; in 1846 was appointed prof. of violin and composition at the Geneva Cons.; in 1856 went to N.Y.; settled in Boston in 1859 as director of the Museum Concerts (till 1866). He also became director of the Boston Cons. and superintendent of music in the public schools; he founded the Eichberg School for Violin.
Works: Light operas: *The Doctor of Alcantara* (Boston, April 7, 1862); *The Rose of Tyrol* (1865); *The 2 Cadis* (Boston, March 5, 1868); studies, duets, and characteristic pieces for violin; trios and quartets for strings; songs.

Eichborn, Hermann, German composer, writer on music, and inventor; b. Breslau, Oct. 30, 1847; d. Gries, near Bozen, April 15, 1918. He studied jurisprudence; then became interested in music and took organ lessons with the organist of the Breslau Cathedral. His income from a wine-brewing business in Gries enabled him to devote himself to writing and the invention of instruments. He also supported a local orch. which performed several of his works. In 1882 he patented his invention of the soprano horn in F, which he called Oktav Waldhorn, and which was adopted in many Silesian bands.
Works: Sonata for Waldhorn and Piano; *Rondo brillant* for Waldhorn and Orch.; *Trompeters Berglied,* "echo piece" for 2 Trumpets; *Trompeter blas! Nur ein Spass!* for 2 Trumpets and Orch.; several operettas.
Writings: *Die Trompete in alter und neuer Zeit* (Leipzig, 1881; new ed., Wiesbaden, 1968); *Das alte Clarinblasen auf Trompeten* (Leipzig, 1894); *Die Dämpfung beim Horn* (Leipzig, 1897); *Militarismus und Musik* (Leipzig, 1909).

Eichheim, Henry, American composer and violinist; b. Chicago, Jan. 3, 1870; d. Montecito, near Santa Barbara, Calif., Aug. 22, 1942. He received his elementary musical training from his father, Meinhard Eichheim, a cellist in the Theodore Thomas Orch.; then studied with C. Becker and L. Lichtenberg at the Chicago Musical College. After a season as a violinist in the Thomas Orch. in Chicago, he was a member of the Boston Sym. Orch. (1890–1912); then devoted himself to concert work and composition. He made 5 trips to the Orient (1915, 1919, 1922, 1928, mid-1930s) and collected indigenous instruments, which he subsequently used in his orch. music. All of his works are on oriental subjects, with their harmonic idiom derived from Debussy and Scriabin.
Works: *Oriental Impressions,* or *The Story of the Bell* (1919–22; Boston, March 24, 1922); *The Rivals,* ballet (1924; Chicago, Jan. 1, 1925; as an orch. piece, under the title *Chinese Legend,* Boston, April 3, 1925); *Malay Mosaic* (1924; N.Y., March 1, 1925); *Impressions of Peking* and *Korean Sketch* for Chamber Orch. (Venice, Sept. 3, 1925); *Burmese Pwé,* incidental music for a play (N.Y., March 16, 1926); *Java* (Philadelphia, Nov. 8, 1929); *Bali* (Philadelphia, April 20, 1933); Violin Sonata (1934); other chamber music.

Eichhorn, Kurt (Peter), German conductor; b. Munich, Aug. 4, 1908. He studied with Hermann Zilcher; made his professional debut at the Bielefeld Opera in 1932. In 1941 he conducted at the Dresden State Opera. After World War II, he returned to Munich as a conductor at the Gärtnerplatz Theater; also conducted at the Bavarian State Opera. From 1967 to 1975 he served as chief conductor of the Munich Radio Orch.

Eichner, Ernst (Dieterich Adolph), German composer and bassoon virtuoso; b. Arolsen, Hesse (baptized), Feb. 15, 1740; d. Potsdam, 1777. He was concertmaster at the court of Duke Christian IV of Pfalz-Zweibrücken from 1769 to 1772; visited Paris with the orch. in 1770, and after a very successful season in London (1773), was appointed a member of the orch. of Prince Frederick William of Prussia.
Works: 31 syms.; piano concertos; piano trios; piano sonatas; duets for violin and viola; quartets for flute, violin, viola, and cello; quintets for flute and string quartet.
Bibl.: A. Volk, *E. E.: Sein Leben und seine Bedeutung für die Kammermusik und das Solokonzert* (diss., Univ. of Cologne, 1943); M. Reissinger, *Die Sinfonien E. E.s (1740–1777)* (diss., Univ. of Frankfurt, 1970; with thematic catalog).

Eijken, Jan Albert van. See **Eyken, Jan Albert van.**

Eilers, Albert, German bass; b. Cöthen, Dec. 21, 1830; d. Darmstadt, Sept. 4, 1896. He studied at the Milan Cons.; made his opera debut in Dresden (1854); sang at the German Theater in Prague (1858–65). In 1876 Wagner selected him to sing the part of the giant Fasolt at Bayreuth. In 1882 he became a member of the Darmstadt Opera. He wrote a fairly successful comic opera, *Die Johannisnacht* (Koblenz, 1889).

Eimert, (Eugen Otto) Herbert, German musicologist and composer; b. Bad Kreuznach, April 8, 1897; d. Cologne, Dec. 15, 1972. He took courses with Abendroth, Bölsche, and Othegraven at the Cologne Cons. (1919–24) and studied musicology with Bücken, Kahl, and Kinsky at the Univ. of Cologne (Ph.D., 1931, with the diss. *Musikalische Formstrukturen im 17. und 18. Jahrhundert;* publ. in Augsburg, 1932). He worked for the Cologne Radio from 1927 until the advent of the Nazis in 1933; after the fall of the Third Reich in 1945 he resumed his activities (until 1965); was founder-director of its electronic music studio (1951–62). He served as a prof. at the Cologne Musikhochschule (1965–71). He composed a number of electronic works. His important writings include *Atonale Musiklehre* (Leipzig, 1924), *Lehrbuch der Zwölftontechnik* (Wiesbaden, 1950; 6th ed., 1966), and *Grundlagen der musikalischen Reihentechnik* (Vienna, 1963). With H. Humpert, he ed. *Das Lexikon der elektronischen Musik* (Regensburg, 1973).

Einem, Gottfried von, outstanding Austrian composer; b. Bern, Switzerland (where his father was attached to the Austrian embassy), Jan. 24, 1918. He went to Germany as a child; studied at Plön, Holstein; then was opera coach at the Berlin State Opera. In 1938 he was arrested by the Gestapo, and spent 4 months in prison. After his release he studied composition with Boris Blacher in Berlin (1941–43); was later (1944) in Dresden, where he became resident composer and music adviser at the Dresden State Opera; was then active in Salzburg. In 1953 he visited the U.S.; then settled in Vienna; in 1965 was appointed prof. at the Hochschule für Musik there. Having absorbed the variegated idioms of advanced techniques, Einem produced a number of successful short operas and ballets; in his music he emphasized the dramatic element by dynamic and rhythmic effects; his harmonic idiom is tense and strident; his vocal line often borders on atonality, but remains singable.
Works: OPERAS: *Dantons Tod* (Salzburg, Aug. 6, 1947); *Der Prozess* (The Trial; Salzburg, Aug. 17, 1953); *Der Zerrissene;* (Hamburg, Sept. 17, 1964); *Der Besuch der alten Dame* (Vienna, May 23, 1971); *Kabale und Liebe* (Vienna, Dec. 17, 1976); *Jesu Hochzeit* (Vienna, May 18, 1980; caused a scandal for depicting Christ as having taken a wife). **BALLETS:** *Prinzessin Turandot* (Dresden, Feb. 5, 1944); *Rondo vom goldenen Kalb* (Hamburg, Feb. 1, 1952); *Pas de cœur* (Munich, July 22, 1952); *Glück, Tod und Traum* (Alpbach, Aug. 23, 1954); *Medusa* (Vienna, Jan. 16, 1957; rev. 1971). **ORCH.:** *Capriccio* (Berlin, March 3, 1943); Concerto for Orch. (1943; Berlin, April 3, 1944); *Orchestra Music* (1947; Vienna, June 21, 1948); *Serenade* for Double String Orch. (1949; Berlin, Jan. 31, 1950);

Hymnus for Alto, Chorus, and Orch. (1949; Vienna, March 31, 1951); *Meditations* (Louisville, Nov. 6, 1954); Piano Concerto (1955; Berlin, Oct. 6, 1956); *Symphonic Scenes* (1956; Boston, Oct. 11, 1957); *Ballade* (1957; Cleveland, March 20, 1958); *Das Stundenlied* for Chorus and Orch. (Hamburg, March 1, 1959); *Dance Rondo* (Munich, Nov. 13, 1959); *Nachtstück* (1960; Kassel, Nov. 16, 1962); *Von der Liebe*, lyrical fantasies for High Voice and Orch. (Vienna, June 18, 1961); *Philadelphia Symphony* (Vienna, Nov. 11, 1961); *Chamber Songs* for Voice and Orch. (1964); Violin Concerto (1966; Vienna, May 31, 1970); *Hexameron* (1969; Los Angeles, Feb. 19, 1970); *Bruckner Dialog* (1971; Linz, March 23, 1974); *Rosa Mystica* for Voice and Orch. (1972; Vienna, June 4, 1973); *An die Nachgeborenen* for Soloists, Chorus, and Orch. (N.Y., Oct. 24, 1975); *Wiener Symphonie* (1976; Minneapolis, Nov. 16, 1977); *Arietten* for Piano and Orch. (1977; Berlin, Feb. 20, 1978); *Ludi Leopoldini*, variations on a theme of Emperor Leopold I (Berlin, Oct. 12, 1980); Organ Concerto (1983); *Müncher Sinfonie* (1985); Sym. No. 4 (1988). **CHAMBER:** Sonata for Violin and Piano (1949); *Sacred Sonata* for Soprano, Trumpet, and Organ (1971); *Die traumenden Knaben* for Chorus, Bassoon, and Clarinet (1972); 3 string quartets (1975, 1977, 1980); Wind Quintet (1975); Sonata for Solo Violin (1976); Sonata for Solo Viola (1980); *Steinbeis Serenade* for 8 Instruments (1981); String Trio (1985); 8 sets of lieder (1944–80).

Einstein, Alfred, eminent German-born American musicologist; b. Munich, Dec. 30, 1880; d. El Cerrito, Calif., Feb. 13, 1952. Although he was friendly with Albert Einstein, the 2 were not related; a search through the genealogies of both revealed no common ancestor. Alfred Einstein 1st studied law, then turned to music and took courses with Sandberger at the Univ. of Munich, receiving a Ph.D. in 1903 with the dissertation *Zur deutschen Literatur für Viola da Gamba im 16. und 17. Jahrhundert* (Leipzig, 1905); from 1918 to 1933 he was ed. of the *Zeitschrift für Musikwissenschaft;* lived in Munich until 1927 as music critic of the *Münchner Post;* from 1927 to 1933 he was an influential critic of the *Berliner Tageblatt;* in 1933 he left Germany; lived in London and Italy (near Florence); in 1938, settled in the U.S.; taught at Smith College (retired, 1950); was naturalized as an American citizen on March 2, 1945. A profound scholar, Einstein was also a brilliant journalist, with a vivid, richly metaphorical style, capable of conveying to the reader an intimate understanding of music of different eras.

WRITINGS: Rev. eds. of Riemann's *Musiklexikon* (9th ed., 1919; 10th ed., 1922; 11th ed., 1929); *Das neue Musiklexikon* (German ed. of A. Eaglefield-Hull's *Dictionary of Modern Music and Musicians,* 1926); *Geschichte der Musik,* with *Beispielsammlung zur älteren Musikgeschichte* (1917–18; 6th ed., rev., 1953); new ed. (3rd) of Köchel's *Mozart Verzeichnis* (Leipzig, 1937; reprint ed. with numerous corrections, Ann Arbor, 1947); *A Short History of Music* (London, 1936; N.Y., 1937; 4th ed., 1954; tr. of *Geschichte der Musik*); *Gluck* (London, 1936); ed. a collection, *The Golden Age of the Madrigal* (N.Y., 1942). His writings in America (publ. in Eng. tr. from his original German) include: *Greatness in Music* (N.Y., 1941; German ed., *Grösse in der Musik,* Zürich, 1951); *Mozart: His Character, His Work* (N.Y., 1945; 4th ed., 1959; German original, 1947); *Music in the Romantic Era* (N.Y., 1947; German ed., *Die Romantik in der Musik,* Vienna, 1950); *The Italian Madrigal* (3 vols., Princeton, 1949; of fundamental importance); *Schubert: A Musical Portrait* (N.Y., 1950; German tr., 1952); *Essays on Music,* ed. by P. Lang (N.Y., 1956; 2nd ed., rev., 1958).

BIBL.: O. Kindeldey, "To A. E.," *Notes,* VIII (1950–51).

Eiríksdóttir, Karólína, Icelandic composer; b. Reykjavík, Jan. 10, 1951. She studied composition with Thorkell Sigurbjornsson at the Reykjavík College of Music and with George Wilson and William Albright at the Univ. of Michigan (M.M., 1978); taught at the Kópavogur School of Music and the Reykjavík College of Music. In 1985 she received an Icelandic Artists'

Grant. Her music is stark and austere, laden with northern Romanticism.

WORKS: ORCH.: *Notes* (Ann Arbor, Mich., March 1, 1979); *Sónans* (Reykjavík, Oct. 15, 1981); 5 *Pieces* for Chamber Orch. (Reykjavík, April 30, 1983); Sinfonietta (Reykjavík, Nov. 3, 1985). **CHAMBER:** *Nabulations* for Paired Winds, Percussion, Violin, and Double Bass (1978); *Brot* (Fragments), nonet (1979); *Ylir* for Bassoon, Brass, String Quartet, and Harpsichord (1980); *In vultus solis* for Solo Violin (1980); *Blaa stulkan* for Clarinet, Violin, and Piano (1983); 6 *Movements* for String Quartet (1983); *Eins konar,* rondo for Piano (1984); *Rhapsodia* (1986); Piano Trio (1987).

Eisenberg, Maurice, outstanding German-born American cellist and pedagogue; b. Königsberg, Feb. 24, 1900; d. (while teaching a cello class at the Juilliard School of Music) N.Y., Dec. 13, 1972. He was taken to the U.S. as a child; studied violin; then, at the age of 12, took up the cello. He played as a youth in café orchs., and studied at the Peabody Cons. in Baltimore; was a cellist of the Philadelphia Orch. (1917–19); then joined the N.Y. Sym. (under Walter Damrosch). He went to Europe in 1927 and studied in Berlin with Hugo Becker; in Leipzig with Julius Klengel; in Paris with Alexanian; and in Spain with Casals; then taught at the École Normale in Paris (1930–37); returning to the U.S., he gave a concert in N.Y. (Dec. 27, 1937) with excellent success; then appeared with major sym. orchs.; taught at various colleges. With M. Stanfield he publ. *Cello Playing of Today* (1957).

Eisenberger, Severin, Polish pianist; b. Krakow, July 25, 1879; d. N.Y., Dec. 11, 1945. He studied with Leschetizky in Vienna; was a prof. at the Krakow Cons. from 1914 to 1921; lived several years in Vienna, and later went to the U.S. He played as a soloist with the Cincinnati Sym. Orch. in 1935, and gave recitals in Cleveland and elsewhere in the U.S.

Eisfeld, Theodor(e), German conductor and composer; b. Wolfenbüttel, April 11, 1816; d. Wiesbaden, Sept. 2, 1882. He conducted at the Wiesbaden Court Theater (1839–43); then in Paris. He occasionally visited Italy; took lessons with Rossini at Bologna. From 1848 to 1866, he lived in N.Y.; conducted the N.Y. Phil. (1852–54), and the Harmonic Soc. from its foundation; established quartet soirées in 1851 with Noll, Reyer, and Eichhorn, joined also by Otto Dresel as pianist. From 1854 to 1865 he alternated with Bergmann in conducting the N.Y. Phil.; retired to Wiesbaden in 1866.

BIBL.: H. Shanet, *Philharmonic: A History of New York's Orchestra* (N.Y., 1975).

Eisler, Hanns (Johannes), remarkable German composer; b. Leipzig, July 6, 1898; d. Berlin, Sept. 6, 1962. He began to study music on his own while still a youth, then studied with Weigl at the New Vienna Cons. and later privately with Schoenberg (1919–23); he also worked with Webern. In 1924 he won the Vienna Arts Prize. He went to Berlin in 1925 and taught at the Klindworth-Scharwenka Cons. In 1926 he joined the German Communist Party; after the Nazis came to power in 1933, he left Germany; made visits to the U.S. and was active in Austria, France, England, and other European countries. He taught at the New School for Social Research in N.Y. (1935–36; 1937–42) and at the Univ. of Calif. in Los Angeles (1942–48); then left the U.S. under the terms of "voluntary deportation" on account of his Communist sympathies. In 1949 he settled in East Berlin and became a prof. at the Hochschule für Musik and a member of the German Academy of the Arts. Under Schoenberg's influence, Eisler adopted the 12-tone method of composition for most of his symphonic works. However, he demonstrated a notable capacity for writing music in an accessible style. His long association with Bertolt Brecht resulted in several fine scores for the theater; he also worked with Charlie Chaplin in Hollywood (1942–47). His songs and choral works have become popular in East Germany. He composed the music for the East German national anthem, *Auferstanden aus Ruinen,* which was adopted in 1949. His writings include *Composing for the Films* (with T. Adorno;

N.Y., 1947), *Reden und Aufsätze* (Berlin, 1959), and *Materialen zu einer Dialektik der Musik* (Berlin, 1973). G. Mayer ed. his *Musik und Politik* (2 vols., Berlin, 1973 and Leipzig, 1982).

WORKS: STAGE: Opera, *Johannes Faustus* (Berlin, March 11, 1953); some 38 scores of incidental music, to works by Brecht (*Rote Revue*, 1932; *Die Rundköpfe und die Spitzköpfe*, 1934–36; *Furcht und Elend des dritten Reiches*, 1945; *Galileo Galilei*, 1947; *Tage der Kommune*, 1950; *Die Gesichte der Simone Machard*, 1957; *Schweyk im zweiten Weltkrieg*, 1943–59), Feuchtwanger (*Kalkutta, 4.Mai*, 1928), Ernst Toller (*Feuer aus den Kesseln*, 1934; *Peace on Earth*, 1934), Ben Jonson (*Volpone*, 1953), Aristophanes (*Lysistrata*, 1954), Shakespeare (*Hamlet*, 1954), Schiller (*Wilhelm Tell*, 1961), etc.; some 42 film scores (*None but the Lonely Heart*, 1944; *Woman on the Beach*, 1947; *Der Rat der Götter*, 1950; *Fidelio*, 1956; *The Witches of Salem*, 1957; *Trübe Wasser*, 1959; etc.). **CHORAL WITH ORCH.**: *Tempe der Zeit*, cantata (1929); *Die Massnahme* (1930); *Die Mutter* (1931); *Kalifornische Ballade*, cantata (1934; based on a radio score); *Deutsche Sinfonie* for Soloists, 2 Speakers, Chorus, and Orch. (Paris, June 25, 1937); *Lenin*, Requiem (1936–37); *Mitte des Jahrhunderts*, cantata (1950); *Bilder aus der "Kriegsfibel"* (1957). **VOICE AND ORCH.**: *Glückliche Fahrt* for Soprano and Orch. (1946); *Rhapsodie* for Soprano and Orch. (1949); *Die Teppichweber von Kujan-Bulak*, cantata for Soprano and Orch. (1957); *Es lächelt der See* for Soprano, Tenor, and Orch. (1961); *Ernste Gesänge*, 7 songs for Baritone and Strings (1936–62); also works for Voice and Smaller Ensembles, including 9 works entitled *Kammerkantate* (1937); many songs with piano; 6 orch. suites drawn from films (1930–33); other orch. works drawn from films and stage pieces, including 5 *Orchesterstücke* (1938) and *Kammersinfonie* (1940). **CHAMBER**: 3 piano sonatas (1923, 1924, 1943); *Divertimento* for Wind Quintet (1923); *Duo* for Violin and Cello (1924); *Piano Sonatine* (1934); *Präludium und Fuge über BACH* for String Trio (1934); Sonata for Flute, Oboe, and Harp (1935); Sonata for Violin and Piano (1937); String Quartet (1938); 2 nonets (1939, 1941); 2 septets (1940, 1947); *14 Arten, den Regen zu beschreiben* for Flute, Clarinet, Violin, Cello, and Piano (1940); piano albums for children, etc. A collected ed. of his compositions and writings was undertaken by the German Academy of the Arts in East Berlin in association with the Hanns Eisler Archive.

BIBL.: H. Brockhaus, *H. E.* (Leipzig, 1961); N. Notowicz, *H. E.: Quellennachweise* (Leipzig, 1966); H. Bunge, *Fragen Sie mehr über Brecht: H. E. im Gespräch* (Munich, 1970); E. Klemm, *H. E.: Für Sie porträtiert* (Leipzig, 1973); A. Betz, *H. E.: Musik einer Zeit* (Munich, 1976; Eng. tr. as *H. E.: Political Musician*, Cambridge, 1982); M. Grabs, *H. E.: Kompositionen, Schriften, Literatur: Ein Handbuch* (Leipzig, 1984).

Eisler, Paul, Austrian pianist, conductor, and composer; b. Vienna, Sept. 9, 1875; d. N.Y., Oct. 16, 1951. He was a pupil of Bruckner at the Vienna Cons.; conducted in Riga, Vienna, and at the Metropolitan Opera in N.Y.; made numerous tours as accompanist for Caruso, Ysaÿe, and other celebrated artists; composed several operettas (*Spring Brides; The Sentinel; The Little Missus; In the Year 1814*).

Eisma, Will (Leendert), Dutch violinist and composer; b. Sungailiat, island of Bangka, Indonesia, May 13, 1929. He learned violin from his father; then studied theory with Kees van Baaren at the Rotterdam Cons. (1948–53); from 1959 to 1961 he took a course with Petrassi at the Accademia di Santa Cecilia in Rome; also studied electronic music in Utrecht. He was an orch. violinist with the Rotterdam Phil. (1953–59) and, since 1961, with the Hilversum Radio Chamber Orch., where he joined a group of avant-garde musicians, Instrumental Circuitry Ensemble. In his works he cultivates a strong polyphonic idiom in an uncompromisingly dissonant counterpoint, while the titles reflect preoccupations with structural abstractions.

WORKS: 3 orch. concertos (1958, 1959, 1960); Concerto for 2 Violins and Orch. (1961); *Taurus* for Orch. (1963); *Volumina* for Orch. (1964); *Diaphora* for 15 Strings, Harpsichord, Marimbaphone, and Percussion (1964); *Pages from Albion Moonlight*

for 2 Mezzo-sopranos, Baritone, Chorus, and Orch. (1968); *5 Roses for Diana* for 16 Amplified Winds (1969); *Orchestral Music with Voice* for Soloists, Chorus, and Orch. (1969); *Vanbridge Concerto* for Horn Player (on 2 different Horns, and Tuba) and Orch. (Einhoven, Nov. 18, 1970); *Little Lane*, concerto for Oboe and Orch. (Hilversum, Feb. 15, 1974); *Le Choix du costume est libre*, concerto for Solo String Trio and Chamber Orch. (1974); *Indian Summer*, concerto for English Horn and Orch. (1981); *Suara-suara pada waktu fajar* (Voices at Daybreak) for Gamelan-Slendro and Orch. (1985); *Silver Plated Bronze* for Double Bass and Orch. (1986); Duo for Violin and Viola (1956); *Concert Piece* for Violin and Piano (1956); Septet (1959); Sonata for Clarinet, Horn, Violin, Viola, and Cello (1959); Solo Flute Sonatina (1959); Violin Sonatina (1960); 4 Duos for Violins (1961); String Quintet (1961); 2 Madrigals for Violin and Piano (1962); *Diaphonia* for Oboe, Violin, Viola, and Cello (1962); *Archipel* for String Quartet (1964); *Affairs II* for Recorder and Harpsichord (1964), and *III* for Oboe, Clarinet, and Bassoon (1965); *Fontemara* for Wind Quintet (1965); *World within World* for Oboe, Violin, Viola, and Cello (1966); *Klein Protokol* for Violin and Cello (1966); *Non-lecture IV* for Violin (1967); *Hot Powdery Stones* for Alto Recorder (1968); *Because It Is* for Oboe, Harpsichord, and Percussion (1968); *Non-lecture III* for Viola (1970); *Gezang XXIII* for Violin and Percussion (1970); *La Sonorité suspendue* for String Trio (1970); *If . . .* for Wind and String Quartets (1970); *Non-lecture II* for Saxophone (1971); *Le Gibet* for Baritone, 7 Instruments, and Live Electronics (1971); *The Light of the Cold Still Moon* for Cello and Piano (1972); *10 Flutes and Tape* (1973); *Collected Papers II* for Solo Instrument, Percussion, and Synthesizer (1973–74); *Concert à vapeur* for Violin, Tape, and Synthesizer (1974); *Helena Is Coming Later* for 2 Violins, Viola, Cello, and Synthesizer (1975); *Le Cheval mort* for Mezzo-soprano, Bass Clarinet, Piano, Percussion, 2 Synthesizers, and Tape (1976); *Mandi* for Brass Ensemble (1981); *À contre-courant* for Violin and Harp (1986); *Kalos* for String Quartet and Piano (1987); tape pieces; songs.

Eitler, Esteban, Austrian-Chilean composer; b. Bolzano, Tirol, June 25, 1913; d. São Paulo, Brazil, June 25, 1960. He studied at the Univ. of Budapest; left Europe in 1936; went to Buenos Aires, where he was associated with modernist music groups; in 1945 he settled in Santiago, Chile.

WORKS: *Microsinfonia politonal* (1943) for Full Orch. and *Policromia* (1950) for String Orch.; *Serie boliviana* for Flute and String Orch. (1941); Concertino for Piano and 11 Instruments (1947); Concertino for Horn and 11 Instruments (1949); Wind Quintet (1945); Quartet for Piccolo, Flute, Trumpet, and Saxophone (1945); Quartet for Flute, Violin, Viola, and Cello (1950); *Microsinfonia atonal* for Orch. (1956).

Eitner, Robert, eminent German musicologist; b. Breslau, Oct. 22, 1832; d. Templin, Feb. 2, 1905. He was a pupil of M. Brosig in Breslan; settled (1853) in Berlin as a teacher, and gave concerts (1857–59) of his own compositions. He established a piano school in 1863, and publ. *Hilfsbuch beim Klavierunterricht* (1871). He devoted himself chiefly to musical literature, and especially to research on works of the 16th and 17th centuries. One of the founders of the Berlin Gesellschaft für Musikforschung, he ed. its *Monatshefte für Musikgeschichte* from 1869 till his death; also the *Publikationen älterer praktischer und theoretischer Musikwerke* (from 1873).

WRITINGS: *Verzeichnis neuer Ausgaben alter Musikwerke aus der frühesten Zeit bis zum Jahre 1800* (1871); *Bibliographie der Musiksammelwerke des 16. und 17. Jahrhunderts* (with Haberl, Lagerberg, and Pohl, 1877); *Die Oper von ihren ersten Anfängen bis 1750* (3 vols., 1881–85); *Quellen- und Hilfswerke beim Studium der Musikgeschichte* (1891). His principal work is the great *Biographisch-bibliographisches Quellen-Lexikon der Musiker und Musikgelehrten der Christlichen Zeitrechnung bis zur Mitte des 19. Jahrhunderts* (10 vols., Leipzig, 1899–1904; additions and corrections publ. from 1913 to 1916 in a quarterly, *Miscellanea Musicae Bio-bibliographica*, ed. by H. Springer, M. Schneider, and W. Wolffheim; rev. and enl. ed.,

1959–60). Among Eitner's compositions are a biblical opera, *Judith;* an overture; a piano fantasia on themes from *Tristan und Isolde;* songs.

Eitz, Carl (Andreas), German music theorist; b. Wehrstedt, near Halberstadt, June 25, 1848; d. Eisleben, April 18, 1924. He originated a new system of solmisation ("Tonwortmethode"), somewhat similar to the English tonic sol-fa system. He also proposed a new unit of musical interval ("Millioktav"), a division of the octave into 1,000 equal parts, which was not adopted.

WRITINGS: *Das mathematisch-reine Tonsystem* (1891); *100 geistliche Liedweisen in Tonsilben gesetzt* (1893); *Deutsche Singfibel* (1899); *Tonwort-Wandtafel* (1907); *Bausteine zum Schulgesangunterricht im Sinne der Tonwortmethode* (Leipzig, 1911; 2nd ed., ed. by F. Bennedik, 1928).

BIBL.: G. Borchers, *C. E.* (1908); O. Messmer, *Die Tonwortmethode von C. E.* (Würzburg, 1911); F. Bennedik, *Historische und psychologisch-musikalische Untersuchungen über die Tonwortmethode von E.* (Langensalza, 1914); M. Koch, *Kurzgefasste Einführung in das Esche Tonwort* (Würzburg, 1925); F. Bennedik and A. Strube, *Handbuch für den Tonwortunterricht* (Leipzig, 1926; 5th ed., 1932); W. Stolte, *C. E. in seiner Bedeutung für Wissenschaft und Schule* (Detmold, 1951).

Ek, (Fritz) Gunnar (Rudolf), Swedish organist, cellist, and composer; b. Åsarum, Blekinge, June 21, 1900; d. Lund, June 21, 1981. He studied organ, cello, and composition at the Stockholm Cons.; played cello in the Swedish film industry orch. (1928–37). In 1942 he went to Lund, where he was employed as an organist.

WORKS: 3 syms. (1928, rev. 1940; 1930; 1932); *Swedish Fantasy* for Orch. (1935); *Fantasy* for Violin and Orch. (1936); Piano Concerto (1944); *Doomsday Cantata* (1946); *Dig vare lov och pris, o Krist,* choral fantasy for Chorus, Organ, and Strings (1950; Malmö, Dec. 13, 1964); *Fantasy and Fugue* for Strings (1940); Suite for Organ (1966); *Dorisk Suite* for Strings and 5 Winds (1966; rev. 1968–69); *Variations on a Chorale Theme* for Strings (1969); Wind Octet (1970); Concertino for Strings (1971); songs.

Ekier, Jan (Stanislaw), Polish pianist and composer; b. Krakow, Aug. 29, 1913. He studied composition with K. Sikorski and piano with Z. Drzewiecki; became a concert pianist; taught piano at the State College of Music in Warsaw. Among his works are *Highland Suite* for Chamber Orch. (1936); *Variations and Fugue* for String Quartet (1937); Piano Concerto (1949); *Melodies in Color* for Mixed Chorus and Orch., to words from folk songs in Polish, Russian, German, French, and English (1951).

Eklund, Hans, prominent Swedish composer and teacher; b. Sandviken, July 1, 1927. He studied at the Stockholm Musikhögskolan with Lars-Erik Larsson (1949–52) and with Ernst Pepping in Berlin (1954). He was prof. of harmony and counterpoint at the Stockholm Musikhögskolan (from 1964). In 1975 he was elected a member of the Royal Swedish Academy of Music; in 1985 he was awarded the degree of Litteris et Artibus from the King of Sweden. His music follows a tradition of neo-Classicism; most of his instrumental works are set in Baroque forms.

WORKS: Radio opera, *Moder Svea* (Mother Svea) for Soloists, Chorus, Trumpet, and Strings (Swedish Radio, Oct. 7, 1972). **ORCH.:** Variations for Strings (1952); *Symphonic Dances* (1954); *Musica da camera:* No. 1 for Cello and Chamber Orch. (1955); No. 2, *Art Tatum in Memoriam,* for Trumpet, Piano, Percussion, and Strings (1956); No. 3 for Violin and Chamber Orch. (1957); No. 4 for Piano and Orch. (1959); No. 5, Fantasia, for Cello and String Orch. (1970); No. 6 for Oboe and Chamber Orch. (1970); 8 syms.: No. 1, *Sinfonia seria* (1958); No. 2, *Sinfonia breve* (1964); No. 3, *Sinfonia rustica* (1967–68); No. 4, *Hjalmar Branting in Memoriam,* for Narrator and Orch. (1973–74); No. 5, *Quadri* (1978); No. 6, *Sinfonia senza speranza* (1983); No. 7, *La Serenata* (1984); No. 8, *Sinfonia grave* (1985); *Music* (1960); *Bocetos españoles* for Chamber Orch. (1961);

Songs from Stahl, cantata (1961); *Variazioni brevi* (1962); *Introduzione-Versioni e Finale* for Strings (1962–63); *Facce* (1964); Toccata (1966); *Interludio* (1967); *Primavera* for Strings (1967); *Pezzo elegiaco* for Cello, Percussion, and Strings (1969); *Introduction and Allegro* for Harpsichord and String Orch. (1972); Concerto for Trombone, Winds, and Percussion (1972); *Variazioni pastorali* for Strings (1974); Chamber Concerto for Violin and Strings (1977); Horn Concerto (1979); Concerto for Clarinet and Strings (1980); Concerto for Tuba and Brass Orch. (1980); Concerto for Clarinet, Cello, and Orch. (1983); *Fantasie breve* (1986); *Divertimento* (1986); *L'estate* for String Orch. (1986); Concerto Grosso for String Quartet and String Orch. (1987); *Due pezzi* (1988). **VOCAL:** *Den fula ankungen,* after H.C. Andersen, for Soloists, Children's Chorus, and Orch. (1976); *Requiem* for 2 Soloists, Chorus, and Orch. (1978; Stockholm, Nov. 24, 1979); *Homofoni* for Chorus (1987); *3 Sea Poems* for Chorus (1988). **CHAMBER:** 4 string quartets (withdrawn, 1954, 1960, 1964); 2 sonatas for Solo Violin (1956, 1982); *Improvisata* for Wind Quintet (1958); Piano Trio (1963); *4 Temperamenti* for 4 Clarinets (1963); *Sommarparafras* for Wind Quintet (1968); *Serenade* for Mixed Quintet (1978); *Omaggio à San Michele* for 4 Saxophones (1981); *5 Pieces* for Solo Clarinet (1983), Solo Oboe (1983), Solo Bassoon (1983), and Solo Double Bass (1984); *Serenade* for 10 Brass Instruments (1986); other chamber works; piano pieces; organ music.

Ekman, Karl, Finnish pianist and conductor; b. Kaarina, near Åbo, Dec. 18, 1869; d. Helsinki, Feb. 4, 1947. He studied in Helsinki (1889–92); from 1892 to 1895, was a pupil of H. Barth in Berlin and A. Grünfeld in Vienna; in 1895, a piano teacher at the Helsinki Cons., and from 1907 to 1911, director there; from 1912 to 1920, he was conductor of the orch. at Åbo. He arranged Swedish and Finnish folk songs, and ed. a piano method; publ. a biography of Sibelius (Stockholm, 1935; Eng. tr., 1936). His wife, Ida (b. Helsinki, April 22, 1875; d. there, April 14, 1942), a concert singer, studied in Helsinki, Paris, and Vienna; she distinguished herself by her performances of Sibelius's songs.

El-Dabh, Halim (Abdul Messieh), Egyptian-born American composer; b. Cairo, March 4, 1921. He studied piano and Western music at the Sulcz Cons. in Cairo (1941–44), then went to the U.S. in 1950 on a Fulbright fellowship, studying with Copland and Irving Fine at the Berkshire Music Center at Tanglewood and taking graduate degrees from the New England Cons. of Music and Brandeis Univ. In 1961 he became a naturalized U.S. citizen, subsequently teaching at Haile Selassie Univ. in Ethiopia (1962–64), Howard Univ. (1966–69), and Kent State Univ. (from 1969), where he later also was co-director of its Center for the Study of World Musics (from 1979). His compositions reveal Afro-Arab influences, especially in their rhythmic structures and their incorporation of unusual percussive devices. He publ. *The Derabucca: Hand Techniques in the Art of Drumming* (1965).

WORKS: **STAGE:** *Clytemnestra,* epic dance drama (for Martha Graham; 1958); *The Egyptian Series: Lament of the Pharaohs, Pyramid Rock to the Sky, Gloria Aton,* and *Prayer to the Sphinx* for Solo Voices, Chorus, and Orch. (1960); *The Islamic Series: Allahu Akbar, Al-khaheera, Ya Leiyly, Saladin and the Citadel,* and *The Nile* for Voices ad libitum and Orch. (1960); *Theodora in Byzantium* (1965); *Black Epic,* opera-pageant (1968); *Opera Flies* (1971); *Ptahmose and the Magic Spell,* opera trilogy: *The Osiris Ritual; Aton, the Ankh, and the World;* and *The 12 Hours Trip* (1972–73); *Drink of Eternity,* opera-pageant (1981). **ORCH.:** 3 syms. (1950, 1952, 1956); Concerto for Darabukka or Timpani, and Strings (1954); *Fantasia-Tahmeel* for Darabukka or Timpani, and Strings (1954); *Bacchanalia* (1958); *Tahmeela* for Flute and Chamber Orch. (1958–59); *Nomadic Waves* for Double Wind Orch. and Percussion; *Unity at the Cross Road;* Concerto for Darabukka, Clarinet, and String Orch. (1981); *Rhapsodia egyptia-brasileira* (1985); also 5 ballet suites; many chamber works.

El-tour, Anna, Russian soprano; b. Odessa, June 4, 1886; d. Amsterdam, May 30, 1954. She studied at the St. Petersburg

Cons. (voice with Mme. von Hecke; piano with Essipova). From 1913 to 1920, she taught in Moscow; then left Russia; from 1922 to 1925 was in Berlin; from 1925 to 1948, she taught at the Cons. International de Paris. After 1948, she was a prof. of singing at the Amsterdam Cons. She traveled widely in the Far East; gave recitals in Israel in 1953.

Elder, Mark (Philip), English conductor; b. Corbridge, June 2, 1947. He was educated at Cambridge Univ. Upon graduation he served as apprentice conductor of several British orchs. In 1970 he was appointed to the music staff of the Royal Opera House, Covent Garden, and the Glyndebourne Festival. In 1974 he became associate conductor of the English National Opera in London, and in 1979 its music director; in 1980 he was engaged as principal guest conductor of the London Mozart Players. In 1981 he made a satisfactory appearance conducting Wagner at the Bayreuth Festival. In 1983 he made his U.S. debut as a guest conductor with the Chicago Sym. Orch. In 1989 he became music director of the Rochester (N.Y.) Phil.

Eldridge, (David) Roy "Little Jazz," outstanding black American jazz trumpeter; b. Pittsburgh, Jan. 30, 1911; d. Valley Stream, N.Y., Feb. 26, 1989. In 1930 he went to N.Y., where he worked with various musicians, including Teddy Hill, and became a featured member of Fletcher Henderson's orch. (1935–36). With his brother Joe Eldridge, the saxophonist and arranger, he formed his own band in Chicago in 1936; then took it to N.Y. in 1939, where he gained fame as one of the master instrumentalists of the swing era. He played with the bands of Gene Krupa (1941–43) and Artie Shaw (1944–45), and also worked with Norman Granz's Jazz at the Philharmonic (from 1948); he later worked with Benny Carter, Johnny Hodges, Ella Fitzgerald, and Coleman Hawkins, and also led his own big band and combos. Although plagued by ill health after 1980, he made occasional appearances as a singer, drummer, and pianist.
BIBL.: J. Evensmo, *The Trumpet of R. E. 1929–1944* (Hosle, Norway, 1979); *Current Biography* (March 1987).

Elgar, Sir Edward (William), great English composer; b. Broadheath, near Worcester, June 2, 1857; d. Worcester, Feb. 23, 1934. He received his earliest music education from his father, who owned a music shop and was organist for the St. George's Roman Catholic Church in Worcester; he also took violin lessons from a local musician. He rapidly acquired the fundamentals of music theory and served as arranger with the Worcester Glee Club, becoming its conductor at the age of 22; simultaneously he accepted a rather unusual position for a young aspiring musician with the County of Worcester Lunatic Asylum at Powick, where he was for several years in charge of the institution's concert band; he was also engaged in various other musical affairs. In 1885 he succeeded his father as organist at St. George's. He married in 1889 and moved to Malvern, where he stayed from 1891 to 1904. During these years he conducted the Worcestershire Phil. (1898–1904); in 1905 he accepted the position of Peyton Prof. of Music at the Univ. of Birmingham, and in 1911–12 served as conductor of the London Sym. Orch. He then settled in Hampstead. His wife died in 1920, at which time he returned to Worcester.

Elgar's 1st signal success was with the concert overture *Froissart* (Worcester, Sept. 9, 1890). His cantata *The Black Knight* was produced at the Worcester Festival (April 18, 1893) and was also heard in London at the Crystal Palace (Oct. 23, 1897); the production of his cantata *Scenes from the Saga of King Olaf* at the North Staffordshire Music Festival (Oct. 30, 1896) attracted considerable attention; he gained further recognition with his *Imperial March* (1897), composed for the Diamond Jubilee of Queen Victoria; from then on, Elgar's name became familiar to the musical public. There followed the cantata *Caractacus* (Leeds Festival, Oct. 5, 1898) and Elgar's great masterpiece, the oratorio *The Dream of Gerontius* (Birmingham Festival, Oct. 14, 1900). He began to give more and more attention to orch. music. On June 19, 1899, Hans Richter presented the 1st performance of Elgar's *Variations*

on an Original Theme (generally known as *Enigma Variations*) in London. This work consists of 14 sections, each marked by initials of fancied names of Elgar's friends; in later years, Elgar issued cryptic hints as to the identities of these persons, which were finally revealed. He also stated that the theme itself was a counterpoint to a familiar tune, but the concealed subject was never discovered; various guesses were advanced in the musical press from time to time; a contest for the most plausible answer to the riddle was launched in America by the *Saturday Review* (1953), with dubious results. The success of the *Enigma Variations* was followed (1901–30) by the production of Elgar's *Pomp and Circumstance* marches, the 1st of which became his most famous piece through a setting to words by Arthur Christopher Benson, used by Elgar in the *Coronation Ode* (1902) as *Land of Hope and Glory;* another successful orch. work was the *Cockaigne Overture* (London, June 20, 1901). Elgar's 2 syms., written between 1903 and 1910, became staples in the English orch. repertoire. His Violin Concerto, 1st performed by Fritz Kreisler (London, Nov. 10, 1910), won notable success; there was also a remarkable Cello Concerto (London, Oct. 26, 1919, Felix Salmond soloist, composer conducting).

The emergence of Elgar as a major composer about 1900 was all the more remarkable since he had no formal academic training. Yet he developed a masterly technique of instrumental and vocal writing. His style of composition may be described as functional Romanticism; his harmonic procedures remain firmly within the 19th-century tradition; the formal element is always strong, and the thematic development logical and precise. Elgar had a melodic gift, which asserted itself in his earliest works, such as the popular *Salut d'amour;* his oratorios, particularly *The Apostles,* were the product of his fervent religious faith (he was a Roman Catholic). He avoided archaic usages of Gregorian chant; rather, he presented the sacred subjects in a communicative style of secular drama. Elgar was the recipient of many honors. He was knighted in 1904. He received honorary degrees of Mus.Doc. from Cambridge (1900), Oxford (1905), and Aberdeen (1906); also an LL.D. from Leeds (1904). During his 1st visit to the U.S., in 1905, he received a D.Mus. degree from Yale Univ.; in 1907 he was granted the same degree from the Univ. of Western Pa. (now the Univ. of Pittsburgh). He received the Order of Merit in 1911; was made a Knight Commander of the Royal Victorian Order in 1928 and a baronet in 1931; was appointed Master of the King's Musick in 1924. He was not a proficient conductor, but appeared on various occasions with orchs. in his own works; during the 3rd of his 4 visits to the U.S. (1905, 1906, 1907, 1911), he conducted his oratorio *The Apostles* (N.Y., 1907); also led the mass chorus at the opening of the British Empire Exhibition in 1924. His link with America was secured when the hymnlike section from his 1st *Pomp and Circumstance* march became a popular recession march for American high school graduation exercises.

WORKS: ORCH.: *Introductory Overture for Christy Minstrels* (Worcester, June 12, 1878, composer conducting); *Minuet-grazioso* (Worcester, Jan. 23, 1879); Suite in D major for Small Orch. (1882; 1st complete perf., Birmingham, March 1, 1888; rev. as *3 Characteristic Pieces,* op. 10 [1899]: No. 1, *Mazurka;* No. 2, *Serenade mauresque;* No. 3, *Contrasts: The Gavotte A.D. 1700 and 1900*); *Sevillana,* op. 7 (Worcester, May 1, 1884; rev. 1889); *Salut d'amour (Liebesgruss),* op. 12 (1888; London, Nov. 11, 1889); *Froissart,* concert overture, op. 19 (Worcester, Sept. 9, 1890, composer conducting); Serenade in E minor for String Orch., op. 20 (1892; 1st complete perf., Antwerp, July 23, 1896); *Sursum corda* for Strings, Brass, and Organ, op. 11 (Worcester, April 9, 1894); *Minuet* for Small Orch., op. 21 (orig. for Piano, 1897; orchestrated 1899; New Brighton, July 16, 1899); *Chanson de matin,* op. 15, No. 1 and *Chanson de nuit,* op. 15, No. 2 (orig. for Violin and Piano, c.1889–90; orchestrated 1901; London, Sept. 14, 1901); *Imperial March,* op. 32 (London, April 19, 1897, A. Manns conducting; for Queen Victoria's Diamond Jubilee); *Variations on an Original Theme (Enigma Variations),* op. 36 (1898–99; London, June

19, 1899, Richter conducting); *Sérénade lyrique* for Small Orch. (London, Nov. 27, 1900); *Pomp and Circumstance*, 5 marches for Sym. Orch., op. 39: No. 1, in D major (1901), and No. 2, in A minor (1901) (Liverpool, Oct. 19, 1901, A. Rodewald conducting), No. 3, in C minor (1904; London, March 8, 1905, composer conducting), No. 4, in G major (London, Aug. 24, 1907, H. Wood conducting), No. 5, in C major (London, Sept. 20, 1930, H. Wood conducting); *Cockaigne (In London Town)*, concert overture, op. 40 (London, June 20, 1901, composer conducting); *Dream Children*, 2 pieces for Small Orch., op. 43 (London, Sept. 4, 1902; also for Piano); *In the South (Alassio)*, concert overture, op. 50 (1903–4; London, March 16, 1904, composer conducting); *Introduction and Allegro* for String Quartet and String Orch., op. 47 (1904–5; London, March 8, 1905, composer conducting); *The Wand of Youth*, 2 suites for Orch., comprising the last revision of his music for a children's play composed c.1867: Suite No. 1, op. 1A (London, Dec. 14, 1907, H. Wood conducting), and Suite No. 2, op. 1B (Worcester, Sept. 9, 1908, composer conducting); Sym. No. 1, in A-flat major, op. 55 (1907–8; Manchester, Dec. 3, 1908, Richter conducting); *Elegy* for String Orch., op. 58 (London, July 13, 1909); Concerto in B minor for Violin and Orch., op. 61 (1909–10; London, Nov. 10, 1910, Fritz Kreisler soloist, composer conducting); *Romance* for Bassoon and Orch., op. 62 (1910; Herefordshire Orch. Soc., Feb. 16, 1911); Sym. No. 2, in E-flat major, op. 63 (1903–10; London, May 24, 1911, composer conducting); *Coronation March*, op. 65 (Westminster Abbey, London, June 22, 1911; for the coronation of King George V); *Carissima* for Small Orch. (1913; 1st public perf., London, Feb. 15, 1914); *Falstaff*, symphonic study in C minor with 2 interludes, op. 68 (1902–13; Leeds Festival, Oct. 1, 1913, composer conducting); *Sospiri* for Strings, Harp, and Organ, op. 70 (London, Aug. 15, 1914, H. Wood conducting); *Carillon*, recitation with Orch., op. 75 (London, Dec. 7, 1914, composer conducting); *Polonia*, symphonic prelude, op. 76 (London, July 6, 1915, composer conducting); *Une Voix dans le désert*, recitation with Orch., op. 77 (1915; London, Jan. 29, 1916, composer conducting); *Le Drapeau belge*, recitation with Orch., op. 79 (London, April 14, 1917, H. Harty conducting); Concerto in E minor for Cello and Orch., op. 85 (London, Oct. 26, 1919, Felix Salmond soloist, composer conducting; later arranged as a viola concerto by Lionel Tertis; Hereford Festival, Sept. 6, 1933, Tertis soloist, composer conducting); *Empire March* (Wembley, April 23, 1924, composer conducting); *Severn Suite* for Brass Band, op. 87 (London, Sept. 27, 1930; also for Orch., 1932; 1st public perf., Worcester, Sept. 7, 1932, composer conducting); *Nursery Suite* (1st public perf., London, Aug. 20, 1931, composer conducting; also arranged as a ballet, *Ninette de Valois*, by C. Lambert; London, March 21, 1932, Lambert conducting); *Mina* for Small Orch. (1933). Also incidental music for *Grania and Diarmid*, op. 42 (Yeats and Moore; Dublin, Oct. 1901); *The Starlight Express*, op. 78 (Blackwood and Pearn; London, Dec. 29, 1915); *King Arthur* (Binyon; London, March 12, 1923); *Beau Brummel* (Matthews; Birmingham, Nov. 5, 1928, composer conducting); other works: a masque, *The Crown of India*, op. 66 (1902–12; London, March 11, 1912; as a suite for Orch., Hereford Festival, Sept. 11, 1912, composer conducting), and a ballet, *The Sanguine Fan*, op. 81 (London, March 20, 1917).
VOCAL: OPERA: *The Spanish Lady*, in 2 acts, to a libretto based on Ben Jonson, op. 89 (unfinished; sketches date from 1878; 15 excerpts orchestrated by Percy M. Young; BBC, London, Dec. 4, 1969). **ORATORIOS:** *The Light of Life (Lux Christi)*, op. 29 (Worcester Festival, Sept. 10, 1896, composer conducting); *The Dream of Gerontius*, op. 38 (1899–1900; Birmingham Festival, Oct. 3, 1900, Richter conducting; although commonly listed as an oratorio, Elgar did not designate it as such); *The Apostles*, op. 49 (Birmingham Festival, Oct. 14, 1903, composer conducting); *The Kingdom*, op. 51 (1901–6; Birmingham Festival, Oct. 3, 1906, composer conducting). **CANTATAS:** *The Black Knight*, op. 25 (Worcester Festival, April 18, 1893, composer conducting); *Scenes from the Saga of King Olaf*, op. 30 (1894–96; North Staffordshire Music Festival, Hanley, Oct. 30, 1896,

composer conducting); *Caractacus*, op. 35 (Leeds Festival, Oct. 5, 1898, composer conducting). **OTHER VOCAL MUSIC:** *Salve Regina* (1878); *Domine salvan fac* (1878); *Tantum ergo* (1878); *O salutaris hostia* for 4–part Chorus (1880); *Credo*, in E minor (1880); *4 Litanies for the Blessed Virgin Mary* for a cappella Choir (1882); *Ave, Verum Corpus (Jesu, Word of God Incarnate)*, op. 2, No. 1 (1887); *Ave Maria (Jesu, Lord of Life and Glory)*, op. 2, No. 2 (1887); *Ave Maris Stella (Jesu, Meek and Lowly)*, op. 2, No. 3 (1887); *Ecce sacerdos magnus* for Chorus and Organ (Worcester, Oct. 9, 1888); *My Love Dwelt in a Northern Land*, part-song for Mixed Voices (Tenbury Musical Soc., Nov. 13, 1890); *Spanish Serenade (Stars of the Summer Night)* for Mixed Voices, op. 23 (1891; with orch. accompaniment, 1892; Herefordshire Phil. Soc., April 7, 1893); *Scenes from the Bavarian Highlands*, 6 choral songs with Piano or Orch., op. 27 (piano version, 1895; orch. version, 1896; Worcester Festival, April 21, 1896, composer conducting); *The Banner of St. George*, ballad for Chorus and Orch., op. 33 (London, March 14, 1895; 2nd version, London, May 18, 1897); *Te Deum and Benedictus* for Chorus and Organ, op. 34 (Hereford Festival, Sept. 12, 1897); *Sea-Pictures*, song cycle for Contralto or Mezzo-soprano and Orch., op. 37 (1897–99; Norwich Festival, Oct. 5, 1899, Clara Butt soloist, composer conducting); *To Her Beneath Whose Steadfast Star*, part-song for Mixed Voices (Windsor Castle, May 24, 1899; dedicated to Queen Victoria); *Weary Wind of the West*, part-song for Mixed Voices (1902; Morecambe Festival, May 2, 1903); *Coronation Ode* for Soloists, Chorus, and Orch., op. 44 (Sheffield Festival, Oct. 2, 1902, composer conducting); *5 Part-Songs from the Greek Anthology* for Men's Voices, op. 45 (1902; London, April 25, 1904); *Evening Scene*, part-song for Mixed Voices (1905; Morecambe Festival, May 12, 1906); *4 Part-Songs* for Mixed Voices, op. 53 (1907); *The Reveille* for Men's Voices, op. 54 (1907; Blackpool Music Festival, Oct. 17, 1908); *Angelus (Tuscany)*, part-song for Mixed Voices, op. 56 (1909; London, Dec. 8, 1910); *Go, Song of Mine* for Chorus, op. 57 (Hereford Festival, Sept. 9, 1909); song cycle with Orch., op. 59, Nos. 3, 5, and 6 (Nos. 1, 2, and 4 not composed; 1909–10; London, Jan. 24, 1910, Muriel Foster soloist, composer conducting); *O hearken thou*, offertory for Chorus and Orch., op. 64 (Westminster Abbey, London, June 22, 1911; for the coronation of King George V); *Great Is the Lord (Psalm 48)*, anthem for Mixed Voices, op. 67 (1910–12; Westminster Abbey, London, July 16, 1912); *The Music Makers*, ode for Soloists, Chorus, and Orch., op. 69 (1902–12; Birmingham Festival, Oct. 1, 1912, composer conducting); *Give unto the Lord (Psalm 29)*, anthem for Mixed Voices, Organ, and Orch., op. 74 (St. Paul's Cathedral, London, April 30, 1914); *2 choral songs for Mixed Voices*, op. 71 (1914); *Death on the Hills*, choral song for Mixed Voices, op. 72 (1914); *2 choral songs for Mixed Voices*, op. 73 (1914); *The Spirit of England* for Soloists, Chorus, and Orch., op. 80 (1915–17; 1st complete perf., London, Nov. 24, 1917, composer conducting); *The Wanderer* for Men's Voices (1923); *Zut, zut, zut* for Men's Voices (1923); also many solo songs.
CHAMBER: *Promenades* for Wind Quintet (1878); *Romance* for Violin and Piano, op. 1 (1878; Worcester, Oct. 20, 1885); *Harmony Music* for Wind Quintet (1879); String Quartet, op. 8 (1887; MS destroyed); Sonata for Violin and Piano, op. 9 (1887; MS destroyed); *Allegretto on GEDGE* for Violin and Piano (1888); *Liebesahnung* for Violin and Piano (1889); *La Capricieuse* for Violin and Piano, op. 17 (1891); *Very Melodious Exercises in the 1st Position* for Solo Violin, op. 22 (1892); *Études caractéristiques pour violon seul*, op. 24 (1882–92); Sonata in E minor for Violin and Piano, op. 82 (1918; 1st public perf., London, March 21, 1919); String Quartet in E minor, op. 83 (1918; 1st public perf., London, May 21, 1919); Quintet in A minor for Strings and Piano, op. 84 (1918–19; 1st public perf., London, May 21, 1919). **PIANO:** *Rosemary* (1882); *May Song* (1901); *Concert Allegro*, op. 46 (London, Dec. 2, 1901); *Skizze* (1903); *In Smyrna* (1905); *Sonatina* (1932); *Adieu* (1932); *Serenade* (1932). **ORGAN:** *11 Vesper Voluntaries*, op. 14 (1889); Sonata in G major, op. 28 (Worcester Cathedral, July 8, 1895). A collected ed. of his works, *The*

Elgar Complete Edition, ed. by Jerrold Northrop Moore and Christopher Kent, commenced publication in 1981.

BIBL.: The Elgar Soc. of England began issuing the *Elgar Society Newsletter* in 1973; it became the *Elgar Society Journal* in 1979. Other writings include the following: R. Buckley, *Sir E. E.* (London, 1904; new ed., 1925); E. Newman, *E.* (London, 1906); J. Porte, *Sir E. E.* (London, 1921); J. Shera, *E.'s Instrumental Works* (London, 1931); B. Maine, *E., His Life and Works* (2 vols., London, 1933); J. Porte, *E. and His Music* (London, 1933); A. Sheldon, *E. E.* (London, 1933); A.H. Fox-Strangways, "*E.*," *Music & Letters* (Jan. 1934); R. Powell, "*E.'s Enigma*," ibid. (July 1934); special Elgar issue of *Music & Letters* (Jan. 1935); C. Barber, "*Enigma Variations*," ibid. (April 1935); W. Reed, *E. as I Knew Him* (London, 1936; new ed., 1973); Mrs. R. Powell, *E. E.: Memories of a Variation* (London, 1937; 2nd ed., 1947); W. Reed, *E.* (London, 1939); W. Anderson, *Introduction to the Music of E.* (London, 1949); D. McVeagh, *E. E., His Life and Music* (London, 1955); P. Young, *E., O.M.* (London, 1955; new ed., 1973); idem, ed., *Letters of E. E. and Other Writings* (London, 1956); idem, ed., *Letters to Nimrod from E. E.* (London, 1965); M. Kennedy, *Portrait of E.* (London, 1968; 2nd ed., rev., 1982); R. Fiske, "The Enigma: A Solution," *Musical Times* (Nov. 1969); M. Hurd, *E.* (London, 1969); E. Sams, "*E.'s Cipher Letter to Dorabella*," *Musical Times* (Feb. 1970); idem, "Variations on an Original Theme (Enigma)," ibid. (March 1970); I. Parrott, *E.* (London, 1971); C. Kent, *E. E.: A Composer at Work: A Study of His Creative Processes as Seen through His Sketches and Proof Corrections* (diss., King's College, Univ. of London, 1978); S. Mundy, *E.: His Life and Times* (Tunbridge Wells, 1980); G. Hodgkins, *Providence and Art: A Study of E.'s Religious Beliefs* (London, 1982); C. Kent, "*E.'s Third Symphony: The Sketches Reconsidered*," *Musical Times* (Aug. 1982); M. De-la-Noy, *E. the Man* (London, 1983); C. Redwood, ed., *An E. Companion* (Ashbourne, 1983); R. Anderson, "E. and Some Apostolic Problems," *Musical Times* (Jan. 1984); D. Bury, *E. and the Two Mezzos* (London, 1984); J. Dibble, "Parry and E.: A New Perspective," *Musical Times* (Nov. 1984); D. Hudson, "*E.'s Enigma*: The Trail of Evidence," ibid.; J. Northrop Moore, *E. E.: A Creative Life* (Oxford, 1984); idem, *Spirit of England: E. E. and His World* (London, 1984); N. Reed, "*E.'s Enigmatic Inamorata*," *Musical Times* (Aug. 1984); M. Portnoy, "The Answer to E.'s Enigma," *Musical Quarterly*, No. 2 (1985); P. Young, "E. and the Spanish Lady," *Musical Times* (May 1986); C. Grogan, "*E.'s Rejected Apostle*," ibid. (Feb. 1988); J. Moore, ed., *E. E.: The Windflower Letters: Correspondence with Alice Caroline Stuart Wortley and Her Family* (Oxford, 1989); C. Weaver, *The Thirteenth Enigma? The Story of E. E.'s Early Love* (London, 1989).

Elías, Alfonso de, Mexican composer, father of **Manuel Jorge de Elías;** b. Cuernavaca, Aug. 30, 1902; d. Mexico City, Aug. 19, 1984. He studied piano and composition at the National Cons. of Mexico, where he later taught. His music is unerringly Romantic and contains no concessions to modern usages.

WORKS: Ballet, *Las biniguendas de plata* (1933); 3 syms. (1926, 1934, 1968); *Tlalmanalco*, suite for Clarinet, Bassoon, Trumpet, Piano, and Strings (1936); 2 string quartets (1930, 1961); Violin Sonata (1932); numerous minor pieces for various instrumental or choral ensembles.

Elías, Manuel Jorge de, Mexican composer, son of **Alfonso de Elías;** b. Mexico City, June 5, 1939. He received his early musical training from his father; he then entered the Autonomous National Univ. of Mexico and the National Cons., where he studied piano, organ, flute, violin, and cello (1959–62); in Mexico City he also attended courses by visiting lecturers: on *musique concrète*, given by Jean-Étienne Marie (1967), and on new music, by Stockhausen (1968); had lessons in conducting with Herrera de la Fuente (1968–72); attended a class in electronic music at Columbia Univ. in N.Y. (1974); then traveled to Belgium and enrolled in a workshop in opera and ballet conducting with Edgar Doneux in Brussels (1974–75); return-

ing to Mexico, he founded in 1976 the Inst. of Music of the Univ. of Veracruz. His music is hedonistically pragmatic and structurally precise, but allows interpolation of aleatory passages.

WORKS: *Pequeños corales* for Chorus a cappella (1954–57); *Suite romántica*, 10 pieces for Piano (1954–56); *Suite de miniaturas* for Wind Quartet (1957); *Sonata breve* for Piano (1958); *Estampas infantiles*, suite for Strings (1959); *Sinfonietta* (1958–61); *Vitral No. 1* for Chamber Orch. (1962), *No. 2* for Chamber Orch. and Tape (1967), and *No. 3* for Orch. (Mexico City, Nov. 7, 1969); *Divertimento* for Percussion (1963); ballet, *Jahel*, for 2 Pianos (1964); *Aforismo No. 1, Pájaros perdidos* for Chorus a cappella (1963); *Aforismo No. 2* for Flute and Tape (1968); *Guanajuato*, overture-divertimento for Orch. (1964); *Impresiones sobre una estampa colonial*, divertimento for Orch. (1965); *Ciclos elementarios* for Wind Quartet (1965); *Speculamen* for 2 Violins, 2 Violas, 3 Cellos, and Double Bass (1967); *Elegía heroica*, symphonic poem (1967); *Memento* for Recorder, Chorus, Strings, and Narrator (1967); String Quartet No. 1 (1967); *Música nupcial* for Contralto, and Brass or Strings (1967); 2 solo violin sonatas (1968, 1969); *Pro pax* for Tape (1968); 3 *Quimeras* for 2 Pianos (1969, 1973, 1974); 3 *Kaleidoscopios* for Organ (1969, 1973, 1974); *Sonante* (Sonority) No. 1 for Piano (1971), *No. 2* for Solo Clarinet (1970), *No. 3* for Trumpet, Trombone, and Horn (1970; version for Orch., 1974), *No. 4* for Orch. (Mexico City, March 26, 1971), *No. 5* for Orch. (Mexico City, Nov. 24, 1972), *No. 6, Homenaje a Neruda*, for String Orch. (1973), and *No. 7* for Orch. (Brussels, Dec. 1974); *Parametros I* for Synthesizer (1971); *Ludus* for 3 Choruses (1972–73); *Concertante No. 1* for Violin and Orch. (1973); *Música domestica* for Recorder and Percussion (1973); *Sine nomine* for String Quartet and Piano (1975); *Jeux* for Horn, Trumpet, and Bassoon (1975); *Obertura-Poema* for Soloists, Chorus, Organ, and Wind Orch. (1975); further choruses; songs.

Elias, Rosalind, American mezzo-soprano; b. Lowell, Mass., March 13, 1930. She studied at the New England Cons. of Music in Boston and at the Accademia di Santa Cecilia in Rome. In 1954 she joined the Metropolitan Opera in N.Y.; on Jan. 15, 1958, she sang the role of Erika in the 1st performance of Samuel Barber's *Vanessa* there; also appeared as a concert singer.

Elias, Salomon (Salomonis), French monk at Sainte-Astère, Périgord. He wrote in 1274 a treatise, *Scientia artis musicae* (printed by Gerbert, *Scriptores ecclesiastici de musica sacra potissimum*, vol. III, 1784), of value as the 1st practical work giving rules for improvised counterpoint.

BIBL.: E. Ferand, *Die Improvisation in der Musik* (Zürich, 1938); idem, "The 'Howling in Seconds' of the Lombards," *Musical Quarterly* (July 1939).

Eliasson, Anders, Swedish composer; b. Borlänge, April 3, 1947. He studied in Stockholm with Ingvar Lidholm and Soderholm. In 1983 he was awarded the Royal Swedish Academy of Music prize in Stockholm. His music emphasizes the structural elements in freely dissonant texture.

WORKS: *In Medias* for Violin (1970); *Kantillation* for Mezzo-soprano and Organ (1970); string quartet, *Melos* (1970); *Picnic* for Wind Quintet (1972); *Tider* for Mezzo-soprano, Trombone, Cello, Electric Organ, Marimba, Vibraphone, and Percussion (1972); *Glasdans* for Orch. (1973; Swedish Television, Jan. 9, 1974); *Inför logos* (In the Presence of Logos), after Kafka, for Chorus and Tape (1973); *Quo vadis* for Mezzo-soprano, Electric Organ, and Tape (1973); church opera, *En av oss* (One of Us; 1974); *Disegno della pioggia* for Piano, 4-hands, Cello, and Xylophone (1974); *Disegno* for String Quartet (1975); *Disegno* for 6 Brasses (2 Trumpets, Horn, 2 Trombones, and Tuba; 1975); *Impronta* for Orch. (1978); *Ombra* for Clarinet and String Quartet (1980); *Anders' Second* for Variable Instrumentation (1983); Sym. No. 1 (1986; Swedish Radio, Feb. 6, 1987); *Fantasia* for Orch. (1988).

Elizalde, Federico, Spanish composer; b. Manila, Philippines (of Spanish parents), Dec. 12, 1908; d. there, Jan. 16, 1979.

He entered the Madrid Cons. as a child and received the 1st prize as pianist at the age of 14. Later he went to California, and studied law at Stanford Univ. At the same time he took composition lessons with Ernest Bloch. He was subsequently active as a conductor of hotel orchs. in England; also visited Germany. Returning to his native islands, he became conductor of the Manila Sym. Orch. (1930). On April 23, 1936, he conducted his *Sinfonia concertante* at the Festival of the ISCM in Barcelona. He was in France during World War II; in 1948 he assumed the post of president of the Manila Broadcasting Co., but continued his travels in both hemispheres. His music is influenced mainly by Mañuel de Falla; beginning with dance-like works in the Spanish vein, Elizalde gradually changed his style toward neo-Classicism. He wrote the opera *Paul Gauguin* for the centennial of Gauguin's birth (1948); a Violin Concerto (1943); a Piano Concerto (1947); much chamber music.

Elizza, Elise (real name, **Elisabeth Letztergroschen**), Austrian soprano; b. Vienna, Jan. 6, 1870; d. there, June 3, 1926. She studied in her native city; then appeared as an operetta singer. In 1895 she joined the Vienna Opera, rapidly becoming one of its principal singers. She retired in 1919; then taught voice. She possessed a fine coloratura voice.

Elkan, Henri, Belgian-American conductor and music publisher; b. Antwerp, Nov. 23, 1897; d. Philadelphia, June 12, 1980. After study at the Antwerp and Amsterdam conservatories, he emigrated to the U.S. in 1920; subsequently conducted performances of the Philadelphia Grand Opera Co. (1928–36). In 1926 he founded the Henri Elkan Music Publishing Co. in Philadelphia; in 1928 he was joined by Adolphe Vogel, a cellist in the Philadelphia Orch., and the company became the Elkan-Vogel Music Publishing Co.; the partnership was dissolved in 1952, and in 1956 Elkan formed a publishing firm once again under his own name.

Elkus, Albert (Israel), American composer and teacher, father of **Jonathan (Britton) Elkus;** b. Sacramento, April 30, 1884; d. Oakland, Feb. 19, 1962. He studied piano with Hugo Mansfeldt in San Francisco, and later with Harold Bauer and Josef Lhévinne; went to Vienna, where he took lessons in conducting with Franz Schalk and counterpoint with Karl Prohaska; then took courses with Robert Fuchs and Georg Schumann in Berlin. Returning to the U.S., he taught at the Dominican College in San Rafael, Calif. (1924–31); was on the faculty of the San Francisco Cons. (1923–25; 1933–37); was its director from 1951 to 1957; he also taught at Mills College in Oakland (1929–44) and at the Univ. of Calif. at Berkeley (1935–51). Among his compositions are *Concertino on Lezione III of Ariosto* for Cello and String Orch. (1917); *Impressions from a Greek Tragedy* for Orch. (San Francisco, Feb. 27, 1921); a chorus for Men's Voices, *I Am the Reaper* (1921).

Elkus, Jonathan (Britton), American conductor, pedagogue, and composer, son of **Albert (Israel) Elkus;** b. San Francisco, Aug. 8, 1931. He started his musical career as a bassoon player; was bassoonist in the Calif. National Guard (1949–57). He studied composition with Cushing and Denny at the Univ. of Calif. in Berkeley (B.A., 1953), Ernst Bacon and L. Ratner at Stanford Univ. (M.A., 1957), and Milhaud at Mills College in Oakland, Calif. (1957). He taught at Lehigh Univ. in Bethlehem, Pa. (1957–73), and also conducted its bands; then was director of music at Cape Cod Academy (from 1979). He publ. a monograph, *Charles Ives and the American Band Tradition: A Centennial Tribute* (Exeter, England, 1974).
Works: operas: *The Outcasts of Poker Flat* (1959; Bethlehem, Pa., April 16, 1960); *Medea* (1963; Milwaukee, Nov. 13, 1970); *The Mandarin* (N.Y., Oct. 26, 1967); *Helen in Egypt* (Milwaukee, Nov. 13, 1970). **musicals:** *Tom Sawyer* (San Francisco, May 22, 1953); *Treasure Island* (1961); *A Little Princess* (1980); incidental music. **band:** *Camino Real* (1955); *Serenade* for Horn, Baritone Horn, and Band (1957); *CC Rag* (1974); *The Apocalypse*, rag (1974); *Pipers on Parade* (1976); *Chiaroscuro*, suite (1977); *Cal Band March* (1978); also many transcriptions and arrangements. **chamber:** *3 Sketches* for 2

Clarinets and Bassoon (1954); *The Charmer*, rag for Clarinet, Trombone, and Piano (1972); piano pieces; organ music; choruses; etc.

Ella, John, English violinist, conductor, and writer on music; b. Leicester, Dec. 19, 1802; d. London, Oct. 2, 1888. He studied violin in London; then enrolled as a harmony student at the Royal Academy of Music there; in 1827 went to Paris to study with Fétis. Returning to London, he played in theater orchs.; was director of Lord Saltoun's musical society until 1846; in 1845 he established the Musical Union, presenting morning concerts of chamber music, and was its director until 1880; in 1850 opened a series of "Music Winter Evenings" which continued until 1859. For these organizations he wrote analytical program notes, of excellent quality for the time. He was a contributor of reviews and music articles to the *Morning Post,* the *Musical World,* and the *Athenaeum.*
Writings: *Lectures on Dramatic Music Abroad and at Home* (1872); *Musical Sketches Abroad and at Home* (3 eds., 1861, 1869, 1878); *Record of the Musical Union* (1845–80); *Personal Memoir of Meyerbeer* (1868).
Bibl.: J. Ravell, "J. E.," *Music & Letters* (Jan. 1953).

Ellberg, Ernst (Henrik), Swedish composer and pedagogue; b. Söderhamn, Dec. 11, 1868; d. Stockholm, June 14, 1948. He studied violin and composition at the Stockholm Cons., and was a teacher there from 1903 to 1933; among his pupils were Hilding Rosenberg, Dag Wiren, and Gunnar de Frumerie. He wrote an opera, *Rassa,* which received a prize; several ballets and concert overtures; some chamber music.

Eller, Heino, noted Estonian composer and pedagogue; b. Tartu, March 7, 1887; d. Tallinn, June 16, 1970. He studied law at St. Petersburg Univ. (1908–11), and later took music courses at the Cons. there, graduating in composition in 1920 in the class of Kalafati. From 1920 to 1940 he taught at the music high school in Tartu; in 1940 he joined the faculty of the Cons. in Tallinn. Together with Artur Kapp, Eller established the modern national school of Estonian music, derived from folk materials but framed in modern harmonic structures. He was also renowned as a pedagogue.
Works: 3 syms. (1936, 1947, 1962); several symphonic poems, including *Öö hüded* (Nocturnal Sounds; 1920; rev. 1960); *Symphonic Scherzo* (1921); Violin Concerto (1933; rev. 1965); *Fantasy* for Violin and Orch. (1916; rev. 1963); 5 string quartets (1925, 1930, 1945, 1954, 1959); 2 violin sonatas (1922, 1946); 4 piano sonatas (1920, 1937, 1944, 1958).

Eller, Louis, Austrian violinist; b. Graz, June 9, 1820; d. Pau, July 12, 1862. He studied with Hysel; from 1836 made tours in central Europe; traveled to Spain and Portugal with Gottschalk. He wrote several effective pieces for the violin: *Valse diabolique, Menuet sentimental,* etc.

Ellerton, John Lodge (real name, **John Lodge**), English poet and prolific composer; b. Chester, Jan. 11, 1801; d. London, Jan. 3, 1873. An Oxford graduate, he studied counterpoint under Pietro Terriani in Rome, where he composed 7 Italian operas; he lived for some time in Germany, where he wrote 2 German operas. Besides his operas, he wrote an oratorio, *Paradise Lost* (1856); 6 syms., 4 concert overtures; 4 string quintets; 50 string quartets; 3 string trios; 8 trios for various instruments; 13 sonatas; 61 glees; 83 vocal duets; songs.

Elleviou, (Pierre-) Jean (-Baptiste-François), French operatic tenor; b. Rennes, June 14, 1769; d. Paris, May 5, 1842. He made his debut in Monsigny's *Le Déserteur* at the Comédie-Italienne in Paris in 1790, and sang there until 1801; then at the Opéra-Comique until 1813. The revival of interest in the works of Grétry in 1801 was largely due to his influence and excellent interpretations; Méhul wrote his *Joseph* (1807) and Boieldieu his *Jean de Paris* (1812) for him.
Bibl.: E.-H.-P. de Curzon, *J. E.* (Paris, 1930).

Elling, Catharinus, Norwegian composer and folklorist; b. Christiania, Sept. 13, 1858; d. there (Oslo), Jan. 8, 1942. He studied music with native teachers; then in Leipzig (1877–

78) and Berlin (1886–87). In 1898 a subvention was granted him by the state for the pursuit of his studies of Norwegian folk songs, on which he publ. various essays; he also wrote biographies of Ole Bull, Grieg, Svendsen, and Kjerulf, and publ. a book, *Norsk Folkemusik* (Oslo, 1922). He composed an opera, *Kosakkerne* (The Cossacks; 1890–94); an oratorio, *The Prodigal Son*; 2 syms.; incidental music to *A Midsummer Night's Dream*; chamber music; many songs.

BIBL.: Ø. Gaukstad, *Melodi- og tekstregister til C. E.s opptegnelser av folkemusikk* (Oslo, 1963).

Ellington, "Duke" (Edward Kennedy), famous black American pianist, bandleader, and composer; b. Washington, D.C., April 29, 1899; d. N.Y., May 24, 1974. He played ragtime as a boy; worked with various jazz bands in Washington, D.C., during the 1910s and early 1920s, and in 1923 went to N.Y., where he organized a "big band" (orig. 10 pieces) that he was to lead for the next half-century, a band that revolutionized the concept of jazz: no longer was jazz restricted to small combos of 4–6 "unlettered" improvisers; with the Ellington band complex arrangements were introduced, requiring both improvising skill and the ability to read scores; eventually these scores were to take on the dimensions and scope of classical compositions while retaining an underlying jazz feeling. In the early days his chief collaborator in composition and arrangements was trumpeter James "Bubber" Miley; baritone saxophonist Harry Carney, another arranger, was with the band from its inception until Ellington's death; from 1939 the main collaborator was pianist-composer Billy Strayhorn. Ellington possessed a social elegance and the gift of articulate verbal expression that inspired respect, and he became known as "Duke" Ellington. He was the 1st jazz musician to receive an honorary degree from Columbia Univ. (1973). He was also the recipient of the Presidential Medal of Freedom. He made several European trips under the auspices of the State Dept.; toured Russia in 1970 and also went to Latin America, Japan, and Australia. So highly was he esteemed in Africa that the Republic of Togo issued in 1967 a postage stamp bearing his portrait. His remarkable career is highlighted in his book *Music Is My Mistress* (Garden City, N.Y., 1973). Since his death, his band has been led by his son Mercer Ellington (b. Washington, D.C., March 11, 1919).

WORKS: More than 1,000 compositions, including *East St. Louis Toodle-Oo* (pronounced "toad-lo"; 1926); *Black and Tan Fantasy* and *Creole Love Song* (1927); *Mood Indigo* (1930); *Sophisticated Lady* (uses a whole-tone scale; 1932); *Diminuendo and Crescendo in Blue* (1937); *Black, Brown and Beige* (a tonal panorama of black history in America; 1943); *Liberian Suite* (1948); *My People*, commissioned for the 100th anniversary of the Emancipation Proclamation (1963); *1st Sacred Concert* (San Francisco, 1965); *2nd Sacred Concert* (N.Y., 1968); *The River*, ballet (1970); *Queenie Pie*, musical (unfinished; completed by others; Philadelphia, Sept. 20, 1986).

BIBL.: B. Ulanov, *D. E.* (N.Y., 1946); P. Gammond, *D. E., His Life and Music* (London, 1958); S. Dance, *The World of D. E.* (N.Y., 1970); D. Jewell, *D., A Portrait of D. E.* (N.Y., 1977); D. George, *The Real D. E.* (London, 1982); M. Tucker, *The Early Years of E.K. "D." E., 1899–1927* (diss., Univ. of Michigan, 1986); R. Frankl, *D. E.* (N.Y., 1988).

Ellinwood, Leonard (Webster), American musicologist; b. Thomaston, Conn., Feb. 13, 1905. He studied at Aurora College in Illinois and at the Eastman School of Music in Rochester, N.Y., where he received the degrees of M.M. and Ph.D. He subsequently held a number of teaching positions until 1939, when he became cataloguer at the Library of Congress in Washington, D.C.; he retired from there in 1975. He compiled *Musica Hermanni Contracti* (Rochester, 1936); ed. works of Francesco Landini (1939), *The History of American Church Music* (N.Y., 1953), and a *Bio-bibliographical Index of Musicians in the U.S.A. Since Colonial Times* (Washington, D.C., 1941; 2nd ed., 1956); also contributed to the Episcopal songbook *The Hymnal Companion* (1951).

Elliott, Paul, English tenor; b. Macclesfield, Cheshire, March 19, 1950. He was a choral scholar at Magdalen College, Oxford (1969–72), later pursuing his education at Oxford Univ. (B.A., 1973; M.A., 1977). His principal vocal teachers were David Johnston and Peter Pears. He served as vicar choral at St. Paul's Cathedral (1972–75) and sang with various choral and early music groups, including the John Alldis Choir (1972–76), the Deller Consort (1973–82), the Monteverdi Choir (1973–78), and the Academy of Ancient Music (from 1973); also was a founding member of the Hilliard Ensemble (1974–84) and the London Early Music Group (1976–79). He toured widely as a solo concert artist, and also sang in opera, scoring success as Handel's Acis in St. Gall (1984) and as Mozart's Belmonte in Chicago (1988). In 1987 he joined the faculty of the Indiana Univ. School of Music in Bloomington.

Ellis (real name, **Sharpe**), **Alexander J(ohn),** English writer on musical science; b. Hoxton (London), June 14, 1814; d. Kensington, Oct. 28, 1890. He studied at Trinity College, Cambridge, graduating in 1837; his subjects were mathematics and philology; he also studied music; was elected Fellow of the Royal Soc. (1864) and was president of the Philological Soc.; publ. valuable papers in the *Proceedings of the Royal Society:* "On the Conditions . . . of a Perfect Musical Scale on Instruments with Fixed Tones" (1864); "On the Physical Constitutions and Relations of Musical Chords" (1864); "On the Temperament of Instruments with Fixed Tones" (1864); and "On Musical Duodenes; or, The Theory of Constructing Instruments with Fixed Tones in Just or Practically Just Intonation" (1874). Papers containing new theories, etc., for the Musical Assoc. are as follows: "The Basis of Music" (1877); "Pronunciation for Singers" (1877); and "Speech in Song" (1878). He was awarded a silver medal for his writings on musical pitch for the *Journal of the Society of the Arts* (1877, 1880, and 1881; publ. separately, 1880–81; and in summary form in the Appendix to the 2nd ed. of his tr. of Helmholtz's *Lehre von den Tonempfindungen* under the title *On the Sensations of Tone, as a Physiological Basis for the Theory of Music*; 1st ed., 1875; 6th ed., 1948); he also wrote "Tonometrical Observations, or Some Existing Non-harmonic Scales" (*Proceedings of the Royal Society*, 1884) and "On the Musical Scales of Various Nations" (*Journal of the Society of the Arts*, 1885).

Ellis, Brent, American baritone; b. Kansas City, Mo., June 20, 1946. He studied with Edna Forsythe (1962–65), Marian Freschl (1965–71), and Daniel Ferro in N.Y. (from 1971), where he also attended classes at the Juilliard School of Music. In 1965 he made his 1st appearance at the Santa Fe Opera, where he later sang regularly (1972–82); also appeared at the Houston Grand Opera (1972–81). In 1973 he won both the WGN Radio Auditions of the Air and the Montreal International Competition, and on April 28, 1974, made his N.Y. City Opera debut as Ottone in *L'incoronazione di Poppea*; then sang with the Chicago Lyric Opera (1974), the San Francisco Opera (1974–78), the Boston Opera (1975–83), the Glyndebourne Festival (1977–78), the Hamburg State Opera (1977–79), and the Vienna State Opera (1977–79). On Oct. 25, 1979, he made his Metropolitan Opera debut in N.Y. as Silvio in *Pagliacci*. Among his other roles are Rossini's Figaro, Belcore, Ford, and Germont.

Ellis, Don(ald Johnson), American trumpet player, bandleader, and jazz music arranger; b. Los Angeles, July 25, 1934; d. there, Dec. 17, 1978. He studied composition at Boston Univ. with Gardner Read, and later at the Univ. of Calif., Los Angeles, with John Vincent; in the interim he took trumpet lessons in Boston, N.Y., and Los Angeles. He played with numerous bands; eventually formed his own group. In his arrangements he boldly introduced asymmetrical meters. His major work is *Contrasts* for 2 Orchs. and Trumpet (1965); he won a Grammy Award for his arrangement of music from the film *The French Connection* (1973).

BIBL.: A. Agostinelli, *D. E.: A Man for Our Time (1934–1978)* (Providence, R.I., 1984).

Elman, Mischa, remarkable Russian-born American violinist; b. Talnoy, Jan. 20, 1891; d. N.Y., April 5, 1967. At the age of 6 he was taken by his father to Odessa, where he became a violin student of Fidelmann and a pupil of Brodsky. His progress was extraordinary, and when Leopold Auer heard him play in 1902, he immediately accepted him in his class at the St. Petersburg Cons. In 1904 he made his debut in St. Petersburg with sensational acclaim; his tour of Germany was equally successful; in 1905 he appeared in England, where he played the Glazunov Violin Concerto. On Dec. 10, 1908, he made his American debut in N.Y. and was hailed as one of the greatest virtuosos of the time; he played with every important sym. orch. in the U.S.; with the Boston Sym. alone he was a soloist at 31 concerts. In the following years he played all over the world, and, with Jascha Heifetz, became a synonym for violinistic prowess. His playing was the quintessence of Romantic interpretation; his tone was mellifluous but resonant; he excelled particularly in the concertos of Mendelssohn, Tchaikovsky, and Wieniawski; but he could also give impressive performances of Beethoven and Mozart. He publ. several violin arrangements of Classical and Romantic pieces, and he also composed some playable short compositions for his instrument. His father publ. a sentimental book, *Memoirs of Mischa Elman's Father* (N.Y., 1933).

Elmendorff, Karl (Eduard Maria), eminent German conductor; b. Düsseldorf, Oct. 25, 1891; d. Hofheim am Taunus, Oct. 21, 1962. He studied at the Hochschule für Musik in Cologne; conducted opera there, then in Munich, Wiesbaden, and Mannheim. From 1927 to 1942 he conducted at the Bayreuth Festival. He appeared infrequently outside Germany, and his reputation rests almost entirely on his interpretations of German operas.

Elmo, Cloe, Italian mezzo-soprano; b. Lecce, April 9, 1910; d. Ankara, May 24, 1962. She studied voice in Rome; made her debut in Cagliari in 1934; from 1936 to 1943, and again after 1951, she was a prominent member of La Scala in Milan; on Nov. 19, 1947, she made an impressive debut at the Metropolitan Opera in N.Y. as Azucena in *Il Trovatore;* in 1949 she returned to Italy. Eventually she made her home in Ankara, where she taught at the Cons. from 1954 until her death.

Elmore, Robert Hall, American organist and composer; b. Ramapatnam, India (of American missionary parents), Jan. 2, 1913; d. Ardmore, Pa., Sept. 22, 1985. He studied organ with Pietro Yon and composition with Harl McDonald; subsequently taught organ at the Clarke Cons. of Music (1936–53) and the Musical Academy (from 1939) in Philadelphia. In 1940 he joined the faculty at the Univ. of Pa. He wrote a commemorative symphonic tone poem, *Valley Forge,* which was performed by the Philadelphia Orch. with Stokowski conducting on April 9, 1937. His *It Began at Breakfast* (Philadelphia, Feb. 8, 1941) was the 1st opera by an American to be televised. He also wrote some organ music, a String Quartet, many sacred compositions, and songs.

Eloy, Jean-Claude, French composer; b. Mont-Saint-Aignan, Seine-Maritime, June 15, 1938. He studied in Paris with Darius Milhaud and in Basel with Pierre Boulez. From his earliest works he adopted the advanced techniques of serialism; his main influences are Boulez, Varèse, and Webern; there is an extreme miniaturization in his instrumental music. He composed *Étude III* for Orch. (1962); *Équivalences* for Chamber Orch. (1963); *Polychronies* for Chamber Orch. (1964), *Macles* for Chamber Orch. (1967), and *Faisceaux-Diffractions* for Chamber Orch. (1970); *Kâmakalâ* for Chorus and 3 Orch. Ensembles (1971); *Kshara-Akshara* for Soprano Chorus and 3-sectioned Orch. with 3 Conductors (1974); *Shanti* (Tibetan for "good fortune"), an electronic work lasting 2½ hours without interruption, among the longest uninterrupted pieces ever composed (Royan, March 23, 1974); *Fluctuante-Immuable* for Orch. (Paris, May 5, 1977); *Yo-In* (Reverberations) for 4 Tapes and Percussion (Bordeaux, Nov. 19, 1980).

Elschek, Oskár, Slovak ethnomusicologist; b. Bratislava, June 16, 1931. He studied musicology and esthetics at Bratislava Univ. (degree, 1954), then became a member of the Musicology Inst. of the Slovak Academy of Sciences. In 1963 he was appointed ed. in chief of *Slovenská Hudba,* and in 1967 he co-ed. the *Annual Bibliography of European Ethnomusicology.* His publications include studies of Slovak and European folk music, organology, and the sociology of music. With his wife Alica Elscheková (b. Bratislava, Nov. 21, 1930), he wrote books on Slovak folk music (1956, 1962) and ed. the 1st vol. of Bartók's folk songs (1959). He publ., with A. Elscheková, *Úvod do štúdia slovenskej l'udovej hudby* (Introduction to the Study of Slovak Folk Music; Bratislava, 1962).

Elsner, Joseph (Anton Franciskus) (Józef Antoni Franciszek), noted Polish pedagogue and composer of German descent; b. Grottkau, Silesia, June 1, 1769; d. Warsaw, April 18, 1854. After singing in the local church choir, he studied at the Breslau Jesuit Gymnasium (1781–88), concurrently singing in the opera chorus, playing violin in chamber music concerts, and beginning to compose. After studying theology and medicine at the Univ. of Breslau and the Univ. of Vienna (1789), he turned decisively to music; he was concertmaster of the Brünn Opera orch. (1791–92) and Kapellmeister in Lemberg (1792–99), then settled in Warsaw, where he served as director of the Opera for 25 years; he was also active as a teacher (Chopin was his most famous student) and founded several music schools, one of which later became the Warsaw Cons. In 1823 he was awarded the Order of St. Stanislaw. His compositions presage the development of the Polish national school.

WRITINGS: *Początki muzyki a szczególniej śpiewania* (The Beginnings of Music, Especially of Singing; Warsaw, 1818–21); *Szkola śpiewu* (School of Singing; Warsaw, 1834; 2nd ed., Leipzig, 1855); *Sumarius moich utworów z objaśnieniami o czynnościach i dzialaniach moich jako artysty muzycznego* (Summary of My Works with Explanations of My Functions and Activities as a Musician; 1840–49; Krakow, 1957).

WORKS (all 1st perf. in Warsaw unless otherwise given): OPERAS: *Amazonki czyli Herminia* (The Amazons, or Herminia; Lemberg, July 26, 1797); *Sultan Wampum czyli Nieroztropne zyczenie* (Sultan Vampum, or The Rash Wish; 1800); *Siedem razy jeden* (7 Times 1; Dec. 14, 1804); *Stary trzpiot i mlody mędrzec* (The Old Dolt and the Young Sage; Feb. 15, 1805); *Wiezczka Urzella czyli To co się damom podoba* (The Soothsayer Urzella, or What Pleases the Ladies; March 7, 1806); *Andromeda* (Jan. 14, 1807); *Chimère et réalité* or *Urojenie i rzeczywistość* (April 22, 1808); *Leszek Bialy czyli Czarownica z-Lysej Góry* (Leszek the White or The Witch of the Bald Mountain; Dec. 2, 1809); *Wawozy Sierra Modena* (The Ravines of the Sierra Modena; Jan. 31, 1812); *Kabalista* (The Cabalist; Jan. 29, 1813); *Król Lokietek czyli Wiśliczanki* (King Lokietek, or The Women of Wislica; April 3, 1818); *Jagiello w Tenczynie* (Jagiello in Tenczyn; Jan. 1, 1820); other works include melodramas, duodramas, ballets, 8 syms., 6 string quartets, Piano Quartet, String Quintet, Septet, 3 violin sonatas, 24 Latin masses, 9 Polish masses, 4 oratorios, offertories, hymns, 55 secular cantatas, and some 100 songs.

BIBL.: J. Reiss, *Ślązak Józef E.: Nauczyciel Chopina* (Silesian J. E.: Chopin's Teacher; Katowice, 1936); J. Prosnak, "Józef E. jako pedagog i organizator polskiego szkolnictwa muzycznego," *Poradnik muzyczny,* VIII (1954); A. Nowak-Romanowicz, *Józef E.* (Krakow, 1957).

Elson, Arthur, American writer on music, son of **Louis (Charles) Elson;** b. Boston, Nov. 18, 1873; d. N.Y., Feb. 24, 1940. He studied with J.K. Paine at Harvard Univ. and at the New England Cons. of Music; received fundamental training from his father. He was a graduate of Harvard (1895) and of the Mass. Inst. of Technology (1897); he served as music critic of the *Boston Advertiser* (from 1920).

WRITINGS: *A Critical History of the Opera* (1901; new ed., 1926, as *A History of Opera); Orchestral Instruments and Their Use* (1902; new ed., 1930); *Woman's Work in Music* (1903; new ed., 1931); *Modern Composers of Europe* (1905; new ed., 1922); *Music Club Programs from All Nations* (1906; new ed.,

1928); *The Musician's Guide* (1913); *The Book of Musical Knowledge* (1915; new ed., 1934); *Pioneer School Music Course* (1917).

Elson, Louis (Charles), American music historian, father of **Arthur Elson;** b. Boston, April 17, 1848; d. there, Feb. 14, 1920. He studied voice with Kreissmann at Boston and music theory with Karl Gloggner Castelli in Leipzig. Returning to Boston, he was music ed. of the *Boston Advertiser* (1886–1920); in 1880 became lecturer on music history at the New England Cons.; was also ed. in chief of the *University Encyclopedia of Music* (10 vols., 1912). In his music criticism he attacked the modernists with vicious eloquence, reserving the choicest invective for Debussy; he called *La Mer* "Le Mal de Mer," and said that the faun of *L'Après-midi d'un faune* needed a veterinary surgeon.

WRITINGS: *Curiosities of Music* (1880); *History of German Song* (1888); *The Theory of Music* (1890; rev. by F. Converse, 1935); *European Reminiscences* (1891; new ed., 1914); *The Realm of Music* (1892); *Great Composers and Their Work* (1898); *The National Music of America and Its Sources* (1899; new ed., rev. by A. Elson, 1924); *Famous Composers and Their Works* (with P. Hale; 1900); *Shakespeare in Music* (1901); *History of American Music* (1904; 2nd ed., 1915; rev. by A. Elson, 1925); *Music Dictionary* (1905); *Pocket Music Dictionary* (1907); *Mistakes and Disputed Points in Music* (1910); *Women in Music* (1918); *Children in Music* (1918).

BIBL.: *Lectures on the History and Art of Music: The L.C. E. Memorial Lectures at the Library of Congress, 1946–1963* (Washington, D.C., 1969).

Elston, Arnold, American composer; b. N.Y., Sept. 30, 1907; d. Vienna, June 6, 1971. He studied harmony and counterpoint with Goldmark in N.Y. and took courses at City College (B.A., 1930) and Columbia Univ. (M.A., 1932); after composition studies with Webern in Vienna (1932–35), he continued his training at Harvard Univ. (Ph.D., 1939), while concurrently studying conducting with Fiedler in Boston (1939). He taught at the Longy School of Music in Cambridge, Mass. (1939–40), the Univ. of Oregon (1941–58), and the Univ. of Calif. at Berkeley (1958–71). He wrote the books *Music and Medicine* (1948) and *A Modern Guide to Symphonic Music* (1966).

WORKS: *Suite* for Orch. (1931); 2 string quartets (1932, 1961); *Variations for String Quartet* (1934); *Sweeney Agonistes*, chamber opera (1948–50); *Chorus for Survival*, chamber cantata for Soprano, Baritone, Chorus, and 7 Instruments (1954–55); *The Love of Don Perlimplin*, opera (1957–58); *Great Age, Behold Us*, cantata for Chorus and Orch. (1965–66); *Prelude, Paean and Furioso* for Orch. (1967–71); Piano Trio (1967); piano music.

Elvey, Sir George (Job), English organist and composer, brother of **Stephen Elvey;** b. Canterbury, March 27, 1816; d. Windlesham, Surrey, Dec. 9, 1893. He studied with Skeats at Canterbury Cathedral, and with Potter and Crotch at the Royal Academy of Music in London. From 1835 until 1882 he served as organist and master of the boys at St. George's Chapel, Windsor; received a Mus.Bac. (1838) and a Mus.Doc. (1840) from Oxford; was knighted in 1871. His widow publ. a memoir, *Life and Reminiscences of George J. Elvey* (London, 1894).

WORKS: 2 oratorios: *The Resurrection and Ascension* (London, Dec. 2, 1840) and *Mount Carmel* (London, June 30, 1886); also many pieces of church music; glees, part-songs; organ pieces.

Elvey, Stephen, English organist and composer, brother of **Sir George (Job) Elvey;** b. Canterbury, June 27, 1805; d. Oxford, Oct. 6, 1860. He was a chorister of Canterbury Cathedral, and a pupil of Skeats there; in 1830 he became organist of New College, Oxford; received a Mus.Bac. (1831) and a Mus.Doc. (1838) from Oxford; was Choragus there from 1840 until his death. He wrote mostly church music, and publ. a successful handbook, *The Psalter, or Canticles and Psalms, Pointed for Chanting, upon a New Principle* (London; 6 eds. to 1866).

Elvira, Pablo, Puerto Rican baritone; b. Santurce, Sept. 24, 1937. He studied voice at the Puerto Rico Cons., becoming a finalist in the Metropolitan Opera auditions in 1966. He taught at the Indiana Univ. School of Music in Bloomington (1966–74), where he made his formal debut as Rigoletto (1968). On Feb. 23, 1974, he made his 1st appearance at the N.Y. City Opera as Germont, where he sang regularly in subsequent seasons. He made his Metropolitan Opera debut in N.Y. as Tonio on Oct. 15, 1979. In addition to his operatic engagements, he also sang frequently in concert. Among his finest roles were Rossini's Figaro, Don Carlo, Renato, Leoncavallo's Tonio, and Puccini's Lescaut.

Elwart, Antoine (-Aimable-Élie), French writer on music and composer; b. Paris, Nov. 18, 1808; d. there, Oct. 14, 1877. A chorister at St.-Eustache when 10 years old, he was apprenticed at 13 to a mechanic, but ran away, and joined a small theater orch. as a violinist. From 1825 to 1834 he studied at the Paris Cons., taking the Grand Prix de Rome in 1834; taught at the Paris Cons. from 1836 to 1871. Among his pupils were Gouvy, Grisar, and Weckerlin.

WORKS: Opera, *Les Catalans* (Rouen, 1840); "oratorio-symphonie," *Noé, ou Le Déluge universel* (Paris, 1845); oratorio, *La Naissance d'Ève* (Paris, 1846); *Les Noces de Cana*, mystery (1853); *Ruth et Booz*, vocal sym. (1850); masses, cantatas, a Te Deum, a Miserere, and other church music; syms., overtures, chamber music, etc.

WRITINGS: *Duprez, sa vie artistique, avec une biographie authentique de son maître A. Choron* (1838); *Théorie musicale* (*Solfège progressif*, etc., 1840); *Feuille harmonique* (1841); *Le Chanteur accompagnateur* (1844); *Traité de contrepoint et de la fugue; Essai sur la transposition; Études élémentaires de musique* (1845); *L'Art de chanter en chœur; L'Art de jouer impromptu de l'alto-viola; Solfège de jeune âge; Le Contrepoint et la fugue appliqués au style idéal; Lutrin et Orphéon* (theoretical and practical vocal studies); *Histoire de la Société des Concerts du Conservatoire* (1860; 2nd ed., 1863); *Manuel des aspirants aux grades de chef et de souschef de musique dans l'armée française* (1862); *Petit manuel d'instrumentation* (1864); *Histoire de concerts populaires* (1864).

Elwell, Herbert, American composer and music critic; b. Minneapolis, May 10, 1898; d. Cleveland, April 17, 1974. He studied at the Univ. of Minnesota; then took courses with Ernest Bloch in N.Y. (1919–21) and Nadia Boulanger in Paris (1921–24); received a Prix de Rome in 1923; from 1924 to 1927 held a fellowship at the American Academy in Rome. Returning to the U.S., he held a post as teacher of composition at the Cleveland Inst. of Music (1928–45); from 1932 to 1964 served as music critic for the Cleveland *Plain Dealer*.

WORKS: Ballet, *The Happy Hypocrite* (an orch. suite drawn from the score was perf. in Rome on May 21, 1927); *Introduction and Allegro* for Orch. (N.Y., July 12, 1942); *I Was with Him*, cantata for Male Chorus, Tenor, and 2 Pianos (1937; Cleveland, Nov. 30, 1942); *Blue Symphony* for Voice and String Quartet (1944; Cleveland, Feb. 2, 1945); *Lincoln: Requiem Aeternam* for Baritone, Chorus, and Orch. (1946; Oberlin, Feb. 16, 1947); *Pastorale* for Voice and Orch. (1947; Cleveland, March 25, 1948); *The Forever Young* for Voice and Orch. (Cleveland, Oct. 29, 1953); 2 string quartets; Piano Sonata; Violin Sonata; etc.

Elwes, Gervase (Cary), noted English tenor; b. Billing Hall, near Northampton, Nov. 15, 1866; d. Boston, Jan. 12, 1921. He began his career as a diplomat; while stationed in Vienna (1891–95), he studied singing; during his sojourn in Paris he took voice lessons with Bouhy, and soon achieved competence as a concert singer. He made a tour of Germany in 1907 and 2 tours in the U.S. (1909 and 1921; died on his 2nd tour, killed by a train in the railroad station in Boston). He excelled in oratorio; sang Elgar's *Dream of Gerontius* about 150 times. Winifred and Richard Elwes publ. an impassioned family monograph, *Gervase Elwes: The Story of His Life* (London, 1935).

Emerson, Luther Orlando, American composer and conductor; b. Parsonsfield, Maine, Aug. 3, 1820; d. Hyde Park, Mass., Sept. 29, 1915. He was a competent composer of church music, a popular conductor of the early musical conventions, and a compiler of numerous successful collections of songs and hymn tunes: *The Romberg Collection* (1853); *The Golden Wreath* (1857); *The Golden Harp* (1860); *The Sabbath Harmony* (1860); *The Harp of Judah* (1863); *Merry Chimes* (1865); *Jubilate* (1866); *The Chorus Wreath.*

Emery, Stephen Albert, American music teacher, writer, and composer; b. Paris, Maine, Oct. 4, 1841; d. Boston, April 15, 1891. His 1st teacher was H.S. Edwards, of Portland, Maine; in 1862 he went to Leipzig, where he studied with Plaidy, Papperitz, Richter, and Hauptmann. He returned to Portland in 1864; went to Boston in 1866; taught at the New England Cons. there from 1867. He publ. 2 textbooks, *Foundation Studies in Pianoforte Playing* (1882) and *Elements of Harmony* (1880; 2nd ed., 1907).

Emery, Walter (Henry James), English organist and writer; b. Tilshead, Wiltshire, June 14, 1909; d. Salisbury, June 24, 1974. He studied organ at the Royal Academy of Music in London; then was engaged as a church organist; from 1937 to 1969 he was an associate at Novello & Co. in the editorial dept.; publ. several valuable books and pamphlets: *The St. Matthew Passion: Its Preparation and Performance* (with Sir Adrian Boult; London, 1949); *Bach's Ornaments* (London, 1953); *Editing Early Music: Notes on the Preparation of Printer's Copy* (with T. Dart and C. Morris; London, 1963); commentaries on Bach's organ works; etc.

Emmanuel, (Marie François) Maurice, eminent French music scholar; b. Bar-sur-Aube, May 2, 1862; d. Paris, Dec. 14, 1938. He received his primary education in Dijon; sang in the church choir in Beaune; then studied at the Paris Cons. (1880–87) with Savard, Dubois, Delibes, and Bourgault-Ducoudray; then specialized in the musical history of antiquity under Gevaert in Brussels; also studied ancient languages at the Sorbonne, becoming a licencié ès lettres (1887) and a docteur ès lettres (1895) with the theses *De saltationis disciplina apud Graecos* (publ. in Latin, Paris, 1895) and *La Danse grecque antique d'après les monuments figurés* (Paris, 1896; in Eng. as *The Antique Greek Dance after Sculptured and Painted Figures,* N.Y., 1916). He was a prof. of art history at the Lycée Racine and Lycée Lamartine (1898–1905); maître de chapelle at Ste.-Clotilde (1904–7); in 1909 he succeeded Bourgault-Ducoudray as prof. of music history at the Paris Cons., and held this post until 1936; he ed. vols. 17 and 18 of the complete works of Rameau; also Bach's works in Durand's ed. of the classical masters.
    Writings: *Histoire de la langue musicale* (2 vols., Paris, 1911; new ed., 1928); *Traité de l'accompagnement modal des psaumes* (Lyons, 1912); *La Polyphonie sacrée* (with R. Moissenet; Dijon, 1923); *Pelléas et Mélisande de Claude Debussy* (Paris, 1926; 2nd ed., 1950); *César Franck* (Paris, 1930); *Anton Reicha* (Paris, 1936).
    Works: Opera, *Salamine* (1921–23; 1927–28; Paris, June 28, 1929); opéra-bouffe, *Amphitryon* (1936; Paris, Feb. 20, 1937); 2 syms. (1919, 1931); 2 string quartets and other chamber music; 6 piano sonatinas; vocal music.
    Bibl.: H. Stewart, "M. E.," *Music & Letters,* XX (1939); special issue of *La Revue Musicale,* no. 26 (1947).

Emmett, Daniel Decatur, American composer of popular songs; b. Mt. Vernon, Ohio, Oct. 29, 1815; d. there, June 28, 1904. He began his career as a drummer in military bands; then joined the Virginia Minstrels, singing and playing the banjo; later was a member of Bryant's Minstrels. He wrote the lyrics and the music of *Dixie* in 1859, and it was performed for the 1st time in N.Y., on April 4, 1859; upon publication, the popularity of the song spread, and it was adopted as a Southern fighting song during the Civil War (even though Emmett was a Northerner). His other songs, *Old Dan Tucker,*

The Road to Richmond, Walk Along, etc., enjoyed great favor for some years, but were eclipsed by *Dixie.*
    Bibl.: C. Galbreath, *D.D. E., Author of Dixie* (Columbus, Ohio, 1904); R. Harwell, *Confederate Music* (Chapel Hill, N.C., 1950); H. Wintermute, *D.D. E.* (Mt. Vernon, 1955); H. Nathan, *Dan E. and the Rise of Early Negro Minstrelsy* (Norman, Okla., 1962).

Emsheimer, Ernst, German-born Swedish ethnomusicologist; b. Frankfurt am Main, Jan. 15, 1905. He studied musicology with Adler and Fischer at the Univ. of Vienna (1924) and the Univ. of Freiburg (Ph.D., 1927), then became musicological consultant in Leningrad at the National Academy for the History of Art, the Hermitage Collection, and the Museum of Ethnography (1932–36), where he led a field recording expedition into the northern Caucasus (1936). He settled in Stockholm in 1937, becoming musicological adviser to the Museum of Ethnography. From 1949 to 1973 he was director of the Museum of Music History in Stockholm; under his direction it became an important center of Swedish musical and musicological activity. He is co-founder of the *Handbücher der Europäischen Volksmusikinstrumente.* He publ. *Studia ethnomusicologica eurasiatica* (Stockholm, 1964– ; collected writings).

Enacovici, George, Rumanian composer; b. Focșani, May 4, 1891; d. Bucharest, Jan. 26, 1965. He studied at the Bucharest Cons. with Kiriac and Castaldi (1905–12); studied composition with d'Indy, and violin at the Schola Cantorum in Paris (1914–18); taught violin at the Bucharest Cons. (1919–54) and was concertmaster of the Bucharest Phil. (1920–21) and the Bucharest Radio Orch. (1928–33). He was a founder-member of the Soc. of Rumanian Composers (1920).
    Works: *Intermezzo* for String Orch. and Harp (1912); *Poem* for Violin and Orch. (1920); *Suite in a Rumanian Style* for Orch. (1928); *Symphonic Episode* (1933); *Rapsodie română* for Orch. (1934); *Amfitrita,* symphonic poem with Violin obbligato (1940); *Arlequinada,* capriccio for 2 Violins and Chamber Orch. (1941); Sym. (1954); Violin Concerto (1956); 3 string quartets; Violin Sonata; Piano Sonata; minor pieces in various genres.

Encina, Juan del, Spanish poet, dramatist, and composer; b. Salamanca, July 12, 1468; d. León, late 1529 or 1530. He was the son of a shoemaker of Salamanca named Juan de Fermoselle; became a chorister at Salamanca Cathedral; studied music under his elder brother, Diego de Fermoselle, and under Fernando de Torrijos; took his degree in law at Salamanca Univ., where he enjoyed the favor of the chancellor, Don Gutiérrez de Toledo. In 1492 he entered the household of the 2nd Duke of Alba, for whom he wrote a series of pastoral eclogues that form the foundation of the Spanish secular drama. These eclogues included "villancicos," or rustic songs, for which Encina composed the music. He went to Rome in 1500; on May 12, 1500, was appointed canon at the Cathedral of Salamanca; from Feb. 2, 1510, until 1512, he was archdeacon and canon of Málaga; on May 2, 1512, he again went to Rome; his *Farsa de Plácida e Vittoriano* was performed there in the presence of Pope Julius II on Jan. 11, 1513. In 1517, he was "subcollector of revenues to the Apostolic Chamber." In 1519 he was appointed prior of León, and that same year made a pilgrimage to Jerusalem, where he was ordained a priest. He described his sacred pilgrimage in *Tribagia o Via Sacra de Hierusalem* (Rome, 1521). After the death of Pope Leo X in 1521, Encina returned to Spain and spent his last years as prior at León. Besides being a leading figure in the development of the Spanish drama, Encina was the most important Spanish composer of the reign of Ferdinand and Isabella; he cultivated with notable artistry a type of part-song akin to the Italian "frottola," setting his own poems to music. Some 62 works are found in H. Anglès, ed., *La música en la corte de los Reyes Catolicos: Cancionero de Palacio,* in Monumentos de la Música Española, V, X, and XIV (1947–65). Another modern ed. was publ. by C. Terni, *Juan del Encina: L'opera musicale* (Florence, 1974–).
    Bibl.: R. Espinosa Maeso, "Nuevos datos biográficos de

J. d.E.," *Boletín de la Real Academia Española*, VII (1921); J. Subirá, *La música en la Casa de Alba* (1927); G. Chase, "Origins of the Lyric Theater in Spain," *Musical Quarterly* (July 1939); idem, "J. d.E., Poet and Musician," *Music & Letters* (Oct. 1939); C. Terni, "J. d.E.," *Chigiana* (1968).

Enckhausen, Heinrich Friedrich, German organist and composer; b. Celle, Aug. 28, 1799; d. Hannover, Jan. 15, 1885. He studied with Aloys Schmitt in Berlin, succeeding him as court organist. He wrote an opera, *Der Savoyard* (Hannover, 1832), and sacred music; publ. a book of chorales.

Enesco, Georges (real name, **George Enescu**), famous Rumanian violinist, conductor, teacher, and composer; b. Liveni-Virnav, Aug. 19, 1881; d. Paris, May 4, 1955. He began to play the piano when he was 4, taking lessons with a Gypsy violinist, Nicolas Chioru, and began composing when he was 5; then studied with Caudella in Iaşi. On Aug. 5, 1889, he made his formal debut as a violinist in Slánic, Moldavia. In the meantime, he had enrolled in the Cons. of the Gesellschaft der Musikfreunde in Vienna (1888), where he studied violin with S. Bachrich, J. Grün, and J. Hellmesberger, Jr.; piano with L. Ernst; harmony, counterpoint, and composition with R. Fuchs; chamber music with J. Hellmesberger, Sr.; and music history with A. Prosnitz, winning 1st prizes in violin and harmony (1892). After his graduation (1894), he entered the Paris Cons., where he studied violin with Marsick and J. White, harmony with Dubois and Thomas, counterpoint with Gédalge, composition with Fauré and Massenet, and early music with Diémer, winning 2nd accessit for counterpoint and fugue (1897) and graduating with the premier prix for violin (1899). At the same time he also studied cello, organ, and piano, attaining more than ordinary proficiency on each. On June 11, 1897, he presented in Paris a concert of his works, which attracted the attention of Colonne, who brought out the youthful composer's op. 1, *Poème roumain*, the next year. Enesco also launched his conducting career in Bucharest in 1898. In 1902 he 1st appeared as a violinist in Berlin and also organized a piano trio; in 1904 he formed a quartet. On March 8, 1903, he conducted the premiere of his 2 *Rumanian Rhapsodies* in Bucharest, the 1st of which was to become his most celebrated work. He soon was appointed court violinist to the Queen of Rumania. In 1912 he established an annual prize for Rumanian composers, which was subsequently won by Jora, Enacovici, Golestan, Otescu, and others. In 1917 he founded the George Enescu sym. concerts in Iaşi. After the end of World War I, he made major tours as a violinist and conductor; he also taught violin in Paris, where his pupils included Menuhin, Grumiaux, Gitlis, and Ferras. He made his U.S. debut in the triple role of conductor, violinist, and composer with the Philadelphia Orch. in N.Y. on Jan. 2, 1923; he returned to conduct the N.Y. Phil. on Jan. 28, 1937. He led several subsequent concerts with it with remarkable success; led it in 14 concerts in 1938, and also appeared twice as a violinist; he conducted 2 concerts at the N.Y. World's Fair in 1939. The outbreak of World War II found him in Rumania, where he lived on his farm in Sinaia, near Bucharest. He visited N.Y. again in 1946 as a teacher. On Jan. 21, 1950, during the 60th anniversary season of his debut as a violinist, he gave a farewell concert with the N.Y. Phil. in the multiple capacity of violinist, pianist, conductor, and composer, in a program comprising Bach's Double Concerto (with Menuhin), a violin sonata (playing the piano part with Menuhin), and his 1st *Rumanian Rhapsody* (conducting the orch.). He then returned to Paris, where his last years were marked by near poverty and poor health. In July 1954 he suffered a stroke and remained an invalid for his remaining days.

Although Enesco severed relations with his Communist homeland, the Rumanian government paid homage to him for his varied accomplishments. His native village, a street in Bucharest, and the State Phil. of Bucharest were named in his honor. Periodical Enesco festivals and international performing competitions were established in Bucharest in 1958. Enesco had an extraordinary range of musical interests. His

compositions include artistic stylizations of Rumanian folk strains; while his style was neo-Romantic, he made occasional use of experimental devices, such as quarter-tones in his opera, *Œdipe*. He possessed a fabulous memory and was able to perform innumerable works without scores. He not only distinguished himself as a violinist and conductor, but he was also a fine pianist and a gifted teacher.

WORKS: OPERA: *Œdipe*, op. 23 (1921–31; Opéra, Paris, March 10, 1936). **ORCH.:** 3 unnumbered syms. (1895, 1896, 1898); 5 numbered syms.: No. 1, op. 13 (1905; Paris, Jan. 21, 1906); No. 2, op. 17 (1912–14; Bucharest, March 28, 1915); No. 3, op. 21, with Chorus (1916–18; Bucharest, May 25, 1919; rev. 1921); No. 4 (1934; unfinished); No. 5, with Tenor and Women's Chorus (1941; unfinished); *Uvertura tragica* (1895); *Ballade* for Violin and Orch. (1896); *Uvertura triumfală* (1896); Violin Concerto (Paris, March 26, 1896); *Fantaisie* for Piano and Orch. (1896; Bucharest, March 26, 1900); Piano Concerto (1897; unfinished); 2 *Suites roumaines:* No. 1 (1896; unfinished); No. 2 (1897); *Poème roumain*, op. 1, with Wordless Chorus (1897; Paris, Feb. 9, 1898); *Pastorale* for Small Orch. (Paris, Feb. 19, 1899); *Symphonie concertante* for Cello and Orch., op. 8 (1901; Paris, March 14, 1909); 2 *Rhapsodies roumaines*, op. 11 (1901; Bucharest, March 8, 1903); 2 *Intermezzi* for Strings, op. 12 (1902–3); Suite No. 1, op. 9 (1903; Paris, Dec. 11, 1904); *Suite châtelaine*, op. 17 (1911; unfinished); Suite No. 2, op. 20 (1915; Bucharest, March 27, 1916); Suite No. 3, op. 27, *Villageoise* (1938; N.Y., Feb. 2, 1939); *Concert Overture*, op. 32, "sur des thèmes dans le caractère populaire roumain" (1948; Washington, D.C., Jan. 23, 1949); *Symphonie de chambre* for 12 Instruments, op. 33 (1954; Paris, Jan. 23, 1955); *Vox maris*, symphonic poem, op. 31 (c.1929–55; Bucharest, Sept. 10, 1964). **CHAMBER:** 2 piano quintets: No. 1 (1895); No. 2, op. 29 (1940); 3 numbered sonatas for Violin and Piano: No. 1, op. 2 (1897); No. 2, op. 6 (1899); No. 3, "dans le caractère populaire roumain" (1926); 2 sonatas for Cello and Piano: No. 1, op. 26 (1898); No. 2, op. 26 (1935); 2 piano trios (1897, 1916); *Aubade* for String Trio (1899); Octet for 4 Violins, 2 Violas, and 2 Cellos, op. 7 (1900); *Dixtuor* for Wind Instruments, op. 14 (1906); *Au soir*, nocturne for 4 Trumpets (1906); *Konzertstück* for Viola and Piano (1906); 2 piano quartets: No. 1, op. 16 (1909); No. 2, op. 30 (1943–44); 2 string quartets: No. 1, op. 22 (1916–20); No. 2, op. 22 (1950–53); other chamber works. **PIANO:** *Introduzione* (1894); *Ballade* (1894); *Praeludium* (1896); *Scherzo* (1896); 3 suites: No. 1, op. 3, "dans le style ancien" (1897); No. 2, op. 10 (1901–3); No. 3, op. 18, *Pièces impromptues* (1913–16); *Variations on an Original Theme* for 2 Pianos, op. 5 (1898); *Impromptu* (1900); *Pièce sur le nom de Fauré* (1922); 2 sonatas: No. 1, op. 24 (1924); No. 2, op. 24 (1933–35; incorrectly publ. as "No. 3"). **VOCAL:** *La Vision de Saul*, cantata (1895); *Ahasverus*, cantata (1895); *L'Aurore*, cantata (1897–98); *Waldgesang* for Chorus (1898); Cantata for Soprano and Orch. (1899); about 25 songs, many to words by the Queen of Rumania, who wrote poetry in German under the pen name Carmen Sylva.

BIBL. (all publ. in Bucharest unless otherwise given): M. Costin, *G. E.* (1938); V. Cheorghiu, *Un muzician genial: G. E.* (1944); F. Brulez, *G. E.* (1947); B. Gavoty, *Yehudi Menuhin—G. E.* (Geneva, 1955); A. Tudor, *G. E.* (1956); L. Voiculescu, *G. E. şi opera sa Oedip* (1956); A. Tudor, *G. E.: Viaţă in imagini* (1959; French tr., 1961); *G. E. on the 80th Anniversary of His Birth* (1961); G. Bălan, *G. E.: Mesajul—estetica* (1962); idem, *E.* (1963; German tr., 1964); F. Foni, N. Missir, M. Voicana, and E. Zottoviceanu, *G. E.* (1964); B. Kotlyarov, *G. E.* (Moscow, 1965); E. Ciomac, *E.* (1968); M. Voicana et al., eds., *G. E.: Monografie* (2 vols., 1971); R. Drăghici, *G. E.* (Bacău, 1973); M. Voicana, ed., *Enesciana*, I (1976; in French, German, and Eng.).

Engel, Carl, German musical historiographer; b. Thiedewiese, near Hannover, July 6, 1818; d. by suicide, London, Nov. 17, 1882. He studied organ with Enckhausen at Hannover and piano with Hummel at Weimar. After residing in Hamburg,

Warsaw, and Berlin, he went to Manchester, England, in 1844, and in 1850 to London. There he became an influential writer, and an authority on musical history and musical instruments.

WRITINGS: *The Pianist's Handbook* (1853); *Piano School for Young Beginners* (1855); *Reflections on Church Music* (1856); his lifework began with *The Music of the Most Ancient Nations, Particularly of the Assyrians, Egyptians, and Hebrews* (1864), followed by *An Introduction to the Study of National Music* (1866); *Musical Instruments of All Countries* (1869); *Catalogue of the Special Exhibition of Ancient Musical Instruments* (2nd ed., 1873); *Descriptive Catalogue of the Musical Instruments in the South Kensington Museum* (1874); *Musical Myths and Facts* (1876); *The Literature of National Music* (1879); *Researches into the Early History of the Violin Family* (1883). Among his unpubl. MSS is a large history of the musical instruments of the world (4 quarto vols. with over 800 illustrations).

BIBL.: C. Engel, "Some Letters to a Namesake," *Musical Quarterly* (July 1942); G. Reese, "More about the Namesake," *A Birthday Offering to C. E.* (N.Y., 1943).

Engel, Carl, distinguished German-born American musicologist and writer on music; b. Paris, July 21, 1883; d. N.Y., May 6, 1944. He was a great-grandson of Josef Kroll, founder of Kroll's Établissement in Berlin, and grandson of J.C. Engel, who made the Kroll Opera famous. Carl Engel was educated at the Univs. of Strasbourg and Munich; studied composition in Munich with Thuille. He went to the U.S. in 1905 and established himself as an ed., musicologist, librarian, and publisher. He was ed. and musical adviser of the Boston Music Co. (1909–21); chief of the Music Division of the Library of Congress (1922–34); president of G. Schirmer, Inc. (1929–32); in 1929 became ed. of the *Musical Quarterly;* remained with it until 1942; from 1934 was again president of G. Schirmer, Inc., and honorary consultant in musicology for the Library of Congress; was U.S. delegate to the Beethoven Centenary, Vienna, 1927; U.S. representative of the International Soc. of Musicology; 1st chairman of the Committee on Musicology, American Council of Learned Socs.; president of the American Musicological Soc. (1937–38); was an honorary member of the Harvard Musical Assoc.; also a Fellow of the American Academy of Arts and Letters; received an honorary Mus.Doc. from Oberlin College (1934); was made a Chevalier of the Légion d'honneur (1937); was a recipient of the Elizabeth Sprague Coolidge medal "for eminent services rendered to chamber music" (1935). A writer with a brilliant style and of wide learning, Engel contributed valuable essays to the *Musical Quarterly* (*Views and Reviews;* articles on Chadwick, Loeffler, etc.); publ. 2 collections of essays: *Alla Breve, from Bach to Debussy* (N.Y., 1921) and *Discords Mingled* (N.Y., 1931). He was also a composer; his music was in the French tradition, in an impressionistic vein; his songs, particularly his settings of poems by Amy Lowell, were often sung (the best known among them is *Sea-Shell*); other works include *Triptych* for Violin and Piano; *Perfumes* for Piano (an album of 5 pieces); *Presque valse* for Piano was publ. posth.

BIBL.: H. Bauer, "C. E.," *Musical Quarterly* (July 1944); G. Reese, "A Postscript," ibid.; H. Putnam and E.S. Coolidge, "Tributes to C. E.," ibid. (April 1945).

Engel, David Hermann, German organist and composer; b. Neuruppin, Jan. 22, 1816; d. Merseburg, May 3, 1877. He studied in Breslau; in 1848 became organist at Merseburg; wrote a comic opera, *Prinz Carneval* (Berlin, 1862); publ. *Beitrag zur Geschichte des Orgelbauwesens* (1855).

Engel, Gabriel, Hungarian-American writer, violinist, and composer; b. Beregszasz, May 4, 1892; d. Vergennes, Vt., Aug. 1, 1952. He was the author of *The Life of Anton Bruckner* (N.Y., 1931) and *Gustav Mahler—Song-Symphonist* (N.Y., 1932); also ed. of *Chord and Discord,* the magazine of the Bruckner Soc. of America. During the last 15 years of his life he was engaged in the rare-books business.

Engel, Hans, eminent German musicologist; b. Cairo, Egypt, Dec. 20, 1894; d. Marburg, May 15, 1970. He studied at the

Akademie der Tonkunst in Munich with Klose and at the Univ. of Munich with Sandberger (Ph.D., 1925, with the diss. *Die Entwicklung des deutschen Klavierkonzertes von Mozart bis Liszt;* publ. in Leipzig, 1927); completed his Habilitation at the Univ. of Greifswald in 1926; then taught there (1926–35). He was on the faculty of the Univ. of Königsberg (1935–46) and Marburg Univ. (1946–63).

WRITINGS: *Carl Loewe* (Greifswald, 1934); *Franz Liszt* (Potsdam, 1936); *Deutschland und Italien in ihren musikgeschichtlichen Beziehungen* (Regensburg, 1944); *Johann Sebastian Bach* (Berlin, 1950); *Musik der Völker und Zeiten* (Hannover, 1952; rev. ed., 1968); *Luca Marenzio* (Florence, 1956); *Musik in Thüringen* (Cologne and Graz, 1966).

Engel, Joel, Russian writer on music and composer; b. Berdiansk, April 16, 1868; d. Tel Aviv, Feb. 2, 1927. He studied at Kharkov; later with Taneyev and Ippolitov-Ivanov in Moscow. In 1922 he went to Berlin, where he organized a publishing house for propaganda of Jewish music; issued a collection of Jewish folk songs in 3 vols. His publications in Russian are: *Pocket Music Dictionary* (Moscow, 1913); *Essays on Music History* (Moscow, 1911); *In the Opera* (1911). He wrote an opera, *Esther* (1894), incidental music, and other works.

Engel, Karl, Swiss pianist; b. Birsfeld, June 1, 1923. He studied in Bern and Paris; his principal teachers were Paul Baumgartner and Alfred Cortot. In 1952 he won 2nd prize at the Queen Elisabeth Competition in Brussels; gave many recitals and played at the leading festivals in Europe. In addition, he became one of the most distinguished accompanists of singers, among them Dietrich Fischer-Dieskau. In 1959 he was appointed prof. at the Hannover Hochschule für Musik.

Engel, Lehman, American composer, conductor, and writer on music; b. Jackson, Miss., Sept. 14, 1910; d. N.Y., Aug. 29, 1982. He began to take piano lessons with local teachers as a child; then studied with Sidney Durst at the Cincinnati College of Music (1927–29) and later with Eduardo Trucco in N.Y.; from 1930 to 1934 he took courses in composition with Rubin Goldmark at the Juilliard School of Music and also took private composition lessons with Roger Sessions (1931–37). While still a student, he began to write music for ballet and theatrical plays; in 1934 he wrote incidental music for Sean O'Casey's play *Within the Gates,* which he conducted. From 1935 to 1939 he led the Madrigal Singers for the Works Progress Administration; later worked with the Mercury Theater as composer and conductor. During World War II Engel enlisted in the U.S. Navy and conducted a military orch. at the Great Lakes Naval Training Station; later was appointed chief composer of the Navy's film division in Washington, D.C. He wrote a great many scores of incidental music for Broadway productions, which he also conducted, among them T.S. Eliot's *Murder in the Cathedral* and Tennessee Williams's *A Streetcar Named Desire.* As a composer, Engel was happiest in writing for the theater; he had a special knack for vivid musical illustration of the action on the stage. Of importance are his numerous books on the American music theater. He was also active as a teacher of composition and led in N.Y. a seminar on musical lyrics. He conducted the 1st American performance of Kurt Weill's *The Threepenny Opera;* also conducted the productions of *Showboat, Brigadoon, Annie Get Your Gun, Fanny, Guys and Dolls,* and *Carousel.* Engel received 2 Antoinette Perry (Tony) Awards, in 1950 for conducting Menotti's opera *The Consul,* and in 1953 for conducting the operettas of Gilbert and Sullivan. In 1971 he received the honorary degree of D.M. from the Univ. of Cincinnati.

WORKS: OPERAS: *Pierrot of the Minuet* (Cincinnati, April 3, 1928); *Malady of Love* (N.Y., May 27, 1954); *The Soldier* (N.Y., Nov. 25, 1956, a concert version); *Golden Ladder,* a musical (Cleveland, May 28, 1953). BALLETS: *Phobias* (N.Y., Nov. 18, 1932); *Ceremonials* (N.Y., May 13, 1933); *Transitions* (N.Y., Feb. 19, 1934); *The Shoebird* (Jackson, Miss., April 20, 1968). INCIDENTAL MUSIC TO SHAKESPEARE'S PLAYS: *Hamlet* (1938); *Macbeth* (1941); *Julius Caesar* (1955); *The Tempest*

(1960); also music to plays by contemporary authors. ORCH.: 2 syms. (1939, 1945); Viola Concerto (1945); *The Creation for Narrator and Orch.* (1947); overture, *Jackson* (Jackson, Miss., Feb. 13, 1961). CHAMBER: Cello Sonata (1945); Violin Sonata (1953). CHORUS: *Rain* (1929); *Rest* (1936); *Chansons innocentes* (1938); *Let Us Now Praise Famous Men* (1955). WRITINGS: *The Bright Day,* autobiography (N.Y., 1956; rev. ed., 1974); *Planning and Producing the Musical Show* (N.Y., 1957; rev. ed., 1966); *The American Musical Theater: A Consideration* (N.Y., 1967; rev. ed., 1975); *The Musical Book* (N.Y., 1971); *Words with Music* (N.Y., 1972); *Their Words Are Music: The Great Lyricists and Their Lyrics* (N.Y., 1975); *Getting the Show On: The Complete Guidebook for Producing a Musical in Your Theater* (N.Y., 1983).

Engelmann, Hans Ulrich, German composer; b. Darmstadt, Sept. 8, 1921. He had piano lessons while in high school; he then took courses in composition with Wolfgang Fortner in Heidelberg (1945–49); from 1948 to 1950 he attended the classes of René Leibowitz and Ernst Krenek in Darmstadt; also enrolled at the Univ. of Frankfurt (1946–52), taking classes in musicology (with Gennrich and Osthoff) and philosophy (with Adorno). In 1952 he received his Ph.D. there with a dissertation on Béla Bartók's *Mikrokosmos* (publ. in Würzburg, 1953). In 1949 he held a Harvard Univ. stipend at the Salzburg Seminar in American Studies; was active in radio programming and in composition for films and for the theater in Iceland (1953–54), and then was theater composer in Darmstadt (1954–61). In 1969 he was appointed an instructor at the Frankfurt Hochschule für Musik. His early works are impregnated by chromaticism with an impressionistic tinge. He adopted the 12-tone method of composition, expanding it into a sui generis "field technique" of total serialism, in which rhythms and instrumental timbres are organized systematically. In his theater music he utilizes aleatory devices, *musique concrète,* and electronic sonorities.

WORKS: THEATER: *Doktor Fausts Höllenfahrt,* chamber opera (1949–50; North German Radio, Hamburg, Jan. 11, 1951); *Verlorener Schatten,* opera (1960); *Der Fall Van Damm,* opera (1966–67; West German Radio, Cologne, June 7, 1968); *Operette,* music theater piece (1959); *Ophelia,* multimedia theater piece (Hannover, Feb. 1, 1969); *Revue,* music theater piece (1972–73); *Ballet coloré* (1948); *Noche de luna,* ballet (1958); *Serpentina,* ballet (1962–63); much incidental music; film scores. ORCH.: *Kaleidoskop,* suite (1941); Concerto for Cello and String Orch. (1948); *Musik* for Strings, Brass, and Percussion (1948); *Impromptu* (1949); *Leopoldskron,* divertimento for Chamber Orch. (1949); *Orchester-Fantasie* (1951; rev. as Sym. No. 1, 1963); Partita (1953); *Strukturen* for Chamber Orch. (1954); *Fünf Orchesterstücke* (1956); *Polifonica* for Chamber Orch. (1957); *Nocturnos* for Soprano and Chamber Orch. (1958); *Ezra Pound Music* (1959); *Trias* for Piano, Orch., and Tape (1962); *Shadows* (1964); *Sonata for Jazz Orch.* (1967); *Capricciosi* (1968); *Sinfonies* (Sym. No. 2; 1968); *Sinfonia da camera* for Chamber Orch. (1981); *Stele für Büchner,* canto sinfonico for Soloists, Chorus, and Orch. (1986). CHAMBER: Sonata for Cello and Piano (1948); String Quartet (1952); *Integrale* for Saxophone and Piano (1954); *Incanto* for Soprano, Soprano Saxophone, and Percussion (1959); *Timbres* for Harp, Celesta, Piano, Percussion, and Tape (1963); *Mobile II* for Clarinet and Piano (1968); *Modelle I oder "I Love You Babi"* for Amplified Instruments (1970); *Modelle II* for Trombone and Percussion Ensemble (1970); *Duettini* for Piano and Percussion (1985); *Inter-Lineas* for Alto Saxophone and Marimba, Vibraphone, or Percussion (1985); other chamber works; choral music; piano pieces. BIBL.: K. Carius et al., *Commedia humana: H.U. E. und sein Werk* (Wiesbaden, 1985).

Engerer, Brigitte, French pianist; b. Tunis, Oct. 27, 1952. She was taken to Paris at an early age, where at 6 she became a pupil of Lucette Descaves and made her public debut; after further training at the Paris Cons., she completed her studies

with Stanislav Neuhaus at the Moscow Cons. (graduated, 1975). She won prizes at the Long-Thibaud Competition in Paris (6th, 1969), the Tchaikovsky Competition in Moscow (6th, 1974), and the Queen Elisabeth of Belgium Competition in Brussels (3rd, 1978); appeared as a soloist with the world's leading orchs. and gave recitals in the major music centers.

Englert, Giuseppe Giorgio, Italian organist and composer; b. Fiesole, near Florence, July 22, 1927. He studied composition with Willy Burkhard at the Zürich Cons. (1945–48); in 1949 went to Paris, where he took organ lessons with André Marchal (1949–56); was his assistant as organist of the St. Eustache Church (1957–62); in 1970 he was appointed a lecturer at the Univ. of Paris at Vincennes.

WORKS: *Rime serie* for Wind Quintet (1958–61); *Au jour ultime liesse,* cantata for Voice and 6 Instruments (1961–63); *Les Avoines folles* for String Quartet (1962–63); *Aria* for Timpani and 13 Instruments (1965); *La Joute des lierres* for String Quartet (1965–66); *Tarok,* musical game for 3–6 String Instruments (1967); *Vagans animula* for Organ and Tape (1969); *Maquillage,* theatrical composition for Voice, Scenic Apparatus, and Tape (1967–71); *Cantus plumbeus* for Organ (1972); *Non pulsando* for Organ (1972); *Caracol* for 15 Instruments (1974).

English, Granville, American composer; b. Louisville, Jan. 27, 1895; d. N.Y., Sept. 1, 1968. He was educated at the Chicago Musical College (Mus.Bac., 1915).

WORKS: Orch: *Ugly Duckling* (1924); *Among the Hills* (Oklahoma City, March 9, 1952); *Mood Tropicale* (Baltimore, Feb. 5, 1955); *Evenings by the Sea,* symphonic poem (Port Washington, N.Y., Jan. 20, 1956); choral works; piano pieces; violin pieces; songs.

Englund, Einar (Sven), prominent Finnish composer, pedagogue, pianist, and music critic; b. Ljugarn, Gotland (Sweden), June 17, 1916. He studied composition with Bengt Carlson and Selim Palmgren, instrumentation with Leo Funtek, and piano with Martti Paavola and Ernst Linko at the Sibelius Academy in Helsinki (1933–41); after military service (1941–45), he was awarded a stipend to continue his training with Aaron Copland at the Berkshire Music Center, Tanglewood (summer 1949). From 1957 to 1976 he was music critic of the Helsinki Swedish newspaper *Hufvudstadsbladet.* He was also active as a pianist, often performing his own works in Finland and abroad. From 1958 to 1982 he was on the music theory faculty of the Sibelius Academy, and in 1978 was elected to membership in the Royal Swedish Academy of Music. He has produced a distinguished body of instrumental music in a well-crafted neo-Classical style.

WORKS: ORCH.: Syms.: No. 1, *The War Symphony* (1946; Helsinki, Jan. 17, 1947); No. 2, *The Blackbird Symphony* (1947; Helsinki, Oct. 8, 1948); No. 3 (1969–71; Helsinki, May 12, 1972); No. 4, *The Nostalgic* (Helsinki, Oct. 26, 1976); No. 5, *Fennica* (Helsinki, Dec. 6, 1977); No. 6, *Aphorisms* for Mixed Choir and Orch. (1984; Helsinki, March 12, 1986); No. 7 (1988); *Epinikia,* symphonic poem (1947); *The Wall of China,* concerto suite from the music to Max Frisch's play (1949); Cello Concerto (1954; Helsinki, May 17, 1955); *4 Dance Impressions* (1954); Piano Concerto No. 1 (1955; Helsinki, March 2, 1956, composer soloist); Piano Concerto No. 2 (1974; Helsinki, Feb. 4, 1975, composer soloist); Violin Concerto (1981; Tampere, March 26, 1982); Serenade for Strings (1983; Kaustinen, Feb. 15, 1984); Flute Concerto (1985; Helsinki, Sept. 16, 1986); *Lahti-fanfaari* (Lahti, Aug. 28, 1986); *Juhlasoitto "1917"* (1986; Turku, Nov. 12, 1987); *Odeion,* overture (1987; Mikkeli, Nov. 18, 1988); also 2 ballets, *Sinuhe* (1953) and *Odysseus* (1959). CHAMBER: Quintet for Piano and Strings (1941); *Divertimento upsaliensis* for Wind Quintet, String Quintet, and Piano (1978); Sonata for Violin and Piano (1979); *De profundis* for 14 Brass Instruments (1980); Concerto for 12 Cellos (1980–81); Sonata for Cello and Piano (1982); Trio for Piano, Violin, and Cello (1982); String Quartet (1985); also works for solo instruments, including Piano Sonata No. 1 (1978); *Arioso interrotto* for Violin (1979); *Pavane e Toccata* for Piano (1983); suite for Cello, *Viimeinen saari* (The Last

Island; 1986); *Intermezzo* for Oboe (1987); also choral pieces and music for films, plays, and radio.

Enna, August (Emil), eminent Danish composer; b. Nakskov, May 13, 1859; d. Copenhagen, Aug. 3, 1939. He was partly of German and Italian blood; his grandfather, an Italian soldier in Napoleon's army, married a German girl, and settled in Denmark. Enna was taken to Copenhagen as a child, and learned to play piano and violin; had sporadic instruction in theory; later became a member of a traveling orch. and played with it in Finland (1880). Upon his return to Copenhagen, he taught piano and played for dancers; in 1883 he became music director of Werner's Theatrical Soc. and wrote his 1st stage work, *A Village Tale,* which he produced the same year. After these practical experiences, he began to study seriously; took lessons with Schjorring (violin), Matthesson (organ), and Rasmussen (composition) and soon publ. a number of piano pieces, which attracted the attention of Niels Gade, who used his influence to obtain a traveling fellowship for Enna; this made it possible for Enna to study in Germany (1888–89) and acquire a complete mastery of instrumental and vocal writing. He followed the German Romantic school, being influenced mainly by Weber's type of opera, and by Grieg and Gade in the use of local color; the 1st product of this period was his most successful work, the opera *Heksen* (The Witch), produced in Copenhagen (Jan. 24, 1892), then in Germany.

WORKS: OPERAS: *Agleia* (1884); *Heksen* (Copenhagen, Jan. 24, 1892); *Cleopatra* (Copenhagen, Feb. 7, 1894); *Aucassin and Nicolette* (Copenhagen, Feb. 2, 1896); *The Match Girl,* after Andersen (Copenhagen, Nov. 13, 1897); *Lamia* (Antwerp, Oct. 3, 1899); *Ung Elskov* (1st produced in Weimar, under the title *Heisse Liebe,* Dec. 6, 1904); *Princess on the Pea,* after Andersen (Århus, Sept. 15, 1900); *The Nightingale,* after Andersen (Copenhagen, Nov. 10, 1912); *Gloria Arsena* (Copenhagen, April 15, 1917); *Comedians,* after Victor Hugo's *L'Homme qui rit* (Copenhagen, April 8, 1920); *Don Juan Mañara* (Copenhagen, April 17, 1925). **BALLETS:** *The Shepherdess and the Chimney Sweep* (Copenhagen, Oct. 6, 1901); *St. Cecilia's Golden Shoe* (Copenhagen, Dec. 26, 1904); *The Kiss* (Copenhagen, Oct. 19, 1927); also a Violin Concerto (1897); 2 syms. (1886, 1908); an overture, *Hans Christian Andersen* (1905); choral pieces.

Eno, Brian (Peter George St. John le Baptiste de la Salle), English composer, musician, and producer; b. Woodbridge, Suffolk, May 15, 1948. Although interested in tape recorders and recorded music at an early age, he received no formal music training, studying art at Ipswich and Winchester art schools (1964–69); he then became involved in avant-garde experiments, performing works by LaMonte Young and Cornelius Cardew. He helped found the art-rock band Roxy Music in 1971, leaving it 2 years later for a solo career that resulted in 4 modestly successful progressive-rock albums during the mid-1970s. In 1975, while confined to bed after being struck by a London taxi, he was also struck by the pleasures of minimalism, shifting his style to what he has termed "ambient," a sort of high-art Muzak. He has collaborated with David Bowie, Talking Heads, and U2. In 1979 he became interested in video, subsequently producing "video paintings" and "video sculptures" used as ambient music in galleries, museums, airport terminals, and private homes. His music has influenced both New Wave and New Age genres. With R. Mills, he publ. *More Dark than Shark* (London, 1986).

WORKS: *Another Green World* (1975); *Discreet Music* (1975); *Before and after Science* (1977); *Music for Airports* (1978); *The Plateaux of Mirror* (with Harold Budd; 1980); *On Land* (1984).

BIBL.: E. Tamm, *B. E.: His Music and the Vertical Color of Sound* (Boston, 1989).

Enríquez, Manuel, Mexican composer and violinist; b. Ocotlán, June 17, 1926. He studied violin with Camarena and composition with Bernal Jiménez at the Guadalajara Cons. (1942–50); then went to N.Y. and took lessons in composition with Peter Mennin and violin with Ivan Galamian at the Juilli-

ard School of Music (1955–57); also had private theory lessons with Stefan Wolpe and attended the Columbia-Princeton Electronic Music Center (1971). Returning to Mexico, he was concertmaster of the Guadalajara Sym. Orch.; later supervised music courses at the Inst. of Fine Arts in Mexico City. In 1975 he went to France under a special commission from the Mexican government. As a composer, he follows the median line of cosmopolitan modernism, making use of a severe constructivist idiom, employing graphic optical notation.

WORKS: *Suite* for Violin and Piano (1949); 2 violin concertos (1955, 1966); Sym. No. 1 (1957); 3 string quartets (1959, 1967, 1974); *Preámbulo* for Orch. (1961); *Divertimento* for Flute, Clarinet, and Bassoon (1962); *4 Pieces* for Viola and Piano (1962); *Obertura lírica* for Orch. (1963); *Pentamúsica* for Wind Quintet (1963); *3 formas concertantes* for Violin, Cello, Clarinet, Bassoon, Horn, Piano, and Percussion (1964); Violin Sonata (1964); *3 invenciones* for Flute and Viola (1964); *Módulos* for 2 Pianos (1965); *Transición* for Orch. (1965); *Poema* for Cello and Small String Orch. (1966); *Ego* for Female Voice, Flute, Cello, Piano, and Percussion (1966); *Trayectorias* for Orch. (1967); *Ambivalencia* for Violin and Cello (1967); *Si libet* for Orch. (1968); *5 Plus 2* for Flute, Viola, Trombone, Piano, and Percussion, with Actress and Director (1969); *Concierto para 8* (1969); *Ixamatl* for Orch. (1969); *Díptico I* for Flute and Piano (1969); *Díptico II* for Violin and Piano (1971); Piano Concerto (1971); *El y Ellos* for Solo Violin and Orch. Ensemble (1973).

Enriquez de Valderrabano, Enrique, 16th-century Spanish lutenist; native of Peñaranda de Duero. He wrote the tablature book *Libro de música de vihuela, intitulado Silva de Sirenas* (Valladolid, 1547), containing transcriptions for vihuela (large 6-stringed guitar) of sacred and secular vocal works (some arranged for 2 vihuelas), also some original pieces.

BIBL.: G. Morphy, *Les Luthistes espagnols du XVIᵉ siècle* (1902); J. Trend, *Luis Milán and the Vihuelistas* (1925); W. Apel, "Early Spanish Music for Lute and Keyboard Instruments," *Musical Quarterly* (July 1934).

Enthoven, (Henri) Emile, Dutch composer; b. Amsterdam, Oct. 18, 1903; d. N.Y., Dec. 26, 1950. He studied composition with Johan Wagenaar in Utrecht, and at the age of 15 wrote an adolescent but well-crafted sym., which Mengelberg performed with the Concertgebouw Orch. in Amsterdam (1918). But this precocious success was not a manifestation of enduring talent; his later works lacked originality. Soon he abandoned composition altogether and took up jurisprudence; for a time he lectured on political science at the Univ. of Leiden; in 1939 emigrated to America and settled in N.Y. Among his works are 3 syms. (1917, 1924, 1931) and a Violin Concerto (1920).

Entremont, Philippe, eminent French pianist and conductor; b. Rheims, June 6, 1934. Both his parents were professional musicians and teachers, and he received his 1st training from them. He subsequently studied piano with Marguerite Long; then entered the Paris Cons.; won 1st prize in solfège at 12, in chamber music at 14, and in piano at 15. In 1951 he was 5th-prize winner of the Belgian State Competition in Brussels. He then toured in Europe; on Jan. 5, 1953, he made his American debut with the National Orch. Assoc. in N.Y.; appeared also as soloist with other American orchs. In 1976 he became music director of the Vienna Chamber Orch.; in 1980 was appointed music adviser and principal conductor of the New Orleans Phil., and from 1981 to 1986 was its music director; in 1982 he took that orch. on a European tour. He was music director–designate (1987–88) and music director (1988–89) of the Denver Sym. Orch.; from 1988 was music director of the Colonne Orch. in Paris.

Eötvös, Peter, Hungarian conductor and composer; b. Székelyudvarhely, Jan. 2, 1944. He studied composition with Pál Kardos at the Budapest Academy of Music (1958–65) and conducting at the Cologne Hochschule für Musik (1966–68). From 1966 he worked closely with Stockhausen, and was also associated with the electronic music studio of Cologne's West German

Radio (1971–79); from 1974 he appeared as a guest conductor in contemporary programs with major European orchs. He became music director of the Ensemble InterContemporain in Paris in 1979, and in 1985 a principal guest conductor of the BBC Sym. Orch. in London.

Works: *Moro Lasso*, comedy madrigal for 5 Soloists (1963; rev. version, 1972; Witten, April 28, 1974); *Hochzeitsmadrigal*, comedy madrigal for 6 Soloists (1963; rev. version, 1976; Metz, Nov. 20, 1976); *Windsequenzen* for Wind Instruments and Amplification (Budapest, Dec. 23, 1975); *Intervalles-Intérieurs* for Various Instruments (1981; La Rochelle, March 11, 1982); *Endless 8* for Voices, Percussion, 2 Organs, and Electric Guitar (Paris, Dec. 5, 1981); *Pierre-Idyll* for Chamber Ensemble (1984; Baden-Baden, March 31, 1985; for Pierre Boulez's 60th birthday); *Chinese Opera* for Chamber Orch. (Paris, Nov. 17, 1986); also works for television and film.

Eppert, Carl, American composer; b. Carbon, Ind., Nov. 5, 1882; d. Milwaukee, Oct. 1, 1961. He studied in Chicago and in Germany; was founder and conductor of the Civic Sym. Orch. in Milwaukee (1921–26).

Works: 7 syms.; *Escapade* for Orch. (Indianapolis, Jan. 3, 1941); symphonic fantasy, *Traffic* (NBC, May 8, 1932); 2 symphonic poems: *City Shadows* and *Speed* (Rochester, N.Y., Oct. 30, 1935); 2 *Symphonic Impressions* (Chicago, Feb. 13, 1941; 1st prize, Chicago Sym. Orch. Golden Jubilee, 1940–41).

Epstein, David M(ayer), American composer, conductor, and writer on music; b. N.Y., Oct. 3, 1930. He learned to play the piano and clarinet and took part in jazz bands. He studied at Antioch College (A.B., 1952); then took courses with Carl McKinley and Francis Judd Cooke at the New England Cons. of Music (M.M., 1953), with Irving Fine, Harold Shapero, and Arthur Berger at Brandeis Univ. (M.F.A., 1954), and with Milton Babbitt and Roger Sessions at Princeton Univ. (M.F.A., 1956; Ph.D., 1968, with the diss. *Schoenberg's Grundgestalt and Total Serialism: Their Relevance to Homophonic Analysis*). In 1955–56 he took lessons in composition with Darius Milhaud at Aspen. In conducting, his mentors were Max Rudolf, Izler Solomon, and George Szell. He taught at Antioch College (1957–62); became an associate prof. of music at the Mass. Inst. of Technology in 1965; was named a prof. there in 1971. He has also served as music director of the M.I.T. Sym. Orch. from 1965. In addition, he was music director of the Harrisburg (Pa.) Sym. Orch. (1974–78). In 1983 he was appointed conductor of the New Orch. of Boston. From 1983 to 1988 he was a member of the Herbert von Karajan Musikgespräche in Vienna and at the Salzburg Easter Festival. He publ. *Beyond Orpheus: Studies in Musical Structure* (Cambridge, Mass., 1979). In his music he follows a serial method, cleansed of impurities and reduced to a euphonious, albeit contrapuntally dissonant, idiom.

Works: orch.: *Movement* (1953); Sym. (1958); *Sonority-Variations* (1968); *Ventures, 3 Pieces for Symphonic Wind Ensemble* (Rochester, N.Y., Dec. 11, 1970); Cello Concerto (1979). chamber: Piano Trio (1953); String Trio (1964); String Quartet (1971). vocal: *Excerpts from a Diary*, song cycle (1953); *The Seasons*, song cycle to poems by Emily Dickinson (1956); *Night Voices* for Narrator, Children's Choir, and Orch. (1974); *The Concord Psalter* for Choir (1979); *The Lament of Job* for Choir (1982); also Piano Variations (1961); film music.

Epstein, Julius, Austrian pianist and pedagogue, father of **Richard Epstein;** b. Agram, Croatia, Aug. 7, 1832; d. Vienna, March 1, 1926. He was a pupil at Agram of Ignaz Lichtenegger, and at Vienna of Anton Halm (piano) and Johann Rufinatscha (composition). From 1867 to 1901 he was a prof. of piano at the Vienna Cons. Among his pupils were Gustav Mahler and Ignaz Brüll.

Bibl.: H. Schuster, *J. E.: Ein tonkünstlerisches Charakterbild zu seinem 70. Geburts-Feste* (Vienna, 1902).

Epstein, Richard, Austrian pianist, son of **Julius Epstein;** b. Vienna, Jan. 26, 1869; d. N.Y., Aug. 1, 1919. He was a pupil at the Vienna Cons. of his father and R. Fuchs (composition); was a prof. of piano at the Vienna Cons.; lived in London

(1904–14); then in N.Y. He excelled as an accompanist, in which capacity he was frequently heard with such artists as Sembrich, Fremstad, Culp, Gerhardt, Destinn, Elman, and Kreisler; and as assisting artist with famous chamber music organizations, including the Joachim, Rosé, and Bohemian Quartets.

Equiluz, Kurt, Austrian tenor; b. Vienna, June 13, 1929. He sang in the Vienna Boys Choir; then studied at the Vienna Academy of Music; sang in the Vienna Akademie-Kammerchor. After winning the Vienna Mozart Competition in 1949, he joined the chorus of the Vienna State Opera; made his solo debut there in 1957. He gained wide recognition as an outstanding concert and oratorio singer; was also a member of the faculty of the Hochschule für Musik in Graz.

Érard, Sébastien, famous Alsatian piano and harp maker; b. Strasbourg, April 5, 1752; d. La Muette, near Paris, Aug. 5, 1831. His family name was orig. **Erhard;** his father was a cabinetmaker by trade, and in his shop Sébastien worked until he was 16, when his father died. He was then engaged by a Paris harpsichord maker, who dismissed him "for wanting to know everything"; under a 2nd employer his ingenuity made a stir in the musical world, and the invention of a "clavecin mécanique" (described by Abbé Roussier, 1776) made him famous. The Duchess of Villeroy became his patroness, and fitted up in her home a workshop for Érard in which (1777) he finished the 1st pianoforte made in France. In the meantime, his brother, Jean-Baptiste, joined him, and they founded an instrument factory in the Rue Bourbon. Their growing success led to a conflict with the fan-makers' guild (to which the brothers did not belong), which tried to prevent them from working. But the Érards obtained a special "brevet" from Louis XVI for the manufacture of "forté-pianos" and this enabled them to continue their trade unmolested. In the following years, Érard invented the "piano organisé" with 2 keyboards, 1 for piano and the other for a small organ; he also became interested in the harp, and invented the ingenious double-action mechanism, perfected in 1811. From 1786 to 1796 he was in London; returning to Paris, he made his 1st grand piano, and employed the English action until his invention, in 1809, of the repetition action, which is regarded as his supreme achievement. An "orgue expressif," built for the Tuileries, was his last important work. His nephew, **Pierre Érard** (1794–1865), succeeded him; he publ. *The Harp in its present improved state compared with the original Pedal Harp* (1821), and *Perfectionnements apportés dans le mécanisme du piano par les Érards depuis l'origine de cet instrument jusqu'à l'exposition de 1834* (1834). Pierre's successor was his wife's nephew, **Pierre Schäffer** (d. 1878); the firm merged with Gaveau in 1859.

Bibl.: F. Fétis, *Notice biographique sur Sébastien Érard* (Paris, 1831).

Eratosthenes, Greek philosopher; b. Cyprene, c.276 B.C.; d. Alexandria, Egypt, c.194 B.C. He wrote on numerous subjects, chiefly mathematics, and was custodian of the Alexandria library. The *Catasterismi*, attributed to Eratosthenes, contain scattered notes on Greek music and instruments, especially the "lyra" (German tr. by Schaubach, 1795; Bernhardy publ. in 1822 an ed. of the original text). His work on music is lost; Ptolemy quotes his division of the tetrachord.

Erb, Donald (James), significant American composer; b. Youngstown, Ohio, Jan. 17, 1927. His family moved to Cleveland when he was a child; he studied cornet with a local musician. After a period of service in the U.S. Navy, he enrolled at Kent State Univ. in Ohio, where he continued to study trumpet and also took courses in composition with Harold Miles and Kenneth Gaburo (B.S., 1950), earning his living by playing trumpet in dance bands. In 1950 he entered the Cleveland Inst. of Music, in the class of Marcel Dick (M.M., 1953). On June 10, 1952, he married Lucille Hyman, and went with her to Paris to study with Nadia Boulanger. Returning to Cleveland, he was engaged as a member of the faculty of the Cleveland Inst. of Music (1953). In 1961 he moved to

Bloomington, Ind., where he studied composition with Bernhard Heiden at Indiana Univ., receiving his doctorate in music in 1964. In 1964–65 he was an assistant prof. of composition at Bowling Green State Univ. In 1965 he received a Guggenheim fellowship grant. From 1965 to 1967 he was a visiting assistant prof. for research in electronic music at Case Inst. of Technology in Cleveland; from 1966 to 1981, composer-in-residence at the Cleveland Inst. of Music; in 1975–76, visiting prof. of composition at Indiana Univ. in Bloomington. From 1969 to 1974 he served as staff composer at the Bennington Composers Conference in Vermont. After holding the chair of Meadows Prof. of Composition at Southern Methodist Univ. in Dallas (1981–84), he was prof. of music at the Indiana Univ. School of Music (1984–87); then was prof. of composition at the Cleveland Inst. of Music (from 1987). From 1982 to 1986 he was president of the American Music Center. From 1988 to 1990 he was composer-in-residence of the St. Louis Sym. Orch. As a composer, he is exceptionally liberal in experimenting in all useful types of composition, from simple folklike monody to the strict dodecaphonic structures; as a former trumpeter in jazz bands, he also makes use of the jazz idiom as freely as of neo-Classical pandiatonic techniques. His most popular composition, *The 7th Trumpet* for Orch., is an epitome of his varied styles. He furthermore applies electronic sound in several of his works. In his band compositions he achieves an extraordinary degree of pure sonorism, in which melody, harmony, and counterpoint are subordinated to the purely aural effect. He also cleverly introduces strange-looking and unusual-sounding musical and unmusical and antimusical instruments, such as euphonious goblets, to be rubbed on the rim, and telephone bells. Thanks to the engaging manner of Erb's music, even when ultradissonant, his works safely traverse their premieres and endure through repeated performances.

Works: orch.: Chamber Concerto for Piano and Strings (1958; Chicago, Feb. 12, 1961); *Spacemusic* for Symphonic Band (1963); *Symphony of Overtures* (1964; Bloomington, Ind., Feb. 11, 1965); Concerto for Solo Percussion and Orch. (Detroit, Dec. 29, 1966); *Christmasmusic* (Cleveland, Dec. 21, 1967); *The 7th Trumpet* (Dallas, April 5, 1969); *Treasures of the Snow* for Youth Orch. (1973; Bergen, N.J., June 8, 1974); Cello Concerto (1975; Rochester, N.Y., Nov. 4, 1976); Trombone Concerto (St. Louis, March 11, 1976); Concerto for Keyboards and Orch. (1978; Akron, Ohio, March 23, 1981); Trumpet Concerto (1980; Baltimore, April 29, 1981); *Sonneries* (1981; Rochester, N.Y., March 18, 1982); *Prismatic Variations* (1983; St. Louis, Jan. 28, 1984); Contrabassoon Concerto (1984; Houston, March 15, 1985); Clarinet Concerto (1984); *Concerto for Orchestra* (Atlanta, Sept. 12, 1985); Concerto for Brass and Orch. (1986; Chicago, April 16, 1987). **chamber:** String Quartet No. 1 (1960); Quartet for Flute, Oboe, Alto Saxophone, and Double Bass (1961); Sonata for Harpsichord and String Quartet (1961); *4 for Percussion* (1962); *Dance Pieces* for Violin, Piano, Trumpet, and Percussion (1963); *Hexagon* for Flute, Alto Saxophone, Trumpet, Trombone, Cello, and Piano (1963); *Antipodes* for String Quartet and Percussion Quartet (1963); *Phantasma* for Flute, Oboe, Double Bass, and Harpsichord (1965); *Diversion for 2 (other than sex)* for Trumpet and Percussion (1966); *Andante* for Piccolo, Flute, and Alto Flute (1966); String Trio for Violin, Electric Guitar, and Cello (1966); *Reconnaissance* for Violin, Double Bass, Piano, Percussion, and 2 Electronic Setups (1967); *Trio for 2* for Alto Flute or Percussion, and Double Bass (1968); *Harold's Trip to the Sky* for Viola, Piano, and Percussion (1972); Quintet for Violin, Cello, Flute, Clarinet, and Piano (1976); Sonata for Clarinet and Percussion (1980); *3 Pieces* for Harp and Percussion (1981); *Déjà vu*, 6 études for Double Bass (1981); *The St. Valentine's Day Brass Quintet* (1981); *Aura* for String Quintet (1981); *The Last Quintet* for Woodwinds (1982); *The Devil's Quickstep* for Flute, Clarinet, Violin, Cello, Percussion, Keyboards, and Harp (1982); *Fantasy for Cellist and Friends* (1982); *Adieu* for Bass Clarinet and 2 Percussionists (1984); *A Book of Fanfares* for Brass Quintet (1987); *Woody* for Clarinet (1988).

vocal: *Cummings Cycle* for Mixed Chorus and Orch. (1963); *Fallout?* for Narrator, Chorus, String Quartet, and Piano (1964); *God Love You Now* for Chorus, Hand Percussion, and Harmonicas (1971); *New England's Prospect* for Choruses, Narrator, and Orch. (Cincinnati, May 17, 1974). **electronic sound:** *Reticulation* for Symphonic Band and Electronic Tape (1965); *Stargazing* for Band and Electronic Tape (1966); *Fission* for Electronic Tape, Soprano Saxophone, Piano, Dancers, and Lights (1968); *In No Strange Land* for Tape, Trombone, and Double Bass (1968); *Basspiece* for Double Bass and 4 tracks of prerecorded Double Bass (1969); *Souvenir* for Tape, Instruments, Lights, etc. (1970); *Klangfarbenfunk I* for Orch., Rock Band, and Electronic Sound (Detroit, Oct. 1, 1970); *Z milosci do Warszawy* for Piano, Clarinet, Cello, Trombone, and Electronic Sound (1971); *The Purple-roofed Ethical Suicide Parlor* for Wind Ensemble and Electronic Sound (1972); *Autumnmusic* for Orch. and Electronic Sound (New Haven, Oct. 20, 1973); *The Towers of Silence* for Electronic Quintet (1974); *Music for a Festive Occasion* for Orch. and Electronic Sound (1975; Cleveland, Jan. 11, 1976); *Views of Space and Time* for Violin, Keyboards, Harp, 2 Percussion, and Amplification (1987).

Erb, John Lawrence, American music pedagogue and author; b. Reading, Pa., Feb. 5, 1877; d. Eugene, Oreg., March 17, 1950. He studied at the Metropolitan College of Music in N.Y.; then was director of the Wooster, Ohio, Cons. (1905–13) and of the School of Music, Univ. of Illinois (1914–21); was lecturer at the American Inst. of Applied Music in N.Y. (1921–24); from 1923 was at the Conn. College for Women. He publ. *Brahms*, a biography (1895; 1905; rev. ed., London, 1934); *Hymns and Church Music* (1911); *Elements of Harmony* (1911); *Elementary Theory* (1911); *Music Appreciation for the Student* (1926); *Select Songs for the Assembly* (1931). He also composed songs, piano pieces, organ music, anthems, and music for pageants.

Erb, Karl, noted German tenor; b. Ravensburg, July 13, 1877; d. there, July 13, 1958. He was self-taught; made his debut in Stuttgart in 1907; then sang in Lübeck (1908–10), Stuttgart (1910–13), and Munich (1913–25); later embarked on a series of appearances as a concert and oratorio singer. He was best known for his portrayal of roles in the works of Mozart; he created the title role in Pfitzner's *Palestrina* (1917). From 1921 to 1932 he was married to **Maria Ivogün.**

Erb, Marie Joseph, Alsatian composer and organist; b. Strasbourg, Oct. 23, 1858; d. Andlau, July 9, 1944. He studied at first in Strasbourg; then (1875–80) in Paris, under Saint-Saëns, Gigout, and Loret, at the École de Musique Classique; returned to Strasbourg as teacher of piano and organ, and organist in the Johanniskirche (Roman Catholic) and at the Synagogue. **Works:** Operas (all 1st perf. in Strasbourg, unless otherwise noted): *Der letzte Ruf* (1895); *Der glückliche Taugenichts* (1897); *Abendglocken* (1900); *Eifersüchtig* (Leipzig, 1901); *Der Riese Schletto* (1901); *Der Zaubermantel* (1901); *Die Vogesentanne* (1904); *Der Heimweg*, ballet-opera (1907); *Prinzessin Flunkerli* (1912); Sym. in G; 3 violin sonatas; Cello Sonata; 2 string quartets; String Trio; Octet for Wind and Strings; *Sonata liturgica* (1919); *Suite liturgique*; *Danses et pièces alsaciennes* (1924, 1925); 8 masses; organ pieces; pieces for piano (2- and 4-hands); songs; also 2 vols. of Alsatian folk songs. **Bibl.:** P. de Bréville, *M.J. E., Sa vie et son œuvre* (Strasbourg, 1948).

Erbach, Christian, noted German organist, teacher, and composer; b. Gaualgesheim, near Mainz, c.1568; d. Augsburg, summer 1635. He went to Augsburg and entered the service of Marcus Fugger, then became organist at the church of St. Moritz, as well as town organist and head of the Stadtpfeifer in 1602. He was made assistant organist at the Cathedral in 1614, and then chief organist in 1625; he also taught organ and composition at the Catholic choir school. Although a Catholic, he was allowed to retain his position at the Cathedral after Swedish troops took control of the town in 1632 during the 30 Years' War; however, he was dismissed on June 9, 1635, when funds could no longer be found to pay him. His music reflects the influence of the Italian masters of his day.

WORKS: VOCAL: *Modi sacri sive cantus musici, ad ecclesiae catholicae usum* for 4 to 10 Voices . . . *liber primus* (Augsburg, 1600); *Mele sive cantiones sacrae ad modum canzonette ut vocant* for 4 to 6 Voices (Augsburg, 1603); *Modorum sacrorum sive cantionum* for 4 to 9 Voices . . . *Lib. secundus* (Augsburg, 1603–4); *Modorum sacrorum tripertitorum* for 5 Voices . . . *pars prima* (Dillingen, 1604); *Modorum sacrorum tripertitorum* for 5 Voices . . . *pars altera* (Dillingen, 1606); *Modorum sacrorum tripertitorum* for 5 Voices . . . *pars tertia* (Dillingen, 1606); *Sacrarum cantionem* for 4 to 5 Voices . . . *liber tertius* (Augsburg, 1611); also *Acht underschiedtliche geistliche teutsche Lieder* for 4 Voices (Augsburg, n.d.); other works in various anthologies of the day. **INSTRUMENTAL:** Many keyboard works, including 35 toccatas, 32 ricercari, 22 canzonas, 11 introits, and 4 fantasias. See A. Grotton, ed., *Christian Erbach: Ausgewählte geistliche Chorwerke* (Mainz, 1943), and C. Raynor, ed., *Christian Erbach (c.1570–1635): Collected Keyboard Compositions* in Corpus of Early Keyboard Music, XXXVI (1971–).

BIBL.: S. Sharpe, *An Introduction to the Keyboard Works of C. E. (1573–1635)* (diss., Indiana Univ., 1961); W. Haldeman, *The Vocal Compositions of C. E. (c.1570–1635)* (diss., Univ. of Rochester, 1962).

Erbse, Heimo, German composer; b. Rudolstadt, Thuringia, Feb. 27, 1924. He studied in Weimar, and in Berlin with Boris Blacher; in 1957 he moved to Salzburg.

WORKS: Sonata for 2 Pianos (1951); *Capriccio* for Piano, Strings, and Percussion (1952); Piano Trio (1953); 12 *Aphorismen* for Flute, Violin, and Piano (1954); *Sinfonietta giocosa* (1955); *Dialog* for Piano and Orch. (1955); *Tango-Variationen* for Orch. (1958); *Julietta,* opera semi-seria (Salzburg, Aug. 17, 1959); Wind Quartet (1961); Piano Concerto (1962); 2 syms. (1963–64; 1969–70); comic opera, *Der Herr in Grau* (1966); 5 *Songs* for Baritone and Orch. (1969); *Musik für Nonett* (1970–71); 4 *Gesänge aus den Anakreontischen Liedern* for Soprano, or Tenor, Flute and Harpsichord (1977); String Quartet No. 2 (1987).

Erdélyi, Miklós, Hungarian conductor; b. Budapest, Feb. 9, 1928. He studied at the Franz Liszt Academy of Music in Budapest; served as music director of the Hungarian Radio Choir (1950–52); from 1951 was a principal conductor of the Hungarian State Opera. He made a successful debut with the Berlin Phil. in 1974; led the Hungarian State Orch. on a tour of England. In 1976 he took the Bamberg Sym. Orch. on an extensive tour of the major European festivals. He made his American debut with the San Antonio Sym. Orch. in 1972. He wrote *Schubert* (1961; 2nd ed., 1979), a biographical study.

Erdmann, Eduard, Latvian pianist and composer; b. Tsezis, Wenden, March 5, 1896; d. Hamburg, June 21, 1958. He studied in Riga; then went to Berlin, where he studied piano with Konrad Ansorge (1914–17) and composition with Heinz Tiessen (1915–18). From 1925 to 1935 he was a prof. at the Cologne Cons.; then was active as a concert pianist (1935–50); in 1950, was appointed prof. of piano at the Hochschule für Musik in Hamburg. He wrote 4 syms.; piano pieces; songs.

Erdmannsdörfer, Max von, German conductor; b. Nuremberg, June 14, 1848; d. Munich, Feb. 14, 1905. He studied at the Leipzig Cons. (1863–67), and in Dresden (1868–69). From 1871 to 1880 he was court conductor at Sondershausen; then was active in Vienna, Leipzig, and Nuremberg. In 1882 he was engaged as conductor of the Imperial Musical Soc. in Moscow; in 1885, became prof. at the Moscow Cons. His sym. concerts in Moscow were of great importance to Russian music; he introduced many new works by Russian composers, and his influence was considerable in Moscow musical circles, despite the mediocrity of his conducting. Returning to Germany, he became conductor of the Bremen Phil. Concerts (until 1895); in 1897 he settled in Munich.

Erede, Alberto, Italian conductor; b. Genoa, Nov. 8, 1908. He studied at the Milan Cons. (piano, cello, theory); then in Basel with Weingartner (conducting). He conducted opera in England (1934–39); from 1950 to 1955, was a guest conductor at the Metropolitan Opera in N.Y.; from 1958 to 1962, was Generalmusikdirektor in Düsseldorf.

BIBL.: L. Rognoni, *A. E.* (Arzignano, 1954).

Erhardt, Otto (real name, **Martin Ehrenhaus**), German opera producer; b. Breslau, Nov. 18, 1888; d. San Carlos de Bariloche, near Buenos Aires, Jan. 18, 1971. He studied violin; took courses in music and art at Breslau, Munich, Oxford, and London. He played violin in various orchs. (1908–11); then became an opera producer; acted in this capacity with the Stuttgart Opera (1920–27), the Dresden State Opera (1927–31), and at the festivals at Salzburg (1933–36). In 1939 he went to Buenos Aires, where he was at the Teatro Colón until 1956; subsequently divided his time between South America, Europe, and the U.S. He publ. a book, *Die Operndichtung der deutschen Romantik* (Breslau, 1911); also a biography of Richard Strauss (Buenos Aires, 1950, in Spanish; German ed., 1953).

Erickson, Robert, American composer; b. Marquette, Mich., March 7, 1917. He studied music with Wesley La Violette at the Chicago Cons.; with Ernst Krenek at Hamline Univ. in St. Paul (B.A., 1943; M.A., 1947); in 1950, attended a seminar in composition under Roger Sessions at the Univ. of Calif., Berkeley; in 1966, held a Guggenheim fellowship. In 1967 he was appointed prof. of composition at the Univ. of Calif., San Diego. In his early works he utilized serial techniques; after exploring electronic music, he resumed non-electronic means of expression. He publ. *The Structure of Music: A Listener's Guide to Melody and Counterpoint* (1955) and *Sound Structure in Music* (1975).

WORKS: *Introduction and Allegro* for Orch. (Minneapolis, March 11, 1949); Piano Sonata (1948); String Quartet No. 1 (1950); Piano Trio (1953); Divertimento for Flute, Clarinet, and Strings (1953); Fantasy for Cello and Orch. (1953); String Quartet No. 2 (1956); Variations for Orch. (1957); Duo for Violin and Piano (1959); *Chamber Concerto* (1960); Concerto for Piano and 7 Instruments (1963); *Sirens and Other Flyers* for Orch. (1965); *Ricercar a 5* for Trombone and Tape (1966); *Scapes,* a "contest for 2 groups" (1966); *Birdland* for Electronic Tape (1967); *Ricercar a 3* for Double Bass and Electronic Tape (1967); *Cardenitas,* dramatic aria for Singer, Mime, Conductor, 7 Musicians, and Stereophonic Prerecorded Tape (1968); *Pacific Sirens* for Instruments and Tape (1969); *The Idea of Order at Key West* for Voice and Instruments (1979); *East of the Beach* for Small Orch. (1980); *Auroras* for Orch. (1982); *Taffytime* for Large Ensemble (1983); *Mountain* for Mezzo-soprano and Chamber Orch. (1983); *Sierra* for Tenor or Baritone, and Chamber Orch. (1984); *Solstice* for String Quartet (1984–85).

Ericson, Eric, Swedish conductor and pedagogue; b. Boras, Oct. 26, 1918. He was educated at the Stockholm Musikhögskolan; then served as organist and choir director in several churches in Stockholm. In 1945 he joined the faculty of the Stockholm Musikhögskolan; was made a prof. in 1968. He made his American debut with the National Sym. Orch. of Washington, D.C., in 1974.

Erigena, John Scotus, Irish philosopher, theologian, and translator; b. Ireland, c.810; d. probably in England, c.877. He went to Gaul about 845; there he was a teacher of grammar and dialectic in Charles the Bald's palace school. His *De divisione naturae* or *Perifiseon* (c.866) contains references to music.

BIBL.: J. Handschin, "Die Musikanschauung des Johannes Scotus (E.)," *Deutsche Vierteljahrsschrift für Literaturwissenschaft und Geistesgeschichte,* V (1927); M. Cappuyns, *Jean Scot Érigène* (Louvain, 1933); E. Wältner, *Organicum melos: Zur Musikanschauung der Iohannes Scottus* (Munich, 1977).

Erk, Ludwig (Christian), German music scholar, conductor, and educator; b. Wetzlar, Jan. 6, 1807; d. Berlin, Nov. 25,

1883. He received good training in music from his father, **Adam Wilhelm Erk** (1779–1820), who was organist at Wetzlar. His further studies were under André in Offenbach. In 1826 he became a prof. at the seminary in Mörs, where he taught until 1835; from 1836 to 1840 he was an instructor in liturgical singing at Berlin, and conducted the Royal Cathedral Choir (from 1836). In 1852, he founded the Erk Gesangverein for mixed voices. During his years as a conductor of choral societies, he became interested in folk songs, and accumulated a great collection of authentic materials on the subject; also publ. songbooks for schools, which attained considerable popularity; some of these were written jointly with his brother Friedrich Erk, and his brother-in-law, Greef. He also publ. *Die deutschen Volkslieder mit ihren Singweisen* (1838–45); *Volkslieder, alte und neue* (1845–46); *Deutscher Liederhort* (folk songs; vol. 1 publ. 1856; MS of the remainder was bought—with the rest of his valuable library—for the Royal Hochschule für Musik in Berlin; continued and ed. by F. Böhme, and publ. in 4 vols., 1893–94); *Mehrstimmige Gesänge* (1833–35); *Volksklänge* (1851–60); *Deutscher Liederschatz* (1859–72); *Vierstimmige Choralgesänge der vornehmsten Meister des 16. und 17. Jahrhunderts* (1845); *J.S. Bachs mehrstimmige Choralgesänge und geistliche Arien* (1850–65); *Vierstimmiges Choralbuch für evangelische Kirchen* (1863); *Choräle für Männerstimmen* (1866); *Methodischer Leitfaden für den Gesangunterricht in Volksschulen* (1834).

BIBL.: *Chronologisches Verzeichnis der musikalischen Werke und literarischen Arbeiten von L. E.* (Berlin, 1867); H. Schmeel, *L. E., Ein Lebensbild* (Giessen, 1908).

Erkel, Franz (Ferenc), distinguished Hungarian pianist, conductor, composer, and pedagogue; b. Gyula, Nov. 7, 1810; d. Budapest, June 15, 1893. He studied in Pozsony at the Benedictine Gymnasium (1822–25) and with Heinrich Klein; then went to Koloszvár, where he began his career as a pianist and became conductor of the Kaschau opera troupe (1834), with which he traveled to Buda (1835). He became conductor of the German Municipal Theater in Pest in 1836; in 1838, was made music director of the newly founded National Theater, an influential post he held until 1874; he was conductor at the Opera House from 1884, and also founded the Phil. concerts (1853), which he conducted until 1871. He was the 1st prof. of piano and instrumentation at the Academy of Music; was its director from 1875 to 1888. He gave his farewell performance as a pianist in 1890 and as a conductor in 1892. Erkel was one of the most significant Hungarian musicians of his era. After successfully producing his opera *Báthory Mária* (1840), he gained lasting fame in his homeland with the opera *Hunyady László* (1844), which is recognized as the 1st truly national Hungarian work for the theater. He composed the Hungarian national anthem in 1844. He later achieved extraordinary success with the opera *Bánk-Bán* (1861), written in collaboration with his sons **Gyula** (b. Pest, July 4, 1842; d. Ujpest, March 22, 1909) and **Sandor** (b. Pest, Jan. 2, 1846; d. Békéscsaba, Oct. 14, 1900). He also collaborated with his other sons, **Elek** (b. Pest, Nov. 2, 1843; d. Budapest, June 10, 1893) and **László** (b. Pest, April 9, 1844; d. Pozsonyi, Dec. 3, 1896), who were successful musicians.

WORKS: Operas: *Báthory Mária* (Pest, Aug. 8, 1840); *Hunyady László* (Pest, Jan. 27, 1844); *Erzsébet* (Pest, May 6, 1857; in collaboration with Franz and Karl Doppler); *Bánk-Bán* (Pest, March 9, 1861; orchestrated with Gyula and Sandor Erkel); *Sarolta*, comic opera (Pest, June 26, 1862; mainly orchestrated by Gyula Erkel); *Dózsa György* (Pest, April 6, 1867; in collaboration with Gyula and Sandor Erkel); *Brankovics György* (Budapest, May 20, 1874; in collaboration with Gyula and Sandor Erkel); *Névtelen hösök* (Budapest, Nov. 30, 1880; in collaboration with Gyula, Sandor, Elek, and László Erkel); *István király* (Budapest, March 14, 1885; generally believed to be principally the work of Gyula Erkel); *Sakk-játék*, ballet (Pest, Feb. 2, 1853; not extant); incidental music; choral music; chamber works; piano pieces; songs. The *Festival Overture* for Orch. (1887) may be mainly the work of Gyula Erkel. A catalog of the works of Franz Erkel was publ. by E. Major (Budapest, 1947; 2nd ed., rev., 1967).

BIBL.: K. Abrányi, *Erkel Franz* (Budapest, 1895); F. Scherer, *Erkel Franz* (Gyula, 1944); a symposium of essays on Erkel was ed. by B. Szabolcsi in *Zenetudományi Tanulmányok*, II (Budapest, 1954); A. Németh, *Erkel Ferenc* (Budapest, 1967); D. Legány, *Erkel Ferenc müvei* (Works of Ferenc E.; Budapest, 1974).

Erkin, Ulvi Cemal, Turkish composer; b. Constantinople, March 14, 1906; d. Ankara, Sept. 15, 1972. He studied piano with Isidor Philipp in Paris and composition with Nadia Boulanger in Fontainebleau. Returning to Turkey, he became a piano instructor at the Ankara Cons.

WORKS: *Bayram*, tone poem (Ankara, May 11, 1934); Sym. No. 1 (Ankara, April 20, 1946); Sym. No. 2 (1948–51); Violin Concerto (Ankara, April 2, 1948); chamber music; piano pieces.

Erlanger, Camille, French composer; b. Paris, May 25, 1863; d. there, April 24, 1919. He was a pupil of the Paris Cons. under Delibes, Durand, and Matthias; in 1888, took the Grand Prix de Rome for his cantata *Velléda*. He earned fame with his opera *Le Juif polonais* (Paris, April 11, 1900); other operas are: *Kermaria* (Paris, Feb. 8, 1897); *Le Fils de l'étoile* (Paris, April 20, 1904); *Aphrodite* (Paris, March 27, 1906); *Bacchus triomphant* (Bordeaux, Sept. 11, 1909); *L'Aube rouge* (Rouen, Dec. 29, 1911); *La Sorcière* (Paris, Dec. 18, 1912); *Le Barbier de Deauville* (1917); *Forfaiture* (Paris, 1921). He also wrote several symphonic poems (*Maître et serviteur*, after Tolstoy, etc.) and a French Requiem.

d'Erlanger, Baron François Rodolphe, French ethnomusicologist; b. Boulonge-sur-Seine, June 7, 1872; d. Sidi bou Said, Tunisia, Oct. 29, 1932. He settled in Tunis in 1910; from 1924, assisted by Arab scholars and musicians, he made intensive study of Arabic music, translating many major theoretical treatises. His most important work, the source collection *La Musique arabe* (6 vols., Paris, 1930–59), was intended to spark a Renaissance of Arab music and its study; the 1st 4 vols. contain translations of writings from the 10th to 16th centuries, and the last 2 vols. codify contemporary theory. Most of his books were publ. posth.; they became primary sources on Arab music, as they include trs., transcriptions, and extended analytic studies. His own compositions were written according to Arab theoretical principles.

WRITINGS: *La Musique arabe* (6 vols., Paris, 1930–59); *Chants populaires de l'Afrique du nord* (Paris, 1931); *Mélodies tunisiennes, hispano-arabes, arabo-berbères, juives, nègres* (Paris, 1937).

d'Erlanger, Baron Frédéric, French-born English composer; b. Paris, May 29, 1868; d. London, April 23, 1943. He was born into the family of French bankers; studied music with Ehmant in Paris; then settled in London, where he was active as a banker and a composer. In 1897 he assumed the pseudonym **Regnal,** formed by reading backward the last 6 letters of his name.

WORKS: Operas: *Jehan de Saintre* (Aix-les-Bains, Aug. 1, 1893); *Inez Mendo* (London, July 10, 1897, under the pseudonym Regnal); *Tess*, after Thomas Hardy (Naples, April 10, 1906); *Noël* (Paris, Dec. 28, 1910); Piano Quintet; String Quartet; Violin Concerto (London, March 12, 1903; Kreisler, soloist); Violin Sonata; *Andante* for Cello and Orch.

Erlebach, Philipp Heinrich, important German composer; b. Esens, East Frisia, July 25, 1657; d. Rudolstadt, April 17, 1714. He was in the service of the Rudolstadt court by the winter of 1678–79; was Hofkapellmeister there from 1681. He was a significant composer of sacred music, especially of cantatas. All of his oratorios and most of his cantatas are lost. His surviving cantatas reveal the influence of Heinrich Schütz. He also composed 4 operas, but only a few arias from 2 of these are extant. His instrumental works number about 120 in all, but only 6 overtures, 6 trio sonatas, and a march are extant. His suites reveal the influence of Lully, while his sonatas follow Italian precepts.

WORKS: 6 overtures (Nuremberg, 1693; 2 in *Organum*, III/15–16, Leipzig, 1926); sonatas for Violin, Viola da Gamba, and Basso Continuo (Nuremberg, 1694; 1 in *Organum*, III/5, Leipzig, 1924, and 2 in Hortus Musicus, CXVII–CXVIII, 1954); a number of secular songs, including *Harmonische Freude musicalischer Freunde* (2 vols., Nuremberg, 1697, 1710); ed. in Denkmäler Deutscher Tonkunst, 46/47, 1914); *Gott-geheiligte Sing-Stunde*, 12 cantatas (Rudolstadt, 1704).

BIBL.: B. Baselt, *Der Rudolstädter Hofkapellmeister P.H. E.* (diss., Univ. of Halle, 1963); K.-H. Wiechers, *P.H. E.* (Aurich, 1964).

Ermatinger, Erhart, Swiss composer; b. Winterthur, Feb. 16, 1900; d. Arnhem, July 14, 1966. He studied at the Zürich Cons. with Jarnach, then at the Berlin Hochschule für Musik; in 1922–23 was chorus master at the Zürich Opera; later a private teacher there; in 1925–26, was a teacher of theory at Freiburg Univ.; lived in Berlin, then in the Netherlands. He wrote an opera, *Gijsbrecht van Amstel* (1947); 3 syms.; 2 string quartets; songs; publ. a book, *Bildhafte Musik: Entwurf einer Lehre von der musikalischen Darstellungskunst* (Tübingen, 1928).

Ernesaks, Gustav (Gustavovich), Estonian composer; b. Chariu, Dec. 12, 1908. He studied composition at the Tallinn Cons. with Arthur Kapp; then was active as a choral conductor. He wrote the music drama *Tormide Rand* (Stormy Coast; Tallinn, Sept. 29, 1949) and a comic opera, *The Bridegroom of Mulgimaa* (1960); also many choruses.

Ernst, Alfred, French writer on music, son of **Heinrich Wilhelm Ernst;** b. Périgueux, April 9, 1860; d. Paris, May 15, 1898. A pupil of the École Polytechnique, he abandoned science for art; was a passionate admirer and defender of Wagner. Besides many contributions to musical journals, he publ. *L'Œuvre dramatique de Berlioz* (1884); *Richard Wagner et le drame contemporain* (1887); *L'Art de Richard Wagner, L'Œuvre poétique* (1893; a projected 2nd vol. on *L'Œuvre musicale* remained unfinished); *Étude sur "Tannhäuser,"* analysis and thematic guide (1895; with E. Poirée). He tr. *Die Meistersinger* and *Der Ring des Nibelungen* into French.

Ernst, Heinrich Wilhelm, famous Moravian violinist and composer, father of **Alfred Ernst;** b. Brünn, May 6, 1814; d. Nice, Oct. 8, 1865. He made his 1st public appearance at age 9; became a student of Böhm at the Vienna Cons. (1825), and also studied composition with Seyfried; later continued his training with Mayseder. After Paganini visited Vienna in 1828, Ernst decided to follow in the footsteps of the legendary Italian virtuoso. He launched his career in 1829; made his Paris debut in 1831, and then toured throughout Europe with enormous success. On July 18, 1843, he made his London debut, and thereafter made regular visits to the British capital before settling there in 1855; subsequently participated in a series of celebrated quartet performances with Joachim, Wieniawski, and Piatti. Ernst was also a distinguished violist; he played Berlioz's *Harold in Italy* under the composer's direction in Brussels (1842), St. Petersburg (1847), and London (1855). Stricken with tuberculosis, he was compelled to abandon his brilliant career in 1859. He spent his last years in Nice. After the death of Paganini in 1840, Ernst was duly acknowledged as the greatest violin virtuoso of his time. Unlike Paganini, he did not restrict himself to virtuoso showpieces. He was also a composer of brilliant works for the violin. Among his approximately 30 compositions are the celebrated *Élégie*, op. 10 (Vienna, 1840); the *Othello Fantasy* on themes of Rossini, op. 11; *Le Carnaval de Venise* (Leipzig, 1844); and the *Concerto pathétique* in F-sharp minor (1st perf. by Ernst in Vienna, 1846; publ. in Leipzig, 1851). He also wrote 6 *Polyphonic Studies* for Solo Violin, as well as a transcription of Schubert's *Erlkönig*, pieces of fiendish difficulty for even the most gifted executant.

BIBL.: A. Heller, *H.W. E. im Urteile seiner Zeitgenossen* (Brünn, 1904; Eng. tr., 1986, as *H.W. E. as Seen by His Contemporaries*); B. Schwarz, *Great Masters of the Violin* (N.Y., 1983).

Ernster, Desző, Hungarian bass; b. Pécs, Nov. 23, 1898; d. Zürich, Feb. 15, 1981. He studied in Budapest and Vienna; then sang in Plauen, Gera, and Düsseldorf; in 1929 he appeared at the Berlin State Opera, in 1931 at the Bayreuth Festival, and in 1933 at the Vienna State Opera; then joined the Graz Opera. He made his 1st visit to the U.S. during the 1938–39 season, when he sang in N.Y. with the Salzburg Opera Guild. On Nov. 20, 1946, he made his Metropolitan Opera debut in N.Y. as Marke in *Tristan und Isolde*; remained on its roster until 1963; was also a member of the Deutsche Oper am Rhein in Düsseldorf (1950–67).

BIBL.: J. Fábián, *E.* (Budapest, 1969).

Erös, Peter, Hungarian conductor; b. Budapest, Sept. 22, 1932. He studied piano with Lajos Hernadi, composition with Zoltán Kodály, conducting with László Somogyi, and chamber music with Leo Weiner in Budapest. After the abortive revolution in Hungary in 1956, he emigrated to the Netherlands. There he served as assistant to Otto Klemperer at the Holland Festival of 1958; from 1958 to 1961, was assistant to Ferenc Fricsay; in 1960 he attended the master classes at Bayreuth. He was assistant conductor of the Concertgebouw Orch. in Amsterdam (1960–65); chief conductor of the Malmö Sym. Orch. (1966–68); permanent guest conductor of the Melbourne Sym. Orch. (1969–70). From 1972 to 1980 he was music director and conductor of the San Diego Sym. Orch. He was also a guest conductor of orchs. all over the world. In 1982 he was appointed conductor of the Peabody Sym. Orch. in Baltimore and chief conductor of the Ålborg Sym. Orch.

Erpf, Hermann (Robert), German musicologist and composer; b. Pforzheim, April 23, 1891; d. Stuttgart, Oct. 17, 1969. He studied at Heidelberg and with Riemann at Leipzig; received his Ph.D. from the Univ. of Leipzig in 1913 with the dissertation *Der Begriff der musikalischen Form* (publ. in Stuttgart, 1914); was in the army (1914–18); taught at Pforzheim (1919–23) and at the Univ. of Freiburg (1923–25); was assistant director at the Academy of Speech and Music in Münster (1925–27); was in charge of the Folkwangschule in Essen (1927–43). From 1943 to 1945, and again from 1952 to 1956, he was director of the Hochschule für Musik in Stuttgart. He composed choral pieces, chamber music, and songs.

WRITINGS: *Entwicklungszüge in der zeitgenössischen Musik* (Karlsruhe, 1922); *Studien zur Harmonie- und Klangtechnik der neueren Musik* (Leipzig, 1927; 2nd ed., 1969); *Harmonielehre in der Schule* (Leipzig, 1930); *Vom Wesen der neuen Musik* (Stuttgart, 1949); *Neue Wege der Musikerziehung* (Stuttgart, 1953); *Gegenwartskunde der Musik* (Stuttgart, 1954); *Form und Struktur in der Musik* (Mainz, 1967).

Ershov, Ivan (Vasilievich), celebrated Russian tenor; b. Maly Nesvetai, near Novocherkassk, Nov. 20, 1867; d. Tashkent, Nov. 21, 1943. He studied voice in Moscow with Alexandrova-Kochetova and in St. Petersburg with Gabel and Paleček. In 1893 he made his operatic debut at the Maryinsky Theater in St. Petersburg as Faust, which became one of his most popular roles; then went to Italy for a year and took voice lessons with Rossi in Milan; appeared in Turin as Don José in *Carmen*. He returned to Russia in 1894 and joined the Kharkov Opera; in 1895 he became a member of the Maryinsky Opera Theater, and served with it until 1929. He achieved fabulous success as the greatest performer of the tenor roles in the Russian repertoire, and he also was regarded by music critics and audiences as the finest interpreter of the Wagnerian operas; he sang Siegfried, Tannhäuser, Lohengrin, and Tristan with extraordinary lyric and dramatic penetration; as an opera tenor in his time he had no rivals on the Russian stage. In 1929, at the age of 62, he sang Verdi's Otello; he also appeared in oratorio and solo recitals. From 1916 to 1941 he taught voice at the Petrograd (Leningrad) Cons. At the beginning of the siege of Leningrad in 1941, Ershov was evacuated with the entire personnel of the Cons. to Tashkent in Central Asia, where he died shortly afterward.

BIBL.: V. Bogdanov-Berezovsky, *I. E.* (Leningrad, 1951).

Erskine, John, American pianist, educator, and writer on music; b. N.Y., Oct. 5, 1879; d. there, June 1, 1951. He studied piano with Carl Walter; composition with MacDowell; then took up an academic and literary career, becoming highly successful as a novelist and essayist. He was educated at Columbia Univ. (B.A., 1900; M.A., 1901; Ph.D., 1903; LL.D., 1929); was a prof. of English there (1909–37), then prof. emeritus. In 1923 he resumed piano study under Ernest Hutcheson; played as soloist with the N.Y. Sym. Orch. and the Baltimore Civic Orch.; was president of the Juilliard School of Music in N.Y. (1928–37); president of the Juilliard Music Foundation from 1948 until his death. He was ed. of *A Musical Companion* (1935). Erskine was an Officer of the French Legion of Honor. He publ. books on music, including *Is There a Career in Music?* (N.Y., 1929); *Song without Words: The Story of Felix Mendelssohn* (1941); *The Philharmonic-Symphony Society of N.Y., Its First Hundred Years* (N.Y., 1943); *What Is Music?* (Philadelphia, 1944); *The Memory of Certain Persons* (Philadelphia, 1947); *My Life as a Teacher* (N.Y., 1948); *My Life in Music* (N.Y., 1950).

Ertel, (Jean) Paul, German pianist and composer; b. Posen, Jan. 22, 1865; d. Berlin, Feb. 11, 1933. He studied with L. Brassin (piano) and later took lessons with Liszt; also studied law; was music critic of the *Berliner Lokal Anzeiger* and ed. of *Deutscher Musikerzeitung* (1897–1905). He wrote several symphonic poems in a general Lisztian vein (*Der Mensch, Die nächtliche Heerschau,* etc.); many ballads for voice and instruments; a Violin Sonata and other chamber music.

Eschenbach (real name, **Ringmann**), **Christoph,** remarkably talented German pianist and conductor; b. Breslau, Feb. 20, 1940. His mother died in childbirth; his father, the musicologist Heribert Ringmann, lost his life in battle soon thereafter; his grandmother died while attempting to remove him from the advancing Allied armies; placed in a refugee camp, he was rescued by his mother's cousin, who adopted him in 1946. He began studying piano at age 8 with his foster mother; his formal piano training commenced at the same age with Eliza Hansen in Hamburg, and continued with her at the Hochschule für Musik there; he also studied piano with Hans-Otto Schmidt in Cologne, and received instruction in conducting from Wilhelm Brückner-Rüggeberg at the Hamburg Hochschule für Musik. In 1952 he won 1st prize in the Steinway Piano Competition; after winning 2nd prize in the Munich International Competition in 1962, he gained wide recognition by capturing 1st prize in the 1st Clara Haskil Competition in Montreux (1965). In 1966 he made his London debut; following studies with George Szell (1967–69), the latter invited him to make his debut as soloist in Mozart's Piano Concerto in F major, K. 459, with the Cleveland Orch. on Jan. 16, 1969. In subsequent years he made numerous tours as a pianist, appearing in all of the major music centers of the world. He also gave duo concerts with the pianist Justus Frantz. In 1972 he began to make appearances as a conductor; made his debut as an opera conductor in Darmstadt with *La Traviata* in 1978. He pursued a successful career as both a pianist and a conductor, sometimes conducting from the keyboard. After serving as Generalmusikdirektor of the Rheinland-Pfalz State Phil. (1979–81), he was 1st permanent guest conductor of the Zürich Tonhalle Orch. (1981–82); then was its chief conductor (1982–85). In 1988 he became music director of the Houston Sym. Orch. He maintains a varied repertoire, as both a pianist and a conductor; his sympathies range from the standard literature to the cosmopolitan avant-garde.
  Bibl.: *Current Biography* (Aug. 1989).

Escher, Rudolf (George), noted Dutch composer; b. Amsterdam, Jan. 8, 1912; d. De Koog, March 17, 1980. He studied harmony, violin, and piano at the Toonkunst Cons. in Rotterdam (1931–37); was a student in composition of Pijper (1934); worked in the electronic music studios in Delft (1959–60) and in Utrecht (1961). He taught at the Amsterdam Cons. (1960–61) and at the Inst. for Musical Science at Utrecht Univ. (1964–75). In 1977 he was awarded the Johan Wagenaar Prize for his compositions. Escher's music was very much influenced by the modern French school.
  Works: orch.: *Sinfonia in memoriam Maurice Ravel* (1940); *Musique pour l'esprit en deuil* (Music for the Soul in Mourning; 1941–43; Amsterdam, Jan. 19, 1947); Passacaglia (1945; withdrawn); Concerto for Strings (1947–48; withdrawn); *Hymne de Grand Meaulnes* (1950–51); 2 syms.: No. 1 (1953–54) and No. 2 (1958; rev. 1964 and 1971); *Summer Rites at Noon* for 2 facing Orchs. (1962–68); orchestration of Debussy's 6 *épigraphes antiques* for Piano Duet (1976–77; Hilversum Radio, July 6, 1978). vocal: *3 poèmes de Tristan Corbière* for Soprano and Piano (1936); *Horcajo* for Mezzo-soprano and Piano (1941); *Lettre du Mexique* for Baritone and Piano (1942); *Protesilaos en Laodamia,* musical comedy for Mezzo-soprano, Tenor, Baritone, and Orch. (1946–48; withdrawn); *De poort van Ishtar,* incidental music for Chorus and Orch. (1947; withdrawn); *Poèmes de Vion Dalibray* for Tenor and Piano (1947–49); *Chants du désir* for Mezzo-soprano and Piano (1951); *Nostalgies* for Tenor and Orch. (1951; rev. 1961); *Strange Meeting,* after Owen, for Baritone and Piano (1952); *Le Vrai Visage de la paix,* after Éluard, for Chorus (1953; rev. 1957); *Song of Love and Eternity,* after Dickinson, for Chorus (1955); *Ciel, air et vents,* after Ronsard, for Chorus (1957); *De Perzen* (The Persians), after Aeschylus, incidental music for Narrator, Men's Choir, and Orch. (1963); *Univers de Rimbaud,* 5 songs after Rimbaud for Tenor and Orch. (1970); *3 Poems by W.H. Auden* for Chorus (1975). chamber: *Sonata concertante* for Cello and Piano (1943); Sonata for 2 Flutes (1944); Solo Cello Sonata (1945); Trio for Oboe, Clarinet, and Bassoon (1946); Solo Flute Sonata (1949); Sonata for Violin and Piano (1950); *Le Tombeau de Ravel* for Flute, Oboe, Violin, Viola, Cello, and Harpsichord (1952); *Air pour charmer un lézard* for Solo Flute (1953); Trio for Violin, Viola, and Cello (1959); Wind Quintet (1966–67); *Monologue* for Solo Flute (1969); Solo Clarinet Sonata (1973); *Sinfonia* for 10 Instruments (1976); Sonata for Flute and Piano (1975–77); Trio for Clarinet, Viola, and Piano (1978). piano: Sonata No. 1 (1935); *Arcana musae dona,* suite (1944); *Habanera* (1945); *Due voci* (1949); *Non troppo,* 10 easy pieces (1949); Sonatina (1951).
  He also wrote a Passacaglia for Organ (1937) and electronic music for *The Long Christmas Dinner,* after Thornton Wilder (1960).
  Writings: *Toscanini en Debussy* (Rotterdam, 1938); "Maurice Ravel," *Groot Nederland* (July 1939); "Debussy and the Musical Epigram," *Key Notes,* 10 (1979/2).
  Bibl.: E. Schönberger, "R. E.: Thinking in and about Music," *Key Notes,* 5 (1977/1).

Eschig, Max(imilian), Czech-born French music publisher; b. Troppau, May 27, 1872; d. Paris, Sept. 3, 1927. He settled in Paris and founded a publishing firm under his name in 1907, prospering continually and forming an impressive catalog of modern works by Ravel, Manuel de Falla, and many other French, Spanish, and English composers.

Eschmann, Johann Karl, Swiss pianist and pedagogue; b. Winterthur, April 12, 1826; d. Zürich, Oct. 27, 1882. He studied in Leipzig with Moscheles, and also had some lessons with Mendelssohn. He then settled in Zürich as a piano teacher; publ. a valuable manual, *Wegweiser durch die Klavierliteratur* (Zürich, 1879; 8th ed., 1914), and *100 Aphorismen aus dem Klavierunterricht* (2nd ed., 1899).

Escobar-Budge, Roberto, Chilean composer; b. Santiago, May 11, 1926. He studied composition with René Amengual and Alfonso Letelier; was active as a music critic; taught at the Catholic Univ. of Chile in Santiago. He publ. *Músicas sin pasado* (Santiago, 1971).
  Works: Wind Quintet (1957); *Diferencias sinfónicas* for Orch. (1962); *Los bisontes,* symphonic suite (1964); Nonet (1965); *Cuarteto estructural* for Strings (1965); *Sinfonía Valparaíso* (1967); *Incógnita* for Harpsichord, Trumpet, Bassoon, Cello, and Percussion (1967); choruses; piano pieces.

Escobar, Luis Antonio, Colombian composer; b. Villapinzón, near Bogotá, July 14, 1925. He studied at the Bogotá Cons.; then took courses with Nicolas Nabokov at the Peabody Cons. in Baltimore and with Boris Blacher in Berlin. He returned to Bogotá in 1953, and received the post of prof. at the Cons., which he held until 1962. His style is brisk and terse in the modern manner; but there is in his music also a melorhythmic pattern of Spanish-American dances.

Works: Flute Concertino (1951); ballet, *Avirama* (1955); *Sinfonía Cero* (1955); *Sinfonía X* (1955); Harpsichord Concertino (1958); Piano Concerto (1959); *Los hampones,* opera for Soloists, Chorus, and Percussion (1961); *Juramento a Bolívar* for Male Chorus and Orch. (1964); *Little Symphony* (Washington, D.C., May 7, 1965); 2 string quartets; 2 violin sonatas; 5 piano sonatinas (1950–59); etc.

Escobedo, Bartolomé de, Spanish singer and composer; b. Zamora province, c.1500; d. between March 21 and Aug. 11, 1563. From 1536 to 1541, and again from 1545 to 1554, he was a singer in the Papal Choir at Rome. He was a judge in the famous dispute between Nicola Vicentino and Vincento Lusitano (1551) over the qualities of Greek modes. He composed 2 masses and a number of motets.

Escot, Pozzi (Olga), Peruvian-born American composer of French-Moroccan descent; b. Lima, Oct. 1, 1931. She studied with Andrés Sás at the Sás-Rosay Academy of Music in Lima (1949–53); she also took courses in mathematics at San Marcos Univ. there (1950–52). She emigrated to the U.S. in 1953, becoming a naturalized citizen in 1963; she studied with William Bergsma at the Juilliard School of Music in N.Y. (B.S., 1956; M.S., 1957) and with Philipp Jarnach at the Hamburg Hochschule für Musik (1957–61). She taught at the New England Cons. of Music in Boston (1964–67; 1980–81) and at Wheaton College in Norton, Mass. (from 1972), where she was director of its electronic music studio; she also lectured at the Univs. of Peking and Shanghai (1984). She ed. the journal *Sonus* (from 1980). With her husband, Robert Cogan, she wrote *Sonic Design: The Nature of Sound and Music* (Englewood Cliffs, N.J., 1976) and *Sonic Design: Practice and Problems* (Englewood Cliffs, N.J., 1981). Her musical idiom follows the tenets of modern structural formalism with modified serial procedures.

Works: 3 syms. (*Little Symphony,* 1952–53; Sym. for Strings, 1955; 1957); *Sands . . .* for 5 Saxophones, Electric Guitar, 17 Violins, 9 Double Basses, and Percussion (1965); Concerto for Piano and Chamber Orch. (1982); *3 Poems of Rilke* for Narrator and String Quartet (1959); *Lamentus: Trilogy No. 1* for Soprano, 2 Violins, 2 Cellos, Piano, and 3 Percussion (1962); *Cristhos: Trilogy No. 2* for Alto Flute, Contrabassoon, 3 Violins, and Percussion (1963); *Visione: Trilogy No. 3* for Soprano, Speaker, Flute or Piccolo, Alto Flute, Alto Saxophone, Double Bass, and Percussion (1964); *Neyrac lux* for 2 Guitars and Electric Guitar (1978); *Trio in memoriam Solrac* for Violin, Cello, and Piano (1984); *Differences,* Group I and II for Piano (1960–61; 1963); *Interra* for Piano, Tape, Lights, and Film (1968); *Interra II* for Piano Left-hand and Tape (1980); *Ainu* for 4 Ensembles of 5 Voices (1970; also for 1 Voice, 1978); *Missa triste* for 3 Women's Choruses and 3 Optional Treble Instruments (1981); *Pluies* for Alto Saxophone and Tape (1981); *Visione* (1987); *Your Kindled Valors Bend* (1989).

Escudier, Léon, French music journalist; b. Castelnaudary, Aude, Sept. 17, 1816; d. Paris, June 22, 1881. He was a brother and partner of **Marie (-Pierre-Yves) Escudier** (b. Castelnaudary, June 29, 1809; d. Paris, April 18, 1880). In 1837, the brothers began publishing the periodical *La France Musicale* and soon afterward established a music shop. Industrious writers, they issued jointly the following works: *Études biographiques sur les chanteurs contemporains* (1840); *Dictionnaire de musique d'après les théoriciens, historiens et critiques les plus célèbres* (2 vols., 1844; reprinted in 1854 as *Dictionnaire de musique, théorique et historique;* 5th ed., 1872); *Rossini, Sa vie et ses œuvres* (1854); *Vie et aventures des cantatrices célèbres, précédées des musiciens de l'Empire, et suivies de la vie anecdotique de Paganini* (1856). Léon broke up partnership with his brother in 1860, retaining the music business; he established a new journal, *L'Art Musical,* which continued to appear until Sept. 27, 1894. Marie retained the publishing and editorial rights to *La France Musicale,* which ceased publication in 1870.

Eshpai, Andrei, Russian composer, son of **Yakov Eshpai;** b. Kozmodemiansk, May 15, 1925. He studied with Aram Khatchaturian in Moscow; during the war he acted as a translator from German. In his music he makes use of folk motifs of the Mari nation from which he descended.

Works: 4 syms. (1959, 1962, 1964, 1982); *Symphonic Dances* (1951); *Hungarian Melodies* for Violin and Orch. (1952); 2 piano concertos (1954, 1972); 2 violin sonatas (1966, 1970); Concerto for Orch., with Solo Trumpet, Vibraphone, Piano, and Double Bass (1967); *Festival Overture* for Chorus, 12 Violins, 8 Cellos, 6 Harps, 4 Pianos, and Orch. (1970); ballet, *The Circle* (Kuibyshev, Feb. 23, 1981); Oboe Concerto (1982).

Bibl.: L. Novosiolova, *The Creative Work of A. E.* (Moscow, 1981).

Eshpai, Yakov, Russian composer of Mari extraction, father of **Andrei Eshpai;** b. near Zvenigorodsk, Oct. 30, 1890; d. Moscow, Feb. 20, 1963. He studied violin and singing in Kazan, and later at the Moscow Cons. He publ. important collections of national songs of the Ural region, particularly of the Mari ethnic group; also wrote vocal and instrumental music on native themes.

Eslava (y Elizondo), (Miguel) Hilarión, Spanish composer and scholar; b. Burlada, Navarra, Oct. 21, 1807; d. Madrid, July 23, 1878. He was a choirboy at the Cathedral of Pamplona; studied organ and violin; in 1827 he went to Calahorra, where he studied with Francisco Secanilla; at the age of 20 he was appointed music director at the Cathedral of Burgo de Osma, where he was ordained a priest. In 1832 he became music director at Seville; in 1844 he obtained the appointment as chapel master to Queen Isabella in Madrid; in 1854 he became a prof. at the Madrid Cons. and in 1866 its director. He also ed. a periodical, *Gaceta Musical de Madrid* (1855–56). He wrote 3 operas with Italian texts: *Il solitario del Monte Selvaggio* (Cádiz, 1841), *La tregua di Ptolemaide* (Cádiz, May 24, 1842), and *Pietro il crudele* (Seville, 1843); his fame rests, however, not on his musical compositions, but on his great collection in 10 vols., *Lira sacro-hispana* (Madrid, 1869), an anthology of Spanish sacred music from the 16th to the 19th century, including some of Eslava's own works (Requiem, Te Deum, etc.). He also publ. *Método de solfeo* (1846) and *Escuela de armonía y composición* (1861).

Bibl.: G. Chase, "M.H. E.," *Musical Quarterly* (Jan. 1938).

Espinosa, Guillermo, Colombian conductor; b. Cartagena, Jan. 9, 1905; d. Washington, D.C., July 5, 1990. He studied music in Milan and in Berlin. After appearing as a guest conductor in Italy, Switzerland, Denmark, and France, he returned to Colombia, and in 1936 founded the National Sym. Orch. at Bogotá, which he led for 10 years. In 1947, he settled in Washington, D.C., as an official of the Division of Music in the Pan American Union; in 1953, succeeded Charles Seeger as chief; retired in 1975.

Bibl.: F.C. Lange, "G. E. y Orquesta la Sinfónica Nacional," *Boletín latinoamericano de Música* (1938).

Esplá (y Triay), Oscar, Spanish music educator and composer; b. Alicante, Aug. 5, 1886; d. Madrid, Jan. 6, 1976. He began his musical studies in Alicante, then studied with Reger in Meiningen and Munich (1912) and Saint-Saëns in Paris (1913). In 1930 he became a prof. at the Madrid Cons., serving as its director (1936–39); was also president of the Junta Nacional de Música y Teatros Líricos (1931–34). He became director of the Laboratoire Musical Scientifique in Brussels in 1946; returning to Spain, he became director of his own cons. in Alicante (1958). He publ. *El arte y la musicalidad* (Alicante, 1912), *Fundamento estético de las actividades del espíritu* (Munich, 1915), and *Función musical y música contemporánea* (Madrid, 1955). His compositions show the influence of Spanish folk music; he utilized his own Levantine scale in his works.

WORKS: OPERAS: *La bella durmiente* (Vienna, 1909); *La balteira* (N.Y., 1935); *Plumes au vent* (1941); *El pirata cautivo* (Madrid, 1974); *Calixto y Melibea* (1974–76); scenic cantata, *Nochebuena del diablo* for Soprano, Chorus, and Orch. (1923). **BALLETS:** *Ciclopes de Ifach* (1920?); *El contrabandista* (Paris, 1928); *Fiesta* (1931; unfinished). **ORCH.:** *El sueño de Eros*, symphonic poem (1904); *Suite levantina* (1911; rev. as *Poema de miños*, 1914); *Don Quijote velando las armas*, symphonic episode (1924); *Schubertiana* (1928); 2 *suites folklóricas* for Chamber Orch. (1932, 1934); *El ámbito de la danza* (1929–34); *Concierto de cámara* (1937); *Sonata del sur* for Piano and Orch. (1943–45); *Sinfonía aitana* (Madrid, Oct. 31, 1964); *Sinfonía de retaguardia* (1969–76). **CHAMBER:** Sonata for Violin and Piano (1915); Piano Trio (1917); 2 string quartets (1920, 1943); *Sonata concertante* (1939); *Lírica española* for Piano and Instruments (1952–54); also several choral works; cantatas; organ music.

BIBL.: A. Iglesias, *O. E., Su obra para piano* (Madrid, 1962); idem, *O. E.* (Madrid, 1973).

Esposito, Michele, Italian composer, pianist, and conductor; b. Castellammare di Stabia, near Naples, Sept. 29, 1855; d. Florence, Nov. 23, 1929. He studied at the Cons. San Pietro e Majella at Naples with Cesi (piano) and Serrao (theory); for a time he gave piano concerts in Italy; from 1878 to 1882 was in Paris; in 1882 he was engaged as a piano teacher at the Royal Irish Academy of Music in Dublin; he organized the Dublin Orch. Soc. in 1899 and conducted it until 1914, and again in 1927. He held the honorary degree of Mus.Doc. of Trinity College, Dublin. He composed several works on Irish subjects: Irish operetta, *The Post Bag* (London, Jan. 27, 1902); incidental music for *The Tinker and the Fairy* (Dublin, 1910); *Suite of Irish Dances* for Orch.; 2 Irish rhapsodies; several arrangements of Irish melodies. He received 1st prizes for his cantata *Deirdre* (Irish Festival, Dublin, 1897); *Irish Symphony* (Irish Festival, Dublin, 1902); also wrote 2 string quartets, 2 violin sonatas, cello sonatas, etc.

BIBL.: K. van Hoek, "M. E., Maestro of Dublin," *Irish Monthly* (June 1943).

Esser, Heinrich, German conductor and composer; b. Mannheim, July 15, 1818; d. Salzburg, June 3, 1872. He studied in Vienna with Sechter. In 1847 he became conductor of the Vienna Court Opera, succeeding Otto Nicolai; in 1869, retired and lived in Salzburg. He was a competent opera conductor; also had a modicum of success as an opera composer; 3 of his operas were performed: *Sitas* (Mannheim, 1840); *Thomas Riquiqui* (Frankfurt, 1843); and *Die zwei Prinzen* (Munich, 1845); also numerous vocal works; 5 syms.; arrangements of Bach's organ works; a String Quartet.

BIBL.: K.-J. Müller, *H. E. als Komponist* (diss., Univ. of Mainz, 1969).

Essipoff (Essipova), Anna, famous Russian pianist and pedagogue; b. St. Petersburg, Feb. 13, 1851; d. there, Aug. 18, 1914. She was a pupil of **Leschetizky,** and married him in 1880 (divorced 1892). She made her debut in St. Petersburg; subsequently made long concert tours throughout Europe and in America; her distinguishing artistic quality was a singing piano tone and "pearly" passage work. From 1870 to 1885 she gave 669 concerts. In 1893 she was engaged as a prof. of piano at the St. Petersburg Cons., and continued to teach there until 1908. Many famous pianists and composers, Prokofiev among them, were her students.

Esswood, Paul (Lawrence Vincent), English countertenor; b. West Bridgford, June 2, 1942. He studied with Gordon Clinton at the Royal College of Music, London; then was lay vicar at Westminster Abbey (1964–71). He made his formal debut as countertenor in 1965 in a performance of *Messiah;* his operatic debut took place in 1968 in Berkeley, Calif., when he

sang in Cavalli's *Erismena.* He was a founder of the Pro Cantione Antiqua, an a cappella male vocal group.

Esteban, Julio, Spanish pianist and pedagogue; b. Shanghai (of Spanish parents), March 18, 1906; d. Baltimore, Dec. 6, 1987. In 1907 he was taken to Spain; gave concerts in Spain from 1919 to 1924; in 1925 went to Manila, where he taught at the Cons. of Music of the Univ. of the Philippines until 1947, when he was appointed director of the Cons. of Music at the Univ. of Santo Tomás there. He traveled through the Orient; gave concerts in Hong Kong and in Japan in 1952; also played for the U.N. troops in Korea. In 1955 he joined the faculty of the Peabody Cons. in Baltimore.

Estes, Simon (Lamont), noted black American bass-baritone; b. Centerville, Iowa, Feb. 2, 1938. He sang in a local Baptist church choir as a child, then studied voice with Charles Kellis at the Univ. of Iowa and on scholarship at N.Y.'s Juilliard School of Music. He made his operatic debut as Ramfis at the Berlin Deutsche Oper (1965); after winning a silver medal at the Tchaikovsky Competition in Moscow (1966), he appeared with the San Francisco Opera and the Chicago Lyric Opera, but was mainly active as a concert artist. On June 10, 1976, he made his 1st appearance with the Metropolitan Opera as Oroveso in *Norma* during the company's visit to the Wolf Trap Farm Park in Vienna, Va. However, it was not until he sang the Dutchman at the Bayreuth Festival in 1978 that his remarkable vocal gifts began to be widely appreciated. He subsequently appeared as the Dutchman throughout Europe to notable acclaim. In 1980 he made his U.S. recital debut at N.Y.'s Carnegie Hall, and in 1981 returned to the Metropolitan Opera roster, singing Wotan opposite Birgit Nilsson's Brünnhilde in a concert performance of Act III of *Die Walküre* in N.Y. He finally made his formal stage debut with the company there as the Landgrave on Jan. 4, 1982. In 1985 he returned to sing Porgy in *Porgy and Bess.* His comprehensive operatic and concert repertoire ranges from Handel to spirituals.

BIBL.: *Current Biography* (Aug. 1986).

Esteve (Estebe) y Grimau, Pablo, Catalonian composer; b. probably in Barcelona, c.1730; d. Madrid, June 4, 1794. He went to Madrid about 1760; was maestro di cappella to the Duke of Osuna; in 1778 was appointed official composer for the municipal theaters of Madrid. He composed over 400 tonadillas, and some zarzuelas. His song *El jilguerito con pico de oro* was arranged for soprano and orch. by Joaquín Nin.

Estévez, Antonio, Venezuelan composer; b. Calabozo, Jan. 3, 1916; d. Caracas, Nov. 26, 1988. He studied composition in Caracas with Vicente Emilio Sojo; played the oboe in the Caracas Sym. Orch. At the age of 50 he became interested in electronic music and obtained a scholarship from the Venezuelan National Inst. of Culture and Fine Arts to study electronic techniques in Paris.

WORKS: *Suite Llanera* for Orch. (1942); Concerto for Orch. (1949–50); *Cantata criolla* for Voices and Orch. (1954); choruses; piano pieces; a group of electronic works under the title *Cosmovibrafonía* (1968).

Estrada, Carlos, Uruguayan conductor, teacher, and composer; b. Montevideo, Sept. 15, 1909; d. there, May 7, 1970. He studied in Paris with Roger-Ducasse and Henri Busser (composition) and with Philippe Gaubert (conducting). Returning to Montevideo, he was associated with the State Radio (1940–54) and was director of the National Cons. in Montevideo (1954–68). He wrote 2 syms. (1951, 1967); chamber music; effective piano pieces.

Estrada, Garcia Juan Agustín, Argentine composer; b. Buenos Aires, Nov. 8, 1895; d. there, 1961. He studied law; then took lessons in composition with Jacques Ibert in Paris. Returning to Argentina, he became a municipal judge.

WORKS: *Tres aires argentinos* for Orch. (Paris, Feb. 28, 1929); opera, *La Cuarterona* (Buenos Aires, Aug. 10, 1951); a number of songs.

Estrada, Julio, Mexican composer, theoretician, historian, and pedagogue; b. Mexico City (of exiled Spanish parents),

April 10, 1943. He studied in Mexico with del Castillo, de Elías, de Tercero, and Julian Orbón (1955–63) in Germany with Gerhard Muench (1963–65), and in Paris (1965–69) with Boulanger, Elsa Barraine, Raffi Ourgandjian, Messiaen, Jean E. Marie, Pousseur, and Xenakis; then returned briefly to Germany, where he studied with Stockhausen at the Kölner Kurse für Neue Musik and with Ligeti at the Darmstadter Musikferienkurse. Upon his return to Mexico in 1970, he worked at Radio Universidad. He created several new-music ensembles, including Pro-Música Nueva and Compañia Musical de Repertorio Nuevo, introducing to Mexico the works of Cage, Ligeti, Oliveros, Riley, Stockhausen, and others. Since 1973 he has taught in the Escuela Nacional de Música at the Universidad Nacional Autónoma de México. He was the 1st full-time music researcher at the Instituto de Investigaciones Estéticas (from 1976) and the 1st music scholar to be appointed by the Mexican Education Ministry as Investigador Nacional (1984–87; 1987–90). He was general ed. of *La música de México* (10 vols., 1984); he also publ. a collection of essays on new Latin American and Mexican music, *Reunión entre tiemps* (1990). His work with Jorge Gil in the Finite Group's Theory and Boolean Algebra Applications in Music (resulting in *Música y teoriá de Grupos Finitos, 3 variables booleanas* [1984]) was the 1st instance in Mexico in which musicians used computers as both a theoretical and a precompositional tool. Estrada also posited his general theory of intervallic cycles as a hierarchical system applied to musical systems based on scales in his *El espectro interválico, una teoría general de la interválica y sus aplicaciones al estudio precomposicional y al análisis musical del gregoriano a la música actual* (1990). He conceives of musical composition as a field where new solutions can be obtained from an objective order and organization according to its inner characteristics of discontinuity or continuity; his own compositions demand the invention of new technical and theoretical models coming out of "the primordial needs of fantasy." Profoundly political, Estrada identifies the act of composition with the act of liberation, with "the permissiveness of musical ideas becoming at the same time the powerful exigency of a true, almost phonographic representation of each detail belonging to sounds already internally experienced."

WORKS: *Persona* (1969); *Solo* (1970); *Memorias, para teclado* (1971); *Melódica* (1973); *Canto mnémico, fuga en 4 dimensiones* (1973; rev. 1983); *Canto tejido* for Piano (1974); *Canto naciente* for 3 Trumpets, 2 Cornets, 2 Trombones, and Tuba (1975–78); *Canto oculto* for Violin (1977); *Canto alterno* for Cello (1978); *Diario* for 15 Stringed Instruments (1980); *eua'on I* for Tape (1981); *eolo'oolin* for 6 Percussionists (1981–82); *eua'on II* for Orch. (1983); *yuunohui'yei* for Cello (1983); *ishini'ioni* for String Quartet (1984–90); *yuunohui'nahui* for Double Bass (1985); *yuunohui'ce* for Violin (1990); *yuunohui'ome* for Viola (1990).

Etcheverry, Henri-Bertrand, French bass-baritone; b. Bordeaux, March 29, 1900; d. Paris, Nov. 14, 1960. He studied in Paris; made his debut at the Paris Opéra in 1932; also sang at the Opéra-Comique; made several appearances at Covent Garden in London. In addition to the French operatic roles, he was one of the best performers of Russian roles, such as Boris Godunov.

Etler, Alvin (Derald), American oboist, teacher, and composer; b. Battle Creek, Iowa, Feb. 19, 1913; d. Northampton, Mass., June 13, 1973. He studied at the Univ. of Illinois, Case Western Reserve Univ., and Yale Univ. He was on the faculty of Yale Univ. (1942–46), Cornell Univ. (1946–47), the Univ. of Illinois (1947–49), and Smith College (1949–73). He held 2 Guggenheim fellowships. His music is marked by stately formality of design.

WORKS: ORCH.: *Music* for Chamber Orch. (1938); 2 sinfoniettas (1940, 1941); *Passacaglia and Fugue* for Orch. (1947); Concerto for String Quartet and String Orch. (1948); Sym. (1951); *Dramatic Overture* (1956); Concerto for Orch. (1957); *Elegy* for Small Orch. (1959); Concerto for Wind Quintet and Orch. (1960; Tokyo, Oct. 18, 1962); *Triptych* (1961); Concerto

for Clarinet and Chamber Ensemble of 3 Trumpets, 3 Trombones, 2 Double Basses, and 3 Percussionists (1962; N.Y., Dec. 20, 1965); Concerto for Brass Quintet, String Orch., and Percussion (1967); Concerto for String Quartet and Orch. (1968; Milwaukee, June 13, 1968); *Convivialities* (1968); Concerto for Cello, with Chamber Group (N.Y., March 2, 1971). **CHAMBER:** Suite for Oboe, Violin, Viola, and Cello (1936); Sonata for Oboe, Clarinet, and Viola (1944); Bassoon Sonata (1951); 2 clarinet sonatas (1952, 1969); Oboe Sonata (1952); 2 wind quintets (1955, 1957); Cello Sonata (1956); Concerto for Violin and Wind Quintet (1958); Sonata for Viola and Harpsichord (1959); 2 string quartets (1963, 1965); Brass Quintet (1963); *Sonic Sequence* for Brass Quintet (1967); also *Onomatopoësis* for Men's Chorus, Winds, Brass, and Percussion (1965).

BIBL.: P. Shelden, *A. E. (1913–1973); His Career and His Two Sonatas for Clarinet* (diss., Univ. of Maryland, 1978).

Eto, Toshiya, Japanese violinist; b. Tokyo, Nov. 9, 1927. After preliminary study in Japan he went to the U.S. and enrolled as a student of Efrem Zimbalist at the Curtis Inst. of Music in Philadelphia; then was on its faculty (1953–61). In 1961 he returned to Japan as a prof. at the Toho School of Music. He continued to appear widely as a soloist, and received praise for his technical ability in performances of contemporary music. He made his American debut as a soloist at Carnegie Hall in N.Y. in 1951.

Ett, Kaspar, German organist and composer; b. Eresing, Jan. 5, 1788; d. Munich, May 16, 1847. From 1816, he was court organist at St. Michael's Church in Munich. He was active in reviving the church music of the 16th and 17th centuries; his own sacred compositions (of which but a few graduals and *cantica sacra* were printed) follow these early works in style. He composed 273 separate works; a complete enumeration is given in F. Bierling, *Kaspar Ett* (1906).

BIBL.: K. von Schafhäutl, "Erinnerungen an K. E.," *Kirchenmusikalisches Jahrbuch* (1891).

Ettinger, Max (Markus Wolf), German composer and conductor; b. Lemberg, Dec. 27, 1874; d. Basel, July 19, 1951. He studied in Berlin and Munich; was active as a conductor in Munich (1900–1920), Leipzig (1920–29), and Berlin (1929–33). In 1938 he went to Switzerland.

WORKS: Operas: *Judith* (Nuremberg, 1921); *Der eifersüchtige Trinker*, after Boccaccio (Nuremberg, 1925); *Juana* (Nuremberg, 1925); *Clavigo*, after Goethe (Leipzig, 1926); *Frühlings Erwachen* (Leipzig, 1928); oratorio, *Weisheit des Orients*, after Omar Khayyám (Nuremberg, 1924); *Jewish Requiem* (1947); also chamber music and songs.

Euclid, famous Greek geometer who lived at Alexandria about 300 B.C. He is the reputed author of a treatise on music, *Katatomè kanonos (Sectio canonis),* following the theories of Pythagoras (new critical ed. by K. von Jan in *Musici scriptores graeci*). For another treatise long ascribed to Euclid, see the entry on Cleonides.

Eulenburg, Ernst (Emil Alexander), German music publisher, father of **Kurt Eulenburg;** b. Berlin, Nov. 30, 1847; d. Leipzig, Sept. 11, 1926. He studied at the Leipzig Cons.; in 1874 established in Leipzig the publishing house bearing his name; after his acquisition of Payne's *Kleine Partitur-Ausgabe* (1891) he enormously increased the scope of that publication so that large orch. scores could be included. Upon his death the firm was taken over by his son.

Eulenburg, Kurt, German music publisher, son of **Ernst (Emil Alexander) Eulenburg;** b. Berlin, Feb. 22, 1879; d. London, April 10, 1982 (at the age of 103!). Apprenticed by his father, he joined the Eulenburg firm in 1911, and upon his father's death in 1926 became its sole owner. He extended the dept. of miniature scores and also publ. the original text ("Urtext") of many of Mozart's works, ed. by Alfred Einstein, Blume, Kroyer, and others. During World War II, he lived in Switzerland. He settled in London in 1945 and took over the management of the London branch of his publishing business. He retired in 1968.

Euler, Leonhard, great Swiss mathematician; b. Basel, April 15, 1707; d. St. Petersburg, Sept. 18, 1783. He was a prof. of mathematics at St. Petersburg (1733) and Berlin (1741); publ. several important works on music theory and acoustics, chief among them being the *Tentamen novae theoriae musicae . . .* (St. Petersburg, 1739). Euler was the 1st to employ logarithms to explain differences in pitch.
BIBL.: Schulz-Euler, *L. E.* (Frankfurt, 1907).

Europe, James Reese, black American conductor and composer; b. Mobile, Ala., Feb. 22, 1881; d. Boston, May 10, 1919 (stabbed to death by a disgruntled drummer in his band). He studied violin and piano in childhood in Washington, D.C.; then went to N.Y., where he was active as a director of musical comedies, founding the Clef Club (1910), a union and contracting agency for black musicians. He also founded the Clef Club sym. orch., which gave performances of works by black composers at Carnegie Hall (1912–14). He was music director and composer for the dancers Irene and Vernon Castle (1914–17), and is credited with composing the 1st fox-trot for them. He also wrote songs for musicals and composed dances and marches for his orchs. and bands.
BIBL.: R. Badger, "J.R. E. and the Prehistory of Jazz," *American Music* (Spring 1989).

Euting, Ernst, English musicologist; b. London, Feb. 7, 1874; d. Berlin, April 21, 1925. From 1892 to 1896 he attended the Hochschule für Musik in Berlin, then devoted himself to musicology at the Univ. there, and became a Ph.D. with the dissertation *Zur Geschichte der Blasinstrumente im 16. und 17. Jahrhundert* (1899); in the same year he founded the *Deutsche Instrumentenbau-Zeitung*, of which he was the editor; also ed. the *Zeitschrift der Internationalen Musikgesellschaft* (1902–3).

Evangelisti, Franco, Italian composer; b. Rome, Jan. 21, 1926; d. there, Jan. 28, 1980. He first studied engineering at the Univ. of Rome; then went to Germany, where he took courses in composition at the Univ. of Freiburg; also attended summer courses with Ernst Krenek and René Leibowitz at Darmstadt. In his music he explored the musical resources of electronics; the titles of his works betray his preoccupation with mathematical terminology, as exemplified by *4!* (factorization of the numbers from 1 to 4) for Violin and Piano (1954); *Ordini* for Orch. (1955); *Random or Not Random* for Orch. (1962); *Proporzioni* for Flute (1958); *Campi integrati* for Tape (1959); *Aleatorio* for String Quartet (1959).
BIBL.: H.-K. Metzger and R. Riehn, eds., *F. E.* (Munich, 1985).

Evans, Anne, English soprano; b. London, Aug. 20, 1939. She was a student of Ruth Packer at the Royal College of Music in London and of Maria Carpi, Herbert Graf, and Lotvi Mansouri at the Geneva Cons. After singing secondary roles at the Geneva Grand Théâtre, she returned to London in 1968 to join the Sadler's Wells Opera (later the English National Opera), where she was notably successful in such roles as Mimi, Tosca, Elsa, the Marschallin, and Sieglinde; she also appeared with the Welsh National Opera in Cardiff as Senta, Chrysothemis, the Empress, Donna Anna, and Brünnhilde (1985). Her Brünnhilde elicited critical acclaim when the company visited London's Covent Garden in 1986.

Evans, Bill (William John), American jazz pianist and composer; b. Plainfield, N.J., Aug. 16, 1929; d. N.Y., Sept. 15, 1980. After taking up the piano, he joined the band of Miles Davis and soon became a leading jazz pianist; after making the classic jazz recording of *Kind of Blue* with the Davis group, he formed his own jazz trio. He received Grammy awards for his recordings *Conversations with Myself* (1963), *Alone* (1970), and *The Bill Evans Album* (1971).
BIBL.: C. Israels, "B. E. (1929–1980): A Musical Memoir," *Musical Quarterly*, No. 2 (1985).

Evans, Dale (Frances Octavia), American country-music singer, songwriter, and actress; b. Uvalde, Texas, Oct. 31, 1912. She received lessons in singing, piano, and dancing in Osceola, Ark., then sang on the radio in Memphis, Dallas, Louisville, and Chicago. She went in 1943 to Hollywood, where she appeared in western films and on radio, often with **Roy Rogers,** who became her husband in 1947; they later starred in their own television series and made many personal appearances. She wrote *Happy Trails*, which the couple adopted as their theme song; her other songs included *The Bible Tells Me So, Happy Birthday Gentle Saviour,* and *San Antone*. She also publ. several books of an inspirational nature.

Evans, David (Emlyn), Welsh music editor and composer; b. near Newscastle Emlyn, Wales, Sept. 21, 1843; d. London, April 19, 1913. He was established in business at Cheltenham, but devoted his leisure hours to music; took part in many Welsh music festivals (Eisteddfodau), his works invariably winning prizes; after the Eisteddfod at Wexham in 1876, when he carried off all 4 prizes, he voluntarily withdrew from further competitions, but frequently acted as judge; at the National Eisteddfod in London in 1887, he was awarded a prize for his *Biography of Welsh Musicians;* for many years he was ed. of *Y Cerddor* (The Musician). His chief work is *Alawon fy ngwlad* (2 vols., 1896), a collection of 500 Welsh airs in piano arrangements; his publ. compositions include 2 cantatas, *The Christian's Prayer* and *The Fairy-tribe;* many glees, anthems, and part-songs.

Evans, Edwin, Jr., English writer on music, son of **Edwin Evans, Sr.;** b. London, Sept. 1, 1874; d. there, March 3, 1945. He studied for a business career; was engaged in telegraphy, railroads, and finance from 1889 to 1913; then devoted himself exclusively to musical pursuits. He was music critic of the *Pall Mall Gazette* (1912–23) and other London papers; was one of the founders of the ISCM (1922); in 1938 was elected its president, retaining this post until his death. He wrote *Tchaikovsky* (London, 1906; 3rd ed., rev., 1966); *The Margin of Music* (London, 1924); *Music and the Dance* (London, 1948).

Evans, Edwin, Sr., English organist and writer on music, father of **Edwin Evans, Jr.;** b. London, 1844; d. there, Dec. 21, 1923. An assiduous and thorough scholar, he publ. basic analytic vols. on Beethoven and Brahms: *Beethoven's 9 Symphonies, Fully Described and Analyzed* (London, 1923–24) and the remarkable 4-vol. ed. (1,581 pages; over 1,000 musical examples) *Historical, Descriptive and Analytical Account of the Entire Works of Johannes Brahms:* vol. I, vocal works (1912); vol. II, chamber and orch. music up to op. 67 (1933; reprinted 1950); vol. III, chamber and orch. music from op. 68 to the end (1935; reprinted 1949); vol. IV, piano works (1936; reprinted 1950). Vols. II, III, and IV were publ. posth. He also wrote *Accompaniment of Plainchant* (1911); *Wagner's Teachings by Analogy* (1915); *How to Compose; How to Accompany at the Piano* (London, 1917); *Method of Instrumentation* (vol. I, *How to Write for Strings*); *Technics of the Organ* (London, 1938).

Evans, Sir Geraint (Llewellyn), distinguished Welsh baritone; b. Pontypridd, South Wales, Feb. 16, 1922. He began to study voice in Cardiff when he was 17, and, after serving in the RAF during World War II, resumed his vocal studies in Hamburg with Theo Hermann; then studied with Fernando Carpi in Geneva and Walter Hyde at the Guildhall School of Music in London. He made his operatic debut as the Nightwatchman in *Die Meistersinger von Nürnberg* at London's Covent Garden (1948); thereafter was a leading member of the company. He also sang at the Glyndebourne Festivals (1949–61). In 1959 he made his U.S. debut with the San Francisco Opera; 1st appearances followed at Milan's La Scala (1960), the Vienna State Opera (1961), the Salzburg Festival (1962), N.Y.'s Metropolitan Opera (debut as Falstaff; March 25, 1964), and the Paris Opéra (1975). In 1984 he made his farewell operatic appearance as Dulcamara at Covent Garden. He was also active as an opera producer. In 1959 he was made a Commander of the Order of the British Empire and was knighted in 1969. With N. Goodwin, he publ. an entertaining autobiography, *Sir Geraint Evans: A Knight at the Opera* (London, 1984). His finest roles included Figaro, Leporello, Papageno, Beckmesser, Falstaff, Don Pasquale, and Wozzeck; he also appeared in contemporary British operas.

Evans, (Ian Ernest) Gil(more Green), Canadian jazz pianist, bandleader, and arranger; b. Toronto, May 13, 1912; d. Cuernavaca, Mexico, March 20, 1988. He went to California in his youth. He was largely self-taught in music; after leading his own band in Stockton (1933–38), he went to N.Y. He made arrangements of popular songs utilizing non-jazz instruments; then became a proponent of cool jazz, and collaborated frequently with Miles Davis (from 1948); he also made arrangements for other groups and recorded his own albums. As he moved toward an increasingly complex modernity, he applied polyharmonic and polyrhythmic procedures to his arrangements.
BIBL.: R. Horricks, *Svengali, or, The Orchestra Called G. E.* (Tunbridge Wells and N.Y., 1984).

Everly, Don, American country-and-western singer; b. Brownie, Ky., Feb. 1, 1937. With his brother, **Phil Everly** (b. Brownie, Ky., Jan. 19, 1939), he appeared at the age of 8 on a radio show managed by their parents at Shenandoah, Iowa. Both brothers then toured with their parents around the country. When they grew up they moved to Nashville, Tenn., and began playing rock 'n' roll in a synthetic style of rhythm-and-blues, pop, and country-and-western. Their hits were *Bye, Bye Love; Wake Up, Little Susie; All I Have to Do Is Dream;* and *Cathy's Clown.* Alas, brotherly love did not last forever; they split apart in 1973; their divergent ways led to a sad impasse, but happily their fraternal records survived, and continued to provide joy to a new generation of bobby-soxers and their hippie mates. They finally patched things up and reunited for a concert at London's Royal Albert Hall in 1983.

Evett, Robert, American composer; b. Loveland, Colo., Nov. 30, 1922; d. Takoma Park, Md., Feb. 3, 1975. He studied with Roy Harris in Colorado Springs (1941–46) and with Persichetti at the Juilliard School of Music in N.Y. (1951–52); settled in Washington, D.C., as a music critic.
WORKS: 4 piano sonatas (1945, 1952, 1953, 1954); Cello Concerto (1954); Piano Quintet (1954); Sonata for Cello and Harpsichord (1955); *Variations* for Clarinet and Orch. (1955); Piano Concerto (1957); Viola Sonata (1958); Sym. No. 1 (1960); Violin Sonata (1960); Concerto for Harpsichord and Orch. (Washington, D.C., April 25, 1961); Piano Quartet (1961); Sonata for Harpsichord (1962); *Anniversary Concerto* for Orch. (Washington, D.C., Oct. 19, 1963); Sonata for Oboe and Harpsichord (1964); Sym. No. 2, *Billy Ascends,* for Voices and Orch., to a text by Melville (Washington, D.C., May 7, 1965); Sym. No. 3 (Washington, D.C., June 6, 1965); *The Windhover,* concerto for Bassoon and Orch. (Washington, D.C., May 20, 1971); songs; piano pieces.

Evseyev, Sergei, Russian composer and pedagogue; b. Moscow, Jan. 24, 1893; d. there, March 16, 1956. He studied piano with Medtner as a youth; then entered the Moscow Cons., where he continued to study piano with Goldenweiser and also attended classes in composition with Taneyev; upon graduation, he devoted himself to teaching music theory at the Moscow Cons., where he introduced a special seminar in modern harmony; he also taught a course of specific Russian folk-song polyphony; furthermore, he conducted classes in musical education by correspondence on an experimental basis (1936–41).
WORKS: 3 syms. (1925, 1933, 1943); 2 piano concertos (1932); Clarinet Concerto (1943); 2 string quartets (1935, 1945); *Dramatic Sonata* for Cello and Piano (1941); many piano pieces (most of them influenced by Medtner).

Ewald, Victor, Russian composer; b. St. Petersburg, Nov. 27, 1860; d. there (Leningrad), April 26, 1935. He studied engineering; from 1895 to 1915 was a prof. at the Inst. of Civil Engineering. Music was his avocation; he played the

cello and the French horn; took part in Belaieff's quartet evenings and wrote a number of chamber music works. After the Revolution he continued to work in his primary profession, as a civil engineer and instructor; also was active as an ethnomusicologist and participated in the expeditions in the north of European Russia collecting folk songs. His daughter **Zinaida** (1894–1942) continued his work in folklore and publ. several collections of Russian songs, in collaboration with her husband, **Evgeny Gippius** (b. 1903).

Ewen, David, prolific Polish-born American writer on music; b. Lemberg, Nov. 26, 1907; d. Miami Beach, Dec. 28, 1985. He went to the U.S. in 1912. He attended the College of the City of N.Y.; studied music theory with Max Persin; was enrolled as a student at the Music School Settlement and at Columbia Univ. He was music ed. of *Reflex Magazine* (1928–29) and *The American Hebrew* (1935); was active as a publisher (1946–49); in 1965, joined the music faculty of the Univ. of Miami, which awarded him in 1974 the honorary degree of D.Mus. In all probability, Ewen publ. more books on music and ed. more reference publications than anyone else in the 20th century (some 85 in all). Some of his publications have been tr. into 17 languages. In 1985 he received the ASCAP Award for Lifetime Achievement in Music.
WRITINGS (not including revisions publ. with the amplificatory modifier "New"): *The Unfinished Symphony* (1931); *Hebrew Music* (1931); *Wine, Women, and Waltz* (1933); *Composers of Today* (1934); *The Man with the Baton* (1936); *Composers of Yesterday* (1937); *Men and Women Who Make Music* (1939); *Musical Vienna* (with Frederic Ewen, 1939); *Living Musicians* (1940); *Pioneers in Music* (1941); *Music Comes to America* (1942; rev. 1947); *Dictators of the Baton* (1943; rev. 1948); *Men of Popular Music* (1944; rev. 1952); *Music for the Millions* (1944; rev. 1946, 1949; publ. under title *Encyclopedia of Musical Masterpieces,* 1950); *American Composers Today* (rev. ed., 1949); *The Story of Irving Berlin* (1950); *The Story of Arturo Toscanini* (1951; in Italian, Milan, 1952); *Fun with Musical Games and Quizzes* (with N. Slonimsky, 1952); *The Complete Book of 20th Century Music* (1952); *European Composers Today* (1953); *The Story of Jerome Kern* (1953); *The Milton Cross Encyclopedia of Great Composers and Their Music* (with Milton Cross, 1953); *Encyclopedia of the Opera* (1955); *A Journey to Greatness, George Gershwin* (1956; rewritten in 1970 under the title *George Gershwin: His Journey to Greatness*); *Panorama of American Popular Music* (1957); *Complete Book of the American Musical Theater* (N.Y., 1958; extremely valuable; brought up to date as *The New Complete Book of the American Musical Theater,* 1970); *Encyclopedia of Concert Music* (N.Y., 1959); *The World of Jerome Kern* (N.Y., 1960); *Leonard Bernstein* (N.Y., 1960; rev. 1967); *History of Popular Music* (N.Y., 1961); *The Story of America's Musical Theater* (N.Y., 1961; rev. 1969); *Ewen's Lighter Classics in Music* (N.Y., 1961); *David Ewen Introduces Modern Music* (N.Y., 1962; rev. 1969); *The Book of European Light Opera* (N.Y., 1962); *Popular American Composers* (N.Y., 1962); *The Complete Book of Classical Music* (N.Y., 1963); *The Life and Death of Tin Pan Alley* (N.Y., 1964); *American Popular Songs: From the Revolutionary War to the Present* (N.Y., 1966); *Great Composers: 1300–1900* (N.Y., 1966); *The World of 20th-Century Music* (N.Y., 1968); *Composers since 1900* (N.Y., 1969); *Great Men of American Popular Songs* (N.Y., 1970); *Composers of Tomorrow's Music* (N.Y., 1971); *New Encyclopedia of the Opera,* a radical revision of *Encyclopedia of the Opera* (1971); *Popular American Composers: First Supplement* (N.Y., 1972); *Mainstreams of Music* (in 4 vols., N.Y., 1972, 1973, 1974, 1975); *All the Years of American Popular Music* (Englewood Cliffs, N.J., 1977); *Musicians since 1900* (N.Y., 1978); *American Composers: A Biographical Dictionary* (N.Y., 1982). He also publ. a number of books for young people (on Gershwin, Bernstein, Haydn, Irving Berlin, Toscanini, Johann Strauss, Jerome Kern, Richard Rodgers, and Cole Porter). He rewrote, rev., and expanded the *Milton Cross Encyclopedia of Great Composers* (N.Y., 1960). Rev. eds. of *The Book of Modern Composers,* orig. publ. in 1943, ap-

peared as *The New Book of Modern Composers* in 1960 and 1967. He further ed. *From Bach to Stravinsky* (1933) and *The World of Great Composers* (Englewood Cliffs, N.J., 1962).

Ewing, Maria (Louise), noted American mezzo-soprano and soprano; b. Detroit, March 27, 1950. She commenced vocal training with Marjorie Gordon, continuing her studies with Eleanor Steber at the Cleveland Inst. of Music (1968–70), and later with Jennie Tourel and O. Marzolla. In 1973 she made her professional debut at the Ravinia Festival with the Chicago Sym. Orch., and subsequently was engaged to appear with various U.S. opera houses and orchs.; she also appeared as a recitalist. On Oct. 14, 1976, she made her Metropolitan Opera debut in N.Y. as Cherubino, and returned there to sing such roles as Rosina, Dorabella, Mélisande, Blanche in *Dialogues des carmélites*, and Carmen. In 1976 she made her 1st appearance at Milan's La Scala as Mélisande; in 1978 she made her Glyndebourne Festival debut as Dorabella, and returned there as a periodic guest. In 1986 she sang Salome in Los Angeles and appeared in *The Merry Widow* in Chicago in 1987. In 1988 she sang Salome at London's Covent Garden, a role she sang to enormous critical acclaim in Chicago that same year; she returned there as Tosca in 1989 and Susanna in 1991. She was married for a time to Sir Peter Hall.
Bibl.: S. Gould, "M. E.: The Art of the Operatic Seductress," *Ovation* (May 1989).

Excestre, William, English singer and composer who flourished c.1390–1410. He was clerk of the Chapel Royal in 1393, and received a prebend in St. Stephen's, Westminster, in 1394. He was one of the composers whose music is contained in the *Old Hall Manuscript;* a Gloria, a Credo, and a Sanctus (all for 3 Voices) are extant.

Eximeno (y Pujades), Antonio, important Spanish writer on music; b. Valencia, Sept. 26, 1729; d. Rome, June 9, 1808. He entered the Soc. of Jesus at the age of 16; became a prof. of rhetoric at the Univ. of Valencia; in 1764, was appointed prof. of mathematics at the military academy in Segovia. When the Jesuits were expelled from Spain in 1767, he went to Rome, and in 1768 began to study music. In 1774 he publ. *Dell' origine e delle regole della musica colla storia del suo progresso, decadenza e rinnovazione* (Rome; Spanish tr. by Gutierrez, 3 vols., 1776), in which he protested against pedantic rules and argued that music should be based on the natural rules of prosody. His theories were strongly controverted, especially by Padre Martini; in answer to the latter, Eximeno publ. *Dubbio di Antonio Eximeno sopra il Saggio fondamentale, pratico di contrappunto del reverendissimo Padre Maestro Giambattista Martini* (Rome, 1775). His dictum that the national song should serve as a basis for the art-music of each country was taken up by Pedrell and led to the nationalist movement in modern Spanish music. Eximeno also wrote a satirical musical novel, *Don Lazarillo Vizcardi*, directed against the theories of Pietro Cerone (publ. by Barbieri, 2 vols., 1872–73).
Bibl.: F. Pedrell, *Padre A. E.* (Madrid, 1920).

Expert, (Isidore Norbert) Henry, eminent French music editor; b. Bordeaux, May 12, 1863; d. Tourettes-sur-Loup (Alpes-Maritimes), Aug. 18, 1952. He attended a Jesuit school in Bordeaux; went to Paris in 1881 and studied with César Franck and Eugène Gigout; taught at the École Nationale de Musique Classique, and lectured at the École des Hautes Études Sociales; from 1909, he was deputy-librarian of the Paris Cons.; became chief of the library in 1921; was the founder (in 1903, with Maury) of the Société d'Études Musicales et Concerts Historiques, also of the choral society Chanterie de la Renaissance (1924). In 1933 he retired. His life work was the editing and publication of Franco-Flemish music of the 15th and 16th centuries, in 6 parts: I. *Les Maîtres-Musiciens de la Renaissance française* (works by Orlando di Lasso, Goudimel, Costeley, Janequin, Brumel, La Rue, Mouton, Fevin, Mauduit, Claude Le Jeune, Regnart, Du Caurroy, Gervaise, and Attaingnant's collection of chansons, all in modern notation, with facsimiles, etc.; 23 vols., publ. 1894–1908); II. *Bibliographie thématique* (2 vols., catalog of publications of

Attaingnant); III. *Les Théoriciens de la musique au temps de la Renaissance* (works of Michel de Menhou); IV. 2 vols. of music by Antoine de Bertrand; V. *Commentaires;* VI. *Extraits des Maîtres Musiciens* (selected single compositions, arranged for modern use; a large number have been publ., including works by some composers not found in Part I, viz.: Bertrand, Bonnet, Certon, De La Grotte, Gardanne, Josquin des Prez, Le Heurteur, Le Pelletier, Passereau, Thoinot-Arbeau). From 1924 to 1929 Expert publ. a new series of French music of the 16th century entitled Monuments de la Musique Française au Temps de la Renaissance (with scores in modern notation), in 10 vols.; these contain works by Le Jeune, in 2 vols. (*Octonaires de la vanité et inconstance du monde*); Certon (3 masses); Le Blanc (*Airs de plusieurs musiciens*); Bertrand, in 4 vols. (*Amours de P. de Ronsard*); Goudimel (*Messes à 4 voix*); L'Estocart (*Octonaires de la vanité du monde*). Expert also ed. *Chansons mondaines des XVIIe et XVIIIe siècles français* (80 songs); *Airs français des XVIe et XVIIe siècles* (Boesset, Guedron, Tessier, Lambert); *Florilège du concert vocal de la Renaissance* (1928–29), in 8 parts (Janequin, Lasso, Costeley, Bonnet, Le Jeune, Mauduit); *Les Maîtres du clavecin des XVIIe et XVIIIe siècles* (Dandrieu, Daquin, Corrette); *Amusements des maîtres français du XVIIIe siècle* (Chédeville, J. Aubert, Baton); *Répertoire de musique religieuse et spirituelle* (Campra, Charpentier, Dumont, Lully, Bernier, Couperin le Grand, Clérambault, Lalande, Rameau, etc.); *La Fleur des musiciens de P. de Ronsard* (1923); instrumental *Fantaisies* by Le Jeune and Du Caurroy; and *Le Pseautier huguenot du XVIe siècle* (the Huguenot Psalter; 1902).

Eybler, Joseph Leopold, Edler von, Austrian composer; b. Schwechat, near Vienna, Feb. 8, 1765; d. Schönbrunn, July 24, 1846. He began his musical training with his father; settling in Vienna, he continued his studies at St. Stephen's choir school and also received instruction from Albrechtsberger (1776–79). Haydn became his friend and mentor, and he was also befriended by Mozart. From 1794 to 1824 he was choirmaster of the Schottenkloster; he also became music teacher at the court (1801) and in 1804 was named deputy Hofkapellmeister under Salieri (1804), succeeding him as Hofkapellmeister (1824). In 1833 he suffered a stroke while conducting Mozart's *Requiem* and was compelled to retire. He was ennobled by the Emperor in 1835.
Works: Opera: *Das Zauberschwert;* oratorios: *Die Hirten bei der Krippe* (1794) and *Die vier letzten Dirge* (1810); cantatas; 32 masses; Mass sections; *Requiem* (1825); 7 *Te Deums;* 33 offertories; 40 graduals; 15 hymns; 2 syms.; Clarinet Concerto (1798); chamber music; piano pieces; songs.
Bibl.: F. Oelsinger, *Die Kirchenmusikwerke J. E.s* (diss., Univ. of Vienna, 1932); R. Ricks, *The Published Works of J. E.* (diss., Catholic Univ. of America, 1967); H. Herrmann, *Thematische Verzeichnis der Werke von J. E.* (Munich and Salzburg, 1976).

Eyken (Eijken), Jan Albert van, Dutch organist, teacher, and composer; b. Amersfoort, April 26, 1823; d. Elberfeld, Sept. 24, 1868. He studied at the Leipzig Cons., and afterward at Dresden with Schneider. In 1848, he became organist of the Remonstrantenkerk in Amsterdam; in 1853, of the Zuyderkerk, and teacher at the music school in Rotterdam; in 1854, he became organist at Elberfeld. His organ pieces (150 chorales with introductions, 25 preludes, a toccata and fugue on B-A-C-H, 3 sonatas, variations, transcriptions, etc.) are well and favorably known.

Eymieu, Henry, French composer and writer on music; b. Saillans, Drôme, May 7, 1860; d. Paris, March 21, 1931. He studied law; turned to music, taking lessons with Widor; settling in Paris, he wrote for *Le Ménestrel* and other musical publications; publ. *Études et biographies musicales* (Paris, 1892); composed a great variety of piano pieces, songs, and duets for piano and violin (58 publ. opus numbers in all); also produced a stage piece, *Un Mariage sous Né ron* (Paris, 1898), and an oratorio, *Marthe et Marie* (Asnières, 1898).

Eyser, Eberhard, Polish-born Swedish violinist, violist, and composer; b. Kwidzyn, Aug. 1, 1932. He studied at the Music Academy in Hannover (1952–57); also attended seminars of Alois Hába in Prague, Hauer in Vienna, and Xenakis. In 1961 he became a violist in the Royal Opera House Orch. in Stockholm.

WORKS: STAGE: 2 one-act operas: *Carmen 36*, after Strindberg, for 2 Singing Voices, Speaking Voice, Chamber Orch., and Tape (1972; Umeå, Nov. 5, 1975) and *Kalifens son* (1970–73); 2 chamber operas, after Strindberg: *Molonne* (Stockholm, Oct. 27, 1970) and *Sista resan* (Last Voyage) for 2 Voices, Clarinet, and Tape (1972–73; Vadstena, July 24, 1974); miniature opera, *Hjärter Kung eller Trägen vinner,* for 9 Voices and Instrumental Ensemble (Vadstena, June 6, 1973); 3 "operettinas": *I, Drömmen om mannen* (Dream of Man) for 7 Voices, Small Girls' Chorus, and Chamber Orch. (1972), *II* for 2 Voices a cappella (1971), and *III* for 4 Voices and 2 Pianists on 1 Piano (1971). His other works include a Toccata for Orch. (1957); *Iberian Suite* for Chamber Orch. (1957); *Serenata spagnola* for English Horn and String Quartet (1959); *Capriccio svedese* for 12 Solo Strings (1964); *Metastrophý* for Orch. (1965); *Podema* for String Quartet (1969); *Capriccio 68* for Orch. (1968); *Colludo* for 3 to 8 String and Wind Instruments (1971); Concertino for Horn and Chamber Orch. (1971); *Constructo* for Optional Instrumental Ensemble (1971); *Solo* for Double Bass (1971); Sonata for Bass Clarinet, Cymbal, and Piano (1972); *Petite nocturne* for Double Bass, Harpsichord, and String Orch. (1972); Sonata for Solo Bassoon (1973); Serenade for Flute, Viola, and Cello (1973); *Stochasta 57–74* for Winds and Percussion (1974); *Symphonie orientale* for Chamber Orch. (1974); Passacaglia for Solo Cello (1974); *Ottoletto* for 8 Clarinets (1975); *Circus Overture* for 12 Winds, Percussion, and Double Bass (1976).

Eysler (originally, **Eisler**), **Edmund,** Austrian composer; b. Vienna, March 12, 1874; d. there, Oct. 4, 1949. He studied at the Vienna Cons.; he produced a great number of stage works; in 1915 he wrote no fewer than 4 operettas (*Leutnant Gustl, Der grosse Gabriel, Ein Tag im Paradies, Die oder Keine*). His most successful operetta was *Bruder Straubinger* (Vienna, Feb. 20, 1903; over 100 perfs. in that year). Other successful operettas: *Pufferl* (Vienna, April 13, 1905); *Künstlerblut* (Vienna, Oct. 20, 1906); *Das Glückschweinchen* (1908); *Der unsterbliche Lump* (1910); *Das Zirkuskind* (1911); *Die goldene Meisterin* (Vienna, Sept. 13, 1927).

BIBL.: R. Prosl, *E. E.* (Vienna, 1947).

Ezaki, Kenjiro, Formosan-born Japanese composer; b. Tainan, Oct. 27, 1926. He studied at the Nihon Univ. in Tokyo (1953–57); also at the Univ. of Illinois Experimental Music Studio, and with Ussachevsky at the Columbia-Princeton Electronic Music Center. Returning to Japan, he operated his own electronic music studio in Tokyo; in 1971 was appointed to the faculty of the Univ. of Tokyo. He uses electronic sound in many of his works.

WORKS: *Discretion* for a Female Voice (1961); *Concretion* for String Trio (1962); *Dim Light* for Chorus and 6 Instruments (1962); *Contention* for Soprano and Guitar (1963); *Presage* for Orch., in mobile configuration (1964); *Omen* for Modified Orch. (1964); Piano Trio (1964); *Pharos No. 1* and *No. 2* for Chorus, Flute, Clarinet, Oboe, and Piano (1965); *Music I* and *II* for Guitar and Tape (1967, 1971); *Ensemble* for a Piano and 2 Playback Devices (1967); *Composition 5* for Flute, 2 Guitars, Cello, Percussion, and Soprano (1968); *Musicronics No. 1* for Piano, Percussion, and Tape (1968); *Zamuzara*, ballet music for Tape (1968); *Requiem 1970* for Soprano and Tape (1969); *Computer Music No. 1* (1969; composed on the FACOM 270–30 computer); *Liaison* for 12-channel Tape (1971).

F

Faber, Heinrich (known as **Magister Henricus Faber**), German music theorist; b. Lichtenfels, c.1500; d. Ölsnitz, Saxony, Feb. 26, 1552. He entered the Univ. of Wittenberg in 1542; received the degree of Master of Liberal Arts in 1545; was rector of the school of St. George's Monastery near Naumburg from 1544; in 1551, was appointed lecturer at Wittenberg Univ.; then was rector at Ölsnitz. He publ. *Compendiolum musicae pro incipientibus* (1548; reprinted many times and also issued in German tr. as *Musica, Kurtzer Inhalt der Singkunst*, 1572; ed. by A. Gumpelzhaimer and publ. as *Compendium musicae pro illius artis tironibus*, 1591). Faber further publ. *Ad musicam practicam introductio* (1550); a *Musica poetica* remains in MS.

Fabini, (Felix) Eduardo, Uruguayan violinist and composer; b. Solís del Mataojo, May 18, 1882; d. Montevideo, May 17, 1950. He studied violin in Montevideo, and later with César Thomson at the Brussels Cons., winning 1st prize; then gave concerts as a violinist in South America and in the U.S. (1926); eventually returned to Montevideo, and was active there as a composer and educator. His music is inspired entirely by South American folklore; the idiom is mildly modernistic, with lavish use of whole-tone scales and other external devices of Impressionism.
WORKS (all 1st perf. in Montevideo): Ballets: *Mburucuyá* (April 15, 1933) and *Mañana de Reyes* (July 31, 1937); symphonic poem, *Campo* (April 29, 1922); overture, *La isla de los Ceibos* (Sept. 14, 1926); *Melga sinfónica* (Oct. 11, 1931); Fantasia for Violin and Orch. (Aug. 22, 1929); choral works; piano pieces; songs.

Fabri, Annibale Pio, famous Italian tenor, known as "Il Bolognese" and "Il Balino"; b. Bologna, 1697; d. Lisbon, Aug. 12, 1760. He studied with Pistocchi; while in the service of Prince Ruspoli in Rome, he sang female roles in operas by Caldara (1711); then made his public debut in Bologna in 1716. He quickly gained renown for his performances throughout Italy (1716–28); then was engaged by Handel for the King's Theatre in London, making his debut there in Handel's *Lotario* on Dec. 2, 1729, creating the role of Berengario. During his 2 seasons in London, he also created the roles of Emilio in *Partenope* (1730) and Alexander in *Poro* (1731), both by Handel. He subsequently appeared throughout Italy again, and then retired in Lisbon as a member of the royal chapel. He was also a composer; was elected to membership in the Accademia Filarmonica in Bologna in 1719 and from 1725 to 1750 served intermittently as its president.

Fabricius, Johann Albert, eminent German bibliographer, son of **Werner Fabricius;** b. Leipzig, Nov. 11, 1668; d. Hamburg, April 30, 1736. A learned man, he was a prof. of elocution; publ. important books of reference, valuable to musicology for the information they contain on musical topics: *Thesaurus antiquitatum hebraicarum* (7 vols., 1713); *Bibliotheca latina mediae et infimae aetatis* (6 vols., 1712–22; 2nd ed., 1734); *Bibliotheca graeca sive notitia scriptorum veterum graecorum* (14 vols., 1705–28).

Fabricius, Werner, German organist and composer, father of **Johann Albert Fabricius;** b. Itzehoe, April 10, 1633; d. Leipzig, Jan. 9, 1679. He began his musical studies with Paul Moth in Flensburg; at age 12 he went to Hamburg to continue his training with Thomas Selle and Heinrich Scheidemann, then studied law, philosophy, and mathematics at the Univ. of Leipzig. He became organist and director of music at the Paulinerkirche of the Univ. there in 1656; also was made organist of the city's Nicolaikirche in 1658. He publ. a treatise on organ building, *Unterricht wie man ein neu Orgelwerk in und auswendig examiniren, und so viel wie möglich probiren soll* (Frankfurt am Main and Leipzig, 1656); also an instruction manual, *Manuductio zum General Bass bestehend aus lauter Excempeln* (Leipzig, 1675).

WORKS: SACRED: 100 melodies in *E.C. Homburgs geistlicher Lieder erster Theil* for 2 Voices and Basso Continuo (Jena, 1659); *Geistliche Arien, Dialogen, und Concerten . . .* for 4 to 6 Voices, Basso Continuo, and Instruments (Leipzig, 1662); other works in contemporary collections; also German and Latin motets in MS. **INSTRUMENTAL:** *Deliciae harmonicae oder Musikalische Ergötzung, von allerhand Paduaenen, Alemanden, Couranten, Balletten, Sarabanden von 5 Stimmen*, Basso Continuo, Viols or Other Instruments (Leipzig, 1656).

BIBL.: R. Mayer, *The Keyboard Tablature by W. F.* (diss., Roosevelt Univ., 1972).

Faccio, Franco (Francesco Antonio), Italian composer and conductor; b. Verona, March 8, 1840; d. near Monza, July 21, 1891. His 1st teacher was G. Bernasconi; from 1855 to 1864 he studied at the Milan Cons.; Arrigo Boito was his fellow pupil and friend; they wrote together a vocal misterio, *Le Sorelle d'Italia*, which was produced by the students; the 2 served together under Garibaldi in 1866. His 1st opera was *I profughi fiamminghi* (La Scala, Milan, Nov. 11, 1863); this was followed by the Shakespearean opera *Amleto*, for which Boito wrote the libretto (Genoa, May 30, 1865). From 1866 to 1868 Faccio made a tour in Scandinavia as a sym. conductor; in 1868 he became a prof. at the Milan Cons., and in 1871 succeeded Terziani as conductor at La Scala; on April 25, 1886, he conducted for the 1,000th time there. His performances of Verdi's operas were regarded as most authentic; he gave the world premiere of *Otello* at La Scala (1887).

BIBL.: R. de Rensis, *F. F. e Verdi* (Milan, 1934).

Fachiri, Adila, Hungarian violinist, grandniece of **Joseph Joachim** and sister of **Jelly d'Aranyi**; b. Budapest, Feb. 26, 1886; d. Florence, Dec. 15, 1962. She studied with Joachim, and received from him a Stradivarius violin. In 1909 she settled in London, where she married Alexander Fachiri, a lawyer (1915). She appeared many times with her sister in duets; on April 3, 1930, the sisters gave in London the 1st performance of Holst's Concerto for 2 Violins, written especially for them.

BIBL.: J. Macleod, *The Sisters d'Aranyi* (London, 1969).

Faelten, Carl, German-American pianist and teacher, brother of **Reinhold Faelten**; b. Ilmenau, Thuringia, Dec. 21, 1846; d. Readfield, Maine, July 20, 1925. He studied in Frankfurt, and profited by advice from Raff. From 1878 to 1882 he taught at the Hoch Cons. in Frankfurt; then was engaged at the Peabody Inst. in Baltimore (1882–85) and at the New England Cons. of Music in Boston (1885–97); was director of the Cons. from 1890 until 1897, when with his brother he founded the Faelten Pianoforte School in Boston. They brought out several didactic vols.

Faelten, Reinhold, German-American pianist and teacher, brother of **Carl Faelten**; b. Ilmenau, Thuringia, Jan. 17, 1856; d. Worcester, Mass., July 17, 1949. He was a pupil of Klughard and Gottschalk at Weimar; taught in Frankfurt, Baltimore, and Boston; in 1897 he founded, with his brother, the Faelten Pianoforte School in Boston. Jointly with his brother, he wrote several books on the Faelten method.

Faerber, Jörg, German conductor; b. Stuttgart, June 18, 1929. He studied at the Stuttgart Hochschule für Musik; then began his career in Stuttgart as a theater conductor. In 1960 he founded the Württemberg Chamber Orch. in Heilbronn, and subsequently established it as one of the finest ensembles of its kind in Europe. He was especially distinguished as an interpreter of the Baroque repertoire.

Fagan, Gideon, South African conductor and composer; b. Somerset West, Cape Province, Nov. 3, 1904; d. Cape Town, March 21, 1980. He studied at the South African College of Music in Cape Town with W.H. Bell (1916–22) and later in London at the Royal College of Music (1922–26), where his teachers were Boult and Sargent (conducting) and Vaughan Williams (composition). With the exception of a brief return to South Africa (1926–27), Fagan established residence in London, where he led theatrical companies, arranged light music for broadcasts and films, and acted as guest conductor with the BBC and other orchs. In 1949 he went back to South Africa, where he became active as arranger and conductor at the Johannesburg Radio (SABC); later was appointed its head of music (1963–66). He also taught composition and conducting at the Univ. of Cape Town (1967–73). In 1979 he received the Medal of Honor of the South African Academy for Science and Art.

WORKS: *Nocturne* for Woodwinds and Strings (1926); *Ilala*, tone poem for Orch. (1941); *South African Folk-tune Suite* for Orch. (1942); symphonic poem, *Ilala* (1942); *5 Orchestral Pieces* (1948–49); Concert Overture in D (1954); *Heuwelkruin* (Hill Crest), suite for Piano and Orch. (1954); *Concert Overture* (1954); *Tears*, symphonic poem, after Whitman, for Soloist, Chorus, and Orch. (1954); *Heuwelkruin*, suite for Piano and Orch. (1954); Nonet (1958); *My Lewe*, 6 poems for Baritone, Flute, Clarinet, Piano, and String Quartet (1969); *Albany*, overture (1970); *Ex unitate vires*, symphonic sketch (1970); Suite for Strings (1974); *Quintics* for 5 Brasses (1975); *Karoosimfonie* (1976–77); *Een vaderland*, oratorio (1977–78); piano pieces; songs; film music.

Fago, (Francesco) Nicola, Italian composer, called "Il virtuosissimo Tarantino" after his place of birth; b. Taranto, Feb. 26, 1677; d. Naples, Feb. 18, 1745. He was a pupil of Provenzale at the Conservatorio della Pietà dei Turchini in Naples (1693–95); he became his assistant in 1697 and his successor in 1705. From 1704 to 1708 he was maestro di cappella at the Conservatorio di S. Onofrio; from 1709 to 1731, maestro di cappella at the Tesoro di S. Gennaro; then at the S. Giacomo degli Spagnuoli Church (1736–45). He was the teacher of Leonardo Leo, Francesco Feo, Jommelli, and Sala. His son **Lorenzo Fago** (b. Naples, Aug. 13, 1704; d. there, April 30, 1793), an organist and composer, was his successor at the Tesoro di S. Gennaro (1731–66 and 1771–80), and taught at the Conservatorio della Pietà dei Turchini for 56 years (1737–93) until his death.

WORKS: 4 operas: *Radamisto* (1707); *Astarto* (1709); *La Cassandra indovina* (1711); *Lo Masillo* (1712); 3 oratorios, including *Faraone sommerso* and *Il monte fiorito*; sacred music.

BIBL.: E. Faustini-Fasini, *N. F., "Il Tarantino" e la sua famiglia* (Taranto, 1931).

Fahrbach, Philipp, Austrian conductor and composer; b. Vienna, Oct. 26, 1815; d. there, March 31, 1885. He was a pupil of Lanner; conducted his own orch. for years, and then a military band. His dances and marches (over 400 works) were very popular. His 3 brothers, his son, and his nephews were all active as band musicians.

BIBL.: O. Schneider, "Die F.s: Eine Wiener Musikerfamilie der Strauss-Zeit," *Österreichische Musikzeitschrift* (Jan. 1967).

Faignient, Noë, Flemish composer; b. c.1540; d. Antwerp, c.1595. His compositions consist of 2 sets of chansons, madrigals, and motets for 4, 5, and 6 voices (1568, 1569).

Failoni, Sergio, Italian conductor; b. Verona, Dec. 18, 1890; d. Sopron, July 25, 1948. He received his musical education in Verona and Milan; conducted opera throughout Italy; from 1932 he made appearances at La Scala in Milan. From 1928 to 1947 he was chief conductor of the State Opera in Budapest. In 1947 he was invited to make his debut at the Metropolitan Opera in N.Y.; however, he suffered a stroke and died the following year. He was regarded as one of the leading interpreters of the Italian repertoire.

Fain (real name, **Feinberg**), **Sammy,** American composer of popular music; b. N.Y., June 17, 1902; d. Los Angeles,

Dec. 6, 1989. He worked in vaudeville and in the music publishing business as a song plugger before achieving success as a full-fledged songwriter on Broadway and in Hollywood. In collaboration with the lyricist Irving Kahal, he produced such hits as *Nobody Knows What a Red-Headed Mama Can Do, Let a Smile Be Your Umbrella on a Rainy Day, When I Take My Sugar to Tea, Dear Hearts and Gentle People, That Old Feeling, I Can Dream, Can't I,* and *I'll Be Seeing You;* later, in collaboration with Paul F. Webster, he composed *Secret Love* and *Love Is a Many-Splendored Thing.*

Fairchild, Blair, American composer; b. Belmont, Mass., June 23, 1877; d. Paris, April 23, 1933. He studied composition with J.K. Paine and Walter Spalding at Harvard Univ. (B.A., 1899); then took courses with Giuseppe Buonamici in Florence. From 1901 till 1903 he was an attaché in the American embassies in Turkey and Persia. From 1905 he lived mostly in Paris, where he continued his musical studies with Charles Widor. Influenced by his travels in the Orient, and fascinated by the resources of exotic melos and rhythm, he wrote a number of pieces for orch. and for piano, and many songs in a pseudo-oriental manner; despite the imitative qualities of his music, Fairchild must be regarded as one of the few Americans who tried to transplant exotic folkways, both in subject matter and in melodic turns.

WORKS: *East and West,* tone poem (1908); *Légende* for Violin and Orch. (1911); *Tamineh,* symphonic poem after a Persian legend (1913); *6 chants nègres* for Piano (also orchestrated, Boston, Dec. 6, 1929); 2 violin sonatas (1908, 1919); 5 sets of *Stornelli Toscani* for Voice and Piano; song cycles.

BIBL.: W. Upton, "Our Musical Expatriates," *Musical Quarterly* (Jan. 1928).

Fairlamb, James Remington, American organist and composer; b. Philadelphia, Jan. 23, 1838; d. Ingleside, N.Y., April 16, 1908. As a youth he played the organ in several Philadelphia churches; in 1858 went to Paris; studied piano there with Marmontel. While in Europe, he was appointed by President Lincoln as American Consul at Zürich (1861) and stayed in Zürich until 1865, when he returned to the U.S. He organized an amateur opera company with which he brought out his 4-act grand opera *Valérie, or Treasured Tokens* (Philadelphia, Dec. 15, 1869). From 1872 to 1898 he was church organist in Philadelphia, Jersey City, and N.Y. He wrote another grand opera, *Lionello,* and 2 light operas: *Love's Stratagem* and *The Interrupted Marriage;* some 50 of his choral works and nearly 150 songs and organ pieces are publ. He was one of the founders of the American Guild of Organists.

Faisst, Immanuel (Gottlob Friedrich), German organist, choral conductor, pedagogue, and composer; b. Esslingen, Württemberg, Oct. 13, 1823; d. Stuttgart, June 5, 1894. He studied theology at Tübingen, and also learned to play the organ; subsequently took lessons with Dehn in Berlin. He became active as a choral conductor and organist; in 1847 organized a society for classical church music in Stuttgart, where he settled. He was the founder of the Schwäbischer Sängerbund (1849); with Lebert, Stark, Brachmann, and others he established the Stuttgart Cons. (1857); became its director in 1859. He received a Dr.Phil. at Tübingen Univ. for his essay *Beiträge zur Geschichte der Claviersonate* (*Cäcilia,* XXV, 1846; reprinted in the *Neues Beethovenjahrbuch,* 1, 1924). He was the editor (with Lebert) of the famous ed. of classical piano works *Instruktive ausgewählte classische Werke;* also (with Stark) of *Elementar- und Chorgesangschule für hohere Lehranstalten* (2 vols., Stuttgart, 1880–82). Faisst was a prolific composer; a number of his songs, ballads, choral works, etc., were publ. during his lifetime, but then were completely forgotten. He also publ. several school manuals on harmony.

Faith, Percy, Canadian-born American conductor and arranger; b. Toronto, April 7, 1908; d. Los Angeles, Feb. 9, 1976. He studied with Louis Waizman and Frank Wellman at the Toronto Cons.; played piano in movie theaters and in dance bands. In 1931 he joined the CBC and conducted the radio orch. in popular programs of Canadian music; in 1940, moved to the U.S. to fill a conducting post for the NBC Carnation Contented Hour; in 1950 he became music director of Columbia Records and made more than 45 albums of his own. He composed numerous film scores for Hollywood movies and in 1955 won an Academy Award nomination for *Love Me or Leave Me.* An amiably disposed composer of music "for listening pleasure," he described his goal as "satisfying the millions of devotees of that pleasant American institution known as the quiet evening at home, whose idea of perfect relaxation is the easy chair, slippers, and good music."

Falabella (Correa), Roberto, Chilean composer; b. Santiago, Feb. 13, 1926; d. there, Dec. 15, 1958. Paralyzed by polio since childhood, Falabella was educated at home; studied privately with Lucila Césped (1945–46), Alfonso Letelier (1949–50), Gustavo Becerra (1952), Miguel Aguilar and Esteban Eitler (1956–57). His music is Classical in form, Romantic in content, and modernistic in technique.

WORKS: Chamber operas: *Epitafios fúnebres* (1952) and *La tirana* (1957); miniature opera, *Del diario morir* (1954); 2 piano sonatas (1951, 1954); *Dueto* for Flute and Violin (1952); *Preludios episódicos* for Piano (1953); ballet, *El peine de oro* (1954); *Palimpsestos* for Contralto, Bassoon, Horn, and Percussion (1954); Violin Sonata (1954); Cello Sonata (1954); *Impresiones* for Piano (1955); Sym. No. 1 (1955); 2 divertimenti for Strings (1955); *Emotional Studies* for Piano (1957; also for Orch., 1957); ballet, *Andacollo,* for Voices, Piano, and Percussion (1957); String Quartet (1957); *Retratos* for Piano (1957); *La Lámpara en la tierra,* cantata for Baritone and Orch. (1958; Santiago, Oct. 21, 1960).

Falchi, Stanislao, Italian composer; b. Terni, Jan. 29, 1851; d. Rome, Nov. 14, 1922. He studied in Rome with C. Maggi and S. Meluzzi; in 1877 he became a teacher at the Accademia di Santa Cecilia there; from 1902 till 1915 was its director. Among his pupils were A. Bonaventura, A. Bustini, V. Gui, B. Molinari, L. Refice, and F. Santoliquido. He wrote the operas *Lorhelia* (Rome, Dec. 4, 1877), *Giuditta* (Rome, March 12, 1887), and *Il Trillo del diavolo* (Rome, Jan. 29, 1899); also a Requiem for the funeral of Victor Emmanuel II (Jan. 17, 1883).

Falcinelli, Rolande, French organist and composer; b. Paris, Feb. 18, 1920. She studied at the Paris Cons. with Samuel-Rousseau and Simone Plé-Caussade; also took courses with Henri Büsser. She received 1st prize in organ playing in the class of Marcel Dupré (1942); also in 1942 she received the Grand Prix de Rome. She subsequently taught at the American Cons. in Fontainebleau; in 1955 she became organ teacher at the Paris Cons. She composed a number of sacred works for chorus and organ pieces, written in an amiable French manner.

Falcon, (Marie-) Cornélie, renowned French soprano; b. Paris, Jan. 28, 1814; d. there, Feb. 25, 1897. She studied with Bordogni and A. Nourrit at the Paris Cons.; made her debut at the Paris Opéra on July 20, 1832, as Alice in *Robert le Diable.* She sang at the Paris Opéra with excellent success; appeared as Valentine in *Les Huguenots* on Jan. 15, 1838, when, though still a very young woman, she unaccountably lost her voice. She made an unsuccessful attempt to return to the stage in a special benefit performance at the Paris Opéra on March 14, 1840; in desperation she resorted to consuming all sorts of quack medicines provided by bogus doctors, but in the end had to give up her career. She retired to her villa near Paris; she lived another 60 years. Still, her singing in the roles of Valentine in *Les Huguenots* and Rachel in *La Juive* became a legendary memory, so that the description "Falcon type" was applied to singers who excelled in her roles.

BIBL.: C. Bouvet, *C. F.* (Paris, 1927).

Falconieri, Andrea, Italian composer and lutenist; b. Naples, 1585 or 1586; d. there, July 19 or 29, 1656. He was in the service of the house of Farnese at Parma; studied with Santino Garsi there until 1614; in 1615, was in Florence; in 1616, in Rome; in 1619, again in Florence; in 1620–21, at the court of Modena; then traveled in Spain and France; from 1629 to

1632, was again at Parma; from 1632 to 1637, was in Genoa as a music teacher; from 1647, was maestro di cappella at the court of Naples. His *Libro primo di villanelle a 1, 2 e 3 voci* (with alphabetical tablature for Spanish guitar) was publ. in Rome in 1616 (reprinted by Gardano at Venice); various other books followed, the *Libro V delle musiche* appearing in 1619; probably one of his last works was the valuable instrumental collection *Primo libro di canzone, sinfonie, fantasie, capricci per violini e viole, overo altri strumenti a 1, 2 e 3 voci con il basso continuo* (Naples, 1650).

Falik, Yuri, greatly talented Russian cellist and composer; b. Odessa, July 30, 1936. He studied cello with A. Strimer at the Leningrad Cons.; in 1962 won 1st cello prize at the International Competition in Helsinki. He composed music from adolescence; in 1955 enrolled in the composition class of Boris Arapov at the Leningrad Cons., graduating in 1964. He subsequently joined the staff of the Leningrad Cons., teaching both cello and composition. In his music Falik reveals a quasi-Romantic quality, making use of tantalizingly ambiguous melodic passages approaching the last ramparts of euphonious dissonance. His angular rhythms, with their frequently startling pauses, suggest a theatrical concept.
Works: Stage: *Till Eulenspiegel,* "mystery ballet" (1967); *Oresteia,* choreographic tragedy (1968); *Les Fourberies de Scapin,* opéra bouffe after Molière (Tartu, Dec. 22, 1984). **Orch.:** Concertino for Oboe and Chamber Orch. (1961); Sym. for String Orch. and Percussion (1963); Concerto for Orch. on the themes of *Till Eulenspiegel* (1967); *Music for Strings* (1968); *Easy Symphony* (1971); Violin Concerto (1971); *Elegiac Music in Memoriam Igor Stravinsky* for Chamber Orch. (1975); Concerto for Orch. No. 2, *Symphonic Études* (1977). **Chamber:** 5 string quartets (1955, 1965, 1974, 1976, 1978); Trio for Oboe, Cello, and Piano (1959); Wind Quintet (1964); *The Tumblers* for 4 Woodwinds, 2 Brasses, and 16 Percussion Instruments (1966); *Inventions* for Vibraphone, Marimba, and 5 Tam-tams (1972); *English Divertimento* for Flute, Clarinet, and Bassoon (1978). **Vocal:** *Solemn Song,* cantata (1968); *Winter Songs* for Chorus a cappella (1975); solo songs.

Falkner, Sir (Donald) Keith, English bass-baritone; b. Sawston, Cambridgeshire, March 1, 1900. He was a chorister at New College School, Oxford, and Perse School, Cambridge; then served in the Royal Naval Air Service during World War I. It was only after the Armistice that he began to study singing in earnest, taking lessons first with Plunkett Greene in London, then far afield, with Lierhammer in Vienna, with Grenzebach in Berlin, and with Dossert in Paris. Returing to England, he made it a specialty to sing Elizabethan songs in recital. He also appeared with the British National Opera Co. During World War II, he served in the Royal Air Force. In 1950 he went to the U.S., and taught voice at Cornell Univ. In 1960 he returned to England, and was appointed director of the Royal College of Music in London, retiring in 1974. He was knighted in 1967.

Fall, Leo(pold), Austrian composer; b. Olomouc, Feb. 2, 1873; d. Vienna, Sept. 16, 1925. His father was a military bandmaster, and it was from him that Leo Fall received his training in practical music making; then he took up academic courses at the Vienna Cons. with N. and R. Fuchs and others. For some years he was a theater conductor in Berlin, Hamburg, and Cologne, but lived for most of his life in Vienna. The list of his operettas includes *Der fidele Bauer* (Mannheim, July 25, 1907), *Eternal Waltz* (London, Dec. 22, 1911), *Die Rose von Constantinople* (Vienna, Dec. 2, 1916), and *Mme. Pompadour* (Berlin, Sept. 9, 1922). His operetta *Der Rebell,* a failure at its 1st production (Vienna, Nov. 28, 1905), was revised and staged under the new title *Der liebe Augustin* (Berlin, Feb. 3, 1912), scoring excellent success.
Bibl.: W. Zimmerli, *L. F.* (Zürich, 1957).

Falla (y Matheu), Manuel (Maria) de, great Spanish composer; b. Cádiz, Nov. 23, 1876; d. Alta Gracia, Córdoba province, Argentina, Nov. 14, 1946. He studied piano with his mother;

after further instruction from Eloisa Galluzo, he studied harmony, counterpoint, and composition with Alejandro Odero and Enrique Broca; then went to Madrid, where he studied piano with José Tragó and composition with Felipe Pedrell at the Cons. He wrote several zarzuelas, but only *Los amores de la Inés* was performed (Madrid, April 12, 1902). His opera *La vida breve* won the prize of the Real Academia de Bellas Artes in Madrid in 1905, but it was not premiered until 8 years later. In 1905 he also won the Ortiz y Cussó Prize for pianists. In 1907 he went to Paris, where he became friendly with Debussy, Dukas, and Ravel, who aided and encouraged him as a composer. Under their influence, he adopted the principles of Impressionism without, however, giving up his personal and national style. He returned to Spain in 1914 and produced his tremendously effective ballet *El amor brujo* (Madrid, April 2, 1915). It was followed by the evocative *Noches en los jardines de España* for Piano and Orch. (Madrid, April 9, 1916). In 1919 he made his home in Granada, where he completed work on his celebrated ballet *El sombrero de tres picos* (London, July 22, 1919). Falla's art was rooted in both the folk songs of Spain and the purest historical traditions of Spanish music. Until 1919 his works were cast chiefly in the Andalusian idiom, and his instrumental technique was often conditioned by effects peculiar to Spain's national instrument, the guitar. In his puppet opera *El retablo de maese Pedro* (1919–22), he turned to the classical tradition of Spanish (especially Castilian) music. The keyboard style of his Harpsichord Concerto (1923–26), written at the suggestion of Wanda Landowska, reveals in the classical lucidity of its writing a certain kinship with Domenico Scarlatti, who lived in Spain for many years. Falla became president of the Instituto de España in 1938. When the Spanish Civil War broke out, and General Franco overcame the Loyalist government with the aid of Hitler and Mussolini, Falla left Spain and went to South America, never to return to his homeland. He went to Buenos Aires, where he conducted concerts of his music. He then withdrew to the small locality of Alta Gracia, where he lived the last years of his life in seclusion, working on his large scenic cantata *Atlántida.* It remained unfinished at his death and was later completed by his former pupil Ernesto Halffter.
Writings: *Escritos sobre música y músicos* (ed. by F. Sopeña; Madrid, 1950; 3rd ed., 1972; Eng. tr., 1979, as *On Music and Musicians*); *Cartas a Segismondo Romero* (ed. by P. Recuero; Granada, 1976); *Correspondencia de Manuel de Falla* (ed. by E. Franco; Madrid, 1978).
Works: Stage: *La vida breve,* opera (1904–5; Nice, April 1, 1913); *El amor brujo,* ballet (1914–15; Madrid, April 2, 1915; concert version, 1916); *El corregidor y la molinera,* farsa mimica (1916–17; Madrid, April 7, 1917; rev. and expanded as *El sombrero de tres picos*); *El sombrero de tres picos,* ballet (rev. and expanded from *El corregidor y la molinera*; 1918–19; 2 orch. suites, 1919; London, July 22, 1919); *El retablo de maese Pedro,* puppet opera (1919–22; concert perf., Seville, March 23, 1923; private stage perf. in the salon of Princess de Poligna, Paris, June 25, 1923; public stage perf., Paris, Nov. 13, 1923); *Atlántida,* cantata escenica (1925–46; unfinished; completed by E. Halffter; Milan, June 18, 1962; rev. and perf. in concert form, Lucerne, Sept. 9, 1976); also several zarzuelas, including *Los amores de la Inés* (Madrid, April 12, 1902); incidental music, and a comic opera, *Fuego fatuo* (1918–19). **Orch.:** *Noches en los jardines de España* for Piano and Orch. (1909–15; Madrid, April 9, 1916); Concerto for Harpsichord or Piano, Flute, Oboe, Clarinet, Violin, and Cello (1923–26; Barcelona, Nov. 4, 1926); *Homenajes,* 4 pieces: 1, *à Cl. Debussy* (orig. for Guitar as *Le Tombeau de Claude Debussy,* 1920); 2, *Fanfare sobre el nombre de E.F. Arbós* (1933); 3, *à Paul Dukas* (orig. for Piano as *Pour le tombeau de Paul Dukas,* 1935); 4, *Pedrelliana* (1924–39); 1st performance of entire suite, Buenos Aires, Nov. 18, 1939. **Chamber:** *Melodía* for Cello and Piano (1897–99); *Mireya* for Flute and Piano Quartet (1899); Piano Quartet (1899); *Romanza* for Cello and Piano (1899); *Serenata andaluza* for Violin and Piano (1899; not extant); *Fanfare pour une fête* (1921). **Piano:** *Nocturno* (1899);

Serenata andaluza (1899); *Canción* (1900); *Vals-capricho* (1900); *Cortejo de gnomos* (1901); *Suite fantástica* (1901; not extant); *Hoja de album* (1902); *Allegro de concierto* (1903); *Pièces espagnoles: Aragonesa, Cubana, Montanesa,* and *Andaluza* (1902–8); *Fantasía bética* (1919); *Canto de los remeros del Volga* (1922); *Pour le tombeau de Paul Dukas* (1935; orch. version in *Homenajes*). GUITAR: *Homenaje "Le Tombeau de Claude Debussy"* (1920; orch. version in *Homenajes*). VOCAL: *Dos rimas* (1899–1900); *Preludios* (1900); *Tus ojillo negros* (1902); *Trois mélodies* (1909); *Siete canciones populares españolas* (1914–15); *Oracion de las madres que tienen a sus hijos en brazos* (1914); *El pan de ronda* (1915); *Psyché* for Voice, Flute, Harp, and String Trio (1924); *Soneto a Córdoba* for Voice and Harp or Piano (1927).
BIBL.: E. Istel, "M. d.F.," *Musical Quarterly* (Oct. 1926); J. Trend, *M. d.F. and Spanish Music* (N.Y., 1929; new ed., 1934); Roland-Manuel, *M. d.F.* (Paris, 1930); G. Chase, "F.'s Music for Piano Solo," *Chesterian* (1940); A. Sagardia, *M. d.F.* (Madrid, 1946); J. Thomas, *M. d.F. en la Isla* (Palma, 1947); J. Jaenisch, *M. d.F. und die spanische Musik* (Zürich and Freiburg, 1952); L. Campodonico, *F.* (Paris, 1959); R. Arizaga, *M. d.F.* (Buenos Aires, 1961); E. Molina Fajardo, *M. d.F. y el "cante jondo"* (Granada, 1962); J. Viniegra, *M. d.F.: Su vida intima* (Cádiz, 1966); A. Saeardia, *Vida y Obra de M. d.F.* (Madrid, 1967); J. Grunfeld, *M. d.F.: Spanien und die neue Musik* (Zürich, 1968); M. Orozco, *M. d.F.: Biografía illustrada* (Barcelona, 1968); A. Campoamor Gonzalez, *M. d.F., 1876–1946* (Madrid, 1976); R. Crichton, *M. d.F.: Descriptive Catalogue of His Works* (London, 1976); B. James, *M. d.F. and the Spanish Musical Renaissance* (London, 1979); R. Crichton, *F.* (London, 1982); G. Chase and A. Budwig, *M. d.F.: A Bibliography and Research Guide* (N.Y., 1986).

Faller, Nikola, Croatian conductor and composer; b. Varaždin, April 22, 1862; d. Zagreb, Feb. 28, 1938. He studied with Bruckner in Vienna and with Massenet in Paris. He was active as an opera conductor in Split and Zagreb; composed choral works and dances.

Famintsyn, Alexander (Sergeievich), Russian music critic and composer; b. Kaluga, Nov. 5, 1841; d. Ligovo, near St. Petersburg, July 6, 1896. He studied with Jean Vogt in St. Petersburg, and then with Hauptmann and Richter in Leipzig. He taught music history at the St. Petersburg Cons. (1865–72); tr. into Russian the textbooks *Allgemeine Musiklehre* by Marx and *Harmonielehre* by Richter. However, he soon abandoned his teaching activities and devoted himself chiefly to music criticism, taking a very conservative attitude; he indulged in frequent polemics against the Russian composers of the National School; Mussorgsky caricatured him in his satirical song *The Classicist* and in a section of his burlesque *Rayok*. Famintsyn's publications on Russian instruments are valuable; he publ. essays on the gusli (1890) and the domra (1891). His opera *Sardanapal* was produced in St. Petersburg on Dec. 5, 1875, but without any success; his other opera, *Uriel Acosta* (1883), was not performed. He further wrote a Piano Quintet, a String Quartet, and some songs.

Fanciulli, Francesco, Italian-American conductor and composer; b. Porto San Stefano, July 17, 1850; d. N.Y., July 17, 1915. He studied in Florence; after some years as an opera conductor in Italy, he went to America (1876) and earned his living as an organist and theatrical conductor; in 1893 he succeeded Sousa as conductor of the Marine Band in Washington, D.C.; was then bandmaster of the 71st Regiment in N.Y. (1898–1904); after that, conducted his own band. He wrote 5 operas, including *Priscilla* (Norfolk, Va., Nov. 1, 1901); a number of marches and other pieces for Band; orch. music; choral works; chamber music; songs; piano pieces.
BIBL.: F. Cipolla, "F. F., Turn-of-the-Century American Bandmaster," *Instrumentalist,* XXX/7 (1979).

Fanelli, Ernest, French composer; b. Paris, June 29, 1860; d. there, Nov. 24, 1917. He played drums in orchs. as a small boy; entered the Paris Cons. in 1876, in the class of Delibes.

He worked as a copyist and music engraver for many years; in 1912 he applied to Gabriel Pierné for work, submitting the score of his symphonic poem *Thèbes* as a specimen of his handwriting. This score, composed by Fanelli as early as 1883, seemed to anticipate the instrumental and harmonic usages of Debussy and other composers of impressionist music, and Pierné decided to perform it as a curiosity; he conducted it at a Colonne concert in Paris (March 17, 1912), and the novelty created a mild sensation in French musical circles; other works by Fanelli (*Impressions pastorales; L'Effroi du Soleil; Suite rabelaisienne;* etc.), all written before 1893, were also found interesting. However, the sensation proved of brief duration, and the extravagant claims for Fanelli's talent collapsed.

Faning, Eaton, English conductor and composer; b. Helston, Cornwall, May 20, 1850; d. Brighton, Oct. 28, 1927. He studied at the Royal Academy of Music in London with Sterndale Bennett and Arthur Sullivan, winning the Mendelssohn Scholarship (1873) and the Lucas medal (1876); received the degrees of Mus.Bac. (1894) and Mus.Doc. (1899) from Cambridge Univ. From 1878 he taught piano at the Royal Academy of Music; in 1885 became music director at Harrow School (until 1901); thereafter occupied various educational posts. He wrote a Sym., some chamber music, and several operettas.

Fano, (Aronne) Guido Alberto, Italian composer and writer on music; b. Padua, May 18, 1875; d. Tauriano di Spilimbergo, Friuli, Aug. 14, 1961. He studied with Pollini in Padua and Martucci in Bologna; at the same time he took courses in law; received the degree of Dr.Juris from Bologna Univ. in 1901. From 1900 to 1905 he was a teacher of piano at the Liceo Musicale in Bologna; was director of the Cons. of Parma (1905–12), Naples (1912–16), and Palermo (1916–22); taught piano at the Milan Cons. (1922–38; 1945–47). He wrote an opera, *Juturna,* and a symphonic poem, *La tentazione di Gesù;* also publ. several books: *Pensieri sulla musica* (Bologna, 1903); *Nella vita del ritmo* (Naples, 1916); *Lo studio del pianoforte* (3 vols., Milan, 1923–34).

Fara, Giulio, Italian writer on music and composer; b. Cagliari, Sardinia, Dec. 3, 1880; d. Pesaro, Oct. 9, 1949. He studied singing and composition; became an instructor in public schools of Sardinia; collected Sardinian folk songs and used some of them in his own compositions, notably in the opera *Elia.* He publ. a biography of Rossini (1915) and a collection of essays, *L'anima musicale d'Italia* (1921); contributed to the *Rivista Musicale Italiana* and other Italian publications. His collection of Sardinian songs was publ. by Ricordi (1924).

Farberman, Harold, American conductor and composer; b. N.Y., Nov. 2, 1929. He studied at the Juilliard School of Music in N.Y. and the New England Cons. of Music in Boston; served as percussion player with the Boston Sym. Orch. (1951–63); from 1971 to 1979 he conducted the Oakland (Calif.) Sym. Orch. In 1975 he founded and was president of the Conductors' Guild; in 1980 he organized the Conductors' Inst. at the Univ. of West Virginia, which removed to the Univ. of South Carolina in 1987. In his music he often cultivates the idiom of jazz and rock.
WORKS: *Medea,* chamber opera (Boston, March 26, 1961); *The Losers,* opera (N.Y., March 26, 1971); *Evolution* for Soprano, Horn, and Percussion (1954); Timpani Concerto (1962); Trio for Violin, Piano, and Percussion (1963); Concerto for Bassoon and String Orch.; *5 Images* for Brass Quintet (1964); *Elegy, Fanfare and March* for Orch. (1964–65); Concerto for Saxophone and String Orch. (1965); Sym. (1956–57); *Greek Scene* for Mezzo-soprano and Orch. (1957); *Progressions* for Flute and Percussion (1961); *Variations* for Piano and Percussion (1954); *If Music Be* for Jazz Vocalist, Rock Group, and Orch. (1965); Violin Concerto (1976); *Impressions* for Oboe, Strings, and Percussion (1959–60); *War Cry on a Prayer Feather* for Soprano, Baritone, and Orch. (Colorado Springs, Nov. 11, 1976); Duo for English Horn and Percussion (1981); *Shapings* for English Horn, Strings, and Percussion (1984);

A Summer's Day in Central Park for Orch. (1987; N.Y., Jan. 21, 1988).

Fariñas, Carlos, Cuban composer; b. Cienfuegos, Las Villas province, Nov. 28, 1934. He studied with José Ardévol in Havana, Copland at the Berkshire Music Center at Tanglewood (1956), and Alexander Priumov at the Moscow Cons. (1961–63). Returning to Cuba in 1963, he became head of the Conservatorio Alejandro Garcia Corturia and director of the Council for National Culture in the dept. of music education. He is a prominent avant-garde composer in Cuba; many of his works utilize graphic or spatial notation that allows for considerable freedom in performance.

WORKS: *Pregón y variaciones* for Flute and String Quartet (1955); a ballet, *Despertar* (1960); 2 string quartets: No. 1 (1963–64) and No. 2, *Tatomaite* (1972); *Oda a Camilo* for Orch. (1966); *Tiento No. 1* for Clarinet, Electric Guitar, Piano, and Percussion (1966) and *No. 2* for 2 Pianos and Percussion (1969).

Farinelli (real name, **Carlo Broschi**), celebrated Italian castrato soprano; b. Andria, Jan. 24, 1705; d. Bologna, July 15, 1782. His father, Salvatore Broschi, was a musician and most likely Carlo's earliest instructor in music. He later adopted the name Farinelli to honor his benefactor, Farina. He studied with Porpora in Naples, making his 1st public appearance there in his teacher's serenata *Angelica e Medoro* in 1720; subsequent appearances brought him great success, and he soon became famous as "il ragazzo" ("the boy"). He also sang in Rome, appearing in Porpora's opera *Eumene* at the age of 16. His repeated successes brought him renown throughout Italy and abroad, and led to his 1st appearance in Vienna (1724). He met the celebrated castrato alto Bernacchi in Bologna in 1727; in a singing contest with him, Farinelli acknowledged defeat and persuaded Bernacchi to give him lessons to achieve virtuosity in coloratura. After further visits to Vienna in 1728 and 1731, Porpora called him to London to sing with the Opera of the Nobility; he made his London debut in Hasse's *Artaserse* on Oct. 27, 1734, appearing with Senesino and Cuzzoni; he remained with the company until the summer of 1736, when he went to Paris; then returned to it for the 1736–37 season. Having amassed a fortune in London, Farinelli went to Madrid in 1737. He attained unparalleled success as court singer to King Philip V; his duty was to sing arias every night to cure the King's melancholy, and his influence on the ailing monarch, and on the Queen, was such that he was able to command considerable funds to engage famous performers for the Madrid court. When his voice began to fail, he served as impresario, decorator, and stage director. He continued to enjoy the court's favor under Philip's successor, Ferdinand VI, who made him a knight of the order of Calatrava in 1750. However, when Carlos III became King in 1759, Farinelli was dismissed. He then returned to Italy in possession of great wealth. He built a palatial villa for himself near Bologna and spent the last years of his life in contentment.

BIBL.: C. Burney, *The Present State of Music in France and Italy* (London, 1771; 2nd ed., 1773; ed. by P. Scholes as *Dr. Burney's Musical Tours*, London, 1959); G. Sacchi, *Vita del Cavaliere Don Carlo Broschi, detto F.* (Venice, 1784); C. Ricci, *Burney, Casanova, e. F. in Bologna* (Milan, 1890); J. Desastre, *Carlo Broschi* (Zürich, 1903); G. Monadi, *Cantanti evirati celebri* (Rome, 1919); F. Haböck, *Die Gesangskunst der Kastraten* (Vienna, 1923); R. Bouvier, *F., le chanteur des rois* (Paris, 1943); R. Freeman, "F. and His Repertory," *Studies in Renaissance and Baroque Music in Honor of Arthur Mendel* (Kassel and Hackensack, N.J., 1974).

Farinelli (real name, **Finco**), **Giuseppe (Francesco),** prolific Italian composer; b. Este, May 7, 1769; d. Trieste, Dec. 12, 1836. In 1785 he entered the Conservatorio della Pietà dei Turchini at Naples, his teachers being La Barbiera, Fago, Sala, and Tritto; his 1st opera, *Il dottorato di Pulcinella,* produced in 1792, was followed by 50 or 60 others, not original, but in very happy imitation of Cimarosa's style and chiefly comic. During the years 1810–17 he lived at Turin; then went

to Trieste as maestro di cappella and organist at the Cathedral of San Giusto. He also wrote several oratorios, cantatas, 5 masses, 2 Te Deums, and other church music.

Farjeon, Harry, English composer; b. Hohokus, N.J. (of English parents), May 6, 1878; d. London, Dec. 29, 1948. He was a son of the English novelist B.L. Farjeon, and grandson of the famous actor Joseph Jefferson. He was educated in England, taking music lessons with Landon Ronald and John Storer; then studied composition with Corder at the Royal Academy of Music; won the Lucas Medal and other prizes. In 1903 he became an instructor at the Academy.

WORKS: Opera, *Floretta* (1899), and 2 operettas, *The Registry Office* (1900) and *A Gentleman of the Road* (1902), all performed in London; Piano Concerto (1903); *Hans Andersen Suite* for Small Orch. (London, 1905); 2 song cycles: *Vagrant Songs* and *The Lute of Jade.* The score of a symphonic poem, *Summer Vision* (regarded by the composer as his best work), was sent to Germany shortly before World War I and was lost.

Farkas, Edmund (Ödön), Hungarian pedagogue, conductor, and composer; b. Puszta-Monostor, 1851; d. Klausenburg, Sept. 11, 1912. He studied engineering at the Univ. of Budapest; then took courses at the Budapest Academy of Music with Erkel, Volkmann, and others. Upon graduation he was appointed director at the Klausenburg Cons. There he organized an orch., established a musical journal, and promoted national Hungarian music.

WORKS: Operas (all 1st perf. in Budapest): *Bayadere* (Aug. 23, 1876); *Valentin Balassa* (Jan. 16, 1896); *The Inquest* (Oct. 5, 1900); *The World of Kurucz* (Oct. 26, 1906); several symphonic poems in a Romantic vein (*Dusk, Storm,* etc.); church music; 5 string quartets; several piano pieces in the Hungarian style.

Farkas, Ferenc, prominent Hungarian composer; b. Nagykanizsa, Dec. 15, 1905. He began to study piano as a child; took courses with Leo Weiner and Albert Siklós at the Academy of Music in Budapest (1922–27); a state scholarship enabled him to study with Respighi at the Accademia di Santa Cecilia in Rome (1929–31); later he was engaged as conductor of incidental music to films in Vienna and Copenhagen (1933–35). Returning to Hungary, he was a music teacher at the municipal school in Budapest (1935–41); from 1941 to 1944 he taught at the Cluj Cons.; was director of the music school in Székesfehérvár (1946–48); from 1949 to 1975 was a prof. of composition at the Academy of Music in Budapest. In 1950 he was awarded the Kossuth Prize and in 1960 the Erkel Prize; was made Merited Artist (1965) and Honored Artist (1970) of the Hungarian People's Republic. He also received the Herder Prize of Hamburg (1979) and was made a Cavaliere dell'Ordine della Repubblica Italiana (1985).

WORKS: STAGE: *The Magic Cupboard,* comic opera (1938–42; Budapest, April 22, 1942; also a separate overture, 1952); *The Sly Students,* ballet (1949); *Csinom Palkó,* musical play (1950; rev. 1960); *Vidróczki,* opera (1964); *Piroschka,* musical comedy (1967); *Story of Noszty Junior with Mari Tóth,* musical comedy (1971); *Panegyricus,* ballet with Narrator and Chorus (1972); *A Gentleman from Venice,* opera (1980). **ORCH.:** Fantasy for Piano and Orch. (1929); Divertimento (1930); Harp Concertino (1937; rev. 1956); *Dinner Music* for Chamber Orch. (1938); *Rhapsodia carpathiana* (1940); *Marionette's Dance Suite* (1940–41); *Musica pentatonica* for String Orch. (1945); Prelude and Fugue (1947; orig. titled *Musica dodecatonica*); Piano Concertino (1947–49); *Lavotta,* suite (1951); Sym. (1951–52); *Scherzo sinfonico* (1952); *Symphonic Overture* (1952); *Sketches from the Bükk* (1955); *Piccola musica di concerto* for String Orch. (1961); *Trittico concertato* for Cello and String Orch. (1964); *Gyász és vígasz* (*Planctus et Consolationes;* 1965); *Concerto all'Antica* for Baryton or Viola da Gamba, and String Orch. (1965); *Serenata concertante* for Flute and String Orch. (1967); *Ouverture philharmonique* (1977–78); *Musica serena* for Strings (1982); *Musica giocosa,* suite (1982); Concertino for Trumpet and Strings (1984). **CHORAL AND OTHER VOCAL:** *Can-*

tata lirica (1945); *Cantus pannonicus,* cantata to the Latin verses of the 15th-century Hungarian archbishop Janus Pannonius (Budapest, April 3, 1959); *Laudatio szigethiana,* oratorio (1967); other works for voice and/or chorus and orch. CHAMBER: 3 violin sonatinas (1930, 1931, 1959); String Quartet (1970–72); other chamber pieces. PIANO: Sonata (1930); Toccata (1945); *Correspondences* (1957); *Hybrids* (1957); 3 *Monograms* (1962); *Naptár* (Calendar) for Soprano, Tenor, and Piano or Chamber Ensemble (1956) and other songs; incidental music.

BIBL.: J. Ujfalussy, *F. F.* (Budapest, 1969).

Farkas, Philip (Francis), American horn player and teacher; b. Chicago, March 5, 1914. After study with Louis Defrasne in Chicago, he was 1st horn player in the Kansas City Phil. (1933–36), the Chicago Sym. Orch. (1936–41; 1947–60), the Cleveland Orch. (1941–45; 1946–47), and the Boston Sym. Orch. (1945–46). He taught at the Indiana Univ. School of Music in Bloomington (1960–82) and founded his own publishing company, Wind Music, Inc.; also authored *The Art of French Horn Playing* (1956), *The Art of Brass Playing* (1962), and *A Photographic Study of 40 Virtuoso Horn Players' Embouchures* (1970).

Farley, Carole Ann, talented American soprano; b. Le Mars, Iowa, Nov. 29, 1946. She studied at the Indiana Univ. School of Music (Mus.B., 1968), with Cornelius Reid in N.Y., and on a Fulbright scholarship with Marianne Schech at the Munich Hochschule für Musik (1968–69). In 1969 she made her debut at the Linz Landestheater and also her U.S. debut at N.Y.'s Town Hall; subsequently appeared as a soloist with major orchs. of the U.S. and Europe, and sang with the Welsh National Opera, the Cologne Opera, the Strasbourg Opera, the N.Y. City Opera, and the Lyons Opera. She made her Metropolitan Opera debut in N.Y. as Lulu on March 18, 1977, and continued to sing there in later seasons; she also sang at the Zürich Opera (1979), the Deutsche Oper am Rhein in Düsseldorf (1980–81; 1984), the Chicago Lyric Opera (1981), and the Florence Maggio Musicale (1985). In addition to her esteemed portrayal of Lulu, which she essayed over 80 times in various operatic centers, she also sang Poppea, Donna Anna, Violetta, Massenet's Manon, Mimi, and various roles in Richard Strauss's operas. She married **José Serebrier** in 1969.

Farmer, Henry George, eminent Irish musicologist; b. Birr, Jan. 17, 1882; d. Law, Scotland, Dec. 30, 1965. He studied piano and violin, and as a boy joined the Royal Artillery Orch. in London, playing the violin and clarinet at its concerts. He then studied philosophy and languages at Glasgow Univ. An extremely prolific writer, he publ. a number of original works, dealing with such varied subjects as military music and Arabic musical theories. He was the founder and conductor of the Glasgow Sym. Orch. (1919–43); wrote a ballet and other works for the theater, several overtures, and some chamber music.

WRITINGS: *Memoirs of the Royal Artillery Band* (1904); *The Rise and Development of Military Music* (1912); *The Arabian Influence on Musical Theory* (1925); *Byzantine Musical Instruments in the 9th Century* (1925); *The Arabic Musical MSS. in the Bodleian Library* (1925); *A History of Arabian Music to the 13th Century* (1929); *Music in Medieval Scotland* (1931); *Historical Facts for the Arabian Musical Influence* (1930); *The Organ of the Ancients from Eastern Sources, Hebrew, Syriac and Arabic* (1931); *Studies in Oriental Musical Instruments* (1931); *An Old Moorish Lute Tutor* (1933); *Al-Farabi's Arabic-Latin Writings on Music* (1934); *Turkish Instruments of Music in the 17th Century* (1937); *A History of Music in Scotland* (1947); *Music Making in the Olden Days* (1950); *Oriental Studies, Mainly Musical* (1953); *The History of the Royal Artillery Band* (1954); *British Bands in Battle* (1965).

Farmer, John, English organist and composer, active from 1591 to 1601. In 1595 he was organist at the Christ Church Cathedral in Dublin; in 1599 he left Dublin and went to London. Among his madrigals the best known are *Faire Phyllis I saw sitting all alone, You pretty flowers,* and *A little pretty bonny lass,* included in his *First Set of English Madrigals to Foure Voices* (London, 1599; reprinted in vol. 8 of E.H. Fellowes's The English Madrigalists). He contributed a 6-part madrigal, *Fair Nymphs, I heard one telling,* to *The Triumphes of Oriana,* and several canticles and hymns to Thomas East's *Whole Booke of Psalmes* (1592). Farmer was also the author of *Divers and sundry waies of two parts in one* (London, 1591).

BIBL.: E.H. Fellowes, *English Madrigal Verse, 1588–1632* (London, 1920; 3rd ed., rev., 1967); idem, *The English Madrigal Composers* (Oxford, 1921; 2nd ed., 1948).

Farmer, John, English organist and composer; b. Nottingham, Aug. 16, 1836; d. Oxford, July 17, 1901. He studied at the Leipzig Cons. and later with Andreas Späth at Coburg; then lived in Switzerland, returning to England in 1862; taught at Harrow School (1862–85). He composed an oratorio, *Christ and His Soldiers* (1878); fairy opera, *Cinderella* (1882); comic cantata, *Froggy Would A-wooing Go* (1887); settings of nursery rhymes for chorus and orch.; church music; chamber music.

Farnaby, Giles, significant English composer; b. c.1563; d. London (buried), Nov. 25, 1640. He graduated from Oxford in 1592, receiving the degree of B.Mus.; later moved to London, where he remained until his death. Farnaby's son, Richard Farnaby, was also a gifted composer.

WORKS: *Canzonets to Fowre Voyces* (1598; includes an added madrigal for 8 Voices, one of the few such works in the English school; reprint by E.H. Fellowes in vol. 20 of The English Madrigalists); vocal religious works in various collections, and motets, Psalms, etc.; more than 50 virginal pieces in the *Fitzwilliam Virginal Book* (ed. by J.A. Fuller Maitland and W. Barclay Squire, London, 1899).

BIBL.: E.H. Fellowes, *The English Madrigal Composers* (Oxford, 1921; 2nd ed., 1948); R. Marlow, *The Life and Music of G. F.* (diss., Cambridge Univ., 1966).

Farnadi, Edith, Hungarian pianist; b. Budapest, Sept. 25, 1921; d. Graz, Dec. 14, 1973. She entered the Budapest Academy of Music at the age of 9; studied with Bartók and Weiner; made her debut at 12; was granted her diploma at 16. She made appearances with the violinists Hubay and Huberman; taught at the Budapest Academy of Music; then became a teacher in Graz.

Farnam, W(alter) Lynnwood, Canadian-American organist; b. Sutton, Quebec, Jan. 13, 1885; d. N.Y., Nov. 23, 1930. He studied with his mother and local teachers; went to America in 1904; was organist at several churches in N.Y. and Boston. He was a teacher at the Curtis Inst. of Music in Philadelphia (from 1927); his students included Harold Gleason, Carl Weinrich, and Robert Noehren.

BIBL.: W. Hawk, "L. F.: His Life," *American Organist,* XLVII/7 (1964).

Farncombe, Charles (Frederick), English conductor; b. London, July 29, 1919. He first studied engineering at the Univ. of London; after military service in World War II he enrolled at the Royal School of Church Music, Canterbury, and the Royal Academy of Music, London. In 1955 he organized the Handel Opera Soc., serving as its music director and conductor. From 1970 to 1979 he was chief conductor of the Drottningholm Court Theater in Stockholm; then was music director of the London Chamber Opera (from 1983). In 1977 he was made a Commander of the Order of the British Empire.

Farquhar, David (Andross), New Zealand composer and teacher; b. Cambridge, New Zealand, April 5, 1928. He studied with Douglas Lilburn, at Canterbury College, and at Victoria College (B.A., B.Mus., 1948); went to England and took his M.A. at Emmanuel College, Cambridge, completing his training with Benjamin Frankel at the Guildhall School of Music in London (1951–52). Returning to New Zealand, he was a lecturer (1953–76) and prof. of music (from 1976) at Victoria Univ. of Wellington; in 1974 he was founding president of the Composers Assoc. of New Zealand. His music is contrapuntal in structure and neo-Romantic in mood.

WORKS: OPERAS: *A Unicorn for Christmas* (1962); *Shadow* (1970; Wellington, Sept. 19, 1988); incidental music. **ORCH.:** *Epithalamion Overture* (1954); *Ring round the Moon*, dance suite (1957); *Evocation* (1957); 3 syms.: No. 1 (1959; Wellington, Aug. 13, 1960; 1st sym. by a New Zealand composer given a public premiere); *Bells in Their Seasons*, choral sym. (1974); No. 2 (Wellington, Nov. 5, 1983); *Harlequin Overture* (1959); *Anniversary Suite No. 1* (1961) and *No. 2* (1965); *Elegy for Strings* (1961); *Echoes and Reflections* for String Orch. (1974); *March* for Clarinet and String Orch. (1984). **CHAMBER:** 2 string quartets (1949, 1989); *Serenade* for Wind Quartet (1951); *Elegy* for Wind Trio (1965); *Notturno* for Brass Quintet (1966); *Ostinato-Capriccio-Epilogo* for Guitar (1967); *Scenes and Memories* for Violin, Piano, and Percussion (1972); *3 Pieces for Double Bass* (1976); *Concerto for 6* for Flute, Clarinet, Vibraphone, Piano, Violin, and Cello (1987); piano pieces; choruses; songs.

Farrant, John, English organist and composer, active in the 16th century. He served as lay clerk (1571–78) and subsequently organist at the Salisbury Cathedral (1587–92); he was briefly organist at Hereford (1593). Contemporary records testify to his intractable temper, which resulted in physical clashes with the dean of the Salisbury Cathedral, and led to his expulsion from there. As a composer, Farrant is chiefly distinguished for his Service in D minor (misattributed in a 19th-century ed. to Richard Farrant). His son, also named **John Farrant** (baptized in Salisbury, Sept. 28, 1575; d. there, 1618), was a chorister at the Salisbury Cathedral in 1585, and organist there from 1598 till his death. Another John Farrant, possibly related to the preceding, was organist at Christ Church, Newgate, London; he was the author of a Magnificat; this work, sometimes referred to as "Farrant in G minor," is often confused with Richard Farrant's Cathedral Service in A minor.

Farrant, Richard, English organist and composer; b. c.1525; d. London, Nov. 30, 1580. He was a Gentleman of the Chapel Royal; then became master of the choristers (1564) at St. George's Chapel, Windsor; also served as a lay clerk and organist there. Beginning with 1567 Farrant presented a play annually before the Queen. In 1569 he became master of the choristers of the Chapel Royal while retaining his Windsor post. Farrant wrote mainly church music; his Cathedral Service in A minor and 2 anthems, *Hide Not Thou Thy Face* and *Call to Remembrance,* are regarded as beautiful examples of English sacred music of the 16th century. A Service in D minor was publ. as by Richard Farrant, but this was a misattribution, the real author being John Farrant of Salisbury.

Farrar, Ernest (Bristow), English organist and composer; b. London, July 7, 1885; d. in the battle of the Somme, France, Sept. 18, 1918. He studied at the Royal College of Music in London with Stanford and Parratt; served as organist of the English Church in Dresden (1909); then at various churches in England (1910–14). His orch. suite *English Pastoral Impression* won the Carnegie Award; he further wrote the orch. pieces *The Open Road, Lavengro, The Forsaken Merman,* and *Heroic Elegy;* also 3 *Spiritual Studies* for Strings; variations on an old English sea song, for Piano and Orch.; the cantatas *The Blessed Damozel* and *Out of Doors;* chamber music (*Celtic Suite* for Violin and Piano, etc.); songs; preludes for organ; etc.

Farrar, Geraldine, celebrated American soprano; b. Melrose, Mass., Feb. 28, 1882; d. Ridgefield, Conn., March 11, 1967. She studied music with Mrs. J.H. Long of Boston; at 17, she went to Europe; took lessons with Emma Thursby in N.Y., Trabadello in Paris, and Graziani in Berlin; made a successful debut at the Berlin Opera on Oct. 15, 1901, as Marguerite, under the direction of Karl Muck; then studied with Lilli Lehmann. She sang at the Monte Carlo Opera (1903–6). Her career in Europe was well established before her American debut as Juliette at the Metropolitan Opera (Nov. 26, 1906); she remained on the staff for 16 years; made her farewell appearance in *Zaza* on April 22, 1922, but continued to sing in concert; gave her last public performance at Carnegie Hall in 1931; then retired to Ridgefield, Conn. Her greatest success was

Madama Butterfly, which she sang with Caruso in its American premiere at the Metropolitan on Feb. 11, 1907; subsequently sang this part in America more than 100 times. Her interpretation of Carmen was no less remarkable. She also appeared in silent motion pictures between 1915 and 1919; her film version of *Carmen* aroused considerable interest. On Feb. 8, 1916, she married the actor Lou Tellegen, from whom she was subsequently divorced. She made adaptations of pieces by Kreisler, Rachmaninoff, and others, for which she publ. the lyrics. She wrote an autobiography, *Such Sweet Compulsion* (N.Y., 1938; reprinted in 1970), which had been preceded in 1916 by *Geraldine Farrar: The Story of an American Singer.* Her scrapbooks, many letters, the fan she used in *Madama Butterfly,* etc., are in the Music Division of the Library of Congress in Washington, D.C.

BIBL.: E. Wagenknecht, *G. F.: An Authorized Record of Her Career* (Seattle, 1929); E. Nash, *Always First Class: The Career of G. F.* (Washington, D.C., 1982).

Farrell, Eileen, brilliant American soprano; b. Willimantic, Conn., Feb. 13, 1920. Her parents were vaudeville singers; she received her early vocal training with Merle Alcock in N.Y., and later studied with Eleanor McLellan. In 1940 she sang on the radio; in 1947–48 made a U.S. tour as a concert singer; toured South America in 1949. Her song recital in N.Y. on Oct. 24, 1950, was enthusiastically acclaimed and secured her immediate recognition. She was soloist in Beethoven's 9th Sym. with Toscanini and the NBC Sym. Orch.; also appeared many times with the N.Y. Phil. She made her operatic debut as Santuzza with the San Carlo Opera in Tampa, Fla., in 1956. In 1958 she joined the San Francisco Opera and in 1957 became a member of the Lyric Opera of Chicago. On Dec. 6, 1960, she made a successful debut with the Metropolitan Opera in N.Y., as Gluck's Alcestis; she remained on its roster until 1964; then returned in 1965–66; was a distinguished Prof. of Music at the Indiana Univ. School of Music in Bloomington from 1971 to 1980; then held that title at the Univ. of Maine in Orono (from 1984).

Farrenc, (Jacques Hippolyte) Aristide, French flutist and music editor; b. Marseilles, April 9, 1794; d. Paris, Jan. 31, 1865. He studied flute; went to Paris in 1815, and studied at the Cons.; at the same time was engaged as 2nd flutist at the Théâtre-Italien. In 1821 he established a music shop and printing press; publ. French eds. of Beethoven; also composed music for the flute. He married Louise Dumont ([Jeanne-] **Louise Farrenc),** a talented musician in her own right. He diligently collected material for the rectification of existing biographies, but generously turned it over to Fétis for use in the 2nd ed. of his great work, of which Farrenc also read proofs. Jointly with Fétis's son, Édouard, he began the publication of *Le Trésor des pianistes* (23 vols., 1861–74; reprinted N.Y., 1977, foreword by Bea Friedland), a collection of piano music from the 16th century to Mendelssohn, with historical notes; it was continued after his death by his wife. From 1854 he contributed articles to *La France Musicale* and other journals.

Farrenc, (Jeanne-) Louise (née **Dumont**), French pianist and composer; b. Paris, May 31, 1804; d. there, Sept. 15, 1875. She studied music with Reicha; in 1821, married **(Jacques Hippolyte) Aristide Farrenc,** but was not entirely eclipsed by his acknowledged eminence. Her 3 syms. had respectable performances: No. 1 in Brussels, Feb. 23, 1845; No. 2 in Paris, May 3, 1846; No. 3 in Paris, April 22, 1849; the last received an accolade in the prestigious, and definitely male-oriented, *Gazette Musicale,* which conceded that "she revealed, alone among her sex in musical Europe, genuine learning, united with grace and taste." She also wrote a Piano Concerto; 30 études in all major and minor keys for Piano; 2 piano trios; Cello Sonata; 2 violin sonatas; 2 piano quintets; a Sextet and a Nonet for Winds and Strings; one of her overtures (1840) was reviewed by Berlioz, who remarked that it was orchestrated "with a talent rare among women." She was a brilliant pianist; she taught piano at the Paris Cons. from 1842 till 1872, the only woman ever to hold a permanent position as an instrumentalist there in the 19th century. Her daughter **Victorine** (b. Paris, Feb. 23, 1826; d. there, Jan. 3, 1859) was also a talented pianist whose promising career was cut short by an early death. After the death of her husband in 1865, Louise Farrenc assumed the editorship of the monumental collection *Le Trésor des pianistes* begun by him.

BIBL.: B. Friedland, "L. F., Composer, Performer, Scholar (1804–1875)," *Musical Quarterly* (April 1974).

Farrow, Norman D., Canadian baritone; b. Regina, May 6, 1916; d. Greensboro, N.C., Sept. 22, 1984. He studied at the Juilliard School of Music and at N.Y. Univ.; took voice lessons with Mack Harrell and others; was one of the organizers of the Bach Aria Group. He toured as soloist with choral ensembles; in 1960 he was engaged as artist-in-residence at Southern Methodist Univ. in Dallas.

Farwell, Arthur (George), American composer and music educator; b. St. Paul, Minn., April 23, 1872; d. N.Y., Jan. 20, 1952. He studied at the Mass. Inst. of Technology, graduating in 1893; then studied music with Homer Norris in Boston, Humperdinck and Pfitzner in Berlin, and Guilmant in Paris. He was a lecturer on music at Cornell Univ. (1899–1901); from 1909 to 1914 was on the editorial staff of *Musical America;* then directed municipal concerts in N.Y. City (1910–13); was director of the Settlement Music School in N.Y. (1915–18); in 1918 he went to California; lectured on music there; was acting head of the music dept. at the Univ. of Calif., Berkeley (1918–19); in 1919 he founded the Santa Barbara Community Chorus, which he conducted until 1921; was the 1st holder of the composers' fellowship of the Music and Art Assoc. of Pasadena (1921–25); taught music theory at Michigan State College in East Lansing (1927–39); eventually settled in N.Y. Farwell was a pioneer in new American music, and tirelessly promoted national ideas in art. He contributed to various ethnological publications. From 1901 to 1911 he operated the Wa-Wan Press (Newton, Mass.), a periodical (quarterly, 1901–7; monthly, 1907–11) that printed piano and vocal music of "progressive" American composers of the period, the emphasis being on works that utilized indigenous (black, Indian, and cowboy) musical materials (reprinted N.Y., 1970, under the direction of Vera Lawrence Brodsky). Disillusioned about commercial opportunities for American music, including his own, he established at East Lansing, in April 1936, his own lithographic handpress, with which he printed his music, handling the entire process of reproduction, including the cover designs, by himself.

WRITINGS: *A Letter to American Composers* (N.Y., 1903); *Music in America* in *The Art of Music,* IV (with W. Dermot Darby; N.Y., 1915).

WORKS: Orch.: *Symbolistic Study No. 3,* after Walt Whitman (1905; rev. 1921; Philadelphia, March 30, 1928); *The Gods of the Mountain* (Minneapolis, Dec. 13, 1929); music for pageants, including Percy MacKaye's *Caliban by the Yellow Sands* (N.Y., May 1916; written for the Shakespeare tercentenary); *The Pilgrimage Way* (Los Angeles, 1921); *Symphonic Song on "Old Black Joe"* (Los Angeles, 1923); *Symphonic Hymn on "March! March!"* (1921); also *The Hako* for String Quartet (1922); Violin Sonata (1927; rev. 1935); Concerto for 2 Pianos and String Orch., a version of *Symbolistic Study No. 6* (1931; CBS, May 28, 1939); numerous school choruses and vocal compositions; piano pieces (many of them arranged for various instrumental ensembles); several collections of American Indian melodies and folk songs of the South and West; arrangements of Indian melodies (*Dawn,* a fantasy on Indian themes, in various versions, dated between 1901 and 1926, is characteristic of these works).

BIBL.: E. Kirk, *Toward American Music: A Study of the Life and Music of A.G. F.* (diss., Univ. of Rochester, 1958); B. Farwell et al., *Guide to the Music of A. F. and to the Microfilm Collection*

of His Work (Briarcliff Manor, N.Y., 1971); E. Culbertson, "A. F.'s Early Efforts on Behalf of American Music, 1889–1921," *American Music* (Summer 1987).

Fasano, Renato, Italian conductor; b. Naples, Aug. 21, 1902; d. Rome, Aug. 3, 1979. He studied piano and composition at Naples, specializing in Renaissance music; in 1941 he founded the Collegium Musicum Italicum of Rome; in 1947 he organized the distinguished chamber group I Virtuosi di Roma, and led its performances on European tours. In 1957 he also founded the Piccolo Teatro Musicale Italiano; in 1960 he was named director of the Accademia di Santa Cecilia in Rome. Fasano was greatly esteemed for his effort to revive a proper appreciation of Italian music of the Renaissance period.

Fasch, Johann Friedrich, important German composer, father of **Karl Friedrich Christian Fasch;** b. Buttelstädt, near Weimar, April 15, 1688; d. Zerbst, Dec. 5, 1758. At age 13 he entered the Leipzig Thomasschule, where he came under the tutelage of Kuhnau; later studied at the Univ. of Leipzig and with Graupner and Grunewald in Darmstadt (1713). He was active as a violinist and organist, then was Kapellmeister to Count Václav Morzin in Prague (1721–22) and court Kapellmeister in Zerbst (from 1722). Although none of his music was publ. in his lifetime, his church cantatas and festival pieces for the Zerbst court were performed in many German cities. His friend Telemann gave performances of his church music in Hamburg, and J.S. Bach prepared several transcriptions of his overtures for performances with the Leipzig Collegium Musicum. Fasch's innovative orch. writing foreshadowed the Classical style of Haydn and Mozart. Although much of his vocal output is not extant, many of his orch. works have survived. Two of his operas were performed in 1711; he also composed 12 cantata cycles, 16 masses and mass movements, 5 Psalms, 19 syms., some 90 overtures (suites), and about 70 concertos. His autobiography appeared in vol. III of F.W. Marpurg's *Historisch-kritische Beyträge zur Aufnahme der Musik* (Berlin, 1757).

BIBL.: P. Tryphon, *Die Symphonien von J.F. F.* (diss., Free Univ. of Berlin, 1954); G. Küntzel, *Die Instrumentalkonzerte von J.F. F.* (diss., Univ. of Frankfurt, 1965); D. Sheldon, *The Chamber Music of J.F. F.* (diss., Indiana Univ., 1968).

Fasch, Karl Friedrich Christian (baptized **Christian Friedrich Carl**), noted German harpsichordist, choral conductor, and composer, son of **Johann Friedrich Fasch;** b. Zerbst, Nov. 18, 1736; d. Berlin, Aug. 3, 1800. He studied keyboard playing and theory with his father, then violin with Karl Höckh, concertmaster of the Zerbst Court Orch.; from the age of 14 he received a thorough music education from Johann Wilhelm Hertel in Strelitz. While in Strelitz, he impressed the violinist Franz Benda, who recommended him to the court of Friedrich the Great in Berlin as 2nd harpsichordist (1756). He was also active as a teacher and composer in Berlin. When C.P.E. Bach left the Berlin court for Hamburg in 1767, Fasch was named his successor as principal harpsichordist. He also served as conductor of the Royal Opera (1774–76). In later years his work at the court was greatly diminished, and he devoted himself to teaching, conducting, and composing. In 1789 he organized his own choral society, which soon became known as the Singakademie. He composed a great amount of sacred vocal music, much of which he discarded. A supposedly complete ed. of his works was publ. by the Singakademie (7 vols., Berlin, 1839).

BIBL.: K. Zelter, *K.F.C. F.* (Berlin, 1801); C. von Winterfeld, *Über K.F.C. F.'s geistliche Gesangwerke* (Berlin, 1829); M. Blumner, *Geschichte der Sing-Akademie zu Berlin* (Berlin, 1891); G. Schünemann, *Die Singakademie zu Berlin* (Regensburg, 1941).

Fassbänder, Brigitte, noted German mezzo-soprano, daughter of **Willi Domgraf-Fassbänder;** b. Berlin, July 3, 1939. She studied with her father; made her debut at the Bavarian State Opera, Munich, in 1961; soon established herself as one of its leading singers. She also made appearances at La Scala, Milan, the Vienna State Opera, Covent Garden, London, etc. She made her Metropolitan Opera debut in N.Y. as Octavian on Feb. 16, 1974. Her repertoire ranges from Gluck to Richard Strauss in opera; she is also adept in lieder.

Fassbender, Zdenka, Bohemian soprano; b. Děčín, Dec. 12, 1879; d. Munich, March 14, 1954. She studied voice in Prague; made her operatic debut in Karlsruhe in 1899; from 1906 to 1919 she was one of the principal singers at the Munich Opera; she also sang at Covent Garden in London (1910, 1913). The famous conductor **Felix Mottl** married her on his deathbed to sanction a lifelong alliance.

Fattorini, Gabriele, Italian composer; b. Faenza in the latter part of the 16th century; place and date of death unknown. He was maestro di cappella at Faenza, and possibly in Venice. His compositions include *Sacri concerti a due voci* (Venice, 1600; further eds., 1602, 1608); *Completorium romanum* (Venice, 1602); motets, madrigals, etc. Several of his works appeared in contemporaneous collections between 1605 and 1622 (Bodenschatz, Donfried, Diruta, etc.). Two of his ricercari for organ are in vol. III of Torchi's *L'arte musicale in Italia.* Banchieri mentions Fattorini in his *Conclusioni del suono dell'Organo* (Lucca, 1591; Bologna, 1609).
BIBL.: C. Wilkinson, "G. F.: Rival of Viadana," *Music & Letters* (Oct. 1984).

Fauchet, Paul Robert, French composer; b. Paris, June 27, 1881; d. there, Nov. 12, 1937. He studied at the Paris Cons., and later taught harmony there; also was maître de chapelle of St.-Pierre de Chaillot in Paris. He wrote a number of sacred works, but is remembered mainly for his *Symphonie* for Band, the earliest example of a classical sym. written for the medium (1936); its *Scherzo* is profusely enmeshed with whole-tone scales.

Fauchey, Paul, French composer; b. Paris, March 18, 1858; d. there, Nov. 15, 1936. He was active in the theater as a chorus master and then began to compose light operas, of which *La Carmagnole* (Paris, 1897) was quite popular for a time.

Faull, Ellen, American soprano and teacher; b. Pittsburgh, Oct. 14, 1918. She studied at the Curtis Inst. of Music in Philadelphia and at Columbia Univ.; made her debut as Donna Anna in *Don Giovanni* with the N.Y. City Opera on Oct. 23, 1947, establishing herself as one of its principals, singing there regularly until 1979. She also appeared in San Francisco, Boston, and Chicago, and as a soloist with many U.S. orchs. She taught at N.Y.'s Manhattan School of Music (from 1971) and the Juilliard School (from 1981). She was particularly noted for her roles in Italian opera.

Fauré, Gabriel (-Urbain), great French composer and pedagogue; b. Pamiers, Ariège, May 12, 1845; d. Paris, Nov. 4, 1924. His father was a provincial inspector of primary schools; noticing the musical instinct of his son, he took him to Paris to study with Louis Niedermeyer; after Niedermeyer's death in 1861, Fauré studied with Saint-Saëns, from whom he received thorough training in composition. In 1866 he went to Rennes as organist at the church of St.-Sauveur; returned to Paris on the eve of the Franco-Prussian War in 1870, and volunteered in the light infantry. He was organist at Notre Dame de Clignancourt (1870), St.-Honoré d'Elyau (1871), and St.-Sulpice (1871–74). He then was named deputy organist (to Saint-Saëns, 1874), choirmaster (1877), and chief organist (1896) at the Madeleine. In 1896 he was appointed prof. of composition at the Paris Cons. He was an illustrious teacher; among his students were Ravel, Enesco, Koechlin, Roger-Ducasse, Florent Schmitt, and Nadia Boulanger. In 1905 he succeeded Théodore Dubois as director and served until 1920. Then, quite unexpectedly, he developed ear trouble, resulting in gradual loss of hearing. Distressed, he made an effort to conceal it but was eventually forced to abandon his teaching position. From 1903 to 1921 he wrote occasional music reviews in *Le Figaro* (a selection was publ. as *Opinions musicales,* Paris, 1930). He was elected a member of the Académie des Beaux Arts in 1909, and in 1910 was made a Commander of

the Légion d'honneur. Fauré's stature as a composer is undiminished by the passage of time. He developed a musical idiom all his own; by subtle application of old modes he evoked the aura of eternally fresh art; by using unresolved mild discords and special coloristic effects, he anticipated procedures of Impressionism; in his piano works he shunned virtuosity in favor of the Classical lucidity of the French masters of the clavecin; the precisely articulated melodic line of his songs is in the finest tradition of French vocal music. His great Requiem and his *Élégie* for Cello and Piano have entered the general repertoire.

WORKS: STAGE: *Barnabé,* opéra-comique (1879; unfinished; not perf.); *Caligula,* op. 52, incidental music to a play by A. Dumas père (Paris, Nov. 8, 1888); *Shylock,* incidental music to a play by E. de Haraucourt, after Shakespeare, op. 57 (Paris, Dec. 17, 1889); *La Passion,* incidental music to a play by Haraucourt (Paris, April 21, 1890); *Le Bourgeois Gentilhomme,* incidental music to a play by Molière (1893); *Pelléas et Mélisande,* incidental music to a play by Maeterlinck, op. 80 (London, June 21, 1898); *Prométhée,* tragédie lyrique, op. 82 (Béziers, Aug. 27, 1900); *Le Voile du bonheur,* incidental music to a play by Clémenceau, op. 88 (Paris, Nov. 4, 1901); *Pénélope,* drame lyrique (Monte Carlo, March 4, 1913); *Masques et bergamasques,* comédie musicale, op. 112 (Monte Carlo, April 10, 1919). ORCH.: *Suite d'orchestre,* op. 20 (1865–74; 1st movement publ. in 1895 as *Allegro symphonique,* op. 68, in an arrangement for Piano, 4-hands, by L. Boëllmann); Violin Concerto, op. 14 (1878–79; 2nd movement destroyed); *Berceuse* for Violin and Orch., op. 16 (1880; original version for Violin and Piano, 1879); *Ballade* for Piano and Orch., op. 19 (Paris, April 23, 1881; original version for Solo Piano, 1877–79); *Romance* for Violin and Orch., op. 28 (1882; original version for Violin and Piano, 1877); Sym. in D minor, op. 40 (1884; Paris, March 15, 1885); *Pavane,* with Chorus ad libitum, op. 50 (1887; Paris, March 28, 1888); *Shylock,* suite from the incidental music, op. 57 (1890); *Menuet* in F major (1893); *Élégie* for Cello and Orch., op. 24 (1896?; original version for Cello and Piano, 1880); *Pelléas et Mélisande,* suite from the incidental music, op. 80 (1898); *Jules César,* suite after *Caligula,* op. 52 (1905); *Dolly,* suite, op. 56 (an orchestration by H. Rabaud [1906] of the pieces for Piano, 4-hands, 1894–97); *Fantaisie* for Piano and Orch., op. 111 (1918–19; Paris, March 14, 1919); *Masques et bergamasques,* suite from the comédie musicale, op. 112 (1919); *Chant funéraire* (1921). CHORAL: SACRED: *Super flumina* for Chorus and Orch. (1863); *Cantique de Jean Racine* for Chorus and Organ, op. 11 (1865; rev. version for Chorus, Harmonium, and String Quintet, 1866); *Cantique à St. Vincent de Paul* (1868; not extant); *Tu es Petrus* for Baritone, Chorus, and Organ (1872?); *Messe basse* for Soloists, Female Chorus, Harmonium, and Violin (1881); *Messe de Requiem* (1886–87; orig. in 5 movements for Soprano, Chorus, Organ, String Ensemble, and Timpani; Madeleine, Paris, Jan. 16, 1888; expanded to 7 movements, adding a Baritone Solo, Horns, and Trumpets, c.1889; full orch. version, c.1900); *Tantum ergo* in E major for Chorus, 3 Children's Voices, Solo Voices, and Organ, op. 65, no. 2 (1894); *Sancta mater* for Tenor, Chorus, and Organ (1894); *Tantum ergo* in F major for Soprano, Chorus, and Organ (1904). SECULAR: *Les Djinns* for Chorus and Orch., op. 12 (1875?); *La Naissance de Vénus* for Soloists, Chorus, and Orch., op. 29 (1882; Paris, April 3, 1886); etc. CHAMBER (all 1st perf. in Paris, op. 89 excepted): Violin Sonata No. 1, op. 13 (1875–76; Jan. 27, 1877); Piano Quartet No. 1, op. 15 (1876–79; Feb. 14, 1880; rev. 1883); *Romance* for Violin and Piano, op. 28 (1877; Feb. 3, 1883; 2nd version for Violin and Orch., 1882); *Berceuse* for Violin and Piano, op. 16 (1879; Feb. 14, 1880; 2nd version for Violin and Orch., 1880); *Élégie* for Cello and Piano, op. 24 (1880; Dec. 15, 1883; 2nd version for Cello and Orch., 1896?); *Papillon* for Cello and Piano, op. 77 (1884?); Piano Quartet No. 2, op. 45 (1885–86; Jan. 22, 1887); *Petite pièce* for Cello, op. 49 (1887?); *Romance* for Cello and Piano, op. 69 (1894); *Andante* for Violin and Piano, op. 75 (1897; Jan. 22, 1898); *Sicilienne* for Cello or Violin, and Piano, op. 78 (1898); *Fantaisie* for

Flute and Piano, op. 79 (July 28, 1898; orchestrated by L. Aubert, 1957); Piano Quintet No. 1, op. 89 (1887–95; 1903–5; Brussels, March 23, 1906); *Sérénade* for Cello and Piano, op. 98 (1908); Violin Sonata No. 2, op. 108 (1916–17; Nov. 10, 1917); Cello Sonata No. 1, op. 109 (1917; Jan. 19, 1918); Piano Quintet No. 2, op. 115 (1919–21; May 21, 1921); Cello Sonata No. 2, op. 117 (1921; May 13, 1922); Piano Trio, op. 120 (1922–23; May 12, 1923); String Quartet, op. 121 (1923–24; June 12, 1925). **SONGS:** *Le Papillon et la fleur*, op. 1, no. 1 (V. Hugo; 1861); *Mai*, op. 1, no. 2 (Hugo; 1862); *Rêve d'amour*, op. 5, no. 2 (Hugo; 1862); *L'Aube nait* (Hugo; 1862); *Puisque j'ai mis lèvre* (Hugo; 1862); *Tristesse d'Olympio* (Hugo; 1865); *Dans les ruines d'une abbaye*, op. 2, no. 1 (Hugo; 1866); *Les Matelots*, op. 2, no. 2 (T. Gautier; 1870); *Lydia*, op. 4, no. 2 (Leconte de Lisle; 1870); *Hymne*, op. 7, no. 2 (C. Baudelaire; 1870); *Seule!*, op. 3, no. 1 (Gautier; 1871); *L'Absent*, op. 5, no. 3 (Hugo; 1871); *L'Aurore* (Hugo; 1871); *La Rançon*, op. 8, no. 2 (Baudelaire; 1871); *Chant d'automne*, op. 5, no. 1 (Baudelaire; 1871); *La Chanson de pêcheur*, op. 4, no. 1 (Gautier; 1872); *Aubade*, op. 6, no. 1 (L. Pomey; 1873); *Tristesse*, op. 6, no. 2 (Gautier; 1873); *Barcarolle*, op. 7, no. 3 (M. Monnier; 1873); *Ici-bas!*, op. 8, no. 3 (S. Prudhomme; 1874); *Au bord de l'eau*, op. 8, no. 1 (Prudhomme; 1875); *Sérénade toscane*, op. 3, no. 2 (1878); *Après un rêve*, op. 7, no. 1 (1878); *Sylvie*, op. 6, no. 3 (P. de Choudens; 1878); *Nell*, op. 18, no. 1 (Leconte de Lisle; 1878); *Le Voyageur*, op. 18, no. 2 (A. Silvestre; 1878); *Automne*, op. 18, no. 3 (Silvestre; 1878); *Poème d'un jour*, op. 21 (C. Grandmougin; 1878); *Les Berceaux*, op. 23, no. 1 (Prudhomme; 1879); *Notre amour*, op. 23, no. 2 (Silvestre; 1879); *Le Secret*, op. 23, no. 3 (Silvestre; 1880–81); *Chanson d'amour*, op. 27, no. 1 (Silvestre; 1882); *La Fée aux chansons*, op. 27, no. 2 (Silvestre; 1882); *Aurore*, op. 39, no. 1 (Silvestre; 1884); *Fleur jetée*, op. 39, no. 2 (Silvestre; 1884); *Le Pays des rêves*, op. 39, no. 3 (Silvestre; 1884); *Les Roses d'Ispahan*, op. 39, no. 4 (Leconte de Lisle; 1884); *Noël*, op. 43, no. 1 (V. Wilder; 1886); *Nocturne*, op. 43, no. 2 (Villiers de l'Isle Adam; 1886); *Les Présents*, op. 46, no. 1 (Villiers de l'Isle Adam; 1887); *Clair de lune*, op. 46, no. 2 (P. Verlaine; 1887); *Larmes*, op. 51, no. 1 (J. Richepin; 1888); *Au cimetière*, op. 51, no. 2 (Richepin; 1888); *Spleen*, op. 51, no. 3 (Verlaine; 1888); *La Rose*, op. 51, no. 4 (Leconte de Lisle; 1890); *Chanson and Madrigal*, op. 57 (Haraucourt; 1889); *En prière* (S. Bordèse; 1889); *Cinq mélodies "de Venise,"* op. 58 (Verlaine): *Mandoline; En sourdine; Green; À Clymène; C'est l'extase* (1891); *Sérénade du Bourgeois gentilhomme*, op. posth. (Molière; 1893); *La Bonne Chanson*, op. 61 (Verlaine): *Une Sainte en son auréole; Puisque l'aube grandit; La Lune blanche luit dans les bois; J'allais par des chemins perfides; J'ai presque peur, en vérité; Avant que tu ne t'en ailles; Donc, ce sera par un clair jour d'été; N'est-ce pas?; L'Hiver a cessé* (1892–94); *Prison*, op. 83, no. 1 (Verlaine; 1894); *Soir*, op. 83, no. 2 (A. Samain; 1894); *Le Parfum inpérissable*, op. 76, no. 1 (Leconte de Lisle; 1897); *Arpège*, op. 76, no. 2 (Samain; 1897); *Melisande's Song*, op. posth. (Maeterlinck; tr. by Mackail; 1898); *Dans la forêt de septembre*, op. 85, no. 1 (C. Mendès; 1902); *La Fleur qui va sur l'eau*, op. 85, no. 2 (Mendès; 1902); *Accompagnement*, op. 85, no. 3 (Samain; 1902); *Le Plus Doux Chemin*, op. 87, no. 1 (Silvestre; 1904); *Le Ramier*, op. 87, no. 2 (Silvestre; 1904); *Le Don silencieux*, op. 92 (J. Dominique; 1906); *Chanson*, op. 94 (H. de Regnier; 1906); *Vocalise-étude* (1907); *La Chanson d'Ève*, op. 95 (C. Van Lerberghe; 1906–10); *Le Jardin clos*, op. 106 (Van Lerberghe; 1914); *Mirage*, op. 113 (Baronne A. de Brimont; 1919); *C'est la paix*, op. 114 (G. Debladis; 1919); *L'Horizon chimérique*, op. 118 (J. de la Ville de Mirmont; 1921). **PIANO** (all for Solo Piano unless otherwise given): *3 romances sans paroles*, op. 17 (1863); *Intermède symphonique* for Piano, 4-hands (1869; included as the Ouverture in *Masques et bergamasques*, op. 112); *Gavotte* (1869; also in the Sym., op. 20, and *Masques et bergamasques*, op. 112); *Prélude et fugue* (1869; fugue the same as op. 84, no. 6); *Nocturne* No. 1, op. 33, no. 1 (1875); *Ballade*, op. 19 (1877–79; 2nd version for Piano and Orch., 1881); *Mazurka*, op. 32 (1878); *Nocturne* No. 2, op. 33, no. 2 (1880); *Barcarolle* No. 1, op. 26 (1880); *Impromptu*

No. 1, op. 25 (1881); *Valse-caprice* No. 1, op. 30 (1882); *Nocturne* No. 3, op. 33, no. 3 (1882); *Impromptu* No. 2, op. 31 (1883); *Impromptu* No. 3, op. 34 (1883); *Nocturne* No. 4, op. 36 (1884); *Nocturne* No. 5, op. 37 (1884); *Valse-caprice* No. 2, op. 38 (1884); *Barcarolle* No. 2, op. 41 (1885); *Barcarolle* No. 3, op. 42 (1885); *Barcarolle* No. 4, op. 44 (1886); *Valse-caprice* No. 3, op. 59 (1887–93); *Souvenirs de Bayreuth: Fantaisie en forme de quadrille sur les thèmes favoris de l'Anneau de Nibelung* for Piano, 4-hands, op. posth. (with Messager; 1888); *Valse-caprice* No. 4, op. 62 (1893–94); *Dolly*, pieces for Piano, 4-hands, op. 56 (1894–97; orchestrated by H. Rabaud, 1906); *Nocturne* No. 6, op. 63 (1894); *Barcarolle* No. 5, op. 66 (1894); *Allegro symphonique* for Piano, 4-hands, op. 68 (an arrangement by L. Boëllmann [1895] of the 1st movement of the *Suite d'orchestre*, op. 20 [c.1865]); *Thème et variations*, op. 73 (1895; orchestrated by Inghelbrecht, 1955); *Barcarolle* No. 6, op. 70 (1896); *Nocturne* No. 7, op. 74 (1898); *8 pièces brèves*, op. 84 (1869–1902); *Barcarolle* No. 7, op. 90 (1905); *Impromptu* No. 4, op. 91 (1905–6); *Barcarolle* No. 8, op. 96 (1906); *Nocturne* No. 9, op. 97 (1908); *Nocturne* No. 10, op. 99 (1908); *Barcarolle* No. 9, op. 101 (1909); *Impromptu* No. 5, op. 102 (1909); *9 préludes*, op. 103 (1909–10); *Nocturne* No. 11, op. 104, no. 1 (1913); *Barcarolle* No. 10, op. 104, no. 2 (1913); *Barcarolle* No. 11, op. 105 (1913); *Barcarolle* No. 12, op. 106bis (1915); *Nocturne* No. 12, op. 107 (1915); *Barcarolle* No. 13, op. 116 (1921); *Nocturne* No. 13, op. 119 (1921).

BIBL.: Special issue of *Musica*, no. 77 (1909); L. Vuillemin, *G. F. et son œuvre* (Paris, 1914); special issue of *La Revue Musicale*, III/11 (1922); L. Aguettant, *La Génie de G. F.* (Lyons, 1924); A. Copland, "G. F.: A Neglected Master," *Musical Quarterly* (Oct. 1924); A. Bruneau, *La Vie et les œuvres de G. F.* (Paris, 1925); C. Koechlin, *G. F.* (Paris, 1927; Eng. tr., 1945; 2nd ed., 1949); P. Fauré-Fremiet, *G. F.* (Paris, 1929; 2nd ed., augmented, 1957); G. Servières, *G. F.* (Paris, 1930); V. Jankélévitch, *G. F. et ses mélodies* (Paris, 1938; 3rd ed., augmented, 1974, as *G. F. et l'inexprimable*); G. Faure, *G. F.* (Paris, 1945); C. Rostand, *L'Œuvre de F.* (Paris, 1945); special issue of *La Revue Musicale* (May 1945); N. Suckling, *F.* (London, 1946); M. Favre, *G. F.s Kammermusik* (Zürich, 1949); V. Jankélévitch, *Le Nocturne: F., Chopin et la nuit, Satie et le matin* (Paris, 1957); E. Vuillermoz, *G. F.* (Paris, 1960; Eng. tr., 1969); M. Long, *Au piano avec G. F.* (Paris, 1963); J.-M. Nectoux, *F.* (Paris, 1972; 2nd ed., augmented, 1986); idem, *Phonographie de G. F.* (Paris, 1979; documents, articles, and iconography); R. Orledge, *G. F.* (London, 1979); J.-M. Nectoux, ed., *G. F.: Correspondance* (Paris, 1980); idem, *G. F.: His Life through His Letters* (London, 1984); J. Rutter, "In Search of the Real F. Requiem," *American Organist* (Nov. 1984; provides an in-depth chronology of the *Requiem* as it is known today); J. Barrie Jones, translator and ed., *G. F.: A Life in Letters* (London, 1989); R. Tait, *The Musical Language of G. F.* (N.Y. and London, 1989).

Faure, Jean-Baptiste, famous French baritone; b. Moulins, Jan. 15, 1830; d. Paris, Nov. 9, 1914. He was a choirboy in Paris; entered the Paris Cons. in 1851; on Oct. 20, 1852, he made his operatic debut at the Opéra-Comique as Pygmalion in Massé's *Galathée*. He subsequently created the roles of Malipieri in Auber's *Haydée* (July 5, 1853) and Hoël in Meyerbeer's *Dinorah, ou Le Pardon de Ploërmel* (April 4, 1859) there. It was as Hoël that he made his Covent Garden debut in London on April 10, 1860; he continued to sing there, as well as at Drury Lane and Her Majesty's Theatre, until 1877. He made his debut at the Paris Opéra as Julien in Poniatowsky's *Pierre de Médicis* on Oct. 14, 1861; he continued to sing there until 1869, and then again from 1872 to 1876 and in 1878. Among the roles he created at the Opéra were Nelusko in Meyerbeer's *L'Africaine* (April 28, 1865), Posa in Verdi's *Don Carlos* (March 11, 1867), and Hamlet in Thomas's opera (March 9, 1868). In later years he appeared in concerts, garnering notable acclaim in Vienna and London. He excelled in dramatic roles in French and Italian operas, and was particularly renowned for his portrayals of Don Giovanni, Méphistophélès, and Guillaume Tell. He publ. 2 books on singing, and also taught at the Paris Cons. (1857–60). He was married to the singer **Constance Caroline Lefèbvre** (1828–1905).

BIBL.: H. de Curzon, "J.-B. F.," *Musical Quarterly* (April 1918); idem, *J.-B. F.* (Paris, 1923).

Favart, Charles-Simon, French librettist and impresario; b. Paris, Nov. 13, 1710; d. Belleville, near Paris, March 12, 1792. He publ. satirical plays as a youth; after a successful performance of one of his vaudevilles at the Opéra-Comique, he was appointed stage manager there; in 1758 he became its director. In 1745 he married **Marie Favart.** He wrote about 150 librettos for operas by Duni, Philidor, and Gluck; he was also the author of *Les Amours de Bastien et Bastienne* (1753), used by Mozart in a German version for his early opera (1768).

Favart, Marie (original name, **Marie-Justine-Benoît Duronceray**), French soprano; b. Avignon, June 15, 1727; d. Paris, April 21, 1772. She married **Charles-Simon Favart** in 1745; went with him to Paris, where she sang soubrette roles at the Théâtre-Italien (from 1751) with notable success, often appearing in works for which her husband had prepared the librettos. She became involved in various theatrical intrigues in Paris; an account of these was publ. by Pougin in his book *Madame Favart* (1912). Offenbach's operetta *Mme. Favart* (1878) was based on her life.

Favero, Mafalda, Italian soprano; b. Portamaggiore, near Ferrara, Jan. 6, 1905; d. Milan, Sept. 3, 1981. She studied in Bologna; then sang in Cremona and Parma. In 1929 Toscanini invited her to sing at La Scala in Milan. She was engaged by Covent Garden in London in 1937; on Nov. 24, 1938, she sang Mimi at her Metropolitan Opera debut in N.Y. From 1945 to 1950 she once again sang at La Scala. She was at her best in Italian and French roles.

BIBL.: I. Buscaglia, *M. F. nella vita e nell'arte* (1946).

Fay, Amy (Amelia Muller), American pianist, teacher, and writer on music; b. Bayou Goula, La., May 21, 1844; d. Watertown, Mass., Feb. 28, 1928. She studied in Berlin with Tausig and Kullak; then became a pupil of Liszt in Weimar. She gained recognition as a pianist in Boston (1875–78); then went to Chicago, where she was active as a lecturer, writer on music, and teacher, as well as a pianist. She promoted the cause of women in American music; served as president of the N.Y. Women's Phil. Soc. (1903–14). She publ. a vivid book of impressions, *Music-Study in Germany* (1880), which went through more than 25 printings and was tr. into French and German.

Fay, Maude, American soprano; b. San Francisco, April 18, 1878; d. there, Oct. 7, 1964. She studied in Dresden; became a member of the Munich Opera (1906–14); appeared at Covent Garden in London in 1910, and with the Beecham Opera Co. in 1914. After the outbreak of World War I, she returned to America; sang with the Metropolitan Opera in 1916; also appeared with the Chicago Opera Co. She was particularly distinguished in Wagnerian roles.

Fayer, Yuri, Russian conductor; b. Kiev, Jan. 17, 1890; d. Moscow, Aug. 3, 1971. He studied violin at the Kiev Cons.; played in various orchs.; in 1909–10, conducted opera in Riga; in 1916, joined the orch. of the Bolshoi Theater in Moscow; from 1923 to 1963 conducted ballet there; toured Europe, America, and China with the ballet troupe. He publ. an autobiography, *Of Me, of Music, of Ballet* (1970).

Fayolle, François (-Joseph-Marie), French writer on music and literature; b. Paris, Aug. 15, 1774; d. there, Dec. 2, 1852. A man of brilliant faculties, he was equally proficient in mathematics and poetry; also studied harmony and cello; after 1814 he lived in London; returned to Paris in 1830; he died in an almshouse. He contributed a number of articles to Fétis's *Biographie universelle;* together with Choron, he publ. *Dictionnaire historique des musiciens . . .* (Paris, 1810–11); his other writings on music include *Notices sur Corelli, Tartini, Gaviniès, Pugnani et Viotti* (Paris, 1810); *Sur les drames lyriques et leur exécution* (Paris, 1813); *Paganini et Bériot* (Paris, 1830).

Fayrfax, Robert, English composer; b. Deeping Gate, Lincolnshire (baptized), April 23, 1464; d. St. Alban, Hertfordshire, Oct. 24, 1521. He was a Gentleman of the Chapel Royal in 1496, and organist at St. Alban's Abbey and at King's Chapel (1497–98); received a B.Mus. (1501) and a D.Mus. (1504) from Cambridge Univ. and a D.Mus. from Oxford Univ. (1511; with his Mass *O quam glorifica*). In 1520 he led the Royal Singers accompanying King Henry VIII to the Field of the Cloth of Gold in France. Of his works, 29 are extant: 6 masses (4 are in the Oxford Museum School Collection), 2 Magnificats, 10 motets, 8 part-songs, 3 instrumental pieces. His sacred and secular vocal works are in the *Fayrfax Book* (British Library MS Add. 5465); lute arrangements of several sacred compositions and an instrumental piece for 3 parts are in the British Library. E. Warren ed. *Robert Fayrfax: Collected Works,* in Corpus Mensurabilis Musicae, XVII/1–3 (1959–66).

BIBL.: Dom A. Hughes, "An Introduction to F.," *Musica Disciplina* (1952); E. Warren, *Life and Works of R. F., 1464–1521,* in Musicological Studies and Documents, XXII (1969).

Feather, Leonard (Geoffrey), English-born American writer on music; b. London, Sept. 13, 1914. He studied at St. Paul School in London; in 1935 he went to the U.S.; was naturalized in 1948. He held various jobs as an arranger, lyricist, adviser for jazz festivals, radio commentator, and lecturer; specialized in the field of jazz and folk music; publ. *Inside Bebop* (N.Y., 1949); *The Encyclopedia of Jazz* (N.Y., 1955; 2nd ed., rev., 1960); *The Encyclopedia of Jazz in the 60's* (1966); *The Encyclopedia of Jazz in the '70s* (1976); *The Passion for Jazz* (1980); *The Jazz Years: Earwitness to an Era* (1987).

Fechner, Gustave Theodor, German music theorist; b. Gross-Särchen, Niederlausitz, April 19, 1801; d. Leipzig, Nov. 18, 1887. He was a prof. of physics at the Univ. of Leipzig from 1834. He publ. *Repertorium der Experimentalphysik,* in which musical phenomena are treated; also *Elemente der Psychophysik* (2 vols., 1860) and *Vorschule der Aesthetik* (2 vols., 1870), valuable as establishing a basis of musical esthetics.

Fedeli, Vito, Italian composer; b. Foglimo, June 19, 1866; d. Novara, June 23, 1933. He was a pupil of Terziani in Rome; was director of the Novara Cons. from 1904. He contributed valuable historical articles to the *Rivista Musicale Italiana* and the *Zeitschrift der Internationalen Musik-Gesellschaft;* also wrote a book, *Giacomo e Gaudenzio Battistini* (1932).

WORKS: Operas: *La Vergine della Montagna* (Reggio-Calabria, Sept. 6, 1897) and *Varsovia* (Rome, Dec. 15, 1900); several masses a cappella; also pieces for Orch.

BIBL.: G. Bustico, *Bibliografia di un musico novarese, V. F.* (1925).

Feder, (Franz) Georg, German musicologist; b. Bochum, Nov. 30, 1927. He studied composition in Bochum; then served as director of stage music at the local Schauspielhaus; subsequently studied musicology at the Univs. of Tübingen, Göttingen, and Kiel; received his Ph.D. from the Univ. of Kiel in 1955 with the dissertation *Bachs Werke in ihren Bearbeitungen 1750–1950, I: Die Vokalwerke.* In 1957 he became assistant to Jens Peter Larsen at the Joseph-Haydn-Inst. in Cologne; he succeeded Larsen as its director in 1960; as such, he became chief ed. of the complete edition of Haydn's works; he also served as ed. of the publication *Haydn-Studien* from 1965. He publ. *Musikphilologie: Eine Einführung in die musikalische Textkritik, Hermeneutik und Editionstechnik* (Darmstadt, 1987).

Federhofer, Hellmut, eminent Austrian musicologist; b. Graz, Aug. 6, 1911. He studied piano and theory in Graz; then continued his studies at the Vienna Academy of Music with Stöhr and Kabasta, graduating in 1936 with a diploma in conducting. He also took private lessons in composition with Alban Berg, Ernst von Sauer, and Oswald Jonas. He took courses in musicology with Alfred Orel and Robert Lach at the Univ. of Vienna; received his Ph.D. there in 1936 with the dissertation *Akkordik und Harmonik in frühen Motetten der Trienter Codices.* From 1937 to 1944 he was State Librarian.

He completed his Habilitation in 1944 at the Univ. of Graz with his *Musikalische Form als Ganzheit* (publ. as *Beiträge zur musikalische Gestaltanalyse*, Graz, 1950). He became Privatdozent at the Univ. of Graz in 1945; in 1951 prof. of musicology. In 1962 he became director of the Musicological Inst. at the Johannes Gutenberg Univ. in Mainz. That same year he became ed. of *Acta Musicologica*. His publications range widely, covering the history of Austrian court music, biographical data of little-known composers of the Renaissance, and abstruse points of old and new music theory. He has also ed. works by Fux and Mozart. His books include *Musikpflege und Musiker am Grazer Habsburgerhof der Erzherzöge Karl und Ferdinand von Innerösterreich (1564–1619)* (Mainz, 1967), *Neue Musik: Ein Literaturbericht* (Tutzing, 1977), *Akkord und Stimmführung in den Musiktheoretischen Systemen von Hugo Riemann, Ernst Kurth und Heinrich Schenker* (Vienna, 1981), and *Musikwissenschaft und Musikpraxis* (Vienna, 1985). He also contributed a great number of articles to various publications dealing with the musical history of Graz.

Federici, Vincenzo, Italian composer; b. Pesaro, 1764; d. Milan, Sept. 26, 1826. He became an orphan at 16; lived in Turin, where he produced his 1st opera, *L'Olimpiade* (Dec. 26, 1789). He then made his way to London, where he became cembalist at the Italian Opera; returned to Italy in 1802; in 1808 he became a teacher of harmony at the Milan Cons.

Fedorov, Vladimir, Russian-born French music librarian and historian; b. near Chernigov, Aug. 18, 1901; d. Paris, April 9, 1979. He studied at the Univ. of Rostov; emigrated to Turkey in 1920; then settled in Paris, where he studied art, archeology, and music; took lessons with Gédalge and Vidal; later took additional courses in Germany. In 1933 he became librarian at the Sorbonne; later took a post in the music division of the Bibliothèque Nationale in Paris (1946–66). He publ. *Moussorgsky, Biographie critique* (Paris, 1935); contributed numerous articles on musical subjects to French publications; was ed. of *Fontes Artis Musicae* from 1954 to 1976.

Fedoseyev, Vladimir, prominent Russian conductor; b. Leningrad, Aug. 5, 1932. He studied with N. Reznikov at the Gnesin Inst. in Moscow (graduated, 1957) and with L. Ginzburg at the Moscow Cons. (graduated, 1971); he conducted an orch. of native instruments (1959–74) and was principal conductor of the Grand Orch. of the All-Union Radio and Television in Moscow (from 1974). He is distinguished for his interpretations of 19th-century Russian music as well as for his work with indigenous music. In 1970 he was awarded the Glinka Prize, and in 1973 was made a National Artist of the Russian S.F.S.R.

Fehr, Max, Swiss musicologist; b. Bülach, near Zürich, June 17, 1887; d. Winterthur, April 27, 1963. He studied at the Univ. of Zürich with Eduard Bernoulli (Ph.D., 1912). In 1917 he became librarian, and in 1923 president, of the Allgemeine Musikgesellschaft of Zürich; retired as librarian in 1957.

WRITINGS: *Spielleute im alten Zürich* (Zürich, 1916); *Die Meistersinger von Zürich,* satirical novelette (Zürich, 1916); *Unter Wagners Taktstock* (Winterthur, 1922); *Geschichte des Musikkollegiums Winterthur, I. Teil: 1629–1830* (1929); *Richard Wagners Schweizer Zeit,* in 2 vols. (Aarau, 1934, 1953); *Die Familie Mozart in Zürich* (Zürich, 1942); *Die wandernden Theatertruppen in der Schweiz: Verzeichnis der Truppen, Aufführungen und Spieldaten für das 17. und 18. Jahrhundert* (Einsiedeln, 1949); *Der junge Mozart in Zürich* (with L. Caflisch; Zürich, 1952); *Musikalische Jagd* (Zürich, 1954).

BIBL.: E. Nievergelt, *M. F.* (Zürich, 1968).

Feicht, Hieronim, Polish musicologist; b. Mogilno, near Poznan, Sept. 22, 1894; d. Warsaw, March 31, 1967. He studied theology; then turned to music and took courses in composition with Wallek-Walewski in Krakow, and with Chybiński in Lwow (Ph.D., Univ. of Lwow, 1925). He taught at the Krakow Cons. from 1927 to 1930 and again from 1935 to 1939; in the interim was a prof. at State College of Music in Warsaw (1930–32). From 1946 to 1952 he was chairman of the musicology dept.

at the Univ. of Wroclaw; subsequently was rector of the State College of Music in Wroclaw (1948–52), and a prof. of music history at the Univ. of Warsaw (1952–64). He publ. important essays on Polish music: *Musik-historische Bemerkungen über die Lemberger Handschriften des Bogarodzica-Liedes* (Poznan, 1925); *Wojciech Debolecki, Ein polnischer Kirchenkomponist aus der 1. Hälfte des 17. Jahrhunderts* (Lwow, 1926); *Polifonia renesansu* (Krakow, 1957); also ed. works by Polish composers. A Festschrift was publ. in honor of his 70th birthday in 1964.

Feinberg, Samuel, eminent Russian pianist and composer; b. Odessa, May 26, 1890; d. Moscow, Oct. 22, 1962. He moved to Moscow in 1894; studied piano with Goldenweisser at the Cons.; also took theory lessons with Zhilayev; graduated in 1911. In 1922 he was appointed prof. of piano at the Cons., holding this post until his death; also gave piano recitals in Russia in programs emphasizing new Russian music; he performed all of Beethoven's sonatas and the complete set of Bach's *Wohl-temperiertes Clavier,* as well as Chopin and Schumann. As a composer he limited himself almost exclusively to piano music, which was influenced mainly by Chopin and Scriabin in its fluidity and enhanced tonality.

WORKS: 3 piano concertos (1931; 1944; 1947, rev. 1951); 12 piano sonatas (1915, 1916, 1917, 1918, 1921, 1923, 1924, 1933, 1939, 1940, 1954, 1960); 2 fantasias for Piano (1916–17; 1924); 4 preludes for Piano (1922); 3 preludes for Piano (1923); 2 suites for Piano (1926, 1936); 10 songs to words by Pushkin (1922, 1937); 7 songs to Lermontov's words; and 13 songs to words by Alexander Blok.

BIBL.: V. Belayev, *S. F.* (Moscow, 1927; in Russian and German); D. Gojowy, *Neue sowjetische Musik der 20er Jahre* (Regensburg, 1980).

Feinhals, Fritz, distinguished German baritone; b. Cologne, Dec. 4, 1869; d. Munich, Aug. 30, 1940. He studied in Milan and Padua; made his operatic debut in Essen in 1895; in 1898 he joined the Munich Court (later State) Opera, where he remained until his retirement in 1927. On Nov. 18, 1908, he made his debut at the Metropolitan Opera in N.Y. as Wotan in *Die Walküre,* but was on its roster for only the 1908–9 season. He also made appearances in London, Paris, and Vienna. He was a Wagnerian singer par excellence; his portrayal of Wotan was imperious in its power; he was also successful in the role of Hans Sachs. He also excelled in operas by Mozart and Verdi.

Feinstein, Michael (Jay), American singer and remarkably facile pianist of popular music; b. Columbus, Ohio, Sept. 7, 1956. He began playing piano by ear when he was 5, later being largely self-taught via the huge record collection he acquired while growing up. After graduating from high school, he worked in various Columbus locales before moving to Los Angeles (1976), where he became assistant to Ira Gershwin (1977–83), who proved an inspiring mentor. In 1984 he accompanied Liza Minnelli on Johnny Carson's "The Tonight Show," later pursuing a highly lucrative solo career on the supper club circuit, making appearances at posh social events, on television, and with U.S. orchs. He was a significant contributor to the revitalized interest in the 1980s in the songs of Gershwin, Berlin, and other composers of the era between the two world wars.

BIBL.: *Current Biography* (April 1988).

Fel, Marie, famous French soprano; b. Bordeaux, Oct. 24, 1713; d. Paris, Feb. 2, 1794. She studied with Christina VanLoo in Paris, making her debut as Venus in the prologue to La Coste's *Philomèle* at the Opéra on Oct. 29, 1734; she subsequently sang with notable success there, and also at court and at the Concert Spirituel. She retired from the operatic stage in 1758. She was renowned for her performances of roles in French operas. Sophie Arnould was one of her pupils. Her brother, **Antoine Fel** (b. Bordeaux, 1694; d. Bicêtre, June 27, 1771), was a singer at the Paris Opéra as well as a composer.

BIBL.: J.-G. Prod'homme, "M. F. (1713–1794)," *Sammelbände der Internationalen Musik-Gesellschaft,* IV (1902–3).

Felciano, Richard (James), American composer; b. Santa Rosa, Calif., Dec. 7, 1930. He studied with Darius Milhaud at Mills College; subsequently took courses at the Paris Cons. In 1958–59 he took private lessons with Luigi Dallapiccola in Florence. He holds a Ph.D. from the Univ. of Iowa (1959). He was the recipient of a Guggenheim fellowship in 1969 and 2 fellowships from the Ford Foundation (1964; 1971–73). He is also the holder of the American Academy of Arts and Letters Award (1974). From 1967 to 1971 he was resident composer at the National Center for Experiments in Television in San Francisco. At the same time he was also on the music faculty of the Univ. of Calif. at Berkeley.

Works: Opera, *Sir Gawain and the Green Knight* (San Francisco, April 4, 1964); *4 Poems from the Japanese* for 5 Harps, Women's Voices, and Percussion (1964); *The Captives* for Chorus and Orch. (1965); *Contractions*, theatrical mobile for Woodwind Quintet (1965); *Mutations* for Orch. (1966); *Aubade* for String Trio, Harp, and Piano (1966); *Glossolalia* for Organ, Baritone, Percussion, and Tape (1967); *Spectra* for Double Bass and Flute (1967); *Noösphere I* for Alto Flute and Tape (1967); *Noösphere II* for Electronic Tape (1967); *Trio* for Speaker, Screen, and Viewer, a videotape (1968); Quintet for Piano, Strings, and Electronic Tape (1970); *Lamentations for Jani Christou* for 12 Instruments and Electronic Tape (1970); *Soundspace for Mozart* for Flute, Electronics, and Tape (1970); *Galactic Rounds* for Orch. (1972); *Chod* for Violin, Cello, Double Bass, Piano, Percussion, and Electronics (1975); *The Passing of Enkidu* for Chorus, Piano, Percussion, and Tape (1975); *In Celebration of Golden Rain* for Indonesian Gamelan and Occidental Pipe Organ (1977); *Lumen*, duo for Soprano and Organ (1980); *Orchestra* for Orch. (San Francisco, Sept. 24, 1980); *Crystal* for String Quartet (1981); *Salvadore Allende* for String Quartet, Clarinet, and Percussion (1983); *Alleluia to the Heart of Stone* for Reverberated Recorder (1984); Organ Concerto (1986); piano pieces. **Bibl.:** S. Christiansen, *The Sacred Choral Music of R. F.: An Analytic Study* (diss., Univ. of Illinois, Urbana, 1977).

Feld, Jindřich, Czech composer; b. Prague, Feb. 19, 1925. He studied violin with his father; took composition with Hlobil at the Prague Cons. (1945–48) and with Řídký at the Prague Academy of Music (1948–52); also studied musicology at Charles Univ. (Ph.D., 1952). During the academic year 1968–69 he was a visiting prof. at the Univ. of Adelaide in Australia; returning to Prague, he was appointed to the staff of the Prague Cons. His early music is in a neo-Baroque manner, but he soon adopted a variety of modern techniques.

Works: Children's opera, *Postácká pohadka* (The Postman's Tale), after Čapek (1956); *Divertimento* for String Orch. (1950); *Furiant* for Orch. (1950); Concerto for Orch. (1951; rev. 1957); *Comedy Overture* (1953); Flute Concerto (1954; Czech Radio, Oct. 26, 1956); *Rhapsody* for Violin and Orch. (1956); Concerto in C for Chamber Orch. (1956–57); Cello Concerto (1958); Bassoon Concerto (1958–59); *May 1945*, dramatic overture (1959–60); Suite for Chamber String Orch. (1960–61); *Thuringian Ouverture* (1961); *3 Frescoes* for Orch. (Prague, Feb. 21, 1964); *Concert Music* for Oboe, Bassoon, and Orch. (1964); *Serenata giocosa* for Chamber Orch. (1966); *Concert Piece* for Horn and Orch. (1966); Sym. No. 1 (Prague, Jan. 23, 1969); *Dramatic Fantasy* for Orch. (1968–69); Oboe Concerto (1970); Piano Concerto (1973); Saxophone Concerto (1980); Harp Concerto (1982); Sym. No. 2 (1983); Suite for Clarinet and Piano (1948–49); 5 string quartets (1949; 1952; 1962; 1965; 1978–79); 2 wind quintets (1949, 1968); Sonatina for 2 Violins (1952–53); 2 *Compositions* for Cello and Piano (1954–55); Viola Sonata (1955); *Rhapsody* for Violin and Piano (1956); Flute Sonata (1957); *Chamber Suite* for Nonet (1960); String Trio (1961); Trio for Flute, Violin, and Cello (1963); *Capriccio* for Wind Quartet and Guitar (1964); Suite for Accordion (1965); *4 Intermezzos* for Accordion (1967); *Miniatures* for Violin, Guitar, and Accordion (1967–68); Brass Quintet (1969–70); *Concertante Suite* for Bass Clarinet and Piano (1971); Cello Sonata (1972); Prelude and Toccata for 2 Pianos (1960); Piano Sonata

(1971–72); *Mockery of Names* for Women's Chorus, Oboe, Clarinet, Bass Clarinet, Ocarina, Double Bass, Piano, and Percussion (1974); *Elegy* for Saxophone and Piano (1981); Oboe Sonata (1981–82); *Concert Music* for Viola and Piano (1983); Sonata for Violin and Piano (1985); many educational pieces.

Feldbrill, Victor, Canadian conductor; b. Toronto, April 4, 1924. He studied violin with Kathleen Parlow in Toronto and conducting with Monteux in Maine; later took lessons in conducting with Otterloo in Hilversum and Zallinger in Salzburg. He was assistant conductor of the Toronto Sym. (1956–57); then was music director of the Winnipeg Sym. (1958–68); in 1968 he joined the staff of the Univ. of Toronto, where he became conductor of its sym. orch. He also served as acting music director of the London, Ontario, Sym. in 1979–80. In 1990–91 he was interim music adviser of the Hamilton (Ontario) Phil. In most of his programs he included works by contemporary Canadian composers.

Feldbusch, Eric, Belgian cellist and composer; b. Grivegnée, March 2, 1922. He studied cello at the Liège Cons. (1934–39); later took courses in composition with Quinet and Legley (1947–48). He divided his time between concert activity as a cellist and teaching; was director of the Mons Cons. (1963–72) and of the Brussels Cons. (1974–87).

Works: stage: Opera, *Orestes* (1969); ballet, *El Diablo Cojuelo* (1972). **orch.:** *Variations sur un air connu* (1955); *Contrastes* (1956); *5 Brief Pieces* for String Orch. and Piano (1957); *Les Moineaux de Baltimore*, suite (1958; also as a radio play); *Adagio* for String Orch. (1958); *Adagio* for 3 Cellos and String Orch. (1960); *Mosaïque* for String Orch. (1961); *Overture* for String Orch. (1961); *Shema Israël* for String Orch. (1962); *Choral* for a group of Wind Instruments (1963); *3 poèmes de Federico García Lorca* for Voice and Orch. (1964); *Ode à des enfants morts* (1965–66); Violin Concerto (1967); *Fantaisie-Divertissement* (1967); *Cantique des cantiques* for Soprano and Orch. (1970); *Piccola musica* for String Orch. (1971); *Kadisch* for Baritone, Violin, and Strings (1974); *Triade* for Chamber Orch. (1977); *Dichroisme II* (1983); Concertante for 2 Pianos and Orch. (1986); Cello Concerto (1988). **chamber:** *Aquarelles* for Wind Quintet (1947); Sonata for Violin and Cello (1955); *Cadence and Allegro* for Cello and Piano (1956); Violin Sonata (1957); *3 pièces* for Viola, Cello, and Oboe (1957); Duo for Violin and Piano (1958); 4 string quartets (1955, 1958, 1963, 1971); *Mosaïque* for Cello (1958); Piano Trio (1958); Duo for Flute and Piano (1959); *Variations extra-formelles* for Cello and Piano (1959); Trio for Flute, Violin, and Cello (1959); Duo for Flute and Viola (1963); Septet for Soprano, 2 Violins, Double Bass, Flute, Trumpet, and Percussion (1969); *Arabesques* for Piano; *3 Movements* for Piano; *Dicht am Flüsschen*, variations for Piano (1960); *Cheminement* for Violin and Violin Ensemble (1984); incidental music for theater plays.

Felderhof, Jan (Reindert Adriaan), Dutch composer; b. Bussum, near Amsterdam, Sept. 25, 1907. He studied theory and composition with Sem Dresden at the Amsterdam Cons. In 1934 he was appointed to its faculty; remained there until 1954; taught at the music school in Bussum (1944–54) and at the Utrecht Cons. (1956–67), and was director of the Rotterdam Cons. (1954–55); in 1958 he was named chief theory teacher at the Amsterdam Cons., and then was its adjunct director (1968–73). His works have an agreeable veneer of simple musicality, and all are excellently written.

Works: opera: *Vliegvuur* (Wildfire; 1959–64; Dutch Radio, Nov. 10, 1965). **orch.:** *Music for 15 Winds and Percussion* (1930); *5 Dance Sketches* (1930); 2 sinfoniettas (1932, 1962); Suite for Flute and Small Orch. (1933); *Rhapsodie* for Oboe and Small Orch. (1937); Sym. (1949); *Ouverture* (1955); Concerto for Flute, String Orch., and Percussion (1955); *Omaggio* (1974); *Complimento* for String Orch. (1975); *Introduction and Rondo* (1980); *Chanterelle* (1985); *Nostalgic Suite* (1989). **chamber:** 3 violin sonatas (1932, 1939, 1965); 4 string quartets (1932, 1936, 1938, 1957); Suite for Flute and Piano (1933); String Trio (1934); Cello Sonata (1935); Piano Trio (1936);

Divertimento for Brass Quartet (1950); Violin Sonatina (1953); *Rondo* for Oboe, Clarinet, and Bassoon (1960); Trio for 3 Different Clarinets (1968); Suite for Flute, Oboe, and Piano (1974); Sonata for 2 Violins and Piano (1977); *Andante* for Flute, Oboe, and Harp (1983); *Music* for 15 Winds and Percussion (1986); Sonatine for Flute, Oboe, and Harp (1988); also several vocal works; 5 piano sonatinas (1933–62); piano and organ pieces; songs.

Feldhoff, Gerd, German baritone; b. Radervormwald, near Cologne, Oct. 29, 1931. He studied at the Northwest German Music Academy in Detmold; made his operatic debut in Essen in 1959 as Figaro in *Le nozze di Figaro;* then sang at the Städtische Oper in Berlin, the Hamburg State Opera, and the Frankfurt Opera. He made his Metropolitan Opera debut in N.Y. as Kaspar in *Der Freischütz* on Sept. 28, 1971. He was especially noted as a dramatic baritone; apart from opera he also made tours as a concert artist.

Feldman, Ludovic, Rumanian violinist and composer; b. Galati, June 6, 1893; d. Bucharest, Sept. 11, 1987. He studied with R. Klenck at the Bucharest Cons. (1910–11) and F. Ondříček at the New Vienna Cons. (1911–13), and later served as violinist with the Bucharest Phil. and State Opera Orch. (1926–40); he then studied composition with Mihail Jora (1941–42). He wrote a number of works in the neo-Classical style that had some performances in Bucharest but hardly anywhere else. Among his works were a Sym., several orch. suites, pieces for Violin and Orch., and several playable pieces of chamber music.

Feldman, Morton, American composer of the avant-garde; b. N.Y., Jan. 12, 1926; d. Buffalo, Sept. 3, 1987. He studied piano with Vera Maurina-Press in N.Y. and composition with Wallingford Riegger (1941) and Stepan Wolpe (1944). Profoundly impressed by the Abstract Expressionism of modern paintings and his friendship with John Cage, he evolved a congenial set of musical concepts based on the seemingly oxymoronic principle of predetermined indeterminacy, as exemplified in his *Projections I–IV* for aleatory instrumental combinations, with only an approximation of the notes in a work, performing a musical "action," indicating the instrumental range and the number of notes per specified time unit. In their immarcescible fidelity to the ideals of new music, his works left a profound impression on the theories and practices of the young composers of the waning years of the 20th century, so that even after his early death (of cancer of the pancreas), his works continued to enjoy frequent performances in America and Europe. In his geometric directness and expressive lucidity of technical devices, Feldman is the De Kooning of musical composition. He held a Guggenheim fellowship (1966); taught at the State Univ. of N.Y. in Buffalo (from 1972), where he held the Edgard Varèse Chair.

Works: *Projections I–IV* (1950–51); *Intersections I* for Orch. (1951), *II* and *III* for Piano (1952, 1953), and *IV* for Cello (1953); *Marginal Intersection* for Orch. (1951); *Extensions I and II* for Violin and Piano (1951), *III* for Piano (1952), *IV* for 3 Pianos (1952–53), and *V* for 2 Cellos (1953); *Structures* for String Quartet (1951); *2 Pieces* for 2 Pianos (1954); *3 Pieces* for String Quartet (1954–56); *Piece* for 4 Pianos (1957); *2 Pianos* for 2 Pianos (1957); *Atlantis* for Orch. (1958); Trio for 3 Pianos (1959); *Ixion (Summerspace),* ballet for 10 Instruments or 2 Pianos (1960; N.Y., April 14, 1966); *Structures* for Orch. (1960–62); *For Franz Kline* for Soprano, Violin, Cello, Horn, Chimes, and Piano (1962); *The Straits of Magellan* for 7 Instruments (1963); *De Kooning* for Piano, Violin, Cello, Horn, and Percussion (1963); *Vertical Thoughts I–IV* for Different Instrumental Combinations (1963); *Numbers* for 9 Instruments (1964); *The King of Denmark* for Percussion (1965); *1st Principles* for Large Instrumental Ensemble (1966–67); *False Relationships and the Extended Ending* for Instrumental Ensemble (1968); *On Time and the Instrumental Factor* for Orch. (1969); *Madame Press Died Last Week at 90* for Chamber Ensemble (St. Paul de Vence, July 20, 1970); *The Viola in My Life I* for Solo Viola and 6 Instrumentalists, *II* for Solo Viola and 7 Instrumentalists, *III* for Viola and Piano, and *IV* for Viola and Orch. (1970–71); *The Rothko Chapel* for Solo Viola, Voice, and Percussion (1971); *Pianos and Voices I* for 5 Pianists that hum, and *II* for 5 Pianos and 5 Voices (1972); *For Frank O'Hara* for 7 Instrumentalists (1973); *Routine Investigations* for Oboe, Trumpet, Piano, Viola, Cello, and Double Bass (1976); *Neither,* monodrama after an original text by Beckett, for Soprano and Orch. (Rome, May 13, 1977); *Piano* (1977); *Principal Sound* for Organ (1980); *The Turfan Fragments* for Chamber Orch. (1980); Trio for Violin, Viola, and Piano (1980); *Triadic Memories* for Piano (1981); untitled composition for Cello and Piano (1981); *For John Cage* for Violin and Piano (1982); *3 Voices* for 3 Sopranos or 3 Solo Violins and Tape (1982); *Clarinet and String Quartet* (1983); *Crippled Symmetry* for Flute, Bass Flute, Vibraphone, Glockenspiel, Piano, and Celesta (1983); String Quartet No. 2 (1983); *For Philip Guston* for Flute, Alto Flute, Percussion, Piano, and Celesta (1984); *For Bunita Marcus* for Piano (1985); *Violin and String Quartet* (1985).

Bibl.: K. Potter, *An Introduction to the Music of M. F.* (diss., Univ. of Wales, Cardiff, 1973); A. Brown, "An Introduction to the Music of M. F.," *Asterisk,* I/1 (1974); T. DeLio, *Circumscribing the Open Universe: Essays on Cage, F., Wolff, Ashley and Lucier* (Washington, D.C., 1984); W. Zimmermann, ed., *M. F. Essays* (Kerpen, 1985).

Feliciano, José, blind Puerto Rican singer, guitarist, and songwriter; b. Lares, Sept. 10, 1945. His family moved to N.Y. when he was 5; he taught himself to play the guitar, and then appeared in Greenwich Village clubs; his self-exclamatory record album *Feliciano!* brought him fame (it included his soulful version of the song *Light My Fire,* notable for its sexual and narcotic overtones). His blues rendition of *The Star-Spangled Banner* at the 1968 World Series in Detroit caused a furor, leading many radio stations to boycott him. After a hiatus of several years, he was able to renew his career. He toured in the U.S. and in Europe.

Felix, Hugo, Austrian composer of operettas; b. Vienna, Nov. 19, 1866; d. Los Angeles, Aug. 24, 1934. He produced several operettas in Vienna: *Husarenblut* (1894); *Das Kätzchen* (1892); etc.; and several in Berlin (*Madame Sherry,* 1902; etc.). After World War I he settled in America; wrote an operetta with an English text, *The Sweetheart Shop* (Chicago, 1920); also incidental music to Otis Skinner's *Sancho Panza,* and other plays.

Felix, Václav, prominent Czech composer and pedagogue; b. Prague, March 29, 1928. He studied composition with P. Bořkovec and V. Dobiáš at the Prague Academy of Music (graduated, 1953), then did postgraduate study in theory with K. Janeček (1953–56); he completed his education at the Charles Univ. in Prague (Ph.D. in philosophy, 1957; Candidatus scientiarum, 1961). He was ed. of *Hudebni Rozhledy* in Prague (1959–61). In 1960 he joined the faculty of the Prague Academy of Music, where he was head of the theory and music history dept. (1979–85) and dean (from 1985). From 1978 to 1989 he was vice president of the central committee of the Union of Czech Composers and Concert Artists. He received the prize of the Czech Minister of Culture (1976), was made an Artist of Merit (1978), and received the prize of the Union of Czech Composers and Concert Artists (1980) and the National Prize (1986). His music follows the golden mean of agreeable Central European modernism.

Works (all 1st perf. in Prague unless otherwise given): **operas:** *Nesmělý Kasanova aneb Čím zrají muži* (Shy Casanova or What Makes Men Ripe; 1966; Dec. 13, 1967); *Inzerát* (The Advertisement; Brno, April 25, 1975); *Mariana* (1982; April 11, 1985). **orch.:** *Concerto romantico* for Violin, Clarinet or Viola, Harp, and Strings (Oct. 19, 1953); *Fantasy* for Clarinet and Orch. (1959; March 30, 1960); *Concertant Variations* (1962; Feb. 17, 1963); Suite for String Orch. (1969); *Joyful Overture* (1971; March 8, 1972); *Concert Waltz* (1973); 5 syms.: No. 1 for Female Voice and Orch. (1974; May 25, 1975); No. 2 for Small Orch. (1981; Karlovy Vary, March 19, 1982); No.

3 for Choir and Orch. (1986; March 10, 1988); No. 4 (Nov. 12, 1987); No. 5 for Chamber Orch. (1987); Concertino for Flute and String Orch. (1976; Jan. 18, 1977); *Labor Victorious,* gala overture for Large Wind Orch. (1977; March 8, 1978); Double Concerto for Cello or Bass Clarinet, Piano, and String Orch. (1978; March 17, 1979); *Symphonic Variations on a Czech Recruit Song* for Large Wind Orch. (1979; March 23, 1980); *Summer Day Romance* for Clarinet and Orch. (1979; Teplice, July 3, 1980); Trumpet Concerto (1984; Poděbrady, May 20, 1986). **CHAMBER:** 3 piano trios (1955, 1956, 1962); Cello Sonata (1960); String Trio (1961); *The Story of Snow White,* quintet for Harp and String Quartet (1963); *Sonata a tre* for Violin, Viola, and Harp (1967); *Sonata da Requiem* for Horn or Bass Clarinet, and Piano (1969); Wind Quintet (1972); Brass Quintet (1972); Trio for Violin, Horn, and Piano (1973); Trio for Clarinet, Cello, and Piano (1977); *Quartetto amoroso* for 2 Violins, Viola, and Cello (1979); *We Have a Baby at Home,* suite for Flute, Violin, and Piano (1984); *A Small Afternoon* for Flute, Viola, and Cello (1985); *Sonata concertante* for Viola and Piano (1989); piano pieces, including 3 sonatinas (1969) and *Sonata poetica* (1988); also many vocal works, including choruses, songs, and the cantatas *The Celebration* (1963), *Where Do the Months Come From?* (1965), and *Always Generous* (1980; Olomouc, Sept. 3, 1981).

Fellegara, Vittorio, Italian composer; b. Milan, Nov. 4, 1927. He studied physics and mathematics at the Univ. of Milan (1945–50); concurrently took lessons in music theory with Luciano Chailly at the Verdi Cons. in Milan, graduating in 1951. He subsequently taught at the Donizetti Cons. in Bergamo. His music follows neo-Baroque models.
    WORKS: A ballet, *Mutazioni* (1962; La Scala, Milan, Jan. 27, 1965); 4 symphonic fragments (Copenhagen ISCM Festival, May 28, 1964); *Invenzioni* for Piano (1949); *Ricercare Fantasia* for Piano (1951); Concerto for Orch. (1952; Turin, Feb. 28, 1957); *Preludio, Fuga e Postludio* for Piano (1952–53); *Ottetto* for Winds (1953); *Concert breve* for Chamber Orch. (1956); *Sinfonia 1957* (Rome, June 28, 1958); *Requiem di Madrid* for Chorus and Orch. (1958; Turin, Oct. 17, 1959); *Dies irae* for Chorus, 6 Trumpets, Cymbals, and 7 Percussionists (1959); *Frammenti I* for Chamber Orch. (1960); *Serenata* for Chamber Orch. or 9 Instruments (1960); *Variazioni (Frammenti II)* for Chamber Orch. (1961); *Epitaphe* for 2 Sopranos and 5 Instrumentalists (1964); *Cantata* for 2 Female Voices and Orch. (Donaueschingen, Oct. 23, 1966); *Madrigale* for Vocal Quintet and 14 Instruments (1969); *Chanson* for Soprano and Chamber Orch. (1974; Milan, Nov. 29, 1975); *Omaggio a Bach* for Piano (1975).

Fellerer, Karl Gustav, eminent German musicologist and editor; b. Freising, July 7, 1902; d. Munich, Jan. 7, 1984. He studied at the Regensburg School of Church Music and took courses in composition with Heinrich Schmid and Joseph Haas in Munich; then studied musicology at the Univ. of Munich with Sandberger and at the Univ. of Berlin with Hornbostel, Abert, Wolf, and Sachs; received his Ph.D. in 1925 from the Univ. of Munich with the dissertation *Beiträge zur Musikgeschichte Freisings von den ältesten christlichen Zeiten bis zur Auflösung des Hofes 1803* (Freising, 1926); completed his Habilitation in 1927 at the Univ. of Münster with his *Der Palestrina stil und seine Bedeutung in der vokalen Kirchenmusik des 18. Jahrhunderts* (Augsburg, 1929). In 1927 he became a lecturer at the Univ. of Münster; in 1931 prof. in Freiburg, Switzerland; in 1934 he became head of the dept. of musicology at the Univ. of Münster; in 1939 he succeeded Theodor Kroyer as prof. of music history at the Univ. of Cologne; he retired in 1970. Fellerer distinguished himself as an outstanding authority on the history of music of the Roman Catholic church; he contributed valuable studies on the music of the Middle Ages, the Renaissance, and the 19th century; he also served as ed. of several important music journals and other publications. His 60th birthday was honored by the publication of 3 Festschrifts.
    WRITINGS: *Die Deklamationsrhythmik in der vokalen Polypho-*

nie des 16. Jahrhunderts (Düsseldorf, 1928); *Orgel und Orgelmusik; Ihre Geschichte* (Augsburg, 1929); *Palestrina* (Regensburg, 1930; 2nd ed., rev., 1960); *Studien zur Orgelmusik des ausgehenden 18. und frühen 19. Jahrhunderts* (Kassel, 1932); *Beiträge zur Choralbegleitung und Choralverarbeitung in der Orgelmusik des ausgehenden 18. und beginnenden 19. Jahrhunderts* (Leipzig, 1932); *Die Aufführung der katholischen Kirchenmusik in Vergangenheit und Gegenwart* (Einsiedeln, 1933); *Mittelalterliches Musikleben der Stadt Freiburg im Uechtland* (Regensburg, 1935); *Der gregorianische Choral im Wandel der Jahrhunderte* (Regensburg, 1936); *Giacomo Puccini* (Potsdam, 1937); *Geschichte der katholischen Kirchenmusik* (Düsseldorf, 1939); *Deutsche Gregorianik im Frankenreich* (Regensburg, 1941); *Edvard Grieg* (Potsdam, 1942); *Einführung in die Musikwissenschaft* (Berlin, 1942; 2nd ed., rev., 1953); *Georg Friedrich Händel: Leben und Werk* (Hamburg, 1953); *Mozarts Kirchenmusik* (Salzburg, 1955); *Soziologie der Kirchenmusik* (Cologne, 1963); *Bearbeitung und Elektronik als musikalisches Problem in Urheberrecht* (Berlin and Frankfurt, 1965); *Klang und Struktur in der abendländischen Musik* (Cologne, 1967); *Das Problem Neue Musik* (Krefeld, 1967); *Monodie und Polyphonie in der Musik des 16. Jahrhunderts* (Brussels, 1972); *Der Stilwandel in der abendländischen Musik um 1600* (Cologne, 1972); *Geschichte der katholischen Kirchenmusik* (Kassel, 1972–76); *Max Bruch* (Cologne, 1974); *Der Akademismus in der deutschen Musik des 19. Jahrhunderts* (Opladen, 1976); *Die Kirchenmusik W.A. Mozarts* (Laaber, 1985).

Fellowes, E(dmund) H(orace), eminent English musicologist and editor; b. London, Nov. 11, 1870; d. Windsor, Dec. 20, 1951. He was educated at Winchester College and Oriel College, Oxford (B.Mus. and M.A., 1896); his teachers in music were P. Buck, Fletcher, and L. Straus. He was ordained in 1894, and then served as assistant curate in Wandsworth, London (until 1897); after serving as minor canon and precentor of Bristol Cathedral (1897–1900), he became minor canon at St. George's Chapel, Windsor Castle, a position he held until his death; he was also choirmaster there (1924–27). He was honorary librarian of St. Michael's College, Tenbury Wells (1918–48); was also a lecturer at various English univs. His importance rests upon his valuable writings on and eds. of early English music. He received honorary Mus.D. degrees from the Univs. of Dublin (1917), Oxford (1939), and Cambridge (1950); was made a Companion of Honour by King George VI in 1944.
    EDITIONS: The English Madrigal School (36 vols., 1913–24; 2nd ed., rev., 1956, by T. Dart as The English Madrigalists); The English School of Lutenist Song Writers (32 vols., 1920–32; 2nd ed., partly rev., 1959–66, by T. Dart as The English Lutesongs; 3rd ed., rev., 1959–); with P. Buck, A. Ramsbotham, and S. Warner, Tudor Church Music (10 vols., 1922–29; appendix, 1948, by Fellowes); The Collected Works of William Byrd (20 vols., London, 1937–50; 2nd ed., rev., 1962– , by T. Dart, P. Brett, and K. Elliott).
    WRITINGS: *English Madrigal Verse, 1588–1632* (Oxford, 1920; 3rd ed., rev. and enl., 1967); *The English Madrigal Composers* (Oxford, 1921; 2nd ed., 1948); *William Byrd: A Short Account of His Life and Work* (Oxford, 1923; 2nd ed., 1928); *The English Madrigal School: A Guide to Its Practical Use* (London, 1924); *Orlando Gibbons: A Short Account of His Life and Work* (Oxford, 1925; 2nd ed., 1951, as *Orlando Gibbons and His Family*); *The English Madrigal* (Oxford, 1925); *The Catalogue of Manuscripts in the Library of St Michael's College, Tenbury* (Paris, 1934); *William Byrd* (a different and much larger study than the monograph of 1923; Oxford, 1936; 2nd ed., 1948); *Organists and Masters of the Choristers of St George's Chapel in Windsor Castle* (London and Windsor, 1939); *English Cathedral Music from Edward VI to Edward VII* (London, 1941; 5th ed., rev., 1969); with E. Pine, *The Tenbury Letters* (London, 1942); *Memoirs of an Amateur Musician* (London, 1946).
    BIBL.: W. Shaw, "E.H. F., 1870–1951," *Musical Times,* CXI (1970).

Felsenstein, Walter, influential Austrian opera producer; b. Vienna, May 30, 1901; d. East Berlin, Oct. 8, 1975. He studied at a Graz technical college; then went to Vienna, where he enrolled in drama courses at the Burgtheater. In 1923 he appeared as an actor in Lübeck; in 1924 went to Mannheim. In 1925 he became dramatic adviser and producer in Beuthen, Silesia; in 1927 he was called to Basel to become chief opera and drama producer at the Stadttheater; in 1929 he went to Freiburg im Breisgau as both actor and dramatic adviser and producer. He served as chief producer at the Cologne Opera in 1932 and at the Frankfurt Opera in 1934. Despite his differences with the policies of the Nazi authorities, he was able to continue producing operas and dramas. From 1938 to 1940 he produced plays in Zürich; he then served as producer in Berlin (1940–44); he was drafted by the military despite his age, and served for a year. After the war he was director of the Komische Oper in East Berlin, a position he held from 1947 until his death. During his tenure, the Komische Oper established itself as one of the best opera houses of Europe; his productions of *Die Fledermaus, Carmen, Le nozze di Figaro, Otello, Les Contes d'Hoffmann,* and *Die Zauberflöte* were artistically of the 1st rank. He also made operatic films and gave courses on theater arts. Among his students were the opera producers Götz Friedrich and Joachim Herz. With S. Melchinger, he compiled *Musiktheater* (Bremen, 1961); with G. Friedrich and J. Herz, he publ. *Musiktheater: Beiträge zur Methodik und zu Inszenierungs-Konzeptionen* (ed., S. Stomper; Leipzig, 1970).

BIBL.: R. Münz, *Untersuchungen zum realistischen Musiktheater W. F.s* (diss., Humboldt Univ., Berlin, 1964); G. Friedrich, *W. F.: Weg und Werk* (Berlin, 1967); P. Fuchs, ed. and translator, *The Music Theater of W. F.: Collected Articles, Speeches and Interviews by F. and Others* (N.Y., 1975).

Felsztyna (Felsztyn, Felstin, Felstinensis, Felsztynski), Sebastian z (von), noted Polish music theorist and composer; b. Felsztyn, Galicia, c.1490; d. c.1543. He studied at the Univ. of Krakow (1507–9); he also studied theology, and was made a priest in Felsztyn c.1528; he most likely served in that capacity in Przemysl, then became parish priest in Sanok c.1536. He wrote the 1st Polish treatise on mensural theory, *Opusculum musice mensuralis* (Krakow, 1517), and a compendium on Gregorian chant, *Opusculum musice compilatum noviter* (Krakow, 1517; 3rd ed., augmented, 1534, as *Opusculum musices noviter congestum*). His manual for church singing, *Directiones musicae ad cathedralis ecclesiae Premisliensis usum* (Krakow, 1543), is not extant. He also publ. a vol. of hymns, *Aliquot hymni ecclesiastici vario melodiarum genere editi* (Krakow, 1522; not extant). His significance as a composer lies in the fact that he was the 1st Polish musician to employ consistent 4–part writing; 3 sacred motets are extant: *Prosa ad Rorate tempore paschali virgini Mariae laudes* in Surzynski's *Monumenta musices sacrae in Polonia,* vol. II (1887), *Alleluia ad Rorate cum prosa Ave Maria* in Szweykoski's *Muzyka w dawnym Krakowie* (Krakow, 1964), and *Alleluia, Felix es sacro virgo Maria* in Feicht's *Muzyka staropolska* (Krakow, 1966).

BIBL.: S. Lobaczewska, "O utworach Sebastiana z Felsztyna" (The Works of S. z F.), *Kwartalnik muzyczny,* no. 3 (1929); A. Chybiński, "Do biografi S. z F.," ibid., nos. 14–15 (1932).

Feltsman, Vladimir, prominent Russian pianist; b. Moscow, Jan. 8, 1952. He was born into a musical family; his father, Oskar Feltsman, was a composer of popular music. He began taking piano lessons at the age of 6 from his mother, and then enrolled at Moscow's Central Music School, completing his training with Yakov Flier at the Moscow Cons. At 11 he made his debut as a soloist with the Moscow Phil., and later won 1st prize in the Prague Concertino Competition. After capturing joint 1st prize in the Long-Thibaud Competition in Paris in 1971, he pursued a successful career as a soloist with major Soviet and Eastern European orchs.; he made particularly successful appearances in works in the Romantic repertoire, his specialty, in Japan (1977) and France (1978). His auspicious career was interrupted by the Soviet authorities

when, in 1979, he applied for a visa to emigrate to Israel with his wife. His application was denied and he subsequently was allowed to give concerts only in remote outposts of the Soviet Union. With the support of the U.S. ambassador, he gave several private concerts at the ambassador's official residence in Moscow; in 1984, one of these was surreptitiously recorded and later released by CBS Masterworks. When his plight became a cause célèbre in the West, Feltsman was allowed to give his 1st Moscow recital in almost a decade (April 21, 1987). In June 1987 he was granted permission to emigrate, and in Aug. 1987 went to the U.S., where he accepted an appointment at the State Univ. of N.Y. at New Paltz. On Sept. 27, 1987, he gave a special concert at the White House for President Reagan, and on Nov. 11, 1987, gave his 1st N.Y. recital in Carnegie Hall.

BIBL.: J. von Rhein, "V. F.," *Ovation* (April 1986); *Current Biography* (April 1988); C. Passy, "V. F.," *Ovation* (Jan. 1989).

Felumb, Svend Christian, Danish oboist and conductor; b. Copenhagen, Dec. 25, 1898; d. there, Dec. 16, 1972. He studied in Copenhagen with L. Nielsen and Bruce, and in Paris with Blenzel and Vidal; from 1924 till 1947 he was an oboist in the Danish Royal Orch.; from 1947 to 1962 he conducted the Tivoli Orch. He was the founder of the Ny Musik society in Copenhagen and a leader of the movement for modern national Danish music.

Fenaroli, Fedele, Italian music theorist, pedagogue, and composer; b. Lanciano, April 25, 1730; d. Naples, Jan. 1, 1818. He studied with his father, who was a church organist; then went to Naples, where he became a pupil of Francesco Durante and P.A. Gallo at the Cons. of S. Maria di Loreto; in 1762 became 2nd maestro di cappella there, and in 1777 the 1st; also taught at the Conservatorio della Pietà. He trained many famous musicians (Cimarosa, Conti, Mercadante, Zingarelli, etc.); his theoretical manuals were highly regarded; he publ. *Partimento ossia Basso numerato* (Rome, 1800); *Studio del contrappunto* (Rome, 1800); *Regole musicali per i principianti di cembalo* (Naples, 1775). He was a prolific composer of church music, which, however, did not sustain its initial renown; composed 3 oratorios and 2 operas.

BIBL.: T. Consalvo, *La teoria musicale del F.* (Naples, 1826); G. de Napoli, "F. F. nel secondo centenario della nascita," *Musica d'Oggi* (March 1930).

Fenby, Eric (William), English composer; b. Scarborough, April 22, 1906. He studied piano and organ; after a few years as an organist in London, he went (1928) to Grez-sur-Loing, France, as amanuensis for Frederick Delius, taking down his dictation note by note, until Delius's death in 1934. He publ. his experiences in a book entitled *Delius as I Knew Him* (London, 1936; 4th ed., N.Y., 1981). He was director of music of the North Riding Training School (1948–62); from 1964, was a prof. of composition at the Royal Academy of Music. In 1964 he was made an Officer of the Order of the British Empire. Because of the beneficent work he undertook, he neglected his own compositions; however, he wrote some pleasant music for strings.

BIBL.: C. Redwood, ed., *A Delius Companion: A 70th Birthday Tribute to E. F.* (London, 1976).

Fennell, Frederick, noted American conductor and teacher; b. Cleveland, July 2, 1914. He began conducting during the summers of 1931 to 1933 at the National Music Camp at Interlochen, Mich.; went on to study at the Eastman School of Music in Rochester, N.Y. (B.M., 1937; M.M., 1939); then served on its faculty as conductor of the Little Sym. and Symphonic Band (1939–65). In 1952 he founded the Eastman Wind Ensemble, with which he made numerous record albums; he was also a guest conductor at the Boston Pops. From 1965 to 1980 he was conductor-in-residence of the Univ. of Miami School of Music at Coral Gables, Fla.; he also made European tours with the School Orch. of America (1965, 1966) and produced a series of specially recorded concerts at the Library of Congress, using 19th-century band instruments and music (1972, 1973, 1977). He is the recipient of an honorary Mus.D. degree from the Univ. of Oklahoma City; in 1958 was made an Honorary Chief by the Kiowa Indian tribe. He publ. *Time and the Winds* (Kenosha, Wis., 1954) and *The Drummer's Heritage* (Rochester, N.Y., 1956).

Fennelly, Brian, American composer; b. Kingston, N.Y., Aug. 14, 1937. He attended Union College in Schenectady (1954–58), earning a bachelor's degree in mechanical engineering; served in the Air Force (1958–61); upon discharge, returned to Union College, obtaining the degree of B.A. in 1963. He then took postgraduate courses at the Yale Univ. School of Music, where he studied with Mel Powell, Gunther Schuller, and Allen Forte (M.M., 1965; Ph.D., 1968); also took cello lessons. As a doctoral student, he wrote the dissertation *A Descriptive Notation for Electronic Music.* In 1968 he was appointed to the faculty of the School of Arts and Sciences at N.Y. Univ. He traveled widely as a pianist, conductor, and lecturer. He held a Guggenheim fellowship (1980–81). He is extremely liberal in his choice of idiom for his music, free of fashionable elitism, willing and eager to use all effective means of composition, ranging from stark homophony to dodecaphonic structuralism, traversing on the way through the unblushing expression of soulful Romanticism. For purely practical purposes he produced 9 pieces, each for a solo instrument, under the general title *Tesserae* (that is, regularly shaped pieces of stone or glass used for mosaic material; the word itself, meaning "4" in Greek, refers to a 4-cornered plate). He also made use of electronic sound.

WORKS: ORCH.: *In Wildness Is the Preservation of the World,* fantasy after Thoreau (1975; Davenport, Iowa, Nov. 5, 1976); *Concert Piece* for Trumpet and Orch. (1976); *Quintuplo* ("five-fold 5") for Brass Quintet and Orch. (1977–78); *Scintilla prisca* for Cello and Orch. (1980); *Tropes and Echos* for Clarinet and Orch. (1981); Concerto for Saxophone and Strings (1983–84). **CHAMBER:** Duo for Violin and Piano (1964); *2 Movements* for Oboe, Clarinet, Trumpet, and Trombone (1965); Wind Quintet (1967); *Evanescences* for Alto Flute, Clarinet, Violin, Cello, and Electronic Tape (1969); String Quartet (1971); *Prelude and Elegy* for Brass Quintet (1973); *Consort I* for Trombone Quintet (1976); *Empirical Rag* for Brass Quintet (1977); *Scintilla prisca* for Cello and Piano (1979); *Canzona* for Clarinet, Violin, Viola, Cello, and Piano (1981–82); *3 Intermezzi* for Bass Clarinet and Marimba (1983). **SOLO INSTRUMENTS:** Suite for Double Bass (1963; rev. 1981); *For Solo Flute* (1964; rev. 1976); *Divisions* for Solo Violin (1968; rev. 1981); *Sonata seria* for Piano (1976); *Empirical Rag* for Piano (1978; also for other instruments); 9 pieces entitled *Tesserae* (i.e., mosaics), numbered in Roman numerals: I for Harpsichord (1971), II for Cello (1972), III for Viola (1976), IV for Double-bass Trombone (1976), V for Tuba (1980), VI for Trumpet (1976), VII for Clarinet (1979), VIII for Alto Saxophone (1980), IX for Percussion (1981); Brass Quintet (1987). **VOCAL:** *Songs with Improvisation* for Mezzo-soprano, Clarinet, and Piano, to texts by e.e. cummings (1964; rev. 1969); Psalm XIII for Chorus and Brass (1965); *Sunyata* for 4-channel Magnetic Tape (1970); *Festive Psalm* for Chorus, Narrator, Organ, and Electronic Tape (1972); *Praise Yah* for Chorus and Organ (1974); *Winterkill* for Chorus and Piano (1981).

Feo, Francesco, celebrated Italian composer and pedagogue; b. Naples, 1691; d. there, Jan. 18, 1761. He studied with Andrea Basso and Nicola Fago at the Conservatorio S. Maria della Pietà dei Turchini (1704–12), subsequently serving as maestro (with Ignazio Prota) at the Conservatorio S. Onofrio (1723–39) and as primo maestro at the Conservatorio dei Poveri di Gesù Cristo (1739–43). His most famous pupil was Nicolò Jommelli, who studied with him at the Conservatorio S. Onofrio. He composed over 150 works, including much sacred music. His works for the stage include *L'amor tirannico, ossia Zenobia,* opera (Naples, Jan. 18, 1713); *La forza della virtù,* opera (Naples, Jan. 22, 1719); *Teuzzone,* opera (Naples, Jan. 20, 1720); *Siface, re di Numidia,* opera (Naples, Nov. 4, 1720); *Morano e Rosina,* intermezzo (Naples, 1723), *Don Chisciotte della Man-*

cia, intermezzo (Rome, Carnival 1726); *Coriando lo speciale,* intermezzo (Rome, Carnival 1726); *Ipermestra,* opera (Rome, Jan. 1728); *Arianna,* opera (Turin, Carnival 1728); *Tamase,* opera (Naples, 1729); *Il vedovo,* intermezzo (Naples, 1729); *Andromaca,* opera (Rome, Feb. 5, 1730); *L'Issipile,* opera (Turin, 1733?); and *Arsace,* opera (Turin, Dec. 26, 1740). He also composed the serenatas *Oreste* (Madrid, Jan. 20, 1738) and *Polinice* (Madrid, June 19, 1738).

Ferand, Ernst (Thomas), Hungarian music scholar; b. Budapest, March 5, 1887; d. Basel, May 29, 1972. He studied at the Budapest Academy of Music, graduating in 1911; then collaborated with Jaques-Dalcroze in Hellerau and Geneva; taught at the Fodor Cons. of Music in Budapest (1912–19) and at the Dalcroze School in Hellerau (1920–25); directed the Hellerau-Laxenburg College, near Vienna (1925–38). In 1938 he emigrated to the U.S. and taught at the New School for Social Research in N.Y. (1939–65); then went to Basel. He publ. a textbook on harmony in Hungarian (Budapest, 1914); *Die Improvisation in Beispielen aus neun Jahrhunderten abendländischer Musik* (Cologne, 1956; 2nd ed., rev., 1961; Eng. tr., 1961, in Das Musikwerk, XII).

Ferchault, Guy, French musicologist; b. Mer, Loire-et-Cher, Aug. 16, 1904. He studied music at the Cons. and philosophy at the Sorbonne (graduated, 1942) in Paris; held teaching positions in music education in Paris, Orléans (1941), Poitiers (1942–49), Tours (1948–51), and Roubaix (from 1952); from 1943 to 1967 he was also a prof. of music history at the Cons. Régional de Musique in Versailles.

WRITINGS: *Henri Duparc, Une Amitié mystique, d'après ses lettres à Francis Jammes* (Paris, 1944); *Les Créatures du drame musical: De Monteverdi à Wagner* (Paris, 1944); *Introduction à l'esthétique de la mélodie* (Gap, 1946); *Claude Debussy, musicien français* (Paris, 1948); *Faust, J.-S. Bach et l'esthétique de son temps* (Zürich, 1950).

Fere, Vladimir, Russian composer and ethnomusicologist; b. Kamyshin, May 20, 1902; d. Moscow, Sept. 2, 1971. He studied piano with Goldenweiser and composition with Glière and Miaskovsky at the Moscow Cons. (1921–29). In 1936 he went to Frunze, Kirghizia; composed (in collaboration with Vlasov) a number of operas based on native folk motifs; all were first produced there: *Golden Girl* (May 1, 1937); *Not Death but Life* (March 26, 1938); *Moon Beauty* (April 15, 1939); *For People's Happiness* (May 1, 1941); *Patriots* (Nov. 6, 1941); *Son of the People* (Nov. 8, 1947); *On the Shores of Issyk-Kul* (Feb. 1, 1951); *Toktogul* (July 6, 1958); *The Witch* (1965); *1 Hour before Dawn* (1969). He also wrote several symphonic pieces on Kirghiz themes; numerous choruses; chamber music.

Ferencsik, János, noted Hungarian conductor; b. Budapest, Jan. 18, 1907; d. there, June 12, 1984. He studied organ and theory at the Budapest Cons.; became répétiteur at the Hungarian State Opera (1927), and subsequently conductor there (from 1930); he was also an assistant at the Bayreuth Festivals (1930, 1931). He was chief conductor of the Hungarian Radio and Television Sym. Orch. (1945–52), the Hungarian State Sym. Orch. (1952–84), and the Budapest Phil. (1953–76); also appeared as a guest conductor in Europe and North America. He was awarded the Kossuth Prize (1951, 1961); the Order of the Banner was bestowed upon him by the Hungarian government on his 70th birthday. He was a persuasive interpreter of the Hungarian repertoire.

Ferenczy, Oto, Slovak composer; b. Brezovica nad Torysou, March 30, 1921. He studied philosophy, esthetics, and musicology at the Comenius Univ. in Bratislava (Ph.D., 1945); was mainly self-taught in composition. In 1951 he joined the staff of the Bratislava Academy of Music and Dramatic Arts; from 1962 to 1966 was its rector. His music is entrenched well within the inoffensive idiom of Central European neo-Classicism; it is expertly crafted.

WORKS: Comic opera, *Nevšedná humoreska* (An Uncommon Humoresque; 1966–67); *Merry-Making,* dance suite for Orch. (1951); *Hurbanovská,* overture (1952); *Serenade* for Harp,

Flute, Clarinet, Bassoon, and String Orch. (1955); *Capriccio* for Piano and Orch. (1957); *Elegy* for Orch. (1957); *Finale* for Orch. (1958); *Partita* for Chamber Orch. (1963–65); *Symphonic Prologue* (1975); *The Star of the North*, cantata (1960); *Music for 4 String Instruments* (1947; rev. 1973); Concerto for 9 Instruments (1949); String Quartet (1962); Violin Sonata (1964); Concertino for 12 Instruments (1965); piano pieces; choruses; solo songs.

Ferguson, Donald (Nivison), American music educator; b. Waupun, Wis., June 30, 1882; d. Minneapolis, May 11, 1985. He studied at the Univ. of Wisconsin (B.A., 1904); then went to London, where he studied composition with Josef Holbrooke and piano with Michael Hambourg. In 1913 he joined the faculty of the Univ. of Minnesota; was named full prof. in 1927; retired in 1950, but returned to teach as prof. emeritus there from 1953 to 1956. Concurrently he was head of the music dept. at Macalester College in St. Paul (1950–59). From 1930 to 1960 he served as program annotator for the Minneapolis Sym. Orch. He celebrated his centennial in 1982 but, ignoring the connotations of melancholy longevity, persevered in bringing to completion his final book, *The Forgotten Purpose of Music Making.*
    WRITINGS: *A History of Musical Thought* (N.Y., 1935; 3rd ed., rev., 1959); *A Short History of Music* (N.Y., 1943); *Piano Music of 6 Great Composers* (N.Y., 1947); *Masterworks of the Orchestral Repertoire* (Minneapolis, 1954); *Music as Metaphor; The Elements of Expression* (Minneapolis, 1960); *Image and Structure in Chamber Music* (Minneapolis, 1964); *The Why of Music* (Minneapolis, 1969).
    BIBL.: J. Slettom, "D. F. at 100: A Life in Music," *Minnesota Monthly* (Sept. 1982).

Ferguson, Howard, Irish composer and music editor; b. Belfast, Oct. 21, 1908. He studied composition with R.O. Morris at the Royal College of Music in London; piano with Harold Samuel; conducting with Sargent. From 1948 to 1963 he was a prof. at the Royal Academy of Music in London. His music is neo-Classical in its idiom; in some of his compositions he makes use of English, Scottish, and Irish folk songs.
    EDITIONS: *W. Tisdall: Complete Keyboard Works* (London, 1958); *Style and Interpretation: An Anthology: Early Keyboard Music: England and France; Early Keyboard Music: Germany and Italy; Classical Piano Music; Romantic Piano Music; Keyboard Duets* (2 vols., London, 1963–71); *Style and Interpretation: Sequels: Early French Keyboard Music, I, II; Early Italian Keyboard Music, I, II; Early German Keyboard Music, I, II; Early English Keyboard Music, I, II* (8 vols., London, 1966–71); with C. Hogwood, *W. Croft: Complete Harpsichord Works* (2 vols., London, 1974); *Anne Cromwell's Virginal Book, 1638* (London, 1974); *F. Schubert, Piano Sonatas* (London, 1979); *Keyboard Works of C.P.E. Bach* (4 vols., London, 1983).
    WORKS: 5 *Irish Folktunes* for Cello or Viola, and Piano (1927); 2 *Ballads* for Baritone, Chorus, and Orch. (1928–32); Violin Sonata No. 1 (1931); 3 *Medieval Carols* for Voice and Piano (1932–33); Octet for Clarinet, Bassoon, Horn, String Quartet, and Double Bass (1933); 5 *Pipe Pieces* for 3 Bamboo Pipes (1934–35); *Partita* for Orch. (1935–36; also for 2 Pianos); 4 *Short Pieces* for Clarinet or Viola, and Piano (1932–36); 4 *Diversions on Ulster Airs* for Orch. (1939–42); Flute Sonata (1938–40); 5 *Bagatelles* for Piano (1944); Violin Sonata No. 2 (1946); *Chauntecleer*, ballet (1948); Concerto for Piano and Strings (1950–51; London, May 29, 1952; Myra Hess, soloist); *Discovery* for Voice and Piano (1951); 3 *Sketches* for Flute and Piano (1932–52); 2 *Fanfares* for 4 Trumpets and 3 Trombones (1952); *Overture for an Occasion* for Orch. (1952–53); 5 *Irish Folksongs* for Voice and Piano (1954); *Amore langueo* for Tenor, Chorus, and Orch. (1955–56); *The Dream of the Rood* for Soprano or Tenor, Chorus, and Orch. (1958–59); piano pieces.
    BIBL.: A. Burn, "The Music of H. F.," *Musical Times* (Aug. 1983); H. Cobbe, "H. F. at 80," ibid. (Oct. 1988).

Ferguson, Maynard, Canadian jazz trumpeter and bandleader; b. Montreal, May 4, 1928. He played violin and piano as a child; then learned to play wind instruments; subsequently studied at the Montreal Cons. He began his career by playing in the bands of Boyd Ferguson, Jimmy Dorsey, Charlie Barnet, and Stan Kenton; in 1956 he formed his own band, and led it until 1967; then spent some time in India and England. He was adept in the pop and the rock genres as well as in traditional jazz.

Fernándes, Armando José, Portuguese composer; b. Lisbon, July 26, 1906; d. there, May 3, 1983. After study at the National Cons. of Lisbon, he went to Paris, where he took piano lessons with Cortot and studied composition with Nadia Boulanger (1933–36). Returning to Lisbon, he taught at the Cons. and pursued the ideal of descriptive music, writing an effective symphonic poem, *O terramoto de Lisboa*, inspired by the devastating earthquake of 1765; another effective piece was his *Fantasia sobre temas populares portugueses* for Piano and Orch. (1945); his piano pieces also reflect Portuguese formulas.

Fernández Arbós, Enrique. See **Arbós, Enrique Fernández.**

Fernández Bordas, Antonio, Spanish violinist; b. Orense, Jan. 12, 1870; d. Madrid, Feb. 18, 1950. He studied at the Madrid Cons. with Jesús de Monasterio, and, at the age of 11, won 1st prize for violin; gave concerts in England, France, and other European countries; returning to Spain, he became a prof. of violin at the Madrid Cons.; in 1921 he was elected director.

Fernández Caballero, Manuel, Spanish composer; b. Murcia, March 14, 1835; d. Madrid, Feb. 20, 1906. He was a precocious musician; learned to play the violin, piano, and piccolo as a child, and at the age of 7, played in a school band. He then studied violin with Soriano Fuertes in Murcia; in 1850 he entered the Madrid Cons., where his teachers were Eslava and Pedro Albéniz; in 1856 he received 1st prize in composition; then conducted various orchs. and became interested in theatrical composition. During his career as a conductor and composer, he wrote more than 200 zarzuelas, several of which attained great popularity: *Los dineros del Sacristan* and *Los Africanistas* (Barcelona, 1894); *El cabo primero* (Barcelona, 1895); *La rueda de la fortuna* (Madrid, 1896); *Los estudiantes* (Madrid, 1900). He also wrote sacred music.

Ferneyhough, Brian, English composer; b. Coventry, Jan. 16, 1943. He studied at the Birmingham School of Music (1961–63); then took courses with Lennox Berkeley and Maurice Miles at the Royal Academy of Music in London (1966–67); furthermore, received instruction in advanced composition with Ton de Leeuw in Amsterdam and Klaus Huber in Basel (1969–73). From 1971 to 1986 he was on the faculty at the Hochschule für Musik in Freiburg im Breisgau; in 1976, 1978, and 1980, lectured at the Darmstadt summer courses. He also taught at the Royal Cons. of The Hague (from 1986) and at the Univ. of Calif. at San Diego (from 1987).
    WORKS: 4 *Miniatures* for Flute and Piano (1965); *Coloratura* for Oboe and Piano (1966); Sonata for 2 Pianos (1966); *Prometheus* for Wind Sextet (1967); *Sonatas* for String Quartet (1967); *Epicycle* for 20 Strings (Hilversum, Sept. 7, 1969); *Missa brevis* for 12 Solo Voices (1971); *Firecycle Beta* for Orch., with 5 Conductors (1969–71); 7 *Sterne* for Organ (1971); *Time and Motion Study I* for Solo Bass Clarinet (1971–77), *II* for Cello and Electronics (1973–75), and *III* for 16 Solo Voices and Percussion (1974); *Transit* for 6 Amplified Voices and Chamber Orch. (1972–75; London Sinfonietta in Royan, France, March 25, 1975; 1st British perf., London, Nov. 16, 1977); *Perspectivae corporum irregularum* for Oboe, Viola, and Piano (1975); *Unity Capsule* for Solo Flute (1975–76); *Funérailles*, version I, for String Sextet, Double Bass, and Harp (1969–77); *La Terre est un homme* for Orch. (1976–79); *Funérailles*, version II, for 7 Strings and Harp (1980); String Quartet No. 2 (1980); *Lemma-Icon-Epigram* for Piano (1981); *Superscriptio* for Piccolo (1981); *Carceri d'invenzione I* for 16 Instruments (1981–82); *Adagissimo* for String Quartet (1983); *Carceri d'invenzione II* for Flute and Chamber Orch. (1984); *Études transcendan-*

tales for Mezzo-soprano, Flute, Oboe, Cello, and Harpsichord (1982–85); *Carceri d'invenzione III* for 15 Wind Instruments and 3 Percussionists (1986); String Quartet No. 3 (1986–87).

BIBL.: R. Toop, "F.'s Dungeons of Invention," *Musical Times* (Nov. 1987).

Ferni-Giraldoni, Carolina, Italian soprano; b. Como, Aug. 20, 1839; d. Milan, June 4, 1926. She studied violin in Paris and Brussels; later took voice lessons with Pasta; made her debut as Leonora in *La Favorita* in Turin in 1862; sang at La Scala in Milan (1866–68); retired in 1883 and taught voice. She was married to the baritone **Leone Giraldoni**; their son **Eugenio Giraldoni** was the famous baritone; Caruso was one of her pupils.

Fernström, John (Axel), Swedish conductor and composer; b. I-Chang, Hupei, China (the son of a Swedish missionary), Dec. 6, 1897; d. Lund, Oct. 19, 1961. He studied first at the Cons. in Malmö, then took violin lessons in Copenhagen, where he also studied with P. Gram (1923–30). He took courses in conducting at Sonderhausen, Germany; was conductor of the Malmö Radio (1939–41) and the Lund Orch. Soc. (1948–61). He publ. an autobiographical book, *Confessions* (1946).

WORKS: 3 operas: *Achnaton* (1931); *Isissystrarnas bröllop* (1942); *Livet en dröm* (1946); 12 syms.: No. 1 (1920); No. 2 (1924); No. 3, *Exotica* (1928); No. 4 (1930); No. 5 (1932); No. 6 (1938); No. 7, *Sinfonietta in forma di sonata de chiesa* (1941); No. 8, *Amore studiorum* (1942); No. 9, *Sinfonia breve* (1943); No. 10, *Sinfonia discrète* (1944); No. 11, *Utan mask* (1945); No. 12 (1951); *Symphonic Variations* (1930); 2 violin concertos (1938, 1952); Chaconne for Cello and Orch. (1936); Clarinet Concerto (1936); Viola Concerto (1937); Concertino for Flute, Female Chorus, and Small Orch. (1941); Bassoon Concerto (1946); Cello Concertino (1949); *Ostinato* for Strings (1952); Mass for Soli, Chorus, and Orch. (1931); *Stabat Mater* for Soli, Chorus, and Strings (1936); *Songs of the Sea*, suite for Soprano and Strings (1943); *Den mödosamma vä gen*, profane oratorio (1947); 8 string quartets (1920, 1925, 1931, 1942, 1945, 1947, 1950, 1952); many other chamber works; songs and choral works.

Ferrabosco, Alfonso, the Elder, Italian composer, son of **Domenico Maria Ferrabosco** and father of **Alfonso Ferrabosco, the Younger;** b. Bologna (baptized), Jan. 18, 1543; d. there, Aug. 12, 1588. From 1562 to 1564 he was in the service of Queen Elizabeth I in England; was again in England from 1572 to 1578. He entered the service of the Duke of Savoy in Turin (1582), accompanying him to Spain; he died while on a visit to his native city. His influence on the English court as a representative of the Italian style was considerable. Of his sacred works, 79 compositions are extant; many are housed in MS collections in English and American libraries. They include 110 Italian madrigals, 73 motets, 4 Lamentations, an anthem, 5 French chansons, 3 English songs, 2 secular Latin songs, 17 pieces for solo lute, 2 fantasias for keyboard, and a pavan for a mixed consort. A number of his madrigals were publ. in anthologies of his time. R. Charteris ed. *Alfonso Ferrabosco the Elder (1543–1588): Opera omnia* in Corpus Mensurabilis Musicae, XCVI/1–9 (1984–88).

BIBL.: G. Arkwright, "Un Compositore italiano alla corte di Elisabetta, A. F. di Bologna," *Rivista Musicale Italiana*, IV (1897); J. Kerman, "Master A. and the English Madrigal," *Musical Quarterly* (April 1952); J. Cockshoot, *The Sacred Music of A. F., Father (1543–88), with Critical Commentary* (diss., Oxford Univ., 1963); R. Charteris, *A. F. the Elder (1543–1588): A Thematic Catalogue of His Music with a Biographical Calendar* (N.Y., 1984).

Ferrabosco, Alfonso, the Younger, Italian-English composer, illegitimate son of **Alfonso Ferrabosco, the Elder;** b. probably in Greenwich, England, c.1575; d. there (buried), March 11, 1628. He was reared by a musician at the English court; he received an annuity from 1592 to 1601, and then entered the service of King James I. He became teacher to the Prince of Wales in 1604; he was granted an annual pension

in 1605, and continued as an active musician in the royal service; he was named Composer of Music in ordinary and Composer of Music to the King in 1626. Ferrabosco was a friend of the dramatist Ben Jonson, for whom he wrote music for several masques produced at the court. He publ. a book of *Ayres* (dedicated to Prince Henry; London, 1609) and a book of *Lessons for 1, 2 and 3 Viols* (London, 1609). His works for viol demonstrate extraordinary ability in contrapuntal writing while preserving the rhythmic quality of the dance forms and the free ornamental style of the fantasies.

BIBL.: G. Arkwright, "A. F., the Younger," *Musician*, I (1897); J. Duffy, *The Songs and Motets of A. G., the Younger (1575–1628)* (Ann Arbor, Mich., 1980).

Ferrabosco, Domenico Maria, Italian composer, father of **Alfonso Ferrabosco, the Elder;** b. Bologna, Feb. 14, 1513; d. there, Feb. 1574. He was maestro di cappella at S. Petronio in Bologna; in 1546 he was at the Vatican, returning to Bologna in 1547; was again at the Vatican from 1551 until 1555; eventually returned to Bologna. He is chiefly known as a composer of madrigals; his book of 45 madrigals, *Il primo libro de' madrigali a 4 voci*, was publ. by Gardano in 1542; Gardano also publ. motets (1554) and other madrigals (1557) by Ferrabosco; some madrigals and a 4-voiced canzona, the latter in lute tablature, appeared in 1584 (publ. by Scotto).

BIBL.: G. Livi, "The F. Family," *Musical Antiquary*, IV (1912–13).

Ferrani (original name, **Zanaggio**), **Cesira,** noted Italian soprano; b. Turin, May 8, 1863; d. Pollone, near Biella, May 4, 1943. She studied with Antonietta Fricci in Turin; was chosen to create the roles of Manon Lescaut (1893) and Mimi in *La Bohème* (1896); from 1894 she sang at La Scala in Milan; retired in 1909. In addition to her Italian repertoire, she was also renowned for her Wagnerian roles.

Ferrara, Franco, Italian conductor; b. Palermo, July 4, 1911; d. Florence, Sept. 6, 1985. He studied piano, violin, organ, and composition at the conservatories of Palermo and Bologna; made his debut as a conductor in Florence in 1938; in 1959 went to the Netherlands, where he gave courses in conducting with the Holland Radio Phil. Among his students was Edo de Waart.

Ferrari, Benedetto, Italian librettist and composer, called "Dalla Tiorba" for his proficiency on the theorbo; b. Reggio Emilia, c.1603; d. Modena, Oct. 22, 1681. He studied music in Rome; served as a choirboy at the Collegio Germanico in Rome (1617–18); subsequently was a musician at the Farnese court in Parma (1619–23). In 1637 he proceeded to Venice; there he wrote the libretto for Manelli's opera *L'Andromeda*, produced at the Teatro di San Cassiano in 1637; it was the 1st Venetian opera performed in a theater open to the public. He then wrote librettos for *La Maga fulminata* by Manelli (1638); *L'inganno d'Amore* by Bertali (Regensburg, 1653); *La Licasta* by Manelli (Parma, 1664); and 4 of his own operas, all produced in Venice: *L'Armida* (Feb. 1639), *Il Pastor regio* (Jan. 23, 1640), *La Ninfa avara* (1641), and *Il Principe giardiniero* (Dec. 30, 1643). From 1651 to 1653 he was in Vienna. From 1653 to 1662 he served as court choirmaster in Modena; after a hiatus of employment, he was reinstated in 1674, remaining in this post until his death. In Modena he produced the opera *L'Erosilda* (1658) and 2 cantatas, *Premo il giogo delle Alpi* and *Voglio di vita uscir* (reprinted in Riemann's *Kantaten Frühling*, vol. 1, Leipzig, 1909). Six of Ferrari's librettos were publ. in Milan in 1644 under the title *Poesie drammatiche*.

Ferrari, Carlotta, Italian composer; b. Lodi, Jan. 27, 1837; d. Bologna, Nov. 23, 1907. She studied with Strepponi and Mazzucato at the Milan Cons.; then devoted herself to the composition of operas to her own librettos. The following operas were produced: *Ego* (Milan, 1857), *Sofia* (Lodi, 1866), and *Eleanora d'Armorea* (Cagliari, 1871).

Ferrari, Domenico, famous Italian composer and violinist; b. Piacenza, c.1722; d. Paris, 1780. He studied with Tartini;

traveled as a concert violinist, obtaining great success; in 1753 he joined the orch. of the Duke of Württemberg in Stuttgart; in 1754 he went to Paris, where he became extremely successful; he excelled as a virtuoso; his employment of passages in octaves, and particularly of harmonics, was an innovation at the time. He publ. 36 sonatas for Violin and Bass, opp. 1 to 6 (Paris, 1758–62); 6 trio sonatas for 2 Violins, or Flute and Basso Continuo (London, c.1758–65); and 6 sonatas or duets for 2 Violins (London, c.1765; 1st 2 sonatas by Nardini).

BIBL.: V. Kock, *The Works of D. F., 1722–1780* (diss., Tulane Univ., 1969).

Ferrari, Gabrielle, French pianist and composer; b. Paris, Sept. 14, 1851; d. there, July 4, 1921. She studied at the Milan Cons. and later in Paris, where she had lessons with Gounod. She wrote a number of effective piano pieces (*Rapsodie espagnole, Le Ruisseau, Hirondelle,* etc.) and songs (*Larmes en songe, Chant d'exil, Chant d'amour,* etc.); finally ventured to compose operas, producing *Le Dernier Amour* (Paris, June 11, 1895), *Sous le masque* (Vichy, 1898), *Le Tartare* (Paris, 1906), and *Le Cobzar,* which proved to be her most successful opera (Monte Carlo, Feb. 16, 1909).

Ferrari, Giacomo (Gotifredo), Italian composer; b. Rovereto, Tirol (baptized), April 2, 1763; d. London, Dec. 1842. He studied harpsichord at Verona with Marcola and theory with Marianus Stecher at the Monastery of Mariaberg in Switzerland. He then went to Naples, where he studied with Latilla. There he met Chevalier Campan, household master for Marie-Antoinette; he was then appointed as court musician at the Tuileries in Paris in 1787; after the Revolution he went to London (1792), where he settled as a singing teacher. He produced in London the operas *I due Svizzeri* (May 14, 1799), *Il Rinaldo d' Asti* (March 16, 1802), *L'Eroina di Raab* (April 8, 1813), and *Lo sbaglio fortunato* (May 8, 1817); he also wrote 2 ballets and several instrumental works (4 septets, 2 piano concertos, etc.). He publ. *Studio di musica pratica, teorica* (1830) and a book of reminiscences, *Anedotti piacevoli e interresanti occorsi nella vita G.G. F. da Rovereto* (1830; contains some vivid recollections of Haydn and other celebrities).

BIBL.: G. de Saint-Foix, "A Musical Traveler, G.G. F. (1759–1842)," *Musical Quarterly* (Oct. 1939).

Ferrari, Gustave, Swiss pianist and composer; b. Geneva, Sept. 28, 1872; d. there, July 29, 1948. He studied at the Geneva Cons., and later in Paris. In 1900 he went to London, where he remained for many years. From 1917 to 1925 he conducted operetta in America; then returned to Europe and toured with Yvette Guilbert, as her accompanist in a repertoire of French folk songs; later on he gave song recitals himself, singing with his own accompaniment folk songs of France and French Canada; also lectured on the subject, and ed. collections of French folk music. As a composer, he wrote mostly incidental music for the stage; composed a cantata for the Rousseau Festival (Geneva, 1912); *The Wilderness,* a Greek dance ballad (London, 1915); other choral works; a song cycle, *Le Livre pour toi.*

Ferrari-Fontana, Edoardo, Italian tenor; b. Rome, July 8, 1878; d. Toronto, July 4, 1936. As a young man he served in the Italian consulate in South America; also studied singing. Returning to Italy in 1908, he sang in operetta; given a chance to appear as Tristan in Turin (Dec. 23, 1909), he scored a signal success, and in a few years became well known as a principal Italian tenor in Wagner's repertoire. He sang in the U.S. during the 1913–14 season of the Boston Opera Co. and with the Metropolitan Opera in N.Y., and at the Chicago Opera (1915–16). In 1926 he settled in Toronto as a singing teacher. He was married (June 26, 1912) to **Margarete Matzenauer,** but they separated after a few years.

Ferrari-Trecate, Luigi, Italian composer; b. Alessandria, Piedmont, Aug. 25, 1884; d. Rome, April 17, 1964. He studied with Antonio Cicognani at the Pesaro Cons., and also with Mascagni. Subsequently he was engaged as a church organist; was prof. of organ at the Liceo Musicale in Bologna (1928–

31); from 1929 to 1955, was director of the Parma Cons. He wrote several operas which had considerable success: *Pierozzo* (Alessandria, Sept. 15, 1922); *La Bella e il mostro* (Milan, March 20, 1926); *Le astuzie di Bertoldo* (Genoa, Jan. 10, 1934); *Ghirlino* (Milan, Feb. 4, 1940); *Buricchio* (Bologna, Nov. 5, 1948); *L'Orso Re* (Milan, Feb. 8, 1950); *La capanna dello Zio Tom* (Uncle Tom's Cabin; Parma, Jan. 17, 1953); *La fantasia tragica; Lo spaventapasseri* (1963); he also wrote music for a marionette play, *Ciottolino* (Rome, Feb. 8, 1922); a sacred cantata, *In hora calvarii* (1956); and *Contemplazioni* for Orch. (1950).

Ferras, Christian, outstanding French violinist; b. Le Touquet-Paris-Plage, June 17, 1933; d. Paris, Sept. 15, 1982. He received his musical education in Nice and Paris. He then began his career as a soloist with many European orchs. His performances were marked by stylistic fidelity to the music and a fine virtuosity.

Ferrata, Giuseppe, Italian-American composer; b. Gradoli, Romagna, Jan. 1, 1865; d. New Orleans, March 28, 1928. At the age of 14 he won a scholarship to study at the Accademia di Santa Cecilia in Rome, where he took courses with Sgambati and Terziani, graduating in 1885; then had the good fortune of benefiting from the last lessons that Liszt gave; in 1892 went to the U.S.; taught at Tulane Univ. in New Orleans. He wrote a Sym., a Piano Concerto, a String Quartet, numerous songs to Italian and English texts (*Night and the Curtains Drawn, A Song of Thanksgiving, On Music, Alla musa,* etc.); piano pieces (*Humoresque, A Wave, An Eagle, Leonard Serpent, Serenade triste*); compiled a book of scales and *Esthetic Exercises of Technique.*

Ferrer, Mateo, famous Spanish organist, teacher, and composer; b. Barcelona, Feb. 25, 1788; d. there, Jan. 4, 1864. He studied with Francisco Queralt and Carlos Baguer, then became organist (1808) and maestro de capilla (1830) at the Barcelona Cathedral, where he was active until his death; in addition, he became director of the Teatro de la Cruz in 1827, holding that post for some 30 years. He was renowned for his improvisations on the organ, and was also esteemed as a teacher. He composed a large body of music for the church and the theater, but many works are lost. His Piano Sonata (1814), publ. by J. Nín in his collection *Seize sonates anciennes d'auteurs espagnols* (Paris, 1925), shows a certain affinity with early Beethoven.

Ferrer, Rafael, Spanish conductor; b. St.-Celoni, near Barcelona, May 22, 1911. He studied with Luis Millet and Enrique Morera (composition) and Eduardo Toldrá (violin). He played the violin in various orchs. in Spain; then devoted himself mainly to conducting. He specialized in Spanish music, and revived many little-known works of Granados, Turina, and other Spanish composers.

Ferrero, Lorenzo, Italian composer; b. Turin, Nov. 17, 1951. As a child he was largely self-taught in music, later studying privately with Massimo Bruni and at the Giuseppe Verdi Cons. in Milan. He studied esthetics with Gianni Battimo at the Univ. of Turin (degree, 1974, with a study of the writings of John Cage). He then began working on electronic music and multimedia theater at IRCAM (Paris), the GMEB (Bourges), and Music/Dia/Licht/Film/Gallerie (Munich). From 1982 to 1988 he was artistic director of the concert series Unione Musicale of Turin.

WORKS: OPERAS: *Marilyn* (1980); *Salvatore Giuliano* (1986); *Carlotta Corday* (1988); *Siglied* for Chamber Orch. (1975); *Thema 44* for Small Orch. (1982); *My Rock, My Rag, My Blues* for Piano (1984); *Ostinato* for 6 Cellos (1987); *Non parto, non resto* for Chorus (1987).

Ferrero, Willy, Italian conductor; b. Portland, Maine, May 21, 1906; d. Rome, March 24, 1954. He was taken to Italy in his infancy; as a child of 6 he conducted a performance at the Teatro Costanzi in Rome; at age 8 he conducted sym. concerts in European capitals with sensational success, and was the object of extravagant praise as a phenomenal musician. World War I interrupted his career; he continued to conduct operas and concerts in Italy, but failed to fulfill the extraordinary promise of his early youth. He received an excellent academic education; studied at the Vienna Academy of Music (graduated, 1924); composed a symphonic poem, *Il mistero dell' aurora*, and some chamber music.

BIBL.: A. de Angelis, "W. F.," *Noi e il Mondo* (Rome, 1919).

Ferretti, Dom Paolo, eminent Italian musicologist; b. Subiaco, Dec. 3, 1866; d. Bologna, May 23, 1938. He studied theology at the Benedictine College of San Anselmo in Rome; then taught in Malta, Genoa, and Parma; was abbot of the Benedictine Monastery of San Giovanni in Parma; in 1922, was appointed by Pope Pius XI director of the Scuola Pontificia (until 1931, when it became the Pontifical Inst. of Sacred Music). During the summers of 1925, 1927, and 1928 he taught courses in Gregorian chant at the Pius X School of Liturgical Music in N.Y. The importance of his investigations lies in a scholarly analysis of the rhythmic treatment and especially the forms of Gregorian chant. He publ. *Principii teorici e practici del canto gregoriano* (Rome, 1905); *El Cursus Metrico e il ritmo delle melodie del canto gregoriano* (Rome, 1913); *Estetica gregoriana ossia Trattato delle forme musicali del canto gregoriano, I* (Rome, 1934; also in French, Tournai, 1938).

Ferri, Baldassare, celebrated Italian castrato soprano; b. Perugia, Dec. 9, 1610; d. there, Nov. 18, 1680. He was a choirboy in Orvieto, where he entered the service of Cardinal Crescenzio in 1622; then studied in Naples and with Vincenzo Ugolini in Rome. He entered the service of Prince Wladyslaw of Poland in Warsaw in 1625 and continued in his employ when he became King Wladyslaw IV Vasa in 1632. In 1655 he went to Vienna, where he served the emperors Ferdinand III and Leopold I until about 1665; he then returned to Italy. He gained public renown with his appearances in major music centers; his travels took him as far as London. According to contemporary accounts, he possessed a phenomenal voice and accumulated a great fortune.

BIBL.: G. Conestabile, *Notizie biografiche di B. F. musico celebratissimo* (Perugia, 1846); G. Monaldi, *Cantati evirati celebri* (Rome, 1919).

Ferrier, Kathleen (Mary), remarkable English contralto; b. Higher Walton, Lancashire, April 22, 1912; d. London, Oct. 8, 1953. She grew up in Blackburn, where she studied piano; also began voice lessons there with Thomas Duerden; for a time she was employed as a telephone operator. In 1937 she won 1st prizes for piano and singing at the Carlisle Competition; she then decided on a career as a singer, and subsequently studied voice with J.E. Hutchinson in Newcastle upon Tyne and with Roy Henderson in London. After an engagement as a soloist in *Messiah* at Westminster Abbey in 1943, she began her professional career in full earnest. Britten chose her to create the title role in his *Rape of Lucretia* (Glyndebourne, July 12, 1946); she also sang Orfeo in Gluck's *Orfeo ed Euridice* there in 1947 and at Covent Garden in 1953. She made her American debut with the N.Y. Phil. on Jan. 15, 1948, singing *Das Lied von der Erde*, with Bruno Walter conducting. She made her American recital debut in N.Y. on March 29, 1949. Toward the end of her brief career, she acquired in England an almost legendary reputation for vocal excellence and impeccable taste, so that her untimely death (from cancer) was greatly mourned. In 1953 she was made a Commander of the Order of the British Empire; she also received the Gold Medal of the Royal Phil. Soc.

BIBL.: N. Cardus, ed., *K. F., A Memoir* (London, 1955; 2nd ed., rev., 1969); W. Ferrier, *The Life of K. F.* (London, 1955); C. Rigby, *K. F.* (London, 1955); W. Ferrier, *K. F., Her Life* (London, 1959); P. Lethbridge, *K. F.* (London, 1959); M. Leonard, *K.: The Life of K. F.: 1912–1953* (London, 1988).

Ferris, William (Edward), American organist, choral conductor, and composer; b. Chicago, Feb. 26, 1937. He studied composition with Alexander Tcherepnin at the De Paul Univ. School of Music (1955–60) and took private lessons with Leo Sowerby in Chicago (1957–62). In 1960 he founded the William

Ferris Chorale, specializing in the music of the Renaissance and that of 20th-century composers. He served as organist of Holy Name Cathedral in Chicago (1954–58; 1962–64) and as director of music at Sacred Heart Cathedral in Rochester, N.Y. (1966–71); in 1973 he joined the faculty of the American Cons. of Music in Chicago. His compositions are mostly liturgical.

WORKS: *Concert Piece* for Trumpet, Horn, and String Orch. (1960); *October–November,* symphonic movement (1962; Rochester, N.Y., Nov. 6, 1968); *Concert Piece* for Organ and String Orch. (1963; Boston Sym., Worcester, Mass., Nov. 19, 1967); *Celebrations,* overture (1966); Trio for Flute, Bassoon, and Piano (1957); String Trio (1958); Piano Sonata (1976). Vocal: *De profundis* (Fordham Univ., Nov. 22, 1964); *Ed e subito sera,* solo cantata for Tenor and String Quartet (1965); *The Angelic Salutation: Glory to God in the Highest* for Chorus, Organ, and Orch. (Rochester, Nov. 6, 1968); *Durobrivae,* music for Tenors, Basses, 5 Brasses, and Kettledrums (1970); *A Canticle of Celebration* for Chorus, Brasses, and Kettledrums (1971); *Make We Joy,* cantata (Chicago, Dec. 12, 1976); *A Song of Light,* cantata (Chicago, Oct. 11, 1977); *Acclamations* for Organ and Orch. (1981–82; Chicago, Jan. 27, 1983); numerous works for Chorus and Organ; a cappella choruses; songs.

Ferroni, Vincenzo (Emidio Carmine), Italian composer and educator; b. Tramutola, Feb. 17, 1858; d. Milan, Jan. 10, 1934. He studied at the Paris Cons. (1876–83) with Savard and Massenet; in 1888 returned to Italy, where he became a prof. of composition at the Milan Cons., succeeding Ponchielli; resigned in 1929. He wrote 3 operas: *Rudello* (Milan, 1892); *Ettore Fieramosca* (Como, 1896); *Il Carbonaro* (Milan, 1900); 2 syms.; a symphonic poem, *Risorgimento;* many works in smaller forms.

Ferroud, Pierre-Octave, French composer; b. Chasselay, near Lyons, Jan. 6, 1900; d. in an automobile accident near Debrecen, Hungary, Aug. 17, 1936. He attended the Univ. of Lyons, and studied there and in Strasbourg with Ropartz; subsequently returned to Lyons to study with Florent Schmitt. In 1923 he settled in Paris, where he developed varied activities as a composer, music critic, and adviser for radio broadcasting. He first attracted attention with the performance of his ballet *Le Porcher* (Paris, Nov. 15, 1924); there followed the symphonic poem *Foules* (Paris, March 21, 1926); an operatic sketch, *Chirurgie,* after Chekhov (Monte Carlo, March 20, 1928); and Sym. in A (Paris, March 8, 1931); other works are the ballets *Jeunesse* (Paris, April 29, 1933) and *Vénus ou L'Équipée planétaire* (1935); Cello Sonata (1933); *Andante cordial* for Violin, Cello, and Piano; Trio for Oboe, Clarinet, and Bassoon (1934); also several song cycles and piano pieces. Ferroud's music is distinguished by an adroit application of contrapuntal methods to compositions of an essentially popular style; his chief influence was Florent Schmitt, about whom he wrote a book, *Autour de Florent Schmitt* (Paris, 1927).

BIBL.: C. Rostand, *L'Œuvre de P.-O. F.* (Paris, 1958).

Fesca, Alexander (Ernst), German pianist and composer, son of **Friedrich (Ernst) Fesca;** b. Karlsruhe, May 22, 1820; d. Braunschweig, Feb. 22, 1849. He studied with his father, and later with Taubert in Berlin. He was extremely successful as a concert pianist from 1839; in 1841 he became chamber musician to Prince Fürstenberg; in 1842 settled in Braunschweig, where he brought out his opera *Der Troubadour* (July 25, 1847); he also wrote 3 other operas, a Piano Sextet, 2 piano trios, a Violin Sonata, and many songs, some of which became popular. His early death at the age of 28 was regretted by many admirers who believed that he was a composer of uncommon talent.

Fesca, Friedrich (Ernst), German composer, father of **Alexander (Ernst) Fesca;** b. Magdeburg, Feb. 15, 1789; d. Karlsruhe, May 24, 1826. He studied violin; made his debut in his own Violin Concerto in Magdeburg at the age of 11; in 1806 he joined the orch. of the Duke of Oldenburg; in 1808 he obtained a similar position at the Westphalian court at

Kassel; in 1813 he was in Vienna; in 1814, became a member of the Grand Duke of Baden's Chapel orch. in Karlsruhe. He was a prolific composer of chamber music (16 quartets and 4 quintets); also wrote 2 operas, *Cantemire* (Karlsruhe, April 27, 1820) and *Omar und Leila* (Karlsruhe, Feb. 26, 1824); 3 syms.; overtures; etc.

Festa, Costanzo, important Italian composer; b. c.1480; d. Rome, April 10, 1545. He was a singer in the Pontifical Chapel from 1517. He was a composer of much importance, being regarded as a forerunner of Palestrina, whose works were strongly influenced by those of Festa; was the 1st important Italian musician who successfully fused the Flemish and Italian styles, melodically and harmonically. He may well be considered one of the 1st, if not the 1st, of the native Italian madrigalists. Of his numerous compositions, many sacred works were publ. in various collections during his lifetime. A. Main ed. *Costanzo Festa, Opera omnia,* in Corpus Mensurabilis Musicae, XXV (1962–68).
    BIBL.: H. Musch, *C. F. als Madrigalistkomponist* (Baden-Baden, 1977).

Festing, Michael (Christian), English violinist and composer; b. London, c.1680; d. there, July 24, 1752. He was a pupil of Richard Jones and Geminiani. In 1735 he became Master of the King's Musick; in 1737, was appointed director of the Italian Opera; in 1742, conductor at Ranelagh Gardens. In 1738 he established, with Maurice Greene and others, the Soc. of Musicians, for the maintenance of impoverished musicians and their families. He wrote numerous solos and concertos for violin; cantatas; songs; many solos for Violin and Basso Continuo.

Fétis, Adolphe (-Louis-Eugène), Belgian-French pianist, teacher, and composer, son of **François-Joseph** and brother of **Édouard (-Louis-François) Fétis;** b. Paris, Aug. 20, 1820; d. there, March 20, 1873. He studied music with his father and then at the Brussels Cons.; subsequently studied piano with Herz and composition with Halévy in Paris. After living in Brussels and Antwerp, he settled in Paris in 1856 as a music teacher and composer. He wrote several comic operas and music for the piano.

Fétis, Édouard (-Louis-François), Belgian music editor, son of **François-Joseph** and brother of **Adolphe (-Louis-Eugène) Fétis;** b. Bouvignes, near Dinant, May 16, 1812; d. Brussels, Jan. 31, 1909. He ed. his father's *La Revue Musicale* (1833–35); was for years librarian of the Brussels Library. He publ. *Les Musiciens belges* (1848) and *Les Artistes belges à l'étranger* (1857–65), and compiled a catalog of his father's library.

Fétis, François-Joseph, erudite Belgian music theorist, historian, and critic, father of **Édouard (-Louis-François)** and **Adolphe (-Louis-Eugène) Fétis;** b. Mons, March 25, 1784; d. Brussels, March 26, 1871. He received primary instruction from his father, an organist at the Mons Cathedral; learned to play the violin, piano, and organ when very young, and in his 9th year wrote a Concerto for Violin, with Orch.; as a youth, was organist to the Noble Chapter of Ste.-Waudru. In 1800 he entered the Paris Cons., where he studied harmony with Rey and piano with Boieldieu and Pradher; in 1803 he visited Vienna, there studying counterpoint, fugue, and masterworks of German music. Several of his compositions (a Sym., an overture, sonatas and caprices for Piano) were publ. at that time. In 1806 he began the revision of the plainsong and entire ritual of the Roman Church, a vast undertaking, completed, with many interruptions, after 30 years of patient research. A wealthy marriage in the same year, 1806, enabled him to pursue his studies at ease for a time; but the fortune was lost in 1811, and he retired to the Ardennes, where he occupied himself with composition and philosophical researches into the theory of harmony; in 1813 he was appointed organist for the collegiate church of St.-Pierre at Douai. In 1818 he settled in Paris; in 1821 became a prof. of composition at the Paris Cons.; in 1824 his *Traité du contrepoint et de la*

fugue was publ. and accepted as a regular manual at the Cons. In 1827 he became librarian of the Cons., and in the same year founded his unique journal *La Revue Musicale,* which he ed. alone until 1832 (his son Édouard ed. it from 1833 until 1835, when its publication ceased). He also wrote articles on music for *Le National* and *Le Temps.* In 1828 he competed for the prize of the Netherlands Royal Inst. with the treatise *Quels ont été les mérites des Néerlandais dans la musique, principalement aux XIVe–XVIe siècles . . . ;* Kiesewetter's essay on the same subject won, but Fétis's paper was also printed by the Inst. In 1832 he inaugurated his famous series of historical lectures and concerts. In 1833 he was called to Brussels as maître de chapelle to King Leopold I, and director of the Cons.; during his long tenure in the latter position, nearly 40 years, the Cons. flourished as never before. He also conducted the concerts of the Academy, which elected him a member in 1845. He was a confirmed believer in the possibility of explaining music history and music theory scientifically; in his scholarly writings he attempted a thorough systematization of all fields of the art; he was opinionated and dogmatic, but it cannot be denied that he was a pioneer in musicology. He publ. the 1st book on music appreciation, *La Musique mise à la portée de tout le monde* (Paris, 1830; numerous reprints and trs. into Eng., German, Italian, Spanish, Russian); further pedagogical writings are: *Solfèges progressifs* (Paris, 1837); *Traité complet de la théorie et de la pratique de l'harmonie* (Brussels, 1844). As early as 1806 Fétis began collecting materials for his great *Biographie universelle des musiciens et bibliographie générale de la musique* in 8 vols. (Paris, 1833–44; 2nd ed., 1860–65; supplement of 2 vols., 1878–80; edited by A. Pougin). This work of musical biography was unprecedented in its scope; entries on composers and performers whom he knew personally still remain prime sources of information. On the negative side are the many fanciful accounts of composers' lives taken from unreliable sources; in this respect Fétis exercised a harmful influence on subsequent lexicographers for a whole century. His *Histoire générale de la musique,* in 5 vols., goes only as far as the 15th century (Paris, 1869–76; reprint, Hildesheim, 1983); this work exhibits Fétis as a profound scholar, but also as a dogmatic philosopher of music propounding opinions without convincing evidence to support them. Of interest are his *Esquisse de l'histoire de l'harmonie considerée comme art et comme science systématique* (Paris, 1840); *Notice biographique de Nicolo Paganini* (Paris, 1851; with a short history of the violin); *Antoine Stradivari* (Paris, 1856; with a commentary on bowed instruments); reports on musical instruments at the Paris Expositions of 1855 and 1867; etc. He was also a composer; between 1820 and 1832 he wrote 7 operas, serious and light, for the Opéra-Comique; composed church music, 3 string quartets, 3 string quintets, 2 syms., and a Flute Concerto. His valuable library of 7,325 vols. was acquired after his death by the Bibliothèque Royale of Brussels; a catalog was publ. in 1877.
    BIBL.: K. Gollmick, *Herr F., Vorstand des Brüsseler Conservatoriums als Mensch, Kritiker, Theoretiker und Componist* (Leipzig and Brussels, 1852); L. Alvin, *Notice sur F.-J. F.* (Brussels, 1874); R. Wangermée, *F.-J. F., musicologue et compositeur* (Brussels, 1951); B. Huys et al., *F.-J. F. et la vie musicale de son temps: 1784–1871* (Brussels, 1972).

Fetler, Paul, American composer and teacher; b. Philadelphia, Feb. 17, 1920. His family moved to Europe when he was a child; he had early music studies in Latvia, the Netherlands, Sweden, and Switzerland; he composed 2 dozen small works and part of a sym. that were later discarded. In 1939 he returned to the U.S. and studied briefly at the Chicago Cons. of Music; he also studied composition with David Van Vactor at Northwestern Univ. (graduated, 1943). Drafted into military service, he was sent at the end of World War II to Berlin as a liaison officer and Russian interpreter assigned to the Allied Control Council. It was during this time that he became a student of Sergiu Celibidache, who arranged the premiere of his *Prelude* for Orch. with members of the Berlin Phil. (July 13, 1946, composer conducting). In 1946 he returned to the U.S. to study with Quincy Porter and Hindemith at Yale Univ. (M.M., 1948). In 1948 he was appointed to the music faculty of the Univ. of Minnesota, which became his permanent position and where he earned his Ph.D. degree in 1956. He returned to Berlin in 1953 to study with Boris Blacher under a Guggenheim fellowship. His 2nd Guggenheim fellowship (1960) took him to Kreuth, Bavaria, where he composed his *Soundings* for Orch. (Minneapolis, Oct. 12, 1962). One of his most successful scores, *Contrasts* for Orch. (Minneapolis, Nov. 7, 1958), was widely performed. He received 3 N.E.A. grants (1975, 1977, 1980).

WORKS: DRAMATIC: *Sturge Maclean*, opera for youth (St. Paul, Minn., Oct. 11, 1965). **ORCH.:** *Symphonic Fantasia* (1941); *Passacaglia* (1942); *Dramatic Overture* (1943); *Berlin Scherzo* (1945); *Prelude* (Berlin, July 13, 1946); 4 syms.: No. 1 (1948); No. 2 (Rochester, N.Y., Nov. 5, 1951); No. 3 (1954; Minneapolis, Nov. 25, 1955); No. 4 (Minneapolis, May 1, 1968); *Orchestral Sketch* (Minneapolis, Aug. 15, 1949); *Comedy Overture* (Minneapolis, March 2, 1952); *Gothic Variations*, after a Machaut theme (Minneapolis, Nov. 13, 1953); *Contrasts* (Minneapolis, Nov. 7, 1958); *Soundings* (Minneapolis, Oct. 12, 1962); *Cantus tristis*, in memory of President John F. Kennedy (Minneapolis, Nov. 20, 1964); 2 violin concertos: No. 1 (St. Paul, March 27, 1971); No. 2 (1980; Minneapolis, March 18, 1981); *Celebration* (1976; Indianapolis, Dec. 16, 1977); *3 Impressions* for Guitar and Orch. (1977; Minneapolis, May 31, 1978); *Serenade* (Minneapolis, July 26, 1981; rev. 1982); Piano Concerto (Minneapolis, Oct. 4, 1984); *Capriccio* for Flute, Winds, and Strings (Minneapolis, June 6, 1985); *3 Excursions*, concerto for Percussion, Piano, and Orch. (1987; Buffalo, Dec. 10, 1988). **CHAMBER:** Sextet for String Quartet, Clarinet, and Horn (1942); 2 string quartets (1947, 1989); 2nd Violin Sonata (Minneapolis, March 6, 1952); *Cycles* for Percussion and Piano (Washington, D.C., May 31, 1970); *Pastoral Suite* for Piano Trio (St. Paul, April 11, 1976; *Rhapsody* for Violin and Piano (1985; rev. 1987); 6 Pieces for Flute and Guitar (1985; rev. 1987); many vocal works, including the cantatas *Of Earth's Image* for Soprano, Chorus, and Orch. (1958), *This Was the Way* for Mixed Chorus and Orch. (St. Paul, May 7, 1969), and *The Hour Has Come* for 2 Choruses, Organ, and Brass (1981); incidental music to plays; film scores.

Feuermann, Emanuel, greatly gifted Austrian-born American cellist; b. Kolomea, Galicia, Nov. 22, 1902; d. N.Y., May 25, 1942. As a child he was taken to Vienna, where he first studied cello with his father; subsequently studied cello with Friedrich Buxbaum and Anton Walter; made his debut in Vienna in 1913 in a recital. He went to Leipzig in 1917 to continue his studies with Julius Klengel; his progress was so great that he was appointed to the faculty of the Gürzenich Cons. in Cologne by Abendroth at the age of 16; he also was 1st cellist in the Gürzenich Orch. and was a member of the Bram Eldering Quartet. In 1929 he was appointed prof. at the Hochschule für Musik in Berlin; as a Jew he was forced to leave Germany after the advent of the Nazis to power; he then embarked on a world tour (1934–35). He made his American debut on Dec. 6, 1934, with the Chicago Sym. Orch.; then appeared as soloist with many of the leading American orchs.; also played chamber music with Schnabel and Huberman, and later with Rubinstein and Heifetz.

BIBL.: S. Itzkoff, *E. F., Virtuoso: A Biography* (University, Ala., 1979).

Févin, Antoine de, French composer; b. probably in Arras, c.1470; d. Blois, late 1511 or early 1512. He was a younger contemporary of Josquin des Prez, whose style he emulated. He composed 9 masses, motets, 3 Magnificats, and 3 Lamentations.

BIBL.: J. Delporte, "A. d.F. (1470–1512)," *Revue Liturgique et Musicale* (Jan.–Feb. 1935); E. Clinkscale, *The Complete Works of A. d.F.* (diss., N.Y. Univ., 1965).

Fevin, Robert, French composer who flourished in the early 16th century. He was a native of Cambrai, probably a relative of **Antoine de Févin.** He was maestro di cappella to the Duke of Savoy in Cambrai. He composed several masses.

Février, Henri, French composer; b. Paris, Oct. 2, 1875; d. there, July 6, 1957. He studied at the Paris Cons. with Fauré, Leroux, Pugno, and Massenet; also privately with Messager. He publ. a monograph on the latter (Paris, 1948).

WORKS: Operas: *Le Roi aveugle* (Paris, May 8, 1906); *Monna Vanna* (Paris, Jan. 13, 1909); *Gismonda* (Chicago, Jan. 14, 1919; Paris, Oct. 15, 1919); *La Damnation de Blanche-Fleur* (Monte Carlo, March 13, 1920); *La Femme nue* (Monte Carlo, March 23, 1929); operettas: *Agnès, dame galante* (1912); *Carmosine* (1913); *Île désenchantée* (Paris, Nov. 21, 1925); etc.

Fewkes, Jesse Walter, pioneering American ethnologist; b. Newton, Mass., Nov. 14, 1850; d. Forest Glen, Md., May 31, 1930. He studied biology at Harvard Univ. (Ph.D., 1877), then did postgraduate work at Leipzig and at the Univ. of Arizona. He was field director of the Hemenway Southwestern Archaeological Expedition (1889–94), on which he used a phonograph to preserve songs of the Passamaquoddy Indians of Maine (1890). These were followed by Zuni (1890) and Hopi (1891) Pueblo Indian recordings, which were analyzed by Benjamin Gilman. From 1895 he was an ethnologist at the Bureau of American Ethnology in Washington, D.C.; he became chief in 1918, retiring in 1928. He is important to ethnomusicology as the 1st researcher to record non-Western music for scientific study; his studies of the Pueblo Indians of Arizona, which include extensive observation of music along with relevant ritual, folklore, and language considerations, are still of value. He did extensive field work in ethnology, archeology, and zoology, and authored some 228 articles and publications. Among them are "On the Use of the Phonograph in the Study of Languages of American Indians," *Science*, XV (1890); "Additional Studies of Zuni Songs and Rituals with the Phonograph," *American Naturalist*, XXIV (1890); and "Tusayan Flute and Snake Ceremonies," *Annual Report of the Bureau of American Ethnology*, XIX (1900).

Ffrangcon-Davies, David (Thomas) (real name, **David Thomas Davis;** the surname Ffrangcon was taken from the Nant-Ffrangcon mountain range near his birthplace), prominent Welsh baritone; b. Bethesda, Caernarvon, Dec. 11, 1855; d. London, April 13, 1918. He was ordained a priest in 1884, but later left the church to take up a musical career; studied singing with Richard Latter, Shakespeare, and Randegger in London; made his concert debut in Manchester (Jan. 6, 1890), his stage debut at Drury Lane Theatre in London (April 26, 1890). From 1896 to 1898, he sang in festivals throughout the U.S. and Canada; then lived in Berlin (1898–1901); from 1903, he was a prof. of singing at the Royal College of Music in London. After a nervous breakdown in 1907, he gave up public singing. His book, *The Singing of the Future* (London, 1905), was republ. by his daughter, Marjorie Ffrangcon-Davies, as Part II of *David Ffrangcon-Davies, His Life and Book* (London, 1938).

Fiala, George (Joseph), Russian-born Canadian composer; b. Kiev, March 31, 1922. He took piano lessons at the music school for gifted children in Kiev; then studied composition at the Kiev Cons. with Revutsky, Liatoshinsky, and others (1939–41). When the Germans occupied Kiev in 1942, he went to Berlin, where he continued his studies despite wartime difficulties; also took courses in conducting with Furtwängler. In 1947 he moved to Belgium, where he became a student of Léon Jongen at the Brussels Cons. In 1949 he emigrated to Canada; settled in Montreal; became a Canadian citizen in 1955. Besides his activities as a composer, pianist, and teacher, he also became a music producer with the Russian section of Radio-Canada International. His compositions still retain traces of Russian and Ukrainian modalities; the settings are formally in a Classical vein.

WORKS: ORCH.: Piano Concerto (1946); *Autumn Music* for Orch. (1949); Sym. in E minor (1950); Concertino for Solo Piano, Trumpet, Timpani, and Strings (1950); *Suite concer-*

tante for Oboe and Strings (1956); *Introduction and Fugato* for English Horn and Strings (1961); *Capriccio* for Piano and Orch. (1962); *Shadows of Our Forgotten Ancestors,* symphonic poem (1962); *Divertimento concertante* for Violin and Orch. (1965); *Eulogy,* in memory of President Kennedy, for Orch. (1965); *Canadian Credo* for Chorus and Orch. (1966); *Montréal,* symphonic suite (1968); *Musique concertante* for Piano and Orch. (1968); *Serenada concertante* for Cello and Strings (1968); *Sinfonietta concertata* for Solo Free-bass Accordion, Harpsichord, and Strings (1971); *Overture Burlesque* (1972); *5 Ukrainian Songs* for Voice and Orch. (1973); Violin Concerto (1973); Sym. No. 4, *Ukrainian* (1973; Toronto, Nov. 21, 1982); *Overtura buffa* (1981); *The Kurelek Suite* (1982); *Festive Overture* (1983).

CHAMBER: *Ukrainian Suite* for Cello and Piano (1948); Wind Quintet (1948); Trio for Oboe, Cello, and Piano (1948); Woodwind Octet (1948); 2 saxophone quartets (1955, 1961); String Quartet (1956); Quartet for 4 Cellos (1957); Piano Quartet (1957); Violin Sonatina (1959); Cello Sonata (1969); Violin Sonata (1969); *Musique à trois* for String Trio (1970); Saxophone Sonata (1970); *Duo Sonata* for Violin and Harp (1971); *Sonata Fantasia* for Cello and Piano (1971); *Sonata da camera* for Soprano Saxophone and Free-bass Accordion (1971); *Musique à quatre* for String Quartet (1972); *Concertino canadese* for 4 Harps (1972); *Sonata breve* for Clarinet and Harp (1972); Piano Quintet (1982); Quartet No. 3 for Saxophone Quartet (1983); Trio Sonata for Violin, Cello, and Piano (1987). **PIANO:** 8 sonatas (No. 7, 1947; No. 8, 1970); *10 Postludes* (1947; rev. 1968); *Australian Suite* (1963); *3 Bagatelles* (1968); 2-piano Sonata (1970); *Concerto da camera* for Piano, 4-hands (1978); 2nd 2-piano Sonata (1983); *Piano Music No. 2* (1987). **VOCAL:** *Concerto Cantata* for Chorus, Piano, and Chimes obbligato (1984); *The Millennium Liturgy* for Chorus (1985).

Fialkowska, Janina, Canadian pianist; b. Montreal, May 7, 1951. She began piano lessons at age 5 with her mother, subsequently training with Yvonne Hubert and Yvonne Lefébure in Paris (1968) and Sascha Gorodnitzki at the Juilliard School in N.Y. (1969). She pursued an international career from 1975. On May 3, 1990, she was soloist with the Chicago Sym. Orch. in the 1st performance of the reputedly newly discovered E-flat-major Concerto by Liszt.

Fibich, Zdeněk (Zdenko) (Antonín Václav), important Czech composer; b. Všebořice, Dec. 21, 1850; d. Prague, Oct. 15, 1900. He studied piano with Moscheles and theory with E.F. Richter at the Leipzig Cons. (1865–66), and then composition privately with Jadassohn (1866–67) and in Mannheim with V. Lachner (1869–70). Upon his return to Prague (1871), he was deputy conductor and chorus master at the Provisional Theater (1875–78) and director of the Russian Orthodox Church Choir (1878–81). He was a fine craftsman and facile melodist, and one of the leading representatives of the Czech Romantic movement in music. His extensive output reveals the pronounced influence of Weber, Schumann, and especially Wagner. His operas *Nevěsta mesinská* (The Bride of Messina) and *Pád Arkuna* (The Fall of Arkun) are recognized as significant achievements, although they have not gained a place in the standard repertoire. He remains best known for his effective music for piano.

WORKS (all 1st perf. in Prague unless otherwise given): **OPERAS:** *Bukovín* (1870–71; April 16, 1874); *Blaník* (1874–77; Nov. 25, 1881); *Nevěsta mesinská* (The Bride of Messina, after Schiller; 1882–83; March 28, 1884); *Bouře* (The Tempest, after Shakespeare; 1893–94; March 1, 1895); *Hedy,* after Byron's *Don Juan* (1894–95; Feb. 12, 1896); *Šárka* (1896–97; Dec. 28, 1897); *Pád Arkuna* (The Fall of Arkun; 1898–99; Nov. 9, 1900); also the stage melodrama trilogy *Hippodamie* (Hippodamia), after Sophocles and Euripides: *Námluvy Pelopovy* (The Courtship of Pelops; 1888–89; Feb. 21, 1890), *Smír Tantaluv* (The Atonement of Tantalus; 1890; June 2, 1891), and *Smrt Hippodamie* (Hippodamia's Death; Nov. 8, 1891); **CONCERT MELODRAMAS FOR RECITER AND PIANO:** *Štědrý den* (Christmas Day; 1875; orchestrated 1899); *Pomsta květin* (The Revenge

of the Flowers; 1877); *Věčnost* (Eternity; 1878); *Královna Ema* (Queen Emma; 1883). **CONCERT MELODRAMAS FOR RECITER AND ORCH.:** *Vodník* (The Water Goblin; 1883); *Hakon* (1888). **ORCH.:** 7 syms. including No. 1 (1877–83), No. 2 (1892–93; Prague, April 9, 1893), and No. 3 (1898; Prague, March 7, 1899); 7 symphonic poems (1873–1900; 6 extant); 4 overtures (1873–98). **SACRED CHORAL:** *Meluzina* for Soloists, Chorus, and Orch. (1872–74); *Svatební scéna* (Wedding Scene) for 7 Soloists, Chorus, and Orch. (1872–74); *Jarní romance* (A Springtime Tale) for Soprano, Bass, Chorus, and Orch. (1880–81); *Missa brevis* for Chorus and Organ (1885); secular choral music; part-songs; songs. **CHAMBER:** Piano Trio (1872); Piano Quartet (1874); 2 string quartets (1874, 1878); 2 violin sonatas (1874, 1875); Piano Quintet (1893); etc.; many piano works, including 376 pieces publ. as *Nálady, dojmy a upomínky* (Moods, Impressions, and Reminiscences; 1892–99). A critical ed. of his works was publ. in Prague (1950–67).

BIBL.: J. Bartoš, Z. F. (Prague, 1914); J. Plavec, Z. F., *mistr české balady* (Z. F., Master of the Czech Ballad; Prague, 1940); K. Jirák, Z. F. (Prague, 1947); G. Abraham, "The Operas of Z. F.," *19th Century Music* (Fall 1985).

Ficher, Jacobo, Russian-Argentine composer; b. Odessa, Jan. 15, 1896; d. Buenos Aires, Sept. 9, 1978. He studied violin with Stolarsky and Korguev in Odessa and composition with Kalafati and Steinberg at the St. Petersburg Cons., graduating in 1917. In 1923 he emigrated to Argentina. In 1956 he was appointed prof. of composition at the National Cons. of Music in Buenos Aires. His music is characterized by a rhapsodic fluency of development and a rich harmonic consistency. A prolific composer, he wrote for the stage, for orch., and for voice; he particularly excelled in chamber music.

WORKS: STAGE: Chamber operas: *The Bear* (1952) and *Proposal in Marriage* (1955), both after Chekhov; ballets: *Colombina de Hoy* (1933); *Los Invitados* (1933); *Golondrina* (1942). **ORCH.:** 8 syms. (1932; 1933; 1938–40; 1947; 1948; 1956; 1958–59; 1965); *Sulamita,* symphonic poem (Buenos Aires, July 20, 1929); *Obertura patética* (Buenos Aires, May 17, 1930); Violin Concerto (1942); 3 piano concertos (1945, 1954, 1960); Harp Concerto (1956); Flute Concerto (1965). **CHAMBER:** 4 string quartets (1927, 1936, 1943, 1952); Piano Quintet (1961); Wind Quintet (1967); 3 violin sonatas (1929, 1945, 1959); *Suite en estilo antiguo* for Woodwind Quintet (1930); Sonata for Viola, Flute, and Piano (1931); Sonatina for Saxophone, Trumpet, and Piano (1932); Piano Trio (1935); Flute Sonata (1935); Clarinet Sonata (1937); Oboe Sonata (1940); Cello Sonata (1943); Sonata for Flute and Clarinet (1949); Sonata for Flute, Oboe, and Bassoon (1950); Viola Sonata (1953); 8 piano sonatas; several sets of piano pieces (including 2 groups of effective "fables," descriptive of animals). **CANTATAS:** *Salmo de alegría* (1949); *Mi aldea* (1958); *Kadisch* (1969).

BIBL.: B. Zipman, *J. F.* (Buenos Aires, 1966).

Fickénscher, Arthur, American pianist, teacher, and composer; b. Aurora, Ill., March 9, 1871; d. San Francisco, April 15, 1954. He studied at the Munich Cons.; toured the U.S. as accompanist to famous singers, among them Bispham and Schumann-Heink. From 1920 till 1941 he was head of the music dept. of the Univ. of Virginia, Charlottesville. In 1947 he settled in San Francisco. A musician of an inquisitive mind, he elaborated a system of pure intonation; contrived the "Polytone," an instrument designed to play music in which the octave is subdivided into 60 tones; publ. an article, "The Polytone and the Potentialities of a Purer Intonation," *Musical Quarterly* (July 1941). His major work was the *Evolutionary Quintet,* evolved from a violin sonata and an orch. scherzo written in the 1890s; the MSS were burned in the San Francisco earthquake and fire of 1906; the musical material was then used from memory for a quintet for piano and strings, in 2 movements; the 2nd movement, entitled *The 7th Realm,* became a separate work. He also wrote *Willowwave and Wellowway* for Orch. (1925); *The Day of Judgment* for Orch. (1927; Grand Rapids, Feb. 10, 1934); *Out of the Gay Nineties* for Orch. (Richmond, Va., Dec. 4, 1934, composer conducting);

Variations on a Theme in Medieval Style for String Orch. (1937); *Dies irae* for Chamber Orch. (1927); *The Chamber Blue,* mimodrama for Orch., Soli, Women's Chorus, and Dancers (1907–9; rev. 1935; Univ. of Virginia, April 5, 1938); *The Land East of the Sun* for Chorus and Orch. (unfinished); Piano Quintet (1939).

BIBL.: W. Jones, *A Biographical Sketch and Catalogue of the Works of A. F.* (MS, 1957).

Ficker, Rudolf von, distinguished German musicologist; b. Munich, June 11, 1886; d. Igls, near Innsbruck, Aug. 2, 1954. From 1905 to 1912 he studied at the Univ. of Vienna with Adler (musicology), and in Munich with Thuille and Courvoisier (composition); received his Ph.D. from the Univ. of Vienna in 1913 with the dissertation *Die Chromatik im italienischen Madrigal des 16. Jahrhunderts.* He taught at the Univ. of Innsbruck from 1920; became a prof. there in 1923; at the Univ. of Vienna in 1927; and in 1931 at the Univ. of Munich. He was a specialist in medieval music. In addition to articles for music journals, he also left unfinished a book entitled *Die Grundlagen der abendländischen Mehrstimmigkeit.*

Fiedler, Arthur, highly popular American conductor; b. Boston, Dec. 17, 1894; d. Brookline, Mass., July 10, 1979. Of a musical family, he studied violin with his father, Emanuel Fiedler, a member of the Boston Sym. Orch.; his uncle, Benny Fiedler, also played violin in the Boston Sym. Orch. In 1909 he was taken by his father to Berlin, where he studied violin with Willy Hess, and attended a class on chamber music with Ernst von Dohnányi; he also had some instruction in conducting with Arno Kleffel and Rudolf Krasselt. In 1913 he formed the Fiedler Trio with 2 other Fiedlers. In 1915, with the war raging in Europe, he returned to America, and joined the 2nd-violin section of the Boston Sym. Orch. under Karl Muck; later he moved to the viola section; he also doubled on the celesta, when required. In 1924 he organized the Arthur Fiedler Sinfonietta, a professional ensemble of members of the Boston Sym. Orch. In 1929 he started a series of free open-air summer concerts at the Esplanade on the banks of the Charles River in Boston, presenting programs of popular American music intermingled with classical numbers. The series became a feature in Boston's musical life, attracting audiences of many thousands each summer. In 1930 Fiedler was engaged as conductor of the Boston Pops, which he led for nearly half a century. Adroitly combining pieces of popular appeal with classical works and occasional modern selections, he built an eager following, eventually elevating the Boston Pops to the status of a national institution. He was seemingly undisturbed by the clinking of beer steins, the pushing of chairs, the shuffling of feet, and other incidental sound effects not provided for in the score but which were an integral part of audience participation at Pops concerts. For Fiedler was a social man, gregarious, fond of extracurricular activities; one of his favorite pastimes was riding on fire engines; this addiction was rewarded by a number of nominations as honorary chief of the fire depts. of several American cities. He became commercially successful and willingly accepted offers to advertise for whisky or for orange juice; this popularity, however, cost him a degradation to a lower rank of music-makers, so that his cherished ambition to conduct guest engagements in the regular subscription series of the Boston Sym. Orch. never materialized. On Jan. 4, 1977, President Ford bestowed upon him the Medal of Freedom. As a mark of appreciation from the city of Boston, a footbridge near the Esplanade was named after him, with the 1st 2 notes of the Prelude to *Tristan und Isolde,* A and F, marking the initials of Arthur Fiedler's name, engraved on the plaque. His death was mourned by Boston music-lovers in a genuine outpouring of public grief.

BIBL.: R. Moore, *F., The Colorful Mr. Pops* (Boston, 1968); C. Wilson, *A. F., Music for the Millions* (N.Y., 1968); J. Holland, *Mr. Pops* (N.Y., 1972); H. Dickson, *A. F. and the Boston Pops* (Boston, 1981).

Fiedler, (August) Max, German conductor and composer; b. Zittau, Dec. 31, 1859; d. Stockholm, Dec. 1, 1939. He was

a piano pupil of his father, and studied the organ and theory with G. Albrecht; attended the Leipzig Cons. (1877–80). In 1882 he was appointed a teacher at the Hamburg Cons.; in 1903, became its director. In 1904 he succeeded Barth as conductor of the Hamburg Phil. Soc.; remained there until 1908. He was guest conductor of the N.Y. Phil. during the season of 1905–6; in 1907, conducted the London Sym. Orch. The climax of his career was the prestigious appointment as conductor of the Boston Sym. Orch., a position he held from 1908 to 1912. In 1916 he was named music director in Essen; after 1933 appeared as conductor with the Berlin Phil. and the Berlin Radio. He composed a Sym., a Piano Quintet, a String Quartet, a *Lustspiel* overture, piano pieces, and songs.

BIBL.: G. Dejmek, *M. F.; Werden und Werken* (Essen, 1940).

Field, John, remarkable Irish pianist and composer; b. Dublin, July 26, 1782; d. Moscow, Jan. 23, 1837. His father was a violinist; his grandfather, an organist; it was from his grandfather that he received his 1st instruction in music. At the age of 9 he began study with Tommaso Giordani, making his debut in Dublin on March 24, 1792. He went to London in 1793, and gave his 1st concert there that same year. He then had lessons with Clementi, and was also employed in the salesrooms of Clementi's music establishment. He began his concert career in earnest with a notable series of successful appearances in London in 1800–1801. He then accompanied Clementi on his major tour of the Continent, beginning in 1802. After visiting Paris in 1802, they proceeded to St. Petersburg in 1803; there Field settled as a performer and teacher, giving his debut performance in 1804. He made many concert tours in Russia. Stricken with cancer of the rectum, he returned to London in 1831 for medical treatment. He performed his Piano Concerto in E-flat major at a Phil. Soc. concert there on Feb. 27, 1832; later that year he played in Paris, and then subsequently toured various cities in France, Belgium, Switzerland, and Italy until his health compelled him to abandon his active career. He eventually returned to Moscow, where he died. Field's historical position as a composer is of importance, even though his music does not reveal a great original talent. He developed the free fantasias and piano recitative, while following the basic precepts of Classical music; he was also the originator of keyboard nocturnes. He composed 7 concertos (1799, 1814, 1816, 1816, 1817, 1819 [rev. 1820], 1822); 4 sonatas (1801, 1801, 1813); about 30 nocturnes (1812–36?); polonaises, etc.; also a Quintet for Piano and Strings (1816) and 2 divertimenti for Piano, Strings, and Flute (c.1810–11).

BIBL.: F. Liszt, *Über J. F.s Nocturnes* (Hamburg, 1859; also in vol. IV of Liszt's *Gesammelte Schriften,* Leipzig, 1882); H. Dessauer, *J. F., Sein Leben und seine Werke* (Langensalza, 1912); W. Grattan Flood, *J. F. of Dublin* (Dublin, 1920); E. von Tideböhl, "Reminiscences of J. F.," *Monthly Musical Record,* LIII (1923); E. Blom, "J. F.," *Chesterian,* XI (1930); A. Nikolaev, *J. F.* (Moscow, 1960; Eng. tr., 1973); C. Hopkinson, *A Bibliographical Thematic Catalogue of the Works of J. F.* (London, 1961); G. Southall, *J. F.'s Piano Concertos: An Analytical and Historical Study* (diss., Univ. of Iowa, 1966); D. Branson, *J. F. and Chopin* (London, 1972); P. Piggott, *The Life and Music of J. F.* (London, 1973; 2nd ed., 1984); R. Langley, "J. F. and the Genesis of a Style," *Musical Times* (Feb. 1982).

Fields, James, American pianist; b. Los Angeles, Nov. 1, 1948; d. there, Nov. 15, 1984. He studied piano with Ethel Leginska and Victor Aller; appeared in public as a child. In 1965 he won a debut grant of the Young Musicians Foundation in California, which catapulted him into a successful concert career.

Fielitz, Alexander von, German conductor and composer; b. Leipzig, Dec. 28, 1860; d. Bad Salzungen, July 29, 1930. He was of partly Slavic origin; his mother was Russian. He studied piano with Julius Schulhoff and composition with Kretschmer in Dresden; in conducting he profited by the advice of Nikisch. He conducted opera in various German towns; a nervous disorder caused him to take a prolonged rest in Italy (1887–97); then he settled in Berlin as a teacher. From 1905 to 1908 he was in Chicago, where he organized an orch. and conducted it for a season; in 1908 he returned to Berlin as a teacher at, and later (1916) director of, the Stern Cons. He wrote a number of songs and piano pieces; his song cycle *Eliland* and his songs based on Tuscan folk music were quite popular; he also wrote 2 operas, *Vendetta* (Lübeck, 1891) and *Das stille Dorf* (Hamburg, March 13, 1900).

Fiévet, Paul, French composer; b. Valenciennes, Dec. 11, 1892; d. Paris, March 15, 1980. His father, **Claude Fiévet** (1865–1938), was a composer in his own right. Paul Fiévet studied piano and music theory at the Paris Cons., where he was a student of Xavier Leroux, Caussade, and Widor, obtaining 1st prize in harmony in 1913, and 1st prize in composition in 1917, 1918, and 1919. He received the Grand Prix International in Ostende in 1931 and the Grand Prix of Paris in 1932. Among his works are an operetta, *Le Joli Jeu* (Lyons, 1933), and several symphonic suites of the type of "landscape music," e.g., *Les Horizons dorés* (Paris, 1932), *Puerta del Sol* (Paris, 1933), *Images de France* (Paris, 1964), *Orient* (Paris, 1929), *En hiver.* He also wrote several string quartets (one of which he whimsically entitled *Sputnik*), a Brass Sextet, and numerous choruses and piano pieces.

Figner, Medea, famous Italian-Russian soprano; b. Florence, April 3, 1858; d. Paris, July 8, 1952. Her complete name was **Zoraide Amedea Mei.** She studied voice with Bianchi, Carlotta Carozzi-Zucchi, and Panofka in Florence; made her debut as Azucena in Sinalunga, near Florence, in 1875; then sang in the opera theaters of Florence. From 1877 to 1887 she toured in Italy, Spain, and South America; she met the celebrated Russian tenor **Nikolai (Nikolaievich) Figner** during her travels, and followed him to Russia; they were married in 1889; she subsequently appeared under the name **Medea Mei-Figner;** they were divorced in 1903. She became extremely successful on the Russian operatic stage; was a member of the Maryinsky Imperial Opera Theater in St. Petersburg until 1912. She then devoted herself mainly to voice teaching. In 1930 she emigrated to Paris. Her voice was described by contemporary critics as engagingly soft, rich, "velvety," and "succulent." She could sing mezzo-soprano roles as impressively as those in the soprano range. She was fortunate in having been coached by Tchaikovsky in the role of Liza in his opera *The Queen of Spades,* which she sang at its premiere in St. Petersburg (Dec. 19, 1890); her husband sang the role of her lover in the same opera. Her other successful roles were Tosca, Mimi, Donna Anna, Elsa, Brünnhilde, Marguerite, Desdemona, Aida, Amneris, and Carmen. In 1912 she publ., in St. Petersburg, her memoirs.

Figner, Nikolai (Nikolaievich), celebrated Russian tenor; b. Nikiforovka, Feb. 21, 1857; d. Kiev, Dec. 13, 1918. He was a lieutenant in the Russian navy before deciding upon a career in music; then studied voice with Prianishnikov and Everardi in St. Petersburg (1881–82), and with De Roxas in Naples, where he made his operatic debut at the Teatro Sannazaro in Gounod's *Philémon et Baucis* in 1882. After singing in various Italian cities and in Latin America, he was a leading member of the Maryinsky Imperial Opera Theater in St. Petersburg (1887–1907). He made his debut at Covent Garden in London on May 26, 1887, as the Duke in *Rigoletto.* After singing in private Russian theaters (1907–10), he served as director of the Narodny Dom in St. Petersburg (1910–15). He was married to the Italian soprano **Medea Mei** (1889–1903); she described their careers in her memoirs (St. Petersburg, 1912). He was the favorite tenor of Tchaikovsky and was selected to create the roles of Hermann in *The Queen of Spades* (Dec. 19, 1890) and Count Vaudémont in *Yolanta* (Dec. 18, 1892) at their St. Petersburg premieres. His other roles included Lensky, Otello, Don José, Faust, Radames, Werther, Lohengrin, and Roméo.

Bibl.: L. Kutateladse, *N. F.: Recollections, Letters, Materials* (Leningrad, 1968).

Figueredo, Carlos, Venezuelan composer; b. Valencia, Aug. 15, 1910. He studied with Vicente Emilio Sojo at the Caracas School of Music, graduating in 1947. In 1948 he entered the diplomatic service as a cultural attaché at the Venezuelan Embassy in Paris, consul in Copenhagen, and then in Madrid. However, he did not abandon music; he wrote 4 competent syms. (1947, 1948, 1951, 1953), some acceptable chamber music, and tolerable choruses.

Figulus (real name, **Töpfer**), **Wolfgang,** German composer and writer on music; b. Naumburg an der Saale, c.1525; d. Meissen, Sept. 1589. He studied in Leipzig; from 1549 to 1551, was cantor at the Thomaskirche in Leipzig; from 1551to 1588, at the Fürstenschule in Meissen. He wrote *Elementa musicae* (1555; many other eds.); rev. Martin Agricola's *Deutsche Musica und Gesängbuchlein* (1560); publ. a book of motets, *Precationes* (Leipzig, 1553); *Cantiones sacrae* (1575); and *Hymni sacri et scholastici* (rev. by his son-in-law, Friedrich Birck, 1604); a collection of Christmas songs, containing works of his own, of Martin Agricola, and others, was publ. posth. in 2 books (1594, 1605).

Figuš-Bystrý, Viliam, Slovak composer; b. Banská Bystrica, Feb. 28, 1875; d. there, May 11, 1937. He spent many years collecting Slovak folk melodies, which he publ. in 5 vols. (1906–15) for voice and piano; also publ. a collection of 1,000 arranged for piano only (1925–31). He further wrote an opera, *Detvan* (1924; Bratislava, Aug. 1, 1928); a cantata, *Slovenská Piesen* (1913); an orch. suite, *From My Youth;* Piano Quartet; Piano Trio; 3 sonatines for Violin and Piano; violin pieces; piano works; choruses and songs.

Filev, Ivan, Bulgarian composer and conductor; b. Kazanluk, June 22, 1941. He studied conducting with Iliev and composition with Goleminov and Raichev at the Bulgarian State Cons. in Sofia, graduating in 1968.

Works: 2 piano concertinos (1963, 1967); String Quartet (1964); *Music* for Strings, Winds, and Piano (1966); Sym. for String Orch. (1967); *5 Pieces* for Orch. (1967); Rondo for String Orch. (1968); Prelude and Fugue for Orch. (1968); *Symphonic Forms* (1970); Concerto for Orch. (1973).

Filiasi, Lorenzo, Italian composer; b. Naples, March 25, 1878; d. Rome, July 30, 1963. He studied at the Conservatorio di S. Pietro a Majella with Nicola d'Arienzo. His 1st success came with the opera *Manuel Menendez,* which won the Sonzogno Competition Prize in 1902 and was produced in Milan (May 15, 1904); his other operas included *Fior di Neve* (La Scala, April 1, 1911) and *Messidoro* (1912). He also wrote a pantomime, *Pierrot e Bluette* (1895); a choral work, with Orch., *La preghiera del marinaio italiano; Visioni romantiche* for Orch.; violin pieces; many songs.

Filippi, Filippo, Italian writer on music and composer; b. Vicenza, Jan. 13, 1830; d. Milan, June 24, 1887. He studied law at Padua, taking his degree in 1853. In 1851 he began his career as a music critic with a warm defense of Verdi's *Rigoletto;* from 1859 till 1862 was ed. of the *Gazzetta Musicale,* and from 1859 to 1862 was music critic of the newly founded *Perseveranza* and then its ed. (1862–87). He publ. a collection of essays on great musicians, *Musica e musicisti* (Milan, 1876); as a zealous Wagnerite he wrote a pamphlet, *Riccardo Wagner* (in German, as *Richard Wagner: Eine musikalische Reise in das Reich der Zukunft,* 1876); also publ. a monograph, *Della vita e delle opere di Adolfo Fumagalli* (Milan, 1857); composed a String Quintet; 9 string quartets; Piano Trio; piano pieces; songs.

Bibl.: A. Della Corte, "Le critiche musicali di F. F.," *Rivista Musicale Italiana,* LVI (1954).

Filke, Max, German composer; b. Steubendorf-Leobschütz, Silesia, Oct. 5, 1855; d. Breslau, Oct. 8, 1911. He studied with Brosig in Breslau and with Haberl at the Kirchenmusikschule in Regensburg (1877); then with Piutti at the Leipzig

Cons. (1880); was engaged as choirmaster at Straubing (1881) and conductor of the Sängerkreis at Cologne (1890); then became director at the Cathedral in Breslau and prof. at the inst. for church music there. He wrote numerous compositions for the church.

Filleul, Henry, French composer; b. Laval, May 11, 1877; d. Saint-Omer, May 1, 1959. He studied at the Paris Cons. with Lavignac and Casadesus; in 1908 became director of the École Nationale de Musique at St. Omer.

WORKS: *Le Jugement de Triboulet*, comic opera (1923); oratorios: *Le Christ vainqueur* (1925); *Le Miracle de Lourdes* (1927); *Les Doulces Joyes de Nostre Dame* (1928); *Jeanne d'Arc* (1929); *Eva* (1931); *Variations symphoniques sur un thème languedocien* (1939); *Fantaisie concertante* for Piano and Orch. (1950); Cello Concerto; violin pieces, with organ; motets; male choruses; etc.

BIBL.: *Hommage à Henri F.* (St. Omer, 1952).

Fillmore, (James) Henry (Jr.), American bandmaster and composer; b. Cincinnati, Feb. 3, 1881; d. Miami, Fla., Dec. 7, 1956. His paternal grandfather was August Damerin Fillmore (2nd cousin of President Millard Fillmore); his father, James Henry Fillmore, and his uncles Fred A. and Charles M. Fillmore were the founders of the Cincinnati music publishing firm of Fillmore Bros. Co. Henry Fillmore was educated at the Miami (Ohio) Military Inst., and later at the Cincinnati College of Music. As a bandmaster, he led the Syrian Shrine Band of Cincinnati to national prominence in the period from 1920 to 1926, making several transcontinental tours; in 1915 he founded the Fillmore Band, which was one of the earliest bands to make regular radio broadcasts (1927–34). In 1938 he moved to Miami, Fla., where he conducted bands at the Orange Bowl. He is best known, however, as the composer of numerous popular marches (*Americans We, Men of Ohio, His Honor* et al.), 2nd only to Sousa's in their tuneful liveliness. He was also the leading proponent of the "trombone smear," a humorous effect of the trombone glissando. He used numerous pseudonyms in his publ. pieces (**Al Hayes, Harry Hartley, Ray Hall, Gus Beans, Henrietta Moore,** and **Harold Bennett,** under which name he publ. the popular *Military Escort March*). He was also a compiler of sacred songs and tune books. In 1956 he received an honorary D.Mus. degree from the Univ. of Miami (Fla.).

BIBL.: P. Bierley, *Hallelujah Trombone: The Story of H. F.* (Columbus, Ohio, 1982); idem, *The Music of H. F. and Will Huff* (Columbus, Ohio, 1982).

Fillmore, John Comfort, American music educator; b. Franklin, Conn., Feb. 4, 1843; d. Norwich, Conn., Aug. 14, 1898. He was a pupil of G.W. Steele at Oberlin College in Ohio; then at the Leipzig Cons. (1865–67). He was director of the music dept. at Oberlin College (1867–68); Ripon College in Wisconsin (1868–78); Milwaukee College for Women (1878–84). He founded (1884) the Milwaukee School of Music, of which he was director until 1895, when he took charge of the School of Music of Pomona College in Claremont, Calif.

WRITINGS: *Pianoforte Music: Its History, with Biographical Sketches and Critical Estimates of Its Greatest Masters* (Chicago, 1883); *New Lessons in Harmony* (Philadelphia, 1887); *Lessons in Music History* (Philadelphia, 1888); *A Study of Omaha Indian Music* (with Alice C. Fletcher and F. La Flesche, 1893).

BIBL.: J. McNutt, "J.C. F.: A Student of Indian Music Reconsidered," *American Music*, II/1 (1984).

Filtz, (Johann) Anton, talented German composer; b. Eichstätt (baptized), Sept. 22, 1733; d. Mannheim (buried), March 14, 1760. He was a pupil of J. Stamitz; from 1754, 2nd cellist in the Mannheim Orch. He belongs to the school of Mannheim Symphonists, early practitioners of classic instrumental style. That his works must have enjoyed great popularity seems to be proved by the numerous reprints issued at London and Amsterdam, pirated from the original Paris eds. He was exceptionally prolific; in the span of his brief life he completed 60 syms., many trio sonatas, string trios, sonatas for violin, cello, flute, etc., and concertos for various instruments. Riemann publ. 4 syms. by Filtz in Denkmäler der Tonkunst in Bayern (4 and 13; formerly 3.i and 7.ii); 2 trios (ibid., 27; formerly 15); and 1 trio in *Collegium Musicum*.

Finck, Heinrich, German composer, great-uncle of **Hermann Finck;** b. probably in Bamberg, 1444 or 1445; d. Vienna, June 9, 1527. He grew up in Poland; was educated at the Univ. of Leipzig (matriculated in 1482); was in the service of Prince Alexander of Vilnius, Lithuania, as Kapellmeister by 1498, and continued in his service when Alexander became king of Poland in 1501, being active at the court in Krakow until at least 1505. He left Poland in 1510, and then was Singemeister at the ducal Kapelle in Stuttgart until 1514; subsequently served the court in Augsburg until being appointed composer of the cathedral chapter in Salzburg in 1519; he formally assumed the position of Hofkapellmeister to the court in Vienna on Jan. 1, 1527. A large portion of his output has not survived; 113 pieces are known to be by him, some incomplete. Among his works are 7 masses, 40 motets, motet cycles for the Proper of the Mass, 28 hymns, 38 songs, and instrumental pieces. See L. Hoffmann-Erbrecht, ed., *Heinrich Finck: Ausgewählte Werke*, I, in Das Erbe Deutscher Musik (1962).

BIBL.: L. Hoffmann-Erbrecht, "H. F. in Polen," *Gesellschaft für Musikforschung Kongressbericht* (Kassel, 1962); idem, *Henricus F., musicus excellentissimus* (1445–1527) (Cologne, 1982).

Finck, Henry T(heophilus), prominent American music critic and editor; b. Bethel, Mo., Sept. 22, 1854; d. Rumford Falls, Maine, Oct. 1, 1926. He was brought up in Oregon; then entered Harvard Univ., where he studied with J.K. Paine. After graduation in 1876 he went to Germany; studied comparative psychology in Berlin and Vienna, and publ. a book, *Romantic Love and Personal Beauty* (1887), propounding a theory that romantic love was unknown to the ancient nations. He was music critic of the N.Y. *Evening Post* and the *Nation* from 1881 to 1924, and occasionally wrote for other journals. Finck was a brilliant journalist; in his books on music he stressed the personal and psychological elements. He married the pianist Abbie Cushman in 1890; a fine literary stylist, she succeeded in copying her husband's style and even wrote music reviews for him.

WRITINGS: *Chopin, and Other Musical Essays* (1889); *Wagner and His Works* (2 vols., 1893; reprinted 1968); with others, *Anton Seidl: A Memorial by His Friends* (1899); *Songs and Song Writers* (1900); *Edvard Grieg* (1906); *Grieg and His Music* (1909); *Success in Music and How It Is Won* (1909); *Massenet and His Operas* (1910); *Richard Strauss* (1917); *Musical Progress* (1923).

Finck, Hermann, German organist, music theorist, and composer, great-nephew of **Heinrich Finck;** b. Pirna, Saxony, March 21, 1527; d. Wittenberg, Dec. 28, 1558. He was educated at the court chapel of King Ferdinand I of Hungary and Bohemia; studied at Wittenberg Univ. (1545); then taught music there (1554); was appointed town organist in 1557. His major work is the treatise *Practica musica* (1556).

BIBL.: P. Matzdorf, *Die Practica musica H. F.s* (Frankfurt, 1957); F. Kirby, *H. F.'s Practica musica: A Comparative Study in 16th Century German Musical Theory* (diss., Yale Univ., 1957).

Findeisen, Nikolai (Fyodorovich), Russian music historian and editor; b. St. Petersburg, July 23, 1868; d. there (Leningrad), Sept. 20, 1928. He studied with Nicolai Sokolov; in 1893 he founded the *Russian Musical Gazette* and remained its ed. until it ceased publication in 1917. His writings include monographs on Verstovsky (1890), Serov (1900; 2nd ed., augmented, 1904), Dargomyzhsky (1902), Anton Rubinstein (1905), and Rimsky-Korsakov (1908); he publ. a series of brochures and books on Glinka; the 1st vol. of a projected large biography, *Glinka in Spain*, appeared in 1896; a catalog of

Glinka's MSS, letters, and portraits was publ. in 1898; he also ed. Glinka's correspondence (2 vols., 1907–8). Findeisen's major achievement was the extensive history of Russian music up to the year 1800, publ. in 2 vols. (partly posth.) in Leningrad (1928–29), under the title *Sketches of Music in Russia from the Most Ancient Times until the End of the 18th Century.*

Findeisen, Otto, German composer and conductor; b. Brünn, Dec. 23, 1862; d. Leipzig, Jan. 23, 1947. He conducted in Magdeburg from 1890, and produced 2 of his operettas there: *Der alte Dessauer* (1890) and *Hennigs von Treffenfeld* (1891). Other light operas were: *Frau Holle* (Berlin, 1904); *Kleopatra* (Hamburg, 1897); *Der Spottvogel* (Bremen, 1898); *Der Sühneprinz* (Leipzig, 1904); *Sonnenguckerl* (Vienna, 1908); *Meister Pinkebank* (Vienna, 1909); etc.

Fine, Irving (Gifford), remarkable American composer; b. Boston, Dec. 3, 1914; d. there, Aug. 23, 1962. He studied with Walter Piston at Harvard Univ. (B.A., 1937; M.A., 1938) and with Nadia Boulanger in Cambridge, Mass. (1938), and in France (1939); studied choral conducting with A.T. Davison; also conducting with Koussevitzky at the Berkshire Music Center at Tanglewood. He taught at Harvard Univ. (1939–50), then was prof. at Brandeis Univ. (from 1950); he also taught at the Berkshire Music Center (1946–57). He was at first influenced by Stravinsky and Hindemith, adopting a cosmopolitan style of composition in which contrapuntal elaboration and energetic rhythm were his main concerns; he later developed a distinctive style of his own, with a lyrical flow of cohesive melody supported by lucid polyphony.
Works: *Toccata concertante* for Orch. (Boston, Oct. 22, 1948); *Notturno* for Strings and Harp (1950–51); *Serious Song,* lament for Strings (1955); *Diversions* for Orch. (1959–60); *Blue Towers* for Orch. (1959); *Symphony 1962* (Boston, March 23, 1962); 3 choruses from *Alice in Wonderland* for 3 to 4 Voices, and Piano or Orch. (1942; 2nd set for Chorus and Piano, 1953); Violin Sonata (1946); *Music* for Piano (1947); Partita for Wind Quintet (1948); String Quartet (1952); Fantasia for String Trio (1956–57); *Hommage à Mozart* for Piano (1956); *Romanza* for Wind Quintet (1958).
Bibl.: R. Wise, *Scoring in the Neoclassic Woodwind Quintets of Hindemith, F., Etler, and Wilder* (diss., Univ. of Wisconsin, 1967).

Fine, Vivian, American composer, teacher, and pianist; b. Chicago, Sept. 28, 1913. She became a scholarship student in piano at the age of 5 at the Chicago Musical College; she studied piano with Djane Lavoie-Herz, harmony and composition with Ruth Crawford and Adolf Weidig, and composition with Henry Cowell; in 1931 she went to N.Y., where she studied piano with Abby Whiteside, composition with Roger Sessions, and orchestration with George Szell; she also appeared as a pianist. She held teaching positions at N.Y. Univ. (1945–48), the Juilliard School of Music in N.Y. (1948), the State Univ. of N.Y. at Potsdam (1951), the Conn. College School of Dance (1963–64), and Bennington (Vt.) College (1964–87). In 1980 she received a Guggenheim fellowship and was elected to the American Academy and Inst. of Arts and Letters. She was particularly adept at writing vocal and instrumental works in a dissonant but acceptable style. In 1935 she married the sculptor Benjamin Karp.
Works: **Theater:** *Alcestis* for Orch. (N.Y., April 29, 1960); *The Women in the Garden,* chamber opera for 5 Voices and Chamber Ensemble (1977; San Francisco, Feb. 12, 1978). **Orch.:** *Elegiac Song* for String Orch. (1937; Lenox, Mass., Aug. 8, 1971); Concertante for Piano and Orch. (1944); *Meeting for Equal Rights 1866* for Soprano, Baritone, Narrator, Chorus, and Orch. (N.Y., April 23, 1976); *Drama for Orchestra* (1982; San Francisco, Jan. 5, 1983); *Poetic Fires* for Piano and Orch. (1984; N.Y., Feb. 21, 1985, composer soloist); *Dancing Winds* (1987); *After the Tradition* for Chamber Orch. (1988). **Choral:** *Valedictions* for Soprano, Tenor, Chorus, and 10 Instruments (1959); *Morning* for Narrator, Chorus, and Organ (1962); *Paean* for Narrator, Women's Voices, and Brass Ensemble (1969); *Sounds of the Nightingale* for Soprano, Women's

Voices, and 9 Instruments (1971); *Oda a las ranas* for Women's Voices, Flute, Oboe, Cello, and Percussion (1980). **Chamber:** String Trio (1930); *Prelude* for String Quartet (1937); *Capriccio* for Oboe and String Trio (1946); Violin Sonata (1952); String Quartet (1957); 3 Pieces for Flute, Bassoon, and Harp (1961); *Dreamscape* for 3 Flutes, Cello, Piano, and Percussion Ensemble (1964); Chamber Concerto for Solo Cello, Oboe, Violin, Viola, Cello, Double Bass, and Piano (1966); Quintet for String Trio, Trumpet, and Harp (1967); Brass Quintet (1978); Piano Trio (1980); Quintet for Oboe, Clarinet, Violin, Cello, and Piano (1984); Cello Sonata (1986); also piano pieces; other works for solo instruments.

Finger, Gottfried, Moravian composer; b. probably in Olomouc, c.1660; d. Mannheim (buried), Aug. 31, 1730. After traveling in Italy, he made his way to England, where he was an instrumentalist in the Roman Catholic chapel of King James II (1687–88); subsequently was active as a composer of incidental music for the London stage, and also wrote operas. He left England in 1704, in 1706 entering the service of Duke Karl Philipp of Neuburg in Breslau, where he remained until 1723.
Works: Operas: *The Rival Queens, or The Death of Alexander* (also known as *Alexander the Great;* London, 1696 or 1703; with D. Purcell); *The Virgin Prophetess, or The Fate of Troy* (London, May 15, 1701); *Der Sieg der Schönheit über die Helden* (Berlin, 1706; with Greber and Stricker; not extant); incidental music to plays by Congreve, Dryden, Shakespeare, Cibber, and others; masques, odes, and serenades; much instrumental music, including numerous sonatas.

Fink, Christian, German organist and composer; b. Dettingen, Aug. 9, 1822; d. Esslingen, near Stuttgart, Sept. 5, 1911. He studied at the Leipzig Cons.; became organist there (1856–60); in 1863 was appointed church organist at Esslingen; publ. numerous organ works. He was greatly esteemed in Germany; his choral works and organ pieces were often performed.

Fink, (Christian) Gottfried Wilhelm, German writer on music and editor; b. Sulza, Thuringia, March 8, 1783; d. Leipzig, Aug. 27, 1846. He studied history and theology in Leipzig; wrote criticism in the *Allgemeine Musikalische Zeitung* from 1808; in 1828 he became ed. of this influential publication (until 1841); also contributed articles on music and musicians to various German encyclopedias. His extensive music history remains in MS.

Fink, Michael Jon, American composer, performer, and teacher; b. Los Angeles, Dec. 7, 1954. He studied composition at the Calif. Inst. of the Arts with Harold Budd, William Kraft, Barney Childs, and Mel Powell (B.F.A., 1976; M.F.A., 1980). He performed with the Negative Band and Stillife; several of his chamber works are included on the album *Vocalise* (1982). In 1982 he joined the faculty of the Calif. Inst. of the Arts. In 1985 he was composer-in-residence at North Michigan Univ. His music is unusually spare and quiet and meticulously crafted, achieving a graceful sense of timelessness. Among his compositions are 2 *Pieces* for Piano (1983), an untitled work for Small Orch. (1986), *Living to Be Hunted by the Moon* for Clarinet, Bass Clarinet, and Electronics (1987), *A Temperament for Angels* for Computer-controlled Electronics and 3 Electronic Keyboards (1989), *Sound Shroud Garden* (sound installation, with Jim Fox; 1989), and *Epitaph* for Bass Clarinet (1990). He publ. *Inside the Music Business: Music in Contemporary Life* (N.Y., 1989).

Finke, Fidelio F(ritz; Friedrich), significant German composer and pedagogue; b. Josefsthal, Northern Bohemia, Oct. 22, 1891; d. Dresden, June 12, 1968. He studied with Vítězslav Novák at the Prague Cons.; from 1915, was on its faculty. He was head of the master classes in composition at the German Academy of Music in Prague from 1927 to 1945; also served as national inspector of the German music schools in Czechoslovakia (1920–38). After World War II, he settled in East Germany; was the director and a teacher of a master class in composition at the Dresden Akademie für Musik und Theater from 1946 to 1951; then was a prof. of composition at the Leipzig Hochschule für Musik from 1951 to 1959. As a composer, he followed the evolutionary path of German music, from the classicism of Brahms through the deeply contrapuntal constructions of Max Reger, finally adopting the liberating precepts of the New Vienna School, with its integration of thematic elements and concomitant emancipation of dissonance.

WORKS: OPERAS: *Die versunkene Glocke* (1915–18); *Die Jakobsfahrt* (Prague, 1936); *Der schlagfertige Liebhaber* (1950–54); *Der Zauberfisch* (Dresden, June 3, 1960). **ORCH.:** *Pan*, a sym. (1919); Piano Concerto (1930); Concerto for Orch. (1931); *Das Lied der Zeit*, choreographic tone poem (1946); 2 *Symphonische Märsche* (1960); *Festliche Musik* (1964); 8 suites for various Instrumental Groupings (1947–61). **CHAMBER:** 5 string quartets (1914–64); Sonata for Harp Solo (1945); Horn Sonata (1946); Clarinet Sonata (1949); Viola Sonata (1954); Wind Quintet (1955); *Primula veris* for Violin and Piano (1957); also numerous choruses; Toccata for Piano, Left-hand; organ works; songs.

BIBL.: G. Hofmeyer, *Vorläufiges Verzeichnis der Kompositionen von F.F. F.* (1966); D. Härtwig, *F.F. F., Leben und Werk* (Leipzig, 1970).

Finko, David, Russian pianist, composer, and conductor; b. Leningrad, May 15, 1936. He studied at the Leningrad School of Performing Arts (1950–58), and subsequently at the Leningrad Cons. (1960–65). In 1979 he emigrated to the U.S.; was then a visiting lecturer in the history and theory of Russian music at the Univ. of Pa. (1979–81). In 1981 he became a lecturer and composer-in-residence at the Univ. of Texas at El Paso. He was awarded a number of grants and fellowships, including ones from ASCAP, the Fromm Foundation, and the Memorial Foundation for Jewish Culture. Some of his works reflect the tragic aspects of Jewish history.

WORKS: OPERAS: *Polinka*, after Anton Chekhov (1965; El Paso, Feb. 26, 1983); *In a Torture Chamber of the Gestapo* (1970); *The Lodger from the Garret* (1976–78; score lost); *The Enchanted Tailor*, after Sholem Aleichem (1983). **ORCH.:** 6 tone poems (1965, 1967, 1968, 1970, 1975, 1978); *Holocaust*, overture (1965; rev. 1983); Sym. No. 1 (1969); Concerto for Piano and Orch. (1971); Concerto for Viola and Orch. (1971); Sym. No. 2 (1972); Double Concerto for Violin, Viola, and Orch. (1973); Double Concerto for Viola, Double Bass, and Orch. (1975); Concerto for Harp and Orch. (1976); Concerto for Viola d'Amore, Lute, and Orch. (1978); Concerto for 3 Violins and Orch. (1981); *Pilgrimage to Jerusalem* (Detroit, April 20, 1983); *The Wailing Wall* (1983). **CHAMBER:** *Mourning Music* for Violin, Viola, and Cello (1968); *Mass without Words* for Violin and Organ (1968); *Lamentations of Jeremiah* for Solo Violin (1969); *Fromm Septet* for Oboe, Clarinet, Bass Clarinet, Violin, Cello, Double Bass, and Percussion (Philadelphia, April 24, 1983). **PIANO:** *Russia in Darkness*, poem for Piano (1961); Piano Sonata (1964).

Finney, Ross Lee, distinguished American composer and teacher, brother of **Theodore M(itchell) Finney;** b. Wells, Minn., Dec. 23, 1906. He studied at the Univ. of Minnesota with Donald Ferguson; received a B.A. in 1927 from Carleton College. In 1928 he went to Paris, where he took lessons with Nadia Boulanger; returning to America, he enrolled at Harvard Univ., where he studied with Edward Burlingame Hill; in 1935 had instructive sessions with Sessions. From 1929 to 1949 he was on the faculty of Smith College; concurrently taught at Mt. Holyoke College (1938–40). In 1931–32 he was in Vienna, where he took private lessons with Alban Berg; in 1937 he studied with Gian Francesco Malipiero in Asolo. He then taught composition at the Hartt School of Music in Hartford, Conn. (1941–42), and at Amherst College (1946–47). In the interim he served with the Office of Strategic Services in Paris; was slightly injured when he stepped on a land mine while working in the war zone; this earned him the Purple Heart and Certificate of Merit. His professional career was facilitated by 2 Guggenheim fellowships (1937, 1947) and a

Pulitzer traveling fellowship (1937). In 1948–49 he was a visiting lecturer at the Univ. of Michigan in Ann Arbor; from 1949 to 1973 he was a prof. there, and also served as chairman of the dept. of composition; furthermore, he established there an electronic music laboratory. Because of the wide diversification of his stylistic propensities, Finney's works represent a veritable encyclopedic inventory of styles and idioms, from innocently pure modalities to highly sophisticated serialistic formations. About 1950 he devised a sui generis dodecaphonic method of composition which he called "complementarity." In it a 12-tone row is formed by 2 mutually exclusive hexachords, often mirror images of each other; tonal oases make their welcome appearances; a curious air of euphony of theoretically dissonant combinations is created by the contrapuntal superposition of such heterophonic ingredients, and his harmonies begin to sound seductively acceptable despite their modernity.

WORKS: STAGE: Opera, *Weep Torn Land* (1984); dance pieces: *Heyoka* (N.Y., Sept. 14, 1981) and *The Joshua Tree* (N.Y., Oct. 10, 1984). **ORCH.:** 4 syms.: No. 1, *Communiqué* (1942; Louisville, Dec. 8, 1964); No. 2 (1958; Philadelphia, Nov. 13, 1959); No. 3 (1960; Philadelphia, March 6, 1964); No. 4 (1972; Baltimore, March 31, 1973); Violin Concerto No. 1 (1933; rev. 1952); *Barbershop Ballad* (CBS Radio, Feb. 6, 1940); *Overture for a Drama* (Rochester, N.Y., Oct. 28, 1941); *Slow Piece* for String Orch. (1940); *Hymn, Fuguing, and Holiday*, based on a hymn tune of William Billings (1943; Los Angeles, May 17, 1947); Piano Concerto No. 1 (1948); *Variations* for Orch. (1957; Minneapolis, Dec. 30, 1965); 3 *Pieces* for Chamber Orch. and Tape (1962); Concerto for Percussion and Orch. (1965); Symphonie Concertante (1967); Piano Concerto No. 2 (1968); *Landscapes Remembered* (1971); *Summer in Valley City* for Concert Band (Ann Arbor, April 1, 1971); *Spaces* (1971; Fargo, N.Dak., March 26, 1972); Violin Concerto No. 2 (1973; Dallas, March 31, 1976; rev. 1977); Concerto for Alto Saxophone, with Wind Orch. (1974); *Variations on a Memory* for 10 Players (1975); *Narrative* for Cello and 14 Instruments (1976); Concerto for Strings (N.Y., Dec. 5, 1977); Chamber Concerto for 7 Players (1981). **CHAMBER:** 8 string quartets (1935–60); 2 piano trios (1938, 1954); Piano Quartet (1948); 2 piano quintets (1953, 1961); *Chromatic Fantasy* for Cello (1957); String Quintet (1958); *Fantasy in 2 Movements* for Violin (commissioned by Yehudi Menuhin and 1st perf. by him at the World's Fair in Brussels, June 1, 1958); *Divertissement* for Piano, Clarinet, Violin, and Cello (1964); 3 *Studies in 4* for 4 Solo Percussionists (1965); 2 *Acts for 3 Players* for Clarinet, Percussion, and Piano (1970); 2 *Ballades* for Flute and Piano (1973); *Tubes I* for 1 to 5 Trombones (1974); *Quartet* for Oboe, Cello, Percussion, and Piano (1979); 2 *Studies* for Saxophones and Piano (1981); also 2 viola sonatas; 2 cello sonatas; 3 violin sonatas. **SOLO PIANO:** 5 sonatas (1933–61); *Fantasy* (1939); *Nostalgic Waltzes* (1947); *Variations on a Theme by Alban Berg* (1952); *Sonata quasi una fantasia* (1961); *Waltz* (1977); *Lost Whale Calf* (1980); *Youth's Companion* (1980); *Narrative in Retrospect* (1983). **CHORAL:** *Pilgrim Psalms* (1945); *Spherical Madrigals* (1947); *Edge of Shadow* for Chorus and Orch. (1959); *Earthrise: A Trilogy Concerned with the Human Dilemma*: 1, *Still Are New Worlds* for Baritone, Chorus, Tape, and Orch. (1962; Ann Arbor, Mich., May 10, 1963); 2, *The Martyr's Elegy* for High Voice, Chorus, and Orch. (Ann Arbor, Mich., April 23, 1967); 3, *Earthrise* for Soloists, Chorus, and Orch. (1978; Ann Arbor, Dec. 11, 1979); *The Remorseless Rush of Time* for Choir and Orch. (1969).

BIBL.: P. Cooper, "The Music of R.L. F.," *Musical Quarterly* (Jan. 1967); D. Amman, *The Choral Music of R.L. F.* (diss., Univ. of Cincinnati, 1972); E. Borroff, *Three American Composers* (1986).

Finney, Theodore M(itchell), American music educator and historian, brother of **Ross Lee Finney;** b. Fayette, Iowa, March 14, 1902; d. Pittsburgh, May 19, 1978. He studied at the Univ. of Minnesota (B.A., 1924), then at the American Cons. at Fontainebleau and in Berlin. Returning to the U.S., he served as an assistant prof. of music at Carleton College (1925–32) and lecturer at the Smith College Summer School (1930–32). From 1936 to 1968 he was head of the music dept. at the Univ. of Pittsburgh. Among his publications is the practical textbook *A History of Music* (N.Y., 1935; 2nd ed., rev., 1947).

Finnilä, Birgit, Swedish contralto; b. Falkenberg, Jan. 20, 1931. She studied in Göteborg; later took courses at the Royal Academy of Music in London with Roy Henderson; made her concert debut in Göteborg in 1963; then made numerous appearances with the major orchs. of Europe; later sang in America, Australia, and Israel.

Finnissy, Michael (Peter), English composer; b. London, March 17, 1946. He studied composition with Bernard Stevens and Humphrey Searle at the Royal College of Music in London (1964–66) and with Roman Vlad in Rome. In 1969 he organized the music dept. of the London School of Contemporary Dance, where he taught until 1974.

WORKS: MUSIC THEATER: *Mysteries,* in 8 parts, for Vocal and Instrumental Forces, some with Dancers and Mimes: 1, *The Parting of Darkness from Light;* 2, *The Earthly Paradise;* 3, *The Great Flood;* 4, *The Prophecy of Daniel;* 5, *The Parliament of Heaven;* 6, *The Annunciation;* 7, *The Betrayal and Crucifixion of Jesus of Nazareth;* 8, *The Deliverance of Souls* (1972–79); *Circle, Chorus, and Formal Act* for Baritone, Women's Chorus, Percussion, Chorus, 6 Sword Dancers, 4 Mimes, and Small Ensemble (1973); *Mr. Punch* for Speaker, 5 Instruments, and Percussion (1976–77); *Vaudeville* for Mezzo-soprano, Baritone, 2 Mimes, 6 Instruments, and Percussion (1983); *The Undivine Comedy,* opera for 5 Singers and 9 Instruments (1988). **ORCH.:** Piano Concertos with Orch.: No. 1 (1975); No. 2 (1975–76); No. 3 (1978); No. 7 (1981); *Sea and Sky* (1979–80); *Red Earth* (London, Aug. 2, 1988). **INSTRUMENTAL ENSEMBLE:** *As when upon a tranced summer night* for 3 Cellos, 2 Pianos, and 2 Percussionists (1966–68); *Transformations of the Vampire* for Clarinet, Violin, Viola, and 3 Percussionists (1968–71); *Evening* for 6 Instruments and Percussion (1974); *Long Distance* for Piano and 14 Instruments (1977–78); *Alongside* for 13 Instruments and Percussion (1979); *Keroiylu* for Oboe, Bassoon, and Piano (1981); *Banumbirr* for Flute, Clarinet, Violin, Cello, and Piano (1982); *Australian Sea Shanties II* for Recorder Consort (1983); *Câtana* for 8 Instruments and Percussion (1984); pieces for solo instruments, including piano; numerous vocal works. **BIBL.:** A. Clements, "F.'s Undivine Comedy," *Musical Times* (July 1988).

Fino, Giocondo, Italian composer; b. Turin, May 2, 1867; d. there, April 19, 1950. He studied oriental languages and theology; concurrently took music lessons with Giovanni Bolzoni; he remained in Turin practically all his life. He wrote the operas *La festa del grano* (Turin, 1910) and *Campana a gloria* (Turin, 1916); several stage works in the Piedmont dialect; biblical cantata, *Noemi e Ruth* (Bergamo, 1908); ballets, pantomimes, choral works; chamber music, piano pieces.

Finscher, Ludwig, distinguished German musicologist; b. Kassel, March 14, 1930. He studied with Rudolf Gerber at the Univ. of Göttingen (Ph.D., 1954), completing his Habilitation at the Univ. of Saarbrücken (1967). He taught at the Univs. of Kiel (1960–65), Saarbrücken (1965–68), Frankfurt (1968–81), and Heidelberg (from 1981); was president of the Gesellschaft für Musikforschung (1974–77) and of the International Musicological Soc. (1977–82). He ed. the complete musical works of Gaffurius in Corpus Mensurabilis Musicae (2 vols., 1955, 1960) and a collected edition of the works of Compère in the same series (4 vols., 1958–72); with K. von Fischer, also ed. the complete works of Hindemith (Mainz, 1976–).

Finzi, Gerald (Raphael), English composer; b. London, July 14, 1901; d. Oxford, Sept. 27, 1956. He began his study of music with Ernest Farrar (1914–16) and Edward Bairstow (1917–22); studied counterpoint with R.O. Morris in 1925. He was a teacher of composition at the Royal Academy of Music in London (1930–33); in 1939 he organized the Newbury String Players, which did much to develop interest in 18th-century English music. He ed. overtures by Boyce for the Musica Britannica series. Finzi's own music reflects the influence of Elgar and Vaughan Williams, while the basic materials are rooted in English folk songs.

WORKS: *A Severn Rhapsody* (1923; Bournemouth, June 4, 1924); *By Footpath and Stile,* song cycle for Baritone and String Quartet to poems by Thomas Hardy (1921–22; London, Oct. 23, 1923); *Introit,* for Violin and Small Orch. (1925; London, May 4, 1927; rev. 1935 and 1942); *Interludium* for Oboe and String Quartet (1936); *Dies Natalis,* cantata for Soprano or Tenor Solo, and Strings (1938–39; London, Jan. 26, 1940); *Prelude and Fugue* for String Trio (1942); *Farewell to Arms* for Tenor and Chamber Orch. (1944; Manchester, April 1, 1945); *Let Us Garlands Bring,* 5 Shakespeare songs for Baritone and Strings (1929–42; BBC, London, Oct. 18, 1942); 5 cycles for Voice and Piano of settings of poems by Thomas Hardy: *Before and after Summer* (1932), *Earth and Air and Rain* (1928–32), *I Said to Love* (1928), *Till Earth Outwears* (1927), and *A Young Man's Exhortation* (1926–29); *Intimations of Immortality,* ode after Wordsworth for Tenor, Chorus, and Orch. (1949–50; Gloucester, Sept. 5, 1950); *Nocturne: New Year Music* for Orch. (1949); *For St. Cecilia,* ceremonial ode for Tenor, Chorus, and Orch. (London, Nov. 22, 1947); Concerto for Clarinet and Strings (1948–49; Hereford, Sept. 9, 1949); *Grand Fantasia and Toccata* for Piano and Orch. (1953); Cello Concerto (1951–55; Cheltenham, July 19, 1955); *In terra pax,* Christmas scene for Soprano, Baritone, Chorus, Strings, and Antique Cymbals (1954; rev. 1956).

Finzi, Graciane, French composer; b. Casablanca, Morocco, July 10, 1945. She enrolled in the Paris Cons. and studied theory with Elsa Barraine and Tony Aubin. Returning to Casablanca, she became active as an organizer of music festivals. Among her works are a Cello Concerto, a Wind Quintet, a Piano Trio, an Oboe Sonata, piano pieces, and songs.

Fiocco, Jean-Joseph, Belgian organist and composer, 2nd son of **Pietro Antonio Fiocco** (of his 1st marriage); b. Brussels (baptized), Dec. 15, 1686; d. there, March 30, 1746. He succeeded his father as music master at the ducal chapel (1714–44); wrote 5 oratorios, 8 Psalms, 9 répons de mort, motets, etc. He publ. *Sacri concentus* for 4 Voices and 3 Instruments. **BIBL.:** C. Stellfeld, *Les F.: Une Famille de musiciens belges aux XVIIe et XVIIIe siècles* (Brussels, 1941).

Fiocco, Joseph-Hector, Belgian organist, harpsichordist, and composer, 8th child of **Pietro Antonio Fiocco** (of his 2nd marriage); b. Brussels, Jan. 20, 1703; d. there, June 22, 1741. He was sous-maître at the royal chapel c.1729–31; from 1731 to 1737, was maître de chapelle at the Antwerp Cathedral; was master of the collegiate church of SS. Michel and Gudule in Brussels until his death. He wrote numerous sacred works, publ. in Monumenta Musicae Belgicae (vol. III); also wrote *Pièces de clavecin* (2 suites of 12 pieces each). **BIBL.:** C. Stellfeld, *Les F.: Une Famille de musiciens belges aux XVIIe et XVIIIe siècles* (Brussels, 1941).

Fiocco, Pietro Antonio, Italian-born Belgian composer, father of **Jean-Joseph** and **Joseph-Hector Fiocco;** b. Venice, c.1650; d. Brussels, Sept. 3, 1714. He traveled to Germany, then settled in Brussels, marrying a Belgian lady in 1682; she died in 1691, and Fiocco remarried in 1692. He was music master of the ducal chapel in Brussels from 1687; in 1694 he established an opera enterprise; until 1698 was director, with Giovanni Paolo Bombarda, of the Opéra du Quai du Forn; wrote special prologues for the operas of Lully; also wrote music for the court; his pastoral play *Le Retour du printemps* was produced in 1699. A collection of his sacred concertos was publ. in Antwerp (1691). Among his instrumental works only a few, including *Sonate à 4,* are extant. **BIBL.:** C. Stellfeld, *Les F.: Une Famille de musiciens belges aux XVIIe et XVIIIe siècles* (Brussels, 1941).

Fioravanti, Valentino, Italian composer, father of **Vincenzo Fioravanti;** b. Rome, Sept. 11, 1764; d. Capua, June 16, 1837. He studied in Rome with Jannacconi and with Sala in Naples. Returning to Rome in 1782, he began his career as a prolific composer of operas. He visited Naples quite often; succeeded Zingarelli as maestro di cappella at St. Peter's in Rome in 1816; between 1784 and 1824 he composed 77 operas; during his last period he wrote much church music. His earliest work, an intermezzo, was *Le avventure di Bertoldino* (Rome, 1784); he produced a comic opera, *Gl' inganni fortunati,* in Naples (1786); there followed *Il furbo contro al furbo* (Venice, Dec. 29, 1796). His greatest success was achieved by his comic opera *Le Cantatrici villane,* first produced in Naples (1799) and then in Venice in a new version under the title *Le Virtuose ridicole* (Dec. 28, 1801); there were performances all over Europe, including Russia; the opera was particularly in favor with German audiences (under the title *Die Dorfsängerinnen*); other operas were *La capricciosa pentita* (Milan, Oct. 2, 1802) and *I Virtuosi ambulanti* (Paris, Sept. 26, 1807). His autobiographical sketch was reprinted by G. Roberti in *La Gazzetta Musicale* (1895).

Fioravanti, Vincenzo, Italian composer, son of **Valentino Fioravanti;** b. Rome, April 5, 1799; d. Naples, March 28, 1877. He studied with his father, and also with his father's teacher, Jannacconi; he also took lessons with Donizetti. He wrote a number of operas in the Neapolitan dialect; only a few of them (tr. into conventional Italian) were produced outside Italy. He also composed sacred works, including 2 oratorios.

Fiorillo, Federigo, Italian violinist and composer, son of **Ignazio Fiorillo;** b. Braunschweig (baptized), June 1, 1755; d. after 1823. He was taught by his father, then he traveled as a violinist and conductor; appeared as a violinist in St. Petersburg in 1777, then in Poland (1780–81); conducted in Riga (1782–84); in 1785 he went to Paris, where he participated in the Concert Spirituel; in 1788 he was in London, where he played the viola in Salomon's quartet. He probably remained in London until c.1815; then he was in Amsterdam and again in Paris. He was a prolific composer for violin and various combinations of string instruments; he is known chiefly through his useful collection *Études de violon,* comprising 36 caprices, which was frequently reprinted.

Fiorillo, Ignazio, Italian composer, father of **Federigo Fiorillo;** b. Naples, May 11, 1715; d. Fritzlar, near Kassel, June 1787. He studied with Durante and Leo in Naples; composed his 1st opera, *Mandane,* at the age of 20 (Venice, 1736). Other operas were *Artimene* (Milan, 1738), *Partenope nell'Adria* (Venice, 1738), and *Il Vincitor di se stesso* (Venice, 1741). He traveled as a theater conductor; was appointed court conductor at Braunschweig (1754); in 1762 he received a similar post at Kassel, retiring in 1780. He wrote a number of German operas in Braunschweig and 3 Italian operas in Kassel. An oratorio, *Isacco;* a Requiem; and other church works are also noteworthy.

Fiqué, Karl, German-American organist and composer; b. St. Magnus, near Bremen, April 17, 1867; d. N.Y., Dec. 7, 1930. After studying at the Leipzig Cons. with Carl Reinecke, he emigrated to the U.S. (1887) and settled in Brooklyn, where he served as church organist and lectured at the Brooklyn Inst. of Arts and Sciences (1897–1915). He wrote 2 comic operas in German: *Priesewitz* (Brooklyn, 1893) and *Der falsche Mufti* (N.Y., 1901); a String Quartet; several choral works; and numerous piano pieces. Shortly before his death, he finished an operetta, *Merry Madrid.*

Firkušný, Rudolf, eminent Czech-born American pianist and pedagogue; b. Napajedla, Feb. 11, 1912. He studied composition with Janáček in 1919 and piano with Růžena Kurzová at the Brno Cons. (1920–27); also attended the Univ. of Brno. His further instructors were Vilém Kurz and Rudolf Karel (theory) at the Prague Cons., Suk (composition; 1929–30), and Artur Schnabel in N.Y. (1932). He made his debut as a child

pianist in Prague on June 14, 1920, playing a Mozart piano concerto. He first performed in London in 1933; on Jan. 13, 1938, he made his U.S. debut in N.Y., where he settled in 1940 and became a naturalized citizen. In 1943–44 he made a tour of Latin America and in 1946 participated in the Prague Festival; in subsequent years he also toured Europe, Israel, and Australia. He often played the music of his teacher Janáček; he also gave the 1st performances of Martinů's 3rd (Dallas, Nov. 20, 1949) and 4th (N.Y., Oct. 4, 1956) piano concertos. He likewise gave the 1st performances of piano concertos of Menotti (No. 1; Boston, Nov. 2, 1945) and Howard Hanson (Boston, Dec. 31, 1948). His technical equipment was of the highest caliber; his lyrical talent enhanced his virtuosity. He was also a composer; he wrote a Piano Concerto, a String Quartet, and a number of attractive piano études and miniatures. In 1979 he began publication, with the violinist Rafael Druian, of a complete ed. of the Mozart violin sonatas. An excellent teacher, Firkušný gave master classes at the Juilliard School of Music in N.Y. and at the Aspen Music School in Colorado.

Fischer, Ádám, Hungarian conductor, brother of **Iván Fischer;** b. Budapest, Sept. 9, 1949. He studied at the Béla Bartók Cons. in Budapest, later taking conducting courses with H. Swarowsky at the Vienna Academy of Music and with F. Ferrara in Venice and Siena (1970–71). In 1973 he won 1st prize in the Cantelli Competition in Milan. He was conductor of the Finnish National Opera in Helsinki (1974–77), 1st conductor at the Karlsruhe Opera (1977–78), and Generalmusikdirektor in Freiburg im Breisgau (1981–83) and in Kassel (from 1987). In 1989 he made his conducting debut at London's Covent Garden.

Fischer, Annie, distinguished Hungarian pianist; b. Budapest, July 5, 1914. She studied at the Franz Liszt Cons. in Budapest with Ernst von Dohnányi; in 1933 she won 1st prize in the International Liszt Competition in Budapest. Her career was interrupted by World War II, but she eventually resumed her concert activities. She became well known for her performances of the piano music of Mozart and Beethoven.

Fischer, Carl, German-American music publisher; b. Buttstädt, Thuringia, Dec. 7, 1849; d. N.Y., Feb. 14, 1923. He studied music in Gotha; entered a partnership in an instrument manufacturing business with his brother August Emil Fischer in Bremen. In 1872 he went to N.Y. and opened a music store at 79 East 4th St.; in 1923 the store was moved to 62 Cooper Square. He secured the rights for republishing orch. scores and parts by German composers, eventually creating one of the most important of American music publishing firms. From 1907 to 1931 the firm publ. a monthly periodical, the *Musical Observer,* ed. by Gustav Sänger; in 1923 the business was incorporated and Carl Fischer's son **Walter S. Fischer** (b. N.Y., April 18, 1882; d. there, April 26, 1946) became president; after his death, Frank H. Connor (1903–77) was elected president; upon his death he was succeeded by his son. In 1909 the firm established a branch in Boston, which was expanded in 1960 through the purchase of the Charles Homeyer Music Co. of Boston; in 1935 a branch was also opened in Los Angeles, and in 1969 one in San Francisco. In 1947 the firm occupied a new building in N.Y. at 165 West 57th St., which also housed a concert hall. The catalog of the firm is representative of all genres of musical composition; early acquisitions were works by composers living in America, including Rachmaninoff and Ernest Bloch; in the last quarter of the century, the firm publ. a number of instrumental and vocal works by composers of the avant-garde, including some in graphic notation.

Fischer, Edwin, eminent Swiss pianist, conductor, and pedagogue; b. Basel, Oct. 6, 1886; d. Zürich, Jan. 24, 1960. He studied with Hans Huber in Basel and Martin Krause in Berlin; then taught at the Stern Cons. in Berlin (1905–14); taught at the Berlin Hochschule für Musik from 1931; between 1926 and 1932 he was also engaged as a conductor in Lübeck, Munich, and Berlin. In 1942 he returned to Switzerland. He was renowned as one of the most intellectual pianists of his time and a distinguished pedagogue. He founded the Edwin-Fischer-Stiftung to assist needy and young musicians. He also publ. several valuable books on music: *J.S. Bach* (Potsdam, 1945); *Musikalische Betrachtungen* (Wiesbaden, 1949; in Eng. as *Reflections on Music,* London, 1951); *Beethovens Klaviersonaten* (Wiesbaden, 1956; Eng. tr., 1959); and *Von den Aufgaben des Musikers* (Wiesbaden, 1960).

BIBL.: B. Gavoty, *E. F.* (Geneva, 1954); H. Haid, ed., *Dank an E. F.* (Wiesbaden, 1962).

Fischer, Emil (Friedrich August), distinguished German bass; b. Braunschweig, June 13, 1838; d. Hamburg, Aug. 11, 1914. He received his vocal training entirely from his parents, who were opera singers; made his debut in Graz in 1857; then was with the Danzig Opera (1863–70), in Rotterdam (1875–80), and with the Dresden Opera (1880–85); made his debut with the Metropolitan Opera in N.Y. on Nov. 23, 1885, as King Heinrich, and remained on the staff for 5 years; then sang with the Damrosch Opera Co. (1894–98); lived mostly in N.Y. as a vocal teacher; returned to Germany shortly before his death. On March 15, 1907, a testimonial performance was held in his honor at the Metropolitan Opera, at which he sang one of his greatest roles: that of Hans Sachs (Act 3, Scene 1). He was particularly famous for his Wagnerian roles.

Fischer, Erich, German music editor and composer; b. Kreuzlingen, April 8, 1887; d. Wahlwies, Jan. 22, 1977. He studied musicology in Berlin at the Univ. under Kretzschmar, Stumpf, and Friedländer; received his Ph.D. in 1909 with the dissertation *Über die Musik der Chinesen;* in 1914 he founded in Berlin the Musikalische Hauskomödien, a society for the performance of little-known music by German composers, arranged as singspiels with new words; for this venture he organized his own company of singers.

Fischer, Irwin, American composer, organist, and conductor; b. Iowa City, July 5, 1903; d. Wilmette, Ill., May 7, 1977. He graduated in 1924 from the Univ. of Chicago; studied organ with Middelschulte, piano with Robyn, and composition with Weidig at the American Cons. in Chicago (M.M., 1930); later studied composition briefly with Nadia Boulanger in Paris (1931) and Kodály in Budapest (1936); took lessons in conducting with Paumgartner and Malko at the Salzburg Mozarteum (1937). In 1928 he joined the faculty of the American Cons. in Chicago; conducted several community orchs. As a composer, he held fast to the historically justified tonal techniques; but upon occasion he ventured into the alluring field of serialism.

WORKS: ORCH.: *Rhapsody of French Folk Tunes* (1933); Piano Concerto (1935; Chicago, Feb. 23, 1936); *Marco Polo,* fantasy overture (1937); *Hungarian Set* (1938); *Lament* for Cello and Orch. (1940); *Chorale Fantasy* for Organ and Orch. (1940); Sym. No. 1 (1943); *Variations on an Original Theme* (1950); *Legend* (1956); *Poem* for Violin and Orch. (1959); *Passacaglia and Fugue* (1961); *Overture on an Exuberant Tone Row* (1964–65); *Short Symphony* (1970–71; Hinsdale, April 16, 1972; orchestration of Piano Sonata); *Concerto giocoso* for Clarinet and Orch. (1971; Hinsdale, Jan. 21, 1973); *Orchestral Adventures of a Little Tune* for Narrator and Orch. (1974; Chicago, Nov. 16, 1974). **VOCAL:** *5 Symphonic Psalms* for Soprano, Chorus, and Orch. (1967); *Statement 1976* for Soprano, Chorus, Brass, Strings, and Percussion (1976; New Haven, April 25, 1976); choruses; songs. **CHAMBER:** *Divertimento* for Flute, Clarinet, Bassoon, Horn, Trumpet, Violin, Cello, and Double Bass (1963); *Fanfare* for Brass and Percussion (1976). **PIANO:** *Introduction and Triple Fugue* (1929); *Rhapsody* (1940); Piano Sonata (1960).

BIBL.: E. Borroff, *Three American Composers* (1986).

Fischer, Iván, Hungarian conductor, brother of **Ádám Fischer;** b. Budapest, Jan. 20, 1951. He studied cello and composition at the Béla Bartók Cons. in Budapest (1965–70); then took lessons in conducting with Hans Swarowsky at the Vienna Academy of Music; during the 1975–76 season he conducted concerts in Milan, Florence, Vienna, and Budapest; beginning in 1976, he filled engagements with the BBC Sym. Orch. in London and the BBC regional orchs. From 1979 to 1982 he was co-conductor of the Northern Sinfonia Orch. in Newcastle upon Tyne. In 1983 he became music director of the Budapest Festival Orch. Also in 1983 he made his 1st appearance in the U.S., as a guest conductor with the Los Angeles Phil.; was music director of the Kent Opera (1984–88), and then its artistic director. From 1989 he was principal guest conductor of the Cincinnati Sym. Orch.

Fischer, Jan (Frank), Czech composer; b. Louny, Sept. 15, 1921. He studied at the Prague Cons. (1940–45) and took lessons in composition from Řídký at the master class there (1945–48). His music occupies the safe ground of Central European Romanticism, not without some audacious exploits in euphonious dissonance.

WORKS: STAGE: 6 operas: *Ženichové* (Bridegrooms; 1956; Brno, Oct. 13, 1957); *Romeo, Julie a tma* (Romeo, Juliet, and Darkness; 1959–61; Brno, Sept. 14, 1962); *Oh, Mr. Fogg,* comic chamber opera after Jules Verne's *Around the World in 80 Days* (1967–70; Saarbrücken, June 27, 1971); *Miracle Theater,* radio opera (1970); *Decamerone,* chamber opera (1975–76); *Copernicus* (1981); ballet, *Eufrosyne* (1951; Pilsen, 1956). **ORCH.:** *Pastoral Sinfonietta* (1944); Violin Concerto (1946); *Essay* for Jazz Orch. and Solo Piano (1947); *Popular Suite* for Wind Orch. and Piano (1950); *Dance Suite* (1957); *Fantasia* for Piano and Orch. (1953); Sym. No. 1, *Monothematic* (1959); Clarinet Concerto (1965); *Obrazy* (Pictures) *I* and *II* (1970, 1973); Harp Concerto (1972); *Tryzna* (Commemoration 1973); *Večerní hudba* (Night Music) for Strings (1973); Concerto for Orch. (1980); Partita for String Orch. (1982). **CHAMBER:** Flute Sonata (1944); Suite for Wind Sextet (1944); Suite for English Horn and Piano (1945); *Ballada* for String Quartet and Clarinet (1949); Piano Quintet (1949); *Ut stellae* for Soprano, 2 Pianos, Flute, Bass Clarinet, Percussion, and Tape (1966); *Amoroso* for Clarinet and Piano (1970); Wind Quintet (1971); *4 Studies* for Solo Harp (1971); *Conversation with Harp,* quintet for Flute, Violin, Viola, Cello, and Harp (1979); Brass Quintet (1983).

Fischer, Johann Caspar Ferdinand, significant German composer; b. c.1665; d. Rastatt, Aug. 27, 1746. He was in the service of the Margrave of Baden (1696–1716), and continued when the court moved to Rastatt in 1716. He adopted Lully's style in his compositions, and thereby influenced other German composers. His *Ariadne musica neo-organoedum* (1702), a collection of 20 organ preludes and fugues in 20 different keys, foreshadowed Bach's *Well-Tempered Clavier.*

WORKS: *Le Journal du printemps,* 8 suites for 5 Strings and 2 Trumpets ad libitum, op. 1 (Augsburg, 1695; ed. in Denkmäler Deutscher Tonkunst, X, 1902); *Les Pièces de clavessin,* 8 suites for Keyboard, op. 2 (Schlackenworth, 1696; reprinted as *Musikalisches Blumen-Büschlein,* 1698); *Ariadne musica neo-organoedum,* 20 preludes and fugues in 20 different keys for Organ, op. 4 (Schlackenworth, 1702); *Blumen Strauss . . . in 8 Tonos Ecclesiasticos eingetheilet* for Organ (Augsburg, 1732); *Musicalischer Parnassus,* 9 suites for Keyboard (Augsburg, 1738); all of the preceding works were ed. by E. von Werra (Leipzig, 1901). Fischer also publ. several of his vocal works.

BIBL.: F. Ludwig, "Neue Forschungen über . . . J.K.F. F.," *Mitteilung des Vereins für die Geschichte der Deutschen in Böhmen,* XLIX (1911); A. Einstein, "Ein Kirchenwerk J.C.F. F.s," *Acta Musicologica,* XXIII (1951); L. Hoffmann-Erbrecht, "J.K.F. F. der Jüngere," *Die Musikforschung,* V (1952); W. Lebermann, "J.C.F. der Jüngere," ibid., XXIII (1970).

Fischer, (Johann Ignaz) Ludwig, renowned German bass; b. Mainz, Aug. 18, 1745; d. Berlin, July 10, 1825. He studied voice with Anton Raaff in Mannheim, then obtained the post of virtuoso da camera at the Mannheim court (1772); also taught voice at the Mannheim Seminario Musico from 1775, continuing in the court's service when it moved to Munich in 1778. He then proceeded to Vienna (1780), where he first gained recognition as a leading opera singer; became a friend of Mozart, who wrote the role of Osmin in his *Die Entführung aus dem Serail* (July 16, 1782) for him. In 1783 he went to Paris, where he was notably successful at the Concert Spirituel; subsequently toured Italy, and then sang in Vienna, Prague, and Dresden (1785). After serving the Prince of Thurn und Taxis in Regensburg (1785–89), he received an appointment for life in Berlin. He continued to make guest appearances in other cities, including London (1794, 1798), giving his last public performance in Berlin in 1812; he was pensioned in 1815. The MS of his autobiography, which covers his life to 1790, is in the Berlin Staatsbibliothek.

BIBL.: J. Reichardt, "L. F.," *Musikalische Monatsschrift*, I (1792).

Fischer, Joseph, German-American music publisher; b. Silberhausen, April 9, 1841; d. Springfield, Ohio, Nov. 24, 1901. He emigrated to the U.S. as a youth, and in 1864 established the firm of J. Fischer & Bro. in Dayton, Ohio, with his brother Ignaz Fischer; in 1875 the firm moved to N.Y. Joseph Fischer was succeeded, at his death, by his sons George and Carl; the sons of George Fischer, Joseph and Eugene, became proprietors of the firm in 1920. During its early years, J. Fischer & Bro. specialized in music for the Roman Catholic church, but later expanded its activities to include instrumental music by contemporary composers, organ works, and also light opera. The firm was purchased by Belwin-Mills Publishing Co. in 1970.

Fischer, Kurt von, distinguished Swiss musicologist; b. Bern, April 25, 1913. He studied piano at the Bern Cons. with F.J. Hirt and with Czeslaw Marek; later took the courses in musicology with Kurth and Gurlitt at the Univ. of Bern, where he received his Ph.D. in 1938 with the dissertation *Griegs Harmonik und die nordländische Folklore* (publ. in Bern, 1938); subsequently completed his Habilitation in 1948 there with *Die Beziehungen von Form und Motiv in Beethovens Instrumentalwerken* (publ. in Strasbourg, 1948; 2nd ed., 1972). He taught piano at the Bern Cons. (1939–57), and concurrently was lecturer in musicology at the Univ. of Bern (1948–57). In 1957 he became prof. of musicology and chairman of the dept. at the Univ. of Zürich. In 1965 he assumed the post of co-ed. of the *Archiv für Musikwissenschaft*. From 1967 to 1972 he served as president of the International Musicological Soc.

WRITINGS: *Studien zur italienischen Musik des Trecento und frühen Quattrocento* (Bern, 1956); *Arthur Honegger* (Zürich, 1977).

BIBL.: H.H. Eggebrecht and M. Lütolf, eds., *Studien zur Tradition in der Musik: K. v.F. zum 60. Geburtstag* (Munich, 1973).

Fischer, Michael Gottard, German organist and composer; b. Alach, near Erfurt, June 3, 1773; d. Erfurt, Jan. 12, 1829. He was a pupil of Kittel; was an organist, conductor, and teacher in Erfurt. He wrote about 50 organ pieces, plus syms., concertos, chamber music, piano pieces, motets, chorales, etc.; publ. *Evangelisches Choral-Melodienbuch*.

Fischer, (Maria) Res (Theresia), German contralto; b. Berlin, Nov. 8, 1896; d. Stuttgart, Oct. 4, 1974. She studied in Stuttgart and Prague; then took lessons in Berlin with Lilli Lehmann; made her debut in 1927 in Basel, where she sang until 1935; then appeared with the Frankfurt Opera (1935–41); in 1941 she joined the Stuttgart Opera, remaining on its roster until 1961; was made its honorary member in 1965. She also sang at the festivals of Salzburg and Bayreuth, and with the state operas in Vienna, Hamburg, and Munich. She created the title role in Orff's *Antigonae* (Salzburg, 1949) and sang in the 1st performance of Wagner-Régeny's *Bergwerk von Falun* (Salzburg, 1961).

Fischer, Wilhelm, eminent Austrian musicologist; b. Vienna, April 19, 1886; d. Innsbruck, Feb. 26, 1962. He studied with Guido Adler at the Univ. of Vienna, where he received his Ph.D. with the dissertation *Matthias Georg Monn als Instrumentalkomponist* in 1912; he completed his Habilitation there with his *Zur Entwicklungsgeschichte des Wiener klassischen*

Stils in 1915; then joined the faculty of the Univ. of Vienna in 1919; subsequently was lecturer in musicology at the Univ. of Innsbruck from 1928 until the Anschluss of 1938, when he was removed from this position and was conscripted as a forced laborer; after World War II, he was restored to the faculty of the Univ. of Innsbruck as a prof., serving there from 1948 until his retirement in 1961. In 1951 he was elected president of the Central Inst. of Mozart Research at the Mozarteum in Salzburg; he publ. numerous essays on Mozart and other Classical composers; among his most important writings, apart from his *Habilitationsschrift*, are *Zur Geschichte des Fugenthemas* (Leipzig, 1925) and *Beethoven als Mensch* (Regensburg, 1928). In 1956 he was presented with a Festschrift on the occasion of his 70th birthday.

Fischer, William G(ustavus), American hymn-tune writer; b. Baltimore, Oct. 14, 1835; d. Philadelphia, Aug. 13, 1912. He sang in a Baltimore German church; was a bookbinder by trade and a choral conductor by avocation; then entered the retail piano business and, under its imprint, Gould & Fischer, printed a number of Sunday-school leaflets. Of his songs, *Coming to the Cross*, first sung at a National Camp meeting at Hamilton, Mass., June 22, 1870, is the best known.

BIBL.: R. McCutchan, *Our Hymnody* (N.Y., 1937).

Fischer-Dieskau, (Albert) Dietrich, celebrated German baritone; b. Berlin, May 28, 1925. The surname of the family was orig. Fischer; his paternal grandmother's maiden surname of Dieskau was legally conjoined to it in 1937. His father, a philologist and headmaster, was self-taught in music; his mother was an amateur pianist. He began to study piano at 9, and voice at 16; he then studied voice with Hermann Weissenborn at the Berlin Hochschule für Musik (1942–43). In 1943 he was drafted into the German army. He was made a prisoner of war by the Americans while serving in Italy in 1945; upon his release in 1947, he returned to Germany and made his 1st professional appearance as a soloist in the Brahms *Requiem* in Badenweiler. He continued his vocal training with Weissenborn in Berlin, where he soon was heard on radio broadcasts over the RIAS. On May 6, 1948, he made his operatic debut in the bass role of Colas in an RIAS broadcast of Mozart's *Bastien und Bastienne*. On Nov. 18, 1948, he made his stage debut as Rodrigo, Marquis of Posa, in Verdi's *Don Carlos* at the Berlin Städtische Oper, where he remained an invaluable member for 35 years. He also pursued his operatic career with appearances at leading opera houses and festivals in Europe. It was as a lieder and concert artist, however, that he became universally known. On April 5, 1955, he made his U.S. debut with the Cincinnati Sym. Orch.; his U.S. recital debut followed at N.Y.'s Town Hall on May 2, 1955. In subsequent years he made tours all over the world to enormous critical acclaim. His finest operatic roles included Count Almaviva, Don Giovanni, Papageno, Macbeth, Falstaff, Hans Sachs, Mandryka, Mathis der Maler, and Wozzeck. He created the role of Mittenhofer in Henze's *Elegy for Young Lovers* (1961) and the title role in Reimann's *Lear* (1978). His honors include membership in the Berlin Akademie der Künste (1956), the Mozart Medal of Vienna (1962), Kammersänger of Berlin (1963), the Grand Cross of Merit of the Federal Republic of Germany (1978), honorary doctorates from Oxford Univ. (1978) and the Sorbonne in Paris (1980), and the Gold Medal of the Royal Phil. Soc. of London (1988). In 1978 he married his 4th wife, the soprano **Julia Varady.**

WRITINGS: *Texte deutscher Lieder: Ein Handbuch* (Munich, 1968; Eng. tr. as *The Fischer-Dieskau Book of Lieder*, London, 1976); *Auf den Spuren der Schubert-Lieder: Werden-Wesen-Wirkung* (Wiesbaden, 1971; Eng. tr. as *Schubert: A Biographical Study of His Songs*, London, 1976; U.S. ed. as *Schubert's Songs: A Biographical Study*, N.Y., 1977); *Wagner und Nietzsche: Der Mystagoge und sein Abtrünniger* (Stuttgart, 1974; Eng. tr. as *Wagner and Nietzsche*, N.Y., 1976, and London, 1978); *Robert Schumann: Das Vokalwerk* (Munich, 1985); *Töne sprechen, Worte klingen: Zur Geschichte und Interpretation des Gesangs* (Stuttgart and Munich, 1985); *Nachklang: Ansich-*

ten und Erinnerungen (Stuttgart, 1987; Eng. tr. as *Reverberations: The Memoirs of Dietrich Fisher-Dieskau*, N.Y., 1989).

BIBL.: K. Whitton, *D. F.-D.—Mastersinger: A Documented Study* (London and N.Y., 1981); W.-E. von Lewinski, *D. F.-D.* (Munich and Mainz, 1988).

Fischhof, Joseph, Austrian pianist, teacher, and composer; b. Butschowitz, Moravia, April 4, 1804; d. Vienna, June 28, 1857. He studied piano with Anton Halm in Vienna; then became a private teacher there, with growing success, and in 1833 was appointed a prof. at the Cons. He publ. *Versuch einer Geschichte des Klavier-Baus* (Vienna, 1853). He gathered a remarkable collection of musical MSS, including one of Bach's *Wohltemperierte Clavier,* and authentic materials for a Beethoven biography collected by Hotschewar (the guardian of Beethoven's nephew); these MSS were given, after Fischhof's death, to the Berlin Hofbibliothek (now Staatsbibliothek). He composed many pieces for the piano.

Fišer, Luboš, outstanding Czech composer; b. Prague, Sept. 30, 1935. He studied composition with Hlobil at the Prague Cons. (1952–56) and with Bořkovec at the Prague Academy of Music, graduating in 1960. In 1971 he emigrated to the U.S.; was a composer-in-residence with the American Wind Sym. Orch. in Pittsburgh. His music is often associated with paintings, archeology, and human history; his style of composition employs effective technical devices without adhering to any particular doctrine.

WORKS: STAGE: Chamber opera, *Lancelot* (1959–60; Prague, May 19, 1961); musical, *Dobrý voják Švejk* (The Good Soldier Schweik; Prague, 1962); ballet, *Changing Game* (1971). **ORCH.:** *Suite* (1954); 2 syms. (1956; 1958–60); *Symphonic Fresco* (1962–63); *Chamber Concerto* for Piano and Orch. (1964; rev. 1970); *15 Prints after Dürer's Apocalypse* (1964–65; Prague, May 15, 1966; his most successful work; winner of a UNESCO prize in Paris, 1967; *Pietà* for Chamber Ensemble (1967); *Riff* (1968); *Double* (1969); *Report* for Wind Instruments (1971; commissioned by the American Wind Sym. Orch.); *Kreutzer Étude* for Chamber Orch. (1974); *Labyrinth* (1977); *Serenade for Salzburg* for Chamber Orch. (1978); *Albert Einstein,* portrait for Organ and Orch. (1979); *Piano Concerto* (1980); *Meridian* (1980); *Romance* for Violin and Orch. (1980); *Centaures* (1983). **CHAMBER:** *4 Compositions* for Violin and Piano (1955); *String Quartet* (1955); *Sextet for Wind Quintet and Piano* (1956); *Ruce* (Hands), sonata for Violin and Piano (1961); *Crux* for Violin, Kettledrums, and Bells (1970); *Cello Sonata* (1975); *Variations on an Unknown Theme* for String Quartet (1976); *Piano Trio* (1978); *Sonata for 2 Cellos and Piano* (1979); *Testis* for String Quartet (1980); *Sonata for Solo Violin* (1981). **VOCAL:** *Caprichos* for Vocalists and Chorus, after a text drawn from Goya's paintings (1966); *Requiem* for Soprano, Baritone, 2 Choruses, and Orch. (Prague, Nov. 19, 1968); *Lament over the Destruction of the City of Ur,* after Ur-Sumerian tablets, for Soprano, Baritone, 3 Narrators, Chorus, Children's and Adult's Speaking Choruses, 7 Timpani, and 7 Bells (1969; as a ballet, 1978); *Ave Imperator* for Solo Cello, Male Chorus, 4 Trombones, and Percussion (1977); *The Rose* for Chorus a cappella (1977); *Per Vittoria Colona* for Solo Cello and Female Chorus (1979); *Istanu,* melodrama for Narrator, Alto Flute, and 4 Percussionists (1980); *Znameni* (The Sign) for Soloists, Chorus, and Orch. (1981); *Address to Music,* melodrama for Narrator and String Quartet (1982). **PIANO:** 6 sonatas: No. 1 (1955); No. 2 (1957); No. 3, *Fantasia* (1960); No. 4 (1962–64); No. 5 (1974); No. 6, *Fras* (1978).

Fisher, Avery (Robert), American pioneer in audio equipment and munificent patron of music; b. N.Y., March 4, 1906. He was educated at N.Y. Univ. (B.S., 1929); then worked for the publishing house of Dodd, Mead as a graphics designer (1933–43). In 1937 he founded the Phil. Radio firm, later known as Fisher Radio; it became one of the foremost manufacturers of audio equipment in the world, producing high-fidelity and stereophonic components. Having amassed a substantial fortune, he sold the firm in 1969. In 1973 he gave the N.Y. Phil. $10 million to renovate the interior of Phil. Hall; in 1976

it was inaugurated at a gala concert in which it was officially renamed Avery Fisher Hall in his honor. He also created the Avery Fisher Prize, which is awarded to outstanding musicians of the day.

Fisher, Eddie (Edwin Jack), American singer of popular music; b. Philadelphia, Aug. 10, 1928. He won an Arthur Godfrey Talent Scouts contest in 1948; then sang successfully on radio and television. His career was highlighted by his romantic marriages and sensational divorces successively to the movie stars Debbie Reynolds, Elizabeth Taylor, and Connie Stevens. His autobiography aptly appeared under the title of *Eddie: My Life, My Loves* (N.Y., 1981).

Fisher, Sylvia (Gwendoline Victoria), admired Australian soprano; b. Melbourne, April 18, 1910. She studied at the Melbourne Cons.; then sang in local productions. In 1949 she became a member of the Covent Garden Opera in London, remaining on its roster until 1958. In 1958 she sang in Chicago; then was a member of the English Opera Group (1963–71). She created the role of Miss Wingrave in Britten's *Owen Wingrave* (London, BBC, May 16, 1971); also sang in other contemporary operas.

Fisher, William Arms, American music editor and publisher; b. San Francisco, April 27, 1861; d. Boston, Dec. 18, 1948. He studied theory with Horatio Parker; singing with William Shakespeare in London. When Dvořák went to N.Y. in 1892, Fisher became his pupil. In 1897 he settled in Boston as ed. and director of music publication for O. Ditson & Co.; was its vice-president (1926–37). He ed. several vocal albums, among them *60 Irish Folksongs* (Boston, 1915) and *Ye Olde New England Psalm Tunes* (Boston, 1930). He wrote the words of the song *Goin' Home,* to the melody of the slow movement of Dvořák's *New World Symphony,* a setting that became enormously popular.

WRITINGS: *Notes on Music in Old Boston* (1918); *The Music That Washington Knew* (1931); *One Hundred and Fifty Years of Music Publishing in the U.S.* (1933); *Music Festivals in the U.S.* (1934).

Fisk, Eliot (Hamilton), outstanding American guitarist; b. Philadelphia, Aug. 10, 1954. He studied with Oscar Ghiglia at the Aspen School of Music (1970–76); also studied with Ralph Kirkpatrick and Albert Fuller at Yale Univ. (B.A., 1972; M.M., 1977). He was on the faculty at the Aspen School of Music (1973–82), at Yale (1977–82), and at the Mannes College of Music in N.Y. (1978–82); in 1982 he became a prof. at the Cologne Hochschule für Musik.

Fiske, Roger (Elwyn), English musicologist; b. Surbiton, Sept. 11, 1910; d. London, July 22, 1987. He attended Wadham College, Oxford (B.A. in English, 1932), then received instruction in composition from Herbert Howells at the Royal College of Music in London and at Oxford Univ. (D.Mus., 1937). He was active as a BBC broadcaster (1939–59), and served as general ed. of the Eulenburg miniature scores (1968–75).

WRITINGS (all publ. in London): *Beethoven's Last Quartets* (1940); *Listening to Music* (1952); *Ballet Music* (1958); *Score Reading* (1958–65); *Chamber Music* (1969); *Beethoven's Concertos and Overtures* (1970); *English Theatre Music in the Eighteenth Century* (1973; 2nd ed., 1986); *Scotland in Music* (1983).

Fissot, Alexis-Henri, French pianist and composer; b. Airaines, Somme, Oct. 24, 1843; d. Paris, Jan. 28, 1896. He entered the Paris Cons. as a child of 9, and studied piano with Marmontel, organ with Benoist, and composition with Ambroise Thomas until 1860, taking successively all 1st prizes. He then taught piano at the Paris Cons. from 1887. He wrote many effective piano pieces: *12 préludes; 2 ballades; 3 feuillets d'album; 12 pièces de genre;* etc.

Fistoulari, Anatole, Russian-born English conductor; b. Kiev, Aug. 20, 1907. He studied with his father, the opera conductor Gregory Fistoulari; a child prodigy, he conducted Tchaikovsky's 6th Sym. at the age of 8; in 1920 went to Rumania and Germany; was in Paris as a ballet conductor in 1933; later toured with the Ballet Russe de Monte Carlo in the U.S. (1937). He was in the French army in 1939; in 1940 made his way to London, where he settled as an orch. and theatrical conductor.

Fitelberg, Gregor (Grzegorz), eminent Latvian-born Polish conductor and composer, father of **Jerzy Fitelberg;** b. Dvinsk, Oct. 18, 1879; d. Katowice, June 10, 1953. He studied at the Warsaw Cons. with Barcewicz and Noskowski; then played the violin in the Warsaw Phil.; became its concertmaster, and eventually (1908) conductor. After the outbreak of World War I, he went to Russia as a conductor of sym. concerts; in 1921 he went to Paris; conducted performances of Diaghilev's Ballets Russes; he returned to Poland and conducted the Warsaw Phil. (1923–34); then founded and led the Polish Radio Sym. Orch. in Warsaw from 1934 to 1939; in 1940 he was in Buenos Aires, after fleeing Warsaw via Vienna, Italy, and Paris; from 1942 to 1945 he was in the U.S.; in 1947 he went back to Poland, and became conductor at the Polish Radio Sym. Orch. in Katowice. At his sym. concerts he gave many performances of works by Polish composers; was one of the best interpreters of Szymanowski. In 1951 the Polish government awarded him a state prize. Fitelberg wrote 2 syms. (1903, 1906); 2 Polish rhapsodies for Orch. (1913, 1914); symphonic poem, *In der Meerestiefe* (1913); Violin Concerto (1901); and some chamber music; his Violin Sonata received the Paderewski prize in 1896.

Fitelberg, Jerzy, talented Polish composer, son of **Gregor (Grzegorz) Fitelberg;** b. Warsaw, May 20, 1903; d. N.Y., April 25, 1951. He received his musical education mainly from his father; then took courses at the Hochschule für Musik in Berlin. In 1933 he went to Paris; in 1940 he went to the U.S., where he remained until his death. In 1936 he received an Elizabeth Sprague Coolidge award for his String Quartet No. 4, which was performed at the Coolidge Festival of Chamber Music in Washington, D.C. (1937); his orch. and chamber music was often performed in Europe; much of it was publ. His works are couched in the neo-Classical style, and are cosmopolitan in thematic substance; they are distinguished by energetic rhythm and strong contrapuntal texture; only a few of his compositions reflect Polish melos.
  Works: 3 suites for Orch. (1925–30); Concerto for String Orch. (1928; arrangement of the 2nd String Quartet); Violin Concerto No. 1 (1928; Vienna, June 20, 1932); Violin Concerto No. 2 (1935; Paris, June 22, 1937); 2 piano concertos (1929, 1934); *The Golden Horn* for String Orch. (1942); *Nocturne* for Orch. (N.Y., March 28, 1946); Octet for Wind Instruments; 5 string quartets; Sonata for 2 Violins and 2 Pianos; Sonatina for 2 Violins; *3 Polish Folksongs* for Women's Voices (1942).
  Bibl.: E. Elsner, "J. F.," *Chesterian* (Sept.–Oct. 1939).

Fitzenhagen, (Karl Friedrich) Wilhelm, eminent German cellist and pedagogue; b. Seesen, Sept. 15, 1848; d. Moscow, Feb. 14, 1890. He studied piano, violin, and cello in his youth; then studied cello with Plock and Theodore Müller, and finally with Grützmacher in Dresden (1867–68); subsequently was a member of the Hofkapelle there. In 1870 he went to Moscow, where he became prof. of cello at the Imperial Cons.; thereafter gained great renown as a virtuoso and teacher. Tchaikovsky composed his *Variations on a Rococo Theme* for Cello and Orch. for him.

Fitzgerald, Ella, remarkable black American jazz singer; b. Newport News, Va., April 25, 1918. She began singing in small clubs in Harlem in the early 1930s; discovered by Chick Webb (one of Harlem's most popular musicians) in 1935, she joined his band; upon his death in 1939, she became its leader; in 1942 she became a free-lance singer and subsequently worked with most major jazz musicians and groups. She was particularly adept at scat singing and improvising, frequently creating new melodies over given harmonies much in the manner of a jazz instrumentalist. Stylistically, she was equally at ease in swing and bebop; developing, over the years, a superlative blend of musicianship, vocal ability, and interpretive insight, she achieved a popularity and respect rarely acquired by jazz singers. In 1987 she was awarded the National Medal of Arts.

Bibl.: S. Colin, *E.: The Life and Times of E. F.* (London, 1987); B. Kliment, ed., *E. F.* (N.Y., 1988).

Fitzwilliam, Viscount Richard, wealthy English collector of paintings, engravings, books, and musical MSS; b. Richmond, Surrey, Aug. 1745; d. London, Feb. 4, 1816. He bequeathed his library to Cambridge Univ. The musical MSS include especially valuable works: the immensely important *Fitzwilliam Virginal Book* (often wrongly termed *Virginal Booke of Queen Elizabeth*), anthems in Purcell's hand, sketches by Handel, and many early Italian compositions. Vincent Novello ed. and publ. 5 vols. of the Italian sacred music as *The Fitzwilliam Music* (London, 1825); J.A. Fuller Maitland and A.H. Mann made a complete catalog of it (1893). The entire contents of the *Fitzwilliam Virginal Book* were ed. and publ. by J.A. Fuller Maitland and William Barclay Squire (2 vols., Leipzig and London, 1894–99; facsimile reprint, N.Y., 1954).
  Bibl.: E. Naylor, *An Elizabethan Virginal Book* (London, 1905).

Fiume, Orazio, Italian composer; b. Monopoli, Jan. 16, 1908; d. Trieste, Dec. 21, 1976. He studied piano and theory in Palermo and Naples; was later a student of Pizzetti (composition) and Molinari (conducting) in Rome. He taught harmony at the Parma Cons. (1941–51), in Milan (1951–59), and in Pesaro (1959–60); was director of the Trieste Cons. (from 1961). His music follows the tradition of expansive Italian Romanticism. He wrote 3 *Pieces* for Chamber Orch. (1937); Sym. (1956); opera, *Il tamburo di panno* (Rome, April 12, 1962); 2 concertos for Orch. (1945, 1956); cantata, *Ajace* (1940); songs.

Fizdale, Robert, American pianist; b. Chicago, April 12, 1920. He studied with Ernest Hutcheson at the Juilliard School of Music; formed a piano duo with Arthur Gold; they made a professional debut at N.Y.'s New School for Social Research in 1944, in a program devoted entirely to John Cage's music for prepared pianos. They toured widely in the U.S., Europe, and South America; works were written specially for them by Samuel Barber, Milhaud, Poulenc, Auric, Virgil Thomson, Norman Dello Joio, and Ned Rorem. With Arthur Gold he publ. a successful book, *Misia* (N.Y., 1979), on the life of Maria Godebska, a literary and musical figure in Paris early in the century. He retired in 1982.

Fjeldstad, Øivin, Norwegian conductor; b. Christiania, May 2, 1903; d. there (Oslo), Oct. 16, 1983. He studied at the Christiania Cons.; then went to Leipzig and Berlin for further studies. He began his career as a violinist. In 1931 he made his debut as conductor with the Oslo Phil. In 1946 he became chief conductor of the Norwegian State Broadcasting Orch. in Oslo, a position he held until 1962; also conducted at the Oslo Opera. In 1962 he was named chief conductor of the Oslo Phil., a post he held until 1969.

Flack, Roberta, black American pop singer; b. Black Mountain, N.C., Feb. 10, 1939. Her mother was a church organist who taught her the rudiments of piano playing. The family moved to Arlington, Va., and she began taking music lessons with Alma Blackmon of Washington, D.C. She then enrolled in Howard Univ. (B.A., 1958), and upon graduation started a teaching career in public schools. Concurrently, she served as voice coach and accompanist. A complete change in her musical direction came in 1968, when she received an opportunity to perform in nightclubs; she suddenly revealed herself as a stunningly successful interpreter of popular songs; in this field she frequently teamed with the brilliant black singer Donny Hathaway. Among her most popular renditions were *The First Time Ever I Saw Your Face* (1972) and *Killing Me Softly with His Song* (1973).

Flackton, William, English organist and composer; b. Canterbury (baptized), March 1709; d. there, Jan. 5, 1798. He was organist at Faversham (1735–52); wrote church music; 6 "overtures" for Harpsichord; 6 sonatas for 2 Violins and Cello.

Flagello, Ezio (Domenico), American bass; b. N.Y., Jan. 28, 1931. He studied with Friedrich Schorr; in 1957 he won the Metropolitan Opera Auditions of the Air and sang there in the same year; also appeared at La Scala in Milan, the Vienna State Opera, the San Francisco Opera, and the Deutsche Oper in Berlin. He created the role of Enobarbus in Barber's *Antony and Cleopatra* at the opening performance of the new Metropolitan Opera house (1966).

Flagello, Nicolas (Oreste), American composer and conductor; b. N.Y., March 15, 1928. He was of Italian antecedents; his father, a professional dress designer, loved music and played the oboe; his mother assisted him tastefully in his successful shop, and also sang. His maternal grandfather, Domenico Casiello, was a musician in Naples. With such genetic endowment, it was inevitable that Flagello should become a musician. He began his piano lessons at the incredible age of 3, and played in public at 5. At 6 he began taking violin lessons with Francesco di Giacomo. He also learned to play the oboe, and was a member of the school band, performing on these instruments according to demand. In 1945–46 he played the violin in Stokowski's All-American Youth Orch. in N.Y. In 1946 he entered the Manhattan School of Music (B.M., 1949; M.M., 1950), studying with a variety of teachers in multifarious subjects (Harold Bauer, Hugo Kortschak, Hugh Ross, Vittorio Giannini). He also took conducting lessons with Mitropoulos. It was with Giannini that he had his most important training in composition, for 15 years, from 1935 to 1950, and it was Giannini who influenced him most in his style of composition—melodious, harmonious, euphonious, singingly Italianate, but also dramatically modern. After obtaining his master's degree, Flagello went to Italy, where he took lessons with Ildebrando Pizzetti at the Accademia di Santa Cecilia in Rome (Mus.D., 1956). Returning to the U.S., he taught composition and conducting at the Manhattan School of Music until 1977; appeared as a guest conductor with the Chicago Lyric Opera and the N.Y. City Opera; also toured as accompanist to Tito Schipa, Richard Tucker, and other singers.

WORKS: *Beowulf* for Orch. (1949); Piano Concerto No. 1 (1950); *Mirra,* opera (1953); *The Wig,* opera (1953); Piano Concerto No. 2 (1956); *Rip Van Winkle,* children's operetta (1957); *Missa sinfonica* for Orch. (1957); *The Sisters,* opera (1958; N.Y., Feb. 23, 1961); Concerto for Strings (1959); *The Judgment of St. Francis,* opera (1959; N.Y., March 18, 1966); *Divertimento* for Piano and Percussion (1960); *Burlesca* for Flute and Guitar (1961); *Capriccio* for Cello and Orch. (1962); Piano Concerto No. 3 (1962); Concertino for Piano, Brass, and Timpani (1963); Violin Sonata (1963); *Lautrec,* ballet suite (1965); *Te Deum for All Mankind* for Chorus and Orch. 1967); Sym. No. 1 (1968); *Passion of Martin Luther King* for Soloists, Orch., and Chorus (1968); *The Piper of Hamelin,* children's opera to Flagello's libretto (1970); Sym. No. 2, *Symphony of the Winds,* for Wind Instruments and Percussion (1970); *Ricercare* for Brass and Percussion (1971); *Remembrance* for Soprano, Flute, and String Quartet (1971); *Credendum* for Violin and Orch. (1974); *Prisma* for Horn Septet (1974); Piano Concerto No. 4 (1975); *Canto* for Soprano and Orch. (1978); *Diptych* for Brass Trio (1979); *Odyssey* for Band (1981); *Quattro amori,* song cycle for Mezzo-soprano and Piano (1983); *Beyond the Horizon,* opera (1983); *Concerto sinfonico* for Saxophone Quartet and Orch. (Buffalo, Nov. 1, 1985).

Flagg, Josiah, American bandmaster; b. Woburn, Mass., May 28, 1737; d. probably in Boston, Jan. 2, 1795(?). He organized and drilled the 1st regular militia band of Boston (most probably the 1st group of that nature in America); on June 29, 1769, presented its 1st concert, and on Oct. 28, 1773, gave a "final Grand Concert" at Faneuil Hall with about 50 players. Subsequently he settled in Providence and served there as lieutenant colonel during the Revolution; little is known of his other activities. He publ. *A Collection of the best Psalm Tunes in 2, 3 and 4 parts . . . To which is added some Hymns and Anthems, the Greater part of them never before printed in America* (1764; introduced the anthem to the English colonies; engraved by Paul Revere) and *Sixteen Anthems . . . To which is added a few Psalm Tunes* (1766). Flagg was the 1st in America to

establish a connection between sacred and secular music. That he was an educated practical musician and was acquainted with European music is evidenced by the type of programs he conducted.

BIBL.: O. Sonneck, *Early Concert Life in America* (Leipzig, 1907); D. Music, "J. F.," *American Music* (Summer 1989).

Flagstad, Kirsten (Malfrid), famous Norwegian soprano; b. Hamar, July 12, 1895; d. Oslo, Dec. 7, 1962. She studied voice with her mother and with Ellen Schytte-Jacobsen in Christiania, then made her operatic debut there as Nuri in d'Albert's *Tiefland* (Dec. 12, 1913). During the next 2 decades, she sang throughout Scandinavia, appearing in operas and operettas, and in concert. In 1933 she sang a number of minor roles at Bayreuth, and then scored her 1st major success there in 1934 when she appeared as Sieglinde. She made an auspicious Metropolitan Opera debut in N.Y. in that same role on Feb. 2, 1935, and was soon hailed as the foremost Wagnerian soprano of her time. On May 18, 1936, she made her 1st appearance at London's Covent Garden, as Isolde. While continuing to sing at the Metropolitan Opera, she made guest appearances at the San Francisco Opera (1935–38) and the Chicago Opera (1937), and also gave concerts with major U.S. orchs. She returned to her Nazi-occupied homeland in 1941 to be with her husband, a decision that alienated many of her admirers. Nevertheless, after World War II, she resumed her career with notable success at Covent Garden. In 1951 she also returned to the Metropolitan Opera, where she sang Isolde and Leonore; made her farewell appearance there in Gluck's *Alceste* on April 1, 1952. She retired from the operatic stage in 1954, but continued to make recordings; from 1958 to 1960 she was director of the Norwegian Opera in Oslo. Among her other celebrated roles were Brünnhilde, Elisabeth, Elsa, and Kundry. She narrated an autobiography to L. Biancolli, which was publ. as *The Flagstad Manuscript* (N.Y., 1952).

BIBL.: E. McArthur, *F.: A Personal Memoir* (N.Y., 1965); T. Gunnarson, *Sannheten om K. F.: En dokumentarbiografi* (Oslo, 1985); H. Vogt, *F.* (London, 1987).

Flament, Édouard, French bassoonist, conductor, and composer; b. Douai, Aug. 27, 1880; d. Bois-Colombes, Seine, Dec. 27, 1958. He studied at the Paris Cons. with Bourdeau (bassoon), Lavignac, Caussade, and Lenepveu (composition). After graduation (1898), he played the bassoon in the Lamoureux Orch. (1898–1907) and in the Société des Instruments à Vent (1898–1923); conducted opera and concerts in Paris (1907–12), Algiers (1912–14), and Marseilles (1919–20); summer concerts at Fontainebleau (1920–22); then with the Diaghilev ballet in Monte Carlo, Berlin, London, and Spain (1923–29). In 1930 he became conductor at the Paris Radio.

WORKS: Operas: *La Fontaine de Castalie, Le Cœur de la rose,* and *Lydéric et Rosèle;* 8 syms.; *Oceano Nox,* symphonic poem; *Variations radio-phoniques;* 5 piano concertos; *Concert-stück* for Bassoon and Orch.; Divertimento for 6 Bassoons; Quintet for 5 Bassoons; Quartet for 4 Bassoons; 3 string quartets; Violin Sonata, Viola Sonata, 2 cello sonatas, etc.; about 180 film scores.

Flanagan, Tommy (Lee), black American jazz pianist; b. Detroit, March 16, 1930. He commenced clarinet studies at 6 and piano training at 11, working throughout his adolescence in local jazz haunts with various senior musicians, including Milt Jackson, Thad Jones, and Elvin Jones. In 1956 he went to N.Y., where he subsequently was pianist and music director for Ella Fitzgerald; also performed with Oscar Pettiford, J.J. Johnson, Miles Davis, and others.

Flanagan, William (Jr.), American composer and music critic; b. Detroit, Aug. 14, 1923; d. N.Y., Aug. 31, 1969 (found dead in his apartment, a victim of an overdose of barbiturates). He studied composition at the Eastman School of Music in Rochester, N.Y., with Burrill Phillips and Bernard Rogers; then at the Berkshire Music Center in Tanglewood with Arthur Honegger, Arthur Berger, and Aaron Copland; also, in N.Y., with David Diamond. Concurrently, he became engaged in musical journalism; was a reviewer for the *N.Y. Herald Tribune* (1957–60) and later wrote for *Stereo Review*. His style of composition is characterized by an intense pursuit of an expressive melodic line, projected on polycentric but firmly tonal harmonies.

WORKS: Opera, *Bartleby*, after Melville (1952–57; N.Y., Jan. 24, 1961); *A Concert Ode* for Orch. (1951; Detroit, Jan. 14, 1960); *A Concert Overture* (1948; N.Y., Dec. 4, 1959); *Divertimento for Classical Orchestra* (1948; Toledo, Ohio, Jan. 9, 1960); *Notations* for Large Orch. (1960); *Chapter from Ecclesiastes* for Mixed Chorus and String Quintet (N.Y., March 21, 1963); *Narrative* for Orch. (Detroit, March 25, 1965); *Divertimento for String Quartet* (1947); *Chaconne for Violin and Piano* (1948); *Passacaglia for Piano* (1947); *Piano Sonata* (1950); song cycles. He wrote background music for Edward Albee's plays *The Sandbox* (1961) and *The Ballad of the Sad Café* (1963).

BIBL.: L. Trimble, "W. F. (1923–1969), an Appreciation," *Stereo Review*, XXIII/5 (1969).

Flatt, Lester (Raymond), American country-music singer and guitarist; b. Overton County, Tenn., June 19, 1914; d. Nashville, May 11, 1979. He joined Bill Monroe's Blue Grass Boys as a singer in 1944; then formed a duo with Earl Scruggs, the banjo player; they organized their own band, the Foggy Mountain Boys, and soon established themselves as leading figures in country music. Flatt became famous for his "Lester Flatt G Run" on the guitar, accompanied by Scruggs's 3-finger banjo style. After their partnership came apart in 1969, Flatt played with the remaining members of the band, which later adopted the name The Nashville Brass. Among the best-known songs of Flatt and Scruggs were *Roll in My Sweet Baby's Arms, Old Salty Dog Blues, The Ballad of Jed Clampett* (from the inane television comedy series "The Beverly Hillbillies"), and *Foggy Mountain Breakdown* (the theme song of the film *Bonnie and Clyde*).

BIBL.: J. Lambert and C. Seckler, *The Good Things Outweigh the Bad: A Biography of L. F.* (Hendersonville, Tenn., 1982).

Flaxland, Gustave-Alexandre, French music publisher; b. Strasbourg, Jan. 26, 1821; d. Paris, Nov. 11, 1895. He studied at the Paris Cons.; founded a music publishing business in 1847, and, by acquiring copyrights of compositions of Schumann and Wagner, made it prominent. He sold his firm to Durand et Schönewerk in 1869, and commenced making pianos.

Flecha, Mateo, Spanish composer; b. Prades, Tarragona, c.1530; d. Solsona, Lérida, Feb. 20, 1604. He received his musical education from his uncle, also named **Mateo Flecha** (1481–1553); was boy chorister in the court chapel at Arevalo. In 1564 he entered the imperial chapel in Vienna; by 1579 was in Prague with the Emperor; Philip III made it possible for him to return to Spain as abbot of Portella in 1599. He publ. a book of madrigals in Venice (1568), and the collection *Las ensaladas* (Prague, 1581), containing "ensaladas" (quodlibets, comic songs) by his uncle, and some by himself. This collection was brought out in a modern ed. by Higinio Anglés, with an introductory essay on the Flechas (Barcelona, 1954).

Fleetwood, Mick, English pop musician; b. Redruth, June 24, 1942. He began his career as a drummer in a local band; then played with John Mayall's Bluesbreakers. In 1967 he teamed up with the string bass player **John McVie** (b. London, Nov. 26, 1942) and, annexing his Scottish prefix "Mc," formed a band named Fleetwood Mac. The personnel of Fleetwood Mac was anything but stable. A procession of British rockers, most notably **Peter Green** (b. London, Oct. 29, 1946), came and went as though through a revolving door into the body of Fleetwood Mac; McVie married a woman providentially named **Christine Perfect** (b. Greenodd, Lancashire, July 12, 1943), who became an integral part of the group. The group flew to California and took shape with the addition of **Stephanie "Stevie" Nicks** (b. Phoenix, Ariz., May 26, 1948) and **Lindsey Buckingham** (b. Palo Alto, Calif., Oct. 3, 1949).

Following the Zeitgeist of the United Kingdom and the disunited state of California, the band drifted away from blues into cosmopolitan pop. In this Anglo-Californian incarnation Fleetwood Mac reached the empyrean heights of the pop charts in the ultra-platinum category. Songs: *Future Games, Over My Head, Say You Love Me, Rhianon, Go Your Own Way, You Make Loving Fun*. Their albums *Fleetwood Mac* and *Rumours* sold over 14 million copies.

Flégier, Ange, French composer; b. Marseilles, Feb. 25, 1846; d. there, Oct. 8, 1927. He studied at the Marseilles Cons. and the Paris Cons. (1866–69), returning to Marseilles in 1870. He wrote *Fatima*, comic opera; *Ossian*, lyric poem for Soli, Chorus, and Orch.; *Françoise de Rimini*, cantata; miscellaneous orch. pieces (*Valse du rêve, Badinage, Habanera, Minuet, Berceuse, Mignardise*, etc.); many songs, of which *Le Cor* is the best known.

Fleischer, Anton, Hungarian conductor and composer; b. Makó, May 30, 1891; d. Budapest, Oct. 30, 1945. He studied in Budapest with Kodály; conducted at the Budapest Municipal Theater (1913–15), then conducted at the Budapest Opera (1915) and taught at the National Cons. from 1918; won the Hungarian State Prize with his sym. on Oscar Wilde's *The Nightingale and the Rose* (1915).

Fleischer, Oskar, eminent German musicologist; b. Zörbig, Nov. 2, 1856; d. Berlin, Feb. 8, 1933. He studied philology at Halle (1878–83); then musicology in Berlin under Spitta. In 1892 he became Privatdozent at the Univ. of Berlin; promoted to prof. in 1895. He was a founder and 1st president of the Internationale Musik-Gesellschaft (1899); with Johannes Wolf he ed. its publications, *Zeitschrift* and *Sammelbände*, until 1904.

WRITINGS: *Führer durch die königliche Sammlung alter Musikinstrumente* (Berlin, 1892); *Musikinstrumente aus deutscher Urzeit* (1893); *W.A. Mozart* (1899); *Führer durch die Bachausstellung im Festsaale des Berliner Rathauses* (Berlin, 1901); *Neumen-Studien* (4 vols.: 1895; 1897; 1904, with facsimiles of late Byzantine notation; 1923, *Die germanischen Neumen als Schlüssel zum altchristlichen und gregorianischen Gesang*).

Fleischmann, Ernest (Martin), German-born American music administrator; b. Frankfurt am Main, Dec. 7, 1924. His family moved to South Africa, where he studied accounting at the Univ. of the Witwatersrand. He then devoted himself to music studies, obtaining a B.Mus. at the Univ. of Cape Town (1954). He was ambitious and took lessons in conducting with the then-resident British conductor, Albert Coates; also acted as an organizer of musical events, including the Van Riebeeck Festival in Cape Town (1952). Furthermore, he served as director of music and drama for the Johannesburg Festival (1956). In the process he learned Afrikaans, and acquired a literary fluency in English. Seeking ever wider fields of endeavor, he went to London, becoming a naturalized citizen in 1959; he acted as general manager of the London Sym. Orch. until 1967 and also made a number of conducting appearances in England. He finally emigrated to the U.S., which became the main center of his activities; in 1969 he was appointed executive director of the Los Angeles Phil. as well as general manager of the Hollywood Bowl. Ever sure of his direction, he was a powerful promoter of the orch. he headed, so that the Los Angeles Phil. became actively involved in extensive national and international tours, garnering profitable recording contracts in addition to television and radio broadcasts, youth programs, and special festivals. Well-educated and fluent in several European languages, Fleischmann acquired an international reputation as a highly successful entrepreneur; he was repeatedly offered new jobs, which he declined. In personal relationships he was known for his abrasive manners. In this respect he revived the style of musical promotion of yore, as if following European impresarios of the previous century. That he created opposition and sometimes even open enmity was to be expected, but he invariably defeated opposition by assuming a genially patronizing attitude toward all adversaries. Courteous but always effective in the difficult trade of musical politics, he has through the years continued to enhance his reputation and influence.

Fleisher, Edwin A(dler), American patron of music; b. Philadelphia, July 11, 1877; d. there, Jan. 9, 1959. He studied at Harvard Univ. (B.A., 1899). He founded a Sym. Club in Philadelphia (1909) and engaged conductors to rehearse an amateur orch. there; at the same time he began collecting orch. scores and complete sets of parts, which became the nucleus of the great Edwin A. Fleisher Collection, presented by him to the Free Library of Philadelphia. A cumulative catalog covering the period from 1929 to 1977 was publ. in Boston in 1979.

Fleisher, Leon, distinguished American pianist, conductor, and teacher; b. San Francisco, July 23, 1928, of Jewish-Russian immigrant parents. His father was a tailor; his mother a singing teacher. He received the rudiments of music from his mother; then studied piano with Lev Shorr. He played in public at the age of 6; then was sent to Europe for studies with Artur Schnabel at Lake Como, Italy; continued his studies with him in N.Y. At the age of 14 he appeared as soloist in the Liszt A-major Piano Concerto with the San Francisco Sym. Orch.; at 16 he was soloist with the N.Y. Phil. (Nov. 4, 1944); in 1952 he became the 1st American to win 1st prize at the Queen Elisabeth of Belgium International Competition in Brussels; this catapulted him into a brilliant career. He made several European tours; also gave highly successful recitals in South America. In 1961–62 he was a soloist with the San Francisco Sym. Orch. to observe its 50th anniversary. At the peak of his career, a pianistic tragedy befell him; in 1964 he was stricken with a mysterious and mystifying neurological ailment that made the fingers of his right hand curl up on itself, completely incapacitating him as a pianist; this condition was diagnosed as carpal-tunnel syndrome. Disabled as he was, Fleisher turned to piano works written for left hand alone commissioned to Ravel, Prokofiev, and others by Paul Wittgenstein, the Austrian pianist who lost his right arm during World War I. Fleisher learned these concertos and performed them successfully. He also began to conduct. He had studied conducting with Pierre Monteux in San Francisco and at the conducting school established by Monteux in Hancock, Maine; he also profited from advice from George Szell. In 1968 he became artistic director of the Theater Chamber Players in Washington, D.C.; in 1970 he became music director of the Annapolis Sym. Orch. as well. From 1973 to 1977 he was associate conductor of the Baltimore Sym. Orch.; then was its resident conductor in 1977–78. He appeared as a guest conductor at the Mostly Mozart Festival in N.Y., and also with the Boston Sym., San Francisco Sym., Cincinnati Sym., and the Los Angeles Chamber Orch. A treatment with cortisone injections and even acupuncture and the fashionable biofeedback to control the electrophysiological motor system did not help. In 1981 he decided to undergo surgery; it was momentarily successful, and on Sept. 16, 1982, he made a spectacular comeback as a bimanual pianist, playing the *Symphonic Variations* by César Franck with Sergiu Comissiona and the Baltimore Sym. Orch. In 1985 he became artistic director–designate of the Berkshire Music Center at Tanglewood, and fully assumed his duties as artistic director in 1986. Fleisher devoted much time to teaching; he joined the faculty of the Peabody Cons. of Music in Baltimore in 1959, and subsequently was named to the Andrew W. Mellon Chair in Piano; was also a visiting prof. at the Rubin Academy of Music in Jerusalem. Among his brilliant pupils were André Watts and Lorin Hollander.

Fleming, Robert (James Berkeley), Canadian pianist and composer; b. Prince Albert, Saskatchewan, Nov. 12, 1921; d. Ottawa, Nov. 28, 1976. He studied piano with Arthur Benjamin and composition with Herbert Howells at the Royal College of Music in London (1937–39); served in the Canadian Air Force during World War II; after the war, he continued his musical education at the Toronto Cons. with Healey Willan

and others. He subsequently joined the National Film Board of Canada in 1946 and was its music director from 1958 to 1970; taught at Carleton Univ. in Ottawa from 1970 until his death. He wrote music for some 250 films.

WORKS: Ballets: *Chapter 13* (1948); *Shadow on the Prairie* (1951); *Ballet Introduction* (1960); 3 puppet plays; *Around the House,* suite for Orch. (1942); *Rondo* for Orch. (1942); *6 Variations on a Liturgical Theme* for String Orch. (1946); *Kaleidoscope* for Small Orch. (1949); *Red River Country* for Small Orch. (1953); *Hymn to War* for Baritone and Strings (1954); *Recollections* for Violin and Strings (1954); *Summer Suite* for Orch. (1957); *Suite Short and Simple* for Piano and Strings (1959); Piano Concerto (1963); *3 Contrasts* for School Orch. (1964); *Concerto '64* for Piano and Orch. (1964); Tuba Concerto (1966); *4 Fantasias on Canadian Folk Themes* for Orch. or Symphonic Band (1966); Divertimento for Organ, 2 Oboes, and Strings (1970); *Hexad* for Small Orch. (1972); *Our Mind Was the Singer,* cycle for Baritone and Orch. (1972); *3 Scenarios* for Symphonic Band (1974); *Of a Timeless Land* for Contralto and Orch. (1974); *Bella Bella Sonatina* for Violin and Piano (1943); Violin Sonata (1944); *Colors of the Rainbow* for Wind Quartet, String Quartet, and Harp (1962); *Maritime Suite* for Wind Quartet, String Quartet, and Harp (1962); *3 Miniatures* for Brass Quintet (1962); *Go for Baroque* for Flute, Oboe, and Harpsichord (1963); *3 Dialogues* for Flute or Oboe, and Piano or Harpsichord (1964); *A Quartet for Strings* (1969); *Threo* for Soprano Saxophone and Piano (1972); piano pieces; choruses.

Fleming, Shirley (Moragne), American music critic and editor; b. N.Y., Dec. 2, 1931. She was educated at Smith College in Northampton, Mass. (B.A., 1952; M.A., 1954); was assistant music ed. of *Hi-fi Music at Home* (1958–60) and of *High Fidelity* (1960–64); then was ed. of *Musical America* (1964–91); also wrote for other periodicals.

Flesch, Carl, celebrated Hungarian violinist and pedagogue; b. Moson, Oct. 9, 1873; d. Lucerne, Nov. 14, 1944. He began to study the violin at the age of 6 in his native town of Moson, then continued his training with Jakob Grün at the Vienna Cons. (1886–90), and with Sauzay (1890–92) and Marsick (1892–94) at the Paris Cons., graduating with the premier prix. While still a student, he played in the Lamoureux Orch. in Paris and made his formal debut in Vienna (1895); went to Bucharest (1897), where he was active as a performer and as a prof. at the Cons. until 1902; he subsequently went to Amsterdam, where he taught at the Cons. (1903–8). Eventually, in 1908, he made his home in Berlin, where he engaged in private teaching. In 1913 he made his N.Y. debut; then served as head of the violin dept. at the Curtis Inst. of Music in Philadelphia (1924–28). Returning to Berlin in 1928, he joined the faculty of the Hochschule für Musik. With the advent of Hitler, he went to London (1934). He was in the Netherlands when World War II erupted in 1939, and lived there until the Nazi invasion in 1940; then made his way to Hungary, finally settling in Lucerne in 1943. He acquired an outstanding reputation as an interpreter of the German repertoire. However, his greatest legacy remains his work as a pedagogue. His *Die Kunst des Violin-Spiels* is an exhaustive treatise on violin technique and interpretation, and is duly recognized as the standard work of its kind. He also prepared eds. of the violin concertos of Beethoven, Mendelssohn, and Brahms, the violin sonatas of Mozart (with A. Schnabel), 20 études of Paganini, and the études of Kreutzer. In 1945 the Flesch Competition was organized in London to honor his memory; it later became part of the City of London International Competition for Violin and Viola, which awards the Flesch Medal.

WRITINGS: *Urstudien* (Berlin, 1911); *Die Kunst des Violin-Spiels* (vol. I, Berlin, 1923; 2nd ed., 1929; Eng. tr., Boston, 1924; vol. II, Berlin, 1928; Eng. tr., Boston, 1934); *Das Klangproblem im Geigenspiel* (Berlin, 1931; Eng. tr., N.Y., 1934); H. Keller and C.F. Flesch, eds., *The Memoirs of Carl Flesch* (London, 1957; 3rd ed., 1974; German ed. as *Erinnerungen eines Geigers,* Freiburg im Breisgau, 1960); *Die hohe Schule* *des Fingersetzes auf der Geige* (MS; 1st publ. in Italian as *Alta scuola di diteggiature violinistica*, Milan, 1960; Eng. tr. as *Violin Fingering: Its Theory and Practice*, London, 1966). **BIBL.:** W. Brederode, *C. F.* (Haarlem, 1938); B. Schwarz, *Great Masters of the Violin* (N.Y., 1983).

Fleta, Miguel, Spanish tenor, father of **Pierre Fleta;** b. Albalate, Dec. 28, 1893; d. La Coruña, May 30, 1938. He studied at the Barcelona and Madrid conservatories; also took vocal lessons in Italy with Louisa Pierrick, who became his wife. He made his debut in Trieste on Nov. 14, 1919. After several busy tours in Europe, Mexico, and South America, he made his debut at the Metropolitan Opera in N.Y. on Nov. 8, 1923, as Cavaradossi in *Tosca;* remained on its roster until 1925; from 1923 to 1926 sang at La Scala in Milan, where he appeared in the premiere of *Turandot.* In 1926 he returned to Spain.

Fleta, Pierre, French tenor, son of **Miguel Fleta;** b. Villefranche-sur-Mer, July 4, 1925. He studied with his mother, Louise Pierrick-Fleta; then sang as a boy soprano at Cannes; went to London, where he was engaged as a professional singer before making his opera debut in Barcelona in 1949. He made a concert tour in the Middle East in 1951; then was engaged as 1st tenor at the Théâtre de la Monnaie in Brussels (1952). He also developed a repertoire of French, Italian, Spanish, and English folk songs.

Fletcher, Alice Cunningham, American ethnologist; b. Cuba (of American parents), March 16, 1838; d. Washington, D.C., April 6, 1923. She devoted her life to the study of North American Indians, among whom she lived for a number of years; became president of the American Anthropological Soc. (1903) and the American Folk Lore Soc. (1905). She was the author of *Indian Story and Song from North America* (1900); *A Study of Omaha Indian Music* (1903); *Indian Games and Dances* (1915); numerous articles in the *Journal of American Folk Lore;* etc.

Fletcher, (Horace) Grant, American composer; b. Hartsburg, Ill., Oct. 25, 1913. He studied music theory with Bessie Louise Smith at Illinois Wesleyan Univ. (1932–35); took a course in conducting with Thor Johnson; for 3 summers (1937–39) attended composition classes with Ernst Krenek at the Univ. of Michigan; then took classes with Healy Willan in Toronto; later studied at the Eastman School of Music in Rochester, N.Y., where his teachers were Bernard Rogers and Howard Hanson (1947–49; Ph.D., 1951); also had private lessons with Herbert Elwell in Cleveland. From 1945 to 1948 he was conductor of the Akron (Ohio) Sym. Orch.; from 1949 to 1951 he was on the faculty of the Chicago Musical College; later taught at Arizona State Univ. at Tempe (1956–78). In his music he follows the median line of modern techniques; he adopts the Baroque forms in most of his compositions while diversifying the contrapuntal and harmonic ingredients, achieving considerable originality. He is ingenious in combining instrumental ensembles. **WORKS: STAGE:** Buffa-fantasy opera, *The Carrion Crow* (1948); ballet-pantomime, *Lomotawi* (1957); opera, *The Sack of Calabasas* (1964–66). **ORCH.:** *Rhapsody* for Flute and Strings (1935; withdrawn); *A Rhapsody of Dances* for Chamber Orch. (1935; for Wind Instruments, 1970; for Full Orch., 1972); *Nocturne* (1938); *Song of Honor,* on Yugoslav themes (1944; 1st perf. as *A Song for Warriors,* Rochester, N.Y., Oct. 25, 1945); *An American Overture* (1945; Duluth, April 23, 1948); *Panels from a Theater Wall* (1949; Rochester, N.Y., April 27, 1949); Sym. No. 1 (1950; Rochester, N.Y., April 24, 1951); Sym. No. 2 (1982–83); *The Pocket Encyclopedia of Orchestral Instruments,* with optional Narrator (1953; also perf. as *Dictionary of Musical Instruments*); 4 concertos: No. 1 for Piano and Orch. (1953); No. 2, *Regency Concerto,* for Piano and Strings (1966); No. 3, *Concerto for Winds* (1969); No. 4, *Multiple Concerto for 5 Solo Winds,* for 1 Soloist playing on 5 different Wind Instruments, with Wind Ensemble (1970); *Sumare* and *Wintare* (1956); *7 Cities of Cibola* (1961); *Retrospection (Rhapsody III)* for Flute, 9 Strings, and Tape (1965; revision of

Rhapsody of 1935); *Dances from the Southwest* for Strings and Piano (1966); *Glyphs* for Band (1970); *Diversion III* for Strings (1971; *I* and *II* are for Piano); ballet suite, *The 5th of May* (1972); *Aubade* for Wind Instruments (1974); *Celebration of Times Past* (1976); *A More Proper Burial Music for Wolfgang* for Wind Instruments (1977); *Saxsōn II* for Saxophone and Strings (1977; *I* is for Solo Saxophone); *Serenade* (1979); *Symphonic Suite* (1980); *Partita* for Chamber Orch. (1985). **VOCAL:** *The Crisis,* after Thomas Paine, for Chorus and Orch. (1945; Walla Walla, Wash., Feb. 22, 1976); *House Made of Dawn* for Alto, Piano, Flute, Indian Drum, and Rattle (1957); 4 sacred cantatas: No. 1, *O Childe Swete* (1965); No. 2 (1967); No. 3, *The Branch* (1970); No. 4, *Judas* (1970); *Who Is Sylvia?* for Baritone, Flute, Oboe, Bassoon, and Guitar (1969); *Psalm I* for Chorus and Organ (1979); choruses; songs. **CHAMBER:** *Musicke for Christening:* No. 1 for Cello and Piano (1945); No. 2 for Saxophone and Piano (1979); No. 3 for Clarinet and Piano (1979); *Heralds* for Brass and Timpani (1949); *Tower Music* for Brass (1957); 5 sonatas: No. 1 for Clarinet and Piano (1958); No. 2, *Sōn,* for Cello and Piano (1972); No. 3 for Saxophone and Piano (1974); No. 4 for Solo Viola (1977); No. 5 for Solo Violin (1983); *PrognosIs* No. 1, *PrognosIIs* No. 2, and *PrognosIIIs* No. 3 for Brass Quintet (1965–67); *Uroboros* for Percussion (1967); *Octocelli* for 8 Solo Cellos or their multiples (1971); Trio for Flute, Guitar, and Piano (1973); *Toccata II* for Marimba (1979; *I* is for Piano); *Quadra* for Percussion (1975); String Quartet (1975; 4 earlier quartets were withdrawn); *Zortzicos* No. 2 for Double Bass and Piano (1977); *Zortzicos* No. 3 for Bassoon and Piano (1979); *Zortzicos* No. 4 for Cello and Piano (1979); *Zortzicos* No. 5 for Clarinet and Piano (1980); *Zortzicos* No. 6 for Viola and Piano (1980; *Zortzicos* No. 1 is the last movement of the piano piece *Izquierdas*); *Saxsōn I* for Saxophone Solo (1977); *Trio Bulgarico* for Flute, Oboe, and Bassoon (1980); *Palimpsest* for Flute Choir (1980); *Madrigals* for Clarinet Choir (1981). **PIANO:** 2 Books of Nocturnes (1935); *4 American Dance Pieces* (1944); *Openend Triptych* (1957); *Izquierdas* for Left Hand (1967); *Toccata I* (1974); also *Dodecachordon* for Organ (1967). **WRITINGS:** *Fundamental Principles of Counterpoint* (Rock Hill, S.C., 1942); *Syllabus for Advanced Integrated Theory* (Tempe, Ariz., 1962; 4th ed., rev., 1976); *Rhythm: Notation and Production* (Tempe, 1967).

Fletcher, Percy (Eastman), English conductor and composer; b. Derby, Dec. 12, 1879; d. London, Sept. 10, 1932. He went to London in 1899 as a conductor at various theaters there; he composed many works in a light, melodious style, including the orch. pieces *Woodland Pictures, Sylvan Scenes, Parisian Sketches, 3 Frivolities,* and the overture *Vanity Fair;* also a short sacred cantata, *Passion of Christ.*

Fleury, André (Édouard Antoine Marie), French organist and composer; b. Neuilly-sur-Seine, July 25, 1903. He studied with his father; later with Gigout, Marcel Dupré, and Louis Vierne. In 1930 he became organist at St. Augustin, Paris; in 1943 he was appointed prof. of organ playing at the École Normale de Musique; he taught at the Cons. of Dijon (1949–71); then was co-organist at St. Eustache in Paris. Fleury wrote 2 syms. for Organ (1947, 1949) and numerous other works for his instrument.

Fleury, Louis (François), eminent French flutist; b. Lyons, May 24, 1878; d. Paris, June 11, 1926. He studied at the Paris Cons.; from 1905 until his death was head of the famous Société Moderne d'Instruments à Vent, also (from 1906) of the Société des Concerts d'Autrefois, with which he gave concerts in England; made appearances with Melba and Calvé. Debussy composed *Syrinx* for Unaccompanied Flute for him. He ed. much early flute music, including sonatas and other pieces by Blavet, Naudet, Purcell, J. Stanley, etc., and contributed to French and English periodicals ("Souvenirs d'un flûtiste," *Le Monde Musical;* etc.).

Flipse, Eduard, Dutch conductor; b. Wissekerke, Feb. 26, 1896; d. Etten-Leur, Sept. 11, 1973. He studied piano and composition in Rotterdam and conducting in Utrecht. In 1930 he became chief conductor of the Rotterdam Phil., a post he retained until 1965. In 1952 he became chief conductor of the Holland Festival, and was later chief conductor of the Antwerp Phil. (1961–70). During his long tenure in Rotterdam, he introduced works of numerous contemporary composers. He was also a passionate propagandist of the music of Gustav Mahler.

Flodin, Karl (Theodor), Finnish composer; b. Vaasa, July 10, 1858; d. Helsinki, Nov. 30, 1925. He studied music with Faltin in Helsinki (1877–83), and with Jadassohn at the Leipzig Cons. (1890–92). In 1908 he went to Buenos Aires as music critic for a German paper there; returned to Finland in 1921. He publ. numerous essays on Finnish music (in Finnish and German; wrote a biography of Martin Wegelius (1922); composed a *Cortège* for Horn and Orch., as well as incidental music to various plays; publ. some 80 piano pieces. He was married to the singer **Adée Leander** (1873–1935).

Floersheim, Otto, German editor and composer; b. Aachen, March 2, 1853; d. Geneva, Nov. 30, 1917. He was a pupil of Ferdinand Hiller at Cologne; went to N.Y. in 1875; became ed. of the *Musical Courier* in 1880, and from 1894 to 1904 was manager of its Berlin branch. As a music journalist and a man of musical affairs, he was very influential in America; he was also a composer of competently put together piano pieces and songs in a German Romantic vein.

Flood, W(illiam) H(enry) Grattan, Irish organist and music historian; b. Lismore, Nov. 1, 1859; d. Enniscorthy, Aug. 6, 1928. He served as a church organist in Dublin; achieved recognition as a writer on Irish music and musicians. He publ. *History of Irish Music* (1895; 4th ed., 1927); *The Story of the Harp* (1905); *The Story of the Bagpipe* (1911); *William Vincent Wallace, A Memoir* (1912); *John Field of Dublin* (Dublin, 1920); *Introductory Sketch of Irish Musical History* (1921); *Early Tudor Composers* (1925); *Late Tudor Composers* (1929); was the editor of *Songs and Airs of O'Carolan, Moore's Irish Melodies, Armagh Hymnal,* and *The Spirit of the Nation.*

Floquet, Étienne Joseph, French composer; b. Aix-en-Provence, Nov. 23, 1748; d. Paris, May 10, 1785. After studying in his native town, he went to Paris; there he wrote the opera-ballet *L'Union de l'amour et des arts,* produced with great success at the Académie Royale de Musique (Sept. 7, 1773); his 2nd opera, *Azolan, ou Le Serment indiscret* (Nov. 22, 1774, also at the Académie), was a fiasco. Floquet then went to Italy, where he perfected his knowledge by studying with Sala in Naples and with Martini in Bologna. Returning to Paris, he had 2 operas performed at the Académie: *Hellé* (Jan. 5, 1779) and *Le Seigneur bien-faisant* (Dec. 14, 1780). He also wrote a comic opera, *La Nouvelle Omphale* (Comédie-Italienne, Nov. 22, 1782). In an attempt to challenge Gluck's superiority, Floquet wrote the opera *Alceste* on the same subject as Gluck's famous work, but it was never produced.
BIBL.: A. Pougin, *É.-J. F.* (Paris, 1863); F. Huot, *Étude biographique sur É.-J. F.* (Aix, 1903).

Flor, Claus Peter, German conductor; b. Leipzig, March 16, 1953. He studied violin and clarinet at the Zwickau Cons. and the Weimar Hochschule für Musik; completed his violin training at the Leipzig Hochschule für Musik, where he also studied conducting with Rolf Reuter and Kurt Masur. He was awarded the Mendelssohn-Stipendium by the Ministry of Culture in 1979, subsequently winning conducting prizes in Poland and Denmark. He was chief conductor of the Suhler Phil. (1981–84) and of the (East) Berlin Sym. Orch. (1984–85); was made its Generalmusikdirektor in 1985. In 1985 he made his U.S. debut at the Hollywood Bowl.

Flores, Bernal, Costa Rican composer; b. San José, July 28, 1937. After acquiring the rudiments of music in Costa Rica, he enrolled at the Eastman School of Music in Rochester, N.Y. (M.M., 1962; Ph.D., 1964). Returning to Costa Rica, he became a prof. at the San José Cons.

WORKS: Sym. No. 1 for Strings (1965); Sym. No. 2 (1966); Concerto for Piano, Percussion, and Orch. (1963); Clarinet Concerto (1968); piano pieces; songs.

Floridia, Pietro, Italian composer; b. Modica, Sicily, May 5, 1860; d. N.Y., Aug. 16, 1932. He studied in Naples with Cesi (piano) and Lauro Rossi (composition); while at the Naples Cons. he publ. several piano pieces which became quite popular. On May 7, 1882, he brought out in Naples a comic opera, *Carlotta Clepier.* From 1888 to 1892 he taught at the Palermo Cons.; then lived in Milan. In 1904 he emigrated to the U.S.; taught at the Cincinnati College of Music (1906–8); in 1908 settled in N.Y.; in 1913 organized and conducted an Italian Sym. Orch. there. His music (mostly for the stage) is written in a competent manner, in the style of the Italian *verismo.* Floridia ed. a valuable collection in 2 vols., *Early Italian Songs and Airs* (Philadelphia, 1923).
WORKS: Operas: *Maruzza* (Venice, Aug. 23, 1894); *La colonia libera* (Rome, May 7, 1899); *Paoletta* (Cincinnati, Aug. 29, 1910); also *The Scarlet Letter* (1902; not produced) and *Malia* (completed in 1932; not produced).

Florimo, Francesco, Italian music historian; b. S. Giorgio Morgeto, Calabria, Oct. 12, 1800; d. Naples, Dec. 18, 1888. In 1817 he entered the Collegio di Musica at Naples; Furno, Elia, Zingarelli, and Tritto were his teachers; from 1826 to 1851 he was librarian there. He was Bellini's closest friend; in 1876 he escorted the latter's remains from Paris to Catania, and publ. the pamphlet "Trasporto delle ceneri di Bellini a Catania"; composed *Sinfonia funebre per la morte di Bellini;* founded the Bellini Prize, a competition open to Italian composers not over 30.
WRITINGS: His chief work is *Cenno storico sulla scuola musicale di Napoli* (2 vols., Naples, 1869–71; republ. 1880–84, in 4 vols., as *La scuola musicale di Napoli e i suoi Conservatori*), a complete musical history of Naples and its conservatories, their teachers and pupils, etc.; despite numerous errors, it remains an extremely valuable guide; also, *Riccardo Wagner ed i Wagneristi* (Naples, 1876); *Bellini, Memorie e lettere* (Florence, 1882); *Album Bellini* (Naples, 1886), containing opinions by many eminent musicians on Bellini's works; and *Metodo di canto,* adopted by the Paris Cons. and described as "magistrale" by Rossini. Florimo was also an excellent singing teacher.
BIBL.: G. Megali del Giudice, *F. F.* (Naples, 1901).

Florio, Caryl (real name, **William James Robjohn**), English-American organist and composer; b. Tavistock, Devon, Nov. 3, 1843; d. Morganton, N.C., Nov. 21, 1920. He left England at the age of 14 and settled in N.Y.; was engaged as a singer and organist at various churches in N.Y., Baltimore, Indianapolis, etc.; conducted choral societies in N.Y.; eventually settled in Asheville, N.C. He wrote 2 operas to his own texts: *Guilda* (1879) and *Uncle Tom's Cabin* (1882); several operettas; cantatas: *Song of the Elements* (1872) and *The Night at Bethlehem* (1891); 2 syms.; Quintet for Piano and 4 Saxophones (the 1st work written for such an ensemble); Piano Concerto; 4 violin sonatas; 2 piano sonatas.

Floros, Constantin, distinguished Greek musicologist; b. Thessalonika, Jan. 4, 1930. He studied composition with Uhl and conducting with Swarowsky and Kassowitz at the Vienna Academy of Music, graduating in 1953; he concurrently studied musicology with Schenck at the Univ. of Vienna (Ph.D., 1955, with the diss. *C.A. Campioni als Instrumentalkomponist*) and then continued his training with Husmann at the Univ. of Hamburg, where he completed his Habilitation in 1961; in 1967 he became ausserplanmässiger prof. and in 1972 prof. of musicology there. P. Petersen ed. a Festschrift in honor of his 60th birthday (Wiesbaden, 1990).
WRITINGS: *Universale Neumenkunde* (3 vols., Kassel, 1970); *Gustav Mahler* (3 vols., Wiesbaden, 1977–85); *Beethovens Eroica und Prometheus-Musik: Sujet Studien* (Wilhelmshaven, 1978); *Mozart-Studien I: Zu Mozarts Sinfonik, Opern- und Kirchenmusik* (Wiesbaden, 1979); *Brahms und Bruckner: Studien zur musikalischen Exegetik* (Wiesbaden, 1980); *Einführung*

in die Neumenkunde (Wilhelmshaven, 1980); *Musik als Botschaft* (Wiesbaden, 1989).

Flosman, Oldřich, Czech composer; b. Plzeň, April 5, 1925. He studied composition with K. Janeček at the Prague Cons. and with Bořkovec at the Prague Academy of Music, graduating in 1950. In his music he follows the neo-Romantic tradition of the Czech school of composition, with strong formal design and an animating rhythmic pulse; the influence of Prokofiev's lyrical dynamism is much in evidence.

Works: Ballets: *Pierrot and Columbine* (1957); *The Woman Partisan* (1959); *The Taming of the Shrew* (1960); *The Salted Fairy-Tale* (1982); Double Concerto for Harp, Clarinet, and Orch. (1950); Clarinet Concerto (1954); Bassoon Concertino (1956); 2 violin concertos (1958, 1972); *Dances* for Harp, and String Quartet or String Orch. (1961); *Cuban Overture* (1962); 3 syms. (1964, 1974, 1984); *3 Studies* for Strings and Piano (1965); *Concertant Music* for Wind Quintet and Chamber Orch. (1965); Sonata for Soprano and Strings (1967); Flute Concerto (1969); Horn Concerto (1970); Fugues for Strings (1970); *Fires on the Hills,* overture (1973); *Rural Partita* for Chamber Orch. (1976); *Symphonic Fugue* for Orch. (1977); *Philharmonic Variations* for Orch. (1980); *Symphonic Plays* for Bass Clarinet, Piano, and Orch. (1983); *Nuptial Dances of Charles IV* for Piano and Chamber Orch. (1984); 2 wind quintets (1948, 1962); *Bagatelles* for Winds and Piano (1950); Sonatina for Clarinet and Piano (1952); *Jesenik Suite* for Viola and Piano (1956); 3 string quartets (1956, 1963, 1966); *Dreaming about a Violin* for Violin and Piano (1962); *Romance and Scherzo* for Flute and Harp (1962); Nonet No. 2 (1967); Sonata for Wind Quintet and Piano (1970); *Chamber Music* for Flute, Oboe, Violin, Viola, and Cello (1971); Sonata for Violin, Cello, and Piano (1971); *Letters to You,* 4 songs for Soprano, Flute, and Piano (1973); *Music* for Double Bass and String Quartet (1980); Serenade for Brass Quintet (1981); *Music* for Flute and Piano or Guitar (1984); *Motýli zde nežijí* (Butterflies Don't Live Here Any Longer), piano sonata inspired by the film about children's drawings from a Nazi concentration camp (1961); *4 Fugues* for Piano (1967); *5 Madrigals* for Chorus a cappella (1965).

Flothuis, Marius (Hendrikus), eminent Dutch composer; b. Amsterdam, Oct. 30, 1914. He received his rudimentary musical education at home from his uncle, who taught him piano; then had piano lessons with Arend Koole and studied music theory with Brandts-Buys. He took academic courses at the Univ. of Amsterdam, and musicology at the Univ. of Utrecht (1932–37); served as assistant manager of the Concertgebouw Orch. After the occupation of the Netherlands by the Germans in 1940 he was dismissed from his job (his wife was half Jewish). On Sept. 18, 1943, he was arrested by the Nazis on the charge of hiding Jews, and transported to the concentration camp in Vught, the Netherlands, and a year later to a German labor camp. His liberation came on May 4, 1945, in a forest near Schwerin; he returned to Amsterdam and was reinstated at his managerial job at the Concertgebouw in 1953. From 1955 till 1974 he was artistic director of the Concertgebouw. In 1974 he was appointed prof. of musicology at the Univ. of Utrecht. He publ. several books, including a monograph on W.A. Mozart (The Hague, 1940) and the essay *Mozarts Bearbeitungen eigener und fremder Werke* (Kassel, 1969). In his compositions he adopted the motivic method of melodic writing and its concomitant form of variations in freely dissonant counterpoint and largely neo-Classical format. Dissatisfied with his youthful works, he destroyed his MSS dating before 1934, including some perfectly acceptable symphonic pieces.

Works: *4 Songs* for Soprano, and Small Orch. or Piano (1937–38); Concertino for Small Orch. (1940); *Sonnet* for Mezzo-soprano and Small Orch. (1939–40); *Small Overture* for Soprano and Orch. (1942); *Dramatic Overture* (1943–46); Flute Concerto (Utrecht, Dec. 19, 1945); *2 Sonnets* for Mezzo-soprano and Orch. (1945); Concerto for Horn and Small Orch. (1945); *Valses sentimentales* for Small Orch. (1946; also for

Piano, 4-hands); Concerto for Piano and Small Orch. (1946–48); *To an Old Love* for Mezzo-soprano and Orch. (1948); *4 Trifles* for High Voice and Small Orch. (1948–50); *Capriccio* for Wind Orch. or String Orch. (1949); Concerto for Violin and Small Orch. (1950; Utrecht, Jan. 14, 1952); Fantasia for Harp and Small Orch. (1953; Amsterdam, May 26, 1955); *Sinfonietta concertante* for Clarinet, Saxophone, and Small Orch. (1954–55; Amsterdam, June 2, 1955); *Concert Overture* (1955); *Rondo festoso* for Orch. (Amsterdam, July 7, 1956); Clarinet Concerto (1957); *Symphonic Music* for Orch. (1957); *Spes patriae,* sinfonietta for Small Orch. (1962); *Espressioni cordiali,* 7 bagatelles for String Orch. (1963); *Canti e Giouchi* (Songs and Games) for Wind Quintet and String Orch. (1964); *Celdroom,* radiophonic scene for Speakers, Chorus, and Orch. (1964); *Hymnus* for Soprano and Orch. (1965); Concertino for Oboe and Small Orch. (1968); *Fantasia quasi una cantate* for 12 Strings, Harpsichord, and Soprano (1968); *Per Sonare ed Ascoltare,* 5 canzonas for Flute and Orch. (1971); *Nocturne* for Orch. (1977); *Cantus amoris* for String Orch. (1979); *Vrijheid* for Choir and Orch. (1983); *Santa Espina* for Mezzo-soprano and Orch. (1985–86); *Cantata silesiana* for Chorus, Flute, String Quartet, and Harpsichord (1946); *Love and Strife,* cantata for Contralto, Flute, Oboe d'Amore, Viola, and Cello (1948–49); *Een Amsterdams lied,* cantata for Solo Soprano and Baritone, Flute, Clarinet, 2 Violins, Viola, Cello, Double Bass, and Piano (1951); *Negro Lament,* after Langston Hughes, for Contralto, Saxophone, and Piano (1953); *Odysseus and Nausikaa,* madrigal for Soprano, Contralto, Tenor, Baritone, and Harp (1958–60); Solo Cello Sonata (1937–38); Nocturne for Flute, Oboe, and Clarinet (1941); Quintet for Flute, Oboe, Clarinet, Bass Clarinet, and Bassoon (1941–42); *Sonata da camera* for Flute and Piano (1943); *2 Pieces* for Guitar (1944); *Aria* for Trumpet and Piano (1944); *Aubade* for Flute (1944); *3 Pieces* for 2 Horns (1945); *Ronde champêtre* for Flute and Harpsichord (1945); Solo Violin Sonata (1945); Sonatina for Horn, Trumpet, and Trombone (1945); Partita for Violin and Piano (1950); *Pour le tombeau d'Orphée* for Harp (1950); *Trio serio* for Piano Trio (1950–51); *Sonata da camera* for Flute and Harp (1951); *Small Suite* for 12 Harps (1951; in collaboration with Lex Van Delden); String Quartet (1951–52); *Small Suite* for Oboe, Trumpet, Clarinet or Saxophone, and Piano (1952); Divertimento for Clarinet, Bassoon, Horn, Violin, Viola, and Double Bass (1952); *4 invenzioni* for 4 Horns (1963); Partita for 2 Violins (1966); Concertino for Oboe, Violin, Viola, and Cello (1967); *Allegro vivace* for 2 Harps (1969); *Caprices roumains* for Oboe and Piano (1975); *Adagio* for Piano, 4-hands, and Percussion (1975); *Romeo's Lament* for Horn (1975); *Canzone* for 4 Wind Instruments (1978); *Hommage à Mallarmé* for Voice, Flute, Cello, and Piano (1980); *Capriccio* for 4 Saxophones (1985–86); Sonata for Oboe, Horn, and Harpsichord (1986); *Preludio e Fughetta* for 3 Trumpets (1986); Sonata for Flute and Alto Flute (1975); Suite for Piano (1937–38); *Divertimento on a Theme of Kees Stokvis* for 2 Pianos (1946); *6 moments musicaux* for Piano (1946–47); *5 Epigrams and a Capriccio* for Piano (1970); songs.

Flotow, Friedrich (Adolf Ferdinand) von, famous German opera composer; b. Teutendorf, April 27, 1813; d. Darmstadt, Jan. 24, 1883. He was a scion of an old family of nobility; he received his 1st music lessons from his mother; then was a chorister in Güstrow. At the age of 16 he went to Paris, where he entered the Cons. to study piano with J.P. Pixis and composition with Reicha. After the revolution of 1830, he returned home, where he completed his 1st opera, *Pierre et Cathérine,* set to a French libretto; it was premiered in a German tr. in Ludwigslust in 1835. Returning to Paris, he collaborated with the Belgian composer Albert Grisar on the operas *Lady Melvil* (1838) and *L'Eau merveilleuse* (1839). With the composer Auguste Pilati, he composed the opera *Le Naufrage de la Méduse* (Paris, May 31, 1839; perf. in a German tr. as *Die Matrosen,* Hamburg, Dec. 23, 1845). He scored a decisive acclaim with his romantic opera *Alessandro Stradella,* based on the legendary accounts of the life of the Italian composer;

it was first performed in Hamburg on Dec. 30, 1844, and had numerous subsequent productions in Germany. He achieved an even greater success with his romantic opera *Martha, oder Der Markt zu Richmond* (Vienna, Nov. 25, 1847); in it he demonstrated his ability to combine the German sentimental spirit with Italian lyricism and Parisian elegance. The libretto was based on a ballet, *Lady Henriette, ou La Servante de Greenwich* (1844), for which Flotow had composed the music for Act I; the ballet in turn was based on a vaudeville, *La Comtesse d'Egmont;* the authentic Irish melody *The Last Rose of Summer* was incorporated into the opera by Flotow, lending a certain nostalgic charm to the whole work. Flotow's aristocratic predilections made it difficult for him to remain in Paris after the revolution of 1848; he accepted the post of Intendant at the grand ducal court theater in Schwerin (1855–63); then moved to Austria; he returned to Germany in 1873, settling in Darmstadt in 1880.

WORKS: OPERAS: *Pierre et Cathérine* (1st perf. in a German version, Ludwigslust, 1835); *Die Bergknappen; Alfred der Grosse;* *Rob-Roy* (Royaumont, Sept. 1836); *Sérafine* (Royaumont, Oct. 30, 1836); *Alice* (Paris, April 8, 1837); *La Lettre du préfet* (Paris, 1837; rev. 1868); *Le Comte de Saint-Mégrin* (Royaumont, June 10, 1838; rev. as *Le Duc de Guise,* Paris, April 3, 1840; in German, Schwerin, Feb. 24, 1841); *Lady Melvil* (with Albert Grisar; Paris, Nov. 15, 1838); *L'Eau merveilleuse* (with Grisar; Paris, Jan. 30, 1839); *Le Naufrage de la Méduse* (with Auguste Pilati; Paris, May 31, 1839; in German as *Die Matrosen,* Hamburg, Dec. 23, 1845); *L'Esclave de Camoëns* (Paris, Dec. 1, 1843; subsequent revisions under different titles); *Alessandro Stradella* (Hamburg, Dec. 30, 1844); *L'Âme en peine* (*Der Förster;* Paris, June 29, 1846); *Martha, oder Der Markt zu Richmond* (Vienna, Nov. 25, 1847); *Sophie Katharina, oder Die Grossfürstin* (Berlin, Nov. 19, 1850); *Rübezahl* (Retzien, Aug. 13, 1852, private perf.; Frankfurt, Nov. 26, 1853, public perf.); *Albin, oder Der Pflegesohn* (Vienna, Feb. 12, 1856; rev. as *Der Müller von Meran,* Königsberg, 1859); *Herzog Johann Albrecht von Mecklenburg, oder Andreas Mylius* (Schwerin, May 27, 1857); *Pianella* (Schwerin, Dec. 27, 1857); *La Veuve Grapin* (Paris, Sept. 21, 1859; in German, Vienna, June 1, 1861); *La Châtelaine* (*Der Märchensucher,* 1865); *Naida* (St. Petersburg, Dec. 11, 1865); *Zilda, ou La Nuit des dupes* (Paris, May 28, 1866); *Am Runenstein* (Prague, April 13, 1868); *L'Ombre* (Paris, July 7, 1870; in German as *Sein Schatten,* Vienna, Nov. 10, 1871); *Die Musikanten,* or *La Jeunesse de Mozart* (Mannheim, June 19, 1887). **BALLETS:** *Lady Henriette, ou La Servante de Greenwich* (Act II by R. Burgmüller and Act III by E. Deldevez; Paris, Feb. 21, 1844); *Die Libelle,* or *La Demoiselle, ou Le Papillon ou Dolores* (Schwerin, Aug. 8, 1856); *Die Gruppe der Thetis* (Schwerin, Aug. 18, 1858); *Der Tannkönig* (Schwerin, Dec. 22, 1861); *Der Königsschuss* (Schwerin, May 22, 1864). **INSTRUMENTAL:** Sym. (1833; not extant); 2 piano concertos (1830, 1831); *Jubel-Ouverture* (1857); also *Trio de salon* for Violin, Piano, and Cello (1845); Violin Sonata (1861); songs.

BIBL.: G. von Flotow, *Beiträge zur Geschichte der Familie von F.* (Dresden, 1844); A. Bussensius, *F. v.F.: Eine Biographie* (Kassel, 1855); F. von Flotow, "Erinnerungen aus meinem Leben," in J. Lewinsky, ed., *Vor den Coulissen* (Berlin, 1882); B. Bardi-Poswiansky, *F. als Opernkomponist* (diss., Univ. of Königsberg, 1924); J. Weissmann, *F.* (London, 1950); R. Stockhammer, "F. v.F.s Beziehungen zu Wien," *Österreichische Musikzeitschrift,* XVII (1962).

Flower, Sir (Walter) Newman, noted English publisher and writer on music; b. Fontmell Magna, Dorset, July 8, 1879; d. Blandford, Dorset, March 12, 1964. He joined the firm of Cassel & Co. in 1906; purchased it in 1927. He became deeply interested in music; publ. an extensive biography, *George Frideric Handel: His Personality and His Times* (London, 1923; 2nd ed., rev., 1947); also *Sir Arthur Sullivan: His Life, Letters and Diaries* (London, 1927; 2nd ed., rev., 1950); *Franz Schubert: The Man and His Circle* (London, 1928; 2nd ed., rev., 1949); also prepared a *Catalogue of a Handel Collection Formed by*

Newman Flower (Sevenoaks, 1921); publ. a vol. of memoirs, *Just As It Happened* (London, 1950). He was knighted in 1938.

BIBL.: A. Walker, *George Frideric Handel: The N. F. Collection* (Manchester, 1972).

Floyd, Carlisle (Sessions, Jr.), American composer; b. Latta, S.C., June 11, 1926. He studied at Syracuse Univ. with Ernst Bacon (Mus.B., 1946; Mus.M., 1949); also took private piano lessons with Rudolf Firkušný and Sidney Foster. In 1947 he joined the staff of the School of Music of Florida State Univ., Tallahassee; in 1976, became a prof. of music at the Univ. of Houston. His musical drama *Susannah* was produced in Tallahassee (Feb. 24, 1955); it was later staged at the City Center in N.Y. (Sept. 27, 1956); received the N.Y. Music Critics Circle Award as the best opera of the year. Floyd's other works include *Slow Dusk,* a musical play in 1 act (1949); *Fugitives,* a musical drama in 3 acts (1951); operas: *Wuthering Heights* (Santa Fe, July 16, 1958); *The Passion of Jonathan Wade* (N.Y., Oct. 11, 1962); *The Sojourner and Mollie Sinclair* (Raleigh, N.C., Dec. 2, 1963); *Markheim* (New Orleans, March 31, 1966); *Of Mice and Men,* after John Steinbeck's novel (Seattle, Jan. 22, 1970); *Bilby's Doll,* for the Bicentennial (Houston, Feb. 29, 1976); *Willie Stark* (Houston, April 24, 1981). He further wrote the ballet *Lost Eden* for 2 Pianos (1952); *Pilgrimage,* a cycle of 5 songs (1955); *The Mystery* (5 *Songs of Motherhood*) for Soprano and Orch. (1962); *In Celebration: An Overture* (1970); other vocal and instrumental pieces.

Flummerfelt, Joseph, American conductor; b. Vincennes, Ind., Feb. 24, 1937. He studied at DePauw Univ. (B.Mus., 1958), the Philadelphia Cons. of Music (M.Mus., 1962), and the Univ. of Illinois (D.M.A., 1971); also had private lessons with Julius Herford in San Diego (1958) and Nadia Boulanger in Fontainebleau (1964). He was director of choral activities at DePauw Univ. (1964–68) and Florida State Univ. (1968–71); in 1971 was appointed choral director at Westminster Choir College; in 1982 he became artistic director and principal conductor there. He served as choral director of the Spoleto Festival in Italy (from 1971) and in the U.S. (from 1976); also held the posts of director of the N.Y. Choral Artists and chorus master of the N.Y. Phil. In 1990 he became director of choral activities at the New England Cons. of Music in Boston.

Flury, Richard, Swiss composer; b. Biberist, March 26, 1896; d. there, Dec. 23, 1967. He studied musicology in Basel, Bern, and Geneva, then theory and composition with Kurth, Hubert, Lauber, and Marx; conducted orchs. and choral societies in Switzerland (Zürich, Bern, and Solothurn); taught at the Solothurn Canton School. He wrote an autobiography, *Lebenserinnerungen* (1950; with a list of works).

WORKS: OPERAS: *Eine florentinische Tragödie* (1926); *Die helle Nacht* (1932); *Casanova e l'Albertolli* (1937); ballet, *Die alte Truhe* (1945); several festival music scores. **ORCH.:** 7 syms.: No. 1 (1923); *Fastnachts-Symphonie* (1928); *Tessiner Symphonie* (No. 2, 1936); *Waldsymphonie* (1942); *Bucheggbergische Symphonie* (No. 3, 1946); *Liechtensteinische Symphonie* (No. 4, 1951); No. 5 (1955–56); 6 symphonic overtures; 4 violin concertos (1933, 1940, 1944, 1965); 2 piano concertos (1927, 1943); *Caprice* for Violin and Orch. (1967). **CHAMBER:** Oboe Sonata (1926); 3 cello sonatas (1937, 1941, 1966); 7 string quartets (1926, 1929, 1938, 1940, 1955, 1958, 1964); Piano Quintet (1948); 11 violin sonatas (Nos. 5–11, 1940–61); Piano Sonata (1920); *50 romantische Stücke* for Piano; 24 preludes for Piano; also 15 military marches and other music for Band; choruses; about 150 songs.

Flynn, George (William), American composer; b. Miles City, Mont., Jan. 21, 1937. He studied composition with Ussachevsky (1960–64), Beeson (1964–66), and Luening at Columbia Univ. (D.M.A., 1972). He was on the faculty at his alma mater (1966–73) and also taught at City College of the City Univ. of N.Y. (1973–76). In 1977 he was appointed chairman of the composition dept. at DePaul Univ. in Chicago; he was a co-founder of Chicago Soundings, a performing group for contemporary music. His own music is of a quaquaversal nature, disdaining nothing, absorbing anything of modernistic applicability.

Works: STAGE: Ballet, *Mrs. Brown,* for Chamber Orch. and Tape (1965). **ORCH.:** 2 syms.: No. 1, *Music for Orchestra* (1966); No. 2 (Chicago, May 19, 1981); *Lammy* for Strings (1973); *Javeh* (1973); *Meditations, Praises* (Chicago, June 20, 1981); *Focus* for Chamber Orch. (1983); *Coloration* for Chamber Orch. (1983); *Quietude* for Chamber Orch. (1983); *Lost and Found* for Youth Orch. (1984). **VOCAL:** *Tirades and Dreams* for Actress, Soprano, and Chamber Orch. (1972); *Songs of Destruction,* 5 duos for Soprano and Piano (1973–74); *American Songs,* 6 settings for Chorus, Horn, and Piano (1983–84); choruses. **CHAMBER:** Piano Quartet (1963); *Solo and Duos* for Violin and Piano (1964); Wind Quintet (1965; rev. 1983); *4 Pieces* for Violin and Piano (1965); *Duo* for Clarinet and Piano (1966); *Duo* for Trumpet and Piano (1974); *Duo* for Viola and Piano (1974); *American Rest* for Clarinet, Viola, Cello, and Piano (1975; rev. 1982); *American Festivals and Dreams* for String Quartet (1976); *Duo* for Cello and Piano (1977); *Celebration* for Violin and Piano (1980); Saxophone Quartet (1980); *4 Fantasy-Études* for Solo Violin (1981); *Diversion* for Flute, Clarinet, Violin, Cello, and Piano (1984). **PIANO:** *Fuguing* (1962); *4 Preludes* (1965); *Fantasy* No. 1 (1966); *Music* for Piano, 4-hands (1966); *Wound* (1968); *Canal* (1976); *Fantasy* No. 2 (1980–82); also *Drive* for Harpsichord (1973).

Foch (real name, **Fock**), **Dirk,** Dutch composer and conductor; b. Batavia, Java (where his father was governor general of the Dutch East Indies), June 18, 1886; d. Locarno, Switzerland, May 24, 1973. He studied in the Netherlands and Germany; began his career in Sweden; conducted the Göteborg Sym. Orch. (1913–15); was guest conductor of the Concertgebouw Orch. in Amsterdam and of the orch. at The Hague (1917–19). He made his American debut as conductor with a specially assembled orch. at Carnegie Hall in N.Y., April 12, 1920; also conducted orch. groups elsewhere in the U.S., and in Vienna.

Works: *Ein hohes Lied,* 5 fragments from the Bible for Recitation and Orch. (Amsterdam, 1931); a musical pageant in the style of the medieval mystery plays, *From Aeon to Aeon;* 3 ballades for Piano (1913); a cycle of songs from the Chinese (1921); *Java Sketches* for Piano (1948).

Fodi, John, Hungarian-born Canadian composer; b. Nagyteval, March 22, 1944. He emigrated to Canada from Germany with his family in 1951, becoming a naturalized citizen in 1961. He studied theory and composition with Lorne Betts in Hamilton (1964–66), composition with John Weinzweig and John Beckwith and electronic music with Gustav Ciamaga at the Univ. of Toronto (B.Mus., 1970), and composition with Istvan Anhalt and electronic music with Paul Pedersen at McGill Univ. in Montreal (1970–71); then returned to the Univ. of Toronto to complete his training in composition with Weinzweig (M.Mus., 1972). He subsequently had some lessons with Mario Davidovsky at Johnson State College (1973) and later took his M.L.S. degree at the Univ. of Toronto (1990). In 1967 he founded the Contemporary Music Group at the Univ. of Toronto, serving as its artistic director until 1970; while at McGill Univ., he was co-founder of the New Music Group and in 1971 helped to organize ARRAY, a contemporary music group, later serving as its president and artistic director (1976–79). In 1974 he joined the staff of the Edward Johnson Music Library at the Univ. of Toronto. His compositions partake of multifarious techniques of ultramodern music; the titles alone point to a preoccupation with abstract textures and mathematical processes, e.g., *Contrasts 4, Pi, Divisions, Signals,* and *Segments.*

Works: DRAMATIC: *Music Bockxd* for 3 Actors or Dancers, 7 Music Boxes, and Tape (1969). **ORCH.:** 2 syms.: No. 1 (1964–66); No. 2 (1987–); *Symparanekromenoi* (1969–71; Toronto, July 25, 1974); Concerto for Viola and 2 Wind Ensembles (1972); *Dragon Day Adagio* for String Orch. (1980); Concertino for Bassoon and Chamber Orch. (1983); Concerto Grosso for Chamber Ensemble (1984); *Kootenay* for Chamber Orch. (1986); Suite for Junior String Orch. (1988–89). **CHAMBER:** 7

string quartets: No. 1 (1963); No. 2, *Short* (1963); No. 3 (1965); No. 4, *Fantasia* (1967); No. 5, *Concerto a quattro* (1973); No. 6, *Aus tiefer Not* (1981); No. 7, *Purcell* (1987–89); Piano Sonata (1964–66); Chamber Sym. for Flute, Horn, Piano, and String Quartet (1967); *Tetrares* for Percussion Quartet (1968); Harpsichord Sonata (1968); *4 for 4* for Clarinet Quartet (1968); *Signals* for Soprano Saxophone, Tenor Saxophone, Trombone, Percussion, and Piano (1969); *Ch'ien* for String Quartet (1969); *Elements* for 1 to 5 Melody Instruments (1972); *Variations II* for Woodwind Quintet (1975); *In campo aperto* for Flute, Oboe, Percussion, 2 Pianos, and Cello (1976); *Concerto in 4 Parts* for Accordion (1978); *Dum transisset, "sonata for 5 instruments"* for Flute, Trombone, Piano, Viola, and Cello (1978–); *Birds,* 4 pieces for Various Instruments (1978–79); Wind Octet for 2 Oboes, 2 Clarinets, 2 Bassoons, and 2 Horns (1980–81); Partita for Brass Quintet (1981–82); Sonata for Double Wind Quintet (1982–83); Tuba Quartet for 2 Euphoniums and 2 Tubas (1984); also vocal works; choruses.

Fodor, Eugene (Nicolas, Jr.), American violinist of Hungarian-Italian extraction; b. Turkey Creek, Colo., March 5, 1950. His great-great-grandfather founded the Fodor Cons. in Hungary. He studied violin with Harold Wippler in Denver; in 1967 he went to N.Y. and studied with Galamian; then with Gingold at the Indiana Univ. School of Music in Bloomington (diploma, 1970); later took lessons in the master class of Jascha Heifetz at the Univ. of Southern Calif. In 1972 he won the Paganini Competition in Genoa, Italy. In 1974 he shared 2nd prize with 2 Soviet violinists (no 1st prize was awarded) at the Tchaikovsky Competition in Moscow. Returning to America, he was given the honors of the state of Colorado, and on Sept. 12, 1974, played at a state dinner at the White House for the premier of Israel, Rabin. In subsequent years he appeared as a soloist with a number of major orchs., and also was active as a recitalist. His seemingly successful career took a bizarre twist in 1989 when he was arrested and jailed for cocaine and heroin possession, cocaine trafficking, and breaking-and-entering on Martha's Vineyard in Massachusetts.

Fodor-Mainvielle, Joséphine, famous French soprano; b. Paris, Oct. 13, 1789; d. Saint-Génis, near Lyons, Aug. 14, 1870. She made her debut in 1808 in St. Petersburg in Fioravanti's *Le Cantatrici villane;* gained renown for her performances in the operas of Mozart and Rossini at the King's Theatre in London (1816–18); was likewise successful in her many engagements in Paris, Naples, and Vienna. During a performance of the title role of *Sémiramide* in Paris on Dec. 9, 1825, she suddenly lost her voice and was eventually compelled to quit the stage. She went to Naples in the hopes of recovery under the warm sun, but her attempts to renew her career in 1828 and 1831 failed, and she spent the rest of her long life in retirement.

Foerster, Adolph Martin, American composer; b. Pittsburgh, Feb. 2, 1854; d. there, Aug. 10, 1927. He owed his 1st musical training to his mother; studied at the Leipzig Cons. with Richter; then returned to Pittsburgh, where he was active as a teacher of singing and piano. He composed *Dedication March* for the opening of the Carnegie Music Hall in Pittsburgh (Nov. 7, 1895); symphonic poem, *Thusnelda;* Violin Concerto; 2 piano trios; 2 piano quartets; 2 string quartets; numerous piano works; songs.

Foerster, Josef Bohuslav, eminent Czech composer and teacher, son of **Josef Förster;** b. Prague, Dec. 30, 1859; d. Nový Vestec, near Stará Boleslav, May 29, 1951. He studied at the Prague Organ School (1879–82), then was organist at St. Vojtěch (1882–88) and choirmaster of Panna Marie Sněžná (1889–94). He married the soprano **Berta Foerstrová-Lautererová** in 1888; when she became a member of the Hamburg Opera in 1893, he settled there as a music critic and later became a prof. of piano at the Cons. in 1901. After his wife became a member of the Vienna Court Opera in 1903, he became a prof. of composition at the New Vienna Cons. He returned to Prague in 1918; then taught composition at the

Cons. (1919–22), at its master school (1922–31), and at the Univ. of Prague (1920–36). He served as president of the Czech Academy of Sciences and Art (1931–39), and was awarded the honorary title of National Artist of the Czech government in 1945. He continued to teach privately and to compose during the last years of his long life. He taught many distinguished Czech composers of the 20th century. He publ. a detailed autobiography (Prague, 1929–47), as well as several vols. of essays and articles. Of his numerous compositions, the most important are his operas, instrumental music, and choral pieces written before World War I. His works from this period are suffused with lyric melos, and reveal characteristic national traits in Foerster's treatment of melodic and rhythmic material; his harmonic idiom represents the general style of Central European Romanticism.

WORKS: OPERAS (all 1st perf. in Prague): *Debora* (1890–91; Jan. 27, 1893); *Eva* (1895–97; Jan. 1, 1899); *Jessika* (1902–4; April 16, 1905); *Nepřemoženi* (Invincibilities; 1917; Dec. 19, 1918); *Srdce* (Hearts; 1921–22; Nov. 15, 1923); *Bloud* (The Fool; 1935–36; Feb. 28, 1936). ORCH.: 5 syms.: No. 1, in D minor (1887–88); No. 2, in F major (1892–93); No. 3, in D major (1894); No. 4, in C minor (1905); No. 5, in D minor (1929); *Mé mládí* (My Youth), symphonic poem (1900); *Cyrano de Bergerac*, suite (1903); *Ze Shakespeara* (From Shakespeare), suite (1908–9); *Legenda o štěstí* (Legend of Happiness), symphonic poem (1909); 2 violin concertos (1910–11; 1925–26); *Jaro a touha* (Spring and Longing), symphonic poem (1912); *Jičínská suita* (1923); Cello Concerto (1930); Capriccio for Flute and Small Orch. (1945–46). CHAMBER: 5 string quartets (1888; 1893; 1907–13; 1944; 1951); 3 piano trios (1883; 1894; 1919–21); String Quintet (1886); Wind Quintet (1909); Piano Quintet (1928); Nonet (1931); Sonata for Violin and Piano (1925); 2 sonatas for Cello and Piano (1898, 1926); *Sonata quasi fantasia* for Violin (1943); also incidental music for various plays; songs; piano pieces; choral works.
BIBL.: Z. Nejedlý, *J.B. F.* (Prague, 1910); J. Bartoš, *J.B. F.* (Prague, 1923); J. Bartoš, P. Pražák, and J. Plavec, eds., *J.B. F.: Jeho životní pout a tvorba: 1859–1949* (on his life and work; Prague, 1949); F. Pala, *J.B. F.* (Prague, 1962).

Foerstrová-Lautererová, Berta, Czech soprano; b. Prague, Jan. 11, 1869; d. there, April 9, 1936. She studied in Prague; made her debut as Agathe in *Der Freischütz* at the Prague National Theater in 1887; during her tenure there, she created roles in Dvořák's operas *Jakobín* and *Dimitrij*; was a member of the Hamburg Opera (1893–1901); then sang with the Vienna Court Opera (1901–13), appearing under the name of **Foerster-Lauterer;** she retired in 1914. Her husband was the composer **Josef Bohuslav Foerster.**

Fogg, (Charles William) Eric, English organist and composer; b. Manchester, Feb. 21, 1903; d. London, Dec. 19, 1939. He studied organ with his father; composition with Granville Bantock. He was active as an organist in Manchester; then was on the staff of the BBC. He wrote an overture to the *Comedy of Errors* (1922); *Poem* for Cello and Piano; Suite for Violin, Cello, and Harp; songs (*Love and Life, The Little Folk,* etc.); piano pieces; choral works; etc.
BIBL.: L. Foreman, "F. out of the mists . . . ," *Music and Musicians International* (Sept. 1989).

Foggia, Francesco, Italian composer; b. Rome, 1604; d. there, Jan. 8, 1688. He was a pupil of A. Cifra and P. Agostini; served at several German courts; returning to Rome, he was maestro di cappella at the Lateran (1636–61); at S. Lorenzo in Damaso (1661); and, from 1677, at S. Maria Maggiore. A prolific and masterly composer, he continued the traditions of the Roman School. He wrote the oratorios *David fugiens a facie Saul* and *San Giovanni Battista* (1670); numerous masses a cappella (also a few with organ); litanies, motets, etc.

Fogliani (Fogliano), Giacomo, Italian organist and composer, brother of **Ludovico Fogliani (Fogliano);** b. Modena, 1468; d. there, April 10, 1548. He was chorister in the Papal Chapel in Rome (1513–14); later was choirmaster of the Modena Cathedral.

Fogliani (Fogliano), Ludovico, Italian music theorist, brother of **Giacomo Fogliani (Fogliano);** b. Modena, 2nd half of the 15th century; d. there, 1538. He was famous for his book *Musica theorica . . .* (Venice, 1529; modern facsimile ed., Bologna, 1970), in which he preceded Zarlino in declaring the correct proportion of the major third to be 4:5, and in distinguishing between the major and minor (greater and lesser) semitones. In Petrucci's *Frottole* (1504–8) are some specimens of his compositions.
BIBL.: J. Barbour, *Tuning and Temperament* (East Lansing, Mich., 1951; 2nd ed., 1953).

Foldes, Andor, Hungarian-born American pianist; b. Budapest, Dec. 21, 1913. He was given piano lessons by his mother as a child, and at the age of 8 played a Mozart concerto with the Budapest Phil. From 1922 to 1932 he studied composition with Leo Weiner, conducting with Ernst Unger, and piano with Dohnányi at the Liszt Academy of Music in Budapest; in 1933 he received the Liszt Prize, and in 1934 began his 1st European tour. In 1939 he went to N.Y., and became a naturalized American citizen in 1948; then he returned to Europe; lived in Germany and in Switzerland. In 1969 he toured India and Japan; also gave concerts in Argentina and South Africa. Apart from the regular piano repertoire, Foldes played almost all the piano works by Bartók. With his wife, Lili Foldes, he publ. an entertaining booklet, *Two on a Continent* (N.Y., 1947); he further publ. a lively piano manual, *Keys to the Keyboard* (N.Y., 1948), which was tr. into German, Hungarian, Italian, Spanish, Norwegian, Polish, Dutch, Japanese, and Korean, and *Gibt es einen Zeitgenössischen Beethoven-Stil und andere Aufsätze* (Wiesbaden, 1963).
BIBL.: W.-E. von Lewinski, *A. F.* (Berlin, 1970).

Foley, "Red" (Clyde Julian), American country-music singer; b. Blue Lick, Ky., June 17, 1910; d. Fort Wayne, Ind., Sept. 19, 1968. He studied briefly at Georgetown (Ky.) College; in 1937 he formed the "Renfro Valley Barn Dance" radio program, and appeared regularly at the Grand Ole Opry in Nashville. He made popular such country-music classics as *Chattanooga Shoeshine Boy, Peace in the Valley,* and *Beyond the Sunset.* In 1967 he was elected to the Country Music Hall of Fame in recognition of his prominent place among modern country-music performers. He died while on tour with the Grand Ole Opry.

Foli (real name, Foley), A(llan) J(ames), Irish bass; b. Cahir, Tipperary, Aug. 7, 1835; d. Southport, Oct. 20, 1899. He was a pupil of Bisaccia in Naples. Following a widespread fashion among aspiring English opera singers, he changed his name to an Italian-sounding homonym, Foli, and made a career as "Signor Foli." He made his professional debut as Elmiro in Rossini's *Otello* in Catania in 1862; then sang throughout Italy; appeared in London at Her Majesty's Theatre in 1865; and later at Covent Garden and Drury Lane; toured the U.S. with Mapleson's opera company (1878–79); also traveled in South Africa, Australia, and Russia.

Folville, Eugénie-Émilie Juliette, Belgian pianist and composer; b. Liège, Jan. 5, 1870; d. Dourgne, France, Oct. 28, 1946. She studied piano with her father and violin with César Thomson; took lessons in composition with Radoux at the Liège Cons. She was only 17 when her *Chant de Noël* was performed at the Liège Cathedral. In 1898 she was appointed prof. at the Liège Cons. After the outbreak of World War I in 1914 she lived in Bournemouth, England; later returned to the Continent. She wrote an opera, *Atala* (Lille, 1892), a Violin Concerto, a Piano Concerto, piano pieces, and songs.

Fomin, Evstignei, Russian composer; b. St. Petersburg, Aug. 16, 1761; d. there, April 27, 1800. He was sent to Bologna to study with Padre Martini; returned to St. Petersburg in 1785; then became a singing teacher and operatic coach at the theatrical school there. He composed about 10 operas, including *Novgorod Hero Vassily Boyeslavich* (St. Petersburg, Dec. 8,

1786); *Yamshchiki* (Coachmen; St. Petersburg, Jan. 13, 1787); *Orpheus and Eurydice* (St. Petersburg, Jan. 13, 1792); and *The Americans* (St. Petersburg, Feb. 19, 1800; the title refers to the Russians in Alaska; vocal score publ. in 1893; the opera was revived in a perf. at Moscow, Jan. 17, 1947). A number of other operas were erroneously attributed to Fomin, among them the popular *Miller, Wizard, Cheat, and Marriage-Broker,* produced in Moscow on Jan. 31, 1779, the music of which was actually written by an obscure violinist named Sokolovsky. **BIBL.:** A. Finagin, "E. F.," *Music in Old Russia* (Leningrad, 1927); N. Findeisen, "The Earliest Russian Operas," *Musical Quarterly* (July 1933); A. Rabinovich, *Russian Opera before Glinka* (Moscow, 1948); B. Dobrokhotov, *E. F.* (Moscow, 1949; 2nd ed., 1968).

Fongaard, Björn, prolific Norwegian composer; b. Christiania, March 2, 1919; d. there (Oslo), Oct. 26, 1980. He played guitar at an early age; began his formal music education in 1942 at the Oslo Cons. with Per Steenberg and Bjarne Brustad; later took a course in advanced techniques with Karl Andersen. He then taught guitar at the Oslo Cons., and also gave guitar recitals. As a composer, he became interested in the potentialities of fractional intervals, and devised special guitars for playing microtonal music with the aid of electronic techniques; he dubbed the resulting sound "orchestra microtonalis." His fascination with science is reflected in titles such as *Uran 235, Galaxy, Kosmos, The Solar System,* and *M.1 Crab Nebula in Taurus.* Possessed with indefatigable energy and astounding diligence, he continued to work to the end of his life, producing an enormous number of works in every conceivable genre. **WORKS: STAGE:** *Skapelse II* (Creation II), church opera, with Lights, Dancers, and Tape (1972); *Andromeda,* ballet music for Tape (orch. microtonalis; San Diego, Calif., 1972); *Dimensions,* ballet music for Tape (orch. microtonalis; 1974). **ORCH.:** 2 sinfoniettas (1951, 1968); *3 Pieces* for Strings, op. 10 (1953); Concertino for Piano and Strings (1953); *3 Pieces* for Strings, op. 22 (1954); *3 Novelettes* (1954); Sonata Concertante for Guitar and Orch. (1963); *Uran 235,* symphonic poem glorifying the energy of the fissionable isotope (1963); *Visions* for Strings (1964); *Kosmos* for Strings and Percussion (1964); *3 Novasjoner* for Chamber Orch. (1966); Serenade for Strings (1967); *Ochestra Antiphonalis* for Orch. divided into 2 groups (1968); *Legende* (1968); *Fantasia* for Strings (1968); *Klangbilder* for Strings (1968); *Symphony of Space I–III* (all 1969); cycle of 5 symphonic poems: *Mare tranquillitatis, Callisto, Titan, Triton,* and *Sinus iridum* (1969); *Sinfonia geo-paleontologica I–V* (1970); *Universum,* symphonic poem (1970); *Relativity: Symphony I–III* (1970); *Angelicum,* symphonic poem (1970); *Sanheten* (The Verity), symphonic poem (1971); *Die Pflanzenwelt,* sym. (1971); *Naturen,* symphonic poem (1971); *Livet* (Life), symphonic poem (1971); 23 piano concertos (1973–76); 7 violin concertos (1973–77); Viola Concerto (1977); 3 cello concertos (1977); Double-bass Concerto (1977); Concerto for Piccolo and Orch. (1973); 3 flute concertos (1973–76); 2 oboe concertos (1976); English Horn Concerto (1976); 2 clarinet concertos (1976); Bass-clarinet Concerto (1976); Saxophone Concerto (1976); Bassoon Concerto (1976); 3 horn concertos (1973–77); 2 trumpet concertos (1977); Trombone Concerto (1977); 5 organ concertos (1977–78); Harp Concerto (1977); Guitar Concerto (1977); Accordion Concerto (1977); Percussion Concerto (1977); 3 serenades for Orch. (1978); *Svalbard. Nasjonal-epos* (1979); *Frans av Assisi* (1979); *Hjemmefronten* (1979); 7 syms. for Strings (1980). **CHAMBER:** 2 *Lyrical Suites* for Guitar (1945, 1955); 2 sonatas for Guitar (1947, 1963); Suite for Solo Horn (1953); Suite for Violin and Cello (1953); Serenade for String Trio (1953); *Vision* for Cello and Piano (1959); *3 Aleatory Pieces* for Chamber Ensemble (1964); 3 concertinos for Quarter-tone Guitar and Percussion (1964); 2 sonatas for Microtonal Guitar (1965, 1975); *Galaxy* for 3 Quarter-tone Guitars, electronically altered (1965); Sonata for Solo Oboe, op. 52, No. 1 (1967); Sonata for Oboe and Organ, op. 52, No. 2 (1967); Sonata for a Single Tam-tam, electronically metamorphosed (1968); Sonata for

Solo Oboe, op. 70, No. 1 (1968); Sonata for Saxophone and Microtonal Guitar (1970); *Microtonal Structures* for Organ, Microtonal Guitar, Percussion, Violin, Viola, and Cello (1971); Sonata for Solo Bassoon (1972); Sonata for Oboe and Organ, op. 109, No. 3 (1970); Harp Sonata (1971); Trio for Flute, Viola, and Harp (1971); 120 preludes for Harp (1972); Solo Saxophone Sonata (1973); 21 string quartets (1973; some with Tape); 57 solo sonatas, for virtually every instrument (1973); *Microtonal syntèse* for String Quartet and Tape (1974); 9 wind quintets (1974); 31 sonatinas for Solo Instrument and Piano (1974); 17 duos for Various Instruments (1974); Suite for Vibraphone (1975); 9 wind trios (1975); 6 wind quartets (1975); 12 string trios (1975); Sonata for Violin and Piano, op. 134 (1975); 41 concertos for Solo Instrument and Tape (orch. microtonalis; 1976–77); *Capriccio* for Accordion (1977); Sonata for Renaissance Instruments, Percussion, and Tape (1977); Sonata for Accordion Duo (1978). **PIANO:** *Tonal Studies,* 341 instructive pieces (1953); 2 sonatas and a suite, op. 9, Nos. 1–3 (1953); 12 sonatinas (1954); *24 Novelettes* (1954); *12 Lyrical Pieces* (1954); 6 sonatinas (1954); *12 Inventions* (1954); Concerto No. 1 (*Space Concerto*) for Piano and Tape (orch. microtonalis; 1971), No. 2 (1973), and No. 3 (1975); *6 peintures* (1970); Sonata, op. 110, No. 1 (1972); *Ex flora et fauna,* 37 sonatas (1969–72); *Fantasia* for Piano and Tape (1975); 28 suites (1975). **ORGAN:** 16 sinfonias, with subtitles such as *Messier 31 i Andromeda, M.42 i Oreon, Cluster of Nebulae in Corona Borealis, M.1 Crab Nebula in Taurus,* etc. (1969–72); *Sinfonia per organum* (1972); *Caritas* (1973); *En kirkes historie* (1974); *Fantasia* (1974); *Peintures sur verre,* 34 liturgical character studies (1974); 12 suites (1976); *Aeternitas,* sym. (1976); *Symphonic Variations* (1976). **VOCAL:** 24 songs, with Piano, each for various soloists, after Norwegian writers (1953); organi and motets to scientific texts, for a cappella Chorus (1953); *2 Reflections* for Narrator and Quarter-tone Guitar (1964); *Orafoni I* for Male Speaking Chorus, Percussion, and Strings (1964) and *II* for Male Speaking Chorus and Electronics (1965); *The Solar System,* after Willy Ley, for Solo Baritone (1964); *Reflections* for Narrator, Percussion, and Tape (orch. microtonalis; 1967); *Skapelsen* (Creation) for Narrator and Tape (orch. microtonalis; 1970); *Mora parva infinitatis* for Soprano, String Quartet, and Tape (1970); *Die Erkentnis* for Soprano, Violin, and Percussion (1976). **TAPE ALONE:** *Homo Sapiens* for Orch. Microtonalis (1966); *Epos* for Orch. Microtonalis (1967); *Elektrofonia I–VII* for Orch. Microtonalis (1970); *Sinfonia Microtonalis I–V* (1970); *Legend* for Orch. Microtonalis (1978).

Fonseca, Julio, Costa Rican composer; b. San José, May 22, 1885; d. there, June 22, 1950. He received elementary musical training at home from his father, a military band musician. A government grant enabled him to pursue serious study in Europe, at the Milan Cons. and in Brussels. Returning to Costa Rica, he became active as a teacher at music schools in San José and as a church organist. His works consist mostly of pleasant salon music for piano and effective band pieces, much of it based on native folk rhythms, such as his band pieces *Suite tropical* (1934) and *Gran fantasia sinfónica sobre motivos folklóricos* (1937).

Fontanelli, Alfonso, eminent Italian composer; b. Reggio Emilia, Feb. 15, 1557; d. Rome, Feb. 11, 1622. He entered the service of Cesare d'Este, a nephew of Duke Alfonso II d'Este in Ferrara, in 1586; then was in the service of the latter (1588–97); in 1598 re-entered the service of Cesare d'Este, who had become the Duke of Modena in the interim; remained in his service until Nov. 1601, when he was found guilty of murdering a man, punished, and banned from the ducal states; was pardoned in 1602. He then was in the service of Cardinal Alessandro in Rome (1602–8); subsequently was active at the court in Florence (1608–10); later was an emissary for Duke Cesare (1611–14), traveling as far as Spain; returned to Rome in 1620 and took Holy Orders. He was greatly esteemed as a composer of madrigals. He publ. *Primo libro de' madrigali* *senza nome* for 5 Voices (Ferrara, 1595; reprint, Venice, 1603) and *Secondo libro de' madrigali senza nome* for 5 Voices (Venice, 1604; reprints 1609 and 1619).

BIBL.: A. Newcomb, "A. F. and the *Seconda Pratica* in Ferrara: Some Newly Uncovered Music and Letters," *International Musicological Society Congress Report*, XI, Copenhagen 1972; idem, "A. F. and the Ancestry of the Seconda Practica Madrigal," in R. Marshall, ed., *Studies in Renaissance and Baroque Music in Honor of Arthur Mendel* (Kassel, 1974).

Fontyn, Jacqueline, Belgian composer and teacher; b. Antwerp, Dec. 27, 1930. She studied piano with Ignace Bolotine in her native city, and later with Marcel Maas; took theory, orchestration, and composition lessons with Marcel Quinet in Brussels and Max Deutsch in Paris; then completed her study of composition at the Chapelle Musicale Reine Elisabeth in Brussels (graduated, 1959). She taught at the Royal Flemish Cons. (1963–70); then was a prof. of composition at the Brussels Cons. (from 1970); won many prizes for her compositions, including the Koopal Prize of the Belgian Ministry of Culture (1961, 1979), the Camille Huismans Prize of Antwerp (1974), and the Arthur Honegger Prize of Paris (1987). In 1961 she married **Camille Schmitt.**

WORKS: BALLET: *Piedigrotta* (1958). ORCH.: *Petite suite* (1951); *Divertimento* for Strings (1953); *Danceries* (1956); *Prelude and Allegro* (1957); *Mouvements concertants* for 2 Pianos and Strings (1957); *Deux estampies* (1961); *Digressions* for Cello and Chamber Orch. (1962); *Six ébauches* (1963); *Digressions* for Chamber Orch. (1964); *Galaxie* for Chamber Orch. (1965); Piano Concerto (1967); *Colloque* for Wind Quintet and Strings (1970); *Pour II archets* (1971); *Evolution* (1972); *Per archi* for String Orch. (1973); Violin Concerto (1975); *Frises* (1975); *Frises II* (1976); *Halo* for Harp and 16 Instruments or Chamber Orch. (1978); *Creneaux* (1982); *Arachne* (1985); *In the Green Shade* (1988). CHAMBER: Wind Quintet (1954); Trio for Violin, Cello, and Piano (1956); String Quartet (1958); *Mosaico* for 4 Clarinets (1965); *Musica a quattro* for Violin, Clarinet, Cello, and Piano (1966); Nonet (1969); *Strophes* for Violin and Piano (1970); *Six climats* for Violin and Piano (1972); *Horizons* for String Quartet (1977); *Zones* for Flute, Clarinet, Cello, Percussion, and Piano (1979); *Rhumbs* for 2 Trumpets, Horn, Trombone, and Tuba (1980); *Analecta* for 2 Violins (1981); *Controverse* for Bass Clarinet or Tenor Saxophone, and Percussion (1983); *Either . . . or entweder . . . oder* for String Quintet, or Clarinet and String Quartet (1984); *Cheminement* for 9 Instrumentalists (1986); other chamber works. PIANO SOLO: 2 *Impromptus* (1950); *Capriccio* (1954); *Ballade* (1964); *Mosaica* (1964); *Le Gong* (1980); *Bulles* (1980); *Aura* (1982). 2 PIANOS: *Spirales* (1971). HARPSICHORD: *Shadows* (1973). VOCAL: *La Trapéziste qui a perdu son cœur* for Mezzosoprano and Chamber Orch. (1953); *Deux rondels de Charles d'Orléans* for Soprano and Piano (1956); *Psalmus Tertius* for Baritone, Chorus, and Orch. (1959); *Éphémères* for Mezzosoprano and 11 Instruments (1979); *Alba* for Soprano and 4 Instruments (1981); *Pro & Antiverbe(e)s* for Soprano and Cello (1984).

Foote, Arthur (William), distinguished American composer; b. Salem, Mass., March 5, 1853; d. Boston, April 8, 1937. He studied harmony with Stephen Emery at the New England Cons. of Music in Boston (1867–70) and took courses in counterpoint and fugue with John Knowles Paine at Harvard College (1870–74), where he received the 1st M.A. degree in music granted by an American univ. (1875). He also studied organ and piano with B.J. Lang, and later with Stephen Heller in France (1883). Returning to the U.S., he taught piano, organ, and composition in Boston; was organist at Boston's Church of the Disciples (1876–78) and at the 1st Unitarian Church (1878–1910); frequently appeared as a pianist with the Kneisel Quartet (1890–1910), performing several of his own works; was a founding member and president (1909–12) of the American Guild of Organists. He taught piano at the New England Cons. of Music (1921–37). He was elected a member of the National Inst. of Arts and Letters (1898). His music, a product

of the Romantic tradition, is notable for its fine lyrical élan. His Suite in E major for Strings (1907) enjoyed numerous performances and became a standard of American orch. music. He publ. *Modern Harmony in Its Theory and Practice* (with W.R. Spalding; 1905; rev. ed., 1959; republ. as *Harmony*, 1969), *Some Practical Things in Piano-Playing* (1909), and *Modulation and Related Harmonic Questions* (1919). His autobiography was privately printed (Norwood, Mass., 1946) by his daughter, Katharine Foote Raffy.

WORKS: ORCH.: *In the Mountains*, overture (1886; Boston, Feb. 5, 1887; rev. 1910); *Francesca da Rimini*, symphonic prologue (1890; Boston, Jan. 24, 1891); *Serenade* for Strings (1891; based on the earlier Suites, opp. 12 and 21); Cello Concerto (1887–93); *Suite* in D minor, op. 36 (1894–95; Boston, March 7, 1896); 4 *Character Pieces after the Rubáiyát of Omar Khayyám* (1900; based on a set of piano pieces); *Suite* in E major for Strings, op. 63 (1907; rev. 1908; Boston, April 16, 1909); *A Night Piece* for Flute and Strings (1922; derived from the *Nocturne and Scherzo* for Flute and String Quartet, 1918). VOCAL: *The Farewell of Hiawatha* for Men's Chorus and Orch. (1885); *The Wreck of the Hesperus* for Chorus and Orch. (1887–88); *The Skeleton in Armor* for Chorus and Orch. (1891); *O Fear the Immortals, Ye Children of Men* for Mezzo-soprano and Orch. (1900); *Lygeia* for Women's Chorus and Orch. (1906); some 100 songs, 52 part-songs, and 35 anthems. CHAMBER: 3 string quartets (1883; 1893; 1907–11); 2 piano trios (1882; rev. 1883; 1907–8); Violin Sonata (1889); *Romance and Scherzo* for Cello and Piano (1890); Piano Quartet (1890); Piano Quintet (1897); Sonata for Cello or Viola and Piano (n.d.); also various piano pieces; organ music.

BIBL.: F. Kopp, *A. F.: American Composer and Theorist* (diss., Univ. of Rochester, 1957); D. Alviani, *The Choral Church Music of A.W. F.* (diss., Union Theological Seminary, 1962); D. Moore, *The Cello Music of A. F., 1853–1937* (diss., Catholic Univ. of America, 1977); W. Cipolla, *A Catalog of the Works of A. F. (1853–1937)* (Detroit, 1980).

Foote, George (Luther), American composer; b. Cannes, France (of American parents), Feb. 19, 1886; d. Boston, March 25, 1956. He studied with E.B. Hill at Harvard Univ.; then in Berlin with Koch and Klatte. Upon his return to the U.S., he was a member of the staff in the music dept. of Harvard Univ. (1921–23) and president of the South End Music School in Boston (until 1943).

WORKS: *Variations on a Pious Theme* for Orch. (Boston, Feb. 11, 1935); *In Praise of Winter*, symphonic suite (Boston, Jan. 5, 1940); *98th Psalm* for Chorus and Organ (1934); religious pantomime, *We Go Forward* (1943); Trio for Flute, Harp, and Violin; other chamber music; piano pieces.

Forbes, Elliot, American choral conductor, musicologist, and music educator; b. Cambridge, Mass., Aug. 30, 1917. He studied at Harvard Univ. (B.A., 1941; M.A., 1947); also took courses at the Mozarteum in Salzburg (1937). He subsequently joined the staff of the music dept. of Princeton Univ. (1947–57). From 1958 to 1984 he was a prof. at Harvard Univ., and from 1958 to 1970 conductor of the Harvard Glee Club and Radcliffe Choral Soc.; conducted the Harvard Glee Club in a tour around the world in 1961 and the Harvard-Radcliffe Chorus in a North American tour in 1964. He is the ed. of the revision of Thayer's *Life of Beethoven* (Princeton, 1964; 2nd ed., rev., 1967), of *Harvard-Radcliffe Choral Music*, and of the *Harvard Song Book* (Boston, 1965); publ. *A History of Music at Harvard to 1972* (Cambridge, Mass., 1988).

Forbes, Henry, English organist and composer; b. London, 1804; d. there, Nov. 24, 1859. He studied with George Smart in London, and with Moscheles and Hummel in Germany; was engaged as a church organist, and publ. a collection of Psalm tunes, *National Psalmody* (1843). His opera *The Fairy Oak* was produced in London (Oct. 18, 1845) with considerable success.

Forbes, Sebastian, English organist, choral conductor, and composer; b. Amersham, Buckingham, May 22, 1941. He studied with Howard Ferguson at the Royal Academy of Music in London (1958–60) and with Philip Radcliffe and Thurston Dart at King's College, Cambridge (1960–64). He subsequently held positions as conductor of the Aeolian Singers (1965–69) and Seiriol Singers (1969–72), and was a univ. lecturer at Bangor (1968–72) and Surrey (from 1972). **WORKS:** *Pageant of St. Paul,* suite for Orch. (1964); Piano Trio (1964); *Antiphony* for Violin and Piano (1965); Partita for Clarinet, Cello, and Piano (1966); Chaconne for Orch. (1967); *Sequence of Carols* for Chorus a cappella (1967); *2nd Sequence of Carols* for Male Chorus, String Orch., and Organ (London, May 1, 1968); String Quartet (1969); *Essay* for Clarinet and Orch. (London, July 28, 1970); *3rd Sequence of Carols* for Chorus a cappella (1971); Sym. in 2 movements (Edinburgh Festival, Sept. 2, 1972); *Fantasy* for Solo Cello (1974); Sonata for 8 Instruments (1978).

Ford, Ernest, English conductor and composer; b. London, Feb. 17, 1858; d. there, June 2, 1919. He was a pupil of Arthur Sullivan at the Royal Academy of Music in London and of Lalo in Paris; was conductor at the Royal English Opera House (where he conducted the premiere of Sullivan's *Ivanhoe* in 1891), then at the Empire Theatre, and from 1897 to 1908 of the Royal Amateur Orch. Soc.; from 1916, was a prof. of singing at the Guildhall School of Music in London; was a Fellow of the Royal Academy of Music from 1899. He wrote operas and operettas; a motet, *Domine Deus* (for the 250th anniversary of Harvard Univ.); songs, duets, etc.; publ. *Short History of Music in England* (1912).

Ford, "Tennessee Ernie" (Ernest Jennings), American country-music singer; b. Bristol, Tenn., Feb. 13, 1919. He studied at the Cincinnati Cons. of Music; then was a bombardier during World War II; after his discharge, he spent a period of time as a disc jockey in California; finally launched a career as a country-music singer. He gained enormous success in 1955 with his recording of *16 Tons.* He became especially successful as a singer of gospel music, capturing a Grammy Award for his album *Great Gospel Songs* (1964). He wrote an autobiography, *This Is My Song, This Is My Story* (1963).

Ford, Thomas, English lutenist and composer; b. c.1580; d. London (buried), Nov. 17, 1648. He was appointed musician to Prince Henry in 1611, and to Charles I in 1626. He was especially successful in the "ayre," a type of composition developed by Dowland, in which melodic prominence is given to the upper voice. These "ayres" appear in alternative settings, either as solo songs with lute accompaniment or as 4-part a cappella songs. He wrote *Musicke of Sundrie Kindes* (1607; the 1st part contains 11 ayres); 2 anthems in Leighton's *Teares;* canons in Hilton's *Catch that catch can;* and the famous madrigal *Since first I saw your face.* MSS are at Christ Church, Oxford, and at the British Library.

Fordell, Erik, Finnish composer; b. Kokkola, July 2, 1917; d. Kaarlela, Dec. 21, 1981. He studied at the Sibelius Academy and the Helsinki Inst. of Church Music. He was unquestionably the most prolific symphonic composer in Finland. He wrote 45 syms. in 32 years: No. 1 (1949); No. 2 (1949); No. 3 (1952); Nos. 4–9 (1956); No. 10 (1956); Nos. 11–13 (1957); No. 14 (1958); No. 15 (1961); No. 16 (1955; rev. 1966); No. 17 (1966); No. 18 (1955; rev. 1966); No. 19 (1967); Nos. 20–21 (1968); Nos. 22–25 (1969); No. 26, *Kaustby* (1970); No. 27 (1973–74); No. 28, *Chou-En-lai* (1974); No. 29 (1974); No. 30, *China's Folk* (1974); Nos. 31–34 (1976); No. 35 (1977); Nos. 36–39 (1978); No. 40 (1978–79); Nos. 41–42 (1979); No. 43 (1980); and 2 unnumbered syms.: *Nature Symphony* (1970–71) and Sym. in 1 Movement (1981). He also wrote 2 violin concertos (1955, 1959); 4 piano concertos (1961, 1962, 1962, 1962); Horn Concerto (1956); *Oratorium profanum* (1968); *Trilogy* for Orch. (1969); *Symphonic Trilogy* (1970); 8 suites for Strings; 5 cantatas; 4 wind quintets; 7 string quartets; Violin Sonata; Flute Sonata; songs; choral music; piano pieces.

Forkel, Johann Nikolaus, erudite German music historian; b. Meeder, near Coburg, Feb. 22, 1749; d. Göttingen, March 20, 1818. He was a chorister at Lüneburg (1762–66) and Schwerin (1766). In 1769 he began the study of law in Göttingen, supporting himself by teaching music. He served as a church organist; in 1778 was appointed music director at the Univ. of Göttingen. His publ. compositions include piano sonatas and songs; in MS are the oratorio *Hiskias;* 2 cantatas: *Die Macht des Gesangs* and *Die Hirten an der Krippe zu Bethlehem;* syms., trios, choruses, etc.
WRITINGS: *Über die Theorie der Musik, sofern sie Liebhabern und Kennern derselben nothwendig und nützlich ist* (1774); *Musikalischkritische Bibliothek* (3 vols., Gotha, 1778–79); *Über die beste Einrichtung öffentlicher Concerte* (1779); *Genauere Bestimmung einiger musikalischer Begriffe* (1780); *Musikalischer Almanach für Deutschland* (1782, 1783, 1784, and 1789); *Allgemeine Geschichte der Musik* (2 vols., Leipzig, 1788, 1801, covering the period up to 1550; his materials for later times went to the publisher Schwickert); *Allgemeine Literatur der Musik, oder Anleitung zur Kenntniss musikalischer Bücher* (1792; important as the pioneer work of its class); *Über Johann Sebastian Bachs Leben, Kunst und Kunstwerke* (Leipzig, 1802; the 1st full biography of Bach, based on information supplied by Bach's sons; in Eng., London, 1820; new tr., London, 1920, by Terry).
BIBL.: H. Edelhoff, *J. F.: Ein Beitrag zur Geschichte der Musikwissenschaft* (Göttingen, 1935); W. Franck, "Musicology and Its Founder, J. F.," *Musical Quarterly* (Oct. 1949).

Formes, Karl Johann, German bass, brother of **Theodor Formes;** b. Mülheim, Aug. 7, 1815; d. San Francisco, Dec. 15, 1889. He made his opera debut as Sarastro in Cologne on Jan. 6, 1842; from 1843 to 1848 he was engaged at Vienna; appeared at Drury Lane in London in 1849; made his Covent Garden debut as Caspar in *Der Freischütz* on March 16, 1850; sang there until 1868; from 1852 to 1857 also sang at the Royal Italian Opera in London; in 1857 he made his 1st American tour; then divided his time between Europe and America. He wrote an autobiography, *Aus meinem Kunst- und Bühnenleben: Erinnerungen des Bassisten* (Cologne, 1888; in Eng., San Francisco, 1891).

Formes, Theodor, German tenor, brother of **Karl Johann Formes;** b. Mülheim, June 24, 1826; d. Endenich, near Bonn, Oct. 15, 1874. He made his debut at Ofen (1846); then sang in Vienna (1848) and Berlin (1851–66); made a tour in America with his brother. He lost his voice temporarily; returned to the stage for a few years; then suffered a setback, became insane, and died in an asylum.

Formichi, Cesare, Italian baritone; b. Rome, April 15, 1883; d. there, July 21, 1949. He studied in Rome; made his debut at the Teatro Lirico in Milan in 1911; then sang at the Teatro Colón in Buenos Aires, in Madrid, in Barcelona, and at the Paris Opéra; appeared with the Chicago Opera Co. (1922–32); sang at Covent Garden in London (1924). He was particularly effective in dramatic roles, such as Rigoletto, Iago, and Scarpia.

Fornerod, Alöys, Swiss violinist and composer; b. Montet-Cudrefin (Vaud), Nov. 16, 1890; d. Fribourg, Jan. 8, 1965. He studied violin and theory at the Lausanne Cons. and at the Schola Cantorum in Paris. Returning to Switzerland, he was a member of the Lausanne Sym. Orch.; in 1954 he was appointed director of the Fribourg Cons. As a composer, he followed the French modern style, in the spirit of fin-de-siècle Impressionism. He publ. *Les Tendances de la musique moderne* (Lausanne, 1924); was for 40 years a critic for *La Tribune de Lausanne.*
WORKS: *Geneviève,* comic opera (Lausanne, May 20, 1954); *Te Deum* for Soloists, Chorus, and Orch. (1955); *Hymne à la Très Sainte Trinité* for Chorus and Brass (1961); *Le Voyage de printemps,* symphonic suite (1943); Piano Concerto (1944); Violin Sonata (1925); Concerto for 2 Violins and Piano (1927); Cello Sonata (1934); choruses and songs.
BIBL.: J. Viret, *A. F., ou, Le Musicien et le pays* (Lausanne, 1982).

Fornia-Labey, Rita (Regina) (née **Newman**), American soprano, later mezzo-soprano; b. San Francisco, July 17, 1878; d. Paris, Oct. 27, 1922. She adopted the name Fornia from her native state of California; married J.P. Labey in 1910. She studied in Paris with Jean de Reszke; began her career as a coloratura soprano; then changed to mezzo-soprano. She made her debut in Hamburg (1901); went to the U.S. in 1906 as a member of H.W. Savage's Opera Co.; from 1907 to 1922 was on the staff of the Metropolitan Opera in N.Y.; also made appearances at Covent Garden in London. She was particularly effective in Wagnerian roles.

Foroni, Jacopo, Italian conductor and composer; b. Verona, July 25, 1825; d. Stockholm, Sept. 8, 1858 (of cholera). He settled in Stockholm in 1849, and became court conductor there; was very successful at his public concerts, and also as a composer. He wrote several operas, among them *I Gladiatori* (Milan, Oct. 7, 1851) and *Advokaten Patelin,* performed posth. in Stockholm (Dec. 4, 1858).

Forqueray, Antoine, French viola da gambist and composer; b. Paris, 1672; d. Mantes, June 28, 1745. He held an appointment as royal chamber musician to Louis XIV from 1690; publ. pieces for his instrument and also *Pièces de clavecin* (ed. by C. Tilney, 1970). His brother, **Michel Forqueray** (b. Chaumes-en-Brie, Feb. 15, 1681; d. Montfort l'Amaury, May 30, 1757), was a Paris organist. **Jean Baptiste (-Antoine) Forqueray** (b. Paris, April 3, 1699; d. there, Aug. 15, 1782), his son, was also a player on the viola da gamba; transcribed for the harpsichord some of his father's pieces. **Nicolas-Gilles Forqueray** (b. Chaumes-en-Brie, Feb. 15, 1703; d. there, Oct. 22, 1761), another son, was a church organist.

Forrest, Hamilton, American composer; b. Chicago, Jan. 8, 1901; d. London, Dec. 26, 1963. He studied with A. Weidig at the American Cons. of Music in Chicago (M.M., 1926), and soon embarked on a successful, though brief, career as an opera composer; his 1st opera, *Yzdra* (1925), received the Bispham Memorial Medal. He then obtained a commission to write an opera on the proverbial subject of Camille; it was produced by the Chicago Civic Opera, with Mary Garden in the title role, on Dec. 10, 1930, with great acclaim. It was a brief success, however, which failed to establish Forrest's position as an American opera composer. His other operas were even less durable; 2 of them, *Don Fortunio* and *Daelia,* were produced during the summers of 1952 and 1954 at Interlochen, Mich. More successful were his settings of American folk songs, frequently performed by Marian Anderson. He also wrote some stage music; other works included 2 piano concertos, *Panorama* for Piano and Orch., *Watercolors* for 14 Wind Instruments and Harp, and *Alamari* for 2 Pianos.

Forrester, Maureen (Kathleen Stewart), outstanding Canadian contralto; b. Montreal, July 25, 1930. She studied voice with Sally Martin in Montreal, and later with Frank Rowe and Bernard Diamant; made her professional debut in a Montreal recital (March 29, 1953). After her U.S. debut at N.Y.'s Town Hall (Nov. 12, 1956), she scored a remarkable success as soloist in Mahler's *Resurrection Symphony* with Bruno Walter and the N.Y. Phil. (Feb. 17, 1957); thereafter pursued an international career as a concert artist. She made her operatic debut as Gluck's Orfeo in Toronto (1961); was a member of the Bach Aria Group (1965–74), and also served as head of the voice dept. at the Philadelphia Musical Academy (1966–71). On Feb. 10, 1975, she made her Metropolitan Opera debut in N.Y. as Erda in *Das Rheingold.* In 1982 she toured the U.S. as soloist with the Montreal Sym. Orch. She publ. the book *Out of Character: A Memoir* (with M. McDonald; Toronto, 1985).

Forsell, (Carl) John (Johan Jacob), famous Swedish baritone; b. Stockholm, Nov. 6, 1868; d. there, May 30, 1941. He was in the Swedish army before embarking on his vocal studies. He made his debut in 1896 at the Stockholm Royal Opera as Rossini's Figaro; sang there from 1896 to 1901, and again from 1903 to 1909. He was on the roster of the Metropolitan Opera in N.Y. during the season of 1909–10. In 1923 he

was appointed director of the Stockholm Royal Opera, a post he held until 1939; also taught singing at the Stockholm Cons. from 1924 until 1931. His outstanding students included Jussi Björling, Set Svanholm, and Askel Schiøtz. A jubilee collection of essays, *Boken om J. Forsell,* was publ. on his 70th birthday (Stockholm, 1938).
BIBL.: E. Ljungberger, *J. F.* (Stockholm, 1916); K. Liliedahl, *J. F.: A Discography* (Trelleborg, 1972).

Förster, Alban, German violinist, conductor, and composer; b. Reichenbach, Oct. 23, 1849; d. Neustrelitz, Jan. 18, 1916. He was a pupil, in Reichenbach, of R. Blume; later studied at the Dresden Cons.; from 1871, was court musician at Neustrelitz, also conducting the Singakademie; from 1881, was a teacher at the Dresden Cons., and conductor of the Liedertafel; from 1882 to 1908, was court Kapellmeister at Neustrelitz. He wrote a ballet, *Träumerei in der Waldmühle* (Zwickau, 1896); orch. and chamber music (string trios and quartets); violin music; instructive piano pieces; songs.

Förster, Emanuel Aloys, German composer; b. Niederstein, Silesia, Jan. 26, 1748; d. Vienna, Nov. 12, 1823. After service in the Prussian army, during which he played the oboe in a band, he went to Vienna for a thorough course in music, eventually becoming a teacher himself, although without a school position. He became friendly with Beethoven, who expressed esteem for him. Förster was a prolific composer; he wrote 48 string quartets, 5 oboe concertos, 10 violin sonatas, 21 piano sonatas, etc. His variations on arias from operas by Mozart, Sarti, and others enjoyed great popularity. He also publ. a manual, *Anleitung zum Generalbass* (1805; several later eds.).
BIBL.: N. Saltscheff, *E. Alois F.* (diss., Univ. of Munich, 1911).

Förster, Georg, German composer and editor; b. Amberg, c.1510; d. Nuremberg, Nov. 12, 1568. He sang at the Heidelberg chapel in 1521, matriculating in classical studies at the Univ. of Heidelberg in 1528. In 1531 he undertook medical studies at Ingolstadt; from 1534 to 1539, studied humanities in Wittenberg with Melanchthon. In 1544 he received his degree of doctor of medicine at Tübingen Univ.; then was a medical practitioner in Amberg (1544–47). He ed. the valuable collection *Ein Ausszug guter alter und neuer teutscher Liedlein* (5 parts; Nuremberg, 1539–56). The 1st 3 parts were publ. in Das Erbe Deutscher Musik: XX (1942), LX (1969), and LXI (1976).
BIBL.: H. Kallenbach, *G. F.s Frische teutsche Liedlein* (diss., Univ. of Giessen, 1931).

Förster, Josef, Bohemian organist, teacher, and composer, father of **Josef Bohuslav Foerster;** b. Osojnitz, Feb. 22, 1833; d. Prague, Jan. 3, 1907. He was organist in several churches in Prague, and a prof. of theory at the Prague Cons. He wrote organ pieces, church music, and a treatise on harmony.

Forsyth, Cecil, English composer and writer on music; b. Greenwich, Nov. 30, 1870; d. N.Y., Dec. 7, 1941. He received his general education at the Univ. of Edinburgh; then studied at the Royal College of Music in London with Stanford and Parry. He joined the viola section in the Queen's Hall Orch.; also was connected with the Savoy Theatre, where he produced 2 of his comic operas, *Westward Ho!* and *Cinderella.* After the outbreak of World War I he went to N.Y., where he remained for the rest of his life. He composed a Viola Concerto and *Chant celtique* for Viola and Orch.; also songs, sacred music, and instrumental pieces. He was the author of a comprehensive manual, *Orchestration* (N.Y., 1914; 2nd ed., 1935; reprinted 1948); *Choral Orchestration* (London, 1920); also a treatise on English opera, *Music and Nationalism* (London, 1911). He publ. (in collaboration with Stanford) *A History of Music* (London, 1916) and a collection of essays, *Clashpans* (N.Y., 1933).

Forsyth, Malcolm (Denis), South African–born Canadian composer, trombonist, conductor, and teacher; b. Pietermaritzburg, Dec. 8, 1936. He was educated at the Univ. of Cape Town (M.Mus., 1966; D.Mus., 1972); among his mentors were Stefans Grove, Mátyás Seiber, and Gideon Fagan (composition), George Hurst and Georg Tintner (conducting), and Hans Grin (trombone). He was co-principal trombonist in the Cape Town Municipal Orch. (1961–67) before settling in Canada; in 1974 he became a naturalized Canadian citizen. He played in the Edmonton Sym. Orch. (from 1968), serving as its principal trombone (1973–80); also was a member of the Univ. of Alberta Brass Quintet (1975–83), and founder-leader of the Malcolm Forsyth Trombone Ensemble (1976–83). He served as conductor of the St. Cecilia Orch. in Edmonton (1977–86). In 1968 he joined the faculty of the Univ. of Alberta, becoming artistic director of its music dept. in 1986. As a composer he successfully applied both African and North American folk elements.

WORKS: ORCH.: *Erewhon*, overture (1962); *Jubilee Overture* (Cape Town, May 5, 1964; rev. 1966); *Essay for Orchestra '67* (Cape Town, Dec. 15, 1967); 3 syms.: No. 1 (1968–72; Cape Town, Sept. 5, 1972); No. 2, ". . . a host of nomads . . ." (1976; Edmonton, March 11, 1977); No. 3, *African Ode* (1980–87; Edmonton, Jan. 30, 1987); *Sketches from Natal* (CBC, March 23, 1970); Piano Concerto (1973–75; Edmonton, March 30, 1979); 3 concerti grossi: No. 1, *Sagittarius* (Banff, Aug. 16, 1975); No. 2, *Quinquefid* (Edmonton, April 6, 1977); No. 3, *The Salpinx* (1981; Edmonton, Feb. 5, 1982); *Images of Night* (1982); *Rhapsody* for 14 Strings (1982; Edmonton, April 18, 1983); *Ukuzalwa* (1983); *Springtide* (Banff, April 3, 1984); *Atayoskewin*, suite (Edmonton, Nov. 16, 1984); *Serenade* for Strings (Toronto, May 12, 1986); Trumpet Concerto (1987; Montreal, Jan. 11, 1988); *Songs from the Qu'appelle Valley* for Brass Band (1987); *Little Suite* for Strings (1988); *Valley of a Thousand Hills* (1989). **CHAMBER:** *Quartet '61* for Brass (1961); *Pastorale and Rondo* for Flute, Clarinet, Horn, Bassoon, and Piano (1968–69); *Quartet '74* for Brass (1974); *6 Episodes after Keats* for Violin, Viola, and Piano (1979–81); *Music for Wit and Science* for Recorder, Lute, and Viola da Gamba, or Flute, Guitar, and Cello (1982); Wind Quintet (1986); *Soliloquy, Epitaph, and Allegro* for Trombone and Organ (1988); *Zephyrus* for Brass (1989); also vocal works.

Forte, Allen, American music theorist; b. Portland, Oreg., Dec. 23, 1926. He was educated at Columbia Univ. (B.S., 1950; M.A., 1952), then taught at Teachers College of Columbia Univ. (1953–59), the Mannes College of Music (1957–59), and Yale Univ. (from 1959). He was ed. of the *Journal of Music Theory* (1960–67). His most important contribution to music theory is an analytic method designed for the explication of atonal music. His *Tonal Harmony in Concept and Practice* represents an original and sophisticated approach to traditional harmony.

WRITINGS: *Contemporary Tonestructures* (1955); *The Compositional Matrix* (Baldwin, N.Y., 1961); *Tonal Harmony in Concept and Practice* (N.Y., 1962; 3rd ed., 1979); *The Structure of Atonal Music* (New Haven, Conn., 1973); *The Harmonic Organization of "The Rite of Spring"* (New Haven, 1978).

Forti, Anton, famous Austrian tenor and baritone; b. Vienna, June 8, 1790; d. there, June 16, 1859. He first sang in Esterháza (1807–11); then went to Vienna, where he appeared at the Theater an der Wien (1811–13); in 1813 he joined the Court Theater, singing both tenor and baritone roles; also sang in Prague, Hamburg, and Berlin; continued to sing until late in his life. He was particularly esteemed for his performances in the roles of Figaro and Don Giovanni.

Fortner, Wolfgang, important German composer; b. Leipzig, Oct. 12, 1907; d. Heidelberg, Sept. 5, 1987. He studied composition with Hermann Grabner at the Leipzig Cons., and musicology with Theodor Kroyer at the Univ. there (1927–31). Upon graduation he was engaged for 22 years as instructor in music theory at the Inst. of Sacred Music in Heidelberg; then was a prof. of composition at the North West German Music Academy in Detmold (1954–57) and held a similar position at the Hochschule für Musik in Freiburg im Breisgau (1957–73). Concurrently he led the concerts of Music Viva in Heidelberg, Freiburg, and Munich; and after 1954 was also a lecturer at the Academy of the Arts in West Berlin. His music is marked by exceptional contrapuntal skills, with the basic tonality clearly present even when harmonic density reaches its utmost; in some of his works from 1947, Fortner gave a dodecaphonic treatment to melodic procedures; in his textures he often employed a "rhythmic cell" device. He was equally adept in his works for the musical theater and purely instrumental compositions; the German tradition is maintained throughout, both in the mechanics of strong polyphony and in rational innovations.

WORKS: STAGE: 5 operas: *Bluthochzeit* (after García Lorca's *Bodas de Sangre*, 1956; Cologne, June 8, 1957; rev. 1963), which is a reworking of a dramatic scene, *Der Wald*, for Voices, Speaker, and Orch. (Frankfurt, June 25, 1953); *Corinna*, opera buffa (Berlin, Oct. 3, 1958); *In seinem Garten liebt Don Perlimlín Belisa* (also after García Lorca's *Bodas de Sangre*, 1961–62; Schwetzingen, May 10, 1962); *Elisabeth Tudor* (1968–71; Berlin, Oct. 23, 1972); *That Time (Damals)*, after Beckett, for Mime, Narrator, Mezzo-soprano, Baritone, Harpsichord, Guitar, Piano, and Live Electronics (Baden-Baden, April 24, 1977); 3 ballets: *Die weisse Rose* (after Wilde's *The Birthday of the Infants*, 1949; concert perf., Baden-Baden, March 5, 1950; stage premiere, Berlin, April 28, 1951) a pantomime, *Die Witwe von Ephesus* (Berlin, Sept. 17, 1952); *Carmen*, a Bizet-collage (1970; Stuttgart, Feb. 28, 1971).

ORCH.: *Suite*, on music of Sweelinck (1930); Concerto for Organ and String Orch. (1932; reused as a Harpsichord Concerto, 1935); Concerto for String Orch. (1933); Concertino for Viola and Small Orch. (1934); *Capriccio und Finale* (1939); *Ernste Musik* (1940); Piano Concerto (1942); *Streichermusik II* for String Orch. (1944); Violin Concerto (1946; Baden-Baden, Feb. 16, 1947); Sym. (1947; Baden-Baden, May 2, 1948; his 1st use of dodecaphony); *Phantasie über die Tonfolge B-A-C-H* for 2 Pianos, 9 Solo Instruments, and Orch. (1950); Cello Concerto (Cologne, Dec. 17, 1951); *Mouvements* for Piano and Orch. (1953; Baden-Baden, Feb. 6, 1954; as a ballet, Essen, Feb. 26, 1960); *La Cecchina*, Italian overture after Piccini (1954); *Impromptus* (Donaueschingen, Oct. 20, 1957); *Ballet blanc* for 2 Solo Violins and String Orch. (1958; as a ballet, Wuppertal, Dec. 30, 1959); *Aulodie* for Oboe and Orch. (1960; rev. 1966); *Triplum* for Orch. and 3 Obbligato Pianos (1965–66; Basel, Dec. 15, 1966; as a ballet, Munich, 1969); *Immagini* for Small or Large String Orch. (1966–67; also version for Large String Orch. and Soprano); *Marginalien* (1969; Kiel, Jan. 12, 1970); *Zyklus* for Cello, Winds, Harp, and Percussion (1969; orig. for Cello and Piano, 1964); *Prolegomena* (concert suite from the opera *Elisabeth Tudor*, 1973; Nuremberg, April 19, 1974); *Prismen* for Flute, Oboe, Clarinet, Harp, Percussion, and Orch. (1974; Basel, Feb. 13, 1975); *Triptychon* (1976–77; consists of 3 parts: *Hymnus I* for 6 Brasses; *Improvisation* for Large Orch., and *Hymnus II* for 18-voice String Orch.; 1st complete perf., Düsseldorf, April 6, 1978); *Variations* for Chamber Orch. (1979; Basel, March 27, 1980); *Madrigal* for 12 Cellos (1979).

VOCAL: *Fragment Maria*, chamber cantata (1969); *Grenzen der Menschheit*, cantata (1930); *Nuptiae Catulli* for Tenor, Chamber Chorus, and Chamber Orch. (1937; Basel, April 5, 1939); *An die Nachgeborenen*, cantata (1947; Baden-Baden, April 4, 1948); *2 Exerzitien* for 3 Female Voices and 15 Instruments (1948); *Mitte des Lebens*, cantata for Soprano and 5 Instruments (1951); *Isaaks Opferung*, oratorio-scene for 3 Soloists and 40 Instruments (Donaueschingen, Oct. 12, 1952); *The Creation*, after James Weldon Johnson's poem, for Voice and Orch. (1954; Basel, Feb. 18, 1955; Fischer-Dieskau, soloist); *Chant de naissance*, cantata for Soprano, Chorus, Solo Violin, Strings, Winds, Percussion, and Harp (1958; Hamburg, April 12, 1959); *Berceuse royale* for Soprano, Solo Violin, and String Orch. (a section from *Chant de naissance*, 1958; rev. in 1975 for Soprano and 7 Instruments); *Prélude und Elegie*, parergon to the Orch.; *Impromptus* for Soprano and Orch., after Hölderlin (1959); *Die Pfingstgeschichte nach Lukas* for Tenor, Chorus, 11 Instruments or Chamber Orch., and Organ (1962–63; Düsseldorf, May 7, 1964); *Der 100. Psalm* for Chorus, 3 Horns, 2 Trumpets, and 2 Trombones (1962); *"Versuch* *eines Agon um . . . ?"* for 7 Singers and Orch. (Hannover, Nov. 8, 1973); *Gladbacher Te Deum* for Baritone, Chorus, Tape, and Orch. (1973; Mönchengladbach, June 6, 1974); *Machaut-Balladen* for Voice and Orch. (1973; Saarbrücken, Jan. 19, 1975); choruses; songs.

CHAMBER: 4 string quartets (1929, 1938, 1948, 1975); *Suite* for Solo Cello (1932); Violin Sonata (1945); *Serenade* for Flute, Oboe, and Bassoon (1945); Flute Sonata (1947); Cello Sonata (1948); String Trio (1952); *6 Madrigals* for Violins and Cellos (1954); *New-Delhi-Musik* for Flute, Violin, Cello, and Harpsichord (1959); *5 Bagatelles* for Wind Quintet (1960); *Zyklus* for Cello and Piano (1964); *Theme and Variations* for Solo Cello (1975); *9 Inventionen und ein Anhang* for 2 Flutes (1976); Trio for Violin, Cello, and Piano (1978); *Capricen* for Flute, Oboe, and Bassoon (1979).

PIANO: Sonatina (1935); *Kammermusik* (1944); *7 Elegies* (1950); *Epigramme* (1964).

ORGAN: *Toccata and Fugue* (1930); *Preamble and Fugue* (1935); *Intermezzi* (1962).

Fortunato, D'Anna, American mezzo-soprano; b. Pittsburgh, Feb. 21, 1945. She studied with Frederick Jagel, Gladys Miller, and John Moriarty at the New England Cons. of Music in Boston (1965–72) and with Phyllis Curtin at the Berkshire Music Center in Tanglewood (1971, 1972). She made her European opera debut with the Boston Camerata as Dido in Purcell's *Dido and Aeneas* in Paris in 1980, and her U.S. opera debut at the N.Y. City Opera as Ruggiero in Handel's *Alcina* in 1983. From 1974 to 1982 she taught at the Longy School of Music in Cambridge, Mass. Her operatic and concert repertoire is extensive, ranging from early music to contemporary works.

Fortune, Nigel (Cameron), noted English musicologist; b. Birmingham, Dec. 5, 1924. He studied at the Univ. of Birmingham (B.A., 1950); received his Ph.D. in 1954 from Gonville and Caius College, Cambridge, with the dissertation *Italian Secular Song from 1600 to 1635: The Origins and Development of Accompanied Monody*. He was music librarian at the Univ. of London (1956–59); in 1959 he became a lecturer at the Univ. of Birmingham; from 1969 to 1986 he was a reader in music there. He was a senior consulting ed. of *The New Grove Dictionary of Music and Musicians* (1980). With D. Arnold, he ed. *The Monteverdi Companion* (London, 1968; 2nd ed., rev., 1985, as *The New Monteverdi Companion*) and *The Beethoven Companion* (London, 1971). He also ed. *Music and Theatre: Essays in Honour of Winton Dean* (Cambridge, 1987).

Foss, Hubert J(ames), English writer on music; b. Croydon, May 2, 1899; d. London, May 27, 1953. He attended Bradfield College; in 1921 became a member of the educational dept. of the Oxford Univ. Press, and in 1924 founded the music dept., which he headed until 1941. He composed *7 Poems by Thomas Hardy* for Baritone, Male Chorus, and Piano; instrumental pieces; songs. He was the author of *Music in My Time* (1933); *The Concertgoer's Handbook* (London, 1946); *Ralph Vaughan Williams* (London, 1950); collected and ed. *The Heritage of Music, Essays . . .* (2 vols., London, 1927–34). His book *London Symphony: Portrait of an Orchestra* remained unfinished at his death, and was completed by Noël Goodwin (London, 1954).

Foss (real name, **Fuchs**), **Lukas,** brilliant German-born American pianist, conductor, and composer; b. Berlin, Aug. 15, 1922. He was a scion of a cultural family; his father was a prof. of philosophy; his mother, a talented modern painter. He studied piano and music theory with Julius Goldstein-Herford. When the dark shadow of the Nazi dominion descended upon Germany, the family prudently moved to Paris; there Foss studied piano with Lazare Lévy, composition with Noël Gallon, and orchestration with Felix Wolfes. He also took flute lessons with Louis Moÿse. In 1937 he went to the U.S. and enrolled at the Curtis Inst. of Music in Philadelphia, where he studied piano with Isabelle Vengerova, composition with Rosario Scalero, and conducting with Fritz Reiner; spent several summers at Tanglewood, Mass., where he studied conduct-

ing with Koussevitzky at the Berkshire Music Center; in 1939–40 he took a course in advanced composition with Hindemith at Yale Univ. He became a naturalized American citizen in 1942. Foss began to compose at a very early age; was awarded a Guggenheim fellowship (1945); in 1960 he received his 2nd Guggenheim fellowship. His 1st public career was that of a concert pianist, and he elicited high praise for his appearances as a piano soloist with the N.Y. Phil. and other orchs. He made his conducting debut with the Pittsburgh Sym. Orch. in 1939. From 1944 to 1950 he was pianist of the Boston Sym. Orch.; then traveled to Rome on a Fulbright fellowship (1950–52). From 1953 to 1962 he taught composition at the Univ. of Calif. in Los Angeles, where he also established the Improvisation Chamber Ensemble to perform music of "controlled improvisation." In 1960 he traveled to Russia under the auspices of the U.S. State Dept. In 1963 he was appointed music director of the Buffalo Phil.; during his tenure he introduced ultramodern works, much to the annoyance of some regular subscribers; he resigned his position in 1970. In 1964–65 he led in N.Y. a series of "Evenings for New Music." In 1965 he served as music director of the American-French Festival at Lincoln Center, N.Y. In 1971 he became principal conductor of the Brooklyn Philharmonia; also established the series "Meet the Moderns" there. From 1972 to 1975 he conducted the Jerusalem Sym. Orch. He became music director of the Milwaukee Sym. Orch. in 1981; relinquished his position in 1986 after a tour of Europe, and was made its conductor laureate; continued to hold his Brooklyn post until 1990. He was elected a member of the American Academy and Inst. of Arts and Letters in 1983. Throughout the years he evolved an astounding activity as conductor, composer, and lately college instructor, offering novel ideas in education and performance. As a composer he traversed a protean succession of changing styles, idioms, and techniques. His early compositions were marked by the spirit of Romantic lyricism, adumbrating the musical language of Mahler; some other works reflected the neo-Classical formulas of Hindemith; still others suggested the hedonistic vivacity and sophisticated stylization typical of Stravinsky's productions. But the intrinsic impetus of his music was its "pulse," which evolves the essential thematic content into the substance of original projection. His earliest piano pieces were publ. when he was 15 years old; there followed an uninterrupted flow of compositions in various genres. Foss was fortunate in being a particular protégé of Koussevitzky, who conducted many of his works with the Boston Sym. Orch.; and he had no difficulty in finding other performers. As a virtuoso pianist he often played the piano part in his chamber music, and he conducted a number of his symphonic and choral works.

WORKS: OPERAS: *The Jumping Frog of Calaveras County*, after Twain (1949; Bloomington, Ind., May 18, 1950); *Griffelkin* (NBC-TV, Nov. 6, 1955); *Introductions and Goodbyes* (1959; N.Y., May 5, 1960). BALLETS: *The Heart Remembers* for Piano (1944); *Within These Walls* for Piano (1944); *Gift of the Magi* for Orch. (Boston, Oct. 5, 1945). INCIDENTAL MUSIC: *The Tempest*, to Shakespeare's play (N.Y., March 31, 1940). ORCH.: 2 symphonic pieces (1939–40; not extant); 2 pieces, *Dance Sketch* and *Allegro concertante* (1941); Clarinet Concerto (1941–42; rev. as Piano Concerto No. 1, 1944); Suite from *The Prairie*, after the cantata (N.Y., May 15, 1944); Sym. in G (1944; Pittsburgh, Feb. 4, 1945); *Ode* (N.Y., March 15, 1945; rev. 1958); *Pantomime*, after *Gift of the Magi* (1946); *Recordare* (Boston, Dec. 31, 1948); Oboe Concerto (1948; radio premiere, N.Y., Feb. 6, 1950); *Elegy* for Clarinet and Orch., after Piano Concerto No. 1 (1949); Piano Concerto No. 2 (1949; Venice, Oct. 7, 1951; rev. 1953); *Symphony of Chorales*, based on Bach's chorales (1956–58; Pittsburgh, Oct. 24, 1958); *Baroque Variations* (1967; 3rd variation as *Phorion* for Strings, Harpsichord, Electric Organ, and Electric Guitar, N.Y., April 21, 1967); *Concert* for Cello and Orch. (N.Y., March 5, 1967); *Geod* for 4 Orch. Groups (Hamburg, Dec. 6, 1969); *Orpheus* for Violin, Viola or Cello, and Small Orch. (1972; rev. as *Orpheus and Euridice* for 2 Violins and Orch., 1984); *Fanfare* for Chamber

Orch. with a "percussionist/magician" perambulating about the stage telling the players what to do and a "mechanical metronomic conductor" (1974); *Folksong* (1975; Baltimore, Jan. 21, 1976); *Solomon Rossi Suite* (1975); *Quintets for Orchestra*, after Brass Quintet (Cleveland, May 2, 1979); *Night Music for John Lennon* for Brass Quintet and Orch. (1979–80); *Exeunt* (1982); *200 Cellos, a Celebration* (1982); *Renaissance Concert* for Flute and Orch. (Buffalo, May 9, 1986); *Celebration*, for the 50th anniversary of the Berkshire Music Center at Tanglewood (July 6, 1990). **OTHER INSTRUMENTAL:** Violin Sonata (1934); 3 pieces: *Dedication, Early Song*, and *Composer's Holiday* for Violin and Piano (1944); 3 string quartets: No. 1 (1947); No. 2, *Divertissement "pour Mica"* (1973); No. 3 (1975); Concerto for 5 Improvising Instruments (1960); *Echoi* for Clarinet, Cello, Piano, and Percussion (1961–63; N.Y., Nov. 11, 1963); *Elytres* for Flute, 2 Violins, and Ensemble (Los Angeles, Dec. 8, 1964); *For 24 Winds (Stillscape)* (1966); *Non-improvisation* for 4 Instruments (1967); *Paradigm* for Percussion, Conductor, Electric Guitar, and 3 Instruments (1968); *Waves* for Ensemble (1969; withdrawn); *The Cave of Winds* for Wind Quintet (1972); *Ni bruit, ni vitesse* for 2 Pianos and 2 Percussion (1972); *MAP* (Musicians at Play) for 4 Instruments (1973); *Curriculum Vitae* for Accordion (1977; rev. as *Curriculum Vitae with Time Bomb* for Speaker and 2 String Quartets, 1980); Brass Quintet (1978); *Round a Common Center* for Mezzo-soprano ad libitum and Piano Quartet or Piano Quintet (1979; Lake Placid, N.Y., Jan. 30, 1980); *Solo Observed* for Piano, Cello, Electric Organ, and Vibraphone (1982); Percussion Quartet (1983); Trio for Violin, Horn, and Piano (1984); *Tashi* for 6 Instruments (1986; Washington, D.C., Feb. 16, 1987). **PIANO SOLO:** 4 Two-part Inventions (1938); *Grotesque Dance* (1938); Sonatina (1939); *Passacaglia* (1941); *Fantasy Rondo* (1944); *Prelude* in D major (1950); *Scherzo ricercato* (1953); Solo (1981). **CHORAL:** *Cool Prayers* (1944); *The Prairie* for Soprano, Alto, Tenor, Bass, Chorus, and Orch., after Sandburg (N.Y., May 15, 1944); *Behold I Build an House* for Chorus, and Organ or Piano (1950); *Adon olom* for Cantor, Chorus, and Organ (1951); *A Parable of Death* for Narrator, Tenor, Chorus, and Orch. (1952); *Psalms* for Chorus and Orch. or 2 Pianos (1955–56); *Fragments or Archilochos* for Contralto, Male Speaker, Female Speaker, 4 Small Choruses, Large Chorus ad libitum, Mandolin, Guitar, and 3 Percussion (1965); *3 Airs for Frank O'Hara's Angel* for Soprano, Women's Chorus, Flute, Piano, and 2 Percussion (1972); *Lamden mi* (Teach Me) for Chorus and 6 Instruments (1973); *American Cantata* for Tenor, Chorus, and Orch. (1976; N.Y., Dec. 1, 1977); *And Then the Rocks on the Mountain Began to Shout*, after Brass Quintet (1978); *De profundis* (1982); other vocal works.

BIBL.: H. Kupferberg, "L. F.," *Ovation* (April 1984).

Foster, Fay, American pianist and composer; b. Leavenworth, Kans., Nov. 8, 1886; d. Bayport, N.Y., April 17, 1960. She studied at the Munich Cons. with Schwartz (piano) and Jadassohn (composition); studied piano further with M. Rosenthal and Sophie Menter; won a prize at the International Waltz Competition (Berlin, 1910); 1st prize in the American Composers' Contest (N.Y., 1913); made several tours as a pianist; eventually settled in N.Y. She wrote 3 operettas; over 100 songs (*The Americans Come!, My Journey's End*, etc.); piano studies; etc.

Foster, Lawrence (Thomas), American conductor; b. Los Angeles, Oct. 23, 1941. He studied conducting with F. Zweig in Los Angeles; made his 1st conducting appearance with the Young Musicians Foundation Debut Orch. in Los Angeles in 1960. At the age of 24 he was appointed assistant conductor of the Los Angeles Phil.; in 1966, received the Koussevitzky Memorial Conducting Prize at the Berkshire Music Center at Tanglewood. From 1969 to 1974 he was chief guest conductor of the Royal Phil. in London. From 1971 to 1978 he was conductor-in-chief of the Houston Sym. Orch. From 1979 he was chief conductor of the Opéra and the Orch. National de Monte Carlo (called Orch. Philharmonique de Monte Carlo from 1980). He also became Generalmusikdirektor in the city of

Duisburg in 1981, remaining in that position until 1988. He was also music director of the Lausanne Chamber Orch. (1985–90) and the Jerusalem Sym. Orch. (from 1988). He is particularly notable for his dynamic interpretations of modern works, but has also been acclaimed for his precise and intelligent presentations of the Classical and Romantic repertoire.

Foster, Sidney, American pianist and pedagogue; b. Florence, S.C., May 23, 1917; d. Boston, Feb. 7, 1977. He began playing piano when he was 4 years old, and at the age of 10 was admitted to the Curtis Inst. of Music in Philadelphia, where he studied with Isabelle Vengerova and David Saperton. In 1940 he won the 1st Leventritt Foundation Award, which entitled him to an appearance as soloist with the N.Y. Phil. This was the beginning of a fine international career. In 1964 he played 16 concerts in Russia. He taught piano at Florida State Univ. (1949–51); from 1952 to 1977 was on the piano faculty of Indiana Univ. at Bloomington.

Foster, Stephen C(ollins), famous American song composer; b. Lawrenceville, Pa., July 4, 1826; d. N.Y., Jan. 13, 1864. He learned to play the flute as a child, but was essentially autodidact as a musician. He publ. his 1st song, *Open Thy Lattice, Love,* when he was 18. While working as a bookkeeper for his brother Dunning Foster in Cincinnati (1846–50), he became interested in songwriting. His song *Old Folks at Home* (1851), sometimes known as *Swanee Ribber* from its initial line "Way down upon de Swanee ribber," established him as a truly American composer. It was publ. on Oct. 21, 1851, with the subtitle "Ethiopian Melody as sung by Christy's Minstrels." E.P. Christy, the minstrel troupe leader, was listed as the composer of the song in consideration of a small payment to Foster, whose name was not attached to it until the expiration of the copyright in 1879. About 40,000 copies of the song were sold during the year after publication. Foster married Jane McDowell in Pittsburgh in 1850, but the marriage proved unhappy, and he left her to live alone in N.Y. (1853–54); he settled there permanently in 1860. His last years were darkened by an addiction to alcohol, and death overtook him as a penniless patient at Bellevue Hospital. Yet his earnings were not small; he received about $15,000 during the last 15 years of his life. Among Foster's most notable songs were *Oh! Susanna* (1848), *Sweetly She Sleeps, My Alice Fair* (1851), *Massa's in de Cold Ground* (1852), *My Old Kentucky Home, Good Night!* (1853), *Jeanie with the Light Brown Hair* (1854), *Camptown Races* (1854), *Gentle Annie* (1856), *Old Black Joe* (1860), and *Beautiful Dreamer* (1864). His other works include hymns, piano pieces, and arrangements of popular melodies in an anthology, *The Social Orchestra* (N.Y., 1854). O. Sonneck and W. Whittlesey prepared a *Catalogue of First Editions of Stephen C. Foster (1826–1864)* (Washington, D.C., 1915). R. Jackson ed. *The Stephen Foster Songbook* (N.Y., 1974) and E. List ed. *S. Foster: Complete Piano Music* (N.Y., 1984).

BIBL.: M. Foster (his brother), *Biography, Songs and Musical Compositions of S. F.* (1896); H. Milligan, *S.C. F.* (N.Y., 1920); J. Howard, *S. F., America's Troubadour* (N.Y., 1934; 3rd ed., rev., 1962); idem, *Newly Discovered F.iana* (N.Y., 1935); R. Walters, *S. F.: Youth's Golden Dream* (Princeton, N.J., 1936); J. Howard, "The Literature on S. F.," *Notes,* I (1943–44); E. Foster Morneweck, *Chronicles of S. F.'s Family* (2 vols., Pittsburgh, 1944); H. Gaul, *The Minstrel of the Alleghenies* (Pittsburgh, 1952); G. Chase, "America's Minstrel," *America's Music* (N.Y., 1955; 2nd ed., rev., 1966); H. Wiley Hitchcock, "S. F.," *Hi Fi/Stereo Review* (Jan. 1967); W. Austin, *"Susanna," "Jeanie," and "The Old Folks at Home": The Songs of S.C. F. from His Time to Ours* (N.Y., 1975); C. Elliker, *S.C. F.: A Guide to Research* (N.Y., 1988).

Fotek, Jan, Polish composer; b. Czerwinsk, Nov. 28, 1928. He studied composition with Wiechowicz at the State College of Music in Krakow and with Szeligowski at the State College of Music in Warsaw.

WORKS: *Opus concertante* for Organ, Piano, and Percussion (1959); *Gregorian Hymn* for Chorus and Orch. (1963); *A Cycle of Verses* for Children's Chorus and Orch. (1963); *Trimorphie*

for 3 Flutes, Harpsichord, and Piano (1966); *Epitasis* for Orch. (1967); *Galileo*, musical drama (1969); *The Last War*, rhapsody for Narrator, Chorus, and Orch. (1971); *Cantata copernicana* (1973); *Partita* for 12 Bassoons and 3 Double Bassoons (1973); *A Forest King's Daughter*, opera-ballet (1977); *Musica chromatica* for String Chamber Orch. (1982); *Anyone*, opera-mystery (1983); Sonata for Tuba and Piano (1984); *Czarnolas Suite* for String Chamber Orch. (1986); *Ecloga* for Countertenor and Ensemble of Early Instruments (1987).

Fougstedt, Nils-Eric, Finnish conductor and composer; b. Raisio, near Turku, May 24, 1910; d. Helsinki, April 12, 1961. He studied composition in Helsinki with Furuhjelm, in Italy with Carlo Felice Boghen, and in Berlin with Max Trapp. Upon returning to Finland in 1932, he lectured in music theory at the Music Inst. in Helsinki; was also active as a conductor; led the Finnish Radio Orch. from 1951 until his death.
    Works: Suite for Orch. (1936); Violin Concertino (1937); 2 syms. (1938, 1949); String Quartet (1940); Cello Concerto (1942); Piano Concerto (1944); *Tulukset* (The Tinderbox), cantata after Hans Christian Andersen (1950); *Trittico sinfonico* (1958); many choruses and songs.

Foulds, John (Herbert), significant English composer and music theorist; b. Manchester, Nov. 2, 1880; d. Calcutta, April 24, 1939. He was precocious and began to compose at a single-digit age; learned to play cello; earned a living by playing in theater orchs. In 1900 he joined the Hallé Orch. in Manchester; then moved to London, where he served as music director for the London Central YMCA (1918–23); also conducted the Univ. of London Music Soc. (1921–26). In 1935 he went to India; undertook a thorough study of Indian folk music; served as director of European music for the All-India Radio at Delhi and Calcutta (1937–39); also formed an experimental "Indo-European" orch., which included both European and Asian instruments. He was the 1st English composer to experiment with quarter-tones, and as early as 1898 wrote a string quartet with fractional intervals; he also composed semi-classical pieces using traditional Indian instruments. Unfortunately, many of his MSS are lost.
    Works: STAGE: Concert opera, *The Vision of Dante* (1905–8); miniature opera, *Cleopatra* (1909; lost); *The Tell-Tale Heart*, melodrama after Edgar Allan Poe, for Actor and Chamber Orch. (1910); 3-act opera, *Avatara* (1919–30; lost); music for the ritual play *Veils* (1926; unfinished). **ORCH.:** *Undine Suite* (c.1899); *Epithalamium* (London, Oct. 9, 1906); *Lento e scherzetto* for Cello and Orch. (c.1906); 2 cello concertos: No. 1 (1908–9; Manchester, March 16, 1911); No. 2 (c.1910; lost); *Apotheosis* for Violin and Orch. (1908–9); *Mirage*, symphonic poem (1910); *Suite française* (1910); *Keltic Suite* (1911); *Music Pictures (Group III)*, suite (London, Sept. 4, 1912); *Hellas* for Double String Orch., Harp, and Percussion (1915–32); *Miniature Suite* (1915); *Peace and War*, meditation (1919); *3 Mantras* (1919–30); *Le Cabaret*, overture to a French comedy (1921); *Suite fantastique* (1922); *Music Pictures (Group IV)* for Strings (c.1922); *Saint Joan Suite* (1924–25); *Henry VIII Suite* (1925–26); *April-England*, tone poem (1926–32); *Dynamic Triptych* for Piano and Orch. (1929; Edinburgh, Oct. 15, 1931); *Keltic Overture* (1930); *Indian Suite* (1932–35); *Pasquinades symphoniques*, sym. in 3 movements (1935; finale left unfinished); *Deva-Music* (1935–36; only fragments remain); *Chinese Suite* (1935); *3 Pasquinades* (c.1936); *Symphony of East and West* for European and Indian Instruments (1937–38; lost); *Symphonic Studies* (1938; lost). **VOCAL:** *The Song of Honor* for Speaker, Chamber Orch., and ad libitum Female Chorus (1918); *A World Requiem* for 4 Soloists, Small Boys' Chorus, Mixed Chorus, and Orch. (1919–21; London, Nov. 11, 1923); choruses; songs. **CHAMBER:** 10 string quartets: Nos. 1–3 (before 1899; lost); No. 4 (1899); No. 5 (lost); No. 6, *Quartetto romantico* (1903); No. 7 (lost); No. 8 (1907–10); No. 9, *Quartetto intimo* (1931–32); No. 10, *Quartetto geniale* (1935; only the 3rd movement, *Lento quieto*, is extant); Cello Sonata (1905; rev. 1927); *Impromptu on a Theme of Beethoven* for 4 Cellos (1905); *Music Pictures (Group I)* for Piano Trio (1910; lost);

Ritornello con variazioni for String Trio (1911); *Aquarelles (Music Pictures—Group II)* for String Quartet (c.1914); *Sonia* for Violin and Piano (1925). **PIANO:** *Dichterliebe*, suite (1897–98); *Essays in the Modes*, 6 studies (1920–27); *Egotistic*, modal essay (1927); *2 Landscapes* (c.1928); *Scherzo chromatico* (1927; lost).
    WRITINGS: *Music To-Day: Its Heritage from the Past, and Legacy to the Future* (London, 1934).
    BIBL.: M. MacDonald, *J. F.: His Life in Music* (London, 1975); idem, *J. F., A centenary brochure from Musica Viva* (1979); idem, "J. F. and the String Quartet," *Tempo* (Feb. and March 1980); idem, *J. F. and His Music* (N.Y. and London, 1990).

Fountain, "Pete" (Peter Dewey, Jr.), American jazz clarinetist and saxophonist; b. New Orleans, July 3, 1930. Growing up in the jazz milieu of New Orleans, he mastered the clarinet in his youth; in 1949 he joined the Dukes of Dixieland, remaining with them until 1954; was then a member of Lawrence Welk's Orch. (1957–60); then founded his own group, with which he toured widely in the U.S. With the aid of an experienced ghostwriter he publ. the book *A Closer Walk: The Pete Fountain Story* (Chicago, 1972).

Fountain, Primous, III, black American composer; b. St. Petersburg, Fla., Aug. 1, 1949. He studied at De Paul Univ. and at the Berkshire Music Center. In 1974 he won a Guggenheim fellowship. His music shows quaquaversal influences, in a spectrum ranging from Stravinskian neo-Classicism to hot jazz.
    Works: *Evolutio quaestionis* for Soprano and Ensemble (1967); *3 Pieces* for Flute, Violin, and Piano (1967); *Will* for Flute, Clarinet, Horn, and Piano (1967); *Meditation on a Theme* for Piano (1967); a ballet, *Manifestation* (1968; Chicago, March 13, 1970); *Ritual Dances of the Amaks* for Orch. (1972); *Exiled* for Orch. (1974); *Osiris* for Orch. (1975); *Ricia* for Piano Trio (1977); Cello Concerto (1976; Minneapolis, Dec. 28, 1977); *Poème* for 17 Wind Instruments (1978); *Caprice* for Orch. (1978; N.Y., May 12, 1980); Concerto for Harp and Chamber Orch. (1981).

Fourdrain, Félix, French composer; b. Nice, Feb. 3, 1880; d. Paris, Oct. 22, 1923. He studied with Widor; wrote operas: *Écho* (Paris, 1906); *La Légende du point d'Argentan* (Paris, April 17, 1907); *La Glaneuse* (Lyons, 1909); *Vercingétorix* (Nice, 1912); *Madame Roland* (Rouen, 1913); *Les Contes de Perrault* (Paris, 1913); *Les Maris de Ginette; La Mare au diable; La Griffe*; operettas: *Dolly* (Paris, 1922); *L'Amour en cage; Le Million de Colette; La Hussarde* (Paris, 1925); incidental music to Cain's *Le Secret de Polichinelle* (Cannes, 1922); *Anniversaire* for Orch.; many songs (*Le Papillon, Sérénades, Revanche d'amour, Pays des cours*, etc.).

Fourestier, Louis (Félix André), French conductor, pedagogue, and composer; b. Montpellier, May 31, 1892; d. Boulogne-Billancourt, Sept. 30, 1976. He studied at the Paris Cons. under Gédalge and Leroux; won the Rossini Prize in 1924 (for his cantata *Patria*), the Grand Prix de Rome in 1925 (for the cantata *La Mort d'Adonis*), and the Heugel Prize in 1927 (for the symphonic poem *Polynice*); served as a conductor in Marseilles and Bordeaux; from 1938 to 1945 was conductor at the Paris Opéra; from 1945 to 1963 was a prof. at the Paris Cons.; on Nov. 11, 1946, he made his conducting debut at the Metropolitan Opera in N.Y.; conducted there until 1948; then returned to Paris.

Fouret, Maurice, French composer; b. St.-Quentin, Nov. 28, 1888; d. Paris, Jan. 22, 1962. He studied with Ravel, Charpentier, and Busser. He composed several symphonic poems on exotic subjects, among them *Aladdin* (Paris, Nov. 28, 1920) and *Danse de Sita* (1922); the ballets *Le Rustre imprudent* (1931) and *La Jeune Fille aux joues roses* (1934); a group of symphonic suites inspired by Alsatian folklore; songs.

Fournet, Jean, distinguished French conductor; b. Rouen, April 14, 1913. He studied at the Paris Cons., graduating with the highest honors. He then was music director at the Opéra-Comique in Paris (1944–57). Concurrently he taught conducting at the École Normale de Musique. In 1961 he was appointed a permanent conductor of the Radio Phil. at Hilversum, the Netherlands. He also was chief conductor of the Rotterdam Phil. (1968–73). From 1973 to 1982 he was music director of l'Orch. de l'Île de France; also appeared as a guest conductor in Japan. On March 28, 1987, he made his Metropolitan Opera debut in N.Y. conducting *Samson et Dalila*. He is especially renowned for his interpretations of new French music, tempering its orch. brilliance with Classical restraint.

Fournier, Émile-Eugène-Alix, French composer; b. Paris, Oct. 11, 1864; d. Joinville-le-Pont, Sept. 12, 1897. He was a pupil of Delibes and Dubois at the Paris Cons.; took the 2nd Grand Prix de Rome in 1891 and the Prix Cressent in 1892 for the 1-act opera *Stratonice* (Paris, 1892); publ. a number of songs.

Fournier, Pierre (Léon Marie), famous French cellist; b. Paris, June 24, 1906; d. Geneva, Jan. 8, 1985. He first studied piano with his mother; stricken by polio at age 9, he turned to the cello, studying with Paul Bazelaire and André Hekking, at the Paris Cons., and at the École Normale de Musique. He made his debut in 1925 and subsequently appeared both as a soloist with orchs. and as a chamber music artist; taught at the Paris Cons. (1941–49). After World War II, he made major tours throughout the world; he appeared regularly in the U.S. from 1948. He was made a Chevalier of the Legion of Honor in 1953; was promoted to Officier in 1963. In 1970 he settled in Switzerland, where he gave master classes. He was renowned for his elegant tone and impeccable musicianship; his repertoire was comprehensive, ranging from Bach to contemporary music. Several composers wrote works for him; he gave 1st performances of works by Roussel, Martin, Poulenc, and Martinů.
    BIBL.: B. Gavoty, *P. F.* (Geneva, 1957).

Fournier, Pierre-Simon, French cutter and founder of music type; b. Paris, Sept. 15, 1712; d. there, Oct. 8, 1768. Instead of the lozenge-shaped types in the style of Hautin's (1525), Fournier introduced round-headed notes, described in his *Essai d'un nouveau caractère de fonte . . .* (1756); he also publ. a *Traité historique sur l'origine et le progrès des caractères de fonte pour l'impression de la musique* (Paris, 1765).

Fou Ts'ong, Chinese pianist; b. Shanghai, March 10, 1934. He studied piano in his native city; then won 3rd prizes in the Bucharest Piano Competition (1953) and the Warsaw International Chopin Competition (1955); continued his studies at the Warsaw Cons. In 1958 he decided to make his home in London; appeared with many of the major orchs. of Europe and the U.S.; also gave many recitals. He was particularly noted for his expressive playing of works by Chopin and Debussy.

Fowler, Jennifer, Australian composer; b. Bunbury, Western Australia, April 14, 1939. She attended the Univ. of Western Australia, graduating in the arts (1961) and in music (1968); studied electronic music at the Univ. of Utrecht (1968–69); then went to England.
    WORKS: *Variations* for Voice, Violin, Clarinet, and Percussion (1966); String Quartet (1967); *Fanfare* for Brass and Strings (1968); *Sculpture in 4 Dimensions* for Orch. (1969); *Chimes, Fractured* for Antiphonally Placed Chamber Ensemble (1970); *Hours of the Day* for 4 Mezzo-sopranos, 2 Oboes, and 2 Clarinets (1970); *Revelation* for String Quintet (1970–71); *Look on This Oedipus* for Orch. (1973); *Piece for an Opera House* for 2 Pianos, or for Piano and Tape (1973); *Chant with Garlands* for Orch. (1974); *The Arrows of Saint Sebastian II* for Bass Clarinet, Cello, and Tape (1981); *The Arrows of Saint Sebastian I* for 13 Instruments (1982); *Echoes from an Antique Land* for 5 Percussion Players (1983; also for Flute, Clarinet, Piano, and Bass).

Fox, Charles Warren, American musicologist; b. Glovers-

ville, N.Y., July 24, 1904; d. there, Oct. 15, 1983. He took courses in psychology at Cornell Univ. (B.A., 1926; Ph.D., 1933); also studied musicology there with Otto Kinkeldey. In 1932 he became a part-time instructor in psychology at the Eastman School of Music in Rochester, N.Y.; in 1933 began giving courses in music history and musicology; he retired in 1970. From 1952 to 1959 he was ed. of the *Journal of the American Musicological Society*. From 1954 to 1956 he served as president of the Music Library Assoc.

Fox, Felix, German-American pianist and teacher; b. Breslau, May 25, 1876; d. Boston, March 24, 1947. He studied at the Leipzig Cons. with Reinecke (piano) and Jadassohn (theory); then with Isidor Philipp in Paris, where he gave several recitals introducing works by MacDowell. In 1897 he settled in Boston as a pianist and teacher; in 1898 he established, with C. Buonamici, a piano school which enjoyed an excellent reputation; after Buonamici's death in 1920 it became the Felix Fox School of Pianoforte Playing; it was discontinued in 1935. Fox wrote many piano pieces and songs; made transcriptions of MacDowell's works; also ed. numerous piano works.

Fox, Fred(erick Alfred), American composer; b. Detroit, Jan. 17, 1931. He studied with Ruth Shaw Wylie at Wayne State Univ. (B.Mus., 1953), Ross Lee Finney at the Univ. of Michigan (1953–54), and Bernhard Heiden at Indiana Univ. (M.Mus., 1957; D.Mus., 1959). In 1974 he was appointed to the faculty there.
    WORKS: ORCH.: Violin Concerto (1971); *Ternion* for Oboe and Orch. (1973); *Variables No. 5* (1974); *Beyond Winterlock* (1977); *Night Ceremonies* (1979); *Tracings* (1981); *Januaries* (1984). **CHAMBER:** *BEC Nos. 1 to 10* for Chamber Ensemble (1967–68); *Quantic* for Woodwind Quintet (1969); *Ad rem* for Guitar (1970); *Variables Nos. 1 to 4 and 6* for 1 to 6 Instruments (1972–75); Quartet for Violin, Piano, and Percussion (1974); *Ambient Shadows* for 8 Instruments (1978); *S.A.X.* for Alto Saxophone and Saxophone Quartet (1979); *Sonaspheres Nos. 1 to 5* for Chamber Ensemble (1980–83); *Bren* for 13 Brass Instruments (1982). **VOCAL:** *A Stone, a Leaf, an Unfound Door* for Soprano, Clarinet, Percussion, and Small Chorus (1966); *The Crystal* for Chorus (1967); *Time Excursions* for Soprano, Speaker, and 8 Instruments (1976); *A Threat* for Soprano and Viola, or Mezzo-soprano and Cello (1981).

Fox, Virgil (Keel), famous American organist; b. Princeton, Ill., May 3, 1912; d. West Palm Beach, Fla., Oct. 25, 1980. He studied piano as a child, but soon turned to the organ as his favorite instrument. He played the organ at the 1st Presbyterian Church in his hometown at the age of 10, and gave his 1st public recital in Cincinnati at 14. He then enrolled in the Peabody Cons. in Baltimore, graduating in 1932. To perfect his playing he went to Paris, where he took lessons with Marcel Dupré at St. Sulpice and Louis Vierne at Notre Dame. He returned to the U.S. in 1938 and became head of the organ dept. at the Peabody Cons. From 1946 to 1965 he was organist at the Riverside Church in N.Y., where he played on a 5-manual, 10,561-pipe organ specially designed for him. He then launched a remarkable career as an organ soloist. He was the 1st American to play at the Thomaskirche in Leipzig, and also played at Westminster Abbey in London. As a solo artist, he evolved an idiosyncratic type of performance in which he embellished Baroque music with Romantic extravaganza; he also took to apostrophizing his audiences in a whimsical mixture of lofty sentiment and disarming self-deprecation. This type of personalized art endeared him to the impatient, emancipated musical youth of America, and he became one of the few organists who could fill a concert hall. He also displayed a robust taste for modern music; he often played the ear-stopping, discordant arrangement of *America* by Charles Ives. Wracked by cancer, he gave his last concert in Dallas on Sept. 26, 1980.

Fox Strangways, A(rthur) H(enry), noted English writer on music and editor; b. Norwich, Sept. 14, 1859; d. Dinton, near Salisbury, May 2, 1948. He studied at Wellington College, London; received his M.A. in 1882 from Balliol College, Oxford;

then was a schoolmaster at Dulwich College (1884–86) and Wellington College (1887–1910). From 1911 to 1925 he wrote music criticism for the *Times* of London; in 1925 he became music critic of the *Observer.* In 1920 he founded the quarterly journal *Music & Letters,* which he ed. until 1937. He was a specialist on Indian music and wrote several books on the subject, including *The Music of Hindostan* (Oxford, 1914); also publ. a collection of essays, *Music Observed* (London, 1936), and a biography of Cecil Sharp (with M. Karpeles; London, 1933; 2nd ed., 1955). He contributed the article "Folk-Song" to the introductory vol. of *The Oxford History of Music* (London, 1929).

BIBL.: Special issues of *Music & Letters* (Oct. 1939 and July 1948); F. Howes, "A.H. F.S.," ibid. (1969).

Fracassi, Américo, Italian composer, brother of **Elmérico Fracassi**; b. Lucito, Campobasso, Feb. 29, 1880; d. Goya, Argentina, Aug. 15, 1936. With his brother, he left his native Italy as a very young man and settled in Buenos Aires, where he taught at a music school. He composed some songs and piano pieces.

Fracassi, Elmérico, Italian composer, brother of **Américo Fracassi**; b. Lucito, Campobasso, Dec. 19, 1874; d. Buenos Aires, Oct. 12, 1930. He was taken to Buenos Aires as a boy, but returned to Italy in 1890 for his musical training (Naples Cons., with Rossomandi and D'Arienzo); toured Europe twice as a concert pianist; in 1904 was appointed director (together with G. d'Andrea) of the Almagro Cons. in Buenos Aires. He composed 2 operas, *Finlandia* (Turin, 1914) and *Merletti di Burano;* Piano Concerto; Violin Sonata; piano studies; songs; and 4 Argentine anthems, 1 of which, *Himno al Centenario,* won a prize from the Argentine government.

Frackenpohl, Arthur (Roland), American composer; b. Irvington, N.J., April 23, 1924. He studied with Bernard Rogers at the Eastman School of Music in Rochester, N.Y. (B.A., 1947; M.A., 1949); took courses with Milhaud at the Berkshire Music Center in Tanglewood (1948) and with Boulanger in Fontainebleau (1950); completed his studies at McGill Univ. in Montreal (D.M.A., 1957). He became a teacher at the Crane School of Music at the State Univ. of N.Y. at Potsdam (1949); was a prof. there (from 1961). He publ. *Harmonization at the Piano* (1962; 4th ed., 1981).

WORKS: Chamber opera: *Domestic Relations* ("To Beat or Not to Beat"), after O. Henry (1964); *Allegro giocoso* for Band (1956); *A Jubilant Overture* for Orch. (1957); *Allegro scherzando* for Orch. (1957); *Overture* (1957); Sym. for Strings (1960); *Largo and Allegro* for Horn and Strings (1962); *Short Overture* (1965); Concertino for Tuba and Strings (1967); Suite for Trumpet and Strings (1970); *American Folk Song Suite* for Band (1973); *Flute Waltz* for 3 Flutes and Orch. (1979); *The Natural Superiority of Men,* cantata for Women's Voices and Piano (1962); [7] *Essays on Women,* cantata for Soloists, Chorus, and Piano (1967); *Meet Job,* 3 litanies for 4 Voices and Winds (1978); *A Child This Day,* cantata for Soloists, Chorus, Narrator, Brass Quartet, and Organ (1980); Brass Quartet (1950); 2 brass quintets (1963, 1972); Trombone Quartet (1967); Brass Trio (1967); String Quartet (1971); *Breviates* for Brass Ensemble (1973); Trio for Oboe, Horn, and Bassoon (1982); Tuba Sonata (1983); piano pieces; song cycles.

Fradkin, Fredric, American violinist and teacher; b. Troy, N.Y., April 2, 1892; d. N.Y., Oct. 3, 1963. At the age of 5 he became a pupil of Schradieck; later studied with Max Bendix and Sam Franko in N.Y.; then went to Paris; studied at the Cons. there with Lefort, graduating in 1909 with 1st prize. He was concertmaster of the Bordeaux Opera Orch.; then took instruction with Ysaÿe in Brussels. Returning to America, he made his debut as a concert violinist in N.Y. on Jan. 10, 1911; then gave concerts in Europe; in 1918–19 he was concertmaster of the Boston Sym. Orch.; later settled in N.Y. as a teacher.

Fraenkel, Wolfgang, German composer; b. Berlin, Oct. 10, 1897; d. Los Angeles, March 8, 1983. He studied violin, piano, and music theory at the Klindworth-Scharwenka Cons. in Berlin; at the same time took courses in jurisprudence and was a judge in Berlin until the advent of the Nazi regime in 1933; he was interned in the Sachsenhausen concentration camp, but as a 50 percent Jew (his mother was an Aryan, as was his wife), he was released in 1939, and went to China, where he enjoyed the protection of Chiang Kai-shek, who asked him to organize music education in Nanking and Shanghai. In 1947 he emigrated to the U.S. and settled in Los Angeles. He earned a living by composing background music for documentary films in Hollywood, supplementing his income by copying music (he had a calligraphic handwriting). Fraenkel's own music was evolved from the standard German traditions, but at a later period he began to experiment with serial methods of composition.

WORKS: Opera, *Der brennende Dornbusch* (1924–27); 3 string quartets (1924, 1949, 1960; the 3rd received the Queen Elisabeth of Belgium Prize); Flute Concerto (1930); *Der Wegweiser,* cantata (1931); Cello Sonata (1934); Violin Sonata (1935); *Filippo* for Speaker and Orch. (1948); Sonata for Solo Violin (1954); *Variations and a Fantasy on a Theme by Schoenberg* for Piano (1954); *Frescobaldi,* transcription for Orch. of 5 organ pieces by Frescobaldi (1957); Viola Sonata (1963); *Klavierstück* for Tape and Piano (1964); *Symphonische Aphorismen* for Orch. (1965; awarded 1st prize at the International Competition of the City of Milan); *Joseph* for Baritone and Orch., to a text by Thomas Mann (1968); *Missa aphoristica* for Chorus and Orch. (1973); String Quintet (1976). All his works, both publ. and in MS, are deposited in the Moldenhauer Archive in Spokane, Wash.

Frager, Malcolm (Monroe), outstanding American pianist; b. St. Louis, Jan. 15, 1935; d. Pittsfield, Mass., June 20, 1991. He studied languages at Columbia Univ.; majored in Russian, graduating in 1957. He studied piano with Carl Friedberg in N.Y. (1949–55); received various prizes in the U.S. In 1960 he won the Queen Elisabeth of Belgium International Competition, which marked the beginning of his worldwide career; he was particularly successful in Russia. He was a brilliant virtuoso endowed with a capacity for profound sensitivity, whose repertoire ranged from Haydn to Prokofiev. Among the rare works in his repertoire were the original versions of the Schumann Concerto and the Tchaikovsky 1st Concerto.

Framery, Nicolas Étienne, French composer, writer on music, and poet; b. Rouen, March 25, 1745; d. Paris, Nov. 26, 1810. He composed the text and music for the comic opera *La Sorcière par hasard* (1768); its performance at Villeroy earned him the position of superintendent of music with the Count of Artois. The opera was performed at the Comédie-Italienne (Paris, Sept. 3, 1783), but suffered a fiasco because of the antagonism against Italian opera generated by the adherents of Gluck. He also wrote librettos for Sacchini, Salieri, Paisiello, Anfossi, and other Italian composers; ed. the *Journal de Musique* (1770–78) and *Calendrier Musical Universel* (1788–89) in Paris; compiled, together with Ginguène and Feytou, the musical part of vol. I of *Encyclopédie méthodique* (1791; vol. II by Momigny, 1818); besides smaller studies, he wrote *De la nécessité du rythme et de la césure dans les hymnes ou odes destinées à la musique* (1796); tr. into French Azopardi's *Musico prattico,* as *Le Musicien pratique* (2 vols., 1786).

BIBL.: J. Carlez, F., *Littérateur-musicien* (Caen, 1893).

Frampton, Peter (Kenneth), English rock singer and guitarist; b. Beckenham, Kent, April 20, 1950. He learned to play the guitar and began working with several rock groups, becoming a sort of rock celebrity himself by the age of 16. He formed the band Humble Pie with Steve Marriott, and toured with it throughout England and the U.S. In 1976 he issued a sensational album titled, with egotistical narcissism, *Frampton Comes Alive!,* which sold something like 12 million copies.

Françaix, Jean, talented and historically significant French composer; b. Le Mans, May 23, 1912. He first studied at the Le Mans Cons., of which his father was director, and later took courses at the Paris Cons. with Isidor Philipp (piano) and Nadia Boulanger (composition). In his music, he associated himself with the new French school of composers, pursuing the twofold aim of practical application and national tradition; his instrumental works represent a stylization of Classical French music; in this respect he comes close to Ravel.

WORKS: OPERAS: *Le Diable boiteux*, comic chamber opera (1937; Paris, June 30, 1938); *L'Apostrophe*, musical comedy, after Balzac (1940; Amsterdam, July 1, 1951); *Paris à nous deux (ou Le Nouveau Rastignac)*, comic opera (Fontainebleau, Aug. 7, 1954); *La Princesse de Clèves* (Rouen, Dec. 11, 1965). **BALLETS:** *Scuola de Ballo*, on themes of Boccherini (1933); *Les Malheurs de Sophie* (1935; Paris, Feb. 25, 1948); *Le Roi nu* (1935; Paris, June 15, 1936); *Le Jeu sentimental* (Brussels, July 8, 1936); *La Lutherie enchantée* (Antwerp, March 21, 1936); *Le Jugement d'un fou* (1938; London, Feb. 6, 1939); *Verreries de Venise* (1938; Paris, June 22, 1939); *Les Demoiselles de la nuit* (Paris, May 20, 1948); *Les Zigues de mars* (1950); *La Dame dans la lune* (Paris, Feb. 18, 1958); *Pierrot ou Les Secrets de la nuit* (1980). **ORCH.:** Sym. (Paris, Nov. 6, 1932); Suite for Violin and Orch. (1934); *Sérénade* for Chamber Orch. (1934); *Divertissement* for Violin, Viola, Cello, and Orch. (Paris, Dec. 22, 1935); Quadruple Concerto for Flute, Oboe, Clarinet, Bassoon, and Orch. (1935); *Au musée Grévin*, suite (1936); Piano Concerto (Berlin, Nov. 3, 1936); *Musique de cour*, duo concertante for Flute, Violin, and Orch. (1937); *Divertissement* for Bassoon and String Orch. (1942; Schwetzingen, May 5, 1968); *Rhapsodie* for Viola and Small Orch. (1946); *L'Heure du berger* for Piano and Strings (1947); *Symphonie d'archets* for String Orch. (1948); *Les Zigues de mars*, "petit ballet militaire" (Paris, Feb. 19, 1950); *Variations de Concert* for Cello and String Orch. (1950); Sym. (La Jolla, Calif., Aug. 9, 1953); Harpsichord Concerto (1959; Paris, Feb. 7, 1960); *L'Horloge de Flore* for Oboe and Orch. (1959; Philadelphia, April 1, 1961); *Le Dialogue des carmélites*, symphonic suite (1960; Paris, April 4, 1969); *Sei preludi* for String Chamber Orch. (1963; Lucerne, Sept. 3, 1964); 2-piano Concerto (Maastricht, Nov. 26, 1965); Flute Concerto (1966; Schwetzingen, May 13, 1967); Clarinet Concerto (1967; Nice, July 30, 1968); 2 violin concertos: No. 1 (1968; Quebec, Jan. 26, 1970); No. 2 (Braunschweig, Nov. 30, 1979); *La Ville mystérieuse*, fantaisie (Nuremberg, March 15, 1974); *Thème et variations* (Bochum, Dec. 12, 1974); Double-bass Concerto (Frankfurt am Main, Nov. 1, 1974); *Le Gay Paris* for Trumpet and Winds (1974; Wiesbaden, April 6, 1975); *Cassazione* for 3 Orchs. (Salzburg, Aug. 12, 1975); *Chaconne* for Harp and 11 String Instruments (1976); *Ouverture anacréontique* (1978; Recklinghausen, Feb. 22, 1981); *Tema con variazioni* for Clarinet and String Orch. (Florence, Sept. 14, 1978); Concerto for 2 Harps and 11 String Instruments (1978; Schwetzingen, May 11, 1979); Bassoon Concerto (1979; Frankfurt, May 20, 1980); Concerto for Guitar and String Orch. (1983); other orch. works. **CHAMBER:** Quartet for Flute, Oboe, Clarinet, and Bassoon (1933); Quartet for 2 Violins, Viola, and Cello (1934); Quintet for Flute, Oboe, Clarinet, Bassoon, and Horn (1948); Quartet for English Horn, Violin, Viola, and Cello (1971); Octet for Clarinet, Horn, Bassoon, 2 Violins, Viola, Cello, and Double Bass (1972); *Aubade* for 12 Cellos (1975); Quintet for Clarinet and String Quartet (1977); *Danses exotiques* for 12 Instrumentalists (1981); *Dixtour* for Wind and String Quintet (1986); Wind Quintet No. 2 (1987); Quintet for Flute, 2 Violins, Cello, and Harpsichord (1988); other chamber works; piano pieces, including a Sonata (1960); organ music. **VOCAL:** *Trois épigrammes* for Chorus, and String Quintet or String Orch. (1938); *L'Apocalypse selon St. Jean*, oratorio for 4 Soli, Chorus, and 2 Orchs. (1939; Paris, June 11, 1942); *La Cantate de Méphisto* for Bass and String Orch. (1952; N.Y., Jan. 25, 1953); *Déploration de Tonton, chien fidèle*, deploring the death of "the faithful dog Tonton," humorous cantata for Mezzo-soprano and String Orch. (1956); *Les Inestimables Chroniques du bon géant Gargantua* for Speaker and String Orch. (1971); *Trois poèmes de Paul Valéry* for Chorus (1984); other vocal works.

BIBL.: M. Lanjean, *J. F.* (Paris, 1961).

Francescatti, Zino (René), brilliant French violinist; b. Marseilles, Aug. 9, 1902. His father, a Frenchman of Italian extraction, was a violin pupil of Paganini; prodded by him, Zino Francescatti appeared in public as a violinist at the age of 5, and played the Beethoven Violin Concerto with an orch. at 10. In 1927 he went to Paris, where he began teaching at the École Normale de Musique; also conducted occasional performances of the Paris sym. organization Concerts Poulet. Between 1931 and 1939 he made several world tours. He made his U.S. debut on Nov. 1, 1939, with the N.Y. Phil.

Francesch, Homero, Uruguayan pianist; b. Montevideo, June 12, 1947. He studied piano with Santiago Baranda Reyes; then went to Germany and took piano lessons in Munich with Maria Hindemith-Landes and Steurer. Following concerts in West Germany, he began an international career; appeared as soloist with the Berlin Phil., London Sym., Vienna Sym., Orch. National de France of Paris, and other leading orchs.

Franchetti, Alberto, Italian composer; b. Turin, Sept. 18, 1860; d. Viareggio, Aug. 4, 1942. He studied in Turin with Niccolò Coccon and Fortunato Magi; then with Rheinberger in Munich and with Draeseke in Dresden. He devoted his entire life to composition, with the exception of a brief tenure as director of the Cherubini Cons. in Florence (1926–28).

WORKS: Operas: *Asrael* (Reggio Emilia, Feb. 11, 1888); *Cristoforo Colombo* (Genoa, Oct. 6, 1892); *Fior d'Alpe* (Milan, March 15, 1894); *Il Signor di Pourceaugnac* (Milan, April 10, 1897); *Germania* (his most successful opera; Milan, March 11, 1902); *La Figlia di Jorio* (Milan, March 29, 1906); *Notte di leggenda* (Milan, Jan. 14, 1915); *Giove a Pompei* (with Umberto Giordano; Rome, June 5, 1921); *Glauco* (Naples, April 8, 1922); Sym. (1886); symphonic poems: *Loreley* and *Nella selva nera*; *Inno* for Soli, Chorus, and Orch. (for the 800th anniversary of the Univ. of Bologna); several pieces of chamber music and songs.

Franchi-Verney, Giuseppe Ippolito, Conte della Valetta, Italian composer and writer on music; b. Turin, Feb. 17, 1848; d. Rome, May 15, 1911. He studied jurisprudence, but gave up his law career for music. He was one of the founders of the Società del Quartetto (1875); under the pen name of Ippolito Valetta he wrote for the *Gazzetta del Popolo*; later for *Il Risorgimento* and other newspapers. In 1889 he married the violinist **Teresina Tua.** Among his compositions (most of them in a Wagnerian vein) are a "lyric sketch," *Il Valdese* (Turin, 1885), and a ballet, *Il Mulatto* (Naples, 1896).

Franchomme, Auguste (-Joseph), famous French cellist; b. Lille, April 10, 1808; d. Paris, Jan. 21, 1884. He studied at the Lille Cons.; then with Levasseur and Norblin at the Paris Cons.; then played cello in various opera houses; in 1828 became solo cellist of the Royal Chapel and was a founding member of the Société des Concerts du Conservatoire. In 1846 he was appointed prof. at the Paris Cons. He was an intimate friend of Chopin; established evenings of chamber music in Paris with Hallé and Alard. He wrote cello pieces, mostly in variation form, and operatic potpourris.

Franci, Benvenuto, Italian baritone, father of **Carlo Franci;** b. Pienza, July 1, 1891; d. Rome, Feb. 27, 1985. He studied in Rome; made his debut there in 1918; from 1923 to 1936 he made regular appearances at La Scala in Milan; was a member of the Rome Opera (1928–49); also sang at Covent Garden, London; he retired in 1955. He excelled in dramatic roles in Italian operas.

Franci, Carlo, Italian conductor, son of **Benvenuto Franci;** b. Buenos Aires, July 18, 1927. His family moved to Italy and he studied composition with Turchi and Petrassi at the Rome Cons., and conducting with Previtali at the Accademia di Santa Cecilia. He went to Ireland, and conducted the Radio Eireann Sym. Orch. in Dublin (1955–57); returning to Rome, he was conductor of the RAI (1961–63). He made his American debut as guest conductor at the Metropolitan Opera in N.Y. in 1969.

Franck, César (-Auguste-Jean-Guillaume-Hubert), great

Belgian composer and organist, brother of **Joseph Franck;** b. Liège, Dec. 10, 1822; d. Paris, Nov. 8, 1890. He studied first at the Royal Cons. of Liège with Daussoigne and others; at the age of 9 he won 1st prize for singing, and at 12 1st prize for piano. As a child prodigy, he gave concerts in Belgium. In 1835 his family moved to Paris, where he studied privately with Anton Reicha; in 1837 he entered the Paris Cons., studying with Zimmerman (piano), Benoist (organ), and Leborne (theory). A few months after his entrance examinations he received a special award of "grand prix d'honneur" for playing a fugue a third lower at sight; in 1838 he received the 1st prize for piano; in 1839, a 2nd prize for counterpoint; in 1840, 1st prize for fugue; and in 1841, 2nd prize for organ. In 1842 he was back in Belgium; in 1843 he returned to Paris, and settled there for the rest of his life. On March 17, 1843, he presented there a concert of his chamber music; on Jan. 4, 1846, his 1st major work, the oratorio *Ruth*, was given at the Paris Cons. On Feb. 22, 1848, in the midst of the Paris revolution, he married; in 1851 he became organist of the church of St.-Jean-St.-François; in 1853, maître de chapelle and in, 1858, organist at Ste.-Clotilde, which position he held until his death. In 1872 he succeeded his former teacher Benoist as prof. of organ at the Paris Cons. Franck's organ classes became the training school for a whole generation of French composers; among his pupils were d'Indy, Chausson, Bréville, Bordes, Duparc, Ropartz, Pierné, Vidal, Chapuis, Vierne, and a host of others, who eventually formed a school of modern French instrumental music. Until the appearance of Franck in Paris, operatic art dominated the entire musical life of the nation, and the course of instruction at the Paris Cons. was influenced by this tendency. By his emphasis on organ music, based on the contrapuntal art of Bach, Franck swayed the new generation of French musicians toward the ideal of absolute music. The foundation of the famous Schola Cantorum by d'Indy, Bordes, and others in 1894 realized Franck's teachings. After the death of d'Indy in 1931, several members withdrew from the Schola Cantorum and organized the École César Franck (1938).

Franck was not a prolific composer, but his creative powers rose rather than diminished with advancing age; his only sym. was completed when he was 66; his remarkable Violin Sonata was written at the age of 63; his String Quartet was composed in the last year of his life. Lucidity of contrapuntal design and fullness of harmony are the distinguishing traits of Franck's music; in melodic writing he balanced the diatonic and chromatic elements in fine equilibrium. Although he did not pursue innovation for its own sake, he was not averse to using unorthodox procedures. The novelty of introducing an English horn into the score of his Sym. aroused some criticism among academic musicians of the time. Franck was quite alien to the Wagner-Liszt school of composition, which attracted many of his own pupils; the chromatic procedures in Franck's music derive from Bach rather than from Wagner.

WORKS: OPERAS: *Le Valet de Ferme* (1851–53); *Hulda* (1882–85; Monte Carlo, March 8, 1894); *Ghisèle* (unfinished; orchestration completed by d'Indy, Chausson, Bréville, Rousseau, and Coquard; 1st perf., Monte Carlo, March 30, 1896). **ORATORIOS:** *Ruth* (1843–46; Paris, Jan. 4, 1846; rev. 1871); *La Tour de Babel* (1865); *Les Béatitudes* (1869–79; Dijon, June 15, 1891); *Rédemption* (1st version, Paris, April 10, 1873; final version, Paris, March 15, 1875); *Rébecca* (Paris, March 15, 1881; produced as a 1-act sacred opera at the Paris Opéra, May 25, 1918). **SYMPHONIC POEMS:** *Les Éolides* (Paris, May 13, 1877); *Le Chasseur maudit* (Paris, March 31, 1883); *Les Djinns* (Paris, March 15, 1885); *Psyché* (Paris, March 10, 1888). **OTHER WORKS FOR ORCH.:** *Variations symphoniques* for Piano and Orch. (Paris, May 1, 1886); Sym. in D minor (Paris, Feb. 17, 1889). **CHAMBER:** 4 piano trios (early works; 1841–42); *Andante quietoso* for Piano and Violin (1843); *Duo pour piano et violon concertants*, on themes from Dalayrac's *Gulistan* (1844); Quintet in F minor for Piano and Strings (1879); Violin Sonata (1886); String Quartet (1889). **ORGAN:** 6 *pièces* (*Fantaisie; Grande pièce symphonique; Prélude, Fugue, et Variations;*

Pastorale; Prière; Finale); *3 pièces* (*Fantaisie; Cantabile; Pièce héroïque*) *Andantino; 3 chorales;* an album of 44 *Petites pièces;* an album of 55 pieces, entitled *L'Organiste;* etc. **SACRED:** *Messe solennelle* (1858); *Messe à 3 voix* (1860); *Panis angelicus* for Tenor, Organ, Harp, Cello, and Double Bass; offertories, motets, etc.; 16 songs, among them *La Procession* (also arranged for Voice and Orch.). **PIANO:** 4 *fantaisies; Prélude, Choral et Fugue; Prélude, Aria et Final; 3 petits riens; Danse lente;* etc.

BIBL.: A. Coquard, *C. F.* (Paris, 1890; new ed., 1904); E. Destranges, *L'Œuvre lyrique de C. F.* (Paris, 1896); G. Servières, *La Musique française moderne* (Paris, 1897); G. Derepas, *C. F.: Étude sur sa vie, son enseignement, son œuvre* (Paris, 1897); A. Meyer, *Les Critiques de C. F.* (Orléans, 1898); P. Locard, *Les Maîtres modernes de l'orgue* (Paris, 1900); P. Garnier, *L'Héroïsme de C. F.: Psychologie musicale* (Paris, 1900); F. Baldensperger, *C. F., L'Artiste et son œuvre* (Paris, 1901); R. Canudo, *C. F. e la giovane scuola musicale francesa* (Rome, 1905); C. Van den Borren, *L'Œuvre dramatique de C. F.* (Brussels, 1906); V. d'Indy, *C. F.* (Paris, 1906; in Eng., London, 1910); O. Séré, *Musiciens français d'aujourd'hui* (Paris, 1911); J. Rivière, *Études* (Paris, 1911); J. Hinton, *C. F., Some Personal Reminiscences* (London, 1912); M. de Rudder, *C. F.* (Paris, 1920); E. Closson, *C. F.* (Charleroi, 1923); R. Jardillier, *La Musique de chambre de C. F.* (Paris, 1929); M. Emmanuel, *C. F.* (Paris, 1930); C. Tournemire, *C. F.* (Paris, 1931); T. Lynn, *C. F.: A Bio-bibliography* (N.Y., 1934); H. Haag, *C. F. als Orgelkomponist* (Kassel, 1936); P. Kreutzer, *Die sinfonische Form C. F.s* (Düsseldorf, 1938); M. Kunel, *La Vie de C. F.* (Paris, 1947); J. Horton, *C. F.* (London, 1948); N. Demuth, *C. F.* (London, 1949); N. Dufourcq, *C. F.: Le Milieu, l'œuvre, l'art* (Paris, 1949); L. Vallas, *La Véritable Histoire de C. F.* (Paris, 1950; in Eng., London, 1951); C. Taube, *C. F. und wir: Eine Biographie* (Berlin, 1951); N. van der Elst, *Organist van de Sinte Clotilde* (Tilburg, 1953); E. Buenzod, *C.A. F.* (Paris, 1966); W. Mohr, *C. F.* (Tutzing, 1969); L. Davies, *C. F. and His Circle* (Boston, 1970); S. Roe, "The Manuscripts of *C. F.*," *Musical Times* (Nov. 1980); R. Smith, *Toward an Authentic Interpretation of the Organ Works of C. F.* (N.Y., 1983).

Franck, Eduard, German pianist, pedagogue, and composer, father of **Richard Franck;** b. Breslau, Oct. 5, 1817; d. Berlin, Dec. 1, 1893. At the age of 17 he studied with Mendelssohn; later he met Schumann and became his friend. These associations were the formative factor in the development of his career; he wrote piano pieces and songs in a Romantic vein, closely adhering to the style of Mendelssohn and, to some extent, of Schumann. As a piano teacher, he enjoyed great renown. He taught in Cologne (1851–58), Bern (1859–67), and Berlin (1867–92). Among his works are 2 piano concertos, 2 violin concertos, much chamber music, and numerous collections of piano pieces.

BIBL.: R. Franck, *Musikalische und unmusikalische Erinnerungen* (Heidelberg, 1928).

Franck, Johann Wolfgang, German composer; b. Unterschwaningen (baptized), June 17, 1644; d. c.1710. He was brought up in Ansbach, and served there as court musician from 1665 until 1679; produced 3 operas at the Ansbach court: *Die unvergleichliche Andromeda* (1675); *Der verliebte Föbus* (1678); and *Die drei Töchter Cecrops* (1679). On Jan. 17, 1679, in a fit of jealousy, he allegedly killed the court musician Ulbrecht, and was forced to flee. He found refuge in Hamburg with his wife, Anna Susanna Wilbel (whom he had married in 1666), and gained a prominent position at the Hamburg Opera; between 1679 and 1686 he wrote and produced 17 operas, the most important of which was *Diokletian* (1682). His private life continued to be stormy; he deserted his wife and their 10 children, and went to London, where he remained from 1690 to about 1702. The exact place and date of his death are unknown. In London he organized (with Robert King) a series of Concerts of Vocal and Instrumental Music; publ. *Geistliche Lieder* (Hamburg, 1681, 1685, 1687, 1700; republ. in 1856 by D.H. Engel, with new words by Osterwald;

newly ed. by W. Krabbe and J. Kromolicki in vol. 45 of Denkmäler Deutscher Tonkunst); *Remedium melancholiae* (25 secular solo songs with Basso Continuo; London, 1690); arias; etc.

BIBL.: F. Zelle, *J.W. F., Ein Beitrag zur Geschichte der ältesten deutschen Oper* (Berlin, 1889); A. Werner, "J.W. F.s Flucht
aus Ansbach," *Sammelbände der Internationalen Musik-Gesellschaft*, XIV/2; W. Barclay Squire, "J.W. F. in England,"
Musical Antiquary (July 1912); R. Klages, *J.W. F., Untersuchungen zu seiner Lebensgeschichte und zu seinen geistlichen
Kompositionen* (Hamburg, 1937); G. Schmidt, *Die Musik am
Hofe der Markgrafen von Brandenburg-Ansbach* (Munich,
1953).

Franck, Joseph, Belgian-French organist and composer,
brother of **César(-Auguste-Jean-Guillaume-Hubert)
Franck;** b. Liège, Oct. 31, 1825; d. Issy, near Paris, Nov.
20, 1891. He studied organ with Benoist at the Paris Cons.,
obtaining the 1st prize (1852); then was organist at the church
of St. Thomas d'Aquin in Paris. He composed sacred music
and piano works, and publ. several manuals on harmony, piano
technique, and other pedagogical subjects.

Franck, Melchior, German composer; b. Zittau, c.1579; d.
Coburg, June 1, 1639. He went to Nuremberg in 1601, and
in 1602 obtained the post of Kapellmeister at Coburg, where
he remained to the end of his life. He was an excellent contrapuntist; composed sacred and secular vocal music, and exerted
considerable influence on his contemporaries. Selections from
his instrumental works, ed. by F. Bölsche, constitute vol. XVI
of Denkmäler Deutscher Tonkunst; vol. XVII of the *Monatshefte für Musikgeschichte* contains a careful description of
his printed works. Reprints of some of his sacred vocal works
have been publ. by F. Commer, E. Mauersberger, and F. Jöde;
secular works in the *Staatliches Liederbuch, Kaiser-Liederbuch,*
and other collections.

BIBL.: A. Obrist, *M. F.: Ein Beitrag zur Geschichte der weltlichen Composition in Deutschland* (Berlin, 1892).

Franck, Richard, German pianist, son of **Eduard Franck;**
b. Cologne, Jan. 3, 1858; d. Heidelberg, Jan. 22, 1938. He
studied with his father in Berlin and also attended the Leipzig
Cons. (1878–80). He was in Basel from 1880 to 1883 and
again from 1887 till 1900, and was active there as a pianist
and teacher. He later lived in Kassel, and finally in Heidelberg.
He was highly regarded as an interpreter of Beethoven's sonatas; publ. a book of memoirs, *Musikalische und unmusikalische
Erinnerungen* (Heidelberg, 1928).

Franckenstein, Clemens von, German composer; b. Wiesentheid, July 14, 1875; d. Hechendorf, Aug. 19, 1942. He spent
his youth in Vienna; then went to Munich, where he studied
with Thuille; later took courses with Knorr at the Hoch Cons.
in Frankfurt. He traveled with an opera company in the U.S.
in 1901; then was a theater conductor in London (1902–7).
From 1912 to 1918 and from 1924 to 1934 he was Intendant
at the Munich Opera. He wrote several operas, the most successful of which was *Des Kaisers Dichter* (on the life of the
Chinese poet Li-Tai Po), performed in Hamburg (Nov. 2, 1920).
Other operas are *Griselda* (Troppau, 1898), *Fortunatus* (Budapest, 1909), and *Rahab* (Hamburg, March 25, 1911). He also
wrote several orch. works.

BIBL.: W. Zentner, "C. v.F.," *Zeitschrift für Musik* (1929).

Franco (real name, **L'Okanga La Ndju Pene Luambo Ma-
kiadi**), influential African singer, songwriter, guitarist, and
bandleader; b. Sona-Bata, Congo, 1938; d. there (Zaire), Oct.
12, 1989. His fame grew to legendary proportions in Zaire
both as a guitar virtuoso and as founder (1956) of O.K. Jazz (for
the initials of an early sponsor and also Orch. Kinois), later
renamed T.P.O.K. Jazz (for Tout Poussant, "all powerful"),
with which Franco made over 100 recordings. The personnel
of the group ranged from 10 to 30 members and included in
its 30-plus-year life virtually every major performing musician
in Zaire; its sound was predominated by horns and guitars,
seasoned with extensive vocals and fortified by a variety of
percussion instruments. Franco's musical interests and activi-

ties followed the political trends of his country; Zaire became
independent in 1960, and in 1972 saw a nationwide cultural
campaign toward "authentic" expression in an effort to recapture African traditions. While early influences upon the group
and upon Franco's compositions came from Cuban music, they
later shifted to Congolese traditions; the Cuban rumba became
"rumba odemba" (odemba being a bark used to make an aphro-
disiac brew), and distinctly Cuban melodies became elongated
and sinuous, more akin to the speech-melodies of Lingala, a
native tonal language. He was generally supportive of Zaire's
nationalism, and his song lyrics (in both Lingala and French)
spoke forcefully on issues ranging from AIDS and equal rights
to world peace; nonetheless,the social commentary heard in the
songs *Helene* and *Jackie* was deemed "immoral" in 1978,
causing him to be jailed; he was soon pardoned, however,
and subsequently was decorated by President Mobutu; he was
later dubbed "Le Grand Maître" of Zairian music, the 2nd
native musician (after Kabaselle) to be so honored. T.P.O.K.
Jazz made its 1st U.S. tour in 1983, returning in 1989, shortly
before Franco's death, to give a sold-out performance in N.Y.
In the 1980s he spent much time in Brussels; he established
a 2nd band to accompany him in his European performances,
and also organized a nightclub/hotel and record label in Zaire.
Although Franco remains relatively unknown in the U.S., his
stature in his own country grew to phenomenal proportions;
the nation of Zaire, by presidential decree, went into a 5-day
mourning at his death, during which his music was heard
continuously on the radio. Among his most popular albums
are *En Colere Vol. 1, 24 Ans d'Âge Vol. 4, Ekaba-Kaba, Le Response de Mario,* and *Live en Hollande.*

BIBL.: J. Pareles, "The Influential and Joyous Legacy of
Zaire's F.," *N.Y. Times* (Oct. 29, 1989).

Franco of Cologne, German music theorist of the 13th century. His identity is conjectural; there was a learned man known
as Magister Franco of Cologne who flourished as early as the
11th century; several reputable scholars regard him as identical
with the music theorist Franco; against this identification is
the improbability of the emergence of theories and usages
found in Franco's writings at such an early date. The generally
accepted period for his activities is 1250 to about 1280. The
work on which the reputation of Franco of Cologne rests is
the famous treatise *Ars cantus mensurabilis.* Its principal significance is not so much the establishment of a new method
of mensural notation as the systematization of rules that had
been inadequately or vaguely explained by Franco's predecessors. The treatise is valuable also for the explanation of usages
governing the employment of concords and discords. It was
reprinted from different MSS, in Gerbert's *Scriptores* (vol. III)
and in Coussemaker's *Scriptores* (vol. I). Gerbert attributes it
to a Franco of Paris, a shadowy figure who may have been
the author of a treatise and 3 summaries, all beginning with
the words "Gaudent brevitate moderni." The *Ars cantus mensurabilis* is reproduced in English in O. Strunk's *Source Readings in Music History* (N.Y., 1950).

BIBL.: O. Koller, "Versuch einer Rekonstruktion der Notenbeispiele zum 11. Kapitel von F.s *Ars cantus mensurabilis,*"
Vierteljahrsschrift für Musikwissenschaft, VI (1890); H. Riemann, *Geschichte der Musiktheorie* (Leipzig, 1898); J. Stainer,
"The Notation of Mensurable Music," *Proceedings of the Musical Association of London*, 26 (1900); J. Wolf, *Handbuch der
Notationskunde* (vol. I, Leipzig, 1913); G. Reese, *Music in
the Middle Ages* (N.Y., 1940); W. Apel, *The Notation of Polyphonic Music, 900–1600* (Cambridge, Mass., 1942); Y. Rokseth,
Polyphonies du XIIIe siècle (Paris, 1948); F. Gennrich, *F. von
Köln, Ars cantus mensurabilis* (Darmstadt, 1955); W. Frobenius, "Zur Datierung von F.s *Ars cantus mensurabilis,*" *Archiv
für Musikwissenschaft*, XXVII (1970).

Franco, Johan (Henri Gustav), Dutch-born American composer; b. Zaandam, July 12, 1908; d. Virginia Beach, Va., April
14, 1988. He studied at the Amsterdam Cons. (1929–34); went
to the U.S. when the dark shadow of Hitler encroached on
his native Netherlands. He became a U.S. citizen in 1942

and served in the U.S. Army during World War II. In his works, Franco followed the ideal of symmetrical construction, adhering to the models of neo-Classical music. Among his compositions are 5 syms., 5 lyric concertos, 6 string quartets, and a number of works for carillon.

Francœur, François, French violinist and composer, uncle of **Louis-Joseph Francœur;** b. Paris, Sept. 8, 1698; d. there, Aug. 5, 1787. He was a member of the orch. of the Paris Opéra, a chamber musician to the King, and one of the "24 violons du roi." Conjointly with his inseparable friend François Rebel (1743–53), he was inspecteur adjoint, then director of the Opéra (1757–67) and Superintendent of the King's Music (1744–76). He wrote 2 books of violin sonatas; produced numerous operas (in collaboration with Rebel).

Francœur, Louis-Joseph, French violinist, conductor, and composer, nephew of **François Francœur;** b. Paris, Oct. 8, 1738; d. there, March 10, 1804. He entered the orch. of the Paris Opéra at the age of 14; became its conductor in 1767. During the Revolution he was imprisoned as a suspect, but was released after the Thermidor coup d'état (1794) and was administrator of the Paris Opéra until 1799. He wrote an act for the opera *Lindor et Ismène* (Paris, Aug. 29, 1766); publ. a treatise, *Diapason général de tous les instruments à vent* (1772).

François, Samson, French pianist; b. Frankfurt am Main (son of the French consul there), May 18, 1924; d. Paris, Oct. 22, 1970. He received a prize at the Nice Cons. at the age of 11; studied in Paris with Alfred Cortot. He traveled widely as a pianist; made his American debut in 1947; played in N.Y. in 1960 and 1961. In 1964 he made a concert tour of China. He was particularly noted for his interpretations of Debussy.

Frandsen, John, respected Danish conductor; b. Copenhagen, July 10, 1918. He was educated at the Royal Danish Cons. in Copenhagen; then was organist at the Domkirke there (1938–53); also made appearances as a conductor. After serving as conductor with the Danish Radio Sym. (1945–46), he became a conductor at the Royal Danish Theater; also made appearances with the Royal Danish Orch. In 1958 he toured the U.S. with the Danish Radio Sym. He was also active as a teacher, at both the Royal Danish Cons. and the Opera School of the Royal Danish Theater. In 1980 he was named orch. counselor of the Danish Radio. He was particularly noted for his outstanding performances of contemporary Danish music.

Frank, Alan (Clifford), English music scholar; b. London, Oct. 10, 1910. He studied the clarinet, conducting, and composition. At the age of 17 he joined the staff of the Oxford Univ. Press; during the war was in the Royal Air Force. In 1947 he was appointed music ed. of the Oxford Univ. Press; in 1954 became head of its music dept.; retired in 1975. In 1935 he married **Phyllis Tate,** the composer. He publ. *The Playing of Chamber Music* (with George Stratton; London, 1935; 2nd ed., 1951) and *Modern British Composers* (London, 1953); he was also co-author (with Frederick Thurston) of *A Comprehensive Tutor for the Boehm Clarinet* (London, 1939).

Frank, Claude, esteemed German-American pianist; b. Nuremberg, Dec. 24, 1925. In 1938 he moved to Paris, and in 1940 went to N.Y.; there he took lessons in piano with Artur Schnabel and in composition with Paul Dessau (1941–44); later studied composition with Normand Lockwood (1946–48); also attended classes in conducting under Koussevitzky at Tanglewood (1947). He taught at Bennington College in Vermont (1948–55); eventually joined the staff of the Mannes School of Music in N.Y. A pianist of a grand envergure, he has earned merited encomiums for his sensitive interpretations of the classics. In 1959 he married the pianist **Lilian Kallir,** with whom he frequently appeared in duo-piano concerts.

Frank, Ernst, German conductor and composer; b. Munich, Feb. 7, 1847; d. Oberdöbling, near Vienna, Aug. 17, 1889. He studied with M. de Fontaine (piano) and F. Lachner (composition); in 1868, was conductor at Würzburg; in 1869, chorus master at the Vienna Court Opera; from 1872 to 1877, conductor at Mannheim; from 1877 to 1879, at Frankfurt; from 1879 to 1887, at the Hannover Court Opera. He wrote the operas *Adam de la Halle* (Karlsruhe, April 9, 1880), *Hero* (Berlin, Nov. 26, 1884), and *Der Sturm* (after Shakespeare; Hannover, Oct. 14, 1887); completed H. Götz's opera *Francesca da Rimini* and produced it at Mannheim (1877). Frank was a friend of Brahms. Mental illness led to his being committed to an asylum in April 1887.

BIBL.: A. Einstein, "Briefe von Brahms an E. F.," *Zeitschrift für Musikwissenschaft* (April 1922).

Frankel, Benjamin, noted English composer; b. London, Jan. 31, 1906; d. there, Feb. 12, 1973. He worked as an apprentice watchmaker in his youth; then went to Germany to study music; returning to London, he earned his living by playing piano or violin in restaurants. It was only then that he began studying composition seriously. In the interim he made arrangements, played in jazz bands, and wrote music for films; some of his film scores, such as that for *The Man in the White Suit,* are notable for their finesse in musical characterization. In 1946 he was appointed to the faculty of the Guildhall School of Music and Drama in London. Frankel also took great interest in political affairs; was for many years a member of the British Communist Party and followed the tenets of socialist realism in some of his compositions.

WORKS: 8 syms.: No. 1 (1952); No. 2 (Cheltenham, July 13, 1962); No. 3 (1964); No. 4 (London, Dec. 18, 1966); No. 5 (1967); No. 6 (London, March 23, 1969); No. 7 (London, June 4, 1970); No. 8 (1971); *The Aftermath* for Tenor, Trumpet, Harp, and Strings (1947); Violin Concerto (dedicated "to the memory of the 6 million"; Stockholm Festival, June 10, 1956); Bagatelles for 11 Instruments (1959); *Serenata concertante* for Piano Trio and Orch. (1961); Viola Concerto (1966); *A Catalogue of Incidents* for Chamber Orch. (1966); *Overture for a Ceremony* (1970); *Pezzi melodici* for Orch. (Stroud Festival, Oct. 19, 1972); Quintet for Clarinet and String Quartet (1953); 5 string quartets (1944, 1945, 1947, 1948, 1965); Piano Quartet (1953); *Pezzi pianissimi* for Clarinet, Cello, and Piano (1964); pieces for solo instruments; songs.

Frankenstein, Alfred (Victor), American writer on music and art; b. Chicago, Oct. 5, 1906; d. San Francisco, June 22, 1981. He played clarinet in the Civic Orch. of Chicago before turning to writing; from 1935 to 1975 he was music critic of the *San Francisco Chronicle;* concurrently served as its principal art critic; from 1937 to 1963 he was program annotator of the San Francisco Sym. He publ., besides innumerable special articles, a book of essays, *Syncopating Saxophones* (Chicago, 1925); *Modern Guide to Symphonic Music* (N.Y., 1966); and several publications dealing with modern American art. He was the 1st to publ. the sketches of Victor Hartmann that inspired Mussorgsky's *Pictures at an Exhibition* (*Musical Quarterly,* July 1939).

Frankl, Peter, brilliant Hungarian-born English pianist; b. Budapest, Oct. 2, 1935. He studied at the Franz Liszt Academy of Music in Budapest; his teachers included Zoltán Kodály, Leo Weiner, and Lajos Hernadi. In 1957 he won 1st prize in the Marguerite Long Competition; also won prizes at competitions in Munich and Rio de Janeiro, which catapulted him into an international career. He made his debut in America in a Dallas recital in 1965. Eventually he moved to London, and became a British subject in 1967. In England he formed the Frankl-Pauk-Kirshbaum Trio. His repertoire is extensive, ranging from Classical music to contemporary works.

Franklin, Aretha, black American "soul" singer; b. Memphis, Tenn., March 25, 1942. Her father was a Baptist preacher; the family settled in Detroit, where he established a pastorate; his church became a hearth of gospel songs and evangelical group singing. At 18 she went to N.Y., where she quickly attracted attention; her singing at the Newport Jazz Festival in 1963 led to numerous important and lucrative engagements; the sales of her recordings skyrocketed to the million mark. In 1967 she toured Europe; in 1968 she made a sensation with her "soul" version of *The Star-Spangled Banner* at the ill-fated Democratic National Convention in Chicago. Among her outstanding recordings were the albums *I Never Loved a Man the Way I Love You* (1967), *Amazing Grace* (1972), *Young, Gifted and Black* (1972), *Something He Can Feel* (1976), *Jump to It* (1982), and *Who's Zoomin' Who?* (1985). In 1987 she recorded the 2-disc *One Lord, One Faith, One Baptism* in her father's church, which featured Jesse Jackson delivering a sermon against drug abuse among young black people.

Franklin, Benjamin, great American statesman; b. Boston, Jan. 17, 1706; d. Philadelphia, April 17, 1790. An amateur musician, he invented (1762) the "armonica," an instrument consisting of a row of glass discs of different sizes, set in vibration by light pressure. A string quartet mistakenly attributed to him came to light in Paris in 1945, and was publ. there (1946); the parts are arranged in an ingenious "scordatura"; only open strings are used, so that the quartet can be played by rank amateurs. Franklin wrote entertainingly on musical subjects; his letters on Scottish music are found in vol. VI of his collected works.
    Bibl.: O. Sonneck, *Suum cuique: Essays in Music* (N.Y., 1916); L. de la Laurencie, "B. F. and the Claveciniste Brillon de Jouy," *Musical Quarterly* (April 1923); "L'Harmonica de B. F.," *Dissonances* (July–Aug. 1944); W. Lichtenwanger, "B. F. on Music," *Church Music and Musical Life in Pennsylvania in the Eighteenth Century*, III/2 (Philadelphia, 1947); K. Stolba, "B. F. y la musica," *Heterofonia* (July–Aug. 1971); M. Granander, "B. F.'s String Quartet," *Early American Literature* (Fall 1972); W. Marrocco, "The String Quartet Attributed to B. F.," *Proceedings of the American Philosophical Society* (1972).

Franko, Nahan, American violinist and conductor, brother of **Sam Franko;** b. New Orleans, July 23, 1861; d. Amityville, N.Y., June 7, 1930. As a child prodigy, he toured with Adelina Patti; then studied in Berlin with Joachim and Wilhelmj. Returning to America, he joined the orch. of the Metropolitan Opera; was its concertmaster from 1883 to 1905; made his debut there as a conductor on April 1, 1900; was the 1st native-born American to be engaged as conductor there (1904–7).

Franko, Sam, American violinist, brother of **Nahan Franko;** b. New Orleans, Jan. 20, 1857; d. N.Y., May 6, 1937 (from a skull fracture resulting from a fall). He studied in Berlin with Joachim, Heinrich de Ahna, and Eduard Rappoldi. Returning to the U.S. in 1880, he joined the Theodore Thomas Orch. in N.Y., and was its concertmaster from 1884 to 1891; in 1883 he toured the U.S. and Canada as a soloist with the Mendelssohn Quintette Club of Boston. In order to prove that prejudice against native orch. players was unfounded, he organized in 1894 the American Sym. Orch., using 65 American-born performers; this orch. was later used for his Concerts of Old Music (1900–1909). In 1910 he went to Berlin and taught at the Stern Cons.; he returned to N.Y. in 1915 and remained there for the rest of his life. He publ. for piano: *Album Leaf* (1889); *Viennese Silhouettes* (a set of 6 waltzes, 1928); etc.; several violin pieces; practical arrangements for violin and piano. His memoirs were publ. posth. under the title *Chords and Discords* (N.Y., 1938).

Frantz, Ferdinand, German bass-baritone; b. Kassel, Feb. 8, 1906; d. Munich, May 26, 1959. He made his debut at the opera in Kassel in 1927 as Ortel in *Die Meistersinger von Nürnberg;* then sang in Halle and Chemnitz; was a leading member of the Hamburg State Opera (1937–43) and the Bavarian State Opera in Munich (1943–59). He made a fine impression at his Metropolitan Opera debut in N.Y. on Dec. 12, 1949, as Wotan in *Die Walküre;* sang there until 1951 and again in 1953–54; he also appeared at Covent Garden in London. He was primarily known as an effective interpreter of Wagnerian roles.

Frantz, Justus, German pianist; b. Hohensalza, May 18, 1944. He studied piano with Eliza Hansen at the Hamburg Hochschule für Musik; later took private courses with Wilhelm

Kempff. After winning a prize in the Munich Competition in 1967, he began appearing with the leading European orchs., including the Berlin Phil., the Royal Phil. of London, the Orch. de Paris, and the London Phil. He made his U.S. debut with the N.Y. Phil. in 1975; subsequently appeared with many other American orchs. He also toured with Christoph Eschenbach in duo-piano concerts. In 1986 he founded the Schleswig-Holstein festival; he also became a prof. at the Hamburg Hochschule für Musik.

Franz, Paul (real name, **François Gautier**), French tenor; b. Paris, Nov. 30, 1876; d. there, April 20, 1950. After private voice studies, he made his debut at the Paris Opéra in 1909 as Lohengrin; remained on its roster until 1938. From 1937 he taught voice at the Paris Cons.

Franz (originally, **Knauth**), **Robert,** famous German song composer; b. Halle, June 28, 1815; d. there, Oct. 24, 1892. His father, Christoph Franz Knauth, legally adopted the name Franz in 1847. The parents did not favor music as a profession, but Franz learned to play the organ and participated as an accompanist in performances in his native city. In 1835 he went to Dessau, where he studied with Friedrich Schneider; in 1837 he returned to Halle. He publ. his 1st set of songs in 1843; they attracted immediate attention and were warmly praised by Schumann. In 1841 he received an appointment as organist at the Ulrichskirche in Halle, and also as conductor of the Singakademie there in 1842; later he received the post of music director at Halle Univ. (1851–67), which conferred on him the title of Mus.Doc. in 1861. The successful development of his career as a musician was interrupted by a variety of nervous disorders and growing deafness, which forced him to abandon his musical activities in 1867. Liszt, Joachim, and others organized a concert for his benefit, collecting a large sum of money (about $25,000); admirers in America (Otto Dresel, S.B. Schlesinger, B.J. Lang) also contributed funds for his support. He publ. *Mitteilungen über J.S. Bachs Magnificat* (Leipzig, 1863); *Offener Brief an Ed. Hanslick über Bearbeitungen älterer Tonwerke, namentlich Bachscher und Händelscher Vokalwerke* (Leipzig, 1871); both were reprinted by R. Bethge as *Gesammelte Schriften über die Wiederbelebung Bachscher und Händelscher Werke* (Leipzig, 1910). Franz was undoubtedly one of the finest masters of the German lied. He publ. about 350 songs; among the best known are *Schlummerlied, Die Lotosblume, Die Widmung,* and *Wonne der Wehmuth.*
    Bibl.: F. Liszt, *R. F.* (Leipzig, 1855; reprinted in *Gesammelte Schriften,* vol. IV, Leipzig, 1882); H. Schuster, *R. F.* (Leipzig, 1874); La Mara, *R. F.,* in vol. III of *Musikalische Studienköpfe* (Leipzig, 1868–82; publ. separately, 1911); R. Procházka, *R. F.* (Leipzig, 1894); W. Golther, *R. F. und Arnold Freiherr Senfft von Pilsach: Ein Briefwechsel 1861–89* (Berlin, 1907); R. Bethge, *R. F.: Ein Lebensbild* (Halle, 1908); H. Kleemann, "R. F.," *Musical Quarterly* (Oct. 1915); O. Lessmann, "Persönliche Erinnerungen an R. F.," *Allgemeine musikalische Zeitung* (1915); S. Barbak, *Die Lieder von R. F.* (Vienna, 1922); H. von der Pfordten, *R. F.* (Leipzig, 1923); J. Boonin, *An Index to the Solo Songs of R. F.* (Hackensack, N.J., 1970).

Fränzl, Ferdinand (Ignaz Joseph), German violinist, conductor, and composer, son of **Ignaz (Franz Joseph) Fränzl;** b. Schwetzingen, May 25, 1767; d. Mannheim, Oct. 27, 1833. He studied with his father; later was a pupil in composition of F.X. Richter and Pleyel at Strasbourg, and of Mattei at Bologna. He entered the Mannheim Court Orch. at the age of 22; in 1785 began to travel on concert tours with his father. He was appointed conductor of the Munich Opera in 1806, but continued his tours; retired in 1826; finally settled in Mannheim. As a master violinist, he enjoyed great renown. A prolific composer, he wrote 9 violin concertos; Double Concerto for 2 Violins; operas; string quartets; string trios; syms.; overtures; songs.
    Bibl.: R. Würtz, "F. F.," *Mannheimer Hefte,* 2 (1967).

Fränzl, Ignaz (Franz Joseph), German violinist, conductor, and composer, father of **Ferdinand (Ignaz Joseph) Fränzl;** b. Mannheim, June 3, 1736; d. there, Sept. 3, 1811. He entered the Mannheim Court Orch. as a boy of 11; became co-concert-master in 1774, and was conductor from 1790 to 1803. He made several concert tours with his son; composed syms. and music for the violin, and also wrote for the stage. His singspiel *Die Luftbälle* was produced in Mannheim with excellent success (April 15, 1787); he also wrote music for Shakespeare's plays.

BIBL.: R. Würtz, " '. . . ein sehr solider Geiger'. Mozart und I. F.," *Acta Mozartiana* (Nov. 1969); idem, *I. F.* (Mainz, 1970).

Fraschini, Gaetano, noted Italian tenor; b. Pavia, Feb. 16, 1816; d. Naples, May 23, 1887. He studied with F. Moretti; made his debut in Pavia in 1837; subsequently sang in Milan, Venice, Trieste, Rome, and other Italian cities; also appeared in London at Her Majesty's Theatre (1847) and Drury Lane (1868). He created the role of Genaro in Donizetti's *Caterina Cornaro;* much esteemed by Verdi, he sang in the premieres of *Attila, Il Corsaro, La battaglia di Legnano, Alzira, Stiffelio,* and *Un ballo in maschera.* The opera house in Pavia is named for him.

Fraser, Norman, Chilean-born English pianist; b. Valparaiso, Nov. 26, 1904. He pursued his musical studies in Chile; in 1917 he went to England, and attended classes at the Royal Academy of Music in London; then took piano lessons with Isidor Philipp in Paris. He subsequently made several tours in South America as a representative of various British organizations. From 1954 to 1971 he was engaged as European music supervisor at the BBC; gave numerous joint recitals with his wife, **Janet Fraser,** the English mezzo-soprano (b. Kirkealdy, May 22, 1911). In 1973 he settled at Seaford, England. He composed a number of attractive piano pieces and some chamber music.

Frazzi, Vito, Italian composer; b. San Secondo Parmense, Aug. 1, 1888; d. Florence, July 8, 1975. He studied organ at the Parma Cons.; also took courses in piano and theory. From 1912 to 1958 he taught at the Florence Cons.; also taught at the Accademia Chigiana in Siena (1932–63). He wrote a music drama, *Re Lear,* after Shakespeare (Florence, 1939); an opera, *Don Quixote* (Florence, April 27, 1952); several symphonic poems; chamber music; orchestrated Monteverdi's stage works.

Freccia, Massimo, Italian conductor; b. Florence, Sept. 19, 1906. He studied at the Florence Cons. and later in Vienna with Franz Schalk. From 1933 to 1935 he conducted the Budapest Sym. Orch.; was guest conductor at the Lewisohn Stadium in N.Y. (1938–40); then was conductor of the Havana Phil. (1939–43), the New Orleans Sym. Orch. (1944–52), and the Baltimore Sym. Orch. (1952–59). He returned to Italy in 1959, and conducted the Rome Radio Orch. until 1963.

Frederick II (Frederick the Great), King of Prussia; b. Berlin, Jan. 24, 1712; d. Potsdam, Aug. 17, 1786. He was an enlightened patron of music, a flute player of considerable skill, and an amateur composer. He studied flute with Quantz; in 1740, when he ascended to the throne, he established a Court Orch. and an opera house; Bach's son Carl Philipp Emanuel was his harpsichordist until 1767. In 1747 J.S. Bach was invited to Potsdam; the fruit of this visit was Bach's *Musical Offering,* written on a theme by Frederick II. A collection of 25 flute sonatas and 4 concertos by Frederick was publ. by Spitta (3 vols., Leipzig, 1889; reprinted, N.Y., 1967); other works were publ. in vol. XX of *Die Musik am preussischen Hofe.* Besides instrumental works, Frederick contributed arias to several operas: *Demofoonte* by Graun (1746); *Il Re pastore* (1747; with Quantz and others); *Galatea ed Acide* (1748; with Hasse, Graun, Quantz, and Nichelmann); and *Il trionfo della fedelità* (1753; with Hasse and others).

BIBL.: K. Müller, *Friedrich der Grosse als Kenner und Dilettant auf dem Gebiete der Tonkunst* (Potsdam, 1847); W. Kothe, *Friedrich der Grosse als Musiker* (Leipzig, 1869); G. Thouret, *Friedrichs des Grossen Verhältniss zur Musik* (Berlin, 1895);

idem, *Friedrich der Grosse als Musikfreund und Musiker* (Leipzig, 1898); K. von Forstner, *Friedrich der Grosse, Künstler und König* (Berlin, 1932); G. Müller, *Friedrich der Grosse, Seine Flöten und sein Flötenspiel* (Berlin, 1932); G. Fitzgibbon, "Of Flutes and Soft Recorders," *Musical Quarterly* (April 1934); J. Bourke, "F. the Great as Music Lover and Musician," *Music & Letters* (Jan. 1947); E. Helm, *Music of the Court of F. the Great* (Norman, Okla., 1960); C. Wolf, "Überlegungen zum *Thema Regium," Bach-Jahrbuch* (1973).

Freed, Alan, American disc jockey and passionate popularizer of rock 'n' roll; b. Johnstown, Pa., Dec. 15, 1922; d. Palm Springs, Calif., Jan. 20, 1965. His greatest achievement was to desegregate black music by introducing it into white-sponsored radio stations. He was also credited with originating the term rock 'n' roll in 1951, although it had been used long before in a musical about a pleasure-boat cruise. He began broadcasting in Cleveland; then went to N.Y. in 1954 to take command of the radio station WINS, which became one of the most popular purveyors of rock 'n' roll. He also acted in the movie *Rock around the Clock.* He began having trouble when stabbings and riots occurred at some of his public concerts in 1958; he was even accused of encouraging such shenanigans for the sake of publicity. Then, with a horrifying peripeteia fit for a Greek tragedy, he suffered a monumental downfall in 1963, when he was convicted of "payola," accepting bribes from commercial record companies for putting their songs on the air. On top of that, he was charged with income-tax evasion. He quit the oppressive city of N.Y. and fled to the more tolerant, laid-back state of California, but he soon died, ignored by enemies and friends alike, in the vacuous spa of Palm Springs.

Freed, Isadore, American composer; b. Brest-Litovsk, Russia, March 26, 1900; d. Rockville Centre, N.Y., Nov. 10, 1960. He went to the U.S. at an early age; graduated from the Univ. of Pa. in 1918 (Mus.Bac.); then studied with Ernest Bloch and with Vincent d'Indy in Paris; returned to the U.S. in 1934; held various teaching positions; in 1944 was appointed head of the music dept. at Hartt College of Music in Hartford, Conn.

WORKS: STAGE: *Vibrations,* ballet (Philadelphia, 1928); operas: *Homo Sum* (1930) and *The Princess and the Vagabond* (Hartford, May 13, 1948). **ORCH.:** *Jeux de timbres* (Paris, 1933); Sym. No. 1 (1941); *Appalachian Symphonic Sketches* (Chautauqua, N.Y., July 31, 1946); *Festival Overture* (San Francisco, Nov. 14, 1946); Rhapsody for Trombone and Orch. (radio premiere, N.Y., Jan. 7, 1951); Sym. No. 2 for Brass (San Francisco, Feb. 8, 1951, composer conducting); Violin Concerto (N.Y., Nov. 13, 1951); Cello Concerto (1952); Concertino for English Horn and Orch. (1953). **CHAMBER:** 3 string quartets (1931, 1932, 1937); Trio for Flute, Viola, and Harp (1940); *Triptych* for Violin, Viola, Cello, and Piano (1943); Passacaglia for Cello and Piano (1947); Quintet for Woodwinds and Horn (Hartford, Dec. 2, 1949); Sonatina for Oboe and Piano (Boston, March 31, 1954); also choral works; piano and organ pieces; songs.

BIBL.: E. Steinhauer, *A Jewish Composer by Choice, I. F.: His Life and Work* (N.Y., 1961).

Freed, Richard D(onald), distinguished American music critic, annotator, and broadcaster; b. Chicago, Dec. 27, 1928. He was educated at the Univ. of Chicago (graduated, 1947). After working for various newspapers, he was a contributor to the *Saturday Review* (1959–71) and a critic for the *N.Y. Times* (1965–66). He served as assistant to the director of the Eastman School of Music in Rochester, N.Y. (1966–70); was a contributing ed. to *Stereo Review* (from 1973) and *Opus* (from 1984); was also a record critic for the *Washington Star* (1972–75), the *Washington Post* (1976–84), and radio station WETA-FM in Washington, D.C. (from 1985); likewise was program annotator for the St. Louis Sym. Orch. (from 1973), the Philadelphia Orch. (1974–84), the Houston Sym. Orch. (1977–80), the National Sym. Orch. in Washington, D.C. (from 1977), and the Baltimore Sym. Orch. (from 1984). From 1974 to 1989 he was executive director of the Music Critics Assoc.; was named consultant to the music director of the National Sym. Orch. in 1981. He received the ASCAP–Deems Taylor

Award in 1984 for his erudite and engagingly indited program annotations, and again in 1986 for his equally stylish record annotations. He occasionally wrote under the names Paul Turner, Gregory Phillip, and Priam Clay.

Freedman, Harry, Polish-born Canadian composer; b. Lodz, April 5, 1922. He was taken to Canada as a child and became a naturalized citizen in 1931; after clarinet lessons, he studied oboe with Perry Bauman and composition with John Weinzweig at the Royal Cons. of Music of Toronto (1945–51); also attended Olivier Messiaen's class in composition at the Berkshire Music Center in Tanglewood (summer 1949). He began his career performing with and composing for dance bands and jazz ensembles; played English horn in the Toronto Sym. Orch. (1946–70), then served as its composer-in-residence (1970–71); was a founder and president (1975–78) of the Canadian League of Composers. In 1985 he was made an Officer of the Order of Canada. In his works, he reveals a fine command of writing in various idioms, ranging from symphonic to jazz scores.

WORKS: STAGE: Opera, *Abracadabra* (1979); ballets: *Rose Latulippe* (Stratford, Aug. 16, 1966); *5 over 13* (1969); *Oiseaux exotiques* (1984–85); *Heroes of Our Time* (1986); incidental music; film and television scores. **ORCH.:** *Nocturne I* (1949) and *II* (1975); *Matinée Suite* (1951–55); *Fantasia and Dance* for Violin and Orch. (1955; rev. 1959); *Images*, symphonic suite (1957–58); 3 syms.: No. 1 (1954–60; Washington, D.C., April 23, 1961); No. 2, *A Little Symphony* (1966); No. 3 (1983; rev. 1985); *Chaconne* (1964); *Armana* (1967); *Tangents*, symphonic variations (Montreal, July 21, 1967); *Klee Wych* (The Laughing One [Indian name of the artist Emily Carr]; 1970); *Scenario* for Saxophone, Electric Bass Guitar, and Orch. (Toronto, May 29, 1970); *Graphic I (Out of Silence . . .)* for Orch. and Tape (Toronto, May 29, 1970); *Preludes* (1971; orchestrated from Debussy); *Tapestry* for Small Orch. (1973); *Tsolum Summer* for Flute, Percussion, and Strings (1976); *Royal Flush*, concerto grosso for Brass Quintet and Orch. (1981); *Chalumeau* for Clarinet, and String Orch. or String Quartet (1981); *Concerto for Orchestra* (1982); *Accord* for Violin and Orch. (1982); *The Sax Chronicles* for Saxophone and Orch. (1984); *Passacaglia* for Jazz Band and Orch. (1984); *Graphic VI (Town)*, after the painting of Harold Town (1986); *A Dance on the Earth* (1988); *Sonata* for Symphonic Winds (1988). **CHAMBER:** Wind Quintet (1962); *The Tokaido* for Chorus and Wind Quintet (1964); *Variations* for Oboe, Flute, and Harpsichord (1965); *Graphic II* for String Quartet (1972); Quartet for Trombones, Bassoons, or Cellos (1973); *5 Rings* for Brass Quintet (1976); *Monday Gig* for Woodwind Quintet (1978); *Opus Pocus* for Flute, Violin, Viola, and Cello (1979); *Blue* for String Quartet (1980); *A Little Girl Blew* for Bass Clarinet (1988); other chamber works. **VOCAL:** *3 poèmes de Jacques Prévert* for Soprano and String Orch. (1962); *2 Sonnets of Love and Age* for Soprano, Baritone, Woodwind Quintet, and Brass Quintet (1975); *Fragments of Alice* for Soprano, Alto, Baritone, and Chamber Orch. (1976); *Nocturne III* for Chorus and Orch. (1980); *A Time Is Coming* for Voices (1982); *Rhymes from the Nursery* for Children's Chorus (1986); other vocal works.

Freeman, Betty (née **Wishnick**), American music patroness, photographer, and record producer; b. Chicago, June 2, 1921. She studied music and English literature at Wellesley College (B.A., 1942), then took piano lessons with Johanna Harris at the Juilliard School of Music in N.Y. and at the New England Cons. of Music in Boston. She also studied privately in N.Y. with Erich Itor Kahn (harmony) and Beveridge Webster (piano). She moved in 1950 to Los Angeles, where she began collecting American avant-garde art; in 1960 she became a founding member of the Contemporary Art Council of the Los Angeles County Museum of Art, and between 1962 and 1964 she completed monographs on Clyfford Still and Sam Francis. From 1964 to 1973 she led the music program of the Pasadena Art Museum, during which period she became interested in the uniquely authentic music of Harry Partch, who became the subject of her prize-winning documentary *The Dreamer That Remains* (1972). She then took up still photography, many of her subjects being the American composers and performing artists who were also her beneficiaries. Her premiere photo exhibit took place at the Otis-Parsons Gallery in Los Angeles in 1985; other shows were held at the Decalage Gallery in Milan (1987), the Los Angeles Phil. (1988), the Brooklyn Academy of Music (1988), the Univ. of Calif. at Irvine (1989), the Berlin Phil. (1990), and various locations throughout Japan (1990). From 1981 she established and financed monthly musicales at her home in Los Angeles with the music critic Alan Rich. She is a particularly active supporter of West Coast composers, including Robert Erickson, Paul Dresher, Morton Subotnick, Dane Rudhyar, Peter Garland, Daniel Lentz, and John Adams. She served on the Inter-Arts Panel of the N.E.A. (1983–84), and received the Cunningham Dance Foundation award for "distinguished support of the arts" (1984). She further received an award from the American Music Center (1986) and the Gold Baton from the American Sym. Orch. League (1987). She has great admirers in the artists she supports; she was the dedicatee of John Cage's *Freeman Etudes* (1977) and of John Adams's opera *Nixon in China* (1987). In 1989 she was elected to the board of directors of the Los Angeles Phil. She had 2 marriages, first to Stanley Freeman, with whom, straight out of college, she busily produced 4 children in 6 years. Divorced in 1971, she later married, in *second lit* (as the French say), the Italian "futurist" artist Franco Assetto.

Freeman, "Bud" (Lawrence), American jazz tenor saxophonist; b. Chicago, April 13, 1906; d. there, March 15, 1991. He began his career in Chicago playing with the Austin High School Gang, then went to N.Y., where he worked with Ben Pollack, Red Nichols, Paul Whiteman, Tommy Dorsey, and Benny Goodman. He was active with various combos from 1939, including the World's Greatest Jazz Band (1969–71), and made many recordings; also publ. the books *You Don't Look Like a Musician* (Detroit, 1974), *If You Know a Better Life, Please Tell Me* (Dublin, 1976), and *Crazeology: The Autobiography of a Chicago Jazzman* (Urbana, 1989).

Freeman, Harry Lawrence, black American composer; b. Cleveland, Oct. 9, 1869; d. N.Y., March 24, 1954. He studied theory with J.H. Beck and piano with E. Schonert and Carlos Sobrino; taught at Wilberforce Univ. (1902–4) and the Salem School of Music (1910–13); organized and directed the Freeman School of Music (1911–22) and the Freeman School of Grand Opera (from 1923); conducted various theater orchs. and opera companies. In 1920 he organized the Negro Opera Co.; in 1930 received the Harmon Gold Award; conducted a pageant, *O Sing a New Song*, at the Chicago World's Fair in 1934. He was the 1st black composer to conduct a sym. orch. in his own work (Minneapolis, 1907), and the 1st of his race to write large operatic compositions. All his music is written in folk-song style; his settings are in simple harmonies; his operas are constructed of songs and choruses in simple concatenation of separate numbers.

WORKS: Grand operas (all on Negro, oriental, and Indian themes): *The Martyr* (Denver, 1893); *Valdo* (Cleveland, May 1906); *Zuluki* (1898); *African Kraal* (Chicago, June 30, 1903, with an all-black cast, composer conducting; rev. 1934); *The Octoroon* (1904); *The Tryst* (N.Y., May 1911); *The Prophecy* (N.Y., 1912); *The Plantation* (1914); *Athalia* (1916); *Vendetta* (N.Y., Nov. 12, 1923); *American Romance*, jazz opera (1927); *Voodoo* (N.Y., Sept. 10, 1928); *Leah Kleschna* (1930); *Uzziah* (1931); *Zululand*, a tetralogy of music dramas: *Nada, The Lily* (1941–44; vocal score contains 2,150 pp.), *Allah* (1947), and *The Zulu King* (1934); *The Slave*, ballet for Choral Ensemble and Orch. (Harlem, N.Y., Sept. 22, 1932); songs (*Whither, If thou did'st love*, etc.).

Freeman, Paul (Douglas), black American conductor; b. Richmond, Va., Jan. 2, 1936. He studied piano, clarinet, and cello in his youth; continued his musical training at the Eastman School of Music in Rochester, N.Y. (B.Mus., 1956; M.Mus., 1957; Ph.D., 1963); then took courses at the Berlin Hochschule für Musik (1957–59). Returning to the U.S., he took conducting lessons with Richard Lert and Pierre Monteux.

He subsequently held the post of conductor with the Opera Theater of Rochester (1961–66), the San Francisco Cons. Orch. (1966–67), and the San Francisco Little Sym. Orch. (1967–68); then was associate conductor of the Dallas Sym. Orch. (1968–70) and resident conductor of the Detroit Sym. Orch. (1970–79); also served as principal guest conductor of the Helsinki Phil. Orch. (1974–76). In 1979 he became music director of the Victoria (B.C.) Sym. Orch.; from 1987 was also music director of the Chicago Sinfonietta. In his concert programs he made it a point to include works by black composers.

Freeman, Robert (Schofield), American oboist, pianist, musicologist, and educator; b. Rochester, N.Y., Aug. 26, 1935. He began his musical studies at the Curtis Inst. in Philadelphia; then studied oboe with Fernand Gillet; piano with Gregory Tucker, Artur Balsam, and Rudolf Serkin; and conducting with Lukas Foss and Leonard Bernstein; he subsequently took courses at Harvard College (1953–57), at Princeton Univ. (1958–60), and at the Univ. of Vienna on a Fulbright grant (1960–62); he received his Ph.D. at Princeton in 1967 with the dissertation *Opera without Drama: Currents of Change in Italian Opera, 1675–1725* (Ann Arbor, 1981). He taught at Princeton (1963–68) and at the Mass. Inst. of Technology (1968–72). In 1972 he was named director of the Eastman School of Music and prof. of musicology.

Freer, Eleanor (née **Everest**), American composer; b. Philadelphia, May 14, 1864; d. Chicago, Dec. 13, 1942. She studied singing in Paris (1883–86) with Mathilde Marchesi; then took a course in composition with Benjamin Godard. Upon her return to the U.S., she taught singing at the National Cons. of Music in N.Y. (1889–91). On April 25, 1891, she married Archibald Freer of Chicago; they lived in Leipzig from 1892 to 1899; then settled in Chicago, where she studied theory with Bernhard Ziehn (1902–7). She publ. some light pieces under the name Everest while still a young girl, but most of her larger works were written after 1919. She also wrote an autobiography, *Recollections and Reflections of an American Composer* (Chicago, 1929).

Works: 9 operas, of which the following were performed: *The Legend of the Piper* (South Bend, Ind., Feb. 28, 1924); *The Court Jester* (Lincoln, Nebr., 1926); *A Christmas Tale* (Houston, Dec. 27, 1929); *Frithiof* (Chicago, Feb. 1, 1931; in concert form); *A Legend of Spain* (Milwaukee, June 19, 1931; in concert form); a song cycle (settings of Elizabeth Barrett Browning's entire *Sonnets from the Portuguese*); about 150 songs; piano pieces.

Bibl.: A. Foster, *E. F. and Her Colleagues* (Chicago, 1927).

Freire (actually, **Pinto Freire**), **Nelson (José),** Brazilian pianist; b. Boa Esperanza, Oct. 18, 1944. After studies in his native country, he went to Vienna to pursue his musical education. He made his concert debut at the age of 15 in 1959. After 1964 he appeared widely in Europe, the U.S., and Japan. He is known for the bravura he brings to the interpretation of the Romantic school of composition.

Freitas (Branco), Frederico (Guedes) de, Portuguese conductor and composer; b. Lisbon, Nov. 15, 1902; d. there, Jan. 12, 1980. He studied piano with Aroldo Silva, composition with A.E. da Costa Ferreira, musicology with Luís de Freitas Branco, and violin at the National Cons. in Lisbon (1919–24); won the National Composition prize (1926). He conducted the Lisbon Emissora National Orch. (from 1934), the Lisbon Choral Soc. (1940–47), the Oporto Sym. Orch. (1949–53), and the Orquesta de Concierto (from 1955). In his Violin Sonata (1923) he made the 1st known use of linear polyphony by a Portuguese composer.

Works: operas: *O eremita* (1952); *A igreja do mar,* radio opera (1957; Lisbon, Feb. 5, 1960); *Don João e a máscara,* radio opera (1960). **ballets:** *Muro do derrete* (1940); *A dança da Menina Tonta* (1941); *Imagens da terra e do mar* (1943). **orch.:** *Nazaré* (1948); *A lenda dos bailarins,* symphonic poem (1926); *Quarteto concertante* for 2 Violins, 2 Cellos, and String Orch. (1945); Flute Concerto (1954); *Suite Medieval* (1958);

Os Jerónimos, sym. (1962); *Missa solene* for 4 Soloists, Chorus, and Orch. (1940); *As sete palavras de Nossa Senhora,* cantata (1946). **chamber:** *Nocturno* for Cello and Piano (1926); Violin Sonata (1946); String Quartet (1946); Wind Quintet (1950); *3 Peças sem importância* for Violin and Piano (1959). **piano:** *Dança* (1923); *Ingenuidades* (1924); Sonata (1944); *Ciranda* (1944); *6 Pieces* (1946); *Bagatelles* (1953); *Variations* (1954); Organ Sonata (1963); songs.

Freitas Branco, Luís de, significant Portuguese composer; b. Lisbon, Oct. 12, 1890; d. there, Nov. 27, 1955. He studied with Tomás Borba, Désiré Pâque, Augusto Machado, and Luigi Mancinelli; then in Berlin with Humperdinck, and later in Paris with Gabriel Grovlez. He was active as a teacher in Lisbon from 1916, serving on the faculty of the National Cons.; he also was involved in musicological undertakings and wrote music criticism. His early compositions, cast in an Impressionistic vein, eventually gave way to neo-Classicism.

Works: 5 syms. (1924, 1926, 1943, 1949, 1952); *Manfredo,* dramatic sym. after Byron for Soloists, Chorus, Organ, and Orch. (1905); symphonic poems: *Antero do Quental* (1908); *Os paraisos artificiais* (1910); *Vathek,* after W. Beckford (1913); *Viriato* (1916); *Solemnia verba* (1952); Violin Concerto (1916); *Balada* for Piano and Orch. (1917); *Cena lírica* for Cello and Orch. (1917); *Suite alentejana* for Orch., No. 1 (1919) and No. 2 (1927); *Variaçoes e fuga tríplice sobre um tema original* for Organ and Strings (1947); *Homenagem a Chopin (Polaca sobre um tema de Chopin)* for Orch. (1949); 2 sonatas for Violin and Piano (1907, 1928); String Quartet (1911); Sonata for Cello and Piano (1913); sacred choral works; piano pieces; organ music; songs.

Frémaux, Louis, French conductor; b. Aire-sur-la-Lys, Aug. 13, 1921. He attended the Cons. in Valenciennes, but his education was interrupted by World War II. He served in the Résistance during the Nazi occupation. After the war he studied conducting at the Paris Cons. with Louis Fourestier, graduating in 1952 with the 1st prize. From 1956 to 1966 he was chief conductor of the Orch. National de Monte Carlo, and then music director of the Orch. Philharmonique Rhône-Alpes in Lyons (1968–71). From 1969 to 1978 he was music director of the City of Birmingham Sym. Orch. From 1979 to 1981 he was chief conductor of the Sydney (Australia) Sym. Orch.

Fremstad, Olive, famous Swedish-born American soprano; b. Stockholm, March 14, 1871 (entered into the parish register as the daughter of an unmarried woman, Anna Peterson); d. Irvington-on-Hudson, N.Y., April 21, 1951. She was adopted by an American couple of Scandinavian origin, who took her to Minnesota; she studied piano in Minneapolis; went to N.Y. in 1890 and took singing lessons with E.F. Bristol; then held several church positions; in 1892 she sang for the 1st time with an orch. (under C. Zerrahn), in Boston. In 1893 she went to Berlin to study with Lilli Lehmann; made her operatic debut in Cologne as Azucena in *Il Trovatore* (1895); sang contralto parts in Wagner's operas at Bayreuth during the summer of 1896; in 1897 made her London debut; also sang in Cologne, Vienna, Amsterdam, and Antwerp. From 1900 to 1903 she was at the Munich Court Opera. She made her American debut as Sieglinde at the Metropolitan Opera in N.Y. on Nov. 25, 1903. Subsequently she sang soprano parts in Wagnerian operas; at first she was criticized in the press for her lack of true soprano tones; however, she soon triumphed over these difficulties, and became known as a soprano singer to the exclusion of contralto parts. She sang Carmen with great success at the Metropolitan (March 5, 1906), with Caruso; her performance of Isolde under Mahler (Jan. 1, 1908) produced a deep impression; until 1914 she was one of the brightest stars of the Metropolitan Opera, specializing in Wagnerian roles, but she was also successful in *Tosca* and other Italian operas. She sang Salomé at the 1st American performance of the Strauss opera (N.Y., Jan. 22, 1907) and in Paris (May 8, 1907). After her retirement from the Metropolitan, she appeared with the Manhattan Opera, the Boston Opera, and the Chicago Opera, and in concerts; presented her last song recital in N.Y.

on Jan. 19, 1920. In 1906 she married Edson Sutphen of N.Y. (divorced in 1911); in 1916 she married her accompanist, Harry Lewis Brainard (divorced in 1925). In Willa Cather's novel *The Song of the Lark*, the principal character was modeled after Fremstad.

French, Jacob, American composer of Psalm tunes; b. Stoughton, Mass., July 15, 1754; d. Simsbury, Conn., May 1817. He was co-founder, with William Billings, of the Stoughton Music Soc. in 1774; fought at the battle of Bunker Hill in the Revolutionary War; was one of the few survivors of the Cherry Valley Massacre. After the war he became a singing teacher, retiring in 1814. He publ. *New American Melody* (1789), *Psalmodist's Companion* (1793), and *Harmony of Harmony* (1802).
Bibl.: M. Genuchi, *The Life and Music of J. F. (1754–1817), Colonial American Composer* (diss., Univ. of Iowa, 1964).

Freni (real name, **Fregni**), **Mirella,** noted Italian soprano; b. Modena, Feb. 27, 1935. Curiously enough, her mother and the mother of the future celebrated tenor Luciano Pavarotti worked for a living in the same cigarette factory; curiouser still, the future opera stars shared the same wet nurse. Freni studied voice with her uncle, Dante Arcelli; made her 1st public appearance at the age of 11; her accompanist was a child pianist named Leone Magiera, whom she married in 1955. She later studied voice with Ettore Campogalliani; made her operatic debut in Modena on Feb. 3, 1955, as Micaela in *Carmen*; then sang in provincial Italian opera houses. In 1959 she sang with the Amsterdam Opera Co. at the Holland Festival; then at the Glyndebourne Festival (1960), Covent Garden in London (1961), and La Scala in Milan (1962). She gained acclaim as Mimi in the film version of *La Bohème*, produced at La Scala on Jan. 31, 1963, with Herbert von Karajan conducting; when La Scala toured Russia in 1964, Freni joined the company and sang Mimi at the Bolshoi Theater in Moscow. She also chose the role of Mimi for her American debut, with the Metropolitan Opera in N.Y. on Sept. 29, 1965. She subsequently sang with the Vienna State Opera, the Bavarian State Opera in Munich, the Teatro San Carlo in Naples, and the Rome Opera. In 1976 she traveled with the Paris Opéra during its 1st American tour. In addition to Mimi, she sang the roles of Susanna in *Le nozze di Figaro*, Zerlina in *Don Giovanni*, Violetta in *La Traviata*, Amelia in *Simon Boccanegra*, and Manon. She won acclaim for her vivid portrayal of Tatiana in *Eugene Onegin*; sang this role with many major opera companies, including the Metropolitan Opera in 1989. In 1990 she appeared as Lisa in *Pique Dame* at La Scala. She married **Nicolai Ghiaurov** in 1981, and subsequently appeared frequently with him in opera performances around the world.

Freschi, (Giovanni) Domenico, Italian composer; b. Bassano del Grappa, c.1625; d. Vicenza, July 2, 1710. He was a singer and priest at the Cathedral of Vicenza; publ. 2 masses and a number of Psalms (1660, 1673). In 1677 he went to Venice, remaining there for 8 years; wrote 15 operas, which were successfully produced there, and a series of short pieces for an opera house in Piazzola, near Padua. He also wrote at least 3 oratorios, including *Giuditta* and *Il Miracolo del mago*.

Frescobaldi, Girolamo, great Italian organist and composer; b. Ferrara (baptized), Sept. 9, 1583; d. Rome, March 1, 1643. He studied with Luzzasco Luzzaschi in Ferrara; by the age of 14 was organist at the Accademia della Morte in Ferrara; in early 1607 became organist of S. Maria in Trastevere; then, in June 1607, traveled to Brussels in the retinue of the Papal Nuncio; publ. his 1st work, a collection of 5-part madrigals, in Antwerp in 1608, printed by Phalèse. Returning to Rome in the same year, he was appointed organist at St. Peter's as successor to Ercole Pasquini. He retained this all-important post until his death, with the exception of the years 1628 to 1634, when he was court organist in Florence. A significant indication of Frescobaldi's importance among musicians of his time was that Froberger, who was court organist in Vienna, came to Rome especially to study with him (1637–41). Fresco-

baldi's place in music history is very great; particularly as a keyboard composer, he exercised a decisive influence on the style of the early Baroque; he enlarged the expressive resources of keyboard music so as to include daring chromatic progressions and acrid passing dissonances, "durezze" (literally, "harshnesses"); in Frescobaldi's terminology "toccata di durezza" signified a work using dissonances; he used similar procedures in organ variations on chorale themes, "fiori musicali" ("musical flowers"). His ingenious employment of variations greatly influenced the entire development of Baroque music.
Works: *Fantasie a 2, 3 e 4* (Milan, 1608, Book I); *Ricercari et canzoni francese* (Rome, 1615); *Toccate e partite d'intavolatura di cembalo* (Rome, 1615); *Il 2° libro di toccate, canzoni, versi d'inni, magnificat, gagliarde, correnti ed altre partite d'intavolatura di cembalo ed organo* (Rome, 1616); *Capricci sopra diversi soggetti* (Rome, 1624); *Arie musicale a più voci* (Florence, 1630); *Fiori musicali di diverse compositioni Toccate, Kirie, Canzoni, Capricci e Recercari in partitura* (Venice, 1635); *Canzoni alla francese* was publ. posth. in Venice, 1645. A complete ed. of organ and other keyboard works by Frescobaldi was issued in 5 vols., edited by P. Pidoux in Kassel (1950–54); *Keyboard Compositions Preserved in Manuscripts*, No. 30 of Corpus of Early Keyboard Music (3 vols., 1968); selected organ works, in 2 vols., were publ. in Leipzig from 1943 to 1948; *Fiori musicale & Toccate e Partite* in 2 vols. was publ. in Rome in 1936–37; *Fiori musicale* was also brought out by J. Bonnet and A. Guilmant (Paris, 1922); *25 Canzoni, 7 Toccate & Correnti* was edited by F. Boghen (Milan, 1918); *Toccate, Ricercari, Canzoni*, etc. was issued by Casella in *I classici della musica italiana* (Milan, 1919); numerous other eds. of selected pieces are also available. A "complete works" ed. was publ. (1975–77) under the auspices of the Comune di Ferrara and the Società Italiana di Musicologia.
Bibl.: N. Bennati, ed., *Ferrara a G. F.* (Ferrara, 1908); L. Ronga, *G. F.* (Turin, 1930); W. Apel, "Neapolitan Links between Cabezón and F.," *Musical Quarterly* (Oct. 1938); A. Machabey, *G. F.: La Vie, l'œuvre* (Paris, 1952); R. Jackson, "On F.'s Chromaticism and Its Background," *Musical Quarterly* (April 1971); F. Hammond, *G. F.* (Cambridge, Mass., 1983); J. Harper, "F.: New Perspectives after 400 Years," *Musical Times* (Oct. 1983); C. Gallico, *G. F.: L'affetto, l'ordito, le metamorfosi* (Florence, 1986); A. Silbiger, ed., *F. Studies* (Durham, N.C., 1987); F. Hammond, *G. F.: A Guide to Research* (N.Y., 1988).

Frešo, Tibor, Slovak conductor and composer; b. Spišský, Nov. 20, 1918. He studied composition with A. Moyzes and conducting with J. Vincourek at the Bratislava Cons., graduating in 1938; then studied with Pizzetti at the Accademia di Santa Cecilia in Rome (1939–42). Returning to Czechoslovakia, he served as conductor of the Slovak National Theater in Bratislava (1942–49) and the Košice Opera (1949–52); in 1953 he was appointed chief opera conductor of the Slovak National Opera.
Works: Children's opera, *Martin and the Sun* (Bratislava, Jan. 25, 1975); *Poor François*, opera (1982–84); 3 cantatas: *Stabat Mater* (1940); *Mother* (1959); *Hymn to the Fatherland* (1961); *Little Suite* for Orch. (1938); *Concert Overture* (1940); *Symphonic Prolog* (1943); symphonic poems: *A New Morning* (1950) and *Liberation* (1955); *Little Concerto* for Piano and Orch. (1976); *Meditation* for Soprano and Orch. (1942); *Song about Woman* for Alto, Narrator, Children's and Mixed Choruses, and Orch. (1975); Wind Quintet (1983).

Freudenberg, Wilhelm, German composer and conductor; b. Raubacher Hütte, near Neuwied, March 11, 1838; d. Schweidnitz, May 22, 1928. He studied at the Leipzig Cons. with Moscheles and others; in 1870 he went to Wiesbaden, where he was active as a choral conductor; in 1886 he settled in Berlin, where he was a theater conductor and teacher. He wrote several light operas: *Die Pfahlbauer* (Mainz, 1877); *Die Mühle im Wispertale* (Magdeburg, 1883); *Das Jahrmarktsfest* *zu Plundersweilen* (Bremen, 1908); etc.; also choruses, songs, and chamber music.

Freund, John Christian, English-American music journalist; b. London, Nov. 22, 1848; d. Mt. Vernon, N.Y., June 3, 1924. He studied music in London and Oxford; in 1871 went to N.Y., where he became ed. of the *Musical and Dramatic Times;* in 1890 began publishing a commercial magazine, *Music Trades.* In 1898 he founded the weekly magazine *Musical America* and was its ed. until his death. In his editorials he fulminated against the rival magazine *Musical Courier,* and also wrote sharp polemical articles denouncing composers and music critics who disagreed with his viewpoint; in this respect he was a typical representative of the personal type of musical journalism of the time.

Freund, Marya, remarkable German soprano; b. Breslau, Dec. 12, 1876; d. Paris, May 21, 1966. She first studied violin, taking lessons with Sarasate; then began to study singing; made successful appearances in Europe and America with sym. orchs. and in recital. Her career as a singer was mainly significant for her devotion to modern music. She sang the principal vocal works by Schoenberg, Stravinsky, Ravel, Bloch, Milhaud, and many others; eventually settled in Paris as a singing teacher.

Freundt, Cornelius, German organist and composer; b. Plauen, c.1535; d. Zwickau (buried), Aug. 26, 1591. He was a cantor at Borna; in 1565, became cantor of St. Marien and a teacher and organist at Zwickau, where he remained until his death. His compositions were designed for use in church and school; most of his sacred works remain in MS. G. Göhler wrote a dissertation on him (Leipzig, 1896).

Frey, Emil, eminent Swiss pianist and composer, brother of **Walter Frey;** b. Baden, April 8, 1889; d. Zürich, May 20, 1946. He studied musical subjects with Otto Barblan at the Geneva Cons.; at the age of 15 was accepted as a student of Louis Diémer in piano and Widor in composition; in 1907 went to Berlin, and later to Bucharest, where he became a court pianist. In 1910 he won the Anton Rubinstein prize for his Piano Trio in St. Petersburg; on the strength of this success he was engaged to teach at the Moscow Cons. (1912–17). Returning to Switzerland after the Russian Revolution, he joined the faculty of the Zürich Cons.; he continued his concert career throughout Europe and also in South America. He wrote 2 syms. (the 1st with a choral finale), Piano Concerto, Violin Concerto, Cello Concerto, *Swiss Festival Overture,* Piano Quintet, String Quartet, Piano Trio, Violin Sonata, Cello Sonata, several piano sonatas, piano suites, and sets of piano variations; publ. a piano instruction manual, *Bewusst gewordenes Klavierspiel und seine technischen Grundlagen* (Zürich, 1933).

Frey, Walter, Swiss pianist, brother of **Emil Frey;** b. Basel, Jan. 26, 1898; d. Zürich, May 28, 1985. He studied piano with F. Niggli and theory with Andreae. From 1925 to 1958 he was an instructor in piano at the Zürich Cons.; concurrently evolved an active concert career in Germany and Scandinavia; specialized in modern piano music and gave 1st performances of several piano concertos by contemporary composers. He publ. (with W. Schuh) a collection, *Schweizerische Klaviermusik aus der Zeit der Klassik und Romantik* (Zürich, 1937).

Fribec, Krešimir, Croatian composer; b. Daruvar, May 24, 1908. He studied with Zlatko Grgošević in Zagreb; later was active as music ed. of the Zagreb Radio (1943–64); also served as director of the Croatian Music Soc. Most of his large output was composed in an accessible style. **WORKS: OPERAS:** *Sluga Jernej* (1951); *Krvava svadba* (Blood Wedding; 1958); *Prometej* (1960); *Jerma* (1960); *Maljiva* (1962); *Cehovljev humoristicon* (1962); *Nova Eva* (1963); *Juduška Golovljiev* (1964); *Adagio melancolico* (1965); *Dolazi revisor* (The Government Inspector; 1965); *Dunja u kovčegu* (1966); *Veliki val* (The Large Wave; 1966); *Heretik* (1971); *Ujak Vanja* (Uncle Vanya; 1972); many ballets; cantatas. **ORCH.:** *Ritmi drammatici* for Chamber Orch. (1960); *Accenti tragici* (1961); *Kosmička kretanja* (Cosmic Movements; 1961); Piano Concerto (1964); *Canto* for Strings (1965); *Ekstaza,* symphonic

suite (1965); *Simfonija* (1965); *Lamento* for Strings (1967); *Koncertantna muzika* for Violin and Orch. (1970); Cello Concerto (1971); *Covjek,* sym. (1972). **CHAMBER:** 7 string quartets (1962–72); *Musica aleatorica* for Flute, Cello, Vibraphone, and Piano (1961); Sonata for Cello (1966); Sonata for Viola and Piano (1967); *Divertimento* for Viola and Percussion (1970); *Alterations,* piano trio (1971).

Fricci (real name, **Frietsche**), **Antonietta,** Austrian soprano; b. Vienna, Jan. 8, 1840; d. Turin, Sept. 7, 1912. She studied with Marchesi in Vienna; made her debut in 1858 in Pisa as Violetta; was a principal singer at La Scala in Milan (1865–73); retired in 1878; then taught voice in Florence and Turin.

Frick, Gottlob, German bass; b. Olbronn, Württemberg, July 28, 1906. He studied at the Stuttgart Cons.; took vocal lessons with Neudörfer-Opitz; after singing in the Stuttgart Opera chorus, he made his operatic debut as Daland in *Der fliegende Holländer* in Colburg (1934); then sang in Freiburg and Königsberg, and subsequently was a leading member of the Dresden State Opera (1941–52). He appeared at the Städtische Oper in West Berlin (from 1950), the Bavarian State Opera in Munich (from 1953), and the Vienna State Opera (from 1953); made his debut at London's Covent Garden (1951), and later sang there regularly (1957–67). On Dec. 27, 1961, he made his Metropolitan Opera debut in N.Y. as Fafner in *Das Rheingold;* also sang at Bayreuth, Milan's La Scala, and Salzburg. He gave his farewell performance in 1970, but continued to make a few stage appearances in later years. A fine Wagnerian, he excelled as Gurnemanz and Hagen; was also admired for his portrayal of Rocco in *Fidelio.*

Fricker, Herbert (Austin), English organist and composer; b. Canterbury, Feb. 12, 1868; d. Toronto, Nov. 11, 1943. He studied organ with W.H. Longhurst, and composition with Sir Frederick Bridge and Edwin Lemare. After filling posts as organist in Canterbury, Folkstone, and Leeds, he moved to Toronto in 1917, and conducted the Mendelssohn Choir there until 1942. He composed sacred and secular choruses and organ pieces.

Fricker, Peter Racine, significant English composer and pedagogue; b. London, Sept. 5, 1920; d. Santa Barbara, Calif., Feb. 1, 1990. He studied with R.O. Morris at the Royal College of Music in London and later with Mátyás Seiber. In 1952 he was appointed music director at Morley College in London; taught composition at the Royal College of Music from 1955. In 1964 he went to Santa Barbara, Calif., as a visiting prof. at the Univ. of Calif.; was full prof. from 1965; from 1970 to 1974 was chairman of the music dept. there. In his compositions, he utilized various techniques as the need arose; his output reveals a fascination for the development of small cells, either melodically, harmonically, or rhythmically.

WORKS: *Rondo scherzoso* for Orch. (1948); Sym. No. 1 (1949; Cheltenham Festival, July 5, 1950; awarded the Koussevitzky prize); Sym. No. 2 (Liverpool, July 26, 1951); *Canterbury Prologue,* ballet (1951); Concerto for Viola and Orch. (Edinburgh, Sept. 3, 1953); Piano Concerto (London, March 21, 1954); *Rapsodia concertante* for Violin and Orch. (Cheltenham Festival, July 15, 1954); *Litany* for Double String Orch. (1955); *Concertante* for 3 Pianos, Strings, and Timpani (London, Aug. 10, 1956); *The Death of Vivien,* radio opera (1956); *A Vision of Judgment,* oratorio (Leeds, Oct. 13, 1958); *Comedy Overture* (1958); *Toccata* for Piano and Orch. (1959); Sym. No. 3 (London, Nov. 8, 1960); *O longs désirs,* song cycle for Soprano and Orch. (1964); Sym. No. 4, "in memoriam Mátyás Seiber" (Cheltenham, Feb. 14, 1967); *3 Scenes* for Orch. (Santa Barbara, Feb. 26, 1967); *7 Counterpoints* for Orch. (Pasadena, Oct. 21, 1967); *Magnificat* for Soloists, Chorus, and Orch. (Santa Barbara, May 27, 1968); *The Roofs* for Coloratura Soprano and Percussion (1970); *Nocturne* for Chamber Orch. (1971); *Introitus* for Orch. (Canterbury, June 24, 1972); Sym. No. 5 (1975); *Rondeaux* for Horn and Orch. (1982); *Whispers at These Curtains,* oratorio (1984); *Concerto for Orchestra* (1986); *Walk by Quiet Waters* for Orch. (1989). Chamber:

Wind Quintet (1947); *3 Sonnets of Cecco Angiolieri* for Tenor, Wind Quintet, Cello, and Double Bass (1947); String Quartet in 1 Movement (1948); *Prelude, Elegy and Finale* for Strings (1949); Concerto for Violin and Chamber Orch. (1950); Violin Sonata (1950); *Concertante* for English Horn and Strings (1950); String Quartet No. 2 (1953); Horn Sonata (1955); Suite for Recorders (1956); Cello Sonata (1957); Octet for Wind and String Instruments (1958); *Serenade No. 1* for 6 Instruments (1959); *Serenade No. 2* for Flute, Oboe, and Piano (1959); *4 Dialogues* for Oboe and Piano (1965); *5 Canons* for 2 Flutes and 2 Oboes (1966); Fantasy for Viola and Piano (1966); *Concertante No. 4* for Flute, Oboe, Violin, and Strings (1969); *Some Superior Nonsense* for Tenor, Flute, Oboe, and Harpsichord (1969); *Serenade No. 3* for Saxophone Quartet (1969); *3 Arguments* for Bassoon and Cello (1969); Suite for Harpsichord (1957); *14 Aubades* for Piano (1958); 12 studies for Piano (1961); *Commissary Report* for Men's Voices (1965); *Refrains* for Solo Oboe (1968); *Paseo* for Guitar (1969); *Concertante No. 5* for Piano and String Quartet (1972); *Come Sleep* for Contralto, Alto, and Bass Clarinet (1972); *The Groves of Dodona* for 6 Flutes (1973); *Spirit Puck* for Clarinet and Percussion (1974); *Trio-Sonata* for Organ (1974); String Quartet No. 3 (1975); Sonata for 2 Pianos (1978); *Aspects of Evening* for Cello and Piano (1985); Violin Sonata No. 2 (1988).

Fricsay, Ferenc, distinguished Hungarian conductor; b. Budapest, Aug. 9, 1914; d. Basel, Feb. 20, 1963. He received his early musical training from his father, a military-band leader; he was barely 6 years old when he was accepted as a pupil in the music class for beginners at the Budapest high school; as he grew up he took piano lessons with Bartók and composition with Kodály. He also learned to play almost all orch. instruments. At the age of 15 he conducted a radio performance of his father's military band; in 1933 he became orch. conductor at Szeged, and in 1936 of the opera there. In 1947 he conducted at the Salzburg Festival; subsequently made a European tour as guest conductor; also toured South America. From 1948 to 1952 he was Generalmusikdirektor of the Berlin City Opera; from 1949 to 1954, was artistic director of the radio orch. RIAS in the American sector of divided Berlin, and was regular conductor there until 1961. On Nov. 13, 1953, he made a highly successful American debut with the Boston Sym. Orch.; in 1954, was engaged as conductor of the Houston Sym. Orch., but soon resigned, owing to disagreement on musical policy with the management. He was Generalmusikdirektor of the Bavarian State Opera in Munich from 1956 to 1958. He then settled in Switzerland, continuing to conduct occasional guest engagements, until illness (leukemia) forced him to abandon all activities. **BIBL.:** F. Herzfeld, *F. F. Ein Gedenkbuch* (Berlin, 1964).

Frid, Géza, Hungarian-born Dutch composer and pianist; b. Máramarossziget, Jan. 25, 1904; d. Beverwijk, Sept. 13, 1989. He studied composition with Kodály and piano with Bartók at the Budapest Cons. (1912–24); settled in Amsterdam in 1929, becoming a Dutch citizen in 1948. In 1964 he joined the faculty of the Utrecht Cons.; remained there until 1969. **WORKS:** Opera, *De zwarte bruid* (1959); 2 ballets: *Luctor et Emergo* (1953) and *Euridice* (1961); *Podium-Suite* for Violin and Orch. (1928); Suite for Orch. (1929); Violin Concerto (1930); *Tempesta d'orchestra* (1931); Divertimento for String Orch. or String Quintet (1932); Sym. (1933); *Romance and Allegro* for Cello and Orch. (1935); *Abel et Cain,* symphonic tableau for Low Voice and Orch. (1938); *Schopenhauer Cantata* (1944); Nocturnes for Flute, Harp, and String Orch. or String Quintet (1946); *Paradou,* symphonic fantasy (1948); *Variations on a Dutch Folk Song* for Wind Orch., or Chorus and Orch. (1950); *Fête champêtre,* suite of dances for String Orch. and Percussion (1951); *Hymne aan de Arbeid* (Hymn to Labor) for Male Chorus and Orch. (1951); 2-violin Concerto (1952); *Caecilia Ouverture* (1953); *Études symphoniques* (1954); *South African Rhapsody* for Orch. or Wind Orch. (1954); *3 Romances* for Soprano and Orch. (1955); *Das Sklavenschiff* for Tenor and Baritone, Male Chorus, Brass, Percussion, and Piano

(1956); Serenade for Chamber Orch. (1956); 2-piano Concerto (1957); *Rhythmic Studies* for Chamber Orch. or 2 Pianos (1959); Concertino for Violin, Cello, Piano, and Orch. (1961); *Sinfonietta* for String Orch. (1963); *7 pauken en een koperorkest,* concerto for 7 Percussionists and Brass Orch. (1964; Amsterdam, May 14, 1965); *Ballade* for Chorus and Wind Orch. (1965; version for Chorus, String Orch., Percussion, and Piano, 4-hands, 1968); *4 Sketches* for Wind Orch. (1966); 3-violin Concerto (The Hague, July 4, 1970); Concerto for 4 different Clarinets (1 Soloist) and String Orch. (1972); Toccata for Orch. or 2 Pianos (1973); 5 string quartets (1926, 1939, 1949, 1956, 1984); String Trio (1926); Serenade for Wind Instruments (1928); Cello Sonata (1931); Concerto for Piano and Mixed Chorus (1934); Solo Violin Sonata (1936); Viola Sonatina (1946); Piano Trio (1947); *20 Duos* for 2 Violins (1951); *Frühlingsfeier* for Soprano, Alto, Flute, Clarinet, Bassoon, Horn, Violin, Viola, Cello, and Piano (1952); Violin Sonata (1955); *12 Metamorphoses* for 2 Flutes and Percussion (1957); *Fuga* for 3 Harps (1961); Sextet for Wind Quintet and Piano (1965); *Dubbeltrio* for Wind Instruments (1967); *Chemins divers* for Flute, Bassoon, and Piano (1968; also arranged for 2 Violins and Piano); *Paganini Variations* for 2 Violins (1969); *Houdt den Tijd!* for Male Chorus and Percussion (1971); Duo for Violin and Piano (1972) *Caprices roumains* for Oboe and Piano (1975); *Sons roumains* for Flute, Viola, Harp, and Percussion (1975); Little Suite for Saxophone and Piano (1975); *Music* for 2 Violins and Viola (1977); *Vice Versa* for Alto Saxophone and Marimba (1982); Piano Sonata (1929); *4 Etudes* for Piano (1932); *Foxtrot* for 2 Pianos (1975); songs; choruses.

Friderici, Daniel, German composer and music theorist; b. Klein-Eichstedt, near Querfurt, 1584; d. Rostock, Sept. 23, 1638. He served as a choirboy; then studied music in Magdeburg; settled in Rostock, where he was cantor of St. Mary's Church from 1618 till his death. He died of pestilence. He publ. in Rostock a number of sacred and secular songs to German words, and a theoretical work, *Musica figuralis oder Newe Unterweisung des Singe Kunst* (1618; 6th ed., 1677). **BIBL.:** W. Voll, *D. F.: Sein Leben und Seine geistlichen Werke* (Kassel and Hannover, 1936).

Fried, Alexej, Czech composer; b. Brno, Oct. 13, 1922. He studied piano and composition at the Brno Cons., and then composition with Hlobil and Bořkovec at the Prague Academy of Music (graduated, 1953). He first gained notice as an arranger for various Czech jazz groups in 1947; also led his own orchs., lectured, and composed. Many of his works are in the "3rd-stream" manner, fusing jazz with Classical styles. **WORKS: ORCH.:** Triple Concerto for Flute, Clarinet, Horn, and Orch. (1971); Concerto (1974); Concerto No. 2 for Clarinet and Orch. (1976); Concerto for Horn and Orch. (1977); *Concerto di Freiberg* for Chamber Orch. (1977). **CHAMBER:** *Sonatina drammatica* for Violin and Piano (1975); *Moravian Trio* for Flute, Marimba, and Harp (1978); *Guernica,* quintet for Soprano Saxophone and String Quartet (1978); Quintet for Flute, Violin, Viola, Cello, and Piano (1979). **JAZZ WORKS FOR BIG BAND:** *Akt* (The Act) for Trumpet, Flute, and Big Band (1968); Jazz Concerto for Clarinet and Big Band (1970); *Souvenir* (1970); *Jazz Ballet Etudes* for Clarinet and Big Band (1970); *Sidonia* for Trumpet and Big Band (1971); *The Solstice,* concerto for 2 Big Bands (1973); Concertino for Clarinet and Big Band (1974); *Dialogue* for 2 Alto Saxophones and Big Band (1974); *Paraphrases to Motives of Blue Skies* for Soprano Saxophone and Big Band (1975); Concerto (1976); *Jazz Composition* for Trombone and Big Band (1977); *Polyphone* (1978); *Song* for Trumpet and Big Band (1979).

Fried, Miriam, Rumanian violinist; b. Satu Mare, Sept. 9, 1946. She went to Israel while very young; studied at the Rubin Academy of Music in Tel Aviv. She then settled in America, her teachers being Josef Gingold at Indiana Univ. and Ivan Galamian at the Juilliard School of Music in N.Y. She appeared with many orchs. in Europe and America; was also active as a recitalist.

Fried, Oskar, German conductor and composer; b. Berlin, Aug. 10, 1871; d. Moscow, July 5, 1941. He studied with Humperdinck in Frankfurt and P. Scharwenka in Berlin; played the horn in various orchs. until the performance of his choral work with orch. *Das trunkene Lied,* given by Muck in Berlin (April 15, 1904), attracted much favorable attention; he continued to compose prolifically; wrote *Verklärte Nacht* for Solo Voices and Orch.; *Andante und Scherzo* for Wind Instruments, 2 Harps, and Kettledrums; *Präludium und Doppelfuge* for String Orch.; etc. At the same time he began his career as a conductor, achieving considerable renown in Europe; he was conductor of the Stern Choral Soc. in Berlin (from 1904), of the Gesellschaft der Musikfreunde in Berlin (1907–10), and of the Berlin Sym. Orch. (1925–26); left Berlin in 1934 and went to Russia; became a Soviet citizen in 1940. For several years he was conductor of the Tbilisi Opera; later was chief conductor of the All-Union Radio Orch. in Moscow.

BIBL.: P. Bekker, *O. F.* (Berlin, 1907); P. Stefan, *O. F.* (Berlin, 1911); D. Rabinovitz, *O. F.* (Moscow, 1971).

Friedberg, Carl, German pianist; b. Bingen, Sept. 18, 1872; d. Merano, Italy, Sept. 8, 1955. He studied piano at the Frankfurt Cons. with Kwast, Knorr, and Clara Schumann; also took a course in composition with Humperdinck; subsequently taught piano at the Frankfurt Cons. (1893–1904) and at the Cologne Cons. (1904–14). In 1914 he made his 1st American tour, with excellent success; taught piano at the Inst. of Musical Art in N.Y.; was a member of the faculty of the Juilliard School of Music in N.Y. Among his pupils were Percy Grainger, Ethel Leginska, Elly Ney, and other celebrated pianists.

BIBL.: J. Smith, *Master Pianist: The Career and Teaching of C. F.* (N.Y., 1963).

Friedheim, Arthur, German pianist; b. St. Petersburg (of German parents), Oct. 26, 1859; d. N.Y., Oct. 19, 1932. He was a pupil of Anton Rubinstein and Liszt, and became particularly known as an interpreter of Liszt's works. He made his 1st American tour in 1891; taught at the Chicago Musical College in 1897; then traveled; lived in London, Munich, and (after 1915) N.Y. as a teacher and pianist; composed a Piano Concerto and many pieces for solo piano, as well as an opera, *Die Tänzerin* (Karlsruhe, 1897). His memoirs, *Life and Liszt: The Recollections of a Concert Pianist,* were publ. posth. (N.Y., 1961).

Friedhofer, Hugo (William), American composer of film music; b. San Francisco, May 3, 1901; d. Los Angeles, May 17, 1981. He played cello in theater orchs.; studied composition with Domenico Brescia. In 1929 he went to Hollywood, where he worked as an arranger and composer for early sound films. In 1935 he was engaged as an orchestrator for Warner Brothers, and received valuable instruction from Erich Wolfgang Korngold and Max Steiner. In Los Angeles he attended Schoenberg's seminars and took additional lessons in composition with Ernst Toch and Kanitz; he also had some instruction with Nadia Boulanger during her sojourn in California. He wrote his 1st complete film score for *The Adventures of Marco Polo* in 1938, and in the following years composed music for about 70 films. His film music for *The Best Years of Our Lives* won the Academy Award in 1946. His other film scores included *Vera Cruz, Violent Saturday, The Sun Also Rises,* and *The Young Lions.* Friedhofer was highly esteemed by the Hollywood theatrical community and by his colleagues in the film studios for his ability to create a congenial musical background, alternatively lyrical and dramatic, for the action on the screen, never sacrificing the purely musical quality for the sake of external effect. He was the only California native of all the famous film composers in Hollywood, the majority of whom were Germans and Austrians. When a Hollywood mogul told Friedhofer to use numerous French horns since the film in question was taking place in France, he acquiesced and, by extension of the dictum, used an English-horn solo to illustrate the approach to the cliffs of Dover of the film characters fleeing the French Revolution.

BIBL.: F. Sternfeld, "Music and the Feature Film," *Musical Quarterly* (Oct. 1947); L. Morton, "Film Music Profile:

H. F.," *Film Music Notes* (1950); I. Atkins, *H. F.* (Los Angeles, 1974).

Friedlaender, Max, eminent German musicologist; b. Brieg, Silesia, Oct. 12, 1852; d. Berlin, May 2, 1934. He was first a bass; studied voice with Manuel García in London and Julius Stockhausen in Frankfurt; appeared at the London Monday Popular Concerts in 1880. He returned to Germany in 1881 and took a course at Berlin Univ. with Spitta; obtained the degree of Ph.D. at Rostock with the dissertation *Beiträge zur Biographie Franz Schuberts* (1887; publ. in Berlin, 1887); then was Privatdozent at Berlin Univ. in 1894, and a prof. and director of music there from 1903. He was exchange prof. at Harvard Univ. in 1911; lectured at many American univs. and received the degree of LL.D. from the Univ. of Wisconsin; retired in 1932. He discovered the MSS of more than 100 lost songs by Schubert and publ. them in his complete ed. (7 vols.) of Schubert's songs. Together with Johann Bolte and Johann Meier, he searched for years in every corner of the German Empire in quest of folk songs still to be found among the people; some of these he publ. in a vol. under the title *100 deutsche Volkslieder* in *Goethe Jahrbuch* (1885); was ed. of *Volksliederbuch für gemischten Chor* (1912); edited songs of Mozart, Schumann, and Mendelssohn, Beethoven's "Scotch Songs," the 1st version of Brahms's *Deutsche Volkslieder* (1926), *Volksliederbuch für die deutsche Jugend* (1928), etc.

WRITINGS: *Das Deutsche Lied im 18. Jahrhundert* (2 vols., 1902); *Brahms Lieder* (1922; in Eng., London, 1928); *Franz Schubert, Skizze seines Lebens und Wirkens* (1928).

BIBL.: E. Dent, "M. F.," *Monthly Musical Record* (June 1934).

Friedman, Erick, distinguished American violinist and teacher; b. Newark, N.J., Aug. 16, 1939. He first studied violin with his father, an amateur violinist; at the age of 10 he enrolled at the Juilliard School of Music in N.Y., in the class of Ivan Galamian; at 17 he commenced studies with Jascha Heifetz; he also received guidance from Nathan Milstein. His progress was rapid, and he soon garnered prizes in several violin competitions; he then appeared as soloist with the Boston Sym., Chicago Sym., Pittsburgh Sym., N.Y. Phil., Philadelphia Orch., Berlin Phil., Orch. de Paris, and other orchs.; made many extensive concert tours, playing in Europe, the Far East, and South America. Friedman's performances are characterized by a careful regard for the composer's intentions and a technical skill that rank him among the finest violinists of his generation. He was Mischa Elman Prof. at the Manhattan School of Music in N.Y. from 1975.

Friedman, Ignaz, famous Polish pianist; b. Podgorze, near Krakow, Feb. 14, 1882; d. Sydney, Australia, Jan. 26, 1948. He studied music theory with Hugo Riemann in Leipzig and piano with Leschetizky in Vienna. In 1904 he launched an extensive career as a concert pianist; gave about 2,800 concerts in Europe, America, Australia, Japan, China, and South Africa. In 1941 he settled in Sydney. He was renowned as an interpreter of Chopin; prepared an annotated ed. of Chopin's works in 12 vols., publ. by Breitkopf & Härtel; also edited piano compositions of Schumann and Liszt for Universal Edition in Vienna. Friedman was himself a composer; he wrote a hundred or so pieces for piano in an effective salon manner, among them a group of *Fantasiestücke.*

Friedman, Ken, American avant-garde composer; b. New London, Conn., Sept. 19, 1939. He became associated with Richard Maxfield, who initiated him into the arcana of modern music. Friedman developed feverish activities in intellectual and musical fields; ed. ephemeral magazines; directed an underground radio program, "Garnisht Kigele," in Mt. Carroll, Ill.; was a founder of the avant-garde group Fluxus. As an avant-garde artist and designer, he exhibited his products in Brno, Nice, Cologne, Copenhagen, Trieste, and San Diego; staged happenings and audiovisual events in California, announcing himself as "The Truly Incredible Friedman." Most of his works are verbal exhortations to existentialist actions, e.g., *Scrub Piece* (scrubbing a statue in a public square), *Riverboat Brawl* (starting a brawl in a riverboat at Disneyland), *Goff Street* (a "theft event," transplanting a street sign), *Come Ze Revolution* (chanting pseudo-Greek songs), *Watermelon* (splitting a watermelon with a karate blow), etc. He also composed a *Quiet Sonata* (1969) for 75 Truncated Guitar Fingerboards with no strings attached; realized for Nam June Paik his alleged *Young Penis Symphony* for 10 ditto, and had it performed at a hidden retreat in San Francisco.

Friedman, Richard, American composer; b. N.Y., Jan. 6, 1944. He received his formal education in exact sciences, specializing in electronics. He worked at the Intermedia Electronic Music Studio at N.Y. Univ. (1966–68) in collaboration with Morton Subotnick; prepared electronic tape pieces, mostly of scientific inspiration: *Lumia Mix* (1967); *Crescent* (1967); and *To the Star Messenger* (1968), a melodrama depicting the discovery of the moons of Jupiter by Galileo. Another piece of the period was *Alchemical Manuscript* (1968), inspired by the arcane lore of the searchers for the philosopher's stone. In 1968 he moved to California; worked with the music dept. of the radio station KPFA in Berkeley; arranged numerous broadcasts of electronic materials, notably *Serenade* for Viola on Tape and *4-Pole Neuro-Magnet with Double Cross*, composed in 1970. Taking advantage of the techniques of amplification, he was able to create the sound of an orch. of violas with a single viola player. In most of his works he applies the avant-garde philosophy of tonal frugality, limiting his resources to a few notes. Apart from his radio work, he conducted information/media performances at the San Francisco Museum of Art under the general title "Outside/Inside," utilizing closed-circuit television, inflatable structures, and sculptures activated by light beams.

Friedrich, Götz, German opera producer and administrator; b. Naumburg, Aug. 4, 1930. He was educated in Weimar; in 1953 was appointed an assistant to Walter Felsenstein at the East Berlin Komische Oper; became a producer there in 1959 and chief producer from 1968 to 1972; was also active as a producer in West Germany. In 1976 he was named principal producer at Covent Garden, London. In 1981 he became Generalintendant of the Deutsche Oper in West Berlin. His productions reflected his adherence to Marxist doctrine. He publ. *Wagner-Regie* (ed. by S. Jaeger; Zürich, 1983) and *Musiktheater: Ansichten, Einsichten* (Frankfurt, 1986). He was married to the American soprano **Karan Armstrong.**

Friedrich, Karl, Austrian tenor; b. Vienna, Jan. 15, 1905; d. there, March 8, 1981. He received his musical education at the Academy of Music in Vienna; sang operatic engagements in Düsseldorf and Hamburg; in 1938, joined the roster of the Vienna State Opera, retiring in 1969.

Friedrich II (der Grosse). See Frederick II (Frederick the Great).

Friemann, Witold, Polish composer; b. Konin, near Kalisch, Aug. 20, 1889; d. Laski, near Warsaw, March 22, 1977. He studied at the Warsaw Cons. and later was a student of Max Reger in Leipzig. Returning to Poland, he dedicated himself to teaching. An exceptionally industrious composer, he wrote nearly 1,000 works, including 4 operas, 3 syms., 24 concertos (among them 5 for Piano, 3 for Trombone, 2 for Viola, 2 for Clarinet, and 1 each for Cello, Violin, Double Bass, 2 Pianos, Flute, Bassoon, Horn, and Trumpet), and 80 instrumental sonatas. During his last years he taught at a school for the blind in Laski.

Fries, Wulf (Christian Julius), German-American cellist and teacher; b. Garbeck, Jan. 10, 1825; d. Roxbury, Mass., April 29, 1902. As a cellist, he played in Norway, in the Bergen theater orch. (from 1842), and at Ole Bull's concerts. In 1847 he went to Boston, where he became a founding member of the Mendelssohn Quintette Club, with A. Fries (1st violin), Gerloff (2nd violin), Edward Lehmann (1st viola), Oscar

Greiner (2nd viola), and himself as cellist. He belonged to it for 23 years; also figured in the Musical Fund Soc. and the Harvard Musical Assoc.; played in trios with Anton Rubinstein, and until 1901 took part in concerts in New England. He held teaching appointments at the New England Cons. of Music (1869), Carlyle Petersilea's Music School (1871), and the Boston Cons. of Music (1889).

Frijsh, Povla (real name, **Paula Frisch**), Danish-American soprano; b. Århus, Aug. 3, 1881; d. Blue Hill, Maine, July 10, 1960. She first studied piano and theory in Copenhagen with O. Christensen, later voice in Paris with Jean Périer; made her debut in Paris at the age of 19; appeared in concert and recital in Paris and briefly in opera in Copenhagen; made her American debut in 1915; gave many 1st performances of modern vocal music (Bloch's *Poèmes d'automne*, Loeffler's *Canticle of the Sun*, songs by Griffes, etc.), and made a specialty of the modern international song literature. She introduced Negro spirituals to Paris and Copenhagen.

Friml (actually, **Frimel**), **(Charles) Rudolf,** famous Bohemian-American operetta composer; b. Prague, Dec. 2, 1879; d. Los Angeles, Nov. 12, 1972. He was a pupil at the Prague Cons. of Juranek (piano) and Foerster (theory and composition); toured Austria, England, Germany, and Russia as accompanist to Kubelik, the violinist, going with him to the U.S. in 1900 and again in 1906; remained in the U.S. after the 2nd tour; gave numerous recitals, appeared as soloist with several orchs. (played his Piano Concerto with the N.Y. Sym. Orch.), and composed assiduously; lived in N.Y. and Hollywood, composing for motion pictures.

WORKS: Operettas: *The Firefly* (Syracuse, Oct. 14, 1912); *High Jinks* (Syracuse, Nov. 3, 1913); *Katinka* (Morristown, N.Y., Dec. 2, 1915); *You're in Love*, musical comedy (Stamford, Conn., 1916); *Glorianna* (1918); *Tumble In* (1919); *Sometime* (1919); *Rose Marie* (N.Y., Sept. 2, 1924; very popular); *Vagabond King* (N.Y., Sept. 21, 1925; highly successful); also wrote a great number of piano pieces in a light vein. In 1937 M-G-M made a film of *The Firefly*, the popular *Donkey Serenade* being added to the original score.

Frimmel, Theodor von, Austrian writer on music; b. Amstetten, Dec. 15, 1853; d. Vienna, Dec. 25, 1928. He first studied medicine in Vienna; then became interested in art and maintained an art gallery; taught the history of art at the Athenäum in Vienna and served as assistant curator of the Hofmuseum (1884–93). In music his main research concentrated on Beethoven.

WRITINGS: *Beethoven und Goethe: Eine Studie* (Vienna, 1883); *Neue Beethoveniana* (Vienna, 1888; 2nd ed., 1890); *Beethovens Wohnungen in Wien* (Vienna, 1894); "Beethoven," in *Berühmte Musiker* (Berlin, 1901; 6th ed., 1922); *Beethoven Studien* (vol. I, *Beethovens äussere Erscheinung*, and vol. II, *Bausteine zu einer Lebensgeschichte des Meisters*; Munich and Leipzig, 1905–6); *Beethoven-Forschung, Lose Blätter* (10 issues, Vienna and Mödling, 1911–25); *Beethoven im zeitgenössischen Bildnis* (Vienna, 1923); *Beethoven-Handbuch* (2 vols., Leipzig, 1926).

Frisch, Paula. See Frijsh, Povla.

Frischenschlager, Friedrich, Austrian composer and musicographer; b. Gross Sankt Florian, Styria, Sept. 7, 1885; d. Salzburg, July 15, 1970. He studied music in Graz; in 1909 went to Berlin, where he studied musicology with J. Wolf and Kretzschmar, and also attended Humperdinck's master classes in composition. In 1918 he was engaged as a music teacher at the Mozarteum in Salzburg; remained there until 1945; also ed. its bulletin. An industrious composer, he wrote the fairy-tale operas *Der Schweinehirt*, after Hans Christian Andersen (Berlin, May 31, 1913); *Die Prinzessin und der Zwerg* (Salzburg, May 12, 1927); and *Der Kaiser und die Nachtigall*, after Andersen (Salzburg, March 27, 1937); also several choral works; *Symphonische Aphorismen* for Orch.; and teaching materials for voice.

Friskin, James, Scottish-American pianist and composer; b.

Glasgow, March 3, 1886; d. N.Y., March 16, 1967. He studied with E. Dannreuther (piano) and Stanford (composition) at the Royal College of Music in London; then taught at the Royal Normal College for the Blind (1909–14). In 1914 he went to the U.S. In 1934 he gave 2 recitals in N.Y. consisting of the complete *Wohltemperierte Clavier* of Bach. In 1944 he married Rebecca Clarke. Among his works were *Phantasie* for String Quartet; *Phantasie* for Piano Trio; *Phantasy* for Piano, 2 Violins, Viola, and Cello (1912); Quintet for Piano and Strings; Violin Sonata. He publ. *The Principles of Pianoforte Practice* (London, 1921; new ed., N.Y., 1937); also (with I. Freundlich) *Music for the Piano* (N.Y., 1954).

Frizzell, "Lefty" (William Orville), American country-music singer and guitarist; b. Corsicana, Texas, March 31, 1928; d. Nashville, Tenn., July 19, 1975. He took up the guitar in his youth; later worked the country-music circuits in Texas and New Mexico; eventually gained fame with several hit recordings. He was a regular member of the Grand Ole Opry in Nashville.

BIBL.: C. Wolfe, *L. F.: His Life, His Music* (1984).

Froberger, Johann Jakob, famous German organist and composer; b. Stuttgart, May 18, 1616; d. Héricourt, Haute-Saône, May 7, 1667. About 1634 he went to Vienna, where he entered the Inst. of Singer oder Canthoreyknaben; there it was the custom to allow the choirboys, when their voices had changed and when they had attained a certain degree of musical scholarship, to serve as apprentices to famous masters of the time on stipends given by Emperor Ferdinand II. Froberger, however, did not apply for the subvention until late 1636, when it was refused him; thereupon, he held the position of 3rd organist at the court from Jan. 1 to Oct. 30, 1637. He then again applied, with success, and was granted a stipend of 200 gulden; in Oct. of that year he left to study under Frescobaldi in Rome. In 1641 he returned to Vienna, where he again was organist (1641–45 and 1653–58); after this he made long concert tours (including Paris and London). He spent his last years in the service of Princess Sybille of Württemberg at her château near Héricourt. Although 2 collections of toccatas, canzoni, and partitas were publ. long after his death (1693 and 1696), there is internal evidence that the majority of these works were written before 1650. Among his organ works are 25 toccatas, 15 ricercari, 8 fantasias, 6 canzonas, and 17 capriccios. Publications of his works followed after his death: *Diverse ingegnosissime, rarissime, et non maj più viste curiose partite di toccate, canzoni, ricercari, capricci,* etc. (1693; reprinted at Mainz, 1695) and *Diverse curiose e rare partite musicali,* etc. (1696); also a vol. of suites for clavecin (Amsterdam, c.1697). His works were ed. by G. Adler in Denkmäler der Tonkunst in Österreich (vols. 8, 13, 21; formerly vols. 4.i, 6.ii, 10.ii; 1897–1903). See also H. Schott, *A Critical Edition of the Works of J.J. F. with Commentary* (diss., Oxford Univ., 1978).

BIBL.: K. Seidler, *Untersuchungen über Biographie und Klavierstil J.J. F.s* (1930); A. Somer, *The Keyboard Music of J.J. F.* (diss., Univ. of Michigan, 1963); G. Sharp, "J.J. F. (1616–1667): A Link between the Renaissance and the Baroque," *Musical Times* (Dec. 1967); H.-A. Timmerman, "J.J. F.," *De Praestant,* 16/3 (1967); G. Leonhardt, "J.J. F. and His Music," *L'Organo* (Jan.–June 1968); U. Scharlau, "Neue Quellenfunde zur Biographie J.J. F.s," *Die Musikforschung* (Jan.–March 1969); G. Beechey, "J.J. F.," *Consort* (July 1972); D. Starke, *F.s Suiten tänze* (Darmstadt, 1972); H. Siedentop, *J.J. F.: Leben und Werk* (Stuttgart, 1977).

Froidebise, Pierre (Jean Marie), important Belgian composer, organist, and teacher; b. Ohey, May 15, 1914; d. Liège, Oct. 28, 1962. He began studies in harmony and organ playing with Camille Jacquemin (1932–35); then entered the classes at the Namur Cons. with René Barbier, and at the Brussels Cons. with Moulaert and Léon Jongen. His chosen specialty was the history of organ music; he publ. in 1958 a monumental *Anthologie de la musique d'orgue des primitifs à la Renaissance.* But he also was deeply interested in the techniques of new

music, particularly Schoenberg's method of composition with 12 tones; in 1949 he formed in Liège a progressive society under the name Variation. As a teacher of composition in Liège, he attracted many students of the avant-garde, among them Henri Pousseur.

WORKS: 2 radio operas: *La Bergère et le ramoneur* and *La Lune amère* (both 1957); *De l'aube à la nuit* for Orch. (1934–37); *Antigona* for Soli, Chorus, and Orch. (1936); Violin Sonata (1938); *La Légende de Saint-Julien l'Hospitalier,* symphonic poem after Flaubert (1941); *3 poèmes japonais* for Voice and Piano (1942–43); *5 comptines* for Voice and 11 Instruments (1947; ISCM Festival, Brussels, June 27, 1950); *Amerœur,* cantata for Voice, Wind Quintet, and Piano (1948); *Stèle pour sei Shonagon* for Soprano and 19 Instruments (1958); *Justorum animae* and *Puer natus est* for Chorus and Orch.

Frölich, (Friedrich) Theodor, Swiss composer; b. Brugg (Aargau), Feb. 20, 1803; d. (suicide) Aarau, Oct. 16, 1836. He studied composition with Zelter in Berlin; returning to Switzerland, was active mainly as an educator. He is remembered chiefly through his colorful songs, *Persische Lieder,* to Rückert's words, and his choruses, *Lieder im Volkston;* one of these choruses, *Wem Gott will rechte Gunst erweisen,* became popular.

Froment, Louis (Georges François) de, French conductor; b. Toulouse, Dec. 5, 1921. He studied at the Paris Cons.; won the Premier Prix de Direction d'Orch. there (1948); conducted the orch. of Radiodiffusion Française; was music director at the Casinos in Cannes, Deauville, and Vichy (1950–54); conducted at various festivals in France; toured in Germany, England, Sweden, the Netherlands, Spain, Russia, and South America. From 1958 to 1981 he was chief conductor of the Luxembourg Radio Orch.

Fromm, Andreas, German composer; b. Plänitz, near Wusterhausen, 1621; d. Prague, Oct. 16, 1683. A son of a Lutheran pastor, he studied theology; in 1649, became a cantor in Stettin; he was subsequently in Rostock (1651), Wittenberg (1668), and Prague, where he turned to the Roman Catholic Church. His principal musical work was an "actus musicus," *Die Parabel von dem reichen Mann und dem armen Lazarus* (1649); the opinion that it was the 1st German oratorio (cf. R. Schwartz, "Das erste deutsche Oratorium," *Jahrbuch der Musikbibliothek Peters 1899*) is discounted by later analysts.

Fromm, Herbert, German-American composer; b. Kitzingen, Feb. 23, 1905. He studied privately with A. Reuss in Munich; was conductor at the Civic Theater in Bielefeld (1930) and at Würzburg (1931–33). He went to the U.S. in 1937; was organist at Temple Beth Zion in Buffalo (1937–41); from 1941 to 1973 was music director at Temple Israel in Boston. He publ. 12 choral works for the Hebrew service; also a Violin Sonata; String Quartet; Flute Concerto; cantatas: *The Stranger* (N.Y., March 12, 1957); *Light Is Sown; Transience; Psalm Cantata* (1962); *Memorial Cantata* (1973); *Festival Cantata* (Boston, Oct. 27, 1973).

Fromm, Paul, prominent German-born American music patron; b. Kitzingen, Sept. 28, 1906; d. Chicago, July 4, 1987. He was born into a family of vintners; emigrated to the U.S. in 1938, becoming a naturalized citizen in 1944. He founded the Great Lakes Wine Co. in Chicago in 1940, subsequently organizing the Fromm Music Foundation (1952), which assumed a leading role in commissioning and sponsoring performances of contemporary music, including those at the Berkshire Music Center in Tanglewood (from 1956), the annual Festival of Contemporary Music there (1964–83), and the Aspen Music Festival (from 1985).

Frontini, Francesco Paolo, Italian composer; b. Catania, Aug. 6, 1860; d. there, July 26, 1939. He was a pupil of his father, Martino Frontini, who was also an opera composer, and of Lauro Rossi at Naples; was director of the Catania Cons. until 1923.

WORKS: Operas: *Nella* (Catania, March 30, 1881); *Malia* (Bologna, May 30, 1893); *Il Falconiere* (Catania, Sept. 15, 1899); oratorio, *Sansone e Dalila* (Catania, Aug. 23, 1882);

numerous choral pieces and songs. Ricordi publ. his collection of Sicilian songs, *Eco di Sicilia* (1883), and of Sicilian dances, *Antiche danze di Sicilia* (3 vols., 1936).

BIBL.: G. Balbo, *Note critico-biografiche su F.P. F.* (Catania, 1905).

Froschauer, Johann, German printer who flourished at the end of the 15th century. He was long thought to have been the 1st to print music with movable type, in Michael Keinspeck's *Lilium musicae planae* (1498); however, it is now known that wood blocks were employed for the music illustrations in that work; it also appears fairly certain that music printing with movable type preceded Froschauer's work.

Frotscher, Gotthold, German musicologist; b. Ossa, near Leipzig, Dec. 6, 1897; d. Berlin, Sept. 30, 1967. He studied in Bonn and Leipzig; received his Ph.D. from the Univ. of Leipzig in 1922 with the dissertation *Die Ästhetik des Berliner Liedes;* was univ. instructor in Danzig (1924–32); completed his Habilitation at the Technische Hochschule there with his *Hauptprobleme der Musikästhetik im 18. Jahrhundert* (1924; publ. in Danzig, 1924); was a prof. at the Univ. of Berlin (1935–45); from 1950, taught at the Pedagögische Hochschule in Berlin. He wrote a valuable history of organ playing, *Geschichte des Orgelspiels und der Orgelkomposition* (2 vols., Berlin, 1935; 3rd ed., rev., 1966); also publ. *Aufführungspraxis alter Musik* (Wilhelmshaven, 1963; 4th ed., 1977) and *Orgeln* (Karlsruhe, 1968).

Frotzler, Carl, Austrian organist and composer; b. Stockerau, April 10, 1873; d. there, July 8, 1960. Of very precocious talent, he wrote a Grand Mass at 14; then entered the Vienna Cons., where he studied with Franz Krenn. He later occupied various posts as organist until his retirement in 1953.

Frugatta, Giuseppe, Italian pianist and composer; b. Bergamo, May 26, 1860; d. Milan, May 30, 1933. He studied with A. Bazzini (composition) and C. Andreoli (piano) at the Milan Cons., where he became a prof. He composed a number of effective piano pieces (*Polonaise de concert, Moments poétiques,* etc.). He publ. *Preparazione al "Gradus ad Parnassum" di Clementi* (1913).

Frugoni, Orazio, Italian pianist and pedagogue; b. Davos, Switzerland, Jan. 28, 1921. He studied at the Geneva Cons. and the Verdi Cons. in Milan; his piano teachers included Alfredo Casella and Dinu Lipatti. In 1945 he won the Prix de Virtuosité at the Geneva Cons. He made his American debut at Town Hall in N.Y. in 1947; later joined the faculty of the Eastman School of Music in Rochester, N.Y. (1951–67). He then taught master classes at the Graduate School of Fine Arts in Florence until 1975; also taught at the Cherubini Cons. there (from 1972).

Frühbeck de Burgos (originally, **Frühbeck**), **Rafael,** eminent Spanish conductor; b. Burgos, Sept. 15, 1933. His father was German, his mother Spanish. He studied violin before pursuing musical training at the Bilbao Cons. and the Madrid Cons. (1950–53); then received instruction in conducting from Eichhorn at the Munich Hochschule für Musik (1956–58). He was conductor of the Bilbao Municipal Orch. (1958–62), chief conductor of the Orquesta Nacional de España in Madrid (1962–77), Generalmusikdirektor of the Düsseldorf Sym. Orch. (1966–71), and music director of the Orch. Symphonique de Montréal (1975–76). He appeared as a guest conductor with major European and North American orchs.; served as principal guest conductor of the National Sym. Orch. in Washington, D.C. (from 1980); was also music director of the Yomiuri Nippon Sym. Orch. in Tokyo (1980–85). In 1990 he was named chief conductor of the Vienna Sym. Orch. His idiomatic performances of Spanish music have won him many accolades; he has also demonstrated expertise as an interpreter of the standard orch. repertoire.

Frumerie, (Per) Gunnar (Fredrik) de, Swedish pianist and composer; b. Nacka, near Stockholm, July 20, 1908; d. Mörby, Sept. 9, 1987. He studied at the Stockholm Cons. and later went to Vienna to take advanced courses in piano with Emil von Sauer; then went to Paris to continue his piano studies with Alfred Cortot. Returning to Sweden, he was engaged as a piano teacher at the Stockholm Musikhögskolan (1945–74). He was a prolific composer and applied native Scandinavian modalities to some of his works.

WORKS: *Singoalla,* opera (Stockholm, March 16, 1940); 2 piano concertos (1929, 1932); 2 piano trios (1932, 1952); Violin Concerto (1936; rev. 1976); *Symphonic Variations* (1941); 2 piano quartets (1941, 1963); Concerto for Clarinet, String Orch., Harp, and Percussion (1958); Trumpet Concerto (1959); 2 piano sonatas (1968); Horn Concerto (1971–72); String Quintet (1974); Cello Concerto (1984; orchestration of his Sonata No. 2 for Cello and Piano, 1947; also orchestrated as a Trombone Concerto, 1986); several choral works and solo songs.

Fry, William Henry, American composer and journalist; b. Philadelphia, Aug. 10, 1813; d. Santa Cruz, West Indies, Dec. 21, 1864. He was one of the most vociferous champions of American music, and particularly of opera on American subjects in the English language. Ironically, his own opera *Leonora* (Philadelphia, June 4, 1845), for which he claimed the distinction of being the 1st grand opera by a native American composer, was a feeble imitation of Italian vocal formulas in the manner of Bellini, with a libretto fashioned from a novel by Bulwer-Lytton, *The Lady of Lyons. Leonora* ran for 16 performances before closing; a revival of some numbers in concert form was attempted in N.Y. on Feb. 27, 1929, but was met with puzzled derision. Fry continued his campaign in favor of American opera in English, and composed 3 more operas, 1 of which, *Notre Dame de Paris,* after Victor Hugo, was produced in Philadelphia on May 3, 1864; 2 other operas, *The Bridal of Dunure* and *Aurelia the Vestal,* were not performed. He also wrote several syms., including *The Breaking Heart* (1852); *Santa Claus* (*Christmas Symphony*) (N.Y., Dec. 24, 1853); *A Day in the Country* (1853?; not extant); *Childe Harold* (N.Y., May 31, 1854; not extant); as well as a symphonic poem, *Niagara* (N.Y., May 4, 1854). Fry's various proclamations, manifestos, and prefaces to publ. eds. of his works are interesting as illustrations of the patriotic bombast and humbug that agitated American musicians in the mid-19th century.

BIBL.: W. Upton, *The Musical Works of W.H. F.* (Philadelphia, 1946); idem, *W.H. F., American Journalist and Composer-Critic* (N.Y., 1954).

Frye, Walter, English composer who flourished in the 15th century. Nothing is known regarding his life, but from indirect indications, it appears that he was attached to the court of Burgundy. Of his 3 masses (in MS at the Royal Library in Brussels), 2 are without a Kyrie, a lack characteristic of the English school; his *Ave Regina* is an early example of the "song motet." His works have been ed. by S. Kenney in *Walter Frye: Collected Works,* in Corpus Mensurabilis Musicae, XIX (1960).

BIBL.: M. Bukofzer, "An Unknown Chansonnier of the 15th Century," *Musical Quarterly* (Jan. 1942; reproduces a chanson by Frye); D. Plamenac, "A Reconstruction of the French Chansonnier in the Bibl. Colombina, Seville," ibid. (Oct. 1951).

Fryer, George Herbert, English pianist, pedagogue, and composer; b. London, May 21, 1877; d. there, Feb. 7, 1957. He studied at the Royal Academy of Music, at the Royal College of Music with F. Taylor in London, and with Busoni in Weimar. He made his debut as a pianist in London (Nov. 17, 1898); then traveled in Europe; in 1914 he made a tour in the U.S.; in 1917 returned to London; taught at the Royal College of Music (1917–47). He wrote miscellaneous pieces for piano; also publ. a book, *Hints on Pianoforte Practice* (N.Y., 1914).

Fryklöf, Harald (Leonard), Swedish composer and teacher; b. Uppsala, Sept. 14, 1882; d. Stockholm, March 11, 1919. He studied theory with J. Lindegren at the Stockholm Cons. and piano with P. Scharwenka in Berlin; in 1908 he became a prof. of harmony at the Stockholm Cons. With G. Sandberg, A. Hellerström, and H. Palm, he ed. the choral series Musica Sacra (1915); also publ. *Koralharmonisering-Kyrkotonarterna* (Choral Harmonizations–Church Modes; 1915); wrote a concert overture, songs, piano pieces.

Fryklund, (Lars Axel) Daniel, Swedish musicologist; b. Västerås, May 4, 1879; d. Hälsingborg, Aug. 25, 1965. He studied Romanic philology at the Univ. at Uppsala; taught at the Univ. of Hälsingborg (1921–44). He was a specialist in the history and etymology of musical instruments; publ. many articles and books, and also amassed a collection of over 800 musical instruments and 10,000 MSS.

Fuchs, (Leonard Johann Heinrich) Albert, German composer and pedagogue; b. Basel, Aug. 6, 1858; d. Dresden, Feb. 15, 1910. He studied with Selmar Bagge in Basel, and later at the Leipzig Cons. with Reinecke and Jadassohn (1876–79). He conducted in Trier (1880–83); was director of the Wiesbaden Cons. (1889–98). In 1898 he joined the staff of the Dresden Cons.; was also conductor at the Schumann Singakademie (from 1901). He was a prolific composer, and publ. a number of choral works and songs; wrote 2 oratorios: *Selig sind, die in dem Herrn sterben* (1906) and *Das tausendjähriges Reich* (1908); several instrumental concertos; publ. *Taxe der Streichinstrumente* (1907; many reprints).
BIBL.: F. Geissler, *A. F.*, in vol. III of *Monographien moderner Musiker* (Leipzig, 1909).

Fuchs, Carl (Dorius Johannes), distinguished German organist and writer on music; b. Potsdam, Oct. 22, 1838; d. Danzig, Aug. 27, 1922. He studied piano with Bülow, thoroughbass with Weitzmann, and composition with Kiel; took his Ph.D. in Greifswald, with the dissertation *Präliminarien zu einer Kritik der Tonkunst* (1871). In 1868 he became a teacher at the Kullak Academy in Berlin; then gave piano concerts in Germany. In 1874 he went to Hirschberg; in 1879, to Danzig, where he was organist at the Petrikirche and music critic of the *Danziger Zeitung* (1887–1920); was also organist for many years at the Synagogue in Danzig.
WRITINGS: *Betrachtungen mit und gegen Arthur Schopenhauer* (1868); *Ungleiche Verwandte unter den Neudeutschen* (1868); *Virtuos und Dilettant* (Leipzig, 1871); *Die Zukunft des musikalischen Vortrags* (Danzig, 1884); *Die Freiheit des musikalischen Vortrags* (Danzig, 1885); *Praktische Anleitung zum Phrasieren* (Berlin, 1886, with H. Riemann; Eng. tr., N.Y., 1892); *Künstler und Kritiker* (1898); *Takt und Rhythmus im Choral* (Berlin, 1911); *Der taktgerechte Choral, Nachweisung seiner 6 Typen* (Berlin, 1923). His letters were publ. by his son, Hans Fuchs, in *Ostdeutsche Monatshefte* (Sept. 1923).

Fuchs, Johann Nepomuk, Austrian conductor and composer, brother of **Robert Fuchs;** b. Frauenthal, Styria, May 5, 1842; d. Vöslau, near Vienna, Oct. 5, 1899. He studied with Sechter at Vienna; conducted the Pressburg Opera in 1864; held similar positions at Brünn, Kassel, Cologne, Hamburg, Leipzig, and (from 1880) the Vienna Court Opera. In 1894 he succeeded Hellmesberger as director of the Vienna Cons. He produced the opera *Zingara* (Brünn, 1892) and several others.

Fuchs, Joseph (Philip), American violinist and teacher, brother of **Lillian Fuchs;** b. N.Y., April 26, 1900. He studied violin with Franz Kneisel at the Inst. of Musical Art; was concertmaster of the Cleveland Orch. (1926–40); made his N.Y. debut in 1943; joined the faculty of the Juilliard School of Music in 1946; toured Europe in 1954, South America in 1957, and Russia in 1965.
BIBL.: F. Selch, "J. F., 88 Years Young," *Ovation* (Oct. 1988).

Fuchs, Lillian, American violinist, violist, and teacher, sister of **Joseph (Philip) Fuchs;** b. N.Y., Nov. 18, 1903. She studied violin with Svecenski and Kneisel and composition with Goetschius at the Inst. of Musical Art; made her N.Y. debut as a violinist in 1926 but later played viola parts; was a member of the Perolé String Quartet; also appeared in concerts with her brothers Joseph and Harry Fuchs; later taught at the Man-

hattan School of Music and the Juilliard School of Music. She wrote several works for solo viola.

Fuchs, Lukas. See **Foss, Lukas.**

Fuchs, Marta, German soprano; b. Stuttgart, Jan. 1, 1898; d. there, Sept. 22, 1974. She was educated in Stuttgart, Munich, and Milan; made her operatic debut in Aachen in 1928. In 1930 she became a member of the Dresden State Opera, where she appeared until 1945; she was also a fine concert singer.

Fuchs, Robert, renowned Austrian composer and pedagogue, brother of **Johann Nepomuk Fuchs;** b. Frauenthal, Styria, Feb. 15, 1847; d. Vienna, Feb. 19, 1927. He studied at the Vienna Cons.; from 1875 to 1912 was a prof. of harmony there, and established himself as a teacher of historical importance; among his students were Gustav Mahler, Hugo Wolf, and Schreker. His own compositions are, however, of no consequence, and there is no evidence that he influenced his famous pupils stylistically or even technically; the only pieces that were at all successful were his 5 serenades for String Orch. He also wrote 2 operas, 5 syms., Piano Concerto, 2 piano trios, 3 string quartets, 2 piano quartets, Piano Quintet, and numerous pieces for piano solo and for piano, 4-hands.
BIBL.: A. Mayr, *Erinnerungen an R. F.* (Graz, 1934).

Fučik, Julius (Arnošt Vilém), Bohemian bandmaster and composer; b. Prague, July 18, 1872; d. Leitmeritz, Sept. 25, 1916. He was a bassoon player at the German Opera in Prague (1893) and later in Zagreb and Budapest; studied composition with Dvořák; was bandmaster of the 86th and 92nd Austrian regiments. He wrote a great number of dances and marches for band, including the immensely popular march *Entrance of the Gladiators.*

Fuenllana, Miguel de, blind Spanish vihuela virtuoso and composer; b. Navalcarnero, Madrid, early in the 16th century; place and date of death unknown. He was chamber musician to the Marquesa de Tarifa, and later at the court of Philip II, to whom he dedicated his *Libro de música para vihuela, intitulado Orphenica Lyra* (1554; modern ed. by C. Jacobs, London, 1979). From 1562 to 1568 he was chamber musician to Queen Isabel de Valois, 3rd wife of Philip II. The *Libro* gives evidence of a high state of musical art in Spain during the 16th century; besides fantasias and other compositions for vihuela by Fuenllana and old Spanish ballads (such as the famous *Ay de mi, Alhama*), it contains arrangements for vihuela of works by Vásquez, Morales, P. and F. Guerrero, Flecha, Bernal, and several Flemish masters.
BIBL.: G. Morphy, *Les Luthistes espagnols* (Leipzig, 1902); A. Koczirz, "Die Gitarrekompositionen in M. d.F.'s Orphenica Lyra," *Archiv für Musikwissenschaft* (1922); H. Anglès, "Dades desconegudes sobre M. d.F., vihuelista," *Revista Musical Catalana* (April 1936).

Fuentes, Juan Bautista, Mexican composer; b. Guadalajara, Jalisco, March 16, 1869; d. Leon, Guanajuato, Feb. 11, 1955. He studied in Mexico City; then taught music in various schools there. He publ. the manuals *Teoría de la música* (1899); *Tratado de intervalos y trasposición* (1909); *Método de armonía* (1920); composed a number of piano pieces in a salon style; also some orch. works, among them *Sinfonia mexicana.*

Fuerstner, Carl, German-born American pianist, conductor, teacher, and composer; b. Strasbourg, June 16, 1912. He studied composition and conducting at the Cologne Hochschule für Musik (1930–34), where his teachers were Hermann Abendorth, Walter Braunfels, Philipp Jarnach, and Ernst Klussmann. While still a student, he composed incidental music for theatrical plays. In 1939 he went to the U.S. as assistant conductor of the San Francisco Opera; he became a naturalized citizen in 1945. From 1945 to 1950 he was head of the opera dept. at the Eastman School of Music in Rochester, N.Y.; then served on the faculty of Brigham Young Univ. in Provo, Utah (1951–61), where he was resident pianist, opera conductor, principal piano teacher, and head of the composition dept. (1955–61); also toured widely as a piano accompanist to many celebrated artists of the day and conducted an impressive repertoire of standard and modern operas in the U.S. and Europe. From 1963 to 1982 he was principal opera coach at the Indiana Univ. School of Music in Bloomington, where he also conducted operas. He also was on the faculty of the Summer Academy of the Salzburg Mozarteum (1973–82); then was active with the American Inst. of Musical Studies in Graz (1983–85); concurrently was associated with the "Festa Musica Pro" in Assisi, Italy. From 1981 to 1989 he was music director of the Bloomington (Ind.) Sym. Orch.

WORKS: *Concerto rapsodico* for Cello and Orch. (Rochester, N.Y., May 11, 1947); *Metamorphoses on a Chorale Theme* for 20 Trombones, 2 Tubas, and Percussion (Rochester, N.Y., April 5, 1949); *Symphorama* for Orch. (1960); *Overture* (1954), *Allegro ritmico* (1958), and many other pieces for Concert Band, as well as band transcriptions of Classical and Romantic works; *Divertimento* for String Quartet (1950); Clarinet Sonata (1950); *Allegro concertante* for Trombone and 10 Instruments (1966); Sonata for Bass Clarinet and Piano or Cello (1977); *Conjurations* for Soprano Saxophone and Piano (1985); piano pieces; choral works, including the *46th Psalm* for Mixed Choir, 4 Trumpets, 4 Trombones, and Organ (1983).

Fuga, Sandro, Italian pianist, teacher, and composer; b. Mogliano Veneto, Nov. 26, 1906. He studied piano, organ, and composition at the Verdi Cons.; was a concert pianist until 1940; became a lecturer at the Turin Cons. in 1933, and in 1966 its director.

WORKS: STAGE: *La croce deserta* (Bergamo, 1950); *Otto Schnaffs* (Turin 1950); *Confessione* (RAI Radio, 1962). **ORCH.:** *Ode in memoria* for Orch. (1945; Turin, March 5, 1948); *Passacaglia* for Orch. (1950); Toccata for Piano and Orch. (1952); Trumpet Concertino (1953); Cello Concerto (1955); Violin Concerto (1959); Concerto for Strings and Percussion (1963); Oboe Concertino (1964); Sym. (1967); Piano Concerto (Rome, Jan. 14, 1970); *Concerto sacro I* for Chorus and Orch. (1938; Turin, Feb. 3, 1939), *II* for Baritone, Male Chorus, and Orch. (1951), *III* for Orch. (1954), and *IV* for Tenor and Double Chorus (1956). **OTHER:** Piano Trio (1943); 4 string quartets (1943, 1945, 1948, 1965); Violin Sonata (1951).

Fugère, Lucien, French baritone; b. Paris, July 22, 1848; d. there, Jan. 15, 1935. He studied at the Paris Cons.; began as a singer in cabarets; then sang in light opera; in 1877, joined the Opéra-Comique, remaining there until 1910; subsequently appeared at the Paris Gaîté Lyrique (1910–19); returned to the Opéra-Comique; continued to sing until his 80th year. He acquired a great following as a brilliant performer of comic parts; his best roles were Leporello, Papageno, Figaro, and Bartolo. He was also well known as a teacher; among his pupils was Mary Garden.

BIBL.: R. Duhamel, *L. F.* (Paris, 1929).

Führer, Robert (Johann Nepomuk), Bohemian composer and organist; b. Prague, June 2, 1807; d. Vienna, Nov. 28, 1861. He studied with Johann Vitásek; was an organist in provincial towns before succeeding his teacher as Kapellmeister at the Prague Cathedral in 1839. He became involved in fraudulent transactions and was dismissed from his post in 1845. He then held various positions as an organist and choral conductor in Vienna, Salzburg, Munich, Augsburg, and Gmunden. A series of embezzlements and other criminal offenses perpetrated by him resulted in his dismissal from several of his positions, but he continued to compose and perform; in 1856 he was Bruckner's competitor for the post of organist in Linz, arousing great admiration for his skill, even though Bruckner was selected. He served a prison term in 1859, but was given full freedom to write music. He publ. numerous sacred works and many organ pieces; also handbooks on harmony and organ playing. Despite his notoriously dishonest acts and professional untrustworthiness (he publ. one of Schubert's masses under his own name), he enjoyed a fine reputation for his musicianship.

Fujikawa, Mayumi, Japanese violinist; b. Asahigawa, July 27, 1946. She studied at the Toho School of Music in Tokyo and at the Antwerp Cons.; later took lessons with Leonid Kogan in Nice. In 1970 she won 2nd prize in the Tchaikovsky Competition in Moscow; then appeared as soloist with major orchs. in Europe and America.

Fukai, Shiro, Japanese composer; b. Akita-City, April 4, 1907; d. Kyoto, July 2, 1959. He studied composition in Tokyo with Sugawara. Perhaps his most notable score is a large choral work, *Prayer for Peace* (Tokyo, Aug. 15, 1949). His other works are the ballets *A City* (Tokyo, June 18, 1936) and *Ocean* (Tokyo, Jan. 30, 1938), and several symphonic suites of "landscape music."

Fukushima, Kazuo, Japanese composer; b. Tokyo, April 11, 1930. Autodidact in composition, he became determined to effect an esthetic and idiomatic synthesis between the traditional Japanese style of court music and the serial organization of Western modernism.

WORKS: *Kadha Hi-Haku* (The Flying Spirit) for Chamber Orch. (1959); *Tsuki-shiro* (The Moon Spirit) for String Orch. and Percussion (1964); *Hi-Kyo* for Flute, Strings, and Percussion (1961; Cologne Radio, Nov. 9, 1962); *3 Pieces from Chu-U* for Flute and Piano; *A Ring of the Wind* for Piano (1968), *Rankei* for Solo Oboe (1970); *Suien* for Piano (1972).

Fuleihan, Anis, Cypriot-born American pianist, conductor, and composer; b. Kyrenia, April 2, 1900; d. Palo Alto, Calif., Oct. 11, 1970. He studied at the English School in Kyrenia; went to the U.S. in 1915 and continued his study of the piano in N.Y. with Alberto Jonás; toured the U.S., also the Near East, from 1919 to 1925; then lived in Cairo, returning to the U.S. in 1928; was on the staff of G. Schirmer, Inc. (1932–39); in 1947, became a prof. at Indiana Univ.; in 1953, director of the Beirut Cons. in Lebanon. In 1962 he went to Tunis under the auspices of the State Dept.; in 1963, organized the Orch. Classique de Tunis; remained there until 1965.

WORKS: Opera, *Vasco* (1960). Orch.: *Mediterranean Suite* (1930; Cincinnati, March 15, 1935); *Preface to a Child's Story Book* (1932); Sym. No. 1 (N.Y., Dec. 31, 1936); Concerto No. 1 for Piano and String Orch. (Saratoga Springs, N.Y., Sept. 11, 1937, composer soloist); Concerto No. 2 for Piano and Orch. (N.Y., 1938); Fantasy for Viola and Orch. (1938); Violin Concerto (1930); *Fiesta* (Indianapolis, Dec. 1, 1939); *Symphonie concertante* for String Quartet and Orch. (N.Y., April 25, 1940); Concerto for 2 Pianos and Orch. (Hempstead, N.Y., Jan. 10, 1941); *Epithalamium* for Piano and Strings (Philadelphia, Feb. 7, 1941); Concerto for Theremin and Orch. (N.Y., Feb. 26, 1945); *Invocation to Isis* (Indianapolis, Feb. 28, 1941); Concerto for Violin, Piano, and Orch. (1943); Ondes Martenot Concerto (1944); *3 Cyprus Serenades* (Philadelphia, Dec. 13, 1946); Rhapsody for Cello and String Orch. (Saratoga Springs, Sept. 12, 1946); *Overture for 5 Winds* (N.Y., May 17, 1947); *The Pyramids of Giza*, symphonic poem (1952); Toccata for Piano and Orch. (1960); *Islands*, symphonic suite (1961); Flute Concerto (1962); Piano Concerto No. 3 (1963); Cello Concerto (1963); Viola Concerto (1963); Violin Concerto No. 2 (1965); Sym. No. 2 (N.Y., Feb. 16, 1967); Violin Concerto No. 3 (1967); *Le Cor anglais s'amuse*, diversions for English Horn and Strings (1969); also Piano Quintet (1967); Piano Trio (1969); 5 string quartets (1940–67); 14 piano sonatas (1940–68); Horn Quintet (1959); Clarinet Quintet; Violin Sonata; Viola Sonata; Cello Sonata; choral pieces; songs.

Fulkerson, Gregory (Locke), American violinist; b. Iowa City, May 9, 1950. He studied at Oberlin College (1967–71) and with Dorothy DeLay, Robert Mann, and Ivan Galamian at the Juilliard School in N.Y. (1975–79); also played in the Cleveland Orch. (1971–74) and later was concertmaster of the Honolulu Sym. Orch. (1979–81). After winning 1st prize in the International American Music Competition in Washington, D.C., in 1980, he pursued a career as a soloist. An adventurous artist, he maintains an enormous repertoire, which includes a number of neglected works; among posthumous premieres was Roy Harris's Violin Concerto (Wilmington, N.C., March 21, 1984). Other premieres of works by contemporary composers include Richard Wernick's Violin Concerto (Philadelphia, Jan. 17, 1986).

Fulkerson, James (Orville), American composer and trombonist; b. Streator, Ill., July 2, 1945. He studied at Wesleyan Univ. (B.A., 1966) and the Univ. of Illinois (M.M., 1969); took lessons in trombone playing with Carmine Caruso and John Silber; studied composition with Gaburo, Hiller, Johnston, and Martirano. He was a creative associate of the Center for the Creative and Performing Arts at the State Univ. of N.Y. in Buffalo (1969–72); composer-in-residence at the Deutscher Akademischer Austauschdienst in Berlin (1973), the Victorian College of the Arts in Melbourne (1977–79), and Dartington College in Devon, England (from 1981). He is a virtuoso on the trombone, and he makes a specialty of playing the most fantastically difficult modern pieces. His own compositions are no less advanced.

WORKS: STAGE: *Vicarious Thrills* for Amplified Trombone and Pornographic Film (1978–79); *Cheap Imitations II: Madwomen* for Soloist, Tape, and Films (1980); *Rats Tale* for 6 Dancers, Trombone, Speaker, Saxophone, Guitar, Banjo, and Piano (1983). ORCH.: *Globs* for Small Orch., Live Electronics, and Tape (1968); *About Time* (1969); *Something about Mobiles* (1969); *Planes* for 4 Orch. Groups (1969); *Behind Closed Doors* for Violin and Orch. (1971); *Patterns IX* (1972); *To See a Thing Clearly* (1972); *For We Don't See Anything Clearly* (1972); Guitar Concerto (1972); Trombone Concerto, with Tape (1973); *Orchestra Piece* (1974); *Stations, Regions, and Clouds* for Bass Trombone and Orch. (1977); Sym. (1980); Concerto (*. . . fierce and coming from far away*) (1981). CHAMBER: *Chamber Musics I–V* for Various Chamber Ensembles (1975–77); *Co-ordinative Systems 1–10* for Various Chamber and Solo Instrumental Combinations (1971–76); *Music for Brass* (1975); *Patterns 1–8* and *11* for Various Solo Instruments (1967–77); *Patterns and Processes* for Percussion (1971); *Stations, Regions, Clouds I* for Trombone, Piano, and Tape (1975); *Bombs* for Bass Trombone and Prepared Piano (1975).

Fuller, Albert, American harpsichordist; b. Washington, D.C., July 21, 1926. He studied organ with Paul Callaway at the National Cathedral in Washington, D.C.; then attended classes at the Peabody Cons. and at Georgetown and Johns Hopkins Univs. He studied harpsichord with Ralph Kirkpatrick at Yale Univ. and also theory there with Hindemith, graduating with a M.Mus. in 1954. He then went to Paris on a Ditson fellowship; upon his return to the U.S., he made his N.Y. recital debut in 1957; his European debut followed in 1959. In 1964 he became a prof. of harpsichord at the Juilliard School of Music in N.Y. From 1972 to 1983 he was founder–artistic director of the Aston Magna Foundation.

Fuller Maitland, J(ohn) A(lexander), eminent English music scholar; b. London, April 7, 1856; d. Carnforth, Lancashire, March 30, 1936. He studied at Westminster School and Trinity College in Cambridge (M.A., 1882); then took piano lessons with Dannreuther and W.S. Rockstro. He was music critic of the *Pall Mall Gazette* (1882–84) and of the *Manchester Guardian* (1884–89); lectured extensively on the history of English music; appeared as a pianist with the Bach Choir and as a performer on the harpsichord in historical concerts. He contributed to the 1st ed. of *Grove's Dictionary of Music and Musicians* and edited the Appendix; was editor-in-chief of the 2nd ed. (1904–10); was also editor of various other works, including the *Fitzwilliam Virginal Book* (1899; with W. Barclay Squire).

WRITINGS: *Schumann* (1884); *Masters of German Music* (1894); *The Musician's Pilgrimage* (1899); *English Music in the 19th Century* (1902); *The Age of Bach and Handel* (vol. IV of *The Oxford History of Music*, 1902; new ed., 1931); *Joseph Joachim* (1905); *Brahms* (1911; in German, 1912); *The Concert of Music* (1915); *The "48"—Bach's Wohltemperiertes Clavier* (2 vols., 1925); *The Keyboard Suites of J.S. Bach* (1925); *The Spell of Music* (1926); *A Door-Keeper of Music* (1929); *Bach's*

Brandenburg Concertos (1929); *Schumann's Concerted Chamber Music* (1929); *The Music of Parry and Stanford* (1934).

Fulton, (Robert) Norman, English composer; b. London, Jan. 23, 1909; d. Birmingham, Aug. 5, 1980. He studied composition with Demuth at the Royal Academy of Music in London. In 1936 he joined the staff of the BBC; in 1966 he was appointed to the faculty of the Royal Academy of Music.

WORKS: ORCH.: *Sinfonia pastorale* (1950); Sym. No. 2 (1955); Sym. No. 3 (1971–73). CHAMBER: Piano Trio (1950); *Scottish Suite* for Recorder and Piano (1954); Sonatina for Oboe and Piano (1962); *Night Music* for Flute and Piano (1969); piano pieces; songs.

Fumagalli, 4 musical brothers, natives of Inzago, Italy: **Disma,** b. Sept. 8, 1826; d. Milan, March 9, 1893. He was a pupil at, and from 1857 a prof. of, the Milan Cons.; was a prolific composer of piano music (over 250 numbers). **Adolfo,** b. Oct. 19, 1828; d. Florence, May 3, 1856, at the age of 27. He was a pianist, pupil of Gaetano Medaglia, and later of Angeleri and Ray at the Milan Cons.; then undertook tours throughout Italy, France, and Belgium, earning the sobriquet "the Paganini of the pianoforte." During his brief lifetime he publ. about 100 elegant and effective piano pieces, which obtained an extraordinary vogue. Filippo Filippi wrote a sketch, *Della vita e delle opere di Adolfo Fumagalli* (Milan, 1857). **Polibio,** b. Oct. 26, 1830; d. Milan, June 21, 1900. He was a pianist and a composer for piano and for organ. **Luca,** b. May 29, 1837; d. Milan, June 5, 1908. He was a pupil at the Milan Cons.; played with great success in Paris (1860), and publ. salon music for piano; also produced an opera, *Luigi XI* (Florence, 1875).

Fumet, Dynam-Victor, French organist and composer; b. Toulouse, May 4, 1867; d. Paris, Jan. 2, 1949. He studied with Franck and Guiraud at the Paris Cons. At an early age he became involved in the political activities of French anarchists and was forced to leave school. For a time he earned his living as a piano player in Paris nightclubs; in 1910 became organist of St. Anne's Church in Paris. His music follows the precepts of French Wagnerism; the influence of Franck is also noticeable. He wrote several orch. works on mystic themes, among them *Magnetisme céleste* for Cello and Orch. (1903); *Trois âmes* (1915); *Transsubstantiation* (1930); *Notre mirage, notre douleur* (1930). During the German occupation he wrote *La Prison glorifiée* (1943).

Fumi, Vinceslao, Italian conductor and composer; b. Montepulciano, Tuscany, Oct. 20, 1823; d. Florence, Nov. 20, 1880. He conducted opera in various Italian cities; also in Constantinople, Montevideo, and Buenos Aires; finally at Florence. His compositions include the opera *Atala* (Buenos Aires, 1862); a Sym.; other orch. works. A collection of folk songs of all times and nations which he undertook remained unfinished.

Furno, Giovanni, Italian composer and pedagogue; b. Capua, Jan. 1, 1748; d. Naples, June 20, 1837. He studied at the Conservatorio di S. Onofrio in Naples, and in 1775 became a teacher of theory of composition there; retired in 1835. Among his pupils were Bellini and Mercadante. He wrote 2 operas, sacred choral music, and some instrumental pieces.

Fürsch-Madi(er), Emma or **Emmy,** French soprano; b. Bayonne, 1847; d. Warrenville, N.J., Sept. 19, 1894. She studied at the Paris Cons., making her operatic debut as Marguerite in Paris (1868); then sang with the French Opera Co. in New Orleans (1873–74); made her 1st appearance at London's Covent Garden as Valentine in *Les Huguenots* (May 9, 1881); after adopting the name Fürsch-Madi (1882), she sang there again (1883–88). She made her Metropolitan Opera debut in N.Y. as Ortrud on Nov. 7, 1883, appearing again on its roster in 1893–94. She was particularly noted for her portrayals of Donna Anna, Lucrezia Borgia, and Aida.

Fürstenau, Moritz, German writer on music and flutist; b. Dresden, July 26, 1824; d. there, March 25, 1889. He was a member of the Dresden Court Orch. from 1842; was librarian of the music section of the Royal Library from 1852; from 1856, was a flute teacher at the Cons.

WRITINGS: *Beiträge zur Geschichte der königlich-sächs. musikalischen Kapelle* (1849); *Zur Geschichte der Musik und des Theaters am Hofe zu Dresden* (2 vols., 1861–62; supplement by H. van Brescius, *Die königliche sachs. musikalische Kapelle von Reissiger bis Schuch, 1826–98*, Dresden, 1898); *Die Fabrikation musikalischer Instrumente im königlich sächsischen Vogtland* (1876; with T. Berthold); also essays and articles in musical journals.

Fürstner, Adolph, German music publisher; b. Berlin, April 3, 1833; d. Bad Nauheim, June 6, 1908. He was a member of a family of merchants; although lacking in musical education, he showed a keen understanding of the commercial value of good music. He founded a music publishing firm under his own name in Berlin in 1868; in 1872 he acquired the catalog of the Dresden firm of C.F. Meser, which owned several operas by Wagner and some works of Liszt; he subsequently purchased the rights of operas by Massenet, and later demonstrated his business acumen by securing *Pagliacci*. His firm distinguished itself as the earliest publisher of Richard Strauss. Fürstner was succeeded after his death by his son **Otto** (b. Berlin, Oct. 17, 1886; d. London, June 18, 1958); in 1933 Otto Fürstner was compelled to leave Germany; he went to England, where he resumed his business and gradually won back the German rights to the original eds. of the firm. After the death of Otto his widow, Ursula, took over the ownership of the firm; in 1970, it was incorporated as Fürstner, London.

Furtwängler, (Gustav Heinrich Ernst Martin) Wilhelm, celebrated German conductor; b. Berlin, Jan. 25, 1886; d. Ebersteinburg, Nov. 30, 1954. His father, Adolf Furtwängler, was a noted archeologist. He grew up in Munich, where he received a private education; his musical studies were with Schillings, Rheinberger, and Beer-Walbrunn; he also studied piano with Conrad Ansorge. He later served as répétiteur with Mottl in Munich (1908–9). In 1910 he became 3rd conductor at the Strasbourg Opera; then conducted the sym. concerts in Lübeck (1911–15); in 1915 he was engaged as conductor in Mannheim. From 1919 to 1924 he conducted the Vienna Tonkünstler Orch.; concurrently (from 1921) he served as director of the Gesellschaft der Musikfreunde in Vienna. He led the Berlin Staatskapelle (1920–22); also served as conductor of the Frankfurt Museum concerts. A decisive turn in his career was his appointment in 1922 as chief conductor of the Berlin Phil. as successor to Nikisch; he also assumed Nikisch's post of Kapellmeister of the Leipzig Gewandhaus Orch., which he held until 1928. On Jan. 3, 1925, he made his American debut with the N.Y. Phil., which was greeted with general acclaim; he conducted this orch. again in 1926 and 1927. In 1927 he was elected conductor of the Vienna Phil. in succession to Weingartner, holding the post of artistic director until 1930, and continuing as guest conductor later on. In 1927 the Univ. of Heidelberg conferred upon him the title of Dr.Phil.; in 1928 the city of Berlin named him Generalmusikdirektor. In 1931 he conducted at the Bayreuth Festival for the 1st time. In 1932, he was awarded the prestigious Goethe Gold Medal. In 1933 he was appointed director of the Berlin State Opera and vice-president of the Reichsmusikkammer. He maneuvered adroitly to secure his independence from the increasing encroachment of the Nazi authorities on both his programs and the personnel of the Berlin Phil., and succeeded in retaining several Jewish players. On March 12, 1934, he conducted Hindemith's sym. *Mathis der Maler* and was sharply berated by Goebbels, who called Hindemith a "cultural Bolshevist" and "spiritual non-Aryan" (this with reference to Hindemith's half-Jewish wife). In the face of continued Nazi interference, Furtwängler decided to resign all of his posts on Dec. 4, 1934; however, a few months later, he made an uneasy peace with the Nazi authorities and agreed to return as a conductor with the Berlin Phil., giving his 1st concert on April 25, 1935. In 1936 he was offered a contract as permanent conductor of the N.Y. Phil. in succession to Toscanini, but had to decline

the prestigious offer to quiet the rising accusations, on the part of American musicians, of his being a Nazi collaborator. In 1937 he went to London to participate in the musical celebrations in honor of the coronation of King George VI; in 1939 he was made a Commander of the Legion of Honor by the French government. After the outbreak of World War II, he confined his activities to Germany and Austria. Continuing to be loyal to Germany but with ambivalent feelings toward the Nazi government, Furtwängler in Jan. 1945 went to Switzerland, where he remained during the last months of the war. He returned to Germany in 1946; faced the Allied Denazification Court, and was absolved from the charges of pro-Nazi activities (Dec. 17, 1946). On May 25, 1947, he conducted the Berlin Phil. for the 1st time since the end of the war, leading an all-Beethoven concert to great acclaim; he also renewed his close association with the Vienna Phil. and the Salzburg Festival. He was tentatively engaged to conduct the Chicago Sym. Orch. in 1949, but the project was canceled when public opinion proved hostile. In Western Europe, however, he took both the Vienna and Berlin phil. orchs. on a number of major tours and was received most enthusiastically; he also became a regular conductor with the Philharmonia Orch. of London. In 1951 he reinaugurated the Bayreuth Festival by conducting Beethoven's 9th Sym.; in 1952 he resumed his post as chief conductor of the Berlin Phil. His last years of life were clouded by increasing deafness, so that his podium had to be wired for sound. He was to conduct the Berlin Phil. on its 1st American tour in the spring of 1955, but death intervened, and Herbert von Karajan was elected his successor.

Furtwängler was a perfect embodiment of the great tradition of the German Romantic school of conducting; his interpretations of the music of Beethoven, Schubert, Schumann, Brahms, Bruckner, and Wagner were models of formal purity. He never strove to achieve personal magic with the audience, and never ranked with such charismatic conductors as Stokowski or Koussevitzky in this respect. But to professional musicians he remained a legendary master of the orch. sound and symmetry of formal development of symphonic music. Furtwängler was also a composer; quite naturally, the style of his works followed the Romantic tradition, with potential exuberance controlled by a severe sense of propriety. He left behind 3 syms. (1903, 1947, 1954), a Te Deum (1910), Piano Quintet (1935), Sym. Concert for Piano and Orch. (1937), 2 violin sonatas (1937, 1940), and some minor pieces. He publ. a critical essay, *Johannes Brahms und Anton Bruckner* (Leipzig, 1941; 2nd ed., 1952); *Gespräche über Musik* (Zürich, 1948; in Eng. as *Concerning Music*, London, 1953); *Ton und Wort* (Wiesbaden, 1954); *Der Musiker und sein Publikum* (Zürich, 1954); *Vermächtnis* (Wiesbaden, 1956). Newsletters and bulletins were issued by the Wilhelm Furtwängler Soc. of Los Angeles, the Société Wilhelm Furtwängler of Paris, and the Wilhelm Furtwängler Associates of Urawa City, Japan.

BIBL.: R. Specht, *W. F.* (Vienna, 1922); A. Einstein, "W. F.," *Monthly Musical Record* (Jan. 1934); O. Schrenck, *W. F.* (Berlin, 1940); F. Herzfeld, *W. F., Weg und Wesen* (Leipzig, 1941); B. Geissmar, *Two Worlds of Music* (N.Y., 1946); W. Siebert, *F., Mensch und Künstler* (Buenos Aires, 1950); C. Riess, *F.; Musik und Politik* (Bern, 1953); D. Gillis, ed., *F. Recalled* (Tuckahoe, N.Y., 1966); H. Schonberg, *The Great Conductors* (N.Y., 1967); D. Gillis, *F. and America* (Woodhaven, N.Y., 1970); E. Furtwängler, *Über W. F.* (Wiesbaden, 1979); K. Hoecker, *Die nie vergessenen Klänge: Erinnerungen an W. F.* (Berlin, 1979); P. Pirie, *F. and the Art of Conducting* (London, 1980); J. Hunt, *The F. Sound* (London, 1985); J. Squire and J. Hunt, *F. and Great Britain* (London, 1985); J. Matzner, *F.: Analyse, Dokument, Protokoll* (Zürich, 1986); H.-H. Schönzeler, *F.* (London, 1987); S. Whiteside, translator, and M. Tanner, ed., *Notebooks 1924–1954 by W. F.* (London, 1989).

Furuhjelm, Erik Gustaf, Finnish composer; b. Helsinki, July 6, 1883; d. there, June 13, 1964. He studied violin; then took lessons in composition with Sibelius and Wegelius; continued his studies in Vienna with Robert Fuchs. From 1909 to 1935 he lectured on music theory at the Helsinki School of Music, and from 1920 to 1935 served as assistant director there. He founded the magazine *Finsk Musikrevy*; in 1916 he wrote the 1st book-length biography of Sibelius.

WORKS: Piano Quintet (1906); 2 syms. (1906–11; 1925–26); *Romantic Overture* (1910); *Konzertstück* for Piano and Orch. (1911); *Intermezzo and Pastorale* for Orch. (1920–24); *Fem bilder* (5 Pictures) for Orch. (1924–25); *Phantasy* for Violin and Orch. (1925–26); *Folklig svit* (Rustic Suite) for Orch. (1939); *Solitude* for Orch. (1940); String Quartet.

Fussan, Werner, German composer; b. Plauen, Dec. 25, 1912; d. Mainz, Aug. 16, 1986. He studied at the Hochschule für Musik in Berlin; served in the German army during World War II; after the war, he taught composition at the Cons. of Wiesbaden; in 1948 was appointed to the faculty of the Hochschule für Musik in Mainz; later was active at the Univ. of Mainz, serving as a prof. of composition from 1966 to 1978.

Fussell, Charles C(lement), American composer and conductor; b. Winston-Salem, N.C., Feb. 14, 1938. He received lessons in piano from Clemens Sandresky in Winston-Salem; in 1956 he enrolled in the Eastman School of Music in Rochester, N.Y., where he studied composition (B.M., 1960) with Thomas Canning, Wayne Barlow, and Bernard Rogers, piano with José Echaniz, and conducting with Herman Genhart; in 1962 he received a Fulbright grant and studied with Boris Blacher at the Berlin Hochschule für Musik; attended Friedelind Wagner's Bayreuth Festival Master Class in opera production and conducting in 1963; then completed his training in composition at the Eastman School of Music (M.M., 1964). In 1966 he joined the faculty of the Univ. of Mass. in Amherst; also founded its Group for New Music in 1974 (later renamed Pro Musica Moderna). He taught composition at the North Carolina School of the Arts in Winston-Salem (1976–77) and at Boston Univ. (1981); in 1981–82 he conducted the Longy School Chamber Orch. in Cambridge, Mass. In his music he adopts a prudent modernistic idiom and favors neo-Romantic but never overladen sonorities, without doctrinaire techniques of the currently prevailing factions.

WORKS: OPERA: *Caligula* (1962). **ORCH.:** 3 syms.: No. 1, *Symphony in 1 Movement* (1963); No. 2 for Soprano and Orch. (1964–67); No. 3, *Landscapes*, for Chorus and Orch. (1978–81); *3 Processionals* (1972–73; Springfield, Mass., April 25, 1974); *Northern Lights*, 2 portraits for Chamber Orch., portraying Leoš Janáček and Edvard Munch (1977–79); *Virgil Thomson Sleeping*, portrait for Chamber Orch. (1981); *4 Fairy Tales*, after Oscar Wilde (1980–81); *Maurice Grosser Cooking*, portrait No. 2 for Chamber Orch. (1982–83); *Jack Larson*, portrait No. 3 for Chamber Orch. (1986). **CHAMBER:** Trio for Violin, Cello, and Piano (1962); *Dance Suite* for Flute, Trumpet, Viola, and 2 Percussionists (1963); *Ballades* for Cello and Piano (1968; rev. 1976); *Greenwood Sketches: Music for String Quartet* (1976); *Free Fall* for 7 Players (N.Y., May 9, 1988). **VOCAL:** *Saint Stephen and Herod*, drama for Speaker, Chorus, and Winds (1964); *Poems* for Chamber Orch. and Voices (1965); *Voyages* for Soprano, Tenor, Women's Chorus, Piano, Winds, and Recorded Speaker (Amherst, Mass., May 4, 1970); *Julian*, drama for Soprano, Tenor, Chorus, and Orch. (1969–71; Winston-Salem, N.C., April 15, 1972); *Eurydice* for Soprano and Chamber Ensemble (1973–75; Winston-Salem, N.C., Jan. 30, 1976); *Résumé*, cycle of 9 songs for Soprano, Clarinet, String Bass, and Piano (1975–76); *Cymbeline*, romance for Soprano, Tenor, Narrator, and Chamber Ensemble (Boston, April 2, 1984); *A Song of Return* for Chorus and Orch. (1989); *Wilde*, 2 monologues for Baritone and Orch. (1989–90); other vocal works.

Füssl, Karl Heinz, Czech-born Austrian composer; b. Jablonec, March 21, 1924. He entered the Berlin Hochschule für Musik in 1939; studied with Uhl at the Vienna Academy (1949–50), and had private studies with Polnauer and Ratz. He became co-ed. of the Urtext Editions publ. by Universal Edition in Vienna.

WORKS: Operas: *Dybuk* (1967–70; Karlsruhe, Sept. 26,

1970) and *Celestina* (1973); *Kain* (1988); *Dialogue in Praise of the Owl and the Cuckoo*, after Shakespeare, for Tenor and 7 Instruments, or for Baritone and 4 Instruments (1948; rev. 1961–68); Divertimento for Orch. (1948); *Szenen* for String Orch. (1954); Cello Sonata (1954); *Epitaph und Antistrophe*, 2 movements for Orch. (1956–65); *Concerto rapsodico*, after G.M. Hopkins, for Alto or Mezzo-soprano, and Orch. (1957); *Miorita*, Rumanian folk ballads for Soprano or Tenor, and 5 Instruments (1963); *Refrains* for Piano and Orch. (1972; rev. 1987); *Bilder der Jahreszeit* for Soprano and Orch. (1983); *Moments musicaux*, 8 pieces for Orch. (1988); *Perpetuum mobile* for Oboe and Piano (1988); Saxophone Quartet (1988).

Futterer, Carl, Swiss composer; b. Basel, Feb. 21, 1873; d. Ludwigshafen, Nov. 5, 1927. He studied to be a lawyer; then began taking lessons in composition with Hans Huber; wrote operas and other works but kept them hidden until late in life. His comic opera *Don Gil mit den grünen Hosen* (1915) was produced in Freiburg im Breisgau in 1922; another opera, *Der Geiger von Gmünd* (1917), was produced in Basel in 1921. He further wrote a Sinfonietta (1917); Octet (1921); Quartet for Oboe, Clarinet, Horn, and Bassoon (1921); Trio for Clarinet, Cello, and Piano (1924); Piano Trio (1927); Violin Sonata (1927); Piano Concerto (1927).

Fux, Johann Joseph, renowned Austrian organist, music theorist, pedagogue, and composer; b. Hirtenfeld, near St. Marein, Styria, 1660; d. Vienna, Feb. 13, 1741. He was born into a peasant family; enrolled in the Jesuit Univ. in Graz as a "grammatista" in 1680, then in 1681 entered the Ferdinandeum there, a Jesuit residential school made up mostly of musically gifted students. He also studied at the Jesuit Univ. of Ingolstadt, being listed as logica studiosus in 1683; served as organist at St. Moritz there until 1688. By 1696 he was in Vienna, where he was organist at the Schottenkirche until 1702; was made court composer by the Emperor in 1698; about 1700 the latter is believed to have sent him to Rome, where he studied composition. He became vice-Kapellmeister at St. Stephen's Cathedral in Vienna in 1705; was then its principal Kapellmeister from 1712 to 1715; became vice-Kapellmeister to the court in 1713; was named Ziani's successor as principal Kapellmeister to the court in 1715. Among his noted students were Gottlieb Muffat, G.C. Wagenseil, and J.D. Zelenka. Fux was the last representative of the Baroque tradition in composition and music theory in Austria. As a composer, he was an outstanding contrapuntist. He found inspiration in the a cappella polyphonic mastery of Palestrina, which led to his adoption of 2 contrasting styles in his sacred music: the stylus a cappella (without instruments) and the stylus mixtus (with instruments). In his solo motets, operas, and oratorios, he prepared the way for the Viennese Classicists. More than 200 works have been added to the original 405 cataloged by Köchel. As a music theorist, he produced the classic treatise on counterpoint, *Gradus ad Parnassum* (1725). It had a profound influence on his successors, and remains an invaluable textbook.

WRITINGS: *Gradus ad Parnassum* (Vienna, 1725; partial Eng. tr. as *Steps to Parnassus: The Study of Counterpoint*, N.Y., 1943; 2nd ed., rev., 1965, as *The Study of Counterpoint*); *Singfundament* (Vienna, c.1832); *Exempla dissonantiarum ligatarum et non ligatarum* (publ. in H. Federhofer, "Drei handschriftliche Quellen zur Musiktheorie in Österreich um 1700," *Musa—mens—musici: Im Gedenken an Walther Vetter* (Leipzig, 1969).

WORKS: OPERAS (all 1st perf. at the Hoftheater, Vienna, unless otherwise given): *Il fato monarchico*, festa teatrale (Feb. 18, 1700; music not extant; *Neo-exoriens phosphorus, id est neo-electus et infulatus praesul Mellicensis*, Latin school opera (1701; music not extant); *L'offendere per amare ovvero La Telesilla*, dramma per musica (June 25, 1702; music not extant); *La clemenza d'Augusto*, poemetto drammatico (Nov. 15, 1702); music not extant; *La clemenza d'Augusto* (Nov. 15, 1702; music not extant); *Julo Ascanio, rè d'Alba*, poemetto drammatico (March 19, 1708); *Pulcheria*, poemetto drammatico (June 21, 1708); *Il mese di Marzo, consecrato a*

Marte, componimento per musica (March 19, 1709); *Gli ossequi della notte,* componimento per musica (July 15, 1709); *La decima fatica d'Ercole, ovvero La Sconfitta di Gerione in Spagna,* componimento pastorale-eroico (Oct. 1, 1710); *Dafne in Lauro,* componimento per camera (Oct. 1, 1714); *Orfeo ed Euridice,* componimento da camera per musica (Oct. 1, 1715); *Angelica vincitrice di Alcina,* festa teatrale (Sept. 14, 1716); *Diana placata,* componimento da camera (Nov. 19, 1717); *Elisa,* festa teatrale per musica (Laxenburg, Aug. 28, 1719); *Psiche,* componimento da camera per musica (Nov. 19, 1720); *Le nozze di Aurora,* festa teatrale per musica (Oct. 6, 1722); *Costanza e Fortezza,* festa teatrale (Prague, Aug. 28, 1723); *Giunone placata,* festa teatrale per musica (Nov. 19, 1725); *La corona d'Arianna,* festa teatrale (Aug. 28, 1726); *Enea negli Elisi, ovvero Il tempio dell'Eternità,* festa teatrale (Aug. 28, 1731). ORA-TORIOS: *Die Heilige Dimpna, Infantin von Irland* (1702; only part 2 extant); *La fede sacrilega nella morte del Precursor S. Giovanni Battista* (1714); *La donna forte nelle madre de' sette Maccabei* (1715); *Il trionfo della fede* (1716); *Il disfacimento di Sisara* (1717); *Cristo nell'orto* (1718); *Gesù Cristo negato da Pietro* (1719); *Santa Geltrude* (1719); *La cena del Signore* (1720); *Ismaele* (1721); *Il testamento di nostro Signor Gesù Cristo sul calvario* (1726); *Oratorium germanicum de passione Domini* (1731); music not extant. His other sacred music includes *Il fonte della salute, aperto dalla grazia nel calvario,* componimento sacro (1716); *La deposizione dalla croce di Gesù Cristo Salvator Nostro,* componimento sacro per musica al SS.

Sepolcro (1728); about 80 masses; Te Deum for Double Choir (1706); motets; vespers and Psalms; antiphons; offertories; hymns; etc. His instrumental music includes about 50 church sonatas, some 80 partitas and overtures, *Concentus musico-instrumentalis* (1701), and keyboard works. A complete edition of his works, ed. by H. Federhofer and O. Wessely under the auspices of the J.J. Fux-Gesellschaft, began publication in 1959.

BIBL.: L. von Köchel, *J.J. F.* (Vienna, 1872; includes thematic catalog and list of works); C. Schnabl, "J.J. F., der österreichische Palestrina," *Jahrbuch der Leo-Gesellschaft* (Vienna, 1895); H. Rietsch, "Der 'Concentus' von F.," *Studien zur Musikwissenschaft,* IV (1916); K. Jeppesen, "J.J. F. und die moderne Kontrapunkttheorie," *Kongressbericht: Leipzig 1925;* A. Liess, *Die Triosonaten von J.J. F.* (Berlin, 1940); idem, *F.iana* (Vienna, 1958); H. Federhofer, "Unbekannte Kirchenmusik von J.J. F.," *Kirchenmusikalisches Jahrbuch,* XLIII (1959); J. van der Meer, *J.J. F. als Opernkomponist* (3 vols., Bilthoven, 1961); F. Riedel, "J.J. F. und die römische Palestrina-Tradition," *Die Musikforschung,* XIV (1961); H. Federhofer, "J.J. F. als Musiktheoretiker," *Hans Albrecht in memoriam* (Kassel, 1962); E. Wellesz, *F.* (London, 1965); C. Rutherford, *The Instrumental Music of J.J. F.* (diss., Colorado State Univ., 1967); H. Seifert, "Die Aufführungen der Opern und Serenate mit Musik von J.J. F.," *Studien zur Musikwissenschaft,* XXIX (1978); R. Flotzinger, *F. Studien* (Graz, 1985); B. Habla, ed., *J.J. F. und die barocke Bläsertradition* (Tutzing, 1987).

G

Gabichvadze, Revaz, Russian composer; b. Tiflis, June 11, 1913. He graduated in composition from the Tiflis Cons. in 1935; in 1938 joined its faculty.

WORKS: Operas: *Nana* (1949) and *We, Mothers of Peace* (1966); operetta, *Grasshopper* (1953); ballet, *Hamlet* (1971); oratorio, *Knight in a Leopard's Skin* (1938); *3 Monologues about Lenin* for Bass, Women's Chorus, and Orch. (1970); 3 syms. (1963, 1971, 1972); 2 chamber syms. (1965, 1968); *9 Variations* for 8 Instruments (1971); Violin Concerto (1947); Cello Concerto (1950); *4 Sketches* for Chamber Orch. (1969); *2 Factures* for Chamber Orch. (1960); Piano Sonata (1964); 3 string quartets; songs; cinema music.

Gabold, Ingolf, German-born Danish composer; b. Heidelberg, March 31, 1942. He studied theory and music history at the Royal Danish Cons. of Music in Copenhagen, and composition with Nørgård at the Århus Cons. His stated goal is to "combine music with Jung's depth psychology."

WORKS: Opera, *Syv scener til Orfeus* (7 Visions to Orpheus) for 4 Singers, 1 Actor, Dancers, and Orch. (1969–70; Danish television, Sept. 28, 1970); a television play, *Mod Vandmandens tegn* (Toward Aquarius) for Soprano, Bass, Chorus, and Organ (1971–72; Copenhagen, Nov. 11, 1973); *Für Louise* for Soprano and Chamber Orch. (1966; Copenhagen, Aug. 18, 1967); *Atlantis* for Rock Group and Orch. (1971; Danish Radio, Feb. 4, 1972); *Visione* for 4 Vocal Soloists and Mixed Chorus (1962); *Your Sister's Drown'd* for Soprano and Male Chorus (1968; to a text from *Hamlet*); *Written in Sand* for Chorus a cappella (1973).

Gabriel, Charles H(utchinson), American composer and music editor; b. Wilton, Iowa, Aug. 18, 1856; d. Los Angeles, Sept. 14, 1932. He went to Chicago in 1892 and became active as a composer of gospel hymns for various evangelists; then worked for Homer A. Rodeheaver's publishing company (1912–32), and ed. the journal *Gospel Choir* (1915–23), for which he wrote his memoirs (IV, 1918), 35 gospel songbooks, 19 anthem collections, and 8 vols. of Sunday-school songs. He also authored the book *Gospel Songs and Their Writers* (Chicago, 1915). He was a prolific composer; included in his more than 8,000 works are gospel hymns, Christmas cantatas, sacred cantatas, children's cantatas, and secular operettas.

Gabriel, Mary Ann Virginia, English composer; b. Banstead, Surrey, Feb. 7, 1825; d. London, Aug. 7, 1877. She studied with Pixis, Döhler, Thalberg, and Molique; married George E. March (1874), who wrote most of her librettos.

WORKS: 3 cantatas: *Evangeline* (Brighton Festival, Feb. 13, 1873); *Dreamland*; *Graziella*; 6 operettas: *Widows Bewitched* (London, Nov. 13, 1867); *Grass Widows*; *Shepherd of Cornouailles*; *Who's the Heir?*; *Follies of a Night*; *A Rainy Day*; piano pieces.

Gabrieli, Andrea (also known as **Andrea di Cannaregio**), eminent Italian organist and composer, uncle of **Giovanni Gabrieli;** b. Venice, c.1510; d. there, 1586. He was a pupil of Adrian Willaert at S. Marco and chorister there (1536); was organist at S. Geremia in Cannaregio in 1557–58; was in Frankfurt for the coronation of Maximilian II as court organist of Duke Albrecht V of Bavaria. In 1566 he returned to

Venice and was appointed 2nd organist at S. Marco; became 1st organist on Jan. 1, 1585, succeeding Merulo. He enjoyed a great reputation as an organist (his concerts with Merulo, on 2 organs, were featured attractions). Among his pupils were his nephew and Hans Leo Hassler. A prolific composer, he wrote a large number of works of varied description, many of which were publ. posth., ed. by his nephew. His versatility is attested by the fact that he was equally adept in sacred music of the loftiest spirit and in instrumental music, as well as in madrigals, often of a comic nature.

Works: sacred vocal: *Sacrae cantiones vulgo motecta appellatae, liber primus* for 5 Voices and Instruments (Venice, 1565); *Primus liber missarum* for 6 Voices (Venice, 1572); *Ecclesiasticarum cantionum omnibus sanctorum solemnitatibus deservientium liber primus* for 4 Voices (1576); *Psalmi Davidici, qui poenitentiales nuncupantur* for 6 Voices and Instruments (1583); *Concerti . . . continenti musica di chiesa, madrigali, & altro . . . liber primo di madrigali* for 6 to 8, 10, 12, and 16 Voices and Instruments (1587). **madrigals:** *Il primo libro di madrigali* for 5 Voices (1566); *Il secondo libro di madrigali* for 5 and 6 Voices, & *uno dialogo* for 8 Voices (1570; 3rd ed., augmented, 1588); *Greghesche e justiniane . . . libro primo* for 3 Voices (1571); *Il primo libro de madrigali* for 6 Voices (1574); *Libro primo di madrigali* for 3 Voices (1575); *Il secondo libro de madrigali* for 6 Voices (1580); *Il terzo libro de madrigali* for 5 Voices (1589); *Madrigali e ricercari* for 4 Voices (1589); also *Chori in musica . . . sopra li chori della tragedia di Edippo Tiranno* (1588) and *Mascherate* for 3 to 6 and 8 Voices (1601). **instrumental:** *Canzoni alla francese per sonar sopra stromenti da tasti* (1571; not extant); *Madrigali et ricercari* for 4 Voices (1589); *Intonationi d'organo . . . libro primo* (1593); *Ricercari . . . composti e tabulati per ogni sorte di stromenti da tasti . . . libro secondo* (1595); *Il terzo libro de ricercari* for Keyboard (1596); *Canzoni alla francese per sonar sopra instrumenti da tasti . . . libro sesto* (1605); 3 organ masses and other pieces. Many of his works have been publ. in modern eds.

Bibl.: G. Benvenuti, "A. e Giovanni G. e la musica strumentale in S. Marco," Istituzioni e Monumenti dell'Arte Musicale Italiana, II (1932); I. Zerr-Becking, *Studien zu A. G.* (Prague, 1933); F. Degrada, *A. G. e il suo tempo* (Florence, 1988).

Gabrieli, Giovanni, celebrated Italian organist, composer, and teacher, nephew of **Andrea Gabrieli;** b. Venice, between 1554 and 1557; d. there, Aug. 12, 1612. He lived in Munich from 1575 to 1579. On Nov. 1, 1584, he was engaged to substitute for Merulo as 1st organist at S. Marco in Venice; on Jan. 1, 1585, was permanently appointed as 2nd organist (his uncle meanwhile took charge of the 1st organ); retained this post until his death. As a composer, he stands at the head of the Venetian school; he was probably the 1st to write vocal works with parts for instrumental groups in various combinations, partly specified, partly left to the conductor, used as accompaniment as well as interspersed instrumental *sinfonie* (*Sacrae symphoniae*). His role as a composer and teacher is epoch-making; through his innovations and his development of procedures and devices invented by others (free handling of several choirs in the many-voiced vocal works, "concerted" solo parts and duets in the few-voiced vocal works, trio-sonata texture, novel dissonance treatment, speech rhythm, root progressions in fifths, use of tonal and range levels for structural purposes, coloristic effects) and through his numerous German pupils (particularly Schütz) and other transalpine followers, he gave a new direction to the development of music. His instrumental music helped to spark the composition of German instrumental ensemble music, which reached its apex in the symphonic and chamber music works of the Classical masters. Of interest also is the fact that one of his ricercari, a 4-part work in the 10th tone (1595), is an early example of the "fugue with episodes" (reprinted in Riemann's *Musikgeschichte in Beispielen*, no. 52, Leipzig, 1913).

Works: sacred vocal: *Concerti . . . continenti musica di chiesa, madrigali, & altro . . . libro primo et secondo* for 6 to 8, 10, 12, and 16 Voices, and Instruments (Venice, 1587); *Sacrae symphoniae* for 6 to 8, 10, 12, and 14 to 16 Voices, and Instruments (Venice, 1597); *Symphoniae sacrae . . . liber secundus* for 7, 8, 10 to 17, and 19 Voices, and Instruments (Venice, 1615). **secular vocal:** *Concerti . . . continenti musica di chiesa, madrigali, & altro . . . primo et secondo* for 6 to 8, 10, 12, and 16 Voices, and Instruments (Venice, 1587). **instrumental:** *Sacrae symphoniae* for 6 to 8, 10, 12, and 14 to 16 Voices, and Instruments (Venice, 1597); *Intonationi d'organo . . . libro primo* (Venice, 1593); *Canzoni et sonate* for 3, 5 to 8, 10, 12, 14, 15, and 22 Instruments, with Basso Continuo (organ) (Venice, 1615). Many of his works also appeared in various collections of the period. The *Opera Omnia*, ed. by D. Arnold, began publication in 1956 in the Corpus Mensurabilis Musicae series.

Bibl.: G. Bedbrook, "The Genius of G. G.," *Music Review* (Jan. 1947); J. Flower, *G. G.'s Sacrae Symphoniae* (1597) (diss., Univ. of Michigan, 1955); W. Yeomans, "The Canzoni (1615) of G. G.," *Monthly Musical Record*, LXXXVI (1956); S. Kunze, *Die Instrumentalmusik G. G.s* (Tutzing, 1963); E. Kenton, *Life and Works of G. G.*, Musicological Studies and Documents, XVI (1967); D. Arnold, *G. G.* (London, 1974); idem, *G. G. and the Music of the Venetian High Renaissance* (Oxford, 1979); P. Manzini, *G. G.: Il suo linguaggio musicale* (Genoa, 1984); R. Charteris, "Another keyboard canzona by G. G.?," *Early Music* (Nov. 1987); idem, "Newly Discovered Works by G. G.," *Music & Letters* (Oct. 1987).

Gabrielli, Caterina, famous Italian soprano; b. Rome, Nov. 12, 1730; d. there, Feb. 16, 1796. Her father served as a cook to Prince Gabrielli; the prince made it possible for her to pursue vocal training, and she thus took his name in appreciation; her nickname "La Coghetta" ("Little Cook") derives from her father's position. She most likely studied with Porpora in Venice (1744–47), then sang throughout Italy with notable success. She subsequently went to Vienna, where she made her concert debut at the Burgtheater on Feb. 16, 1755; she found a friend and mentor in Metastasio, and quickly established herself as one of the leading singers of the day. In 1758 she went to Milan, where she found another mentor in the castrato Gaetano Guadagni; that same year she was in Padua and Lucca, and later appeared in Parma (1759–60). She then returned to Vienna, where she created the title roles in Gluck's *Tetide* (Oct. 8, 1760) and Traetta's *Armide* (Jan. 3, 1761). Following further appearances in Italy, she sang in St. Petersburg (1772–75) and in London (1775–76); she then returned to Italy, singing in Naples, Venice, Lucca, and Milan until her 1780 retirement. Her reputed beauty and scandalous liaisons made her a legendary figure in operatic lore.

Bibl.: H. de Koch, *La G.* (Paris, 1878).

Gabrielli, Domenico, renowned Italian cellist and composer, called the "Menghino dal violoncello" ("Mignàn dal viulunzaal" in Bolognese dialect), the 1st part of his nickname being the diminutive of Domenico; b. Bologna, April 15, 1651; d. there, July 10, 1690. He studied composition with Legrenzi in Venice and cello with Petronio Franceschini in Bologna. He was elected a member of the Accademia Filarmonica in Bologna in 1676; became its president in 1683. He became cellist at S. Petronio in Bologna in 1676; his fame as a virtuoso led him to travel often, a circumstance that resulted in his dismissal in 1687; however, he was restored to his post in 1688. He was one of the 1st great masters of the cello, both as a performer and as a composer for the instrument; he was also a distinguished composer of vocal music, both sacred and secular.

Gabrielli, Nicolò, Italian composer; b. Naples, Feb. 21, 1814; d. Paris, June 14, 1891. He was a pupil of Buonamici, Conti, Donizetti, and Zingarelli at the Naples Cons.; from 1854 he lived in Paris. He wrote about 20 operas and 60 ballets, produced at Naples, Paris, and Vienna.

Gabrilowitsch, Ossip (Salomonovich), notable Russian-American pianist and conductor; b. St. Petersburg, Feb. 7, 1878; d. Detroit, Sept. 14, 1936. From 1888 to 1894 he was a pupil at the St. Petersburg Cons., studying piano with A. Rubinstein and composition with Navrátil, Liadov, and Glazunov; graduated as winner of the Rubinstein Prize, and then spent 2 years (1894–96) in Vienna studying with Leschetizky; then toured Germany, Austria, Russia, France, and England. His 1st American tour (debut Carnegie Hall, N.Y., Nov. 12, 1900) was eminently successful, as were his subsequent visits (1901–16). During the season 1912–13 he gave in Europe a series of 6 historical concerts illustrating the development of the piano concerto from Bach to the present day; on his American tour in 1914–15 he repeated the entire series in several of the larger cities, meeting with an enthusiastic reception. On Oct. 6, 1909, he married the contralto Clara Clemens (daughter of Mark Twain), with whom he frequently appeared in joint recitals. He conducted his 1st N.Y. concert on Dec. 13, 1916; was appointed conductor of the Detroit Sym. Orch. in 1918. From 1928 he also conducted the Philadelphia Orch., sharing the baton with Leopold Stokowski, while retaining his Detroit position.

BIBL.: C. Clemens, *My Husband G.* (N.Y., 1938).

Gaburo, Kenneth (Louis), American composer and teacher; b. Somerville, N.J., July 5, 1926. He studied composition, piano, and theory at the Eastman School of Music in Rochester, N.Y. (B.M., 1944; M.M., 1949), composition and conducting at the Conservatorio di Santa Cecilia in Rome (1954–55), and composition, theater, and linguistics at the Univ. of Illinois, Urbana (D.M.A., 1962); he also studied composition at the Berkshire Music Center at Tanglewood (summer 1956), and attended the Princeton Seminar in Advanced Musical Studies (summer 1959). After teaching at Kent State Univ. (1950), he was associate prof. at McNeese State Univ. (1950–54); then was a prof. at the Univ. of Illinois (1955–67) and at the Univ. of Calif. at San Diego (1967–75); also was founder-director of the Studio for Cognitive Studies in San Diego (1975–83) and a prof. at the Univ. of Iowa (from 1983). He is the recipient of a Fulbright fellowship (1954), ASCAP awards (from 1960), a Guggenheim fellowship (1967), and an N.E.A. award (1975); in 1985 he received the Milhaud Chair fellowship at Mills College in Oakland, Calif. His music is quaquaversal.

WORKS: OPERAS: *The Snow Queen* (Lake Charles, La., May 5, 1952); *Blur* (Urbana, Ill., Nov. 7, 1956); *The Widow* (Urbana, Ill., Feb. 26, 1961). ORCH.: *3 Interludes* for String Orch. (Rochester, N.Y., May 27, 1948); Concertante for Piano and Orch. (Rochester, N.Y., April 29, 1949); *On a Quiet Theme* (1950; N.Y., Feb. 26, 1955); *Elegy* for Small Orch. (1956; N.Y., April 3, 1959); *Shapes and Sounds* (1960); *Antiphony IX* (—a dot is no mere thing—) for Orch., Children, and Tape (1984–85; Kansas City, Mo., Oct. 13, 1985). CHAMBER: *Music for 5 Instruments* for Flute, Clarinet, Trumpet, Trombone, and Piano (1954); *Ideas and Transformations* No. 1 for Violin and Viola, No. 2 for Violin and Cello, No. 3 for Viola and Cello, and No. 4 for Violin, Viola, and Cello (all 1955); String Quartet (1956); *Line Studies* for Flute, Clarinet, Viola, and Trombone (N.Y., Dec. 15, 1957). ELECTRONIC AND TAPE: *Antiphony I* (Voices) for 3 String Groups and Tape (1958); *Antiphony II* (Variations on a Poem of Cavafy) for Soprano, Chorus, and Tape (1962); *Antiphony III* (Pearl-White Moments) for Chamber Chorus and Tape (1963); *Antiphony IV* (Poised) for Piccolo, Trombone, Double Bass, and Tape (1967); *Antiphony V* for Piano and Tape (1968–89); *Antiphony VI* (Cogito) for String Quartet, Slides, and 2- and 4-channel Tape (1971); *Antiphony VII* (—And) for 4 Video Systems and 4-channel Tape (1974–89); *Antiphony VIII* (Revolution) for Percussionist and Tape (1983–84); *Antiphony X* (Winded) for Organ and Tape (1985–89); numerous other works involving tape, actors, slides, film, lighting, and various acoustic instruments.

Gabussi, Giulio Cesare, Italian composer; b. Bologna, 1555; d. Milan, Sept. 12, 1611. He was a pupil of Costanzo Porta; in 1582 he was called to Milan as singer and composer at the Cathedral, and remained in that post until his death, with the exception of a brief stay in Poland in the service of Sigismund III (1601–2). He publ. 2 books of madrigals for 5 Voices

(Venice, 1580 and 1598); motets for 5 and 6 Voices (Venice, 1586); *Te Deum* for 4 Voices (Milan, 1589); etc. He was one of the 1st composers whose works in the Ambrosian ritual (litanies, etc.) appeared in print.

Gade, Axel Willy, Danish violinist, son of **Niels Gade;** b. Copenhagen, May 28, 1860; d. there, Nov. 9, 1921. He studied with his father and with Joachim; was active in Copenhagen as a theater conductor and teacher. He wrote a Violin Concerto and an opera, *Venezias Nat* (Copenhagen, Jan. 18, 1919).

Gade, Jacob, Danish conductor and composer; b. Vejle, Nov. 29, 1879; d. Copenhagen, Feb. 21, 1963. He studied violin; was a member of the N.Y. Sym. Orch. (1919–21); then returned to Copenhagen and was active there as a conductor. Among his light compositions, *Jalousie* (1925) attained great popularity. He also wrote several symphonic poems (*Den sidste Viking, Leda and the Swan*, etc.).

BIBL.: K. Bjarnjof, *Tango Jalousie* (Copenhagen, 1969).

Gade, Niels (Wilhelm), greatly significant Danish composer, conductor, and pedagogue, father of **Axel Willy Gade;** b. Copenhagen, Feb. 22, 1817; d. there, Dec. 21, 1890. The son of a maker of instruments, he studied violin with F.T. Wexschall and theory and composition with A.P. Berggreen. After making his debut as a violinist in 1833, he joined the Royal Orch. in 1834. He first came to prominence as a composer with his concert overture *Efterklange af Ossian* (1840), which won the prize of the Copenhagen Musical Soc. This popular score was followed by his outstanding 1st Sym. (1841–42), which Mendelssohn conducted in its premiere performance in Leipzig at a Gewandhaus concert on March 2, 1843, with extraordinary success. Gade was appointed assistant conductor to Mendelssohn and the Gewandhaus Orch.; he also joined the faculty of the Leipzig Cons. Upon Mendelssohn's death in 1847, Gade was named Gewandhaus Kapellmeister. However, with the outbreak of the Schleswig-Holstein War in 1848, he returned to Copenhagen and quickly assumed a preeminent place in the musical life of his homeland. He reorganized the Copenhagen Musical Soc. and became its chief conductor in 1850, leading its orch. and choir in distinguished performances of his own music as well as that of other composers. In 1866 he helped to organize the Copenhagen Cons., and thereafter served as one of its directors; also taught composition and music history there. In 1876 the Danish government awarded him a life pension. Gade was an ardent admirer of Mendelssohn and Schumann and thus adopted the prevalent German Romantic style in his own works; his influence was nonetheless great in Denmark. His activities as a conductor and teacher were also extremely important.

WORKS: STAGE: *Mariotta*, singspiel (1848–49). BALLETS: *Faedrelandets muser* (The Muses of Our Fatherland; 1840); *Napoli* (1842; Act 2 only); *Et folkesagn* (1853–54; Act 2 by J.P.E. Hartmann); incidental music. ORCH.: 8 syms.: No. 1, "Paa Sjolunds fagre sletter" (1841–42; Leipzig, March 2, 1843, Mendelssohn conducting); No. 2 (1843; Leipzig, Jan. 18, 1844); No. 3 (1846; Leipzig, Dec. 9, 1847); No. 4 (Copenhagen, Nov. 16, 1850); No. 5 (Copenhagen, Dec. 11, 1852); No. 6 (Copenhagen, March 17, 1857); No. 7 (Leipzig, March 2, 1865, Reinecke conducting); No. 8 (Copenhagen, Dec. 7, 1871); *I højlandene* (In the Highlands), overture (1844); *Nordisk soeterrejse* (A Mountain Trip in the North), overture (1850); *Festmarsch ved Kong Christian IX.'s regjerings-jubilaeum* (1850); *Hamlet*, overture (1861); *Michel Angelo*, overture (1861); *Sørgemarsch ved Kong Frederik d. 7des* (Funeral March for King Frederik VII; 1863); *Novelletter* in F major for String Orch. (1874); *Capriccio* for Violin and Orch. (1878); *En sommerdag paa landet* (A Summer's Day in the Country), 5 pieces (1879); Violin Concerto (1880); *Novelletter* in E major (1883; rev. 1886); *Holbergiana*, suite (1884); *Ulysses-marsch: Forspil til Holberg's Ulysses von Ithaca* (1888–90). CANTATAS: *Comala* (1846); *Mindekantate over Fru Anna Nielsen* (Cantata in Memory of Fru Anna Nielsen; 1856); *Baldurs drøn* (Baldur's Dream; 1858); *Frühlings-Botschaft* (1858); *Mindekantate over Overhofmarschal Chamberlain Levetzau* (Cantata in Memory of Count Chamberlain

Levetzau; 1859); *Mindekantate over skuespiller Nielsen* (Cantata in Memory of the Actor Nielsen; 1860); *Die heilige Nacht* (1862); *Ved solnedgang* (At Sunset; 1863); *Korsfarerne* (The Crusader; 1865–66); *Kalanus* (1869); *Gefion* (1869); *Zion* (1874); *Den bjergtagne* (The Mountain Thrall; 1873); *Psyche* (1881–82); *Der Strom* (1889). OTHER VOCAL: *Frühlings-Fantasie* for Solo Voices and Orch. (1852); *Elverskud* (Elf-King's Daughter) for Solo Voices, Chorus, and Orch. (1853); etc. CHAMBER: 3 violin sonatas (1842, 1849, 1885); 2 string quartets (n.d., 1889); 2 string quintets (1845, 1851); Octet (1848); String Sextet (1863); *Fantasiestücke* for Clarinet and Piano (1864); *Folkesdanse* for Violin and Piano (1888); etc. PIANO: Sonata (1840; rev. 1854); *Foraarstoner* (Spring Flowers; 1841); *Akvareller* (1850); *Albumsblade* (1850); *Arabeske* (1854); *Folkedanse* (1855); *Idyller* (1857); also organ pieces; songs.
BIBL.: R. Henriques, *N.W. G.* (Copenhagen, 1891); D. Gade, *N.W. G.: Optengenelser og breve* (Copenhagen, 1892; German tr., 1894); C. Kjerulf, *N.W. G.* (Copenhagen, 1917); W. Behrend, *Minder om N.W. G.* (Copenhagen, 1930); J. Gade, *Omkring N.W. G.: Breve fra fader og søn* (Copenhagen, 1967); L. Brix, "N.W. G. als Klavierkomponist," *Die Musikforschung,* XXVI (1973); *N.W. G.—Katalog* (Copenhagen, 1986).

Gadsby, Henry (Robert), English organist, composer, and music teacher; b. Hackney, London, Dec. 15, 1842; d. London, Nov. 11, 1907. He was a chorister at St. Paul's from 1849 to 1858; organist at St. Peter's, Brockley; in 1884 succeeded Hullah as prof. of harmony at Queen's College, London; was prof. at the Guildhall School of Music from its founding (1880) until his death. He wrote 3 syms., overtures, songs, etc.

Gadski, Johanna (Emilia Agnes), celebrated German soprano; b. Anklam, June 15, 1872; d. as a result of an automobile accident, Berlin, Feb. 22, 1932. She studied with Schroeder-Chaloupka in Stettin; made her operatic debut as Lortzing's Undine at Berlin's Kroll Opera (1889), continuing to appear there until 1893; also sang in Mainz, Stettin, and Bremen. On March 1, 1895, she made her U.S. debut as Elsa in *Lohengrin* with the Damrosch Opera Co. in N.Y.; continued to sing with it until 1898, appearing in such roles as Elisabeth, Eva, and Sieglinde. She made her 1st appearance at London's Covent Garden as Elisabeth on May 15, 1899, and sang there until 1901; also appeared as Eva in Bayreuth (1899). On Jan. 6, 1900, she made her Metropolitan Opera debut in N.Y. as Senta, and quickly established herself there as an outstanding interpreter of such compelling roles as Brünnhilde and Isolde. She made 2 transcontinental concert tours of the U.S. (1904–6), then returned to the Metropolitan Opera (1907), making her farewell performance there as Isolde on April 13, 1917. Having married Lt. Hans Tauscher on Nov. 11, 1892, she returned to Germany in 1917 when her husband was deported as an enemy alien. She sang opera again in the U.S. with a touring German company from 1929 to 1931.

Gadzhibekov, Sultan, Azerbaijani conductor, pedagogue, and composer; b. Shusha, May 8, 1919; d. Baku, Sept. 19, 1974. He studied composition with B. Zeidman at the Baku Cons. (graduated, 1946), where he later taught instrumentation and composition (from 1965); also conducted the Azerbaijan Phil. (1955–62). He received state prizes for his ballet *Gulshen* (1952) and his Concerto for Orch. (1970), and was named a People's Artist of the Azerbaijan S.S.R. (1960).
WORKS: STAGE: *The Red Rose,* musical comedy (1940); *Iskender and the Shepherd,* children's opera (1947); *Gulshen,* ballet (1950). ORCH.: *Variations* (1941); 2 syms. (1944, 1946); *Caravan,* symphonic picture (1945); Violin Concerto (1945); Overture (1956); Concerto (1964); suites: *Gulshen* (1953); *Bulgarian* (1957); *Indian* (1970). CHAMBER: String Quartet (1943); 2 scherzos (1949). SOLO PIANO: Sonata (1940); 6 Preludes (1941); also vocal works.
BIBL.: D. Danilov, *S. G.* (Baku, 1956); E. Abasova, *S. G.* (Baku, 1965); A. Tagizade, *S. G.* (Baku, 1967).

Gadzhibekov, Uzeir, Azerbaijani composer; b. Agdzhabedy, near Shusha, Sept. 17, 1885; d. Baku, Nov. 23, 1948. He studied

in Shusha; then lived in Baku, where he produced his 1st opera on a native subject, *Leyly and Medzhnun* (Jan. 25, 1908). His comic opera *Arshin Mal Alan* (Baku, Nov. 27, 1913) had numerous performances; another opera, *Kyor-Oglu* (A Blind Man's Son), was produced at the Azerbaijan Festival in Moscow (April 30, 1937).

Gadzhiev, (Akhmed) Jevdet, Azerbaijani composer; b. Nukha, June 18, 1917. He studied with M. Rudolf and U. Gadzhibekov at the Baku Cons. (1936–38), and with Anatoli Alexandrov, S. Vasilenko, and Shostakovich at the Moscow Cons. (1938–41; graduated, 1947); then taught composition at the Baku Cons. (from 1963). He received state prizes for his opera *Veten* (1946) and the *Symphonic Poem for Peace* (1952), and was made a People's Artist of the Azerbaijan S.S.R. (1960).
WORKS: STAGE: *Veten,* opera (with K. Karayev; 1945); *Ghazal My Flower* (1956); *The Maiden Gathering Apples* (1957). ORCH.: Sinfonietta (1938); *Azerbaijan Suite* (1941); 5 syms. (1944; 1946; 1947; 1956, "In Memory of Lenin"; 1971, "Man, Earth, Universe"); symphonic poems: *Azerbaijan* (1936); *Epistle to Siberia* (1937); *For Peace* (1951). CHAMBER: *Fugue* (1940); *3 Fugues* (1941); String Quartet (1941); *Quartet Poem* (1961). SOLO PIANO: *24 Preludes* (1935); *Ballade* (1950); Sonata (1956); *Scherzo* (1957); *Children's Corner Suite* (1962); vocal works.
BIBL.: E. Muradova, *J. G.* (Baku, 1962); K. Abezgauz, *J. G.* (Baku, 1965); E. Abasova, *J. G.* (Baku, 1967).

Gaffurius (Gafurius, Gaffurio, etc.), **Franchino (Franchinus),** celebrated Italian music theorist and composer; b. Lodi, Jan. 14, 1451; d. Milan, June 24, 1522. He studied theology and music; lived in Mantua, Verona, and Genoa (1477); he formed an intimacy with the Doge Prospero Adorno (then in exile) and fled with him to Naples (1478). There he met various distinguished musicians, and held public disputation with Johannes Tinctoris, Guarnier, and Hycart. The plague and the Turkish invasion compelled him to return to Lodi (1480). He was a teacher and choirmaster at Monticello for 3 years; made a short visit to Bergamo in 1483; from 1484 until his death was maestro di cappella at the Milan Cathedral, and 1st singer in the choir of Duke Lodovico Sforza. In addition to his cathedral and court duties, he wrote music and his most important treatises: *Theorica musicae* (1492); his magnum opus, entitled *Practica musicae* (1496); and *De harmonia musicorum instrumentorum opus* (1518). His last years were marked by a controversy with the theorist Giovanni Spataro of Bologna. His sacred music, mainly masses and motets, reveal his mastery of the Franco-Netherlands and Italian styles. The MSS of these, as well as works by other composers, are extant and known as the Gaffurius Codices. His works have been ed. by A. Bortone, F. Fano, and L. Migliavacca in the Archivium Musices Metropolitantum Mediolanese series (5 vols., Milan, 1958–60).
BIBL.: A. Cretta, L. Cremascoli, and L. Salamina, *F. Gaffurio* (Lodi, 1951); A. Gallo, "Le traduzioni dal Greco per F. Gaffurio," *Acta Musicologica,* XXXV (1963); C. Miller, "G.'s Practica Musicae: Origin and Contents," *Musica Disciplina,* XXII (1968).

Gage, Irwin, American pianist; b. Cleveland, Sept. 4, 1939. He studied with Eugene Bossart at the Univ. of Michigan, at Yale Univ., and with Erik Werba, Hilde Langer-Rühl, Kurt Schmidek, and Klaus Vokurka in Vienna; then devoted himself mainly to a career as an accompanist, becoming well known for his master classes.

Gagliano, famous family of violin makers in Naples. **Alessandro,** who worked from 1695 to 1725, was a pupil of Stradivari, and he, as well as his sons **Nicola** (1695–1758) and **Gennaro** (1700–1788), followed largely the Stradivari model. The instruments of **Ferdinando Gagliano** (c.1724–81), a son of Nicola, exhibit less skillful workmanship than those of the older members of the family.

Gagliano, Marco da, significant Italian composer; b. Florence, May 1, 1582; d. there, Feb. 25, 1643. He studied with Luca Bati, and became his assistant at S. Lorenzo in 1602; concurrently studied with the Compagnia dell'Arcangelo Raf-

Gagnebin–Galajikian

592

faello, serving as maestro di cappella in 1607 and 1609; also took Holy Orders. In 1607 he went to Mantua, where his opera *La Dafne* was given with great success in 1608. After returning to Florence, he succeeded Bati as maestro di cappella at the Cathedral in 1608; was later in the service of the Medici court; was made canon in 1610 and Apostolic Protonotary in 1615; founded the Accademia degli Elevati in 1607. With Jacopo Peri, he wrote the opera *Lo sposalizio di Medoro e Angelica,* which was performed in honor of the election of Emperor Ferdinand III at the Palazzo Pitti on Sept. 25, 1619. He also composed the opera *La Flora,* for which Peri wrote the role of Clori; it was performed in honor of the wedding of Margherita de' Medici and Duke Odoardo Farnese of Parma at the Palazzo Pitti on Oct. 14, 1628. Gagliano was one of the earliest composers to write in the *stile rappresentativo,* which he developed further by ornamentation.

WORKS: Operas: *La Dafne* (Mantua, 1608); *Lo sposalizio di Medoro e Angelica* (Palazzo Pitti, Florence, Sept. 25, 1619; in collaboration with J. Peri); *La Flora, overo Il natal di Fiori* (Palazzo Pitti, Florence, Oct. 14, 1628; major portion by Gagliano, with the role of Clori by Peri). Another dramatic work, *La liberazione di Tirreno e d'Arnea* (Florence, Feb. 6, 1617), may be by Gagliano; he may have collaborated with Peri on the score, or it may be entirely the work of Peri. Additional secular works include books of madrigals for 5, 6, 7, and 8 Voices (1602–17) and *Musiche* for 1 to 3 and 5 Voices (1615). His sacred music includes *Officium defunctorum* for 4 to 8 Voices (Venice, 1607–8); *Missae et sacrarum cantionum* for 6 Voices (Florence, 1614); *Sacrarum cantionum . . . liber secundus* for 1 to 4 and 6 Voices (1622); *Responsoria maioris hebdomadae* for 4 Voices (1630–31).

BIBL.: D. Butchart, *I Madrigali di M. d.G.* (Florence, 1982).

Gagnebin, Henri, Swiss composer and pedagogue; b. Liège (of Swiss parents), March 13, 1886; d. Geneva, June 2, 1977. He studied organ with Vierne and composition with d'Indy at the Schola Cantorum in Paris; served as a church organist in Paris (1910–16) and in Lausanne (1916–25); was director of the Geneva Cons. from 1925 to 1957. He publ. the books *Entretiens sur la Musique* (Geneva, 1943), *Musique, mon beau souci* (Paris, 1968), and *Orgue, musette et bourbon* (Neuchâtel, 1975).

WORKS: 4 syms. (1911; 1918–21; 1955; 1970); 3 *Tableaux symphoniques d'après F. Hodler* (1942); *Suite d'orchestre sur des Psaumes huguenots* for Orch. (1950); Piano Concerto (1951); Clarinet Concerto (1971); Concerto for Oboe, Bassoon, and String Orch. (1972); String Trio (1968); Wind Octet (1970); Brass Quintet (1970); Wind Sextet (1971); other chamber music, including several string quartets; many organ pieces.

Gaigerova, Varvara, Russian pianist and composer; b. Oryekhovo-Zuyevo, Oct. 17, 1903; d. Moscow, April 6, 1944. She studied piano at the Moscow Cons. with Neuhaus and composition with Miaskovsky. In most of her compositions she cultivated folk materials of the constituent republics of the U.S.S.R., including those of the Mongol populations of Siberia and Central Asia.

WORKS: 3 syms. (1928, 1934, 1937); 3 suites for Domra Ensembles on folk themes of Kazakhstan, Turkestan, Uzbekistan, etc. (1932, 1934, 1935); 2 string quartets (1927, 1947); piano pieces; some 150 songs; cantata, *The Sun of Socialism* (1932).

Gailhard, Pierre, noted French bass and opera manager; b. Toulouse, Aug. 1, 1848; d. Paris, Oct. 12, 1918. He began his vocal studies in his native city, and entered the Paris Cons. in 1866. After 1 year of study under Révial he graduated in 1867, winning 3 1st prizes. He made his debut at the Opéra-Comique (Dec. 4, 1867) as Falstaff in Thomas's *Songe d'une nuit d'été;* on Nov. 3, 1871, he made his debut at the Opéra as Méphistophélès in Gounod's *Faust.* At the height of his powers and success he gave up the stage when, in 1884, he accepted, jointly with M. Ritt, the management of the famous institution; on the appointment of M. Bertrand as successor to Ritt, in 1892, he retired, but joined Bertrand the following

year as co-director; after the latter's death, in 1899, he remained sole director until 1908. His administration was remarkably successful, considering both the novelties produced and the engagement of new singers (Melba, Eames, Bréval, Caron, Ackté, Alvarez, Saléza, Renaud, the 2 de Reszkes, etc.). Against violent opposition he introduced, and maintained in the repertoire, *Lohengrin* (1895), *Die Walküre* (1893), *Tannhäuser* (1895; the 1st perf. after the notorious fiasco of 1861), *Meistersinger* (1897), and *Siegfried* (1902). His son, **André Gailhard** (b. Paris, June 29, 1885; d. Ermont, Val d'Oise, July 3, 1966), composed the operas *Amaryllis* (Toulouse, 1906), *Le Sortilège* (Paris, 1913), and *La Bataille* (Paris, 1931).

Gaillard, Marius-François, French composer and conductor; b. Paris, Oct. 13, 1900; d. Evecquemont, Yvelines, July 23, 1973. He studied with Diémer and Leroux at the Paris Cons. He began his career as a pianist; then started a series of sym. concerts in Paris, which he conducted from 1928 to 1949. He traveled all over the world, collecting examples of primitive music. His compositions follow a neo-impressionist trend.

WORKS: *La Danse pendant le festin* (1924) and *Détresse,* ballets (1932); 3 syms.; *Guyanes,* symphonic suite (1925); *Images d'Épinal* for Piano and Orch. (1929); Violin Sonata (1923); String Trio (1935); *Sonate baroque* for Violin and Piano (1950); *Concerto classique* for Cello and Orch. (1950); *Tombeau romantique* for Piano and Orch. (1954); *Concerto leggero* for Violin and Orch. (1954); *Concerto agreste* for Viola and Orch. (1957); Harp Concerto (1960); many songs and piano pieces.

Gaito, Constantino, Argentine composer; b. Buenos Aires, Aug. 3, 1878; d. there, Dec. 14, 1945. He studied in Naples with Platania; lived in Buenos Aires as a teacher; wrote the operas (all produced in Buenos Aires) *Shafras* (1907), *I Doria* (1915), *I paggi di Sua Maestà* (1918); *Caio Petronio* (Sept. 2, 1919), *Flor de nieve* (Aug. 3, 1922), *Ollantay* (July 23, 1926), *Lázaro* (1929), and *La sangre de las guitarras* (Aug. 17, 1932); the ballet *La flor del Irupé* (Buenos Aires, July 17, 1929); oratorio, *San Francisco Solano* (1940); symphonic poem, *El ombú* (1924); songs; piano pieces.

Gál, Hans, Austrian composer and music scholar; b. Brunn, near Vienna, Aug. 5, 1890; d. Edinburgh, Oct. 3, 1987. He studied at the Univ. of Vienna with Mandyczewski and Adler; from 1919 to 1929 he lectured there, then went to Germany; was director of the Mainz Cons. from 1929 to 1933; returned to Vienna in 1933; after the advent of the Nazi government, was compelled to leave Vienna in 1938, and settled in Edinburgh, where he became a lecturer on music at the Univ. (1945–65) while continuing to compose.

WRITINGS: *Anleitung zum Partiturlesen* (Vienna, 1923; Eng. tr. as *Directions for Score-Reading,* 1924); *The Golden Age of Vienna* (London, 1948); *Johannes Brahms* (Frankfurt, 1961; Eng. tr., 1964); *Richard Wagner* (Frankfurt, 1963); *The Musician's World: Great Composers in Their Letters* (London, 1965; German tr., 1966); *Franz Schubert, oder Die Melodie* (Frankfurt, 1970; Eng. tr., 1974); *Giuseppe Verdi und die Oper* (Frankfurt, 1982).

WORKS: Operas: *Der Arzt der Sobeide* (Breslau, 1919); *Die heilige Ente* (Düsseldorf, April 29, 1923); *Das Lied der Nacht* (Breslau, April 24, 1926); *Der Zauberspiegel* (Breslau, 1930; also as an orch. suite); *Die beiden Klaas* (1933); 4 syms. (1928, 1949, 1952, 1975); *A Pickwickian Overture* (1939); Violin Concerto (1931); Cello Concerto (1944); Piano Concerto (1947); *Idyllikon* for Small Orch. (1969); Triptych for Orch. (1970); 4 string quartets (1916, 1929, 1969, 1971); String Trio (1931); Piano Quartet (1915); Piano Trio (1948); Violin Sonata (1921); numerous choral works, sacred and secular.

BIBL.: W. Waldstein, *H. G.* (Vienna, 1965).

Galajikian, Florence Grandland, American pianist and composer; b. Maywood, Ill., July 29, 1900; d. River Forest, Ill., Nov. 16, 1970. She studied at Northwestern Univ. and Chicago Musical College; her teachers were Oldberg, Lutkin, Rubin Goldmark, Carl Beecher, and Noelte. She toured as a pianist; composed a number of songs which enjoyed favor among sopranos; she also wrote orch. pieces; her *Symphonic Intermezzo* was awarded NBC's 4th prize, and was performed by the NBC Sym. Orch. on May 8, 1932.

Galamian, Ivan (Alexander), eminent Armenian-born American violinist and pedagogue; b. Tabriz, Persia (of Armenian parents), Feb. 5, 1903; d. N.Y., April 14, 1981. He studied with Konstantin Mostras at the school of Moscow's Phil. Soc. (1916–22); then attended Lucien Capet's master course in Paris (1922–23), making his formal debut there (1924); taught at the Russian Cons. (1925–39) and at the École Normale de Musique (1936–39) there. He settled in N.Y. (1939), becoming a teacher at the Henry St. Settlement School (1941); was later named to the faculty of the Curtis Inst. of Music in Philadelphia (1944) and of the Juilliard School of Music in N.Y. (1946); was also founder of the Meadowmount School for string players in Westport, N.Y. (1944). Among his numerous students were such gifted artists as Itzhak Perlman, Michael Rabin, Kyung-Wha Chung, Erick Friedman, Miriam Fried, Pinchas Zuckerman, Young-Uck Kim, and Jaime Laredo. He publ. *Principles of Violin Playing and Teaching* (with E. Green; Englewood Cliffs, N.J., 1962; 2nd ed., rev., 1985) and *Contemporary Violin Technique* (with F. Neumann; 2 vols., N.Y., 1966, 1977).
BIBL.: R. Schmidt, "The Legacy of I. G.," *American String Teacher*, XXXV/2 (1985).

Galas, Diamanda (Dimitria Angeliki Elena), remarkable American avant-garde composer and vocalist of Greek extraction; b. San Diego, Aug. 29, 1955. She studied biochemistry, psychology, music, and experimental performance at the Univ. of Calif. at San Diego (1974–79); she also took private vocal lessons. In her scientific studies she and a group of medical students began investigating extreme mental states, using themselves as subjects in a series of bizarre mind-altering experiments; her resultant understanding of psychopathology (notably schizophrenia and psychosis) became an underlying subject in most of her work. After some success as a jazz pianist, she began a vocal career, in which her remarkable precision and advanced technique attracted attention. Although she has performed such demanding works as Xenakis's microtonal *N'Shima* (Brooklyn Phil., Jan. 15, 1981) and Globokar's *Misère* (West German Radio Orch., Cologne, 1980), she is best known for her theatrical performances of her own solo vocal works, given at venues ranging from the Donaueschingen Festival to the N.Y. rock club Danceteria. Her compositions, most of which employ live electronics and/or tape, are improvised according to rigorous, complex "navigation(s) through specified mental states." Her performances have stringent requirements for lighting and sound and possess a shattering intensity. Her brother Philip Dimitri Galas, a playwright whose works were as violent as is his sister's music, died of AIDS in the late 1980s; her increasing emotional and political involvement in what she regards as this "modern plague" led to her 4-part work *Masque of the Red Death* (1986–). She publ. an esthetic statement as "Intravenal Song" in *Perspectives of New Music*, XX (1981).
WORKS: *Medea tarantula* for Voice (1977); *Les Yeux sans sang* for Voice and Electronics (1978); *Tragouthia apo to aima exoun fonos* (Song from the Blood of Those Murdered) for Voice and Tape (1981); *Wild Women with Steak Knives* for Tape and Live Electronics (1981–83); *Litanies of Satan* for Voice, Tape, and Live Electronics (1982); *Panoptikon* for Voice, Tape, and Live Electronics (1982–83); *Masque of the Red Death* for Voice, Electronics, and Instrument (*The Divine Punishment, Saint of the Pit, You Must Be Certain of the Devil,* and a 4th work in progress; 1986–).
BIBL.: L. Morra, "D. G.: Rebellious Soprano," *East Village Eye* (March 1983); S. Holden, "D. G., Avant-garde Diva," *N.Y. Times* (July 19, 1985); J. Johnson and B. Coley, "D. G.: Tura Satana without Cleavage," *Forced Exposure*, XV (1989).

Galeffi, Carlo, esteemed Italian baritone; b. Malamocco, near Venice, June 4, 1882; d. Rome, Sept. 22, 1961. After private vocal studies, he made his debut at the Teatro Adriano in Rome in 1903. On Nov. 29, 1910, he made his Metropolitan Opera debut in N.Y. as Germont in *La Traviata;* sang there again in 1920–21; for years was a member of La Scala in Milan (1912–38); he retired in 1954. He was renowned for his roles of Rigoletto, Boccanegra, and Nabucco in Verdi's operas.
BIBL.: A. Marchetti, *C. G.: Una vita per el canto* (Rome, 1973).

Galeotti, Cesare, Italian composer; b. Pietrasanta, June 5, 1872; d. Paris, Feb. 19, 1929. He studied piano with Sgambati and composition with Guiraud at the Paris Cons. Several of his symphonic works were performed in Paris; his opera *Anton* was staged at La Scala, Milan (Feb. 17, 1900). Another opera, *Dorisse,* was first given in Brussels (April 18, 1910).

Gales, Weston, American organist and conductor; b. Elizabeth, N.J., Nov. 5, 1877; d. Portsmouth, N.H., Oct. 21, 1939. He studied composition with Horatio Parker at Yale Univ. and organ with Gaston-Marie Déthier in N.Y.; held various posts as church organist in Boston; then took additional instruction with Widor and Vierne in Paris. Returning to America, he was active as a choral conductor. In 1914 he organized the Detroit Sym. Orch.; conducted it until 1918; became associate conductor of the N.Y. State Sym. Orch. (1924). In 1928 he was made répétiteur at the Bayreuth Festivals, returning to the U.S. in 1933.

Galilei, Vincenzo, celebrated Italian lutenist, composer, and music theorist, father of the great astronomer Galileo Galilei; b. S. Maria a Monte, near Florence, c.1520; d. Florence (buried), July 2, 1591. A skillful lutenist and violinist, and a student of ancient Greek theory, he was a prominent member of the artistic circle meeting at Count Bardi's house known as the Florentine Camerata; his compositions for solo voice with lute accompaniment may be regarded as the starting point of the monody successfully cultivated by Peri, Caccini, etc., the founders of the "opera in musica." A zealous advocate of Grecian simplicity, in contrast with contrapuntal complexity, he publ. a *Dialogo . . . della musica antica et della moderna* (Florence, 1581; to the 2nd ed. [1602] is appended a polemical *Discorso . . . intorno all' opere di messer Gioseffo Zarlino da Chioggia,* which had appeared separately in 1589) and *Fronimo. Dialogo . . .* (in 2 parts: Venice, 1568 and 1569; new ed., 1584), all of considerable historical interest. Vol. IV of Istituzioni e Monumenti dell' Arte Musicale Italiana (Milan, 1934), ed. by F. Fano, is devoted entirely to Galilei; it contains a large selection of music reprints from his *Fronimo. Dialogo* (lute transcriptions by Galilei and original compositions), *Libro d'intavolatura di liuto* (1584), *Il secondo libro de madrigali a 4 et a 5 voci* (1587), and a 4-part *Cantilena,* together with biographical details, list of works, notes about extant MSS, reprints, transcriptions, etc. His *Contrapunti a due voci* (1584) was ed. by Louise Read (Smith College Music Archives, vol. VIII, 1947).
BIBL.: O. Fleissner, *Die Madrigale V. G.s und sein Dialogo della musica antica e moderna* (Munich, 1922); S. Drake, "V. G. and Galileo," *Galileo Studies* (Ann Arbor, 1970); D. Walker, "Some Aspects of the Musical Theory of V. G. and Galileo Galilei," *Proceedings of the Royal Musical Association,* C (1973–74).

Galimer, Felix, Austrian-born American violinist and pedagogue; b. Vienna, May 12, 1910. He studied with Adolf Bak at the Vienna Cons. (diploma, 1928) and with Carl Flesch in Berlin and Baden-Baden (1929–30). In 1929 he founded the Galimir String Quartet in Vienna. Emigrating to the U.S. in 1938, he made his debut at N.Y.'s Town Hall, and also organized a new Galimir String Quartet, which subsequently acquired a fine reputation for its performances of contemporary music. He became a naturalized U.S. citizen in 1944. He was 1st violinist of the NBC Sym. Orch. (1939–54), concertmaster of the Sym. of the Air (1954–56) in N.Y., and a performer and teacher at the Marlboro (Vt.) Festival and Music School (from 1954). He held teaching positions at the Juilliard School of Music in N.Y. (from 1962), the Curtis Inst. of Music in Philadelphia (from 1972), and the Mannes College of Music in N.Y. (from 1977), where his quartet was in residence.

Galin, Pierre, French music pedagogue; b. Samatan, Gers, 1786; d. Bordeaux, Aug. 31, 1821. He was a mathematics teacher at the Lycée in Bordeaux, and conceived the idea of simplifying music instruction by a method which he termed the "Méloplaste" and explained in his work *Exposition d'une nouvelle méthode pour l'enseignement de la musique* (1818; 3rd ed., 1831). The method attracted attention, and was energetically promoted by Chevé.

Galindo (Dimas), Blas, Mexican composer; b. San Gabriel, Jalisco, Feb. 3, 1910. He studied harmony, counterpoint, and fugue with Rolón, musical analysis with Huízar, composition with Chávez, and piano with Rodriguez Vizcarra at the National Cons. in Mexico City (1931–42); had special composition lessons with Aaron Copland at the Berkshire Music Center in Tanglewood, Mass. (1941–42); in 1934 he formed, together with Ayala, Contreras, and Moncayo, the Grupo de los Cuatro for the presentation of modern music (disbanded after a few years). He was a prof. of music and director of the National Cons. in Mexico City from 1942 to 1961; in 1955 became director of the orch. of the Mexican Inst. of Social Security; was pensioned by the government in 1965 and devoted himself mainly to composition thereafter. In his music he stresses native elements, while adhering to classical forms; in his later works he made use of electronic sound.
WORKS: BALLETS: *Entre sombras anda el fuego* (Among Shadows Walks Fire; Mexico City, March 23, 1940); *Danza de las fuerzas nuevas* (Dance of the New Forces; 1940); *El Zanate* (Mexico City, Dec. 6, 1947); *La Manda* (Mexico City, March 31, 1951); *El sueño y la presencia* (Mexico City, Nov. 24, 1951); *La hija del Yori* (Mexico City, 1952); *El maleficio* (Mexico City, Oct. 28, 1954). ORCH.: *Sones de mariachi* (1940); 2 piano concertos: No. 1 (Mexico City, July 24, 1942); No. 2 (Mexico City, Aug. 17, 1962); *Nocturno* (1945); *Don Quijote* (1947); *Homenaje a Cervantes,* suite (1947); *Astucia* (1948); *Poema de Neruda* for String Orch. (1948); *Pequeñas variaciones* (1951); *Los signos del zodíaco* for Small Orch. (1951); 3 syms.: No. 1, *Sinfonía breve,* for Strings (Mexico City, Aug. 22, 1952); No. 2 (Caracas, March 19, 1957; shared 1st prize at the Caracas Festival); No. 3 (Washington, D.C., April 30, 1961); *Obertura mexicana* (1953); Flute Concerto (1960; New Orleans, April 3, 1965); *4 Pieces* (1961; Mexico City, Nov. 15, 1963); *Edipo Rey* (1961; incidental music for Sophocles' *Oedipus Rex*); Violin Concerto (1962; Mexico City, Sept. 13, 1970); *3 Pieces* for Clarinet and Orch. (1962); *Obertura* for Organ and Strings (1963); *3 Pieces* for Horn and Orch. (1963); Concertino for Electric Guitar and Orch. (1973; Mexico City, June 12, 1977); *En busca de un muro* (1973). VOCAL: *Jicarita* for Voice and Orch. (1939); *Primavera,* youth cantata for Wind Orch. and Children's Chorus (1944); *Arrullo* for Voice, and Small Orch. or Piano (1945); *La Montana* for Chorus a cappella (1945); *A la Patria,* cantata (1946); *3 canciones de la Revolución* for Orch. and Chorus (1953); *Homenaje a Juárez,* cantata with Narrator (1957); *A la Independencia,* cantata (Mexico City, Nov. 24, 1960); *Quetzalcoatl* for Orch. and Narrator (1963); *Tríptico Teotihuacán* for Wind Orch., Indigenous Mexican Percussion Instruments, Chorus, and Soloists (Teotihuacán, Sept. 14, 1964); *Letanía erótica para la paz* for Orch., Organ, Chorus, Soloists, Narrator, and Tape (1963–65; Mexico City, May 2, 1969); *La ciudad de los dioses* (*Luz y Sonido*) for Orch., Chorus, and Narrators (1965); *Homenaje a Rubén Dario* for Narrator and String Orch. (1966); choruses; songs. CHAMBER: Suite for Violin and Cello (1933); Quartet for 4 Cellos (1936); *Bosquejos* for Wind Instruments (1937); 2 *Preludes* for Oboe, English Horn, and Piano (1938); *Obra para orquesta mexicana* for Indigenous Instruments (1938); Sextet for Flute, Clarinet, Bassoon, Horn, Trumpet, and Trombone (1941); Violin Sonata (1945); Cello Sonata (1949); Suite for Violin and Piano (1957); Quintet for Piano and String Quartet (1960); *3 sonsonetes* for Wind Quintet and Electronic Sound (1967); String Quartet (1970); *Titoco-tico* for Indigenous Percussion Instruments

(1971); *Tríptico* for Strings (1974). PIANO: *Llano Alegre* (1938); 5 *preludios* (1945); 7 *piezas* (1952); Sonata (1976); numerous small pieces. ORGAN: *Estudio* (1971). A list of his works up to 1965 is found in *Composers of the Americas,* vol. 11 (Washington, D.C., 1965).

Galkin, Elliott W(ashington), American conductor, music critic, and educator; b. N.Y., Feb. 22, 1921; d. Baltimore, May 24, 1990. He studied at Brooklyn College (B.A., 1943); then served with the U.S. Air Force (1943–46); was stationed in France, and received conducting diplomas from the Paris Cons. (1948) and the École Normale de Musique (1948). Returning to the U.S., he studied at Cornell Univ. (M.A., 1950; Ph.D., 1960, with the diss. *The Theory and Practice of Orchestral Conducting from 1752*). During 1955–56 he was an apprentice conductor with the Vienna State Opera; in 1956 he joined the faculty of Goucher College in Towson, Md.; served as prof. there from 1964 to 1977. In 1957 he joined the faculty of the Peabody Cons. of Music in Baltimore as a conductor; was chairman of the music history and literature dept. (1964–77); also was director of musical activities and a prof. at Johns Hopkins Univ. (from 1968). From 1977 to 1982 he served as director of the Peabody Cons. of Music, and subsequently was director of its graduate program in music criticism. He also was active as conductor of the Baltimore Chamber Orch. (from 1960) and served as music ed. and critic of the *Baltimore Sun* (1962–77). In 1972 and 1975 he received ASCAP–Deems Taylor Awards, and in 1982 was awarded the George Foster Peabody Medal for outstanding contributions to music. He publ. the valuable study *A History of Orchestral Conducting* (Stuyvesant, N.Y., 1988).

Gall (real name, **Galle**), **Yvonne,** French soprano; b. Paris, March 6, 1885; d. there, Aug. 21, 1972. She studied at the Paris Cons.; made her debut at the Paris Opéra in 1908, and remained on its roster until 1935; also sang at the Opéra-Comique (1921–34). From 1918 to 1921 she was a member of the opera in Chicago, then sang in San Francisco (1931). After her retirement, she taught voice at the Paris Cons. She was highly successful in the French and Italian operatic repertoire. In 1958 she married the French composer and conductor **Henri Paul Busser,** who, although much older, outlived her and reached the age of 101.

Galla-Rini, Anthony, American accordionist and composer; b. Manchester, Conn., Jan. 18, 1904. He learned music from his father, a bandmaster; toured the U.S. and Canada from the age of 6, playing accordion, cornet, mandolin, piccolo, oboe, French horn, contrabassoon, euphonium, and sarrusophone, as well as several other instruments. He was the 1st accordionist to appear with an orch. in a concerto of his own composition (Oklahoma City, Nov. 15, 1941); invented many technical improvements for his instrument; was the 1st to omit the fifth in the dominant-seventh row. In 1921 he introduced the 160-bass system in an extended left-hand range model. He publ. a number of transcriptions of classical and popular music for accordion. He also publ. a *Method for Accordion* (1931), an *Accordion Course* (1955–56), the *Galla-Rini Accordion Primer* (1958), and *A Collection of Lectures* (1981). He composed 2 accordion concertos (1941, 1976), a Sonata for Accordion (1982), and pieces for solo accordion.

Gallenberg, Wenzel Robert, Graf von, Austrian composer; b. Vienna, Dec. 28, 1783; d. Rome, March 13, 1839. He studied under Albrechtsberger; in 1803 he married Countess Giulietta Guicciardi (to whom Beethoven dedicated his Sonata No. 2, op. 27). In Naples shortly thereafter, he made the acquaintance of the impresario Barbaja; wrote numerous successful ballets for him, and in 1822–23 was his partner when Barbaja was director of opera in Vienna. He attempted the management of the Kärnthnertortheater (1828–30) but failed, and was obliged to return to Italy, rejoining Barbaja. He wrote about 50 ballets; a Sonata, marches, fantasies, and other works for piano. Beethoven wrote a set of variations on one of his themes.

Gallès, José, Catalan organist and composer; b. Casteltersol, 1761; d. Vich, 1836. He was organist of the Vich Cathedral;

was ordained a priest. J. Nin publ. his Piano Sonata (1800) in the collection *17 sonates et pièces anciennes d'auteurs espagnols* (Paris, 1929).

Galli, Amintore, Italian composer; b. Talamello, near Rimini, Oct. 12, 1845; d. Rimini, Dec. 8, 1919. He was a pupil of Mazzucato at the Milan Cons. (1862–67); was music editor for the publisher Sonzogno, and critic of *Il Secolo;* later ed. *Il Teatro Illustrato* and *Musica Popolare.* He publ. *Musica e musicisti dal secolo X sino ai nostri giorni* (1871); *Estetica della musica* (1900); *Storia e teoria del sistema musicale* (1901); *Piccolo lessico di musica* (1902).

WORKS: Operas: *Il corno d'oro* (Turin, Aug. 30, 1876) and *David* (Milan, Nov. 12, 1904); oratorios: *Espiazione* (after Moore's *Paradise and Peri*) and *Cristo al Golgota; Totentanz* (after Goethe) for Baritone Solo and Orch.; String Quintet; etc.

Galli, Filippo, celebrated Italian bass; b. Rome, 1783; d. Paris, June 3, 1853. He made his debut as a tenor in Naples in 1801; after an interruption caused by an illness, he returned to the stage as a bass in Padua in 1811, singing in the premiere of Rossini's *La cambiale di matrimonio;* his success was so great that Rossini wrote several other roles for him, including Fernando in *La gazza ladra* and the title role in *Maometto II;* Donizetti wrote the role of Henry VIII for him in *Anna Bolena.* He sang in London at the King's Theatre (1827–33). His voice began to decline about 1840, and he abandoned the stage; was then active as a chorus master in Lisbon and Madrid; taught voice at the Paris Cons. (1842–48).

Galli-Curci, Amelita, brilliant Italian soprano; b. Milan, Nov. 18, 1882; d. La Jolla, Calif., Nov. 26, 1963. She studied in Milan and intended to be a pianist; graduated in 1903 from the Milan Cons., winning 1st prize. She then had a few voice lessons with Carignani and Dufes, and received advice from Mascagni and William Thorner. She made her debut in Trani as Gilda (Dec. 26, 1906), then sang in various opera houses in Italy and in South America (1910). She continued her successful career as an opera singer in Europe until 1915; after the entry of Italy into World War I, she went to America; made a sensationally successful debut with the Chicago Opera Co. as Gilda (Nov. 18, 1916); made her 1st appearance with the Metropolitan Opera in N.Y. as Violetta (Nov. 14, 1921); remained as a member of the Metropolitan until 1930; then gave concert recitals; eventually retired to California. She was married twice: to the painter Luigi Curci (1910; divorced 1920) and to Homer Samuels, her accompanist.

BIBL.: C. LeMassena, *G.-C.'s Life of Song* (N.Y., 1945).

Galli-Marié, Célestine (Laurence; née **Marié de l'Isle),** French mezzo-soprano; b. Paris, Nov. 1840; d. Vence, near Nice, Sept. 22, 1905. Her father, an opera singer, was her only teacher. She made her debut at Strasbourg (1859); sang in Toulouse (1860) and in Lisbon (1861). She sang *La Bohème* at Rouen (1862) with such success that she was immediately engaged for the Paris Opéra-Comique; made her debut there (1862) as Serpina in *La Serva padrona.* She created the roles of Mignon (1866) and Carmen (1875).

Galliard, Johann Ernst, German oboist, organist, and composer; b. Celle, c.1680; d. London, 1749. He was a pupil of A. Steffani in Hannover. A skillful oboist, he went to London (1706) as chamber musician to Prince George of Denmark; succeeded Draghi as organist at Somerset House; in 1713, played in the Queen's Theatre orch.; from 1717 to 1736, engaged in writing music for the stage productions at Covent Garden and Lincoln's Inn Fields. He last appeared as an oboist probably in 1722. Besides the music to numerous plays, masques, and pantomimes, he wrote several operas, including *Calypso and Telemachus* (London, Queen's Theatre, May 17, 1712), *Circe* (London, Lincoln's Inn Fields, April 11, 1719; 3 songs extant), and *The Happy Captive* (London, Little Theatre in the Haymarket, April 16, 1741; music not extant). He also composed cantatas, a Te Deum, a Jubilate, anthems, soli for Flute and Cello, etc.; set to music the *Morning Hymn of Adam and Eve,* from Milton's *Paradise Lost.*

BIBL.: S. Lincoln, "J.E. G. and *A Critical Discourse,*" *Musical Quarterly* (July 1967).

Gallico, Paolo, Italian-American composer and pianist; b. Trieste, May 13, 1868; d. N.Y., July 6, 1955. At the age of 15, he gave a recital at Trieste; then studied at the Vienna Cons. under Julius Epstein, graduating at 18 with highest honors. After successful concerts in Italy, Austria, Russia, Germany, etc., he settled in N.Y. in 1892 as a concert pianist and teacher; toured the U.S. frequently as pianist in recitals and as a soloist with the principal orchs. He won the prize of the National Federation of Music Clubs in 1921 with his dramatic oratorio *The Apocalypse* (N.Y., Nov. 22, 1922). His symphonic episode, *Euphorion,* was performed in Los Angeles (April 6, 1923), N.Y., and Detroit; his Sextet was performed by the Soc. of the Friends of Music in N.Y. He also wrote an opera, *Harlekin* (1926); piano pieces; and songs. His son, Paul Gallico, was a well-known writer.

Galliera, Alceo, Italian conductor and composer; b. Milan, May 3, 1910. He studied piano, organ, and composition at the Milan Cons., and then was on its faculty. After World War II, he appeared as a conductor throughout Europe and South America; was music director of the Victorian Sym. Orch. in Melbourne (1950–51), at the Teatro Carlo Felice in Genoa (1957–60), and of the Strasbourg Phil. (1964–71). He wrote a ballet, orch. pieces, chamber music, and songs.

Gallignani, Giuseppe, Italian composer and writer on music; b. Faenza, Jan. 9, 1851; d. (suicide) Milan, Dec. 14, 1923. He studied at the Milan Cons.; was then choir leader at the Milan Cathedral; ed. the periodical *Musica Sacra* (1886–94); was director of the Parma Cons. (1891–97); from 1897, was director of the Milan Cons. He produced the operas *Il Grillo del focolare* (Genoa, Jan. 27, 1873), *Atala* (Milan, March 30, 1876), and *Nestorio* (Milan, March 31, 1888), which were unsuccessful; but his church music was greatly appreciated (particularly his Requiem for King Umberto I).

Gallo, Fortune, Italian-American impresario; b. Torremaggiore, May 9, 1878; d. N.Y., March 28, 1970. He studied piano in Italy; migrated to the U.S. in 1895; first directed the tours of a number of famous bands (1901–9), then founded the San Carlo Opera Co. (1909); in 1920, brought Anna Pavlova and her Russian Ballet to America; in 1923, organized an opera season in Havana, Cuba; in 1925, was director of the tour of Eleanora Duse; in 1926, built and operated the Gallo Theater; in 1928, made a film version of *Pagliacci;* presented performances of operetta in N.Y. and elsewhere.

Gallois-Montbrun, Raymond, French violinist, composer, and administrator; b. Saigon, Aug. 15, 1918. He studied composition with Büsser, theory with Gallon, and violin with Touche at the Paris Cons.; won the Prix de Rome for his *Louise de la miséricorde* in 1944. He then toured throughout Europe as a violinist, and also played in Japan and Africa. He was director of the Versailles Cons. (1957–62), then of the Paris Cons. (1962–84). His compositions include *Le Rossignol et l'empereur,* a chamber opera after Andersen (1959); *Symphonie japonaise* (1951); Violin Concerto (1957); Cello Concerto (1961); Piano Concerto (1964); chamber music.

Gallon, Jean, French composer and pedagogue, brother of **Noël Gallon;** b. Paris, June 25, 1878; d. there, June 23, 1959. He studied piano with Diémer and theory with Lavignac and Lenepveu at the Paris Cons.; was chorus director of the Société des Concerts du Conservatoire (1906–14) and at the Paris Opéra (1909–14). From 1919 to 1949 he taught harmony at the Paris Cons. Among his pupils were Robert Casadesus, Marcel Delannoy, Henri Dutilleux, Olivier Messiaen, and Jean Rivier. He publ. harmony exercises for use at the Cons.; with his brother, he composed several pieces of theater music, among them a ballet, *Hansli le Bossu* (1914); also composed some chamber music and songs.

Gallon, Noël, French composer, brother of **Jean Gallon;** b. Paris, Sept. 11, 1891; d. there, Dec. 26, 1966. He studied piano with I. Philipp and Risler; theory with Caussade and Lenepveu at the Paris Cons., and also with Rabaud. In 1910 he received the 1st Prix de Rome. From 1920 he was on the faculty of the Paris Cons. as an instructor in solfège, counterpoint, and fugue. As a composer, he was influenced by his brother, who was his 1st tutor in music; with him he wrote a ballet, *Hansli le Bossu* (1914); his own works comprise a few symphonic pieces; Suite for Flute and Piano (1921); Quintet for Horn and Strings (1953); teaching pieces.

Gallus (Petelin), Jacobus, important Slovenian composer; b. Carniola (probably in Ribniča), between April 15 and July 31, 1550; d. Prague, July 24, 1591. His Slovenian name was Petelin (which means "cockerel"); its Germanic equivalent was **Handl,** or **Hähnel** (diminutive of Hahn, "rooster"); he publ. most of his works under the corresponding Latin name Gallus ("rooster"). As a master of polychoral counterpoint, Gallus was highly regarded in his time; he held several important positions as an organist and music director; was Kapellmeister to the Bishop of Olmütz (1579–85), and later was employed at the church of St. Johannes in Vado in Prague. A number of his works were publ. during his lifetime. Of these there are several masses: *Selectiores quaedam Missae* (Prague, 1580), containing 4 books of 16 masses, from 4 to 8 Voices; a modern ed. by P. Pisk was publ. in Denkmäler der Tonkunst in Österreich (Vienna, 1935; reprinted in 1959, 1967, and 1969); 4 books of motets were publ. in Prague between 1586 and 1591 under the title *Opus musicum*: 1st part (1586) from 4 to 8 Voices (exact title, *Tomus primus musici operis harmonium quatuor, quinque, sex, octo et pluribus vocum*); 2nd and 3rd were publ. in 1587, and 4th in 1591; 5 additional motets were printed individually from 1579 to 1614. *Opus musicum* was reprinted in a modern ed. by E. Bezecny and J. Mantuani in Denkmäler der Tonkunst in Österreich (Vienna, 1899, 1905, 1908, 1913, 1917, 1919; all reprinted again in 1959); *Moralia 5, 6 et 8 vocibus concinnata*, orig. publ. in 1596, was reprinted in a modern ed. by D. Cvetko (Ljubljana, 1968) and A. Skei (Madison, Wis., 1970). His secular works include *Harmoniae morales* (Prague, 1589–90; modern ed. by D. Cvetko, Ljubljana, 1966) and *Moralia* (Prague, 1596). A motet by Gallus, *Ecce quomodo moritur justus*, was borrowed by Handel for his *Funeral Anthem*.

BIBL.: P. Pisk, "Die Parodieverfahren in den Messen des J. G.," *Studien zur Musikwissenschaft*, V (1918); A. Skei, "Jacob Handl's *Moralia*," *Musical Quarterly* (Oct. 1966); idem, "Jacob Handl's Polychoral Music," *Music Review* (May 1968); D. Cvetko, *J. G., Sein Leben und Werk* (Munich, 1972).

Gallus, Johannes (Jean le Cocq, Maître Jean, Mestre Jhan), Flemish composer; d. c.1543. He was maestro di cappella to Duke Ercole of Ferrara in 1534 and 1541. Many of his pieces were publ. in collections and in a vol. of motets printed by Scotto (1543). He was long confused with Jhan Gero.

Galpin, Francis W(illiam), English writer on music; b. Dorchester, Dorset, Dec. 25, 1858; d. Richmond, Surrey, Dec. 30, 1945. He graduated with classical honors from Trinity College, Cambridge (B.A., 1882; M.A., 1885); received his music education from Garrett and Sterndale Bennett; held various posts as vicar and canon (1891–1921); wrote many articles on the viola pomposa and other early instruments in *Music & Letters* and *Monthly Musical Record* (1930–33). A Galpin Soc. was formed in London in 1946 with the object of bringing together all those interested in the history of European instruments and to commemorate the pioneer work of Galpin; it publishes the *Galpin Society Journal* (1948–).

WRITINGS: *Descriptive Catalogue of the European Instruments in the Metropolitan Museum of Art, N.Y.* (1902); *The Musical Instruments of the American Indians of the North West Coast* (1903); *Notes on the Roman Hydraulus* (1904); *The Evolution of the Sackbut* (1907); *Old English Instruments of Music* (1910; 4th ed., rev., 1965, by T. Dart); *A Textbook of European Musical Instruments* (London, 1937); *The Music of the Sumerians, Babylonians and Assyrians* (1937); *The Music of Electricity*

(1938). Galpin was the editor of the revised and augmented ed. of Stainer's *Music of the Bible* (1913).

Galston, Gottfried, Austrian-American pianist; b. Vienna, Aug. 31, 1879; d. St. Louis, April 2, 1950. He was a pupil of Leschetizky in Vienna, and of Jadassohn and Reinecke at the Leipzig Cons.; from 1903 to 1907 he taught at the Stern Cons. in Berlin. On his extended concert tours, he proved himself a player of keen analytical powers and intellectual grasp; in 1902, he toured Australia; then Germany, France, and Russia; in 1912–13, he toured America; toured Russia 11 times (last, in 1926); returned to the U.S. in 1927 and settled in St. Louis. He publ. a *Studienbuch* (1909; 3rd ed., Munich, 1920) and analytical notes to a series of 5 historical recitals.

Galuppi, Baldassare, celebrated Italian composer, called "Il Buranello" after his birthplace; b. on the island of Burano, near Venice, Oct. 18, 1706; d. Venice, Jan. 3, 1785. He began his musical training with his father, a barber and violinist, writing his 1st opera, *La fede nell'incostanza ossia Gli amici rivali*, when he was 16; it failed at its premiere in Vicenza in 1722, so he pursued a thorough course of instruction in composition and keyboard playing with Antonio Lotti. He garnered his 1st unqualified success as a composer with the opera *Dorinda* (Venice, June 9, 1729), written in collaboration with G.B. Pescetti, and subsequently wrote numerous operas for the leading Italian opera houses. From 1740 to 1751 he was maestro di musica of the Ospedale dei Mendicanti in Venice. He was active as a composer in London at the King's Theatre at the Haymarket (1741–43); also visited Vienna in 1748. He was named vice-maestro of the cappella ducale of S. Marco in Venice in 1748; was made Venice's maestro di cappella in 1762. Turning to the new form of opera buffa, he established himself as a master of the genre with his *L'Arcadia in Brenta* (Venice, May 14, 1749), sealing his fame with his *Il Filosofo di campagna* (Venice, Oct. 26, 1754), which was performed with great acclaim all over Europe. He was called to Russia in 1765 to serve as music director of the court chapel of Catherine the Great in St. Petersburg; his opera seria *Ifigenia in Tauride* was given at the court on May 2, 1768. He returned to Venice in 1768, and resumed his post at S. Marco; that same year he also became maestro di coro of the Ospedale degli Incurabili. Galuppi was a pivotal figure in the development and refinement of opera buffa. His effective vocal and orch. writing, combined with Goldoni's innovative librettos, ensured popular success. He was also a distinguished composer for the keyboard; his sonatas confirm his contemporary renown as a harpsichord virtuoso.

WORKS: OPERAS (all 1st perf. in Venice unless otherwise given): **SERIA:** *Gl'odj delusi dal sangue* (1728; in collaboration with G.B. Pescetti); *L'odio placato* (1729); *Argenide* (1733); *L'ambizione depressa* (1733); *Tamiri* (1734); *Elisa regina di Tiro* (1736); *Ergilda* (1736); *L'Alvilda* (1737); *Issipile* (Turin, 1737); *Alessandronelle Indie* (Mantua, 1738); *Adriano in Siria* (Turin, 1740); *Gustavo primo re di Svezia* (1740); *Oronte re de' Sciti* (1740); *Didone abbandonata* (Modena, 1741); *Penelope* (London, 1741); *Scipione in Cartagine* (London, 1742); *Enrico* (London, 1743); *Sirbace* (London, 1743); *Ricimero* (Milan, 1745); *Antigono* (London, 1746); *Scipione nelle Spagne* (1746); *Evergete* (Rome, 1747); *L'Arminio* (1747); *Vologeso* (Rome, 1748); *Demetrio* (Vienna, 1748); *Clotilde* (1748); *Demofoonte* (Madrid, 1749); *Olimpia* (Naples, 1749); *Alcimena principessa dell'Isole Fortunate, ossia L'amore fortunato ne' suoi disprezzj* (1749); *Antigona* (Rome, 1751); *Dario* (Turin, 1751); *Lucio Papirio* (Reggio Emilia, 1751); *Artaserse* (Padua, 1751); *Le Virtuose ridicole* (1752); *La calamità de' cuori* (1752); *I bagni d'Abano* (1753; in collaboration with Bertoni); *Sofonisba* (Rome, 1753); *Siroe* (Rome, 1754); *Attalo* (Padua, 1755); *Idomeneo* (Rome, 1756); *Ezio* (Milan, 1757); *Sesostri* (1757); *Ipermestra* (Milan, 1758); *Adriano in Siria* (Livorno, 1758); *Meilite riconosciuto* (Rome, 1759); *La clemenza di Tito* (1760); *Solimano* (Padua, 1760); *Antigono* (1762); *Il Re pastore* (Parma, 1762); *Siface*, later known as *Viriate* (1762); *Il Muzio Scevola* (Padua, 1762); *Arianna e Teseo* (Padua, 1763); *Sonofisba* (Turin, 1764);

Cajo Mario (1764); *Ifigenia in Tauride* (St. Petersburg, 1768); *Montezuma* (1772). DRAMMAS GIOCOSO: *L'Arcadia in Brenta* (1749); *Il Conte Caramella* (Verona, 1749?); *Arcifanfano re dei matti* (1749); *Il paese della Cuccagna* (1750); *Il mondo alla roversa, ossia Le Donne che comandano* (1750); *La mascherata* (1750); *Il Filosofo di campagna* (1754); *Il Povero superbo* (1755); *Le nozze* (Bologna, 1755); *La Diavolessa* (1755); *L'Amante di tutte* (1760); *Li tre amanti ridicoli* (1761); *Il caffè di campagna* (1761); *Il Marchese villano* (1762); *L'Uomo femmina* (1762); *Il puntiglio amoroso* (1762); *Il Re alla caccia* (1763); *La Donna di governo* (Rome, 1761; rev. version, Prague, 1763); *La partenza il ritorno de' marinari* (1764); *La Cameriera spiritosa* (Milan, 1764); *Il Villano geloso* (1769); *Amor lunatico* (1770); *L'inimico delle donne* (1771); *La Serva per amore* (1773; Act 1 unfinished); also several other dramatic works, including farsettas, pastorales, intermezzos, serenatas, and cantatas. His sacred works include oratorios, masses, Requiems, Magnificats, motets, and a number of pieces for the Russian Orthodox church. Among his instrumental works are numerous sonatas, toccatas, divertimenti, and other pieces for keyboard.

BIBL.: P. Molmenti, "Il Buranello," *Gazzetta Musicale di Milano*, I (1899); F. Piovano, "B. G.: Note bio-bibliografiche," *Rivista Musicale Italiana*, XIII (1906), XIV (1907), and XV (1908); C. van den Borren, "Contribution au catalogue thématique des sonates de G.," ibid., XXX (1923); F. Raabe, *G. als Instrumentalkomponist* (diss., Univ. of Munich, 1926); W. Bollert, *Die Buffoopern B. G.s* (diss., Univ. of Berlin, 1935); A. Chiuminatto, *The Liturgical Works of B. G.* (diss., Northwestern Univ., 1959); D. Pullmann, *A Catalogue of the Keyboard Sonatas of B. G. (1706–1785)* (diss., American Univ., 1972); R. Holmes, *A Critical Edition of Selected Keyboard Sonatas by B. G. (1706–1785)* (diss., Texas Technical Univ., 1976); R. Wiesend, *Studien zur Opera Seria von B. G.* (2 vols., Tutzing, 1984); D. Arnold, "G.'s Religious Music," *Musical Times* (Jan. 1985).

Galvani, Giacomo, noted Italian tenor; b. Bologna, Nov. 1, 1825; d. Venice, May 7, 1889. He studied in Bologna with Gamberini and Zamboni; made his debut in *I Masnadieri* in Spoleto in 1849; subsequently sang in Bologna, Milan, London, Barcelona, and other cities with great success; after his retirement, he taught voice in Venice and at the Moscow Cons. (1869–87). He was acclaimed for his performances in the operas of Rossini and Donizetti.

Galway, James, famous Irish flute virtuoso; b. Belfast, Dec. 8, 1939. His 1st instrument was the violin, but he soon began to study the flute. At the age of 14 he went to work in a piano shop in Belfast; a scholarship enabled him to go to London, where he continued to study flute, and also took academic courses in music at the Royal College of Music and the Guildhall School of Music and Drama. He then received a grant to go to Paris, where he studied with Gaston Crunelle at the Cons. and privately with Marcel Moyse. His 1st professional job as a flutist was with the wind band at the Royal Shakespeare Theatre in Stratford-upon-Avon. He subsequently played with the Sadler's Wells Opera Co., the Royal Opera House Orch., and the BBC Sym. Orch.; then was appointed principal flutist of the London Sym. Orch., and later with the Royal Phil. As his reputation grew, he was engaged in 1969 by Herbert von Karajan as 1st flutist in the Berlin Phil., a post he held until 1975. Abandoning his role as an orch. flutist, he devoted himself to a career as a concert artist; in a single season, 1975–76, he appeared as a soloist with all 5 major London orchs.; also toured in the U.S., Australia, and the Orient, as well as in Europe. He became successful on television, playing his 18-karat-gold flute. He publ. *James Galway: An Autobiography* (N.Y., 1979) and *Flute* (London, 1982).

BIBL.: W. Mann, *J. G.'s Music in Time* (London, 1982); D. Adler, "J. G. Pipes Up," *Ovation* (June 1987).

Gamba, Piero (Pierino), Italian conductor; b. Rome, Sept. 16, 1936. From a musical family (his father was a professional violinist), he was trained in music at home; his precocity was so remarkable that he was reportedly able to read an orch.

score at the age of 8, and at 9 was actually allowed to conduct a regular sym. concert in Rome. He also composed. Unlike the talent of so many child musicians, his gift did not evaporate with puberty; he became a professional artist. According to ecstatic press reports, he conducted in 40 countries and 300 cities, so that his name became familiar to uncounted multitudes (including a billion people in China). From 1970 to 1981 he served as music director of the Winnipeg Sym. Orch.; from 1982 to 1987 he conducted the Adelaide (Australia) Sym. Orch.

Ganche, Édouard, French writer on music; b. Baulon, Ille-et-Vilaine, Oct. 13, 1880; d. Lyons, May 31, 1945. He studied with Imbert, Henry Expert, and others in Paris. He devoted his life to the study of Chopin and publ. *La Vie de Chopin dans son œuvre: Sa liaison avec George Sand* (1909); *Frédéric Chopin, Sa vie et ses œuvres, 1810–1849* (1909; 3rd ed., 1949). He also ed. the Oxford edition of Chopin's works (3 vols., 1928–32).

Gandini, Gerardo, Argentine composer and pianist; b. Buenos Aires, Oct. 16, 1932. He studied with Pía Sebastini, Roberto Caamaño, and Alberto Ginastera in Buenos Aires (1956–59); completed studies in Rome with Petrassi (1966–67). He taught at various schools in Buenos Aires, and in 1970 was appointed to the faculty of the American Opera Center at the Juilliard School of Music in N.Y.; has concertized widely, specializing in contemporary repertoire; founded the Group for Musical Experimentation in Buenos Aires.

WORKS: Piano Concerto (1960); Variations for Orch. (1962); *Concertino I* for Clarinet, String Trio, and Percussion, *II* for Flute and Instruments, and *III* for Harpsichord and Instruments (1962–63); *Música nocturna I* for Flute, Piano, and String Trio (1964), and *II* for Chamber Orch. (1965); *Cadencias I* for Violin and Chamber Orch. (1966), and *II* for Chamber Orch. (1967); *Mutantes I* for Chamber Orch. (1966); *Fuggevole* for Chamber Orch. (1967); *L'Adieu* for Piano, Vibraphone, 3 Percussionists, and Conductor (1967); *A Cow in a Mondrian Painting* for Flute and Instruments (1967); *Soria Moria* for Variable Instrumental Ensemble (1968); *Contrastes* for 2 Pianos and Orch. (1968); *Fases* for Clarinet and Orch. (1969); *Play* for Piano and an Instrument (1969); *Fantasie-Impromptu*, an "imaginary portrait of Chopin," for Piano and Orch. (1970); *Piange e sospira* for Flute, Violin, Clarinet, and Piano (1970); *Il concertino* for Flute and Instruments (1971); Guitar Concerto (1975; Washington, D.C., May 18, 1976).

Gandolfi, Riccardo (Cristoforo Daniele Diomede), Italian composer; b. Voghera, Piedmont, Feb. 16, 1839; d. Florence, Feb. 5, 1920. He was a pupil of Carlo Conti at the Naples Cons., then of Mabellini in Florence; was appointed inspector of studies at the Real Istituto di Musica in Florence (1869), chief librarian in 1889; was pensioned in 1912. He began as a dramatic composer, then turned to the larger instrumental and vocal forms, and finally abandoned composition altogether, devoting himself to historical studies, which won him distinction.

WORKS: Operas: *Aldina* (Milan, 1863); *Il Paggio* (Turin, 1865); *Il Conte di Monreale* (Genoa, 1872); *Caterina di Guisa* (Catania, 1872); *Messa da Requiem*; cantata, *Il Battesimo di S. Cecilia*; several overtures; chamber music.

WRITINGS: *Sulla relazione della poesia colla musica melodrammatica* (1868); *Una riparazione a proposito di Francesco Landino* (1888); *Commemorazioni di W.A. Mozart* (1891); *Illustrazioni di alcuni cimeli concernanti l'arte musicale in Firenze* (1892); *Appunti di storia musicale* (1893); *Onoranze Fiorentine a G. Rossini* (1902).

Ganelin, Viacheslav, Russian pianist and composer; b. Kraskovo, 1944. He graduated from the Vilnius Cons. and was music director of the Russian Dramatic Theater. He wrote much theater music, film scores, an opera, *The Red-Haired Liar and the Soldier*, and a rock musical, *The Devilish Bride*. When he met the percussionist **Vladimir Tarasov** (b. Archangelsk, 1947) in Vilnius, the 2 formed what was to be the basis of the Ganelin Trio; after playing at the Jazz Club in Sverdlovsk in the early 1960s, they were joined by **Chaksin** (b. Sverdlovsk, 1947), a graduate of the Sverdlovsk Cons. The Ganelin Trio has an eclectic and ironic style synthesizing strong formal structural ideas with improvisation; it stresses constant innovation and Ganelin's conviction that the 2 most important elements of jazz are "swing and improvisation." Ganelin himself plays the piano and basset horn, providing harmony and bassline; Tarasov, on percussion, states the rhythms; Chaksin controls the melodic line, strongly influenced by Ornette Coleman and John Coltrane, on an assortment of reeds, flute, trombone, and violin. Because of their uncompromising musical stance, their music has not been widely available; only recently has the official music publishing house, Melodiya, unbent sufficiently to produce scores and recordings. The trio's work has most often been heard on recordings made at jazz festivals across Europe, where they are widely acclaimed; select recordings were also produced by an expatriate Russian, Leo Feigin (Leo Records, London).

Gange, Fraser, distinguished Scottish-American baritone; b. Dundee, June 17, 1886; d. Baltimore, July 1, 1962. He studied in Dundee with his father; later was a pupil of Amy Sherwin in London; made his debut as a basso at the age of 16; toured England, Scotland, Australia, and New Zealand twice; taught singing at the Royal Academy of Music in London; made his American debut in N.Y. (Jan. 18, 1924); from 1932 to 1946 was a prof. of voice at the Juilliard Summer School in N.Y.; from 1931 to 1957 taught at the Peabody Cons. in Baltimore. His repertoire included 40 oratorios and more than 2,000 songs; he presented in Baltimore a concert of songs on his 70th birthday, in 1956.

Gann, Kyle (Eugene), American music critic and composer; b. Dallas, Nov. 21, 1955. His mother was a piano teacher and his 1st teacher; he studied formally with Randolph Coleman at the Oberlin Cons. (B.Mus., 1977) and with Peter Gena at Northwestern Univ. (M.Mus., 1981; D.Mus., 1983); also privately with Ben Johnston and Morton Subotnick. He began writing free-lance music criticism for a variety of Chicago newspapers, and in 1986 joined the staff of the *Village Voice* in N.Y., where he became especially well known as a provocative and insightful reviewer of contemporary music. His compositions are written in a minimalistic fashion and often incorporate native American elements; he has also been influenced by astrology and Jungian psychology. In 1990 he joined the music faculty of Bucknell Univ.

WORKS: *Long Night* for 3 Pianos (1981); *Mountain Spirit* for 2 Flutes, Synthesizer, and 2 Drums (1982–83); *Baptism* for 2 Flutes, Synthesizer, and 2 Drums (1983); *The Black Hills Belong to the Sioux* for Trumpet or Saxophone, Accordion or Synthesizer, Flute, and Drum (1984); *I'itoi Variations* for 2 Pianos (1985); *Cyclic Aphorisms* for Violin and Piano (1986–88); *Paris Intermezzo* for Toy Piano (1989); *The Convent at Tepoztlan (Homage to Nancarrow)* for 2 Pianos and Tape (1989).

Ganne, Louis Gaston, French composer; b. Buxières-les-Mines, Allier, April 5, 1862; d. Paris, July 13, 1923. He was a pupil of T. Dubois, Massenet, and César Franck at the Paris Cons. He was conductor of the balls at the Opéra, and at the municipal Casino at Monte Carlo; wrote successful comic operas, ballets, and divertissements.

WORKS: Operas: *Rabelais* (Paris, Oct. 25, 1892); *Les Colles des femmes* (Paris, 1893); *Les Saltimbanques* (Paris, Dec. 30, 1899); *Miss Bouton d'or* (Paris, Oct. 14, 1902); *Hans le joueur de flûte* (his most successful operetta; Monte Carlo, April 14, 1906); *Les Ailes* (Paris, Sept. 1, 1910); ballets: *Au Japon* (1903; very successful) and *Kermesse flamande* (1917); many orch. dances, of which *La Czarine* and *La Tsigane* became favorites; the patriotic tunes *La Marche Lorraine* and *Le Père de la Victoire,* immensely popular in France; about 150 piano pieces.

Gänsbacher, Johann (Baptist), Austrian composer; b. Sterzing, Tirol, May 8, 1778; d. Vienna, July 13, 1844. He studied

with Abbé Vogler (1803–4) and Albrechtsberger in Vienna (1806); then continued study under Vogler, at Darmstadt (Weber and Meyerbeer were his fellow pupils). He served in the war of 1813, led a roving life for several years, and finally settled in Vienna as Kapellmeister of the Cathedral in 1823. He wrote masses, Requiems, orch. works, piano pieces, songs, etc.

BIBL.: C. Fischnaler, *J. G.* (Innsbruck, 1878); J. Woerz, *J. G.* (Innsbruck, 1894).

Ganz, Rudolph, distinguished Swiss-American pianist, conductor, and pedagogue; b. Zürich, Feb. 24, 1877; d. Chicago, Aug. 2, 1972. He studied music assiduously, first as a cellist (with Friedrich Hegar), then as a pianist (with Robert Freund) in Zürich; also took composition lessons with Charles Blanchet at the Lausanne Cons.; in 1897–98 he studied piano with F. Blumer in Strasbourg, and in 1899 took a course in advanced piano playing with Ferruccio Busoni in Berlin. He made his 1st public appearance at the age of 12 as a cellist, and at 16 as a pianist. In 1899, he was the soloist in Beethoven's *Emperor Concerto* and Chopin's E-minor Concerto with the Berlin Phil.; and in May 1900 the Berlin Phil. performed his 1st Sym. In 1901 he went to the U.S. and was engaged as a prof. of piano at the Chicago Musical College; between 1905 and 1908 he made several tours of the U.S. and Canada, and from 1908 to 1911 toured Europe, playing 16 different piano concertos. After 1912 he divided his time touring in Europe and America; in 1921 he added one more profession to his career, that of a sym. conductor; from 1921 to 1927 he was music director and conductor of the St. Louis Sym. Orch.; from 1938 to 1949 he conducted a highly successful series of Young People's Concerts with the N.Y. Phil.; concurrently (1929–54) he served as director of the Chicago Musical College. He played 1st performances of many important works by modern composers, including Ravel, Bartók, and Busoni. He was a highly successful pedagogue, and continued to teach almost to the time of his death, at the age of 95. Besides the early sym., he wrote a lively suite of 20 pieces for Orch., *Animal Pictures* (Detroit, Jan. 19, 1933, composer conducting); Piano Concerto (Chicago Sym. Orch., Feb. 20, 1941, composer soloist); *Laughter—Yet Love, Overture to an Unwritten Comedy* (1950); solo piano pieces; and a couple of hundred songs to words in German, French, English, and Swiss and Alsatian dialects. He publ. *Rudolph Ganz Evaluates Modern Piano Music* (N.Y., 1968).

Ganz, Wilhelm, German-born English pianist, violinist, and conductor; b. Mainz, Nov. 6, 1833; d. London, Sept. 12, 1914. He studied piano and conducting with his father, **Adolf Ganz** (b. Mainz, Oct. 14, 1796; d. London, Jan. 11, 1870), and with Karl Anschütz. He settled in England in 1850; was active as an accompanist to Jenny Lind and other musicians, and was also a violinist in Henry Wylde's New Phil. Orch. in London (from 1852); was then joint conductor with Wylde (1874–79) and subsequently sole conductor, organizing his own "Mr. Ganz's Orchestral Concerts" in 1880; after their discontinuance in 1883, he taught voice at the Guildhall School of Music. He publ. *Memories of a Musician* (London, 1913).

Ganzarolli, Wladimiro, Italian bass-baritone; b. Venice, Jan. 9, 1936. He studied in his native city; made his operatic debut in Spoleto; in 1959 became a member of La Scala, Milan. In 1964 he made his debut at the Vienna State Opera; then sang at Covent Garden in London, in N.Y., and in Buenos Aires. In addition to the Italian repertoire, he gained recognition in the parts of Figaro and Leporello in Mozart's operas.

Garaguly, Carl von, Hungarian-born Swedish violinist and conductor; b. Budapest, Dec. 28, 1900; d. Stockholm, Oct. 8, 1984. He studied violin with Hubay in Budapest and with Marteau in Lichtenberg. He was then a violinist in the Berlin Phil. Orch.; in 1923 went to Sweden; was concertmaster of the Göteborg Orch. (1923–30), then of the Stockholm Phil. (1930–40). From 1941 to 1953 he conducted the Stockholm Orch., and from 1953 to 1958 was conductor of the Bergen (Norway) Phil. He was artistic director of the Het Gelders

Orch. in Arnhem from 1959 to 1970; from 1965 to 1980 was conductor of the Sønderborg Sym. Orch.

Garant, (Albert Antonio) Serge, Canadian composer; b. Quebec City, Sept. 22, 1929; d. Sherbrooke, Quebec, Nov. 1, 1986. He studied composition in Montreal with Claude Champagne. In 1951 he went to Paris to take a course in musical analysis with Messiaen. Returning to Canada in 1953, he worked as a pianist and music arranger; with the composers Morel and Joachim and the pianist Jeanne Landry he organized in Montreal a modern group, Musique de Notre Temps, dedicated to the presentation of new European and American music; in 1967 he was appointed to the music faculty of the Univ. of Montreal. His music is constructed with formal precision and developed along classical lines.

Works: *Musique* for Saxophone and Winds (1948–50); *Canon VI* for 10 Players (1957); *Asymétries* No. 1 for Piano (1958) and No. 2 for Clarinet and Piano (1959); *Ouranos* for Orch. (1963); *Jeu à quatre* for 4 Instrumental Groups (1968); a group of 5 works based on mathematical proportions taken from the theme of Bach's *Musical Offering: Offrande I* for 19 Musicians and Prerecorded Voice (1969; alternative title, *Cérémonial du corps*; Montreal, March 6, 1970), *Offrande II* for Orch. (Toronto, July 29, 1970), *Offrande III* for 3 Cellos, 2 Harps, Piano, and 2 Percussionists (1971), *Circuit I* for 6 Percussionists (1972), and *Circuit II* for 14 Players (1972); *Circuit III* for 18 Players (1973); songs, including *Cage d'oiseau* for Soprano and Piano (1962).

Garat, (Dominique) Pierre (Jean), famous French singer and teacher; b. Ustaritz, Bas-Pyrénées, April 25, 1762; d. Paris, March 1, 1823. His talent was discovered early, and he studied theory and singing with Franz Beck in Bordeaux; his father wished him to become a lawyer, and sent him to the Univ. of Paris in 1782. However, he neglected his legal studies, and, aided by the Count d'Artois, he was introduced to Marie Antoinette, whose special favor he enjoyed up to the Revolution. He earned his livelihood as a concert singer; accompanied Rode, in 1792, to Rouen, where he gave numerous concerts before being arrested as a suspect during the Terror; subsequently he went to Hamburg. He returned to Paris in 1794, and sang (1795) at the Feydeau Concerts, where his triumphs speedily procured him a professorship of singing in the newly established Cons. For 20 years longer, his fine tenor-baritone voice, trained to perfection, made him the foremost singer on the French concert stage. Nourrit, Levasseur, and Ponchard were his pupils.

Bibl.: P. Lafond, *G.* (Paris, 1899); B. Miall, *P. G., Singer and Exquisite; His Life and His World* (London, 1913); I. de Fagoaga, *P. G., le chanteur* (Bayonne, 1944).

Garaudé, Alexis (Adélaide-Gabriel) de, French singer and composer; b. Nancy, March 21, 1779; d. Paris, March 23, 1852. He studied theory under Cambini and Reicha, and singing under Crescentini and Garat; was a singer in the royal choir (1808–30) and prof. of singing at the Cons. (1816–41). He publ. 3 string quintets; many ensemble pieces for violin, flute, clarinet, and cello; sonatas and variations for piano; a solemn Mass; vocalises, arias, duets, and songs; also a *Méthode de chant* (1809, op. 25; rev. ed. as *Méthode complète de chant*, op. 40); *Solfège, ou Méthode de musique; Méthode complète de piano;* and *L'Harmonie rendue facile, ou Théorie pratique de cette science* (1835).

Garay Narciso, Panamanian violinist, composer, and diplomat; b. Panama, June 12, 1876; d. there, March 27, 1953. He studied at the Brussels Cons., graduating with a premier prix; later attended the Schola Cantorum in Paris. He publ. a Violin Sonata and a valuable treatise on Panamanian folk music, *Tradiciones y cantares de Panama* (1930). He also occupied diplomatic posts and was Minister of Foreign Affairs.

Garbarek, Jan, Norwegian jazz saxophonist and composer; b. Oslo, March 4, 1947. An autodidact in music, he was influenced mainly by Coltrane, George Russell (notably Russell's Lydian Chromatic System), Miles Davis, and Keith Jarrett. On the majority of the albums he has produced, he plays his own compositions. He has appeared with the Bobo Stenson Quartet in Norway and as a sideman with an eclectic assortment of major jazz players, among them Jarrett and Egberto Gismonti (*Sol do Meio Dia*, 1978). He has been said to "spiritualize rock phrases in terms of free jazz."

Garbin, Edoardo, Italian tenor; b. Padua, March 12, 1865; d. Brescia, April 12, 1943. He studied with Alberto Selva and Vittorio Orefice in Milan; made his debut in 1891 in Vicenza as Alvaro in *La forza del destino;* also sang in Milan (Teatro dal Verme), Naples, and Genoa; in 1893 he created the role of Fenton in Verdi's *Falstaff* at La Scala in Milan; made guest appearances in Rome, Vienna, Berlin, London, Russia, and South America. He married the soprano **Adelina Stehle.** He was particularly distinguished in *verismo* roles.

Garbousova, Raya, Russian-American cellist; b. Tiflis, Oct. 10, 1905. She studied at the Tiflis Cons., graduating in 1923; later studied with Hugo Becker, Felix Salmond, and Pablo Casals. After many concerts in Europe, she settled in the U.S. (1939); appeared as a soloist with major American orchs. She played the 1st performance of the Cello Concerto by Samuel Barber (Boston, April 5, 1946) and the Cello Concerto by Rieti (1960).

García, Eugénie, French soprano, wife and pupil of **Manuel Patricio Rodríguez García;** b. Paris, 1818; d. there, Aug. 12, 1880. She sang for several years in Italian theaters, then at the Opéra-Comique in Paris (1840) and in London (1842); finally, after separating from her husband, she lived as a singing teacher in Paris.

Garcia, Jerry, American rock musician; b. San Francisco, Aug. 1, 1942. He was a school dropout, and served in the U.S. Army before associating himself with various rock groups, especially those cultivating the new electronic sound. Garcia's most successful creation was a group bearing the puzzling name The Grateful Dead. (One theory is that the name was taken from signs on trucks: "Grateful, for proper passing on the left, and Dead, for illegal passing on the right.") He engaged a harmonica player named **"Pig Pen" McKernan** (b. San Bruno, Calif., Sept. 8, 1945; d. of drug-cum-alcohol ingestion, in Marin County, Calif., March 8, 1973), and also brought in a violinist named **Phil Lesh** (b. Berkeley, Calif., March 15, 1940); another acquisition was a keyboard player who doubled as a vocalist, **Keith Godchaux** (b. San Francisco, July 19, 1948; d. an unnatural death, Ross, Calif., July 23, 1980). The immediate predecessor of The Grateful Dead was a group named the Warlocks. The mortuary connotations of the group continued with such albums as *Workingman's Dead*, but there were also in its repertoire some antonyms, such as *American Beauty*. Garcia's innovative use of electronic amplification established a state of the art for clean, loud, psychedelic rock sound. The Grateful Dead made so much money that they could make a sensational tour to Egypt to play at the foot of the Pyramids for the benefit of the mummified ungrateful dead once buried there, and incidentally contributed funds to the Egyptian Dept. of Antiquities.

García, Manuel (del Popolo Vicente Rodríguez), famous Spanish tenor, singing teacher, and composer, father of **Manuel Patricio Rodríguez García;** b. Seville, Jan. 21, 1775; d. Paris, June 9, 1832. A chorister in the Seville Cathedral at 6, he was taught by Ripa and Almarcha, and at 17 was already well known as a singer, composer, and conductor. After singing in Cadiz, Madrid, and Málaga, he proceeded (1807) to Paris, and sang to enthusiastic audiences at the Théâtre-Italien; in 1809, at his benefit, he sang his own monodrama *El poeta calculista* with extraordinary success. From 1811 to 1816 he was in Italy. On his return to Paris, his disgust at the machinations of Catalani, the manageress of the Théâtre-Italien, caused him to break his engagement and go to London (1817), where his triumphs were repeated. From 1819 to 1824 he was again the idol of the Parisians at the Théâtre-Italien; sang as 1st tenor at the Royal Opera in London (1824) and in 1825 embarked for N.Y. with his wife, his son Manuel, and his daughter Maria (Malibran), and the distinguished artists Crivelli *fils*, Angrisani, Barbieri, and de Rosich; from Nov. 29, 1825, to Sept. 30, 1826, they gave 79 performances at the Park and Bowery theaters in N.Y.; the troupe then spent 18 months in Mexico. García returned to Paris, and devoted himself to teaching and composition. His operas, all forgotten, comprise 17 in Spanish, 18 in Italian, and 8 in French, besides a number never performed, and numerous ballets. He was a preeminently successful teacher; his 2 daughters, Mme. Malibran and Pauline Viardot-García, as well as Nourrit, Rimbault, and Favelli, were a few of his best pupils.

BIBL.: G. Malvern, *The Great G.s* (N.Y., 1958).

García, Manuel Patricio Rodríguez, distinguished Spanish vocal teacher, son of **Manuel (del Popolo Vicente Rodríguez) García;** b. Madrid, March 17, 1805; d. London, July 1, 1906 (aged 101). He was intended to be a stage singer; in 1825 went to N.Y. with his father, but in 1829 adopted the vocation of a singing teacher (in Paris), with conspicuous success. An exponent of his father's method, he carefully investigated the functions of the vocal organs; in 1855 he invented the laryngoscope, for which the Königsberg Univ. made him a Dr.Phil. In 1840 he sent to the Academy a *Mémoire sur la voix humaine,* a statement of the conclusions arrived at by various investigators, with his own comments. He was appointed prof. at the Paris Cons. in 1847, but resigned in 1848 to accept a similar position at the London Royal Academy of Music, where he taught uninterruptedly until 1895. Among García's pupils were his 1st wife, **Eugénie García,** Jenny Lind, Henriette Nissen, and Stockhausen. His *Traité complet de l'art du chant* was publ. in 1847 (Eng. ed., 1870; rev. ed. by García's grandson Albert García as *García's Treatise on the Art of Singing,* London, 1924). He also publ. (in Eng.) *Hints on Singing* (London, 1894).

BIBL.: M. Sterling Mackinlay, *G., the Centenarian, and His Time* (Edinburgh, 1908); J. Levien, *The G. Family* (London, 1932); G. Malvern, *The Great G.s* (N.Y., 1958).

García, Pauline Viardot-. See **Viardot-García, Pauline.**

García Fajer, Francisco Javier, Spanish composer; b. Nalda, 1730; d. Saragossa, Feb. 26, 1809. He lived for some years in Rome as a student and singing teacher; in 1756 he was appointed maestro at Saragossa Cathedral. His works show a marked contrast to the fugal style prevailing before, being more natural and simple. He wrote the componimento sacro *Il Tobia* (Rome, 1752); the operas *La finta schiava* (Rome, 1754), *Pompeo Magno in Armenia* (Rome, 1755), *La Pupilla* (Rome, 1755), and *Lo Scultore deluso* (Rome, 1756); masses; motets, chiefly in 8 parts.

BIBL.: J. Carreras López, *La musica en las catedrales durante el siglo XVIII: F.J. G. "El Españoleto" (1730–1809)* (Saragossa, 1983).

García Mansilla, Eduardo, American-born French-Argentine composer; b. Washington, D.C., March 7, 1870; d. Paris, May 9, 1930. He studied composition with Massenet, Saint-Saëns, and d'Indy in Paris and with Rimsky-Korsakov in St. Petersburg. His opera *Ivan* was produced in St. Petersburg in 1905, and another opera, *La angelica Manuelite,* in Buenos Aires in 1917. He also wrote choruses.

García Navarro, (Luis Antonio). See **Navarra, (Luis Antonio) García.**

Gardano, Antonio, one of the earliest and most celebrated Italian music-printers; b. 1509; d. Venice, Oct. 28, 1569. From 1537 he reprinted many current publications as well as important novelties, and compositions of his own, e.g., *Motetti del frutto* (1538) and *Canzoni franzese* (1539). His works also appeared in various collections of the time. After his death his sons Alessandro and Angelo carried on the business until 1575, when they separated; the former later set up for himself in Rome (1582–91), while the latter remained in Venice until his death (1610); his heirs continued publishing under his name until 1677.

BIBL.: M. Lewis, *A. G., Venetian Music Printer, 1538–1569: A Descriptive Bibliography and Historical Study* (4 vols., 1988–89).

Gardel, Carlos, Uruguayan popular singer; b. Tacuarembó, Dec. 11, 1887; d. in an aerial accident, Medellín, Colombia, June 24, 1935. His early years are a matter of conjecture; he apparently was a natural son of Berthe Gardés of Toulouse, France. The identity of his father is concealed in the self-generated mist of fearful illegitimacy; he could have been a Frenchman, or a Uruguayan army colonel named Carlos Escayola; earnest genealogists are at sixes and sevens about this weighty problem. However that might be, Gardel became popular in Argentina as a singer at carnivals around Montevideo and Buenos Aires. In 1912 he formed with Francisco Martino and José Razzano a vocal trio in a repertoire of native songs. Gardel was a pioneer in performances of tangos, which before him were considered unfit for public presentation. He further appeared in Paris, Madrid, and Barcelona. In 1934 and 1935 he sang in the musicals *El Tango en Broadway* and *Tango Bar* in N.Y.

BIBL.: F. Jiménez, *Vida de C. G.* (Buenos Aires, 1936).

Gardelli, Lamberto, distinguished Italian conductor; b. Venice, Nov. 8, 1915. He studied at the Liceo Musicale Rossini in Pesaro; after a brief career as a concert pianist he went to Stockholm as a guest conductor of sym. concerts there (1946–55). He then conducted concerts of the Danish Radio Sym. Orch. in Copenhagen (1955–61) and the Hungarian State Opera in Budapest (1961–65). He made his Metropolitan Opera debut in N.Y. conducting *Andrea Chénier* on Jan. 30, 1966. He was chief conductor of the Munich Radio Orch. (1983–88) and of the Danish Radio Sym. Orch. in Copenhagen (1986–89).

Garden, Mary, celebrated Scottish soprano; b. Aberdeen, Feb. 20, 1874; d. Inverurie, Jan. 3, 1967. She went to the U.S. as a child; studied violin and piano; in 1893 she began the study of singing with Mrs. Robinson Duff in Chicago; in 1895 she went to Paris, where she studied with many teachers (Sbriglia, Bouhy, Trabadello, Mathilde Marchesi, and Lucien Fugère). Her funds, provided by a wealthy patron, were soon depleted, and Sybyl Sanderson, an American soprano living in Paris, introduced her to Albert Carré, director of the Opéra-Comique. Her operatic debut was made under dramatic circumstances on April 10, 1900, when the singer who performed the title role of Charpentier's *Louise* at the Opéra-Comique was taken ill during the performance, and Garden took her place. She revealed herself not only as a singer of exceptional ability, but also as a skillful actress. She subsequently sang in several operas of the general repertoire; also created the role of Diane in Pierné's *La Fille de Tabarin* (Opéra-Comique, Feb. 20, 1901). A historic turning point in her career was reached when she was selected to sing Mélisande in the premiere of Debussy's opera (Opéra-Comique, April 30, 1902); she became the center of a raging controversy when Maurice Maeterlinck, the author of the drama, voiced his violent objection to her assignment (his choice for the role was Georgette Leblanc, his common-law wife) and pointedly refused to have anything to do with the production. Garden won warm praise from the critics for her musicianship, despite the handicap of her American-accented French. She remained a member of the Opéra-Comique; also sang at the Grand Opéra, and at Monte Carlo. She made her U.S. debut as Thaïs at the Manhattan Opera House, N.Y. (Nov. 25, 1907), and presented there the 1st U.S. performance of *Pelléas et Mélisande* (Feb. 19, 1908). In 1910 she joined the Chicago Opera Co.; she became its impresario in the season 1921–22, during which the losses mounted to about $1,000,000. After 1930 she made sporadic appearances in opera and concerts; in 1935, she gave master classes in opera at the Chicago Musical College; acted as technical adviser for opera sequences in motion pictures in Hollywood; in 1939 she returned to Scotland; made a lecture tour in the U.S. in 1947. With Louis Biancolli she wrote a book of memoirs, *Mary Garden's Story* (N.Y., 1951).

Gardes, Roger, French tenor; b. Paris, March 4, 1922. He sang in the chorus of the Opéra-Comique in Paris in 1950; in 1954, won 1st Grand Prix at a contest of tenors in Cannes, and was engaged as soloist at the Opéra-Comique (debut, Aug. 14, 1954, in *La Bohème*); subsequently sang tenor roles in *Lakmé, Eugene Onegin, Les Pêcheurs de perles,* etc.

Gardiner, H(enry) Balfour, English composer; b. London, Nov. 7, 1877; d. Salisbury, June 28, 1950. He was a pupil of Iwan Knorr in Frankfurt; taught singing for a short time in Winchester, but then devoted himself to composition. He was also an ardent collector of English folk songs; his compositions reflect the authentic modalities of the English countryside. He wrote a *Fantasy* for Orch. (1908; not extant); *English Dance* (1904); Sym. in D major (1908; not extant); *News from Wydah* for Soli, Chorus, and Orch. (1912); piano pieces; songs. His most successful piece was *Shepherd Fennel's Dance* for Orch. (1911).
Bibl.: S. Lloyd, *H.B. G.* (Cambridge, 1984).

Gardiner, John Eliot, English conductor; b. Springhead, Dorset, April 20, 1943. He was educated at King's College, Cambridge; while still a student there, he founded the Monteverdi Choir (1964); then went to France to study with Nadia Boulanger; upon his return to England, took postgraduate courses with Thurston Dart at King's College, London. He made his 1st major conducting appearance at the Promenade Concerts in London in 1968; also conducted at the Sadler's Wells Opera and at Covent Garden. He continued giving concerts with his Monteverdi Choir; also founded the English Baroque Soloists, a group which played works of the Baroque on original instruments. From 1980 to 1983 he was principal conductor of the CBC Radio Orch. in Vancouver; from 1981 he served as artistic director of the Göttingen Handel Festival, and from 1982 to 1989 of the Orch. de l'Opéra de Lyon. In 1991 he was made chief conductor of the North German Radio Sym. Orch. in Hamburg. He prepared performing eds. of a number of scores by Rameau and others; he is credited with the discovery (in Paris in 1971) of the MS of Rameau's opera *Les Boréades,* which he conducted at Aix-en-Provence in 1982.
Bibl.: D. Stearns, "The Genteel Revolution of J.E. G.," *Ovation* (March 1986).

Gardiner, William, English writer on music; b. Leicester, March 15, 1770; d. there, Nov. 16, 1853. His father, a hosiery manufacturer, was an amateur musician from whom he acquired the rudiments of music. During his travels on the Continent on his father's business he gathered materials for a collection, *Sacred Melodies* (1812–38), adapted to English words from works by Mozart, Haydn, and Beethoven. His book *The Music of Nature* (London, 1832) enjoyed a certain vogue; he also publ. memoirs, *Music and Friends, or Pleasant Recollections of a Dilettante* (3 vols.; I–II, London, 1838; III, 1853); *Sights in Italy, with some Account of the Present State of Music and the Sister Arts in that Country* (London, 1847).
Bibl.: J. Wilshire, *W. G. of Leicester, 1770–1853* (London, 1970).

Gardner, John (Linton), English composer; b. Manchester, March 2, 1917. He studied at Exeter College, Oxford, with Sir Hugh Allen, Ernest Walker, R.O. Morris, and Thomas Armstrong (Mus.B., 1939). From 1946 to 1952 he was opera coach at Covent Garden; in 1952 was appointed instructor at Morley College; served as its director of music (1965–69); concurrently was director of music at St. Paul's Girls' School (1962–75), and taught at the Royal Academy of Music in London (from 1956); retired in 1975. His style is characteristically fluent and devoid of attempts at experimentation; modernistic devices are used sparingly. He was made a Commander of the Order of the British Empire in 1976.
Works: Operas: *The Moon and Sixpence,* after Somerset Maugham (London, May 24, 1957); *The Visitors* (Aldeburgh Festival, June 10, 1972); *Bel and the Dragon* (1973); *The Entertainment of the Senses* (London, Feb. 2, 1974); *Tobermoray* (1976). Orch.: Sym. (Cheltenham, July 5, 1951); *A Scots Overture* (London, Aug. 16, 1954); Piano Concerto No. 1 (1957); *Sinfonia piccola* for Strings (1974); *An English Ballad* (1969); *3 Ridings* (1970); Sonatina for Strings (1974). Chamber: *Rhapsody* for Oboe and String Quartet (1935); Oboe Sonata (1953); *Concerto da camera* for 4 Instruments (1968); *Chamber Concerto* for Organ and 11 Instruments (1969); also sacred and secular choruses; piano pieces; songs.

Gardner, Samuel, Russian-American violinist and composer; b. Elizavetgrad, Aug. 25, 1891; d. N.Y., Jan. 23, 1984. He went early to the U.S. and studied violin with Felix Winternitz and Franz Kneisel; composition with Goetschius, and later with Loeffler in Boston. He was a member of the Kneisel String Quartet (1914); also played in American orchs. From 1924 to 1941 he taught violin at the Inst. of Musical Art in N.Y. He wrote a number of pleasant pieces: *Country Moods* for String Orch. (N.Y., Dec. 10, 1946); a tone poem, *Broadway* (Boston, April 18, 1930); *From the Canebrake* (1918); he also publ. *Essays for Advanced Solo Violin* (1960).

Garfunkel, Art, American soft-rock composer and singer; b. N.Y., Nov. 5, 1941. With his classmate at high school **Paul Simon** he started a song duo; at the age of 16, they produced together a fairly successful record, *Hey, Schoolgirl,* under the group name Tom and Jerry. Their next common effort, *Sounds of Silence,* was a major hit when it was issued as a single in 1965. They demonstrated their dual versatility by writing the sound track for the film *The Graduate,* which featured a song, *Mrs. Robinson,* destined to become very popular. Their album *Bridge over Troubled Water* was praised in pop circles; then the 2 went their separate ways in 1970. Art Garfunkel became interested in acting and appeared in *Catch-22, Carnal Knowledge,* and *Bad Timing/A Sensual Obsession.* He also tried his hand at writing poetry. Garfunkel was reunited with Simon in 1982, producing a fine album, *The Concert in Central Park.*

Garland, Judy (real name, **Frances Ethel Gumm**), famous American singer of popular music and actress; b. Grand Rapids, Minn., June 10, 1922; d. London, June 22, 1969. Having been reared in a family of vaudeville entertainers, she made her stage debut at the age of 2 and then toured with her sisters before breaking into films in 1936; subsequently gained wide recognition for her film appearances with Mickey Rooney. She won a special Academy Award as well as film immortality for her portrayal of Dorothy in *The Wizard of Oz* (1939), adopting its *Over the Rainbow* as her theme song. She later appeared in such musical films as *For Me and My Gal* (1942), *Meet Me in St. Louis* (1944), *Easter Parade* (1948), and *In the Good Old Summertime* (1949). In succeeding years she concentrated mainly on nightclub and concert hall performances; however, she made several more compelling film appearances, most notably in *A Star Is Born* (1954) and *Judgment at Nuremberg* (1961). In spite of many successes, her private life became public when a string of misfortunes, including marital difficulties, drug dependency, and suicide attempts, overwhelmed her. Her fans remained steadfastly loyal until her early death at the age of 47. Her daughter **Liza Minnelli** also became a successful singer and actress but managed to stay relatively even-tempered.
Bibl.: M. Torme, *The Other Side of the Rainbow* (N.Y., 1971); M. Deans and A. Pinchot, *Weep No More, My Lady: J. G. by Her Last Husband* (London, 1972); A. Edwards, *J. G.* (N.Y., 1975); T. Watson and B. Chapman, *J: Portrait of an American Legend* (N.Y., 1986).

Garland, Peter, American composer, publisher, and writer on music; b. Portland, Maine, Jan. 27, 1952. He studied with James Tenney and Harold Budd at the Calif. Inst. of the Arts (B.F.A., 1972), then (from 1972) began editing and publishing *Soundings,* a journal comprising scores and writings by a variety of American composers. During the 1970s he lived in Mexico, where he did field recordings; since 1980 he has lived in Santa Fe, N.Mex., where he directs his own performing ensemble. In 1984 he was guest composer at the Darmstadt Ferienkurse. As a composer, he is influenced by native American and Mexican cultures and by his teacher Budd; his works are spare and lyrical, often using exotic instruments.

WRITINGS (all publ. in Santa Fe): *Music Is Dangerous* (1973); *Magic Animals* (1975); *Americas: Essays on American Music and Culture* (1982).

WORKS: *Apple Blossom* for 2–4 Marimbas (1972); *Dreaming of Immortality in a Thatched Cottage* for Voices, Angklung, Marimba, Harpsichord, and Percussion (1977); *The Conquest of Mexico*, theater work for Dancers, Shadow Puppets, Soloists, Recorder, Harp, Harpsichord, and Percussion (1977–80); *Matachin Dances* for 2 Violins and Gourd Rattles (1980–81).

Garlandia, Johannes de (sometimes called **Johannes de Garlandia the Elder** to distinguish him from a hypothetical Joh. Garlandia the Younger, proposed by H. Riemann on rather suppositional grounds), English writer on mathematics, theology, and alchemy; b., c.1195. He studied at Oxford; in 1217 went to Paris; joined the Crusade against the Albigenses; was probably still living in 1272. He is the author of several tracts on music, among them *De musica mensurabili positio,* a valuable treatise on mensural music; 2 versions were printed by Coussemaker in his *Scriptores,* vol. I; a modern ed. was prepared by F. Reimer (Wiesbaden, 1972). There are 4 works printed under his name in Gerbert and Coussemaker.

BIBL.: R. Rasch, *J. d.G. en de ontwikkeling van de voor-Franconische notatie* (Brooklyn, N.Y., 1969; with summaries in Eng. and German).

Garner, Erroll (Louis), famous black American jazz pianist and composer; b. Pittsburgh, June 15, 1921; d. Los Angeles, Jan. 2, 1977. Completely untutored and unlettered, he composed tunes extemporaneously, singing and accompanying himself at the piano, with an amanuensis to put down the notes. He also played drums and slap-bass. His nervous rubato style won acclaim from the cognoscenti and jazz aficionados. Incredibly precocious, he played regularly over radio station KDKA in Pittsburgh at the age of 7 with a group called the Candy Kids; as an adolescent, he played piano on riverboats cruising the Allegheny River; then was a featured piano player in nightclubs and restaurants. He went to N.Y. in 1944; formed his own trio in 1946. In 1948 he went to Paris; made further European tours in 1962, 1964, 1966, and 1969. His whimsical piano style especially appealed to French jazz critics, who called him "The Picasso of the Piano" and, alluding to his digital dexterity, "The Man with 40 Fingers." In 1971 the Republic of Mali issued a postage stamp in his honor. Among his own songs, the plangent *Misty* became greatly popular; many of his other songs (he composed about 200 of them) reflect similar wistful moods, exemplified by such titles as *Dreamy, Solitaire,* and *That's My Kick.*

BIBL.: J. Doran, *E. G., The Most Happy Piano* (Metuchen, N.J., 1985).

Garreta, Julio, Catalan composer; b. San Feliu, March 12, 1875; d. there, Dec. 2, 1925. Entirely self-taught, he learned piano and composition. He wrote a great number of "sardanas" (the Catalan national dance); a friendship with Casals stimulated several larger works; his *Impressions symphoniques* for String Orch. was performed in Barcelona on Oct. 29, 1907. His *Suite Empordanesa* for Orch. received 1st prize at the Catalan Festival in 1920. He also wrote a Cello Sonata, a Piano Sonata, and a Piano Quartet.

Garrett, George (Mursell), English composer and organist; b. Winchester, June 8, 1834; d. Cambridge, April 8, 1897. A pupil of Elvey and Wesley, he was assistant organist at Winchester Cathedral (1851–54); organist of Madras Cathedral (1854–56) and of St. John's College, Cambridge (1857); and organist to the Univ. (1873), succeeding Hopkins. He took degrees of Mus.Bac. (1857) and Mus.D. (1867); also received the degree of M.A. *propter merita* (1878). From 1883, he was a Univ. lecturer on harmony and counterpoint; also was an examiner in music at Cambridge Univ. He wrote 5 cantatas, 4 services, and other church music.

Garrido, Pablo, Chilean composer and ethnomusicologist; b. Valparaiso, March 26, 1905; d. Santiago, Sept. 14, 1982.

He studied in Santiago; conducted concerts of Chilean music and gave lectures; publ. a valuable monograph, *Biografía de la Cueca Chilena* (Santiago, 1942). He composed an opera, *La sugestión* (Santiago, Oct. 18, 1961); a ballet, *El Guerrillero* (1963); *Rapsodía chilena* for Piano and Orch. (1938); Piano Concerto (1950); *Fantasía antillana* for Cello and Orch. (1950); *13 & 13* for String Quartet (1951); piano pieces and songs based on Chilean folklore.

Garrido-Lecca, Celso, Peruvian composer; b. Piura, March 9, 1926. He studied music theory with Andrés Sas and Rodolfo Holzmann in Lima; then went to Santiago, Chile, where he took courses in composition with Domingo Santa Cruz. In 1964 he received a Guggenheim fellowship. In 1967 he was appointed to the faculty of the Univ. of Chile.

WORKS: Sinfonia (Washington, D.C., April 22, 1961); *Laudes* for Orch. (1963); *Elegía a Machu Picchu* (1965; N.Y., March 23, 1967); *Música* for 6 Instruments and Percussion (1957); Divertimento for Wind Quintet (1965); String Quartet (1963); *Antaras* for String Nonet (1969); choruses; piano pieces; songs.

Garrison, Lucy McKim, American collector of slave songs; b. Philadelphia, Oct. 30, 1842; d. West Orange, N.J., May 11, 1877. During a visit to the South Carolina Sea Islands in 1862, she collected the slave songs of the freedmen she met; with her husband, Wendell Phillips Garrison, and William Francis Allen and Charles Pickard Ware, she publ. the valuable book *Slave Songs of the United States* (1867).

BIBL.: D. Epstein, "L.M. G., American Musician," *Bulletin of the New York Public Library,* LXVII (1963).

Garrison, Mabel, American soprano; b. Baltimore, April 24, 1886; d. N.Y., Aug. 20, 1963. She was a pupil of W.E. Heimendahl and P. Minetti at the Peabody Cons. of Music in Baltimore (1909–11); then of O. Saenger (1912–14) and H. Witherspoon (1916) in N.Y. She made her debut as Filina (*Mignon*) in Boston, April 18, 1912; was a member of the Metropolitan Opera in N.Y. from 1914 to 1921; made a world tour; from 1933 she taught singing at Smith College; retired in 1939.

Gaspari, Gaetano, Italian librarian and historiographer; b. Bologna, March 15, 1807; d. there, March 31, 1881. He entered the Liceo Musicale in 1820; took 1st prize in composition in 1827. He served as maestro di cappella at various churches; then devoted himself to historical research.

WRITINGS: *Ricerche, documenti e memorie risguardanti la storia dell'arte musicale in Bologna* (1867); *Ragguagli sulla cappella musicale della Basilica di S. Petronio in Bologna* (1869); *Memorie dell'arte musicale in Bologna al XVI secolo* (1875); etc.

BIBL.: F. Parisini, *Elogio funebre del professore G. G.* (1882).

Gasparini, Francesco, eminent Italian composer and pedagogue; b. Camaiore, near Lucca, March 5, 1668; d. Rome, March 22, 1727. He became a member of the Accademia Filarmonica in Bologna in 1685, then studied with Legrenzi in Venice in 1686; subsequently went to Rome (1689), where he became a member of the Accademia di Santa Cecilia; he may have received further instruction from Corelli and Pasquini. In 1701 he became maestro di coro of the Ospedale della Pietà in Venice; in 1713 returned to Rome, where he became maestro di cappella of S. Lorenzo in Lucina in 1717; he was appointed to the same position at St. John Lateran in 1725, but ill health prevented him from assuming his duties. He distinguished himself as a composer of both secular and sacred music; he wrote about 50 operas in all. He was also an esteemed teacher, numbering Domenico Scarlatti, Quantz, and Benedetto Marcello among his students. He publ. the valuable treatise *L'armonico pratico al cimbalo* (Venice, 1708; many subsequent eds.; Eng. tr. by F. Stillings as *The Practical Harmonist at the Keyboard,* New Haven, 1963).

WORKS: OPERAS (all 1st perf. in Venice unless otherwise given): *Il Roderico* (Rome, 1694); *L'Ajace* (Rome, 1697); *Mirena e Floro* (Naples, 1699); *Tiberio Imperatore d'Oriente* (Venice?, 1702); *Gli imenei stabiliti dal caso* (1702); *Il più fedel fra i*

vassalli (1703); *Il miglior d'ogni amore per il peggiore d'ogni odio* (1703); *La fede tradita e vendicata* (1704); *La maschera levata al vitio* (1704); *La Fredegonda* (1704); *Ambleto* (1705); *Il principato custodito dalla frode* (1705); *Statira* (1705); *Antioco* (1705); *Flavio Anicio Olibrio* (1707); *Anfitrione* (1707); *L'amor generoso* (1707); *Taican Rè della Cina* (1707); *Engelberta* (1708); *Atenaide* (Vienna, 1709; Act 1 by A.S. Fiore, Act 2 by Caldara, and Act 3 by Gasparini); *Sesostri Rè d'Egitto* (1709); *La Ninfa Apollo* (1709); *Alciade, overo La violenza d'amore* (Bergamo, 1709; Act 1 by Gasparini, Act 2 by C.F. Pollarolo, and Act 3 by G. Ballarotti); *La Principessa fedele* (1709); *Tamerlano* (1710); *L'amor tirannico* (1710); *Merope* (1711); *Costantino* (1711); *Amor vince l'odio, overo Timocrate* (Florence, 1715); *Il Tartaro nella Cina* (Reggio Emilia, 1715); *Il comando non inteso ed ubbedito* (Florence, 1715); *Ciro* (Rome, 1716); *Teodosio ed Eudossa* (Braunschweig, 1716; in collaboration with J. Fux and A. Caldara); *Il trace in catena* (Rome, 1716–17); *Intermezzi in derisione della setta maomettana* (Rome, 1717?); *Pirro* (Rome, 1717); *Il gran Cid* (Naples, 1717); *Democrito* (Turin, 1718); *Lucio Vero* (Rome, 1719); *Astianatte* (Rome, 1719); *L'oracolo del fato* (Vienna, 1719); *La pace fra Seleuco e Tolomeo* (Milan, 1720); *Nino* (Reggio Emilia, 1720; Act 1 by G.M. Capelli, Act 2 by Gasparini, and Act 3 by A.M. Bononcini); *L'Avaro* (Florence, 1720?); *Il Faramondo* (Rome, 1720); *Dorinda* (Rome, 1723); *Gl'equivoci d'amore e d'innocenza* (1723); *Tigrane* (Rome, 1724). His other secular vocal music includes *Cantate da camera a voce sola,* op. 1 (Rome, 1695); cantatas; arias; etc. **ORATORIOS:** *Santa Maria egittiaca, piacere, pentimento, e Lucifero* (n.d.); *Moisé liberato dal Nilo* (Vienna, 1703?); *L'Atalia* (n.d.); *La nascita di Cristo* (1724); *Le nozze di Tobia* (1724); also masses and motets.
    BIBL.: G. Marotti, "Quasi un incognito: Il Camaiorese F. G.," *Cenobio,* XV (1966); A. Bonaccorsi, "F. G.," *Maestri di Lucca* (Florence, 1967).

Gasparo da Salò (family name, **Bertolotti**), Italian instrument maker; b. Polpenazzi (baptized in Salò, May 20), 1540; d. Brescia (buried), April 14, 1609. He went to Brescia in 1562, and settled there as a maker of viols, viole da gamba, and contrabass viols, which gained much celebrity; his violins were less valued. His pupils were his eldest son, Francesco; Giovanni Paolo Maggini; and Giacomo Lafranchini. Dragonetti's favorite double bass was an altered "viola contrabassa" of Gasparo's.
    BIBL.: V. Rhò-Guerriero, *G. d.S.* (Rome, 1892); P. Bettoni, "G. d.S. e l'invenzione del violino," *Commentari del Ateneo di Brescia* (1901); M. Butturini, *G. d.S.: Studio critico* (Salò, 1901); G. Bignami, "G. d.S.," *Musica d'Oggi* (Feb. 1940); A. Mucchi, *G. d.S.* (Milan, 1940).

Gasperini, Guido, Italian musicologist; b. Florence, June 7, 1865; d. Naples, Feb. 20, 1942. He was a pupil of Tacchinardi (composition) and Sbolci (cello); from 1902 to 1924 was librarian and a teacher of music history at the Parma Cons.; later, librarian at the Naples Cons. (1924–35); in 1908 he founded the Associazione dei Musicologi Italiani, one of the main purposes of which was the examination and cataloguing of all books on music and musical MSS in the Italian libraries; in 1909 it was affiliated with the Internationale Musik-Gesellschaft (as its Italian branch), and began issuing a quarterly *Catalogo delle opere musicali . . . esistenti . . . nelle biblioteche e negli archivi pubblici e privati d'Italia.*
    WRITINGS: *Storia della musica* (1899; a series of 10 lectures); *Dell' arte d'interpretare la scrittura della musica vocale del Cinquecento* (1902); *Storia della Semiografia musicale* (1905); *I caratteri peculiari del Melodramma italiano* (1913); *Musicisti alla Corte dei Farnesi;* "L'Art italien avant Palestrina," *Mercure Musical,* II, 6–8; *Noterelle su due liutiste al servizio di Casa Farnese* (1923).

Gassmann, Florian Leopold, important Bohemian composer; b. Brüx, May 3, 1729; d. Vienna, Jan. 20, 1774. He studied voice, violin, and harp with Johann Woborschil (Jan Voboril), the regens chori in Brüx; his father opposed his inter-

est in music, so he ran away from home, eventually making his way to Italy, where he may have studied with Padre Martini in Bologna. His 1st opera, *Merope,* was given in Venice in 1757. After serving Count Leonardo Veneri there, he was invited to Vienna to become ballet composer at the court in 1763. He soon established himself as an opera composer, gaining fame with his comic operas *L'amore artigiano* (Vienna, April 26, 1767) and *La Contessina* (Mährisch-Neustadt, Sept. 3, 1770). In 1772 he was appointed court composer and also founded and served as 1st vice-president of the Tonkünstler-Sozietät, a benevolent society for musicians. In addition to his operas, he distinguished himself as an accomplished symphonist. He was highly esteemed by Mozart, Gerber, Burney, and Salieri, the last having been his student in Vienna. His 2 daughters, **Maria Anna Fux** (b. Vienna, 1771; d. there, Aug. 27, 1852) and **(Maria) Therese Rosenbaum** (b. Vienna, April 1, 1774; d. there, Sept. 8, 1837), were pupils of Salieri; both were active as singers.
    WORKS: OPERAS: *Merope* (Venice, Carnival 1757; only the overture and Act 1 extant); *Issipile* (Venice, Carnival 1758); *Gli Uccellatori,* dramma giocoso (Venice, Carnival 1759); *Filosofia ed amore,* dramma giocoso (Venice, Carnival 1760); *Catone in Utica* (Venice, 1761; only 1 aria extant); *Un Pazzo ne fa cento,* dramma giocoso (Venice, 1762); *L'Olimpiade* (Vienna, 1764); *Il trionfo d'amore,* azione teatrale (Vienna, 1765); *Achille in Sciro* (Venice, 1766); *Il Viaggiatore ridicolo,* dramma giocoso (Vienna, 1766); *L'amore artigiano,* dramma giocoso (Vienna, 1767); *Amore e Psiche* (Vienna, 1767); *La notte critica,* dramma giocoso (Vienna, 1768); *L'opera seria,* commedia per musica (Vienna, 1769); *Ezio* (Rome, Carnival 1770); *La Contessina,* dramma giocoso (Mährisch-Neustadt, 1770; ed. in Denkmäler der Tonkunst in Österreich, XLII–XLIV, Jg. XXI/1, 1914); *Il Filosofo inamorato,* dramma giocoso (Vienna, 1771); *Le Pescatrici,* dramma giocoso (Vienna, 1771); *Don Quischott von Mancia,* comedy (Vienna, 1771; Acts 1 and 2 by Paisiello, Act 3 by Gassmann); *I rovinati,* comedy (Vienna, 1772); *La casa di campagna,* dramma giocoso (Vienna, 1773). **SACRED:** *La Betulia liberata,* oratorio (Vienna, 1772); masses; motets; offertories; graduals; hymns; etc.; see F. Kosch, ed., *F.L. G.: Kirchenwerke,* in Denkmäler der Tonkunst in Österreich, LXXXIII, Jg. XLV (1938). **INSTRUMENTAL:** About 60 syms. (1 ed. by K. Geiringer, Vienna, 1933; 1 ed. by L. Somfai in Musica Rinata, XVIII, 1970); 27 opera overtures; Flute Concerto; 37 string quartets; 8 string quintets; 10 wind quintets; 37 wind trios; 7 string duos; etc.
    BIBL.: F. Kosch, *F.L. G. als Kirchenkomponist* (diss., Univ. of Vienna, 1924); E. Leuchter, *Die Kammermusik F.L. G.s* (diss., Univ. of Vienna, 1926); E. Girach, *F.L. G.* (Reichenberg, 1930); G. Hill, *A Thematic Catalog of the Instrumental Music of F.L. G.* (Hackensack, N.J., 1976).

Gassner, Ferdinand Simon, Austrian violinist; b. Vienna, Jan. 6, 1798; d. Karlsruhe, Feb. 25, 1851. From 1816, he was violinist at the National Theater in Mainz; in 1818, he became music director at Giessen Univ., which in 1819 made him Dr.Phil. and lecturer on music. In 1826 he joined the Court Orch. at Karlsruhe, where he became music director in 1830. He publ. the *Musikalischer Hausfreund* (Mainz, 1822–35); ed. (1841–45) the *Zeitschrift für Deutschlands Musikvereine und Dilettanten.* He wrote *Partiturkenntniss, Ein Leitfaden zum Selbstunterricht* (1838; French ed., 1851, as *Traité de la partition*) and *Dirigent und Ripienist* (1846); contributed to the Supplement of Schilling's *Universallexikon der Tonkunst* (1842) and ed. an abridgment of the entire work (1849). He composed 2 operas, several ballets, 3 cantatas, songs, etc.

Gast, Peter. See **Köselitz, Johann Heinrich.**

Gastaldon, Stanislas, Italian composer; b. Turin, April 7, 1861; d. Florence, March 7, 1939. At the age of 17 he began publishing nocturnes, *ballabili,* and other pieces for piano; was music critic for the *Nuovo Giornale* in Florence. He wrote about 300 songs, some of which were popular (*La musica proibita; Ti vorrei rapire; Frate Anselmo; Donna Clara*); he was fairly successful with his operas *Mala Pasqua* (Rome,

1890), *Il Pater* (Milan, 1894), *Stellina* (Florence, 1905), *Il sonetto di Dante* (Genoa, 1909), and *Il Reuccio di Caprilana* (Turin, 1913). He also wrote marches for military band; a piano fantasia, *La dansa delle scimmie;* etc.

Gastinel, Léon-Gustave-Cyprien, French composer; b. Villers, near Auxonne, Aug. 13, 1823; d. Fresnes-les-Rurgis, Oct. 20, 1906. He was a pupil of Halévy at the Paris Cons., taking 1st Grand Prix de Rome for his cantata *Vélasquez* in 1846. A successful composer of operas, he produced *Le Miroir* (1853), *L'Opéra aux fenêtres* (1857), *Titus et Bérénice* (1860), *Le Buisson vert* (1861), *Le Barde* (Nice, 1896), and the ballet *Le Rêve* (Paris Opéra, 1890), besides other stage works: *La Kermesse, Eutatès, Ourania,* and *La Tulipe bleue;* also 4 oratorios and 3 solemn masses, orch. compositions, chamber music, choruses, etc.
BIBL.: F. Boisson, *L. G.* (1893).

Gastoldi, Giovanni Giacomo, eminent Italian composer; b. Caravaggio, date unknown; d. c.1622. He was active mainly in Mantua; was a sub-deacon (1572) and deacon (1573–74) at S. Barbara, later serving as maestro di contrappunto to the young priests (1579–87) and as maestro di cappella (1592–1608); then went to Milan. He contributed part of the score of *L'Idropica* for performance at the Mantuan court (June 2, 1608). He composed numerous sacred and secular vocal works, the finest being his *ballettos,* which include *Balletti* for 5 Voices, *con li suoi versi per cantare, sonare, & ballare; con una mascherata de cacciatori* for 6 Voices, & *un concerto de pastori* for 8 Voices (1591; ed. in Le Pupitre, X, Paris, 1968, and by H. Schmidt, N.Y., 1970) and *Balletti, con la intavolatura del liuto, per cantare, sonare, & ballare* for 3 Voices (1594).
BIBL.: D. Arnold, "G. and the English Ballet," *Monthly Musical Record,* LXXXVI (1956); R. Rasch, "The *Balletti* of G. G. and the Musical History of the Netherlands," *Tijdschrift van de Vereniging voor Nederlandse muziekgeschiedenis,* XXIV/2 (1974).

Gaston, E(verett) Thayer, American music educator and music therapist; b. Woodward, Okla., July 4, 1901; d. Springfield, Mo., June 3, 1970. He took premed courses at Sterling (Kans.) College (B.A., 1923), then studied music there (B.M., 1936) and at the Univ. of Kansas (M.A. in music education, 1938; Ph.D. in educational psychology, 1940). He was a prominent figure in the fields of music education and music therapy in the U.S.; was founder of the National Assoc. for Music Therapy, serving for a season as its president (1952–53). He prepared the *Gaston Test of Musicality* (1941; 4th ed., 1957) and ed. the textbook *Music in Therapy* (1968).
BIBL.: R. Johnson, *E.T. G.: Contributions to Music Therapy and Music Education* (diss., Univ. of Michigan, 1973); idem, "E.T. G.: Leader in Scientific Thought on Music in Therapy and Education," *Journal of Research in Music Education,* XXIX (1981).

Gastoué, Amédée (-Henri-Gustave-Noël), French organist and music scholar; b. Paris, March 19, 1873; d. there, June 1, 1943. He studied piano and harmony with A. Deslandres (1890), harmony with Lavignac (1891), then organ with Guilmant and counterpoint and composition with Magnard. From 1896 to 1905 he was ed. of *Revue du Chant Grégorien;* in 1897 began to contribute to the *Tribune de St.-Gervais;* became its ed. in 1904 and, in 1909, ed. in chief and director. He was prof. of Gregorian chant at the Schola Cantorum from its foundation (1896); also music critic of *La Semaine Littéraire* in 1905. For many years he was organist and maître de chapelle at St.-Jean-Baptiste-de-Belleville, Paris, where he also gave concerts; was a lecturer at the Catholic Univ. and the École des Hautes Études Sociales, a laureate of the Académie des Inscriptions et Belles-Lettres, and a Commander of the Order of St. Gregory the Great; in 1925, became a member of the Académie des Beaux Arts.
WRITINGS: *Cours théorique et pratique de plain-chant romain grégorien* (1904); *Historie du chant liturgique à Paris* (vol. I: *Des Origines à la fin des temps carolingiens,* 1904; 2nd ed., 1917); *Les Origines du chant romain, l'antiphonaire grégorien* (1907); *Catalogue des manuscrits de musique byzantine de la Bibliothèque Nationale de Paris et des bibliothèques publiques de France* (1907; with facsimiles); *Nouvelle méthode pratique de chant grégorien* (1908); *Traité d'harmonisation du chant grégorien* (1910); *L'Art grégorien* (1911; 3rd ed., 1920); *La Musique de l'église* (1911); *Variations sur la musique d'église* (1912); *Musique et liturgie. Le Graduel et l'Antiphonaire romain* (Lyons, 1913); *L'Orgue en France de l'antiquité au début de la période classique* (1921); *Les Primitifs de la musique française* (1922); *Le Cantique populaire en France: Ses sources, son histoire* (Lyons, 1924); *La Vie musicale de l'église* (1929); *La Liturgie et la musique* (1931); *Le Manuscrit de musique polyphonique du trésor d'Apt, XIVe–XVe siècles* (1936); *L'Église et la musique* (Paris, 1936).

Gatlin, Larry, American country-music singer and songwriter; b. Seminole, Texas, May 2, 1948. He was educated at the Univ. of Texas (1966–70); in 1971 he launched his career as a country-music artist, active mainly in Nashville; made numerous appearances as a singer with his brothers in a group dubbed Larry Gatlin and the Gatlin Brothers Band, which enjoyed excellent success.

Gatti, Guido M(aggiorino), eminent Italian music critic and writer; b. Chieti, May 30, 1892; d. Grottaferrata, near Rome, May 10, 1973. He was ed. of *La Riforma Musicale* (Turin, 1913–15) and *Il Pianoforte* (Turin, 1920–27), which changed its name in 1927 to *La Rassegna Musicale.*
WRITINGS: *Guida musicale della Giovanna d'Arco di Enrico Bossi; Biografia critica di Bizet* (1914); *Musicisti moderni d'Italia e di fuori* (Bologna, 1920; 2nd ed., 1925); *Le Barbier de Séville de Rossini* (Paris, 1925); *Debora e Jaele di I. Pizzetti* (1922); *Dizionario musicale* (in collaboration with A. della Corte; 1925; 2nd ed., 1930; rev. ed., 1952); *Ildebrando Pizzetti* (Turin, 1934; 2nd ed., 1955; in Eng., London, 1951); *Alfredo Casella* (with F. D'Amico; Milan, 1958); *Victor de Sabata* (Milan, 1958).

Gatti-Casazza, Giulio, Italian impresario; b. Udine, Feb. 3, 1868; d. Ferrara, Sept. 2, 1940. He was educated at the Univs. of Ferrara and Bologna, and graduated from the Naval Engineering School at Genoa; abandoned his career as engineer and became director of the opera in Ferrara in 1893. His ability attracted the attention of the Viscount di Modrone and A. Boito, who, in 1898, offered him the directorship of La Scala at Milan. During the 10 years of his administration the institution came to occupy 1st place among the opera houses of Italy. From 1908 to 1935 he was general director of the Metropolitan Opera in N.Y., and the period of his administration was, both artistically and financially, the most flourishing in the history of the house; he vastly improved the orch., chorus, and all the mechanical depts.; one of his 1st suggestions to the board of directors was to offer a $10,000 prize for the encouragement of native operatic composers (won by Horatio Parker with *Mona,* 1912); the doors were opened to American composers (starting with Converse, Damrosch, and Herbert), and eminent foreign composers gladly accepted invitations to have the world premiere of new works take place at the Metropolitan (Humperdinck's *Königskinder,* Puccini's *Girl of the Golden West,* Granados's *Goyescas,* Giordano's *Madame Sans-Gêne,* etc.); the list of novelties produced is a long one, numbering 110 works; besides, there were noteworthy revivals of older works, e.g., Gluck's *Iphigénie en Tauride* (rev. by Richard Strauss), etc. During this period, Giulio Setti was chorus master and set a high standard for the opera chorus. Gatti-Casazza procured the services of the best conductors available, bringing with him from La Scala the master Arturo Toscanini, and such able conductors as Polacco and Panizza. He resigned in 1935, Giulio Setti leaving with him, and went to Italy, where he lived in retirement. On April 3, 1910, Gatti-Casazza married the soprano **Frances Alda;** they were divorced in 1929; in 1930 he married Rosina Galli (d. April 30, 1940), premiere danseuse and ballet mistress. Gatti-Casazza's *Memories of the Opera* was posth. publ. in Eng. in 1941.

BIBL.: I. Kolodin, *The Metropolitan Opera, 1883–1935* (N.Y., 1936; 4th ed., rev., 1966).

Gatty, Nicholas Comyn, English composer; b. Bradfield, Sept. 13, 1874; d. London, Nov. 10, 1946. He was educated at Downing College, Cambridge (B.A., 1896; Mus.B., 1898); then studied with Stanford at the Royal College of Music; was organist to the Duke of York's Royal Military School at Chelsea, and music critic of *Pall Mall Gazette* (1907–14); also acted as assistant conductor at Covent Garden.

WORKS: 1-act operas (all produced in London): *Greysteel* (1906); *Duke or Devil* (1909); *The Tempest* (April 17, 1920); *Prince Ferelon* (1921; received the Carnegie Award); *Macbeth*, 4-act opera (MS); *King Alfred and the Cakes; Ode on Time* for Soli, Chorus, and Orch., after Milton; *3 Short Odes*; Variations for Orch. on *Old King Cole;* Piano Concerto; Piano Trio; String Quartet; waltzes for piano; songs.

Gaubert, Philippe, French conductor and composer; b. Cahors, July 3, 1879; d. Paris, July 8, 1941. He studied flute with Taffanel at the Paris Cons.; in 1905, won the 2nd Prix de Rome; from 1919 to 1938, was conductor of the Paris Cons. concerts; from 1920, principal conductor at the Paris Opéra.

WORKS: Operas: *Sonia* (Nantes, 1913) and *Naïla* (Paris, April 7, 1927); ballet, *Philotis* (Paris, 1914); oratorio, *Josiane* (Paris, Dec. 17, 1921). Orch.: *Rhapsodie sur des thèmes populaires* (1909); *Poème pastoral* (1911); *Le Cortège d'Amphitrite* (Paris, April 9, 1911); *Fresques*, symphonic suite (Paris, Nov. 12, 1923); *Les Chants de la mer*, 3 symphonic pictures (Paris, Oct. 12, 1929); Violin Concerto (Paris, Feb. 16, 1930); *Les Chants de la terre* (Paris, Dec. 20, 1931); *Poème romanesque* for Cello and Orch. (Paris, Jan. 30, 1932); *Inscriptions sur les portes de la ville*, 4 symphonic tableaux (Paris, Nov. 18, 1934); Sym. in F (Paris, Nov. 8, 1936); *Poème des champs et des villages* (Paris, Feb. 4, 1939). Chamber: *Médailles antiques* for Flute, Violin, and Piano; *Divertissement grec* for Flute and Harp; *Sur l'eau* for Flute and Piano; *Intermède champêtre* for Oboe and Piano; Violin Sonata; songs; *Méthode complète de flûte* in 8 parts (1923); many transcriptions for flute.

Gaudimel, Claude. See Goudimel, Claude.

Gauk, Alexander, Russian conductor and composer; b. Odessa, Aug. 15, 1893; d. Moscow, March 30, 1963. He studied composition with Kalafati and Vitols, and conducting with N. Tcherepnin, at the Petrograd Cons., where he graduated in 1917; then conducted at the State Opera and Ballet Theater there (1920–31). He was chief conductor of the Leningrad Phil. (1930–34), the U.S.S.R. State Sym. Orch. of Moscow (1936–41), and the All-Union Radio Sym. Orch. of Moscow (1953–63). He also taught conducting at the conservatories of Leningrad (1927–33), Tbilisi (1941–43), and Moscow (1939–63). His pupils included such distinguished conductors as Mravinsky, Melik-Pashayev, Simeonov, and Svetlanov. He championed the music of Russian composers; restored Rachmaninoff's 1st Sym. to the active Russian repertoire from orch. parts found in the archives of the Moscow Cons. He wrote a Sym., a Harp Concerto, a Piano Concerto, and songs.

Gaul, Alfred (Robert), English composer; b. Norwich, April 30, 1837; d. Worcestershire, Sept. 13, 1913. A chorister in the Cathedral at 9, he was apprenticed to Z. Buck; was organist at Fakenham, Birmingham, and Edgbaston; graduated (1863) as Mus.Bac. from Cambridge; became conductor of the Walsall Phil. in 1887, then teacher and conductor at the Birmingham and Midland Inst., and teacher at King Edward's High School for Girls. He wrote an oratorio, *Hezekiah* (1861); several sacred cantatas, some of which (*Ruth* and *The Holy City*) were popular in the U.S.; vocal trios and duets; songs and part-songs; etc.

Gaultier (Gautier, Gaulthier), Denis, French lutenist and composer, cousin of **Ennemond Gaultier;** b. Marseilles?, 1603; d. Paris, late Jan. 1672. He spent most of his life in Paris as a lutenist. With his cousin, he was a leading composer of lute music and a major influence on the keyboard style of Froberger.

WORKS: *La Rhétorique des dieux* (Paris, c.1652; ed. by A. Tessier in Publications de la Société Française de Musicologie, VI–VII, 1932); *Pièces de luth sur trois differens modes nouveaux* (Paris, c.1670; reprint, 1978); *Livre de tablature des pièces de Mr. Gaultier Sr. de Neve et de Mr. Gaultier son cousin* (Paris, c.1672; reprint, 1978). **BIBL.:** E. Häffner, *Die Lautenstücke des D. G.* (Endingen, 1939); A. Souris and M. Rollin, eds., *Œuvres du vieux Gautier* (Paris, 1966).

Gaultier (Gaulthier, Gautier), Ennemond, French lutenist and composer, cousin of **Denis Gaultier;** b. Villette, Dauphoné, 1575; d. Nèves, near Villette, Dec. 11, 1651. He was valet de chambre to Henri IV's queen (1600–1631). Several of his lute works were publ. in collections of his day. See A. Souris and M. Rollin, eds., *Œuvres du vieux Gautier* (Paris, 1966).

Gauthier, (Ida Josephine Phoebe) Eva, Canadian mezzo-soprano; b. Ottawa, Sept. 20, 1885; d. N.Y., Dec. 26, 1958. She studied voice in Ottawa with Frank Buels, in Paris with Jacques Bouhy and Auguste-Jean Dubulle, and in London with William Shakespeare; in 1909 she made her operatic debut as Micaela in Pavia, Italy; in 1910, appeared at Covent Garden, London (Yniold in *Pelléas et Mélisande*); later devoted herself to a concert career; performed many works of contemporary composers; during her world tours she also made a study of Javanese and Malayan folk songs. **BIBL.:** I. Kolodin, "The Art of E. G.," *Saturday Review* (May 28, 1966).

Gautier, (Jean-François-) Eugène, French violinist, conductor, and composer; b. Vaugirard, near Paris, Feb. 27, 1822; d. Paris, April 1, 1878. He was a pupil of Habeneck (violin) and Halévy (composition) at the Paris Cons.; in 1848, became 2nd conductor at the Théâtre-Italien; in 1864 became a prof. of harmony at the Cons. and, in 1872, a prof. of history. He composed 16 comic operas; an oratorio, *La Mort de Jesus;* a cantata, *Le 15 août;* an *Ave Maria;* etc.

Gavazzeni, Gianandrea, Italian conductor and composer; b. Bergamo, July 25, 1909. He studied at the Accademia di Santa Cecilia in Rome (1921–24); then at the Milan Cons. (1925–31), where his principal teacher was Pizzetti. He then became engaged in musical journalism and, later, in conducting; he conducted concerts in England, Moscow, and Canada (1965–67). He was music director of La Scala, Milan, from 1965 to 1972; on Oct. 11, 1976, made his American debut at the Metropolitan Opera in N.Y. He is also a prolific writer on music; among his publications are *Musicisti d'Europa* (Milan, 1954); *La casa di Arlecchino* (autobiographical; 1957); *Trent'anni di musica* (1958); *Le campane di Bergamo* (Milan, 1963); *I Nemici della musica* (1965).

WORKS: *Concerto Bergamasco* for Orch. (1931); scenic melodrama, *Paolo e Virginia* (1932); ballet, *Il furioso nell' Isola di San Domingo* (1933); several orch. works and pieces of chamber music.

Gaviniès, Pierre, noted French violinist and composer; b. Bordeaux, May 11, 1728; d. Paris, Sept. 8, 1800. He learned to play the violin as a child in the workshop of his father, a violin maker. In 1734, the family moved to Paris. Gaviniès made his 1st public appearance at a Concert Spirituel at the age of 13; he reappeared at these concerts as a youth of 20; his success with the public was such that Viotti described him as "the French Tartini." From 1773 to 1777 he was director (with Gossec) of the Concert Spirituel. When the Paris Cons. was organized in 1795, he was appointed prof. of violin. His book of technical exercises, *Les 24 Matinées* (violin studies in all the 24 keys), demonstrates by its transcendental difficulty that Gaviniès must have been a virtuoso; he attracted numerous pupils, and is regarded as the founder of the French school of violin pedagogy. His compositions are of less importance; he wrote 3 sonatas for Violin accompanied by Cello (publ. posth.; the one in F minor is known as *Le Tombeau de Gaviniès*); his most celebrated piece is an air, *Romance de Gaviniès*, which has been publ. in numerous arrangements; he also wrote 6 sonatas for 2 Violins and 6 violin concertos, and a comic opera, *Le Prétendu* (Paris, Nov. 6, 1760).

BIBL.: C. Pipelet, *Éloge historique de P. G.* (Paris, 1802); L. de La Laurencie, *L'École française de violon de Lully à Viotti* (Paris, 1923).

Gavoty, Bernard, French organist and writer on music; b. Paris, April 2, 1908; d. there, Oct. 24, 1981. He took courses in philosophy and literature at the Sorbonne; also studied organ and composition at the Paris Cons. In 1942 he was appointed organist at Saint-Louis des Invalides in Paris; in 1945 he became music critic for *Le Figaro*, under the nom de plume Clarendon, a position he continued to hold until his death. He publ. *Louis Vierne, La Vie et l'œuvre* (Paris, 1943); *Jehan Alain, musicien français* (Paris, 1945); *Les Souvenirs de Georges Enesco* (Paris, 1955); *Pour ou contre la musique moderne?* (with Daniel-Lesur; Paris, 1957); *Chopin amoureux* (with Émile Vuillermoz; Paris, 1960); *Vingt grands interprètes* (Lausanne, 1966; also in German); a number of lavishly illustrated monographs about contemporary artists, under the general title *Les Grands Interprètes* (Geneva, 1953, et seq.), containing biographies of Gieseking, Furtwängler, Menuhin, etc.; also made documentary films on famous musicians.

Gavrilin, Valery, Russian composer; b. Vologda, Aug. 17, 1939. He studied composition with Evlahov at the Leningrad Cons., graduating in 1964. From the very first he devoted himself to vocal music on folkloric Russian themes, as well as popular songs. Among his choral cycles, the most successful is *Letters from Soldiers* (1970). He also wrote some piano pieces in an engaging salon manner.

Gavrilov, Andrei, outstanding Russian pianist; b. Moscow, Sept. 21, 1955. He studied piano with his mother, then entered the Central Music School in Moscow when he was 6 and studied with Tatiana Kestner; subsequently trained with Lev Naumov at the Moscow Cons. He won 1st prize at the Tchaikovsky Competition in Moscow in 1972, and thereafter pursued a distinguished career, making an impressive N.Y. recital debut in 1985. His superlative technique and interpretive insights are revealed in his remarkable performances of a comprehensive repertoire, ranging from the Baroque to the avant-garde.

Gawronski, Adalbert (Wojciech), Polish pianist and composer; b. Seimony, near Vilnius, April 27, 1868; d. Kowanónak, near Posen, Aug. 5, 1910. He studied with Noskowski at the Warsaw Music Inst. and later in Berlin and Vienna; then went to Russia, where he organized a music school in Orel, returning to Warsaw after a few years. He wrote 3 operas: *Samuel Zborowski, Marja,* and *Pojata;* a Sym.; 3 string quartets; piano pieces; songs; etc.

Gay, John, English poet and dramatist, librettist of *The Beggar's Opera;* b. Barnstaple, Devon (baptized), Sept. 16, 1685; d. London, Dec. 4, 1732. *The Beggar's Opera* was premiered in London on Jan. 29, 1728, and was immensely popular for a century, chiefly because of its sharp satire and the English and Scots folk melodies it used. It has had a number of successful revivals. The government disliked it, and forbade the performance of its sequel, *Polly,* the score of which was printed in 1729. When *Polly* was finally performed in London on June 19, 1777, it was a fiasco, because the conditions satirized no longer prevailed.

BIBL.: C. Pearce, *Polly Peachum: The story of "Polly" and "The Beggar's Opera"* (London, 1923); W. Schultz, *G.'s Beggar's Opera* (New Haven, Conn., 1923); O. Sherwin, *Mr. G.; Being a Picture of the Life and Times of the Author of The Beggar's Opera* (N.Y., 1929); C. Tolksdorf, *J. G.'s Beggar's Opera und Bert Brechts Dreigroschenoper* (Rheinberg, 1934); P. Gaye, *Ballad Opera* (N.Y., 1937).

Gay, Maria (née **Pitchot**), Spanish contralto; b. Barcelona, June 13, 1879; d. N.Y., July 29, 1943. She studied sculpture and the violin; became a singer almost by chance, when Pugno,

traveling in Spain, heard her sing and was impressed by the natural beauty of her voice. She sang in some of his concerts; also with Ysaÿe in Brussels; made her operatic debut there as Carmen (1902), a role that became her finest. She then studied in Paris with Ada Adiny, and when she returned to the operatic stage, made an international reputation. After tours in Europe, she made her American debut at the Metropolitan Opera in N.Y. as Carmen on Dec. 3, 1908, with Toscanini conducting. She sang with the Boston Opera Co. from 1910 to 1912 and with the Chicago Opera Co. from 1913 to 1927, when she retired from the stage. She and her husband, the tenor **Giovanni Zenatello,** whom she married in 1913, settled in N.Y. as teachers (1927).

Gayarre, Julián (real name, **Gayarre Sebástian**), famous Spanish tenor; b. Valle de Roncal, Jan. 9, 1844; d. Madrid, Jan. 2, 1890. He studied in Madrid; attracted attention at his appearance at Covent Garden, in London, in 1877; continued to sing there until 1880, and again in 1886–87. He was generally regarded as one of the finest lyrico-dramatic tenors of his time, and was described by enthusiasts as having "the voice of an angel." He created the role of Enzo in *La Gioconda* (1876) and the title role in *Il Duca d'Alba* (1882).

BIBL.: F. Hernandel Girbal, *J. G., El tenor de la voz de ángel* (1955).

Gaye, Marvin (Pentz), black American rhythm-and-blues singer; b. Washington, D.C., April 2, 1939; d. (murdered by his father, a retired Pentecostal preacher) Los Angeles, April 1, 1984. The family name was **Gay,** but a mute "e" was added to the end to avoid the slang connotation of the original surname. He sang in the choir of his father's church, and also beat the drums at school. In 1956 he sang with the group called Rainbows, which split, and he joined a separate group, The Marquees, which later became the Moonglows. In 1961 he was recruited by Motown in Detroit; he made duet recordings with Tammi Terrell, including *Ain't No Mountain High Enough* (1967) and *Ain't Nothing Like the Real Thing* (1968). Among his early hits was *I Heard It through the Grapevine* in 1968: his successful individual albums included *What's Going On* (1970) and *Midnight Love* (1983), on which he also performed almost every instrumental part. His career was broken up by his divorces (he was married thrice) and bouts with cocaine and other narcotics. Although he earned a sizable fortune, he squandered it; he was shot twice in the chest by his father during an altercation about money, and was pronounced D.O.A. at the hospital.

BIBL.: D. Ritz, *Divided Soul: The Life of M. G.* (N.Y., 1985).

Gayer (Ashkenasi), Catherine, American soprano; b. Los Angeles, Feb. 11, 1937. She studied at the Univ. of Calif. at Los Angeles and in Berlin; made her operatic debut in Venice in the premiere of *Intolleranza* as the Companion on April 13, 1961; then joined the Deutsche Oper in West Berlin; also made guest appearances in Vienna, Salzburg, and Milan. She excelled in the modern operatic repertoire.

Gayle, Crystal (real name, **Brenda Gail Webb**), American country-music singer, sister of **Loretta Lynn;** b. Paintsville, Ky., Jan. 9, 1951. She was reared in Wabash, Ind., where she took up the guitar; began making appearances as a singer on tour with her sister in 1967, adopting the name Crystal Gayle. She cut her 1st single before graduating from high school; then went to Nashville to pursue her career as a country-music singer and soon expanded her horizons to include popular numbers, ballads, and soft-rock staples. After producing the albums *Crystal Gayle* (1975), *Somebody Loves You* (1976), and *Crystal* (1976), she scored a major success with the album *We Must Believe in Magic* (1978), which contained her hit rendition of *Don't It Make My Brown Eyes Blue*; it hit the top of the charts in both country-western and pop categories and won her a Grammy award as best female vocalist of the year. She subsequently brought out such successful albums as *When I Dream* (1979), *Miss the Mississippi* (1979), *True Love* (1982), and *Cage the Songbird* (1984). She also toured widely and appeared on many television shows, including several of her own specials.

BIBL.: *Current Biography* (March 1986).

Gaztambide (y Garbayo), Joaquín (Romualdo), Spanish conductor and composer; b. Tudela, Navarre, Feb. 7, 1822; d. Madrid, March 18, 1870. He studied at Pamplona and at the Madrid Cons. with Pedro Albéniz (piano) and Ramón Carnicer (composition). After a stay in Paris, he returned to Madrid as manager of several theaters and director of the Cons. concert society in 1862. He was best known, however, for his zarzuelas, the satiric musical productions which are identified with the Madrid stage. He wrote 44 zarzuelas, many of which became popular; one, *El juramento*, 1st produced in 1858, was revived in Madrid in 1933. His most popular work was *Catalina* (Madrid, Oct. 23, 1854). He took his own zarzuela company to Mexico and Havana in 1869–70.

Gazzaniga, Giuseppe, Italian composer; b. Verona, Oct. 5, 1743; d. Crema, Feb. 1, 1818. He studied with Porpora, first in Venice and then at the Conservatorio di S. Onofrio a Capuana in Naples (1760–66); subsequently studied with Piccinni. He composed 47 operas; his *Don Giovanni Tenorio osia Il Convitato di pietra* (Venice, Feb. 5, 1787; ed. by S. Kunze, Kassel and Basel, 1974) anticipated Mozart's great masterpiece *Don Giovanni*.

Gazzelloni, Severino, Italian flutist; b. Roccasecca, Frosinone, Jan. 5, 1919. He studied at the Accademia di Santa Cecilia in Rome, graduating in 1942; was then employed as an orch. musician; later launched a major career as a concert flutist. His repertoire ranged from the classics to works of the modern school.

Gebel, Georg, German composer; b. Brieg, Silesia, Oct. 25, 1709; d. Rudolstadt, Sept. 24, 1753. He studied with his father; was organist at St. Maria Magdalene in Breslau, and Kapellmeister to the Duke of Oels. In 1735 he joined Count Brühl's orch. at Dresden, where he met Hebenstreit, the inventor of the "Pantaleon," and learned to play that instrument. In 1747 he was appointed Kapellmeister to the Prince of Schwarzburg-Rudolstadt. He wrote a number of light operas (to German rather than Italian librettos, thus upholding the national tradition), and more than 100 syms., partitas, and concertos.

Gebhard, Heinrich, German-American pianist, composer, and teacher; b. Sobernheim, July 25, 1878; d. North Arlington, N.J., May 5, 1963. As a boy of 8, he went with his parents to Boston, where he studied with Clayton Johns; after a concert debut in Boston (April 24, 1896), he went to Vienna to study with Leschetizky. He gave 1st American performances of works by Vincent d'Indy; his most notable interpretation was Loeffler's work for Piano and Orch., *A Pagan Poem*, which he played nearly 100 times with U.S. orchs. His own works are also in an impressionistic vein: Fantasy for Piano and Orch. (N.Y. Phil., Nov. 12, 1925, composer soloist); symphonic poem, *Across the Hills* (1940); Divertimento for Piano and Chamber Orch. (Boston, Dec. 20, 1927); String Quartet; *Waltz Suite* for 2 Pianos; song cycle, *The Sun, Cloud and the Flower*; many piano pieces. He also arranged Loeffler's *A Pagan Poem* for 2 Pianos. His book *The Art of Pedaling* was publ. posth. with an introduction by Leonard Bernstein, who was one of his students (N.Y., 1963).

Gédalge, André, eminent French music theorist, composer, and pedagogue; b. Paris, Dec. 27, 1856; d. Chessy, Feb. 5, 1926. He began to study music rather late in life, and entered the Paris Cons. at the age of 28. However, he made rapid progress, and obtained the 2nd Prix de Rome after a year of study (with Guiraud). He then elaborated a system of counterpoint, later publ. as *Traité de la fugue* (Paris, 1901; Eng. tr., 1964), which became a standard work. In 1905, he became engaged as a prof. of counterpoint and fugue at the Paris Cons.; among his students were Ravel, Enesco, Koechlin, Roger-Ducasse, Milhaud, and Honegger. He also publ. *Les Gloires musicales du monde* (1898) and other pedagogic works. As a composer, he was less significant. Among his works are a

pantomime, *Le Petit Savoyard* (Paris, 1891); an opera, *Pris au piège* (Paris, 1895); and 3 operas that were not performed: *Sita, La Farce du Cadi,* and *Hélène;* he also wrote 3 syms., several concertos, some chamber music, and songs.

BIBL.: "Hommage à G.," *Revue Musicale* (March 1, 1926).

Gedda, Giulio Cesare, Italian conductor and composer; b. Turin, April 16, 1899; d. Callegno, near Turin, Sept. 7, 1970. He studied composition with Alfano in Turin; played cello and organ; began conducting in 1932; lived mostly in Turin. He wrote an opera, *L'amoroso fantasma* (Turin, 1933); 2 violin concertos (1930, 1954); a Viola Concerto (1940); Cello Concerto; Concerto for 4 Saxophones (1952). He ended his days in a mental institution.

Gedda (real name, **Ustinov**), **Nicolai (Harry Gustav),** noted Swedish tenor; b. Stockholm, July 11, 1925, of Russian-Swedish extraction. Gedda was his mother's name, which he assumed in his professional life. His father was a Russian who went to Sweden after the Civil War. He studied at the opera school at the Stockholm Cons.; on April 8, 1952, he made his operatic debut as Chapelou in *Le Postillon de Longjumeau*. In 1953 he made his debut at La Scala in Milan; in 1954 he sang Faust at the Paris Opéra; then had an engagement at Covent Garden in London; in 1957 he sang Don José in *Carmen* at the Vienna State Opera. He made his U.S. debut as Faust with the Pittsburgh Opera on April 4, 1957; his Metropolitan Opera debut followed in N.Y. on Nov. 1, 1957; he created the role of Anatol in Barber's *Vanessa* at the Metropolitan on Jan. 15, 1958. Because of his natural fluency in Russian and his acquired knowledge of German, French, Italian, and English, he was able to sing with total freedom the entire standard operatic repertoire. In 1980 and 1981 he made highly successful appearances in Russia, both in opera and on the concert stage, in programs of Russian songs. His memoirs were publ. as *Gåvan är inte gratis* (Stockholm, 1978).

Gedike, Alexander. See **Goedike, Alexander.**

Gedzhadze, Irakly, Russian composer; b. Mtskheta, Oct. 26, 1925. He studied with Matchavariani at the Tbilisi Cons.; graduated in 1957. His works include the opera *Sunrise* (Tbilisi, Nov. 23, 1961); *Lake Palestomi,* symphonic poem (1956); piano pieces.

Geehl, Henry Ernest, English composer; b. London, Sept. 28, 1881; d. Beaconsfield, Buckinghamshire, Jan. 14, 1961. A pupil of R.O. Morgan, he was appointed a prof. at Trinity College of Music, London, in 1919. He wrote a Sym.; Violin Concerto; Piano Concerto; pieces for brass band, including *Cornwall* and *Cornish Rhapsody;* pedagogic piano pieces; songs.

Gefors, Hans, Swedish composer; b. Stockholm, Dec. 8, 1952. He studied composition with Per-Gunnar Alldahl and Maurice Karkoff, with Ingvar Lidholm at the Stockholm Musikhögskolan (1972), and with Per Nørgård at the Århus Cons.; also wrote music criticism and worked as an ed. In 1988 he joined the faculty at the Univ. of Lund.

WORKS: *Aprahishtita* for Cello, Piano, and Tape (1970–71); *Matutino* for Flute, Violin, Viola, Cello, and Piano (1973); *Visviter* for String Orch. (1973); *Reveille* for Voice and 5 Instruments (1974–75); *Orpheus singt,* cantata for Choir and Orch. (1976–77); *Poeten och glasmästaren* (The Poet and the Glazier), chamber opera (1979; Århus, April 26, 1980); *Me morire en Paris* for Baritone and 4 Instruments (1979); *Syndabocken,* theater music (1979); Trio for Voice, Guitar, and Violin (1981); *Slits* for Orch. (1981; Hälsingborg, Feb. 18, 1982); *Galjonsfiguren* for Soprano, Electric Guitar, and Tape (1983); *Christina,* opera (1985; Stockholm, Oct. 18, 1986); piano music; organ pieces.

Gehlhaar, Rolf (Rainer), Polish-born American composer; b. Breslau, Dec. 30, 1943. He emigrated to the U.S. in 1953; studied at Yale Univ. (B.A., 1965) and the Univ. of Calif., Berkeley (1965–67); was an assistant to Stockhausen in his course in new music in Cologne (1967–70). In 1974 and 1976 he taught at the annual summer courses in new music in Darmstadt, and in 1976–77 at England's Dartington College of Arts. He helped to organize the Electro-Acoustic Assoc. of Great Britain (1979) and worked at IRCAM in Paris, where he created the 1st digital reproductions of "3-dimensional" sounds (1981). **WORKS:** *Cello Solo* (1966); *Piano Pieces 1–2* and *2–2* (1970); *Wege* for 2 String Instruments, Piano, and Electronics (1971); *Musi-ken* for String Quartet (1972); *Phase* for Orch. (1971–72; Saarbrücken, May 4, 1972); *Der gelbe Klang* for Small Chorus and Chamber Ensemble (1973); *Tachys* for String Instruments (1973); *Solipse* for Cello (1973); *Prototypen* for Orch. (1973); *Liebeslied* for Alto and Orch. (Graz, Oct. 9, 1974); *Resonanzen* for 8 Orch. Groups (1976); *Lamina* for Trombone and Orch. (1977); *Pixels* for 8 Winds (1981); *Tokamak* for Piano and Orch. (1982); *Copernic Opera F6,* live electronic dance piece (1987).

Gehot, Jean or **Joseph,** Belgian violinist and composer; b. Brussels, April 8, 1756; d. in the U.S., c.1820. He went to London after 1780; there he publ. *A Treatise on the Theory and Practice of Music* (1784), *The Art of Bowing the Violin* (1790), and *Complete Instructions for Every Musical Instrument* (1790). In 1792, he went to America; gave concerts in N.Y., where he presented his *Overture in 12 movements, expressive of a voyage from England to America.* He then played violin at the City Concerts in Philadelphia, under the management of Reinagle and Capron. However, he failed to prosper in America; most of his works were publ. in London, among them 17 string quartets, 12 string trios, and 24 "military pieces" for 2 Clarinets, 2 Horns, and Bassoon.

Gehrkens, Karl (Wilson), American music educator; b. Kelleys Island, Ohio, April 19, 1882; d. Elk Rapids, Mich., Feb. 28, 1975. After graduation from Oberlin (Ohio) College (B.A., 1905; M.A., 1912), he became a prof. of school music at the Oberlin Cons. of Music in 1907; retired in 1942. He was ed. of *School Music* from 1925 to 1934; co-ed., with Walter Damrosch and George Gartlan, of the Universal School Music Series, teachers' manuals for grade and high schools (1923–36); etc. During his tenure as president of the Music Supervisors National Conference (1923), he coined the slogan "Music for every child, and every child for music." **BIBL.:** F. Lendrim, *Music for Every Child: The Story of K.W. G.* (diss., Univ. of Michigan, 1972).

Geiringer, Karl (Johannes), eminent Austrian-American musicologist; b. Vienna, April 26, 1899; d. Santa Barbara, Calif., Jan. 10, 1989. He studied composition with Hans Gál and Richard Stöhr, and musicology with Guido Adler and Wilhelm Fischer in Vienna; continued his musicological studies with Curt Sachs and Johannes Wolf in Berlin; received his Ph.D. from the Univ. of Vienna with the dissertation *Die Flankenwirbelinstrumente in der bildenden Kunst (1300–1550)* in 1923 (publ. in Tutzing, 1979). In 1930 he became librarian and museum curator of the Gesellschaft der Musikfreunde in Vienna. He left Austria in 1938 and went to London, where he worked for the BBC; also taught at the Royal College of Music (1939–40); he then emigrated to the U.S.; was a visiting prof. at Hamilton College, Clinton, N.Y. (1940–41); in 1941 he became a prof. at Boston Univ. and head of graduate studies in music; in 1962 he was made a prof. at the Univ. of Calif., Santa Barbara; he retired in 1972. In 1955–56 he was president of the American Musicological Soc. In 1959 he was elected a Fellow of the American Academy of Arts and Sciences; also was an honorary member of the Österreichische Gesellschaft für Musikwissenschaft and of the American chapter of the Neue Bach-Gesellschaft; in addition, was a member of the Joseph Haydn Inst. of Cologne. A music scholar and writer of great erudition, he contributed valuable publications on the Bach family, Haydn, and Brahms. As a member of the editorial board of Denkmäler der Tonkunst in Österreich, he ed. the collected works of Paul Peuerl and the instrumental works of Isaac Posch (vol. LXX); also, with E. Mandyczewski, selected works by Antonio Caldara (vol. XXXIX). He ed. Gluck's opera *Telemaco, Sämtliche Werke,* I/2; Haydn's opera *Orlando Paladino, Werke,* XXV/11; and 100 arrangements of Scottish folk

songs by Haydn, *Werke,* XXXII/1. He was general editor of the Harbrace History of Musical Forms and of the Univ. of Calif., Santa Barbara, Series of Early Music; ed. Isaac Posch's *Harmonia concertans 1623.* **WRITINGS:** *Führer durch die Joseph Haydn Kollektion im Museum der Gesellschaft der Musikfreunde in Wien* (with H. Kraus; Vienna, 1930); "Joseph Haydn," in Bücken's *Grosse Meister* (Potsdam, 1932); *Wiener Meister um Mozart und Beethoven* (a collection of piano works; Vienna, 1935); *Johannes Brahms: Leben und Schaffen eines deutschen Meisters* (a major study; Vienna, 1935; Eng. tr., London and N.Y., 1936; 3rd ed., rev. and enl., N.Y., 1981); *Musical Instruments: Their History in Western Culture from the Stone Age to the Present Day* (London, 1943; 3rd ed., rev. and enl., as *Instruments in the History of Western Music,* N.Y., 1978); *Haydn: A Creative Life in Music* (N.Y., 1946; 3rd ed., 1983); *A Thematic Catalogue of Haydn's Settings of Folksongs from the British Isles* (Superior, Wis., 1953); *The Bach Family: Seven Generations of Creative Genius* (an important study; N.Y., 1954); *Music of the Bach Family: An Anthology* (a valuable collection; Cambridge, Mass., 1955); *Johann Sebastian Bach: The Culmination of an Era* (an excellent study; N.Y., 1966). **BIBL.:** A. Silver, ed., *K. G.: A Checklist of His Publications in Musicology* (Santa Barbara, Calif., 1969); H.C. Robbins Landon and R. Chapman, *Studies in Eighteenth-Century Music: A Tribute to K. G. on His 70th Birthday* (N.Y. and London, 1970).

Geiser, Walther, Swiss composer and pedagogue; b. Zofingen, May 16, 1897. He studied violin with Hirt and composition with Suter at the Basel Cons.; then went to Berlin, where he took lessons with Busoni. After Busoni's death, he returned to Basel, and taught violin and composition at the Cons. (1924–63); was director of the Basel Bach-Chorus (1954–72). He composed 2 syms. (1953, 1967); a Violin Concerto (1930); Horn Concerto (1934); *Konzertstück* for Organ and Chamber Orch. (1941); *Stabat Mater* for Baritone, Chorus, Orch., and Organ (1938); *Te Deum* for 4 Soloists, Chorus, Orch., and Organ (1960); *Concerto da camera* for 2 Solo Violins, Harpsichord, and String Orch. (1957); Piano Concerto (1959); 2 flute concertos (1921, 1963); several choral works and solo piano pieces.

Geisler, Paul, German conductor and composer; b. Stolp, Aug. 10, 1856; d. Posen, April 3, 1919. He was a pupil of his grandfather, who was a conductor at Marienburg, and also of Constantine Decker. As a conductor, Geisler was associated with the Leipzig musical theater (1881) and A. Neumann's traveling Wagner company (1882–83); for the following 2 years he was a conductor at Bremen. He lived in Leipzig and Berlin for most of his career before going to Posen, where he became director of the Cons. He wrote 7 operas, 2 cyclic cantatas, symphonic poems, incidental stage music, etc.

Geissler, Fritz, German composer; b. Wurzen, near Leipzig, Sept. 16, 1921; d. Bad Saarow, Jan. 11, 1984. He studied at the Hochschule für Musik in Leipzig with Max Dehnert and Wilhelm Weismann (1948–50); later taught there (1962–70); then joined the faculty of the Dresden Cons.; was named a prof. there in 1974. His music is dialectical and almost Hegelian in its syllogistic development and climactic synthesis; the ground themes are carefully adumbrated before their integration in a final catharsis; formal dissonances are emancipated by a freely modified application of the Schoenbergian method of composition with 12 tones related only to one another. The human quality of the tightly elaborate polyphonic structure of his works is expressed with considerable élan by means of variegated rhythmic designs and quasi-aleatory instrumental soliloquies. The formal element remains strictly observed; he favors Classical paradigms of sym. and concerto. **WORKS: STAGE:** *Der verrückte Jourdain,* a "Rossiniada" in 3 acts (1971); *Der Schatten,* fantastic opera (1975); *Die Stadtpfeifer,* opera in 4 scenes (1977); *Das Chagrinleder,* opera in 7 scenes (1978); 3 ballets: *Pigment* (1960); *Sommernachtstraum* (1965); *Der Doppelgänger* (1969). **ORCH.:** *Italienische*

Lustspielouvertüre, after Rossini (1958); *November 1918*, suite in 3 movements, commemorating the 40th anniversary of the German Revolution (1958); 9 syms.: No. 1 (1961); No. 2, composed in celebration of the 800th anniversary of the city of Leipzig (1963); No. 3 (1965–66); No. 4 for Strings (1968); No. 5, to mark the 20th anniversary of the German Democratic Republic (1969); No. 6, *Sinfonia concertante*, for Wind Quintet and Strings (1971); No. 7 (1973); No. 8 for Soloists, Chorus, and Orch. (1974); No. 9 (1978); 2 chamber syms. (1954, 1970); *Sinfonietta giocosa* (1963); *The Adventures of the Good Soldier Schweik*, symphonic burlesque (1963); *Essay* (1969); 2 *Symphonic Scenes* (1970); Piano Concerto (1970); *Beethoven-Variationen* (1971); Cello Concerto (1974); *Offenbach-Metamorphosen* (1977); Concerto for Flute, Strings, Harpsichord, and Percussion (1977); Concerto for Organ, Percussion, and Strings (1979). **CHAMBER:** String Quartet (1951); Suite for Wind Quintet (1957); *Chamber Concerto* for Harpsichord, Flute, and 10 Instruments (1967); *Ode to a Nightingale* for Nonet (1967–68); Viola Sonata (1969); Piano Trio (1970). **VOCAL:** *Gesang vom Menschen*, oratorio (1968); *Nachtelegien*, romance for High Voice and Instruments (1969); *Die Liebenden*, romance for Tenor and 2 Instrumental Groups (1969); *Schöpfer Mensch*, oratorio (1973); *Die Glocke von Buchenwald*, cantata (1974); *Die Flamme von Mansfeld*, oratorio (1978); also piano works; choruses; songs.

Gelatt, Roland, American writer on music; b. Kansas City, Mo., July 24, 1920; d. Philadelphia, Dec. 3, 1986. He studied at Swarthmore College, then served in the U.S. Army (1943–46); in 1947 he joined *Saturday Review* as music critic. From 1958 to 1968 he was ed. in chief of *High Fidelity*. He publ. the informative book *The Fabulous Phonograph* (1955); he also wrote articles on a variety of other subjects, including travel and the arts.

Gelber, Bruno-Leonardo, Argentine pianist; b. Buenos Aires, March 19, 1941. He received his early musical training in Buenos Aires; then went to Paris for advanced training with Marguerite Long; eventually developed a successful international career, cultivating mainly the Romantic repertoire.

Gelbrun, Artur, Polish-born Israeli composer; b. Warsaw, July 11, 1913; d. Tel Aviv, Dec. 24, 1985. He studied at the Warsaw Cons.; then went to Italy, where he took courses with Molinari and Casella at the Accademia di Santa Cecilia in Rome; later he studied composition with W. Burkhard and conducting with Scherchen in Zürich. He was an orch. and solo violinist in Warsaw, Lausanne, and Zürich (1936–47). In 1949 he emigrated to Israel and joined the staff of the Tel Aviv Academy of Music as prof. of conducting and composition. **WORKS:** A radiophonic oratorio, *Le Livre du Feu* (1964; Jerusalem, 1966; Prix Italia, 1966); 4 ballets: *Hedva* (1951; concert version, Ein-Gev, May 27, 1951; stage premiere, St. Gallen, 1958); *Miadoux* (1966–67); *Prologue to the Decameron* (1968; Jerusalem, 1968); *King Solomon and the Hoopoes* (1976); *Lieder der Mädchen* for Voice and Orch. (1945); *Suite* for Orch. (1947); *Prelude, Passacaglia and Fugue* for Orch. (1954); *Variations* for Piano and Orch. (1955); *Prologue Symphonique* (1956); 5 *Capriccios* for Orch. (1957); 3 syms. (1957–58; 1961; *Jubilee*, 1973); *Song of the River* for Soprano and Orch. (1959); Cello Concerto (1962); *Piccolo Divertimento* for Youth Orch. (1963; also perf. as a ballet); 4 *Pieces* for String Orch. (1963); *Concerto-Fantasia* for Flute, Harp, and String Orch. (1963); *Salmo e Alelujah* for Soprano and Orch. (1968); Concertino for Chamber Orch. (1974); *Adagio* for String Orch. (1974); *Holocaust and Revival*, cantata for Narrator, Chorus, and Orch. (1977–78); *Hommage à Rodin* for Orch. (1979–81); Concerto for Oboe and Strings (1985; rev. and orchestrated by L. Biriotti, 1986); also chamber music; piano pieces; songs.

Gelineau, Joseph, French composer and editor; b. Champsur-Layon, Maine-et-Loire, Oct. 31, 1920. At the age of 21 he entered the Order of the Jesuits; studied organ and composition at the École César Franck in Paris; also obtained a doctorate in theology. He publ. *Chant et musique dans le culte chrétien* (Paris, 1962); composed *Missa plebs sancta* (1960), Psalms, etc.; tr. and set to music the Psalmody of the Bible of Jerusalem.

Gelinek (Jelinek), Joseph, Bohemian pianist and composer; b. Seltsch, near Beroun, Dec. 3, 1758; d. Vienna, April 13, 1825. He studied philosophy in Prague and at the same time took lessons in music with Seger; became a good pianist (Mozart praised him); was ordained a priest in 1786, but did not abandon music; went to Vienna and settled there as a piano teacher; c.1810 became music master to Prince Esterhazy. He was a prolific composer; wrote 120 sets of variations for keyboard, as well as fantasias and dances, chamber music, etc.

Gellman, Steven, Canadian composer and teacher; b. Toronto, Sept. 16, 1947. He studied composition with Dolin at the Royal Cons. of Music in Toronto; then studied with Berio, Sessions, and Persichetti at the Juilliard School of Music in N.Y. (1965–68), with Milhaud at Aspen, Colo. (summers 1965 and 1966), and with Messiaen at the Paris Cons. (1974–76). In 1976 he joined the faculty of the Univ. of Ottawa. He adopted an uncompromisingly modernistic idiom in most of his music, while safeguarding the formal design of Classical tradition. **WORKS: ORCH.:** Piano Concerto (1964); *Mural* (1965); *Movement* for Violin and Orch. (1967); *Symphony in 2 Movements* (Ottawa, July 15, 1971); *Odyssey* for Rock Group, Solo Piano, and Orch. (Hamilton, Ontario, March 9, 1971); *Symphony II* (Toronto, Dec. 2, 1972); *Encore (Mythos I Revisited)* (1972); *Overture for Ottawa* (1972); *Chori* (1974; rev. 1976); *Animus-Anima* (Paris, April 28, 1976); *Awakening* (1982); *The Bride's Reception: A Symphonic Contemplation* (1981–83); *Universe Symphony* (1985; Toronto, Jan. 8, 1986). **CHAMBER:** 2 *Movements* for String Quartet (1963); *Soliloquy* for Cello (1966; rev. 1982); *After Bethlehem* for String Quartet (1966); *Quartets: Poems of G.M. Hopkins* for Voice, Flute, Cello, and Harp (1966–67); *Mythos II* for Flute and String Quartet (1968); *Sonate pour sept* for Flute, Clarinet, Cello, Guitar, Piano, and 2 Percussionists (1975); *Wind Music* for 2 Trumpets, Horn, Trombone, and Bass Tuba (1978); *Trikáya* for Violin, Clarinet, Percussion, and Piano (1981); *Chiaroscuro* for Flute, Clarinet, Violin, Viola, Cello, Piano, and Percussion (1988). **PIANO:** 2 sonatas (1964, 1973); *Fantasy* (1967); *Melodic Suite* (1971–72); *Fantasia on a Theme by Robert Schumann* (1983); *Keyboard Triptych* (Montreal, Oct. 19, 1986).

Gelmetti, Gianluigi, Italian conductor; b. Rome, Sept. 11, 1945. He received training in Rome and then studied conducting with Sergiu Celibidache and Hans Swarowsky; after appearing as a guest conductor with Italian opera houses and orchs., he served as chief conductor of the Orchestra Sinfonia della RAI in Rome (1980–84); in 1984 he was named music director of the Teatro dell'Opera in Rome, in 1989 chief conductor of the Stuttgart Radio Sym. Orch., and in 1990 chief conductor of the Orch. Philharmonique de Monte Carlo.

Geminiani, Francesco (Xaverio), eminent Italian violinist, composer, and music theorist; b. Lucca (baptized), Dec. 5, 1687; d. Dublin, Sept. 17, 1762. He studied with Carlo Ambrogio Lonati in Milan; then studied violin with Arcangelo Corelli and composition with Alessandro Scarlatti in Rome. He was a violinist in the orch. of the Signoria theater in Lucca from 1707 to 1710; became concertmaster of the Naples Orch. in 1711. In 1714 he went to London, where he gained fame as a violin virtuoso, composer, and teacher. During the 1731–32 season, he presented a series of subscription concerts in London; in 1733–34 he maintained a concert room in Dublin, and also sold paintings; from 1737 to 1740 he was again in Dublin, giving concerts and teaching. He spent most of the succeeding years in England, but also made trips to the Continent. He returned to Ireland in 1759 as music master to Charles Coote (later the Earl of Bellamont) at Cootehill, County Cavan; that same year he went to Dublin, where he gave his last concert in 1760. Geminiani composed a number of fine sonatas and concertos in a distinctive and assured style. He also wrote the valuable treatise *The Art of Playing on the Violin* (1751), which effectively carried forward the Italian tradition of Corelli while setting the course for succeeding generations.

WRITINGS: *Rules for Playing in a True Taste . . .*, op. 8 (London, 1748; with 4 tunes); *A Treatise of Good Taste in the Art of Musick* (London, 1749; facsimile ed. by R. Donnington, 1969; with 4 songs and 7 "Airs"); *The Art of Playing on the Violin*, op. 9 (London, 1751; facsimile ed. by D. Boyden, London, 1952; with 12 works and 24 examples); *Guida armonica . . .*, op. 10 (London, c.1754); *The Art of Accompaniament . . .*, op. 11 (2 parts, London, c.1754); *A Supplement to the Guida Armonica* (London, c.1754); *The Art of Playing the Guitar or Cittra . . .* (Edinburgh, 1760; with 11 sonatas). He also publ. a periodical, *The Harmonical Miscellany* (London, 1758; Part 1: 14 works "in the Tone Minor"; Part 2: 16 works "in the Tone Major").
BIBL.: W.H. Gratton Flood, "G. in England and Ireland," *Sammelbände der Internationalen Musik-Gesellschaft,* XII (1910–11); A. Betti, *F. G.* (Lucca, 1934); R. Hernreid, "F. G.'s Concerti Grossi Op. 3," *Acta Musicologica,* IX (1937); A. Betti, "F. G.," *Violins and Violinists,* X/6 (1949); M. McArtor, *F. G.* (diss., Univ. of Michigan, 1951); T. Dart, "F. G. and the Rule of Taste," *Consort,* XIX (1962); N. Jenkins, "G.'s 'The Enchanted Forest': A Conspectus," *Chigiana,* XXIV (1967).

Gemünder, August (Martin Ludwig), German-American violin maker; b. Ingelfingen, Württemberg, March 22, 1814; d. N.Y., Sept. 7, 1895. He established a shop at Springfield, Mass., in 1846; then moved to Boston, where he was joined by his brother **Georg** (b. April 13, 1816; d. Jan. 15, 1899), also a violin maker, a pupil of J.B. Vuillaume in Paris. In 1852, the brothers settled in N.Y., where they established themselves as the foremost manufacturers of musical instruments; between 1860 and 1890 they received numerous medals for excellence at expositions in Europe and America. After the death of August Gemünder, the business was continued by 3 of his sons, as August Gemünder & Sons. Georg Gemünder wrote an autobiographical sketch with an account of his work, *Georg Gemünder's Progress in Violin Making* (1881).

Gencer, Leyla, Turkish soprano; b. Constantinople, Oct. 10, 1924. She studied in Istanbul; made her operatic debut in Ankara in 1950; then continued her musical studies in Italy; sang at the Arena Flegrea in Naples in 1953; became a member of La Scala in Milan in 1956; also made guest appearances in San Francisco, Salzburg, and London.

Gendron, Maurice, eminent French cellist and pedagogue; b. Nice, Dec. 26, 1920; d. Grez-sur-Loing, Aug. 20, 1990. He studied at the Nice Cons., and later at the Paris Cons. with G. Hekking. In 1945 he played in London with the London Phil., creating a favorable impression with his performance of Prokofiev's Cello Concerto; then appeared with major European orchs. and taught at the Paris Cons.

Genée, (Franz Friedrich) Richard, German conductor and composer; b. Danzig, Feb. 7, 1823; d. Baden, near Vienna, June 15, 1895. He studied under Stahlknecht in Berlin; was a theater conductor (1847–67) at Riga, Cologne, Düsseldorf, Danzig, Amsterdam, and Prague; from 1868 to 1878, was conductor at the Theater an der Wien in Vienna; then retired to his villa at Pressbaum, near Vienna. He wrote several of his own librettos (some with F. Zell); he also wrote librettos for Strauss, Suppé, and Millöcker.
WORKS: Operettas: *Der Geiger aus Tirol* (1857); *Der Musikfeind* (1862); *Die Generalprobe* (1862); *Rosita* (1864); *Der schwarze Prinz* (1866); *Am Runenstein* (with Flotow; 1868); *Der Seekadett* (1876); *Nanon* (1877); *Im Wunderlande der Pyramiden* (1877); *Die letzten Mohikaner* (1878); *Nisida* (1880); *Rosina* (1881); *Die Zwillinge* (1885); *Die Piraten* (1886); *Die Dreizehn* (1887).

Generali (real name, **Mercadetti**), **Pietro,** Italian composer; b. Masserano, Oct. 23, 1773; d. Novara, Nov. 3, 1832. He studied in Rome; began to compose sacred music at an early age, but soon turned to opera. He traveled all over Italy as producer of his operas, and also went to Vienna and Barcelona. Returning to Italy, he became maestro di cappella at the Cathedral of Novara. He anticipated Rossini in the effective use of dynamics in the instrumental parts of his operas, and was generally praised for his technical knowledge. He wrote about 50 stage works, in both the serious and comic genres, but none survived in the repertoire after his death. The following were successful at their initial performances: *Pamela nubile* (Venice, April 12, 1804); *Le lagrime di una vedova* (Venice, Dec. 26, 1808); *Adelina* (Venice, Sept. 16, 1810); *L'Impostore* (Milan, May 21, 1815); *I Baccanali di Roma* (Venice, Jan. 14, 1816; his best work); *Il Servo padrone* (Parma, Aug. 12, 1818); *Il divorzio persiano* (Trieste, Jan. 31, 1828).
BIBL.: Piccoli, *Elogio del maestro P. G.* (1833).

Genetz, Emil, Finnish composer; b. Impilahti, Oct. 24, 1852; d. Helsinki, May 1, 1930. He studied at the Dresden Cons. (1875–77); devoted himself chiefly to vocal music; many of his male choruses were well known in Finland.

Gennrich, Friedrich, German musicologist; b. Colmar, March 27, 1883; d. Langen, Sept. 22, 1967. He studied Roman philology at the Univ. of Strasbourg; took courses in musicology with F. Ludwig. In 1921 he went to Frankfurt, where he taught musicology at the Univ. (1921–64). He was a leading authority on music of the troubadours, trouvères, and Minnesinger.
WRITINGS: *Musikwissenschaft und romanische Philologie* (Halle, 1918); *Der musikalische Vortrag der altfranzösischen Chansons de geste* (Halle, 1923); *Die altfranzösiche Rotrouenge* (Halle, 1925); *Das Formproblem des Minnesangs* (Halle, 1931); *Grundriss einer Formenlehre des mittelalterlichen Liedes* (Halle, 1932; a comprehensive work); *Die Strassburger Schule für Musikwissenschaft* (Würzburg, 1940); *Abriss der frankonischen Mensuralnotation* (Nieder-Modau, 1946; 2nd ed., Darmstadt, 1956); *Abriss der Mensuralnotation des XIV. und der 1. Hälfte des XV. Jahrhunderts* (Nieder-Modau, 1948); *Melodien altdeutscher Lieder* (Darmstadt, 1954); *Franco von Köln, Ars Cantus Mensurabilis* (Darmstadt, 1955); *Die Wimpfener Fragmente der Hessischen Landesbibliothek* (Darmstadt, 1958); *Der musikalische Nachlass der Troubadours* (Darmstadt, 1960).

Gentele, Goeran, brilliant Swedish opera manager; b. Stockholm, Sept. 20, 1917; d. in an automobile crash near Olbia, Sardinia, July 18, 1972. He studied political science in Stockholm, and art at the Sorbonne in Paris. He was first engaged as an actor, then was stage director at the Royal Drama Theater in Stockholm (1941–52) and at the Royal Opera (1952–63), where he was appointed director in 1963. In 1970 he became engaged as general manager of the Metropolitan Opera in N.Y., effective June 1972; great expectations for his innovative directorship in America were thwarted by his untimely death during a vacation in Italy.

Gentry, Bobbie (née **Roberta Streeter**), American country-music singer and guitarist; b. Chickasaw County, Miss., July 27, 1944. She learned to play piano, guitar, banjo, and other instruments; determined to get some real education in classical music, she attended classes at the Univ. of Calif. in Los Angeles and learned to write notes. In 1967 she produced her 1st hit song, *Ode to Billy Joe*. She made successful tours across the U.S. and also ventured to give concerts in Europe.

Genzmer, Harald, German composer and pedagogue; b. Blumenthal, near Bremen, Feb. 9, 1909. He studied piano and organ in Marburg; then took courses in composition with Hindemith in Berlin. He spent the war years there; from 1946 to 1957 he taught at the Hochschule für Musik in Freiburg im Breisgau; from 1957 to 1974 he was on the faculty of the Hochschule für Musik in Munich. A prolific composer, he wrote music in a utilitarian manner, adhering closely to classical forms while allowing for dissonant counterpoint. He took interest in the electronic instrument Trautonium and wrote 2 concertos for it (1939, 1952).
WORKS: *Bremer Sinfonie* (1942); Sym. No. 1 (1957); Sym. No. 2 (1958); Sym. No. 3 (1986); 3 piano concertos (1942–74); Cello Concerto (1950); Flute Concerto (1954); Violin Concerto (1959); Viola Concerto (1967); 2 organ concertos (1970, 1980); Chamber Concerto for Viola and Strings (1973); *Musik für Orchester* (1977–78); Concerto for 2 Clarinets and Strings

(1983); Concerto for Cello, Double Bass, and Strings (1985); *Cassation* for Strings (1987); much chamber music, including a String Quartet; 2 piano trios; Trio for Harp, Flute, and Viola; 3 violin sonatas, 2 flute sonatas, Sonata for Viola Solo; several works for piano and for organ; also cantatas and other choral works.

George, Earl, American composer, conductor, music critic, and teacher; b. Milwaukee, May 1, 1924. He studied composition at the Eastman School of Music in Rochester, N.Y., with Howard Hanson and Bernard Rogers (1942–46); in the summer of 1946 he attended seminars of Martinu and Lopatnikoff at the Berkshire Music Center at Tanglewood, and in 1947 studied with Martinu again in N.Y. He subsequently held a teaching position at the Univ. of Minnesota (1948–56). From 1959 to 1988 he was on the music faculty at Syracuse Univ.; conducted the Syracuse Univ. Sym. Orch. there (1971–80). From 1961 he served as music critic of the Syracuse *Herald-Journal.* In his music he follows an astute median course of prudent American modernism, embellished by occasional satirical touches.
WORKS: STAGE: *Birthdays,* 2 1-act operas, individually titled *Pursuing Happiness* and *Another 4th of July* (Syracuse, April 23, 1976); *Genevieve,* opera (Berea, Ohio, Feb. 10, 1984). **ORCH.:** Concerto for Strings (1948); *A Thanksgiving Overture* (1949); *A Currier and Ives Set* (1953); Violin Concerto (1953); Piano Concerto (1958); *Introduction, Variations, and Finale* (1959); *Declamation* for Wind Instruments and Percussion (1965). **VOCAL:** *Missa Brevis* (1948); *Abraham Lincoln Walks at Midnight,* oratorio (1949); *3 Poems of Wordsworth* for Narrator, Chorus, and Piano (1960); *War Is Kind* for Male Chorus, Percussion, Trumpet, and Piano (1966); *Voyages,* cantata after a poem by Hart Crane (1967); *The Dust of Timas,* cantata after Sappho (1969); *Voices* for Soprano, Chorus, 2 Pianos, and Percussion (1974); *Humdrum Heaven* for Narrator, Soprano, Chorus, Piano, and Percussion (1978); *Valentines and Graffiti,* after e.e. cummings, for Soprano, Chorus, Clarinet, and Piano (1980). **CHAMBER:** *3 Pieces* for Violin, Cello, and Piano (1949); String Quartet (1961); *Tuckets and Sennets* for Trumpet and Piano (1973); *Lonesome Music* for Clarinet (1973). **PIANO:** Sonata (1948); *Prelude, Aria and Burlesca* for 2 Pianos (1950); *3 Intermezzi* (1971); *3 Pieces about Marches* (1975).

Georges, Alexandre, French organist and composer; b. Arras, Feb. 25, 1850; d. Paris, Jan. 18, 1938. He studied at the Niedermeyer School in Paris, and later became a teacher of harmony there. He occupied various posts as organist in Paris churches, and was a successful organ teacher. As a composer, he was mainly interested in opera; the following operas were produced in Paris: *Le Printemps* (1888), *Poèmes d'amour* (1892), *Charlotte Corday* (March 6, 1901), *Miarka* (Nov. 7, 1905; his most successful work; revived and shortened, 1925), *Myrrha* (1909), and *Sangre y sol* (Nice, Feb. 23, 1912). He also wrote the oratorios *Notre Dame de Lourdes, Balthazar,* and *Chemin de Croix;* the symphonic poems *Léila, La Naissance de Vénus,* and *Le Paradis perdu.* He wrote some chamber music for unusual combinations: *À la Kasbah* for Flute and Clarinet; *Kosaks* for Violin and Clarinet, etc. He is best known, however, for his melodious *Chansons de Miarka* for Voice and Piano (also with Orch.) and his arrangement of *Chansons champenoises à la manière ancienne,* by G. Dévignes.

Georgescu, Dan Corneliu, Rumanian composer; b. Craiova, Jan. 1, 1938. He studied at the Popular School for the Arts (1952–56) and with Ion Dumitrescu, Ciortea, Olah, and Mendelsohn at the Bucharest Cons. (1956–61). From 1962 to 1983 he was head of research at the Ethnography and Folklore Inst. of the Rumanian Academy; then pursued research at the Inst. for the History of Art (from 1984). His music employs folksong motifs in a modern manner.
WORKS: Piano Sonata (1958); Trio for Flute, Clarinet, and Bassoon (1959); *3 Pieces* for Orch. (1959); *Motive maramureşene,* suite for Orch. (1963; Bucharest, Dec. 3, 1967); 4 pieces for Orch.: *Jocuri I* (1963); *II, Dialogue rythmique* (1964); *III, Danses solennelles* (1965); and *IV, Collages* (1966); Partita for

Orch. (1966); a cycle of 4 pieces for various orch. groupings: *Alb-negru* (1967), *Zig-Zag* (1967), *Continuo* (1968), and *Rubato* (1969); *Chorals I, II,* and *III* for Flute, Violin, Viola, Cello, and Piano (1970); *Model mioritic,* opera-ballet (1973; Cluj, Oct. 1, 1975); *Schiţe pentru o frescă,* cantata (1976); 3 syms.: No. 1, *Armoniile simple* (1976); No. 2, *Orizontale* (1980); No. 3, *Privirile culorilor* (1985); 3 string quartets (1982; 1983–84; 1985).

Georgescu, Georges, Rumanian conductor; b. Sulina, Sept. 12, 1887; d. Bucharest, Sept. 1, 1964. He studied at the Bucharest Cons.; then took cello lessons with Hugo Becker in Berlin; returning to Bucharest, he founded the George Enesco State Phil. Orch. in 1919, and led it until his death; also conducted guest appearances with European orchs.

Georgiades, Thrasybulos, Greek musicologist; b. Athens, Jan. 4, 1907; d. Munich, March 15, 1977. He studied piano in Athens; then studied musicology with Rudolf von Ficker at the Univ. of Munich, where he received his Ph.D. in 1935 with the dissertation *Englische Diskanttraktate aus der ersten Hälfte des 15. Jahrhunderts* (publ. in Würzburg, 1937); he also studied composition with Carl Orff. In 1938 he became a prof. at the Athens Odeon; was its director from 1939 to 1941. He completed his Habilitation at the Univ. of Munich in 1947 with his *Der griechische Rhythmus: Musik, Reigen, Vers und Sprache* (publ. in Hamburg, 1949; Eng. tr., N.Y., 1956). In 1948 he joined the faculty of the Univ. of Heidelberg; in 1956 he became a prof. at the Univ. of Munich, retiring in 1972. He contributed valuable papers to German music journals on ancient Greek, Byzantine, and medieval music. His other writings include *Volkslied als Bekenntnis* (Regensburg, 1947); *Musik und Sprache* (Berlin, 1954; Eng. tr., Cambridge, 1983); *Musik und Rhythmus bei den Griechen; Zum Ursprung der abendländischen Musik* (Hamburg, 1958); *Das musikalische Theater* (Munich, 1965); *Schubert, Musik und Lyrik* (Göttingen, 1967).

Georgiadis, Georges, Greek pianist and composer; b. Salonika, Sept. 8, 1912; d. Athens, May 8, 1986. He studied piano and composition at the Athens Cons.; in 1943 was appointed prof. of piano there. His music, in a traditional mold, is inspired chiefly by Greek folk resources.
WORKS: Sym. in E minor, *De la paix* (1960); Concertino for Piano and Orch. (1959); 2 violin sonatas; songs; many piano pieces; incidental music for *Demeter and Persephone, Medea,* etc.

Georgii, Walter, German pianist and pedagogue; b. Stuttgart, Nov. 23, 1887; d. Tübingen, Feb. 23, 1967. He studied piano in Stuttgart and music theory in Leipzig, Berlin, and Halle. From 1914 to 1945 he taught piano in Cologne. He publ. *Weber als Klavierkomponist* (Leipzig, 1914); *Geschichte der Musik für Klavier zu 2 Hände* (Zürich, 1941; rev. ed., 1950, with added material on piano music for 1, 3, 5, and 6 hands); *Klavierspielerbüchlein* (Zürich, 1953); also an anthology of piano music, *400 Jahre europäischer Klavier Musik* (Cologne, 1950).

Gérardy, Jean, Belgian cellist; b. Spa, Dec. 6, 1877; d. there, July 4, 1929. At the age of 5 he began to study cello with R. Bellmann; was a pupil of Alfred Massau at the Liège Cons. from 1885 to 1889. In 1888 he played as a student in a trio with Ysaÿe and Paderewski; he became noted as an ensemble player; with Ysaÿe and Godowsky, he formed a trio and toured the U.S. in 1913–14. Gérardy's instrument was a Stradivari made in 1710.

Gerber, Ernst Ludwig, celebrated German lexicographer, son of the organist and composer Heinrich Nikolaus Gerber; b. Sondershausen, Sept. 29, 1746; d. there, June 30, 1819. He studied organ and theory with his father; then law and music in Leipzig, becoming a skillful cellist and organist, in which latter capacity he became (1769) his father's assistant, and succeeded him in 1775. He visited Weimar, Kassel, Leipzig, and other cities, and gradually gathered together a large collection of musicians' portraits; to these he appended brief biographical notices, and finally conceived the plan of writing a biographical dictionary of musicians. Though his resources (in a small town without a public library, and having to rely in great measure on material sent him by his publisher, Breitkopf) were hardly adequate to the task he undertook, his *Historisch-biographisches Lexikon der Tonkünstler* (Leipzig, 2 vols., 1790–92; reprinted 1976) was so well received, and brought in such a mass of corrections and fresh material from all quarters, that he prepared a supplementary ed., *Neues historisch-biographisches Lexikon der Tonkünstler* (4 vols., 1812–14; reprinted 1966). Though the former was intended only as a supplement to Walther's dictionary, and both are, of course, out of date, they contain much material still of value, and have been extensively drawn upon by more recent writers. The Viennese Gesellschaft der Musikfreunde purchased his large library.

Gerber, René, Swiss composer; b. Travers, June 29, 1908. He studied with V. Andreae in Zürich and with Boulanger and Dukas in Paris. Upon his return to Switzerland he devoted himself to teaching; in 1947 was appointed director of the Neuchâtel Cons., occupying this post until 1951.
Works: *3 suites françaises* for Orch. (1933–45); 2 sinfoniettas for String Orch. (1949, 1968); 2 harp concertos (1931, 1969); 2 piano concertos (1933; 1966–70); Clarinet Concerto (1932); Flute Concerto (1934); Bassoon Concerto (1935–39); Trumpet Concerto (1939); Violin Concerto (1941); 3 string quartets (1947–70); opera, *Roméo et Juliette* (1957–61); 3 *Visions espagnoles* for Voice and Small Ensemble (1973).

Gerber, Rudolf, German musicologist; b. Flehingen, Baden, April 15, 1899; d. Göttingen, May 6, 1957. He attended the Univs. of Halle and Leipzig, receiving his Ph.D. from the latter in 1922. He went as Abert's assistant to the Univ. of Berlin in 1923; in 1928, Gerber joined the faculty at Giessen Univ., where he completed his Habilitation (1928) and became a prof. (1937); he was head of the Music-Historical Inst. there from 1937 to 1943, when he became a prof. at Göttingen Univ. An authority on German music, he publ. *Johannes Brahms* (Potsdam, 1938); *Christoph Willibald Ritter von Gluck* (Potsdam, 1941; 2nd ed., rev., 1950); *Bachs Brandenburgische Konzerte* (Kassel, 1951). He ed. works by Schütz, J.S. Bach, and Gluck.

Gerbert, Martin, Freiherr von Hornau, eminent German music scholar; b. Hornau, near Horb am Neckar, Aug. 11, 1720; d. St.-Blasien, May 13, 1793. A student in the Benedictine monastery at St.-Blasien, he joined the order in 1737, became a priest in 1744, then prof. of theology there; from 1759 to 1762 he made trips to Germany, France, and throughout Italy, collecting old MSS, particularly those on music history, of which he later made valuable use in his own works; also visited Padre Martini in Bologna, corresponding with him from 1761 until Martini's death in 1784; in 1764 he was elected Prince-Abbot of the monastery at St.-Blasien. His writings on music are *De cantu et musica sacra* (2 vols., 1774; reprint, 1968), *Vetus liturgia alemannica* (2 vols., 1776; reprint, 1967), *Monumenta veteris liturgiae alemannicae* (2 vols., 1777–79), and *Scriptores ecclesiastici de musica sacra potissimum* (3 vols., 1784; reprint, 1905).
Bibl.: J. Bader, *Fürstabt M. G.* (Freiburg, 1875); F. Niecks, "M. G.: Priest, Prince, Scholar and Musican," *Musical Times* (Nov.–Dec. 1882); A. Lamy, *M. G.* (Rheims, 1898); A. Brinzinger, "Zu M. G.s . . . 200-jährigem Geburtsfest," *Neue Musik-Zeitung* (Sept. 2, 1920); G. Pfeilschifter, *Die Korrespondenz des Fürstabtes M. G. von St. Blasien* (vol. I, 1752–73; 1931); E. Hegar, *Die Anfänge der neueren Musikgeschichtsschreibung um 1770 bei G., Burney and Hawkins* (Strasbourg, 1932); G. Pfeilschifter, A. Allgeler, and W. Müller, eds., *Briefe und Akten des Fürstabts M. II. G. von St. Blasien, 1764–1793* (Karlsruhe, 1957).

Gerelli, Ennio, Italian conductor and composer; b. Cremona, Feb. 12, 1907; d. there, Oct. 5, 1970. He studied at the Bologna Cons.; conducted ballet and opera in Italy; was on the staff of La Scala in Milan (1935–40); in 1961 founded the Camerata di Cremona. He also wrote some chamber music.

Gerhard, Roberto, eminent Spanish-born English composer; b. Valls, near Tarragona, Sept. 25, 1896; d. Cambridge, Jan. 5, 1970. Although of Swiss parentage and nationality, he was prominently associated with the Catalonian musical movement. He studied piano in Barcelona with Granados (1915–16) and was the last composition student of Felipe Pedrell (1916–22). The currents of Central European music were already becoming apparent in his music even before he joined Schoenberg's master classes in Vienna and Berlin (1923–28). He held a brief professorship in Barcelona, and served as head of the music dept. of the Catalan Library there until the defeat of the Republic in the Spanish Civil War; lived in Paris until June 1939, then settled in England and became a British subject in 1960. He was a guest prof. of composition at the Univ. of Michigan in the spring of 1960 and at the Berkshire Music Center, Tanglewood, during the summer of 1962. In 1967 he was made a Commander of the Order of the British Empire. In his music written in England, Gerhard makes use of serialistic procedures, extending the dodecaphonic principle into the domain of rhythms (12 different time units in a theme, corresponding to the intervallic distances of the notes in the tone row from the central note).
Works: Opera, *The Duenna,* after Sheridan's play (1945–47; perf. in concert form, Wiesbaden, June 27, 1951); 5 ballets: *Ariel* (1934; ballet suite, Barcelona, April 19, 1936); *Soirées de Barcelona* (1936–38); *Don Quixote* (1940–41; London, Feb. 20, 1950); *Alegrías, Divertissement Flamenco* for 2 Pianos (also an orch. suite, BBC, April 4, 1944); *Pandora* for 2 Pianos and Percussion (1943–44; also for Orch., Cambridge, Jan. 26, 1944); 2 cantatas: *L'Alta Naixença del Rei en Jaume* (1931) and *The Plague,* after Camus (London, April 1, 1964). He also wrote *Albade, Interludi i Dansa* for Orch. (1936; London, June 24, 1938); a sym., *Pedrelliana (Homenaje a Pedrell),* based on themes from Pedrell's opera *La Celestina* (1941); Violin Concerto (1942; rev. 1945 and 1949; Florence, June 16, 1950); Concerto for Piano and Strings (1950); 5 numbered syms.: No. 1 (1952–53; Baden-Baden, June 21, 1955); No. 2 (London, Oct. 28, 1959; rev. 1967–68 and retitled *Metamorphoses*); No. 3, *Collages* for Orch. and Tape (London, Feb. 8, 1961); No. 4, *New York* (N.Y., Dec. 14, 1967); No. 5 (1969; unfinished); Concerto for Harpsichord, Strings, and Percussion (1955–56); *Concerto for Orchestra* (Boston, April 25, 1965); *Epithalamion* for Orch. (Valdagno, Italy, Sept. 17, 1966); *L'Infantament meravellós de Schahrazade,* song cycle for Voice and Piano (1918); Piano Trio (1918); *Dos Apunts* for Piano (1922); 7 *Hai-Kai* for Voice, 4 Winds, and Piano (1922–23); 2 *Sardanas* for 11 Instruments (1928); 6 *cançons populars catalanes* for Soprano and Piano (1928; orchestrated in 1931; Vienna, June 16, 1932, Webern conducting); Wind Quintet (1928); *Cancionero de Pedrell,* 8 songs for Soprano and Chamber Orch. (1941); *Capriccio* for Solo Flute (1949); *Impromptus* for Piano (1950); Viola Sonata (1950); 2 string quartets (1950–55; 1961–62); *The Akond of Swat,* after Edward Lear, for Voice and 2 Percussionists (London, Feb. 7, 1956); Nonet for 4 Woodwinds, 4 Brasses, and Accordion (1956); *Chaconne* for Solo Violin (1958); *Concert for 8* for Flute, Clarinet, Guitar, Mandolin, Double Bass, Accordion, Piano, and Percussion (London, May 17, 1962); *Hymnody* for 7 Winds, Percussion, and 2 Pianos (London, May 23, 1963); Cello Sonata (BBC, Oct. 10, 1964); *Gemini* for Violin and Piano (1966; orig. titled *Duo Concertante*); *Libra* for Flute, Clarinet, Violin, Guitar, Piano, and Percussion (BBC, Oct. 26, 1968); *Leo,* chamber sym. (Hanover, N.H., Aug. 23, 1969). He wrote an electronic sound track for a medical film, *Audiomobile No. 2 "DNA,"* and electronic music to accompany a reading of García Lorca's *Lament for the Death of a Bullfighter;* incidental music to Shakespeare's plays (*Romeo and Juliet, Taming of the Shrew, Midsummer Night's Dream, King Lear*); film music; harmonizations of Catalan melodies; etc.
Bibl.: *Score* (Sept. 1956); K. Potter, *The Life and Works of R. G.* (diss., Univ. of Birmingham, 1972).

Gerhardt, Elena, celebrated German-born English mezzo-soprano; b. Leipzig, Nov. 11, 1883; d. London, Jan. 11, 1961. She studied at the Leipzig Cons. (1899–1903) with Marie Hedmont; made her public debut on her 20th birthday in a recital, accompanied by Nikisch; toured Europe as a lieder singer with great success; made her English debut in London in 1906, and her American debut in N.Y., Jan. 9, 1912. In 1933 she settled in London, making appearances as a singer, and teaching. She compiled *My Favorite German Songs* (1915), ed. a selection of Hugo Wolf's songs (1932), and wrote her autobiography, *Recital* (London, 1953).

Gericke, Wilhelm, noted Austrian conductor; b. Schwanberg, April 18, 1845; d. Vienna, Oct. 27, 1925. He studied with Dessoff at the Vienna Cons. (1862–65); after a number of engagements as guest conductor in provincial theaters, he became conductor of the municipal theater in Linz. In 1874 he joined the staff of the Vienna Court Opera as an assistant conductor; in 1880 he took charge of the Gesellschaft der Musikfreunde concerts, and also led the Singverein. From 1884 to 1889 he was conductor of the Boston Sym. Orch.; returning to Vienna, he once again served as conductor of the Gesellschaft der Musikfreunde concerts (1890–95). He was called again to America in 1898 to lead the Boston Sym. Orch., conducting its concerts until 1906; then returned to Vienna. Gericke did much to make it a fine ensemble, for he was a remarkably able conductor and a highly efficient drillmaster.
    BIBL.: J. Burk, "W. G.: A Centennial Retrospect," *Musical Quarterly* (April 1945).

Gerl, Franz Xaver, German bass and composer; b. Andorf, Nov. 30, 1764; d. Mannheim, March 9, 1827. He sang in the choir at Salzburg; in 1789 became principal bass at the Theater auf der Wieden in Vienna, remaining on its roster until 1793; he created the role of Sarastro in Mozart's *Die Zauberflöte* in 1791; his wife, **Barbara Reisinger** (1770–1806), created the role of Papagena in that production. He composed several works for the stage, collaborating with Bendikt Schack.

Gerlach, Theodor, German conductor and composer; b. Dresden, June 25, 1861; d. Kiel, Dec. 11, 1940. He studied with Wüllner; then was a conductor in several provincial towns. He wrote an *Epic Symphony* (1891) and the opera *Matteo Falcone* (Hannover, 1898); of particular interest were his experiments with "spoken opera," utilizing inflected speech, most notably in his *Liebeswogen* (Bremen, Nov. 7, 1903; rev. as *Das Seegespenst*, Altenburg, April 24, 1914); he also used the spoken word over an instrumental accompaniment in his *Gesprochene Lieder*.

Gerle, Hans, German lutenist; b. Nuremberg, c.1500; d. there, 1570. He was well known in his time, both as a performer on the lute and as a manufacturer of viols and lutes. His works in tablature are of considerable historic value: *Musica Teusch auf die Instrument der grossen unnd kleinen Geygen, auch Lautten* (Nuremberg, 1532; 2nd ed., 1537; 3rd ed., under the title *Musica und Tabulatur*, 1546); *Tabulatur auff die Laudten* (Nuremberg, 1533); *Ein newes sehr künstlichs Lautenbuch* (Nuremberg, 1552; with pieces by Francesco da Milano, A. Rotta, Joan da Crema, Rosseto, and Gintzler). Reprints of his works have been ed. by W. Tappert in *Sang und Klang aus alter Zeit* (1906) and by H.D. Bruger in *Schule des Lautenspiels*, I/2, and *Alte Lautenkunst I.*
    BIBL.: W. Tappert, "Die Lautenbücher des H. G.," *Monatshefte für Musikgeschichte*, XVIII (1886).

Gerle, Robert, Hungarian violinist and conductor; b. Abbazia, Italy, April 1, 1924. He was educated at the Franz Liszt Academy of Music and the National Cons. in Budapest; received the Hubay Prize in 1942; played in recital and with major orchs. in Europe. He eventually settled in the U.S.; headed the string dept. of the Univ. of Oklahoma (1950–54); then was on the staff of the Peabody Cons. in Baltimore (1955–68), the Mannes College of Music in N.Y. (1959–70), the Manhattan School of Music (1967–70), and Ohio State Univ. (1968–

72). In 1972 he was named head of the Instrumental Program of the Univ. of Maryland, Baltimore County; was active as a conductor there and also continued his career as a violinist. He publ. *The Art of Practicing the Violin* (London, 1983).

German, Sir Edward (real name, **German Edward Jones**), English composer; b. Whitchurch, Feb. 17, 1862; d. London, Nov. 11, 1936. He began serious music study in 1880 under W.C. Hay at Shrewsbury; entered the Royal Academy of Music in London (1880–87), studying organ (Steggall), violin (Weist-Hill and Burnett), theory (Banister), and composition and orchestration (Prout); was elected a Fellow there in 1895. In 1888–89 he conducted the orch. at the Globe Theatre, where his incidental music to Richard Mansfield's production of *King Richard III* was so successful that Sir Henry Irving commissioned him to write the music to *Henry VIII* (1892). German was then enabled to give up teaching and to devote himself entirely to composition. He was knighted in 1928; awarded the gold medal of the Royal Phil. Soc. in 1934.
    WORKS: ORCH.: 2 syms. (1890, 1893); *Gypsy Suite* (1892); Suite in D minor (1895); English fantasia, *Commemoration* (1897); symphonic poem, *Hamlet* (1897); symphonic suite, *The Seasons* (1899); *Rhapsody on March-Themes* (1902); *Funeral March* in D minor for Orch.; *Welsh Rhapsody* (1904); *Coronation March and Hymn* (1911); *Theme and 6 Variations* (1919); *The Willow Song* (1922); Serenade for Voice, Piano, Oboe, Clarinet, Bassoon, and Horn; *The Guitar; Bolero* for Violin and Orch.; incidental music to *Richard III* (1889), *Henry VIII* (1892), *As You Like It* (1896), *Much Ado about Nothing* (1898), *Nell Gwyn* (1900), *The Conqueror* (1905). **OPERAS:** *The Emerald Isle* (completing the score of Arthur Sullivan; 1901); *Merrie England* (London, April 2, 1902); *A Princess of Kensington* (1903); *Tom Jones* (London, April 17, 1908); *Fallen Fairies* (1909; the last libretto written by Sir W.S. Gilbert); operetta, *The Rival Poets* (1901). Also, many piano solos (incl. a suite) and duets; chamber music, organ pieces, etc.; Te Deum in F; a patriotic hymn, *Canada*; intercessory hymn, *Father Omnipotent*; *Three Albums of Lyrics* (with Harold Boulton); *The Just So Song Book* (words by Rudyard Kipling); other songs; etc.
    BIBL.: W. Scott, *Sir E. G.: An Intimate Biography* (London, 1932); B. Rees, *A Musical Peacemaker: The Life and Works of Sir E. G.* (Bourne End, Buckinghamshire, 1987).

Germani, Fernando, Italian organist; b. Rome, April 5, 1906. He studied with Bajardi (piano), Dobici (theory), Respighi (composition), and Manari (organ) at the Accademia di Santa Cecilia in Rome. He taught organ at the Curtis Inst. of Music in Philadelphia (1936–38), and at various institutions in Italy. He served as 1st organist at St. Peter's Cathedral in Rome (1948–59); also made numerous tours of Europe and North America. He ed. Frescobaldi's *Opere per organo e cembalo* (3 vols., Rome, 1964).

Gernsheim, Friedrich, German pianist, conductor, and composer; b. Worms, July 17, 1839; d. Berlin, Sept. 11, 1916. He studied at the Leipzig Cons. with Moscheles (piano) and Hauptmann (theory); then was in Paris (1855–61). Returning to Germany, he became a prof. at the Cologne Cons. (1865–72); then conducted choral concerts in Rotterdam (1872–80); subsequently taught at the Stern Cons. in Berlin (1890–97). His works are marked by a Romantic flair, as an epigone of Schumann; he was also influenced by Brahms, who was his friend. He wrote 4 syms., overtures, a Piano Concerto, a Violin Concerto, 5 string quartets, 3 piano quartets, 2 piano trios, a String Quintet, 3 violin sonatas, 2 cello sonatas, choral works, songs, and piano pieces.
    BIBL.: K. Holl, *F. G., Leben, Erscheinung und Werk* (Leipzig, 1928).

Gero, Jhan (Jehan), Flemish composer who flourished in the 16th century. He was a fine madrigalist; publ. 2 books of madrigals for 4 Voices (Venice, 1549), 2 books of madrigals for 3 Voices (Venice, 1553), and a book of madrigals for 2 Voices (Venice, 1541; modern ed. by S. Bernstein and J. Haar,

N.Y., 1977); he also wrote motets. He was at one time confused with Johannes Gallus.

Bibl.: A. Einstein, *The Italian Madrigal* (Princeton, 1949).

Gérold, (Jean) Théodore, eminent Alsatian music scholar; b. Strasbourg, Oct. 26, 1866; d. Allenwiller, Feb. 15, 1956. He studied voice, violin, and theory at the Strasbourg Cons., and musicology with Gustaf Jacobsthal and theology at the German Univ. of Strasbourg (Ph.D., 1910). In 1890 he went to Frankfurt to study singing with Jules Stockhausen; then took courses at the Paris Cons. He was a lecturer on music at the Univ. of Basel from 1914 to 1918; returned to Strasbourg in 1919 to lecture on music at the new French Univ., from which in 1921 he received his doctorat *ès lettres,* and in 1931 his doctorat d'État. He retired from the Univ. in 1937; occupied an ecclesiastical lecturing position in Allenwiller until his death.

Writings: *Kleine Sänger-Fiebel: Sprachliche Übungen für Sänger* (Mainz, 1908; 2nd ed., 1911); *Das Liederbuch einer französischen Provinzdame um 1620* (Frankfurt, 1912); *Chansons populaires des XVe et XVIe siècles avec leurs mélodies* (Strasbourg, 1913); *Clément Marot: Les Psaumes avec leurs mélodies* (Strasbourg, 1919); *La Musicologie médiévale* (Paris, 1921); *François Schubert* (Paris, 1923); *Jean Sébastien Bach* (Paris, 1925); *Les Pères de l'église et la musique* (Paris, 1931); *La Musique au moyen âge* (Paris, 1932); *Histoire de la musique des origines à la fin du XIVe siècle* (Paris, 1936); *Marie-Joseph Erb: Sa vie, son œuvre* (Strasbourg and Paris, 1948).

Bibl.: F. Münch, "In memoriam T. G. (1866–1956)," *Revue d'histoire et de philosophie religieuses,* XXXVII (1956).

Gerschefski, Edwin, American composer; b. Meriden, Conn., June 10, 1909. He studied piano with Bruce Simons and composition at Yale Univ.; then went to London, where he took courses at the Tobias Matthay Piano School; he further had lessons with Schnabel in Como, Italy. Returning to N.Y. in 1935, he studied the Schillinger system of composition with Schillinger (1936–38). From then on he occupied various teaching posts; in 1960 was appointed to the faculty of the Univ. of Georgia; retired in 1972. His works are of a pleasing modernistic type, showing knowledge and ability in handling instrumental and vocal idioms.

Works: Piano Quintet (1935); *Discharge in E* and *Streamline* for Band (1935); 8 Variations for String Quartet (1937); Brass Septet (1938); cantata, *Half Moon Mountain,* for Baritone, Women's Chorus, and Orch., after a story in *Time* magazine (Spartanburg, S.C., April 30, 1948); Toccata and Fugue for Orch. (1954); Rhapsody for Violin, Cello, and Piano (1963); *Celebration* for Violin and Orch. (1964); *Psalm C,* cantata for Soprano, Baritone, Chorus, Percussion, and Piano (1965); *The Alexander Suite* for 2 Cellos (1971); *Letter from BMI* for Chorus and Small Orch. (1981); also 2 piano sonatas (1936, 1968) and many other piano pieces; songs; music for films; etc.

Gershfeld, David, Moldavian composer; b. Bobrinets, Aug. 28, 1911. He studied French horn and music theory in Odessa; then moved to Kishinev, where he produced 2 operas on Moldavian subjects: *Grozovan* (June 9, 1956) and *Aurelia* (April 26, 1959); also a Violin Concerto (1951) and a ballad for Unaccompanied Chorus, *26 Commissars of Baku* (commemorating the Bolshevik representatives in Azerbaijan martyred by the British expeditionary force). In 1966 he moved to Sochi in the Caucasus.

Gershwin, George, immensely gifted American composer, brother of **Ira Gershwin;** b. N.Y., Sept. 26, 1898; d. Los Angeles, July 11, 1937. His real name was **Jacob Gershvin,** according to the birth registry; his father was an immigrant from Russia whose original name was Gershovitz. Gershwin's extraordinary career began when he was 16, playing the piano in music stores to demonstrate new popular songs. His studies were desultory; he took piano lessons with Ernest Hutcheson and Charles Hambitzer in N.Y.; studied harmony with Edward Kilenyi and Rubin Goldmark; later on, when he was already a famous composer of popular music, he continued to take private lessons; he studied counterpoint with Henry Cowell

and Wallingford Riegger; during the last years of his life, he applied himself with great earnestness to studying with Joseph Schillinger in an attempt to organize his technique in a scientific manner; some of Schillinger's methods he applied in *Porgy and Bess.* But it was his melodic talent and a genius for rhythmic invention, rather than any studies, that made him a genuinely important American composer. As far as worldly success was concerned, there was no period of struggle in Gershwin's life; one of his earliest songs, *Swanee,* written at the age of 19, became enormously popular (more than a million copies sold; 2,250,000 phonograph records). He also took time to write a lyrical *Lullaby* for String Quartet (1920). Possessing phenomenal energy, he produced musical comedies in close succession, using fashionable jazz formulas in original and ingenious ways. A milestone in his career was *Rhapsody in Blue* for Piano and Jazz Orch., in which he applied the jazz idiom to an essentially classical form. He played the solo part at a special concert conducted by Paul Whiteman at Aeolian Hall in N.Y. on Feb. 12, 1924. The orchestration was by Ferde Grofé, a circumstance that generated rumors of Gershwin's inability to score for instruments; these rumors, however, were quickly refuted by his production of several orch. works, scored by himself in a brilliant fashion. He played the solo part of his Piano Concerto in F, with Walter Damrosch and the N.Y. Sym. Orch. (Dec. 3, 1925); this work had a certain vogue, but its popularity never equaled that of the *Rhapsody in Blue.* Reverting again to a more popular idiom, Gershwin wrote a symphonic work, *An American in Paris* (N.Y. Phil., Dec. 13, 1928, Damrosch conducting). His *Rhapsody No. 2* was performed by Koussevitzky and the Boston Sym. on Jan. 29, 1932, but was unsuccessful; there followed a *Cuban Overture* (N.Y., Aug. 16, 1932) and Variations for Piano and Orch. on his song *I Got Rhythm* (Boston, Jan. 14, 1934, composer soloist). In the meantime, Gershwin became engaged in his most ambitious undertaking: the composition of *Porgy and Bess,* an American opera in a folk manner, for black singers, after the book by Dubose Heyward. It was first staged in Boston on Sept. 30, 1935, and in N.Y. on Oct. 10, 1935. Its reception by the press was not uniformly favorable, but its songs rapidly attained great popularity (*Summertime; I Got Plenty o' Nuthin'; It Ain't Neccessarily So; Bess, You Is My Woman Now*); the opera has been successfully revived in N.Y. and elsewhere; it received international recognition when an American company of black singers toured with it in South America and Europe in 1955. Gershwin's death (of a gliomatous cyst in the right temporal lobe of the brain) at the age of 38 was mourned as a great loss to American music. The 50th anniversary of his death brought forth a number of special tributes in 1987, including a major joint broadcast of his music by the PBS and BBC television networks. His musical comedies include *Our Nell* (1922); *Sweet Little Devil* (1924); *Lady, Be Good!* (1924); *Primrose* (1924); *Tip-Toes* (1925); *Oh Kay!* (1926); *Strike Up the Band* (1927); *Funny Face* (1927); *Rosalie* (1928); *Treasure Girl* (1928); *Show Girl* (1929); *Girl Crazy* (1930); *Of Thee I Sing* (1931; a political satire which was the 1st musical to win a Pulitzer Prize); *Pardon My English* (1933); *Let 'Em Eat Cake* (1933); for motion pictures: *Shall We Dance, A Damsel in Distress,* and *The Goldwyn Follies* (left unfinished at his death; completed by Vernon Duke). A collection of his songs and piano transcriptions, *George Gershwin's Song Book,* was publ. in 1932 and reprinted as *Gershwin Years in Song* (N.Y., 1973).

Bibl.: I. Goldberg, *G. G., A Study in American Music* (N.Y., 1931; 2nd ed., rev., 1958); V. Thomson, "G. G.," *Modern Music* (Nov. 1935); M. Armitage, ed., *G. G.* (N.Y., 1938); O. Levant, *A Smattering of Ignorance* (N.Y., 1938); D. Ewen, *A Journey to Greatness; G. G.* (N.Y., 1956; 2nd ed., rev. as *G. G., His Journey to Greatness,* 1970); E. Jablonski and L. Stewart, *The G. Years* (Garden City, N.Y., 1958; 2nd ed., rev., 1973); C. Schwartz, *G.: His Life and Music* (Indianapolis, 1973); idem, *G. G.: A Selective Bibliography and Discography* (Detroit, 1974); C. Hamm, "The Theatre Guild Production of Porgy and Bess," *Journal of the American Musicological Soci-*

ety (Fall 1987); E. Jablonski; *G.: A Biography* (Garden City, N.Y., 1987); A. Kendall, *G. G.: A Biography* (N.Y., 1987); P. Kresh, *An American Rhapsody: The Story of G. G.* (N.Y., 1988); R. Wyatt, "The Seven Jazz Preludes of G. G.: A Historical Narrative," *American Music* (Spring 1989).

Gershwin, Ira, talented American librettist and lyricist, brother of **George Gershwin;** b. N.Y., Dec. 6, 1896; d. Beverly Hills, Calif., Aug. 17, 1983. He attended night classes at the College of the City of N.Y., wrote verses and humorous pieces for the school paper, and served as cashier in a Turkish bath of which his father was part owner. He began writing lyrics for shows in 1918, using the pseudonym Arthur Francis. His 1st full-fledged show as a lyricist was the musical comedy *Be Yourself,* for which he used his own name for the 1st time. He achieved fame when he wrote the lyrics for his brother's musical comedy *Lady, Be Good!* (1924). He remained his brother's collaborator until George Gershwin's death in 1937, so that his lyrics became an inalienable part of the whole, so that the brothers George and Ira Gershwin became artistic twins, like Gilbert and Sullivan, indissolubly united in some of the greatest productions of the musical theater in America: *Strike Up the Band* (1927), *Of Thee I Sing* (1931), and the culminating product of the brotherly genius, the folk opera *Porgy and Bess* (1935). He also wrote lyrics for other composers, among them Vernon Duke (*The Ziegfeld Follies of 1936*), Kurt Weill (*Lady in the Dark,* and several motion pictures), and Jerome Kern (the enormously successful song *Long Ago and Far Away* from the film *Cover Girl*).

Gerson-Kiwi, (Esther) Edith, German-born Israeli musicologist; b. Berlin, May 13, 1908. She studied musicology with W. Gurlitt at the Univ. of Freiburg, Kroyer at the Univ. of Leipzig, and Besseler at the Univ. of Heidelberg (Ph.D., 1933, with the diss. *Studien zur Geschichte des italienischen Liedmadrigals im 16. Jahrhundert;* publ. in Würzburg, 1938). In 1935 she went to Palestine, where she was active in research and teaching; in 1969 she joined the faculty of the Univ. of Tel Aviv. She is a prolific and versatile writer; her subjects have included Renaissance, Classical, Romantic, and contemporary music, and the ethnic music of the Middle East, on which she is an outstanding authority. Her books include *The Persian Doctrine of Dastgah Composition: A Phenomenological Study in the Musical Modes* (Tel Aviv, 1963), *The Legacy of Jewish Music through the Ages of Dispersion* (Jerusalem, 1963–64), and *Migrations and Mutations of the Music in East and West* (Tel Aviv, 1980). **Bibl.:** S. Burstyn, ed., *Essays in Honor of E. G.-K.* (Tel Aviv, 1986).

Gerstberger, Karl, German music scholar and composer; b. Neisse, Feb. 12, 1892; d. Bremen, Oct. 30, 1955. He studied in Cologne with Othegraven and in Munich with Courvoisier. In his music he endeavored to revive the spirit of Lutheran polyphony. He wrote choral works, lieder, a String Quartet, 2 string trios, etc.; publ. a collection of essays, *Zum Schicksal der Musik.*

Gerster, Etelka, noted Hungarian soprano; b. Kaschau, June 25, 1855; d. Pontecchio, near Bologna, Aug. 20, 1920. She studied with Mathilde Marchesi in Vienna, then made her debut in Venice as Gilda in *Rigoletto,* Jan. 8, 1876. Her great success resulted in engagements in Berlin and Budapest in Italian opera under the direction of Carlo Gardini. She married Gardini on April 16, 1877. She then continued her successful career, making her London debut on June 23, 1877, as Amina in *La Sonnambula,* and her U.S. debut in the same role on Nov. 11, 1878, at the N.Y. Academy of Music. She returned to London for 2 more seasons (1878–80), then sang again in N.Y. from 1880 to 1883 and in 1887. After retiring, she taught singing in Berlin (1896–1917). She wrote the treatise *Stimmführer* (1906; 2nd ed., 1908).

Gerster, Ottmar, eminent German violinist, composer, and pedagogue; b. Braunfels, June 29, 1897; d. Leipzig, Aug. 31, 1969. He studied music theory with Bernhard Sekles at the Frankfurt Cons. (1913–16); then was mobilized during the last years of World War I; after the war, studied violin with Adolf Rebner (1919–21); played the viola in string quartets (1923–27), and concurrently was concertmaster of the Frankfurt Museumgesellschaft Orch. From 1927 to 1939 he taught violin and theory at the Folkwang-Schule in Essen; then was again in the army. After World War II he was on the faculty of the Hochschule für Musik in Weimar (1947–52) and in Leipzig (1952–62). His music is marked by melodious polyphony in a neo-Classical vein; in his operas he used folklike thematic material.

Works: Operas: *Madame Liselotte* (Essen, 1933); *Enoch Arden* (Düsseldorf, 1936); *Die Hexe von Passau* (Düsseldorf, 1941); *Das Verzauberte Ich* (Wuppertal, 1949); *Der fröhliche Sünder* (Weimar, 1963); ballet, *Der ewige Kreis* (Duisburg, 1939); *Kleine Sinfonie* (1931); *Thüringer Sinfonie* (1952); *Leipziger Sinfonie* (1965); *Oberhessische Bauerntänze* for Orch. (1937); Cello Concerto (1946); Piano Concerto (1956); Horn Concerto (1962); 2 string quartets (1923, 1954); String Trio (1957); *Ballade vom Manne Karl Marx (und der Veränderung der Welt)* for Baritone Solo, Chorus, and Orch. (1961); many other choruses, some to words of political significance; songs. **Bibl.:** O. Goldhammer, *O. G.* (Berlin, 1953); R. Malth, *O. G.: Leben und Werk* (Leipzig, 1988).

Gerstman, Blanche, South African pianist and composer; b. Cape Town, April 2, 1910; d. there, Aug. 11, 1973. She was of British extraction, but adopted the family name of her adoptive parents. She studied music theory with Hely-Hutchinson and later with William Henry Bell at the South African College of Music. She was subsequently active as a radio pianist; in 1950 she went to London, where she took additional courses at the Royal College of Music with Howard Ferguson. Returning to South Africa in 1952, she taught at the College of Music in Cape Town. She composed pleasurable piano pieces, singable choruses, and some playable chamber music.

Gertler, André, Hungarian violinist and pedagogue; b. Budapest, July 26, 1907. He studied violin with Hubay and composition with Kodály at the Budapest Academy of Music (diploma, 1925). He toured as a soloist; also appeared in recitals with Bartók (1925–38) and was violinist in his own Quatuor Gertler in Brussels (1931–51); was a prof. at the Brussels Cons. (1940–54), the Cologne Hochschule für Musik (1954–59), and the Hannover Hochschule für Musik (1964–78). He became well known as a sympathetic interpreter of contemporary music.

Gervaise, Claude, French composer who flourished in the 16th century. He was a violist and chamber musician to François I and Henri II. He composed many dances and chansons; 6 vols. of his *Danceries à 4 et 5 parties* were publ. by Attaignant from about 1545 to 1556, but only 3 vols. remain; a selection of his dances is included in vol. 23 (Danceries) of *Les Maîtres Musiciens,* ed. by H. Expert (1908). Several chansons by Gervaise appear in 16th-century collections. **Bibl.:** L. Bernstein, "C. G. as Chanson Composer," *Journal of the American Musicological Society,* XVIII (1965).

Gerville-Réache, Jeanne, French contralto; b. Orthez, March 26, 1882; d. N.Y., Jan. 5, 1915. She spent her childhood in Guadeloupe, French West Indies, where her father was governor. In 1898 she was sent to Paris to study singing with Mme. Viardot-García. She made her debut at the Opéra-Comique in Paris in 1899; continued to sing there until 1903. She created the role of Geneviève in *Pelléas et Mélisande* there on April 30, 1902; went to N.Y., where she became a member of the Manhattan Opera Co. (1907–10); subsequently sang in Chicago, Boston, Philadelphia, and Montreal. In 1908 she married Dr. Georges Rambaud, director of the Pasteur Inst. in N.Y.

Gesensway, Louis, Latvian-American violinist and composer; b. Dvinsk, Feb. 19, 1906; d. Philadelphia, March 11, 1976. The family moved to Canada when he was a child; he studied violin; in 1926, joined the Philadelphia Orch., remaining with it until 1971. He was a prolific composer of some originality;

he developed a system of "color harmony" by expanding and contracting the intervals of the diatonic scale into fractions, establishing a difference between enharmonically equal tones; such a scale in his projection contained 41 degrees.

WORKS: ORCH.: Flute Concerto (Philadelphia, Nov. 1, 1946); *The 4 Squares of Philadelphia* for Narrator and Orch. (Philadelphia, Feb. 25, 1955); *Ode to Peace* (Philadelphia, April 15, 1960); *Commemoration Symphony* (1966–68; Philadelphia, Feb. 25, 1971); *A Pennsylvania Overture* (1972); Cello Concerto (1973). **CHAMBER:** Concerto for 13 Brass Instruments (1942); Quartet for Clarinet and Strings (1950); Quartet for Oboe, Bassoon, Violin, and Viola (1951); Sonata for Solo Bassoon; Duo for Oboe and Guitar (1959); Duo for Viola and Bassoon (1960); Duo for Violin and Cello (1970).

Gesualdo, Carlo, Prince of Venosa and Count of Conza, Italian lutenist and composer; b. probably in Naples, c.1560; d. there, Sept. 8, 1613. In 1590, his unfaithful wife and 1st cousin, Maria d'Avalos, and her lover were murdered at Gesualdo's orders; in 1594, he was at the court of the Estensi in Ferrara, where he married his 2nd wife, Leonora d'Este, in that year; sometime after the death of the Duke of Ferrara, in 1597, Carlo returned to Naples, where he remained till death. Living in the epoch when the "new music" (the homophonic style) made its appearance, he was one of the most original musicians of the time. Like Rore, Banchieri, and Vincentino, he was a so-called chromaticist; his later madrigals reveal a distinctly individual style of expression and are characterized by strong contrasts, new (for their time) harmonic progressions, and a skillful use of dissonance; he was a master in producing tone color through the use of different voice registers and in expressing the poetic contents of his texts. He publ. 6 vols. of madrigals *a* 5 (1594–1611; modern ed. by F. Vatielli and A. Bizzelli, 1956–58). A complete edition of his works was ed. by W. Weisman and G. Watkins (10 vols., 1957–67).

BIBL.: F. Keiner, *Die Madrigale G.s von Venosa* (diss., Univ. of Leipzig, 1914); C. Gray and P. Heseltine, *C. G., Prince of Venosa, Musician and Murderer* (London, 1926); F. Vatielli, *Il Principe di Venosa e Leonora d'Este* (Milan, 1941); G. Watkins, *G., The Man and His Music* (London, 1973).

Geszty (real name, **Witkowsky**), **Sylvia,** Hungarian soprano; b. Budapest, Feb. 28, 1934. She studied at the Budapest Cons.; made her debut at the Budapest State Opera in 1959; was a member of the Berlin State Opera (1961–70), the Berlin Komische Oper (1963–70), the Hamburg State Opera (1966–72; 1973), the Württemberg State Theater in Stuttgart (from 1970). She sang the Queen of the Night at London's Covent Garden in 1966, and repeated the role at the Salzburg Festival in 1967; at the Munich Opera Festival she also sang Zerbinetta, a favorite soubrette role, which she chose for her Glyndebourne Festival debut in 1971. She made her North American debut as Sophie in *Der Rosenkavalier* with the N.Y. City Opera during its visit to Los Angeles on Nov. 19, 1973; she also appeared with the Berlin Städtische Oper, the Paris Opéra, La Scala in Milan, and the Teatro Colón in Buenos Aires, and in concerts and recitals.

Getty, Gordon, American composer who bears the unique brunt of being a scion of a billionaire; b. Los Angeles, Dec. 20, 1933. In 1945 he was taken to San Francisco, where he studied English literature at San Francisco State College (graduated, 1956) and took courses at the San Francisco Cons. of Music. From his earliest attempts at composition, he proclaimed faith in the primacy of consonance and a revival of Romantic ideals. His preference lay with vocal music, and he possessed a natural gift for writing a fetching melodic line. For his songs and choruses he selected the poems of Housman, Tennyson, Poe, and Emily Dickinson. He also produced an opera, *Plump Jack*, based on the character of Shakespeare's Falstaff (excerpts only; San Francisco, March 13, 1985). The inevitable headline in one of several newspaper reviews was "Billionaire Has a Hit in *Plump Jack*!" Every music critic writing about Getty must deal with the inescapable suspicion that his music is the accidental outgrowth of his material for-

tune, and must conquer conscious or subliminal prejudice in favor or disfavor of a work. Getty deserves full credit for braving this test courageously, ignoring bouquets and brickbats and persevering in writing his kind of music. Among his other works are the piano pieces *Homework Suite, 3 Diatonic Waltzes,* and *Tiefer und Tiefer* (all 1986), and a vocal work, *The White Election* for Soprano and Piano, to poems by Emily Dickinson (1986).

Getz, Stan(ley), American jazz tenor saxophonist; b. Philadelphia, Feb. 2, 1927. While still a teenager, he joined Jack Teagarden's group; then played with Stan Kenton, Jimmy Dorsey, and Benny Goodman; after a stint with Woody Herman, he embarked upon a series of recordings with Gerry Mulligan, Dizzy Gillespie, and other noted jazz musicians. He joined the faculty of Stanford Univ. in 1984. He was an impressive exponent of "cool" jazz.

Gevaert, François Auguste, eminent Belgian musicologist and composer; b. Huysse, near Audenarde, July 31, 1828; d. Brussels, Dec. 24, 1908. He was a pupil of De Somère (piano) and Mengal (composition) at the Ghent Cons. (1841–47), taking the Grand Prix de Rome for composition; from 1843 he was also organist at the Jesuit church. He lived in Paris (1849–50), and was commissioned to write an opera for the Théâtre-Lyrique; then spent a year in Spain, his *Fantasía sobre motivos españoles* winning him the Order of Isabella la Católica. After visits to Italy and Germany, he returned to Ghent in 1852 and brought out 9 operas in quick succession. In 1857 his festival cantata *De nationale verjaerdag* won him the Order of Léopold. From 1867 to 1870 he was music director at the Paris Opéra; from 1871 he was director of the Brussels Cons., succeeding Fétis. As conductor of the "Concerts du Conservatoire," he exerted a far-reaching influence through his historical concerts, producing works of all nations and periods. In 1873 he was elected a member of the Academy, succeeding Mercadante; in 1907 he was made a baron.

WORKS: 12 operas; 8 cantatas; a *Missa pro defunctis* and *Super flumina Babylonis* (both for Male Chorus and Orch.); overture, *Flandre au lion;* ballads (*Philipp van Artevelde,* etc.); songs (many in the collection *Nederlandsche Zangstukken*).

WRITINGS: *Leerboek van den Gregoriaenschen Zang* (1856); *Traité d'instrumentation* (1863; rev. and enl. as *Nouveau traité de l'instrumentation,* 1885; German tr. by Riemann, 1887; Spanish tr. by Neuparth, 1896; Russian tr. by Rebikov, 1899); *Histoire et théorie de la musique de l'antiquité* (2 vols., 1875, 1881); *Les Origines du chant liturgique de l'église latine* (1890; German tr. by Riemann; threw new light on the Gregorian tradition); *Cours méthodique d'orchestration* (2 vols., 1890; complement of *Nouveau traité*); *La Mélopée antique dans l'église latine* (1895; a monumental work); *Les Problèmes musicaux d'Aristote* (3 vols., 1899–1902; adopts the theories of Westphal, certain of which were later proved untenable); *Traité d'harmonie théorique et pratique* (2 vols., 1905, 1907). He ed. *Les Gloires de l'Italie* (a collection of vocal numbers from operas, oratorios, cantatas, etc., of the 17th and 18th centuries); *Recueil de chansons du XVᵉ siècle* (transcribed in modern notation); *Vademecum de l'organiste* (classic transcriptions).

BIBL.: F. Dufour, *Le Baron F.A. G.* (Brussels, 1909); E. Closson, *G.* (Brussels, 1928).

Geyer, Stefi, Hungarian-born Swiss violinist; b. Budapest, Jan. 28, 1888; d. Zürich, Dec. 11, 1956. She studied with Hubay at the Royal Academy of Music in Budapest; toured in Europe and the U.S. at an early age. In 1919 she settled in Zürich and married the composer **Walter Schulthess.** She taught at the Zürich Cons. (1923–53). She was an object of passion on the part of Béla Bartók, who wrote a violin concerto for her (1907).

Ghedini, Giorgio Federico, Italian composer; b. Cuneo, July 11, 1892; d. Nervi, March 25, 1965. He studied piano and organ with Evasio Lovazzano, cello with S. Grossi, and composition with G. Cravero at the Turin Cons.; then at the Liceo Musicale in Bologna with M.E. Bossi, graduating in 1911. From 1918 to 1937, he was an instructor at the Turin Cons.;

taught composition at the Parma Cons. (1938–41) and in 1941 took a similar post at the Milan Cons., where he was later its director (1951–62).

WORKS: STAGE: OPERAS: *Gringoire* (1915); *Maria d'Alessandria* (Bergamo, Sept. 9, 1937); *Re Hassan* (Venice, Jan. 26, 1939); *La pulce d'oro* (Genoa, Feb. 15, 1940); *Le Baccanti* (Milan, Feb. 21, 1948); *Billy Budd* (after the Melville novel; Venice, Sept. 7, 1949); *Lord Inferno,* "harmonious comedy" for radio (after Beerbohm's *The Happy Hypocrite;* RAI, Oct. 22, 1952; rev. as *L'Ipocrita felice,* La Scala, Milan, March 10, 1956); *La Via della Croce* (Venice, April 9, 1961). **BALLET:** *Girotondo,* mime play for children (Venice, 1959). **ORCH.:** *Partita* (1926); *Concerto grosso* for Wind Quintet and Strings (1927); *Pezzo concertante* for 2 Violins, Viola obbligato, and Orch. (1931); *Marinaresca e baccanale* (1933; Rome, Feb. 2, 1936); Sym. (1938); *Architetture,* concerto for Orch. (1940; Rome, Jan. 19, 1941); *Invenzioni,* concerto for Cello, Strings, Kettledrums, and Cymbals (1940); Piano Concerto (1946); *Musica Notturna* for Chamber Orch. (1947); Concerto for 2 Pianos and Chamber Orch. (1947; Milan, Jan. 24, 1948); *Il Belprato,* concerto for Violin and Strings (1947); *Canzoni* (1948); *L'Alderina,* concerto for Flute, Violin, and Orch. (1951); *L'Olmeneta,* concerto for 2 Cellos and Orch. (1951); *Musica da concerto* for Viola and Strings (1953); *Concentus Basiliensis* for Violin and Chamber Orch. (1954); *Vocalizzo da concerto* for Cello or Baritone Voice, and Orch. (1957); *Composizione* (1958); *Fantasie* for Piano and Strings (1958); *Sonata da concerto* for Flute, Strings, and Percussion (1958); *Divertimento* for Violin and Orch. (1960); *Studi per un affresco di battaglia* (1962); *Contrappunti* for Violin, Viola, Cello, and Strings (1962); *Musica concertante* for Cello and Strings (1962); *Appunti per un credo* for Chamber Orch. (1962); *Concert Overture* (1963). **VOCAL:** *Il pianto della Madonna,* sacred cantata (1921); *Ecco il Re forte,* cantata (1923); *Litanie della Vergine* for Soprano, Women's Chorus, and Orch. (1926); *Le Messa del Venerdi santo* (Good Friday Mass), oratorio (1929; Perugia, Italy, Sept. 27, 1949); *Cantico del sole* for Men's Chorus and Strings (1932); *Antigone,* cantata (1933); *Lectio Libri Sapientiae,* spiritual cantata for Voice, Trumpet, Piano, and Strings (1938); *Concerto spirituale* for 2 Sopranos or Women's Chorus, and 9 Instruments or Chamber Orch. (1943); *Antifona per Luisa* for Soprano Chorus, Boy's Voice, and Organ or Strings (1944); *Concerto dell'Albatro* for Narrator and Small Orch. (Rome, Dec. 11, 1945); *Corona di Sacre Canzoni, o, Laudi Spirituali* for Voice, Chorus, Piano, and Strings (1946); *Concerto funebre per Duccio Galimberti* for Tenor, Bass, 2 Trombones, Strings, and Timpani (1948; Rome, June 8, 1949); *Il Rosero,* concerto for Women's Chorus, Piano, Harp, and Strings (1950); *Lectio Jeremiae prophetae,* cantata da camera for Soprano, Chorus, and Small Orch. (1960); *Credo di Perugia* for Chorus and Orch. (1962); masses and motets; songs. **CHAMBER:** Wind Quintet (1910); Piano Quartet (1917); Double Quartet for 5 Winds, 5 Strings, Harp, and Piano (1921); Violin Sonata (1922); Cello Sonata (1924); 2 string quartets (1927, 1959); *Adagio e allegro da Concerto* for Flute, Clarinet, Horn, Viola, Cello, and Harp (1936); *Concertato* for Flute, Viola, and Harp (1942); *7 Ricercari* for Piano Trio (1943); *Canons* for Violin and Cello (1946); *Concentus* for String Quartet (1948); *Music* for Flute, Cello, and Piano (1963). **PIANO:** *Pastorale elegiaca* (1926) and *Capriccio* (1934); also several orch. transcriptions for modern performance of works by Bach, Gabrieli, Monteverdi, Schütz, and Frescobaldi, most notably of Frescobaldi's *Quattro pezzi* (orig. for Organ) in 1931.

BIBL.: N. Castiglioni, *G.F. G* (Milan, 1955).

Gheluwe, Leon van, Belgian composer; b. Wanneghem-Lede, Sept. 15, 1837; d. Ghent, July 14, 1914. He studied in Ghent with Gevaert and others; became a prof. at the Ghent Cons. (1869–71), and later was director of the École de Musique in Bruges (1871–1900). He wrote a Flemish opera, *Philippine van Vlaanderen* (Brussels, 1876), and a number of songs.

Ghent, Emmanuel, American composer; b. Montreal, May 15, 1925. He studied bassoon and music theory at McGill Univ.; also took courses in psychology and psychoanalysis; eventually settled in N.Y. as a practicing psychiatrist. In 1964, with the aid of an engineer, he constructed the Polynome, a device capable of accurate reproduction of multiple rhythms by click signals transmitted to a performer's ear through a tiny earphone; he applied this instrument in several compositions.

WORKS: *Movement* for Wind Quintet (1944); *3 Duos* for Flutes (1944); *Lament* for String Quartet (1958); Quartet for Flute, Oboe, Clarinet, and Bassoon (1960); *2 Duos* for Flute and Clarinet (1962); *Dance Movement* for Trumpet and String Quartet (1962); *Entelechy* for Viola and Piano (1963); *Triality I* and *II* for Violin, Trumpet, and Bassoon, in conjunction with the Polynome (1964); *Dithyrambos* for Brass Quintet (1965); *Hex, an Ellipsis* for Trumpet, 11 Instruments, and Synchronized Tape (1966); *Helices* for Violin, Piano, and Tape (1969). Electronic compositions include *Lady Chatterley's Lover* (1969); *L'Après-midi d'un Summit Meeting* (1970); *Our Daily Bread* (1970); *12 Electronic Highlights* (1970).

Gheorghiu, Valentin, Rumanian composer; b. Galaţi, March 21, 1928. He studied composition with Jora and Andricu at the Bucharest Cons.; then studied piano with Lazare Lévy and harmony at the Paris Cons. (1937–39). His works include 2 syms. (1949; 1953, rev. 1974); a Piano Concerto (1959); *Imagini din copilărie* (Images of Youth), suite for Orch. (1961); *Burlesca* for Piano and Orch. (1964); String Quartet (1946); Piano Sonata (1946); Cello Sonata (1950); Piano Trio (1950); songs.

Gheyn, Matthias van den, Flemish organist and composer; b. Tirlemont, Brabant, April 7, 1721; d. Louvain, June 22, 1785. From 1741, he was organist at St. Peter's, Louvain, and from 1745, town "carillonneur"; he was celebrated in both capacities. He composed pieces for organ and for carillon.

WRITINGS: *Fondements de la basse continue* (lessons and sonatinas for organ and violin); *6 divertissements pour clavecin* (c.1760).

BIBL.: S. van Elewyck, *M. v.d.G.* (Louvain, 1862).

Ghezzo, Dinu, Rumanian-born American conductor and composer; b. Tuzla, July 2, 1941. He studied music at the Bucharest Cons., graduating in 1966; then went to the U.S., where he enrolled at the Univ. of Calif., Los Angeles (Ph.D., 1973). From 1974 to 1978 he was on the faculty of Queens College. In 1975 he organized in N.Y. the New Repertory Ensemble, for the purpose of presenting programs of new music. In 1977 he became an associate prof. at N.Y. Univ. His works are of a distinctly modern character, making use of electronic instruments.

WORKS: Clarinet Sonata (1967); String Quartet (1967); *Segmenti* for Clarinet, Cello, and Piano (1968); *Music* for Flutes and Tapes (1971); *Kanones* for Flutes, Cello, Harpsichord, and Tapes (1972); *Images* for Bass Flute, Divider, and Echoplex (1972); *Thalla* for Piano, Electric Piano, and 16 Instruments (1974); *Concertino* for Clarinet and Winds (1975); *Ritualen* for Prepared Piano (1969); *Ritualen II* for Prepared Piano and Tape (1970); *Cantos nuevos,* ballet (1977); *Sketches* for Clarinet and Chamber Orch. (1981); *From Here to . . . There,* 6 interrelated songs for 6 Players (1983); *Echoes of Brazil* for Prepared Piano (1984–85); *Dantesca,* a multimedia production for a Triple Trio (1985).

Ghiaurov, Nicolai, Bulgarian bass; b. Lydjene, near Velingrad, Sept. 13, 1929. He studied violin and piano at the Sofia Cons.; then went to Moscow, where he received his vocal training. He made his debut in Sofia as Don Basilio in *The Barber of Seville* in 1955; then appeared at La Scala in Milan (1959), London's Covent Garden (1962), the Vienna State Opera (1962), and the Chicago Lyric Opera (1964). He soon established himself as a fine singer; he sang Méphistophélès in *Faust* at his debut with the Metropolitan Opera in N.Y. (Nov. 8, 1965). In 1981 he married **Mirella Freni.**

Ghiglia, Oscar, Italian guitarist; b. Livorno, Aug. 13, 1938. He studied at the Accademia di Santa Cecilia in Rome; also took lessons with Segovia at the Accademia Chigiana in Siena. After winning a guitar competition in Paris, he received a scholarship to the Schola Cantorum, where he studied music history with Jacques Chailley. He made his American debut in N.Y. in 1966; subsequently toured in America and in Europe.

Ghignone, Giovanni Pietro. See **Guignon, Jean-Pierre.**

Ghis, Henri, French pianist and composer; b. Toulon, May 17, 1839; d. Paris, April 24, 1908. He studied at the Paris Cons. with Marmontel (piano); received 1st prize in 1854; also studied organ with Benoist; graduated in 1855. He became a fashionable piano teacher in Paris; many aristocratic ladies (to whom he dedicated his pieces) were his pupils. He was also the 1st teacher of Ravel. He publ. salon music for piano: waltzes, mazurkas, polonaises, polkas, gavottes, caprices, etc., often with superinduced titles, as *Séduction, Menuet de la petite princesse, La Marquisette*, etc.; but is mostly known for his popular arrangement of an early aria, which he publ. for piano as *Air Louis XIII* (1868); the actual melody was definitely not by Louis XIII; in all probability it is an old French folk song.

Ghiselin, Johannes, important Flemish composer who flourished in the late 15th and early 16th centuries. He also used the name Verbonnet as an alias. He was active at the court in Ferrara; was a singer at S. Giovanni in Florence (1492–93); later was a singer to the King of France in Paris. He returned to Ferrara in 1503, but fled to the Netherlands after an outbreak of the plague in 1505; was last reported in Bergen op Zoom in 1507. Petrucci publ. a vol. of Ghiselin's masses in 1503. His extant works include 9 masses, 13 motets, and secular vocal works. These compositions reveal him as a worthy contemporary of Josquin Desprez and Jacob Obrecht. A complete edition of his works was ed. by C. Gottwald in Corpus Mensurabilis Musicae, XXIII/1–4 (1961–68).
    BIBL.: C. Gottwald, *J. G.—Johannes Verbonnet: Stilkritische Untersuchung zum Problem ihrer Identität* (Wiesbaden, 1962); M. Staehelin, "Quellenkundliche Beiträge zum Werk von J. G.-Verbonnet," *Archiv für Musikwissenschaft*, XXIV (1967).

Ghisi, Federico, Italian musicologist and composer; b. Shanghai, China (of Italian parents), Feb. 25, 1901; d. Luzerna San Giovanni, July 18, 1975. His father was a member of the diplomatic corps in China; the family returned to Italy in 1908, and settled in Milan. Ghisi studied music with Ghedini at the Turin Cons.; in 1937, became instructor at the Univ. of Florence, leaving that position in 1940. He subsequently taught at the Università per Stranieri in Perugia (1945–74) and at the Univ. of Pisa (1963–70).
    WORKS: Operas: *Il dono dei Re Magi* (1959); *Il Vagabondo e la guardia* (1960); *L'ultima visione*, oratorio after Plato's *Republic* and Cicero (1967–72).
    WRITINGS: *I canti carnascialeschi* (Florence, 1937); *Le feste musicali della Firenze Medicea* (Florence, 1939); *Alle Fonti della Monodia* (Milan, 1940).

Ghislanzoni, Antonio, Italian writer and dramatic poet; b. Barco, near Lecco, Nov. 25, 1824; d. Caprino-Bergamasco, July 16, 1893. He was intended for the church, but his fine baritone voice led him to adopt the career of a stage singer (Lodi, 1846), which he speedily abandoned, however, for literary work. He became the manager of *Italia Musicale*, and was for years the ed. of the Milan *Gazzetta Musicale*, to which he remained a faithful contributor until his death. He wrote over 80 opera librettos, that of *Aida* being the most famous; publ. *Reminiscenze artistiche* (contains an episode entitled *La casa di Verdi a Sant' Agata*).
    BIBL.: T. Mantovani, "Librettisti Verdiani, VI: A. G.," *Musica d'Oggi* (March–April 1929).

Ghitalla, Armando, distinguished American trumpeter; b. Alfa, Ill., June 1, 1925. He studied at the Juilliard School of Music in N.Y. with William Vacchiano; in 1949 he joined the Houston Sym. Orch.; in 1951 he was engaged by the Boston Sym. Orch.; from 1965 to 1979 was its 1st trumpet.

Ghys, Joseph, Belgian violinist and composer; b. Ghent, 1801; d. St. Petersburg, Aug. 22, 1848. A pupil of Lafont at the Brussels Cons., he later taught in Amiens and Nantes, and, beginning in 1832, made concert tours in France, Belgium, Germany, Austria, and northern Europe. He wrote *Le Mouvement perpétuel* for Violin, with String Quartet; a Violin Concerto; and other music for the violin.

Giacomelli, Geminiano, Italian composer; b. Piacenza, c.1692; d. Loreto, Jan. 25, 1740. He studied with Capelli at Parma, and wrote his 1st opera, *Ipermestra*, in 1724. It was the 1st of 19 operas he wrote for Venice, Parma, Naples, and other Italian towns; the most popular was *Cesare in Egitto* (Milan, 1735). He was maestro di cappella at the court of Parma and the Chiesa della Steccata from 1719 to 1727; returned to both posts from 1732 to 1737; was maestro di cappella for the church of S. Giovanni in Piacenza from 1727 to 1732; he held a similar post at the Santa Casa in Loreto from 1738. His many church compositions include an oratorio, *La conversione di Santa Margherita*, and a setting of Psalm VIII for 2 Tenors and Bass.
    BIBL.: G. Tebaldini, *L'Archivio musicale della Cappella Lauretana* (Loreto, 1921); C. Anguisola, *G. G. e Sebastiano Nasolini, musicisti piacentini* (Piacenza, 1935).

Gialdini, Gialdino, Italian conductor and composer; b. Pescia, Nov. 10, 1843; d. there, March 6, 1919. He was a pupil of T. Mabellini in Florence. His 1st opera, *Rosamunda* (prize opera in a competition instituted by the Pergola Theater, Florence), given in 1868, was unsuccessful; after producing 2 "opere buffe," *La Secchia rapita* (Florence, 1872) and *L'Idolo cinese* (1874), in collaboration with other musicians, he devoted himself to conducting. Later he again turned to dramatic composition, producing the operas *I due soci* (Bologna, Feb. 24, 1892), *La Pupilla* (Trieste, Oct. 23, 1896), and *La Bufera* (Pola, Nov. 26, 1910). He also publ. *Eco della Lombardia*, a collection of 50 folk songs.

Gianettini (or **Zanettini**), **Antonio,** Italian organist and composer; b. Fano, 1648; d. Munich, July 12, 1721. He was organist at S. Marco, Venice (1677–86); produced 3 operas in Venice, winning a reputation that led to his appointment as maestro di cappella at the court of Modena; was organist at Modena from 1686 to 1721, except during 1695, when he brought out 3 operas in Hamburg. He moved to Munich with his family in 1721. He composed operas; 9 oratorios; several cantatas; a Kyrie *a* 5; and Psalms *a* 4, with Instruments (Venice, 1717).
    BIBL.: E. Luin, *A. G. e la musica a Modena alla fine del secolo 17* (Modena, 1931).

Gianneo, Luis, Argentine composer; b. Buenos Aires, Jan. 9, 1897; d. there, Aug. 15, 1968. He studied composition with Gaito and Fornarini. From 1923 to 1943 he taught at the Inst. Musical in Tucumán; then was a prof. of music at various schools in Buenos Aires. He was especially interested in the problems of musical education of the very young; in 1945 he organized and conducted the Orquesta Sinfónica Juvenil Argentina; from 1955 to 1960 he was director of the Buenos Aires Cons.
    WORKS: Ballet, *Blanca nieves* (1939); 3 syms. (1938, 1945, 1963); *Turay-Turay*, symphonic poem (Buenos Aires, Sept. 21, 1929); *Obertura para una comedia infantil* (1939); Piano Concerto (1941); Sinfonietta (Buenos Aires, Sept. 20, 1943); Violin Concerto (Buenos Aires, April 13, 1944); *Cantica Dianae* for Chorus and Orch. (1949); *Variaciones sobre tema de tango* for Orch. (1953); *Angor Dei* for Soprano and Orch. (1962); *Poema de la Saeta* for Soprano and Orch. (1966); 4 string quartets (1936, 1944, 1952, 1958); 2 piano trios; String Trio; Violin Sonata; Cello Sonata; teaching pieces for piano; 3 Piano Sonatas (1917, 1943, 1957); songs.

Giannetti, Giovanni, Italian composer; b. Naples, March 25, 1869; d. Rio de Janeiro, Dec. 10, 1934. He studied in Naples, Trieste, and Vienna; in 1912–13, was director of the Liceo Musicale, Siena; in 1915, was in Rome, where (from 1920) he was music director of the Teatro dei Piccoli, with which he toured Europe and South America.

Works: Operas: *L'Erebo* (Naples, April 9, 1891); *Padron Maurizio* (Naples, Sept. 26, 1896); *Milena* (Naples, Nov. 15, 1897); *Il Violinaro di Cremona* (Milan, Nov. 23, 1898); *Don Marzio* (Venice, March 2, 1903); *Il Cristo alla festa di Purim* (Rio de Janeiro, Dec. 16, 1904); *Il Nazareno* (Buenos Aires, Jan. 20, 1911); *La Serenata di Pierrot,* pantomime (Rome, April 18, 1917); *Cuore e beutte* (Rome, June 5, 1918); *Il Principe Re,* operetta (Rome, July 7, 1920).

Giannini, Dusolina, American soprano, daughter of **Ferruccio** and sister of **Vittorio Giannini;** b. Philadelphia, Dec. 19, 1900; d. Zürich, June 26, 1986. She received her early musical training at home, then studied voice with Sembrich in N.Y., where she made her concert debut on March 14, 1920. She made her operatic debut as Aida with the Hamburg Opera on Sept. 12, 1925, then sang in Berlin, Vienna, and London. She made her Metropolitan Opera debut in N.Y. as Aida on Feb. 12, 1936, and remained on its roster until 1941; she also appeared with other American opera houses. She sang again in Europe (1947–50), then taught voice. She created the role of Hester in her brother's *The Scarlet Letter* (Hamburg, June 2, 1938).

Giannini, Ferruccio, Italian-American tenor, father of **Dusolina** and **Vittorio Giannini;** b. Ponte d'Arnia, Nov. 15, 1868; d. Philadelphia, Sept. 17, 1948. He emigrated to the U.S. in 1885; studied with Eleodoro De Campi in Detroit. He made his debut in Boston in 1891, then toured the U.S. with the Mapleson Opera Co. (1892–94); made the 1st operatic recordings, which were issued by Emile Berliner in 1896. He later settled in Philadelphia, where he presented operas, concerts, and plays in his own theater.

Giannini, Vittorio, American composer, son of **Ferruccio** and brother of **Dusolina Giannini;** b. Philadelphia, Oct. 19, 1903; d. N.Y., Nov. 28, 1966. Brought up in a musical family, he showed a precocious talent. He was sent to Italy at the age of 10, and studied at the Cons. of Milan (1913–17). After returning to the U.S., he took private lessons with Martini and Trucco in N.Y.; in 1925 he entered the Juilliard graduate school, where he was a pupil of Rubin Goldmark in composition and Hans Letz in violin; in 1932 he won the American Prix de Rome; was in Rome for a period of 4 years. Upon his return to N.Y., he was appointed to the faculty of the Juilliard School of Music in 1939 as a teacher of composition and orchestration; in 1941 he also became an instructor in music theory; furthermore, he was appointed prof. of composition at the Curtis Inst. of Music in Philadelphia in 1956. As a composer, Giannini was at his best in opera, writing music of fine emotional éclat, excelling in the art of bel canto and avoiding extreme modernistic usages; in his symphonic works he also continued the rich Italian tradition; these qualities endeared him to opera singers, but at the same time left his music out of the mainstream of contemporary music making.

Works: operas: *Lucedia* (Munich, Oct. 20, 1934); *Flora* (1937); *The Scarlet Letter* (Hamburg, June 2, 1938); *Beauty and the Beast* (1938; concert version, CBS Radio, Nov. 24, 1938; stage premiere, Hartford, Conn., Feb. 14, 1946); *Blennerhasset,* radio opera (CBS Radio, Nov. 22, 1939); *The Taming of the Shrew* (his most appreciated opera; in concert form, Cincinnati Sym. Orch., Jan. 31, 1953; in color telecast, NBC opera theater, March 13, 1954); *The Harvest* (Chicago, Nov. 25, 1961); *Rehearsal Call,* opera buffa (N.Y., Feb. 15, 1962); *The Servant of 2 Masters* (posthumous, N.Y., March 9, 1967). **orch.:** Sym., subtitled "In Memoriam Theodore Roosevelt" (1935; N.Y., NBC Orch., Jan. 19, 1936, composer conducting); *I.B.M. Sym.,* commissioned for the N.Y. World's Fair (1939); 4 numbered syms.: No. 1, *Sinfonia* (Cincinnati, April 6, 1951); No. 2 (St. Louis, April 16, 1956); No. 3 for Band (1958); No. 4 (N.Y., May 26, 1960); 3 divertimentos (1953, 1961, 1964); *Psalm 130,* concerto for Double Bass and Orch. (Brevard, N.C., Aug. 9, 1963); *The Medead,* monodrama for Soprano and Orch. (Atlanta, Ga., Oct. 20, 1960); Piano Concerto (1937); Organ Concerto (1937); Concerto for 2 Pianos (1940); several sacred works for chorus; *Canticle of the Martyrs* (commissioned for

the 500th anniversary of the Moravian Church, 1957, at Winston-Salem, N.C.); Concerto Grosso for Strings (1931); Piano Quintet (1931); Woodwind Quintet (1933); Piano Trio (1933); 2 violin sonatas (1926, 1945); Piano Sonata; many songs.

Giarda, Luigi Stefano, Italian cellist and composer; b. Pavia, March 19, 1868; d. Viña del Mar, Chile, Jan. 3, 1953. He was a pupil at the Milan Cons.; a teacher at the Padua music school (1893–97); an instructor at the Royal Cons. in Naples (1897–1910); then went to Santiago, Chile, where he was vice-director of the Cons.; also taught theory there.

Works: Operas: *Reietto* (Naples, 1898) and *Giorgio Byron* (Santiago, Chile, 1910); symphonic poems: *Loreley; La vida; Triptico* (*Civilization, War, Peace*) for 3 Voices and Orch.; concert pieces for Cello and Orch.; a String Quartet; *Adagio* for 4 Cellos; 2 cello sonatas; Prelude and Scherzo for Violin and Cello.

Giardini, Felice de', Italian violinist and composer; b. Turin, April 12, 1716; d. Moscow, June 8, 1796. He was a chorister at the Cathedral of Milan; studied singing and harpsichord with Paladini and violin with Somis in Turin. As a young man he played in various theater orchs. in Rome and Naples; often improvised cadenzas at the end of operatic numbers. He acquired popularity in Italy and made a tour in Germany (1748); then went to London (1750), where he made a series of successful appearances as a concert violinist. In 1752 he joined the Italian opera in London as concertmaster; became its impresario in 1755, and was connected with the management, with interruptions, for some 40 years. He was concertmaster at the Pantheon Concerts (1774–80). From 1784 to 1789 he was in Italy; returned to London in 1790 and led 3 seasons of Italian opera. In 1796 he was engaged as a violinist in Russia and gave his initial concert in Moscow, on March 24, 1796, but soon became ill, and died shortly afterward. As a violinist, he was eclipsed in London by Salomon and Cramer, but he left his mark on musical society there. Among operas entirely by him were *Rosmira* (April 30, 1757), *Siroe* (Dec. 13, 1763), *Enea e Lavinia* (May 5, 1764), and *Il Re pastore* (March 7, 1765); he also wrote music for various pasticcios; also wrote several overtures, concertos, string quartets, and violin sonatas.

Bibl.: R. Mooser, *Annales de la musique et des musiciens en Russie au XVIIIᵉ siècle* (vol. II, Lausanne, 1950); S. McVeigh, *The Violinist in London's Concert Life, 1750–1784; F. G. and His Contemporaries* (diss., Oxford Univ., 1980).

Giazotto, Remo, Italian musicologist; b. Rome, Sept. 4, 1910. He studied piano at the Milan Cons., and later took courses in literature at the Univ. of Genoa; was on the staff of the *Rivista Musicale Italiana* from 1932 to 1949; from 1967, was co-ed. of *Nuova Rivista Musicale Italiana;* from 1957, a prof. at the Univ. of Florence. He undertook a detailed study of the musical history of Genoa, and publ. a work of fundamental value, *La musica a Genova nella vita pubblica e privata dal XIII al XVIII secolo* (Genoa, 1952). He is also the author of a biography of Tomaso Albinoni (Milan, 1945), containing newly discovered materials as well as a thematic catalogue. He further publ. a monograph, *Ferruccio Busoni, La vita nell'opera* (Milan, 1948), and biographies on Giovanni Battista Viotti (Milan, 1956) and Vivaldi (Milan, 1965).

Gibbons, Christopher, English organist and composer, son of **Orlando Gibbons;** b. London (baptized), Aug. 22, 1615; d. there, Oct. 20, 1676. He was a pupil at the Chapel Royal; from 1638 to 1642 he was organist at Winchester Cathedral; in 1660 was appointed organist of the Chapel Royal, private organist to Charles II, and organist at Westminster Abbey. He received the degree of Mus.D. from Oxford in 1664, at the special request of the King. He wrote verse anthems, motets, and many string fantasies. He also collaborated with M. Locke in the music for Shirley's masque *Cupid & Death.* C. Rayner prepared the modern ed. *Christopher Gibbons: Keyboard Compositions,* in Corpus of Early Keyboard Music, XVIII (1967).

Bibl.: C. Rayner, *A Little-known 17th-century Composer, C. G.* (diss., Indiana Univ., 1963).

Gibbons, Edward, English composer, brother of **Ellis** and **Orlando Gibbons;** b. Cambridge, 1568; d. probably in Exeter, c.1650. He received a B.Mus. degree from both Oxford and Cambridge; after serving as a lay clerk at King's College, Cambridge, he became master of choristers in 1593, and kept the post until 1598; then he went to the Exeter Cathedral, where he served for many years, with the titles of "priest-vicar" and succentor, though he remained a layman. Little of his music is extant.

Gibbons, Ellis, English composer and organist, brother of **Edward** and **Orlando Gibbons;** b. Cambridge, 1573; d. May 1603. The only compositions of his which are known to exist are 2 madrigals included by Morley in his collection *The Triumphes of Oriana* (London, 1601): *Long live fair Oriana* and *Round about her charret.*

Gibbons, Orlando, celebrated English composer and organist, father of **Christopher** and brother of **Edward** and **Ellis Gibbons;** b. Oxford (baptized), Dec. 25, 1583; d. Canterbury, June 5, 1625. He was taken to Cambridge as a small child; in 1596 he became chorister at King's College there; matriculated in 1598; composed music for various occasions for King's College (1602–3). In 1605 he was appointed organist of the Chapel Royal, retaining this position until his death. He received the degree of B.Mus. from Cambridge Univ. in 1606, and that of D.Mus. from Oxford in 1622. In 1619 he became chamber musician to the King; in 1623, organist at Westminster Abbey. He conducted the music for the funeral of James I (1625); died of apoplexy 2 months later. His fame as a composer rests chiefly on his church music; he employed the novel technique of the "verse anthem" (a work for chorus and solo voices, the solo passages having independent instrumental accompaniment, for either organ or strings); other works followed the traditional polyphonic style, of which he became a master. He was also one of the greatest English organists of the time. **WORKS:** *Fantasies of 3 Parts . . . composed for viols* (1610); pieces for the virginal, in *Parthenia* (1611); *The First Set of Madrigals and Mottets of 5 Parts* (1612); 9 Fancies, appended to *20 konincklijke Fantasien op 3 Fiolen* by T. Lupo, Coperario, and W. Daman (Amsterdam, 1648). His madrigals and motets were ed. by E.H. Fellowes in The English Madrigal School, V (1921; 2nd ed., rev., 1964 by T. Dart), his services and anthems by P. Buck and others in Tudor Church Music, IV (1925), his keyboard music by G. Hendrie in Musica Britannica, XX (1962), and his verse anthems by D. Wulstan in Early English Church Music, III (1964). **BIBL.:** E.H. Fellowes, *The English Madrigal Composers* (1921; 2nd ed., 1948); M. Glyn, *About Elizabethan Virginal Music and Its Composers* (1924); E.H. Fellowes, *O. G., A Short Account of His Life and Work* (1925; 2nd ed., 1951, as *O. G. and His Family*); G. Hendrie, "The Keyboard Music of O. G.," *Proceedings of the Royal Musical Association,* LXXXIX (1962–63).

Gibbs, Cecil Armstrong, English composer; b. Great Braddow, near Chelmsford, Aug. 10, 1889; d. Chelmsford, May 12, 1960. He studied at Trinity College, Cambridge (B.A., 1911; Mus.B., 1913); took courses in composition with Charles Wood and Vaughan Williams and conducting with Boult at the Royal College of Music in London, where he also taught (1921–39). In 1934 he received the Cobbett Gold Medal for his services to British chamber music. His style adhered to the Romantic school; he was best known for his songs, many to texts by Walter De la Mare. **WORKS: STAGE:** *The Blue Peter,* comic opera (London, 1923); *The Sting of Love,* comic opera (1926); *When One Isn't There,* operetta (1927); *Twelfth Night,* opera (1946–47); *The Great Bell of Burley,* children's opera (1952); also incidental music. **ORCH.:** 3 syms.; Oboe Concerto; *Essex Suite* for String Quartet and Strings; *The Enchanted Wood,* dance phantasy for Piano and Strings (1919); *Fancy Dress,* dance suite (1935); *A Spring Garland,* suite for Strings (1937); Concertino for Piano and Strings (1942); *Prelude, Andante, and Finale* for Strings (1946);

Dale and Fell, suite for Strings (1954); *A Simple Concerto* for Piano and Strings (1955); *Threnody for Walter De la Mare* for String Quartet and Strings (1956); *A Simple Suite* for Strings (1957); Suite for Strings (1958–59); *Shade and Shine,* suite for Strings (1958); *Suite of Songs from the British Isles* (1959); 4 Orch. Dances (1959). **CHORAL:** *La Belle Dame sans merci* for Chorus and Orch. (1928); *The Birth of Christ* for Soloists, Chorus, and Orch. (1929); *The Highwayman* for Chorus and Orch. (1932); *The Ballad of Gil Morrice* for Chorus and Orch. (1934); *Deborah and Barak* for Soloists, Chorus, and Orch. (1936); *Odysseus* for Soloists, Chorus, and Orch. (1937–38); *The Passion According to St. Luke* for Chorus and Organ (1945); *Pastoral Suite* for Baritone, Chorus, and Orch. (1948–49); also anthems, motets, Psalms, part-songs, carols, and about 150 songs. **CHAMBER:** 11 string quartets; 2 sonatas for Cello and Piano; *Country Magic,* piano trio (1922); *Lyric Sonata* for Violin and Piano (1928); Piano Trio (1940); Suite for Violin and Piano (1943); also a number of piano pieces. **BIBL.:** D. Brown, "A. G. and His 'Odysseus' Symphony," *Music and Musicians International* (Oct. 1987); idem, "A Paradoxical Figure: A. G. (1889–1960)," ibid. (Aug. 1989).

Gibbs, Terry (real name, **Julius Gubenko**), American jazz percussionist and bandleader; b. N.Y., Oct. 13, 1924. He began to play the drums and timpani in his youth; won a Major Bowes contest at the age of 12; later played with Tommy Dorsey, Buddy Rich, Woody Herman, Benny Goodman, and other musicians; also was successful as a bandleader.

Gibson, Sir Alexander (Drummond), distinguished Scottish conductor; b. Motherwell, Feb. 11, 1926. He was educated at the Univ. of Glasgow and the Royal College of Music in London; also took courses at the Salzburg Mozarteum and in Siena. He made his debut as conductor at the Sadler's Wells Opera in London in 1952; was subsequently associate conductor of the BBC Scottish Sym. Orch. in Glasgow (1952–54). From 1959 to 1984 he was principal conductor of the Scottish National Orch. in Glasgow. In 1962 he founded that city's Scottish Opera, becoming its 1st music director and serving until 1987. In 1977 Queen Elizabeth II knighted him for his services in behalf of the musical life of his native Scotland and Great Britain. From 1981 to 1983 he was principal guest conductor of the Houston Sym. Orch. He is mainly renowned for his congenial performances of the works of Romantic composers, particularly those of the English school.

Gideon, Miriam, American composer and teacher; b. Greeley, Colo., Oct. 23, 1906. She studied piano with Hans Barth in N.Y. and with Felix Fox in Boston; then enrolled at Boston Univ. (B.A., 1926) and took courses in musicology at Columbia Univ. (M.A., 1946); studied composition privately with Lazare Saminsky and Roger Sessions. She served on the music faculty of Brooklyn College (1944–54); in 1955 became a prof. of music at the Jewish Theological Center; in 1967 joined the faculty at the Manhattan School of Music; was a prof. of music at the City Univ. of N.Y. (1971–76); was elected to the American Academy and Inst. of Arts and Letters in 1975, and in 1986 was honored with a special concert in N.Y. on her 80th birthday. She wrote music in all genres, in a style distinguished by its attractive modernism. **WORKS:** Opera, *Fortunato* (1958). **ORCH.:** *Lyric Piece* for String Orch. (1941); *Symphonia brevis* (2 *Movements for Orchestra*) (N.Y., May 16, 1953); *Songs of Youth and Madness* for Voice and Orch. on poems of Friedrich Hölderlin (N.Y., Dec. 5, 1977). **CHAMBER:** String Quartet (1946); Viola Sonata (1948); *Fantasy on a Javanese Motive* for Cello and Piano (1948); Divertimento for Woodwind Quartet (1948); *Biblical Masks* for Violin and Piano or Organ Solo (1960); Suite for Clarinet or Bassoon, and Piano (1972); *Fantasy on Irish Folk Motives* for Oboe, Viola, Bassoon, and Vibraphone (1975). **CHORAL:** *Sonnets from "Fatal Interview,"* after Edna St. Vincent Millay, for Voice, Violin, Viola, and Cello (1952); *The Condemned Playground* for Soprano and Instruments (1963); *Questions on Nature* for Voice, Oboe, Piano, Tam-tam, and Glockenspiel (1964); *Rhymes from the Hill*, after the *Galgenlieder* of Christian Morgenstern, for Voice, Clarinet, Cello, and Marimba (1966); *The Seasons of Time*, after Japanese poetry, for Voice, Flute, Cello, and Piano (1969); *Nocturnes* for Voice, Flute, Oboe, Violin, Cello, and Vibraphone (1976); *Where Wild Carnations Blow—A Song to David* for Solo Voices, Chorus, and Instrumental Ensemble (1984); also individual songs.

Giebel (Kanders), Agnes, Dutch soprano of German descent; b. Heerlen, Aug. 10, 1921. She was educated at the Folkwangschule in Essen; began a career as a concert singer in 1947. She gained wide recognition for her radio broadcasts of the Bach cantatas over the RIAS in Berlin in 1950. At a later period she promoted modern music; her performances of works by Schoenberg, Alban Berg, Hindemith, and Henze were praised by informed critics. She made several tours as a concert artist in the U.S.

Gieburowski, Waclaw, eminent Polish musicologist; b. Bydgoszcz, Feb. 6, 1876; d. Warsaw, Sept. 17, 1943. He was a student of theology in Regensburg, where he also took courses in church music with Haberl; then studied in Berlin with Wolf and Kretzschmar and in Breslau with Otto Kinkeldey; obtained a doctorate from the Univ. of Breslau with the dissertation *Die Musica Magistri Szydlowitae, Ein polnischer Choraltraktat des 15. Jahrhunderts und seine Stellung in der Choraltheorie des Mittelalters* (1913; publ. Posen, 1915). He settled in Posen; was a prof. of church music at the Univ. (1925–39); in 1916 was appointed choir conductor at the Posen Cathedral; wrote church music. From 1928 to 1939 he publ. the valuable series Cantica Selecta Musices Sacrae in Polonia; restored to use many sacred works by Polish composers of the Renaissance; publ. several treatises on this subject; also composed several sacred choral works.

Giegling, Franz, Swiss musicologist; b. Buchs, near Aarau, Feb. 27, 1921. He studied piano and theory at the Zürich Cons. with Cherbuliez; received his Ph.D. from the Univ. of Zürich in 1947 with the valuable dissertation *Giuseppe Torelli, Ein Beitrag zur Entwicklungsgeschichte des italienischen Konzerts* (publ. in Kassel, 1949); was music critic of the *Neue Zürcher Zeitung* (1947–53); subsequently worked for Radio Zürich and Radio Basel; was one of the eds. of the 6th edition of the Köchel catalogue of Mozart's works; contributed articles to *Die Musik in Geschichte und Gegenwart.*

Gielen, Michael (Andreas), noted German conductor; b. Dresden, July 20, 1927. His father, Josef Gielen, was an opera director who settled in Buenos Aires in 1939; his uncle was **Eduard Steuermann.** Gielen studied piano and composition with Erwin Leuchter in Buenos Aires (1942–49); was on the staff of the Teatro Colón there (1947–50), then continued his training with Polnauer in Vienna (1950–53). In 1951 he became a répétiteur at the Vienna State Opera, and later was its resident conductor (1954–60). He was principal conductor of the Royal Opera in Stockholm (1960–65), a regular conductor with the Cologne Radio Sym. Orch. (1965–69), and chief conductor of the Orch. National de Belgique in Brussels (1968–73) and the Netherlands Opera in Amsterdam (1973–75). From 1977 to 1987 he was artistic director of the Frankfurt Opera and chief conductor of its Museumgesellschaft concerts; also was chief guest conductor of the BBC Sym. Orch. in London (1979–82) and music director of the Cincinnati Sym. Orch. (1980–86). In 1986 he became chief conductor of the South-West Radio Sym. Orch. in Baden-Baden; he also was a prof. of conducting at the Salzburg Mozarteum (from 1987). Gielen has acquired a fine reputation as an interpreter of contemporary music; he has also composed a number of works of his own, including a Violin Sonata (1946); a Trio for Clarinet, Viola, and Bassoon (1948); *Variations* for String Quartet (1949); *Variations* for 40 Instruments (1959); *Pentaphonie* for Piano, 5 Soloists, and 5 Quintets (1960–63); a String Quartet (1983); and *Pflicht und Neigung* for 22 Players (1988).

Gieseking, Walter (Wilhelm), distinguished German pianist; b. Lyons, France (of German parents), Nov. 5, 1895; d. London, Oct. 26, 1956. He studied with Karl Leimer at the Hannover Cons., graduating in 1916; then served in the German army during World War I; began his concert career with extensive tours of Europe; made his American debut at Aeolian Hall, N.Y., Feb. 22, 1926, and after that appeared regularly in the U.S. and Europe with orchs. and in solo recitals. He became the center of a political controversy when he arrived in the U.S. in 1949 for a concert tour; he was accused of cultural collaboration with the Nazi regime, and public protests forced the cancellation of his scheduled performances at Carnegie Hall. However, he was later cleared by an Allied court in Germany and was able to resume his career in America. He appeared again at a Carnegie Hall recital on April 22, 1953, and until his death continued to give numerous performances in both hemispheres. He was one of the most extraordinary pianists of his time. A superb musician capable of profound interpretations of both Classical and modern scores, his dual German-French background enabled him to project with the utmost authenticity the masterpieces of both cultures. He particularly excelled in the music of Mozart, Beethoven, Schubert, and Brahms; his playing of Debussy and Ravel was also remarkable; he was also an excellent performer of works by Prokofiev and other modernists. He composed some chamber music and made piano transcriptions of songs by Richard Strauss. His autobiography, *So Wurde ich Pianist*, was publ. posth. in Wiesbaden (1963).

BIBL.: B. Gavoty, *G.* (Geneva, 1955).

Gigli, Beniamino, celebrated Italian tenor; b. Recanati, March 20, 1890; d. Rome, Nov. 30, 1957. He was a chorister at Recanati Cathedral; commenced serious vocal studies with Agnese Bonucci in Rome, and continued his training with Cotogni and Rosati as a scholarship student at the Liceo Musicale there; after winning 1st prize in the Parma competition in 1914, he made his operatic debut as Enzo in *La Gioconda* in Rovigo on Oct. 14, 1914; subsequently sang in various Italian theaters, including Milan's La Scala in 1918 as Boito's Faust, a role he repeated in his Metropolitan Opera debut in N.Y. on Nov. 16, 1920. He remained on the Metropolitan roster as one of its leading singers until 1932, then returned for the 1938–39 season. He made his Covent Garden debut in London as Andrea Chénier on May 27, 1930; sang there again in 1931, 1938, and 1946. He spent the years during World War II in Italy; then resumed his operatic appearances, making his farewell to the stage in 1953; however, he continued to give concerts, making a final, impressive tour of the U.S. in 1955. Gigli's voice, with its great beauty and expressivity, made him one of the foremost tenors of his era; he was famous for such roles as the Duke of Mantua, Nemorino, Lionel, Des Grieux, Nadir, and Gounod's Faust, as well as for the leading roles in Puccini's operas. His memoirs were publ. in an Eng. tr. in London in 1957.

BIBL.: R. Rosner, *B. G.* (Vienna, 1929); D. Silvestrini, *B. G.* (Bologna, 1937); R. Gigli, *B. G. mio padre: A cura di Celso Minestroni* (Parma, 1986).

Gigout, Eugène, esteemed French organist, pedagogue, and composer; b. Nancy, March 23, 1844; d. Paris, Dec. 9, 1925. He began music studies in the *maîtrise* of Nancy Cathedral; at 13 he entered the Niedermeyer School at Paris, in which he subsequently taught (1863–85 and 1900–1905); for a time, was a pupil of Saint-Saëns. From 1863, Gigout was organist at the church of St.-Augustin; he won fame as a concert organist in France, England, Germany, Switzerland, Spain, and Italy; he was especially famous for his masterly improvisations. In 1885 he founded at Paris an organ school subsidized by the government, from which many excellent pupils graduated (Boëllmann, Fauré, Messager, A. Georges, A. Roussel, C. Terrasse, etc.); from 1911, he was a prof. of organ and improvisation at the National Cons., Paris. He was also an esteemed writer on music and a critic; he was a Commander of the Order of Isabella la Católica; Officer of Public Instruction (from 1885); and Chevalier of the Legion of Honor (from 1895).

WORKS: ORGAN: *100 pièces brèves* (Gregorian); *Album grégo-*

rien (3 vols., each containing 100 pieces in the church modes); many secular pieces for organ; also sacred choruses; songs.

BIBL.: G. Fauré, *Hommage à E. G.* (Paris, 1923).

Gil-Marchex, Henri, French pianist; b. St. Georges d'Espérance (Isère), Dec. 16, 1894; d. Paris, Nov. 22, 1970. He studied at the Paris Cons., then with L. Capet and A. Cortot; toured Europe, Russia, and Japan, and performed modern works at various festivals in Europe. From 1956 he was director of the Cons. at Poitiers.

Gilardi, Gilardo, Argentine composer; b. San Fernando, May 25, 1889; d. Buenos Aires, Jan. 16, 1963. He studied with Pablo Berutti, then devoted himself to teaching and composing. Two of his operas were produced at the Teatro Colón in Buenos Aires: *Ilse* (July 13, 1923) and *La leyenda de Urutaú* (Oct. 25, 1934). He also wrote *Sinfonia cíclico* (1961), 3 piano trios, 2 string quartets, *Sonata Popular Argentina* for Violin and Piano (1939), and many dances and songs based on native melodies.

Gilbert, Anthony (John), English composer and teacher; b. London, July 26, 1934. He studied composition with Anthony Milner, Alexander Goehr, and Mátyás Seiber in London both privately and at Morley College (1958–63); studied conducting at Morley with Norman Del Mar (1967–69); also received training in composition from Luigi Nono and Luciano Berio at the Dartington Summer School (1961, 1962) and from Gunther Schuller, Seymour Shifrin, Elliott Carter, and Roger Sessions at the Berkshire Music Center in Tanglewood (summer 1967); studied piano with Denis Holloway at London's Trinity College of Music; completed his training at the Univ. of Leeds (M.A., 1984; Mus.D., 1990). He taught at Goldsmiths' College, Univ. of London (1968–73); served as composer-in-residence (1970–71) and visiting lecturer (1971–72) at the Univ. of Lancaster; then taught at Morley College (1971–74). In 1973 he joined the faculty of the Royal Northern College of Music in Manchester; in 1978–79 he also was senior lecturer in composition at the New South Wales State Conservatorium of Music in Sydney, and in 1981 was composer-in-the-community of Bendigo, Australia. A modernist by nature, he nevertheless writes music in Classical forms and is not averse to representational music; on the purely structural side, he adopts various attenuated forms of serial music, and in thematic development uses disparate agglutinative blocks.

WORKS: OPERAS: *The Scene Machine* (1970; Kassel, April 1, 1971); *The Chakravaka-bird,* radio opera (1977; BBC, Jan. 1982). **ORCH.:** *Sinfonia* for Chamber Orch. (London, March 30, 1965); *Regions* for 2 Orchs. (1966); *Peal II* for Big Band (1968); Sym. (Cheltenham, July 12, 1973); *Ghost and Dream Dancing* (Birmingham, Sept. 19, 1974); *Crow-cry* for Chamber Orch. (1976; London, March 16, 1977); *Welkin* for Student Orch. (1976); *Towards Asavari* for Piano and Chamber Orch. (1978; Manchester, Jan. 26, 1979); *Koonapippi* for Youth Orch. (1981); *Dream Carousels* for Wind Band (1988; London, Feb. 26, 1989). **CHAMBER:** 2 piano sonatas (1962, 1966); *Brighton Piece* for Clarinet, Horn, Trumpet, Trombone, Cello, and 3 Percussion (1967); *Spell Respell* for Electric Bassett Clarinet and Piano (1968); *O'Grady Music* for Clarinet, Cello, and Toy Instruments (1971); *String Quartet with Piano Pieces* (1972); *Canticle I: Rock-song* for 2 Clarinets, Bass Clarinet, 2 Horns, 2 Trumpets, and Trombone (1973); *Vasanta with Dancing* for Flute or Alto Flute, Oboe or English Horn, Violin, Viola, Harp, Percussion, and Optional Dancer (1981); *Quartet of Beasts* for Flute, Oboe, Bassoon, and Piano (1984); *6 of the Bestiary* for Saxophone Quartet (1985); *Fanfarings* for 6 and 8 Brass Instruments (1986); String Quartet II (1987) and III (1987); other chamber works. **VOCAL:** *Love Poems* for Soprano, Clarinet, Cello, Accordion or Soprano, Bass Clarinet, and Chamber Organ (1970); *Inscapes* for Soprano, Speaker, and Small Ensemble (1975); *Chant of Cockeye Bob* for Children's Voices and Instruments (1981); *Beastly Jingles* for Soprano and Instrumental Ensemble (1984); *Certain Lights Reflecting* for Soprano and Orch. (Cheltenham, July 14, 1989); also choruses.

Gilbert, Henry F(ranklin Belknap), remarkable American composer; b. Somerville, Mass., Sept. 26, 1868; d. Cambridge, Mass., May 19, 1928. He studied at the New England Cons. and with E. Mollenhauer; from 1889 to 1892, was a pupil of MacDowell (composition) in Boston. Rather than do routine music work to earn his livelihood (he had previously been a violinist in theaters, etc.), he took jobs of many descriptions, becoming, in turn, a real estate agent, a factory foreman, a collector of butterflies in Florida, etc., and composed when opportunity afforded. In 1893, at the Chicago World's Fair, he met a Russian prince who knew Rimsky-Korsakov and gave him many details of contemporary Russian composers whose work, as well as that of Bohemian and Scandinavian composers which was based on folk song, influenced Gilbert greatly in his later composition. In 1894 he made his 1st trip abroad and stayed in Paris, subsequently returning to the U.S.; when he heard of the premiere of Charpentier's *Louise,* he became intensely interested in the work because of its popular character, and, in order to hear it, earned his passage to Paris, in 1901, by working on a cattle boat; the opera impressed him so much that he decided to devote his entire time thereafter to composition. In 1902 he became associated with Arthur Farwell, whose Wa-Wan Press publ. Gilbert's early compositions. From 1903 he employed Negro tunes and rhythms extensively in his works. The compositions of his mature period (from 1915) reveal an original style, not founded on any particular native American material but infused with elements from many sources, and are an attempt at "un-European" music, expressing the spirit of America and its national characteristics.

WORKS: OPERA: *The Fantasy in Delft* (1915). **ORCH.:** 2 *Episodes* (Boston, Jan. 13, 1896); *Humoresque on Negro-Minstrel Tunes* (orig. entitled *Americanesque,* 1903; Boston Pops, May 24, 1911); *Comedy Overture on Negro Themes* (1905; N.Y., Aug. 17, 1910); symphonic poem, *The Dance in Place Congo* (1906; perf. as a ballet at the Metropolitan Opera, N.Y., March 23, 1918); *Strife* (1910); *Negro Rhapsody* (Norfolk [Conn.] Festival, June 5, 1913, composer conducting); symphonic prologue for Synge's *Riders to the Sea* (1904; MacDowell Festival, Peterboro, N.H., Aug. 20, 1914; rev. version, N.Y. Phil., Nov. 11, 1917); *American Dances* (1915); *Indian Sketches* (Boston, March 4, 1921); Suite from *Music to Pilgrim Tercentenary Pageant* (Boston, March 31, 1922); *Symphonic Piece* (Boston, Feb. 26, 1926); Nocturne, a "symphonic mood" after Walt Whitman (Philadelphia, March 16, 1928); Suite for Chamber Orch. (commissioned by the E.S. Coolidge Foundation; Boston, April 28, 1928, Slonimsky conducting); *To Thee, America,* hymn for Chorus and Orch. (MacDowell Festival, Peterboro, N.H., Jan. 25, 1915); *Salammbô's Invocation to Tänith,* aria for Soprano and Orch. (N.Y., March 10, 1906). **CHAMBER:** String Quartet. **PIANO:** *Negro Episode, Mazurka, Scherzo, 2 Verlaine Moods, The Island of the Fay* (also for Orch.), *Indian Scenes, A Rag Bag, Negro Dances.* **SONGS:** *Pirate Song,* after Stevenson; *Celtic Studies,* cycle of 4 songs to poems by Irish poets; *The Lament of Deirdre; Faery Song; 2 South American Gypsy Songs; Fish Wharf Rhapsody; Give Me the Splendid Sun; The Owl; Orlamonde; Zephyrus; Homesick; Tell Me Where Is Fancy Bred?; Croon of the Dew; 8 Simple Songs; Perdita; The Curl; School Songs.*

BIBL.: A. Farwell, "*Wanderjahre* of a Revolutionist," *Musical America* (April 10, 1909); "An American Composer's Triumph in Russia," *Current Opinion* (May 1916); E. Ranck, "The Mark Twain of American Music," *Theatre Magazine* (Sept. 1917); O. Downes, "An American Composer," *Musical Quarterly* (Jan. 1918); J. Howard, *Our American Music* (N.Y., 1939, and subsequent eds.); O. Downes, "H. G.: Nonconformist," in *A Birthday Greeting to Carl Engel* (N.Y., 1943); E. Carter, "American Figure," *Modern Music* (1943); H. Sear, "H.F. G.," *Music Review* (1944); G. Chase, *America's Music* (N.Y., 1955; 2nd ed., 1966); K. Longyear, *H.F. G.: His Life and Works* (diss., Univ. of Rochester, 1968).

Gilbert, Kenneth, Canadian harpsichordist, organist, and musicologist; b. Montreal, Dec. 16, 1931. He studied organ in Montreal with Conrad Letendre; also piano with Yvonne Hubert, and theory with Gabriel Cusson at the Montreal Cons.;

he won the Prix d'Europe for organ in 1953, and subsequently studied in Europe with Nadia Boulanger (theory), Gaston Litaize (organ), and Gustav Leonhardt and Ruggero Gerlin (harpsichord). From 1952 to 1967 he was organist and music director of the Queen Mary Road United Church in Montreal; gave concerts as organist and harpsichordist. He taught at the Montreal Cons. (1957–74), McGill Univ. (1964–72), and Laval Univ. (1969–76). He ed. the complete harpsichord works of François Couperin (4 vols., 1969–72); also the complete sonatas of Domenico Scarlatti (11 vols., 1971–85). In 1986 he was made an Officer of the Order of Canada.

Gilbert, L. Wolfe, Russian-born American songwriter; b. Odessa, Aug. 31, 1886; d. Beverly Hills, Calif., July 12, 1970. His family went to Philadelphia when he was an infant; at the age of 14 he went to N.Y. and sang in vaudeville, burlesque theaters, and nightclubs; he also toured as an entertainer with John L. Sullivan, the prizefighter. In 1912 he wrote his 1st hit song, *Waitin' for the Robert E. Lee.* In 1929 he settled in Hollywood, where he formed his own publishing company. He composed some 250 songs, of which several became perennial favorites: *Ramona* (written for a motion picture in 1927); *Peanut Vendor; Down Yonder;* and *Lucky Lindy,* inspired by Lindbergh's transatlantic flight of 1927.

Gilbert, Pia, spirited German-born American composer and pedagogue; b. Kippenheim, June 1, 1921. She began her career as a dance accompanist in the N.Y. studios of Lotte Goslar, Doris Humphreys, and Martha Graham; then found her niche as a composer for dance and theater. She served in various capacities during her lengthy tenure as prof. in the dance dept. at the Univ. of Calif., Los Angeles (1947–85), including resident composer and music director of its dance company; in 1986 she joined the music faculty at the Juilliard School in N.Y. As a teacher she is distinguished by her commitment to the musical literacy of dancers, as well as for her interdisciplinary approach. Her compositions, whether for dance, theater, or simply "music per se," are always subtly dramatic, and a certain sly humor invades several of her vocal works; *Vociano,* 1st performed by Jan DeGaetani at the 1978 Aspen Music Festival, is pleasing for its use of imaginary languages. With A. Lockhart, she publ. *Music for the Modern Dance* (1961).
WORKS: DANCE: *In 2s It's Love* (1949); *Songs of Innocence and Experience* (1952); *Trio for Piano, Dancer, and Lights* (1956); *Valse for Lotte Goslar* (1959); *Bridge of the 7th Moon* (1960); *Freke-Phreec-Freake-Phreaque-Freak* (1969); *Irving, the Terrific* (1971); *Requiem for Jimmy Dean* (1972); *Legend* (1985). THEATER (all 1st perf. by the Mark Taper Forum Theatre Group, Los Angeles): *The Deputy* (R. Hochhuth, 1966); *Murderous Angels* (C.C. O'Brien, 1970); *Tales from Hollywood* (C. Hampton, 1982). ORCH.: *Gestures* (1988). CHAMBER: *Transmutations* for Organ and Percussion (1975); *Spirals and Interpolations* for Small Ensemble (1976); *Interrupted Suite* for Clarinet and 3 Pianos (1978); *Tri, dispute, dialogue, diatribe* for Cello and Piano (1978); *Volatile* for Solo Piano (1987). VOCAL: *Vociano* for Mezzo-soprano and Piano (1978); *Food,* to texts by John Cage, for Soprano, Baritone, Trumpet, Piano, and Snare Drum (1981); *Bells* for Soprano and Piano (1983); *Das Lied der Gefallenen,* to a poem by Lion Feuchtwanger, for Voice and Piano (1984).

Gilbert, Sir W(illiam) S(chwenck), English playwright and creator, with Sir Arthur (Seymour) Sullivan, of the famous series of comic operas; b. London, Nov. 18, 1836; d. Harrow Weald, Middlesex, May 29, 1911 (of cardiac arrest following a successful attempt to rescue a young woman swimmer from drowning). He was given an excellent education (at Boulogne and at King's College, London) by his father, who was a novelist. After a routine career as a clerk, Gilbert drifted into journalism, contributing drama criticism and humorous verse to London periodicals. His satirical wit was 1st revealed in a theater piece, *Dulcamara* (1866), in which he ridiculed grand opera. He met Sullivan in 1870, and together they initiated the productions of comic operas, which suited them so perfectly. Some plots borrow ludicrous situations from actual Italian and French

operas; Gilbert's librettos, in rhymed verse, were nonetheless unmistakably English. This insularity of wit may explain the enormous popularity of the Gilbert & Sullivan operas in English-speaking countries, while they are practically unknown on the Continent. Despite the fact that the targets of Gilbert's ridicule were usually the upper classes of Great Britain, the operas were often performed at court. He was knighted in 1907. After 20 years of fruitful cooperation with Sullivan, a conflict developed, and the 2 severed their relationship for a time. A reconciliation was effected, but the subsequent productions fell short of their greatest successes. See the biography of Sullivan for complete details on the operas and a full bibliography.

Gilberté, Hallett, American song composer; b. Winthrop, Maine, March 14, 1872; d. N.Y., Jan. 5, 1946. He studied piano with J. Orth and C. Barmann and composition with E. Nevin in Boston. He wrote about 250 songs, some of which were quite successful (*Spanish Serenade, Mother's Cradle Song, In Reverie, 2 Roses, Song of the Canoe, Ah, Love But a Day, Spring Serenade, Minuet La Phyllis, Moonlight and Starlight*).

Gilboa, Jacob, Czech-born Israeli composer; b. Košice, May 2, 1920. He grew up in Vienna and went to Palestine in 1938. He studied composition with Tal in Jerusalem and Ben-Haim in Tel Aviv (1944–47); then traveled to Germany and attended courses of new music with Stockhausen, Pousseur, Alois Kontarsky, and Caskel. His music represents a blend of oriental and Eastern Mediterranean idioms, basically lyrical, but technically ultramodern.
WORKS: *7 Little Insects,* piano pieces for children (1955); *Wild Flowers,* 4 lyrical pieces for Female Voice, Horn, Harp, and String Orch. (1957); *Passing Clouds* for Female Voice, Clarinet, Cello, and Piano (1958); Violin Sonata (1960); *The 12 Jerusalem Chagall Windows* for Voices and Instruments (1966); *Crystals* for Flute, Viola, Cello, Piano, and Percussion (1967); *Horizons in Violet and Blue,* ballet scene for 6 Players (1970); *Pastels* for 2 Prepared Pianos (1970); *Thistles,* theater piece for Singing and Speaking Voices, Horn, Cello, Piano, and Percussion (1970); *Cedars* for Orch. (1971); *From the Dead Sea Scrolls* for Chorus, Children's Chorus, 2 Organs, Tape, and Orch. (1971; Hamburg, Jan. 11, 1972); *14 Epigrams for Oscar Wilde* for Female Voice, Piano, and Tape (1973); *Bedu,* metamorphoses on a Bedouin call, for Male Voice, Cello, Flute, and Piano (1975); *The Beth Alpha Mosaic* for Female Voice, Chamber Ensemble, and Tape (1975; Chicago, Jan. 24, 1976); *3 Red Sea Impressions* for Violin, Piano, Harp, Electric Guitar, Organ, and Tape (1976); *3 Vocalises for Peter Breughel* for Mezzo-soprano, Tape, and 13 Instruments (1976); *7 Ornaments on a Theme of Ben-Haim* for Piano and Orch. (1981); String Quartet (1984); *3 Lyric Pieces in the Mediterranean Style* for Chamber Orch. (1984).

Gilchrist, William Wallace, American composer; b. Jersey City, N.J., Jan. 8, 1846; d. Easton, Pa., Dec. 20, 1916. He studied organ with H.A. Clarke at the Univ. of Pa., which conferred on him the degree of Mus.D. in 1896. He was a choirmaster at various Philadelphia churches; from 1882, taught at the Philadelphia Music Academy. He formed the Mendelssohn Club and later was its conductor. He wrote cantatas, a Christmas oratorio, 2 syms., chamber music, church music, and songs.
BIBL.: M. Schleifer, *W.W. G., 1846–1916: A Moving Force in the Musical Life of Philadelphia* (Metuchen, N.J., 1985).

Gilels, Elizabeta, Russian violinist, sister of **Emil (Grigorievich) Gilels;** b. Odessa, Sept. 30, 1919. She studied with Stoliarsky at his school for gifted youths in Odessa and later graduated from the Moscow Cons., where she took lessons from A. Yampolsky. She received 3rd place in the Ysaÿe Competition (Brussels, 1937); taught at the Moscow Cons. (from 1967). She played duets with her husband, **Leonid Kogan;** their son, Pavel Kogan, was also a talented violinist.

Gilels, Emil (Grigorievich), eminent Russian pianist, brother of **Elizabeta Gilels;** b. Odessa, Oct. 19, 1916; d. Moscow, Oct. 14, 1985. He entered the Odessa Cons. at the age of 5 to study with Yakov Tkatch, making his 1st public appearance at 9, followed by his formal debut at 13; after further studies with Bertha Ringbald at the Cons., he went to Moscow for advanced studies with Heinrich Neuhaus (1935–38). He won 1st prize at the Moscow Competition in 1933; after taking 2nd prize at the Vienna Competition in 1936, he won 1st prize at the Brussels Competition in 1938; that same year he became a prof. at the Moscow Cons. Following World War II, he embarked upon an esteemed international career. He was the 1st Soviet musician to appear in the U.S. during the Cold War era, making his debut in Tchaikovsky's 1st Piano Concerto with Ormandy and the Philadelphia Orch. (Oct. 3, 1955). He subsequently made 13 tours of the U.S., the last in 1983. A member of the Communist party from 1942, he received various honors from the Soviet government. Gilels was one of the foremost pianists of his time. He was especially renowned for his performances of Beethoven, Schubert, Schumann, Chopin, Liszt, Tchaikovsky, and Brahms.

BIBL.: V. Delson, *E. G.* (Moscow, 1959); S. Hentova, *E. G.* (Moscow, 1967).

Giles, Nathaniel, English organist and composer; b. Worcester, c.1558; d. Windsor, Jan. 24, 1634. He studied at Oxford; was organist at Worcester Cathedral from 1581 to 1585, when he became clerk, organist, and choirmaster at St. George's Chapel, Windsor; in 1597, became Gentleman and Master of the Children. He wrote 3 services for the church; many anthems; several motets and 2 madrigals for 4 and 5 Voices.

BIBL.: J. Pulver, "N. G.," *Monthly Musical Record* (Nov. 1933).

Gilibert, Charles, French baritone; b. Paris, Nov. 29, 1866; d. N.Y., Oct. 11, 1910. He sang at the Paris Opéra-Comique, and then went to the Théâtre de la Monnaie in Brussels, where he became a great favorite; from 1900 to 1903 he was a member of the Metropolitan Opera in N.Y.; at his debut on Dec. 18, 1900, and throughout the entire season, he failed to make a decided impression, but on his appearance in the 2nd season he took the public by storm; from 1906 to 1910, he was at the Manhattan Opera House in N.Y.; he was then reengaged for the Metropolitan, and was to have created Jack Rance in *The Girl of the Golden West*, but died just before the opening of the season. He was also a distinguished concert singer and interpreter of early French songs.

Gille, Jacob Edvard, Swedish composer; b. Stockholm, Aug. 10, 1814; d. there, Nov. 8, 1880. He was a notary public; learned to play the piano and organ; served as choral master at the Catholic church in Stockholm, where he wrote 9 masses. As a composer he acquired a solid technique; his style of composition closely adhered to the German school. His works include 4 operas, 5 syms., 5 string quartets, 4 piano trios, 2 string trios, 3 piano sonatas, 3 organ sonatas, and many minor pieces.

Gilles, Jean, French composer; b. Tarascon, near Avignon, Jan. 8, 1668; d. Toulouse, Feb. 5, 1705. He received his musical training in the choir school of the Cathedral of St. Sauveur at Aix-en-Provence; in 1688 became 2nd instructor and organist there; later he received an appointment as maître de musique at St. Étienne at Toulouse. His most famous work was *Messe des morts*, which became part of the regular services at funerals; it was performed at services for Louis XV in 1774. That Gilles possessed an excellent technique is proved by the erudite fugue in the final Requiem of his *Messe des morts*. He also wrote 32 choral motets and other sacred works.

BIBL.: M. Prada, *Un Maître de musique en Provence et en Languedoc: J. G., 1668–1705: L'Homme et l'œuvre* (Beziers, 1986).

Gillespie, "Dizzy" (John Birks), famous black American jazz trumpeter and bandleader; b. Cheraw, S.C., Oct. 21, 1917. He picked up the rudiments of music from his father; at the age of 18 he went to Philadelphia, where he joined a local jazz band; in 1939 he became a member of the Cab Calloway orch., and in 1944 he was with the Billy Eckstine band. In 1945 he formed his own band, and emerged as one of the true jazz innovators of his era. With Charlie "Bird" Parker, he was one of the founders of the style variously known as bebop, bop, and rebop. He received the nickname "Dizzy" because of his wild manner of playing, making grimaces and gesticulating during his performances. He was doubtless one of the greatest trumpeters in jazz history and practice, a true virtuoso on his instrument, extending its upper ranges and improvising long passages at breakneck speed. With A. Fraser, he publ. *To Be or Not to Bop* (N.Y., 1979). In 1989 he was awarded the National Medal of Arts.

BIBL.: M. James, *D. G.* (London, 1959); R. Horricks, *D. G. and the Be-Bop Revolution* (Tunbridge Wells and N.Y., 1984).

Gillet, Ernest, French composer; b. Paris, Sept. 13, 1856; d. there, May 6, 1940. He studied cello at the Paris Cons., and was for many years a cellist in the orch. of the Paris Opéra. He publ. a number of melodious pieces, of which *Loin du bal* for Piano became a perennial drawing-room favorite.

Gillis, Don, American composer and arranger; b. Cameron, Mo., June 17, 1912; d. Columbia, S.C., Jan. 10, 1978. He played trumpet and trombone in school bands; graduated from the Christian Univ. at Fort Worth, Texas, in 1936; later from North Texas State Univ. (M.M., 1943). From 1944 to 1954 he was a producer for NBC, and became associated with Toscanini, who was then conductor of the NBC Sym. Orch. Gillis acquired a facility for arranging, and also composed music on his own. From 1968 to 1973 he was chairman of the division of arts at Dallas (Texas) Baptist College; later was director of the Center for Media Art Studies at the Univ. of South Carolina (1973–78). He wrote 12 syms. (2 being unnumbered), supplemented with an intercalatory work which he called *Symphony No. 5½* and subtitled "Symphony for Fun." It so amused Toscanini that he performed it in 1947 with the NBC Sym.; among his other orch. works with similarly whimsical titles are *The Panhandle, Thoughts Provoked on Becoming a Prospective Papa,* etc. He also wrote 10 short operas to his own librettos, among them *The Park Avenue Kids* (Elkhart, Ind., May 12, 1957), *Pep Rally* (Interlochen, Mich., Aug. 15, 1957), *The Libretto* (Norman, Okla., Dec. 1, 1961), *The Gift of the Magi* (Fort Worth, Texas, Dec. 7, 1965), *The Legend of the Star Valley Junction* (N.Y., Jan. 7, 1969); patriotic pieces for orch., among them *The Alamo* (1947) and *The Secret History of the Birth of the Nation* with Narrator and Chorus (York, Pa., Nov. 14, 1976); 2 piano concertos; *Rhapsody* for Trumpet and Orch.; 6 string quartets; other chamber music.

Gilly, Dinh, French baritone; b. Algiers, July 19, 1877; d. London, May 19, 1940. He studied at the Toulouse Cons. and with Cotogni in Rome; after completing his studies at the Paris Cons., he made his debut as the Priest in *Sigurd* at the Paris Opéra in 1899; continued to sing there until 1908. He made his Metropolitan Opera debut in N.Y. as Alfio in *Cavalleria rusticana* on Nov. 24, 1909, and remained on its roster until 1914; he 1st appeared at London's Covent Garden as Amonasro in *Aida* on May 15, 1911; sang there until 1914 and again from 1919 to 1924. He also made appearances with the Beecham, Carl Rosa, and British National Opera companies. He made London his home and was active in later years as a teacher; among his pupils was John Brownlee.

Gilman, Benjamin Ives, American psychologist and ethnomusicologist; b. N.Y., Feb. 19, 1852; d. Boston, March 18, 1933. He studied at Williams College (A.B., 1872), Johns Hopkins Univ. (1881–82), the Univ. of Berlin (1882), and the Univ. of Paris (1886); also did graduate work in psychology at Harvard Univ. (1883–85). He lectured on the psychology of music at Princeton Univ., Columbia Univ., and at Harvard (1883); was assistant prof. of psychology at Clark Univ. (1892–93); then became secretary of the Boston Museum of Fine Arts, where he remained until his retirement in 1925. In 1890 Mary Hemenway commissioned J. Walter Fewkes to record Zuni speech and song; Gilman was engaged to do the analysis, and he became the 1st ethnomusicologist to use the phonograph in analyzing ethnic music. In 1891 he and Fewkes worked together on Hopi transcriptions; for these, Gilman invented a graphic notation. At the World's Columbian Exposition in Chicago in 1893, he recorded over 100 cylinders of music, including the earliest extant recordings of music from Java, Samoa, and Serbia. These cylinders were rediscovered in 1976 and provide evidence of change in this music during the 20th century. Gilman was internationally recognized in the field of ethnomusicological research; he also publ. studies on psychology, comparative musicology, museology, and art criticism. Among his important articles are "On Some Psychological Aspects of the Chinese Musical System," *Philosophical Review*, I (1892), and "Hopi Songs," *Journal of American Archaeology and Ethnology*, V (1908).

Gilman, Lawrence, American music critic; b. Flushing, N.Y., July 5, 1878; d. Franconia, N.H., Sept. 8, 1939. He was self-taught in music; from 1901 to 1913 he was music critic of *Harper's Weekly*; from 1915 to 1923, music, dramatic, and literary critic of the *North American Review*; from 1921 to 1939, author of the program notes of the N.Y. Phil. and Philadelphia Orch. concerts; from 1923 to 1939, was music critic of the *N.Y. Herald Tribune*; was a member of the National Inst. of Arts and Letters.

Writings: *Phases of Modern Music* (1904); *Edward MacDowell* (1905; 2nd ed., rev. and enl., 1909, as *Edward MacDowell: A Study*); *The Music of To-Morrow* (1906); *Stories of Symphonic Music* (1907); *Aspects of Modern Opera* (1909); *Nature in Music* (1914); *A Christmas Meditation* (1916); *Music and the Cultivated Man* (1929); *Wagner's Operas* (1937); *Toscanini and Great Music* (1938).

Bibl.: C. Engel, "L. G.," *Musical Quarterly* (Jan. 1940).

Gilmore, Patrick S(arsfield), Irish-American bandmaster; b. Ballygar, County Galway, Dec. 25, 1829; d. St. Louis, Sept. 24, 1892. He went to Canada with an English band, but soon settled in Salem, Mass., where he conducted a military band. In 1859 in Boston he organized the famous Gilmore's Band. As bandmaster in the Federal army at New Orleans (1864), he gave a grand music festival with several combined bands, introducing the novel reinforcement of strong accents by cannon shots. He won wide renown through the National Peace Jubilee (1869) and the World's Peace Jubilee (1872), 2 monster music festivals held in Boston; in the former, he led an orch. of 1,000 and a chorus of 10,000; in the latter, an orch. of 2,000 and a chorus of 20,000; the orch. was reinforced by a powerful organ, cannon fired by electricity, anvils, and chimes of bells. After the 2nd jubilee, Gilmore went to N.Y., and, as a popular bandmaster, traveled throughout the U.S. and Canada, and also (1878) to Europe. He composed military music, dance music, and many arrangements for band. Some of his songs were popular. He claimed to be the composer of *When Johnny Comes Marching Home* (1863), a song that remained a favorite long after the Civil War. The song bears the name of Louis Lambert as composer; this may have been one of Gilmore's many aliases—at any rate, he introduced the song and started it on its way to popularity.

Bibl.: M. Darlington, *Irish Orpheus: The Life of P. G.* (Philadelphia, 1950); F. Cipolla, "P.S. G.: The Boston Years," *American Music* (Fall 1988).

Gilse, Jan van, Dutch conductor and composer; b. Rotterdam, May 11, 1881; d. Oegstgeest, near Leyden, Sept. 8, 1944. He studied with Wüllner at the Cologne Cons. (1897–1902) and with Humperdinck in Berlin (1902–3). He was a conductor of the Bremen Opera (1905–8) and of the Dutch Opera at Amsterdam (1908–9); was music director of the City of Utrecht (1917–22). He lived again in Berlin (1922–33); then was director of the Utrecht Cons. (1933–37). His music is heavily imbued with German Romanticism.

Works: 2 operas: *Frau Helga von Stavern* (1911) and *Thijl* (1938–40; 1st complete perf., Amsterdam, Sept. 21, 1976; a symphonic extract, *Funeral Music*, is often heard separately); *Concert Overture* (1900); 4 syms.: No. 1 (1900–1901); No. 2 (1902–3); No. 3, *Erhebung*, with Soprano (1907); No. 4 (1914); No. 5 (1922–23; unfinished sketch only); *Eine Lebensmesse*,

oratorio (1904); *Variaties over een St. Nicolaasliedje* (Variations on a St. Nicholas Song) for Orch. or Piano (1909); *3 Songs*, after Tagore's "Gitanjali," for Soprano and Orch. (1915); *3 Songs*, after Tagore's "Der Gartner," for Soprano and Orch. (1923); *3 Tanzkizzen* (Dance Sketches) for Piano and Small Orch. (1926); *Der Kreis des Lebens*, oratorio (1928); *Prologus brevis* for Orch. (1928); *Kleine Vals* for Small Orch. (1936); Nonet (1916); Trio for Flute, Violin, and Viola (1927); songs.

Gilson, Paul, noted Belgian composer, critic, and educator; b. Brussels, June 15, 1865; d. there, April 3, 1942. He studied with Auguste Cantillon and Charles Duyck; took lessons from Gevaert at the Brussels Cons., where, in 1889, he won the Belgian Prix de Rome with his cantata, *Sinaï*. His subsequent works, both choral and orch., won him a foremost place among modern Flemish composers. His most successful score was *La Mer* for Orch. (1892). In addition to his composing, he wrote numerous books and articles on music, and taught, beginning in 1899, as a prof. of harmony at the Brussels Cons.; from 1904, he was also on the faculty of the Antwerp Cons.; in 1909, he left both posts to become music inspector in the Belgian schools. He was also an important music critic: for *Soir* from 1906 to 1914, for *Le Diapason* from 1910 to 1914, and later for *Midi*. A group of his students banded together in 1925 to form the Synthétistes to carry out his ideals; they also founded the *Revue Musicale Belge* that same year. In 1942, he publ. his memoirs, *Notes de musique et souvenirs*. He also publ. *Les Intervalles*, *Le Tutti orchestral*, *Quintes et octaves*, *Traité d'harmonie*, and *Traité d'orchestre militaire*.

Works: **choral:** *Inaugural Cantata* (for the Brussels Exhibition, 1897); *Francesca da Rimini*, after Dante (Brussels, 1892); *Le Démon*, after Lermontov; *Que la lumière soit*; *Hymne à l'Art*; *Ludus pro Patria*. **ballets:** *La Captive* (1896–1900); *Les Deux Bossus* (1910–21); *Légende rhénane*; also incidental music for E. Hiel's drama *Alva*. **operas:** *Princesse Rayon de Soleil* (1901); *Zeevolk* (Antwerp, 1904); *Rooversliefde* (*Les Aventuriers*; Antwerp, 1906); *Mater Dolorosa*. **orch.:** 3 symphonic poems: *La Mer* (Brussels, 1892); *Italia*; *La Destinée*; *Variations symphoniques* (1903); 8 suites; *Danses écossaises*; *Rapsodie écossaise*; *Andante et presto sur un thème brabançon*; *Rapsodie canadienne*; also 2 string quartets; String Trio; pieces for military band; choruses; piano pieces; instrumental pieces; songs.

Bibl.: G. Brenta, *P. G.* (Brussels, 1965).

Giltay, Berend, Dutch composer; b. Hilversum, June 15, 1910; d. Utrecht, March 21, 1975. He studied violin and viola with Dick Waleson and composition with Badings; was a violinist with the Hilversum Radio Phil. and with various other Dutch orchs. From 1963 to 1966 he attended courses in electronic music at the Utrecht Univ. and worked in Bilthoven at the Gaudeamus electronic studio.

Works: Violin Concerto (1950); *4 Miniatures* for Viola and Piano (1952); *Sonata a tre* for Oboe, Clarinet, and Bassoon (1953); Concerto for Viola and Chamber Orch. (1955); Wind Quintet (1956); Oboe Concerto (1956–57); *Sinfonia* (1956–57); String Quintet (1957); Horn Concerto; Concerto for Orch. (1960); 2 duos for 2 Violins (1962, 1966); Divertimento for 5 Flutes (1963); *Scherzo* for 2 Violins (1963); 6 *studi concertante* for Solo Viola (1963); *Phonolieten* for Tape (1965); *Polychromie I* for Tape (1966) and *II* for a Solo Trio of Piccolo, Flute and Alto Flute, 4 Flutes or other Instruments, and Tape (1972); *Kurucz Változatok Zenekarra*, variations for Orch. (1966–67); 2-violin Concerto (1966–67); *Elegy* for Alto Flute and 4 Flutes (1969); *Gossauer Symphonie* (Utrecht, Oct. 3, 1972); Trio for 2 Violins and Cello (1971); *Kosmochromie I* for 4 Loudspeakers and Orch. (Utrecht, Feb. 22, 1974); *Kosmochromie II* for String Quartet, Chamber Orch., and Tape (1974).

Giménez (Jiménez) (y Bellido), Jerónimo, Spanish conductor and composer; b. Seville, Oct. 10, 1854; d. Madrid, Feb. 19, 1923. He studied with Alard, Savard, and A. Thomas at the Paris Cons.; was conductor of the Sociedad de Conciertos in Madrid. He wrote over 100 zarzuelas.

Gimpel, Bronislaw, Austrian-born American violinist, brother of **Jakob Gimpel**; b. Lemberg, Jan. 29, 1911; d. Los

Angeles, May 1, 1979. He studied with R. Pollack in Vienna (1922–26) and Carl Flesch in Berlin (1928–29). From 1929 to 1931 he was concertmaster at the Radio Orch. in Königsberg; from 1931 to 1936 was in Göteborg, Sweden. In 1937 he emigrated to the U.S.; from 1937 to 1942 he was concertmaster of the Los Angeles Phil. In 1962 he organized the Warsaw String Quartet and toured with it in the U.S., Europe, and Japan. In 1968 he also became the concertmaster of the New England Quartet. He was to play a joint recital with his brother in Los Angeles on May 9, 1979, but died 8 days before the scheduled concert; instead, his brother played a piano recital in his memory.

Gimpel, Jakob, esteemed Austrian-born American pianist and teacher, brother of **Bronislaw Gimpel;** b. Lemberg, April 16, 1906; d. Los Angeles, March 12, 1989. He received his earliest musical training at home. After preliminary study at the Lemberg Cons., he went to Vienna, where he took piano lessons with Eduard Steuermann; also had private instruction in music theory with Alban Berg. He made his concert debut in Vienna in 1923; then engaged in a brilliant concert career; he was especially successful in Germany; in one particular season he gave 80 concerts there. His specialty was Romantic music; he infused the works of Beethoven, Schumann, and Chopin with a peculiarly lyrico-dramatic poetry which seemed to re-create the zeitgeist to perfection. When Germany was usurped by the Nazis, he went to Palestine, where he became closely associated with the violinist Bronislaw Huberman, the founder of the Israel Phil. In 1938 he emigrated to America, settling in Los Angeles, where he became active as an artist and a teacher. He received the Ben-Gurion Award of the State of Israel and the Order of Merit, First Class, of the Federal Republic of Germany for his "great services as an interpreter of German music," an exquisitely ironic but all the more precious gesture of the country that during its period of darkness closed its doors to Gimpel as a Jew. In 1971 he joined the music faculty of Calif. State Univ., Northridge, as Distinguished Prof.-in-Residence. On May 9, 1979, he was to give a joint recital in Los Angeles with his brother, who died suddenly 8 days before the scheduled concert. Instead, he played a solo recital in memory of his brother.

Ginastera, Alberto (Evaristo), greatly talented Argentine composer; b. Buenos Aires, April 11, 1916; d. Geneva, June 25, 1983. His father was of Catalan descent, and Ginastera often preferred to pronounce his name with a soft "g," as in the Catalan language; the standard pronunciation, however, is with a hard "g". His mother was of Italian origin. He took private lessons in music as a child; then entered the National Cons. of Music in Buenos Aires, where he studied composition with José Gil, Athos Palma, and José André; also took piano lessons with Argenziani. He began to compose in his early youth; in 1934 won 1st prize of the musical society El Unisono for his *Piezas infantiles* for Piano. His next piece of importance was *Impresiones de la Puna* for Flute and String Quartet, in which he made use of native Argentine melodies and rhythms; he discarded it, however, as immature; he withdrew a number of his other works, some of them of certain value, for instance, his *Concierto argentino,* which he wrote in 1935, and *Sinfonía Porteña,* his 1st Sym. (which may be identical in its musical material with *Estancia*). Also withdrawn was his 2nd Sym., the *Sinfonía elegíaca,* written in 1944, even though it was successfully performed. In 1946–47 Ginastera traveled to the U.S. on a Guggenheim fellowship. Returning to Argentina, he was appointed to the faculty of his alma mater, the National Cons. in Buenos Aires, where he taught intermittently from 1948 to 1958; he also served as dean of the faculty of musical arts and sciences at the Argentine Catholic Univ.; also was a prof. at the Univ. of La Plata. In 1968 he left Argentina and lived mostly in Geneva, Switzerland. From his earliest steps in composition, Ginastera had an almost amorous attachment for the melodic and rhythmic resources of Argentine folk music, and he evolved a fine harmonic and contrapuntal setting congenial with native patterns. His 1st significant work in the Argen-

tine national idiom was *Panambí,* a ballet, composed in 1935 and performed at the Teatro Colón in Buenos Aires on July 12, 1940. There followed a group of *Danzas argentinas* for Piano, written in 1937; in 1938 he wrote 3 songs; the 1st one, *Canción al árbol del olvido,* is a fine evocation of youthful love; it became quite popular. In 1941 he was commissioned to write a ballet for the American Ballet Caravan, to be called *Estancia;* the music was inspired by the rustic scenes of the pampas; a suite from the score was performed at the Teatro Colón on May 12, 1943, and the complete work was brought out there on Aug. 19, 1952. A series of works inspired by native scenes and written for various instrumental combinations followed, all infused with Ginastera's poetic imagination and brought to realization with excellent technical skill. Soon, however, he began to search for new methods of musical expression, marked by modern and sometimes strikingly dissonant combinations of sound, fermented by asymmetrical rhythms. Of these works, one of the most remarkable is *Cantata para América Mágica,* scored for dramatic soprano and percussion instruments, to apocryphal pre-Columbian texts, freely arranged by Ginastera; it was first performed in Washington, D.C., on April 30, 1961, with excellent success. An entirely new development in Ginastera's evolution as composer came with his 1st opera, *Don Rodrigo* (1964), produced on July 24, 1964, at the Teatro Colón. In it he followed the general formula of Berg's *Wozzeck,* in its use of classical instrumental forms, such as rondo, suite, scherzo, and canonic progressions; he also introduced a *Sprechstimme.* In 1964 he wrote the *Cantata Bomarzo* on a commission from the Elizabeth Sprague Coolidge Foundation in Washington, D.C. He used the same libretto by Manuel Mujica Láinez in his opera *Bomarzo,* which created a sensation at its production in Washington on May 19, 1967, by its unrestrained spectacle of sexual violence. It was announced for performance at the Teatro Colón on Aug. 9, 1967, but was canceled at the order of the Argentine government because of its alleged immoral nature. The score of *Bomarzo* reveals extraordinary innovations in serial techniques, with thematical employment not only of different chromatic sounds, but also of serial progressions of different intervals. His last opera, *Beatrix Cenci,* commissioned by the Opera Soc. of Washington, D.C., and produced there on Sept. 10, 1971, concluded his operatic trilogy. Among instrumental works of Ginastera's last period, the most remarkable was his 2nd Piano Concerto (1972), based on a tone-row derived from the famous dissonant opening of the finale of Beethoven's 9th Sym.; the 2nd movement of the concerto is written for the left hand alone. He was married to the pianist Mercedes de Toro in 1941; they had a son and a daughter. He divorced her in 1965 and married the Argentine cellist Aurora Natola, for whom he wrote the Cello Sonata, which she played in N.Y. on Dec. 13, 1979, and his 2nd Cello Concerto, which she performed in Buenos Aires on July 6, 1981.

WORKS: OPERAS: *Don Rodrigo* (1963–64; Buenos Aires, July 24, 1964); *Bomarzo* (1966–67; Washington, D.C., May 19, 1967); *Beatrix Cenci* (Washington, D.C., Sept. 10, 1971). **BALLETS:** *Panambí* (1935; Buenos Aires, July 12, 1940); *Estancia* (1941; Buenos Aires, Aug. 19, 1952). **ORCH.:** Suite from the ballet *Panambí* (Buenos Aires, Nov. 27, 1937); *Primer concierto argentino* (Montevideo, July 18, 1941; withdrawn); *Primera sinfonía* (*Porteña*) (1942; withdrawn); *Dances* from the ballet *Estancia* (Buenos Aires, May 12, 1943); *Obertra para el "Fausto" Criollo* (1943; Santiago, Chile, May 12, 1944); *Sinfonía elegíaca* (2nd Sym.; Buenos Aires, May 31, 1946; withdrawn); *Ollantay,* 3 symphonic movements after an Inca poem (1947; Buenos Aires, Oct. 29, 1949); *Variaciones concertantes* for Chamber Orch. (Buenos Aires, June 2, 1953); *Pampeana No. 3,* symphonic pastoral (Louisville, Ky., Oct. 20, 1954); Harp Concerto (1956; Philadelphia, Feb. 18, 1965); Piano Concerto No. 1 (Washington, D.C., April 22, 1961); Violin Concerto (N.Y., Oct. 3, 1963); Concerto for Strings (1965; Caracas, May 14, 1966); Suite from *Bomarzo* (1967); *Estudios sinfónicos* (1967; Vancouver, March 31, 1968); Cello Concerto No. 1 (Dartmouth College, July 7, 1968; rev. 1971–

72 and 1977); Piano Concerto No. 2 (1972; Indianapolis, March 22, 1973); *Popul Vuh* (1975–83; unfinished; St. Louis, April 7, 1989); *Glosses sobre temes de Pau Casals* for String Orch. and String Quintet "in lontano" (San Juan, Puerto Rico, June 14, 1976; rev. for Full Orch. and 1st perf. in Washington, D.C., Jan. 24, 1978); Cello Concerto No. 2 (Buenos Aires, July 6, 1981; Aurora Natola, soloist); *Iubilum* (1979–80; Buenos Aires, April 12, 1980).

CHAMBER: *Impresiones de la Puna* for Flute and String Quartet (1942; withdrawn); *Dúo* for Flute and Oboe (1945); *Pampeana No. 1* for Violin and Piano (1947); 4 string quartets: No. 1 (1948); No. 2 (1958); No. 3, with Soprano (1973); No. 4, with Baritone, to the text of Beethoven's Heiligenstadt Testament (1974; unfinished); *Pampeana No. 2* for Cello and Piano (1950); Piano Quintet (1963); *Puneña No. 2* for Cello Solo (1976); Guitar Sonata (1976); Cello Sonata (N.Y., Dec. 13, 1979; Aurora Natola, cellist); *Fanfare* for 4 Trumpets in C (from *Iubilum*, 1980); *Serenade* for Cello Solo, Flute, Oboe, Clarinet, Bassoon, Horn, Double Bass, Harp, and Percussion (1980).

VOCAL: 2 *Canciones:* No. 1, *Canción al árbol del ovido;* No. 2, *Canción a la luna lunanca* (1938); *Cantos del Tucumán* for Voice, Violin, Harp, and 2 Indian Drums (1938); *Psalm 150* for Mixed Choir, Boys' Choir, and Orch. (1938; Buenos Aires, April 7, 1945); *5 Canciones populares argentinas* for Voice and Piano (1943); *Las horas de una estancia* for Voice and Piano (1943); *Hieremiae prophetae lamentatiónes* for Mixed Choir a cappella (1946); *Cantata para América Mágica* for Dramatic Soprano and Percussion, to an apocryphal pre-Columbian text (1960; Washington, D.C., April 30, 1961); *Sinfonía Don Rodrigo* for Soprano and Orch. (Madrid, Oct. 31, 1964); *Cantata Bomarzo* for Speaker, Baritone, and Chamber Orch. (Washington, D.C., Nov. 1, 1964); *Milena,* cantata for Soprano and Orch., to texts from Kafka's letters (1971; Denver, April 16, 1973); *Serenata* for Cello, Baritone, and Chamber Ensemble, to texts of Pablo Neruda (1973; N.Y., Jan. 18, 1974); *Turbae ad Passionem Gregorianam* for Tenor, Baritone, Bass, Boys' Chorus, Mixed Chorus, and Orch. (1974; Philadelphia, March 20, 1975).

PIANO: *Piezas infantiles* (1934); *Danzas argentinas* (1937); *3 piezas* (1940); *Malambo* (1940); *12 Preludios americanos* (1944); *Suite de Danzas criollas* (1946); *Rondó sobre temas infantiles argentinos* (1947); Sonata No. 1 (1952); *Pequeña danza* from *Estancia* (1955); *Toccata,* arranged from *Toccata per organo* by Domenico Zipoli (1972); Sonata No. 2 (1981); Sonata No. 3 (1982); also *Toccata, Villancico y Fuga* for Organ (1947); *Variazioni e Toccata* for Organ (1980); film music.

BIBL.: P. Suárez Urtubey, *A. G.* (Buenos Aires, 1967); *A. G.: A Catalogue of His Published Works* (London, 1976); F. Spangemacher, ed., *A. G.* (Bonn, 1984); L. Tan, "An Interview with A. G.," *American Music Teacher* (Jan. 1984).

Gingold, Josef, distinguished Russian-born American violinist and pedagogue; b. Brest-Litovsk, Oct. 28, 1909. He went to the U.S. in 1920. He studied violin in N.Y. with Vladimir Graffman, and later in Brussels with Eugène Ysaÿe. He then served as 1st violinist in the NBC Sym. Orch. (1937–43); was concertmaster of the Detroit Sym. Orch. (1943–46) and the Cleveland Orch. (1947–60). He taught at Case Western Reserve Univ. (1950–60) and was prof. of chamber music at the Meadowmount School of Music (1955–81). In 1960 he was appointed to the faculty of the Indiana Univ. School of Music in Bloomington; was made a distinguished prof. of music there in 1965. He also gave master classes at the Paris Cons. (1970–81), in Tokyo (1970), in Copenhagen (1979), and in Montreal (1980); held the Mischa Elman Chair at the Manhattan School of Music in N.Y. (1980–81). He was a guiding force in establishing the International Violin Competition of Indianapolis; was its 1st honorary chairman and president of the jury in 1982, positions he held again in 1986 and 1990.

Ginguené, Pierre Louis, French historian of literature and writer on music; b. Rennes, April 25, 1748; d. Paris, Nov. 16, 1816. He studied at Rennes College; then went to Paris; was an original member of the Institut de France; served in government posts, then wrote extensively on the history of French and Italian literature. He was an ardent advocate of Piccinni in the Gluck-Piccinni controversy; his attacks on Gluck are contained in his *Lettres et articles sur la musique, insérés dans les journaux sous le nom de Mélophile, pendant nos dernières querelles musicales, en 1780, 1781, 1782 et 1783* (Paris, 1783). He also wrote *Notice sur la vie et les ouvrages de Piccinni* (Paris, 1800); contributed historical articles to the *Dictionnaire de musique* of the *Encyclopédie méthodique.*

BIBL.: D. Garat, *Notice sur la vie et les ouvrages de P.L. G.* (Paris, 1817).

Ginsburg, Lev, Russian music scholar, cellist, and pedagogue; b. Mogilev, Jan. 28, 1907; d. Moscow, Nov. 21, 1981. He studied cello at the Moscow Cons., graduating in 1931; subsequently was appointed to its faculty, teaching cello and later the methodology of string playing. He publ. a number of valuable works on the subject, among them a basic compendium, *History of the Art of Cello Playing* in 3 vols. (Moscow, 1950, 1957, 1965). He publ. monographs on cello virtuosos: *Pablo Casals* (Moscow, 1958), *Mstislav Rostropovich* (Moscow, 1963), and *Maurice Maréchal* (Moscow, 1972); also contributed numerous articles on string instrumental techniques to Russian and foreign publications.

Ginsburg, Semion, Russian musicologist and pedagogue; b. Kiev, May 23, 1901. He studied art history and musicology in Petrograd; in 1925 was appointed to the faculty of the Leningrad Cons.; in his scientific pursuits, he explored the sociological foundation of national musical resources. He publ. *Fundamentals of Musical Culture* (Leningrad, 1935) and *Russian Music on the Threshold of the 20th Century* (Moscow, 1966).

Giordani, Giuseppe, Italian composer, called Giordanello; b. Naples, Dec. 9, 1743; d. Fermo, Jan. 4, 1798. He studied with Fenaroli at the S. Loreto Cons., Naples; Cimarosa and Zingarelli were fellow students. His 2nd opera, *Epponina,* was given in Florence in 1779. He continued to write operas for various Italian towns, but they were not outstanding, and few of the 30-odd he wrote have survived. He also wrote several oratorios and church music. From 1791 until his death he was maestro di cappella at the Fermo Cathedral. He is sometimes credited with *Il bacio* and other operas and works produced in London by Tommaso Giordani; Giuseppe was not related to Tommaso, and never left Italy. The famous song *Caro mio ben,* popularized in London by Pacchierotti, was probably written by Giuseppe.

Giordani, Tommaso, Italian composer; b. Naples, c.1730; d. Dublin, Feb. 23 or 24, 1806. His family formed a strolling opera company, with the father as impresario and singer and the rest of the family, except Tommaso, as singers. Tommaso was probably a member of the orch. and the arranger of music. They left Naples about 1745 and moved northward, appearing in Italian towns, then in Graz (1748), Frankfurt (1750), Amsterdam (1752), and Covent Garden, London (Dec. 17, 1753); returned in 1756, at which time Tommaso first appeared as a composer, with his comic opera *La Comediante fatta cantatrice* (Covent Garden, Jan. 12, 1756). The Giordani company next went to Dublin, appearing there in 1764; Tommaso continued to be active both in Dublin and in London; he was conductor and composer at the King's Theatre, London, in 1769 and many following seasons, and in Dublin, where he lived after 1783, was conductor and composer at the Smock Alley and Crow St. theaters; he also taught piano. In 1794 he was elected president of the Irish music fund. He played an important part in Irish music circles, and wrote altogether more than 50 English and Italian operas, including pasticcios and adaptations. The most notable were *L'Eroe cinese* (Dublin, 1766), *Il Padre e il figlio rivali* (London, 1770), *Artaserse* (London, 1772), *Il Re pastore* (London, 1778), and *Il bacio* (London, 1782). He also wrote several cantatas, including *Aci e Galatea* (London, 1777); an oratorio, *Isaac* (Dublin, 1767); songs for the original production of Sheridan's *The Critic* (Drury Lane, London, Oct. 29, 1779); many Italian and English songs that were popular for a long time; concertos; string quartets; trios; many piano pieces.

Giordano, Umberto, noted Italian composer; b. Foggia, Aug. 28, 1867; d. Milan, Nov. 12, 1948. He studied with Gaetano Briganti at Foggia, and then with Paolo Serrao at the Naples Cons. (1881–90). His 1st composition performed in public was a symphonic poem, *Delizia* (1886); he then wrote some instrumental music. In 1888 he submitted a short opera, *Marina*, for the competition established by the publisher Sonzogno; Mascagni's *Cavalleria rusticana* received 1st prize, but *Marina* was cited for distinction. Giordano then wrote an opera in 3 acts, *Mala vita*, which was performed in Rome, Feb. 21, 1892; it was only partly successful; was revised and presented under the title *Il voto* in Milan (Nov. 10, 1897). There followed a 2-act opera, *Regina Diaz* (Rome, Feb. 21, 1894), which obtained a moderate success. Then he set to work on a grand opera, *Andrea Chénier*, to a libretto by Illica. The production of this opera at La Scala in Milan (March 28, 1896) was a spectacular success, which established Giordano as one of the best composers of Italian opera of the day. The dramatic subject gave Giordano a fine opportunity to display his theatrical talent; but the score also revealed his gift for lyric expression. Almost as successful was his next opera, *Fedora* (Teatro Lirico, Milan, Nov. 17, 1898), but it failed to hold a place in the world repertoire after the initial acclaim; there followed *Siberia*, in 3 acts (La Scala, Dec. 19, 1903; rev. 1921; La Scala, Dec. 5, 1927). Two short operas, *Marcella* (Milan, Nov. 9, 1907) and *Mese Mariano* (Palermo, March 17, 1910), were hardly noticed and seemed to mark a decline in Giordano's dramatic gift; however, he recaptured the attention of the public with *Madame Sans-Gêne*, produced at a gala premiere at the Metropolitan Opera in N.Y. on Jan. 25, 1915, conducted by Toscanini, with Geraldine Farrar singing the title role. With Franchetti, he wrote *Giove a Pompei* (Rome, July 5, 1921); then he produced *La cena delle beffe* in 4 acts, which was his last signal accomplishment; it was staged at La Scala, Dec. 20, 1924. He wrote 1 more opera, *Il Re*, in 1 act (La Scala, Jan. 10, 1929). During his lifetime he received many honors, and was elected a member of the Accademia Luigi Cherubini in Florence and of several other institutions. Although not measuring up to Puccini in musical qualities or to Mascagni in dramatic skill, Giordano was a distinguished figure in the Italian opera field for some 4 decades.

Bibl.: G. Paribeni, *Madame Sans-Gêne di U. G.* (Milan, 1923); D. Cellamare, *U. G.: La vita e le opere* (Milan, 1949); R. Giazotto, *U. G.* (Milan, 1949); G. Confalonieri, *U. G.* (Milan, 1958); D. Cellamare, *U. G.* (Rome, 1967); M. Morini, ed., *U. G.* (Milan, 1968).

Giorni, Aurelio, Italian pianist and composer; b. Perugia, Sept. 15, 1895; d. (suicide) Pittsfield, Mass., Sept. 23, 1938. He studied piano with Sgambati at the Accademia di Santa Cecilia in Rome (1909–11) and composition with Humperdinck in Berlin (1911–13). He emigrated to the U.S. in 1914 and was active mainly as a teacher; he was on the faculty at Smith College, the Philadelphia Cons. of Music, and the Hartford School of Music. He was also a fairly prolific composer; his Sym. in D minor was performed in N.Y. on April 25, 1937, but had such exceedingly bad reviews that he sank into a profound state of depression; several months later he threw himself into the Housatonic River.

Bibl.: E. Giorni Burns (his daughter), *The Broken Pedal* (Whittier, Calif., 1986).

Giornovichi (real name, **Jarnowick**), **Giovanni Mane,** Italian violinist and composer; b. Raguso or Palermo, c.1735; d. St. Petersburg, Nov. 23, 1804. He may have been a pupil of Antonio Lolli in Palermo; gave successful concerts in Europe; on the strength of his reputation, he was engaged as court musician to Catherine II (1783–86). He was in Russia again from 1789 to 1791; then appeared in London (1791–96), Hamburg, and Berlin. He returned to Russia in 1803, and was a member of the Court Orch. in St. Petersburg until his death.

In his old age he devoted himself to playing billiards for money. Among his works are 25 violin concertos (17 extant); 3 string quartets; *Fantasia e Rondo* for Piano. He was probably the 1st to introduce the "romance" into the violin concerto as a slow movement, and he helped to set the rondo as the finale.

Bibl.: R. Aloys Mooser, *Annales de la musique et des musiciens en Russie au XVIIIe siècle* (vol. II, Geneva, 1950); C. White, "The Violin Concertos of G.," *Musical Quarterly* (Jan. 1972; includes a concordance of eds.).

Giorza, Paolo, Italian composer; b. Milan, Nov. 11, 1832; d. Seattle, May 5, 1914. He was especially known for his ballet music; wrote more than 70 ballets, 2 operas, sacred music, marches, dances, songs, etc. He lived in N.Y., London, and San Francisco; in 1906, settled in Seattle.

Giovannelli, Ruggiero, Italian composer; b. Velletri, near Rome, c.1560; d. Rome, Jan. 7, 1625. He served as maestro di cappella of S. Luigi de' Francesi at Rome; later was maestro in the Collegico Germanico (1591–94); he succeeded Palestrina as maestro at St. Peter's, and in 1599 joined the Pontifical Chapel. He was one of the most famous masters of the Roman School; of his works there have been printed 3 books of madrigals *a* 5 (1586, 1587, 1589; completely reprinted 1600); 2 of *Madrigali sdruccioli a* 4 (1585 [7th ed., 1613], 1589 [5th ed., 1603]); 2 books of motets *a* 5–8 (1589, 1604); *Canzonette* and *Villanelle a* 3 (1592, 1593); also scattered works in collections publ. from 1583 to 1620 (Scotto, Phalèse, Schadaeus, etc.). K. Proske's *Musica divina* contains a Psalm (vol. III, 1859); L. Torchi's *L'arte musicale in Italia* includes a motet and Psalm *a* 8 and a madrigal *a* 5 (vol. II). In the Vatican Library are many sacred works in MS. To Giovannelli was entrusted, by Pope Paul V, the preparation of a new ed. of the Gradual (2 vols., 1614, 1615).

Bibl.: C. Winter, *R. G. (c.1560–1625), Nachfolger Palestrinas zu St. Peter in Rom* (Munich, 1935).

Giovanni da Cascia (Giovanni de Florentia), Italian composer who flourished in the 14th century. According to his younger contemporary Filippo Villani, in *Liber de civitatis Florentiae famosis civibus*, he was the initiator of the stylistic reform which spread from Florence shortly after 1300. He was organist and probably chorus master at S. Maria del Fiore at Florence; lived at the court of Mastino II della Scala, Verona, c.1329–51. His extant compositions include 16 madrigals and 3 *cacce;* MSS may be found in libraries at Florence and Paris, and in the British Museum. For modern editions of his works, see N. Pirrotta, ed., *The Music of 14th Century Italy,* in Corpus Mensurabilis Musicae, VIII/1 (1954), and W. Marrocco, ed., *Italian Secular Music,* in Polyphonic Music of the Fourteenth Century, VI (1967).

Bibl.: J. Wolf, "Florenz in der Musikgeschichte des 14. Jahrhunderts," *Sammelbände der Internationalen Musik-Gesellschaft,* III (1901–2); A. Morini, "Un celebre musico dimenticato, G. d.C.," *Bollettino della Regia Deputazione di Storia Patria per l'Umbria* (Perugia, 1926); M. Martinez, *Die Musik des frühen Trecento* (Munich, 1963).

Gipps, Ruth (Dorothy Louisa), English conductor and composer; b. Bexhill-on-Sea, Sussex, Feb. 20, 1921. She studied at the Royal College of Music in London with Vaughan Williams, Gordon Jacob, and R.O. Morris (1937–42), and attended the Matthay Piano School (1942–43); obtained a B.Mus. in 1941 and a D.Mus. in 1948. She began her performing career as a pianist and oboist; after serving as director of the City of Birmingham Choir (1948–50), she was conductor of the London Repertoire Orch. (1955–86); also was founder-conductor of the London Chanticleer Orch. (from 1961), and music director of the Rondel Ensemble, a wind group. She taught at Trinity College, London (1959–66), the Royal College of Music (1967–77), and Kingston Polytechnic (1977–79). In 1981 she was made a Member of the Order of the British Empire. Her works include 5 syms. (1942, 1945, 1965, 1972, 1982); Clarinet Concerto (1940); Oboe Concerto (1941); Violin Concerto (1943); Horn Concerto (1968; London, Nov. 15, 1969); Piano Concerto

(1948); Concerto for Violin, Viola, and Orch. (1957); Trio for Oboe, Clarinet, and Piano (1940); Quintet for Oboe, Clarinet, Violin, Viola, and Cello (1941); *Leviathan* for Double Bassoon and Chamber Orch. (1969; London, Feb. 13, 1971); *Ambarvalia* for Orch. (1988); Sinfonietta for 10 Wind Instruments (1989); also many other chamber works; vocal pieces.

Giraldoni, Eugenio, famous Italian baritone, son of **Leone Giraldoni** and **Carolina Ferni-Giraldoni;** b. Marseilles, May 20, 1871; d. Helsinki, June 23, 1924. He made his debut in Barcelona as Don José in 1891; then sang in Buenos Aires and in Italy (at La Scala and other theaters); made his debut at the Metropolitan Opera in N.Y. as Barnaba in *La Gioconda* on Nov. 28, 1904; remained there only 1 season (1904–5); eventually settled in Russia.

Giraldoni, Leone, Italian baritone, father of **Eugenio Giraldoni;** b. Paris, 1824; d. Moscow, Oct. 1, 1897. He studied in Florence with Ronzi; made his debut in 1847 in Lodi; created the title roles of *Il Duca d'Alba* by Donizetti, *Simone Boccanegra* by Verdi, and Renato in Verdi's *Un ballo in maschera.* He retired from the stage in 1885; then taught voice in Italy. From 1891 to 1897 he was on the staff of the Moscow Cons. Among his students were Nikolai and Medea Figner. He publ. *Guida teorico-practico ad uso dell'artista cantante* (Bologna, 1864).

Giraud, Fiorello, Italian tenor; b. Parma, Oct. 22, 1870; d. there, March 29, 1928. He was the son of the tenor **Lodovico Giraud** (1846–82). He studied with Babacini in Parma; made his debut as Lohengrin in 1891 in Vercelli; then sang in Barcelona, Lisbon, and South America, and at La Scala in Milan. He created the role of Canio in Leoncavallo's *Pagliacci;* was a fine interpreter of other *verismo* roles.

Giraudet, Alfred-Auguste, French bass and pedagogue; b. Étampes, March 29, 1845; d. N.Y., Oct. 17, 1911. He studied with Delsarte; made his operatic debut at the Théâtre-Lyrique in Paris as Méphistophélès (1868); then sang at the Théâtre-Italien, the Opéra-Comique, and the Opéra; in 1883 he retired from the stage and devoted himself to teaching; eventually settled in N.Y.

Girdlestone, Cuthbert (Morton), English music scholar; b. Bovey-Tracey, Sept. 17, 1895; d. St. Cloud, France, Dec. 10, 1975. He was educated at the Sorbonne (licence ès lettres, 1915) and the Schola Cantorum in Paris; then entered Trinity College, Cambridge; became a lecturer at Cambridge in 1922; from 1926 to 1960 he was prof. of French at the Univ. of Durham, Newcastle division (later the Univ. of Newcastle upon Tyne). He publ. a valuable analysis of Mozart's piano concertos under the title *Mozart et ses concertos pour piano* (Paris, 1939; Eng. tr., 1948; 2nd ed., 1964); also the important monograph *Jean-Philippe Rameau: His Life and Work* (London, 1957; 2nd ed., rev., 1969). He further wrote *La Tragédie en musique (1673–1750) considérée comme genre littéraire* (Paris, 1972). **BIBL.:** N. Suckling, ed., *Essays Presented to C.M. G.* (Newcastle upon Tyne, 1960).

Giro, Manuel, Spanish composer; b. Lérida, Catalonia, Sept. 5, 1848; d. Barcelona, Dec. 20, 1916. He studied organ and composition at the cathedral school in Lérida and later in Barcelona and Paris. In 1884 he settled in Barcelona, where in 1885 he brought out his opera *Il rinegato Alonso García,* which proved a popular success. Another opera, *El sombrero de tres picos* (Madrid, 1893), was also well received. He further wrote ballets, choral music, chamber music, and piano pieces.

Gistelinck, Elias, Belgian composer; b. Beveren Leie, May 27, 1935. He received his training at the Brussels Cons. and the Paris Cons., then served as a producer for the Belgian Radio and Television (from 1961). He received the Italia Prize (1969) and a prize from the Fondation de France (1984). **WORKS: BALLETS** (titles in the Flemish language): *Terpsichore en Euterpe* (1971); *De Bijen* (1972). **ORCH.:** *Ad Maiorem Limburgiae Fodientium Gloriam* for Alto Saxophone, Bass Clarinet, and String Orch. (1970); *Drie Middelheimsculpturen* for Trumpet, Bass, Drums, Brass, and Winds (1972); *Weest gelukkig* for Tenor Saxophone, Trombone, Vibraphone, and Jazz Orch. (1974); *Muziek* for 3 Brass Groups and Percussion (1975); *Elegie voor Jan* (1976); *Drie bewigingen* for Jazz Quintet and Orch. (1985); Violin Concerto (1986); Sinfonietta for Chamber Orch. (1988). **CHAMBER:** Suite for Flute, Oboe, Clarinet, Horn, and Bassoon (1962); *5 Portraits* for Clarinet (1965); *Antieke alchemie* for String Quartet (1967); *Koan* for Clarinet Quartet (1971); *Cantus* for Oboe (1973); *Kleine treurmuziek voor "Che"* for Flute and Piano (1974); *Treurmuziek voor Ptak IV* for Violin, Cello, and Piano (1975); *So What, Brother* for Alto Saxophone (1981); *Lullaby for Nathaly* for Violin and Piano (1984); *Music for RGIP* for Violin and Piano (1987); *Memories of Childhood* for Trumpet and 4 Groups of Trumpets (1988); piano pieces; vocal works.

Giteck, Janice, American composer and pianist; b. N.Y., June 27, 1946. She studied with Milhaud and Subotnick at Mills College in Oakland, Calif. (B.A., 1968; M.A., 1969), and with Messiaen at the Conservatoire National Supérieur de Musique in Paris (1969–70). She also studied electronic music with Lowell Cross and Anthony Gnazzo, Javanese gamelan with Daniel Schmidt, and West African drumming with Obo Addy. Since 1979 she has taught at the Cornish Inst. in Seattle. Her compositions, variously scored, reflect interest in the language and lore of American Indians; her best-known work is the ceremonial opera *A'agita* (orig. and sacrilegiously entitled *Wi'igita*), which is based on the legends and mythologies of the Pima and Papago, a native American tribe living in southwestern Arizona and Mexico. **WORKS:** String Quartet No. 1 (1963); Quintet for Piano and Strings (1965); *How to Invoke a Garden/How to Invoke the Same Garden,* cantata for Soloists and 10 Instruments (1969); *Messalina,* mini-opera for Male Voice, Cello, and Piano (1973); *Helixes* for Flute, Trombone, Violin, Cello, Guitar, Piano, and Percussion (1974); *A'agita,* ceremonial opera for 3 Singing Actors, 1 Dancing Actor, and 8 Instrumentalists/Actors (1976; orig. titled *Wi'igita*); *8 Sandbars on the Takano River* for 5 Women's Voices, Flute, Bassoon, and Guitar (1976); *Thunder, Like a White Bear Dancing,* ritual performance for Soprano, Flute, Piano, Hand Percussion, and Slide Projections (based on the Mide Picture Songs of the Ojibwa Indians; 1977); *Callin' Home Coyote,* burlesque for Tenor, Steel Drums, and String Bass (1977); *Peter and the Wolves* for Trombonist/Actor and Prepared Tape (1978); *Far North Beast Ghosts the Clearing* for Chorus (after Swampy Creek Indians; 1978); *When the Crones Stop Counting* for 60 Flutes (1980); *Tree,* chamber sym. (1982); *Loo-wit* for Viola and Orch. (1983); also other chamber and vocal works; a film score, *Hopi: Songs of the 4th World* (1983).

Gitlis, Ivry, Israeli violinist; b. Haifa, Aug. 22, 1922. He began violin lessons at a very early age; he entered the École Normale de Musique in Paris at 10 and won the premier prix at 13; then studied with Enesco, Thibaud, and Flesch. He subsequently made appearances with the leading London orchs.; won the Thibaud Prize in 1951. He then returned to Israel; also made tours of Europe; made his U.S. debut in 1955. Gitlis has consistently cultivated contemporary violin music in his recital programs.

Giuffre, Jimmy (James Peter), American jazz clarinetist, saxophonist, and composer; b. Dallas, April 26, 1921. He studied at North Texas State Teachers College (B.Mus., 1942), then played in a U.S. Army band; subsequently joined the bands of Jimmy Dorsey, Buddy Rich, and Woody Herman. While he played flute and tenor saxophone, he was primarily known for his cool tone, *sans* vibrato, on the clarinet, especially in the lower register of the instrument. He wrote an influential score for Woody Herman, *4 Brothers* (1947), which explored the expressive potential of timbre and became known as the "Four Brothers sound." He was an important figure in avant-garde jazz of the late 1950s and '60s, especially as a proponent of the free-jazz style; he worked in a series of different combos, including those of Jim Hall and Ralph Pena (1956); he also played with Paul Bleg and Steve Swallow. He was also active as a teacher, serving on the faculty of the New School for Social Research in N.Y. and the School of Jazz in Lenox, Mass.; he publ. an influential text, *Jazz Phrasing and Interpretation* (N.Y., 1969). His compositions include *Hex* for Jazz Orch. (1960); *Orb*, quintet for Clarinet and Strings (1969); several pieces for solo instruments and orch.; and film scores. Well-known recordings of his work include *The Giuffre Clarinet* (1956), *Free Fall* (1962), and *Music for People, Birds, Butterflies and Mosquitoes* (1972).

Giuglini, Antonio, Italian tenor; b. Fano, 1827; d. Pesaro, Oct. 12, 1865. He studied with Cellini; made his debut in Fermo; was highly successful in London when he sang at Her Majesty's Theatre in 1857; also sang at Drury Lane and the Lyceum there; in 1865 he was in St. Petersburg, where he displayed symptoms of mental aberrations. Upon his return to London, he was committed to an asylum; in the same year he was taken to Pesaro, where he died.

Giuliani, Mauro (Giuseppe Sergio Pantaleo), famous Italian guitarist and composer; b. Bisceglie, near Bari, July 27, 1781; d. Naples, May 8, 1829. He was entirely self-taught; at the age of 19 undertook a highly successful tour in Europe; in 1806 settled in Vienna, where he became associated with Hummel, Moscheles, and Diabelli; Beethoven became interested in him, and wrote some guitar music expressly for his performances. In 1823 he visited London, where he won extraordinary acclaim; a special publication, named after him *The Giulianiad* and devoted to reports about his activities, was initiated there, but only a few issues appeared. He publ. over 200 works for guitar; he also perfected a new guitar with a shorter fingerboard ("la ghitarra di terza").

BIBL.: T. Heck, *The Birth of the Classic Guitar and Its Cultivation in Vienna, Reflected in the Career and Compositions of M. G. (d. 1829)* (diss., Yale Univ., 1970); idem, "M. G.," *Guitar Review* (1972).

Giulini, Carlo Maria, eminent Italian conductor; b. Barletta, May 9, 1914. He began to study the violin as a boy; at 16 he entered the Conservatorio di Musica di Santa Cecilia in Rome, where he studied violin and viola with Remy Principe, composition with Alessandro Bustini, and conducting with Bernardino Molinari; also received instruction in conducting from Casella at the Accademia Chigiana in Siena; then joined the Augusteo Orch. in Rome in the viola section, under such great conductors as Richard Strauss, Bruno Walter, Mengelberg, and Furtwängler. He was drafted into the Italian army during World War II, but went into hiding as a convinced anti-Fascist; after the liberation of Rome by the Allied troops in 1944, he was engaged to conduct the Augusteo Orch. in a special concert celebrating the occasion. He was then engaged as assistant conductor of the RAI Orch. in Rome, and was made its chief conductor in 1946. In 1950 he helped to organize the RAI Orch. in Milan; in 1952 he conducted at La Scala as an assistant to Victor de Sabata; in 1954 he became principal conductor there; his performance of *La Traviata*, with Maria Callas in the title role, was particularly notable. In 1955 he conducted Verdi's *Falstaff* at the Edinburgh Festival, earning great praise. On Nov. 3, 1955, he was a guest conductor with the Chicago Sym. Orch. and later was its principal guest conductor (1969–72); during its European tour of 1971, he was joint conductor with Sir Georg Solti. From 1973 to 1976 he was principal conductor of the Vienna Sym. Orch., and in 1975 he took it on a world tour, which included the U.S., Canada, and Japan. On Oct. 24, 1975, he led it at a televised concert from the United Nations. In 1978 he succeeded Zubin Mehta as music director of the Los Angeles Phil., and succeeded in maintaining it at a zenith of orchestral brilliance until 1984. His conducting style embodies the best traditions of the Italian school as exemplified by Toscanini, but is free from explosive displays of temper. He is above all a Romantic conductor who can identify his musical Weltanschauung with the musical essence of Beethoven, Verdi, Mahler, and Tchaikovsky; he leads the classics with an almost abstract contemplation. In the music of the

20th century, he gives congenial interpretations of works by Debussy, Ravel, and Stravinsky; the expressionist school of composers lies outside of his deeply felt musicality, and he does not actively promote the experimental school of modern music. His behavior on the podium is free from self-assertive theatrics, and he treats the orch. as comrades-in-arms, associates in the cause of music, rather than subordinate performers of the task assigned to them. Yet his personal feeling for music is not disguised; often he closes his eyes in fervent self-absorption when conducting without score the great Classical and Romantic works.

BIBL.: *Le Grand Baton* (Sept. 1977; includes articles and discography).

Giulini, Giorgio, Italian composer; b. Milan, 1716; d. there, 1780. He was the author of several instrumental works of considerable merit.

BIBL.: G. Cesari, "G. G., musicista," *Rivista Musicale Italiana* (1917).

Giustini, Lodovico, Italian organist and composer; b. Pistoia, Dec. 12, 1685; d. there, Feb. 7, 1743. He became organist of the Congregazione della Spirito Santo in 1725; was the 1st to publ. sonatas for Cristofori's pianoforte (*12 Sonate da Cimbalo di piano e forte*, Florence, 1732).

Gladstone, Francis Edward, English organist, teacher, and composer; b. Summertown, near Oxford, March 2, 1845; d. Hereford, Sept. 6, 1928. He was a pupil of S. Wesley (1859–64); filled positions as organist at Weston-super-Mare, Llandaff, Chichester, Brighton, London, and Norwich. After embracing the Catholic religion, he was choir director at St. Mary of the Angels, Bayswater, until 1894. In 1876 he took the degree of Mus.Bac. at Cambridge; in 1879, Mus.Doc.; was a prof. of harmony and counterpoint at the Royal College of Music from 1883 to 1910.

WORKS: Oratorio, *Philippi* (1883); much church music; an overture; some chamber music (all in MS); also publ. organ pieces, *The Organ-Student's Guide* and *A Treatise on Strict Counterpoint* (1906); wrote an a cappella chorus, *In Paradisium*, for his own funeral and trained 4 monks to sing it.

Glanville-Hicks, Peggy, Australian-born American composer and critic; b. Melbourne, Dec. 29, 1912; d. Sydney, June 25, 1990. She studied composition with Fritz Hart at the Melbourne Cons.; in 1931 went to London, where she took courses in piano with Arthur Benjamin, theory with R.O. Morris and C. Kitson, composition with Ralph Vaughan Williams, orchestration with Gordon Jacob, and conducting with Constant Lambert and Malcolm Sargent. She obtained a traveling scholarship, which enabled her to go to Paris for lessons with Nadia Boulanger and to Vienna, where she took a course in musicology and advanced composition with Egon Wellesz. In 1939 she went to the U.S.; became an American citizen; from 1938 to 1948 was married to the English composer **Stanley Bate;** from 1948 to 1958 she wrote music criticism for the *N.Y. Herald Tribune*. From 1956 to 1958 she received 2 Guggenheim fellowships; in 1959 she made her residence in Athens. There she produced her opera *Nausicaa*, to the text of Robert Graves (Aug. 19, 1961), which was well received. As a pragmatic composer of functional music with human connotations, Glanville-Hicks shunned the monopolistic fashion of mandatory dissonance, but explored attentively the resources of folk music, making use of Greek melos in her opera *Nausicaa*, of Hindu rhythmic modes in the opera *The Transposed Heads*, and of allusions to non-Western modalities in *Letters from Morocco*.

WORKS: STAGE: OPERAS: *The Transposed Heads* (Louisville, March 27, 1954); *The Glittering Gate* (N.Y., May 14, 1959); *Nausicaa* (Athens, Aug. 19, 1961); *Sappho* (1963); *Beckett* (1990). **BALLETS:** *The Masque of the Wild Man* (1958); *Saul and the Witch of Endor* (1959); *Tragic Celebration* (1966); *A Season in Hell* (1967). **ORCH.:** *Letters from Morocco* for Voice and Orch., to texts from actual letters she received from the composer Paul Bowles (N.Y., Feb. 22, 1953); *Sinfonia da Paci-*

fica (1953); *Tapestry* (1956); *Etruscan Concerto* for Piano and Chamber Orch. (N.Y., Jan. 25, 1956); *Concerto romantico* for Viola and Orch. (1957); *Drama* (1966). CHAMBER: *Concertino da camera* for Flute, Clarinet, Bassoon, and Piano (Amsterdam, June 10, 1948); other works inspired by ancient Greek modalities; choral pieces; songs.

Glareanus, Henricus or **Heinrich Glarean** (real name, **Heinrich Loris;** Latinized: **Henricus Loritus**), Swiss music theorist; b. Mollis, Glarus canton, June 1488; d. Freiburg, March 28, 1563. He studied with Rubellus at Bern, and later with Cochläus at Cologne, where he was crowned poet laureate by Emperor Maximilian I in 1512, as the result of a poem he composed and sang to the Emperor. He first taught mathematics at Basel (1514); from 1517 to 1522 he was in Paris, where he taught philosophy; in 1522 returned to Basel, where he stayed till 1529, when he settled in Freiburg. There he was a prof. of poetry, then of theology. His 1st important work, *Isagoge in musicen,* publ. at Basel in 1516 (Eng. tr. in the *Journal of Music Theory,* III, 1959), dealt with solmization, intervals, modes, and tones. A still more important vol., the *Dodecachordon,* was publ. in 1547; in it, Glareanus advanced the theory that there are 12 church modes, corresponding to the ancient Greek modes, instead of the commonly accepted 8 modes. The 3rd part of the *Dodecachordon* contains many works by 15th- and 16th-century musicians. A copy of the *Dodecachordon,* with corrections in Glareanus's own handwriting, is in the Library of Congress, Washington, D.C. A German tr., with the musical examples in modern notation, was publ. by P. Bohn in vol. 16 of *Publikationen der Gesellschaft für Musikforschung* (Leipzig, 1888); Eng. tr. and commentary by C. Miller in Musicological Studies and Documents, 6 (1965); facsimile ed. in Monuments of Music and Music Literature in Facsimile, 2/65 (N.Y., 1967). A complete index of Glareanus's works is contained in P. Lichtenthal's *Dizionario e bibliografia della musica,* IV, pp. 274–76 (Milan, 1826). J. Wonegger publ. *Musicae epitome ex Glareani Dodekachordo* (1557; 2nd ed., 1559; in German as *Uss Glareani Musik ein Usszug,* 1557).
BIBL.: O. Fritzsche, *Glarean, Sein Leben und seine Schriften* (Frauenfeld, 1890); A. Schering, "Die Notenbeispiele in Glareanus Dodecachordon," *Sammelbände der Internationalen Musik-Gesellschaft,* XIV (1912); E. Refardt, *Musikerlexikon der Schweiz* (1928); E. Kirsch, "Studie zum Problem des Heinrich Loriti (Glarean)," *Festschrift A. Schering zum 60.sten Geburtstag* (Berlin, 1937); B. Meier, "Heinrich Loriti Glareanus als Musiktheoretiker," *Aufsätze zur Freiburger Wissenschaft- und Universitätsgeschichte,* XXI (1960); C. Miller, "The *Dodecachordon;* Its Origin and Influence on Renaissance Thought," *Musica Disciplina,* XV (1961).

Glasenapp, Carl Friedrich, German music scholar; b. Riga, Oct. 3, 1847; d. there, April 14, 1915. He studied philology at Dorpat; from 1875, was headmaster at Riga. An ardent admirer of Wagner's art, he devoted his entire life to the study of the master's works, and was one of the principal contributors to the *Bayreuther Blätter* from their foundation. His great work is the monumental *Richard Wagners Leben und Wirken* (2 vols., Leipzig, 1876–77; 3rd ed., rev. and enl., as *Das Leben Richard Wagners,* 6 vols., Leipzig, 1894–1911; Eng. tr. by W. Ellis as *Life of Richard Wagner,* 6 vols., London, 1900–1908; vols. I–III based on Glasenapp; reprinted N.Y., 1977, with new introduction by G. Buelow; 5th German ed., rev., 1910–23). Though Glasenapp's work was considered the definitive biography of its time, its value is diminished by the fact that he publ. only materials approved by Wagner's family; as a result, it was superseded by later biographies. His other works include *Wagner-Lexikon* with H. von Stein (1883); *Wagner-Encyklopädie* (2 vols., 1891); *Siegfried Wagner* (1906); *Siegfried Wagner und seine Kunst* (1911), with sequels, *Schwarzschwanenreich* (1913) and *Sonnenflammen* (1919); he also ed. *Bayreuther Briefe, 1871–73* (1907) and *Familienbriefe an Richard Wagner, 1832–74* (1907).

Gläser, Franz (Joseph), Bohemian composer and conductor; b. Obergeorgenthal, April 19, 1798; d. Copenhagen, Aug. 29,

1861. He studied at the Prague Cons.; was active in Vienna as a composer for the theater from 1817. In 1830 he went to Berlin, where he produced the successful opera *Des Adlers Horst* (Dec. 29, 1832); in 1842 he settled in Copenhagen, where he became court conductor (1845). His Danish operas were *Bryllupet vet Como-soen* (The Wedding by Lake Como; Copenhagen, Jan. 29, 1849), *Nokken* (The Water Sprites; Copenhagen, Feb. 12, 1853), and *Den forgyldte svane* (The Golden Swan; Copenhagen, March 17, 1854). Hans Christian Andersen prepared the librettos for the 1st 2 for the Danish capital.
BIBL.: W. Neumann, *F. G.* (Leipzig, 1859); N. Pfeil, *F. G.* (Leipzig, 1870).

Glaser, Werner Wolf, German-born Swedish pianist, conductor, teacher, and composer; b. Cologne, April 14, 1910. He studied with Jarnach at the Cologne Hochschule für Musik, where he also received training in piano and conducting; later studied composition with Hindemith at the Berlin Hochschule für Musik, art history at the Univ. of Bonn, and psychology at the Univ. of Berlin, receiving a Ph.D. After conducting the Chemnitz Opera orch. (1929–31) and serving as chorus master in Cologne (1931–33), he went to Copenhagen as a teacher at the Fredricksberg Cons. (1936–43); with I. Skovgaard, he founded the Lyngby School of Music in 1939. He settled in Sweden, becoming a naturalized citizen in 1951; was conductor of the Södra Västmanland Orch. Soc. (1944–59) and was active as a music critic. With I. Andrén and G. Axén, he founded the Västerås School of Music in 1945, and was its director of studies from 1954 until his retirement in 1975. A man of wide interests, he studied modern art and literature and wrote poetry; he also investigated the potentialities of music therapy. A prolific composer, he followed the neo-Classical line.
WORKS: OPERAS: *Kagekiyo,* chamber opera (1961); *Encounters,* chamber opera (Västerås, Dec. 13, 1970); *A Naked King* (1971; Göteborg, April 6, 1973); *Cercatori,* chamber opera (1972); *The Boy and the Voice,* children's opera (1973); *Freedom Bells* (1980). BALLETS: *Persefone* (1960); *Les Cinq Pas de l'homme* (1973). ORCH.: 11 syms. (1934; 1936; 1936; 1943; 1949; 1957; 1961; 1964; 1976; 1974–80; 1983); Flute Concerto (1934); Concertino for Alto Saxophone and String Orch. (1935); *Trilogia I* (1939) and *II* (1981); *3 Pieces* for String Orch. (1947); *Idyll, Elegy, and Fanfare* (1954); Concerto No. 2 (1957); *Music* for String Orch. (1957); *Concerto della Capella* for Winds, Percussion, and Piano (1960); *Le tre gradi* for String Orch. (1961); *Capriccio No. 3* for Piano and Orch. (1962); Concertino for Clarinet and Small Orch. (1962); Concerto for Violin, Winds, and Percussion (1962); Violin Concerto (1964); *4 Dance Scenes* (1964); *3 pezzi* for Oboe d'Amore and Chamber Orch. (1964); *Conflitti* (1966); Oboe Concerto (1966); *Transformations* for Piano and Orch. (1966); *Modi gestus* for String Orch. (1966); *Syringa* for 3 Flutes and String Orch. (1966); Concerto for 20 Wind Instruments and Percussion (1966); *Paradosso* for 2 String Orchs. (1967); Concerto for Flute and String Orch. (1967); Horn Concerto (1969); *Arioso e Toccata No. 2* for Piano and Orch. (1969); *Canto* for Soprano Saxophone and String Orch. (1970); *Concerto lirico* for Soprano, Piano, Timpani, and String Orch. (1971); *3 Symphonic Dances* (1975); Cello Concerto (1976); *Adagio* for Strings (1977); Divertimento No. 2 for Wind Quintet and String Orch. (1979); Concerto for Soprano Saxophone and String Orch. (1980); Concerto for Tenor Saxophone and String Orch. (1981); Divertimento No. 3 (1983); *5 Serious Short Songs* for String Orch. (1984); *Concerto breve* for Violin, Strings, and Percussion (1986); *Nigeria* (1986); *5 Choreographic Scenes* for Chamber Orch. (1987); *Theme and Variations* (1987); Piano Concerto (1988). CHAMBER: 12 string quartets (1934, 1937, 1946, 1947, 1948, 1948, 1954, 1967, 1967, 1978, 1980, 1988); *Quartetto piccolo* for Strings (1938); Quartet for Saxophone, Violin, Viola, and Cello (1950); *Chamber Music* for Clarinet, Cello, and Piano (1952); Quartet for Flute, Clarinet, Cello, and Piano (1960); *Musica sacra* for Flute, Clarinet, Organ, and Strings (1960); *Intrada* for String Quartet (1964); Sonata for Solo Flute (1966); *Music* for Clarinet, Violin, and Double Bass (1967); 2 string trios (1969, 1975); 2 wind

quintets (1970, 1970); Sonata for Solo Violin (1971); *Paysages sonores* for Piano Trio (1973); *Variations and Interlude* for 8 Cellos (1978); *3 Pieces* for 11 Saxophones (1982); Quintet for Piano and String Quartet (1984); Saxophone Quartet (1984); *Linda Quartet* for Baritone Saxophone and String Trio (1985); Sonata for Oboe and Piano (1986); Sonata for Baritone Saxophone and Piano (1986); *Trezze* for Oboe and String Quartet (1987); *Fantasia all antico* for Violin (1988); also piano pieces, organ music, and various vocal works, including cantatas, choruses, and songs.

Glass, Louis (Christian August), Danish composer; b. Copenhagen, March 23, 1864; d. there, Jan. 22, 1936. He was a pupil of his father, **Christian Hendrik** (1821–93); then, at the Brussels Cons., of J. de Zarembski and J. Wieniawski (piano) and of J. Servais (cello); he appeared as both a pianist and a cellist.
    Works: 6 syms.: No. 1 (1893); No. 2 (1898–99); No. 3, *Skavsymfoni* (Wood Sym.; 1901); No. 4 (1910–11); No. 5, *Sinfonia svastica* (1919); No. 6, *Skoldungeaet* (Bird of the Scyldings; 1926); 2 overtures, *Der Volksfeind* and *Dänemark; Sommerliv*, suite for Orch.; dance poem, *Artemis* (Copenhagen, Oct. 27, 1917); Concerto for Oboe and Orch.; 4 string quartets; Piano Trio; 2 violin sonatas; numerous works for piano.

Glass, Philip, remarkable American composer; b. Baltimore, Jan. 31, 1937. He entered the Peabody Cons. of Music in Baltimore as a flute student when he was 8; then took courses in piano, mathematics, and philosophy at the Univ. of Chicago (1952–56); subsequently studied composition with Persichetti at the Juilliard School of Music in N.Y. (M.S., 1962). He received a Fulbright fellowship in 1964 and went to Paris to study with Boulanger; much more important to his future development was his meeting with Ravi Shankar, who introduced him to Hindu ragas. During a visit to Morocco, Glass absorbed the modalities of North African melo-rhythms, which taught him the art of melodic repetition. When he returned to N.Y. in 1967, his style of composition became an alternately concave and convex mirror image of Eastern modes, undergoing melodic phases of stationary harmonies in lieu of modulations. He formed associations with modern painters and sculptors who strove to obtain maximum effects with a minimum of means. He began to practice a similar method in music, which soon acquired the factitious sobriquet of Minimalism. Other Americans and some Europeans followed this practice, which was basically Eastern in its catatonic homophony; Steve Reich was a close companion in minimalistic pursuits of maximalistic effects. Glass formed his own phonograph company, Chatham Square, which recorded most of his works. He also organized an ensemble of electrically amplified instruments, which became the chief medium of his compositions. On April 13, 1968, he presented the 1st concert of the Philip Glass Ensemble at Queens College in N.Y. He subsequently toured widely with it, making visits abroad as well as traveling throughout the U.S. His productions, both in America and in Europe, became extremely successful among young audiences, who were mesmerized by his mixture of rock realism and alluring mysticism; undeterred by the indeterminability and interminability of his productions, some lasting several hours, these young people accepted him as a true representative of earthly and unearthly art. The mind-boggling titles of his works added to the tantalizing incomprehensibility of the subjects that he selected for his inspiration. The high point of his productions was the opera *Einstein on the Beach* (in collaboration with Robert Wilson), which involved a surrealistic communition of thematic ingredients and hypnotic repetition of harmonic subjects. It was premiered at the Avignon Festival on July 25, 1976, and was subsequently performed throughout Europe. It was given on Nov. 21, 1976, at the Metropolitan Opera in N.Y., where it proved something of a sensation of the season; however, it was not produced as part of the regular subscription series. In Rotterdam on Sept. 5, 1980, he produced his opera *Satyagraha*, a work based on Gandhi's years in South Africa. "Satyagraha" was Gandhi's slogan, composed of 2 Hindu words: *satya*

(truth) and *āgraha* (firmness). Another significant production was a film, *Koyaanisqatsi*, a Hopi Indian word meaning "life out of balance." The music represented the ultimate condensation of the basic elements of Glass's compositional style; here the ritualistic repetition of chords arranged in symmetrical sequences becomes hypnotic, particularly since the screen action is devoid of narrative; the effect is enhanced by the deep bass notes of an Indian chant. His mixed-media piece *The Photographer: Far from the Truth*, based on the life of the photographer Eadweard Muybridge, received its 1st U.S. performance in N.Y. on Oct. 6, 1983. It was followed by the exotic opera *Akhnaton*, set in ancient Egypt, with a libretto in ancient Akkadian, Egyptian, and Hebrew, with an explanatory narration in English; it was produced in Stuttgart on March 24, 1984. In collaboration with Robert Moran, he produced the opera *Juniper Tree* (Cambridge, Mass., Dec. 11, 1985). After bringing out the dance-theater piece *A Descent into the Maelstrom* (1986) and the dance piece *In the Upper Room* (1986), he wrote a Violin Concerto (1987). His symphonic score *The Light* was first performed in Cleveland on Oct. 29, 1987. It was followed by his opera *The Making of the Representative for Planet 8* (to a text by Doris Lessing), which received its premiere in Houston on July 8, 1988. His next opera, *The Fall of the House of Usher*, was first performed in Cambridge, Mass., on May 18, 1988. The music theater piece *1000 Airplanes on the Roof* was produced in Vienna in 1988. On Nov. 2, 1989, his *Itaipu* for Chorus and Orch. was premiered in Atlanta. Among his other works are *Music with Changing Parts* (N.Y., Nov. 10, 1972); *Music in 12 Parts* (N.Y., June 1, 1974), and *North Star* for 2 Voices and Instruments (1975). With R. Jones, he publ. *Music by Philip Glass* (N.Y., 1987; new ed., with supplement, 1988 as *Opera on the Beach: On His New World of Music Theatre*).
    Bibl.: M. Swed, "P. G.'s Operas," *Musical Times* (Nov. 1988).

Glaz (Glatz), Herta, Austrian-American contralto; b. Vienna, Sept. 16, 1908. She made her debut at the Breslau Opera in 1931, presaging a successful career, but in 1933 was forced to leave Germany. She toured Austria and Scandinavia as a concert singer; sang at the German Theater in Prague during the season 1935–36; in 1936 she took part in the American tour of the Salzburg Opera Guild; subsequently sang at the Chicago Opera (1940–42); on Dec. 25, 1942, she made her debut with the Metropolitan Opera in N.Y., and remained on its roster until 1956; then taught voice at the Manhattan School of Music, retiring in 1977.

Glazer, David, American clarinetist and teacher; b. Milwaukee, May 7, 1913. He studied at Milwaukee State Teachers College (B.Ed., 1935) and the Berkshire Music Center in Tanglewood (summers, 1940–42). After teaching at the Longy School of Music in Cambridge, Mass. (1937–42), he played in the Cleveland Orch. (1946–51); then joined the N.Y. Woodwind Quintet (1951–85). He also taught at the Mannes College of Music, the N.Y. College of Music, N.Y. Univ., and the State Univ. of N.Y. at Stony Brook.

Glazunov, Alexander (Konstantinovich), eminent Russian composer; b. St. Petersburg, Aug. 10, 1865; d. Neuilly-sur-Seine, March 21, 1936. Of a well-to-do family (his father was a book publisher), he studied at a technical high school in St. Petersburg, and also took lessons in music with N. Elenkovsky. As a boy of 15, he was introduced to Rimsky-Korsakov, who gave him weekly lessons in harmony, counterpoint, and orchestration. He made rapid progress, and at the age of 16 completed his 1st Sym., which was conducted by Balakirev on March 29, 1882, in St. Petersburg. So mature was this score that Glazunov was hailed by Stasov, Cui, and others as a rightful heir to the masters of the Russian national school. The music publisher Belaiev arranged for publication of his works, and took him to Weimar, where he met Liszt. From that time Glazunov composed assiduously in all genres except opera. He was invited to conduct his syms. in Paris (1889) and London (1896–97). Returning to St. Petersburg, he conducted concerts of Russian music. In 1899 he was engaged as an instructor in composition and orchestration at the St. Petersburg Cons. He resigned temporarily during the revolutionary turmoil of 1905 in protest against the dismissal of Rimsky-Korsakov by the government authorities, but returned to the staff after full autonomy was granted to the Cons. by the administration. In 1905 Glazunov was elected director and retained this post until 1928, when he went to Paris. In 1929 he made several appearances as conductor in the U.S. He was the recipient of honorary degrees of Mus.D. from Cambridge and Oxford Univs. (1907). Although he wrote no textbook on composition, his pedagogical methods left a lasting impression on Russian musicians through his many students who preserved his traditions. His music is often regarded as academic, yet there is a flow of rhapsodic eloquence that places Glazunov in the Romantic school. He was for a time greatly swayed by Wagnerian harmonies, but resisted this influence successfully; Lisztian characteristics are more pronounced in his works. Glazunov was one of the greatest masters of counterpoint among Russian composers, but he avoided extreme polyphonic complexity. The national spirit of his music is unmistakable; in many of his descriptive works, the programmatic design is explicitly Russian (*Stenka Razin, The Kremlin*, etc.). His most popular score is the ballet *Raymonda*. The major portion of his music was written before 1906, when he completed his 8th Sym.; after that he wrote mostly for special occasions. He also completed and orchestrated the overture to Borodin's *Prince Igor* from memory, having heard Borodin play it on the piano.

WORKS (all 1st perf. in St. Petersburg [Petrograd] unless otherwise given): **STAGE:** Introduction and Dance of Salome for *Salome* by O. Wilde (1912); incidental music to *The King of the Jews* by K. Romanov (Jan. 9, 1914). **BALLETS:** *Raymonda* (1896; Jan. 19, 1898); *The Ruses of Love* (1898; 1900); *The Seasons* (1899; Feb. 20, 1900). **ORCH.:** 9 syms.: No. 1, in E major (1881; March 29, 1882; rev. 1885, 1929); No. 2, in F-sharp minor (1886; Paris, June 29, 1889); No. 3, in D major (Dec. 20, 1890); No. 4, in E-flat major (1893; Feb. 3, 1894); No. 5, in B-flat major (1895; London, Jan. 28, 1897); No. 6, in C minor (1896; Feb. 21, 1897); No. 7, in F major (1902; Jan. 3, 1903); No. 8, in E-flat major (Dec. 22, 1906); No. 9, in D major (1910; completed by G. Yudin, 1948). **SOLO WITH ORCH.:** *Melody and Spanish Serenade* for Cello (1888); *Song of a Minstrel* for Cello (1900; also for Cello and Piano); Violin Concerto (1904; March 4, 1905; L. Auer, soloist); Piano Concerto No. 1 (1910); Piano Concerto No. 2 (Nov. 11, 1917); *Mazurka-Oberek* for Violin (1917; orchestration by I. Yampolsky of work for Violin and Piano); *Concerto-Ballata* for Cello (1931; Paris, Oct. 14, 1933; Maurice Eisenberg, soloist); Saxophone Concerto (1931; Nykoping, Nov. 25, 1934; Sigurd Rascher, soloist). **OTHER:** 2 *Overtures on Greek Themes* (1881, 1883); 2 *Serenades* (1883, 1884); *Lyric Poem* (1884); *Stenka Razin*, symphonic poem (1885); *To the Memory of a Hero* (1885); *Characteristic Suite* (1885); *Idyll and Oriental Reverie* (1885); *The Forest*, symphonic poem (1887); *Mazurka* (1888); *Slavonic Festival* (1888; from String Quartet No. 3); *Wedding March* (1889); *The Sea*, symphonic fantasy (1889); *Oriental Rhapsody* (1890); *The Kremlin*, musical picture (1891); *Spring*, musical picture (1891); *Chopiniana*, suite on themes by Chopin (1893); *Carnaval*, overture (1893); 2 *Concert Waltzes* (1894); 2 *Solemn Processionals* (1894, 1910); *Ballet Suite* (1894); *From Darkness to Light*, fantasy (1894); *Fantasy* (1895); *Suite* (1898) and *Characteristic Dance* (1900) from *Raymonda*; *Romantic Intermezzo* (1900); *Festival Overture* (1900); *March on a Russian Theme* (1901); *Ballade* (1902); *From the Middle Ages*, suite (1902; Jan. 3, 1903); *Ballet Scene* (1904); *Russian Fantasy* for Balalaika Orch. (March 11, 1906); 2 *Preludes*: No. 1, *In Memory of V. Stasov* (1906), and No. 2, *In Memory of Rimsky-Korsakov* (1908); *The Song of Destiny*, overture (1908); *In Memory of N. Gogol* (1909); *Finnish Fantasy* (1909; March 27, 1910); *Finnish Sketches* (1912); *Karelian Legend*, musical picture (1914); *Paraphrase on National Anthems of the Allies* (1915); *Variations* for Strings (1918); *Epic Poem* (1934). **VO-**

CAL: *Triumphal March* for Chorus and Orch. (for the Chicago Columbian Exposition; 1893); Coronation Cantata (1894); *Cantata in Memory of Pushkin's 100th Birthday* (1899); *Hymn to Pushkin* for Female Chorus and Piano (1899); *Love* for Chorus (1907); *Prelude-Cantata for the 50th Anniversary of the St. Petersburg Cons.* (1912); 21 songs. **CHAMBER:** 7 string quartets: No. 1, in D major (1882); No. 2, in F major (1884); No. 3, in G major (*Quatuor Slave;* 1888); No. 4, in A minor (1894); No. 5, in D minor (1898); No. 6, in B-flat major (1921); No. 7, in C major (1930); 5 *Novelettes* for String Quartet (1886); Suite for String Quartet (1891); String Quintet (1895); *Elegy* for String Quartet (1928); *Elegy to the Memory of F. Liszt* for Cello and Piano (1886); *Reverie* for Horn and Piano (1890); *Meditation* for Violin and Piano (1891); *In modo religioso* for Brass Quartet (1892); *Elegy* for Viola and Piano (1893); *Mazurka-Oberek* for Violin and Piano (1917); Saxophone Quartet (1932). **PIANO:** 2 sonatas (1901, 1901); *Suite on the Theme "Sacha"* (1883); *Barcarolle* and *Novelette* (1889); *Prelude* and 2 *Mazurkas* (1889); *Nocturne* (1889); 3 *Études* (1890); *Little Waltz* (1892); *Grand Concert Waltz* (1893); 3 *Miniatures* (1893); *Salon Waltz* (1893); 3 *Pieces* (1894); 2 *Impromptus* (1895); *Prelude and Fugue* (1899); *Theme and Variations* (1900); 4 *Preludes and Fugues* (1918–23); *Idylle* (1926); *Prelude and Fugue* (1926); *Suite* for 2 Pianos (1920).

BIBL.: A. Ossovsky, *G.: His Life and Works* (St. Petersburg, 1907); M. Montagu-Nathan, *Contemporary Russian Composers* (N.Y., 1917); V. Belaiev, *G.* (vol. 1, Petrograd, 1922); V. Derzhanovsky, *A. G.* (Moscow, 1922); I. Glebov, *G.* (Leningrad, 1924); M. Calvocoressi and G. Abraham, *Masters of Russian Music* (N.Y., 1936); G. Fedorova, *G.* (Moscow, 1947; 2nd ed., 1961); H. Gunther, *A. G.* (Bonn, 1956); M. Ganina, *G.: Life and Works* (Leningrad, 1961); D. Gojowy, *A. G.: Sein Leben in Bildern und Dokumenten: Unter Ein beziehung des biographischen Fragments von G.s Schwiegersohn Herbert Günther* (Munich, 1986).

Gleason, Frederick Grant, American organist, composer, and critic; b. Middletown, Conn., Dec. 17, 1848; d. Chicago, Dec. 6, 1903. He studied in Hartford with Dudley Buck; later at the Leipzig Cons., in Berlin, and in London. Upon his return to the U.S., he was active as a church organist, teacher, and music critic. He wrote 2 operas, *Otho Visconti* (1877–90; Chicago, June 4, 1907) and *Montezuma;* 4 cantatas; a symphonic poem, *Edris* (1896); a Piano Concerto; 3 piano trios; organ and piano pieces; songs; 2 Episcopal church services.

Gleason, Harold, American organist, musicologist, and teacher; b. Jefferson, Ohio, April 26, 1892; d. La Jolla, Calif., June 28, 1980. He studied organ with Farnam in Boston, and in Paris with Bonnet; took a course in composition with Herbert Inch at the Eastman School of Music in Rochester, N.Y.; was head of the organ dept. there from 1921 to 1953; also taught musicology. He publ. *Method of Organ Playing* (1937; 7th ed., 1987); *Examples of Music before 1400* (1942); and *Music in America* (with W.T. Marrocco; N.Y., 1964).

Glebov, Evgeny, Russian composer; b. Roslavl, near Smolensk, Sept. 10, 1929. He studied at the Belorussian Cons. in Minsk with Bogatyrev; later was appointed to its faculty. Several of his compositions reflect the events of World War II, which devastated Belorussia in 1941.

WORKS: Opera, *Our Spring* (1963); ballet, *A Vision* (1961); cantata, *We Will Fight for Truth* (1956); cantata, *The Communists Lead Us* (1963); *Partisan Symphony* (1958); Concerto for Voice and Orch. (1965); several pieces for native Belorussian instruments.

BIBL.: L. Mukharinskaya, *E. G.* (Moscow, 1959); E. Rakova, *E. G.* (Minsk, 1971).

Glebov, Igor. Pen name of **Boris Asafiev.**

Glen, John, Scottish manufacturer of bagpipes and music researcher; b. Edinburgh, June 13, 1833; d. there, Nov. 29, 1904. His father, **Thomas Glen** (1804–73), the inventor of the "Serpentcleide," had established himself as a manufacturer of musical instruments, and the son succeeded to the business in 1866; he confined himself to the manufacture of bagpipes, of which he was soon recognized as the foremost manufacturer in Great Britain. He was equally noted for his research in Scottish music; compiled *The Glen Collection of Scottish Dance Music, Strathspeys, Reels and Jigs . . . containing an Introduction on Scottish Dance Music* (2 vols., 1891, 1895) and *Early Scottish Melodies: including examples from MSS. and early printed works, along with a number of comparative tunes, notes on former annotators, English and other claims, and Biographical Notices, etc.* (1900).

Glick, Srul Irving, Canadian composer; b. Toronto, Sept. 18, 1934. He studied composition with Weinzweig at the Univ. of Toronto (M.M., 1958); attended classes of Darius Milhaud in Aspen, Colo. (summers 1956, 1957), and later took lessons with him and with Louis Saguer and Max Deutsch in Paris (1959–60). Returning to Canada, he taught theory and composition at the Royal Cons. of Music in Toronto (1963–69). His catalogue of works contains scores of 2 distinct types: those of a traditional Hebraic nature, direct and recognizable, and those that are abstract, written in a highly advanced idiom. **WORKS: ORCH.:** *Heritage,* dance sym. (Toronto, Dec. 9, 1967); 2 *Essays* for Orch. (1957); Sonata for String Orch. (1957); *Sinfonietta* (1958); *Sinfonia concertante* No. 1 for String Orch. (1961); *Sinfonia concertante* No. 2, *Lamentations,* for String Quartet and Orch. (1972); *Suite hébraïque* (1961); *Dance Concertante No. 1* for Small Orch. (1963); *Symphonic Dialogues* for Piano and Orch. (Toronto, Dec. 20, 1964); *Pan* (1966); Sym. No. 1 for Chamber Orch. (Toronto, April 24, 1966); . . . *i never saw another butterfly . . . ,* to a text of children's poems written in the Terezin concentration camp, for Alto and Chamber Orch. (1968); Sym. No. 2 (Toronto, Jan. 24, 1969); *Gathering In,* "symphonic concept" for Strings (Montreal, March 26, 1970); *Psalm* (Hamilton, Oct. 17, 1971); *Symphonic Elegy,* with line drawing and funeral march (Toronto, April 20, 1974); Violin Concerto, *Shir Hamaalot* (Songs of Ascents; Victoria, British Columbia, Nov. 14, 1976); Concerto for Viola and String Orch. (1981); *Devequt,* sonata for Orch. (1982); *The Hour Has Come* for Chorus and Orch. (1984; Toronto, Feb. 25, 1985); *The Vision of Ezekiel,* fantasy for Violin and Orch. (1987); *Divertimento* for String Orch. (1988). **CHAMBER:** *Divertimento Sextet* for Flute, Clarinet, Bassoon, and String Trio (1958); Trio for Clarinet, Piano, and Cello (1958–59); String Trio (1963); *Dance Concertante No. 2* for Flute, Clarinet, Trumpet, Cello, and Piano (1964); Sonata for Jazz Quintet (1964); Sonatina for Jazz Sextet (1965–66); *Divertissement* for 7 Instruments and Conductor (1968); *Suite hébraïque* No. 2 for Clarinet, Piano, and String Trio (1969); *Suite hébraïque* No. 3 for String Quintet (1975); *Prayer and Dance* for Cello and Piano (1975); *Suite hébraïque* No. 4 for Alto Saxophone or Clarinet or Viola, and Piano (1979); *Suite hébraïque* No. 5 for Flute, Clarinet, Violin, and Cello (1980); String Quartet No. 1 (Toronto, June 25, 1984); *Suite hébraïque* No. 6 for Violin and Piano (1984); Sonata for Oboe and Piano (1987); piano pieces; also songs; liturgical choruses for Hebrew services.

Glière, Reinhold (Moritsovich), eminent Russian composer; b. Kiev, Jan. 11, 1875; d. Moscow, June 23, 1956. He studied violin with Hrimaly at the Moscow Cons., where he also took courses with Arensky, Taneyev, and Ippolitov-Ivanov (1894–1900), graduating with a gold medal. In 1905 he went to Berlin, where he remained for 2 years; returning to Russia, he became active as a teacher; was appointed prof. of composition at the Kiev Cons., and was its director from 1914 to 1920; then was appointed to the faculty of the Moscow Cons., a post he retained until 1941. He traveled extensively in European and Asiatic Russia, collecting folk melodies; conducted many concerts of his own works; he made his last tour a month before his death, conducting in Odessa, Kishinev, and other cities. He was a prolific composer, and was particularly distinguished in symphonic works, in which he revealed himself as a successor of the Russian national school. He never transgressed the natural borderline of traditional harmony, but he was able to achieve effective results. His most impressive work

is his 3rd Sym., subtitled *Ilya Muromets,* an epic description of the exploits of a legendary Russian hero. In his numerous songs Glière showed a fine lyrical talent. He wrote relatively few works of chamber music, most of them early in his career. In his opera *Shah-Senem,* he made use of native Caucasian songs. Glière was the teacher of 2 generations of Russian composers; among his students were Prokofiev and Miaskovsky. He received Stalin prizes for the String Quartet No. 4 (1948) and the ballet *The Bronze Knight* (1950). **WORKS: OPERAS:** *Shah-Senem* (Baku, May 4, 1934); *Leily and Medzhnun* (Tashkent, July 18, 1940); *Rachel,* 1-act opera after Maupassant's *Mademoiselle Fifi* (Moscow, April 19, 1947); *Ghulsara* (Tashkent, Dec. 25, 1949). **BALLETS:** *Chrysis* (Moscow, Nov. 30, 1912); *Cleopatra* (Moscow, Jan. 11, 1926); *Red Poppy* (Moscow, June 14, 1927); *Comedians* (Moscow, April 5, 1931); *The Bronze Knight* (Leningrad, March 14, 1949). **INCIDENTAL MUSIC:** *King Oedipus* of Sophocles (1921); *Lysistrata* of Aristophanes (1923); *Marriage of Figaro* of Beaumarchais (1927). **ORCH.:** Sym. No. 1 (Moscow, Jan. 3, 1903); Sym. No. 2 (Berlin, Jan. 23, 1908, Koussevitzky conducting); *The Sirens,* symphonic poem (Moscow, Jan. 30, 1909); Sym. No. 3, *Ilya Muromets* (Moscow, March 23, 1912); 2 *Poems* for Soprano and Orch. (1924); *Cossacks of Zaporozh,* symphonic poem (1921; Odessa, Dec. 23, 1925); *Trizna,* symphonic poem (1915); *For the Festival of the Comintern,* fantasy for Wind Orch. (1924); *March of the Red Army* for Wind Orch. (1924); *Imitation of Jezekiel,* symphonic poem for Narrator and Orch. (1919); Concerto for Harp and Orch. (Moscow, Nov. 23, 1938); *Friendship of Nations,* overture (1941); Concerto for Coloratura Soprano and Orch. (Moscow, May 12, 1943); *For the Happiness of the Fatherland,* overture (1942); *25 Years of the Red Army,* overture (1943); *Victory,* overture (Moscow, Oct. 30, 1945); Cello Concerto (Moscow, Feb. 18, 1947); Horn Concerto (Moscow, Jan. 26, 1952, composer conducting); an unfinished Violin Concerto. **CHAMBER:** 5 string quartets (No. 4 won the Stalin Prize, 1948; No. 5 left unfinished at his death); 3 string sextets; String Octet. **OTHER:** 20 pieces for Violin and Piano; 12 duos for 2 Violins; Ballad for Cello and Piano; 4 pieces for Double Bass and Piano; 8 pieces for Violin and Cello; 12 pieces for Cello and Piano; 10 duos for 2 Cellos; miscellaneous pieces for different instruments. He also wrote about 200 songs and 200 piano pieces. **BIBL.:** I. Boelza, *R.M. G.* (Moscow, 1955; 2nd ed., 1962).

Glinka, Mikhail (Ivanovich), great Russian composer, often called "the father of Russian music" for his pioneering cultivation of Russian folk modalities; b. Novospasskoye, Smolensk district, June 1, 1804; d. Berlin, Feb. 15, 1857. A scion of a fairly rich family of landowners, he was educated at an exclusive school in St. Petersburg (1817–22); he also took private lessons in music; his piano teacher was a resident German musician, Carl Meyer; he also studied violin; when the pianist John Field was in St. Petersburg, Glinka had an opportunity to study with him, but he had only 3 lessons before Field departed. He began to compose even before acquiring adequate training in theory. As a boy he traveled in the Caucasus; then stayed for a while at his father's estate; at 20 he entered the Ministry of Communications in St. Petersburg; he remained in government employ until 1828; at the same time, he constantly improved his general education by reading; he had friends among the best Russian writers of the time, including the poets Zhukovsky and Pushkin. He also took singing lessons with an Italian teacher, Belloli. In 1830 he went to Italy; he continued irregular studies in Milan (where he spent most of his Italian years); he also visited Naples, Rome, and Venice. He met Donizetti and Bellini. He became enamored of Italian music, and his early vocal and instrumental compositions are thoroughly Italian in melodic and harmonic structure. In 1833 he went to Berlin, where he took a course in counterpoint and general composition with Dehn; thus he was nearly 30 when he completed his theoretical education. In 1834 his father died, and Glinka went back to Russia to take care of the family affairs. In 1835 he was married; the marriage was unhappy, and he soon became separated from his wife, finally divorcing her in 1846. The return to his native land led him to consider the composition of a truly national opera on a subject (suggested to him by Zhukovsky) depicting a historical episode in Russian history: the saving of the 1st czar of the Romanov dynasty by a simple peasant, Ivan Susanin. (The Italian composer Cavos wrote an opera on the same subject 20 years previously, and conducted it in St. Petersburg.) Glinka's opera was produced in St. Petersburg on Dec. 9, 1836, under the title *A Life for the Czar.* The event was hailed by the literary and artistic circles of Russia as a milestone of Russian culture, and indeed the entire development of Russian national music received its decisive creative impulse from Glinka's patriotic opera. It remained in the repertoire of Russian theaters until the Revolution made it unacceptable, but it was revived, under the original title, *Ivan Susanin,* on Feb. 27, 1939, in Moscow, without alterations in the music, but with the references to the czar eliminated from the libretto, the idea of saving the country being substituted for that of saving the czar. Glinka's next opera, *Ruslan and Ludmila,* after Pushkin's fairy tale, was produced in St. Petersburg on Dec. 9, 1842; this opera, too, became extremely popular in Russia. Glinka introduced into the score many elements of oriental music; 1 episode contains the earliest use of the whole-tone scale in an opera. Both operas retain the traditional Italian form, with arias, choruses, and orch. episodes clearly separated. In 1844 Glinka was in Paris, where he met Berlioz; he also traveled in Spain, where he collected folk songs; the fruits of his Spanish tour were 2 orch. works, *Jota Aragonesa* and *Night in Madrid.* On his way back to Russia, he stayed in Warsaw for 3 years; the remaining years of his life he spent in St. Petersburg, Paris, and Berlin.

WORKS: STAGE: Operas: *A Life for the Czar* (1st perf. as *Ivan Susanin,* St. Petersburg, Dec. 9, 1836); *Ruslan and Ludmila* (St. Petersburg, Dec. 9, 1842); sketches for 3 unfinished operas; *Chao-Kang,* ballet (1828–31); incidental music for Kukolnik's tragedy *Prince Kholmsky* (1840) and for the play *The Moldavian Gypsy* (1836). **ORCH.:** *Andante Cantabile and Rondo;* Larghetto; 2 overtures; Sym. in B-flat; *Trumpet March* (1828); *Overture-Symphony on Russian Themes* (1834; completed in 1938 by V.I. Shebalin); *Valse* (1839); *Polonaise* (1839); *Valse-Fantaisie* (1839); *Capriccio brillante* on the *Jota Aragonesa* (1845; afterward renamed *Spanish Overture No. 1*); *Summer Night in Madrid: Spanish Overture No. 2* (1848); *Kamarinskaya* (1848); symphonic poem on Gogol's *Taras Bulba* (unfinished; part of 1st movement only, 1852); *Festival Polonaise* on a bolero melody (1855). **CHAMBER:** Septet in E-flat (1824); 2 string quartets (1824, 1830); *Trio pathétique* (1827); 2 serenades (1832); Sonata for Piano and Viola (1825–28); about 40 piano numbers (5 valses, 7 mazurkas, nocturnes, etc.); much vocal music, including choral works, quartets, duets, arias, and about 85 songs with piano accompaniment, many set to poems by Pushkin and Zhukovsky.

BIBL.: Glinka's autobiographical sketch intended for inclusion in the *Biographie universelle des musiciens* by Fétis was publ. for the 1st time in *Muzikalnaya Letopis'* in 1926; his collected letters, ed. by N. Findeisen, were publ. in 1907. See also C. Cui, *La Musique en Russie* (Paris, 1880); O. Fouque, *G.* (Paris, 1880); K. Albrecht, *Catalogue of G.'s Vocal Works* (Moscow, 1891); P. Weimarn, *M.I. G.* (Moscow, 1892); L. Shestakova, *G. as He Was* (St. Petersburg, 1894); N. Findeisen, *M.I. G.* (St. Petersburg, 1896); idem, *G. in Spain and the Spanish Folk Songs Recorded by Him* (St. Petersburg, 1896); idem, *Catalogue of the Musical Manuscripts, Letters, and Portraits of M.I. G. in the Manuscript Section of the Imperial Public Library in St. Petersburg* (St. Petersburg, 1898); V. Avenarius, *G., the Creator of Russian Opera* (St. Petersburg, 1903); A. Pougin, *Essai historique sur la musique en Russie* (Paris, 1904); M.D. Calvocoressi, *G.* (Paris, 1913); M. Montagu-Nathan, *G.* (London, 1916); K. Kuznetzov, *G. and His Contemporaries* (1926); M.D. Calvocoressi and G. Abraham, *Masters of Russian Music* (N.Y., 1936); D. Brook, *Six Great Russian Composers* (London, 1946); I. Martinov, *M.I. G.* (Moscow, 1947); B. Asafiev, *G.* (Moscow, 1947); E. Kann-Novikova, *M.I. G., New Mate-* rials and Documents (Moscow, 1951); A. Orlova, *M.I. G., Chronicle of Life and Work* (Moscow, 1952; ed. by M. Brown and tr. by R. Hoops, Ann Arbor, 1988); P. Dippel, *Klingende Einkehr; G. und Berlin* (Berlin, 1953); A. Orlova, *G. in St. Petersburg* (Leningrad, 1970); D. Brown, *G.: A Biographical and Critical Study* (London, 1974); R. Taruskin, "G.'s Ambiguous Legacy and the Birth Pangs of Russian Opera," *19th Century Music* (Nov. 1977).

Gliński, Mateusz, Polish conductor, musicologist, and composer; b. Warsaw, April 6, 1892; d. Welland, Ontario, Jan. 3, 1976. He studied at the Warsaw Cons. with Barcewicz (violin) and Statkowski (composition); then took courses in Leipzig with Max Reger, Riemann, and Schering; also had lessons in conducting with Nikisch. He went to St. Petersburg in 1914; studied composition with Glazunov and Steinberg, and conducting with Nikolai Tcherepnin. In 1918 he went to Warsaw; from 1924 to 1939 was ed. of the periodical *Muzyka.* At the outbreak of World War II he went to Rome, where he engaged in various activities as music critic and ed. In 1949 he established in Rome the Istituto Internazionale Federico Chopin. In 1956 he went to America; from 1959 to 1965 he taught at Assumption Univ. in Windsor, Ontario. In 1965 he established the Niagara Sym. Orch., which he conducted. His works include an opera, *Orlotko,* after Rostand's play *L'Aiglon* (1918–27); a symphonic poem, *Wagram* (1932); choral works; songs; piano pieces. He publ., in Polish, a monograph on Scriabin (Warsaw, 1933); *Chopin's Letters to Delfina Potocka* (Windsor, 1961), in which he subscribes to the generally refuted belief that these letters, which came to light in 1945, are indeed genuine; and *Chopin the Unknown* (Windsor, 1963).

Globokar, Vinko, French composer of Slovenian descent; b. Anderny, July 7, 1934. He studied trombone in Ljubljana (1949–54) and at the Paris Cons. (1955–59); took composition lessons in Paris with René Leibowitz (1959–63) and Luciano Berio (1965). He was a trombonist and composer at the Center for Creative Arts at the State Univ. of N.Y. at Buffalo in 1965–66. In 1968 he was appointed trombone instructor at the Cologne Hochschule für Musik; was active at IRCAM in Paris (from 1975). As a composer, he follows the most modern ideas of serial music in aleatory distribution. His works include *Plan for a Persian Drum and 4 Instruments* (1965); *Fluide* for 9 Brasses and 3 Percussion Instruments (1967); *Traumdeutung,* a "psychodrama" (Amsterdam, Sept. 7, 1968); *Étude pour folklore I* for 19 Soloists (1968); *Étude pour folklore II* for Orch. (1968); Concerto Grosso (Cologne, Nov. 6, 1970; rev. 1975); *Airs de voyages vers l'intérieur* for Ensemble (Stuttgart, Nov. 3, 1972); *Carroussel* for 4 Singers and 16 Instrumentalists (1977); *Realities/Augenblick* for Vocalists, Orch., and Film Projection (1984); *Dos a dos* for 2 Performers (1988); *Atemstudie* for Oboe (1988).

Glock, Sir William (Frederick), English music critic and broadcasting administrator; b. London, May 3, 1908. He studied at Gonville and Caius College, Cambridge; then took piano lessons with Artur Schnabel in Berlin (1930–33). He made some appearances as a concert pianist, but devoted most of his time and effort to music criticism. In 1934 he joined the staff of the *Observer;* served as its chief music critic from 1939 to 1945. In 1949 he founded the magazine the *Score,* and ed. it until 1961. In 1948 he established the Summer School of Music at Bryanston, Dorset, which relocated to Dartington Hall, Devon, in 1953; he continued as its music director until 1979. In 1959 he assumed the important post of controller of music of the BBC, retaining it until 1973. In 1964 he was made a Commander of the Order of the British Empire; was knighted in 1970.

Glodeanu, Liviu, Rumanian composer; b. Dirja, Aug. 6, 1938; d. Bucharest, March 31, 1978. He studied at the Cluj Cons., and later at the Bucharest Cons., with Ion Dumitrescu, Martian Negrea, Alfred Mendelsohn, and Tudor Ciortea. He subsequently taught at the School of Arts in Bucharest (1961–63); then was artistic adviser of the Bucharest Phil. (1963–71).

Works: Radio opera, *Zamolxe* (Bucharest, Oct. 8, 1969); 4 cantatas: *The Young Dead Soldiers,* to a text by Archibald MacLeish (1958; Cluj, March 31, 1962); *Inscriptions on the Cradle* (1959); *Bright Horizons* (1960); *Cantata 1933* (1961); an oratorio, *Un pămînt numit România* (1977). Other vocal works: *Suite* for Children's Chorus, Wind Instruments, and Percussion (1961); *2 Madrigals* for Chorus and Percussion (1963); *Incantation* for Chorus, Flute, Clarinet, and Percussion (1965); *Gloire* for Children's Chorus and Percussion (1967); *Ulysses* for Soprano or Tenor, and Orch. or Piano (1967). **orch.:** Concerto for String Orch. and Percussion (1959); Piano Concerto (1960); Symphonic Movement (1961); Flute Concerto (1962); Violin Concerto (1966); *Studies* (1967); *Ricercari* (1971); *Symphonies* for Wind Ensemble (1971); *Pintea Vinteazul* (Pintea the Brave), symphonic poem (1976); Concerto for Organ and Brass (1978). **chamber:** Clarinet Sonata (1959); 2 string quartets (1959, 1970); *Inventions* for Wind Quintet and Percussion (1963); Violin Sonatina (1963); *Mélopée* for Flute, Clarinet, Violin, and Tape (1971).

Glorieux, François, Belgian pianist, composer, teacher, and conductor; b. Courtrai, Aug. 27, 1932. He studied at the Royal Cons. in Ghent (graduated, 1953), then toured as a pianist; he taught chamber music at the Royal Cons. in Ghent, and was head of the summer courses in piano at the Royal Cons. in Antwerp. He became especially successful in presenting entertaining improvisational recitals in 5 languages; also conducted his own 25-member orch. from 1979. His compositions run the gamut from serious works to popular scores and arrangements, the last including pieces by Stan Kenton and Michael Jackson. He also prepared a new version of the Belgian national anthem (1981).

Works: television musical: *Rip van Winkel* (1969). ballets: *L'Énigme* (1964); *Ritus paganus* (1972); *The Dream* (1982). other: *Manhattan* for Piano and Orch. (1973–74; Antwerp, March 28, 1974); *Walking on the Street* for Big Band (1975); *Evolution* for African Percussion Instruments, Piano, Electric Guitar, and Drums (1975); *Tribute to Stan Kenton* for Piano, Flute, Brass, Bass Guitar, and Percussion (1976); *Fanfare for Europe* for Brass and Percussion Ensemble (1977–78); *In memoriam Stan Kenton* for Piano, Flute, Brass, Bass Guitar, and Percussion (1979); *Hello Mister Joplin* for Synthesizers (1982); *Tribute to Michael Jackson,* instrumental suite in 8 parts (1984–88); *The Legend of Bruce Lee* for Flute, Synthesizers, Brass, and Percussion (1986); *Glorieux Hymn* for Organ or Synthesizer, Brass, Percussion, and Choir ad libitum (1988); *6 Pieces* for 8 Trumpets (1988); *Contrasts* for Tenor Trombone and Orch. (1988); other chamber works; film scores.

Glossop, Peter, English baritone; b. Sheffield, July 6, 1928. He was educated privately as a singer; was a member of the Sadler's Wells Opera Co. (1953–62). In 1966 he joined the Royal Opera, Covent Garden. His American debut at the Metropolitan Opera in N.Y. took place on Aug. 18, 1967, in *Rigoletto.* He is notable principally for his performances of dramatic roles in Verdi's operas.

Glover, Jane (Alison), English conductor and musicologist; b. Helmsley, Yorkshire, May 13, 1949. She was educated at St. Hugh's College, Oxford (Ph.D., 1978, with a diss. on Cavalli); made her professional conducting debut at the Wexford Festival in 1975 with her own performing ed. of Cavalli's *Eritrea,* which she later presented in London (1982); in 1980 she became chorus master at the Glyndebourne Festival, and from 1982 to 1985 served as music director of the Glyndebourne Touring Opera; she also served as music director of the London Choral Soc. (from 1983) and was artistic director of the London Mozart Players (from 1984). She appeared as a guest conductor in England and on the Continent; in 1988 she made her Covent Garden debut in London conducting *Die Entführung aus dem Serail.* She also engaged in research and teaching; was a research fellow (1973–75) and lecturer in music (1976–84) at St. Hugh's College, Oxford; likewise lectured at St. Anne's College (1976–80) and Pembroke College (1979–84) there; in 1979 she was elected to the music faculty of Oxford Univ.

In her performing eds., she endeavors to preserve the authenticity of the original scores.

Glover, John William, Irish composer; b. Dublin, June 19, 1815; d. there, Dec. 18, 1899. He studied in Dublin; from 1848 he taught vocal music at the Normal Training School of the Irish National Education Board and was also director of music in the Roman Catholic procathedral. He was noted for his promotion of choral music in Ireland. He ed. Moore's *Irish Melodies* (1859).

Works: Opera, *The Deserted Village,* after Goldsmith (London, 1880); 2 Italian operas to librettos by Metastasio; cantata, *St. Patrick at Tara* (1870); *Erin's Matin Song* (1873); ode to Thomas Moore, *100 years ago* (1879); also concertos; piano pieces; songs; church music.

Glover, Sarah Anna, English piano pedagogue; b. Norwich, Nov. 13, 1786; d. Malvern, Oct. 20, 1867. She was the originator of the tonic sol-fa system of notation, a method later modified and developed by John Curwen. She devised a pictorial chart called the "Norwich Sol-fa Ladder." She wrote *Scheme to Render Psalmody Congregational* (1835; 2nd ed., 1850), *Manual of the Norwich Sol-fa System* (1845), and *Manual containing a Development of the Tetrachordal System* (1850).

Glover, William Howard, English conductor and composer; b. London, June 6, 1819; d. N.Y., Oct. 28, 1875. He played the violin in the Lyceum Theater orch. in London; conducted opera in Manchester, Liverpool, and London. In 1868 he went to N.Y., where he was conductor at Niblo's Garden until his death.

Works: Opera, *Ruy Blas* (London, Oct. 21, 1861); operettas: *Aminta* (London, Jan. 26, 1852); *Once Too Often* (London, Jan. 20, 1862); *Palomita, or The Veiled Songstress* (publ. in N.Y., 1875); cantata, *Tam o' Shanter* (London, July 4, 1855, Berlioz conducting); overtures; piano music; songs.

Gluck, Alma (née **Reba Fiersohn**), famous Rumanian-American soprano; b. Iaşi, May 11, 1884; d. N.Y., Oct. 27, 1938. She was taken to America as a small child and was educated at public schools in N.Y. Her early marriage to Bernard Gluck in 1902 ended in divorce, but they had a talented daughter, Abigail, born in 1903, who became a successful author; in her novel *Of Lena Geyer* (1936) and in her autobiography, *Too Strong for Fantasy* (1967), publ. under her assumed name, Marcia Davenport, she gives many revealing glimpses of her mother's career. From 1906 to 1909 Alma Gluck studied voice with Arturo Buzzi-Peccia, who arranged for her to appear in the role of Sophie in Massenet's opera *Werther* on the stage of the New Theater in N.Y. on Nov. 16, 1909. Shortly afterward, on Nov. 28, 1909, she sang at a Sunday concert at the Metropolitan Opera in N.Y. On Dec. 23, 1909, she appeared in a revival of *Orfeo ed Euridice* at the Metropolitan, with Toscanini conducting. Her success led to further engagements in such diversified roles as Marguerite in *Faust,* Venus in *Tannhäuser,* Gilda in *Rigoletto,* and Mimi in *La Bohème.* On Oct. 10, 1910, she gave a recital in N.Y. Her divorce became final in 1912, and she went to Europe to complete her vocal studies; she coached with Jean de Reszke in Paris and with Marcella Sembrich in Switzerland. Returning to the U.S., she resumed her career, appearing at Sunday concerts under the auspices of the Metropolitan Opera. She rapidly became a favorite with both opera and concert audiences; she also satisfied public demand by recording popular songs such as *Carry Me Back to Old Virginny,* a disc which reportedly sold 2 million copies. On June 15, 1914, she married in London the Russian violinist **Efrem Zimbalist;** their combined artistic genes produced a son, Efrem Zimbalist, Jr., who became a famous actor and whose daughter Stefanie also swam into thespian popularity.

Gluck, Christoph Willibald, Ritter von, renowned German composer; b. Erasbach, near Weidenwang, in the Upper Palatinate, July 2, 1714; d. Vienna, Nov. 15, 1787. His father was a forester at Erasbach until his appointment as forester to Prince Lobkowitz of Eisenberg about 1729. Gluck received his elementary instruction in the village schools at Kamnitz and Albersdorf near Komotau, where he also was taught singing and instrumental playing. Some biographers refer to his study at the Jesuit college at Komotau, but there is no documentary evidence to support this contention. In 1732 he went to Prague to complete his education, but it is doubtful that he took any courses at the Univ. He earned his living by playing violin and cello at rural dances in the area; also sang at various churches. He met Bohuslav Čzernohorsky, and it is probable that Gluck learned the methods of church music from him. He went to Vienna in 1736, and was chamber musician to young Prince Lobkowitz, son of the patron of Gluck's father. In 1737 he was taken to Milan by Prince Melzi; this Italian sojourn was of the greatest importance to Gluck's musical development. There he became a student of G.B. Sammartini and acquired a solid technique of composition in the Italian style. After 4 years of study, he brought out his 1st opera, *Artaserse*, to the text of the celebrated Metastasio; it was produced in Milan (Dec. 26, 1741) with such success that he was immediately commissioned to write more operas. There followed *Demetrio*, or *Cleonice* (Venice, May 2, 1742), *Demofoonte* (Milan, Jan. 6, 1743), *Il Tigrane* (Crema, Sept. 9, 1743), *La Sofonisba*, or *Siface* (Milan, Jan. 13, 1744), *Ipermestra* (Venice, Nov. 21, 1744), *Poro* (Turin, Dec. 26, 1744), and *Ippolito*, or *Fedra* (Milan, Jan. 31, 1745). He also contributed separate numbers to several other operas produced in Italy. In 1745 he received an invitation to go to London; on his way, he visited Paris and met Rameau. He was commissioned by the Italian Opera of London to write 2 operas for the Haymarket Theatre, as a competitive endeavor to Handel's enterprise. The 1st of these works was *La Caduta dei giganti*, a tribute to the Duke of Cumberland on the defeat of the Pretender; it was produced on Jan. 28, 1746; the 2nd was a pasticcio, *Artamene*, in which Gluck used material from his previous operas; it was produced March 15, 1746. Ten days later, he appeared with Handel at a public concert, despite the current report in London society that Handel had declared that Gluck knew no more counterpoint than his cook (it should be added that a professional musician, Gustavus Waltz, was Handel's cook and valet at the time). On April 23, 1746, Gluck gave a demonstration in London, playing on the "glass harmonica." He left London late in 1746 when he received an engagement as conductor with Pietro Mingotti's traveling Italian opera company. He conducted in Hamburg, Leipzig, and Dresden; on June 29, 1747, he produced a "serenata," *Le nozze d'Ercole e d'Ebe*, to celebrate a royal wedding; it was performed at the Saxon court, in Pillnitz. He then went to Vienna, where he staged his opera *Semiramide riconosciuta*, after a poem of Metastasio (May 14, 1748). He then traveled to Copenhagen, where he produced a festive opera, *La Contesa dei Numi* (March 9, 1749), on the occasion of the birth of Prince Christian; his next productions (all to Metastasio's texts) were *Ezio* (Prague, 1750), *Issipile* (Prague, 1752), *La clemenza di Tito* (Naples, Nov. 4, 1752), *Le Cinesi* (Vienna, Sept. 24, 1754), *La danza* (Vienna, May 5, 1755), *L'innocenza giustificata* (Vienna, Dec. 8, 1755), *Antigono* (Rome, Feb. 9, 1756), and *Il Re pastore* (Vienna, Dec. 8, 1756).

In 1750 Gluck married Marianna Pergin, daughter of a Viennese merchant; for several years afterward he conducted operatic performances in Vienna. As French influence increased there, he wrote several entertainments to French texts, containing spoken dialogue, in the style of opéra comique; of these, the most successful were *Le Cadi dupé* (Dec. 1761) and *La Rencontre imprévue* (Jan. 7, 1764; perf. also under the title *Les Pèlerins de la Mecque*), his most popular production in this genre). His greatest work of the Vienna period was *Orfeo ed Euridice*, to a libretto by Calzabigi (in a version for male contralto; Oct. 5, 1762, with the part of Orfeo sung by the famous castrato Gaetano Guadagni). Gluck revised it for a Paris performance, produced in French on Aug. 2, 1774, with Orfeo sung by a tenor. There followed another masterpiece, *Alceste* (Vienna, Dec. 16, 1767), also to Calzabigi's text. In the preface to *Alceste*, Gluck formulated his esthetic credo, which elevated the dramatic meaning of musical stage plays above a mere

striving for vocal effects: "I sought to reduce music to its true function, that of seconding poetry in order to strengthen the emotional expression and the impact of the dramatic situations without interrupting the action and without weakening it by superfluous ornaments." Among other productions of the Viennese period were *Il trionfo di Clelia* (Vienna, May 14, 1763), *Il Parnaso confuso* (Schönbrunn Palace, Jan. 24, 1765), *Il Telemacco* (Vienna, Jan. 30, 1765), and *Paride ed Elena* (Vienna, Nov. 30, 1770).

The success of his French operas in Vienna led Gluck to the decision to try his fortunes in Paris, yielding to the persuasion of François du Roullet, an attaché at the French embassy in Vienna, who also supplied him with his 1st libretto for a serious French opera, an adaptation of Racine's *Iphigénie en Aulide* (Paris, April 19, 1774). He set out for Paris early in 1773, preceded by declarations in the Paris press by du Roullet and Gluck himself, explaining in detail his ideas of dramatic music. These statements set off an intellectual battle in the Paris press and among musicians in general between the adherents of traditional Italian opera and Gluck's novel French opera. It reached an unprecedented degree of acrimony when the Italian composer Nicola Piccinni was engaged by the French court to write operas to French texts, in open competition with Gluck; intrigues multiplied, even though Marie Antoinette never wavered in her admiration for Gluck, who taught her singing and harpsichord playing. However, Gluck and Piccinni themselves never participated in the bitter polemics unleashed by their literary and musical partisans. The sensational successes of the French version of Gluck's *Orfeo* and of *Alceste* were followed by the production of *Armide* (Sept. 23, 1777), which aroused great admiration. Then followed his masterpiece, *Iphigénie en Tauride* (May 17, 1779), which established Gluck's superiority to Piccinni, who was commissioned to write an opera on the same subject but failed to complete it in time. Gluck's last opera, *Echo et Narcisse* (Paris, Sept. 24, 1779), did not measure up to the excellence of his previous operas. By that time, his health had failed; he had several attacks of apoplexy, which resulted in partial paralysis. In the autumn of 1779 he returned to Vienna, where he lived as an invalid. His last work was a *De profundis* for Chorus and Orch., written 5 years before his death.

Besides his operas, he wrote several ballets, of which *Don Juan* (Vienna, Oct. 17, 1761) was the most successful; he also wrote a cycle of 7 songs to words by Klopstock, 7 trio sonatas, several overtures, etc. Wagner made a complete revision of the score of *Iphigénie en Aulide*; this arrangement was so extensively used that a Wagnerized version of Gluck's music became the chief text for performances during the 19th century. A complete ed. of Gluck's works was begun by the Bärenreiter Verlag in 1951. A thematic catalogue was publ. by A. Wotquenne (Leipzig, 1904; German tr. with supplement by J. Liebeskind). See also C. Hopkinson, *A Bibliography of the Printed Works of C.W. von Gluck, 1714–1787* (2nd ed., N.Y., 1967).

BIBL.: F. Riedel, *Über die Musik des R.s C. v.G.* (Vienna, 1775); C. Coqueau, *Entretiens sur l'état actuel de l'opéra de Paris* (Paris, 1779; dialogue on the Gluck-Piccinni controversy); G. Leblond, *Mémoires pour servir à l'histoire de la révolution opérée dans la musique par M. le Chevalier G.* (Paris, 1781; German tr., 1823; 2nd ed., 1837); J. Siegmeyer, *Über den R. G. und seine Werke* (Berlin, 1837); E. Miel, *Notice sur G.* (Paris, 1840); A. Schmid, *C.W. R. v.G.* (Leipzig, 1854); W. Neumann, *C.W. G.* (Kassel, 1855); J. Baudoin, *L'Alceste de G.* (Paris, 1861); A. Marx, *G. und die Oper* (Berlin, 1863); L. Nohl, *G. und Wagner* (Munich, 1870); G. Desnoiresterres, *G. et Piccinni* (Paris, 1875); A. Jullien, *La Cour et l'opéra sous Louis XVI* (Paris, 1878); E. Thoinan, *Notes bibliographiques sur la guerre musicale des G.istes et Piccinnistes* (Paris, 1878); H. Barbedette, *G.* (Paris, 1882); A. Reissmann, *C.W. v.G.* (Berlin, 1882); K. Bitter, *Die Reform der Oper durch G. und Wagner* (Braunschweig, 1884); H. Welti, *G.* (Leipzig, 1888); E. Newman, *G. and the Opera* (London, 1895); J. d'Udine, *G.* (Paris, 1906); J. Tiersot, *G.* (Paris, 1910); E. Kurth, "Die Jugendopern

G.," *Studien zur Musikwissenschaft,* I (1913); S. Wortsmann, *Die deutsche G.-Literatur* (Nuremberg, 1914); W. Squire, "G.'s London Operas," *Musical Quarterly* (July 1915); J.-G. Prod'homme, "G.'s French Collaborators," ibid. (April 1917); idem, "Les Portraits français de G.," *Rivista Musicale Italiana,* XXV, 1 (1918); M. Arend, *G.* (1921); W. Vetter, "Die Arie bei G.," *Zeitschrift für Musikwissenschaft,* III (1921); R. Haas, "Die Wiener Ballet-Pantomime im 18. Jahrhundert und G.s *Don Juan,*" *Studien zur Musikwissenschaft,* X (1923); E. Müller, "Zwei unveröffentlichte Briefe G.s an Carl August," *Die Musik* (Stuttgart, 1923); G. Scuderi, *C. G.: Orfeo* (Milan, 1924); R. Haas, *G. und Durazzo im Burgtheater* (Vienna, 1925); P. Brück, "G.s *Orpheus und Eurydike,*" *Archiv für Musikwissenschaft,* VIII/4 (1926); M. Cauchie, "G. et ses éditeurs parisiens," *Le Ménestrel* (1927); T. Veidl, "Neues über G.s Jugend," *Auftakt,* VIII/3 (1928); J. Tiersot, "G. and the Encyclopaedists," *Musical Quarterly* (July 1930); E. Istel, "G.'s Dramaturgy," ibid. (April 1931); K. Huschke, "G. und seine deutsche Zeitgenossen," *Zeitschrift für Musikwissenschaft,* XV (1933); L. de la Laurencie, *G., Orphée: Étude et analyse musicale* (Paris, 1934); D. Tovey, "C.W. G. and the Musical Revolution," in H. Foss, *The Heritage of Music,* vol. 2 (London, 1934); M. Cooper, *G.* (London, 1935); A. Einstein, *G.* (London, 1936); R. Tenschert, *C.W. G. (1714–1787); Sein Leben in Bildern* (Leipzig, 1938); P. Landormy, *G.* (Paris, 1941); A. Della Corte, *G.* (Turin, 1942); W. Brandl, *C.W. R. v.G.* (Wiesbaden, 1948); A. Della Corte, *G. e i suoi tempi* (Florence, 1948); J.-G. Prod'homme, *G.* (Paris, 1948; rev. ed., 1985, by J. Faquet); R. Gerber, *C.W. R. v.G.* (Potsdam, 1950); R. Tenschert, *C.W. G.: Der grosse Reformator der Oper* (Freiburg, 1951); A.A. Abert, *C.W. G.* (Munich, 1959); *The Collected Correspondence and Papers of C.W. G.* (London, 1962); P. Howard, *G. and the Birth of Modern Opera* (N.Y., 1964); W. Vetter, *C.W. G.* (Leipzig, 1964); D. Heartz, "From Garrick to G.: The Reform of Theatre and Opera in the Mid-Eighteenth Century," *Proceedings of the Royal Musical Association* (1967–68); G. Croll, "G.forschung und G.-Gesamtausgabe," in R. Baum and W. Rehm, eds., *Musik und Verlag* (Kassel, 1968); H.C.R. Landon, *Essays on the Viennese Classical Style* (N.Y., 1970); K. Hortschansky, "*Arianna* (1762)—Ein Pasticcio von G.," *Die Musikforschung* (Oct.–Dec. 1971); B. Brown, "'Le Mandarin': An Unknown G. Opera?," *Musical Times* (Nov. 1987); P. Howard, *C.W. G.: A Guide to Research* (N.Y., 1987); J. Rushton, "The Musician G.," *Musical Times* (Nov. 1987).

Glyn, Margaret H(enrietta), English musicologist; b. Ewell, Surrey, Feb. 28, 1865; d. there, June 3, 1946. She studied in London under C.J. Frost and Yorke Trotter; became an authority on keyboard music of the Tudor period. She ed. organ and virginal music by Byrd, Orlando Gibbons, John Bull, and other composers, and publ. *The Rhythmic Conception of Music* (1907); *Analysis of the Evolution of Musical Form* (1909); *About Elizabethan Virginal Music and Its Composers* (1924; 2nd ed., 1934); *Theory of Musical Evolution* (1924). She also composed a number of works for organ.

Gnattali, Radamés, Brazilian composer; b. Pôrto Alegre, Jan. 27, 1906. He studied piano, violin, composition, and conducting at the Pôrto Alegre Cons. of Music and the National School of Music in Rio de Janeiro; also appeared as a concert pianist and violist. His music is imbued with indigenous rhythms and harmonies popularized in the 1960s as the "bossa nova sound." **Works:** 12 *Brasilianas:* 1–3 for Orch. (1945, 1948, 1948); 4 and 5 for Piano (1949, 1950); 6 for Piano and Orch. (1960); 7 for 2 Pianos (1957); 8 for Saxophone and Piano (1957); 9 and 10 for Orch. (1962); 11 for 8 Cellos and Piano (1968; orchestrated 1970); 12 for 2 Pianos and String Orch. (1968); 3 *Sinfonias populares* (1955, 1962, 1969); 4 piano concertos (1934, 1936, 1960, 1967); Cello Concerto (1941); 3 violin concertos (1947, 1962, 1969); 2 *Concêrtos românticos* for Piano and Orch. (1949, 1964); 3 *Concêrtos cariocas* for Various Instrumental Soloists and Orch. (1950–70); 4 guitar concertinos (1952, 1953, 1955, 1968); Harp Concerto (1958); 2 harmonica

concertos (1958, 1968); chamber music; 2 piano sonatas (1948, 1963).

Gnazzo, Anthony J(oseph), American composer; b. Plainville, Conn., April 21, 1936. He studied music theory at the Hartt School of Music in Hartford, Conn. (B.A., 1957), and with Krenek, Berger, and Shapero at Brandeis Univ. (M.F.A., 1965; Ph.D., 1970). He was an instructor in electronic system design at the Univ. of Toronto (1965–66), and director of the tape-music center at Mills College in Oakland, Calif. (1967–69); in 1974 he became an audio technician at the electronic music studio at Calif. State Univ. at Hayward. His compositions include text-sound pieces, electronic scores, environmental pieces, and kinetic sculpture. **Works: instrumental:** *Music* for 2 Pianos and Electronic Sound (1964); *Chamber Music* for 13 Instruments (1965); *Cross-cut for Paul Hertelendy* for 3 Electric Saws and String Orch. (1969); *Tighten Up* for 4 Rock Groups (1970); *Music for Cello and Tape I* (1971) and *II* (1974); *Music for Piano and Instruments* (1974). **vocal:** *Eden* for Narrator and 7 Instruments (1964); *Music for Large Vocal Groups* (1966; rev. 1969); *The Question,* oratorio for Chorus (1969); *Prime Source Nos. 1–23* (1971–79). **tape:** *Stereo Radio I* and *II* (1970), *III* (1971), *IV* and *V* (1972); *The Art of Canning Music* (1976); *Image/Delusion* (1980). **mixed-media:** *Theater Piece I–XXVI* (1967–71); *10 Pieces for Pauline Oliveros* (1969); *Compound Skull Fracture* for Actor, Tape, and Slides (1975; in collaboration with J. Cuno); *Waiting for JB* (1980); *Lontano* for Narrator, Tape, and Slides (1982); also incidental music; dance scores; film and television music.

Gnecchi, Vittorio, Italian composer; b. Milan, July 17, 1876; d. there, Feb. 1, 1954. He studied at the Milan Cons. His opera *Cassandra* was performed at Bologna on Dec. 5, 1905; some years later, after the premiere of Strauss's *Elektra,* there was considerable discussion when the Italian musicologist Giovanni Tebaldini pointed out the identity of some 50 themes in both *Cassandra* and *Elektra* ("Telepatia Musicale," *Rivista Musicale Italiana,* Feb.–March 1909). Gnecchi also wrote the operas *Virtù d'amore* (1896) and *La rosiera,* after a comedy by Alfred de Musset (in German, Gera, Feb. 12, 1927; in Italian, Trieste, Jan. 24, 1931).

Gnessin, Mikhail (Fabianovich), Russian composer; b. Rostov-on-the-Don, Feb. 2, 1882; d. Moscow, May 5, 1957. He studied at the St. Petersburg Cons. with Rimsky-Korsakov and Liadov (1901–8); went to Germany in 1911; in 1914 returned to Rostov, where he composed, taught music, and interested himself in various socialist activities. He made a trip to Palestine in 1921 to study Jewish music; some of his subsequent work reflected this visit. After 1923, he composed and taught alternately in Moscow and Leningrad. In addition to his Jewish music, he composed a number of works in the Romantic vein. He publ. his reflections and reminiscences of Rimsky-Korsakov in Moscow in 1956. **Works: dramatic:** *Balagan,* by Blok (1909); *The Rose and the Cross,* by Blok (1914); *Antigone,* by Sophocles (1909–15); *The Phoenician Women,* by Euripides (1912–16); *Oedipus Rex,* by Sophocles (1914–15); *The Story of the Red-Haired Motele,* by Utkin (1926–29); *The Inspector-General,* by Gogol (1926). **operas:** *Abraham's Youth* (1921–23) and *The Maccabees.* **voice and orch.:** *Ruth* (1909); *Vrubel* (1912); *The Conqueror Worm* (1913); symphonic movement for Solo Voices, Chorus, and Orch., *1905–1917* (1925). **orch.:** Symphonic fragment, *After Shelley* (1906–8); *Songs of Adonis* (1919); symphonic fantasy, *Songs of the Old Country* (1919); suite, *Jewish Orchestra at the Town Bailiff's Ball* (1926). **chamber:** Requiem, in memory of Rimsky-Korsakov, for String Quartet and Piano (1913–14); *Variations on a Jewish Theme* for String Quartet (1916); *Azerbaijan Folksongs* for String Quartet (1930); *Adygeya* for Violin, Viola, Cello, Clarinet, Horn, and Piano (1933); *Sonata-Fantasia* for Piano, Violin, Viola, and Cello (1945); *Theme with Variations* for Cello and Piano (1955); several song cycles; piano pieces; arrangements of Jewish folk songs.

BIBL.: L. Sabaneyev, *Modern Russian Composers* (N.Y., 1927); A. Drozdov, *G.* (Moscow, 1927; in Russian and German).

Gobbaerts, Jean-Louis, Belgian pianist and composer; b. Antwerp, Sept. 28, 1835; d. Saint-Gilles, near Brussels, May 5, 1886. He studied at the Brussels Cons. He wrote more than 1,000 light piano pieces, some quite popular, using the pseudonyms "Streabbog" (Gobbaerts reversed), "Ludovic," and "Lévi." His *Little Fairy Waltz* was a favorite of President Harry S Truman.

Gobbi, Tito, famous Italian baritone; b. Bassano del Grappa, near Venice, Oct. 24, 1913; d. Rome, March 5, 1984. He received vocal lessons from Barone Zanchetta in Bassano del Grappa before going to Rome to train with Giulio Crimi; made his operatic debut as Count Rodolfo in *La Sonnambula* in Gubbio (1935); during the 1935–36 season, he was an understudy at Milan's La Scala, where he made a fleeting stage appearance as the Herald in Pizzetti's *Oreseolo* (1935). In 1936 he won 1st prize in the male vocal section of the Vienna International Competition; then went to Rome, where he sang Germont *père* at the Teatro Adriano (1937); that same year he made his 1st appearance at the Teatro Reale, in the role of Lelio in Wolf-Ferrari's *Le Donne curiose;* after singing secondary roles there (1937–39), he became a principal member of the company; appeared as Ford in *Falstaff* during its visit to Berlin in 1941. He also sang on the Italian radio and made guest appearances with other Italian opera houses; in Rieti in 1940 he first essayed the role of Scarpia, which was to become his most celebrated characterization. In 1942 he made his formal debut at La Scala as Belcore in *L'elisir d'amore*. In 1947 he appeared as Rigoletto in Stockholm, and in 1948 he sang in concerts in London and also made his U.S. debut as Figaro in *Il Barbiere di Siviglia* at the San Francisco Opera. In 1950 he made his Covent Garden debut in London as Renato in *Un ballo in maschera*. He made his 1st appearance at the Chicago Opera as Rossini's Figaro in 1954. On Jan. 13, 1956, he made his Metropolitan Opera debut in N.Y. as Scarpia. In subsequent years his engagements took him to most of the principal music centers of the world. He was also active as an opera producer from 1965. In 1979 he bade farewell to the operatic stage. He was the brother-in-law of **Boris Christoff**. Gobbi was acclaimed as an actor as well as a singer; his mastery extended to some 100 roles. He publ. *Tito Gobbi: My Life* (1979) and *Tito Gobbi and His World of Italian Opera* (1984).

Godard, Benjamin (Louis Paul), French composer; b. Paris, Aug. 18, 1849; d. Cannes, Jan. 10, 1895. He studied violin with Richard Hammer and Vieuxtemps; composition with Reber at the Paris Cons. He publ. his 1st work, a Violin Sonata, at the age of 16 and wrote several other chamber music pieces, obtaining the Prix Chartier. In 1878 he received a municipal prize for an orch. work; in the same year he produced his 1st opera, *Les Bijoux de Jeannette*. His 2nd opera was *Pedro de Zalamea* (Antwerp, Jan. 31, 1884), but it left little impact; then came his masterpiece, *Jocelyn*, after Lamartine's poem (Brussels, Feb. 25, 1888). The famous *Berceuse* from this opera became a perennial favorite, exhibiting Godard's lyric talent at its best. There followed the opera *Dante et Béatrice*, produced at the Opéra-Comique in Paris on May 13, 1890. His opera *La Vivandière* was left unfinished at his death, and the orchestration was completed by Paul Vidal; it was staged in Paris on April 1, 1895; another posthumous opera, *Les Guelphes*, was produced in Rouen (Jan. 17, 1902). Godard wrote 3 programmatic syms.: *Symphonie gothique* (1883), *Symphonie orientale* (1884), and *Symphonie légendaire* (1886); and a *Concerto Romantique* for Violin and Orch. (1876); he also wrote 3 string quartets, 5 violin sonatas, a Cello Sonata, and 2 piano trios; piano pieces; and more than 100 songs. A 2-vol. collection of Godard's piano works was publ. by G. Schirmer (N.Y., 1895); another collection of piano pieces was ed. by Paolo Gallico (N.Y., 1909).
BIBL.: M. Clerjot, *B. G.* (Paris, 1902); M. Clavié, *B. G.* (Paris, 1906).

Goddard, Arabella, French pianist of English descent; b. St.-Servan, St.-Malo, Jan. 12, 1836; d. Boulogne, April 6, 1922. She began study with Kalkbrenner in Paris at the age of 6; made her 1st public appearance at the age of 14, in London, at a Grand National Concert. After 3 years of study with the critic J.W. Davison (whom she married in 1859), she made tours of Europe; later toured the U.S., Australia, and India (1872–76); retired in 1882. She was particularly known for her performances of the late Beethoven sonatas at her recitals in London.

Godfrey, Dan(iel), English bandmaster, father of **Sir Dan(iel) Eyers) Godfrey;** b. Westminster, Sept. 4, 1831; d. Beeston, Nottinghamshire, June 30, 1903. He was a pupil and Fellow of the Royal Academy of Music, in which he was later a prof. of military music. He was also bandmaster of the Grenadier Guards from 1856; traveled with his band in the U.S. in 1872; retired in 1896. He wrote popular waltzes (*Mabel, Guards, Hilda,* etc.), and made many arrangements for military band.

Godfrey, Sir Dan(iel Eyers), English conductor, son of **Dan(iel) Godfrey;** b. London, June 20, 1868; d. Bournemouth, July 20, 1939. He studied at the Royal College of Music; was conductor of the London Military Band (a civilian group in reality) from 1889 to 1891. In 1893, he settled in Bournemouth as conductor of the Winter Gardens orch.; founded the Sym. Concerts there in 1894; directed them until his retirement in 1934; he brought the concerts to a high level, and used all his efforts to promote the works of British composers. He was knighted in 1922 for his services to orch. music. He wrote his memoirs, *Memories and Music* (London, 1924).

Godfrey, George. See **Müller, Georg Gottfried.**

Godfrey, Isidore, English conductor; b. London, Sept. 27, 1900; d. Sussex, Sept. 12, 1977. He was educated at the Guildhall School of Music in London. In 1925 he joined the D'Oyly Carte Opera Co. as a conductor; from 1929 to 1968 he served as its music director. In 1965 he was named an Officer of the Order of the British Empire.

Godimel, Claude. See **Goudimel, Claude.**

Godowsky, Leopold, famous Polish-born American pianist; b. Soshly, near Vilnius, Feb. 13, 1870; d. N.Y., Nov. 21, 1938. He played in public as a child in Russia; at 14, was sent to Berlin to study at the Hochschule für Musik, but after a few months there, proceeded to the U.S.; gave his 1st American concert in Boston on Dec. 7, 1884; in 1885, played engagements at the N.Y. Casino; in 1886, toured Canada with the Belgian violinist Ovide Musin. He then played in society salons in London and Paris, and became a protégé of Saint-Saëns. In 1890 he joined the faculty of the N.Y. College of Music; in 1891 became an American citizen. He taught at the Broad St. Cons. in Philadelphia (1894–95); was head of the piano dept. of the Chicago Cons. (1895–1900); then embarked on a European tour; gave a highly successful concert in Berlin (Dec. 6, 1900), and remained there as a teacher; from 1909 to 1914, conducted a master class at the Vienna Academy of Music; made tours in the U.S. from 1912 to 1914, and settled permanently in the U.S. at the outbreak of World War I. After the war, he toured Europe, South America, and Asia as a concert pianist; his career was greatly restricted after 1930, when he suffered a stroke. Godowsky was one of the outstanding masters of the piano; possessing a scientifically inclined mind, he developed a method of "weight and relaxation"; applying it to his own playing, he became an outstanding technician of his instrument, extending the potentialities of piano technique to the utmost, with particular attention to the left hand. He wrote numerous piano compositions of transcendental difficulty, yet entirely pianistic in style; also arranged works by Weber, Brahms, and Johann Strauss. Particularly remarkable are his 53 studies on Chopin's études, combining Chopin's themes in ingenious counterpoint; among his original works, the most interesting are *Triakontameron* (30 pieces; 1920; no. 11 is the well-known *Alt Wien*) and *Java Suite* (12 pieces; 1924–25). He also wrote simple pedagogical pieces, e.g., a set of 46 *Miniatures* for Piano, 4-hands, in which the pupil is given a part within the compass of 5 notes only (1918); ed. piano studies by Czerny, Heller, Köhler, etc.; composed music for the left hand alone (6 *Waltz Poems, Prelude and Fugue*, etc.); and publ. an essay, "Piano Music for the Left Hand," *Musical Quarterly* (July 1935). Maurice Aronson publ. a musical examination paper, providing an analysis of Godowsky's *Miniatures* (N.Y., 1935).

BIBL.: L. Saxe, "The Published Music of L. G.," *Notes* (March 1957; with an annotated list of original works, arrangements, and eds.); C. Hopkins, "G's 'Phonoramas': A 20th-century 'Wanderlust,'" *Musical Times* (July 1989); J. Nicholas, *G.—The Pianists' Pianist: A Biography of L. G.* (Hexham, 1989).

Godron, Hugo, Dutch composer; b. Amsterdam, Nov. 22, 1900; d. Zoelmond, Dec. 6, 1971. He studied violin at the music school in Bussum, and composition with Sem Dresden in Amsterdam (1921–22). He taught composition and harmony at music schools in Bussum, Hilversum, and Utrecht; from 1939 to 1969 was active as a sound engineer in Hilversum and Amsterdam. His music is generally joyful, almost playful, in character.

WORKS: Radio fairy tale, *Assepoes* (Cinderella; 1946–47); Sinfonietta for Small Orch. (1932–33); 7 *Miniatures* for Piano and Strings (1933); Piano Concerto (1938–39); *Sérénade occidentale* for Orch. (1942–48); *Amabile Suite* for Clarinet, Piano, and Strings (1943); Concerto Grosso for Clarinet and Small Orch. (1944–45); *Concert Suite* for Piano and String Orch. (1945–47); *Miniatuur symphonie* (1949–50; orchestration of *Gardenia Suite* for Piano); 2 *Polkas* for Orch. (1950–51; 1957–58); Suite for String Orch. and Harpsichord (1950); *Hommage à Chabrier* for Orch. (1950–51); *Hommages classiques* for Flute, Piano, and Strings (1950); Concerto for Orch. (1953–54); *Variations traditionnelles* for Small Orch. (1954); *Promenades*, suite for Orch. (1954–55); 4 *impressies* for Chamber Orch. (1956–57); *Aubade Gaudeamus*, suite for Piano, String Orch., and Percussion (1966–68); *Hommage à Bizet* for Small Orch. (1971); String Trio (1937); Serenade for Piano and Wind Quintet (1947); Sonatina for Flute, Violin, Viola, and Piano (1948); Piano Trio (1948); *Sonata facile* for Cello and Piano (1950); Divertimento for 2 Violins and Piano (1956); *Nouvelles* for Piano Trio (1963); *Quatuor bohémien* for Piano Quartet (1970); also piano pieces.

Godwin, Joscelyn, English-born American musicologist, composer, and painter; b. Kelmscott, Jan. 16, 1945. He was educated at Christ Church Cathedral Choir School, Oxford (1952–58); Radley College (1958–62); and Magdalene College, Cambridge (B.A., 1965; M.A., 1968). He became a Fellow of the Royal College of Organists in 1965. He also studied at Cornell Univ. (Ph.D., 1969, with a diss. on the music of Henry Cowell). He was an instructor in music at Cleveland State Univ. (1969–71); then joined the faculty of Colgate Univ. (from 1982). He has lectured widely in the U.S. and the United Kingdom; he became a U.S. citizen in 1980. While his compositions are occasionally performed, and he himself performs frequently as a conductor and an instrumentalist, he is best known as the author of numerous books, articles, and trs. dealing with mysticism and ancient philosophies in relation to music.

WRITINGS: *Music, Mysticism and Magic: A Sourcebook* (London, 1986); *Harmonies of Heaven and Earth* (London, 1987); *The Mystery of the Seven Vowels in Theory and Practice* (Grand Rapids, Mich., 1991).

Goeb, Roger (John), American composer; b. Cherokee, Iowa, Oct. 9, 1914. He studied agriculture at the Univ. of Wisconsin, graduating in 1936; in 1938 went to Paris, where he took lessons with Nadia Boulanger. Returning to America in 1939, he was a pupil of Otto Luening, pursued graduate work at N.Y. Univ., was a pupil of Herbert Elwell at the Cleveland Inst. of Music (M.Mus., 1942), and obtained his Ph.D. at the Univ. of Iowa (1945); occupied teaching posts at the Univ. of Oklahoma (1942–44), Iowa State Univ. (1944–45), and the Juilliard School of Music (1947–50). He held 2 Guggenheim fellowships (1950, 1952); taught music at Stanford Univ.

(1954–55); then became director of the American Composers' Alliance (1956–62). Personal misfortunes (both his wife and his son died of multiple sclerosis) caused him to interrupt his professional activities in 1964; but he resumed composition in 1979.

WORKS: ORCH.: 6 syms.: No. 1 (1941; withdrawn); No. 2 (1945); No. 3 (1950; N.Y., April 3, 1952, Stokowski conducting); No. 4 (1955; Pittsburgh, Feb. 24, 1956); No. 5 (1981); No. 6 (1987); *Lyric Piece* for Trumpet and Orch. (1942); *Fantasy* for Oboe and Strings (1947); 4 *Concertantes*: No. 1 for Flute, Oboe, Clarinet, and Strings (1948); No. 2 for Bassoon or Cello, and Strings (1950); No. 3 for Viola and Orch. (1951); No. 4 for Clarinet, Strings, Piano, Timpani, and 2 Percussion (1951); *Romanza* for String Orch. (1948); 2 concertinos: No. 1 (1949) and No. 2 (Louisville, Ky., Nov. 28, 1956); 5 *American Dances* (1952; 1–3 for Strings; 4 and 5 for Orch.); Violin Concerto (1953; N.Y., Feb. 1954); Piano Concerto (1954); 2 *Sinfonias* (1957, 1962); *Iowa Concerto* for Small Orch. (1959); *Caprice* (1982); *Memorial* (1982); *Divertissement* (1982); *Fantasia* (1983); *Essay* (1984); *Gambol* (1984). **CHAMBER:** 4 string quartets (1942, withdrawn; 1948; 1954; 1980); Solo Viola Sonata (1942); *Suite* for Woodwind Trio (1946); Brass Septet (1949); Quintet for Trombone and String Quartet (1949); 4 wind quintets (1949–82); 2 *Divertimenti* for Flute (1950); 3 *Processionals* for Organ and Brass Quintet (1951); Solo Violin Sonata (1957); *Running Colors* for String Quartet (1961); Quartet for Oboe and String Trio (1964); Quintet for Cello and String Quartet (1980); Flute Quartet (1983); *Black on White* for Clarinet and Strings (1985); *Nuances* for Clarinet and Viola (1986).

Goebel, Reinhard, esteemed German violinist; b. Siegen, Westphalia, July 31, 1952. He commenced violin lessons in his youth, receiving principal training in Cologne and Amsterdam from Maier, Gawriloff, and Leonhardt. In 1973 a passion for early music led him to organize the Musica Antiqua Köln, an ensemble dedicated to performing works on original instruments or modern replicas; after a major tour of Europe in 1978, the ensemble toured widely in North and South America, the Far East, and Australia, acquiring an international reputation through its exacting but spirited performances. He plays a Jacobus Stainer violin built in 1665.

Goedike, Alexander, Russian pianist and composer; b. Moscow, March 4, 1877; d. there, July 9, 1957. He was a member of a musical family of German extraction; his father was an organist and a cons. teacher. He entered the Moscow Cons., where he studied piano with Safonov and composition with Arensky; graduated in 1898. In 1900 he won the Rubinstein Prize for his pieces for violin at the international competition in Vienna; in 1909 he was appointed prof. of piano at the Moscow Cons. His 80th birthday was celebrated in Moscow at a gala banquet, a few months before his death.

WORKS: 4 operas to his own librettos: *Virineya* (1915), *At the Crossing* (1933), *Jacquerie* (1937), and *Macbeth* (1944); 3 syms. (1903, 1905, 1922); Piano Concerto (1900); Violin Concerto (1951); Horn Concerto; Trumpet Concerto; Piano Quintet; 2 piano trios; String Quartet; numerous teaching pieces for piano; many arrangements of Russian songs.

BIBL.: V. Yakovlev, *A. G.* (Moscow, 1927; in Russian and German); K. Adzhemov, *A. G.* (articles and reminiscences; Moscow, 1960).

Goehr, (Peter) Alexander, English composer, son of **Walter Goehr**; b. Berlin, Aug. 10, 1932. He studied at the Royal Manchester College of Music (1952–55); then took courses with Messiaen and Loriod in Paris (1955–56). From 1960 to 1966 he was in charge of the production of orch. concerts for the BBC. In 1968–69 he was composer-in-residence at the New England Cons. in Boston; in 1969–70, taught at Yale Univ. Returning to England, he joined the faculty of Leeds Univ. (1971–76). In 1976 he was appointed prof. of music at Cambridge Univ. In 1989 he was made an honorary member of the American Academy and Inst. of Arts and Letters. His compositions are marked with a severe, at times austere, polyphony, tending toward integral serialism.

WORKS: Piano Sonata (1952); *Fantasias* for Clarinet and Piano (1955); *Fantasia* for Orch. (1955); *Narration* for Voice and Piano (1955); String Quartet (1958); *The Deluge*, cantata (1958); *4 Seasons from the Japanese* for Soprano and Orch. (1959); *Sutter's Gold*, cantata (1960); *Hecuba's Lament* for Orch. (1960); Suite for Flute, Clarinet, Horn, Violin, Viola, Cello, and Harp (1961); Violin Concerto (1962); *Little Symphony* (1963); *Pastorals* for Orch. (1965); Piano Trio (1966); *Arden muss sterben*, opera (Hamburg, March 5, 1967); String Quartet No. 2 (1967); *Romanza* for Cello and Orch. (1968); *Konzertstück* for Piano and Orch. (1969); *Nonomiya* for Piano (1969); Sym. (London, May 9, 1970); *Triptych*, theater piece for Actors, Singers, and Instruments, consisting of *Naboth's Vineyard* (1968), *Shadowplay* (1970; after Plato's *Republic*), and *Sonata about Jerusalem* (1970); Concerto for 11 Instruments (Brussels, Jan. 25, 1971); Piano Concerto (Brighton Festival, May 14, 1972); *Chaconne* for Wind Instruments (Leeds, Nov. 3, 1974); *Lyric Pieces* for Chamber Ensemble (London, Nov. 15, 1974); *Metamorphosis/Dance* for Orch. (London, Nov. 17, 1974); String Quartet No. 3 (London, June 28, 1976); *Psalm 4* for Female Soloists, Chorus, Viola, and Organ (London, July 8, 1976); *Fugue on the 4th Psalm* for Strings (1976); *Babylon the Great Is Fallen* for Chorus and Orch. (1979); *Das Gesetz der Quadrille* for Baritone and Piano (1979); *Sinfonia* for Orch. (1980); *2 études* (1981); *Behold the Sun*, concert aria for Soprano, Vibraphone, and Chamber Ensemble (1981; London, Feb. 9, 1982); *Behold the Sun*, opera (1st perf. in German as *Die Wiedertäufer*, Duisburg, April 19, 1985); *Symphony with Chaconne* for Orch. (1987); *Eve Dreams in Paradise* for 2 Vocal Soloists and Orch. (Birmingham, March 15, 1989).

BIBL.: B. Northcott, ed., *The Music of A. G.: Interviews and Articles* (London, 1980); idem, "On—and from—G.," *Musical Times* (Aug. 1982).

Goehr, Walter, German-born English conductor and composer, father of **(Peter) Alexander Goehr;** b. Berlin, May 28, 1903; d. Sheffield, Dec. 4, 1960. He studied theory with Schoenberg in Berlin; then became conductor of Berlin Radio (1925–31). In 1933 he went to England; from 1945 to 1948, was conductor of the BBC Theatre Orch.; was conductor of the Morley College concerts from 1943 until his death.

Goepfart, Karl Eduard, German pianist, conductor, and composer; b. Weimar, March 8, 1859; d. there, Feb. 8, 1942. He studied with his father, **Christian Heinrich Goepfart** (1835–90); also had lessons with Liszt. He toured as a theater conductor in the U.S. and in Germany; wrote several operas, of which only 1, *Der Müller von Sans Souci*, was produced (Weimar, 1907). He further wrote 2 syms., sacred music, and many songs.

Goepp, Philip H(enry), American organist, writer on music, and composer; b. N.Y., June 23, 1864; d. Philadelphia, Aug. 25, 1936. He studied in Germany (1872–77); graduated from Harvard with honors in music in 1884; while there, he studied composition with J.K. Paine; graduated from the Univ. of Pa. Law School in 1888, and practiced law until 1891. He then devoted himself to music in Philadelphia, as an organist, teacher, and writer; from 1900 to 1921 he wrote the program notes for the Philadelphia Orch.; publ. *Annals of Music in Philadelphia* (1896) and *Symphonies and Their Meaning* (3 vols., 1898, 1902, 1913); composed orch. music, pieces for piano and organ, a *Christmas Cantata*, an operetta, *The Lost Prince*, etc.

Goethals, Lucien (Gustave Georges), Belgian composer and conductor; b. Ghent, June 26, 1931. He studied with Rosseau at the Royal Cons. in Ghent (1947–56) and took courses at the Ghent Inst. for Psycho-Acoustics and Electronic Music at Ghent Univ.; also worked in an electronic studio in Germany; in 1971 became a teacher of analysis at the Ghent Cons. In 1964 he organized the Belgian group Spectra, devoted to the promotion of new music. In 1981 he was awarded the Culture Prize of the City of Ghent. His own compositions explore the problems of modernistic constructivism.

WORKS: *Vensters*, audio-visual play for 2 Narrators, Cello, Piano, Percussion, Recorded Sounds, and Film Projections (Brussels, Sept. 16, 1967); *Hé*, audio-visual production for 10 Instruments, Tapes, and Film Projections (1971; in collaboration with Herman Sabbe and Karel Goeyvaerts); *5 Impromptus* for Chamber Orch. (1959); *Dialogos* for String Orch., Wind Quintet, 2 String Quintets, Percussion, and Tape (Ghent, Sept. 3, 1963); *Dialogos Suite* for Chamber Orch. (1963); *Sinfonia in Gris Mayor* for 2 Orchs., Percussion, and Tape (Brussels, June 14, 1966); *Enteuxis* for String Orch., Oboe, and Flute (Ghent, Sept. 2, 1968); Concerto for Orch. (1972); *4 Pieces* for Orch. (1976); Concerto for 2 Clarinets and Orch. (1980–83); Violin Sonata (1959); *Rituele Suite* for Wind Quintet (1959); *Endomorfie I* for Violin, Piano, and Tape (1964); *Endomorfie II* for Flute, Oboe, Clarinet, Bassoon, 2 Trumpets, Trombone, and Tuba (1964); *Cellotape* for Cello, Piano, Tape, and Contact Microphone (1965); *Movimientos y acciones* for Flute, Clarinet, String Quartet, Chromatic Harp, and Percussion (1965); *Lecina* for Mezzo-soprano, Flute, Violin, and Cello (1966); *Mouvement* for String Quartet (1967); *Cascaras*, chamber cantata for Mezzo-soprano, Flute, Clarinet, Violin, Cello, and Piano (1969); *Quebraduras* for Piano Quartet (1969); *Ensimismamientos* for Violin, Cello, Bassoon, Piano, and Tape (1969); *Superposiciones* for Violin, Cello, Bassoon, and Piano (1970); *Suma* for an undefined number of Instruments, and Tape (1971); *3 paisajes sonores* for Flute, Oboe, Cello, Trombone, Double Bass, and Harpsichord (1973); *Diferencias* for 10 Instruments (1974); *Musica con cantus firmus triste* for Flute, Violin, Viola, and Cello (1978); *Pampa* for Mezzo-soprano and 8 Instruments (1979); *Rituel* for Cheng, Percussion, and Tape (1979); *Beweging* for Clarinet Quartet (1981); *Duelos* for Xylorimba and Percussion (1984); for Piano, *Musica dodecafonica* (1957) and *Pentagoon* (1963); for Organ, *Sinfonia* (1959) and *Klankstrukturen* (1962); several works for Tape alone.

Goethe, Johann Wolfgang von, illustrious German poet and dramatist; b. Frankfurt am Main, Aug. 28, 1749; d. Weimar, March 22, 1832. Although he could not comprehend Beethoven, and even snubbed him, he had ideas of his own on music (see *Briefwechsel zwischen Goethe und Zelter*, Berlin, 1833; Ferdinand Hiller also shows this in his *Goethes musicalisches Leben*, Cologne, 1883). In recent years, Goethe's attitude toward music has been made the subject of investigation by several scholars, as evidenced in the present bibliography.

BIBL.: K. Mendelssohn-Bartholdy, *G. und Felix Mendelssohn-Bartholdy* (Leipzig, 1871; in Eng., with additions, London, 2nd ed., 1874); A. Julien, *G. et la musique: Ses jugements, son influence, les œuvres qu'il a inspirées* (Paris, 1880); J. von Wasielewski, *G.'s Verhältnis zur Musik* (Leipzig, 1880); H. Blaze de Bury, *G. et Beethoven* (Paris, 1892); W. Nagel, *G. und Beethoven* (Langensalza, 1902); idem, *G. und Mozart* (Langensalza, 1904); J. Chantavoine, *G. musicien* (Paris, 1905); J. Simon, *Faust in der Musik* (Berlin, 1906); E. Segnitz, *G. und die Oper in Weimar* (Langensalza, 1908); W. Bode, *Die Tonkunst in G.s Leben* (2 vols., Berlin, 1912); idem, *G.s Schauspieler und Musiker: Erinnerungen von Eberwein und Lobe* (1912); H. Abert, *G. und die Musik* (1922); P. Frenzel, *R. Schumann und G.* (1926); H. John, *G. und die Musik* (1928); W. Nohl, *G. und Beethoven* (1929); R. Rolland, *G. et Beethoven* (Paris, 1930; in Eng., N.Y. and London, 1931); W. Engelsmann, *G. und Beethoven* (1931); A. Della Corte, *La vita musicale di G.* (Turin, 1932); F. Küchler, *G.s Musikverständnis* (Leipzig, 1935); F. Sternfeld, *G. and Music* (N.Y., 1954); W. Gerstenberg, *G.s Dichtung und die Musik* (Leipzig, 1966); R. Spaethling, *Music and Mozart in the Life of G.* (Columbia, S.C., 1987).

Goetschius, Percy, renowned American music pedagogue; b. Paterson, N.J., Aug. 30, 1853; d. Manchester, N.H., Oct. 29, 1943. He studied at the Stuttgart Cons., and taught various classes there; returned to the U.S. in 1890; was on the faculty of Syracuse Univ. (1890–92) and at the New England Cons.

of Music in Boston (1892–96). In 1905 he was appointed head of the dept. of music at the N.Y. Inst. of Musical Art; he retired in 1925. Goetschius was a product of the fossilized Germanic tradition; convinced that the laws of harmony as set by old German pedagogues were unalterable and inviolate, he stood in horror before any vestige of unresolved dissonances.

Writings: *The Material Used in Musical Composition* (Stuttgart, 1882; N.Y., 1889; 14th ed., 1913); *The Theory and Practice of Tone-relations* (Boston, 1892; 17th ed., 1917); *Models of Principal Musical Forms* (Boston, 1895); *Syllabus of Music History* (1895); *The Homophonic Forms of Musical Composition* (N.Y., 1898; 10th ed., 1921); *Exercises in Melody Writing* (N.Y., 1900; 9th ed., 1923); *Applied Counterpoint* (N.Y., 1902); *Lessons in Music Form* (Boston, 1904); *Exercises in Elementary Counterpoint* (N.Y., 1910); *Essentials in Music History* (N.Y., 1914; with T. Tapper); *The Larger Forms of Musical Composition* (N.Y., 1915); *Masters of the Symphony* (Boston, 1929); *The Structure of Music* (Philadelphia, 1934).

Bibl.: A. Shepherd, " 'Papa' G. in Retrospect," *Musical Quarterly* (July 1944).

Goetz, Hermann (Gustav), German composer; b. Königsberg, Dec. 7, 1840; d. Hottingen, near Zürich, Dec. 3, 1876. He studied in Berlin (1860–63), with von Bülow in piano and H. Ulrich in composition. In 1863 he took the post of organist at Winterthur, Switzerland; then lived in Zürich; gave private lessons; conducted a singing society. His most famous work is the opera *Der Widerspenstigen Zähmung,* based on Shakespeare's play *The Taming of the Shrew,* which was given in Mannheim, Oct. 11, 1874. His other works include the opera *Francesca da Rimini* (Mannheim, Sept. 30, 1877; unfinished; 3rd act completed by Ernst Frank); incidental music for Widmann's play *Die heiligen drei Könige* (Winterthur, Jan. 6, 1866); Piano Concerto (Basel, Dec. 1, 1867); Violin Concerto (1868); Sym. in F (1873); choral music; String Quartet (1865); other chamber music; several pieces for piano; songs.

Bibl.: A. Steiner, *H. G.* (Zürich, 1907); E. Kreuzhage, *H. G.: Sein Leben und seine Werke* (Leipzig, 1916); G. Kruse, *H. G.* (Leipzig, 1920); G. Puchelt, "H. G. (1840–1876)," *Schweizerische Musikzeitung/Revue Musicale Suisse,* CXVI (1976).

Goetze, Walter W., German composer; b. Berlin, April 17, 1883; d. there, March 24, 1961. He began as a composer of popular ballads; then produced numerous operettas, among them *Der liebe Pepi* (1913), *Ihre Hoheit, die Tänzerin* (Stettin, May 8, 1919; highly popular; about 700 perfs. in Berlin alone), *Adrienne* (1926), *Der Page des Königs* (1933), *Akrobaten des Glücks* (1933), *Der goldene Pierrot* (Berlin, March 31, 1934), *Sensation im Trocadero* (1936), and *Liebe im Dreiklang* (1951).

Goeyvaerts, Karel (August), significant Belgian composer; b. Antwerp, June 8, 1923. He studied at the Antwerp Cons. (1943–47), and with Milhaud, Messiaen, and Maurice Martenot in Paris (1947–50); received the Lili Boulanger Award in 1949. He taught music history at the Antwerp Cons. (1950–57); organized the Ghent Inst. of Psycho-Acoustics and Electronic Music (IPEM) in 1970. Goeyvaerts was one of the pioneers of serialism, spatial music, and electronic techniques. His works bear pointedly abstract titles with structural connotations; he also applies aleatory devices in audio-visual collages.

Works: *3 lieder per sonare a venti-sei* for 6 Solo Instruments (1948–49); Sonata for 2 Pianos, op. 1 (1950–51); *Opus 2* for 13 Instruments (1951); *Opus 3 aux sons frappés et frottés* (with Striking and Rubbing Sounds) for 7 Instruments (1952); *Opus 4 aux sons morts* (with Dead Sounds) for Tape (1952); *Opus 5 aux sons purs* (with Pure Sounds) for Tape (1953); *Opus 6* for 180 Sound Objects (1954); *Opus 7 aux niveaux convergents et divergents* (with Converging and Diverging Levels) for Tape (1955); *Diaphonie,* suite for Orch. (1957); *Improperia,* cantata for Good Friday, for Alto, Double Chorus, and 6 Instruments (1958); *Piece for 3* for Flute, Violin, and Piano (1960); *Jeux d'été* for 3 Orch. Groups (1961); *La Passion* for Orch. (1962); *Cataclysme,* ballet for Orch. and ad libitum Narration (1963); *Piece* for Piano, with Tape (1964); *Goathe-*

mala for Mezzo-soprano and Flute (1966); *Parcours* for 2 to 6 Violins (1967); *Mass in Memory of John XXIII* for Chorus and 10 Winds (1968); *Actief-Reactief* for 2 Oboes, 2 Trumpets, and Piano (1968); *Catch à quatre,* verbal composition for 4 Wandering Musicians (1969); *Al naar gelang* for 5 Instrumental Groups (1971); *Hé,* audio-visual production (1971; in collaboration with Herman Sabbe and Lucien Goethals); Piano Quartet, mobile composition for Violin, Viola, Cello, and Tape (1972); *Belise dans un jardin* (Belise in a Garden) for Chorus and 6 Instruments (1972); *Nachklänge aus dem Theater* for Tape (1972); *Op acht paarden wedden* (To Bet on 8 Horses), electronic mobile composition for 8 Sound Tracks (1973); *Landschap,* mobile composition for Harpsichord (1973); *You'll Never Be Alone Anymore* for Bass Clarinet and Electronics (1974); *Mon doux pilote s'endort aussi* for Choral Ensemble (1976); *Litanie III,* ballet (1980); *Litanie IV* for Soprano, Flute, Clarinet, Violin, Cello, and Piano (1981); *Zum Wassermann* for Chamber Ensemble (1984); *De Heilige Stad* for Chamber Ensemble (1986).

Gogorza, Emilio (Edoardo) de, American baritone; b. Brooklyn, May 29, 1874; d. N.Y., May 10, 1949. After singing as a boy soprano in England, he returned to the U.S. and studied with C. Moderati and E. Agramonte in N.Y.; made his debut in 1897 with Marcella Sembrich in a concert; sang throughout the country in concerts and with leading orchs. Beginning in 1925, he was an instructor of voice at the Curtis Inst. of Music in Philadelphia. He married the American soprano **Emma Eames** in 1911.

Goh, Taijiro, Japanese composer; b. Dairen, Manchuria, Feb. 15, 1907; d. Shizuoka, July 1, 1970. He studied in Tokyo; organized the Soc. of Japanese Composers, and created the Japan Women's Sym. Orch. (1963). His music follows the European academic type of harmonic and contrapuntal structure.

Works: 3 operas: *Madame Rosaria* (1943), *Tsubaki saku koro* (When Camellias Blossom; 1949; unfinished), and *Tais* (1959; unfinished); ballet, *Oni-Daiko* (Devil Drummers; 1956); 2 choreographic plays, *Koku-sei-Ya* and *Rashômon* (both 1954); 8 syms.: No. 1 (1925); No. 2 (1930); No. 3, *Kumo* (Clouds; 1938); No. 4 (1938); No. 5, *Nippon* (1939); No. 6, *Asia* (1939); No. 7, *Sokoku* (Motherland; 1942); No. 8, *Chô jô Banri* (The Long Wall; 1945; only the 1st movement was completed); 3 violin concertos (1935, 1937, 1962); 2 piano concertos (1936, 1940); *Movement* for Cello, Temple Blocks, and Orch. (1937); Theme and Variations for Orch. (1938); 2 overtures: *Otakebi* (War Cry; 1939) and *Over the Tan-Shan Southern Path* (1941); 3 symphonic marches: *Eiyû* (Hero; 1940); *Taiiku* (Gymnastics; 1940); *Akeyuku Azia* (Asia Dawning; 1942); *Shimpi-shu* (Mysteries; 1942); *Nemuri no Serenâde* (Serenade for Slumber) for Vocal Solo and Orch. (1944); *The Flow of the River Dalny* for Chorus and Orch. (1950); *Seija to Eiyû* (The Saint and the Hero), symphonic dance piece (1961); *Brasil,* symphonic poem, with Narration and Chorus (1967); numerous short symphonic works, including *Konchû* (Insects; 1941) and *Gekiryû* (Torrent; 1952); several pieces for Vocal Soloist or Narrator, and Orch.; Theme and Variations for String Trio (1933); 2 string quartets (1935, 1938); *Imayo* for Cello and Piano (1954); 5 piano sonatas (1915, 1919, 1920, 1927, 1927); *November in Manchuria,* rhapsody for Piano (1926); Fantasy for Piano (1927); Variations for Piano (1931); *8 Chinese Dances* for Piano (1941); *Katyusha,* choreographic poem for Piano (1954); over 100 songs.

Göhler, (Karl) Georg, German conductor and composer; b. Zwickau, June 29, 1874; d. Lübeck, March 4, 1954. He was a pupil of Vollhardt in Zwickau; then studied at the Leipzig Univ. and Cons.; obtained his Ph.D. with a dissertation on the 16th-century composer Cornelius Freundt; he then pursued a career as a conductor, becoming best known as a champion of Bruckner and Mahler. He wrote an opera, *Prinz Nachtwächter* (1922); several syms.; a Clarinet Concerto; 2 violin concertos; a Cello Concerto; *Quartetto enimmatico* for Piano and Strings; a String Trio; more than 200 songs; and numerous choral works; also 24 bagatelles for Piano.

Gold, Arthur, Canadian pianist; b. Toronto, Feb. 6, 1917; d. N.Y., Jan. 3, 1990. He studied with Josef and Rosina Lhévinne at the Juilliard School of Music; upon graduation, formed a piano duo with Robert Fizdale; together they gave numerous concerts in Europe and America, in programs of modern music, including works specially written for them by such celebrated composers as Barber, Milhaud, Poulenc, Auric, and Thomson. They also pioneered performances of works by John Cage for prepared piano. With Fizdale he publ. a successful book, *Misia* (N.Y., 1979), on the life of Maria Godebska, a literary and musical figure in Paris early in the century. Gold retired in 1982, and in a spirit of innocent but practical amusement he publ., with Fizdale, *The Gold and Fizdale Cookbook* (1983).

Gold (real name, **Goldner**), **Ernest,** Austrian-born American composer and conductor; b. Vienna, July 13, 1921. He studied piano and violin at home, and later piano, conducting, and composition at the Vienna Academy of Music (1937–38); he went to the U.S. in 1938 and became a naturalized citizen in 1946; studied harmony with Otto Cesana and conducting with Leon Barzin in N.Y. Moving to Hollywood, he worked as an arranger and took lessons with George Antheil (1946–48); he became particularly successful as a composer for films, winning an Academy Award for his score for *Exodus* (1960). He was music director of the Santa Barbara Sym. Orch. (1958–60) and founder-conductor of Los Angeles's Senior Citizens' Orch.

Works: Many film scores, including *The Defiant Ones* (1958); *On the Beach* (1959); *Exodus* (1960); *Inherit the Wind* (1960); *Judgment at Nuremberg* (1961); *It's a Mad, Mad, Mad, Mad World* (1963); *Ship of Fools* (1965); *The Secret of Santa Vittoria* (1969); 2 musicals: *Too Warm for Furs* (1956) and *I'm Solomon* (1968); *Pan American Symphony* (1941); Piano Concerto (1943); *Ballad* for Orch. (1944); *Symphonic Preludes* (1944); *Allegorical Overture* (1947); Sym. No. 2 (1947); *Band in Hand* for Narrator and Band (1966); *Boston Pops March* (1966); chamber music; piano pieces; songs.

Goldbeck, Robert, German-American pianist, teacher, and composer; b. Potsdam, April 19, 1839; d. St. Louis, May 16, 1908. He studied piano and harmony with his uncle, Louis Köhler, then continued his training with Henry Litolff in Braunschweig; after a period in Paris and London, he went to N.Y. (1857); in 1867 he went to Boston, where he helped Eben Tourjée organize the New England Cons. of Music; subsequently went to Chicago and founded his own cons. (1868); in 1873 he proceeded to St. Louis, where he became co-director of the Beethoven Cons., conductor of the Harmonic Soc., and later founder of the St. Louis College of Music (1880). He lived in N.Y., Königsberg, London, St. Louis, and Chicago (from 1886), finally settling in St. Louis (1903). He wrote an opera, *Newport* (London, 1889); an operetta, *The Soldier's Return* (London, 1856); several *Morceaux symphoniques* for Piano and Orch.; and various pedagogical pieces for piano. He publ. an *Encyclopedia of Music Education* (3 vols., 1903).

Goldberg, Albert, American music critic; b. Shenandoah, Iowa, June 2, 1898; d. Memphis, Tenn., Feb. 4, 1990. He studied at the Chicago Musical College (1920–22); taught there (1924–26); was music critic of the *Chicago Herald Examiner* (1925–36) and of the *Chicago Tribune* (1943–46). In 1947 he was appointed to the staff of the *Los Angeles Times;* after his official retirement in 1965, he wrote occasional articles for the paper until 1989.

Goldberg, Johann Gottlieb, German organist, harpsichordist, and composer; b. Danzig (baptized), March 14, 1727; d. Dresden, April 13, 1756. As a child, he was taken to Dresden by his patron, Count Hermann Karl von Keyserlingk; he is reported to have studied with Wilhelm Friedemann Bach, and later with J.S. Bach (1742–43); in 1751 he became musician to Count Heinrich Brühl, a post he held till his death. His name is immortalized through the set of 30 variations for keyboard by Bach, the so-called *Goldberg Variations,* which were believed to have been commissioned by Keyserlingk for Goldberg. Although this account is now doubted, it is known that Bach gave Goldberg a copy of the score. Goldberg's own compositions include 2 concertos; polonaises; a Sonata with Minuet and 12 variations for Harpsichord; 6 trios for Flute, Violin, and Bass; a Motet; a Cantata; etc.

Bibl.: E. Dadder, *J.G. G.: Leben und Werke* (Bonn, 1923).

Goldberg, Reiner, German tenor; b. Crostau, Oct. 17, 1939. He studied in Dresden with Arno Schellenberg; made his debut in Radebeul in 1966; in 1969 he joined the Dresden State Opera, and in 1973 the (East) Berlin State Opera. On Feb. 22, 1982, he appeared at Covent Garden in London in the role of Walther in *Die Meistersinger von Nürnberg;* he subsequently had guest engagements in Hamburg, Vienna, Madrid, and Leningrad, in the roles of Florestan, Cavaradossi, Bacchus, Siegmund, and Tannhäuser; he also sang the title role in Syberberg's movie version of *Parsifal.*

Goldberg, Szymon, eminent Polish-born American violinist and conductor; b. Wloclawek, June 1, 1909. He played violin as a child in Warsaw; in 1917 he went to Berlin and took regular violin lessons with Carl Flesch. After a recital in Warsaw in 1921, he was engaged as concertmaster of the Dresden Phil. Orch. (1925–29); in 1929 he was appointed concertmaster of the Berlin Phil., but was forced to leave in 1934 despite Furtwängler's vigorous attempts to safeguard the Jewish members of the orch.; he then toured Europe. He made his American debut in N.Y. in 1938; while on a tour of Asia, he was interned in Java by the Japanese from 1942 to 1945; eventually he went to the U.S.; became an American citizen in 1953. From 1951 to 1965 he taught at the Aspen Music School; concurrently was active as a conductor. In 1955 he founded the Netherlands Chamber Orch. in Amsterdam, which he led with notable distinction for 22 years; he also took the ensemble on tours. He taught at Yale Univ. (1978–82), the Juilliard School in N.Y. (from 1978), the Curtis Inst. of Music in Philadelphia (from 1980), and the Manhattan School of Music in N.Y. (from 1981).

Bibl.: B. Gavoty, *S. G.* (Geneva, 1961).

Goldberg, Theo, German composer; b. Chemnitz, Sept. 29, 1921. He studied in Berlin (1945–50); in 1954, settled in Canada and taught in Vancouver; received his doctorate in composition from the Univ. of Toronto (1972). He composed the chamber operas *Minotauros; Schwere Zeiten für Engel* (Berlin, Sept. 20, 1952), *Galatea elettronica* (1969), and *Jeanne des anges* (1972); a ballet, *Nacht mit Kleopatra* (Karlsruhe, Jan. 20, 1952); *La Femme Cent Têtes* for Orch. (1950); *Variations on a Theme by Strauss* for Orch. (1952); Double Concerto for Oboe, Bassoon, and Orch. (1952); Cantata (1953); Divertissement No. 3 for Orch. (1957); *Sinfonia concertante* for Flute, Clarinet, Trumpet, Violin, Cello, and Orch. (1967); String Quartet (1949); Clarinet Quintet (1952); Quartet for Alto Flute, Viola, Cello, and Harp (1962); *Calliope* for Bassoon, Trombone, Piano, Violin, Tape, and Sound-related Images (1973).

Golde, Walter, American pianist, vocal teacher, and composer; b. Brooklyn, Jan. 4, 1887; d. Chapel Hill, N.C., Sept. 4, 1963. He studied at Dartmouth College, graduating in 1910; then went to Vienna, where he took vocal lessons and studied counterpoint and composition with Robert Fuchs at the Cons. Returning to the U.S., he became a professional accompanist; played for Casals, Mischa Elman, Mary Garden, and Melchior. From 1944 to 1948 he headed the voice dept. of Columbia Univ.; in 1953 he was appointed director of the Inst. of Opera at the Univ. of North Carolina. He composed a number of attractive songs and piano pieces.

Goldenweiser, Alexander (Borisovich), Russian piano pedagogue; b. Kishinev, March 10, 1875; d. Moscow, Nov. 26, 1961. He studied piano with Siloti and Pabst and composition with Arensky, Ippolitov-Ivanov, and Taneyev at the Moscow Cons.; in 1906 became a prof. of piano there, holding this post for 55 years, until his death. Two generations of Russian pianists were his pupils, among them Kabalevsky and Berman.

As a pedagogue, he continued the traditions of the Russian school of piano playing, seeking the inner meaning of the music while achieving technical brilliance. He was a frequent visitor at Tolstoy's house near Moscow, and wrote reminiscences of Tolstoy (Moscow, 1922); publ. several essays on piano teaching; also composed chamber music and piano pieces.

Goldman, Edwin Franko, eminent American bandmaster and composer, father of **Richard Franko Goldman;** b. Louisville, Ky., Jan. 1, 1878; d. N.Y., Feb. 21, 1956. He was the nephew of **Sam** and **Nahan Franko;** studied composition with Dvořák, and cornet with J. Levy and C. Sohst in N.Y. He became solo cornetist of the Metropolitan Opera orch. when he was 21, remaining there for 10 years. For the next 13 years he taught cornet and trumpet; he formed his 1st band in 1911. In 1918 the Goldman Band outdoor concerts were inaugurated. His band was noted not only for its skill and musicianship but for its unusual repertoire, including modern works especially commissioned for the band. Goldman was a founder and 1st president of the American Bandmasters' Assoc.; he received honorary D.Mus. degrees from Phillips Univ. and Boston Univ., and medals and other honors from governments and associations throughout the world. He wrote more than 100 brilliant marches, of which the best known is *On the Mall;* also other band music; solos for various wind instruments; studies and methods for cornet and other brass instruments; several songs. He was the author of *Foundation to Cornet or Trumpet Playing* (1914); *Band Betterment* (1934); and *The Goldman Band System* (1936).

Goldman, Richard Franko, distinguished American bandmaster, writer on music, teacher, and composer, son of **Edwin Franko Goldman;** b. N.Y., Dec. 7, 1910; d. Baltimore, Jan. 19, 1980. He graduated from Columbia Univ. in 1931; later studied composition with Nadia Boulanger in Paris. He became an assistant of his father in conducting the Goldman Band in 1937; on his father's death in 1956, he succeeded him as conductor; continued to conduct the band into the summer of 1979, when ill health forced him to retire and allow the band to dissolve. He taught at the Juilliard School of Music (1947–60); was a visiting prof. at Princeton Univ. (1952–56); in 1968 was appointed director of the Peabody Cons. of Music in Baltimore, serving as its president from 1969 to 1977. He was the N.Y. critic for the *Musical Quarterly* (1948–68) and ed. of the *Juilliard Review* (1953–58). He wrote many works for various ensembles: *A Sentimental Journey* for Band (1941); 3 duets for Clarinets (1944); Sonatina for 2 Clarinets (1945); Duo for Tubas (1948); Violin Sonata (1952); etc.; many arrangements for band. A progressive musician, Goldman experimented with modern techniques, and his music combines highly advanced harmony with simple procedures accessible to amateurs. **WRITINGS:** *The Band's Music* (N.Y., 1938); *Landmarks of Early American Music, 1760–1800* (N.Y., 1943); *The Concert Band* (N.Y., 1946); *The Wind Band: Its Literature and Technique* (Boston, 1961); *Harmony in Western Music* (N.Y., 1965); D. Klotzman, ed., *Richard Franko Goldman: Selected Essays and Reviews, 1948–1968* (N.Y., 1980).

Goldmann, Friedrich, German composer; b. Siegmar-Schönau, April 27, 1941. He studied composition with Thilman at the Dresden Hochschule für Musik (1959–62); then attended the master classes of Wagner-Régeny at the Akademie der Künste in East Berlin (1962–64); later entered Humboldt Univ. in East Berlin to study musicology (1964–68). In 1973 he received the Hanns Eisler Prize.
WORKS: STAGE: *R. Hot bzw. die Hitze,* opera fantasy (1976). **ORCH.:** *Essay I–III* (1963–64; 1968; 1971); 3 syms. (1972–73; 1976; 1986); *Musik für Kammerorchester* (1973); Concerto for Trombone and 3 Instrumental Groups (1977); Violin Concerto (1977); Oboe Concerto (1978); Piano Concerto (1979); *Inclinatio temporum* (1981); *Orchesterstück* (1988). **CHAMBER:** Trio for Flute, Percussion, and Piano (1966–67); String Trio (1967); Sonata for Wind Quintet and Piano (1969–

70); *So und So* for English Horn, Trombone, and Double Bass (1972); *Cellomusik* (1974); String Quartet (1975); *Zusammenstellung,* music for Wind Instruments (1976); Piano Trio (1978); *Für P.D.* for 15 Strings (1975); Oboe Sonata (1980). **VOCAL:** *Odipus Tyrann: Kommentar* for Chorus and Orch. (1968–69); *Sing' Lessing* for Baritone, Flute, Oboe, Clarinet, Horn, Bassoon, and Piano (1978).

Goldmark, Karl (Károly), eminent Hungarian composer, uncle of **Rubin Goldmark;** b. Keszthely, May 18, 1830; d. Vienna, Jan. 2, 1915. The son of a poor cantor, he studied at the school of the Musical Soc. of Sopron (1842–44); the talent he showed there as a violinist resulted in his being sent to Vienna, where he studied with L. Jansa (1844–45); later studied at the Vienna Cons., as a pupil of Preyer (harmony) and Böhm (violin). He spent most of his life in Vienna, where the 1st concert of his compositions was given on March 20, 1857. Landmarks in his career were the 1st performance of his *Sakuntala* overture by the Vienna Phil. on Dec. 26, 1865, and the premiere of his 1st opera, *Die Königin von Saba,* at the Vienna Court Opera on March 10, 1875; both were very successful. He publ. an autobiography, *Erinnerungen aus meinem Leben* (Vienna, 1922; in Eng. as *Notes from the Life of a Viennese Composer,* N.Y., 1927).
WORKS: OPERAS: *Die Königin von Saba* (Vienna, March 10, 1875); *Merlin* (Vienna, Nov. 19, 1886); *Das Heimchen am Herd,* based on Dickens's *The Cricket on the Hearth* (Vienna, March 21, 1896); *Die Kriegsgefangene* (Vienna, Jan. 17, 1899); *Götz von Berlichingen,* based on Goethe's play (Budapest, Dec. 16, 1902); *Ein Wintermärchen,* based on Shakespeare's *A Winter's Tale* (Vienna, Jan. 2, 1908). **ORCH.:** 7 overtures: *Sakuntala, Penthesilea, Im Frühling, Der gefesselte Prometheus, Sappho, In Italien, Aus Jugendtagen;* a symphonic poem, *Ländliche Hochzeit* (Rustic Wedding; Vienna, March 5, 1876); 2 syms.; symphonic poem, *Zrinyi* (1903); Violin Concerto No. 1 (Nuremberg, Oct. 28, 1878); other instrumental concertos. **CHAMBER:** 2 piano trios; Piano Quintet; Cello Sonata; Violin Sonata; also piano pieces; songs; choral works.
BIBL.: O. Keller, *K. G.* (Leipzig, 1901); H. Schwarz, *Ignaz Brüll und sein Freundeskreis: Erinnerungen an Brüll, G. und Brahms* (Vienna, 1922); L. Koch, ed., *K. G.* (Budapest, 1930); P. Várnai, *Károly G.* (Budapest, 1957); H. Truscott, "C. G.," *Monthly Musical Record,* XC (1960).

Goldmark, Rubin, American composer and teacher, nephew of **Karl (Károly) Goldmark;** b. N.Y., Aug. 15, 1872; d. there, March 6, 1936. He studied at the Vienna Cons. with A. Door (piano) and J.N. Fuchs (composition); from 1891 to 1893 he was a student at the National Cons. in N.Y. with Joseffy (piano) and Dvořák (composition). He taught at the Colorado Springs College Cons. (1895–1901). Returning to N.Y. in 1902, for the next 20 years he gave private lessons in piano and theory. In 1924 he was appointed head of the composition dept. of the Juilliard School in N.Y., and remained there until his death; among his pupils were Copland, Chasins, and Jacobi. He was active in promoting such musical clubs as The Bohemians (of N.Y.), of which he was a founder and president (1907–10); the Beethoven Assoc.; and the Soc. for the Publication of American Music.
WORKS: Overture, *Hiawatha* (Boston, Jan. 13, 1900); tone poem, *Samson* (Boston, March 14, 1914); Requiem, suggested by Lincoln's Gettysburg Address (N.Y., Jan. 30, 1919); *A Negro Rhapsody* (his most popular work; N.Y., Jan. 18, 1923); Piano Quartet (Paderewski Prize, 1909; N.Y., Dec. 13, 1910); Piano Trio; *The Call of the Plains* for Violin and Piano (1915); songs.
BIBL.: A. Copland, "R. G.: A Tribute," *Juilliard Review,* III/3 (1956); D. Tomatz, *R. G., Postromantic: Trial Balances in American Music* (diss., Catholic Univ. of America, 1966).

Goldovsky, Boris, Russian-American pianist, conductor, opera producer, lecturer, and broadcaster, son of **Lea** and nephew of **Pierre Luboshutz;** b. Moscow, June 7, 1908. He studied piano with his uncle and took courses at the Moscow Cons. (1918–21); in 1921 he made his debut as a pianist with the

Berlin Phil., and continued his studies with Schnabel and Kreutzer at the Berlin Academy of Music (1921–23); after attending Dohnányi's master class at the Budapest Academy of Music (graduated, 1930), he received training in conducting from Reiner at the Curtis Inst. of Music in Philadelphia (1932). He served as head of the opera depts. at the New England Cons. of Music in Boston (1942–64), the Berkshire Music Center at Tanglewood (1946–61), and the Curtis Inst. of Music (from 1977). In 1946 he founded the New England Opera Theater in Boston, which became the Goldovsky Opera Inst. in 1963; he also toured with his own opera company until 1984. He was a frequent commentator for the Metropolitan Opera radio broadcasts (from 1946) and also lectured extensively; he prepared Eng. trs. of various operas.

WRITINGS: *Accents on Opera* (1953); *Bringing Opera to Life* (1968); with A. Schoep, *Bringing Soprano Arias to Life* (1973); with T. Wolf, *Manual of Operatic Touring* (1975); with C. Cate, *My Road to Opera* (1979); *Good Afternoon, Ladies and Gentlemen!: Intermission Scripts from the Met Broadcasts* (1984).

Goldsand, Robert, Austrian pianist and teacher; b. Vienna, March 17, 1911. He studied with A. Manhart, M. Rosenthal, Camillo Horn, and Joseph Marx. He played in public at the age of 10; then toured in Europe and South America; made his U.S. debut at Carnegie Hall, March 21, 1927; then was again in Europe, but settled permanently in the U.S. in 1939.

Goldschmidt, Adalbert von, Austrian composer; b. Vienna, May 5, 1848; d. Hacking, near Vienna, Dec. 21, 1906. He studied at the Vienna Cons.; from his earliest efforts in composition, he became an ardent follower of Wagner. At the age of 22, he wrote a cantata, *Die sieben Todsünden* (Berlin, 1875); this was followed by a music drama, *Helianthus* (Leipzig, 1884), for which he wrote both words and music. A dramatic trilogy, *Gaea* (1889–92), was his most ambitious work along Wagnerian lines. He also brought out a comic opera, *Die fromme Helene* (Hamburg, 1897); wrote about 100 songs and a number of piano pieces.

BIBL.: E. Friedegg, *Briefe an einen Komponisten: Musikalische Korrespondenz an A. v.G.* (Berlin, 1909).

Goldschmidt, Berthold, German-born English composer and conductor; b. Hamburg, Jan. 18, 1903. He studied at the Univ. of Hamburg and at the Friedrich Wilhelm Univ. in Berlin; also at the Berlin State Academy of Music with Schreker. He was an assistant conductor at the Berlin State Opera (1926–27) and conductor at the Darmstadt Opera (1927–29); then was a conductor with the Berlin Radio and the Städtische Oper. In 1935 he went to England; became a British citizen in 1947. He made numerous guest appearances in England with various orchs.; conducted the 1st complete performance of Deryck Cooke's performing version of Mahler's 10th Sym. in 1964; also conducted opera. He composed 2 operas: *Der gewaltige Hahnrei* (Mannheim, Feb. 14, 1932) and *Beatrice Cenci* (1949–50); a ballet, *Chronica* (1938); Sym. (1944); Concertino for Violin (1933); Concertino for Cello (1933); Concertino for Harp (1949); and Concertino for Clarinet (1955); also works for piano.

Goldschmidt, Hugo, German writer on music; b. Breslau, Sept. 19, 1859; d. Wiesbaden, Dec. 26, 1920. He studied with Hirschberg and Schäffer in Breslau; obtained his Ph.D. in law at the Univ. of Breslau (1884); then studied singing with Stockhausen in Frankfurt (1887–90); was co-director of the Klindworth-Scharwenka Cons. in Berlin (1893–1905).

WRITINGS: *Die italienische Gesangsmethode des 17. Jahrhunderts* (1890); *Der Vokalismus des neuhochdeutschen Kunstgesangs und der Bühnensprache* (1892); *Handbuch der deutschen Gegangspädagogik* (1896); *Studien zur Geschichte der italienischen Oper im 17. Jahrhundert* (2 vols., 1901, 1904; reprint, 1967); *Die Lehre von der vokalen Ornamentik* (1907); *Die Musikästhetik des 18. Jahrhunderts und ihre Beziehungen zu seinem Kunstschaffen* (1915; reprint, 1968).

Goldschmidt, Otto (Moritz David), German pianist, conductor, and composer; b. Hamburg, Aug. 21, 1829; d. London,

Feb. 24, 1907. He was at first a pupil of Jakob Schmitt and F.W. Grund in Hamburg; then of Mendelssohn, Bülow, Hauptmann, and Plaidy in Leipzig. In 1848 he played in London at a concert given by **Jenny Lind;** accompanied her on her American tour (1851) and married her at Boston, Feb. 5, 1852; from 1852 to 1855 they lived in Dresden; from 1858 until her death (1887), in London. He founded the Bach Choir in 1875, and conducted it till 1885. He composed an oratorio, *Ruth* (Hereford, 1867); a choral song, *Music,* for Soprano and Women's Chorus (Leeds, 1898); piano music, including a Concerto, piano studies, 2 duets for 2 Pianos, etc.

Goldsmith, Jerry, American composer; b. Los Angeles, Feb. 10, 1929. He studied piano with Jakob Gimpel and theory and composition with Castelnuovo-Tedesco; then studied music at Los Angeles City College; also sat in on Rosza's sessions on film music at the Univ. of Southern Calif. He wrote music for various CBS radio and television programs (1950–60); then devoted himself mainly to writing music for films. Among his works are the scores for *Freud* (1962); *7 Days in May* (1964); *A Patch of Blue* (1966); *Seconds* (1966); *Planet of the Apes* (1967); *Patton* (1970); *Papillon* (1973); *The Cassandra Crossing* (1976); *Islands in the Stream* (1977); *MacArthur* (1978); *Poltergeist* (1982); *Rambo* (1985); etc. He also wrote chamber music and vocal works.

Goldstein, Mikhail, brilliant Russian violinist, composer, and musicologist; b. Odessa, Nov. 8, 1917; d. Hamburg, Sept. 7, 1989. He was a proverbial *wunderkind* who seemed to have been born with an extra limb shaped like a violin; as an infant he began to study with the renowned Odessa violin teacher Pyotr Stoliarsky, known among Russian-Jewish musicians as a "talent manufacturer." He was sent to Moscow and at 13 entered the Cons., where he studied composition with Miaskovsky and conducting with Saradzhev. During the war of 1941–45, he was active in the entertainment division of the Red Army; during the battle of Stalingrad, he played Bach over a powerful loudspeaker for the benefit of the German soldiers, and the Germans urged him to play more, promising not to shoot; they did not realize that the Bach player was a lowly Jew. He was discriminated against by the Soviets because he was married to a German woman; for that reason, none of his works were publ. In a spirit of witty retaliation, he perpetrated a hoax, claiming the discovery of a sym. allegedly composed in 1810 by a mythical Russian musician named Ovsianiko-Kulikovsky; the work was hailed as a proof that syms. were written in Russia in Beethoven's time; the score was publ. and recorded; the Soviet musicologist Valerian Dovzhenko wrote a learned dissertation on the subject. When Goldstein publicly admitted his deception, he was denounced as an impostor trying to appropriate a historically important Russian work. In eclipse as a result of this episode, Goldstein left Russia in 1964; lived first in East Berlin; in 1967 went to Israel and taught violin at the Musical Academy in Jerusalem. In 1969 he settled in Hamburg, where he resumed his career as a concert violinist and a pedagogue. He also did valuable research in musical biography, establishing important facts about Russian and German composers of the 18th and 19th centuries. In 1969 he was appointed a prof. at the Hamburg Hochschule für Musik, leading master classes. He was an inventive composer; one of his most original compositions is a Quartet for 4 Violas, without precedent in instrumental music. He also wrote 4 syms. and other instrumental music.

Goléa, Antoine, Rumanian-French music critic; b. Vienna, Aug. 30, 1906; d. Paris, Oct. 12, 1980. He studied at the Bucharest Cons.; then emigrated to France, where he became active as a journalist, specializing in lively monographs on contemporary composers.

WRITINGS: *Rencontres avec Pierre Boulez* (Paris, 1958); *Georges Auric* (Paris, 1958); *Rencontres avec Olivier Messiaen* (Paris, 1959); *La Musique dans la société européenne depuis le moyen âge jusqu'à nos jours* (Paris, 1960); *Claude Debussy* (Paris, 1965); *Richard Strauss* (Paris, 1965); *Entretiens avec*

Wieland Wagner (Paris, 1967; in German, Salzburg, 1968); *Histoire du ballet* (Lausanne, 1967).

Goleminov, Marin, Bulgarian composer and pedagogue; b. Kjustendil, Sept. 28, 1908. He studied at the Sofia State Academy of Music (graduated, 1931), then went to Paris; there he took courses in composition with d'Indy and in conducting with Marcel Labé at the Schola Cantorum, in composition with Dukas at the École Normale de Musique, and in esthetics and music history at the Sorbonne (1931–34); subsequently studied composition with J. Haas and conducting with H. Knappe and E. Erenberg at the Munich Akademie der Tonkunst (1938–39). In 1943 he joined the faculty of the Bulgarian State Cons. in Sofia, where he served as a prof. of orchestration, conducting, and composition; was also its rector; from 1965 to 1967 he was director of the National Opera. He received various honors from the Bulgarian government, and in 1976 was awarded the Gottfried von Herder Prize of the Univ. of Vienna. His music utilizes folk elements, particularly the asymmetrical rhythms of Bulgarian folk motifs, in a fairly modern but still quite accessible idiom.
WORKS: OPERAS: *Ivailo* (1958; Sofia, Feb. 13, 1959); *Zahari the Icon Painter* (1971; Sofia, Oct. 17, 1972); *Thracian Idols* (1981); and the operatic fairy tale *Zlatnata ptica* (The Golden Bird; Sofia, Dec. 20, 1961). BALLETS: *Nestinarka* (1940; Sofia, Jan. 4, 1942) and *The Daughter of Kaloyan* (Sofia, Dec. 23, 1973). OTHER STAGE: *The Titan*, oratorio (Sofia, June 25, 1972); *Father Paissy*, cantata (1966). ORCH.: *Night*, symphonic poem (1932); Cello Concerto (1949–50); *Prelude, Aria and Toccata* for Piano and Orch. (1959); Concerto for String Quartet and String Orch. (1963; Moscow, Feb. 11, 1964); 4 syms.: No. 1, *Children's Symphony* (1963); No. 2 (1967; Sofia, March 6, 1968); No. 3, *Peace in the World* (1970; Sofia, April 21, 1971); No. 4, *Shopophonia* (1978); Violin Concerto No. 1 (1968); *Aquarelles* for String Orch. (1973); Piano Concerto (1975); *3 Miniatures* for Soprano and Chamber Orch. CHAMBER: 7 string quartets (1934; 1938; 1944; *Micro-quartet*, 1967; 1969; 1975; 1977); 2 wind quintets (1936, 1946); Trio for Oboe, Clarinet, and Bassoon (1964); Cello Sonata (1969); also choruses; songs; incidental music.
BIBL.: B. Arnaudova, *M. G.* (Sofia, 1968); S. Lazarov, *M. G.* (Sofia, 1971).

Golestan, Stan, Rumanian composer; b. Vaslui, June 7, 1875; d. Paris, April 21, 1956. He studied composition and orchestration with Vincent d'Indy, Albert Roussel, and Paul Dukas at the Schola Cantorum in Paris (1895–1903). Subsequently he wrote music criticism for *Le Figaro.*
WORKS: ORCH.: *La Dembovitza* (1902); *Lăutarul și Cobzarul*, Rumanian dances (1902); Sym. (1910); *Rapsodie roumaine* (1912); *Rapsodie concertante* for Violin and Orch. (1920); *Concerto roumain* for Violin and Orch. (1933); *Concerto moldave* for Cello and Orch. (1936); Piano Concerto, subtitled *Sur les cîmes des Carpathes* (1935–38). CHAMBER: Violin Sonata (1908); 2 string quartets; *Arioso* and *Concert Allegro* for Viola and Piano (1932); Flute Sonatina (1932). PIANO: *Poèmes et paysages* (1922); also *Thème, variations et danses;* vocal pieces.

Golitzin, Nikolai (Borisovich), Russian nobleman and patron of music; b. St. Petersburg, Dec. 19, 1794; d. Tambov district, Nov. 3, 1866. He was a talented cello player, but his name is remembered mainly because of his connection with Beethoven, who dedicated the overture op. 124 and the string quartets opp. 127, 130, and 132 to him. Golitzin was also responsible for the 1st performance of Beethoven's *Missa solemnis* (St. Petersburg Phil. Soc., April 7, 1824).
BIBL.: L. Ginzburg, "Beethoven und N. G.," *Beethoven Jahrbuch* (Bonn, 1962).

Göllerich, August, Austrian writer on music; b. Linz, July 2, 1859; d. there, March 16, 1923. He was a pupil of Liszt; studied composition with Bruckner; acquired Ramann's music school in Nuremberg in 1890, and established branches in Erlangen, Fürth, and Ansbach; from 1896, he was conductor of the Musikverein and director of the Linz Cons.; his wife, Gisela Pászthory-Voigt (also a pupil of Liszt), supervised the

other schools. He publ. *A. Reissmann als Schriftsteller und Komponist* (1884); *Beethoven* (1904); *Franz Liszt* (1908). His chief work, a biography of Bruckner (who himself selected Göllerich for this task), in 4 vols., was completed by Max Auer (1st vol., Regensburg, 1924; 2nd, 1928; remaining vols., 1932 and 1937).

Gollmick, Adolf, German pianist, teacher, and composer, son of **Karl Gollmick;** b. Frankfurt am Main, Feb. 5, 1825; d. London, March 7, 1883. He studied with his father and other teachers in Frankfurt; in 1844 he settled in London as a pianist and teacher. He composed 3 comic operas: *Dona Constanza, The Oracle,* and *Balthasar;* 2 "operatic cantatas": *The Blind Beggar's Daughter of Bethnal Green* and *The Heir of Lynne;* also several symphonic works, piano pieces, and songs.

Gollmick, Karl, German writer on music and composer, father of **Adolf Gollmick;** b. Dessau, March 19, 1796; d. Frankfurt am Main, Oct. 3, 1866. He was of a musical family; his father, **Friedrich Karl Gollmick** (1774–1852), was an opera tenor. He studied theology in Strasbourg; in 1817 he settled in Frankfurt, where he taught French and served as chorus master. He wrote mostly for piano; publ. potpourris, etc. His writings include *Kritische Terminologie für Musiker und Musikfreunde* (1833; 2nd ed., 1839); *Fétis als Mensch, Kritiker, Theoretiker und Komponist* (1852); *Handlexikon der Tonkunst* (1858); etc. He also wrote an autobiography (1866).

Golovanov, Nikolai (Semyonovich), Russian conductor, composer, and pedagogue; b. Moscow, Jan. 21, 1891; d. there, Aug. 28, 1953. He studied choral conducting with Kastalsky at the Synodal School in Moscow, graduating in 1909; then entered the composition classes of Ippolitov-Ivanov and Vassilenko at the Moscow Cons. After graduation in 1914 he was engaged as assistant chorus conductor at the Bolshoi Theater in Moscow; was its chief conductor (1919–28; 1948–53); was also chief conductor of the Moscow Phil. (1926–29), the U.S.S.R. All-Union Radio Sym. Orch. (1937–53), and the Stanislavsky Opera Theater (1938–53). He was awarded the Order of the Red Banner in 1935, and was 4 times recipient of the 1st Stalin Prize (1946, 1948, 1950, 1951). He wrote an opera, *Princess Yurata;* a Sym.; a symphonic poem, *Salome,* after Oscar Wilde; numerous piano pieces; songs.
BIBL.: N. Anosov, "N. G.," *Sovetskaya Musyka* (May 1951).

Golschmann, Vladimir, renowned French-born American conductor; b. Paris (of Russian parents), Dec. 16, 1893; d. N.Y., March 1, 1972. He studied violin and piano at the Schola Cantorum in Paris; in 1919 he organized the Concerts Golschmann in Paris, in programs featuring many 1st performances of modern works. In 1923 he conducted ballet orchs. in the U.S.; then was conductor of the Scottish Orch. in Glasgow (1928–30). In 1931 he was engaged as conductor of the St. Louis Sym. Orch., and held this post for more than a quarter of a century (until 1958); from 1964 to 1970, was conductor of the Denver Sym. Orch.; also appeared as guest conductor with other American orchs. He became an American citizen in 1947.
BIBL.: J. Titzler, "V. G., Conductor," *Le Grand Baton* (Sept.– Dec. 1979).

Goltermann, Georg (Eduard), German cellist, conductor, and composer; b. Hannover, Aug. 19, 1824; d. Frankfurt am Main, Dec. 29, 1898. He studied cello with A.C. Prell in Hannover; then studied cello with J. Menter and composition with I. Lachner in Munich. After touring as a cellist and serving briefly as a music director in Würzburg, he was assistant music director (1853–74) and music director (1874–98) of the Frankfurt Stadttheater. He wrote a Sym., 3 overtures, 8 cello concertos, much piano music, and songs.

Goltz, Christel, German soprano; b. Dortmund, July 8, 1912. She studied in Munich; from 1936 to 1950 she was a member of the Dresden State Opera; also sang with the Berlin State Opera and the Berlin City Opera. From 1951 to 1970 she made many appearances with the Vienna State Opera; in 1952 she was named a Kammersängerin. On Dec. 15, 1954, she made her Metropolitan Opera debut in N.Y. as Salome. She sang in many productions of modern operas.

Golubev, Evgeny, Russian composer and pedagogue; b. Moscow, Feb. 16, 1910; d. there, Dec. 25, 1988. He studied composition with Miaskovsky at the Moscow Cons., graduating in 1936, and piano with Feinberg. He joined the faculty of his alma mater upon graduation and taught special courses in polyphonic composition. Several well-known Soviet composers were his students, among them Khrennikov, Eshpai, and Schnittke.

Works: 7 syms. (1933, 1937, 1942, 1947, 1960, 1966, 1972); 3 piano concertos (1944, 1948, 1956); Cello Concerto (1958); Viola Concerto (1962); Violin Concerto (1970); 19 string quartets; 2 string quintets; 10 piano sonatas; oratorios: *Return of the Sun* (1936) and *Heroes Are Immortal* (1946); ballet, *Odysseus* (1965); many choruses.

Golyscheff, Jefim, Russian composer; b. Kherson, Sept. 20, 1897; d. Paris, Sept. 25, 1970. He studied violin in Odessa; in 1909, in the wake of anti-Jewish pogroms in Russia, he went to Berlin, where he studied chemistry as well as music theory; at the same time he began to paint in the manner of Abstract Expressionism. He played a historic role in the development of the serial methods of composition; his String Trio, written about 1914 and publ. in 1925, contains passages described by him as "Zwölftondauer-Komplexen," in which 12 different tones are given 12 different durations in the main theme. As both a painter and a musician, he was close to the Dada circles in Berlin, and participated in futuristic experiments. On April 30, 1919, he presented at a Dada exhibition his *Anti-Symphonie*, subtitled *Musikalische Kreisguillotine*, with characteristic titles of its movements: 1, *Provocational Injections;* 2, *Chaotic Oral Cavity, or Submarine Aircraft;* 3, *Clapping in Hyper F-sharp Major*. On May 24, 1919, he appeared at a Dada soirée with a piece entitled *Keuchmaneuver*. All this activity ceased with the advent of the Nazis in 1933. Golyscheff fled to Paris, but after the fall of France in 1940 was interned by the Vichy authorities. His life was probably spared because of his expertise as a chemist; he was conscripted as a cement laborer. In 1956 he went to Brazil, where he devoted himself exclusively to painting. In 1966 he returned to Paris, where he remained until his death.

Bibl.: D. Gojowy, "J. G., der unbequeme Vorläufer," *Melos* (May–June 1975).

Gombert, Nicolas, important Flemish composer; b. southern Flanders, possibly between Lille and St. Omer, c.1495; d. c.1560. He was one of the most eminent pupils of Josquin des Prez, on whose death he composed a funeral dirge. The details of his early life are obscure and uncertain. The physician Jerome Cardan reported that Gombert violated a boy and was sentenced to the galleys on the high seas. He is first positively accounted for in 1526, when his name appears on the list of singers at the court chapel of Charles V that was issued at Granada in that year; the restless Emperor traveled continually throughout his extensive domain—Spain, Germany, and the Netherlands—and his retinue was obliged to follow him in his round of his courts at Vienna, Madrid, and Brussels; Gombert probably was taken into the service of the Emperor on one of the latter's visits to Brussels. He is first mentioned as "maistre des enffans de la chapelle de nostre sr empereur" ("master of the boys of the royal chapel") in a court document dated Jan. 1, 1529; he remained in the Emperor's employ until 1538–40, during which time he took an active part in the various functions of the court, composing assiduously. After his retirement from his post in the royal chapel, he seems to have returned to his native Netherlands (Tournai), and there continued to compose until his death. He held a canonship at Notre Dame, Courtrai, from June 23, 1537, without having to take up residence there, and was also a canon at the Cathedral of Tournai from June 19, 1534. Despite his many trips abroad and the natural influence of the music of other countries, Gombert remained, stylistically, a Netherlander. The chief feature of his sacred works is his use of imitation, a principle

which he developed to a high state of perfection. The parts are always in motion, and pauses appear infrequently; when they do occur, they are very short. In his handling of dissonance he may be regarded as a forerunner of Palestrina. His secular works, of which the earliest known printed examples (9 4-part chansons) are included in Attaignant's collection of 1529–49, are characterized by a refreshing simplicity and directness. Gombert's greatest contributions to the development of 16th-century music lay in his recognizing the peculiarities of Netherlandish polyphony and his developing and spreading it abroad. His extant works include 10 masses, over 160 motets, and 70 chansons, many of which appeared in contemporary (mostly Spanish) lute and guitar arrangements, a fact which shows the great vogue they had. Gombert's *Opera omnia*, ed. by J. Schmidt-Görg, was publ. in Corpus Mensurabilis Musicae, VI/1–11 (1951–75).

Bibl.: D. Bartha, "Probleme der Chansongeschichte im 16. Jahrhundert: N. G.—Benedictus Appenzeller," *Zeitschrift für Musikwissenschaft*, XIII (1930–31); H. Eppstein, *N. G. als Motettenkomponist* (Würzburg, 1935); J. Schmidt-Görg, "Die acht Magnifikat des N. G.," *Gesammelte Aufsätze zur Kulturgeschichte Spaniens*, V (1935); idem, *N. G., Kapellmeister Karls V: Leben und Werk* (Bonn, 1938); R. Maniates, "The Sacred Music of N. G.," *Canadian Music Journal*, VI (1962); C. Miller, "Jerome Cardan on G., Phinot, and Carpentras," *Musical Quarterly* (July 1972).

Gombosi, Otto (János), eminent Hungarian musicologist; b. Budapest, Oct. 23, 1902; d. Natick, Mass., Feb. 17, 1955. He studied at the Academy of Music in Budapest; then musicology with Hornbostel, Sachs, and Wolf at the Univ. of Berlin (Ph.D., 1925, with the diss. *Jacob Obrecht: Eine stilkritische Studie;* publ. in Leipzig, 1925); from 1926 to 1928 he ed. the progressive Hungarian music periodical *Crescendo*. In 1939 he went to the U.S.; was a lecturer in music at the Univ. of Washington, Seattle (1940–46); then taught at Michigan State College and the Univ. of Chicago (1949–51); from 1951 to 1955, was a prof. at Harvard Univ. He contributed numerous valuable papers to various periodicals, in Hungarian, German, Italian, and English; among his most important writings are *Tonarten und Stimmungen der antiken Musik* (Copenhagen, 1939) and a treatise on V. Bakfark in *Musicologia Hungarica* (Budapest, 1935).

Gomes, (Antônio) Carlos, Brazilian composer; b. Campinas (of Portuguese parents), July 11, 1836; d. Belém, Sept. 16, 1896. He studied with his father, then at the Rio de Janeiro Cons., where he produced 2 operas, *A Noite do Castello* (Sept. 4, 1861) and *Joana de Flandres* (Sept. 15, 1863). The success of these works induced Emperor Don Pedro II to grant him a stipend for further study in Milan; there he soon made his mark with a humorous little piece entitled *Se sa minga* (a song from this work, *Del fucile ad ago*, became popular), produced in 1867. After another piece in the same vein (*Nella Luna*, 1868), he made a more serious bid for fame with the opera *Il Guarany*, produced at La Scala on March 19, 1870, with brilliant success; this work, in which Amazon Indian themes are used, quickly went the round of Italy, and was given in London (Covent Garden) on July 13, 1872. Returning to Rio de Janeiro, Gomes brought out a very popular operetta, *Telegrapho elettrico*. His other operas are *Fosca* (La Scala, Milan, Feb. 16, 1873), *Salvator Rosa* (Genoa, March 21, 1874), *Maria Tudor* (La Scala, Milan, March 27, 1879), *Lo Schiavo* (Rio de Janeiro, Sept. 27, 1889), and *Condor* (La Scala, Milan, Feb. 21, 1891). He wrote the hymn *Il saluto del Brasile* for the centenary of American independence (Philadelphia, July 19, 1876); also the cantata *Colombo*, for the Columbus Festival (Oct. 12, 1892). In 1895 he was appointed director of the newly founded Belém Cons., but he died soon after arriving there. Besides his operas, he composed songs (3 books), choruses, and piano pieces.

Bibl.: S. Boccanera Júnior, *Um artista brasileiro: In memoriam* (Bahia, 1904); H.P. Vieira, *C. G.: Sua arte e sua obra* (São Paulo, 1934); I. Gomes Vaz de Carvalho, *A vida de*

C. G. (Rio de Janeiro, 1935; Italian tr., Milan, 1935); R. Seidl, *C. G.*, *Brasileiro e patriota* (Rio de Janeiro, 1935); L.F. Vieira Souto, *A.C. G.* (Rio de Janeiro, 1936); centenary issue of *Revista Brasileira de Musica* (1936); J. Prito, *C. G.* (São Paulo, 1936); R. Almeida, *C. G.* (Rio de Janeiro, 1937); M. de Andrade, *C. G.* (Rio de Janeiro, 1939); P. Cerquera, *C. G.* (São Paulo, 1944).

Gomes de Araújo, João, Brazilian composer; b. Pindamonhangaba, Aug. 5, 1846; d. São Paulo, Sept. 8, 1942. He studied at São Paulo and Milan; in 1905, became a teacher at the São Paulo Cons., and remained there almost to the end of his long life. **WORKS:** 4 operas: *Edmea; Carminosa* (Milan, 1888); *Maria Petrowna* (1904; São Paulo, 1929); *Helena* (São Paulo, 1910); also 6 syms., 6 masses, and vocal and instrumental works.

Gómez, Calleja. See **Calleja, Gómez Rafael.**

Gomez, Jill, English soprano; b. New Amsterdam, British Guiana, Sept. 21, 1942. She studied at the Royal Academy of Music in London, and also at the Guildhall School of Music; made her debut in 1967 in a Cambridge Univ. opera production; in 1968 she appeared with the Glyndebourne Touring Opera; then sang at Covent Garden (1970). Her other engagements were with the English Opera Group, the Aldeburgh Festival, the Scottish Opera, and the Welsh National Opera.

Gomezanda, Antonio, Mexican pianist and composer; b. Lagos, Jalisco, Sept. 3, 1894; d. Mexico City, March 26, 1961. He studied composition in Berlin. Returning to Mexico, he taught piano at the National Cons. (1921–29) and at the Univ. of Mexico (1929–32). Among his works is an "Aztec ballet," *Xiuhtzitzquilo,* which was produced in Berlin on Feb. 19, 1928.

Gomez Martínez, Miguel Angel, Spanish conductor; b. Granada, Sept. 17, 1949. He studied piano with his mother; then enrolled at the Granada Cons.; also studied composition, piano, and violin at the Madrid Cons.; later attended the conducting classes of Boult and Leinsdorf at Tanglewood; then studied with Markevitch in Madrid and Swarowsky in Vienna. He was music director of the St. Pölten Stadttheater (1971–72) and principal conductor of the Lucerne Stadttheater (1972–74); in 1973 he conducted at the Deutsche Oper in Berlin; was subsequently its resident conductor (1974–77). In 1976 he was made resident conductor at the Vienna State Opera; also conducted in Berlin, Munich, Hamburg, London (at Covent Garden), Geneva, and Paris; in 1980 he made his U.S. debut, conducting at the Houston Grand Opera. From 1984 to 1987 he was principal conductor of the Orquestra Sinfónica de Radiotelevisión Española in Madrid. In 1990 he became Generalmusikdirektor in Mannheim.

Gomólka, Michal, Polish musician, son of **Mikolaj Gomólka;** b. Sandomierz, 1564; d. Jazlowiec, March 9, 1609. He was active as a conductor at various palaces of Polish noblemen; little is known of his life, except that he enjoyed the favor of Polish aristocratic society.

Gomólka, Mikolaj, Polish composer, father of **Michal Gomolka;** b. probably in Sandomierz, c.1535; d. c.1591. He was a chorister at Krakow (1545); then played trumpet and flute in the Court Orch. In 1566 he returned to his native town, where he married and served as a judge. His chief work was *Melodiae na psalterz polski* (Krakow, 1580), containing 150 melodies to words from the Psalms, tr. by the poet Jan Kochanowski; a new ed. was publ. by J.W. Reiss in 1923; several pieces are included in the anthology by Jachimecki and Lissa, *Music of the Polish Renaissance* (Warsaw, 1954). **BIBL.:** J. Reiss, *Melodye psalmowe M. Gomolki* (Krakow, 1912); M. Perz, *M. G., monografia* (Krakow, 1969).

Gondimel, Claude. See **Goudimel, Claude.**

Gönnenwein, Wolfgang, German conductor; b. Schwäbisch-Hall, Jan. 29, 1933. He studied music in Stuttgart; in 1959 became conductor of the South German Madrigal Choir there. In 1973 he became director of the Hochschule für Musik und Darstellende Kunst in Stuttgart; in 1985, Intendant of the Württemberg State Theater in Stuttgart. He is best known as a conductor of the choral works of Bach, Haydn, and Mozart.

González-Avila, Jorge, Mexican composer; b. Mérida, Yucatán, Dec. 10, 1925. He studied composition with Rodolfo Halffter, harmony with Blas Galindo, piano with Francisco Agea Hermosa, and theory with Hernández Moncada at the National Cons. (1949–53); had a course in musical orientation with Jesús Bal y Gay in 1952, and a year later a similar course with Chávez at the National College. He devoted himself to teaching; in 1972 was appointed director of the Audiotranscription Division of the Centro Nacional de Investigación, Documentación y Información Musical (CENIDIM) of the National Inst. of Fine Arts in Mexico City. He wrote an impressive quantity of piano pieces, and other instrumental music. **WORKS:** 3 *Inventions* for Solo Violin (1955); *Impromptus* for String Quartet (1960); *Invention* for Soprano, Piano, and Orch. (1964); *Invention interpolar* for Piano and Orch. (1974); 2 sonata trios for Flute, Cello, and Piano (1965, 1977); Solo Violin Sonata (1966); Suite for Solo Guitar (1968); 2 *Interludes* for Violin and Piano (1968); *Recitativo* for Violin and Piano (1969); *Inventions quasi Fantasia* for Viola and Piano (1970); *Invention concertante No. 1* for Piano and Orch. (1973); *Impromptu* for Solo Viola (1974); 2 *Preludes* for Horn and Piano (1974); *Invention* for Tuba and Piano (1974); *Fantasia* for Organ (1974); *Invention* for English Horn, Piano, and Orch. (1975); *Prelude and Invention* for String Orch. (1976); Violin Sonata (1977); Duo for Viola and Piano (1977); Piano: 17 sonatas; 2 sonatinas (1975, 1976); 20 suites (1953–75); 7 partitas (1953–73); 14 fantasias (1956–75); 8 studies (1959–76); 12 impromptus (1960–75); 16 preludes in 3 sets (1969–73); 2 *Symphonic Studies* (1970); 2 ballets (1973, 1975); 8 *Preludes and Inventions* (1974); 5 *Bagatelles* (1975); 24 *Inventions* (1959); 5 *Variation Studies* (1960); 77 *Miniature Studies* (1973); *Prelude and Invention* for 2 Pianos (1975); 2-piano Sonata (1977).

Goodall, Sir Reginald, greatly esteemed English conductor; b. Lincoln, July 13, 1901.; d. near Canterbury, May 5, 1990. He studied at the Royal College of Music in London; from 1936 to 1939 was assistant conductor at Covent Garden; then was engaged as an assistant to Furtwängler at the Berlin Phil.; also led many operatic performances, including the premiere of Britten's *Peter Grimes* in 1945. He was regarded as a foremost interpreter of Wagner's music dramas; in 1973 he conducted the entire cycle of the *Ring of the Nibelung* at Sadler's Wells Opera in London. In 1975 he was made a Commander of the Order of the British Empire; was knighted in 1985.

Goode, Richard (Stephen), American pianist; b. N.Y., June 1, 1943. He became a pupil of Elvira Szigeti (1949–52) and Claude Frank (1952–54); subsequently was an extension student at the Mannes College of Music in N.Y. (1954–56), where he trained with Nadia Reisenberg (piano), Carl Schachter (theory), and Carl Bamberger (conducting). He studied with Rudolf Serkin in Marlboro, Vt., and then privately (1960) and at the Curtis Inst. of Music in Philadelphia (1961–64), where he also studied with Mieczyslaw Horszowski. After attending the City College of the City Univ. of N.Y. (1964–67), he completed his training at the Mannes College of Music (1967–69; B.S., 1969). On Feb. 12, 1962, he made his formal debut in N.Y.; his European debut followed, at the Festival of Two Worlds in Spoleto, Italy, in 1964. In 1967 he became a member of the Boston Sym. Chamber Players; from 1969 to 1979 he was a member of the Chamber Music Soc. of Lincoln Center in N.Y. His career as a solo artist was enhanced with his capture of the 1st prize at the Clara Haskil competition in 1973; in 1980 he was awarded the Avery Fisher Prize. He made various appearances as a soloist with orchs. and as a recitalist; also appeared with the Chamber Music Soc. of Lincoln Center again from 1983 to 1989. A non-specialist, he won praise as a virtuoso soloist, compelling recitalist, committed chamber music performer, and sensitive accompanist. His repertoire ranges from the standard literature to contemporary scores.

BIBL.: K. Campbell, "R. G.," *Ovation* (Jan. 1987); *Current Biography* (Nov. 1988).

Goodman (real name, **Guttmann**), **Alfred,** German-American composer; b. Berlin, March 1, 1920. He studied at the Berlin Cons.; in 1939 went to England, and in 1940 settled in America; was in the U.S. Army during World War II. In 1946 he was an arranger with several dance bands; at the same time he studied with Henry Cowell and Otto Luening at Columbia Univ., receiving his B.S. in 1952 and his M.A. in 1953. In 1960 he returned to Germany; was active as a composer and broadcaster with the Bavarian Radio in Munich; from 1971 to 1985 was its music adviser. He received his Ph.D. from the Free Univ. of Berlin in 1973; in 1976 was appointed to the faculty of the Hochschule für Musik in Munich. Among his compositions are the operas *The Audition* (1948–54; Athens, Ohio, July 27, 1954), *Der Läufer* (1969), and *The Lady and the Maid* (1984); 2 syms. (1949, 1962); other orch. works; and numerous chamber works. He publ. a music lexicon, *Musik von A–Z* (Munich, 1971) and *Sachwörterbuch der Musik* (Munich, 1982).

Goodman, Benny (Benjamin David), famous American clarinetist and bandleader; b. Chicago, May 30, 1909; d. N.Y., June 13, 1986. He acquired a taste for syncopated music as a child by listening to phonograph recordings of ragtime; was playing professionally by the age of 12 (1921), and in 1926 was working with Ben Pollack, one of the leading Chicago jazz musicians of the period. In 1929 he went to N.Y. as a clarinetist in various bands. In 1934 he formed his own band, which became known nationwide from its weekly appearances on the "Let's Dance" radio program. Both as the leader of a large dance band and for his virtuoso performances in various jazz combos, Goodman was the best-known and most successful musician of the swing era; was called the King of Swing. He also played clarinet parts in classical works in concert and for records, appearing as soloist in Mozart's Clarinet Concerto with the N.Y. Phil. (Dec. 12, 1940), and recording works by Copland, Bartók, Stravinsky, Morton Gould, and Leonard Bernstein. His autobiography, *The Kingdom of Swing*, was publ. in 1939; a biographical movie, *The Benny Goodman Story*, was made in 1955.

BIBL.: D. Connor, *The Record of a Legend—B. G.* (N.Y., 1984); idem, *B. G.: Listen to His Legacy* (Metuchen, N.J., 1988); J. Collier, *B. G.* (N.Y., 1989).

Goodrich, (John) Wallace, American organist, conductor, and writer on music; b. Newton, Mass., May 27, 1871; d. Boston, June 6, 1952. He studied at the New England Cons. in Boston (organ with Dunham, composition with Chadwick); then in Munich with Rheinberger (1894–95) and with Widor in Paris. In 1897 he returned to Boston and became an instructor at the New England Cons. of Music; was appointed dean in 1907, and in 1931 director, a post he held until 1942. He was organist of the Boston Sym. Orch. from 1897 to 1909. He founded the Choral Art Soc. in 1902, and was its conductor until 1907; was also, at various periods, conductor of the Cecilia Soc., the Boston Opera Co., and the Worcester County Choral Assoc. He composed an *Ave Maria* for Chorus and Orch. (Munich, 1895) and other choral music; wrote *The Organ in France* (Boston, 1917).

Goodson, Katharine, English pianist; b. Watford, Hertfordshire, June 18, 1872; d. London, April 14, 1958. From 1886 to 1892 she was a pupil of O. Beringer at the Royal Academy of Music in London, and from 1892 to 1896 of Leschetizky in Vienna; made her debut in London at a Saturday Popular Concert, Jan. 16, 1897, with signal success; then made tours of England, France, Austria, and Germany, which established her reputation; her American debut, with the Boston Sym., took place on Jan. 18, 1907; she subsequently made many tours of the U.S., the Netherlands, Belgium, and Italy. In 1903 she married the English composer **Arthur Hinton.**

Goossens, prominent family of English musicians of Belgian descent:

(1) Eugène Goossens, conductor; b. Bruges, Feb. 25, 1845; d. Liverpool, Dec. 30, 1906. He studied violin at the Bruges Cons. and violin and composition at the Brussels Cons.; in 1873 went to London, where he appeared as an operetta conductor; was 2nd conductor (1883–89) and principal conductor (1889–93) of the Carl Rosa Opera Co., then settled in Liverpool, where he was founder-conductor of the Goossens Male Voice Choir (from 1894).

(2) Eugène Goossens, violinist and conductor, son of the preceding; b. Bordeaux, Jan. 28, 1867; d. London, July 31, 1958. He studied in Bruges and at the Brussels Cons. (1883–86); then went to England, where he worked as a violinist, répétiteur, and assistant conductor under his father with the Carl Rosa Opera Co.; also continued his studies at London's Royal Academy of Music (1891–92); after conducting various traveling opera companies, he served as principal conductor of the Carl Rosa Opera Co. (1899–1915); later was a conductor with the British National Opera Co. He had the following 4 children, who became musicians:

(3) Sir (Aynsley) Eugene Goossens, distinguished conductor and composer; b. London, May 26, 1893; d. there, June 13, 1962. He first studied at the Bruges Cons. (1903–4), then at the Liverpool College of Music. After winning a scholarship to the Royal College of Music in London in 1907, he studied there with Rivarde (violin), Dykes (piano), and C. Wood and Stanford (composition). He was a violinist in the Queen's Hall Orch. (1912–15), then was assistant conductor to Beecham (1915–20). In 1921 he founded his own London orch.; conducted opera and ballet at Covent Garden (1921–23). After serving as conductor of the Rochester (N.Y.) Phil. (1923–31), he greatly distinguished himself as conductor of the Cincinnati Sym. Orch. from 1931 to 1947. He then was conductor of the Sydney (Australia) Sym. Orch. and director of the New South Wales Conservatorium (1947–56). In 1955 he was knighted. He was a discriminating interpreter of the late 19th- and early 20th-century repertoire of the Romantic and Impressionist schools. As a composer, he wrote prolifically in all genres, including opera, ballet, symphonic, and chamber music; his style became a blend of impressionistic harmonies and neo-Classical polyphony; while retaining a clear tonal outline, he often resorted to expressive chromatic melos bordering on atonality. He publ. *Overture and Beginners: A Musical Autobiography* (London, 1951).

WORKS: *Variations on a Chinese Theme* for Orch. (1911); *Miniature Fantasy* for String Orch. (1911); Suite for Flute, Violin, and Harp (1914); *5 Impressions of a Holiday* for Flute, Cello, and Piano (1914); symphonic poem, *Perseus* (1914); symphonic prelude, *Ossian* (1915); *Phantasy Quartet* for Strings (1915); String Quartet No. 1 (1916); 2 sketches for String Quartet: *By the Tarn* and *Jack o' Lantern* (1916); *Kaleidoscope,* suite of piano pieces in a humorous vein (1917–18); Violin Sonata No. 1 (1918); Prelude to Verhaeren's *Philip II* (1918); *The Eternal Rhythm* for Orch. (London, Oct. 19, 1920); *4 Conceits* for Piano (1918); Piano Quintet (1919); *Lyric Poem* for Violin and Piano (1921; also arranged for Violin and Orch.); ballet, *L'École en crinoline* (1921); *Silence* for Chorus and Piano (1922); incidental music to W. Somerset Maugham's *East of Suez* (1922); *Sinfonietta* (London, Feb. 19, 1923); String Sextet (1923); *Pastoral and Harlequinade* for Flute, Oboe, and Piano (1924); Fantasy for Wind Instruments (1924); opera, *Judith* (1925; London, June 25, 1929); *Rhythmic Dance* for Orch. (Rochester, N.Y., March 12, 1927); Concertino for Double String Orch. (1928); Oboe Concerto (London, Oct. 2, 1930; L. Goossens, soloist); Violin Sonata No. 2 (1930); opera, *Don Juan de Mañana* (1934; London, June 24, 1937); Sym. No. 1 (Cincinnati, April 12, 1940); 2nd String Quartet (1942); *Phantasy-Concerto* for Piano and Orch. (Cincinnati, Feb. 25, 1944; José Iturbi, soloist; composer conducting); Sym. No. 2 (BBC, Nov. 10, 1946); oratorio, *Apocalypse* (1951; Sydney, Nov. 22, 1954, composer conducting).

(4) Marie (Henriette) Goossens, harpist; b. London, Aug. 11, 1894. She studied at the Royal College of Music in London; made her debut in Liverpool in 1910, then was principal harpist at Covent Garden, the Diaghilev Ballet, the Queen's Hall Orch. (1920–30), the London Phil. (1932–39), the London Sym. Orch. (1940–59), and the London Mozart Players (from 1972). She was also prof. of harp at the Royal College of Music (1954–67); was made an Officer of the Order of the British Empire (1984).

(5) Leon Goossens, eminent oboist; b. Liverpool, June 12, 1897; d. Tunbridge Wells, Feb. 13, 1988. He studied at the Royal College of Music in London (1911–14); played in the Queen's Hall Orch. (1914–24), and later in the orchs. of Covent Garden and the Royal Phil. Soc.; subsequently was principal oboe of the London Phil. (1932–39); was also prof. of oboe at the Royal Academy of Music (1924–35) and the Royal College of Music (1924–39). In succeeding years he appeared as a soloist with major orchs. and as a chamber music artist; in 1962 he suffered injuries to his lips and teeth as a result of an automobile accident, but after extensive therapy he was able to resume his virtuoso career. He commissioned works from several English composers, among them Elgar and Vaughan Williams. In 1950 he was made a Commander of the Order of the British Empire.

(6) Sidonie Goossens, harpist; b. Liscard, Cheshire, Oct. 19, 1899. She studied at the Royal College of Music in London; made her orch. debut in 1921; was principal harpist of the BBC Sym. Orch. in London (1930–80); served as prof. of harp at the Guildhall School of Music there (from 1960); was made a Member of the Order of the British Empire in 1974 and an Officer of the Order of the British Empire in 1981.

Goovaerts, Alphonse (Jean Marie André), Belgian musicologist; b. Antwerp, May 25, 1847; d. Brussels, Dec. 25, 1922. He was a member of a literary family; as a youth he became greatly interested in Flemish literature and in church music. He arranged and publ. a collection of Flemish songs (1868–74); composed several pieces of church music, and performed them with a chorus he established in Antwerp; also made transcriptions for chorus of works by Palestrina and Flemish contrapuntists. He publ. several papers propounding a reform in church music, which aroused opposition from conservative circles (*La Musique de l'église,* 1876; in Flemish as *De kerkmuziek*); also publ. a valuable book, *Histoire et bibliographie de la typographie musicale dans le Pays-Bas* (1880; awarded the gold medal of the Belgian Academy); a monograph on the Belgian music printer Pierre Phalèse; and other studies relating to Flemish music.

Gorchakov (real name, **Zweifel**), **Sergei,** Russian composer and arranger; b. Moscow, Feb. 10, 1905; d. there, July 4, 1976. He studied conducting with Saradzhev at the Moscow Cons., graduating in 1929. From 1939 to 1952 he conducted the orch. of the All-Union Soviet Radio; from 1960 he taught orchestration at the Inst. of Military Band Conducting. He became particularly interested in the problem of orch. arrangements; in 1959 submitted a dissertation, *Specific Problems of Transcribing Piano Music for Wind Orchestra,* for which he received the degree of candidate of arts and sciences. He also publ. *Practical Manual of Orchestration for Wind Orchestra* (Moscow, 1962). He made numerous orch. arrangements of piano music; of these, particularly notable was his orchestration of Mussorgsky's *Pictures at an Exhibition,* which enjoyed a number of performances in Russia and abroad.

Gorczycki, Grzegorz Gerwazy, important Polish composer; b. Bytom, Silesia, c.1647; d. Krakow, April 30, 1734. He studied at the Univ. of Prague; was rector of the Congregatio Missionis in Chelmno (1674–76), and studied theology at the Univ. of Vienna (1689); he received a doctorate in philosophy from 1 of the 2 aforementioned Univs. He may have been in the service of King Jan III Sobieski (1674–96); was chapel master at Wawel Cathedral in Krakow (1698–1734), where he caught a fatal cold while conducting at the coronation of August III and Maria Josepha (Jan. 17, 1734). He was a significant figure in Polish religious music. His works to Latin texts include motets, hymns, Psalms, and masses, some with instrumental accompaniment.

BIBL.: H. Feicht, "Do biografi G.G.G.," *Polski Rocznik Muzykologicany,* II (1936); M. Kaczorowska-Gúnkiewicz, "Do biografii G.G.G.," *Muzyka,* XVIII/4 (1973); S. Skrzypczak, "Notes towards a biography of the Polish composer G.G.G.," *Musicology Australia,* VIII (1985).

Gordeli, Otar, Russian composer; b. Tiflis, Nov. 18, 1928. He studied composition with Andrei Balanchivadze; later took courses at the Moscow Cons., graduating in 1955. In 1959 he was appointed instructor at the Tbilisi Cons. In his music he applies resources of native folk songs; his polyphonic structure is considerably advanced.

WORKS: Piano Concerto (1952); cantata, *The Seasons,* for Narrator, Boys' Chorus, and Chamber Orch. (1955); Concertino for Flute and Orch. (1958); *Festive Overture* (1959); *Georgian Dance* for Orch. (1961); Sym. (1964); film music; jazz pieces.

Gordigiani, Luigi, Italian composer; b. Florence, June 21, 1806; d. Modena, May 1, 1860. He is chiefly known for his more than 300 songs for voice and piano; these *canzonette* and *canti populari* were based on Italian folk tunes; Gordigiani wrote the words for many himself. He also publ. a collection of songs based on Tuscan folk poems. Other works include 10 operas, 3 cantatas, a ballet, and an oratorio.

Gordon, Dexter (Keith), prominent black American jazz tenor saxophonist; b. Los Angeles, Feb. 27, 1923; d. Philadelphia, April 25, 1990. He studied clarinet; took up the alto saxophone at the age of 15; then turned to the tenor saxophone and soon began to play in a local band. He worked with Lionel Hampton (1940–43) and Louis Armstrong (1944); then went to N.Y., where he played in Billy Eckstine's band (1944–46); after returning to Los Angeles, he appeared with Wardell Gray (1947–52). In 1962 he moved to Copenhagen, and continued his career in Europe; then returned to the U.S.; was elected a member of the Jazz Hall of Fame in 1980. He was generally acknowledged as the most influential tenor saxophonist of the bop period.

Gordon, Jacques, Russian-American violinist and teacher; b. Odessa, March 7, 1899; d. Hartford, Conn., Sept. 15, 1948. He made his debut in Odessa at age 7; after graduating from the Odessa Cons. (1913), he emigrated to the U.S., where he studied with Kneisel (violin) and Goetschius (theory) at N.Y.'s Inst. of Musical Art. He played in the Russian Sym. Orch. in N.Y. and then was concertmaster of the Chicago Sym. Orch. (1921–31); also played in the Berkshire String Quartet (1917–20). He founded the Gordon String Quartet (1930), and led it until 1947; also was conductor of the Hartford (Conn.) Sym. Orch. (1936–39). He taught at the American Cons. of Music in Chicago (from 1921) and at the Eastman School of Music in Rochester, N.Y. (from 1942).

Gordon, James Carel Gerhard, flute maker; b. Cape Town, May 22, 1791; d. Lausanne, c.1845. He was born of a Dutch captain and a Swiss mother. He joined the Swiss Guards of Charles X in Paris in 1814; concurrently, studied flute with Tulou; worked on improvements of its mechanism more or less at the same time as Böhm, so that the priority of the invention became a matter of insoluble controversy. He escaped with his life during the attack on the Swiss Guards in the Revolution of 1830; was pensioned and retired to Switzerland when his mind became deranged.

BIBL.: C. Welch, *History of the Boehm Flute* (London, 1896); P. Kirby, "Captain G., The Flute Maker," *Music & Letters* (July 1957).

Gordy, Berry Jr., significant black American record producer, creator of the Motown sound (so named after the Motor Town, that is, Detroit; b. Detroit, Nov. 28, 1929. He trained as a featherweight boxer; then was drafted into the U.S. Army; after discharge, he worked on the assembly line for Ford, and began writing songs. However, his significance in popular American music was connected not with songwriting but with his recording enterprise. He attracted a number of talented groups, composers, and singers to record for Motown, among them Smokey Robinson and The Miracles, Mary Wells, Martha and The Vandellas, The Supremes, Jr. Walker and The All Stars, Gladys Knight and The Pips, Diana Ross, Marvin Gaye, The O Jays, Stevie Wonder, and The Jackson Five. He contributed to the final desegregation of so-called "race music" and its integration into the mainstream of American popular music, which included rhythm-and-blues, soul-and-gospel, and semi-classical pop.

Górecki, Henryk (Mikolaj), significant Polish composer; b. Czernica, Dec. 6, 1933. He studied composition with Boleslaw Szabelski at the Katowice Cons. (1955–60); in 1968 was appointed to its faculty. In his music he makes use of the entire arsenal of modern techniques while preserving traditional formal design.

WORKS: *Toccata* for 2 Pianos (1955); Piano Sonata (1956); *Pieśń o radości i rytmie* (Song of Joy and Rhythm) for Orch. (1956); Sonata for 2 Violins (1957); Concerto for 5 Instruments and String Quartet (1957); *Epitaph* for Chorus and Instrumental Ensemble (1958); *5 Pieces* for 2 Pianos (1959); Sym. No. 1 for String Orch. and Percussion (1959); *3 Diagrams* for Solo Flute (1959); *Monologhi* for Soprano and 3 Instrumental Groups (1960); *Zderzenia* (Collisions) for Orch. (1960); *Genesis,* cycle of 3 works: *Elementi* for String Trio (1962), *Canti strumentali* for 15 Performers (1962), and *Monodram* for Soprano, Metal Percussion, and 6 Double Basses (1963); *Chôros I* for 56 Strings (1964); *Refren* (Refrain) for Orch. (1965); *La Musiquette I* for 2 Trumpets and Guitar (1967), *II* for Brass and Percussion (1967), *III* for Violas (1969), and *IV* for Clarinet, Trombone, Cello, and Piano (1970); *Muzyka staropolska* (Old Polish Music), 3 pieces for Orch. (Warsaw, Sept. 24, 1969); Sym. No. 2, *Copernican Symphony,* for Soprano, Baritone, Chorus, and Orch. (Warsaw, June 22, 1973); *Amen* for Chorus a cappella (1975); Sym. No. 3 (1976); *Beatus vir* for Baritone, Chorus, and Orch. (1979); Harpsichord Concerto (1980); *Already It Is Dusk* for String Quartet (1988).

Gorin, Igor, Russian-born American baritone; b. Grodek, Ukraine, Oct. 26, 1908; d. Tucson, Ariz., March 24, 1982. His family moved to Vienna after the Russian Revolution; there he studied medicine and music; entered the Cons., graduating in 1930; made his professional operatic debut at the Volksoper in 1930. In 1933 he went to the U.S.; became a naturalized citizen in 1939. He launched a successful career as a radio singer, without forsaking his operatic ambitions. He made his debut at the Metropolitan Opera in N.Y. as Germont *père* in *La Traviata* (Feb. 10, 1964). In his last years he taught voice at the Univ. of Arizona in Tucson.

Gorini, Gino (actually, **Luigino**), Italian composer and pianist; b. Venice, June 22, 1914; d. there, Jan. 27, 1989. He studied piano with Tagliapietra (diploma, 1931) and composition with Agostini (diploma, 1933) at the Venice Cons.; later studied composition with Malipiero; in 1940 was appointed prof. of piano at the Venice Cons.; made many tours in Italy and abroad, including 2-piano team tours in Italy with Sergio Lorenzi.

WORKS: *3 omaggi* for Orch. (1933); Suite for Piano and Orch. (1934); Violin Concerto (1934); Sym. (1935); *Introduction and Arioso* for Orch. (1937); *Concertino* for 7 Instruments (1933); *Contrasti* for 5 Instruments (1933); Divertimento for Chamber Orch. (1935); Piano Sonata (1936); String Quartet (1936); Cello Sonata (1939); Quintet for Piano and Strings (1939); Piano Concerto (1948; Rome, March 16, 1952); *5 studi* for 2 Pianos, Strings, and Timpani (1960); *Serenata* for String Orch., Harpsichord or Piano, and Timpani (1966); Concerto for Viola, Piano, and Orch. (1968).

Goritz, Otto, German baritone; b. Berlin, June 8, 1873; d. Hamburg, April 11, 1929. He received his musical education from his mother; made his debut on Oct. 1, 1895, as Matteo (*Fra Diavolo*) at Neustrelitz; his success led to an immediate engagement for 3 years; from 1898 to 1900 he was in Breslau; from 1900 to 1903, in Hamburg. On Dec. 24, 1903, he made his American debut at the Metropolitan Opera in N.Y. as Klingsor in the 1st production of *Parsifal* outside Bayreuth; remained

there until 1917. In 1924 he returned to Germany, where he sang in Berlin and Hamburg.

Gorme, Eydie, American singer of popular music; b. N.Y., Aug. 16, 1932. She began her professional career as a vocalist with the bands of Tommy Tucker and Tex Beneke; also sang with the orch. of Ray Eberle; then began a solo career as a singer in nightclubs and on radio and television. In 1957 she married the singer **Steve Lawrence.**

Gorney, Jay, Polish-American composer; b. Bialystok, Dec. 12, 1896; d. N.Y., June 14, 1990. He emigrated to the U.S. as a child; studied music at the Univ. of Michigan. Beginning in 1924 he wrote a number of scores and separate songs for Broadway. In 1933 he went to Hollywood. He composed the celebrated song *Brother, Can You Spare a Dime?,* which became a musical symbol of the Depression era.

Gorno, Albino, Italian-American pianist and composer; b. Casalmorano (Cremona), March 10, 1859; d. Cincinnati, Oct. 29, 1945. He studied at the Milan Cons., where he took 3 gold medals, and where his opera, *Cuore e Patria,* was produced. He was accompanist to Adelina Patti on her American tour (1881–82); stayed in the U.S., and became head of the piano dept. and dean of the faculty at the Cincinnati College of Music. He wrote a cantata, many pieces for piano, and songs.

Gorodnitzki, Sascha, Russian-born American pianist; b. Kiev, May 24, 1904; d. N.Y., April 4, 1986. He was taken to the U.S. as an infant; studied at the Inst. of Musical Art and the Juilliard Graduate School in N.Y.; appeared as a child prodigy at 9; toured the U.S. and Canada in recitals; in 1930, won the Schubert Memorial Prize; was appointed prof. of piano at the Juilliard Graduate School in 1932.

Gorr, Rita (real name, **Marguerite Geirnaert**), noted Belgian mezzo-soprano; b. Zelzaete, Feb. 18, 1926. She was educated in Ghent and Brussels. After local appearances in Belgium, she sang in London and Edinburgh. On Oct. 17, 1962, she made her debut at the Metropolitan Opera in N.Y. as Amneris in *Aida.* She excelled in the Wagnerian repertoire, and made several appearances at the Bayreuth Festivals.

Goss, Sir John, English organist and composer; b. Fareham, Hampshire, Dec. 27, 1800; d. London, May 10, 1880. A son of Joseph Goss, the Fareham organist, he became a child chorister of the Chapel Royal; then studied under Attwood. He was successively organist of Stockwell Chapel (1821), St. Luke's, Chelsea (1824), and St. Paul's Cathedral (1838–72). In 1856 he was appointed a composer to the Chapel Royal; he was knighted in 1872, and received the degree of Mus.Doc. from Cambridge Univ. in 1876. His music includes church services, anthems, chants, Psalms, etc.; some orch. pieces; songs and glees. He ed. a collection of hymns, *Parochial Psalmody* (1826–27); *Chants, Ancient and Modern* (1841); *Church Psalter and Hymnbook* (1855; with W. Mercer). He publ. *The Organist's Companion,* 4 vols. of voluntaries and interludes and *An Introduction to Harmony and Thorough-bass* (1833; many eds.).

BIBL.: D. Gedge, "J. G., 1800–1880," *Musical Times* (May and July 1980).

Gossec, François-Joseph, significant South Netherlands composer; b. Vergnies, Jan. 17, 1734; d. Paris, Feb. 16, 1829. He showed musical inclinations at an early age; as a child, studied at the collegiate church in Walcourt and sang in the chapel of St. Aldegonde in Maubeuge; then joined the chapel of St. Pierre there, where he studied violin, harpsichord, harmony, and composition with Jean Vanderbelen; in 1742 was engaged as a chorister at the Cathedral of Notre Dame in Antwerp; received some instruction with André-Joseph Blavier in violin and organ there. In 1751 he went to Paris, and in 1754 joined a private musical ensemble of the rich amateur La Poupliniére. There he wrote chamber music and little syms., in which he seems to have anticipated Haydn; several works for string quartet followed in 1759. After the death of La Poupliniére in 1762, Gossec became director of the private theater of Louis-Joseph de Bourbon, Prince of Condé, in Chantilly. In 1760 he wrote a Requiem; then turned his attention to stage music; produced a 3-act opéra comique, *Le Faux Lord* (Paris, June 27, 1765); obtained a decisive success with another short opéra comique, *Les Pêcheurs* (Paris, April 23, 1766). In 1769 he organized a performing society, Concerts des Amateurs; became a director of the Concert Spirituel (1773–77); was also an associate director of the Paris Opéra (1780–85) and director of the École Royale de Chant (1784–89); when this school became the Cons. in 1795, Gossec became one of the inspectors, and also taught composition there; he publ. a manual, *Exposition des principes de la musique*, for use at the Cons. In 1795 he became a member of the newly founded Académie des Beaux-Arts of the Institut de France. Gossec welcomed the French Revolution with great enthusiasm, and wrote many festive works to celebrate Revolutionary events, among them *L'Offrande à la Liberté* (1792), *Le Triomphe de la République* (1793), and numerous marches and hymns. During his long life he saw many changes of regime, but retained his position in the musical world and in society throughout the political upheavals. He retired to Passy, then a suburb of Paris, at the age of 80. Gossec's historic role consists in his creation of a French type of symphonic composition, in which he expanded the resources of instrumentation so as to provide for dynamic contrasts; he experimented with new sonorities in instrumental and choral writing; his string quartets attained a coherence of style and symmetry of form that laid the foundation of French chamber music. In his choral works, Gossec was a bold innovator, presaging in some respects the usages of Berlioz; his *Te Deum* (1790), written for a Revolutionary festival, is scored for 1,200 singers and 300 wind instruments; in his oratorio *La Nativité* (1774), he introduced an invisible chorus of angels placed behind the stage; in other works, he separated choral groups in order to produce special antiphonal effects.

WORKS: STAGE: *Le Périgourdin*, intermezzo (private theater of the Prince of Conti, Paris, June 7, 1761); *Le Tonnelier*, opéra comique (Comédie-Italienne, Paris, March 16, 1765); *Le Faux Lord*, opéra comique (Comédie-Italienne, June 27, 1765); *Les Pêcheurs*, opéra comique (Comédie-Italienne, April 23, 1766); *Toinon et Toinette*, opéra comique (Comédie-Italienne, June 20, 1767); *Le Double Déguisement*, opéra comique (Comédie-Italienne, Sept. 28, 1767); *Les Agréments d'Hylas et Sylvie*, pastorale (Comédie-Française, Dec. 10, 1768); *Sabinus*, tragédie lyrique (Versailles, Dec. 4, 1773); *Berthe*, opera (Théâtre Royal de la Monnaie, Brussels, Jan. 18, 1775; not extant); *Alexis et Daphné*, pastorale (Opéra, Paris, Sept. 26, 1775); *Philémon et Baucis*, pastorale (Opéra, Sept. 26, 1775); *Annette et Lubin*, ballet (Opéra, 1778); *La Fête de village*, intermezzo (Opéra, May 26, 1778); *Mirza*, ballet (Opéra, Nov. 18, 1779; rev. 1788); *La Fête de Mirza*, ballet-pantomime (Opéra, Feb. 17, 1781); *Thésée*, tragédie lyrique (Opéra, March 1, 1782); *Électre*, incidental music (1782); *Nitocris*, opera (1783); *Le Premier Navigateur, ou Le Pouvoir de l'amour*, ballet (Opéra, July 26, 1785); *Athalie*, incidental music (Fontainebleau, Nov. 3?, 1785); *Rosine, ou L'Épouse abandonnée*, opera (Opéra, July 14, 1786); *Le Pied de bœuf*, divertissement (Opéra, June 17, 1787); *Les Sabots et le cerisier*, opera (Théâtre des Jeunes Élèves, Paris, 1803). **ORCH.:** About 50 syms., other orch. pieces, and Revolutionary works for Wind Band. **CHORAL:** *Missa pro defunctis* (1760; publ. as *Messe des morts* in 1780); oratorios: *La Nativité* (1774; ed. by D. Townsend, N.Y., 1966) and *L'Arche d'alliance* (1781; not extant); motets and other sacred works. **REVOLUTIONARY WORKS FOR VOICES:** About 40 such pieces, including a *Te Deum* (1790); *Le Chant du 14 juillet* (1791); *Chœur à la liberté* (1792); *L'Offrande à la Liberté* (1792); *Hymne à la liberté* (1792); *Le Triomphe de la république, ou Le Camp de Grandpré* (1793); *Hymne à la liberté* (*Hymne à la nature*) (1793); *Hymne à l'humanité* (1795); *La Nouvelle au camp de l'assassinat . . . ou Le Cri de vengeance* (1799). **CHAMBER:** 6 trio sonatas (c.1753); 6 duos for Flutes or Violins (c.1754); 6 duets for 2 Violins (1765); 6 trios for 2 Violins and Bass with Horns ad libitum (1766); 12 string quartets (2 books, 1769 and 1772).

BIBL.: P. Hédouin, *G.: Sa vie et ses ouvrages* (Valenciennes, 1852); É. Gregoir, *Notice biographique sur F.-J. Gossé dit G., compositeur de musique* (Mons, 1878); F. Hellouin, *G. et la musique française à la fin du XVIIIᵉ siècle* (Paris, 1903); A. Gastoué, "F.-J. G., professeur et compositeur de musique (1734–1829)," *Les Contemporains*, I–XVI (1911); L. Dufrane, *G.: Sa vie, ses œuvres* (Paris, 1927); F. Tonnard, "F.J. G.," *La Vie wallonne*, XIV (1934); A. Gastoué, "G. et Gluck à l'Opéra de Paris," *Revue de Musicologie*, XVI (1935); F. Tonnard, *F.-J. G., musicien hennuyer de la Révolution française* (Brussels, 1938); J.-G. Prod'homme, "F.-J. G.," *Euterpe* (Paris, 1940); B. Brook, *La Symphonie française* (Paris, 1962); R. Macdonald, *F.-J. G. and French Instrumental Music in the Second Half of the Eighteenth Century* (diss., Univ. of Michigan, 1968); W. Thibaut, *F.-J. G., Chantre de la Révolution française* (Gilly, 1970).

Gossett, Philip, esteemed American musicologist; b. N.Y., Sept. 27, 1941. He was educated at Amherst College (B.A., 1963), Columbia Univ. (1961–62), and Princeton Univ. (M.F.A., 1965; Ph.D., 1970, with the diss. *The Operas of Rossini: Problems of Textual Criticism in Nineteenth-Century Opera*); held a Fulbright fellowship (1965–66) and a Guggenheim fellowship (1971–72). He joined the faculty at the Univ. of Chicago in 1968. He ed. and tr. Rameau's *Traité de l'harmonie* as *Treatise on Harmony by Jean-Philippe Rameau* (N.Y., 1971); with C. Rosen, he ed. *Early Romantic Opera* (44 vols., N.Y., 1977–83); also ed. *Italian Opera 1810–1840* (58 vols., N.Y., 1984–); also served as general editor of *The Works of Giuseppe Verdi*. He publ. *The Tragic Finale of Tancredi* (Pesaro, 1977), *Le Sinfonie di Rossini* (Pesaro, 1981), and *Anna Bolena and the Artistic Maturity of Gaetano Donizetti* (Oxford, 1985), for which he received the ASCAP–Deems Taylor Award in 1986.

Gostuški, Dragutin, Serbian composer and musicologist; b. Belgrade, Jan. 3, 1923. He studied art history at the Univ. of Belgrade (Ph.D., 1965); also took courses in composition and conducting at the Belgrade Academy of Music; subsequently was active as a music critic. In 1952 he was engaged as a member of the staff of the Musicological Inst. of the Serbian Academy of Arts and Sciences; in 1974 became its director. His works include a symphonic poem, *Belgrade* (Belgrade, June 11, 1951); *Concerto accelerato* for Violin and Orch. (Belgrade, Nov. 14, 1961); a fantastic ballet, *Remis* (1955; 1st stage perf., Zagreb, May 15, 1963); chamber music; piano pieces; songs.

Gotovac, Jakov, Croatian conductor and composer; b. Split, Oct. 11, 1895; d. Zagreb, Oct. 16, 1982. He studied law at Zagreb Univ., and music with Antun Dobronić in Zagreb and with Joseph Marx in Vienna. In 1923 he was appointed conductor of the Croatian National Opera in Zagreb, retaining this post until 1958. He composed mostly for the theater; his instrumental music is imbued with the folkways of Croatia, enhancing the simple native materials by carefully proportioned modernistic mutations while preserving the impulsive asymmetrical patterns of the original songs. His music was often performed in Yugoslavia and at occasional Central European festivals, but rarely beyond.

WORKS: OPERAS: *Dubravka*, pastoral opera (1928); *Morana* (Brno, Nov. 29, 1930); *Ero s onoga svijeta* (A Rogue from the World Beyond; Zagreb, Nov. 2, 1935; in German as *Ero der Schelm*, Karlsruhe, April 3, 1938); *Kamenik* (The Quarry; Zagreb, Dec. 11, 1946); historical music drama, *Mila Gojsalica* (Zagreb, May 18, 1952); *Stanac* (Zagreb, Dec. 6, 1959); *Dalmaro*, opera-legend (Zagreb, Dec. 20, 1964); *Petar Svačiç*, opera-oratorio (1969). **ORCH.:** *Simfonijsko kolo*, a symphonic national dance (Zagreb, Feb. 6, 1927); *Orači* (Ploughmen; 1937); *Pjesme i ples za Balkana* (Balkan Song and Dance) for String Orch. (1939); *Guslar* (Gusla Player; Zagreb, Oct. 7, 1940); *Bunjevačka igra* (1960); *Dalmatinsko pastirče* (Dalmatian Shepherd) for Recorders (1962). **OTHER VOCAL:** *Anakreontske pjesme* (2 Anacreontic Songs) for Baritone and Piano (1918); *Jadovanka za teletom* (Elegy for a Dead Calf) for Chorus (1924); *Koleda*, peasant dance for Male Chorus, Wind Instruments, and Percussion (1925); *Pjesme Cežnuča* (Songs of Desire) for Mezzo-soprano and Chamber Orch. (1939); *Intima*, 5 songs for Baritone and Piano (1945); *Zvonimirova ladja* (Zvonimir's Ship) for Chorus (1952); *Gjerdam* (The Necklace), play with music (1955).

Gottlieb, Jack, American composer; b. New Rochelle, N.Y., Oct. 12, 1930. He studied with Karol Rathaus at Queens College (B.A., 1953) and with Irving Fine at Brandeis Univ. (M.F.A., 1955); at the Berkshire Music Center in Tanglewood with Boris Blacher and Aaron Copland, and at the Univ. of Illinois with Burrill Phillips and Robert Palmer (D.M.A., 1964). From 1958 to 1966 he served as assistant to Bernstein at the N.Y. Phil.; was music director of the Congregation Temple Israel in St. Louis (1970–73), and in 1973 was appointed composer-in-residence at the School of Sacred Music, Hebrew Union College, N.Y. He retired from teaching in 1977; in 1979 he formed his own publishing company.

WORKS: OPERAS: *Tea Party* (1955; Athens, Ohio, Aug. 4, 1957); *Public Dance* (1964; withdrawn); *The Song of Songs, Which Is Solomon's* (1968–76); *Death of a Ghost* (N.Y., Dec. 13, 1988). MUSICALS: *Mouse* (1988–90); *Bellwether* (1989–90). OTHER: Quartet for 3 Clarinets and Bass Clarinet (1952); String Quartet (1954); *Twilight Crane*, fantasy for Woodwind Quintet (1961); *Pieces of 7*, overture (Jacksonville, Fla., Oct. 23, 1962); Piano Sonata (1960); *The Silent Flickers*, 12 diversions for Piano, 4-hands (1968); *4 Affirmations* for Chorus and Brass Sextet (N.Y., April 17, 1976); other chamber and orch. works; much vocal music, both sacred and secular.

Gottschalk, Louis Moreau, celebrated American pianist and composer; b. New Orleans, May 8, 1829; d. Tijuca, near Rio de Janeiro, Dec. 18, 1869. His father, an English businessman, emigrated to New Orleans; his mother was of noble Creole descent, the granddaughter of a governor of a Haitian province. His talent for music was developed early; at the age of 4, he began studying violin with Félix Miolan, concertmaster of the opera orch., and piano with François Letellier, organist at the St. Louis Cathedral; at the age of 7, he substituted for Letellier at the organ during High Mass, and the next year played violin at a benefit for Miolan. In 1841 he was sent to Paris, where he studied piano with Charles Hallé and Camille Stamaty and harmony with Pierre Maleden. He also later studied composition with Berlioz. On April 2, 1845, he gave a concert at the Salle Pleyel, which attracted the attention of Chopin. His piano compositions of the period, including *Bamboula*, *Le Bananier*, and *La Savane*, were influenced by Liszt and Chopin, but also inspired by childhood recollections of Creole and Negro dances and songs. In 1846–47 he appeared in a series of concerts with Berlioz at the Italian Opera, and in 1850 concertized throughout France and Switzerland, playing his own compositions. In 1851 he appeared in Madrid at the invitation of the Queen and was given the Order of Isabella; during his stay there, he developed the "monster concerts," for which he wrote a Sym. for 10 Pianos, *El Sitio de Zaragosa*, later transformed into *Bunker's Hill* by replacing the Spanish tunes with American ones.

Gottschalk returned to give a highly praised concert in N.Y. on Feb. 11, 1853, followed by many concerts throughout the U.S., Cuba, and Canada during the next 3 years. During the winter of 1855–56, he gave 80 concerts in N.Y. alone. His compositions from this period, including *La Scintilla*, *The Dying Poet*, and *The Last Hope*, written to display his talents, used many novel techniques of the "style pianola." After playing Henselt's Piano Concerto with the N.Y. Phil. on Jan. 10, 1857, he went to Cuba with the pubescent singer Adelina Patti. He then lived in the West Indies, writing works influenced by its indigenous music. In Havana, on Feb. 17, 1861, he introduced his most famous orch. work, *La Nuit des tropiques*. He also produced several grand "monster concerts" modeled after those of Jullien.

Though he was born in the antebellum South, Gottschalk's sympathies were with the North during the American Civil War; he had manumitted the slaves he inherited after his father's death in 1853. He resumed his U.S. concert career with a performance in N.Y. on Feb. 11, 1862, and from then

until 1865 toured the North and the West with Max Strakosch, playing (by his estimation) over a thousand concerts. His notebooks from this era, posth. publ. as *Notes of a Pianist* (Philadelphia, 1881; reprinted 1964), perceptively reveal life in Civil War America. After becoming involved in a scandal with a teenage girl in San Francisco, he was forced to flee to South America (Sept. 18, 1865); he appeared in concert throughout South America, and composed new works based on local melodies and rhythms. During a festival of his music in Rio de Janeiro on Nov. 25, 1869, he collapsed on stage after playing the appropriately titled *Morte!!*; he died within a month. His remains were exhumed and reburied with great ceremony in Brooklyn on Oct. 3, 1870.

Gottschalk was a prolific composer of bravura, pianistic works that enjoyed great popularity for some time even after his death; ultimately they slipped into the uniquitous centenary oblivion. As a pianist he was one of the most adulated virtuosos of his era. His concerts, featuring his own compositions, emphasized his prodigious technique but were criticized by some as being superficial. A definitive catalog of his works is difficult to assemble, since many of the works referred to in his copious correspondence have not been found, there are revisions of one and the same work using different titles, and several works were publ. using the same opus number. Two catalogs of his music are R. Offergeld, *The Centennial Catalogue of the Published and Unpublished Compositions of Louis Moreau Gottschalk* (N.Y., 1970), and J. Doyle, *Louis Moreau Gottschalk 1829–1869: A Bibliographical Study and Catalog of Works* (Detroit, 1983). The latter is especially useful, since it lists each publ. work using the linguistic nominal variants. Gottschalk publ. some of his works using the pseudonyms Steven Octaves, Oscar Litti, A.B.C., and Paul Ernest. Among modern editions of his music, the most notable are *The Piano Works of Louis Moreau Gottschalk* (5 vols., N.Y., 1969), ed. by V. Lawrence and R. Jackson, and *The Little Book of Louis Moreau Gottschalk* (N.Y., 1976), ed. by R. Jackson and N. Ratliff.

BIBL.: H. Didimus, *Biography of L.M. G., the American Pianist and Composer* (Philadelphia, 1853); O. Hensel, *Life and Letters of L.M. G.* (Boston, 1870); L. Fors, *G.* (Havana, 1880); "G. edition," *Musician* (Oct. 1908); J. Cooke, *L.M. G.* (Philadelphia, 1928); F. Lange, *Vida y muerte de L.M. G. en Rio de Janeiro (1869)* (Mendoza, Argentina, 1951); J. Doyle, *The Piano Music of L.M. G. (1829–1869)* (diss., N.Y. Univ., 1960); R. Stevenson, "G. in Buenos Aires" and "G. in Western South America," *Inter-American Music Bulletin* (Nov. 1969); J. Gray, *A Study and Edition of Recently Discovered Works of L.M. G.* (diss., Univ. of Rochester, 1971); W. Korf, *The Orchestral Music of L.M. G.* (diss., Univ. of Iowa, 1974); L. Rubin, *G. in Cuba* (diss., Columbia Univ., 1974).

Gottwald, Clytus, German conductor, musicologist, and composer; b. Bad Salzbrunn, Silesia, Nov. 20, 1925. He studied singing, choral conducting, and musicology at the Univs. of Tübingen and Frankfurt, with sociology, theology, and folklore as subsidiary subjects. He received a doctorate from the Univ. of Frankfurt (1961), his dissertation proving through style analysis that Ghiselin and Verbonnet were the same person; he also ed. the complete works of that composer. In 1960 he founded the Stuttgart Schola Cantorum, which under his direction became a fine avant-garde vocal group; in 1967 he became adviser for new music for the South German Radio in Stuttgart. His numerous recordings are exemplary, particularly his performances of difficult works by such composers as Schnebel, Kagel, and Bussotti; his articles include, in addition to various MS studies, sophisticated explorations of the philosophy of contemporary music. He publ. *Codices musici: Die Handschriften der Württembergischen landesbibliothek Stuttgart* (Wiesbaden, 1964–65).

Götze, Johann Nikolaus Konrad, German violinist and composer; b. Weimar, Feb. 11, 1791; d. there, Feb. 5, 1861. He studied with Kreutzer in Paris; returning to Weimar, he became music director to the Grand Duke (1826–48). He played concerts in Germany and Austria; also wrote operas (some of which he produced in Weimar) and chamber music.

Götze, Karl, German conductor and composer; b. Weimar, 1836; d. Magdeburg, Jan. 14, 1887. He was a pupil of Töpfer and Gebhardi, later of Liszt; then was active as a theater conductor.

WORKS: Operas: *Die Korsen* (Weimar, 1866); *Gustav Wasa, Der Held des Nordens* (Weimar, 1868); *Judith* (Magdeburg, 1887); symphonic poem, *Eine Sommernacht*; piano pieces; songs.

Goudimel, Claude (also rendered as **Gaudimel, Gaudiomel, Godimel, Gondimel, Goudmel, Gudmel,** etc.), celebrated French composer and music theorist; b. Besançon, c.1510; d. (killed in the St. Bartholomew massacre) Lyons, Aug. 27, 1572. In 1549 Goudimel studied at the Univ. of Paris; he publ. a book of chansons as a joint publisher with Du Chemin. He lived in Metz between 1557 and 1568; there he became a Huguenot; in 1568 he returned to Besançon, then lived in Lyons, where he perished. Most of his music was publ. by Du Chemin in Paris; other contemporary publishers were Adrien Le Roy and Robert Ballard, who publ. his complete Huguenot psalter in 1564 under the title *Les CL Pseaumes de David, nouvellement mis en musique à quatre parties*; it was publ. in Geneva in 1565 as *Les Pseaumes mis en rime françoise par Clément Marot et Th. de Bèze, mis en musique à 4 parties*; it was reprinted in a facsimile ed. in Kassel, 1935. Goudimel also composed 5 masses, 1 publ. by Du Chemin (1554) and 4 by Le Roy and Ballard (1558), together with other sacred music. Two 4-part motets were included in T. Susato's *Ecclesiasticarum cantionum* (Antwerp, 1553–55). Publication of the Complete Works, under the direction of L. Dittmer and P. Pidoux (Inst. of Medieval Music), began in 1967 and concluded in 1983.

BIBL.: G. Becker, *Goudimel et son œuvre* (1885); M. Brenet, *Claude Goudimel, Essai bio-bibliographique* (Besançon, 1898); H. Kling, "Les Compositeurs de la musique du Psautier Huguenot Genevois," *Rivista Musicale Italiana* (1899); J. Tiersot, *Ronsard et la musique de son temps* (1901); G. Woodward, "The Genevan Psalter of 1562; Set in 4-part Harmony by Claude Goudimel in 1565," *Proceedings of the Musical Association* (London, 1918); E. Müller, "Claude Goudimel zum 350. Todestage," *Neue Musikalische Zeitung* (1922); C. Schneider, *La Restauration du Psautier huguenot d'après les sources de 1562 et de 1565* (Neuchâtel, 1930); G. Thibault, *Bibliographie des éditions d'Adrien Le Roy et Robert Ballard* (Paris, 1955).

Goudoever, Henri Daniel van, Dutch cellist, conductor, and composer; b. Utrecht, Nov. 12, 1898; d. The Hague, March 3, 1977. He studied cello privately; then attended classes in composition with Johan Wagenaar at the Utrecht Cons. (1913–16); completed his cello studies with Charles van Isterdael in Utrecht (1916–18) and Gérard Hekking in Paris (1918–21). He appeared as soloist in some of his own works with the N.Y. Phil. (1921–22); was then 1st cellist of the Amsterdam Concertgebouw Orch. (1922–24); then served as conductor in Coburg, Bavaria, at the behest of the exiled King Ferdinand of Bulgaria (1924–32); subsequently conducted the Utrecht Municipal Orch. (1932–37). In 1937 he abandoned music and became a disciple of Rudolf Steiner, founder of the Anthroposophical Soc.; traveled as a speaker and monitor of anthroposophy until his death. He composed *La Fête bleue*, symphonic poem for Cello and Orch. (1917); *Sphynx*, nocturne for Orch. (1919); pieces for cello.

Gould, Glenn (Herbert), remarkably individualistic Canadian pianist; b. Toronto, Sept. 25, 1932; d. there, Oct. 4, 1982. His parents were musically gifted and gladly fostered his precocious development; he began to play piano, and even compose, in his single-digit years. At the age of 10, he entered the Royal Cons. of Music in Toronto, where he studied piano with Alberto Guerrero, organ with Frederick C. Silvester, and music theory with Leo Smith; he received his diploma as a graduate at 13, in 1945. He made his debut in Toronto on May 8, 1946. As he began practicing with total concentration on the mechanism of the keyboard, he developed mannerisms that were to become his artistic signature. He reduced the use of the pedal to a minimum in order to avoid a harmonic haze; he cultivated "horizontality" in his piano posture, bringing his head down almost to the level of the keys. He regarded music as a linear art; this naturally led him to an intense examination of Baroque structures; Bach was the subject of his close study rather than Chopin; he also cultivated performances of the early polyphonists Sweelinck, Gibbons, and others. He played Mozart with emphasis on the early pianoforte techniques; he peremptorily omitted the Romantic composers Chopin, Schumann, and Liszt from his repertoire. He found the late sonatas of Beethoven more congenial to his temperament, and, remarkably enough, he played the piano works of the modern Vienna school—Schoenberg, Berg, and Webern—perhaps because of their classical avoidance of purely decorative tonal formations. Following his U.S. debut in Washington, D.C. (Jan. 2, 1955), he evoked unequivocal praise at his concerts, but in 1964 he abruptly terminated his stage career and devoted himself exclusively to recording, which he regarded as a superior art to concertizing. This enabled him to select the best portions of the music he played in the studio, forming a mosaic unblemished by accidental mishaps. A great part of the interest he aroused with the public at large was due to mannerisms that marked his behavior on the stage. He used a 14-inch-high chair that placed his eyes almost at the level of the keyboard; he affected informal dress; he had a rug put under the piano and a glass of distilled water within reach. He was in constant fear of bodily injury; he avoided shaking hands with the conductor after playing a concerto; and he sued the Steinway piano company for a large sum of money when an enthusiastic representative shook his hand too vigorously. But what even his most ardent admirers could not palliate was his unshakable habit of singing along with his performance; he even allowed his voice to be audible on his carefully wrought, lapidary phonograph recordings. Socially, he was a recluse; he found a release from his self-imposed isolation in editing a series of radio documentaries for the CBC. He called 3 of them a "solitude tragedy." Symbolically, they were devoted to the natural isolation of the Canadian Arctic, the insular life of Newfoundland, and the religious hermetism of the Mennonite sect. He also produced a radio documentary on Schoenberg, treating him as a musical hermit. Other activities included conducting a chamber orch. without an audience. Needless to add, Gould never married. See T. Page, ed., *The Glenn Gould Reader* (N.Y., 1985).

BIBL.: G. Paysant, *G. G.: Music and Mind* (Toronto, 1978; rev. ed., 1984); J. Cott, *Conversations with G. G.* (Boston, 1984); W. Matheis, *G. G.: Der Unheilige am Klavier* (Munich, 1987); O. Friedrich, *G. G.: A Life and Variations* (N.Y., 1989).

Gould, Morton, extraordinarily talented and versatile American composer and conductor; b. Richmond Hill, N.Y., Dec. 10, 1913. His father was an Austrian; his mother came from Russia; both fostered his early addiction to music. If the affectionate family memories are to be accepted as facts, Gould composed a piano waltz at the age of 6 (indeed, it was ultimately publ. under the title *Just 6*). Being a prodigy did not harm him. He was bent on learning what music really is. He had piano lessons with Joseph Kardos and Abby Whiteside; later enrolled in the composition class of Vincent Jones at N.Y. Univ.; there, at the age of 16, he presented a concert of his works. To keep body and soul together he played the piano in silent movies and in loud jazz bands, accompanied dancers, and gave demonstrations of musical skill on college circuits. In 1931–32 he served as staff pianist at Radio City Music Hall in N.Y.; from 1934 to 1946 was in charge of the series "Music for Today" on the Mutual Radio network, and in 1943 became music director of the lucrative "Chrysler Hour" on CBS Radio. These contacts gave great impetus to his bursting talent for composing singable, playable, and enjoyable light pieces; he was pregnant with the fertile sperm of musical Americana; his *American Symphonette No. 1* (1933) became a popular success; equally accessible to the musical youth of the day was the *Chorale and Fugue in Jazz* for 2 Pianos and Orch. (1934); no less a musical magus than Stokowski put it on the program of the Philadelphia Orch. (Jan. 2, 1936). Gould then produced 3 more symphonettes (1935, 1938, 1941). No. 3 disgorged the luscious *Pavanne* (sic); the misspelling was a concession to public illiteracy; the piece cloned several arrangements. There followed the *Latin-American Symphonette* (1940), an engaging tetrad of Latin dances (Rhumba, Tango, Guaracha, Conga). His *Spirituals* for Strings and Orch. (1941) is Gould's interpretation of the religious aspect of the American people. His other works touch on American history, as exemplified by *A Lincoln Legend* (1941), which Toscanini placed on his program with the NBC Sym. on Nov. 1, 1942; there followed the rambunctious orch. *Cowboy Rhapsody* (1943). In 1945 Gould conducted a whole program of his works with the Boston Sym. Orch. He then turned to ballet in his *Fall River Legend* (1947), based on the story of the notorious New England old maid Lizzie Borden, who may or may not have given her mother 40 whacks and "when she saw what she had done she gave her father 41." Gould's *Symphony of Spirituals*, written for the American bicentennial (1976), was a reverential offering; his other bicentennial work, *American Ballads* (1976), is a symphonic florilegium of American songs. Gould wrote the music for the Broadway show *Billion Dollar Baby* (1945), several scores for Hollywood films, and also background music for the historical television productions *Verdun* (1963), *World War I* (1964–65), and *Holocaust* (1978). But Gould was not so much seduced by public success as not to test his powers in absolute music. He studied ways and means of Baroque techniques, and wrote several concertos, 1 for piano (1937), 1 for violin (1938), 1 for viola (1944); *Variations* for 2 Pianos and Orch. (1952); and *Inventions* for 4 Pianos and Orch. (1953). On top of these "classical" works he produced a unique shtick, *Concerto for Tap Dancer*, with Orch. (1953). Gould was a conductor of excellent skills; he toured Australia in 1977, Japan in 1979, Mexico in 1980, and Israel in 1981. In 1983 he received the National Arts Award. He was elected a member of the American Academy and Inst. of Arts and Letters in 1986. He was president of ASCAP from 1986.

WORKS: STAGE: Musicals: *Billion Dollar Baby* (N.Y., Dec. 21, 1945) and *Arms and the Girl* (N.Y., Feb. 2, 1950); ballets: *Interplay* (N.Y., Oct. 17, 1945); *Fall River Legend* (N.Y., April 22, 1947); *Fiesta* (Cannes, March 17, 1957); *I'm Old Fashioned* (1983). **ORCH.:** *3 American Symphonettes* (1933, 1935, 1937); *Chorale and Fugue in Jazz* for 2 Pianos and Orch. (1934; N.Y., Jan. 2, 1936); Piano Concerto (1937; radio perf., June 16, 1938); Violin Concerto (1938); *Stephen Foster Gallery* (Pittsburgh, Jan. 12, 1940); *Spirituals* (N.Y., Feb. 9, 1941); *Latin-American Symphonette* (N.Y., Feb. 22, 1941); *Lincoln Legend* (1942); *Cowboy Rhapsody* (1942); *American Salute* (1943); Sym. No. 1 (Pittsburgh, March 5, 1943); Viola Concerto (1943); *Symphony on Marching Tunes*, No. 2 (N.Y., June 2, 1944); Concerto for Orch. (Cleveland, Feb. 1, 1945); *Harvest* for Harp, Vibraphone, and Strings (St. Louis, Oct. 27, 1945); *Minstrel Show* (Indianapolis, Dec. 21, 1946); *Holiday Music* (1947); Sym. No. 3 (Dallas, Feb. 16, 1947; rev. 1948); *Philharmonic Waltzes* (1948); *Serenade of Carols* (1949); *Tap Dance Concerto* (1952); *Dance Variations* for 2 Pianos and Orch. (N.Y., Oct. 24, 1953); *Showpiece* (Philadelphia, May 7, 1954); *Jekyll and Hyde Variations* (N.Y., Feb. 2, 1957); *Dialogues* for Piano and String Orch. (N.Y., Nov. 3, 1958); *Festive Music* (N.Y., Jan. 16, 1965); *Columbia: Broadsides for Orchestra* (1967); *Venice* for Double Orch. and Brass Bands (Seattle, May 2, 1967); *Vivaldi Gallery* (Seattle, March 25, 1968); *Soundings* (1969); *Troubadour Music* for 4 Guitars and Orch. (San Diego, March 1969); *Symphony of Spirituals* (Detroit, April 1, 1976); *American Ballads* (N.Y., April 24, 1976); *Cheers* (Boston, May 1, 1979); *Burchfield Gallery* (Cleveland, April 9, 1981); *Housewarming* (Baltimore, Sept. 16, 1982); *Apple Waltzes* (1983); *Flourishes and Galop* (1983); Flute Concerto (1984; Chicago, April 18, 1985); *Classical Variations on Colonial Themes* (Pittsburgh, Sept. 11, 1986); *Chorales and Rags* (1988);

Concerto Grosso (N.Y., Dec. 4, 1988). **FILM SCORES:** *Delightfully Dangerous* (1945); *Cinerama Holiday* (1955); *Windjammer* (1958). **TELEVISION SCORES:** *World War I* (1964–65); *Holocaust* (1978; suite for Orch., 1979, and for Band, 1980); *Celebration '81* (1981). **CHAMBER:** Suite for Violin and Piano (1945); Tuba Suite (1965); Suite for Cello and Piano (1981); *Concerto Concertante* for Violin, Woodwind Quintet, and Piano (1983). **PIANO:** *Boogie Woogie Etude* (1943); *Dance Gallery* (1952); *Abby Variations* (1964); *At the Piano* (2 books, 1964); *10 for Deborah* (1965); *Patterns* (1985); *2 Pianos* (Miami, Dec. 22, 1987); also works for band; choral works.

BIBL.: L. Evans, *M. G.: His Life and Music* (diss., Columbia Univ., Teachers College, 1978); S. Flatow, "M. G.," *Musical America* (Jan. 1989).

Gould, Nathaniel Duren, American singing-school teacher and tune-book compiler; b. Bedford, Mass., Nov. 26, 1781; d. Boston, May 28, 1864. His father was the church builder Reuben Duren; after being adopted by a maternal uncle in 1792, he took the name Gould in 1806. He studied vocal music with Reuben Emerson; organized his 1st singing school in Stoddard, N.H. (1798). He then formed the New Ipswich military band (1804), and was conductor of the Middlesex (Mass.) Musical Soc. (from 1805). From 1819 he lived mainly in Boston, where he was active as a teacher of vocal music and chirography. He publ. 8 anthologies for singing-school use, including *National Church Harmony* (1832; 4th ed., 1836). His study *Church Music in America* (Boston, 1853) remains a standard work in spite of its inaccuracies.

BIBL.: J. Ingalls, *N.D. G. 1781–1864* (thesis, Univ. of Lowell [Mass.], 1980).

Goulet, Robert (Gerard), American singer of popular music and actor; b. Lawrence, Mass., Nov. 26, 1933. His family moved to Edmonton, Canada; he then won a scholarship to the opera school of the Royal Cons. of Music in Toronto; made a successful American debut as Lancelot in the Broadway musical *Camelot* in 1960; subsequently appeared in a number of films.

Gounod, Charles (François), famous French composer; b. St. Cloud, June 17, 1818; d. Paris, Oct. 18, 1893. His father, Jean François Gounod, was a painter, winner of the 2nd Grand Prix de Rome, who died when Gounod was a small child. His mother, a most accomplished woman, supervised his literary, artistic, and musical education, and taught him piano. He completed his academic studies at the Lycée St. Louis; in 1836 he entered the Paris Cons., studying with Halévy, Le Sueur, and Paër. In 1837 he won the 2nd Prix de Rome with his cantata *Marie Stuart et Rizzio*; in 1839 he won the Grand Prix with his cantata *Fernand*. In Rome, he studied church music, particularly the works of Palestrina; composed a Mass for 3 Voices and Orch., which was performed at the church of San Luigi dei Francesi. In 1842, during a visit to Vienna, he conducted a Requiem of his own; upon his return to Paris, he became precentor and organist of the Missions Étrangères; studied theology for 2 years, but decided against taking Holy Orders; yet he was often referred to as l'Abbé Gounod; some religious choruses were publ. in 1846 as composed by Abbé Charles Gounod. Soon he tried his hand at stage music. On April 16, 1851, his 1st opera, *Sapho*, was produced at the Opéra, with only moderate success; he revised it much later, extending it to 4 acts from the original 3, and it was performed again on April 2, 1884; but it was unsuccessful. His 2nd opera, *La Nonne sanglante*, in 5 acts, was staged at the Opéra on Oct. 18, 1854; there followed a comic opera, *Le Médecin malgré lui*, after Molière (Jan. 15, 1858), which also failed to realize his expectations. In the meantime, he was active in other musical ways in Paris; he conducted the choral society Orphéon (1852–60) and composed for it several choruses. Gounod's great success came with the production of *Faust*, after Goethe (Théâtre-Lyrique, March 19, 1859; perf. with additional recitatives and ballet at the Opéra, March 3, 1869); *Faust* remained Gounod's greatest masterpiece, and indeed the most successful French opera of the 19th century, triumphant all over the world without any sign of diminishing effect through a century of changes in musical tastes. However, it was widely criticized for the melodramatic treatment of Goethe's poem by the librettists, Barbier and Carré, and for the somewhat sentimental style of Gounod's music. The succeeding operas *Philémon et Baucis* (Paris, Feb. 18, 1860), *La Colombe* (Baden-Baden, Aug. 3, 1860), *La Reine de Saba* (Paris, Feb. 29, 1862), and *Mireille* (Paris, March 19, 1864) were only partially successful, but with *Roméo et Juliette* (Paris, April 27, 1867), Gounod recaptured universal acclaim. In 1870, during the Franco-Prussian War, he went to London, where he organized Gounod's Choir, and presented concerts; when Paris fell, he wrote an elegiac cantata, *Gallia*, to words from the Lamentations of Jeremiah, which he conducted in London on May 1, 1871; it was later performed in Paris. He wrote some incidental music for productions in Paris: *Les Deux Reines*, to a drama by Legouvé (Nov. 27, 1872), and *Jeanne d'Arc*, to Barbier's poem (Nov. 8, 1873). In 1874, he returned to Paris; there he produced his operas *Cinq-Mars* (April 5, 1877), *Polyeucte* (Oct. 7, 1878), and *Le Tribut de Zamora* (April 1, 1881), without signal success. The last years of his life were devoted mainly to sacred works, of which the most important was *La Rédemption*, a trilogy, first performed at the Birmingham Festival in 1882; another sacred trilogy, *Mors et vita*, also written for the Birmingham Festival, followed in 1885. He continued to write religious works in close succession, including a *Te Deum* (1886); *La Communion des saints* (1889); *Messe dite le Clovis* (1890); *La Contemplation de Saint François au pied de la croix* (1890); *Tantum ergo* (1892). A Requiem (1893) was left unfinished, and was arranged by Henri Büsser after Gounod's death. One of his most popular settings to religious words is *Ave Maria*, adapted to the 1st prelude of Bach's *Well-tempered Clavier*, but its original version was *Méditation sur le premier Prélude de Piano de J.S. Bach* for Violin and Piano (1853); the words were added later (1859). Other works are: 2 syms. (1855); *Marche funèbre d'une marionnette* for Orch. (1873); *Petite symphonie* for Wind Instruments (1888); 3 string quartets; a number of piano pieces; songs. Among his literary works were *Ascanio de Saint-Saëns* (1889); *Le Don Juan de Mozart* (1890; in Eng., 1895); and an autobiography, *Mémoires d'un artiste* (Paris, 1896; Eng. tr. by W. Hutchenson, N.Y., 1896).

BIBL.: M. de Bovet, *C. G.* (Paris, 1890; in Eng., London, 1891); L. Pagnerre, *C. G., Sa vie et ses œuvres* (Paris, 1890); C. Saint-Saëns, *C. G. et le Don Juan de Mozart* (Paris, 1893); T. Dubois, *Notice sur C. G.* (Paris, 1894); P. Voss, *C. G.: Ein Lebensbild* (Leipzig, 1895); H. Tolhurst, *G.* (London, 1905); P. Hillemacher, *C. G.* (Paris, 1906); C. Bellaigue, *G.* (Paris, 1910); J.-G. Prod'homme and A. Dandelot, *G.: Sa vie et ses œuvres* (2 vols., Paris, 1911); H. Soubiès and H. de Curzon, *Documents inédits sur le Faust de G.* (Paris, 1912); J. Tiersot, "C. G., A Centennial Tribute," *Musical Quarterly* (July 1918); R. d'Ollone, "G. et l'opéra comique," *Revue Musicale* (Nov. 1933); M. Cooper, "C. G. and His Influence on French Music," *Music & Letters* (1940); P. Landormy, *G.* (Paris, 1942); idem, *Faust de G.: Étude et analyse* (Paris, 1944); H. Wagener, "Die Messen C. G.s," *Kirchenmusikaliches Jahrbuch*, 51 (1967; reprinted in *Musica Sacra*, July–Aug. and Sept.–Oct. 1970); idem, "C.F. G. Ein Beitrag zur Kirchenmusik des 19. Jahrhunderts," *Musica Sacra* (Jan. 1968); A. Lebois, "La Reine de Saba ou Amour et Franc-Maçonnerie," *Annales Publiées par la Faculté des Lettres de Toulouse. Littératures* (Oct. 1968); J. Harding, *G.* (London, 1973); S. Huebner, "Mireille Revisited," *Musical Times* (Dec. 1983); M. Rustman, *Lyric Opera: A Study of the Contribution of C. G.* (diss., Univ. of Kansas, 1986); S. Huebner, *The Operas of G.* (Oxford, 1990).

Gouvy, Louis Théodore, French composer; b. Goffontaine, near Saarbrücken, July 5, 1819; d. Leipzig, April 21, 1898. The son of French parents, he graduated from the college at Metz; went to Paris to study law, but turned to music; presented a concert of his works in Paris in 1847; also made frequent trips to Germany, where his music was received with great favor. He composed about 200 works, including an opera, *Der*

Cid (1863); 7 syms. (1846–92); Wind Nonet; Wind Octet; Sextet for Flute and Strings; Piano Quintet; String Quintet; 5 string quartets; 5 piano trios; numerous piano pieces in an ingratiating salon manner; songs.

BIBL.: O. Klauwell, *L.T. G., Sein Leben und seine Werke* (Berlin, 1902).

Gow, Nathaniel, Scottish violinist, arranger, and music publisher, son of **Niel Gow**; b. Inver, near Dunkeld, May 28, 1763; d. Edinburgh, Jan. 19, 1831. He played the trumpet in Scottish bands; then changed to violin. In 1788 he opened a music shop in Edinburgh; publ. numerous arrangements of Scottish tunes by his father and also his own arrangements of Scottish dances; became a commercial music publisher in 1796, but was bankrupt by 1827. He also led a band for various aristocratic assemblies. Among his original pieces was an interesting instrumental composition, *Caller Herrin'*, based on a street vendor's cry.

Gow, Niel, Scottish violinist and composer, father of **Nathaniel Gow**; b. Strathbrand, Perthshire, March 22, 1727; d. Inver, near Dunkeld, March 1, 1807. He played Scottish reels on the violin, and as a young man earned his living by performing at social gatherings in Edinburgh and London. He publ. a number of "Strathspey Reels"; however, many of them were not original compositions but arrangements of old dance tunes.

BIBL.: J. Glen, *The Glen Collection of Scottish Dance Music* (vol. 2, Edinburgh, 1895).

Graben-Hoffmann, Gustav (Heinrich) (properly, **Gustav Heinrich Hoffmann**), German composer; b. Bnin, near Posen, March 7, 1820; d. Potsdam, May 20, 1900. He studied with his father and with other teachers in Posen; then taught music in various localities in eastern Germany; in 1843, settled in Berlin; in 1850, founded a Musikakademie für Damen; then went to Leipzig, where he studied composition with Moritz Hauptmann; in 1869, returned to Berlin, where he taught singing. He composed industriously; wrote a number of songs, but was compelled to publ. them at his own expense, despite economic hardships; of these, *500,000 Teufel* had a great vogue. He also publ. singing manuals: *Die Pflege der Singstimme* (1865); *Das Studium des Gesangs* (1872); *Praktische Methode als Grundlage für den Kunstgesang* (1874).

Grabner, Hermann, Austrian composer and music theorist; b. Graz, May 12, 1886; d. Bolzano, Italy, July 3, 1969. He took his degree in law at Graz Univ. in 1909; then studied music with Reger and Hans Sitt at the Leipzig Cons.; he became a lecturer in theory at the Strasbourg Cons. in 1913; served in the German army in World War I; after the Armistice, taught at the Mannheim Cons.; from 1924 to 1938 was prof. of composition at the Leipzig Cons.; then taught at the Hochschule für Musik in Berlin (1938–46), and later at the Berlin Cons. (1950–51). He wrote an opera, *Die Richterin* (Barmen, May 7, 1930); *Perkeo Suite* and *Burgmusik* for Wind Orch.; Concerto for 3 Violins; organ pieces; songs; etc.

WRITINGS: *Die Funktionstheorie Hugo Riemanns und ihre Bedeutung für die praktische Analyse* (Munich, 1923); *Allgemeine Musiklehre* (Stuttgart, 1924; 5th ed., 1949); *Lehrbuch der musikalischen Analyse* (Leipzig, 1925); *Der lineare Satz; Ein Lehrbuch des Kontrapunktes* (Stuttgart, 1930; rev. ed., 1950); *Handbuch der Harmonielehre* (Berlin, 1944).

Grabovsky, Leonid, Russian composer; b. Kiev, Jan. 28, 1935. He studied at the Kiev Cons. with Revutsky and Liatoshinsky, graduating in 1959. His music is marked by modern tendencies, making use of dissonant counterpoint and asymmetric polyrhythmic combinations.

WORKS: *Intermezzo* for Orch. (1958); String Quartet (1958); *4 Ukrainian Songs* for Chorus and Orch. (1959); Sonata for Unaccompanied Violin (1959); *Symphonic Frescoes* (1961); 2 comic operas, after Chekhov: *The Bear* (1963) and *Marriage Proposal* (1964); Trio for Violin, Double Bass, and Piano (1964); *Microstructures* for Oboe Solo (1964); *Constants* for 4 Pianos, 6 Percussion Groups, and Solo Violin (1964); *From Japanese Haiku* for Tenor, Piccolo, Bassoon, and Xylophone (1964); *La*

Mer for Narrator, 2 Choruses, Organ, and Orch. (1964–70; Rotterdam, Sept. 10, 1971); *Pastels* for Female Voice, Violin, Viola, Cello, and Double Bass (1964); *Little Chamber Music No. 1* for 15 String Instruments (1966); *Homeomorphia I, II, and III* for 1 or 2 Pianos (1968); *Ornaments* for Oboe, Viola, and Harp (1969); *Homeomorphia IV* for Orch. (1969); *Little Chamber Music No. 2* for Oboe, Harp, and 12 Solo String Instruments (1971); *2 Pieces* for String Orch. (1972); *Concorsuono* for Solo Horn (1974); *St. John's Eve*, symphonic legend for Orch., after Gogol (1976).

Grace, Harvey, English organist and writer on music; b. Romsey, Jan. 25, 1874; d. Bromley, Kent, Feb. 15, 1944. He studied with M. Richardson at Southwark Cathedral, London; was organist at various churches in London; directed the St. Cecilia Festivals; from 1918 to his death, he was editor of the *Musical Times* and wrote editorial articles for it under the name "Feste"; also ed. the *New Musical Educator* (London, 1934). He also composed 20 organ pieces; made 30 transcriptions from Bach, mostly for organ; ed. Rheinberger's 20 sonatas for organ.

Writings: *French Organ Music, Past and Present* (N.Y., 1919); *The Complete Organist* (London, 1920; 4th ed., 1956); *The Organ Works of Bach* (London, 1922); *The Organ Works of Rheinberger* (London, 1925); *Ludwig van Beethoven* (London, 1927); *A Musician at Large* (collection of articles from the *Musical Times*; London, 1928); *A Handbook for Choralists* (London, 1928); with Sir Walford Davies, *Music and Worship* (London, 1935; 2nd ed., 1948); *The Organ Works of César Franck* (London, 1948).

Gracis, Ettore, Italian conductor; b. La Spezia, Sept. 24, 1915. He studied violin at the Parma Cons. and piano and composition at the Venice Cons.; also took courses in composition with Gian Francesco Malipiero in Siena. He made his conducting debut in 1942; from that time appeared with many opera houses of Italy. He also conducted sym. concerts. He was active in bringing out contemporary scores; conducted a number of works by Malipiero and other leading Italian composers.

Grad, Gabriel, Lithuanian composer; b. Retovo, near Kovno, July 9, 1890; d. Tel Aviv, Dec. 9, 1950. He studied in Ekaterinoslav and in Berlin; founded a Jewish music school in Kovno (1920–22); went to Palestine in 1924; from 1925 was founder and director of the Benhetov Cons. in Tel Aviv. He wrote an opera, *Judith and Holofernes*, and about 250 other works, including chamber music, piano pieces, choruses, and songs, many of which are based on Jewish folk melodies.

Grädener, Carl (Georg Peter), German cellist, conductor, and composer, father of **Hermann (Theodor Otto) Grädener;** b. Rostock, Jan. 14, 1812; d. Hamburg, June 10, 1883. He studied cello with Mattstedt; from 1838 was music director at Kiel Univ. for 10 years; in 1851 established an academy for vocal music in Hamburg; after 3 years at the Vienna Cons. (1862–65) he returned to Hamburg, and became a teacher at the Cons. there, until 1873; was also co-founder and a president of the Hamburger Tonkünstlerverein. He wrote *System der Harmonielehre* (Hamburg, 1877); his articles for music periodicals were collected and publ. as *Gesammelte Aufsätze* (Hamburg, 1872).

Works: 2 operas, *König Harald* and *Der Mullerin Hochzeit*; oratorio, *Johannes der Täufer*; 2 syms.; *Fiesco*, overture; Piano Concerto; *Romance* for Violin and Orch.; String Octet; 5 piano quintets; 3 string quartets; String Trio; 2 piano trios; 3 violin sonatas; Cello Sonata; many piano pieces.

Grädener, Hermann (Theodor Otto), German violinist, conductor, and composer, son of **Carl (Georg Peter) Grädener;** b. Kiel, May 8, 1844; d. Vienna, Sept. 18, 1929. He studied at the Vienna Cons.; was violinist in the Court Orch. in Vienna; then taught theory at the Horaksche Klavierschule in 1873, and at the Cons. of the Gesellschaft der Musikfreunde in Vienna from 1877 to 1913; was also a prof. at the Univ. of Vienna (from 1882); in 1899 succeeded Bruckner there. He wrote 2 operas, *Der Richter von Zalamea* and *Die heilige Zita*; 2 syms.; concertos for Violin, for Cello, and for Piano; String

Octet; String Quintet; Piano Quintet; 2 string quartets; 5 *Impromptus* for Piano and Strings; 5 *Intermezzi* for Violin and Piano; Sonata for 2 Pianos.

Gradenwitz, Peter (Werner Emanuel), German-born Israeli musicologist; b. Berlin, Jan. 24, 1910. He took courses in musicology, literature, and philosophy at the Univs. of Berlin and Freiburg im Breisgau (1928–33); also was a student at the Berlin Hochschule für Musik; was a pupil in composition of Hanns Eisler and Josef Rufer in Berlin, Julius Weismann in Freiburg im Breisgau, and Darius Milhaud in Paris (1934); completed his training in musicology at the German Univ. in Prague (Ph.D., 1936, with the diss. *Johann Stamitz: Das Leben*; publ. in Brno, 1936; 2nd ed., greatly augmented, as *Johann Stamitz: Leben, Umwelt, Werke*, 2 vols., Wilhelmshaven, 1984). In 1936 he settled in Palestine, and was active as a writer, lecturer, and concert organizer; was founder, ed., and director of Israeli Music Publications, Ltd. (1949–82); also taught at the Univ. of Tel Aviv (1968–77). He lectured in Europe and the U.S.; in 1980 he was made an honorary prof. at the Univ. of Freiburg im Breisgau, where he subsequently led annual seminars. He contributed numerous articles to various journals and other publications. He also composed; among his works are a Sym.; a Serenade for Violin and Orch.; a String Quartet; a Trio for Flute, Viola, and Cello; *Palestinian* (later *Biblical) Landscapes* for Oboe and Piano; and songs.

Writings: *Toldot hamusika* (Jerusalem, 1939; 8th ed., 1969); *The Music of Israel* (N.Y., 1949); *Olam hasimofonia* (Tel Aviv, 1945; 9th ed., 1974); *Olaf hapsantran* (Tel Aviv, 1952); *Die Musikgeschichte Israels* (Kassel, 1961); *Wege zur Musik der Gegenwart* (Stuttgart, 1963; 2nd ed., rev., 1974); *Wege zur Musik der Zeit* (Wilhelmshaven, 1974); *Musik zwischen Orient und Okzident: Eine Geschichte der Wechselbeziehungen* (Wilhelmshaven, 1977); *Das Heilige Land in Augenzeugenberichten* (Munich, 1984); *Leonard Bernstein: Eine Biographie* (Zürich, 1984; 2nd ed., 1990; Eng. tr., Oxford, 1986); *Kleine Kulturgeschichte der Klaviermusik* (Munich, 1986).

Gradstein, Alfred, Polish composer; b. Czestochowa, Oct. 30, 1904; d. Warsaw, Sept. 9, 1954. He studied with Statkowski (composition) and Melcer (conducting) at the Warsaw Cons. (1922–25) and with Marx (composition) and Krauss (conducting) at the Vienna Academy of Music; from 1928 to 1947 he lived in Paris; then returned to Poland. He wrote mostly for piano; his Piano Concerto was publ. in 1932.

Graener, Paul, significant German composer; b. Berlin, Jan. 11, 1872; d. Salzburg, Nov. 13, 1944. He studied composition with Albert Becker at the Veit Cons. in Berlin. He traveled in Germany as a theater conductor; in 1896 went to London, where he taught at the Royal Academy of Music (1897–1902). He was then in Vienna as a teacher at the Neues Konservatorium; subsequently directed the Mozarteum in Salzburg (1910–13); then lived in Munich; in 1920 he succeeded Max Reger as a prof. of composition at the Leipzig Cons. (until 1925); was director of the Stern Cons. in Berlin (1930–33). He wrote music in all genres, and was fairly successful as an opera composer; in his style, he followed the Romantic movement, but also emphasized the folk element.

Works: operas: *Don Juans letztes Abenteuer* (Leipzig, June 11, 1914); *Theophano* (Munich, June 5, 1918); *Schirin und Gertraude* (Dresden, April 28, 1920); *Hanneles Himmelfahrt* (Dresden, Feb. 17, 1927); *Friedemann Bach* (Schwerin, Nov. 13, 1931); *Der Prinz von Homburg* (Berlin, March 14, 1935); *Schwanhild* (Cologne, Jan. 4, 1941). **orch.:** Sym.; *Romantische Phantasie; Waldmusik; Gothische Suite;* Piano Concerto; Cello Concerto. **chamber:** 6 string quartets; Piano Quintet; 3 violin sonatas.

Bibl.: G. Graener, *P. G.* (Leipzig, 1922); P. Grümmer, *Verzeichnis der Werke P. G.s* (Berlin, 1937).

Graeser, Wolfgang, Swiss composer; b. Zürich, Sept. 7, 1906; d. (suicide) Nikolassee, June 13, 1928. He went to Berlin in 1921; studied violin with Karl Klingler, and quickly acquired erudition in general music theory; also made a serious study of various unrelated arts and sciences (mathematics, oriental languages, painting). His signal achievement was an orchestration of Bach's *Kunst der Fuge* (Leipzig Thomaskirche, June 26, 1927). He publ. *Körpersinn* (Munich, 1927).

BIBL.: H. Zurlinden, *W. G.* (Munich, 1935).

Graetzer, Guillermo, Austrian-Argentine composer; b. Vienna, Sept. 5, 1914. He studied in Vienna with Paul Pisk; in 1930 moved to Buenos Aires, devoting himself mainly to educational activities; also ed. musical anthologies.

WORKS: *Concierto para orquesta* (1939); *La Parábola* for Orch. (1947); *Sinfonía brevis* (1951); Bassoon Concerto (1952); *Concierto de cámara* (1953); *Los burgueses de Calais* for Male Chorus and Orch. (1954–55); Cello Concerto (1957); *Cantos de la eternidad* for Orch. (1958); arrangements of folk dances of Argentina and Brazil for Recorder and Percussion (1968).

Graf, Herbert, Austrian-born American opera producer and director, son of **Max Graf;** b. Vienna, April 10, 1903; d. Geneva, April 5, 1973. He studied at the Univ. of Vienna with Guido Adler; received his Ph.D. in 1925. He then was a producer at the opera houses in Münster, Breslau, Frankfurt, and Basel. In 1934 he went to the U.S.; was associated with the Philadelphia Opera in 1934–35; in 1936 he was appointed producer of the Metropolitan Opera in N.Y.; in 1949, became head of the opera dept. at the Curtis Inst. of Music, Philadelphia. In 1958 he returned to Europe, where he was director of the Zürich Opera (1960–62) and the Grand Théâtre in Geneva (1965–73). He publ. *The Opera and Its Future in America* (N.Y., 1941), *Opera for the People* (Minneapolis, 1951), and *Producing Opera for America* (Zürich, 1961).

Graf, Max, Austrian music critic, teacher, and musicologist, father of **Herbert Graf;** b. Vienna, Oct. 1, 1873; d. there, June 24, 1958. He studied with Hanslick at the Univ. of Vienna (Ph.D., 1896, with the diss. *Die Musik der Frau in der Renaissancezeit;* publ. in Vienna, 1905). From 1900 to 1938 he wrote music criticism for the *Wiener Allgemeine Zeitung;* he lectured on music history at the Cons. of the Gesellschaft der Musikfreunde (1902–9); then was on the staff of the Academy of Music (1909–38). In 1938, when Austria was incorporated into the Greater German Reich, he went to the U.S. He returned to Vienna in 1947. A brilliant writer in his homeland, he lapsed into speculative journalism in his books publ. in America, which are rendered worthless because of blatant inaccuracies.

WRITINGS: *Deutsche Musik im 19. Jahrhundert* (Berlin, 1898); *Wagner-Probleme und andere Studien* (Vienna, 1900); *Die innere Werkstatt des Musikers* (Stuttgart, 1910); *Vier Gespräche über deutsche Musik* (Regensburg, 1931); *Legend of a Musical City* (N.Y., 1945; 2nd ed., 1969); *Composer and Critic* (N.Y., 1946; 2nd ed., 1969); *Modern Music* (N.Y., 1946; 2nd ed., 1969; also in German as *Geschichte und Geist der modernen Musik,* Vienna, 1953); *From Beethoven to Shostakovich* (N.Y., 1947; 2nd ed., 1969); *Die Wiener Oper* (Vienna, 1955).

Graf, Walter, Austrian ethnomusicologist; b. St. Pölten, June 20, 1903; d. Vienna, April 11, 1982. He studied musicology with Lach, Adler, and Wellesz, as well as anthropology, philosophy, psychology, and phonetics, at the Univ. of Vienna (Ph.D., 1933, with a diss. on German influences on Estonian folk song; Habilitation, 1952, with a study of the music of New Guinea). He became lecturer (1958) and then assistant prof. (1962) at the Univ. of Vienna; concurrently was head of the Austrian Academy of Sciences recording archive, which he greatly expanded. In his articles he continued Lach's anthropological concept of music; he also attempted to define the characteristics of sound that are important in the hearing and understanding of music. Among his writings are "Die ältesten deutschen Überlieferungen estnischer Volkslieder," *Musik des Ostens,* I (1962), *Die musikalische Klangforschung: Wege zur Erfassung der musikalischen Bedeutung der Klangfarbe* (Karlsruhe, 1969), and "Zur Rolle der Teiltonreihe in der Gestaltung klingend tradiertet Musik," *Festschrift Kurt Blaukopf* (Vienna, 1975).

Graffigna, Achille, Italian composer; b. S. Martino dall' Argine, near Mantua, May 5, 1816; d. Padua, July 19, 1896. He studied with Alessandro Rolla in Milan; wrote church music and theatrical cantatas; then devoted himself to opera; his *Ildegonda e Rizzardo* (La Scala, Milan, Nov. 3, 1841) was accepted with favor. In 1842 he went to Verona, where he produced *Eleonora di San Bonifacio* (March 11, 1843); there followed *Maria di Brabante* (Trieste, Oct. 16, 1852), *L'assedio di Malta* (Padua, July 30, 1853), *Gli Studenti* (Milan, Feb. 7, 1857), *Veronica Cibo* (Mantua, Feb. 13, 1858; rev. and produced at the Théâtre-Italien, Paris, March 22, 1865, as *La Duchessa di San Giuliano*), *Il Barbiere di Siviglia* (Padua, May 17, 1879; intended as an homage to Rossini), *Il matrimonio segreto* (Florence, Sept. 8, 1883), and *La buona figliuola* (Milan, May 6, 1886).

Graffman, Gary, outstanding American pianist; b. N.Y., Oct. 14, 1928. He won a scholarship to the Curtis Inst. of Music in Philadelphia when he was 8, and studied with Isabelle Vengerova. He was only 10 when he gave a piano recital at Town Hall in N.Y. After graduating in 1946, he was a scholarship student at Columbia Univ. (1946–47). In 1946 he won the 1st regional Rachmaninoff competition, which secured for him his debut with the Philadelphia Orch. in 1947. In 1949 he was honored with the Leventritt Award. Subsequently he received a Fulbright grant to go to Europe (1950–51). Returning to the U.S., he had lessons with Horowitz in N.Y. and Rudolf Serkin in Marlboro, Vt. He was on his way to establishing himself as a pianist of the 1st rank when disaster struck; about 1979 he began to lose the use of his right hand through a rare ailment, designated by some doctors as carpal-tunnel syndrome, that attacks instrumentalists. (Leon Fleisher suffered from it. Schumann had to discontinue his career as a pianist owing to a similar impedimentum, but he applied primitive treatments, such as exercising his weak fingers with a sling and a pulley, which in the end strained the tendons, further weakening the hand.) He was appointed to the faculty of the Curtis Inst. of Music in 1980; was made its artistic director in 1986. He brought out an autobiography under the title *I Really Should Be Practicing* (Garden City, N.Y., 1981).

Grahn, Ulf, Swedish composer; b. Solna, Jan. 17, 1942. He studied piano, violin, and composition with Hans Eklund at the Stockholm Citizen's School (1962–66); then took various courses at the Stockholm Musikhögskolan (1966–70). In 1972 he and his wife, the pianist Barbro Dahlman, went to America; he enrolled at the Catholic Univ. of America (M.M., 1973); with his wife he founded the Contemporary Music Forum (1974), presenting programs of modern music by American and European composers. After teaching at Northern Virginia Community College (1975–80), he joined the faculty of George Washington Univ. in Washington, D.C. (1983); he also served as artistic and managing director of the Lake Siljan Music Festival in Sweden (1988–89). In his own music he maintains the golden mean of contemporary idioms, without doctrinaire deviations, scrupulously serving the tastes of the general audience.

WORKS: *Musica da camera* for Chamber Orch. (1964); *Serenade* for 2 Oboes (1965); *Fancy* for Orch. (1965); *Elegy* for Oboe, Horn, and Cello (1967); Trio for Flute, Oboe, and Clarinet (1967); Suite for 2 Violins and Viola (1967); *Lamento* for Strings (1967); Sym. No. 1 (1967); *Hommage à Charles Ives* for String Orch. (1968; Trondheim, Feb. 13, 1969); Chamber Concerto for Double Bass (1968; Santa Barbara, Calif., Feb. 7, 1973); *Dialogue* for Flute and Clarinet (1969); *Joy* for Symphonic Band (1969; Stockholm, Feb. 2, 1970); *Ancient Music* for Piano and Chamber Orch. (1970; Copenhagen, March 20, 1972); *A Dream of a Lost Century* for Chamber Orch. (1971; Stockholm, June 1, 1972); *Lux,* ballet (1972; Stockholm, April 6, 1972); *Alone* for Flute (1972); *This Reminds Me of . . .* for Flute, Clarinet, Horn, Trombone, and Percussion (1972; Washington, D.C., Dec. 15, 1975); Concerto for Orch. (1973; Philadelphia, April 10, 1981); *Soundscapes I* for Flute, Bass Clarinet, English Horn, and Percussion (1973; Washington, D.C., Oct. 28, 1973);

Soundscapes II for Instruments (1974); *Soundscapes III* for Flute, Clarinet, Percussion, and Tape (1975); *Soundscapes IV* for Soprano, Flute, Bass Clarinet, Percussion, and Piano (1975); Chamber Concerto for Viola d'Amore and 10 Instruments (1975; Washington, D.C., Jan. 17, 1977); *Order-Fragments-Mirror* for Flute, Bass Clarinet, Percussion, and Piano (1975); Flute Sonata (1976); *Magnolias in Snow* for Flute and Piano (1976); Concertino for Piano and Strings (1979; Northern Virginia Sym., Feb. 28, 1981; Barbro Dahlman, soloist); String Quartet No. 2 (1979); *Floating Landscape* for 8 Flutes (1979); Piano Sonata (1980); *Rondeau* for Chamber Orch. (1980); Piano Quartet (1980); *Summer Deviation* for Flute, Violin, Viola, Cello, and Piano (1981); *Images* for Bass Clarinet and Marimba (1981); *Eldorado* for Flute, Violin, Clarinet, Piano, and Baryton (1982); Violin Sonata (1983); Sym. No. 2 (1983; Stockholm, June 20, 1984); Guitar Concerto (Reston, Va., June 15, 1985); *Un Coup de dés* for Soprano and Chamber Ensemble (Washington, D.C., April 20, 1987); *Celebration* for Marimba (1988); *Trosa Bilder* for Accordion (1989).

Grainger, (George) Percy (Aldridge), celebrated Australian-born American pianist and composer; b. Melbourne, July 8, 1882; d. White Plains, N.Y., Feb. 20, 1961. He received his early musical training from his mother; at the age of 10, appeared as pianist at several public concerts; then had lessons with Louis Pabst; in 1894 went to Germany, where he studied with Kwast in Frankfurt; also took a few lessons with Busoni. In 1901 he began his concert career in England; then toured South Africa and Australia. In 1906 he met Grieg, who became enthusiastic about his talent; Grainger's performances of Grieg's Piano Concerto were famous. In 1914 Grainger settled in the U.S.; made a sensational debut in N.Y., on Feb. 11, 1915; gave summer sessions at the Chicago Musical College from 1919 to 1931; was for 1 academic year (1932–33) chairman of the music dept. of N.Y. Univ. In 1935 he founded a museum in Melbourne, in which he housed all his MSS and his rich collection of musical souvenirs. He married Ella Viola Ström in 1928 in a spectacular ceremony staged at the Hollywood Bowl, at which he conducted his work *To a Nordic Princess,* written for his bride. Grainger's philosophy of life and art calls for the widest communion of peoples and opinions; his profound study of folk music underlies the melodic and rhythmic structure of his own music; he made a determined effort to re-create in art music the free flow of instinctive songs of the people; he experimented with "gliding" intervals within the traditional scales and polyrhythmic combinations with independent strong beats in the component parts. In a modest way he was a pioneer of electronic music; as early as 1937 he wrote a quartet for electronic instruments, notating the pitch by zigzags and curves. He introduced individual forms of notation and orch. scoring, rejecting the common Italian designations of tempi and dynamics in favor of colloquial English expressions. An eccentric to the last, he directed that his skeleton, after the removal and destruction of the flesh, be placed for preservation and possible display in the Grainger Museum at the Univ. of Melbourne, but his request was declined and he was buried in an ordinary manner.

WORKS: ORCH.: *Mock Morris* for Strings (1911); *Irish Tunes from County Derry* (1909); *Molly on the Shore; Shepherd's Hey; Colonial Song* (1913); *The Warriors* for 3 Pianos and Orch. (1916); *English Dance* for Orch. and Organ (1925); *Ye Banks and Braes o' Bonnie Doon* (1932); *Harvest Hymn* (1932); *Danish Folk-song Suite* (1937). **CHAMBER ORCH.:** *The Nightingale and the 2 Sisters* (1931). **CHORUS AND ORCH.:** *Marching Song of Democracy* (1901–17); *The Merry Wedding* (1916); *Father and Daughter; Sir Eglamore; The Camp; The March of the Men of Harlech; The Hunter in His Career; The Bride's Tragedy; Love Verses from "The Song of Solomon"; Tribute to Foster* (1931). **CHORUS AND BRASS BAND:** *I'm 17 Come Sunday; We Have Fed Our Seas for a Thousand Years* (1912); *Marching Tune.* **A CAPPELLA CHORUS:** *Brigg Fair; The Innuit; Morning Song in the Jungle; A Song of Vermland; At Twilight; Tiger-Tiger!; The Immovable Do; etc.* **CHAMBER:** *Handel in the Strand* (1913);

octet, *My Robin Is to the Greenwood Gone; Walking Tune* for Woodwind Quintet (1900–1905); *Green Bushes* (1921); *Hill-Song No. 1* (1923); *Shallow Brown* (1924); *Hill-Song No. 2* (1929); *Spoon River* (1930); *Free Music for Strings* (1935). **MILITARY BAND:** *Children's March* (1918); march, *The Lads of Wamphrey; Lincolnshire Posy,* 6 folk songs from Lincolnshire, England; settings, in various combinations, of 20 of Kipling's poems (1911–38); 32 settings of British folk songs (1911–38); piano pieces; etc.

BIBL.: D. Parker, *P.A. G., A Study* (N.Y., 1918); T. Slattery, *P. G.: The Inveterate Innovator* (Evanston, Ill., 1974); *A Complete Catalogue of Works of P. G.* (Nedlands, 1975); J. Bird, *P. G.* (London, 1976); L. Foreman, ed., *The P. G. Companion* (London, 1981); D. Tall, ed., *P. G.: A Catalogue of the Music* (London, 1982); R. Simon, *P. G.: The Pictorial Biography* (N.Y., 1984); K. Dreyfus, ed., *The Farthest North of Human Kindness: Letters of P. G. 1901–14* (London, 1985; unexampled in their perverse frankness in proclamation of sado-masochism, supported by illustrations); J. Blacking, "A Commonsense View of All Music": Reflections on P. G.'s Contribution to Ethnomusicology and Music Education (Cambridge, 1987).

Gram, Hans, Danish-born American organist, writer on music, and composer; b. Copenhagen, May 20, 1754; d. Boston, April 28, 1804. He studied philosophy at the Univ. of Copenhagen, and also had some training in music. About 1785 he went to America, and settled in Boston, where he became organist of the Brattle St. Church. He contributed various musical pieces to the *Massachusetts Magazine,* including a curious composition entitled *The Death Song of an Indian Chief* for Voice, 2 Clarinets, 2 Horns, and Strings, which was publ. in the March 1791 issue; it was apparently the 1st orch. score publ. in the U.S.; he also wrote *Sacred Lines for Thanksgiving Day* (1793) and some other vocal works for the same magazine. He was a co-ed. of *The Massachusetts Compiler* (Boston, 1795), a rather progressive collection on Psalmody, which also contained a music dictionary.

BIBL.: F. Metcalf, *American Writers and Compilers of Sacred Music* (N.Y., 1925).

Gram, Peder, Danish conductor and composer; b. Copenhagen, Nov. 25, 1881; d. there, Feb. 4, 1956. After graduation from the Univ. of Copenhagen, he studied music theory at the Leipzig Cons. with Sitt and Krehl and conducting with Nikisch (1904–7). Returning to Copenhagen, he was chief conductor of the Danish Concert Soc. (1918–32) and head of the music dept. of the Danish Radio (1937–51). He publ. *Musikens formlaere i grundtraek* (1916), *Moderne musik* (1934), and *Analytisk harmonilaere* (1947), all in Copenhagen.

WORKS: 3 syms. (1913, 1925, 1954); *Symphonic Fantasy* (1908); *Poème lyrique* for Orch. (1911); *Romance* for Violin and Orch. (1909); *Festouverture* (1927); *Avalon* for Soprano and Orch. (1916); Violin Concerto (1919); *Prologue to a Shakespearean Drama* (1928); *Ballet Suite* (1944); *Intrada seria* for Orch. (1946); 3 string quartets (1907, 1928, 1941); Piano Trio (1914); Cello Sonata (1914); Oboe Sonatina (1935); Wind Quintet (1943); piano pieces; songs.

Gramatges, Harold, Cuban composer; b. Santiago de Cuba, Sept. 26, 1918. He studied with José Ardévol and Amadeo Roldán in Havana; in 1942 went to the U.S. and took a summer course in composition with Copland at the Berkshire Music Center at Tanglewood. Returning to Havana, he founded, with several other modern Cuban composers, the Grupo de Renovación Musical (1943). From 1961 to 1964 he was a member of the Cuban Embassy in Paris. Once again in Havana, he organized the music dept. of the Casa de las Américas. In his own works he pursues the aim of enlightened functionalism in an effective modern style.

WORKS: *Invenciones* for Chamber Orch. (1941); ballet, *Icaro* (1943); *Mensaje al futuro* for Wind Orch. (1944); Sym. (1945); *Móvil* for 7 Instruments (1969); Wind Quintet (1957); *La muerte del guerrillero* for Speaker and Orch. (1969).

Gramm (real name, **Grambasch**), **Donald (John),** American bass-baritone; b. Milwaukee, Feb. 26, 1927; d. N.Y., June 2,

1983. He studied piano and organ at the Wisconsin College-Cons. of Music (1935–44); also studied voice with George Graham. He made his professional debut in Chicago at the age of 17 when he sang the role of Raimondo in Donizetti's *Lucia di Lammermoor;* he continued his vocal studies at the Chicago Musical College and at the Music Academy of the West in Santa Barbara, where he was a student of Martial Singher. On Sept. 26, 1952, he made his debut at the N.Y. City Opera, as Colline in *La Bohème,* and continued to appear with the company for the rest of his life. He was extremely versatile in his roles; he sang Méphistophélès in *Faust,* Leporello in *Don Giovanni,* Figaro in *Le nozze di Figaro,* Falstaff in Verdi's opera, Baron Ochs in *Der Rosenkavalier,* and Scarpia in *Tosca;* on Jan. 10, 1964, he made his debut at the Metropolitan Opera in N.Y., in the minor role of Truffaldino in *Ariadne auf Naxos;* he also distinguished himself as an interpreter of such difficult parts as Dr. Schön in Berg's *Lulu* and Moses in Schoenberg's *Moses und Aron.*

Grammann, Karl, German composer; b. Lübeck, June 3, 1844; d. Dresden, Jan. 30, 1897. He studied at the Leipzig Cons.; spent some years in Vienna; in 1885, settled in Dresden. As a youth, he wrote 2 operas, *Die Schatzgräber* and *Die Eisjungfrau,* which were not produced; the following operas were staged with some success: *Melusine* (Wiesbaden, 1875), *Thusnelda und der Triumphzug des Germanicus* (Dresden, 1881), *Das Andreasfest* (Dresden, 1882), and 2 short operas, *Ingrid* and *Das Irrlicht* (Dresden, 1894). His last opera, *Auf neutralem Boden,* was produced posth. (Hamburg, 1901). He further wrote several cantatas, syms., string quartets, violin sonatas, and other chamber music works.

BIBL.: F. Pfohl, *K. G. Ein Künstlerleben* (Berlin, 1910).

Granados (y Campiña), Eduardo, Spanish conductor and composer, son of **Enrique Granados (y Campiña);** b. Barcelona, July 28, 1894; d. Madrid, Oct. 2, 1928. He studied in Barcelona with his father; then at the Madrid Cons. with Conrado del Campo; taught at the Granados Academy in Barcelona; was also active as a conductor; presented many works by his father. He wrote several zarzuelas, of which the 1st, *Bufon y Hostelero,* was performed with some success in Barcelona (Dec. 7, 1917); other stage works were *Los Fanfarrones,* comic opera; *La ciudad eterna,* mystery play; *Los Cigarrales,* operatic sketch; also musical comedies (*Cocktails del Nuevo,* etc.).

Granados (y Campiña), Enrique, outstanding Spanish composer, father of **Eduardo Granados (y Campiña);** b. Lérida, July 27, 1867; d. at sea, March 24, 1916 (victim of the sinking by a German submarine of the S.S. *Sussex* in the English Channel). He studied piano at the Barcelona Cons. with Jurnet and Pujol, winning 1st prize (1883); then studied composition there with Pedrell (1883–87); in 1887 went to Paris to study with Charles de Beriot; made his recital debut in Barcelona in 1890. He first supported himself by playing piano in restaurants and giving private concerts. He attracted attention as a composer with his zarzuela *Maria del Carmen* (Madrid, Nov. 12, 1898); in 1900 he conducted a series of concerts in Barcelona; also established a music school, the Academia Granados (1901). He then wrote 4 operas, which were produced in Barcelona with little success: *Picarol* (Feb. 23, 1901), *Follet* (April 4, 1903), *Gaziel* (Oct. 27, 1906), and *Liliana* (1911). He undertook the composition of a work that was to be his masterpiece, a series of piano pieces entitled *Goyescas* (1911), inspired by the paintings and etchings of Goya; his fame rests securely on these imaginative and effective pieces, together with his brilliant *Danzas españolas.* Later, Fernando Periquet wrote a libretto based on the scenes from Goya's paintings, and Granados used the music of his piano suite for an opera, *Goyescas.* Its premiere took place, in the presence of the composer, at the Metropolitan Opera in N.Y., on Jan. 28, 1916, with excellent success; the score included an orch. *Intermezzo,* one of his most popular compositions. It was during his return voyage to Europe that he lost his life. Granados's music is essentially Romantic, with an admixture of specific Spanish rhythms and rather elaborate ornamentation. Other works include an inter-

mezzo to *Miel de la Alcarría* (1893); symphonic poems, *La nit del mort* and *Dante; Suite arabe; Suite gallega; Marcha de los vencidos; Serenata;* orch. suites, *Elisenda* and *Navidad;* Piano Trio; String Quartet; *Serenata* for 2 Violins and Piano; *Oriental* for Oboe and Strings; *Trova* for Cello and Piano; *Cant de les Estrelles* for Chorus, Organ, and Piano. Piano works: *Danzas españolas* (4 vols.); *Goyescas:* (Part I) *Los Requiebros, Coloquio en la Reja, El fandango del Candil, Quejas o la Maja y el Ruiseñor;* (Part II) *El Amor y la Muerte* (*Ballade*), *Epílogo* (*Serenade of the Specter*), *El Pelele* (*Escena goyesca*); *Escenas romanticas;* 6 pieces on Spanish popular songs; *Valses poéticos; Cuentos para la juventud; Marche militaire* and *A la Cubana* (also arranged for Orch.); 2 *danses caractéristiques: Danza gitana* and *Danza aragonesa.* Songs: *Colección de Tonadillas, escritas en estilo antiguo; Colección de canciones amatorias.*

BIBL.: Special issue of *Revista Musical Catalana* (June 15, 1916); G. Jean-Aubry, "E. G.," *Musical Times* (Dec. 1916); E. Newman, "The G. of the *Goyescas,*" ibid. (Aug. 1917); G. Boladeres Ibern, *E. G., Recuerdos de su vida y estudio crítico de su obra* (Barcelona, 1921); H. Collet, *Albéniz et G.* (Paris, 1926); J. Subira, *E. G.* (Madrid, 1926); E. Mason, "E. G.," *Music & Letters* (1933); A. Livermore, "G. and the 19th Century in Spain," *Musical Review* (1946); F. Vicens, *E. G.* (Barcelona, 1958).

Grancini (Grancino), Michel'Angelo, Italian organist and composer; b. Milan, 1605; d. there, April 17, 1669. He was organist at the Paradiso Church in Milan as a youth of 17; then was appointed organist at S. Sepolcro (1624) and later at S. Ambrogio (1628). In 1630 he became maestro di cappella of the Milan Cathedral, and retained this post until his death. During his lifetime he publ. some 20 vols. of his works, which included madrigals, motets, and *concerti sacri.*

Grancino, family of Italian violin makers, active in the 17th and early 18th centuries. **Andrea Grancino** established a workshop in Milan in 1646. His son, **Paolo,** worked in Milan between 1665 and 1692; he belonged to the Amati school, and several violins attributed to Amati are apparently the work of Paolo Grancino. Paolo's son, **Giovanni,** began making violins in 1677; he is reputed to have been the best of the family. His sons, **Giovanni Battista** and **Francesco,** were active between 1715 and 1746; their labels are marked **Fratelli Grancini.**

Grandert, Johnny, Swedish composer; b. Stockholm, July 11, 1939. He studied under Lidholm at the Stockholm Musikhögskolan (1959–64); also took music courses in Germany, Italy, and America; was mainly antodidact in music; also was active as a painter. In 1972 he became principal and in 1986 director of music at the Norrtälje School of Music. The titles of his compositions betray a desire to puzzle and tantalize, but the music itself is not forbidding, despite the application of startling effects.

WORKS: *Chamber Music* for Chamber Ensemble (1961); 2 string quartets (40,2°, 1963; 1977); Nonet for Winds, Euphonium, and Cello (1964); *86 T* for Chamber Ensemble (Stockholm, June 4, 1965); *Mirror 25* for Chorus and Orch. (Stockholm, Feb. 11, 1966; the score calls for a machine gun, and the chorus is invited to belch at some points); *10 an' 30* for Chamber Ensemble (1966); Octet for 3 Voices, Flute, Trombone, Viola, Double Bass, and Harp (1966); *The D. of B.* for Orch. (1967); *Barypet,* concerto for Trumpet and Baritone Saxophone, with 16 Flutes, Percussion, and Strings (1968); *Prego I* for Cello and Horn (1968); *Non omesso* for Chamber Ensemble (1969); *Skorogovorka* (Russian for "tongue twister") for Wind Orch. and Percussion (Swedish Radio, April 18, 1971); *Non lo so* (*I do not know it* in Italian) for Flute, Cello, and Piano (1970); wind quintet, *Pour Philippe* (1970); *Pour Pjotr* for Voice, Piano, Cello, Clarinet, and Percussion (1971); 6 syms.: No. 1 (1971); No. 2 (1973); No. 3, *Sinfonia Calamagrostis* (1974); No. 4 (1974; Stockholm, Nov. 29, 1975); No. 5 (1976; Swedish Radio, Feb. 22, 1977); No. 6 (1982; Helsinki, March 3, 1983); Quartet for Recorders (1972); *Jerikos murar* for Flute, Slide Flute, 3 Bass Recorders, 3 Clarinets, 15 Trombones, Percussion, Organ, and Strings (Norrtälje, Nov. 25, 1972); Saxophone Quintet (1975); *Temptation*, essay for String Quartet (1979); *Gyllene jord*, opera (1984); *Midtwedt*, canon for 8 Violins (1986); *Isola Sale* for Chamber Ensemble (1989).

Grandi, Alessandro, significant Italian composer; b. c.1577; d. Bergamo, 1630. He was maestro di cappella at the Accademia della Morte (1597–1604), the Accademia dello Spirito Santo (1610–15), and the cathedral in Ferrara (1615–17); then became a singer (1617) and 2nd maestro di cappella (1620) at S. Marco in Venice; subsequently was maestro di cappella at S. Maria Maggiore in Bergamo from 1627 until his death from the plague. His sacred music is of great importance; he excelled in the new concertato style. He also composed secular solo cantatas and arias, as well as concertato madrigals of great merit.

WORKS (all publ. in Venice unless otherwise given): **SACRED:** *Il primo libro de* (21) *motetti* for 2 to 5 and 8 Voices, *con una messa* for 4 Voices and Basso Continuo (1610); *Il secondo libro de* (12) *motetti* for 2 to 4 Voices and Basso Continuo (1613; 2nd ed., augmented, 1617); (16) *Motetti* for 5 Voices and Basso Continuo, *con le Letanie della beata vergine* (Ferrara, 1614; 3rd ed., augmented, 1620, for 2 to 5 and 8 Voices and Basso Continuo [organ]); *Il terzo libro de* (26) *motetti* for 2 to 4 Voices, *con le Letanie della beata vergine* for 5 Voices and Basso Continuo (1614; not extant; 2nd ed., 1618); *Il quarto libro de* (17) *motetti* for 2 to 4 and 7 Voices and Basso Continuo (1616); *Celesti fiori . . . de suoi* (16) *concerti* for 2 to 4 Voices and Basso Continuo, *con alcune cantilene* (1619; 2nd ed., 1620, for 1 to 4 Voices); (18) *Motetti* for Voice and Basso Continuo (1621); (15) *Motetti* for 1 and 2 Voices and Basso Continuo, *con sinfonie* (1621); (14) *Motetti* for 1 and 2 Voices and Basso Continuo, *. . . libro II* (2nd ed., 1625); (19) *Motetti* for 1 and 2 Voices and Basso Continuo, *con sinfonie . . . libro III* (1629); *Salmi brevi* for 8 Voices and Basso Continuo (1629); *Messa, e salmi* for 3 Voices and Basso Continuo (1630); *Raccolta terza . . . de messa et salmi . . .* for 2 to 4 and 6 Voices ad libitum, Cornett, 4 Trombones, Violin, and Basso Continuo (1630); *Il sesto libro de* (19) *motetti* for 2 to 4 Voices and Basso Continuo (1630; 3rd ed., Antwerp, 1640, for 2 to 4 Voices and Basso Continuo); (2) *Messe* for 8 Voices and Basso Continuo (1637). **SECULAR:** (3) *Madrigali* for 2 to 4 Voices and Basso Continuo (1615); (42) *Cantade et arie* for Voice and Basso Continuo (2nd ed., 1620; not extant); (20) *Madrigali* for 2 to 4 Voices and Basso Continuo *. . . libro II* (1622); *Cantade et arie* for Voice and Basso Continuo *. . . libro III* (1626); *Arie, et cantade* for 2 and 3 Voices, 2 Violins, and Basso Continuo (1626; only 2nd-violin part extant); *Cantade et arie* for Voice and Basso Continuo *. . . libro IV* (1629; not extant). **BIBL.:** D. Arnold, "A. G., a Disciple of Monteverdi," *Musical Quarterly* (April 1957); M. Seelkopf, *Das geistliche Schaffen von A. G.* (diss., Julius-Maximilian Univ., Würzburg, 1973); J. Roche, "A. G.: A Case Study in the Choice of Texts for Motets," *Journal of the Royal Musical Association*, 113/2 (1988).

Grandi, Margherita (original name, **Margaret Garde**), Australian soprano; b. Hobart, Oct. 4, 1894. She studied with Calvé in Paris; made her debut under the name of **Djema Vécla** (an anagram of Calvé) in 1919 at the Paris Opéra-Comique in *Werther;* after marrying the scenic designer Giovanni Grandi, she used her married name; later sang in Monte Carlo, Milan, Glyndebourne, and London. She was best known for her performances in the Italian repertoire.

Grandjany, Marcel (Georges Lucien), French-born American harpist; b. Paris, Sept. 3, 1891; d. N.Y., Feb. 24, 1975. He studied at the Paris Cons., winning 1st prize for harp (1905); made his Paris debut on Jan. 24, 1909; his American debut in N.Y., Feb. 7, 1924; taught at the Fontainebleau Cons. (1921–35); in 1936 settled in N.Y.; became an American citizen in 1945. In 1938 he joined the staff of the Juilliard School of Music; remained there until shortly before his death; also taught at the Montreal Cons. from 1943 to 1963. He composed a *Poème symphonique* for Harp, Horn, and Orch., and several

other works for harp; also songs to French texts. He publ. *First Grade Harp Pieces* (N.Y., 1964).

Grandjean, Axel Karl William, Danish composer; b. Copenhagen, March 9, 1847; d. there, Feb. 11, 1932. He began his career as an opera singer, but gave up the stage for teaching and composition; also conducted several choral societies in Copenhagen. He wrote the operas *Colomba* (Copenhagen, Oct. 15, 1882), *Oluf* (Copenhagen, April 7, 1894), and others; many choral works.

Grandval, Marie Félicie Clémence de Reiset, French composer; b. Saint-Rémy-des-Monts, Sarthe, Jan. 21, 1830; d. Paris, Jan. 15, 1907. She studied composition with Flotow and Saint-Saëns; under various pen names she wrote the operas *Le Sou de Lise* (Paris, 1859), *Les Fiancés de Rose* (Paris, May 1, 1863), *La Comtesse Eva* (Paris, Aug. 7, 1864), *La Pénitente* (Paris, May 13, 1868), *Piccolino* (Paris, Jan. 5, 1869), and *Mazeppa* (Bordeaux, 1892); the oratorio *St. Agnès* (Paris, April 13, 1876); *La Forêt*, lyric poem for Soli, Chorus, and Orch. (Paris, March 30, 1875); songs.

Granichstaedten, Bruno, Austrian composer; b. Vienna, Sept. 1, 1879; d. N.Y., May 20, 1944. He began his career as a cabaret singer; in 1908 he turned to composing light opera; produced 16 stage works before 1930; of these, *Der Orlow* (Vienna, April 3, 1925) was the most successful; other operettas are *Bub oder Mädel, Auf Befehl der Kaiserin, Evelyne, Walzerliebe*, etc. In 1938 he settled in the U.S.

Grant, Clifford (Scantlebury), Australian bass; b. Randwick, Sept. 11, 1930. He studied at the Sydney Cons.; later had voice lessons with Otakar Kraus in London. In 1951 he made his operatic debut with the New South Wales Opera; in 1966 he became a member of the Sadler's Wells Opera in London; also sang with the San Francisco Opera and the Welsh National Opera, at Covent Garden, and at the Glyndebourne Festival.

Grant, (William) Parks, American composer; b. Cleveland, Jan. 4, 1910. He studied at Capital Univ. in Columbus, Ohio, graduating with a B.Mus. (1932); received a Ph.D. from the Eastman School of Music in Rochester, N.Y. (1948). He retired in 1974, culminating a 40-year teaching career at various institutions. He was an ed. for the International Gustav Mahler Soc. in Vienna (1965–66; 1970; 1972–73), for whose *Critical Collected Edition* he corrected the new editions of Mahler's 2nd, 3rd, 8th, and 9th syms. and *Das klagende Lied*.

WORKS: *The Dream of the Ballet-Master*, ballet for Piano Quintet (1934); 3 syms. (1936, 1947, 1961); *The Masque of the Red Death*, symphonic poem (1938); Horn Concerto (1940); 6 overtures; Clarinet Concerto (1944); *Integrated Concerto* for Double Bass and Orch. (1946); *Scherzo* for Flute and Small Orch. (1950); 3 suites for String Orch.; 2 string quartets; *Essay for Horn and Organ* (1948); 3 suites for Brass Quintet (1949, 1951, 1953); *Varied Obstinacy* for 2 Saxophones (1974); *Pensive Monologue* for Solo Cello (1976); choruses; songs. **WRITINGS:** *Music for Elementary Teachers* (N.Y., 1951; rev. ed., 1960) and *Handbook of Music Terms* (Metuchen, N.J., 1967).

Grantham, Donald, American composer; b. Duncan, Okla., Nov. 9, 1947. He studied composition at the Univ. of Oklahoma (B.Mus., 1970). In 1974 he entered the Univ. of Southern Calif. in the composition classes of Robert Linn and Halsey Stevens (M.M., 1974; D.M.A., 1980). In the summers of 1973 and 1974 he studied with Nadia Boulanger at the Conservatoire Américain in Fontainebleau.

WORKS: ORCH.: *Música para "Los desastres de la guerra"* (1974); 5 *Variations and Double Fugue on "L'Homme armé"* (1970); *El album de los duendecitos* (1983). **CHAMBER:** Brass Quintet (1970); Piano Trio (1971); *Intrada* for Trumpet, Horn, and Trombone (1973); Chamber Concerto for Harpsichord and String Quartet (1974); *4 caprichos de Francisco Goya* for Solo Violin (1976); *Fanfare festiva* for 2 Trumpets, 2 Trombones, Timpani, and Organ (1978); *Sonata in 1 Movement* for Bass Trombone and Piano (1979); *Concerto* for Bass Trombone and

Wind Ensemble (1979); *Caprichos II* for Solo Cello (1979); *3 Epigrams* for Clarinet, Bassoon, and Piano (1980); *Duendecitos!* for Flute and Piano (1981); *Caprichos III* for Solo Double Bass (1982). VOCAL: *The War Prayer*, to words by Mark Twain, for Baritone, and Orch. or Piano (1974); *La noche en la isla* for Baritone, and Chamber Orch. or Piano, to words by Pablo Neruda (1980); *To the King Celestial* for Soprano and Chamber Orch., to a 14th-century Eng. text (1981).

Grappelli (Grappelly), Stéphane, outstanding French jazz violinist; b. Paris, Jan. 26, 1908. He was trained as a classical musician, but turned to jazz in the late 1920s; then organized the Quintette du Hot Club de France with the guitarist Django Reinhardt in 1934; subsequently toured widely and made recordings; made his U.S. debut at the Newport (R.I.) Jazz Festival in 1969. He appeared regularly in concert with Yehudi Menuhin from 1973, and later with Nigel Kennedy. In 1974 he made his Carnegie Hall debut in N.Y.; played there for a special 80th-birthday concert in 1988. He was the foremost jazz violinist in the European style of "Le Jazz hot."
  BIBL.: R. Horricks, *S. G., or the Violin with Wings: A Profile* (N.Y., 1983); G. Smith, *S. G.: A Biography* (London, 1987); *Current Biography* (Aug. 1988).

Gräsbeck, Gottfrid (Gustaf Unosson), Finnish conductor, musicologist, and composer; b. Turku, Feb. 15, 1927. He graduated with a philosophy degree from the Turku Academy; traveled on study trips to West Germany and America. Upon his return to Finland, he taught at Turku; also founded his own concert agency. Among his works are *Toccata dodecafonica* for Orch. (1959); Concerto for Orch. and Tape (1964); *Visan från molnet* (Song about the Cloud), cantata for Female Chorus and Orch. (1967); *Sinfonia da camera* (1969); *Lucia musik* for Solo Voices, Chorus, Organ, and Orch. (1971); Sonata for Guitar (1974).

Grasse, Edwin, American violinist and composer; b. N.Y., Aug. 13, 1884; d. there, April 8, 1954. Blind from infancy, he dictated his compositions to an accompanist. He studied violin with Carl Hauser in N.Y.; then went to Brussels for study with César Thomson at the Cons., where he won 1st prize in 1900, and diplôme de capacité in 1901; toured Europe and America. His works include *American Fantasie* for Violin and Orch.; Violin Sonata and other violin pieces; organ pieces.

Grassi, Eugène, French composer; b. Bangkok (of French parents), July 5, 1881; d. Paris, June 8, 1941. He went to France as a youth and studied with d'Indy; he revisited Siam from 1910 to 1913 to collect materials on indigenous music; his works reflect this study as well as, in harmonic idiom, the influence of Debussy. Among his compositions, all with oriental flavor, are *Le Réveil de Bouddha,* symphonic poem (Paris, Feb. 20, 1920); *Poème de l'univers* for Orch. (Paris, April 9, 1922); *Les Sanctuaires* (Paris, March 25, 1926); also songs in the impressionist manner.

Grassini, Josephina (Giuseppina) (Maria Camilla), Italian contralto; b. Varese, April 8, 1773; d. Milan, Jan. 3, 1850. She studied in Varese with Domenico Zucchinetti and in Milan with Antonio Secchi. She made her operatic debut in Parma in 1789 in Guglielmi's *La Pastorella nobile;* sang at La Scala in Milan in 1790, and soon attained popularity on all the leading Italian stages; in 1800 she sang in Milan before Napoleon, and became his mistress; he took her with him to Paris, where she sang at national celebrations. She was in London from 1804 to 1806; then returned to Paris and sang at the French court; she was noted for her beauty and her acting, as well as her voice.
  BIBL.: P. Cambiasi, "Una famosa cantante varesina," *Gazzetta Musicale di Milano* (Feb. 20, 1902); A. Pougin, *Une Cantatrice "amie" de Napoléon: G. G.* (Paris, 1920); A. Gavoty, *La G.* (Paris, 1947).

Grau, Maurice, Bohemian-born American operatic impresario; b. Brünn, 1849; d. Paris, March 14, 1907. He was taken to the U.S. at the age of 5; studied law at Columbia Univ. In 1872 he was a co-manager of the American tours of Anton Rubinstein; in 1873 he organized the Kellogg Opera Co.; was instrumental in bringing Offenbach to the U.S. In 1890 he presented a special season of 21 performances at the Metropolitan Opera in N.Y., with such famous artists as Patti, Albani, Nordica, and Tamagno. From 1891 to 1897 the Metropolitan was leased to the partnership of Abbey, Schoeffel, and Grau, and upon Abbey's death, to the Maurice Grau Opera Co. (1898–1903). The secret of Grau's success as an impresario was his understanding of public taste in opera; he frankly subordinated the repertoire to the favorite roles of the great European stars; he did not produce Wagner's operas until Wagnerian cycles presented by Damrosch had shown that American audiences were ripe for them. In fact, the growing popularity of Wagner contributed greatly toward the financial success of Grau's last seasons.

Graudan, Nicolai, Russian-American cellist; b. Libau, Sept. 5, 1896; d. Moscow, Aug. 9, 1964. He studied cello with Abbiate at the St. Petersburg Cons.; subsequently was an instructor there; left Russia in 1922 and went to Germany; was 1st cellist of the Berlin Phil. (1926–35). In 1935 he went to London, and in 1938 to the U.S.; from 1939 to 1944 was 1st cellist of the Minneapolis Orch.; from 1944 to 1950 lived in N.Y.; in 1950 settled in Los Angeles; gave duo-recitals with his wife, the pianist Joanna Freudberg; was a member of the Festival Quartet. He taught at Black Mountain College, at Santa Barbara's Music Academy of the West, at Aspen, and at the Univ. of Calif., Los Angeles. In 1964 he went to Moscow for a visit, and died there.

Graun, August Friedrich, German organist and composer, brother of **Carl Heinrich** and **Johann Gottlieb Graun;** b. Wahrenbrück, near Dresden, 1699; d. Merseburg, May 5, 1765. He was active as an organist and cantor at Merseburg, where he settled in 1729. Only 1 of his works is preserved, *Kyrie et Gloria* for 4 Voices with Instruments.

Graun, Carl Heinrich, noted German composer, brother of **August Friedrich** and **Johann Gottlieb Graun;** b. Wahrenbrück, near Dresden, May 7, 1704; d. Berlin, Aug. 8, 1759. He studied voice with Grundig and Benisch, keyboard playing with Pezold, and composition with Johann Christoph Schmidt at the Dresden Kreuzschule (1713–21); also sang in the chorus of the Dresden Court Opera. He became a tenor at the Braunschweig court in 1725; was made Vice-Kapellmeister about 1727, and wrote several operas for the Court Theater. He then joined the court establishment of Crown Prince Ferdinand (later Frederick II the Great) in Ruppin in 1735, becoming his Kapellmeister in Rheinsberg in 1736. After Frederick became king, Graun went to Berlin as Royal Kapellmeister (1740); the new opera house was inaugurated with his opera *Cesare e Cleopatra* on Dec. 7, 1742; many others followed, several with librettos by the King. Graun enjoyed royal favor and public esteem throughout his career in Berlin, his only serious challenger being Hasse. His operas were firmly rooted in the Italian tradition; although not without merit, they vanished from the repertoire after he passed from the scene. His gifts were more strikingly revealed in his sacred music, particularly in his *Te Deum* (written to commemorate Frederick's victory at the battle of Prague in 1756) and his Passion oratorio, *Der Tod Jesu;* the latter, his finest and most famous work, was performed in Germany regularly until the end of the 19th century.
  WORKS: OPERAS (all 1st perf. in Berlin unless otherwise given): *Sancio und Sinilde* (Braunschweig, 1727); *Polydorus* (Braunschweig, 1726 or 1728); *Iphigenia in Aulis* (Braunschweig, 1731); *Scipio Africanus* (Wolfenbüttel, 1732); *Lo specchio della fedeltà* or *Timareta* (Braunschweig, 1733); music not extant); *Pharao Tubaetes* (Braunschweig, 1735); *Rodelinda, regina de' langobardi* (Potsdam, Dec. 13, 1741); *Venere e Cupido* (Potsdam, 1742); *Cesare e Cleopatra* (1742); *Artaserse* (1743); *Catone in Utica* (1744); *La festa del Imeneo* (1744); *Lucio Papirio* (1745); *Adriano in Siria* (1746); *Demofoonte, rè di Tracia* (1746; 3 arias by Frederick II); *Cajo Fabricio* (1746); *Le feste galanti* (1747); *Il Rè pastore* (Charlottenburg, 1747; recitative, duet, and 2 choruses by Graun; remainder by Frederick

II, Nichelmann, and Quantz); *L'Europa galante* (Schloss Monbijou, 1748); *Galatea ed Acide* (Potsdam, 1748; overture, 1 recitative, and 1 aria by Quantz; arias by Frederick II); *Ifigenia in Aulide* (1748); *Angelica e Medoro* (1749); *Coriolano* (1749); *Fetonte* (1750); *Il Mitridate* (1750); *L'Armida* (1751); *Britannico* (1751); *L'Orfeo* (1752); *Il giudizio di Paride* (Charlottenburg, 1752); *Silla* (1753; libretto by Frederick II); *Il trionfo della fedeltà* (Charlottenburg, 1753; major portion of the work by G. Benda and Hasse); *Semiramide* (1754); *Montezuma* (1755; libretto by Frederick II; ed. in Denkmäler Deutscher Tonkunst, XV, 1904); *Ezio* (1755); *I Fratelli nemici* (1756; libretto by Frederick II); *La Merope* (1756; libretto by Frederick II). **SACRED:** *Cantata in obitum Friderici Guilielmi regis borussorum beati defuncti* (publ. in Berlin, 1741); Passion oratorio, *Der Tod Jesu* (Berlin, 1755; ed. by H. Serwer, Madison, Wis., 1974); *Te Deum* (publ. in Leipzig, 1757); 4 masses; a number of settings of the Missa Brevis; 2 Magnificats; cantatas; motets; Psalms. He also composed much secular vocal music, including Italian and German cantatas, songs, arias, etc. **INSTRUMENTAL:** About 40 concertos, some 35 trio sonatas, keyboard music, etc.

BIBL.: E. Prout, "G.'s Passion Oratorio and Handel's Knowledge of It," *Monthly Musical Record*, XXIV (1894); A. Mayer-Reinach, "C.H. G. als Opernkomponist," *Sammelbände der Internationalen Musik-Gesellschaft*, I (1899–1900); C. Mennicke, "Zur Biographie der Brüder G.," *Neue Zeitschrift für Musik*, LXXI (1904); idem, *Hasse und die Brüder G. als Symphoniker* (Leipzig, 1906); E. Schenk, "Zur Bibliographie der Triosonaten von J. G. und C.H. G.," *Zeitschrift für Musikwissenschaft*, XI (1928–29).

Graun, Johann Gottlieb, distinguished German composer, brother of **August Friedrich** and **Carl Heinrich Graun**; b. Wahrenbrück, near Dresden, c.1703; d. Berlin, Oct. 27, 1771. He began his musical studies while at the Dresden Kreuzschule; studied violin and composition with Pisendel in Dresden, then went to Prague, where he studied with Tartini. In 1726 he became Konzertmeister in Merseburg, where he numbered among his students Wilhelm Friedemann Bach. He was appointed Konzertmeister to Crown Prince Frederick (later Frederick II the Great) in Ruppin in 1732; continued in his service in Rheinsberg (1736–40), and then in Berlin in the newly founded Royal Opera under his brother **Carl Heinrich**, its Kapellmeister. He was a notable composer of instrumental music; he wrote about 95 sinfonias, 17 French overtures, 80 concertos (60 for violin), some 175 trio sonatas, and other chamber works.

BIBL.: C. Mennicke, "Zur Biographie der Brüder G.," *Neue Zeitschrift für Musik*, LXXI (1904); idem, *Hasse und die Brüder G. als Symphoniker* (Leipzig, 1906); E. Schenk, "Zur Bibliographie der Triosonaten von J. G. und C.H. G.," *Zeitschrift für Musikwissenschaft*, XI (1928–29).

Graunke, Kurt, German violinist, conductor, and composer; b. Stettin, Sept. 30, 1915. He studied violin with Gustav Havemann at the Berlin Hochschule für Musik, composition with Adolf Lessle and Hermann Grabner, violin with Hanns Weisse and Hans Dunschede, and conducting with Felix Husadel. During World War II, he studied in Vienna with Wolfgang Schneiderhan and played violin in the radio orch. In Munich in 1945 he founded his own orch., which he conducted for over 40 years and which made many recordings of scores for movies and television; it also gave several concerts each year, playing the world premieres of many works. His compositions are firmly rooted in Germanic modern Romanticism.

WORKS (all 1st perf. in Munich): 8 syms.: No. 1 (May 14, 1969); No. 2 (Sept. 9, 1972); No. 3 (for Strings, Nov. 7, 1975; for Orch., May 12, 1976); No. 4 (Jan. 25, 1978); No. 5 (May 13, 1981); No. 6 (May 12, 1982); No. 7 (May 11, 1983); No. 8 (Sept. 11, 1985); Violin Concerto (Sept. 17, 1959); *Air for Harp and Orch.*; 2 *Symphonic Dances*; *Novelette*; *Perpetuum mobile*; *Valse Anastasia*.

Graupner, (Johann) Christoph, German composer; b. Kirchberg, Saxony, Jan. 13, 1683; d. Darmstadt, May 10, 1760.

He studied music in Kirchberg with the cantor Michael Mylius and the organist Nikolaus Kuster, and later at the Thomasschule in Leipzig with Johann Kuhnau and Johann Schelle; he then went to Hamburg, where he became harpsichordist at the Oper-am-Gänsemarkt (1707–9); during this time he composed 5 operas. In 1709 he was called to Darmstadt as Vice-Kapellmeister to the Landgraf Ernst Ludwig; in 1712 he was appointed Kapellmeister, a post he held until his death. Graupner was a highly industrious composer; he wrote 8 operas, some 1,400 church cantatas, 24 secular cantatas, about 100 syms., 50 concertos, 80 overtures, and many instrumental sonatas and keyboard works. Several of his compositions were publ. during his lifetime, including *8 Partien auf das Clavier . . . erster Theil* (Darmstadt, 1718), the *Monatliche Clavier Früchte . . . meistenteils für Anfänger* (Darmstadt, 1722), and *Vier Partien auf das Clavier, unter der Benennung der Vier Jahreszeiten* (Darmstadt, 1733); he also brought out a *Neu vermehrtes Darmstädtisches Choralbuch* (Darmstadt, 1728). He was proficient as an engraver, and printed several keyboard pieces in his own workshop. His operas include *Dido, Königin von Carthago* (Hamburg, 1707); *Il fido amico, oder Der getreue Freund Hercules und Theseus* (Hamburg, 1708; not extant); *L'amore ammalato: Die Krankende Liebe, oder Antiochus und Stratonica* (Hamburg, 1708); *Bellerophon, oder Das in die preussisch Krone verwandelte Wagenstirn* (Hamburg, Nov. 28, 1708; not extant); *Der Fall des grossen Richters in Israel, Simson, oder Die abgekühlte Liebesrache der Deborah* (Hamburg, 1709); not extant); *Berenice und Lucilla, oder Das tugendhafte Lieben* (Darmstadt, March 4, 1710; not extant); *Telemach* (Darmstadt, Feb. 16, 1711; not extant); *La costanza vince l'inganno* (Darmstadt, 1715). Denkmäler Deutscher Tonkunst, LI/LII (1926), contains 17 of his cantatas; an incomplete edition of his works was ed. by F. Noack (4 vols., Kassel, 1955–57).

BIBL.: W. Kleefeld, "Bach und G.," *Jahrbuch der Musikbibliothek Peters 1897*; W. Nagel, "C. G. als Sinfoniker," *Musikalisches Magazin*, XLIX (Langensalza, 1912); F. Noack, "Bachs und G.s Kompositionen aus Bewerbung um das Thomaskantorat in Leipzig," *Bach-Jahrbuch 1913*; idem, *C. G.s Kirchenmusiken* (Leipzig, 1916); L. Hoffmann-Erbrecht, "J.C. G. als Klavierkomponist," *Archiv für Musikwissenschaft*, X (1953); M. Witte, *Die Instrumentalkonzerte von C. G.* (diss., Univ. of Göttingen, 1963); A. McCredie, "C. G. as Opera Composer," *Miscellanea Musicologica*, I (1966); C. Lawson, "J.C. G.: Bach's Rival for the Thomaskantorat," *Musical Times* (Jan. 1983).

Graupner, (Johann Christian) Gottlieb, German-born American oboist and composer; b. Verden, near Hannover, Oct. 6, 1767; d. Boston, April 16, 1836. He was the son of the oboist Johann Georg Graupner, and became himself an oboist in military bands. In 1788 he was in London, and played in Haydn's orch. in 1791. About 1795, he emigrated to America, settling in Charleston, S.C.; played his Oboe Concerto there on March 21, 1795; early in 1796, he went to Boston; in 1800 he opened a music store; also taught piano, and all orch. instruments, on which he was fairly proficient; publ. works by himself and other composers; he became an American citizen in 1808. In 1810 he organized the Boston Phil. Soc., which was the 1st semiprofessional orch. in Boston; it gave performances of Haydn's syms., Handel's *Messiah* in 1818, and Haydn's *Creation* in 1819; the orch. continued its activity until Nov. 1824. In 1815 he was a co-founder of a musical organization which became the Handel and Haydn Soc. of Boston, and which greatly influenced the development of choral music in New England. In view of these accomplishments, Graupner is referred to by some writers as the "father of American orchestral music." In 1806, he publ. *Rudiments of the Art of Playing the Piano Forte, Containing the Elements of Music* (reprinted 1819, 1825, and 1827). He was married to **Catherine Hillier** (1770–1821), a professional singer; in Boston on Dec. 30, 1799, she sang a Negro ballad; this fact led to erroneous reports that Graupner himself appeared as a blackface minstrel. Typescript copies of a memoir on Graupner, compiled by his granddaughter, Catherine Graupner Stone (1906), are available in the Library of Congress, the N.Y. Public Library, and the Boston Public Library.

Bibl.: O. Sonneck, *Early Concert Life in America* (Leipzig, 1907); J. Howard, *Our American Music* (N.Y., 1931; 4th ed., N.Y., 1965); H. Johnson, *Musical Interludes in Boston* (N.Y., 1943).

Graveure, Louis (real name, **Wilfred Douthitt**), English baritone; b. London, March 18, 1888; d. Los Angeles, April 27, 1965. He studied voice with Clara Novello-Davies; went to the U.S. and sang in the operetta *The Lilac Domino* in N.Y. on Oct. 28, 1914. In 1915 he reappeared in N.Y. as Louis Graveure (after his mother's maiden name) and became a popular concert artist, singing all types of music. On Feb. 5, 1928, he gave a concert in N.Y. as a tenor; from 1931 to 1938 he was in Germany; from 1938 to 1940, in France; from 1940 to 1947, in England. In 1947 he returned to the U.S.; taught in various music schools.

Bibl.: "The Case of a Beardless Baritone," N. Slonimsky, *A Thing or Two about Music* (N.Y., 1948).

Gray, Alan, English organist and composer; b. York, Dec. 23, 1855; d. Cambridge, Sept. 27, 1935. He took degrees in law and music from Trinity College, Cambridge (Mus.D., 1889); was music director of Wellington College (1883–92); conductor of the Cambridge Univ. Musical Soc. (1892–1912); also organist at Trinity College (1892–1930). He wrote 5 cantatas; a *Coronation March*; chamber music; many organ works. He was also an ed. for the Purcell Soc. Vaughan Williams was one of his students.

Gray, Cecil, Scottish writer on music and composer; b. Edinburgh, May 19, 1895; d. Worthing, Sept. 9, 1951. He studied at the Univ. of Edinburgh and with Bantock in Birmingham; was co-ed. (with Philip Heseltine) of the periodical *The Sackbut* from 1920; was music critic for the *National and Athenaeum* (1925–30), the *Daily Telegraph* (1928–33), and the *Manchester Guardian* (1932); wrote the operas (to his own texts) *Deirdre, Temptation of St. Anthony,* and *The Trojan Women*; also other works.

Writings: *A Survey of Contemporary Music* (1924; 2nd ed., 1927); with P. Heseltine, *Carlo Gesualdo, Prince of Venosa; Musician and Murderer* (1926); *The History of Music* (1928); *Sibelius* (1931; 2nd ed., 1934); *Peter Warlock* (1934); *Sibelius: The Symphonies* (1935); *Predicaments, or Music and the Future* (1936); *The 48 Preludes and Fugues of Bach* (1938); *Contingencies and Other Essays* (1947); *Musical Chairs or Between Two Stools* (memoirs, 1948).

Bibl.: R. Gorer, "The Music of C. G.," *Musical Review* (Aug. 1947); H. Davies, "Bernard van Dieren, Philip Heseltine and C. G.: A Significant Affiliation," *Music & Letters* (Jan. 1988).

Gray, Jerry, American bandleader, composer, and arranger; b. Boston, July 3, 1915; d. Dallas, Texas, Aug. 10, 1976. He studied violin with Ondriček in Boston; at the age of 13, was concertmaster of the Boston Junior Sym. Orch.; then became a jazz-band leader. He played in nightclubs and other locales of musical subculture; in 1936 joined the Artie Shaw Orch. as arranger; during World War II was arranger for the fabled Glenn Miller band, which he took over after Miller's death in 1944. He had his own radio show (1946–52); led dance orchs.; also wrote several songs that became popular, among them *String of Pearls*.

Gray, Linda Esther, Scottish soprano; b. Greenock, May 29, 1948. She studied at the Scottish Academy of Music and in London with Eva Turner; won the Kathleen Ferrier and John Christie awards in 1973. She made her debut with the Glyndebourne Touring Opera in 1972 as Mimi; sang with the Glyndebourne Festival in 1974 and with the Scottish Opera in 1975 in the roles of Donna Elvira, Ariadne, Eva, and Amelia. Her 1st role with the English National Opera was Micaela in 1978; she later sang Aida, Tosca, and Isolde there. She also sang Isolde with the Welsh National Opera in 1979 and Sieglinde at Covent Garden. She made her U.S. debut in Dallas as Sieglinde in 1981; then appeared as Beethoven's Leonore with the same company in Mexico.

Graziani, Bonifazio, significant Italian composer; b. probably in Marino, near Rome, 1604 or 1605; d. Rome, June 15, 1664. He was maestro di cappella in Rome at the church of the Gesù and at the Roman Seminary from 1648. His sacred motets are notable.

Works (all publ. in Rome, all with Basso Continuo [Organ]): *Motetti* for 2 to 6 Voices, op. 1 (1650); *Il secondo libro de motetti* for 2 to 6 Voices, op. 2 (1652); *Motetti a voce sola,* op. 3 (1652); *Psalmi vespertini . . . Liber I* for 5 Voices, op. 4 (1652); *Psalmi vespertini* for 5 Voices, op. 5 (1653); *Il secondo libro de motetti a voce sola,* op. 6 (1655); *Motetti* for 2 to 3 and 5 Voices, libro terzo, op. 7 (1657); *Il terzo libro de motetti a voce sola,* op. 8 (1658); *Responsoria hebdomadae sanctae* for 4 Voices, op. 9 (1663); *Il quarto libro de motetti a voce sola,* op. 10 (1665); *Litanie della madonna* for 4 to 5 and 7 to 8 Voices, op. 11 (1665); *Motetti* for 2 to 5 Voices, op. 12 (1673); *Antifone della Beatissima Vergine Maria* for 4 to 6 Voices, op. 13 (1665); *Antifone per diverse festività* for 2 to 6 Voices, op. 14 (1666); *Sacri concerti* for 2 to 5 Voices, op. 15 (1668); *Partitura del quinto libro de motetti a voce sola,* op. 16 (1669); *Psalmi vespertini binis choris,* op. 17 (1670); *Il primo libro delle messe* for 4 to 5 Voices, op. 18 (1671); *Sacrae cantiones* for Voice, *liber sextus,* op. 19 (1672); *Motetti* for 2 to 5 Voices, *libro sesto,* op. 20 (1672); *Hinni vespertini* for 3 to 5 Voices, op. 21 (1673); *Il secondo libro delle messe* for 4 to 5 and 8 Voices, op. 22 (1674); *Motetti* for 2 to 4 Voices, op. 23 (1674); *Motetti* for 2 to 5 Voices, op. 24 (1676); *Musiche sagre* for 1 to 4 Voices, op. 25 (1678); also 2 oratorios, *Adae* and *Filii prodigi.*

Graziani, Francesco, Italian baritone, brother of **Lodovico Graziani;** b. Fermo, April 26, 1828; d. there, June 30, 1901. He studied with Cellini; made his debut in 1851 in Ascoli Piceno; sang in Paris (1853–61) and the U.S. (1854); made many appearances at Covent Garden in London (1855–80); also sang in St. Petersburg, where he created the role of Don Carlo in Verdi's *La forza del destino* (1862).

Graziani, Lodovico, Italian tenor, brother of **Francesco Graziani;** b. Fermo, Nov. 14, 1820; d. there, May 15, 1885. He studied with Cellini; made his debut in Cambiaggio's *Don Procopio* in Bologna in 1845; created the role of Alfredo in Verdi's *La Traviata* (1853); also sang at La Scala in Milan. He was greatly esteemed for his performances in the operas of Verdi.

Greatorex, Thomas, English organist, singer, and conductor; b. North Wingfield, Derby, Oct. 5, 1758; d. Hampton, near London, July 18, 1831. He was the son of an organist; the family moved to Leicester in 1767. He studied with B. Cooke (1772); was befriended by Lord Sandwich, and became music director of his household for a time. He sang at the Concerts of Antient Music in London (from 1776) and was organist at Carlisle Cathedral (1781–84). He then traveled in the Netherlands, Italy, and France. Settling in London, he became a highly popular singing teacher (in 1 week he gave 84 lessons at a guinea each). In 1793 he was appointed conductor of the Concerts of Antient Music, a post he held until his death, never missing a single concert. He assisted in the revival of the Vocal Concerts in 1801; from 1819 he was organist at Westminster Abbey; he conducted festivals throughout England, and was 1 of the founders of the Royal Academy of Music in London (1822). He publ. *A Selection of Tunes* (London, 1829); the collection *Parochial Psalmody* (1825); *12 Glees* (1832); anthems; Psalms; and chants. His son, **Henry Wellington Greatorex** (b. Burton upon Trent, Dec. 24, 1813; d. Charleston, S.C., Sept 10, 1858), was also an organist and composer. He publ. a *Collection of Sacred Music* (1851), which included hymn tunes by his grandfather and father, as well as 37 of his own.

Greef, Arthur de, Belgian pianist and composer; b. Louvain, Oct. 10, 1862; d. Brussels, Aug. 29, 1940. He studied at the Brussels Cons. with L. Brassin (piano) and Gevaert (composition); then traveled as a pianist in Europe; in 1885 he became a prof. of piano at the Brussels Cons., retaining that post until 1930.

WORKS: Opera in Flemish, *De Marketenster* (Louvain, 1879); Sym.; Ballad for Strings; 2 piano concertos; 2 violin sonatas; *4 vieilles chansons flamandes* for Piano; a number of piano études; songs.

BIBL.: F. Rasse, "Notice sur A. d.G.," *Annuaire de l'Académie Royale de Belgique* (1949).

Green, Adolph, American musician, playwright, and lyricist; b. N.Y., Dec. 2, 1915. After graduating from high school, he sang, danced, and acted with The Revuers. With the dramatist Betty Comden, he entered a long-standing and highly successful collaboration; their 1st success came with *On the Town* (1944; music by Leonard Bernstein), which was followed by *Billion Dollar Baby, Two on the Aisle, Bells Are Ringing,* etc. He received Tony awards for his contributions to *Applause* (1970) and *On the 20th Century* (1978).

Green (Greene), Al, black American soul singer and songwriter; b. Forrest City, Ark., April 13, 1946. The family moved to Grand Rapids, Mich., and Al Green sang in local churches with his brothers. He was barely 18 years old when he formed a pop group named The Creations, which scored considerable success. He toured on the "chitlin circuit" in the South, then moved to Memphis and produced his 1st hit, *Tired of Being Alone.* It was followed by another hit, *Let's Stay Together.* He was also successful as a solo soul singer of gospel songs, which eventually led him to found his own church in Memphis, where he became a regular preacher; from 1979 he concentrated his attention on singing religious music.

Green, Elizabeth A(dine) H(erkimer), American string and conducting pedagogue; b. Mobile, Ala., Aug. 21, 1906. She began violin lessons at age 4 with her father, Albert Wingate Green, then studied at Wheaton (Ill.) College (Mus.B., 1924; B.S., 1928); later received instruction in conducting from Nicolai Malko in Chicago (1940–42), and completed violin studies with Ivan Galamian at the Meadowmount School in N.Y. From 1942 to 1954 she taught in the Ann Arbor (Mich.) public schools, then at the Univ. of Michigan, retiring in 1974. She became well known as a teacher of string instruments and of conducting, and appeared as a conductor of various ensembles in the U.S. She publ. the widely consulted textbook *The Modern Conductor* (1961; 4th ed., 1987).

WRITINGS: *Orchestral Bowings and Routines* (1949; 2nd ed., 1957); *The Modern Conductor* (1961; 4th ed., 1987); *Teaching Stringed Instruments in Classes* (1966); with N. Malko, *The Conductor and His Score* (1975; 2nd ed., 1985, as *The Conductor's Score*); *The Dynamic Orchestra: Principles of Orchestral Performance for Instrumentalists, Conductors and Audiences* (1987).

BIBL.: D. Smith, *E.A.H. G.: A Biography* (diss., Univ. of Michigan, 1986).

Green, John (Waldo), American pianist, conductor, arranger, and composer; b. N.Y., Oct. 10, 1908; d. Beverly Hills, Calif., May 15, 1989. He studied economics at Harvard Univ. (B.A., 1928), where he also received instruction in music theory from W.R. Spalding; later studied piano with Ignace Hilsberg, orchestration with Adolf Deutsch, and conducting with Frank Tours. Working as an arranger for Guy Lombardo, he produced his 1st hit song, *Coquette* (1928); while working as accompanist to Gertrude Lawrence, he wrote the popular *Body and Soul* (1930). He became an arranger for Paramount in Hollywood (1930); made recordings with his own dance band and performed on the radio. He settled in Hollywood as a member of the music staff of MGM (1942), serving as head of its music dept. (1949–58). He prepared award-winning adaptations of the original scores for film versions of *Easter Parade* (1948), *An American in Paris* (1951), *West Side Story* (1961), and *Oliver!* (1968); he also wrote the score for the film *Raintree County* (1957). He was associate conductor of the Los Angeles Phil. (1959–61); also appeared as a guest conductor with several of the major U.S. orchs.

Green, Ray (Burns), American composer; b. Cavendish, Mo., Sept. 13, 1909. He began piano study at 14, winning a composition scholarship to the San Francisco Cons., where he studied with Ernest Bloch (1927–33); after further studies with Elkus and Stricklen at the Univ. of Calif. in Berkeley (1933–35), he won a scholarship to Paris to study with Milhaud (composition) and Monteux (conducting). He returned to the U.S. (1937); was active with the WPA and served as director of the Federal Music Project of Northern Calif. (1939–41); then was chief of music for the Veterans Administration in Washington, D.C. (1946–48); subsequently was executive director of the American Music Center in N.Y. (1948–61). He also founded his own music publishing company, American Music Editions (1951). His works are often modal in harmonic settings; rhythmic animation is much in evidence in his pieces based on American rural songs.

WORKS: ORCH.: *Sunday Sing Symphony* for Flute, Clarinet, Bassoon, and Orch. (1939–40); *3 Short Symphonies* (1945–53; 1970; 1974); Concertino for Piano and Orch. (1937); *Prelude and Fugue* (1937); *3 Pieces for a Concert* for Chamber Orch. (1947); *Jig Theme and 3 Changes* for Piano and Strings (1948); Violin Concerto (1952). CHAMBER: Suite for Violin and Piano (1929); Suite for Viola and Piano (1930); *5 Epigrammic Portraits* for String Quartet (1933; rev. 1950–52); Wind Quintet (1933); *Holiday for 4* for Viola, Violin, Bassoon, and Piano (1936; rev. 1939); *Concertante* for Viola or Clarinet, and Piano (1940; also for Viola and Orch., 1946); *Concert Set* for Trumpet, Piano, and Drums (1941); piano music, including a Sonata (1933) and *12 Short Sonatas* (1948–62).

BIBL.: S. Vise, *R. G.: His Life and Stylistic Elements of His Music from 1938–1962* (diss., Univ. of Missouri, 1976).

Greenawald, Sheri (Kay), American soprano; b. Iowa City, Nov. 12, 1947. After completing her vocal studies, she quickly rose to prominence through her appearances with the Santa Fe Opera, Cincinnati Opera, San Francisco Opera, Houston Grand Opera, Washington Opera, and others. In addition to her roles in the standard Italian and French operatic repertoires, she sang in the world premieres of Pasatieri's *Signor Deluso* (1974) and *Washington Square* (1976) and Bernstein's *A Quiet Place* (1983). She was also a soloist with the Boston Sym., Philadelphia Orch., San Francisco Sym., Cleveland Orch., and St. Louis Sym.

Greenberg, Noah, American conductor; b. N.Y., April 9, 1919; d. there, Jan. 9, 1966. He studied music privately; served in the U.S. Merchant Marine (1944–49); organized choruses in N.Y. In 1952 he founded the N.Y. Pro Musica Antiqua, an organization specializing in Renaissance and medieval music, performed in authentic styles and on copies of early instruments; he revived the medieval liturgical music dramas *The Play of Daniel* (1958) and *The Play of Herod* (1963); traveled with his ensemble in Europe in 1960 and 1963. It was primarily through the efforts of this group (later known as the N.Y. Pro Musica) that early music, formerly known only to musicologists, became a viable idiom available to modern audiences. He held a Guggenheim fellowship in 1955 and Ford fellowships in 1960 and 1962.

Greene, Maurice, important English organist and composer; b. London, Aug. 12, 1696; d. there, Dec. 1, 1755. He served as a choirboy in St. Paul's Cathedral; became proficient as an organist; was appointed organist of St. Paul's in 1718. In 1727 he succeeded Croft as organist and composer to the Chapel Royal; in 1730 he was Tudway's successor as prof. of music at Cambridge Univ., receiving the title of Mus.Doc. In 1735 he became Master of the King's Musick. Beginning in 1750, he accumulated and collated a great number of English sacred works; he willed this material to Boyce, who made use of it in his monumental collection, *Cathedral Music.* Greene was one of the most distinguished composers of vocal music in his day, excelling in both sacred and secular works.

WORKS: 3 oratorios: *The Song of Deborah and Barak* (1732); *Jephtha* (1737); *The Force of Truth* (1744); dramatic pastoral, *Florimel, or Love's Revenge* (1734); *The Judgment of Hercules,* masque (1740); *Phoebe,* pastoral opera (1747); a collection of 12 English songs, *The Chaplet* (London, 1738); an album of 25 sonnets for Voice, with Harpsichord and Violin, *Spenser's Amoretti* (London, 1739); he collected *40 Select Anthems in Score* (2 vols., 1743); composed numerous catches and canons, organ voluntaries, harpsichord pieces, etc.

BIBL.: E. Walker, "The Bodleian MSS of M. G.," *Musical Antiquarian* (April–July 1910); E. Janifer, *The English Church Music of M. G. and His Contemporaries: A Study of Traditional and Contemporary Influences* (diss., Univ. of London, 1959); J. Moore, *The Church Music of M. G.* (diss., Univ. of Nottingham, 1961); H. Johnstone, *The Life and Works of M. G. (1696–1755)* (diss., Oxford Univ., 1967).

Greene, (Harry) Plunket, noted Irish bass-baritone; b. Old Connaught House, County Wicklow, June 24, 1865; d. London, Aug. 19, 1936. He studied in Florence with Vannuccini, and in London under J.B. Welsh and A. Blume; made his debut in Handel's *Messiah* at Stepney (Jan. 21, 1888) and soon became a popular concert artist. He made the 1st of several tours of the U.S. in 1893; also appeared in Canada. He was noted for his interpretations of Schumann and Brahms; publ. a valuable instruction book for singers, *Interpretation in Song* (London, 1912); a biography of Stanford (London, 1935); and a vol. of musical reminiscences, *From the Blue Danube to Shannon* (London, 1934).

Greenhouse, Bernard, esteemed American cellist and pedagogue; b. Newark, N.J., Jan. 3, 1916. He studied cello with Felix Salmond at the Juilliard School of Music in N.Y.; subsequently took lessons with Feuermann and Casals. He made his debut in N.Y. in a recital in 1946; from 1955 to 1987 he was a founding member of the Beaux Arts Trio, which gradually acquired a fine reputation in its genre. He was also active as a teacher; taught at the Juilliard School of Music (1951–61), the Manhattan School of Music (1950–82), the Indiana Univ. School of Music (summers 1956–64), the Hartt Cons. in Hartford, Conn. (1956–65), the State Univ. of N.Y. at Stony Brook (1960–85), the New England Cons. of Music in Boston (from 1986), and the State Univ. of N.J. at Rutgers (from 1987); also gave master classes worldwide.

BIBL.: N. Delbanco, *The Beaux Arts Trio: A Portrait* (N.Y. and London, 1985).

Grefinger, Wolfgang, important Austro-German composer; b. between 1470 and 1480; d. after 1515. He studied with Paul Hofhaimer; at the beginning of the 16th century he went to Vienna, where he attended the Univ. (1509) and was ordained, serving as organist at St. Stephen's Cathedral. His historical significance rests upon his Tenorlieder, which are a vital link between the works of Erasmus Lapicida and Arnold von Bruck. He also composed sacred music, being especially admired for his 4-voice settings of hymns by Prudentius, *Cathemerinon: Hoc est Diurnarum rerum opus varium* (Vienna, 1515). He ed. the liturgical hymnbook *Psalterium pataviense antiphonis, responsoriis, hymnisque in notis musicalibus* (Vienna, 1512). His works were ed. by L. Nowak in *Das deutsche Gesellschaftslied in Österreich von 1480–1550* in Denkmäler der Tonkunst in Österreich, LXXII, Jg. XXXVII/2 (1930).

Gregh, Louis, French composer and music publisher; b. Philippeville, Algeria, March 16, 1843; d. St. Mesme, Seine-et-Oise, Jan. 21, 1915. He began his musical career with the production of a light opera, *Un Lycée de jeunes filles* (Paris, 1881), which won a decided success; this was followed by several other operettas, including *Le Présomtif* (1884) and *Le Capitaine Roland* (1895), and ballets. He then turned to publishing; the firm was continued by his son, **Henri Gregh,** who established it as Henri Gregh & Fils (1902); Henri Gregh's son, **André,** succeeded him as director in 1934.

Gregoir, Édouard (Georges Jacques), Belgian pianist, composer, and writer on music, brother of **Jacques (Mathieu Joseph) Gregoir;** b. Turnhout, near Antwerp, Nov. 7, 1822; d. Wyneghem, June 28, 1890. He studied piano, and was a professional accompanist; in 1851 he settled in Antwerp. He

was a prolific composer; wrote over 150 works in all. His Flemish opera, *Willem Beukels,* was produced in Brussels (July 21, 1856); he also wrote incidental music to various patriotic plays: *De Belgen in 1848; La Dernière Nuite du Comte d'Egmont;* etc.; a symphonic oratorio, *Le Déluge* (1849); a historical sym., *Les Croisades* (1846).

WRITINGS: *Essai historique sur la musique et les musiciens dans les Pays-Bas* (1861); *Histoire de l'orgue* (1865; with biographical notes on Belgian and Dutch organists and organ builders); *Galerie biographique des artistes-musiciens belges du XVIIIe et du XIXe siècles* (1862; 2nd ed., 1885); *Notice sur l'origine du célèbre compositeur Louis van Beethoven* (1863); *Les Artistes-Musiciens néerlandais* (1864); *Du chant choral et des festivals en Belgique* (1865); *Notice historique sur les sociétés de musique d'Anvers* (1869); *Recherches historiques concernant les journaux de musique depuis les temps les plus reculés jusqu'à nos jours* (1872); *Notice biographique d'Adrian Willaert; Réflexions sur la regénération de l'ancienne école de musique flamande et sur le théâtre flamand; Les Artistes-Musiciens au XIXe siécle; Réponse à un critique de Paris* (1874); *Documents historiques relatifs à l'art musical et aux artistes-musiciens* (4 vols., 1872–76); *Panthéon musical populaire* (6 vols., 1876–77); *Notice biographique sur F.J. Gossé dit Gossec* (1878); *L'Art musical en Belgique sous les règnes de Léopold I et Léopold II* (1879); *Les Gloires de l'Opéra et la musique à Paris* (4 vols., 1880–83; vol. I embraces the period 1392–1750); *A.-E.-M. Grétry* (1883); *Souvenirs artistiques* (3 vols., 1888–89).

Gregoir, Jacques (Mathieu Joseph), Belgian pianist and composer, brother of **Édouard (Georges Jacques) Gregoir;** b. Antwerp, Jan. 19, 1817; d. Brussels, Oct. 29, 1876. He studied with Henri Herz in Paris and with Rummel in Biebrich. He gave a number of successful piano recitals in Belgium, Germany, and Switzerland; wrote salon pieces for piano and several practical methods of piano playing; publ. duets for violin and piano in collaboration with Vieuxtemps; he also wrote an opera, *Le Gondolier de Venise* (1848).

Gregor, Bohumil, Czech conductor; b. Prague, July 14, 1926. He studied at the Prague Cons.; then conducted in Prague (1947–49), Brno (1949–51), and Ostrava (1958–62). Returning to Prague in 1963, he conducted at the National Theater there. He was also a regular guest conductor at the Royal Opera in Stockholm and at the Hamburg State Opera, where he frequently performed Czech music. He made his U.S. debut with the San Francisco Opera conducting *Jenůfa* in 1969.

Gregor, Čestmír, Czech composer; b. Brno, May 14, 1926. He studied composition with Kvapil at the Brno Cons.; from 1959 until 1972, was music director of Ostrava Radio.

WORKS: Ballet, *Závrat* (Vertigo; 1963; Ostrava, May 9, 1964; ballet version of the *Choreographic Symphony*); *Joyous Overture* (1951); *No One Is Alone,* rhapsody for Piano and Orch. (1955); *Prosím o slovo* (May I Speak?), overture (1956); *Tragic Suite* for Chamber Orch. (1957); *Concerto semplice* for Piano and Orch. (1958); *Polyfonietta* for Orch. (1961); *The Children of Daidalos,* symphonic poem (1961); *Choreographic Symphony* (1963); *Prague Walker,* 2 nocturnes for 16 Strings (1963); Violin Concerto (1965); *Symfonie mého města* (Symphony of My Town; 1970); Sinfonietta (1973); Cello Concerto, subtitled *Complimento alla musica di ogni giorno* (1974); *Overture giocosa* (1975); *Sinfonia notturna di Praga* (1976); *Concerto da camera* for Clarinet and Strings (1977); *Concerto giocondo* for Piano and Orch. (1979); Trio for Flute, Viola, and Bass Clarinet (1959); String Quartet (1965); *Experiment* for Piano (1946); *Sonata brevis* for Piano (1946); *3 movimenti* for Piano (1966); *Sonata in 3 tempi* for Piano (1966).

Gregor, Christian Friedrich, organist, music director, composer, and hymnologist; b. Dirsdorf, Silesia, Jan. 1, 1723; d. Zeist, the Netherlands, Nov. 6, 1801. He was the most important musician of the international Moravian Church (Unitas Fratrum) of the 18th century. Joining the Moravian Brethren in Herrnhut, Saxony, in 1742, he soon assumed leading positions in its management: was financial agent of Zinzendorf, member of the Unity Elders Conference (1764–1801), and bishop (1789–1801). He made numerous business trips to Germany, the Netherlands, England, Russia, and North America (Pennsylvania, 1770–72); while in Pennsylvania, he gave instruction in composition to Johann Friedrich Peter. During his stay at Herrnhut as organist, he compiled the 1st hymnal publ. by the Moravians (*Choral-Buch, enthaltend alle zu dem Gesangbuche der Evangelischen Brüder-Gemeinen vom Jahre 1778 gehörige Melodien*; Leipzig, 1784), and arranged the musical liturgies. He wrote 308 hymns (*Gesangbuch zum Gebrauch der evangelischen Brüder-Gemeinen*; Barby, 1778 et seq.), about 100 chorale tunes, and approximately 200 anthems and arias. The last are preserved in MS in the Moravian Church Archives at Bethlehem, Pa., and Winston-Salem, N.C. Several of his anthems were republ. frequently in 19th-century American tune books.

BIBL.: *Historische Nachricht vom Brüder-Gesangbuche des Jahres 1778, und von dessen Lieder-Verfassern* (Gnadau, 1835); J. and K. Hamilton, *History of the Moravian Church* (Bethlehem, Pa., 1967).

Gregory I, "the Great"; b. Rome, c.540; d. there, March 12, 604. He was Pope from 590 to 604; was celebrated in music history as the reputed reformer of the musical ritual of the Roman Catholic Church. It is traditionally believed that by his order, and under his supervision, a collection was made in 599 of the music employed in the different churches; that various offertories, antiphons, responses, etc., were revised and regularly and suitably distributed over the entire year in an arrangement which came to be known as Gregorian chant. While for centuries the sole credit for the codification, which certainly took place, had been ascribed to Gregory, investigations by such scholars as Gevaert, Riemann, P. Wagner, Frere, Houdard, Gastoué, Mocquereau, and others have demonstrated that some of Gregory's predecessors had begun this reform and even fixed the order of certain portions of the liturgy, and that the work of reform was definitely completed under some of his immediate successors. Evidence in favor of Gregory's leading part in the reform is marshaled in E. Wyatt's *Saint Gregory and the Gregorian Music* (1904); evidence against his participation is given in Paul Henry Lang's *Music in Western Civilization* (N.Y., 1941). See also G. Morin, *Les Véritables Origines du Chant grégorien* (Maredsous, 1890; 2nd ed., 1904); W. Brambach, *Gregorianisch* (Leipzig, 1895); F. Duddin, *Gregory the Great* (2 vols., London, 1905); F. Tarducci, *Storia di S. Gregorius e del suo tempo* (Rome, 1909); P. Vivell, *Der gregorianische Gesang: Eine Studie über die Echtheit der Tradition* (Graz, 1904); J. Deshusses, *Le Sacramentaire grégorien* (Fribourg, 1971).

Gregson, Edward, English conductor, teacher, and composer; b. Sunderland, July 23, 1945. He was a pupil in composition of Alan Bush at the Royal Academy of Music in London (1963–67), later becoming principal lecturer in music at the Univ. of London Goldsmiths' College (from 1976) and prof. of composition at the Royal Academy of Music (from 1986). As a conductor, he was an advocate of contemporary scores.

WORKS: ORCH.: *Music for Chamber Orchestra* (1968); Concerto for Horn and Brass Band (1971; also for Horn and Orch.); Concerto for Tuba and Brass Band (Manchester, April 24, 1976); *Flourish* (1978; rev. 1986); Trombone Concerto (London, July 25, 1979); Trumpet Concerto (London, April 20, 1983); *Contrasts* (1st perf. as *Greenwich Dances*, London, May 7, 1983). **BRASS BAND:** *Essay* (1970); Concerto Grosso (1973); *Connotations* (1976); *Dances and Arias* (1984); *Occasion* (1986). **CHAMBER:** Oboe Sonata (1965); *Divertimento* for Trombone and Piano (1967); *Prelude and Capriccio* for Trumpet and Piano (1972). **VOCAL:** *In the Beginning* for Chorus and Piano (1966; rev. 1981); *Missa Brevis Pacem* for Baritone, Treble Voices, and Large Symphonic Wind Ensemble (1988).

Greindl, Josef, German bass; b. Munich, Dec. 23, 1912. He studied with Paul Bender and Anna Bahr-Mildenburg in Munich; made his debut in Krefeld (1936); then sang in Düssel-

dorf, at the Berlin State Opera, the Berlin City Opera, and the Vienna State Opera, and in Bayreuth and Salzburg. He made his American debut as Heinrich in *Lohengrin* at the Metropolitan Opera in N.Y., on Nov. 15, 1952. In 1961 he became a prof. at the Hochschule für Musik in Saarbrücken, and in 1973 at the Vienna Hochschule für Musik. He was particularly renowned for his excellent renditions of the heroic bass roles in Wagner's operas.

Greissle, Felix, Austrian-American music editor and scholar; b. Vienna, Nov. 15, 1894; d. Manhasset, N.Y., April 26, 1982. He studied with Guido Adler at the Univ. of Vienna and privately with Schoenberg and Berg; from 1925 to 1937 he conducted the cantata society of the Vienna State Opera. After the Anschluss in 1938 he went to the U.S. and worked as an ed. and arranger with various publishers in N.Y. In 1925 he contributed an exposition of Schoenberg's method of composition with 12 tones to the Austrian periodical *Anbruch*.

Greiter, Matthaeus or **Matthias,** German poet and composer; b. Aichach, Bavaria, c.1490; d. Strasbourg, Dec. 20, 1550. He wrote the texts and melodies of Psalm-Lieder for Lutheran services, and settings, for 4 voices, of German songs. He also wrote a tract, *Elementale musicum inventuti* (Strasbourg, 1544). A modern ed. of his works was publ. by H.-C. Müller, *Matthaeus Greiter: Sämtliche Weltliche Lieder,* in *Das Chorwerk,* LXXXVII (1962).

BIBL.: T. Gérold, *Les Plus Anciennes Mélodies de l'église protestante de Strasbourg et leurs auteurs* (Paris, 1928); E. Lowinsky, "Matthaeus G.'s Fortuna; An Experiment in Chromaticism and in Musical Iconography," *Musical Quarterly* (Oct. 1956 and Jan. 1957).

Grell, (August) Eduard, German organist, conductor, and composer; b. Berlin, Nov. 6, 1800; d. Steglitz, near Berlin, Aug. 10, 1886. He studied organ with his father, piano with J.C. Kaufmann, and theory with Zelter; later studied organ with M. Fischer in Erfurt; at the age of 17, he became a member of the Singakademie and was connected with it for 59 years, until his death; he was director from 1853 to 1876. Grell held the view that only vocal music was true art; consequently, he wrote almost exclusively for voice. His works include a *Missa solemnis* (in 16 parts a cappella); an oratorio, *Die Israelitin in der Wüste;* and other church music. H. Bellermann ed. Grell's essays, *Aufsätze und Gutachten* (Berlin, 1887).

BIBL.: H. Bellermann, *A.E. G.* (Berlin, 1899).

Grešák, Jozef, Slovak composer; b. Bardejov, Dec. 30, 1907. He had training in piano and organ, but was largely autodidact in composition; after his youthful opera *Prichod Slovákov* (The Arrival of the Slovaks; 1925), he had a hiatus in his work as a composer, and did not resume composition until much later, with a ballet, *Radúz and Mahuliena* (1954–55), and an interesting ethnic work, *The Emigrant Songs* for Soloists, Male Chorus, and Orch. (1961). There followed a Piano Concerto (1963); *Concertino-Pastorale* for Oboe, English Horn, Horn, and Orch. (1965); *Zemplin Variations* for Soloists, Chorus, and Orch. (1965); *Morceau I* for Violin and Orch. (1965); *Morceau II* for Violin and Piano (1966); *Rotors I* for Piano (1966); *Rotors II* for Orch. (1969); *Hexody* for Clarinet and Piano (1967); *Workers' Songs* for Soloist, Chorus, and Orch. (1971); *Amoebae,* overture (1971); an opera, *With Rosary* (1970–73); *Zuzanka Hraškovie,* monodrama for Soprano, Organ, and Orch. (1973; Bratislava, Jan. 15, 1975); and *Concertant Symfonietta* for Orch. (1975; Košice, May 5, 1976).

Gresnick, Antoine-Frédéric, Belgian composer; b. Liège (baptized), March 2, 1755; d. Paris, Oct. 16, 1799. He was a chorister at the St. Lambert Church in Liège, and studied in Naples under Sala. He made several trips to London, where he produced his operas *Demetrio, Alessandro nell'Indie, Donna di Cattiva Umore,* and *Alceste* with considerable success. He was in Lyons from 1789 to 1793; his opera *L'Amour exilé de Cythère* was produced there in 1793. He returned to Paris in 1794, and had varying success; he died there in poverty.

BIBL.: P. Mercier, *A.-F. G., compositeur liégeois* (Louvain, 1977).

Gretchaninoff, Alexander (Tikhonovich), Russian-born American composer; b. Moscow, Oct. 25, 1864; d. N.Y., Jan. 3, 1956. He studied at the Moscow Cons. (1881–91) with Safonov (piano) and Arensky (composition); then entered the St. Petersburg Cons. as a pupil of Rimsky-Korsakov (1891–1903); was a prof. of composition at the Moscow Inst. until 1922; then lived in Paris; visited the U.S., where he appeared with considerable success as guest conductor of his own works (1929–31); went to the U.S. again in 1939, settling in N.Y. He became an American citizen on July 25, 1946. He continued to compose until the end of his long life. A concert of his works was presented on his 90th birthday at Town Hall in N.Y. (Oct. 25, 1954) in the presence of the composer. His music is rooted in the Russian national tradition; influences of both Tchaikovsky and Rimsky-Korsakov are in evidence in his early works; toward 1910 he attempted to inject some impressionistic elements into his vocal compositions, but without signal success. His masterly sacred works are of historical importance, for he introduced a reform into Russian church singing by using nationally colored melodic patterns; in several of his masses he employed instrumental accompaniment contrary to the prescriptions of the Russian Orthodox faith, a circumstance that precluded the use of these works in Russian churches. His *Missa oecumenica* represents a further expansion toward ecclesiastical universality; in this work he makes use of elements pertaining to other religious music, including non-Christian. His instrumental works are competently written, but show less originality than his vocal music. His early *Lullaby* (1887) and the song *Over the Steppes* still retain their popularity, and have been publ. in numerous arrangements. He publ. a book of reminiscences, *My Life* (Paris, in Russian, 1934; in Eng., with additions and introduction by N. Slonimsky, N.Y., 1952; contains a complete catalogue of works).

Works: operas: *Dobrinya Nikititch* (Moscow, Oct. 27, 1903); *Sister Beatrice* (Moscow, Oct. 25, 1912; suppressed after 3 perfs. as being irreverent); *The Dream of a Little Christmas Tree,* children's opera (1911); *The Castle Mouse,* children's opera (1921); *The Cat, the Fox, and the Rooster,* children's opera (1919); *Marriage,* comic opera after Gogol (1945–46; Berkshire Music Festival, Aug. 1, 1948); *Idylle forestière,* ballet divertissement for Orch. (N.Y., 1925); incidental music to Ostrovsky's *Snegoruchka* (Moscow, Nov. 6, 1900), A. Tolstoy's *Tsar Feodor* (Moscow, Oct. 26, 1898), and *Death of Ivan the Terrible* (1899). **orch.:** Concert Overture in D minor (1892; St. Petersburg, March 1893); *Elegy in Memory of Tchaikovsky* (1893; St. Petersburg, Dec. 31, 1898, Rimsky-Korsakov conducting); 5 syms: No. 1 (1893; St. Petersburg, Jan. 26, 1895); No. 2 (1909; Moscow, March 14, 1909); No. 3 (1920–23; Kiev, May 29, 1924); No. 4 (1923–24; N.Y., April 9, 1942); No. 5 (1936; Philadelphia, April 5, 1939); *Poème élégiaque* (Boston, March 29, 1946); *Festival Overture* (Indianapolis, Nov. 15, 1946); *Poème lyrique* (1948). **vocal:** *Liturgy of St. John Chrysostom* (Moscow, Oct. 19, 1898); *Laudate Deum* (Moscow, Nov. 24, 1915); *Liturgia domestica* (Moscow, March 30, 1918); *Missa oecumenica* for Soli, Chorus, and Orch. (Boston, Feb. 25, 1944); 84 choruses; 14 vocal quartets; 8 duets; 258 songs (some with Orch.). **chamber:** 4 string quartets; 2 trios; Violin Sonata; Cello Sonata; 2 clarinet sonatas; 2 *Miniatures* for Saxophone and Piano. **piano:** 2 sonatas (2nd in 1944); *Petits tableaux musicaux* (1947); etc. After the Revolution, Gretchaninov wrote a new Russian national anthem, *Hymn of Free Russia* (sung in N.Y. at a concert for the benefit of Siberian exiles, May 22, 1917), but it was never adopted by any political Russian faction.

Bibl.: J. Yasser, "G.'s 'Heterodox' Compositions," *Musical Quarterly* (July 1942).

Grétry, André-Ernest-Modeste, greatly significant French composer; b. Liège, Feb. 8, 1741; d. Montmorency, near Paris, Sept. 24, 1813. He was a choirboy and 2nd violinist at the collegiate church of St. Denis in Liège (1750–60), where his father served as violinist; he subsequently studied voice with François Leclerc, thoroughbass with H.F. Renkin, and compo-

sition with Henri Moreau. About 1754 an Italian opera company gave a season in Liège, and young Grétry thus received his 1st impulse toward dramatic music. His early works were instrumental; his 1st syms. were performed at the home of his patron, Canon Simon de Harlez; the latter helped him to obtain a scholarship to the Collège de Liège in Rome, where he studied harmony with G.B. Casali (1761–65). While in Rome, he composed mainly sacred music; however, he did write 2 intermezzos entitled *La Vendemmiatrice* for Carnival 1765. He was in Geneva in 1766 as a music teacher; there he met Voltaire, who advised him to go to Paris; before his departure, he produced the opéra comique *Isabelle et Gertrude* (Dec. 1766), to a libretto by Favart, after Voltaire. He arrived in Paris in the autumn of 1767; he sought the patronage of aristocrats and diplomats; the Swedish ambassador, the Count de Creutz, gave him the 1st encouragement by obtaining for him Marmontel's comedy *Le Huron;* it was performed with Grétry's music at the Comédie-Italienne (Aug. 20, 1768). From then on, he produced operas one after another, without interruption, even during the years of the French Revolution.

The merit of Grétry's operas lies in their melodies and dramatic expression. He was not deeply versed in the science of music; yet despite this lack of craftsmanship, he achieved fine effects of vocal and instrumental writing. His operas suffered temporary eclipse when Méhul and Cherubini entered the field, but public interest was revived by the magnificent tenor Elleviou in 1801. The changes in operatic music during the next 30 years caused the neglect of his works. Nevertheless, Grétry—the "Molière of music," as he was called—founded the school of French opéra comique, of which Boieldieu, Auber, and Adam were worthy successors. He was greatly honored; he was elected a member of many artistic and learned institutions in France and abroad; the Prince-Bishop of Liège made him a privy councillor in 1784; a street in Paris was named for him in 1785; he was admitted to the Institut de France in 1795, as one of the 1st 3 chosen to represent the dept. of musical composition; he was also appointed inspector of the Paris Cons. in 1795, but resigned after just a few months; Napoleon made him a Chevalier of the Legion of Honor in 1802, and granted him a pension of 4,000 francs in compensation for losses during the Revolution. His daughter, **Lucille** (real name, **Angélique-Dorothée-Lucie;** b. Paris, July 15, 1772; d. there, Aug. 25, 1790), was a gifted musician; at the age of 13, with some assistance from her father, she composed an opera, *Le Mariage d'Antonio,* which was produced at the Opéra-Comique on July 29, 1786; her 2nd opera, *Toinette et Louis,* was produced on March 23, 1787.

Works: stage (all 1st perf. in Paris unless otherwise given): **opéras comiques:** *Isabelle et Gertrude, ou Les Sylphes supposés* (Geneva, Dec. 1766); *Le Huron* (Comédie-Italienne, Aug. 20, 1768); *Lucile* (Comédie-Italienne, Jan. 5, 1769); *Le Tableau parlant* (Comédie-Italienne, Sept. 20, 1769); *Silvain* (Comédie-Italienne, Feb. 19, 1770); *Les Deux Avares* (Fontainebleau, Oct. 27, 1770); *L'Amitié à l'épreuve* (Fontainebleau, Nov. 13, 1770); *L'Ami de maison* (Fontainebleau, Oct. 26, 1771); *Zémire et Azor* (Fontainebleau, Nov. 9, 1771); *Le Magnifique* (Comédie-Italienne, March 4, 1773); *La Rosière de Salency* (Fontainebleau, Oct. 23, 1773); *La Fausse Magie* (Comédie-Italienne, Feb. 1, 1775); *Matroco* (Nov. 3, 1777); *Le Jugement de Midas* (March 28, 1778); *Les Fausses Apparences, ou L'Amant jaloux* (Versailles, Nov. 20, 1778); *Les Événements imprévus* (Versailles, Nov. 11, 1779); *Aucassin et Nicolette, ou Les Mœurs du bon vieux temps* (Versailles, Dec. 30, 1779); *Théodore et Paulin* (Versailles, March 5, 1784); *Richard Cœur-de-lion* (Comédie-Italienne, Oct. 21, 1784); *Les Méprises par ressemblance* (Fontainebleau, Nov. 7, 1786); *Le Comte d'Albert* (Fontainebleau, Nov. 13, 1786); *Le Prisonnier anglais* (Comédie-Italienne, Dec. 26, 1787); *Le Rival confident* (Comédie-Italienne, June 26, 1788); *Raoul Barbe-bleue* (Comédie-Italienne, March 2, 1789); *Pierre le Grand* (Comédie-Italienne, Jan. 13, 1790); *Guillaume Tell* (Comédie-Italienne, April 9, 1791); *Cécile et Ermance, ou Les Deux Couvents* (Comédie-Italienne, Jan. 16, 1792); *Basile, ou À trompeur, trompeur et demi* (Comédie-Italienne, Oct. 17, 1792); *Le Congrès des rois*

(Opéra-Comique; Feb. 26, 1794; in collaboration with others); *Joseph Barra* (Opéra-Comique, June 5, 1794); *Callias, ou Nature et patrie* (Opéra-Comique, Sept. 19, 1794); *Lisbeth* (Opéra-Comique, Jan. 10, 1797); *Le Barbier du village, ou Le Revenant* (Théâtre Feydeau, May 6, 1797); *Elisca, ou L'Amour maternel* (Opéra-Comique, Jan. 1, 1799). OTHER STAGE WORKS: *La Vendemmiatrice*, 2 intermezzos (Rome, Carnival 1765); *Les Mariages samnites*, opéra (Jan. 1768?; rev. version, Comédie-Italienne, June 12, 1776); *Céphale et Procris, ou L'Amour conjugal*, opéra-ballet (Versailles, Dec. 30, 1773); *Amour pour amour*, 3 divertissements (Versailles, March 10, 1777); *Les Trois Âges de l'opéra*, prologue (Opéra, April 27, 1778); *Andromaque*, opéra (June 6, 1780); *Emilie, ou La Belle Esclave*, opéra-ballet (Opéra, Feb. 22, 1781); *L'Embarras des richesses*, opéra (Opéra, Nov. 26, 1782); *Thalie au nouveau théâtre*, prologue (Comédie-Italienne, April 28, 1783); *La Caravane du Caire*, opéra-ballet (Fontainebleau, Oct. 30, 1783); *Panurge dans l'île des lanternes*, opéra (Opéra, Jan. 25, 1785); *Amphitryon*, opéra (Versailles, March 15, 1786); *Aspasie*, opéra (Opéra, March 17, 1789); *Denys le tyran, maître d'école à Corinthe*, opéra (Opéra, Aug. 23, 1794); *La Fête de la raison*, later called *La Rosière républicaine, ou La Fête de la vertu*, opéra (Opéra, Sept. 2, 1794); *Anacréon chez Polycrate*, opéra (Opéra, Jan. 17, 1797); *Le Casque et les colombes*, opéra-ballet (Opéra, Nov. 7, 1801); *Le Ménage*, later called *Delphis et Mopsa*, opéra (Opéra, Feb. 15, 1803). Several other stage works listed by Grétry were either never performed or were left unfinished. He also composed a number of vocal romances, some sacred music, Revolutionary songs, and several instrumental works. F.A. Gevaert, E. Fétis, A. Wotquenne, and others ed. a *Collection complète des œuvres* (Leipzig, 1884–1936).

BIBL.: Comte de Livry, *Recueil de lettres écrites à G., ou à son sujet* (Paris, 1809); A.J. Grétry, *G. en famille . . . précédées de son oraison funèbre par M. Bouilly* (Paris, 1814); F. Van Hulst, *G.* (Liège, 1842); L. de Saegher, *Notice biographique sur A. G.* (Brussels, 1869); E. Gregoir, *G., célèbre compositeur belge* (Brussels, 1883); J. Rongé and F. Delhasse, *G.* (Brussels, 1883); C. Gheude, *G.* (Liège, 1906); H. de Curzon, *G.* (Paris, 1907); H. Fierens-Gevaert, *Maison G.: Catalogue illustré* (Liège, 1913; supplement, 1930); E. Closson, *A.-M. G.* (Turnhout and Brussels, 1920); P. Long des Clavières, *La Jeunesse de G. et ses débuts à Paris* (Besançon, 1921); H. Wichmann, *G. und das musikalische Theater in Frankreich* (Halle, 1929); J. Bruyr, *G.* (Paris, 1931); J. Sauvenier, *A. G.* (Brussels, 1934); M. Degey, *A.-M. G.* (Brussels, 1939); S. Clercx, *G., 1741–1813* (Brussels, 1944); G. de Froidcourt, *G., Rouget de Lisle et la Marseillaise* (Liège, 1945); idem ed., *La Correspondance générale de G.* (Brussels, 1962); R. Jobe, *The Operas of A.-E.-M. G.* (diss., Univ. of Michigan, 1965); D. Charlton, *G. and the Growth of Opéra Comique* (Cambridge, 1986).

Grevillius, Nils, Swedish conductor; b. Stockholm, March 7, 1893; d. Mariefred, Aug. 15, 1970. He studied at the Stockholm Cons. (1905–11), receiving 1st prize for violin and the Prix Marteau; from 1911 to 1914 was concertmaster of the Royal Theater orch.; conducted the Swedish ballet season in Paris in 1922–23; then returned to Stockholm to conduct the Radio Orch. (1927–39); also served as court music director (1931–53).

Grey, Madeleine, French soprano; b. Villaines-la-Juhel, Mayenne, June 11, 1896. She made her debut in Paris in 1919 in the 1st performance of Fauré's *Mirages*; thereafter she was identified with modern French music; was chosen to present French art songs at 3 international festivals (Venice, 1930; Siena, 1932; Florence, 1934); also toured South America. She retired in 1952.

Grider, Rufus, American Moravian musician and historian; b. Bethlehem, Pa., 1817; date and place of death unknown (sometime after 1873 he wandered away from home and was never heard from again). Raised in the exceedingly rich musical culture of the American Moravians, Grider was a flutist in the Bethlehem orch. and a leading tenor; he was also a poet, artist, and antiquarian. His claim to remembrance stems from his unique and detailed portrayal of Moravian musical life in *Historical Notes on Music in Bethlehem, Pennyslvania, from 1741 to 1871* (Bethlehem, 1873; reprint, 1957).

Griebling-Long, Karen Jean, American composer and violist; b. Akron, Ohio, Dec. 31, 1957. She studied at the Eastman School of Music in Rochester, N.Y. (B.M., 1980), the Univ. of Houston (M.M., 1982), and the Univ. of Texas in Austin (D.M.A., 1986). She was violist in the Houston Ballet Orch. (1980–82), the Texas Chamber Orch. (1980–82), and the Corpus Christi Sym. Orch. (1985–86). Her works include an opera, *The House of Bernarda Alba* (1986); a ballet, *Johnny Appleseed* (1983); 4 string quartets (1970–73); Trio for 2 Violins and Viola (1973); Trio for Flute, Clarinet, and Bassoon (1976); Viola Sonata (1976); songs.

Grieg, Edvard (Hagerup), celebrated Norwegian composer; b. Bergen, June 15, 1843; d. there, Sept. 4, 1907. The original form of the name was **Greig.** His great-grandfather, Alexander Greig, of Scotland, emigrated to Norway about 1765, and changed his name to Grieg. Edvard Grieg received his 1st instruction in music from his mother, an amateur pianist. At the suggestion of the Norwegian violinist Ole Bull, young Grieg was sent to the Leipzig Cons. (1858), where he studied piano with Plaidy and Wenzel, and later with Moscheles; and theory with E.F. Richter, Robert Papperitz, Moritz Hauptmann, and Reinecke. He became immersed in the atmosphere of German Romanticism, with the esthetic legacy of Mendelssohn and Schumann; Grieg's early works are permeated with lyric moods related to these influences. In 1863 he went to Copenhagen, where he took a brief course of study with Niels Gade. In Copenhagen, he also met the young Norwegian composer Rikard Nordraak, with whom he organized the Euterpe Soc. for the promotion of national Scandinavian music, in opposition to the German influences dominating Scandinavian music. The premature death of Nordraak at the age of 23 (1866) left Grieg alone to carry on the project. After traveling in Italy, he returned to Norway, where he opened a Norwegian Academy of Music (1867), and gave concerts of Norwegian music; he was also engaged as conductor of the Harmonic Soc. in Christiania. In 1867 he married his cousin, the singer **Nina Hagerup.** At that time he had already composed his 2 violin sonatas and the 1st set of his *Lyric Pieces* for Piano, which used Norwegian motifs. On April 3, 1869, Grieg played the solo part in the world premiere of his Piano Concerto, which took place in Copenhagen. Thus, at the age of 25, he established himself as a major composer of his time. In 1874–75 he wrote incidental music to Ibsen's *Peer Gynt;* the 2 orch. suites arranged from this music became extremely popular. The Norwegian government granted him an annuity of 1,600 crowns, which enabled him to devote most of his time to composition. Performances of his works were given in Germany with increasing frequency; soon his fame spread all over Europe. On May 3, 1888, he gave a concert of his works in London; he also prepared recitals of his songs with his wife. He revisited England frequently; received the honorary degree of Mus.Doc. from Cambridge (1894) and Oxford (1906). Other honors were membership in the Swedish Academy (1872), the French Academy (1890), etc. Despite his successes, Grieg was of a retiring disposition, and spent most of his later years in his house at Troldhaugen, near Bergen, avoiding visitors and shunning public acclaim. However, he continued to compose at a steady rate. His death, of heart disease, was mourned by all Norway; he was given a state funeral and his remains were cremated, at his own request, and sealed in the side of a cliff projecting over the fjord at Troldhaugen.

Grieg's importance as a composer lies in the strongly pronounced nationalism of his music; without resorting to literal quotation from Norwegian folk songs, he succeeded in re-creating their melodic and rhythmic flavor. In his harmony, he remained well within the bounds of tradition; the lyric expressiveness of his best works and the contagious rhythm of his dancelike pieces imparted a charm and individuality which contributed to the lasting success of his art. His unassuming personality made friends for him among his colleagues; he was admired by Brahms and Tchaikovsky. The combination of lyricism and nationalism in Grieg's music led some critics to describe him as "the Chopin of the North." He excelled in miniatures, in which the perfection of form and the clarity of the musical line are remarkable; the unifying purpose of Grieg's entire creative life is exemplified by his lyric pieces for piano. He composed 10 sets of these pieces in 34 years, between 1867 and 1901. His songs are distinguished by the same blend of Romantic and characteristically national inflections. In orch. composition, Grieg limited himself almost exclusively to symphonic suites, and arrangements of his piano pieces; in chamber music, his 3 violin sonatas, a Cello Sonata, and a String Quartet are examples of fine instrumental writing.

WORKS: STAGE: Incidental music to Bjørnson's *Sigurd Jørsalfar* for Voice, Men's Chorus, and Orch., op. 22 (Christiania, April 10, 1872), and to Ibsen's *Peer Gynt* for Solo Voices, Chorus, and Orch., op. 23 (1874–75; Christiania, Feb. 24, 1876; rev. 1885 and 1891–92); *Szenen aus Olav Trygvason*, op. 50 (1873; rev. and orchestrated 1889).

ORCH.: Sym. in C minor (1864); *Im Herbst*, overture, op. 11 (1866; rev. and orchestrated 1887; orig. for Piano, 4-hands); *Trauermarsch zum Andenken an Richard Nordraak* for Military Band (1866; rev. 1878; orig. for Piano, 2-hands); Piano Concerto in A minor, op. 16 (1868; Copenhagen, April 3, 1869; rev. 1906–7); *Zwei nordische Weisen* for String Orch., op. 63 (1869; orchestrated 1895; 1, *Im Volkston* [from the piano piece, op. 17, no. 22]; 2, *Kuhreigen* [from the piano piece, op. 17, no. 18]); *Drei Orchesterstücke aus Sigurd Jørsalfar*, op. 56 (1872; rev. 1892); *Peer Gynt Suite* No. 1, op. 46 (1874–75; rev. 1888); *Peer Gynt Suite* No. 2, op. 55 (1874–75; rev. 1891 and 1892); *Zwei elegische Melodier* for String Orch., op. 34 (1881; 1, *Herzwunden* [from the song, op. 33, no. 3]; 2, *Letzter Frühling* [from the song, op. 33, no. 2]); Piano Concerto in B minor (1882–83; unfinished); *Aus Holbergs Zeit*, suite for String Orch., op. 40 (1884; orchestrated 1885; orig. for Piano, 2-hands); *Altnorwegische Romanze mit Variationen*, op. 51 (1891; orchestrated 1900; orig. for 2 Pianos); *Zwei Melodien* for String Orch., op. 53 (1891; 1, *Norwegisch* [from the song, op. 33, no. 12]; 2, *Erstes Begegnen* [from the song, op. 21, no. 1]); *Lyrische Suite*, op. 54 (1891; orchestrated 1904; based on the piano pieces, op. 54, nos. 1, 2, 4, and 3); (4) *Symphonische Tänze*, op. 64 (1896–97; also for Piano, 4-hands); *Zwei lyrische Stücke* (1898; orig. for Piano, 2-hands, op. 68, nos. 4 and 5).

VOICE AND ORCH.: Cantata for the unveiling of the Christie monument in Bergen, for Men's Voices and Military Band (1868); *Foran sydens kloster* (At a Southern Convent's Gate) for Soprano, Alto, Women's Voices, and Orch., op. 20 (1871); *Bergliot*, melodrama for Declamation and Orch., op. 42 (1871; orchestrated 1885); *Landkjending* (Land-sighting) for Baritone, Men's Chorus, Orch., and Organ ad libitum, op. 31 (1872; rev. 1881); *Den bergtekne* (The Mountain Thrall) for Baritone, 2 Horns, and Strings, op. 32 (1877–78); (6) Lieder for Voice and Orch. (1874–95).

CHORAL: For men's voices unless otherwise given: *Børneskytten* (The Bear Hunt; 1867); *Aftenstemning* (Evening Mood; 1867); *Valgsang; Hvad siger du dog om dig* (Election Song: What Are They Saying about You; 1868); *Den norske sjømand* (The Norwegian Sailor; 1868–70); *Ved Welhavens baare* (At Welhaven's Bier; 1873); *Opsang til frihedsfolket i Norden* (Ballad of the Scandinavian Freedom Lovers; 1874); *Ved Halfdan Kjerulfs mindestøtte* (At Halfdan Kjerulf's Monument), cantata for Tenor and Men's Voices (1874); *Album for mandssang*, arrangements of Norwegian folk songs, op. 30 (1877–78); *Min dejligste tanke* (My Loveliest Thoughts; 1881); *Vort løsen* (Our Solution; 1881); *Sangerhilsen* (Salute in Song; 1883); *Holbergkantate* for Baritone and Men's Voices (1884); *Flagvise* (Flag Song; 1893); *Vestanveir faedervise* (Wind from the West; 1896); *Kristianiasernes sangerhilsen* (Salute in Song from Christiania) for Baritone and Chorus (1896); *Till Ole Bull: Hvor sodt at

favnes (To Ole Bull: How Sweet to Be Embraced; 1901); *Fire salmer* (4 Psalms) for Baritone and Mixed Voices, op. 74 (1906); also a few unpubl. works.

CHAMBER: String Quartet in D minor (1861; not extant); Violin Sonata No. 1, in F major, op. 8 (1865); Violin Sonata No. 2, in G major, op. 13 (1867); Intermezzo in A minor for Cello and Piano (1867); *Veed mandjaevningen* (Trial of Strength), march for Violin and Piano (1874; arranged from *Sigurd Jørsalfar*, op. 22, no. 2); String Quartet in G minor, op. 27 (1877–78); *Andante con moto* in C minor for Violin, Cello, and Piano (1878; 2nd movement from an unfinished piano trio); Cello Sonata in A minor, op. 36 (1883); Violin Sonata No. 3, in C minor, op. 45 (1886–87); String Quartet in F major (1891; unfinished).

SONGS: *Vier Lieder für Altstimme*, op. 2 (1861); *Sex digte*, op. 4 (1863–64); *Hjertets melodier* (The Heart's Melodies), op. 5 (1863–64); *Romancer og ballader*, op. 9 (1863–66); *Fire Romancer*, op. 10 (1864); *Min lille fugl* (My Little Bird; 1865); *Romancer*, op. 15 (1864–68); *Romancer og sange*, op. 18 (1865–69); *Odalisken synger* (Song of the Odalisque; 1870); *Prinsessen* (The Princess; 1871); *Fire digte*, op. 21 (1870–72); *Til Generalkonsul Tønberg* (1873); *Sex digte*, op. 25 (1876); *Fem digte*, op. 26 (1876); *Tolv melodier*, op. 33 (1873–80); *Romancer*, op. 39 (1869–84); *Under juletraet* (Under the Christmas Tree; 1885); *Rejseminder: Fra fjeld og fjord* (Reminiscences: From Mountain and Fjord), op. 44 (1886); *Sechs Lieder*, op. 48 (1889); *Sechs Gedichte*, op. 49 (1889); *Norge*, op. 58 (1893–94); *Elegiske digte*, op. 59 (1893–94); *Digte*, op. 60 (1893–94); *Sange*, op. 61 (1894–95); *Haugtussa*, op. 67 (1895); *Ave maria stella* (1899); *Fem digte*, op. 69 (1900); *Fem digte*, op. 70 (1900); *Efterladte sange*, I and II (1865–1905); also several unpubl. songs.

PIANO SOLO: *Vier Stücke*, op. 1 (1861); (6) *Poetiske tonebilleder*, op. 3 (1863); (4) *Humoresker*, op. 6 (1865); Sonata in E major, op. 7 (1865; rev. 1887); *Sørgemarsch over Rikard Nordraak* (Funeral March for Rikard Nordraak), in A minor (1866; also for Orch.); *Lyriske smaastykker* (Lyric Pieces), op. 12 (1864–67); *Norske folkeviser og dandse*, op. 17 (1869); *Folkelivsbilleder* (Pictures from Life in the Country), op. 19 (1870–71); *Sex norske fjeldmelodier* (6 Norwegian Mountain Tunes, as arranged by Grieg; 1874–75; rev. 1886); *Ballade in Form van Variationen über eine norwegische Melodie* in G minor, op. 24 (1875–76); *Fire albumblade*, op. 28 (1864–78); *Improvisata over to norske folkeviser*, op. 29 (1878); *Neue lyrische Stücke*, op. 38 (1883); *Fra Holbergs tid* (From Holberg's Time), op. 40 (1884; also for Orch.); *Klavierstücke nach eigenen Liedern*, op. 41 (1884); *Lyrische Stücke*, op. 43 (1886); *Norwegische Tänze*, op. 35 (1887; arrangement of pieces for Piano, 4-hands, op. 35); *Walzer-Capricen* (1887; arrangement of pieces for Piano, 4-hands, op. 37); *Peer Gynt Suite* No. 1 (1888; arrangement of the orch. suite, op. 46); *Lyrische Stücke*, op. 47 (1885–88); *Lyrische Stücke*, op. 54 (1891; nos. 1 to 4 orchestrated as *Lyrische Suite*, 1904); *Gebet und Tempeltanz* (1893; arrangement from the Olav Trygvason scenes, op. 50); *Peer Gynt Suite* No. 2 (1893; arrangement of the orch. suite, op. 55); *Drei Orchesterstücke aus Sigurd Jørsalfar* (1893; arrangement of the orch. pieces, op. 56); *Lyrische Stücke*, op. 57 (1893); *Lyrische Stücke*, op. 62 (1895); *Zwei nordische Weisen* (1896; arrangement of the orch. pieces, op. 63); *Lyrische Stücke*, op. 65 (1897); *Norske folkeviser*, op. 66 (1897); *Drei Klavierstücke* (1891–98); *Lyrische Stücke*, op. 68 (1898; nos. 4 and 5 also for Orch.); *Lyrische Stücke*, op. 71 (1901); *Slåtter* (Norwegian Peasant Dances), op. 72 (1902–3); *Stimmungen*, op. 73 (1903–5).

PIANO, 4-HANDS: *Deux pièces symphoniques*, op. 14 (1863–64); *I höst* (In Autumn), op. 11 (1866; based on the song *Efteraarsstormen*, op. 18, no. 4); *Sigurd Jørsalfar* (1874; 3 pieces from the incidental music, op. 22); (4) *Norwegische Tänze*, op. 35 (also for Piano, 2-hands); (2) *Walzer-Capricen*, op. 37 (1883; also for Piano, 2-hands); *Peer Gynt Suite* No. 1 (1888; arrangement of the orch. suite, op. 46); *Peer Gynt Suite* No. 2 (1893; arrangement of the orch. suite, op. 55); *Drei Orchesterstücke aus Jørsalfar* (1893; arrangement of the orch. pieces, op. 56); *Brudefølget drager forbi* (The Bridal Procession Passes; 1893; arrangement of the piano piece, op. 19, no. 2); *Zwei nordische Weisen* (1896; arrangement of the orch. pieces, op. 63); (4) *Symphonische Tänze*, op. 64 (1897; arrangement of the orch. pieces, op. 64).

2 PIANOS: *Altnorwegische Romanze mit Variationen*, op. 51 (1891).

A complete ed. of his works commenced publication in Frankfurt am Main in 1977.

BIBL.: J. Foerster, *E.H. G.* (Prague, 1890); E. Closson, *E. G. et la musique scandinave* (Paris, 1892); D. Mason, *From G. to Brahms* (N.Y., 1902; 2nd ed., 1936); G. Schjelderup, *E. G. og hans vaerker* (Copenhagen, 1903); G. Capellen, *Die Freiheit oder Unfreiheit der Töne und Intervalle als Kriterium der Stimmführung nebst einem Anhang: G.-Analysen als Bestätigungsnachweis und Wegweiser der neuen Musiktheorie* (Leipzig, 1904; 2nd ed., 1917); H. Finck, *E. G.* (N.Y. and London, 1905; 2nd ed., rev. and augmented, 1909, as *G. and His Music*); P. Grainger, "Personal Recollections of G.," *Musical Times*, XLVIII (1907); E. Lee, *E. G.* (London, 1908); G. Schjelderup and W. Niemann, *E. G.: Biographie und Würdigung seiner Werke* (Leipzig, 1908); E. Haraszti, *Das Nationalelement in G.s Musik* (Budapest, 1911); R. Stein, *G.: Eine Biographie* (Berlin, 1921); G. Hauch, ed., *Breve fra G.: Et udvalg* (Copenhagen, 1922); M. Beyer, ed., *Breve fra E. G. til Frants Beyer 1872–1907* (Christiania, 1923); P. de Stoecklin, *G.* (Paris, 1926); J. Röntgen, *G.* (The Hague, 1930); W. Bauer, *Die Harmonik in den Werken von E. G.* (diss., Univ. of Vienna, 1931); E. von Zschinsky-Troxler, ed., *E. G.: Briefe an die Verleger der Edition Peters 1866–1907* (Leipzig, 1932); Y. Rokseth, *G.* (Paris, 1933); D. Monrad Johansen, *E. G.* (Oslo, 1934; 3rd ed., 1956; Eng. tr., 1938); K. von Fischer, *G.s Harmonik und die nordländische Folklore* (Bern and Leipzig, 1938); K. Göllner, *Die Vokalmusik Norwegens als Grundlage des Schaffens E. G.s* (diss., Univ. of Vienna, 1940); K. Fellerer, *E. G.* (Potsdam, 1942); A. Bakke, *E. G.* (Bern, 1943); *E. G. 1843–15. juni 1943: Til hundre-årsdagen for Hans Fødsel* (Bergen, 1943); F. Törnblom (Stockholm, 1943); H. Ustvedt, *E. G.: Tondedikteren, nordmannen, demokraten* (Stockholm, 1943); L. Day, *G.* (N.Y., 1945); J. Grieg Cederblad, *E. G.* (Stockholm, 1946); A. Cherbuliez, *E. G.: Leben und Werk* (Zürich, 1947); G. Abraham, ed., *G.: A Symposium* (London, 1948); F. Bøe, *Trekk av E. G.s personlige* (Oslo, 1949); J. Horton, *E. G.* (London, 1950); A. Vos, *Het leven van E. G. 1843–1907* (The Hague, 1951); D. Schjelderup-Ebbe, *A Study of G.'s Harmony: With Special Reference to His Contributions to Musical Impressionism* (Oslo, 1953); S. Jordan, *E. G.: En oversikt over hans liv og werker* (Bergen, 1954; supplement, 1959); H. Hurum, *I E. G.s verden* (Oslo, 1959); S. Torsteinson, *Troldhaugen: Nina og E. G.s hjem* (Oslo, 1959; 2nd ed., 1962); D. Schjelderup-Ebbe, *E. G. 1858–1867: With Special Reference to the Evolution of His Harmonic Style* (Oslo and London, 1964); B. Kortsen, *Four Unknown Cantatas by G.* (Bergen, 1972); J. Horton, *G.* (London, 1974); B. Schlotel, *G.* (London, 1986); C. Steel, *G.* (Kent, 1987).

Grieg, Nina (née **Hagerup**), Norwegian singer; b. near Bergen, Nov. 24, 1845; d. Copenhagen, Dec. 9, 1935. Her father, Herman Hagerup, was a brother of Grieg's mother. Nina Hagerup studied singing with Helsted; she met **Edvard Grieg** in Copenhagen, and married him on June 11, 1867. Her interpretations of his songs elicited much praise from the critics.

Griend, Koos van de, Dutch pianist, conductor, music critic, and composer; b. Kampen, near Zwolle, Dec. 11, 1905; d. Amsterdam, Jan. 12, 1950. He studied in Amsterdam and in Berlin. Returning to Amsterdam in 1933, he developed energetic activities as a pianist, conductor, and music critic. He wrote 2 syms., a Cello Concerto, and 3 string quartets; also a Quartet for 4 Horns.

Griepenkerl, Wolfgang Robert, German music theorist, son of the music editor **Friedrich (Conrad) Griepenkerl;** b. Hofwyl, May 4, 1810; d. Braunschweig, Oct. 16, 1868. He studied philosophy and literature at Berlin Univ.; taught art history at the Carolinum, Braunschweig (1839), and at the Braunschweig Cadet School (1840–48). He wrote the dramas *Robespierre* (which inspired Litolff's well-known overture) and *Girondistes.* He also publ. *Das Musikfest, oder Die Beethovener,* a novel (1838; 2nd ed., 1841); *Ritter Berlioz in Braunschweig* (1843); and *Die Oper der Gegenwart* (1847).

BIBL.: O. Sievers, *R. G.* (Braunschweig, 1879); T. Werner, "W.R. G.s Schriften über Musik," *Zeitschrift für Musikwissenschaft,* II (1920).

Griesbach, John Henry, English composer; b. Windsor, June 20, 1798; d. London, Jan. 9, 1875. He studied cello with his father, and played in the court band. His major work was a sacred opera, *Belshazzar's Feast* (1835; rev. as the oratorio *Daniel,* London, June 30, 1854); also wrote a number of overtures and cantatas.

Griesbacher, Peter, German priest and composer; b. Egglham, March 25, 1864; d. Regensburg, Jan. 28, 1933. He studied theology; was ordained a priest in 1886; was an instructor at the Franciscan church in Regensburg (from 1894); ed. various publications for Catholic church music; wrote 40 masses, secular cantatas, and songs (about 250 opus numbers). He began as a composer in the strict style of contrapuntal writing; his later works, in which he applied modern harmonies to Gregorian melodies, aroused considerable opposition. He publ. several manuals: *Lehrbuch des Kontrapunkts* (1910); *Kirchenmusikalische Stilistik und Formenlehre* (3 vols., 1912–13); *Glockenmusik* (1926).

BIBL.: M. Tremmel, *P. G.* (Passau, 1935).

Griffes, Charles T(omlinson), outstanding American composer; b. Elmira, N.Y., Sept. 17, 1884; d. N.Y., April 8, 1920. He studied piano with a local teacher, Mary S. Broughton; also took organ lessons. In 1903 he went to Berlin, where he was a pupil of Gottfried Galston (piano) and of Rüfer and Humperdinck (composition). To eke out his living, he gave private lessons; also played his own compositions in public recitals. In 1907 he returned to the U.S., and took a music teacher's job at the Hackley School for Boys at Tarrytown, N.Y.; at the same time he continued to study music by himself; he was fascinated by the exotic art of the French Impressionists, and investigated the potentialities of oriental scales. He also was strongly influenced by the Russian school, particularly Mussorgsky and Scriabin. A combination of natural talent and determination to acquire a high degree of craftsmanship elevated Griffes to the position of a foremost American composer in the impressionist genre; despite changes of taste, his works retain an enduring place in American music.

WORKS: *The White Peacock* for Piano (1917; also for Orch., Philadelphia, Dec. 19, 1919); tone poem, *The Pleasure Dome of Kubla Khan,* after Coleridge (Boston, Nov. 28, 1919); *The Kairn of Koridwen,* dance drama for 5 Woodwinds, Celesta, Harp, and Piano (N.Y., Feb. 10, 1917); *Shojo,* Japanese pantomimic drama for 4 Woodwinds, 4 Muted Strings, Harp, and Percussion (1917); *Poem* for Flute and Orch. (N.Y., Nov. 16, 1919); *2 Sketches on Indian Themes* for String Quartet (1922); for Piano: *3 Tone Pictures* (*The Lake at Evening, The Vale of Dreams,* and *The Night Winds;* 1915); *Fantasy Pieces* (*Barcarolle, Notturno,* and *Scherzo;* 1915); *Roman Sketches* (*White Peacock, Nightfall, The Fountain of Acqua Paola,* and *Clouds;* 1917); Sonata in F (Feb. 26, 1918); vocal works: *These Things Shall Be* for Unison Chorus (1917); songs to German texts (*Auf geheimen Waldespfade, Auf dem Teich,* etc.); songs to Eng. words: *The 1st Snowfall, The Half-ring Moon, Evening Song; Tone Images* (*La Fuite de la lune, Symphony in Yellow,* and *We'll to the Woods, and Gather May;* 1915); *2 Rondels* (*Come, love, across the sunlit land* and *This book of hours;* 1915); *3 Poems* (*In a Myrtle Shade, Waikiki,* and *Phantoms;* 1916); *5 Poems of Ancient China and Japan* (*So-Fei gathering flowers, Landscape, The Old Temple, Tears,* and *A Feast of Lanterns;* 1917); *3 Poems* (*The Lament of Ian the Proud, Thy Dark Eyes to Mine,* and *The Rose of the Night;* 1918); *An Old Song Re-sung* (1920).

BIBL.: W. Upton, "The Songs of C.T. G.," *Musical Quarterly* (July 1923); M. Bauer, "C.T. G. as I Remember Him," ibid. (July 1943); E. Maisel, *C.T. G.* (N.Y., 1943; reprinted with new preface by D. Anderson, N.Y., 1972; rev. ed., 1984); D. Boda, *The Music of C. G.* (diss., Florida State Univ., 1962); idem, *The Works of C.T. G.: A Descriptive Catalogue* (Ann Arbor, 1984).

Griffes, Elliot, American pianist, teacher, and composer; b. Boston, Jan. 28, 1893; d. Los Angeles, June 8, 1967. He studied at Ithaca College (graduated, 1913), then with Horatio Parker at the Yale Univ. School of Music (1915–16), and with Chadwick, Stuart Mason, and Pattison at the New England Cons. of Music in Boston (1917–18); won a Juilliard scholarship (1922) and a Pulitzer scholarship (1931). He was active as a recitalist; also taught in various institutions, including Grinnell College in Iowa (1920–22), the Brooklyn Settlement School (1923–24), the St. Louis School of Music (head of theory dept., 1935–36), and the Westchester Cons. in White Plains, N.Y. (director, 1942–43); settled in Los Angeles as a composer of film scores. He wrote works in ingratiatingly Romantic colors.
WORKS: Operetta, *The Blue Scarab* (1934); opera, *Port of Pleasure* (Los Angeles, June 29, 1963); *A Persian Fable* for Orch. (1925); *Paul Bunyan, Colossus,* symphonic poem (1926–34); Sym. No. 1 (1931); *Fantastic Pursuit,* sym. for Strings (1941); *Yon Green Mountain,* suite for Orch. (1943); 3 string quartets (1926, 1930, 1937); Sonata for Violin and Piano (1931); *To the Sun,* symphonic fragment for Piano Trio (1940); Suite for Piano Trio (1941); *The Aztec Flute* for Flute and Piano Trio (1942); *Montevallo,* concerto grosso for Organ, Piano, and Strings (1945); *The Fox and the Crow* for Chamber Ensemble (1950); song cycles; songs; piano pieces.

Grignon, Ricard Lamote de. See **Lamote de Grignon, Ricard.**

Grigny, Nicolas de, French organist and composer; b. Rheims (baptized), Sept. 8, 1672; d. there, Nov. 30, 1703. He was born into a musical family; his father and grandfather were organists in Rheims; after going to Paris, he served as organist at the abbey church of St. Denis (1693–95); he then returned to Rheims, where he became cathedral organist about 1697. He publ. *Premier livre d'orgue contenant une messe et les hymnes des principalles festes de l'année* (Paris, 1699; modern ed. by N. Dufourcq and N. Pierront, Paris, 1953).
BIBL.: W. Maul, *The Organ Works of N. d.G.* (diss., Univ. of Washington, 1965).

Grigoriu, Theodor, Rumanian composer; b. Galaţi, July 25, 1926. He studied violin with Enacovici at the Bucharest Cons. and composition with Jora; then went to Moscow, where he had lessons with Khatchaturian and Golubev (1954–55).
WORKS: 2 cantatas: *Cantată pentru 23 August* (1951) and *Odă oraşului meu* (Ode to My City; 1963; rev. 1971); *Sinfonia cantabile* (1950; rev. 1966); *Dans tătar,* choreographic piece for Orch. (1953); *Theatrical Suite in the Classical Style* for Chamber Orch. (1956); *Symphonic Variations,* on a melody by Anton Pann, for Orch. (1955; Bucharest, Jan. 21, 1956); Concerto for Double Chamber Orch. and Solo Oboe (1957); *Vis cosmic* (Cosmic Dream), symphonic poem, with Vocalizing Tenor or Electronic Instrument (1959; Bucharest, Oct. 28, 1965); *Hommage to Enesco* for 4 Groups of Violins (1960); *Melodic infinită* for Chamber String Orch. (1969); *Elegie pontică,* to verses by Ovid, for Bass-Baritone, Female Chorus, and Chamber Orch. (Bucharest, June 24, 1969); *Vocalizele mării,* choral sym. (1984); *Pastorale şi idile transilvane* for Orch. (1984; 2nd version, 1986); String Quartet (1943); Piano Trio (1943); *Pe Argeş în sus* (The River Arges Flows On), suite for String Quartet (1953); choral music; songs; film music.

Grimaldi, Nicolo. See **Nicolini.**

Grimm, Carl Hugo, American organist and composer; b. Zanesville, Ohio, Oct. 31, 1890; d. Cincinnati, Oct. 25, 1978.

He studied music with his father; subsequently held positions as organist in Cincinnati; taught composition at the Cincinnati Cons. (1907–31).
WORKS: *Erotic Poem* for Orch. (1927); *Thanatopsis* for Orch. (1928); *Abraham Lincoln,* "character portrait" for Orch. (1930); *Montana,* symphonic poem (Cincinnati, March 26, 1943); *An American Overture* (Cincinnati, Feb. 15, 1946); Trumpet Concerto (1948); Sym. in F minor (1950); *Pennsylvania Overture* (1954); Gothic Mass (1970); *Byzantine Suite* for 10 Instruments (1930); *Little Serenade* for Wind Quintet (1934); Cello Sonata (1945); many anthems, songs, and organ pieces; also works for multiple flutes (ensembles of 4, 8, and 12 flutes).

Grimm, Friedrich Melchior, Baron von, German writer on music; b. Regensburg, Sept. 25, 1723; d. Gotha, Dec. 19, 1807. He went to Paris in 1750 and remained there until the Revolution, frequenting literary and musical circles and taking an active part in all controversies; his "Lettre sur Omphale" in the *Mercure de France* (1752) took the side of Italian opera in the "guerre des bouffons," but some years later he upheld Gluck against the Italian faction supporting Piccinni. He ed. the *Correspondance littéraire, philosophique et critique,* which offers important data on French opera (16 vols., Paris, 1877–82). He befriended the Mozarts on their 1st visit to Paris (see the many references to him in E. Anderson, *Letters of Mozart and His Family,* London, 1938; 2nd ed., rev., rev., 1966, by A. Hyatt King and M. Carolan; 3rd ed., rev., 1985). He also wrote a satire on J. Stamitz, *Le Petit Prophète de Boehmisch-Broda;* reproduced in Eng. in O. Strunk's *Source Readings in Music History* (N.Y., 1950).
BIBL.: Carlez, *G. et la musique de son temps* (1872); J.-L.-A. Jullien, *La Musique et les philosophes* (1873); E. Schérer, *M. G.* (1887); E. Hirschberg, *Die Encyklopädisten und die französische Oper im 18. Jahrhundert* (1903); H. Kretzschmar, "Die *Correspondance littéraire* als musikgeschichtliche Quelle," *Jahrbuch Peters* (1903); P. Nettl, *Der kleine Prophète de Boehmisch-Broda* (Esslingen, 1951).

Grimm, Heinrich, German composer; b. Holzminden, c.1593; d. Braunschweig, July 10, 1637. He studied with Michael Praetorius; then studied theology at the Univ. of Helmstedt; in 1619, became rector of the Magdeburg town school; in 1631, when the town was destroyed, he fled with his family to Braunschweig, where he became a cantor at the church of St. Catherine; subsequently was a cantor at St. Andreas's church (1632–37). He was an exponent of the concerted style, with thoroughbass, at that time still a novel technique in Germany. His extant works include masses, Psalms, Passions, motets, and several pedagogical works; he publ. *Unterricht, wie ein Knabe nach der alten Guidonischen Art zu solmisieren leicht angeführt werden kann* (Magdeburg, 1624) and *Instrumentum Instrumentorum, hoc est, Monochordum, vel potius Dodecachordum* (MS, 1629); prepared a combined ed. of *Melopoeia seu melodiae condendae ratio* by Calvisius and *Pleiades Musicae* by Baryphonus (Magdeburg, 1630).
BIBL.: H. Lorenzen, *Der Cantor H. G.* (1593–1637); *Sein Leben und seine Werke mit Beitrag zur Musikgeschichte Magdeburgs und Braunschweigs* (diss., Univ. of Hamburg, 1940).

Grimm, Julius Otto, German conductor and composer; b. Pernau, Latvia, March 6, 1827; d. Münster, Dec. 7, 1903. He studied philosophy at the Univ. of Dorpat; then lived in St. Petersburg; in 1851 he went to Leipzig, where he studied with Moscheles and Hauptmann; there he formed close friendships with Brahms and Joachim. In 1855 he went to Göttingen; in 1860, obtained a position as conductor in Münster. He wrote a Sym. (1874); a Suite for String Orch. in canon form; several cycles of songs; albums of piano pieces.
BIBL.: *Brahms im Briefwechsel mit J.O. G.* (Berlin, 1912); F. Ludwig, *J.O. G.* (Leipzig, 1925).

Grimm, Karl, German cellist and composer; b. Hildburghausen, April 28, 1819; d. Freiburg, Jan. 9, 1888. He was for half a century 1st cellist at the Wiesbaden Opera; composed many cello pieces, some of which attained considerable popularity.

Grimm, (Karl Konstantin) Louis (Ludwig), German harpist and composer; b. Berlin, Feb. 17, 1820; d. there, May 23, 1882. He studied with Josef Hasselmans at the Stuttgart Cons. and Elias Parish Alvars in Leipzig. In 1844 he was made principal harpist of the royal chapel in Berlin; in 1869 was named Königliche Concertmeister. He enjoyed a considerable reputation as a harp soloist; also wrote various pieces for his instrument.

Grinblat, Romuald, Russian composer; b. Tver, April 11, 1930. He studied at the Latvian Cons. in Riga; after graduation in 1955, he devoted himself to composition and teaching. His works include 4 syms. (1955, 1957, 1964, 1967); *Youth Overture* (1958); Piano Concerto (1963); Flute Concerto (1970); Piano Quintet (1954); Nocturne for 17 Strings (1966); a ballet, *Rigonda* (1959); children's opera, *Barber's Daughter* (1972); piano pieces; and a curious work for voices, *Exercises in Phonetics* (1969).

Grisar, Albert, Belgian composer; b. Antwerp (of German-Belgian parents), Dec. 26, 1808; d. Asnières, near Paris, June 15, 1869. He studied for a short time (1830) with Reicha in Paris. Returning to Antwerp, he brought out his opera *Le Mariage impossible* (Brussels, March 4, 1833), and obtained a government subsidy for further study in Paris. On April 26, 1836, he produced *Sarah* at the Opéra-Comique; then *L'An mille* (June 23, 1837), *La Suisse à Trianon* (March 8, 1838), *Lady Melvil* (Nov. 15, 1838, with Flotow), *L'Eau merveilleuse* (Jan. 31, 1839, with Flotow), *Le Naufrage de la Méduse* (May 31, 1839, with Flotow and Pilati), *Les Travestissements* (Nov. 16, 1839), and *L'Opéra à la cour* (July 16, 1840, with Boieldieu, Jr.). In 1840 he went to Naples for further serious study under Mercadante; returning to Paris in 1848, he brought out *Gilles ravisseur* (Feb. 21, 1848), *Les Porcherons* (Jan. 12, 1850), *Bonsoir, M. Pantalon* (Feb. 19, 1851), *Le Carillonneur de Bruges* (Feb. 20, 1852), *Les Amours du diable* (March 11, 1853), *Le Chien du jardinier* (Jan. 16, 1855), *Voyage autour de ma chambre* (Aug. 12, 1859), *Le Joaillier de St. James* (9 songs from *Lady Melvil*; Feb. 17, 1862), *La Chatte merveilleuse* (March 18, 1862), *Les Bégaiements d'amour* (Dec. 8, 1864), and *Les Douze Innocentes* (Oct. 19, 1865). He left, besides, 12 finished and unfinished operas; also dramatic scenes, over 50 romances, etc. His statue (by Brackeleer) was placed in the vestibule of the Antwerp Theater in 1870.
Bibl.: A. Pougin, *A. G.* (Paris, 1870).

Grisart, Charles Jean Baptiste, French composer; b. Paris, Sept. 29, 1837; d. Compiègne, March 11, 1904. He is known for his light operas, the most popular of which were *La Quenouille de verre* (1873), *Les Trois Margots* (1877), *Le Pont d'Avignon* (1878), *Les Poupées de l'Infante* (1881), *Le Bossu* (1888), *Le Petit Bois* (1893), and *Voilà le roi!* (1894). He also wrote many piano pieces, masses, *mélodies,* etc., and a quantity of transcriptions.

Griselle, Thomas, American composer; b. Upper Sandusky, Ohio, Jan. 10, 1891; d. Los Angeles, Dec. 27, 1955. He studied at the Cincinnati College of Music; later took courses in Europe with Nadia Boulanger and Arnold Schoenberg; in 1928, won the $10,000 prize of the Victor contest for American composers with his *2 American Sketches.* In 1939 he settled in Hollywood. He wrote a number of semipopular pieces, often with humorous intent, such as *A Keyboard Symphony* for 6 Pianos (Providence, March 27, 1928); *Tutti-Frutti* and *Czerny Pilots a Flying Saucer* for Piano; etc.

Grishkat, Hans (Adolf Karl Willy), German choral conductor; b. Hamburg, Aug. 29, 1903; d. Stuttgart, Jan. 10, 1977. He studied at the Univ. of Tübingen and at the Hochschule für Musik in Stuttgart. In 1924 he organized the Reutlingen Chorale; in 1931 he formed the Swabian Chorale, and in 1936 the Grishkat Chorale in Stuttgart; gained a fine reputation as a choral conductor in Germany. From 1945 to 1950 he led

the Swabian Sym. Orch. in Reutlingen. In 1946 he was appointed instructor of choral conducting at the Hochschule für Musik in Stuttgart; from 1968 until his death he led the orch. conducting classes there.

Grisi, Giuditta, Italian mezzo-soprano, sister of **Giulia Grisi;** b. Milan, July 28, 1805; d. Robecco d'Oglio, near Cremona, May 1, 1840. She studied at the Milan Cons.; made her 1st appearance in Vienna in 1826; afterward sang with success in Italy and in Paris at the Théâtre-Italien under Rossini's management; retired in 1838, after her marriage to Count Barni. Bellini wrote for her the part of Romeo in *I Capuleti ed i Montecchi* (Venice, March 11, 1830); her sister sang Juliet.

Grisi, Giulia, celebrated Italian soprano, sister of **Giuditta Grisi;** b. Milan, July 28, 1811; d. Berlin, Nov. 29, 1869. She studied with her sister, and with Filippo Celli and Pietro Guglielmi; also with Marliani in Milan and with Giacomelli in Bologna; made her 1st appearance at 17 as Emma in Rossini's *Zelmira* in Milan; won the admiration of Bellini, who wrote for her the part of Juliet in *I Capuleti ed i Montecchi* (Venice, March 11, 1830); she sang in Milan until 1832; dissatisfied with her contract and unable to break it legally, she fled to Paris, where she joined her sister at the Théâtre-Italien; she made her Paris debut in the title role of Rossini's *Semiramide* (Oct. 16, 1832); her success was phenomenal, and for the next 16 years she sang there regularly. She made her London debut in Rossini's *La gazza ladra* (April 8, 1834), and continued to visit London annually for 27 years. With Rubini, Tamburini, and Lablache, she appeared in Bellini's *I Puritani* and other operas; when the tenor Giovanni Mario replaced Rubini, Grisi sang with him and Tamburini; she lived with Mario from 1839; toured the U.S. with him in 1854; retired in 1861, and lived mostly in London, making occasional visits to the Continent; on one visit to Berlin, she died of pneumonia.
Bibl.: E. Forbes, *Mario and G.* (London, 1985).

Grist, Reri, black American soprano; b. N.Y., 1934. She studied at the High School of Music and Art and at Queens College; began her professional career on Broadway, appearing in *West Side Story* (1957); made her operatic debut with the Santa Fe Opera as Blonde in *Die Entführung aus dem Serail* in 1959; in 1960 sang at the Cologne Opera as the Queen of the Night. She made her Metropolitan Opera debut in N.Y. on Feb. 25, 1966, as Rosina in *Il Barbiere di Siviglia.*

Griswold, Putnam, American bass-baritone; b. Minneapolis, Dec. 23, 1875; d. N.Y., Feb. 26, 1914. He studied with A. Randegger in London, Bouhy in Paris, Stockhausen in Frankfurt, and Emerich in Berlin; sang at Berlin's Royal Opera in 1904; in 1904–5 toured the U.S. with Savage's company, appearing in the English version of *Parsifal;* from 1906 to 1911, was a popular singer at the Berlin Royal Opera; made his Metropolitan Opera debut on Nov. 23, 1911, in N.Y. in the role of Hagen in *Götterdämmerung.* He was identified with the bass parts in Wagner's works until his death; German critics pronounced him the greatest foreign interpreter of these roles, and he was twice decorated by the Kaiser.

Grob-Prandl, Gertrud, Austrian soprano; b. Vienna, Nov. 11, 1917. She was educated in Vienna; made her debut at the Volksoper in 1938. In 1947 she became a member of the Vienna State Opera, remaining on its roster until 1964. She then toured Europe and South America. She was particularly effective in Wagnerian roles.

Grocheo, Johannes de, French music theorist who flourished in the 13th and early 14th centuries. He wrote the treatise *Ars musice* or *Theoria* (c.1300), important as a source of information on secular music of the Middle Ages. It is printed in the original Latin with German tr. by J. Wolf in *Sammelbände der Internationalen Musik-Gesellschaft,* I (1899–1900); emendations were provided by H. Müller (op. cit., vol. IV).
Bibl.: E. Rohloff, *Studien zum Musiktraktat des J. d. G.* (Leipzig, 1930); J. Maddrell, "*Mensura* and the Rhythm of Medi-

eval Monodic Song," *Current Musicology*, 10 (1970); H. Vander-werf, "Concerning the Measurability of Medieval Music," ibid.; J. Maddrell, "G. and the Measurability of Medieval Music," ibid., 11 (1971); E. Rohloff, *Die Quellenhandschriften zum Musiktraktat des J. d.G.* (Leipzig, 1972).

Grofé, Ferde (Ferdinand Rudolph von), American composer, pianist, and arranger; b. N.Y., March 27, 1892; d. Santa Monica, Calif., April 3, 1972. He studied music with Pietro Floridia; then was engaged as viola player in the Los Angeles Phil., at the same time working as pianist and conductor in theaters and cafés; joined Paul Whiteman's band in 1920 as pianist and arranger; it was his scoring of Gershwin's *Rhapsody in Blue* (1924) that won him fame. In his own works, Grofé successfully applied jazz rhythms, interwoven with simple ballad-like tunes; his *Grand Canyon Suite* (Chicago, Nov. 22, 1931, Whiteman conducting) became very popular. Other light pieces in a modern vein include a Piano Concerto (1932–59); *Broadway at Night; Mississippi Suite; 3 Shades of Blue; Tabloid Suite* (N.Y., Jan. 25, 1933); *Symphony in Steel* (N.Y., Jan. 19, 1937); *Hollywood Suite; Wheels Suite; New England Suite; Metropolis; Aviation Suite; San Francisco Suite* for Orch. (San Francisco, April 23, 1960); *Niagara Falls Suite* for Orch. (Buffalo, Feb. 1961); *World's Fair Suite* for Orch. (N.Y., April 22, 1964); *Virginia City: Requiem for a Ghost Town*, symphonic poem (Virginia City, Nev., Aug. 10, 1968).

Grøndahl, Launy, Danish conductor and composer; b. Ordrup, near Copenhagen, June 30, 1886; d. Copenhagen, Jan. 21, 1960. He studied violin with Anton Bloch and Axel Gade, and theory with Ludolf Nielsen; later took music courses in Paris, Italy, Vienna, and elsewhere. Returning to Denmark, he became president of the Soc. of Young Musicians; then was appointed conductor of the Danish State Radio Orch., giving his 1st concert on Oct. 28, 1925.
WORKS: Sym. (1919); Violin Concerto (1917); Trombone Concerto (1924); Bassoon Concerto (1943); 2 string quartets; Violin Sonata; numerous piano pieces and songs.

Groningen, Stefan van, Dutch pianist and pedagogue; b. Deventer, June 23, 1851; d. Laren, March 25, 1926. He studied with Kiel in Berlin; gave concerts; taught in various music schools in The Hague, Utrecht, and Leiden. He wrote mostly piano music; also a Piano Quartet.

Groot, Cor de, Dutch pianist and composer; b. Amsterdam, July 7, 1914. He studied composition with Sem Dresden at the Amsterdam Cons.; in 1936 won the international piano contest in Vienna; then gave concerts in Europe and America. He taught piano in The Hague; also served as librarian and archivist in Hilversum.
WORKS: Piano Concerto (1931); *Concerto classico* for Piano and Orch. (1932); 2-piano Concerto (1939); 2-oboe Concerto (1939); Piano Concertino (1939); Clarinet Concerto (1940); Flute Concerto (1940); Violin Concerto (1940); Divertimento for Orch. (1949); *Wilhelmus ouverture* (1950); *Minuten Concerto* for Piano and Orch. (1950); *Ouverture energico* (1951); *Capriccio* for Piano and Orch. (1955); *Variations imaginaires* for Piano, left-hand, and Orch. (1960–62); Concertino for Clarinet and Small Orch. (1971); "*Bis*" (Evocation) for Piano and Orch. (1972); *Les Chatons de Paris* for Accordion and Orch. (1978); String Quartet (1947); Serenade for Oboe and Bassoon (1949); *Apparition* for Violin and Piano (1960); *2 Figures* for Oboe and Piano (1968); *Solitude* for Cello and Piano (1968); *Invocation* for Cello and Piano (1974); *Cloches dans le matin* for 1 or 2 Pianos (1972); *Zit-liedjes en spring-dansjes* for Irish Harp (1982); *Music for the Party* for 2 Harps (1983).

Grosheim, Georg Christoph, German writer on music and composer; b. Kassel, July 1, 1764; d. there, Nov. 18, 1841. He played viola in the Court Orch. at Kassel; ed. the magazine *Euterpe* in 1797–98; wrote biographical articles on composers, and corresponded with Beethoven. His autobiography was publ. by G. Heinrichs (1926). He composed 3 operas: *Titania, oder Liebe durch Zauberei* (1792), *Das heilige Kleeblatt* (1793; Oct. 1794), and *Les Esclaves d'Alger* (Kassel, Oct. 14, 1808; not extant).

Grosjean, Ernest, French organist and composer, nephew of **Jean Romary Grosjean;** b. Vagney, Dec. 18, 1844; d. Versailles, Dec. 28, 1936. He studied in Paris with Boëly and Stamaty; was organist at Verdun Cathedral from 1868 to 1916; then at St. Antoine, Versailles; from 1888 to 1914 was ed. of the *Journal des Organistes.* He wrote many works for organ and a *Théorie et pratique de l'accompagnement du plainchant.*

Grosjean, Jean Romary, French organist and composer, uncle of **Ernest Grosjean;** b. Épinal, Jan. 12, 1815; d. St. Dié, Feb. 13, 1888. He was organist at the St. Dié Cathedral from 1839; he publ. a 2-vol. collection of organ works, *Album d'un organiste catholique*, which included some of his own compositions; also ed. a complete collection of noëls and folk songs of Lorraine.

Grosskopf, Erhard, German composer; b. Berlin, March 17, 1934. He studied with Pepping at the Berlin Church Music School (1957–59) and with Blacher and others at the Berlin Hochschule für Musik (1959–64); afterward engaged in teaching. In his compositions he explores highly complex abstract constructivism.
WORKS: 3 sonatas: No. 1 for Piano Trio (1965); No. 2 for Solo Violin (1965); No. 3 for Flute, Viola, and Cello (1967); *Sonata concertante No. 1* for Small Orch. (1966) and *No. 2* for Violin and Orch. (1967); *Konzertante Aspekte II* for Flute, Cello, Piano, and Orch. (1967); *Nexus* for Flute, Percussion, and Chamber Ensemble or Tape (1968); *Konzert: Flecktreue Raritätenkunst P* for Clarinet and Instrumental Ensemble (1969); *Dialectics 1969* for 3 Instruments and Tape (1969); *Stop* for 5 Choral Groups (1971); *Hörmusik* for Cello, 5 Orch. Groups, and Electronics (1970–71; West Berlin, Sept. 30, 1971); *Sun Music* for 3 Instrumental Groups (West Berlin, July 16, 1972); *Balance JENC* for Violin and Tape (1972); *Looping* for 5 Performers and Tape, *Looping III* for 5–7 Performers and Tape, and *Looping IV* for 5 Performers (all 1973); *Arbeiter und Bauer müssen sich erheben . . . (Looping II)* for Ensemble (1974).

Grossmann, Ferdinand, Austrian conductor; b. Tulln, July 4, 1887; d. Vienna, Dec. 5, 1970. He studied music in Linz; later took a course in conducting with Weingartner in Vienna. In 1923 he founded a Volkskonservatorium in Vienna; in 1946 organized the Chamber Chorus of the Vienna Academy of Music and toured with it in Europe and America. He was also a composer; wrote a *German Mass* a cappella (1952) and some chamber music.

Grout, Donald J(ay), eminent American musicologist; b. Rock Rapids, Iowa, Sept. 28, 1902; d. Skaneateles, N.Y., March 9, 1987. He studied philosophy at Syracuse Univ. (A.B., 1923) and musicology at Harvard Univ. (A.M., 1932; Ph.D., 1939). He studied piano in Boston, and took a course in French music in Strasbourg and in the history of opera in Vienna. In 1935–36 he was a visiting lecturer in music history at Mills College in California, from 1936 to 1942 he was in the music dept. at Harvard Univ.; from 1942 to 1945, was at the Univ. of Texas in Austin; from 1945 to 1970, was a prof. of musicology at Cornell Univ. He held a Guggenheim Foundation grant in 1951. He served as president of the American Musicological Soc. (1952–54; 1960–62); in 1966, became curator of the Accademia Monteverdiana in N.Y. He was the author of *A Short History of Opera* (2 vols., N.Y., 1948; 3rd ed., 1988); *A History of Western Music* (N.Y., 1960; 4th ed., 1988); *Mozart in the History of Opera* (Washington, D.C., 1972); and *Alessandro Scarlatti: An Introduction to His Operas* (Berkeley, 1979). In his honor a Festschrift was issued: W. Austin, ed., *New Looks at Italian Opera: Essays in Honor of Donald J. Grout* (Ithaca, N.Y., 1968).

Grove, Sir George, eminent English musicographer; b. Clapham, South London, Aug. 13, 1820; d. Sydenham, May 28, 1900. He studied civil engineering; graduated in 1839 from the Institution of Civil Engineers, and worked in various shops in Glasgow, and then in Jamaica and Bermuda. He returned to England in 1846, and became interested in music; without abandoning his engineering profession, he entered the Soc. of Arts, of which he was appointed secretary in 1850; this position placed him in contact with the organizers of the 1851 Exhibition; in 1852 he became secretary of the Crystal Palace. He then turned to literary work; was an ed., with William Smith, of the *Dictionary of the Bible;* traveled to Palestine in 1858 and 1861 in connection with his research; in 1865 he became director of the Palestine Exploration Fund. In the meantime, he accumulated a private music library; began writing analytical programs for Crystal Palace concerts; these analyses, contributed by Grove during the period 1856–96, established a new standard of excellence in musical exegesis. His enthusiasm for music led to many important associations; with Arthur Sullivan he went to Vienna in 1867 in search of unknown music by Schubert, and discovered the score of *Rosamunde.* In 1868 he became ed. of *Macmillan's Magazine;* remained on its staff for 15 years. He received many honors for his literary and musical achievements, among them the D.C.L., Univ. of Durham (1875), and LL.D., Univ. of Glasgow (1885). In 1883 he was knighted by Queen Victoria. When the Royal College of Music was formed in London (1882), Grove was appointed director, and retained this post until 1894. His chief work, which gave him enduring fame, was the monumental *Dictionary of Music and Musicians,* which Macmillan began to publ. in 1879. It was first planned in 2 vols., but as the material grew, it was expanded to 4 vols., with an appendix, its publication being completed in 1889. Grove contributed voluminous articles on his favorite composers, Beethoven, Schubert, and Mendelssohn; he gathered a distinguished group of specialists to write the assorted entries. The 2nd edition was ed. by Fuller Maitland (5 vols., 1904–10), the 3rd edition (1927–28), by H.C. Colles; an American supplement, first publ. in 1920, ed. by W.S. Pratt and C.H.N. Boyd, was expanded and republ. in 1928; the 4th edition, also ed. by H.C. Colles, was publ. in 5 vols., with a supplementary vol. in 1940. E. Blom was entrusted with the preparation of an entirely revised and greatly enlarged 5th ed., which was publ. in 9 vols. in 1954. An entirely new 6th ed. was edited by S. Sadie as *The New Grove Dictionary of Music and Musicians* (20 vols., 1980).

BIBL.: C. Graves, *The Life and Letters of Sir G. G.* (London, 1904); idem, "G. G.: A Centenary Study," *Music & Letters* (1920); P. Young, *G. G., 1820–1900* (London, 1980).

Grové, Stefans, South African composer; b. Bethlehem, Orange Free State, July 23, 1922. He studied piano with his mother and his uncle; later took courses with Cameron Taylor at the South African College of Music, with W.H. Bell in Cape Town, and with Walter Piston at Harvard Univ. (1953–55), where he received his M.A. In 1956 he was appointed instructor at the Peabody Cons., Baltimore, where he founded the Pro Musica Rara group for performance of Baroque music; in 1972 he was appointed senior lecturer in composition at the Univ. of Cape Town, and in 1973 took a similar post at the Univ. of Pretoria. He ed. the orch. score of the newly discovered (1971) Concerto for 2 Pianos and Orch. of Max Bruch. Grové's music is distinguished by clarity of formal presentation and a free flow of melodic line; the contrapuntal structure is often complex, but it is invariably cast within clearly outlined harmonies.

WORKS: Clarinet Sonata (1947); String Trio (1948); *Elegy* for String Orch. (Cape Town, July 9, 1948); Duo for Violin and Cello (1950); *Die Dieper Reg,* ballet (1950); Piano Trio (1952); Trio for Oboe, Clarinet, and Bassoon (1952); Quintet for Flute, Oboe, Viola, Bass Clarinet, and Harp (1952); *Tower Music* for Brass Ensemble (1954); Flute Sonata (1955); Sinfonia Concertante (Johannesburg, Oct. 23, 1956); Quartet for Flute, Oboe, Clarinet, and Bassoon (1956); Violin Concerto (1959); *Alice in Wonderland* for Viola, Piccolo, Alto Flute, Wind Ensemble, and Percussion (1959); *Symphony 1962;* Partita for Orch. (1964); *Ritual,* fantasy for Organ (1969); *An Experience in Style,* 14 imitative pieces for Harpsichord and Piano (1971); *Kaapse Draaie* for Chorus, Piano, Guitar, Marimba,

Flute, Clarinet, and Saxophone (1974); Concerto Grosso for Violin, Cello, Piano, and Youth Orch. (1974); *Maya,* concerto for Violin, Piano, and Youth String Orch. (1976); *Warata,* ballet for Young Dancers (1976); *For a Winter Day,* fantasy for Bassoon and Piano (1977); *Chain Rows* for Orch., with Instrumental Soloists (1978); *Rendezvous* for Piccolo and Tuba (1978).

Groven, Eivind, Norwegian composer and musicologist; b. Lårdal, Telemark, Oct. 8, 1901; d. Oslo, Feb. 8, 1977. He studied at the Christiania (Oslo) Cons. (1923–25). In 1931 he was appointed a consultant on folk music for Norwegian Radio; remained there until 1946; in 1940 he received a state composer's pension. His many theoretical studies include *Naturskalaen* (The Natural Scale; Skein, 1927); *Temperering og renstemning* (Temperament and Non-tempered Tuning, dealing with a new system of piano tuning according to natural intervals; Oslo, 1948; Eng. tr., 1970); *Eskimomelodier fra Alaska* (Eskimo Melodies from Alaska; Oslo, 1955). He collected about 1,800 Norwegian folk tunes, several of which he used as thematic foundation for his own compositions. In 1965 he patented an electronic organ, with special attachments for the production of non-tempered intervals.

WORKS: ORCH.: Symphonic poems: *Renaissance* (1935); *Historiske syner* (Historical Visions; 1936); *Fjelltonar* (Tunes from the Hills; 1938); *Skjebner* (The Fates; 1938); *Bryllup i skogen* (Wedding in the Wood; 1939); 2 syms.: No. 1, *Innover viddene* (Toward the Mountains; 1937; rev. 1951); No. 2, *Midnattstimen* (The Midnight Hour; 1946); *Hjalarljod,* overture (1950); Piano Concerto (1950); *Symfoniske slåtter* (Norwegian Folk Dances), 2 sets: No. 1 (1956) and No. 2, *Faldafeykir* (1967). **VOCAL:** *Brudgommen* (The Bridegroom) for Soprano, 2 Altos, Tenor, Chorus, and Orch. (1928–31); *Naturens tempel* (The Temple of Nature) for Chorus and Orch. (1945); *Ivar Aasen,* suite for Soprano, Bass, Chorus, and Orch. (1946); *Soga om ein by* (The Story of a Town) for Soprano, Tenor, Bass, Chorus, and Orch. (1956); *Margjit Hjukse* for Chorus and Hardanger Fiddle (1963); *Draumkaede* for Soprano, Tenor, Baritone, Chorus, and Orch. (1965); *Ved foss og fjord* (By Falls and Fjord) for Male Chorus and Orch. (1966); among his many songs for solo voice, most scored with piano and later rescored with orch., are: *Moen* (The Heath; 1926; orchestrated 1934); *Neslandskyrkja* (The Nesland Church; 1929; orchestrated 1942); *Moderens korstegn* (The Mother's Sign of the Cross; 1930; orchestrated 1942); *På hospitalet om natten* (In the Hospital at Night; 1930; orchestrated 1946); *Høstsanger* (The Autumn Song; orchestrated 1946). **CHAMBER:** *Solstemning* (Sun Mood) for Solo Flute, or Flute and Piano (1946); *Balladetone* for 2 Hardanger Fiddles (1962); *Regnbogen* (The Rainbow) for 2 Hardanger Fiddles (1962).

Groves, Sir Charles (Barnard), distinguished English conductor; b. London, March 10, 1915. He was educated at the Royal College of Music in London. In 1938 he joined the BBC as a choral conductor. He then was music director of the Bournemouth Sym. Orch. (1951–61) and the Welsh National Opera (1961–63). From 1963 to 1977 he was music director of the Royal Liverpool Phil. Orch. In 1978 he became music director of the English National Opera in London, resigning in 1979. He was knighted by Queen Elizabeth II in 1973. He was especially fond of the music of Elgar and Delius, which he performed with great élan, and was also noted for his sensitive readings of the syms. of Sibelius. He was instrumental in launching the careers of several English conductors of the younger generation, especially in his sponsorship of the Liverpool International Conductors' Competition.

Grovlez, Gabriel (Marie), French conductor and composer; b. Lille, April 4, 1879; d. Paris, Oct. 20, 1944. He studied at the Paris Cons. under Diémer, Lavignac, Gédalge, and Fauré; won 1st prize in piano there (1899); then taught piano at the Schola Cantorum (1899–1909); was conductor at the Paris Opéra (1914–34); also conducted the Chicago Opera Co., among others. He ed. the collection *Les Plus Beaux Airs de l'Opéra français* (8 vols., Paris, 1924); also publ. a book, *L'Initiation à l'orchestration* (Paris, 1944).

WORKS: Operas: *La Princesse au jardin* (Monte Carlo, 1920); *Psyché*; *Cœur de rubis* (Nice, 1922); opéra bouffe, *Le Marquis de Carabas* (1925); 2 ballets: *Maïmouna* (Paris Opéra, April 25, 1921) and *Le Vrai Arbre de Robinson* (Chicago, 1921); symphonic poems: *Madrigal lyrique*; *La Vengeance des fleurs*; *Reposoir des amants*; *Dans le jardin* for Soprano, Women's Chorus, and Orch. (1907); Violin Sonata; Cello Sonata; more than 50 songs, and many piano pieces, including *Recuerdos*, *2 études*, *A Child's Garden*, *Nocturne*, *Le Royaume puéril*, *2 impressions*, and the sets *Almanach aux images* and *London Voluntaries*.

Grozăvescu, Trajan, Rumanian tenor; b. Lugoj, Nov. 21, 1895; d. (murdered) Vienna, Feb. 15, 1927. He studied in Bucharest and Cluj; made his debut in Cluj as Pinkerton in *Madama Butterfly* in 1920; continued his vocal studies in Vienna with F. Steiner; made appearances with the Vienna Volksoper, the Prague National Theater, and the Vienna State Opera. He was shot to death by his wife.

BIBL.: M. Demeter-Grozăvescu and I. Voledi, *T. G.* (1965).

Grua, Carlo Luigi Pietro, Italian composer; b. Florence, c.1665; place and date of death unknown. He most likely was the father of **Carlo (Alisio) Pietro Grua.** He was in Dresden from 1691 to 1694, first as singer in the electoral chapel, then as assistant Kapellmeister; his opera *Camillo generoso* was produced in Dresden in 1693; he next went to the Palatine court at Düsseldorf as assistant Kapellmeister; his opera *Telegono* was given there during the 1697 Carnival; he then went to Venice, where he produced 2 operas: *Il Pastor fido* (1721) and *Romolo e Tazio* (1722).

Grua, Carlo (Alisio) Pietro, Italian composer, father of **Franz Paul (Francesco da Paula or Paolo) Grua;** b. probably in Milan, c.1700; d. Mannheim (buried), April 11, 1773. He may have been a son of **Carlo Luigi Pietro Grua.** He was Kapellmeister at Mannheim from about 1734 until his death; during this time, wrote 2 operas, *Meride* (1742) and *La clemenza di Tito* (1748); also 5 oratorios.

Grua, Franz Paul (Francesco da Paula or Paolo), German composer of Italian descent, son of **Carlo (Alisio) Pietro Grua;** b. Mannheim (baptized), Feb. 1, 1753; d. Munich, July 5, 1833. He studied with Holzbauer in Mannheim; then went to Bologna, where he was a pupil of Padre Martini, and to Parma, where he studied with Traetta. Returning to Mannheim, he became a member of the electoral orch.; in 1778, accompanied the court to Munich; became court conductor there in 1784. He wrote 1 opera, *Telemaco*, given at the Munich Carnival in 1780; also much church music.

Gruber, Franz Xaver, Austrian composer, great-great-grand-father of **H(einz) K(arl) Gruber;** b. Unterweizburg, near Hochburg, Nov. 25, 1787; d. Hallein, near Salzburg, June 7, 1863. He acquired fame as the composer of the Christmas carol *Stille Nacht, Heilige Nacht.* Of a poor family, Gruber had to do manual work as a youth, but managed to study organ; by dint of perseverance he obtained, at the age of 28, his 1st position, as church organist and schoolmaster at Oberndorf. It was there, on Christmas Eve of 1818, that a young curate, Joseph Mohr, brought him a Christmas poem to be set to music, and Gruber wrote the celebrated song.

BIBL.: K. Weinmann, *Stille Nacht, Heilige Nacht* (Regensburg, 1918); J. Mühlmann, *F.X. G.* (Salzburg, 1966); A. Schmaus and L. Kriss-Rettenbeck, *Stille Nacht, Heilige Nacht* (Innsbruck, 1967).

Gruber, Georg, Austrian conductor; b. Vienna, July 27, 1904. He studied music at the Univ. of Vienna; received his Ph.D. in 1928. In 1930 he became conductor of the famous Vienna Choirboys, and toured with them throughout Europe, South America, and the U.S. He also arranged for his choir folk songs and choral works of the Renaissance period. In 1953 he was appointed prof. of music at Rhodes Univ. in Grahamstown, South Africa.

Gruber, H(einz) K(arl), Austrian composer, great-great-grandson of **Franz Xaver Gruber;** b. Vienna, Jan. 3, 1943. He studied composition with Uhl and Jelinek; also played double bass and horn; took courses in film music at the Hochschule für Musik in Vienna (1957–63); in 1963–64 attended master classes there held by Einem. He played principal double bass in the Niederösterreiches Tonkünstler-Orch. in Vienna (1961–69); was a co-founder, with Schwertsik and Zukan, of an avant-garde ensemble, MOB art & tone ART (1968). In 1961 he joined the Vienna ensemble *die reihe* as a double-bass player; in 1969 was engaged as double-bass player in the ORF (Austrian Radio) Sym. Orch. there and also performed as an actor. In his music Gruber maintains a wide amplitude of styles, idioms, and techniques, applying the dodecaphonic method of composition in works of a jazz and pop nature. His "pandemonium," *Frankenstein!!*, which is a megamultimedia affair, with children's verses recited in a bizarre and mock-scary manner, became quite popular.

WORKS: STAGE: Melodrama, *Die Vertreibung aus dem Paradies* (The Expulsion from Paradise) for Speakers and 6 Solo Instruments (1966); "pandemonium," *Frankenstein!!*, after H.C. Artmann, for Baritone Chansonnier and Orch. (1976–77; London, Nov. 25, 1978; U.S. premiere, Tanglewood, Aug. 13, 1980; version for Vocalist and 12-player Ensemble, Berlin Festival, Sept. 30, 1979); opera, *Gomorra* (1984–90). **ORCH.:** Concerto for Orch. (1960–64); *Manhattan Broadcasts* for Light Orch. (1962–64); *fürbass,* concerto for Double Bass and Orch. (1965); *Revue* for Chamber Orch. (1968); *Vergrösserung* (Magnification; 1970); *Arien* for Violin and Orch. (1974–75); *Phantom-Bilder* (Photo-Fit Pictures) for Chamber Ensemble (1977); . . . *aus Schatten duft gewebt* (. . . of shadow fragrance woven) for Violin and Orch. (1977–78; Berlin Festival, Sept. 29, 1979); *Entmilitärisierte Zonen* (Demilitarized Zones), march-paraphrases (1979); *Charivari,* subtitled *An Austrian Journal* (1981); *Rough Music,* concerto for Percussion and Orch. (1982–83); Cello Concerto (Tanglewood, Aug. 3, 1989). **CHAMBER:** *Suite* for 2 Pianos, Wind Instruments, and Percussion (1960); *Improvisation* for Wind Quintet (1961); Concerto No. 1 for Flute, Vibraphone, Xylophone, and Percussion (1961); Concerto No. 2 for Tenor Saxophone, Double Bass, and Percussion (1961); *4 Pieces* for Solo Violin (1963); *Gioco a tre* for Piano Trio (1963); *Spiel* for Wind Quintet (1967); *3 "MOB" Pieces* for 7 interchangeable Instruments and Percussion (1968; rev. 1977); *Bossa Nova* for Ensemble (1968); *Die wirkliche Wut über den verlorenen Groschen* (A Real Rage over a Lost Penny) for 5 Players (1972). **VOCAL:** Mass for Mixed Chorus, 2 Trumpets, English Horn, Double Bass, and Percussion (1960); *Drei Lieder* for Baritone, Ensemble, and Tape (1961); *Frankenstein-Suite* for Voice and Ensemble (1970; incorporated into *Frankenstein!!*); *Reportage aus Gomorrah* for 5 Singers and 8 Players (1975–76). **PIANO:** *Episodes* for 2 Pianos (1961); *6 Episodes from a Discontinued Chronicle* (1967); *Luftschlösser* (Castles in the Air), cycle in 4 movements (1981).

Gruberová, Edita, Czech soprano; b. Bratislava, Dec. 23, 1946. She received her musical education in Prague and Vienna; made her debut with the Slovak National Theater in Bratislava in 1968; in 1972 she made a successful appearance at the Vienna State Opera; she also sang at the Bayreuth Festivals, the Hamburg State Opera, the Frankfurt Opera, the Bavarian State Opera in Munich, and other major opera houses, establishing herself as one of the finest coloratura sopranos of her generation.

Gruenberg, Erich, Austrian-born English violinist; b. Vienna, Oct. 12, 1924. After studying in Vienna, he was awarded a scholarship to enroll in the Jerusalem Cons. in 1938; subsequently was engaged as concertmaster of the radio orch. there. In 1946 he went to London; became an English citizen in 1950. He served as concertmaster of the Boyd Neel Orch.; then of the Stockholm Phil. (1956–58), the London Sym. Orch. (1962–65), and the Royal Phil. (1972–76); also made appearances as a soloist.

Gruenberg, Eugene, Austrian-American violinist and composer; b. Lemberg, Oct. 30, 1854; d. Boston, Nov. 11, 1928. He studied violin with Heissler and ensemble playing with

Hellmesberger at the Vienna Cons.; took a course in composition with Bruckner. He went to Leipzig, where he played in the Gewandhaus Orch. In 1891 he emigrated to America and taught at the New England Cons. of Music in Boston. He publ.*The Violinist's Manual* (N.Y., 1897; rev. ed., 1919, as *Violin Teaching and Violin Studies*, with a preface by Fritz Kreisler). He composed a Sym. and a Violin Sonata, and wrote a cadenza for Brahms's Violin Concerto.

Gruenberg, Louis, eminent Russian-born American composer; b. near Brest Litovsk, Aug. 3, 1884; d. Los Angeles, June 9, 1964. He was taken to the U.S. as an infant; studied piano with Adele Margulies in N.Y.; then went to Berlin, where he studied with Busoni (piano and composition); in 1912 made his debut as a pianist with the Berlin Phil.; intermittently took courses at the Vienna Cons., where he also was a tutor. In 1919 he returned to the U.S. and devoted himself to composing. He was one of the organizers and active members of the League of Composers (1923); became a champion of modern music, and one of the earliest American composers to incorporate jazz rhythms in works of symphonic dimensions (*Daniel Jazz, Jazzettes,* etc.); from 1933 to 1936 he taught composition at the Chicago Music College; then settled in California.
    WORKS: STAGE: *The Emperor Jones,* opera after O'Neill's play (Metropolitan Opera, N.Y., Jan. 7, 1933; awarded the David Bispham Medal); *The Witch of Brocken* (1912); *The Bride of the Gods* (1913); *Dumb Wife* (1921); *Jack and the Beanstalk* (libretto by John Erskine; N.Y., Nov. 19, 1931); *Queen Helena* (1936); *Green Mansions,* radio opera (CBS, Oct. 17, 1937); *Volpone,* opera (1945); *The Miracle of Flanders,* mystery play (1950); *Anthony and Cleopatra,* opera (1940–60). ORCH.: 5 syms.: No. 1 (1919; rev. 1929; won the $5,000 RCA-Victor prize, 1930; Boston, Feb. 10, 1934); Nos. 2–5 (1942–48); *Vagabondia* (1920); *The Hill of Dreams,* symphonic poem (won the Flagler prize; N.Y., Oct. 23, 1921); *Jazz Suite* (Cincinnati, March 22, 1929); *The Enchanted Isle,* symphonic poem (Worcester Festival, Oct. 3, 1929); *9 Moods* (1929); *Music for an Imaginary Ballet,* 2 sets (1929, 1944); *Serenade to a Beauteous Lady* (Chicago, April 4, 1935); 2 piano concertos (1914; 1938, rev. 1961); Violin Concerto (Philadelphia, Dec. 1, 1944); *Americana,* suite for Orch. (1945). VOCAL: *Daniel Jazz* for Tenor and 8 Instruments (N.Y., Feb. 22, 1925); *Creation* for Baritone and 8 Instruments (N.Y., Nov. 27, 1926); *Animals and Insects* for Voice and Piano; *4 Contrasting Songs; A Song of Faith,* spiritual rhapsody for Speaker, Voices, Chorus, Orch., and a Dance Group, dedicated to the memory of Mahatma Gandhi (1952–62; Los Angeles, Nov. 1, 1981); also publ. 4 vols. of Negro spirituals. CHAMBER: Suite for Violin and Piano (1914); 3 violin sonatas (1912, 1919, 1950); *Indiscretions* for String Quartet (1922); *Diversions* for String Quartet (1930); 2 string quartets (1937, 1938); *Jazzettes* for Violin and Piano (1926); 2 piano quintets (1929, 1937); *Poem in Form of a Sonatina* for Cello and Piano (1925); *4 Whimsicalities* for String Quartet (1923). PIANO: *Jazzberries, Polychromatics, Jazz Masks, 6 Jazz Epigrams, 3 Jazz Dances,* etc.
    BIBL.: R. Nisbett, *L. G.: His Life and Work* (diss., Ohio State Univ., 1979); idem, "L. G.'s American Idiom," *American Music,* III/1 (1985).

Gruhn (originally **Grunebaum**), **Nora,** English soprano of German descent; b. London, March 6, 1905. She studied at the Royal College of Music in London and with Hermine Bosetti in Munich. She made her debut in Kaiserslautern in 1928; sang for a season with the Cologne Opera (1929–30); appeared at Covent Garden in London (1929–33; 1936–37) and Sadler's Wells (1946–48). She sang the part of Gretel in an English production of Humperdinck's *Hänsel und Gretel* reportedly more than 400 times.

Grumiaux, Arthur, eminent Belgian violinist; b. Villers-Perwin, March 21, 1921; d. Brussels, Oct. 16, 1986. He studied violin and piano with Fernand Quinet at the Charleroi Cons. and violin with Alfred Dubois at the Royal Cons. in Brussels; also took private lessons in composition with Enesco in Paris.

In 1940 he was awarded the Prix de Virtuosité from the Belgian government. In 1949 he was appointed prof. of violin at the Royal Cons. In 1973 he was knighted by King Baudouin for his services to music; he thus shared the title of baron with Paganini. His performances were characterized by a studied fidelity to the composer's intentions, assured technical command, and a discerning delineation of the inner structure of the music.

Grümmer, Elisabeth, famous German soprano; b. Niederjeutz, near Diedenhofen, Alsace-Lorraine, March 31, 1911; d. Berlin, Nov. 6, 1986. She first pursued a career as an actress. In 1941 Herbert von Karajan invited her to sing at the Aachen Opera, which marked the beginning of a successful career. In 1951 she appeared at London's Covent Garden; in 1957 at Bayreuth. In 1959 she became a prof. at the Hochschule für Musik in West Berlin; in 1961 toured South America; in 1964 gave concerts in Korea and Japan. It was not until April 20, 1967, at the age of 56, that she sang for the 1st time at the Metropolitan Opera in N.Y., as Elsa in *Lohengrin.* Her acting ability greatly redounded to her success in opera.

Grümmer, Paul, eminent German cellist, viola da gambist, and pedagogue; b. Gera, Feb. 26, 1879; d. Zug, Oct. 30, 1965. He studied with Klengel at the Leipzig Cons. and with Becker in Frankfurt; began his career as a cellist in 1898, appearing regularly in London from 1902. He became solo cellist of the Vienna Opera and Konzertverein (1905), and was a founding member of the Busch Quartet (1913); also toured with his own chamber orch. He taught at the Vienna Academy of Music (1907–13; 1940–46), the Cologne Hochschule für Musik (1926–33), and the Berlin Hochschule für Musik (1933–40). He publ. pedagogical works, including a *Viola da Gamba Schule* (Leipzig, 1928), and ed. Bach's unaccompanied cello suites (Vienna, 1944). His autobiography was publ. as *Begegnungen* (Munich, 1963).

Grün, Jakob, Austrian violinist and teacher; b. Budapest, March 13, 1837; d. Baden, near Vienna, Oct. 1, 1916. He was a pupil of J. Böhm in Vienna and M. Hauptmann in Leipzig; in 1858 he became a member of the Weimar Court Orch.; went to Vienna in 1868, as concertmaster at the Court Opera (until 1897); from 1877 until he retired in 1909 he was a prof. at the Vienna Cons.

Grünbaum (originally **Müller**), **Therese,** famous Austrian soprano; b. Vienna, Aug. 24, 1791; d. Berlin, Jan. 30, 1876. She studied with her father, **Wenzel Müller,** the composer and conductor; appeared on stage while still a child; in 1807 went to Prague; in 1816 joined the Kärnthnertortheater in Vienna, remaining as a principal member there until 1826; while in Vienna, she gained fame for her Rossini roles; also created the role of Eglantine in Weber's *Euryanthe;* after appearances in Berlin (1828–30), she taught voice. She married the tenor **Johann Christoff** (b. Haslau, Oct. 28, 1785; d. Berlin, Oct. 10, 1870); a daughter, **Caroline** (b. Prague, March 18, 1814; d. Braunschweig, May 26, 1868), was also a soprano.

Grund, Friedrich Wilhelm, German conductor and composer; b. Hamburg, Oct. 7, 1791; d. there, Nov. 24, 1874. He was brought up in a musical family, his father having been a theater conductor. He studied cello, but after a brief concert career devoted himself mainly to conducting. In 1819 he founded in Hamburg the Gesellschaft der Freunde des Gesanges, which later became the Hamburg Singakademie. In 1828 he was engaged to lead the newly established Phil. Concerts, a post he held until 1862. In 1867 he organized (with Karl Grädener) the Hamburg Tonkünstlerverein. He wrote several operas; a cantata, *Die Auferstehung und Himmelfahrt Christi;* chamber music; and many piano pieces, which enjoyed considerable success and were praised by Schumann.

Grunenwald, Jean-Jacques, distinguished French organist and composer; b. Cran-Gevrier, near Annecy (of Swiss parentage), Feb. 2, 1911; d. Paris, Dec. 19, 1982. He studied organ with Dupré at the Paris Cons.; received 1st prize in 1935; studied composition with Henri Busser, obtaining another 1st prize in 1937. From 1936 to 1945 he was the assistant of Dupré at St.-Sulpice in Paris; from 1955 to 1970, organist at St.-Pierre-de-Montrouge. He was a prof. at the Schola Cantorum in Paris from 1958 to 1961, and from 1961 to 1966 was on the faculty of the Geneva Cons. Through the years he played more than 1,500 concerts, presenting the complete organ works of Bach and César Franck. He also became famous for the excellence of his masterly improvisations, which rivaled those of his teacher Dupré. His compositions include *Fêtes de la lumière* for Orch. (1937); Piano Concerto (1940); *Concert d'été* for Piano and String Orch. (1944); lyric drama, *Sardanapale*, after Byron (1945–50); *Ouverture pour un Drame sacre* for Orch. (1954); *Cantate pour le Vendredi Saint* (1955); *Psalm 129 (De profundis)* for Chorus and Orch. (1959); *Fantaisie en dialogue* for Organ and Orch. (1964); Sonata for Organ (1964); piano pieces; etc.

Grüner-Hegge, Odd, Norwegian conductor; b. Christiania, Sept. 23, 1899; d. there (Oslo), May 11, 1973. He studied piano and compostion at the Christiania Cons.; then took courses in conducting with Weingartner. He was conductor of the Olso Phil. (1931–61) and of the Norwegian Opera there (1961–69). He appeared as a guest conductor throughout Europe. He composed some orch. works; a Violin Sonata (1915); a Piano Trio (1918; rev. 1959); piano pieces; etc.

Grünfeld, Alfred, Austrian pianist and composer, brother of **Heinrich Grünfeld;** b. Prague, July 4, 1852; d. Vienna, Jan. 4, 1924. He studied in Prague, and at Kullak's Academy in Berlin; settled in Vienna in 1873, and established himself as a pianist and teacher; also made tours in other European countries. He composed an operetta, *Der Lebemann* (Vienna, Jan. 16, 1903), and the comic opera *Die Schönen von Fogaras* (Dresden, 1907); made brilliant arrangements for piano of waltzes by Johann Strauss, Jr.; also publ. piano studies and various other pieces.

Grünfeld, Heinrich, Austrian cellist and teacher, brother of **Alfred Grünfeld;** b. Prague, April 21, 1855; d. Berlin, Aug. 26, 1931. He studied at the Prague Cons.; went to Berlin in 1876, and taught at Kullak's Academy; also played chamber music. He publ. a book of memoirs, *In Dur und Moll* (Berlin, 1924).

Grunn, John Homer, American pianist and composer; b. West Salem, Wis., May 5, 1880; d. Los Angeles, June 6, 1944. He studied piano with E. Liebling in Chicago and then at the Stern Cons. in Berlin; taught piano at the Chicago Musical College (1903–7), then settled in Los Angeles as a piano teacher in 1910. He wrote a number of pieces based on Indian motifs: the ballets *Xochitl* and *The Flower Goddess* (both on Aztec subjects); *Hopi Indian Dance* for Orch.; *Zuni Indian Suite* for Orch.; many songs (*From Desert and Pueblo*, etc.).

Grützmacher, Friedrich (Wilhelm Ludwig), renowned German cellist and teacher; b. Dessau, March 1, 1832; d. Dresden, Feb. 23, 1903. He received his musical training from his father, a chamber musician at Dessau; at the age of 16 he went to Leipzig, and produced such a fine impression that Ferdinand David secured for him the post of 1st cellist of the Gewandhaus Orch. (1849). In 1860 he went to Dresden, where he remained for more than 40 years, until his death, as a teacher and chamber music player. Among his pupils were Hugo Becker and several other well-known cellists. He wrote a Cello Concerto; *Hohe Schule des Violoncellspiels* (Leipzig, 1891); several books of cello studies, and numerous arrangements for cello of works by classical composers; also ed. cello works by Beethoven, Mendelssohn, Chopin, and Schumann.

Guadagni, Gaetano, famous Italian castrato contralto, later soprano; b. Lodi or Vicenza, c.1725; d. Padua, Nov. 1792. He began his career in Parma (1746); in 1748, went to London, where he attracted the attention of Handel, who gave him contralto parts in *Messiah* and *Samson;* after many successful appearances in London, he sang in Dublin (1751–52); then went to Paris (1754) and to Lisbon (1755), where he studied with Gizziello. He then returned to Italy; in 1762, Gluck se-

cured an engagement for him in Vienna to sing Orfeo in Gluck's opera. In 1769 Guadagni was again in London. In 1770 he sang in Munich; in 1772 he appeared in Venice; in 1776 he was summoned by Frederick the Great to Potsdam, receiving great acclaim; in 1777, he settled in Padua, where he sang mainly at the Basilica del Santo. He was not only a fine singer but an excellent actor; also wrote various arias, 1 of which, *Pensa a serbarmi, o cara,* is preserved in the Bologna library.

Guadagnini, family of famous Italian violin makers. **Lorenzo** (1689–1748) used the label "Laurentius Guadagnini, alumnus Antonius Stradivarius," and he may have studied with Stradivarius in Cremona shortly before the latter's death in 1737. Lorenzo's son, **Giovanni Battista** (b. Cremona, 1711; d. Turin, Sept. 18, 1786), received his training presumably from his father, and may have been with him at the shop of Stradivarius; he followed his father from Cremona to Piacenza (1740–49); worked in Milan (1749–58); was in Parma (1759–71); then settled in Turin. His violins are regarded as the finest of the Guadagninis. His 2 sons, **Giuseppe** (1736–1805) and **Gaetano** (1745–1831), continued the family tradition and manufactured some good instruments, but failed to approach the excellence of their father's creations. Violin-making remained the family's occupation through 4 more generations in Turin; the last representative, **Paolo Guadagnini,** perished in the torpedoing of an Italian ship, on Dec. 28, 1942.

BIBL.: W. von Lütgendorff, *Die Geigen- und Lautenmacher vom Mittelalter bis zur Gegenwart* (Frankfurt, 1904); E. Doring, *The G. Family of Violin Makers* (Chicago, 1949).

Guadagno, Anton, Italian-born American conductor; b. Castellammare del Golfo, May 2, 1925. He studied at the Accademia di Santa Cecilia in Rome and at the Salzburg Mozarteum. His teachers in conducting were Ferrara, Molinari, C. Zecchi, and Karajan. He appeared in many of the regional opera houses of Italy; then served as an assistant conductor at the Metropolitan Opera in N.Y. (1958–59) and as music administrator of the Philadelphia Lyric Opera (1966–72). Returning to Europe, he was named chief conductor of the Vienna Volksoper; then became conductor of the Palm Beach (Fla.) Opera (1984).

Gualdo, John (Giovanni), Italian musician and wine merchant; place and date of birth unknown; d. Philadelphia, Dec. 20, 1771. He arrived in Philadelphia from London in 1767 and opened a store; among other things, he sold instruments and taught violin, flute, guitar, etc.; also arranged music; presented concerts; the 1st of these, given in Philadelphia on Nov. 16, 1769, was devoted largely to Gualdo's own compositions, and may well be regarded as the earliest "composer's concert" in America. He died insane. His *6 easy evening entertainments for 2 mandolins or 2 violins with a thorough bass for the harpsichord or violincello* are in MS in the Library of Congress, Washington, D.C.; the printed op. 2, *6 Sonates for 2 German flutes with a thorough bass* (his name appears as **Giovanni Gualdo da Vandero**), is in the British Museum.

BIBL.: O. Sonneck, *Early Concert-Life in America* (Leipzig, 1907).

Guami, Francesco, Italian trombonist and composer, brother of **Gioseffo (Giuseppe) Guami;** b. Lucca, c.1544; d. there, Jan. 30, 1602. He was trombonist at the court chapel in Munich (1568–80), and maestro di cappella at Baden-Baden (1580–88), Venice (1593), and Lucca (1598). He wrote madrigals on the Venetian model, and some church music.

BIBL.: P. Crabtree, *The Vocal Works of Gioseffo and F. G.* (diss., Univ. of Cincinnati, 1971).

Guami, Gioseffo (Giuseppe), Italian organist and composer, brother of **Francesco Guami;** b. Lucca, c.1540; d. there, 1611. He was organist at the court in Munich (1568–79) and maestro di cappella at the court in Genoa (1585). From 1588 to 1591 he was 1st organist at S. Marco in Venice (while Giovanni Gabrieli was 2nd organist); in 1591 he returned to Lucca as church organist. His surviving compositions include madrigals, motets, and toccatas; in his madrigals, he followed the Venetian school.

BIBL.: A. Bonaccorsi, *Maestri di Lucca: i G. e altri musicisti* (Florence, 1967); P. Crabtree, *The Vocal Works of G. and Francesco G.* (diss., Univ. of Cincinnati, 1971).

Guarino, Carmine, Italian composer; b. Rovigo, Oct. 1, 1893; d. Genoa, June 5, 1965. He studied violin and composition at the Naples Cons. His 1st opera, *Madama di Challant,* set in a Verdian tradition, was produced there on March 9, 1927, attracting favorable comments. He was also the composer of the 1st Italian radio opera, *Cuore di Wanda* (Radio Italiano, Dec. 20, 1931). Other works for the stage are an operetta, *Gaby* (San Remo, March 20, 1924); a musical fable, *Tabarano alla Corte di Nonesiste* (1931); the operas *Balilla* (Rome, March 7, 1935) and *Sogno di un mattino d'autunno* (Cluj, March 30, 1936); and a ballet, *El Samet, il silenzioso* (1958).

Guarino, Piero, Italian conductor and composer; b. Alexandria, Egypt, June 20, 1919. He studied at the Athens Cons. and the Accademia di Santa Cecilia in Rome. He then conducted opera and sym. throughout Italy. In 1960 he returned to Alexandria as director of the Cons.; also taught at the Salzburg Mozarteum. In 1962 he was named chief conductor of the Orch. of the Academy of Music in Naples, with which he toured in Europe and the U.S. In 1969 he was appointed director of the Cons. at Sassari in Sardinia. Among his works are *Chamber Music,* to words of James Joyce, set for Middle Strings and Piano (1963), and a 1-act opera, *Vettura-Letto,* after Thornton Wilder (1969).

Guarneri, famous Italian family of violin makers. The Italian form of the name was **Guarnieri;** Guarneri was derived from the Latin spelling, **Guarnerius;** the labels invariably used the Latin form. **Andrea,** head of the family (b. Cremona, c.1625; d. there, Dec. 7, 1698), was a pupil of Nicolo Amati; he lived in Amati's house from 1641 to 1646, and again from 1650 to 1654, when, with his wife, he moved to his own house in Cremona and began making his own violins, labeling them as "alumnus" of Amati and, after 1655, "ex alumnus," often with the additional words of "sub titolo Sanctae Theresiae." Andrea's son **Pietro Giovanni,** known as **Peter of Mantua** (b. Cremona, Feb. 18, 1655; d. Mantua, March 26, 1720), worked first at Cremona; then went to Mantua, where he settled; he also used the device "sub titolo Sanctae Theresiae." Another son of Andrea, **Giuseppe Giovanni Battista,** known as **Silius Andreae** (b. Cremona, Nov. 25, 1666; d. there, c.1740), worked in his father's shop, which he eventually inherited; in his own manufactures, he departed from his father's model and followed the models of Stradivarius. Giuseppe's son **Pietro** (b. Cremona, April 14, 1695; d. Venice, April 7, 1762) became known as **Peter of Venice;** he settled in Venice in 1725, and adopted some features of the Venetian masters Montagnana and Serafin. Another son of Giuseppe, **(Bartolomeo) Giuseppe Antonio,** known as **Giuseppe del Gesù,** from the initials IHS often appearing on his labels (b. Cremona, Aug. 21, 1698; d. there, Oct. 17, 1744), became the most celebrated member of the family; some of his instruments bear the label "Joseph Guarnerius Andreae Nepos Cremonae," which establishes his lineage as a grandson of Andrea. His violins are greatly prized, rivaling those of Stradivarius in the perfection of instrumental craftsmanship; he experimented with a variety of wood materials, and also made changes in the shapes of his instruments during different periods of his work. Such great virtuoso violinists as Heifetz, Stern, Szeryng, Grumiaux, and Paganini used his instruments.

BIBL.: G. de Piccolellis, *Liutai antichi e moderni, genealogia degli Amati et dei Guarnieri* (Florence, 1886); W. Lütgendorff, *Die Geigen- und Lautenmacher vom Mittelalter bis zur Gegenwart* (Frankfurt, 1904; 6th ed., 1922); H. Petherick, *Joseph Guarnerius, His Work and His Master* (London, 1906); H. Wenstenberg, *Joseph Guarnerius del Gesù Abbildungen und Beschreibungen seiner Instrumente aus seinen drei Perioden* (Berlin, 1921); W. Hill, *Violin Makers of the G. Family, 1626–1762: Their Life and Work* (London, 1931).

Guarnieri, Antonio, Italian conductor; b. Venice, Feb. 1, 1880; d. Milan, Nov. 25, 1952. He studied cello; was a member of the Martucci Quartet. In 1922 he conducted at La Scala in Milan; in 1929 he became one of its regular conductors, remaining there until his death. He excelled in the Italian repertoire.

Guarnieri, (Mozart) Camargo, outstanding Brazilian composer; b. Tiété, Feb. 1, 1907. He studied piano and composition in São Paulo before going, in 1938, to Paris, where he took a course in composition with Charles Koechlin and one in conducting with Rühlmann. In 1942 and 1946 he visited the U.S. as a conductor of his own works. He later returned to Brazil, where he taught at various institutions. His music is permeated with "Brasilidad," a syndrome that is Brazilian in its melody and rhythm; his *Dansa brasileira* is typical in its national quality.

WORKS: *Pedro Malazarte,* comic opera (1931); opera, *Um homem só* (1960); 4 syms. (1944, 1946, 1952, 1963); 5 piano concertos (1936, 1946, 1964, 1967, 1970); 2 violin concertos (1940, 1953); *Overture concertante* (1943); *Dansa brasileira* for Orch. (São Paulo, March 7, 1941; orig. for Piano, 1931); *Dansa negra* for Orch. (1947); *Chôro* for Violin and Orch. (1951); *Variations on a Northeast Brazilian Theme* for Piano and Orch. (1953); *Suite IV Centenário* for Orch. (1954; Louisville, Jan. 15, 1955); *Chôro* for Clarinet and Orch. (1956); *Chôro* for Piano and Orch. (1957); *Sêca,* cantata (1957); *Suite Vila Rica* for Orch. (1958); *Chôro* for Cello and Orch. (1961); Piano Concertino (1961); *Seresta* for Piano and Chamber Orch. (1965); *Guaná bará,* cantata (1965); *Homage to Villa-Lobos* for Wind Orch. (1966); *Següencia, Coral e Ricercare* for Chamber Orch. (1966); 3 string quartets (1932, 1944, 1962); 5 violin sonatas (1930, 1933, 1950, 1959, 1962); many songs and piano pieces.

Guarrera, Frank, American baritone; b. Philadelphia, Dec. 3, 1923. He studied voice with Richard Bonelli in Philadelphia. On Dec. 14, 1948, he made his Metropolitan Opera debut in N.Y. as Escamillo in *Carmen;* was invited by Toscanini to sing at La Scala in Milan; also made guest appearances in San Francisco, Chicago, Paris, and London. He was best known for his performances of Italian roles.

Guastavino, Carlos, Argentine composer; b. Santa Fé, April 5, 1912. He studied chemistry; then took a course in composition with Athos Palma. He cultivates miniature forms, mostly for piano; of these, the suites *10 cantilenas argentinas* (1958) and *Las presencias* (1961) radiate a certain melorhythmic charm. He also wrote a ballet, *Fué una vez* (1942); *Romance de Santa Fé* for Piano and Orch. (1952); Violin Sonata (1952); choruses on Argentine themes; many songs.

Guba, Vladimir, Russian composer; b. Kiev, Dec. 22, 1938. He studied at the Kiev Cons. with Liatoshinsky; became interested in modern techniques of composition; applied the 12-tone method in his piano pieces *Deformation* and *Echo* (1961); also wrote a series of 30 piano pieces, *In the World of Childhood,* and a cycle of 24 piano pieces, *Sonorous Exhibits.*

Gubaidulina, Sofia, remarkable Russian composer of unique individuality; b. Chistopol, Oct. 24, 1931. She was descended of a Tatar father (her grandfather was a mullah) and of a mother who had both Russian and Jewish blood (she once said that she was the place where East and West met). Her sources of inspiration in composition were similarly diverse, extending from mystical Eastern elements to Catholic and Russian Orthodox conformations. She studied at the Kazan Cons. (graduated, 1954); then enrolled at the Moscow Cons. to study composition with Peiko and Shebalin. From her very 1st essays in composition she followed vectorially divergent paths without adhering to any set doctrine of modern techniques. Perhaps her most astounding work is the Concerto for Bassoon and Low String Instruments, in 5 movements (1975); in it, the bassoon is embedded in a net of 4 cellos and 3 double basses, creating a claustrophobic syndrome of congested low sonorities, while the solo instrument is forced to perform acrobatic feats to escape constriction, including such effects as labial glissandos and explosive iterations of a single thematic note. Her music soon penetrated into the music world far beyond the Soviet frontiers, and her works became solicited by performers in Europe and the U.S. She made several voyages to the U.S. to hear performances of her works, and was a guest at the Boston Festival of Soviet Music in 1988; but it took a decisive change in official Soviet policy before her music received full recognition in her own country.

WORKS: ORCH.: Sym. (1958); Piano Concerto (1959); *Intermezzo* for 16 Harps, 8 Trumpets, and Drums (1961); *Fairy Tale* (1971); *Concordanza* for Chamber Orch. (1971); *Music for Harpsichord and Instruments from the Collection of Mark Pekarsky* (1972; Pekarsky is a Russian percussionist); *Intervals* (1972); *Detto II* for Cello and Chamber Orch. (1972); Concerto for Bassoon and Low String Instruments (1975; Moscow, May 6, 1976); *Percussio per Pekarsky,* concerto for Percussion, Mezzo-soprano, and Orch. (1976); Concerto for Orch. and Jazz Band (1976); Concerto for Piano and String Orch. (1978); *Introitus,* concerto for Piano and Chamber Orch. (Moscow, Feb. 22, 1978); *Offertorium,* concerto for Violin and Orch. (1980–86); *The 7 Words* for Cello, Bayan, and String Orch. (1982; a contemplation of Christ's 7 last words on the cross); *Stimmen . . . verstummen . . . ,* sym. (1986); *Pro et Contra* (Louisville, Nov. 24, 1989). **VOCAL:** *Fazelija* for Soprano and Orch. (1956); *Night in Memphis* for Mezzo-soprano, Men's Chorus, and Orch. (1968); *Rubaiyat* for Bass and Chamber Orch. (1969); *Laudatio pacis* for Choirs and Orch. (1975); *Perception* for Soprano, Bass, 2 Violins, 2 Violas, 2 Cellos, Double Bass, and Tape (1983); *Homage to Marina Tsvetaeva* for Unaccompanied Chorus (1984); *Homage to T.S. Eliot* for Soprano and 8 Instruments (1987). **CHAMBER:** Piano Quintet (1957); *Allegro rustico* for Flute and Piano (1963); Piano Sonata (1965); *5 Études* for Harp, Double Bass, and Percussion (1965); Sonata for Percussion (1966); *Pantomimes* for Double Bass and Piano (1966); *Musical Tog* for Piano (1969); 3 string quartets (1971, 1987, 1987); *10 Preludes* for Cello (1974); *Humore e silenzio* for Percussion, and Harpsichord or Cello (1974; Moscow, April 16, 1975); Sonata for Double Bass and Piano (1975); *Misterioso* for 7 Percussion (1977); *Detto I* for Organ and Percussion (1978); *Jubilatio* for 4 Percussion (1979); *In croce* for Cello and Organ (Kazan, March 26, 1979); *Garden of Joy and Sorrow* for Flute, Viola, and Harp (1980); Sonata for Violin and Cello (1981); *Descensio* for 3 Trombones, 3 Percussion, Harp, Harpsichord or Celesta, and Celesta or Piano (Paris, April 30, 1981); *Quasi hoquetus* for Viola, Bassoon, and Piano (1984); *In the Beginning Was Rhythm* for 7 Percussion (1984); Accordion Sonata (1985).
BIBL.: G. McBurney, "Encountering G.," *Musical Times* (March 1988).

Gubrud, Irene (Ann), American soprano; b. Canby, Minn., Jan. 4, 1947. She studied at St. Olaf College in Northfield, Minn. (B.M., 1969), and with Marion Freschel at the Juilliard School of Music in N.Y. She won the Naumburg International Voice Competition (1980), and made her operatic debut as Mimi in St. Paul, Minn., in 1981; she taught at Washington Univ. in St. Louis (1976–81). She is successful in a comprehensive repertoire, extending from early music to the avant-garde.

Gudehus, Heinrich, distinguished German tenor; b. Altenhagen, near Celle, March 30, 1845; d. Dresden, Oct. 9, 1909. He first studied organ, and also taught school; then took up singing; made his debut in Berlin in Spohr's *Jessonda* (Jan. 7, 1871). After several engagements in various German towns, he sang Parsifal in Bayreuth (July 28, 1882) with excellent success; was with the Dresden Opera from 1880 to 1890; appeared in London (1884) in Wagnerian roles; was with the Metropolitan Opera in N.Y. (1890–91); then returned to Germany, where he sang at the Berlin Royal Opera (1891–96). He settled in Dresden as a voice teacher.

Gudmel, Claude. See Goudimel, Claude.

Gudmundsen-Holmgreen, Pelle, Danish composer; b. Copenhagen, Nov. 21, 1932. He studied theory and composition

with Finn Höffding, and with Svend Westergaard at the Royal Danish Cons. in Copenhagen (1953–58); served as stage manager of the Royal Theater there (1959–64); taught composition at the Århus Academy of Music (1967–73). He then devoted himself mainly to composition. In 1973 he received the Carl Nielsen Prize, and in 1980 won the Nordic Council Music Prize for his sym. *Antifoni.* He followed serial techniques; then experimented with a "new simplicity" achieved through persistent repetition of notes and patterns; employed optical notation, in which the distance between notes in a score equals the "time span" between the playing of those notes.

WORKS: BALLET: *Flight* (1981). **ORCH.:** *Ouverture* for Strings (1955); *Chronos* for 22 Instrumentalists (1962); 3 syms.: No. 1 (1962–65); No. 2, *På Rygmarven* (1966); No. 3, *Antifoni* (1974–77); *Collegium Musicum Concerto* for Chamber Orch. (1964); *Mester Jakob* (*Frère Jacques*) for Chamber Orch. (1964); *Repriser* (Recapitulations) for 15 Instrumentalists (1965); *5 Pieces* (1966); *Rerepriser* (Rerecapitulations) for 13 Instruments (1967); *Stykke for stykke* (Piece by Piece) for Chamber Orch. (1968); *3 Movements* for String Orch. and Cowbells (1968); *Tricolore IV* (Copenhagen, Sept. 11, 1969); *Spejl II* (Mirror II; Copenhagen, Feb. 24, 1974); *Triptykon,* concerto for Percussion and Orch. (1985); *Concord* for Chamber Orch. (1988). **CHAMBER:** 8 string quartets (1959–86); *In terra pax* for Clarinet, Piano, and 2 Percussionists (1961); *Canon* for 9 Instruments (1967); *Plateaux pour 2* for Cello and Percussion (1970); *Terrace,* in 5 stages, for Wind Quintet (1970); *Solo* for Electric Guitar (1972); *The Old Man* for 2 Flutes, Harp, Viola, and Cello (1976); *Ritual Dances* for 6 Percussionists, or 5 Percussionists and Electric Guitar (1976). **PIANO/ORGAN:** Variations for Piano (1959); *Udstillingsbilleder* (Pictures at an Exhibition) for Piano (1968); *Spejl III* for Organ (1974). **VOCAL:** *5 Songs* for Soprano, Flute, Violin, and Cello (1958); *3 Songs to Texts from Politiken* (a Danish newspaper) for Alto, Violin, Viola, Cello, Guitar, and Percussion (1967); *Songs Without* for Mezzo-soprano and Piano (1976); other vocal works; a cappella choruses, including *Examples* (1975).

Gueden, Hilde, noted Austrian soprano; b. Vienna, Sept. 15, 1917; d. Klosterneuburg, Sept. 17, 1988. She studied with Wetzelsberger at the Vienna Cons., then made her debut in operetta at the age of 16. She made her operatic debut as Cherubino in 1939 in Zürich, where she sang until 1941. After appearing in Munich (1941–42) and Rome (1942–46), she sang at the Salzburg Festival (1946); subsequently was a leading member of the Vienna State Opera until 1973. She 1st appeared at London's Covent Garden with the visiting Vienna State Opera in 1947; her Metropolitan Opera debut followed in N.Y. on Nov. 15, 1951, when she appeared as Gilda; she continued to sing there until 1960. In 1951 she was made an Austrian Kammersängerin. She maintained a wide-ranging repertoire, singing roles from Mozart to contemporary composers such as Britten and Blacher; she also was a fine operetta singer. She particularly excelled as Despina, Sophie, Zerbinetta, and Daphne.

Guédron, Pierre, important French composer; b. Beauce province, Normandy, between 1570 and 1575; d. probably in Paris, 1619 or 1620. He was a chorister in the service of Cardinal de Guise, Louis II of Lorraine, by 1585; following the cardinal's assassination in 1588, he entered the service of the royal chapel; was given 1st place as maître des chanteurs de la chambre about 1590, then was made compositeur de la chambre du Roi (1601) and valet de chambre to the king and maître des enfants de la musique (1603); his son-in-law, Antoine Boësset, succeeded him in 1613 while he took up the post of intendant des musiques de la chambre du Roy et de la Reyne Mère (he is listed as surintendant in court records of 1617 and 1619). He was one of the most significant composers of airs de cour and ballets de cour of his era; some of these were included in a number of the ballets he wrote for the court.

WORKS: BALLETS (all 1st perf. in Paris): *Ballet sur la naissance de Monseigneur le duc de Vendosme* (1602); *Ballet de* *la Reyne* (1609); *Ballet de Monseigneur le duc de Vendosme, ou Ballet d'Alcine* (1610); *Ballet du maître à danser* (c.1612); *Ballet de Madame, soeur du Roy* (1613); *Ballet des Argonautes* (1614); *Ballet du triomphe de Minerve* (1615); *Ballet de Monsieur le Prince Condé* (1615); *Ballet du Roy, ou Ballet de la délivrance de Renaud* (1617); *Ballet des princes* (1618); *Ballet du Roy sur l'aventure de Tancrède en la forest enchantée* (1619).

AIRS: *Airs de cour* for 4 and 5 Voices (Paris, 1602; 1 part-book not extant); *Airs de cour* for 4 and 5 Voices (Paris, 1608); *Second livre d'airs de cour* for 4 and 5 Voices (Paris, 1613); *Troisième livre d'airs de cour* for 4 and 5 Voices (Paris, 1617); *Quatrième livre d'airs de cour* for 4 and 5 Voices (Paris, 1618; 1 part-book not extant); *Cinquième livre d'airs de cour* for 4 and 5 Voices (Paris, 1620; 4 part-books not extant). Airs were also arranged for voice and lute and were publ. in various contemporary anthologies; several were also arranged for instruments.

BIBL.: H. Quittard, "L'Air de cour: P. G.," *Revue Musicale* (1905); H. Prunières, *Le Ballet de cour en France avant Benserade et Lully* (Paris, 1914); T. Gérold, *L'Art du chant en France au XVIIᵉ siècle* (Strasbourg, 1921); L. de La Laurencie, "Un Musicien dramatique du XVIIᵉ siècle: P. G.," *Rivista Musicale Italiana*, XXIX (1922); D. Walker, "The Influence of *Musique mesurée à l'antique*, particularly on the *Airs de cour* of the Early Seventeenth Century," *Musica Disciplina*, II (1948); A. Verchaly, "Un Précurseur de Lully: P. G.," *XVIIᵉ siècle*, XXI–XXII (1954); M. McGowan, *L'Art du ballet de cour en France, 1581–1643* (Paris, 1963); D. Royster, *P. G. and the Air de cour, 1600–1620* (diss., Yale Univ., 1972).

Guelfi, Giangiacomo, Italian baritone; b. Rome, Dec. 21, 1924. He studied law in Florence; then began voice studies with Titta Ruffo; made his debut in Spoleto in 1950 as Rigoletto; in 1952 joined La Scala in Milan; also sang in Chicago and in London. On Feb. 5, 1970, he made his Metropolitan Opera debut in N.Y. as Scarpia.

Guénin, Marie-Alexandre, French violinist and composer; b. Maubeuge, Feb. 20, 1744; d. Étampes, Jan. 22, 1835. He showed a precocious talent, and was sent to Paris for study with Gaviniès (violin) and Gossec (composition). In 1771 he joined the orch. of the Paris Opéra; later was active in the Concert Spirituel; taught at the École Royale de Chant (later, Paris Cons.), and about 1808 went to Spain, where he was in the service of Charles IV; later was in Marseilles; then was 2nd violin in the Musique du Roi (1814–16). Several of his works were publ. in his lifetime: 6 syms., 6 violin duos, 6 string trios, etc.

Guéranger, Dom Prosper Louis Pascal, French ecclesiastic scholar; b. Sable-sur-Sarthe, April 4, 1805; d. Solesmes, Jan. 30, 1875. As abbot of the Benedictine monastery at Solesmes, he carried out research and produced writings that gave the impetus to and laid the foundations for scholarly investigations leading to the restoration of Gregorian melodies. Dom Guéranger and the Benedictines of Solesmes played a role of prime importance in the accomplishment of this work. He wrote *Institutions liturgiques* (3 vols., 1840–53; 2nd ed., 4 vols., 1878–85); *L'Année liturgique* (15 parts, 1840–1901; continued by Fromage); *Ste. Cécile et la Société Romaine* (1873; 8th ed., 1898).

BIBL.: G. Guépin, *Prosper G.* (Le Mans, 1876); *Bibliographie des Bénédictins de la Congrégation de France* (Solesmes, 1889); Chamard, *G. et l'abbé Bernier* (Angers, 1901); P. Delatte, *Dom G., abbé de Solesmes* (2 vols., Paris, 1909).

Guerra-Peixe, César, Brazilian composer; b. Petropolis, March 18, 1914. He studied composition with Newton Pádua at the Conservatorio Brasileiro in Rio de Janeiro (1938–43) and also with H.J. Koellreutter; played violin in theater orchs. and in the National Sym. Orch.; arranged music for radio. As a composer, he plunged headlong into the torrent of dodecaphony, but about 1949 changed his orientation and returned to his Brazilian roots, nurtured by melorhythmic folk-song resources. He wrote 2 syms. (1946, 1960); Nonet (1945); 2 string

quartets (1947, 1958); Violin Sonata (1950); Piano Trio (1960); Guitar Sonata (1969); *Duo* for Clarinet and Bassoon (1970); pieces for guitar.

Guerrero, Francisco, Spanish composer; b. Seville, 1528 (probably on St. Francis Day, Oct. 4); d. there, Nov. 8, 1599. He was a pupil of his brother, Pedro, and for a short time of Morales. In 1546 he became maestro de capilla of Jaén Cathedral; in 1549 he went to Seville as cantor at the Cathedral there. In both 1551 and 1554 he was offered a similar post at the Cathedral of Malaga, but declined it. In 1556 he was in Lisbon; in 1567, in Cordova; in 1570, in Santander; in 1581–82 he went to Rome; in 1588 he was in Venice, whence he undertook a pilgrimage to Palestine. His account of his journey, *El viaje de Jerusalem que hizo Francisco Guerrero*, was publ. in 1611, and went through numerous eds. As a composer he was greatly appreciated by his contemporaries, but the comparisons with Morales or Victoria overestimate his importance.

WORKS: *Sacrae cantiones vulgo moteta* (1555); *Psalmorum, Liber I, accedit Missa defunctorum* (1559; 2nd ed., with Italian title, 1584); *Canticum beatae Mariae quod Magnificat nuncupatur, per octo musicae modos variatum* (1563); *Liber I missarum* (1566; contains 9 masses for 4–5 Voices and 3 motets for 4–8 Voices); *Motteta* (1570); *Missarum Liber II* (1582; contains 7 masses and a *Missa pro defunctis*); *Liber vesperarum* (1584; includes 7 Psalms, 24 hymns, 8 Magnificats, Te Deum, etc.); *Passio . . . secundum Matthaeum et Joannem more Hispano* (1585); *Canciones y villanescas espirituales* (1589); *Mottecta* (1589); *Missa Saeculorum Amen* (1597); etc. Reprints have been made by Eslava (2 *Passiones*) in *Lira sacro-hispana* and by Pedrell in *Hispaniae schola musica sacra* (in vol. II: *Magnificat, Officium defunctorum*, Passions, antiphonals, etc.; in vol. VI: a *Falso bordone*). The *Libro de música para vihuela, intitulado Orphénica Lyra* of Miguel de Fuenllana contains some works by Guerrero arranged for vihuela. Two vols. of Guerrero's *Opera omnia* (unfinished), ed. by V. Garcia and M.Q. Garalda (1955–57), containing *Canciones y villanescas espirituales*, constitute vols. 16 and 19 of Monumentos de la Música Española.

BIBL.: R. Mitjana y Gordon, *F. G. (1528–1599): Estudio crítico-biográfico* (Madrid, 1922); R. Stevenson, *Spanish Cathedral Music in the Golden Age* (Berkeley and Los Angeles, 1961).

Guerrini, Guido, Italian composer; b. Faenza, Sept. 12, 1890; d. Rome, June 13, 1965. He was a pupil of Consolini (violin) and of Toschi and Busoni (composition) at the Liceo Musicale at Bologna; was prof. of harmony there (1920–24); prof. of composition at the Parma Cons. (1925–28); director of the Florence Cons. (1928–47); director of the Bologna Cons. (1947–49); in 1950 was appointed director of the Santa Cecilia Cons. in Rome; retired in 1960. He wrote the books *Ferruccio Busoni, La vita, la figura, e l'opera* (Florence, 1941) and *A. Vivaldi: La vita e l'opera* (Florence, 1951).

WORKS: Operas: *Zalebì* (1915); *Nemici* (Bologna, Jan. 19, 1921); *La vigna* (1923–25; Rome, March 7, 1935); *Enea*, after Virgil (Rome, Feb. 11, 1953); *Missa pro defunctis*, in memory of Marconi, for Solo Voices, Chorus, and Orch. (1938–39); *La città beata, la città perduta*, biblical cantata (1942); *Tre liriche* for Voice and Orch. (1947); Cello Concerto (1914); *Canzonetta* for 4 Saxophones (1938); *Arcadia* for Oboe and Piano; Piano Quintet; 3 string quartets (1920, 1922, 1959); *Le Suore*, 3 pieces for Harp; vocal works: *Le fiamme su l'altare* for Voice, Double String Quartet, and 2 Harps; songs.

Guerrini, Paolo (Antigono), Italian music historian; b. Bagnolo Mella, Brescia, Nov. 18, 1880; d. Brescia, Nov. 19, 1960. He specialized in Italian sacred music; ed. the periodical *Brixia Sacra* (1910–25); in 1930 he began publication of the historical studies *Memorie storiche della Diocesi di Brescia*; served further as archivist and librarian in Brescia. In 1936 he was appointed canon of the Brescia Cathedral. He revived and tr. into Italian the music books of Cardinal Katschthaler as *Storia della musica sacra* (Turin, 1910; 3rd ed., 1936).

Guest, George (Howell), Welsh organist and conductor; b. Bangor, Caernarvon, Feb. 9, 1924. He was a chorister at the cathedrals in Bangor and Chester; studied organ at the latter with Boyle; then was an organ scholar at St. John's College, Cambridge (Mus.B., 1951), under Robin Orr, whom he succeeded as organist and choirmaster. Under his discriminating direction, the choir of St. John's College attained international renown through numerous recordings and tours.

Guézec, Jean-Pierre, French composer; b. Dijon, Aug. 29, 1934; d. Paris, March 9, 1971. He enrolled at the Paris Cons., where he attended classes of Messiaen, Milhaud, and Rivier; received the premier prix in 1963; joined the faculty of the Paris Cons. in 1969.

WORKS: Concerto for Violin and 14 Instruments (1960); *Concert en trois parties* for 11 Instruments (1961); *Suite pour Mondrian* for Orch. (1962); *Architectures colorées* for 15 Instruments (1964); *Ensemble multicolore 65* for 18 Instruments (1965); *Formes* for Orch. (1966); *Textures enchaînées* for 13 Wind Instruments (1967); *Assemblages* for 28 Instruments (1967); String Trio (1968); *Reliefs polychromés* for Chorus (1969); *Couleurs juxtaposées* for 2 Percussion Groups (1969); *Onze pour cinq* for Percussionists (1970).

Guglielmi, Pietro Alessandro, noted Italian composer, father of **Pietro Carlo Guglielmi**; b. Massa di Carrara, Dec. 9, 1728; d. Rome, Nov. 18, 1804. He began his musical training with his father, Jacopo Guglielmi, then studied with Durante at the S. Maria di Loreto Cons. in Naples. His 1st opera, *Lo solachianello 'mbroglione*, was given in Naples in 1757. During the next decade, he wrote no fewer than 25 operas; these included such popular works as *Il ratto della sposa* (Venice, 1765) and *La Sposa fedele* (Venice, 1767), which, along with *L'impresa d'opera* (Venice, 1769), were performed throughout Europe with notable success. In 1767 he went to London, where he brought out several operas; his wife, known as Maria Leli or Lelia Acchiapati (or Acchiappati), sang in his *Ezio* at the King's Theatre (Jan. 13, 1770). He returned to Italy in 1772, and continued to compose stage works with abandon; among the most popular were *La Villanella ingentilita* (Naples, Nov. 8, 1779), *La Quakera spiritosa* (1782), *Le vicende d'amore* (Rome, 1784), *La Virtuosa di Mergellina* (Naples, 1785), *La Pastorella nobile* (Naples, April 15, 1788), *La bella pescatrice* (Naples, Oct. 1789), and *La Serva innamorata* (Naples, 1790). His oratorios were also highly successful, and were often performed in stage versions; *La morte di Oloferne* (Rome, April 22, 1791) was a great favorite. In 1793 he was appointed maestro di cappella at S. Pietro in the Vatican; in 1797 he also assumed the post of maestro di cappella at S. Lorenzo Lucina. Guglielmi was one of the major Italian composers of his day. His productivity and facility were remarkable, making it possible for him to write for the stage or the church with equal aplomb.

WORKS: OPERAS (all 1st perf. in Naples unless otherwise given): COMIC: *Lo solachianello 'mbroglione* (1757); *Il Filosofo burlato* (1758); *I capricci di una vedova* (1759); *La Moglie imperiosa* (1759); *I du soldati* (1760); *L'Ottavio* (1760); *Il finto cieco* (1761); *La Donna di tutti i caratteri* (1762); *La Francese brillante* (1763); *Li Rivali placati* (1764); *Il ratto della sposa* (Venice, 1765); *La Sposa fedele* (Venice, 1767); *I Viaggiatori ridicoli tornati in Italia* (London, 1768); *L'impresa d'opera* (Venice, 1769); *Il Disertore* (London, 1770); *L'Amante che spende* (Venice, 1770); *Le pazzie di Orlando* (London, 1771); *Il carnevale di Venezia, o sia La Virtuosa* (London, 1772); *L'assemblea* (London, 1772); *Mirandolina* (Venice, 1773); *Il matrimonio in contrasto* (1776); *I fuoriusciti* (1777); *Il raggiratore di poca fortuna* (1779); *La Villanella ingentilita* (1779); *La Dama avventuriera* (1780); *La Serva padrona* (1780); *Le nozze in commedia* (1781); *Mietitori* (1781); *La semplice ad arte* (1782); *La Quakera spiritosa* (1783); *La Donna amante di tutti, e fedele a nessuno* (1783); *I finti amori* (1784); *La Virtuosa di Mergellina* (1785); *L'inganno amoroso* (1786); *Le astuzie villane* (1786); *Lo scoprimento inaspettato* (1787); *La Pastorella nobile* (1788); *Gl'inganni delusi* (1789); *La bella pescatrice*

(1789); *La Serva innamorata* (1790); *L'azzardo* (1790); *Le false apparenze* (1791); *La Sposa contrastata* (1791); *Il Poeta di campagna* (1792); *Amor tra le vendemmie* (1792); *La lanterna di Diogene* (Venice, 1793); *La Pupilla scaltra* (Venice, 1795); *L'amore in villa* (Rome, 1797). SERIOUS: *Tito Manlio* (Rome, 1763); *L'Olimpiade* (1763); *Siroe re di Persia* (Florence, 1764); *Farnace* (Rome, 1765); *Tamerlano* (Venice, 1765); *Adriano in Siria* (Venice, 1765); *Sesostri* (Venice, 1766); *Demofoonte* (Treviso, 1766); *Antigono* (Milan, 1767); *Il Re pastore* (Venice, 1767); *Ifigenia in Aulide* (London, 1768); *Alceste* (Milan, 1768); *Ruggiero* (Venice, 1769); *Ezio* (London, 1770); *Demetrio* (London, 1772); *Tamas Kouli-Kan nell'Indie* (Florence, 1774); *Merope* (Turin, 1775); *Vologeso* (Milan, 1775); *La Semiramide riconosciuta* (1776); *Artaserse* (Rome, 1777); *Ricimero* (1777); *Enea e Lavinia* (1785); *Laconte* (1787); *Arsace* (Venice, 1788); *Rinaldo* (Venice, 1789); *Ademira* (1789); *Alessandro nell'Indie* (1789); *Il trionfo di Camilla* (1795); *La morte di Cleopatra* (1796); *Ippolito* (1798); *Siface e Sofonisba* (1802). He also composed many other stage works and vocal works.

BIBL.: G. Bustico, *Pier A. G.: Appunti biografici* (Massa, 1898); idem, *Un musicista massese: Pier A. G.* (Barga, 1926).

Guglielmi, Pietro Carlo, Italian composer, son of **Pietro Alessandro Guglielmi**; b. Rome or Naples, c.1763; d. Naples, Feb. 21, 1817. After study at the S. Maria di Loreto Cons. in Naples, he went to Spain; his 1st opera was performed at Madrid in 1794; he then lived in Italy, producing operas in Naples, Florence, and Rome. He went to London in 1809; presented several operas at the King's Theatre; returned to Italy in 1811, and was appointed maestro di cappella to the Duchess Beatrice at Massa di Carrara. A list of his works, including some 40 operas, oratorios, and cantatas, was publ. by Francesco Piovano in the *Rivista Musicale Italiana* (1909–10). Although several works were popular in their day, their lack of intrinsic worth doomed them to eventual oblivion.

Gui, Vittorio, eminent Italian conductor; b. Rome, Sept. 14, 1885; d. Florence, Oct. 16, 1975. He studied at the Liceo Musicale di Santa Cecilia in Rome; began his career as an opera conductor; then conducted in Parma and Naples, and at La Scala in Milan (1923); eventually settled in Florence; was founder of the Maggio Musicale Fiorentino in 1933. From 1947 to 1965 he conducted opera in England; was counselor of Glyndebourne Festival Opera (1960–65). Among his compositions are the opera *Fata Malerba* (Turin, May 15, 1927) and the symphonic works *Giulietta e Romeo* (1902), *Il tempo che fu* (1910), *Scherzo fantastico* (1913), *Fantasia bianca* (1919); an orch. experiment making use of films), and *Giornata di festa* (1921). He publ. the books *Nerone di Arrigo Boito* (Milan, 1924) and *Battute d'aspetto*, a vol. of critical essays (Florence, 1944).

Guidetti, Giovanni Domenico, Italian ecclesiastic scholar; b. Bologna (baptized), Jan. 1, 1531; d. Rome, Nov. 30, 1592. After taking Holy Orders, he went to Rome, where he became Palestrina's pupil and in 1575 was appointed "cappellano" and chorister in the papal choir. From 1576 to 1581 he worked with Palestrina on a revised ed. of the Gradual and Antiphonary, but this work being forestalled by the publication of Leichtenstein's ed. (Venice, 1580), he obtained permission to publ. the services for everyday use: *Directorium chori ad usum sacrosanctae basilicae Vaticanae* (Rome, 1582, and several reprints); *Cantus ecclesiaticus passionis Domini Nostri Jesu Christi* (Rome, 1586); *Cantus ecclesiasticus officii majoris* (Rome, 1587; new ed., 1619); he also publ. *Praefationes in cantu firmo* (Rome, 1588).

Guido d'Arezzo or **Guido Aretinus,** famous Italian reformer of musical notation and vocal instruction; b. c.991; d. after 1033. He received his education at the Benedictine abbey at Pomposa, near Ferrara. He left the monastery in 1025, as a result of disagreements with his fellow monks, who were envious of his superiority in vocal teaching; he was then summoned by Bishop Theobald of Arezzo to the cathedral school there;

it was because of this association that he became known as Guido d'Arezzo. The assertions that he traveled in France and spent several years at the monastery of Saint-Maur des Fossés, near Paris (see, for example, Dom G. Morin in *Revue de l'art chrétien*, 1888) are not borne out by documentary evidence. Still more uncertain are the claims of his travels in Germany, and even in England. However this may be, his fame spread and reached the ears of Pope John XIX, who called him to Rome to demonstrate his system of teaching (1028). In his last years, he was a prior of the Camaldolite fraternity at Avellano. Guido's fame rests on his system of solmization, by which he established the nomenclature of the major hexachord Ut, Re, Mi, Fa, Sol, La, from syllables in the initial lines of the Hymn of St. John:

> *Ut* queant laxis *Re*sonare fibris
> *Mi*ra gestorum *Fa*muli tuorum,
> *Sol*ve polluti *La*bii reatum,
>   Sancte Joannes.

No less epoch-making was Guido's introduction of the music staff of 4 lines, retaining the red *f*-line and the yellow *c*-line of his predecessors, and drawing between them a black *a*-line, above them a black *e*-line, and writing the plainsong notes (which he did *not* invent) in regular order on these lines and in the spaces:

New black line e———————
Old yellow line c———————
New black line a———————
Old red line   f———————

He also added new lines above or below these, as occasion required; thus, Guido's system did away with all uncertainty of pitch. Another invention credited to Guido is the so-called Guidonian hand, relating the degrees of the overlapping hexachords to various places on the palm of the left hand, a device helpful in directing a chorus by indicating manually the corresponding positions of the notes. Opinions differ widely as to the attribution to Guido of all these innovations; some scholars maintain that he merely popularized the already-established ideas and that solmization, in particular, was introduced by a German abbot, Poncius Teutonicus, at the abbey of Saint-Maur des Fossés. Guido's most essential treatises are *Micrologus de disciplina artis musicae* (c.1026; ed. by J. Smits van Waesberghe in Corpus Scriptorum de Musica, IV, 1955) and *Epistola de ignoto cantu* (c.1028–29; Eng. tr. in O. Strunk, *Source Readings in Music History*, N.Y., 1950).

BIBL.: L. Angeloni, *Sopra la vita, le opere ed il sapere di G. d'A.* (Paris, 1811); R. Kiesewetter, *G. von A.* (1840); G. Ristori, *Biografia di G. Monaco d'A.* (2nd ed., 1868); M. Falchi, *Studi su G. Monaco di San Benedetto* (1882); H. Wolking, *G.s Micrologus de disciplina artis musicae und seine Quellen* (Emsdetten, 1930); J. Smits van Waesberghe, *De musicopaedogogico et theoretico Guidone Aretino eiusque vita et moribus* (in Latin; Florence, 1953); H. Oesch, *G. von A.* (Bern, 1954); J. Smits van Waesberghe, *Musikerziehung. Lehre und Theorie der Musik im Mittelalter*, Musikgeschichte in Bildern, 3/3 (Leipzig, 1969); D. Harbinson, "The Hymn *Ut queant laxis*," *Music & Letters* (Jan. 1971).

Guignon, Jean-Pierre (real name, **Giovanni Pietro Ghignone**), famous Italian-born French violinist and composer; b. Turin, Feb. 10, 1702; d. Versailles, Jan. 30, 1774. He went to Paris in his youth; was engaged as music tutor to the Dauphin, and persuaded the King to revive and bestow on him the title of Roi des Violons et Ménétriers, which had last been used in 1695; every professional musician in France was required to join a guild and to pay a fee to Guignon as holder of the title; so much opposition was aroused by this requirement that Parliament considered the case and deprived Guignon of this prerogative. He wrote 2 violin concertos, 6 sets of sonatas, and several duos.

Guilbert, Yvette, famous French *diseuse* and folksinger; b. Paris, Jan. 20, 1865; d. Aix-en-Provence, Feb. 2, 1944. She made her debut in Paris as an actress in 1877; in 1890 began her career as a café singer; later toured Europe and the U.S.,

where she became noted for her interpretations of French folk songs; she regarded herself as primarily an actress. She wrote her memoirs, *La Chanson de ma vie* (Paris, 1927) and *Autres temps, autres chants* (Paris, 1946).

BIBL.: B. Knapp and M. Chipman, *That Was Y.* (London, 1966).

Guillemain, Louis-Gabriel, French violinist and composer; b. Paris, Nov. 7, 1705; d. (suicide) Chaville, near Paris, Oct. 1, 1770. He was a member of the King's orch. and gave concerts as a virtuoso. He was one of the 1st French composers to write violin sonatas with a developed clavichord accompaniment. He also wrote several ballets, and instrumental music for various combinations.

Guillou, Jean, French organist, pianist, and composer; b. Angers, April 4, 1930. He began playing the piano and organ as a child; in 1952 he went to study with Dupré, Messiaen, and Duruflé at the Paris Cons.; upon graduation, he taught organ playing in Lisbon (1955–58); then moved to Berlin, where he was active as a concert pianist and organist (1958–63). Returning to France, he was appointed organist of the St. Eustache Church in Paris; from 1972 he conducted annual master classes in Zürich. As a solo organist he has given concerts in Poland, Russia, Japan, and the U.S.; he often concludes his concerts with improvisations on themes proposed by members of the audience. He has made numerous effective transcriptions for organ of works by Bach, Vivaldi, Mozart, and other composers; also a transcription of Stravinsky's *Petrouchka*. His own compositions, especially those before 1960, are written in a neo-Baroque idiom.

WORKS: Oratorio, *Le Jugement dernier* (1958; Krakow, June 16, 1968); 3 concertos for Organ and Orch.: No. 1, *Inventions* (1956); No. 2 (1966; Leningrad, Oct. 10, 1972); No. 3 (1967; Rouen, Jan. 16, 1972); *Triptyque* for Strings (1957); 3 syms.: *Judith* (No. 1), with Soprano (1968; Paris, Feb. 25, 1971); No. 2 for Strings (1971; Paris, Nov. 30, 1972); No. 3 (1974); Piano Concerto (1970); 5 *Colloques*: No. 1 for Flute, Oboe, Violin, and Piano (1954); No. 2 for Piano and Organ (1960); No. 3 for Oboe, Harp, Celesta, Vibraphone, Xylophone, Timpani, Percussion, 4 Cellos, and 2 Double Basses (1961); No. 4 for Piano, Organ, and Percussion (1965); No. 5 for Piano and Organ (1975); *Cantilia* for Piano, Harp, Timpani, and 4 Cellos (1961); Oboe Quartet (1975); 2 piano sonatas (1967, 1975). Organ: 18 Variations (1954); Sinfonietta (1958); *Fantaisie* (1962); Toccata (1963); *Pour le Tombeau de Colbert* (1963); *Symphonie initiatique* for 3 Organs (1965; 1 live, 2 on tape); *Allen* (1966); 6 *Sagas* (1968); *La Chapelle des Abîmes* (1973); *Scènes d'enfants* (1973).

Guilmant, (Félix) Alexandre, eminent French organist and composer; b. Boulogne, March 12, 1837; d. Meudon, near Paris, March 29, 1911. He studied organ with his father, Jean-Baptiste Guilmant (1793–1890); took harmony lessons with Gustave Carulli in Boulogne. In 1860 he took an advanced course in organ playing with Lemmens in Brussels; then played organ in various churches in Paris, including St.-Sulpice (1862) and Notre Dame (1868); in 1871 he was appointed organist of Ste. Trinité, remaining at this post for 30 years. He was one of the founders of the Schola Cantorum (1894); in 1896 he was appointed prof. of organ at the Paris Cons.; also appeared as organ soloist with Paris orchs. and subsequently all over Europe and in the U.S. (1893–97). He was not only a virtuoso of the 1st rank, but a master in the art of improvisation; he formed a great school of students, among whom were René Vierné, Joseph Bonnet, Nadia Boulanger, Marcel Dupré, and the American organist William Carl. He was a prolific composer of works for organ, which include 8 sonatas, 2 syms. for Organ and Orch., 25 books of organ pieces, and 10 books of *L'Organiste liturgiste;* he also wrote Psalms, vespers, motets, etc. He ed. *Archives des maîtres de l'orgue* (10 vols., Paris, 1898–1914) and *École classique de l'orgue* (1898–1903).

BIBL.: *À la mémoire de A. G.* (by his friends of the Schola; Paris, 1911); A. Eaglefield-Hull, "The Organ Works of G.," *Monthly Musical Record* (Oct.–Nov. 1914); N. Dufourcq, *La*

Musique d'orgue française (Paris, 1949); F. Sabatier, *Pour une approche d'A. G.* (Paris, 1986).

Guion, David (Wendell Fentress), American composer; b. Ballinger, Texas, Dec. 15, 1892; d. Dallas, Oct. 17, 1981. He studied piano with Leopold Godowsky in Vienna; returning to the U.S. in 1915, he occupied various teaching posts in Texas; then lived in N.Y., while continuing to gravitate toward Texas; was commissioned to write a musical panorama, *Cavalcade of America,* for the 1936 Texas centennial; his *Texas Suite* for Band followed in 1952. He devoted many years to collecting and arranging American folk songs for various folk ensembles. Of these arrangements, the most famous were *Turkey in the Straw, Arkansas Traveler,* and *Home on the Range.* He also wrote an African ballet suite, *Shingandi,* and several orch. suites, among them *Southern Nights Suite, Sheep and Goat Walking to the Pasture, Alley Tunes,* and *Mother Goose Suite.*

Guiraud, Ernest, French composer; b. New Orleans, June 23, 1837; d. Paris, May 6, 1892. He studied with his father, Jean Baptiste Guiraud; produced his 1st opera, *Le Roi David,* in New Orleans at the age of 15. He then went to Paris, which was his home for the rest of his life; studied at the Cons. with Marmontel (piano) and Halévy (composition); won the Grand Prix de Rome in 1859 with his cantata *Bajazet et le joueur de flûte.* He stayed in Rome for 4 years; then returned to Paris, where his 1-act opera *Sylvie* was produced at the Opéra-Comique (May 11, 1864). He was appointed a prof. at the Cons. in 1876; among his students were Debussy, Gédalge, and Loeffler. He wrote the recitatives to Bizet's *Carmen* and completed the orchestration of Offenbach's *Les Contes d'Hoffmann.* His operas (all 1st perf. in Paris) include *En prison* (March 5, 1869), *Le Kobold* (July 2, 1870), *Madame Turlupin* (Nov. 23, 1872), *Piccolino* (April 11, 1876; his most popular stage work), *Galante aventure* (March 23, 1882), and *Frédégonde* (completed by Saint-Saëns; Dec. 18, 1895). He also wrote a ballet, *Gretna Green* (Paris, May 5, 1873); 2 suites for Orch. (c.1871, 1886); *Caprice* for Violin and Orch. (c.1885). He publ. a treatise on instrumentation (Paris, 1892).

Gulak-Artemovsky, Semyon Stepanovich, Russian baritone and composer; b. Gorodishche, Feb. 16, 1813; d. Moscow, April 17, 1873. He studied voice with Glinka in St. Petersburg; sang at the Imperial Opera there (1842–64); then lived in Moscow. His opera *Zaporozhets za Dunayem* (A Cossack beyond the Danube) was produced in St. Petersburg on April 26, 1863, and subsequently acquired considerable popularity in Russia.
Bibl.: L. Kaufman, *S.S. G.-A.* (Kiev, 1962; in Ukrainian).

Gulbranson, Ellen (née **Norgren**), esteemed Swedish soprano; b. Stockholm, March 4, 1863; d. Oslo, Jan. 2, 1947. She studied at the Stockholm Cons., then with Mathilde Marchesi in Paris; returning to Stockholm, she made her concert debut in 1886; in 1896 she sang the part of Brünnhilde at Bayreuth, with great success; she also sang in Berlin, Paris, Moscow, Amsterdam, and London.

Gulda, Friedrich, remarkable Austrian pianist; b. Vienna, May 16, 1930. He studied piano with Felix Pazofsky; then enrolled at the Vienna Academy of Music as a piano student of Bruno Seidlhofer. At the age of 16 he won 1st prize at the International Pianists' Contest in Geneva, and immediately embarked on a concert career, giving recitals in Europe (1947–48), South America (1949), and the U.S., making a brilliant American debut in Carnegie Hall, N.Y., on Oct. 11, 1950. He was praised for his intellectual penetration of the music of Bach, Beethoven, and Mozart. About 1955 he became intensely fascinated by jazz, particularly in its improvisatory aspect, which he construed as corresponding to the freedom of melodic ornamentation in Baroque music. He often included jazz numbers (with drums and slap bass) at the end of his recitals; he learned to play the saxophone, began to compose for jazz, and organized the Eurojazz Orch. As a further symptom of his estrangement from musical puritanism he returned the Beethoven Bicentennial ring given to him by the Vienna Academy of Music in appreciation of his excellence in playing Bee-

thoven's music, and gave a speech explaining the reasons for his action. He composed and performed jazz pieces, among them *Music* Nos. 1 and 2 for Piano and Big Band (1962, 1963); *Music* for 3 Jazz Soloists and Band (1962); Sym. in F for Jazz Band and Orch.; *The Veiled Old Land* for Jazz Band (1964); *The Excursion* for Jazz Orch., celebrating the flight of the American spaceship *Gemini 4* (1965); *Concertino for Players and Singers* (1972). He made a bold arrangement of Vienna waltzes in the manner of the blues; also composed a jazz musical, *Drop-out oder Gustav der Letzte* (1970), freely after Shakespeare's *Measure for Measure;* publ. a book of essays, *Worte zur Musik* (Munich, 1971).
Bibl.: E. Jantsch, *F. G.: Die Verantwortung des Interpreten* (Vienna, 1953); K. Geitel, *Fragen an F. G.* (Berlin, 1973).

Gulli, Franco, distinguished Italian violinist; b. Trieste, Sept. 1, 1926. He studied violin with his father, making his debut in 1933; then went to the Trieste Cons.; also studied in Siena and Paris; his teachers included Arrigo Serato and Joseph Szigeti. He married the pianist **Enrica Cavallo;** in 1947 they formed the noted Gulli-Cavallo Duo, which made several successful tours. In 1968 he was soloist with the Dallas Sym.; subsequently played with several American orchs. In 1972 he was appointed prof. at the Indiana Univ. School of Music. An artist of integrity, he secures fine performances of Classical and modern music faithful to the style of the period.

Gumbert, Ferdinand, German composer; b. Berlin, April 22, 1818; d. there, April 6, 1896. After a short study of singing, he appeared at the Cologne Opera (1840–42); in 1842 he settled in Berlin as a voice teacher and also began to compose. His songs, written in a facile, eclectic style, enjoyed a considerable vogue; the song *An des Rheines grünen Ufern* was used as an insert in Lortzing's opera *Undine.* He produced several operettas in Berlin, including *Der kleine Ziegenhirt* (Jan. 21, 1854) and *Bis der Rechte kommt* (Nov. 20, 1856). He publ. *Musik, Gelesenes und Gesammeltes* (Berlin, 1860).
Bibl.: W. Neumann, *F. G.* (Kassel, 1856).

Gumpelzhaimer, Adam, German composer, writer on music, and teacher; b. Trostberg, Upper Bavaria, 1559; d. Augsburg, Nov. 3, 1625. He studied music with Jodocus Entzenmüller at the Benedictine cloister of St. Ulrich and St. Afra in Augsburg; was Kantor and Präzeptor of the school and church of St. Anna there from 1581; was made a citizen of Augsburg in 1590. He publ. the treatise-textbook *Compendium musicae,* which went through 13 eds.; it included compositions by Gumpelzhaimer as well as by other composers; the canons he wrote for it are particularly noteworthy.
Works (all publ. in Augsburg): *Compendium musicae* (1591; 2nd ed., augmented, 1595, as *Compendium musicae latino-germanicum;* 13th ed., 1681; facsimile, Ann Arbor, 1965); (27) *Neue teutsche geistliche Lieder . . . nach Art der welschen Villanellen* for 3 Voices (1591; 3rd ed., 1611, as *Lustgärtlins teutsch und lateinischer geistlicher Lieder erster Theil*); (29) *Neue teutsche geistliche Lieder nach Art der welschen Canzonen* for 4 and 5 Voices (1594; 3rd ed., 1619, as *Wirtzgärtlins teutsch und lateinischer geistlicher Lieder, erster Theil*); *Contrapunctus* for 4 and 5 Voices (1595); (27) *Sacrorum concentuum . . . liber primus* for 8 Voices (1601); *Psalmus LI* for 5 Voices (1604); *Lustgärtlins* (28) *teutsch und lateinischer geistlicher Lieder ander Theil* for 3 Voices (1611); (25) *Sacrorum concentuum . . . cum duplici basso ad organorum usum . . . liber secundus* for 8 Voices (1614); *Zwai schöne Weihenächt Lieder* for 4 Voices (1618); *Wirtzgärtlins* (31) *teutsch und lateinischer geistlicher Lieder, ander Theil* for 4 and 5 Voices (1619); *Christliches Weihenacht Gesang* for 4 Voices (1620). O. Mayr ed. *Adam Gumpelzhaimer: Ausgewählte Werke* in Denkmäler der Tonkunst in Bayern, XIX, Jg. X/2 (1909).
Bibl.: O. Mayr, *A. G.: Ein Beitrag zur Musikgeschichte der Stadt Augsburg im 16. und 17. Jahrhundert* (Augsburg, 1908).

Gumpert, Friedrich Adolf, German horn player; b. Lichtenau, April 27, 1841; d. Leipzig, Dec. 31, 1906. He studied with Hammann in Jena; from 1864, played 1st horn in the Gewandhaus Orch., Leipzig; was also a prof. at the Cons. there. He publ. valuable manuals for horn and other instruments: *Praktische Hornschule* (1879); a *Solobuch* for horn (difficult passages from operas, syms., etc.); *Hornquartette* (2 books); *Hornstudien*; and orch. studies for clarinet, oboe, bassoon, trumpet, and cello.

Gundry, Inglis, English composer; b. London, May 8, 1905. He studied law at Balliol College, Oxford; in 1935 entered the Royal College of Music in London, where he took a music course with Vaughan Williams. In 1942 he was appointed Royal Marines Schoolmaster; then taught music history at London Univ. In 1960 he became music director of the Sacred Music Drama Soc. He wrote the operas (all to his own librettos) *Naaman, The Leprosy of War* (1938), *The Return of Odysseus* (1941; rev. 1957), *The Partisans* (London, May 28, 1946), *Avon* (London, April 11, 1949), *The Logan Rock* (Portchurno, Aug. 15, 1956), *The Prince of the Coxcombs* (London, Feb. 3, 1965), *The 3 Wise Men* (London, Jan. 11, 1968), and *The Prisoner Paul* (1969); a ballet, *Sleep* (1943); *Symphonic Fantasy* for Orch. (1948); and the song cycles *The Black Mountains* (1956) and *The Year of the Firebird* (1957). He also arranged several early English music dramas.

Gungl, Joseph (József), famous Hungarian bandmaster and composer; b. Zsámbék, Dec. 1, 1810; d. Weimar, Jan. 31, 1889. He studied in Buda; played the oboe in the band of an artillery regiment in the Austrian army, and later became that band's conductor; he wrote a number of marches and dances, which became extremely popular; traveled with his band all over Germany. In 1843 he established his own orch. in Berlin; made an American tour in 1849; then returned to Europe and lived mostly in Munich and Frankfurt.

Gunn, Glenn Dillard, American pianist, conductor, and music critic; b. Topeka, Kans., Oct. 2, 1874; d. Washington, D.C., Nov. 22, 1963. He studied at the Leipzig Cons. with Carl Reinecke (piano); appeared as a pianist in German cities; returning to the U.S. in 1900, he taught at the Chicago Musical College (1901–5). In 1915 he founded the American Sym. Orch., whose object was the performance of American works and the engagement of American soloists. He was music critic for the *Chicago Tribune* (1910–15), the *Chicago Herald and Examiner* (1922–36), and the *Washington Times-Herald* (1940–54). He publ. *A Course of Lessons on the History and Esthetics of Music* (Chicago, 1912) and *Music, Its History and Enjoyment* (N.Y., 1930).

Gunn, John, Scottish cellist and writer on music; b. Edinburgh, c.1765; d. there, c.1824. In 1789 he went to London, where he taught cello and flute; returned to Edinburgh in 1802.

WRITINGS: *40 Scotch Airs arranged as trios for flute, violin and violoncello; The Art of Playing the German Flute on New Principles; The Theory and Practice of Fingering the Violoncello* (London, 1793); *An Essay, Theoretical and Practical, on the Application of Harmony, Thorough-Bass, and Modulation to the Violoncello* (Edinburgh, 1801); *An Historical Inquiry respecting the Performance on the Harp in the Highlands of Scotland from the earliest Times until it was discontinued about the year 1734* (Edinburgh, 1807).

Gunsbourg, Raoul, Rumanian-French impresario; b. Bucharest, Dec. 25, 1859; d. Monte Carlo, May 31, 1955. After directing opera companies in Russia, he became the director of the Grand Theatre in Lille (1888–89), the Nice Opera (1889–91), and the Monte Carlo Opera (1893–1950), where he produced several of his own operas (he wrote the piano scores, and the orchestration was done by L. Jehin); of these, *Le Vieil Aigle,* after Maxim Gorky's fable (Feb. 13, 1909), had a modicum of success.

Gura, Eugen, distinguished German bass-baritone, father of **Hermann Gura;** b. Pressern, near Saatz, Bohemia, Nov. 8, 1842; d. Aufkirchen, Bavaria, Aug. 26, 1906. He studied in

Vienna and in Munich; sang in Munich (1865–67), Breslau (1867–70), and Leipzig (1870–76), obtaining extraordinary success; then was in Hamburg (1876–83) and Munich (1883–96). He was particularly impressive in Wagnerian roles; his performance of Hans Sachs was greatly praised. He publ. *Erinnerungen aus meinem Leben* (Leipzig, 1905).

Gura, Hermann, German baritone, son of **Eugen Gura;** b. Breslau, April 5, 1870; d. Bad Wiessee, Bavaria, Sept. 13, 1944. He studied with Hasselbeck and Zenger in Munich, making his debut as the Dutchman in Weimar in 1890; then sang throughout Europe (1890–96). He subsequently was a singer and producer at the Schwerin Hoftheater in Munich (1896–1908), then director of the Berlin Komische Opera (from 1911); also worked at London's Covent Garden as a producer in 1913. After producing opera in Helsinki from 1920 to 1927, he taught voice in Berlin.

Guridi (Bidaola), Jésus, Spanish organist and composer; b. Vitoria, Alava province, Sept. 25, 1886; d. Madrid, April 7, 1961. He studied harmony with Valentín Arín, and then with José Sainz Besabé in Bilbao; took courses in piano with Grovlez, organ with Decaux, composition with Sérieyx, and counterpoint and fugue with d'Indy at the Paris Schola Cantorum; studied organ and composition with Jongen in Liège; finally took a course in instrumentation with Neitzel in Cologne. He was an organist in Bilbao (1909–29); also conducted the Bilbao Choral Soc. (1911–26). In 1939 he settled in Madrid, where he became prof. of organ at the Cons. in 1944. During his years in Bilbao, he promoted the cause of Basque folk music; publ. an album of 22 Basque songs. His zarzuelas make frequent use of Basque folk music; of these, *El caserio* (Madrid, 1926) attained enormous success in Spain. Other stage works include *Mirentxu,* idyll in 2 acts (Madrid, 1915); *Amaya,* lyric drama in 3 acts (Bilbao, 1920); and *La Meiga* (Madrid, 1928). He also wrote a symphonic poem, *Una aventura de Don Quijote* (1916); *Sinfonia pirenáica; Basque Sketches* for Chorus and Orch.; an orch. suite, *10 Basque Melodies* (very popular in Spain); a number of a cappella choral works on Basque themes; 4 string quartets; pieces for piano; songs.

BIBL.: J. de Arozamena, *J. G.* (Madrid, 1967).

Gurlitt, Cornelius, German organist and composer; b. Altona, Feb. 10, 1820; d. there, June 17, 1901. He studied piano with Johann Peter Reinecke in Altona, and with Weyse in Copenhagen. In 1845 he made a journey through Europe; he met Schumann, Lortzing, Franz, and other eminent composers. In 1864 he was appointed organist of the Altona Cathedral, retaining this post until 1898; also taught at the Hamburg Cons. (1879–87). He wrote an opera, *Die römische Mauer* (Altona, 1860); another opera, *Scheik Hassan,* was not performed. He also composed 3 violin sonatas, 3 cello sonatas, several cycles of songs, etc. He is chiefly remembered, however, for his numerous piano miniatures, in Schumann's style; a collection of these was publ. by W. Rehberg, under the title *Der neue Gurlitt* (2 vols., Mainz, 1931).

Gurlitt, Manfred, German conductor and composer; b. Berlin, Sept. 6, 1890; d. Tokyo, April 29, 1972. He studied in Berlin with Humperdinck (composition) and Karl Muck (conducting); rapidly progressed as a professional conductor; was a conductor in Essen, Augsburg, and Bremen (1914–27). After 1933, he was deprived of his position by the Nazi regime; in 1939 he settled in Japan as a teacher and conductor; organized the Gurlitt Opera Co. in Tokyo.

WORKS: Operas: *Die Heilige* (Bremen, Jan. 27, 1920); *Wozzeck* (Bremen, April 22, 1926), *Soldaten* (1929); *Nana* (1933); *Seguidilla Bolero* (1937); *Nordische Ballade; Wir schreiten aus; 3 politische Reden* for Baritone, Men's Chorus, and Orch.; *Goya Symphony* (1950); *Shakespeare Symphony* (1954) for 5 Solo Voices and Orch.; songs with Orch.; concertos for Piano, for Violin, for Cello; Piano Quartet; songs.

Gurlitt, Wilibald, eminent German musicologist and editor; b. Dresden, March 1, 1889; d. Freiburg im Breisgau, Dec. 15, 1963. He studied musicology at the Univ. of Heidelberg with Philipp Wolfrum; also with Hugo Riemann and Arnold Schering at the Univ. of Leipzig, where he received his Ph.D. in 1914 with the dissertation *Michael Praetorius (Creuzbergensis): Sein Leben und seine Werke* (publ. in Leipzig, 1915); subsequently was an assistant to Riemann. He served in World War I, and was taken prisoner in France. After the Armistice, he became a lecturer at the Univ. of Freiburg; directed its dept. of musicology from 1920; was made a full prof. in 1929, but was removed from his position by the Nazi regime in 1937; resumed his professorship in 1945; retired in 1958. Gurlitt's investigations of the organ music of Praetorius led him to construct (in collaboration with Oscar Walcker) a "Praetorius organ," which was to reproduce the tuning of the period. This gave impetus in Germany to performance of historic works on authentic or reconstructed instruments. Gurlitt's other interests included the problem of musical terminology, resulting in the publication of his *Handwörterbuch der musikalischen Terminologie*. In 1952 he revived the moribund *Archiv für Musikwissenschaft*. He edited the 1st 2 vols. of the 12th ed. of Riemann's *Musik-Lexikon* (Mainz, 1959 and 1961). He also publ. *Johann Sebastian Bach: Der Meister und sein Werk* (Berlin, 1936; 4th ed., 1959; in Eng., St. Louis, 1957).

BIBL.: A. Schmitz, "W. G.," *Jahrbuch der Akademie der Wissenschaften und der Literatur* (Mainz, 1964).

Gurney, Ivor (Bertie), English poet and composer; b. Gloucester, Aug. 28, 1890; d. Dartford, Kent, Dec. 26, 1937. He was a chorister at Gloucester Cathedral; studied at the Royal College of Music in London with Stanford and Vaughan Williams; served in World War I, was wounded and gassed, and never recovered his physical and mental health; the 2 vols. of his war poems illustrate the turmoil of his inner life. After the Armistice, Gurney began to compose songs; 27 were publ. before his death, and several more were included in a 2-vol. ed. of his melodies publ. posth. Gurney's gift was not for larger forms; he was at his best in his songs; he also wrote 5 *Western Watercolors*, 5 preludes for Piano, and some violin pieces.

BIBL.: C. Moore, *Maker and Lover of Beauty: I. G., Poet and Songwriter* (Rickmansworth, 1976); M. Hurd, *The Ordeal of I. G.* (Oxford, 1978); M. Pilkington, *G., Ireland, Quilter and Warlock* (London, 1989).

Guschlbauer, Theodor, Austrian conductor; b. Vienna, April 14, 1939. He was educated at the Vienna Academy of Music and in Salzburg; then was conductor of the Vienna Baroque Ensemble (1961–69); subsequently served as chief conductor of the Salzburg Landestheater (1966–68); then went to Lyons as conductor of the Opera. In 1975 he was appointed chief conductor of the Landestheater in Linz; concurrently assumed the post of chief conductor of the Linz-Bruckner Sym. Orch. and director of the annual Bruckner Festival. In 1983 he became chief conductor of the Strasbourg Phil. and also of the Oper am Rhein in Düsseldorf.

Gusikoff, Michel, American violinist and composer; b. N.Y., May 15, 1893; d. there, July 10, 1978. He was the great-grandson of **Michal Jozef Guzikov,** a famous performer on the xylophone. He studied violin with Kneisel and composition with Goetschius; served as concertmaster with the Russian Sym. Orch. in N.Y., the N.Y. Sym. Orch., the Philadelphia Orch., and the NBC Sym. Orch. He subsequently became concertmaster and associate conductor of the Pittsburgh Sym. Orch. He made violin arrangements of songs by Gershwin; also wrote an *American Concerto* for Violin and Orch. (1931).

Gussakovsky, Apollon, Russian composer; b. Akhtyrka, 1841; d. St. Petersburg, March 9, 1875. He was educated as a chemist and served on the science faculty of the Univ. of St. Petersburg. He became acquainted with Balakirev as early as 1857, and became an associate of the nationalist school of Russian composers; both Balakirev and Mussorgsky thought highly of his talents. The majority of his works were written between 1857 and 1861; among these were *Allegro* for Orch. and "Let There Be Light," the 1st movement of a projected sym. (St. Petersburg, Jan. 27, 1861); a String Quartet; "Foolish or Comical Scherzo"; piano works; and songs.

BIBL.: A. Gozenpud, "Lost Talent (A.S. G.)," *Sovetskaya Muzyka*, no. 4 (1951); L. Lisich, "Forgotten Composers of 'Moguchaya kuchka,' A. G.," *Muzykalnaya zhizn*, no. 3 (1973).

Gutchë, Gene (real name, **Romeo Maximilian Eugene Ludwig Gutsche**), German-born American composer; b. Berlin, July 3, 1907. He studied in Germany; then went to the U.S., where he undertook additional academic work at the Univ. of Minnesota with Donald Ferguson and at the Univ. of Iowa with Philip Greeley Clapp (Ph.D., 1953); held 2 Guggenheim fellowships (1961, 1964). His music is marked by a fairly advanced idiom and a neo-Romantic treatment of programmatic subject matter. In some of his orch. works he applies fractional tones by dividing the strings into 2 groups tuned at slightly differing pitches.

WORKS: Sym. No. 1 (Minneapolis, April 11, 1950); Sym. No. 2 (1950–54); Sym. No. 3 (1952); *Rondo capriccioso* (1953; N.Y., Feb. 19, 1960; with the application of fractional tones); Piano Concerto (Minneapolis, June 19, 1956); Cello Concerto (1957); Sym. No. 4 (1960; Albuquerque, March 8, 1962); Sym. No. 5 for Strings (Chautauqua, N.Y., July 29, 1962); *Bongo Divertimento* for Solo Percussionist and Orch. (1962); *Timpani Concertante* (Oakland, Calif., Feb. 14, 1962); Violin Concerto (1962); *Genghis Khan*, symphonic poem (Minneapolis, Dec. 6, 1963); *Rites in Tenochtitlán* for Small Orch. (St. Paul, Jan. 26, 1965); *Gemini* for Orch., with microtones (Minneapolis, July 26, 1966); *Classic Concerto* for Orch. (St. Paul, Nov. 11, 1967); Sym. No. 6 (1968); *Epimetheus USA* for Orch. (Detroit, Nov. 13, 1969); *Icarus*, suite for Orch. (1975); *Bi-Centurion* for Orch. (1975; Rochester, N.Y., Jan. 8, 1976); *Perseus and Andromeda XX* for Orch. (1976; Cincinnati, Feb. 25, 1977); *Akhenaten* for Chorus and Orch. (St. Louis, Sept. 23, 1983); 4 string quartets; 3 piano sonatas; choruses.

Gutheil-Schoder, Marie, prominent German mezzo-soprano; b. Weimar, Feb. 16, 1874; d. Bad Ilmenau, Oct. 4, 1935. She was largely self-taught, although she received some coaching from Richard Strauss in Weimar, where she made her operatic debut (1st Lady in *Die Zauberflöte*, 1891). After singing in Berlin and Leipzig, she was engaged by Mahler for the Vienna Hofoper (debut as Nedda, Feb. 16, 1900); in her early performances, she was criticized for her small voice; Mahler made note of her "disagreeable middle register," but he also declared that she was a musical genius; her strong dramatic characterizations made her a favorite there until 1926. She was successful as Carmen, Elektra, Eva, and the 3 principal soprano roles in *Les Contes d'Hoffmann*; her Mozart roles included Pamina, Elvira, Susanna, and Cherubino. Her only London appearance was at Covent Garden as Oktavian in 1913; 3 years later she sang the role of the Composer, under Strauss's direction, in a Zürich production of the revised version of *Ariadne aux Naxos*. She was closely associated with the music of Schoenberg; took part in the premiere of his 2nd String Quartet (Vienna, Feb. 5, 1907), and later frequently performed in his *Pierrot Lunaire*; Schoenberg conceived the part of The Woman in his monodrama *Erwartung* as a "Gutheil part"; she appeared in its 1st performance (Prague, June 6, 1924). After her retirement, she was active as a teacher and producer in Vienna and Salzburg. She was successively married to the violinist and composer Gustav Gutheil and the Viennese photographer Franz Setzer.

Guthrie, Woody (Woodrow Wilson), legendary American folksinger and songwriter; b. Okemah, Okla., July 14, 1912; d. N.Y., Oct. 3, 1967. He left home with his guitar and harmonica when he was 15, riding the rails of freight trains across the U.S. and playing in hobo and migrant camps, bars, and labor meetings during the Great Depression, becoming famous as a champion of disadvantaged Americans and as a supporter of various leftist causes. Among the songs he wrote or arranged were *So Long, It's Been Good to Know Yuh; This Train Is Bound for Glory; Hard Traveling; Blowing Down This Old Dusty Road*; and *This Land Is Your Land*. In later years he joined Pete Seeger and others as a member of the Almanac Singers in N.Y. His career was cut short in 1957 when he was stricken with Huntington's chorea. In spite of his freely professed radical convictions, the U.S. government bestowed upon him an award of merit in 1966 as "a poet of the American landscape." He publ. the books *Bound for Glory* (N.Y., 1943) and *American Folksong* (N.Y., 1947; with memoirs). W. Doerflinger ed. his *Seeds of Man: An Experience Lived and Dreamed* (N.Y., 1976). His son, **Arlo Guthrie** (b. N.Y., July 10, 1947), followed in his father's footsteps as a folksinger and songwriter; he became famous for his ballad *Alice's Restaurant* (1969); this became the title of a film in which he starred.

BIBL.: R. Reuss, ed., *A W. G. Bibliography, 1912–1967* (N.Y., 1968); H. Yurchenco, *A Mighty Hard Road: The W. G. Story* (N.Y., 1970); H. Wood, ed., *A Tribute to W. G.* (N.Y., 1972); J. Klein, *W. G.: A Life* (N.Y., 1980).

Gutiérrez, Gonzalo, Spanish organist and composer; b. c.1540; d. Granada, 1605. He was appointed organist at the Cathedral of Granada in 1569, and held this post until his death.

BIBL.: J. Lopez Calo, *La música en la catedral de Granada en el siglo XVI* (Granada, 1963; vol. I, pp. 205–10; vol. II includes several of his works).

Gutiérrez, Horacio, brilliant Cuban-born American pianist; b. Havana, Aug. 28, 1948. He studied in Havana; made his concert debut there as a young child; continued his studies in Los Angeles and at the Juilliard School of Music in N.Y. He gained fame in 1970, after winning 2nd prize in the world's most prestigious musical arena, the International Tchaikovsky Competition in Moscow. Subsequently, he appeared with major American and European orchs. In 1976 he became a naturalized American citizen.

Gutiérrez Heras, Joaquín, Mexican composer; b. Tehuacán, Sept. 28, 1927. He attended classes in architecture at the National Univ. of Mexico and then studied composition with Blas Galindo and Rodolfo Halffter at the National Cons. of Mexico (1950–52). A scholarship from the French Inst. of Mexico enabled him to go to Paris, where he took courses in composition with Messiaen, Rivier, and Dandelot at the Paris Cons. (1952–53); on a Rockefeller Foundation scholarship, he studied composition with Bergsma and Persichetti at the Juilliard School of Music in N.Y. (1960–61). Upon his return to Mexico, he gave radio lectures and taught music theory. As a composer, he professes a "voluntary lack of complexity."

WORKS: Divertimento for Piano and Orch. (1949); satirical ballet, *El deportista* (1957); *Variations on a French Song* for Piano or Harpsichord (1958–60); *Chamber Cantata on Poems by Emilio Prados* for Soprano, 2 Flutes, Harp, and 4 Strings (1961); a symphonic scene, *Los Cazadores* (The Hunters; 1962); Duo for Alto Flute and Cello (1964); *Sonata simple* for Flute and Piano (1965); Trio for Oboe, Clarinet, and Bassoon (1965); *2 Pieces for 3 Brasses* (1967); *Night and Day Music* for Wind Sym. Orch. (1973); *De profundis* for a cappella Chorus (1977); several scores for theater and film.

Gutmann, Adolph, German pianist and composer; b. Heidelberg, Jan. 12, 1819; d. Spezia, Oct. 27, 1882. He lived mostly in Paris, where he studied with Chopin, and became a close friend of his. He publ. an album of *Études caractéristiques* which were quite popular in the 19th century, and much salon music for piano. He was also a successful performer whose virtuoso technique made him popular with audiences.

Gutsche, Romeo Maximilian Eugene Ludwig. See **Gutché, Gene.**

Güttler, Ludwig, noted German trumpeter, conductor, and pedagogue; b. Sosa, June 13, 1943. He commenced music studies when he was 5, and began playing the trumpet at 14; after obtaining a degree in architecture, he studied trumpet with Armin Mennel at the Leipzig Hochschule für Musik (1961–65). From 1965 he was solo trumpeter of the Handel Festival Orch. in Halle, and later, of the Dresden Phil. (1969–81). In 1976 he founded the Leipziger Bach-Collegium, in 1978 the Blechbläserensemble Ludwig Güttler, and in 1985 the Virtuosi Saxoniae; made many tours with these groups,

appearing as a trumpeter and conductor. In 1972 he joined the faculty of the Dresden Hochschule für Musik, taking charge of its master classes in wind instruments in 1982; also served as a guest teacher at the Weimar International Music Seminar (from 1977) and in Austria, Japan, and the U.S. Güttler discovered many scores for his instrument in various German archives, libraries, and castles, and made a special effort to bring them before the public. He won renown for his performances of Baroque and Classical works on period instruments. In 1978 he won the National Prize of the German Democratic Republic and in 1989 was awarded the Music Prize of the City of Frankfurt.

Guy-Ropartz. See **Ropartz, (Joseph) Guy (Marie).**

Guyonnet, Jacques, Swiss composer; b. Geneva, March 20, 1933. He studied at the Geneva Cons. (1950–58); had courses in new music with Boulez at the summer sessions held in Darmstadt (1958–61); in 1959 he founded the Studio de Musique Contemporaine in Geneva; from 1976 to 1981 was president of the ISCM.

WORKS: *Monades I* for Chamber Ensemble (1958); *Monades II–III* for Orch. (1960, 1961); *Polyphonie I* for Flute and Piano (1961); *Polyphonie II* for 2 Pianos (1959); *Polyphonie III* for Flute, Viola, and 2 Pianos (1964); *Chronicles* for Piano (1964–71); *En 3 éclats!* for Piano and Chamber Orch. (1964); *Stèle in memoriam J.F. Kennedy* for Chamber Orch. and Tape (1964); *The Approach to the Hidden Man I* for Solo Cello and 6 Instruments (1966), and *II* for Mezzo-soprano, Chamber Orch., and Electronic Sound (1967); *7 portes du temps* for Orch. (1966–69); *Entremonde,* ballet for Flute, Piano, 4 Percussionists, and Tape (1967); *Let There Be Events!* for 17 Instrumental Soloists (1968–71); *Good Grief Jerry!* for Soprano and Chamber Orch. (1970–71); *Modèles I–II* for any number of Instrumental Soloists (1970); *A Single R* for Viola and Chamber Orch. (1971); *Le Chant remémoré* for 4 Vocal Soloists and Orch. (1972); *Die Wandlung* for Orch. (1973); *Les Enfants du désert* for String Orch. (1974); *Mémorial* for 4 Trumpets and 4 Trombones (1974); *Zornagore* for Orch. (1976); *Ombre* for Orch. (1979); *Harmonique-Souffle* for Chamber Orch. (1980); *Electric Sorcerers,* rock opera (1980–81).

Guyot, Jean, South Netherlands composer, also known as **Jean de Châtelet** and **Johannes Castileti;** b. Châtelet, Hainaut, 1512; d. Liège, March 11, 1588. He studied at the Univ. of Louvain, and received the degree of licencié-ès-arts on March 22, 1537; in 1546 he was chaplain at St. Paul's in Liège; publ. his 1st motets in Antwerp that year; about 1557 assumed the duties of maître de chapelle at the Cathedral of St. Lambert in Liège; on Nov. 1, 1563, was appointed music master at the Imperial Court in Vienna; he returned to Liège in Aug. 1564, and remained maître de chapelle at the Cathedral of St. Lambert to his death.

BIBL.: C. Lyon, *J. G.* (Charleroi, 1876); B. Even, *J. G. de Châtelet et son œuvre* (diss., Univ. of Liège, 1974).

Guzikov, Michal Jozef, famous Polish xylophonist and composer; b. Szklow, Sept. 14, 1806; d. Aachen, Oct. 21, 1837. Of a Jewish musical family, he showed precocious talent; with 4 relatives he traveled all over Europe; his virtuosity on the xylophone was extraordinary, and elicited praise from the public as well as from celebrated musicians, among them Mendelssohn. His programs consisted of arrangements of well-known works and also his own pieces; his most successful number was a transcription of Paganini's *La Campanella.*

BIBL.: M. Schlesinger, *Über G.* (Vienna, 1936).

Gyrowetz, Adalbert (Mathias) (original name, **Vojtěch Matyáš Jírovec**), noted Bohemian composer and conductor; b. Budweis, Feb. 19, 1763; d. Vienna, March 19, 1850. He studied piano, violin, and composition with his father, a local choirmaster, and began to compose while a student at the Piarist Gymnasium in his native town; then studied philosophy and law in Prague. He subsequently became secretary to Count Franz von Fünfkirchen, to whom he dedicated his 1st syms., a set of 6 in Haydnesque style (1783); was also a member of his private orch. In 1784 he went to Vienna, where he was befriended by Mozart; the latter arranged for 1 of his syms. to be performed in 1785. He then became secretary and music master to Prince Ruspoli, who took him to Italy. While in Rome (1786–87), he composed a set of 6 string quartets, the 1st of his works to be publ. After leaving Ruspoli's service, he studied with Sala in Naples. He made a brief visit to Paris in 1789, and then proceeded to London, where he met and befriended Haydn, who was also visiting the British capital. During his London sojourn, Gyrowetz was commissioned by the Pantheon to write an opera, *Semiramis*; however, before the work could be mounted, both the theater and his MS were destroyed by fire (1792). He returned to the Continent in 1793; in 1804 he became composer and conductor of the Vienna Hoftheater, where he produced such popular operas as *Agnes Sorel* (Dec. 4, 1806) and *Der Augenarzt* (Oct. 1, 1811). He also wrote *Il finto Stanislao* (Milan, July 5, 1818), to a libretto by Romani, which Verdi subsequently used for his *Un giorno di regno*. He likewise anticipated Wagner by writing the 1st opera on the subject of Hans Sachs's life in his *Hans Sachs im vorgerückten Alter* (Dresden, 1834). He retired from the Hoftheater in 1831, and his fame soon dissipated; he spent his last years in straitened circumstances and relative neglect, having outlived the great masters of the age. He composed a variety of stage works, including operas, singspiels, and melodramas; he also composed about 40 syms., 2 piano concertos (1796, 1800), and 3 concertantes (for Violin, Viola, and Cello, 1792; for 2 Violins and Viola, 1798; and for Flute, Oboe, Bassoon, Violin, and Cello, 1798). Among his sacred compositions are 11 masses, a Te Deum, a Tantum Ergo, and 2 vesper services. He also composed much chamber music, including about 45 string quartets (1788–1804) and some 46 piano trios (1790–1814).

BIBL.: K. Mey, "A. G. und seine neu aufgefundene Hans Sachs-Oper," *Die Musik*, II (1902–3); E. Doernberg, "A. G.," *Music & Letters*, XLIV (1963).

Gyzi, Fritz, Swiss music critic and musicologist; b. Zofingen, Feb. 18, 1888; d. Zürich, March 5, 1967. He studied at the Basel Cons., and then took courses in musicology and art history at the Univs. of Zürich, Berlin, and Bern (Ph.D., 1913, with the diss. *Die Entwicklung der kirchlichen Architektur in der deutschen Schweiz im 17. und 18. Jahrhundert*; publ. in Zürich, 1914); subsequently (1921) completed his Habilitation in music history at the Univ. of Zürich, where he was made a titular prof. in 1931; he was also a music critic for the *Basler Nachrichten* and the Basel *National-Zeitung* (from 1915), and the Zürich *Tagesanzeiger* (from 1928).

WRITINGS: *Mozart in seinen Briefen* (Zürich, 1919–21); *Max Bruch* (Zürich, 1922); *Claude Debussy* (Zürich, 1926); *Richard Wagner und die Schweiz* (Frauenfeld, 1929); *Richard Wagner und Zürich* (Zürich, 1933); *Richard Strauss* (Potsdam, 1934); *Hans Georg Nägeli* (Zürich, 1936).

H

Haapanen, Toivo (Elias), Finnish musicologist and conductor; b. Karvia, May 15, 1889; d. Asikkala, July 22, 1950. He studied violin and music theory in Helsinki, Berlin, and Paris; he studied musicology with I. Krohn at the Univ. of Helsinki (M.A., 1918; Ph.D., 1925, with the diss. *Die Neumenfragmente der Universitätsbibliothek Helsingfors*). In 1925 he became a lecturer at the Univ. of Helsinki; was a prof. there from 1946. From 1929 to 1946 he was head of the music division of the Finnish Broadcasting Co.; was chief conductor of its Radio Sym. Orch. from 1929 until his death. He publ. a valuable *Verzeichnis der mittelalterlichen Handschriftenfragmente in der Universitätsbibliothek zu Helsingfors* (3 vols., Helsinki, 1922; 1925; 1932). He further publ. *Suomen säveltaide* (The Art of Music in Finland; Helsinki, 1940) and ed. a dictionary of music (Helsinki, 1948).

Haar, James, American musicologist; b. St. Louis, July 4, 1929. He studied at Harvard Univ. (B.A., 1950) and at the Univ. of North Carolina (M.A., 1954); then returned to Harvard to complete his training under John Ward and Nino Pirrotta (Ph.D., 1961, with the diss. *Musica mundana: Variations on a Pythagorean Theme*); served on its faculty (1960–67). He taught at the Univ. of Pa. (1967–69), N.Y. Univ. (1969–78), and the Univ. of North Carolina (from 1978); was general ed. of the *Journal of the American Musicological Society* (1966–69), later serving as the society's president (1976–78). With L. Bernstein, he ed. *The Duos of Jhan Gero* (1977); publ. *The Tugendsterne of Harsdorffer and Staden* (1965) and *Essays on Italian Poetry and Music in the Renaissance, 1350–1600* (1986). With I. Fenlon, he publ. *The Italian Madrigal in the Early Sixteenth Century: Sources and Interpretation* (1989).

Haarklou, Johannes, Norwegian organist and composer; b. Førde, Sunnfjord, near Bergen, May 13, 1847; d. Oslo, Nov. 26, 1925. He studied at the Leipzig Cons.; then in Berlin with Haupt, Kiel, and Bungert; for 40 years (1880–1920) he was organist at the Akers Church in Christiania; also conducted sym. concerts there for 3 seasons. His 5 operas have not made their way beyond Norway, but among works more generally known is an oratorio, *Skapelsen* (The Creation; 1891; Christiania, 1924). He wrote 4 syms. (1883–88) and *Olafs-Legende* for Orch.; a Violin Sonata; piano pieces; choruses; organ works.

BIBL.: F. Benestad, *J. H., Mannen og verket* (Oslo, 1961).

Haas, Joseph, eminent German composer and pedagogue; b. Maihingen, March 19, 1879; d. Munich, March 30, 1960. He studied composition with Max Reger in Munich and organ with Karl Straube in Leipzig. In 1911 he was appointed composition teacher at the Stuttgart Cons.; in 1921 became a prof. in the Catholic church music dept. at the Akademie der Tonkunst in Munich. From 1945 to 1950 he was president of the Hochschule für Musik in Munich. Through the long years of his pedagogical activities, Haas established himself as one of the most reputable teachers in Germany. As a composer, he was equally estimable, but his music failed to gain popularity outside his circle. He wrote more than 100 opus numbers. At the time of his retirement in 1950, a Joseph Haas Soc. was organized in Munich, with the aim of promoting his works. He publ. a biography of Max Reger (Bonn, 1949); contributed articles to various publications. A collection of his speeches and articles was publ. posthumously, as *Reden und Aufsätze* (Mainz, 1964).

Works: Operas: *Tobias Wunderlich* (Kassel, Nov. 24, 1937) and *Die Hochzeit des Jobs* (Dresden, July 2, 1944); oratorios: *Die heilige Elisabeth* (1931); *Christnacht* (1932); *Das Lebensbuch Gottes* (1934); *Das Lied von der Mutter* (1939); *Das Jahr im Lied* (1952); *Die Seligen* (Kassel, April 12, 1957); *Deutsche Kindermesse* (1958); *Marienkantate* (1959); *Variations on a Rococo Theme* for Orch.; *Ouvertüre zu einem frohen Spiel* (1943); 2 string quartets (1908, 1919); Trio for 2 Violins and Piano (1912); many song cycles. A catalog of his works was compiled by K. Fellerer (1950; 2nd ed., 1953).

Bibl.: K. Laux, *J. H.* (Mainz, 1931; 2nd ed., 1954); special issue of the *Zeitschrift für Musik* (March 1954).

Haas, Karl (Wilhelm Jacob), German conductor and musicologist; b. Karlsruhe, Dec. 27, 1900; d. London, July 7, 1970. He studied at the Univs. of Munich and Heidelberg; then worked for the Karlsruhe and Stuttgart radios; was active as a collector of valuable early instruments; made microfilms of early music. In 1939 he emigrated to England; in 1943 he organized the London Baroque Ensemble; led it until 1966 in performances of little-known Baroque music. He also ed. works by Haydn, Boccherini, and Cherubini.

Haas, Monique, French pianist; b. Paris, Oct. 20, 1906; d. there, June 9, 1987. She studied at the Paris Cons. with Lazare Lévy; became greatly interested in modern music, and gave numerous concerts all over Europe in programs of 20th-century composers; also appeared with orchs. in modern concertos. She was married to the composer **Marcel Mihalovici.**

Haas, Pavel, Czech composer; b. Brünn, June 21, 1899; put to death in the concentration camp at Auschwitz (Oświęcim), Oct. 17, 1944. He studied piano and composition in Brünn; was a soldier in the Austrian army in World War I; after the Armistice, continued his study with Petrželka at the Brno Cons. (1919–21) and at the master class there with Janáček (1920–22). He tried to leave Czechoslovakia after its occupation by the Nazi hordes, but the outbreak of World War II made this impossible; in 1941 he was placed in a concentration camp in Terezín, where he continued to compose until, in Oct. 1944, he was sent to Auschwitz and put to death.

Works: Opera, *Šarlatán* (The Charlatan), to his own libretto (1934–37; Brno, April 2, 1938); *Zesmutnělé Scherzo* (Mournful Scherzo) for Orch. (1921); *Předehra pro rozhlas* (Overture for Radio) for Orch., Male Chorus, and Narrator (1930); Sym. (1941; unfinished); *Studie* for String Orch. (1943; Theresienstadt, Sept. 13, 1944); Variations for Piano and Orch. (1944); cantata, *Introduction and Psalm XXIX* (1931); 3 string quartets (1920, 1925, 1938); *Fata morgana*, piano quintet, with Tenor Solo (1923); Wind Quintet (1929); Suite for Oboe and Piano (1939); Suite for Piano (1935); songs. His extant MSS are preserved in the Moravian Museum in Brno.

Haas, Robert (Maria), distinguished Austrian musicologist; b. Prague, Aug. 15, 1886; d. Vienna, Oct. 4, 1960. He received his primary education in Prague; then studied music history at the Univs. of Prague, Berlin, and Vienna; obtained his Ph.D. in 1908 from the Univ. of Prague with his dissertation *Das Wiener Singspiel.* He then was an assistant to Guido Adler at the Inst. for Music History in Vienna (1908–9). During World War I he was in the Austrian army; then joined the staff of the Nationalbibliothek in Vienna, becoming chief of the music division in 1920. He completed his Habilitation at the Univ. of Vienna in 1923 with his *Eberlins Schuldramen und Oratorien;* then became a lecturer there; also devoted much of his time to the music of the Baroque and Classical eras. After the founding of the International Bruckner Soc., he became ed. of the critical edition of Bruckner's works; he also edited works for Denkmäler der Tonkunst in Österreich. He retired in 1945.

Writings: *Gluck und Durazzo im Burgtheater* (Vienna, 1925); *Die estensischen Musikalien: Thematisches Verzeichnis mit Einleitung* (Regensburg, 1925); *Die Wiener Oper* (Vienna, 1926); *Wiener Musiker vor und um Beethoven* (Vienna, 1927); *Die Musik des Barocks* (Potsdam, 1928); *Aufführungspraxis der Musik* (Potsdam, 1931); *W.A. Mozart* (Potsdam, 1933; 2nd ed., 1950); *Anton Bruckner* (Potsdam, 1934); *Bach und Mozart in Wien* (Vienna, 1951); *Ein unbekanntes Mozart-Bildnis* (Vienna, 1955).

Bibl.: G. Reichert, "R. H.," *Österreichische Musikzeitschrift,* XIII (1958); H. Federhofer, "In memoriam R. H.," *Acta Musicologica,* XXXII (1960).

Haas, Werner, talented German pianist; b. Stuttgart, March 3, 1931; d. Nancy, Oct. 13, 1976. He studied at the Hochschule für Musik in Stuttgart and at the Saarbrücken Cons. Following the example of Walter Gieseking, whose master courses he had attended, Haas developed a particular interest in French music, and became a fine interpreter of works of Debussy and Ravel.

Haase, Hans, German musicologist; b. Neumünster, Schleswig-Holstein, May 12, 1929. He studied with Blume and Albrecht at the Univ. of Kiel (1950–55); from 1954 to 1958 was editorial contributor to *Die Musik in Geschichte und Gegenwart;* then did valuable work in various archives and libraries; also wrote music criticism for newspapers. He publ. the monographs *Jobst vom Brandt* (Kassel, 1967) and *Heinrich Schütz* (Wolfenbüttel, 1972), and numerous valuable articles on German composers of the Reformation. He also became interested in applied psychology; lectured on this subject in Zürich and Vienna; publ. *Die harmonikalen Wurzeln der Musik* (Vienna, 1969) and *Aufsätze zur harmonikalen Naturphilosophie* (Graz, 1974).

Hába, Alois, notable Czech composer and pedagogue, brother of **Karel Hába;** b. Vizovice, Moravia, June 21, 1893; d. Prague, Nov. 18, 1973. He studied with Novák at the Prague Cons. (1914–15); then privately with Schreker in Berlin (1918–22); returned to Prague in 1923; taught there from 1924 to 1951. He became interested in the folk music of the Orient, which led him to consider writing in smaller intervals than the semitone. His 1st work in the quarter-tone system was the 2nd String Quartet (op. 7, 1920); in his 5th String Quartet (op. 15, 1923) he first applied the sixth-tones; in his 16th String Quartet (op. 98, 1967) he introduced the fifth-tones. He notated these fractional intervals by signs in modified or inverted sharps and flats. The piano manufacturing firm A. Förster constructed for him 3 types of quarter-tone pianos (1924–31), a quarter-tone (1928) and a sixth-tone harmonium (1936), and a quarter-tone guitar (1943); other firms manufactured at his request a quarter-tone clarinet (1924) and trumpet (1931). From 1924 to 1951 he led a class of composition in fractional tones at the Prague Cons., attracting a large number of students, among them his brother, Karel, the conductors Ančerl and Susskind, and the composers Dobiáš, Ježek, Kowalski, Kubín, Lucký, Ponc, Karel Reiner (who, along with E. Schulhoff, specialized in quarter-tone piano playing and premiered 10 of Hába's works), Seidel, Srnka, Constantin Iliev of Bulgaria, Slavko Osterc of Yugoslavia, and Necil Kâzim Akses of Turkey. Hába publ. an important manual of modern harmony, *Neue Harmonielehre des diatonischen, chromatischen, Viertel-, Drittel-, Sechstel-, und Zwölfteltonsystems* (New Principles of Harmony of the Diatonic, Chromatic, Fourth-, Third-, Sixth-, and Twelfth-Tone Systems; Leipzig, 1927), detailing new usages introduced by him in his classes; he further publ. *Harmonicke základy čtvrttónové soustavy* (Harmonic Foundation of the Quarter-Tone System; Prague, 1922) and *Von der Psychologie der musikalischen Gestaltung, Gesetzmässigkeit der Tonbewegung und Grundlagen eines neuen Musikstils* (On the Psychology of Musical Composition; Rules of Tonal Structure and Foundation of New Musical Style; Vienna, 1925); also *Mein Weg zur Viertel- und Sechstetonmusik* (Düsseldorf, 1971). As a composer, he cultivated a "non-thematic" method of writing, without repetition of patterns and devoid of development.

Works: operas: *Matka* (Mother; 1927–29), in quarter-tones, to his own text; 1st perf. in Munich as *Die Mutter* on May 17, 1931, and subsequently in Czech (Prague, May 27, 1947); *Nová Země* (The New Land; 1934–36), written in the traditional tempered scale; never perf., except for the overture, in Prague on April 8, 1936; *Přijd království Tvé* (Thy Kingdom Come), in fractional tones, to Hába's own text (1937–40; unperf.); cantata, *Za mír* (For Peace; Prague, Nov. 1, 1950). ORCH.: Overture (Berlin, Dec. 9, 1920); *Symphonic Fantasy for Piano and Orch.* (1921); *Cesta života* (The Path of Life; Winterthur, March 15, 1934); *Valašská suita* (Prague, Oct. 29, 1953); Violin Concerto (1955; Prague, Feb. 17, 1963); Viola Concerto (1955–57). CHAMBER (the following are in the tempered scale): 4 nonets for Wind and String Instruments (1931, based on a 12-tone row; 1932, based on a 7-tone row; 1953; 1963); string quartets Nos. 1, 7, 8, 9, 13, and 15 (1919; 1951; 1951; 1952; *Astronautic*, 1961; 1964); Violin Sonata (1915); Fantasy for Flute or Violin and Piano, op. 34 (1928; op. 34a, version for Bass Clarinet and Piano, 1967); Sonata for Guitar Solo (1943); Sonata for Chromatic Harp, op. 59 (1944); Sonata for Diatonic Harp, op. 60 (1944); *Intermezzo and Preludium* for Diatonic Harp (1945); Suite for Solo Bassoon (1950; op. 69a, version for Bass Clarinet, 1968); Suite, quartet for Bassoons (1951); *Fantasy* and *Fantasy and Fugue* for Organ (both 1951); Solo Clarinet Sonata (1952); Suite for Solo Violin, op. 81a (1955); Suite for Solo Cello, op. 81b (1955); Suite for Solo Cymbalom (1960); Suite for Solo Bass Clarinet, op. 96 (1964); Suite for Solo Saxophone (1968); Suite for Bass Clarinet and Piano (1969); *Observations from a Journal* for Narrator and String Quartet (1970); Suite for Violin and Piano, op. 103 (1972; his last work); *Fugue Suite* for Piano (1918); *Variations on a Canon by Schumann* for Piano (1918); 2 *morceaux* for Piano (1917–18; arranged for String Orch. by R. Kubín, 1930); Piano Sonata, op. 3 (1918); 6 *Pieces* for Piano (1920); 4 *Modern Dances* for Piano (1927); *Toccata quasi una Fantasia* for Piano (1931); 6 *Moods* for Piano (1971). Works in quartertones: String quartets Nos. 2, 3, 4, 6, 12, and 14 (1920, 1922, 1922, 1950, 1960, 1963); Fantasy for Solo Violin (1921); *Music* for Solo Violin (1922); Fantasy for Solo Cello (1924); Fantasy for Violin and Piano, op. 21 (1925); Suite No. 1 for Clarinet and Piano (1925); Fantasy for Viola and Piano (1926); Fantasy for Cello and Piano (1927); 2 suites for Solo Guitar (1943, 1947); Suite No. 2 for Solo Clarinet (1943–44); Suite for Trumpet and Trombone (1944); Suite for 4 Trombones (1950); Suite for Solo Violin, op. 93 (1961–62); 6 suites for Piano (1922, rev. 1932; 1922, rev. 1932; 1923; 1924; 1925; 1959); 11 fantasies for Piano (Nos. 1–10, 1923–26; No. 11, 1959); Piano Sonata, op. 62 (1947). Works in fifth-tones: String Quartet No. 16 (1967). Works in sixth-tones: String quartets Nos. 5, 10, and 11 (1923, 1952, 1958); Duo for 2 Violins (1937); Suite for Solo Violin, op. 85a (1955); Suite for Solo Cello, op. 85b (1955); 6 *Pieces* for Harmonium (1928). He also wrote songs and choral pieces, many of them in the quarter-tone system. BIBL.: J. Vysloužil, *A. H.: Život a dílo* (Prague, 1974).

Hába, Karel, Czech composer, brother of **Alois Hába;** b. Vizovice, Moravia, May 21, 1898; d. Prague, Nov. 21, 1972. He studied violin with Karel Hoffmann and Jan Mařák, and music theory with V. Novák, J. Křička, and J.B. Foerster at the Prague Cons.; also attended his brother's class in quarter-tone music (1925–27). He wrote only 3 pieces in quarter-tones, but he faithfully followed the athematic method of composing that was the cornerstone of his brother's esthetics. He was a violinist in the orch. of Prague Radio (1929–36); was later a music critic and lecturer in music education at Charles Univ. (1951–63). He wrote *Modern Violin Technique* (2 vols., Prague, 1928).

WORKS: 4 operas: *Jánošík* (1929–32; Prague, Feb. 23, 1934; 1st operatic treatment of this famous historical Czech figure), *Stará historia* (The Old Story; 1934–37; unperf.), *Smoliček,* children's radio opera (Prague, Sept. 28, 1950), and *Kalibův zločin* (Kaliba's Crime; 1957–61; Košice, May 16, 1968); cantata, *To Those Who Build Up Ostrava* (1950–51); Overture (1922); Violin Concerto (Prague, March 6, 1927); *Scherzo* for Orch. (1928); Cello Concerto (Prague, Sept. 1, 1935); 2 syms. (1947–48; 1953–54); *Brigand's Suite* for Orch. (1955); Suite for Orch. (1963); 4 string quartets (1922, 1924, 1943, 1969); Trio for Violin, Cello, and Quarter-tone Piano

(1926); 3 *Pieces* for Violin and Piano in quarter-tones (1927); Flute Sonatina (1927); Septet for Violin, Clarinet, Viola, Horn, Cello, Bassoon, and Piano (1928–29); Duo for Violin and Cello (1935); Piano Trio (1940); Wind Quintet (1944); 3 *Inventions* for Harp (1945); Nonet (1950); Trio for 2 Violins and Viola (1952); 15 *Concert Études* for Violin (1956); Sonatina for 3 Violins (1960); Sonatina for 3 Clarinets (1960); 3 *Instructive Duos* for 2 Violins (1968); 2 Suites for Piano (1920, 1929); Suite for Quarter-tone Piano (1925); Piano Sonata (1942); choral pieces; songs.

Habeneck, François-Antoine, eminent French conductor; b. Mézières, Jan. 22, 1781; d. Paris, Feb. 8, 1849. His father, a native of Mannheim and a member of a regimental band, taught him the violin. In 1800 he entered the Paris Cons., studying violin with Baillot. In 1804 he became a violinist in the orch. of the Opéra-Comique; shortly thereafter he joined the orch. of the Paris Opéra, becoming principal violin in 1817. From 1806 to 1815 he conducted the student orch. at the Paris Cons., and also taught violin there (1808–16; 1825–48). From 1824 to 1831 he was *premier chef* (with Valentino) of the Paris Opéra, holding that post alone from 1831 to 1846; during his tenure there he conducted the premieres of *Guillaume Tell, La Juive, Les Huguenots,* and *Benvenuto Cellini.* In 1828 he founded the Société des Concerts du Conservatoire de Paris, which initially consisted of an orch. of 86 musicians and a chorus of 79 singers (the average complement of orch. members was 60). At his 1st concert on March 9, 1828, he conducted Beethoven's *Eroica* Sym.; he subsequently championed Beethoven's syms. in his concerts, giving the 1st Paris performance of the 9th Sym. on March 27, 1831. Under his guidance the orch. became the finest in its day, gaining the praise of such musicians as Mendelssohn and Wagner. He led it for 20 years, conducting his last concert on April 16, 1848. A pioneering figure among conductors, Habeneck retained many of the characteristics of the earlier violin-leader type of conductor (for instance, he used the violin part, with other instruments cued in, instead of a full score; directed with a violin bow; and, at the beginning of his career, played along with his musicians); nevertheless, he assumed a foremost place among the conductors of his era. He was also a composer, but his works are not significant. With Isouard and Benincori he wrote an opera, *Aladin ou La Lampe merveilleuse* (Paris Opéra, Feb. 6, 1822); he composed 2 violin concertos and other violin music; also publ. a *Méthode théorique et pratique de violon* (Paris, 1835). BIBL.: H. Schonberg, *The Great Conductors* (N.Y., 1967).

Haberbier, Ernst, German pianist and composer; b. Königsberg, Oct. 5, 1813; d. while giving a concert in Bergen, Norway, March 12, 1869. He studied with his father, an organist; left home in 1832; went to Russia and became a court pianist in St. Petersburg in 1847; gave concerts in London in 1850; in 1852 appeared in Paris, where he scored a sensational success; in 1866 he settled in Bergen. He perfected what he considered a novel system of piano technique, dividing difficult passages between the 2 hands (however, this had been done by Scarlatti and Bach long before). He wrote a number of effective piano pieces, of which *Études-Poésies* (op. 53) are the best known.

Haberl, Franz Xaver, eminent German organist, music theorist, music editor, and historiographer; b. Oberellenbach, Lower Bavaria, April 12, 1840; d. Regensburg, Sept. 5, 1910. He studied in the Boys' Seminary at Passau, and took Holy Orders in 1862; was Cathedral Kapellmeister and music director at the Seminary (1862–67); organist at S. Maria dell'Anima in Rome (1867–70); from 1871 to 1882 he was Cathedral Kapellmeister at Regensburg, where he founded, in 1875, a world-renowned school for church music. He was an authority on Catholic church music. In 1872 he assumed the editorship of the collection Musica Divina, and ed. the periodical *Musica Sacra* in 1888. In 1876 he began to publ. the *Cäcilienkalender,* the scope of which was greatly widened until, after 1885, it was issued under the more appropriate name of *Kirchenmusikalisches Jahrbuch;* as such it has become one of the most important publications for historical studies concerning the church music of the 15th, 16th, and 17th centuries; Haberl continued as ed. until 1907, when he resigned and was succeeded by Karl Weinmann. He founded the Palestrina Soc. in 1879, and (beginning with vol. X) was ed. in chief of Breitkopf & Härtel's complete edition of Palestrina's works (33 vols., completed on the tercentenary of Palestrina's death, 1894), which he aided not only by his experience and learning, but also by rare MSS from his private collection. In 1899 he was elected president of the Allgemeiner Cäcilienverein, and became ed. of its official organ, *Fliegende Blätter für Katholische Kirchenmusik*. In 1889 he was made Dr.Theol. *honoris causa* by the Univ. of Würzburg; in 1908, "Monsignore." Under his general supervision, a new ed. of the *Editio Medicea* (1614) of the plainchant melodies was issued, with papal sanction, at Regensburg (1871–81). When modern scholarship proved that the original ed. had not been publ. with papal sanction and had not been revised by Palestrina—that, in fact, it contained the old melodies in badly distorted and mutilated form—the papal sanction was withdrawn, and the ed. suppressed and replaced by a new *Editio Vaticana* in 1904. The result of this was that Haberl's books dealing with plainchant (which had been held in the highest esteem, and had passed through many eds.) fell into desuetude. The books thus affected are *Praktische Anweisung zum harmonischen Kirchengesang* (1864), *Magister Choralis* (1865; 12th ed., 1899; tr. into Eng., French, Italian, Spanish, Polish, and Hungarian), *Officium hebdomadae sanctae* (1887, in German), and *Psalterium vespertinum* (1888). His other writings, the value of which remains unimpaired, are *Bertalotti's Solfeggien* (1880), *Wilhelm Dufay* (1885), *Die römische "Schola Cantorum" und die päpstlichen Kapellsänger bis zur Mitte des 16. Jahrhunderts* (1887), and *Bibliographischer und thematischer Musikkatalog des päpstlichen Kapellarchivs im Vatikan zu Rom* (1888).

Habert, Johannes Evangelista, Bohemian organist, composer, and writer on music; b. Oberplan, Oct. 18, 1833; d. Gmunden, Sept. 1, 1896. He was organist at Gmunden from 1861; wrote sacred music and organ pieces; a complete ed. of his works was publ. by Breitkopf & Härtel. He was founder and ed. of the *Zeitschrift für katholische Kirchenmusik* (1868–83); also publ. *Beiträge zur Lehre von der musikalischen Komposition* (4 vols., 1889 et seq.).
BIBL.: A. Hartl, *J.E. H., Organist in Gmunden* (Vienna, 1900).

Habich, Eduard, German baritone; b. Kassel, Sept. 3, 1880; d. Berlin, March 15, 1960. He studied in Frankfurt; made his debut in Koblenz in 1904; then sang in Posen, Halle, and Düsseldorf, at the Berlin Royal (later State) Opera (1910–30) and at the Bayreuth Festivals (1911–31). He made his Metropolitan Opera debut in N.Y. on Dec. 20, 1935, as Peter in *Hänsel und Gretel;* returned to Germany in 1937; then taught voice in Berlin.

Hacker, Alan (Ray), English clarinetist, conductor, and pedagogue; b. Dorking, Sept. 30, 1938. He studied at Dulwich College and the Royal Academy of Music in London; continued his training in Paris, Vienna, and Bayreuth. He played clarinet in the London Phil. (1959–66), and in 1965 was a founding member of the Pierrot Players, which became the Fires of London in 1970. In 1971 he founded his own group, Matrix, and in 1977, the Classical Orch. He taught at the Royal Academy of Music (1960–76) and the Univ. of York (from 1976). In 1988 he was made an Officer of the Order of the British Empire. His extensive repertoire ranges from early music to contemporary scores.

Hackett, Bobby (Robert Leo), American jazz cornetist and guitarist; b. Providence, R.I., Jan. 31, 1915; d. West Chatham, Mass., June 7, 1976. He started playing guitar at the age of 8, and later picked up the violin. After playing in a Chinese restaurant as a youth, he changed to the trumpet and earned a living working in speakeasies and other dives in Boston and N.Y. He hit the big time when he appeared with Benny Good-

man at Carnegie Hall in N.Y. in 1938. Following a stint with Glenn Miller (1941–42), he worked as a staff musician for NBC and ABC; he resumed his career by leading his own combos, excelling in hot, cool, lukewarm, and tepid jazz. He became a favorite with young enthusiasts of jazz and pop music, but grew inexorably old and died peacefully in bed, of an irrelevant heart failure.

Hackett, Charles, American tenor; b. Worcester, Mass., Nov. 4, 1889; d. N.Y., Jan. 1, 1942. He studied voice 1st in Boston, and then in Florence; made his opera debut in Genoa; then sang at La Scala in Milan; subsequently appeared in South America, London, Paris, etc. On Jan. 31, 1919, he made his American debut as the Count in *Il Barbiere di Siviglia* with the Metropolitan Opera Co., remaining until 1921; was a member of the Chicago Civic Opera (1923–33); in 1934 rejoined the Metropolitan, and remained on its staff until 1939.

Hackh, Otto (Christoph), German-American music teacher and composer; b. Stuttgart, Sept. 30, 1852; d. N.Y., Sept. 21, 1917. He studied at the Stuttgart Cons.; traveled as a concert pianist in Europe; settled in N.Y. as head of the Grand Cons. (1880–89); then taught piano privately. He publ. some 200 pieces for piano, in a modern salon style, and also many songs, some of which became extremely popular.

Hadden, J(ames) Cuthbert, Scottish writer on music; b. Banchory-Ternan, near Aberdeen, Sept. 9, 1861; d. Edinburgh, May 1, 1914. He studied organ in London; was an organist in Aberdeen and Edinburgh; ed. the *Scottish Musical Monthly* (1893–96); publ. several biographies: *Handel* (1888; new ed., 1904); *Mendelssohn* (1888; new ed., 1904); *George Thomson, The Friend of Burns* (1898); *Haydn* (1899; 2nd ed., rev., 1903); *Chopin* (1899; 2nd ed., rev., 1902); also *The Operas of Wagner; Their Plots, Music and History* (1908); *Master Musicians* (1909); *Favourite Operas from Mozart to Mascagni* (1911); *Composers in Love and Marriage* (1913); *Modern Musicians* (1914); ed. *The Lays of Caledonia,* a collection of Scottish airs (Glasgow, 1883).

Hadley, Henry (Kimball), noted American composer and conductor; b. Somerville, Mass., Dec. 20, 1871; d. N.Y., Sept. 6, 1937. He studied piano and violin with his father and then with S. Emery and G.W. Chadwick at the New England Cons. in Boston; in 1894, studied theory with Mandyczewski in Vienna. Returning to America, he became director of music at St. Paul's School in Garden City, N.Y. (1895–1902); toured various cities in Germany, conducting his own works (1905–9); conducted at the Stadttheater in Mainz (1908–9) and brought out there his 1-act opera *Safié.* In 1909 he was engaged as conductor of the Seattle Sym. Orch.; from 1911 to 1915 he was conductor of the San Francisco Sym. Orch., and from 1920 to 1927, associate conductor of the N.Y. Phil. Orch. He traveled extensively; conducted his own works in Japan and Argentina; spent his last years mostly in N.Y. He received a Mus.D. from Tufts College (1925); was a member of the National Inst. of Arts and Letters and the American Academy of Arts and Letters; received the Order of Merit from the French government. Hadley occupied a position of prominence among American composers. In his style, he frankly adhered to programmatic writing. Although he shunned the unresolved dissonances of the ultramodern school, he was not averse to using fairly advanced harmonies in an impressionistic vein; he often applied exotic colors when the subject matter justified it. He was an excellent craftsman, both as composer and conductor, and contributed much to the growth of American music culture.
WORKS: Comic opera, *Nancy Brown;* operas: *Safié* (Mainz, April 4, 1909); *Azora, the Daughter of Montezuma* (Chicago, Dec. 26, 1917); *Bianca* (N.Y., Oct. 15, 1918, composer conducting); *The Fire-Prince,* operetta (1917); *Cleopatra's Night* (N.Y., Jan. 31, 1920); *A Night in Old Paris* (N.Y., Feb. 22, 1933); festival play, *The Atonement of Pan* (San Francisco, Aug. 10, 1912); 5 syms.: No. 1, *Youth and Life* (N.Y., Dec. 2, 1897); No. 2, *The 4 Seasons* (N.Y., Dec. 20, 1901; won the Paderewski prize and one offered by the New England Cons.); No. 3 (Berlin,

Dec. 27, 1907, composer conducting); No. 4, *North, East, South, West* (Norfolk [Conn.] Festival, Jan. 6, 1911, composer conducting); No. 5, *Connecticut* (Norfolk [Conn.] Festival, 1935); overtures: *Hector and Andromache; In Bohemia* (Boston, Dec. 16, 1901); *Herod; Othello* (Philadelphia, Dec. 26, 1919); *Youth Triumphant; Aurora Borealis* (1931); *Academic Overture; Alma Mater* (1932); *The Enchanted Castle* (1933); tone poems: *Salome* (composed in 1905, before the production of *Salome* by Richard Strauss; publ. in 1906; Boston, April 12, 1907); *Lucifer* (Norfolk [Conn.] Festival, June 2, 1914, composer conducting); *The Ocean* (N.Y., Nov. 17, 1921, composer conducting); orch. rhapsody, *The Culprit Fay* (Grand Rapids, Mich., May 28, 1909, composer conducting; won a $1,000 prize of the National Federation of Music Clubs); orch. suites: *Oriental* (1903); *Ballet of the Flowers* (1925); *Suite ancienne* (1926); *Silhouettes, San Francisco* in 3 movements (Robin Hood Dell, July 17, 1932, composer conducting); *Streets of Pekin* (Tokyo, Sept. 24, 1930, composer conducting); *Scherzo diabolique* for Orch., "to recall a harrowing personal experience during a terrifying automobile ride at night, exceeding all speed limits" (Century of Progress Exposition, Chicago, Aug. 1934, composer conducting); incidental music to *The Daughter of Hamilcar* and *Audrey; Konzertstück* for Cello and Orch. (1937); Piano Quintet (1920); 2 string quartets; 2 piano trios; Violin Sonata; Elegy for Cello and Piano; choral works with Orch.: *In Music's Praise* (1899; won the Oliver Ditson Prize); *Merlin and Vivien; The Fate of Princess Kiyo; The Nightingale and the Rose; The Golden Prince; The Fairy Thorn; Ode to Music* (1917); *The New Earth* (1919); *Resurgam* (Cincinnati Music Festival, May 1923); *Mirtil in Arcadia* (Harrisburg [Pa.] Festival, May 17, 1928); *Belshazzar* (1932); 6 ballads (*The Fairies; In Arcady; Jabberwocky; Lelawala, a Legend of Niagara; The Princess of Ys; A Legend of Granada*); many anthems; piano pieces; over 150 songs to German and Eng. words. A Henry Hadley Foundation for the Advancement of American Music was organized in 1938.

BIBL.: H. Boardman, *H. H., Ambassador of Harmony* (diss., Emory Univ., 1932); P. Berthoud, *The Musical Works of Dr. H. H.* (N.Y., 1942).

Hadley, Patrick (Arthur Sheldon), English composer; b. Cambridge, March 5, 1899; d. King's Lynn, Norfolk, Dec. 17, 1973. He studied at the Royal College of Music in London with Vaughan Williams and others (1922–25); then taught there (1925–62); from 1938 to 1946 held a fellowship at Gonville and Caius College, Cambridge; held a chair there from 1946 to 1962. He composed mostly vocal music; among his works are the cantatas *The Trees So High* (1931); *La Belle Dame sans merci* (1935); *Travelers* (1940); *The Hills* (1944); *Fen and Flood* (1954); *Connemara* (1958); *Cantata for Lent* (1960).

BIBL.: W. Todds, *P. H.; A Memoir* (London, 1974; with catalog of works).

Hadow, Sir W(illiam) H(enry), English music educator, writer on music, and composer; b. Ebrington, Gloucestershire, Dec. 27, 1859; d. London, April 8, 1937. He studied at Malvern College (1871–78) and Worcester College, Oxford (1878–82); received the degrees of M.A. (1885) and Mus.B. (1890). He held various positions in English univs. from 1885 to 1919; was knighted in 1918. He wrote a cantata, *The Soul's Pilgrimage;* a String Quartet; 2 violin sonatas; a Viola Sonata; and a number of anthems. These, however, are of little significance; Hadow's importance lies in his books, written in a lively journalistic style. His book *A Croatian Composer* (London, 1897), claiming that Haydn was of Slavonic origin, aroused considerable controversy; modern research proves the claim fanciful and devoid of foundation. Of more solid substance are his other writings: *Studies in Modern Music* (2 vols., 1892–95; 10th ed., 1921); *Sonata Form* (1896; 2nd ed., 1915); *The Viennese Period* (vol. 5 of the *Oxford History of Music*, 1904; 2nd ed., 1931); *William Byrd* (1923); *Music* (1924; 3rd rev. ed., by G. Dyson, 1949); *Church Music* (1926); *A Comparison of Poetry and Music* (1926); *Collected Essays* (1928); *English Music* (1931); *The Place of Music among the Arts* (1933); *Ri-*

chard Wagner (1934). He also ed. songs of the British Isles (1903); was editor in chief of the *Oxford History of Music* (1901–5 and 1929).

Hadzidakis, Manos, Greek composer; b. Xanthi, Macedonia, Oct. 23, 1925. He wrote piano pieces in an advanced idiom, recalling Prokofiev; then turned to film music. He wrote the theme song for the film released in America under the title *Never on Sunday* (1960).

Haebler, Ingrid, esteemed Austrian pianist; b. Vienna, June 20, 1926. She was educated in Vienna, Salzburg, and Geneva. After winning 1st prize in the International Competition in Munich and the Schubert Competition in Geneva, she developed a fine career as a soloist with orchs. and as a concert artist. She excels in the music of Haydn, Mozart, Schubert, and Schumann. In 1969 she was appointed to the faculty of the Salzburg Mozarteum.

Haeffner, Johann Christian Friedrich, German organist, conductor, and composer; b. Oberschönau, near Suhl, March 2, 1759; d. Uppsala, May 28, 1833. He was a pupil of Vierling in Schmalkalden; studied at the Univ. of Leipzig, and served as proofreader for Breitkopf; then became conductor of a traveling opera troupe; in 1781 he arrived in Stockholm, where he was an organist at St. Gertrud until 1793. He composed several operas in the style of Gluck which had a favorable reception: *Electra* (July 22, 1787), *Alcides inträde i Världen* (Nov. 11, 1793), and *Renaud* (Jan. 29, 1801). In 1792 he was appointed director of the Swedish Royal Orch.; in 1808 he went to Uppsala, where he remained for the rest of his life, acting as organist of the Cathedral and music director of the Univ. He took great interest in Swedish national music; publ. Swedish folk songs with accompaniment, and revised the melodies of the Geijer-Afzelius collection; ed. a *Svenska Choralbok* (2 parts, 1819–21), in which he restored the choral melodies of the 17th century, and added preludes (1822); also arranged a collection of old Swedish songs in 4 parts (1832–33; he finished only 2 books).

Haefliger, Ernst, Swiss tenor; b. Davos, July 6, 1919. He studied at the Univ. of Zürich; also with Julius Patzak in Vienna and Fernando Carpi in Geneva. His appearance at the Salzburg Festival (1949) catapulted him onto an international career. He made many concert appearances with the leading orchs. of Europe; was also a fine lieder singer in solo recitals. His repertoire is most extensive; he is best known for his Mozart interpretations. He publ. *Die Singstimme* (Bern, 1983).

Haendel, Ida, Polish-born violinist; b. Chelm, Dec. 15, 1923. She studied at the Warsaw Cons., receiving its gold medal; made a remarkable London debut when she was only 14 years old, appearing with Sir Henry Wood at a Proms concert in the Brahms Violin Concerto. She then continued her studies with Carl Flesch and Georges Enesco. She settled in England and became a British subject; after her 1st tour of the U.S. in 1946–47, she settled in Canada (1952). She was a soloist with the London Phil. on its tour of China in 1973. A facile writer, she publ. an interesting account of her life and career in *Woman with Violin* (London, 1970).

Hafez (Shabana), Abdel Halim, renowned Egyptian singer; b. Zakazik, Sharkia, 1929; d. London, March 30, 1977. He rose to prominence in Egypt, and the Arab world in general, as the foremost interpreter of romantic and nationalistic songs; won renown for his renditions of *Safini Marra* and *Ala Kad el Shouk.* He used Western instruments in his performances, and even utilized the Moog synthesizer. So widespread was his fame at the time of his death that 100,000 Egyptians lined the streets of the funeral procession in Cairo.

Hafgren, Lily (Johana Maria), Swedish soprano; b. Stockholm, Oct. 7, 1884; d. Berlin, Feb. 27, 1965. She was educated in Frankfurt; began her career as a pianist; Siegfried Wagner encouraged her to consider an operatic career, and she studied voice in Stuttgart with Max Fleisch; made her debut at the Bayreuth Festival in 1908; then sang in Mannheim (1908–

12) and at the Royal (later State) Opera in Berlin (1912–21); also appeared in Paris, Rome, and Milan. She retired in 1934. In later years she used her married names, Hafgren-Waag and Hafgren-Dinkela.

Hagegård, Håkan, outstanding Swedish baritone; b. Karlstad, Nov. 25, 1945. After initial training in Karlstad, he studied at the Musikhögskolan and with Erik Werba and Gerald Moore in Salzburg; made his operatic debut at the Royal Theater in Stockholm as Papageno in *Die Zauberflöte* (1968); after further study with Tito Gobbi, he made his 1st venture outside his homeland at the Glyndebourne Festival in 1973. He gained wide recognition through his notable portrayal of Papageno in the film version of *Die Zauberflöte* by Ingmar Bergman (1975); subsequently appeared throughout Europe in opera and concert. On Dec. 7, 1978, he made his Metropolitan Opera debut in N.Y. as Dr. Malatesta in *Don Pasquale.* He particularly distinguished himself in operas by Mozart, Rossini, Donizetti, and Verdi; also became highly esteemed as a concert singer, excelling as an interpreter of lieder.

BIBL.: *Current Biography* (May 1985).

Hageman, Maurits (Leonard), Dutch violinist, conductor, and composer, father of **Richard Hageman;** b. Zutfen, Sept. 25, 1829; d. Nijmegen, April 16, 1906. He studied with Bériot and Fétis at the Brussels Cons., graduating in 1852. After playing violin in the Italian Opera orch. at Brussels, he became a conductor at Groningen; then was director of the Cons. of Batavia, Java (1865–75), and conductor of the orch. there. Returning to the Netherlands, he founded a music school in Leeuwarden. He wrote an oratorio, *Daniel;* several other choral works; piano pieces; songs.

Hageman, Richard, distinguished Dutch-American pianist, conductor, and composer, son of **Maurits (Leonard) Hageman;** b. Leeuwarden, July 9, 1882; d. Beverly Hills, March 6, 1966. He studied music with his father, then took courses at the Brussels Cons. with Gevaert and Arthur de Greef. He held an auxiliary position as conductor at the Royal Opera in Amsterdam (1899–1903). After playing accompaniments for Mathilde Marchesi in Paris (1904–5), he went to the U.S. as accompanist for Yvette Guilbert in 1906; from 1913 to 1921 and again in 1936 was on the conducting staff of the Metropolitan Opera; also conducted the summer opera at Ravinia Park in Chicago and taught voice at the Chicago Musical College. In 1938 he settled in Hollywood, where he was engaged as a composer of film music. He wrote 2 operas: *Caponsacchi* (1931; produced in Freiburg im Breisgau as *Tragödie in Arezzo,* Feb. 18, 1932; at the Metropolitan Opera, N.Y., Feb. 4, 1937; received the David Bispham Memorial Medal) and *The Crucible* (Los Angeles, Feb. 4, 1943). He achieved a lasting reputation mainly through his solo songs, of which *Do Not Go My Love* (to words by Rabindranath Tagore; 1917) and *At the Well* (1919) became extremely popular.

Hagen, Francis Florentine, American Moravian minister and composer; b. Salem, N.C., Oct. 30, 1815; d. Lititz, Pa., July 7, 1907. He served as a teacher and minister in various Moravian congregations; ed. and compiled the *Church and Home Organist's Companion.* He wrote a number of anthems, in which a definite sense for distinguished popular melody is noticeable; also a cantata and an overture. His *Morning Star,* a Christmas carol, which in Moravian communities stood in continuous favor for almost a century, was reprinted in 1939.

BIBL.: A. Rau and H. David, *A Catalogue of Music by American Moravians* (Bethlehem, Pa., 1938).

Hagen, Friedrich Heinrich von der, German scholar; b. in the Ukraine, Feb. 19, 1780; d. Berlin, June 11, 1856. He was a prof. of German literature at the Univ. of Berlin. He publ. the valuable collection *Minnesinger* (5 vols., 1838–56); in vol. III are *Minnegesänge* in notation according to the Jena Codex and other sources, with a treatise on the music of the Minnesinger); *Melodien zu der Sammlung deutscher, vlämischer und französicher Volkslieder* (1807; with Büsching).

Hagen-Groll, Walter, German choral conductor; b. Chemnitz, April 15, 1927. He was educated at the Hochschule für Musik in Stuttgart; in 1952 he became conductor of the choir at the Stuttgart Opera; obtained a similar position at the Heidelberg Opera in 1957. In 1961 he was appointed conductor of the Deutsche Oper Chorus in West Berlin; also became director of the choir of the Berlin Phil. Orch. concerts. Furthermore, he served as chorus leader at Bayreuth and Salzburg; appeared in London as conductor of the Philharmonia Orch. Chorus. He was conductor of the Vienna State Opera chorus (1984–86); served as director of the Wiener Singakademie (from 1987).

Hager, Leopold, Austrian conductor; b. Salzburg, Oct. 6, 1935. He was educated at the Salzburg Mozarteum; then served as an assistant conductor in Mainz (1957–62) and Linz (1962–64). He was 1st conductor of the Cologne Opera (1964–66) and Generalmusikdirektor in Freiburg im Breisgau (1965–69); then returned to Salzburg as chief conductor of the Mozarteum Orch.; left this post in 1981. He was also chief conductor of the Luxembourg Radio Orch. (from 1981). He appeared as a guest conductor throughout Europe and the U.S.

Hagerup Bull, Edvard, Norwegian composer; b. Bergen, June 10, 1922. He studied composition in Norway with Bjarne Brustad and Ludvig Irgens Jensen; in 1947 went to Paris, where he took courses with Koechlin, Rivier, Messiaen, and Milhaud; continued his studies in Berlin with Boris Blacher.

WORKS: OPERAS: *Fyrtøjet* (1973–74) and *Den Grimme Aelling* (1972–77). **BALLET:** *Munchhausen* (1961). **ORCH.:** *Le Soldat de plomb,* ballet suite (1948–49); *Serenade* (1950); *Morceaux rapsodiques,* divertimento (1950); 2 trumpet concertos (1950, 1960); *Sinfonia di teatro,* symphonic prelude (1950–51); *Petite suite symphonique* for Small Orch. (1951); *Escapades,* suite (1952); Divertimento for Piano and Orch. (1954); 6 syms.: No. 1, *3 mouvements symphoniques* (1955); No. 2, *In modo d'una sinfonia* (1958–59); No. 3, *Sinfonia espressiva* (1964); No. 4, *Sinfonia humana* (1968); No. 5, *Sinfonia in memoriam* (1971–72); No. 6, *Lamentazione, Sinfonia da camera pour la Pologne, Solidarité et Lech Walesa* (1981–82); *3 morceaux brefs* for Saxophone and Orch. (1955); *Cassation* for Chamber Orch. (1959); *Epilogue* for Strings (1961); *Undecim Sumus* for Chamber Orch. of Soloists (1962); *Dialogue* for Flute, Strings, and Piano (1965); *6 épigrammes* for Chamber Ensemble (1969); Concerto for Flute and Chamber Orch. (1969); *Air solennel,* symphonic movement (1972); Alto Saxophone Concerto (1980); *Movimenti* (1985). **CHAMBER:** Clarinet Sonata (1950); *3 bucoliques* for Oboe, Clarinet, and Bassoon (1953); Duo for Violin and Piano (1956); *Ad usum amicorum* for Flute, Violin, Cello, and Piano (1957); *Marionnettes sérieuses* for Wind Quintet (1960); *Quadrige* for 4 Clarinets (1964); Sextet for Saxophone and Wind Quintet (1965); *Sonata cantabile* for Flute, Violin, Cello, and Piano (1966); *Concert* for Trumpet, Horn, and Trombone (1966); *Accents* for Piano (1968); *Sonata con spirito* for Piano Quartet (1970).

Hägg (Peterson), Gustaf Wilhelm, eminent Swedish organist and composer; b. Visby, Nov. 28, 1867; d. Stockholm, Feb. 7, 1925. Hägg was his mother's name, which he legally adopted; his father's name was Peterson. He was a remote relative of **Jakob Adolf Hägg.** He studied organ at the Stockholm Cons.; in 1893 he was appointed organist at the Klara Church in Stockholm, retaining this position for the rest of his life. In the interim he traveled for further study in Germany and France (1897–1900). In 1904 he joined the staff of the Stockholm Cons., as a teacher of harmony and organ playing. He enjoyed a distinguished reputation in Sweden as an organist, and gave numerous recitals in which he played the works of César Franck and other organ composers. He also composed 5 organ concertos and other organ pieces; several cantatas; songs. He arranged and publ. collections of Swedish songs (Stockholm, 1908), and an album, *Songs of Sweden* (N.Y., 1909).

Hägg, Jakob Adolf, Swedish composer; b. Oestergarn, June 27, 1850; d. Hudiksvall, March 1, 1928. He was a remote relative of **Gustaf Wilhelm Hägg (Peterson).** He studied at the Stockholm Cons.; then received a stipend to take courses in Denmark with Gade, who exercised a decisive influence on his style of composition; he further studied piano with Anton Door in Vienna and music theory with Kiel in Berlin. Ambition to learn and relentless diligence in his studies upset his mental equilibrium so that he had to spend 15 years in a sanatorium (1880–95). He recovered but retired to the country, reducing his activity to a minimum. Despite this misadventure he was able to leave a considerable legacy of works, among them 5 syms., of which *Nordische Symphonie* (1870; rev. 1890) was the best known; 3 overtures; Cello Sonata, Piano Trio, String Quartet, and other chamber music; piano pieces; songs.

BIBL.: G. Hetsch, *J.A. H.* (Leipzig, 1903).

Haggard, Merle (Ronald), American country-western singer, fiddler, and guitarist; b. Bakersfield, Calif., April 6, 1937. His impoverished family moved to California, where they lived in an abandoned boxcar near Bakersfield. He started early on a criminal career; escaped 7 times from reform schools, stole cars and held up a bar, and finally ended up at San Quentin as prisoner No. 845,200. There he met the notorious "red-light bandit" Caryl Chessman, eventually executed for a series of brutal rapes; Chessman exercised a profound intellectual influence on Haggard, who began improvising songs of destitution, despair, and crime, exemplified by the autobiographical ballad "Did you ever steal a quarter when you was 10 years old?" In due time he completed his term and in 1972 was pardoned by Ronald Reagan, then governor of California. No longer did he have to steal money, for he commanded a fee of $15,000 per concert, sold millions of record albums to his own lyrics and music, and won awards galore in the city of Nashville. He married 3 times and made more successful recordings, gradually reaching the topnotch rank as a country-western singer with such hits as *Okie from Muskogee, Workin' Man Blues, Daddy Frank (the Guitar Man),* and *Hungry Eyes.* He authored an autobiography with P. Russell titled *Sing Me Back Home.* And—supreme reward—he made the *Time* magazine cover story (March 11, 1977).

Haggin, B(ernard) H., iconoclastic American music critic; b. N.Y., Dec. 29, 1900; d. there, May 29, 1987. An aggressive writer who held unalterable opinions on musical matters, he adopted a polemical manner of personal journalism, disregarding all conventional amenities. He was music critic for the *Brooklyn Daily Eagle* (1934–37) and for the *Nation* (1936–57). He collected many of his articles in book form. He publ. *Music for the Man Who Enjoys Hamlet* (N.Y., 1944); *Music in The Nation* (N.Y., 1949); *Music Observed* (N.Y., 1964; reprinted 1974 under the title *35 Years of Music*); and *The New Listener's Companion and Record Guide* (N.Y., 1967; new eds., 1968, 1971). In his *The Toscanini Musicians Knew* (N.Y., 1967) and *Conversations with Toscanini* (N.Y., 1959; 2nd ed., enl., 1979), he fired some Parthian shots at Toscanini's less Olympian colleagues. However contentious, his books have the virtue of readability.

Hahn, Reynaldo, Venezuelan-born French conductor, music critic, and composer; b. Caracas, Aug. 9, 1874; d. Paris, Jan. 28, 1947. His father, a merchant from Hamburg, settled in Venezuela c.1850; the family moved to Paris when Reynaldo was 5 years old. He studied singing and apparently had an excellent voice; a professional recording he made in 1910 testifies to that. He studied music theory at the Paris Cons. with Dubois and Lavignac and composition with Massenet, who exercised the most important influence on Hahn's own music. He also studied conducting, achieving a high professional standard as an opera conductor. In 1934 he became music critic of *Le Figaro.* He remained in France during the Nazi occupation at a considerable risk to his life, since he was Jewish on his father's side. In 1945 he was named a member of the Institut de France and in 1945–46 was music director of the Paris Opéra. Hahn's music is distinguished by a facile, melodious flow and a fine Romantic flair. Socially, he was known in Paris for his brilliant wit. He maintained a passionate youthful friendship with Marcel Proust, who portrayed him as a poetic genius

in his novel *Jean Santeuil;* their intimate correspondence was publ. in 1946. He was a brilliant journalist; his articles were publ. as *Du Chant* (Paris, 1920; 2nd ed., 1957), *Notes. Journal d'un musicien* (Paris, 1933), *L'Oreille au guet* (Paris, 1937), and *Thèmes variés* (Paris, 1946). **WORKS: OPERAS:** *L'Île du rêve,* "Polynesian idyll," after Pierre Loti (Opéra-Comique, Paris, March 23, 1898); *La Carmélite* (Opéra-Comique, Paris, Dec. 16, 1902); *Nausicaa* (Monte Carlo, April 10, 1919); *Fête triomphale* (Paris Opéra, July 14, 1919); *La Colombe de Bouddah* (Cannes, March 21, 1921); *Ciboulette,* light opera (Théâtre des Variétés, Paris, April 7, 1923); *Le Marchand de Venise,* after Shakespeare (Paris Opéra, March 25, 1935). **OPERETTAS:** *Miousic* (Paris, March 22, 1914); *Mozart,* after a play by Sascha Guitry (Paris, Dec. 2, 1925); *Brummel* (Paris, Jan. 20, 1931); *O mon bel inconnu* (Paris, Oct. 5, 1933); *Malvina* (Gaîté Lyrique, Paris, March 25, 1935). **INCIDENTAL MUSIC:** To Daudet's *L'Obstacle* (1890); Croisset's *Deux courtisanes* (1902); Racine's *Esther* (1905); Hugo's *Angelo* (1905) and *Lucrèce Borgia* (1911); Wolff and Duvernois's *Le Temps d'aimer* (1926). **BALLETS:** *Fin d'amour* (1892); *Le Bal de Béatrice d'Este* (Paris, April 11, 1907); *La Fête chez Thérèse* (Paris, Feb. 16, 1910); *Medusa* (Monte Carlo, Dec. 24, 1911); *Le Dieu bleu* (Diaghilev's Ballets Russes, Paris, May 14, 1912); *Le Bois sacré* (1912); 2 symphonic poems: *Nuit d'amour bergamasque* (1897) and *Prométhée triomphant* (1911); Christmas mystery, *La Pastorale de Noël* (1908); lyric comedy, *Le Oui des jeunes filles* (unfinished; completed and orchestrated by Henri Busser; Opéra-Comique, Paris, June 21, 1949); Violin Concerto (Paris, Feb. 26, 1928); Piano Concerto (Paris, Feb. 4, 1931); Cello Concerto; Piano Quintet; String Quartet; a number of piano pieces, among them a suite, *Portraits de peintres,* inspired by poems of Marcel Proust.

BIBL.: D. Bendahan, *R. H. Su vida y su obra* (Caracas, 1973); B. Gavoty, *R. H.: Le Musicien de la belle époque* (Paris, 1976).

Hahn, Ulrich. See Han, Ulrich.

Haibel, (Johann Petrus) Jakob, Austrian tenor and composer; b. Graz, July 20, 1762; d. Djakovar, March 24, 1826. He was engaged in Vienna as a tenor; in 1806 settled in Djakovar; there he married Sophie Weber, sister of Mozart's widow. He produced several stage works in Vienna, among them the ballet *Le nozze disturbate* (May 18, 1795) and a singspiel, *Der Tyroler Wastl* (May 14, 1796), which became very popular.

Haieff, Alexei (Vasilievich), Russian-American composer; b. Blagoveshchensk, Siberia, Aug. 25, 1914. He received his primary education at Harbin, Manchuria; in 1931 went to the U.S.; studied with Rubin Goldmark and Frederick Jacobi at the Juilliard School of Music in N.Y.; during 1938–39 he studied with Nadia Boulanger in Cambridge, Mass. He held a Guggenheim fellowship in 1946 and again in 1949; was a Fellow at the American Academy in Rome (1947–48), a prof. at the Univ. of Buffalo (1962–68), and composer-in-residence at the Univ. of Utah (1968–70). In his music Haieff follows Stravinsky's type of neo-Classical writing, observing an austere economy of means, but achieving modernistic effects by a display of rhythmic agitation, often with jazzy undertones. **WORKS:** Ballets: *The Princess Zondilda and Her Entourage* (1946) and *Beauty and the Beast* (1947); 3 syms.: No. 1 (1942); No. 2 (Boston, April 11, 1958; received the American International Music Fund Award); No. 3 (New Haven, Conn., April 11, 1961); Divertimento for Orch. (N.Y., April 5, 1946); Violin Concerto (1948); Piano Concerto (N.Y., April 27, 1952; received the Award of the N.Y. Music Critics Circle); Sonatina for String Quartet (1937); 3 *Bagatelles* for Oboe and Bassoon (1939); Serenade for Oboe, Clarinet, Bassoon, and Piano (1942); *Eclogue* for Cello and Piano (1947); *La Nouvelle Héloïse* for Harp and String Quartet (1963); Cello Sonata (1963); *Éloge* for Chamber Orch. (1967); *Caligula* for Baritone and Orch., after Robert Lowell (N.Y., Nov. 5, 1971); *Rhapsodies* for Guitar and Harpsichord (1980); Wind Quintet (1983); Sonata for 2 Pianos (1945); Piano Sonata (1955); songs.

Haig, Al(lan Warren), American jazz pianist; b. Newark, N.J., July 22, 1924; d. N.Y., Nov. 16, 1982. He served in the

U.S. Coast Guard in World War II; in 1945 he joined the band of Dizzy Gillespie, and also was a member of the Charlie Parker Quintet. His piano style was influenced by the popular bebop technique. He was a colorful figure in the new jazz world, but his career was interrupted when he had to stand trial on the charge of having murdered his 1st wife, Bonnie. Fortunately, he was acquitted and was able to resume piano playing; he also found another woman to marry.

Haile, Eugen, German-American composer; b. Ulm, Feb. 21, 1873; d. Woodstock, N.Y., Aug. 14, 1933. He studied at the Stuttgart Cons.; emigrated to America in 1903. He wrote about 200 songs to German texts, some of them of excellent quality (*Herbst, Der Todesengel singt, Teufelslied, Soldaten kommen,* etc.). His musical setting to a spoken drama ("gesprochene Oper"), *The Happy Ending,* produced in N.Y. on Aug. 21, 1916, is an interesting attempt to combine spoken words in the play with pitch inflections in the vocal parts, in the manner of *Sprechtstimme.* His other opera, *Harold's Dream,* was produced in Woodstock on June 30, 1933.

Hailstork, Adolphus (Cunningham), black American composer and teacher; b. Rochester, N.Y., April 17, 1941. He studied composition with Mark Fax at Howard Univ. in Washington, D.C. (B.Mus., 1963); Nadia Boulanger at the American Cons. in Fontainebleau (summer 1963); Ludmila Ulehla, Nicolas Flagello, Vittorio Giannini, and David Diamond at the Manhattan School of Music in N.Y. (B.Mus., 1965; M.Mus., 1966); and H. Owen Reed at Michigan State Univ. in East Lansing (Ph.D., 1971). He also attended sessions on synthesizer and computer music given by John Appleton and Herbert Howe at the New Hampshire Electronic Music Inst. (summer 1972), and on contemporary music at the State Univ. of N.Y. at Buffalo (summer 1978). In 1987 he held a Fulbright fellowship for study in Guyana. He taught at Michigan State Univ. (1969–71), Youngstown (Ohio) State Univ. (1971–76), and Norfolk (Va.) State Univ. (from 1977). Several of his works reflect his Afro-American experience. He has received various commissions, and a number of his works have been performed by major U.S. orchs.

WORKS: ORCH.: *Phaedra,* tone poem (1966); *SA-1* for Jazz Ensemble (1971); *Bellevue* (1974); Concerto for Violin, Horn, and Orch. (1975); *American Landscape No. 1* for Concert Band (1977); *Epitaph: In Memoriam: Martin Luther King, Jr.* (1979); *Norfolk Pride,* march for Concert Band (1980); *American Landscape No. 3* (1982); *American Guernica* for Piano and Concert Band (1983); *An American Port of Call* (1984); Sym. No. 1 (1988). CHAMBER: Horn Sonata (1966); *Capriccio for a Departed Brother: Scott Joplin* for Strings (1969); Violin Sonata (1971); *Spiritual* for Brass Octet (1975); *American Landscape No. 2* for Violin and Cello (1978); *Variations* for Trumpet (1981); *Music* for 10 Players (1982); Trio for Violin, Cello, and Piano (1985); *3 Preludes* for Guitar (1989). PIANO: *Ignis Fatuus* (1976); *5 Friends* (1978); 2 sonatas (1980, 1989); *Reflections* (1981); Sonata for 2 Pianos (1987); also choral pieces.

Hainl, François, French cellist and conductor; b. Issoire, Nov. 16, 1807; d. Paris, June 2, 1873. After graduating as a cellist from the Paris Cons. with a 1st prize (1830), he went to Lyons, where he conducted theater music (1841–63); then conducted at the Paris Opéra (1863–72). He wrote several pieces for cello, as well as an orch. fantasy on Rossini's *William Tell;* publ. a valuable account, *De la musique à Lyon depuis 1713 jusqu'à 1852.*

Haitink, Bernard (Johann Herman), eminent Dutch conductor; b. Amsterdam, March 4, 1929. He studied violin at the Amsterdam Cons.; then played in the Radio Phil. Orch. in Hilversum. In 1954–55 he attended the conducting course of Ferdinand Leitner, sponsored by the Netherlands Radio; in 1955 he was appointed to the post of 2nd conductor of the Radio Phil. Orch. in Hilversum, becoming its principal conductor in 1957. In 1956 he made his 1st appearance as a guest conductor with the Concertgebouw Orch. of Amsterdam. He made his U.S. debut with the Los Angeles Phil. Orch. on

Jan. 2, 1958. In 1959 he conducted the Concertgebouw Orch. in England. In 1961 he became co–principal conductor of the Concertgebouw Orch., sharing his duties with Eugen Jochum; that same year he led it on a tour of the U.S., followed by one to Japan in 1962. In 1964 he became chief conductor of the Concertgebouw Orch., a position he held with great distinction until 1988. In 1967 he also assumed the post of principal conductor and artistic adviser of the London Phil. Orch., becoming its artistic director in 1969; he resigned from this post in 1978. He made his 1st appearance at the Glyndebourne Festival in 1972, and from 1978 to 1988 was its music director. In 1987 he became music director of the Royal Opera House at London's Covent Garden. He also acted as a guest conductor with the Berlin Phil., Vienna Phil., N.Y. Phil., Chicago Sym., Boston Sym., and Cleveland Orch. In 1982 he led the Concertgebouw Orch. on a transcontinental tour of the U.S. In his interpretations Haitink avoids personal rhetoric, allowing the music to speak for itself. Yet he achieves eloquent and colorful effect; especially fine are his performances of the syms. of Bruckner and Mahler; equally congenial are his projections of the Classical repertoire. He has received numerous international honors, including the Netherlands' Royal Order of Orange-Nassau (1969), the Medal of Honor of the Bruckner Soc. of America (1970), and the Gustav Mahler Soc. Gold Medal (1971); he was named a Chevalier de l'Ordre des Arts et des Lettres of France (1972). He received the rare distinction of being made an Honorary Knight Commander of the Order of the British Empire by Queen Elizabeth II in 1977.

BIBL.: S. Mundy, *B. H.: A Working Life* (London, 1987).

Haizinger (Haitzinger), Anton, Austrian tenor; b. Wilfersdorf, Liechtenstein, March 14, 1796; d. Vienna, Dec. 31, 1869. He studied in Vienna; made his opera debut there in 1821; then sang in Prague, Frankfurt, Paris, and London; retired in 1850, and returned to Vienna. In his prime he enjoyed an excellent reputation, and was equally successful in the Italian and German repertoires. He publ. a song, *Vergiss mein nicht,* and a manual of singing.

Hajdu, André, Hungarian-born Israeli composer; b. Budapest, March 5, 1932. He studied with Kodály, Szabó, Szervánszky, and Kosá at the Budapest Music Academy; then took seminars in Paris with Milhaud and Messiaen (1957–59). For 2 years he taught at the Tunis Cons. (1959–61); emigrated to Israel in 1966, and in 1967 became a teacher at the Tel Aviv Academy of Music. His music is folkloristic in its sources of inspiration, while the harmonic idiom is fairly advanced.

WORKS: *Gypsy Cantata* (1956); *A Little Hell* for Orch. (1960); *Babeliana* for Orch. (1964); Piano Concerto (1968); *Ludus Paschalis* for 8 Soloists, Children's Chorus, and 9 Instruments (1970); *Terouath Melech,* Jewish rhapsody for Clarinet and String Orch. (1973); *Military Diary (The Art of the Canon),* 50 canons for different instrumental combinations (1976); *Stories about Mischievous Boys* for Orch. (1976); *5 Sketches in a Sentimental Mood* for Piano Quartet (1976); *The Prophet of Truth and the Prophet of Deceit* for Narrator and String Orch. (1977); *Concerto for 10 Little Pianists and Grand Orchestra* (1978; also arranged for 2 Pianos); *Plasmas* for 10 Players (1982); *Overture in the Form of a Kite* for Orch. (1985).

Hajdú, Mihály, Hungarian composer; b. Orosháza, Jan. 30, 1909. He studied composition with Kodály and piano with Thomán at the Academy of Music in Budapest; from 1949 to 1960 taught at the Budapest Cons., and from 1960 to 1977 at the Academy of Music.

WORKS: Opera, *Kádár Kata* (1957; Budapest, 1959); 2 *scherzi* for Piano (1931); Suite for Orch. (1934); 2 string quartets (1936, 1970); Piano Sonata (1940); Piano Sonatina (1952); 2 violin sonatas (1953, 1977); Variations and Rondo for Cello and Piano (1955); Piano Trio (1957); *A munka dicsérete* (In Praise of Work), symphonic poem (1958); Trio for Winds (1958); Concertino for Cello and Strings (1966); Piano Concerto (1968); Cello Sonatina (1969); *Capriccio all'ongarese* for Clarinet and Orch. (1969); 8 *Études* for String Orch. (1970); 3 *Pieces* for 2 Pianos (1971); *30 Little Pieces* for Cello and Piano, or 2 Cellos (1973); *Herendi porcelánok* (Herend Porcelain), orch. suite (1976); Divertimento for Chamber Orch. (1978); *4 Movements* for Wind Quintet (1979).

Håkansson, Knut (Algot), Swedish composer; b. Kinna, Nov. 4, 1887; d. Göteborg, Dec. 13, 1929. He studied philosophy and philology at the Univ. of Uppsala; later traveled in Germany. He wrote a ballet, *Mylitta* (1918); several orch. suites on Swedish themes; a String Quartet, a String Trio, and other chamber music. His most significant works are for chorus, many of them derived from the melodic patterns of Swedish folk songs; among the finest were (4) *Fyra madrigaler* (1929) and *Brusala* (1929).

Hakim, Talib Rasul (real name, **Stephen Alexander Chambers**), black American composer; b. Asheville, N.C., Feb. 8, 1940; d. New Haven, Conn., March 31, 1988. He studied at the Manhattan School of Music, the N.Y. College of Music, and the New School for Social Research (1958–65), where his teachers included Starer, Sydeman, Overton, Feldman, Chou Wen-Chung, Whittenberg, and the jazz saxophonist Ornette Coleman. He taught at Pace Univ. (1970–72) and Adelphi Univ. (1972–79). Hakim received an N.E.A. grant for 1973–74 and for 1975; received the ASCAP Composers' Award 3 times and the Bennington Composers' Conference Fellowship 4 times. He employed in his music a series of dissonant blocks of sound moving along in asymmetrical progressions.
WORKS: *Mutations* for Bass Clarinet, Trumpet, Horn, Viola, and Cello (1964); *Peace-Mobile* for Wind Quintet (1964); *Ode to Silence* for Soprano and Piano (1964); *Encounter* for Wind Quintet, Trumpet, and Trombone (1965); *4* for Clarinet, Trumpet, Trombone, and Piano (1965); *A Piano Piece* (1965); *Shapes* for Chamber Orch. (1965); *Portraits* for Flute, Bass, Clarinet, Piano, and 3 Percussionists (1965); *Titles* for Wind Quartet (1965); *Contours* for Oboe, Bassoon, Horn, Trumpet, Cello, and Double Bass (1966); *Inner-Sections* for Flute, Clarinet, Trombone, Piano, and Percussion (1967); *Roots and Other-things* for Flute, Oboe, Clarinet, Horn, Trumpet, Trombone, Viola, Cello, and Double Bass (1967); *Sound-Gone*, "philosophical sketch" for Piano (1967); *Currents* for String Quartet (1967); *Quote-Unquote* for Baritone, Oboe, Trumpet, and 2 Percussionists (1967); *Sound-Image* for Female Voices, Brass, Strings, and Percussion (1969); *Placements* for Piano and 5 Percussionists (1970); *Set-3* for Soprano, Cello, and Piano (1970); *Visions of Ishwara* for Orch. (N.Y., Oct. 10, 1970); *Reflections on the 5th Ray* for Narrator and Chamber Orch. (1972); *Sketchy Blue-bop* for Jazz-band Ensemble (1973); *Tone-Prayers* for Chorus, Piano, and Percussion (1973); *Re/Currences* for Orch. (Washington, D.C., June 7, 1975); *Concepts* for Orch. (1976); *Music* for Soprano and 9 Players (1977); *Arkan-5* for Tape and Orch. (1980); *Quote-Unquote* for Tenor, Oboe, Trumpet, and Percussion (1983).

Halász, László, Hungarian-born American conductor; b. Debrecen, June 6, 1905. He studied piano, theory, and conducting at the Budapest Cons., graduating in 1929; toured Europe as a concert pianist (1928–31), but devoted himself mainly to conducting. After numerous conducting engagements in Budapest, Prague, and Vienna, he emigrated to America in 1936; became a naturalized American citizen in 1943. He was music director of the St. Louis Grand Opera (1937–42); in 1944 was appointed music director of the N.Y. City Opera Co., where he established an audacious policy of producing modern operas, but became embroiled in personal difficulties with the management, and resigned in 1951. From 1949 to 1952 he conducted opera in Chicago, and from 1955 to 1959 was conductor of the German repertoire at the Barcelona Opera; served as artistic director of N.Y.'s Empire State Music Festival (1957–65) and the National Grand Opera (from 1983). He was head of the conducting dept. at the Eastman School of Music in Rochester, N.Y. (1965–67); then was on the faculty of the State Univ. of N.Y. College at Old Westbury (1968–71) and at Stony Brook (1971–75).

Hale, Adam de la. See **Adam de la Halle.**

Hale, Philip, eminent American music critic; b. Norwich, Vt., March 5, 1854; d. Boston, Nov. 30, 1934. He took music lessons in his early youth, and as a boy played the organ in the Unitarian Church at Northampton, Mass.; went to Yale Univ. to study law, and was admitted to the bar in 1880. He then took organ lessons with Dudley Buck; subsequently went to Europe (1882–87), where he studied organ with Haupt in Berlin, and composition with Rheinberger in Munich and with Guilmant in Paris. Returning to America, he served as a church organist in Albany and Troy, N.Y., and in Boston, but soon abandoned this employment for his true vocation, that of drama and music criticism. He was a forceful and brilliant writer; his articles were often tinged with caustic wit directed against incompetent performers and, regrettably, against many modern composers; he also disliked Brahms, and was credited with the celebrated but possibly apocryphal quip that the exits in the newly opened Sym. Hall in Boston should have been marked not "Exit in Case of Fire," but "Exit in Case of Brahms." Another verbal dart attributed to Philip Hale was his dismissal of a singer with the concluding sentence "Valuable time was consumed." Hale was music critic for the *Boston Home Journal* (1889–91), the *Boston Post* (1890–91), the *Boston Journal* (1891–1903), and the *Boston Herald*, of which he was also drama ed. (1904–33). He was also ed. of the *Boston Musical Record* (1897–1901). From 1901 to 1933 he compiled the program books of the Boston Sym. Orch., setting a standard of erudition and informative annotation. He ed. *Modern French Songs* for The Musician's Library (1904); was joint author, with L. Elson, of *Famous Composers and Their Works* (1900). Hale was succeeded as the program annotator of the Boston Sym. by John N. Burk, who publ. a selection of Hale's articles under the title *Philip Hale's Boston Symphony Programme Notes* (N.Y., 1935; 2nd ed., rev., 1939). Hale's voluminous archives and collections of newspaper articles are preserved in the Music Division of the Boston Public Library.

Halévy (real name, **Levy**), **(Jacques-François-) Fromental (-Elie),** celebrated French composer; b. Paris, May 27, 1799; d. Nice, March 17, 1862. The family changed its name to Halévy in 1807. He entered the Paris Cons. at age 9 as a student of Cazot; then studied with Lambert (piano), Berton (harmony), and Cherubini (counterpoint); he also studied with Méhul, winning the 2nd Prix de Rome in 1816 and 1817 and the Grand Prix de Rome in 1819 with his cantata *Herminie*. He became chef du chant at the Théâtre-Italien in 1826. His 1st stage work to be performed was the opéra-comique *L'Artisan* (Opéra-Comique, Jan. 30, 1827), which had a modicum of success. He gained further notice with his *Clari*, introduced to Paris by Malibran (Théâtre-Italien, Dec. 9, 1828). His 1st major success came with *Le Dilettante d'Avignon* (Opéra-Comique, Nov. 7, 1829). He then was chef du chant at the Paris Opéra (1829–45); there he scored his greatest triumph with *La Juive* (Feb. 23, 1835), which established his name and was performed throughout Europe and the U.S. His next opera, *L'Éclair* (Opéra-Comique, Dec. 16, 1835), also enjoyed a favorable reception. Among later operas that were retained in the repertoire were *La Reine de Chypre* (Dec. 22, 1841), *Charles VI* (March 15, 1843), and *La Magicienne* (March 17, 1858), all 1st performed at the Opéra. He was also active as a teacher at the Paris Cons., being made a prof. of harmony and accompaniment (1827), of counterpoint and fugue (1833), and of composition (1840). His students included Gounod, Bizet (who became his son-in-law), and Saint-Saëns. He was elected to membership in the Institut in 1836, and served as its secretary from 1854. Halévy was an extremely apt composer for the stage; he won the admiration of both Berlioz and Wagner. Yet he could never equal Meyerbeer in popular success; as time went by, only *La Juive* gained a permanent place in the world repertoire.
WRITINGS: *Leçons de lecture musicale . . . pour les écoles de la ville de Paris* (Paris, 1857); *Souvenirs et portraits* (Paris, 1861); *Derniers souvenirs et portraits* (Paris, 1863).
WORKS: OPERAS (all 1st perf. in Paris unless otherwise

given): *L'Artisan*, opéra-comique (Opéra-Comique, Jan. 30, 1827); *Le Roi et le batelier*, opéra-comique (Opéra-Comique, Nov. 8, 1827; in collaboration with L. Rifaut); *Clari*, opera semi-seria (Théâtre-Italien, Dec. 9, 1828); *Le Dilettante d'Avignon*, opéra-comique (Opéra-Comique, Nov. 7, 1829); *Attendre et courir*, opéra-comique (Opéra-Comique, May 28, 1830; in collaboration with H. de Ruolz); *La Langue musicale*, opéra-comique (Opéra-Comique, Dec. 11, 1830); *La Tentation*, ballet-opera (Opéra, June 20, 1832; in collaboration with C. Gide); *Les Souvenirs de Lafleur*, opéra-comique (Opéra-Comique, March 4, 1833); *Ludovic*, opéra-comique (Opéra-Comique, May 16, 1833; completion of an opera by Hérold); *La Juive* (Opéra, Feb. 23, 1835); *L'Éclair*, opéra-comique (Opéra-Comique, Dec. 16, 1835); *Guido et Ginevra, ou La Peste de Florence* (Opéra, March 5, 1838); *Les Treize*, opéra-comique (Opéra-Comique, April 15, 1839); *Le Sherif*, opéra-comique (Opéra-Comique, Sept. 2, 1839); *Le Drapier* (Opéra, Jan. 6, 1840); *Le Guitarrero*, opéra-comique (Opéra-Comique, Jan. 21, 1841); *La Reine de Chypre* (Opéra, Dec. 22, 1841); *Charles VI* (Opéra, March 15, 1843); *Le Lazzarone, ou Le Bien vient en dormant* (Opéra, March 23, 1844); *Les Mousquetaires de la reine*, opéra-comique (Opéra-Comique, Feb. 3, 1846); *Les Premiers Pas*, prologue (Opéra-National, Nov. 15, 1847; in collaboration with Adam, Auber, and Carafa); *Le Val d'Andorre*, opéra-comique (Opéra-Comique, Nov. 11, 1848); *La Fée aux roses*, opéra-comique (Opéra-Comique, Oct. 1, 1849); *La Tempestà*, opéra italien (Her Majesty's Theatre, London, June 8, 1850); *La Dame de pique*, opéra-comique (Opéra-Comique, Dec. 28, 1850); *Le Juif errant* (Opéra, April 23, 1852); *Le Nabab*, opéra-comique (Opéra-Comique, Sept. 1, 1853); *Jaguarita l'indienne*, opéra-comique (Théâtre-Lyrique, May 14, 1855); *L'Inconsolable*, opéra-comique (Théâtre-Lyrique, June 13, 1855; perf. under the nom de plume Alberti); *Valentine d'Aubigny*, opéra-comique (Opéra-Comique, April 26, 1856); *La Magicienne* (Opéra, March 17, 1858); *Noé* (unfinished; completed by Bizet and perf. as *Le Déluge*, Karlsruhe, April 5, 1885); *Vanina d'Ornano* (unfinished). **BALLET:** *Manon Lescaut* (Opéra, May 3, 1830). **OTHER WORKS:** *Les Derniers Moments du Tasse*, cantata (won 2nd Prix de Rome, 1816); *La Mort*, cantata (won 2nd Prix de Rome, 1817); *Herminie*, cantata (won Grand Prix de Rome, 1819); *Marche funèbre et De profundis* for 3 Voices and Orch. (1820); *Ouverture* for Orch. (1822); *Les Cendres de Napoléon* for Military Band (1840); *Les Plages du Nil* for Voice and Piano (1846); *Prométhée enchaîné* for Solo Voices, Chorus, and Orch. (1849); *Ave verum* for Solo Voices, Chorus, and Orch. (1850); *Messe de l'Orphéon* for 4 Male Voices, Sopranos, and Organ ad libitum (1851; *Agnus Dei* and *Sanctus* by Halévy; remainder by Adam and Clapisson); Cantata (1856); *Italie*, cantata (1859); *La Nouvelle Alliance* for 4 Male Voices (1860); *France et Italie* for 4 Male Voices (1860); *Come dolce a me favelli*, cavatina for Voice and Orch.; other vocal works; piano pieces. **BIBL.:** C. de Lorbac, *Fromenthal H.: Sa vie, ses œuvres* (Paris, 1862); L. Halévy, *F. H.: Sa vie et ses œuvres* (Paris, 1862; 2nd ed., 1863); A. Catelin, *F. H.: Notice biographique* (Paris, 1863); E. Monnais, *F. H.: Souvenirs d'un ami* (Paris, 1863); A. Pougin, *F. H., écrivain* (Paris, 1865); M. Curtiss, "F. H.," *Musical Quarterly* (April 1953); J. Klein, "J.F. H. (1799–1862)," *Music Review*, XXIII (1962).

Haley, Bill (William John Clifton, Jr.), popular American singer, guitarist, and bandleader; b. Highland Park, Mich., July 6, 1925; d. Harlingen, Texas, Feb. 9, 1981. He began to play guitar as a youth, and at the age of 15 embarked on a tour with country-and-western groups; soon formed his own band, The Saddlemen; in 1952 it was renamed The Comets, to impart a more cosmological beat to the music. Haley precipitated the rock-'n'-roll era with his rendition of *Crazy Man Crazy* in 1953; there followed his hit version of Joe Turner's *Shake, Rattle and Roll*, which combined the elements of the blues, country music, and urban pop. His fame skyrocketed in 1955 with his strident projection of *Rock around the Clock*. Immortalized in the motion picture *Blackboard Jungle*, it became the banner of the rising generation of long-haired, wide-eyed, loose-

eared, spaced-out, stoned American youth; 22 million albums of this song were sold. But like so many instinctual musicians of the period, Haley gradually sank into a state of oblivious torpor, and his once-agile style gave way to the irresistible ascent of the more sexually explicit art of Elvis Presley. **BIBL.:** J. Swenson, *B. H.: The Daddy of Rock and Roll* (N.Y., 1982).

Halffter (Jiménez), Cristóbal, significant Spanish composer and conductor, nephew of **Ernesto Halffter (Escriche)** and **Rodolfo Halffter (Escriche);** b. Madrid, March 24, 1930. He studied composition with Conrado del Campo at the Madrid Cons. (1947–51); then had private lessons with Tansman in Paris. He taught at the Madrid Cons. (1960–67) and was associated with the Radio Nacional de España; traveled as a conductor and lecturer in Europe; visited the U.S. in 1966. In his music he adopted a radical modern idiom; evolved a modified technique of dodecaphonic writing, and explored electronic sound. **WORKS: STAGE:** Opera, *Don Quichotte* (Düsseldorf, 1970); ballet, *Saeta* (Madrid, Oct. 28, 1955). **ORCH.:** *Scherzo* (1951); Piano Concerto (Madrid, March 13, 1954); 2 *Movements* for Timpani and Strings (Madrid, June 26, 1957); Concertino for String Orch. (1956; expanded version of his 1st String Quartet); 5 *Microformas* (1960); *Rhapsodia española de Albeniz* for Piano and Orch. (1960); Sinfonia for 3 Instrumental Groups (1963); *Sequencias* (Madrid, June 16, 1964); *Lineas y puntos* for 20 Winds and Tape (Donaueschingen, Oct. 22, 1967); *Anillos* (1967–68; perf. as a ballet, Lyons, April 13, 1971); *Fibonaccana*, concerto for Flute and String Orch. (Lisbon, May 30, 1970); *Planto por las victimas de la violencia* (Plaint for the Victims of Violence) for Chamber Ensemble and Tape (Donaueschingen, Oct. 17, 1971); *Requiem por la libertad imaginada* (1971); *Pinturas negras* for Orch. and Concertante Organ (1972); *Procesional* for 2 Pianos, Winds, and Percussion (Strasbourg, June 8, 1974); *Tiempo para espacios* for Harpsichord and 12 Strings (1974); 2 cello concertos: No. 1 (1974; Granada, June 24, 1975); No. 2, *No queda mas quel el silencio* (1984); *Elegias a la muerte de tres poetas españoles* (1974–75); *Pourquoi* for 12 Strings (1974–75); Violin Concerto (1979; Madrid, Nov. 29, 1980); *Tiento* (1980); *Sinfonia Ricercata* for Organ and Orch. without violins and percussion (Vienna, Jan. 30, 1983); *Versus* (1983); *Tiento del primer tono y Batalla Imperial* (1986). **VOCAL:** *Antifona Pascual a la Virgen* (*Regina coeli*) for Soprano, Contralto, and Orch. (1951); *Misa ducal* for Chorus and Orch. (Madrid, May 14, 1956); *In exspectatione resurrectionis Domini*, cantata (1962); *Brecht-Lieder* for Voice and Orch. (1967); *In memoriam Anaick* for Child Narrator, Children's Chorus, and ad libitum Instruments (1967); *Symposion* for Baritone, Chorus, and Orch. (1968); *Yes Speak Out Yes*, cantata, after a text by Norman Corwin, in honor of the 20th anniversary of the United Nations' declaration of human rights (N.Y., Dec. 12, 1968); *Noche pasiva del sentido* for Soprano, 2 Percussionists, and Tapes (1971); *Gaudium et Spes* for 32 Voices and Tapes (1972); *Oración a Platero* for Narrator, Chorus, Children's Chorus, and 5 Percussionists (1975); *Officium Defunctorum* for Chorus and Orch. (1977); 3 *Poemas de la Lirica Española* for Baritone and Orch. (1984–86). **CHAMBER:** 3 string quartets: No. 1, 3 *Pieces* (1955); No. 2, *Memories, 1970* (1970); No. 3 (1978); 3 *Pieces* for Solo Flute (1959); Solo Violin Sonata (1959); *Codex* for Guitar (1963); *Espejos* (Mirrors) for 4 Percussionists and Tape (1963); *Antiphonismoi* for 7 Players (1967); *Oda* for 8 Players (1969); *Noche activa del espiritu* for 2 Pianos and Electronics (1973); *Mizar* for 2 Flutes, 9 Strings, and Percussion (1977) and *Mizar II* for 2 Flutes and Electronic Transformation (1979). **PIANO:** Sonata (1951); *Formantes* for 2 Pianos (1961).

Halffter (Escriche), Ernesto, important Spanish composer and conductor, brother of **Rodolfo Halffter (Escriche);** b. Madrid, Jan. 16, 1905; d. there, July 5, 1989. He studied composition with Manuel de Falla and Adolfo Salazar; 1st attracted attention with his *Sinfonietta*, which was included in the program of the Oxford Festival of the ISCM (July 23, 1931). In his music he continued the tradition of Spanish modern nationalism, following the stylistic and melorhythmic formations of his teacher Manuel de Falla; he also completed and orchestrated Falla's unfinished scenic cantata, *Atlántida*, which was 1st performed at La Scala in Milan on June 18, 1962. Among his works are *Fantaisie portugaise* for Orch. (Paris, March 23, 1941) and the ballets *Dulcinea* (1940), *Cojo enamorado* (1954), and *Fantasía galaica* (1955; Milan, 1967). He also composed a Guitar Concerto (1968) and several cantatas.

Halffter (Escriche), Rodolfo, eminent Spanish-born Mexican composer, brother of **Ernesto Halffter (Escriche)** and uncle of **Cristóbal Halffter (Jiménez);** b. Madrid, Oct. 30, 1900; d. Mexico City, Oct. 14, 1987. He acquired a considerable technique of composition, mainly by the study of classical works; received some instruction and advice from Manuel de Falla in Granada (1929). As a young man he was a member of a group of Spanish composers promoting national Spanish music in a modern idiom. From 1934 to 1936 he was a music critic of *La Voz.* During the Spanish Civil War, he occupied important positions in the cultural sections of the Loyalist government; was chief of the Music Section of the Ministry of Propaganda (1936) and then became a member of the Central Music Council of the Spanish Republic (1937); after the Loyalist defeat, he fled to France and then to Mexico, where he settled in 1939 and became a naturalized citizen. In 1940 he founded the 1st Mexican company for contemporary ballet, La Paloma Azul; founded the publishing house Ediciones Mexicanas de Música in 1946; ed. the journal *Nuestra Música* (1946–52); was director of the music dept. of the National Inst. of Fine Arts (1959–64). His early music is influenced by Manuel de Falla and is imbued with Spanish melorhythm; he experimented with dodecaphonic structures; his *3 hojas de álbum* (1953) were the earliest pieces of 12-tone music publ. in Mexico. The scores of his opera buffa *Clavileño* (1934–36) and an *Impromptu* for Orch. (1931–32) were lost when a bomb hit the house where he stayed on the Spanish border during the Civil War.

WORKS: BALLETS: *Don Lindo de Almería* (1935; Mexico City, Jan. 9, 1940); *La madrugada del Panadero* (The Baker's Morning; Mexico City, Sept. 20, 1940); *Elena la Traicionera* (Mexico City, Nov. 23, 1945). ORCH.: Suite (1924–28; Madrid, Nov. 5, 1930); *Obertura concertante* for Piano and Orch. (1932; Valencia, May 23, 1937); Divertimento for 9 Instruments (1935; Mexico City, Nov. 18, 1943); Violin Concerto (1939–40; Mexico City, June 26, 1942); an orch. scoring of *3 sonatas* of Antonio Soler (1951); *Obertura festiva* (Mexico City, May 25, 1953); *3 piezas* for String Orch. (Mexico City, Aug. 10, 1955); *Tripartita* (Mexico City, July 15, 1960); *Diferencias* (Mexico City, Sept. 13, 1970); *Alborada* (Mexico City, May 9, 1976). CHAMBER: *Giga* for Solo Guitar (1930); *Pastorale* for Violin and Piano (1940); *3 piezas breves* for Solo Harp (1944); String Quartet (1957–58); Cello Sonata (1960); *3 movimientos* for String Quartet (1962); *8 tientos* (*Fantasias*) for String Quartet (1973). PIANO: *2 sonatas de El Escorial* (1928); *Preludio y fuga* (1932); *Danza de Ávila* (1936); *Pequeñas variaciones elegiacas* (1937); *Homenaje a Antonio Machado* (1944); 3 sonatas (1947, 1951, 1967); *11 bagatelles* (1949); *3 hojas de álbum* (1953); *Música para 2 Pianos* (1965); *Laberinto: Cuatro intentos de acertar con la salida* (Labyrinth: 4 Attempts to Locate the Exit; 1971–72); *Homenaje a Arturo Rubinstein* (1973); *Facetas* (1976). VOCAL: *La nuez* for Children's Chorus (1944); *3 epitafios* for Chorus a cappella (1947–53); *Pregón para una Pascua pobre* for Chorus, 3 Trumpets, 2 Tenor Trombones, Bass Trombone, and Percussion (Mexico City, April 6, 1969); 3 song cycles: *Marinero en tierra* (1925); *2 sonetos* (1940–46); *Desterro* (1967).

Halíř, Carl (born **Karel Halíř**), Bohemian violinist; b. Hohenelbe, Feb. 1, 1859; d. Berlin, Dec. 21, 1909. He was a pupil of Bennewitz at the Prague Cons., and of Joachim in Berlin. In 1883 he was appointed concertmaster of the Court Orch. at Weimar; in 1893 he obtained a similar post in Berlin; was also appointed prof. at the Hochschule für Musik there; for a time he was a member of the Joachim Quartet, but later formed

his own quartet, which became famous. His tour of the U.S. (1896–97) was very successful. His pedagogic exercises for the violin, *Tonleiterstudien,* are still in use. In 1888 he married Theresa Zerbst, a fine soprano.

Hall, David, American writer on music; b. New Rochelle, N.Y., Dec. 16, 1916. He was educated at Yale Univ. (B.A., 1939) and Columbia Univ. (graduate study in psychology, 1939–40); then worked for Columbia Records and NBC; from 1948 to 1956 he was music director of the classics division of the Mercury Record Corp., where he pioneered in the development of high-fidelity recordings; then was music ed. of *Stereo Review* (1957–62); later was named president of Composers Recordings, Inc. (1963–66). From 1967 to 1980 he was head of the Rodgers and Hammerstein Archives of Recorded Sound at the N.Y. Public Library, and from 1980 its curator. He publ. several annotated guides to recordings; also contributed countless articles and record reviews to leading publications.

Hall, Edmond, black American jazz clarinetist; b. New Orleans, May 15, 1901; d. Boston, Feb. 11, 1967. He performed in the bands of Buddy Petit (1921–23), Claude Hopkins (1929–35), Teddy Wilson (1941–44), and Eddie Condon (from 1944), and with Louis Armstrong's All Stars (1955–58); then pursued a career as a free-lance artist. He was one of the foremost Dixieland clarinetists of his day.

BIBL.: B. McRae, "E. H.," *Jazz Journal,* XXIII/12 (1970); M. Selchow and K. Lohmann, *E. H.: A Discography* (Lübbecke, Germany, 1981).

Hall, Frederick Douglass, black American music educator and composer; b. Atlanta, Dec. 14, 1898; d. there, Dec. 28, 1982. He studied at Morehouse College in Atlanta (B.A., 1921), Chicago Musical College (B.Mus., 1924), Columbia Univ. Teachers College (M.A., 1929; D.Mus. Ed., 1952), Royal Academy of Music in London (licentiate), and Univ. of London (1933–35); taught at various institutions, including Dillard Univ. in New Orleans (1936–41; 1960–74), where he led a male quartet, and Alabama State College in Montgomery (1941–55). His compositions include an oratorio, *Deliverance* (1938); a song-cycle, *Afro-American Religious Work Songs* (1952); and some 20 art songs; he also prepared choral arrangements of spirituals (6 vols., 1929–55).

Hall, Jim (James Stanly), American jazz guitarist; b. Buffalo, N.Y., Dec. 4, 1930. He spent his early years in Cleveland, working in local bands from the age of 13; later moved to Los Angeles and worked with a variety of ensembles and senior performers, beginning with Jimmy Giuffre. His collaborations with Sonny Rollins and Bill Evans had major influence on his work. He has been described as a "blue flame player, playing low, not too obtrusive, but burning hot." An interesting example of the universal admiration of Hall's musicianship is Itzhak Perlman's enthusiastic endorsement on the album *The Jim Hall Trio* (1981), in which Perlman recounts his pleasure in playing jazz in a group comprising Hall, André Previn, Shelly Maure, and Red Mitchell. Hall popularized the rhythms of bossa nova in the U.S. with his collaborative album (with Sonny Rollins) *What's New,* which was produced after a visit to Brazil in May of 1960. An example of his powers of improvisational expression is recorded on *Jim Hall Live!* (Bourbon St. Cafe, Toronto, June 1975), which offers the unselfconsciously free, loose, and often witty improvisations which are the heart and soul of live jazz.

Hall, John, English physician and writer on medicine and religion; b. c.1529; d. c.1566. He was a surgeon by profession and a musician by avocation. A collection consisting of 30 melodies and 1 song in 4 parts has been preserved, entitled *The Court of Vertu* (London, 1565; modern ed. publ. by R. Fraser, London, 1961).

Hall, Marie (Mary Paulina), English violinist; b. Newcastle upon Tyne, April 8, 1884; d. Cheltenham, Nov. 11, 1956. As a small child she gave performances in the homes of music-lovers in Newcastle, Malvern, and Bristol with her father, an amateur harp player, her uncle (violin), her brother (violin), and her sister (harp). Elgar heard her, and was impressed by her talent; he sent her to Wilhelmj in London for regular study; she also studied with Johann Kruse. At the age of 15 she won the 1st Wessely Exhibition at the Royal Academy of Music. She was recommended by Jan Kubelik to Ševčik in Prague (1901), from whom she received a rigorous training; she made her professional debut in Prague (1902); then played in Vienna. After a highly successful London concert (Feb. 16, 1903), she made her American debut as soloist with the N.Y. Sym. Orch., Walter Damrosch conducting (Nov. 8, 1905); toured Australia (1907) and India (1913). On Jan. 27, 1911, she married her manager, Edward Baring, and settled in Cheltenham; she continued to appear in concerts in England until 1955, with her daughter, Pauline Baring, as her accompanist.

BIBL.: J. Cuthbert Hadden, "M. H.," in *Modern Musicians* (Edinburgh, 1913).

Hall, Pauline (Margarete), Norwegian composer; b. Hamar, Aug. 2, 1890; d. Oslo, Jan. 24, 1969. She studied piano with Johan Backer Lunde (1908–10) and theory and composition with Catharinus Elling (1910–12) in Christiania; completed her studies in Paris and Dresden (1912–14). She was the Berlin music and drama correspondent for the Norwegian newspaper *Dagbladet* (1926–32), then was its music critic in Oslo (1934–42; 1945–64). In her early works, she was greatly influenced by French Impressionism; she later evolved a neo-classical style seasoned by disturbing dissonance.

WORKS: BALLET: *Markisen* (The Marquise; 1950). **ORCH.:** *Poème élégiaque* (1920); *Verlaine Suite* (1929); *Cirkusbilder* (1939). **CHAMBER:** Suite for Wind Quintet (1945); *Little Dance Suite* for Oboe, Clarinet, and Bassoon (1958); *4 tosserier* for Soprano, Clarinet, Bassoon, Horn, and Trumpet (1961); *Variations on a Classical Theme* for Flute (1961); choral music; incidental music; piano pieces; songs.

Hall, Sir Peter (Reginald Frederick), noted English theater and opera producer; b. Bury St. Edmunds, Nov. 22, 1930. He was educated at St. Catharine's College, Cambridge. In 1955–56 he was director of the Arts Theatre, London. He was managing director of the Royal Shakespeare Theatre from 1960 to 1968; from 1973 to 1988 he was director of the National Theatre; worked also at the Royal Opera House, Covent Garden. In 1970 he began a long and fruitful association as an opera producer at Glyndebourne, serving as its artistic director from 1984 to 1990. He was head of his own Peter Hall Production Co. (from 1988). For several years he was married to **Maria Ewing.** He was knighted in 1977. He is known for his versatility, having produced operas by Cavalli, Mozart, Wagner, Tchaikovsky, Schoenberg, and Tippett. In 1983 he produced the new *Ring* cycle at Bayreuth for the 100th anniversary of Wagner's death, with Solti conducting.

Hall, Robert Browne, American cornetist, bandmaster, and composer; b. Bowdoinham, Maine, June 30, 1858; d. Portland, Maine, June 8, 1907. He began cornet studies in childhood, and after playing in bands in Maine and Boston, was made director of the Bangor (Maine) Band (1882); later became director of the Waterville (Maine) Military Band (c.1890). He wrote a number of marches, which led to his being described as the "New England March King."

BIBL.: T. Bardwell, "R.B. H. (the New England March King)," in R. Cummings, ed., *Music Journal Anthology 1968* (N.Y., 1968); idem, "The New England March King," *Fanfare,* I/10 (1977); R. Swift, "Credit Overdue: R.B. H.," *Woodwind, Brass & Percussion,* XXI/7 (1982).

Hall, Tom T., American country-music singer and songwriter; b. Olive Hill, Ky., May 25, 1936. He sang on a local radio station as a youth; then served in the army. He made many appearances on television, often giving vent to his liberal views in the form of social commentary. Of his songs, *Harper Valley P.T.A.* achieved popular success in 1968.

Hallberg, Björn Wilho, Norwegian-born Swedish composer; b. Oslo, July 9, 1938. He studied with Brustad and Mortensen; in 1962 went to Sweden, where he studied with Lidholm, Bo

Wallner, and Blomdahl at the Musikhögskolan in Stockholm; also took sporadic lessons with Ligeti. His compositions are exploratory in techniques.

WORKS: Operas: *Evakueringen* (The Evacuation; 1969; Stockholm, Dec. 9, 1969) and *Majdajar* (May Days; Stockholm, Dec. 16, 1989); *Felder* for Flute and Percussion (Vienna Festival, June 17, 1961); String Quartet (1963); *Ur dagboken* (From the Diary) for Percussion Ensemble (1964); *Études for Chamber Ensemble* (1966); *Missa pro defunctis,* in memory of Dag Hammarskjöld, for Soprano, Chorus, Tape, and Orch. (Stockholm, May 17, 1968); *Conversation/Vide* for 5 Singers, 5 Woodwinds, Tape, and Loudspeakers (1968); *États* for Soprano, Flute, Double Bass, Piano, and Percussion (1970); *Aspiration* for Orch. (Östersund, July 11, 1971); *Novelletten* for Orch. (1973); *Die Drohung,* ballet music for Wind Orch. (1973).

Halle, Adam de la. See **Adam de la Halle.**

Hallé, Sir Charles (original name, **Carl Halle**), renowned German-born English pianist and conductor; b. Hagen, April 11, 1819; d. Manchester, Oct. 25, 1895. A child prodigy, he began to play the piano at age 4, making his formal debut in a recital when he was 9; made his conducting debut in Hagen at 11. He subsequently studied harmony and counterpoint with Rinck in Darmstadt (1835–36) and piano with George Osborne in Paris, where he moved in the circles of Chopin, Liszt, Berlioz, and Wagner; made his debut in Paris as a pianist in a trio with Alard and Franchomme in 1840. In 1842 he made a concert tour of Germany, which was followed by his London debut in 1843; he was the 1st pianist to play all the Beethoven piano sonatas in Paris. After the Revolution of 1848 he went to England, where he founded a series of chamber music concerts in Manchester; he then reorganized the Gentlemen's Concerts in 1849 and formed a choral society in 1850; in 1857 he established subscription concerts with his own orch., which developed into the famous Charles Hallé's Orch. (inaugural concert, Jan. 30, 1858); the ensemble endured after his death, eventually becoming the esteemed Hallé Orch. He conducted the Bristol Festivals (1873–93) and the Liverpool Phil. Soc. (1883–95); served as the 1st principal of the Royal Manchester College of Music (1893–95), where he was also a prof. of piano. He was a champion of Berlioz in England, and gave several complete performances of Berlioz's *Damnation de Faust.* His 1st wife was Désirée Smith de Rilieu; with his 2nd wife, the violinist **Wilma Neruda,** he made 2 Australian tours (1890, 1891). He was knighted in 1888. Hallé established a very high standard of excellence in orch. performance, which greatly influenced musical life in England. He publ. a *Pianoforte School* (1873) and ed. a *Musical Library* (1876). M. Kennedy ed. *The Autobiography of Charles Hallé* (London, 1972).

BIBL.: L. Engel, *From Handel to H.* (London, 1890); C. and M. Hallé, *Life and Letters of Sir C. H.* (London, 1896); C. Rigby, *Sir C. H.* (Manchester, 1952); C. Rees, *100 Years of the H.* (London, 1957); M. Kennedy, *H. Orchestra* (Manchester, 1968; rev. ed., 1976); idem, *The H. 1858–1983* (Manchester, 1983); A. Kersting, *C. H.: Ein europäischer Musiker* (Hagen, 1986).

Hallén, (Johannes) Andreas, Swedish conductor and composer; b. Göteborg, Dec. 22, 1846; d. Stockholm, March 11, 1925. He studied with Reinecke in Leipzig, Rheinberger in Munich, and Rietz in Dresden; upon his return to Sweden, conducted in Göteborg (1872–78 and 1883–84); then was conductor of the Phil. Concerts in Stockholm (1885–95) and of the Royal Opera (1892–97). From 1908 to 1919 he was a prof. of composition at the Stockholm Cons. He composed in a Wagnerian style.

WORKS: Operas: *Harald der Wiking* (Leipzig, Oct. 16, 1881); *Häxfällan* (Stockholm, March 16, 1896); *The Treasure of Waldemar* (Stockholm, April 8, 1899); *Walpurgis Night* (rev. version of *Häxfällan;* Stockholm, March 15, 1902); symphonic poems: *En Sommarsaga* (1889) and *Die Toteninsel* (1898); *Sphärenklänge* (1905); cantatas; overtures.

BIBL.: P. Vretblad, *A. H.* (Stockholm, 1918).

Haller, Michael, German composer and writer on music; b. Neusaat, Jan. 13, 1840; d. Regensburg, Jan. 4, 1915. He was educated at Matten monastery; took Holy Orders in 1864; was appointed prefect of the Regensburg Cathedral Choristers' Inst.

WORKS: 14 masses; Psalms; litanies; a Te Deum; melodramas; string quartets; etc. He completed the 3rd-choir parts of 6 compositions *a* 12 of Palestrina, which had been lost.

WRITINGS: *Vademecum für den Gesangsunterricht* (1876; 12th ed., 1910); *Kompositionslehre für den polyphonen Kirchengesang* (1891); *Modulation in den Kirchentonarten*; *Exempla polyphoniae ecclesiasticae* (in modern notation, with explanatory notes).

Hallgrímsson, Haflidi (Magnus), Icelandic composer and cellist; b. Akureyri, Sept. 18, 1941. He graduated from the Reykjavik College of Music in 1962; then studied at the Accademia di Santa Cecilia in Rome and the Royal Academy of Music in London; also took private lessons with Bush and Davies. Returning to Iceland, he was active as a cello player. He also played with the London Sinfonietta, the English Chamber Orch., and the Scottish Chamber Orch. His *Poemi* for Violin and Strings won the Nordic Prize in 1985.

WORKS: 2 string quartets (1962, 1964); Fantasia for Cello (1969); *Elegy* for Mezzo-soprano, Piano, Celesta, Flute, and 2 Cellos (1971); Duo for Viola and Cello (1972); *Hoa-Haka-Nana-Ia* for Clarinet, Strings, and Percussion (1972); *7 Icelandic Folk Songs* for Cello and Piano (1973); Divertimento for Harpsichord and String Trio (1974); *2 Icelandic Folk Songs* for Mezzo-soprano, Clarinet, Flute, Cello, and Piano (1974); *Fimma* for Cello and Piano (1976); *Poemi* for Violin and Strings (1983); *Daydreams in Numbers* for String Orch. (1986); *Words in Winter* for Soprano and Orch. (1987).

Hallnäs, (Johan) Hilding, Swedish organist and composer; b. Halmstad, May 24, 1903; d. Stockholm, Sept. 11, 1984. He studied at the Stockholm Cons. (1924–29); subsequently served as church organist in Göteborg, where he was also active as a teacher. His early works reflect the prevalent Romantic style of Scandinavian music; in later compositions he applied modified serial techniques.

WORKS: He wrote 9 syms., but withdrew the 1st 2 and renumbered the others No. 1, *Sinfonia pastorale* (1944; Göteborg, March 22, 1945); No. 2, *Sinfonia notturna* (Göteborg, March 4, 1948); No. 3, *Little Symphony*, for Strings and Percussion (Göteborg, Oct. 3, 1948); No. 4, *Metamorfose sinfonische* (Göteborg, April 17, 1952; rev. 1960); No. 5, *Sinfonia aforistica* (Göteborg, Jan. 24, 1963); No. 6, *Musica intima*, for Strings and Percussion (Malmö, Nov. 7, 1967); No. 7, *A Quite Small Symphony*, for Chamber Orch. (Minneapolis, June 12, 1974). Ballets: *Kärlekens ringdans* (Love's Dance in the Round; 1955–56) and *Ifigenia* (1961–63; also a suite); Divertimento for Orch. (1937); 2 violin concertos (1945, 1965); *Symphonic Ballet Suite* (1955–56); Piano Concerto (1956); *Cantica lyrica* for Tenor, Chorus, and Orch. (1957); 2 concertos for Flute, Strings, and Percussion (1957, 1962); Concerto for String Orch. and Percussion (1959); *Epitaph* for Strings (1963); *Rapsodie* for Chamber Orch. and Soprano (1963); *En grekisk saga* (A Greek Saga) for Orch. (1967–68; dedicated to Melina Mercouri, Mikis Theodorakis, and the Greek people); *Momenti bucolichi* for Oboe and Orch. (1969); *Horisont och linjespel* for String Orch. (1969); *Triple Concerto* for Violin, Clarinet, Piano, and Orch. (1972–73); Viola Concerto (1976–78); Cello Concerto (1981); 3 string quartets (1949; 1967; with Soprano, 1976); Quintet for Flute, Oboe, Viola, Cello, and Piano (1954); *Cantata* for Soprano, Flute, Clarinet, Cello, and Piano (1955); 2 violin sonatas (1957, 1975); piano trio, *Stanze sensitive* (1959); 4 piano sonatas (1963–83); organ sonata, *De Profundis* (1965); *24 Preludes* for Guitar (1967); *Passionsmusik*, 15 pieces for Organ (1968); *3 momenti musicali* for Violin, Horn, and Piano (1971); *Invocatio* for Chorus and String Quartet (1971); *Confessio*, trio for Clarinet, Cello, and Piano (1973); *Triptykon* for Violin, Clarinet, and Piano (1973); *4 Monologues* for Clarinet (1974); *Trauma* for 4 Strings and Piano (1979); String Quartet (1980); *Musikaliska aforismer* for String Trio (1982).

Hallström, Ivar (Christian), Swedish composer; b. Stockholm, June 5, 1826; d. there, April 11, 1901. He studied jurisprudence at the Univ. of Uppsala; there he became a friend of Prince Gustaf, who was himself a musical amateur; on April 9, 1847, jointly with Gustaf, he produced in Stockholm an opera, *Hvita frun på Drottningholm* (The White Lady of Drottningholm); in 1853 he became librarian to Prince Oscar; from 1861 to 1872 he was director of Lindblad's music school in Stockholm. His opera *Hertig Magnus och sjöjungfrun* (Duke Magnus and the Mermaid) was produced at the Royal Opera in Stockholm on Jan. 28, 1867, but had only 6 performances in all, purportedly because it contained more arias in minor keys (10, to be exact) than those in major (only 8). He then produced another opera, *Den förtrollade Katten* (The Enchanted Cat; Stockholm, April 20, 1869), which was more successful. With his next opera, *Den Bergtagna* (The Bewitched One), produced in Stockholm on May 24, 1874, he achieved his greatest success; it had repeated performances not only in Sweden, but also in Germany and Denmark. In this work Hallström made use of Swedish folk motifs, a pioneering attempt in Scandinavian operatic art. His next opera, *Vikingarna* (Stockholm, June 6, 1877), was but moderately successful; there followed *Neaga* (Stockholm, Feb. 24, 1885), to a libretto by Carmen Sylva (Queen Elisabeth of Rumania). He also wrote several ballets, cantatas, and arrangements of Swedish folk songs for piano.

Halm, August Otto, German writer on music and composer; b. Gross-Altdorf, Württemberg, Oct. 26, 1869; d. Saalfeld, Feb. 1, 1929. A member of a family of scholars, he received an excellent general education; then studied theology at Tübingen. In 1892 he went to Munich, where he took courses with Rheinberger. Subsequently he devoted himself mainly to musical pedagogy; taught in various schools in Thuringia; conducted choral societies and wrote music criticism. He wrote 2 syms.; a Piano Concerto; 8 string quartets; 2 suites for String Trio; piano studies. He publ. *Harmonielehre* (Berlin, 1905); *Von zwei Kulturen der Musik* (Munich, 1913; 3rd ed., 1947); *Die Symphonien Anton Bruckners* (Munich, 1914; 2nd ed., 1923); *Von Grenzen und Ländern der Musik: Gesammelte Aufsätze* (Munich, 1916); *Einführung in die Musik* (Berlin, 1926); *Beethoven* (Berlin, 1927).

Halpern, Steven, American composer, performer, and producer; b. N.Y., April 18, 1947. He played trumpet and guitar in jazz and rock bands as a youth, and in the late 1960s began to explore the effects of music on the listener. He studied at the State Univ. of N.Y. at Buffalo (B.A., 1969), Lone Mountain College in San Francisco (M.A., 1973), and Sierra Nevada Univ. in Barcelona (Ph.D., 1977). He became absorbed in musical therapy, and developed a study curriculum of healing through music. In 1976 he began distributing his music to bookshops and health food stores, creating what has become Sound R$_x$ Productions, a distribution company, which promoted therapeutic methods in music. He is a pioneer of New Age music, particularly the variety that is intended to be therapeutic; many of his recordings include subliminal suggestions for physical and mental improvement. Among his many solo and collaborative recordings, both audio and video, are *Spectrum Suite* (1975), *Dawn* (1981), and *Radiance* (1988). From 1986 to 1988 he ed. *New Frontier Magazine*; he also publ. *Tuning the Human Instrument* (Belmont, Calif., 1978) and *Sound Health* (N.Y., 1985).

Halvorsen, Johan, Norwegian violinist, conductor, and composer; b. Drammen, March 15, 1864; d. Oslo, Dec. 4, 1935. He studied violin with Lindberg at the Stockholm Cons.; was concertmaster of the Bergen Orch.; then went to Leipzig to study with Brodsky; subsequently studied with César Thomson in Belgium; returning to Norway in 1892, he became conductor of a theater orch. in Bergen; in 1899 was appointed conductor at the National Theater in Christiania (Oslo). He was married to a niece of Grieg, and his music reflects Grieg's influence very strongly. He wrote incidental music to Björnson's *Vasan-*

tasena and *The King*, Drachmann's *Gurre*, Eldegard's *Fossegrimen* and *Dronning Tamara*, and other works. He further wrote 3 syms. (1923; *Fatum*, 1924, rev. 1928; *Sommer*, 1929), a Violin Concerto, 2 Norwegian rhapsodies, and several orch. suites on Norwegian themes. His most popular works are the march *Triumphant Entry of the Boyars* and an arrangement of Handel's Passacaglia for Violin, and Viola or Cello.

Halvorsen, Leif, Norwegian violinist, conductor, and composer; b. Christiania, July 26, 1887; d. there (Oslo), Dec. 28, 1959. He studied violin with local teachers; then went to St. Petersburg, where he became a pupil of Auer. Upon his return to Norway, he served as concertmaster in the National Theater Orch., Christiania (1915–17), then was an opera conductor (1918–21); also led the Fredrikstad Singing Soc. (1925–47). He wrote much incidental music; an orch. suite, *Peasant's Legend*; piano pieces; songs.

Hamal, Henri-Guillaume, Belgian organist and composer; b. Liège, Dec. 3, 1685; d. there, Dec. 3, 1752. He studied with Lambert Pietkin, maître de chapelle of St. Lambert. As a youth, he excelled as a harpsichordist, cellist, and singer; wrote songs to texts in many languages, all of which are lost. His son, **Jean-Noël Hamal** (b. Liège, Dec. 23, 1709; d. there, Nov. 26, 1778), studied with his father, becoming a chorister at St. Lambert (1716); where he studied with Canon Henri Dupont; he also studied with Giuseppe Amadori at the Liège College of Rome (1728–31). He then became a Cathedral musician in Liège, where he was made director of music in 1738. His 6 *ouvertures de camera, a 4,* op. 1 (Paris, 1743), presage the Classical school; he also wrote 4 operas, 3 oratorios, 33 masses, 32 grands motets, 51 petits motets, etc. His nephew, **Henri Hamal** (b. Liège, July 20, 1744; d. there, Sept. 17, 1820), studied with his uncle, then at the Liège College of Rome (1763–69). He was deputy director of music to his uncle at the Liège Cathedral (1770–78), and then director (1778–93). He wrote much sacred choral music.
BIBL.: L. de Lavalleye, *Les H. de Liège* (Liège, 1860); M. de Smet, *Jean-Noël H. (1709–1778), chanoine impérial et Directeur de la Musique de la Cathédrale Saint-Lambert de Liège: Vie et œuvre* (Brussels, 1959).

Hamari, Julia, Hungarian mezzo-soprano; b. Budapest, Nov. 21, 1942. She was educated at the Academy of Music in Budapest and at the Stuttgart Hochschule für Musik. She then appeared in concerts and lieder recitals, to great acclaim; also made appearances in opera, singing in Stuttgart and Düsseldorf and at the Salzburg and Holland festivals.

Hambourg, noted family of Russian-born musicians:
(1) Michael (Mikhail) Hambourg, pianist and teacher; b. Yaroslavl, July 12, 1855; d. Toronto, June 18, 1916. He studied with N. Rubinstein and Taneyev in St. Petersburg and at the Moscow Cons.; was prof. at the latter (1880–90), and then at the Guildhall School of Music in London (1890–1910). He went to Toronto in 1911 and founded the Hambourg Cons. of Music with his son Boris. All of his sons were musicians:
(2) Mark Hambourg, pianist; b. Bogutchar, June 12, 1879; d. Cambridge, Aug. 26, 1960. He studied with his father, making his debut in Moscow at age 9; then studied with Leschetizky in Vienna. After international tours, he settled in England and became a British citizen. He publ. *How to Play the Piano* (Philadelphia, 1922), *From Piano to Forte: A Thousand and One Notes* (London, 1931), and *The Eighth Octave* (London, 1951).
(3) Jan Hambourg, violinist; b. Voronezh, Aug. 27, 1882; d. Tours, Sept. 29, 1947. He studied with Sauret and Wilhelmj in London, Sevčik in Prague, and Ysaÿe in Brussels; played in a trio with his brothers. He died during a concert tour in France.
(4) Boris Hambourg, cellist; b. Voronezh, Jan. 8, 1885; d. Toronto, Nov. 24, 1954. He studied with his father and with H. Walenn in London, H. Becker at the Frankfurt Cons. (1898–1903), and Ysaÿe (1904); played in a trio with his brothers. He went to Toronto in 1911 and founded the Hambourg Cons.

of Music with his father, serving as its director until 1951; he also played in the Hart House Quartet (1924–46).

Hamboys, John. See **Hanboys, John.**

Hambraeus, Bengt, prominent Swedish composer and pedagogue; b. Stockholm, Jan. 29, 1928. He took organ lessons with Alf Linder (1944–48); then entered Uppsala Univ. (M.A., 1956); also attended the summer courses in modern music at Darmstadt (1951–55). In 1957 he joined the music dept. of the Swedish Broadcasting Corp.; in 1972 was appointed to the faculty of McGill Univ. in Montreal. His style of composition oscillates between modernistic constructivism based on strong dissonant polyphony and sonoristic experimentalism; he is regarded as a leader of the Swedish musical avant-garde. He publ. a book, *Om notskifter* (On Notation; Stockholm, 1970).
WORKS: 2 chamber operas: *Experiment X*, making use of Electronic Sound (Stockholm, March 9, 1971), and a church opera, *Se människan* (Stockholm, May 15, 1972); radio opera, *Sagan* (1978–79); Concerto for Organ and Harpsichord (1947–51); 3 string quartets (1948–64); *Diptychon* for Flute, Oboe, Viola, Celesta, and Harpsichord (1952); *Spectogram* for Soprano and Instrumental Ensemble (1953); *Giuoco del cambio* (Play of Changes) for 5 Instruments and Percussion (1952–54); *Antiphones en rondes* for Soprano and 24 Instruments (1953); *Crystal Sequence* for Soprano Choir and Instrumental Ensemble (1954); *Cercles* for Piano (1955); *Constellations I–III: I* for Organ (1958); *II* for Taped Organ Sounds (1959); *III* includes tape from *II*, plus new, superimposed live organ score (1961); *Introduzione—Sequenze—Coda* for 3 Flutes, 6 Percussion, and Amplifier (1958–59); *Segnali* for 7 String Instruments (1956–60); *Notazioni* for Harpsichord, 10 Wind Instruments, Celesta, and Percussion (1961); *Mikrogram* for Alto Flute, Viola, Harp, and Vibraphone (1961); *Interferences* for Organ (1962); a 5-work cycle of compositions: *Rota I* for 3 Orchs. (Stockholm, May 27, 1964); *Rota II* for Electronically Modulated Organ and Bell Sounds (1963); *Transit I* for Tape (1963); *Transit II* for Horn, Piano, Trombone, and Electric Guitar (1963); *Transfiguration* for Orch. (1962–63; Swedish Radio, Feb. 20, 1965); *Responsorier* for Tenor, Chorus, 2 Organs, and Church Bells (1964); *Tetragon (Homenaje a Pablo Picasso)* for Electronically Modulated Soprano and Chamber Ensemble (1965); *Klassiskt spel* (Classical Play), electronic ballet (1965); *Praeludium, Kyrie, Sanctus* for Solo Voice, 2 Choruses, 2 Organs, and Church Bells (1966); *Motetum Archangeli Michaelis* for Chorus and Organ (1967); *Movimento—Monodia—Shogaku* for Organ (1967); *Fresque sonore* for Electronically Modulated Soprano and Chamber Ensemble (1965–67); *Inventions II* for Piano (1967–68); *Rencontres* for Orch. (Swedish Radio, Aug. 8, 1971); *Pianissimo in due tempi* for 20 String Instruments (1970–72); *Récit de deux* for Soprano (vocalizing and playing percussion), Flute, and Piano (1973); *Ricercare* for Organ (1974); *Carillon (Le Récital oublié)* for 2 Pianos (1974); *Icons* for Organ (1974–75); *Advent* for Organ and 10 Brasses (1975); *Continuo—A partire da Pachelbel* for Organ and Orch. without Violins (1975; Nuremberg, June 5, 1976); *Ricordanza* for Orch. (1976); *Relief—haut et bas* for 10 Instruments (1979); *Constellations V* for Organ, Chorus, and 2 Amplified Sopranos (1982–83); *Quodlibet re BACH* for Orch. (1984; Toronto, March 15, 1985); *Symphonia sacra* for Soli, Chorus, Winds, and Percussion (1986; Montreal, March 6, 1987); *Echoes of Loneliness* for 4 Choirs, Viola, and Percussion (1988).

Hämeenniemi, Eero, Finnish composer; b. Valkeakoski, April 29, 1951. He studied with Heininen at the Sibelius Academy in Helsinki (1973–78), Schaeffer in Krakow, Donatoni in Italy (1979), and Schwantner and Warren Benson at the Eastman School of Music in Rochester, N.Y. (1980–81). In 1975 he became active with Korvat Auki, the Finnish society for the promotion of contemporary music; served as its chairman (until 1979; 1981–82). He also taught at the Sibelius Academy (from 1977).
WORKS: BALLET: *Loviisa* (1985–86). ORCH.: . . . *Only the Earth and Mountains* (1981); 2 syms.: No. 1 (1982–83); No. 2 (Helsinki, Aug. 31, 1988); *Soitto* (1984); *Dialogi* for Piano

and Orch. (1985). CHAMBER: *Duo I* for Flute and Cello (1976); *Dedicato . . .* for 12 Instruments (1978); *Aria* for Horn (1978); Piano Sonata (1979); Sonata for Clarinet and Piano (1983); *Efisaes* for Piano and 12 Solo Strings (1983); *Canterai . . .* for Flute (1983).

Hamel, Fred, German musicologist; b. Paris, Feb. 19, 1903; d. Hamburg, Dec. 9, 1957. He studied chemistry in Bonn and Berlin and musicology in Berlin and Giessen; in 1930 received his Ph.D. from the Univ. of Giessen with the dissertation *Form- und Stilprinzipien in der Vokalmusik Johann Rosenmüllers;* also publ. a monograph on J.S. Bach, *Geistige Welt* (Göttingen, 1951), and contributed numerous articles to German music journals. From 1948 he served as production manager for Deutsche Grammophon Gesellschaft; founded its prestigious Archiv-Produktion of recordings of early music in authentic performances.

Hamel, Marie-Pierre, French judge and organ builder; b. Auneuil, Oise, Feb. 24, 1786; d. Beauvais, July 25, 1879. He was from a family of jurists, and himself pursued a legal career; in 1817 he became a judge at Beauvais. Apart from his professional activities, he was from his childhood interested in music; he built a small organ of 3 octaves at the age of 13. In 1826 he rebuilt the grand organ of the Cathedral of Beauvais. He publ. several manuals and descriptions of organs in various French cities. His principal writings were *Rapport sur les travaux du grand orgue de l'Église de la Madeleine à Paris* (Paris, 1846) and *Nouveau manuel complet du facteur d'orgues* (3 vols., Paris, 1849; new ed. by Guédon, 1903).

Hamerik (real name, **Hammerich**), **Asger,** Danish composer, father of **Ebbe Hamerik** and brother of **Angul Hammerich;** b. Frederiksberg, April 8, 1843; d. there, July 13, 1923. He studied with Gade in Copenhagen and with Bülow in Berlin. He met Berlioz in Paris in 1864, and accompanied him to Vienna in 1866, studying orchestration. Hamerik was probably the only pupil that Berlioz had. He received a gold medal for his work *Hymne de la paix,* at the contest for the Paris Exposition. His opera *Tovelille* was performed in Paris in concert form (May 6, 1865); another opera, *Hjalmar and Ingeborg,* was not performed in its entirety. In 1870 he visited Italy and produced his Italian-language opera, *La vendetta* (Milan, Dec. 23, 1870). He then received an invitation to become director of the newly organized Peabody Cons. in Baltimore. He accepted, and remained in Baltimore until 1898, when he returned to Copenhagen. His other works include 8 syms. (1881–98), 5 *Nordic Suites* (1872–77), and the opera *Den rejsende* (1871).

BIBL.: R. Hove, "A. H., en dansk symphoniker," *Nordisk Musikkultur,* VI (1957).

Hamerik (real name, **Hammerich**), **Ebbe,** Danish conductor and composer, son of **Asger Hamerik** and nephew of **Angul Hammerich;** b. Copenhagen, Sept. 5, 1898; d. there, Aug. 11, 1951 (drowned in the Kattegat). He studied with his father; was active mainly as a conductor. He held the post of 2nd conductor at the Royal Danish Theater in Copenhagen (1919–22) and conductor of the Copenhagen music society (1927–31) and the State Radio Sym. Orch. He composed the operas *Stepan* (Mainz, Nov. 30, 1924), *Leonardo da Vinci* (Antwerp, March 28, 1939), *Marie Grubbe* (Copenhagen, May 17, 1940), *Rejsekammeraten,* after Andersen (Copenhagen, Jan. 5, 1946), and *Drømmerne* (posthumous, Århus, Sept. 9, 1974); 5 syms.; *Ur cantus firmus I–V* (1937; 1947; 1947–48; 1949; 1949); Wind Quintet (1942); 2 string quartets (1917, 1917); piano pieces; songs.

Hamilton, Clarence Grant, American organist and music educator; b. Providence, R.I., June 9, 1865; d. Wellesley, Mass., Feb. 14, 1935. He studied piano with Arthur Foote in Boston and Matthay in London; composition with Chadwick. He occupied various positions as an organist in and around Boston; taught at Wellesley College (1904–34); wrote piano pieces and songs.

WRITINGS: *Outlines of Music History* (1908; new ed., 1924);

Piano Teaching (1910); *Sound and Its Relation to Music* (1911); *Music Appreciation, Based upon Methods of Literary Criticism* (1920); *Piano Music, Its Composers and Characteristics* (1925); *Epochs in Musical Progress* (1926); *Touch and Expression in Piano Playing* (1927); *What Every Piano Pupil Should Know* (1928); *Ornaments in Classical and Modern Music* (1929).

Hamilton, David (Peter), American music critic; b. N.Y., Jan. 18, 1935. He was educated at Princeton Univ. (1952–56; A.B., 1956; M.F.A., music history, 1960); then was music and record librarian there (1961–65); in 1965 he became assistant music ed. of W.W. Norton & Co. in N.Y.; was music ed. from 1968 to 1974. In 1967 he became a contributing ed. of *High Fidelity,* and in 1968, music critic of the *Nation;* also served as N.Y. music correspondent for the *Financial Times* of London (1969–74) and associate ed. of the *Musical Newsletter* (1971–77). He wrote *The Listener's Guide to Great Instrumentalists* (N.Y., 1981) and *Metropolitan Opera Encyclopedia: A Comprehensive Guide to the World of Opera* (N.Y., 1987); also publ. *The Music Game: An Autobiography* (London, 1986).

Hamilton, George, IV, American country-music singer; b. Winston-Salem, N.C., July 19, 1937. He was educated at the Univ. of North Carolina and at the American Univ.; while still in college, he began to make appearances as a singer of popular music; made several tours abroad; sang many of his songs in German, Japanese, and other languages for his appearances overseas.

Hamilton, Iain (Ellis), remarkable Scottish composer; b. Glasgow, June 6, 1922. He was taken to London at the age of 7, and attended Mill Hill School; after graduation he became an apprentice engineer, but studied music in his leisure time. He was 25 years old when he decidedly turned to music; won a scholarship to the Royal Academy of Music, where he studied piano with Harold Craxton and composition with William Alwyn; concurrently studied at the Univ. of London (B.Mus., 1950). He made astonishing progress as a composer, and upon graduation from the Royal Academy of Music received the prestigious Dove Prize; other awards included the Royal Phil. Soc. Prize for his Clarinet Concerto, the Koussevitzky Foundation Award for his 2nd Sym., the Edwin Evans Prize, the Butterworth Award, the Arnold Bax Gold Medal, and the Vaughan Williams Award. From 1951 to 1960 he was a lecturer at Morley College in London; he also lectured at the Univ. of London (1952–60). He served as Mary Duke Biddle Prof. of Music at Duke Univ. in Durham, N.C. (1961–78), where he was chairman of its music dept. (1966–67); also was composer-in-residence at the Berkshire Music Center at Tanglewood, Mass. (summer 1962). In 1970 he received an honorary D.Mus. from the Univ. of Glasgow. His style of composition is marked by terse melodic lines animated by a vibrant rhythmic pulse, creating the impression of kinetic lyricism; his harmonies are built on a set of peculiarly euphonious dissonances, which repose on emphatic tonal centers. For several years he pursued a sui generis serial method, but soon abandoned it in favor of a free modern manner; in his operas he makes use of thematic chords depicting specific dramatic situations.

WORKS: STAGE: *Clerk Saunders,* ballet (1951); *The Royal Hunt of the Sun,* opera (1966–68; 1975; London, Feb. 2, 1977); *Agamemnon,* dramatic narrative (1967–69); *Pharsalia,* dramatic commentary (1968); *The Cataline Conspiracy,* opera (1972–73; Stirling, Scotland, March 16, 1974); *Tamburlaine,* lyric drama (1976; BBC, London, Feb. 14, 1977); *Anna Karenina,* opera (1977–78; London, May 7, 1981); *Dick Whittington,* lyric comedy (1980–81); *Lancelot,* opera (1982–83; Arundel, England, Aug. 24, 1985); *Raleigh's Dream,* opera (1983; Durham, N.C., June 3, 1984). ORCH.: 4 syms.: No. 1 (1948); No. 2 (1951); No. 3, *Spring* (1981; London, July 24, 1982); No. 4 (1981; Edinburgh, Jan. 21, 1983); *Variations on an Original Theme* for Strings (1948); 2 piano concertos: No. 1 (1949); No. 2 (1960; rev. 1967, 1987; BBC, Glasgow, May 1989); Clarinet Concerto (1950); Sinfonia Concertante for Violin, Viola, and Chamber Orch. (1950); 2 violin concertos: No. 1 (1952); No. 2, *Amphion* (1971); *Scottish Dances* (1956); *Sonata per orchestra da camera* (1956); *Overture: 1812* (1957); Concerto for Jazz Trumpet and Orch. (1957); *Sinfonia for 2 Orchestras* (1958); *Écossaise* (1959); *Arias for Small Orch.* (1962); *The Chaining of Prometheus* for Wind Instruments and Percussion (1963); *Cantos* (1964); Concerto for Organ and Small Orch. (1964); *Circus* for 2 Trumpets and Orch. (1969); *Alastor* (1970); *Voyage* for Horn and Chamber Orch. (1970); *Commedia*, concerto (London, May 4, 1973); *Aurora* (N.Y., Nov. 21, 1975); *The Alexandrian Sequence* for Chamber Orch. (1976). CHAMBER: 2 quintets for Clarinet and String Quartet: No. 1 (1948); No. 2, *Sea Music* (1974); 4 string quartets (1949, 1965, 1984, 1984); Quartet for Flute and String Trio (1951); Piano Trio (1954); 2 octets: No. 1 for Strings (1954); No. 2 for Winds (1983); 2 sonatas for Cello and Piano (1958, 1974); Sextet for Flute, 2 Clarinets, Violin, Cello, and Piano (1962); *Sonatas and Variants* for 10 Wind Instruments (1963); Brass Quintet (1964). VOCAL: *The Bermudas* for Baritone, Chorus, and Orch. (1956); *Cinque canzone d'amore* for Tenor and Orch. (1957); *Epitaph for This World and Time* for 3 Choruses and 3 Organs (1970); *Cleopatra*, dramatic scene for Soprano and Orch. (1977); *The Passion of Our Lord According to St. Mark* for Soloists, Chorus, and Orch. (1982; London, May 6, 1983); *The Bright Heavens Sounding* for Soloists, Chorus, and Instrumental Ensemble (1985; London, June 27, 1986); *Prometheus* for Soloists, Chorus, and Orch. (1986); *La Mort de Phèdre* for Voice and Orch. (1987); other vocal works; also piano pieces, including 3 sonatas (1951, rev. 1971; 1973; 1978) and works for Solo Organ, including *Threnos—In Time of War* (1966) and *Le Tombeau de Bach* (1986).

Hamlisch, Marvin (Frederick), American composer of popular music; b. N.Y., June 2, 1944. His father, an accordionist, trained him in music; he studied piano at the Juilliard School of Music and at Queens College (B.A., 1967). He began writing songs at the age of 15. His 1st signal success came in 1974, when he won 3 Academy Awards for the music scores for the movies *The Way We Were* and *The Sting.* (For the latter, his award was won for a score written mostly by others: the piano music was by Scott Joplin, composed 60–70 years earlier, and the orchestrations were by Gunther Schuller, adapted from 60-year-old stock arrangements.) In 1975 he wrote the score for the musical *A Chorus Line,* which received the Pulitzer Prize for the play and a Tony award for the best musical score; Universal Pictures bought the cinema rights for $5.5 million. The Broadway production opened on July 25, 1975, to a chorus line of hosannas from otherwise sobersided critics; an international touring company was started in Toronto in May 1976, and a national company began its cross-country tour a few days later.

Hamm, Charles (Edward), American musicologist; b. Charlottesville, Va., April 21, 1925. He studied at the Univ. of Virginia (B.A., 1947) and Princeton Univ. (M.F.A., 1950; Ph.D., 1960, with the diss. *A Chronology of the Works of Guillaume Dufay,* publ. in Princeton, 1964). He taught at Princeton Univ. (1948–50 and 1958), at the Cincinnati Cons. of Music (1950–57), and at Tulane Univ. (1959–63). In 1963 he was appointed prof. of musicology at the Univ. of Illinois; in 1976 joined the faculty of Dartmouth College. He served as president of the American Musicological Soc. from 1973 to 1974. A versatile scholar, he publ. books on a variety of subjects; these include *Opera* (Boston, 1966); *Yesterdays: Popular Song in America* (N.Y., 1979); *Music in the New World* (N.Y., 1983); *Afro-American Music, South Africa, and Apartheid* (N.Y., 1988).

Hammer, Heinrich (Albert Eduard), German-American violinist, conductor, and composer; b. Erfurt, Germany, Oct. 27, 1862; d. Phoenix, Ariz., Oct. 28, 1954. He studied violin with A. Pott and theory with H. Ritter; also took singing lessons with Viardot-García in Paris. He conducted the Lausanne Sym. Orch. (1901–5); in 1905 he organized a sym. orch. in Göteborg, Sweden. In 1908 he settled in America; conducted his own orch. in Washington, D.C., until 1921, when he went to California. He continued to compose until the end of his long life; at the age of 90 he married his pupil Arlene Hammer, who

helped him to edit his autobiography. Among his works are a Sym.; 3 American Indian rhapsodies for Orch.; a symphonic poem, *Sunset at Sea;* an orch. ode, *Columbia Triumphant in Peace* (1915); and much church music.

Hammerich, Angul, Danish musicologist, brother of **Asger** and uncle of **Ebbe Hamerik;** b. Copenhagen, Nov. 25, 1848; d. Frederiksberg, April 26, 1931. He studied cello with Rudinger and Neruda, and piano and theory with C.F.E. Horneman; he received the 1st Ph.D. awarded by a Danish univ., from the Univ. of Copenhagen (1892; with the diss. *Musikken ved Christian den Fjerdes hof;* publ. in Copenhagen, 1892); he subsequently was its 1st reader in music history (1896–1922); also was founder-director of the Museum of the History of Music in Copenhagen (1899–1931).

WRITINGS: *Musikforeningens historie 1836–1886* (Copenhagen, 1886); *Kjøbenhavns Musikkonservatorium 1867–1892* (Copenhagen, 1892); *Kammermusikforeningen 1868–1893* (Copenhagen, 1893); *Musikmindesmaerker fra middelalderen i Danmark* (Leipzig, 1912; Eng. tr., 1912, as *Mediaeval Musical Relics of Denmark);* J.P.E. Hartmann: *Biografiske essays* (Copenhagen, 1916); *Kammermusikforeningen 1868–1918* (Copenhagen, 1918); *Dansk musikhistorie indtil ca. 1700* (Copenhagen, 1921).

Hammerschlag, János, organist, conductor, writer on music, and composer; b. Prague, Dec. 10, 1885; d. Budapest, May 21, 1954. He studied composition with Kodály and organ at the Budapest Academy of Music. He taught at the Budapest Cons. from 1919; also conducted choral concerts there; in 1920 he founded a chamber music group for the performance of early music; it developed into the Motet and Madrigal Soc. in 1923. He publ. a book on Bach (Budapest, 1926).

Hammerschmidt, Andreas, important Bohemian-born organist and composer; b. Brüx, 1611 or 1612; d. Zittau, Nov. 8, 1675. He received his musical training in Freiberg, Saxony; was organist to Count Rudolf von Bünau at his castle in Weesenstein, Saxony (1633–34), and at St. Petri in Freiberg (1634–39); then was organist at St. Johannis in Zittau from 1639 until his death. During his tenure in Zittau, he became one of the most celebrated musicians of the day. He wrote a large body of sacred vocal music, some 400 works publ. in 14 collections. His compositions for the Lutheran liturgy are of great significance. He was one of the earliest composers to adopt the new Italian style of writing elaborate instrumental accompaniments to polyphonic vocal works.

WORKS: SACRED VOCAL: *Musicalischer Andacht, erster Theil, das ist, Geistlische Concerten* for 1 to 4 Voices and Basso Continuo (Freiberg, 1639); *Musicalischer Andachten, ander Theil, das ist, Geistliche Madrigalien* for 4 to 6 Voices, Chorus for 5 Voices ad libitum, and Basso Continuo (Freiberg, 1641); *Musicalischer Andachten, dritter Theil, das ist, Geistliche Symphonien* for 1 and 2 Voices, 2 Violins, Cello, and Basso Continuo (Freiberg, 1642); *Dialogi, oder Gespräche zwischen Gott und einer gläubigen Seelen, erster Theil* for 2 to 4 Voices and Basso Continuo (Dresden, 1645; ed. in Denkmäler der Tonkunst in Österreich, XVI, Jg. VIII/1, 1901); *Geistlicher Dialogen ander Theil, darinnen Herrn Opitzens Hohes Lied Salomonis* for 1 and 2 Voices, 2 Violins, Cello, and Basso Continuo (Dresden, 1645); *Vierter Theil, Musicalischer Andachten, geistlicher Moteten und Concerten* for 5 to 10, 12, and more Voices, and Basso Continuo (Freiberg, 1646); *Motettae* for 1 and 2 Voices and Basso Continuo (Dresden, 1649); *Chormusic auff Madrigal Manier: Fünffter Theil Musicalischer Andachten* for 5 to 6 Voices and Basso Continuo (Freiberg and Leipzig, 1652–53); *Musicalische Gespräche über die Evangelia* for 4 to 7 Voices and Basso Continuo (Dresden, 1655); *Ander Theil geistlicher Gespräche über die Evangelia* for 5 to 8 Voices and Basso Continuo (Dresden, 1656); *Fest-, Buss- und Danklieder* for Voices and 5 Instruments ad libitum (Zittau and Dresden, 1658–59); *Kirchen- und Tafel-Music* for 1 to 3 Voices, 4 to 6 Instruments, and Basso Continuo (Zittau, 1662); *Missae, tam vivae voci, quam instrumentis variis accommodatae* for 5 to 12 and more Voices (Dresden, 1663); *Fest- und Zeit-Andachten* for 6 Voices and Basso Continuo (Dresden, 1671). **OCCASIONAL WORKS:** *Hertzliche Aufmerkung und heiligen Weihnachtsgruss zu Ehren Matthia Albert und Jacob Rüdiger* for 4 Voices (Freiberg, 1639; not extant); *Stölichen Schiessen bei der Hochzeit Herrn Rothens zu Zittau und Christine Stoll,* 29 Oct. 1640 (Görlitz, 1640; not extant); *Der auff den . . . seligen Hintritt des . . . Herrn M. Michaelis Theophili Lehmanns . . . erwehlte Leichen-Text: Ich bin gewiss, dass weder Tod noch Leben* for 5 Voices (Freiberg, 1650); *Lob- und Danck Lied aus dem 84. Psalm . . . auff die rümliche Einweihung der wider erbauten Kirche S. Elisabeth in Breslau* for 9 Voices, 5 Trumpets, 3 Trombones, 5 Violas, and Basso Continuo (Freiberg, 1652); *Bussfertiges Friedens-Seuffzerlein . . . Ihr Jungen und ihr Alten hört* (M. Francke) for 3 Voices (Coburg, 1658); also hymn melodies publ. in various collections. **SECULAR VOCAL:** *Erster Theil weltlicher Oden oder Liebesgesänge* for 1 and 2 Voices, Violin Obbligato, and Viola da Gamba or Theorbo (Freiberg, 1642; ed. in *Das Erbe Deutscher Musik,* 1st series, XLIII, 1962); *Ander Theil weltlicher Oden oder Liebesgesänge* for 1 to 3 Voices, Violin Obbligato, and Viola da Gamba or Theorbo (Freiberg, 1643; ed. in *Das Erbe Deutscher Musik,* 1st series, XLIII, 1962); *Dritter Theil geist- und weltlicher Oden und Madrigalien* for 1 to 5 Voices and Basso Continuo (Leipzig, 1649; ed. in *Das Erbe Deutscher Musik,* 1st series, XLIII, 1962). **INSTRUMENTAL:** *Erster Fleiss allerhand neuer Paduanen, Galliarden, Balletten, Mascharaden, françoischen Arien, Courenten und Sarabanden* for 5 Viols and Basso Continuo (Freiberg, 1636; ed. in *Das Erbe Deutscher Musik,* 1st series, XLIX, 1957); *Ander Theil neuer Paduanen, Canzonen, Galliarden, Balletten, Mascharaden* for 3 and 5 Viols and Basso Continuo (Freiberg, 1639; ed. in *Das Erbe Deutscher Musik,* 1st series, XLIX, 1957); *Dritter Theil neuer Paduanen* for 3 to 5 Instruments and Basso Continuo (Leipzig and Freiberg, 1650). H. Leichtentritt, ed., *Andreas Hammerschmidt: Ausgewählte Werke* in Denkmäler Deutscher Tonkunst, XL (1910). **BIBL.:** A. Tobias, "A. H.," *Mitteilungen des Vereins für die Geschichte der Deutschen in Böhmen,* IX/7–8 (1870); P. Stöbe, "A. H.," *Mitteilungen der Gesellschaft für Zittauer Geschichte,* I (1900); G. Schünemann, "Beiträge zur Biographie H.'s," *Sammelbände der Internationalen Musik-Gesellschaft,* XII (1910–11); S. Temesvári, *H.s "Dialogi"* (diss., Univ. of Vienna, 1911); F. Blume, *Das monodische Prinzip in der protestantischen Kirchenmusik* (Leipzig, 1925); P. Stöbe, "A. H.," *Zeitschrift für Evangelische Kirchenmusik,* IV (1926); H. Mueller, *The "Musikalische Gespräche über die Evangelia" of A. H.* (diss., Univ. of Rochester, N.Y., 1956).

Hammerstein, Oscar, celebrated German-American impresario, grandfather of **Oscar (Greeley Clendenning) Hammerstein, II;** b. Stettin, May 8, 1846; d. N.Y., Aug. 1, 1919. At the age of 16 he ran away from home; spent some time in England; then went to America, where he worked in a N.Y. cigar factory. Possessing an inventive mind, he patented a machine for shaping tobacco leaves by suction; later ed. a tobacco trade journal. At the same time, he practiced the violin; learned to write music, and dabbled in playwriting; in 1868 he produced in N.Y. a comedy in German; also wrote the libretto and music of an operetta, *The Kohinoor* (N.Y., Oct. 24, 1893). His main activity, however, was in management. He built the Harlem Opera House (1888), the Olympia Music Hall (1895), and the Republic Theater (1900), and presented brief seasons of plays and operas in all 3. In 1906 he announced plans for the Manhattan Opera House in N.Y., his crowning achievement. The enterprise was orig. planned as a theater for opera in English, but it opened with an Italian company in Bellini's *I Puritani* (Dec. 3, 1906). Hammerstein entered into bold competition with the Metropolitan Opera, and engaged celebrated singers, among them Melba, Nordica, Tetrazzini, and Garden; among the spectacular events presented by him were the 1st U.S. performances of 5 operas by Massenet, Charpentier's *Louise,* and Debussy's *Pelléas et Mélisande.* The new venture held its own for 4 seasons, but in the end Hammerstein was compelled to yield; in April 1910, he sold the Manhattan Opera House to the management of the Metropolitan for $1.2 million, and agreed not to produce grand opera in N.Y. for 10 years. He also sold to the Metropolitan (for $100,000) his interests in the Philadelphia Opera House, built by him in 1908. Defeated in his main ambition in the U.S., he transferred his activities to England. There he built the London Opera House, which opened with a lavish production of *Quo Vadis* by Nouguès (Nov. 17, 1911). However, he failed to establish himself in London, and after a season there, returned to N.Y. In contravention of his agreement with the Metropolitan, he announced a season at the newly organized American Opera House in N.Y., but the Metropolitan secured an injunction against him, and he was forced to give up his operatic venture. **BIBL.:** V. Sheean, *O. H., I: The Life and Exploits of an Impresario* (N.Y., 1956); J. Cone, *O. H.'s Manhattan Opera Company* (Norman, Okla., 1966).

Hammerstein, Oscar (Greeley Clendenning), II, outstanding American lyricist, grandson of **Oscar Hammerstein;** b. N.Y., July 12, 1895; d. Highland Farms, Doylestown, Pa., Aug. 23, 1960. He studied law at Columbia Univ., graduating in 1917; then became interested in the theater. He collaborated on the librettos for Friml's *Rose Marie* (1924), Romberg's *The Desert Song* (1926), and Kern's *Show Boat* (1927; included the celebrated song *Ol' Man River*). In 1943 he joined forces with the composer Richard Rodgers, and together they produced some of the most brilliant and successful musical comedies in the history of the American theater: *Oklahoma!* (1943; Pulitzer Prize); *Carousel* (1945); *Allegro* (1947); *South Pacific* (1949; Pulitzer Prize, 1950); *The King and I* (1951); *Me and Juliet* (1953); *Pipe Dream* (1955); *The Flower Drum Song* (1958); *The Sound of Music* (1959). His lyrics are characterized by a combination of appealing sentiment and sophisticated nostalgia, making them particularly well suited to the modern theater. **BIBL.:** D. Taylor, *Some Enchanted Evenings: The Story of Rodgers and H.* (N.Y., 1953); M. Wilk, *They're Playing Our Song* (N.Y., 1973); H. Fordin, *Getting to Know Him, A Biography of O. H. II* (N.Y., 1977).

Hammond, Frederick (Fisher), American musicologist and harpsichordist; b. Binghamton, N.Y., Aug. 7, 1937. He received his B.A. and Ph.D. from Yale Univ., where he studied harpsichord with Kirkpatrick. He taught at the Univ. of Chicago (1962–65) and at Queens College (1966–68), then joined the faculty at the Univ. of Calif. in Los Angeles (1968). In 1989 he became Irma Brandeis Prof. of Romance Studies at Bard College. He has performed and recorded as a harpsichordist; made his N.Y. recital debut in 1969. He was assistant music director of the Castelfranco Veneto Festival (1975–80), assistant music director of the Clarion Music Soc. (from 1978), and director of the Nakamichi Festival of Baroque Music (from 1986). His research focuses on Italian harpsichord composers; his *Girolamo Frescobaldi* (Cambridge, Mass., 1983) is the definitive biography. He also publ. *Girolamo Frescobaldi: A Guide to Research* (N.Y., 1988). His honors include a Rome Prize fellowship (1965–66) and the Cavaliere al merito della Repubblica (1986).

Hammond, Dame Joan (Hood), prominent New Zealand soprano; b. Christchurch, May 24, 1912. She studied at the Sydney Cons.; made her operatic debut in Sydney in 1929; then went to London, where she continued vocal studies with Dino Borgioli; also studied in Vienna. She made her London debut in 1938; then sang with the Vienna State Opera; was a member of the Carl Rosa Opera Co. (1942–45). She made her Covent Garden debut in London in 1948; also sang with the Sadler's Wells Opera; appeared in the U.S. with the N.Y. City Center Opera in 1949; she retired in 1965. In 1974 she was made a Dame Commander of the Order of the British Empire. She wrote an autobiography, *A Voice, a Life* (London, 1970).

Hammond, John Hays, Jr., American organist and manufacturer of organs; b. San Francisco, April 13, 1888; d. N.Y.,

Feb. 12, 1965. He studied at Yale Univ. (B.S., 1910), then devoted himself to improving pipe-organ mechanisms.

Hammond, Laurens, American manufacturer of keyboard instruments; b. Evanston, Ill., Jan. 11, 1895; d. Cornwall, Conn., July 1, 1973. He studied engineering at Cornell Univ.; then went to Detroit to work on the synchronization of electrical motor impulses, a principle which he later applied to the Hammond Organ (1933), an electronic keyboard instrument, resembling a spinet piano, which suggests the sound of the pipe organ. Still later, he developed a newfangled electrical device which he called the Novachord and which was designed to simulate the sound of any known or hypothetical musical instrument; he gave the 1st demonstration of the Novachord in the Commerce Dept. auditorium in Washington, D.C., on Feb. 2, 1939. In 1940 he introduced the Solovox, an attachment to the piano keyboard which enables an amateur player to project the melody in organlike tones. A further invention was the "chord organ," which he introduced in 1950, and which is capable of supplying basic harmonies when a special button is pressed by the performer.

Hammond-Stroud, Derek, English baritone; b. London, Jan. 10, 1929. He studied with Elena Gerhardt in London and Gerhard Hüsch in Vienna and Munich. He made his debut in London in 1955; in 1961 he joined the Sadler's Wells Opera; was a leading member of the Royal Opera, Covent Garden. He made his American debut with the Houston Grand Opera in 1975, and on Dec. 5, 1977, his Metropolitan Opera debut as Faninal in *Der Rosenkavalier.* He was made an Officer of the Order of the British Empire in 1987. He was known for his vivid portrayals of the Wagnerian roles of Alberich and Beckmesser; was also a distinguished concert singer.

Hampson, Thomas, American baritone; b. Elkhart, Ind., June 28, 1955. He studied at Eastern Washington Univ. (B.A., 1977), Fort Wright College (B.F.A., 1979), the Univ. of Southern Calif., and the Music Academy of the West at Santa Barbara, where he won the Lotte Lehmann award (1978). In 1980 he took 2nd prize at the 's Hertogenbosch International Vocal Competition, and in 1981 1st place in the Metropolitan Opera Auditions. In 1981 he appeared with the Deutsche Oper am Rhein in Düsseldorf, and in 1982 attracted wide notice as Guglielmo in *Così fan tutte* with the Opera Theatre of St. Louis. In subsequent seasons he appeared with opera companies in Santa Fe, Cologne, Lyons, and Zürich. On Oct. 9, 1986, he made his Metropolitan Opera debut in N.Y. as Almaviva in *Le nozze di Figaro.* He won particular success for roles in operas by Mozart, Rossini, Donizetti, Verdi, and Puccini.

Hampton, Calvin, esteemed American organist, choirmaster, and composer; b. Kittanning, Pa., Dec. 31, 1938; d. Port Charlotte, Fla., Aug. 5, 1984. He studied organ at the Oberlin (Ohio) College Cons. of Music (B.M., 1960) and composition at Syracuse Univ. (M.M., 1962); was organist-choirmaster at N.Y.'s Calvary Episcopal Church (later combined with Holy Communion and St. George's; 1963–83). On March 2, 1980, at St. George's, he conducted what is thought to be the 1st complete U.S. performance, in French, of Franck's oratorio *Les Béatitudes.* His compositions fuse popular and classical influences; his anthems are found in supplements to the Episcopal hymnal.

Works: *Prisms* for Piano (1963); *Catch-Up* for Tape and 2 Quarter-tone Pianos (1967); *Prelude and Variations on Old 100th* for Organ (1970); *Transformation and Despair* for Organ (1971); *The Road to Leprachaunia* for Soprano, Synthesizer, and Organ (1973); *O Lord, Support Us* for Chorus and Prerecorded Synthesizer (1974); *Pentecost Cantata* for Soli, Chorus, and Percussion (1977); *Candlelight Carol Service* for Soli, Chorus, Dancers, Pantomime, Organ, and Orch. (1978); Concerto for Organ and Strings (St. Paul, June 18, 1980); *Cantata for Palm Sunday* for Tenor, Chorus, and Organ (1981); *It Happened in Jerusalem,* music drama for Soli, Speakers, Actors, Dancers, Chorus, Organ, Percussion, and Tape (1982); *Variations on "Amazing Grace"* for English Horn and Organ (1983); songs and anthems.

Bibl.: L. King, "C. H.: A Twenty-Year Ministry," *American Organist* (Oct. 1983).

Hampton, Lionel "Hamp," black American jazz vibraphonist, drummer, pianist, and bandleader; b. Louisville, Ky., April 12, 1909. He played drums in Chicago nightclubs; then moved to Los Angeles. He was a pioneer in introducing to jazz the vibraphone, on which he is a virtuoso performer; made the 1st recording of a jazz vibes solo with Louis Armstrong in *Memories of You* (1930). He gained nationwide prominence as a member of the Benny Goodman Quartet (1936–40). From then on he usually led his own bands, most often playing vibes, but occasionally performing on other instruments; he is the originator of the "trigger-finger" method of piano playing (2 forefingers drumming upon a single note *prestissimo*). Beginning in 1956, he made several successful European tours. In 1965 he founded a sextet called the Jazz Inner Circle.

Han (Hahn), Ulrich (known as **Udalricus Gallus**), German music printer; b. Ingolstadt, c.1425; d. Rome, after 1478. He is believed to be the 1st to print music with movable type, in his *Missale secundum consuetudinem curie romane* (Rome, 1476). In this work the double-process method was employed, i.e., 2 impressions were made; 1st, the lines of the staff were printed, then the note forms (mostly square black heads with a stem at the right side) were superimposed over them.

Bibl.: O. Kinkeldey, "Music and Music Printing in Incunabula," *Papers of the Bibliographic Society of America* (1932).

Hanboys (or **Hamboys**), **John,** English music theorist who flourished in the 15th century. He held an ecclesiastic rank. His Latin treatise *Summa super musicam continuam et discretam,* which describes the musical notation of his time, was printed by Coussemaker in his *Scriptorum de musica medii aevi* (Vol. I, Paris, 1864).

Bibl.: J. Bale, *Illustrium Maioris Britanniae Scriptorum Catalogus* (1559); J. Pulver, "The English Theorists, VI; J. Hanboys," *Musical Times* (March 1934).

Hanchett, Henry Granger, American organist, music pedagogue, and inventor; b. Syracuse, N.Y., Aug. 29, 1853; d. Siasconset, Mass., Aug. 19, 1918. He studied at the N.Y. Homeopathic Medical College (M.D., 1884); at the same time he pursued pianistic studies with various teachers; held teaching positions in music schools in N.Y. and elsewhere; also was organist at many churches (1884–98). In 1874 he obtained a patent for the sustaining piano pedal, now in use on all grand pianofortes. He publ. *Teaching as a Science* (1882), *The Art of the Musician* (1905), and *An Introduction to the Theory of Music* (1918); also wrote several church services and anthems.

Hancock, Herbie (Herbert Jeffrey), black American jazz pianist and composer; b. Chicago, April 12, 1940. A precocious musician, he made an appearance with the Chicago Sym. Orch. at 11; growing to maturity, he studied engineering at Grinnell (Iowa) College (1956–60); then took courses at the Manhattan School of Music and The New School for Social Research in N.Y. While still in school, he led his own band; also made appearances with such jazz artists as Coleman Hawkins, Donald Byrd, and Miles Davis. In 1968 he organized the Herbie Hancock Sextet, which later was reduced to the Herbie Hancock Quartet; with it he appeared in pop concerts. In addition to jazz piano he became adept as a player on an electric piano. In 1972 he went to Los Angeles, and in 1973 converted to a Californian brand of Buddhism. Among his most popular recordings were the albums *Headhunters* (1973), *V.S.O.P.: The Quintet* (1977), and *Future Shock* (1983).

Bibl.: *Current Biography* (April 1988).

Handel, George Frideric (the Anglicized form of the name, adopted by Handel in England; the original German spelling was **Georg Friedrich Händel;** other forms used in various branches of the family were Hendel, Hendeler, Händler, and Hendtler; the early spelling in England was Hendel; in France it is spelled Haendler; the Russian transliteration of the name from the Cyrillic alphabet, which lacks the aspirate, is Gendel), great German-born English composer; b. Halle, Feb. 23, 1685;

d. London, April 14, 1759. His father was a barber-surgeon and valet to the Prince of Saxe-Magdeburg; at the age of 61 he took a 2nd wife, Dorothea Taust, daughter of the pastor of Giebichenstein, near Halle; Handel was the 2nd son of this marriage. As a child, he was taken by his father on a visit to Saxe-Weissenfels, where he had a chance to try out the organ of the court chapel. The Duke, Johann Adolf, noticing his interest in music, advised that he be sent to Halle for organ lessons with Friedrich Wilhelm Zachau, the organist of the Liebfrauenkirche there. Zachau gave him instruction in harpsichord and organ playing and also introduced him to the rudiments of composition. Handel proved to be an apt student, and was able to substitute for Zachau as organist whenever necessary; he also composed trio sonatas and motets for church services on Sundays. After the death of his father in 1697, he entered the Univ. of Halle in 1702, and was named probationary organist at the Domkirche there. In 1703 he went to Hamburg, where he was engaged as "violino di ripieno" by Reinhard Keiser, the famous composer and director of the Hamburg Opera. There he met Johann Mattheson; in 1703 the 2 undertook a journey to Lübeck together, with the intention of applying for the post of organist in succession to Buxtehude, who was chief organist there. It was the custom for an incoming organist to marry a daughter of the incumbent as a condition of appointment; neither Mattheson nor Handel availed themselves of this opportunity. (Bach made the same journey in 1704, and also returned without obtaining the succession.) There was apparently a quarrel between Mattheson and Handel at a performance of Mattheson's opera *Cleopatra*, in which he sang the leading male role of Antonio, while Handel conducted from the keyboard as maestro al cembalo. When Mattheson completed his stage role, he asked Handel to yield his place at the keyboard to him; Handel declined, and an altercation ensued, resulting in a duel with swords, which was called off when Mattheson broke his sword on a metal button of Handel's coat. There is no independent confirmation of this episode, however, and the 2 apparently reconciled.

Handel's 1st opera, *Almira*, was produced at the Hamburg Opera on Jan. 8, 1705; his next opera, *Nero*, was staged there on Feb. 25, 1705. He was then commissioned to write 2 other operas, *Florindo* and *Daphne*, orig. planned as a single opera combining both subjects. In 1706 he undertook a long voyage to Italy, where he visited Florence, Rome, Naples, and Venice. The 1st opera he wrote in Italy was *Rodrigo*, presented in Florence in 1707. Then followed *Agrippina*, produced in Venice on Dec. 26, 1709; it obtained an excellent success, being given 27 performances. In Rome, he composed the serenata *Il trionfo del Tempo e del Disinganno*, which was performed there in the spring of 1707. Handel's oratorio *La Resurrezione* was given in Rome on April 8, 1708. On July 19, 1708, he brought out in Naples his serenata *Aci, Galatea, e Polifemo*; its score was remarkable for a bass solo that required a compass of 2 octaves and a fifth. During his Italian sojourn he met Alessandro and Domenico Scarlatti. In 1710 he returned to Germany and was named Kapellmeister to the Elector of Hannover, as successor to Agostino Steffani. Later that year he visited England, where he produced his opera *Rinaldo* at the Queen's Theatre in London on Feb. 24, 1711; it received 15 performances in all. After a brief return to Hannover in June 1711, he made another visit to London, where he produced his operas *Il Pastor fido* (Nov. 22, 1712) and *Teseo* (Jan. 10, 1713). He also wrote an ode for Queen Anne's birthday, which was presented at Windsor Palace on Feb. 6, 1713; it was followed by 2 sacred works, his *Te Deum* and *Jubilate*, performed on July 7, 1713, to celebrate the Peace of Utrecht; these performances won him royal favor and an annuity of 200 pounds sterling.

An extraordinary concurrence of events persuaded Handel to remain in London, when Queen Anne died in 1714 and Handel's protector, the Elector of Hannover, became King George I of England. The King bestowed many favors upon the composer and augmented his annuity to 400 pounds sterling. Handel became a British subject in 1727, and Anglicized his name to George Frideric Handel, dropping the original German umlaut. He continued to produce operas, invariably to Italian librettos, for the London stage. His opera *Silla* was produced in London on June 2, 1713; it was followed by *Amadigi di Gaula* on May 25, 1715. In 1716 Handel wrote *Der für die Sünden der Welt gemarterte und sterbende Jesus*, to the text of the poet Heinrich Brockes. In 1717 he produced one of his most famous works, written expressly for King George I, his *Water Music*. On July 17, 1717, an aquatic fête on the Thames River was held by royal order; the King's boat was followed by a barge on which an orch. of 50 musicians played Handel's score, or at least a major portion of it. The final version of the *Water Music* combines 2 instrumental suites composed at different times: one was written for the barge party; the other is of an earlier provenance. In 1717 Handel became resident composer to the Duke of Chandos, for whom he wrote the so-called *Chandos Anthems* (1717–18), 11 in number; the secular oratorio *Acis and Galatea* (1718); and the oratorio *Esther* (1718). He also served as music master to the daughters of the Prince of Wales; for Princess Anne he composed his 1st collection of *Suites de pièces pour le clavecin* (1720), also known as *The Lessons*, which includes the famous air with variations nicknamed *The Harmonious Blacksmith*; the appellation is gratuitous, and the story that Handel was inspired to compose it after he visited a blacksmith shop, where he was impressed by the steady beat of the artisan's hammer, was a persistent figment of anonymous imagination. In 1719 he was made Master of Musick of a new business venture under the name of the Royal Academy of Music, established for the purpose of presenting opera at the King's Theatre. The 1st opera he composed for it was *Radamisto* (April 27, 1720). In the fall of 1720 the Italian composer Giovanni Bononcini joined the company. A rivalry soon developed between him and Handel that was made famous by a piece of doggerel by the poet John Byrom ("Some say, compar'd to Bononcini, that Mynheer Handel's but a ninny. Others aver that he to Handel is scarcely fit to hold a candle. Strange all this difference should be twixt tweedledum and tweedledee"). Handel won a Pyrrhic victory when Bononcini had the unfortunate idea of submitting to the London Academy of Music a madrigal which he had appropriated *in extenso* from a choral piece by the Italian composer Antonio Lotti; Lotti discovered it, and an embarrassing controversy ensued, resulting in Bononcini's disgrace and expulsion from London (he died in obscurity in Vienna, where he sought refuge). The irony of the whole episode is that Handel was no less guilty of plagiarism. An article on Handel in the 1880 ed. of the *Encyclopædia Britannica* spares no words condemning Handel's conduct: "The system of wholesale plagiarism carried on by Handel is perhaps unprecedented in the history of music. He pilfered not only single melodies but frequently entire movements from the works of other masters, with few or no alterations, and without a word of acknowledgment." Between 1721 and 1728 he produced the following operas at the King's Theatre: *Florindante, Ottone, Flavio, Giulio Cesare, Tamerlano, Rodelinda Scipione, Alessandro, Admeto, Riccardo Primo, Siroe*, and *Tolomeo*; of these, *Giulio Cesare* and *Rodelinda* became firmly established in the operatic repertoire and had numerous revivals. In 1727 he composed 4 grand anthems for the coronation of King George II and Queen Caroline. In the spring of 1728 the Royal Academy of Music ceased operations, and Handel became associated with the management of the King's Theatre. The following year, he went to Italy to recruit singers for a new Royal Academy of Music. Returning to London, he brought out the operas *Lotario, Partenope, Poro, Ezio, Sosarme*, and *Orlando*; only *Orlando* proved to be a lasting success. On May 2, 1732, Handel gave a special performance of a revised version of his oratorio *Esther* at the King's Theatre; it was followed by the revised version of *Acis and Galatea* (June 10, 1732) and the oratorio *Deborah* (March 17, 1733). On July 10, 1733, he produced his oratorio *Athalia* at Oxford, where he also appeared as an organist; he was offered the degree of Mus.Doc. (*honoris causa*), but declined the honor.

Discouraged by the poor reception of his operas at the King's

Theatre, Handel decided to open a new season under a different management. But he quarreled with the principal singer, the famous castrato Senesino, who was popular with audiences, and thus lost the support of a substantial number of his subscribers, who then formed a rival opera company called Opera of the Nobility. It engaged the famous Italian composer Porpora as director, and opened its 1st season at Lincoln's Inn Fields on Dec. 29, 1733. Handel's opera *Arianna in Creta* had its premiere at the King's Theatre on Jan. 26, 1734, but in July of that year both Handel's company and the rival enterprise were forced to suspend operations. Handel set up his own opera company at Covent Garden, inaugurating his new season with a revised version of *Il Pastor fido* (Nov. 9, 1734); this was followed by *Ariodante, Alcina, Atalanta, Arminio, Giustino,* and *Berenice,* all staged between 1735 and 1737; only *Alcina* sustained a success; Handel's other operas met with an indifferent reception. On Feb. 19, 1736, he presented his ode *Alexander's Feast* at Covent Garden, and on March 23, 1737, he brought out a revised version of his oratorio *Il trionfo del Tempo e della Verità.* His fortunes improved when he was confirmed by the Queen as music master to Princesses Amelia and Caroline. He continued to maintain connections with Germany, and traveled to Aachen in 1737. Upon his return to London, he suffered from attacks of gout, an endemic illness of British society at the time, but he managed to resume his work. On Jan. 3, 1738, he produced his opera *Faramondo,* and on April 15, 1738, presented his opera *Serse* (a famous aria from this opera, *Ombra mai fù,* became even more famous in an instrumental arrangement made by parties unknown, under the title "Handel's Celebrated Largo"). There followed a pasticcio, *Giove in Argo* (May 1, 1739), and *Imeneo* (Nov. 22, 1740). On Jan. 10, 1741, he produced his last opera, *Deidamia,* which marked the end of his operatic enterprise.

In historical perspective, Handel's failure as an operatic entrepreneur was a happy turn of events, for he then directed his energy toward the composition of oratorios, in which he achieved greatness. For inspiration, he turned to biblical themes, using English texts. On Jan. 16, 1739, he presented the oratorio *Saul;* on April 4, 1739, there followed *Israel in Egypt.* He also wrote an *Ode for St. Cecilia's Day,* after Dryden (Nov. 22, 1739), and his great set of 12 *Concerti grossi,* op. 6. Milton's *L'Allegro* and *Il Penseroso* inspired him to write *L'Allegro, il Penseroso, ed il Moderato* (Feb. 27, 1740). In 1741 he was invited to visit Ireland, and there he produced his greatest masterpiece, *Messiah;* working with tremendous concentration of willpower and imagination, he completed Part I in 6 days, Part II in 9 days, and Part III in 6 days. The work on orchestration took him only a few more days; he signed the score on Sept. 14, 1741. The 1st performance of *Messiah* was given in Dublin on April 13, 1742, and its London premiere was presented on March 23, 1743. If contemporary reports can be trusted, King George II rose to his feet at the closing chords of the "Hallelujah" chorus, and the entire audience followed suit. This established a tradition, at least in England; since then every performance of *Messiah* has moved the listeners to rise during this celebratory chorus. Handel's oratorio *Samson,* produced in London on Feb. 18, 1743, was also successful, but his next oratorio, *Semele* (Feb. 10, 1744), failed to arouse public admiration. Continuing to work, and alternating between mythological subjects and religious themes, he produced *Joseph and His Brethren* (March 2, 1744), *Hercules* (Jan. 5, 1745), and *Belshazzar* (March 27, 1745). His subsequent works, composed between 1746 and 1752, were the *Occasional Oratorio, Judas Maccabaeus, Joshua, Alexander Balus, Susanna, Solomon, Theodora, The Choice of Hercules,* and *Jephtha.* Of these, *Judas Maccabaeus, Solomon,* and *Jephtha* became favorites with the public. Besides oratorios, mundane events also occupied his attention. To celebrate the Peace of Aachen, he composed the remarkable *Music for the Royal Fireworks,* which was heard for the 1st time in Green Park in London on April 27, 1749. In 1750 he revisited Germany. But soon he had to limit his activities on account of failing eyesight, which required the removal of cataracts; the operation

proved unsuccessful, but he still continued to appear in performances of his music, with the assistance of his pupil John Christopher Smith. Handel's last appearance in public was at the London performance of *Messiah* on April 6, 1759; 8 days later, on April 14, the Saturday between Good Friday and Easter, he died. He was buried at Westminster Abbey; a monument by Roubiliac marks his grave. (It should be noted that the year of birth on Handel's gravestone is marked as 1684 rather than 1685; this discrepancy is explained by the fact that at that time the calendar year in England and other European countries began in March, and not in Jan.)

A parallel between the 2 great German contemporaries, Bach and Handel, is often drawn. Born a few months apart, Bach in Eisenach, Handel in Halle, at a distance of about 130 kilometers, they never met. Bach visited Halle at least twice, but Handel was then away, in London. The difference between their life's destinies was profound. Bach was a master of the Baroque organ who produced religious works for church use, a schoolmaster who regarded his instrumental music as a textbook for study; he never composed for the stage, and traveled but little. By contrast, Handel was a man of the world who dedicated himself mainly to public spectacles, and who became a British subject. Bach's life was that of a German burgher; his genius was inconspicuous; Handel shone in the light of public admiration. Bach was married twice; survivors among his 20 children became important musicians in their own right. Handel remained celibate, but he was not a recluse. Physically, he tended toward healthy corpulence; he enjoyed the company of friends, but had a choleric temperament, and could not brook adverse argument. Like Bach, he was deeply religious, and there was no ostentation in his service to his God. Handel's music possessed grandeur of design, majestic eloquence, and lusciousness of harmony. Music-lovers did not have to study Handel's style to discover its beauty, while the sublime art of Bach could be fully understood only after knowledgeable penetration into the contrapuntal and fugal complexities of its structure.

Handel bequeathed the bulk of his MSS to his amanuensis, John Christopher Smith, whose son presented them in turn to King George III. They eventually became a part of the King's Music Library; they comprise 32 vols. of operas, 21 vols. of oratorios, 7 vols. of odes and serenatas, 12 vols. of sacred music, 11 vols. of cantatas, and 5 vols. of instrumental music. Seven vols. containing sketches for various works are in the Fitzwilliam Collection at Cambridge.

WORKS: OPERAS: *Almira* (Theater am Gänsemarkt, Hamburg, Jan. 8, 1705; part of music not extant); *Nero* (Theater am Gänsemarkt, Feb. 25, 1705; music not extant); *Rodrigo* (Accademia degli Infuocata, Florence, 1706 or 1707; part of music not extant); *Florindo* and *Daphne* (presented as 2 separate operas, Theater am Gänsemarkt, Jan. 1708; only a small part of music extant); *Agrippina* (Teatro San Giovanni Grisostomo, Venice, Dec. 26, 1709); *Rinaldo* (Queen's Theatre, London, Feb. 24, 1711; major rev., King's Theatre, London, April 6, 1731); *Il Pastor fido* (Queen's Theatre, Nov. 22, 1712; rev. versions, King's Theatre, May 18, 1734, and Nov. 9, 1734 [the latter with ballet *Terpsicore*]); *Teseo* (Queen's Theatre, Jan. 10, 1713); *Silla* (Queen's Theatre, or Burlington House, June 2, 1713); *Amadigi di Gaula* (King's Theatre, May 25, 1715); *Radamisto* (King's Theatre, April 27, 1720; rev. versions there, Dec. 28, 1720, and Jan.–Feb. 1728); *Floridante* (King's Theatre, Dec. 9, 1721; rev. version there, March 3, 1733); *Ottone, rè di Germania* (King's Theatre, Jan. 12, 1723; rev. versions there, Feb. 8, 1726, and Nov. 13, 1733); *Flavio, rè di Longobardi* (King's Theatre, May 14, 1723; major rev. there, April 18, 1732); *Giulio Cesare in Egitto* (King's Theatre, Feb. 20, 1724; rev. versions there, Jan. 2, 1725, and Jan. 17, 1730); *Tamerlano* (King's Theatre, Oct. 31, 1724); *Rodelinda, regina de' Longobardi* (King's Theatre, Feb. 13, 1725); *Scipione* (King's Theatre, March 12, 1726; rev. version there, Nov. 3, 1730); *Alessandro* (King's Theatre, May 5, 1726); *Admeto, rè di Tessaglia* (King's Theatre, Jan. 31, 1727; rev. version there, Dec. 7, 1731); *Riccardo Primo, rè d'Inghilterra* (King's Theatre, Nov.

11, 1727); *Siroe, rè di Persia* (King's Theatre, Feb. 17, 1728); *Tolomeo, rè di Egitto* (King's Theatre, April 30, 1728; major rev. there, May 19, 1730); *Lotario* (King's Theatre, Dec. 2, 1729); *Partenope* (King's Theatre, Feb. 24, 1730; rev. version there, Dec. 12, 1730; later rev. for Covent Garden, London, Jan. 29, 1737); *Poro, rè dell'Indie* (King's Theatre, Feb. 2, 1731; rev. versions there, Nov. 23, 1731, and Dec. 8, 1736); *Ezio* (King's Theatre, Jan. 15, 1732); *Sosarme, rè di Media* (King's Theatre, Feb. 15, 1732); *Orlando* (King's Theatre, Jan. 27, 1733); *Arianna in Creta* (King's Theatre, Jan. 26, 1734; rev. for Covent Garden, Nov. 27, 1734); *Oreste*, a pasticcio with music by Handel (Covent Garden, Dec. 18, 1734); *Ariodante* (Covent Garden, Jan. 8, 1735); *Alcina* (Covent Garden, April 16, 1735); *Atalanta* (Covent Garden, May 12, 1736); *Arminio* (Covent Garden, Jan. 12, 1737); *Giustino* (Covent Garden, Feb. 16, 1737); *Berenice* (Covent Garden, May 18, 1737); *Faramondo* (King's Theatre, Jan. 3, 1738); *Alessandro Severo*, pasticcio with music by Handel (King's Theatre, Feb. 25, 1738); *Serse* (King's Theatre, April 15, 1738); *Giove in Argo*, pasticcio (King's Theatre, May 1, 1739); *Imeneo* (Lincoln's Inn Fields, London, Nov. 22, 1740); *Deidamia* (Lincoln's Inn Fields, Jan. 10, 1741). Also *Muzio Scevola* (Act 3 by Handel; Act 1 by F. Amadei and Act 2 by G. Bononcini; King's Theatre, April 15, 1721); *Genserico* (only part of Act 1 drafted); *Tito* (only scenes 1–3 of Act 1 composed); *Alceste* (greater part of music used in the oratorio *The Choice of Hercules*; see below).

ORATORIOS: *Oratorio per la Resurrezione di Nostro Signor Gesù Cristo* (Palazzo Ruspoli, Rome, April 8, 1708); *Acis and Galatea* (Cannons, 1718; major rev., King's Theatre, June 10, 1732; also subsequent revs.); *Esther* (Cannons, 1718; major rev., King's Theatre, May 2, 1732; also subsequent additions); *Deborah* (King's Theatre, March 17, 1733; also subsequent revs.); *Athalia* (Sheldonian Theatre, Oxford, July 10, 1733; major rev., Covent Garden, April 1, 1735); *Il Parnasso in festa* (greater part of music from *Athalia*; King's Theatre, March 13, 1734); *Saul* (King's Theatre, Jan. 16, 1739; also subsequent revs.); *Israel in Egypt* (King's Theatre, April 4, 1739; also subsequent extensive changes); *Messiah* (New Music Hall, Dublin, April 13, 1742; also numerous revs. made for many subsequent perfs.); *Samson* (Covent Garden, Feb. 18, 1743; also subsequent revs.); *Semele* (Covent Garden, Feb. 10, 1744); *Joseph and His Brethren* (Covent Garden, March 2, 1744; also subsequent revs.); *Hercules* (King's Theatre, Jan. 5, 1745); *Belshazzar* (King's Theatre, March 27, 1745; rev. version, Covent Garden, Feb. 22, 1751); *Occasional Oratorio*, pasticcio (Covent Garden, Feb. 14, 1746); *Judas Maccabaeus* (Covent Garden, April 1, 1747; also many subsequent revs.); *Alexander Balus* (Covent Garden, March 23, 1748; rev. version, March 1, 1754); *Susanna* (Covent Garden, Feb. 10, 1749); *Solomon* (Covent Garden, March 17, 1749); *Theodora* (Covent Garden, March 16, 1750); *The Choice of Hercules* (greater part of music from *Alceste*; Covent Garden, March 1, 1751); *Jephtha* (Covent Garden, Feb. 26, 1752); *The Triumph of Time and Truth* (greater part of music from *Il trionfo del Tempo e della Verità*; Covent Garden, March 11, 1757).

PASSIONS: *Passion According to St. John* (most likely spurious; Hamburg, Feb. 17, 1704); *Der für die Sünden der Welt gemarterte und sterbende Jesus*, the so-called *Brockes Passion* (Hamburg?, 1716).

SERENATAS: *Il trionfo del Tempo e del Disinganno* (Rome, 1707?; major rev. as *Il trionfo del Tempo e della Verità*, Covent Garden, March 23, 1737); *Aci, Galatea, e Polifemo* (Naples, July 19, 1708).

ODES: *Ode for the Birthday of Queen Anne* (Windsor, Feb. 6, 1713); *Ode for St. Cecilia's Day* or *Alexander's Feast* (Covent Garden, Feb. 19, 1736).

OTHER VOCAL: *ENGLISH CHURCH MUSIC:* Te Deum and Jubilate in D major, "Utrecht," (for the Peace of Utrecht; St. Paul's, London, July 7, 1713); Te Deum in D major, "Caroline" (Chapel Royal, London, Sept. 26, 1714); *11 Chandos Anthems: As pants the hart; Have mercy upon me, O God; In the Lord put I my trust; I will magnify thee, O God; Let God arise; My song shall be alway; O be joyful; O come let us sing unto the Lord; O praise the Lord with one consent; O sing unto the Lord; The*

Lord is my light (1717–18); Te Deum in B-flat major, "Chandos" (c.1718); Te Deum in A major (based upon the "Chandos" Te Deum; 1721–26); *4 Coronation Anthems: Let thy hand be strengthened; My heart is inditing; The king shall rejoice; Zadok the priest* (for the coronation of King George II; Westminster Abbey, London, Oct. 11, 1727); *Funeral Anthem: The ways of Zion do mourn* (for the funeral of Queen Caroline; Westminster Abbey, Dec. 17, 1737); Te Deum and Anthem in D major, "Dettingen" (for the victory at Dettingen; Chapel Royal, Nov. 27, 1743); *Anthem on the Peace: How beautiful are the feet* (for the Peace of Aix-la-Chapelle; Chapel Royal, April 25, 1749); *Foundling Hospital Anthem: Blessed are they that considereth the poor* (Foundling Hospital, London, May 27, 1749). *LATIN CHURCH MUSIC: Laudate pueri Dominum* in F major (c.1706); *O qualis de caelo sonus* in G major, motet (Vignanello, June 12, 1707); *Coelestis dum spirat aura* in D/G major, motet (Vignanello, June 13, 1707); *Laudate pueri Dominum* in D major (1707); *Dixit Dominus* in G minor (1707); *Nisi Dominus* in G major (1707); *Silete venti* in B-flat major, motet (c.1729).

SECULAR CANTATAS, DRAMATIC (unless otherwise indicated, date is unknown): *Aminta e Fillide* (1708); *Clori, Tirsi e Fileno* (1707); *Il duello amoroso* (1708); *Apollo e Dafne* (c.1708); *Olinto, Il Tebro, Gloria* (1708); etc. **SOLO AND DUO CANTATAS WITH INSTRUMENTS:** *Agrippina condotta a morire* (c.1708); *Ah! crudel nel pianto mio* (c.1707); *Alpestre monto; Armida abbandonata* (1707); *Cantata spagnuola* (1707); *Carco sempre di gloria* (1737); *Cecilia, volgi un sguardo* (1736); *Clori, mia bella Clori; Crudel tiranno amor* (1721); *Cuopre tal volta; Il delirio amoroso* (1707); *Diana cacciatrice* (1707); *Figlio d'alte speranze; Languia di bocca lusinghiera; Mi palpita il cor; Pensieri notturni di Filli; Notte placida e cheta* (1708); *Qual ti riveggio, oh Dio; Spande ancor; Splende l'alba in oriente; Tra le fiamme; Tu fedel? tu costante?* (1707); *Un alma innamorata* (1707); *Venus and Adonis* (c.1711). **SOLO CANTATAS WITH BASSO CONTINUO:** *Ah, che pur troppo e vero; Allor ch'io dissi; Aure soavi e liete* (1707); *Bella ma ritrosetta; Care selve; Chi rapi la pace* (1709); *Clori, degli occhi miei; Clori, ove sei; Clori, si ch'io t'adoro* (may not be by Handel); *Clori, vezzosa Clori* (1708); *Dal fatale momento; Dalla guerra amorosa* (1709); *Da sete ardente afflitto* (1709); *Deh! lasciate e vita e volo; Del bel idolo mio* (1709); *Dimmi, o mio cor; Dite, miepiante* (1708); *Dolce pur d'amor l'affanno; E partirai, mia vita?; Figli del mesto cor; Filli adorata e cara* (1709); *Fra pensieri quel pensiero; Fra tante pene* (1709); *Hendel, non puo mia musa* (1708); *Ho fuggito amore; Irene, idolo mio; L'aure grate, il fresco rio; Lungi dal mio bel nume* (1708); *Lungi da me pensier tiranno* (1709); *Lungi da voi, che siete poli* (1708); *Lungi n'ando Fileno* (1708); *Manca pur quanto sai* (1708); *Mentre il tutto e in furore* (1708); *Menzognere speranze* (1707); *Mi, palpita il cor; Nel dolce tempo; Nell-africane selve; Nella stagion, che di viole* (1707); *Ne' tuoi lumi, o bella Clori* (1707); *Nice che fa? che pensa?; Ninfe e pastori* (1709); *Non sospirar, non piangere; Occhi miei, che faceste?; O lucenti, o sereni occhi; O numi eterni* (1709); *Parti, l'idolo mio; Poichè giuraro amore* (1707); *Qual fior che all'alba ride* (rev.1739); *Qualor crudele si mia vaga Dori; Qualor l'egre pupille* (1707); *Qual sento io non conosciuto* (may not be by Handel); *Quando sperasti, o core* (1708); *Sans y penser; Sarai contenta un di; Sarei troppo felice* (1707); *Sei pur bella, pur vezzosa* (1707); *Sento là che ristretto* (1709); *Se pari è la tua fe* (1708); *Se per fatal destino* (1707); *Siete rose rugiadose; S'il ne falloit; Solitudini care, amata libertà; Son gelsomino; Stanco di più soffrire* (1708); *Stelle, perfide stelle; Torna il core al suo diletto; Udite il meo consiglio* (1707); *Un sospir a chi si muove; Vedendo amor; Venne voglia ad amore; Zeffiretto, arresta il volo* (1709). Also 22 duets and trios with Continuo; more than 30 English songs; 9 German arias; Italian songs; French songs.

CHAMBER: Twenty trio sonatas: op. 2, no. 1, in B minor, for Flute or Violin, Violin, and Basso Continuo; op. 2, no. 2, in G minor, for 2 Violins and Basso Continuo; op. 2, no. 3, in E-flat major, for 2 Violins and Basso Continuo; op. 2, no. 4, in F major, for Flute or Recorder or Violin, Violin, and

Basso Continuo; op. 2, no. 5, in G minor, for 2 Violins and Basso Continuo; op. 2, no. 6, in G minor, for 2 Violins and Basso Continuo; op. 5, no. 1, in A major, for 2 Violins and Basso Continuo; op. 5, no. 2, in D major, for 2 Violins and Basso Continuo; op. 5, no. 3, in E minor, for 2 Violins and Basso Continuo; op. 5, no. 4, in G major, for 2 Violins and Basso Continuo; op. 5, no. 5, in G minor, for 2 Violins and Basso Continuo; op. 5, no. 6, in F major, for 2 Violins and Basso Continuo; op. 5, no. 7, in B-flat major, for 2 Violins and Basso Continuo; in C minor, for Recorder or Flute, Violin, and Basso Continuo; in F major, for 2 Violins and Basso Continuo; in E major, for 2 Violins and Basso Continuo; in E minor, for 2 Flutes and Basso Continuo; in F major, for 2 Violins and Basso Continuo; in C major, for 2 Violins and Basso Continuo; 17 solo sonatas with Basso Continuo: No. 1, in A minor, for Recorder; No. 2, in B-flat major, for Recorder; No. 3, in C major, for Recorder; No. 4, in D minor, for Recorder; No. 5, in F major, for Recorder; No. 6, in G minor, for Recorder; No. 7, in E minor, for Flute; No. 8, in B-flat major, for Oboe; No. 9, in C minor, for Oboe; No. 10, in F major, most likely for Oboe; No. 11, in A major, for Violin; No. 12, in D major, for Violin; No. 13, in D minor, for Violin; No. 14, in G major, for Violin; No. 15, in G minor, for Violin; No. 16, in G minor, for Viola da Gamba; No. 17, in A major, for Violin. Also *Suites de pièces pour le clavecin* (2 books, London, 1720 and 1733) and additional works for keyboard.

ORCH.: Six Concerti Grossi, op. 3: No. 1, in B-flat major; No. 2, in B-flat major; No. 3, in G major; No. 4, in F major; No. 5, in D minor; No. 6, in D major/D minor (publ. as a set in London, 1734); 12 Concerti Grossi, op. 6: No. 1, in G major; No. 2, in F major; No. 3, in C minor; No. 4, in A minor; No. 5, in D major; No. 6, in G minor; No. 7, in B-flat major; No. 8, in C minor; No. 9, in F major; No. 10, in D minor; No. 11, in A major; No. 12, in B minor (publ. as a set in London, 1740). Also 19 organ concertos; 3 *Concerti a due cori* (mostly arranged from other works); *Water Music* (greater part of music perf. during the royal barge excursion on the Thames River, July 17, 1717); *Music for the Royal Fireworks* (Green Park, London, April 27, 1749); overtures; sinfonie; many marches.

BIBL.: COLLECTED EDITIONS, SOURCE MATERIAL: The 1st ed. of Handel's collected works was edited by S. Arnold in 180 installments in 54 vols. (1787–97). It was superseded by the monumental ed. prepared by F. Chrysander under the title *G.F. H.s Werke: Ausgabe der deutschen Händelgesellschaft* (100 vols., Leipzig and Bergedorf bei Hamburg, 1858–94; 6 supplementary vols., 1888–1902). In 1955 the *Hallische H.-Ausgabe* was begun as a supplement to the Chrysander ed.; however, it soon became a new critical ed. in its own right, being edited by M. Schneider and R. Steglich as the *Hallische H.-Ausgabe im Auftrage der Georg Friedrich H.-Gesellschaft*, and publ. in Kassel. A. Bell ed. a *Chronological Catalogue of H.'s Work* (Greenock, Scotland, 1969). Other sources include the following: R. Streatfeild, "The Granville Collection of H. Manuscripts," *Musical Antiquary*, II (1910–11); N. Flower, *Catalogue of a H. Collection Formed by Newman Flower* (Sevenoaks, 1920); W. Squire, *Catalogue of the King's Music Library, I: The H. Manuscripts* (London, 1927); F. Zobeley, "Werke H.s in der Gräfl. von Schönbornschen Musikbibliothek," *H.-Jahrbuch 1931*; K. Taut, "Verzeichnis des Schriftums über G.F. H.," *H.-Jahrbuch 1933*; J. Coopersmith, "H.ian Lacunae: A Project," *Musical Quarterly* (April 1935); idem, "The First Gesamtausgabe: Dr. Arnold's Edition of H.'s Works," *Notes*, IV (1946–47); P. Hirsch, "Dr. Arnold's H. Edition," *Music Review*, VIII (1947); W. Smith, "Verzeichnis der Werke G.F. H.s," *H.-Jahrbuch 1956*; F. Hudson, "Concerning the Watermarks in the Manuscripts and Early Prints of G.F. H.," *Music Review*, XX (1959); H. Shaw, *A First List of Word-books of H.'s "Messiah," 1742–83* (Worcester, 1959); R. Ewerhart, "Die H.-Handschriften der Santini-Bibliothek in Münster," *H.-Jahrbuch 1960*; W. Smith and C. Humphries, *H.: A Descriptive Catalogue of the Early Editions* (London, 1960; 2nd ed., rev., 1970); H. Federhofer, *Unbekannte Kopien von Werken G.F. H.s* (Kassel, 1963); K. Sasse, *H.-Bibliographie* (Leipzig, 1963; new ed., 1967; with supplement,

1969); L. Duck, "The Aylesford H. Manuscripts," *Manchester Review*, X (1965); M. Picker, "H.iana in the Rutgers University Library," *Journal of the Rutgers University Library*, XXIX (1965); W. Smith, *A H.ian's Notebook* (London, 1965); P. Krause, *Handschriften und ältere Drucke der Werke G.F. H.s in der Musikbibliothek der Stadt Leipzig* (Leipzig, 1966); J. Hall, "The Importance of the Aylesford H. Manuscripts," *Brio*, IV/1 (1967); A. Hyatt King, *H. and His Autographs* (London, 1967); H. Lenneberg and L. Libin, "Unknown H. Sources in Chicago," *Journal of the American Musicological Society*, XXII (1969); A. Mann and J. Knapp, "The Present State of H. Research," *Acta Musicologica*, XLI (1969); W. Meyerhoff, ed., *50 Jahre Göttinger H.-Festspiele. Festschrift* (Kassel, 1970); H. Clausen, *H.s Direktionspartituren ("Handexemplare")* (Hamburg, 1972); A. Walker, *G.F. H.: The Newman Flower Collection in the Henry Watson Music Library* (Manchester, 1972); J. Knapp, "The Hall H. Collection," *Princeton University Library Chronicle*, XXXVI (1974); F. Hudson, "The Earliest Paper Made by James Whatman the Elder (1702–1759) and Its Significance in Relation to G.F. H. and John Walsh," *Music Review*, XXXVIII (1977); H. Marx, *Göttinger H.-Beiträge I* (Kassel, 1984); B. Baselt, *Verzeichnis der Werke G.F. H.s (HWV)* (Leipzig, 1986); M. Parker-Hale, *G.F. H.: A Guide to Research* (N.Y., 1988).

BIOGRAPHICAL: J. Mattheson, *Grundlage einer Ehren-Pforte . . .* (contains 8 pages on H.; Hamburg, 1740; reprint ed. by M. Schneider, Berlin, 1910); J. Mainwaring, *Memoirs of the Late G.F. H.* (London, 1760; reprint, 1967); J. Mattheson, *G.F. H.s Lebensbeschreibung* (based almost entirely on Mainwaring's biography; Hamburg, 1761; reprint, 1976); C. Burney, *An Account of the Musical Performances in Westminster Abbey and the Pantheon May 26th, 27th, 29th; and June the 3rd and 5th, 1784: In Commemoration of H.* (London, 1785; reprint, 1965); W. Coxe, *Anecdotes of G.F. H. and John Christopher Smith* (London, 1799; reprint, 1980); R. Clark, *Reminiscences of H.* (London, 1836); K. Förstemann, *G.F. H.s Stammbaum* (Leipzig, 1844); W. Callcott, *A Few Facts in the Life of H.* (London, 1850); H. Townsend, *An Account of H.'s Visit to Dublin: With Incidental Notices of His Life and Character* (Dublin, 1852); V. Schoelcher, *The Life of H.* (London, 1857); A. Stothard, *H.: His Life, Personal and Professional* (London, 1857); F. Chrysander, *G.F. H.* (an important source in its day; incomplete, bringing the life down only to 1740; 3 vols., Leipzig, 1858–67; reprint, 1966); M. Delany, *Autobiography and Correspondence of Mary Granville, Mrs. Delany* (contains a detailed account of Handel's death; London, 1861–62); F. van Kempen, *G.F. H.: Een Leven* (Leyden, 1868); J. Marshall, *H.* (London, 1881; 3rd ed., 1912); W. Rockstro, *The Life of G.F. H.* (London, 1883); J. Opel, *Mitteilungen zur Geschichte der Familie des Tonkünstlers H.* (Leipzig, 1885); A. Ademollo, *G.F. H. in Italia* (Milan, 1889); F. Volbach, *G.F. H.* (Berlin, 1897; 3rd ed., 1914); W. Cummings, *H.* (London, 1904); F. Williams, *H.* (London, 1904); J. Hadden, *Life of H.* (London, 1905); R. Streatfeild, *H.* (London, 1909; reprint, 1964); idem, "H. in Italy," *Musical Antiquary*, I (1909–10); R. Rolland, *H.* (Paris, 1910; 2nd ed., 1974; Eng. tr., 1916; reprint, 1975); M. Brenet, *H.* (Paris, 1912); H. Davey, *H.* (London, 1912); G. Thormälius, *G.F. H.* (Stuttgart, 1912); R. Streatfeild, *H., Canons and the Duke of Chandos* (London, 1916); N. Flower, *G.F. H.: His Personality and His Times* (London, 1923; 3rd ed., rev., 1959); H. Leichtentritt, *H.* (Stuttgart, 1924); H. Moser, *Der junge H. und seine Vorgänger in Halle* (Halle, 1929); J. Coopersmith, "A List of Portraits, Sculptures, etc., of H.," *Music & Letters*, XII (1932); J. Müller-Blattau, *G.F. H.* (Potsdam, 1933); E. Dent, *H.* (London, 1934); L. Liebeman, *G.F. H. und Halle* (Halle, 1935); E. Müller, ed., *The Letters and Writings of G.F. H.* (London, 1935); C. Williams, *H.* (London, 1935); H. Weinstock, *H.* (N.Y., 1946; 2nd ed., rev., 1959); P. Young, *H.* (London, 1946; 3rd ed., rev., 1975); W. Smith, *Concerning H., His Life and Works* (London, 1948); A.-E. Cherbuliez, *G.F. H.: Leben und Werk* (Olten, 1949); H. and E.H. Müller von Asow, *G.F. H.: Briefe und Schriften* (Lindau, 1949); W. Smith, "H.iana," *Music & Letters*, XXXI (1950) and XXXIV (1953); O. Deutsch, *H., A*

Documentary Biography (N.Y., 1954, and London, 1955); W. Siegmund-Schultze, *G.F. H.: Leben und Werke* (Leipzig, 1954; 3rd ed., rev., 1962); W. Serauky, *G.F. H.: Sein Leben, sein Werk* (only vols. III–V publ.; Kassel, 1956–58); E. Flessa, *Ombra mai fu: Die H. Chronik des Christopher Smith* (Biberbach, 1958); P. Nettl, *G.F. H.* (Berlin, 1958); R. Friedenthal, *G.F. H. in Selbstzeugnissen und Bilddokumenten* (Hamburg, 1959; 3rd ed., Reinbeck, 1967); B. Matthews, "Unpublished Letters Concerning H.," *Music & Letters* (July 1959); J. Müller-Blattau, *G.F. H.: Der Wille zur Volldendung* (Mainz, 1959); M. Nicolescu, *H.* (Bucharest, 1959); B. Matthews, "H.: More Unpublished Letters," *Music & Letters* (April 1961); W. Rackwitz and H. Steffens, *G.F. H., Persönlichkeit, Umwelt, Vermächtnis* (Leipzig, 1962); S. Sadie, *H.* (London, 1962); P. Lang, *G.F. H.* (N.Y., 1966); K. Sasse, *Bildsammlung; Hogarth-Grafik; Darstellung zur Geschichte, H.-pflege und Musikkunde* (Halle, 1967); M. Szentkuthy, *H.* (Budapest, 1967); W. Ober, "Bach, H., and 'Chevalier' John Taylor, M.D., Opthalmiater," *New York State Journal of Medicine* (June 1969); M. Foss, *The Age of Patronage: The Arts in England 1660–1750* (Ithaca, N.Y., 1971); C. Timms, "H. and Steffani," *Musical Times* (April 1973); R. Strohm, "H. in Italia: Nuovi contributi," *Rivista Italiana di Musicologia,* IX (1974); W. Siegmund-Schultze, ed., *G.F. H.: Beiträge zu seiner Biographie aus dem 18. Jahrhundert* (Leipzig, 1977); M. Keynes, "H. and His Illnesses," *Musical Times* (Sept. 1982); C. Hogwood, *H.* (London, 1984); H.C. Robbins Landon, *H. and His World* (Boston, 1984); J. Keates, *H.: The Man and His Music* (London, 1985); H.C. Robbins Landon, "G.F. H. 1685–1759," *Ovation* (Jan. 1985); P. Lang, "H.: 300 Years On," *Musical Times* (Feb. 1985); W. Rackwitz, *G.F. H.: Lebensbeschreibung in Bildern* (Wiesbaden, 1986); C. Ludwig, *G.F. H.: Composer of Messiah* (Milford, Mich., 1987).

CRITICAL, ANALYTICAL (in addition to the writings listed below, important articles may be found in the *H.-Jahrbuch* [1928–33; 1955–]): J. Weissebeck, *Der grosse Musikus H. im Universalruhme* (Nuremberg, 1809); H. Chorley, *H.-Studies* (2 vols., London, 1859); G. Gervinus, *H. und Shakespeare: Zur Ästhetik der Tonkunst* (Leipzig, 1868); R. Franz, *Über Bearbeitungen älterer Tonwerke, namenlich Bachscher und Händelscher Vokalmusik* (Leipzig, 1871; reprinted by R. Bethge as *Gesammelte Schriften über die Wiederbelebung Bachscher und Händelscher Werke,* Leipzig, 1910); E. Frommel, *H. und Bach* (Berlin, 1878); F. Chrysander, *H.s biblische Oratorien in geschichtlicher Betrachtung* (Hamburg, 1897); F. Volbach, *Die Praxis der H.-Aufführung* (Charlottenburg, 1900); J. Shedlock, "H.'s Borrowings," *Musical Times,* XLII (1901); G. Vernier, *L'Oratorio biblique de H.* (Cahors, 1901); J. Garat, *La Sonate de H.* (Paris, 1905); E. Bernoulli, *Quellen zum Studium Händelscher Chorwerke* (Leipzig, 1906); S. Taylor, *The Indebtedness of H. to Works by Other Composers* (Cambridge, 1906); P. Robinson, *H. and His Orbit* (London, 1908); A. Schering, *Geschichte des Oratoriums* (Leipzig, 1911); H. Abert, *H. als Dramatiker* (Göttingen, 1921); J. Benson, *H.'s "Messiah": The Oratorio and Its History* (London, 1923); E. Bairstow, *The Messiah* (London, 1928); F. Kahle, *H.s Cembalo-Suiten* (Berlin, 1928); E. Bredenfoerder, *Die Texte der H.-Oratorien* (Leipzig, 1934); F. Ehrlinger, *H.s Orgelkonzerte* (Erlangen, 1934); G. Abraham, "H.'s Clavier Music," *Music & Letters* (Oct. 1935); E. Dent, "H. on the Stage," ibid. (July 1935); H. Leichtentritt, "H.'s Harmonic Art," *Musical Quarterly* (April 1935); V. Redway, "H. in Colonial and Post-Colonial America," ibid.; E. Völsing, *G.F. H.s englische Kirchenmusik* (Leipzig, 1940); J. Eisenschmidt, *Die szenische Darstellung der Opern H.s auf der Londoner Bühne seiner Zeit* (Wolfenbüttel, 1940–41); J. Herbage, *Messiah* (London, 1948); R. Myers, *H.'s Messiah, A Touchstone of Taste* (N.Y., 1948); P. Young, *The Oratorios of H.* (London, 1949); G. Cuming, "The Text of 'Messiah,'" *Music & Letters* (July 1950); W. Dean, "The Dramatic Element in H.'s Oratorios," *Proceedings of the Royal Musical Association,* LXXIX (1952–53); G. Abraham, ed., *H.: A Symposium* (London, 1954); R. Myers, *H., Dryden and Milton* (London, 1956); J. Larsen, *H.'s Messiah: Origins, Composition, Sources* (London, 1957; 2nd ed., rev., 1972); H. Wolff, *Die H.-Oper auf der modernen Bühne* (Leipzig, 1957); W. Dean, *H.'s Dramatic Oratorios*

and Masques (London, 1959); J. Knapp, "H., the Royal Academy of Music, and Its First Opera Season in London (1720)," *Musical Quarterly* (April 1959); H. Dietz, *Die Chorfuge bei G.F. H.* (Tutzing, 1961); B. Trowell, "H. as a Man of the Theatre," *Proceedings of the Royal Musical Association,* XXXVIII (1961–62); H. Shaw, *The Story of H.'s Messiah* (London, 1963); J. Tobin, *H. at Work* (London, 1964); H. Shaw, *A Textual and Historical Companion to H.'s Messiah* (London, 1965); D. Kimbell, *A Critical Study of H.'s Early Operas* (diss., Oxford Univ., 1968); W. Dean, *H. and the Opera Seria* (Berkeley, Calif., 1969); J. Tobin, *H.'s Messiah* (London, 1969); T. Best, "H.'s Keyboard Music," *Musical Times* (Sept. 1971); S. Sadie, *H. Concertos* (London, 1972); D. Burrows, "H.'s Performances of 'Messiah': The Evidence of the Conducting Score," *Music & Letters* (July–Oct. 1975); H. Friedrichs, *Das Verhältnis von Text und Musik in den Brockespassionen Keisers, H.s, Telemanns und Mattthesons* (Munich and Salzburg, 1975); A. Hicks, "H.'s Early Musical Development," *Proceedings of the Royal Musical Association,* CIII (1976–77); G. Beeks, *The Chandos Anthems and Te Deum of G.F. H.* (diss., Univ. of Calif., Berkeley, 1977); D. Burrows, "H. and the Foundling Hospital," *Music & Letters* (July 1977); E. Harris, *H. and the Pastoral Tradition* (London, 1980); D. Burrows, "H. and 'Alexander's Feast,'" *Musical Times* (April 1982); J. Knapp, "H.'s Second Song on the London Stage," ibid.; H. Hoffmann, *G.F. H.: Vom Opernkomponisten zum Meister des Oratoriums* (Marburg an der Lahn, 1983); J. Milhous and R. Hume, "New Light on H. and the Royal Academy of Music in 1720," *Theater Journal,* XXXV (1983); D. Burrows, *H. and the Chapel Royal* (London, 1984); T. Best, "H.'s Chamber Music," *Early Music* (Nov. 1985); idem, "H.'s Overtures for Keyboard," *Musical Times* (Feb. 1985); D. Burrows, "The Autographs and Early Copies of 'Messiah': Some Further Thoughts," *Music & Letters* (July 1985); idem, "H.'s London Theatre Orchestra," *Early Music* (Aug. 1985); E. Salzman, "H.: Man of the Opera," *Ovation* (Jan. 1985); W. Shaw, "H.'s Vesper Music: 1: Some MS Sources Rediscovered," and G. Dixon, "2: Towards a Liturgical Reconstruction," *Musical Times* (July 1985); R. Strohm, *Essays on H. and Italian Opera* (Cambridge, 1985); T. Towe, "In Search of the True 'Messiah' with Christopher Hogwood," *Ovation* (Jan. 1985); P. Williams, ed., *Bach, H. and Scarlatti: Tercentenary Essays* (Cambridge, 1985); D. Chisholm, "H.'s Lucio Cornelio Silla: Its Problems and Context," *Early Music* (Feb. 1986); R. Hume, "H. and Opera Management in London in the 1730's," *Music & Letters* (Oct. 1986); H. Diack Johnstone, "H.'s Organ Voluntaries," *Musical Times* (Jan. 1986); J. Milhous and R. Hume, "A Prompt Copy of H.'s 'Radamisto,'" ibid. (June 1986); H. Meynell, *The Art of H.'s Operas* (Lewiston, N.Y., 1986); P. Brett and G. Haggerty, "H. and the Sentimental: The Case of 'Athalia,'" *Music & Letters* (April 1987); D. Burrows, "Four New H. Songs," *Musical Times* (April 1987); W. Dean and J. Knapp, *H.'s Operas 1704–1726* (Oxford, 1987); G. Dixon, "H.'s Music for the Carmelites: A Study in Liturgy and Some Observations on Performance," *Early Music* (Feb. 1987); N. Pirrotta and A. Zino, eds., *H. e gli Scarlatti a Roma: Atti del convegno internazionale di studi* (Roma, 12–14 giugno 1985) (Florence, 1987); J. Roberts, "H. and Vinci's 'Didone abbandonata': Revisions and Borrowings," *Music & Letters* (April 1987); J. Fuld, "Songs from Messiah Published during H.'s Lifetime," *Notes* (Dec. 1988); J. Larsen, *Essays on H., Haydn, and the Viennese Classical Style* (tr. by U. Krämer; Ann Arbor, 1988); H. Marx, "The Instrumentation of H.'s Early Italian Works," *Early Music* (Nov. 1988); P. Rogers, *Continuo Realization in H.'s Music* (Ann Arbor, 1988); S. Sadie and A. Hicks, eds., *H. Tercentenary Collection* (Ann Arbor, 1988); R. Fenton, "H.'s 'La Resurrezione': Is Lucifer a Comic Character?," *Musical Times* (Aug. 1989); J. Johnson, "The Rules for 'Thorough Bass' and for Tuning Attributed to H.," *Early Music* (Feb. 1989).

Handford, Maurice, English conductor; b. Salisbury, April 29, 1929; d. Warminster, Dec. 16, 1986. He studied at the Royal Academy of Music in London; then went to Manchester as principal horn player in the Hallé Orch. (1949–61). He made his conducting debut with that ensemble in 1960; in 1964 was named its assistant conductor; in 1966 its associate conductor; he resigned in 1971. From 1970 to 1974 he was conductor of the City of Birmingham Sym. Orch.; from 1971 to 1975, music director of the Calgary (Alberta) Phil.

Handl, Jacob. See **Gallus, Jacob Handl.**

Handley, Vernon (George), English conductor; b. London, Nov. 11, 1930. He was educated at Balliol College, Oxford, and the Guildhall School of Music in London. He made his debut with the Bournemouth Sym. Orch. in 1961. From 1962 to 1983 he was principal conductor of the Guildford Phil.; was also a prof. at the Royal College of Music in London (1966–72). In 1982 he was appointed associate conductor of the London Phil.; in 1983 he became principal guest conductor of the BBC Scottish Sym. Orch. in Glasgow. He was also principal conductor of the Ulster Orch. in Belfast (1985–89) and the Malmö Sym. Orch. (1985–91); in 1988 he was named principal guest conductor of the Royal Liverpool Phil.

Handrock, Julius, German piano pedagogue and composer; b. Naumburg, June 22, 1830; d. Halle, Jan. 5, 1894. He publ. several collections of piano studies which retained their popularity among teachers and students for many years (*Moderne Schule der Geläufigkeit; 50 Melodisch-technische Klavier-Etuden*, etc.).

Handschin, Jacques (Samuel), eminent Swiss organist and musicologist; b. Moscow, April 5, 1886; d. Basel, Nov. 25, 1955. He studied organ in Moscow; in 1905 he studied mathematics and history at the Univ. of Basel; then went to Munich to pursue his academic studies; also studied organ and theory with Reger; he later attended some of the lectures in musicology given in Leipzig by Riemann and in Berlin by Hornbostel; took additional courses in organ with Straube in Leipzig and with Widor in Paris. Returning to Russia, he taught organ at the St. Petersburg Cons. (1909–20); gave numerous organ recitals in Russia, and promoted contemporary organ works by Russian composers, among them Glazunov and Taneyev; included these works in his anthology *Les Maîtres contemporains de l'orgue* (Paris, 1913–14). In 1920 he returned to Switzerland; in 1921 he received his Ph.D. from the Univ. of Basel with the dissertation *Choralbearbeitungen und Kompositionen mit rhythmischem Text in der mehrstimmigen Musik des 13. Jahrhunderts*; completed his Habilitation there in 1924 with his *Über die mehrstimmige Musik der St. Martial-Epoche sowie die Zusammenhänge zwischen Notre Dame und St. Martial und die Zusammenhänge zwischen einem dritten Stil und Notre Dame und St. Martial.* In 1924 he became Privatdozent at the Univ. of Basel; later was a prof. of musicology there (1935–55). He also served as a church organist in Zürich and Basel. He was greatly esteemed for his erudition and the soundness of his analytical theories; he evolved philosophical principles of musical esthetics seeking the rational foundations of the art. His most important work is *Der Toncharakter: Eine Einführung in die Tonpsychologie* (Zürich, 1948), which sets down his principles of musical esthetics; other works include *La Musique de l'antiquité* (Paris, 1946) and *Musikgeschichte im Überblick* (Lucerne, 1948).
BIBL.: H. Oesch, *Gedenkschrift J. H.: Aufsätze und Bibliographie* (Bern and Stuttgart, 1957); H. Anglés et al., eds., *In memoriam J. H.* (Strasbourg, 1962).

Handt, Herbert, American tenor and conductor; b. Philadelphia, May 26, 1926. He studied at the Juilliard School of Music in N.Y. and the Vienna Academy of Music, making his operatic debut at the Vienna State Opera (1949). After making his conducting debut in Rome (1960), he prepared performing eds. of rarely heard Italian scores; he later settled in Lucca, where he was founder-director of the Associazione Musicale Lucchese, the Lucca Chamber Orch., and the Marilia International Festival.

Handy, W(illiam) C(hristopher), noted black American composer, known as the "father of the blues"; b. Florence, Ala., Nov. 16, 1873; d. N.Y., March 28, 1958. His father and grandfather were ministers. In 1892 he graduated from the Teachers' Agricultural and Mechanical College in Huntsville, Ala.; became a schoolteacher and also worked in iron mills; learned to play the cornet and was a soloist at the Chicago World's Fair (1893); became bandmaster of Mahara's Minstrels. From 1900 to 1902 he taught at the Agricultural and Mechanical College; then conducted his own orch. and toured the South (1903–21). He received the award of the National Assoc. for Negro Music, St. Louis (1937). On Jan. 1, 1954, he married his secretary, Irma Louise Logan. His famous song *Memphis Blues* (publ. 1912; the 2nd piece to be publ. as a "blues," and the 1st blues work to achieve popularity) was orig. written as a campaign song for the mayor of Memphis, E.H. Crump (1909); this song, along with his more celebrated *St. Louis Blues* (1914), opened an era in popular music, turning the theretofore prevalent spirit of ragtime gaiety to ballad-like nostalgia, with the lowered third, fifth, and seventh degrees ("blue notes") as distinctive melodic traits. He followed these with more blues: *Yellow Dog; Beale Street; Joe Turner;* the march *Hail to the Spirit of Freedom* (1915); *Ole Miss* for Piano (1916); the songs *Aunt Hagar's Children* (1920), *Loveless Love* (1921), and *Aframerican Hymn;* etc. He publ. *Blues: An Anthology* (also publ. as *A Treasury of the Blues;* N.Y., 1926; 2nd ed., 1949; 3rd ed., rev. by J. Silverman, 1972); *Book of Negro Spirituals* (N.Y., 1938); *Negro Music and Musicians* (N.Y., 1944); *Negro Authors and Composers of the U.S.* (N.Y., 1936); wrote an autobiography, *Father of the Blues* (N.Y., 1941). A commemorative stamp depicting Handy was issued in 1969 in Memphis, Tenn., the birthplace of his "blues."

Handy, Will, pseudonym for the songwriting team Cole and Johnson Bros. See **Johnson, James Weldon** and **Johnson, J(ohn) Rosamond.**

Hanff, Johann Nikolaus, German organist and composer; b. Wechmar, near Mühlhausen, 1665; d. Schleswig, 1711 or 1712. He was organist in Eupin; later in Hamburg (1706–11). A few months before his death, he was appointed organist at the Cathedral of Schleswig. He was a master of the chorale prelude, and his works considerably influenced J.S. Bach's style in this form. Only 6 of his chorale preludes are extant (publ. 1907 by K. Straube in his 45 *Choralvorspiele alter Meister;* reprinted by E. White in Masterpieces of Organ Music, N.Y., 1949); also extant are 3 cantatas.
BIBL.: H. Schillings, *Tobias Eniccelius, Friedrich Meister, N. H.: Ein Beitrag zur Geschichte der evangelischen Frühkantate in Schleswig-Holstein* (Kiel, 1934).

Hanfstängel, Marie (née **Schröder**), German soprano; b. Breslau, April 30, 1846; d. Munich, Sept. 5, 1917. She studied at Baden-Baden with Viardot-García; made her debut as Agathe in *Der Freischütz* at the Théâtre Lyrique in Paris (Feb. 27, 1867). On the declaration of the Franco-Prussian War, she returned to Germany, and was engaged at the Stuttgart Opera (1870). She publ. *Meine Lehrweise der Gesangskunst* (1902).

Hanisch, Joseph, German organist and composer; b. Regensburg, March 24, 1812; d. there, Oct. 9, 1892. He studied with his father, and with Proske, with whom he went to Italy as an assistant (1834). In 1839 he became organist at the Regensburg Cathedral. He wrote *Missa auxilium Christianorum, Quatuor hymni pro festo corporis Christi;* also composed pieces for organ solo. He was a master of improvisation, and was regarded as one of the greatest in this field in his time.

Hanke, Karl, German composer; b. Rosswald, Silesia, c.1750; d. Flensburg, June 10, 1803. As a young man he was sent to Vienna to pursue his music studies; there he briefly associated himself with Gluck, and profited by the master's advice. He then held the post of music director in Brünn (1778–81), Warsaw (1781–83), and Hamburg (1783–86); was in Schleswig from 1786 to 1792. In 1792 he settled in Flensburg, where he remained until the end of his life. He composed several pieces for the stage; his singspiel *Der Wunsch mancher Mädchen* (1781), dedicated to Gluck, was performed on various occasions with some success; 2 albums of his songs were publ. in 1796–97.

Hann, Georg, remarkable Austrian bass; b. Vienna, Jan. 30, 1897; d. Munich, Dec. 9, 1950. He enlisted in the Austrian army in World War I; after demobilization, he began to study singing with Theodor Lierhammer at the Vienna Academy of Music. In 1927 he joined the Bavarian State Opera in Munich; made guest appearances in Brussels, Berlin, Paris, and London; also sang at La Scala in Milan. He was equally successful in such dramatic roles as Pizarro in *Fidelio*, Sarastro in *Die Zauberflöte*, and Rigoletto, as well as in buffo parts such as Falstaff and Leporello. He performed all his roles in German, even in the Italian repertoire, and continued to sing and record to the very last months of World War II.

Hanna, Sir Roland, black American jazz pianist; b. Detroit, Feb. 10, 1932. He began taking piano lessons as a child but soon turned to jazz; commenced his career as a performer in local clubs. During service in the U.S. Army, he played in an army band (1950–52); after his discharge, he took courses at the Eastman School of Music in Rochester, N.Y., and at the Juilliard School of Music in N.Y. He formed his own trio in 1959, was a leading member of the Thad Jones–Mel Lewis Orch. (1966–74), and then played with the N.Y. Jazz Quartet. In 1970 he was knighted by the government of Liberia.

Hannan, Michael (Francis), Australian composer, pianist, and writer on music; b. Newcastle, New South Wales, Nov. 19, 1949. Endowed by nature and unique intellectual inheritance (his father is a mathematician), he went through the rules and regulations of classical music in record time, easily obtaining the requisite degrees at the Univ. of Sydney (B.A., 1972; Ph.D., 1979). He plunged headlong into the wilderness of ultramodern music, absorbing the novel tonal, metric, and rhythmic innovations with easy penetration, adorning his own works with engaging titles, such as *Riff Madness* for Jazz Piano, borrowing concepts from oriental philosophy as in *Zen Variations*, or geometric art forms as in *Improvisatory Mobiles* and occasionally indulging in iconoclastic fantasies as in *Beethoven Deranged*. Yet advanced logic reigned in all of his creations and recreations. An excellent pianist, he is able to give a full account of modern pieces in his repertoire. As an instructor, he held positions at the Univ. of Sydney, the New South Wales and Queensland Cons. of Music, and the Northern Rivers College of Advanced Education (later Univ. of New England, Northern Rivers) in Lismore, New South Wales (from 1986), where he became head of the Performing Arts and Music Divisions (1987). He obtained enviable awards and grants; traveled to California in 1983 on a Fulbright fellowship, and was a visiting prof. at the Univ. of Southern Calif. in 1990. Exceptionally gifted for the exploration of tonal, polytonal, and atonal techniques of composition, Hannan also possesses a saving grace of humor, as revealed in such works, recorded on electronic tape, as *Alphabeat* [sic] and *Slonimsky Variations*. In his purely scholarly pursuits he compiled the section on musical terms to the *Macquarie Dictionary* (1981). He also contributed essays on Australian music to various publications and compiled the critical biography *Peter Sculthorpe: His Music and Ideas, 1929–79* (1982).
WORKS: CHAMBER: *Eliza Survivor* for Speaker, Piano, Flute, and Live Electronics (1978); *Garland Piece* for Large Ensemble (1979); *Occasional Medley* for String Quartet (1981); *Island Song* for Large Recorder Ensemble, Percussion, and Organ (1983); *Interaction I* for Ensemble (1987). **PIANO:** *Piano Collage I* (1978) and *II* (1979) for Piano and Tapes; *7 Studies for Single Hands* (1981); *Riff Madness* for Jazz Pianist (1981); *3 Improvisatory Mobiles* (1981); *Zen Variations* (1982); *3 Meditations for Dane Rudhyar* (1983–84); *Resonances I* (1986–87) and *II* (1989); *Beethoven Deranged* (1987); *Mysterious Flowers* (1990); *Romantic Suggestions* (1990); *Minimal Study I* (1990); also *Bracefell's Story* for Voice and Piano (1990); numerous works with dancers.

Hannay, Roger D(urham), talented American composer; b. Plattsburg, N.Y., Sept. 22, 1930. He studied composition with F. Morris and D. Newlin at Syracuse Univ. (1948–52), H. Norden at Boston Univ. (1952–53), Bernard Rogers and Hanson at the Eastman School of Music in Rochester, N.Y. (1954–56; Ph.D., 1956), and Foss and Copland at the Berkshire Music Center at Tanglewood (1959); had sessions with Sessions and attended lectures by Carter at the Princeton Seminar for Advanced Studies (1960). He taught at various colleges; in 1966 joined the music faculty of the Univ. of North Carolina at Chapel Hill; was founder and director of the New Music Ensemble (1967–82), and also served as chairman of the Division of Fine Arts there (1979–82). An unprejudiced and liberal music-maker, he makes use of varied functional resources, from neo-Classical pandiatonism to dodecaphony; resorts also to the device of "objets trouvés," borrowing thematic materials from other composers.
WORKS: STAGE: *2 Tickets to Omaha, The Swindlers,* chamber opera (1960); *The Fortune of St. Macabre,* chamber opera (1964); *The Journey of Edith Wharton,* opera (1982). **ORCH.:** 5 syms.: No. 1 (1953; rev. 1973); No. 2 (1956); No. 3, *The Great American Novel,* with Chorus and Tape-recorded Sound (1976–77); No. 4, *American Classic* (1977); No. 5 (1987–88); *Cantata* (1952); *Dramatic Overture,* homage to Schoenberg (1955); *Lament* for Oboe and Strings (1957); *Requiem,* after Whitman's "When Lilacs Last in the Dooryard Bloom'd" (1961); Sym. for Band (1963); *Sonorous Image* (1968); *Sayings for Our Time,* to a text from the "current news media," for Chorus and Orch. (Winston-Salem, N.C., Aug. 2, 1968); *Fragmentation* for Orch. or Chamber Orch. (1969); *The Inter-Planetary Aleatoric Serial Factory* for Soprano, String Quartet, Rock Band, Actors, Dancers, Tapes, Film, and Slides (1969); *Listen* (1971; Greensboro, N.C., July 7, 1973); *Celebration* for Tape and Orch. (N.Y., May 19, 1975); *Suite-Billings* for Youth Orch. (1975); *American Colonial* for Concert Band (1979); *Introduction and Allegro* for Symphonic Band (1981); *Pastorale,* "from Olana," for Horn and Strings (1982); *The Age of Innocence,* orch. suite arranged from *The Journey of Edith Wharton* (1983). **CHAMBER:** Sonata for Brass Ensemble (1957); Divertimento for Wind Quintet (1958); *Concerto da camera* for Recorder, Violin, Viola, Cello, Harpsichord, and Soprano (1958; rev. 1975); 4 string quartets: No. 1 (1962); No. 2, *Lyric* (1962); No. 3, *Designs* (1963); No. 4, *Quartet of Solos* (1974; comprising the simultaneous perfs. of the 4 solo pieces *Grande Concerte, 2nd Fiddle, O Solo Viola,* and *Concert Music*); *The Fruit of Love,* after St. Vincent Millay, for Soprano, and Piano or Chamber Orch. (1964, 1969); *Spectrum* for Brass Quintet (1964); *Structure* for Percussion Ensemble (1965; rev. 1974); *Marshall's Medium Message* for Mod Girl Announcer and Percussion Quartet (1967); *Live and in Color!* for Mod Girl Announcer, Percussion Quartet, 2 Action Painters, Tape, Films, and Slides (1967); *Squeeze Me* for Chamber Ensemble and Film (1970); *Tuonelan Joutsen,* vocalise after Sibelius's *Swan of Tuonela* for Soprano, English Horn, and Film (1972); *4 for 5* for Brass Quintet (1973); *Oh Friends!* for Chamber Wind Ensemble and Pitched Percussion (1976); *Festival Trumpets* for 10 Trumpets and Conductor (1978); *Nocturnes,* a woodwind quintet (1979); Sonata for Trumpet and Piano (1980); *La Ronde* for Flute, Clarinet, Cello, and Piano (1980); Suite for Flute, Clarinet, Cello, and Piano (1981); *Masquerade* for Synthesizer (1982); *Souvenir* for Flute, Clarinet, Violin, Cello, Percussion, Piano, and Conductor (1984); *Trio-Rhapsody* for Flute, Cello, and Piano (1984); *Sic Transit Spiritus* for Wind Ensemble (1985); *Consorting Together* for Viola da Gamba Consort (1986); *Souvenir II* for Flute, Clarinet, Violin, Cello, and Piano (1986); *Modes of Discourse* for Flute, Violin, and Cello (1988). **PIANO:** Suite (1954); *Abstractions* (1962); Sonata (1964); *Sonorities* (1966); *The Episodic Refraction* for Tape and Piano (1971); *Mere Bagatelle* for Piano, 4-hands, and Synthesizer (1978); *Serenade* for Piano and Synthesizer (1979); *Dream Sequence* for Piano and Electronic Tape (1980); *Luminere* (1988); also *Scarlatti on Tour* for Harpsichord (1989); choruses; songs.

Hannikainen, distinguished family of Finnish musicians:
(1) Pekka (or **Pietari**) **(Juhani) Hannikainen,** conductor and composer; b. Nurmes, Dec. 9, 1854; d. Helsinki, Sept. 13, 1924. He was self-taught; was active as a choral conductor and teacher of choral singing in Helsinki; wrote a number of choral works and songs that became popular in his native country. His wife, **Alli** (née Laura Alfhild; b. Helsinki, June 21, 1867; d. there, April 12, 1949), was a teacher of singing and conductor of a women's choir. Their sons also became prominent musicians:
(2) (Toivo) Ilmari Hannikainen, pianist and composer; b. Jyväskylä, Oct. 19, 1892; d. Kuhmoinen, July 25, 1955. He studied piano and composition at the Helsinki music school (1911–13); then with Schreker in Vienna (1913–14) and Siloti and Steinberg in Petrograd (1916–17). He made his debut in Helsinki in 1914 and later toured with his brothers Tauno (Heikki) and Arvo (Sakari) in a trio; also taught piano at his alma mater and at the Sibelius Academy (1939–55). He wrote a folk play, *Talkoottanssit* (1930); a Piano Concerto; a Piano Quartet; and many pieces for solo piano.
(3) Tauno (Heikki) Hannikainen, cellist and conductor; b. Jyväskylä, Feb. 26, 1896; d. Helsinki, Oct. 12, 1968. He studied cello with O. Forström in Helsinki, making his debut there as a soloist in 1920; then took lessons with Casals in Paris (1921). After making his conducting debut in 1921, he served as conductor of the Finnish Opera in Helsinki until 1927; also played in a trio with his brothers (Toivo) Ilmari and Arvo (Sakari). He was conductor of the Turku Sym. Orch. (1929–39); then went to the U.S., where he became music director of the Duluth (Minn.) Sym. Orch. (1942–46). Subsequently he was conductor of the Chicago Civic Orch. (1947–50), then assistant conductor (1947–49) and associate conductor (1949–50) of the Chicago Sym. Orch. From 1950 to 1963 he was conductor of the Helsinki Phil.
(4) Arvo (Sakari) Hannikainen, violinist and conductor; b. Jyväskylä, Oct. 11, 1897; d. Helsinki, Jan. 8, 1942. He studied violin in Helsinki (1915–17), in Berlin and Weimar (1920–23), and with Thibaud and Ysaÿe in Paris. In 1917 he became a member of the Helsinki orch., then was 1st violinist in 1923; he also played in a trio with his brothers (Toivo) Ilmari and Tauno (Heikki). He taught at the Sibelius Academy, and was conductor of its student orch.
(5) Väinö (Aatos) Hannikainen, harpist and composer; b. Jyväskylä, Jan. 12, 1900; d. Kuhmoinen, Aug. 7, 1960. He studied in Helsinki and Berlin; was 1st harpist in the Helsinki orch. (1923–57). He wrote several symphonic poems, a Harp Concerto, a Harp Sonata, and songs.

Hanon, Charles-Louis, French pianist and pedagogue; b. Renescure, near Dunkerque, July 2, 1819; d. Boulogne-sur-Mer, March 19, 1900. Next to Czerny, Hanon was the most illustrious composer of piano exercises, embodied in his chef d'œuvre, *Le Pianiste-virtuose,* which for over a century has been the vademecum for many millions of diligent piano students all over the face of the musical globe. He further wrote a collection of 50 instructive piano pieces under the title *Méthode élémentaire de piano;* a useful compilation, *Extraits des chefs-d'œuvres des grands maîtres;* as well as a selection of 50 ecclesiastical chants, *50 cantiques choisis parmi les plus populaires.* He also attempted to instruct uneducated musicians in the art of accompanying plainchant in a curious didactic publication, *Système nouveau pour apprendre à accompagner tout plainchant sans savoir la musique.*

Hansen, (Emil) Robert, Danish cellist, conductor, and composer; b. Copenhagen, Feb. 25, 1860; d. Århus, July 18, 1926. He received his 1st instruction from his father; then studied with F. Neruda at the Copenhagen Cons., and with Friedrich Grützmacher in Dresden; was a member of the Court Orch. in Copenhagen (1877–89). After a stay in London, he settled in 1891 in Leipzig, where he joined the Gewandhaus Orch. and became a prof. at the Cons. From 1918 he was conductor of the Århus Orch.
Works: Opera, *Frauenlist* (Sondershausen, 1911); operetta,

Die wilde Komtesse (Eisenach, 1913); Sym.; Symphonic Suite for Strings and 2 Horns; Piano Concerto; Cello Concerto; Piano Quintet; String Quartet.

Hansen, Wilhelm, Danish music publishing firm founded in Copenhagen in 1857 by Jens Wilhelm Hansen (1821–1904). His sons, Jonas Wilhelm (1850–1919) and Alfred Wilhelm Hansen (1854–1922), were also active in the business. Alfred's sons, Asger Wilhelm (1889–1965) and Svend Wilhelm Hansen (1890–1959), and, later, Svend's daughters, Hanne Wilhelm (b. 1927) and Lone Wilhelm Hansen (b. 1930), carried on the business. The firm publ. many works by Scandinavian composers, as well as many by Europeans. It has branches in Frankfurt, London, N.Y., Oslo, Stockholm, Århus, and Odense.

Hanslick, Eduard, greatly renowned Austrian music critic of Czech descent; b. Prague, Sept. 11, 1825; d. Baden, near Vienna, Aug. 6, 1904. He studied law in Prague and Vienna; took the degree of Dr.Jur. in 1849, qualifying himself for an official position. But having already studied music under Tomaschek at Prague, in 1848–49 he served as music critic for the *Wiener Zeitung,* and soon adopted a literary career. His 1st work, *Vom Musikalisch-Schönen: Ein Beitrag zur Revision der Aesthetik der Tonkunst* (Leipzig, 1854; in French, 1877; Spanish, 1879; Italian, 1884; Eng., 1891; Russian, 1895), brought him worldwide fame. Its leading idea is that the beauty of a musical composition lies wholly and specifically in the music itself; i.e., it is immanent in the relations of the tones, without any reference whatever to extraneous (non-musical) ideas, and can express no others. Such being his point of view through life, it follows logically that he could not entertain sympathy for Wagner's art; his violent opposition to the music-drama was a matter of profound conviction, not personal spite; he in fact wrote a moving tribute after Wagner's death. On the other hand, he was one of the very 1st and most influential champions of Brahms. From 1855 to 1864 Hanslick was music ed. of the *Presse;* thereafter of the *Neue Freie Presse;* he became a lecturer on music history and esthetics at Vienna Univ., prof. extraordinary in 1861, and full prof. in 1870, retiring in 1895 (succeeded by Guido Adler). What gives his writings permanent value is the sound musicianship underlying their brilliant, masterly style. Yet in music history he is chiefly known as a captious and intemperate reviler of genius; Wagner caricatured him in the part of Beckmesser (in an early version of *Die Meistersinger von Nürnberg* the name was to have been Veit Hanslich). A collection of Hanslick's articles in the *Neue Freie Presse* was publ. in Eng. tr. under the title *Vienna's Golden Years of Music, 1850–1900* (N.Y., 1950).
Writings: *Geschichte des Concertwesens in Wien* (1869); *Aus dem Concertsaal* (1870); a series begun with *Die moderne Oper* (1875) and followed by 8 more vols.: II, *Musikalische Stationen* (1880); III, *Aus dem Opernleben der Gegenwart* (1884); IV, *Musikalisches Skizzenbuch* (1888); V, *Musikalisches und Litterarisches* (1889); VI, *Aus dem Tagebuch eines Musikers* (1892); VII, *Fünf Jahre Musik* (1896); VIII, *Am Ende des Jahrhunderts* (1899); IX, *Aus neuer und neuester Zeit* (1900); *Suite, Aufsätze über Musik und Musiker* (1885); *Konzerte, Komponisten und Virtuosen der letzten fünfzehn Jahre* (1886); *Aus meinem Leben* (2 vols., 1894).
Bibl.: R. Schafke, *E. H. und die Musikästhetik* (1922); S. Deas, *In Defence of H.* (London, 1940); A. Wilhemer, *Der junge H.* (Klagenfurt, 1959); D. Glatt, *Zur geschichtlichen Bedeutung der Musikästhetik E. H.s* (Munich, 1972); W. Abegg, *Musikästhetik und Musikkritik bei E. H.* (Regensburg, 1974).

Hanson, Howard (Harold), important American composer, conductor, and educator; b. Wahoo, Nebr., Oct. 28, 1896; d. Rochester, N.Y., Feb. 26, 1981. His parents emigrated from Sweden to America and made their home in Nebraska, which had a large population of Scandinavian settlers; Hanson's northern ancestry played an important part in his spiritual outlook and his own music. His mother taught him piano; he began to compose very early in life; he also learned to play the cello. He attended the Luther College in Wahoo and played piano and organ in local churches; in 1912 he enrolled in the Univ. of Nebraska; in 1913 he went to N.Y., where he took piano lessons with Friskin and studied composition with Goetschius at the Inst. of Musical Art. In 1915 he enrolled at Northwestern Univ. in Evanston, Ill., where his teachers in composition were Arne Oldberg and P.C. Lutkin; he graduated in 1916 with a B.A. degree. He progressed rapidly as a composer; his *Symphonic Prelude* was performed by the Chicago Sym. Orch.; he also wrote a Piano Quintet and other works. In 1916, at the age of 20, he received an appointment to teach music at the College of the Pacific in San Jose, Calif.; was named its dean in 1919. In 1921 he became the 1st American to win the prestigious Prix de Rome, which enabled him to spend 3 years at the American Academy there. He composed copiously; the major part of his works reflected his profound sentiment for his ancestral land; his *Scandinavian Suite* for Piano (1919) exemplified this devotion. He believed in music as a function of the natural environment. During his stay in the West, he wrote the score for a *California Forest Play* (1920). The work that gained him admission to Rome was a symphonic poem, *Before the Dawn;* in 1923 he completed a piece for chorus and orch. entitled *North and West.* All these works clearly indicated his future path as a composer; they were permeated with the spirit of the northern country, inspired by both Scandinavia and the American West. There followed his 1st important work, Sym. No. 1, subtitled *Nordic;* he conducted its 1st performance in Rome on May 30, 1923. In it he expressed, as he himself said, "the solemnity, austerity, and grandeur of the North, of its restless surging and strife, and of its somberness and melancholy." Hanson was often described as an American Sibelius; indeed, he professed profound admiration for the great Finn, with whom he shared an affinity for slowly progressing lyrical modalities and somber harmonies anchored in deep organ points. In 1924 he conducted the U.S. premiere of his *Nordic Symphony* in Rochester, and met George Eastman, the inventor of Kodak film. Eastman, who knew next to nothing about music, had nonetheless a keen appreciation of ability among artists and composers; in 1924 he offered Hanson the position of director of the Eastman School of Music; Hanson was not quite 28 years old at that time. Eastman's insight was justified; Hanson elevated the Eastman School of Music from a provincial conservatory to one of the most important musical institutions in America. He retained his post as director for 40 years; apart from his teaching, he inaugurated annual festivals of American music in Rochester; as director and conductor of these festivals, he showed an extraordinary measure of liberal choice, programming not only musical compositions that were naturally congenial to him, but also modern works in dissonant harmonies; and he maintained a friendly attitude toward his students even when they veered away into the field of cosmopolitan abstractions. All told, during his tenure in Rochester, Hanson presented works by 700 composers and something like 1,500 different compositions. In 1925 he completed one of his most significant works, *The Lament for Beowulf,* for Chorus and Orch., based on an Old English saga. In 1930 he wrote his 2nd Sym., entitled *Romantic,* on commission from Koussevitzky and the Boston Sym. Orch. on its 50th anniversary; Koussevitzky conducted its 1st performance on Nov. 28, 1930. Hanson's 3rd Sym. (1936–37) glorified the pioneer spirit of Swedish immigrants; it was presented over the NBC Radio network on March 26, 1938, with Hanson himself conducting. In his Sym. No. 4, subtitled *The Requiem,* written in 1943, Hanson paid tribute to the memory of his father; he conducted its 1st performance with the Boston Sym. Orch. on Dec. 3, 1943; in 1944 the work received the Pulitzer Prize in music. There followed the 5th Sym., *Sinfonia Sacra,* in a single movement (1954); in it Hanson invoked his deep-rooted Christian faith; it was 1st performed by the Philadelphia Orch. on Feb. 18, 1955. Hanson wrote his 6th Sym. to commemorate the 125th anniversary of the N.Y. Phil.; Leonard Bernstein conducted it on leap-year day of 1968. Hanson's 7th Sym., *A Sea Symphony,* with Chorus, derived from Whitman's poem, was 1st performed on Aug. 7, 1977, at the National Music Camp at Interlochen. Whitman's poetry was close to Hanson's creative imagination; he wrote several other works based on Whitman's poems, among them 3 *Songs from "Drum Taps"* (1935); *Song of Democracy,* which Hanson conducted in Philadelphia on April 9, 1957; and *The Mystic Trumpeter,* performed in Kansas City on April 26, 1970. Hanson remained faithful to his musical and philosophical convictions throughout his long career. Like Sibelius, he wrote music of profound personal feeling, set in an idiom which reflected the triumphs and laments of his life and of his double inheritance. In 1933 he composed his opera, *Merry Mount,* based on *The Maypole Lovers of Merry Mount* by Nathaniel Hawthorne. Hanson dedicated the work to the memory of George Eastman, who had committed suicide 2 years before. Hanson conducted its 1st performance in concert form in Ann Arbor on May 20, 1933; on Feb. 10, 1934, it was produced by the Metropolitan Opera in N.Y., conducted by Tullio Serafin. It was one of the few operas by an American composer staged at the Metropolitan, and the production was very successful; according to reports, there was a total of 50 curtain calls for Hanson and the singers after its 4 acts. Despite this popular reception and favorable critical reviews, the opera had only 4 performances, and was not retained in the repertoire, a fate not unlike that of other American operas produced at the Metropolitan. A symphonic suite drawn from the score enjoyed frequent performances at summer sym. concerts and on the radio.

In the meantime, Hanson continued an active career as a conductor. In 1932 he led several concerts of American music in major cities of Europe. During 1961–62 he took the Eastman School Phil. Orch. on a grand European tour, under the auspices of the State Dept.; Hanson received a most gratifying success; he was praised as both a composer and an able conductor; his school orch. also received its share of appreciation. As an educator, Hanson enjoyed great prestige; many talented American composers studied under him. He received numerous honorary degrees. In 1935 he was elected a member of the National Inst. of Arts and Letters; in 1938 he became a fellow of the Royal Academy of Music in Sweden. He held, at various times, a presidency of the National Assoc. of Schools of Music; served also as president of the Music Teachers National Assoc. and of the National Music Council. He was awarded 19 honorary doctorates in music, among them from Syracuse Univ., Univ. of Nebraska, Northwestern Univ., New England Cons. of Music, and Univ. of Michigan. In 1945 he received the Ditson Award, and in 1946 was given the George Foster Peabody Award. But with the radical changes in contemporary composition, Hanson's music seemed to recede into an old-fashioned irrelevance; the number of performances of his music dwindled; only occasionally were his syms. broadcast from old recordings. Hanson never tried to conceal his bitterness at this loss of appreciation in his country for whose artistic progress he labored so mightily. Yet his music cannot in all fairness be judged as unredeemingly obsolete. His array of sonorous harmonies, often in modulations at a tritone's distance of their respective tonics, reaches the borderline of pungent bitonality; his bold asymmetrical rhythms retain their vitality; his orchestration is masterly in its instrumental treatment. True, Hanson never accepted the modern techniques of serialism or a total emancipation of dissonance; yet he maintained a liberal attitude toward these new developments. Many of his conservative conservatory admirers were surprised by the publication of his book, *Harmonic Materials of Modern Music* (1960), in which he presented an exhaustive inventory of advanced harmonic formulas, tabulating them according to their combinatory potentialities.

WORKS: STAGE: *California Forest Play of 1920,* ballet, with Solo Voices, Chorus, and Orch. (1919; Calif. State Redwood Park, 1920); *Merry Mount,* opera in 3 acts (1933, commissioned by the Metropolitan Opera; concert perf., Ann Arbor, May 20, 1933; 1st stage perf., Metropolitan Opera, N.Y., Feb. 10, 1934); *Nymph and Satyr,* ballet (1978; Chautauqua, N.Y., Aug. 9, 1979).

ORCH.: *Symphonic Prelude* (1916); *Symphonic Legend* (San Francisco, 1917); *Symphonic Rhapsody* (1920; Los Angeles, May 26, 1921); *Before the Dawn*, symphonic poem (Los Angeles, 1920); *Exultation*, symphonic poem with Piano obbligato (San Francisco, 1920); Concerto for Organ, Strings, and Harp (1921); 7 syms.: No. 1, *Nordic Symphony* (1922; Rome, May 30, 1923, composer conducting; 1st U.S. perf., Rochester, N.Y., March 19, 1924); No. 2, *Romantic Symphony* (1928–30; commissioned for the 50th anniversary of the Boston Sym. Orch., Koussevitzky conducting, Nov. 28, 1930); No. 3 (1937–38; 1st complete perf., NBC Sym. Orch., March 26, 1938, composer conducting; 1st public perf., Boston Sym. Orch., Nov. 3, 1939, composer conducting); No. 4, *Requiem* (Boston Sym. Orch., Dec. 3, 1943, composer conducting; won Pulitzer Prize of 1944); No. 5, *Sinfonia Sacra* (1954; Philadelphia Orch., Feb. 18, 1955); No. 6 (1967; N.Y. Phil., Feb. 29, 1968, Bernstein conducting); No. 7, *A Sea Symphony*, after Whitman, for Chorus and Orch. (Interlochen, Mich., Aug. 7, 1977; for the 50th anniversary of the National Music Camp there); *North and West*, symphonic poem with Choral obbligato (1923; N.Y., 1924); *Lux Aeterna*, symphonic poem with Viola obbligato (1923); *Pan and the Priest*, symphonic poem with Piano obbligato (1925–26; London, Oct. 26, 1926); Concerto for Organ and Orch. (1926; Rochester, N.Y., Jan. 6, 1927; uses themes from *North and West*); *Merry Mount Suite* (1937; from the opera); *Fantasy* for String Orch. (1939; based on the String Quartet of 1923); *Serenade* for Flute, Harp, and Strings (1945; also arranged for Flute and Piano); Piano Concerto (Boston Sym. Orch., Dec. 31, 1948, composer conducting); *Pastorale* for Oboe, Harp, and Strings (1949; also arranged for Oboe and Piano); *Fantasy-Variations on a Theme of Youth* for Piano and Strings (for the Northwestern Univ. Centennial, Feb. 18, 1951); *Elegy in Memory of My Friend, Serge Koussevitzky* (Boston Sym. Orch., Jan. 20, 1956); *Mosaics* (1957; Cleveland Orch., Jan. 23, 1958); *Summer Seascape I* for Orch. (New Orleans, March 10, 1959); *Summer Seascape II* for Strings (1965); *Bold Island Suite* (1959–61; Cleveland Orch., Jan. 25, 1962); *For the 1st Time* (Rochester Univ., 1963); *Dies Natalis I* (1967); *Young Composer's Guide to the 6-tone Scale*, suite for Piano, Winds, and Percussion (1971–72). **BAND:** *March Carillon* (1920; arranged for Band by Erik Leidzen); *Chorale and Alleluia* (1953); *Centennial March* (1968); *Dies Natalis II* (1972); *Laude* (1974). **VOCAL:** *The Lament for Beowulf* for Chorus and Orch. (1923–25; Ann Arbor Festival, 1926); *Heroic Elegy* for Orch. and Chorus without words (for the Beethoven centenary, 1927); *3 Songs from "Drum Taps,"* after Whitman, for Baritone, Chorus, and Orch. (1935); *Hymn to the Pioneers* for Men's Voices a cappella (1938); *The Cherubic Hymn* for Chorus and Orch. (1948–49); *Centennial Ode* for Narrator, Baritone, Chorus, and Orch. (1950); *How Excellent Thy Name* for Chorus and Piano (1952); *The Song of Democracy* for Chorus and Orch. (1956; Philadelphia, April 9, 1957); *The Song of Human Rights*, cantata for Speaking Chorus and Orch., to the Universal Declaration of Human Rights (Washington, D.C., Dec. 10, 1963); *4 Psalms* for Baritone, Solo Cello, and String Sextet (Washington, D.C., Oct. 31, 1964); *2 Psalms: Psalm 150 (A Jubilant Song)* for Chorus and Orch. (1965) and *Psalm 121* for Chorus and Orch. (1968); *Streams in the Desert* for Chorus and Orch. (1969); *The Mystic Trumpeter* for Narrator, Chorus, and Orch. (1969; Kansas City, Mo., April 26, 1970); *New Land, New Covenant* for Soloist, Children's Chorus, Mixed Chorus, and Orch., to words by Isaac Watts, T.S. Eliot, and John Newton, and from the Bible and the Declaration of Independence (1976; Bryn Mawr, Pa., May 2, 1976); *Prayer for the Middle Ages* for Chorus a cappella (1976); songs. **CHAMBER:** Piano Quintet (1916); *Concerto da Camera* for Piano and String Quartet (1916–17; version for Strings Alone, Rome, March 20, 1922); String Quartet (1923). **PIANO:** *Prelude and Double Concert Fugue* for 2 Pianos (1915); *4 Poems* (1917–18); Sonata (1918); *3 Miniatures* (1918–19); *Scandinavian Suite* (1919); *3 Études* (1920); *2 Yule-Tide Pieces* (1920).

WRITINGS: *Harmonic Materials of Modern Music: Resources of the Tempered Scale* (N.Y., 1960).

BIBL.: E. Royce, "H. H.," in H. Cowell's *American Composers on American Music* (Stanford, 1933); B. Tuthill, "H. H.," *Musical Quarterly* (April 1936); M. Alter, "H. H.," *Modern Music* (Jan.–Feb. 1941); R. Watanabe, "H. H.'s Manuscript Scores," *The University of Rochester Library Bulletin*, vol. V, no. 2 (Winter 1950); B. Wehrung, "A Life in American Music," *Le Grand Baton* (March 1981; with discography by N. Brown).

Hanssens, Charles-Louis, Belgian cellist, conductor, and composer; b. Ghent, July 12, 1802; d. Brussels, April 8, 1871. As a child of 10 he played in the orch. of the National Theater in Amsterdam; was 1st cellist of the orch. in the Brussels theater (1824–27); then taught harmony at the Brussels Cons.; subsequently conducted opera at The Hague and in Ghent. From 1848 to 1869 he was conductor at the Théâtre de la Monnaie in Brussels.

WORKS: 8 operas; 15 ballets; 9 syms.; overtures; orch. fantasies; Violin Concerto; Cello Concerto; Clarinet Concerto; several piano concertos; string quartets; masses; cantatas; a cappella choruses.

BIBL.: L. de Burbure, *Notice sur C.-L. H.* (Antwerp, 1872); L. Bäwolf, *C.-L. H.* (Brussels, 1895).

Hanuš, Jan, Czech composer; b. Prague, May 2, 1915. He studied composition privately with Jeremiáš (1932–40), and conducting with Pavel Dědeček at the Prague Cons. (1940). He then devoted himself to editorial work in music publishing houses; was an assistant in preparing the complete critical ed. of Dvořák's collected works; also completed the instrumentations of the unfinished operas *Tkalci* by Nejedlý and *Balada o lásce* by Doubrava. His own music is marked by lyrical Romanticism, not without stringent dissonant textures.

WORKS: 4 operas: *Plameny* (Flames; 1942–44; Pilsen, 1956), *Sluha dvou pánů* (Servant of 2 Masters; 1958; Pilsen, 1959), *Pochodeň Prometheova* (The Torch of Prometheus; 1961–63; Prague, 1965), *Pohádka jedné noci* (The Story of 1 Night; 1965–68); 2 ballets: *Sůl nad zlato* (Salt Is Worth More than Gold; 1953) and *Othello* (1956); 2 cantatas: *The Country Speaks* (1940) and *The Song of Hope* (1945–48); *Rondo capriccio* for Orch. (1937); 6 syms. (with Solo Alto, 1942; 1951; 1957; 1960; 1965; 1978); *The Eulogy*, sinfonietta for Soprano and Orch. (1945); *Concertante Symphony* for Organ, Harp, Timpani, and Strings (1954); *Petr a Lucie* (Peter and Lucia), symphonic fantasy (1955); *Overture*, after Walt Whitman's "The Bugler's Secret" (1961); Double Concerto for Oboe, Harp, and Orch. (1965); *Relay Race*, symphonic allegro (1968); *Pražská nokturna* (Prague Nocturne) for Chamber Orch. (1972–73); *3 Essays* for Orch. (1975–76); *Variations and Collage* for Orch. (1982–83); Fantasy for String Quartet (1939); *Sonata-Rhapsody* for Cello and Piano (1941); *Suite to Paintings by Mánes* for Violin and Piano (1948); *A Year in Bohemia* for Children's Chorus, and Piano or Chamber Orch. (1949–52); Serenade for Nonet (1953); Viola Sonatina (1958); *Suita dramatica* for String Quartet (1959); *3 Portraits from "Othello"* for Violin and Piano (1960); *Frescoes*, piano trio (1961); *Suita domestica* for Wind Quintet (1964); *Poselství* (The Message), triptych for Baritone, Chorus, 2 Prepared Pianos, Electric Guitar, Percussion, and Tape (1969); *Musica concertante* for Cello, Piano, Winds, and Percussion (1969–70); Concertino for 2 Percussionists and Tape (1972); *The Swallow*, concerto piccolo for Chorus, Flute, and Cello (1973); *Tower Music* for Brass Quintet (1976); *In Praise of Chamber Music*, sextet for Flute, Oboe, Violin, Viola, Cello, and Harpsichord (1979); *Meditations* for Piano (1938–39; rev. 1974); Preludes for Piano (1949); *Suita lyrica* for Organ (1957); *Contemplazioni* for Organ (1969); Canons for Children's Chorus (1971–72); *Ecce Homo*, oratorio (1980); *Glagolitic Mass* for Bass, Chorus, Organ, and Bells (1985); songs.

Hanuszewska-Schaeffer, Mieczyslawa Janina, Polish writer on music; b. Borszów, Oct. 1, 1929. She studied musicology with Jachimecki at the Jagiello Univ. in Krakow. In 1963 she joined the staff of Krakow's *Zycie Literackie*, producing a weekly chronicle on the world's music, and also extensive articles on modern music; she was a contributor to *Wielka Encyklopedia Muzyczna* and *The New Grove Dictionary of Music and Musicians* (1980). With her husband, **Boguslaw Schaeffer,** she ed. *Almanach wspólszesnych kompozytorów polskich* (Almanac of Modern Polish Composers; Krakow, 1966; new ed., 1989); she also edited *1000 kompozytorów* (1,000 Composers; 5th ed., Krakow, 1986).

Harasiewicz, Adam, Polish pianist; b. Chodziez, July 1, 1932. He studied with Kazimierz Mirski until 1950; then at the Krakow State College of Music. He entered the Chopin Contest in 1949, but failed to win a prize. In 1955 he competed again and won 1st prize.

Harasowski, Adam, Polish pianist and writer on music; b. Delatyn, Sept. 16, 1904. He was brought up in a musical family. He studied at the Lwow Cons. with Adam Soltys (1923–29); also took private lessons in composition with Szymanowski during his frequent visits at Lwow. Concurrently he studied mechanical engineering, graduating from the Lwow Polytechnic in 1931, and subsequently earned his living mainly as an engineering draftsman. At the outbreak of World War II he went to England with the Polish Air Force, and remained with the Royal Air Force of Great Britain as a flight lieutenant (1943–58); then devoted himself to journalism, both in Polish and in English; publ. *The Skein of Legends around Chopin* (Glasgow, 1967); also compiled collections of Polish songs.

Harászti, Emile, Hungarian musicologist; b. Nagyvárad, Nov. 1, 1885; d. Paris, Dec. 27, 1958. He studied composition and musicology in Vienna, Munich, Leipzig, Berlin, and Paris. Returning to Budapest, he served as the music critic of the *Budapest Hirlap* (1908–30); lectured on music at the Budapest Cons. (1918–27). In 1945 he went to Paris. Among his publications are *La Musique hongroise* (Paris, 1933), *Béla Bartók, His Life and Works* (Oxford, 1938), and *Un Centenaire romantique: Berlioz et la Marche Hongroise d'après des documents inédits* (Paris, 1946).

Harbach (real name, **Hauerbach**), **Otto (Abels),** American lyricist and librettist; b. Salt Lake City, Aug. 18, 1873; d. N.Y., Jan. 24, 1963. He studied at Knox College and Columbia Univ. In 1908 he collaborated with the composer Karl Hoschna on the successful musical *Three Twins;* subsequently wrote more than 40 works for Broadway, with such composers as Oscar Hammerstein II, Rudolf Friml, Vincent Youmans, Jerome Kern, and Sigmund Romberg; he also wrote for films. His most popular lyrics included *Rose-Marie* and *Indian Love Call* from Friml's *Rose-Marie* (with Hammerstein; 1924), *The Night Was Made for Love* from Kern's *The Cat and the Fiddle* (1931), and *Smoke Gets in Your Eyes* from Kern's *Roberta* (1932).

Harbison, John (Harris), significant American composer; b. Orange, N.J., Dec. 20, 1938. He grew up in a highly intellectual environment; his father was a prof. of history at Princeton Univ. and his mother was a magazine writer; both were musically endowed. Exceptionally versatile, Harbison studied violin, viola, piano, voice, and tuba at Princeton High School and also took lessons in music theory. In 1956 he entered Harvard Univ. as a composition student of Piston (B.A., 1960), receiving a Paine Traveling Fellowship for a season of study with Boris Blacher in Berlin. Returning to the U.S., he studied composition privately with Roger Sessions and with Earl Kim at Princeton Univ. (M.F.A., 1963). From 1963 to 1968 he was a member of the Soc. of Fellows at Harvard, and from 1969 to 1982 taught at the Mass. Inst. of Technology; was composer-in-residence of the Pittsburgh Sym. Orch. (1982–84) and of the Los Angeles Phil. (1985–88). He also made numerous appearances as a conductor; led the Cantata Singers (1969–73; 1980–82). In 1977 he held a Guggenheim fellowship, and in 1987 received the Pulitzer Prize in Music for his vocal work *The Flight into Egypt* (1986). Equipped with a thorough knowledge of modern compositional technique, Harbison wrote music free from doctrinaire pedestrianism; yet in his melodic structures he adumbrated dodecaphonic procedures. In his Shakespearean opera, *The Winter's Tale,* he introduced innovative "dumb shows" acted in pantomime on the stage; in his opera *Full Moon in March,* he made use of the "prepared piano," by which the sonorities are altered by manipulating the strings of the piano. He further made use of ready-made recordings for special effects. **WORKS: OPERAS:** *The Winter's Tale,* after Shakespeare (1974; San Francisco, Aug. 20, 1979); *Full Moon in March,* after Yeats (1977; Cambridge, Mass., April 30, 1979). **BALLETS:** *Ulysses' Bow* (1983; Pittsburgh, May 11, 1984); *Ulysses' Raft* (1983; New Haven, Conn., March 6, 1984). **ORCH.:** *Sinfonia* for Violin and Double Orch. (1963); *Descant-Nocturne* (1976); *Diotima* (1976; Boston, March 10, 1977); *Piano Concerto* (1978; N.Y., May 12, 1980); *Violin Concerto* (1980; N.Y., Jan. 24, 1981); *Sym. No. 1* (1981; Boston, March 22, 1984); *Sym. No. 2* (San Francisco, May 13, 1987); *Concerto for Oboe, Clarinet, and Strings* (Sarasota, Fla., June 14, 1985); *Remembering Gatsby* (Atlanta, Sept. 11, 1986); *Viola Concerto* (Princeton, N.J., May 18, 1990). **CHAMBER:** *Serenade* for 6 Players (1968); *Bermuda Triangle* for Tenor Saxophone, Amplified Cello, and Electric Organ (1970); *Woodwind Quintet* (1979); *Piano Quintet* (1981); *Variations* for Clarinet, Violin, and Piano (1982); *String Quartet No. 1* (1985); *Music for 18 Wind Instruments* (Boston, April 18, 1986); *Christmas Concerto* for Brass Quintet (1987); *String Quartet No. 2* (1987). **VOCAL:** *Autumnal* (1965); *Shakespeare Series* (1965); *Elegiac Songs* for Mezzo-soprano and Chamber Orch., to poems by Emily Dickinson (1973; N.Y., Jan. 12, 1974); *Book of Hours and Seasons* (1975); *Moments of Vision* (1975); *Samuel Chapter,* to biblical texts (1978); *The Flower-fed Buffaloes* for Baritone and Chorus (1976; N.Y., Feb. 27, 1978); *Mottetti di Montale* (1980); *Mirabai Songs* (1982); *The Flight into Egypt,* to biblical texts (Boston, Nov. 21, 1986; Pulitzer Prize); *The Natural World* for Mezzo-soprano and 5 Instruments (1987; Los Angeles, Nov. 13, 1989).

Harburg, E.Y. (Edgar "Yip"), American lyricist; b. N.Y., April 8, 1898; d. Los Angeles (in a car accident), March 5, 1981. He graduated from the City College of N.Y. in 1921; then was co-proprietor of an electrical appliance company, which failed during the Depression; he then began to write lyrics for Broadway; with Jay Gorney he produced the famous song *Brother, Can You Spare a Dime.* In 1939 he won an Academy Award for *Over the Rainbow* from *The Wizard of Oz;* his other lyrics included *We're Off to See the Wizard, It's Only a Paper Moon,* and *April in Paris* (to music by Vernon Duke). He was lyricist and co-author, with Burton Lane and Fred Saidy, of *Finian's Rainbow.*

d'Harcourt, Eugène, French conductor and composer; b. Paris, May 2, 1859; d. Locarno, March 4, 1918. He studied at the Paris Cons. with Massenet, Durand, and Savard (1882–86); then took courses in Berlin with Bargiel. In 1892 he built the Salle d'Harcourt in Paris, where he presented 3 seasons of Concerts Éclectiques Populaires. He wrote an unsuccessful opera, *Le Tasse* (Monte Carlo, 1903), in addition to 3 unnecessary syms. and some passable chamber music.

d'Harcourt, Marguerite (née **Béclard**), French folk-song collector and composer; b. Paris, Feb. 24, 1884; d. there, Aug. 2, 1964. She studied composition with Vincent d'Indy and Maurice Emmanuel; composed 2 syms.; *Rapsodie péruvienne* for Oboe, Clarinet, and Bassoon; and many songs. With her husband, Raoul d'Harcourt, she publ. a valuable treatise, *Musique des Incas et ses survivances* (2 vols., Paris, 1925), based on materials gathered during their journeys in Peru; another valuable publication which she compiled was a collection of 240 songs, *Chansons folkloriques françaises au Canada* (Quebec, 1956).

Hardegg, Grad, Austrian pianist and composer; b. Vienna, April 24, 1834; d. there, March 22, 1867. He was a piano pupil of Czerny, and composed a number of pieces of salon music which became popular.

d'Hardelot, Guy (Mrs. W.I. Rhodes, née **Helen Guy),** French song composer; b. 1858 at the Château d'Hardelot,

Boulogne-sur-Mer; d. London, Jan. 7, 1936. She studied at the Paris Cons.; traveled with Emma Calvé in the U.S. in 1896; then married, and settled in London. She wrote many melodious songs: *Sans toi; Because* (very popular); *Tristesse;* etc.

Harding, A(lbert) A(ustin), American bandmaster; b. Georgetown, Ill., Feb. 10, 1880; d. Champaign, Ill., Dec. 3, 1958. At 14 he began to play cornet, then trombone and other wind instruments. After graduation from high school in Paris, Ill., he conducted the local concert band. In 1902 he enrolled as an engineering student at the Univ. of Illinois, acquiring his bachelor's degree in 1906. At the same time he developed many campus music contacts, and in 1905 was made acting leader of the Univ. Band; in 1907 he was appointed director, a post he held until 1948. Harding was the 1st to succeed in raising college bands to a "symphonic" level in which oboes, saxophones, and other reed instruments supplied variety to the common brass-heavy contingent; thanks to this sonic enhancement, he was able to arrange orch. works of the general repertoire and perform them in a satisfactory musical manner; he was credited with 147 such transcriptions. John Philip Sousa, who greatly admired Harding, bequeathed to him and his band his own entire music library. Harding was a charter founder of the American Bandmasters' Assoc. in 1929 and was its president in 1937–38; was honorary life president from 1956 until his death. He also was active in founding the College Band Directors' Assoc., of which he was honorary life president from its founding in 1941.

BIBL.: C. Weber, "A.A. H.: Pioneer College Bandmaster," *Journal of Band Research* (Autumn 1966).

Harewood, Sir George (Henry Hubert Lascelles), 7th Earl of, distinguished English arts administrator, music critic, and music editor; b. London, Feb. 7, 1923. He was educated at Eton and King's College, Cambridge; served as captain in the Grenadier Guards in World War II; was wounded and taken prisoner in 1944. He was founder and ed. of the magazine *Opera* (1950–53); was on the board of directors of the Royal Opera, Covent Garden (1951–53; 1969–72); served as chairman of the Music Advisory Committee of the British Council (1956–66), artistic director of the Edinburgh International Festival (1961–65), and chancellor of the Univ. of York (1962–67). In 1972 he was appointed managing director of the Sadler's Wells Opera (known after 1974 as the English National Opera); retained this position until 1985. He was knighted in 1986. He ed. Kobbé's *Complete Opera Book* in 1954, 1963, and 1972; it was publ. as *The New Kobbé's Complete Opera Book* in 1976, then as *The Definitive Kobbé's Opera Book* (1987).

Harich-Schneider, Eta (Margarete), German musicologist and harpsichordist; b. Oranienburg, Nov. 16, 1897; d. Vienna, Oct. 16, 1986. She studied piano and musicology in Berlin, making her debut in 1924 with the 1st performance of Hindemith's *1922 Suite.* She then studied harpsichord with Landowska (1929–35), subsequently forming an early-music ensemble; then became a prof. at the Berlin Hochschule für Musik, but was dismissed in 1940 when she refused to join the Nazi party. She then fled to Tokyo, where she directed the music dept. of the U.S. Army College and also taught Western music at the imperial court (1947–49). After her move to N.Y. in 1949, she pursued Japanese studies at Columbia Univ.; she also took courses in sociology at the New School for Social Research (M.A., 1955). From 1955 to 1961 she taught harpsichord at the Vienna Academy of Music. She wrote important books on harpsichord technique and repertoire and on Japanese art music; also made notable recordings of works by the Baroque masters and of collections of Japanese music. She received a Guggenheim fellowship in 1955.

WRITINGS: *Die Kunst des Cembalospiels* (Kassel, 1939; 3rd ed., 1970); *Gendai ongaku to Nippon no sakkyokusha* (Contemporary Music and Japanese Composers, Tokyo, 1950); *The Harpsichord: An Introduction to Technique, Style and the Historical Sources* (Kassel, 1954; 3rd ed., 1973); *A History of Japanese Music* (London, 1973).

Harline, Leigh, American composer; b. Salt Lake City, March 26, 1907; d. Long Beach, Calif., Dec. 10, 1969. He studied music at the Univ. of Utah; went to Los Angeles in 1928 and became arranger for Walt Disney (1931–42); then worked as a film-music composer in Hollywood; his song *When You Wish upon a Star* received an Academy Award in 1940.

Harling, William Franke, English-American composer; b. London, Jan. 18, 1887; d. Sierra Madre, Calif., Nov. 22, 1958. He was taken to the U.S. in his infancy; filled various jobs as a church organist. Eventually he settled in Hollywood. He wrote a 1-act opera, *A Light from St. Agnes* (Chicago, Dec. 26, 1925); a "native opera with jazz," *Deep River* (Lancaster, Pa., Sept. 18, 1926; N.Y., Oct. 4, 1926); some instrumental music; and more than 100 songs. He was also the composer of the march *West Point Forever.*

Harman, Carter, American music critic, recording-firm executive, and composer; b. N.Y., June 14, 1918. He studied with Sessions at Princeton Univ. (B.A., 1940) and continued his studies at Columbia Univ. (M.A., 1949). He was a music critic for the *N.Y. Times* (1947–52) and later music ed. of *Time* magazine (1952–57); from 1958 to 1967 he lived in Puerto Rico, where he became president of the West Indies Recording Corp. In 1967 Harman became producer and executive vice-president of Composers Recordings, Inc., in N.Y., devoted mainly to recording contemporary American music; was its executive director from 1976 to 1984. He publ. *A Popular History of Music from Gregorian Chant to Jazz* (N.Y., 1956; rev. 1968).

WORKS: Ballet, *Blackface* (N.Y., May 18, 1947); children's operas: *Circus at the Opera* (1951) and *Castles in the Sand* (1952); a group of 34 songs for children. In 1974 he began experiments with the total electronic synthesizing of nursery rhymes (with vocal parts accomplished by using a Sonovox and "artificial larynx") for an "entertainment" called *Alex and the Singing Synthesizer,* completed in 1977.

Harmat, Artur, Hungarian composer; b. Nyitrabajna, June 27, 1885; d. Budapest, April 20, 1962. He studied at the Budapest Academy of Music and later took courses in Prague and Berlin. From 1920 to 1946 he was an inspector of singing in the Budapest schools; from 1924 to 1959 he was a prof. of religious music at the Budapest Academy of Music. He wrote 2 valuable manuals on counterpoint (1947, 1956) and composed a great quantity of church music, based on the lines of Palestrina's polyphony.

WORKS: *Te Deum* for Chorus and Organ (1912–29); *Tu es Petrus* for Chorus and Orch. (1929); *Psalm 150* for Chorus and Instruments (1929); *De Profundis* for a cappella Chorus (1932); *Szép Ilonka* (Fair Helen), cantata (1954); Organ Sonata (1956).

Harmati, Sándor, Hungarian-American violinist, conductor, and composer; b. Budapest, July 9, 1892; d. Flemington, N.J., April 4, 1936. He studied at the Budapest Academy of Music; went to the U.S. in 1914 and became a member of the Letz Quartet (1917–21), then of the Lennox Quartet (1922–25); from 1925 to 1930 he was conductor of the Omaha Sym. Orch. He composed a Symphonic Poem, a String Quartet, and several works for violin, as well as piano pieces and songs; his song *Bluebird of Happiness* became popular.

Harnoncourt, Nikolaus, eminent Austrian cellist, conductor, and musicologist; b. Berlin, Dec. 6, 1929. His father, an engineer, also played the piano and composed; the family settled in Graz. He began to study the cello at the age of 9, later training with Paul Grümmer and at the Vienna Academy of Music with Emanuel Brabec. He was a cellist in the Vienna Sym. Orch. (1952–69); founded the Vienna Concentus Musicus (1953), which began giving concerts in 1957, playing on period instruments or modern copies; the group made its 1st tour of England, the U.S., and Canada in 1966. From the mid-1970s he also appeared internationally as a guest conductor, expanding his repertoire to include music of later eras. His writings include *Musik als Klangrede: Wege zu einem neuen*

Musikverständnis (Salzburg and Vienna, 1982; Eng. tr., 1988, as *Baroque Music Today: Music as Speech; Ways to a New Understanding of Music*) and *Der musikalische Dialog: Gedanken zu Monteverdi, Bach und Mozart* (Salzburg, 1984; Eng. tr., 1989, as *The Musical Dialogue: Thoughts on Monteverdi, Bach, and Mozart*). His wife, **Alice Harnoncourt** (b. Vienna, Sept. 26, 1930), studied violin with Feist and Moraves in Vienna and with Thibaud in Paris; she became concertmistress of the Vienna Concentus Musicus at its founding.

BIBL.: T. Towe, "N. H.," *Ovation* (May 1985).

Harnoy, Ofra, Israeli-born Canadian cellist; b. Hadera, Jan. 31, 1965. She began cello lessons as a child; in 1972 she emigrated with her family to Canada, where she studied with Vladimir Orloff in Toronto. In 1978 she won 1st prize in the Montreal Sym. Orch. competition, and in 1982 the Concert Artists Guild Award of N.Y. In 1983 she was soloist in the world premiere of a recently discovered Cello Concerto by Offenbach in N.Y. Her performances are marked by excellent technique and compelling musicianship.

BIBL.: R. Matthew-Walker, "O. H.," *Music and Musicians International* (July 1987).

Harper, Edward (James), English composer, pianist, and teacher; b. Taunton, March 17, 1941. After studies at Christ Church, Oxford (1959–63), he received instruction in composition from Gordon Jacob at the Royal College of Music in London (1963–64) and with Donatoni in Milan (1968). From 1964 he lectured on music at the Univ. of Edinburgh, and in 1975 became director of the New Music Group of Scotland.

WORKS: OPERAS: *Fanny Robin* (1974; Edinburgh, Feb. 5, 1975); *Hedda Gabler* (1984–85; Glasgow, June 5, 1985); *The Mellstock Quire* (1987). ORCH.: Piano Concerto (1969; Edinburgh, Jan. 29, 1970); *Sonata* for Chamber Orch. (1971; Edinburgh, Feb. 25, 1973); *Bartók Games* (Edinburgh, Nov. 26, 1972); *Fantasia I* for Chamber Orch. (Edinburgh, March 27, 1976); *Fern Hill* for Chamber Orch. (St. Andrews, Feb. 23, 1977); Sym. (1978–79; Edinburgh, March 1979); Clarinet Concerto (1981–82; Llandaff, June 3, 1982); *Intrada after Monteverdi* for Chamber Orch. (1982; Edinburgh, Oct. 6, 1983); *Fantasia V*, passacaglia for Chamber Orch. (St. Magnus Festival, June 24, 1985). CHAMBER: Quintet for Flute, Clarinet, Violin, Cello, and Piano (Glasgow, May 1974); *Ricercari in Memoriam Luigi Dallapiccola* for Chamber Group (Edinburgh, Aug. 30, 1975); *Fantasia III* for Brass Quintet (Edinburgh, Nov. 3, 1977); String Quartet No. 2 (London, Dec. 17, 1986); also works for chorus.

Harper, Heather (Mary), distinguished Irish soprano; b. Belfast, May 8, 1930. She studied at Trinity College of Music in London and also took voice lessons with Helene Isepp and Frederic Husler; made her debut as Lady Macbeth with the Oxford Univ. Opera in 1954. She was a member of the English Opera Group (1956–75); 1st sang at the Glyndebourne Festival in 1957, at Covent Garden as Helena in *A Midsummer Night's Dream* in 1962, and at the Bayreuth Festival as Elsa in 1967; also sang in the U.S. and South America. In 1990 she made her last public appearance as a singer. From 1985 she was a prof. at the Royal College of Music in London; she also was director of singing studies at the Britten-Pears School in Snape (from 1986). Her notable roles included Arabella, Marguerite, Antonia, Gutrune, Hecuba, Anne Trulove in *The Rake's Progress*, The Woman in *Erwartung*, and Ellen Orford in *Peter Grimes*; she also created the role of Nadia in Tippett's *The Ice Break* (1977). An esteemed concert artist, she sang in the premieres of Britten's *War Requiem* (1962) and Tippett's 3rd Sym. (1972). In 1965 she was made a Commander of the Order of the British Empire.

Harrell, Lynn, outstanding American cellist, son of **Mack Harrell;** b. N.Y., Jan. 30, 1944. He studied at the Juilliard School of Music in N.Y. with Leonard Rose and at the Curtis Inst. of Music in Philadelphia with Orlando Cole; also attended master classes with Piatigorsky in Dallas (1962) and Casals

in Marlboro, Vt. (1963). He made his debut at a young people's concert of the N.Y. Phil. in 1961; then was 1st cellist of the Cleveland Orch. (1965–71). In 1975 he was named co-recipient (with the pianist Murray Perahia) of the 1st Avery Fisher Prize. He taught at the Univ. of Cincinnati College–Cons. of Music from 1971 to 1976; then joined the faculty of Juilliard; subsequently was appointed to the newly established Gregor Piatigorsky Chair at the Univ. of Southern Calif. in Los Angeles (1986). His playing is marked by ingratiating tonal mellowness and a facile, unforced technical display.

BIBL.: H. Kupferberg, "L. H.," *Ovation* (March 1986).

Harrell, Mack, noted American baritone, father of **Lynn Harrell;** b. Celeste, Texas, Oct. 8, 1909; d. Dallas, Jan. 29, 1960. He studied violin and voice at the Juilliard School of Music in N.Y.; after some concerts as a soloist he joined the staff of the Metropolitan Opera (1939–45) and continued to make appearances there between 1946 and 1954; also taught voice at the Juilliard School (1945–56). He publ. a book, *The Sacred Hour of Song* (N.Y., 1938).

Harris, Sir Augustus (Henry Glossop), celebrated English impresario; b. Paris, 1852; d. Folkestone, June 22, 1896. An actor by profession, he became a stage manager and producer (with his brother Charles) with the Mapleson Co. in Manchester in 1873. In 1879 he leased the Drury Lane Theatre in London; in 1887 took up the promotion of Italian opera and secured control of Her Majesty's Theatre, Covent Garden, the Olympia, and various provincial stages. He introduced to the English public many of the most famous singers of his time, among them Melba, Maurel, and the de Reszkes. He was knighted in 1891.

Harris, Donald, American composer and educator; b. St. Paul, Minn., April 7, 1931. He studied composition with Finney at the Univ. of Michigan (B.M., 1952; M.M., 1954), Blacher and Foss at the Berkshire Music Center in Tanglewood (1954–55), Boulanger in Paris, and Jolivet at Aix-en-Provence (1960). In 1968 he joined the faculty and administrative staff of the New England Cons. of Music in Boston, where he was vice-president for academic affairs (1971–74) and executive vice-president (1974–77); in 1977 he became prof. and chairman and in 1980 dean of the composition and theory dept. of the Hartt School of Music in Hartford, Conn. In 1988 he became dean of the College of the Arts at Ohio State Univ. He received a Fulbright fellowship (1956), a Guggenheim fellowship (1966), numerous ASCAP Awards (from 1973), and the ASCAP/Deems Taylor Award (1989) for his co-editorship (with C. Hailey and J. Brand) of the Berg-Schoenberg correspondence (N.Y., 1987). His music follows the trends of the cosmopolitan avant-garde.

WORKS: *The Little Mermaid*, opera (1985–90); *The Legend of John Henry*, ballet (1954; rev. 1979); *The Golden Deer*, ballet (1955); *Intervals*, dance score for Chamber Ensemble (1959); incidental music to Shakespeare's *Twelfth Night* (1989); *Symphony in 2 Movements* (1958–61); *On Variations* for Chamber Orch. (1976); *Prelude to a Concert in Connecticut* (1981); String Quartet (1965); *Ludus* for 10 Instruments (1966) and *Ludus II* for 5 Instruments (1973); *Canzona and Carol* for Double Brass Quintet and Timpani (1986); *Charmes* for Soprano and Orch. (1971–80); *Pierrot Lieder* for Soprano and Chamber Ensemble (1988); other works.

Harris, Emmylou, American singer of country and pop songs; b. Birmingham, Ala., April 12, 1947. She studied drama at the Univ. of North Carolina; then made appearances as a successful singer of folk music, extending her repertoire in the kindred genres of country and pop music.

Harris, Roy (Leroy Ellsworth), significant American composer; b. Chandler, Okla., Feb. 12, 1898; d. Santa Monica, Calif., Oct. 1, 1979. His parents, of Irish and Scottish descent, settled in Oklahoma; in 1903 the family moved to California, where Harris had private music lessons with Henry Schoenfeld and Arthur Farwell. In 1926 he went to Paris, where he studied composition with Nadia Boulanger; was able to continue his stay in Paris thanks to 2 consecutive Guggenheim fellowship awards (1927, 1928). Upon return to the U.S. he lived in California and in N.Y.; several of his works were performed and attracted favorable attention; Farwell publ. an article in the *Musical Quarterly* (Jan. 1932) in which he enthusiastically welcomed Harris as an American genius. In his compositions, Harris showed a talent of great originality, with a strong melodic and rhythmic speech that is indigenously American. He developed a type of modal symbolism akin to Greek ethos, with each particular mode related to a certain emotional state. Instrumental music is the genre in which he particularly excelled. He never wrote an opera or an oratorio, but made astute use of choral masses in some of his works. He held the following teaching positions: Westminster Choir School, Princeton (1934–35); Cornell Univ. (1941–43); Colorado College (1943–48); Utah State Agricultural College in Logan (1948–49); Peabody College for Teachers at Nashville (1949–51); Sewanee, Tenn. (1951); Pa. College for Women (1951–56); Univ. of Southern Illinois (1956–57); Indiana Univ. (1957–60); Inter-American Univ., San Germán, Puerto Rico (1960–61); Univ. of Calif., Los Angeles (1961–73). In 1973 he was appointed composer-in-residence at Calif. State Univ., Los Angeles, a post he held until his death. He received honorary D.Mus. degrees from Rutgers Univ. and the Univ. of Rochester in N.Y.; in 1942 he was awarded the Elizabeth Sprague Coolidge Medal "for eminent services to chamber music." In 1936 he married the pianist **Johana Harris** (née **Beula Duffey; b.** Ottawa, Ontario, Jan. 1, 1913); she assumed her professional name Johana in honor of J.S. Bach; the single *n* is used owing to some esoteric numerologic considerations to which Harris was partial. After his death, she married, on Dec. 18, 1982, her 21-year-old piano student John Heggie.

WORKS: ORCH.: 13 syms.: No. 1 (Boston, Jan. 26, 1934); No. 2 (Boston, Feb. 28, 1936); No. 3 (Boston, Feb. 24, 1939; his best-known and most frequently perf. work; it was the 1st American sym. to be played in China, during the 1973 tour of the Philadelphia Orch. under the direction of Eugene Ormandy); No. 4, *Folksong Symphony,* with Chorus (Cleveland, Dec. 26, 1940); No. 5 (Boston, Feb. 26, 1943); No. 6, *Gettysburg Address* (Boston, April 14, 1944); No. 7 (Chicago, Nov. 20, 1952); No. 8 (San Francisco, Jan. 17, 1962); No. 9 (Philadelphia, Jan. 18, 1963); No. 10, *Abraham Lincoln Symphony* for Chorus, Brass, 2 Amplified Pianos, and Percussion (Long Beach, Calif., April 14, 1965); No. 11 (N.Y., Feb. 8, 1968); No. 12, *Pere Marquette Symphony,* for Tenor/Speaker and Orch. (1968–69; final version, Milwaukee, Nov. 8, 1969); No. 13, *Bicentennial Symphony 1976,* for Chorus and Orch. (1975; premiered as No. 14, Washington, D.C., Feb. 10, 1976); Sym. for Band (West Point, N.Y., May 30, 1952); *When Johnny Comes Marching Home,* symphonic overture (Minneapolis, Jan. 13, 1935); *Farewell to Pioneers,* symphonic elegy (Philadelphia, March 27, 1936); Concerto for 2 Pianos and Orch. (Denver, Jan. 21, 1947); *Kentucky Spring* (Louisville, Ky., April 5, 1949); Violin Concerto (1949–51; Wilmington, N.C., March 21, 1984); Piano Concerto (Louisville, Dec. 9, 1953); *Fantasy* for Piano and Orch. (Hartford, Conn., Nov. 17, 1954); *Epilogue to Profiles in Courage: J.F.K.* (Los Angeles, May 10, 1964); *These Times* for Orch., with Piano (1962); Concerto for Amplified Piano, Wind Instruments, and Percussion (1968). **VOCAL:** *Whitman Triptych* for Women's Voices and Piano (1927); *A Song for Occupations,* after Whitman, for Chorus a cappella (1934); *Symphony for Voices,* after Whitman, for Chorus a cappella (Princeton, May 20, 1936); *American Creed* for Chorus and Orch. (Chicago, Oct. 30, 1940); Mass for Men's Voices and Organ (N.Y., May 13, 1948); *Canticle to the Sun* for Coloratura Soprano and Chamber Orch., after St. Francis (Washington, D.C., Sept. 12, 1961); *Jubilation* for Chorus, Brasses, and Piano (San Francisco, May 16, 1964). **CHAMBER:** Concerto for Clarinet, Piano, and String Quartet (Paris, May 8, 1927); 3 string quartets (1930, 1933, 1939); String Sextet (1932); Fantasy for Piano, Flute, Oboe, Clarinet, Bassoon, and Horn (Pasadena, Calif., April 10, 1932); Piano Trio (1934); Quintet for Piano and Strings (1936); *Soliloquy and Dance* for Viola and Piano

(1939); String Quintet (1940). **PIANO:** Sonata (1929); *Variations on an Irish Theme* (1938); *Little Suite* (1938); *American Ballads* (1942).

BIBL.: A. Farwell, "R. H.," *Musical Quarterly* (Jan. 1932); H. Cowell, "R. H.," *American Composers on American Music* (Stanford, Calif., 1933); W. Piston, "R. H.," *Modern Music* (Jan.–Feb. 1934); N. Slonimsky, "R. H.," *Musical Quarterly* (Jan. 1947); D. Stehman and C. Gibbs, "R. H.," *Ovation* (July 1984); D. Stehman, *R. H.: An American Musical Pioneer* (Boston, 1984).

Harris, (William) Victor, American pianist, conductor, and composer; b. N.Y., April 27, 1869; d. there, Feb. 15, 1943. He studied voice and organ; music theory with Fred K. Schilling, and conducting with Anton Seidl. He subsequently served as organist at various churches in N.Y., and was conductor of the St. Cecilia Club in N.Y. (1902–36). He publ. about 150 songs, some of which enjoyed considerable popularity.

Harrison, Beatrice, English cellist, sister of **May Harrison;** b. Roorkee, India, Dec. 9, 1892; d. Smallfield, Surrey, March 10, 1965. She was taken to England in infancy; entered the Royal College of Music in London; won a prize at the age of 10; she was 14 when she made her 1st public appearance as a soloist with an orch. (London, May 29, 1907); then went to Berlin, where she took lessons with Hugo Becker; was the winner of the prestigious Mendelssohn Prize. She made several European tours, most of them in company with her sister; toured the U.S. in 1913 and 1932.

Harrison, Frank (Francis) Ll(ewellyn), Irish musicologist; b. Dublin, Sept. 29, 1905; d. Tunbridge Wells, Dec. 31, 1987. He studied in Dublin at the Royal Irish Academy of Music and at Trinity College (Mus.B., 1926; Mus.D., 1929); later was a postdoctoral fellow under Schrade and Hindemith at Yale Univ. (1946). He taught at Queen's Univ., Kingston, Ontario (1935–46); Colgate Univ. (1946–47); Washington Univ. in St. Louis (1947–52); Oxford Univ. (1952–70); and the Univ. of Amsterdam (1970–76). He helped launch the Early English Church Music series, serving as its general ed. from 1961 to 1972; held a similar position with the Polyphonic Music of the Fourteenth Century series from 1962 to 1974. In 1981 he was made a corresponding member of the American Musicological Soc.

WRITINGS: *Music in Medieval Britain* (1958; 2nd ed., 1963); with J. Westrup, ed. *Collins Music Encyclopedia* (1959; U.S. edition as *The New College Encyclopedia of Music,* 1960); with M. Hood and C. Palisca, *Musicology* (1963); with J. Rimmer, *European Musical Instruments* (1964); *Time, Place and Music: An Anthology of Ethnomusicological Observations c. 1550–c. 1800* (1973); with E. Dobson, *Medieval English Songs* (1979).

Harrison, George, English rock singer, member of the celebrated group The Beatles; b. Liverpool, Feb. 25, 1943. Like his co-Beatles, he had no formal musical education, and learned to play the guitar by osmosis and acclimatization. Not as extroverted as John Lennon, not as exhibitionistic as Paul McCartney, and not as histrionic as Ringo Starr, he was not as conspicuously projected into public consciousness as his comrades-in-rock. Yet he exercised a distinct influence on the character of the songs that The Beatles sang. He became infatuated with the mystical lore of India; sat at the feet of a hirsute guru; introduced the sitar into his rock arrangements. He is the author of *Something,* one of the greatest successes of The Beatles. When the group broke up in 1970, Harrison proved sufficiently talented to impress his individual image in his own music; he also collaborated on songs of social consciousness with Bob Dylan. He brought out the successful albums *All Things Must Pass* (1970) and *The Concert for Bangla Desh* (1972). In 1973 his album *Living in the Material World* quickly attained gold status. In 1981 he scored a hit with his single *All Those Years Ago.* His album *Cloud 9* (1987) also proved a success.

BIBL.: H. Davies, *The Beatles: The Authorized Biography* (N.Y., 1968); E. Davies, "The Psychological Characteristics of Beatle Mania," *Journal of the History of Ideas* (April–June 1969); P. McCabe and R. Schonfeld, *Apple to the Core: The Unmaking of the Beatles* (N.Y., 1972); W. Mellers, *Twilight of the Gods: The Music of the Beatles* (N.Y., 1973); T. O'Grady, *The Beatles: A Musical Evolution* (Boston, 1983); *Current Biography* (Jan. 1989).

Harrison, Guy Fraser, English-American conductor; b. Guildford, Surrey, Nov. 6, 1894; d. San Miguel de Allende, Mexico, Feb. 20, 1986. He studied at the Royal College of Music, where he won an organ scholarship; served as an organist of the Episcopal Cathedral in Manila (1914–20); then emigrated to America; was organist of St. Paul's Cathedral in Rochester, N.Y. (1920–24); then was conductor of the Eastman Theater Orch. in Rochester (1924–29) and the Rochester Civic Orch. (1930–51); also was associate conductor of the Rochester Phil. (1930–51). From 1951 to 1973 he was conductor of the Oklahoma City Sym. Orch.

Harrison, Jimmy (James Henry), black American jazz trombonist and singer; b. Louisville, Oct. 17, 1900; d. N.Y., July 23, 1931. He grew up in Detroit, and started playing the trombone when he was 15; then toured with minstrel shows and played with groups in Atlantic City and Detroit. In 1922 he went to N.Y., where he worked with June Clark, James P. Johnson, and others; was a member of Bill Fowler's orch. (1925–26) and Fletcher Henderson's orch. (from 1927). In 1930 he was stricken with stomach cancer, and died within a year. He is acknowledged as the "father of the swing trombone."

BIBL.: R. Stewart, "The Father of Swing Trombone (J. H.)," *Jazz Masters of the Thirties* (N.Y., 1972).

Harrison, Julius (Allan Greenway), English conductor and composer; b. Stourport, Worcestershire, March 26, 1885; d. Harpenden, Hertfordshire, April 5, 1963. He studied music with Granville Bantock; subsequently was active mainly as a conductor; filled in engagements with the Beecham Opera Co., the Scottish Sym. Orch., the Handel Soc., the Hastings Orch. (1930–40), etc. In his music he makes competent use of English folk songs. He wrote an opera, *The Canterbury Pilgrims;* an orch. suite, *Worcestershire Pieces;* cantatas; some chamber music; many songs.

Harrison, Lou, inventive American composer and performer; b. Portland, Oreg., May 14, 1917. He studied with Cowell in San Francisco (1934–35) and with Schoenberg at the Univ. of Calif. at Los Angeles (1941). He taught at Mills College in Oakland, Calif. (1937–40; 1980–85), the Univ. of Calif. at Los Angeles (1942), Reed College in Portland, Oreg. (1949–50), Black Mountain College in North Carolina (1951–52), and San Jose State Univ. (from 1967). He also was a music critic for the *New York Herald-Tribune* (1945–48). He held 2 Guggenheim fellowships (1952, 1954). His interests are varied: he invented 2 new principles of clavichord construction; built a Phrygian aulos; developed a process for direct composing on a phonograph disc; in 1938 proposed a theory in interval control, and in 1942 supplemented it by a device for rhythm control; also wrote plays and versified poematically. He was one of the earliest adherents of an initially small group of American musicians who promoted the music of Ives, Ruggles, Varèse, and Cowell; he prepared for publication Ives's 3rd Sym., which he conducted in its 1st performance in 1946. He visited the Orient in 1961, fortifying his immanent belief in the multiform nature of music by studying Japanese and Korean modalities and rhythmic structures. Seeking new sources of sound production, he organized a percussion ensemble of multitudinous drums and such homely sound makers as coffee cans and flowerpots. He also wrote texts in Esperanto for some of his vocal works. He later composed for the Indonesian gamelan; many of these instruments were constructed by his longtime associate and friend William Colvig.

WORKS: OPERAS: *Rapunzel* (Rome, 1954); *Young Caesar,* puppet opera (Aptos, Calif., Aug. 21, 1971). **BALLETS:** *Changing World* (1936); *Green Mansions* (1939); *Something to Please*

Everybody (1939); *Johnny Appleseed* (1940); *Omnipotent Chair* (1940); *Perilous Chapel* (1948); *Western Dance* (1948); *The Marriage at the Eiffel Tower* (1949); *Solstice* (1949); *Almanac of the Seasons* (1950); *Io and Prometheus* (1951); *Praises for Hummingbirds and Hawks* (1951); *Orpheus* (1941–69); other works, including *Jeptha's Daughter* (1940–63; Cabrillo College, March 9, 1963); incidental music to plays; film scores. **ORCH.:** *Alleluia* (1944); Suite No. I (1947) and II (1948) for Strings; Suite for Violin, Piano, and Small Orch. (1951; N.Y., Jan. 11, 1952); *Symphony on G* (1948–61; Aptos, Calif., 1964); *Pacifika rondo* for Chamber Orch. (1963); Concerto for Organ, Percussion, and Orch. (1972–73); Sym. No. 3 (1937–82); Piano Concerto (N.Y., Oct. 20, 1985). **CHAMBER:** Concerto No. 1 for Flute and Percussion (1939); *Canticle No. 1* for 5 Percussion (1940); *Song of Queztecoatl* for Percussion Quartet (1940); *Canticle No. 3* for Flute or Ocarina, Guitar, and Percussion (1941; rev. 1989); *Double Music* for Percussion Quartet (1941; in collaboration with John Cage); *Fugue for Percussion* for Percussion Quartet (1941); *Labyrinth* for 11 Players and 91 Percussion Instruments (1941); *Schoenbergiana* for 6 Woodwinds (1945); *Siciliana* for Wind Quintet (1945); *Motet for the Day of Ascension* for 7 Strings (1946); String Trio (1946); Suite for Cello and Harp (1949); Suite No. 2 for String Quartet (1949–50); *7 Pastorales* for 4 Woodwinds, Harp, and Strings (1952); *Koncherro* for Violin and 5 Percussion (1959); *Concerto in slendro* for Violin, Cello, 2 Tack Piano, and Percussion (1961); *Quintal taryung* for Flute and Changgo (1961); *Majestic Fanfare* for Trumpets and Percussion (1963); *Avalokiteshvara* for Harp and Jaltarang (1965); *Music for Violin with Various Instruments* (1967–69); *Beverly's Troubadour Piece* for Harp and 2 Percussion (1968); *In Memory of Victor Jowers* for Clarinet and Piano (1968); *Arion's Leap* for Justly Tuned Instruments and Percussion (1974); *String Quartet Set* (1978–79); Suite for Guitar and Percussion (1978–79); *Ariadne* for Flute and Percussion (1987); *Varied Trio* for Violin, Piano, and Percussion (1987). **GAMELAN:** Suite for Violin and Gamelan (1972–73; in collaboration with R. Dee); *Gending Pak Chakro* (1976); *Lagu socisknum* (1976); *Lancaran Daniel* (1976); *Main bersama-sama* for Gamelan and Horn (1978); *Serenade for Betty Freeman and Franco Assetto* for Gamelan and Suling (1978); *Threnody for Carlos Chávez* for Gamelan and Violin (1979); *Scenes from Cavafy* for Baritone, Men's Voices, and Gamelan (1979–80); *Gending Alexander* (1981); *Gending Demeter* (1981); *Gending Hermes* (1981); *Gending Hephaestus* (1981); *Ladrang Epikuros* (1981); *Ladrang Samuel* (1981); Double Concerto for Violin, Cello, and Gamelan (1981–82); *Gending Claude* (1982); *Gending Dennis* (1982); *Gending Palladio* (1982); *Gending Pindar* (1982); *Lancaran Molly* (1982); *The Foreman's Song Tune* for Chorus and Gamelan (1983); *For the Pleasure of Ovid's Changes* (1983); *Gending James and Joel* (1983); *Gending Sinan* (1983); *Ketawang Wellington* (1983); *Lagu lagu Thomasan* (1983); *Lagu Victoria* (1983); *Gending William Colvig* (1984); *Ladrang Pak Daliyo* (1984); *Lagu Elang Yusuf* (1984). **VOCAL: CHORAL:** *Easter Cantata* for Soloists, Chorus, and Orch. (1943–46); *A Political Primer* for Soloists, Chorus, and Orch. (1951); *Mass* for Chorus, Trumpet, Harp, and Strings (1939–54); *4 Strict Songs* for 8 Baritones and Orch. (1955); *A Joyous Procession and a Solemn Procession* for Chorus, Trombones, and Percussion (1962); *Nova odo* for Chorus and Orch. (1962); *Haiku* for Unison Voices, Xiao, Harp, and Percussion (1968); *Peace Pipe 1* for Unison Voices, Trombone, 3 Percussion, 2 Harps, Organ, and String Quintet (1968); *La koro sutro* for Chorus, Gamelan, and Percussion Orch. (1972). **SOLO:** *May Rain* for Voice, Tack Piano, and Tam-tam (1941); *Pied Beauty* for Voice, Trombone or Cello, Flute, and Percussion (1941); *Fragment from Calamus* for Alto or Bass, and Piano (1946); *Sanctus* (1946); *Alma redemptoris mater* for Baritone, Violin, Trombone, and Tack Piano (1949); *Holly and Ivy* for Voice, Harp, and Strings (1951); *Peace Piece 3* for Voice, Violin, Harp, and Strings (1953); *Peace Piece 2* for Tenor, 3 Percussion, 2 Harps, and String Quintet (1968); *A Summerfield Set* for Piano (1988).

WRITINGS: *About Carl Ruggles* (N.Y., 1946); *Music Primer:*

Various Items about Music to 1970 (N.Y., 1971); with others, *Soundings: Ives, Ruggles, Varèse* (Sante Fe, N.Mex., 1974); P. Garland, ed., *A Lou Harrison Reader* (Santa Fe, N.Mex., 1987).

BIBL.: V. Rathbun, *L. H. and His Music* (thesis, San Jose State Univ., 1976); C. Rutman, *The Solo Piano Works of L. H.* (diss., Peabody Cons. of Music, 1983).

Harrison, May, English violinist, sister of **Beatrice Harrison;** b. Roorkee, India, March 1891; d. South Nutfield, Surrey, June 8, 1959. She attended the Royal College of Music in London; like her sister, she was a precocious talent; at the age of 10 she won a gold medal of the Royal College of Music, competing against some 3,000 contestants. She then went to St. Petersburg, where she took lessons with Leopold Auer; returning to England, she made several concert tours, often in the company of her sister.

Harrison, William, English tenor and operatic impresario; b. London, June 15, 1813; d. there, Nov. 9, 1868. He studied at the Royal Academy of Music in London; made his debut in 1839 at Covent Garden; then made many appearances at Drury Lane. With the soprano Louisa Pyne, he organized an opera company in 1856; presented seasons of opera at Covent Garden (1858–64), producing works by Wallace, Balfe, Benedict, and other British composers.

Harriss, Charles (Albert Edwin), English-Canadian organist and composer; b. London, Dec. 16–17 (midnight), 1862; d. Ottawa, July 31, 1929. He studied at St. Michael's College, Tenbury; then was an organist in Ottawa (1882–83) and Montreal (1882–94). He was founder-director of Montreal's McGill Cons. (1904–7). Having married into wealth, he subsequently devoted himself to organizing music festivals in Canada. He wrote an opera, *Torquil* (Montreal, 1896); cantatas; organ music; and songs.

Harsányi, Tibor, Hungarian composer; b. Magyarkanizsa, June 27, 1898; d. Paris, Sept. 19, 1954. He studied at the Budapest Academy of Music with Kodály; in 1923 he settled in Paris, where he devoted himself to composition. The melodic material of his music stems from Hungarian folk melos; his harmonic idiom is largely polytonal; the rhythms are sharp, often with jazzlike syncopation; the form remains classical. **WORKS: STAGE:** Chamber opera, *Les Invités* (Gera, Germany, 1930); radio opera, *Illusion* (Paris, June 28, 1949); 4 ballets: *Le Dernier Songe* (Budapest, Jan. 27, 1920); *Pantins* (Paris, 1938); *Chota Roustaveli* (in collaboration with Honegger and A. Tcherepnin; Monte Carlo, 1945); *L'Amour et la vie* (1951); puppet show, *L'Histoire du petit tailleur* for 7 Instruments and Percussion (1939). **ORCH.:** *La Joie de vivre* (Paris, March 11, 1934, composer conducting); 2 divertissements (1940–41; 1943); Violin Concerto (Paris Radio, Jan. 16, 1947); *Figures et rythmes* (Geneva, Nov. 19, 1947, composer conducting); *Danses variées* (Basel, Feb. 14, 1950, composer conducting); Sym. (Salzburg Festival, June 26, 1952). **CHAMBER:** Sonatina for Violin and Piano (1918); *3 Pieces* for Flute and Piano (1924); 2 string quartets (1918, 1935); Cello Sonata (1928); Nonet for String and Wind Instruments (Vienna Festival, June 21, 1932); Rhapsody for Cello and Piano (1939); *Picnic* for 2 Violins, Cello, Double Bass, and Percussion (1951); many piano pieces, among them 5 *études rythmiques* (1934), *3 pièces lyriques,* and albums for children; also several choral works, including *Cantate de Noël* for Voices, Flute, and Strings (Paris, Dec. 24, 1945).

Harshaw, Margaret, outstanding American mezzo-soprano, later soprano; b. Narberth, Pa., May 12, 1909. She was a scholarship student at the Juilliard Graduate School of Music in N.Y., where she studied voice with Anna Schoen-René, graduating in 1942. Shortly after graduation, she won the Metropolitan Opera Auditions of the Air and made her debut with the company in N.Y. as a mezzo-soprano in the role of the 2nd Norn in *Götterdämmerung* on Nov. 25, 1942; subsequently sang contralto and mezzo-soprano roles in German, Italian, and French operas; she also acquitted herself brilliantly as a

dramatic soprano in her appearance as Senta in *Der fliegende Holländer* at the Metropolitan Opera on Nov. 22, 1950; was particularly successful in Wagnerian roles; she sang Isolde, Sieglinde, Kundry, Elisabeth, and all 3 parts of Brünnhilde. She also excelled as Donna Anna in *Don Giovanni* and Leonore in Beethoven's *Fidelio.* She was a guest soloist with the opera companies of Philadelphia, Cincinnati, San Francisco, and Covent Garden in London, and at the Glyndebourne Festivals. In 1962 she joined the faculty of the Indiana Univ. School of Music in Bloomington; she retired from the Metropolitan Opera in 1964.

Hart, Frederic Patton, American composer; b. Aberdeen, Wash., Sept. 5, 1894. He studied at the American Cons. in Chicago and at the Art Inst. there; later took courses with Rubin Goldmark, with Ernest Hutcheson, and at the Diller-Quaile School in N.Y. He taught at Sarah Lawrence College (1929–47) and at the Juilliard School of Music (1947–60); then settled in Los Angeles. **WORKS:** Opera, *The Wheel of Fortune* (1943); opera-ballet, *The Romance of Robot* (1937); *The Farewell Supper,* opera (posthumous; N.Y., Feb. 3, 1984); chamber music; piano pieces; songs.

Hart, Fritz (Bennicke), English conductor and composer; b. Brockley, Kent, Feb. 11, 1874; d. Honolulu, July 9, 1949. He studied at the Royal College of Music in London (1893–96); in 1908 he went to Australia and settled there; in 1915 he became director of the Melbourne Cons.; in 1927 was appointed joint artistic director of the Melbourne Sym. Orch.; conducted the Honolulu Sym. Orch. (1932 until his death); settled in Honolulu in 1936 when appointed prof. of music at the Univ. of Hawaii; retired in 1942. He wrote operas, operettas, orch. works, chamber music, choruses, and over 500 songs.

Hart, James, English bass and composer; b. York, 1647; d. London, May 8, 1718. He was a singer in York Minster until 1670; was then appointed Gentleman of the Chapel Royal and lay-vicar of Westminster Abbey; settled in London and composed songs, publ. in *Choice Ayres and Songs* (1673–84), *The Theater of Music* (1685–87), *Banquet of Musick* (1688–90), and *Comes amoris* (1687–94). He wrote *Adieu to the pleasures and follies of love* for Shadwell's operatic adaptation of *The Tempest* (1674), publ. as one of 6 "Ariel's Songs."

Hart, Lorenz (Milton), American lyricist; b. N.Y., May 2, 1895; d. there, Nov. 22, 1943. He began as a student of journalism at Columbia Univ. (1914–17); then turned to highly successful theatrical writing. During his 24-year collaboration with Richard Rodgers, he wrote the lyrics for *Connecticut Yankee* (1927); *On Your Toes* (1936); *Babes in Arms* (1937); *The Boys from Syracuse* (1938); *I Married an Angel* (1938); *Too Many Girls* (1939); *Pal Joey* (1940); *By Jupiter* (1942). Some of their best songs (*Manhattan, Here in My Arms, My Heart Stood Still, Small Hotel, Blue Moon, Where or When, I Married an Angel*) are publ. in the album *Rodgers & Hart Songs* (N.Y., 1951). **BIBL.:** S. Marx and J. Clayton, *Rodgers and H.* (N.Y., 1976); D. Hart, *Thou Swell, Thou Witty: The Life and Lyrics of L. H.* (N.Y., 1976).

Hart, Philip, English organist and composer; b. London, c.1674; d. there, July 17, 1749. He was assistant organist (1696–97) and organist (1697–1749) at St. Andrew, Undershaft; was also organist at St. Michael, Cornhill (1704–23) and St. Dionis, Backchurch (1724–49). He wrote a number of keyboard pieces and vocal works; his finest work was the *Ode in Praise of Musick* or *Ode to Harmony* (1702). He also wrote *The Morning Hymn* for 2 Voices, Cello, and Harpsichord, after Milton's *Paradise Lost,* Book V (London, c.1729). **BIBL.:** F. Dawes, "*P. H.,*" *Musical Times,* CVI (1965); idem, "The Music of P. H. (c.1676–1749)," *Proceedings of the Royal Musical Association,* XCIV (1967–68).

Hart & Sons, a firm of London violin makers, founded in 1825 by John Hart. His son, **John Thomas Hart** (b. Dec. 17, 1805; d. London, Jan. 1, 1874), a pupil of Gilkes, made a complete study of Cremonese and other violins of Italian make, establishing a reputation as an expert in his field. His son, **George Hart** (b. London, March 23, 1839; d. near Newhaven, April 25, 1891), succeeded him and publ. *The Violin: Its Famous Makers and Their Imitators* (London, 1875; French ed., Paris, 1886) and *The Violin and Its Music* (London, 1881). His sons, George and Herbert Hart, inherited the business.

Hart, Weldon, American composer; b. Place-Bear Spring, Tenn., Sept. 19, 1911; d. (suicide) East Lansing, Mich., Nov. 20, 1957. He studied in Nashville, at the Univ. of Michigan, and at the Eastman School of Music in Rochester, N.Y., with Howard Hanson and Bernard Rogers, receiving his Ph.D. in 1946. He was head of the music dept. of Western Kentucky State College (1946–49) and director of the School of Music of the Univ. of West Virginia (1949–57). In 1957 he was engaged as head of the music dept. of Michigan State Univ. at East Lansing; upon arrival there he became despondent over his inability to produce an impression with a concert of his works, and killed himself with carbon monoxide exhaust in his car. Yet his music, although not innovative, is well crafted. He wrote *Sinfonietta* (1944); symphonic poem, *The Dark Hills* (1939); Sym. (1945); Violin Concerto (1951); 3 *West Virginia Folk Songs* for Chorus and Orch. (1954); several violin pieces and choruses.

Harth, Sidney, American violinist, conductor, and pedagogue; b. Cleveland, Oct. 5, 1929. He studied at the Cleveland Inst. of Music (Mus.B., 1947); then took lessons with Joseph Fuchs and Georges Enesco; was a recipient of the Naumburg prize in 1948; made his debut at Carnegie Hall in N.Y. in 1949. He later served as concertmaster and assistant conductor of the Louisville Orch. (1953–58); he was concertmaster of the Chicago Sym. Orch. (1959–62) and of the Casals Festival Orch. in San Juan (1959–65; 1972). From 1963 to 1973 he was a prof. of music and chairman of the music dept. at Carnegie-Mellon Univ. in Pittsburgh. He then served as concertmaster and associate conductor of the Los Angeles Phil. (1973–79); was interim concertmaster of the N.Y. Phil. in 1980; also served as music director of the Puerto Rico Sym. Orch. (1977–79). From 1981 to 1984 he was director of orch. studies at the Mannes College of Music; also was a prof. of violin at the State Univ. of N.Y. at Stony Brook (from 1981) and Yale Univ. (from 1982), and director of orch. studies at Carnegie-Mellon Univ. (from 1989). With his wife, Teresa Testa Harth, he gave duo-violin concerts.

Harthan, Hans, German composer; b. Bavaria, Feb. 23, 1855; d. Glendale, Calif., March 14, 1936. He studied with Lachner and Rheinberger in Germany. In 1883 he obtained a post of prof. of music in Odessa; in 1896 he went to Chile, where he became director of the National Cons. of Music in Santiago. In 1903 he emigrated to the U.S., eventually settling in California, the final destination of so many retiring European musicians. During his extended lifetime he wrote and publ. an astounding number of vocal and instrumental compositions, particularly for piano, expertly imitating the models of Schumann and Mendelssohn.

Hartig, Heinz (Friedrich), German composer; b. Kassel, Sept. 10, 1907; d. Berlin, Sept. 16, 1969. He studied piano at the Kassel Cons., and musicology at the Univ. of Vienna. Unable to hold a teaching post under the Nazi regime, he occupied himself with performances as a harpsichord player; in 1948 he joined the Hochschule für Musik in Berlin. In his compositions he applied varied techniques of modern music, from neo-Classicism to serialism, with formal unity achieved by the principle of free variations. He wrote a ballet, *Schwarze Sonne* (1958); chamber opera, *Escorial* (1961); Violin Concerto (1952); *Concertante Suite* for Guitar and Orch. (1954); Piano Concerto (1959); *Mass after a Holocaust,* after Dylan Thomas, for Baritone, Chorus, and Orch. (1960); *Wohin,* oratorio (1965); *Immediate* for Flute, Clarinet, Piano, and 2 Cellos (1966); *Concerto strumentale* for Violin and Orch. (1969); *Komposition in 5 Phasen* for Cello, Orch., Chorus, and Tape (1969).

BIBL.: W. Burde, *H. H.* (Berlin, 1967).

Hartley, Walter S(inclair), American composer, pianist, and teacher; b. Washington, D.C., Feb. 21, 1927. He studied with Burrill Phillips, Bernard Rogers, and Howard Hanson at the Eastman School of Music in Rochester, N.Y. (B.M., 1950; M.M., 1951; Ph.D., 1953). He taught at the National Music Camp in Interlochen, Mich. (1956–64), and at Davis and Elkins College in W.Va. (1958–69); then was prof. of music at the State Univ. of N.Y. College at Fredonia (from 1969); was also active as a pianist, especially in chamber music settings. His works for brass and saxophones have been widely performed.

WORKS: ORCH.: Sinfonietta (1950); *3 Patterns* for Small Orch. (1951); *Triptych* (1951); *Elegy* for Strings (1952); Sonatina for Trumpet and Small Orch. (1952); Piano Concerto (1952); *Concert Overture* (1954); Chamber Sym. (1954); *Scenes from Lorca's Blood Wedding* (1956); *Elizabethan Dances* (1962); *Festive Music* (1963); *Psalm* for Strings (1964); Partita for Chamber Orch. (1964); *Variations* (1973); Sym. No. 3 (1983); Sinfonia No. 7 (1986); Concerto No. 2 for Alto Saxophone and Small Orch. (1989). **BAND:** Concerto for 23 Winds (1957); 4 sinfonias (1961, 1963, 1965, 1977); Alto Saxophone Concerto (1966); 2 syms. for Winds (1970, 1978); *Southern Tier Suite* (1972); *Bacchanalia* (1975); *Coast Guard Overture* (1981); *Catskill Suite* (1982). **CHAMBER:** 2 string quartets (1950, 1962); Woodwind Quartet (1950); Sonata for Violin and Piano (1951); Sonata for Viola and Piano (1952); Trio for Violin, Viola, and Cello (1953); Divertimento for Cello and Woodwind Quintet (1956); Trio for Piano, Violin, and Cello (1960); Serenade for Woodwind Quintet and String Bass (1963); Sonata for Tuba and Piano (1967); Suite for Saxophone Quartet (1972); Concerto for Tuba and 6 Percussion Players (1974); Sonata for Baritone Saxophone and Piano (1976); Quintet No. 2 for Brass (1977); Quintet for Saxophones (1981); Trio for Saxophones (1984); Sinfonia No. 8 for 5 Percussion Players (1987); Quartet for 4 Guitars (1987); Chamber Concerto for Baritone Saxophone and Wind Octet (1988); also various vocal works.

Hartmann, family of eminent Danish musicians of German descent:

(1) Johann Ernst (Joseph) Hartmann, violinist and composer; b. Gross Clogau, Silesia, Dec. 24, 1726; d. Copenhagen, Oct. 21, 1793. He was a member of the orch. of the Prince-Bishop of Breslau (1754–57); in 1761 he was at the Rudolstadt court and at the ducal court in Plön Holstein, where he became Konzertmeister. He then was a member of Sarti's Italian opera orch. in Copenhagen (1762–64), where he settled as a member of the Royal Chapel (1766), becoming 1st violinist (1767) and music director (1768). He is recognized as the founder of the Danish national school of Romantic opera. His most notable singspiels, among the many composed for the Royal Theater, are *Balders død* (The Death of Balder; Copenhagen, Jan. 30, 1779) and *Fiskene* (The Fishermen; Copenhagen, Jan. 31, 1780); the latter includes the final stanza of the Danish national anthem, *Kong Christian stod ved højen mast;* however, the present melody was not in the original score, so Hartmann may not have composed it. Most of his other MSS were destroyed in the Christiansborg Palace fire of 1794. The MSS of his Violin Concerto (composed in collaboration with his pupil Claus Schall; 1780), 3 cantatas, and VI *sonates à deux violons et basse,* op. 1, are extant; also his publ. works, *Simphonie périodique* (No. 7; Amsterdam, 1770) and *Air favori varié pour le clavecin ou harpe avec un violon obligé* (Copenhagen, 1792). He prepared a *Violin-Schule* (MS, 1777).

(2) August Wilhelm Hartmann, violinist, organist, and composer, son of the preceding; b. Copenhagen, Nov. 6, 1775; d. there, Nov. 15, 1850. He studied with his father; was 1st violinist in the Royal Chapel (1796–1817) and then organist and choirmaster at Copenhagen's Garnisonskirke (1817–24).

(3) Johann Peter Emilius Hartmann, celebrated organist and composer, son of the preceding; b. Copenhagen, May 14, 1805; d. there, March 10, 1900. He studied piano, organ, violin, and theory with his father, and began to compose when still a child; he succeeded his father as organist at Copenhagen's Garnisonskirke (1824), and then studied law at the Univ. of Copenhagen (graduated, 1828). While retaining a government post (1828–70), he pursued an active career as a musician. He joined the faculty of Siboni's cons. in 1827; helped to organize the Musikforening in 1836; also was active with the Studentersanforening from 1839, serving as its president from 1868. He expanded his musical horizons with trips abroad; visited Germany, Switzerland, Austria, and France in 1836, meeting such famous musicians as Marschner, Cherubini, Chopin, Rossini, Paer, Spohr, and Spontini; met Franz Berwald and Clara Wieck in Berlin and Mendelssohn and Schumann in Leipzig in 1839; he won the critical admiration of Schumann, who wrote about him in the pages of the *Neue Zeitschrift für Musik*; subsequently met Liszt in Hamburg in 1841; was a guest conductor with the Leipzig Gewandhaus Orch. in 1844. He was appointed organist of Vor Frue Kirke, Copenhagen's cathedral, in 1843, and continued in that capacity until his death. He was also a founder of the Copenhagen Cons. (1866), serving as joint director with Gade (his son-in-law) and Paulli. As the leading representative of the Danish Romantic movement in music, he was held in the greatest esteem by his countrymen; he received an honorary Ph.D. from the Univ. of Copenhagen in 1874.

WORKS: OPERAS: *Ravnen, eller Broderprøven* (The Raven, or The Brother Test; Copenhagen, Oct. 29, 1832; rev. version, Copenhagen, April 23, 1865); *Korsarerne* (The Corsairs; Copenhagen, April 23, 1835); *Liden Kirsten* (Little Christina; Copenhagen, May 12, 1846; rev. version, Copenhagen, Oct. 29, 1858). BALLETS: *Et folkesagn* (A Folk Tale; Copenhagen, March 20, 1854; in collaboration with Gade); *Valkyrien* (Copenhagen, Sept. 13, 1861); *Thrymskviden* (The Legend of Thrym; Copenhagen, Feb. 21, 1868); *Arcona* (Copenhagen, May 7, 1875); also a melodrama, *Guldhornene* (The Golden Horns; 1834), and incidental music to more than 15 plays. ORCH.: 2 syms.: No. 1, in G minor, op. 17 (Copenhagen, April 17, 1836; rev. version, Copenhagen, May 17, 1851); No. 2, in E major, op. 48b (Copenhagen, 1849). OVERTURES: D minor (1825); *Gejstlig Ouverture* in C minor (1827); C major (1852); *En efteraarsjagt* (An Autumn Hunt; 1863); also overtures to Oehlenschlaeger's *Axel og Valborg* (1856) and *Correggio* (1858). CHAMBER: Sonata for Flute or Clarinet (1825); 3 violin sonatas (1826, 1846, 1886); Suite for Violin or Clarinet (1864); *Fantasi-Allegro* for Violin or Clarinet (1889); many cantatas; choruses; songs; works for organ; piano pieces.
BIBL.: E. Grieg, "J.P.E. H.," *Musikbladet* (May 14, 1885); W. Behrend, *J.P.E. H.* (Copenhagen, 1895); A. Hammerich, *J.P.E. H.: Biografiske essays* (Copenhagen, 1916); W. Behrend, *J.P.E. H.* (Copenhagen, 1918); R. Hove, *J.P.E. H.* (Copenhagen, 1934); V. Bitsch, *J.P.E. H.* (Hellerup, 1955); L. Brix, *Die Klaviermusik von J.P.E. H.* (diss., Univ. of Göttingen, 1971); J. Thornberg, "J.P.E. H.s ouverturer," *Musik og forskning*, I (1975).

(4) Emil (Wilhelm Emilius Zinn) Hartmann, organist and composer, son of the preceding; b. Copenhagen, Feb. 21, 1836; d. there, July 18, 1898. He studied organ and theory with his father and piano with Anton Rée; later studied in Leipzig. He began composing songs as a child; his 1st mature work was the *Passionssalme* (1858), followed by the ballet *Fjeldstuen* (The Mountain Cottage; Copenhagen, May 13, 1859), written in collaboration with his brother-in-law August Winding. Although he continued to write for the stage, he became best known as a composer of instrumental music. He was organist of St. John's (1861–71) and of the Christiansborg Palace Church (1871–98).

WORKS (all 1st perf. in Copenhagen): OPERAS: *En nat mellem fjeldene* (A Night in the Mountains; April 11, 1863); *Elverpigen* (The Elf Girl; Nov. 5, 1867); *Korsikaneren* (The Corsican; April 7, 1873); *Ragnhild* (Runic Spell; 1896); *Det store lod* (The Big Prize; 1897; probably not perf.). BALLETS: *Fjeldstuen* (The Mountain Cottage; May 13, 1859; in collaboration with A. Winding); *En bryllupsfest i Hardanger* (A Wedding Feast in Hardanger; 1897; not perf.). ORCH.: 7 syms.; *Hakon Jarl*, symphonic poem; Piano Concerto; Violin Concerto; Cello Concerto; etc.; much vocal music, including *Passionssalme* for

Soprano, Chorus, and Orch. (Maundy Thursday, 1858); choruses; songs.

Hartmann, Arthur (Martinus), American violinist, teacher, and composer; b. Philadelphia, July 22, 1881; d. N.Y., March 30, 1956. He was a pupil of Loeffler (violin) and Homer Norris (composition). He made his debut in Philadelphia (1887) as a child prodigy; by the time he was 12, he had played practically the entire modern violin repertoire. He toured the U.S., Canada, and Scandinavia; played in Paris in recitals with Debussy, and became his intimate friend. In 1939 he settled in N.Y.; retired in 1954. He made numerous transcriptions and arrangements; discovered and ed. 6 sonatas of Felice de' Giardini; wrote an essay on Bach's Chaconne which has been tr. into 14 languages.

Hartmann, Carl, German tenor; b. Solingen, May 2, 1895; d. Munich, May 30, 1969. He studied with Senff in Düsseldorf; made a successful debut in Elberfeld as Tannhäuser (1928), then sang all over Germany, in Vienna, in Paris, and in Stockholm. In 1930 he toured the U.S. with Gadski's Opera Co., appearing in Wagnerian tenor roles; from 1937 to 1940 was a member of the Metropolitan Opera in N.Y.; then returned to Germany and lived mostly in Munich.

Hartmann, Karl Amadeus, outstanding German composer; b. Munich, Aug. 2, 1905; d. there, Dec. 5, 1963. He studied with Joseph Haas at the Music Academy in Munich (1923–27) and later with Scherchen. He began to compose rather late in life; his 1st major work was a Trumpet Concerto, which was performed in Strasbourg in 1933. During World War II he studied advanced musical composition and analysis with Anton von Webern in Vienna (1941–42). After the war he organized in Munich the society Musica Viva. He received a prize from the city of Munich in 1948; in 1952, was elected a member of the German Academy of Fine Arts, and soon after became president of the German section of the ISCM. Despite his acceptance of a highly chromatic, atonal idiom and his experimentation in the domain of rhythm (patterned after Blacher's "variable meters"), Hartmann retained the orthodox form and structural cohesion of basic Classicism. He was excessively critical of his early works, and discarded many of them, but some were retrieved and performed after his death.

WORKS: Chamber opera, *Des Simplicius Simplicissimus Jugend* (1934–35; Cologne, Oct. 20, 1949; a rev., reduced scoring of the work was made in 1955 and retitled *Simplicius Simplicissimus*); 9 syms.: No. 1, *Versuch eines Requiems* (Attempt at a Requiem), to words by Walt Whitman, for Soprano and Orch. (1936–40; Vienna, June 22, 1957); *Sinfonia tragica* (1940; Munich, May 20, 1989); No. 2, *Adagio* (1941–46; Donaueschingen, Sept. 10, 1950); No. 3 (1948–49; Munich, Feb. 10, 1950); No. 4 for String Orch. (1946–47; Munich, April 2, 1948); No. 5, *Symphonie concertante*, for Wind Instruments, Cellos, and Double Basses (1950; Stuttgart, April 21, 1951; based on "variable meters"); No. 6 (1951–53; Munich, April 24, 1953); No. 7 (1958; Hamburg, March 15, 1959); No. 8 (1960–62; Cologne, Jan. 25, 1963); Trumpet Concerto (Strasbourg, 1933); *Miserae* (Prague, Sept. 1, 1935); *Concerto funebre* for Violin and String Orch. (1939; rev. 1959; Braunschweig, Nov. 12, 1959); *Symphonischen Hymnen* (1942; Munich, Oct. 9, 1975); symphonic overture, *China kämpft* (China at War; 1942; Darmstadt, July 1947); Concerto for Piano, Winds, and Percussion (Donaueschingen, Oct. 10, 1953); Concerto for Viola, Piano, Winds, and Percussion (Frankfurt, May 25, 1956); *Gesangsszene*, on German texts of Jean Giraudoux's "Sodome et Gomorrhe," for Baritone and Orch. (1962–63; unfinished; Frankfurt, Nov. 12, 1964); *Kammerkonzert* for Clarinet, String Quartet, and String Orch. (Zürich, June 17, 1969); *Jazz-Toccata und -Fugue* for Piano (1928); *Tanzsuite* for Wind Quintet (1931; Frankfurt, April 20, 1975); Piano Sonatina (1931); 2 string quartets (*Carillon*, 1933; 1945–46); *Burleske Musik* for 6 Winds, Percussion, and Piano (c.1933; Rotterdam, June 30, 1967); *Friede Anno 48*, after Gryphius, for Soprano, Chorus, and Piano (1937; Cologne, Oct. 22, 1968; the sections for soprano and piano also exist as a separate piece called *Lamento*, a cantata for

Soprano and Piano); *Kleines Konzert* for String Quartet and Percussion (version for String Orch. and Percussion, Braunschweig, Nov. 29, 1974).

BIBL.: R. Wagner, ed., *K.A. H. und die Musica Viva* (Munich, 1980); A. Jaschinski, *K.A. H.: Symphonische Tradition und ihre Auflösung* (Munich, 1982); A. McCredie, ed., *K.A. H.: Catalogue of His Work* (Wilhelmshaven and N.Y., 1982); idem, *K.A. H.: Sein Leben und Werk* (1982).

Hartmann, Pater (real name, **Paul Eugen Josef von An der Lan-Hochbrunn**), German organist and composer; b. Salurn, near Bozen, Dec. 21, 1863; d. Munich, Dec. 5, 1914. He entered the Franciscan order at the age of 16; studied theology and music in various monasteries; then completed his musical studies with Josef Pembaur in Innsbruck; was ordained a priest in 1886; was appointed organist at the Church of the Redeemer in Jerusalem (1893) and at the Church of the Holy Sepulchre (1894); in 1895 he was transferred to Rome as organist of the monastery Ara Coeli and director of the Scuola Musicale Cooperativa. From 1906 until his death he lived in the Franciscan monastery of St. Anna at Munich.

WORKS: Oratorios: *Petrus* (1900); *Franziskus* (1902); *Das letzte Abendmahl* (1904); *Der Tod des Herrn* (1905); *Septem ultima verba Christi in Cruce* (1908); *Te Deum* (1913); masses; organ works.

Hartmann, Rudolf, German opera producer and administrator; b. Ingolstadt, Oct. 11, 1900; d. Munich, Aug. 26, 1988. He studied in Munich; then became an opera producer successively in Altenburg (1924–27), in Nuremberg (1928–34), and at the State Opera in Berlin (1934–37). From 1937 to 1944 he worked at the Bavarian State Opera in Munich; then was Intendant of the Bavarian State Opera (1952–67). His productions were noteworthy for their fusion of traditional and contemporary stage practices. He publ. *Richard Strauss: The Staging of His Operas and Ballets* (Oxford, 1982).

Hartmann, Thomas (Alexandrovich de), Russian composer; b. Khoruzhevka, Ukraine, Sept. 21, 1885; d. Princeton, N.J., March 26, 1956. He studied piano with Anna Essipova at the St. Petersburg Cons.; composition with Taneyev and Arensky. His 1st important work, the ballet *The Little Crimson Flower*, was produced at the Imperial Theater in St. Petersburg in 1907 with Pavlova, Karsavina, Nijinsky, and Fokine. After the Revolution he went to the Caucasus; taught at the Tiflis Cons. (1919); then went to Paris, where he remained until 1951, when he settled in N.Y. His early music is in the Russian national style, influenced particularly by Mussorgsky; from about 1925, he made a radical change in his style of composition, adopting many devices of outspoken modernism.

WORKS: Ballets: *The Little Crimson Flower* (St. Petersburg, Dec. 16, 1907) and *Babette* (Nice, March 10, 1935); opera, *Esther* (not perf.); 4 syms. (1915; 1944; 1953; 1955, unfinished); Cello Concerto (1935; Boston, April 14, 1938); Piano Concerto (1940; Paris, Nov. 8, 1942); Double-bass Concerto (1943; Paris, Jan. 26, 1945); Harp Concerto (1944); Violin Concerto (Paris, March 16, 1947); Flute Concerto (Paris, Sept. 27, 1950); *12 Russian Fairy Tales* for Orch. (Houston, April 4, 1955); Violin Sonata (1937); Cello Sonata (1942); Trio for Flute, Violin, and Piano (1946); 3 song cycles to words by Verlaine, Proust, and James Joyce; other songs; piano pieces. His music to Kandinsky's spectacle *The Yellow Sound*, arranged by Gunther Schuller from Hartmann's sketches, was played in N.Y. in a series of performances beginning Feb. 9, 1982.

Hartog, Eduard de, Dutch pianist and composer; b. Amsterdam, Aug. 15, 1829; d. The Hague, Nov. 8, 1909. He studied in Germany with Hoch and Dulcken, and in Paris with Elwart. He lived many years in Paris, where he produced the opera *Le Mariage de Don Lope* (1865); another opera by him, *L'Amour et son Hôte*, was produced in Brussels (1873). He also wrote several symphonic works, chamber music, and piano pieces.

Härtwig, Dieter, distinguished German musicologist; b. Dresden, July 18, 1934. He studied musicology at the Univ. of Leipzig (Ph.D., 1963, with the diss. *Der Opernkomponist Rudolf*

Wagner-Régeny: Leben und Werke; publ. in Berlin in 1965 in an enl. ed. as *Rudolf Wagner-Régeny: Der Opernkomponist*); then completed his Habilitation there in 1970 with *Fidelio F. Finke: Leben und Werk*. He was a dramaturge at the Schwerin State Theater (1959–60), then at the Radebeul Theater in Dresden (1960–65); lectured in music history at the Dresden Hochschule für Musik from 1960 to 1962, and again from 1973. In 1965 he also assumed the positions of chief dramaturge and deputy artistic director of the Dresden Phil. Orch. He publ. a valuable history of the Dresden Phil., *Die Dresdner Philharmonie: Eine Chronik des Orchesters 1870 bis 1970* (Leipzig, 1970); also publ. *Kurt Masur* (Leipzig, 1976), *Die Dresdner Philharmonie* (Leipzig, 1985; 2nd ed., 1989), and *Carl Maria von Weber* (Leipzig, 1986; 2nd ed., 1989).

Harty, Sir (Herbert) Hamilton, eminent Irish conductor and composer; b. Hillsborough, County Down, Dec. 4, 1879; d. Brighton, Feb. 19, 1941. He received his entire education from his father, an organist; so well grounded was he as a performer that on Feb. 12, 1894, at the age of 14, he was formally appointed as organist at Magheragall Church, in County Antrim; later he also filled positions as church organist in Belfast and in Bray, outside Dublin. In 1901 he went to London, where he began to compose; his Piano Quintet, String Quartet, and *Irish Symphony* won prizes; he also began to conduct. On July 15, 1904, he married **Agnes Nicholls.** In 1920 he was appointed conductor of the renowned Hallé Orch. in Manchester, remaining at that post for 13 seasons. From 1932 to 1934 he was conductor of the London Sym. Orch. In 1931 he made his 1st American tour, during which he conducted in Boston, Chicago, and Cleveland, and at the Hollywood Bowl. In 1934 he conducted in Australia. He was knighted in 1925. Harty's arrangements of Handel's *Water Music* and *Royal Fireworks Music* became standard repertoire pieces; of his original works, only *An Irish Symphony*, 1st performed under his direction in Manchester on Nov. 13, 1924, received praise; he also wrote *Comedy Overture* (1906; rev. 1908); *Ode to a Nightingale*, after Keats, for Soprano and Orch. (1907); Violin Concerto in D major (1908–9); *With the Wild Geese*, symphonic poem (1910); *The Mystic Trumpeter* for Baritone, Chorus, and Orch. (1913); *The Children of Lir*, symphonic poem (London, March 1, 1939). He also arranged *A John Field Suite* for Orch., based on piano pieces by Field.

BIBL.: D. Greer, ed., *H. H.: His Life and Music* (Belfast, 1978; with discography and list of works).

Hartzell, Eugene, American-born Austrian composer; b. Cincinnati, May 21, 1932. He studied at Kent State Univ. (B.S., 1953) and Yale Univ. (B.M., 1954; M.M., 1955), and with H.E. Apostel in Vienna (1956–58). He then lived in Vienna, working in various positions only peripherally connected with music. He adopted the 12-tone method of composition; his works in this idiom include *14 Monologues* for Assorted Instruments (1957–84) and *10 Workpoints* (1977–82).

WORKS: ORCH.: Sym. No. 1 for Strings (1965); Sym. No. 2 for Wind Quintet and Strings (1968); *Synopsis for Symphony* (1970); Sinfonietta for Strings (1980). CHAMBER: Trio for Flute, Bass Clarinet, and Piano (1969); *Projections* for Wind Quintet (1970); *Companion Pieces to a Wind Quintet* (1973); Sonata for Clarinet and Piano (1981). VOCAL: *A Keats Songbook* for Tenor and Guitar (1978); *4 Latin Lyrics* for Tenor and Orch. (1981); songs.

Harvey, Jonathan (Dean), significant English composer; b. Sutton Coldfield, Warwickshire, May 3, 1939. He was a scholarship student at St. John's College, Cambridge, and also received private instruction from Erwin Stein and Hans Keller; after obtaining his Ph.D. from the Univ. of Glasgow (1964), he attended the Darmstadt summer courses in new music (1966) and studied with Milton Babbitt at Princeton Univ. He subsequently taught at the Univ. of Southampton (1964–77) and at the Univ. of Sussex (from 1977). In 1985 he received the Koussevitzky Foundation Award. In his ultimate style of composition he astutely synthesized a number of quaquaversal idioms and techniques ranging from medieval modalities to ultramodern procedures, occasionally making use of electronic resources.

WORKS: CHURCH OPERA: *Passion and Resurrection* (Winchester Cathedral, March 21, 1981). ORCH.: Sym. (1966); Chaconne on *Iam dulcis amaica* (1967); *Benedictus* (1970); *Persephone's Dream* (1972; London, Jan. 18, 1973); *Smiling Immortal* for Chamber Ensemble and Tape (London, July 11, 1977); *Whom Ye Adore* (Glasgow, Sept. 19, 1981); *Bhakti* for Chamber Orch. and Tape (Paris, Dec. 3, 1982); *Easter Orisons* for Chamber Orch. (1983; Newcastle upon Tyne, Jan. 15, 1984); *Gong-Ring* for Chamber Ensemble and Electronics (Edinburgh, Sept. 1, 1984); *Madonna of Winter and Spring* for Orch., Synthesizers, and Electronics (London, Aug. 27, 1986); *Lightness and Weight* for Tuba and Orch. (Poole, Feb. 18, 1987); *Timepieces* (1987; Saarbrücken, Sept. 23, 1988). CHAMBER: *Inner Light I* for 7 Players (London, Nov. 26, 1973); *Quantumplation* for Instrumental Ensemble (1973); 2 string quartets: No. 1 (1977; Southampton, March 6, 1979); No. 2 (1988; Brussels, March 17, 1989); *Concelebration* for Chamber Ensemble (1979; London, Jan. 6, 1980; rev. 1981); *Ricercare una melodia* for Trumpet or Flute or Oboe, and Tape Delay (1985); *Tendril* for 11 Instruments (London, June 10, 1987); *The Valley of Aosta* for 13 Players (1988; Radio France, March 7, 1989). VOCAL: Cantata I for Soloists, Chorus, Organ, and Strings (1965); Cantata II, *3 Lovescapes*, for Soprano and Piano (1967); Cantata III for Soprano and 6 Players (1968); Cantata IV, *Ludus Amoris*, for Soloists, Speaker, Chorus, and Orch. (1969); Cantata V for Soloists and Wind Quintet (1970); Cantata VI, *On Faith*, for Chorus and Strings (1970); Cantata VII, *On Vision* (1971); Cantata VIII (1971); Cantata IX (1973); Cantata X, *Spirit Music*, for Soprano, 3 Clarinets, and Piano (Sheffield, Feb. 20, 1976); *Inner Light II* for Soloists, Instruments, and Tape (Cheltenhan, July 8, 1977); *Hymn* for Chorus and Orch. for the 900th anniversary of Winchester Cathedral (Winchester Cathedral, July 12, 1979); *The Path of Devotion* for Chorus and Small Orch. (1983; London, Feb. 16, 1985); *Song Offerings* for Soprano and 8 Players (London, March 22, 1985); *Lauds* for Chorus and Cello (Winchester, July 23, 1987); *From Silence* for Soprano, Violin, Viola, Percussion, 3 Synthesizers, and Tape (1988; Cambridge, Mass., Feb. 2, 1989); also *Mortuos Plango, Vivos Voco* for Computer-manipulated Concrete Sounds on Tape (Lille, Nov. 30, 1980).

Harwood, Basil, English organist and composer; b. Woodhouse, Gloucestershire, April 11, 1859; d. London, April 3, 1949. He studied piano with J.L. Roeckel and organ with George Risely; also studied with Reinecke and Jadassohn at the Leipzig Cons. Returning to England, he occupied various posts as an organist: at St. Barnabas Church, Pimlico (1883–87); Ely Cathedral (1887–92); and Christ Church, Oxford (1892–1909). He ed. the *Oxford Hymn Book* (1908); wrote a number of sacred works for chorus; organ pieces (2 sonatas, Organ Concerto, Christmastide, *Dithyramb*, etc.); a cantata, *Ode on May Morning,* after Milton (Leeds Festival, 1913).

Harwood, Elizabeth (Jean), English soprano; b. Barton Seagrave, May 27, 1938; d. Ingatestone, June 21, 1990. She studied at the Royal Manchester College of Music; won the Kathleen Ferrier Memorial Prize in 1960. In 1961 she joined the Sadler's Wells Opera; was a winner of the Verdi Sesquicentennial Competition in Busetto in 1963; sang with the Scottish Opera, Covent Garden, and the English Opera Group; also made guest appearances at La Scala in Milan and at the Salzburg Festival. She made her Metropolitan Opera debut in N.Y. on Oct. 15, 1975, as Fiordiligi in *Così fan tutte.*

Häser, August Ferdinand, German composer, brother of **Charlotte (Henriette) Häser;** b. Leipzig, Oct. 15, 1779; d. Weimar, Nov. 1, 1844. He was educated at the Thomasschule in Leipzig, and studied theology at Leipzig Univ. In 1817 he was engaged in Weimar as music teacher to Princess Augusta (the future German empress); also conducted the chorus at the Court Opera there; was a church organist and a teacher of Italian. He publ. *Versuch einer systematischen Übersicht der Gesanglehre* (Leipzig, 1822) and *Chorgesangschule für Schul- und Theaterchöre* (Mainz, 1831). He composed 3 operas; an oratorio, *Die Kraft des Glaubens;* many sacred choruses; 4 overtures; several instrumental works in salon style.

Häser, Charlotte (Henriette), German soprano, sister of **August Ferdinand Häser;** b. Leipzig, June 24, 1784; d. Rome, May 1, 1871. She studied with her father, the composer Johann Georg Häser (1729–1809); then sang in Dresden; in 1806 she went to Italy, where she enjoyed tremendous success; she was also one of the 1st women to sing male roles. After she left the stage, she settled in Rome.

Haskil, Clara, brilliant Rumanian pianist; b. Bucharest, Jan. 7, 1895; d. Brussels, Dec. 7, 1960. A precocious musician, she played in public at the age of 7; then entered the Paris Cons., where she studied piano with Cortot and won a 1st prize at the age of 14. Busoni heard her in Basel and invited her to study with him in Berlin. She played programs of Beethoven sonatas with Enesco, Ysaÿe, and Casals; subsequently gave piano recitals and appeared as a soloist with major sym. orchs. in Europe and America. A muscular deficiency severely impeded her concert career; however, she continued playing concerts during periods of remission of her ailment. Music critics praised her fine musicianship and her penetrating interpretation of Classical and early Romantic works.

BIBL.: R. Wolfensberger, *C. H.* (Bern, 1961); J. Spycket, *C. H.* (Paris, 1975).

Haslinger, Tobias, Austrian music publisher; b. Zell, March 1, 1787; d. Vienna, June 18, 1842. He went to Vienna in 1810 after studying music in Linz; was a bookkeeper in Steiner's music establishment; later became a partner and, after Steiner's retirement in 1826, sole proprietor. A gregarious and affable person, he made friends with many musicians, and was on excellent terms with Beethoven, who seemed to enjoy Haslinger's company; many letters to him from Beethoven are extant, among them the humorous canon *O Tobias Dominus Haslinger.* He was succeeded by his son **Carl Haslinger** (b. Vienna, June 11, 1816; d. there, Dec. 26, 1868). The latter studied with Czerny and became a brilliant pianist as well as an industrious composer; he publ. more than 100 works of various kinds. Continuing the tradition of his father, he publ. several syms., piano concertos, overtures, and other works by Beethoven, and later Liszt's Piano Concerto in E-flat; he was also the publisher of many Strauss waltzes. In 1875 the firm was bought from his widow by Schlesinger of Berlin (subsequently, R. & W. Lienau).

Hasse, Faustina (née **Bordoni**), famous Italian mezzo-soprano; b. Venice, c.1700; d. there, Nov. 4, 1781. She found patrons in Alessandro and Benedetto Marcello, who entrusted her vocal training to M. Gasparini; made her debut in Pollarolo's *Ariodante* in Venice in 1716, and then entered the service of the Elector Palatine. In addition to appearances in Venice until 1725, she also sang in Reggio (1719), Modena (1720), Bologna (1721–22), Naples (1721–23), and Rome (1722). She made her 1st appearance in Germany in P. Torri's *Griselda* in Munich in 1723 with notable success, returning in 1724, 1728, and 1729. She created a number of roles in operas by Handel, including Rossane in *Alessandro* (London debut, May 5, 1726), Alcestis in *Ameto* (Jan. 31, 1727), Pulcheria in *Riccardo Primo* (Nov. 11, 1727), Emira in *Siroe* (Feb. 17, 1728), and Elisa in *Tolomeo* (April 30, 1728). Her rivalry with Cuzzoni became a public scandal, culminating in a physical altercation during a performance of *Astianatte* on June 6, 1727. Her other performances were in Florence (1728–29), Parma (1729–30), Turin (1729, 1731), Venice (1729–32), Milan (1730), and Rome (1731). She sang in the premieres of **Johann Adolf Hasse**'s *Dalisa* and *Arminio* in Venice in 1730, and married the composer that same year. Her career thereafter was closely related to her husband's, and she frequently appeared in his operatic and concert works. In 1731 they were called to the Saxon court in Dresden, where she became prima donna assoluta and her husband Kapellmeister; she also made frequent visits to Italy to sing in the principal music centers. She made her farewell stage appearance in the premiere performance of her husband's *Ciro riconosciuto* in Dresden on Jan. 20, 1751. She continued to receive her salary of 3,000 thaler and retained her title of virtuosa da camera until 1763, when she and her husband were dismissed by the new elector. They lived in Vienna until 1773, and then retired to Venice. According to contemporary accounts, she possessed one of the finest voices of the day. She also possessed great physical beauty, which greatly enhanced her dramatic gifts.

BIBL.: A. Niggli, *F. B.-H.* (Leipzig, 1880); G. Urbani de Gheltof, *La "Nuova Sirena" ed il "Caro Sassone"* (Venice, 1890); M. Högg, *Die Gesangskunst der F. H. und das Sängerinnenwesen ihrer Zeit in Deutschland* (Berlin, 1931).

Hasse, Johann Adolf, celebrated German composer; b. Bergedorf, near Hamburg (baptized), March 25, 1699; d. Venice, Dec. 16, 1783. He studied in Hamburg (1714–17), and then was engaged as a tenor at the Opera there (1718); he was a member of the Braunschweig Opera (1719–21), where he sang in the premiere of his opera *Antioco* (Aug. 11, 1721). He then went to Naples, where he studied with Alessandro Scarlatti. The success of his serenata *Antonio e Cleopatra* (Naples, Sept. 1725), sung by the famous castrato Farinelli and Vittoria Tesi, brought him a commission from the Teatro San Bartolomeo. There he produced his opera *Il Sesostrate* (Naples, May 13, 1726), which launched his career as a major dramatic composer. His *Artaserse* (Venice, Feb. 1730) was a particular favorite of Farinelli, who was later called upon to sing the arias *Per questo dolce amplesso* and *Pallido il sole* while in the service of the ailing King Philip V of Spain (1737–46). Hasse married the mezzo-soprano **Faustina Hasse** (née **Bordoni**) in 1730, the same year in which she sang in the premieres of his *Dalisa* and *Arminio* in Venice. He went to the Saxon court in Dresden in 1731 as Kapellmeister; his wife joined him there as prima donna. His 1st opera for Dresden was *Cleofide* (Sept. 13, 1731). As his fame increased, the court allowed him frequent leaves of absence to produce his operas in other major music centers, often with his wife singing leading roles. He scored a major success with *Seroe, rè de Persia* (Bologna, May 2, 1733). His admiration for the renowned librettist Metastasio led to their remarkable personal and professional relationship from 1743. During this period, Hasse was acknowledged as the preeminent composer of opera seria in Germany, Austria, and Italy. Although Porpora served the Dresden court as Kapellmeister from 1748 to 1751, Hasse succeeded in maintaining his own position and was elevated to the post of Oberkapellmeister in 1750. His wife made her farewell appearance in opera in the premiere of his *Ciro riconosciuto* (Jan. 20, 1751). His *Solimano* (Feb. 5, 1753), with its huge cast of singers, actors, and even animals, proved a major court event. His last opera written for Dresden was *L'Olimpiade* (Feb. 16, 1756); he remained in the court's service until the advent of the new elector in 1763. In the meantime, he found an appreciative court in Vienna, where he produced the operas *Alcide al bivio* (Oct. 8, 1760), *Zenobia* (Carnival 1761), and *Il trionfo di Clelia* (April 27, 1762). Following the success of these works, he settled in Vienna; after bringing out his opera *Egeria* there (April 24, 1764), he wrote *Romolo ed Erisilia* for the Innsbruck court (Aug. 6, 1765). His success in Vienna continued with the productions of his *Partenope* (Sept. 9, 1767) and *Piramo e Tisbe* (Nov. 1768). But his *Il Ruggiero ovvero L'eroica gratitudine* (Milan, Oct. 16, 1771) failed to please the Italian public, and he decided to cease composing for the stage. In 1773 he retired to Venice. Hasse was a master of bel canto writing; his extraordinary craftsmanship is revealed in his command of harmony and orchestration; in addition to his dramatic works, he also distinguished himself as a composer of sacred music.

WORKS: OPERAS: *Antioco* (Braunschweig, Aug. 11, 1721); *Antonio e Cleopatra*, serenata (Naples, Sept. 1725); *Il Sesostrate* (Naples, May 13, 1726); *La Semele o sia La richiesta fatale*, serenata (Naples, 1726); *L'Astarto* (Naples, Dec. 1726); *Enea in Caonia*, serenata (Naples, 1727); *Gerone tiranno di Siracusa*

(Naples, Nov. 19, 1727); *Attalo, re di Bitinia* (Naples, May 1728); *L'Ulderica* (Naples, Jan. 29, 1729); *La Sorella amante, commedia per musica* (Naples, 1729); *Tigrane* (Naples, Nov. 4, 1729; rev. version, Naples, Nov. 4, 1745); *Artaserse* (Venice, Feb. 1730; rev. version, Dresden, Sept. 9, 1740); *Dalisa* (Venice, May 1730); *Arminio* (Milan, Aug. 28, 1730); *Ezio* (Naples, 1730; rev. version, Dresden, Jan. 20, 1755); *Cleofide* (Dresden, Sept. 13, 1731; rev. version, Venice, Carnival 1736; subsequent revs. 1738 and 1743); *Catone in Utica* (Turin, Dec. 26, 1731); *Cajo Fabricio* (Rome, Jan. 12, 1732; subsequent revs. for Naples, 1733; Dresden, July 8, 1734; Berlin, Sept. 1766); *Demetrio* (Venice, Jan. 1732; subsequent revs. for Vienna [as *Cleonice*], Feb. 1734; Venice, Carnival 1737; Dresden [as *Cleonice*], Feb. 8, 1740; Venice, Carnival 1747); *Euristeo* (Venice, May 1732); *Issipile* (Naples, Oct. 1, 1732; rev. version by Leo, Naples, Dec. 19, 1742; 2nd rev. version by P. Cafaro, Naples, Dec. 26, 1763; *Siroe rè di Persia* (Bologna, May 2, 1733; subsequent revs. for Naples, Nov. 4, 1747; Warsaw, Carnival 1763); *Sei tu, Lidippe, ò il sole*, serenata (Dresden, Aug. 4, 1734); *Senz'attender che di maggio*, cantata (Dresden, 1734); *Tito Vespasiano* (Pesaro, Sept. 24, 1735; subsequent revs. for Dresden, Jan. 17, 1738; Naples, Jan. 20, 1759); *Senocrita* (Dresden, Feb. 27, 1737); *Atalanta* (Dresden, July 26, 1737); *Asteria*, favola pastorale (Dresden, Aug. 3, 1737); *Irene* (Dresden, Feb. 8, 1738); *Alfonso* (Dresden, May 11, 1738); *Viriate* (Venice, Carnival 1739); *Numa Pompilio* (Hubertusburg, Oct. 7, 1741); *Lucio Papirio* (Dresden, Jan. 18, 1742; rev. version by G. de Majo, Naples, Nov. 4, 1746; 2nd rev. version by Hasse or Graun, Berlin, Jan. 24, 1766); *Asilio d'amore*, festa teatrale (Naples, July 1742); *Didone abbandonata* (Hubertusburg, Oct. 7, 1742; rev. version by N. Logroscino, Naples, Jan. 20, 1744; subsequent revs. for Berlin, Dec. 29, 1752; Versailles, Aug. 28, 1753); *Endimione*, festa teatrale (Naples, July 1743); *Antigono* (Hubertusburg, Oct. 10, 1743?; rev. version by A. Palella, Naples, Dec. 19, 1744); *Ipermestra* (Vienna, Jan. 8, 1744; rev. version by A. Palella, Naples, Jan. 20, 1746; 2nd rev. version, Hubertusburg, Oct. 7, 1751); *Semiramide riconosciuta* (Naples, Nov. 4, 1744; subsequent revs. for Dresden, Jan. 11, 1747; Warsaw, Oct. 7, 1760); *Arminio* (Dresden, Oct. 7, 1745; rev. version, Dresden, Jan. 8, 1753); *La Spartana generosa, ovvero Archidamia* (Dresden, June 14, 1747); *Leucippo*, favola pastorale (Hubertusburg, Oct. 7, 1747; subsequent revs. for Venice, May 1749; Dresden, Jan. 7, 1751; Berlin, Jan. 7, 1765); *Demofoonte* (Dresden, Feb. 9, 1748; subsequent revs. for Venice, Carnival 1749; Naples, Nov. 4, 1758); *Il natal di Giove*, serenata (Hubertusburg, Oct. 7, 1749); *Attilio Regolo* (Dresden, Jan. 12, 1750); *Ciro riconosciuto* (Dresden, Jan. 20, 1751); *Adriano in Siria* (Dresden, Jan. 17, 1752); *Solimano* (Dresden, Feb. 5, 1753; rev. version, Dresden, Jan. 7, 1754); *L'Eroe cinese* (Hubertusburg, Oct. 7, 1753; rev. version, Potsdam, July 18, 1773); *Artemisia* (Dresden, Feb. 6, 1754); *Il Rè pastore* (Hubertusburg, Oct. 7, 1755); *L'Olimpiade* (Dresden, Feb. 16, 1756; subsequent revs. for Warsaw, Carnival 1761; Turin, Dec. 26, 1764); *Nitteti* (Venice, Jan. 1758; rev. version, Vienna, 1762); *Il sogno di Scipione*, azione teatrale (Warsaw, Oct. 7, 1758); *Achille in Sciro* (Naples, Nov. 4, 1759); *Alcide al bivio*, festa teatrale (Vienna, Oct. 8, 1760); *Zenobia* (Vienna, Carnival 1761); *Il trionfo di Clelia* (Vienna, April 27, 1762; rev. version by G. de Majo, Naples, Jan. 20, 1763); *Egeria*, festa teatrale (Vienna, April 24, 1764); *Romolo ed Ersilia* (Innsbruck, Aug. 6, 1765); *Partenope*, festa teatrale (Vienna, Sept. 9, 1767; rev. version, Berlin, July 18, 1775); *Piramo e Tisbe*, intermezzo tragico (Vienna, Nov. 1768; rev. version, Vienna, Sept. 1770); *Il Ruggiero ovvero L'eroica gratitudine* (Milan, Oct. 16, 1771).

INTERMEZZOS: *Miride e Damari* (Naples, May 13, 1726); *Larinda e Vanesio* (Naples, Dec. 1726; subsequent revs. for Dresden, July 8, 1734; Venice, Carnival 1739); *Grilletta e Porsugnacco* (Venice, May 1727; subsequent revs. for Naples, Nov. 19, 1727; Dresden, Aug. 4, 1747); *Carlotta e Pantaleone* (Naples, May 1728; subsequent revs. for Naples, Carnival 1734; Potsdam, 1749); *Scintilla e Don Tabarano* (Naples, 1728; subsequent revs. for Venice, 1731; Dresden, July 26, 1737); *Merlina e Galoppo* (Naples, Jan. 29, 1729; subsequent revs. for Venice,

1741; Dresden, 1749); *Dorilla e Balanzone* (Naples, Nov. 4, 1729; rev. version, Venice, 1732); *Lucilla e Pandolfo* (Naples, 1730; subsequent revs. for Dresden, 1738; Venice, 1739; Dresden, 1755); *Arrighetta e Cespuglio* (Naples, c.1730); *Pimpinella e Marcantonio* (Hubertusburg, Oct. 7, 1741; subsequent revs. for Dresden, Jan. 14, 1743); *Versailles*, Aug. 28, 1753); *Rimario e Grilantea* (Nov. 3, 1741).

ORATORIOS: *Daniello* (Vienna, Feb. 15, 1731); *Serpentes ignei in deserto* (Venice, c.1731); *S. Petrus et S. Maria Magdalena* (Venice, c.1731); *Il cantico de'tre fanciulli* (Dresden, April 23, 1734); *Le virtù appiè della croce* (Dresden, April 19, 1737); *Giuseppe riconosciuto* (Dresden, March 31, 1741); *I Pellegrini al sepolcro de Nostro Signore* (Dresden, March 23, 1742); *La caduta di Gerico* (Dresden, April 12, 1743); *La deposizione dalla croce di Gesu Cristo, salvatore nostro* (Dresden, April 4, 1744); *S. Elena al Calvario* (Dresden, April 9, 1746); *La conversione di S. Agostino* (Dresden, March 28, 1750). Additional sacred works include about 90 cantatas, some 15 masses, several Requiem masses, various mass movements, 10 offertories, 23 Psalms, over 20 antiphons, many hymns, some 40 solo motets, and various other works, including arias.

INSTRUMENTAL: Twelve Concertos in 6 parts for Flute, 2 Violins, Viola, and Harpsichord or Cello, op. 3 (London, 1741); 6 Concertos for Harpsichord or Organ (London, 1743; keyboard reduction of pieces from op. 3); 6 Concertos in 6 parts for Flute, 2 Violins, Viola, and Harpsichord or Cello, op. 6 (London, c.1745); various other concertos; 3 quartets; many trio sonatas; numerous keyboard sonatas; etc.

BIBL.: F. Kandler, *Cenni storico-critici intorno alla vita ed alle opere del cel. Gio. Adolfo H. detto il Sassone* (Venice, 1820); R. Eitner, "J.A. H.'s Werke auf der König. Bibliothek zu Berlin," *Monatshefte für Musikgeschichte*, XI (1879); U. de Gheltof, *La "nuova Sirena" e il "caro Sassone"* (Venice, 1890); B. Zeller, *Das Recitativo accompagnato in den Opern J.A. H.s* (Halle, 1911); W. Müller, *J.A. H. als Kirchenkomponist* (Leipzig, 1911; with a thematic catalog); L. Kamienski, *Die Oratorien von J.A. H.* (Leipzig, 1912); O. Sonneck, "Die drei Fassungen des H.'schen Artaserse," *Sammelbände der Internationalen Musik-Gesellschaft*, XIV (1912–13); R. Gerber, *Der Operntypus J.A. H. und seine textlichen Grundlagen* (Leipzig, 1925); S. Hansell, *The Solo Cantatas, Motets and Antiphons of J.A. H.* (diss., Univ. of Illinois, 1966); idem, *Works for Solo Voice of J.A. H.* (Detroit, 1968; a catalog); idem, "Sacred Music at the *Incurabili* in Venice at the Time of J.A. H.," *Journal of the American Musicological Society*, XXIII (1970); P. Drummond, "The Concertos of J.A. H.," *Proceedings of the Royal Musical Association*, XCIX (1972–73); K.-H. Viertel, "Neue Dokumente zu Leben und Werk J.A. H.s," *Analecta Musicologica*, no. 12 (1973); F. Millner, "H. and London's Opera of the Nobility," *Music Review*, XXXV (1974); D. Heartz, "H., Galuppi and Metastasio," *Venezia e il melodramma nel settecento: Venezia 1975*; R. Strohm, "H., Scarlatti, Rolli," *Analecta Musicologica*, no. 15 (1975); F. Millner, *The Operas of J.A. H.* (Ann Arbor, 1979); F. Lippmann, ed., "Colloquium 'J.A. H. und die Musik seiner Zeit' (Siena 1983)," *Analecta Musicologica*, no. 25 (1987).

Hasse, Karl, German composer and musicologist; b. Dohna, near Dresden, March 20, 1883; d. Cologne, July 31, 1960. He studied with Kretzschmar and Riemann at the Univ. of Leipzig, and with Straube and Nikisch at the Leipzig Cons.; later took courses in Munich with Reger and Mottl. He was music director and a prof. at Tübingen Univ. from 1919; in 1923 received his Ph.D. there. He was director of the Staatliche Musikhochschule in Cologne from 1935 to 1945. He wrote a number of works for orch., chamber groups, organ, and voice, aggregating 120 opus numbers; publ. books on Max Reger (Leipzig, 1921; Berlin, 1936; Leipzig, 1948; Dortmund, 1951); 3 books on Bach (Leipzig, 1925; Cologne, 1938; Leipzig, 1949); contributed numerous articles to German music magazines.

Hassell, Jon, American composer; b. Memphis, Tenn., March 22, 1937. He was trained as a trumpet player; then studied composition with Bernard Rogers at the Eastman School of Music in Rochester, N.Y. (B.M., 1969; M.M., 1970). Progress-

ing away from traditional arts, he took courses in advanced electronic techniques with Stockhausen and Pousseur in Cologne (1965–67); returning to the U.S., he was composer-in-residence and a performer at the Center for Creative and Performing Arts in Buffalo (1967–69). In 1969 he moved to N.Y., where he pursued independent activities in music and in sculpture. Among his compositions from this period are *Goodbye Music* for Mixed Media (Buffalo, May 4, 1969), *Superball* for 4 Players with Hand-held Magnetic Tape Heads (Ithaca, Oct. 29, 1969), and *Map 1 and Map 2* for Hand-held Magnetic Playback Heads (exhibited in Buffalo as sculptures, 1969). In the 1970s he studied Indian music with Pandit Pran Nath, and developed a vocal style of trumpet playing; he combined this with avant-garde and jazz backgrounds to create a series of works marked by their remarkable syntheses of African, Asian, and Western music. His popular works in this style appear on the recordings *Earthquake Island* (1978), the synthetically sampled *Aka/Darbari/Java–Magic Realism* (1983), *Power Spot* (1986), and *The Surgeon of the Nightsky Restores Dead Things by the Power of Sound* (1987). On the recording *Flash of the Spirit* (1989), he performs with the West African group Farafina.

Hasselmans, family of Belgian-French musicians:
(1) Josef H. Hasselmans, Belgian harpist, violinist, and conductor; b. Antwerp, 1814; d. 1902. He studied harp with Antoine Prumier; also learned to play the violin. He was 1st violinist in the Antwerp theater orch., and subsequently its conductor; then was conductor of the Strasbourg theater orch. and director of the Cons. (from 1854).

(2) Alphonse (Jean) Hasselmans, Belgian-born French harpist and composer, son of the preceding; b. Liège, March 5, 1845; d. Paris, May 19, 1912. He began harp studies with his father; then continued his training with Gottlieb Krüger in Stuttgart, Xavier Désargus *fils* in Brussels, and Ange-Conrad Prumier in Paris. He began his career as a harpist in the orch. of Brussels's Théâtre de la Monnaie; then settled in Paris, where he attracted notice with a series of solo concerts in 1877; subsequently was principal harpist in the orchs. of the Opéra, the Opéra-Comique, and the Cons.; was prof. of harp at the Cons. from 1884. He became a French citizen in 1903. Many composers wrote works for him; his own compositions include some 50 works and numerous transcriptions.

BIBL.: W. Trezise, Jr., "A. H.," *American Harp Journal*, i/1 (1967).

(3) Louis Hasselmans, French cellist and conductor, son of the preceding; b. Paris, July 15, 1878; d. San Juan, Puerto Rico, Dec. 27, 1957. He studied with Godard, Lavignac, and Massenet; also studied cello with Jules Delsart at the Paris Cons., winning the premier prix in 1893. He was a member of the Capet Quartet (1904–9); made his conducting debut with the Lamoureux Orch. (1905); then conducted at the Opéra-Comique (1909–11; 1919–22), the Montreal Opera and Marseilles Concerts Classiques (1911–13), and the Chicago Civic Opera (1918–19); later conducted the French repertoire at the Metropolitan Opera in N.Y. (1921–36). From 1936 to 1948 he taught at the Louisiana State Univ. School of Music.

Hassler, eminent family of German musicians:
(1) Isaak Hassler, organist; b. Joachimsthal, c.1530; d. Nuremberg (buried), July 14, 1591. He studied in Joachimsthal with Johann Matthesius, the local headmaster, and with Nicolaus Herman, the Kantor; then in 1554 settled in Nuremberg, where he was active as both a lapidary and a musician. He was highly esteemed as a musician, as were his 3 sons:
(2) Caspar Hassler, organist, editor, and composer; b. Nuremberg (baptized), Aug. 17, 1562; d. there, Aug. 19, 1618. He studied with his father; in 1586 he became organist of the Egidienkirche and then of St. Lorenz, where he remained until 1616, when he became organist of St. Sebald. He was renowned as an organist and as an authority on organ design; restored the organ at St. Sebald in 1617. He was ennobled by Emperor Rudolf II in 1595. He ed. valuable collections of works by the leading Italian masters, which included some works by

his brother Hans Leo Hassler and other German composers (1598, 1600, 1600, 1613). His only extant work is a 4–part *Fantasia* in German organ tablature (ed. in Denkmäler der Tonkunst in Bayern, VII, Jg. IV/2, 1903).

(3) Hans (Johann) Leo Hassler, celebrated organist and composer; b. Nuremberg (baptized), Oct. 26, 1564; d. Frankfurt am Main, June 8, 1612. He began his musical training with his father; then in 1584 continued his education in Venice, where he was a pupil of Andrea Gabrieli. He was named chamber organist to Octavian II Fugger in Augsburg in Jan. 1586, and quickly established himself as one of the leading musicians in Germany. In 1591 the emperor granted him the privilege of copyrighting his compositions. He was ennobled by the emperor in 1595, and was given a coat of arms and the title of Hassler von Roseneck in 1604. While in Augsburg, he also became active as a manufacturer of mechanical musical instruments, an enterprise that led to numerous litigations with business rivals. After Octavian's death in 1600, he was made director of the town music in Augsburg; also served as Kaiserlicher Hofdiener to the court of Emperor Rudolf II, a position which may have been purely honorary. He obtained a year's leave of absence from Augsburg for a stay in Ulm in 1604, and then decided to remain there the following year; became a citizen of Ulm in 1607 and a member of its merchants' guild in 1608. He was appointed the Saxon electoral chamber organist in Dresden in 1608, and later assumed the duties of Kapellmeister. Following his move to Dresden, he was stricken with tuberculosis. He died during the visit of the court chapel to Frankfurt for the election and coronation of Emperor Matthias. Hassler excelled as a composer of both sacred and secular vocal works; his sacred compositions reflect the influence of Lassus and others of the Venetian school, while his secular compositions display a pronounced individuality. His organ music follows the precepts of Andrea and Giovanni Gabrieli.

WORKS: *Canzonette* for 4 Voices, *libro I* (Nuremberg, 1590); *Cantiones sacrae de festis praecipuis totius anni* for 4 to 8 *et plurium vocum* (Augsburg, 1591); *Madrigali* for 5 to 8 Voices (Augsburg, 1596); *Neüe teütsche Gesang nach Art der welschen Madrigalien und Canzonetten* for 4 to 8 Voices (Augsburg, 1596); *Missae* for 4 to 8 Voices (Nuremberg, 1599); *Lustgarten neuer teutscher Gesäng, Balletti, Gaillarden und Intraden* for 4 to 8 Voices (Nuremberg, 1601); *Sacri concentus* for 4 to 12 Voices (Augsburg, 1601; 2nd ed., augmented, 1612); *Psalmer und christliche Gesänge* for 4 Voices, *auff die Melodeyen fugweiss componiert* (Nuremberg, 1607); *Kirchengesänge: Psalmen und geistlicher Lieder, auff die gemeinen Melodeyen* for 4 Voices, *simpliciter gesetzet* (Nuremberg, 1608); *Venusgarten: oder neue lustige liebliche Täntz* for 4 to 6 Voices (Nuremberg, 1615); *Litaney teütsch* for 7 Voices (Nuremberg, 1619); also vocal works in various contemporary collections. The *Sämtliche Werke*, ed. by C. Crosby, commenced publication in Wiesbaden in 1961.

BIBL.: A. Sanderberger, "Bemerkungen zur Biographie H.L. H.s und seiner Brüder sowie zur Musikgeschichte der Städte Nürnberg und Augsburg im 16. und Anfang des 17. Jahrhunderts," Denkmäler der Tonkunst in Bayern, VIII, Jg. V (1904); R. Schwartz, "Zur H.-Forschung," *Jahrbuch der Musikbibliothek Peters 1905*; H. Leichtentritt, *Geschichte der Motette* (Leipzig, 1908); J. Neyses, *Studien zur Geschichte der deutschen Motette des XVI. Jahrhunderts: I. Die Form der H.schen Motette* (diss., Univ. of Bonn, 1926); M. Jarvis, *The Latin Motets of H.L. H.* (diss., Univ. of Rochester, 1959); H. Moser, "Das Opus sacrum des 400jährigen H.L. H.," *Musik und Kirche*, XXXIV (1964); F. Hartmann, *H.L. H.: Gedenkschrift* (Frankfurt, 1969); W. Dupont, *Werkausgaben Nürnberger Komponisten in Vergangenheit und Gegenwart* (Nuremberg, 1971; with list of editions); H. Harrasowitz, *Geschichte der Kirchenmusik an St. Lorenz in Nürnberg* (Nuremberg, 1973).

(4) Jakob Hassler, organist and composer; b. Nuremberg (baptized), Dec. 18, 1569; d. probably in Eger, between April and Sept. 1622. He studied with his father; was apprenticed as a town wait in Augsburg in 1585; then received a stipend from his patron, Christoph Fugger. He was ennobled by Emperor Rudolf II in 1595. In 1595–96 he became entangled in legal problems, culminating in his incarceration; he was released through the efforts of his brother Hans Leo Hassler. He was organist at the Hohenzollern court in Hechingen (1597–1601), and later imperial court organist to Emperor Rudolf II in Prague. Following the emperor's death in 1612, he pursued mining in Eger.

WORKS: *Madrigali* for 6 Voices (Nuremberg, 1600); *Magnificat 8 tonorum* for 4 Voices, *cum missa* for 6 Voices, *et psalmo li* for 8 Voices (Nuremberg, 1601); also keyboard works, some of which were ed. by E. von Werra in Denkmäler Tonkunst in Bayern, VII, Jg. IV/2 (1903).

Hässler, Johann Wilhelm, German organist, composer, and pianist; b. Erfurt, March 29, 1747; d. Moscow, March 29, 1822. His father was a maker of men's headwear; he followed his father's trade while studying organ with his uncle, Johann Christian Kittel. At the age of 14, he was able to earn his living as organist at an Erfurt church. After his father's death, in 1769, he maintained for some years a manufactory of fur muffs. A meeting in Hamburg with C.P.E. Bach gave him a fresh impetus toward continuing his musical activities. He gave concerts as a pianist, and publ. several piano sonatas. On Feb. 8, 1779, he married his pupil Sophie Kiel. In 1780 he opened public winter concerts in Erfurt; his wife appeared there as a singer and choral director. In 1789 he played in Berlin and Potsdam; in Dresden he took part in a contest with Mozart, as organist and pianist, without producing much impression either on Mozart himself or on the listeners. In 1790 he went to London, where he performed piano concertos under the direction of Haydn. In 1792 he went to Russia, where he remained until his death. In Moscow he became greatly renowned as a pianist, as a composer, and particularly as a teacher. Most of his works were publ. in Russia; these included sonatas, preludes, variations, fantasies, etc., and also pieces for piano, 4-hands. His style represents a transition between Bach and Beethoven, without attaining a degree of the imagination or craftsmanship of either. However, his piano pieces in the lighter vein have undeniable charm. His *Grande gigue* was well known. His autobiography is included in W. Kahl, *Selbstbiographien deutscher Musiker* (Cologne, 1948).

BIBL.: H. Strobel, *J.W. H.s Leben und Werke* (diss., Univ. of Munich, 1922); R.-A. Mooser, *Annales de la musique et des musiciens en Russie au XVIIIᵉ siècle* (vol. II, Geneva, 1951); H. Hamann, "W.A. Mozart—J.W. H.: Der Dresdener Orgelwettstreit im Jahre 1789," *Musik und Kirche*, XXXIII (1963).

Hastings, Thomas, American composer of hymn tunes; b. Washington, Litchfield County, Conn., Oct. 15, 1784; d. N.Y., May 15, 1872. The family moved to Clinton, N.Y., when Hastings was 12; he became interested in practical music and was a leader of a village chorus. He collected hymns, which were later publ. in a collection, *Musica Sacra* (Utica, N.Y., 1815; 2nd ed., 1816); it was later combined with S. Warriner's *Springfield Collection* (Boston, 1813) as *Musica Sacra: or, Springfield and Utica Collection* (Utica, 1818; 9 subsequent eds. to 1830). He moved to Utica in 1823 and was a member of a Handel and Haydn society there; he also ed. a religious weekly publication, *The Western Recorder*. In 1832 he settled in N.Y., where he was connected with the Normal Inst., in association with Lowell Mason. He received the honorary degree of D.Mus. from N.Y. Univ. (1858). Among his many publications were *Musical Reader* (1817); *Dissertation on Musical Taste* (in which he discourses on the superiority of German music; Albany, 1822; 2nd ed., 1853); *The Union Minstrel* (1830); *Spiritual Songs for Social Worship* (with Lowell Mason; 1831); *Devotional Hymns and Religious Poems* (1850); *History of Forty Choirs* (1854); and *Sacred Praise* (1856). His own hymn tunes have been estimated to number more than 1,000, and, next to those of Lowell Mason, are regarded as the finest of his time in America. These include the tune to which the celebrated hymn *Rock of Ages* is sung; the words are by Augustus Toplady, and Hastings entitled his tune simply *Toplady* to honor the author of the words. Other well-known hymn tunes are *Retreat, Zion,* and *Ortonville.* He publ. many of his melodies under foreign-sounding names, and it is not always possible to ascertain their authorship.

Bibl.: F. Metcalf, *American Writers and Compilers of Sacred Music* (N.Y., 1925); M. Scanlon, "T. H.," *Musical Quarterly* (April 1946); J. Dooley, *T. H.: American Church Musician* (diss., Florida State Univ., 1963); R. Stevenson, *Protestant Church Music in America* (N.Y., 1966).

Hathaway, Donny, black American jazz singer and composer; b. Chicago, Oct. 1, 1945; d. N.Y., Jan. 13, 1979. He played piano and sang gospel songs as a youth; studied at Howard Univ. in Washington, D.C.; while in college, he played organ in churches and acted as an entertainer in nightclubs; also arranged music. He composed for films and television; his best-known songs were *The Ghetto* and *You've Got a Friend.* His early death was a grievous loss to black music.

Hatrík, Juraj, Slovak composer; b. Orkučany, May 1, 1941. He studied with Alexander Moyzes at the Bratislava Music Academy (1958–62); then taught esthetics and psychology of music there.

Works: Sinfonietta (1962); *Contrasts* for Violin and Piano (1963); *Canto responsoriale* for Double Chorus and 4 Kettle-drums (1964); *Čakanie* (Waiting) for Narrator, Flute, Harp, Strings, and Percussion (1965); *Monumento malincolico* for Organ and Orch. (1965); *Concertino in modo classico* for Piano and Orch. (1968); *Introspection* for Soprano, Flute, Violin, Cello, Clarinet, Horn, and Vibraphone (1968); *Domov sú ruky,* cantata (1968); *Sonata ciacona* for Piano (1970); *Da capo al fine,* symphonic poem (1975; Bratislava, Feb. 19, 1976); *Choral Fantasia* for Accordion and Chamber Ensemble (1976).

Hatton, John Liptrot, English composer; b. Liverpool, Oct. 12, 1808; d. Margate, Sept. 20, 1886. He acquired facility as a pianist and singer, and appeared on the vaudeville stage as a musical comedian. He publ. a great number of songs, among which *Anthea* and *Good-bye, sweetheart, good-bye* became extremely popular. In 1832 he went to London; produced his operetta, *The Queen of the Thames, or The Anglers* (Feb. 25, 1842). He then went to Vienna, where he staged his opera *Pascal Bruno* (March 2, 1844). For some of his numbers he used the punning pseudonym Czapek (genitive plural of the Hungarian word for "hat"). From 1848 to 1850 he made an extensive American tour. Returning to England, he was music director at the Princess's Theatre (1853–59); wrote music for several Shakespeare plays there; wrote a cantata, *Robin Hood* (Bradford Festival, Aug. 26, 1856); a grand opera, *Rose, or Love's Ransom* (London, Nov. 26, 1864); and a sacred drama, *Hezekiah* (Dec. 15, 1877); ed. collections of old English songs.

Hatze, Josip, Croatian composer; b. Split, March 21, 1879; d. there, Jan. 30, 1959. He studied with Mascagni in Italy, and belongs to a generation of Croatian composers entirely influenced by Italian music. He wrote the operas *Povratak* (The Return; Zagreb, March 21, 1911) and *Adel i Mara* (Zagreb, March 1, 1933); many songs.

Haubenstock-Ramati, Roman, Polish composer of experimental music; b. Krakow, Feb. 27, 1919. He studied philosophy at the Univ. of Krakow; also took music lessons with Arthur Malawski and Josef Koffler. From 1947 to 1950 he was music director of Radio Krakow; then went to Israel, where he was director of the State Music Library in Tel Aviv (1950–56). In 1957 he settled in Vienna, where he was for a time employed by Universal Edition as reader and adviser for publications of new music; he also was a prof. of composition at the Vienna Academy of Music (from 1973); in 1981 he was awarded the Austrian State Prize. In 1959 he organized in Donaueschingen the 1st exhibition of musical scores in graphic notation; he evolved an imaginative type of modern particella in which the right-hand page gives the outline of musical action for the conductor while the left-hand page is devoted to instrumental and vocal details. This type of notation combined the most advanced type of visual guidance with an aide-mémoire of traditional theater arrangements. Several of his works bear the subtitle "Mobile" to indicate the flexibility of their architectonics.

Works: *Ricercari* for String Trio (1950); *Blessings* for Voice and 9 Players (1952); *Recitativo ed Aria* for Harpsichord and Orch. (1954); *Papageno's Pocket-Size Concerto* for Glockenspiel and Orch. (1955); *Les Symphonies des timbres* for Orch. (1957); *Chants et Prismes* for Orch. (1957, rev. 1967); *Séquences* for Violin and Orch. in 4 groups (1957–58); *Interpolation,* "mobile" for Solo Flute (1958); *Liaisons,* "mobile" for Vibraphone and Marimbaphone (1958); *Petite musique de nuit,* "mobile" for Orch. (1958); *Mobile for Shakespeare* for Voice and 6 Players (1960); *Credentials or "Think, Think Lucky,"* after Beckett, for Speech-voice and 8 Players (1960); *Decisions,* 10 pieces of musical graphics for Variable Instrumentation (1960–68); *Jeux 6,* "mobile" for 6 Percussionists (1960); opera, *Amerika,* after Kafka's novel (1962–64; Berlin, Oct. 8, 1966); *Vermutungen über ein dunkles Haus,* 3 pieces for 3 Orchs., 2 of which are on tape (1963; material from the opera); *Klavierstücke I* for Piano (1963–65); *Jeux 2* and *4,* "mobiles" for 2 and 4 Percussionists (1965, 1966); *Hotel Occidental* for Speech-chorus, after Kafka (in 3 versions, 1967); an anti-opera, *La Comédie,* after Beckett, for 1 Male and 2 Female Speech-singers, and 3 Percussionists (St. Paul-de-Vence, Alpes-Maritimes, France, July 21, 1969; German version as *Spiel,* Munich, 1970; Eng. version as *Play*); *Tableau I, II,* and *III* for Orch. (1967, 1968, 1970); *Symphonie "K"* (1967; material from the opera *Amerika*); *Psalm* for Orch. (1967); *Divertimento,* text collage for Actors, Dancer, and/or Mime, and 2 Percussionists (1968; after *Jeux 2*); *Catch I* for Harpsichord (1969), *II* for 1 or 2 Pianos (1970), and *III* for Organ (1971); *Multiple I–VI* for Various Instrumental Combinations (1969); *Alone* for Trombone and Mime (1969); *Describe* for Voice and Piano (1969); *Hexachord I* and *II* for 2 Guitars (1972); *Concerto a tre* for Piano, Trombone, and Percussion (1973); 2 string quartets (1973, 1978); *Shapes (in Memory of Stravinsky) I* for Organ and Tape, and *II* for Organ, Piano, Harpsichord, and Celesta (both 1973); *Endless,* endless "mobile" for 7 Players and Conductor (1974); Solo Cello Sonata (1975); *Musik* for 12 Instruments (1976); *Ulysses,* ballet (1977); *Concerto per archi* (1977; Graz, Oct. 11, 1977); *Symphonien* (1977; Baden-Baden, May 10, 1978); *Song* for Percussion (1978); *Self I* for Bass Clarinet or Clarinet (1978) and *II* for Saxophone (1978); *3 Nocturnes* for Orch. (1981, 1982, 1985); *Mirrors/Miroirs,* "mobile" for 16 Pianos (1984); *Mirrors/Miroirs II,* "mobile" for 8 Pianos (1984); *Mirrors/Miroirs III,* "mobile" for 6 Pianos (1984); String Trio No. 2 (1985); *Sotto voce* for Chamber Orch. (1986).

Haubiel (real name, **Pratt**), **Charles Trowbridge,** American composer; b. Delta, Ohio, Jan. 30, 1892; d. Los Angeles, Aug. 26, 1978. His father's last name was Pratt, but he adopted his mother's maiden name, Haubiel, as his own. He had piano lessons with his sister Florence Pratt, an accomplished pianist. In 1911 he went to Europe, where he studied piano with Rudolph Ganz in Berlin; also took composition lessons with Alexander von Fielitz in Leipzig. Returning to the U.S. in 1913, he taught music at various schools in Oklahoma. When the U.S. entered World War I in 1917, he enlisted in the field artillery and served in France. After the Armistice he resumed serious study of composition with Rosario Scalero at the David Mannes Music School in N.Y. (1919–24), while continuing piano lessons with Rosina and Josef Lhévinne. Intermittently he taught musical subjects at the Inst. of Musical Art in N.Y. (1921–31) and at N.Y. Univ. (1923–47). In 1935 he organized the Composers Press, Inc., with the purpose of promoting the publication of American music, and served as its president until 1966. His compositions reveal an excellent theoretical and practical grasp of harmony, counterpoint, instrumentation, and formal design. In his idiom he followed the models of the Romantic school of composition, but he embroidered the basic patterns of traditional music with winsome coloristic touches, approaching the usage of French Impressionism. He was extremely prolific; many of his works underwent multiple transformations from a modest original, usually for solo piano or a chamber group, to a piece for full orch.; in all these forms his compositions remain eminently playable.

WORKS: STAGE: Mexican folk opera, *Sunday Costs 5 Pesos* (Charlotte, N.C., Nov. 6, 1950). **ORCH.:** *Gothic Variations* (orig. for Violin and Piano, 1919; rev. 1942; adapted for Full Orch., Los Angeles, June 9, 1970); *Vox Cathedralis* (orig. for Organ, 1925; arranged for 2 Pianos, 1928; finally transcribed for Orch., 1934; N.Y., May 6, 1938); *Rittrati* (Portraits; orig. for Piano, 1919; orch. transcription 1st perf., Chicago, Dec. 12, 1935); *Karma*, symphonic variations (1928; received 1st prize in the Schubert Centennial contest by Columbia Records; rev. 1968 and retitled *Of Human Destiny*); *Suite Passacaglia* (Los Angeles, Jan. 31, 1936; orig. for 2 Pianos); *Symphony in Variation Form* (1937); *Miniatures* for String Orch. (N.Y., April 23, 1939); *American Rhapsody* (1948); *Pioneers*, symphonic saga of Ohio (1946; rev. 1956; Los Angeles, Feb. 19, 1960); *Metamorphosis* (1926; set of 29 variations on Stephen Foster's *Swanee River*; filmed as a short subject and produced under the title *Swanee River Goes Hi-Hat*); *1865 A.D.* (1943; rev. 1958, under the title *Mississippi Story*; Los Angeles, April 24, 1959). **CHAMBER:** *Ecchi classici* for String Quartet (1924); *Duo Forms* for Cello and Piano (1929–31); *Cryptics* for Bassoon and Piano (1932); *Lodando la danza* for Oboe, Violin, Cello, and Piano (1932); *Nuances*, suite for Flute and Piano (1938); Cello Sonata (1941); *In the French Manner* for Flute, Cello, and Piano (1942); String Trio (1943); Violin Sonata (1945); *Shadows* for Violin and Piano (1947); *Pastoral Trio* for Flute, Cello, and Piano (1949); *Epochs* for Violin and Piano (1954–55); *Threnody for Love* for 6 Instruments (1965); *Ohioana*, cycle for Violin and Piano (1966); Trio for Clarinet, Cello, and Piano (1969). Also numerous choral works: *Vision of Saint Joan* (1941); *Jungle Tale* (1943); *Father Abraham* (1944); etc.; piano suite, *Solari* (1932–34); other pieces for piano solo.

Haudebert, Lucien, French composer; b. Fougères, April 10, 1877; d. Paris, Feb. 24, 1963. He studied organ; then went to Paris, where he took lessons in composition with Fauré. He followed in his music the traditions of César Franck, preferring large sonorities and clear tonal harmonies. He stood aloof from modern developments in France and had little recognition even among traditional musicians, despite praise from Romain Rolland. His most effective work is the oratorio *Dieu Vainqueur* (1916–22); other significant works are the oratorio *Moïse* (1928); *Symphonie bretonne* (1936); *Symphonie française* (1941); *Voyage en Bretagne* for Orch. (1953); *Chants de la mer* for Voices and Orch. (1950); also chamber music, including a Quartet for Saxophones.

Hauer, Josef Matthias, significant Austrian composer and music theorist; b. Wiener-Neustadt, near Vienna, March 19, 1883; d. Vienna, Sept. 22, 1959. After attending a college for teachers, he became a public-school instructor; at the same time he studied music. An experimenter by nature, with a penchant for mathematical constructions, he developed a system of composition based on "tropes," or patterns, which aggregated to thematic formations of 12 different notes. As early as 1912 he publ. a piano piece, entitled *Nomos* (Law), which contained the germinal principles of 12-tone music; in his theoretical publications he elaborated his system in greater detail. These were *Über die Klangfarbe*, op. 13 (Vienna, 1918; augmented as *Vom Wesen des Musikalischen*, Leipzig and Vienna, 1920; 3rd ed., rev. and augmented, 1966); *Deutung des Melos: Eine Frage an die Künstler und Denker unserer Zeit* (Leipzig, Vienna, and Zürich, 1923); *Vom Melos zur Pauke: Eine Einführung in die Zwölftonmusik* (Vienna, 1925; 2nd ed., 1967); and *Zwölftontechnik: Die Lehre von den Tropen* (Vienna, 1926; 2nd ed., 1953), in which the method of composing in the 12-tone technique was illustrated with practical examples. Hauer vehemently asserted his priority in 12-tone composition; he even used a rubber stamp on his personal stationery proclaiming himself the true founder of the 12-tone method. This claim was countered, with equal vehemence but with more justification, by Schoenberg; indeed, the functional basis of 12-tone composition in which the contrapuntal and harmonic structures are derived from the unifying tone row did not appear until Schoenberg formulated it and put it into practice in 1924. Hauer lived his entire life in Vienna, working as a composer, conductor, and teacher. Despite its forbidding character, his music attracted much attention.

WORKS: 2 operas: *Salambo* (1930; Austrian Radio, Vienna, March 19, 1983) and *Die schwarze Spinne* (1932; Vienna, May 23, 1966); oratorio, *Wandlungen*, for 6 Soloists, Chorus, and Chamber Orch. (1927; Baden-Baden, April 16, 1928); cantatas: *Emilie vor ihrem Brauttag* for Alto and Orch. (1928) and *Der Menschen Weg*, in 7 sections, to poems by Hölderlin, for 4 Soloists, Chorus, and Orch. (1934; reduced in 1952 to 5 sections; Vienna, June 1953); *Lateinische Messe* for Chorus, Chamber Orch., and Organ (1926, unfinished; Vienna, June 18, 1972); *Vom Leben*, after Hölderlin, for Narrator, Small Chorus, and Small Orch. (1928). **OTHER WORKS:** *Nomos* (Sym. No. 1), in 7 parts, for 1 or 2 Pianos, or Orch. (1912–13; version for 2 Pianos, Sankt Pölten, June 7, 1913); *Nomos* (Sym. No. 2), in 5 parts, for Piano or Small Orch. (1913); *Nomos*, 7 little piano pieces (1913); *Apokalyptische Phantasie* (Sym. No. 3) for 2 Pianos or Orch. (1913; version for 2 Pianos, Wiener-Neustadt, May 9, 1914; version for Orch., Graz, Oct. 21, 1969); *Oriental Tale* for Piano (1916); *Nomos* for Piano and String Ensemble (1919); Quintet for Clarinet, Violin, Viola, Cello, and Piano (1924); 6 string quartets (1924–26); 8 suites for Orch. (1924; 1924; 1925, with Baritone Solo; 1926; 1926; 1926, also for String Quartet; 1926; 1927); *Romantische Fantasie* for Small Orch. (1925); 7 *Variations* for Flute, Clarinet, Violin, Viola, Cello, and Double Bass (1925); *Symphonische Stücke* (*Kammerstücke*) for String Orch., Piano, and Harmonium (1926); Sinfonietta (1927; Berlin, Dec. 13, 1928); Violin Concerto (1928; Berlin, Nov. 12, 1929); Piano Concerto (1928); *Divertimento* for Small Orch. (1930); *Konzertstücke* for Orch. (1932; from the opera *Die schwarze Spinne*); *Tanzphantasien* Nos. 1 and 2 for 4 Soloists and Orch. (1933) and Nos. 3–7 for Chamber Orch. (1934); 2 *Tanzsuiten* for 9 Solo Instruments (1936); *Labyrinthischer Tanz* for Piano, 4-hands (1952); *Langsamer Walzer* for Orch. (1953); *Chinesisches Streichquartett* (1953); *Hausmusik* for Piano, 4-hands (1958). From 1940, Hauer was primarily concerned with composing a series of pieces, each ostentatiously bearing the subtitle *Zwölftonspiel*, for orch. and chamber combinations of all descriptions—their total number exceeding 100—with each one designated by the month and year composed, as, for example, *Zwölftonspiel* for Orch. (Aug. 1940), *Zwölftonspiel* for Violin and Harpsichord (July 1948), *Zwölftonspiel* for Orch. (Sept. 1957), and *Zwölftonspiel* for String Sextet (May 1958).

BIBL.: W. Reich, "J.M. H.," *Die Musik* (May 1931); H. Picht, *J.M. H., Ein Vorkämpfer geistiger Musikauffassung* (Stuttgart, 1934); M. Lichtenfeld, *Untersuchungen zur Theorie der Zwölftontechnik bei J.M. H.* (Regensburg, 1964); W. Szmolyan, *J.M. H.* (Vienna, 1965); J. Sengstschmid, "Anatomie eines Zwölftonspiels, Ein Blick in die Werkstatt J.M. Hs.," *Zeitschrift für Musiktheorie* (April 1971); H. Schöny, "Die Vorfahren des Komponisten J.M. H.," *Genealogie* (Aug. 1971); M. Keyton, *A Mathematical Construction of the "Tropen" Occurring in H.'s Musical System* (thesis, Louisiana State Univ., 1976); R. Gustafson, "J.M. H.," *Tempo* (Sept. 1979); idem, "J.M. H.: A List of Works," ibid. (Sept. 1987).

Haug, Gustav, Swiss organist, teacher, and composer; b. Strasbourg, Nov. 30, 1871; d. St. Gallen, April 22, 1956. He studied at the Strasbourg Cons.; then settled in St. Gallen, where he was active as a church organist and voice teacher. As a composer, he produced a number of singable choral anthems, several works for solo voice with orch. accompaniment, and many songs to German texts.

Haug, Hans, Swiss conductor and composer; b. Basel, July 27, 1900; d. Lausanne, Sept. 15, 1967. He studied piano with Egon Petri and Ernst Levy in Basel, and later with Busoni at the Munich Academy of Music. Returning to Switzerland, he became choral conductor at the Municipal Theater in Basel

(1928–34); from 1935 to 1938 he conducted the orch. of the Radio Suisse Romande and also taught at the Lausanne Cons. As a composer, he was most successful in writing for the theater.

Works: Operas: *Don Juan in der Fremde* (Basel, Jan. 15, 1930), *Madrisa* (Basel, Jan. 15, 1934), *Tartuffe* (Basel, May 24, 1937), *Le Malade imaginaire*, after Molière (Zürich, Feb. 8, 1947), *Der Spiegel der Agrippina* (1954), and *Justice du roi* (1963); radio operas: *Gardien vigilant* (1967) and *Le Souper de Venise* (1967); oratorio, *Michelangelo* (Solothurn, Feb. 28, 1943); operettas: *Barbara* (1938) and *Gilberte de Courgenay* (1939); several radio operettas; ballets: *L'Indifférent* and *Pan und Apollo;* incidental music for theatrical plays; numerous cantatas, including a humorous *Cantate gastronomique* for Soli, Chorus, and Orch.; Sym. (1948); *Capriccio* for Wind Instruments and Piano (1957); Concertino for Flute and Small Orch. (1943); Concertino for Oboe, Viola, and Small Orch.; Concertino for Piano and Orch.; Guitar Concerto (1952); 2 piano concertos (1938, 1962); Double Concerto for Oboe and Viola (1953); 3 string quartets; Wind Quartet; Wind Quintet; also a curious symphonic poem entitled *Charlie Chaplin* (1930).

Haugland, Aage, Danish bass-baritone; b. Copenhagen, Feb. 1, 1944. He studied with Mogens Wöldike and Kristian Riis in Copenhagen, making his operatic debut as the Brewer in Martinů's *Veselohra na mostě* at the Norwegian Opera in Oslo in 1968; then sang with the Royal Opera in Copenhagen (from 1973); also made guest appearances with other major European opera houses, including London's Covent Garden as Hunding (1975), Milan's La Scala as the King in *Lohengrin* (1981), in Salzburg as Rocco (1982), and in Bayreuth as Hagen (1983). In 1979 he made his U.S. debut as Boris Godunov in St. Louis, as well as his Metropolitan Opera debut in N.Y. (Dec. 13, 1979) as Baron Ochs; at the Metropolitan he later sang several Wagnerian roles. His other roles include Leporello, Sarastro, Gounod's Méphistophélès, and the Grand Inquisitor.

Hauk, Minnie (real name, **Amalia Mignon Hauck**), celebrated American soprano; b. N.Y., Nov. 16, 1851; d. Triebschen, near Lucerne, Switzerland, Feb. 6, 1929. Her father was a German carpenter who became involved in the political events of 1848, emigrated to America, and married an American woman; he named his daughter Mignon after the character in Goethe's *Wilhelm Meister.* The family moved to Atchison, Kans., when Minnie was very young; her mother maintained a boarding house at a steamboat landing on the Missouri. In 1860 they moved to New Orleans; there Minnie began to sing popular ballads for entertainment. She made her operatic debut at the age of 14 in Brooklyn, in *La Sonnambula* (Oct. 13, 1866); then took lessons with Achille Errani in N.Y. On Nov. 15, 1867, she sang Juliette at the American premiere of Gounod's opera in N.Y. She attracted the attention of the rich industrialist Leonard Jerome and the music publisher Gustave Schirmer, who financed her trip to Europe. She sang in opera in Paris during the summer of 1868; made her London debut at Covent Garden on Oct. 26, 1868; in 1870 she sang in Vienna. She sang the title roles in the 1st American performances of *Carmen* (N.Y., Oct. 23, 1878) and Massenet's *Manon* (N.Y., Dec. 23, 1885); made her debut at the Metropolitan Opera in N.Y. as Selika in *L'Africaine* on Feb. 10, 1891; continued to appear there for that season, but following a disagreement with the management, decided to organize her own opera group; with it, she gave the 1st Chicago performance of *Cavalleria rusticana* (Sept. 28, 1891). She then settled in Switzerland with her husband, Baron Ernst von Hesse-Wartegg, whom she had married in 1881; after his death she lived mostly in Berlin; lost her fortune in the depreciation of her holdings in Germany. In 1919 Geraldine Farrar launched an appeal to raise funds for her in America. Hauk's autobiography, collated by E. Hitchcock, was publ. as *Memories of a Singer* (London, 1925).

Haupt, Karl August, German organist, pedagogue, and composer; b. Kuhnau, Silesia, Aug. 25, 1810; d. Berlin, July 4, 1891. He studied with Dehn in Berlin; played in various

churches and became famous for his masterly improvisations in the style of Bach. He was one of the experts consulted for the specifications in building the grand organ at the Crystal Palace in London. He had many distinguished pupils, including about 40 American organists. He publ. a valuable *Choralbuch* (1869); many of his compositions for organ remain in MS.

Hauptmann, Moritz, eminent German music theorist, pedagogue, and composer; b. Dresden, Oct. 13, 1792; d. Leipzig, Jan. 3, 1868. His father was an architect and hoped to bring up his son in that profession; however, there was no parental opposition to music studies. Hauptmann took lessons with Scholz (violin), Grosse (piano and harmony), and Morlacchi (composition) in Dresden; later studied with Weinlig; in 1811 he went to Gotha to study violin and composition with Spohr, and became his lifelong friend; went to Vienna in 1813 as a violinist in Spohr's orch. at the Theater an der Wien. In 1812 he joined the Dresden Court Orch. as violinist; in 1815 he became music teacher in the family of the Russian military governor of Dresden, Prince Repnin, and went with them to Russia, where he remained for 5 years. In 1820 he returned to Dresden; in 1822 Spohr engaged him as violinist in the Court Orch. at Kassel. In 1842, at Mendelssohn's recommendation, he was appointed cantor at the Thomasschule and prof. of composition at the Leipzig Cons., retaining these posts until his death. He became greatly renowned as a teacher of violin and composition. Among his pupils were Ferdinand David, Joachim, Hans von Bülow, Jadassohn, and Arthur Sullivan. A master of classical form, he was a polished composer, in the tradition of Spohr and Mendelssohn; the architectonic symmetry of his instrumental works and the purity of part-writing in his vocal music aroused admiration among his contemporaries; yet his music failed to endure, and rapidly went into decline after his death. He publ. about 60 works, among them 3 violin sonatas, 4 violin sonatinas, 2 string quartets, piano pieces, sacred works, and a number of lieder, a genre in which he excelled. His theoretical work *Die Natur der Harmonik und Metrik* (Leipzig, 1853; 2nd ed., 1873; Eng. tr., London, 1888) is an attempt to apply Hegel's dialectical philosophy to the realm of music. It exercised considerable influence on the later development of German theory of harmony; among other German scholars, Riemann was influenced by it. Hauptmann's other writings are *Erläuterungen zu J.S. Bachs Kunst der Fuge* (Leipzig, 1841; 2nd ed., 1861); *Die Lehre von der Harmonik* (ed. by O. Paul; Leipzig, 1868; 2nd ed., 1873); *Opuscula* (miscellaneous writings, ed. by E. Hauptmann; Leipzig, 1874). His letters to Spohr and others were ed. by F. Hiller (Leipzig, 1876). A. Coleridge publ. a selection, in Eng., of Hauptmann's correspondence as *Letters of a Leipzig Cantor* (1892).

Bibl.: O. Paul, *M. H., Eine Denkschrift zur Feier seines Siebzigjährigen Geburtstages am 13. Oktober 1862* (Leipzig, 1862); S. Krehl, *M. H.; Ein Dank- und Gedenkwort* (Leipzig, 1918); P. Rummenhöller, *M. H. als Theoretiker* (Wiesbaden, 1963); D. Jorgenson, *M. H. of Leipzig* (Lewiston, N.Y., 1986).

Hauschka, Vincenz, gifted Bohemian cellist and composer; b. Mies, Jan. 21, 1766; d. Vienna, Sept. 13, 1840. He was a pupil of his father, a schoolteacher; became chorister in the Prague Cathedral; studied composition with Zöger and cello with Christ. He was appointed cellist to Count Joseph von Thun in Prague (1782); made successful concert tours through Germany performing not only on the cello, but also on the baryton (a popular instrument at the time). He publ. 9 sonatas for cello and a book of vocal canons; in MS are several pieces for the baryton.

Hausegger, Friedrich von, Austrian musicologist, father of **Siegmund von Hausegger;** b. St. Andrä, Carinthia, April 26, 1837; d. Graz, Feb. 23, 1899. He was a pupil of Salzmann and Dessoff; also studied law and became a barrister at Graz. In 1872 he became a teacher of history and theory of music at the Univ. of Graz. He contributed to music periodicals.

Writings: *Musik als Ausdruck* (Vienna, 1885); *Richard Wagner und Schopenhauer* (1890); *Vom Jenseits des Künstlers* (1893); *Die künstlerische Persönlichkeit* (1897); *Unsere deut* *schen Meister* (ed. by R. Louis; 1901); his *Gesammelte Schriften* was brought out by his son in 1939.

Hausegger, Siegmund von, esteemed Austrian conductor and composer, son of **Friedrich von Hausegger;** b. Graz, Aug. 16, 1872; d. Munich, Oct. 10, 1948. He was trained by his father. At the age of 16 he composed a grand Mass, which he himself conducted; at 18 he brought out in Graz an opera, *Helfrid.* Richard Strauss thought well enough of Hausegger as a composer to accept for performance his comic opera *Zinnober,* which he conducted in Munich on June 19, 1898. Hausegger began his own conducting career in Graz as a theater conductor in 1895; in 1897 he was guest conductor in Bayreuth; was conductor of the Volk-Symphonie-Konzerte in Munich (1899–1902), the Museum Concerts in Frankfurt (1903–6), and the Phil. Concerts in Hamburg (1910–20). From 1918 to 1934 he was director of the Academy of Musical Art in Munich; in 1920 was named Generalmusikdirektor of the Munich Konzertverein, which became the Munich Phil. in 1928; remained there until his retirement in 1938. He acquired a fine reputation as a conductor in Germany, becoming a champion of Bruckner's syms. in their original versions. As a composer, he wrote in a late German Romantic style. He publ. a monograph, *Alexander Ritter, Ein Bild seines Charakters und Schaffens* (Berlin, 1907), and his father's correspondence with Peter Rosegger (Leipzig, 1924). His collected articles appeared under the title *Betrachtungen zur Kunst* (Leipzig, 1921).
  WORKS: Operas: *Helfrid* (Graz, 1890) and *Zinnober* (Munich, June 19, 1898, R. Strauss conducting); *Dionysische Fantasie* for Orch. (1899); symphonic poems: *Barbarossa* (1900) and *Wieland der Schmied* (1904); *Natursymphonie,* with a choral finale (1911); several works for Chorus and Orch.; symphonic variations on a children's song, *Aufklänge* (1919); etc.

Hauser, Miska, Austrian violinist and composer; b. Pressburg, 1822; d. Vienna, Dec. 8, 1887. He studied with Kreutzer in Vienna, and traveled as a child prodigy in Europe; from 1853 to 1858 made a grand tour of America and Australia. He wrote an operetta, *Der blinde Leiermann;* numerous violin pieces, of which his meretricious *Rapsodie hongroise* and *Lieder ohne Worte* enjoyed undeserved popularity; and *American Rhapsody* for Violin and Piano (1855). During his American tour he sent correspondence to the *Ostdeutsche Post* which was collected and publ. in 2 vols., *Aus dem Wanderbuch eines österreichischen Virtuosen* (Leipzig, 1858–59). *History of Music in San Francisco* (San Francisco, 1939) contains Eng. trs. of some of these reports, which are not devoid of interest.

Hausmann, Robert, German cellist; b. Rottleberode, Harz, Aug. 13, 1852; d. Vienna, Jan. 18, 1909. He studied cello with Theodor Müller in Berlin; was the cellist of the Hochberg quartet in Dresden (1872–76); then joined the Joachim quartet (1879), with which he remained until its dissolution after Joachim's death (1907).

Haussermann, John (William, Jr.), American composer; b. Manila, Philippines, Aug. 21, 1909; d. Denver, May 5, 1986. He was taken to New Richmond, Ohio, as a child and studied piano with local teachers; in 1924 he enrolled in the Cincinnati Cons. of Music, studying organ with Parvin Titus and music theory with George Leighton. In 1930 he went to Paris, where he studied organ with Marcel Dupré and composition with Paul Le Flem. In 1934 he was again in Manila, where he was active as an organist; then lived in Cincinnati; dedicated himself mainly to composing. His music is marked by a pragmatic sense of formal cohesion, which does not exclude a flair for innovation, as exemplified by his Concerto for Voice and Orch.
  WORKS: ORCH.: Syms.: No. 1 (1938; partial perf., N.Y., May 28, 1939); No. 2 (1941; Cincinnati, March 31, 1944); No. 3 (1947; Cincinnati, April 1, 1949); *The After Christmas Suite* (Cincinnati, March 22, 1938); Concerto for Voice and Orch. (Cincinnati, April 24, 1942); *Ronde carnavalesque* (N.Y., Feb. 6, 1949); *Stanza* for Violin and Orch. (Mallorca, Spain, Feb. 22, 1956); *Sacred Cantata* for Baritone and Orch. (Cincinnati,

Jan. 31, 1965); Concerto for Organ and Strings (1985). **CHAMBER:** Quintet for Flute, Oboe, Clarinet, Bassoon, and Harpsichord (1935); String Quartet (1937); *Serenade* for Theremin and Strings (1945); Violin Sonata (1941). **PIANO:** *24 préludes symphoniques* (1932–33); *Sonatine fantastique* (1932); *Pastoral fantasie* for 2 Pianos, 4-hands (1933); *Ballade, Burlesque, et Légende* (1936); *7 Bagatelles* (1948); *9 Impromptus* (1958); *5 Harmonic Études* (1968); a great number of organ pieces; songs.

Haussmann, Valentin, significant German composer; b. Gerbstedt, near Eisleben, c.1565; d. c.1614. He studied at the Regensburg Gymnasium Poeticum, receiving instruction in music from the Kantor, Andreas Raselius; then traveled extensively throughout Germany, serving various courts, municipalities, and private patrons. He was also active in collecting and editing music; tr. Italian texts for several anthologies, which helped to spread Italian music in Germany. His most important contribution to German music was his instrumental music, which included intradas, pavanes, galliards, and the *Fuga prima.* A musician named Valentin Haussman and 2 others named Valentin Bartholomaeus Haussmann were apparently related to him.
  WORKS (all publ. in Nuremberg unless otherwise given): **SECULAR VOCAL:** *Neue teutsche weltliche Lieder . . . lieblich zu singen, und auff Instrumenten wol zu gebrauchen* for 5 and 6 Voices (1592); *Eine fast liebliche art derer noch mehr teutschen weltlichen Lieder* for 4 and 5 Voices (1594); *Neue teutsche weltliche Canzonette, lieblich zu singen, und auff Instrumenten zugebrauchen* for 4 Voices (1596); *Neue teutsche weltliche Lieder, mit höfelichen kurtzweiligen Texten, lieblich zu singen, und auff Instrumenten zugebrauchen* for 5 Voices (1597); *Andere noch mehr neue teutsche weltliche Lieder, nach art der Canzonetten, auff schöne lustige Text gesetzt* (1597); *Neue liebliche Melodien unter neue teutsche weltliche Texte, deter jeder einen besondern Namen anzeiget, dess mehrern theils zum Täntze zugebrauchen* for 4 Voices (1598; not extant; 2nd ed., 1600); *Neue artige und liebliche Täntze, zum theil mit Texten, dass man kan mit Menschlicher Stimme zu Instrumenten singen, zum Theil ohne Text gesetzt* for 5 Voices (1598; not extant; 2nd ed., 1599); *Fragmenta, oder, 35 noch übrige neue weltliche teutsche Lieder* for 4 and 5 Voices (1602); *Venusgarten, darinnen 100 ausserlesene gantz liebliche mehrerntheils polnische Täntze, unter welche ersten 50 feine höfliche amorosische Texte, von ihme Haussmann gemacht und untergelegt seind* (1602); *Fasciculus neuer Hochzeit und Braut Lieder* for 4 to 6 Voices (1602); *Extract auss . . . fünff Theilen der teutschen weltlichen Lieder . . . mit lustigen kurtzen lateinischen lemmatibus gezieret: Der erste Theil* for 5 Voices (1603); *Der ander Theil dess Extracts auss . . . fünff Theilen der teutschen weltliche Lieder . . . diser Theil* for 4 Voices (1603); *Rest von polnischen und andern Täntzen, nach art, wie im Venusgarten zu finden, colligirt, und zume Theil gemacht, auch mit weltlichen amorosischen Texten unterlegt* for 5 Voices (1603); *Ausszug auss . . . zweyen unterschiedlichen Wercken . . . mit und ohne Text* for 5 Voices (1608); *Melodien unter weltliche Texte, da jeder einen besondern Namen anzeiget, umb ein guten Theil vermehret und von neuem auffgelegt* for 5 Voices (1608); *Musicalische teutsche weltliche Gesänge, nach art der italianischen Canzonen und Madrigalien* for 4 to 8 Voices (1608). **SACRED VOCAL:** *Manipulus sacrarum cantionum* for 5 and 6 Voices (1602); *Ad imitationem cantionis italicae Fuggi pur se sai &c. missam* for 8 Voices . . . *cum duabus motectis* for 10 and 14 Voices (1604); also a Magnificat for 8 Voices; a Mass for 8 Voices; motets. **OCCASIONAL WORKS:** *Psalmus XLVI, Magnifico, nobilibus, amplissimis . . . viris, Dn. Burgrabio regio, coss: & reliquis senatorij ordinis viris inclytae Reipub: Elbingensis* for 5 Voices (Königsberg, 1588); *Threnodia (Justorum animae) in obitum reverendi et clarissimi viri D. Ludovict Rabus* for 6 Voices (Tübingen, 1592); *Ode sapphica adv. Turcae immanitatem* for 6 Voices (Magdeburg, 1597; not extant); *Epithalamium nuptiis Keckii* for 6 Voices (Magdeburg, 1597; not extant); *Harmonia melica (Tempus adest) nuptiis Georgii Rei-*

manni . . . *et Catharinae . . . Ketneri* for 5 Voices (Königsberg, 1598); *Hochzeit Lied zu Ehren dem D. Schitzing* for 5 Voices (Königsberg, 1598; not extant); *Teutsche Villanel aus dem 10: capitel der Sprüche Salomonis, auff den Nahmen des Herrn Zacharias Kreelen in Elbing* for 5 Voices (Königsberg, 1598; not extant); *2 Brautlieder zu Ehren dem L. Levit* for 5 Voices (Königsberg, 1598; not extant; in collaboration with Emmelius); *Harmonia melica pro felicissimi novi anni viris* (Königsberg, 1599); *Urbs Mariaeburgum fortissima* for 5 Voices (Königsberg, 1599; not extant); *Villanellae nuptiales duae* for 4 Voices (Frankfurt an der Oder, n.d.). **INSTRUMENTAL:** *Neue Intrade . . . fürnemlich auff Fiolen lieblich zugebrauchen: nach disen sind etliche englische Paduan und Galliarde anderer Composition zu finden, a* 5 and 6 (1604); *Neue paduane und Galliarde . . . fürnemlich auff Fiolen lieblich zugebrauchen, a* 5 (1604). See F. Boelsche, ed., *Valentin Haussmann: Ausgewählte Instrumentalwerke* in Denkmäler Deutscher Tonkunst, XVI (1904).

EDITIONS: *Ausszugauss L. Marentii 4 Theilen seiner italienischen Villanellen und Neapolitanen, mit teutschen Texten gezierest* for 3 Voices (1606); *Canzonette Horatii Vecchi und Gemignani Capi Lupi . . . mit teutschen Texten beleget* for 3 Voices (1606); *Johann-Jacobi Gastoldi und anderer Autorn Tricinia . . . mit teutschen weltlichen Texten* for 3 Voices (1607; including 5 works by Haussmann); *Liebliche frölice Ballette welche zuvor von T. Morlei unter italienische Texte gesetzt . . . mit unterlegung teutscher Texte* for 5 Voices (1609); *Die erste Class der Canzonetten Horatii Vecchi . . . mit Unterlegung teutscher Texte* for 4 Voices (1610; including 1 work by Haussmann); *Die ander Class der Canzonetten Horatii Vecchi . . . mit Unterlegung teutscher Texte* for 4 Voices (1610); *Die dritte Class der Canzonetten Horatii Vecchi . . . mit Unterlegung teutscher Texte* for 4 Voices (1610).

BIBL.: C. Morricone and A. Salottolo, "V. H. trascrittore e le canzonette italiane in Germania," *Rivista Italiana di Musicologia,* V (1970).

Hausswald, Günter, distinguished German musicologist; b. Rochlitz an der Mülde, March 11, 1908; d. Stuttgart, April 23, 1974. He studied piano with Max Pauer and composition with Karg-Elert in Leipzig; theory with Grabner at the Leipzig Hochschule für Musik; musicology with Kroyer and others at the Univ. of Leipzig, where he took his Ph.D. in 1937 with the dissertation *Johann David Heinichens Instrumentalwerke* (publ. in Wolfenbüttel and Berlin, 1937); he completed his Habilitation in 1949 at the Dresden Technical College with his *Mozarts Serenaden* (publ. in Leipzig, 1951). From 1933 to 1945 he taught school in Dresden; then was dramaturge at the Dresden State Opera (1947–53); he also lectured at the Dresden Hochschule für Musik and at the Univ. of Jena from 1950 to 1953. He then settled in West Germany, where he ed. the monthly *Musica* (1958–70); was also program director for the South German Radio at Stuttgart (1960–68). His important monographs include *Heinrich Marschner* (Dresden, 1938); *Die deutsche Oper* (Cologne, 1941); *Die Bauten des Staatstheater Dresden* (Dresden, 1948); *Das neue Opernbuch* (Dresden, 1951; 5th ed., 1956); *Richard Strauss* (Dresden, 1953); *Dirigenten: Bild und Schrift* (Berlin, 1966). He also contributed exemplary eds. to the complete works of Telemann, Gluck, Bach, and Mozart.

Hautzig, Walter, Austrian-born American pianist and teacher; b. Vienna, Sept. 28, 1921. He studied at the Vienna Academy of Music; left Austria after the rise of the Nazis to power, and went to Jerusalem; studied at the Cons. there. He eventually settled in America; continued his musical education at the Curtis Inst. of Music in Philadelphia with Harry Kaufmann and Mieczyslaw Munz; also in N.Y. with Artur Schnabel. He became an American citizen in 1945. In 1979 he represented the U.S. in the 1st visit of an American pianist to the People's Republic of China since the Cultural Revolution. He taught at the Peabody Cons. in Baltimore from 1960 to 1987; also gave master classes at the Hartt School of Music in Hartford, Conn. (from 1969).

Havelka, Svatopluk, Czech composer; b. Vrbice, May 2, 1925. He began composing as a child; studied violin, piano, and harmony; took courses in history and philosophy at the Univ. of Prague; studied privately with K.B. Jirák; later was active as director of music programs at the Ostrava Radio (1949–51) and with the Army Artistic Ensemble in Prague (1951–54). His music follows folkloric trends, with some sonoristic and generally modernistic deflections from the nationalistic formulae.

WORKS: *Mort et Redemption* for Orch. (1944); *4 Baroque Songs* for Medium Voice and Piano (1944; retitled *Růže ran* [Rose of Wounds] and scored with instrumental accompaniment, 1974); Suite for Small Orch. (1947); *2 Pastorales* for Orch. (1948, 1951); *4 Suites to Moravian Folk Texts* for Narrator, Soli, Chorus, and Chamber Orch. (1948, 1949, 1949, 1951); cantata, *Spring* (1949); Sym. No. 1 (Prague, Nov. 5, 1956); cantata, *Chvála světla* (In Praise of Light; Prague, May 4, 1960); *Heptameron,* subtitled *A Poem of Nature and Love,* for Narrator, 4 Soli, and Orch. (Prague, March 25, 1964); *Pěna* (Foam), to the poem by H.M. Enzensberger, for Orch. (1965; Olomouc, Feb. 9, 1966); *Ernesto Ché Guevara,* symphonic poem in memory of the fallen Cuban revolutionary (1969); ballet, *Pyrrhos* (1970); *Hommage à Hieronymus Bosch,* symphonic fantasy (1974); Nonet (1976); songs; film music.

Havemann, Gustav, German violinist; b. Güstrow, March 15, 1882; d. Schöneiche, near Berlin, Jan. 2, 1960. He studied with his father; then at the Berlin Hochschule für Musik, where he was a pupil of Joachim. As a youth he played in the Court Orch. in Schwerin; then was concertmaster in Lübeck, Darmstadt, and Hamburg. In 1911 he joined the faculty of the Leipzig Cons.; subsequently was concertmaster at the Dresden State Opera (1915–20); from 1920 to 1945 was a prof. at the Berlin Hochschule für Musik. He was 1st violinist in the prestigious Havemann String Quartet, which performed much modern music. He composed a Violin Concerto (1938) and publ. a useful manual, *Die Violintechnik bis zur Vollendung* (1928).

Havingha, Gerhardus, Dutch organist and music theorist; b. Groningen, Nov. 15, 1696; d. Alkmaar, March 6, 1753. He studied with his father, a church organist at Groningen; then became an organist at various churches in the Netherlands; publ. *Oorspronk en Voortgang der orgelen* (Alkmaar, 1727; reprinted 1973), an apologia defending his reconstruction of the Alkmaar organ utilizing equal temperament. He publ. a vol. of Suites for Harpsichord (Amsterdam, 1724; ed. by J. Watelet in Monumenta Musicae Byzantinae, VII, 1951).

Hawel, Jan Wincenty, Polish composer and conductor; b. Pszów, July 10, 1936. He studied composition and conducting at the Katowice State College of Music, graduating in 1967; then became a member of its faculty; also conducted the Silesian Chamber Orch. (from 1981).

WORKS: *Profiles* for Male Chorus and Orch. (1962); 4 syms. (1962–77); *Contrasts* for Orch. (1964); *Constructions* for Orch. (1965); Divertimento for Trombone, Piano, and Percussion (1968); *Woodland Impressions* for Narrator, Chorus, and Orch. (1969); *Sinfonia concertante* for Organ and Orch. (1972); 4 string quartets (1971–82); *Stained Glass Windows* for Piano (1972); *Polish Oratorio* for Soloists, Narrator, 2 Choruses, and Orch. (Katowice, April 29, 1983); *Magnificat* for Vocal Ensemble and Orch. (Poznan, March 30, 1989).

Hawes, William, English composer and conductor; b. London, June 21, 1785; d. there, Feb. 18, 1846. As a boy he was a chorister at the Chapel Royal (1793–1801); then violinist at Covent Garden (1802–5); became Gentleman of the Chapel Royal (1805), vicar-choral and master of choristers at St. Paul's Cathedral (1812), master of the children of the Chapel Royal (1817), and lay-vicar of Westminster Abbey (1817–20). He was director of English opera at the Lyceum (1824–36); it was at his suggestion that Weber's *Der Freischütz* was given for the 1st time in England (July 22, 1824; he contributed some airs of his own composition to this production). Subsequently, he adapted and produced many Italian, French, and German operas for the English stage; he wrote and staged several light operas, among them *Broken Promises* (1825), *The Quartette, or Interrupted Harmony* (1828), and *The Sister of Charity* (1829).

Hawkins, Coleman (Randolph), "Bean" or **"Hawk,"** outstanding black American jazz tenor saxophonist; b. St. Joseph, Mo., Nov. 21, 1904; d. N.Y., May 19, 1969. He joined the Kansas City group Jazz Hounds in 1921; from 1923 to 1934 was a member of Fletcher Henderson's band in N.Y.; his full tone and heavy vibrato became the standard for tenor saxophone, and he was considered the foremost performer on the instrument. From 1934 to 1939 he worked in Europe; upon his return to the U.S. in 1939 he made his most influential recording, *Body and Soul*; departing from the usual paraphrase approach of swing improvisation, his extemporized solo became an inspiration to the new generation of jazz musicians and paved the way for the bebop of the 1940s. **BIBL.:** A. McCarthy, *C. H.* (London, 1963); B. James, *C. H.* (N.Y., 1984).

Hawkins, Sir John, eminent English music historian; b. London, March 29, 1719; d. there, May 21, 1789. He studied law while serving as a clerk, and soon was able to act as an attorney. An ardent devotee of music, he entered the musical society of the time and was on friendly terms with Handel; he also participated in literary clubs, and knew Samuel Johnson, Goldsmith, and others. A wealthy marriage (1753) enabled him to devote his leisure to literature and music. In 1761 he became a magistrate; in 1763, chairman of the Quarter Sessions; he was knighted in 1772. His 1st publication dealing with music was *Memoirs of the Life of Sig. Agostino Steffani* (1758). He then brought out *An Account of the Institution and Progress of the Academy of Ancient Music* (1770). The culmination of 16 years of labor was his monumental *A General History of the Science and Practice of Music*, publ. in 1776 in 5 vols. The 1st vol. of Burney's *General History of Music* appeared at the same time; thus, Hawkins undoubtedly held priority for the 1st general history of music publ. in England; however, its reception was rather hostile; Burney himself derided Hawkins in an unpubl. poem. Yet the Hawkins work contained reliable information, particularly dealing with musical life in London in the 18th century. Hawkins died of a paralytic stroke and was buried in Westminster Abbey. **BIBL.:** R. Stevenson, " 'The Rivals'—H., Burney, and Boswell," *Musical Quarterly* (Jan. 1950); P. Scholes, *The Life and Activities of Sir J. H.* (London, 1953); B. Davis, *A Proof of Eminence: The Life of Sir J. H.* (Bloomington, Ind., and London, 1973).

Hawkins, John, Canadian composer; b. Montreal, July 26, 1944. He studied piano at the Montreal Cons. (premier prix, 1967) and composition with Anhalt at McGill Univ.; then attended a course in modern music given by Boulez in Basel (1969). Returning to Canada in 1970, he taught music theory at the Univ. of Toronto. He won the Jules Léger Prize for new chamber music in 1983. **WORKS:** *3 Cavatinas* for Soprano, Violin, Cello, Vibraphone, and Celesta (1967); *Sequences for 2 Groups* for 18 Instruments (1968); *Remembrances* for Piano, Harp, Horn, Trumpet, and Trombone (1969); Variations for Orch. (1969–70; Montreal, June 4, 1975); *Études* for 2 Pianos (1974); Trio for Flute, Xylophone, and Cello (1975); Quintet for Winds (1977); *Prelude for Tenor and Orch.* (1979–80); *Dance Variations* for Percussion Quartet (1983); *3 Archetypes* for String Quartet: *Dance, Invocation, Hymn* (1984); *Light to Dark* for Soprano, Clarinet, and Piano (1987); *The 1st Fable* for Oboe, Percussion, Cello, Piano, Soprano, Mezzo-Soprano, Mimes/Dancers, and Storyteller (1988).

Hawkins, Micah, American composer; b. Head of the Harbor, near Stony Brook, N.Y., Jan. 1, 1777; d. N.Y., July 29, 1825. In 1798 he settled in N.Y. City, where he worked as a carriage builder, grocer, and innkeeper. He was also a member of amateur music groups, such as the Euterpian and Apollo societies; wrote the dialect song *Backside Albany* (1815), which became notably successful, and *Massa Georgee Washington and General LaFayette*, to celebrate Lafayette's visit to the U.S. in 1824. His opera, *The Saw-Mill, or A Yankee Trick* (1824), is the earliest work of its kind by an American on an American subject. **BIBL.:** O. Wegelin, *M. H. and The Saw-Mill* (N.Y., 1917); V. Lawrence, "M. H., the Pied Piper of Catherine Slip," *New York Historical Society Quarterly*, LXII (1978).

Hawley, Charles Beach, American organist and composer; b. Brookfield, Mass., Feb. 14, 1858; d. Red Bank, N.J., Dec. 29, 1915. He studied organ at the Cheshire Military Academy; took composition lessons in N.Y. with Dudley Buck; then served as organist in various churches; publ. some songs, showing a facile melodic invention.

Hay, Edward Norman, Irish composer and organist; b. Faversham, April 19, 1889; d. Belfast, Sept. 10, 1943. He studied organ with Koeller and Eaglefield-Hull; was organist of various churches in Ireland. He won the Feis Ceoil Prize in 1916 with his Cello Sonata on Irish folk tunes, the Cobbett Prize (1917) with his *Folksong Phantasy* for String Quartet, and the Carnegie Award (1918) with his String Quartet in A. He also wrote the orch. compositions *The Gilly of Christ, Dunluce* (1921), etc.; organ works; songs.

Hay, Frederick Charles, Swiss composer; b. Basel, Sept. 18, 1888; d. Langau, July 18, 1945. He was a medical student; then studied with Huber in Basel, Widor in Paris, and F. Schalk in Vienna; conducted the Univ. of Bern orch. (1912) and oratorio concerts in Geneva (1920–25); taught musicology at the Univ. of Geneva. He wrote the orch. works *Heaven and Earth* and *Der Dom*; concertos for oboe, violin, piano, and viola; *Notturno, intermezzo e capriccio* for Piano and Woodwind Orch.; choral works; hymns; piano pieces.

Hayasaka, Fumio, Japanese composer, b. Sendai-City, Aug. 19, 1914; d. Tokyo, Oct. 15, 1955. He studied in Tokyo with A. Tcherepnin; won the Weingartner Prize (1938). He was particularly successful in writing for Japanese motion pictures; wrote the score for the film *Rashomon*, which received 1st prize at the International Festival in Venice (1952). **WORKS:** Overture in D major (Tokyo, March 17, 1940); Piano Concerto No. 1 (Tokyo, June 22, 1948); *The Ancient Dance* (Tokyo, May 15, 1939); *Yukara*, suite (Tokyo, June 9, 1955).

Hayashi, Hikaru, Japanese composer; b. Tokyo, Oct. 22, 1931. He studied at the Tokyo Music Academy with H. Otaka and T. Ikenouchi. **WORKS:** *Variations* for Orch. (1955; Tokyo, Nov. 17, 1955); radio opera, *The Naked King* (1955); television opera, *Amanjaku and Urikohime* (1958); 2-act opera, *The Wife in the Picture* (1961); ballet, *White-haired Woman* (1961); oratorio, *Beggar's Song* (1962); *Movement* for Orch. (1953); Sym. in G (1953); *Allegro* for Strings (1954); *The Humid Area* for Orch. (1960); Music for Orch. (1965); *Étude* for 2 Guitars (1960); *Rhapsody* for Violin and Piano (1965); *Contrasts* for 2 Marimbas (1965); Flute Sonata (1967); *Duo* for Violin and Piano (1968); *Winter on 72nd Street (Rhapsody No. 2)* for Violin and Piano (1968); *AYA* for Flute and Harp (1970) and *AYA II* for Solo Harp (1972); *Play I* for 10 Players (1971) and *II* for Voice, Violin, and Piano (1971–72); *Wonderland I* for Flute, Violin, and Piano (1972); *Shirabe* for 3 Flutes (1974); Piano Sonata (1965); Piano Sonatina (1966); choruses; songs.

Hayashi (Nagaya), Kenzō, Japanese musicologist; b. Osaka, May 1, 1899; d. Nara, June 9, 1976. He graduated from the Tokyo Arts School in 1924, and became a moderately successful sculptor. He also wrote some music for brass instruments. In 1928 he met the Chinese scholar Kuo Mo-jo, who encouraged him to write about his findings in the field of ancient Asian music. His 1st book, on music of the Sui and T'ang dynasties, was tr. into Chinese by Kuo (Shanghai, 1936). In 1948 he was commissioned to begin what became his life's work, research on early Chinese instruments kept in the imperial storehouse in Hara dating as far back as the 8th century. He publ.

some theoretical findings, among them *Ming yüen pa-tiao yen-chiu* (8 Musical Modes of the Ming Dynasty; Shanghai, 1957), *T'un-huang p'i-pa pu ti chieh-tu yen-chiu* (An Attempt to Interpret the T'un-huang Pipa Notation; Shanghai, 1957), and *Higashi Ajia gakki kō* (Musical Instruments of East Asia; Tokyo, 1973).

Haydn, (Franz) Joseph, illustrious Austrian composer, brother of **(Johann) Michael Haydn;** b. Rohrau, Lower Austria, probably March 31, 1732 (baptized, April 1, 1732); d. Vienna, May 31, 1809. He was the 2nd of 12 children born to Mathias Haydn, a wheelwright, who served as village sexton, and Anna Maria Koller, daughter of the market inspector and a former cook in the household of Count Harrach, lord of the village. Their 2nd son, Michael, also became a musician. On Sundays and holidays music was performed at home, the father accompanying the voices on the harp, which he had learned to play by ear. When Haydn was a small child his paternal cousin Johann Mathias Franck, a choral director, took him to Hainburg, where he gave him instruction in reading, writing, arithmetic, and instrumental playing. When Haydn was 8 years old, Karl Georg Reutter, Kapellmeister at St. Stephen's Cathedral in Vienna, engaged him as a soprano singer in the chorus. After his voice began to break, he moved to the household of Johann Michael Spangler, a music teacher. He obtained a loan of 150 florins from Anton Buchholz, a friend of his father's, and was able to rent an attic room where he could use a harpsichord. In the same house lived the famous Italian poet and opera librettist Pietro Metastasio, who recommended Haydn to a resident Spanish family as a music tutor. He was also engaged as accompanist to students of Nicolò Porpora, for whom he performed various menial tasks in exchange for composition lessons. He made a diligent study of *Gradus ad Parnassum* by Fux and *Der vollkommen Capellmeister* by Mattheson. Soon he began to compose keyboard music. In 1751 he wrote the singspiel *Der krumme Teufel*. A noblewoman, Countess Thun, engaged him as harpsichordist and singing teacher; he met Karl Joseph von Fürnburg, for whom he wrote his 1st string quartets. In 1759 Haydn was engaged by Count Ferdinand Maximilian von Morzin as Kapellmeister at his estate in Lukaveč. On Nov. 26, 1760, he married Maria Anna Keller, the eldest daughter of his early benefactor, a Viennese wigmaker.

A decided turn in Haydn's life was his meeting with Prince Paul Anton Esterházy. Esterházy had heard one of Haydn's syms. during a visit to Lukaveč, and engaged him to enter his service as 2nd Kapellmeister at his estate in Eisenstadt; Haydn signed his contract with Esterházy on May 1, 1761. Prince Paul Anton died in 1762, and his brother, Prince Nikolaus Esterházy, known as the "Magnificent," succeeded him. He took Haydn to his new palace at Esterháza, where Haydn was to provide 2 weekly operatic performances and 2 formal concerts. Haydn's service at Esterháza was long-lasting, secure, and fruitful; there he composed music of all descriptions, including most of his known string quartets, about 80 of his 104 syms., a number of keyboard works, and nearly all his operas; in 1766 he was elevated to the rank of 1st Kapellmeister. Prince Nikolaus Esterházy was a cultural patron of the arts, but he was also a stern taskmaster in his relationship to his employees. His contract with Haydn stipulated that each commissioned work had to be performed without delay, and that such a work should not be copied for use by others. Haydn was to present himself in the "antichambre" of the palace each morning and afternoon to receive the Prince's orders, and he was obliged to wear formal clothes, with white hose and a powdered wig with a pigtail or a hairbag; he was to have his meals with the other musicians and house servants. In particular, Haydn was obligated to write pieces that could be performed on the baryton, an instrument which the Prince could play; in consequence, Haydn wrote numerous pieces for the baryton. He also wrote 3 sets of 6 string quartets each (opps. 9, 17, and 20), which were brought out in 1771–72. His noteworthy syms. included No. 49, in F minor, *La pas-*

sione; No. 44, in E minor, known as the *Trauersinfonie*; No. 45, in F-sharp minor; and the famous *Abschiedsinfonie* (the *Farewell* Sym.), performed by Haydn at Esterháza in 1772. The last movement of the *Farewell* Sym. ends in a long slow section during which one musician after another ceases to play and leaves the stage, until only the conductor and a single violinist remain to complete the work. The traditional explanation is that Haydn used the charade to suggest to the Prince that his musicians deserved a vacation after their arduous labors, but another and much more plausible version, found in *Anedotti piacevoli ed interessanti*, publ. in 1830 by G.G. Ferrari, who personally knew Haydn, is that the Prince had decided to disband the orch. and that Haydn wished to impress on him the sadness of such a decision; the known result was that the orch. was retained. In 1780 Haydn was elected a member of the Modena Phil. Soc.; in 1784 Prince Henry of Prussia sent him a gold medal; in 1785 he was commissioned to write a "passione istrumentale," *The 7 Last Words*, for the Cathedral of Cádiz; in 1787 King Friedrich Wilhelm II gave him a diamond ring; many other distinctions were conferred upon him. During his visits to Vienna he formed a close friendship with Mozart, who was nearly a quarter of a century younger, and for whose genius Haydn had great admiration. If the words of Mozart's father can be taken literally, Haydn told him that Mozart was "the greatest composer known to me either in person or by name." Mozart reciprocated Haydn's regard for him by dedicating to him a set of 6 string quartets. Prince Nikolaus Esterházy died in 1790, and his son Paul Anton (named after his uncle) inherited the estate. After he disbanded the orch., Haydn was granted an annuity of 1,000 florins; nominally he remained in the service of the new Prince as Kapellmeister, but he took up permanent residence in Vienna.

In 1790 Johann Peter Salomon, the enterprising London impresario, visited Haydn and persuaded him to travel to London for a series of concerts. Haydn accepted the offer, arriving in London on Jan. 1, 1791. On March 11 of that year he appeared in his 1st London concert in the Hanover Square Rooms, presiding at the keyboard. Haydn was greatly feted in London by the nobility; the King himself expressed his admiration for Haydn's art. In July 1791 he went to Oxford to receive the honorary degree of Mus.D. For this occasion, he submitted his Sym. No. 92, in G major, which became known as the *Oxford* Sym.; he composed a 3-part canon, *Thy Voice, O Harmony, Is Divine*, as his exercise piece. It was also in England that he wrote his Sym. No. 94, in G major, the *Surprise* Sym. The surprise of the title was provided by the loud drum strokes at the end of the main theme in the slow movement; the story went that Haydn introduced the drum strokes with the sly intention of awakening the London dowagers, who were apt to doze off at a concert. On his journey back to Vienna in the summer of 1792 Haydn stopped in Bonn, where young Beethoven showed him some of his works, and Haydn agreed to accept him later as his student in Vienna. In 1794 Haydn went to London once more. His 1st concert, on Feb. 10, 1794, met with great success. His *London* syms., also known as the *Salomon* syms., because Haydn wrote them at Salomon's request, were 12 in number, and they included No. 99, in E-flat major; No. 100, in G major, known as the *Military* Sym.; No. 101, in D major, nicknamed *The Clock* because of its pendulum-like rhythmic accompanying figure; No. 102, in B-flat major; No. 103, in E-flat major, known as the *Drum Roll* Sym.; and No. 104, in D major. A philatelic note: Haydn sent the MS of his oratorio *The Creation* to Salomon in London for its 1st performance there. The package was delivered on March 23, 1800, by stagecoach and sailboat from Vienna, and the postage was £30 16s. 0d., a sum equal to £650 today, c.$1,000. In 1800, this sum was enough to buy a horse, or to pay the living expenses for a family of 4 for a year.

Returning to Vienna, Haydn resumed his contact with the Esterházy family. In 1794 Prince Paul Anton died and was succeeded by his son Nikolaus; the new Prince revived the orch. at Eisenstadt, with Haydn again as Kapellmeister. Conforming to the new requirements of Prince Nikolaus, Haydn turned to works for the church, including 6 masses. His Mass in C major was entitled *Missa in tempore belli* (1796), for it was composed during Napoleon's drive toward Vienna. The 2nd Mass, in B-flat major, the *Heiligmesse*, also dates from 1796. In 1798 he composed the 3rd Mass, in D minor, which is often called the *Nelsonmesse*, with reference to Lord Nelson's defeat of Napoleon's army at the Battle of the Nile. The 4th Mass, in B-flat major (1799), is called the *Theresienmesse*, in honor of the Austrian Empress Maria Theresa. The 5th Mass, in B-flat major, written in 1801, is known as the *Schöpfungsmesse*, for it contains a theme from the oratorio *Die Schöpfung* (*The Creation*). The 6th Mass, in B-flat major (1802), is referred to as the *Harmoniemesse*, for its extensive use of wind instruments; the word "harmonie" is here used in the French meaning, as the wind instrument section. Between 1796 and 1798 Haydn composed his great oratorio *Die Schöpfung*, which was 1st performed at a private concert for the nobility at the Schwarzenburg Palace in Vienna on April 29, 1798. In 1796 he wrote the Concerto in E-flat major for Trumpet, which became a standard piece for trumpet players. In 1797 Haydn was instructed by the Court to compose a hymn-tune of a solemn nature that could be used as the national Austrian anthem. He succeeded triumphantly in this task; he made use of this tune as a theme of a set of variations in his String Quartet in C major, op. 76, no. 3, which itself became known as the *Emperor* Quartet. The original text for the hymn, written by Lorenz Leopold Haschka, began "Gott erhalte Franz den Kaiser." This hymn had a curious history: a new set of words was written by August Heinrich Hoffmann during a period of revolutionary disturbances in Germany preceding the general European revolution of 1848; its 1st line, "Deutschland, Deutschland über alles," later assumed the significance of German imperialism; in its original it meant merely, "Germany above all (in our hearts)." Between 1799 and 1801 Haydn completed the oratorio *Die Jahreszeiten*; its text was tr. into German from James Thomson's poem *The Seasons*. It was first performed at the Schwarzenburg Palace in Vienna on April 24, 1801. In 1802, beset by illness, Haydn resigned as Kapellmeister to Prince Nikolaus.

Despite his gradually increasing debility, Haydn preserved the saving grace of his natural humor; in response to the many salutations of his friends, he sent around a quotation from his old song *Der Alte*, confessing his bodily weakness. Another amusing musical jest was Haydn's reply to a society lady who identified herself at a Vienna party as a person to whom Haydn had dedicated a lively tune ascending on the major scale; she sang it for him, and he replied wistfully that the tune was now more appropriate in an inversion. Haydn made his last public appearance at a concert given in his honor in the Great Hall of the Univ. of Vienna on March 27, 1808, with Salieri conducting *Die Schöpfung*. When Vienna capitulated to Napoleon, he ordered a guard of honor to be placed at Haydn's residence. Haydn died on May 31, 1809, and was buried at the Hundsturm Cemetery. In consequence of some fantastic events, his skull became separated from his body before his reinterment at Eisenstadt in 1820; it was actually exhibited under glass in the hall of the Gesellschaft der Musikfreunde in Vienna for a number of years, before being reunited with his body in the Bergkirche in Eisenstadt on June 5, 1954, in a solemn official ceremony.

Haydn was often called "Papa Haydn" by his intimates in appreciation of his invariable good humor and amiable disposition. Ironically, he never became a papa in the actual sense of the word. His marriage was unsuccessful; his wife was a veritable termagant; indeed, Haydn was separated from her for most of his life. Still, he corresponded with her and sent her money, even though, according to a contemporary report, he never opened her letters.

In schoolbooks Haydn is usually described as "father of the symphony," the creator of the classical form of the sym. and string quartet. Historically, this absolute formulation cannot be sustained; the symphonic form was established by Stamitz and his associates at the Mannheim School; the string quartet was of an even earlier provenance. But Haydn's music was not limited to formal novelty; its greatness was revealed in the variety of moods, the excellence of variations, and the contrast among the constituent movements of a sym.; string quartets, as conceived by Haydn, were diminutions of the sym.; both were set in sonata form, consisting in 3 contrasting movements, *Allegro, Andante, Allegro*, with a *Minuet* interpolated between the last 2 movements. It is the quality of invention that places Haydn above his contemporaries and makes his music a model of classical composition. A theory has been put forward that Haydn's themes were derived from the folk melodies of Croatian origin that he had heard in the rural environment of his childhood, but no such adumbrations or similarities can be convincingly proved. Genius is a gift bestowed on a musician or poet without external urgencies.

The intimate *Volkstümlichkeit*, a popular impressiveness of Haydn's music, naturally lent itself to imaginative nicknames of individual compositions. There are among his syms. such appellations as *Der Philosoph* and *Der Schulmeister*; some were titled after animals: *L'Ours* and *La Poule*; others derived their names from the character of the main theme, as in *Die Uhr* (The Clock), the *Paukenschlag* (Surprise), and the *Paukenwirbel* (Drum Roll). Among Haydn's string quartets are *La Chasse*, so named because of the hunting horn fanfares; the *Vogelquartett*, in which one hears an imitation of birdcalls; the *Froschquartett*, which seems to invoke a similarity with frog calls in the finale; and the *Lerchenquartett*, containing a suggestion of a lark call. The famous *Toy* Sym., scored for an ensemble which includes the rattle, the triangle, and instruments imitating the quail, cuckoo, and nightingale, was long attributed to Haydn but is actually a movement of a work by Leopold Mozart.

Haydn played a historic role in the evolution of functional harmony by adopting 4-part writing as a fundamental principle of composition, particularly in his string quartets. This practice has also exercised a profound influence on the teaching of music theory.

WORKS: The precise extent of Haydn's vast output will probably never be known. Many works are lost; others, listed in various catalogs, may never have existed or were duplications of extant works; some are of doubtful authenticity, and some are definitely spurious. The following list of his works attempts to be comprehensive in scope, but it is not an exhaustive compilation.

SYMS.: The generally accepted list of Haydn's authentic syms. numbers 104. For detailed information, consult the monumental study by H.C. Robbins Landon, *The Symphonies of J. H.* (London, 1955; supplement, 1961); see also his exhaustive biography *H.: Chronicle and Works* (5 vols., Bloomington, Ind., and London, 1976–80). The numbering follows the thematic catalog prepared by Anthony van Hoboken. Also included are the descriptive titles, whether authorized by Haydn or not. No. 1, in D major (1759); No. 2, in C major (1761); No. 3, in G major (1762); No. 4, in D major (1760); No. 5, in A major (1760); No. 6, in D major, *Le Matin* (1761); No. 7, in C major, *Le Midi* (1761); No. 8, in G major, *Le Soir* (1761); No. 9, in C major (1762); No. 10, in D major (1761); No. 11, in E-flat major (1760); No. 12, in E major (1763); No. 13, in D major (1763); No. 14, in A major (1764); No. 15, in D major (1761); No. 16, in B-flat major (1763); No. 17, in F major (1762); No. 18, in G major (1764); No. 19, in D major (1760); No. 20, in C major (1763); No. 21, in A major (1764); No. 22, in E-flat major, *The Philosopher* (1764); No. 23, in G major (1764); No. 24, in D major (1764); No. 25, in C major (1761); No. 26, in D minor, *Lamentatione* (1770); No. 27, in G major (1761); No. 28, in A major (1765); No. 29, in E major (1765); No. 30, in C major, *Alleluja* (1765); No. 31, in D major, *Hornsignal* (1765); No. 32, in C major (1760); No. 33, in C major (1760); No. 34, in D minor/D major (1767); No. 35, in B-flat major (1767); No. 36, in E-flat major (1765); No. 37, in C major (1758); No. 38, in C major (1769); No. 39, in G minor (1765); No. 40, in F major (1763); No. 41, in C major (1770); No. 42, in D major (1771); No. 43, in E-flat major,

Mercury (1772); No. 44, in E minor, *Trauersinfonie* (1772); No. 45, in F-sharp minor, *Abschiedsinfonie* (1772); No. 46, in B major (1772); No. 47, in G major (1772); No. 48, in C major, *Maria Theresia* (1769); No. 49, in F minor, *La passione* (1768); No. 50, in C major (1773); No. 51, in B-flat major (1774); No. 52, in C minor (1774); No. 53, in D major, *Imperial* or *Festino* (1778); No. 54, in G major (1774); No. 55, in E-flat major, *The Schoolmaster* (1774); No. 56, in C major (1774); No. 57, in D major (1774); No. 58, in F major (1768); No. 59, in A major, *Fire* (1769); No. 60, in C major, *Il Distratto* (1774); No. 61, in D major (1776); No. 62, in D major (1780); No. 63, in C major, *La Roxelane* or *Roxolana* (1779); No. 64, in A major, *Tempora mutantur* (1773); No. 65, in A major (1773); No. 66, in B-flat major (1776); No. 67, in F major (1776); No. 68, in B-flat major (1774); No. 69, in C major, *Laudon* or *Loudon* (1776); No. 70, in D major (1779); No. 71, in B-flat major (1779); No. 72, in D major (1765); No. 73, in D major, *La Chasse* (1782); No. 74, in E-flat major (1781); No. 75, in D major (1781); No. 76, in E-flat major (1782); No. 77, in B-flat major (1782); No. 78, in C minor (1782); No. 79, in F major (1784); No. 80, in D minor (1784); No. 81, in G major (1784); *Paris* syms.: No. 82, in C major, *L'Ours* or *The Bear* (1786); No. 83, in G minor, *La Poule* or *The Hen* (1785), No. 84, in E-flat major (1786), No. 85, in B-flat major, *La Reine* or *The Queen* (1785), No. 86, in D major (1786), and No. 87, in A major (1785); No. 88, in G major (1787); No. 89, in F major (1787); No. 90, in C major (1788); No. 91, in E-flat major (1788); No. 92, in G major, *Oxford* (1789); *London* or *Salomon* syms.: No. 93, in D major (1791; London, Feb. 17, 1792), No. 94, in G major, *Mit dem Paukenschlag* or *The Surprise* (1791; London, March 23, 1792), No. 95, in C minor (1791; London, 1791), No. 96, in D major, *The Miracle* (1791; London, 1791), No. 97, in C major (1792; London, May 3 or 4, 1792), No. 98, in B-flat major (1792; London, March 2, 1792), No. 99, in E-flat major (1793; London, Feb. 10, 1794), No. 100, in G major, *Militär* or *Military* (1793–94; London, March 31, 1794), No. 101, in D major, *Die Uhr* or *The Clock* (1793–94; London, March 3, 1794), No. 102, in B-flat major (1794; London, Feb. 2, 1795), No. 103, in E-flat major, *Paukenwirbel* or *Drum Roll* (1795; London, March 2, 1795), and No. 104, in D major, *London* or *Salomon* (1795; London, May 4, 1795); also the Concertante (now called Sinfonia Concertante) in B-flat major, listed in the Hoboken catalog as No. 105 (1792; London, March 9, 1792). Hoboken also lists No. 106, in D major (1769; only 1st movement extant; may have been composed as the overture to *Le Pescatrici*); No. 107, in B-flat major (1761; may be by Wagenseil); and No. 108, in B-flat major (1761).

CONCERTOS: 4 for Violin: No. 1, in C major (1765); No. 2, in D major (1765; not extant); No. 3, in A major (1770); No. 4, in G major (1769); 2 for Cello: No. 1, in C major (1765), and No. 2, in D major (1783); another cello concerto may be lost or has been confused with No. 1; 2 for Organ or Harpsichord: C major (1756) and D major (1767); also most likely by Haydn are 3 others for Organ or Harpsichord, all in C major (1763, 1766, 1771); 1 for Violin, and Harpsichord or Organ, in F major (1766); 3 for Harpsichord: in F major (1771), G major (1770; also for Piano), and D major (1784; also for Piano); 1 for Trumpet, in E-flat major (1796); 5 for 2 Lire Organizzate: in C major (1787), F major (1786), G major (1787), F major (1787), and G major (1787); also divertimenti, notturni, etc. Several other concertos for oboe, flute, horn, and bassoon are either lost or spurious.

Haydn also composed several miscellaneous orch. works, including overtures to his dramatic pieces: G minor (to *L'isola disabitata*); D major (to *L'incontro improvviso*); G major (to *Lo speziale*); B-flat major (to *La vera costanza*); C major (to *L'infedeltà delusa*); C minor/C major (to *Il ritorno di Tobia*); also the *Musica instrumentale sopra le 7 ultime parole del nostro Redentore in croce ossiano 7 sonate con un'introduzione ed al fine un terremoto* (1786; for Cadiz).

DRAMATIC WORKS: *Der krumme Teufel*, singspiel (1751?; 1st confirmed perf., Vienna, May 29, 1753; not extant); *Der neue krumme Teufel* (*Asmodeus, der krumme Teufel*), singspiel (1758?; music not extant); *Acide*, festa teatrale (1762; Eisenstadt, Jan. 11, 1763; only fragment and libretto extant; rev. version, 1773; only fragment extant); *Marchese* (*La Marchesa Nespola*), comedia (1762?; only fragment extant; dialogues not extant); *Il Dottore*, comedia (1765?; not extant); *La Vedova*, comedia (1765?; not extant); *Il scanarello*, comedia (1765?; not extant); *La Canterina*, intermezzo in musica (1766; Bratislava, Sept. 11?, 1766); *Lo speziale* (*Der Apotheker*), dramma giocoso (1768; Esterháza, Autumn 1768); *Le Pescatrici* (*Die Fischerinnen*), dramma giocoso (1769; Esterháza, Sept. 16?, 1770); *L'infedeltà delusa* (*Liebe macht erfinderisch; Untreue lohnt sich nicht; Deceit Outwitted*), burletta per musica (1773; Esterháza, July 26, 1773); *Philemon und Baucis oder Jupiters Reise auf die Erde*, singspiel/marionette opera (1773; Esterháza, Sept. 2, 1773); *Hexenschabbas*, marionette opera (1773?; not extant); *L'incontro improvviso* (*Die unverhoffte Zusammenkunft; Unverhofftes Begegnen*), dramma giocoso (1775; Esterháza, Aug. 29, 1775); *Dido*, singspiel/marionette opera (1776?; Esterháza, March ?, 1776; music not extant); *Opéra comique vom abgebrannten Haus* (not extant; may be identical with the following work); *Die Feuerbrunst*, singspiel/marionette opera (1775?–78?; may be by Haydn; dialogues not extant); *Il mondo della luna* (*Die Welt auf dem Monde*), dramma giocoso (1777; Esterháza, Aug. 3, 1777); *Die bestrafte Rachbegierde*, singspiel/marionette opera (1779?; Esterháza, 1779; music not extant); *La vera costanza*, dramma giocoso (1778?; Esterháza, April 25, 1779; only music extant appears in the rev. version of 1785); *L'isola disabitata* (*Die wüste Insel*), azione teatrale (1779; Esterháza, Dec. 6, 1779; rev. 1802); *La fedeltà premiata* (*Die belohnte Treue*), dramma pastorale giocoso (1780; Esterháza, Feb. 25, 1781); *Orlando paladino* (*Der Ritter Roland*), dramma eroicomico (1782; Esterháza, Dec. 6, 1782); *Armida*, dramma eroico (1783; Esterháza, Feb. 26, 1784); *L'anima del filosofo ossia Orfeo ed Euridice*, dramma per musica (1791; composed for London but not perf.; 1st confirmed perf., Florence, June 10, 1951); *Alfred, König der Angelsachsen, oder Der patriotische König* (1796; perf. as the incidental music to *Haldane, König der Dänen*, Eisenstadt, Sept. 1796).

MASSES: *Missa Rorate coeli desuper*, in G major (date unknown; not extant, or identical with the following); Mass in G major (date unknown; composed by G. Reutter, Jr., Arbesser, and Haydn; publ. in London, 1957); *Missa brevis* in F major (1749?); *Missa Cellensis in honorem Beata Maria Virgine*, in C major, *Cäcilienmesse* (1766); *Missa Sunt bona mixta malis*, in D minor (1769?); *Missa in honorem Beata Maria Virgine*, in E-flat major, *Missa Sancti Josephi; Grosse Orgelmesse* (1769?); *Missa Sancti Nicolai*, in G major, *Nicolaimesse; 6/4-Takt-Messe* (1772); *Missa brevis Sancti Joannis de Deo*, in B-flat major, *Kleine Orgelmesse* (1775?); *Missa Cellensis*, in C major, *Mariazeller Messe* (1782); *Missa Sancti Bernardi von Offida*, in B-flat major, *Heiligmesse* (1796); *Missa in tempore belli*, in C major, *Kriegsmesse; Paukenmesse* (1796; Vienna, Dec. 26, 1796?); *Missa* in D minor, *Nelsonmesse; Imperial Mass; Coronation Mass* (1798; Eisenstadt, Sept. 23, 1798?); *Missa* in B-flat major, *Theresienmesse* (1799); *Missa* in B-flat major, *Schöpfungsmesse* (1801; Eisenstadt, Sept. 13, 1801); *Missa* in B-flat major, *Harmoniemesse* (1802; Eisenstadt, Sept. 8, 1802).

ORATORIOS: Stabat Mater (1767); *Applausus* (*Jubilaeum virtutis Palatium*), allegorical oratorio/cantata (1768; Zwettl, April 17, 1768); *Il ritorno di Tobia* (1774–75; Vienna, April 2 and 4, 1775, in 2 parts; rev. 1784); *Die sieben letzten Worte unseres Erlösers am Kreuze* (1795–96; Vienna, 1796); *Die Schöpfung* (The Creation; 1796–98; 1st private perf., Schwarzenburg Palace, Vienna, April 29, 1798; 1st public perf., Kärnthnertortheater, Vienna, March 19, 1799); *Die Jahreszeiten* (The Seasons; 1799–1801; Schwarzenburg Palace, Vienna, April 24, 1801).

Haydn's other vocal works include 2 Te Deums (both in C major); offertories; secular cantatas; secular vocal works for orch.; more than 50 songs with keyboard accompaniment; vocal duets, trios, and quartets with keyboard accompaniment; more than 50 canons; arrangements of Scottish and other songs; and *Gott erhalte Franz den Kaiser* (God Save the Emperor Franz; 1797; was the Austrian national anthem until 1918).

STRING QUARTETS: Op. 1 (c.1757–59): No. 1, in B-flat major, *La Chasse;* No. 2, in E-flat major; No. 3, in D major; No. 4, in G major; No. 5, in E-flat major; No. 6, in C major; op. 2 (c.1760–62): No. 1, in A major; No. 2, in E major; No. 4, in F major; No. 6, in B-flat major; op. 9 (1771): No. 1, in C major; No. 2, in E-flat major; No. 3, in G major; No. 4, in D minor; No. 5, in B-flat major; No. 6, in A major; op. 17 (1771): No. 1, in E major; No. 2, in F major; No. 3, in E-flat major; No. 4, in C minor; No. 5, in G major, *Recitative;* No. 6, in D major; *Sun Quartets,* op. 20 (1772): No. 1, in E-flat major; No. 2, in C major; No. 3, in G minor; No. 4, in D major; No. 5, in F minor; No. 6, in A major; *Russian Quartets; Jungfern-quartette,* op. 33 (1781): No. 1, in B minor; No. 2, in E-flat major, *The Joke;* No. 3, in C major, *The Bird;* No. 4, in B-flat major; No. 5, in G major, *How do you do?;* No. 6, in D major; op. 42, in D minor (1785); *Prussian Quartets,* op. 50 (1787): No. 1, in B-flat major; No. 2, in C major; No. 3, in E-flat major; No. 4, in F-sharp minor; No. 5, in F major, *Ein Traum;* No. 6, in D major, *The Frog; Tost Quartets,* op. 54 (1788): No. 1, in G major; No. 2, in C major; No. 3, in E major; *Tost Quartets,* op. 55 (1788): No. 1, in A major; No. 2, in F minor, *The Razor;* No. 3, in B-flat major; *Tost Quartets,* op. 64 (1790): No. 1, in C major; No. 2, in B minor; No. 3, in B-flat major; No. 4, in G major; No. 5, in D major, *The Lark;* No. 6, in E-flat major; *Apponyi Quartets,* op. 71 (1793): No. 1, in B-flat major; No. 2, in D major; No. 3, in E-flat major; *Apponyi Quartets,* op. 74 (1793): No. 1, in C major; No. 2, in F major; No. 3, in G minor, *The Rider; Erdödy Quartets,* op. 76 (1797): No. 1, in G major; No. 2, in D minor, *Fifths;* No. 3, in C major, *Emperor;* No. 4, in B-flat major, *Sunrise;* No. 5, in D major; No. 6, in E-flat major; *Lobkowitz Quartets,* op. 77 (1799): No. 1, in G major; No. 2, in F major; op. 103, in D minor (1803?; unfinished; only movements 2 and 3 finished). Haydn also arranged the orch. version of the *Musica instrumentale sopra le 7 ultime parole del nostro Redentore in croce . . .* for String Quartet (1787), as well as pieces from the operas *La vera costanza* and *Armida.*

Other works by Haydn include 21 string trios (3 not extant); a great number of works for baryton, written for Prince Ester-házy, who was an avid baryton player: about 125 baryton trios (divertimentos), various works for 1 or 2 barytons, etc.; 29 keyboard sonatas (3 listed as trios), most of them for harpsi-chord or piano, with violin and cello; 47 solo keyboard sonatas (7 not extant, 1 not complete), almost all of them for harpsi-chord; etc.

BIBL.: COLLECTED EDITIONS, SOURCE MATERIAL: The 1st at-tempt to publ. a complete edition was made by Breitkopf & Härtel; *J. H.s Werke,* ed. by G. Adler, H. Kretzschmar, E. Mandy-czewski, M. Seiffert, and others, reached only 10 vols. in its coverage (Leipzig, 1907–33). An attempt to continue it after World War II as *J. H.: Kritische Gesamtausgabe,* under the editorship of Jens Peter Larsen and the sponsorship of the Haydn Soc. of Boston, also failed; only 4 vols. were issued (Boston, Leipzig, and Vienna, 1950–51). Finally, in 1955, through the efforts of Friedrich Blume and the publisher Gün-ter Henle, the Joseph Haydn-Institut of Cologne was founded to sponsor a monumental critical ed. The new ed., *J. H.: Werke,* also includes accompanying Kritische Berichte. Jens Peter Lar-sen ed. the 1st series of vols. (Munich, 1958–61); he was succeeded as editor by Georg Feder. Expected to be completed by the year 2000, this exhaustive ed. will contain more than 100 vols. H.C. Robbins Landon has ed. all of the syms. in a separate series, issued in miniature score as *J. H.: Kritische Ausgabe sämtlicher Symphonien* (I–XII, Vienna, 1965–68). A. van Hoboken prepared a thematic catalog, *J. H.: Thematisch-bibliographisches Werkverzeichnis* (2 vols., Mainz, 1957 and 1971).

Invaluable articles may be found in the *H. Yearbook* (1962–) and *H. Studien* (Joseph Haydn-Institut, Cologne, 1965–).

Other sources include the following: A. Csatkai, *J. H.: Katalog der Gedächtnisausstellung in Eisenstadt 1932* (Eisenstadt, 1932); R. Lachmann, "Die H.-Autographen der Staatsbi-bliothek zu Berlin," *Zeitschrift für Musikwissenschaft,* XIV (1932); A. Orel, *Katalog der H.-Gedächtnisausstellung Wien 1932* (Vienna, 1932); G. de Saint-Foix, "Les Manuscrits et les copies d'œuvres de J. H. à la Bibliothèque du Conservatoire (Fonds Malherbe)," *Revue de Musicologie,* XIII (1932; supple-ment by Y. Rokseth, ibid., XIV, 1933); J. Larsen, *Die H.-Überlieferung* (Copenhagen, 1939); J. Larsen, ed., *Drei H. Kata-loge in Faksimile: Mit Einleitung und ergänzenden Themenver-zeichnissen* (Copenhagen, 1941; 2nd ed., rev., 1979); R. Feuchtmüller, F. Hadamowsky, and L. Nowak, *J. H. und seine Zeit: Ausstellung Schloss Petronell (N. Ö.) Mai bis Oktober 1959* (Vienna, 1959); H.C. Robbins Landon, "Survey of the H. Sources in Czechoslovakia," *Internationale Konferenz zum Andenken J. H.s:* Budapest 1959; L. Nowak, ed., *J. H.: Ausstel-lung zum 150. Todestag: Vom 29. Mai bis 30. September 1959* (Vienna, 1959); A. Brown, C. Brown, and J. Berkenstock, "J. H. in Literature: A Bibliography," *H.-Studien* (July 1974, Bd. III, Heft 3/4, pp. 173–352; an alphabetical list, chiefly by author, of 2,285 books, monographs, periodical and *Festschrift* articles, and some unpubl. dissertations, with full bibliographical infor-mation and indexes by name, topic, and work); see also their "J. H. in Literature: A Survey," *Notes* (March 1975); S. Bryant and G. Chapman, *A Melodic Index to H.'s Instrumental Music* (N.Y., 1982); E. Badura-Skoda, ed., *Congress Report: Interna-tional F.J. H. Congress: Vienna 1982* (Munich, 1987).

CORRESPONDENCE: H.C. Robbins Landon, ed., *The Collected Correspondence and London Notebooks of J. H.* (London, 1959); D. Bartha, ed., *J. H.: Gesammelte Briefe und Aufzeichnungen: Unter Benützung der Quellensammlung von H.C. Robbins Lan-don* (Kassel, 1965).

BIOGRAPHICAL: G. Griesinger, "Biographische Notizen über J. H.," *Allgemeine Musikalische Zeitung,* XI (Leipzig, 1809; also publ. separately, Leipzig, 1810; 2nd ed., 1819; modern ed. by F. Grasberger, Vienna, 1954; Eng. tr. in V. Gotwals, ed., *J. H.: Eighteenth-century Gentleman and Genius,* Madison, Wis., 1963; 2nd ed., 1968, as *H.: Two Contemporary Portraits,* including Eng. tr. of Dies [see below]); S. Mayr, *Brevi notizie istoriche della vita e delle opere di H.* (Bergamo, 1809); A. Dies, *Biographische Nachrichten von J. H.: Nach mündlichen Erzählungen desselben entworfen und herausgegeben von Albert Christoph Dies, Landschaftmahler* (Vienna, 1810; modern ed. by H. Seeger, Berlin, 1959; 4th ed., 1976; Eng. tr. in V. Gotwals, ed., *J. H.: Eighteenth-century Gentleman and Genius,* Madison, 1963; 2nd ed., 1968, as *H.: Two Contemporary Portraits,* includ-ing Eng. tr. of Griesinger [see above]); G. Carpani, *Le Haydine, ovvero Lettere su la vita e le opere del celebre maestro Giuseppe H.* (Milan, 1812; 2nd ed., 1823; Eng. tr. as *The Life of H. in Letters,* 1839); T. von Karajan, *J. H. in London, 1791 und 1792* (Vienna, 1861); C. von Wurzbach, *J. H. und sein Bruder Mi-chael: Zwei bio-bibliographische Künstler-Skizzen* (Vienna, 1861); C. Pohl, *Mozart und H. in London:* Vol. II, *H. in London* (Vienna, 1867); idem, *J. H.* (incomplete; 2 vols.; Vol. I, Berlin, 1875; 2nd ed., 1878; Vol. II, Leipzig, 1882; Vol. III, completed by H. Botstiber, Leipzig, 1927); J. Hadden, *H.* (London and N.Y., 1902; 2nd ed., rev., 1934); F. Artaria and B. Botstiber, *J. H. und das Verlagshaus Artaria: Nach den Briefen des Meisters an das Haus Artaria & Compagnie dargestellt* (Vienna, 1909); M. Brenet, *H.* (Paris, 1909; 2nd ed., 1910; Eng. tr., 1926); H. von Hase, *J. H. und Breitkopf & Härtel* (Leipzig, 1909); F. Scherber, "J. H.s Tod," *Neue Musik-Zeitung,* XXX (1909); A. Schnerich, *J. H. und seine Sendung* (Zürich, 1922; 2nd ed., 1926, with supplement by W. Fischer); O. Deutsch, "H. und Nelson," *Die Musik,* XXIV (1931–32); H. Botstiber, "H. and Luigia Polzelli," *Musical Quarterly* (April 1932); K. Geiringer, *J. H.* (Potsdam, 1932); J. Muller, "H. Portraits," *Musical Quar-terly* (April 1932); E. Schmid, "J. H. in Eisenstadt: Ein Beitrag zur Biographie des Meisters," *Burgenländische Heimatblätter,* I (Eisenstadt, 1932); M. Scott, "H. in England," *Musical Quar-terly* (April 1932); E. Schmid, *J. H.: Ein Buch von Vorfahren und Heimat des Meisters* (Kassel, 1934); D. Bartha, "Zur Abstammung J. H.s," *Acta Musicologica*, VII (1935); K. Geiringer, *H.: A Creative Life in Music* (N.Y., 1946; 3rd ed., rev., 1983); R. Hughes, *H.* (London, 1950; 6th ed., rev., 1989); L. Nowak, *J. H.: Leben, Bedeutung und Werk* (Zürich, 1951; 3rd ed., rev., 1966); R. Sondheimer, *H., A Historical and Psychological Study Based on His Quartets* (London, 1951); E. Schmid, "J. H.s Jugendliebe," in *Festschrift Wilhelm Fischer* (Innsbruck, 1956); J. Larsen, "H. und Mozart," *Österreichische Musikzeitschrift*, XIV (1959); D. Bartha and L. Somfai, *H. als Opernkapellmeister: Die H.-Dokumente der Esterházy-Opernsammlung* (Budapest, 1960; rev. ed. in *New Looks at Italian Opera: Essays in Honor of Donald J. Grout*, Ithaca, N.Y., 1968); H. Seeger, *J. H.* (Leipzig, 1961); A. van Hoboken, *Discrepancies in H. Biographies* (Washington, D.C., 1962); L. Somfai, *J. H.: Sein Leben in zeitgenössischen Bildern* (Budapest and Kassel, 1966; Eng. tr., 1969); J. Chailley, "J. H. and the Freemasons," in *Studies in Eighteenth-century Music: A Tribute to Karl Geiringer* (N.Y., 1970); G. Feder, "J. H. als Mensch und Musiker," *Jahrbuch für österreichische Kulturgeschichte*, 1/2: *Beiträge zur Musikgeschichte des 18. Jahrhunderts*, II (1972); H.C. Robbins Landon, *H.* (London, 1972); B. Redfern, *H.: A Biography, with a Survey of Books, Editions and Recordings* (London, 1972); H.C. Robbins Landon, *H.: Chronicle and Works* (a monumental study of his life and music; 5 vols., Bloomington, Ind., and London; Vol. I, *H.: The Early Years, 1732–1765* [1980]; Vol. II, *H. at Esterháza, 1766–1790* [1978]; Vol. III, *H. in England, 1791–1795* [1976]; Vol. IV, *H.: The Years of "The Creation," 1796–1800* [1977]; Vol. V, *H.: The Late Years, 1801–1809* [1977]; idem, *H.: A Documentary Study* (London, 1981); J. Webb, "J. H.—Freemason and Musician," *Ars Quatuor Coronatorum*, 94, Transactions of Quatuor Coronatorum Lodge No. 2076, London (Lodge of Research; 1981); J. Webster, "Prospects for H. Biography," *Musical Times* (March 1982); N. Butterworth, *H.* (Sydney, 1983); H.C. Robbins Landon and D. Jones, *H.: His Life and Music* (London, 1988).

CRITICAL, ANALYTICAL: L. Wendschuh, *Über J. H.'s Opern* (Halle, 1896); A. Sandberger, "Zur Geschichte des H.schen Streichquartetts," *Altbayerische Monatshefte* (1900; rev. ed. in *Ausgewählte Aufsätze zur Musikgeschichte*, I, Munich, 1921); H. Abert, "J. H.s Klavierwerke," *Zeitschrift für Musikwissenschaft*, II (1919–20); F. Blume, "J. H.s künstlerische Persönlichkeit in seinen Streichquartetten," *Jahrbuch der Musikbibliothek Peters 1931*; G. Adler, "H. and the Viennese Classical School," *Musical Quarterly* (April 1932); K. Geiringer, "H.'s Sketches for 'The Creation,' " ibid.; M. Herter Norton, "H. in America (before 1820)," ibid.; O. Strunk, "H.'s Divertimenti for Baryton, Viola, and Bass," ibid.; C. Smith, "H.'s Chamber Music and the Flute," ibid. (July and Oct. 1933); B. Rywosch, *Beiträge zur Entwicklung in J. H.'s Symphonik, 1759–1780* (Turbenthal, 1934); O. Strunk, "Notes on a H. Autograph," *Musical Quarterly* (April 1934); J. Larsen, "H. und das 'kleine Quartbuch,' " *Acta Musicologica*, VII (1935; for reply, see A. Sandberger in the *Zeitschrift für Musik*, 1935); H. Wirth, *J. H. als Dramatiker: Sein Bühnenschaffen als Beitrag zur Geschichte der deutschen Oper* (Wolfenbüttel and Berlin, 1940); C. Brand, *Die Messen von J. H.* (Würzburg, 1941); H. Therstappen, *J. H.s sinfonisches Vermächtnis* (Wolfenbüttel, 1941); M. Scott, "H.: Fresh Facts and Old Fancies," *Proceedings of the Royal Musical Association*, LXVIII (1941–42); P. Radcliffe, "The Piano Sonatas of J. H.," *Music Review*, VII (1946); M. Scott, "The Opera Concerts of 1795," ibid., XII (1951); H. Wirth, *J. H.: Orfeo ed Euridice; Analytical Notes* (Boston, 1951); H.C. Robbins Landon, "H. and Authenticity: Some New Facts," *Music Review*, XVI (1955); idem, *The Symphonies of J. H.* (includes a thematic catalog, with exhaustive commentaries on their authenticity, chronology, and availability; London, 1955; supplement, 1961; for additional information, consult his *H.: Chronicle and Works*, Bloomington, Ind., and London, 5 vols., 1976–80); J. Larsen, "Zu H.s künstlerischer Entwicklung," in *Festschrift Wilhelm Fischer* (Innsbruck, 1956); D. Arnold, "H.'s Counterpoint and Fux's *Gradus*," *Monthly Musical Record*, LXXXVII (1957); H.C. Robbins Landon, "Doubtful and Spurious Quartets and Quintets Attributed to H.," *Music*

Review, XVIII (1957); H. Keller, "The Interpretation of the H. Quartets," *Score*, no. 23 (1958); E. Schenk, "Das Weltbild J. H.s'," *Österreichische Akademie der Wissenschaften: Almanach*, CIX (1959); J. Larsen, "Probleme der chronologischen Ordnung von H.s Sinfonien," in *Festschrift Otto Erich Deutsch* (Kassel, 1963); A. Tyson and H.C. Robbins Landon, "Who Composed H.'s Op. 3?," *Musical Times* (July 1964); R. Hughes, *H. String Quartets* (London, 1966); H.C. Robbins Landon, *H. Symphonies* (London, 1966); I. Saslav, *Tempos in the String Quartets of J. H.* (diss., Indiana Univ., 1969); A. Brown, *The Solo and Ensemble Keyboard Sonatas of J. H.: A Study of Structure and Style* (diss., Northwestern Univ., 1970); D. Cushman, *J. H.'s Melodic Materials: An Exploratory Introduction to the Primary and Secondary Sources Together with an Analytical Catalogue and Tables of Proposed Melodic Correspondence and/or Variance* (diss., Boston Univ., 1972); H.C. Robbins Landon, "The Operas of H.," in *The New Oxford History of Music* (vol. VII, London, 1973); W. Steinbeck, *Das Menuett in der Instrumentalmusik J. H.s* (Munich, 1973); J. Webster, *The Bass Part in H.'s Early String Quartets and in Austrian Chamber Music, 1756–1780* (diss., Princeton Univ., 1973); L. Somfai, "The London Revision of H.'s Instrumental Style," *Proceedings of the Royal Musical Association*, C (1973–74); R. Barrett-Ayres, *J. H. and the String Quartet* (London and N.Y., 1974); L. Finscher, *Studien zur Geschichte des Streichquartetts, Vol. I: Die Entstehung des klassischen Streichquartetts: Von den Vorformen zur Grundlegung durch J. H.* (Kassel, 1974); O. Moe, "Texture in H.'s Early Quartets," *Music Review*, XXV (1974); J. Drury, *H.'s Seven Last Words: An Historical and Critical Study* (diss., Univ. of Illinois, 1975); G. Feder, "Opera seria, opera buffa und opera semiseria bei H.," in *Opernstudien: Anna Amalie Abert zum 65. Geburtstag* (Tutzing, 1975); W. Koller, *Aus der Werkstatt der Wiener Klassiker: Bearbeitung H.s* (Tutzing, 1975); B. Wackernagel, *J. H.s frühe Klaviersonaten: Ihre Beziehungen zur Klaviermusik um die Mitte des 18. Jahrhunderts* (Tutzing, 1975); J. Webster, "The Chronology of H.'s String Quartets," *Musical Quarterly* (Jan. 1975); A. Brown, "Critical Years for H.'s Instrumental Music: 1787–90," ibid. (July 1976); I. Lowens, *H. in America* (Detroit, 1979); C. Wolff, ed., *The String Quartets of H., Mozart, and Beethoven: Studies of the Autograph Manuscripts* (a valuable investigation; Cambridge, Mass., 1980); G. Feder, "From the Workshop of the H. Edition," *Musical Times* (March 1982); J. Larsen, "H.: Repertory, Interpretation, Image," ibid.; D. McCaldin, "H. as Self-Borrower," ibid.; M. Huss, *J. H.: Klassiker zwischen Barock und Biedermeier* (Eisenstadt, 1984); S. Fisher, *H.'s Overtures and Their Adaptations as Concert Orchestral Works* (diss., Univ. of Pa., 1985); A. Peter Brown, *Performing H.'s Creation* (Bloomington, Ind., 1986); H. Keller, *The Great H. Quartets: Their Interpretation* (London, 1986); M. Bandur, *Form und Gehalt in den Streichquartetten J.H.s: Studien zur Theorie der Sonatenform* (Pfaffenweiler, 1988); S. Fruehwald, *Authenticity Problems in J. H.'s Early Instrumental Works: A Stylistic Investigation* (N.Y., 1988); J. Larsen, *Essays on Handel, H., and the Viennese Classical Style* (tr. by U. Krämer; Ann Arbor, 1988); J. Taggart, *F.J. H.'s Keyboard Sonatas: An Untapped Gold Mine* (Lewiston, N.Y., 1988).

MISCELLANEOUS: W. Hadow, *A Croatian Composer: Notes toward the Study of J. H.* (London, 1897; an attempt to prove H.'s Slavic origin; modern research has disproved Hadow's theory); J. Tandler, "Über den Schädel H.s'," *Mitteilungen der Anthropologischen Gesellschaft*, XXXIX (1909); V. Gotwals, "J. H.'s Last Will and Testament," *Musical Quarterly* (July 1961).

Haydn, (Johann) Michael, distinguished Austrian composer, brother of **(Franz) Joseph Haydn;** b. Rohrau, Lower Austria (baptized), Sept. 14, 1737; d. Salzburg, Aug. 10, 1806. He went to Vienna about 1745 and became a chorister at St. Stephen's Cathedral; his voice was remarkable for its wide range, extending 3 octaves. In addition to the academic and musical training he received as a chorister, he also studied composition on his own by absorbing the theories of Fux as propounded in his treatise on counterpoint, *Gradus ad Parnassum*. He then obtained the post of Kapellmeister to the Bishop of Grosswardein in 1757, and subsequently was named a court musician and Konzertmeister to Archbishop Sigismund Schrattenbach of Salzburg in 1762. In 1768 he married Maria Magdalen Lipp (1745–1827), the daughter of the court organist Franz Ignaz Lipp; she was a soprano in the archbishop's service. Haydn also became principal organist of the Dreifatigkeitskirche in 1777, and was Mozart's successor as cathedral organist in 1781. Part of his time he devoted to teaching; Carl Maria von Weber and Anton Diabelli were among his students. When Archbishop Hieronymus Colloredo abdicated in 1800 and the French took control of Salzburg, Haydn lost his positions. Although his last years were made difficult by this change in his fortunes, he turned down the post of Vice-Kapellmeister to Prince Nikolaus Esterházy, his famous brother's patron. He was a prolific composer of both sacred and secular music, and particularly esteemed for his mastery of church music. His outstanding Requiem in C minor, *Pro defuncto Archiepiscopo Sigismundo*, was composed in memory of his patron in 1771; it was also performed at Joseph Haydn's funeral. He also wrote a fine Mass, the *Sotto il titulo di S. Teresia*, for the Empress Maria Theresia, who sang the soprano solos under his direction in Vienna in 1801. His secular output included dramatic works, syms., serenades, divertimentos, chamber music, etc. His Sym. in G major (1783) was long attributed to Mozart (who composed an introduction to its 1st movement) as K.444/425a.

WORKS: SACRED: Over 400 works, including 38 masses; among the most notable are Requiem in C minor, the *Pro defuncto Archiepiscopo Sigismundo* (Salzburg, Dec. 31, 1771; ed. in Accademia Musicale, VIII [Vienna, 1970]), *S. Hieronymi* (Salzburg, Sept. 14, 1777; ed. in Accademia Musicale, VII [Vienna, 1970]), *S. Aloysii* (Salzburg, Dec. 21, 1779; publ. in Zürich, 1942); *A due cori* or *Missa hispanica* (Salzburg, Aug. 4, 1786; ed. by C. Sherman, Vienna, 1966), *Sotto il titulo di S. Teresia* (Vienna, Aug. 3, 1801), and *S. Leopoldi* (Salzburg, Dec. 22, 1805; ed. by W. Reinhart, Zürich, 1952); 6 settings of the Te Deum, 4 of the *Litaniae lauretanae*, 4 vespers, 6 responsories, 130 gradual motets, 65 offertory motets, 20 settings of the *Tantum ergo*, 13 settings of the *Salve Regina*, etc.; also 8 German masses, 9 German offertory motets, etc. **DRAMATIC SINGSPIELS:** *Rebekka als Braut* (Salzburg, April 10, 1766); *Die Hochzeit auf der Alm* (Salzburg, May 6, 1768); *Die Wahrheit der Natur* (Salzburg, July 7, 1769); *Der Bassgeiger zu Wörgl* (c.1773–75); *Abels Tod* (c.1778; only fragment extant); *Der englische Patriot* (c.1779); *Die Ährenleserin* (Salzburg, July 2, 1788). **OPERA SERIA:** *Andromeda e Perseo* (Salzburg, March 14, 1787). **ORATORIOS:** *Die Schuldigkeit des ersten Gebots* (1767; part 2 by Haydn; remainder in collaboration with Mozart and Adlgasser; not extant); *Der Kampf der Busse und Bekehrung* (Salzburg, Feb. 21, 1768); *Kaiser Constantin I. Feldzug und Sieg* (Salzburg, Feb. 20, 1769; part 3 by Haydn, part 1 by Adlgasser, and part 2 by Scheicher); *Der reumütige Petrus* (Salzburg, March 11, 1770); *Der büssende Sünder* (Salzburg, Feb. 15, 1771); *Oratorium de Passione Domini nostri Jesu Christi* (c.1775); *Figura: In emigratione nostra* (Salzburg, Aug. 24, 1782); also incidental music to Voltaire's *Zaïre* (Salzburg, Sept. 29, 1777; ed. by K. Geiringer, Vienna, 1934), cantatas, songs, canons, part-songs, etc. **INSTRUMENTAL:** About 40 syms. composed between 1759 and 1789; 3 violin concertos (1759–61; 1760; 1775–76); 2 flute concertos (1766, 1771); Trumpet Concerto (1764); Horn Concerto (1775–76); etc. He also wrote about 30 divertimentos, 2 serenatas, 3 notturnos, dances, marches, and other pieces. **CHAMBER:** 12 string quartets (1776–1802); sonatas; etc. Much of his instrumental music is available in modern eds.

BIBL.: [J.]G. Schinn and [F.]J. Otter, *Biographische Skizze von M. H.* (Salzburg, 1808); C. von Wurzbach, *Joseph Haydn und sein Bruder M.* (Vienna, 1861); A. Schnerich, *Der Messentypus von H. bis Schubert* (Vienna, 1892); J. Engl, *Zum Gedenken J.M. H.s* (Salzburg, 1906); O. Schmid, *J.M. H. . . . Sein Leben und Wirken* (Langensalza, 1906); E. Istel, "Hoffmann und das Requiem von M. H.," *Kirchenmusikalisches Jahrbuch*, XXI (1908); A. Klafsky, "M. H. als Kirchenkomponist," *Studien zur Musikwissenschaft*, III (1915); B. Wallner, "M. H. zu seinem 200. Geburtstage," *Deutsche Musikkultur*, II (1937–38); H. Jancik, *M. H.: Ein vergessener Meister* (Vienna, 1952); R. Pauly, *M. H.'s Latin "Proprium Missae" Compositions* (diss., Yale Univ., 1956); idem, "The Motets of M. H. and Mozart," *Journal of the American Musicological Society*, IX (1956); idem, "Some Recently Discovered M. H. Manuscripts," ibid., X (1957); R. Hess, *Serenade, Cassation, Notturno und Divertimento bei M. H.* (Mainz, 1963); C. Sherman, *The Masses of M. H.: A Critical Survey of Sources* (diss., Univ. of Michigan, 1967); special issue of *Österreichische Musikzeitschrift*, XXVII/1 (1972); G. Croll and K. Vössing, *J.M. H.: Sein Leben—sein Schaffen—seine Zeit: Eine Bildbiographie* (Vienna, 1987).

Haydon, Glen, eminent American musicologist; b. Inman, Kans., Dec. 9, 1896; d. Chapel Hill, N.C., May 8, 1966. He studied at the Univ. of Calif., Berkeley (B.A., 1918; M.A., 1921); he then went to Paris, where he studied clarinet and composition; then enrolled at the Univ. of Vienna, where he obtained his Ph.D. in 1932 with the dissertation *Zur Entwicklungsgeschichte des Quartsextakkordes; The Evolution of the Six-Four Chord: A Chapter in the History of Dissonance Treatment* (publ. in Berkeley, 1933). Returning to America, he became head of the dept. of music at the Univ. of North Carolina at Chapel Hill (1934), and held this post until his death. Among Haydon's publications are *Introduction to Musicology* (N.Y., 1941) and a *Graded Course of Clarinet Playing* (N.Y., 1927).

BIBL.: J. Pruett, ed., *Studies in Musicology: Essays in the History, Style and Bibliography of Music in Memory of G. H.* (Chapel Hill, 1969).

Hayes, Isaac, black American singer and songwriter of soul and popular music; b. Covington, Tenn., Aug. 6, 1938. He learned to play saxophone and piano; after singing with local groups, he went to Memphis as a studio saxophonist and pianist. He teamed up with David Porter in 1964, and subsequently penned such successful songs as *Hold On, I'm Coming; Soul Man;* and *B-A-B-Y.* After recording his hits *Walk on By* (1969), *By the Time I Get to Phoenix* (1969), and *Never Can Say Goodbye* (1971), he made waves with his music for the film *Shaft* (1972), which garnered him an Academy Award, a Golden Globe, and 2 Grammy Awards; he also won a Grammy for his album *Black Moses* (1972).

Hayes, Philip, English organist and composer, son of **William Hayes;** b. Oxford (baptized), April 17, 1738; d. London, March 19, 1797. He studied mainly with his father; received a Mus.B. from Oxford (May 18, 1763); became a Gentleman of the Chapel Royal in 1767; organist of New College, Oxford (1776); succeeded his father as organist of Magdalen College, and prof. of music at the univ. (1777); also received his Mus.D. the same year; also became organist of St. John's College (1790). He ed. *Harmonia Wiccamica* (London, 1780).

WORKS: Oratorio, *Prophecy* (Oxford, 1781); masque, *Telemachus;* odes; anthems; services; Psalms; glees; 6 concertos for Organ, Harpsichord, or Piano (1769); also some numbers in Dibdin's *The 2 Misers* and Arnold's *2 to 1.*

Hayes, Roland, distinguished black American tenor; b. Curryville, Ga., June 3, 1887; d. Boston, Jan. 1, 1977. His parents were former slaves. He studied singing with A. Calhoun in Chattanooga, Tenn., and later at Fisk Univ. in Nashville; subsequently continued vocal studies in Boston and in Europe. He made his concert debut in Boston on Nov. 15, 1917, in a program of German lieder and arias by Mozart; then made a successful tour in the U.S. In 1920 he went to London, where he studied the German repertoire with Sir George Henschel. A grand European tour followed, with appearances in Paris, Vienna, Leipzig, Munich, Amsterdam, Madrid, and Copenhagen. In 1924 he gave more than 80 concerts in the U.S., obtaining a veritable triumph for his interpretation of lyrical German and French songs, and most particularly for his poignant rendition of Negro spirituals. In 1925 he was awarded the Spingarn Medal for "most outstanding achievement among colored people," and in 1939 he received the honorary degree of Mus.D.

from Wesleyan Univ. in Delaware, Ohio. He publ. expert arrangements of 30 Negro spirituals, *My Songs* (N.Y., 1948).

BIBL.: M. Helm, *Angel Mo' and Her Son, R. H.* (Boston, 1942); F. Woolsey, "Conversation with R. H.," and W. Marr, II, "R. H.," both in *Black Perspectives in Music* (Fall 1977).

Hayes, William, English organist and composer, father of **Philip Hayes;** b. Gloucester, Dec. 1707 (baptized, Jan. 26, 1708); d. Oxford, July 27, 1777. He was a chorister at Gloucester Cathedral; was organist of St. Mary's, Shrewsbury (1729–31), then of Worcester Cathedral (1731–34). In 1734 he became organist and master of the choristers of Magdalen College, Oxford; received a Mus.Bac. (Oxford, 1735); was univ. prof. of music (1742); in 1749 received a Mus.D. He conducted the Gloucester music festival in 1757, 1760, and 1763. His canons *Allelujah* and *Miserere nobis* and his glee *Melting airs soft joys inspire* won prizes offered by the Catch Club in 1763; he also wrote a masque, *Circe;* Psalms; odes; glees; canons; ballads; cantatas. He wrote *Remarks on Mr. Avison's Essay on Musical Expression* (1762) and *Anecdotes of the Five Music-Meetings* (1768), and was co-ed. of Boyce's *Cathedral Music.*

Haym (Haim), Nicola Francesco, Italian cellist, composer, and librettist of German descent; b. Rome, July 6, 1678; d. London, Aug. 11, 1729. He was a violone player in the private orch. of Cardinal Ottoboni in Rome under Corelli (1694–1700); then went to London, where he was composer and cellist to the 2nd Duke of Bedford (1701–11); later was a bass player in the employ of the Duke of Chandos. He was a major figure in organizing performances of Italian opera in London. In 1722 he became the official librettist and Italian secretary of the Royal Academy of Music, the business venture responsible for presenting Italian opera in London. His works include 2 oratorios, *David sponsae restitutus* (1699) and *Santa Costanza* (1700); a serenata, *Il reciproco amore di Tirsi e Clori* (1699); a secular cantata, *Lontan del idol mio* (1704); instrumental pieces, including *12 Sonate a tre* (1703) and *12 Sonate a tre* (1704). His historical importance, however, rests upon his adaptations for Handel's scores, including *Teseo* (1713), *Radamisto* (1720), *Ottone* (1723), *Flavio* (1723), *Giulio Cesare* (1724), *Tamerlano* (1724), *Rodelinda* (1725), *Siroe* (1728), and *Tolomeo* (1728).

Hayman, Richard, American composer of the extreme avant-garde; b. Sandia, N.Mex., July 29, 1951. He studied humanities and philosophy at Columbia Univ.; attended classes of Vladimir Ussachevsky in electronic music; also studied flute with Eleanor Laurence at the Manhattan School of Music and had sessions on Indian vocal music with Ravi Shankar; consulted with Philip Corner and John Cage on the problems of ultra-modern music; attended Pierre Boulez's conducting seminars at the Juilliard School of Music. He eked out a meager living by intermittent employment as a construction worker, gardener, operating-room assistant in a hospital, and church pipe-organ renovator; earned an occasional few dollars as a subject in sleep-laboratory experiments; as a last resort, boldly peddled earplugs in the N.Y. subway. He arranged exhibitions of his graffiti at the Univ. of Buffalo; organized assemblages of objects and sounds at the Avant-Garde Festival at Shea Stadium in N.Y.; wrote provocatively titled articles. In 1975 he was appointed an ed. of *Ear* magazine. Perhaps his most mind-boggling musical work is *Dali,* composed at the command of Salvador Dali, scored for large orch., and notated on a toothpick, with instructions to "ascend chromatically in slow pulse." It was "performed" on March 23, 1974. Another work is *it is not here,* a light-and-sound piece, realized in Morse code at the Museum of Modern Art in N.Y. on June 14, 1974. Other pieces are *heartwhistle,* with the audience beating their collective pulses and whistling continuous tones (Aug. 3, 1975); *sleep whistle,* with the composer whistling while asleep in a store window during a paid sleep exhibition (Dec. 7, 1975); *roll,* with the composer rolling, lying down, in the street, covered with bells as a token of Hindu devotion (April 9, 1975); *dreamsound,* a sleep event in which the composer makes various sounds for the benefit of slumbering participants (Berkeley,

Calif., Feb. 20, 1976); *home* for a Telephone; *Boo Boo* for Piano; *Buff Her Blind* for Musical Toys and Electronic Instruments; *spirits* for Transduced Piano.

Hayman, Richard (Warren Joseph), American composer, arranger, and conductor; b. Cambridge, Mass., March 27, 1920. He studied composition with Alfred Newman and Max Steiner and conducting with Arthur Fiedler; then pursued a highly successful career as a composer and arranger of light musical fare; also appeared extensively as a guest conductor throughout North America.

Haymes, Dick, American singer of popular music; b. Buenos Aires (of English parents), Sept. 13, 1918; d. Los Angeles, March 28, 1980. After making his home in the U.S., he became a singer with the bands of Tommy Dorsey, Harry James, Benny Goodman, and Bunny Berrigan; later succeeded Frank Sinatra as the leading vocalist with the Dorsey and James bands. He gained particular success with his dulcet recordings of *It Had to Be You, Little White Lies,* and *It Might as Well Be Spring;* also appeared in 35 films. Although he was a millionaire several times over, his private life proved disastrous; he became an alcoholic, the subject of deportation proceedings, a bankrupt, and a husband 6 times; numbering among his wives were the actresses Rita Hayworth and Joanne Dru. He managed to survive all these misfortunes only to die from cancer at the age of 61.

Haynes, Roy (Owen), black American jazz drummer; b. Roxbury, Mass., March 13, 1926. After taking up the drums in Boston, he went to N.Y., where he worked with Lester Young, Miles Davis, and Charlie Parker. He had a particularly successful association with Stan Getz and Gary Burton, and also led his own group, the Hip Ensemble. He is regarded as one of the most gifted jazz drummers of his generation.

Haynes, Walter Battison, English organist and composer; b. Kempsey, near Worcester, Nov. 21, 1859; d. London, Feb. 4, 1900. He studied 1st with his uncle, an organist, then with F. Taylor and E. Prout; also studied with C. Reinecke and S. Jadassohn at the Leipzig Cons., where he won the Mozart scholarship. In 1884 he was appointed organist at St. Philip's Church, Sydenham; from 1890, also taught at the Royal Academy of Music in London.

WORKS: Sym.; Concert Overture; *Idyll* for Violin and Orch.; Piano Trio; organ pieces; 2 cantatas for Women's Voices: *Fairies' Isle* and *A Sea Dream.*

Hays, Lee, American folksinger; b. Little Rock, Ark., 1914; d. Tarrytown, N.Y., Aug. 26, 1981. He was a co-founder, with Pete Seeger, of the folk-song group The Weavers, with which he sang bass; made appearances with this group from 1949 to 1963. He collaborated on writing such successful songs as *Kisses Sweeter than Wine* and *If I Had a Hammer.*

BIBL.: D. Willens, *Lonesome Traveler: The Life of L. H.* (N.Y., 1988).

Hays, Sorrel (actually, **Doris Ernestine**), American composer, pianist, and mixed-media artist; b. Memphis, Tenn., Aug. 6, 1941. She was educated at the Univ. of Chattanooga (B.M., 1963), the Munich Hochschule für Musik (piano and harpsichord diploma, 1966), the Univ. of Wisconsin (M.M., 1968), and the Univ. of Iowa (composition and electronic music, 1969). In 1971 she won 1st prize in the International Competition for Interpreters of New Music in Rotterdam, and subsequently toured as a performer of contemporary music; was prof. of theory at Queens College of the City Univ. of N.Y. (1974–75), and a guest lecturer and performer at various institutions. In 1984 she adopted Sorrel as her 1st name.

WORKS: OPERAS: *Love in Space,* radio opera/music theater (1986); *The Glass Woman* (1989); *Touch of Touch,* video opera (1989); film scores; various works for radio. **INSTRUMENTAL:** *Scheveningen Beach* for Flute Quintet (1972); *Pieces from Last Year* for 16 Instruments (1976); *SensEvents* for 6 Instruments and Tape (1970–77); *Characters,* concerto for Harpsichord, String Quartet, and 3 Woodwinds (1978); *Segment/Junctures* for Viola, Clarinet, and Piano (1978); *Tunings* for Double Bass

(1978), for Flute, Clarinet, and Bassoon (1979), for Flute, Clarinet, Violin, and Soprano (1979), for Clarinet, Piano, and Soprano (1979), for String Quartet (1980), for Viola (1980), for 2 Violins (1980), and for Violin, Cello, Piano, and Soprano (1981); *UNI*, dance suite for String Quartet, Flute, Chorus, and Tape (1978); *Lullabye* for Flute, Violin, and Piano (1979); *Tommy's Trumpet* for 2 Trumpets (1979); *Fanfare Study* for Horn, Trumpet, and Trombone (1980); *Southern Voices* for Orch. and Soprano (1982); *Harmony* for String Orch. (1983); *Rocking* for Flute, Violin, and Viola (1983); *After Glass* for 10 Percussionists (1984); *Juncture Dance III* for 7 Percussionists (1989); other chamber works; piano pieces. VOCAL: *Star Music* for Chorus, Tape, and Bells (1974); *Hands Full* for 2-part Chorus, Drums, and Tape (1977); *In-de-pen-dance* for Chanter and Nylon String (1979); *Hush* for Voice, Reco-reco, and Sand Block (1981); *Rest Song* for Chorus and Optional Flute (1981); *Something (to Do) Doing* for Scat Singer, 15 Chanters, and 2 Actors (1984); *Hei-Ber-Ny-Pa-To-Sy-Bei-Mos* for Percussion, Flute, and Voice (1989); other vocal works. ELECTRONIC AND MIXED MEDIA: *Hands and Lights* for Piano and Lights (1971); *Duet* for Pianist and Audience (1971); *Certain: Change* for Piccolo, Bass Flute, and Tape (1978); *Reading Richie's Paintings* for Synthesizer, Flute, and Slides (1979); *The Gorilla and the Girl* for Tape (1981); *Only* for Piano, 2 Tapes, Slides, and Film (1981); *Water Music* for Soprano, Tape, Water Pump, Slides, Optional Violin, and Optional Baby Pool (1981); *Celebration of No* for Tape, Film, and Optional Violin or Soprano or Piano Trio (1983); *The Needy Sound* for Tape (1983); *M.O.M. 'n P.O.P.* for 3 Pianos, Tape, Film, Slides, and Mime (1984); *Weaving (Interviews)* for Optional Soprano, Piano, Film, and Slides (1984); other tape pieces; sound structures.

Hays, W(illiam) S(hakespeare), American composer; b. Louisville, Ky., July 19, 1837; d. there, July 22, 1907. He worked on Ohio and Mississippi riverboats; later wrote the "River" column for the *Louisville Courier-Journal*. He became successful as a writer of verse and a composer of songs, in spite of the fact that he had no formal training. Some 20 million copies of his songs were publ., including such popular numbers as *Evangeline* (1857), *The Drummer Boy of Shiloh* (1862), and *Mollie Darling* (1873).
    BIBL.: F. Stoll, *W.S. H.: Kentucky Composer, Marine Editor, Poet* (thesis, Univ. of Kentucky, 1943); G. Grise, *W.S. H.: His Life and Works* (thesis, Western Kentucky State Teachers College, 1947); M. Chrisman, *W.S. H.: A Biography* (thesis, Univ. of Minnesota, 1980).

Hayton, Lennie (Leonard George), American jazz pianist, arranger, and conductor; b. N.Y., Feb. 13, 1908; d. Palm Springs, Calif., April 24, 1971. He played piano in various jazz groups in N.Y.; then went to California, where he was music director for Metro-Goldwyn-Mayer and for the 20th Century-Fox Film Corp. (1940–53). He composed several semi-classic instrumental numbers and orchestrated scores for films. He married the singer **Lena Horne** in 1947, and acted as song arranger for her.

Head, Michael (Dewar), English singer, pianist, and composer; b. Eastbourne, Jan. 28, 1900; d. Cape Town, South Africa, Aug. 24, 1976. He studied composition with Frederick Corder at the Royal Academy of Music in London, and in 1927 joined its faculty as a piano instructor. In 1947 he made a grand tour through Asia, Canada, and Australia, performing both as singer and pianist. He publ. several collections of English songs; also wrote 2 children's operas, *The Bachelor Mouse* (1954) and *Key Money* (1966); Trio for Oboe, Bassoon, and Piano (1966); Suite for Recorders (1968); cantata, *Daphne and Apollo* (1964).

Headington, Christopher (John Magenis), English pianist, writer on music, and composer; b. London, April 28, 1930. He studied piano with Percy Waller and composition with Lennox Berkeley at the Royal Academy of Music in London; also received private instruction in composition from Britten

(1947–54) and studied piano with Lefebure and composition with Lutoslawski at the Dartington International Summer School (1963). He was deputy director of music at Lancing College, Sussex (1954–64); was also active with the BBC in London (1964–65); toured as a pianist in Europe, the Middle East, and the Far East.
    WRITINGS: *The Orchestra and Its Instruments* (1965); *The Bodley Head History of Western Music* (1974; 2nd ed., rev., 1980); *Illustrated Dictionary of Musical Terms* (1980); *The Performing World of the Musician* (1981); *Britten* (1981); *Listener's Guide to Chamber Music* (1982); *Opera: A History* (1987); *Sweet Sleep* (lullaby anthology). 1990.
    WORKS: *Variations* for Piano and Orch. (1950); *Introduction and Allegro* for Chamber Orch. (1951); Sonata for Cello and Piano (1953); 3 string quartets (1953, 1972, 1982); 3 piano sonatas (1955, 1974, 1985); *Chanson de l'éternelle tristesse*, ballet (1957); Violin Concerto (1959); *Towards a Pindaric Ode* for Soprano, Mezzo-soprano, and Piano (1965); *A Bradfield Mass* for Choir, Congregation, and Organ (1977); Piano Quartet (1978); *The Healing Fountain: In memoriam Benjamin Britten* for Medium Voice and Orch. (1978); Sinfonietta for Chamber Orch. (1985); Sonata for Bassoon and Piano (1988); Piano Concerto (1990).

Healey, Derek, English composer; b. Wargrave, May 2, 1936. He studied organ (with Darke) and composition with Howells at Durham Univ. (B.Mus., 1961); then took courses in flute, organ, and piano at the Royal College of Music in London; then went to Italy; took courses in composition with Petrassi and conducting with Celibadache at the Accademia Chigiana in Siena (summers of 1961–63 and 1966), and composition with Porena in Rome (1962–66). Settling in Canada, he taught at the Univ. of Victoria, British Columbia (1969–71), and at the Univ. of Toronto (1971–72); from 1972 to 1978 was on the faculty of the College of Arts at the Univ. of Guelph. In 1979 he joined the faculty of the Univ. of Oregon as prof. of theory and composition. In 1980 he was awarded the International Composition Prize of the Univ. of Louisville. His style of composition was influenced at 1st by Britten and Hindemith; later he began to experiment with large and discordant blocks of sonorities.
    WORKS: Opera: *Seabird Island* (Guelph, May 7, 1977); children's opera, *Mr. Punch* (1969); 2 ballets: *Il Carcerato* (1965) and *The 3 Thieves* (1967); *The Willow Pattern Plate* for Orch. (1957); Concerto for Organ, Strings, and Timpani (1960); *Ruba'i* for Orch. (1968); *Butterflies* for Mezzo-soprano and Small Orch. (Victoria, July 20, 1970); *Arctic Images* for Orch. (Vancouver, Sept. 21, 1971); *Noh*, triple concerto for Flute, Piano, Synthesizer, and Orch. (1974); *Primrose in Paradise*, fantasy on a shape-note hymn, for Chamber Orch. (1975; last movement of a projected sym.); *Tribulation* for Orch. (1977; 1st movement of a projected sym.); Sym. III, *Music for a Small Planet* (1984); Sym. II, *Mountain Music*, for Large Wind Ensemble and Percussion (1985); String Quartet (1961); Cello Sonata (1961); *Partita bizzara* for Oboe and Piano (1962); *Divisions* for Brass Quintet (1963); *Mobile* for Flute, Vibraphone, Celesta, Harp, 2 Percussionists, and Cello (1963); 6 *Epigrams* for Violin and Piano (1963); *Movement* for Flute, Oboe, Clarinet, and String Trio (1965); *Laudes* for Flute, Horn, Percussion, Harp, 2 Violins, and Cello (1966); *Maschere* for Violin and Piano (1967); *Stinging* for Alto Recorder, Cello, Harpsichord, and Tape (1971); *Wood II* for Soprano and String Quartet (1978; rev. 1981); *Solana Grove* for Wind Quintet (1982). Piano: *October's Dream* (1957); *Partita moderna* (1959); *12 Preludes* (1960); *Lieber Robert*, with musical phrases quoting from Schumann (1974). Organ: *Voluntaries 1–6* (1956–62); Sonata (1961); *Variants* (1964); *The Lost Traveler's Dream* (1970); also songs.

Heap, Charles Swinnerton, English pianist, organist, conductor, and composer; b. Birmingham, April 10, 1847; d. there, June 11, 1900. He studied at the Leipzig Cons.; returning to England, took courses at Cambridge; obtained the degree of Mus.D. in 1872. He was then engaged in conducting choral societies in Birmingham; also led the Birmingham Phil. Union. He wrote several cantatas and orch. overtures and a number of works of chamber music, as well as organ pieces and songs.

Heartz, Daniel (Leonard), American musicologist; b. Exeter, N.H., Oct. 5, 1928. He studied at the Univ. of New Hampshire in Durham (A.B., 1950) and at Harvard Univ. (A.M., 1951; Ph.D., 1957, with the diss. *Sources and Forms of the French Instrumental Dance in the Sixteenth Century*). From 1957 to 1960 he was on the faculty of the Univ. of Chicago; in 1960 he was appointed to the music faculty of the Univ. of Calif., Berkeley. In 1967–68 and 1978–79 he held Guggenheim fellowships. He publ. a valuable monograph, *Pierre Attaingnant, Royal Printer of Music: A Historical Study and Bibliographical Catalogue* (Berkeley, 1969); ed. *Preludes, Chansons, and Dances for Lute, Published by P. Attaingnant, Paris (1529–1530)* (Neuilly-sur-Seine, 1964) and *Keyboard Dances of the Earlier Sixteenth Century*, in Corpus of Early Keyboard Music, VIII (1965); also contributed numerous articles on Renaissance music to various music journals.

Hebenstreit, Pantaleon, German musician; b. Eisleben, 1667; d. Dresden, Nov. 15, 1750. In his early years, he was engaged variously as a violinist and a dancing master in Leipzig, but fled from his creditors to Merseburg. There the idea of improving the dulcimer was suggested to him, and he invented the instrument with which he made long and brilliant concert tours, and which Louis XIV named the Pantaleon, after its originator's Christian name. As a precursor of the piano, it has disappeared in the process of evolution. In 1706 Hebenstreit was appointed Kapellmeister and dancing master to the court at Eisenach; in 1714, "pantaleon chamber musician" at the Dresden court.

Heckel, Emil, German music publisher and piano manufacturer; b. Mannheim, May 22, 1831; d. there, March 28, 1908. He was trained by his father, Karl Ferdinand Heckel (1800–1870), in piano manufacturing. He was a great admirer of Wagner, was one of the most important supporters of the Bayreuth Festivals, and maintained a voluminous correspondence with Wagner, which was publ. by his son Karl Heckel as *Briefe Richard Wagners an E. H.* (Berlin, 1899; Eng. tr. by W. Ellis, London, 1899). Emil Heckel had an enormous bust of Wagner, sculpted by J. Hoffart, installed in his palatial residence at Mannheim, but the bust was busted during the anti-Wagnerian air bombardment in World War II.

Heckel, Johann Adam, German manufacturer of musical instruments; b. Adorf, July 14, 1812; d. Biebrich, April 13, 1877. From 1824 to 1835 he worked with the bassoonist Carl Almenräder on experiments for improving the clarinet and the bassoon. His son and successor, **Wilhelm** (b. Biebrich, Jan. 25, 1856; d. there, Jan. 13, 1909), continued his experiments with success and constructed the "Heckelphone" (a baritone oboe; used by Strauss in the score of *Salome*) in 1904; also made various changes in the construction of other woodwind instruments. He wrote *Der Fagott. Kurzgefasste Abhandlung über seine historische Entwicklung, seinen Bau und seine Spielweise* (1899; new ed., 1931).

Heckscher, Céleste de Longpré (née **Massey**), American composer; b. Philadelphia, Feb. 23, 1860; d. there, Feb. 18, 1928. Of an artistic family (her grandfather was the artist Louis de Longpré), she studied piano and participated in the musical affairs of her native city. She wrote the operas *The Flight of Time* and *Rose of Destiny* (Philadelphia, May 2, 1918); *Dances of the Pyrenees,* an orch. suite (Philadelphia, Feb. 17, 1911); a fantasy, *To the Forest,* for Violin and Piano (1902); songs; piano pieces. Her style, melodious and without pretensions, is akin to Chaminade's.

Hedges, Anthony (John), English composer; b. Bicester, March 5, 1931. He studied at Keble College, Oxford, graduating in 1953, and at the Royal Academy of Music in London; taught at the Royal Scottish Academy of Music (1957–63), and in 1968 was appointed senior lecturer at the Univ. of Hull.
  Works: Opera, *Shadows in the Sun* (1976); *Minotaur,* musi-

cal (1978); *The Birth of Freedom,* ballet (1961); Sinfonietta (1955); *Comedy Overture* (1962; rev. 1967); *Sinfonia Semplice* (1963); *Expressions* for Orch. (1964); *Concertante Music* for Piano and Orch. (1965); *Variations on a Theme of Rameau* for Orch. (1969); *4 Diversions* for Strings (1971); Sym. (1972–73); *Celebrations* for Orch. (1973); *4 Breton Sketches* for Orch. (1980); *Sinfonia Concertante* (1981); *A Cleveland Overture* (1984); *Cantiones Festivals* for Chorus and Orch. (1960); *Epithalamium* for Chorus and Orch. (1969); *To Music* for Chorus and Orch. (1972); *A Manchester Mass* for Chorus, Brass Band, and Orch. (1974); *The Temple of Solomon* for Chorus and Orch. (1979); *The Jackdaw of Rheims* for Chorus and Orch. (1980); *I Sing the Birth* for Chorus and Orch. (1985); *Rondo Concertante* for Clarinet, Horn, Violin, and Cello (1967); Sonata for Violin and Harpsichord (1967); String Quartet (1970); Piano Sonata (1974); Piano Trio (1977); Cello Sonata (1983); *Variations on a Tyneside Air* for Wind Quintet (1984).

Hedley, Arthur, English musicologist; b. Dudley, Northumberland, Nov. 12, 1905; d. Birmingham, Nov. 8, 1969. He studied French literature at the Federal Univ. of Durham (1923–27), and music with W.G. Whittaker at Newcastle. An ardent Chopinist, he learned the Polish language to be able to study Chopin documentation in the original; publ. a biography, *Chopin* (London, 1947; 3rd ed., rev., 1974, by M.J.E. Brown); edited and tr. *Selected Correspondence of Fryderyk Chopin* (London, 1962); helped to dispel cumulative misconceptions and deceptions relating to Chopin's life; was instrumental in exposing the falsity of the notorious Potocka-Chopin correspondence produced by Mme. Czernicka (who killed herself in 1949 on the 100th anniversary of Chopin's death, after the fraudulence of her claims was irrefutably demonstrated by Hedley at the Chopin Inst. in Warsaw). Hedley's Chopinolatry was carried to the point of fetishism; he acquired Chopin's cuff links and a lead pencil; proved the authenticity of Chopin's silk waistcoat, which came to light in Paris.

Hédouin, Pierre, French lawyer and littérateur; b. Boulogne, July 28, 1789; d. Paris, Dec. 20, 1868. He studied law in Paris from 1809; became an attorney, and for 30 years practiced in Boulogne. He settled in Paris in 1842, when he was appointed head of the Ministry of Public Works. His relationship with Monsigny fostered a predilection for music and the arts, and he occupied his leisure moments with literature, especially that of music, and in composition. He wrote novels; contributed to the *Annales Archéologiques, Annales Romantiques,* and several musical periodicals; composed nocturnes, romances, and songs, also writing the words; furnished the librettos of several operas.
  Writings: *Notice historique de Monsigny* (1821); *Gossec, Sa vie et ses ouvrages* (1852); *Mosaïque* (1856; a collection of his miscellaneous articles).

Hedwall, Lennart, Swedish conductor and composer; b. Göteborg, Sept. 16, 1932. He studied composition with Bäck and Blomdahl; in 1957 attended the Darmstadt composition courses. Returning to Sweden, he conducted at the Göteborg Theater (1962–65), at the Royal Theater in Stockholm (1967–68), and in Örebro (1968–74); was on the faculty of the Göteborg College of Speech and Drama (1963–67) and the School of the Royal Theater in Stockholm (1968–70; from 1974). The idiom of his music ranges from the traditional to the audaciously dissonant.
  Works: Operas: *Herr Sleeman kommer* (1976–78; Örebro, March 16, 1979); *Amerika, Amerika* (1980–81); 4 pieces for String Orch., noncommittally entitled *Music* (1950–69); *Metamorphoses* for Chamber Ensemble (1955); Oboe Concerto (1956; Swedish Radio, Dec. 21, 1961); *Variazioni piccoli* for Orch. (1958); *Lyric Music* for Soprano and Orch. (1959); *Canzona* for Strings (1965); Concerto for Cello and String Orch. (1970); *Fantasia on Veni redemptor gentium* for String Orch. (1972); *Uvertyr till Fortunios visa* for Orch. (1980); *Sagan,* symphonic fantasy (Örebro, Sept. 13, 1986); 2 string trios (1952, 1960); Solo Flute Sonata (1954); Trio for Flute, Viola, and Cello (1955); Duo for Clarinet and Bassoon (1955); Solo

Violin Sonata (1957); 2 suites for Organ (1958–59; 1970); Piano Sonata (1960); Partita for 13 Winds (1961); Trio for Flute, Clarinet, and Bassoon (1962); Wind Quintet (1965); String Quartet (1965); 6 *Monologues* for Solo Oboe (1965); 3 *Dialogues* for Clarinet and Cello (1969); Organ Sonata (1971); Sonata for Solo Bassoon (1977); *Diptyk* for Flute and Organ (1983); *Une Petite Musique de soir*, sextet for Winds (1984); liturgical cantatas; a cappella choral pieces; songs.

Heermann, Hugo, distinguished German violinist and teacher; b. Heilbronn, Württemberg, March 3, 1844; d. Merano, Italy, Nov. 6, 1935. As a boy he was taken to Rossini in Paris for advice; then studied with Bériot and Meerts at the Brussels Cons., graduating in 1861; subsequently took lessons with Joachim. In 1865 he became 1st violinist of the Frankfurt String Quartet; also taught at the Hoch Cons. In 1904 he founded his own violin school; made extended tours as a concert violinist in Europe, the U.S., and Australia; from 1906 to 1909 he taught violin at the Chicago Musical College; returning to Europe, he taught at the Stern Cons. in Berlin, and at the Geneva Cons. (1911–22). He had the distinction of having been the 1st to play the Violin Concerto of Brahms in Paris, N.Y., and Australia. He publ. a book of memoirs, *Meine Lebenserinnerungen* (Leipzig, 1935).

Hegar, Friedrich, Swiss composer and conductor; b. Basel, Oct. 11, 1841; d. Zürich, June 2, 1927. He studied at the Leipzig Cons. with Hauptmann, Richter, Ferdinand David, Rietz, and Plaidy. In 1862 he established himself in Zürich, where he was active as a violinist, conductor, and pedagogue. He conducted the Choral Soc. (1864–1901) and the concerts of the Tonhalle Orch. (1865–1906); also led various other choral organizations. He was a founder of the Zürich Music School (later the Zürich Cons.) in 1876, and its director until 1914. He received many honors, including membership in the Berlin Academy of Arts in 1917. As a composer, he contributed a great deal to Swiss choral music, particularly in the field of romantic ballads. His most successful work was the oratorio *Manasse* for Male Voices (Zürich, Oct. 25, 1885; rev. version, Jan. 10, 1888); other works are *Hymne an die Musik* for Chorus and Orch. (1870); *Das Herz von Douglas* for Soli, Male Chorus, and Orch. (1905); *Festival Overture* (1895); Cello Concerto (1919); Ballade for Violin and Orch. (1922); String Quartet; Violin Sonata; songs; etc.
BIBL.: A. Steiner, *F. H., Sein Leben und Wirken* (Zürich, 1928); W. Jerg, *H.: Ein Meister des Männerchorliedes* (Lachen, 1946).

Hegedüs, Ferenc, Hungarian violinist; b. Fünfkirchen, Feb. 26, 1881; d. London, Dec. 12, 1944. His precocious talent was carefully fostered by his father, a professional cellist (his mother was also a musician); he then studied at the Budapest Cons. with Hubay. His style of playing had the manner of the Hungarian school, but his performances of Beethoven and other classics were entirely traditional. He lived in Switzerland after 1930; then went to London.

Heger, Robert, Alsatian-born German conductor and composer; b. Strasbourg, Aug. 19, 1886; d. Munich, Jan. 14, 1978. He studied composition with Max Schillings in Berlin; then engaged in opera conducting. He conducted at Nuremberg from 1913 to 1921; was subsequently engaged at the State Opera in Vienna (1925–33); was at the Berlin State Opera (1933–45), and at the Berlin City Opera (1945–50); he subsequently led the Bavarian State Opera in Munich.
WORKS: Operas: *Ein Fest auf Haderslev* (Nuremberg, Nov. 12, 1919), *Der Bettler Namenlos* (Munich, April 8, 1932), *Der verlorene Sohn* (Dresden, March 11, 1936), and *Lady Hamilton* (Nuremberg, Feb. 11, 1951); 3 syms.; symphonic poem, *Hero und Leander;* Violin Concerto; Cello Concerto; chamber music; choral works; songs.

Hegner, Otto, Swiss pianist; b. Basel, Nov. 18, 1876; d. Hamburg, Feb. 22, 1907. He studied piano with Eugene d'Albert; at the age of 12 made an American tour and was hailed as one of the most phenomenal young pianists. His early death,

at the age of 30, cut short his brilliant career. His sister **Anna Hegner** (b. Basel, March 1, 1881; d. there, Feb. 3, 1963) was a violinist.

Hegyesi (real name, **Spitzer**), **Louis,** noted Hungarian cellist; b. Arpad, Nov. 3, 1853; d. Cologne, Feb. 27, 1894. He studied with Demis in Vienna and with Franchomme in Paris. In 1888 he was appointed to the faculty of the Cologne Cons. He publ. several brilliant cello pieces and a valuable theoretical manual, *Neue rhythmische Tonleiter- und Akkordstudien*.

Heiden, Bernhard, German-born American composer; b. Frankfurt am Main, Aug. 24, 1910. He studied piano, clarinet, violin, theory, and harmony; from 1929 to 1933 studied at the Hochschule für Musik in Berlin, where his principal teacher was Paul Hindemith. In 1935 he emigrated to the U.S.; became a naturalized citizen in 1941; taught at the Art Center Music School in Detroit; was also conductor of the Detroit Chamber Orch., as well as pianist, harpsichordist, and chamber music artist. He served in the U.S. Army (1943–45); then studied musicology with Donald Grout at Cornell Univ. (A.M., 1946). In 1946 he joined the faculty of the Indiana Univ. School of Music in Bloomington; retired in 1981. His music is neo-Classical in its formal structure, and strongly polyphonic in texture; it is distinguished also by its impeccable sonorous balance and effective instrumentation.
WORKS: STAGE: Incidental music to *Henry IV* (1940) and *The Tempest* (1942); *Dreamers on a Slack Wire*, dance drama for 2 Pianos and Percussion (1953); *The Darkened City*, opera (1962; Bloomington, Ind., Feb. 23, 1963). **ORCH.:** Sym. No. 1 (1938); *Euphorion: Scene for Orch.* (1949); Concerto for Small Orch. (1949); Sym. No. 2 (1954); *Memorial* (1955); Concerto for Piano, Violin, Cello, and Orch. (1956); *Philharmonic Fanfare* (1958); *Variations* (1960); *Envoy* (1963); Concerto for Cello and Orch. (1967); Concertino for String Orch. (1967); Concerto for Horn and Orch. (1969); *Partita* (1970); Concerto for Tuba and Orch. (1976); Concerto for Trumpet and Wind Orch. (1981); *Triptych* for Baritone and Orch. (1983); *Recitative and Aria* for Cello and Orch. (1985; Pittsburgh, May 8, 1986); *A Bestiary* for Soprano, Tenor, and Chamber Orch. (1986); *Fantasia concertante* for Alto Saxophone, Winds, and Percussion (1987); Concerto for Recorder and Chamber Orch. (1987). **CHAMBER:** Sonata for Alto Saxophone and Piano (1937); Sonata for Horn and Piano (1939); String Quartet No. 1 (1947); Sinfonia for Woodwind Quintet (1949); String Quartet No. 2 (1951); Quintet for Horn and String Quartet (1952); Sonata for Violin and Piano (1954); Quintet for Clarinet and Strings (1955); Serenade for Bassoon, Violin, Viola, and Cello (1955); Trio for Violin, Cello, and Piano (1956); Sonata for Cello and Piano (1958); Sonata for Viola and Piano (1959); Quintet for Oboe and Strings (1962); *Intrada* for String Quartet (1962); 7 *Pieces* for String Quartet (1964); Woodwind Quintet (1965); 4 *Dances* for Brass Quintet (1967); *Intrada* for Woodwind Quintet and Saxophone (1970); 5 *Canons* for 2 Horns (1971); *Variations* for Tuba and 9 Horns (1974); Quintet for Flute, Violin, Viola, Bassoon, and Contrabass (1975); 4 *Movements* for Saxophone Quartet and Timpani (1976); variations on *Lilliburlero* for Cello Solo (1976); *Terzetto* for 2 Flutes and Cello (1979); Quartet for Horns (1981); Sextet for Brass Quintet and Piano (1983); Quartet for Piano, Violin, Cello, and Horn (1985); Trio Serenade for Violin, Clarinet, and Piano (1987); *Preludes* for Flute, Bass, and Harp (1988). **KEYBOARD:** Piano Sonata No. 1 (1941); Sonata for Piano, 4-hands (1946); Variations on *The Cruel Ship's Carpenter* for Organ (1950); Piano Sonata No. 2 (1952); Variations for Piano (1959); Fantasia for 2 Pianos (1971); *Hommage à Scarlatti* for Piano (1971). **VOCAL:** 2 *Songs of Spring* for Women's Chorus (1947); 4 *Songs from the Song of Songs* for Soprano and Orch. or Piano (1948); *Divine Poems* for Mixed Chorus, after John Donne (1949); *In Memoriam* for Mixed Chorus (1964); *Advent Song* for Mixed Chorus (1965); *Riddles of Jonathan Swift* for Women's Chorus (1975); *Sonnets of Louise Labe* for Soprano and String Quartet (1977).

Heidingsfeld, Ludwig, German composer; b. Jauer, March 24, 1854; d. Danzig, Sept. 14, 1920. He studied at the Stern

Cons. in Berlin, and later taught there. He subsequently settled in Danzig, and founded a cons. (1899). He wrote 2 operettas, *Der neue Dirigent* (Danzig, 1907) and *Alle Burchenherrlichkeit* (Danzig, 1911); the symphonic poems *King Lear* and *Der Totentanz*; piano pieces; songs.

Heifetz, Daniel (Alan), American violinist; b. Kansas City, Mo., Nov. 20, 1948. He studied with several teachers in Los Angeles; then went to Philadelphia, where he had advanced training with Zimbalist, Galamian, and Jascha Brodsky at the Curtis Inst. of Music (1966–71). On Jan. 20, 1970, he made a significant debut in Tchaikovsky's Violin Concerto with the National Sym. Orch. of Washington, D.C. He then entered the Tchaikovsky Competition in Moscow, winning 4th prize (1978). Later he concertized in Europe and throughout the Americas; from 1980 he taught at the Peabody Cons. in Baltimore. He is not related to Jascha Heifetz.

Heifetz, Jascha, celebrated Russian-born American violinist; b. Vilnius, Feb. 2, 1899; d. Los Angeles, Dec. 10, 1987. His father, Ruben Heifetz, an able musician, taught him the rudiments of violin playing at a very early age; he then studied with Ilya Malkin at the Vilnius Music School, and played in public before he was 5 years old; at the age of 6, he played Mendelssohn's Concerto in Kovno. In 1910 he was taken by his father to St. Petersburg, and entered the Cons. there in the class of Nalbandian; after a few months, he was accepted as a pupil by Leopold Auer. He gave his 1st public concert in St. Petersburg on April 30, 1911. The following year, with a letter of recommendation from Auer, he went to Berlin; his 1st concert there (May 24, 1912), in the large hall of the Hochschule für Musik, attracted great attention: Artur Nikisch engaged him to play the Tchaikovsky Concerto with the Berlin Phil. (Oct. 28, 1912), and Heifetz obtained sensational success as a child prodigy of extraordinary gifts. He then played in Austria and Scandinavia. After the Russian Revolution of 1917, he went to America, by way of Siberia and the Orient. His debut at Carnegie Hall in N.Y. (Oct. 27, 1917) won for him the highest expression of enthusiasm from the public and in the press. Mischa Elman, the prime violinist of an older generation, attended the concert in the company of the pianist Leopold Godowsky. When Elman complained that it was too hot in the hall, Godowsky retorted, "Not for pianists." Veritable triumphs followed during Heifetz's tour of the U.S., and soon his fame spread all over the world. He made his 1st London appearance on May 5, 1920; toured Australia (1921), the Orient (1923), Palestine (1926), and South America. He revisited Russia in 1934, and was welcomed enthusiastically. He became a naturalized American citizen in 1925, and made his home in Beverly Hills, Calif.; in subsequent years he continued to travel as a concert violinist, visiting virtually every country in the world, but from 1974 ceased to appear in public as a soloist; he participated in a trio (with Piatigorsky and Pennario) and also taught classes of exceptionally talented pupils at the Univ. of Southern Calif., Los Angeles (1962–72).

The quality of his playing was unique in luminous transparency of texture, tonal perfection, and formal equilibrium of phrasing; he never allowed his artistic temperament to superimpose extraneous elements on the music; this inspired tranquillity led some critics to characterize his interpretations as impersonal and detached. Heifetz made numerous arrangements for violin of works by Bach, Vivaldi, and contemporary composers; his most famous transcription is *Hora Staccato* by Grigoraş Dinicu, made into a virtuoso piece by adroit ornamentation and rhythmic elaboration. In his desire to promote modern music, he commissioned a number of composers (Walton, Gruenberg, Castelnuovo-Tedesco, and others) to write violin concertos for him, and performed several of them. Herbert R. Axelrod ed. and publ. an "unauthorized pictorial biography" of Heifetz (Neptune City, N.J., 1976; 2nd ed., augmented, 1981); Heifetz filed a lawsuit for $7.5 million against the publisher and compiler, claiming invasion of privacy. Upon sober reflection, the suit was withdrawn.

BIBL.: A. Weschler-Vered, *J. H.* (London, 1986); D. Soria,

"H.: Aloof, Awe-inspiring," *Musical America* (May 1988); I. Stern, "Remembering J. H.," *Ovation* (March 1988).

Heiller, Anton, significant Austrian organist and composer; b. Vienna, Sept. 15, 1923; d. there, March 25, 1979. He studied piano and organ at the Vienna Cons.; in 1952 won 1st prize at the International Organ Contest in Haarlem, the Netherlands; in 1969 he received the Austrian Grand Prize for Music; in 1971 was appointed prof. at the Hochschule für Musik in Vienna. His music is rooted deeply in the tradition of the Renaissance, while his contrapuntal technique adopts modern procedures. He particularly excelled in sacred works, to Latin texts; in these he occasionally made use of the 12-tone method of composition.

WORKS: Chamber oratorio, *Tentatio Jesu* (1952); *Psalmenkantate* (1955); Concerto for Organ and Orch. (1963); cantata, *In principio erat verbum* (1965); *Stabat Mater* for Chorus and Orch. (1968); several masses, including *Kleine Messe über Zwölftonmodelle*, a cappella (1962); *English Mass* (1965); *Adventsmusik* for Chorus and Organ (1971).

Heilman, William Clifford, American composer; b. Williamsport, Pa., Sept. 27, 1877; d. there, Dec. 20, 1946. He studied at Harvard Univ. (B.A., 1900) and in Europe with Rheinberger and Widor. He was a member of the music dept. of Harvard Univ. from 1905 till 1930. Among his works are a symphonic poem, *By the Porta Catania* (1916); Piano Trio; Romance for Cello and Piano; a number of character pieces for piano; choruses. He also made arrangements of Negro spirituals.

Heinefetter, family of German opera singers:

(1) Sabine Heinefetter, soprano; b. Mainz, Aug. 19, 1809; d. Illemau, Nov. 18, 1872. She made her operatic debut in Ritter's *Der Mandarin* in Frankfurt in 1822; Spohr then engaged her for Kassel, but she broke her contract to continue vocal study with Banderali and Tadolini in Paris. After appearances at the Théâtre-Italien there, she sang with brilliant success all over Europe. She created the role of Adina in *L'elisir d'amore* (Milan, 1832); made her farewell appearances in Marseilles in 1846. She died insane.

(2) Clara Heinefetter, soprano, sister of the preceding; b. Mainz, Sept. 7, 1813; d. Vienna, Feb. 23, 1857. She studied with her sister Sabine and with Ciccimarra in Vienna, making her debut there in 1831; subsequently sang under the name of Mme. Stöckl-Heinefetter; appeared in London (1840–42). She also died insane.

(3) Kathinka Heinefetter, soprano, sister of the preceding; b. Mainz, Sept. 12, 1819; d. Freiburg, Dec. 20, 1858. She studied with her sister Sabine and with Ponchard in Vienna, making her debut in Frankfurt in 1836; retired from the stage in 1853. Three other Heinefetter sisters, Fatima, Eva, and Nanetta, also appeared professionally on the operatic stage.

Heinemann, Alfred, German composer; b. Bückeburg, April 10, 1908. He played piano as a child, and began to compose at the age of 10. In 1936 he went to Johannesburg, South Africa. In 1944 he moved to Cape Town; was active mainly as a teacher. In 1949 he settled in the U.S.; in 1967 joined the staff of Broadcast Music Inc. His music follows the tenets of enlightened functionalism, without transgressing the natural capacities of the instruments.

WORKS: Opera, *Torso* (1958); ballets: *Galaxy* (1941); *Roulette* (1946); *La Manie des titres et des abbréviations* (1953); *Kobold* (1963); Piano Concerto (1941); Violin Concerto (1942); *March of the Neanderthal Men* (Cape Town, April 7, 1946); Sym. (1959–64).

Heinemeyer, Ernst Wilhelm, outstanding German flutist; b. Hannover, Feb. 25, 1827; d. Vienna, Feb. 12, 1869. He studied with his father, Christian Heinemeyer (1796–1872), who was the chamber flutist at Hannover. In 1847 he went to Russia, where he played the flute in the Imperial Orch. at St. Petersburg; in 1859 he returned to Hannover; in 1866 he went to Vienna. He wrote several concertos for the flute.

Heinichen, Johann David, notable German composer and music theorist; b. Krössuln, near Weissenfels, April 17, 1683;

d. Dresden, July 16, 1729. He was educated at the Thomasschule in Leipzig, studying with Schell and Kuhnau; at the same time, he studied law, and practiced as a lawyer in Weissenfels. His 1st opera, *Der Karneval von Venedig, oder Der angenehme Betrug*, was performed in Leipzig in 1709; he then held a position as conductor at Zeitz. Councillor Buchta of Zeitz supplied the funds for Heinichen to accompany him to Italy (1710–16), where he produced several operas. In Venice he joined the Elector of Saxony, Frederick Augustus, and followed him to Dresden as Kapellmeister of the Italian opera company there (1717). However, as a result of confusion brought about by a violent quarrel between Heinichen and the singer Berselli, the Dresden opera was dissolved. Heinichen remained in Dresden as director of church and chamber music. He was a prolific composer; a thematic catalog of his works is found in G. Seibel, *Das Leben des J.D. H.* (Leipzig, 1913), listing, besides his operas, 2 oratorios, 16 masses, 63 cantatas, more than 100 other sacred works, 4 syms., 2 overtures, 30 concertos, 17 sonatas, 7 pieces for flute, many separate airs, etc. Most of them were preserved in the Dresden Court (later State) Library, but unfortunately many perished in the fire-bombing of Dresden in 1945. Few of his works have been publ. Heinichen's importance lies not so much in his compositions as in his basic theoretical work, *Neu erfundene und gründliche Answeisung zu vollkommener Erlernung des General-Basses* (Hamburg, 1711; 2nd ed., rev. and greatly augmented, as *Der General-Bass in der Composition*, Dresden, 1728).

BIBL.: R. Tanner, *J.D. H. als dramatischer Komponist* (Leipzig, 1916); G. Hausswald, *J.D. H.s Instrumentalwerke* (Wolfenbüttel and Berlin, 1937); G. Buelow, *Thorough-Bass Accompaniment According to J.D. H.* (Berkeley, Calif., 1966; 2nd ed., rev., 1986).

Heininen, Paavo (Johannes), significant Finnish composer and teacher; b. Helsinki, Jan. 13, 1938. After studying privately with Usko Merilainen, he took courses with Aarre Merikanto, Einojuhani Rautavaara, Einar Englund, and Joonas Kokkonen at the Sibelius Academy in Helsinki (composition diploma, 1960); later took courses with Bernd Alois Zimmermann in Cologne (1960–61), and with Persichetti and Steuermann at the Juilliard School of Music in N.Y. (1961–62); also worked with Lutoslawski in Poland, and attended theory classes at the Univ. of Helsinki. In 1962–63 he was on the faculty of the Sibelius Academy; taught in Turku (1963–66); resumed his position at the Sibelius Academy, where he was mentor to a generation of Finnish composers. He was also active as a pianist, conductor, and program annotator. He developed a highly complex compositional style, employing styles and techniques ranging from neo-Classicism to dodecaphonic and serial procedures culminating in "stream of consciousness" modality.

WORKS: STAGE: *Silkkirumpu* (The Silken Drum), concerto for Singers, Players, Words, Images, and Movements (1981–83; Helsinki, April 5, 1984); *Veitsi* (The Knife), opera (1985–88; Helsinki, July 3, 1989). **ORCH.:** 4 syms.: No. 1 (1958; rev. 1960; Helsinki, March 24, 1964); No. 2, *Petite symphonie joyeuse* (Helsinki, Dec. 7, 1962); No. 3 (1969; rev. 1977; Helsinki, Jan. 24, 1978); No. 4 (1971; Oslo, Sept. 4, 1972); *Preambolo* (1959); *Tripartita* (1959; Helsinki, Nov. 11, 1960); Concerto for String Orch. (1959; Helsinki, April 19, 1960; rev. 1963; Turku, May 30, 1963); *Soggetto* (1963; Helsinki, Jan. 12, 1965); *Adagio . . . concerto per orchestra in forma di variazioni . . .* (1963; Helsinki, Jan. 24, 1964; rev. 1966; Camden Festival, Feb. 19, 1967); 3 piano concertos: No. 1 (1964; Turku, Jan. 23, 1965); No. 2 (Turku, Dec. 1, 1966); No. 3 (1981; Helsinki, March 13, 1982); *Arioso* for Strings (Helsinki, May 21, 1967); *Cantico delle creature* for Baritone and Orch. (1968); *Deux chansons* for Cello and Orch. (1976; Tampere, Feb. 25, 1977); *Tritopos* (1977; Helsinki, March 7, 1978); *Dia* (Helsinki, Sept. 12, 1979); *Attitude* (Helsinki, Dec. 10, 1980); *. . . floral view with maidens singing . . .* for Chamber Orch. (1982; Kokkola, April 8, 1983); *Dicta*, "Nonette avec milieu" for 9 plus 14 Players in the Audience (Helsinki, March 25, 1983); Saxophone Concerto (Helsinki, Aug. 29, 1983); *KauToKei* for Double String

Orch. (1985; Helsinki, Feb. 12, 1986); Cello Concerto (1985; Helsinki, Feb. 26, 1986). **CHAMBER:** Quintet for Flute, Saxophone, Piano, Vibraphone, and Percussion (1961); Violin Sonata (1970; Helsinki, Feb. 18, 1973); *Poesia squillante ed incandescente*, piano sonata (1974; Helsinki, Feb. 14, 1979); String Quartet (1974; Helsinki, Jan. 21, 1976); *Gymel* for Bassoon and Tape (1978; Hameenlinna, July 3, 1979); *Cinq moments de jour* for Piano (1984); other works. **CHORAL:** *The Autumns* (1970); *. . . cor meum . . .* (1976–79); *Virsi-81* (Hymn-81) for Chorus and Organ (1981); *4 Lullabies* for Men's Voices (1986); songs; also the electro-acoustic *Maiandros* (Finnish Radio, Helsinki, March 23, 1977).

Heiniö, Mikko, Finnish composer; b. Tampere, May 5, 1948. He studied musicology at the Univ. of Helsinki; took courses in composition with Joonas Kokkonen and in piano with Liisa Pohjola at the Sibelius Academy (1971–75); from 1975 to 1977 studied composition with Witold Szalonek at the Hochschule der Künste in West Berlin; also took lessons in piano with Martin Krause and in conducting with Hans Hildorf. In 1977 he joined the musicology dept. of the Univ. of Helsinki, taking his Ph.D. in 1984.

WORKS: Trio for Flute, Violin, and Guitar (1971); String Quartet No. 1 (1972); Piano Concerto No. 1 (Tampere, Nov. 17, 1972); *Luominen* (The Creation) for Soprano, Baritone, Chorus, and Orch. (1972); Suite for Flute and 2 Guitars (1974); *4 romantische Lieder* for Soprano and Orch. (1974); Piano Concerto No. 2 (Helsinki, Feb. 26, 1975); *Tredicia* for Orch. (1976); Bassoon Concerto (1977); Horn Concerto (1978); Concerto for Orch. (Turku, Nov. 11, 1982); Piano Concerto No. 3 (1981); *". . . in spe"* for Saxophone, and Marimba or Vibraphone (1984); *Mannerkantaatti* (Cantata of Continent) for Soprano, Baritone, Mixed Chorus, and Orch. (1985); songs.

Heinitz, Wilhelm, German musicologist; b. Hamburg-Altona, Dec. 9, 1883; d. Hamburg, March 31, 1963. He studied the bassoon, and played in various orchs.; then became interested in phonetics; studied primitive music and the languages of Africa and Polynesia; took a Ph.D. in psychology at the Univ. of Kiel (1920), and completed his Habilitation at the Univ. of Hamburg (1931) with his *Strukturprobleme in primitiver Musik* (publ. in Hamburg, 1931); then became a member of the Phonetic Laboratory at the Univ. of Hamburg, and led a seminar in comparative musicology until his retirement in 1949. He wrote a number of valuable papers on the structural problems of speech, which he publ. in specialized journals; also the books *Klangprobleme im Rundfunk* (Berlin, 1926), *Neue Wege der Volksmusikforschung* (Hamburg, 1937), and *Physiologische Reaktion und Pulsationsmessung* (Hamburg, 1958).

Heinrich, Anthony Philip (Anton Philipp), American violinist and composer of German-Bohemian birth; b. Schönbüchel, March 11, 1781; d. N.Y., May 3, 1861. As a boy he acquired proficiency on the piano and violin, but began adult life as a wholesale merchant and banker; in 1810 he emigrated to America, settling in Philadelphia as a merchant and as unpaid music director of the Southwark Theatre. After business reverses in 1817 he moved to the wilds of Kentucky, 1st to Bardstown and then to nearby Lexington, where he managed to find enough musicians to conduct in a performance of a Beethoven sym. Without any knowledge of harmony, he began to compose in 1818; these 1st songs and choral and instrumental pieces he publ. later as op. 1, *The Dawning of Music in Kentucky, or The Pleasures of Harmony in the Solitudes of Nature*, and op. 2, *The Western Minstrel* (both 1820; reprinted N.Y., 1972). He became music director at the Southwark Theatre in Philadelphia; later, in Louisville, Ky. The year 1827 found him in London, playing violin in a small orch.; there he also studied theory, and about 1830 began to write for orch.; returned to the U.S. in 1832. In 1834 he again visited England, as well as Germany and Austria (1835), and had some of his works produced at Dresden, Prague, Budapest, and Graz (his sym. *The Combat of the Condor* was perf. at Graz in 1836; also in France); in Vienna he entered a competition with a sym., but the prize was awarded to Franz Lachner;

disappointed, he returned to America and settled in N.Y., where he soon gained immense popularity, becoming known as "Father Heinrich." He was a commanding figure in the musical affairs of the U.S., publishing many of his piano pieces and songs; grand festivals of his works were arranged in N.Y., Philadelphia, and Boston; critics spoke of him as the "Beethoven of America." But a tour of Germany in 1857–58 was a dismal failure; he died in extreme poverty. The quality of his works is dubious at best; he wrote for an enormous orch., *à la* Berlioz, and his musical ideas, out of all proportion to the means employed, recall the style of Haydn's imitators; nevertheless, he is historically important, as the 1st to employ American Indian themes in works of large dimensions and to show decided nationalist aspirations. In 1917 the Library of Congress acquired Heinrich's "Memoranda" (letters, programs, newspaper clippings, etc.), many publ. works, and almost all the orch. scores, enumerated in a list made by Heinrich himself in 1857. A perusal of the titles is amusing and instructive: *Grand American Chivalrous Symphony; The Columbiad, or Migration of American Wild Passenger Pigeons; The Ornithological Combat of Kings, or The Condor of the Andes and the Eagle of the Cordilleras; Pocahontas, the Royal Indian Maid and the Heroine of Virginia, the Pride of the Wilderness; The Wild-wood Spirit's Chant or Scintillations of "Yankee Doodle," forming a Grand National Heroic Fantasia scored for a Powerful Orch. in 44 Parts; Manitou Mysteries, or The Voice of the Great Spirit; Gran Sinfonia Misteriosa-Indiana* (U.S. perf., N.Y., Dec. 2, 1975). Reprints (in addition to opp. 1 and 2): *Songs without Words*, vol. I of Piano Music in Nineteenth Century America (Chapel Hill, N.C., 1975); *Yankeedoodle* (for Piano) in W. Marrocco and H. Gleason, *Music in America* (N.Y., 1964); *The Maiden's Dirge*, in E. Gold, *The Bicentennial Collection of American Music* (Dayton, Ohio, 1975). **BIBL.:** F. Mussik, *Skizzen aus dem Leben des . . . A.P. H.* (Leipzig, 1843); O. Sonneck, "Musical Landmarks in New York," *Musical Quarterly* (April 1920); W. Upton, *A.P. H.* (N.Y., 1939); D. Barron, *The Early Vocal Works of A.P. H.* (diss., Univ. of Illinois, 1972); L. Filbeck, *The Choral Works of A.P. H.* (diss., Univ. of Illinois, 1973); W. Maust, *The Symphonies of A.P. H. Based on American Themes* (diss., Indiana Univ., 1973).

Heinroth, Johann August Günther, German composer and writer on music; b. Nordhausen, June 19, 1780; d. Göttingen, June 2, 1846. He studied with his father, an able organist. He then attended the Univs. of Leipzig and Halle. In 1804 he became attached to the School of Jewish Studies organized by Israel Jacobson. This was the beginning of a lifelong study of the Jewish liturgy, which he reorganized, adding numerous original melodies that became part of the Jewish service. He also attempted to introduce a simplified musical notation by figures. From 1818 he served as music director of the Univ. of Göttingen, in succession to Forkel. WRITING (all publ. in Göttingen): *Gesangunterrichts-Methode für höhere und niedere Schulen* (3 parts; 1821–23); *Volksnoten oder vereinfachte Tonschrift* (1828); *Kurze Anleitung, das Klavier oder Forte-Piano spielen zu lehren* (1828); *Musikalisches Hilfsbuch für Prediger, Kantoren und Organisten* (1833). **BIBL.:** W. Boetticher, *Die Musik an der Georgia Augusta-Universität zu Göttingen* (1958).

Heinsheimer, Hans (Walter), German-born American publishing executive and writer on music; b. Karlsruhe, Sept. 25, 1900. He studied law in Heidelberg, Munich, and Freiburg im Breisgau (Juris Dr., 1923); then joined Universal Edition in Vienna, where he was in charge of its opera dept. (1924–38), and supervised the publication of such important stage works as Berg's *Wozzeck*, Krenek's *Jonny spielt auf*, Weinberger's *Schwanda*, Weill's *Aufstieg und Fall der Stadt Mahagonny*, and Antheil's *Transatlantic*. He went to the U.S. in 1938 and was associated with the N.Y. branch of Boosey & Hawkes. In 1947 he was appointed director of the symphonic and operatic repertoire of G. Schirmer, Inc.; in 1957 became director of publications and in 1972 vice-president of the firm; in these capacities he promoted the works of Barber, Menotti, Bernstein,

and Carter. He retired in 1974 and devoted himself mainly to writing. A brilliant stylist in both German and English, he contributed numerous informative articles to *Melos, Musical Quarterly, Holiday, Reader's Digest,* etc. He publ. the entertaining books *Menagerie in F-sharp* (N.Y., 1947) and *Fanfare for Two Pigeons* (1952); the 2 works were publ. in German in a single vol. entitled *Menagerie in Fis-dur* (Zürich, 1953); he also wrote *Best Regards to Aida* (publ. in German as *Schönste Grüsse an Aida*; Munich, 1968).

Heintze, Gustaf (Hjalmar), Swedish pianist, organist, and composer; b. Jönköping, July 22, 1879; d. Saltsjöbaden, March 4, 1946. His grandfather, Gustaf Wilhelm Heintze (1825–1909), and father, Georg Wilhelm Heintze (1849–95), were well-known organists. He studied organ in Lund and Stockholm; also studied composition and instrumentation with Joseph Dente (1897–1900) and piano with Richard Andersson (1901) in Stockholm; then taught piano at Andersson's school (1901–18). He subsequently founded his own piano school, and was also organist at the Maria Magdalena Church. He wrote 2 piano concertos (1917, 1926), 2 violin concertos (1921, 1932), a Concerto for 2 Pianos and Orch. (1933), 3 cantatas (1923, 1934, 1940), and piano pieces.

Heinze, Sir Bernard (Thomas), eminent Australian conductor; b. Shepparton, near Melbourne, July 1, 1894; d. Sydney, June 9, 1982. He studied at the Univ. of Melbourne and the Royal College of Music in London, and attended classes of d'Indy at the Schola Cantorum in Paris. He also took violin lessons in Berlin with Willy Hess. Returning to Australia after service in the Royal Artillery during World War I, he became a teacher at the Melbourne Conservatorium in 1924; was named a prof. in 1925 and remained on its faculty until 1956. He also served as director of the New South Wales Cons. (1956–66). In 1938 he made a European tour as conductor; from 1932 until 1949 he was also conductor of the Melbourne Sym. Orch. He was knighted in 1949, and in 1976 was made a Companion of the Order of Australia. **BIBL.:** T. Radic, *B. H.: A Biography* (South Melbourne, 1986).

Heinze, Gustav Adolf, German conductor and composer; b. Leipzig, Oct. 1, 1820; d. Muiderberg, near Amsterdam, Feb. 20, 1904. He received his early musical education from his father, a clarinetist in the Gewandhaus Orch. in Leipzig, and joined that orch. as clarinetist at the age of 16. He then conducted at the Breslau City Theater (1844–49), where he successfully produced 2 operas: *Loreley* (1846) and *Die Ruinen von Tharandt* (1847). In 1850 he went to Amsterdam, where he founded a singing school (1862–69); he later founded a music school in Bussum (1885). He composed, besides his operas, several oratorios and other choral works. He publ. an autobiography (Amsterdam, 1905).

Heise, Peter (Arnold), esteemed Danish composer; b. Copenhagen, Feb. 11, 1830; d. Stockkerup, Sept. 12, 1879. He studied music with Berggreen in Copenhagen and with Hauptmann at the Leipzig Cons. Returning to Denmark, he became a music teacher and organist at Sorö, where he remained until 1865. He then settled in Copenhagen; produced 2 successful operas, *Paschaens datter* (The Pasha's Daughter; Sept. 30, 1869) and *Drot og marsk* (King and Marshal; Sept. 25, 1878). He also wrote a Sym., chamber music, etc. It was in his many lieder to Danish texts that Heise achieved enduring fame. **BIBL.:** G. Hetsch, *P. H.* (Copenhagen, 1926).

Heiss, Hermann, German composer; b. Darmstadt, Dec. 29, 1897; d. there, Dec. 6, 1966. He studied with Bernhard Sekles in Frankfurt (1921); then took a course in 12-tone music with Hauer (1925). He was active as a teacher in Frankfurt and Vienna; beginning in 1946 he taught at the Darmstadt summer courses for new music. In his compositions he adopted ultra-modern techniques. **WORKS: ORCH.:** *Sinfonia atematica* (1950); *Sinfonia giocosa* (1954); *Configurationen I–II* (1956–59); *Polychromatica* (1959); *Bewegungsspiele* (1959). **BALLETS:** *Herz auf bürger-*

liche Art (1953); *Der Manager* (1954); also chamber music; electronic pieces.

BIBL.: B. Reichenbach, *H. H.* (Mainz, 1975).

Heiss, John, American composer; b. N.Y., Oct. 23, 1938. He studied flute as a youth; then took his formal education at Columbia Univ. (1960–65) and at Princeton Univ. (M.F.A., 1967), where his principal mentors were Babbitt, Kim, Luening, and Milhaud. He held teaching positions at Barnard College, at Columbia Univ., and at the New England Cons. of Music (from 1967). He received several N.E.A. grants and a Guggenheim fellowship.

WORKS: ORCH.: *4 Short Pieces* (1962); *Music for Orchestra* (1968); *Flute Concerto* for Chamber Orch. (1977); *Festival Prelude* (1983). **CHAMBER:** *4 Movements for 3 Flutes* (1969); Quartet for Flute, Clarinet, Violin, and Piano (1971); *Capriccio* for Flute, Clarinet, and Percussion (1976); *Eloquy* for Flute, Oboe, Clarinet, and Bassoon (1978); *So-nar-ity* for Piano, 4-hands, Harp, Percussion, Flute, and Clarinet (1982); *A Place in New England* for Brass Quartet or Brass Choir, and Organ (1982); *Epigrams* for Flute and Percussion (1985); *Mosaics No. 1* for a Very Large Array of Flutists (1986); *Mosaics No. 2* for Large Cello Choir (1987); *Mosaics No. 3* for Trombone Choir (1990). **CHORAL:** *3 Songs from Sandburg* for Treble Choir, Piano, and Bassoon (1963); *Rejoice in the Lord* for Treble or Mixed Choir, and Keyboard (1964); *From Infinity Full Circle,* chamber cantata for Treble Choir and Piano (1979); also vocal settings and a variety of pieces for solo instruments.

Hekking, André, French cellist of Dutch descent, brother of **Anton Hekking;** b. Bordeaux, July 30, 1866; d. Paris, Dec. 14, 1925. He was the son of the Dutch-born French cellist Robert Gérard Hekking (1820–75), who settled in France; received his training from him. From 1909 he lived in Paris; in 1919 was appointed prof. at the Paris Cons.; also taught at the American Cons. in Fontainebleau. He publ. a practice book for cellists, *Violoncelle, Exercices quotidiens* (Paris, 1927).

Hekking, Anton, Dutch cellist, brother of **André Hekking;** b. The Hague, Sept. 7, 1856; d. Berlin, Nov. 18, 1935. He was the son of the Dutch-born French cellist Robert Gérard Hekking (1820–75). He studied at the Paris Cons. with Joseph Giese; then undertook an American tour with the pianist Essipoff. Returning to Europe, he was 1st cellist of the Berlin Phil. (1884–88; 1898–1902). After another American tour, he became 1st cellist of the Boston Sym. Orch. (1889–91) and later of the N.Y. Sym. Orch. (1895–98). He returned to Berlin in 1898; taught at the Stern Cons. there, and became a member of a trio with Schnabel and Wittenberg (1902).

Hekking, Gérard, French cellist, cousin of **André** and **Anton Hekking;** b. Nancy, Aug. 22, 1879; d. Paris, June 5, 1942. He studied at the Paris Cons., winning 1st prize (1899). He was 1st cellist of the Concertgebouw Orch. in Amsterdam (1903–14) and taught at the Amsterdam Cons.; also made tours in Russia, Spain, Germany, and France. He was in the French army during World War I; from 1921 to 1927 was again in the Netherlands; in 1927 became a prof. at the Paris Cons. He wrote several cello pieces; also revised *Principes de la technique du violoncelle* of François Gervais (Paris, 1930).

Hekster, Walter, Dutch clarinetist and composer; b. Amsterdam, March 29, 1937. He studied composition and clarinet at the Amsterdam Cons., graduating in 1961; then went to the U.S., where he was engaged as clarinetist with the Sym. Orch. (1962–65); attended classes of Sessions at Tanglewood in the summer of 1966; from 1965 to 1971 he taught clarinet and composition at Brandon Univ. in Manitoba; then returned to the Netherlands and assumed teaching posts at the Utrecht Cons. and the Arnhem Cons.

WORKS: *Epitaphium (In Memoriam Eduard van Beinum)* for Strings (1959); *Foci* for Violin and Chamber Ensemble (1965–66); *Facets* for Orch. (1967–68); *Branches* for 15 Strings (1969; rev. 1979); *Nocturnal Conversation* for Orch. in 4 groups (1970–71); *Early 1 Morning* for 15 Winds (1972); *Mobiles* for Orch. in 4 groups (1973); *The Auroras of Autumn* for Oboes and Orch. (1975); *Sunday* for Orch. (1976); *Sea Surface Full of Clouds* for String Orch. (1978); *Primavera,* "a Spring Concerto" for Piano and Orch. (1979); Guitar Concerto (1981); Clarinet Concerto (1982); *Pentagram* for Wind Quintet (1961); *Reflections* for Clarinet, Horn, Cello, Vibraphone, Celesta, and Percussion (1964); *Dialogues* for Flute and Clarinet (1965); *Music for Bassoon and Piano* (1965); 2 sonatas: No. 1 for Piano (1966) and No. 2 for Solo Cello (1967); *Interpolations* for Violin and Piano (1967); *Fluxus* for Solo Flute (1968); *Fluxions* for Clarinet and Piano (1968); *5 Reliefs* scored for Various Instrumental Combinations (1968–69); *The Snow Man* for Soprano, Percussion, and Bass Clarinet (1969); *Windsong* for Trumpet, Flute, and Saxophone (1970); *Reedmusic* for Oboe, Clarinet, and Bassoon (1970); *Incenter* for Flute, Oboe, and Cello (1970); *Fresco* for Clarinet and String Trio (1970); *Diversities* for Flute, Clarinet, Horn, Bassoon, and Piano (1970); *Ambage* for String Quartet (1970); *Credences of Summer* for Violin, Clarinet, and Piano (1974; rev. 1977); *Tropos* for Flute, Oboe, Violin, Viola, Cello, and Piano (1974–75); *Map* for Solo Ondes Martenot (1975); *Epicycle I* for Flute, Guitar, and Double Bass (1975); *Epicycle II* for Trumpet, Bass Clarinet, Accordion, and Percussion (1975); *Echoes of Summer* for Oboe, Clarinet, and Bassoon (1975); *Graffiti* for Ondes Martenot, Percussion, and Piano (1975); *Ideas of Order* for Wind Quintet (1980); Quintet (1982); *Japanese Settings* for Voice, Flute, Cello, Percussion, and Guitar (1985); *Nightmirrors* for Guitar (1986); *Derivations* for Piano (1965); *Studies in Spatial Notation* for Piano (1970).

Helder, Bartholomäus, German composer; b. Gotha, 1585; d. Remstedt, near Gotha, Oct. 28, 1635. He studied theology in Leipzig; was a schoolteacher at a village near Gotha (1607–16); then was for 20 years a pastor at Remstedt. He died of the plague. He publ. a collection of Christmas and New Year's songs, *Cymbalum genethliacum* (1614), and a book of Psalm tunes, *Cymbalum Davidicum*; many of his secular songs are included in contemporary anthologies. His New Year's song *Das alte Jahr vergangen ist* became very popular.

Helfer, Walter, American composer; b. Lawrence, Mass., Sept. 30, 1896; d. New Rochelle, N.Y., April 16, 1959. He studied at Harvard Univ.; then took courses in composition with Caussade in Paris and with Respighi in Rome. Returning to the U.S., he joined the staff of Hunter College in N.Y. He wrote an orch. *Fantasy on Children's Tunes* (1935); *Symphony on Canadian Airs* (1937); Concertino for Piano and Chamber Orch. (1947); *Soliloquy* for Cello and Piano; String Quartet; String Trio; *Elegiac Sonata* for Piano; minor piano pieces; songs.

Helfert, Vladimír, distinguished Czech musicologist; b. Plánice, near Klatovy, March 24, 1886; d. Prague, May 18, 1945. He studied musicology with Kretzschmar, Stumpf, and Wolf at the Univ. of Berlin (1906–7); completed his studies with Hostinský at the Univ. of Prague (Ph.D., 1908, with the diss. *Jiří Benda a Jean Rousseau).* He was active as a history and geography teacher in Prague until 1919; then moved to Brno, where he became a lecturer (1921), docent (1926), and prof. of musicology (1931) at the Univ. He was founder-ed. of the Musica Antiqua Bohemica series, as well as ed. of several journals; founded the Baroque, Classical, and Janáček collections at the Moravian Museum; also conducted the amateur Brno Orchestrální Sdružení. He was arrested by the Nazis in 1940 and held in Breslau until 1943; then was rearrested in 1945 and taken to the Terezin concentration camp, where he contracted typhus; he died a few days after his liberation.

WRITINGS: *Smetanismus a wagnerismus* (Prague, 1911); *Hudebni barok na českých zámcích* (The Musical Baroque in Czech Castles; Prague, 1916); *Smetanovské kapitoly* (Chapters on Smetana; Prague, 1917; 2nd ed., 1954); *Naše hudba a český stát* (Our Music and the Czech State; Prague, 1918; 2nd ed., 1970); *Hudba na Jaroměřickém zámku: František Míča 1696–1745* (Music in the Jaromerice Castle: František Míča 1696–1745; Prague, 1924); *Tvůrči rozvoj Bedřicha Smetany,* I (Smetana's Creative Development; Prague, 1924; 2nd ed., 1953; German tr., 1956); *Jiří Benda* (Brno, 1929–34); ed. with G. Černušák, *Pazdírkův hudební slovník naučný* (Pazdírek's Scientific Music Dictionary; Brno, 1929; 1933–41); *Základy hudební výchovy na nehudebnich školách* (Principles of Musical Education in Secondary Schools; Prague, 1930); *Česka moderní hudba* (Czech Modern Music; Olomouc, 1936; French and German trs., 1938); with E. Steinhard, *Histoire de la musique dans la république Tchecoslovaque* (Prague, 1936; German tr., 1936; 2nd ed., rev., 1938, as *Die Musik in der tschechoslovakischen Republik*); *Útok na Českou moderní hudbu* (The Attack on *Česká moderní hudba*; Olomouc, 1937); *Leoš Janáček*, I (Brno, 1939); *Státní hudebně historický ústav* (The State Inst. of Music History; ed. by G. Černušák; Prague, 1945); *O Janáčkovi* (ed. by B. Štědroň; Prague, 1949); *O Smetanovi* (ed. by B. Štědroň; Prague, 1950); *O české hudbě* (On Czech Music; ed. by B. Štědroň and I. Poledňák; Prague, 1957); *Vybrané studie, I: O hudebni tvořivosti* (Selected Studies, I: On Musical Creativity; ed. by F. Hrabal; Prague, 1970).

BIBL.: Special issue of *Index*, VIII/3 (1936); B. Štědroň, *Dr. V. H.* (Prague, 1940); I. Poledňák, "K některým otázkám H. ovy estetiky" (Some Questions concerning H.'s Esthetics), *Hudebni Rozhledy*, V (1957); A. Sychra, "V. H. a smysl české hudby" (V. H. and the Meaning of Czech Music), ibid., XIV (1961); M. Černý, "Hudebně historické dílo V. H.'s" (V. H.'s Works on Music History), *Hudebni Věda*, III (1966); R. Pečman and J. Vysloužil, eds., *V. H.: Pokrokový vedec a člověk* (V. H.: Progressive Scholar and Man; Brno, 1975); special issue of *Opus Musicum*, VII, no. 10 (1975).

Helfman, Max, Polish-born American choral conductor and composer; b. Radzin, May 25, 1901; d. Dallas, Aug. 9, 1963. He was taken to the U.S. in 1909; studied at the David Mannes School of Music in N.Y. and at the Curtis Inst. in Philadelphia, where his teachers were Rosario Scalero in composition and Fritz Reiner in conducting. He subsequently was active mainly as a conductor of Jewish choral groups; was in charge of choral singing at Temple Emanuel in Paterson, N.J. (1926–39), Temple B'nai Abraham in Newark (1940–53), and Temple Sinai in Los Angeles (1954–57); was music director at the Brandeis Inst. in Santa Susanna, Calif., and dean of the arts at the Univ. of Judaism in Los Angeles (1958–62). He wrote a dramatic cantata, *New Hagadah* (1949), and several pieces of Jewish liturgical music; ed. a series of choral works for the Jewish Music Alliance.

BIBL.: P. Moddel, *M. H.* (Berkeley, 1974).

Helfritz, Hans, German ethnomusicologist and composer; b. Hilbersdorf, July 25, 1902. He studied with Hindemith at the Hochschule für Musik in Berlin, and with Egon Wellesz in Vienna. In 1936 he went to South America; lived mostly in Chile, where he worked on problems of musical folklore. In 1956 he undertook a journey along the west coast of Africa and made recordings of native songs. In 1962 he settled in Ibiza in the Balearic Islands. He composed 2 string quartets, a Violin Sonata, a Saxophone Concerto, and various short orch. pieces; in some of them he makes use of South American and African motifs.

WRITINGS: *Amerika, Land der Inka, Maya und Azteken* (Vienna, 1965); *Die Götterburgen Mexikos* (Cologne, 1968); *Mexiko, Land der drei Kulturen* (Berlin, 1968).

Hellendaal, Pieter, Dutch-born English organist, violinist, and composer; b. Rotterdam (baptized), April 1, 1721; d. Cambridge, April 19, 1799. He was taken as a child to Utrecht, where he became organist at St. Nicolas Church; when the family went to Amsterdam in 1737, he found a patron in the city secretary Mattheus Lestevenon, who helped him to study with Tartini in Italy. In 1751 he went to London, where he was organist at St. Margaret's Church, King's Lynn (1760); Pembroke Hall Chapel, Cambridge (1762); and Peterhouse Chapel, Cambridge (1777). He was also active as a violinist and a composer. His concerti grossi and violin sonatas are skillfully written.

WORKS: (6) *Sonate* for Violin and Basso Continuo, op. 1 (Amsterdam, c.1745); *VI Sonate* for Violin and Basso Continuo, op. 2 (Amsterdam, c.1750); *6 Grand Concertos* for Strings and

Basso Continuo, op. 3 (London, c.1758; ed. in Monumenta Musicae Neerlandicae, I, 1959); *6 Solos* for Violin and Basso Continuo, op. 4 (London, c.1777); *8 Solos* for Cello and Basso Continuo, op. 5 (Cambridge, c.1780); *3 Grand Lessons* for Harpsichord or Piano, Violin, and Cello, op. 6 (London, c.1790); *Hellendaal's Celebrated Rondo* for Violin and Basso Continuo (Cambridge, c.1790); also 11 sonatas for Violin and Basso Continuo in MS. His other works include the cantata *Strephon and Myrtilla* for Voice, Violin or Flute, and Basso Continuo (Cambridge, c.1785); *A Collection of Psalms and Hymns . . .* for 3 to 4 Voices and Basso Continuo (Cambridge, 1790); glees; catches; etc.

BIBL.: J. Parkinson, "Peter H.," *Monthly Musical Record*, LXXXII (1952); W. Newman, *The Sonata in the Classic Era* (Chapel Hill, 1963; 3rd ed., rev., 1983).

Heller, Hans Ewald, German-American composer; b. Vienna, April 17, 1894; d. N.Y., Oct. 1, 1966. He studied with J.B. Foerster and Camillo Horn; was engaged in Vienna as a music critic and teacher. In 1938 he settled in the U.S. Among his compositions are the light operas *Satan* (Vienna, 1927), *Messalina* (Prague, 1928), and *Der Liebling von London* (Vienna, 1930); an overture, *Carnival in New Orleans* (1940); a cantata, *Ode to Our Women* (1942); 2 string quartets; Suite for Clarinet and Piano; about 150 songs.

Heller, James G., American composer; b. New Orleans, Jan. 4, 1892; d. Cincinnati, Dec. 19, 1971. He studied at Tulane Univ. in New Orleans (B.A., 1912), the Univ. of Cincinnati (M.A., 1914), the Hebrew Union College (Rabbi, 1916), and the Cincinnati Cons. (Mus.D., 1934); for 12 years wrote the program notes for the Cincinnati Sym. Orch.; then taught musicology at the Cincinnati Cons. Among his works are *Elegy and Pastorale* for Voice and String Orch. (Cincinnati, Dec. 30, 1934); String Quartet; Violin Sonata; Jewish services (New Union Hymnal, 1930–32).

Heller, Stephen (István), celebrated Hungarian pianist and composer; b. Pest, May 15, 1813; d. Paris, Jan. 14, 1888. He was of a Jewish family, but was converted to Christianity as a youth. He studied piano with Franz Brauer and showed such extraordinary ability that he was sent to Vienna to continue his studies; he studied briefly with Czerny before taking lessons with Anton Halm. In 1828 he began a tour through Austria and Germany. However, the exertion of travel proved too much for him; in Augsburg he became ill, and decided to remain there for a time; financial means were provided by a wealthy family. In 1838 he went to Paris, where he became friendly with Berlioz, Chopin, and Liszt. Soon he became very successful as a pianist; some critics even judged him as superior to Chopin. He began to compose piano pieces somewhat akin to Schumann's: brilliant salon dances, studies, and character pieces that became exceedingly popular. In 1849 he visited London, where his concerts charmed a large circle of music-lovers. A nervous ailment forced him to curtail his appearances; in 1862 he revisited England and played with Hallé at London's Crystal Palace. He then returned to Paris, where he remained for the rest of his life. He wrote in all several hundred piano pieces, arranged in groups in 158 opus numbers; of these, the most effective are *Traumbilder; Promenades d'un solitaire; Nuits blanches; Dans les bois; Voyage autour de ma chambre; Tablettes d'un solitaire; Tarentelles;* admirable études; ballades (notably *La Chasse*); 4 sonatas; 3 sonatinas; waltzes; mazurkas; caprices; nocturnes; variations; etc.

BIBL.: M. Hartmann, "S. H.," *Monatshefte* (1859); H. Barbedette, *S. H.* (Paris, 1876; Eng. tr., London, 1877); R. Schütz, *S. H.* (Leipzig, 1911); I. Philipp, "Some Recollections of S. H.," *Musical Quarterly* (Oct. 1935); R. Booth, *The Life and Music of S. H.* (diss., Univ. of Iowa, 1969); J.-J. Eigeldinger, ed., *S. H.: Lettres d'un musicien romantique à Paris* (Paris, 1981).

Hellinck, Lupus (Wulfaert), important Flemish composer; b. c.1496; d. Bruges, Jan. 14?, 1541. He was a choirboy at St. Donatian in Bruges (1506–11); was verger there (1513–15); after studying for the priesthood, he returned there as an installed cleric (1519); then was maître de chapelle at Notre Dame there (1521–23), and subsequently at St. Donatian from 1523. His output was widely dispersed in his day. Among his finest works are 13 parody masses; he also composed motets, chorales, chansons, and Flemish songs. See J. Wolf, ed., *Newe deudsche geistliche Gesenge, 1544* in Denkmäler Deutscher Tonkunst, XXXIV (1908).

BIBL.: J. Graziano, "L. H.: A Survey of Fourteen Masses," *Musical Quarterly*, LVI (1970); B. Blackburn, *The L. Problem* (diss., Univ. of Chicago, 1970); idem, "Johannes Lupi and L. H.: A Double Portrait," *Musical Quarterly*, LIX (1973).

Hellmesberger, family of famous Austrian musicians:

(1) Georg Hellmesberger, Sr., violinist, conductor, and composer; b. Vienna, April 24, 1800; d. Neuwaldegg, near Vienna, Aug. 16, 1873. His father, a country schoolmaster, gave him his 1st instruction in music; he succeeded Schubert as a chorister in the Hofkapelle. After making his concert debut on Dec. 9, 1819, he studied violin with Böhm and composition with E. Förster at the Vienna Cons.; then was made assistant to Böhm in 1821; subsequently was titular prof. (1826–33) and prof. (1833–67). He became concertmaster of the Hofoper in 1830, and also a member of the Hofkapelle; served as conductor of the Vienna Phil. with Nicolai (1845–47), and then was its sole conductor (1847–48). He made appearances as a violinist in London in 1847; was also active as a teacher; in addition to his sons, he taught Ernst, Auer, and Joachim. He composed 2 violin concertos, some chamber music, and some pieces for solo violin. His 2 sons became musicians of distinction:

(2) Joseph Hellmesberger, Sr., violinist and conductor; b. Vienna, Nov. 3, 1828; d. there, Oct. 24, 1893. He studied violin with his father at the Vienna Cons.; was named soloist in the orch. of the Hofoper when he was 17; was artistic director and conductor of the Gesellschaft der Musikfreunde concerts (1851–59); concurrently taught violin at the Vienna Cons. (1851–77); then was its director until 1893; was also concertmaster of the Vienna Phil. (1855–77) and the Hofoper (1860–77); was named Hofkapellmeister in 1877. In 1849 he founded the renowned Helmesberger Quartet, in which he played 1st violin, retiring in 1891.

BIBL.: A. Barthlmé, *Vom alten H.* (Vienna, 1908); R. Prosl, *Die H.: Hundert Jahre aus dem Leben einer Wiener Musikerfamilie* (Vienna, 1947).

(3) Georg Hellmesberger, Jr., violinist and composer; b. Vienna, Jan. 27, 1830; d. Hannover, Nov. 12, 1852. He studied violin and music theory with his father and composition with Rotter; then toured Germany, and subsequently accompanied his father to London in 1847; was named Hofkonzertmeister in Hannover in 1850. Among his 9 operas were *Die Bürgschaft* and *Die beiden Königinnen;* he also wrote syms., chamber music, violin pieces, and songs. His promising career was tragically cut short by tuberculosis.

(4) Joseph Hellmesberger, Jr., violinist, conductor, and composer, son of **Joseph Hellmesberger, Sr.;** b. Vienna, April 9, 1855; d. there, April 26, 1907. He studied with his father, making his debut at a Vienna Cons. concert when he was 8 and becoming 2nd violinist in his father's quartet when he was 15. He was concertmaster of the Vienna Phil. (1870–84); was also made solo violinist of the Hofkapelle and the Hofoper in 1878, and prof. of violin at the Cons. He became conductor of the new Ringtheater in 1881, but his tenure was cut short by a disastrous fire (Dec. 8, 1881), which destroyed the building. He then became conductor of the Carltheater in 1882, and subsequently (1884) was made concertmaster and music director of the ballet at the Hofoper; was named Vizehofkapellmeister in 1889, and then Hofkapellmeister in succession to Richter in 1890; also succeeded his father as 1st violin in the Hellmesberger Quartet in 1891; later served as conductor of the Vienna Phil. (1901–3) and of the Stuttgart Opera (1904–5). He wrote 10 operettas, the most celebrated being *Das Veilchenmädel* (Vienna, Feb. 27, 1904).

(5) Ferdinand Hellmesberger, cellist and conductor, son of **Joseph Hellmesberger, Sr.;** b. Vienna, Jan. 24, 1863; d.

there, March 15, 1940. He studied at the Vienna Cons.; became a member of the Hofkapelle in 1879; also played in his father's quartet (from 1883). He taught cello at the Vienna Cons. (1884–1902), and was solo cellist in the orch. of the Hofoper (1886–1902). He then was conductor of the Volksoper (1902–5), and subsequently ballet conductor at the Berlin Hofoper (1905–10); later conducted various spa orchs.

Hellwig, Karl (Friedrich) Ludwig, German organist and composer; b. Wriezen, July 23, 1773; d. Berlin, Nov. 24, 1838. He learned to play all the string instruments and piano; then studied theory with Zelter and others; at the same time, he was engaged in the manufacture of paint, which enabled him to pursue his musical studies as an avocation. He became a member of the Singakademie in 1793; was a conductor with it from 1803, serving as joint deputy conductor (1815–33). In 1813 he became organist of the Berlin Cathedral; was its director of music from 1815. He wrote 2 operas, *Die Bergknappen* (Dresden, April 27, 1820) and *Don Sylvio di Rosalbo* (unperf.); much church music; and a number of German lieder, which show a certain poetic sensitivity and a ballad-like quality in the manner of Zelter and other early German Romanticists.

Helm, Anny, Austrian soprano; b. Vienna, July 20, 1903. She studied in Vienna and Berlin; made her debut in Magdeburg in 1924. She sang at the Berlin State Opera (1926–33); also at Bayreuth. In 1933 she settled in Italy; subsequently made professional appearances under her married name, Anny Helm-Sbisa (her husband, Giuseppe Sbisa, was the director of the Teatro Giuseppe Verdi in Trieste).

Helm, E(rnest) Eugene, American musicologist; b. New Orleans, Jan. 23, 1928. He was educated at Southeastern Louisiana College (B.M.E., 1950), Louisiana State Univ. (M.M.E., 1955), and North Texas State Univ. (Ph.D., 1958, with the diss. *The Musical Patronage of Frederick the Great*). He taught at Louisiana College (1953–55), Wayne (Nebr.) State College (1958–59), the Univ. of Iowa (1960–68), and the Univ. of Maryland (from 1968), where he was also chairman of the musicology division (1971–87). He served as coordinating ed. of the Carl Philipp Emanuel Bach Edition (from 1982).

WRITINGS: *Music at the Court of Frederick the Great* (1960); with A. Luper, *Words and Music* (1971; 2nd ed., 1982); *A New Thematic Catalog of the Works of Carl Philipp Emanuel Bach* (1987).

Helm, Everett (Burton), American composer and musicologist; b. Minneapolis, July 17, 1913. He studied at Harvard Univ. (M.A., 1936; Ph.D., 1939); then went to Europe, where he took courses with Malipiero in Italy and Vaughan Williams in London. Returning to the U.S., he taught at Western College in Oxford, Ohio (1943–44); then toured South America (1944–46). From 1948 to 1950 he was a music officer under the U.S. military government in Germany; then lived mostly in Germany, Austria, and Italy. In 1963 he made his home in Asolo, near Venice. A linguist, he contributed articles to various music magazines in several languages; he made a specialty of the music of Yugoslavia and was a guest lecturer at the Univ. of Ljubljana (1966–68).

WRITINGS: *Béla Bartók in Selbstzeugnissen und Biddokumenten* (Reinbek-bei-Hamburg, 1965; reduction and Eng. tr., N.Y., 1972); *Composer, Performer, Public: A Study in Communication* (Florence, 1970); *Franz Liszt* (Hamburg, 1972); *Music and Tomorrow's Public* (Wilhelmshaven, 1981).

WORKS: Piano Concerto (N.Y., April 24, 1954); *Adam and Eve,* an adaptation of a medieval mystery play (Wiesbaden, Oct. 28, 1951, composer conducting); Concerto for 5 Instruments, Percussion, and String Orch. (Donaueschingen, Oct. 10, 1953); *The Siege of Tottenburg,* radio opera (1956); *Le Roy fait battre tambour,* ballet (1956); *500 Dragon-Thalers,* singspiel (1956); Piano Concerto No. 2 (Louisville, Ky., Feb. 25, 1956); Divertimento for Flutes (1957); *Sinfonia da camera* (1961); Concerto for Double Bass and String Orch. (1968); 2 string quartets; Woodwind Quintet (1967); numerous piano pieces and songs.

Helm, Theodor (Otto), Austrian music critic; b. Vienna, April 9, 1843; d. there, Dec. 23, 1920. He studied jurisprudence in Vienna and became a government employee; in 1867 he began writing music criticism for various Viennese publications; in 1874 became a music teacher at Horák's music school; from 1875 to 1901 he was ed. of Fromme's *Kalender für die Musikalische Welt;* publ. *Beethovens Streichquartette: Versuch einer technischen Analyse im Zusammenhang mit ihrem geistigen Gehalt* (Leipzig, 1885; 2nd ed., 1910).

Helmholtz, Hermann (Ludwig Ferdinand) von, celebrated German scientist and acoustician; b. Potsdam, Aug. 31, 1821; d. Berlin, Sept. 8, 1894. He studied medicine at the Friedrich Wilhelm Medical Inst. in Berlin (M.D., 1843); also learned to play the piano. He was an assistant at Berlin's Anatomical Museum and prof. extraordinary at the Academy of Fine Arts (1848–49), assistant prof. and director of Königsberg's Physiological Inst. (1849–55), and prof. of anatomy and physiology at the Univ. of Bonn (1855–58) and the Univ. of Heidelberg (1858–71). He became prof. of physics at the Univ. of Berlin in 1871, and from 1888 served as the 1st director of the Physico-Technical Inst. in Berlin. He was ennobled in 1882. His most important work for those interested in music was his *Lehre von den Tonempfindungen als physiologische Grundlage für die Theorie der Musik* (Braunschweig, 1863; Eng. tr. by A. Ellis as *On the Sensations of Tone as a Physiological Basis for the Theory of Music,* London, 1875; new ed., N.Y., 1948), in which he established a sure physical foundation for the phenomena manifested by musical tones, either single or combined. He supplemented and amplified the theories of Rameau, Tartini, Wheatstone, Corti, and others, furnishing impregnable formulae for all classes of consonant and dissonant tone effects, and proving with scientific precision what Hauptmann and his school sought to establish by laborious dialectic processes. His labors resulted primarily in instituting the laws governing the differences in quality of tone (tone color) in different instruments and voices, covering the whole field of harmonic, differential, and summational tones, and those governing the nature and limits of music perception by the human ear.
Bibl.: S. Epstein, *H. v.H. als Mensch und Gelehrter* (Stuttgart, 1896); L. Königsberger, *H. v.H.* (3 vols., Braunschweig, 1902–3; 1 vol., 1911); E. Waetzman, *Zur H.schen Resonanztheorie* (Breslau, 1907); L. Lloyd, "H. and the Musical Ear," *Musical Quarterly* (April 1939); H. Ebert, *H. v.H.* (Stuttgart, 1949).

Helps, Robert (Eugene), American pianist, teacher, and composer; b. Passaic, N.J., Sept. 23, 1928. He studied at the Juilliard School of Music in N.Y.: piano with Abby Whiteside and composition with Roger Sessions (1943–56); also took courses at Columbia Univ. (1947–49) and the Univ. of Calif. in Berkeley (1949–51); received a Guggenheim fellowship in 1966. He occupied teaching posts at Princeton Univ., the San Francisco Cons. of Music (1968–70), Stanford Univ., and the Univ. of Calif. at Berkeley. From 1970 to 1972 he was on the staff of the New England Cons. of Music in Boston; then taught at the Manhattan School of Music (1973–76) and, from 1978, at the Univ. of Southern Florida. His natural pianism helps Helps to write idiomatically for his instrument.
Works: Fantasy for Piano (1952); Sym. No. 1 (1955); Piano Trio (1957); *Image* for Piano (1958); *Recollections* for Piano (1959); *Portrait* for Piano (1960); *Cortège* for Orch. (1963); Serenade in 3 parts: (1) Fantasy for Violin and Piano, (2) Nocturne for String Quartet, and (3) *Postlude* for Piano, Violin, and Horn (1964); 2 piano concertos (1966, 1976); *Saccade* for Piano, 4-hands (1967); *Quartet* for Piano Solo, divided into 4 equal parts, each numbering 22 keys (1971); Quintet for Flute, Clarinet, Violin, Cello, and Piano (1976); *Gossamer Noons* for Soprano and Orch. (1977); other piano pieces.

Helsted, Gustaf, Danish organist, teacher, and composer; b. Copenhagen, Jan. 30, 1857; d. there, March 1, 1924. He was a pupil of Hartmann and Gade; from 1892 was a prof. of theory, and from 1904 also a prof. of organ, at the Copenhagen Cons.; from 1915 was organist of the Frauenkirche. He wrote

2 syms.; a Decimet for Woodwinds and Strings; a String Sextet; 3 string quartets; a Piano Trio; 2 violin sonatas; 2 cantatas: *Gurresänge* (Copenhagen, April 18, 1904) and *Vort Land* (Copenhagen, April 19, 1909).

Hemberg, (Bengt Sven) Eskil, Swedish conductor, operatic administrator, and composer; b. Stockholm, Jan. 19, 1938. He studied organ and conducting (with Herbert Blomstedt) at the Stockholm Musikhögskolan (1957–64); conducted the choir of the Univ. of Stockholm (from 1959), which he led on tours of Europe and the U.S. (1963–70). He was president of the Swedish Soc. of Composers (1971–83), and served as artistic director of the Göteborg Opera (1984–87) and of Stockholm's Royal Theater (from 1987). In 1974 he was elected a member of the Royal Swedish Academy of Music in Stockholm. Most of his works are for vocal groups; he maintains the main lines of classical polyphony in sacred music, while in his instrumental writing he ventures into modern harmony.
Works: Operas: *Love* (1969–70); *The Pirates in the Deep Green Sea* (1975–77); *St. Erik's Crown,* church opera (1979); *3 Jerusalem Choruses* (1958); *2 Evangelical Motets* (1960); *Zoo,* 5 nonsense songs for Chorus (1965); *Paradise,* cantata (1965); *En natt som lyste,* cantata (1966); *18 Movements,* choreographic choral suite (Stockholm, April 30, 1968); *Signposts* for Chorus (1968); *The Gallery,* after E.A. Robinson, for Bass and Male Chorus (1969); *Messa d'oggi* for 5 Solo Voices and Chorus (1968–70); *Jesu lidande, död och uppståndelse,* St. Mark Passion for Soli, Chorus, and Orch. (Stockholm, March 26, 1972); *Cantica* for Soli, Chorus, and Orch. (Bergen, Nov. 29, 1973); *En gammal saga* (An Old Tale), cantata for Soprano, Harp, and Harpsichord (1973); *Migraine* for Orch. (1973); *Zona rosa* for String Quartet (1973); *Between Happenings* for 4 Singers and 4 Percussion (1974); *Songbook from Österbotten* for Men's Voices, English Horn, Clarinet, Small Drum, and Double Bass (1975); *With God and His Friendship,* a "Mass about belief and politics" for Priest, Congregation, Chorus, Trumpet, and Organ (1976); *Women,* scenic cantata for Soli, Women's Chorus, and Orch. (1978–79); *Concerning My Negotiations with Myself—and with God* for Solo Quartet, Double Chorus, and Organ (1980); *Love Fancies* for Baritone and String Orch. (1980); *Sad Waltz* for Soprano, Live Electronics, Kettledrums, and Gran Cassa (1980); *Canticles I–III,* dramatic scenes for Soprano, Tenor, Bass, and Instruments (1981); *Lützener Te Deum* for Double Chorus and 3 Trombones (1982); *Les Adieux* for String Quartet (1982); *Magnificat* for Double Chorus (1982); *To the Light,* cantata for Soli, Men's Chorus, and Chamber Orch. (1984); Trio for Violin, Viola, and Cello (1984; also for Flute, Violin, and Cello, 1986); *Psalm 150 (The Psalter)* for Chorus, Viola d'Amore, and Cello (1985); *A Monthly Journal in the Middle of the 80s* for Chorus (1986); *Requiem Aeternam* for Chorus (1987).

Hemel, Oscar van, Dutch composer; b. Antwerp, Aug. 3, 1892; d. Hilversum, July 9, 1981. He studied with Lodewijk Mortelmans and de Boeck at the Royal Flemish Cons. in Antwerp; settled in the Netherlands in 1914; took lessons in composition with Pijper in Rotterdam (1931–33), but did not begin to write music until late in life; he compensated for this delay by composing prolifically. His style oscillates between the Romantic trends of German and Austrian music of the early 20th century and the more complex technical structures favored by Dutch modernists.
Works: Radio opera, *Viviane* (Hilversum Radio, 1950); *Maria Magdalena,* sacred cantata (1941); *De bruid* (The Bride) for Soprano, Male Chorus, and Orch. (1946); *Dat liet van Alianora* for Soprano, Male Chorus, and Orch. (1947); *Hart van Nederland* (Heart of Holland) for Male Chorus, Winds, and Percussion (1952); *Ballade van Brabant* for Narrator, Boys' Chorus, Male Chorus, and Orch. (1952); *Le Tombeau de Kathleen Ferrier* for Alto and Orch. (1954); *Herdenkingshymne 1940–1945* (Memorial Hymn 1940–1945) for Mixed Chorus, Children's Chorus, Brass, and Percussion (1955; for Full Orch., 1970); *Les Mystères du Christ,* 5 Psalms for Alto, Baritone, Male Chorus, and Orch. (1958); *Te Deum* for 4 Soloists, Chorus,

and Orch. (1958); *Tuin van Holland* for Soprano, Baritone, Chorus, and Orch. (1958); *Ballade van Kapitein Joos de Decker* for Alto, Bass, Chorus, and Orch. (1943–59); *Trittico liturgico* for Soprano and Strings (1959); *Huwelijks Cantata* (1966); *Song of Freedom* for Speaking Chorus, Mixed Chorus, and Orch. (1968–69); 5 syms.: No. 1 (1935); No. 2 (1948); No. 3, *Sinfonietta* for Small Orch. (1952); No. 4 (1962); No. 5 (1963–64; rev. 1967); Suite for Chamber Orch. (1936); Suite for Flute, and Chamber Orch. or Piano (1937); Piano Concerto (1941–42); Ballade for Orch. (1942); 3 violin concertos (1945, 1968, 1977); *De stad* (The City), symphonic poem (1949); *Divertimento Ballet* for Orch. (1950; drawn from his opera *Viviane*); Viola Concerto (1951); *Feestelijke ouverture* (1952); *Olof Suite* for Orch. (1953); *Entrada festante* (1953); *Tema con variazioni* for Orch. (1953); Oboe Concerto (1955); Concerto for Wind Orch. (1960); *Concerto da camera* for Flute and String Orch. (1962); Violin Concertino (1963); Cello Concerto (1963); *3 Contrasts* for Winds and Percussion (1963); Divertimento for Strings (1964); *Entrada* for Orch. (1964); Serenade for 3 Solo Winds and String Orch. (1965); Polonaise for Orch. (1966); Concerto for 2 Violins and String Orch. (1970–71); Divertimento for Orch. and Piano (1974); 2 violin sonatas (1933, 1945); 6 string quartets (Nos. 3–6: 1946–47; 1953; 1956; 1961); Piano Trio (1937); Piano Quartet (1938); Viola Sonata (1942); String Trio (1951); Concertino for Trumpet and Piano (1953); *Canticum psalmorum* for Contralto, Chorus, 2 Pianos, and Percussion (1954); *4 Koperkwartetten* for Horn, 2 Trumpets, and Trombone (1955); Clarinet Quintet (1958); *Divertimento II* for 12 Winds and Piano (1959); Trio for Flute, Oboe, and Bassoon (1959); *Rondeau et Ballade* for Female Chorus, Flute, String Quartet, and Harp (1959); *Capriccio* for Clarinet and Piano (1960); Sextet for Piano and Wind Quintet (1962); *Donquichotterie* for 4 Trombones (1962); Suite for 2 Violins (1966); *About Commedia dell'arte* for Oboe Quartet (1967); Wind Quintet (1972).

Hemke, Frederick (LeRoy), American saxophonist and teacher; b. Milwaukee, July 11, 1935. He studied at the Univ. of Wisconsin (1953–55); then with Marcel Mule at the Paris Cons., becoming the 1st American to win a premier prix for saxophone (1956). He then continued his studies with Joseph Mariano and Robert Sprenkle at the Eastman School of Music in Rochester, N.Y., and at the Univ. of Wisconsin (D.M.A., 1975). He taught at Northwestern Univ. (from 1962), serving as chairman of the dept. of wind and percussion instruments (from 1964); was also a member of the Chicago Sym. Orch. (1962–82). He publ. *The Early History of the Saxophone* (1975) and *The Teacher's Guide to the Saxophone* (1977). He commissioned Pettersson's Sym. No. 16 for Alto Saxophone and Orch., and played in its premiere (Stockholm, Feb. 24, 1983).

Hempel, Frieda, brilliant German soprano; b. Leipzig, June 26, 1885; d. Berlin, Oct. 7, 1955. In 1900 she entered the Leipzig Cons. as a piano pupil; she studied singing with Nicklass-Kempner in Berlin (1902–5); made her debut in Breslau in 1905; made her Berlin Opera debut in Nicolai's *Merry Wives of Windsor* (Aug. 22, 1905); from 1905 to 1907 was at the Court Opera in Schwerin; from 1907 to 1912 was a member of the Royal Opera in Berlin; from 1912 to 1919 was one of the foremost members of the Metropolitan Opera in N.Y., where she made her debut as the Queen in *Les Huguenots* on Dec. 27, 1912; sang there until 1919. In 1920 she impersonated Jenny Lind in the Lind centenary celebrations in N.Y. and throughout the U.S. (70 concerts). She was married to William B. Kahn in 1918 (divorced in 1926). From 1940 to 1955 she lived in N.Y. A few months before her death, knowing that she was incurably ill, she returned to Berlin. Her memoirs, *Mein Leben dem Gesang*, were publ. posthumously (Berlin, 1955).

Hemsi (Chicurel), Alberto, Italian conductor, ethnomusicologist, and composer of Jewish descent; b. Cassaba, Turkey, Dec. 23, 1896; d. Aubervilliers, near Paris, Oct. 7, 1975. He studied music in Izmir, and later took courses in piano, theory, and composition at the Milan Cons. He was music director

of the Grand Synagogue in Alexandria, Egypt (1927–57), and founder-conductor of the Alexandria Phil. Orch. (1928–40); also founded the Édition Orientale de Musique (1929) and was active as a teacher. In 1957 he settled in Paris as prof. at the Jewish Seminary. He was particularly interested in Sephardic Jewry. His compositions were of an oriental flavor, the most characteristic being the symphonic suite *Croquis égyptiens* (1930); other works include *Poème biblique* for Voice and Orch., *Suite Séfardie* for Violin and Piano, *6 danses turques* for Piano, and a number of songs.

Hemsley, Thomas, English baritone; b. Coalville, April 12, 1927. He studied voice with Lucie Manén; made his professional debut in London (1951). He then sang at Aachen (1953–56) and Düsseldorf (1957–63). From 1953 he made regular appearances at Glyndebourne; also sang at Bayreuth, where he distinguished himself as one of the few English singers in the Wagnerian repertoire.

Henderson, Alva, American composer; b. San Luis Obispo, Calif., April 8, 1940. He studied voice and music theory at San Francisco State College; devoted himself mainly to vocal works. His 1st opera, *Medea,* based on the play by Robinson Jeffers, was produced with a modicum of critical favor in San Diego, on Nov. 29, 1972; his 2nd opera was adapted from Shakespeare's play *The Tempest.* He obtained his most decisive success with his 3rd opera, *The Last of the Mohicans,* after the novel of James Fenimore Cooper, produced by the Wilmington (Del.) Opera Soc. on June 12, 1976.

Henderson, (James) Fletcher "Smack," black American jazz pianist, bandleader, and arranger; b. Cuthbert, Ga., Dec. 18, 1897; d. N.Y., Dec. 28, 1952. He studied piano as a child and chemistry as a youth; received a degree in chemistry from Atlanta Univ. College. In 1920 he went to N.Y.; formed the Fletcher Henderson band, which rapidly advanced into the front ranks of jazzdom; a number of famous jazz figures played in it. He made arrangements for other jazz bands as well as for his own.
  BIBL.: W. Allen, *H.ia: The Music of F. H. and His Musicians* (Highland Park, N.J., 1973).

Henderson (real name, **Brost**), **Ray(mond),** American composer of popular songs; b. Buffalo, Dec. 1, 1896; d. Greenwich, Conn., Dec. 31, 1970. He studied music at the Univ. of Southern Calif.; played organ in churches and piano in jazz groups in Buffalo; then went to N.Y. as a song plugger in Tin Pan Alley, and soon began writing songs of his own. His 1st success was *Georgette* (1922); this was followed by *Sonny Boy,* which he wrote for Al Jolson's early talkie *The Singing Fool;* subsequent hits were *You're the Cream in My Coffee, Button Up Your Overcoat, Alabamy Bound, Hold Everything,* and *3 Cheers;* some of these songs were written in collaboration with B.G. DeSylva. Unlike most Broadway composers, Henderson could read and write music; he even took private lessons with Benjamin Britten. His film biography, *The Best Things in Life Are Free,* was made in 1966.

Henderson, Roy (Galbraith), Scottish baritone; b. Edinburgh, July 4, 1899. He studied at the Royal Academy of Music in London (1920–25); made his London debut as Zarathustra in *A Mass of Life* by Delius in 1925; his operatic debut followed in 1929, as Donner in Wagner's *Das Rheingold* at Covent Garden; he also sang at the Glyndebourne Festivals (1934–39). He was founder and conductor of the Nottingham Oriana Choir (1936–52); was a prof. of singing at the Royal Academy of Music (1940–74). He was made a Commander of the Order of the British Empire in 1970.

Henderson, "Skitch" (Lyle Russell Cedric), English-born American pianist, conductor, composer, and arranger; b. Birmingham, Jan. 27, 1918. He went to the U.S. in his youth; took up the organ and piano, then played on a radio station in North Dakota; moving to Hollywood, he was accompanist to Judy Garland and worked at MGM. During World War II he served as a fighter pilot in the Royal Air Force and the U.S. Air Force; after the war, he returned to Hollywood as a conductor for radio and films; also studied with Ernst Toch. In 1949 he joined the music staff of NBC; later was music director for several television shows; also had guest engagements with provincial orchs. In 1983 he organized his own N.Y. Pops Orch., which made its 1st appearance at Carnegie Hall.

Henderson, W(illiam) J(ames), noted American music critic; b. Newark, N.J., Dec. 4, 1855; d. (suicide) N.Y., June 5, 1937. He was a graduate of Princeton Univ. (M.A., 1886); studied piano with Carl Langlotz (1868–73) and voice with Torriani (1876–77); was chiefly self-taught in theory. He wrote many librettos of light operas, and also *Cyrano de Bergerac* for Walter Damrosch (1913). He was 1st a reporter (1883), then music critic of the *N.Y. Times* (1887–1902) and the *N.Y. Sun* (1902–37); lectured on music history at the N.Y. College of Music (1889–95; 1899–1902); from 1904, lectured on the development of vocal art at the Inst. of Musical Art in N.Y. A brilliant writer, Henderson was an irreconcilable and often venomous critic of modern music; he loved Wagner, but savagely attacked Debussy and Richard Strauss. Henderson, in turn, was the butt of some of Charles Ives's caustic wit.

WRITINGS: *The Story of Music* (N.Y., 1889; 2nd ed., enl., 1912); *Preludes and Studies* (N.Y., 1891); *How Music Developed* (N.Y., 1898); *What Is Good Music?* (N.Y., 1898; 6th ed., 1935); *The Orchestra and Orchestral Music* (N.Y., 1899); *Richard Wagner, His Life and His Dramas* (N.Y., 1901; 2nd ed., 1923); *Modern Musical Drift* (N.Y., 1904); *The Art of the Singer* (N.Y., 1906; 2nd ed., augmented, 1938, as *The Art of Singing*); *Some Forerunners of Italian Opera* (N.Y., 1911); *Early History of Singing* (N.Y., 1921).

BIBL.: O. Thompson, "An American School of Criticism: The Legacy Left by W.J. H., R. Aldrich and Their Colleagues of the Old Guard," *Musical Quarterly* (Oct. 1937).

Hendl, Walter, American conductor; b. West New York, N.J., Jan. 12, 1917. He studied conducting with Fritz Reiner at the Curtis Inst. of Music in Philadelphia. He was associate conductor of the N.Y. Phil. (1945–49), then music director of the Dallas Sym. (1949–58). From 1964 to 1972 he was director of the Eastman School of Music in Rochester, N.Y.; in 1976 he was appointed music director of the Erie (Pa.) Phil.

Hendricks, Barbara, greatly admired black American soprano; b. Stephens, Ark., Nov. 20, 1948. She sang in church and school choirs before majoring in chemistry and mathematics at the Univ. of Nebraska (graduated, 1969); during the summer of 1968 she began vocal training with Jennie Tourel at the Aspen (Colo.) Music School, continuing under her guidance at the Juilliard School in N.Y. (1969–71); she also attended Maria Callas's master class there. In 1971 she won the Geneva International Competition, and in 1972 both the International Concours de Paris and the Kosciuszko Foundation Vocal Competition. On Feb. 20, 1973, she made her debut in Virgil Thomson's *4 Saints in 3 Acts* in the Mini-Metropolitan Opera production presented at the Lincoln Center Forum Theatre in N.Y.; later that year she made her 1st concert tour of Europe. In 1974 she appeared as Erisbe in Cavalli's *Ormindo* at the San Francisco Spring Opera, and in the title role of Cavalli's *La Calisto* at the Glyndebourne Festival. On Feb. 26, 1975, she made her formal N.Y. debut as Inez in a concert performance of *La Favorite* at Carnegie Hall. In 1976 she sang Amor in Gluck's *Orfeo ed Euridice* with the Netherlands Opera at the Holland Festival, and on Nov. 14 of that year made her N.Y. recital debut at Town Hall. At the Berlin Deutsche Oper in 1978 she appeared as Mozart's Susanna, a role she quickly made her own. In 1980 she sang Gilda and in 1981 Pamina at the Orange Festival in France; in 1982 she appeared as Gounod's Juliet at both the Paris Opéra and London's Covent Garden. On Oct. 30, 1986, she made her Metropolitan Opera debut in N.Y. as Strauss's Sophie. In 1988 she sang at the 70th-birthday celebration for Leonard Bernstein at the Tanglewood Festival, and also starred as Mimi in Luigi Comencini's film version of *La Bohème*. In 1989 she appeared at the Bolshoi

Theater in Moscow. In addition to her operatic career, she has won notable distinction as a recitalist. Her interpretations of the German and French lieder repertoire, as well as of Negro spirituals, have won accolades. In 1986 she was made a Commandeur des Arts et des Lettres of France. Her unswerving commitment to social justice led the High Commissioner for Refugees at the United Nations to name her a goodwill ambassador of the world body in 1987.

BIBL.: *Current Biography* (March 1989); L. Marum, "B. H.: A Singular Soprano," *Ovation* (April 1989).

Hendrix, Jimi (James Marshall), black American rock guitarist, singer, and songwriter; b. Seattle, Nov. 27, 1942; d. as a result of asphyxiation while unconscious after taking an overdose of barbiturates in London, Sept. 18, 1970. Being left-handed, he taught himself to play the guitar upside down; played in a high school band before dropping out of school during his senior year to join the U.S. Army paratroopers. Following his discharge (1961), he worked with groups in Nashville, Vancouver, and Los Angeles. In 1964 he went to N.Y., where he joined the Isley Brothers and found a ready response for his wild attire and erotic body locomotions; after working with Curtis Knight's group (1964–65), he formed his own outfit, Jimmy James and the Blue Flames. He then went to England, where he organized the Jimi Hendrix Experience (1966) with bass guitarist Noel Redding and drummer Mitch Mitchell. The live Hendrix experience was replete with the most provocative stage manner, which he frequently culminated by setting his guitar on fire. After recording his 1st album, *Are You Experienced?* (1967), he made his 1st appearance in the U.S. with his group at the Monterey (Calif.) Pop Festival that same year. He then recorded the albums *Axis: Bold as Love* (1968) and *Electric Ladyland* (1968), followed by a knockout appearance at the Woodstock Festival (1969). Several of his albums were released posthumously.

BIBL.: D. Henderson, *'Scuse Me While I Kiss the Sky: The Life of J. H.* (Toronto, 1981); J. Hopkins, *Hit and Run: The J. H. Story* (N.Y., 1983).

Hengeveld, Gerard, Dutch pianist and composer; b. Kampen, Dec. 7, 1910. He studied piano with Carl Friedberg; appeared as a soloist with European orchs. and in recital; then was appointed to the piano faculty at The Hague Cons. He composed a Violin Sonata (1944); Concertino for Piano and Orch. (1946); Piano Concerto (1947); Cello Sonata (1965); *Musica concertante* for Oboe and Chamber Orch. (1968); numerous teaching pieces for piano.

Henkel, Heinrich, German pianist, son of **(Johann) Michael Henkel;** b. Fulda, Feb. 17, 1822; d. Frankfurt am Main, April 10, 1899. He was a pupil of his father; also studied with Aloys Schmitt. He settled in Frankfurt in 1849, as a teacher. He publ. a piano method, *Vorschule des Klavierspiels,* an abridged ed. of A. André's *Lehrbuch der Tonsetzkunst* (1875); *Mitteilungen aus der musikalischen Vergangenheit Fuldas* (1882); piano pieces and songs.

Henkel, (Johann) Michael, German organist and composer, father of **Heinrich Henkel;** b. Fulda, June 18, 1780; d. there, March 4, 1851. He studied with Vierling; then served as a local music teacher. He wrote a great number of sacred works, organ pieces, and instrumental works.

Henkemans, Hans, Dutch pianist and composer; b. The Hague, Dec. 23, 1913. He took lessons in piano and composition with Bernhard van den Sigtenhorst-Meyer and Willem Pijper (1930–36); made his debut as a pianist in his own Piano Concerto at 19. Concurrently he studied medicine at the Univ. of Utrecht, and was active as a practicing psychiatrist. As a composer, he follows the stylistic manner of the modern French school, cultivating sonorous harmonies supporting melodic lines of a modal character.

WORKS: 2 piano concertos (1932, 1936); Sym. (1934); *Voorspel* (Prelude) for Orch. (1935–36); *Ballade* for Alto and Chamber Orch. (1936); *Driehonderd waren wij* (300 Were We . . .), cantata (1933–40); *Passacaglia and Gigue* for Piano and Orch. (1941–42; Amsterdam, Dec. 2, 1945); *Primavera* for 12 Instruments (1944; rev. 1959); Flute Concerto (1945–46); Violin Concerto (1948–50); Viola Concerto (1954); Harp Concerto (1955); Partita for Orch. (Scheveningen, Dec. 8, 1960); *Barcarola fantastica* for Orch. (Groningen, Nov. 13, 1962); *Dona Montana,* 3 pieces for Orch. (1964); *Bericht aan de Levenden* (Message to the Living) for Chorus, Narration, and Orch. (1964; Amsterdam, May 4, 1965); *Villonnerie* for Baritone and Orch., after Villon's poems (1965); *Élégies* for 4 Flutes and Orch. (Utrecht, Oct. 18, 1967); *Tre aspetti d'amore* for Chorus and Orch. (1967–68; Amsterdam, July 5, 1971); *Canzoni amorose* for Soprano, Baritone, Piano, and Orch. (1972–73); Horn Concerto (1981); *Riflessioni* for Strings (1985–86); 2 wind quintets (1934, 1962); 3 string quartets; Cello Sonata (1936); Violin Sonata (1944); *Epilogue* for Flute and Piano (1947); *4 Pieces* for Harp and Flute (1963); *Aere festivo* for 3 Trumpets and 2 Trombones (1965); *2 Études* for Piano (1937); 2-piano Sonata (1943); Piano Sonata (1958); songs, including *De Tooverfluit* (The Magic Flute; 1946) and *3 Liederen* (1964); choruses. In 1971 he orchestrated 12 of Debussy's preludes (Amsterdam, July 5, 1971).

Henneberg, (Carl) Albert (Theodor), Swedish composer, son of **Richard Henneberg;** b. Stockholm, March 27, 1901. He studied composition in Stockholm (1920–24) and later in Vienna and Paris (1926–30). Returning to Stockholm in 1931, he became active as a conductor.

WORKS: 5 operas: *Inka* (1935–36); *Det jäser i Småland* (1937–38); *Den lyckliga staden* (1940–41); *Bolla och Badin* (1942–44); *I madonnans skugga* (1946); Chamber Sym. (1927); 6 syms.: No. 1, *På ledungsfärd* (1925); No. 2, with Baritone Solo (1927); No. 3, *Vårvindar* (1927); No. 4, *Pathétique* (1930–31); No. 5 (1935); No. 6, *Vinterskärgård* (1953–54); Piano Concerto (1925); *Valborgsmässonatt,* symphonic poem (1928); Serenade for String Orch. (1931; also for String Quartet); *Sommar,* suite for Orch. (1932); *Det ljusa landet* for Soloists, Chorus, and Orch. (1933); Trumpet Concerto (1934); Trombone Concerto (1935); *I brytningstider,* symphonic suite (1943); *Gustavianska kapriser* for Orch. (1943); Concertino for Flute and Strings (1944); Cello Concerto (1948); Concertino for Bassoon and Strings (1956); Concertino for Clarinet, Strings, Piano, and Percussion (1960); 2 string quartets (1931); *Little Quartet* for Flute, Oboe, Bassoon, and Horn; Violin Sonata.

Henneberg, Johann Baptist, Austrian organist, conductor, and composer; b. Vienna, Dec. 6, 1768; d. there, Nov. 26, 1822. He conducted at Vienna theaters (1790–1803); then became a member of the orch. of Count Esterházy; in 1818, returned to Vienna, where he became choirmaster at the Am Hof Church; was named court organist in 1818. He wrote a great number of singspiels, of which the most successful were *Die Waldmänner* (Vienna, Oct. 14, 1793) and *Liebe macht kurzen Prozess* (Leipzig, 1799).

BIBL.: E. Komorzynski, "J.B. H., Schikaneders Kapellmeister (1768–1822)," *Mozart Jahrbuch 1955.*

Henneberg, Richard, German conductor and composer, father of **(Carl) Albert (Theodor) Henneberg;** b. Berlin, Aug. 5, 1853; d. Malmö, Oct. 19, 1925. He studied piano with Liszt; then traveled as accompanist with various artists, including Wieniawski; held posts as operatic coach at the Italian Opera in London, and at various theaters in Berlin and Stockholm; from 1885 to 1907 conducted at the Stockholm Opera; from 1914 to 1920 was conductor of the Malmö Orch. Henneberg gave the 1st performance of *Tannhäuser* in Stockholm (1876) and the 1st complete production of the *Ring of the Nibelung* in Sweden (1907), and was an ardent propagandist of Wagner's music. He wrote a comic opera, *Drottningens Vallfart* (Stockholm, 1882); incidental music to Ibsen's *Brand;* various Shakespearean pieces; a ballet, *Undine;* some choral works and songs.

Hennerberg, Carl Fredrik, Swedish organist and musicologist; b. Älgaras, Jan. 24, 1871; d. Stockholm, Sept. 17, 1932. As a young man, he was an organist at Varola; then went to Stockholm, where he studied at the Cons. (1899–1903) and

remained on the faculty as a harmony teacher. In 1909 he was appointed organist at the Royal Chapel. He specialized in the study of organ manufacture; traveled in European countries to collect information; publ. *Die schwedischen Orgeln des Mittelalters* (Vienna, 1909) and *Orgelns byggnad och vård* (Uppsala, 1912; 2nd ed., 1928).

Hennes, Aloys, German pianist; b. Aachen, Sept. 8, 1827; d. Berlin, June 8, 1889. He studied with Hiller and Reinecke in Cologne; then taught piano in various provincial towns; in 1872 settled in Berlin. He publ. *Klavierunterrichtsbriefe,* containing ingenious teaching pieces. His daughter, Therese, was a child prodigy, who made an exceptionally successful tour in England in 1877.

Hennessy, Swan, American composer; b. Rockford, Ill., Nov. 24, 1866; d. Paris, Oct. 26, 1929. He was the son of an Irish-American settler; studied general subjects at Oxford, and music in Germany; then traveled in Italy, France, and Ireland, eventually settling in Paris. He wrote about 70 compositions, several of which are derived from Irish folk melos; his technical equipment was thorough; his idiom, impressionistic. Among his Irish-inspired works are *Petit trio celtique* for Violin, Viola, and Cello; *Rapsodie celtique* for Violin and Piano; *Rapsodie gaélique* for Cello and Piano; *Sonata in Irish Style* for Violin and Piano; several piano albums "à la manière de . . ."; characteristic piano pieces in a humorous vein, such as *Épigrammes d'un solitaire, Impressions humoristiques,* etc.; 4 string quartets.

Hennig, Carl, German organist, choral conductor, and composer, father of **Carl Rafael Hennig;** b. Berlin, April 23, 1819; d. there, April 18, 1873. He began to conduct choral groups at an early age; then became a church organist at the Sophienkirche in Berlin; also was conductor of the Lyra Choral Soc. He wrote a great number of miscellaneous pieces, sacred works, and cantatas, as well as popular dances for piano.

Hennig, Carl Rafael, German organist, choral conductor, music theorist, and composer, son of **Carl Hennig;** b. Berlin, Jan. 4, 1845; d. Posen, Feb. 6, 1914. He studied music with his father; then with Richter in Leipzig and Kiel in Berlin; at the same time, studied law. After a brief period of teaching in Berlin, he went to Posen, where he founded the Hennig Vocal Soc.; he also served as a church organist. He composed several cantatas, choruses, songs, and instrumental pieces, but it is as a writer on theoretical subjects that he is mainly remembered.

WRITINGS: *Die Methodik des Schulgesang-Unterrichts* (Leipzig, 1885); *Die Unterscheidung der Gesangregister auf physiologischer Grundlage* (Leipzig, 1892); *Beitrag zur Wagner-Sache* (Leipzig, 1893); *Ästhetik der Tonkunst* (Leipzig, 1896); *Über die Entstehung der "hohen Resonanz"* (Leipzig, 1902); *Musiktheoretisches Hilfsbuch* (Leipzig, 1903; 2nd ed., 1906); *Einführung in das Wesen der Musik* (Leipzig, 1906); excellent analyses of Beethoven's 9th Sym. and *Missa Solemnis.*

Henning, Ervin Arthur, American composer; b. Marion, S.Dak., Nov. 22, 1910; d. Boston, July 27, 1982. He studied music in Chicago with **Roslyn Brogue,** whom he subsequently married. In 1944 he entered the New England Cons. of Music in Boston, graduating in 1946. He wrote mostly for chamber music combinations; in his later works he adopted the 12-tone method of composition.

WORKS: Quintet for Flute, Horn, Violin, Viola, and Cello (1946); Partita for String Quartet (1948); Suite for Viola Concertante, 2 Violins, and Cello (1950); Divertimento for Unaccompanied Bassoon (1950); Trio for Clarinet, Viola, and Piano (1959); Piano Sonata (1959); pieces for recorders; arrangements of Bach for various woodwind ensembles.

Henriot, Nicole, French pianist; b. Paris, Nov. 23, 1925. She studied with Marguerite Long; entered the Paris Cons. at the age of 12, graduating with a 1st prize 2 years later. She toured Europe (1946–49), appearing with major orchs.; made her American debut on Jan. 29, 1948.

Henriques, Fini (Valdemar), Danish violinist, conductor, and composer; b. Copenhagen, Dec. 20, 1867; d. there, Oct. 27, 1940. He studied violin with Valdemar Tofte in Copenhagen, and with Joachim at the Hochschule für Musik in Berlin; studied composition with Svendsen; returning to Copenhagen, he was a violinist in the Court Orch. (1892–96); also appeared as a soloist. He organized his own string quartet, and traveled with it in Europe; also conducted orchs. As a composer, he followed the Romantic school; he possessed a facile gift of melody; his *Danish Lullaby* became a celebrated song in Denmark. He also wrote an opera, *Staerstikkeren* (Copenhagen, May 20, 1922); several ballets (*The Little Mermaid,* after Hans Andersen; *Tata;* etc.); *Hans Andersen Overture;* 2 syms.; String Quartet; Quartet for Flute, Violin, Cello, and Piano; Violin Sonata; a number of piano pieces (several cycles, *Lyrik, Erotik,* etc.).
BIBL.: S. Berg, *F.V. H.* (Copenhagen, 1943).

Henriques, Robert, Danish cellist, conductor, and composer; b. Copenhagen, Dec. 14, 1858; d. there, Dec. 29, 1914. He studied cello with Popper, and composition with Kretschmer in Dresden. Upon his return to Copenhagen, he conducted orch. concerts; wrote music criticism; composed an overture, *Olaf Trygvason;* a symphonic sketch, *Aquarellen;* a number of pieces for the cello.

Henry, Leigh Vaughan, English conductor, writer on music, and composer; b. Liverpool, Sept. 23, 1889; d. London, March 8, 1958. He received his earliest training from his father, John Henry, a singer and composer; then studied with Granville Bantock in London, Ricardo Viñes in France, and Buonamici in Italy; taught music at Gordon Craig's Theatrical School in Florence (1912); then was in Germany, where he was interned during World War I. Returning to England, he ed. a modern-music journal, *Fanfare* (1921–22); also was active in various organizations promoting modern music; in 1930 he went to the U.S.; lectured at various colleges. He was music director of the Shakespeare Festival Week in London in 1938, 1945, and 1946; organized and conducted orch. concerts of British music, and the National Welsh Festival Concerts; also conducted at the BBC. Among his compositions are *The Moon Robber,* opera; *Llyn-y-Fan,* symphonic poem; various pieces on Welsh themes.
WRITINGS: *Music: What It Means and How to Understand It* (London, 1920); *The Growth of Music in Form and Significance* (1921); *The Story of Music* (1935); *Dr. John Bull* (largely fictional; London, 1937); *My Surging World,* autobiography (with R. Hale; 1937).

Henry, Michel, a member of the 24 "violons du roi" under Henry IV and Louis XIII; b. Paris, Feb. 1555; date of death unknown. He wrote ballets for the court. His younger brother, known as Le Jeune, also in the "violons du roi," composed some very interesting instrumental music: a *Fantaisie* for 5 Violins; another *Fantaisie,* for 5 *cornetti; Pavane* for 6 Oboes; some of this is reproduced by P. Mersenne in his *Harmonie universelle* (vol. 3, pp. 186–277). Dolmetsch made a modern arrangement of the *Fantaisie* for 5 Violins.
BIBL.: F. Lesure, "Le Recueil de ballets de M. H.," in *Les Fêtes de la Renaissance* (Paris, 1956).

Henry, Pierre, French composer and acoustical inventor; b. Paris, Dec. 9, 1927. He studied with Messiaen at the Paris Cons.; also took courses with Nadia Boulanger; in 1950 was a founder of the Groupe de Recherche de Musique Concrète with Pierre Schaeffer, but in 1958 separated from the group to experiment on his own projects in the field of electro-acoustical music and electronic synthesis of musical sounds. In virtually all of his independent works he applied electronic effects, often with the insertion of prerecorded patches of concrete music and sometimes "objets trouvés" borrowed partially or in their entirety from pre-existent compositions.
WORKS: In collaboration with Schaeffer he wrote *Symphonie pour un homme seul* (1950) and the experimental opera *Orphée 53* (1953); independently he wrote *Microphone bien tempéré* (1952); *Musique sans titre* (1951); *Concerto des ambiguïtés*

(1951); *Astrologie* (1953); *Spatiodynamisme* (1955); 4 ballets: *Haut voltage* (1956); *Coexistence* (1959); *Investigations* (1959); *Le Voyage* (1962); also *Messe de Liverpool* (1967); *Ceremony* (1970); *Futuristie 1,* "electro-acoustical musical spectacle," with the reconstruction of the "bruiteurs" introduced by the Italian futurist Luigi Russolo in 1909 (Paris, Oct. 16, 1975).

Henry V, English king; b. Monmouth, Sept. 1387; d. Bois de Vincennes, Aug. 31, 1422. During his reign (1413–22), he established a flourishing musical service at the Chapel Royal; was a musician himself; probably was the author of a Gloria and a Sanctus for 3 Voices in the Old Hall MS (transcribed into modern notation, and publ. by the Plainsong and Medieval Music Soc., Vols. I and III, 1933–38, where they are ascribed to Henry VI).

Henry VI, English king; b. Windsor, Dec. 6, 1421; d. London, May 21, 1471. He reigned from 1422 to 1471. For a long time, he was regarded as the "Roy Henry" who was the author of a Gloria and a Sanctus in the Old Hall MS; however, research by M. Bukofzer tends to indicate that the works may actually be by Henry V.

Henry VIII, English king; b. Greenwich, June 28, 1491; d. Windsor, Jan. 28, 1547. He reigned from 1509 to 1547. He received regular instruction in music. Of his 34 extant works, 33 are found in Henry VIII's MS, which also includes works by other composers of England and the Continent. Actually, of the 20 vocal works given as his, some are merely arrangements. The MS also includes 13 instrumental works. His only extant sacred work is the motet *Quam pulchra es* for 3 Voices (Baldwin MS). All of his vocal music was ed. by Lady Mary Trefusis in *Songs, Ballads and Instrumental Pieces Composed by King Henry the Eighth* (Oxford, 1912); all of his secular vocal and instrumental music was ed. by J. Stevens in Musica Britannica, XVIII (London, 1962).
BIBL.: J. Stevens, *Music and Poetry in the Early Tudor Court* (London, 1961).

Henschel, Sir (Isidor) George (Georg), esteemed German-born English conductor, composer, and baritone; b. Breslau, Feb. 18, 1850; d. Aviemore, Scotland, Sept. 10, 1934. Both his parents were of Polish-Jewish descent, but he was converted to Christianity when young. He studied with Julius Shäffer in Breslau; with Moscheles (piano), Götze (singing), and Reinecke (theory) at the Leipzig Cons. (1867–70); then with Friedrich Kiel (composition) and Adolf Schulze (singing) in Berlin. He was a boy soprano; when his voice broke, he gave concerts as a tenor; made his debut in Leipzig (1868) as Hans Sachs (baritone) in a concert performance of *Die Meistersinger von Nürnberg;* he then toured throughout Europe; later gave recitals as a bass, and in 1914 appeared in London singing as a basso profundo. At the age of 78 he sang a group of Schubert lieder in London (at the Schubert centennial, 1928). An important turning point in his career came when he was selected as the 1st conductor of the Boston Sym. Orch., which he led for 3 seasons (1881–84); he also gave concerts in Boston and N.Y. as a singer. Settling in England, he founded the London Sym. Concerts (inaugural concert, Nov. 17, 1886), and conducted them until the series was concluded in 1897. He was a vocal teacher at the Royal College of Music (1886–88) and conductor of the Scottish Orch. (1891–95). From 1905 to 1908 he was a prof. of singing at the Inst. of Musical Art in N.Y. In 1931, at the age of 81, he was engaged to conduct a commemorative concert on the 50th anniversary of the Boston Sym. Orch., identical (except for 1 number) with his inaugural Boston concert of 1881. In 1881 Henschel married **Lillian June Henschel** (née **Bailey**), with whom he gave concerts; she died in 1901. In 1907 he was married for a 2nd time, to Amy Louis. In 1890 he became a British subject. He was knighted in 1914. He was the author of *Personal Recollections of Johannes Brahms* (1907) and *Musings and Memories of a Musician* (1918). His musical compositions (mostly vocal) are in the German Romantic tradition. They include the opera *Nubia* (Dresden, Dec. 9, 1899); *Stabat Mater* (Birmingham, Oct. 4, 1894); *Requiem,* in memory of his 1st wife (Boston, Dec. 2,

1902); Mass for 8 Voices (London, June 1, 1916); String Quartet; about 200 songs.

BIBL.: M.A. de Wolfe Howe, *The Boston Symphony Orchestra, 1881–1931* (Boston, 1931); H. Earle Johnson, *Symphony Hall* (Boston, 1950).

Henschel, Lillian June (née **Bailey**), American soprano; b. Columbus, Ohio, Jan. 17, 1860; d. London, Nov. 4, 1901. She made her professional debut in Boston at 16; then went to Paris to study with Viardot-García. On April 30, 1879, she appeared in London, at a Phil. concert, when she sang, besides her solo number, a duet with **George Henschel.** She then studied with him and on March 9, 1881, married him. When Henschel was appointed 1st conductor of the Boston Sym. Orch., she appeared as a soloist with him accompanying her at the piano, also in duets at Boston Sym. concerts. Until her untimely death, the Henschels were constantly associated in American artistic life. Her well-trained voice and fine musical feeling won her many admirers.

BIBL.: H. Henschel, *When Soft Voices Die: A Musical Biography* (London, 1944).

Hensel, Fanny (Cäcilie) (née **Mendelssohn-Bartholdy**), German pianist and composer, sister of **(Jacob Ludwig) Felix Mendelssohn (-Bartholdy)**; b. Hamburg, Nov. 14, 1805; d. Berlin, May 14, 1847. She began her musical training with her mother, then studied piano with Berger and composition with Zelter; subsequently studied with Marie Bigot in Paris (1816). She later attended Humboldt's lectures on physical geography and Holtei's lectures on experimental physics in Berlin (1825), but music remained her great love. She married the painter W. Hensel on Oct. 3, 1829. From 1843 she oversaw the Sunday morning concerts at Berlin's Elternhaus. Her untimely death was a great shock to Mendelssohn, who died a few months afterward. She was a talented composer; 6 of her songs were publ. under her brother's name in his opp. 8 and 9 (*Heimweh, Italien, Suleika und Hatem, Sehnsucht, Verlust,* and *Die Nonne*); other works publ. under her own name, including some posthumously, include 4 books of songs, a collection of part-songs entitled *Gartenlieder,* and *Lieder ohne Worte* for Piano.

BIBL.: S. Hensel, *Die Familie M. 1729–1847, nach Briefen und Tagebüchern* (Berlin, 1879; 18th ed., 1924; 19th ed., rev. and abridged, 1959; Eng. tr., 1882); J. Werner, "Felix and F. M.," *Music & Letters,* XXVIII (1947); *F. H.: Dokumente ihres Lebens,* Ausstellungskatalog der Staatsbibliothek Preussicher Kulturbesitz, II (Berlin, 1972); M. Citron, ed., *The Letters of F. H. to Felix Mendelssohn* (Stuyvesant, N.Y., 1987).

Hensel, Heinrich, German tenor; b. Neustadt, Oct. 29, 1874; d. Hamburg, Feb. 23, 1935. He studied in Vienna and Milan; was a member of the Frankfurt Opera (1900–1906), then at Wiesbaden (1906–11), where Siegfried Wagner heard him and engaged him to create the chief tenor part in his opera *Banadietrich* (Karlsruhe, 1910) and also to sing Parsifal at the Bayreuth Festival. He obtained excellent success; subsequently sang at Covent Garden, London (1911–14). He made his American debut at the Metropolitan Opera in N.Y. as Lohengrin (Dec. 22, 1911) and was hailed by the press as one of the finest Wagnerian tenors; he also appeared with the Chicago Opera; returned to Germany and sang at the Hamburg Opera (1912–29). He was married to the soprano Elsa Hensel-Schweitzer (1878–1937), who sang in Dessau (1898–1901) and then in Frankfurt (from 1901).

Hensel, Walther (real name, **Julius Janiczek**), Bohemian-born music educator; b. Moravska Trebova, Sept. 8, 1887; d. Munich, Sept. 5, 1956. He studied in Vienna, Prague, and Freibourg, where he obtained his Ph.D. (1911); taught languages in Prague (1912–18). He traveled in Europe (1918–25) as an organizer of folk-song activities, with the aim of raising the standards of choral music for the young. From 1925 to 1929 he was head of the Jugendmusik School at the Dortmund Cons. In 1930 he went to Stuttgart, where he organized an educational program for the promotion of folk music.

In 1938 he returned to Prague; taught at the German Univ. there. After 1945 he went to Munich. He ed. a number of folk-song collections; publ. *Lied und Volk, Eine Streitschrift wider das falsche deutsche Lied* (1921); *Im Zeichen des Volksliedes* (1922; 2nd ed., 1936); *Musikalische Grundlehre* (Kassel, 1937); *Auf den Spuren des Volksliedes* (Kassel, 1944; reprint, 1964).

Henselt (Hänselt), (Georg Martin) Adolf (Adolph), distinguished German pianist and composer; b. Schwabach, May 9, 1814; d. Warmbrunn, Silesia, Oct. 10, 1889. The family moved to Munich when he was still an infant, and he studied piano there with Mme. von Fladt. In 1831 an allowance from King Ludwig I enabled him to continue piano study with Hummel at Weimar; he then took a course of theory under Sechter in Vienna. After a highly successful tour in Germany (1836), he went to St. Petersburg (1838), where he established himself as a piano teacher; was appointed chamber pianist to the Empress, and inspector of music at Imperial Institutes for girls in principal Russian cities. He remained in Russia for 40 years; a generation of Russian pianists studied under him. He was a virtuoso of the 1st rank; like Liszt (whose intimate friend he became), he developed an individual manner of playing, designed to express a personal feeling for the music. His technical specialty was the artful execution, in legato, of widely extended chords and arpeggios, for the achievement of which he composed extremely difficult extension studies. As a composer of piano pieces, he was praised by Schumann and Liszt. His principal works are a Piano Concerto, 2 sets of études, and a number of effective piano pieces (*Frühlingslied, La gondola,* etc.); altogether, he publ. 54 works. He publ. a long-winded but historically and didactically interesting paper entitled *Instructions for Teaching of Playing the Fortepiano, Based on Experience of Many Years, a Manual for the Teachers and Pupils of the Educational Institutions Entrusted to Him by the Government* (in Russian; St. Petersburg, 1868).

BIBL.: W. von Lenz, *Die grossen Pianoforte Virtuosen unserer Zeit aus persönlicher Bekanntschaft: Liszt, Chopin, Tausig, H.* (Berlin, 1872; Eng. ed., N.Y., 1899, rev. 1971); La Mara, "A. H.," *Musikalische Studienköpfe* (vol. III, 1909; reprinted separately, 1911); H. Schonberg, *The Great Pianists* (N.Y., 1963).

Hentschel, Franz, German conductor and composer; b. Berlin, Nov. 6, 1814; d. there, May 11, 1889. He studied with A.W. Bach; after conducting theater orchs. in provincial towns, he settled in Berlin as a music teacher. He wrote an opera, *Die Hexenreise,* and numerous marches for military band.

Hentschel, Theodor, German conductor and composer; b. Schirgiswalde, March 28, 1830; d. Hamburg, Dec. 19, 1892. He studied with Reissiger and Ciccarelli in Dresden; was active as a theater conductor in Bremen (1860–90), and then at Hamburg. He wrote the operas *Matrose und Sänger* (Leipzig, 1857); *Der Königspage* (Bremen, 1874); *Die Braut von Lusignan, oder Die schöne Melusine* (Bremen, 1875); *Lancelot* (Bremen, 1878); *Des Königs Schwerdt* (Hamburg, 1891); overtures and symphonic marches for orch.; piano music; songs.

Henze, Hans Werner, outstanding German composer of the modern school; b. Gütersloh, Westphalia, July 1, 1926. His early studies at the Braunschweig School of Music (1942–44) were interrupted by military service, and for a year he was in the German army on the Russian front. In 1946 he took music courses at the Kirchenmusikalisches Inst. in Heidelberg; at the same time he studied privately with Wolfgang Fortner. He became fascinated with the disciplinary aspects of Schoenberg's method of composition with 12 tones, and attended the seminars on the subject given by Leibowitz at Darmstadt. A musician of restless temperament, he joined a radical political group and proclaimed the necessity of writing music without stylistic restrictions in order to serve the masses. In search of natural musical resources, he moved to Italy; lived in Ischia from 1953 to 1956; then stayed in Naples and finally settled in Marino. He successfully integrated musical idioms and mannerisms of seemingly incompatible techniques; in his vocal works he freely adopted such humanoid effects as screaming, bellowing, and snorting; he even specified that long sustained tones were to be sung by inhaling as well as exhaling. Nonetheless, Henze manages to compose music that is feasible for human performance. But political considerations continued to play a decisive role in his career. In 1967 he withdrew from the membership of the Academy of the Arts of West Berlin, in a gesture of protest against its artistic policies. During his stay in Italy he joined the Italian Communist Party. His political stance did not preclude his acceptance in "bourgeois" musical centers, for his works were performed widely in Europe. He held the International Chair of Composition Studies at the Royal Academy of Music in London from 1986. In 1989 he helped found the Munich Biennale.

WORKS: STAGE: *Das Wundertheater*, opera for Actors, after Cervantes (1948; Heidelberg, May 7, 1949; rev. for Singers, 1964; Frankfurt, Nov. 30, 1965); *Ballet Variations* (concert premiere, Düsseldorf, Oct. 3, 1949; stage premiere, Wuppertal, Dec. 21, 1958); *Jack Pudding*, ballet (1949; Wiesbaden, Jan. 1, 1951); *Rosa Silber*, ballet (1950; concert premiere, Berlin, May 8, 1951; stage premiere, Cologne, Oct. 15, 1958); *Labyrinth*, choreographic fantasy (1951; concert perf., Darmstadt, May 29, 1952); *Die schlafende Prinzessin*, ballet after Tchaikovsky (1951; Essen, June 5, 1954); *Ein Landarzt*, radio opera after the story by Kafka (Hamburg, Nov. 19, 1951; broadcast, Nov. 29, 1951; rev. as a monodrama for Baritone and Orch., 1964; Berlin, Oct. 12, 1965; Fischer-Dieskau, soloist; radio opera rev. for the stage, 1964; Frankfurt, Nov. 30, 1965); *Boulevard Solitude*, opera (1951; Hannover, Feb. 17, 1952); *Der Idiot*, ballet pantomime after Dostoyevsky (Berlin, Sept. 1, 1952); *Pas d'action*, ballet (Munich, 1952; withdrawn by the composer and rev. as *Tancredi*, 1964; Vienna, May 14, 1966); *Das Ende einer Welt*, radio opera (Hamburg, Dec. 4, 1953; rev. for the stage, 1964; Frankfurt, Nov. 30, 1965); *König Hirsch*, opera (1952–55; Berlin, Sept. 23, 1956; rev. as *Il Re cervo*, 1962; Kassel, March 10, 1963); *Maratona*, ballet (1956; Berlin, Sept. 24, 1957); *Ondine*, ballet (1956–57; London, Oct. 27, 1958); *Der Prinz von Homburg*, opera (1958; Hamburg, May 22, 1960); *L'Usignolo dell'Imperatore*, pantomime after Andersen (Venice, Sept. 16, 1959); *Elegy for Young Lovers*, chamber opera (1959–61; in German, Schwetzingen, May 20, 1961; 1st perf. to Auden's original Eng. libretto, Glyndebourne, July 13, 1961); *Der junge Lord*, comic opera (1964; Berlin, April 7, 1965); *The Bassarids*, opera seria (1965; in German, Salzburg, Aug. 6, 1966; 1st perf. to the original Eng. libretto by Auden and Kallman, Santa Fe, N. Mex., Aug. 7, 1968); *Moralities*, scenic cantatas after Aesop, to texts by Auden (1967; Cincinnati, May 18, 1968); *Der langwierige Weg in die Wohnung der Natascha Ungeheuer*, show (RAI, Rome, May 17, 1971); *La cubana, oder Ein Leben für die Kunst*, vaudeville (1973; NET Opera Theater, N.Y., March 4, 1974; stage premiere, Munich, May 28, 1975); *We Come to the River*, actions for music (1974–76; London, July 12, 1976); *Don Chisciotte*, opera, arrangement of Paisiello (Montepulciano, Aug. 1, 1976); *Orpheus*, ballet in 2 acts by Edward Bond (1978; Stuttgart, March 17, 1979); *Pollicino*, fairy-tale opera (1979–80; Montepulciano, Aug. 2, 1980); *The English Cat*, chamber opera (1980–83; Schwetzingen, June 2, 1983); *Il ritorno d'Ulisse in patria*, realization of Monteverdi's opera (1981; Salzburg, Aug. 18, 1985); *Ödipus der Tyrann oder Der Vater vertreibt seinen Sohn und Schickt die Tochter in die Küche* (Kindberg, Oct. 30, 1983); *Das verratene Meer*, opera (Berlin, May 5, 1990).

ORCH.: Chamber Concerto for Piano, Flute, and Strings (Darmstadt, Sept. 27, 1946); Concertino for Piano and Winds, with Percussion (Baden-Baden, Oct. 5, 1947, Egk conducting); Sym. No. 1 (Bad Pyrmont, Aug. 25, 1948, Fortner conducting; rev. version, Berlin, April 9, 1964, composer conducting); Violin Concerto No. 1 (Baden-Baden, Dec. 12, 1948); Sym. No. 2 (Stuttgart, Dec. 1, 1949); Symphonic Variations (1950); Piano Concerto No. 1 (1950; Düsseldorf, Sept. 14, 1952, composer conducting); Sym. No. 3 (Donaueschingen, Oct. 7, 1951); *Ode to the West Wind* for Cello and Orch., to the poem by Shelley (Bielefeld, April 30, 1954); *4 poemi* (Frankfurt, May 31, 1955, Stokowski conducting); Sym. No. 4, in 1 movement (1955;

Berlin, Oct. 9, 1963, composer conducting); *In Memoriam: Die weisse Rose* for Chamber Orch. (1956); Sonata for Strings (Zürich, March 21, 1958, Sacher conducting); *3 Symphonic Studies* (1955–64; 1st version perf. as *Symphonic Studies*, Hamburg, Feb. 14, 1956); *3 Dithyrambs* for Chamber Orch. (Cologne, Nov. 27, 1958); *Jeux des Tritons*, divertimento from the ballet *Ondine*, for Piano and Orch. (Zürich, March 28, 1960); *Antifone* (1960; Berlin, Jan. 20, 1962, Karajan conducting); Sym. No. 5 (1962; N.Y., May 16, 1963, Bernstein conducting); *Los Caprichos*, fantasia for Orch. (1963; Duisburg, April 6, 1967); *Doppio Concerto* for Oboe, Harp, and Strings (Zürich, Dec. 2, 1966, Sacher conducting); *Telemanniana* (Berlin, April 4, 1967); Fantasia for Strings, from the film *Junge Torless* (Berlin, April 1, 1967); Concerto for Double Bass and Orch. (Chicago, Nov. 2, 1967); Piano Concerto No. 2, in 1 movement (1967; Bielefeld, Sept. 29, 1968); Sym. No. 6 (Havana, Nov. 24, 1969); *Compases para Preguntas Ensimismadas* (Basel, Feb. 11, 1971, Sacher conducting); *Heliogabalus Imperator*, "allegoria per musica" (Chicago, Nov. 16, 1972, Solti conducting); *Tristan* for Piano, Tape, and Mixed Orch. (1973; London, Oct. 20, 1974, C. Davis conducting); *Ragtimes and Habaneras* for Brass Instruments (London, Sept. 13, 1975); Concert Suite from the film *Katharina Blum* (Brighton, May 6, 1976, composer conducting); *Aria de la folia española* for Chamber Orch. (St. Paul, Sept. 17, 1977); *Il Vitalino raddoppiato* for Violin Concertante and Chamber Orch. (Salzburg, Aug. 2, 1978); *Barcarola* (1979; Zürich, April 22, 1980); *Apollo trionfante*, suite from *Orpheus* (1979; Gelsenkirchen, Sept. 1, 1980); dramatic scenes from *Orpheus* (1979; Zürich, Jan. 6, 1981, composer conducting); *I sentimenti di Carl Philip Emmanuel Bach*, transcriptions for Flute, Harp, and Strings (Rome, April 14, 1982); *Le Miracle de la rose* for Clarinet and 13 Players (1981; London, May 26, 1982); *Cinque piccoli concerti* (1980–82; Cabrillo Music Festival, Aug. 26, 1983); Sym. No. 7 (1983–84; Berlin, Dec. 1, 1984); *Sieben Liebeslieder* for Cello and Orch. (1984–85; Cologne, Dec. 12, 1986); *Fandango* (1985; Paris, Feb. 5, 1986); *12 kleine Elegien* for Renaissance Instruments (Cologne, Dec. 13, 1986); *Allegro brillante* (Dallas, Sept. 14, 1989).

CHAMBER: Violin Sonata (1946); Sonatina for Flute and Piano (1947); String Quartet No. 1 (1947); Serenade for Solo Cello (1949); Variations for Piano (1949); Chamber Sonata for Piano, Violin, and Cello (1948; Cologne, March 16, 1950; rev. 1963); *Apollo et Hyazinthus* for Harpsichord, Alto, and 8 Instruments (Frankfurt, June 26, 1949); String Quartet No. 2 (Baden-Baden, Dec. 16, 1952); Wind Quintet (1952; Bremen, Feb. 15, 1953); *Concerto per il Marigny* for Piano and 7 Instruments (Paris, March 9, 1956); Sonata for Piano (1959); *Chamber Music 1958* for Tenor, Guitar, and 8 Instruments (Hamburg, Nov. 26, 1958); *Lucy Escott Variations* for Piano (1963; Berlin, March 21, 1965); Divertimento for 2 Pianos (N.Y., Nov. 30, 1964); *Royal Winter Music*, 2 sonatas on Shakespearean characters, for Guitar (1975–79); String Quartet No. 3 (Berlin, Sept. 12, 1976); *Amicizia* for Clarinet, Cello, and Percussion Instruments (Montepulciano, Aug. 6, 1976); String Quartets Nos. 4 and 5 (Schwetzingen, May 25, 1977); Sonata for Violin Solo (Montepulciano, Aug. 10, 1977); *L'autunno* for Wind Instruments (London, Feb. 28, 1979); Sonata for Viola and Piano (Witten, April 20, 1980); *Canzona* for 7 Instruments (1982); Sonata for Wind Ensemble (Berlin, Sept. 17, 1983); Sonata for 6 Players (London, Sept. 26, 1984); *Selbst- und Zwiegespräche*, trio for Viola, Guitar, and Small Organ (1984–85); *Serenade* for Solo Violin (1986).

VOCAL: 5 madrigals, to poems by François Villon, for Mixed Chorus and 2 Solo Instruments (1947; Frankfurt, April 25, 1950); *Chorus of the Captured Trojans*, from *Faust*, Part 2, for Mixed Chorus and Large Orch. (1948; Bielefeld, Feb. 6, 1949; rev. 1964); *Whispers from Heavenly Death*, cantata from the poem by Walt Whitman, for High Voice and 8 Solo Instruments (1948); *Der Vorwurf* (The Reproach), concert aria to words by Franz Werfel, for Baritone, Trumpet, and Strings (Darmstadt, July 29, 1948); 5 Neapolitan songs for Baritone and Orch. (Frankfurt, May 26, 1956; Fischer-Dieskau, soloist);

Nocturnes and Arias for Soprano and Orch. (Donaueschingen, Oct. 20, 1957); *Novae de Infinito Laudes,* cantata to text by Giordano Bruno (1962; Venice, April 24, 1963); *Ariosi,* to poems by Tasso, for Soprano, Violin, and Orch. (1963; Edinburgh Festival, Aug. 23, 1964); *Being Beauteous,* cantata from the poem by Arthur Rimbaud, for Soprano, Harp, and 4 Cellos (1963; Berlin, April 12, 1964); *Cantata della Fiaba Estrema* for Soprano, Small Chorus, and 13 Instruments (1963; Zürich, Feb. 26, 1965); Choral Fantasy for Small Chorus, 5 Instruments, and Percussion (1964; Berlin, Jan. 23, 1967); *Muses of Sicily* for Chorus, 2 Pianos, Winds, and Timpani (Berlin, Sept. 20, 1966); *Versuch über Schweine* (Essay on Pigs) for Baritone and Chamber Orch. (London, Feb. 14, 1969; the title is an ironic reference to certain revolting students, active during the 1960s); *Das Floss der Medusa* (The Raft of the Medusa), oratorio to the memory of Ché Guevara (1968; concert premiere, Vienna, Jan. 29, 1971; stage premiere, Nuremberg, April 15, 1972); *El Cimarrón* for Baritone, Flute, Guitar, and Percussion, to texts from *The Autobiography of a Runaway Slave* by Esteban Montejo (Aldeburgh Festival, June 22, 1970); *Voices* for Mezzo-soprano, Tenor, and Instrumental Group, to 22 revolutionary texts (London, Jan. 4, 1974, composer conducting); *Jephtha,* oratorio by Carissimi, realized by Henze (London, July 14, 1976, composer conducting); *The King of Harlem* for Mezzo-soprano and Instrumental Ensemble, to a text by Federico García Lorca (Witten, April 20, 1980); *3 Auden Pieces* for Voice and Piano (Aldeburgh, June 15, 1983).
    WRITINGS: *Musik und Politik: Schriften und Gespräche, 1955–1975* (Munich, 1976; also in Eng., as *Music and Politics: Collected Writings, 1953–81,* London and Ithaca, N.Y., 1982).
    BIBL.: K. Geitel, *H.W. H.* (Berlin, 1968); H.H. Stuckenschmidt, "H.W. H. und die Musik unserer Zeit," *Universitas,* XXVII/2 (1972); E. Restagno, ed., *H.* (Turin, 1986); D. Rexroth, ed., *Der Komponist H.W. H.: Ein Buch der Alten Oper Frankfurt, Frankfurt Feste '86* (Mainz and N.Y., 1986); P. Peterson, *H.W. H., ein politischer Musiker: Zwölf Vorlesungen* (Hamburg, 1988).

Heppener, Robert, Dutch composer; b. Amsterdam, Aug. 9, 1925. He took piano lessons with Jan Öde and Johan van den Boogert at the Amsterdam Cons.; later studied composition with Bertus van Lier. He then joined the staff of the Cons. of the Music Lyceum Soc. in Amsterdam. In his compositions he observes the rational boundaries of modern harmony.
    WORKS: *Cantico delle creature di S. Francesco d'Assisi* for Soprano, Harp, and Strings (1952; rev. 1954); Nocturne for Piano (1953); Sym. (1957); Septet (1958); *Derivazioni* for String Orch. (1958; rev. 1980); *Arcadian Sonatina* for 2 Recorders and Violin (1959); *À fond de fleurettes* for String Quartet (1961); Sinfonietta for Small Orch. (1961); *Het derde land* (The 3rd Country), 3 songs for Chorus and Chamber Orch. (1962); *Cavalcade,* overture and rondo for Orch. (1963); *Eglogues* for Orch. (1963); *Scherzi* for Strings (1965); *Canti carnascialeschi* (Carnival Songs), 5-movement cycle for a cappella Chorus (1966); *Fanfare trionfale* for Chorus, Winds, Timpani, and Piano (1967); Quartet for Alto Flute, Violin, Viola, and Cello (1967); *Air et sonneries* for Orch. (1969); *Canzona* for Saxophone Quartet (1969); *Hymns and Conversations* for 28 Harps (1969; Amsterdam, July 8, 1969); *4 Songs,* after Pound, for Middle Voice and Piano (1968–70); *Muziek voor straten en pleinen* (Music for Streets and Squares) for Orch. (Amsterdam, Oct. 31, 1970); *Del iubilo del core che esce in voce* for a cappella Chorus (1974); *Pas de quatre-mains* for Piano, 4-hands (1975); *Nachklänge* for Chamber Chorus (1977); *Sweelinck Fanfare* for Orch. (1978); Viola Concerto (Amsterdam, Oct. 6, 1979); *Memento,* dramatic scene for Soprano and 8 Instruments (1984); *Spinsel* for Piano (1986).
    BIBL.: W. Paap, "R. H.," *Sonorum Speculum,* 39 (1969).

Herbage, Julian (Livingston), English musicologist; b. Woking, Sept. 4, 1904; d. London, Jan. 15, 1976. He studied harmony and counterpoint with Charles Wood at St. John's College, Cambridge. In 1927 he became a member of the music staff of the BBC; from 1940 to 1946 was assistant director of music there. With his wife, Anna Instone, he ed. the BBC "Music Magazine" radio program from 1944 to 1973. He also made appearances as a conductor of music by Baroque composers. He wrote the book *Handel's Messiah* (London, 1948).

Herbart, Johann Friedrich, German philosopher, educator, writer on music, and composer; b. Oldenburg, May 4, 1776; d. Göttingen, Aug. 14, 1841. He studied in Jena with Fichte. In 1805 he was appointed prof. of philosophy at Göttingen; from 1809 to 1835 he was at Königsberg; from 1835 to his death he was again at Göttingen. Of importance to music theory is his *Psychologische Bemerkungen zur Tonlehre* (1811). He composed a Piano Sonata (Leipzig, 1808) and other works.
    BIBL.: W. Kahl, *H. als Musiker* (Langensalza, 1926).

Herbeck, Johann (Franz), Ritter von, Austrian conductor and composer; b. Vienna, Dec. 25, 1831; d. there, Oct. 28, 1877. He was a boy chorister at the Heiligenkreuz monastery, where he had instruction in piano; then studied composition with Ludwig Rotter in Vienna; he also studied philosophy and law at the Univ. of Vienna; from 1858 to 1870, and from 1875 to his death, he was conductor of the Gesellschaft der Musikfreunde choral society; in 1863 he became Vice-Kapellmeister and in 1866 Kapellmeister of the Hofkapelle; in 1869–70, was co-conductor of the Hofoper; in 1870 was named its director as well, remaining there until 1875. He was particularly successful as conductor and organizer of several choral societies in Vienna. Herbeck publ. numerous choral works of considerable worth, if not of any originality. His son, Ludwig Herbeck, publ. a biography, *Johann Herbeck, Ein Lebensbild* (Vienna, 1885), which contains a complete catalog of his works. See also the sketch on Herbeck in Hanslick's *Suite* (Vienna, 1885).
    BIBL.: J. Braun, *J. R. v.H. und das Wiener Hofoperntheater* (diss., Univ. of Vienna, 1949).

Herberigs, Robert, Belgian composer; b. Ghent, June 19, 1886; d. Oudenaarde, Sept. 20, 1974. He studied singing at the Ghent Cons. and made his debut as a baritone at the Flemish Opera in Antwerp (1908), but soon abandoned his operatic aspirations and began an assiduous study of composition. He succeeded swiftly, and won the Belgian Grand Prix in 1909 with his cantata *La Légende de St. Hubert.* He also pursued an interest in literature, and publ. several novels. His music reflects the manner of French Romanticism.
    WORKS: 2 comic operas: *Le Mariage de Rosine,* after Beaumarchais (1919; Ghent, Feb. 13, 1925), and *L'Amour médecin,* after Molière (1920); radio play, *Antoine et Cleopatra,* after Shakespeare, for 6 Speakers, Chorus, and Orch. (1949); open-air play, *Lam Godsspel* or *Jeu de l'Agneau Mystique* (Pageant of the Mystic Lamb; 1948; Ghent, 1949); a play of "light and sound in stereorama," *Le Château des comtes de Gand* (1960); 2 piano concertos (1932, 1952); 2 suites for Brass Ensemble (1946); *Sinfonia breve* (1947; 2 earlier syms. were withdrawn); Organ Concerto (1957); numerous symphonic poems and orch. suites: *Cyrano de Bergerac,* with Solo Horn, in the form of a concerto (Brussels, April 12, 1912); *Le Chant d'Hiawatha,* after Longfellow (1921); *Vlaanderen, O Welig Huis* (Flanders, the Well-Beloved; 1949); *De Vrolijke Vrouwtjes van Windsor* (The Merry Wives of Windsor; 1950); *Rapsodia alla Zingara* (1952); *À la Fontaine Bellerie* (1954; orig. for Piano, 1923); *Échos et mirages* (1954); *Esquisses et impromptus* (1954); *La Chanson d'Ève,* 2 suites (1955, 1959; orig. a cycle of 40 songs, 1922–24); *4 ballades* (1955); *La Petite Sirène,* after Hans Christian Andersen (1955); *Odes aux Muses* (1955); *4 saisons,* after Breughel (1956); *4 odes à Botticelli* (1958); *Commedia dell'arte* (1958); *De Nachtelijke Wapenschouw* (Nocturnal Parade; 1961); *Hamlet* (1962); *Roméo et Juliette* (1963); *Reinaut et Armida* (1967); *Cantata* to the memory of Jan Willems (1946); *Te Deum laudamus* for Chorus and Organ (1912); *Missa pro defunctis* for Chorus a cappella (1926); 7 other masses for Chorus and Organ, including *Messe in nativitate* (1926) and *Messe pour la Paix* (1938); String Quartet (1921); *Poème* for Piano Trio (1923); Violin Sonata (1932); *Concert champêtre*

for Wind Quintet (1938); Clarinet Sonatina (1939); Piano Quartet (1939); *Suite miniature* and Sonatine for Flute and String Trio (both 1954); 21 piano sonatas and sonatinas (1941–45); piano pieces; songs.

Herbert, Victor (August), famous Irish-born American composer; b. Dublin, Feb. 1, 1859; d. N.Y., May 26, 1924. He was a grandson of Samuel Lover, the Irish novelist; his father died when he was an infant; his mother married a German physician and settled in Stuttgart (1867), taking the boy with her. He entered the Stuttgart high school, but did not graduate; his musical ability was definitely pronounced by then, and he selected the cello as his instrument, taking lessons from Bernhard Cossmann in Baden-Baden. He soon acquired a degree of technical proficiency that enabled him to take a position as cellist in various orchs. in Germany, France, Italy, and Switzerland; in 1880 he became a cellist of the Eduard Strauss waltz band in Vienna; in 1881, he returned to Stuttgart, where he joined the Court Orch., and studied composition with Max Seifritz at the Cons. His earliest works were for cello with orch.; he performed his Suite with the Stuttgart orch. on Oct. 23, 1883, and his 1st Cello Concerto on Dec. 8, 1885. On Aug. 14, 1886, he married the Viennese opera singer **Therese Förster** (1861–1927); in the same year she received an offer to join the Metropolitan Opera in N.Y., and Herbert was engaged as an orch. cellist there, appearing in N.Y. also as a soloist (played his own Cello Concerto with the N.Y. Phil., Dec. 10, 1887). In his early years in N.Y., Herbert was overshadowed by the celebrity of his wife, but soon he developed energetic activities on his own, forming an entertainment orch. which he conducted in a repertoire of light music; he also participated in chamber music concerts; was a soloist with the Theodore Thomas and Seidl orchs. He was the conductor of the Boston Festival Orch. in 1891; Tchaikovsky conducted this orch. in Philadelphia in a miscellaneous program, and Herbert played a solo. He was associate conductor of the Worcester Festival (1889–91), for which he wrote a dramatic cantata, *The Captive* (Sept. 24, 1891). In 1893 he became bandmaster of the famous 22nd Regiment Band, succeeding P.S. Gilmore. On March 10, 1894, he was soloist with the N.Y. Phil. in his 2nd Cello Concerto. In the same year, at the suggestion of William MacDonald, the manager of the Boston Ideal Opera Co., Herbert wrote a light opera, *Prince Ananias*, which was produced with encouraging success in N.Y. (Nov. 20, 1894). From 1898 to 1904, Herbert was conductor of the Pittsburgh Sym. Orch., presenting some of his own compositions: *Épisodes amoureuses* (Feb. 2, 1900); *Hero and Leander* (Jan. 18, 1901); *Woodland Fancies* (Dec. 6, 1901); *Columbus* (Jan. 2, 1903). In 1900 he directed at Madison Square Garden, N.Y., an orch. of 420 performers for the benefit of the sufferers in the Galveston flood. On April 29, 1906, he led a similar monster concert at the Hippodrome for the victims of the San Francisco earthquake. In 1904 he organized the Victor Herbert N.Y. Orch., and gave concerts in N.Y. and neighboring communities.

But it is as a composer of light operas that Herbert became chiefly known. In the best of these he unites spontaneous melody, sparkling rhythm, and simple but tasteful harmony; his experience as a symphonic composer and conductor imparted a solidity of texture to his writing that placed him far above the many gifted amateurs in this field. Furthermore, he possessed a natural communicative power in his music, which made his operettas spectacularly successful with the public. In the domain of grand opera, he was not so fortunate. When the production of his 1st grand opera, *Natoma*, took place in Philadelphia on Feb. 25, 1911, it aroused great expectations; but the opera failed to sustain lasting interest. Still less effective was his 2nd opera, *Madeleine*, staged by the Metropolitan Opera in N.Y. on Jan. 24, 1914. Herbert was one of the founders of ASCAP in 1914, and was vice-president from that date until his death. In 1916 he wrote a special score for the motion picture *The Fall of a Nation*, in synchronization with the screenplay.

Works: Operettas: *Prince Ananias* (N.Y., Nov. 20, 1894); *The Wizard of the Nile* (Chicago, Sept. 26, 1895); *The Gold Bug* (N.Y., Sept. 21, 1896); *The Serenade* (Cleveland, Feb. 17, 1897); *The Idol's Eye* (Troy, N.Y., Sept. 20, 1897); *The Fortune Teller* (Toronto, Sept. 14, 1898); *Cyrano de Bergerac* (Montreal, Sept. 11, 1899); *The Singing Girl* (Montreal, Oct. 2, 1899); *The Ameer* (Scranton, Pa., Oct. 9, 1899); *The Viceroy* (San Francisco, Feb. 12, 1900); *Babes in Toyland* (Chicago, June 17, 1903); *Babette* (Washington, D.C., Nov. 9, 1903); *It Happened in Nordland* (Harrisburg, Pa., Nov. 21, 1904); *Miss Dolly Dollars* (Rochester, N.Y., Aug. 31, 1905); *Wonderland* (Buffalo, Sept. 14, 1905); *Mlle. Modiste* (Trenton, Oct. 7, 1905); *The Red Mill* (Buffalo, Sept. 3, 1906); *Dream City* (N.Y., Dec. 25, 1906); *The Tattooed Man* (Baltimore, Feb. 11, 1907); *The Rose of Algeria* (Wilkes-Barre, Sept. 11, 1909); *Little Nemo* (Philadelphia, Sept. 28, 1908); *The Prima Donna* (Chicago, Oct. 5, 1908); *Old Dutch* (Wilkes-Barre, Nov. 6, 1909); *Naughty Marietta* (Syracuse, Oct. 24, 1910); *When Sweet 16* (Springfield, Mass., Dec. 5, 1910); *Mlle. Rosita* (later called *The Duchess*; Boston, March 27, 1911); *The Enchantress* (Washington, D.C., Oct. 9, 1911); *The Lady of the Slipper* (Philadelphia, Oct. 8, 1912); *The Madcap Duchess* (Rochester, N.Y., Oct. 13, 1913); *Sweethearts* (Baltimore, March 24, 1913); *The Débutante* (Atlantic City, Sept. 21, 1914); *The Only Girl* (Atlantic City, Oct. 1, 1914); *Princess Pat* (Atlantic City, Aug. 23, 1915); *Eileen* (Cleveland, Jan. 1, 1917, as *Hearts of Erin*); *Her Regiment* (Springfield, Mass., Oct. 22, 1917); *The Velvet Lady* (Philadelphia, Dec. 23, 1918); *My Golden Girl* (Stamford, Conn., Dec. 19, 1919); *The Girl in the Spotlight* (Stamford, Conn., July 7, 1920); *Oui, Madame* (Philadelphia, March 22, 1920); *Orange Blossoms* (Philadelphia, Sept. 4, 1922); *The Dream Girl* (New Haven, April 22, 1924). Operas: *Natoma* (Philadelphia, Feb. 25, 1911) and *Madeleine* (Metropolitan Opera, N.Y., Jan. 24, 1914). Other stage productions: *Cinderella Man* (1915); *The Century Girl* (1916); *Ziegfeld Follies* (1917; 1920–23); *The Willow Plate*, marionette play by Tony Sarg (1924). Non-stage works: Serenade, op. 12; 1st Cello Concerto (Stuttgart, Dec. 8, 1885); 2nd Cello Concerto, op. 30 (N.Y. March 10, 1894); *Pan-Americana; Suite of Serenades* (composed for Paul Whiteman's orch.; perf. 1924); *Golden Days; Dramatic Overture;* orch. arrangements; men's choruses; songs; many pieces for piano, violin and piano, and cello and piano.

Bibl.: J. Kaye, *V. H.* (N.Y., 1931); E. Waters, *V. H.* (N.Y., 1955).

Herbig, Günther, noted German conductor; b. Ustí-nad-Labem, Czechoslovakia, Nov. 30, 1931. He studied conducting with Abendroth at the Weimar Hochschule für Musik, and received further training from Scherchen, Yansons, and Karajan. He was conductor of the German National Theater in Weimar (1957–62), music director of the Hans Otto Theater in Potsdam (1962–66), and conductor of the (East) Berlin Sym. Orch. (1966–72). He was Generalmusikdirektor (1970–72) and chief conductor (1972–77) of the Dresden Phil.; then was chief conductor of the (East) Berlin Sym. Orch. (1977–83), and principal guest conductor of the Dallas Sym. Orch. (1979–81) and BBC Northern Sym. Orch. in Manchester (1981–83). From 1984 to 1990 he was music director of the Detroit Sym. Orch., and from 1990 of the Toronto Sym.

Herbst, Johannes, German-American Moravian minister and composer; b. Kempten, Swabia, July 23, 1735; d. Salem, N.C., Jan. 15, 1812. He went to the U.S. in 1786 to serve as minister at Lancaster, Pa., and later at Lititz. In 1811 he was elevated to the episcopate and transferred to the Southern Province of the Moravian Church at Salem. When he emigrated to the U.S. he brought with him a large number of musical MSS, this being the practice of those traveling to the American Moravian settlements. During the following years, in which he was a performing musician, composer, and teacher, he added to his collection, copying MSS brought from Europe by other Moravians, and music composed by American Moravians; altogether there are almost 12,000 pages in his hand, constituting the most extensive individual collection of 18th- and 19th-century Moravian (and non-Moravian) music in the U.S. The Herbst Collection is in the Archives of the Moravian Music Foundation in Winston-Salem, N.C., and is available on either microfiche or roll microfilm: A. 493 MS scores of about 1,000 vocal-instrumental pieces (Congregation Music); B. 45 MS scores or parts of larger vocal works by C.P.E. Bach, Mozart, Haydn, and others, including Herbst and other Moravians; C. 6 miscellaneous vols. of keyboard works, texts, etc.; the entire collection totals 11,676 pages. An itemized *Catalog of the Johannes Herbst Collection*, prepared by M. Gombosi, was publ. in Chapel Hill, N.C., in 1970 and includes a biographical sketch of Herbst and a short history of the collection. Herbst was the most prolific of all the American Moravian composers, having to his credit some 127 choral anthems and songs. Many of his works show him to have been a highly skilled musical craftsman.

BIBL.: A. Rau and H. David, *A Catalogue of Music by American Moravians* (Bethlehem, Pa., 1938); H. David, "Background for Bethlehem: Moravian Music in Pennsylvania," *Magazine of Art* (April 1939); idem, "Musical Life in the Pennsylvania Settlements of the Unitas Fratrum," *Transactions of the Moravian Historical Society* (1942; reprinted as Moravian Music Foundation Publication No. 6, 1959); D. McCorkle, *Moravian Music in Salem: A German-American Heritage* (diss., Indiana Univ., 1958); J. Falconer, *Bishop J. H. (1735–1812), An American Moravian Musician, Collector and Composer* (2 vols., diss., Columbia Univ., 1969).

Hercigonja, Nikola, Croatian composer; b. Vinkovcim, Feb. 19, 1911. He studied in Zagreb; in 1950 became a prof. of the Music Academy in Belgrade. In his music he follows a general trend of realistic composition, inspired by national folk songs.

WORKS: *Vječni Žid u Zagrebu* (The Wandering Jew in Zagreb), musical burlesque (1942); *Gorski vijenac* (Mountain Wreath), opera-oratorio (Belgrade, Oct. 19, 1957); *Planetarium*, scenic action for Voices, Speaking Chorus, and Orch. (1960); numerous choruses.

Herford (real name, **Goldstein**), **Julius,** German-American pianist, choral conductor, and pedagogue; b. Anklam, Feb. 21, 1901; d. Bloomington, Ind., Sept. 17, 1981. He studied at the Stern Cons. in Berlin; then pursued a rather successful career as a choral conductor and concert pianist. He emigrated to the U.S. in 1939 and devoted himself mainly to teaching; was on the faculty of Columbia Univ., the Juilliard School of Music, and Westminster Choir College. From 1964 to 1980 he was prof. of music at Indiana Univ. Among his students were Lukas Foss, Robert Shaw, and Robert Wagner. With H. Decker, he ed. *Choral Conducting* (1973; 2nd ed., rev., 1988, as *Choral Conducting Symposium*).

Herincx, Raimund (Frederick), English bass-baritone; b. London, Aug. 23, 1927, of Belgian parentage. He studied voice in Belgium and Italy; made his operatic debut in 1950 with the Welsh National Opera; then sang at the Sadler's Wells Opera (1957–66) and at Covent Garden (from 1968). He also made guest appearances in America.

Hering, Karl Gottlieb, German music pedagogue and composer; b. Bad Schandau, Oct. 25, 1765; d. Zittau, Jan. 4, 1853. He studied academic subjects at Leipzig Univ.; studied music with J.G. Schicht. In 1811 he was appointed music teacher at the Zittau seminary, and remained there until 1836, when he retired. He publ. *Praktisches Handbuch zur leichten Erlernung des Klavier-Spielens* (Halberstadt, 1796) and *Praktische Violin-Schule* (Leipzig, 1810); also compiled *Zittauer Choralbuch* (Leipzig, 1822) and other collections, including original compositions. Some of his pieces for children became celebrated in Germany and elsewhere, particularly *Steckenpferd* ("Hopp, hopp, hopp, Pferdchen lauf Galopp"), *Weihnachtsfreude* ("Morgen, Kinder, wird's was geben"), and (most famous of them all) *Grossvaterlied*, which was used by Schumann in his *Carnaval*.

BIBL.: L. Gelber, "K.G. H.," *Die Liederkomponisten* (Berlin, 1936).

Héritte-Viardot, Louise-Pauline-Marie, French voice teacher and composer, daughter of **Pauline Viardot-García;** b. Paris, Dec. 14, 1841; d. Heidelberg, Jan. 17, 1918. She was for many years a singing teacher at the St. Petersburg Cons.; then taught in Frankfurt, Berlin, and Heidelberg. She was also a composer; her opera *Lindoro* was performed in Weimar (1879); she further wrote the cantatas *Das Bacchusfest* (Stockholm, 1880) and *Le Feu de ciel;* some chamber music; and vocal exercises. Her memoirs (tr. from the original German) were publ. in Eng. as *Memories and Adventures* (London, 1913).

Herman, Jerry (Gerald), American composer and lyricist of popular music; b. N.Y., July 10, 1933. He played piano by ear; it was only after becoming a professional musician that he took up the study of theory and harmony; he also studied drama at the Univ. of Miami. He worked as a pianist in nightclubs and wrote for television in N.Y.; composed the revues *I Feel Wonderful* (1954), *Nightcap* (1958), and *Parade* (1960); then won a Tony Award for his Broadway show *Milk and Honey* (1961). After the failure of *Madame Aphrodite* (1961), he came roaring back with the smash hit *Hello, Dolly!* (N.Y., Jan. 16, 1964), which garnered 10 Tony Awards. It was followed by another highly successful score, *Mame* (N.Y., May 24, 1966), which also won a Tony. Following the non-success of *Dear World* (1969), *Mack & Mabel* (1974), and *The Grand Tour* (1979), he again won a Tony with the wonderfully eccentric *La Cage aux folles* (1983).

Herman, Vasile, Rumanian composer; b. Satu-Mare, June 10, 1929. He studied piano in his hometown, and composition with Demian, Toduță, and Comes at the Cluj Cons. (1949–57); subsequently was appointed to its staff. His music is cautiously modernistic, with occasional overflow into aleatoric indeterminacy.

WORKS: ORCH.: *Variante* for 2 Clarinets, Piano, and Percussion (1963–64); *4 Ritornele* (1964); *Cantilații* (1967); *Polifonie* for 7 Instrumental Groups (1968); *Episoade* (1968); *Postludiu* (1971); *Syntagma I* for 14 Instruments and Piano (1971); Double Concerto for Flute, Oboe, and Orch. (1973); *Simfoniisi fantezii* (1974–75); 3 syms.: No. 1 (1976); No. 2, *Memorandum* (1980); No. 3, *Metamorfoze* (1982); *Unison* (1977–78); Concerto for String Orch. (1979); Concertino for Trombone, Double Bass, and Orch. (1981). VOCAL: 6 cantatas (1969, 1970, 1974, 1977, 1980, 1983); songs. CHAMBER: 2 string quartets: No. 1, *Omagiu lui Enescu* (1971); No. 2, *Refrene* (1977); *Sonata-Baladă* for Oboe and Piano (1961); *Triptic* for Violin (1964); *Melopee* for Flute (1965); Sonata for Flute and Piano (1965–66); *Aforisme* for Oboe and Piano (1970); *3 Pieces* for Violin and Piano (1974); *Syntagma II* for Chamber Ensemble (1975); *Monofonii* for Oboe (1975); Trio for Violin, Cello, and Piano (1979); *Neanes* for Chamber Ensemble (1979); *Sonata de camera* for Flute, Oboe, Cello, and Harpsichord (1981); *Panrhytmicon* for 5 Percussion Groups (1982). PIANO: 2 sonatas: No. 1, *Sonata da ricercar* (1958); No. 2 (1967); *Partita* (1961); *Microforme* (1965); *Grafică* for 1 or 2 Pianos (1969); etc.

Herman, Woody (Woodrow Charles), noted American clarinetist, saxophonist, and bandleader; b. Milwaukee, May 16, 1913; d. Los Angeles, Oct. 29, 1987. He studied at Marquette Univ. In 1931 he joined a jazz band as a clarinet player, and in 1937 formed his 1st band; had several thereafter, most called "Herds"; i.e., the 1st Herd, 2nd Herd, etc. In the mid-1940s Herman's was the 1st prominent big band to make the transition from swing to a more advanced, bebop-influenced idiom characterized by "progressive" harmonies; it became known as "progressive jazz." On March 25, 1946, he presented in Carnegie Hall in N.Y. the 1st performance of Stravinsky's *Ebony Concerto*, written specially for him. He also composed popular songs. With S. Troup, he wrote *The Woodchopper's Ball: The Autobiography of Woody Herman* (N.Y., 1990).

BIBL.: E. Edwards, *W. H. and the Swinging Herd, 1959–*

1966 (Los Angeles, 1966); J. Treichel, *W. H.: The Second Herd* (Spottswood, N.J., 1980).

Hermann, Hans, German composer; b. Leipzig, Aug. 17, 1870; d. Berlin, May 18, 1931. He studied with W. Rust in Leipzig, E. Kretschmer in Dresden, and H. von Herzogenberg in Berlin; from the age of 18, played the double bass in various European orchs.; then taught at the Klindworth-Scharwenka Cons. in Berlin (1901–7). He publ. some 100 songs, of which several became fairly well known (*Drei Wanderer, Alte Landsknechte,* etc.); he had a flair for imitating the simple style of the folk ballad; he further wrote a Sym., *Lebensepisoden;* a stage work, *Der rote Pimpernell;* pieces for clarinet with piano; etc.

Hermann, Robert, Swiss composer; b. Bern, April 29, 1869; d. Ambach, Bavaria, Oct. 22, 1912. He studied in Frankfurt; as a youth, developed an original approach to composition; he met Grieg, who encouraged him; studied briefly with Humperdinck; his Sym. was performed by the Berlin Phil. (Nov. 7, 1895), and other works followed.
  BIBL.: W. Niemann, "R. H.," *Monographien Moderner Musiker,* III (Leipzig, 1909).

Hermannus (surnamed **Contractus** on account of his paralyzed limbs), Swabian theoretician and composer; b. Saulgau, July 18, 1013; d. Altshausen, near Biberach, Sept. 24, 1054. He was the son of Hermann, Count of Vehringen. He was a student in the Reichenau monastery; under the guidance of his tutor, Abbot Berno, he acquired wide learning. In 1043 he entered the Benedictine order. His best-known work (containing valuable historical notices on music) is a chronology from the time of Christ to 1054. It has been republ. several times, and is to be found in Peres's (Pertz's) *Monumenta* (vol. V). Hermannus was the author of *Opuscula musica,* in which he gives a thorough discussion of the church modes and criticizes the Daseian notation used in the 10th-century tract *Musica enchiriadis.* He proposed his own notation by Greek and Latin letters. In the indication of a change in pitch, it had an advantage over neume notation. His notation is written above the neume notation in some MSS of the 11th and 12th centuries in the Munich Library. The sequence *Grates, honis, hierarchia* and an office for St. Afra, *Glorioso et beatissima,* are the only compositions which have been definitely established as being by Hermannus. L. Ellinwood ed. *Musica Hermanni Contracti* (Rochester, N.Y., 1936), which gives the Latin text (prepared from the Vienna MS and an 11th-century MS at the Eastman School of Music in Rochester, N.Y.), an Eng. tr., and commentary.
  BIBL.: W. Brambach, *Hermanni Contracti Musica* (Leipzig, 1884); H. Oesch, *Berno und Hermann von Reichenau als Musiktheoretiker* (Bern, 1961); R. Crocker, "Hermann's Major Sixth," *Journal of the American Musicological Society* (Spring 1972).

Hermanson, Åke (Oscar Werner), Swedish composer, pianist, and organist; b. Mollösund, June 16, 1923. He studied piano and organ in Göteborg and Stockholm; took courses in composition with Hilding Rosenberg (1950–52). He was chairman of the Swedish Soc. of Composers (1967–71). In his music he follows a type of concentrated brevity marked by an alternation of short contrasting motifs; he defines this usage as "pendulum dynamics."
  WORKS: *Lyrical Metamorphoses* for String Quartet (1954–57); *A due voci* for Flute and Viola (1957–58); *Invoco* for Strings (1958–60); *Norrköping,* May 24, 1961); *Stadier* for Soprano, Flute, Bass Clarinet, Viola, and Percussion (1960–61); *Suoni d'un flauto* for Alto Flute (1961); *In nuce* (In a Nutshell) for Orch. (1962–63; the title is justified, for the piece takes barely 3 minutes to play; Stockholm, Oct. 9, 1964); *Nenia bahusiensis* for Children's Chorus a cappella (1963); Sym. No. 1 (1964–67; Stockholm, Oct. 29, 1967); *Appel I–IV* for Orch. (1968–69; 1st complete perf., Swedish Radio, Dec. 12, 1970); *Alarme* for Horn (1969); *In sono* for Flute, Oboe or English Horn, Viola, and Cello (1970); *Ultima* for Orch. (1971–72; Swedish Radio, Nov. 18, 1972); *Flauto d'inverno* for Bass Flute (1976);

Sym. No. 2 (1973–75; Stockholm, Sept. 26, 1976); *Ars lineae* for 6 Wind Instruments (1976); *Utopia* for Orch. (1977–78); *Thrice* for Oboe, Clarinet, and Trombone (1976–79); *Bild* for Tenor and Trombone (1978–79); *Äggjakten* for Narrator, Tenor Saxophone, Guitar, and Percussion (1979); Sym. No. 3 (1980); *La Strada* for Horn and Organ (1979–80); String Quartet (1982–83); Sym. No. 4, *Oceanus* (1981–84; Stockholm, Dec. 19, 1984).

Hermesdorff, Michael, German organist, musicologist, and composer; b. Trier, March 4, 1833; d. there, Jan. 1885. He entered the priesthood, and was appointed organist of Trier Cathedral. He founded the Choral Soc., chiefly for the exposition of Gregorian plainchant, on which he was an authority by virtue of his study of original sources. He ed. the *Graduale ad usum Romanum cantus S. Gregorii* (Leipzig, 1876–82, 10 nos.) in the monthly supplements of the *Cäcilia* journal, but died before its completion. He publ. a *Kyriale; Harmonica cantus choralis a* 4; a *Graduale;* several anthems and *Praefatio* (prayers used in the Trier diocese); and 3 masses of his own.

Hermstedt, (Johann) Simon, famous German clarinetist; b. Langensalza, Dec. 29, 1778; d. Sondershausen, Aug. 10, 1846. He was educated at the Annaberg school for soldiers' children; studied with Knoblauch and Baer; was a court musician in Sondershausen. He made improvements in his instrument; composed concertos, variations, and other pieces for clarinet. Spohr wrote a Clarinet Concerto for him.

Hernández, Hermilio, Mexican composer; b. Autlán, Jalisco, Feb. 2, 1931. He studied music with José Valadez and Domingo Lobato at the Escuela Superior Diocesana de Música Sagrada in Guadalajara, graduating in 1956; then studied in Italy and Paris.
  WORKS: *Cantata Adviento* (1953); *5 Pieces* for Orch. (1955); Violin Concerto (1960); *Sonata* for Chamber Orch. (1964); *Suite* for Violin and Piano (1952); String Quartet (1954); Piano Trio (1955); Cello Sonata (1962); Wind Quintet (1965); *Poliédros* for Oboe, Bassoon, and Piano (1969); *Music for 4 Instruments* for Flute, Violin, Cello, and Piano (1970); 2 piano sonatinas (1955, 1971); *Tema transfigurado* for Piano (1962); *6 Inventions* for Piano (1968); Piano Sonata (1970); *Diálogos* for 2 Pianos (1970); *Fantasia* for Organ (1970); songs.

Hernández-López, Rhazés, Venezuelan composer and musicologist; b. Petare, June 30, 1918. He studied in Caracas with Vicente Emilio Sojo and Juan Bautista Plaza. Apart from composition, he engaged in teaching and radio work. In his series of piano pieces *Casualismo,* he applies the 12-tone method of composition. Other works include *Las Torres desprevenidas,* symphonic poem (1951); *Sonorritmo* for Orch. (1953); *Mérida, geografía celeste,* symphonic suite (1958); *Expansión tres* for Orch. (1965); *Tres dimensiones* for Strings (1967); *Cuadros* for Flute, Violin, Viola, Cello, and Harp (1950); Viola Sonata (1952); *Tres espacios* for Violin, Cello, and Piano (1965); *Horizontal* for Flute and Strings (1966); piano pieces; songs.

Hernández Moncada, Eduardo, Mexican conductor and composer; b. Jalapa, Sept. 24, 1899. He studied with Rafael Tello at the National Cons. in Mexico City. He conducted theater orchs.; in 1933 became assistant conductor of the Orquesta Sinfónica in Mexico; then was conductor of the Sym. Orch. of the National Cons. (1947–49). As a composer he made an impression with his Sym., 1st performed in Mexico City (July 31, 1942). His ballet *Ixtepec* (1945) employs Mexican rhythms.

Hernández Sales, Pablo, Spanish composer; b. Saragossa, Jan. 25, 1834; d. Madrid, Dec. 10, 1910. He was 1st a church chorister; at 14 played organ at the San Gil church in Saragossa. At 22 he went to Madrid to study with Eslava at the Madrid Cons.; graduated with a gold medal (1861), and joined the faculty in 1863 as a singing teacher. He wrote 2 zarzuelas: *Gimnasio higienico* and *Un Sevillano en la Habana;* also many sacred works.

Hernándo (y Palomar), Rafael (José María), Spanish composer; b. Madrid, May 31, 1822; d. there, July 10, 1888. He studied with Carnicer, Saldoni, and P. Albéniz at the Madrid Cons. (1837–43); then went to Paris, where he took lessons with Auber. His *Stabat Mater* was performed there, and a grand opera, *Romilda*, was accepted for performance at the Théâtre des Italiens, but the revolutionary upheaval of 1848 prevented its production. Hernándo returned to Madrid, where he produced a number of zarzuelas, of which the most successful was *El duende* (June 6, 1849); others were *Palo de ciego* (Feb. 15, 1849); *Colegialas y soldados* (March 21, 1849); *Bertoldo y Comparsa* (May 23, 1850); *Cosas de Juan* (Sept. 9, 1854); *El tambor* (April 28, 1860); *Aurora*; etc.; he also collaborated with Barbieri, Oudrid, and Gaztambide in *Escenas de Chamberí* (Nov. 19, 1850) and *Don Simplicio Bobadilla* (May 7, 1853). In 1852 he became secretary of the Madrid Cons.; also taught harmony there.

Hernried, Robert (Franz Richard), Austrian-born American musicologist and composer; b. Vienna, Sept. 22, 1883; d. Detroit, Sept. 3, 1951. He studied at the Univ. of Vienna; conducted opera at provincial theaters (1908–14); taught theory at the Mannheim Academy of Music (1919–22), at the Heidelberg Cons. (1923), in Erfurt, and at the Stern Cons. in Berlin. In 1934 he went to Vienna; in 1939, to the U.S.; he taught in N.Y., in Davenport, Iowa, in Dickinson, N.Dak., and in Fort Wayne, Ind. In 1946 he became a prof. of music at the Detroit Inst. of Musical Art. He publ. a monograph on Jaques-Dalcroze (Geneva, 1929); a biography of Brahms (Leipzig, 1934); and 2 theoretical works, *Allgemeine Musiklehre* (Berlin, 1932) and *Systematische Modulationslehre* (Berlin, 1935; 2nd ed., 1948). He wrote 2 operas, *Francesca da Rimini* and *Die Bäuerin;* about 75 choral works; a Mass; some characteristic pieces for orch.; etc.

Hérold, (Louis-Joseph) Ferdinand, celebrated French composer; b. Paris, Jan. 28, 1791; d. Thernes, near Paris, Jan. 19, 1833. His father, **François-Joseph Hérold** (b. Seltz, Bas-Rhin, March 18, 1755; d. Paris, Oct. 1, 1802; pupil of C.P.E. Bach), a piano teacher and composer, did not desire his son to become a musician, and sent him to the Hix school, where his aptitude for music was noticed by Fétis, then assistant teacher there. After his father's death, Hérold began to study music seriously; in 1806 he entered the Paris Cons., taking piano lessons with Louis Adam, and winning 1st prize for piano playing in 1810. He studied harmony under Catel, and (from 1811) composition under Méhul; in 1812 his cantata *Mlle. de la Vallière* won the Prix de Rome. From Rome he went to Naples, where he became pianist to Queen Caroline; he produced his 1st opera, *La gioventù di Enrico Quinto* (Jan. 5, 1815), which was well received. From Naples he went to Vienna, and after a few months' stay returned to Paris, where he brought out the score of Boieldieu's *Charles de France,* an "opéra d'occasion" (Opéra-Comique, June 18, 1816), and where all the rest of his operas were produced. The flattering reception of *Charles de France* led to the successful production of *Les Rosières* (Jan. 27, 1817), *La Clochette* (Oct. 18, 1817), *Le Premier Venu* (Sept. 28, 1818), *Les Troqueurs* (Feb. 18, 1819), and *L'Auteur mort et vivant* (Dec. 18, 1820); the failure of the last-named opera caused him to distrust his natural talent, and to imitate, in several succeeding stage works, the style then in vogue—that of Rossini. With the comic opera *Marie* (Aug. 12, 1826) Hérold returned, however, to his true element, and won instant and brilliant success. Meantime he had obtained the post of chorus master at the Italian Opera (1824); during this period he brought out *Le Muletier* (May 12, 1823), *Lasthénie* (Sept. 8, 1823), *Vendôme en Espagne* (Dec. 5, 1823), *Le Roi René* (Aug. 24, 1824), and *Le Lapin blanc* (May 21, 1825). In 1826 he was appointed to the staff of the Grand Opéra, for which he wrote several melodious and elegant ballets: *Astolphe et Jaconde* (Jan. 29, 1827); *La Somnambule* (Sept. 19, 1827); *Lydie* (July 2, 1828); *La Fille mal gardée* (Nov. 17, 1828); *La Belle au bois dormant* (April 27, 1829); *La Noce de village* (Feb. 11, 1830). *La Somnambule* furnished Bellini with the subject of his popular opera. On July 18, 1829, Hérold produced *L'Illusion,* a 1-act opera full of charming numbers.

Emmeline, a grand opera (Nov. 28, 1829), was a failure, but his next opera, *Zampa* (May 3, 1831), was sensationally successful and placed him in the 1st rank of French composers. He then wrote *L'Auberge d'Aurey* (May 11, 1830) jointly with Carafa; *La Marquise de Brinvilliers* (Oct. 31, 1831) in collaboration with Auber, Batton, Berton, Blangini, Boieldieu, Carafa, Cherubini, and Paër; also produced *La Médecine sans médecin* (Oct. 15, 1832). His last completed work, *Le Pré aux clercs* (Dec. 15, 1832), had a remarkable vogue. He died of tuberculosis shortly before his 42nd birthday. His unfinished opera *Ludovic* was completed by Halévy and produced posthumously at the Opéra-Comique on May 16, 1833. Hérold's piano music (55 opus numbers) consists of sonatas, caprices, rondos, divertissements, fantasies, variations, and potpourris.

BIBL.: B. Jouvin, *H., Sa vie et ses œuvres* (Paris, 1868); A. Pougin, *H.* (Paris, 1906).

Herold, Vilhelm (Kristoffer), Danish tenor; b. Hasle, March 19, 1865; d. Copenhagen, Dec. 15, 1937. He studied in Copenhagen and Paris; made his debut at the Royal Danish Theater in Copenhagen in 1893 as Faust; was a member of the Royal Theater in Stockholm (1901–3; 1907–9); also made guest appearances in London, Berlin, Dresden, and Hamburg. He served as director of Copenhagen's Royal Theater (1922–24).

Herrera de la Fuente, Luis, Mexican conductor and composer; b. Mexico City, April 26, 1916. He studied piano and violin; took composition lessons with Rodolfo Halffter. From 1955 to 1972 he served as principal conductor of the National Sym. Orch. in Mexico City; in the interim he led the National Sym. Orch. of Peru (1965–71); was guest conductor of orchs. in the U.S., Canada, Europe, and New Zealand; from 1978 to 1988 was music director of the Oklahoma Sym. Orch. in Oklahoma City.

WORKS: Opera, *Cuauhtemoc;* ballets, *La Estrella y la Sirena* and *Fronteras.*

Herreweghe, Philippe, esteemed Belgian conductor; b. Ghent, May 2, 1947. He received instruction in piano from Marcel Gazelle, in organ from Gabriel Verschraegen, and in harpsichord from Johan Huys at the Ghent Cons.; he also took courses in medicine at the Univ. there before turning decisively to music. In 1977 he organized in Paris the Ensemble Vocal de l'Orch. de la Chapelle Royale, which acquired an international reputation. He also appeared as a guest conductor throughout Europe and North America. In his repertoire he emphasizes works of the great masters from the Renaissance to the 19th century.

Herrmann, Bernard, American conductor and outstanding composer for films; b. N.Y., June 29, 1911; d. Los Angeles, Dec. 24, 1975. He won a composition prize at the age of 13; then enrolled at N.Y. Univ., where he studied with Philip James and Percy Grainger; later took courses with Wagenaar in composition and Albert Stoessel in conducting at the Juilliard Graduate School of Music. In 1934 he was appointed to the staff of CBS as a composer of background music for radio programs and conductor of the CBS Sym. Orch. summer radio series; from 1942 to 1959 he was chief conductor of the CBS Sym. Orch. in boldly progressive programs of modern works, including those by Charles Ives. He became associated with Orson Welles and wrote several scores for the radio broadcasts of the Mercury Theater. His music for *Citizen Kane* (1940), the 1st of his 61 film scores, is still regarded as a classic of the genre. His use of an electric violin and electric bass in the score for *The Day the Earth Stood Still* (1951) is an example of early application of electronic music in films. He subsequently wrote film scores for the thrillers of Alfred Hitchcock, succeeding in capturing the eerie spirit of Hitchcock's peculiar art by the use of atonal devices; of these, the score for *Psycho* (1960), for strings only, was particularly apt. Among Herrmann's other film scores were *The Devil and Daniel Webster* (1941; also known as *All That Money Can Buy);* received an Academy Award); *Jane Eyre* (1942); *Anna and the King of Siam* (1946); *The Ghost and Mrs. Muir* (1948); *Snows of Kilimanjaro* (1952); *Garden of Evil* (1954); *The Trouble with Harry*

(1955); *The Man Who Knew Too Much* (1956); *The Wrong Man* (1957); *Vertigo* (1958); *North by Northwest* (1959); *The Man in the Gray Flannel Suit* (1956); *The 7th Voyage of Sinbad* (1958); *Journey to the Center of the Earth* (1959); *The Birds* (1963); *Fahrenheit 451* (1966); *La Mariée était en noir* (The Bride Wore Black; 1967); *Sisters* (1973); and *Obsession* (1975). Herrmann spent the last 10 years of his life in England, but was in Los Angeles in Dec. 1975 to conduct the score for his last film, *Taxi Driver;* he died in his sleep shortly after completing the final recording session. His other works include the opera *Wuthering Heights* (1941–50; recorded in England in 1966; 1st complete stage perf., Portland, Oreg., Nov. 6, 1982); 2 Christmas operas for television: *A Christmas Carol* (CBS Television, N.Y., Dec. 23, 1954) and *A Child Is Born;* 2 cantatas: *Moby Dick* (N.Y., April 11, 1940) and *Johnny Appleseed* (1940); *The City of Brass,* symphonic poem (1934); *Sinfonietta* for Strings (1935); *Currier and Ives,* suite (1935); *Nocturne and Scherzo* (1936); *Fiddle Concerto* (1940); Sym. No. 1 (1940; N.Y., Nov. 12, 1942); *For the Fallen* (N.Y., Dec. 16, 1943, composer conducting); *The Fantasticks* for Vocal Quartet and Orch. (1944); String Quartet (1932); *Aubade* for 14 Instruments (1933); *Echoes* for String Quartet (1966); clarinet quintet, *Souvenirs de Voyage* (1967).

Herrmann, Eduard, German-American violinist, conductor, and composer; b. Oberrotweil, Dec. 18, 1850; d. Miami, Fla., April 24, 1937. He studied violin with Joachim in Berlin; played in various German orchs.; from 1878 to 1881 he was concertmaster of the Imperial Orch. in St. Petersburg. In 1881 he settled in N.Y.; formed a quartet with Schenck, Lilienthal, and Hauser, which enjoyed an excellent reputation; 1 of their features was the annual performance of all of Beethoven's quartets. He wrote a Violin Concerto; String Quintet; String Quartet; Sextet for Oboe, Clarinet, and Strings; etc.

Herrmann, Hugo, German composer; b. Ravensburg, April 19, 1896; d. Stuttgart, Sept. 7, 1967. He acquired primary knowledge of music without systematic study; was drafted into the German army during World War I and severely wounded in 1918. After the Armistice he took courses in composition with Schreker and Gmeindl in Berlin. In 1923 he went to the U.S. and was employed as a church organist; in 1925 he returned to Germany; from 1935 to 1962 he was director of a music school in Trossingen. A believer in practical art, he promoted community music; took especial interest in the accordion and wrote several works for this instrument; he also composed pieces for the mouth organ. He wrote several operas: *Gazellenhorn; Picknick; Vasantasena; Das Wunder; Paracelsus; Der Rekord; Der Überfall; Die Heinzelmännchen;* 5 syms.; 5 string quartets; etc. He publ. a manual, *Einführung in die Satztechnik für Mundharmonika-Instrumente* (Trossingen, 1958), containing instructions for performance on the mouth organ.

BIBL.: A. Fett, ed., *H. H., Leben und Werk* (Trossingen, 1956).

Herschel, Sir (Frederick) William (Friedrich Wilhelm), eminent German-born English astronomer, violinist, organist, and composer; b. Hannover, Nov. 15, 1738; d. Slough, near Windsor, Aug. 25, 1822. The son of a military musician, he was brought up to be a musician; he became an oboist and violinist in the regimental Hannoverian band at age 14 and was sent with it to Durham in 1755. He became director of the Leeds subscription concerts in 1762; was organist at Halifax Parish Church (1766) and at Octagon Chapel, Bath (1766–82). Long interested in astronomy, he constructed the great "Herschel" telescope, which led to his discovery of the planet Uranus in 1781. He subsequently abandoned music and was made "Astronomer Royal" to King George III in 1781. He became a British citizen in 1802, and was knighted in 1816. Among his compositions are 24 syms., a number of concertos, chamber music, organ pieces, and sacred works, including many anthems.

Herseth, Adolph, outstanding American trumpeter; b. Lake Park, Minn., July 25, 1921. He studied with Marcel LaFosse

and Georges Mager in Boston (1946–48); in 1948 he was appointed 1st trumpeter of the Chicago Sym. Orch., a position he held with distinction for more than 40 years. He also made many appearances as a soloist, as in the premiere of Husa's Trumpet Concerto (Chicago, Feb. 11, 1988), and was active as a teacher.

Hertel, Johann Wilhelm, distinguished German violinist, harpsichordist, and composer; b. Eisenach, Oct. 9, 1727; d. Schwerin, June 14, 1789. His father, **Johann Christian Hertel** (b. Oettingen, 1699; d. Strelitz, Oct. 1754), was an accomplished violist and composer. Johann Wilhelm studied with J.H. Heil; began touring as harpsichord accompanist to his father when he was 12; after violin studies with Carl Höckh in Zerbst, he served as violinist and harpsichordist at the Strelitz court (1744–53); also studied with Franz Benda in Berlin; then was court composer in Schwerin from 1754. He wrote much vocal music, including masses, Passions, sacred and secular cantatas, and lieder; he also composed syms. and keyboard concertos. Between 1752 and 1784 he wrote 2 autobiographical accounts of his life; they were ed. and publ. by E. Schenk (Graz and Cologne, 1957).

Hertog, Johannes den, Dutch conductor and composer; b. Amsterdam, Jan. 20, 1904. He studied with his father, Herman Johannes den Hertog; then with Cornelis Dopper. He was director and conductor of the Wagner Soc. in Amsterdam; from 1938 to 1941 was assistant conductor of the Concertgebouw Orch.; also conducted at The Hague; in 1948 he was appointed conductor of the Flemish Opera in Antwerp, and from 1960 to 1965 was artistic director of the Netherlands Opera in Amsterdam. He wrote an opera, *Pygmalion* (1957); a musical play, *Pandora* (1968); a number of songs; some orch. pieces.

Hertz, Alfred, eminent German-born American conductor; b. Frankfurt am Main, July 15, 1872; d. San Francisco, April 17, 1942. After completing his academic studies, he entered the Hoch Cons. in Frankfurt, where he studied with Anton Urspruch; then held positions as an opera conductor in Halle (1891–92), Altenburg (1892–95), Barmen-Elberfeld (1895–99), and Breslau (1899–1902). In 1902 he was engaged as conductor of the German repertoire at the Metropolitan Opera in N.Y.; he conducted the 1st American performance of *Parsifal* (Dec. 24, 1903), which took place against the wishes of the Wagner family; consequently, Hertz could no longer obtain permission to conduct Wagner in Germany. He made his Covent Garden debut in London in 1910. From 1915 to 1930 he led the San Francisco Sym. Orch.; also founded the summer series of concerts at the Hollywood Bowl (1922), and conducted more than 100 concerts there; he was affectionately known as the "Father of the Hollywood Bowl." His autobiography was publ. in the *San Francisco Chronicle* (May 3–14, 1942).

BIBL.: J. Toczek, "A. H.," *Le Grand Baton* (June 1981).

Hertzka, Emil, Austrian music publisher; b. Budapest, Aug. 3, 1869; d. Vienna, May 9, 1932. He was engaged on the staff of the music publisher Weinberger in Vienna (1893); then joined Universal Edition in 1901. In 1907 he became its director, and remained in that capacity until his death. He purchased the catalogs of the Wiener Philharmonischer Verlag and the Albert J. Gutmann Co. (which publ. Bruckner and Mahler), and acquired the publication rights to works by many celebrated modern composers (Bartók, Schoenberg, Berg, Weill, Krenek); also represented Soviet composers. An impassioned believer in the eventual worth of experimental music, he encouraged young composers, took active part in the organization of concerts of modern music, etc. An Emil Hertzka Foundation was established by his family after his death, for the purpose of helping unknown composers secure performances and publication of their works.

Hertzmann, Erich, German-American musicologist; b. Krefeld, Dec. 14, 1902; d. Berkeley, Calif., March 3, 1963. He studied at the Hoch Cons. in Frankfurt; then took courses with several eminent teachers (J. Wolf, Abert, Schering, Sachs,

Hornbostel, and Friedrich Blume) at the Univ. of Berlin, where he obtained his doctorate with a dissertation on Willaert (1931). In 1938 he emigrated to the U.S., and joined the faculty of Columbia Univ.; also lectured at Princeton Univ. (1946–49). In 1949 he held a Guggenheim fellowship; in 1955 received a stipend from Columbia Univ. to study the creative processes of Beethoven. Apart from his dissertation, he publ. numerous articles in German and American music journals, mostly dealing with structural analysis of classical scores.

Hervé (real name, **Florimond Ronger**), French organist, singer, and composer; b. Houdain, near Arras, June 30, 1825; d. Paris, Nov. 3, 1892. He was a chorister at St.-Roch; then studied with Elwart at the Paris Cons.; became organist at various churches in Paris. In 1848 he sang in *Don Quichotte et Sancho Pansa*, an interlude of his own composition, at the Opéra National. In 1851 he conducted at the Palais Royal; in 1854 he opened the Folies-Concertantes, a small theater for the production of pantomimes, *saynètes* (musical comediettas for 2 persons), etc., and, with phenomenal activity, he developed the light French operetta from these diminutive and frivolous pieces, writing both librettos and music, conducting the orch., and often appearing as an actor on the stage. From 1856 to 1869 he led this feverish life in Paris, producing his works at various theaters, and responding to failures by doubling his efforts. In 1870–71, when the Franco-Prussian War and the Commune stopped theatrical activities in Paris, he went to London, where he produced several of his light operas; he revisited London many times afterward; was music director of the Empire Theater there from 1886. He wrote about 50 operettas, of which only 1 became a universal success, *Mam'zelle Nitouche* (Paris, Jan. 26, 1883, followed by numerous productions in European cities); other fairly successful works were *L'Œil crevé* (Paris, Oct. 12, 1867) and *Le Petit Faust* (Paris, April 28, 1869). He also wrote a grand opera, *Les Chevaliers de la table ronde* (Paris, Nov. 17, 1866); the ballets *Sport, La Rose d'Amour, Les Bagatelles*, etc. **BIBL.:** L. Schneider, *Les Maîtres de l'opérette française, H. et Charles Lecocq* (Paris, 1924).

Hervey, Arthur, Irish writer on music and composer; b. Paris, Jan. 26, 1855; d. London, March 10, 1922. At 1st intended for the diplomatic service, he embraced a musical career in 1880; was a critic for *Vanity Fair* (1889–92); then was on the staff of the London *Morning Post* (1892–1908). **WRITINGS** (all publ. in London): *Masters of French Music* (1894); *French Music in the XIXth Century* (1904); *Alfred Bruneau* (1907); *Franz Liszt and His Music* (1911); *Meyerbeer* (1913); *Rubinstein* (1913); *Saint-Saëns* (1921).

Hervig, Richard (Bilderback), American composer; b. Story City, Iowa, Nov. 24, 1917. He studied composition with Philip Greeley Clapp at the Univ. of Iowa (M.A., 1941; Ph.D., 1947). He taught at the Univ. of Iowa (1947–52), Long Beach State College (1952–55), and the Univ. of Iowa School of Music (from 1955), where he also was co-director of its Center for New Music (1966–84). He wrote 2 syms. (1947, 1960); 2 clarinet sonatas (1953, 1971); a Violin Sonata (1979); *Airs and Roulades* for Clarinet and Wind Ensemble (1983); *The Tree* for 9 Instruments (1984); *Epitaph* for Chorus (1985).

Herz, Henri (actually, **Heinrich**), famous Austrian pianist, teacher, and composer; b. Vienna, Jan. 6, 1803; d. Paris, Jan. 5, 1888. He was taught by his father, and by Hünten at Coblenz; later (1816) by Pradher, Reicha, and Dourlen at the Paris Cons.; he won 1st piano prize; improved himself in Moscheles's style after that virtuoso's visit in 1821; was in high repute as a fashionable teacher and composer, his compositions realizing 3 and 4 times the price of those of his superior contemporaries. In 1831 he made a tour of Germany with the violinist Lafont; visited London in 1834, where at his 1st concert Moscheles and Cramer played duets with him. From 1842 to 1874 he was a piano prof. at the Paris Cons. He suffered financial losses through partnership with a piano manufacturer, Klepfer,

and thereupon undertook a concert tour through the U.S., Mexico, and the West Indies (1845–51). He then established a successful piano factory, his instruments receiving 1st prize at the Paris Exhibition of 1855. As a composer, he acknowledged that he courted the popular taste; his numerous works (over 200) include piano concertos, variations, sonatas, rondos, nocturnes, dances, marches, fantasias, etc. He publ. an interesting and vivid book, *Mes voyages en Amérique* (1866), a reprint of his letters to the *Moniteur Universel.* **BIBL.:** A. Loesser, *Men, Women, and Pianos* (N.Y., 1954); H. Schonberg, *The Great Pianists* (N.Y., 1963; 2nd ed., rev., 1987); R. Lott, *The American Concert Tours of Leopold de Myer, H. H., and Sigismond Thalberg* (diss., City Univ. of N.Y., 1986).

Herz, Joachim, German opera producer and administrator; b. Dresden, June 15, 1924. He was educated at the Hochschule für Musik in Dresden; also studied in Berlin. From 1953 to 1956 he was assistant producer to Walter Felsenstein at the Berlin Komische Oper. In 1957 he joined the Leipzig Opera as producer; from 1959 to 1976 was its director. In 1976 he was named director of the Berlin Komische Oper. From 1981 he was chief producer at the Dresden State Opera. With Walter Felsenstein, he wrote the book *Musiktheater: Beiträge zur Methodik und zu Inszenierungskonzeptionen* (Leipzig, 1976). **BIBL.:** H.-J. Irmer and W. Stein, *J. H., Regisseur im Musiktheater* (Berlin, 1977).

Herzog, Emilie, Swiss soprano; b. Ermatingen, Dec. 17, 1859; d. Aarburg, Sept. 16, 1923. She studied in Zürich and Munich; made her debut in a minor role at the Munich Court Opera in 1880, and afterward sang in other German opera houses, including Bayreuth. In 1889 she was engaged at the Berlin Royal Opera, where she became one of the best interpreters of soubrette roles; she also gave recitals in Germany as a lieder artist. She made guest appearances in the opera houses of London, Paris, Vienna, and Brussels, and in 1896 sang at the Bolshoi Theater in Moscow; she made her Metropolitan Opera debut in N.Y. as a Flower Maiden in *Parsifal* on Nov. 24, 1904. Returning to Europe, she continued to sing at the Berlin Royal Opera (until 1910); then taught at the Zürich Cons. (1910–22).

Herzog, George, Hungarian-born American ethnomusicologist; b. Budapest, Dec. 11, 1901; d. Indianapolis, Nov. 4, 1983. He studied musicology and anthropology in Budapest and Berlin; in 1925 he went to America; became a research associate in anthropology at the Univ. of Chicago in 1929; was a member (1930–31) of its expedition to Liberia, where he made a thorough study of West African music; then was on the faculty of Yale Univ. (1932–35); was a visiting lecturer at Columbia Univ. in 1936–37, and took his Ph.D. there in 1937; subsequently was a visiting assistant prof. there (1937–38), and then an assistant prof. of anthropology (1939–48). In 1948 he was appointed prof. of anthropology and folk music at Indiana Univ. in Bloomington; was made prof. emeritus in 1962. He publ. *Research in Primitive and Folk Music in the United States: A Survey* (Washington, D.C., 1936). **BIBL.:** B. Krader, "G. H.: A Bibliography," *Ethnomusicology Newsletter,* 1 (1956).

Herzog, Johann Georg, German organist, pedagogue, and composer; b. Hummendorf, near Kronach, Aug. 5, 1822; d. Munich, Feb. 3, 1909. He studied at the music school in Schmölz, in Bavaria, and at the age of 11 began to earn a living playing the organ. In 1843 he went to Munich, where he was a church organist, and later (from 1850) a prof. at the Cons.; among his pupils was Rheinberger. In 1854 he went to Erlangen; established a series of historical organ concerts there (1861–65); then returned to Munich. He wrote a great number of organ works; also practical manuals. **BIBL.:** M. Herzog, *Erinnerungen an Dr. J.G. H.* (Munich, 1915).

Herzogenberg, (Leopold) Heinrich (Picot de Peccaduc), Freiherr von, Austrian composer; b. Graz, June 10, 1843;

d. Wiesbaden, Oct. 9, 1900. He entered the Univ. of Vienna as a student of philosophy and law in 1861; then studied composition at the Cons. with Dessoff (1862–64), through whom he met and became a close friend of Brahms. He went to Leipzig in 1872; was one of the founders of the Bach-Verein (1874) and served as its director (1875–85). He then became prof. of composition at the Berlin Hochschule für Musik (1885), taking charge of its master class (1889); his activities were halted by ill health for a time, but he resumed teaching in 1892, retiring in 1900. As a composer, he was greatly influenced by Schumann, Wagner, and Brahms. His wife, **Elisabeth** (née **von Stockhausen;** b. Paris, April 13, 1847; d. San Remo, Jan. 7, 1892), was a fine pianist and, like her husband, a close friend of Brahms. See M. Kalbeck, ed., *Johannes Brahms im Briefwechsel mit Heinrich und Elisabeth von Herzogenberg* (Berlin, 1907).

Works: orch.: 3 syms.: No. 1, *Odysseus* (1876); No. 2 (1885); No. 3 (1890); Concerto for Flute, Oboe, Clarinet, 2 Bassoons, 2 Horns, and String Orch. (1879). **sacred choral:** Requiem for Chorus and Orch. (1891); *Totenfeier,* cantata for Soloists, Chorus, and Orch. (1894); Mass for Soloists, Chorus, and Orch. (1895); *Die Geburt Christi,* oratorio for Soloists, Chorus, Children's Chorus, Oboe, Harmonium, Organ, and Strings (1895); *Die Passion,* oratorio for Soloists, Chorus, Harmonium, Organ, and Strings (1896); *Erntefeier,* oratorio for Soloists, Chorus, Organ, and Orch. (1899); *Gott ist gegenwärtig,* cantata for Chorus and Orch. (1901); 2 biblical scenes: *Der Seesturm* for Baritone, Chorus, Organ, and Strings (1903) and *Das kananäische Weib* for Soprano, Baritone, Male Voices, and Organ (1903); also motets, Psalms, liturgical songs, etc. **secular choral:** *Columbus,* dramatic cantata for Soloists, Male Voices, and Orch. (c.1870); *Der Stern des Lieds,* ode for Chorus and Orch. (1887); *Die Weihe der Nacht* for Alto, Chorus, and Orch. (1887); *Nannas Klage* for Soprano, Alto, Chorus, and Orch. (1888); also various works with piano accompaniment or unaccompanied. **chamber:** Piano Quintet (1876); Quintet for Piano, Oboe, Clarinet, Horn, and Bassoon (1888); Quintet for 2 Violins, 2 Violas, and Cello (1892); 2 piano quartets (1892, 1897); 5 string quartets (1876, 1884, 1884, 1884, 1890); 2 piano trios (1877, 1884); Trio for Piano, Oboe, and Horn (1889); 2 string trios (1879); piano pieces; organ music; songs.

Bibl.: C. Krebs, "H. v.H.," *Deutsche Rundschau,* CV (1900); F. Spitta, "H. v.H.," *Monatsschrift für Gottesdienst und kirchliche Kunst,* V (1900); W. Altmann, "H. v.H.: Sein Leben und Schaffen," *Die Musik,* XIX (1903); F. Spitta, "H. v.H.s Bedeutung für die evangelische Kirchenmusik," *Jahrbuch der Musikbibliothek Peters 1919.*

Hesch, Wilhelm (real name, **Vilém Heš**), Bohemian bass; b. Týnec nad Labem, July 3, 1860; d. Vienna, Jan. 3, 1908. He made his debut in Brünn in 1880; then sang in Prague (1882–93) and Hamburg (1893); was a principal member of the Vienna Court Opera (1896–1908). He gained distinction for his outstanding performances in buffo roles.

Heseltine, Philip (Arnold), brilliant English composer and writer who used the pen name Peter Warlock; b. London, Oct. 30, 1894; d. (suicide) there, Dec. 17, 1930. He studied at Eton with Colin Taylor (1908–10), in Germany, and at Oxford; a meeting with Delius in France in 1910 influenced him profoundly in the direction of composition; he adopted a style that was intimately connected with English traditions of the Elizabethan period and yet revealed impressionistic undertones in harmonic writing. Another influence was that of Bernard van Dieren, from whom he absorbed an austerely contrapuntal technique. He publ. all his musical works under his pen name. He was a conscientious objector during World War I; in 1917–18 he was in Ireland; after the Armistice he returned to London; in 1920 he founded the progressive journal of musical opinion the *Sackbut;* wrote criticism; made transcriptions of early English music; participated in organizing the Delius Festival in 1929. Suffering from depression, he committed suicide by gas in his London flat. He ed. (with P. Wilson) 300 early songs

(*English Ayres, Elizabethan and Jacobean; French Ayres*); was co-editor of Oxford Choral Songs and the Oxford Orchestral Series, a collection of early English and Italian dances.

Writings (all publ. in London): *Frederick Delius* (1923); *Carlo Gesualdo, Prince of Venosa: Musician and Murderer* (1926); *The English Ayre* (1926); *Thomas Whythorne* (1929). **Works: orch.:** *An Old Song* (1917); *Serenade for Delius on his 60th Birthday* for Strings (1921–22); *Capriol,* suite for Strings (1926; for Orch., 1928). **other works:** *The Curlew,* song cycle for Tenor, Flute, English Horn, and String Quartet (1920–21; rev. 1922); *Corpus Christi* for Soprano, Baritone, and String Quartet (1919–23); *3 Carols* for Chorus and Orch. (1923); also other choral works and solo songs.

Bibl.: C. Gray, *Peter Warlock: A Memoir of P. H.* (London, 1934); K. Avery, "The Chronology of Warlock's Songs," *Music & Letters* (Oct. 1948); F. Tomlinson, *A Peter Warlock Handbook* (2 vols., Rickmansworth, 1974, 1977); I. Copley, *The Music of Peter Warlock: A Critical Survey* (London, 1979); M. Pilkington, *Gurney, Ireland, Quilter, and Warlock* (London, 1989).

Hess, Ludwig, German tenor and composer; b. Marburg, March 23, 1877; d. Berlin, Feb. 5, 1944. He studied singing with Vidal in Milan; gave concerts of German lieder throughout Europe, specializing in the modern repertoire; made a successful tour of the U.S. and Canada in 1911; conducted a choral society in Königsberg (1917–20); then settled in Berlin. He wrote the operas *Abu und Nu* (Danzig, 1919) and *Vor Edens Pforte* (after Byron); *Kranion* (Erfurt, 1933); a Sym.; symphonic poem, *Himmelskönig mit musizierenden Engeln* (after Hans Memling); *Ariadne,* a cantata; many choral works; numerous songs. He publ. *Die Behandlung der Stimme vor, während und nach der Mutation* (Marburg, 1927).

Hess, Dame Myra, distinguished English pianist; b. London, Feb. 25, 1890; d. there, Nov. 25, 1965. She studied at the Royal Academy of Music in London with Tobias Matthay; made her concert debut in London on Nov. 14, 1907, at the age of 17, playing Beethoven's G-major Concerto with Beecham. She then embarked on a successful career; made several tours in Germany and France; played recitals in America in 1922, repeating her American tours at regular intervals. She organized the National Gallery Concerts in 1939, continuing them through World War II and the blitz. It was mainly for her work during this period that she was created a Dame Commander of the Order of the British Empire by King George VI in 1941. Her playing was marked by classical precision and poetic imagination; although she was never attracted to the modern repertoire of her time, she occasionally performed piano music by contemporary British composers.

Bibl.: D. Lassimonne and H. Ferguson, eds., *M. H., By Her Friends* (London, 1966); M. McKenna, *M. H.: A Portrait* (London, 1976).

Hess, Willy, German violinist and teacher; b. Mannheim, July 14, 1859; d. Berlin, Feb. 17, 1939. His 1st teacher was his father, who was a pupil of Spohr. As a child of 6, he was taken to the U.S.; at the age of 9, he played with the Thomas Orch. He then studied with Joachim in Berlin (1876); was concertmaster in Frankfurt (1878–86), in Rotterdam, where he taught at the Cons. (1886–88), and in Manchester, England, with the Hallé Orch. (1888–95). From 1895 to 1903 he was a prof. of violin at the Cologne Cons.; then taught at the Royal Academy of Music in London (1903–4); in 1904 he was engaged as concertmaster of the Boston Sym. Orch., and remained in that position until 1910; also organized the Hess Quartet in Boston. From 1910 to 1928 he taught at the Hochschule für Musik in Berlin.

Bibl.: F. Bonavia, "W. H. as Teacher," *Monthly Musical Record,* LXI (1931).

Hess, Willy, noted Swiss musicologist; b. Winterthur, Oct. 12, 1906. He studied piano and music theory at the Zürich Cons. and musicology at the Univ. of Zürich. He played bassoon in the Winterthur Stadtorchester (1942–71). As a musicologist, he devoted most of his effort to the compilation of a Beethoven catalog. He ed. a valuable *Verzeichnis der nicht* *in der Gesamtausgabe veröffentlichten Werke Ludwig van Bee-thovens* (Wiesbaden, 1957); also ed. the extensive supplement *Ludwig van Beethoven: Sämtliche Werke: Supplement zur Ges-amtausgabe* (14 vols., Wiesbaden, 1959–71). His other impor-tant writings include *Ludwig van Beethoven* (Geneva, 1946); *Beethovens Oper Fidelio und ihre drei Fassungen* (Zürich, 1953); *Beethoven* (Zürich, 1956; 2nd ed., rev., 1976); *Die Har-monie der Künste* (Vienna, 1960); *Die Dynamik der musikalis-chen Formbildung* (2 vols., Vienna, 1960; 1964); *Vom Doppe-lantlitz des Bösen in der Kunst, dargestellt am Beispiel der Musik* (Munich, 1963); *Vom Metaphysischen im Künstlerischen* (Winterthur, 1963); *Parteilose Kunst, parteilose Wissenschaft* (Tutzing, 1967); *Beethoven-Studien* (Munich, 1972); also an autobiography, *Aus meinem Leben: Erlebnisse, Bekenntnisse, Betrachtungen* (Zürich, 1976). He was also a prolific composer; wrote several fairy-tale operas, a Sym., a Sonata for Bassoon and Small Orch., a Horn Concerto, and numerous pieces of chamber music, including a curious work for double bassoon and string quartet.

Hesse, Adolph (Friedrich), German organist, conductor, and composer; b. Breslau, Aug. 30, 1808; d. there, Aug. 5, 1863. His father was an organ builder, and Hesse received his 1st instruction from him; he further profited by the advice of Hum-mel and Spohr. He was church organist at Breslau; was also active as a conductor. He wrote 6 syms., 5 overtures, the oratorio *Tobias,* and much organ music.

Hesse, Ernst Christian, German viola da gambist and com-poser; b. Grossgottern, April 14, 1676; d. Darmstadt, May 16, 1762. He studied the viola da gamba, first at Darmstadt, then in Paris; gave successful demonstrations of his virtuosity in various European towns. From 1707 to 1714 he was Kapelldi-rektor in Darmstadt. In 1713 he married **Johanna Döbricht.** He wrote an Italian opera, *La fedeltà coronata* (c.1712); a diver-timento, *Apollo in tempe;* a Flute Sonata; and many works for viola da gamba.

Hesse, Max, German music publisher; b. Sondershausen, Feb. 18, 1858; d. Leipzig, Nov. 24, 1907. In 1880 he founded a publishing house, with headquarters in Leipzig; in 1915 the firm moved to Berlin. Among its most important publica-tions were the 3rd through 11th eds. of Riemann's *Musik Lexi-kon* (1887–1929) and H.J. Moser's *Musik-Lexikon.* Great devas-tation was wreaked on the physical materials of the firm by air bombardment during World War II. After the war the firm was re-established in Berlin.
BIBL.: *80 Jahre M. H.s Verlag* (Berlin, 1960).

Hesse-Bukowska, Barbara, Polish pianist; b. Lodz, June 1, 1930. She studied piano with Margerita Trombini-Kazuro; con-tinued her musical education at the Warsaw Academy of Music. In 1949 she won 2nd prize in the Chopin Competition in Warsaw; in 1953 she was awarded the Chopin Prize at the Long-Thibaud Competition. From that time she made regular appearances in London, Paris, Moscow, Vienna, and Rome; also made extensive tours of India, Egypt, and Japan. In 1963 she became a member of the faculty of the Academy of Music in Wroclaw; in 1973 she joined the Academy of Music in Warsaw. She is regarded as a fine interpreter of Chopin and also a leading champion of contemporary Polish music.

Hesselberg, Edouard Gregory, Latvian-American pianist, teacher, and composer; b. Riga, May 3, 1870; d. Los Angeles, June 12, 1935. He studied at the Cons. of the Moscow Phil. Soc. (1888–92); later was a private pupil of Anton Rubinstein. In 1892 he went to the U.S.; taught at the Ithaca Cons. (1895–96), the Music Academy in Denver (1896–1900), the Cons. of Music at Wesleyan College (1900–1905), Belmont College in Nashville (1905–12), and the Toronto Cons. (1912–18). He wrote *Russian Suite* and *Russian Rhapsody* for Orch.; also piano pieces; made arrangements for 2 pianos of works by Bach, Chopin, and Schubert.

Hessen, Alexander Friedrich, Landgraf von, German com-poser; b. Copenhagen, Jan. 25, 1863; d. Fronhausen, March 26, 1945. In 1888 he became landgrave of the House of Hessen.

Although blind from childhood, he studied music with admira-ble diligence; took violin lessons in Berlin with Joachim and Bruch; studied composition with Draeseke in Dresden and with Fauré in Paris. By an extraordinary effort he managed to compose a number of works, mostly chamber music and lieder.
BIBL.: P. Hiller, *Der Liederzyklus von A.F. v.H.* (1910).

Hessenberg, Kurt, German composer; b. Frankfurt am Main, Aug. 17, 1908. He studied in Leipzig with Raphael (composi-tion) and Teichmüller (piano). In 1933 he was appointed to the faculty of the Hoch Cons. in Frankfurt. Possessing great facility in composition, Hessenberg evolved an effective idiom, fundamentally Classical, but containing Wagnerian elements in dramatic passages, with occasional infusion of prudential modernistic devices. His most successful work was *Struw-welpeter* (1933), a suite for Small Orch. based on a well-known German children's tale. He further wrote 3 syms. (1936, 1943, 1954); Concerto for Orch. (1958); Piano Concerto (1940); Con-certo for 2 Pianos and Orch. (1950); 2 flute sonatas (1932); Cello Sonata (1941); Violin Sonata (1942); String Trio (1949); Piano Trio (1950); 5 string quartets (1934–67); numerous piano pieces; a number of cantatas; a multitude of lieder.
BIBL.: K. Laux, *K. H.* (Essen, 1949).

Hetsch, (Karl) Ludwig Friedrich, German conductor; b. Stuttgart, April 26, 1806; d. Mannheim, June 28, 1872. He studied with Abeille; was attached to the court of the King of Württemberg; then conducted in Heidelberg (1846–56) and in Mannheim (from 1856 until his death). He wrote an opera, *Ryno* (Stuttgart, 1833); orch. works; chamber music.

Hétu, Jacques (Joseph Robert), Canadian composer and teacher; b. Trois-Rivières, Quebec, Aug. 8, 1938. He studied piano, harmony, and Gregorian chant at the Univ. of Ottawa (1955–56); then took courses in composition and counterpoint with Clermont Pépin, in harmony with Isabelle Delorme, and in fugue with Jean Papineau-Couture at the Montreal Cons. (1956–61; premier prix in composition, 1961); also received instruction in composition from Foss at the Berkshire Music Center in Tanglewood, Mass. (summer 1959); completed his training in Paris with Dutilleux (composition diploma, 1963) at the École Normale de Musique and with Messiaen (analy-sis) at the Cons. (1962–63). He taught at Laval Univ. in Que-bec (1963–77) and at the Univ. of Montreal (1972–73; 1978–79); then was a prof. at the Univ. of Quebec in Montreal (from 1979). In his music he makes use of permissible mod-ern devices, while hewing to Classical formal conventions.
WORKS: ORCH.: 3 syms.: No. 1 for String Orch. (1959); No. 2 (1961); No. 3 (1971); *Adagio et Rondo* for String Orch. or String Quartet (1960); *Rondo* for Cello and String Orch. (1965); Double Concerto for Violin, Piano, and Chamber Orch. (1967); *L'Apocalypse* (1967); Piano Concerto (1969); *Passacaille* (1970); *Fantaisie* for Piano and Orch. (1973); *Antinomie* (1977); Bassoon Concerto (1979); *Mirages* (1981); Symphonie concertante for Flute, Oboe, Clarinet, Bassoon, Horn, and String Orch. (1986); Clarinet Concerto (1987); Trumpet Con-certo (1987); *Images de la Révolution* for the bicentennial of the French Revolution (1988); *Poème* for String Orch. (1989). **CHAMBER:** Trio for Flute, Oboe, and Harpsichord (1960); Wind Quintet (1967); String Quartet (1972); *Suite* for Guitar (1986); *Sérénade* for Flute and String Quartet (1988); other works for solo instruments; piano pieces; organ music. **VOCAL:** *Les Clartés de la Nuit* for Soprano and Piano (1972; also for Soprano and Orch., 1987); *Les Djinns* for Chorus, 6 Percussion, and Piano (1975); *Les Abîmes du Rêve* for Bass and Orch. (1982); *Missa pro trecentesimo anno* for Chorus and Orch. (1985); *Les Illusions fanées* for Chorus (1988).

Heuberger, Richard (Franz Joseph), Austrian choral con-ductor, music critic, and composer; b. Graz, June 18, 1850; d. Vienna, Oct. 27, 1914. By profession a civil engineer, in 1876 he turned his full attention to music; became choral master of the Vienna Akademischer Gesangverein and con-ductor of the Singakademie (1878); was conductor of the Männergesangverein (1902–9); prof. at the Vienna Cons.

(1902). From 1881 to 1896 he was music critic of the *Wiener Tageblatt*, then of the *Neue Freie Presse* (1896–1901); from 1904 to 1914 he was music critic of the *Neue Musikalische Presse*, and was ed. of the *Musikbuch aus Österreich* (1904–6).

WRITINGS: *Im Foyer: Gesammelte Essays über das Opernrepertoire der Gegenwart* (Lepizig, 1901); *Musikalische Skizzen* (Leipzig, 1901); *Franz Schubert* (Berlin, 1902; 3rd ed., rev., 1920, by H. von der Pfordten); *Anleitung zum Modulieren* (Vienna, 1910).

WORKS: Operas: *Abenteuer einer Neujahrsnacht* (Leipzig, 1886); *Manuel Venegas* (Leipzig, March 27, 1889), remodeled as the 3-act grand opera *Mirjam, oder Das Maifest* (Vienna, Jan. 20, 1894); *Barfüssele* (Dresden, 1905); operettas (all 1st perf. in Vienna): *Der Opernball* (Jan. 5, 1898; exceptionally successful); *Ihre Excellenz* (1899; new version as *Eine entzückende Frau*); *Der Sechsuhrzug* (1900); *Das Baby* (1902); *Der Fürst von Düsterstein* (1909); *Don Quixote* (1910); ballet, *Struwwelpeter* (Dresden, 1897); cantata, *Geht es dir wohl, so denk' an mich*, from *Des Knaben Wunderhorn*; overture to Byron's *Cain*; songs.

BIBL.: H. Hughes, *R. H.'s Erinnerungen an Johannes Brahms: The Life, Work, and Times of Johannes Brahms as Revealed by a Contemporary* (diss., Ball State Univ., 1987).

Heubner, Konrad, German composer; b. Dresden, April 8, 1860; d. Koblenz, June 6, 1905. He studied with Riemann in Leipzig, Nottebohm in Vienna, and Nicodé in Dresden. In 1890 he was appointed director of the Koblenz Cons. He wrote a Sym.; a cantata, *Das Geheimnis der Sehnsucht*; several overtures; and a Violin Concerto.

Heugel, Henry, Swiss-French music theorist, father of **Jacques-Léopold Heugel;** b. Neuchâtel, Switzerland, Sept. 26, 1789; d. Nantes, France, May 2, 1841. He studied in Paris with Galin and Reicha; developed a "méthode de méloplaste" along the lines of Galin's system; publ. *Nouvelle méthode pour l'enseignement de la musique inventée par H. Heugel et développée par lui de manière à permettre d'apprendre sans maître* (1832).

Heugel, Jacques-Léopold, French music publisher, son of **Henry Heugel;** b. La Rochelle, March 1, 1811; d. Paris, Nov. 12, 1883. In 1839 he joined a music publishing establishment founded in Paris in 1812 by J.A. Meissonnier; became its director in 1842. After his death his nephew, Paul Chevalier Heugel (1861–1931), became its owner. The firm is now managed by Philippe and François Heugel, successors to their father, Jacques-Paul Heugel, who was the grandson of Jacques-Léopold Heugel. The firm's list of publications includes the works of celebrated composers (Bizet, Charpentier, Delibes, Fauré, Franck, Honegger, Ibert, d'Indy, Lalo, Massenet, Milhaud, Offenbach, Poulenc, Ravel, Roussel, Widor, etc.), as well as the series of comprehensive practical eds. of early music known as Le Pupitre (from 1967). The firm also publ. the important weekly *Le Ménestrel* (founded by Jules Lovy in 1833; suspended publication during the Franco-Prussian War and during World War I; ceased publishing in 1940). The firm merged with Leduc in 1980.

Heuss, Alfred (Valentin), Swiss-born German musicologist and music critic; b. Chur, Jan. 27, 1877; d. Gaschwitz, July 9, 1934. He studied at the Stuttgart Cons. (1896–98), then at the Akademie der Tonkunst in Munich, attending the Univ. of Munich simultaneously (1898–99); from 1899 to 1902 he studied musicology with Kretzschmar at the Univ. of Leipzig (Ph.D., 1903, with the diss. *Die Instrumentalstücke des "Orfeo" und die venezianischen Opernsinfonien*). He was music critic of the *Signale* (1902–5), *Leipziger Volkszeitung* (1905–12), and *Leipziger Zeitung* (1912–18); ed. of the *Zeitschrift der Internationalen Musik-Gesellschaft* (1904–14), to which he contributed valuable articles; ed. in chief of the *Zeitschrift für Musik* (1921–29). He publ. *J.S. Bachs Matthäuspassion* (1909), *Kammermusikabende* (1919), *Beethoven: Eine Charakteristik* (1921), and *Beethovens Orch.-Crescendo* (Basel, 1924).

Heward, Leslie (Hays), esteemed English conductor; b. Littletown, Liversedge, Yorkshire, Dec. 8, 1897; d. Birmingham, May 3, 1943. He studied with his father, an organist; then continued his training at the Manchester Cathedral Choir School, where he served as assistant cathedral organist; was made organist of St. Andrew's, Ancoats (1914); then won a scholarship in composition to the Royal College of Music in London (1917), where he studied with Stanford and Vaughan Williams. After appearing as a conductor with the British National Opera Co., he was music director of the South African Broadcasting Corp. and conductor of the Cape Town Orch. (1924–27); then was conductor of the City of Birmingham Orch. (from 1930). He was acknowledged as one of England's finest conductors. He was also a composer, but he destroyed many of his MSS; his works included 2 unfinished operas, a symphonic poem, several orch. suites, choral works, chamber music, and songs.

BIBL.: E. Blom, ed., *L. H.: A Memorial Volume* (London, 1944); W. Holmes, "L. H. Discography," *Le Grand Baton* (Dec. 1980).

Hewitt, Harry Donald, unimaginably fecund American composer; b. Detroit, March 4, 1921. His paternal grandmother was a Winnebago Indian. He was completely autodidact in music, and achieved such mastery of composition in quaquaversal directions without stylistic prejudice, that in some 40 years of writing music he produced 3,300 works in every conceivable manner, using every speculative idiom, from jazz to pop, couched in every available tonal, atonal, polytonal, and incommensurate oriental scale. Entirely free from supercilious elitism, he was not ashamed to admit the authorship of a *Hymn to Mickey Mouse* or an *Homage to Bugs Bunny*. None of his 30 syms. were ever performed. The brute weight of his collected MSS is 1½ tons.

WORKS: 8 operas: *The Shadowy Waters, Moby Dick, The Song of Kawas, The Happy Hymadrayad, Doctor Too-Big, Clara's Friend, Remember George, Pierre;* 30 syms., 2 of which are unnumbered, *Amerindian Symphony* and *War Symphony;* over 300 works for Orch., including 19 symphonic poems: *Kabir, The Manchild, The Night, Fairyland, The Mysterious Sea, The Seasons, In the Shade of the Upas Tree, New Year's Eclogue, The House of Sleep, Raggedy Ann, Wa-Kon-Da, The Happy Garden, In a Green Shade, 7, Selene, The Wheel, Aldebaran, Angkor, Anglesley Abbey;* 2 piano concertos; Trombone Concerto; Guitar Concerto; 18 piano sonatas; 23 string quartets; and more than 100 other works for diverse chamber ensembles, e.g., Preludes for Flute and Marimba, Fantasia for Flute and Horn, *Leaf in the Stream* for Oboe and Tuba, etc.; uncountable songs and choruses.

Hewitt, Helen (Margaret), American musicologist; b. Granville, N.Y., May 2, 1900; d. Denton, Texas, March 19, 1977. She studied at the Eastman School of Music in Rochester, N.Y.; then traveled to Paris, and took a course in theory with Nadia Boulanger and organ lessons with Widor. Returning to America, she enrolled in the musicology class of Lang at Columbia Univ. (M.A., 1933); further supplemented her studies at Heidelberg Univ., where she was a student of Besseler. She obtained her Ph.D. from Radcliffe College in 1938 with the dissertation *O. Petrucci: Harmonice Musices Odhecaton A* (publ. in Cambridge, Mass., 1942); received a Guggenheim fellowship in 1947. From 1942 until 1969 she was on the music faculty of North Texas State Univ. in Denton. She publ. the valuable compilation *Doctoral Dissertations in Musicology* (Denton, 1952; 4th ed., 1965); contributed valuable articles on the music of the Renaissance to various periodicals.

Hewitt, James, English-born American composer, publisher, organist, and violinist; b. Dartmoor, June 4, 1770; d. Boston, Aug. 1, 1827. He played in London as a youth. In 1792 he went to America and settled in N.Y., where he was described as one of the "professors of music from the Opera House, Hanover Square, and Professional Concerts under the direction of Haydn, Pleyel, etc., London." On Sept. 21, 1792, he gave a benefit concert with the violinists J. Gehot and B. Bergmann, the flutist W. Young, and a cellist named Phillips, which included Hewitt's *Overture in 9 Movements, expressive of a battle.* Subsequently, Young and Gehot went to Philadelphia, and in 1793 Hewitt, Bergmann, and Phillips gave a series of 6 subscription concerts; at their 5th concert (March 25, 1793) they presented for the 1st time in America Haydn's *Passion of Our Saviour* (i.e., *The 7 Last Words*); in 1794 Henri Capron joined Hewitt in promoting his "City Concerts"; meanwhile, Hewitt became the leader of the Old American Co. Orch., and in 1795 gave up his activities in connection with the subscription concerts. In 1798 he bought out the N.Y. branch of Carr's "Musical Repository" and established a publishing business of his own. In 1811 he went to Boston, where he played organ at Trinity Church and was in charge of the music presented at the Federal St. Theatre. In 1816 he returned to N.Y.; also traveled in the South. In N.Y. he was director of the Park Theatre. He wrote ballad operas: *Tammany* (N.Y., 1794, under the auspices of the Tammany Soc.; only 1 song, *The Death Song of the Cherokee Indians,* survives); *The Patriot or Liberty Asserted* (1794); *The Mysterious Marriage* (1799); *Columbus* (1799); *Pizarro, or The Spaniards in Peru* (1800); *Robin Hood* (1800); *The Spanish Castle* (N.Y., Dec. 5, 1800); *The Wild Goose Chase* (1800); overture, *Demophon;* set of 3 piano sonatas; *Battle of Trenton* for Piano; *The 4th of July— A Grand Military Sonata for the Pianoforte;* etc. His eldest son, **John Hill Hewitt** (b. N.Y., July 12, 1801; d. Baltimore, Oct. 7, 1890), studied at West Point Academy; was a theatrical manager, newspaperman, and drillmaster of Confederate recruits in the Civil War; wrote poems and plays; about 300 songs (*The Minstrel's Return from the War, All Quiet along the Potomac, Our Native Land, The Mountain Bugle,* etc.); cantatas (*Flora's Festival, The Fairy Bridal, The Revelers,* and *The Musical Enthusiast*); ballad operas (*Rip Van Winkle, The Vivandiere, The Prisoner of Monterey, The Artist's Wife*). His admirers dubbed him the "father of the American ballad," but the ballad form existed in America long before him. He wrote a book of memoirs, *Shadows on the Wall* (1877; reprinted 1971). Another son, **James Lang Hewitt** (b. N.Y., Sept. 28, 1803; d. there, March 24, 1853), was associated with the publishing firm of J.A. Dickson in Boston (1825); after his father's death he returned to N.Y. and continued his father's publishing business.

BIBL.: J. Howard, "The H. Family in American Music," *Musical Quarterly* (Jan. 1931); C. Huggins, *John Hill H.: Bard of the Confederacy* (diss., Florida State Univ., 1964); J. Wagner, *James H.: His Life and Works* (diss., Indiana Univ., 1969); W. Winden, *The Life and Music Theater Works of John Hill H.* (diss., Univ. of Illinois, 1972); F. Hoogerwerf, *John Hill H.: Sources and Bibliography* (Atlanta, 1982).

Hewitt, Maurice, French violinist and conductor; b. Asnières, Seine, Oct. 6, 1884; d. Paris, Nov. 7, 1971. He studied at the Paris Cons.; was a violinist in the Capet Quartet (1908–28); taught at the Cleveland Inst. of Music (1930–34); from 1934, was a teacher at the American Cons. of Fontainebleau; was at the Paris Cons. from 1938 to 1954 (chamber music class); in 1928 organized in Paris the Quatuor Hewitt; in 1939 founded the Orch. de Chambre Hewitt.

Hey, Julius, German singing teacher; b. Irmelshausen, April 29, 1832; d. Munich, April 22, 1909. He 1st studied painting, but turned to music, taking courses in harmony and counterpoint with Franz Lachner and Friedrich Schmitt. He became an ardent Wagnerian after his introduction to the master by King Ludwig II, and worked under the direction of Hans von Bülow at the Munich School of Music (established by the King in accordance with Wagner's plans). After Bülow's departure (1869), Hey vainly tried to effect a reform from a German national standpoint in the cultivation of singing, but met with so many obstacles that he resigned when Wagner died (1883), and devoted himself to finishing his method of singing, *Deutscher Gesangsunterricht* (4 vols., Mainz, 1885; ed. by F. Volbach and H. Hey as *Der kleine Hey,* Mainz, 1912; 2nd ed., rev., 1956, by F. Reusch). It contains a complete and logical exposition of Wagner's views on vocal training. His

book *Richard Wagner als Vortragsmeister* (Leipzig, 1911) was publ. posthumously by his son Hans.

Heyden (Heiden, Haiden), Hans, German organist, son of **Sebald Heyden;** b. Nuremberg (baptized), Jan. 15, 1536; d. there (buried), Oct. 22, 1613. He was his father's successor as organist at St. Sebald Church, and was the inventor of the unique "Geigen-Clavicymbel" ("Nürnbergisch Geigenwerk"), which he described in *Musicale instrumentum reformatum* (1605).

BIBL.: G. Kinsky, "H. H.," *Zeitschrift für Musikwissenschaft,* VI (1923–24).

Heyden (Heiden, Haiden), Sebald, important German music theorist, father of **Hans Heyden;** b. Bruck, near Erlangen, Dec. 8, 1499; d. Nuremberg, July 9, 1561. In 1521 he was appointed cantor at the Spitalkirche and rector of its school in Nuremberg; in 1525 became rector of the school at St. Sebald. He was the author of the important theoretical work *Musicae, id est, Artis canendi, libri duo* (Nuremberg, 1537; 2nd ed. as *De arte canendi,* etc., 1540; tr. into Eng. by C. Miller in Musicological Studies and Documents, XXVI, 1972). The famous Passion song *O Mensch, bewein dein Sünde gross* has been ascribed to him.

BIBL.: A. Kosel, *S. H. (1499–1561): Ein Beitrag zur Geschichte der Nürnberger Schulmusik in der Reformationszeit* (Würzburg, 1940).

Heyer, Wilhelm (Ferdinand), German patron of music; b. Cologne, March 30, 1849; d. there, March 20, 1913. A wealthy co-owner of the wholesale paper manufacturing firm Poensgen & Heyer, he was an enthusiastic amateur and was active in the musical affairs of Cologne in advisory capacities. In 1906 he established a historical musical museum in Cologne, in which he assembled more than 2,600 instruments with accessories, about 20,000 autographs of musicians, 3,700 portraits, and a library of books about music, containing many rare eds. Georg Kinsky, curator of the museum from 1909, publ. an illustrated catalog of the Heyer collections. The museum was dissolved in 1927, and the instruments were acquired by the Univ. of Leipzig but sustained heavy damage during World War II.

BIBL.: G. Kinsky, *Musikhistorisches Museum von W. H. in Cöln: Katalog* (Cologne, vol. I, 1910; vol. II, 1912; vol. IV, 1916).

Heyman, Katherine Ruth Willoughby, American pianist; b. Sacramento, Calif., 1877; d. Sharon, Conn., Sept. 28, 1944. She made her debut as soloist with the Boston Sym. Orch. in 1899; from 1905 to 1915 toured the U.S. and Europe with Schumann-Heink, Marcella Sembrich, and others. She became greatly interested in the works of Scriabin, and played recitals of his works in Europe and America; also publ. many articles on Scriabin's theosophic ideas. In 1928 she founded in Paris the Groupe Estival pour la Musique Moderne. She publ. *The Relation of Ultra-Modern to Archaic Music* (Boston, 1921); composed *Studies in Modern Idiom* for the piano, and songs.

Heywood, Eddie (Edward, Jr.), black American jazz pianist, composer, and arranger; b. Atlanta, Dec. 4, 1915; d. North Miami, Jan. 2, 1989. His father was the ragtime pianist and bandleader Eddie Heywood, Sr., with whom he began taking piano lessons as a youth. Later he joined Benny Carter's band (1939–40), then formed his own trio and later his own sextet (1943–47). He scored a notable success with his rendition of Cole Porter's *Begin the Beguine;* he also devoted much time to composing. Among his works were the tone poem *Portrait of Martha's Vineyard* and several songs, including the popular *Canadian Sunset.*

Hickman, Hans (Robert Hermann), German musicologist; b. Rosslau, May 19, 1908; d. Blandford Forum, Dorset, England, Sept. 4, 1968. He studied in Halle and Berlin, where he took courses in musicology with Sachs, Schering, Schünemann, and Wolf. In 1933 he went to Egypt, where he collected materials dealing with ancient Egyptian music. In 1957 he joined the faculty of the Univ. of Hamburg; became director of Deutsche Grammophon Gesellschaft's Archiv Produktion label for early music recordings in 1958. His principal works include the books *Das Portativ* (Ph.D. diss. at the Univ. of Berlin, 1934; publ. in Kassel, 1936); *La Trompette dans l'Égypte ancienne* (Cairo, 1946); *Terminologie arabe des instruments de musique* (Cairo, 1947); *Musikgeschichte in Bildern*, vol. 2, on Egypt (Leipzig, 1961).

Hickox, Richard (Sidney), English conductor; b. Stokenchurch, Buckinghamshire, March 5, 1948. He studied at the Royal Academy of Music in London (1966–67), and was an organ scholar at Queen's College, Cambridge (1967–70). In 1971 he founded in London the Richard Hickox Singers and Orch., with which he gave programs of works ranging from the 14th century to the present era; also was music director of the City of London Sinfonia (from 1971) and organist and master of music at St. Margarets, Westminster (1972–82). He likewise served as conductor of the London Sym. Orch. Chorus (from 1977), artistic director of the Northern Sinfonia in Newcastle upon Tyne (from 1982), and associate conductor of the San Diego Sym. Orch. (1983–85) and the London Sym. Orch. (from 1985). In 1990 he founded, together with Simon Standage, the Collegium Musicum 90 of London. As a guest conductor, he appeared with all the principal British orchs., opera houses, and festivals.

Hidalgo, Juan, eminent Spanish composer; b. Madrid, c.1612; d. there, March 30, 1685. In 1631 he became a member of the Royal Chapel in Madrid as harpist and also as player of the "clavi-harpa," an instrument he is said to have invented. A document of 1677 attests that he was "of superior skill, and had merited the highest honors from Their Majesties at all times." So great was his reputation that the Duke of Infantado called him "unique in the faculty of music." He composed the opera *Celos aun del aire matan,* to a text by Calderón de la Barca (Madrid, Dec. 5, 1660); the music of Act I (voices and basso continuo) was discovered by J. Subirá and publ. by him in 1933 (this is the longest extant specimen of Spanish operatic music from the 17th century). Hidalgo also wrote music for Calderón's comedies *Ni amor se libra de amor* (1662) and *Hado y divisa de Leónido y de Marfisa* (1680), and for *Los celos hacen estrellas* by Juan Vélez (1672). He also composed the opera *La púrpura de la rosa* (1660), text by Calderón. He was likewise known as a composer of sacred and secular songs (some preserved in the National Library, Madrid). Music by Hidalgo is reprinted in Pedrell's *Cancionero* (IV) and *Teatro lírico* (vols. III, IV, and V).

BIBL.: J. Subirá, *"Celos aun del aire matan," Opera del siglo XVII* (Barcelona, 1933); idem, "El operista español Don J. H.," *Las ciencias* I (1934); O. Ursprung, " 'Celos aun del aire matan'; Text von Calderón, Musik von H., die älteste erhaltene spanische Oper," *Schering-Festschrift* (Berlin, 1937); J. Moll, "Nuevos datos para la biografía de J. H.," *Anglés Festschrift* (Barcelona, 1958–61).

Hidas, Frigyes, Hungarian conductor and composer; b. Budapest, May 25, 1928. He studied composition with Viski at the Budapest Academy of Music (1947–52); served as music director and conductor of the National Theater in Budapest (1951–66), later was director of the Budapest Operetta Theater (1974–79). His music derives from national Hungarian modalities, which are dressed up in modernistic harmonies.

WORKS: STAGE: 4 operas: *Asszony és az igazság* (The Woman and the Truth; 1965), *Tökéletes alattvaló* (The Perfect Subject; 1973), *Bösendorfer* (1977), and *Dunakanyar* (Danube Bend; 1984); operetta, *Riviera* (1963); 2 ballets: *Színek* (Colors; 1966) and *Cédrus* (Cedar; 1975). **ORCH.:** Oboe Concerto (1951); Violin Concertino (1957); Viola Concerto (1959); Sym. (1960); Concertino for Strings (1960); 2 flute concertos (1967, 1982); Horn Concerto (1968); Concertino for Winds and Strings (1969); Piano Concerto (1972); *Concerto semplice* for Clarinet and Orch. (1977); *Adagio,* 2 dances (1977; from the ballet

Cédrus); *Merry Music* for Wind Band (1981); *Ballet Music* for Wind Band (Manchester, England, July 26, 1981); *Rhapsody* for Bass Trombone and Small Wind Orch. (1982). **CHAMBER:** 3 string quartets (1954, 1963, 1988); Oboe Sonata (1954); 3 wind quintets (1961, 1969, 1979); *Fantasy* for Clarinet and Piano (1965); Brass Sextet (1972); Brass Quintet (1973); Brass Quartet (1973); Horn Quartet (1974); *Fantasy* for Solo Trombone (1977); *Introduction and Fugue* for 2 Trombones (1977); *Interludio* for 3 Trombones (1977); *Scherzo e chorale* for 4 Trombones (1977); *Meditation* for Bass Trombone (1979); *7 Bagatelles* for 10 Tenor Trombones and 2 Bass Trombones (1980); *3 Sketches* for 15 Clarinets (1981); organ music; songs.

Hier, Ethel Glenn, American pianist, teacher, and composer; b. Cincinnati, June 25, 1889; d. Winter Park, Fla., Jan. 14, 1971. She studied at the Cincinnati Cons. of Music and at the Inst. of Musical Art, N.Y., where she was a pupil of Goetschius; also took lessons with Ernest Bloch. She lived mostly in N.Y. Among her compositions are *Asolo Bells* for Orch. (Rochester, N.Y., Oct. 25, 1939); a cantata, *Mountain Preacher* (N.Y., Dec. 5, 1941); numerous pieces of chamber music; also piano works.

Higginbotham, J.C. (Jay C.), black American jazz trombonist; b. Social Circle, Ga., May 11, 1906; d. N.Y., May 26, 1973. He acquired mastery of the trombone in his youth; in 1928 moved to N.Y., where he played with Chick Webb, Fletcher Henderson, and Benny Carter; later worked with Louis Armstrong (1937–40) and Henry "Red" Allen (1940–47); subsequently led his own groups.

BIBL.: C. Jones, *J.C. H.* (London, 1944); F. Hoffman, *Henry "Red" Allen/J.C. H. Discography* (Berlin, 1982).

Higgins, Dick (Richard Carter), English-born American composer, performer, music publisher, and writer; b. Cambridge, March 15, 1938. He was taken to America as a child; studied piano in Worcester, Mass.; composition with John Cage in N.Y. Eventually he moved to California; became active in the mushrooming avant-garde groups; participated in staging "happenings" across the country; joined the ultramodern group Fluxus in 1961; organized the Something Else Press (1964–73) with the aim of publishing something else; founded Unpublished Editions (1972), which later became Printed Editions (1978). Not averse to academic activities, he taught at the Calif. Inst. of the Arts (1970–71); was a research associate in the visual arts dept. of the State Univ. of N.Y. in Purchase (from 1983). In his productions he pursues the objective of total involvement, in which music is verbalized in conceptual designs without reification, or expressed in physical action; the ultimate in this direction is achieved by his work *The Thousand Symphonies* (1968), in which the composer shoots machine-gun bullets through MS paper; his Sym. No. 585, shot by a sergeant of the army at the composer's behest, was distributed in holographs in No. 6 of the avant-garde magazine *Source* (1969) under the subtitle "The Creative Use of Police Resources." Other compositions include *Graphis,* 146 works for Varying Groups (1958); *A Loud Symphony* (1958); Sym. No. 3½ (duration, 50 seconds; 1959); *In the Context of Shoes,* "happening" for Tape, Vacuum Cleaners, Drills, Gardener's Shears, Piano, and Anti-Dancers (1960); *In Memoriam,* 164-part canon (1960); *Musical Processes,* cycle of 5 pieces for Indeterminate Ensembles (1960); *Constellations and Contributions* for Multimedia (1959–60); *Symphoniae sacrae,* conceptual works without a definite realization (1961); *The Peaceable Kingdom,* spoken opera with Bells (1961); *Danger Musics,* a cycle of 43 conceptual pieces (1961–63); *Litany* for 5 Pianos and Tape Recorder (1962–68); *Requiem for Wagner the Criminal Mayor* for Tape Recorder (1962); *Lavender Blue,* opera (1963); *Hrušalk,* opera (1965); *Egg* for Magnetic Tape (1967); *Sophocles I and II,* fatal pieces for Piano (1970); *26 Mountains for Viewing the Sunset From* for Singers, Dancers, and Chamber Orch. (1980); *Variations on a Natural Theme* for Orch. (1981); *St. Columba* for String Quartet, Orch. or 4 Voices, Chorus, and Tubular Chimes (1983). He publ. *foew&ombwhnw,* "a grammar of the mind and a phenomenology of love and a science of the arts as seen by a stalker of the wild mushroom" (N.Y., 1969). His zodiac parameter is Aries, with the sun in Pisces.

Higginson, Henry Lee, American music patron; b. N.Y., Nov. 18, 1834; d. Boston, Nov. 15, 1919. He studied at Harvard Univ. in 1851; from 1856 to 1860 studied voice, piano, composition, and theory in Vienna; in 1868 became a partner in his father's brokerage firm in Boston (Lee, Higginson & Co.). In 1881, in order to found the Boston Sym. Orch., he assumed the responsibility of providing for about $50,000 yearly of the annual budget of some $115,000, thus clearing the estimated deficit and assuring the organization's successful continuance; the orch., consisting of 67 performers, gave its 1st concert at the old Music Hall on Oct. 22, 1881; in the summer of 1885, the series of concerts of lighter music, famous as the "Pops," was instituted; on Oct. 15, 1900, the Boston Sym. Orch. inaugurated its own permanent home, Sym. Hall; in 1903 the Pension Fund was established, for the benefit of which a special concert is given annually. A firm believer in the superiority of German musicians, Higginson engaged George Henschel as the 1st conductor of the orch. (1881–84); there followed a line of German conductors: Wilhelm Gericke (1884–89), Arthur Nikisch (1889–93), Emil Paur (1893–98), Gericke again (1898–1906), Karl Muck (1906–8), Max Fiedler (1908–12), and again Karl Muck, from 1912 till 1918, when he submitted to arrest as an enemy alien to avoid prosecution under the Mann Act when the U.S. entered World War I. Higginson, distraught over Muck's arrest, resigned his position shortly after and selected a board of directors to control the orch. He died the following year.

BIBL.: M. de Wolfe Howe, *The Boston Symphony Orchestra* (Boston, 1914; 2nd ed., augmented, 1931); H. Earle Johnson, *Symphony Hall* (Boston, 1950); J. Baker-Carr, *Evening at Symphony: A Portrait of the Boston Symphony Orchestra* (Boston, 1977).

Hignard, (Jean-Louis) Aristide, French composer; b. Nantes, May 20, 1822; d. Vernon, March 20, 1898. He studied with Halévy at the Paris Cons., taking the 2nd Grand Prix de Rome. He was an earnest composer of lofty aims, but brought out operas and other works of secondary importance; his best opera, *Hamlet,* composed in 1868, was to be performed in Paris; unluckily for him, *Hamlet* by Ambroise Thomas was produced that same year, with such spectacular success that Hignard could not compete with it; accordingly, he had to be content with a provincial production in his native city (Nantes, April 21, 1888). His other operas included *Le Visionnaire* (Nantes, 1851), *Le Colin-Maillard* (Paris, 1853), *Les Compagnons de la Marjolaine* (Paris, 1855), *M. de Chimpanzé* (Paris, 1858), *Le Nouveau Pourceaugnac* (Paris, 1860), *L'Auberge des Ardennes* (Paris, 1860), and *Les Musiciens de l'orchestre* (Paris, 1861).

Hijman, Julius, Dutch pianist, teacher, and composer; b. Almelo, Jan. 25, 1901; d. N.Y., Jan. 6, 1969. He studied piano privately with Dirk Schaefer, then with Paul Weingartner in Vienna; theory and composition with Sem Dresden in the Netherlands. He went to the U.S. in 1940; was an instructor at the Houston Cons. (1940–42) and at the Kansas City Cons. (1945–49); then taught composition at the Philadelphia Musical Academy and the N.Y. College of Music. He composed mostly chamber music; sonatas for violin, cello, saxophone, oboe, and flute, with piano; 4 string quartets; a Sonata for 2 Violins and Piano.

Hildach, Eugen, German baritone, teacher, and composer; b. Wittenberge-an-der-Elbe, Nov. 20, 1849; d. Zehlendorf, near Berlin, July 29, 1924. He began to study voice at the age of 24; married Anna Schubert, a singer, and went to Dresden, where they both taught at the Cons.; they also toured together in Germany. In 1904 they established their own singing school in Frankfurt. He publ. a number of songs, several of which became well known; particularly popular was *Der Lenz.*

Hildegard von Bingen, German composer, poetess, and mystic; b. Bemersheim, near Alzey, 1098; d. Rupertsberg, near Bingen, Sept. 17, 1179. Her noble parents, Hildebert and Mechtild, promised to consecrate her to the Church since she was their 10th child; accordingly, she began her novitiate as a child; joined with the reclusive mystic Jutta of Spanheim, who with her followers occupied a cell of the Benedictine monastery of Disibodenberg. At 15 Hildegard took the veil, and succeeded Jutta as Mother Superior in 1136. Between 1147 and 1150 she founded a monastery on the Rupertsberg (near Bingen) with 18 sisters; around 1165 she founded another house at Eibingen (near Rüdesheim). She is called "abbess" in letters drawn up by Frederick Barbarossa in 1163. She was known as the "Sybil of the Rhine," and conducted extensive correspondence with popes, emperors, kings, and archbishops. She was thus greatly involved in politics and diplomacy. Several fruitless attempts were made to canonize her, but her name is included in the Roman Martyrology, and her feast is celebrated on Sept. 17. Hildegard is musically important through her monophonic chants, several of which were settings of her lyric and dramatic poetry. She collected her poems in the early 1150s under the title *Symphonia armonie celestium revelationum.* This vol. survives in 2 sources, both in early German neumes; it comprises 70-odd liturgical poems (the exact number varies, depending on classification), all with melismatic music. The poetry is rich with imagery, and it shares the apocalyptic language of her visionary writings. The music is not typical of plainchant, but involves a technique unique to Hildegard; it is made of a number of melodic patterns recurring in different modal positions, which operate as open structures allowing for internal variation in different contexts. She also wrote a morality play in dramatic verse, *Ordo virtutum,* which includes 82 melodies which are similarly structured but distinctly more syllabic in style. She pointed out that her music is written in a range congenial to women's voices, contrasting with the formal Gregorian modes. Hildegard was also known for her literary works, which include prophecy, medical and scientific treatises, and hagiographies, as well as letters.

BIBL.: J. Gmelch, *Die Kompositionen der heiligen H.* (Düsseldorf, 1913); L. Bronarski, *Die Lieder der heiligen H.: Ein Beitrag zur Geschichte der geistlichen Musik des Mittelalters* (Zürich, 1922); M. Davic-Windstosser, *Carmina sanctae H.s: Die Lieder der heiligen H. v.B.* (Munich, 1928); B. Widmer, *Heilsordnung und Zeitgeschehen in der Mystik H.s v.B.* (Basel, 1955); M. Schrader and A. Führkötter, *Die Echtheit des Schriftums der heiligen H. v.B.* (Cologne, 1956); *H. v.B.: Briefwechsel* (Salzburg, 1965).

Hiles, Henry, English organist and composer; b. Shrewsbury, Dec. 31, 1826; d. Worthing, near London, Oct. 20, 1904. He filled various positions as organist and harmony teacher (1846–1904); was ed. of the *Quarterly Musical Review* (1885–88). He composed several oratorios, glees, and part-songs; publ. the manuals *Harmony of Sounds* (1871); *Grammar of Music* (2 vols., 1879); *First Lessons in Singing* (1881); *Part-Writing or Modern Counterpoint* (1884); *Harmony or Counterpoint?* (1889); *Harmony, Choral or Contrapuntal* (1894).

Hill, Alfred (Francis), noted Australian composer; b. Melbourne, Nov. 16, 1870; d. Sydney, Oct. 30, 1960. He played violin in traveling theater orchs.; then studied with Paul, Schreck, and Sitt at the Leipzig Cons. (1887–91); subsequently was active in New Zealand and Australia as a conductor, and later as a prof. at the New South Wales State Conservatorium (1916–34). He was made an Officer of the Order of the British Empire in 1953 and a Companion of the Order of St. Michael and St. George in 1960. He wrote over 500 works, some of which employ Maori and Australian aboriginal materials. He publ. *Harmony and Melody* (London, 1927).

WORKS: OPERAS: *Whipping Boy* (1893); *Lady Dolly* (1898; Sydney, 1900); *Tapu* (1902–3); *A Moorish Maid or Queen of the Riffs* (Auckland, 1905); *Teora—The Weird Flute* (1913; Sydney, 1928); *Giovanni, the Sculptor* (1913–14; Melbourne, 1914); *Rajah of Shivapore* (Sydney, 1914); *Auster* (1919; Sydney, 1922); *The Ship of Heaven* (1923; 1st complete perf., Sydney, 1933). ORCH.: 13 syms., including No. 1, *Maori* (1896–1900); No. 2, *Joy of Life* (1941); No. 3, *Australia* (1951); No. 4, *Pursuit of Happiness* (1955); No. 5, *Carnival* (1955); No. 6, *Celtic* (1956); No. 7 (1956); No. 8, *The Mind of Man* (1957); No. 9, *Melodious* (1958); No. 10 (1958); all transcribed from chamber pieces except No. 1. CHORAL: *The New Jerusalem* (1892); *Hinemoa, a Maori Legend* (1895); *Tawhaki* (1897); Mass (1931); part-songs. CHAMBER: 17 string quartets; 6 sonatas for Violin and Piano; *Life* for 8 Solo Voices and Piano Quintet (1912); piano pieces; songs.

BIBL.: A. McCredie, "A. H. (1870–1960): Some Backgrounds and Perspectives for an Historical Edition," *Miscellanea Musicologica*, III (1968); J. Thomson, *A Distant Music: The Life and Times of A. H., 1870–1960* (Oxford, 1982).

Hill, Bertha "Chippie," black American blues singer; b. Charleston, S.C., March 15, 1905; d. (struck and killed by an automobile) N.Y., May 7, 1950. She was an offspring of a large family, which included 16 children. She made her way to N.Y., where she 1st appeared as a dancer in Harlem; then toured as a dancer and singer with Ma Rainey; subsequently made tours and recordings with Louis Armstrong and others. She was active in Chicago as a singer in nightclubs; in 1948 she appeared at Carnegie Hall in N.Y.

Hill, Edward Burlingame, eminent American composer and teacher; b. Cambridge, Mass., Sept. 9, 1872; d. Francestown, N.H., July 9, 1960. A member of a distinguished family of educators (his father was a prof. of chemistry at Harvard, and his grandfather, president of Harvard), he pursued regular courses at Harvard Univ.; studied music with J.K. Paine; graduated in 1894 summa cum laude; took lessons in piano with B.J. Lang and A. Whiting, in composition with Chadwick and Bullard; also (for 1 summer) studied with Widor in Paris. He became greatly interested in the new tonal resources of the impressionist school of composers; wrote articles in the *Boston Evening Transcript* and other publications dealing with French music; publ. a book, *Modern French Music* (Boston, 1924). In 1908 he joined the faculty of Harvard Univ. as an instructor in music; became associate prof. in 1918, prof. in 1928, then James E. Ditson Prof. (1937–40); was a member of the National Inst. of Arts and Letters and of the American Academy of Arts and Sciences; was a Chevalier of the Légion d'Honneur; lectured at the Univs. of Strasbourg and Lyons (1921). In his music, Hill reveals himself as a follower of the French school; clarity of design and elegance of expression are his chief characteristics. His best works are for orch., but he also composed some fine chamber and choral music.

WORKS: ORCH.: Symphonic poem, *The Parting of Lancelot and Guinevere* (St. Louis, Dec. 31, 1915); *Stevensoniana Suite No. 1* (N.Y., Jan. 27, 1918); symphonic poem, *The Fall of the House of Usher*, after Poe (Boston, Oct. 29, 1920); *Stevensoniana Suite No. 2* (N.Y., March 25, 1923). The following were perf. for the 1st time by the Boston Sym. Orch.: *Waltzes* (Feb. 24, 1922); *Scherzo* for 2 Pianos and Orch. (Dec. 19, 1924); symphonic poem, *Lilacs* (his best work in the impressionist manner; Cambridge, March 31, 1927); Sym. No. 1 (March 30, 1928); *An Ode* (for the 50th anniversary of the Boston Sym. Orch.; Oct. 17, 1930); Sym. No. 2 (Feb. 27, 1931); Concertino for Piano and Orch. (Boston, April 25, 1932); Sinfonietta for String Orch. (N.Y., April 3, 1936); Sym. No. 3 (Dec. 3, 1937); Violin Concerto (Nov. 11, 1938); Concertino for String Orch. (April 19, 1940); *Music for English Horn and Orch.* (March 2, 1945); *Prelude* for Orch. (N.Y., March 29, 1953). *Diversion* for Small Ensemble was perf. at the Saratoga Festival (Sept. 6, 1947). CHAMBER: Flute Sonata (1926); Clarinet Sonata (1927); Sextet for Flute, Oboe, Clarinet, Bassoon, Horn, and Piano (1934); String Quartet (1935); Piano Quartet (1937); Sonata for 2 Clarinets (1938); Quintet for Clarinet and String Quartet (1945); Sonata for Bassoon and Piano (1948); Sonatina for Cello and Piano (1949); Sonatina for Violin and Piano (1951). VOCAL: *Nuns of the Perpetual Adoration*, cantata for Women's Voices, with Orch. or Piano (1908); *Autumn Twilight*

for Soprano and Orch.; *The Wilderness Shall Rejoice*, anthem for Mixed Chorus (1915); 2 pantomimes, with orch. accompaniment: *Jack Frost in Midsummer* (1908) and *Pan and the Star* (1914). PIANO: *Poetical Sketches* (1902); *Country Idyls*, a set of 6 pieces; *Jazz Study* for 2 Pianos (1924).

BIBL.: G. Smith, "E.B. H.," *Modern Music*, XVI (1939); L. Tyler, *E.B. H.: A Bio-Bibliography* (N.Y., 1989).

Hill, Ralph, English writer on music; b. Watford, Oct. 8, 1900; d. London, Oct. 19, 1950. He studied cello with his father at the Guildhall School of Music in London; was then active in music publishing (1920–29); was music ed. of the *Radio Times* (1933–45); also wrote for the *Daily Mail* (1933–39 and 1945–50). He publ. the following works, all in London: *An Outline of Musical History* (1929); *Brahms: A Study in Musical Biography* (1933); *Liszt* (1936; 2nd ed., 1949); *Challenges: A Series of Controversial Essays* (1943); *Music without Fears* (1945); *Prelude to Music* (1951); also ed. *The Symphony* (1949) and *The Concerto* (1952).

Hill, Richard S(ynyer), American music librarian; b. Chicago, Sept. 25, 1901; d. Naples, Fla., Feb. 7, 1961. He was educated at Phillips Exeter Academy; then studied at Cornell Univ. (B.A., 1924) and did post-graduate work at Oxford Univ. (1924–26); held a research fellowship in psychology with Kurt Koffka at Smith College (1927–29); returned to Cornell Univ. for further study in psychology and musicology, the latter under Otto Kinkeldey. He joined the staff of the Music Division of the Library of Congress in Washington, D.C., in 1939; served as ed. of *Notes*, the quarterly journal of the Music Library Assoc., from 1943 to the time of his death; was president of the International Assoc. of Music Libraries (1951–55). In 1946 he was sent by the Library of Congress to Germany and Austria to investigate the conditions of music libraries there and estimate the losses inflicted by World War II; publ. an important account, "The Former Prussian State Library," listing MSS of Mozart, Beethoven, and Haydn which were missing in the aftermath of the war (*Notes*, Sept. 1946). He contributed several important articles to music magazines, one of the most notable being "Schoenberg's Tone Rows and the Tonal System of the Future" (*Musical Quarterly*, Jan. 1936). In collaboration with Kurtz Myers, he ed. a new type of discography, publ. under the title *Record Ratings* (N.Y., 1956).

BIBL.: C. Bradley and J. Coover, eds., *R.S. H.: Tributes from Friends* (Detroit, 1987).

Hill, Ureli Corelli, American violinist and conductor; b. Hartford, Conn.?, c.1802; d. (suicide) Paterson, N.J., Sept. 2, 1875. His father, Uri K. Hill, was a teacher of music in Boston and N.Y., and author of a manual, *Solfeggio Americano, A System of Singing* (N.Y., 1820). An admirer of Corelli, he named his son after him; the first name (Ureli) is a combination of the father's name, Uri, and a friend's name, Eli. Ureli played violin in various theaters in N.Y. as a boy; was a violinist in the orch. of Garcia's opera company in 1825; then joined the N.Y. Sacred Musical Soc., and conducted it in the 1st American performance, with orch. accompaniment, of Handel's *Messiah* (1831). From 1835 to 1837 he was in Germany, where he studied for a year with Spohr. Returning to N.Y., he became a founder and 1st president of the N.Y. Phil. (1842–47); then went West in quest of fortune, which failed to materialize. In N.Y. he exhibited a pianoforte of his own invention, in which he used small bell tuning forks in place of strings, so as to secure perfect intonation; the attempt to promote this instrument met with failure. He played the violin in the N.Y. Phil. from 1850 until 1873, when he retired because of age; continued to play engagements in various theater orchs. throughout his life; then moved to Paterson, N.J., where he engaged (unsuccessfully) in real-estate schemes. Depressed on account of constant setbacks in his ventures of promotion in music and in business, he committed suicide by swallowing morphine.

BIBL.: H. Shanet, *Philharmonic: A History of New York's Orchestra* (Garden City, N.Y., 1975).

Hill, W.E. & Sons, firm of violin makers and music dealers in London. The founder of the firm was Joseph Hill (1715–84); he was an apprentice to Peter Wamsley; established his business in 1750. He had 5 sons, who were violinists. **William Ebsworth Hill,** a great-grandson of the founder (b. London, Oct. 20, 1817; d. Hanley, April 2, 1895), adopted the present name of the firm; his instruments took 1st prize at the expositions in London (1851) and Paris (1867). His sons, **William Henry Hill** (b. London, June 3, 1857; d. there, Jan. 20, 1927), **Arthur Frederick Hill** (b. London, Jan. 24, 1860; d. there, Feb. 5, 1939), and **Alfred Ebsworth Hill** (b. London, Feb. 11, 1862; d. there, April 21, 1940), collaborated in the writing of *Antonio Stradivari, His Life and Work* (London, 1902). William H., Arthur F., and Alfred E. Hill also wrote *The Violin-Makers of the Guarneri Family* (London, 1931). The Ashmolean Museum at Oxford contains a valuable collection of stringed instruments, including a 1716 Stradivari violin with a bow dated 1694, presented by Arthur F. Hill. The firm continued under the direction of the descendants of the founder, **Andrew Hill** (b. London, July 3, 1942) and **David Hill** (b. London, Feb. 28, 1952).

Hill, Wilhelm, German pianist and composer; b. Fulda, March 28, 1838; d. Homburg, June 6, 1902. He studied in Frankfurt, and received a prize for his opera *Alona* in the competition for the opening of a new opera house. He publ. violin sonatas; a Piano Quartet; piano pieces. His song *Es liegt eine Krone im tiefen Rhein* achieved immense popularity.
    BIBL.: K. Schmidt, *W. H., Leben und Werke* (Leipzig, 1910).

Hillebrecht, Hildegard, German soprano; b. Hannover, Nov. 26, 1927. She made her operatic debut as Leonora in *Il Trovatore* in Freiburg im Breisgau (1951); then sang in Zürich (1952–54), Düsseldorf (1954–59), Cologne (1956–61), Munich (from 1961), and again in Zürich (from 1972). She also made guest appearances in Vienna, Hamburg, Berlin, Salzburg, Paris, and Rome. In 1967 she made her Covent Garden debut in London as the Empress in *Die Frau ohne Schatten;* on Nov. 8, 1968, she made her Metropolitan Opera debut in N.Y. as Sieglinde in *Die Walküre.* She was best known for her roles in operas by Mozart, Wagner, Puccini, Strauss, and Verdi; she also sang in the premiere of Dallapiccola's *Ulisse* in Berlin (1968).

Hillemacher, 2 brothers, French composers; **Paul Joseph Guillaume** (b. Paris, Nov. 29, 1852; d. Versailles, Aug. 13, 1933) and **Lucien Joseph Édouard** (b. Paris, June 10, 1860; d. there, June 2, 1909). They studied at the Paris Cons.; Paul won the 2nd Prix de Rome in 1875, and the 1st in 1876, with the cantata *Judith;* Lucien obtained the 2nd Prix de Rome in 1879, and the 1st in 1880, with the lyric scene *Fingal.* After graduation, they decided to write music in collaboration, and adopted a common signature—P.L. Hillemacher. They also wrote a biography of Gounod (Paris, 1905; 2nd ed., 1925). Together they produced the following stage works: *Saint-Mégrin,* opéra-comique (Brussels, March 2, 1886); *Une Aventure d'Arlequin,* opéra-comique (Brussels, March 22, 1888); *Le Régiment qui passe,* opéra-comique (Royan, Sept. 11, 1894); *Le Drac,* lyric drama (in German as *Der Flutgeist,* Karlsruhe, Nov. 14, 1896); *Orsola,* lyric drama (Paris, May 21, 1902); *Circé,* lyric drama (Paris, April 17, 1907). Paul, who survived his brother by 24 years, also wrote a "tableau musical," *Fra Angelico,* which was produced at the Paris Opéra-Comique on June 10, 1924. In addition to their operas, the brothers wrote a symphonic legend, *Loreley,* which won the prize of the City of Paris (1882); 2 orch. suites, *La Cinquantaine* and *Les Solitudes;* an oratorio, *La Légende de Sainte Geneviève* (1886); songs.

Hiller, Ferdinand (von), noted German conductor, composer, and writer on music; b. Frankfurt am Main, Oct. 24, 1811; d. Cologne, May 10, 1885. He studied piano with A. Schmitt, making his public debut at age 10; then went to Weimar to study with Hummel (1825), whom he accompanied to Vienna for a visit with Beethoven (1827); subsequently was in Paris (1828–35), where he was befriended by Chopin, Liszt,

Berlioz, and other famous musicians. He became conductor of Frankfurt's Cäcilien-Verein (1836); after studies in Italy (1841), he devoted himself mainly to conducting, composing, and writing on music. He was a conductor with the Leipzig Gewandhaus Orch. (1843–44), then in Dresden, where he brought out 2 of his operas (1845–47); subsequently conducted in Düsseldorf (1847–50). He settled in Cologne as a conductor (1850), gaining distinction in particular with the Lower Rhine Festival; also reorganized the municipal music school, serving as its director until his death. He appeared as a guest conductor in Paris (1851–52), London (1852–72), and St. Petersburg (1870). A musical conservative, he violently attacked Wagner. His own compositions met with indifferent success, although his career as a conductor and writer on music won him many admirers.
    WORKS: OPERAS: *Romilda* (Milan, 1839); *Der Traum in der Christnacht* (Dresden, 1845); *Konradin* (Dresden, Oct. 13, 1847); *Der Advokat* (Cologne, 1854); *Die Katakomben* (Wiesbaden, Feb. 15, 1862); *Der Deserteur* (Cologne, Feb. 17, 1865). ORATORIOS: *Die Zerstörung Jerusalems* (Leipzig, April 2, 1840) and *Saul;* also cantatas and various other choral works. ORCH.: 3 syms.; 3 overtures; 3 piano concertos. CHAMBER: 5 string quartets; 5 piano quartets; 5 piano trios. Also more than 100 songs and many piano pieces.
    WRITINGS: *Die Musik und das Publikum* (Cologne, 1864); *Aus dem Tonleben unserer Zeit* (2 vols., Leipzig, 1868 and 1871); *Ludwig van Beethoven; Gelegentliche: Aufsätze* (Leipzig, 1871); *Felix Mendelssohn Bartholdy: Briefe und Erinnerungen* (Cologne, 1874); *Musikalisches und Persönliches* (Leipzig, 1876); *Briefe an eine Ungenannte* (Cologne, 1877); *Künstlerleben* (Cologne, 1880); *Wie hören wir Musik?* (Leipzig, 1881); *Goethes musikalisches Leben* (Cologne, 1883); *Erinnerungsblätter* (Cologne, 1884).
    BIBL.: W. Neumann, "F. H.," *Die Componisten der neueren Zeit,* XLIII (Kassel, c.1857); E. Wolff, "F. H.," *Neue Zeitschrift für Musik,* LXXVIII (1911); H. Hering, *Die Klavierwerke F. v.H.s* (diss., Univ. of Cologne, 1928); R. Sietz, ed., *Aus F. H.s Briefwechsel* (7 vols., Cologne, 1958–70); idem, *Der Nachlass F. H.s* (Cologne, 1970).

Hiller, Friedrich Adam, German singer, conductor, and composer, son of **Johann Adam Hiller;** b. Leipzig, c.1767; d. Königsberg, Nov. 23, 1812. He studied music with his father; was a conductor at various provincial theaters in Germany, and wrote a number of light operas: *Biondetta* (Schwerin, 1792); *Das Schmuckkästchen* (Königsberg, 1804); *Die drei Sultaninen* (Königsberg, 1809); etc.; also chamber music.

Hiller, Johann Adam, important German conductor, composer, and writer on music, father of **Friedrich Adam Hiller;** b. Wendisch-Ossig, near Görlitz, Dec. 25, 1728; d. Leipzig, June 16, 1804. He began his musical training as a child; after attending the Görlitz Gymnasium (1740–45), he won a scholarship to the Dresden Kreuzschule, where he studied keyboard playing and thoroughbass with Homilius (1746–51); then studied law at the Univ. of Leipzig (1751). He was active as a bass singer and flutist in Leipzig's Grosses Concert prior to serving as steward to Count Brühl in Dresden (1754–58), and also later in Leipzig (1758–60). Thereafter he assumed a major role in the musical life of Leipzig. He organized his own subscription concert series (1762), and was director of the revived Grosses Concert (1763–71); also founded a singing school, which evolved into a music school. He was the erudite ed. of the *Wöchentliche Nachrichten* (1766–70), the 1st major specialized journal on music. During this same period, he helped to establish the German singspiel in collaboration with the poet Christian Felix Weisse. He mastered the genre in his *Lottchen am Hofe* (Leipzig, April 24, 1767), in which he created effective characterizations by writing simple songs for the country people and arias in the opera seria tradition for the people of means. His finest singspiels were *Die Liebe auf dem Lande* (Leipzig, May 18, 1768) and *Die Jagd* (Weimar, Jan. 29, 1770). He founded the Musikabende Gesellschaft (1775), with which he gave many concerts; then became conductor of the Gewandhaus concerts in 1781, leading them until 1785. This famous series of concerts has continued without interruption for more than 200 years. He also was music director of the Univ.'s Paulinerkirche (1778–85) and of the Neukirche (1783–85); then was Kapellmeister to the Duke of Courland in Mitau (1785–86) and civic music director in Breslau (1787–89). He returned to Leipzig as Kantor of the Thomaskirche in 1789, remaining there until his retirement in 1800.

WORKS: SINGSPIELS (all 1st perf. in Leipzig unless otherwise given): *Die verwandelten Weiber oder Der Teufel ist los, erster Teil* (May 28, 1766; 12 pieces by J. Standfuss); *Der lustige Schuster oder Der Teufel ist los, zweiter Teil* (1766; 7 pieces by Hiller, remainder by Standfuss); *Lisuart und Dariolette oder Die Frage und die Antwort* (Nov. 25, 1766); *Lottchen am Hofe* (April 24, 1767); *Die Muse* (Oct. 3, 1767); *Die Liebe auf dem Lande* (May 18, 1768); *Die Jagd* (Weimar, Jan. 29, 1770); *Der Dorfbalbier* (1771; with pieces by C. Neefe); *Der Aerndtekranz* (1771); *Der Krieg* (1772); *Die Jubelhochzeit* (April 5, 1773); *Die kleine Aehrenleserin*, children's operetta (publ. in Leipzig, 1778); *Das Grab des Mufti oder Die beiden Geitzigen* (Jan. 17, 1779); *Poltis oder Das gerettete Troja* (1777?). **SACRED VOCAL:** (22) *Choralmelodien zu Gellerts geistlichen Oden und Liedern* for Voice and Basso Continuo (1761; 2nd ed., rev., 1792, as *25 neue Choralmelodien* for 4 Voices and Basso Continuo); *50 geistliche Lieder für Kinder* for Voice and Keyboard (1774); *Geistliche Lieder einer vornehmen curländischen Dame* for Voice and Keyboard (1780); *Religiöse Oden und Lieder* for Voice and Keyboard (1790); *3 Melodien zu Wir glauben all an einen Gott* for 4 Voices (1790); *Herr Gott, dich loben wir* for 4 Voices, Trumpets, Trombones, and Timpani (1790); *Gesang zum Charfreytage* for 4 Voices (1793); *Vierstimmige Chor-Arien zum neuen Jahre . . . nebst 4 lateinischen Sanctus* (1794); etc. **SECULAR VOCAL:** *Lieder mit Melodien* (1759); *Melodien zu 6 Romanzen von Löwen* (1760); *Cantate auf die Ankunft der hohen Landesherrschaft* for Soloists, Chorus, and Orch. (1765); *Lieder für Kinder* (1769); *Lieder mit Melodien* (1772); *Der Greis, Mann und Jüngling*, cantata (1778); *Horatii Carmen ad Aelium Lamium* for Soloists, Chorus, and Keyboard (1778); *Die Friedensfeyer oder Die unvermuthete Wiederkunft* (1779); *Cantaten und Arien verschiedener Dichter* for Voice and Keyboard (1781); *Sammlung der Lieder aus dem Kinderfreunde* (1782); *Letztes Opfer in einigen Liedermelodien der comischen Muse* (1790); *Aerntelied* (1797). He also wrote instrumental music, including chamber music and pieces for keyboard.

COLLECTIONS (a number include works by Hiller): *Wöchentlicher musikalischer Zeitvertreib* (1759–60); *Sammlung kleine Klavier- und Singstücke* (4 vols., 1774); *Vierstimmige Motetten und Arien . . . von verschiedenen Komponisten* (6 vols., 1776–91); *Sammlung der vorzüglichsten noch ungedruckten Arien und Duetten des deutschen Theaters* (6 vols., 1777–80); *6 italienische Arien verschiedener Componisten* (1778); (49) *Lieder und Arien aus Sophiens Reise* (1779); *Italienische Duetten* for 2 Sopranos (1781); *Arien und Duetten des deutschen Theaters* (vol. I, 1781); *Duetten zur Beförderung des Studium des Gesanges* (1781); *Elisens geistliche Lieder* (1783); *Deutsche Arien und Duetten von verschiedenen Componisten* (vol. I, 1785); *Meisterstücke des italienischen Gesanges . . . mit deutschen geistlichen Texten* (1791); *Allgemeines Choral-Melodien-Buch* for 4 Voices and Basso Continuo (1793); *Nachtrag* for 4 Voices (1797).

WRITINGS: *Anekdoten zur Lebensgeschichte grosser Regenten und berühmter Staatsmänner* (Leipzig, 1766–72); ed. *Wöchentliche Nachrichten und Anmerkungen die Musik betreffend* (Leipzig, 1766–70; supplement publ. as *Musikalische Nachrichten und Anmerkungen*, Leipzig, 1770); *Anweisung zur Singekunst in der deutschen und italienischen Sprache* (Frankfurt and Leipzig, 1773); *Musikalisches Handbuch für die Liebhaber des Gesanges und Claviers* (Leipzig, 1773); *Anweisung zum musikalisch-richtigen Gesange* (Leipzig, 1774; 2nd ed., augmented, 1798); *Exempelbuch der Anweisung zum Singen* (Leipzig, 1774); *Anweisung zum musikalisch-zierlichen Gesange* (Leipzig, 1780); *Lebensbeschreibungen berühmter Musikgelehrten und Tonkünstler neuerer Zeit* (vol. I, Leipzig, 1784);

Über Metastasio und seine Werke (Leipzig, 1786); *Nachricht von der Aufführung des Händelschen Messias in . . . Berlin den 19. May 1786* (Berlin, 1786); *Fragmente aus Händels Messias, nebst Betrachtungen über die Aufführung Händelscher Singcompositionen* (Leipzig, 1787); *Über Alt und Neu in der Musik* (Leipzig, 1787); *Was ist wahre Kirchenmusik?* (Leipzig, 1789); *Beyträge zu wahrer Kirchenmusik von J.A. Hasse und J.A. Hiller* (Leipzig, 1791); *Kurze und erleichterte Anweisung zum Singen* (Leipzig, 1792); *Anweisung zum Violinspielen für Schulen und zum Selbstunterrichte* (Leipzig, 1792); *Erinnerungen gegen das Melodien-Register in Freyes kleiner Lieder-Konkordanz* (Leipzig, 1798).

BIBL.: C. Naumann, *J.A. H.: Eine bescheidene Würdigung seiner Verdienste als Mensch, Künstler und Schulmann* (Leipzig, 1804); K. Peiser, *J.A. H.* (Leipzig, 1894); G. Calmus, *Die ersten deutschen Singspiele von Standfuss und H.* (Leipzig, 1908); H. von Hase, "J.A. H. und Breitkopfs," *Zeitschrift für Musikwissenschaft*, II (1919–20); A. Schering, *Das Zeitalter J.S. Bachs und J.A. H.s* (Leipzig, 1940); G. Sander, *Das Deutschtum im Singspiel J.A. H.s* (diss., Univ. of Berlin, 1943); K. Kawada, *Studien zu den Singspielen von J.A. H. (1728–1804)* (Marburg, 1969); V. Duckles, "J.A. H.'s *Critical Prospectus for a Music Library*," *Studies in Eighteenth-Century Music: A Tribute to Karl Geiringer* (N.Y. and London, 1970).

Hiller, Lejaren (Arthur, Jr.), American composer and theorist of computer music; b. N.Y., Feb. 23, 1924. He studied chemistry at Princeton Univ. (Ph.D., 1947) and music at the Univ. of Illinois (M.Mus., 1958); began his career as a chemist; was assistant prof. of chemistry at the Univ. of Illinois (1953–58), and subsequently taught music there, until 1968; then became Frederick B. Slee Prof. of Composition at the State Univ. of N.Y. at Buffalo, and also served as co-director of the Center of the Creative and Performing Arts; was made Birge-Cary Prof. of Music in 1980. He publ. (with L. Isaacson) a manual, *Experimental Music* (N.Y., 1959), and numerous articles on the application of computers to musical composition. He composed 2 syms. (1953, 1960); Piano Concerto (1949); 7 string quartets (1949, 1951, 1953, 1957, 1962, 1972, 1979); 6 piano sonatas (1946–72), etc. He achieved notoriety with his computer composition *Illiac Suite* for String Quartet (in collaboration with L. Isaacson; 1957), the name being an abbreviation of *Illinois Accumulator;* the result is a programmed, i.e., dictated, production which includes vast stretches of cadential C-major chords. Encouraged by publicity, Hiller wrote a *Computer Cantata* for Soprano, Magnetic Tape, and Chamber Ensemble (1963). Other works are *Man with the Oboe* (1962); *Machine Music* for Piano, Percussion, and Tape (1964); *An Avalanche* for Pitchmen, Prima Donna, Player Piano, Percussion, and Pre-recorded Playback (1968); *HPSCHD* for 1 to 7 Harpsichords and 1 to 51 Tapes (1968; in collaboration with J. Cage); *A Preview of Coming Attractions* for Orch. (1975); *Midnight Carnival* for a Principal Tape, an Indeterminate Number of Subsidiary Tapes, and Other Events in an Urban Environment (1976); *Fast and Slow* for Saxophone Quartet (1984); *The Fox Trots Again* for Chamber Ensemble (1985).

Hillier, Paul (Douglas), English baritone and conductor; b. Dorchester, Feb. 9, 1949. He trained at the Guildhall School of Music in London, and then served as vicar-choral at St. Paul's Cathedral (1973–74). In 1974 he made his formal concert debut at London's Purcell Room and also founded the Hilliard Ensemble, which he directed in performances of early music. He also gave master classes in early music performance. He publ. *300 Years of English Partsongs* (1983), *Romantic English Partsongs* (1986), and *The Catch Book* (1987).

Hillis, Margaret (Eleanor), American conductor; b. Kokomo, Ind., Oct. 1, 1921. She studied piano as a child; also played the tuba and double bass in school bands. An energetic person, she became a junior golf champion and, fantastically, was a civilian flying instructor for the U.S. Navy during World War II. She then enrolled as a music student at Indiana Univ. (B.A., 1947), and studied choral conducting at the Juilliard School of Music in N.Y. (1947–49). Her teacher, Robert Shaw, engaged her as his assistant (1952–53). She became conductor of the chorus of the American Opera Soc. in N.Y. in 1952, remaining in this post until 1968; also was choral director of the N.Y. City Opera (1955–56). In 1957, at Fritz Reiner's behest, she organized the Chicago Sym. Orch. Chorus, which soon developed into an outstanding choral aggregation. Her various, often synchronous, employments included the following: instructor in choral conducting at the Juilliard School of Music (1951–53); music director of the Kenosha (Wis.) Orch. (1961–68); director of the Cleveland Orch. Chorus (1969–71); resident conductor of the Chicago Civic Orch. (from 1967); director of choral activities at Northwestern Univ. in Chicago (1970–77); music director of the Elgin (Ill.) Sym. Orch. (1971–85). In 1978 she became a visiting prof. of conducting at the Indiana Univ. School of Music in Bloomington. In 1981 she was named music director of the Concert Soc., Libertyville, Ill.; in 1982–83 she was director of choral activities for the San Francisco Sym. She had numerous engagements as a guest conductor. On Oct. 31, 1977, in a sort of coup de théâtre, she substituted on short notice for the temporarily incapacitated Sir Georg Solti to conduct a performance of Mahler's monumental Sym. No. 8 at Carnegie Hall in N.Y. She received many awards of merit from various organizations; she is also the recipient of honorary degrees of Mus.D. from Temple Univ. (1967) and Indiana Univ. (1972).

Hilsberg (real name, **Hillersberg**), **Alexander,** Polish-born American violinist and conductor; b. Warsaw, April 24, 1897; d. Camden, Maine, Aug. 10, 1961. He studied violin with Auer at the St. Petersburg Cons. In 1918 he went on a concert tour in Siberia, eventually reaching Harbin in Manchuria; in 1923 he went to the U.S. via Japan. In 1926 he joined the violin section of the Philadelphia Orch.; became its concertmaster in 1931, and associate conductor in 1945. He was also on the staff of the Curtis Inst. of Music (1927–53). The great success that Hilsberg achieved conducting the Philadelphia Orch. at a Carnegie Hall concert in 1950 led to his engagement as permanent conductor of the New Orleans Sym. Orch. (1952–60); in the spring of 1956 he took this orch. on a tour of Latin America.

Hilton, John (the Elder), English organist and composer, father of **John Hilton (the Younger);** place and date of birth unknown; d. Cambridge, before March 20, 1608. He was a countertenor at Lincoln Cathedral (1584–94), then organist at Trinity College, Cambridge (from 1594). It is not possible to determine which sacred works ascribed to John Hilton are by the Elder or the Younger. The anthem *Call to Remembrance* is ascribed to the Elder in 1 source. His only known secular work is the madrigal *Fair Oriana, Beauty's Queen,* publ. in Morley's *The Triumphes of Oriana* (London, 1601).

Hilton, John (the Younger), English organist and composer, son of **John Hilton (the Elder);** b. probably in Cambridge, 1599; d. Westminster (buried), March 21, 1657. He studied at Trinity College, Cambridge (Mus.B., 1626), then became organist and clerk of St. Margaret's, Westminster (1628). He ed. a popular collection under the title *Catch that Catch Can* for 3 to 4 Voices (London, 1652; 3rd ed., 1667, as *The Musical Companion*), which contains 42 pieces by him. Other secular works include *Ayres or Fa La's* for 3 Voices (London, 1627; ed. by J. Warren, Musical Antiquarian Soc., XIII, London, 1844), 14 fantasias *a 3,* several dance movements, and various songs and dialogues in MS collections (7 ed. in Musica Britannica, XXXIII, 1971). His sacred works, which include 4 Services, a Te Deum, 5 anthems, and 12 verse anthems, are open to much speculation; some may be by his father.

Himmel, Friedrich Heinrich, German composer; b. Treuenbrietzen, Brandenburg, Nov. 20, 1765; d. Berlin, June 8, 1814. He studied theology at the Univ. of Halle; at the same time, he cultivated music. He received a stipend from Friedrich Wilhelm II to study with Naumann in Dresden; subsequently he went to Italy, where he acquired skill in stage music. His

cantata *Il primo navigatore* was performed in Venice (March 1, 1794), and his opera *La morte di Semiramide* in Naples (Jan. 12, 1795). He then returned to Berlin and was appointed court composer. In 1798 he went to St. Petersburg, where he produced his opera *Alessandro* (Jan. 1799). In 1800 he returned from Russia by way of Sweden and Denmark; in Berlin he produced his Italian opera *Vasco di Gama* (Jan. 12, 1801). His subsequent operas, staged in Berlin, were in the nature of singspiels, to German words: *Frohsinn und Schwärmerei* (March 9, 1801), *Fanchon das Leiermädchen* (May 15, 1804; his most successful work; many revivals), *Die Sylphen* (April 14, 1806), etc. His last opera, *Der Kobold,* was produced in Vienna (May 22, 1813). Many of his songs had great vogue (*An Alexis, Es kann ja nicht immer so bleiben,* etc.). He also composed an oratorio, *Isacco figura del Redentore* (Berlin, March 14, 1792); several works of sacred music; a Piano Concerto; Piano Sextet; Piano Quartet; pieces for piano solo.

BIBL.: L. Odendahl, *F.H. H.; Bemerkungen zur Geschichte der Berliner Oper um die Wende des 18. und 19. Jahrhunderts* (diss., Univ. of Bonn, 1914).

Hindemith, Paul, eminent German-born American composer, one of the leading masters of 20th-century music; b. Hanau, near Frankfurt am Main, Nov. 16, 1895; d. Frankfurt am Main, Dec. 28, 1963. He began studying violin at the age of 9; at 14 he entered the Hoch Cons. in Frankfurt, where he studied violin with A. Rebner, and composition with Arnold Mendelssohn and Sekles. His father was killed in World War I, and Hindemith was compelled to rely on his own resources to make a living. He became concertmaster of the orch. of the Frankfurt Opera (1915–23), and later played the viola in the string quartet of his teacher Rebner; from 1922 to 1929 he was violist in the Amar String Quartet; also appeared as a soloist on the viola and viola d'amore; later was engaged as a conductor, mainly in his own works. As a composer, he joined the modern movement and was an active participant in the contemporary music concerts at Donaueschingen, and later in Baden-Baden. In 1927 he was appointed instructor in composition at the Berlin Hochschule für Musik. With the advent of the Hitler regime in 1933, Hindemith began to experience increasing difficulties, both artistically and politically. Although his own ethnic purity was never questioned, he was married to Gertrud Rottenberg, daughter of the Jewish conductor Ludwig Rottenberg, and he stubbornly refused to cease ensemble playing with undeniable Jews. Hitler's propaganda minister, Goebbels, accused Hindemith of cultural Bolshevism, and his music fell into an official desuetude. Unwilling to compromise with the barbarous regime, Hindemith accepted engagements abroad. Beginning in 1934, he made 3 visits to Ankara at the invitation of the Turkish government, and helped to organize the music curriculum at the Ankara Cons. He made his 1st American appearance at the Coolidge Festival at the Library of Congress in Washington, D.C., in a performance of his Unaccompanied Viola Sonata (April 10, 1937); after a brief sojourn in Switzerland, he emigrated to the U.S.; was instructor at the Berkshire Music Center at Tanglewood in the summer of 1940; from 1940 to 1953 he was a prof. at Yale Univ.; he was elected a member of the National Inst. of Arts and Letters; and during the academic year 1950–51 he was Charles Eliot Norton Lecturer at Harvard Univ. He became an American citizen in 1946. He conducted concerts in the Netherlands, Italy, and England during the summer of 1947; in 1949, revisited Germany for the 1st time since the war, and conducted the Berlin Phil. in a program of his own works (Feb. 14, 1949). In 1953 he went to Switzerland; gave courses at the Univ. of Zürich; also conducted orchs. in Germany and Austria. In 1954 he received the prestigious Sibelius Award of $35,000, offered annually to distinguished composers and scientists by a Finnish shipowner. From 1959 to 1961 he conducted guest appearances in the U.S.; in 1963 he visited America for the last time; then went to Italy, Vienna, and finally Frankfurt, where he died. Hindemith's early music reflects rebellious opposition to all tradition; this is noted in such works as the opera *Mörder, Hoffnung der Frauen* (op. 12, 1921) and *Suite 1922* for Piano (op. 26); at the same time, he cultivated the techniques of constructivism, evident in his theatrical sketch *Hin und Zurück* (op. 45a, 1927), in which *Krebsgang* (retrograde movement) is applied to the action on the stage, so that events are reversed; in a work of a much later period, *Ludus Tonalis* (1943), the postlude is the upside-down version of the prelude. Along constructive lines is Hindemith's cultivation of so-called *Gebrauchsmusik,* that is, music for use; he was also an ardent champion of *Hausmusik,* to be played or sung by amateurs at home; the score of his *Frau Musica* (as revised in 1944) has an obbligato part for the audience to sing. A neo-Classical trend is shown in a series of works, entitled *Kammermusik,* for various instrumental combinations, polyphonically conceived, and Baroque in style. Although he made free use of atonal melodies, he was never tempted to adopt an integral 12-tone method, which he opposed on esthetic grounds. Having made a thorough study of early music, he artfully assimilated its polyphony in his works; his masterpiece of this genre was the opera *Mathis der Maler.* An exceptionally prolific composer, Hindemith wrote music of all types for all instrumental combinations, including a series of sonatas for each orch. instrument with piano. His style may be described as a synthesis of modern, Romantic, Classical, Baroque, and other styles, a combination saved from the stigma of eclecticism only by Hindemith's superlative mastery of technical means. As a theorist and pedagogue, he developed a self-consistent method of presentation derived from the acoustical nature of harmonies.

WORKS: OPERAS: *Mörder, Hoffnung der Frauen,* op. 12 (1919; Stuttgart, June 4, 1921); *Das Nusch-Nuschi,* op. 20, marionette opera (1920; Stuttgart, June 4, 1921; rev. version, Königsberg, Jan. 22, 1931); *Sancta Susanna,* op. 21 (1921; Frankfurt, March 26, 1922); *Cardillac,* op. 39 (Dresden, Nov. 9, 1926; rev. version, Zürich, June 20, 1952); *Hin und Zurück,* op. 45a, 1-act sketch (Baden-Baden, July 17, 1927); *Neues vom Tage* (1928–29, rev. 1953; Berlin, June 8, 1929; rev. version, Naples, April 7, 1954, composer conducting); *Mathis der Maler* (1934–35; Zürich, May 28, 1938; Hindemith's best stage work); *Orfeo,* realization of Monteverdi's opera (1943); *Die Harmonie der Welt* (1950–57; Munich, Aug. 11, 1957, composer conducting); *Das lange Weihnachtsmahl* (1960; Mannheim, Dec. 17, 1961); *Tuttifäntchen,* incidental music for a Christmas fairy tale (Darmstadt, Dec. 13, 1922).

BALLETS: *Der Dämon,* op. 28, a pantomime (1922; Darmstadt, Dec. 1, 1923); *Nobilissima visione,* dance legend in 6 scenes (perf. under the title *St. Francis* by the Ballets Russes de Monte Carlo, in London, July 21, 1938, composer conducting); *Theme and Variations: The 4 Temperaments* for String Orch. and Piano (1940; N.Y. City Ballet, Nov. 20, 1946; most often perf. as a concert piece); *Hérodiade,* with recitation, after Mallarmé (produced as *Mirror before Me,* by the Martha Graham Dance Group, Washington, D.C., Oct. 30, 1944; also as a concert piece, with optional narration).

ORCH.: Cello Concerto, op. 3 (1916); *Lustige Sinfonietta,* op. 4 (1916); Piano Concerto, op. 29 (1924); Concerto for Orch., with Oboe, Bassoon, and Violin Soli, op. 38 (Duisburg, July 25, 1925); *Konzertmusik* for Wind Orch., op. 41 (Donaueschingen, July 1926); *Konzertmusik* for Viola and Orch., op. 48 (Hamburg, March 28, 1930, composer soloist); *Konzertmusik* for Piano, Brass, and 2 Harps, op. 49 (Chicago, Oct. 12, 1930); *Konzertmusik* for Strings and Brass, op. 50 (for 50th anniversary of the Boston Sym. Orch.; Boston, April 3, 1931); *Konzertstück* for Trautonium and Strings (1931); *Philharmonisches Konzert,* variations (Berlin, April 15, 1932); *Mathis der Maler,* sym. from the opera (Berlin, March 12, 1934, Furtwängler conducting); *Der Schwanendreher,* concerto for Viola and Small Orch. (Amsterdam, Nov. 14, 1935, composer soloist); *Trauermusik* for Solo Viola or Violin or Cello, and String Orch. (written for a memorial broadcast for King George V, who died on Jan. 20, 1936; London, Jan. 22, 1936, composer soloist); *Symphonic Dances* (London, Dec. 5, 1937); *Nobilissima visione,* suite from the ballet (Venice, Sept. 13, 1938); Violin Concerto (1939;

Amsterdam, March 14, 1940); Cello Concerto (1940; Boston, Feb. 7, 1941; Piatigorsky, soloist); Sym. in E-flat (1940; Minneapolis, Nov. 21, 1941); *Cupid and Psyche,* overture for a ballet (1943; Philadelphia, Oct. 29, 1943); *Symphonic Metamorphosis on Themes of Carl Maria von Weber* (1943; N.Y., Jan. 20, 1944); *Theme and Variations: The 4 Temperaments* for String Orch. and Piano (Boston, Sept. 3, 1944; Foss, soloist; premiered in 1946 as a ballet); Piano Concerto (1945; Cleveland, Feb. 27, 1947; Sanromá, soloist); *Symphonia Serena* (1946; Dallas, Feb. 2, 1947); Clarinet Concerto (1947; Philadelphia, Dec. 11, 1950; Benny Goodman, soloist); Concerto for 4 Winds, Harp, and Small Orch. (N.Y., May 15, 1949); Concerto for Trumpet, Bassoon, and String Orch., in 2 movements (New Haven, Conn., Nov. 4, 1949; 3rd movement added in 1952); Sinfonietta (1949; Louisville, March 1, 1950, composer conducting); Horn Concerto (1949; Baden-Baden, June 8, 1950; Dennis Brain, soloist); Sym. in B-flat for Concert Band (Washington, D.C., April 5, 1951, composer conducting); *Die Harmonie der Welt,* sym. from the opera (1951; Basel, Jan. 24, 1952); *Pittsburgh Symphony* (1958; Pittsburgh, Jan. 30, 1959, composer conducting); Organ Concerto (1962–63; N.Y., April 25, 1963; Heiller, soloist; composer conducting).

CHAMBER: *Andante and Scherzo,* op. 1, trio for Clarinet, Horn, and Piano (1914); unnumbered String Quartet in C, op. 2 (1915); Piano Quintet, op. 7 (1917); *3 Stücke* for Cello and Piano, op. 8 (1917); 1st String Quartet, in F minor, op. 10 (Frankfurt, June 2, 1919); a set of 6 sonatas, opp. 11/1–6, of which 2 are for Violin and Piano (1918), 1 for Cello and Piano (1919), 1 for Viola and Piano (1919), 1 for Solo Viola (1919), and 1 for Solo Violin (1919); 2nd String Quartet, in C, op. 16 (Donaueschingen, Aug. 1, 1921); 3rd String Quartet, op. 22 (Donaueschingen, Nov. 4, 1922); *Kleine Kammermusik,* op. 24/2, for Wind Quintet (1922); a set of 4 sonatas, opp. 25/1–4: for Solo Viola (1922), for Viola d'Amore and Piano (1923), for Solo Cello (1923), and for Viola and Piano (1924; publ. 1977); *"Minimax"—Reportorium für Militärmusik,* parody for String Quartet (1923; publ. 1978); Quintet for Clarinet and String Quartet, op. 30 (Salzburg Festival, Aug. 7, 1923); 4th String Quartet, op. 32 (Vienna, Nov. 5, 1923); a set of 4 sonatas, opp. 31/1–4, of which 2 are for Solo Violin (1924), 1, a *Canonic Sonatina,* for 2 Flutes (1924), and 1 for Solo Viola (1924); 1st Trio for Violin, Viola, and Cello, op. 34 (Salzburg, Aug. 6, 1924); *Rondo* for 3 Guitars (1925); *3 Stücke* for 5 Instruments (1925); 7 numbered pieces titled *Kammermusik: No. 1,* op. 24/1 (Donaueschingen Festival, July 31, 1922); *No. 2,* op. 36/1, for Piano and 12 Instruments (Frankfurt, Oct. 31, 1924); *No. 3,* op. 36/2, for Cello and 10 Instruments (Bochum, April 30, 1925; composer's brother, Rudolf, soloist); *No. 4,* op. 36/3, for Violin and Large Chamber Orch. (Dessau, Sept. 25, 1925); *No. 5,* op. 36/4, for Viola and Large Chamber Orch. (Berlin, Nov. 3, 1927); *No. 6,* op. 46/1, for Viola d'Amore and Chamber Orch. (1927; Cologne, March 29, 1928); *No. 7,* op. 46/2, for Organ and Chamber Ensemble (1927; Frankfurt, Jan. 8, 1928); *8 Pieces* for Solo Flute (1927); Trio for Viola, Heckelphone or Saxophone, and Piano, op. 47 (1928); *2 Canonic Duets* for 2 Violins (1929); *14 Easy Duets* for 2 Violins (1931); 2nd Trio for Violin, Viola, and Cello (Antwerp, March 17, 1933); *Konzertstück* for 2 Saxophones (1933); *Duet* for Viola and Cello (1934); Violin Sonata in E (1935); Flute Sonata (1936); Sonata for Solo Viola (1937); *Meditation* for Violin or Viola or Cello, and Piano (1938); Quartet for Clarinet, Violin, Cello, and Piano (1938); Oboe Sonata (1938); Bassoon Sonata (1938; transcribed for Bass Clarinet in 1959 for Josef Horák); Clarinet Sonata (1939); Horn Sonata (1939); Trumpet Sonata (1939); Solo Harp Sonata (1939); Violin Sonata in C (1939); Viola Sonata in C (1939); English Horn Sonata (1941); Trombone Sonata (1941); *A Frog He Went a-Courting,* variations for Cello and Piano (1941); *Echo* for Flute and Piano (1942); 5th String Quartet, in E-flat (Washington, D.C., Nov. 7, 1943); Sonata for Saxophone (or Alto Horn or French Horn) and Piano (1943); 6th String Quartet (Washington, D.C., March 21, 1946); Cello Sonata (1948); Septet for Winds (1948); Double-bass Sonata (1949); Sonata for 4 Horns (1952); Tuba Sonata

(1955); Octet for Clarinet, Bassoon, Horn, and String Quintet (Berlin, Sept. 23, 1958).

VOCAL: 3 Songs for Soprano and Orch., op. 9 (1917); Melancholie for Contralto and String Quartet, op. 13 (1918); Des Todes Tod, op. 23/1, 3 songs for Female Voice, 2 Violas, and 2 Cellos (1922); Die junge Magd, op. 23/2, 6 poems for Contralto, Flute, Clarinet, and String Quartet (1922); Lieder nach alten Texten for Mixed Chorus a cappella, op. 33 (1923); Die Serenaden, op. 35, little cantata on romantic poems, for Soprano, Oboe, Viola, and Cello (1925); Der Lindenberghflug for Soloists and Orch. (1929); Das Unaufhörliche, oratorio (Berlin, Nov. 21, 1931); 5 Songs on Old Texts for Mixed Chorus a cappella (c.1938; includes revisions of some songs of op. 33); 6 Chansons, after Rilke, for Mixed Chorus a cappella (1939); 3 Choruses for Male Chorus a cappella (1939); The Demon of the Gibbet for Male Chorus a cappella (1939); When Lilacs Last in the Dooryard Bloom'd, an American Requiem after Walt Whitman, for Mezzo-soprano, Baritone, Chorus, and Orch. (N.Y., May 14, 1946); Apparebit Repentina Dies for Chorus and Brass (Harvard Symposium, Cambridge, Mass., May 2, 1947); Das Marienleben, after Rilke, for Soprano and Orch. (1938–48; rev., shortened, and orchestrated version of songs orig. for Voice and Piano, 1923); Ite, angeli veloces, cantata trilogy: Chant de triomphe du roi David, Custos quid de nocte, and Cantique de l'espérance (1953–55; 1st complete perf., Wuppertal, June 4, 1955); 12 Madrigals for 5-part Mixed Chorus a cappella (1958); Der Mainzer Umzug for Soprano, Tenor, Baritone, Mixed Chorus, and Orch. (Mainz, June 23, 1962); Mass for Mixed Chorus a cappella (Vienna, Nov. 12, 1963).

VOICE AND PIANO: 3 Hymnen, op. 14, after Whitman (1919); 8 Songs for Soprano, op. 18 (1920); Das Marienleben, op. 27, a cycle of songs after Rilke (Donaueschingen, June 17, 1923; rev. radically and perf. in Hannover, Nov. 3, 1948); 6 Lieder for Tenor and Piano (1933–35); 9 English Songs (1942–44); 13 Motets (1941–60).

PIANO: 7 Waltzes, op. 6, for 4-hands (1916); In einer Nacht, op. 15, a set of 14 pieces (1920); Sonata, op. 17 (1917); Tanzstücke, op. 19 (1922); Suite "1922," op. 26 (1922); Klaviermusik, op. 37, incorporating Übung in drei Stücken, op. 37/1 (1925) and Reihe kleiner Stücke, op. 37/2 (1927); 3 numbered sonatas (1936); Sonata for 4-hands (1938); Sonata for 2 Pianos (1942); Ludus Tonalis, studies (Chicago, Feb. 15, 1943).

GEBRAUCHSMUSIK: Music for Mechanical Instruments, op. 40: Toccata for Player Piano, and Music for Mechanical Organ (both 1926–27); music for the film Felix the Cat for Mechanical Organ, op. 42 (1927); Spielmusik for Strings, Flutes, and Oboes, op. 43/1 (1927); Lieder für Singkreise for a cappella Voices, op. 43/2 (1927); Schulwerk für Instrumental-Zusammenspiel, op. 44, including the often-performed 5 Pieces for String Orch., op. 44/4 (1927); Sing- und Spielmusiken für Liebhaber und Musikfreunde, including: Frau Musica for Soli, Chorus, and String Orch., op. 45/1 (1928; rev. as In Praise of Music, 1943), 8 Canons for 2 Voices and Instruments, op. 45/2 (1928); Ein Jäger aus Kurpfalz for Strings and Winds, op. 45/3 (1928); Kleine Klaviermusik, op. 45/4 (1929), and Martinslied for Unison Chorus and 3 Instruments, op. 45/5 (1929); Lehrstück, after Brecht, for Male Soli, Narrator, Chorus, Orch., Dance Group, Clowns, and Community Singing (Baden-Baden, July 28, 1929); Wir bauen eine Stadt, play for Children's Soli and Chorus, and Instruments (Berlin, June 21, 1930); Plöner Musiktag, in 4 sections: Morgenmusik for Brass Quintet, Tafelmusik for Strings and Brass, Kantate for Soli, Children's Chorus, Narrator, Strings, Winds, and Percussion, and Abendkonzert, 6 individual pieces for Chamber and Orch. Grouping (all 1932; Plön, June 1932); Wer sich die Musik erkiest for Voices and Instruments (1952). The Auftrag der Hindemith-Stiftung began issuing a collected ed. in 1975. Thematic indexes have been compiled by K. Stone (N.Y., 1954; verified by the composer) and H. Rösner, Paul Hindemith—Katalog seiner Werke, Diskographie, Bibliographie, Einführung in das Schaffen (Frankfurt am Main, 1970).

WRITINGS: Unterweisung im Tonsatz (2 vols., 1937, 1939; in Eng. as The Craft of Musical Composition, N.Y., 1941; rev., 1945); A Concentrated Course in Traditional Harmony (2 vols., N.Y., 1943, 1953); Elementary Training for Musicians (N.Y., 1946); J.S. Bach: Heritage and Obligation (New Haven, Conn., 1952; German ed., J.S. Bach: Ein verpflichtendes Erbe, Wiesbaden, 1953); A Composer's World: Horizons and Limitations (Cambridge, Mass., 1952).

BIBL.: The H.-Jahrbuch began publication in 1971. See also the following: F. Willms, "P. H.," Von neuer Musik (Cologne, 1925); W. Altmann, "P. H.," ibid.; H. Kleemann, "Das Kompositionsprinzip P. H.s," in Gedenkschrift für Hermann Abert (Halle, 1928); H. Strobel, P. H. (Mainz, 1928; 3rd ed., augmented, 1948); W. Reich, "P. H.," Musical Quarterly (Oct. 1931); P. Rosenfeld, "Neo-Classicism and H.," in Discoveries of a Music Critic (N.Y., 1936); H.H. Stuckenschmidt, "H. Today," Modern Music (1937); F. Muser, "The Recent Works of P. H.," Musical Quarterly (Jan. 1944); N. Cazden, "H. and Nature," Music Review (Nov. 1954); R. Stephan, "H.'s Marienleben, An Assessment of Its Two Versions," Zeugnis in Bildern (Mainz, 1955; updated ed. as P. H.: Die letzten Jahre; Ein Zeugnis in Bildern, Mainz, 1965); H. Schilling, P. H.'s Cardillac (Würzburg, 1962); H. Boatwright, "P. H. as a Teacher," Musical Quarterly (July 1964); H. Tischler, "Remarks on H.'s Contrapuntal Technique," Essays in Musicology (Apel Festschrift; Bloomington, Ind., 1968); A. Briner, P. H. (Zürich, 1970; Eng. tr., 1987); I. Kemp, H. (London, 1970); A. Lanza, "Libertà e determinazione formale nel giovane H.," Rivista Italiana di Musicologia, V/1 (1970); E. Zwink, P. H.s Unterweisung im Tonsatz (Göppingen, 1974); G. Skelton, P. H.: The Man behind the Music (London, 1975); G. Metz, Melodische Polyphonie in der Zwölftonordnung: Studien zum Kontrapunkt P. H.s (Baden-Baden, 1976); D. Rexroth, Erprobungen und Erfahrungen: Zu P. H.s Schaffen in den Zwanziger Jahren (Frankfurt, 1978); G. Schubert, H. (Hamburg, 1981); D. Rexroth, P. H. Briefe (Frankfurt, 1982); E. Preussner, P. H.: Ein Lebensbild (Innsbruck, 1984); D. Neumeyer, The Music of P. H. (New Haven, 1986); S. Cook, Opera during the Weimar Republic: The Zeitopern of Ernst Krenek, Kurt Weill, and P. H. (Ann Arbor, 1987); L. Noss, P. H. in the United States (Urbana, 1989).

Hinderas (real name, **Henderson**), **Natalie**, black American pianist; b. Oberlin, Ohio, June 15, 1927; d. Elkins Park, Pa., July 22, 1987. Her father was a jazz musician, and her mother was a music teacher. She was a child prodigy and was accepted at the Oberlin School of Music at the age of 8; graduated at 18 (B.Mus., 1945). She subsequently took lessons with Olga Samaroff at the Juilliard School of Music in N.Y.; then studied piano with Eduard Steuermann and composition with Vincent Persichetti. She made her N.Y. debut in 1954; later toured in Europe and the Far East. In addition to the standard piano repertoire, she included in her concert programs pieces by black composers.

Hine, William, English organist and composer; b. Brightwell, 1687; d. Gloucester, Aug. 28, 1730. He studied with Jeremiah Clarke; then served as organist at Gloucester Cathedral (from 1707). A collection of his anthems under the title Harmonia sacra Glocestriensis was publ. posthumously by his widow.

Hines, Earl (Kenneth) "Fatha," remarkable black American jazz pianist; b. Duquesne, Pa., Dec. 28, 1905; d. Oakland, Calif., April 22, 1983. His father was a professional trumpet player and his mother played piano and organ. He took piano lessons as a child, but became interested mainly in jazz piano. He played with big bands as a young man, and in 1927 joined a quintet led by Louis Armstrong in Chicago. He began recording with Armstrong and under his influence evolved a special type of "trumpet piano style" characterized by sharp accents, octave tremolos in the treble, and insistently repeated melodic notes. In 1928 he organized his own big band in Chicago, and toured with it in the U.S., including the Southern states; his was one of the 1st black big bands to play in the South; its theme song, Deep Forest, became popular. A radio announcer used to introduce him as "Fatha Hines coming through deep forest with his children," and the nickname "Fatha" stuck.

After a hiatus of several years, Hines reappeared on the jazz horizon as a solo pianist and made a hit wherever he appeared. In 1957 he toured Europe; played in Berlin in 1965 and in Russia in 1966; he also played in Japan. During his last years he made his residence in San Francisco, where he played his last engagement just a week before his death.

BIBL.: S. Dance, *The World of E. H.* (N.Y., 1977); L. Moxhet, *A Discography of E. H., 1923–1977* (Sannois, France, 1982).

Hines (real name, **Heinz**), **Jerome (Albert Link),** distinguished American bass; b. Los Angeles, Nov. 8, 1921. He studied mathematics and chemistry at the Univ. of Calif. in Los Angeles, graduating in 1943; at the same time took vocal lessons with Gennaro Curci in Los Angeles, and later with Samuel Margolis in N.Y. After a few performances in light opera, he sang the part of Monterone in *Rigoletto* with the San Francisco Opera, on Oct. 19, 1941. In 1944 he sang Méphistophélès in *Faust* with the New Orleans Opera Co. He was not drafted into the U.S. Army during the war because of his excessive height (6 feet 6 inches), but instead was employed as a chemist in war-related work. On Nov. 21, 1946, he made his debut at the Metropolitan Opera in N.Y. as the Sergeant in *Boris Godunov,* and on Feb. 18, 1954, sang its title role. He made numerous guest appearances with European opera houses, at the Edinburgh Festival in 1953, and at La Scala in Milan and the Bayreuth Festival in 1958. On Sept. 23, 1962, he made history when he sang the role of Boris Godunov, in Russian, at the Bolshoi Theater in Moscow, with the Soviet Premier, Khrushchev, in attendance. He repeated his feat a month later at the Bolshoi Theater, and also performed in Leningrad, Kiev, and Tbilisi. On his return to the U.S., he sang the part of Boris Godunov in the original Mussorgsky version with the Metropolitan Opera in N.Y. on Oct. 14, 1975. His other roles included Don Giovanni, Don Basilio, Sarastro, Des Grieux, Wotan, and Rodolfo. His 40th anniversary with the Metropolitan was observed in 1986. He publ. an autobiography, *This Is My Story, This Is My Song* (Westwood, N.J., 1968), and a book, *Great Singers on Great Singing* (London, 1982). He also composed an opera, *I Am the Way,* based on the life of Christ.

Hingston (also **Hingeston, Hinkstone,** and **Hinkson), John,** English organist, viol player, and composer; b. c.1610; d. London (buried), Dec. 17, 1683. He sang in the choir at York Minster and may have studied with Orlando Gibbons; then was in the service of Charles I. He subsequently was state organist and private musician to Oliver Cromwell (1654–58). After the Restoration, he became viol player and overseer of the court musical instruments (1660). Purcell became his apprentice in 1673. Among his works are fantasias and dances utilizing viols and violins with organ, as well as some for cornetts and sackbut; he also wrote dances for 2 and 3 bass viols.

BIBL.: E. Bock, *The String Fantasies of J. Hingeston c. 1610–1683* (diss., Univ. of Iowa, 1956).

Hinrichs, Gustav, German-American conductor; b. Ludwigslust, Dec. 10, 1850; d. Mountain Lake, N.J., March 26, 1942. He studied violin and piano with his father; composition with E. Marxsen in Hamburg. In 1870 he settled in America; in 1885 he went to Philadelphia, where he organized his own opera company; gave the American premieres of *Cavalleria rusticana* (Philadelphia, Sept. 9, 1891) and *Pagliacci* (N.Y., June 15, 1893). In 1903–4 he conducted at the Metropolitan Opera in N.Y. He was the composer of an opera, *Onti-Ora* (Indian name of the Catskill Mountains; Philadelphia, July 28, 1890).

Hinshaw, William Wade, American baritone; b. Union, Iowa, Nov. 3, 1867; d. Washington, D.C., Nov. 27, 1947. He studied voice with L.G. Gottschalk in Chicago; was choir director at various churches; made his operatic debut as Méphistophélès in Gounod's *Faust* with the H.W. Savage Co. (St. Louis, Nov. 6, 1899); in 1903, opened the Hinshaw School of Opera in Chicago, which was later incorporated into the Chicago Cons.; was president of the combined institutions (1903–7). In 1909 he organized the International Grand Opera Co. of Chicago. He made his debut at the Metropolitan Opera, N.Y., on Nov. 16, 1910, remaining on its roster until 1913; in 1912 he sang in the Wagner festival at Graz, and in 1914, in the special *Ring* festival at Berlin; then returned to America. In 1916 he offered a prize of $1,000 for the best 1-act opera by an American composer (awarded to Hadley for his opera *Bianca*). From 1920 to 1926 he produced Mozart's operas in English with his own company in the U.S., Canada, and Cuba (about 800 perfs. in all). He then settled in Washington, D.C.

Hinton, Arthur, English composer; b. Beckenham, Nov. 20, 1869; d. Rottingdean, Aug. 11, 1941. He studied at the Royal Academy of Music in London; then taught violin there; subsequently went to Munich for further study with Rheinberger. He composed a Sym., which he conducted at one of the concerts of the Munich Cons.; traveled in Italy; returned to London in 1896. He continued to compose; his 2nd Sym. was performed in London in 1903. He married the pianist **Katharine Goodson,** who gave many performances of his piano works, including a concerto. He wrote the children's operettas *The Disagreeable Princess* and *St. Elizabeth's Rose;* also a number of songs.

Hipkins, Alfred (James), English writer on music; b. London, June 17, 1826; d. there, June 3, 1903. He was connected with the Broadwood piano manufacturers; acquired an excellent knowledge of the piano and was Chopin's favorite tuner on his last visit to England. He himself learned to play the piano well enough to give recitals. He publ. works on instruments, among them *Musical Instruments, Historic, Rare, and Unique* (Edinburgh, 1888; contains numerous colored plates; 3rd ed., 1945) and *A Description and History of the Pianoforte, and of the Older Keyboard Stringed Instruments* (London, 1896; 3rd ed., rev., 1929).

Hirai, Kozaburo, Japanese composer; b. Kochi, Sept. 10, 1910. He studied violin with Robert Pollak and composition and conducting with Klaus Pringsheim at the Tokyo Imperial Academy of Music (1929–34); taught at the Academy (1937–47); in 1966 he organized the Assoc. of Composers and Authors (ACA).

WORKS: Operetta, *Taketori-Monogatari* (1949); ballet, *Spirit of the Snow,* for String Orch. (1942; rev. 1968); several cantatas; *Festival of Insects,* suite for Orch. (Tokyo, Sept. 15, 1941); *Pastoral* for Clarinet and String Orch. (1943); *On the Grass,* suite for Orch. (1947); Koto Concerto (Tokyo, Nov. 12, 1950); *Festival,* concerto grosso for 3 Koto Soli and Koto Orch. (1962); *Symphonic Ballad* (1963); *Seaside Sketch* for Chamber Orch. (1967); *Marriage of the Whale,* symphonic chorus for 3 Voices, Chorus, and Orch. (Tokyo, Nov. 27, 1969); *Hakusan* for Shakuhachi, Solo Koto, Chorus, Percussion, and Koto Ensemble (1970); Trio for Flute, Viola, and Guitar (1942); String Quartet No. 1, *Japanese Suite* (1943); String Trio (1946); *Fantasy* for Strings (1954); Cello Sonata (1956); Sonata for Koto and Oboe (1956); *Duet* for Violin and Trombone (1966); 3 *Capriccios* for Solo Violin (1971); *Sakura Sakura,* fantasy for Piano (1971).

Hirao, Kishio, Japanese composer; b. Tokyo, July 8, 1907; d. there, Dec. 15, 1953. He graduated from Keio Univ. in 1930; studied composition with Guy de Lioncourt at the Schola Cantorum in Paris (1931–34); became a prof. at the Tokyo Music Academy.

WORKS: Choreographic drama in 3 acts, *Histoire de Wanasa—Otome* (1943); *Cantilène antique* for Orch. (1937); *Variations on a Japanese Theme* for Orch. (1938); *Suite* for Flute and Orch. (1940); *Kinuta,* symphonic poem (1942); *La Paix,* overture (1951); String Quartet (1940); Flute Sonatina (1941); Octet (1944); Piano Quintet (1945); Trio for Flute, Violin, and Piano (1949); Wind Quintet (1950); Violin Sonata (1947); Oboe Sonata (1951); Piano Sonata (1948).

Hirayoshi, Takekuni, Japanese composer; b. Kobe, July 10, 1936. He studied with Yoshio Hasegawa at the Tokyo Univ. of Arts (1955–61); later attended the graduate school there

(1963–67). In 1970 he was appointed an instructor at the Toho Girls' High School.

WORKS: String Quartet (1960); *Composition* for Orch. (Tokyo, Nov. 5, 1962); *Ballade* for Orch. (1966); *Dialog* for Marimba, Flute, Clarinet, and Cello (1968); Symphonic Variations (Tokyo, Oct. 23, 1969; winner of the 1969 Odaka Prize); Prelude and Fantasia for Solo Guitar (1970); *Monodrama* for Piano (1970); *Impromptu* for Flute, Violin, and Piano (1970); *Epitaph* for Solo Cello (1971); Octet for 4 Japanese Instruments and String Quartet (1972); *Epitaph* for 2 Flutes (1973); *Song of the Wind* for 2 Marimbas (1973); *Ballade* for Organ and Orch. (1974); *Requiem* for Violin and Orch. (1975).

Hirsch, Paul (Adolf), German-English music collector and bibliographer; b. Frankfurt am Main, Feb. 24, 1881; d. Cambridge, Nov. 23, 1951. He began collecting rare musical eds. as a young man, and publ. successive catalogs of his rapidly growing library. In 1936 he left Germany and was able to transport his entire collection to England; it was purchased by the British Museum in 1946; the total number of items was about 20,000. In 1922 he began the publication of new eds. (several in facsimile, and with commentaries) of rare works; these were F. Caza, *Tractato vulgare de canto figurato* (Milan, 1492; ed. J. Wolf, 1922); G. L. Conforto, *Breve et facile maniera d'essercitarsi a far passaggi* (Rome, 1593; ed. J. Wolf, 1922); *Neujahrsgrüsse Seelen; Eine Sammlung von Liedern mit Melodien und Bilderschmuck aus den Jahren 1770–1800* (ed. M. Friedlaender, 1922); G.P. Telemann, *Fantaisies pour le clavessin: 3 douzaines* (ed. M. Seiffert, 1923); H. Bottrigari, *Il desiderio, overo De' concerti di varii strumenti musicali* (Venice, 1594; ed. K. Meyer, 1924); K.F. Zelter, *Fünfzehn ausgewählte Lieder* (ed. M. Bauer, 1924); G. Spataro, *Dilucide et probatissime demonstratione* (Bologna, 1521; ed. J. Wolf, 1925); N. Listenius, *Musica, ab authore denuo recognita* (Nuremberg, 1549; ed. G. Schünemann, 1927); C.P.E. Bach, *Zwölf zwei- und dreistimmige kleine Stücke für die Flöte oder Violine und das Klavier* (1770; ed. R. Hohenemser, 1928); C. Schultze, *Lukas-Passion* (Leipzig, 1653; ed. P. Epstein, 1930); M. Luther, *Deutsche Messe* (1526; ed. J. Wolf, 1934); W.A. Mozart, *The Ten Celebrated String Quartets*, 1st authentic edition in score (ed. A. Einstein, 1945).

BIBL.: P. Muir, "The H. Catalogue," *Music Review* (1948); a list of eds. is found in the Jan. 1951 issue of *Music Review*.

Hirst, Grayson, American tenor; b. Ojai, Calif., Dec. 27, 1939. He studied at the Music Academy of the West in Santa Barbara, Calif., with Singher at the Univ. of Calif. at Los Angeles, and with Tourel at the Juilliard School of Music in N.Y. (1963–72), making his professional debut as Cavalli's Ormindo with the Opera Soc. of Washington, D.C. (1969). His 1st appearance in N.Y. was as Tonio in a concert performance of *La Fille du régiment* at Carnegie Hall (1970); after singing Quint in *The Turn of the Screw* at the N.Y. City Opera (1972), he appeared in opera throughout the U.S. and Europe while also pursuing an extensive concert career. In 1986 he joined the faculty at the Univ. of Arizona. His operatic repertoire includes over 70 roles, ranging from Mozart to contemporary roles.

Hirt, Al(ois Maxwell), popular American trumpeter; b. New Orleans, Nov. 7, 1922. He studied with Frank Simon at the Cincinnati Cons. of Music (1940–42); then served in the U.S. Army, and played in the 82nd Army Air Force Band; after his discharge in 1946, he played with various bands; in 1956 he formed his own band, and began touring with it in 1960. His 1st major recording, in 1961, was the album *The Greatest Horn in the World.* A versatile musician, he came to espouse the "Nashville sound," being equally at ease in the country-western, jazz, and popular music genres.

Hirt, Franz Josef, Swiss pianist; b. Lucerne, Feb. 7, 1899; d. Bern, May 20, 1985. He studied with Hans Huber and Ernst Lévy at the Basel Cons.; later took lessons with Egon Petri and Alfred Cortot. In 1919 he became a teacher at the Bern Cons.; also gave numerous piano recitals in Europe. He

publ. *Meisterwerke des Klavierbaues* (1955; Eng. tr., *Stringed Keyboard Instruments, 1440–1880;* Boston, 1968).

Hirt, Fritz, Swiss violinist; b. Lucerne, Aug. 9, 1888; d. Chigny-sur-Morges, Jan. 5, 1970. He studied in Zürich and had an extended career as a violinist in Europe; was also a member of the Basel String Quartet.

Hitchcock, H(ugh) Wiley, eminent American musicologist and editor; b. Detroit, Sept. 28, 1923. He was educated at Dartmouth College (A.B., 1943) and the Univ. of Michigan (M.Mus., 1948; Ph.D., 1954, with the diss. *The Latin Oratorios of Marc-Antoine Charpentier*); taught music at the Univ. of Michigan (1947–61); then was prof. of music at Hunter College (1961–71); in 1971 became prof. of music at Brooklyn College (named Distinguished Prof. of Music in 1980), where he also served as director of the Inst. for Studies in American Music. A recipient of numerous grants, including Fulbright senior research fellowships in 1954–55 (Italy) and 1968–69 (France), and a Guggenheim fellowship in 1968–69, he also served on the boards of the Music Library Assoc. (1965–72) and the American Musicological Soc. (1966–78), and as president of the Charles Ives Soc. (from 1973); was also ed. of The Prentice-Hall History of Music Series (Englewood Cliffs, N.J., 1965–), *Earlier American Music* (reprints of music; N.Y., 1972–), and Recent Researches in American Music (Madison, Wis., 1976–). He was co-ed. of *The New Grove Dictionary of American Music* (4 vols., N.Y., 1986). His research interests are wide and meritorious, covering French Baroque and American music; his editorial contributions include the works of Caccini, Leonardo Leo, Charpentier, and Lully.

WRITINGS: *Music in the United States: A Historical Introduction* (Englewood Cliffs, N.J., 1969; 2nd ed., rev. and enl., 1974; 3rd ed., 1988); *Charles Ives Centennial Festival-Conference 1974* (program book; N.Y., 1974); *Ives* (London, 1977; rev. 1983); co-ed., with V. Perlis, of *An Ives Celebration: Papers and Panels of the Charles Ives Centennial Festival-Conference* (Urbana, Ill., 1977); *The Phonograph and Our Musical Life* (Brooklyn, 1980); with L. Inserra, *The Music of Ainsworth's Psalter (1612)* (Brooklyn, 1981); *The Works of Marc-Antoine Charpentier: A Catalogue Raisonné* (Paris, 1982); *Ives: A Survey of the Music* (N.Y., 1983); *Marc-Antoine Charpentier* (Oxford, 1990).

BIBL.: R. Crawford, R. Lott, and C. Oja, eds., *A Celebration of American Music: Words and Music in Honor of H.W. H.* (Ann Arbor, 1989).

Hjort Albertsen, Per. See Albertsen, Per Hjort.

Hlobil, Emil, Czech composer; b. Veselí nad Lužnici, Oct. 11, 1901; d. Prague, Jan. 25, 1987. He studied with Křička at the Prague Cons. (1920–23) and in the master classes of Suk there (1924–30); taught at the Cons. (1941–58) and afterward at the Academy of Music and Dramatic Arts in Prague. He was made an Artist of Merit (1972) and a National Artist (1981) for his services to Czech music. He followed the national tradition of the modern Czech school, and also cautiously experimented with serial methods of composition.

WORKS: 3 operas: *Anna Karenina,* after Tolstoy (1962; České Budějovice, April 16, 1972), *Le Bourgeois gentilhomme,* after Molière (1965), and *Král Václav IV* (1981); 7 syms.: No. 1 (1949); No. 2, *The Day of Victory* (1951); No. 3 (1957); No. 4 (1959); No. 5 (1969); No. 6 for Strings (1972); No. 7 (1973); symphonic suites: *Summer in the Giant Mountains* (1950); *Folk Merry-Making* (1950); *Spring in the Gardens of Prague* (1951–53); *In the Valachian Village* (1952); cantata, *On the Gift of Coal* (1952); Violin Concerto (1955); Accordion Concerto (1956); *Labor Holiday* for Orch. (1960); Organ Concerto (1963); *Concerto filharmonico* for Orch. (1965); *Invocazioni* for Orch. (1967); Double-bass Concerto (1968); *The Path of the Living* for Orch. (1974); *Jubilace* for Orch. (1977); Marimba Concerto (1979); Cello Concerto (1983); String Quintet (1925); 4 string quartets (1931, 1936, 1955, 1969); Piano Trio (1938); Wind Quintet (1940); Horn Sonata (1942; rev. 1948);

Quartet for Harpsichord, Violin, Viola, and Cello (1943); Nonet (1946); Wind Octet (1956); Violin Sonata (1959); Quartet for Flute, Oboe, Clarinet, and Bassoon (1964); Flute Sonata (1966); Trumpet Sonata (1967); Bass-clarinet Sonata (1970); Trombone Sonata (1973); Sonata for 2 Cellos (1973); Clarinet Sonata (1978); *Canto pensieroso* for Saxophone (1983); also piano pieces; songs; choruses.

Bibl.: J. Bajer, *E. Hlovil: Hudebni putováni stoletim* (Prague, 1984).

Hoboken, Anthony van, eminent Dutch music collector and bibliographer; b. Rotterdam, March 23, 1887; d. Zürich, Nov. 1, 1983. He studied with Iwan Knorr at the Hoch Cons. in Frankfurt and with Schenker in Vienna (1925–34). In 1927 he founded the Archive for Photographs of Musical Manuscripts in the Austrian National Library in Vienna; he then began to collect 1st eds. of classical works; his Haydn collection is particularly rich. He publ. a complete thematic catalog of Haydn's work (2 vols., 1957, 1971). He also contributed a number of articles on Haydn to music journals. A Festschrift in his honor was publ. on his 75th birthday, ed. by J. Schmidt-Görg (Mainz, 1962). His archive was purchased by the Austrian government in 1974, and officially opened at the Austrian National Library in Vienna on Hoboken's 90th birthday, March 23, 1977, as a tribute to his signal accomplishments in musical bibliography; although frail, Hoboken was present on this occasion.

Hobson, Ian, English pianist; b. Wolverhampton, Aug. 7, 1952. He studied piano and organ at the Royal Academy of Music in London and at Magdalene College, Cambridge (B.A., 1972); and piano with Claude Frank and harpsichord with Ralph Kirkpatrick at Yale Univ. (D.M.A., 1978); made his London debut in 1979. In 1981 he won 1st prize in the Leeds International Pianoforte Competition. He made his U.S. debut in N.Y. in 1983. He has appeared as soloist with major orchs. of Europe and North America. In 1975 he joined the faculty of the Univ. of Illinois.

Hoch, Joseph (Paul Johannes), German musical Maecenas, founder of the celebrated Hoch Conservatorium; b. Frankfurt am Main, May 3, 1815; d. there, Sept. 19, 1874. He was a successful businessman, music being his avocation. He established a music school in Frankfurt in 1856 under the name Hoch Cons. Its 1st director was Joachim Raff, who was succeeded in 1882 by Bernhard Scholz. Hoch's widow continued to contribute funds to maintain the Cons.; the building was expanded and a concert hall was added, but all were destroyed during the aerial assault on Frankfurt in 1944. The Cons. was not restored until some years later. In its best times, the faculty acquired the services of the mezzo-soprano Pauline Viardot-García, the composer Engelbert Humperdinck, and the pianist James Kwast. The faculty also included Iwan Knorr, who was recommended by Brahms as a teacher of composition. Among the graduates of the Hoch Cons. were such eminent composers as Hans Pfitzner, Walther Braunfels, Cyril Scott, Bernhard Sekles, and Paul Hindemith.

Hochberg, Hans Heinrich, XIV, Bolko Graf von, German theater Intendant and composer; b. Fürstenstein Castle, Silesia, Jan. 23, 1843; d. near Salzbrunn, Dec. 1, 1926. He established and for several years maintained the Hochberg Quartet; also founded the Silesian music festivals (1878); was general Intendant of the Berlin Royal Theater (1886–1902). His works include the operas *Claudine von Villabella* (Schwerin, 1864) and *Die Falkensteiner* (Hannover, 1876; rewritten as *Der Wärwolf,* Dresden, 1881); 3 syms.; 3 string quartets; 2 piano trios; a Concerto for Piano; songs; choruses.

Hockh, Carl, outstanding German violinist, composer, and pedagogue; b. Ebersdorf, Jan. 22, 1707; d. Zerbst, Nov. 25, 1773. He studied violin with his father, and voice with the local schoolmaster; then studied with Michael Schade in Pruck. After playing oboe in a military regiment, he was in the service of the governor of Warsaw as 2nd violinist and horn player; subsequently was music director in Zerbst from 1734. He was

one of the founders of the German school of violin playing, and was influential as a virtuoso, composer for the violin, and teacher.

Hoddinott, Alun, Welsh composer; b. Bargoed, Aug. 11, 1929. He studied music at the Univ. College of South Wales in Cardiff; also took private instruction with Arthur Benjamin. In 1951 he was appointed lecturer in music at Cardiff College of Music and Drama; from 1959 to 1987 was on the music faculty of the Univ. College of South Wales. He also served as organizer of the annual Cardiff Music Festival. In 1983 he was made a Commander of the Order of the British Empire. His music follows the judicious line of humanitarian modernism, without blundering into musical chaos.

Works: operas: *The Beach of Falesá* (Cardiff, March 26, 1974); *Murder, the Magician* (Welsh Television, Feb. 11, 1976); *What the Old Man Does Is Always Right* (1975; Fishguard Festival, July 27, 1977); *The Rajah's Diamond* (1979); *The Trumpet Major* (Manchester, England, April 1, 1981). **orch.:** Syms.: No. 1 (National Eisteddfod of Wales; Pwillheli, Aug. 5, 1955); No. 2 (Cheltenham Festival, July 11, 1962); No. 3 (Manchester, Dec. 5, 1968); No. 4 (Manchester, Dec. 4, 1969); No. 5 (London, March 6, 1973); No. 6 (1984); No. 7 for Organ and Orch. (Swansea Festival, Oct. 17, 1989); Concerto No. 1 for Piano, Wind Instruments, and Percussion (London, Feb. 22, 1960); Concerto No. 2 for Piano and Orch. (Cardiff, Aug. 5, 1969); Harp Concerto (Cheltenham Festival, July 16, 1958); Concerto for Clarinet and String Orch. (Cheltenham Festival, July 16, 1954); Concerto for Organ and Orch. (Llandaff Festival, June 19, 1967); Horn Concerto (Llandaff Festival, June 3, 1969); Concertino for Viola and Small Orch. (Llandaff Festival, June 25, 1958); Violin Concerto (Birmingham, March 30, 1961); Concerto Grosso No. 1 (Caerphilly Festival, June 11, 1965); Concerto Grosso No. 2 (1966); *Variants* (London, Nov. 2, 1966); *Fioriture* (London, Nov. 24, 1968); Divertimento (Llandaff, Nov. 14, 1969); *4 Welsh Dances* (London, June 28, 1958); *Investiture Dances* (commissioned to celebrate the investiture of the Prince of Wales; London, June 22, 1969); *Night Music* (Aberystwyth, Jan. 30, 1967); Sinfonia for String Orch. (Bromsgrove Festival, April 19, 1964); *Sinfonietta No. 1* (Cardiff Festival, 1968); *Sinfonietta No. 2* (Cheltenham Festival, July 4, 1969); *Sinfonietta No. 3* (Swansea, March 10, 1970); *Sinfonietta No. 4* (Wales, July 30, 1971); *The Sun, the Great Luminary of the Universe* (Swansea, Oct. 8, 1970); *Sinfonia Fidei* for Soprano, Tenor, Chorus, and Orch. (1977); *Heaventree of Stars* for Violin and Orch. (Cardiff, March 3, 1980); *Lanterne des Morts* (St. Asaph Cathedral, Sept. 21, 1981); Triple Concerto for Piano Trio and Orch. (1986); Concerto (1986); *Star Children* (London, Sept. 7, 1989); *Noctis Equi,* scena for Cello and Orch. (London, Oct. 27, 1989). **chamber:** 4 violin sonatas (1969, 1970, 1971, 1976); 2 cello sonatas (1970, 1977); Clarinet Sonata (1967); Sonata for Harp (1964); Horn Sonata (1971); Divertimenti for 8 Instruments (1968); Divertimento for Oboe, Clarinet, Horn, and Bassoon (1963); Piano Quintet (1972); Septet for Wind Instruments, Strings, and Piano (1956); Sextet for Flute, Clarinet, Bassoon, Violin, Viola, and Cello (1960); 2 string quartets (1966, 1984); Variations for Flute, Clarinet, Harp, and String Quartet (1962); 6 piano sonatas (1959–72); *Ritornelli* for Trombone, Wind Instruments, and Percussion (1974); *Ritornelli 2* for Brass Quintet (1979); 2 piano trios (1981, 1984); *Mask* for Oboe, Bassoon, and Piano (1983); *Bagatelles* for Oboe and Harp (1984); also many vocal works; piano pieces; organ music; choruses; songs.

Bibl.: B. Deane, *A. H.* (Cardiff, 1977); G. Lewis, "H. at 60," *Music and Musicians International* (April 1989); idem, "H. and the Symphony," *Musical Times* (Aug. 1989).

Hodeir, André, French jazz musician, writer on music, and composer; b. Paris, Jan. 22, 1921. He studied at the Paris Cons. with Messiaen and others; in 1954 founded the Jazz Group of Paris, which he led until 1960. He ed. the periodical *Jazz Hot* (1947–50).

Writings: *Le Jazz, cet inconnu* (Paris, 1945); *Introduction à la musique de jazz* (Paris, 1948); *Les Formes de la musique*

(Paris, 1951; 5th ed., 1969; in Eng., N.Y., 1966); *Hommes et problèmes du jazz* (Paris, 1954; in Eng. as *Jazz, Its Evolution and Essence*, N.Y., 1956); *La Musique étrangère contemporaine* (Paris, 1954; 3rd ed., 1971); *La Musique depuis Debussy* (Paris, 1961; in Eng. as *Since Debussy*, N.Y., 1961); *Toward Jazz* (N.Y., 1963); *Les Mondes du jazz* (Paris, 1970; in Eng. as *The Worlds of Jazz*, N.Y., 1972); *Jazzistiques* (Roquevaire, 1984).

Hodemont, Léonard (Collet) de, important South Netherlands composer; b. Liège, c.1575; d. there, Aug. 1636. He received his musical training at Liège Cathedral, where he was senior duodenus (1589–93); then continued his education at the Pédagogie du Lys at the Univ. of Louvain. After being ordained a priest, he became succentor of the collegiate church of St. Pierre in Liège in 1610; was made canon at Liège Cathedral in 1612, and then at St. Materne there in 1616; subsequently was maître de chant at Liège Cathedral from 1619 to 1633. He was a leading composer of sacred music. He publ. *Armonica recreatione: Villanelli* for 3 Voices and Basso Continuo (Antwerp, 1625) and *Sacri concentus* for 1 to 5 Voices, Violin, and Basso Continuo (Organ) (Liège, 1630).

BIBL.: J. Quitin, "Un Musicien liègeois, L. d.H., c. 1575–1636; Notes biographiques," *La Vie Wallonne,* XXV (1951).

Hodges, Edward, English organist and composer; b. Bristol, July 20, 1796; d. Clifton, Sept. 1, 1867. He was an organist at Bristol; received his Mus.Doc. at Cambridge (1825); in 1838, went to North America, where he became an organist in Toronto and then in N.Y. (1839). He returned to England in 1863. His daughter, **Faustina Hasse Hodges** (b. near Malmesbury, Aug. 7, 1823; d. Philadelphia, Feb. 4, 1895), was also an organist in the U.S. She composed songs and instrumental pieces and publ. a biography of her father (N.Y., 1896). His son, **Rev. J(ohn) Sebastian B(ach) Hodges** (b. Bristol, 1830; d. Baltimore, May 1, 1915), an accomplished organist, composed many anthems and services.

Hodges, Johnny (John Cornelius) "Rabbit," black American alto and soprano saxophonist; b. Cambridge, Mass., July 25, 1906; d. N.Y., May 11, 1970. After playing drums and piano, he studied the saxophone with Sidney Bechet; then played with Willie "the Lion" Smith, Bechet, and Chick Webb; from 1928 to 1951 he was a member of Duke Ellington's band; subsequently led his own band and septet for several years; then rejoined Ellington in 1955, remaining with him until his death. He publ. a vol. of his own *Sax Originals* (1945; 2nd ed., 1972). He was one of the most gifted saxophonists of the swing era.

Hodkinson, Sydney P(hillip), Canadian-born American conductor, teacher, and composer; b. Winnipeg, Jan. 17, 1934. He studied composition with Louis Mennini and Bernard Rogers, and conducting with Paul White and Frederick Fennell at the Eastman School of Music in Rochester, N.Y. (M.Mus., 1958); after attending the Seminar in Advanced Musical Studies given by Carter, Sessions, and Babbitt at Princeton Univ. (1960), he studied conducting with Max Rudolf; completed his training in composition with Leslie Bassett, Niccolo Castiglioni, Ross Lee Finney, and George B. Wilson at the Univ. of Michigan (D.M.A., 1968). From 1970 to 1972 he was music director of the St. Paul (Minn.) Chamber Orch.; also served as artist-in-residence in Minneapolis–St. Paul. He taught at the Univ. of Virginia (1958–63), Ohio Univ. (1963–66), and the Univ. of Michigan (1968–73), where he conducted its Contemporary Directions Ensemble. In 1973 he joined the faculty of the Eastman School of Music, where he was also conductor of its Musica Nova Ensemble. From 1984 to 1986 he was a visiting prof. at Southern Methodist Univ. in Dallas. In 1971 he received an award from the American Academy and National Inst. of Arts and Letters; was granted 4 awards from the N.E.A. (1976, 1978, 1980, 1984); in 1978–79 he held a Guggenheim fellowship. In his compositions he explores modern techniques with pragmatic coherence.

WORKS: DRAMATIC: 4 operas: *The Swinish Cult* (1969–75), *The Wall* (1980), *In the Gallery* (1981), and *Catsman* (1985);

Lament, fable with music for Guitar and 2 Lovers (1962); *Taiwa,* myth for Actors, Dancers, and Musicians (1965); *Vox Populous,* active oratorio for 2 Actors, Electronics Technician, 4 Vocal Soloists, and Chorus (1971–72). **ORCH.:** Syms.: No. 1, *Fresco,* mural in 5 panels (1965–68; Buffalo, April 26, 1974); No. 3, *The Celestial Omnibus* (1975); No. 4, *Horae Canonica* for Soprano, Baritone, Narrator, 2 Choirs, and Orch. (1977–83); No. 5, *Sinfonia Concertante,* for Chamber Orch. (1980); No. 6, *Sonata quasi una fantasia* (1982–83); *Stabile* (1970; Milwaukee, Feb. 6, 1972); *Valence* for Chamber Orch. (1970); *Epigrams* (1971); *Celestial Calendar* for String Orch. (1976); *The Edge of the Olde One,* chamber concerto (N.Y., May 13, 1977); *Burning Bell,* symphonic poem for Youth Orch. (1985). **WIND ENSEMBLE OR BAND:** *Litigo* for Winds and Percussion (1959); *Blocks* for Concert Band (1972); *Monolith: Megalith VI* for Wind Ensemble (1974); *Tower* for Concert Band (1974; Buffalo, N.Y., Dec. 12, 1976); *Cortege: Dirge-Canons* for Wind, Brass, and Percussion (1975); *Echo Preludes* for Brass Choir and Cello Obbligato (1983). **CHAMBER:** *Drawings:* Set No. 1 for 4 Percussion (1960); Set No. 3 for Clarinet and Drums (1961); Set No. 4 for 3 Percussion (1961); Set No. 6 for Violin, 2 Clarinets, and Bass Clarinet (1965); Set No. 9 for 3 Percussion (1977); Set No. 10, *Cerberus,* for 4 Tubas (1977); *Mosaic* for Brass Quintet (1964); *Armistice,* truce for Dancers and Musicians (1966); String Quartet No. 1 for 5 Players (1967); *Dissolution of the Serial* for Piano and 1 Instrument, with Tape Excerpt (1967); *1 Man's Meat* for Double Bass and Electronic Tape (1970; Los Angeles, Feb. 9, 1972); Sonata for Double Bass and Piano (1980); Sym No. 2, *Symphonie fantastique,* for Organ, Brass, and Percussion (1974–82); String Trio, *Alla marcia* (1983); Sonata, *Das Lebewohl,* for Piano Trio (1984); *Tsatskes,* potpourri for Woodwind Trio (1984); piano, organ, and harpsichord pieces; vocal works; choruses; songs.

Höeberg, Georg, Danish violinist, conductor, and composer; b. Copenhagen, Dec. 27, 1872; d. Vedbaek, Aug. 3, 1950. He studied at the Copenhagen Cons., and in Berlin; taught at the Copenhagen Cons. (1900–1914), then was conductor at the Royal Danish Theater (1914–30). He wrote the opera *Bryllup i Katakomberne* (The Wedding in the Catacombs; Copenhagen, March 6, 1909); the ballet *The Paris Cathedral* (Copenhagen, Oct. 25, 1912); several pieces for violin and orch.; Sym.; choral works; songs.

Hoelscher, Ludwig, noted German cellist; b. Solingen, Aug. 23, 1907. He studied cello in Leipzig with Julius Klengel and in Berlin with Hugo Becker. In 1930 he won the Mendelssohn Prize; in 1936 was appointed prof. at the Berlin Hochschule für Musik; later gave master classes at the Mozarteum in Salzburg. From 1931 he engaged in far-flung tours in Europe and in the Far East; gave duo-recitals with the pianist Elly Ney. A musician of great culture, he arranged his programs covering both the classical and the modern literature, ranging from Bach to the works of Pfitzner, Krenek, Fortner, and Henze.

BIBL.: E. Valentin, *Cello, Das Instrument und sein Meister L. H.* (Pfullingen, 1955); M. Kaindl-Hönig, *L. H.* (Geneva, 1962); W.-E. von Lewinski, *L. H.* (Tutzing, 1967).

Hoelscher, Ulf, talented German violinist; b. Kitzingen, Jan. 17, 1942. After study in Germany he received a grant which enabled him to go to America and enroll in the classes of Ivan Galamian at the Curtis Inst. of Music in Philadelphia and of Josef Gingold at the Indiana Univ. School of Music in Bloomington. He then developed an international career, touring Europe, Australia, and the Far East, as well as the U.S. In 1981 he became a prof. at the Karlsruhe Hochschule für Musik. His repertoire is commendably large, encompassing works of the Baroque era, the Romantic school, and the contemporary avant-garde.

Hoerburger, Felix, German musicologist; b. Munich, Dec. 9, 1916. He studied composition at the Munich Academy of Music and musicology at the Univ. of Munich (Ph.D., 1941, with a diss. on the music of the Ungoni in East Africa), completing his Habilitation at the Univ. of Erlangen (1963, with a study of dance among Albanian Yugoslavs). He was organist and research assistant at the Music Research Inst. in Regensburg (1947–68) and at the Musicology Research Inst. of the Univ. of Erlangen (1968), where he later became lecturer (1970). He then was a prof. at the Univ. of Regensburg (from 1971). His extensive publications on folk music include studies of the music and dance of Bavaria, Turkey, the Balkans, Nepal, and Afghanistan.

WRITINGS: *Volkstanzkunde* (Kassel, 1961–64); *Musica vulgaris: Legengesetze der instrumentalen Volksmusik* (Erlangen, 1966); *Studien zur Musik in Nepal* (Regensburg, 1975).

Hoérée, Arthur (Charles Ernest), Belgian music critic and composer; b. Saint Gilles, near Brussels, April 16, 1897; d. Paris, June 3, 1986. He studied organ and theory at the Brussels Cons. In 1919 he went to Paris, where he studied composition with Paul Vidal and orchestration with Vincent d'Indy. He then devoted himself mainly to music criticism, without abandoning composition. He gave several courses in composition at the École Normale Supérieure de Musique in Paris and at the French Radio Center. In 1972 he was appointed instructor in musicology at the Sorbonne. His compositions include several ballets and scores of incidental music for theatrical plays; *Pastorale et Danse* for String Quartet (1923); *Septet* (1923); *Pour le premier jour du printemps* for Piano (1949); *Crève-Coeur, le Magicien* for Soli, Chorus, and Orch. (1961). He publ. a monograph, *Albert Roussel* (Paris, 1938); a later major study, *Roussel* (Paris 1969); and *La Musique française au XXᵉ siècle* (Paris, 1974).

Hoesick, Ferdinand, Polish musicologist; b. Warsaw, Oct. 16, 1867; d. there, April 13, 1941. He studied at the Univs. of Heidelberg, Krakow, and Paris, returning to Warsaw in 1891; was ed. and writer on literature; his writings on music deal exclusively with Chopin and include the biography *Chopin* (Warsaw, 1904; rev. and enl. ed. as *Chopin: Life and Letters,* 3 vols., 1910–11; later revision, 4 vols., Krakow, 1962–68).

Hoesslin, Franz von, German conductor; b. Munich, Dec. 31, 1885; d. (in a plane crash in southern France) Sept. 28, 1946. He studied general subjects at the Univ. of Munich; conducting with Mottl, composition with Reger. He held the post of conductor at the Municipal Theater of St. Gallen (1908–11); then conducted in Riga (1912–14); was in the German army during World War I; then conducted in Lübeck (1919–20), Mannheim (1920–22), and at the Berlin Volksoper (1922–23). He was Generalmusikdirektor in Dessau (1923–26), then opera conductor in Barmen-Elberfeld (1926–27); later was engaged as conductor for the Bayreuth Festival; conducted opera in France and Spain. He wrote some orch. works, a Clarinet Quintet, and choruses.

Høffding, (Niels) Finn, Danish composer; b. Copenhagen, March 10, 1899. He studied violin with K. Sandby (1911–21), organ with R.S. Rung-Keller (1919–21), composition and harmony with Knud Jeppesen (1918–21), and music history with Thomas Laub (1920–23); then went to Vienna, where he took lessons with Joseph Marx (1921–22). He subsequently was on the faculty of the Royal Danish Cons. of Music in Copenhagen (1931–69); from 1954 to 1969 he acted as director there. His style of composition is influenced by linear counterpoint as practiced by Carl Nielsen.

WORKS: 3 operas: *Kejserens nye Klaeder* (The Emperor's New Clothes), after Hans Christian Andersen (1926; Copenhagen, Dec. 29, 1928), *Kilderejsen* (The Healing Spring), after Holberg (1931; Copenhagen, Jan. 13, 1942), and a school opera, *Pasteur* (1935; Copenhagen, March 9, 1938); 4 syms.: No. 1, *Sinfonia impetuosa* (1923; Copenhagen, Aug. 22, 1925); No. 2, *Il Canto de Liberato,* to a phonic text devised by the composer, for Coloratura Soprano, Chorus, and Orch. (1924); No. 3 for 2 Pianos and Orch. (1928); No. 4, *Sinfonia concertante,* for Chamber Orch. (1934); 4 symphonic fantasies: No. 1, *Evolution* (1939; Copenhagen, Sept. 4, 1940); No. 2, *Det er ganske vist* (It Is Perfectly True), after Hans Christian Andersen (1940; Copenhagen, March 6, 1944; as a pantomime, Tivoli Gardens,

July 1, 1948); No. 3, *Vår-Höst* (Spring-Autumn), for Baritone and Orch. (1944; Copenhagen Radio, Jan. 24, 1946); No. 4, *The Arsenal at Springfield,* after Longfellow's poem, for 3 Soloists, Chorus, and Orch. (1953; Copenhagen Radio, Sept. 22, 1955); *Overture* for Small Orch. (1930); Concerto for Oboe and String Orch. (1933); *Fanfare,* concert piece for Orch. (1939); *Fire Minespil,* suite for Small Orch. (1944); *Majfest,* fantasy on a Danish folk dance, for Orch. (1945); *Fantasia concertante* for Orch. (Copenhagen Radio, April 1, 1965); *Karls-vognen* for Soloists, Chorus, and Orch. (1924); *Fem Svaner* (The 5 Swans) for Soloists, Chorus, and Orch. (1937; Copenhagen, Sept. 9, 1938); *Christofer Columbus,* chaconne for Male Chorus, Baritone Solo, and Orch. (1937; Copenhagen, March 5, 1941); *Giordano Bruno* for Baritone Solo, Male Chorus, Winds, and Percussion (Univ. of Copenhagen, Dec. 8, 1968); several works for school performance, including *Da solen blev forkølet* (When the Sun Caught a Cold) for Children's Chorus and School Orch. (1977); *Kammermusik* for Soprano, Oboe, and Piano (1927); *Das Eisenbahngleichnis* for Chorus, Piano, and 3 Saxophones (1934); *Fire Satser* for Chorus and Instruments (1965); *Vintersolhverv* for Chorus and Instruments (1965); *Årets kredsgang,* cycle for Chorus and Instruments (1965); *Davids 18 og 23,* 2 Psalms for Voice and Organ (1966); several a cappella choruses, including *Agent* (1969), *2 Songs* (1977), and *4 Songs* (1977). Chamber: 2 string quartets (1920, 1925); *Dialogues* for Oboe and Clarinet (1927); 2 wind quintets (1940; *Familien Vind,* 1954); Oboe Sonata (1943). Piano: Sonatina (1951); Canon (1959); several sets of pieces.

BIBL.: S. Bruhns and D. Fog, *F. H.s Kompositionen* (Copenhagen, 1969).

Höffer, Paul, German composer; b. Barmen, Dec. 21, 1895; d. Berlin, Aug. 31, 1949. He studied piano with Walter Georgii in Cologne; then took courses in composition with Schreker in Berlin. In 1923 he became piano teacher at the Hochschule für Musik in Berlin, and in 1948–49 was director there. In his compositions he adopted a fairly radical idiom, making free use of the modern techniques of polytonality and atonality. However, most of his works preserve the formal unity of the Romantic school; the influence of his teacher Schreker is discernible.

WORKS: Operas: *Borgia* (1931) and *Der Falsche Waldmar* (1934); oratorios: *Der reiche Tag* (1938); *Von edlen Leben* (1941); *Mysterium der Liebe* (1942); *Sinfonie der grossen Stadt* (1937); 2 piano concertos; Oboe Concerto (1946); 3 string quartets; Clarinet Quintet; Wind Sextet.

Höffgen, Marga, German contralto; b. Mülheim an der Ruhr, April 26, 1921. She studied at the Berlin Hochschule für Musik; made her concert debut in Berlin in 1952; in 1953 she made a highly successful appearance in Vienna in a concert conducted by Karajan; she was active as an oratorio singer in Europe; also appeared in opera at Covent Garden in London, at the Vienna State Opera, and at the Bayreuth Festival.

Hoffman, Grace (Goldie), American mezzo-soprano; b. Cleveland, Jan. 14, 1925. She was educated at Western Reserve Univ. in Cleveland; then studied voice with Friedrich Schorr in N.Y. and Mario Basiola in Milan; after appearances in the U.S., she sang in Florence and Zürich; in 1955 became a member of the Württemberg State Theater in Stuttgart. On March 27, 1958, she made her Metropolitan Opera debut in N.Y. as Brangäne in *Tristan und Isolde.* She made many appearances at La Scala in Milan, Covent Garden in London, Bayreuth, and the Vienna State Opera. In 1978 she became a prof. of voice at the Hochschule für Musik in Stuttgart. She was noted for her performances of the music of Wagner and Verdi, particularly for her roles of Brangäne, Kundry, and Eboli; also sang widely in concerts.

Hoffman, Richard, English-American pianist and composer; b. Manchester, May 24, 1831; d. Mt. Kisco, N.Y., Aug. 17, 1909. He received his 1st instruction from his father and then studied with Leopold de Meyer, Pleyel, Moscheles, Rubinstein, Döhler, and Liszt. He spent most of his life in the U.S. and was a major figure in American musical life, but chose to retain his British citizenship. (Perhaps this was due to his having the same birthdate as Queen Victoria; on their joint birthday he would place a British flag on the mantel and play *God Save the Queen* on the piano.) He went to N.Y. in 1847; traveled with Jenny Lind on her American tour (1850–52) as joint artist; appeared often with Gottschalk in duo-piano recitals. He was a prolific composer, mainly of salon music for piano; wrote about 100 opus numbers; also songs, anthems, etc. He publ. *Some Musical Recollections of Fifty Years* (N.Y., 1910).

Hoffmann, Bruno, German player on the glass harmonica; b. Stuttgart, Sept. 15, 1913; d. there, April 11, 1991. He studied piano, organ, and voice. In 1929 he became interested in building a modern "glass harp" and eventually expanded its range to 4 octaves, covering a full chromatic scale. With this instrument he gave several concert tours: in Europe (from 1949), in Asia (from 1962), in the U.S. and Canada (from 1964), and in South America (from 1969); he also composed a number of works for the glass harp.

Hoffmann, E(rnst) T(heodor) A(madeus) (his 3rd Christian name was Wilhelm, but he replaced it with Amadeus, from love of Mozart), famous German writer, who was also a composer; b. Königsberg, Jan. 24, 1776; d. Berlin, June 25, 1822. He studied law at the Univ. of Königsberg; also studied violin with Christian Gladau, piano with Carl Gottlieb Richter, and thoroughbass and counterpoint with Christian Podbielski; after further studies with Gladau, he completed his training by taking a course in composition with J.F. Reichardt in Berlin. He served as music director at the theater in Bamberg; then conducted opera performances in Leipzig and Dresden (1813–14). In 1814 he settled in Berlin. He used the pen name of Kapellmeister Johannes Kreisler (subsequently made famous in Schumann's *Kreisleriana*); his series of articles in the *Allgemeine Musikalische Zeitung* under that name were reprinted as *Phantasiestücke in Callot's Manier* (1814). As a writer of fantastic tales, he made a profound impression on his period, and influenced the entire Romantic school of literature; indirectly, he was also a formative factor in the evolution of the German school of composition. His own compositions are passable from the technical viewpoint, but strangely enough, for a man of his imaginative power, they lack the inventiveness that characterizes his literary productions. His writings on music were ed. by H. von Ende (Cologne, 1896); see also D. Charlton, ed., *E.T.A. Hoffmann's Musical Writings: Kreisleriana, The Poet and the Composer, Music Criticism* (Cambridge, 1989).
WORKS: Operas: *Die Maske* (1799); *Scherz, List und Rache* (Posen, 1801); *Der Renegat* (Plozk, 1803); *Faustine* (Plozk, 1804); *Die ungeladenen Gäste, oder Der Canonicus von Mailand* (Warsaw, 1805); *Lustige Musikanten* (Warsaw, 1805); *Liebe aus Eifersucht* (Warsaw, 1807); *Der Trank der Unsterblichkeit* (Bamberg, 1808); *Das Gespenst* (Warsaw, 1809); *Aurora* (1811; rev. version by L. Böttcher, Bamberg, Nov. 5, 1933); *Undine* (Berlin, Aug. 3, 1816; his best work; vocal score ed. by Pfitzner, 1907); *Julius Sabinus* (unfinished); also a ballet, *Harlekin;* some sacred works; Sym.; Piano Trio; 4 piano sonatas. G. Becking ed. his musical works (2 vols., 1922–23).
BIBL.: E. Istel, "E.T.A. H. als Musikschriftsteller," *Neue Zeitschrift für Musik,* XCIX (1903); H. von Müller, *Das Kreislerbuch* (Leipzig, 1903); H. von Wolzogen, *E.T.A. H. und R. Wagner* (Berlin, 1906); E. Kroll, *E.T.A. H.s musikalische Anschauungen* (Königsberg, 1909); H. Ehinger, *E.T.A. H. als Musiker und Musik-Schriftsteller* (Cologne, 1954); H. Dechant, *E.T.A. H.s Oper Aurora* (1975); R. Murray Schafer, *E.T.A. H. and Music* (Toronto, 1975); W. Keil, *E.T.A. H. als Komponist: Studien zur Kompositionstechnik an ausgewählten Werken* (Wiesbaden, 1986).

Hoffmann, Hans, German conductor and musicologist; b. Neustadt, Silesia, Jan. 26, 1902; d. Bielefeld, Aug. 8, 1949. He studied musicology at the Univ. of Breslau, and later in

Leipzig, Berlin, and Kiel. Concurrently he took instruction in singing and for several years sang in oratorio performances in Germany. In 1933 he became choral conductor in Hamburg, and taught music theory at Hamburg Univ. He was also active as a sym. and opera conductor, and in 1940 was appointed music director of the Bielefeld Opera. Among his publications are *H. Schütz und J.S. Bach* (Kassel, 1940) and *Vom Wesen der zeitgenössischen Kirchenmusik* (Kassel, 1949).

Hoffmann, Heinrich August (also known as **Hoffmann von Fallersleben**), German poet, philologist, literary historian, and composer; b. Fallersleben, near Braunschweig, April 2, 1798; d. Schloss Korvei, near Höxter, Jan. 19, 1874. He received his education at the Univ. of Göttingen; in 1830 he was appointed prof. at Breslau Univ. For some years (1842–48) he was not allowed to teach or reside in Prussia, on account of his dissenting political views; from 1860 he was librarian to Prince Lippe at Korvei. He wrote several important books dealing with music, *Geschichte des deutschen Kirchenlieds* (1832; 3rd ed., 1861), *Schlesische Volkslieder mit Melodien* (1842), etc., but his chief claim to fame is the text of *Deutschland, Deutschland, über alles,* which he wrote to Haydn's hymn *Gott erhalte Franz den Kaiser.*

Hoffmann, Richard, Austrian-born American composer; b. Vienna, April 20, 1925. He studied violin and harmony in Vienna as a child; was in New Zealand from 1935 to 1947; graduated from Auckland Univ. College in 1945. He settled in the U.S. in 1947; studied composition with Arnold Schoenberg, and subsequently became his amanuensis and secretary. In 1954 he joined the faculty of the Oberlin Cons. of Music. He held Guggenheim fellowships in 1970 and 1977; was a Fulbright senior lecturer at the Univ. of Vienna in 1984. He developed a sui generis serial technique, in which intervals, meters, rhythms, timbres, and dynamics are systematically organized, while the tone row is not necessarily dodecaphonic.
WORKS: 4 string quartets (1947; 1950; 1972–74; 1977–78, with computer-generated sounds); Trio for Piano, Violin, and Bass Clarinet (1948); *Fantasy and Fugue, in Memoriam Arnold Schoenberg* for Orch. (1951); Piano Concerto (1954); Cello Concerto (1956–59); String Trio (1963); *memento mori* for Male Chorus and Orch. (1966–69); *Souffleur* for Orch. *sans conductor* (1975–76); *Les Adieux* for Chorus and Orch. (1981–83); choruses; songs.

Hoffmeister, Franz Anton, German composer and music publisher; b. Rothenburg am Neckar, May 12, 1754; d. Vienna, Feb. 9, 1812. He went to Vienna as a law student, but became greatly interested in music, and in 1785 established his publishing firm, of historic significance owing to its publications of Mozart and Beethoven. In 1800 he went to Leipzig, where he organized (with Kühnel) a "Bureau de Musique," which eventually became incorporated into the celebrated firm of C.F. Peters. In 1805 he returned to Vienna, where he devoted himself mostly to composition. Amazingly prolific, he composed 9 operas, more than 66 syms. and overtures, over 150 string quartets, 5 piano quartets, 11 piano trios, 18 string trios, and 12 piano sonatas; in addition he wrote a very great number of compositions for flute with various instruments.
BIBL.: E. Schmid, "F.A. H. und die 'Göttweiger Sonaten,'" *Zeitschrift für Musik,* CIV (1937); A. Weinmann, *Die Wiener Verlagswerke von F.A. H.* (Vienna, 1964).

Hoffstetter, Roman, German composer; b. Laudenbach, near Bad Mergentheim, April 24, 1742; d. Miltenberg, May 21, 1815. He was a member of the Benedictine monastery of Amorbach; was ordained a priest in 1766, and was active as regens chori there; settled in Miltenberg in 1803. He greatly admired the music of Haydn; his chamber music so closely resembled Haydn's that it was long attributed to Haydn; the works in question are the 2 string quartets written c.1765, as well as the publ. 6 String Quartets, op. 1 (Amsterdam, c.1770), and 6 String Quartets, op. 3 (Paris, 1777). He also wrote 3 cello concertos and a number of masses.
BIBL.: A. Tyson and H.C. Robbins Landon, "Who Composed

Haydn's Op. 3?," *Musical Times* (July 1964); H. Unverricht, *Die beiden H.* (Mainz, 1968; includes thematic catalog).

Hofhaimer (also **Hoffhaimer, Hoffheimer, Hofhaymer,** etc.), **Paul,** greatly celebrated Austrian organist, composer, and pedagogue; b. Radstadt, Jan. 25, 1459; d. Salzburg, 1537. Although he is believed to have been self-taught as a musician, he may have received organ instruction at the court of Emperor Frederick III. He entered the service of the court of Duke Sigmund of Tyrol in Innsbruck in 1478, and was made organist for life in 1480. He was also in the service of Emperor Maximilian I from 1489, settling in Augsburg in 1507. He was knighted and ennobled by Maximilian and the Polish king in 1515, and was granted the title of Obrister [principal] Organist by the former. Following Maximilian's death in 1519, he was made organist of the cathedral and to the archbishop of Salzburg. In addition to his fame as a virtuoso, he was renowned as a teacher. He also distinguished himself as a composer of lieder and organ works; among his few extant works are the *Harmoniae poeticae* (Nuremberg, 1539; ed. by I. Achtleithner, Salzburg, 1868; 35 settings of Horatian odes) and 2 liturgical organ pieces, *Recordare* and *Salve Regina.* See H.J. Moser, ed., "Gesammelte Tonwerke," *Paul Hofhaimer* (Stuttgart and Berlin, 1929); K. Gudewill, ed., *G. Forster: Frische teutsche Liedlein (1539–1556),* Das Erbe Deutscher Musik, 1st series, XX (1942); H. Marx, ed., *Tabulaturen des XVI. Jahrhunderts, I: Die Tabulaturen aus dem Besitz des Basler Humanisten Bonifacius Amerbach,* Schweizerische Musikdenkmäler, VI (1967); idem, ed., *Tabulaturen des XVI. Jahrhunderts, II: Die Orgeltabulatur des Clemens Hör,* ibid., VII (1970).

BIBL.: H.J. Moser, *P. H.* (Stuttgart and Berlin, 1929); L. Hoffmann-Erbrecht, "P. H. in Salzburg," *Festschrift Heinrich Besseler* (Leipzig, 1962).

Hofman, Shlomo, Polish-Israeli composer and musicologist; b. Warsaw, April 24, 1909. He studied at the Warsaw Cons., graduating in 1934; then went to Paris, where he studied composition with Roger-Ducasse, Charles Koechlin, and Darius Milhaud (1937–38). He subsequently settled in Palestine; in 1954 became a lecturer in musicology at the Academy of Music in Tel Aviv. Among his works are Oboe Concerto (1950); Hebrew cantata, *Tawashih* (1960); Quintet for Clarinet and Strings (1945). He publ. a valuable thesis, *L'Œuvre de clavecin de François Couperin le Grand* (Paris, 1961); also a polyglot *Dictionary of Musical Terms* (Jerusalem, 1955); *The Music of Israel* (1959); *La Musique arabe en Israël* (1963).

Hofmann, Casimir (Kazimierz), Polish pianist, conductor, and composer, father of **Josef (Casimir) (Józef Kazimierz) Hofmann;** b. Krakow, 1842; d. Berlin, July 6, 1911. He studied with R. Fischof and Gachlechner at the Vienna Cons.; then conducted opera in Krakow. In 1878 he moved to Warsaw, where he taught at the Inst. of Music (1878–86). After the spectacular success of his young son, he followed him on his extended tours throughout Europe and America. From 1886, he lived mainly in Berlin.

Hofmann, Heinrich (Karl Johann), German pianist and composer; b. Berlin, Jan. 13, 1842; d. Gross-Tabarz, Thuringia, July 16, 1902. He studied in Berlin with Grell, Dehn, and Wüerst. He became a concert pianist, then turned to composition after the enormous success of his comic opera *Cartouche* (Berlin, 1869); his *Ungarische Suite* for Orch. (1873) and his *Frithjof-Symphonie* (1874) added to his popularity. Exceptionally productive, he wrote a great deal of operatic, symphonic, and chamber music, choral works, and solo piano pieces, all of which were publ. and frequently performed. His popularity declined precipitously toward the end of his life; his music vanished from concert programs after his death. His style reflected Wagnerian procedures, particularly in heroic moods; he possessed complete mastery of technique, but his music lacked originality or distinction.

WORKS: STAGE: Comic opera, *Cartouche* (Berlin, 1869); heroic opera, *Armin* (Dresden, Oct. 14, 1877); lyric opera, *Aennchen von Tharau* (Hamburg, Nov. 6, 1878); romantic opera, *Wilhelm von Oranien* (Hamburg, Feb. 5, 1882); opera,

Donna Diana (Berlin, Nov. 15, 1886). ORCH.: *Frithjof-Symphony* (1874); *Hungarian Suite* (1873); Cello Concerto (1880); *Konzertstück* for Flute and Orch. (1888). CHAMBER: String Sextet (1875); Piano Quartet (1880); Octet for 2 Violins, Viola, Cello, Flute, Clarinet, Horn, and Bassoon (1883); etc.; also choral works; keyboard pieces.

Hofmann, Josef (Casimir) (Józef Kazimierz), celebrated Polish-born American pianist, son of **Casimir (Kazimierz) Hofmann;** b. Podgorze, near Krakow, Jan. 20, 1876; d. Los Angeles, Feb. 16, 1957. At the age of 4 he began to play the piano, tutored by an older sister and an aunt; at 5 he began taking regular lessons from his father. He was barely 6 when he 1st appeared in public in Ciechocinek; at the age of 10 he played Beethoven's Concerto No. 1 with the Berlin Phil., under Hans von Bülow. He also made a tour of Scandinavia; played in France and England; his concerts as a child prodigy became a European sensation; soon an American offer of a concert tour came from the impresarios Abbey, Schoeffel & Grau. On Nov. 29, 1887, Hofmann appeared at the Metropolitan Opera House, as a soloist in Beethoven's Concerto No. 1; he also played works by Chopin and some of his own little pieces. He electrified the audience, and hardheaded critics hailed his performance as a marvel. He appeared throughout the U.S., giving 42 concerts in all; then agitation was started by the Soc. for the Prevention of Cruelty to Children against the exploitation of his talent. Alfred Corning Clark of N.Y. offered $50,000 to the family for his continued education. The offer was accepted, and he began serious study with Moszkowski (piano) and Urban (composition) in Berlin. Then Anton Rubinstein accepted him as a pupil in Dresden, where Hofmann traveled twice a week for piano lessons. At the age of 18 he resumed his career, giving recitals in Dresden and elsewhere in Germany with enormous success; made his 1st tour of Russia in 1896, attaining huge popularity there; he reappeared in Russia frequently. In 1898 he again played in the U.S.; from then on, he appeared in American cities almost every year. At the peak of his career, he came to be regarded as one of the greatest pianists of the century. He possessed the secret of the singing tone, which enabled him to interpret Chopin with extraordinary delicacy and intimacy. He was also capable of summoning tremendous power playing Liszt and other works of the virtuoso school. His technique knew no difficulties; but in his interpretations, he subordinated technical effects to the larger design of the work. When the Curtis Inst. of Music was founded in Philadelphia (1924), Hofmann was engaged to head the piano dept.; he was director from 1926 to 1938. He became an American citizen in 1926. On Nov. 28, 1937, his golden jubilee in the U.S. was celebrated with a concert at the Metropolitan Opera in N.Y. He performed the D-minor Concerto of Anton Rubinstein, and his own *Chromaticon* for Piano and Orch. From 1938 to his death he lived mostly in California, his concert career coming sadly to a close in 1945 owing to alcoholism. Hofmann was also a composer, under the pen name Michel Dvorsky (a transliteration of the literal translation into Polish of his German name, meaning "courtyard man"). Among his works are several piano concertos; some symphonic works; *Chromaticon* for Piano and Orch. (Cincinnati, Nov. 24, 1916, composer soloist); numerous piano pieces. He publ. a practical manual, *Piano-Playing with Piano-Questions Answered* (1915).

BIBL.: A. Chasins, *Speaking of Pianists* (N.Y., 1957; 2nd ed., 1961); H. Schonberg, *The Great Pianists* (N.Y., 1961; 2nd ed., rev., 1987).

Hofmann, Leopold, Austrian organist, violinist, and composer; b. Vienna, Aug. 14, 1738; d. there, March 17, 1793. He studied piano and violin; held posts as choirmaster in Vienna churches; also served as a court organist. He wrote much church music and a number of instrumental concertos and chamber works, highly competent technically but lacking in invention and polyphonic strength.

BIBL.: V. Kreiner, *L. H. als Sinfoniker* (diss., Univ. of Vienna, 1958).

Hofmann, Peter, outstanding German tenor; b. Marienbad, Aug. 12, 1944. He studied at the Hochschule für Musik in Karlsruhe; made his operatic debut in 1972 in Lübeck as Tamino; in 1973 joined the Württemberg State Theater in Stuttgart. He came to prominence in his performance of the role of Siegmund in the centennial Bayreuth productions of *Der Ring des Nibelungen* (1976); later he appeared as Parsifal at Covent Garden in London. He made his U.S. debut as Siegmund with the San Francisco Opera in 1977; sang Lohengrin with the Metropolitan Opera in N.Y. in 1980. His other roles include Max, Florestan, Alfred in *Die Fledermaus,* Loge, and Bacchus.
BIBL.: M. Müller, *P. H.: Singen ist wie Fliegen* (Bonn, 1983).

Hofmeister, Friedrich, German music publisher; b. Strehlen an der Elbe, Jan. 24, 1782; d. Reudnitz, near Leipzig, Sept. 30, 1864. In 1807 he established in Leipzig the music firm that bears his name; beginning in 1829, he publ. a valuable monthly catalog, the *Musikalisch-litterarischer Monatsbericht.* His son and successor, **Adolf Hofmeister** (b. c.1802; d. Leipzig, May 26, 1870), publ. a 3rd and enl. ed. of Whistling's *Handbuch der musikalischen Litteratur* (1845), with supplementary vols. filled from issues of Hofmeister's *Monatsbericht.* After 1852, the 12 *Monatsberichte* for each complete year were arranged in alphabetical order and issued as a *Jahresbericht.* All these valuable eds. were continued by the firm under the proprietorship of Albert Röthing (b. Leipzig, Jan. 4, 1845; d. there, Aug. 11, 1907). In 1905 Karl Günther became the head of the firm; he was succeeded by Karl Ganzenmüller. In 1935 the firm acquired the catalog of Merseburger (Leipzig); after World War II the firm had offices both in Frankfurt and Leipzig; it was later removed to Hofheim an der Taunus.
BIBL.: R. Elvers and C. Hopkinson, "A Survey of the Music Catalogues of Whistling and H.," *Fontes Artis Musicae,* XIX (1972).

Hogarth, George, Scottish writer on music; b. Carfrae Mill, near Oxton, Berwickshire, 1783; d. London, Feb. 12, 1870. He was a practicing lawyer in Edinburgh, and an amateur musician. He settled in London in 1830; contributed articles to the *Harmonicon;* also wrote reviews for the *Morning Chronicle.* His daughter married Charles Dickens in 1836; when Dickens became ed. of the *Daily News* (1846), Hogarth began writing music criticisms for it; also wrote for other newspapers. From 1850 to 1864 he was secretary to the Phil. Soc. of London.
WRITINGS: *Musical History, Biography, and Criticism* (1835); *Memoirs of the Musical Drama* (1838; 2nd ed., 1851, as *Memoirs of the Opera*); *The Birmingham Festival* (1855); *The Philharmonic Society of London* (1862).

Hogwood, Christopher (Jarvis Haley), prominent English harpsichordist, conductor, and musicologist; b. Nottingham, Sept. 10, 1941. He studied classics as well as music at Pembroke College, Cambridge (B.A., 1964); received instruction in harpsichord from R. Puyana and G. Leonhardt, and also took courses at the Charles Univ. and the Academy of Music in Prague. In 1967 he joined David Munrow in organizing the Early Music Consort, an ensemble devoted to the performance of medieval music. In 1973 he founded the Academy of Ancient Music with the aim of performing music of the Baroque and early Classical periods on original instruments; he toured widely with the ensemble and made many recordings with it, including a complete set of Mozart's syms. utilizing instruments of Mozart's time. He also served as artistic director of the Handel and Haydn Soc. of Boston (from 1986) and music director of the St. Paul (Minn.) Chamber Orch. (from 1988). His guest conducting engagements took him all over Europe and North America. In 1989 he was made a Commander of the Order of the British Empire. He ed. works by J.C. Bach, Purcell, and Croft; was a contributor to *The New Grove Dictionary of Music and Musicians* (1980).
WRITINGS: *Music at Court* (London, 1977); *The Trio Sonata* (London, 1979); *Handel* (London, 1984).
BIBL.: P. Smith, "C. H.," *Ovation* (Dec. 1983).

Hoiby, Lee, talented American composer and pianist; b. Madison, Wis., Feb. 17, 1926. He began piano study at age 5, and

while attending high school received instruction from Gunnar Johansen; then studied at the Univ. of Wisconsin (B.A., 1947); attended Egon Petri's master class in Ithaca, N.Y. (1944), and at Mills College in Oakland, Calif. (M.A., 1952), where he also studied composition with Milhaud; he also received instruction in composition from Menotti at the Curtis Inst. of Music in Philadelphia. He received a Fulbright fellowship (1953), an award from the National Inst. of Arts and Letters (1957), and a Guggenheim fellowship (1958). In addition to his career as a composer, he appeared as a concert pianist; made his N.Y. recital debut on Jan. 17, 1978. He has composed a number of highly successful vocal and instrumental works, being particularly adept in writing operas in a manner reminiscent of Menotti—concise, dramatic, and aurally pleasing, and sometimes stimulating.
WORKS: OPERAS: *The Scarf,* after Chekhov (Spoleto, June 20, 1958); *Beatrice,* after Maeterlinck (Louisville, Oct. 23, 1959; withdrawn); *Natalia Petrovna,* after Turgenev (N.Y., Oct. 8, 1964; rev. as *A Month in the Country,* Boston, Jan. 1981); *Summer and Smoke,* after Tennessee Williams (1970; St. Paul, Minn., June 19, 1971); *Something New for the Zoo* (1979; Cheverly, Md., May 17, 1982); *The Tempest,* after Shakespeare (1982–86; Indianola, Iowa, June 21, 1986); also *The Italian Lesson,* monodrama for Mezzo-soprano and Chamber Orch. (1980; Newport, R.I., 1982); incidental music to various plays. BALLETS: *Hearts, Meadows, and Flags* (1950); *After Eden* (1966); *Landscape* (1968). ORCH.: *Pastoral Dances* for Flute and Small Orch. (New Orleans, Nov. 6, 1956); 2nd Suite for Orch. (1953); Piano Concerto No. 1 (1958); *The Tides of Sleep,* symphonic song for Low Voice and Orch., after Thomas Wolfe (1961); *Design* for Strings (1965); *Music for a Celebration,* overture (1975); Piano Concerto No. 2 (1979). CHAMBER: Sonata for Violin and Piano (1951; rev. 1980); *Diversions* for Woodwind Quartet (1953); Piano Quintet (1974); *Serenade* for Violin and Piano (Washington, D.C., Nov. 4, 1988). CHORAL: *A Hymn of the Nativity* for Soprano, Baritone, Chorus, and Orch. (1960); *Galileo Galilei,* oratorio for Soloists, Chorus, and Orch. (1975); *Psalm 93* for Large Chorus, Organ, Brass, and Percussion (Cathedral of St. John the Divine, N.Y., May 17, 1985); piano pieces; songs.
BIBL.: *Current Biography* (March 1987).

Hol, Richard (Rijk), Dutch composer, conductor, pianist, and organist; b. Amsterdam, July 23, 1825; d. Utrecht, May 14, 1904. He studied organ with Martens and theory with Bertelmann. After traveling in Germany, he taught music in Amsterdam; in 1862, became city music director at Utrecht, succeeding Kufferath; then cathedral organist (1869–87) and director of the School of Music (1875–1904); conducted concerts in The Hague and Amsterdam. From 1886 to 1900 he was ed. of *Het Orgel;* wrote a monograph on Sweelinck (1860).
WORKS: Operas: *Floris V* (Amsterdam, April 9, 1892); *Uit de branding* (Amsterdam, 1894); *De schoone schaapster;* oratorio, *David* (1879); 4 syms.; choral and orch. works; chamber music; songs.
BIBL.: H. Nolthenius, *R. H., Levensschets* (Haarlem, 1904).

Holborne, Antony or **Anthony,** English composer; place and date of birth unknown; d. Nov. 29?, 1602. He publ. *The Cittharn Schoole* (58 pieces; London, 1597) and *Pavans, Galliards, Almains . . . in 5 Parts* (65 pieces; London, 1599), which were popular in their day; other works were publ. in contemporary collections. See *The Complete Works of Anthony Holborne,* Harvard Publications in Music, i, V (1967–73).
BIBL.: B. Jeffery, *The Life and Music of Antony H.* (diss., Oxford Univ., 1964; with thematic index); idem, "Antony H.," *Musica Disciplina,* XXI (1968).

Holbrooke, Joseph (actually, **Josef Charles**), English composer; b. Croydon, July 5, 1878; d. London, Aug. 5, 1958. He received his primary education from his father; then studied at the Royal Academy of Music in London with F. Westlake (piano) and Corder (composition). After graduation, he conducted ballet and various summer orchs. Although he composed prolifically, and had many ardent admirers of his music, he never succeeded in establishing himself as a representative British composer. Perhaps this was owing to the fact that he stood aloof from modernistic developments in European music, and preferred to write for a hypothetical mass audience, which, however, failed to materialize at the infrequent performances of his music. He wrote a book, *Contemporary British Composers* (1925).

WORKS: OPERAS: *Pierrot and Pierrette* (London, Nov. 11, 1909); a trilogy (his main dramatic work), *The Cauldron of Anwyn*: I. *The Children of Don* (London, June 15, 1912), II. *Dylan, Son of the Wave* (London, July 4, 1913), III. *Bronwen, Daughter of Llyr* (Huddersfield, Feb. 1, 1929); *The Enchanter* (Chicago, 1915); *The Snob*, 1-act comic opera. BALLETS: *The Red Masque; The Moth; The Enchanted Garden.* ORCH.: Symphonic poems: *The Raven* (London, 1900); *The Viking; Ulalume* (1904); *Byron*, with Chorus; *Queen Mab*, with Chorus (Leeds Festival, 1904); *Homage to E.A. Poe*, with Chorus; *The Bells*, with Chorus (Birmingham, 1906); *The Skeleton in Armor; The Masque of the Red Death*; 5 syms.; variations on *3 Blind Mice, The Girl I Left behind Me*, and *Auld Lang Syne; Dreamland Suite; Les Hommages*, suite; *The Haunted Palace*, fantasy; *The New Renaissance*, overture. CHAMBER: 5 string quartets; 4 string sextets; 3 violin sonatas; 2 piano quartets; 2 clarinet quintets; Piano Quintet; Trio for Violin, Horn, and Piano.

BIBL.: G. Lowe, *J. H. and His Work* (1920); *J. H.: Various Appreciations by Many Authors* (London, 1937).

Holde, Artur, German-American choral conductor and music critic; b. Rendsburg, Oct. 16, 1885; d. N.Y., June 23, 1962. He studied musicology at the Univ. of Berlin; from 1910 to 1936 was music director of the Frankfurt Synagogue; also was active as a music critic. In 1937 he emigrated to the U.S.; was choirmaster at the Hebrew Tabernacle in N.Y. (1937–43) and music critic of the German periodical *Aufbau* in N.Y. He publ. the books *Jews in Music* (N.Y., 1959) and *A Treasury of Great Operas* (N.Y., 1965); contributed articles to the *Musical Quarterly* and other American publications.

Holden, Oliver, American musician, carpenter, and minister; b. Shirley, Mass., Sept. 18, 1765; d. Charlestown, Mass., Sept. 4, 1844. After serving as a marine in the navy, he settled in Charlestown in 1787 and was active as a justice of the peace and carpenter; then abandoned carpentry and established a music store (about 1790); also offered music lessons; officiated as preacher of the Puritan Church; served in the State House of Representatives (1818–33). He composed Psalm tunes and odes; at least 21 hymns are known to be of his authorship, his best being *Coronation* (set to the words of *All Hail the Power of Jesus' Name*), 1st publ. in vol. I of his *Union Harmony* (1793); it has retained its popularity. His *From Vernon's mount behold the hero rise*, one of the many works written in commemoration of George Washington's death, was sung at the Old South Meeting House, Boston, in Jan. 1800. Other publications: *The American Harmony* (1792); *The Massachusetts Compiler* (1795; with H. Gram and S. Holyoke); *The Worcester Collection* (1797; ed. and rev. by Holden); *Sacred Dirges, Hymns and Anthems* (1800); *Modern Collection of Sacred Music* (1800); *Plain Psalmody* (1800); *Charlestown Collection of Sacred Songs* (1803); *Vocal Companion* (1807); and *Occasional Pieces.*

BIBL.: F. Metcalf, *American Psalmody* (N.Y., 1917); idem, *American Writers and Compilers of Sacred Music* (N.Y., 1925); D. McCormick, *O. H., Composer and Anthologist* (Union Theological Seminary, 1963); R. Patterson, *Three American "Primitives": A Study of the Musical Styles of Samuel Holyoke, O. H., and Hans Gram* (diss., Washington Univ., 1963).

Holewa, Hans, Austrian-born Swedish composer; b. Vienna, May 26, 1905. He studied conducting at the New Cons. of Music in Vienna, and piano and theory with J. Heinz; in 1937 he settled in Stockholm as a pianist and pedagogue; there he introduced Schoenberg's 12-tone technique. From 1949 to 1970 he worked in the music library of the Swedish Broadcasting Corp.

WORKS: OPERA: *Apollos förvandling* (1967–71). ORCH.: *Vier kleine Märsche* (1940); *Variations* for Piano and Orch. (1943);

6 syms.: No. 1 (1948); No. 2 (1976; Stockholm, April 28, 1978); No. 3 for Textless Soprano and Orch. (1977; Stockholm, Oct. 17, 1979); No. 4 (1980; Stockholm, June 7, 1984); No. 5 (1983; Västerås, Nov. 15, 1984); No. 6 (1985–86; Stockholm, April 8, 1988); Violin Concerto (1963; Swedish Radio, Feb. 7, 1965); *Komposition* (1965–66; Swedish Radio, Oct. 8, 1966); *Quattro cadenze* for Cello and Orch. (1968; Swedish Radio, April 12, 1970); *Movimento espressivo* (Stockholm, April 17, 1971); 3 piano concertos: No. 1 (1972; Swedish Radio, April 28, 1973); No. 2 (1980–81; Swedish Radio, Feb. 11, 1983); No. 3 (1984–85; Swedish Radio, Jan. 30, 1987); Concerto for 2 Pianos and String Orch. (1975; Uppsala, April 8, 1976). CHAMBER: 2 string quartets (1939, 1965); Sonata for Solo Cello (1952); 9 concertinos (1960–87); Sonata for Solo Violin (1960); Quintet for Clarinet, Trombone, Cello, Percussion, and Piano (1962); *Chamber Music* for Cello and Piano No. 1 (1964), No. 2 (1973), and No. 3 (1981); *Chamber Concerto* for Viola and 11 Strings (1966); *Lamenti*, 3 pieces for Horn, Alto Saxophone, and Bassoon (1976); Quartet for Oboe, Violin, Viola, and Cello (1979); Octet for Clarinet, Horn, Bassoon, 2 Violins, Viola, Cello, and Double Bass (1982); Wind Quintet (1982); *Sonata Movement* for String Quartet (1984); Sonata for Violin and Piano (1985); Quartet for Flute, Oboe, Cello, and Piano (1988); also numerous piano pieces; choral works; songs.

Holguín, Guillermo. See **Uribe-Holguín, Guillermo.**

Holiday, Billie (Eleanora) "Lady Day," remarkable black American jazz singer; b. Philadelphia, April 7, 1915; d. N.Y., July 17, 1959. She was the illegitimate daughter of Sadie Fagan and the guitarist Clarence Holiday. She began singing in Harlem nightclubs when she was 14; there she was discovered by the impresario John Hammond, who arranged for her to perform and record with Benny Goodman and his band in 1933; she later worked with Teddy Wilson (1935), Fletcher Henderson (1936), Count Basie (1937–38), Artie Shaw, and others before setting out on her own. She gave a solo concert at N.Y.'s Town Hall and appeared in the movie *New Orleans* in 1946. Her otherwise brilliant career was marred by personal tragedies, which included addiction to narcotics and alcohol; she served time for Federal narcotics charges in 1946, but made a comeback at N.Y.'s Carnegie Hall in 1948. She subsequently toured throughout the U.S. and also sang in Europe (1954, 1958). Arrested again on a narcotics charge, she died in N.Y.'s Metropolitan Hospital. Despite the oft-quoted phrase "Lady Day sings the blues," she rarely sang classic blues; with her unique vocal endowments, she made everything she performed—mostly popular tunes of the day—sound "bluesy." She wrote an autobiography, *Lady Sings the Blues* (with W. Duffy; N.Y., 1956), which was later used as the basis of a popular film of the same name starring Diana Ross.

BIBL.: J. Chilton, *B.'s Blues: A Survey of B. H.'s Career, 1933–1959* (N.Y., 1975); J. Millar, *Born to Sing: A Discography of B. H.* (Copenhagen, 1979); B. James, *B. H.* (N.Y., 1984); M.-E. Nabe, *L'Âme de B. H.* (Paris, 1986); J. White, *B. H.: Her Life & Times* (Tunbridge Wells and N.Y., 1987); B. Kliment, *B. H.* (N.Y., 1990).

Hollaender, Alexis, German pianist, choral conductor, and composer; b. Ratibor, Silesia, Feb. 25, 1840; d. Berlin, Feb. 5, 1924. He studied piano with Carl Schnabel and organ with Adolf Hesse in Breslau; then took courses at the Berlin Royal Academy with Greel and others; became an instructor at the Kullak Academy (1861); conducted choral groups. He composed piano works, choruses, songs, etc.; also publ. an instructive ed. of Schumann's piano music and *Methodische Übungen fürs Halten einer tieferen Stimme.*

Hollaender, Gustav, German violinist and composer, brother of **Viktor Hollaender;** b. Leobschütz, Silesia, Feb. 15, 1855; d. Berlin, Dec. 4, 1915. He was taught the violin by his father; then studied at the Leipzig Cons. with F. David, and in Berlin with Joachim. At the age of 20 he embarked on a concert career; gave concerts of chamber music with Scharwenka and Grünfeld in Berlin (1878–81); in 1881 he was appointed a teacher at the Cologne Cons.; from 1894 to 1915 was director of the Stern Cons. in Berlin. He wrote numerous pieces for violin, in an effective virtuoso style.

Hollaender, Viktor (pen name, Arricha del Tolveno), German conductor and composer, brother of **Gustav Hollaender;** b. Leobschütz, April 20, 1866; d. Los Angeles, Oct. 24, 1940. He studied with Kullak; was a theater conductor in Berlin for a number of years; also a theater conductor in London. He lived mostly in Berlin until 1933, when he went to America and settled in Los Angeles. His works include the operettas *Carmosinella* (Leipzig, 1887), *The Bey of Morocco* (London, 1894), *Double Dealings* (London, 1898), *San-Lin* (Berlin, 1898), *Der Sonnenvogel* (1907), *Der Regimentspapa* (Dresden, 1914); songs and piano pieces. His son, **Fredrick Hollaender** (b. London, Oct. 18, 1896; d. Munich, Jan. 18, 1976), was also a composer; he studied at the Berlin Hochschule für Musik, and also with Humperdinck. He composed for films in Germany and Hollywood; wrote his memoirs, *Von Kopf bis Fuss: Mein Leben mit Text und Musik* (Munich, 1965).

Holland, Charles, black American tenor; b. Norfolk, Va., Dec. 27, 1909; d. Amsterdam, Nov. 7, 1987. He studied with May Hamaker Henley, Georges Le Pyre in Los Angeles, and Clyde Burrows in N.Y. He sang with the bands of Benny Carter and Fletcher Henderson, appeared in the film *Hullabaloo* (1941), and had his own concert program on NBC radio. In 1949 he settled in France, where he appeared on radio and television; made his European operatic debut in *Die Zauberflöte* at the Paris Opéra in 1954, and in 1955 became the 1st black artist to sing at the Paris Opéra-Comique. He later sang throughout Europe, Australia, New Zealand, and Canada, making his N.Y. debut in a recital at Carnegie Hall in 1982.

Holland, Dulcie, Australian pianist and composer; b. Sydney, Jan. 5, 1913. She studied at the Sydney Cons. with Alfred Hill, Frank Hutchens, and Roy Agnew. She then went to London, where she took courses with John Ireland at the Royal College of Music. Returning to Australia, she was active as a radio lecturer and concert pianist. Among her works are *Symphony for Pleasure* (1974), some theater music, and songs for children. She also publ. several school manuals.

Holland, Theodore (Samuel), English composer; b. London, April 25, 1878; d. there, Oct. 29, 1947. He studied with F. Corder at the Royal Academy of Music in London and with Joachim at the Hochschule für Musik in Berlin. In 1927 he became prof. of composition at the Royal Academy of Music. He was an estimable composer, particularly proficient in writing for the theater. Among his works are a children's operetta, *King Goldemar;* a musical play, *Santa Claus; Evening on a Lake* for Chamber Orch. (1924); *Cortège* for an Ensemble of Cellos (1939); *Spring Sinfonietta* (1943); 2 string quartets; 2 piano trios; Suite for Viola and Piano; several song cycles.

Hollander, Lorin, talented American pianist; b. N.Y., July 19, 1944. He received his early musical training from his father, a violinist; then studied piano with Steuermann and composition with Giannini at the Juilliard School in N.Y. He earned the reputation of an aggressive pianist to whom technical difficulties, whether in Bach or Prokofiev, did not exist.

Holle, Hugo, German choral conductor, pedagogue, and writer on music; b. Mehlis, Thuringia, Jan. 25, 1890; d. Stuttgart, Dec. 12, 1942. He was a pupil of Max Reger; was director of the Heilbronn Cons. (1919–21) and ed. of the *Neue Musikzeitung* in Stuttgart (1921–25); was a teacher of music theory at the Hochschule für Musik, Stuttgart (1925–42); was conductor of the famous Holle's Madrigal Choir, with which he toured Central Europe; also co-ed. of the Musikalische Volksbücher. He publ. *Goethes Lyrik in Weisen deutscher Tonsetzer bis zur Gegenwart* (1914); *Die Chorwerke Max Regers* (Munich, 1922); and numerous articles in music periodicals.

Höller, Karl, German composer; b. Bamberg, July 25, 1907; d. Hausham, April 14, 1987. He received musical training at the Cathedral of Bamberg; pursued his formal studies at the Würzburg Cons.; later took courses at the Academy of Music

in Munich, where he studied composition with Joseph Haas. He subsequently was engaged as an instructor there (1933–37); then taught at the Hochschule für Musik in Frankfurt until 1946; in 1949 he succeeded Haas as composition teacher at the Hochschule für Musik in Munich; remained there until 1972.

WORKS: 2 syms. (1942–46; 1973); Chamber Concerto for Violin and Orch. (1931); *Hymnen* for Orch. (1932–34); *Symphonic Fantasy on a Theme of Frescobaldi* for Orch. (1935; rev. 1965); 2 violin concertos (1938, 1948); 2 cello concertos (1941, 1949); *Sweelinck Variations* for Orch. (1951); 6 string quartets (1938–50); Clarinet Quintet; Piano Quartet; Piano Trio; 8 violin sonatas; Cello Sonata; 2 flute sonatas; Viola Sonata ("in memoriam Hindemith," 1967); a multitude of piano pieces; some vocal works.

Höller, York (Georg), German composer; b. Leverkusen, Jan. 11, 1944. He studied serial and electronic composition at the Cologne Hochschule für Musik (1963–67), with Boulez in Darmstadt (1965), and with Zimmermann at the Univ. of Cologne (1968–70). He worked at the electronic music studio of the WDR in Cologne (1971–72), and from 1976 taught music theory at the Cologne Hochschule für Musik. Most of his works employ either live or tape electronics. His *Arcus* for 17 Instrumentalists and Electronically Transformed Instruments on Tape was commissioned for the inaugural concert of Paris's Inst. de Recherche et de la Coordination Acoustique/Musique (IRCAM), the musical research center created for Boulez by the French government in 1978.

WORKS: *Decollage* for 2 Speaking Choruses, Electric Guitar, Electric Cello, Electric Organ, and Tape (1972); *Chroma,* "choreographic visions" for Orch. and Electronically Transformed Organ (1972–74); *Tangens* for Cello, Electric Guitar, Electric Organ/Piano (1 player), and 2 Synthesizers (1973); *Median,* symphonic sketch for Orch. and 4-channel Tape (1974–75); *Klanggitter* for 3 Instruments and Tape (1976–77); *Arcus* for 17 Instrumentalists and Electronically Transformed Instruments on Tape (1978); *Mythos* for 13 Instruments, Percussion, and Electronic Sound (1978–80; Cologne, March 22, 1981); *Schwarze Halbinseln* for Orch. and Tape (1982); *Traumspiel* for Orch. and Soprano (1982–83); Clarinet Concerto (1984); *Improvisation sur le nom de Pierre Boulez* for 17 Instruments (1985); *Der Meister und Margarita,* music theater (1989).

Holliger, Heinz, outstanding Swiss oboist, pedagogue, and composer; b. Langenthal, May 21, 1939. He commenced playing the recorder at 4 and the piano at 6; later studied oboe with Cassagnaud and composition with Veress at the Bern Cons., then oboe with Pierlot and piano with Lefébure at the Paris Cons. In 1959 he won 1st prize in the Geneva competition, and then played in the Basel Sym. Orch.; also attended Boulez's master classes in composition in Basel (1961–63). After winning 1st prize in the Munich competition in 1961, he embarked upon a brilliant international career; toured in Europe and the U.S. as soloist with the Lucerne Festival Strings in 1962. He also gave concerts with his wife, the harpist Ursula Hänggi, and his own Holliger Ensemble. In addition to giving master classes, he was a prof. at the Freiburg im Breisgau Hochschule für Musik (from 1965). He is generally recognized as the foremost oboist of his era, his mastery extending from early music to the commissioned works of such modern composers as Penderecki, Henze, Stockhausen, Krenek, Berio, Jolivet, and Lutoslawski. In his own works, he is an uncompromising avant-gardist.

WORKS: STAGE: *Der magische Tänzer* for 2 Singers, 2 Dancers, 2 Actors, Chorus, Orch., and Tape (1963–65; Basel, April 26, 1970); *Come and Go/Va et vient/Kommen und Gehen,* chamber opera, after Samuel Beckett (1976–77; Hamburg, Feb. 16, 1978); *Not I,* monodrama for Soprano and Tape, after Beckett (1978–80; Avignon, July 15, 1980); *What Where,* chamber opera, after Beckett (1988; Frankfurt am Main, May 19, 1989). ORCH.: *Elis—Drei Nachtstücke* (1963; rev. 1973; Basel, May 3, 1973); *Siebengesang* for Oboe, Orch., Voices, and Loudspeakers (1966–67; Rotterdam, June 17, 1968); *Pneuma* for Winds,

Percussion, Organ, and Radios (Donaueschingen, Oct. 18, 1970); *Atembogen* (1974–75; Basel, June 6, 1975); *Ad marginem* for Chamber Orch. and Tape (1983; Baden-Baden, March 8, 1985); *Engführung* for Chamber Orch. (1983–84; Donaueschingen, Oct. 18, 1985); *Der ferne Klang* for Chamber Orch. and Tape (1983–84; Donaueschingen, Oct. 18, 1985); *Schaufelrad* for Chamber Orch. and 4 to 5 Women's Voices ad libitum (1983–84; Donaueschingen, Oct. 18, 1985); *Turm-Musik* for Flute, Small Orch., and Tape (1984; Basel, Jan. 17, 1985); *Tonscherben,* "Orchester-Fragmente in memoriam David Rokeah" (Geneva, Sept. 26, 1985); *Zwei Liszt-Transkriptionen* (1986; Basel, Feb. 12, 1987). **CHAMBER:** Trio for Oboe or English Horn, Viola, and Harp (1966); *h* for Wind Quintet (1968); *Cardiophone* for Oboe and 3 Magnetophones (1971); String Quartet (1973); *Studie II* for Oboe (1981); *Praeludium, Arioso und Passacaglia* for Harp (1987); *Felicity's Shake-Wag* for Violin and Cello (1988); piano pieces; organ music; also vocal works, with and without orch. accompaniment.

BIBL.: *Current Biography* (Jan. 1987); H. Waleson, "H. H.: Musical Renaissance Man," *Ovation* (Feb. 1989).

Hollingsworth, Stanley, American composer; b. Berkeley, Calif., Aug. 27, 1924. He studied at San Jose State College; then with Darius Milhaud at Mills College and with Gian Carlo Menotti at the Curtis Inst. of Music in Philadelphia; subsequently was at the American Academy in Rome (1955–56). He received a Guggenheim fellowship in 1958; also was awarded several grants from the National Endowment for the Arts. From 1961 to 1963 he taught at San Jose State College; in 1963 joined the faculty of Oakland Univ. in Rochester, Mich. His music follows the principles of practical modernism; in this respect he emulates Menotti. He used the pseudonym Stanley Hollier in some of his works.

WORKS: 4 operas: *The Mother,* after Andersen (1949; Philadelphia, March 29, 1954), *La Grande Bretèche,* after Balzac (1954; NBC TV, Feb. 10, 1957), *The Selfish Giant* (1981), and *Harrison Loved His Umbrella* (1981); *Dumbarton Oaks Mass* for Chorus and String Orch.; *Stabat Mater* for Chorus and Orch. (San Jose, May 1, 1957); *Psalm of David* for Tenor, Chorus, and Orch. (1962); Piano Concerto (1980); Divertimento for Orch. (1982); *3 Ladies beside the Sea* for Narrator and Orch. (1983); Chamber: Sonata for Oboe and Piano; 3 impromptus for Flute and Piano (1975); *Ricordanza* for Oboe and String Trio (in memory of Samuel Barber; 1981); *Reflections and Diversions* for Clarinet and Piano (1984).

Hollins, Alfred, blind English pianist, organist, and composer; b. Hull, Sept. 11, 1865; d. Edinburgh, May 17, 1942. He studied piano at several schools for the blind; then studied with Hans von Bülow in Berlin. In 1886 he made a tour of the U.S. playing in an ensemble with other blind musicians; in 1888, appeared in America once more, as soloist with several orchs. Returning to England, he became a church organist in Edinburgh (1897–1904); then toured Australia (1904), South Africa (1907, 1909, and 1916), and the U.S. (1925). He publ. an autobiography, *A Blind Musician Looks Back* (London, 1936).

Hollmann, Joseph, Dutch cellist; b. Maastricht, Oct. 16, 1852; d. Paris, Jan. 1, 1927. He studied with Servais at the Brussels Cons., winning 1st prize (1870); then at the Paris Cons. with Jacquard; played many concerts in Europe and America; lived mostly in Paris. Saint-Saëns wrote his 2nd Cello Concerto for Hollmann.

Holloway, Robin (Greville), English composer, teacher, and writer on music; b. Leamington Spa, Oct. 19, 1943. He studied privately with Goehr (1959–63), and also attended King's College, Cambridge (1961–64); completed his education at New College, Oxford (1965–67; Ph.D., 1971, with a diss. on Debussy and Wagner; publ. in London, 1979); was a lecturer at Cambridge Univ. (from 1975); also contributed various articles to periodicals and anthologies. His music is deeply rooted in the English tradition; he prefers the discipline of neo-medieval counterpoint, adhering to basic tonality and modality. On occasion he audaciously piles tonal Pelion on modal Ossa in his effort to achieve mountainous polyharmony. He also sometimes

makes use of *objets trouvés* from the music of Brahms, Debussy, and Schoenberg, treating such objects as legitimate flotsam and jetsam. His dramatizations, intensifications, and amplifications of Schumann's lieder are notable.

WORKS: OPERA: *Clarissa* (1976; also *Clarissa Symphony* for Soprano, Tenor, and Orch., Birmingham, Dec. 9, 1982). **ORCH.:** 2 concertinos for Small Orch.: No. 1 (1964; rev. 1968–69; London, March 14, 1969); No. 2 (1967, 1974; London, Jan. 8, 1975); Concerto for Organ and Wind Orch. (1965–66; St. Albans, July 1, 1967); 2 concertos for Orch.: No. 1 (1966–69; Glasgow, April 25, 1973); No. 2 (1978–79; Glasgow, Sept. 22, 1979); Divertimento No. 1 for Amateur or Youth Orch., with Piano Obbligato (Cambridge, June 9, 1968); *Scenes from Schumann,* 7 paraphrases (Cheltenham, July 10, 1970); *Domination of Black,* symphonic poem (1973–74; London, Aug. 8, 1974); *Romanza* for Violin and Small Orch. (1976; London, Aug. 8, 1978); *Idyll* for Small Orch. (1979–80; Cheltenham, July 17, 1981); Horn Concerto (1979–80); *Ode* for 4 Winds and Strings (London, June 4, 1980); *Serenata notturna* for 4 Horns, 2 Trumpets, and Strings (1982; London, Dec. 9, 1984); *2nd Idyll* for Small Orch. (1982–83; London, Oct. 10, 1983); *Seascape and Harvest,* 2 pictures (1983–84; Birmingham, April 29, 1986); Viola Concerto (1983–84; London, Sept. 7, 1985); *Romanza* for Oboe and String Orch. (1984; Peterborough, N.H., Aug. 30, 1986); *Ballad* for Harp and Small Orch. (1984–85; Cheltenham, July 28, 1985); Bassoon Concerto (1984–85; Newcastle upon Tyne, Jan. 8, 1986); *Inquietus* for Small Orch. (1986; London, April 3, 1987); Double Concerto for Clarinet, Saxophone, and 2 Chamber Orchs. (1987–88); Violin Concerto (1990). **CHAMBER:** *Garden Music* for 9 Players (1962; rev. 1967, 1982); *Fantasy-Pieces* on Schumann's *Liederkreis* for Piano and 12 Instruments (Oxford, Dec. 11, 1971); *Evening with Angels* for 16 Players (1972; London, Jan. 1, 1973; rev. 1983); Divertimento No. 2 for Wind Nonet (1972; London, May 31, 1975); Concertino No. 3: *Homage to Weill* for 11 Players (1975; Aldeburgh, Jan. 23, 1977); *The Rivers of Hell,* concertante for 7 Players (London, Nov. 1, 1977); Serenade in C for Octet (1978–79); *Aria* for 14 Players (1979–80; London, July 14, 1980); Sonata for Solo Violin (1981); *Showpiece:* Concertino No. 4 for 14 Players (1982–83; London, May 23, 1983); Serenade for Wind Quintet and String Quintet (1983; London, June 26, 1985); Serenade for String Sextet and Double Bass (1986; Keele, May 14, 1987; also for String Orch.); Brass Quintet (1987); works for solo instruments; vocal settings.

Hollreiser, Heinrich, German conductor; b. Munich, June 24, 1913. He studied at the Munich Academy of Music; took lessons in conducting with Elmendorff. He subsequently was engaged as an opera conductor in Wiesbaden, Darmstadt, Mannheim, and Duisburg. From 1945 to 1952 he was Generalmusikdirektor in Düsseldorf. He then was a conductor at the Vienna State Opera (1952–61) and chief conductor of the Deutsche Oper in West Berlin (1961–64); also served as a regular conductor at Bayreuth for several seasons. In 1978 he was engaged as a guest conductor with the Cleveland Orch.

Hollweg, Ilse, German soprano; b. Solingen, Feb. 23, 1922; d. there, Feb. 9, 1990. She was educated at the Cologne Hochschule für Musik; made her debut at the Opera in Saarbrücken in 1943. From 1946 to 1951 she sang in Düsseldorf; later in Berlin, in Hamburg, and at the Vienna State Opera; in 1955 she joined the Düsseldorf Opera. She also made appearances at Salzburg, at Bayreuth, and in England.

Hollweg, Werner (Friedrich), German tenor; b. Solingen, Sept. 13, 1936. He studied at Detmold; made his professional debut with the Vienna Chamber Opera in 1962; then sang in Bonn and Düsseldorf. He made his 1st American appearance in 1968 as a soloist with the N.Y. Phil.; subsequently sang at the Salzburg Festival, the Berlin Deutsche Oper, the Bavarian State Opera, and the Hamburg State Opera.

Holly, Buddy (real name, **Charles Harden Holley**), pioneering American rock musician; b. Lubbock, Texas, Sept. 7, 1936; d. in a plane crash in Clear Lake, Iowa, Feb. 2, 1959. He played the fiddle as a small boy, then switched to guitar. He joined a friend playing western and bop music on a local radio station; then teamed with a guitarist, a drummer, and a bass player to form the group the Crickets to record his 1st song, *That'll Be the Day*; it soon became a hit and after Holly's death was included in an album significantly named *The Great Buddy Holly*. Stylistically, he was distinguished as one of the 1st white performers who used a characteristic "backbeat" of rhythm-and-blues in country-western music. In 1958 he toured in the U.S. and Australia as a guitarist in a trio with 2 other members of the Crickets. His songs have been reissued in record albums many times since his death. A motion picture, *The Buddy Holly Story*, was issued in 1978.

BIBL.: D. Laing, *B. H.* (London, 1971); J. Goldrosen, *B. H.: His Life and Music* (Bowling Green, Ohio, 1975; 2nd ed., rev., 1979); J. Girard, *Changing All Those Changes* (Berkeley, Calif., 1976); J. Goldrosen and J. Beecher, *Remembering B.: The Definitive Biography* (N.Y., 1986).

Holm, Mogens Winkel, Danish composer; b. Copenhagen, Oct. 1, 1936. He studied composition with Jørgen Jersild and oboe with Mogens Andreassen at the Royal Danish Cons. of Music (1955–61); then became music critic on the foremost Danish daily newspaper, *Politiken* (1965–71); was chairman of the Danish Union of Composers (1971–75; 1982–   ).

WORKS: Chamber opera, *Aslak* (Copenhagen, Jan. 27, 1963); textless chamber opera, *Sonata for 4 Opera Singers*, with Jazz Instruments and Electronics (Copenhagen, April 19, 1968); ballets: *Tropismer II* (Copenhagen, May 24, 1964); *Kontradans* (Danish Radio, July 16, 1965); *Chronicle* (Swedish Radio, May 5, 1969); *Galgarien* (Malmö, Nov. 27, 1970); *Rapport* (Danish Radio, March 19, 1972); *Tarantel* (1975); *Eurydike tøver* (1977); *Til Blåskaeg* (1982); *Chamber Concertante* for Bassoon, String Quartet, and String Orch. (1959); *Concerto piccolo* for Orch. (1961); *A Ghost Story* for Soloists, Chorus, and Orch. (1964); *Cumulus* for Orch. (Danish Radio, Aug. 17, 1965); *Alios*, sym. (Danish Radio, March 24, 1972; symphonic version of the ballet *Rapport*); *Cries* for Orch. (1983–84); Trio for Oboe, Clarinet, and Bassoon (1956); Wind Quintet (1957); *Little Chamber Concerto* for 5 Wind Instruments, Violin, and Cello (1958); String Quartet (1959); *ABRACADABRA* for Flute, Trumpet, Cello, and 4 Timpani (1960); *Tropismer I* for Oboe, Bassoon, Horn, and Piano (1961); *Annonce* for Soprano and Chamber Group (1965; to a text from a marriage advertisement in *Politiken*); Sonata for Woodwind Quintet (1965); *Overtoninger I* for Soprano, Cymbalon, and Cello (1971); *Overtoninger II* for Flute, Piano, and Cello (1972); *Adieu* for Flute, Violin, Cello, Harp, and Percussion (1982); *Note-book* for Oboe, Clarinet, and Bassoon (1983); songs; choruses.

Holm, Peder, Danish composer; b. Copenhagen, Sept. 30, 1926. He studied violin with Thorval Nielsen and counterpoint with Jeppesen at the Royal Danish Cons. of Music in Copenhagen (1945–47); became a lecturer at the Esbjerg Cons. in 1949 and in 1964 was named its director.

WORKS: Ballad opera, *Ingen mad i dag, men i morgen* (No Food Today but Tomorrow; 1962); Violin Concerto (1952); Piano Concerto (1953); *Fantasy* for Viola and Orch. (1954); Concerto for Orch. (1955); Sym. No. 1 (1955); *Preludio, Scherzo, and Fantasia* for Orch. (1956); *Symphonic Dance* (1957); *Capriccio* for Orch. (1959); 2 concertos for Piano and Strings (1963, 1967); *Pezzo concertante* for Orch. (1964); 2 *Sketches* for Trumpet, Trombone, and Orch. (1966); 3 *Pieces* for Orch. (1966); String Quartet (1967); *VYL* for Orch. (1967; Esbjerg, May 2, 1968); 2 *Pieces* for Wind Quintet (1968); *KHE-BEB* for 2 Pianos and Orch. (1968); Trumpet Concertino (1970); Clarinet Concertino (1970).

Holm, Renate, German soprano; b. Berlin, Aug. 10, 1931. She studied with Maria Ivogün; made a successful debut in 1958 at the Vienna Volksoper in the operetta *Waltz Dream* by Oskar Strauss. In 1961 she joined the Vienna State Opera; received acclaim for her performances in the operas of Mozart, Rossini, and Richard Strauss. She also continued to appear

in operettas, especially those by Johann Strauss and Franz Lehár.

Holm, Richard, German tenor; b. Stuttgart, Aug. 3, 1912; d. Munich, July 20, 1988. He studied in Stuttgart; in 1937 he became a member of the Kiel Opera; also made guest appearances at other German opera houses; in 1948 he joined the Bavarian State Opera in Munich. On March 15, 1952, he made his Metropolitan Opera debut in N.Y. as David in *Die Meistersinger von Nürnberg*; was on its roster until 1953. He also made successful appearances in London, Vienna, Salzburg, and Bayreuth. In 1967 he became a prof. of voice at the Hochschule für Musik in Munich.

Holmboe, Vagn, eminent Danish composer; b. Horsens, Jutland, Dec. 20, 1909. He studied composition with Jeppesen and Høffding at the Royal Danish Cons. of Music in Copenhagen (1927–29); then took intermittent courses in Berlin (1930–33); traveled in Transylvania (1933–34), where he gained firsthand knowledge of Balkan folk music. Upon return to Copenhagen, he taught at the Royal Danish Inst. for the Blind (1940–49), wrote music criticism for the newspaper *Politiken* (1947–55), and taught at the Royal Danish Cons. (1950–65). He received a government lifetime grant; publ. a book on contemporary music, *Mellemspil* (Interlude; Copenhagen, 1966). His music evolved from the legacy of Sibelius and Carl Nielsen; he then developed a method of composition with "germ themes" that grow metamorphically; his symphonic works give an impression of grandeur, with long, dynamic crescendos in expanded tonality.

WORKS: STAGE: 3-act opera, *Lave og Jon* (Lave and Jon; 1946–48); 1-act chamber opera, *Kniven* (The Knife; 1959–60); symphonic fairy play, *Fanden og borgemesteren* (The Devil and the Mayor; 1940); radio play, *Fløjten* (1946); ballet, *Den galsindede tyrk* (1942–44). **ORCH.:** 11 numbered syms.: No. 1, for Chamber Orch. (1935; Århus, Feb. 21, 1938); No. 2 (Copenhagen, Dec. 5, 1939); No. 3, *Sinfonia rustica* (1941; Copenhagen, June 12, 1948); No. 4, *Sinfonia sacra*, with Chorus (1941; rev. 1945; Copenhagen, Sept. 2, 1945); No. 5 (1944; Copenhagen, June 16, 1945); No. 6 (1947; Copenhagen, Jan. 8, 1948); No. 7 (1950; Copenhagen, Oct. 18, 1951); No. 8, *Sinfonia boreale* (1951–52; Copenhagen, March 5, 1953); No. 9 (Copenhagen, Dec. 19, 1968); No. 10 (1970–71; Detroit, Jan. 27, 1972); No. 11 (Copenhagen, Feb. 17, 1983); *Sinfonia in memoriam* (1954–55); 4 sinfonias for String Orch., known collectively as *Kairos* (1957; 1957; 1958–59; 1962); 3 chamber syms.: No. 1, *Collegium musicum concerto No. 1* (1951); No. 2 (1968); No. 3, *Frise* (1969–70); 3 works representing symphonic metamorphoses: *Epitaph* (1956), *Monolith* (1960), and *Epilogue* (1961–62); *Tempo variabile* (1971–72); Concerto for Orch. (1929); Concerto for Chamber Orch. (1931); Concerto for String Orch. (1933); *Rapsodi* for Flute and Chamber Orch. (1935); Violin Concerto (1938); Cello Concerto (1974); Concerto for Recorder, Celeste, Vibraphone, and Strings (1974); Flute Concerto (1976); Tuba Concerto (1976); 13 chamber concertos: No. 1 for Piano, Strings, and Percussion (1939); No. 2 for Flute, Violin, Celesta, Percussion, and String Orch. (1940); No. 3 for Clarinet, 2 Trumpets, 2 Horns, and Strings (1940); No. 4, *Triple Concerto*, for Violin, Cello, Piano, and Chamber Orch. (1942); No. 5 for Viola and Chamber Orch. (1943); No. 6 for Violin and Chamber Orch. (1943); No. 7 for Oboe and Chamber Orch. (1944–45); No. 8, *Sinfonia concertante*, for Chamber Orch. (1945); No. 9 for Violin, Viola, and Chamber Orch. (1945–46); No. 10, *Træ-messing-tarm*, for Chamber Orch. (1945–46); No. 11 for Trumpet, 2 Horns, and String Orch. (1948); No. 12 for Trombone and Chamber Orch. (1950); No. 13, *Collegium musicum concerto No. 2*, for Oboe, Viola, and Chamber Orch. (1955–56); Concertino No. 1 for Violin, Viola, and String Orch. (1940) and No. 2 for Violin and String Orch. (1940); *Symphonic Overture* for Percussion, Piano, and Strings (1941). **CHAMBER:** 14 string quartets: No. 1 (1948–49); No. 2 (1949); No. 3 (1949–50); No. 4 (1953–54; rev. 1956); No. 5 (1955); No. 6 (1961); No. 7 (1964–65); No. 8 (1965); No. 9 (1965–66; rev. 1969); No. 10 (1969);

No. 11, *Quartetto rustico* (1972); No. 12 (1973); No. 13 (1975); No. 14 (1975); *Musik for fugle og frøer* for 2 Flutes and 16 Bassoons (1971); Sextet for Flute, Clarinet, Bassoon, Violin, Viola, and Cello (1972–73); Wind Quintet (1933); Quintet for Flute, Oboe, Clarinet, Violin, and Viola (1936); *Notturno* for Wind Quintet (1940); *Aspekter* for Wind Quintet (1957); *Tropos* for String Quintet (1960); Brass Quintet (1961–62); *Musik til Morten* for Oboe and String Quartet (1970); Serenade for Flute, Piano, Violin, and Cello (1940); *Primavera* for Flute, Piano, Violin, and Cello (1951); *Quartetto medico* for Flute, Oboe, Clarinet, and Piano (1956); Quartet for Flute, Violin, Viola, and Cello (1966); *Fanden løs i Voldmosen* for Clarinet, 2 Violins, and Double Bass (1971); *Firefir*, quartet for 4 Flutes (1977); *Rhapsody Intermezzo* for Violin, Clarinet, and Piano (1938); Piano Trio (1954); Trio for Flute, Piano, and Cello (1968); *Nuigen*, piano trio (1976); an unnumbered Violin Sonata (1929); 3 numbered violin sonatas (1935, 1939, 1965); *Sonatina capricciosa* for Flute and Piano (1942); sonata for Violin and Viola (1963); *Triade* for Trumpet and Organ (1975). **SOLO INSTRUMENTS:** Violin Sonata (1953); Flute Sonata (1957); Double-bass Sonata (1962); Cello Sonata (1968–69). ***PIANO:*** *Choral Fantasy* (1929); 2 sonatas (1929, 1930); *Allegro affettuoso* (1931); 4 suites (1930–33); *Julen 1931* (1931); 6 *Sketches* (1934); *Rumaensk Suite* (1937–38); 6 *Pieces* (1939); *Sonatina briosa* (1941); *Suono da bardo* (1949–50); *Moto austero* (1965); *I venti* (1972). **ORGAN:** *Fabula I* (1972); *Fabula II* (1973); *Contrasti* (1972). **VOCAL:** *Requiem for Nietzsche* for Tenor, Baritone, Mixed Chorus, and Orch. (1963–64); *Skoven* (The Forest) for Mixed Chorus, Children's Chorus, and Instruments (1960); *3 Inuit sange* (3 Eskimo Songs) for Baritone, Male Chorus, and Percussion (1956); *Beatus parvo* for Chorus and Chamber Orch. (1973); *Edward* for Baritone and Orch. (1971); *The wee-wee man* for Tenor and Orch. (1971); *Zeit* for Alto and String Quartet (1966–67); a cappella choruses, including *Solhymne* (1960) and the Latin motets *Liber Canticorum I* (1951–52), *II* (1952–53), *III* (1953), *IV* (1953), and *V, Beatus vir* (1967); numerous cantatas for ceremonial events; songs. **BIBL.:** P. Rapoport, *V. H.: A Catalogue of His Music, Discography, Bibliography, Essays* (London, 1974; 2nd ed., rev. and enl., Copenhagen, 1979); idem, *V. H.'s Symphonic Metamorphoses* (diss., Univ. of Illinois, 1975); idem, *Opus Est* (1979); R. Layton, "*V. H.*: An Eightieth Birthday Salute," *Nordic Sounds* (Dec. 1989).

Holmes, Alfred, English violinist and composer; b. London, Nov. 9, 1837; d. Paris, March 4, 1876. His only teacher was his father, an amateur violinist; he sang at the Oratory in London as a soprano chorister; appeared as a violinist at the age of 9, playing a duet with his brother, Henry, with whom he went on a European tour, playing in Belgium, Germany, Sweden, Denmark, and the Netherlands (1855–61). He then lived in Paris (1861–64); visited Russia in 1867; then returned to Paris, making occasional visits to London. He composed 4 programmatic syms., entitled *Robinhood, The Siege of Paris, Charles XII,* and *Romeo and Juliet,* and 2 overtures, *The Cid* and *The Muses.* His brother, **Henry Holmes** (b. London, Nov. 7, 1839; d. San Francisco, Dec. 9, 1905), was also a precocious violinist and composer; after 1865 he settled in London, where he taught at the Royal College of Music. In 1894 he went to San Francisco, where he remained until his death. He wrote 4 syms., 2 cantatas, a Violin Concerto (London, Dec. 11, 1875), and chamber music.

Holmès (real name, **Holmes**), **Augusta (Mary Anne),** French composer; b. Paris (of Irish parents), Dec. 16, 1847; d. there, Jan. 28, 1903. She progressed very rapidly as a child pianist, and gave public concerts; also composed songs, under the pen name Hermann Zenta. She studied harmony with H. Lambert, an organist; later became a pupil of César Franck. She then began to compose works in large forms, arousing considerable attention, mixed with curiosity, for she was one of the very few professional women composers of the time. Her music lacks individuality or strength; at best, it represents a conventional by-product of French Roman-

ticism, with an admixture of fashionable exotic elements. **WORKS:** Operas: *La Montagne noire* (Paris Opéra, Feb. 8, 1895); *Héro et Léandre; Astarte; Lancelot du lac;* for Orch.: *Andante pastoral* (Paris, Jan. 14, 1877); *Lutèce* (Angers, Nov. 30, 1884); *Les Argonautes* (Paris, April 24, 1881); *Irlande* (Paris, March 2, 1882); *Ode triomphale* (Paris, March 4, 1888); *Pologne; Andromède; Hymne à Apollon;* cantatas: *La Vision de la Reine; La Chanson de la caravane; La Fleur de Neflier;* piano pieces; 117 songs. **BIBL.:** P. Barillon-Bauché, *A. H. et la femme compositeur* (Paris, 1912); R. Pichard du Page, *A. H.; Une Musicienne versaillaise* (Paris, 1921); R. Myers, "*A. H.*: A Meteoric Career," *Musical Quarterly* (July 1967).

Holmes, Edward, English music critic; b. London, 1797; d. there, Aug. 28, 1859. He studied music with Vincent Novello. In 1826 he became a contributor to a literary journal, *Atlas;* also wrote for *Fraser's Magazine* and the *Spectator* (from 1830) and for the *Musical Times* (1845–49; 1850–59). He publ. *A Ramble among the Musicians of Germany* (1828; reprint, ed. by C. Cudworth, N.Y., 1969) and *The Life of Mozart* (1845; 2nd ed., rev., 1878, by E. Prout; 3rd ed., rev., 1912, by E. Newman). **BIBL.:** E. Mackerness, "*E. H.* (1797–1859)," *Music & Letters,* XLV (1964).

Holmes, Ralph, English violinist; b. Penge, April 1, 1937; d. Beckenham, Sept. 4, 1984. He studied with David Martin at the Royal Academy of Music in London, and later with Enesco in Paris and Galamian in N.Y.; made his London debut at a children's concert of the Royal Phil. (1951); then won prizes at international competitions in Paris (1957) and Bucharest (1958). He pursued a successful career in England before making his U.S. debut with Barbirolli and the Houston Sym. Orch. at N.Y.'s Carnegie Hall in 1966; in subsequent years he toured widely; with Anthony Goldstone and Moray Welsh, he formed his own piano trio in 1972. He was a prof. at the Royal Academy of Music from 1964. His repertoire included all the major 20th-century concertos written for his instrument.

Holmes, Reed K., American composer; b. Oak Ridge, Tenn., Aug. 20, 1952. He studied at the Univ. of Tenn. (B.M., 1974; M.M., 1976) and the Univ. of Texas at Austin (Ph.D., 1981, with the diss. *Relational Systems and Process in Recent Works of Luciano Berio*), where he taught (from 1985) and was director of its Electronic Music Studio. He was a founding member of the Texas Composers Forum (1985); received an ASCAP Award in Composition (1989) and an N.E.A. grant (1990–91). His spirited compositions are often minimalist in design, motivated by rhythmic and timbral processes. **WORKS:** MULTI-MEDIA: *Moiré* for Dancers and Computer-generated Sound (1981); *Nova* for Dissolve Slide Projections and Quadraphonic Sound (1982–83); *Around the Waves* for Dissolve Slide Projections and Quadraphonic Sound (1983); *Drumfire* for Dancers and Computer (1986); *Electric Symphonies* for Dancers and Computer (1988). CHAMBER: *Sound Streams* for Flute Choir (1979); *Patterns* for Any Group of Homogeneous Wind Instruments (1982); *Kaleidoscope* for 23 Musicians (1984); *Pocket Hocket* for 4 Synthesizers (or for Any 4 Parts) (1985); *Circle Sonata* for 5 Percussionists and Tape (1986); *Variations* for 6 Parts Performed by Any Homogeneous Group of Instruments (1988); *Nonet* for Soprano, English Horn or Oboe, Saxophone, Trumpet, Violin, Viola, Cello, Piano, and Mallet Percussion (1991). SOLO, WITH TAPE: *Dream Quest* for Percussion (1975); *Chalumeau Rain* for Clarinet (1980); *Song and Fantasy* for Trombone (1982); *With Wings They Came* for Saxophone (1983); *Cat's Cradle 4* for Cello (1990).

Holoman, D(allas) Kern, American musicologist and conductor; b. Raleigh, N.C., Sept. 8, 1947. He pursued his academic training at Duke Univ. (B.A., 1969) and Princeton Univ. (M.F.A., 1971; Ph.D., 1974, with the diss. *Autograph Musical Documents of Hector Berlioz, c.1818–1840;* publ. in a rev. and corrected ed. as *The Creative Process in the Autograph Musical Documents of Hector Berlioz, c.1818–1840,* Ann Arbor, 1980), receiving a Fulbright fellowship (1972–73). In 1973, after teaching briefly at Westminster Choir College in Princeton, N.J. (1972), he joined the faculty of the Univ. of Calif. at Davis, where he was founder-director of its Early Music Ensemble (1973–77; 1979) and conductor of its sym. orch. (from 1978). With J. Kerman and R. Winter, he was founding ed. of the distinguished journal *19th Century Music* (1977). In 1989 he became general ed. of the series Recent Researches in the Music of the Nineteenth and Twentieth Centuries. His writings are notable for their accessible prose style and engaging, dry wit. An authority on Berlioz, he publ. the 1st thematic catalog of that composer's output and ed. his *Roméo et Juliette* for the New Berlioz Edition.

WRITINGS: Ed., with C. Palisca, *Musicology in the 1980s* (N.Y., 1982); *Dr. Holoman's Handy Guide to Concert-Going* (Sacramento and Davis, 1983); *Catalogue of the Works of Hector Berlioz* (Kassel, 1987); *Writing about Music: A Style-Sheet from the Editors of 19th Century Music* (Berkeley and Los Angeles, 1988); *Berlioz* (Cambridge, Mass., 1989).

Holoubek, Ladislav, Slovak conductor and composer; b. Prague, Aug. 13, 1913. He studied theory with A. Moyzes at the Bratislava Academy of Music (1926–33) and with V. Novák at the Prague Cons. (1934–36). He conducted at the Slovak National Theater in Bratislava (1933–52; 1959–66), and at the State Theater in Košice (1955–58; from 1966).

WORKS: 5 operas, all brought out in Bratislava: *Stella* (March 18, 1939), *Svitanie* (Dawn; March 14, 1941), *Túžba* (Yearning; Feb. 12, 1944), *Rodina* (Fatherland; 1956–60), and *Professor Mamlock* (May 21, 1966); Sym. (1946); Sinfonietta (1950); *10 Variations on an Original Theme* for Orch. (1950); *Defiances and Hopes*, symphonic poem (1973); 2 cantatas: *Mesačná noc* (Moonlight Night; 1951) and *The Promise* (1952); Violin Sonata (1933); 3 string quartets (1936, 1948, 1962); Wind Quintet (1938); Trio for Flute, Violin, and Harp (1939); 2 piano sonatas (1931, 1947); songs.

Holst, Edvard, Danish-American composer; b. Copenhagen, 1843; d. N.Y., Feb. 4, 1899. He emigrated to America in 1874, and was active in N.Y. as an actor, dancing master, etc.; also wrote numerous pieces for military band (*Marine Band March, Battle of Manila*, etc.); a number of songs; and a comic opera, *Our Flats* (N.Y., 1897); in all, more than 2,000 numbers.

Holst, Gustav(us Theodore von), significant English composer, father of **Imogen (Clare) Holst;** b. Cheltenham, Sept. 21, 1874; d. London, May 25, 1934. He was of Swedish descent. He received his primary musical training from his parents. In 1892 he became organist and choirmaster in Wyck Rissington, Gloucestershire; in 1893 he entered the Royal College of Music in London, where he studied composition with Stanford and Rockstro, organ with Hoyte, and piano with Sharpe; also learned to play the trombone. After graduating in 1898, he was a trombonist in the orch. of the Carl Rosa Opera Co. (until 1900) and the Scottish Orch. in Glasgow (1900–1903). His interest in Hindu philosophy, religion, and music during this period led to the composition of his settings from the Sanskrit of *Hymns from the Rig Veda* (1907–8). He worked as a music teacher in a Dulwich girls' school (1903–20); was director of music at St. Paul's Girls' School, Hammersmith (1905–34), and of London's Morley College (1907–24). He became a teacher of composition at the Royal College of Music (1919); was also prof. of music at Univ. College, Reading (1919–23). Plagued by suspicions of his German sympathies at the outbreak of World War I in 1914, he removed the Germanic-looking (actually Swedish) nobiliary particle "von" from his surname; his early works had been publ. under the name Gustav von Holst. He was deemed unfit for military service, but served as YMCA musical organizer among the British troops in the Near East in 1918. After the war, he visited the U.S. as a lecturer and conductor in 1923 and 1932. However, his deteriorating health limited his activities; his daughter described his mind in the last years of his life as "closed in gray isolation." Holst's most celebrated work, the large-scale orch. suite *The Planets*, was inspired by the astrological signifi-

cance of the planets. It consists of 7 movements, each bearing a mythological subtitle: *Mars, the Bringer of War; Venus, the Bringer of Peace; Mercury, the Winged Messenger; Jupiter, the Bringer of Jollity; Saturn, the Bringer of Old Age; Uranus, the Magician; Neptune, the Mystic,* with an epilogue of female voices singing wordless syllables. It was 1st performed privately in London (Sept. 29, 1918); 5 movements were played in public (Feb. 15, 1920); the 1st complete performance followed (Nov. 15, 1920). The melodic and harmonic style of the work epitomizes Holst's musical convictions, in which lyrical, dramatic, and triumphant motifs are alternately presented in coruscatingly effective orch. dress. His music in general reflects the influence of English folk songs and the madrigal. He was a master of choral writing; one of his notable works utilizing choral forces was *The Hymn of Jesus* (1917). His writings were ed. by S. Lloyd and E. Rubbra as *Gustav Holst: Collected Essays* (London, 1974).

WORKS: STAGE: OPERAS: *The Revoke,* op. 1 (1895); *The Youth's Choice,* op. 11 (1902); *Sita,* op. 23 (1899–1906); *Sāvitri,* chamber opera, op. 25 (1908; London, Dec. 5, 1916); *The Perfect Fool,* op. 39 (1918–22; London, May 14, 1923); *At the Boar's Head,* op. 42 (1924; Manchester, April 3, 1925); *The Wandering Scholar,* chamber opera, op. 50 (1929–30; Liverpool, Jan. 31, 1934); *Lansdown Castle,* operetta (Cheltenham, Feb. 7, 1893); *The Idea,* children's operetta (c.1898); *The Vision of Dame Christian,* masque, op. 27a (London, July 22, 1909). **BALLETS:** *The Lure* (1921); *The Golden Goose,* choral ballet, op. 45/1 (BBC, London, Sept. 21, 1926); *The Morning of the Year,* choral ballet, op. 45/2 (1926–27; London, March 17, 1927). **INCIDENTAL MUSIC:** *The Sneezing Charm* (1918) and *The Coming of Christ* (1927; Canterbury, May 28, 1928); 7 choruses from *Alcestis* (1920).

ORCH.: *A Winter Idyll* (1897); *Örnulf's Drapa* for Baritone and Orch., op. 6 (1898); *Walt Whitman,* overture, op. 7 (1899); Sym. in F major, op. 8, *The Cotswolds* (1899–1900; Bournemouth, April 24, 1902); *Suite de ballet* in E-flat major, op. 10 (1899; London, May 20, 1904; rev. 1912); *Indra,* symphonic poem, op. 13 (1903); *The Mystic Trumpeter* for Soprano and Orch., op. 18 (1904; London, June 29, 1905; rev. 1912); *A Song of the Night* for Violin and Orch., op. 19/1 (1905); *Invocation* for Cello and Orch., op. 19/2 (1911); *Songs of the West,* op. 21/1 (1906–7); *A Somerset Rhapsody,* op. 21/2 (1906–7; London, April 6, 1910); *2 Songs without Words: Country Song and Marching Song* for Chamber Orch., op. 22 (1906); *Suite No. 1,* in E-flat major, for Military Band, op. 28/1 (1909); *Suite No. 2,* in F major, for Military Band, op. 28/2 (1911); *Beni Mora,* oriental suite, op. 29/1 (1909–10; London, May 1, 1912); *Phantastes,* suite in F major (1911); *St. Paul's Suite* for Strings, op. 29/2 (1912–13); *The Planets,* op. 32 (1914–16; private perf., London, Sept. 29, 1918; 1st complete public perf., London, Nov. 15, 1920); *Japanese Suite,* op. 33 (1915); *A Fugal Overture,* op. 40/1 (1922; as the overture to *The Perfect Fool,* London, May 14, 1923); *A Fugal Concerto* for Flute, Oboe, and Strings, op. 40/2 (London, Oct. 11, 1923); *Egdon Heath: Homage to Hardy,* op. 47 (1927; N.Y., Feb. 12, 1928); *A Moorside Suite* for Brass Band (London, Sept. 29, 1928); *Double Concerto* for 2 Violins and Orch., op. 49 (1929; London, April 3, 1930); *Hammersmith: Prelude* and *Scherzo* for Military Band, op. 52 (1930; 2nd version for Orch., 1931; London, Nov. 25, 1931); Jazz-band Piece (1932; ed. by I. Holst as *Capriccio,* 1967; London, Jan. 10, 1968); *Brook Green Suite* for Strings (1933); *Lyric Movement* for Viola and Chamber Orch. (1933; BBC, London, March 18, 1934); *Scherzo* (1933–34; London, Feb. 6, 1935).

CHAMBER: *Fantasiestücke* for Oboe and String Quartet, op. 2 (1896; rev. 1910); Quintet in A minor for Piano, Oboe, Clarinet, Horn, and Bassoon, op. 3 (1896); Wind Quintet in A-flat major, op. 14 (1903; London, Sept. 15, 1982); *Terzetto* for Flute, Oboe, and Viola (1925); piano pieces: *Toccata* (1924); *Chrissemas Day in the Morning,* op. 46/1 (1926); 2 folk-song fragments: *O I hae seen the roses blaw* and *The Shoemaker,* op. 46/2 (1927); *Nocturne* (1930); *Jig* (1932).

CHORAL: *Light Leaves Whisper* (c.1896); *Clear and Cool* for

Chorus and Orch., op. 5 (1897); *Clouds o'er the Summer Sky* for Women's Chorus and Piano (c.1898); 5 Part-songs, op. 9a (1897–1900); *Ave Maria* for 8-part Women's Chorus, op. 9b (1900); *I Love Thee* (n.d.); 5 Part-songs, op. 12 (1902–3); *King Estmere* for Chorus and Orch., op. 17 (1903; London, April 4, 1908); *Thou Didst Delight My Eyes* (c.1903); *In Youth Is Pleasure* (n.d.); *Songs from the Princess* for Women's Chorus, op. 20a (1905); 4 *Old English Carols* for Chorus or Women's Chorus, and Piano, op. 20b (1907); 2 carols for Chorus, Oboe, and Cello (1908, 1916); *Pastoral* for Women's Chorus (c.1908); *Choral Hymns from the Rig Veda* for Chorus, and Orch. or Ensemble, op. 26 (1908–10); *O England My Country* for Chorus and Orch. (1909); *The Cloud Messenger* for Chorus and Orch., op. 30 (1909–10); *Christmas Day* for Chorus and Orch. (1910); 4 Part-songs for Women's Chorus and Piano (1910); 2 *Eastern Pictures* for Women's Chorus and Harp (1911); *Hecuba's Lament* for Alto, Women's Chorus, and Orch., op. 31/1 (1911); 2 Psalms for Tenor, Chorus, Strings, and Organ (1912); *The Swallow Leaves Her Nest* for Women's Chorus (c.1912); *The Homecoming* for Men's Chorus (1913); *Hymn to Dionysus* for Women's Chorus and Orch., op. 31/2 (1913); *A Dirge for 2 Veterans* for Men's Chorus, Brass, and Percussion (1914); *Nunc dimittis* (1915); *This I Have Done for My True Love*, op. 34/1 (1916); *Lullay My Liking* for Soprano and Chorus, op. 34/2 (1916); *Of One That Is So Fair* for Soprano, Alto, Tenor, Bass, and Chorus, op. 34/3 (1916); *Bring Us in Good Ale*, op. 34/4 (1916); 3 carols for Chorus and Orch. (1916–17); 3 Festival Choruses with Orch., op. 36a (1916); 6 Choral Folk Songs, op. 36b (1916); *Diverus and Lazarus* (1917); 2 Part-songs for Women's Chorus and Piano (1917); *A Dream of Christmas* for Women's Chorus, and Strings or Piano (1917); *The Hymn of Jesus* for 2 Choruses, Women's Semi-chorus, and Orch., op. 37 (1917; London, March 25, 1920); *Ode to Death* for Chorus and Orch., op. 38 (1919; Leeds Festival, Oct. 6, 1922); Short Festival Te Deum for Chorus and Orch. (1919); *I Vow to Thee, My Country* for Chorus and Orch. (1921; arranged from *The Planets*, no. 4); *1st Choral Symphony* for Soprano, Chorus, and Orch., op. 41 (1923–24; Leeds Festival, Oct. 7, 1925); *The Evening-watch*, op. 43/1 (1924); *Sing Me the Men*, op. 43/2 (1925); 7 Part-songs for Soprano, Women's Chorus, and Strings, op. 44 (1925–26); 2 anthems (1927); *Wassail Song* (1928–30); *A Choral Fantasia* for Soprano, Chorus, Organ, Strings, Brass, and Percussion, op. 51 (1930; Gloucester Festival, Sept. 8, 1931); 12 Welsh Folk Songs (1930–31); 6 choruses, some with accompaniment, op. 53 (1931–32); 8 canons (1932). SONGS: 4 Songs, op. 4 (1896–98); 6 Songs, op. 15 (1902–3); 6 Songs for Soprano and Piano, op. 16 (1903–4); *Hymns from the Rig Veda*, op. 24 (1907–8); *The Heart Worships* (1907); 4 Songs for Soprano or Tenor, and Violin, op. 35 (1916–17); 12 Songs, op. 48 (1929). See I. Holst and C. Matthews, eds., *Gustav Holst: Collected Facsimile Edition of Autograph Manuscripts of the Published Works* (4 vols., London, 1974–83). BIBL.: L. Dyer, *G. H.* (London, 1931); A. Bliss, "G. H.: A Lonely Figure in Music," *Radio Times* (June 15, 1934); A. Boult, "G. H.: The Man and His Work," ibid.; E. Evans, "G. H.," *Musical Times*, LXXV (1934); A. Foster, "G. H.—An Appreciation," *Monthly Musical Record*, LXIV (1934); G. Jacob, "H. the Composer," *R.C.M. Magazine*, XXX (1934); I. Holst, *G. H.: A Biography* (London, 1938; 2nd ed., 1969); E. Rubbra, *G. H.* (Monaco, 1947); I. Holst, *The Music of G. H.* (London, 1951; 3rd ed., rev., 1986, including *H.'s Music Reconsidered*); M. Tippett, "H.—Figure of Our Time," *Listener*, LX (Nov. 13, 1958); U. Vaughan Williams and I. Holst, eds., *Heirs and Rebels* (London, 1959); J. Warrack, "A New Look at G. H.," *Musical Times*, CIV (1963); A. Boult, "Interpreting *The Planets*," ibid., CXI (1970); idem, "G. H.," *R.C.M. Magazine*, LXX (1974); I. Holst, *H.* (London, 1974; 2nd ed., 1981); idem, "H. and the Royal College of Music," *R.C.M. Magazine*, LXX (1974); idem, *A Thematic Catalogue of G. H.'s Music* (London, 1974); H. Ottaway, "H. as an Opera Composer," *Musical Times*, CXV (1974); M. Short, ed., *G. H. (1874–1934): A Centenary Documentation* (London, 1974); J. Warrack, "H. and the Linear Principle," *Musical Times*, CXV (1974); D. Boyer, "H.'s The

Hymn of Jesus: An Investigation into Mysticism in Music," *Music Review*, XXXVI (1975); I. Holst, ed., *A Scrapbook for the H. Birthplace Museum* (Cheltenham, 1978); idem, "H.'s At the Boar's Head," *Musical Times* (May 1982); idem, "H. in the 1980s," ibid. (May 1984); C. Matthews, "Some Unknown H.," ibid.; M. Short, *G. H.: The Man and His Music* (Oxford, 1990).

Holst, Henry, Danish violinist of English parentage; b. Copenhagen, July 25, 1899. He studied with Telmanyi at the Royal Danish Cons. of Music in Copenhagen; then went to Berlin, where he took violin lessons with Willy Hess; subsequently was engaged as concertmaster of the Berlin Phil. (1923–31); then taught at the Royal College of Music in Manchester, England (1931–46; 1950–53); from 1946 to 1954 he was prof. of violin at the Royal College of Music in London; from 1961 to 1963 taught violin classes at the Univ. of Arts in Tokyo.

Holst, Imogen (Clare), English musician, daughter of **Gustav(us Theodore von) Holst;** b. Richmond, Surrey, April 12, 1907; d. Aldeburgh, March 9, 1984. She studied at the Royal College of Music in London. She was a faithful keeper of her father's musical materials and writings. From 1952 to 1964 she was musical assistant to Benjamin Britten; she also conducted the ensemble of the Purcell Singers (1953–67) and served as artistic director of the Aldeburgh Festival (from 1956). In 1975 she was made a Commander of the Order of the British Empire. Her most important writings include *Gustav Holst* (London, 1938; 2nd ed., 1969), *The Music of Gustav Holst* (London, 1951; 3rd ed., rev., 1986, including *Holst's Music Reconsidered*), and *A Thematic Catalogue of Gustav Holst's Music* (London, 1974). With C. Matthews, she ed. *Gustav Holst: Collected Facsimile Edition of Autograph Manuscripts of the Published Works* (London, 1974–83). BIBL.: P. Cox and J. Dobbs, eds., *I. H. at Dartington* (Dartington, 1988).

Holstein, Franz (Friedrich) von, German composer; b. Braunschweig, Feb. 16, 1826; d. Leipzig, May 22, 1878. His father was an army officer; at his behest, Holstein entered the Cadet School; he concurrently studied music theory with Griepenkerl. While a lieutenant, he privately produced his operetta, *Zwei Nächte in Venedig* (1845). He fought in the Schleswig-Holstein campaign; then wrote a grand opera, *Waverley*, after Walter Scott. He sent the score to Hauptmann at the Leipzig Cons.; the latter expressed his willingness to accept Holstein as a student. Accordingly, he resigned from the army (1853) and studied with Hauptmann, H. Richter, and Moscheles at the Leipzig Cons. He then devoted himself to composition. He was also a poet, and wrote his own librettos. The style of his operas was close to the French type, popularized by Auber. He was a man of means, and left a valuable legacy for the benefit of indigent music students. WORKS: Operas: *Der Haideschacht* (Dresden, Oct. 22, 1868); *Der Erbe von Morley* (Leipzig, Jan. 23, 1872); *Die Hochländer* (Mannheim, Jan. 16, 1876); *Marino Faliero* (unfinished); overture, *Frau Aventiure* (sketches only; orchestrated by A. Dietrich; Leipzig, Nov. 13, 1879); *Beatrice*, scene for Soprano, with Orch.; Piano Trio; other chamber music; part-songs for Mixed and Men's Voices; etc. BIBL.: G. Glaser, *F. v.H.: Ein Dichterkomponist des 19. Jahrhunderts* (Leipzig, 1930).

Holt, Henry, Austrian-born American conductor and operatic administrator; b. Vienna, April 11, 1934. He studied with Hugo Strelitzer at Los Angeles City College and with Ingolf Dahl at the Univ. of Southern Calif.; made his conducting debut in *Rigoletto* with the American Opera Co. in Los Angeles in 1961; then was general director of the Portland (Oreg.) Opera (1964–66). In 1966 he was appointed general director of the Seattle Opera; conducted its acclaimed Wagner Festivals. In 1983 he became music director of the Univ. of Southern Calif. Opera; continued to lead the Wagner Festivals in Seattle.

Holt, Simeon ten, Dutch composer; b. Bergen, North Holland, Jan. 24, 1923. He studied piano with Jacob van Domselaer; later took composition lessons with Honegger in Paris. From

1960 to 1970 he was connected with the Inst. for Sonologie in Utrecht; in 1970 opened his own electronic-music studio.

WORKS: Suite for String Quartet (1954); *Diagonal Music* for String Orch. (1956); Divertimento for 3 Flutes (1957); *Epigenese* for Orch. (1964); *Triptichon* for 6 Percussionists (1965); *Sandpipers* for Percussion (1965); String Quartet (1965); *A-talon* for Mezzo-soprano and 36 Playing and Talking Instrumentalists (1967–68); *Differenties* for 3 Clarinets, Piano, and Vibraphone (1969); *Scenario X* for Brass Quintet (1970); *Centrifuga* for Orch. (1979); *Canto ostinato* for Various Instruments (1979); *Une Musique blanche* for Orch. (1982); *Horizon* for Keyboard Instruments (1983–85). Piano: *Compositions I–IV* (1942–45); Suite (1953); 2 sonatas (1953, 1959); *20 Bagatelles* (1954); *Allegro ex machina* (1955); *Diagonal Suite* (1957); *Journal* (1957); *Music for Peter*, 7 little pieces (1958); *20 Epigrams* (1959); *5 Études* (1961); *Natalon in E* (1980). Electronic: *Sevenplay* (1970); *Inferno I* and *II* (1970, 1971); *Modules I–IV* (1971); *I Am Sylvia* (1973); *Recital I* and *II* (1972–74).

Holter, Iver (Paul Fredrik), Norwegian conductor and composer; b. Gausdal, Dec. 13, 1850; d. Oslo, Jan. 25, 1941. He entered the Univ. of Christiania as a student of medicine, but devoted much more time to music, which he studied under Svendsen; then was a pupil of Jadassohn, Richter, and Reinecke at the Leipzig Cons. (1876–78); became Grieg's successor as conductor of the Harmonien in Bergen (1882); from 1886 to 1911 he was conductor of the Musikföreningen in Christiania, and from 1890 to 1905, of the Handvaerkersångföreningen; in 1907, founded (and conducted until 1921) Holters Korförening, a society devoted to the production of large choral works (sacred and secular); was conductor of several of the great Scandinavian festivals; in 1900 he conducted with Svendsen the Northern Concerts in Paris. In 1919 the Norwegian government granted him an artist's stipend. He was ed. of the *Nordisk Musik Revue* (1900–1906). His compositions include a Sym. (1885); a Violin Concerto; several cantatas, as for the 300-year jubilee of Christiania (1924) and for the 900-year Olavs-jubilee (1930); also choruses; chamber music; songs.

Holtzner, Anton, German organist and composer; d. 1635. He was educated in Italy. His keyboard canzonas make use of free rhythmic transformation of themes in the manner of Frescobaldi's "variation canzonas"; 1 of them is reprinted in A. Ritter's *Geschichte des Orgelspiels im 14.–18. Jahrhundert* (1884).

Holý, Alfred, Portuguese harpist; b. Oporto, Aug. 5, 1866; d. Vienna, May 8, 1948. He studied violin and piano; then took harp lessons with Staněk at the Prague Cons. (1882–85). He subsequently was 1st harpist at the German Opera in Prague (1885–96), the Berlin Royal Opera (1896–1903), and the Vienna Court Opera (1903–13). In 1913 he became 1st harpist of the Boston Sym. Orch.; retired in 1928. He publ. studies for harp, arranged from the symphonic works of Richard Strauss, and various other harp transcriptions.

Holyoke, Samuel (Adams), American composer; b. Boxford, Mass., Oct. 15, 1762; d. East Concord, N.H., Feb. 7, 1820. His father was a clergyman, and Holyoke was naturally drawn to composing hymns. Although he received no formal training in music, he began to compose early, following his innate musical instinct. He wrote his most popular hymn tune, *Arnheim*, when he was only 16. He attended Harvard College, graduating in 1789; in 1793 he organized a school of higher education, known as the Groton Academy (later Lawrence Academy). In 1800 he went to Salem, where he was active as a teacher; was also a member of the Essex Musical Assoc. in Salem. Holyoke was among those who did not favor the application of "fuging" tunes in sacred music, as advocated by Billings, and generally omitted that style of composition from his collections; in the preface to his *Harmonia Americana* he states his reason for this as being because of "the trifling effect produced by that sort of music; for the parts . . . confound the sense and render the performance a mere jargon of words." His 1st collection was the *Harmonia Americana* (Boston, 1791);

then followed *The Massachusetts Compiler* (co-ed. with Hans Gram and Oliver Holden; Boston, 1795); *The Columbian Repository of Sacred Harmony* (Exeter, N.H., 1802; contains 734 tunes, many of his own composition); *The Christian Harmonist* (Salem, 1804); *The Instrumental Assistant* (2 vols., Exeter, 1800–1807; includes instructions for violin, German flute, clarinet, bass viol, and hautboy). He also publ. the song *Washington* (1790), and *Hark from the Tombs* (music for the funeral of Washington; 1800).

BIBL.: F. Metcalf, *American Psalmody* (N.Y., 1917); idem, *American Writers and Compilers of Sacred Music* (N.Y., 1925); J. Willhide, *S. H., American Music-Educator* (diss., Univ. of Southern Calif., 1954); R. Patterson, *Three American "Primitives." A Study of the Musical Styles of S. H., Oliver Holden, and Hans Gram* (diss., Washington Univ., 1963).

Holzbauer, Ignaz (Jakob), noted Austrian composer; b. Vienna, Sept. 17, 1711; d. Mannheim, April 7, 1783. He studied law and at the same time received instruction in music from members of the choir at St. Stephen's in Vienna; he also perused *Gradus ad Parnassum* by Fux, whom he met later and who advised him to go to Italy for further studies. He then proceeded to Venice, but soon returned home. For a brief period he served as Kapellmeister to Count Rottal of Holešov in Moravia; in 1737 he married Rosalie Andreides, a singer; shortly thereafter they moved to Vienna, where he became a conductor and she a singer at the Court Theater; they also spent several years in Italy. In 1751 he was named Oberkapellmeister in Stuttgart. In 1753 he became Kapellmeister at the court of the elector Karl Theodor in Mannheim, a post he held until the court moved to Munich in 1778. He visited Rome in 1756, Turin in 1758, and Milan in 1759; during these visits he produced several of his operas. Holzbauer was greatly respected as a composer, especially for his church music; Mozart heard one of his masses in Mannheim in 1777 and found it excellent. He was an important figure among symphonic composers of the Mannheim school; he wrote some 65 works for orch. Of his operas, *Günther von Schwarzburg* (Mannheim, Jan. 5, 1777) is historically significant for its departure from Italian convention; it is thoroughly German in subject and treatment, and is noteworthy for the inclusion of accompanied recitative in place of the dialogue of the singspiel. It was publ. in Mannheim in 1776; reprinted in Denkmäler Deutscher Tonkunst, VIII–IX (1902). His other operas include *Il Figlio delle selve* (Schwetzingen, 1753), *L'isola disabitata* (Schwetzingen, 1754), *L'issipile* (Mannheim, Nov. 4, 1754), *Don Chisciotte* (Schwetzingen, 1755), *I Cinesi* (Mannheim, 1756), *Le nozze d'Arianna* (Mannheim, 1756), *Il Filosofo di campagna* (Mannheim, 1756), *La clemenza di Tito* (Mannheim, Nov. 4, 1757), *La Nitteti* (Turin, 1758), *Alessandro nell'Indie* (Milan, 1759), *Ippolito ed Aricia* (Mannheim, Nov. 4, 1759), *Adriano in Siria* (Mannheim, Nov. 4, 1768), and *Tancredi* (Munich, Jan. 1783). He also wrote ballet music for operas by J.A. Hasse: *L'Ipermestra* (Vienna, Jan. 8, 1744) and *Arminio* (Vienna, May 13, 1747). In addition, he composed 4 oratorios, 21 masses (also a *Deutsche Messe*), 37 motets, a Miserere, and other church music. His instrumental works, in addition to the syms., include concertos, divertimentos, string quartets, string quintets, etc. See U. Lehmann, ed., *Ignaz Holzbauer: Instrumentale Kammermusik*, in Das Erbe Deutscher Musik, 1st series, XXIV (1953).

BIBL.: H. Werner, *Die Sinfonien von I. H.* (diss., Univ. of Munich, 1942).

Homer, Louise (Dilworth) (née **Beatty**), esteemed American contralto; b. Shadyside, near Pittsburgh, April 30, 1871; d. Winter Park, Fla., May 6, 1947. She studied in Philadelphia and at the New England Cons. of Music in Boston, where she received instruction in harmony from **Sidney Homer**, who later became her husband (1895); then went to Paris to study voice with Fidèle Koenig and dramatic acting with Paul Lhérie, making her operatic debut as Leonora in *La Favorite* in Vichy (1898). She made her 1st appearance at London's Covent Garden as Lola in *Cavalleria rusticana* on May 9, 1899, and appeared there again in 1900; was also on the roster of the Théâtre Royal de la Monnaie in Brussels (1899–1900). On Nov. 14, 1900, she made her U.S. debut as Amneris with the touring Metropolitan Opera in San Francisco and again on Dec. 22, 1900, with the company in N.Y. She was acclaimed for her interpretation of Gluck's Orfeo in Paris in 1909, a role she repeated later that year at the Metropolitan Opera under Toscanini; she also created the roles of the Witch in Humperdinck's *Königskinder* (Dec. 28, 1910) and of Mona in Parker's opera (March 14, 1912) there. After singing with opera companies in Chicago (1920–25) and in San Francisco and Los Angeles (1926), she returned to the Metropolitan (1927), continuing on its roster until her farewell performance as Azucena on Nov. 28, 1929. She subsequently appeared in recitals with her daughter, the soprano Louise Homer Stires. Her nephew was the composer **Samuel Barber.**

BIBL.: S. Homer, *My Wife and I* (N.Y., 1939); A. Homer, *L. H. and the Golden Age of Opera* (N.Y., 1973).

Homer, Sidney, American composer; b. Boston, Dec. 9, 1864; d. Winter Park, Fla., July 10, 1953. He studied in Boston, with Chadwick; then in Leipzig and Munich. In 1895 he married **Louise (Dilworth)** (née **Beatty) Homer,** his pupil, and went with her to Paris. He publ. a book of memoirs, *My Wife and I* (N.Y., 1939). He publ. about 100 songs, many of which won great favor, particularly *A Banjo Song;* also *Dearest, Requiem, Prospice, Bandanna Ballads, It was the time of roses, General William Booth Enters into Heaven, The Song of the Shirt, Sheep and Lambs, Sing me a song of a lad that is gone,* and *The Pauper's Drive.* He also composed a Sonata for Organ (1922); Quintet for Piano and Strings (1932); Violin Sonata (1936); String Quartet (1937); Piano Trio (1937).

BIBL.: H. Thorpe, "The Songs of S. H.," *Musical Quarterly* (Jan. 1931).

Homilius, Gottfried August, eminent German organist and composer; b. Rosenthal, Feb. 2, 1714; d. Dresden, June 5, 1785. He studied composition and keyboard playing with J.S. Bach; completed his education at the Univ. of Leipzig in 1735; in 1742 became organist of the Frauenkirche in Dresden; then was appointed music director of 3 main churches there (1755). His publ. works are a Passion (1775); a Christmas oratorio, *Die Freude der Hirten über die Geburt Jesu* (1777); *6 deutsche Arien* (1786). In MS in the Berlin State Library and in the Dresden Kreuzchor archives are a Passion according to St. Mark; motets, cantatas, fugued chorales, a thoroughbass method, 2 chorus books, etc.

BIBL.: R. Fricke, "G.A. H.," *Zeitschrift für Kirchenmusiker,* XVII (1935); H. John, *G.A. H. und die evangelische Kirchenmusik Dresdens im 18. Jahrhundert* (diss., Univ. of Halle, 1973).

Homs (Oller), Joaquín, Catalan composer; b. Barcelona, Aug. 22, 1906. He studied cello; began to compose late in life. He took lessons in music theory with Roberto Gerhard (1931–37); formed a constructivist style with thematic contents derived from Catalan melos.

WORKS: 7 string quartets (1938–68); Duo for Flute and Clarinet (1936); Wind Quintet (1940); Concertino for Piano and Strings (1946); Sextet (1959); String Trio (1968); *Impromptu for 10* (1970).

Honegger, Arthur (Oscar), remarkable French composer; b. Le Havre (of Swiss parents), March 10, 1892; d. Paris, Nov. 27, 1955. He studied violin in Paris with Lucien Capet; then took courses with L. Kempter and F. Hegar at the Zürich Cons. (1909–11). Returning to France in 1912, he entered the Paris Cons., in the classes of Gédalge and Widor; also took lessons with d'Indy. His name 1st attracted attention when he took part in a concert of Les Nouveaux Jeunes in Paris on Jan. 15, 1918. In 1920 the Paris critic Henri Collet publ. an article in *Comoedia* in which he drew a fortuitous parallel between the Russian Five and a group of young French composers whom he designated as Les Six. These Six were Honegger, Milhaud, Poulenc, Auric, Durey, and Tailleferre. The label persisted, even though the 6 composers went their separate ways and rarely gave concerts together. Indeed, only Honegger, Milhaud, and Poulenc became generally known; Auric limited

his activities mainly to the theater and the cinema, while Germaine Tailleferre produced some musical plays and concert pieces; as to Durey, he was known more as a dedicated member of the French Communist Party than as a composer. In the early years of his career, Honegger embraced the fashionable type of urban music, with an emphasis on machine-like rhythms and curt, pert melodies. In 1921 he wrote a sport ballet, *Skating Rink,* and a mock-militaristic ballet, *Sousmarine.* In 1923 he composed the most famous of such machine pieces, *Mouvement symphonique No. 1,* subtitled *Pacific 231.* The score was intended to be a realistic tonal portrayal of a powerful American locomotive, bearing the serial number 231. The music progressed in accelerating rhythmic pulses toward a powerful climax, then gradually slackened its pace until the final abrupt stop; there was a simulacrum of a lyrical song in the middle section of the piece. *Pacific 231* enjoyed great popularity and became in the minds of modern-minded listeners a perfect symbol of the machine age. Honegger's 2nd *Mouvement symphonique,* composed in 1928, was a musical rendering of the popular British sport rugby. His *Mouvement symphonique No. 3,* however, bore no identifying subtitle. This abandonment of allusion to urban life coincided chronologically with a general trend away from literal representation and toward absolute music in classical forms, often of historical or religious character. Among his most important works in that genre were *Le Roi David,* to a biblical subject, and *Jeanne d'Arc au bûcher,* glorifying the French patriot saint on the semimillennium of her martyrdom. Honegger's syms. were equally free from contemporary allusions; the first 2 lacked descriptive titles; his 3rd was entitled *Liturgique,* with a clear reference to an ecclesiastical ritual; the 4th was named *Deliciae Basilienses,* because it was written to honor the city of Basel; the somewhat mysterious title of the 5th, *Di tre re,* signified nothing more arcane than the fact that each of its movements ended on the thrice-repeated note D. Honegger spent almost all of his life in France, but he retained his dual Swiss citizenship, a fact that caused some biographers to refer to him as a Swiss composer. In 1926 he married the pianist-composer **Andrée Vaurabourg** (1894–1980), who often played piano parts in his works. In 1929 he paid a visit to the U.S.; he returned in 1947 to teach summer classes at the Berkshire Music Center at Tanglewood, but soon after his arrival was stricken with a heart ailment and was unable to complete his term; he returned to Paris and remained there until his death. He publ. a book, *Je suis compositeur* (Paris, 1951; Eng. tr., London, 1966).

WORKS: THEATER: *Le Roi David,* dramatic Psalm in 3 parts for Narrator, Soloists, Chorus, and 15 Instruments (Mézières, June 11, 1921; rev. as an oratorio with Full Orch., 1923; Winterthur, Dec. 2, 1923); *Antigone,* opera in 3 acts (1924–27; Brussels, Dec. 28, 1927); *Judith,* biblical drama in 13 scenes (Mézières, June 11, 1925; expanded to a 3-act opera; Monte Carlo, Feb. 13, 1926); *Amphion,* melodrama (1929; Paris, June 23, 1931); *Les Aventures du Roi Pausole,* operetta (1929–30; Paris, Dec. 12, 1930); *Cris du Monde,* stage oratorio for Soprano, Contralto, Baritone, Chorus, and Orch. (1930; Solothurn, May 3, 1931); *La Belle de Moudon,* operetta in 5 acts (Mézières, May 30, 1931); *Jeanne d'Arc au bûcher,* dramatic oratorio in a Prologue and 11 scenes (1934–35; concert version, without Prologue, Basel, May 12, 1938; stage premiere, in German, Zürich, June 13, 1942); *L'Aiglon,* opera in collaboration with Jacques Ibert (1935; Monte Carlo, March 11, 1937); *Les Mille et Une Nuits,* spectacle for Soprano, Tenor, Chorus, and Orch. (Paris Exhibition, 1937); *Les Petites Cardinal,* operetta in collaboration with Jacques Ibert (1937; Paris, Feb. 20, 1938); *Nicolas de Flue,* dramatic legend for Narrator, Mixed Choir, Children's Choir, and Orch. (1939; concert premiere, Solothurn, Oct. 26, 1940; stage premiere, Neuchâtel, Switzerland, May 31, 1941).

BALLETS: *Vérité-Mensonge,* marionette ballet (Paris, Nov. 1920); *Skating Rink* (1921; Paris, Jan. 20, 1922); *Sousmarine* (1924; Paris, June 27, 1925); *Roses de métal* (Paris, 1928); *Sémiramis,* ballet-melodrama (1931; Paris, May 11, 1934); *Un Oiseau blanc s'est envolé* (Paris, June 1937); *Le Cantique des* *cantiques* (1937; Paris, Feb. 2, 1938); *La Naissance des couleurs* (1940; Paris, 1949); *Le Mangeur de rêves* (Paris, 1941); *L'Appel de la montagne* (1943; Paris, July 9, 1945); scenes 1 and 4 of *Chota Roustaveli*, in 4 scenes (also known as *L'Homme à la peau de léopard*; 1945; Monte Carlo, May 5, 1946; scenes 2 and 3 composed by Harsányi and A. Tcherepnin); *De la musique* (1950).

INCIDENTAL MUSIC: *Les Dit des jeux du monde*, in the form of 10 dances, 2 interludes, and epilogue, for Flute, Trumpet, Percussion, and Strings (1918; as a ballet, Paris, Dec. 2, 1918); *La Mort de Sainte Alméenne* (1918); *La Danse macabre* (1919); *Saül* (Paris, June 16, 1922); *Fantasio* (1922); *Antigone* (1922); *La Tempête* (1923); *Liluli* (1923); *Le Miracle de Notre-Dame* (1925); *L'Impératrice aux rochers* (1925; Paris, Feb. 17, 1927); *Phèdre* (1926); *800 mètres* (1941); *Le Soulier de satin* for Soprano, Baritone, and Orch. (Paris, Nov. 17, 1943); *Charles le Téméraire* for Choir, 2 Trumpets, 2 Trombones, and Percussion (1943–44; Mézières, May 27, 1944); *Hamlet* for Narrator, Chorus, and Orch. (Paris, Oct. 17, 1946); *Prométhée* (1946); *L'État de siège* (Paris, Oct. 27, 1948); *Tête d'or* (1948); *Œdipe-Roi* (1948).

ORCH.: *Prélude pour "Aglavaine et Sélysette"* by Maeterlinck (1916–17; Paris Cons. orch. class, April 3, 1917, composer conducting); *Le Chant de Nigamon* (1917; Paris, Jan. 3, 1920); *Entrée, Nocturne et Berceuse* for Piano and Chamber Orch. (Paris, 1919); *Pastorale d'été* (1920; Paris, Feb. 12, 1921); *Horace Victorieux*, "mimed sym." (1920–21; concert premiere, Lausanne, Oct. 30, 1921; mimed premiere, Essen, Dec. 28, 1927); *Marche funèbre* (1 section of *Les Mariés de la Tour Eiffel*, with other individual sections by Auric, Milhaud, Poulenc, and Tailleferre; Paris, June 18, 1921); *Chant de joie* (Paris, April 7, 1923); *Prélude pour "La Tempête,"* after Shakespeare (Paris, May 1, 1923); *Pacific 231* (designated as *Mouvement symphonique No. 1*; 1923; Paris, May 8, 1924); *Concertino for Piano and Orch.* (1924; Paris, May 23, 1925; A. Vaurabourg, soloist); *Suite from incidental music to L'Impératrice aux rochers* (1925); *Suite from incidental music to Phèdre* (1926); *Rugby* (*Mouvement symphonique No. 2*; Paris, Oct. 19, 1928, Ansermet conducting); *Prélude, Fugue et Postlude*, from the melodrama *Amphion* (1929; Geneva, Nov. 3, 1948); *Cello Concerto* (1929; Boston, Feb. 17, 1930); 5 syms.: No. 1 (1929–30; Boston, Feb. 13, 1931); No. 2 for String Orch. and optional Trumpet (1941; Zürich, May 18, 1942); No. 3, *Liturgique* (1945–46; Zürich, Aug. 17, 1946); No. 4, *Deliciae Basilienses* (1946; Basel, Jan. 21, 1947); No. 5, *Di tre re* (1950; Boston, March, 9, 1951); *Mouvement symphonique No. 3* (1932–33; Berlin, March 26, 1933); *Suite from the film Les Misérables* (1934; Paris, Jan. 19, 1935); *Prélude, Arioso et Fughetta sur le nom de BACH* for String Orch. (arranged by A. Hoérée from the piano version, 1936; Paris, Dec. 5, 1936); *Nocturne* (Brussels, April 30, 1936); *La Marche sur la Bastille* for Band, from incidental music for Romain Rolland's pageant *Le Quatorze Juillet* (Paris, July 14, 1936); *La Grande Barrage*, an "image musicale" (1942); *Jour de fête suisse*, suite from music to the ballet *L'Appel de la montagne* (1943; Winterthur, Nov. 14, 1945); 2 extracts from the film *Mermoz* (1943); *Sérénade à Angélique* for Small Orch. (Zürich Radio, Nov. 19, 1945); *Concerto da camera* for Flute, English Horn, and Strings (Zürich, May 6, 1949); *Toccata* (1 section of *La Guirlande de Campra*, with other individual sections by Lesur, Manuel, Tailleferre, Poulenc, Sauguet, and Auric, 1950; complete work, Aix-en-Provence Festival, July 31, 1952); *Suite archaïque* (1950–51; Louisville, Ky., Feb. 28, 1951); *Monopartita* (Zürich, June 12, 1951).

VOCAL: *Cantique de Pâques* for 3 Women's Voices, Women's Chorus, and Orch. (1918; Toulouse, March 27, 1923); *Pâques à New York* for Voice and String Quartet (1920); *Chanson de Ronsard* for Voice, Flute, and String Quartet (1924); *3 chansons de la petite sirène* for Voice, Flute, and Strings or String Quartet (1926); *La Danse des morts*, oratorio for Narrator, Soloists, Chorus, Organ, and Orch. (1938; Basel, March 1, 1940); *Chant de libération* for Baritone, Unison Chorus, and Orch. (1942; Paris, Oct. 22, 1944); *Une Cantate de Noël* for Baritone, Mixed

Chorus, Children's Chorus, Organ, and Orch. (sketched 1941, completed 1953; Basel, Dec. 18, 1953).

CHAMBER: 2 violin sonatas (1916–18; 1919); 3 string quartets (1916–17; 1934–36; 1936–37); *Rapsodie* for 2 Flutes, Clarinet (or 2 Violins, Viola), and Piano (1917); *Danse de la chèvre* for Solo Flute (1919); Sonatina for 2 Violins (1920); Viola Sonata (1920); Cello Sonata (1920); *Hymn* for 10 String Instruments (1920); Sonatina for Clarinet or Cello, and Piano (1921–22); 3 *contrepoints* for Flute, English Horn, Violin, and Cello (1923); *Prélude et Blues* for Quartet of Chromatic Harps (1925); Sonatina for Violin and Cello (1932); *Petite suite* for any 2 Treble Instruments and Piano (1934); Solo Violin Sonata (1940); *Sortilèges* for Ondes Martenot (1946); *Intrada* for Trumpet and Piano (1947); *Romance* for Flute and Piano (1953).

RADIO MUSIC: *Les Douze Coups de minuit*, "radio-mystère" for Chorus and Chamber Orch. (Paris Radio, Dec. 27, 1933); *Radio panoramique* for Tenor, Soprano, Organ, String Quintet, Wind Instruments, and Percussion (Geneva Radio, March 4, 1935; concert premiere, Paris, Oct. 19, 1935); *Christophe Colomb*, radio oratorio for 2 Tenors, Chorus, and Orch. (Lausanne Radio, April 17, 1940); *Les Battements du monde* for Woman's Voice, Child's Voice, Chorus, and Orch. (Lausanne Radio, May 18, 1944); *Saint François d'Assise* for Narrator, Baritone, Chorus, and Orch. (Lausanne Radio, Dec. 3, 1949).

FILM MUSIC: *Les Misérables* (1934); *Mayerling* (1935); *Regain* (1937); *Mlle. Doctor* (1937); *Pygmalion*, after G.B. Shaw's play (1938); *Mermoz* (1943); *Bourdelle* (1950); 36 others.

PIANO: 3 *pièces* (*Scherzo, Humoresque*, and *Adagio espressivo*; 1910); 3 *pièces: Hommage à Ravel* (1915); *Prélude et Danse* (1919); *Toccata et Variations* (1916); 7 *pièces brèves* (1919–20); *Sarabande* (1920); *Le Cahier Romand*, 5 pieces (1921–23); *Hommage à Albert Roussel* (1928); Suite for 2 Pianos (1928); *Prélude, Arioso et Fughetta sur le nom de BACH* (1932; arranged for Strings by A. Hoérée in 1936); *Scenic-Railway* (1937); *Partita* for 2 Pianos (1940; arranged from 3 *contrepoints*); 2 *esquisses*, in Obouhov's simplified notation (1943–44); *Souvenir de Chopin* (1947).

SONGS: 4 *poèmes* (1914–16); 6 *poèmes de Apollinaire* (1915–17; Nos. 1 and 3–6 orchestrated as 5 *poèmes de Apollinaire*, 1916–17); 3 *poèmes de Paul Fort* (1916); 6 *poésies de Jean Cocteau* (1920–23); 2 *chants d'Ariel* (1923; also arranged for Orch.); 3 *poèmes de Claudel* (1939–40); 3 Psalms (1940–41); 5 *mélodies-minute* (1941); 4 Songs for Low Voice and Piano (1944–45). Honegger publ. a book, *Je suis compositeur* (Paris, 1951; in Eng. as *I Am a Composer*, London, 1966).

BIBL.: R. Chalupt, "A. H.," *Revue Musicale* (1922); E. Hill, *Modern French Composers* (N.Y., 1924); Roland-Manuel, *A. H.* (Paris, 1925); A. George, *A. H.* (Paris, 1926); W. Tappolet, *A. H.* (in German, Zürich, 1933; 2nd German ed., Zürich, 1954; French ed., Neuchâtel, 1938; 2nd French ed., Neuchâtel, 1957); C. Gérard, *A. H.: Catalogue succinct des œuvres* (Brussels, 1945); J. Bruyr, *H. et son œuvre* (Paris, 1947); J. Matter, *H. ou La Quête de joie* (Lausanne, 1956); A. Gauthier, *A. H.* (London, 1957); M. Landowski, *H.* (Paris, 1957); W. Reich, ed., *A. H., Nachklang: Schriften, Photos, Dokumente* (Zürich, 1957); J. Feschotte, *A. H.: L'Homme et son œuvre* (Paris, 1966); P. Meylan, *A. H., Humanitäre Botschaft der Musik* (Frauenfeld, 1970); J. Mailliard and J. Nahoum, *Les Symphonies d'A. H.* (Paris, 1974); G. Spratt, *The Music of A. H.* (Cork, 1987).

Honegger, Henri (Charles), Swiss cellist; b. Geneva, June 10, 1904. He studied with Ami Briquet in Geneva; then went to Germany, where he took lessons with Julius Klengel at the Leipzig Cons.; from there he traveled to Paris, where he took lessons with Casals and Alexanian; returning to Switzerland, he became 1st cellist in the Orch. de la Suisse Romande (until 1964), but also continued his tours as a soloist.

Honegger, Marc, French musicologist; b. Paris, June 17, 1926. He studied music history and theory at the Sorbonne with Chailley and P.-M. Masson; in 1954 was appointed to the faculty of the musicological dept. of the Univ. of Paris. In 1958 he joined the faculty of the Univ. of Strasbourg; in 1970 received the degree of Docteur-ès-lettres. He publ. several valuable articles on French music of the late Renaissance; also a historical survey, *La Musique française de 1830 à 1914* (1962). He ed. the valuable 4-vol. encyclopedia *Dictionnaire de la musique* (Strasbourg, 1970–77; 2nd ed., rev., 1986).

Höngen, Elisabeth, esteemed German mezzo-soprano; b. Gevelsberg, Dec. 7, 1906. She was educated at the Hochschule für Musik in Berlin; also studied voice with Hermann Weissenborn. She made her debut at the Wuppertal Opera in 1933, remaining there until she joined the Düsseldorf Opera in 1935; then sang at the Dresden State Opera (1940–43). In 1943 she became a member of the Vienna State Opera. On Jan. 10, 1952, she made her debut at the Metropolitan Opera in N.Y. as Hérodias in *Salome;* then continued her career in Europe. In 1947 she was named an Austrian Kammersängerin.

Hood, George, American minister, writer on music, and composer; b. Topsfield, Mass., Feb. 10, 1807; d. Minneapolis, Sept. 24, 1882. He studied in local singing schools and with Lowell Mason in Boston. After being ordained in Lawrenceville, N.J. (1848), he held pastorates in Bath, N.Y. (1849–50), and Southport, N.Y. (1851–53); subsequently was supply (i.e., substitute) minister in Bethel, N.Y. (1874–78), and Minneapolis (1880), and superintendent of Shakopee Mission, Minn. His most important work was *A History of Music in New England with Biographical Sketches of Reformers and Psalmists* (Boston, 1846); he also wrote *Can All Learn to Sing?* (Boston, c.1840) and *Musical Manual Designed as a Text-book for Classes or Private Pupils in Vocal or Instrumental Music* (Philadelphia, 1864). He also composed congregational hymn tunes.

Hood, Helen, American composer; b. Chelsea, Mass., June 28, 1863; d. Brookline, Mass., Jan. 22, 1949. She studied piano with B.J. Lang and composition with Chadwick; also piano with Moszkowski in Berlin. Among her publ. pieces are *The Robin* (part-song); *5 Pieces for Violin and Piano; Song Etchings* (a set of 6 songs). She also wrote some chamber music.

Hood, Mantle, American ethnomusicologist and composer; b. Springfield, Ill., June 24, 1918. He studied composition privately with Ernst Toch (1945–50); was enrolled at the Univ. of Calif., Los Angeles (B.A., 1951; M.A. in composition, 1951); continued his studies at the Univ. of Amsterdam (Ph.D., 1954, with the diss. *The Nuclear Theme as a Determinant of Patet in Javanese Music;* publ. in Groningen, 1954). In 1954 he joined the faculty at the Univ. of Calif., Los Angeles, becoming a full prof. there in 1962; in 1961 he was appointed director of the Inst. of Ethnomusicology there. In 1956–57 he traveled to Indonesia on a Ford Foundation fellowship, and in 1976 received a Fulbright fellowship for study in India. In 1976 he became an adjunct prof. at the Univ. of Maryland; in 1977 was a visiting prof. at Yale Univ. and at Wesleyan Univ. He publ. *The Ethnomusicologist* (N.Y., 1971) and *The Paragon of the Roaring Sea* (Wilhelmshaven and N.Y., 1988); contributed valuable articles on oriental music to learned journals and musical encyclopedias; also made arrangements of Indonesian melodies. His compositions include a symphonic poem, *Vernal Equinox* (1955); Woodwind Trio (1950); 6 duets for Soprano and Alto Recorder (1954); piano pieces.

Hoof, Jef van, Belgian composer; b. Antwerp, May 8, 1886; d. there, April 24, 1959. He studied composition at the Antwerp Cons. with Gilson, Mortelmas, and Huybrechts; composed 3 operas: *Tycho-Brahe* (1911), *Meivuur* (1916), and *Jonker Lichthart* (1928); 5 syms. (1938, 1941, 1945, 1951, 1956); choruses; lieder; piano pieces. His style of composition is neo-Romantic, with a penchant for expansive sonorities.

Hoogstraten, Willem van, Dutch conductor; b. Utrecht, March 18, 1884; d. Tutzing, Sept. 11, 1965. He studied violin with Alexander Schmuller; then with Bram Eldering at the Cologne Cons. and with Ševčik in Prague; played concerts with the pianist **Elly Ney,** whom he married in 1911 (divorced in 1927). From 1914 to 1918 he conducted the municipal orch. in Krefeld; in 1922 he was engaged as conductor of the summer concerts of the N.Y. Phil. (until 1938); was its associate conductor (1923–25). He was regular conductor of the Portland

(Oreg.) Sym. Orch. from 1925 to 1938. During World War II he was in charge of the Mozarteum Orch. in Salzburg (1939–45). After the war, he appeared as a guest conductor in Europe.

Hook, James, English organist and composer; b. Norwich, June 3, 1746; d. Boulogne, 1827. He exhibited a precocious talent as a boy; took lessons with Garland, organist of the Norwich Cathedral. In 1764 he went to London, where he played organ at various entertainment places. In 1765 he won a prize for his *Parting Catch.* He was subsequently organist and music director at Marylebone Gardens (1769–73) and at Vauxhall Gardens (1774–1820); his last position was at St. John's, Horsleydown. He publ. a manual, *Guida di musica,* in 2 parts (1785, 1794).

WORKS: Theater (all 1st perf. in London): *Cupid's Revenge* (June 12, 1772); *The Lady of the Manor* (Nov. 23, 1778); *The Fair Peruvian* (March 8, 1786); *Jack of Newbury* (May 6, 1795); *Wilmore Castle* (Oct. 21, 1800); *The Soldier's Return* (April 23, 1805); *The Invisible Girl* (April 28, 1806); *The Fortress* (July 16, 1807); *Safe and Sound* (August 28, 1809); etc. Also many oratorios and odes; concertos for harpsichord; sonatas, sonatinas, and divertimentos for piano; songs.

BIBL.: C. Cudworth, "J. H.," *Norwich Journal* (Aug. 24, 1946).

Hope-Jones, Robert, English organ manufacturer; b. Hooton Grange, Cheshire, Feb. 9, 1859; d. (suicide) Rochester, N.Y., Sept. 13, 1914. As a boy, he entered the employ of Laird Bros., engineers at Birkenhead; then became chief electrician of the National Telephone Co.; at the same time, was engaged as a church organist. In 1889 he set up his own business as an organ builder. In 1903 he settled in America; was connected with the E.M. Skinner Co. of Boston; in 1907, founded the Hope-Jones Organ Co. at Tonawanda, N.Y., but sold the plant and his patents in 1910 to the Rudolph Wurlitzer Co. of N.Y. He introduced many innovations into the building of electrical organs; the development of the modern organ in the U.S. owes much to his inventive genius. One of the finest of his organs is in the Auditorium at Ocean Grove, N.J.

BIBL.: G. Miller, *The Recent Revolution in Organ Building* (N.Y., 1913).

Hopekirk, Helen, Scottish-born American pianist, teacher, and composer; b. Edinburgh, May 20, 1856; d. Cambridge, Mass., Nov. 19, 1945. She studied with A.C. Mackenzie; then went to Germany; made her debut with the Gewandhaus Orch., Leipzig (Nov. 28, 1878); took lessons with Leschetizky in Vienna. In 1897 she settled in Boston; taught at the New England Cons. of Music; became an American citizen in 1918. In her recitals she featured works of the modern French school (Debussy, Fauré, etc.). She was also a composer; played her own Piano Concerto with the Boston Sym. Orch. (Dec. 27, 1900). Among her other compositions are Concertstück for Piano and Orch. (1894), 2 violin sonatas and other chamber music, piano pieces, choral works, and about 100 songs. She arranged and ed. *Seventy Scottish Songs* (Boston, 1905).

BIBL.: C. Hall and H. Tetlow, *H. H. 1856–1945* (Cambridge, Mass., 1954).

Hopf, Hans, German tenor; b. Nuremberg, Aug. 2, 1916. He studied in Munich, making his debut there in 1936. He then was engaged with the Opera in Augsburg (1939–42). In 1946 he sang at the Berlin State Opera, and after 1949, was a leading member of the Bavarian State Opera in Munich. He made his debut at the Metropolitan Opera in N.Y. as Walther in *Die Meistersinger von Nürnberg,* on March 15, 1952; sang there intermittently until 1964. His last public appearance was at the Munich Festival in 1988.

Hopkins (real name, **Reynolds**), **Antony,** English pianist, conductor, broadcaster, writer on music, and composer; b. London, March 21, 1921. He was a pupil of Cyril Scott and Gordon Jacob at the Royal College of Music in London (1939–42); then served as music director of the Intimate Opera Co. (from 1952), for which he composed several scores. He also wrote music for films, radio, and the theater, and was active as a radio broadcaster, hosting the series "Talking about Music" (from 1954). His books include *Understanding Music* (1979), *The Nine Symphonies of Beethoven* (1980), and *The Concertgoer's Companion* (2 vols., 1984, 1986). In 1976 he was made a Commander of the Order of the British Empire.

Hopkins, Charles Jerome (1st name is sometimes erroneously given as Edward), American writer on music and composer; b. Burlington, Vt., April 4, 1836; d. Athenia, N.J., Nov. 4, 1898. Self-taught in music (he took only 6 lessons in harmony), he learned to play piano sufficiently well to attain professional status. He studied chemistry at the N.Y. Medical College; played organ in N.Y. churches, and was active in various educational enterprises; in 1856 he founded the American Music Assoc., which promoted concerts of music by Gottschalk, Bristow, and other American composers. In 1868 he founded the *N.Y. Philharmonic Journal*, and was its ed. until 1885. In 1886 he organized several "Free Singing and Opera Schools," for which he claimed nearly 1,000 pupils. In 1889 he went to England on a lecture tour, announcing himself as "the first American Operatic Oratorio composer and Pianist who has ever ventured to invade England with New World Musical theories and practices." Throughout his versatile career, he was a strong advocate of American music; his sensational methods and eccentric professional conduct brought him repeatedly into public controversy; in England he was sued for libel. Hopkins claimed a priority in writing the 1st "musicianly and scientific Kinder-Oper" (*Taffy and Old Munch*, a children's fairy tale, 1880). He further wrote an operatic oratorio, *Samuel*, and a great number of choruses and songs, few of which were publ. He compiled 2 collections of church music and an *Orpheon Class-Book*.
BIBL.: N. Slonimsky, "The Flamboyant Pioneer," *A Thing or Two about Music* (N.Y., 1947).

Hopkins, Claude (Driskett), black American jazz pianist and bandleader; b. Alexandria, Va., Aug. 24, 1903; d. Riverdale, N.Y., Feb. 16, 1984. He studied piano; then enrolled at Howard Univ. in Washington, D.C. (B.A., 1923). He went to Paris, where he acted as music director for Josephine Baker, and led a band that featured the famous saxophone player Sidney Bechet. Returning to the U.S., he presided over bands at the Coconut Grove in Harlem, also filling engagements at the top clubs in N.Y. In his own playing he followed the uninhibited insouciant manner of the famous Harlem jazz pianist "Fats" Waller. Hopkins fell sick in his later years and died in a nursing home.

Hopkins, Edward John, English organist and composer; b. London, June 30, 1818; d. there, Feb. 4, 1901. He was a chorister at the Chapel Royal (1826–33); then studied theory with T.F. Walmisley. In 1834 he became organist at Mitcham Church; from 1838 was at St. Peter's Islington; from 1841, at St. Luke's; and from 1843 to 1898, at the Temple Church, London. Several of his many anthems have become established in the church repertoire (*Out of the Deep, God Is Gone Up, Thou Shalt Cause the Trumpet of the Jubilee to Sound,* etc.). His book, *The Organ: Its History and Construction* (in collaboration with Rimbault; London, 1855; 5th ed., 1887), is a standard work. He contributed articles to *Grove's Dictionary of Music and Musicians* and to various musical publications.
BIBL.: C. Pearce, *The Life and Works of E.J. H.* (London, 1910).

Hopkins, John Henry, American clergyman and writer of hymn tunes; b. Pittsburgh, Oct. 28, 1820; d. Hudson, N.Y., Aug. 13, 1891. He studied at schools of divinity and served as a deacon in several churches. His Christmas carol *We 3 Kings of Orient Are* is a perennial favorite. He publ. a collection, *Carols, Hymns and Songs* (1862).
BIBL.: R. McCutchan, *Our Hymnody* (N.Y., 1937).

Hopkins, Sam "Lightnin'," black American blues singer, guitarist, and songwriter; b. Centerville, Texas, March 15, 1912; d. Houston, Jan. 30, 1982. He worked on a farm in Texas; learned to play the guitar; accompanied the singer Texas

Alexander, a cousin, and developed a style of his own, with deep organ points in the bass and irregular rhythms in the melody; wrote about 600 songs. He was responsive to world events; composed *Happy Blues for John Glenn* after the astronaut's orbital flight. He was a popular singer at the Village Gate in N.Y. and took part in a hootenanny with Joan Baez and Pete Seeger. He was the subject of the film documentary *Blues accordin' to Lightnin' Hopkins* (1970).

Hopkinson, Francis, American statesman, writer, and composer; b. Philadelphia, Sept. 21, 1737; d. there, May 9, 1791. By profession a lawyer, he was deeply interested in music; learned to play the harpsichord; studied theory with James Bremner; was a member of an amateur group in Philadelphia who met regularly in their homes to play music, and also gave public concerts by subscription. He was the composer of the 1st piece of music written by a native American, *Ode to Music,* which he wrote in 1754, and of the 1st original American song, *My days have been so wondrous free* (1759). At least, this is the claim he makes in the preface to his 7 *Songs* [actually 8, the last having been added after the title page was engraved] *for the harpsichord or forte piano,* dated Philadelphia, Nov. 20, 1788, and dedicated to George Washington: "I cannot, I believe, be refused the Credit of being the first Native of the United States who has produced a Musical Composition." Other works: *Ode in Memory of James Bremner* (1780); a dramatic cantata, *The Temple of Minerva* (1781); some songs. Hopkinson's music was couched in the conventional English style, modeled after pieces by T.A. Arne, but he possessed a genuine melodic gift. He also provided Benjamin Franklin's glass harmonica with a keyboard, introduced improvements in the quilling of the harpsichord, and invented the Bellarmonic, an instrument consisting of a set of steel bells. He was probably the compiler of *A Collection of Psalm Tunes with a Few Anthems,* etc. A MS book of songs in Hopkinson's handwriting is in the possession of the Library of Congress. Hopkinson's son, Joseph Hopkinson, wrote the words to *Hail Columbia.*
BIBL.: O. Sonneck, *F. H., The First American Poet Composer . . .* (Washington, D.C., 1905; reprinted, N.Y., 1969); H. Milligan, *The First American Composer: 6 Songs by F. H.* (Boston, 1918); G. Hastings, *The Life and Works of F. H.* (Chicago, 1926); O. Albrecht, "F. H., Musician, Poet and Patriot," *University of Pennsylvania Library Chronicle* (1933, 1937, 1938).

Hoppin, Richard H(allowell), American musicologist; b. Northfield, Minn., Feb. 22, 1913. He studied piano at the École Normale de Musique in Paris (1933–35), and musicology at Harvard Univ. (M.A., 1938; Ph.D., 1952). He was on the music faculty of the Univ. of Texas, Austin (1949–61); in 1961 he was appointed prof. of music at Ohio State Univ. In 1959–60 he was the recipient of a Guggenheim fellowship. He ed. the important collection *The Cypriot-French Repertory of the Manuscript Torino, Biblioteca Nazionale, J. II. 9.,* Corpus Mensurabilis Musicae, XXI (1960–63); publ. *An Introduction to Medieval Music* (N.Y., 1978).

Horák, Adolph, Bohemian pianist and teacher, brother of **Eduard Horák;** b. Jankovic, Feb. 15, 1850; d. Vienna, Jan. 14, 1921. With his brother he established the Horák Pianoforte School in Vienna; in collaboration, they publ. a valuable *Klavierschule;* Adolph alone wrote *Die technische Grundlage des Klavierspiels.*

Horák, Antonin, Czech conductor and composer; b. Prague, July 2, 1875; d. Belgrade, March 12, 1910. He was an opera conductor in Prague and Belgrade; his own opera, *Babička* (Grandmother), was fairly successful at its 1st production, in Prague (March 3, 1900); he also wrote cantatas and other choral works.

Horák, Eduard, Bohemian pianist and teacher, brother of **Adolph Horák;** b. Holitz, April 22, 1838; d. Riva, Lake of Garda, Dec. 16, 1892. With his brother he founded in Vienna the Horák Pianoforte School, which soon acquired a European reputation. In collaboration with F. Spigl, he publ. *Der Klavier-*

unterricht in neue, natürliche Bahnen gelenkt (2 vols., Vienna, 1892), and with his brother, a practical manual, *Klavierschule.*

Horák, Josef, Czech bass clarinetist; b. Znojmo, March 24, 1931. He attended the Brno Cons. (1945–51); was a clarinetist in the Brno State Phil. and Prague Radio Sym. Orch. On Oct. 20, 1955, he made his debut as a performer on the bass clarinet, and began a career as a virtuoso on that instrument; along with the Dutch bass clarinetist Harry Sparnaay, Horák is responsible for the revival of interest in the bass clarinet. In 1963 he and the pianist Emma Kovárnová formed the chamber duo Due Boemi di Praga, and performed nearly 300 specially commissioned works by Alois Hába, André Jolivet, Frank Martin, Messiaen, Stockhausen, and many, many others. In 1972 he was appointed to the faculty of the Prague Cons.

Horak (Horák), Wenzel (Václav) Emanuel, Bohemian organist and composer; b. Mscheno-Lobes, Jan. 1, 1800; d. Prague, Sept. 3, 1871. He studied briefly with Josef Schubert, then received instruction in composition from B.D. Weber, Jan Kuchař, Vitásek, and Tomaschek. He taught voice (1831–32) and theory (1837–38) at the Prague Organ School; taught voice at the Prague teacher-training college (1837–53); was director of the Žofin Academy (1851–53) and was also active as a church organist. He wrote 11 masses, 3 Requiems, 2 Te Deums, and other works; also publ. several theoretical treatises.

Horenstein, Jascha, renowned Russian-born American conductor; b. Kiev, May 6, 1898; d. London, April 2, 1973. His family moved to Germany when he was a child; he studied with Max Brode in Königsberg and Adolf Busch in Vienna; also took courses in composition with Franz Schreker in Berlin, where he became an assistant to Wilhelm Furtwängler. He made his conducting debut with the Vienna Sym. Orch. in 1923; then was a guest conductor with the Berlin Phil. Orch.; from 1925 to 1928 was conductor of the Berlin Sym. Orch.; in 1929 he became chief conductor of the Düsseldorf Opera, a post he held until forced to leave in 1933. In 1940 he went to the U.S.; after World War II, he returned to Europe. He was especially noted for his authoritative interpretations of the syms. of Bruckner and Mahler.
Bibl.: *Le Grand Baton* (June 1976).

Horký, Karel, Czech composer; b. Štěmechy, near Třebíč, Sept. 4, 1909; d. Brno, Nov. 27, 1988. He played in a military band as a boy; studied bassoon; took private lessons in composition with V. Polívka and Pavel Haas; then entered the Prague Cons. as a student of Křička, graduating in 1944. He taught harmony at the Brno Cons. (1945–52) and from 1964 to 1971 was its director.
Works: 5 operas: *Jan Hus* (Brno, May 27, 1950), *Hejtman Šarovec* (Brno, 1953), *Jed z Elsinoru* (The Poison from Elsinor), freely after Shakespeare's *Hamlet* (Brno, Nov. 11, 1969), *Dawn* (Brno, July 4, 1975), and *Atlantida* (1980); 2 ballets: *Lastura* (The Shell; Brno, Oct. 23, 1945) and *Král Ječmínek* (King Ječmínek; Brno, Sept. 21, 1951); cantata, *Český sen* (The Czech Dream; 1961–62); *Klythia,* symphonic poem (1941); *Romantic Sinfonietta* (1944); Cello Concerto (1953); Violin Concerto (1955); 5 syms. (1959, 1964, 1971, 1974, 1977); Serenade for String Orch. (1963); Bassoon Concerto (1966); Horn Concerto (1971); *Fateful Preludes* for Piano and Orch. (1972); *Dimitrov,* symphonic poem with Narrator and Chorus, in memory of the chairman of the Bulgarian Communist Party (1972); 4 string quartets (1938, 1954, 1955, 1963); Violin Sonata (1943); Suite for Wind Quintet (1943); Nonet (1958); Clarinet Quintet (1960); piano pieces; choruses; songs; film music.

Horn, August, German composer and arranger; b. Freiberg, Sept. 1, 1825; d. Leipzig, March 25, 1893. He was a pupil of Mendelssohn at the Leipzig Cons.; wrote overtures and light music; but became principally known as an arranger of syms., operas, etc., for piano, 2- and 4-hands. His comic opera *Die Nachbarn* was produced in Leipzig in 1875.

Horn, Camillo, Bohemian composer; b. Reichenberg, Dec. 29, 1860; d. Vienna, Sept. 3, 1941. He was a pupil of Bruckner at the Vienna Cons.; conducted choruses there, and was also active as a music critic. He wrote a Sym.; a cantata, *Bundeslied der Deutschen in Böhmen; Deutsches Lied* for Chorus and Orch.; many choruses a cappella; piano pieces.

Horn, Charles Edward, English singer, conductor, and composer, son of **Karl Friedrich Horn;** b. London, June 21, 1786; d. Boston, Oct. 21, 1849. He studied with his father, and practiced voice under the guidance of Rauzzini. He made his debut as a singer in a light opera (London, June 26, 1809); sang Kaspar in the English production of *Der Freischütz.* In 1827 he went to N.Y., where he staged several of his operas; returned to London in 1830; in 1832 he emigrated to America; there he wrote several oratorios, including *The Remission of Sin* (later named *Satan*). In 1847 he became conductor of the Handel and Haydn Soc. in Boston. In the U.S., he was notable primarily as a singer and composer of ballads.
Bibl.: R. Montague, *C.E. H.: His Life and Works* (diss., Florida State Univ., 1959).

Horn, Karl Friedrich, German organist and composer, father of **Charles Edward Horn;** b. Nordhausen, April 13, 1762; d. Windsor, Aug. 5, 1830. He settled in England at the age of 20, and with the patronage of Count Brühl, Saxon ambassador in London, became a fashionable teacher. In 1823 he became organist of St. George's Chapel at Windsor. With Wesley, he prepared an English ed. of Bach's *Wohltemperierte Clavier* (1810–13); also wrote *A Treatise on Harmony with Practical Examples* (London, 1821). He composed 12 sets of piano variations, with flute obbligato; 6 piano sonatas; *Military Divertimentos.*

Hornbostel, Erich Moritz von, eminent Austrian musicologist; b. Vienna, Feb. 25, 1877; d. Cambridge, England, Nov. 28, 1935. He studied philosophy in Vienna and Heidelberg; received a Ph.D. in chemistry from the Univ. of Vienna (1900); in 1905–6 was the assistant of Stumpf in Berlin; in 1906 went to the U.S. to record and study Indian music (Pawnee); from 1906 to 1933, was director of the Phonogramm-Archiv in Berlin, and concurrently a prof. at the Univ. of Berlin (1917–33); then went again to the U.S. In 1934 he went to England. He was a specialist in Asian, African, and other non-European music; also investigated the problems of tone psychology; contributed hundreds of articles to scholarly publications on these subjects. He ed. a collection of records, *Musik des Orients* (Lindström, 1932); from 1922 until his death, was co-ed., with C. Stumpf, of the *Sammelbände für vergleichende Musikwissenschaft.* Hornbostel's writings are being prepared for reissue, ed. by K. Wachsmann et al. (The Hague, 1975–).

Horne, Lena (Calhoun), remarkable black American singer of popular music; b. N.Y., June 30, 1917. She left school at 16 to help support her ailing mother; began her career as a chorus girl at Harlem's Cotton Club; after singing with Noble Sissle's orch. (1935–36), she appeared with Charlie Barnet's orch. (1940–41) and made a name for herself via such recordings as *Good for Nothing Joe* and *Haunted Town.* In 1941 she sang at Carnegie Hall in N.Y.; after finding success as a radio vocalist, she went to Hollywood to star in the all-black musical films *Cabin in the Sky* (1943) and *Stormy Weather* (1943), adopting the title song of the latter as her trademark. In subsequent years she pursued a highly successful career as a vocalist in nightclubs and on television. She scored a triumph in N.Y. with her retrospective appearances in *Lena Horne: The Lady and Her Music* (1981–83), which she took on the road to critical acclaim. Her inimitable renditions of such standards as *Bewitched, Bothered, and Bewildered, Can't Help Lovin' Dat Man, Love Me or Leave Me,* and *Believe in Yourself* placed her in the exalted ranks of the leading vocalists of popular music in her time. In 1947 she married **Lennie Hayton.** She publ. the autobiography *Lena* (with R. Schickel; 1965).
Bibl.: J. Haskins, *L. H.* (N.Y., 1983); J. Haskins and K. Benson, *L.: A Personal and Professional Biography of L. H.* (N.Y., 1984); L. Palmer, *L. H.* (N.Y., 1989).

Horne, Marilyn (Bernice), outstanding American mezzo-soprano; b. Bradford, Pa., Jan. 16, 1934. She studied with William Vennard at the Univ. of Southern Calif. in Los Angeles; also attended Lotte Lehmann's master classes. She then went to Europe, where she made her professional operatic debut as Giulietta at the Gelsenkirchen Opera in 1957; remained on its roster until 1960, appearing in such roles as Mimi, Tatiana, Minnie, Fulvia in *Ezio*, and Marie in *Wozzeck*, the role she repeated in her U.S. debut at the San Francisco Opera on Oct. 4, 1960. She married the black American conductor **Henry Lewis** in 1960, and subsequently made a number of appearances under his direction; they were separated in 1976. In 1965 she made her debut at London's Covent Garden, again as Marie. She appeared at Milan's La Scala in 1969, and on March 3, 1970, made her Metropolitan Opera debut in N.Y. as Adalgisa; subsequently became one of the Metropolitan's principal singers. Her notable performances there included Rosina in *Il Barbiere di Siviglia* (Jan. 23, 1971), Carmen (Sept. 19, 1972), Fides in *Le Prophète* (Jan. 18, 1977), Rinaldo (the 1st Handel opera to be staged there, Jan. 19, 1984), and Isabella in *L'Italiana in Algeri* (telecast live by PBS, Jan. 11, 1986). Acclaimed for her brilliant portrayals in roles by Handel, Rossini, and Meyerbeer, she won equal praise as an outstanding concert artist. She publ. an autobiography (with J. Scovell; N.Y., 1983).

BIBL.: B. Zakariasen, "M. H.," *Ovation* (July 1983).

Horneman, Christian Frederik Emil, Danish choral conductor, teacher, and composer, son of **Johan Ole Emil Horneman;** b. Copenhagen, Dec. 17, 1840; d. there, June 8, 1906. He studied at the Leipzig Cons. (1858–60), where he became a friend of Grieg. He composed light music under various pseudonyms; returning to Copenhagen, he organized a concert society there; then was founder-director of the Koncertforeningen (1874–79) and of his own Cons. (1880–1906). He wrote an opera, *Aladdin* (Copenhagen, Nov. 18, 1888), 2 string quartets, and numerous songs.

Horneman, Johan Ole Emil, Danish publisher and composer, father of **Christian Frederik Emil Horneman;** b. Copenhagen, May 13, 1809; d. there, May 29, 1870. He composed music in a popular vein; in 1846, established a publishing firm with Emil Erslev. His collection of piano pieces, *Nordiske sange uden tekst* (Nordic Songs without Text), enjoyed some popularity; he further publ. a piano manual, *Ny praktisk Pianoforteskole.*

Horner, Ralph Joseph, English conductor and composer; b. Newport, Monmouthshire, April 28, 1848; d. Winnipeg, Canada, April 7, 1926. He studied at the Leipzig Cons. (1864–67) with Moscheles, Reinecke, and Plaidy. On his return to England, he was active as a choral conductor; also conducted light opera. From 1906 to 1909 he was in N.Y.; then settled in Winnipeg, where he became director of the Imperial Academy of Music and Arts and conductor of the Oratorio Soc. (1909–12). He wrote the operas *Confucius, Amy Rosbart,* and *The Belles of Barcelona;* the oratorios *St. Peter* and *David's 1st Victory; Torch Dance* for Orch.; many sacred cantatas, anthems, piano pieces, songs.

Hornstein, Robert von, German composer; b. Donaueschingen, Dec. 6, 1833; d. Munich, July 19, 1890. He studied at the Leipzig Cons.; then went to Munich, where he became a teacher at the municipal school of music. He was a close friend of Wagner; composed operas in a Romantic vein; one of these, *Adam und Eva,* was produced in Munich in 1870; other works are a ballet, *Der Blumen Rache;* incidental music to Shakespeare's *As You Like It;* many songs.

Horovitz, Joseph, Austrian-born English conductor, teacher, and composer; b. Vienna, May 26, 1926. He was taken to England after the Anschluss in 1938, and studied music at New College, Oxford, gaining his degree of B.Mus. there; then went to Paris to take a course with Nadia Boulanger; then was active as a theater and sym. conductor, and taught at the Royal College of Music in London (from 1961). He developed a series of mannerisms that, when synthesized, became a recognizable style: modernistic without solemnity, appealing without crudity, and often cachinnogenic.

WORKS: Operas: *Gentleman's Island* (Cheltenham, July 9, 1959) and *The Dumb Wife* (Antwerp, Jan. 10, 1972); 11 ballets; *Fantasia on a Theme of Couperin* for Strings (London, July 29, 1962); Trumpet Concerto (1963); *Horizon Overture* (1972); *Jubilee Toy Symphony* (1977); 5 string quartets; Cello Sonata (1951); Oboe Quartet (1956); *Horrortorio,* a horror oratorio (1959); *Malicious Madrigal* for Voices (1970); *Samson* for Baritone, Chorus, and Brass Band (London, Oct. 8, 1977).

Horowitz, Richard, American composer and instrumentalist; b. Buffalo, Jan. 6, 1949. In 1968 he became a pianist with Alan Sylvia's Orch., playing at European festivals. He returned to America in 1969 to study at Antioch College, but difficulties with the selective service led to a decade-long exodus to Europe and North Africa. From 1970 to 1980 he studied electronic music in Paris, and microtonal modulation and the ney (reed flute) in Morocco with Kasmi Nacquisabundi. He composed for the Mabou Mines and choreographer Alice Farley; he performed with Anthony Braxton, Jon Hassell, and David Byrne. His recordings include *Oblique Sequences/Solo Ney Improvisations No. 1* (1979; recorded at IRCAM) and *Solo Ney Improvisations No. 3* (recorded at the Stanford Computer Music Center); he also collaborated with Daniel Kobialka on the album *Memoire* (1982). His film scores include *The Sheltering Sky* (1990; directed by Bertolucci with screenplay by Paul Bowles). In 1981 he began a remarkable collaboration with the Iranian-born American vocalist, dancer, and composer Sussan Deiheim (b. Teheran, Dec. 14, 1956); their works are based on a dense tangle of Middle Eastern, jazz, and avant-garde styles, and involve improvisation, electronics, and computer processing. The works themselves are hypnotically intense but highly formal, with structures and titles based on complex puns and paradoxes; among their stage works are *Desert Equations* (1984), *Azax/Attra* (1985), *Ibn Sabbah, Ghost of the Assassin* (N.Y., 1988), and *X-Isle Isle X* (1989). They also collaborated on a recording, *Abstract Quotients* (1984).

Horowitz, Vladimir, Russian-born American pianist of legendary fame; b. Berdichev, Oct. 1, 1903; d. N.Y., Nov. 5, 1989. Reared in a musically inclined Jewish family, he began playing piano in his early childhood under the direction of his mother, a professional pianist and later an instructor at the Kiev Cons. His other teachers were Sergei Tarnowsky and Felix Blumenfeld. He made his 1st public appearance in a recital in Kiev on May 30, 1920, that marked the opening of a fantastically successful career. The revolutionary events in Russia did not prevent him from giving concerts in and around Kiev until he decided to leave Russia; his 1st official concert abroad took place in Berlin on Jan. 2, 1926. Arriving in Paris in 1928, he took brief instruction with Alfred Cortot, and on Jan. 12 of that same year, he made his American debut in Tchaikovsky's 1st Piano Concerto with the N.Y. Phil. under the direction of Sir Thomas Beecham; he subsequently appeared as soloist with several other American orchs., earning the reputation of a piano virtuoso of the highest caliber, so that his very name became synonymous with pianistic excellence. He played for President Hoover at the White House in 1931, and in 1933 married Wanda Toscanini, daughter of Arturo Toscanini; he became an American citizen in 1942.

Horowitz seemed to possess every gift of public success; he was universally admired, and his concerts sold out whenever and wherever he chose to appear. His natural affinity was with the Russian repertoire; he formed a sincere friendship with Rachmaninoff, despite the disparity in their ages; Rachmaninoff himself regarded Horowitz as the greatest pianist of the century; Horowitz's performance of Rachmaninoff's 3rd Piano Concerto, which he played numerous times, was his proudest accomplishment. His performances of works by Chopin, Liszt, Schumann, and Tchaikovsky were equally incomparable. Yet amid all these successes, he seemed unable to master his own nervous system. He became subject to irrational fears of failure, and once or twice tried to cancel his engagements at the last minute; it took all the devotion and persuasive powers of his wife for him to overcome his psychological difficulties. Eventually, in 1973, he underwent shock therapy, which appeared to help. In the meantime he underwent an appendectomy, recovering normally.

Horowitz lived for a while in Europe in the hope of a salutary change of environment. During World War II, he appeared with Toscanini in numerous patriotic concerts; it was for such a celebration in N.Y.'s Central Park that he made a vertiginous transcription for piano of Sousa's *Stars and Stripes Forever,* a veritable tour de force of pianistic pyrotechnics, which he performed for years as an encore, to the delight of his audiences. On Dec. 9, 1949, he gave the world premiere of Samuel Barber's Piano Sonata in Havana. On Feb. 25, 1953, the 25th anniversary of his American debut, he gave a recital performance in Carnegie Hall in N.Y. After this recital, he withdrew from the stage, not to return for nearly 12 years. However, he enjoyed making recordings when he was free to change his successive versions in the sanctuary of a studio. He also accepted a few private pupils. He then announced a definite date for a concert in Carnegie Hall: May 9, 1965. Tickets went on sale 2 weeks in advance, and a line formed whose excitement and agitation would equal and surpass that of a queue of fans for a baseball game. Horowitz himself was so touched by this testimony of devotion that he sent hundreds of cups of coffee to the crowd to make the waiting more endurable on a rainy day.

Despite his agonies over solo performances, Horowitz had no difficulty whatsoever appearing as an accompanist to Dietrich Fischer-Dieskau; he also played trios with Mstislav Rostropovich and Isaac Stern. On Feb. 26, 1978, he played at the White House at the invitation of President Carter, a performance that coincided with the 50th anniversary of Horowitz's American debut. On May 22, 1982, at the behest of the Prince of Wales, he gave a recital in the Royal Festival Hall in London, marking his 1st appearance in Europe in 31 years. Through his recordings he formed a large following in Japan; to respond to his popularity there, he gave a series of concerts in Tokyo and other Japanese cities (June 1983). The climax of his career, which became a political event as well, was his decision to accept an invitation to revisit Russia for a series of concerts in 1986. His Steinway grand piano was tuned and cleaned and placed on a special plane to Moscow. Horowitz was accompanied on this trip by his wife, a piano tuner, and his cook. Special foods consisting of fresh sole and other delicacies were airmailed to Moscow every day. Horowitz made a short introductory speech in Russian before he played. The Russian music-lovers who filled the hall listened almost tearfully to his playing on his return to Russia after 61 years of absence. His program included works by Rachmaninoff, Tchaikovsky, and Scriabin, and also pieces by Scarlatti and Chopin.

The Russian trip seemed to give Horowitz the necessary spiritual uplift. Returning to N.Y., he resumed his concert and recording career. He was awarded the U.S. Medal of Freedom by President Reagan in 1986, and the National Medal of Arts in 1989. He made his last recording on Nov. 1 of that year; 4 days later, in the afternoon, he suddenly collapsed and died of a heart attack. His passing created a universal feeling of loss the world over. His body lay in state in N.Y. and was then flown by his wife to Italy, where it was interred in the Toscanini family plot in Milan.

BIBL.: A. Chasins, *Speaking of Pianists* (N.Y., 1957; 2nd ed., 1961); H. Schonberg, *The Great Pianists* (N.Y., 1963; 2nd ed., rev., 1987); G. Plaskin, *H.: A Biography* (highly controversial, containing unauthorized material of dubious authenticity; N.Y., 1983).

Horsley, Charles Edward, English organist and composer, son of **William Horsley;** b. London, Dec. 16, 1822; d. N.Y., Feb. 28, 1876. He was a pupil of his father; then studied with Moscheles. In Leipzig he became friendly with Mendelssohn, who instructed him in composition. Upon his return to London, he obtained a post as organist of St. John's (1853–57); wrote the oratorios *David, Joseph,* and *Gideon;* incidental music to Milton's *Comus.* In 1866 he went to Australia, and served as organist in Melbourne. There he wrote an ode, *Euterpe,* for the opening of the Town Hall (1870). He eventually settled in N.Y. His *Text Book of Harmony* was publ. posthumously (1876).

Horsley, William, English organist and composer, father of **Charles Edward Horsley;** b. London, Nov. 15, 1774; d. there, June 12, 1858. He had little formal study, but his friendly association with John Callcott, the composer of glees, led him to try his hand at the composition of light vocal pieces. He married Callcott's daughter in 1813. He was instrumental in the establishment of the choral society Concentores Sodales (1798–1847), for which he wrote many anthems, catches, and glees; was also a founder of the Phil. Soc. of London (1813); occupied various posts as church organist. Many of his songs (*See the Chariot at Hand, O Nightingale,* etc.) were frequently sung. He further publ. 5 albums of glees (1801–27), hymn tunes, canons, piano pieces, etc.; also *An Explanation of the Musical Intervals* (London, 1825) and *An Introduction to the Study of Practical Harmony and Modulation* (London, 1847).

Horst, Anthon van der, Dutch composer, conductor, and organist; b. Amsterdam, June 20, 1899; d. Hilversum, March 7, 1965. He studied composition with Zweers, and piano and organ with de Pauw at the Amsterdam Cons.; won the Prix d'Excellence for organ in 1919. He served as an organist of the English Reformed Church in Amsterdam (1918–41) and of the Netherlands Protestant League in Hilversum (1944–55); was prof. of organ and conducting at the Amsterdam Cons. (1936–65). In some of his organ and piano works he adopted the scale of alternating tones and semitones known in the Netherlands as "Pijper's scales," which he called "modus conjunctus."

WORKS: 3 syms.: No. 1 (1935–37); No. 2, *Divertimento pittorale* (1954); No. 3, with Chorus (1959); *Choros I–VIII,* 8 separate works for Soloists, Chorus, and Orch., based on various texts (1931–58); *Rembrandt Cantata* (1956); *Nocturne funèbre* for Orch. (1950–51); *Concerto per organo romantico* for Organ and Orch. (1952); *Concerto spagnuolo* for Violin and Orch. (1953; Groningen, May 26, 1965); 3 *études symphoniques* (1954); *Concerto in Baroque Style* for Organ and Strings (1960); *Reflexions sonores* for Orch. (1962); *Ricercar svelato* for Brass, Organ, and Strings (1963); *Salutation joyeuse* for Orch. (1964); *Hymn* for Solo Soprano (1935); Suite for Solo Cello (1941); *Suite in modo conjuncto* for Organ (1943); *Partita diverse sopra Psalm 8* for Organ (1947); *Tema con variazioni in modo conjuncto* for Piano (1950); *Sonata in modo conjuncto* for 2 Pianos (1951); Suite for 31-tone Organ (1953); *Theme, Variations, and Fugue* for Flute, Violin, and Viola (1957); Sextet for Flute and Strings; songs; choruses.

Horst, Louis, American composer; b. Kansas City, Mo., Jan. 12, 1884; d. N.Y., Jan. 23, 1964. He studied violin and piano in San Francisco, and composition with Richard Stöhr in Vienna, as well as with Max Persin and Riegger in N.Y. (1925). From 1915 to 1925 he was music director of the Denishawn Dance Co., and from 1926 to 1948, of Martha Graham's dance company, for which he wrote a number of works that played a crucial role in the development of modern dance. He wrote extensively on the subject of music and dance; founded and ed. the journal *Dance Observer* (1934) and *Modern Dance Forms* (with C. Russell; 1961). He was also active as a teacher at Bennington (Vt.) College (1934–45), Columbia Univ. Teachers College (1938–41), and the Juilliard School of Music in N.Y. (1958–63).

BIBL.: E. Pease, *L. H.: His Theories on Modern Dance Composition* (diss., Univ. of Michigan, 1953).

Horszowski, Mieczyslaw, remarkable Polish pianist; b. Lemberg, June 23, 1892. He was a certified child prodigy who made his 1st public appearance at the age of 9 playing Beethoven's 1st Piano Concerto with the Warsaw Phil. He studied piano with Soltys and Melcer in Lemberg; was then sent to

Vienna, where Leschetizky accepted him as a private pupil. On Feb. 16, 1906, he played a solo recital at La Scala in Milan; he subsequently played privately for the Pope and for the King of England, then undertook an extensive concert tour in Europe; also played chamber music with Casals. In 1941 he joined the faculty of the Curtis Inst. of Music in Philadelphia. Among his most prominent students were Seymour Lipkin, Peter Serkin, and Cecile Licad. In 1981, at the age of 89, he married his longtime companion, the Italian pianist Bice Costa; it was the 1st marriage for both. Indefatigable, Horszowski continued his career as a concert pianist well into his 90s. His performance in Los Angeles on Jan. 31, 1990, in a program of Bach, Beethoven, Schumann, and Chopin, aroused wonderment for its impeccable interpretation and all but faultless technique. Astonished critics await his repeat performance as a full-fledged centenarian.

Horton, Austin Asadata Dafora, Nigerian composer; b. Freetown, Sierra Leone, West Africa, Aug. 4, 1890; d. N.Y., March 4, 1965. As a youth, he became deeply interested in African folk dance festivals and studied the culture of many African tribes. He then organized a dance group in Germany. He settled in the U.S. in 1921, devoting himself to the propagation of African art, coaching singers, dancers, and drummers for performance of African dances. He utilized authentic African melorhythms in several of his stage spectacles, for which he also arranged the musical scores. Of these, *Kykunkor, the Witch,* produced at the Unity Theater Studio in N.Y. on May 7, 1934, attracted considerable attention. He also produced a dance drama, *Tunguru.*

Horvat, Milan, Yugoslav conductor; b. Pakrac, July 28, 1919. He studied piano, composition, and conducting at the Zagreb Academy of Music. In 1946 he became a conductor of the Zagreb Phil. From 1958 to 1969 he was chief conductor of the Belgrade Phil.; later directed the Austrian Radio Sym. Orch. in Vienna (1969–75) and the Zagreb Radio Sym. Orch. (from 1975); also made guest appearances in Europe, conducting both orch. and operatic performances.

Horvat, Stanko, Croatian composer; b. Zagreb, March 12, 1930. He studied composition with Šulek at the Zagreb Academy of Music, graduating in 1956; then took a course with Aubin at the Paris Cons. and private composition lessons with Leibowitz (1958–59); returning to Yugoslavia, he was appointed to the music faculty of the Zagreb Academy in 1961. In his style of composition he traversed successively a period of neo-Classical mannerisms, serialism in its dodecaphonic aspect, aleatory expressionism, and sonorism; eventually he returned to a median technique of pragmatic modernism.
    Works: Television opera, *3 Legends* (Salzburg, 1971); ballet, *Izabranik* (The Chosen One; 1961); Sinfonietta (1954); Sym. (1956); *Concerto rustico* for Strings (1958); Piano Concerto (1966; Zagreb, April 3, 1967); *Choral* for Strings (1967); *Taches* for Piano and Chamber Orch. (Graz, Sept. 26, 1968); *Hymnus* for Orch. (1969); *Perpetuum mobile* for String Orch. (Zagreb, May 9, 1971); *Krik* (The Cry), after García Lorca, for Mezzosoprano and Orch. (1968; Zagreb, March 19, 1969); cantata, *Jama* (The Pit; Zagreb, Dec. 18, 1971); *Choral Variations* for String Quartet (1953); *Contrasts* for String Quartet (1963); *Rondo* for String Quartet (1967); *Variants* for Piano (1965); *Sonnant* for Piano (1970).

Horvath, Josef Maria, Austrian composer of Hungarian descent; b. Pécs, Dec. 20, 1931. He studied piano and composition at the Liszt Academy in Budapest; in 1956 he went to Salzburg, where he studied composition and took instruction in electronic music. Subsequently he became a composition teacher at the Salzburg Mozarteum.
    Works: *Entropia,* sym. in 5 movements (1961); Trio for Violin, Horn, and Piano (1963); a group of works under the generic title *Redundance,* for Wind Octet and/or String Quartet (1970); *Origines* for Chamber Group (1975).

Horwitz, Karl, Austrian composer; b. Vienna, Jan. 1, 1884; d. Salzburg, Aug. 18, 1925. He studied with Schoenberg, and adopted an atonal idiom. He was active in organizing the Donaueschingen Festivals (1921) and other societies devoted to modern music; among his works are a symphonic poem, *Vom Tode;* 2 string quartets; several song cycles. In 1924 he suffered a loss of hearing, as a result of disease, and died shortly afterward.

Hoschna (Hoschner), Karl, Czech-American composer; b. Kuschwarda, Aug. 16, 1876; d. N.Y., Dec. 23, 1911. He studied piano, harmony, and composition at the Vienna Cons.; then played oboe in an Austrian army band before going to the U.S. (1896), where he was an oboist in Victor Herbert's orch. After working as a music copyist and arranger, he turned to composing, turning out a number of successful operettas, mostly in collaboration with the lyricist Otto Harbach.
    Works: operettas: *The Belle of the West* (Chicago, Oct. 29, 1905); *The Girl from Broadway* (Philadelphia, Dec. 3, 1906); *3 Twins* (N.Y., June 15, 1908); *Prince Humbug* (Boston, Sept. 3, 1908); *The Photo Shop* (1910); *Bright Eyes* (N.Y., Feb. 28, 1910); *Madame Sherry* (N.Y., Aug. 30, 1910); *Katie Did* (Chicago, Feb. 18, 1911); *Jumping Jupiter* (N.Y., March 6, 1911); *Dr. Deluxe* (N.Y., April 17, 1911); *The Girl of My Dreams* (N.Y., Aug. 7, 1911); *The Fascinating Widow* (N.Y., Sept. 11, 1911); *The Wall Street Girl* (N.Y., April 15, 1912).

Hosmer, Lucius, American composer; b. South Acton, Mass., Aug. 14, 1870; d. Jefferson, N.H., May 9, 1935. He studied with Chadwick at the New England Cons.; wrote a "romantic comic opera," *The Rose of the Alhambra* (Rochester, N.Y., 1905; N.Y., Feb. 4, 1907); a comic opera, *The Walking Delegate* (rev. and produced under the title *The Koreans*); various light pieces for Orch.: *On Tiptoe, Chinese Wedding Procession, Southern Rhapsody, Northern Rhapsody, Ethiopian Rhapsody,* etc.; also songs.

Hostinský, Otakar, eminent Czech esthetician; b. Martiněves, Jan. 2, 1847; d. Prague, Jan. 19, 1910. He studied law at the Univ. of Prague (1865–66) and philosophy and esthetics at the Univ. of Munich (Ph.D., 1868); then studied composition with Smetana (1871). He was a music critic and an ed. of literary journals before becoming an instructor of esthetics at the Univ. of Prague (1877); was made a prof. there (1892); he also taught music history at the Prague Cons. (1882–86). He developed what he termed concrete formalism (in opposition to Herbart's abstract formalism) in the study of esthetics; he also made important contributions to analytical methods of ethnomusicological research and to the study of harmony.
    Writings: *Das Musikalisch-schöne und das Gesamthkunstwerk vom Standpunkte der formalen Aesthetik* (Leipzig, 1877); *Die Lehre von den musikalischen Klängen* (Prague, 1879); *O významu praktických idejí Herbartových pro všeobecnou esthetiku* (The Importance of Herbart's Practical Ideas for General Esthetics; Prague, 1881); *O české deklamaci hudebni* (Czech Musical Declamation; Prague, 1886); *Herbarts Aesthetik* (Hamburg, 1892); *36 nápěvů světských pisni českého lidu z XVI. stoleti* (36 Melodies from Secular Czech Folk Song of the 16th Century; Prague, 1892; 2nd ed., 1957); *Jan Blahoslav a Jan Josquin* (Prague, 1896); *Hudba v Čechách* (Music in Bohemia; Prague, 1900); *B. Smetana a jeho boj o moderni českou hudbu* (Smetana and His Struggle for Modern Czech Music; Prague, 1901; 2nd ed., 1941); *O socialisaci uměni* (The Socialization of Art; Prague, 1903); *Česká světská piseň lidová* (Czech Secular Folk Song; Prague, 1906); *Uměni a společnost* (Art and Society; Prague, 1907); *Česká hudba 1864–1904* (Czech Music 1864–1904; Prague, 1909).
    Bibl.: J. Racek, "O. H., tvůrce a zakladatel české hudební vědy" (O. H., Creator and Founder of Czech Musicology), *Musikologie,* II (1949); Z. Strejc, *Uměni a společnost v teoretickém díle O. Hostinského* (Art and Society in O. H.'s Theoretical Work; diss., Univ. of Brno, 1969); L. Juřica, *Hostinského nauka o harmonii* (H.'s Theory of Harmony; diss., Univ. of Brno, 1972); Z. Strejc, "O. H. a sociologie uměni" (O.H. and the Sociology of Arts), *Hudební Věda,* X (1973).

Hothby, John, English music theorist and composer; b. c.1415; d. 1487. He was a student at Oxford; was a member of the Carmelite order; lived in Florence, Italy, about 1450, and was known there under the Italianized name Ottobi; was then in Lucca (1467–86), where he taught in canonic schools. In 1486 he was recalled to England by Henry VII. A. Seay ed. *The Musical Works of John Hothby* in Corpus Mensurabilis Musicae, XXXIII (1964).

WRITINGS: *Ars plane musica; Regulae supra proportionem; De canto figurato; Regulae supra contrapunctum; Regulae de monocordo; Quid est proportio?; Tractatus quarundam regularum;* etc. A complete ed. of his theoretical writings is being prepared in the Corpus Scriptorum de Musica series.
BIBL.: U. Kornmüller, "Johann H.," *Kirchenmusikalisches Jahrbuch,* VIII (1893); A. Schmidt, *Die Calliopea legale des J. H.* (Leipzig, 1897).

Hotter, Hans, greatly esteemed German bass-baritone; b. Offenbach am Main, Jan. 19, 1909. He studied voice with Matthäus Roemer, making his debut as the Speaker in *Die Zauberflöte* in Opava in 1929; was a member of the opera there from 1930, and also sang at the German Theater in Prague (1932–34). He then sang at the Hamburg State Opera (1934–45), Bavarian State Opera in Munich (1937–72), Berlin State Opera (1939–42), and the Vienna State Opera (1939–72). He made his 1st appearance at London's Covent Garden with the visiting Vienna State Opera in 1947; made appearances regularly at Covent Garden until 1967; was a principal singer at the Bayreuth Festivals (1952–64), where he became renowned for his portrayal of Wotan; he also distinguished himself in such roles as Kurwenal, Hans Sachs, Amfortas, Gurnemanz, Marke, and Pogner. He made his Metropolitan Opera debut in N.Y. as the Dutchman in *Der fliegende Holländer* on Nov. 9, 1950, remaining on its roster until 1954; also sang at La Scala in Milan, the Paris Opéra, the Salzburg Festival, the Chicago Opera, and the Teatro Colón in Buenos Aires. He became a member of the faculty of the Vienna Hochschule für Musik in 1977. In addition to his Wagnerian roles, Hotter also sang in several 1st performances of operas by Richard Strauss; created the roles of the Kommandant in *Friedenstag* (Munich, July 24, 1938), of Olivier in *Capriccio* (Munich, Oct. 28, 1942), and of Jupiter in *Die Liebe der Danae* (public dress rehearsal, Salzburg, Aug. 16, 1944).
BIBL.: B. Wessling, *H. H.* (Bremen, 1966); P. Turing, *H. H.: Man and Artist* (London, 1983).

Hotteterre, family of French musicians: **Nicolas Hotteterre** (b. 1637; d. Paris, May 10, 1694), a hurdy-gurdy player; his brother **Martin Hotteterre** (d. 1712), also a hurdy-gurdy player and a performer at the court ballets; **Louis Hotteterre** (d. 1719), son of Nicolas, who played flute at the French court (1664–1714); his brother **Nicolas Hotteterre** (d. Paris, Dec. 4, 1727), who played flute and oboe in Lully's orch. at the court of Louis XIV; their cousin **Jacques Hotteterre** (b. Sept. 29, 1674; d. Paris, July 16, 1762), surnamed "le Romain," evidently owing to his long sojourns in Rome, popularized the transverse (German) flute at the French court and publ. several manuals on that instrument and others: *Principes de la flûte traversière ou flûte d'Allemagne, de la flûte à bec ou flûte douce et du hautbois* (Paris, 1707; sometimes attributed to Louis; the 1728 ed. was reprinted in facsimile, Kassel, 1941; Eng. tr. by P. Douglas, N.Y., 1968; 2nd ed., 1983); *L'Art de préluder sur la flûte traversière, sur la flûte à bec, etc.* (Paris, 1712; 2nd ed. under the title *Méthode pour apprendre . . . ,* c.1765); *Méthode pour la musette* (1738); he also wrote sonatas, duos, trios, suites, *rondes (chansons à danser),* and minuets for flute.
BIBL.: J. Carlez, *Les H.* (Caen, 1877); E. Thoinan, *Les H. et les Chédeville* (Paris, 1894); N. Mauger, *Les H., Nouvelles recherches* (Paris, 1912); J. Bowers, "The H. Family of Woodwind Instrument Makers," in R. de Reede Broekmans and V. Poppel, eds., *Concerning the Flute* (Amsterdam, 1984).

Houdard, Georges, French writer on music; b. Neuilly-sur-Seine, March 30, 1860; d. Paris, Feb. 28, 1913. He studied with L. Hillemacher and Massenet at the Paris Cons.; then devoted himself exclusively to writing on early church music; publ. valuable treatises and also composed some sacred music.
WRITINGS: *L'Art dit grégorien d'après la notation neumatique* (1897); *L'Évolution de l'art musical et l'art grégorien* (1902); *Aristoxène de Tarente* (1905); *La Rythmique intuitive* (1906); *Textes théoriques; Vademecum de la rythmique grégorienne des X⁰ et XI⁰ siècles* (1912).

Hough, Stephen (Andrew Gill), English pianist; b. Heswall, Cheshire, Nov. 22, 1961. He began piano lessons at age 6, later becoming a pupil of Gordon Green and Derrick Wyndham at the Royal Northern College of Music in Manchester and of Adele Marcus at the Juilliard School in N.Y. In 1982 he won the 1st Terence Judd Award and made his London debut; in 1983 he won the Naumburg International Piano Competition in N.Y. He made his N.Y. debut in 1984; in subsequent seasons he appeared as a soloist with many of the world's leading orchs. and toured widely as a recitalist. His vast repertoire ranges from early keyboard works to contemporary scores.

Houseley, Henry, English-American organist, conductor, and composer; b. Sutton in Ashfield, Nottinghamshire, Sept. 20, 1852; d. Denver, March 13, 1925. He studied with Michael Costa and E.H. Turpin; was an organist in Derby and Nottingham and was on the faculty at the Univ. of Nottingham. He settled in Denver (1888), becoming organist at the Episcopal Cathedral of St. John in the Wilderness (1888–92) and director of the Denver Choral Soc. (1894); he also founded a sym. orch. (1900). His best-known work was the cantata *Omar Khayyám* (Denver, June 1, 1916); he also wrote 7 operas, some orch. pieces, anthems, ballads, and keyboard music.
BIBL.: S. Linscome, "H. H., Versatile Musician of Early Denver," *Colorado Magazine,* XLIX (1972).

Housman, Rosalie, American composer; b. San Francisco, June 25, 1888; d. N.Y., Oct. 28, 1949. She studied with Arthur Foote in Boston; also took lessons in N.Y. with Ernest Bloch; composed *Color Sequence* for Soprano and Small Orch.; women's choruses; children's pieces; songs.

Houston, Whitney, black American singer of popular music; b. Newark, N.J., Aug. 9, 1963. She joined the choir of the local New Hope Baptist Church when she was 9, later receiving vocal coaching from her mother, the gospel and rhythm-and-blues singer "Cissy" Houston, with whom she sang in clubs and on recordings. After graduating from high school, she attempted to find a niche as a singer, but it was not until the release of the 1983 album *Paul Jabara and Friends,* on which she sang *Eternal Love,* that her career really began. After several television appearances and the release of her single *All at Once,* which proved enormously popular in Europe, she scored a spectacular success with her album *Whitney Houston* (1985). One of its singles, *Saving All My Love for You,* won her a Grammy Award as best female pop vocalist of the year.
BIBL.: *Current Biography* (Nov. 1986); K. Greenberg, *W. H.* (Minneapolis, 1988).

Houtmann, Jacques, French conductor; b. Mirecourt, March 27, 1935. He studied at the Nancy Cons., and at the École Normale de Musique in Paris with Jean Fournet and Henri Dutilleux; then took courses in conducting with Franco Ferrara in Rome. He won 1st prize in the conductors' competition in Besançon (1961) and the Mitropoulos Competition in N.Y. (1964); was for a season an assistant conductor of the N.Y. Phil. (1965–66). He then returned to France, and served as conductor with the Rhône-Alpes Phil. in Lyons (1967–71). In 1971 he went again to the U.S., and was appointed music director of the Richmond (Va.) Sym. Orch. (until 1986); then was music director of the Lorraine Phil. in Metz (from 1986).

Hovhaness (Chakmakjian), Alan (Vaness Scott), prolific and proficient American composer of Armenian-Scottish descent; b. Somerville, Mass., March 8, 1911. He took piano lessons with Adelaide Proctor and with Heinrich Gebhard in Boston; his academic studies were at Tufts Univ.; in 1932 he enrolled in the New England Cons. of Music in Boston as a student of Frederick Converse; then was a scholarship student of Martinů at the Berkshire Music Center at Tanglewood in 1942. From his earliest attempts at composition, he took great interest in the musical roots of his paternal ancestry, studying the folk songs assembled by the Armenian musician Komitas. He gradually came to believe that music must reflect the natural monody embodied in national songs and ancient church hymns. In his music he adopted modal melodies and triadic harmonies. This *parti pris* had the dual effect of alienating him from the milieu of modern composers while exercising great attraction for the music consumer at large. By dint of ceaseless repetition of melodic patterns and relentless dynamic tension, he succeeded in creating a sui generis type of impressionistic monody, flowing on the shimmering surfaces of euphony, free from the upsetting intrusion of heterogeneous dissonance; an air of mysticism pervades his music, aided by the programmatic titles which he often assigns to his compositions. After completion of his studies, he served on the faculty of the New England Cons. of Music (1948–51); then moved to N.Y. He was awarded 2 Guggenheim fellowships (1954 and 1958). In 1959 he received a Fulbright fellowship and traveled to India and Japan, where he collected native folk songs for future use and presented his own works, as pianist and conductor, receiving acclaim. In 1962 he was engaged as composer-in-residence at the Univ. of Hawaii; then traveled to Korea. He eventually settled in Seattle. A composer of relentless fecundity, he produced over 60 syms.; several operas, quasi-operas, and pseudo-operas; and an enormous amount of choral music. The totality of his output is in excess of 370 opus numbers. In a laudable spirit of self-criticism, he destroyed 7 of his early syms. and began numbering them anew so that his 1st numbered sym. (subtitled *Exile*) was chronologically his 8th. He performed a similar auto-da-fé on other dispensable pieces. Among his more original compositions is a symphonic score *And God Created Great Whales*, in which the voices of humpback whales recorded on tape were used as a solo with the orch.; the work was performed to great effect in the campaign to save the whale from destruction by human (and inhuman) predators.

WORKS: STAGE: OPERAS (each to the composer's own libretto): *Etchmiadzin* (1946); *The Blue Flame* (San Antonio, Dec. 13, 1959); *Spirit of the Avalanche* (Tokyo, Feb. 15, 1963); *Wind Drum* and *The Burning House* (both at Gatlinburg, Tenn., Aug. 23, 1964); *Pilate* (Los Angeles, June 26, 1966); *The Travelers* (Foothill College, Los Altos Hills, Calif., April 22, 1967); *Pericles*, grand opera (1975); *Tale of the Sun Goddess Going into the Stone House* (1979). **OPERETTA:** *Afton Water*, on the play of William Saroyan (1951). **BALLETS:** *Killer of Enemies* (1983); *God the Revenger* (1986).

SYMS. (the numbering does not always coincide with the chronological order of composition): No. 1, *Exile* (BBC, London, May 26, 1939); No. 2, *Mysterious Mountain* (Houston, Oct. 31, 1955, Stokowski conducting); No. 3 (N.Y., Oct. 14, 1956); No. 4 for Concert Band (Pittsburgh, June 28, 1959); No. 5, *Short Symphony* (1959); No. 6, *Celestial Gate* (1959); No. 7, *Nanga Parvat*, for Band (1959); No. 8, *Arjuna* (1947; Madras, India, Feb. 1, 1960); No. 9, *St. Vartan* (N.Y., March 11, 1951); No. 10 (1959); No. 11, *All Men Are Brothers* (1960; New Orleans, March 21, 1961; rev. version, New Orleans, March 31, 1970); No. 12, with Chorus (1960); No. 13 (1953); No. 14, *Ararat* (1960); No. 15, *Silver Pilgrimage* (N.Y., March 28, 1963); No. 16, *Korean Kayageum*, for Strings and Korean Percussion Instruments (Seoul, Jan. 26, 1963); No. 17 for Metal Orch., commissioned by the American Metallurgical Congress (Cleveland, Oct. 23, 1963); No. 18, *Circe* (1964); No. 19, *Vishnu* (N.Y., June 2, 1967); No. 20, *3 Journeys to a Holy Mountain*, for Concert Band (1968); No. 21, *Etchmiadzin* (1968); No. 22, *City of Light* (1970); No. 23, *Ani*, for Band (1972); No. 24, *Majnun*, with Chorus (1973; Lubbock, Texas, Jan. 25, 1974); No. 25, *Odysseus*, for Chamber Orch. (1973; London, April 10, 1974); No. 26, *Consolation* (San Jose, Calif., Oct. 24, 1975); No. 27 (1975); No. 28 (1976); No. 29 for Horn and Orch. (Minneapolis, May 4, 1977); No. 30 (1976); No.

31 for Strings (Seattle, Dec. 7, 1977); No. 32 for Chamber Orch. (1977); No. 33 for Chamber Orch. (1978); No. 34 (1977); No. 35 for Korean Instruments and Orch. (Seoul, June 9, 1978); No. 36 for Flute and Orch., op. 312 (Washington, D.C., Jan. 16, 1979; Rampal, soloist; Rostropovich conducting); No. 37 (1978); No. 38 for Soprano and Orch. (1978); No. 39 for Guitar and Orch. (1978); No. 40 for Brass, Timpani, and Orch. (1979; Interlochen, April 9, 1982); No. 41, *Mountain Sunset* (1979); No. 42 (1979); No. 43 (1979; Aptos, Calif., Aug. 20, 1981); No. 44 (1980); No. 45 (1979); No. 46, *To the Green Mountains* (Burlington, Vt., May 2, 1981); No. 47, *Walla Walla, Land of Many Waters*, for Soprano and Orch. (Walla Walla, Wash., Nov. 24, 1981); No. 48, *Vision of Andromeda* (Miami, Fla., June 21, 1982); No. 49, *Christmas*, for Strings (1981); No. 50, *Mount St. Helens* (1982); No. 51 for Trumpet and Strings (1982); No. 52, *Journey to Vega* (1983); No. 53, *Star Dawn*, for Band (1983); No. 54 (1983); No. 55 (1983); No. 56 (1983); No. 57, *Cold Mountain*, for Tenor, Soprano, Clarinet, and Strings (1983); No. 58, *Sacra*, for Soprano, Baritone, Chorus, and Orch. (Valparaiso, Ind., Nov. 10, 1985); No. 59 (Bellevue, Wash., Jan. 28, 1985); No. 60, *To the Appalachian Mountains* (Knoxville, Tenn., April 24, 1985); No. 61 (Boise, Idaho, Oct. 4, 1986); No. 62, *Let Not Man Forget*, for Baritone and Strings (1987); No. 63, *Loon Lake* (1988).

CONCERTOS: Concerto for Cello and Orch. (1936); *Lousadzak* (Coming of Light) for Piano and Strings (1944; Boston, Feb. 4, 1945); *Return and Rebuild the Desolate Places*, concerto for Trumpet and Strings (N.Y., June 17, 1945); *Asori*, concerto for Flute, Cornet, Bassoon, Trumpet, Timpani, and Strings (1946); *Sosi*, concerto for Violin, Piano, Percussion, and Strings (1948; N.Y., March 6, 1949); *Artik*, concerto for Horn and Orch. (1948; Rochester, N.Y., May 7, 1954); *Zertik Parkim*, concerto for Piano and Chamber Orch. (1948); *Elibris* (God of Dawn), concerto for Flute and Strings (1949; San Francisco, Jan. 26, 1950); *Khaldis*, concerto for 4 Trumpets, Piano, and Percussion (1951); *Talin*, concerto for Viola and String Orch. (1952); Accordion Concerto (1959); Concerto for Harp and Strings (1973); Concerto for Euphonium and Orch. (1977); Concerto for Guitar and Orch. (1979); Concerto for Soprano Saxophone and Orch. (1980); Concerto No. 2 for Guitar and Strings (1985). Also 8 numbered concertos: No. 1, *Arevakal* (Season of the Sun), for Orch. (1951; N.Y., Feb. 18, 1952); No. 2 for Violin and Strings (1951–57); No. 3, *Diran*, for Baritone Horn or Trombone, and Strings (1948); No. 4 for Orch. (1952; Louisville, Ky., Feb. 20, 1954); No. 5 for Piano and Strings (1952); No. 6 for Harmonica and Strings (1953); No. 7 for Orch. (1953); No. 8 for Orch. (1953).

OTHER WORKS FOR ORCH.: *Storm on Mt. Wildcat* (1931); *Celestial Fantasy* (1944); *3 Armenian Rhapsodies* (1944); *Khiriam Hairis* for Trumpet and Strings (1944); *Tzaikerk* (Evening Song) for Orch. (1945); *Kohar* for Orch. (1946); *Forest of Prophetic Sounds* for Orch. (1948); *Overture* for Trombone and Strings (1948); *Janabar*, 5 hymns for Violin, Trumpet, Piano, and Strings (1949; N.Y., March 11, 1951); Prelude and Quadruple Fugue for Orch. (1955); *Meditation on Orpheus* for Orch. (1957–58); *Copernicus*, tone poem (1960); *Mountain of Prophecy* for Orch. (1960); *Meditation on Zeami*, symphonic poem (1963; N.Y., Oct. 5, 1964); *Ukiyo, Floating World*, tone poem (1964; Salt Lake City, Jan. 30, 1965); *Fantasy on Japanese Wood Prints* for Xylophone and Orch. (Chicago, July 4, 1964); *The Holy City* for Orch. (Portland, Oreg., April 11, 1967); *Fra Angelico*, symphonic poem (Detroit, March 21, 1968); *Mountain and Rivers without End* for 10 Instruments (1968); *And God Created Great Whales* for Orch., with Voices of Humpback Whales recorded on Tape (1969; N.Y., June 11, 1970); *A Rose for Emily*, ballet for Orch. (1970); *Dawn on Mt. Tahoma* for Orch. (1973); *Fanfare to the New Atlantis* for Orch. (1975); *Ode to Freedom* for Violin and Orch. (Wolf Trap Farm Park, near Washington, D.C., July 3, 1976; Yehudi Menuhin, soloist); *Rubáiyát* for Narrator, Accordion, and Orch. (1975; N.Y., May 20, 1977).

CHAMBER: Piano Quintet No. 1 (1926; rev. 1962); Piano Trio (1935); String Quartet No. 1 (1936); Violin Sonata (1937);

Suite for English Horn and Bassoon (1938); *Varak* for Violin and Piano (1944); *Anahid* for Flute, English Horn, Trumpet, Timpani, Percussion, and Strings (1944); *Saris* for Violin and Piano (1946); *Haroutiun* (Resurrection), aria and fugue for Trumpet and Strings (1948); *Sosi* (Forest of Prophetic Sounds) for Violin, Piano, Horn, Timpani, Giant Tam-tam, and Strings (1948); String Quartet No. 2 (1950); *Khirgiz Suite* for Violin and Piano (1951); *Orbit No. 1* for Flute, Harp, Celesta, and Tam-tam (1952); *Orbit No. 2* for Alto Recorder and Piano (1952); *koke no kiwa* (Moss Garden) for English Horn, Clarinet, Harp, and Percussion (1954); Wind Quintet (1960); *Nagooran* for an Ensemble of South Indian Instruments (1962); String Trio (1962); Piano Quintet No. 2 (1964); Sextet for Violin and 5 Percussionists (1966); *6 Dances* for Brass Quintet (1967); *Spirit of Ink*, 9 pieces for 3 Flutes (1968); String Quartet No. 3 (1968); *Vibration Painting* for 13 String Instruments (1969); String Quartet No. 4 (1970); *The Garden of Adonis* for Flute and Harp (1971); Sonata for 2 Bassoons (1973); Clarinet Quartet (1973); *Night of a White Cat* for Clarinet and Piano (1973); *Fantasy* for Double Bass and Piano (1974); String Quartet No. 5 (1976); Suite for 4 Trumpets and Trombone (1976); Suite for Alto Saxophone and Guitar (1976); Septet for Flute, Clarinet, Bass Clarinet, Trumpet, Trombone, Double Bass, and Percussion (1976); Sonata for 2 Clarinets (1977); *Sunset on Mt. Tahoma* for 2 Trumpets, Trombone, and Organ (1978); Sonata for Clarinet and Harpsichord (1978); Saxophone Trio (1979); 2 Sonatas for 3 Trumpets and 2 Trombones (1979); sextet, *Lake Winnipesaukee* (1982); *Capuan Sonata* for Viola and Piano (1982); *Prelude and Fugue* for Brass Quartet (1983); sonata, *Spirit of Trees*, for Harp and Guitar (1983); Sonata for Clarinet and Piano (1983); *Starry Night* for Flute, Xylophone, and Harp (1984); Sonata for Alto Recorder and Harpsichord (1984); *Mountain under the Sea* for Alto Saxophone, Timpani, Vibraphone, Tam-tam, and Harp (1984).

KEYBOARD (for Piano Solo unless otherwise given): *Mountain Lullaby* (1931); *3 Preludes and Fugues* (1935); *Sonata Ricercare* (1935); *Macedonian Mountain Dance* (1937); *Do you remember the last silence?* (1957); *Poseidon Sonata* (1957); *Child of the Garden* for Piano, 4-hands (1958); *Madras Sonata* (1947; final rev., 1959); *Bardo Sonata* (1959); *Love Song Vanishing into Sounds of Crickets* (1979); *Sonata Catamount* (1980); *Sonata, Journey to Arcturus* (1981); *Hiroshige's Cat* (1982); Sonata No. 5 for Harpsichord (1982); *Sonata on the Long Total Eclipse of the Moon, July 6, 1982* (1982); *Tsugouharu Fujita's Cat* (1982); *Lake Sammamish* (1983); Organ Sonata No. 2, *Invisible Sun* (1984); *Lilydale* (1986); sonata, *Cougar Mountain* (1985); Sonata (1986).

VOCAL: *Ad Lyram* for Solo Voices, Double Chorus, and Chamber Orch. (Houston, March 12, 1957); *To the God Who Is in the Fire*, cantata (Urbana, Ill., April 13, 1957); *Magnificat* for Solo Voices, Chorus, and Chamber Orch. (1957); *Fuji*, cantata for Female Voices, Flute, Harp, and String Orch. (1960); *In the Beginning Was the Word* for Vocal Soloists, Chorus, and Orch. (1963); *Lady of Light* for Solo Voices, Chorus, and Chamber Orch. (1969); *Saturn*, 12 pieces for Soprano, Clarinet, and Piano (1971); *The Way of Jesus*, folk oratorio (St. Patrick's Cathedral, N.Y., Feb. 23, 1975); *Revelations of St. Paul*, cantata (1980; N.Y., Jan. 28, 1981); *The Waves Unbuild the Wasting Shore*, cantata for Tenor, Chorus, and Organ (1983); *Cantata Domino* for Chorus and Organ (1984); innumerable hymns, anthems, sacred and secular choruses; songs.

Hovland, Egil, Norwegian organist, music critic, and composer; b. Mysen, Oct. 18, 1924. He studied organ and composition at the Oslo Cons. (1946–49), later studying privately with Brustad (1951–52, in Oslo), Vagn Holmboe (1954, in Copenhagen), Copland (1957, at Tanglewood), and Dallapiccola (1959, in Florence). In Norway he was active as a music critic and as an organist at a church in Fredrikstad. In 1983 he was made a Knight of the Royal Order of St. Olav for his services to Norwegian music. He cultivates a peculiarly Scandinavian type of neo-Classical polyphony, but is apt to use serial techniques.

WORKS: Church opera, *Brunnen* (The Well; 1971–72; Oslo, March 17, 1982); ballets: *Dona Nobis Pacem* (1982); *Den Heliga Dansen* (1982); *Veni Creator Spiritus* (1984); *Danses de la Mort* (Bergen, June 8, 1983); Passacaglia and Fugue for String Orch. (1949); *Festival Overture* (1951); 3 syms.: No. 1, *Symphonia Veris* (Sym. of Spring; 1952–53; Oslo, Dec. 10, 1954); No. 2 (1954–55; Bergen, Nov. 8, 1956); No. 3 for Narrator, Chorus, and Orch. (1969–70; Oslo, April 9, 1970); Suite for Orch. (1954); Concertino for 3 Trumpets and Strings (1954–55); *Music for 10 Instruments* (1957); Suite for Flute and Strings (1959); *Festival Overture* for Wind Orch. (1962); *Lamenti* for Orch. (Oslo, April 24, 1964); *Rorate* for 5 Sopranos, Organ, Chamber Orch., and Tape (1966–67); *Missa vigilate* for Soprano, Baritone, Chorus, 2 Female Dancers, Organ, and Tape (1967); *Mass to the Risen Christ* for Chorus and Instruments (1968); *Rapsodi 69* for Orch. (1969); *All Saints' Mass* for Soprano, Chorus, Organ, and Instruments (1970); *Den vakreste rosen* (The Most Beautiful Rose), after Hans Christian Andersen, for Narrator, 4 Sopranos, Organ, and Orch. (1970); Trombone Concerto (1972); *Missa verbi* for Chorus, Organ, and Instruments (1972–73); Violin Concerto (1974); *Noël-Variations* for Orch. (1975); Piano Concerto (1976–77; Oslo, Dec. 1, 1977); *Tombeau de Bach* for Orch. (1977–78); *Pilgrim's Mass* for Choir, Organ, Congregation, and 9 Brasses (1982); Concerto for Piccolo, Flute, and String Orch. (1986; Oslo, April 20, 1989); Suite for Flute and Piano (1950); *Motus* for Solo Flute (1961); *Song of Songs* for Soprano, Violin, Percussion, and Piano (1962–63); *Magnificat* for Alto, Flute, and Harp (1964); *Varianti* for 2 Pianos (1964); Piano Trio (1965); 2 wind quintets (1965, 1980); *Elemento* for Organist and 2 Assistants (1965; rev. 1966); Variations for Oboe and Piano (1968–69); *I DAG* for Chorus and Instruments (1974); String Quartet (1981); numerous sacred works and organ pieces.

Howard, Ann, English mezzo-soprano; b. Norwood, July 22, 1936. She studied in London; won a Royal Opera House grant to study with Modesti in Paris; made her operatic debut at the Sadler's Wells Opera in 1964 as Czipra in *Der Zigeunerbaron*; also sang at Covent Garden, the Scottish Opera, the Welsh National Opera, and the Santa Fe Opera.

Howard, John Tasker, eminent American writer on music; b. Brooklyn, Nov. 30, 1890; d. West Orange, N.Y., Nov. 20, 1964. He attended Williams College in Williamstown, Mass.; then studied composition with Howard Brockway and Mortimer Wilson. He then devoted himself primarily to musical journalism; was managing editor of the *Musician* (1919–22); served as educational director of the Ampico Corp. (1922–28); ed. the music section of *McCall's Magazine* (1928–30) and *Cue* (1936–38); taught at Columbia Univ. (1950–54). From 1940 to 1956 he was the curator of the Americana Music Collection at the N.Y. Public Library, which he enriched to a great extent. His major achievement was the publication of several books and monographs on American music and musicians. He was also a composer of modest, but respectable, attainments. He wrote a piece for Piano and Orch., *Fantasy on a Choral Theme* (Orange, N.J., Feb. 20, 1929); also *Foster Sonatina* for Violin and Piano; piano pieces; some songs.

WRITINGS: *Our American Music* (N.Y., 1931; 4th ed., rev., 1965); *Stephen Foster, America's Troubadour* (N.Y., 1934; 2nd ed., rev., 1953); *Ethelbert Nevin* (N.Y., 1935); *Our Contemporary Composers, American Music in the 20th Century* (1941); *This Modern Music* (N.Y., 1942; new ed. by J. Lyons, 1957, under the title *Modern Music*); *The World's Great Operas* (N.Y., 1948); *A Short History of Music in America* (N.Y., 1957; with G. Bellows).

BIBL.: G. Bellows, "J.T. H.," *Notes* (Sept. 1957; with a complete list of his publ. writings).

Howard, Kathleen, Canadian-American contralto; b. Niagara Falls, Ontario, July 17, 1884; d. Los Angeles, Aug. 15, 1956. She studied in N.Y. with Bouhy and in Paris with Jean de Reszke; sang at the Metz Opera (1907–9), at Darmstadt (1909–12), at Covent Garden in London (1913), and with the Century

Opera in N.Y. (1914–15). She made her 1st appearance with the Metropolitan Opera in N.Y. in *Die Zauberflöte* (Nov. 20, 1916); remained on the staff until 1928. After her retirement from the stage, she was engaged in magazine work; was fashion ed. of *Harper's Bazaar* (1928–33); publ. an autobiography, *Confessions of an Opera Singer* (N.Y., 1918).

Howarth, Elgar, English trumpeter and conductor; b. Cannock, Staffordshire, Nov. 4, 1935. He studied at the Univ. of Manchester and the Royal Manchester College of Music; then played trumpet in the orch. of the Royal Opera House, Covent Garden (1958–63), with the Royal Phil. Orch. (1963–69), and with other London ensembles. In 1969 he began his career as a conductor with the London Sinfonietta; became its director in 1973. He also composed music for brass band. With Patrick Howarth, he publ. *What a Performance! The Brass Band Plays . . .* (London, 1988).

Howe, Mary (Carlisle), American pianist and composer; b. Richmond, Va., April 4, 1882; d. Washington, D.C., Sept. 14, 1964. She studied at the Peabody Cons. in Baltimore; was a pupil of Gustav Strube (composition) and Ernest Hutcheson (piano); later toured as a duo-pianist with Anne Hull.
WORKS: Violin Sonata (1922); Suite for String Quartet and Piano (1923); *Sand* for Orch. (1928); *Dirge* for Orch. (1931); *Castellana* for 2 Pianos and Orch. (1935); *Spring Pastoral* for Solo Violin and 13 Instruments (1936); *Stars and Whimsy* for 15 Instruments (1937); *Potomac,* orch. suite (1940); *Agreeable Overture* (1949); *Rock,* symphonic poem (Vienna, Feb. 15, 1955); choral works: *Chain Gang Song* (1925) and *Prophecy, 1792* (1943).

Howell, Dorothy, English pianist and composer; b. Handsworth, Feb. 25, 1898; d. London, Jan. 12, 1982. She studied composition with McEwen and piano with Matthay at the Royal Academy of Music in London; from 1924 to 1970 she taught music theory there. Among her works are a ballet, *Koong Shee;* a symphonic poem, *Lamia;* a Piano Concerto (1923); chamber music.

Howell, Gwynne (Richard), Welsh bass; b. Gorseinon, June 13, 1938. He began his career as a town planner; concurrently studied at the Royal Manchester College of Music and later with Otakar Kraus in London. He made his professional operatic debut as Monterone in *Rigoletto* at the Sadler's Wells Opera in 1968; subsequently sang at Covent Garden, the English National Opera, Aix-en-Provence, and Barcelona. He also continued his career as a concert and oratorio singer in England and America. He made his Metropolitan Opera debut in N.Y. as Lodovico in *Otello* on Jan. 21, 1985.

Howells, Anne (Elizabeth), English mezzo-soprano; b. Southport, Lancashire, Jan. 12, 1941. She studied at the Royal Manchester College of Music; made her operatic debut as Flora in *La Traviata* with the Welsh National Opera in 1966; 1st sang at Covent Garden in 1967. She made her American debut in Chicago in 1972; her Metropolitan Opera debut in N.Y., as Dorabella in *Così fan tutte,* followed on Oct. 15, 1975. She also sang in Paris, Geneva, Lyons, and other opera centers. She married the tenor **Ryland Davies** in 1966.

Howells, Herbert (Norman), distinguished English composer; b. Lydney, Gloucestershire, Oct. 17, 1892; d. Oxford, Feb. 24, 1983. In 1912 he entered the Royal College of Music in London, where he studied composition with Stanford and counterpoint with Charles Wood; in 1920 he was appointed an instructor in composition there, a position he held for more than 40 years. In 1936 he succeeded Holst as music director at St. Paul's Girls' School, remaining there until 1962; he also was a prof. of music at the Univ. of London (1954–64). In 1953 he was made a Commander of the Order of the British Empire and in 1972 a Companion of Honour. The music Howells wrote during his long life was nobly British, in its national references, its melodic outspokenness, and its harmonic opulence; in this it was a worthy continuation of the fine tradition of Elgar and Vaughan Williams. In 1987 the Herbert Howells Soc. was founded to further the cause of his music.

WORKS: ORCH.: Piano Concerto No. 1, in C major (1913; London, July 10, 1914); 3 dances for Violin and Orch. (1915); *The B's,* suite (1915); *Puck's Minuet* and *Merry-eye* (1917–20); *Procession* (1922); *Pastoral Rhapsody* (1923); Piano Concerto No. 2, in C minor (1924); *Paradise Rondel* (1925); *Pageantry* for Brass Band (1934); *Fantasia* for Cello and Orch. (1937); Concerto for Strings (1939); Suite for Strings (1944); *Music for a Prince,* suite (1949); *Triptych* for Brass Band (1960).
CHORAL: *Sine nomine* for 2 Soloists, Chorus, and Orch. (1922); *A Kent Yeoman's Wooing Song* for Soloists, Chorus, and Orch. (1933); *Requiem* for Unaccompanied Chorus (1936); *Hymnus Paradisi* for Soprano, Tenor, Chorus, and Orch. (1938); *A Maid Peerless* for Women's Voices, and Strings or Piano (1949); *Missa Sabrinensis* for Soloists, Chorus, and Orch. (1954; Worcester Festival, Sept. 7, 1954); *An English Mass* (1956); *Stabat Mater* for Tenor, Chorus, and Orch. (1963); *Take him, earth, for cherishing* (Motet on the Death of President Kennedy) (1964); *The Coventry Mass* for Choir and Organ (1968).
CHAMBER: Piano Quartet (1916); *Rhapsodic Quintet* for Clarinet and Strings (1917); *Phantasy String Quartet* (1918); *In Gloucestershire,* string quartet (1923); 3 sonatas for Violin and Piano (1918, 1918, 1923); Sonata for Oboe and Piano (1943); Sonata for Clarinet and Piano (1949).
KEYBOARD: Organ Sonata No. 1 (1911); Organ Sonata No. 2 (1933); *Prelude—De profundis* for Organ (1958); Partita for Organ (1971); 2 sets of pieces for Clavichord: *Lambert's Clavichord* (1926–27) and *Howells' Clavichord* (1951–56); *Sonatina* for Piano (1971).
BIBL.: R. Spearing, *H.H.: A Tribute to H. H. on His Eightieth Birthday* (London, 1972); C. Palmer, *H. H.: A Study* (London, 1978); M. Dreyer, "H. H. at 90: The Cello Fantasia and Its Orchestral Predecessors," *Musical Times* (Oct. 1982); N. Webber, "H. H. 1892–1983," *American Organist* (June 1983); R. Wells, "H.'s Unpublished Organ Works," *Musical Times* (Aug. 1987).

Howes, Frank (Stewart), English music critic, writer, and editor; b. Oxford, April 2, 1891; d. Standlake, Oxfordshire, Sept. 28, 1974. He studied at St. John's College, Oxford. In 1925 he joined the staff of the *Times* of London as music critic, and from 1943 to 1960 was its chief music critic. He was also ed. of the *Folk Song Journal* (later known as *Journal of the English Folk Dance and Song Society*) from 1927 to 1945; taught music history and appreciation at the Royal College of Music in London (1938–70); was Cramb Lecturer at the Univ. of Glasgow (1947 and 1952). In 1954 he was made a Commander of the Order of the British Empire.
WRITINGS: *The Borderland of Music and Psychology* (London, 1926); *The Appreciation of Music* (London, 1928); *William Byrd* (London, 1928); *A Key to the Art of Music* (London, 1935); *A Key to Opera* (in collaboration with P. Hope-Wallace; London, 1939); *Full Orchestra* (London, 1942; 2nd ed., rev. and enl., 1976); *The Music of William Walton* (2 vols., London, 1942–43; new ed., 1965); *Man, Mind and Music* (London, 1948); *Music: 1945–50* (London, 1951); *The Music of Ralph Vaughan Williams* (London, 1954); *Music and Its Meanings* (London, 1958); *The Cheltenham Festival* (London, 1965); *The English Musical Renaissance* (London, 1966); *Oxford Concerts: A Jubilee Record* (Oxford, 1969); *Folk Music of Britain—and Beyond* (London, 1970).

Howland, William Legrand, American composer; b. Asbury Park, N.J., 1873; d. Long Island, N.Y., July 26, 1915. He studied with Philip Scharwenka in Berlin, and lived most of his life in Europe. His 1-act opera *Sarrona,* to his own libretto, was produced in Italian in Bruges (Aug. 3, 1903), and subsequently had a number of performances in Italy; it was staged in N.Y. (in Eng.) on Feb. 8, 1910, and in Philadelphia (in German) on March 23, 1911. He wrote another opera, *Nita;* 2 oratorios, *The Resurrection* and *Ecce Homo;* and some choral works.

Hoyer, Karl, German organist and composer; b. Weissenfels, Saale, Jan. 9, 1891; d. Leipzig, June 12, 1936. He studied at the Leipzig Cons. with Reger, Straube, and Krehl; was organist in Reval (1911), in Chemnitz (1912–26), and at the St. Nicholas Church in Leipzig (from 1926); also taught organ and theory at the Leipzig Cons. He wrote about 50 organ works; selections for organ and string orch.; chamber music; choral works; songs.

Hoyland, Vic(tor), English composer; b. Wombwell, Yorkshire, Dec. 11, 1945. He studied at the Univ. of Hull and with Robert Sherlaw Johnson and Bernard Rands at the Univ. of York, where he served as a visiting lecturer in 1984; then was a lecturer at the Univ. of Birmingham (from 1985).

Works: *Em* for 24 Voices (1970); *Es* for Voices and Ensemble (1971); *Jeux-Theme* for Mezzo-soprano and Ensemble (1972); *Ariel* for Voice and Ensemble (1975); *Esem* for Double Bass and Ensemble (1975); *Serenade* for 14 Players (1979); *Xingu*, music theater piece (1979); *Reed* for Double Reed Instruments (1980); *Fox* for Chamber Ensemble (1983); *Quintet of Brass* (1985); *String Quartet* (1985); *In Transit* for Orch. (1987); *Of Fantasy, Of Dreams, and Ceremonies* for 13 Strings (1989).

Hřimalý, Adalbert (Vojtěch), Czech violinist, conductor, and composer, brother of **Johann (Jan)** and father of **Otakar Hřimalý;** b. Pilsen, July 30, 1842; d. Vienna, June 15, 1908. A member of an exceptionally musical family, he received an early training at home; then studied with Mildner at the Prague Cons. (1855–61); was subsequently active as a conductor, composer, and teacher in various towns in the Netherlands, Sweden, and Rumania. He wrote a great number of works, including an opera, *Zaklety princ* (The Enchanted Prince; Prague, May 13, 1872).

Hřimalý, Johann (Jan), celebrated Czech violinist and teacher, brother of **Adalbert (Vojtěch)** and uncle of **Otakar Hřimalý;** b. Pilsen, April 13, 1844; d. Moscow, Jan. 24, 1915. He studied at the Prague Cons. At the age of 24 he went to Moscow, where he became a prof. of violin at the Cons. (1874). He remained in Moscow for 40 years until his death, and was regarded there as a great teacher; 2 generations of Russian violinists studied under him. He also organized a string quartet in Moscow; publ. *Tonleiterstudien und Übungen in Doppelgriffen für die Violine* (Prague, 1895).

Hřimalý, Otakar, Czech violinist, conductor, and composer, son of **Adalbert (Vojtěch)** and nephew of **Johann (Jan) Hřimalý;** b. Czernowitz, Bukovina, Dec. 20, 1883; d. Prague, July 10, 1945. He studied at the Vienna Cons. In 1909 he went to Moscow upon the recommendation of his uncle; became a prof. at the Moscow Cons., and remained there until 1922; then lived in Rumania; in 1939, went to Prague. He was known not only as a violin teacher but also as a composer; wrote an opera; 7 syms.; chamber music and violin pieces.

Hrisanidis (Hrisanide), Alexandre, Rumanian-born Greek pianist and composer; b. Petrila, June 15, 1936. He studied at the Bucharest Cons. with Paul Constantinescu, Tudor Ciortea, Zeno Vancea, Mihail Jora, and Alfred Mendelsohn (1953–64); continued his studies at the American Cons. in Fontainebleau with Nadia Boulanger (1965); attended the Darmstadt summer courses in new music (1966–67); then taught at the Bucharest Academy of Music (1959–62) and at the Cons. (1962–72). In 1972 he left Rumania; was a visiting prof. of music at the Univ. of Oregon (1972–73); in 1974 settled in the Netherlands. His music follows constructivist tendencies, with the application of modified serial techniques. In 1965 he won the annual award of the Lili Boulanger Memorial Fund, Boston, for his *Volumes—Inventions* and his Clarinet Sonata.

Works: 2 cantatas: *C'était issu stellaire* for Male Chorus, Organ, 3 Trumpets, 4 Trombones, and Percussion (1965; Zagreb, May 16, 1967) and *Les Lumières de la patrie* (1965); *Poem* for Orch. (1958; Bucharest, Feb. 8, 1963); *Passacaglia* for Orch. (1959; Cluj, Nov. 25, 1962); "*Vers-Antiqua*" (*Hommage à Euripide*) for Chamber Orch. (1960; Hannover, Jan. 28, 1966); Concerto for Orch. (1964); *Ad perpetuam rei memoriam*, 3 pieces for Orch. (1966; Bucharest, Dec. 22, 1967); *RO* for Orch. (1968); *I-RO-LA-HAI* for Voice and Orch. (Nurem-

berg, June 8, 1971); *Sonnets*, concerto for Harpsichord and Orch. (Hilversum, March 26, 1973); 3 flute sonatas (1956; 1960–62; 1956); Violin Sonata (1957; its 3 movements can be played as separate pieces: *Hommages à Bartók, Enesco, and Schoenberg*); Trio for Violin, Viola, and Bassoon (1958); String Quartet (1958); Clarinet Sonata (1960–62); *Mers-Tefs* for Solo Violin (1960–68); *Volumes—Inventions* for Cello and Piano (1963); *Music* for Viola and Piano (1965); *À la recherche de la verticale* for Solo Oboe (1965); *M. P.5 (Musique pour 5)* for Violin, Viola, Cello, Saxophone (or Clarinet), and Piano (1966); *Directions* for Wind Quintet (1967–69); *Première musique pour RA* for Piano and Tape (1968–69); *Seconde musique pour RA* for Piano and Tape (1969); *Troisième musique pour RA* for Piano, Varying Percussion Instruments, and Tape, divided into 3 separate pieces: *Das Finale der Unendlichkeit, Vergangenheit schauende Stunde,* and *glorreich ist alles* (all composed in 1970); *Quatrième musique pour RA* for Piano and Tape, in 2 separate pieces: *Maister Manole* and *Blaga* (both written in 1970); *Cinquième musique pour RA* for Piano, Celesta, Harpsichord, and Tape (1973); *Sixième musique pour RA* for Piano, Varying Instruments, and Tape, in 3 separate pieces: *Là où ça passe, "ZED-UE,"* and *Mnemosyne* (all 1970); *Soliloquium × 11* for String Quartet (1970); *Music for 1 to 4 Violins,* quartet for Violins (1970); *Chanson sous les étoiles,* duet for Flute and Oboe (1973); *Du soir venant* for Solo Bass Clarinet (1974–75); *Suite classique* for Piano (1954); *Piano Pieces 1–13* (1955–56); 3 piano sonatas: No. 1 (1955–56; movements can be played independently: *Flames, Duality,* and *Study No. 4*); No. 2, *Sonata piccola* (1959); No. 3, *Picasso Sonata* (1956–64); *Desseins espagnols* for Prepared Piano (1971); *Unda* for Organ (1965); songs.

Hristić, Stevan, Serbian conductor and composer; b. Belgrade, June 19, 1885; d. there, Aug. 21, 1958. He studied in Leipzig, Rome, Paris, and Moscow. Returning to Belgrade, he became conductor of the National Opera Theater (1912–14); then was chief conductor of the Belgrade Phil. (1923–34) and Opera (1924–34); also taught at the Music Academy there. He composed a music drama, *Suton* (Sunset, 1925; rev. 1954); a ballet, *Legend of Okhrid* (1933; rev. 1958); many choral works.

Hrušovský, Ivan, Slovak composer; b. Bratislava, Feb. 23, 1927. In 1947 he began studies of composition with A. Moyzes at the Bratislava Cons.; continued composition studies with Moyzes at the Academy of Musical Arts, graduating in 1957; then joined its faculty. His music represents the common denominator of Central European trends.

Works: *Suite pastorale* for Orch. (1955); Piano Concerto (1957); Sinfonietta for 2 String Orchs. (1959); *The Tatra Poem,* symphonic poem (1960); *Hiro-šima,* cantata (1961–62); *Concertante Overture* for String Orch. (1963); *Combinazioni sonorische* for 9 Instruments (1963); *Sen o člevěku* (A Dream about a Man), cantata (1964); *Passacaglia eroica* for Orch. (1964); *Musica nocturna* for String Orch. (1971); 2 piano sonatas (1965, 1970); Sonata for Solo Violin (1969); *Sonata in modo classico* for Solo Cymbalom (1976); electronic tape pieces: *Invocation* (1974) and *Idée fixe* (1975); choruses.

Hsu, John (Tseng-Hsin), Chinese-born American cellist, viola da gambist, baryton player, and teacher; b. Shantou, April 21, 1931. He emigrated to the U.S. (1949) and became a naturalized U.S. citizen (1961); he studied at Carroll College, the Berkshire Music Center in Tanglewood, and the New England Cons. of Music in Boston (B.Mus., 1953; M.Mus., 1955); his teachers included Josef Schroetter, Alfred Zinghera, and Samuel Mayes for cello, and Eugene Lehner and William Kroll for chamber music performance. From 1955 he taught at Cornell Univ., and toured widely as a recitalist. He was a founding member of the Amadé Trio (1972), dedicated to performing early music on original instruments; also in 1972 he joined the Aston Magna Foundation for Music, serving as its artistic director (from 1985). In 1981 he organized the Haydn Baryton Trio for the purpose of playing Haydn's rarely heard baryton trios. He also ed. the collected works of Marais (1980) and wrote *A Handbook of French Baroque Viol Technique* (1981).

Hsu, Tsang-houei, Chinese composer, musicologist, and teacher; b. Changhau, Taiwan, Sept. 6, 1929. He studied violin in Tokyo from the age of 11, remaining in Japan until 1945, when he returned to Taiwan. He studied violin and composition at the National Univ. (1949–53); in 1954 he went to Paris to study violin at the École César Franck and music history and analysis at the Sorbonne (1956–58). He also studied with Jolivet and Messiaen at the Paris Cons. In 1959 he returned to Taiwan; his 1st concert (1960), which introduced avant-garde ideas to Taiwan audiences, met with both censure and enthusiasm. He taught advanced composition techniques and founded several organizations to promote contemporary music, including the Chinese Composers' Forum (1961) and the Chinese Soc. for Contemporary Music (1969); he also was active in the League of Asian Composers. Hsu made extensive study of Taiwanese folk music, elements of which are integrated into his compositions. He co-founded the Centre for Chinese Folk Music Research (1967), and was appointed examiner in charge of folk-music research by the Taiwanese provincial government (1976). He holds professorships at the National Academy of Arts, Soochow Univ., and the College of Chinese Culture, and has lectured throughout East Asia and the U.S. His early compositions show a variety of influences, including aspects of impressionism, atonality, and serialism, along with traditional Chinese and Taiwanese elements; his later works are less aggressively modern, but have a distinctive identity and unified style.

WRITINGS: *Te-pu-hsi* (Studies on Debussy; Taipei, 1961); *Hsünchao chung-kuo yin-yüeh te chüan-yüan* (In Search of the Sources of Chinese Music; Taipei, 1968); *Kuan-yü T'ai-wan te min-chien yin-yüeh* (On the Folk Music of Taiwan; Taipei, 1975).

WORKS: *Nü kuan tsu* for Soprano, Strings, and Percussion, op. 14 (1963); *Sun-wu-k'ung t'uo t'ien-luo,* dance drama, op. 21 (1967–73); Sym., op. 29 (1975–76).

Huang, Cham-Ber, Chinese-American harmonica player and manufacturer; b. Shanghai, Oct. 17, 1925. He commenced playing the harmonica when he was 6; later studied violin, theory, and composition at the Shanghai School of Music (1945–49) and St. John's Univ. in Shanghai (B.A., 1949). He went to the U.S., where he taught at N.Y.'s Turtle Bay Music School (1958–76) and at the Grand Teton Music Festival in Teton Village, Wyo. (1975–79). He also toured widely as a harmonica virtuoso, from 1979 making regular tours of China, where he helped to make his instrument popular. In 1983 he formed Huang Harmonics, a manufacturing firm in Farmingdale, N.Y.

Hubay, Jenő, celebrated Hungarian violinist, pedagogue, and composer; b. Budapest, Sept. 15, 1858; d. Vienna, March 12, 1937. He received his initial training from his father, Karl Hubay, prof. of violin at the Budapest Cons.; gave his 1st public concert at the age of 11; then studied with Joachim in Berlin (1873–76). His appearance in Paris, at a Pasdeloup concert, attracted the attention of Vieuxtemps, of whom he became a favorite pupil; in 1882 he succeeded Vieuxtemps as prof. at the Brussels Cons. In 1886 he became a prof. at the Budapest Cons. (succeeding his father); from 1919 to 1934 he was its director. In Budapest he formed the celebrated Hubay String Quartet. In 1894 he married the Countess Rosa Cebrain. Among his pupils were Vecsey, Szigeti, Telmányi, Eddy Brown, and other renowned violinists. Hubay was also a prolific composer. He ed. the violin études of Kreutzer (1908), Rode, Mayseder, and Saint Lubin (1910).

WORKS: Operas (all produced in Budapest): *Alienor* (Dec. 5, 1891); *Le Luthier de Crémone* (Nov. 10, 1894); *A Falu Rossza* (The Village Vagabond; March 20, 1896); *Moosröschen* (Feb. 21, 1903); *Anna Karenina* (Nov. 10, 1923); *Az álarc* (The Mask; Feb. 26, 1931); 4 syms.: No. 1 (1885); No. 2, *1914–15* (1915); No. 3, *Vita nuova,* for Soli, Chorus, and Organ (1921); No. 4, *Petőfi-Sinfonie,* for Soli, Chorus, and Orch. (1925); *Biedermeyer Suite* for Orch. (1913); 4 violin concertos; *Scènes de la Csárda,* 14 pieces for Violin and Orch., in the Hungarian manner; *Sonate romantique* for Violin and Piano.

BIBL.: B. Schwarz, *Great Masters of the Violin* (N.Y., 1983).

Hubbard, "Freddie" (Frederick De Wayne), black American jazz trumpeter, pianist, and bandleader; b. Indianapolis, April 7, 1938. After playing with local jazz musicians, including Wes Montgomery, he worked with Art Blakey, Max Roach, Quincy Jones, and others; also played with Friedrich Gulda in Europe.

Hubbell, Frank Allen, American conductor, arranger, and composer; b. Denver, May 9, 1907; d. Kirkland, Wash., April 21, 1971. He was taken to California as a child and was reared on an orange grove. He learned to play the cornet and also began to compose music. In 1936 he arranged a native Hawaiian tune and launched it as *The Hawaiian War Chant;* it became his most popular creation. His reputation was further enhanced by his arrangement of old California songs for band, under the title *California El Dorado Suite.* His later band pieces, all in the "landscape music" genre, included *The San Diego Story* (1957), *The Oregon Story* (1959), and *The Kansas Story* (1961). He was also active on the pageant stage, and was music director of the International Beauty Congress, for which he wrote 2 theme songs, *World of Beauty* and *Sound the Trumpets.*

Hubeau, Jean, French pianist and composer; b. Paris, June 22, 1917. He entered the Paris Cons. at the age of 9; studied piano with Lazare Lévy, and composition with Jean and Noël Gallon and Paul Dukas. He won 1st prize for piano at 13, and for composition at 16; in 1934, at the age of 17, he received the 2nd Grand Prix de Rome with his cantata *La Légende de Roukmani.* He made several European tours as a pianist; from 1942 to 1957 he was director of the Versailles Cons.; then joined the staff of the Paris Cons.

WORKS: BALLETS: *Trois fables de La Fontaine* (Paris, March 2, 1945); *La Fiancée du diable* (Paris, Dec. 8, 1945); *Un Cœur de diamant ou L'Infante* (Monte Carlo, April 7, 1949). **ORCH.:** *Tableaux hindous* (Paris, Oct. 18, 1936); Violin Concerto (Paris, March 30, 1941); Cello Concerto (Paris, Nov. 28, 1942); *Concerto héroïque* for Piano and Orch. (Paris, Dec. 22, 1946). **CHAMBER:** Violin Sonata (1941); *Sonatine-Humoresque* for Horn, Flute, Clarinet, and Piano (1942); Sonata for Trumpet and Piano (1943); *Sonate-Caprice* for 2 Violins (1944); *Air varié* for Clarinet and Piano (1961); *Idylle* for Flute and Piano (1966); Piano Sonata; other piano pieces; songs; choral works.

Huber, Hans, Swiss composer; b. Eppenberg, near Olten, June 28, 1852; d. Locarno, Dec. 25, 1921. He studied at the Leipzig Cons. with Richter, Reinecke, and Wenzel (1870–74); then taught music in Wesserling, Thann (Alsace), and Basel; received an honorary degree of Dr.Phil. from Basel Univ. (1892). In 1896 he became director of the Basel Cons., a post he held until 1917. Huber composed prolifically in all genres; his style combined the rhapsodic form typical of Lisztian technique with simple ballad-like writing. He often used Swiss songs for thematic material. In Switzerland his reputation is very great and his works are frequently performed, but they are virtually unknown elsewhere.

WORKS: Operas: *Weltfrühling* (Basel, March 28, 1894); *Kudrun* (Basel, Jan. 29, 1896); *Der Simplicius* (Basel, Feb. 22, 1912); *Die schöne Bellinda* (Bern, April 2, 1916); *Frutta di mare* (Basel, Nov. 24, 1918); 8 syms. (all except No. 2 perf. 1st in Basel): No. 1, *William Tell* (April 26, 1881); No. 2, *Böcklinsinfonie* (Zürich, July 2, 1900); No. 3, *Heroische* (Nov. 9, 1917); No. 4, *Akademische* (May 23, 1909); No. 5, *Romantische* (Feb. 11, 1906); No. 6 (Nov. 19, 1911); No. 7, *Swiss* (June 9, 1917); No. 8 (Oct. 29, 1921); 4 piano concertos (Basel, 1878, 1891, 1899, 1910); Violin Concerto (1878); Sextet for Piano and Wind Instruments (1900); Quintet for Piano and Wind Instruments (1914); 2 string quintets (1890, 1907); String Quartet; 2 piano quartets; 5 piano trios; 10 violin sonatas; 5 cello sonatas; a number of piano works, among them 48 preludes and fugues for piano, 4-hands.

BIBL.: E. Refardt, *H. H.* (Leipzig, 1906); idem, *H. H., Beiträge* *zu einer Biographie* (1922); C. Bundi, *H. H., Die Persönlichkeit nach Briefen und Erinnerungen* (1925); E. Refardt, *H. H.* (Zürich, 1944).

Huber, Klaus, Swiss composer; b. Bern, Nov. 30, 1924. He studied violin with Stefi Geyer and composition with Willy Burkhard at the Zürich Cons. (1947–49); later took courses in composition with Boris Blacher in Berlin (1955–56). He taught violin at the Zürich Cons. from 1950; from 1960 to 1963 he lectured on music history at the Lucerne Cons.; in 1961 joined the faculty of the Basel Music Academy.

WORKS: Opera: *Tot oder Wann kommt der Herr Zurück* (Berlin, Sept. 27, 1973); *Oratio Mechtildis* for Contralto and Chamber Orch. (Strasbourg Festival, June 9, 1958); *Des Engels Anredung an die Seele,* cantata for Voice and 4 Instruments (Rome, June 13, 1959); *Alveare vernat* for Flute and 12 Solo Strings (1965); *Tenebrae* for Orch. (1966–67); *James Joyce Music* for Harp, Horn, and Chamber Orch. (1966–67); *Tempora,* violin concerto (1969–70); *Im Paradies oder Der Alte vom Berge* (1974–75); *Ohne Grenze und Rand* for Viola and Small Orch. (1976–77); *Von Zeit zu Zeit* for String Quartet (1984–85); *Protuberanzen* for Orch. (1985–86); *Spes contra spem* for Voice, Narrator, and Orch. (1986–88).

Huber, Kurt, eminent German musicologist of Swiss descent; b. Chur, Oct. 24, 1893; d. (executed by the Gestapo) Munich, July 13, 1943. He studied philosophy and psychology with Becher and Külpe and musicology with Kroyer and Sandberger at the Univ. of Munich (Ph.D., 1917, with the diss. *Ivo de Vento: Ein Beitrag zur Musikgeschichte des 16. Jahrhunderts,* 1; publ. in Lindenberg, 1918); then completed his Habilitation in psychology (1920). He became assistant lecturer at the Univ. of Munich's Inst. of Psychology in 1920; was made a Dozent there in 1926. From 1925 he devoted himself to collecting and recording early Bavarian folk songs, which he publ. with Paul Kiem. He actively opposed the Nazi regime, and was imprisoned and executed for his participation in student protests. In addition to his book *Die Doppelmeister des 16. Jahrhunderts* (Munich, 1920), the following vols. have been publ.: O. Ursprung ed. his *Ästhetik* (Ettal, 1954) and *Musikästhetik* (Ettal, 1954), J. Hanslmeier his *Grundbegriffe der Seelenkunde: Einführung in die allgemeine Psychologie* (Ettal, 1955), and C. Huber and O. von Müller his *Volkslied und Volkstanz: Aufsätze zur Volksliedkunde des bajuwarischen Raumes* (Ettal, 1960).

BIBL.: W. Rubsamen, "K. H. of Munich," *Musical Quarterly* (April 1944); C. Huber, ed., *K. H. zum Gedächtnis: Bildnis eines Menschen, Denkers und Forchers* (Regensburg, 1947); E. Grave, *Die ästhetischen Kategorien in K. H.s Ästhetik* (diss., Univ. of Munich, 1957).

Huberman, Bronislaw, famous Polish violinist; b. Częstochowa, Dec. 19, 1882; d. Corsier-sur-Vevey, Switzerland, June 15, 1947. He began to study violin with Michalowicz at age 6, making his debut when he was 7; then studied with Izydor Lotto. When he was 9 he was taken to Berlin, where he studied with Joachim's assistant Markees; he then studied privately with Carl Grigorovich, his most influential mentor; later took some lessons with H. Heermann in Frankfurt and M. Marsick in Paris. He played in the Netherlands and Belgium in 1893, then in Paris and London in 1894. Adelina Patti heard him in London and engaged him for her farewell appearance in Vienna (Jan. 12, 1895), where he scored a brilliant success. He then played the Brahms Violin Concerto there in the presence of the composer (Jan. 29, 1896), who commended him warmly. He made his 1st tour of the U.S. in 1896–97; subsequently made world tours and was active as a teacher in Vienna. He went to Palestine in 1936 and founded the Palestine Sym. Orch., an ensemble composed mainly of Jewish musicians who had lost their positions in the wake of Nazism in Europe. The orch. prospered and became the Israel Phil. Orch. in 1948. He went to the U.S. in 1940, but returned to Europe at the end of World War II (1945). He publ. *Aus der Werkstatt des Virtuosen* (1912) and *Mein Weg zu Paneuropa* (1925).

BIBL.: H. Goetz, *B. H. and the Unity of Europe* (Rome, 1967); I. Ibbeken and T. Avni, eds., *An Orchestra Is Born: The Founding of the Palestine Orchestra as Reflected in B. H.'s Letters, Speeches, and Articles* (Tel Aviv, 1969).

Hubert, Nikolai, Russian conductor and pedagogue; b. St. Petersburg, March 19, 1840; d. Moscow, Oct. 8, 1888. He studied with his father; then at the St. Petersburg Cons. (1863–68) with Zaremba and A. Rubinstein. In 1869 he was in Odessa as an opera conductor; in 1870 was engaged as a prof. of music theory at the Moscow Cons.; he succeeded N. Rubinstein as its director in 1881, resigning in 1883; retired from teaching in 1888. He also wrote music criticism in Moscow newspapers.

Huberti, Gustave (-Léon), Belgian conductor and composer; b. Brussels, April 14, 1843; d. Schaerbeek, June 28, 1910. He studied at the Brussels Cons., where he won the Prix de Rome in 1865 for his cantata *La Fille de Jephté.* He was director of the Mons Cons. (1874–78), then a conductor in Antwerp and Brussels; in 1889 was appointed a prof. at the Brussels Cons.; was also director of the Music School of St.-Joost-ten-Noode from 1893. In 1891 he was elected a member of the Belgian Academy. He publ. a book, *Aperçu sur l'histoire de la musique religieuse des Italiens et des Néerlandais* (Brussels, 1873).

WORKS: 3 oratorios: *Een Laatste Zonnestraal* (1874); *Bloemardinne*; *Willem van Oranjes dood*; dramatic poem, *Verlichting (Fiat lux),* for Soli, Chorus, Organ, and Orch.; symphonic poem, *Kinderlust en Leed,* for Chorus and Orch.; *Symphonie funèbre; Suite romantique; In den Garade; Triomffeest,* with Organ; Piano Concerto; marches; many French, Flemish, and German songs; piano pieces.

Hübler, Klaus K(arl), German composer; b. Munich, July 12, 1956. He studied composition with Peter Kiesewetter (1975–76) and Brian Ferneyhough (1980–82). He received several fellowships and prizes; visited the U.S. as a participant in the Pittsburgh International Music Festival (1986). His compositions are extremely complex, demanding an intricate system of notation.

WORKS: *MUSICA MENSURABILIS* for 2 Violins and Viola (1975–76); 3 string quartets: No. 1, *Hommage à Alban Berg* (1977); No. 2, *sur le premier prélude* (1979–80); No. 3, *Dialektische Fantasie* (1982–84); *CERCAR* for Trumpet (1983); *Kannitverstan: Hörstück für Schallkonserven* for Tape (1985); *sklEros* for Flute, Oboe d'Amore, Clarinet, Bassoon, and Horn Obbligato (1985–86); *Sonetto LXXXIII del Michelangelo* for Piano (1986); *Arie dissolute* for Viola and Chamber Ensemble (1986–87); *Epiphyt* for Flute and Chamber Orch. (1987–88).

Hucbald (Hugbaldus, Ubaldus, Uchubaldus), Flemish monk, music theorist, and composer; b. in or near Tournai, c.840; d. Saint-Amand, near Tournai, June 20, 930. He was a pupil of his uncle Milo, director of the singing school at Saint-Amand; then was himself director of a similar school at Nevers; subsequently returned to Saint-Amand and succeeded his uncle. His only extant treatise is *De Harmonica Institutione,* a guide to chant singing in which he developed a systematic approach to music. Several of his compositions are also extant.

BIBL.: C. de Coussemaker, *Mémoire sur H. et sur ses traités de musique* (1814); E. Grutchfield, "H., A Millenary Commemoration," *Musical Times* (1930; 2 installments); A.H. Fox-Strangways, "A Tenth Century Manual," *Music & Letters* (1932); J. Handschin, "Etwas Greifbares über H.," *Acta Musicologica,* VII (1935); R. Weakland, "H. as Musician and Theorist," *Musical Quarterly* (Jan. 1956); C. Palisca, ed., and W. Babb, tr., *H., Guido, and John on Music: Three Medieval Treatises* (New Haven, 1979).

Hudson, Frederick, English organist and musicologist; b. Gateshead, Durham, Jan. 16, 1913. He studied with Edward Bairstow at the Univ. of Durham and with Gordon Slater at Lincoln Cathedral; specialized as an organist; received the degree of B.Mus. at the Univ. of Durham in 1941, and of D.Mus. in 1950. He served as organist and choirmaster at

Alnwick (1941–48); was a lecturer in music at King's College, Univ. of Durham (1949–70), and at the Univ. of Newcastle upon Tyne (from 1970). He ed. works by Bach, Handel, Giovanni Gabrieli, William Byrd, and others for the new editions of their works; contributed important papers dealing with watermarks of undated MSS and prints, making use of beta-radiography with carbon-14 sources; also compiled a catalog of the works of Charles Villiers Stanford (*Music Review*, May 1976).

Hüe, Georges (-Adolphe), French composer; b. Versailles, May 6, 1858; d. Paris, June 7, 1948. He was a pupil of Reber and Paladilhe at the Paris Cons.; took 1st Grand Prix de Rome in 1879, and the Prix Crescent in 1881; lived in Paris as a teacher and composer; was a member (succeeding Saint-Saëns) of the Académie des Beaux-Arts (1922).

Works: Operas (all 1st perf. in Paris): *Les Pantins* (Opéra-Comique, Dec. 28, 1881); *Le Roi de Paris* (Opéra, April 26, 1901); *Titania*, after Shakespeare (Opéra-Comique, Jan. 20, 1903); *Le Miracle* (Opéra, Dec. 30, 1910); *Dans l'ombre de la cathédrale*, after Blasco Ibañez (Opéra-Comique, Dec. 7, 1921); *Riquet à la houppe*, after Perrault (Opéra-Comique, Dec. 21, 1928); ballet, *Cœur brisé* (Paris, 1890); pantomime, *Siang Sin* (Opéra, March 19, 1924); *Rübezahl*, symphonic legend in 3 parts (Concerts Colonne, 1886); "féerie dramatique," *La Belle au bois dormant* (Paris, 1894); *Résurrection*, "épisode sacré" (1892); *Le Berger*, ballade and fantaisie for Violin and Orch. (1893); Sym.; *Rêverie* and *Sérénade* for Small Orch.; *Romance* for Violin and Orch.; choral works, including the cantata *Médée* (1879); songs.

Hueffer, Francis (real name, **Franz Hüffer**), German-born English writer on music; b. Münster, May 22, 1843; d. London, Jan. 19, 1889. He studied philology and music in London, Paris, Berlin, and Leipzig; received a Dr.Phil. degree from Göttingen Univ. for his 1st publication (1869), a critical ed. of the works of Guillem de Cabestant, troubadour of the 12th century. In 1869 he settled in London as a writer on music, and from 1878 was music critic of the *Times*. He publ. (in London, unless otherwise given) *Richard Wagner and the Music of the Future* (1874); *The Troubadours: A History of Provençal Life and Literature in the Middle Ages* (1878); *Musical Studies* (Edinburgh, 1880; reprints of his articles from the *Times* and *Fortnightly Review*); *Richard Wagner* (1881); *Italian and Other Studies* (1883); *Half a Century of Music in England* (1889; 2nd ed., 1898).

Huehn, Julius, American baritone; b. Revere, Mass., Jan. 12, 1904; d. Rochester, N.Y., June 8, 1971. He studied engineering at the Carnegie Inst. of Technology; later took voice lessons with Anna Schoen-René at the Juilliard School of Music in N.Y. He made his operatic debut with the Metropolitan Opera in N.Y. as the Herald in *Lohengrin* on Dec. 21, 1935, singing there until 1944; then served in the U.S. Air Force and carried out missions in Europe as a bombardier. He sang again at the Metropolitan after the war (1945–46). He was particularly noted for his performances of heroic baritone parts in Wagner's operas.

Huggler, John, American composer; b. Rochester, N.Y., Aug. 30, 1928. He studied at the Eastman School of Music in his hometown (graduated, 1950), and with Charles Warren Fox (musicology) and Dante Fiorillo (composition). He received 2 Guggenheim fellowships (1962, 1969); also served as composer-in-residence of the Boston Sym. Orch. (1964–65).

Works: Orch.: *Elegy to the Memory of Federico García-Lorca* (1952); Horn Concerto (1957); *Ecce Homo* (1959); Divertimento for Viola and Orch. (1961); *Sculptures* for Orch. with Soprano Soloist (1964); *Music in 2 Parts* (1966); Flute Concerto (1967); Trumpet Concerto (1968); *7 Songs on Poems of E.J. Leavenworth* for Soprano and Orch. (1974); Sym. in 3 Movements (1980); *Continuum* (1985). **Chamber:** 9 string quartets (1951–67); 3 string quintets (1958); 7 Bagatelles for Piano (1953); Piano Sonata (1957); 4 brass quintets (1957, 1962, 1973, 1982); *Outdoor Piece for Tanglewood* for Brass and Per-

cussion (1966); *Sinfonia* for 13 Players (1974); *Poem* for Violin and Piano (1985); *Capriccio Sregolato* for Flute, Clarinet, Violin, Viola, and Cello (1986).

Hughes, Dom Anselm, eminent English musicologist; b. London, April 15, 1889; d. Nashdom Abbey, Burnham, Buckinghamshire, Oct. 8, 1974. He studied at Keble College, Oxford (B.A., 1911; M.A., 1915), and at Ely Theological College (1911–12); was ordained a priest (1913). He was a curate and choirmaster in several London churches (1912–22) before joining the Anglican Benedictine community at Pershore Abbey; was professed there (1923) and served as its director of music (1922–45) and prior (1936–45), continuing after its 1926 move to Nashdom Abbey. He was a leading authority on medieval and Renaissance music; contributed articles to the 3rd, 4th, and 5th eds. of *Grove's Dictionary of Music and Musicians* and to the 2nd ed. of *The Oxford History of Music*; edited the 2nd and 3rd (with G. Abraham) vols. of *The New Oxford History of Music*; also edited the *Old Hall Manuscript* (with H. Collins). He composed *Missa Sancti Benedicti* (1918) and other sacred pieces.

Writings: *Latin Hymnody: An Enquiry into the Underlying Principles of the Hymnarium* (London, 1922); *The House of My Pilgrimage* (London, 1929); *Index to the Facsimile Edition of MS Wolfenbüttel 677* (Oxford, 1939); *Liturgical Terms for Music Students* (Boston, 1940); *Medieval Polyphony in the Bodleian Library* (Oxford, 1951); *Catalogue of the Musical Manuscripts at Peterhouse, Cambridge* (Cambridge, 1953); *Septuagesima: Reminiscences of the Plainsong and Mediaeval Music Society* (London, 1959); *Plainsong for English Choirs* (Leighton Buzzard, 1966).

Hughes, Arwel, Welsh conductor and composer, father of **Owain Arwel Hughes**; b. Rhosllanerchrugog, Aug. 25, 1909; d. Cardiff, Sept. 23, 1988. He studied with Kitson and Vaughan Williams at the Royal College of Music in London; then returned to Wales, where he became a member of the music dept. of the BBC in 1935; from 1965 to 1971 was head of music there. He was made an Officer of the Order of the British Empire in 1969. He wrote the operas *Menna* (1950–51) and *Serch yw'r doctor* (Love's the Doctor), after Molière (1959); also a Sym. (1971); choral works; chamber music.

Hughes, Edwin, American pianist and teacher; b. Washington, D.C., Aug. 15, 1884; d. N.Y., July 17, 1965. He studied with S.M. Fabian in Washington, D.C., with Rafael Joseffy in N.Y. (1906–7), and with T. Leschetizky in Vienna (1907–10); taught at the Ganapol School of Musical Art in Detroit (1910–12), the Volpe Inst. of Music in N.Y. (1916–17), and the Inst. of Musical Art in N.Y. (1918–23); lectured at various schools. From 1920 to 1926 he was special ed. of piano music for G. Schirmer, Inc. He toured widely in the U.S. and Europe after the close of World War I; performed duo-recitals with his wife, the pianist Jewel Bethany Hughes, and also gave master classes.

Hughes, Herbert, Irish music critic and composer; b. Belfast, March 16, 1882; d. Brighton, England, May 1, 1937. He studied at the Royal College of Music in London; was one of the founders of the Irish Folksong Soc. and co-ed. of its early journals; was music critic of the *Daily Telegraph*. He collected and ed. many folk songs, including the collections Boosey's *Modern Festival Series*; *Irish Country Songs* (in 4 vols.); *Old Irish Melodies* (3 vols.); *Historical Songs and Ballads of Ireland*; *Songs from Connacht*; *Songs of Uladh*. He composed incidental music to the comedy *And So to Bed*; the film *Irish Hearts*; *Nursery Rhymes*, studies in imitation (2 vols.); *Parodies* for Voice and Orch. (2 vols.); *Brian Boru's March* for Piano; *3 Satirical Songs* for Violin, Flute, Clarinet, and Bassoon; *Shockheaded Peter*, cycle for Soprano, Baritone, and Piano; etc.

Hughes, Owain Arwel, Welsh conductor, son of **Arwel Hughes;** b. Cardiff, March 21, 1942. He 1st studied at Univ. College in Cardiff; then (1964–66) at the Royal College of Music in London, where his teachers included Boult and Harvey Philips; subsequently studied with Kempe in London and Haitink in Amsterdam. He made his London debut in 1968; then appeared as a guest conductor with leading English orchs.; also conducted at the Welsh National Opera and the English National Opera. In 1977 he became music director of the Royal National Eisteddfod of Wales; also was associate conductor of the BBC Welsh Sym. Orch. (from 1980) and music director of the Huddersfield Choral Soc. (1980–86); then was associate conductor of the Philharmonia Orch. of London (from 1987).

Hughes, Robert Watson, Scottish-born Australian composer; b. Leven, Fyfeshire, March 27, 1912. He emigrated to Australia in 1930; worked as a music librarian at the Australian Broadcasting Commission in Melbourne; was chairman of the Australian Performing Right Assoc. (1977–85). In 1978 he was made a Member of the Order of the British Empire. He withdrew most of his early compositions; his extant works include *Festival Overture* (1948); *Farrago*, suite for Orch. (1949); *Serenade for Small Orch.* (1952); Sym. No. 1 (1952); *Essay* for Orch. (1953); ballet, *Xanadu* (1954); *Masquerade Overture* (1956); Sinfonietta (1957; Manchester, England, Nov. 10, 1957); television ballet, *The Forbidden Rite* (1962); *Synthesis* for Orch. (1969); 5 *Indian Poems* for Chorus, Woodwind Instruments, and Percussion (1971); *Sea Spell* for Orch. (1973); *The Intriguers*, opera (1975); 2 *Indian Poems* for Soprano and Chamber Orch. (1979); *Essay II* for Orch. (1982).

Hughes, Rupert, American novelist, writer on music, and composer; b. Lancaster, Mo., Jan. 31, 1872; d. Los Angeles, Sept. 9, 1956. He studied with W.G. Smith in Cleveland (1890–92), E.S. Kelley in N.Y. (1899), and C. Pearce in London (1900–1901). His publications include *American Composers* (Boston, 1900; rev. 1914); *The Musical Guide* (2 vols., N.Y., 1903; republ. as *Music Lovers' Encyclopedia*, in 1 vol., 1912; rev. and newly ed. by Deems Taylor and Russell Kerr as *Music Lover's Encyclopedia*, 1939; rev. 1954); ed. *Thirty Songs by American Composers* (1904). He also composed a dramatic monologue for Baritone and Piano, *Cain* (1919); piano pieces; songs. He was principally known, however, as a novelist.

Hugo, John Adam, American pianist and composer; b. Bridgeport, Conn., Jan. 5, 1873; d. there, Dec. 29, 1945. From 1888 to 1897 he studied at the Stuttgart Cons. with Speidel, Faisst, Doppler, and Zumpe; appeared as a concert pianist in Germany, England, and Italy; returned to the U.S. in 1899. His 1-act opera *The Temple Dancer*, was one of the few operas by American composers presented by the Metropolitan Opera in N.Y. (March 12, 1919); it was also produced in Honolulu (Feb. 19, 1925). His other works are the operas *The Hero of Byzanz* and *The Sun God*; a Sym.; 2 piano concertos; Piano Trio; pieces for violin; pieces for cello; piano pieces; songs.

Hugon, Georges, French composer; b. Paris, July 23, 1904; d. Blauvac, Vaucluse, July 19, 1980. He studied at the Paris Cons.; received the Prix Bizet (1926). He was director of the Boulogne-sur-Mer Cons. (1934–41); in 1941 became a prof. at the Paris Cons.

Works: Oratorio, *Chants de deuil et d'espérance* (1947); 2 syms. (1941, 1949); symphonic poems: *Au nord* (1930) and *La Reine de Saba* (1933); Piano Concerto (1962); Flute Sonata (1965); Piano Trio; String Quartet; various pieces for piano; songs.

Huhn, Bruno, English-born American pianist, conductor, and composer; b. London, Aug. 1, 1871; d. N.Y., May 13, 1950. He studied piano in London and N.Y.; toured in Egypt, India, and Australia (1889–91). In 1891 he settled in N.Y., where he made a successful debut as a pianist (April 17, 1896). Subsequently he held various positions as a conductor of suburban choral groups and as an accompanist to singers. He wrote many sacred choruses and solo songs, of which his setting of Henley's *Invictus* (1910) attained great popularity.

Huízar (García de la Cadena), Candelario, Mexican composer; b. Jerez, Feb. 2, 1883; d. Mexico City, May 3, 1970. He studied violin and composition; in 1917 settled in Mexico City, where he continued his studies with Gustavo Campa. He was a copyist in various music schools (1920–25), and from 1929 to 1948 was librarian of the Mexico Sym. Orch. His compositions reflect Mexican folklore, and often contain authentic Mexican themes.

Works: Orch. (all 1st perf. in Mexico City): *Imágenes*, symphonic poem (Dec. 13, 1929); Sym. No. 1 (Nov. 14, 1930); *Pueblerinas*, symphonic poem (Nov. 6, 1931); *Surco*, symphonic poem (Oct. 25, 1935); Sym. No. 2 (Sept. 4, 1936); Sym. No. 3 (July 29, 1938); Sym. No. 4 (Aug. 7, 1942); Sonata for Clarinet and Bassoon (1931); String Quartet (1938); choral works; songs.

Bibl.: J. Romero, "C. H.," *Nuestra Música* (Jan. 1952).

Hull, Anne, American pianist, teacher, and composer; b. Brookland, Pa., Jan. 25, 1888; d. Westport, Conn., Jan. 31, 1984. She studied at the Peabody Cons. in Baltimore, and upon graduation became active as a piano teacher; made numerous appearances with Mary Howe in duo-piano recitals. Her work for 2 Pianos, *Ancient Ballad*, attained considerable popularity.

Hull, Arthur Eaglefield, English writer on music; b. Market Harborough, March 10, 1876; d. (suicide) London, Nov. 4, 1928. He studied with Matthay and C. Pearce in London; was (from 1912) ed. of the *Monthly Musical Record*. In 1918 he founded the British Music Soc.; was its honorary director until 1921; received his Mus.Doc. from Queen's College, Oxford. In 1906 he married Constance Barratt, an accomplished violinist. A man of broad culture, he was an enthusiast for new music; was an early champion of Scriabin in England. In 1924 he brought out a *Dictionary of Modern Music and Musicians*. This was a pioneer vol. and, despite an overabundance of egregious errors and misconceptions, is of service as a guide; a corrected German tr. was made by A. Einstein (1926); another vol. which still retains its value is *Modern Harmony: Its Explanation and Application* (London, 1914; 3rd ed., 1923; reprinted 1934). In 1927 he publ. a book, *Music: Classical, Romantic and Modern*, which proved to be a pasticcio of borrowings from various English and American writers; this was pointed out by many reviewers, and the book was withdrawn by the publishers in 1928; this episode led directly to Hull's suicide; he threw himself under a moving train at the Huddersfield Railway Station, suffered grave injuries and loss of memory, and died a few weeks later. The list of his publications also includes *Organ Playing, Its Technique and Expression* (1911); *The Sonata in Music* (1916); *Scriabin* (1916); *Modern Musical Styles* (1916); *Design or Construction in Music* (1917); *Cyril Scott* (1918); etc.

Hullah, John (Pyke), English organist, writer on music, teacher, and composer; b. Worcester, June 27, 1812; d. London, Feb. 21, 1884. He was a pupil of William Horsley; in 1833 he studied singing with Crivelli at the Royal Academy of Music in London; as a composer, he was entirely self-taught. At the age of 24 he produced an opera to a story by Charles Dickens, *The Village Coquette* (London, Dec. 6, 1836); 2 other operas followed: *The Barber of Bassora* (London, Nov. 11, 1837) and *The Outpost* (May 17, 1838). In the meantime, he obtained the post of church organist at Croydon. He made several trips to Paris, where he became interested in the new system of vocal teaching established by Wilhem; he modified it to suit English requirements, and, with the sanction of the National Education Committee, he opened his Singing School for Schoolmasters at Exeter Hall (1841). The school became the target of bitter criticism; nonetheless, it prospered; thousands of students enrolled; his wealthy supporters helped him build St. Martin's Hall for performances of vocal music by his students; the hall was inaugurated in 1850; it was destroyed by fire in 1860. From 1844 to 1874 Hullah taught singing at King's College, and later at Queen's College and Bedford College in London. He conducted the student concerts of the Royal Academy of Music (1870–73); in 1872 he became an inspector of training schools. He held the honorary degree of LL.D. from Edinburgh Univ. (1876); was also a member of the Cecilia Soc. in Rome and of the Academy of Music in Florence. He ed. Wilhem's *Method of Teaching Singing Adapted to English Use* (1841); publ. *A Grammar of Vocal Music* (1843); *A Grammar of Harmony* (1852); *A Grammar of Counterpoint* (1864); *The History of Modern Music* (1862); *The Third or Transition Period of Musical History* (1865); *The Cultivation of the Speaking Voice* (1870); *Music in the House* (1877); also brought out useful collections of vocal music: *The Psalter; The Book of Praise Hymnal; Whole Book of Psalms with Chants.* He was the composer of the celebrated song *O that we two were Maying;* other popular songs are *The Storm* and *3 Fishers.* A *Life of John Hullah* was publ. by his wife (London, 1886).

Hüllmandel, Nicolas-Joseph, Alsatian composer; b. Strasbourg, May 23, 1756; d. London, Dec. 19, 1823. He was an illegitimate son of Michel Hüllmandel, organist at the Strasbourg Cathedral and nephew of the composer Jean-Joseph Rodolphe. Around 1776 he went to Paris, where he taught piano and the glass harmonica; among his pupils in composition were Onslow and Aubert. After the French Revolution he went to London, where he remained until his death. There he publ. a manual, *Principles of Music, Chiefly Calculated for the Pianoforte* (1795). He composed in a typical manner of his time; Mozart, in one of his letters to his father, expressed appreciation of Hüllmandel's sonatas. He publ. 25 keyboard sonatas between 1773 and 1790, some with violin accompaniment; also other works for piano or harpsichord.
BIBL.: R. Benton, *N.-J. H. and French Instrumental Music in the Second Half of the 18th Century* (diss., Univ. of Toronto, 1961); W. Newman, *The Sonata in the Classic Era* (Chapel Hill, 1963; 3rd ed., rev., 1983).

Humbert, Georges, Swiss organist and writer on music; b. St. Croix, Aug. 10, 1870; d. Neuchâtel, Jan. 1, 1936. He studied with Huberti at the Brussels Cons. and with Bargiel in Berlin. In 1892 he became a prof. of music history at the Geneva Cons., retaining this post until 1912; from 1898 to 1918 he was an organist at Morges. In 1918 he established the Neuchâtel Cons., and was its director until his death; also conducted various performing societies in Switzerland. He was ed. of *Gazette Musicale de la Suisse Romande* (1894–96) and *La Vie Musicale* (1918–24); publ. *Notes pour servir à l'étude de l'histoire de la musique* (1904).

Humble, (Leslie) Keith, Australian pianist, conductor, and composer; b. Geelong, Victoria, Sept. 6, 1927. He studied at the Melbourne Cons. (1947–49), then with Ferguson at the Royal Academy of Music in London (1950–51); subsequently took courses at the École Normale de Musique in Paris (1951–52) and studied composition and conducting privately there with Leibowitz (1952–54), serving as his assistant (1957–59). He joined the faculty of the Melbourne Cons. (1958); was founder and music director (1959–68) of Le Centre de Musique in Paris, a contemporary music workshop. He was made senior lecturer at the Melbourne Cons. (1966), and established its electronic music studio; also prof. of music at the Univ. of Calif. at San Diego (1971–74), and then Foundation Prof. at La Trobe Univ. in Victoria, Australia (1974). He appeared widely in his native country as a pianist and conductor; was music director of the Australia Contemporary Music Ensemble (1975–78). In 1982 he was made a Member of the Order of Australia. His music reflects British, French, and American avant-garde tendencies.
WORKS: String Trio (1953); *Fragments of War Poems* for Soprano and Instruments (1959); 2 piano sonatas (1959; 1977, rev. 1980); *Music for Monuments* for Instruments and/or Voices and Prepared Tape (1967); *Materials for Larountala* for 22 Solo Strings (1968); a series of works entitled *Nunique* (1968; II, a and b, 1968; III, 1969; IV, 1971; VI, 1971; VII, 1972; IX, 1984); a series of works entitled *Arcade* (I, a and b, 1969; III, a and b, 1969; II, IV, and V, 1969); *Après la légende* for Piano and Orch. (1969); *La Légende,* cantata for Solo Voice, Choir, Instruments, and Electronics (1970); *Statico I* for Organ and 2 Synthesizers (1971), *II* (1972), and *III* for Orch. (1972–73); *A. C. F.* for Chamber Ensemble (1980); Trio No. 2 for Violin, Clarinet, and Piano (1982); Trio No. 3 for Flute, Percussion, and Piano (1985).

Hume, Paul (Chandler), American music critic; b. Chicago, Dec. 13, 1915. He studied at the Univ. of Chicago; took private lessons in piano, organ, and voice; was organist, choirmaster, and baritone soloist at various churches in Chicago and Washington, D.C.; also gave song recitals. From 1946 to 1982 he was music ed. and critic of the *Washington Post;* was an instructor in music history at Georgetown Univ. (1950–77); also a visiting prof. at Yale Univ.; was active as a lecturer and radio commentator on music; publ. *Catholic Church Music* (N.Y., 1956), *Our Music, Our Schools, and Our Culture* (National Catholic Education Assoc., 1957), and *Verdi* (1977). Hume leaped to national fame in 1950, when President Truman, outraged by his unenthusiastic review of Margaret Truman's song recital, wrote him a personal letter threatening him with bodily injury. Hume sold the letter to a Connecticut industrialist for an undisclosed sum of money.

Humel, Gerald, American composer; b. Cleveland, Nov. 7, 1931. He studied at Hofstra Univ. in N.Y. (B.A., 1954), the Royal College of Music in London (A.R.C.M., 1956), Oberlin Cons. (M.M., 1958), and the Univ. of Michigan in Ann Arbor (1958–60); in 1960 went to Berlin, where he took private lessons with Boris Blacher and Rufer; remained in Berlin as a permanent resident. His music at 1st maintained a median line of cosmopolitan modernism, in a neo-Classical direction, but gradually he became oriented toward dodecaphonic techniques.
WORKS: Operas: *The Proposal* (1949) and *The Triangle* (Oberlin, Nov. 14, 1958); ballets: *Devil's Dice* (1957); *1st Love* (1965); *Herodias* (1967); Flute Concerto (1964); Chamber Concerto for Horn, Piano, and Strings (1966); Concerto for Wind Orch. (1968); *Flashes* for Chamber Ensemble (1968); *Fantasie* for 2 Flutes, Cello, and Piano (1968); *Lepini* for Orch. (1977); *Duo* for Viola and Cello (1964); Cello Sonata (1967); Clarinet Sonata (1968); 2 sonatas for Solo Viola (1967, 1968).

Humes, Helen, black American jazz and blues singer; b. Louisville, Ky., June 23, 1913; d. Santa Monica, Calif., Sept. 13, 1981. She 1st gained prominence as a singer with Count Basie's orch. (1938–42). Among her most successful renditions were the songs *If Papa Has Outside Lovin', Do What You Did Last Night, Everybody Does It Now, Sub-Deb Blues,* and *He May Be Your Man but He Comes to See Me Sometimes;* her greatest hit was *Be-Baba-Leba* (1945).

Humfrey, Pelham, English composer; b. 1647; d. Windsor, July 14, 1674. He was among the 1st children appointed to the restored Chapel Royal in 1660, and (together with fellow-choristers John Blow and William Turner) he wrote the famous *Club Anthem.* In 1664 King Charles II sent him to study in France and Italy under the Secret Service Funds; that he worked under Lully remains unverified, nor can it be proved that he got to Italy. He returned to England in 1666 as lutenist of the Chapel Royal, and was appointed Gentleman of the Chapel Royal on Jan. 24, 1667. An entry in Pepys's diary for Nov. 15, 1667, described him as being "full of form, and confidence, and vanity" and disparaging "everything, and everybody's skill but his own." Humfrey's justification of his self-confidence lay in his undoubted mastery of the Italian declamatory style, greater than anyone had yet achieved in England. On July 14, 1672, he was appointed Master of the Children of the Chapel Royal. Two years later he died, at the early age of 27. One of his wards was the young Henry Purcell, whose style clearly shows Humfrey's influence.
WORKS: 22 secular songs; 5 sacred songs; a dialogue, composed with John Blow; songs and vocal ensembles for Shadwell's version of Shakespeare's *The Tempest;* 3 odes, all to Charles II; 26 anthems, of which 19 are extant (1 composed with John Blow and William Turner). A number of his secular songs were publ. in collections of his era. A complete ed. of his sacred music has been prepared by P. Dennison in Musica Britannica, XXXIV–XXXV (London, 1972).

BIBL.: W. Barclay Squire, "The Music of Shadwell's Tempest," *Musical Quarterly* (Oct. 1921); P. Dennison, *The Life and Works of P. H.* (diss., Oxford Univ., 1970; includes an ed. and catalog of complete works); idem, "The Will of P. H.," *R.M.A. Research Chronicle*, 7 (1970); idem, "The Church Music of P. H.," *Proceedings of the Royal Music Association*, 98 (1971–72); idem, *P. H.* (London, 1986).

Hummel, Ferdinand, German harpist and composer; b. Berlin, Sept. 6, 1855; d. there, April 24, 1928. He gave concerts as a child harpist (1864–67); then studied music at Kullak's Academy in Berlin and later at the Hochschule für Musik there. He established himself as a teacher in Berlin, and also became a prolific composer. Much impressed by the realistic school of Italian opera (Mascagni), he wrote several short operas in the same genre: *Mara* (Berlin, 1893); *Angla* (Berlin, 1894); *Assarpai* (Gotha, 1898); *Sophie von Brabant* (Darmstadt, 1899); *Die Beichte* (Berlin, 1900); *Ein treuer Schelm* (Altenburg, 1894); and *Die Gefilde der Seligen* (Altenburg, 1917). He also wrote a Sym., a Piano Concerto, chamber music, and choral works.

Hummel, Johann Nepomuk, celebrated Austrian pianist, composer, and pedagogue; b. Pressburg, Nov. 14, 1778; d. Weimar, Oct. 17, 1837. A child prodigy, he began to study the violin and the piano under his father's tutelage; when he was 8 the family moved to Vienna, where his father became music director of the Theater auf der Wieden. Mozart interested himself in the young musician, took him into his house, and for 2 years instructed him. Hummel made his Vienna debut in 1787; then toured under his father's guidance, visiting Bohemia, Germany, Denmark, Scotland, the Netherlands, and England, where he presented his String Quartet in Oxford. He returned to Vienna in 1793 and studied counterpoint with Albrechtsberger, composition with Salieri, and organ with Haydn. He served as Konzertmeister to Prince Nikolaus Esterházy (1804–11), carrying out the duties of Kapellmeister, although Haydn retained the title. His opera *Mathilde von Guise* was produced in Vienna on March 26, 1810. He returned there in 1811 as a teacher; then resumed his appearances as a pianist in 1814, being particularly successful at the Congress of Vienna; subsequently toured Germany in 1816. He served as court Kapellmeister in Stuttgart (1816–18); then in 1819 became Grand Ducal Kapellmeister in Weimar, a position he held until his death. His years in Weimar were marked by his friendship with Goethe. He traveled widely as a pianist; visited St. Petersburg (1822); Paris (1825), where he was made a Chevalier of the Legion of Honor; and Belgium and the Netherlands (1826). In 1827 he was in Vienna, where he visited Beethoven on the composer's deathbed; he traveled to Warsaw in 1828 and to Paris and London in 1830. He revisited London in 1831 and 1833; during the latter visit, he conducted German opera at the King's Theater. The last years of his life were marred by ill health and much suffering. At the peak of his career as a pianist, he was regarded as one of the greatest virtuosos of his time; both as a pianist and as a composer, he was often declared to be the equal of Beethoven. His compositions were marked by excellent craftsmanship; his writing for instruments, particularly for piano, was impeccable; his melodic invention was rich, and his harmonic and contrapuntal skill was of the highest caliber. Yet with his death, his music went into an immediate eclipse; performances of his works became increasingly rare, until the name of Hummel all but vanished from active musical programs. However, some of his compositions were revived by various musical societies in Europe and America, and as a result, at least his Trumpet Concerto and chamber music were saved from oblivion. He wrote works in all genres except the sym. He also publ. *Anweisung zum Pianofortespiel* (1828), an elaborate instruction book and one of the 1st to give a sensible method of fingering. His wife, Elisabeth Hummel-Rockl (1793–1883), was an opera singer; they had 2 sons, a pianist and a painter.

WORKS: *Il Viaggiator ridicolo*, opera (1797; unfinished);

Dankgefühl einer Geretteten, monodrama (March 21, 1799); *Demagorgon*, comic opera (c.1800; only fragment extant; used in the following opera); *Don Anchise Campione*, opera buffa (c.1800; unfinished); *Le vicende d'amore*, opera buffa (1804; rev. as *Die vereitelten Ränke*, Eisenstadt, Sept. 1806); *Die beyden Genies*, Lustspiel (1805; not extant); *Die Messenier*, grosse heroische Oper (c.1805–10); *Pimmalione*, azione teatrale (c.1805–15); *Mathilde von Guise*, opera (Vienna, March 26, 1810; rev. version, Weimar, Feb. 17, 1821); *Stadt und Land*, singspiel (c.1810; unfinished); *Dies Haus ist zu verkaufen*, singspiel (Vienna, May 5, 1812, based on *Die vereitelten Ränke*); Aria in Castelli's pasticcio *Fünf sind Zwey* (Vienna, March 21, 1813); *Der Junker in der Mühle*, singspiel (Nov. 1813); *Die Eselshaut, oder Die blaue Insel*, Feenspiel (Vienna, March 10, 1814); *Die Rückfahrt des Kaisers*, singspiel (Vienna, June 15, 1814); *Attila*, opera (c.1825–27; not extant); music to operas by others; incidental music to plays; ballets and pantomimes; 12 cantatas; sacred music; at least 8 piano concertos; Trumpet Concerto (1803); Bassoon Concerto; numerous works for solo piano; much chamber music.

BIBL.: K. Benyovszky, *J.N. H., Der Mensch und Künstler* (Bratislava, 1934); D. Zimmerschied, *Thematisches Verzeichnis der Werke von J.N. H.* (1971); J. Sachs, "Authentic English and French Editions of J.N. H.," *Journal of the American Musicological Society* (Summer 1972); idem, "H. and the Pirates: The Struggle for Musical Copyright," *Musical Quarterly* (Jan. 1973); idem, "A Checklist of the Works of J.N. H.," *Notes* (June 1974; corrects and complements Zimmerschied); idem, *Kapellmeister H. in England and France* (Detroit, 1977).

Humperdinck, Engelbert, famous German composer and pedagogue; b. Siegburg, near Bonn, Sept. 1, 1854; d. Neustrelitz, Sept. 27, 1921. He began to study piano at 7; commenced composing at 14, then studied at the Cologne Cons. (1872–76), where his teachers were Hiller, Gernsheim, and Jensen (harmony and composition), Hompesch, Mertke, and Seiss (piano), F. Weber (organ), and Ehlert and Rensburg (cello). After winning the Mozart Prize (1876), he studied counterpoint and fugue with Rheinberger at Munich's Royal Music School (1877); also studied composition privately there with F. Lachner. In 1879 he won the Mendelssohn Prize of Berlin for his choral work *Die Wallfahrt nach Kevelaar* (1878); then went to Italy, where he met Wagner in Naples (1880); at Wagner's invitation, he worked in Bayreuth (1881–82). In 1881 he won the Meyerbeer Prize of Berlin, which enabled him to visit Paris in 1882. He taught at the Barcelona Cons. (1885–86) and the Cologne Cons. (1887–88); subsequently worked for the Schott publishing firm in Mainz (1888–89). After serving as private teacher to Siegfried Wagner (1889–90), he joined the faculty of the Hoch Cons. in Frankfurt in 1890; was made prof. there in 1896, but resigned in 1897. During this period he also was music critic of the *Frankfurter Zeitung*. His fame as a composer was assured with the extraordinary success of his opera *Hänsel und Gretel* (Weimar, Dec. 23, 1893), written to a libretto by his sister Adelheid Wette. This fairy-tale score, with its melodies of ingenuous felicity in a Wagnerian idiom, retains its place in the repertoire. Although he continued to write for the stage, his succeeding works left little impression. He was director of a master class in composition at Berlin's Akademische Meisterschule (1900–1920); was also a member of the senate of the Berlin Academy of Arts.

WORKS: OPERAS: *Hänsel und Gretel* (Weimar, Dec. 23, 1893, R. Strauss conducting); *Dornröschen* (Frankfurt, Nov. 12, 1902); *Die Heirat wider Willen* (Berlin, April 14, 1905); *Königskinder* (N.Y., Dec. 28, 1910; based on his incidental music to Rosmer's *Königskinder*; *Die Marketenderin* (Cologne, May 10, 1914); *Gaudeamus* (Darmstadt, March 18, 1919); also *Die sieben Geislein*, children's fairy play for Voice and Piano (Berlin, Dec. 19, 1895). **INCIDENTAL MUSIC:** To Rosmer's *Königskinder* (Munich, Jan. 23, 1897; later expanded into an opera); for the Berlin productions of Shakespeare's *The Merchant of Venice* (Nov. 5, 1905), *The Winter's Tale* (Sept. 15, 1906), *The Tempest* (Oct. 26, 1906), *Romeo and Juliet* (Jan. 29, 1907), and *Twelfth Night* (Oct. 17, 1907); also to Aristophanes' *Lysistrata* (Berlin, Feb. 27, 1908) and Maeterlinck's *The Blue Bird* (Berlin, Dec. 23, 1912), as well as for Reinhardt's production of *The Miracle* (London, Dec. 23, 1911). His other works include *Die Wallfahrtnach Kevelaar* for Chorus (1878); *Humoreske* for Orch. (1879); *Das Glück von Edenhall* for Chorus (Munich, July 15, 1879; 2nd version, 1882–83); *Die maurische Rhapsodie* for Orch. (1898); *4 Kinderlieder* (1901).

BIBL.: O. Besch, *E. H.* (Leipzig, 1914); H. Kühlmann, *Stil und Form in der Musik von H.s Oper "Hänsel und Gretel"* (Borna and Leipzig, 1930); L. Kirsten, *Motivik und Form in der Musik zu E. H.s Oper "Königskinder"* (diss., Univ. of Jena, 1942); K. Püllen, *Die Schauspielmusiken E. H.s* (diss., Univ. of Cologne, 1951); E. Thamm, *Der Bestand der lyrischen Werke E. H.s* (diss., Univ. of Mainz, 1951); W. Humperdinck, *E. H.* (Frankfurt, 1965); K. Fellerer, "E. H. und seine Stellung im deutschen Musikleben," *Heimatbuch der Stadt Siegburg,* 2 (1967); H. Irmen, *Die Odyssee des E. H.: Eine biographische Dokumentation* (Siegburg, 1975); idem, ed., *E. H.: Briefe und Tagebücher* (Cologne, 1976).

Humperdinck, Engelbert (real name, **Arnold George Dorsey**), English popular-music singer; b. Madras, India, May 3, 1936. As a youth, he showed innate aptitude for raucous sentimentality and unmitigated schmaltz; these propensities attracted the attention of a hustler in search of potential rock singers; dissatisfied with the lackluster name of his chosen candidate for lucre and glory, he brazenly picked up the name Engelbert Humperdinck from a music dictionary, and conferred it on Dorsey. As luck would have it, the rechristened singer (and his manager) prospered, making a quantum leap from his early beginnings as a hapless entertainer in British pubs to a successful crowd-pleaser in England and America. His voice was bland and colorless, but his stance was sincere, and his records sold prodigiously among British and American music fans. *Chacun à son goût.*

Humpert, Hans, German composer; b. Paderborn, April 19, 1901; d. in battle in Salerno, Sept. 15, 1943. He studied at the Frankfurt Cons. and in Berlin; then taught at Paderborn until he was called into the army. His music is marked by a neo-Romantic quality, with a strong contrapuntal structure.

WORKS: 2 syms. (1937, 1942); 3 string quartets; String Trio; Violin Sonata; Viola Sonata; Sonata for Flute Solo; 5 cantatas; 4 masses; 3 motets; 7 Psalms; many choral and organ works.

BIBL.: G. Hoffmann, "H. H.," *Musica* (Sept. 1953).

Huneker, James Gibbons, brilliant American writer on music; b. Philadelphia, Jan. 31, 1857; d. N.Y., Feb. 9, 1921. He studied piano with Michael Cross in Philadelphia, and in 1878 in Paris with Théodore Ritter; later with Joseffy at the National Cons. in N.Y.; then taught piano there (1888–98). He was music and drama critic of the *N.Y. Recorder* (1891–95) and the *Morning Advertiser* (1895–97); music, drama, and art critic for the *N.Y. Sun* (1900–1912). In 1917–18 he was music critic of the *Philadelphia Press;* after 1 season (1918–19) with the *N.Y. Times* he became music critic for the *N.Y. World,* a position he held until his death; also wrote for various journals in N.Y., London, Paris, Berlin, and Vienna. He publ. a novel dealing with artistic life in N.Y., *Painted Veils* (1921), but devoted most of his uncommon gifts to musical journalism. He was capable of rising to true poetic style when writing about Chopin and other composers whom he loved; but he also possessed a talent for caustic invective; his attacks on Debussy were particularly sharp. In addition to his literary publications, Huneker furnished introductory essays for Joseffy's ed. of Chopin's works.

WRITINGS: *Mezzotints in Modern Music* (1899); *Chopin: The Man and His Music* (1900; in German, 1914); *Melomaniacs* (1902); *Overtones, A Book of Temperaments* (1904); *Iconoclasts: A Book for Dramatists* (1905); *Visionaries: Fantasies and Fiction* (1905); *Egoists: A Book of Supermen* (1909); *Promenades of an Impressionist: Studies in Art* (1910); *Franz Liszt: A Study* (1911; in German, 1922); *The Pathos of Distance* (1913); *Old Fogy, His Musical Opinions and Grotesques* (1913); *New Cos-*

mopolis (1915); *Ivory Apes and Peacocks* (1915); *Unicorns* (1917); *The Philharmonic Society of New York and Its 75th Anniversary* (1917); *Bedouins* (1920); *Steeplejack* (his memoirs; 1920); *Variations* (1921).

BIBL.: B. De Casseres, *J.G. H.* (N.Y., 1925); A. Schwab, *J.G. H.: Critic of the Seven Arts* (Stanford, Calif., 1963); idem, ed., *Americans in the Arts, 1890–1920: Critiques by J.G. H.* (N.Y., 1985).

Hungerford, Bruce, Australian pianist; b. Korumburra, Victoria, Nov. 24, 1922; d. in an automobile accident in N.Y., Jan. 26, 1977. He received his initial education in Melbourne; studied piano with Ignaz Friedman in Sydney (1944), and later with Ernest Hutcheson at the Juilliard School of Music in N.Y. (1945–47); took private lessons with Myra Hess in N.Y. (1948–58) and also with Carl Friedberg (1948–55). He gave his 1st piano recital in N.Y. in 1951; from then until 1965 he appeared under the name Leonard Hungerford. Apart from his virtuoso technique, he possessed an extraordinary mastery of dynamic gradations and self-consistent musical phraseology. He also gained recognition as a color photographer and archeologist, specializing in Egyptology; he recorded a 17-part audiovisual lecture entitled "The Heritage of Ancient Egypt" (1971).

Hüni-Mihacsek, Felice, noted Hungarian soprano; b. Pécs, April 3, 1891; d. Munich, March 26, 1976. She studied in Vienna with Rosa Papier; made her debut with the Vienna State Opera in 1919, remaining there until 1926; was then a member of the Bavarian State Opera, Munich (1926–44); she retired from the stage in 1953. She particularly excelled in Mozart's operas.

Hunt, Jerry (Edward), American pianist and composer; b. Waco, Texas, Nov. 30, 1943. He studied piano at North Texas State Univ. in Denton; developed a successful career as a performer of modern music; was on the faculty of Southern Methodist Univ. in Dallas (1967–73) and was artist-in-residence at the Video Research Center in Dallas. The titles of his works indicate a preoccupation with mathematical and abstract concepts, as exemplified by his 8 pieces for varying instrumental groups bearing the generic title *Helix* (1961–71); other works are *Sur Dr. John Dee,* scored for "Zero to 11 performers" (1963); *Tabulatura Soyga,* for Zero to 11 Instruments (1965); *Preparallel* for Orch. Groups (1965); *Unit,* a "solo situation" (1967); *Infrasolo* for 10 Cymbals "or something else" (1970); *Autotransform glissando* (1970); *Symphony* for Electronics (1971); *Haramand Playing: Recursive/Regenerative* for Electronic Audio and Video Generating Systems (1972); *Quaquaversal Transmission,* a theater work (1973); *Cantegral Segments* for Various Instruments (1973–78); *Kernel* for Electronics (1980).

Hünten, Franz, German pianist, pedagogue, and composer; b. Koblenz, Dec. 26, 1793; d. there, Feb. 22, 1878. He studied with his father, an organist; at the age of 26 he went to Paris and took courses at the Cons. with Pradher (piano) and Cherubini (composition); composed salon music for piano (fantasies, variations on opera themes, waltzes, etc.), some 250 opus numbers in all, most of which he succeeded in publishing; also brought out a *Méthode nouvelle pour le piano* and other didactic compilations which became popular among teachers and students; Hünten was very much in demand as a piano teacher in Paris. Having accumulated considerable capital from his enterprises, he returned to Koblenz in 1848, and remained there until his death.

BIBL.: G. Zöllner, *F. H.: Sein Leben und sein Werk* (Cologne, 1959).

Hunter, Alberta, outstanding black American blues singer; b. Memphis, Tenn., April 1, 1895; d. N.Y., Oct. 17, 1984. She went to Chicago; began her career there with appearances in nightclubs; subsequently gained fame as an outstanding blues singer; also worked in Europe as a singer and actress. She retired in 1956; after a silence of 21 years, she resumed her career in 1977 and astonished her auditors as one of the last of the great blues singers. She continued to make public appearances in her 89th year.

BIBL.: F. Taylor and G. Cook, *A. H.: A Celebration in Blues* (Santa Barbara, Calif., 1987).

Hunter, Rita (Nellie), distinguished English soprano; b. Wallasey, Aug. 15, 1933. She studied with Edwin Francis in Liverpool and with Clive Carey and Redvers Llewellyn in London; sang in the Sadler's Wells chorus (1954–56) before touring with the Carl Rosa Opera Co. (1956–58); after further studies with Dame Eva Turner, she joined the Sadler's Wells Opera (1959), singing leading roles there from 1965, including Brünnhilde in the English-language version of *Die Walküre* (June 29, 1970); later sang Brünnhilde in the 1st complete English-language version of the *Ring* (July–Aug. 1973). On Dec. 19, 1972, she made her Metropolitan Opera debut in N.Y. as Brünnhilde; appeared as Norma at the San Francisco Opera in 1975. Her other notable roles included Donna Anna, Aida, Senta, and Santuzza. In 1980 she was made a Commander of the Order of the British Empire. She publ. an autobiography entitled *Wait Till the Sun Shines, Nellie* (London, 1986).

Hupfeld, Herman, American composer of popular music, singer, pianist, and lyricist; b. Montclair, N.J., Feb. 1, 1894; d. there, June 8, 1951. He served in the U.S. Navy in World War I. While in the service, he wrote and performed his songs to his own words. Possessing a natural flair for sentimental melodies and nostalgic lyrics, he contributed successfully to Broadway shows; occasionally employed jazz rhythms, as in his song *When Yuba Plays the Rhumba on the Tuba.* He achieved fame with the theme song for the movie *Casablanca* (with Ingrid Bergman and Humphrey Bogart), *As Time Goes By,* a tune that indelibly impinged on the hearts of millions.

Hupperts, Paul (Henri Franciscus Marie), Dutch conductor; b. Gulpen, Jan. 1, 1919. He studied music in Utrecht; then appeared as a guest conductor in the Netherlands. In 1947 he was appointed conductor of the Limburg Orch. From 1949 to 1977 he was chief conductor of the Utrecht Sym. Orch.; in his programs he often included works by modern Dutch composers.

Hurd, Michael (John), English composer, conductor, broadcaster, and writer on music; b. Gloucester, Dec. 19, 1928. He was a pupil of Thomas Armstrong and Bernard Rose at Pembroke College, Oxford (1950–53), and of Lennox Berkeley (1954–56). He taught at the Royal Marines School of Music (1953–59), and from 1956 was a broadcaster with the BBC. His compositions are written in an accessible style; among his lighter scores, the "pop" cantatas have been particularly successful.

WORKS: STAGE: *Little Billy,* children's opera (1964); *Mr. Punch,* operatic entertainment for young people (1970); *The Widow of Ephesus,* chamber opera (Stroud, Oct. 23, 1971). **ORCH.:** *Concerto to an Unwritten Comedy* (1970); *Dance Diversions* (1972); *Sinfonia Concertante* for Violin and String Orch. (1973); *Concerto da Camera* for Oboe and Small Orch. (1979); *A Little Suite* for String Orch. (1985). **CHAMBER:** Sonata for Violin and Piano (1970; rev. 1986); *Harlequin Suite* for Brass (1971; rev. 1982). **VOCAL:** 9 "pop" cantatas: *Jonah-man Jazz* (1966; rev. 1967); *Swingin' Samson* (1972); *Hip-Hip Horatio* (1974); *Rooster Rag* (1975); *Pilgrim* (1978); *Adam-in-Eden* (1981); *Mrs. Beeton's Book* (1982); *Captain Coram's Kids* (1988); *Prodigal* (1989); also choral works; songs.

WRITINGS: *Immortal Hour: The Life and Period of Rutland Boughton* (1962); *The Composer* (1968); *An Outline of European Music* (1968; 2nd ed., rev., 1988); *Elgar* (1969); *Vaughan Williams* (1970); *Mendelssohn* (1970); *The Ordeal of Ivor Gurney* (1978); *The Oxford Junior Companion to Music* (1979); *Vincent Novello and Company* (1981); *The Orchestra* (1981).

Huré, Jean, French pianist, organist, composer, and writer on music; b. Gien, Loiret, Sept. 17, 1877; d. Paris, Jan. 27, 1930. He received his musical education at a monastery in Angers; went to Paris in 1895; there he founded the École Normale pour Pianistes (1912) and the monthly magazine *L'Orgue et les Organistes* (1923); in 1925 he became church organist at St. Augustin; in 1926 he won the Prix Chartier for composition. His ballet, *Le Bois sacré,* was produced at the Opéra-Comique in Paris on June 28, 1921; he further wrote incidental music to Musset's *Fantasio;* 3 syms.; Violin Concerto; *Andante* for Saxophone and Orch.; 2 string quartets; Piano Quintet; Violin Sonata; 3 cello sonatas; etc. He publ. the manuals *La Technique du piano* (1908); *La Technique de l'orgue* (1918); also *L'Esthétique de l'orgue* (1923) and *Saint Augustin, musicien* (1924).

BIBL.: G. Migot, *J. H.* (1926).

Hurford, Peter (John), noted English organist; b. Minehead, Somerset, Nov. 22, 1930. He studied law and music at Jesus College, Cambridge; later took organ lessons with André Marchal in Paris. In 1958 he was named Master of the Music at St. Albans Abbey; in 1963 he founded the International Organ Festival there. He left St. Albans in 1979 to pursue his international career as a leading interpreter of the music of the Baroque period. He publ. the study *Making Music on the Organ* (Oxford, 1988). In 1984 he was made an Officer of the Order of the British Empire.

Hurley, Laurel, American soprano; b. Allentown, Pa., Feb. 14, 1927. Of a musical family, she studied with her mother, a church organist; at 16, she appeared on Broadway (Aug. 21, 1943) as Kathie in Romberg's operetta *The Student Prince;* then toured with the company that produced it. She was the winner of the Walter W. Naumburg Foundation Award, which enabled her to give a song recital in N.Y. (Nov. 6, 1952). She made her debut at the Metropolitan Opera in N.Y., on Feb. 8, 1955, in a minor role; on Jan. 11, 1957, she appeared in the title role of *La Périchole;* she remained at the Metropolitan until 1967.

Hurlstone, William (Yeates), English pianist and composer; b. London, Jan. 7, 1876; d. there, May 30, 1906. A precocious musician, he composed waltzes as a young child; studied at the Royal College of Music in London with Stanford (composition) and Edward Dannreuther (piano); performed his own Piano Concerto in 1896. In 1905 he was appointed a prof. at the Royal College of Music, but died in the following year; his early death was much regretted.

WORKS: *The Magic Mirror,* fairy suite for Orch.; *Variations on a Hungarian Air* and *Fantasie-Variations on a Swedish Air* for Orch.; Quartet for Flute, Oboe, Horn, and Bassoon; Quintet for Flute, Oboe, Horn, Bassoon, and Piano; Piano Trio; Trio for Clarinet, Bassoon, and Piano; Clarinet Sonata; Bassoon Sonata; several song cycles.

BIBL.: H. Newell, *W.Y. H.: Musician and Man* (London, 1936); K. Hurlstone, ed., *W. H., Musician: Memories and Records by His Friends* (London, 1949).

Hurník, Ilja, Czech pianist and composer; b. Poruba, near Svinov, Nov. 25, 1922. He moved to Prague in 1938; studied composition with Řídký and was the last pupil of Novák (1941–44); later studied piano with Štěpánová at the Prague Academy of Music (1945–51); then made several concert tours in Czechoslovakia. His works are marked with impressionistic flavor, while retaining a classical format.

WORKS: 3 operas: *Dáma a lupiči* (The Lady and the Gangster), after the film *The Ladykillers* (1966), *Mudrci a bloudi* (The Wise and the Foolish; 1968), and *Diogenes* (1974); ballet, *Ondráš* (1950); oratorio, *Noe* (Noah; 1959); 2 cantatas: *Maryka* (1948; rev. 1955) and *Ezop* (Aesop; 1964); *Sulamit,* cycle of songs after the Old Testament, for Female Voice and Orch. (1963); Flute Concerto (1953); Serenade for Strings (1954); Concerto for Winds and Percussion (1956); Concerto for Oboe, String Orch., and Piano (1959); *Musikanti* (The Musicians) for 20 Instruments (1962); *Chamber Music* for Strings (1962); *Kyklopes* (Cyclops) for Orch. (Prague, June 4, 1965); Concerto for Piano and Small Orch. (1972); *Věci,* divertimento for Chamber Orch. (1977); *Ozvěna,* chamber cantata (1981); Wind Quintet (1944); 2 string quartets (1949; 2nd, with Baritone Solo, to Old Testament texts, 1961); Viola Sonata (1952); *Die vier Jahreszeiten* (The 4 Seasons of the Year) for 12 Solo Instruments (1952); *Sonata da camera* for Flute, Oboe, Cello, and Harpsichord (1953); Piano Quintet (1953); *Ballet* for 9 Instruments (1954); *Esercizi* for Flute, Oboe, Clarinet, and Bassoon (1958); *Moments musicaux* for 11 Winds (1962); *Gloria di flauti* for 2 Flutes (1973); Preludes for Piano (1943); Piano Sonatina (1952); 3 organ sonatas (1956); Étude for Piano (1972).

Hurok, Sol(omon Israelovich), Russian-born American impresario; b. Pogar, April 9, 1888; d. N.Y., March 5, 1974. Fleeing the political iniquities of the Czarist regime in regard to Jews, he emigrated to the U.S. in 1906, and became a naturalized citizen in 1914. In 1913 he inaugurated a series of weekly concerts announced as "Music for the Masses" at the Hippodrome in N.Y.; then became an exclusive manager for famous Russian artists, among them Anna Pavlova, Feodor Chaliapin, Artur Rubinstein, Mischa Elman, and Gregor Piatigorsky, as well as numerous other celebrities in the fields of ballet and opera. He negotiated the difficult arrangements with the Soviet government for American appearances of the Bolshoi Ballet, the Ukrainian dance company, and the Leningrad Kirov Ballet; made frequent trips to Russia, helped by his fluency in the language. Ironically, his N.Y. office became the target of a bomb attack by a militant Jewish organization which objected to Hurok's importation of Soviet artists, even though many of the artists were themselves Jewish.

Hurst, George, English conductor; b. Edinburgh, May 20, 1926, of Rumanian-Russian parentage. He 1st studied piano with Isserlis; then took courses in conducting and composition at the Royal Cons. of Music of Toronto; also studied conducting with Monteux. He was a teacher and conductor at the Peabody Cons. of Music in Baltimore (1947–55); then was assistant conductor of the London Phil. Orch. (1955–57) and of the BBC Northern Sym. Orch. at Manchester (1958–68); subsequently conducted the Bournemouth Sinfonietta (until 1978). From 1986 to 1990 he was principal guest conductor of the BBC Scottish Sym. Orch. in Glasgow. In 1990 he became principal conductor of the National Sym. Orch. of Ireland in Dublin.

Hurum, Alf (Thorvald), Norwegian pianist, conductor, composer, and painter; b. Christiania, Sept. 21, 1882; d. Honolulu, Aug. 15, 1972. He studied with Max Bruch at the Hochschule für Musik in Berlin (1905–9); later took additional courses in Paris and in Russia. He was a co-founder of the Soc. of Norwegian Composers in 1917. After touring as a concert pianist, he settled in Hawaii, where he established the Honolulu Sym. Orch. and was its conductor briefly (1924–26). His 2nd career was that of a silk painter in the Japanese manner, which preoccupied him during his later years. In his music he cultivated coloristic harmonies, somewhat in an impressionist mode.
    WORKS: 2 violin sonatas (1911, 1916); *3 Aquarelles* for Piano (1912); String Quartet (1913); *Exotic Suite* for Violin and Piano (1916); *Pastels*, 4 pieces for Piano (1916); *Eventyrland* (Fairy Land), suite for Orch. or Piano (1920); *Gotiske bilder*, 6 pieces for Piano (1920); *Norse Suite* for Orch. (1920); *Bendikt and Aarolilja*, symphonic poem (1923); Sym. (Bergen, 1927); piano pieces; songs; motets.

Hurwitz, Emanuel (Henry), English violinist and conductor; b. London, May 7, 1919. He received a scholarship from Bronislaw Huberman which allowed him to study at the Royal Academy of Music in London. In 1948 he became concertmaster of the Goldsborough (later English) Chamber Orch., a position he held until 1968; was then concertmaster of the New Philharmonia Orch. (1969–71). He was also active as a chamber music artist; was 1st violinist of the Hurwitz String Quartet (1946–51), the Melos Ensemble (1956–72), and the Aeolian Quartet (from 1970). In 1968 he founded the Hurwitz Chamber Orch. (from 1972 known as the Serenata of London), a conductorless

ensemble. He was made a Commander of the Order of the British Empire in 1978.

Hus-Desforges, Pierre Louis, French cellist, conductor, and composer; b. Toulon, March 14, 1773; d. Pont-le-Voy, near Blois, Jan. 20, 1838. He studied at the Paris Cons.; played the cello in various orchs.; held numerous posts as a theatrical conductor and teacher. He was director of the orch. of the Théâtre-Français in St. Petersburg early in the 19th century; returning to France, was cellist at the Théâtre Saint-Martin in Paris; from 1819 to 1822 taught at Metz; in 1823 was in Bordeaux; from 1824, again in Paris. His name as composer appears for the 1st time as Citoyen Desforges, on a song entitled *L'Autel de sa patrie* (Paris, 1798); he also composed a String Quartet and a "Sinfonia concertante" with Violin and Cello obbligato; he publ. a historical novel, *Sapho à Leucade* (Paris, 1818), and a *Méthode de violoncelle à l'usage des commençants* (Paris, 1828).

Husa, Karel, distinguished Czech-born American composer, conductor, and pedagogue; b. Prague, Aug. 7, 1921. He studied violin and piano in his youth; concurrently took courses in engineering; in 1941 he entered the Prague Cons., studying composition with Jaroslav Řidký; in 1945–46 he attended the Academy of Music; in 1946 was awarded a French government grant to continue his studies in Paris at the École Normale de Musique and the Paris Cons.; his teachers included Arthur Honegger and Nadia Boulanger; he also studied conducting with Jean Fournet and André Cluytens. In 1954 he emigrated to the U.S., and joined the music dept. of Cornell Univ. as teacher of composition and conductor of the student orch. He also taught at Ithaca College (1967–86). He became an American citizen in 1959. He appeared widely as a guest conductor, frequently including his own music in his programs. In his early works he followed the modern Czech school of composition, making thematic use of folk tunes; later he enlarged his musical resources to include atonal, polytonal, microtonal, and even occasional aleatory procedures, without following doctrinaire prescriptions to the letter. His music is oxygenated by humanistic Romanticism; as a result, it gains numerous performances. In 1969 Husa received the Pulitzer Prize in Music for his 3rd String Quartet. In 1974 he was elected to membership in the Royal Belgian Academy of the Arts and Sciences. In 1986 he received an honorary Doctor of Music degree from Ithaca College.
    WORKS: ORCH.: Overture for Large Orch. (1st public perf., Prague, June 18, 1946); Sinfonietta for Orch. (Prague, April 25, 1947); *3 fresques* for Orch. (Prague, April 27, 1949; rev. as *Fresque* for Orch., Syracuse, N.Y., May 5, 1963); Divertimento for String Orch. (Paris, Oct. 30, 1949); Concertino for Piano and Orch. (Brussels, June 6, 1952); *Musique d'amateurs*, 4 Easy Pieces for Oboe, Trumpet, Percussion, and Strings (1953); *Portrait* for String Orch. (Donaueschingen, Oct. 10, 1953); Sym. No. 1 (Brussels, March 4, 1954); 4 Little Pieces for Strings (Fürsteneck, March 17, 1957); *Fantasies for Orchestra* (Ithaca, N.Y., April 28, 1957); Divertimento for Brass and Percussion (Ithaca, N.Y., Feb. 17, 1960); Poem for Viola and Chamber Orch. (Cologne, June 12, 1960); *Mosaïques for Orchestra* (Hamburg, Nov. 7, 1961); *Élégie et Rondeau* for Alto Saxophone and Orch. (Ithaca, N.Y., May 6, 1962); Serenade for Woodwind Quintet Solo with String Orch., Xylophone, and Harp (Baltimore, Jan. 7, 1964); *Festive Ode* for Chorus and Orch. (1965); Concerto for Brass Quintet and String Orch. (Buffalo, Feb. 15, 1970); Concerto for Alto Saxophone and Concert Band (Ithaca, N.Y., March 17, 1968); *Music for Prague 1968* (2 versions; for Band: Washington, D.C., Jan. 31, 1969; for Orch.: Munich, Jan. 31, 1970; 1st Czech perf. of orch. version, Prague, Feb. 13, 1990, composer conducting); Concerto for Percussion and Wind Instruments (Waco, Texas, Feb. 7, 1972); *Apotheosis of This Earth* for Wind Instruments (Ann Arbor, Mich., April 1, 1971; 2nd version for Chorus and Orch.: Ithaca, N.Y., April 12, 1973); *2 Sonnets from Michelangelo* for Orch. (Evanston, Ill., April 28, 1972); Trumpet Concerto (Storrs, Conn., Aug. 9, 1974); *The Steadfast Tin Soldier* for

Narrator and Orch. (Boulder, Colo., May 10, 1975); *Monodrama*, ballet for Orch. (Indianapolis, March 26, 1976); *An American Te Deum* for Baritone, Chorus, and Wind Ensemble (Cedar Rapids, Iowa, Dec. 4, 1976; 2nd version for Baritone, Chorus, and Orch.: Washington, D.C., May 10, 1978); Fanfare for Brass Ensemble (1980); Pastoral for Strings (Miami Beach, April 12, 1980); *The Trojan Women*, ballet for Orch. (Louisville, March 28, 1981); Concerto for Wind Ensemble (Lansing, Mich., Dec. 3, 1982); Cantata for Men's Chorus and Brass Quintet (Crawfordsville, Ind., April 20, 1983); Sym. No. 2, *Reflections* (Greensboro, N.C., July 16, 1983); *Smetana Fanfare* for Wind Ensemble (San Diego, April 3, 1984); *Symphonic Suite* (Athens, Ga., Oct. 1, 1984); Concerto for Orch. (N.Y., Sept. 25, 1986); Organ Concerto, *The Sunlights* (Cleveland, Oct. 28, 1987); Trumpet Concerto (Chicago, Feb. 11, 1988); Cello Concerto (1988; Los Angeles, March 2, 1989). **CHAMBER:** String Quartet (1942–43); Suite for Viola and Piano (1945); String Quartet No. 1 (Prague, May 23, 1948); Piano Sonata No. 1 (1950); *Evocations of Slovakia* for Clarinet, Viola, and Cello (Paris, May 4, 1952); String Quartet No. 2 (Paris, Oct. 23, 1954); 2 *Preludes* for Flute, Clarinet, and Bassoon (Ithaca, N.Y., April 21, 1966); Divertimento for Brass Quintet (Ithaca, N.Y., Nov. 20, 1968); String Quartet No. 3 (Chicago, Oct. 14, 1968); Studies for Percussion (1968); Sonata for Violin and Piano (N.Y., March 31, 1974); Piano Sonata No. 2 (1975); *Landscapes* for Brass Quintet (Kalamazoo, Mich., Oct. 17, 1977); 3 *Dance Sketches* for Percussion (Miami Beach, April 12, 1980); *Intradas and Interludes* for 7 Trumpets and Timpani (Columbus, Ohio, June 20, 1980); 3 *Moravian Songs* for Chorus a cappella (1981); *Every Day* for Chorus a cappella (1981); *Sonata a tre* for Violin, Clarinet, and Piano (Hong Kong, March 23, 1982); *Recollections* for Woodwind Quintet and Piano (Washington, D.C., Oct. 28, 1982); *Variations* for Violin, Viola, Cello, and Piano (Atlanta, May 20, 1984); *Intrada* for Brass Quintet (Baltimore, Nov. 15, 1984); String Quartet No. 4 (1989); 12 *Moravian Songs* for Voice and Piano (1956); other vocal pieces. **BIBL.:** L. Hartzell, "K. H.: The Man and the Music," *Musical Quarterly* (May 1976).

Hüsch, Gerhard (Heinrich Wilhelm Fritz), noted German baritone; b. Hannover, Feb. 2, 1901; d. Munich, Nov. 21, 1984. He made his debut in Osnabrück in 1923; then sang in Bremen. From 1927 to 1930 he was a member of the Cologne Opera; then went to Berlin, appearing with the City and State Operas (1930–44); also sang at Bayreuth. In later years he became known as a lieder artist.

Husmann, Heinrich, distinguished German musicologist; b. Cologne, Dec. 16, 1908; d. Brussels, Nov. 8, 1983. He studied musicology with Ludwig at the Univ. of Göttingen, and with Hornbostel, Schering, Wolf, and Blume at the Humboldt Univ. in Berlin; received his Ph.D. there in 1932. In 1933 he was appointed assistant lecturer at the musicological inst. at the Univ. of Leipzig; completed his Habilitation there in 1941, and then was made its acting director in 1944. He completed a 2nd Habilitation at the Univ. of Hamburg in 1948; organized its musicological inst. in 1949; was a reader there from 1956 and a prof. from 1958. In 1960 he became a prof. of musicology at the Univ. of Göttingen. His books include *Fünf- und siebenstellige Centstafeln zur Berechnung musikalischer Intervalle* (Leiden, 1951); *Vom Wesen der Konsonanz* (Heidelberg, 1953); *Einführung in die Musikwissenschaft* (Heidelberg, 1958); *Grundlagen der antiken und orientalischen Musikkultur* (Berlin, 1961). **BIBL.:** H. Becker and R. Gerlach, eds., *Speculum musicae artis: Festgabe für H. H.* (Munich, 1970).

Huss, Henry Holden, American pianist and composer; b. Newark, N.J., June 21, 1862; d. N.Y., Sept. 17, 1953. He was a descendant of Jan Huss, the Bohemian martyr. His mother, Sophia Ruckle Holden Huss, was a granddaughter of Levi Holden, a member of George Washington's staff. Huss studied piano and theory with his father and with O. Boise. In 1882 he went to Germany, and studied organ and composition with Rheinberger at the Munich Cons.; graduated with a *Rhapsody* for Piano and Orch. (1885), which he subsequently performed with several American orchs.; he also played his Piano Concerto in B with the N.Y. Phil., the Boston Sym., etc. In 1904 he married Hildegard Hoffmann, a concert singer; they appeared frequently in joint recitals.
WORKS: *Rhapsody* for Piano and Orch. (1885); *Romance and Polonaise* for Orch. (1889); Piano Concerto (1894); Violin Concerto (1906); symphonic poems: *Life's Conflicts* (1921) and *La Nuit* (orig. for Piano Solo, 1902; orchestrated 1939; Washington, D.C., March 12, 1942); 4 string quartets; Violin Sonata; Cello Sonata; Viola Sonata; choral works.

Huston, (Thomas) Scott (Jr.), American composer; b. Tacoma, Wash., Oct. 10, 1916; d. Cincinnati, March 1, 1991. He studied with Burrill Phillips, Bernard Rogers, and Howard Hanson at the Eastman School of Music in Rochester, N.Y. (B.M., 1941; M.M., 1942; Ph.D., 1952); from 1952 to 1988 he taught at the Univ. of Cincinnati College–Cons. of Music. He leaned toward a modern concept of Romanticism, not without an admixture of decidedly advanced techniques.
WORKS: Toccata for Piano and Orch. (Rochester, May 30, 1951); *Abstract* for Orch. (Cincinnati, Nov. 20, 1955); *The 8th Word of Christ*, cantata (1959); Organ Sonata (1960); *Intensity I* for Wind Ensemble (1962); Concerto for Trumpet, String Orch., Harp, and Timpani (1963); Sym. No. 3, *Phantasms* (Cincinnati, Feb. 2, 1968); *Pro vita* for Piano and Brass Quintet (1965); *The Wisdom of Patriotism* for Chorus, Band, and Orch. (1966); *Penta-Tholoi* for Piano (1966); *Phenomena* for Flute, Oboe, Double Bass, and Harpsichord (1967); *Idioms* for Violin, Clarinet, and Horn (1968); *Love and Marriage*, chamber cantata (1969); *The Oratorio of Understanding* (1969); *The Song of Deborah*, cantata (1969); *Orthographics* for 4 Trombones (1970); *Divinely Superfluous Beauty and Natural Music*, song cycle for Soprano and Chamber Ensemble (1971); *A Game of Circles* for Clarinet, Celesta, and Piano (1971); *Sounds at Night* for Brass Choir (1971); *Life-Styles I* and *II* for Piano Trio, or Clarinet, Cello, and Piano (1972); Sym. No. 4 for String Orch. (Cincinnati, Aug. 10, 1972); *Suite: For Our Times* for Brass Sextet (1973); *Tamar*, monodrama for Soprano and Piano (1974); *Eleatron* for Viola and Piano (1975); *Impressions from Life* for Small Chamber Orch. (1977); *Ecstasies of Janus* for Countertenor and Small Ensemble (1978); *Time/Reflections*, cantata enigmatica for Chorus and Chamber Orch. (1978); *Blind Girl*, opera (1981); Sym. No. 6, *The Human Condition* (1982); *Songs of the Courtesans* for Voice and Chamber Ensemble (1985; Cincinnati; Nov. 20, 1988); *Optimism: A Way of Life* for Brass Quintet (1986); *An Ecumenical Mosaic of Cincinnati* for Chorus, Organ, and Double String Quartet (1987; Cincinnati, May 1, 1988); *The Unpredictable Pendulum of Temperaments* for 3 Women Dancers and Chamber Ensemble (1988).

Hutchens, Frank, New Zealand pianist and composer; b. Christchurch, Jan. 15, 1892; d. Sydney, Australia, Oct. 18, 1965. He studied at the Royal Academy of Music in London with Matthay (piano) and Corder (composition); taught there from 1908 to 1914; in 1915 was appointed a prof. at the New South Wales State Cons. in Sydney. In 1962 he was made an Officer of the Order of the British Empire. His compositions include *Ballade* for Orch. (1938); Concerto for 2 Pianos and Orch. (1940); *Air Mail Palestine* for Voice and Orch. (1942); also piano pieces.

Hutcherson, Bobby (Robert), black American vibraphone and marimba player and composer; b. Los Angeles, Jan. 27, 1941. Inspired by the playing of the great Milt "Bags" Jackson, he took up vibes, soon finding his own voice. In 1962 he went to N.Y., where he worked with Eric Dolphy, Jackie McLean, Archie Shepp, Hank Mobley, Herbie Hancock, and Andrew Hill, all musicians who were beginning to break the boundaries of traditional song forms. He made a series of excellent recordings for Blue Note Records; the album *Medina* (1969), in particular, represents a pure jazz esthetic. In 1985 he began a series of recordings which incorporated strong Afro-Cuban rhythmic elements; these included *Good Bait* (1985), *Color Scheme* (1986), *In the Vanguard* (1987), *Cruisin' the Bird* (1988), and *Ambos Mandos* (1989).

Hutcheson, Ernest, Australian pianist, writer on music, teacher, and composer; b. Melbourne, July 20, 1871; d. N.Y., Feb. 9, 1951. He studied piano in Australia with Max Vogrich; played concerts as a very young child; then was sent to the Leipzig Cons. to study with Reinecke, graduating in 1890. In 1898 he performed his own Piano Concerto with the Berlin Phil. In 1900 he arrived in the U.S.; was head of the piano dept. at the Peabody Cons. in Baltimore (1900–1912). In 1915 he created a sensation in N.Y. by playing 3 concertos (Tchaikovsky, Liszt, and MacDowell) in a single evening; in 1919 he repeated his feat, playing 3 Beethoven concertos in 1 evening. From 1924 to 1945 he was variously associated with the Juilliard School in N.Y., including serving as its dean (1927–37) and its president (1937–45). Among his compositions are several symphonic works and numerous piano pieces. He publ. *The Elements of Piano Technique* (N.Y., 1907); *Elektra by Richard Strauss: A Guide to the Opera* (N.Y., 1910); *A Musical Guide to the Richard Wagner Ring of the Nibelung* (N.Y., 1940); *The Literature of the Piano* (N.Y., 1948; 2nd ed., rev., 1964).

Hutchings, Arthur (James Bramwell), English musicologist; b. Sunbury-on-Thames, July 14, 1906. He studied violin and piano; then was engaged in teaching music and composing; was prof. of music at Durham Univ. (1947–68) and at Exeter Univ. (1968–71). His books include *Schubert* (London, 1945; 4th ed., 1973); *Delius* (London, 1948); *A Companion to Mozart's Piano Concertos* (London, 1948; 3rd ed., 1980); *The Invention and Composition of Music* (London, 1958); *The Baroque Concerto* (London, 1961; 3rd ed., rev., 1973); *Church Music in the Nineteenth Century* (London, 1967); *Mozart: The Man, the Musician* (London, 1976); *Purcell* (London, 1982).

Hutschenruyter (Hutschenruijter), noted family of Dutch musicians:

(1) Wouter Hutschenruyter, conductor and composer; b. Rotterdam, Dec. 28, 1796; d. there, Nov. 18, 1878. He studied violin, horn, and theory; was founder-director of the band of the Rotterdam civic guard (1821) and of the music society Eruditio Musica (1826). He was a teacher at the music school of the Maatschappij tot Bevordering der Toonkunst. Among his compositions are the opera *Le Roi de Bohème* (Rotterdam, 1833), several syms., overtures, a Concertino for 8 Timpani and Orch., much band music, masses, cantatas, chamber music, and songs.

(2) Willem Jacob Hutschenruyter, horn player and conductor, son of the preceding; b. Rotterdam, March 22, 1828; d. there, Jan. 19, 1889. He played the horn in the orchs. of the Rotterdam Opera and his father's Eruditio Musica; was conductor of the municipal band (1865–85).

(3) Wouter Hutschenruyter, conductor, musicologist, and composer, son of the preceding; b. Rotterdam, Aug. 15, 1859; d. The Hague, Nov. 14, 1943. He studied in Rotterdam, where he began his career as a choral conductor and teacher; then was 2nd conductor of the Concertgebouw Orch. in Amsterdam (1890–92); subsequently was conductor of the Utrecht municipal orch. (1892–1917), which he developed into a respected Dutch ensemble; later was director of the music school of Rotterdam's Maatschappij tot Bevordering der Toonkunst (1917–25). He composed a Piano Concerto, a *Nocturne* for Horn and Orch., various other orch. pieces, chamber music, piano pieces, and songs. **WRITINGS:** *Richard Strauss* (Haarlem, 1898); *Orkest en orkestspel na 1600* (Utrecht, 1903); *Felix Weingartner* (Haarlem, 1906); *Het muziekleven in de 17e eeuw* (Baarn, 1909); *Wolfgang Amadeus Mozart* (Rotterdam, 1909; abridged ed., 1927, as *Mozart*; 2nd ed., 1943); *De geschiedenis der toonkunst* (Amsterdam, 1920); *De programma muziek* (Bussum, 1922); *De geschiedenis van het orkest en van zijn instrumenten* (Amsterdam, 1926); *Mahler* (The Hague, 1927); *De symphonieën van Beetho-*

ven geanalyseerd en toegelicht (The Hague, 1928; 2nd ed., 1943); *Wagner* (The Hague, 1928); *Brahms* (The Hague, 1929); with J. Kruseman, *Richard Strauss* (The Hague, 1929); *Een en ander uit de geschiedenis der militaire muziek* (Hilversum, 1930); *Grepen uit geschiedenis van de piano en van het pianospel* (Hilversum, 1930); *De sonates van Beethoven geanalyseerd en toegelicht* (The Hague, 1930); *De dirigent* (Hilversum, 1931; 3rd ed., 1955); *De ontwikkeling der symphonie door Haydn, Mozart en Beethoven* (Hilversum, 1931); *De geschiedenis der kamermuziek* (Hilversum, 1935); with J. Kruseman, *Musiciana* (The Hague, 1938); *Frédéric Chopin* (The Hague, 1939; 3rd ed., 1949); *Bijdrage tot de bibliographie der muziekliteratur* (Leiden, 1941–43); *Grepen uit de geschiedenis van de snaarinstrumenten en van het snarenspel* (Hilversum, 1942); *Franz Schubert* (The Hague, 1944).

Hüttenbrenner, Anselm, Austrian composer; b. Graz, Oct. 13, 1794; d. Ober-Andritz, near Graz, June 5, 1868. At the age of 7 he studied with the organist Gell; studied law at the Univ. of Graz; in 1815 he went to Vienna to study with Salieri. Schubert was his fellow student, and they became close friends. Hüttenbrenner also knew Beethoven intimately, and was present at his death. He was an excellent pianist and a prolific composer; Schubert praised his works. He wrote 6 operas; an operetta; 8 syms.; many overtures; 10 masses; 4 Requiems; 3 funeral marches; 2 string quartets; a String Quintet; piano sonatas; 24 fugues; other piano pieces; some 300 male quartets; 200 songs. One of his songs, *Erlkönig*, was included in the collection *12 Lieder der deutschen Romantik*, ed. by H. Rosenwald (1929). His reminiscences of Schubert (1854) were publ. by Otto Deutsch in 1906. It was Hüttenbrenner who came into the possession of many Schubert MSS after Schubert's death, among them that of the "Unfinished Sym.," which he held until 1865. It has been suggested that Hüttenbrenner lost the 3rd and 4th movements of Schubert's work, and for that reason was reluctant to part with the incomplete MS, but the extant sketches for the Scherzo make that unlikely.
    BIBL.: K. Kurth, *A. H. als Liederkomponist* (diss., Univ. of Cologne, 1932); T. Pritchard, "The Unfinished Symphony," *Music Review* (Jan. 1942); F. Hüttenbrenner, "A. H. und Schuberts H-moll Symphonie," *Zeitschrift des Historischen Vereines für Steiermark*, LII (1961).

Huybrechts, Albert, Belgian composer; b. Dinant, Feb. 12, 1899; d. Woluwe-St.-Pierre, near Brussels, Feb. 21, 1938. He studied at the Brussels Cons. with Martin Lunssens, Paulin Marchand, Léon Dubois, and Joseph Jongen. In 1926 he gained international recognition by winning 2 U.S. prizes, the Elizabeth Sprague Coolidge Prize of the Library of Congress for his Violin Sonata, and the Ojai Valley Prize in California for his String Quartet. In 1937 he was appointed a prof. at the Brussels Cons., but a severe attack of uremia led to his premature death. He wrote in a judiciously modern idiom, seasoned with prudential dissonance.
    WORKS: 2 symphonic poems: *David* (1923) and *Poème féerique* (1923); *Chant funèbre* for Cello and Orch. (1926); *Sérénade* for Orch. (1929); *Chant d'angoisse* for Orch. (1930; his most distinctive work); Nocturne for Orch. (1931); *Divertissement* for Brass and Percussion (1931); Cello Concertino (1932); 2 string quartets (1924, 1927); Violin Sonata (1925); Trio for Flute, Viola, and Piano (1926); Sextet for Wind Quintet, with 2nd Flute (1927); Suite for Flute, Oboe, Clarinet, Bassoon, and Piano (1929); *Choral* for Organ (1930); *Sicilienne* for Piano (1934); *Pastourelle* for Cello and Piano (1934); Sonatine for Flute and Viola (1934); String Trio (1935); Wind Quintet (1936); songs, of which the best known is *Horoscopes* (1926).

Hvorostovsky, Dmitri, Russian baritone, distinguished by tremendous vocal splendor; b. Krasnoyarsk, Oct. 16, 1962. He studied piano before receiving vocal instruction from Ekaterina Yofel; subsequently won the Glinka Prize (1987). He then proceeded to Wales, where he won 1st prize in the BBC Cardiff Singer of the World Competition (1989). His European appearances included Amsterdam, London, Dublin, and Nice. In 1990 he appeared in recital in N.Y. (March 4) and in Washington, D.C. (March 10), obtaining unprecedented acclaim. He enchanted his audiences particularly with his inspiring renditions of songs by Tchaikovsky and Rachmaninoff. He also seemed to have mastered the standard operatic repertoire, fulfilling engagements at La Scala in Milan and other operatic centers. The press did not spare superlatives, comparing him with the finest masters of song.

Hvoslef (Saeverud), Ketil, Norwegian composer, son of **Harald Saeverud;** b. Fana, near Bergen, July 19, 1939. He took his mother's maiden name in 1980. He studied organ and viola at the Bergen Cons., graduating in 1962; studied composition with Blomdahl and Lidholm in Stockholm and with Jersild in Copenhagen. From 1963 to 1979 he was on the faculty of the Bergen Cons. After a period of hesitant serialism he evolved a "motivic assimilation technique," wherein a central motif influences all the other thematic material in the manner of a theme with variations.

WORKS: STAGE: Choral opera, *The Ballad of Narcissus and Echo,* for Mixed Chorus a cappella (1981); much incidental music. **ORCH.:** Sinfonietta (1963); Piano Concertino (1964); Trumpet Concerto (1968–69; Bergen, April 22, 1972); *Mi-Fi-Li,* symphonic poem (Oslo, Sept. 4, 1972); Double-bass Concerto (1973); Cello Concerto (1976); *Variations* for Chamber Orch. (1976); Double Concerto for Flute, Guitar, and String Orch. (1977); Concertino for Orch. (Trondheim, Sept. 20, 1979); Concerto for Bassoon and Strings (1979); *Suite* for School Orch. (1980); *Antigone,* symphonic variations (1981–82); *Il Compleanno* (Bergen, Oct. 8, 1985). **CHAMBER:** Clarinet Quartet (1962); Wind Quintet (1964); *Suite* for Guitar (1966); *Ariseturo,* concerto for Percussion and 8 Wind Instruments (1966); *Duets* for Bassoons (1966); 2 string quartets (1969, 1973); *Flauto Solo* (1970); *Tromba Solo* (1971); *Kim* for 4 Crumhorns, 4 Recorders, Bass Gamba, and Percussion (1975); Trio for Oboe, Violin, and Percussion (1978); Octet for Flutes (1978); *Brass* for 13 Brass Instruments (1978); *Violino Solo* (1980); *Post,* sextet (1980); *Duodu* for Violin and Viola (1982); *Erkejubel* for 2 Trumpets, 2 Trombones, Synthesizer, and Percussion (1982). **VOCAL:** *So einsam ist der Mensch,* after Nelly Sachs, for Chorus or Vocal Quartet (1970); *Or "Håvamål"* (Sayings of the High One), cantata for Chorus and Orch. (1971; rev. 1974); *Kvartoni* for Voice, Recorder, Guitar, and Piano (1974); Trio for Soprano, Alto, and Piano (1974); *Collage in Black/White with Red* for Baritone Narration, Violin, Guitar, Clarinet, and Percussion (1975); Concerto for Choir and Orch. (1977); *Spillemaend* (Fiddlers) for Chorus, Hardanger Fiddle, and Organ (1980); *Dano Tiore,* quintet for Soprano, Violin, Viola, Cello, and Harpsichord (1985). **PIANO:** *Rondo con variazioni* (1970); *Beethoven Fantasy* (1982). **ORGAN:** *Organ Variations* (1972); *Organo Solo* (1974).

BIBL.: L. Reitan, "K. H.—the Champion of Intuition," *Nordic Sounds* (Sept. 1985).

Hwang, Byung-Ki, Korean composer, virtuoso kayagum performer, and pedagogue; b. Seoul, May 31, 1936. He studied traditional Korean music and the kayagum (a 12-stringed Korean zither with movable bridges, dating from the turn of the 7th century) at the National Classical Music Inst. in Seoul (1951–58), his principal teachers being Yong-yun Kim, Yundok Kim, and Sang-gon Sim. He received 1st prize at the National Competition of Traditional Music (1954, 1956), a National Music Prize (1965), and the Korean Cinema Music Award (1973). From 1974 he was prof. of Korean traditional music at the College of Music, Ewha Women's Univ., in Seoul; in 1985–86 he was a visiting scholar at Harvard Univ. Hwang is noted as the 1st Korean composer to write modern works for the kayagum; he is also a distinguished kayagum player, and has appeared in recital in the U.S., West Germany, France, and Austria. His U.S. debut took place in N.Y.'s Carnegie Hall on April 20, 1986, in a program which included a number of his own compositions. His works are translucent and elegant

in their structures, and impressionistic in harmonic and melodic design.

WORKS: KAYAGUM: *The Forest* (1963); *The Pomegranate House* (1965); *Kara Town* (1967); *Chimhyangmu* (1974); *The Silk Road* (1977); *Sounds of the Night* (1985); *Southern Fantasy* (1989). **OTHER INSTRUMENTS:** *Pungyo* for Piri (Korean oboe; 1972); *Mandaeyop-haetan* for Korean Orch. (1976); *Chasi* for Taegum (Korean bamboo flute; 1978); *Unbak* for Korean Orch. (1979); *Harim Castle* for Taegum (1982); *Soyopsanbang* for Komungo (Korean 6-stringed plucked zither with 16 frets; 1989). **VOCAL:** *Beside a Chrysanthemum* for Voice, Komungo, and Changgu (Korean hour-glass drum with 2 heads; 1962); *Chongsando and Kanggangsullae* for Chorus (1974); *The Labyrinth* for Voice and Kayagum (1975); *Nolbujon,* narrative song (1976); *The Evening Chant* for Chorus and Percussion (1983); also dance music; film scores.

Hyde, Walter, English tenor; b. Birmingham, Feb. 6, 1875; d. London, Nov. 11, 1951. He studied with Gustave Garcia; sang in light opera before he undertook Wagnerian roles, which became his specialty. He sang Siegmund at Covent Garden in London in 1908; his other roles included Walther in *Die Meistersinger von Nürnberg* and also Parsifal. He made his Metropolitan Opera debut in N.Y., on March 28, 1910, as Siegmund in *Die Walküre;* then returned to England and made regular appearances at Covent Garden; later sang with the Beecham Opera Co. and the British National Opera Co., serving as a director of the latter. He was a frequent participant at many musical festivals in England.

Hye-Knudsen, Johan, distinguished Danish conductor; b. Nyborg, May 24, 1896; d. Copenhagen, Sept. 28, 1975. He studied cello at the Royal Danish Cons. of Music in Copenhagen with Rudinger; also in Paris with André Hekking; studied conducting in Dresden with Fritz Busch. In 1925 he was named a conductor of the Royal Danish Theater in Copenhagen; concurrently led concerts of the Royal Danish Orch. He was also a composer; wrote a number of orch. works and 2 operas: *Orfeus i underverdenen* (Copenhagen, Jan. 1, 1934) and *Kirke og orgel* (Copenhagen, Nov. 8, 1947).

Hykes, David (Bond), distinctive American composer and vocalist; b. Taos, N.Mex., March 2, 1953. He studied filmmaking at Antioch College, in Ohio (1970–74), and arts administration at Columbia Univ. (M.F.A., 1984). He also studied classical Azerbaijani and Armenian music with Zevulon Avshalomov (1975–77) and north Indian rāga singing with S. Dahr (1982). In 1975 he founded the Harmonic Choir, whose members employ vocal techniques borrowed from Tibetan and Mongolian music in which strongly resonated upper partials are produced in addition to the fundamental tone. From 1979 the ensemble was in residence at the ideal location of the Cathedral of St. John the Divine in N.Y., and from 1980 made tours of the U.S. and Europe. In 1981 Hykes traveled to Mongolia under the auspices of the Asian Cultural Council. His compositions for voice use harmonics to produce rich waves of slowly changing sounds over diatonic melodies; the result resembles a sort of modernized chant with an ethereal haze of overtones. Among such compositions are *Hearing Solar Winds* (1977–83), *Current Circulation* (1983–84), and *Harmonic Meetings* (1986). He has also written several film and television scores and a number of instrumental works.

BIBL.: N. Kenyon, "Tuning the Skies," *New Yorker,* LVIII (1982); J. Reinhard, "An Interview with D. H.," *Ear Magazine East,* VII/5 (1982–83); R. Palmer, "Get Ready for the Music of Harmonics," *N.Y. Times* (July 17, 1983).

Hyllested, August, Swedish pianist and composer; b. Stockholm, June 17, 1856; d. Blairmore, Scotland, April 5, 1946. He played in public as a child; then studied at the Copenhagen Cons. with Niels Gade, and subsequently with Theodor Kullak (piano) and Friedrich Kiel (composition) in Berlin; then had some lessons from Liszt. He gave concerts as a pianist in England (1883) and in America (1885). From 1886 to 1891 he was a prof. and assistant director of the Chicago Musical

College; from 1891 to 1894, he taught piano at the Gottschalk Lyric School in Chicago. After a concert tour in Europe, he returned to Chicago in 1897; he was in Glasgow from 1903 to 1914; then again in the U.S. (1916–19), and in Denmark and Sweden (1919–21); in 1923 he retired to Blairmore, where he died shortly before his 90th birthday. He publ. numerous piano pieces in a Romantic style (*Album Leaf, Valse sentimentale, Suite romantique,* etc.); a suite of Scandinavian dances; a fantasia on Scotch tunes; choral pieces; a symphonic poem, *Elizabeth,* with Double Chorus (London, 1897, composer conducting).

Hynninen, Jorma, distinguished Finnish baritone and operatic administrator; b. Leppävirta, April 3, 1941. He studied at the Sibelius Academy in Helsinki (1966–70); also took courses in Rome with Luigi Ricci and in Salzburg with Kurt Overhoff. He won 1st prize at the singing competition in Lappeenranta in 1969, and in the Finnish division of the Scandinavian singing competition in Helsinki in 1971. In 1970 he made his concert debut in Helsinki, as well as his operatic debut as Silvio in *Pagliacci* with the Finnish National Opera there, and subsequently sang leading roles with the company. He also made 1st appearances at La Scala in Milan (1977), the Vienna State Opera (1977), the Hamburg State Opera (1977), the Bavarian State Opera in Munich (1979), and the Paris Opéra (1980); gave recitals throughout Europe and the U.S. He made his N.Y. debut in a recital in 1980; his operatic debut followed in 1983, when he sang with the Finnish National Opera during its visit to America; made his Metropolitan Opera debut in N.Y. as Rodrigo in *Don Carlo* on March 30, 1984. He was artistic director of the Finnish National Opera from 1984 to 1990. In addition to such traditional operatic roles as Pelléas, Wolfram, Orpheus, and Valentin in *Faust,* he has sung parts in contemporary Finnish operas; he created the role of the King in *The King Goes Forth to France* by Aulis Sallinen, 1st performed at the Savonlinna Opera Festival on July 7, 1984; also created the title role in Rautawaura's *Thomas,* performed in Joensuu on June 21, 1985.

I

Iannaccone, Anthony (Joseph), American composer; b. N.Y., Oct. 14, 1943. He studied composition with Giannini, Diamond, and Flagello at the Manhattan School of Music (M.M., 1968), and with Adler and Benson at the Eastman School of Music in Rochester, N.Y. (Ph.D., 1971). In 1971 he was appointed to the faculty of Eastern Michigan Univ.; he founded there an Electronic Music Studio. In his music he applies serial methods with a certain liberality toward unintentional occurrences of tonal, and even explicitly triadic, elements. In his band music he openly exploits pop devices.

WORKS: ORCH.: *Suite* (1962); 2 syms. (1965, 1966); Concertino for Violin and Orch. (1967); *Lysistrata,* overture (1968); *Variations* for Violin and Orch. (1969); *Interlude* for Wind Instruments (1970); *Antiphonies* for Wind Instruments (1973); *Scherzo* for Band (1976); *Of Fire and Ice* for Band (1977); *After a Gentle Rain* for Band (1980); *Images of Songs & Dance:* No. 1, *Orpheus,* for Wind Instruments (1982); No. 2, *Terpsichore,* for Wind Instruments (1981); *Plymouth Trilogy* for Wind Instruments (1981); *Divertimento* (1983); *Apparitions* for Wind Ensemble or Band (1986); *Sinfonia concertante* for Flute, Violin, Viola, Cello, Piano, and Orch. (1988; rev. 1989); *Whispers of Heavenly Death* (1989). **CHAMBER:** Piano Trio (1959); Viola Sonata (1961); 2 violin sonatas (1964, 1971); String Quartet (1965); *Remembrance* for Viola and Piano (1968); *Hades* for Brass Quartet (1968); *3 Mythical Sketches* for Brass Quintet (1971); *Anamorphoses* for 2 Trumpets, Trombone, and Percussion (1972); *Rituals* for Violin and Piano (1973); *Parodies* for Wind Quintet (1974); *Bicinia* for Flute and Saxophone (1975); Sonatina for Trumpet and Tuba (1975); *Night Song* for Bassoon and Piano (1975); *Aria concertante*

for Cello and Piano (1976); *Invention* for 2 Saxophones (1978); Trio for Flute, Clarinet, and Piano (1979); *Toccata-Fanfares* for Brass Sextet or Brass Choir (2 vols., 1986); *Mobiles* for 3 Brass and 2 Percussion Players (1988; Richmond, Va., July 21, 1989). **PIANO:** *Retail Rags* (1959); *Partita* (1967); *Keyboard Essays* (1972); *Inventions* (1985). **VOCAL:** *The Prince of Peace,* cantata (1970); *Walt Whitman Song No. 2* for Soloists, Chorus, and Winds (1980); numerous choruses; tape pieces.

Ibach, Johannes Adolf, German piano maker; b. Barmen, Oct. 17, 1766; d. there, Sept. 14, 1848. In 1794 he founded a piano factory at Barmen; also manufactured organs from 1834, with his son C. Rudolf Ibach; then traded under the name of Adolf Ibach & Sohn; from 1839, as Rudolf & Söhne, when his son Richard joined the firm. From 1862 the firm was known as C. Rudolf & Richard Ibach, to distinguish it from another business founded by a 3rd son, Gustav J. The same year C. Rudolf died, and in 1869 his son **Rudolf** (d. Herrenalb, Black Forest, July 31, 1892) continued the piano factory alone as Rudolf Ibach Sohn; he established a branch at Cologne, gained medals for the excellence of his pianos, and became purveyor to the Prussian court. Richard Ibach continued the organ factory.

BIBL.: *Das Haus I. 1794–1894* (1895).

Ibert, Jacques (François Antoine), distinguished French composer; b. Paris, Aug. 15, 1890; d. there, Feb. 5, 1962. He studied at the Paris Cons. with Gédalge and Fauré (1911–14); during World War I served in the French navy; returned to the Paris Cons. after the Armistice and studied with Paul Vidal; received the Prix de Rome in 1919 for his cantata *Le*

Poète et la fée; while in Rome, he wrote his most successful work, the symphonic suite *Escales* (Ports of Call), inspired by a Mediterranean cruise while serving in the navy. In 1937 he was appointed director of the Académie de France of Rome, and held this post until 1960; was also administrator of the Réunion des Théâtres Lyriques Nationaux in Paris (1955–56). He was elected a member of the Institut de France (1956). In his music, Ibert combines the most felicitous moods and techniques of Impressionism and neo-Classicism; his harmonies are opulent; his instrumentation is coloristic; there is an element of humor in lighter works, such as his popular orch. *Divertissement* and an even more popular piece, *Le Petit Âne blanc,* from the piano suite *Histoires.* His craftsmanship is excellent; an experimenter in tested values, he never fails to produce the intended effect.

WORKS: OPERAS: *Angélique* (Paris, Jan. 28, 1927); *Persée et Andromède, ou Le Plus Heureux des trois* (1921; Paris, May 15, 1929); *Le Roi d'Yvetot* (Paris, Jan. 15, 1930); *Gonzague* (Monte Carlo, 1935); *L'Aiglon,* with Honegger (Monte Carlo, March 11, 1937); *Les Petites Cardinal,* with Honegger (Paris, 1938); *Barbebleue,* radio opera (Lausanne Radio, Oct. 10, 1943). **BALLETS** (all 1st perf. in Paris): *Les Rencontres* (Nov. 21, 1925); *Diane de Poitiers* (April 30, 1934); *Les Amours de Jupiter* (March 9, 1946); *Le Chevalier errant* (May 5, 1950); *Tropismes pour des Amours Imaginaires* (1957). **ORCH.:** Symphonic poem, *Noël en Picardie* (1914); *Ballade de la geôle de Reading,* after Oscar Wilde (Paris, Oct. 22, 1922); *Escales,* 3 symphonic pictures (Paris, Jan. 6, 1924); *Féerique,* symphonic scherzo (Paris, Dec. 12, 1925); Concerto for Cello and Wind Instruments (Paris, Feb. 28, 1926); *Divertissement,* suite (Paris, Nov. 30, 1930; from incidental music to *Le Chapeau de paille d'Italie*); *Paris,* suite for Chamber Orch. (Venice, Sept. 15, 1932; from incidental music to *Donogoo* by Jules Romains); Flute Concerto (Paris, Feb. 25, 1934); *Concertino da camera* for Saxophone and Chamber Orch. (Paris, May 2, 1935); *Capriccio* (1938); *Ouverture de fête* (Paris, Jan. 18, 1942); *Suite élisabéthaine* (1944); *Symphonie concertante* for Oboe and String Orch. (Basel, Feb. 11, 1949); *Louisville Concerto* (Louisville, Ky., Feb. 17, 1954); *Hommage à Mozart* for Orch. (1957); *Bacchanale* for Orch. (1958); *Bostoniana* for Orch. (1956–61). **VOCAL:** *Le Poète et la fée,* cantata (1919); *Chant de folie* for Solo Voices, Chorus, and Orch. (Boston, April 23, 1926); *3 chansons* for Voice, and Orch. or Piano; *La Verdure dorée* for Voice and Piano; *Chanson du rien* for Voice and Piano; *Quintette de la peur* for Chorus and Piano (1946). **CHAMBER:** *2 mouvements* for 2 Flutes, Clarinet, and Bassoon (1923); *Jeux,* sonatina for Flute and Piano (1924); *3 pièces brèves* for Flute, Oboe, Clarinet, Horn, and Bassoon (1930); *Pastoral* for 4 Fifes (in *Pipeaux,* by various composers, 1934); *Entr'acte* for Flute and Guitar (1935); String Quartet (1944); Trio for Violin, Cello, and Harp (1944); *2 Interludes* for Violin and Harpsichord (1949); also 6 pieces for Harp (1917); a piece for Unaccompanied Flute (1936). **PIANO:** *Histoires* (10 pieces); *Les Rencontres,* arranged from the ballet (5 pieces); *Petite suite en 15 images* (1943).

BIBL.: A. Hoerée, "J. I.," *Revue Musicale* (July 1929); G. Samazeuilh, *Musiciens de mon temps* (Paris, 1947); J. Feschotte, *J. I.* (Paris, 1959); G. Michel, *J. I., L'Homme et son œuvre* (Paris, 1968).

Ichiyanagi, Toshi, Japanese composer, pianist, and conductor; b. Kobe, Feb. 4, 1933. He studied composition with Ikencuchi and piano with Chieko Hara; then went to N.Y., where he took courses at the Juilliard School of Music (1952). Returning to Japan in 1961, he founded the group New Directions (1963) and assisted Takemitsu in the organization of the Orchestral Space Festival (1966); also participated in concerts sponsored by the Soc. for 20th Century Music. In 1966–67 he gave concerts in the U.S. with Cage, Tudor, and other avant-garde musicians. He created various works for Expo '70 in Osaka, including *Music for Living Space* for Chorus and Computer (1969). Among his other works are *Shiki soku ze kū, kū soku ze shiki* (Lust Is Emptiness, Emptiness Is Lust) for Tape (1965), *Voice Act* for Chorus (1973), and

Recurrence for Flute, Clarinet, Harp, Piano, and Percussion (1977).

Idelsohn, Abraham Zevi, eminent Latvian musicologist; b. Pfilsburg, near Libau, July 13, 1882; d. Johannesburg, Aug. 14, 1938. He studied in Königsberg, in Berlin, and with Jadassohn, Krehl, Zoellner, and Kretzschmar at the Leipzig Cons. He possessed a powerful baritone voice and for a time was cantor of the synagogue at Regensburg (1903–5); then went to Johannesburg and later (1906–21) was in Jerusalem, where he founded an Inst. for Jewish Music (1910) and a Jewish music school (1919). In 1921 he returned to Germany; then went to the U.S.; lectured at the Hebrew Union College in Cincinnati (1924–34). In 1934 he suffered a paralytic stroke; was taken to Miami, and in 1937 to Johannesburg, where he finally succumbed. Idelsohn was one of the greatest authorities on Jewish music and contributed much toward its establishment on a scientific basis. He publ. a quantity of studies in English, German, and Hebrew on oriental and Hebrew music, of which the most important are *History of Jewish Music* (in Hebrew, 1924; 2nd ed., 1928, also publ. in Eng.); *The Ceremonies of Judaism* (Cincinnati, 1929); *Diwan of Hebrew and Arabic Poetry of the Yemenite Jews* (in Hebrew; 1930); *Jewish Liturgy and Its Development* (N.Y., 1932). His most important contribution to the study of Jewish music is the monumental *Thesaurus of Hebrew-Oriental Melodies* (10 vols., Leipzig, 1914–32), in which are collected, with the aid of phonograph recordings, Jewish melodies of North Africa, Asia Minor, Palestine, and other parts of the world. He also composed and publ. 6 synagogue services; Hebrew songs (1929); a music drama, *Jephtah* (1922); and a *Jewish Song Book for Synagogue, Home and School* (1929).

Ifukube, Akira, Japanese composer; b. Kushiro, March 7, 1914. As a young man he was trained in forestry; then took lessons from Alexander Tcherepnin. He wrote several ballets based on Japanese melodies. His music is rooted in Japanese modalities, but he adorns them with impressionistic harmonies.

WORKS: BALLETS: *Salome* (1948); *Enchanted Citadel* (Tokyo, Dec. 20, 1949); *Fire of Prometheus* (1950); *Drums of Japan* (Tokyo, Dec. 29, 1951); *The Martyrs of Japan* (Tokyo, March 30, 1972). **ORCH.:** *Japanese Rhapsody* (1935; Boston, April 5, 1936); *Triptyque aborigène* (1937); Piano Concerto (1941; Tokyo, March 3, 1942; music destroyed in an air raid); *Ballade symphonique* (Tokyo, Nov. 20, 1943); *Arctic Forest* (Changchun, Manchuria, April 26, 1944); 2 violin concertos: No. 1 (Tokyo, June 22, 1948); No. 2 (1978); *Bascana* (1949); *Rapsodia concertante* for Violin and Orch. (1951); *Buddha* (1953); *Sinfonia Tapkaara* (1954; Indianapolis, Jan. 21, 1955); *Ritmica ostinata* for Piano and Orch. (1961); *Rondo in Burlesque* for Concert Band (1972); *Lauda concertata* for Marimba and Orch. (1976; rev. 1979); *Eglogue symphonique* for Orch. and Japanese Instruments (1982). **OTHER:** *Okhotsk,* choral ode for Chorus and Orch. (1958); several pieces for solo guitar.

Iglesias (Buga), Julio, Spanish singer and songwriter of popular music; b. Madrid, Sept. 23, 1943. He was 20 before he evinced an interest in music, teaching himself to play the guitar. After studying English at Cambridge, he entered the Benidorm Song Festival in his native country and carried off all of its prizes (1968); he subsequently pursued a successful international career, turning out some 60 albums in 6 languages, which sold over 100 million copies, and for which his name was entered in the *Guinness Book of World Records.*

Igumnov, Konstantin (Nikolaievich), distinguished Russian pianist and pedagogue; b. Lebedyan, near Tambov, May 1, 1873; d. Moscow, March 24, 1948. He studied piano with Zverev and Siloti, and theory with Taneyev, Arensky, and Ippolitov-Ivanov at the Moscow Cons., graduating as a pianist in the class of Pabst (1894). He gave numerous concerts, specializing in Romantic music, and was regarded as an artist of impeccable taste who worked out every detail of the music to the utmost perfection. But great as his artistic reputation was in

Russia (he rarely, if ever, played abroad), his main accomplishment was as a piano pedagogue. He was appointed a prof. of the Moscow Cons. in 1899, and remained on its staff for nearly half a century, until his death. Among his students were Nicolai Orlov, Dobrowen, and Oborin.

BIBL.: Y. Milstein, *K.N. I.* (Moscow, 1975).

Ikebe, Shin-Ichiro, Japanese composer; b. Tokyo, Sept. 15, 1943. He studied with Ikenouchi, Yashiro, and Miyoshi at the Tokyo Univ. of Arts, graduating in 1967.

WORKS: *The Death Goddess,* opera (1971; NHK-TV, July 25, 1971; winner of the 1971 Salzburg Opera Prize); *The Whistling of the Wind,* musical drama (1976); *Hoichi, the Earless,* opera (1982); *Cleopatra, Her Love and Death,* ballet (1983); *Chichibu Bansho,* opera (1988); *Movement* for Orch. (1965); Sonata for Violin (1965); *Crepa in sette capitoli* for Violin, 3 Violas, Cello, and Double Bass (1966); *Construction,* 2 movements for Orch. (1966); Trio for Oboe, Clarinet, and Bassoon (1966); 2 piano concertos: No. 1 (1966–67); No. 2, *Tu M'* (1987); *Raccontino* for Violin and Piano (1967); 3 syms.: No. 1 (1967; Tokyo, March 30, 1968); No. 2, *Trias* (1979); No. 3, *Ego Phano* (1984); *Petite symphonie pour enfants* for Small Orch. (1969); *Lion* for Brass Ensemble (1969); *Un-en* for 2 Kotos, Ju-shichi-gen, Violin, Viola, Cello, and Double Bass (1970); *Energia* for 60 Players (1970); *Clipper by 9* for Nonet (1971); *Trivalence I* for Flute, Violin, and Piano or Organ (1971) and *II* for Harpsichord, Clarinet, and Cello (1973); *Flash!* for Flute Ensemble (1972); *Kusabi* for 11 Players, Female Chorus, and Dance (1972); *Monovalence I* for Marimba (1972) and *III* for Voice (1973); *Dimorphism* for Organ and Orch. (1974); *Quadrants* for Japanese Instruments and Orch. (1974); Violin Concerto (1981); *Spirals* for 9 Horns (1979); *Black Blank Blaze* for 9 Clarinets (1982); *Oedipus' Pilgrimage* for Joruri, Male Chorus, and 10 Players (1984); choruses; songs.

Ikenouchi, Tomojirô, Japanese composer; b. Tokyo, Oct. 21, 1906. In 1927 he became the 1st Japanese student at the Paris Cons., where he studied with Fauchey, Busser, and Caussade; returned to Japan in 1936 and became a prof. of composition at Tokyo Univ.; from 1947, taught at the Tokyo National Univ. of Fine Arts and Music.

WORKS: *Yuya,* music for a Noh drama (Tokyo, Feb. 1, 1943); *3 Pieces* for Orch. (1937); *4 Seasons* for Orch. (1938); *Umaki-Uta* for Orch. (1938); Sym. in 2 movements (Tokyo, Nov. 4, 1951); *Koi no omoni* (Burden of Love) for Baritone, Timpani, and Chorus (1974); 3 string quartets (1937, 1945, 1946); *Fantasy* for Cello and Piano (1940); Flute Sonata (1946); Violin Sonata (1946); Cello Sonatina (1946); Piano Sonatina (1946); *Ceremonial Music* for Piano Duet (1958).

Ikonen, Lauri, Finnish musicologist and composer; b. Mikkeli, Aug. 10, 1888; d. Helsinki, March 21, 1966. He studied at Helsinki Univ. and with Paul Juon in Berlin (1910–13); was ed. of the Finnish music magazine *Suomen Musikkilehti* (1923–29). His music follows the Romantic tradition of Sibelius.

WORKS: 6 syms.: No 1, *Sinfonia inornata* (1922); No. 2 (1937); No. 3, *Lemmin poika* (Son of Lemmi; 1941; rev. 1959); No. 4, *Sinfonia concentrata* (1942); No. 5, *Sinfonia aperta* (1943); No. 6 (1956); *Koulemaantuomitun mielialoja* (Thoughts of a Condemned Man) for Baritone and Orch. (1936); Violin Concerto (1939); Piano Trio (1941); *Concerto meditativo* for Cello and Orch. (1942); *Concerto intimo* for Piano (1956); *Elaman lahja* (The Gift of Life) for Soloists, Chorus, and Orch. (1956); 2 violin sonatas; Piano Sonata; choral works; songs.

Ikonomov, Boyan Georgiev, Bulgarian composer; b. Nikopol, Dec. 14, 1900; d. Sofia, March 27, 1973. He studied in Sofia (1920–26); then went to Paris, where he attended classes of d'Indy and Lioncourt at the Schola Cantorum (1928–32); also took a course in conducting with Weingartner in Basel (1934). Returning to Bulgaria, he was music director of Sofia Radio (1937–48) and of the Bulgarian film center (1948–56); then was head of the music dept. of Sofia Radio (1957–60). His music is rooted in Bulgarian folk songs, with an emphasis on modal melodic progressions and asymmetric rhythms.

WORKS: Opera, *Indje Voivoda* (1960); children's operetta, *The Young Artful Boys* (1960); 3 ballets: *The 7 Mortal Sins* (1933), *The Tragedy of Othello* (1946), and *The Light Floods Everything* (1967); 2 oratorios: *The Legend of Shipka* (1968) and *Vassil Levsky* (1972); 2 cantatas: *George Dimitrov* (1954) and *Poem about Lenin* (1969); *Haidouk Rhapsody* for Orch. (1932); Sinfonietta (1934); *Kaliakra,* symphonic poem (1935); *Pastorale* for Chamber Orch. (1937); 4 syms. (1937, 1947, 1955, 1971); *Pastorale and Dance* for Orch. (1939); *Shar Planina,* symphonic poem (1942); Violin Concerto (1951); Divertimento for String Quartet and Orch. (1956); Piano Concertino (1958); 6 string quartets (1933, 1937, 1941, 1944, 1945, 1949); 2 trios for Oboe, Clarinet, and Bassoon (1935, 1968); Cello Sonata; choral and solo songs; incidental music.

Ilerici, Kemal, Turkish composer; b. Kastamonu, Oct. 15, 1910. He studied composition with Ferit Alnar. Among his works are a symphonic suite, *In My Village* (1945), *Pastoral Fantasy* for Orch. (1951), String Quartet, Suite for Oboe and Piano, and choral works. He wrote a book on Turkish music, *Türk musikisi tonal sistemi ve armonisi* (1948).

Iliev, Konstantin, Bulgarian conductor, teacher, and composer; b. Sofia, March 9, 1924; d. there, March 6, 1988. He studied composition with Khadzhiev and Vladigerov, and conducting with Goleminov, at the Bulgarian State Cons. in Sofia (1942–46); later took courses in composition with Řídký and Alois Hába, and in conducting with Talich, at the Prague Cons. (1946–47). Returning to Bulgaria, he devoted himself mainly to conducting; was a conductor at the National Opera in Sofia (1947–56); then conducted the Varna Sym. Orch. (1956–72) and the Sofia Phil. (1978–85). From 1964 to 1985 he was on the faculty of the State Cons. in Sofia. As a composer, he evolved a rather stimulating idiom, adroitly exploring the asymmetric Balkan rhythms and oriental melismas to create an aura of folkloric authenticity; in non-ethnic pieces he often applied serial principles of melodic formations.

WORKS: Operas: *The Master of Boyana* (Sofia, Oct. 3, 1962) and *The Kingdom of the Deer* (1975); oratorio, *Eulogy to Constantin the Philosopher* (1971); 5 syms. (1947, 1951, 1954, 1958, 1959); *Concerto grosso* for String Orch., Piano, and Percussion (1949); *Symphonic Variations* (1951); *Tempi concertanti I* for String Orch. (1967); *Tempi concertanti II* for Flute, Harpsichord, and 12 Instruments (1969); Violin Concerto (1971); 4 string quartets (1949, 1952, 1953, 1956); Piano Trio (1976); choruses.

Ilitsch, Daniza, Serbian soprano; b. Belgrade, Feb. 21, 1914; d. Vienna, Jan. 15, 1965. She studied at the Stankovic Cons. in Belgrade, then in Berlin; made her debut as Nedda in *Pagliacci* with the Berlin State Opera (Nov. 6, 1936); was on its roster for 2 seasons; then became a member of the Vienna State Opera (1938–41). The German army of occupation put her in a concentration camp in 1944, and she spent 4 months there until the liberation of Vienna. She made her debut with the Metropolitan Opera in N.Y. as Desdemona (March 12, 1947).

Ilyinsky, Alexander Alexandrovich, Russian composer; b. Tsarskoye Selo, Jan. 24, 1859; d. Moscow, Feb. 23, 1920. He graduated from the St. Petersburg Cons. (1885); also studied in Berlin with Kullak (piano) and Bargiel (composition); upon returning to Moscow, was a teacher at the Phil. Inst. (1885–1905). He wrote an opera, *The Fountain of Bakhchisaray* (1911); *3 valses brillantes* for Piano; several orch. works.

Imai, Nobuko, Japanese violist; b. Tokyo, March 18, 1943. She studied at the Toho School of Music in Tokyo and at the Juilliard School of Music in N.Y.; won 1st prize at viola competitions in Munich and Geneva; subsequently played in several chamber music groups.

Imbert, Hugues, French music critic and essayist; b. Moulins-Engilbert, Nièvre, Jan. 11, 1842; d. Paris, Jan. 15, 1905. He studied violin; was on the editorial staff of *Le Guide Musical.* He publ. *Profils des Musiciens* (3 series: 1888, 1892, 1897);

Symphonie (1891); *Portraits et Études* (1894); *Rembrandt et Wagner* (1897); *Charles Gounod, L'Autobiographie et les Mémoires* (1897); *Bizet* (1899); *La Symphonie après Beethoven* (1900); *Médaillons contemporains* (1902); *J. Brahms: Sa vie et son œuvre* (1906).

Imbrie, Andrew (Welsh), notable American composer and teacher; b. N.Y., April 6, 1921. He studied piano with Leo Ornstein (1930–42); then served in the Signal Corps of the U.S. Army during World War II; spent a summer studying composition with Nadia Boulanger at Fontainebleau; intermittently had fruitful sessions with Sessions, 1st privately, then at Princeton Univ. and at the Univ. of Calif. at Berkeley (M.A., 1947). In 1947 he was awarded the American Prix de Rome; after a sojourn in Italy, was appointed a prof. of music at Berkeley, in 1960. He held 2 Guggenheim fellowships (1953–54; 1959–60). He was elected to membership in the National Inst. of Arts and Letters in 1969, and in the American Academy of Arts and Sciences in 1980. His style of composition is marked by a sharp and expressive melodic line, while the polyphony is vigorously motile; harmonic confluence is dissonant but euphoniously tonal. His natural propensity is toward instrumental writing; even his choral pieces possess the texture of chamber music. **WORKS: ORCH.:** *Ballad* (1947; Florence, June 20, 1949); Violin Concerto (1954; Berkeley, April 22, 1958); *Little Concerto for Piano, 4-hands, and Orch.* (1956; Oakland, Calif., Nov. 14, 1961); *Legend* (San Francisco, Dec. 9, 1959); Sym. No. 1 (San Francisco, May 11, 1966); Sym. No. 2 (San Francisco, May 20, 1970); Sym. No. 3 (Manchester, England, Dec. 4, 1970); Cello Concerto (1972; Oakland, Calif., April 30, 1973); Piano Concerto No. 1 (1973); Piano Concerto No. 2 (1974); Flute Concerto (N.Y., Oct. 13, 1977). **CHAMBER:** 4 string quartets (1942, 1953, 1957, 1969); Piano Trio (1946); Piano Sonata (1947); *Divertimento* for 6 Instruments (1948); *Serenade* for Flute, Viola, and Piano (1952); *Impromptu* for Violin and Piano (1960); Cello Sonata (1966); *Pilgrimage* for Flute, Clarinet, Violin, Cello, Piano, and Percussion (1983); *Eulogy* for Piano (1986). **VOCAL:** *On the Beach at Night,* to words by Walt Whitman (1948); *Drum Taps,* cantata to words by Walt Whitman (1961); operas: *Christmas in Peeples Town* (Berkeley, Dec. 3, 1964) and *Angle of Repose,* after Wallace Stegner (San Francisco, Nov. 6, 1976); *3 Campion Songs* for Vocal Quartet and Piano (1981); *Requiem* for Soprano, Chorus, and Orch. (1984).

Inbal, Eliahu, prominent Israeli conductor; b. Jerusalem, Feb. 16, 1936. He was educated at the Cons. and Academy of Music in Jerusalem; then studied conducting with Franco Ferrara in Rome, Louis Fourestier in Paris, and Sergiu Celibidache. In 1963 he won 1st prize in the Cantelli Competition; he then appeared widely in Europe as a guest conductor. From 1974 to 1990 he was chief conductor of the Frankfurt Radio Sym. Orch.; in 1980 took this orch. to the U.S. for the 1st time. From 1983 to 1986 he served as artistic director of the Teatro La Fenice in Venice.

Inch, Herbert Reynolds, American composer; b. Missoula, Mont., Nov. 25, 1904; d. La Jolla, Calif., April 14, 1988. He studied at the Univ. of Montana and then at the Eastman School of Music in Rochester, N.Y., with Howard Hanson (Mus.B., 1925; M.M., 1928); he was a fellow of the American Academy in Rome in 1931. After teaching for several years at the Eastman School, he became a member of the faculty at Hunter College, N.Y. (1937–65). **WORKS:** *Variations on a Modal Theme* (Rochester, April 29, 1927); *3 Pieces* for Small Orch. (Rochester, Oct. 24, 1930); Sym. No. 1 (Rochester, May 5, 1932); Serenade for Small Orch. (Rochester, Oct. 24, 1939); Piano Concerto (1940); *Answers to a Questionnaire* for Orch. (1942); *Northwest Overture* (1943); *Return to Zion* for Women's Chorus (1945); Piano Quintet (1930); *Mediterranean Sketches* for String Quartet (1933); Divertimento for Brass (1934); String Quartet (1936); Cello Sonata (1941); *3 Conversations* for String Quartet (1944); 3 symphoniettas

(1948, 1950, 1955); Piano Trio (1963); 3 piano sonatas (1935, 1946, 1966).

d'India, Sigismondo, outstanding Italian composer; b. Palermo, c.1582; d. probably in Modena, before April 19, 1629. He most likely traveled throughout Italy visiting various courts (1600–1610), then was director of chamber music at the court of Carlo Emanuele I, Duke of Savoy, in Turin (1611–23). After working at the Este court in Modena (1623–24), he was in the service of Cardinal Maurizio of Savoy in Rome (1624–25); subsequently was in the service of the Este court in Modena. He was a master of secular vocal music, excelled only by the great Monteverdi. His output included 84 chamber monodies, polyphonic madrigals, motets, and villanellas, as well as works for the stage and some sacred music. At its finest, his music represents an assured command of the styles of Marenzio, Wert, Gesualdo, and Monteverdi, with a personal style marked by bold harmonic progressions. **WORKS: SECULAR SONGS AND DUETS:** *Le musiche* for 1 to 2 Voices and Basso Continuo (Milan, 1609); *Le musiche* for 2 Voices and Basso Continuo (Venice, 1615); *Le musiche . . . libro III* for 1 to 2 Voices and Basso Continuo (Milan, 1618); *Le musiche* for 1 to 2 Voices and Basso Continuo, *con alcune arie, gue . . . libro IV* (Venice, 1621); *Le musiche* for 1 to 2 Voices and Basso Continuo, *con alcune arie, gui . . . libro V* (Venice, 1623). **MADRIGALS AND OTHER PIECES:** *Il primo libro de madrigali* for 5 Voices (Milan, 1606); *Villanelle alla napolitana* for 3 to 5 Voices, *libro I* (Naples, 1608; not extant; 2nd ed., 1610); *Libro secondo de madrigali* for 5 Voices (Venice, 1611); *Libro secondo delle villanelle alla napolitana* for 3 to 5 Voices (Venice, 1612); *Il terzo libro de madrigali* for 5 Voices, Basso Continuo, and Other Instruments ad libitum, *ma necessariamente per gli 8 ultima* (Venice, 1615); *Il quarto libro de madrigali* for 5 Voices (Venice, 1616); *Il quinto libro de madrigali* for 5 Voices (Venice, 1616); *Le musiche e balli* for 4 Voices and Basso Continuo (Venice, 1621); *Settimo libro de madrigali* for 5 Voices (Rome, 1624); *Ottavo libro de madrigali* for 5 Voices and Basso Continuo (Rome, 1624). **STAGE:** *Zalizura,* pastoral; *Sant'Eustacho,* sacred drama (Rome, 1625; not extant). **SACRED:** *Novi concentus ecclesiastici* for 2 to 3 Voices and Basso Continuo (Venice, 1610); *Liber secundus sacrorum concentuum* for 3 to 6 Voices (Venice, 1610); *Liber primus motectorum* for 4 to 5 Voices and Basso Continuo (Venice, 1627). J. Joyce and G. Watkins ed. his works in Musiche Rinascimentali Siciliane (1980–). **BIBL.:** F. Mompellio, "S. d'I. e il suo primo libro di 'Musiche da cantar solo,'" *Collectanea Historiae Musicae,* I (1953); N. Fortune, "S. d'I.: An Introduction to His Life and Works," *Proceedings of the Royal Musical Association,* LXXXI (1954–55); F. Mompellio, *S. d'I., musicista palermitano* (Milan, 1956); G. Watkins, "The Polyphonic Madrigals of S. d'I.," *Abstracts of Papers Read at the 38th Annual Meeting of the American Musicological Society* (1972); J. Joyce, *The Monodies of S. d'I.* (Ann Arbor, 1981).

d'Indy, (Paul-Marie-Théodore-) Vincent, eminent French composer and pedagogue; b. Paris, March 27, 1851; d. there, Dec. 2, 1931. Owing to the death of his mother at his birth, his education was directed entirely by his grandmother, a woman of culture and refinement who had known Grétry and Monsigny, and who had shown a remarkable appreciation of the works of Beethoven when that master was still living. From 1862 to 1865 he studied piano with Diémer and Marmontel; in 1865 studied harmony with Lavignac. In 1869 he made the acquaintance of Henri Duparc, and with him spent much time studying the masterpieces of Bach, Beethoven, Berlioz, and Wagner; at that time, he wrote his opp. 1 and 2, and contemplated an opera on Victor Hugo's *Les Burgraves* (1869–72; unfinished). During the Franco-Prussian War he served in the Garde Mobile, and wrote of his experiences in *Histoire du 105ᵉ bataillon de la Garde nationale de Paris en l'année 1870–71* (1872). He then began to study composition with Franck (1872); when the latter was appointed prof. of organ at the Paris Cons. (1873), d'Indy joined the class, winning a 2nd *accessit* in 1874 and the 1st the following year. On his 1st visit to Germany in 1873 he met Liszt and Wagner, and was introduced to Brahms; in 1876 he heard the 1st performances of the *Ring* dramas at Bayreuth, and for several years thereafter made regular trips to Munich to hear all the works of Wagner; he also attended the premiere of *Parsifal* in 1882. From 1872 to 1876 he was organist at St. Leu-la-Forêt; from 1873 to 1878, chorus master and timpanist with the Colonne Orch.; for the Paris premiere of *Lohengrin* in 1887 he drilled the chorus and was Lamoureux's assistant. In 1871 he joined the Société Nationale de Musique as a junior member, and was its secretary from 1876 to 1890, when, after Franck's death, he became president. In 1894 he founded, with Bordes and Guilmant, the famous Schola Cantorum (opened 1896), primarily as a school for plainchant and the Palestrina style. Gradually the scope of instruction was enlarged to include all musical disciplines, and the inst. became one of the world's foremost music schools. D'Indy's fame as a composer began with the performance of his *Le Chant de la cloche* at a Lamoureux concert in 1886; the work itself had won the City of Paris Prize in the competition of the preceding year. As early as 1874, Pasdeloup had played the overture *Les Piccolomini* (later embodied as the 2nd part in the *Wallenstein* trilogy), and in 1882 the 1-act opera *Attendez-moi sous l'orme* had been produced at the Opéra-Comique; but the prize work attracted general attention, and d'Indy was recognized as one of the most important of modern French masters. Although he never held an official position as a conductor, he frequently, and with marked success, appeared in that capacity (chiefly upon invitation to direct his own works); thus, he visited Spain in 1897, Russia in 1903 and 1907, and the U.S. in 1905, when he conducted the Boston Sym. Orch. In 1892 he was a member of the commission appointed to revise the curriculum of the Cons., and refused a proffered professorship of composition; but in 1912 he accepted an appointment as prof. of the ensemble class. Besides his other duties, he was, from 1899, inspector of musical instruction in Paris; made his last U.S. visit in 1921. He was made a Chevalier of the Legion of Honor in 1892, an Officer in 1912. Both as teacher and creative artist, d'Indy continued the traditions of Franck. Although he cultivated almost every form of composition, his special talent was in the field of the larger instrumental forms. Some French critics assign to him a position in French music analogous to that of Brahms in German music. His style rests on Bach and Beethoven; however, his deep study of Gregorian chant and the early contrapuntal style added an element of severity, and not rarely of complexity, that renders his approach somewhat difficult, and has prompted the charge that his music is lacking in emotional force. He wrote numerous articles for various journals, which are remarkable for their critical acumen and literary finish.

WRITINGS: *Cours de Composition musicale* (Book I, 1903; Book II: Part 1, 1909, Part 2, 1933); *César Franck* (1906; in Eng., 1910; reprint, N.Y., 1965); *Beethoven: Biographie critique* (1911; Eng. tr. by T. Baker, Boston, 1913; reprint, N.Y., 1970); *La Schola Cantorum en 1925* (1927); *Wagner et son influence sur l'art musical français* (1930); *Introduction à l'étude de Parsifal* (1937).

WORKS: STAGE: *Les Burgraves*, opera (1869–72; unfinished); *Attendez-moi sous l'orme*, op. 14, 1-act comic opera (Opéra-Comique, Paris, Feb. 11, 1882); *Le Chant de la cloche*, op. 18, dramatic legend (Brussels, Nov. 21, 1912); *Fervaal*, op. 40, lyric drama (Brussels, March 12, 1897); *L'Étranger*, op. 53, lyric drama (Brussels, Jan. 7, 1903); *La Légende de Saint-Christophe*, op. 67, lyric drama (Opéra, Paris, June 9, 1920); *Le Rêve de Cynias*, op. 80, lyric comedy (Paris, June 10, 1927).

ORCH.: *Jean Hunyade*, op. 5, sym. (Paris, May 15, 1875); *Antoine et Cléopâtre*, op. 6, overture (Paris, Feb. 4, 1877); *La Forêt enchantée*, op. 8, symphonic legend (Paris, March 24, 1878); *Wallenstein*, op. 12, symphonic trilogy: *Le Camp de Wallenstein* (April 12, 1880), *Max et Thécla* (Jan. 25, 1874; orig. *Les Piccolomini*), and *La Mort de Wallenstein* (April 11,

1884); *Lied,* op. 19, for Cello and Orch. (Paris, April 18, 1885); *Saugefleurie,* op. 21, legend (Paris, Jan. 25, 1885); *Symphonie Cévenole (sur un chant montagnard français),* op. 25, for Orch. and Piano (Paris, March 20, 1887); *Sérénade et Valse,* op. 28 (from opp. 16 and 17), for Small Orch. (1887); *Fantaisie,* op. 31, for Oboe and Orch. (Paris, Dec. 23, 1888); incidental music to Alexandre's *Karadec,* op. 34 (Paris, May 2, 1891); *Tableaux de voyage,* op. 36 (Le Havre, Jan. 17, 1892); *Istar,* op. 42, symphonic variations (Brussels, Jan. 10, 1897); incidental music to Mendès's *Médée,* op. 47 (1898); *Choral varié,* op. 55, for Saxophone and Orch. (Paris, May 17, 1904); 2nd Sym., in B-flat, op. 57 (Paris, Feb. 28, 1904); *Jour d'été à la montagne,* op. 61 (Paris, Feb. 18, 1906); *Souvenirs,* op. 62, tone poem (Paris, April 20, 1907); *La Queste de Dieu,* op. 67, descriptive sym. (from *La Légende de Saint-Christophe;* 1917); 3rd Sym., op. 70, *Sinfonia brevis de bello Gallico* (1916–18; Paris, Dec. 14, 1919); *Le Poème des rivages,* op. 77 (N.Y., Dec. 1, 1921); *Diptyque méditerranéen,* op. 87 (Paris, Dec. 5, 1926); Concerto for Piano, Flute, Cello, and String Orch., op. 89 (Paris, April 2, 1927).

CHAMBER: Piano Quartet in A minor, op. 7 (1878); Suite in D, op. 24, for Trumpet, 2 Flutes, and String Orch. (Paris, March 5, 1887); Trio for Piano, Clarinet, and Cello, op. 29 (1888); String Quartet No. 1, op. 35 (1891); String Quartet No. 2, op. 45 (1898); *Chansons et Danses,* op. 50, divertissement for 7 Wind Instruments (Paris, March 7, 1899); Violin Sonata, op. 59 (1905); Piano Quintet in G minor, op. 81 (1925); Cello Sonata, op. 84 (1926); *Suite en 4 parties,* op. 91, for Flute, Strings, and Harp (Paris, May 17, 1930); String Sextet, op. 92 (1928); String Quartet No. 3, op. 96 (1929); Trio No. 2, op. 98, for Piano, Violin, and Cello (1929).

VOCAL: *Chanson des aventuriers de la mer,* op. 2, for Baritone Solo and Men's Chorus (1870); *La Chevauchée du Cid,* op. 11, for Baritone, Chorus, and Orch. (1879); *Cantate Domino,* op. 22 (1885); *Ste. Marie-Magdeleine,* op. 23, cantata (1885); *Sur la mer,* op. 32, for Women's Voices and Piano (1888); *Pour l'inauguration d'une statue,* op. 37, cantata (1893); *L'Art et le peuple,* op. 39, for Men's Chorus (1894); *Deus Israël,* op. 41, motet (1896); *Ode à Valence,* op. 44, for Soprano and Chorus (1897); *Les Noces d'or du sacerdoce,* op. 46 (1898); *Sancta Maria,* op. 49, motet (1898); 6 *Chants populaires français,* opp. 90 and 100, for a cappella Chorus (1928, 1931); *Le Bouquet de printemps,* op. 93, for Women's Chorus (1929); songs (opp. 3, 4, 10, 13, 20, 43, 48, 52, 56, 58, 64).

PIANO: 3 *romances sans paroles,* op. 1 (1870); *Petite sonate,* op. 9 (1880); *Poème des montagnes,* op. 15: *Le Chant des bruyères, Danses rythmiques, Plein-air* (1881); 4 *pièces,* op. 16 (1882); *Helvetia,* op. 17, 3 waltzes (1882); *Saugefleurie,* op. 21 (1884; also arranged for Orch.); *Nocturne,* op. 26 (1886); *Promenade,* op. 27 (1887); *Schumanniana,* op. 30, 3 pieces (1887); *Tableaux de voyage,* op. 33, 13 pieces (1889); *Petite chanson grégorienne,* op. 60, for Piano, 4-hands (1904); Sonata, op. 63 (1907); *Menuet sur le nom de Haydn,* op. 65 (1909); 13 *Short Pieces,* op. 68; 12 *petites pièces faciles,* op. 69, in old style; 7 *chants de terroir,* op. 73, for Piano, 4-hands; *Pour les enfants de tous les âges,* op. 74, 24 pieces; *Thème varié, fugue et chanson,* op. 85; *Conte de fées,* op. 86, suite (1926); 6 paraphrases on French children's songs, op. 95; *Fantaisie sur un vieil air de ronde française,* op. 99 (1931).

ORGAN: *Prélude et Petit Canon,* op. 38 (1893); *Vêpres du Commun d'un Martyr,* op. 51 (1889); *Prélude,* op. 66 (1913).

WITHOUT OPUS NUMBER: *O gai Soleil,* canon a 2 (1909); incidental music to *Veronica* (1920); 3 *chansons anciennes du Vivarais* (1926); *La Vengeance du mari* for 3 Soli, Chorus, and Orch. (1931).

BIBL.: E. Deniau, *V. d'I.* (Toulouse, 1903); A. Hervey, *French Music in the 19th Century* (London, 1903); F. Starczewski, *La Schola Cantorum de Paris, ou V. d'I. considéré comme professeur* (Warsaw, 1905); O. Séré, *Musiciens français d'aujourd'hui* (2nd ed., Paris, 1911); L. Borgex, *V. d'I.: Sa vie et son œuvre* (Paris, 1913); A. Sérieyx, *V. d'I.* (Paris, 1913); R. Rolland, *Musiciens d'aujourd'hui* (Paris, 1914); E. Hill, "V. d'I., An Estimate," *Musical Quarterly* (April 1915); P. Landormy, "V. d'I.," ibid. (July 1932); M. de Fraguier, *V. d'I.* (Paris, 1933); L. Vallas, "The Discovery of Musical Germany by V. d'I. in 1873," *Musical Quarterly* (April 1939); idem, *V. d'I.: I. La Jeunesse, II. La Maturité, La Vieillesse* (Paris, I, 1946; II, 1950); J. Canteloube, *V. d'I.* (Paris, 1949); N. Demuth, *V. d'I.* (London, 1951); J. Guy-Ropartz, ed., *Le Centenaire de V. d'I., 1851–1951* (Paris, 1952); L. Davies, *Cesar Franck and His Circle* (Boston, 1970); C. Paul, "Rameau, d'I., and French Nationalism," *Musical Quarterly* (Jan. 1972).

Infantas, Fernando de las, Spanish composer and theologian; b. Córdoba, 1534; d. c.1610. He belonged to a noble family and enjoyed the protection of the Emperor Charles V and later of Philip II, who employed him on diplomatic missions in Italy. He went to Venice, and then to Rome, where he lived for 25 years (c.1572–97). He exerted a decisive influence upon the course of Catholic church music by opposing the plan for the reform of the Roman Gradual undertaken by Palestrina in 1578 at the request of Pope Gregory XIII. Backed by the authority of Philip II of Spain, he succeeded in having the project abandoned. He publ. *Sacrarum varii styli cantionum tituli Spiritus Sancti,* a collection of motets in 3 books: I for 4 Voices, II for 5 Voices (both publ. in Venice, 1578), III for 6–8 Voices (Venice, 1579), and *Plura modulationum genera quae vulgo contrapuncta appellantur super excelso gregoriano cantu* (Venice, 1579; contains 100 contrapuntal exercises for 2–8 Voices based on 1 plainsong theme; it pointed the way to a new freedom and elasticity in polyphonic writing); separate compositions were also publ. in various collections of the time. A Sequence for 6 Voices, *Victimae paschali,* was publ. by W. Dehn in *Sammlung älterer Musik aus dem 16. und 17. Jahrhundert,* vol. V (Berlin, 1837–40).

BIBL.: R. Mitjana y Gordón, *Don F. d.l.I., teólogo y músico* (Madrid, 1918); R. Stevenson, *Spanish Cathedral Music in the Golden Age* (Berkeley, Calif., 1961).

Infante, Manuel, Spanish pianist and composer; b. Osuna, near Seville, July 29, 1883; d. Paris, April 21, 1958. He studied piano and composition with Enrique Morera; in 1909 he settled in Paris; gave concerts of Spanish music; wrote numerous pieces for piano, mostly on Spanish themes: *Gitanerias; Pochades andalouses; Sevillana,* fantasy (1922); *El Vito* (variations on a popular theme); also an opera, *Almanza.*

Ingarden, Roman (Witold), important Polish theoretician of musical esthetics; b. Krakow, Feb. 5, 1893; d. there, June 14, 1970. He studied philosophy with Husserl and mathematics with Hilbert at the Univs. of Göttingen and Freiburg im Breisgau (Ph.D., 1918). After completing his Habilitation (1921), he joined the faculty at the Univ. of Lwow. In 1945 he became chairman of philosophy at the Jagellonian Univ. in Krakow, only to be barred from teaching in 1950 by the Communist Polish government because of his adherence to "idealism"; during his forced sabbatical, he tr. Kant's *Critique of Pure Reason.* He regained his academic post in 1956, retiring in 1963. Ingarden is regarded as the ablest of Husserl's students, preserving the cognitive core of Husserl's phenomenology that was lost in Heidegger's and Sartre's emotional reduction of it to existentialism. His *The Work of Music and the Problem of Its Identity* (Berkeley, 1986), an excerpt from his *Studia z estetyki* (Studies in Esthetics; Warsaw, 1957–70), is an important consideration of ontology and epistemology in musical esthetics. His other publications include *Spór o istnienie świata* (Controversy over the Existence of the World; Krakow, 1947–48); *Untersuchungen zur Ontologie der Kunst: Musikwerk, Bild, Architektur, Film* (Tübingen, 1962); *The Literary Work of Art: An Investigation on the Borderlines of Ontology, Logic, and Theory of Literature, with an Appendix on the Functions of Language in the Theater* (Evanston, Ill., 1973); and *Selected Papers in Aesthetics* (Washington, D.C., 1985).

Ingegneri, Marc'Antonio, important Italian composer; b. Verona, c.1547; d. Cremona, July 1, 1592. He was a choirboy at Verona Cathedral, where he most likely studied with its maestro di cappella, Vincenzo Ruffo. Around 1568 he settled in Cremona, where he was prefect of music at the Cathedral from 1578; acted as maestro di cappella from 1579, and was officially named to that position in 1581. Monteverdi was his pupil. He distinguished himself as a composer of both secular and sacred music.

WORKS (all publ. in Venice): **SACRED:** *Liber primus missarum* for 5 and 8 Voices (1573); *Sacrarum cantionum . . . liber primus* for 5 Voices (1576; ed. by M. Duggan in *Marc Antonio Ingegneri: Motets for Four and Five Voices,* diss., Univ. of Rochester, 1968); *Sacrarum cantionum . . . liber primus* for 4 Voices (1586; ed. in the preceding diss.); *Liber secundus missarum* for 5 Voices (1587); *Responsoria hebdomadae sanctae, Benedictus, & improperia . . . & Miserere* for 4 and 6 Voices (1588); *Lamentationes Hieremiae* for 4 Voices (1588); *Liber sacrarum cantionum* for 7 to 10, 12, and 16 Voices and Instruments ad libitum (1589); *Sacrae cantiones . . . liber primus* for 6 Voices (1591); *Liber secundus hymnorum* for 4 Voices (1606). **SECULAR:** *Il primo libro de madrigali* for 5 and 8 Voices (not extant); *Il secondo libro de madrigali* for 5 Voices (1572); *Il primo libro de madrigali* for 4 Voices (1st ed. not extant; 2nd ed., 1578); *Il secondo libro de madrigali . . . con due arie di canzon francese per sonare* for 4 Voices (1579); *Il terzo libro de madrigali . . . con due canzoni francese* for 5 Voices (1580); *Il quarto libro de madrigali* for 5 Voices (1584); *Il primo libro de madrigali* for 6 Voices (1586); *Il quinto libro de madrigali* for 5 Voices (1587); *Il sesto libro de madrigali* for 5 Voices (1606); other madrigals in collections of the day. See G. Cesari, ed., *La musica in Cremona nella seconda metà del secolo XVI e i primordi dell'arte monteverdiana,* Istituzioni e Monumenti dell'Arte Musicale Italiana, VI (1939); and B. Hudson, ed., *M.A. Ingegneri: 7 Madrigale,* Das Chorwerk, CXV (1974).

BIBL.: F. Haberl, "Marcantonio I.: Eine bio-bibliographische Studie," *Kirchenmusikalisches Jahrbuch,* XIII (1898); E. Dohrn, *M.'A. I. als Madrigalkomponist* (Hannover, 1936); M. Duggan, *Marc Antonio I.: Motets for Four and Five Voices* (diss., Univ. of Rochester, 1968).

Ingenhoven, Jan, Dutch composer; b. Breda, May 29, 1876; d. Hoenderlo, May 20, 1951. He studied with L. Brandts-Buys in Rotterdam and Mottl in Munich, where he conducted a madrigal choir (1909–12); then devoted himself mainly to composition. His works are influenced by Debussy, but he preserved an element of peculiarly native melos. Among his works are *Symphonische Fantasie über Zarathustras* for Orch. (1906); a symphonic fantasy, *Brabant and Holland;* 3 symphonic poems (*Lyric; Dramatic; Romantic*); 3 string quartets (1907–8; 1911; 1912); Woodwind Quintet (1911); Clarinet Sonata (1916–17); 2 violin sonatas (1919–20; 1921); 2 cello sonatas (1919, 1922); choral works; songs.

BIBL.: D. Ruyneman, *De componist J. I.* (Amsterdam, 1938).

Inghelbrecht, D(ésiré)-E(mile), noted French conductor and composer; b. Paris, Sept. 17, 1880; d. there, Feb. 14, 1965. He studied at the Paris Cons.; after graduation, conducted at various theaters in Paris; toured as conductor of the Ballets Suédois (1919–23); was director of the Opéra-Comique (1924–25 and 1932–33), the Pasdeloup Orch. (1928–32), and the Algiers Opera (1929–30). From 1945 to 1950 he was conductor of the Paris Opéra; also conducted abroad. He was the founder of the Orch. National de la Radiodiffusion in Paris in 1934; conducted it until 1944, and again from 1951 to 1958. He publ. *Comment on ne doit pas interpréter Carmen, Faust et Pelléas* (1932); *Diabolus in musica* (1933); *Mouvement contraire: Souvenirs d'un musicien* (1947); and *Le Chef d'orchestre et son équipe* (1948; Eng. tr. as *The Conductor's World,* 1953).

WORKS: OPERA: *La Nuit vénitienne,* in 3 acts, after Musset (1908). **BALLETS:** *La Bonne Aventure* (1912); *El Greco* (Ballets Suédois, Paris, Nov. 18, 1920); *Le Diable dans le beffroi* (after Poe; Paris Opéra, June 1, 1927); *Jeux de Couleurs* (Opéra-Comique, Feb. 21, 1933); *Le Chêne et le tilleul,* opera-ballet (Paris, 1961). **ORCH.:** *Automne* (1905); *Pour le jour de la première neige au vieux Japon* (1908); *Rapsodie de printemps* (1910); *3 poèmes dansés* (1925); *La Métamorphose d'Ève* (1925); *La Légende du grand St. Nicolas* (1925); *Iberiana* for Violin and

Orch. (1948); *Vézelay, évocation symphonique* (1952). CHAMBER: *2 esquisses antiques* for Flute and Harp (1902); *Poème sylvestre* for Woodwinds (1905); Quintet for Strings and Harp (1918); pieces for cello and piano, and for viola and piano. CHORAL: *Le Cantique des créatures de Saint François d'Assise* for Chorus and Orch. (1919); Requiem (1940); *4 chansons populaires françaises* for Mixed Chorus. PIANO: *La Nursery*, 4-hand pieces for children, 3 vols. (1905 and 1911); *Suite petite-russienne* (1908); *Paysages* (1918); etc.; also songs (*Mélodies sur des poésies russes*, 1905; *Au jardin de l'infante*, 1910; etc.).

Inghilleri, Giovanni, Italian baritone; b. Porto Empedocle, March 9, 1894; d. Milan, Dec. 10, 1959. He made his debut in Milan at the Teatro Carcano in 1919; then made regular appearances in Italy; he also sang in London and Chicago. Following his retirement from the stage in 1953, he taught voice.

Insanguine, Giacomo (Antonio Francesco Paolo Michele), called **Monopoli,** Italian composer; b. Monopoli, near Bari, March 22, 1728; d. Naples, Feb. 1, 1795. He studied with Abos and Durante at the San Onofrio Cons. in Naples; became a teacher there (1767) and later secondo maestro (1774). From 1785 until his death he was primo maestro. He concurrently was 2nd organist at the Cappella del Tesoro di San Gennaro (1774), 1st organist (1776), and maestro di cappella there (1781). He wrote some 20 operas, about half of which are lost; also wrote masses, cantatas, and other sacred works.
    BIBL.: A. Mondolfi, "Destino e stile di G. I. detto Monopoli," *Gazzetta Musicale di Napoli*, IV (1958).

Inten, Ferdinand, German-American pianist and teacher; b. Leipzig, Feb. 23, 1848; d. N.Y., Jan. 16, 1918. He studied at the Leipzig Cons. (1862–66) with Moscheles, Plaidy, Hauptmann, and Reinecke; made his American debut as piano soloist in N.Y., on Dec. 12, 1868. He organized concerts of chamber music there, which became famous. As a teacher, he also achieved success; among his pupils were Frank and Walter Damrosch.

Inzenga (y Castellanos), José, Spanish composer; b. Madrid, June 3, 1828; d. there, June 28, 1891. He 1st studied with his father, then at the Madrid Cons. and the Paris Cons.; became a prof. at the Madrid Cons. (1860). He was commissioned by the Minister of Public Instruction to make a collection of Spanish folk songs, which he publ. as *Cantos y bailes populares de España* (3 vols., 1874–88); also wrote a treatise on accompaniment (Madrid, 1876) and *La música en el templo católico* (Madrid, 1878). He was very successful as a composer of zarzuelas: *Para seguir una mujer* (Madrid, Dec. 24, 1851); *Don Simplicio Bobadilla* (1853); *Un día de reino* (1854); *El campamento* (Madrid, May 8, 1861); *Si yo fuera rey* (1862); etc.

Ioannidis, Yannis, Greek composer; b. Athens, June 8, 1930. He studied piano in Athens (1946–55), then organ, composition, and harpsichord at the Vienna Academy of Music (1955–63); taught at Pierce College in Athens (1963–68); in 1968 went to Caracas (his family was from Venezuela), where he served as artistic director of the chamber orch. of the National Inst. of Culture and Fine Arts; he was a prof. there from 1969, and at the Caracas Cons. and Univ. from 1971. He returned to Athens in 1976. As a composer, he follows the precepts of the 2nd Vienna School, with a firm foundation of classical forms.
    WORKS: 2 string quartets (1961, 1971); *Triptych* for Orch. (1962); Duo for Violin and Piano (1962); *Peristrophe* for String Octet (1964); *Versi* for Solo Clarinet (1967); *Arioso* for String Nonet (1960); *Tropic* for Orch. (1968); *Schemata* (Figures) for String Ensemble (1968); *Projections* for Strings, Winds, and Piano (1968); *Fragments I* for Cello and Piano (1969) and *Fragments II* for Solo Flute (1970); *Metaplassis A* and *B* for Orch. (1969, 1970); *Actinia* for Wind Quintet (1969); *Transiciones* for Orch. (1971); *Estudio I, II,* and *III* for Piano (1971–

73); *Fancy for 6* for 4 Winds, Cello, and Percussion (1972); *Nocturno* for Piano Quartet (1972); *Orbis* for Piano and Orch. (1975–76); *Dance Vision* for Trombone, Clarinet, Cello, and Piano (1980); transcriptions of Greek folk songs for chorus.

Iparraguirre y Balerdí, José María de, Spanish-Basque composer and poet; b. Villarreal de Urrechu, Aug. 12, 1820; d. Zozobastro de Isacho, April 6, 1881. He led a wandering life; improvised songs, accompanying himself on the guitar; 1 of his songs, *Guernikako arbola,* a hymn to the sacred tree of Guernica, became the national anthem of the Basques. As a result of the unrest in the Basque country, and his own participation in it, he was compelled to leave Spain; spent many years in South America; was enabled to return to Spain in 1877, and even obtained an official pension.

Ipavec, Benjamin, Slovenian composer; b. St. Jurij, Dec. 24, 1829; d. Graz, Dec. 20, 1909. He studied medicine in Vienna and became a professional physician, with music as an avocation; he was the 1st to cultivate national Slovenian motifs systematically. He wrote a national Slovenian opera, *Teharski plemiči* (The Nobles of Teharje; Ljubljana, 1892); an operetta, *Tičnik* (The Aviary; 1862); numerous songs in a Romantic vein; also brought out collections of Slovenian folk songs.

Ippolitov-Ivanov (real name, **Ivanov**), **Mikhail (Mikhailovich),** important Russian composer and pedagogue; b. Gatchina, Nov. 19, 1859; d. Moscow, Jan. 28, 1935. He assumed his mother's name to distinguish himself from Michael Ivanov, the music critic. He studied composition with Rimsky-Korsakov at the St. Petersburg Cons., graduating in 1882. He then received the post of teacher and director of the Music School in Tiflis, in the Caucasus, where he remained until 1893; he became deeply interested in Caucasian folk music; many of his works were colored by the semi-oriental melodic and rhythmic inflections of that region. Upon Tchaikovsky's recommendation, he was appointed prof. of composition at the Moscow Cons. in 1893; in 1906 became its director, retiring in 1922; then taught at the Tiflis Cons. (1924–25). Among his pupils were Glière and Vasilenko. From 1898 to 1906 he was conductor of the Mamontov Opera in Moscow; in 1925 he became conductor of the Bolshoi Theater in Moscow. Outside Russia, he is known mainly for his effective symphonic suite *Caucasian Sketches* (1895). He publ. *The Science of the Formation and Resolution of Chords* (1897, in Russian) and *50 Years of Russian Music in My Memories* (Moscow, 1934; in Eng. in *Musical Mercury*, N.Y., 1937).
    WORKS: OPERAS: *Ruth* (Tiflis, Feb. 8, 1887); *Azra* (Tiflis, Nov. 28, 1890); *Asya* (Moscow, Sept. 28, 1900); *Treason* (1909); *Ole from Nordland* (Moscow, Nov. 21, 1916); *The Last Barricade* (1934); also completed Mussorgsky's unfinished opera *Marriage* (1931). ORCH.: *Symphonic Scherzo* (St. Petersburg, May 20, 1882); *Yar-Khmel,* spring overture (St. Petersburg, Jan. 23, 1883, composer conducting); *Caucasian Sketches* (Moscow, Feb. 5, 1895, composer conducting); *Iveria* (2nd series of *Caucasian Sketches;* Moscow, 1906); Sym. No. 1 (Moscow, 1908); *Armenian Rhapsody* (Moscow, 1909); *On the Volga* (Moscow, 1910); *Mtzyri,* symphonic poem (Moscow, 1922); *Turkish March* (Baku, 1929); *From the Songs of Ossian,* 3 musical pictures (Moscow, 1927); *Episodes of the Life of Schubert* (1929); *In the Steppes of Turkmenistan; Voroshilov March; Musical Scenes of Uzbekistan;* symphonic poem, *Year 1917; Catalan Suite* (1934); suite on Finnish themes, *Karelia* (1935, last work; only the Finale was orchestrated). CHAMBER: Violin Sonata; 2 string quartets; *An Evening in Georgia* for Harp, Flute, Oboe, Clarinet, and Bassoon. VOCAL: *Alsatian Ballad* for a cappella Mixed Chorus; *5 Characteristic Pieces* for Chorus, and Orch. or Piano; *The Legend of a White Swan* for a cappella Mixed Chorus; *Cantata in Memory of Pushkin* for Children's Chorus and Piano; *Cantata in Memory of Zhukovsky* for Mixed Chorus and Piano; *Pythagorean Hymn to the Rising Sun* for Mixed Chorus, 10 Flutes, 2 Harps, and Tuba; *Cantata in Memory of Gogol* for Children's Chorus and Piano; *Hymn to Labor* for Mixed Chorus and Orch.; 116 songs.

Bibl.: S. Boguslavsky, *I.-I.* (Moscow, 1936); L. Podzemskaya, *M.M. I.-I. and Georgian Musical Culture* (Tbilisi, 1963).

Ipuche-Riva, Pedro, Uruguayan composer; b. Montevideo, Oct. 26, 1924. He studied at the Montevideo Cons., and later in Paris with Jean Rivier and Nöel Gallon. Returning to Uruguay, he unfolded energetic activities as a music critic, lecturer, teacher, and radio commentator.

Works: Symphonic poem, *El Arbol solo* (1961); 3 syms. (1962, 1965, 1968); Cello Concerto (1962); *Fantasía concertante* for Trumpet and String Orch. (1963); String Quartet (1962); Quartet for Flute, Violin, Cello, and Piano (1963); *Espejo roto* for Violin, Horn, and Piano (1966); Concerto for Small Orch. (1966); *Sinfonietta-Concertino* for Piano and Orch. (1967); *Animales ilustres,* suite for Wind Quintet (1967); *Pieza* for Oboe and Piano (1969); *Variaciones antipianísticas* for Piano (1969); other piano pieces; choruses; songs.

Iradier, Sebastián de. See **Yradier (Iradier), Sebastián de.**

Ireland, John (Nicholson), eminent English composer; b. Inglewood, Bowdon, Cheshire, Aug. 13, 1879; d. Rock Mill, Washington, Sussex, June 12, 1962. A member of a literary family (both his parents were writers), he received a fine general education. As his musical inclinations became evident, he entered the Royal College of Music in London in 1893, studying piano with Frederick Cliffe and composition with Stanford. His parents died while he was still a student; he obtained positions as organist in various churches; the longest of these was at St. Luke's, Chelsea (1904–26). In 1905 he received the degree of Bac.Mus. at the Univ. of Durham; was awarded an honorary Mus.Doc. there in 1932. He taught at the Royal College of Music (1923–39); Benjamin Britten, Alan Bush, E.J. Moeran, and other British composers were his pupils. He began to compose early in life; during his student years, he wrote a number of works for orch., chamber groups, and voices, but destroyed most of them; 2 string quartets (1895, 1897) came to light after his death. His early compositions were influenced by the German Romantic school; soon he adopted many devices of the French impressionistic school; his rhythmic concepts were enlivened by the new Russian music presented by the Diaghilev Ballet. At the same time, he never wavered in his dedication to the English spirit of simple melody; his music re-creates the plainsong and the usages of Tudor music in terms of plagal modalities and freely modulating triadic harmonies.

Works: ORCH.: *The Forgotten Rite,* symphonic prelude (1913); *Mai-Dun,* symphonic rhapsody (1921); *A London Overture* (1936); *Concertino pastorale* for Strings (1939); *Epic March* (1942); *Satyricon* (1946); Piano Concerto (London, Oct. 2, 1930). CHORAL: *Morning Service* for Voices with Organ (1907–20); motet, *Greater love hath no man* (1912); *Communion Service* (1913); *Evening Service* (1915); *These things shall be* for Baritone Solo, Chorus, and Orch. (1937); a number of 4-part songs a cappella; 2-part songs with piano accompaniment; unison choral songs with piano accompaniment. CHAMBER: 2 string quartets (1895, 1897); *Fantasy Trio* for Piano, Violin, and Cello (1906); Trio for Violin, Clarinet, and Piano (1913; rewritten for Violin, Cello, and Piano, 1915, and rev. again in 1938); Trio No. 2 for Violin, Cello, and Piano (1917); Violin Sonata No. 1 (1909; rev. 1917, 1944); Violin Sonata No. 2 (1917); Cello Sonata (1923); *Fantasy Sonata* for Clarinet and Piano (1943). PIANO: *The Daydream* and *Meridian* (1895; rev. 1941); *Decorations* (1913); *The Almond Trees* (1913); Rhapsody (1915); *London Pieces* (1917–20); *Leaves from a Child's Sketchbook* (1918); *Summer Evening* (1919); Sonata (1920); *On a Birthday Morning* (1922); *Soliloquy* (1922); *Sonatina* (1927); Ballade (1929); *Indian Summer* (1932); *Green Ways* (1937); *Sarnia,* "An Island Sequence" (1941); *3 Pastels* (1941); organ works; about 100 songs. See E. Chapman, *John Ireland: A Catalogue of Published Works and Recordings* (London, 1968).

Bibl.: N. Townshend, "The Achievement of J. I.," *Music & Letters* (April 1943); J. Longmire, *J. I.: Portrait of a Friend* (London, 1969); M. Searle, *J. I.: The Man and His Music* (Tunbridge Wells, 1979); M. Pilkington, *Gurney, I., Quilter and Warlock* (London, 1989).

Irgens Jensen, Ludvig (Paul), Norwegian composer; b. Christiania, April 13, 1894; d. Enna, Sicily, April 11, 1969. He studied philosophy, music theory, and piano in Christiania, but was mainly self-taught in composition; from 1946 was a recipient of the Norwegian State Salary of Art, a government life pension. His output was relatively small; his compositions are influenced mainly by German Romanticism.

Works: *Japanischer Frühling* for Voice and Piano (1918–19); *Der Gott und die Bajadere,* cantata (1921–32); Violin Sonata (1924); *Tema con variazioni* for Orch. (1925); Passacaglia for Orch. (1926); Piano Quintet (1927); *Heimferd* (The Return), dramatic sym. for Soloists, Chorus, and Orch., commemorating the 900th anniversary of the death of St. Olav (1929; Oslo, 1930; recast as an opera and produced in Oslo, Aug. 27, 1947); *Partita sinfonica* (1937); Sym. (1942); *Canto d'omaggio,* festival overture (Oslo, 1950); choruses; songs.

Irino, Yoshirō, Japanese composer; b. Vladivostok, Nov. 13, 1921; d. Tokyo, June 28, 1980. Although of pure Japanese ancestry, he was baptized in the Greek Orthodox faith, which he retained throughout his life. He was sent to Tokyo as a child, and studied economics at Tokyo Univ.; at the same time he took composition lessons with Saburo Moroi. He became a teacher at the Tōhō Gakuen School of Music in 1952; was its director (1960–70); then was prof. at the Tokyo Music College (from 1973). A prolific composer, he wrote music of all categories, adopting a style decidedly modern in character, marked by fine instrumental coloration, with a complete mastery of contemporary techniques. Most of his vocal and stage music is imbued with a pronounced Japanese sensibility, with touches that are almost calligraphic in their rhythmic precision.

Works: An operetta, *The Man in Fear of God* (Tokyo, May 25, 1954); a television opera, *Drum of Silk* (1962); a ballet, *Woman-Mask* (1959); *Adagietto and Allegro vivace* for Orch. (1949); Sinfonietta for Chamber Orch. (1953); *Ricercari* for Chamber Orch. (1954); Double Concerto for Violin, Piano, and Orch. (1955); *Concerto grosso* (1957); Sinfonia (1959); Concerto for String Orch. (1960); Suite for Jazz Ensemble (1960); *Music* for Harpsichord, Percussion, and 19 String Instruments (1963); Sym. No. 2 (1964); 2 *Fantasies* for 17 and 20 Kotos (1969); *Sai-un* (Colorful Clouds) for 15 String Instruments (1972); *Wandlungen* for 2 Shakuhachi and Orch. (1973); 2 string quartets (1945, 1957); Piano Trio (1948); String Sextet (1950); *Chamber Concerto* for 7 Instruments (1951); Quintet for Clarinet, Saxophone, Trumpet, Cello, and Piano (1958); Divertimento for 7 Winds (1958); *Music* for Violin and Cello (1959); *Music* for Vibraphone and Piano (1961); Partita for Wind Quintet (1962); String Trio (1965); 3 *Movements* for 2 Kotos and Jushichi-gen (1966); 7 *Inventions* for Guitar and 6 Players (1967); Violin Sonata (1967); 3 *Movements* for Cello (1969); Sonata for Piano, Violin, Clarinet, and Percussion (1970); Trio for Flute, Violin, and Piano (1970); *A Demon's Bride* for Chorus, Oboe, Horn, Piano, and Percussion (1970); *Globus I* for Horn and Percussion (1970); *Globus II* for Marimba, Double Bass, and Percussion (1971); *Globus III* for Violin, Cello, Piano, Harp, Shō, and 2 Dancers (1975); Suite for Viola (1971); *Cloudscape* for String Ensemble (1972); 3 *Improvisations* for Flute (1972); 3 *Scenes* for 3 Kotos (1972); *Strömung* for Flute, Harp, and Percussion (1973); *Shō-yō* for Japanese Instruments (1973); *Gafu* for Flute, Shō, and Double Bass (1976); *Movements* for Marimba (1977); *Cosmos* for Shakuhachi, Violin, Piano, 2 Kotos, and Percussion (1978); *Shidai* for Shakuhachi, 20-gen, 17-gen, and Shamisen (1979); Duo Concertante for Alto Saxophone and Koto (1979).

Irrgang, Heinrich Bernhard, German organist and composer; b. Zduny, July 23, 1869; d. Berlin, April 8, 1916. He was a church organist and teacher in Berlin; composed organ music and songs.

Irving, Robert (Augustine), English conductor; b. Winchester, Aug. 28, 1913. He studied at Winchester College, at New College, Oxford, and at the Royal College of Music in London.

In 1936 he became a répétiteur at the Royal Opera House, Covent Garden, and also music master of Winchester College. At the outbreak of World War II in 1939 he joined the Royal Air Force. From 1945 to 1948 he was associate conductor of the BBC Scottish Orch.; from 1949 to 1958 he conducted the Royal Ballet at Covent Garden. In 1958 he was appointed conductor of the N.Y. City Ballet. He made guest conducting appearances with orchs. in Europe and the U.S., but it was as a highly efficient ballet conductor that he gained distinction.

Isaac, Adèle, French soprano; b. Calais, Jan. 8, 1854; d. Paris, Oct. 22, 1915. She studied with Duprez in Paris; made her debut at the Théâtre Montmartre in Paris in 1870, in *Noces de Jeannette*; then sang at the Opéra-Comique (1873; 1878–88) and the Paris Opéra (1883–85); retired from the stage in 1894. She was noted for her performances of French operatic roles.

Isaac (Isaak, Izak, Yzac, Ysack), Heinrich, important Flemish composer; b. Flanders, c.1450; d. Florence, March 26, 1517. He was in the service of Lorenzo de'Medici in Florence (1485–92); was also a singer at Ss. Annunziata and a member of the Cantori di S. Giovanni (until 1493). In 1496 he went to Vienna, where he was named court composer (1497); then traveled widely before settling in Florence in 1514. He became known as Arrigo Tedesco (Henry the German; Low Latin, Arrighus), the Italian term "Tedesco" being used at the time for Flemish people as well as Germans. Isaac was a master of cantus firmus technique in both masses and motets; he also wrote French chansons, Italian frottole, and German lieder. His profound influence on German music was continued through his student Senfl, who ed. a voluminous collection of his motets as *Choralis Constantinus* (3 parts, 1550). His other works include about 40 masses and mass movements, 99 cycles of proper settings of the Mass, and various secular vocal works. A complete ed. of his works is being prepared by E. Lerner in Corpus Mensurabilis Musicae, LXV/1– (1974–).
BIBL.: H. Rietsch, "H. Isaak und das Innsbrucklied," *Jahrbuch der Musikbibliothek Peters 1917;* P. Blaschke, "Der Choral in H. Isaacs Choralis constantinus," *Kirchenmusikalisches Jahrbuch,* XXVI (1931); H. Birtner, "H. Isaac und die deutsche Musik," *Zeitschrift für Musikwissenschaft,* XVII (1935); F. Ghisi, "Le musiche di Isaac per il San Giovanni e Paolo di Lorenzo il Magnifico," *La Rassegna Musicale,* XVI (1943); L. Cuyler, "The Sequences of Isaac's Choralis constantinus," *Journal of the American Musicological Society,* III (1950); W. Heinz, *Isaacs und Senfls Propriums-Kompositionen in Handschriften der Bayerischen Staatsbibliothek München* (diss., Univ. of Berlin, 1952); M. Just, *Studien zu H. Isaacs Motetten* (diss., Univ. of Tübingen, 1960); F. D'Accone, "H. Isaac in Florence: New and Unpublished Documents," *Musical Quarterly* (Oct. 1963); F. Ghisi, "Arrigo il Tedesco, musicista fiorentino," *Chigiana,* 24 (1967); S. Novack, "Fusion of Design and Tonal Order in Mass and Motet: Josquin Desprez and H. Isaac," *Music Forum,* 2 (1970); M. Staehelm, *Die Messen H. Isaacs* (3 vols., Bern and Stuttgart, 1977).

Isamitt, Carlos, Chilean composer; b. Rengo, Colchagua, March 13, 1887; d. Santiago, July 2, 1974. He studied both music and painting in Chile; then in Italy, Spain, France, and the Netherlands. As a composer, he became interested in the folk music of the Araucanian Indians, and made use of these authentic materials in several of his works: *4 movimientos sinfónicos* (1960); *Te kuduam mapuche* for Voice, Bassoon, and the Araucanian Drum Kultrún (1958); Harp Concerto (1957); Sonata for Flute Solo (1954).

Isbin, Sharon, American guitarist and teacher; b. Minneapolis, Aug. 7, 1956. She studied with Jeffrey Van in Minneapolis, then took courses at Yale Univ. (B.A., 1978; M.A., 1979); she also received instruction from Rosalyn Tureck and Oscar Ghiglia at the Aspen Music School (1971–75) and from Alirio Diaz at the Banff Music Festival (1972). She won 1st prizes in the Toronto International Guitar Competition (1975), the Mu-

nich International Guitar Competition (1976), and the Queen Sofia Competition in Madrid (1979), subsequently appearing throughout the world as a soloist with orchs. and as a recitalist. She taught at N.Y.'s Manhattan School of Music (from 1979) and Mannes College of Music (from 1984). Her repertoire ranges from the Classical period to jazz, folk, and beyond. She has commissioned works from a variety of composers, including Leo Brouwer, Joan Tower, and Joseph Schwanter.
BIBL.: H. Waleson, "Magnificent Obsession: S. I.'s—with the Guitar—Opens New Horizons," *Musical America* (Jan. 1988).

Iseler, Elmer (Walter), prominent Canadian choral conductor; b. Port Colborne, near Niagara Falls, Ontario, Oct. 14, 1927. He studied piano and organ; then studied church music at Waterloo Lutheran Univ.; subsequently enrolled at the Univ. of Toronto (B.Mus., 1950). He taught music in high schools in Toronto (1952–64); in 1964 he became conductor of the Toronto Mendelssohn Choir; taught choral music at the Univ. of Toronto (1965–68); founded the Elmer Iseler Singers in 1978. He ed. the Festival Singers of Canada Choral Series. Iseler is generally acknowledged as one of Canada's leading choral conductors. In 1975 he was made an Officer of the Order of Canada.

Isepp, Martin (Johannes Sebastian), Austrian pianist and harpsichordist; b. Vienna, Sept. 30, 1930. He went to England; studied at Lincoln College, Oxford, and at the Royal Academy of Music in London; in 1957 he joined the music staff of the Glyndebourne Festival. From 1973 to 1976 he was on the faculty of the Juilliard School of Music in N.Y. He became best known as an accompanist to many of the foremost singers of the day, including Dame Janet Baker, Hans Hotter, Elisabeth Schwarzkopf, and John Shirley-Quirk.

Isham, Mark, American composer and instrumentalist; b. N.Y., Sept. 7, 1951. His mother was a violinist, and his father taught music and art; he studied piano, violin, and trumpet from an early age. After his family moved to California, he played trumpet in the Oakland and San Francisco Syms. and in the San Francisco Opera Orch.; also played in various jazz and rock bands, including the Beach Boys. He became a synthesizer programmer in the early 1970s, and in 1979 he formed (with Peter Maunu, Patrick O'Hearn, and Terry Bozzio) the groundbreaking art-rock Group 87, which produced 2 albums before its demise in 1986. His 1st solo album (1983) was the 1st electronic release by the New Age label Windham Hill. Among his film scores is the important documentary *The Times of Harvey Milk* (1985); also *The Moderns* (1988). His music is slow and delicate, overlapping harmonies and rhythms in a haze of electronics; it is distinct from other New Age music in its nobility, a hieratic effect created by his special use of brass instruments. Among his compositions are *Vapor Drawings* (1983), *Castalia* (1988), and *Tibet* (1989).

Ishii, Kan, Japanese composer, brother of **Maki Ishii;** b. Tokyo, March 30, 1921. He is one of two sons of Baku Ishii, a renowned scholar of modern dance. He studied in Tokyo at the Musashino Music School with Goh, Ikenouchi, and Odaka (1939–43); in 1952 went to Germany and took lessons with Carl Orff at the Hochschule für Musik in Munich. Returning to Japan, he taught at the Tōhō Gakuen School of Music (1954–66) and at the Aichi-Prefectural Arts Univ. in Nagoya (from 1966).
WORKS: 4 operas: *Mermaid and Red Candle* (1961), *Kaguyahime* (Prince Kaguya; 1963), *En-no-Gyojia* (Tokyo, 1964), *Lady Kesa and Morito* (Tokyo, Nov. 24, 1968); 9 ballets: *God and the Bayadere* (Tokyo, Nov. 6, 1950); *Birth of a Human* (Tokyo, Nov. 27, 1954); *Frökln Julie* (1955); *Shakuntara* (1961); *Marimo* (Tokyo, 1963); *Biruma no tategoto* (Harp of Burma; 1963); *Haniwa* (1963); *Hakai* (1965); *Ichiyo Higuchi* (1966); symphonic poem, *Yama* (Mountain; Tokyo, Oct. 7, 1954); *Kappa's Penny* for Youth Orch. (1956); *Sinfonia Ainu* for Soprano, Chorus, and Orch. (1958–59); *The Reef,* cantata for Baritone, Chorus, 4 Pianos, and Percussion (1967); *Akita the Great* for Chorus and Brass (1968); *Music for Percussion* for 8 Players (1970); Viola Sonata (1960); Music for Solo Flute (1972); *Foot-*

steps to Tomorrow, cantata for Solo Soprano (1972); folk songs; choruses; etc.

Ishii, Maki, Japanese composer, brother of **Kan Ishii;** b. Tokyo, May 28, 1936. He received an early training in music from his father, a renowned scholar of modern dance; studied composition with Akira Ifukube and Tomojiro Ikenouchi, and conducting with Akeo Watanabe, in Tokyo (1952–58); then went to Germany, where he took courses at the Berlin Hochschule für Musik with Boris Blacher and Josef Rufer (1958–61); after a brief return to Japan he went back to Germany, where he decided to remain. In his works he attempts to combine the coloristic effects of Japanese instruments with European techniques of serial music and electronic sounds.
    WORKS: Prelude and Variations for 9 Players (1959–60); 7 *Stücke* for Small Orch. (1960–61); *Transition* for Small Orch. (1962); *Aphorismen I* for String Trio, Percussion, and Piano (1963); *Galgenlieder* for Baritone, Male Chorus, and 13 Players (1964); *Characters* for Flute, Oboe, Piano, Guitar, and Percussion (1965); *Hamon* for Violin, Chamber Ensemble, and Tape (1965); *Expressions* for String Orch. (Tokyo, Jan. 11, 1968); 5 *Elements* for Guitar and 6 Players (1967); *Piano Piece* for Pianist and Percussionist (1968); *Kyō-ō* for Piano, Orch., and Tape (Tokyo, Feb. 22, 1969); *Kyō-sō* for Percussion and Orch. (Tokyo, Feb. 7, 1969); *La-sen I* for 7 Players and Tape (1969); *La-sen II* for Solo Cello (1970); *Sō-gū I* for Shakuhachi and Piano (1970); *Music for Gagaku* (1970); *Dipol* for Orch. (1971); *Sō-gū II* for Gagaku and Sym. Orch. (Tokyo, June 23, 1971; work resulting from simultaneous perf. of *Music for Gagaku* and *Dipol*); *Sen-ten* for Percussion Player and Tape (1971); *Aphorismen II* for a Pianist (1972); *Chō-etsu* for Chamber Group and Tape (1973); *Polaritäten* for Soloists and Orch. (1973; work exists in 3 versions, each having different soloists: *I* for Biwa and Harp; *II* for Biwa, Shakuhachi, and Flute; *III* for Shakuhachi and Flute); *Synkretismen* for Marimba, 7 Soloists, Strings, and 3 Percussionists (1973); *Anime Amare* for Harp and Tape (1974); *Jo* for Orch. (1975); *Lost Sounds III,* violin concerto (1978); *Translucent Vision* for Orch. (1981–82); *Afro-Concerto* for Percussion and Orch. (1982); *Kaguya-Hime,* symphonic suite for Percussion Group (1984); *Gioh,* symphonic poem for Yokobue (Japanese Flute) and Orch. (1984); *Gedatsu* for Yokobue and Orch. (1985); *Herbst Variante* for Orch. (1986); *Intrada* for Orch. (1986); *13 Drums* for Solo Percussion (1986); *Concertante* for Marimba and 6 Percussionists (1988).

Isidore of Seville, Spanish cleric; b. probably in Cartagena, c.560; d. Seville, April 4, 636. He was taken to Seville as a child; in 599 became archbishop there. Between 622 and 633 he compiled a treatise on the arts, *Etymologiarum sive originum libri XX;* he expressed the conviction that music can only be preserved through memory, for musical sounds could never be notated (*scribi non possunt*). The text was publ. in Oxford (1911); an Eng. tr. of the pertinent parts is included in Strunk's *Source Readings in Music History* (N.Y., 1950).
    BIBL.: K. Schmidt, *Quaestiones de musicis scriptoribus romanis imprimis Cassiodoro et Isidoro* (Leipzig, 1898); J. Pérez de Urbel, *San Isidoro de Sevilla* (Barcelona, 1945); J. Fontaine, *Isidore de Séville et la culture classique dans l'Espagne wisigothique* (Paris, 1959); J. Madoz, *San Isidoro de Sevilla* (Madrid, 1960).

Isler, Ernst, Swiss organist and music critic; b. Zürich, Sept. 30, 1879; d. there, Sept. 26, 1944. He studied in Zürich and Berlin; served as an organist in Zürich, and taught organ there. He became music critic of the influential daily paper *Neue Zürcher Zeitung* in 1902, and held this position until his death; from 1910 to 1927 he was ed. of the *Schweizerische Musikzeitung.* He publ. monographs on Hans Huber (1923), Max Reger (1917), etc.; also *Das Züricherische Musikleben seit der Eröffnung der neuen Tonhalle* (1895) (2 vols., Zürich, 1935–36).
    BIBL.: H. Grossmann et al., eds., *E. I. zum Gedächtnis* (Zürich, 1944).

Ísólfsson, Páll, Icelandic organist and composer; b. Stokkseyri, Oct. 12, 1893; d. Reykjavík, Nov. 23, 1974. He studied organ at the Leipzig Cons. with Straube (1913–18),

and later in Paris with Bonnet (1925). Returning to Iceland, he served as organist at the Reykjavík Cathedral (1939–68) and director of the Reykjavík Cons. (1930–57) and Icelandic Radio (1930–59). He wrote a number of attractive piano pieces in the manner of Grieg (humoresques, intermezzi, capriccios, etc.), choruses, and a cantata on the millennial anniversary of the Icelandic Parliament (1930); also compiled (with S. Einarsson) a collection of choral pieces by various composers. He wrote an autobiography (2 vols., 1963–64).
    BIBL.: J. Thorarinsson, *P. Í.* (Reykjavík, 1963).

Isouard, Nicolò, important Maltese-born French composer; b. Malta, Dec 6, 1775; d. Paris, March 23, 1818. He was sent to Paris to study at the Pensionnat Berthaud, a preparatory school for engineers and artillerymen; also studied piano there with Pin. With the outbreak of the French Revolution (1789), he returned to Malta, where he worked in a merchant's office and took courses in composition with Michel-Ange Vella and counterpoint with Azzopardi; his father then sent him to Italy to act as his assistant, but he found time to study harmony with Nicolas of Amendola in Palermo; later studied composition with Sala in Naples, where he also received counsel from Guglielmi. His 1st opera, *L'avviso ai maritati* (Florence, 1794), proved so successful that he decided to devote himself fully to composition. In order not to embarrass his family, he used the name Nicolò de Malte, or simply Nicolò, professionally. The singer Senesino commissioned his 2nd opera, *Artaserse* (Livorno, 1794), which also was a success. After serving as organist of the church of St. John of Jerusalem in Malta (1795–98), he went to Paris, gaining his 1st major success with the opera *Michel-Ange* (Opéra-Comique, Dec. 11, 1802) and quickly establishing himself as the leading composer at the Opéra-Comique. His *Cendrillon* (Feb. 22, 1810), *Joconde ou Les Coureurs d'aventures* (Feb. 28, 1814), and *Jeannot et Colin* (Oct. 17, 1814) were popular favorites. In spite of the competition from his friend and rival Boieldieu, he remained a protean figure in the musical life of Paris until his death.
    WORKS: *L'avviso ai maritati,* opera (Florence, 1794); *Artaserse,* opera (Livorno, 1794); *Rinaldo d'Asti,* opera (Malta, c.1796); *Il Barbiere di Siviglia,* opera buffa (Malta, c.1796); *L'improvisata in campagna,* opera buffa (Malta, 1797; rev. as *L'impromptu de campagne,* Paris, 1801); *I due avari,* opera buffa (Malta, c.1797); *Ginevra di Scozia,* opera (Malta, c.1798); *Il Barone d'Alba chiara,* opera (Malta, c.1798); *Le Petit Page ou La Prison d'état,* opéra-comique (Paris, 1800; in collaboration with R. Kreutzer); *Flaminius à Corinthe,* opera (Paris, 1801; in collaboration with Kreutzer); *Le Tonnelier,* opéra-comique (Paris, 1801); *La Statue ou La Femme avare,* opéra-comique (Paris, April 26, 1802); *Michel-Ange,* opera (Paris, 1802); *Les Confidences,* opéra-comique (Paris, 1803); *Le Baiser et la quittance ou Une Aventure de garnison,* opéra-comique (Paris, 1803; in collaboration with Boieldieu, Kreutzer, and Méhul); *Le Médecin turc,* opéra-comique (Paris, 1803); *L'Intrigue aux fenêtres,* opéra-comique (Paris, 1805); *La Ruse inutile ou Les Rivaux par convention,* opéra-comique (Paris, 1805); *Léonce ou Le Fils adoptif,* opéra-comique (Paris, 1805); *La Prise de Passaw,* opéra-comique (Paris, 1806); *Idala ou La Sultane,* opéra-comique (Paris, 1806); *Les Rendez-vous bourgeois,* opéra-comique (Paris, 1807); *Les Créanciers ou Le Remède à la goutte,* opéra-comique (Paris, 1807); *Un Jour à Paris ou La Leçon singulière,* opéra-comique (Paris, 1808); *Cimarosa,* opéra-comique (Paris, 1808); *Cendrillon,* opéra-féerie (Paris, 1810); *La Victime des arts,* opéra-comique (Paris, 1811; in collaboration with Solié and Berton Fils); *La Fête au village,* opéra-comique (Paris, 1811); *Le Billet de loterie,* opéra-comique (Paris, 1811); *Le Magicien sans magic,* opéra-comique (Paris, 1811); *Lully et Quinault,* opéra-comique (Paris, 1812); *Le Prince de Catane,* opera (Paris, 1813); *Les Français à Venise,* opéra-comique (Paris, 1813); *Bayard à Mézières ou Le Siège de Mézières,* opéra-comique (Paris, 1814; in collaboration with Boieldieu, Catel, and Cherubini); *Joconde ou Les Coureurs d'aventures,* opéra-comique (Paris, 1814); *Jeannot et Colin,* opéra-comique (Paris, 1814); *Les Deux Maris,* opéra-comique (Paris, 1816); *L'Une*

pour l'autre ou L'Enlèvement, opéra-comique (Paris, 1816); *Aladin ou La Lampe merveilleuse,* opera (Paris, 1822; completed by A. Benincori); also sacred music, cantatas, airs, and romances.

Bibl.: F. Fétis, "N. I.," *Revue et Gazette Musicale de Paris,* VII (1840); E. Wahl, *N. I.: Sein Leben und sein Schaffen auf dem Gebiet der Opéra Comique* (Munich, 1906).

Israel, Brian M., American composer and pianist; b. N.Y., Feb. 5, 1951; d. Syracuse, N.Y., May 8, 1986. He studied composition with Ulysses Kay at Lehman College in N.Y. (B.A., 1971), and with Robert Palmer, Burrill Phillips, and Karel Husa at Cornell Univ. (M.F.A., 1974; D.M.A., 1975); taught at Cornell (1972–75) and Syracuse Univ. (1975–86). As a performer he advocated contemporary works; his own compositions form an eclectic traversal from Baroque contrapuntal devices to serialism.
Works: STAGE: *Ladies' Voices,* mini-opera for 4 Voices and 4 Instruments (1970); *The Obtaining of Portia,* chamber opera after Shakespeare (Bloomington, Ind., April 13, 1976); *Love and Other Important Nonsense,* after Alberta Phillips, for Soprano, Saxophone, Trombone, and Percussion (1977); *Winnie the Pooh,* children's opera after Milne (Syracuse, June 1, 1979). ORCH.: *Contrasts* for Cello and Orch. (1967); 6 syms., including No. 2 (1974), No. 4, with Women's Chorus (1984), and No. 6, with Soprano and Bass (Syracuse, May 4, 1986); Viola Concerto (1974); *Dorian Variations* for Strings (1981); 2 sinfoniettas (1983, 1985); Mandolin Concerto (1985). CHAMBER: Clarinet Sonata (1969); 3 string quartets (1971; 1976, rev. 1983; 1978); Oboe Sonata (1972); Piano Quintet (1973); 2 sonatas for 2 Tubas (1976, 1977); Sonata for 2 Trombones (1977); Piano Trio, in memoriam Ernest Bloch (1980); *Concertino* for Saxophone Ensemble (1985); Piano Quartet (1985); works for band; choral works; songs.
Bibl.: "In Memoriam: B. I.," *Saxophone Symposium* (Summer 1986).

Isserlis, Julius, Russian pianist; b. Kishinev, Nov. 7, 1888; d. London, July 23, 1968. He studied with Puchalski at the Kiev Cons.; then with Safonov and Taneyev at the Moscow Cons. He taught at the Moscow Phil. Inst. of Music (1913–23), then in Vienna (1923–28); in 1928 he settled in London. He wrote a number of character pieces for piano.

Istel, Edgar, eminent German musicologist; b. Mainz, Feb. 23, 1880; d. Miami, Fla., Dec. 17, 1948. He studied with Thuille at the Munich Hochschule für Musik and Sandberger at the Univ. of Munich (Ph.D., 1900, with the diss. *J.J. Rousseau als Komponist seiner lyrischen Scene "Pygmalion"* (publ. in *Publikationen der International Musikgesellschaft,* I/i, Leipzig, 1901); then settled in Munich as a teacher; in 1919, taught in Berlin; in 1920 he moved to Madrid, where he remained until the outbreak of the civil war in 1936; then went to England, and eventually to the U.S. (1938). He was also a composer; wrote 5 operas, oratorios, and smaller pieces.
Writings: *Das deutsche Weihnachtsspiel und seine Wiedergeburt aus dem Geiste der Musik* (Langensalza, 1901); *Richard Wagner im Lichte eines zeitgenössischen Briefwechsels* (1902); *Peter Cornelius* (1906); *Die Entstehung des deutschen Melodramas* (1906); *Die komische Oper* (1906); *Die Blütezeit der musikalischen Romantik in Deutschland* (1909); *Das Kunstwerk Richard Wagners* (1910); *Das Libretto* (1914; Eng. ed. as *The Art of Writing Opera Librettos,* N.Y., 1922); *Die moderne Oper vom Tode Wagners bis zum Weltkrieg* (Leipzig, 1915); *Niccolo Paganini* (Leipzig, 1919); *Revolution und Oper* (1919); *Das Buch der Oper; Die deutschen Meister von Gluck bis Wagner* (Berlin, 1919); *Bizet und Carmen* (Stuttgart, 1927).

Istomin, Eugene (George), distinguished American pianist; b. N.Y., Nov. 26, 1925. He studied with Rudolf Serkin and Mieczyslaw Horszowski at the Curtis Inst. of Music in Philadelphia; in 1943 he won the Leventritt Award and appeared as a soloist with the N.Y. Phil. (Nov. 21, 1943), playing the 2nd Piano Concerto of Brahms. He developed a highly successful concert career; appeared with a number of American

orchs., and also gave recitals in America and in Europe. On Feb. 15, 1975, he married Martita Casals, widow of Pablo Casals.

Istrate, Mircea, Rumanian pianist and composer; b. Cluj, Sept. 27, 1929. He studied piano and composition at the Cluj Cons. (1945–53) and in Bucharest (1954–57), where he subsequently taught piano. He composed a Flute Sonata (1954); *Burlesca,* chamber concerto for Violin, Oboe, Clarinet, Bassoon, and Double Bass (1955); *Muzică stereofonică* for 2 String Orchs. (1955–57); *Evocare* for Mezzo-soprano, Female Chorus, and Orch. (1960); *Pe o plajă japoneză* (On a Japanese Beach), sequences for Female Chorus, Orch., and Tape (1961); Oboe Sonata (1962); *Algoritm* for Orch. (1964); *Interferente* (Interferences) for Orch. and Electronics (1965); *Evenimente I–II–III,* etc., for Prepared Piano, Percussion within a Piano, Electric Guitar, Double Bass, Vibraphone, Horn, Marimba, and Tape (1966; of variable duration); *Pulsations* for Orch. (1973); songs.

Ištvan, Miloslav, Czech composer; b. Olomouc, Sept. 2, 1928; d. Brno, Jan. 20, 1990. He studied at the Brno Academy of Music with Jaroslav Kvapil (1948–52); subsequently was active as a teacher there (from 1956). Like many of his compatriots he cultivated a national style of composition, thematically derived from folk music, but later adopted the *modus operandi* of the cosmopolitan avant-garde. In 1963 he joined the Creative Group A of Brno, dedicated to free musical experimentation "uninhibited by puritanically limited didactical regulations." He also worked in the electronic music studio of Brno Radio.
Works: Concerto for Horn, String Orch., and Piano (1949); Sym. (1952); *Winter Suite* for Strings, Piano, and Percussion (1956); *Concerto-Symphony* for Piano and Orch. (1957); *Balada o Jihu* (Ballad of the South), 3 symphonic frescoes after Lewis Allan's satirical view of the American South (Brno, Dec. 8, 1960); Concertino for Violin and Chamber Orch. (1961); 6 *Studies* for Chamber Ensemble (1964; rev. for Chamber Orch. and perf. at the ISCM Festival, Prague, Oct. 9, 1967); *Zaklínání času* (Conjuration of Time) for Orch. and 2 Narrators (1967; Ostrava, Jan. 23, 1969); *Ja, Jakob* (I, Jacob), chamber oratorio, with Tape (1968); Sonata for Violin and Chamber Orch. (1970); *In memoriam Josef Berg* for Orch. (1971); *Hymn to the Sun,* small cantata (1971); *Beauty and the Beast,* chamber oratorio (1974); *Shakespearean Variations* for Orch. (1975); *The Games,* 7 pictures for Orch. (1977); *Hard Blues,* chamber cantata after black American folk poetry (1980); Rondos for Viola and Piano (1950); Trio for Clarinet, Cello, and Piano (1950); Clarinet Sonata (1954); Suite for Horn and Piano (1955); Piano Trio (1958); *Rhapsody* for Cello and Piano (1961); String Quartet (1963); *Dodekameron* for 12 Players (1962–64); *Refrains* for String Trio (1965); *Ritmi ed antiritmi* for 2 Pianos and 2 Percussionists (1966); *Lamentations,* 5 songs for Alto, Piano, and Tape (1970); Cello Sonata (1970); 5 *framenti* for Solo Salterio (1971); *Omaggio a J.S. Bach* for Wind Quintet (1971); *Psalmus niger* for 6 Percussionists (1971); *Blacked-out Landscape,* in memory of those fallen in World War II, for String Quartet (1975); *Ad fontes intimas* for Double Bass or Trumpet, and Percussion (1975); *The Micro-Worlds Diptych: Summer Micro-Worlds* for Flute, Harp, and Harpsichord and *Micro-Worlds of My Town* for 2 Violas, Oboe, and Clarinet (1977); Capriccio for Vibraphone, Marimba, and Percussion (1978); *Diptych Canti: Canto I* for Viola (1979) and *II* for Prepared Violas and Female Voice (1980); *Partita* for 16 Strings (1980); 3 piano sonatas (1954, 1959, 1978); *Impromptus* for Piano (1956); *Odyssey of a Child from Lidice* for Piano (1963); *Musica aspera* for Organ (1964); Variations for 2 Pianos (1972); 2 scores of "musique concrète": *Island of Toys* (1968) and *Avete morituri* (1970); many choruses and songs.

Ito, Ryûta, Japanese composer; b. Kure, March 4, 1922. He graduated from the faculty of medicine of the Univ. of Tokyo in 1946 (Doctor of Medical Science, 1955); then studied composition with S. Takata, S. Moroi, T. Ikenouchi, and S. Fukai. Subsequently he divided his interests between music and medicine and became a prof. of pharmacy at the school of medicine of Toho Univ.; also served as secretary and a member of the committee of the Japanese Soc. for Contemporary Music (1952–61).

Works: Chamber opera, *The Court of Judgment* (1954); *Allemand and Aria* for Orch. (1945; Tokyo, May 19, 1950); 2 *Moments* for Orch. (1947; Tokyo, Oct. 29, 1947); *Divertissement* for Orch. (1950); *Festival Music* for Orch. (1953); *Suite* for String Orch. (1954); *Ostinato concertanto* for Piano and Orch. (1957; Tokyo, Oct. 18, 1957); *Temariuta* (Handball Song) for Orch. (1958); Concerto for Japanese Flute and Orch. (1958; Tokyo, Nov. 28, 1958); *Suzuka*, suite for Orch. (1959); *Suite* for Chamber Orch. (1959); *Suite* for Orch. (1961); *Les Cloches*, symphonic suite for Japanese Instruments, Celesta, Percussion, Male Chorus, Viola, Cello, and Double Bass (1971; Tokyo, Nov. 9, 1971); *Abrasion of a Life*, suite for Mixed Chorus (1984); several works for Japanese instruments, including *Duets* Nos. 1 and 2 for Shakuhachi and Jushichi-gen (1987–88).

Iturbi, José, celebrated Spanish pianist and conductor; b. Valencia, Nov. 28, 1895; d. Los Angeles, June 28, 1980. He took piano lessons with Malats in Barcelona; while still a very young boy he earned a living by playing in street cafés. A local group of music-lovers collected a sum of money to send him to Paris for further study; he was accepted as a student at the Paris Cons., and graduated in 1912. He was head of the piano dept. of the Geneva Cons. (1919–23); then developed a brilliant concert career; his performances of Spanish music were acclaimed for their authentic rhythmic spirit. He made a tour of South America; in 1928 he appeared as soloist in the U.S.; during his 2nd American tour, in 1930, he gave 67 concerts. In 1936 he turned to conducting; led the Rochester Phil. until 1944. He wrote a number of pleasing piano pieces in a typical Spanish vein; of these, *Pequeña danza española* exercised considerable attraction. He also appeared in several Hollywood films. His sister, **Amparo Iturbi** (b. Valencia, March 12, 1898; d. Beverly Hills, Calif., April 21, 1969), was also a talented pianist; she played piano duos with José Iturbi on numerous occasions in Europe and America.

Iturriberry, Juan José, Uruguayan composer; b. Pando, Oct. 24, 1936. He studied in Montevideo with Carlos Estrada and Héctor Tosar, and also took a course in electro-acoustical techniques. His works are quaquaversal; some require electronic applications. His *Meditation in F* (1975) is concentrated on the single note F, which is repeated ad nauseam.

Ivanov, Georgi, Bulgarian conductor and composer; b. Sofia, Aug. 23, 1924. He studied with Lubomir Pipkov and Veselin Stoyanov in Sofia; then went to Moscow, where he studied with Shaporin (1946–50). Returning to Bulgaria, he became conductor of the National Youth Theater in Sofia.

Works: 2 symphonic poems: *Legend of the Lopian Forest* (Sofia, Feb. 15, 1951) and *The Mutiny on the S.S. Nadezhda* (1955); Sym. (Sofia, June 22, 1960); Divertimento for Clarinet, Violin, Harpsichord, and Chamber Orch. (1962); *Metamorphosis* for Strings (1967); *Timbres in Rhythm* for Orch. (1968); Variations for Orch. (1969); *Musica concertante* for Orch. (1970).

Ivanov, Konstantin, Russian conductor and composer; b. Efremov, May 21, 1907; d. Moscow, April 15, 1984. He played trumpet in Soviet cavalry orchs.; then enrolled in the conducting class at the Moscow Cons.; after graduation in 1937, served as assistant conductor at various operatic and sym. posts. From 1941 to 1946 he was conductor of the Bolshoi Radio Orch.; from 1946 to 1975 was conductor of the State Sym. Orch. of the U.S.S.R.; made world tours with it, which included the U.S. and Japan, as well as countries of Western Europe. He was also a composer; among his works are several symphonic poems and a Double-bass Concerto.

Ivanov, Mikhail Mikhailovich, Russian music critic and composer; b. Moscow, Sept. 23, 1849; d. Rome, Oct. 20, 1927. He studied mechanical sciences at the Technological Inst. in St. Petersburg, graduating in 1869; then went to Moscow, where he took private harmony lessons with Tchaikovsky; from

1870 to 1875 he lived in Italy, where he took music lessons with Sgambati. In 1875 he returned to St. Petersburg, where he obtained the position of music critic of the influential newspaper *Novoye Vremya*, which he held from 1880 to 1917. After the Revolution he emigrated to Italy, where he remained until his death. A critic of reactionary tendencies, he assailed the composers of the Russian national school; endowed with a lively literary style, he made use of irony against any new musical developments; this in turn earned him the enmity of liberal musicians. He was also a composer of sorts; wrote a ballet, *Vestal Virgin* (St. Petersburg, Feb. 29, 1888); the operas *Zabava Putiatishna* (Moscow, Jan. 15, 1899) and *Potemkin Holiday* (St. Petersburg, Dec. 16, 1902); and a number of songs. He publ. *Pushkin in Music* (St. Petersburg, 1899) and *The Historical Development of Music in Russia* (2 vols., St. Petersburg, 1910–12).

Ivanov, Nikolai (Kuzmich), Russian tenor; b. Voronezh, Oct. 22, 1810; d. Bologna, July 19, 1880. He sang as a child in the Imperial Court Chapel in St. Petersburg; there he attracted the attention of Glinka, who took him to Italy in 1830; he studied with Bianchi in Milan and with Joséphine Fodor-Mainvielle and Nozzari in Naples. He made his debut at the Teatro San Carlo in Naples in 1832 as Percy in Donizetti's *Anna Bolena*; subsequently sang in Paris at the Théâtre-Italien (1833–37); concurrently appeared in London. Later he was a member of La Scala in Milan. He retired in 1852. He was reputed to be one of the best representatives of the Italian school of *bel canto*, and enjoyed the friendship of Rossini and other famous contemporaries.

Bibl.: S. Smolensky, *The Tenor I., Companion of Glinka in Italy* (St. Petersburg, 1904).

Ivanov-Boretzky, Mikhail Vladimirovich, Russian musicologist and composer; b. Moscow, June 16, 1874; d. there, April 1, 1936. He studied jurisprudence at the Univ. of Moscow, graduating in 1896; at the same time he took music lessons; in 1898 he went to St. Petersburg and became a student of composition of Rimsky-Korsakov. From 1921 to 1936 he taught at the Moscow Cons. His music was mainly imitative of Rimsky-Korsakov's works. He wrote the operas *Adolfina* (Moscow, Dec. 10, 1908) and *The Witch* (Moscow, Aug. 14, 1918); a Sym.; piano music; choruses; songs. His importance to Russian music, however, lies in his writings. He publ. monographs on Palestrina, Handel, Schumann, Mendelssohn, and Beethoven; also a useful anthology of music history, with a synoptic table of 18th-century music (Moscow, 1934). A collection of his articles was publ. in Moscow in 1972.

Ivanov-Radkevitch, Nikolai, Russian composer; b. Krasnoyarsk, Siberia, Feb. 10, 1904; d. Moscow, Feb. 4, 1962. He studied composition with Glière and orchestration with Vasilenko at the Moscow Cons., graduating in 1928; subsequently was on its faculty (1929–48). In 1952 he was appointed instructor in orchestration at the Inst. of Military Bandleaders of the Soviet Army. He was particularly successful in writing popular marches for band, of which *Our Own Moscow* and *Victory March* received the State Prize. He also composed 4 syms. (1928, 1932, 1937, 1945); 12 symphonic suites on folk motifs; Violin Sonata; various pieces for other instruments; film music.

Ivanovici, Ion, Rumanian bandleader and composer; b. Banat, 1845; d. Bucharest, Sept. 29, 1902. He played the flute and clarinet in a military band in Galaţi, and in 1880 conducted his own band there. In the same year he wrote the waltz *Valurile Dunării* (The Waves of the Danube), which became a perennial favorite all over the world. He took part in the Paris Exposition of 1889, and conducted there a band of 116 musicians. In 1900 he was appointed Inspector of Military Music in Rumania. He publ. about 150 pieces for piano and dances for band.

Bibl.: V. Cosma, *I.* (Bucharest, 1958).

Ivanovs, Janis, prolific Latvian composer; b. Preili, Oct. 9, 1906; d. Riga, March 27, 1983. He studied composition with Wihtol, piano with Dauge, and conducting with Schneevoigt

at the Riga Cons., graduating in 1931; then worked at the Latvian Radio; in 1944 was appointed to the composition faculty at the Riga Cons. An exceptionally fecund composer, he wrote 20 syms., several of a programmatic nature descriptive of the Latvian countryside: No. 1, *Symphonie-Poème* (1933); No. 2, *Atlantida* (1941); No. 6, *Latgales* (Latvian; 1949); No. 12, *Sinfonia energica* (1967); No. 13, *Symphonia humana* (1969). His symphonic poems also reflect nature scenes; e.g., *Varaviksne* (Rainbow; 1938) and *Padebešu Kalns* (Mountain under the Sky; 1939). He further wrote 3 string quartets (1933, 1946, 1961); a Cello Concerto (1938); Violin Concerto (1951); Piano Concerto (1959); choruses; songs; piano pieces; film music.
BIBL.: N. Grünfeld, *J. I.* (Moscow, 1959); V. Berzina, *Dzives simfonija Jana I.* (Riga, 1964).

Ives, Burl (Icle Ivanhoe), American folksinger; b. Hunt Township, Jasper County, Ill., June 14, 1909. He studied briefly at N.Y. Univ.; traveled through the U.S. and Canada as an itinerant handyman, supplementing his earnings by singing and playing the banjo. He then became a dramatic actor, appearing on the stage and in films, and gave concerts of folk ballads, accompanying himself on the guitar. He publ. an autobiography, *Wayfaring Stranger* (N.Y., 1948), and the anthologies *The Burl Ives Songbook* (1953) and *The Burl Ives Book of Irish Songs* (1958).

Ives, Charles (Edward), one of the most remarkable American composers, whose individual genius created music so original, so universal, and yet so deeply national in its sources of inspiration that it profoundly changed the direction of American music; b. Danbury, Conn., Oct. 20, 1874; d. N.Y., May 19, 1954. His father, George Ives, was a bandleader of the 1st Conn. Heavy Artillery during the Civil War, and the early development of Charles Ives was, according to his own testimony, deeply influenced by his father. At the age of 12, he played the drums in the band and also received from his father rudimentary musical training in piano and cornet playing. At the age of 13 he played organ at the Danbury Church; soon he began to improvise freely at the piano, without any dependence on school rules; as a result of his experimentation in melody and harmony, encouraged by his father, he began to combine several keys, partly as a spoof, but eventually as a legitimate alternative to traditional music; at 17 he composed his *Variations on America* for organ in a polytonal setting; still earlier he wrote a band piece, *Holiday Quick Step*, which was performed by the Danbury Band in 1888. He attended the Danbury High School; in 1894 he entered Yale Univ., where he took regular academic courses and studied organ with Dudley Buck and composition with Horatio Parker; from Parker he received a fine classical training; while still in college he composed 2 full-fledged syms., written in an entirely traditional manner demonstrating great skill in formal structure, fluent melodic development, and smooth harmonic modulations. After his graduation in 1898, Ives joined an insurance company; also played organ at the Central Presbyterian Church in N.Y. (1899–1902). In 1907 he formed an insurance partnership with Julian Myrick of N.Y.; he proved himself to be an exceptionally able businessman; the firm of Ives & Myrick prospered, and Ives continued to compose music as an avocation. In 1908 he married Harmony Twichell. In 1918 he suffered a massive heart attack, complicated by a diabetic condition, and was compelled to curtail his work both in business and in music to a minimum because his illness made it difficult to handle a pen. He retired from business in 1930, and by that time had virtually stopped composing. In 1919 Ives publ. at his own expense his great masterpiece, *Concord Sonata*, for piano, inspired by the writings of Emerson, Hawthorne, the Alcotts, and Thoreau. Although written early in the century, its idiom is so extraordinary, and its technical difficulties so formidable, that the work did not receive a performance in its entirety until John Kirkpatrick played it in N.Y. in 1939. In 1922 Ives brought out, also at his expense, a volume of *114 Songs*, written between 1888 and 1921 and marked by great diversity of style, ranging from lyrical Romanticism to

powerful and dissonant modern invocations. Both the *Concord Sonata* and the *114 Songs* were distributed gratis by Ives to anyone wishing to receive copies. His orch. masterpiece, *3 Places in New England*, also had to wait nearly 2 decades before its 1st performance; of the monumental 4th Sym., only the 2nd movement was performed in 1927, and its complete performance was given posthumously in 1965. In 1947 Ives received the Pulitzer Prize for his 3rd Sym., written in 1911.

The slow realization of the greatness of Ives and the belated triumphant recognition of his music were phenomena without precedent in music history. Because of his chronic ailment, and also on account of his personal disposition, Ives lived as a recluse, away from the mainstream of American musical life; he never went to concerts and did not own a record player or a radio; while he was well versed in the musical classics, and studied the scores of Beethoven, Schumann, and Brahms, he took little interest in sanctioned works of modern composers; yet he anticipated many technical innovations, such as polytonality, atonality, and even 12-tone formations, as well as polymetric and polyrhythmic configurations, which were prophetic for his time. In the 2nd movement of the *Concord Sonata* he specified the application of a strip of wood on the white and the black keys of the piano to produce an echo-like sonority; in his unfinished *Universe Symphony* he planned an antiphonal representation of the heavens in chordal counterpoint and the earth in contrasting orch. groups. He also composed pieces of quarter-tone piano music. A unique quality of his music was the combination of simple motifs, often derived from American church hymns and popular ballads, with an extremely complex dissonant counterpoint which formed the supporting network for the melodic lines. A curious idiosyncrasy is the frequent quotation of the "fate motive" of Beethoven's 5th Sym. in many of his works. Materials of his instrumental and vocal works often overlap, and the titles are often changed during the process of composition. In his orchestrations he often indicated interchangeable and optional parts, as in the last movement of the *Concord Sonata*, which has a part for flute obbligato; thus he reworked the original score for large orch. of his *3 Places in New England* for a smaller ensemble to fit the requirements of Slonimsky's Chamber Orch. of Boston, which gave its 1st performance, and it was in this version that the work was 1st publ. and widely performed until the restoration of the large score was made in 1974. Ives possessed an uncommon gift for literary expression; his annotations to his works are both trenchant and humorous; he publ. in 1920 *Essays before a Sonata* as a literary companion vol. to the *Concord Sonata;* his *Memos* in the form of a diary, publ. after his death, reveal an extraordinary power of aphoristic utterance. He was acutely conscious of his civic duties as an American, and once circulated a proposal to have federal laws enacted by popular referendum. His centennial in 1974 was celebrated by a series of conferences at his alma mater, Yale Univ.; in N.Y., Miami, and many other American cities; and in Europe, including Russia. While during his lifetime he and a small group of devoted friends and admirers had great difficulties in having his works performed, recorded, or publ., a veritable Ives cult emerged after his death; eminent conductors gave repeated performances of his orch. works, and modern pianists were willing to cope with the forbidding difficulties of his works. In terms of the number of orch. performances, in 1976 Ives stood highest among modern composers on American programs, and the influence of his music on the new generation of composers reached a high mark, so that the adjective "Ivesian" became common in music criticism to describe certain acoustical and coloristic effects characteristic of his music. America's youth expressed especial enthusiasm for Ives, which received its most unusual tribute in the commercial marketing of a T-shirt with Ives's portrait. All of the Ives MSS and his correspondence were deposited by Mrs. Ives at Yale Univ., forming a basic Ives archive. The Charles Ives Soc., in N.Y., promotes research and publications. Letters from Ives to Nicolas Slonimsky are reproduced in the latter's book *Music since 1900* (4th ed., N.Y., 1971). A television movie, "A Good Dissonance Like a Man," produced and directed by Theodor W. Timreck in 1977, with the supervision of Vivian Perlis, depicts the life of Ives with fine dramatic impact. See also *Modern Music . . . Analytical Index,* complied by Wayne Shirley and ed. by William and Carolyn Lichtenwanger (N.Y., 1976).

WORKS: ORCH.: 4 syms.: No. 1 (1896–98); No. 2 (1897–1902; N.Y., Feb. 22, 1951); No. 3 (1901–4; N.Y., April 5, 1946); No. 4 (1910–16; 2nd movement only, N.Y., Jan. 29, 1927; 1st perf. in its entirety, N.Y., on April 26, 1965, Stokowski conducting); also incomplete fragments of a *Universe Symphony* (1911–16; 1st perf. of rev. version, Los Angeles, Dec. 13, 1984); *3 Places in New England (Orchestral Set No. 1: The "St. Gaudens" in Boston Common; Putnam's Camp, Redding, Connecticut; The Housatonic at Stockbridge; 1903–14;* N.Y., Jan. 10, 1931, Chamber Orch. of Boston, Nicolas Slonimsky conducting); *Calcium Light Night* for Chamber Orch. (1898–1907); *Central Park in the Dark* (1898–1907; Columbia Univ., N.Y., May 11, 1946); *The Unanswered Question* (1908); *Theater Orchestra Set: In the Cage, In the Inn, In the Night* (1904–11); *The Pond* (1906); *Browning Overture* (1911); *The Gong on the Hook and Ladder, or Firemen's Parade on Main Street* for Chamber Orch. (1911); *Lincoln, the Great Commoner* for Chorus and Orch. (1912); *A Symphony: Holidays,* in 4 parts, also perf. separately: *Washington's Birthday* (1913), *Decoration Day* (1912), *4th of July* (1913), *Thanksgiving and/or Forefathers' Day* (1904); *Over the Pavements* for Chamber Orch. (1913); *Orchestral Set No. 2* (1915); *Tone Roads* for Chamber Orch. (1911–15); *Orchestral Set No. 3* (1919–27). **CHAMBER:** String Quartet No. 1, subtitled *A Revival Service* (1896); *Prelude,* from "Pre-First Sonata," for Violin and Piano (1900); Trio for Violin, Clarinet, and Piano (1902); "Pre-Second String Quartet" (1905); *Space and Duration* for String Quartet and a very mechanical Piano (1907); *All the Way Around and Back* for Piano, Violin, Flute, Bugle, and Bells (1907); *The Innate* for String Quartet and Piano (1908); *Adagio sostenuto* for English Horn, Flute, Strings, and Piano (1910); Violin Sonata No. 1 (1908); Violin Sonata No. 2 (1910); Trio for Violin, Cello, and Piano (1911); String Quartet No. 2 (1913); Violin Sonata No. 3 (1914); *Set* for String Quartet and Piano (1914); Violin Sonata No. 4, subtitled *Children's Day at the Camp Meeting* (1915). **VOCAL:** *Psalm 67* (1898); *The Celestial Country,* cantata (1899); *3 Harvest Home Chorales* for Mixed Chorus, Brass, Double Bass, and Organ (1898–1912); *General William Booth Enters into Heaven* for Chorus with Brass Band (1914); *114 Songs* (1884–1921). **PIANO:** *3-page Sonata* (1905); *Some Southpaw Pitching* (1908); *The Anti-Abolitionist Riots* (1908); Sonata No. 1 (1909); *22* (1912); *3 Protests for Piano* (1914); Sonata No. 2 for Piano, subtitled *Concord, Mass., 1840–1860,* in 4 movements: *Emerson, Hawthorne, The Alcotts, Thoreau* (1909–15; publ. 1919; 1st perf. in its entirety by John Kirkpatrick, N.Y., Jan. 20, 1939; the 2nd movement requires the application of a strip of wood on the keys to produce tone-clusters); *3 Quartertone Piano Pieces* (1903–24).

WRITINGS: As a companion piece to his *Concord Sonata* (Piano Sonata No. 2), Ives wrote *Essays before a Sonata* (N.Y., 1920), commentaries on the Concord writers who inspired his work, and on various musical and philosophical matters; this has been reprinted as *Essays before a Sonata and Other Writings,* ed. by Howard Boatwright (N.Y., 1961). Most of his other expository writings are publ. as *Memos,* ed. by John Kirkpatrick (N.Y., 1972), composed of autobiography, explanation, and criticism.

BIBL.: H. Bellamann, "C. I., The Man and His Music," *Musical Quarterly* (Jan. 1933); H. Cowell, "C. I.," in *American Composers on American Music* (Stanford Univ., 1933); P. Rosenfeld, "I.' Concord Sonata," *Modern Music* (Jan.–Feb. 1939); M. Goss, *Modern Music Makers* (N.Y., 1952); N. Slonimsky, "C. I., America's Musical Prophet," *Musical America* (Feb. 15, 1954); H. and S. Cowell, *C. I. and His Music* (N.Y., 1955); reprinted with additional material, 1969); G. Chase, *America's Music* (N.Y., 1955); J. Kirkpatrick, *A Temporary Mimeographed Catalogue of the Music Manuscripts and Related Materials of C.E.*

I. (New Haven, 1960); S. Charles, "The Use of Borrowed Materials in I.' Second Symphony," *Music Review* (May 1967); D. Marshall, "C. I.' Quotations: Manner or Substance?," *Perspectives of New Music* (Spring–Summer 1968); J. Bernlef and R. de Leeuw, *C. I.* (Amsterdam, 1969); D.-R. de Lerma, *C.E. I., 1874–1954: A Bibliography of His Music* (Kent, Ohio, 1970); R. Warren, Jr., compiler, *C.E. I.: Discography* (Yale Univ. Library, New Haven, 1972); H. Wiley Hitchcock, *Music in the United States: A Historical Introduction* (Englewood Cliffs, N.J., 1969; 2nd ed., 1974); V. Perlis, *C. I. Remembered: An Oral History* (New Haven, 1974); R. Perry, *C. I. and the American Mind* (Kent, Ohio, 1974); D. Wooldridge, *From the Steeples and Mountains: A Study of C. I.* (N.Y., 1974); F. Rossiter, *C. I. and His America* (N.Y., 1975); H. Wiley Hitchcock, *C. I.* (London, 1977); H. Wiley Hitchcock and V. Perlis, *An I. Celebration: Papers and Panels of the C. I. Centennial Festival-Conference* (Urbana, Ill., 1977); H. Sive, *Music's Connecticut Yankee* (N.Y., 1977); B. Chmaj, *Sonata for American Studies: Perspectives on C. I.* (Sacramento, 1978); H. Wiley Hitchcock, *I.: A Survey of the Music* (N.Y., 1983); J. Burkholder, " 'Quotation' and Emulation: C. I.'s Uses of His Models," *Musical Quarterly,* LXXI, no. 1 (1985); idem, *C. I.: The Ideas behind the Music* (New Haven, 1985); M. Solomon, "C. I.: Some Questions of Veracity," *Journal of the American Musicological Society* (Fall 1987); G. Block, *C. I.: A Bio-Bibliography* (Westport, Conn., 1988).

Ives (Ive), Simon, English organist and composer; b. Ware (baptized), July 20, 1600; d. London, July 1, 1662. He was organist in Newgate and a choral master at St. Paul's Cathedral in London; wrote music for masques at the court; in 1633 contributed material to Shirley's masque *The Triumph of Peace.* His songs, catches, and rounds were publ. in several 17th-century collections: Playford's *Select Ayres and Dialogues* (1669) and *Musical Companion* (1672), Hilton's *Catch that Catch can* (1652), etc. He also wrote instrumental music, some of which was included in *Musick's Recreation* (1652 and 1661).

Ivogün, Maria (real name, **Ilse Kempner**), esteemed Hungarian soprano; b. Budapest, Nov. 18, 1891; d. Beatenberg, Lake Thun, Oct. 2, 1987. Her mother was the singer Ida von Günther. She studied voice with Schlemmer-Ambros in Vienna, then with Schöner in Munich, where she made her debut as Mimi at the Bavarian Court Opera (1913). She became renowned there for her portrayal of Zerbinetta, and also created the role of Ighino in Pfitzner's *Palestrina* (1917). In 1925 she joined the Berlin Städtische Oper; also made guest appearances with the touring German Opera Co. in the U.S. (1923), at the Chicago Opera (1923), at London's Covent Garden (1924, 1927), and at the Salzburg Festivals (1925, 1930). She gave her farewell performance as Zerbinetta at the Berlin Städtische Oper (1934); subsequently was active as a teacher, later serving on the faculties of the Vienna Academy of Music (1948–50) and the Berlin Hochschule für Musik (1950–58); her most celebrated pupil was Elisabeth Schwarzkopf. She was married to the tenor **Karl Erb** (1921–32), then to her accompanist Michael Raucheisen (from 1933).

Ivry, Richard d', French composer; b. Beaune, Feb. 4, 1829; d. Hyères, Dec. 18, 1903. He studied music as an avocation; wrote mostly for the stage; also wrote songs and hymns; composed several grand operas: *Les Amants de Vérone,* after *Romeo and Juliet* (Paris, Oct. 12, 1878); *Fatma, Omphale et Pénélope;* etc. He used the anagram Yrvid as a nom de plume.

Iwaki, Hiroyuki, distinguished Japanese conductor; b. Tokyo, Sept. 6, 1932. He was educated in Tokyo at the Academy of Music and at the Univ. of Arts; later received instruction from Herbert von Karajan; then conducted many of the major Japanese orchs. In 1969 he assumed the post of chief conductor of the NHK (Japan Broadcasting Corp.) Sym. Orch.; in 1974 he also became chief conductor of the Melbourne (Australia) Sym. Orch.; in addition, was principal guest conductor of the Atlanta Sym. Orch. In 1988 he became music director of the Kanazawa Sym. Orch.

J

Jacchia, Agide, Italian conductor; b. Lugo, Jan. 5, 1875; d. Siena, Nov. 29, 1932. He studied at the Parma Cons. and at the Pesaro Liceo Musicale; won prizes as a flutist (1896), apprentice conductor (1897), and composer (1898). He made his conducting debut in Brescia on Dec. 26, 1898; then was a theater conductor in Italy. In 1902 he accompanied Mascagni on his American tour; also conducted the Milan Opera Co. on its American tour in 1907–9. He was conductor of the Montreal Opera Co. (1910–13), the Boston National Opera (1915–16), and the Boston Pops (1918–26); then returned to Italy.

Jachet di Mantua (Jacques Colebault), important French-born Italian composer; b. Vitré, 1483; d. Mantua, Oct. 2, 1559. He was in the service of the Rangoni family in Modena as a singer by 1519, then was at the Este court in Ferrara in 1525. Around 1526 he went to Mantua, where he became a citizen in 1534; was titular maestro di cappella at the Cathedral of Ss. Peter and Paul (1534–59). He was one of the leading composers of sacred music of his era.
    WORKS: MASSES: *Messe del fiore . . . libro primo* for 5 Voices (Venice, 1561). **MOTETS:** *Celeberrimi maximeque delectabilis musici Jachet . . . motecta quatuor vocum* (Venice, 1539); *Jacheti musici . . . motecta quinque vocum* (Venice, 1539); *Primo libro di motetti di Jachet a cinque voci* (Venice, 1540); *Celeberrimi . . . Jachet . . . motecta quatuor vocum . . . liber primus* (Venice, 1544); *Jachet . . . motecta quatuor vocum . . . liber primus* (Venice, 1545). A complete edition of his works, ed. by P. Jackson and G. Nugent, was publ. in the Corpus Mensurabilis Musicae series from 1970 to 1982.

BIBL.: P. Jackson, *The Vesper Hymns of J. d.M.* (diss., Univ. of North Carolina, 1965); idem, *The Masses of J. d.M.* (diss., Univ. of North Carolina, 1968); G. Nugent, *The J. Motets and Their Authors* (diss., Princeton Univ., 1973).

Jachimecki, Zdzislaw, eminent Polish musicologist; b. Lemberg, July 7, 1882; d. Krakow, Oct. 27, 1953. He studied music with S. Niewiadomski and H. Jarecki in Lemberg; then musicology with Adler at the Univ. of Vienna (Ph.D., 1906, with the diss. *Psalmy Mikolaja Gomólki*; publ. in an abridged ed., Krakow, 1907); also studied composition with H. Grädener and Schoenberg in Vienna and completed his Habilitation at the Univ. of Krakow in 1911 with his *Wplywy wloskie w muzyce polskiej cześć I. 1540–1560* (Italian Influence on Polish Music, Part 1, 1540–1560; publ. in Krakow, 1911); then was a lecturer in music history there, later being made a reader (1917) and a prof. (1921); was also a guest lecturer at many European univs. He conducted sym. concerts in Krakow (1908–24), and composed a number of orch. pieces and songs.
    WRITINGS: *Ryszard Wagner: Zycie i twórczość* (Richard Wagner: Life and Works; Lemberg, 1911; 2nd ed., augmented, 1922; 4th ed., 1973); *Tabulatura organowa z biblioteki klasztoru Św. Ducha w Krakowie z roku 1548* (Organ Tablature from the Library of the Monastery of the Holy Spirit in Krakow, 1548; Krakow, 1913); *Muzyka na dworze krota Wladyslawa Jagielly 1425–1430* (Music at the Court of Wladyslaw Jagiello 1425–1430; Krakow, 1916); *Pieśń rokoszan z roku 1606* (A Rebel Song from 1606; Krakow, 1916); *Historia muzyki polskiej w zarysie* (The History of Polish Music in Outline; Warsaw, 1920); *Fryderyk Chopin: Zarys zycia i twórczości* (Frédéric

Chopin: An Outline of His Life and Work; Krakow, 1927; 4th ed., augmented, 1957); *Mikolaj Gomólka i jego poprzednicy we historii muzyki polskiej* (Mikolaj Gomólka and His Predecessors in the History of Polish Music; Warsaw, 1946); *Bartlomiej Pekiel* (Warsaw, 1948); *Muzyka polska w rozwoju historycznym od czasów najdawniejszych do doby obecnej* (The Historical Evolution of Polish Music from the Earliest Times to the Present Day; Krakow, 1948–51); *Muzykologia i piśmiennictwo muzyczne w Polsce* (Musicology and Writing on Music in Poland; Krakow, 1948).

Jachino, Carlo, Italian composer; b. San Remo, Feb. 3, 1887; d. Rome, Dec. 23, 1971. He studied with Luporini in Lucca and with Riemann in Leipzig; then taught in Parma (1928–33), Naples (1933–38), and Rome (1938–51). He then went to South America, where he was director of the National Cons. in Bogotá, Colombia (1953–57); returning to Italy, he served as artistic director of the Teatro San Carlo in Naples (1961–69). He publ. *Tecnica dodecafonica* (Milan, 1948) and *Gli strumenti d'orchestra* (Milan, 1950). In his early compositions he followed the Romantic Italian style; after adopting a modified 12-tone method, he finally returned to tonality in his last years.

WORKS: OPERA: *Giocondo e il suo re* (1915–21; Milan, June 24, 1924). **ORCH.:** *Sonata drammatica* for Violin and Orch. (1930); *Pastorale di Natale* (1932); *Fantasia del rosso e nero* (1935); *Pagine di Ramon* (1937); *L'ora inquieta* for Strings (1953); 2 piano concertos (1952, 1957); Cello Concerto (1960); *Variazioni su un tema car a Napoleone I* (1966). **CHAMBER:** Sonata for 9 Instruments (1922); 3 string quartets (1925, 1927, 1930); Trio for Flute, Cello, and Piano (1954); *Quintetto dell'alba* for Clarinet, Horn, and String Trio (1956); also choral music, film scores, keyboard music, and songs.

Jackson, Francis (Alan), English organist, conductor, and composer; b. Malton, Yorkshire, Oct. 2, 1917. He studied with Bairstow in York, then was made a Fellow of the Royal College of Organists (1937) and later studied at Durham Univ. (D.Mus., 1957). He was organist of Malton Parish Church (1933–40), Master of the Music at York Minster (1946–82), and also conductor of the York Sym. Orch. (1947–80); made numerous tours of Europe and North America as an organist. He was made an Officer of the Order of the British Empire (1978). He wrote a Sym., choral works, and much music for the organ.
BIBL.: P. Hardwick, "F. J. at 70," *Musical Times* (Oct. 1987).

Jackson, George K(nowil), English-American organist, editor, and composer; b. Oxford (baptized), April 15, 1757; d. Boston, Mass., Nov. 18, 1822. He was a pupil of James Nares at the Chapel Royal; completed his studies at the Univ. of St. Andrews (D.Mus., 1791). He went to the U.S. (1796), where he was first active in N.Y. (1801–12); then settled in Boston (1812), where he played a leading role in the musical life of the city. He publ. *First Principles, or a Treatise on Practical Thorough Bass* (London, 1795). His works include *Dr. Watts's Divine Songs set to Music* (London, c.1791), *David's Psalms* (Boston, 1804), 53 secular songs, 11 Masonic songs, and 13 instrumental pieces. He ed. *The Choral Companion* (Boston, 1814), *A Choice Collection of Chants in 4 Voices* (Boston, 1816), *The Boston Handel and Haydn Society Collection of Church Music* (Boston, 1820), and 7 instrumental collections.
BIBL.: F. Metcalf, *American Writers and Compilers of Sacred Music* (N.Y., 1925); H. Johnson, "G.K. J., Doctor of Music (1745–1822)," *Musical Quarterly* (Jan. 1943).

Jackson, George Pullen, American folklorist; b. Monson, Maine, Aug. 20, 1874; d. Nashville, Tenn., Jan. 19, 1953. He studied philology in Dresden and at the Univ. of Chicago (Ph.B., 1904; Ph.D., 1911); was a teacher of German at Vanderbilt Univ. (1918–43), founder of the Tennessee State Sacred Harp Singing Assoc., and president of the Tennessee Folklore Soc. (1942).
WRITINGS: *The Rhythmic Form of the German Folk Songs* (1917); *White Spirituals in the Southern Uplands* (1933); *Spiritual Folksongs of Early America* (1937; 3rd ed., 1965); *Down-East Spirituals* (1943; 2nd ed., 1953); *White and Negro Spiritu-*

als (1943); *Story of the Sacred Harp* (1944); *Another Sheaf of White Spirituals* (1952).

Jackson, Isaiah (Allen), black American conductor; b. Richmond, Va., Jan. 22, 1945. He majored in Russian studies at Harvard Univ. (B.A., 1966), then studied conducting at Stanford Univ. (M.A., 1967), and composition with N. Boulanger at the American Cons. in Fontainebleau and at the Juilliard School in N.Y. (M.S., 1969; D.M.A., 1973). He was founder-conductor of the Juilliard String Ensemble (1970–71), and also assistant conductor of the American Sym. Orch. in N.Y. (1970–71); after serving as assistant conductor of the Baltimore Sym. Orch. (1971–73), he was associate conductor of the Rochester (N.Y.) Phil. (1973–87) and music director of the Flint (Mich.) Sym. Orch. (1982–87); then was music director of the Royal Ballet at London's Covent Garden (from 1987) and of the Dayton (Ohio) Phil. (from 1987).

Jackson, Judge, black American composer and tunebook compiler; b. Ozark, Ala., March 12, 1883; d. there, April 7, 1958. He learned shape-note hymn singing from the blacks of southeastern Alabama. He was active as a singing-school teacher. He wrote shape-note religious songs and also compiled *The Colored Sacred Harp* (1934), which proved influential as a tunebook among blacks.
BIBL.: J. Work, "Plantation Meistersinger," *Musical Quarterly*, XXVII (1941); J. Boyd, "J. J.: Black Giant of White Spirituals," *Journal of American Folklore*, LXXXIII (1970).

Jackson, Mahalia, remarkable black American gospel singer; b. New Orleans, Oct. 26, 1911; d. Evergreen Park, Ill., Jan. 27, 1972. The daughter of a minister, she sang in her father's church at an early age; went when she was 16 to Chicago, where she supported herself by menial labor while singing in the choir of the Greater Salem Baptist Church; began touring with the Johnson Gospel Singers in 1932. She revealed an innate talent for expressive hymn singing, and soon was in demand for conventions and political meetings. She steadfastly refused to appear in nightclubs. Her 1947 recording *Move On Up a Little Higher* brought her renown as the "Gospel Queen." She appeared in a series of concerts at N.Y.'s Carnegie Hall (1950–56); made her 1st European tour in 1952, which was a triumphant success. She sang at President Kennedy's inauguration (1961) and at the civil rights march on Washington, D.C. (1963); made her last tour of Europe in 1971. She publ. an autobiography, *Movin' On Up* (N.Y., 1966).
BIBL.: P. Oliver, *M. J.* (Milan, 1968); L. Goreau, *Just M., Baby* (Waco, Texas, 1975).

Jackson, Michael (Joseph), black American rock superstar; b. Gary, Ind., Aug. 29, 1958. He began his career as a rhythm-and-blues singer, then joined his 4 brothers in a group billed as The Jackson Five, which scored immediate success. But Michael Jackson soon outshone his brothers and was accorded superstar status in the field of popular music with his lycanthropic album *Thriller* (1983), also issued on videocassette, in which Jackson turns into a werewolf, scaring his sweet girlfriend out of her wits. The album sold some 30 million copies universe-wide, certified in the *Guinness Book of World Records* in 1984 as the largest sale ever of a single album. According to one enthusiast, Jackson could count on an audience of one-quarter of the entire earth's population (c.2,000,000,000). In 1984 he won a record number of 8 Grammys for his assorted talents. Jackson's androgynous appearance and his penchant for outlandish apparel (he wore a sequined naval commodore's costume at the Grammy show) seem to act like a stream of powerful pheromones on squealing admiring youths of both sexes. Jackson suffered a minor catastrophe when his hair caught fire during the filming of a TV commercial, and he had to be outfitted with an inconspicuous hairpiece to cover the burned spot. In collaboration with Lionel Richie, he penned the song *We Are the World* in support of African famine relief; it won a Grammy Award as best song of 1985. In 1987 he brought out the album *Bad* (which means good), and then launched a major solo tour of the U.S. in 1988. On

Sept. 19, 1986, his *Captain EO* opened at the Disneyland Theme Park in Anaheim, Calif., featuring Jackson as a singing and dancing commander of a motley space crew. His autobiography was publ. as *Moonwalk* (N.Y., 1988).

BIBL.: G. Brown, *M. J.: Body and Soul* (N.Y., 1984); N. George, *The M. J. Story* (N.Y., 1984; new ed., 1987); G. Matthews, *M. J.* (N.Y., 1984).

Jackson, Milt(on) "Bags," black American jazz vibraphonist; b. Detroit, Jan. 1, 1923. He began his career in 1945 with Dizzy Gillespie; after working with several other musicians, he organized the Milt Jackson Quartet in 1951, with John Lewis, Ray Brown, and Kenny Clarke; in 1952 it was renamed the Modern Jazz Quartet, a group that was crucial in the synthesis of "cool" with "classical" jazz which eventually came to be known as Third Stream. The Quartet disbanded in 1974.

BIBL.: J. Blum, "M. J.: Vibes Original," *Jazz Times* (July 1984).

Jackson, Samuel P., English-American organist and composer; b. Manchester, Feb. 5, 1818; d. Brooklyn, July 27, 1885. Son of the organ builder James Jackson, he was taken to America in 1825, and learned his father's trade; was for many years active as a church organist. He publ. a variety of vocal sacred works, the collection *Gems for the Organ*, and 4 books of *Organ-Voluntaries*.

Jackson, William, English organist and composer; b. Exeter, May 29, 1730; d. there, July 5, 1803. He studied music at Exeter Cathedral, and then organ with John Travers in London. After teaching and performing in Exeter (1748–77), he became organist and choirmaster at the Cathedral there. He wrote 2 comic operas: *The Lord of the Manor* (London, Dec. 27, 1780) and *The Metamorphosis* (London, Dec. 5, 1783); also the afterpiece *Lycidas* (Covent Garden, London, Nov. 4, 1767; music not extant). He also wrote sacred music, odes, harpsichord sonatas, and a number of popular songs, elegies, and duets.

WRITINGS: *30 Letters on Various Subjects* (1782); *Observations on the Present State of Music in London* (1791); *The Four Ages, together with Essays on Various Subjects* (1798).

BIBL.: J. Hayes, "W. J. of Exeter: Organist, Composer and Amateur Artist," *The Connoisseur* (Jan. 1970).

Jackson, William, English organist and composer; b. Masham, Yorkshire, Jan. 9, 1815; d. Bradford, April 15, 1866. He left school when he was 13 to work in a mill and bakery; was a self-taught musician, becoming an organist in Masham in 1832. In 1852 he founded a music business and became organist of St. John's Church at Bradford; later was conductor of the Festival Choral Soc. (from 1856). He wrote the oratorio *The Deliverance of Israel from Babylon* (Leeds, 1847).

BIBL.: J. Smith, *The Life of W. J., the Miller Musician* (Leeds, 1926).

Jacob, Benjamin, English organist and composer; b. London, May 15, 1778; d. there, Aug. 24, 1829. He was a pupil of Willoughby, Shrubsole, and Arnold (1796); served as organist at various churches, finally at Surrey Chapel (1794–1825). With Wesley and Crotch, he gave organ recitals (1808–14), which were attended by large crowds; conducted a series of oratorios in 1800, and the Lenten Oratorios at Covent Garden in 1818. Jacob was very active in spreading the Bach cult in London (see O. Mansfield, "J.S. Bach's First English Apostles," *Musical Quarterly*, April 1935). He publ. *National Psalmody* (London, 1819) and other collections; also glees and catches.

Jacob, Gordon (Percival Septimus), distinguished English composer and pedagogue; b. London, July 5, 1895; d. Saffron Walden, June 8, 1984. He studied at Dulwich College and took courses in composition with Stanford, Howells, and Wood at the Royal College of Music in London (D.Mus., 1935). He taught at the Royal College of Music from 1926 to 1966; among his notable students were Malcolm Arnold, Imogen Holst, Elizabeth Maconchy, and Bernard Stevens. In 1968 he was made a Commander of the Order of the British Empire. Jacob produced a significant output of instrumental music, and also publ. several important books.

WRITINGS (all publ. in London): *Orchestral Technique: A Manual for Students* (1931; 2nd ed., 1982); *How to Read a Score* (1944); *The Composer and His Art* (1954); *The Elements of Orchestration* (1962).

WORKS: ORCH.: 2 syms. (1928–29; 1943–44); 2 viola concertos (1925, 1979); 2 piano concertos (1927, 1957); 2 oboe concertos (1933, 1956); *Divertimento* (1938); 3 suites (1941; 1948–49; 1949); 3 sinfoniettas (1942, 1951, 1953); Sym. for Strings (1943); Concerto for Bassoon, Strings, and Percussion (1947); *Rhapsody* for English Horn and Strings (1948); Concerto for Horn and Strings (1951); Flute Concerto (1951); Trombone Concerto (1952); Concerto for Violin and Strings (1953); Violin Concerto (1954); Cello Concerto (1955); Sym. for Small Orch. (1958); 2 overtures (1965); Concerto for Piano Duet, 3-hands (1969); Concerto for Band (1970); *A York Symphony* for Woodwind Instruments (1971); Suite for Tuba and Strings (1972). **CHAMBER:** String Quartet (1928); Quartet for Oboe and Strings (1938); Quintet for Clarinet and Strings (1942); *Serenade* for 8 Woodwind Instruments (1950); Piano Trio (1955); Cello Sonata (1957); Sextet for Wind Quintet and Piano (1962); Suite for 4 Trombones (1968); *Divertimento* for 8 Wind Instruments (1969); Suite for Bassoon and String Quartet (1969); Trio for Clarinet, Viola, and Piano (1969); Piano Quartet (1971); Suite for 8 Violas (1976); Sonata for Viola and Piano (1978); sacred and secular choral works; film scores; band music; songs; piano pieces.

Jacob, Maxime, French composer; b. Bordeaux, Jan. 13, 1906; d. in the Benedictine Abbey in En-Calcat, Tarn, Feb. 26, 1977. He studied with Gédalge, Koechlin, Milhaud, and Nat in Paris. Pursuing a whimsical mode, he became associated with the so-called École d'Arcueil, named after a modest Paris suburb where Erik Satie presided over his group of disciples; then made a 180° turn toward established religion, and in 1930 entered the Benedictine Order, where he served mainly as an organist; also served as a soldier (1939–40) and army chaplain (1944–45) during World War II. He wrote a Piano Concerto (1961); 8 string quartets (1961–69); 3 violin sonatas; 2 cello sonatas; 15 piano sonatas; a curious *Messe syncopée* (1968); over 500 songs, etc. He wrote the books *L'Art et la grâce* (Paris, 1939) and *Souvenirs à deux voix* (Toulouse, 1969).

BIBL.: R. Chalupt, *M. J.* (Paris, 1927); J. Roy, "M. J.," *La Revue Musicale* (July 1939).

Jacobi, Erwin R(euben), Swiss musicologist; b. Strasbourg, Sept. 21, 1909; d. Zürich, Feb. 27, 1979. He studied economics in Berlin, obtaining a diploma of engineering in 1933; from 1934 to 1952 he lived in Israel, where he studied harpsichord with Pelleg and composition with Ben-Haim; in 1952 he went to the U.S. to study with Landowska (harpsichord), Hindemith (composition), and Sachs (music history); completed his studies at the Univ. of Zürich (Ph.D., 1957, with the dissertation *Die Entwicklung der Musiktheorie in England nach der Zeit von Jean-Philippe Rameau*; publ. in Strasbourg, 1957–60; 2nd ed., rev. and augmented, Baden-Baden, 1971); was an assistant lecturer there (from 1961). He was a visiting prof. at the Univ. of Iowa (1970) and at Indiana Univ. (1971–72). He wrote a number of valuable articles on Baroque composers for various music journals; ed. *J.-P. Rameau: Complete Theoretical Writings* (Rome, 1967–72); publ. *Albert Schweitzer und die Musik* (Wiesbaden, 1975).

Jacobi, Frederick, American composer; b. San Francisco, May 4, 1891; d. N.Y., Oct. 24, 1952. He studied piano with Paolo Gallico and Rafael Joseffy, and composition with Rubin Goldmark; then took private lessons with Ernest Bloch and studied with Paul Juon at the Berlin Hochschule für Musik. He was an assistant conductor at the Metropolitan Opera in N.Y. (1913–17); then taught at the Master School of the Arts (1924–36) and at the Juilliard School of Music (1936–50). In his music he often made use of authentic American Indian themes; also drew from jazz, black music, folk songs, and even some Hebraisms.

WORKS: OPERA: *The Prodigal Son* (1944). **ORCH.:** *The Pied Piper*, symphonic poem (1915); *A California Suite* (San Francisco, Dec. 6, 1917); 2 syms.: No. 1, *Assyrian* (San Francisco, Nov. 14, 1924) and No. 2 (San Francisco, April 1, 1948); *Ode for Orchestra* (San Francisco, Feb. 12, 1943); Concertino for Piano and String Orch. (Saratoga Springs, Sept. 3, 1946); *2 Assyrian Prayers* for Voice and Orch. (1923); *The Poet in the Desert* for Baritone Solo, Chorus, and Orch. (1925); *Sabbath Evening Service* for Baritone Solo and Mixed Chorus (1931); 3 string quartets (1924, 1933, 1945); *Impressions from the Odyssey* for Violin and Piano (1947); *Meditation* for Trombone and Piano (1947); miscellaneous piano pieces and songs.

BIBL.: D. Diamond, "F. J.," *Modern Music* (March–April 1937).

Jacobi, Georg, German violinist, conductor, and composer; b. Berlin, Feb. 13, 1840; d. London, Sept. 13, 1906. He studied violin with Eduard and Leopold Ganz in Berlin, Bériot in Brussels (1849–52), and Massart at the Paris Cons. (1852); also composition there with Réber, Gevaert, and Chéri. After graduating with a premier prix in violin (1861), he played in the orchs. of the Opéra-Comique (1861–63) and the Opéra (1863–69); then was conductor of the Bouffes-Parisiens (1869–71). He subsequently settled in London as conductor of the Alhambra Theatre (1871–98); then conducted at the Crystal Palace and also taught at the Royal College of Music (from 1896). He wrote a comic opera, *The Black Crook*, which attained temporary popularity; also 103 ballets and divertissements, 2 violin concertos, a Viola Concerto, violin pieces, and songs.

Jacobs, Arthur (David), English music critic, editor, writer on music, and translator; b. Manchester, June 14, 1922. He studied at Merton College, Oxford; was music critic for the *Daily Express* (1947–52) and deputy ed. of the journal *Opera* (1960–71). He was a prof. at the Royal Academy of Music in London (1964–79) and head of the music dept. at Huddersfield Polytechnic (1979–84); also ed. the *British Music Yearbook* (1971–80). An accomplished linguist, he prepared admirable trs. of some 20 operas into English; he also wrote the libretto for Maw's opera *One Man Show* (1964).

WRITINGS: *Gilbert and Sullivan* (London, 1951); *A New Dictionary of Music* (Harmondsworth, 1958; 4th ed., rev., 1978); with S. Sadie, *The Pan Book of Opera* (London, 1964; rev. ed., 1972, as *Opera: A Modern Guide*; new ed., 1984); *A Short History of Western Music* (Harmondsworth, 1972); *Arthur Sullivan: A Victorian Musician* (Oxford, 1984); *The Pan Book of Orchestral Music* (London, 1988); *The Penguin Dictionary of Musical Performers* (Harmondsworth, 1990).

Jacobs, Paul, American pianist and harpsichordist; b. N.Y., June 22, 1930; d. there, a victim of AIDS (Acquired Immune Deficiency Syndrome), Sept. 25, 1983. He was a prototypical child prodigy, but overcame his musical precocity by an extraordinary intellectual endeavor, specializing in the twin aspects of structural composition, Baroque and avant-garde; he played the former on the harpsichord; by disposition and natural selection he eschewed Romantic music. He studied piano with Ernest Hutcheson; from 1951 to 1960 he was in Europe; gave an unprecedented recital in Paris of a complete cycle of piano music of Schoenberg; became associated with the European centers of avant-garde music, at the Domaine Musical in Paris, at the contemporary music festivals in Darmstadt, and in various other localities. Returning to the U.S., he was appointed official pianist and harpsichordist of the N.Y. Phil. (1962–74); also taught at the Manhattan School of Music and at Brooklyn College until his death. He recorded the piano works of Debussy, Schoenberg, Stravinsky, Elliott Carter, and others.

Jacobs, René, Belgian countertenor; b. Ghent, Oct. 30, 1946. He pursued training in philology at the Univ. of Ghent, then studied voice with Louis Devos in Brussels and Lucie Frateur in The Hague; subsequently pursued an international career as a performer with various early-music groups, as an opera singer, and as a recitalist; also taught at the Schola Cantorum Basiliensis in Basel. He has been particularly successful in works by Cavalli, Monteverdi, Charpentier, Gluck, and Handel.

Jacobs-Bond, Carrie. See **Bond, Carrie Jacobs.**

Jacobsthal, Gustav, German musicologist; b. Pyritz, Pomerania, March 14, 1845; d. Berlin, Nov. 9, 1912. He studied at the Univ. of Strasbourg (1863–70), then at the Univ. of Berlin (Ph.D., 1870, with the diss. *Die Mensuralnotenschrift des 12. und 13. Jahrhunderts*; publ. in Berlin, 1871); subsequently completed his Habilitation at the Univ. of Strasbourg (1872), where he was a reader (1875–97) and prof. of musicology (1897–1905). He publ. *Die chromatische Alteration im liturgischen Gesange der abendländischen Kirche* (1897).

BIBL.: F. Ludwig, "G. J.," *Zeitschrift der Internationalen Musik-Gesellschaft*, XIV (1912–13); F. Gennrich, *Die Strassburger Schule für Musikwissenschaft* (Wuürzburg, 1940).

Jacoby, Hanoch (actually **Heinrich**), German-born Israeli violist and composer; b. Königsberg, March 2, 1909. He studied composition with Hindemith, Bihnke, Mahlke, and Wolfsthal at the Berlin Hochschule für Musik (1927–30); played in Fischer's chamber orch. (1929–30) and the Frankfurt Radio Orch. (1930–33). He emigrated to Jerusalem in 1934, where he taught at the Academy of Music until 1958; also played in the Palestine (later Israel) Broadcasting Sym. Orch. (1936–58) and then in the Israel Phil. Orch.

WORKS: 3 syms. (1940, 1951, 1960); Viola Concerto (1939); Violin Concerto (1942); *7 Miniatures* for Small Orch. (1945); *King David's Lyre* for Small Orch. (1948); *Capriccio israélien* for Orch. (1951); Sinfonietta (1960); *Serio giocoso* for Orch. (1964); *Partita concertata* for Orch. (1970–71); *Mutatio* for Orch. (1975); *Variations* for Orch. (1976); *Jewish Oriental Folklore*, suite for String Orch. (1977); Concertino for String Trio (1932); 2 string quartets (1937, 1938); *Theme, Variations and Finale* for Piano Trio (1940); Wind Quintet (1946); *Canzona* for Solo Harp (1960); *2 Suites of Jewish Oriental Folklore* for Brass Quintet (1975); *Mutatio II* for Oboe, Bassoon, 2 Trumpets, 2 Trombones, 2 Violas, and Double Bass (1976).

Jacopo da Bologna (Jacobus de Bononia; Magister Jachobus de Bononia), Italian composer and music theorist who flourished in the 14th century. He was one of the earliest representatives of the Florentine Ars nova. He wrote madrigals, ballate, and other works; W. Marrocco ed. his complete works (Berkeley and Los Angeles, 1954).

BIBL.: J. Wolf, "L'arte del biscanto misurato secondo el maestro J. d. B.," *Kroyer-Festschrift* (1933); K. von Fischer, " 'Portraits' von Piero, Giovanni da Firenze, und J. d. B. in einer Bologneser Handschrift des 14. Jahrhunderts?," *Musica Disciplina*, 27 (1973).

Jacotin, a name applied to several musicians who flourished in the 1st half of the 16th century. It is now believed that **Jacotin Le Bel** (b. c.1490; d. c.1555), a singer in the Papal Chapel and the church of S. Luigi dei Francesi in Rome (1516–21), was the composer of the esteemed chansons publ. mainly by Attaingnant. A Jacotin Le Bel is also listed as a singer and canon at the French royal chapel (1532–55); he may be identical to the preceding. Some 30 chansons by Jacotin were publ. in contemporary collections; only a few motets and Magnificat settings are extant.

Jacques de Liège (Iacobus Leodiensis), Belgian music theorist; b. Liège, c.1260; d. there, after 1330. He studied in Paris; then was a cleric in Liège. About 1325, already at an advanced age, he wrote the important compendium *Speculum musicae*, in 7 parts and 293 folios (586 pages; approximating some 2,000 pages in modern typography); it was long attributed to Johannes de Muris, but the authorship of Jacques de Liège is proved by the specific indication in the MS in the Bibliothèque Nationale in Paris that the initial letters of the 7 chapters form the name of the author (I-A-C-O-B-U-S). W. Grossmann overlooked this indication in his *Die einleitenden Kapitel des Speculum Musicae von Johannes de Muris* (Leipzig, 1924). The treatise has been ed. by R. Bragard in Corpus Scriptorum de Musica, III (parts 1–5, 1955–68), and by C. de Coussemaker in Scriptorum de musica medii aevi nova series, II (parts 6–7, 1864–76; incorrectly attributed to Johannes de Muris); selections in Eng. tr. are given in O. Strunk's *Source Readings in Music History* (N.Y., 1950).

BIBL.: R. Bragard, "Le 'Speculum musicae' du compilateur J. d. L.," *Musica Disciplina*, VII (1953) and VIII (1954).

Jacquet, (Jean Baptiste) Illinois, black American tenor saxophonist and bassoonist; b. Broussard, La., Oct. 31, 1922. He was reared in Houston, where he learned to play the soprano and alto saxophones; after working in local jazz circles, he played with Lionel Hampton, Cab Calloway, and Count Basie. He led his own bands from 1946; also played bassoon from 1956, becoming a featured performer at jazz festivals.

Jacquillat, Jean-Pierre, French conductor; b. Versailles, July 13, 1935; d. in an automobile accident in Chambo-sur-Lignon, Aug. 6, 1986. He was educated at the Paris Cons., winning premiers prix in harmony, percussion, and piano; also studied conducting with Munch, Cluytens, and Dervaux. He was assistant conductor (1967) and associate conductor (1968) of the Orch. de Paris; toured with it in the Soviet Union, North America, and Mexico. In 1970 he was named resident conductor and music director of the Angers Phil. Orch.; in 1971 he became permanent conductor of the Lyons Opera and the Rhône-Alpes Phil.; then was resident conductor and music adviser to the Lamoureux Orch. in Paris (1975–78); subsequently was chief conductor of the Iceland Sym. Orch. in Reykjavík (1980–86).

Jadassohn, Salomon, German pedagogue, conductor, and composer; b. Breslau, Aug. 13, 1831; d. Leipzig, Feb. 1, 1902. He studied with Brosig, Hesse, and Lüstner in Breslau, at the Leipzig Cons. (1848–49), and with Liszt in Weimar; then studied with Hauptmann in Leipzig, where he settled. He founded a choral society, Psalterion (1866); conducted the concerts of the Euterpe Soc. (1867–69). In 1871 he was appointed instructor at the Leipzig Cons.; was made Ph.D. (honoris causa, 1887) and Royal Prof. (1893). A scholar of the highest integrity and of great industry, he codified the traditional views of harmony, counterpoint, and form in his celebrated manuals. He was a firm believer in the immutability of harmonic laws, and became the Rock of Gibraltar of conservatism in musical teaching; through his many students, who in turn became influential teachers in Germany and other European countries, the cause of orthodox music theory was propagated far and wide. He composed 4 syms., 2 piano concertos, chamber music, choral works, piano pieces, and songs. Although he was a master of contrapuntal forms, his music is totally forgotten.

WRITINGS: *Harmonielehre* (Leipzig, 1883; 7th ed., 1903; Eng. tr. by T. Baker, 1893, as *A Manual of Harmony*); *Kontrapunkt* (1884; 5th ed., 1909); *Kanon und Fuge* (1884; 3rd ed., 1909); *Die Formen in den Werken der Tonkunst* (1889; 4th ed., 1910); *Lehrbuch der Instrumentation* (1889; 2nd ed., 1907); *Die Kunst zu Modulieren und Präludieren* (1890); *Allgemeine Musiklehre* (1892); *Elementar-Harmonielehre* (1895); *Methodik des musiktheoretischen Unterrichts* (1898); *Das Wesen der Melodie in der Tonkunst* (1899); *Das Tonbewusstsein; die Lehre vom musikalischen Hören* (1899); *Erläuterung der in Bachs "Kunst der Fuge" enthaltenen Fugen und Kanons* (1899); *Der Generalbass* (1901).

Jadin, Louis Emmanuel, French pianist, composer, and pedagogue; b. Versailles, Sept. 21, 1768; d. Montfort-l'Amaury, Yvelines, April 11, 1853. He studied music and violin with his father, then was a page in the household of Louis XVI. After the Revolution, he became 2nd keyboard player at the Théâtre de Monsieur (later the Théâtre Feydeau) in 1789, and then chief accompanist in 1791. He joined the music corps of the National Guard about 1792, and was busily engaged in writing festive works for special occasions during the revolutionary period. During the Napoleonic wars, he continued to write patriotic pieces. His orch. overture *La Bataille d'Austerlitz* (1806) enjoyed great popularity for a time. He also composed numerous opéras comiques. He taught solfège (1796–98), singing (1802–4), and piano (1804–16) at the newly established Paris Cons.; was gouverneur des pages of the royal chapel

(1814–30). He was made a Chevalier of the Légion d'honneur (1824). He also wrote pieces for piano.

BIBL.: G. de Saint-Foix, "Les Frères J.," *Revue Musicale* (1925).

Jadlowker, Hermann, distinguished Latvian tenor; b. Riga, July 17, 1877; d. Tel Aviv, May 13, 1953. He studied with J. Gänsbacher at the Vienna Cons., making his debut as Gomez in *Nachtlager von Granada* in Cologne (1897); after appearances in Königsberg, Stettin, Rostock, and Riga, he sang in Karlsruhe (1906–10) and at Berlin's Kroll Opera (from 1907). He made his Metropolitan Opera debut in N.Y. as Gounod's Faust (Jan. 22, 1910), and sang there until 1912; also sang in Boston (1910–12), and at the Berlin Hofoper (1911–12). He created the role of Bacchus in Richard Strauss's *Ariadne auf Naxos* (Stuttgart, Oct. 25, 1912). After guest appearances in Europe and a period with the Berlin State Opera (1922–23), he served as chief cantor of the Riga synagogue (1929–38) and taught at the Riga Cons. (1936–38); then settled in Tel Aviv as a teacher. Among his notable roles were Florestan, Don Carlos, Parsifal, and Lohengrin.

Jaëll, Alfred, Austrian pianist and composer; b. Trieste, March 5, 1832; d. Paris, Feb. 27, 1882. He studied with his father, Eduard Jaëll; appeared as a child prodigy in Venice in 1843, then continued his studies with Moscheles (1844). His subsequent concert tours earned him the nickname "le pianiste voyageur." After touring in the U.S. (1852–54), he was court pianist in Hannover (1856–66). He married **Marie** (née **Trautmann**) **Jaëll** in 1866. He wrote a number of effective virtuoso pieces for piano and also made piano transcriptions of the works of Wagner, Schumann, and Mendelssohn.

Jaëll, Marie (née **Trautmann**), French pianist and teacher; b. Steinseltz, Alsace, Aug. 17, 1846; d. Paris, Feb. 4, 1925. She studied with Hamm in Stuttgart, then with Herz at the Paris Cons., winning the premier prix; also studied composition with Franck and Saint-Saëns. She married **Alfred Jaëll** in 1866. In later years she devoted herself to teaching; her most celebrated pupil was Albert Schweitzer. She wrote characteristic pieces for piano, and publ. pedagogical works: *La Musique et la psycho-physiologie* (1895); *Le Mécanisme du toucher* (1896); *Le Toucher* (1899); *L'Intelligence et le rythme dans les mouvements artistiques* (1905); *Le Rythme du regard et la dissociation des doigts* (1906); *La Coloration des sensations tactiles* (1910); *La Résonance du toucher et la topographie des pulpes* (1912); *La Main et la pensée musicale* (posthumous, 1925).

BIBL.: H. Kiener, *M. J.: Problèmes d'esthétique et de pédagogie musicales* (Paris, 1952).

Jaffee, Michael, American early-music performer and instrument builder; b. N.Y., April 21, 1938. He studied music at N.Y. Univ. (B.A., 1959; M.A., 1963), and learned to play the guitar. While still a student, he married **Kay Cross** (b. Lansing, Mich., Dec. 31, 1937), a keyboard player, in 1961. Their interest in early music led Michael to master the lute and Kay the recorder; they subsequently organized the Waverly Consort, a group dedicated to authentic performances of music from the medieval and Renaissance eras using period instruments and costumes; the group made its formal debut at N.Y.'s Carnegie Hall in 1966. The two founders became highly proficient on a variety of instruments, many of which they built themselves. The Waverly Consort toured extensively, becoming one of the most successful early-music groups in the U.S.

BIBL.: H. Waleson, "The Waverly Consort: New Masters of an Ancient Repertoire," *Ovation* (Nov. 1983).

Jagel, Frederick, American tenor and teacher; b. N.Y., June 10, 1897; d. San Francisco, July 5, 1982. He studied with William Brady in N.Y., then went to Milan; made his operatic debut as Rodolfo in *La Bohème* in Livorno (1924). He made his Metropolitan Opera debut in N.Y. as Radames (Nov. 8, 1927), and remained there until 1950; also made guest appearances with the San Francisco Opera and at the Teatro Colón in Buenos Aires. From 1949 to 1970 he taught voice at the New England Cons. of Music in Boston.

Jagger, Mick (Michael Philip), English rock singer and songwriter, the demonic protagonist of the fantastically popular rock group The Rolling Stones; b. Dartford, Kent, July 26, 1944. He studied at the London School of Economics (1962–64); at the same time, pursued his interest in music, forming The Rolling Stones in 1962; his 1st success came with *Satisfaction* (1965), a song of candid sexual expression composed by Keith Richard with lyrics by Jagger. With this frontal assault upon the social sensibilities of the Establishment, the group earned a reputation as the outlaws of rock; Jagger assumed the role of high priest at their subsequent concerts, which often degenerated into mad orgies among the audience, incited by the plenary obscenity of the words and metaphorical gestures of Jagger and his celebrants. He is responsible for such hallucinogenic psychedelic hits as *Midnight Rambler, Jumpin' Jack Flash,* and *Sympathy for the Devil.*
    Bibl.: S. Booth, *Dance with the Devil: The Rolling Stones and Their Times* (N.Y., 1984); C. Schofield, *J.* (N.Y., 1985).

Jahn, Otto, learned German philologist, archeologist, and music scholar; b. Kiel, June 16, 1813; d. Göttingen, Sept. 9, 1869. He studied languages and antiquities at the Univs. of Kiel, Leipzig, and Berlin. He became a lecturer on philology in Kiel (1839), then was made prof. of archeology in Greifswald (1842); later was director of the Leipzig Archeological Museum (1847–48), but lost this position in the wake of the political upheaval of 1848. In 1855 he was appointed prof. of archeology at the Univ. of Bonn. His magnum opus in the field of music was the biography *Wolfgang Amadeus Mozart* (4 vols., Leipzig, 1856–59; 2nd ed., 1867; Eng. tr. by P. Townsend, London, 1882; German revs. by H. Deiters, 3rd ed., 1891–93 and 4th ed., 1905–7; exhaustively rewritten and rev. by H. Abert as *Wolfgang Amadeus Mozart: Neu bearbeitete und erweiterte Ausgabe von Otto Jahns "Mozart,"* 2 vols., Leipzig, 1919–21, rendering it the standard biography; further rev. by A.A. Abert, 2 vols., Leipzig, 1955–56). Jahn's biography was the 1st musical life written according to the comparative critical method; it reviews the state of music during the period immediately preceding Mozart; this comprehensive exposition has become a model for subsequent musical biographies. He intended to write a biography of Beethoven according to a similar plan, but could not complete the task; Thayer utilized the data accumulated by him in his own work on Beethoven; Pohl used his notes in his biography of Haydn. Numerous essays by Jahn were publ. in his *Gesammelte Aufsätze über Musik* (1866).
    Bibl.: J. Vahlen, *O. J.* (Vienna, 1870); E. Petersen, ed., *O. J. in seinen Briefen* (Leipzig, 1912); J. Pulver, "O. J.," *Musical Times* (April 1913); R. Petzoldt, "Der Mozart-Biograph O. J.," *Allgemeine Musikalische Zeitung,* LXV (1938).

Jahn, Wilhelm, Austrian conductor and opera adminstrator; b. Hof, Moravia, Nov. 24, 1834; d. Vienna, April 21, 1900. At the age of 20 he became a theater conductor in Budapest; then occupied similar posts in Agram, Amsterdam, and Prague. He was in Wiesbaden (1864–80); became music director of the Vienna Court Opera (1880) and conductor of the Vienna Phil. (1882–83). He retired in 1897, and was succeeded by Mahler.

Jähns, Friedrich Wilhelm, German vocal pedagogue, writer on music, and composer; b. Berlin, Jan. 2, 1809; d. there, Aug. 8, 1888. He studied singing with Grell and Detroit; was a boy soprano in the chorus of the Berlin Royal Opera; then studied voice with Stümer and Lemm, and later composition with Gorzizky. He was founder-conductor of the Jähnssche Gesangverein (1845–70). He was made royal music director (1849); from 1881, taught declamation at the Scharwenka Cons. He was very successful as a vocal teacher; taught some 1,000 pupils. His admiration for Weber impelled him to collect all the available materials pertaining to Weber's life and works; his collection, containing 300 autograph letters, documents, pamphlets, essays, and 1st editions, was acquired in 1883 by

the Berlin Royal Library. He publ. a treatise on Weber, with a thematic catalog, *Carl Maria von Weber in seinen Werken* (Berlin, 1871). Apart from exhaustive biographical data, this book is historically interesting because in the preface he introduced, for the 1st time in print, the Wagnerian term "Leitmotiv"; this was later popularized by Wolzogen and others. He composed a Piano Trio, a Grand Sonata for Violin and Piano, a book of *Schottische Lieder,* and many other vocal pieces.

Jairazbhoy, Nazir (Ali), American ethnomusicologist and instrumentalist; b. Clifton, England (of North Indian parents), Oct. 31, 1927. After schooling in England and India, he studied at the Univ. of Washington (B.A., 1951) and at the School of Oriental and African Studies in London (Ph.D., 1971, with the diss. *The Rāgas of North Indian Music: Their Structure and Evolution;* publ. in London, 1971), where he lectured on Indian music (1962–69). He was associate prof. of Asian studies at the Univ. of Windsor, Ontario (1969–75), and prof. of ethnomusicology at the Univ. of Calif., Los Angeles (from 1975), where he later became the chairman of its Department of Ethnomusicology and Systematic Musicology (1988). His study of the evolution of different rāgas and scales contributed greatly to knowledge about North Indian music.

Jakowicka-Friderici, Teodozja. See **Friderici-Jakowicka, Teodozja.**

Jalas (real name, **Blomstedt**), **Jussi,** Finnish conductor; b. Jyväskylä, June 23, 1908. He studied at the Helsinki Cons. and with Ilmari Krohn at the Univ. of Helsinki; later studied in Paris with Rhené-Baton and Monteux. He was active as a theater conductor in Helsinki (1930–45); subsequently conducted at the Finnish National Opera, serving as its music director until 1973; also made guest conducting appearances throughout Europe, the U.S., and Japan. He was highly regarded as an interpreter of the music of **Sibelius,** his father-in-law; also excelled in performances of 20th-century works, ranging from Puccini to Shostakovich.

James, Dorothy, American composer; b. Chicago, Dec. 1, 1898; d. St. Petersburg, Fla., Dec. 1, 1982. She studied with Louis Gruenberg and Adolf Weidig at the Chicago Musical College and at the American Cons. of Music in Chicago (M.M., 1927); also with Howard Hanson at the Eastman School of Music in Rochester, N.Y., Healey Willan in Toronto, and Ernst Krenek at the Univ. of Michigan. For 41 years (1927–68) she valiantly taught music appreciation at Eastern Michigan Univ. in Ypsilanti, before retiring to Florida. She publ. *Music of Living Michigan Composers* (1976). She composed an opera, *Paolo and Francesca* (partial concert perf., Rochester, N.Y., April 2, 1931, on the same program with her *3 Symphonic Fragments*); also *The Jumblies,* children's cantata, to a text by Edward Lear (1935); *Paul Bunyan,* children's cantata (1938); *Tone-Row,* piano suite (1962); chamber music.

James, Harry (Haag), popular American jazz trumpeter and bandleader; b. Albany, Ga., March 15, 1916; d. Las Vegas, July 5, 1983. His father was a trumpeter and his mother a trapeze artist with the Mighty Haag Circus; he took up the drums at the age of 4 and the trumpet at 8; became leader of a circus band at 12. He worked as a contortionist until going with his family to Texas, where he played trumpet in local dance bands. After playing with Ben Pollack's band (1935–37), he became a featured member of Benny Goodman's orch. (1937–39), being featured in such songs as *One O'Clock Jump, Sing, Sing, Sing,* and *Life Goes to a Party.* His virtuoso technique was striking; he could blow *dolce* and even *dolcissimo,* but when needed he blew with deafening *fortissimo;* could also perform ultra-chromatic glissando. He struck out on his own as a bandleader in 1939, producing a sensation with his trumpet version of *You Made Me Love You* in 1941; subsequently was a leading figure of the big band era, bringing out many hit recordings and touring extensively; one of his hit songs, *Ciribiribin,* became his theme song. Several of his albums, including the self-proclamatorily-titled *Wild about Harry,* sold into the millions, even in wartime, when shellac, from which disks were manufactured, was rationed. In 1943 he married Betty Grable, the pin-up girl of the G.I.s in World War II, famous for the lissome beauty of her nether limbs. She was his 2nd wife, out of a total of 4. They were divorced in 1965. Faithful to the slogan that "the show must go on," James, wracked with the pain of fatal lymphatic cancer, continued to perform; he played his last gig in Los Angeles, on June 26, 1983, nine days before his death. He observed, as he was dying, "Let it just be said that I went up to do a one-nighter with Archangel Gabriel."

BIBL.: F. Stacy, *H. J.'s Pin-Up Life Story* (N.Y., 1944).

James, Philip (Frederick Wright), American organist, conductor, composer, and teacher; b. Jersey City, N.J., May 17, 1890; d. Southampton, N.Y., Nov. 1, 1975. He received rudimentary instruction in music from his sister; later studied composition with Rubin Goldmark, Homer Norris, Elliot Schenck, and Rosario Scalero; also studied organ with J. Warren Andrews, and later with Joseph Bonnet and Alexandre Guilmant in Paris. He served in the U.S. Army during World War I; after the Armistice, was appointed bandmaster of the American Expeditionary Force General Headquarters Band. Returning to the U.S., he held various posts as organist and choirmaster in several churches in N.Y., and also conducted the Victor Herbert Opera Co. (1919–22). He then was founder-conductor of the New Jersey Sym. Orch. (1922–29); also conducted the Brooklyn Orch. Soc. (1927–30) and the Bamberger Little Sym. (WOR Radio, N.Y., 1929–36). He won numerous prizes, among them one from NBC for his orch. suite *Station WGZBX*. In 1923 he joined the faculty of N.Y. Univ., becoming chairman of its music dept. in 1933; retired in 1955. In 1933 he was elected a member of the National Inst. of Arts and Letters.

WORKS: STAGE: *Judith*, dramatic reading with Ballet and Chamber Orch. (1927; N.Y., Feb. 18, 1933). **ORCH.:** *Overture in Olden Style on French Noëls* (1926; rev. 1929; N.Y., Feb. 23, 1930); *Sea Symphony* for Bass-baritone and Orch. (1928; Frankfurt am Main, July 14, 1960); *Song of the Night*, symphonic poem (1931; N.Y., March 15, 1938); *Station WGZBX*, satirical suite (NBC Sym. Orch., May 1, 1932); Suite for Strings (N.Y. Univ., April 28, 1934); *Gwalia, a Welsh Rhapsody* (N.Y., Nov. 14, 1935); *Bret Harte Overture No. 3* (N.Y., Dec. 20, 1936); *Brennan on the Moor* for Chamber Orch. (N.Y., Nov. 28, 1939); Sinfonietta (N.Y., Nov. 10, 1941; rev. 1943); Sym. No. 1 (1943; rev. 1961); 2nd Suite for Strings (1943; Saratoga Springs, Sept. 5, 1946); Sym. No. 2 (1946; Rochester, N.Y., May 7, 1966); *Miniver Cheevy* and *Richard Cory* for Narrator and Orch. (Saratoga, N.Y., Sept. 9, 1947); *Chaumont*, symphonic poem for Chamber Orch. (1948; N.Y., May 2, 1951). **CHAMBER:** String Quartet (1924; rev. 1939); Suite for Woodwind Quintet (1936); Piano Quartet (1937; rev. 1948). **CHORAL:** *The Nightingale of Bethlehem*, cantata (1920; rev. 1923); *Shirat ha-Yam*, cantata (1920; rev. 1933–58); *Song of the Future* for Mixed Chorus a cappella (1922); *Missa Imaginum* for Mixed Chorus and Orch. (1929); *General William Booth Enters into Heaven* for Tenor, Male Voices, and Chamber Orch. (1932); *World of Tomorrow* for Mixed Chorus and Orch. (1938); *Psalm 150* for Mixed Chorus and Orch. (1940; rev. 1956); *Chorus of Shepherds and Angels*, cantata (1956); *To Cecilia*, cantata for Chorus and Chamber Orch. (1966); choruses; hymns; songs. **BAND:** *Perstare et Perstare*, festal march (N.Y., June 10, 1942; arr. for Orch., 1946); *E.F.G. Overture* (1944; N.Y., June 13, 1945); *Fanfare and Ceremonial* (1955; N.Y., June 20, 1956; rev. 1962). **ORGAN:** *Méditation à Sainte Clotilde* (1915); *Dithyramb* (1921); *Fête* (1921); Sonata No. 1 (1929); *Pantomime* (1941); *Galarnad* (1946); *Novelette* (1946); *Solemn Prelude* (1948); *Alleluia-Toccata* (1949); *Pastorale* (1949); *Requiescat in pace* (1949; rev. 1955); *Passacaglia on an Old Cambrian Bass* (1951; arr. for Orch., 1956; for Band, 1957); *Sortie* (1973); piano pieces.

BIBL.: H. James, *A Catalog of the Musical Works of P. J. (1890–1975)* (N.Y., 1980).

Janáček, Leoš, greatly significant Czech composer; b. Hukvaldy, Moravia, July 3, 1854; d. Moravská Ostrava, Aug. 12, 1928. He grew up in a musical household; his father was a choirmaster. At the age of 11 he was sent to Brno to serve as a chorister at the Augustinian Queen's Monastery, where he was schooled under its choirmaster, Křížkovský. He then went to the German College in Brno (1869–72); subsequently occupied a teaching post and also served as choirmaster of the men's chorus, Svatopluk (1873–77), taking an opportunity to study organ with Skuherský at the Prague Organ School (1874–75). He conducted the Beseda Choral Soc. in Brno (1876–88), and also pursued studies at the Leipzig Cons., where he took music history courses with Oskar Paul and composition courses with Leo Grill (1879–80). He continued his composition studies with Franz Krenn at the Vienna Cons.; returning to Brno, he was appointed the 1st director of the new organ school (1881). His social position in Brno was enhanced by his marriage to Zdenka Schulzová, the daughter of the director of the teachers' training college. He also engaged in scholarly activities; from 1884 to 1886 was ed. of the music journal *Hudební Listy* (Music Bulletins); he further became associated with František Bartoš in collecting Moravian folk songs. From 1886 to 1902 he taught music at the Brno Gymnasium. In 1919 he retired from his directorship of the Brno Organ School, and then taught master classes in Brno (1920–25). Throughout all these busy years he worked diligently on his compositions, showing particular preference for operas.

Janáček's style of composition underwent numerous transformations, from Romantic techniques of established formulas to bold dissonant combinations. He was greatly influenced by the Russian musical nationalism exemplified by the "realistic" speech inflections in vocal writing. He visited St. Petersburg and Moscow in 1896 and 1902, and publ. his impressions of the tour in the Brno press. From 1894 to 1903 he worked assiduously on his most important opera, *Její pastorkyňa* (Her Foster Daughter), to a highly dramatic libretto set in Moravia in the mid-19th century, involving a jealous contest between 2 brothers for the hand of Jenůfa (the innocent heroine), and infanticide at the hands of a foster mother, with an amazing outcome absolving Jenůfa and her suitors. The opera encountered great difficulty in securing production in Prague because of its grisly subject, but was eventually produced on various European stages, mostly in the German text, and under the title *Jenůfa*. Another opera by Janáček that attracted attention was *Výlet pana Broučka do XV stoleti* (Mr. Brouček's Excursion to the 15th Century), depicting the imaginary travel of a Czech patriot to the time of the religious struggle mounted by the followers of the nationalist leader Hus against the established church. There followed an operatic fairy tale, *Příhody Lišky Bystroušky* (The Adventures of the Vixen Bystrouška, or The Cunning Little Vixen), and a mystery play, *Věc Makropulos* (The Makropulos Affair). Janáček's great interest in Russian literature was reflected in his opera *Kát'a Kabanová*, after the drama *The Storm* by the Russian playwright Ostrovsky, and one after Dostoyevsky, *Z mrtvého domu* (From the House of the Dead). He further composed a symphonic poem, *Taras Bulba* (the fictional name of a Ukrainian patriot, after a story by Gogol). Like most artists, writers, and composers of Slavic origin in the old Austro-Hungarian Empire, Janáček had a natural interest in the Pan-Slavic movement, with an emphasis on the common origins of Russian, Czech, Slovak, and other kindred cultures; his *Glagolitic Mass*, to a Latin text tr. into the Czech language, is an example. Janáček lived to witness the fall of the old Austrian regime and the national rise of the Slavic populations. He also showed great interest in the emerging Soviet school of composition, even though he refrained from any attempt to join that movement. Inevitably, he followed the striking innovations of the modern school of composition as set forth in the works of Stravinsky and Schoenberg, but he was never tempted to experiment along those revolutionary lines. He remained faithful to his own well-defined style, and it was as the foremost composer of modern

Czech music that he secured for himself his unique place in history.

WORKS: STAGE: OPERAS: *Šárka* (1887–88; rev. 1918–19, with Act 3 orchestrated by O. Chlubna; rev. 1924–25; Brno, Nov. 11, 1925); *Počátek romanu* (The Beginning of a Romance; 1891; Brno, Feb. 10, 1894); *Její pastorkyňa* (Her Foster Daughter; generally known by its German title, *Jenůfa*; 1894–1903; Brno, Jan. 21, 1904; several subsequent revisions, including final version by K. Kovařovic, 1916; Prague, May 26, 1916); *Osud* (Fate; 1903–5; rev. 1906–7; 1st complete perf., Brno Radio, Sept. 18, 1934; 1st stage perf., National Theater, Brno, Oct. 25, 1958); *Výlet pana Broučka do měsíce* (Mr. Brouček's Excursion to the Moon; 1908–17; National Theater, Prague, April 23, 1920); a sequel to the preceding, *Výlet pana Broučka do XV století* (Mr. Brouček's Excursion to the 15th Century; 1917; National Theater, Prague, April 23, 1920); *Káťa Kabanová* (1919–21; Brno, Nov. 23, 1921); *Příhody Lišky Bystroušky* (The Adventures of the Vixen Bystrouška; The Cunning Little Vixen; 1921–23; Brno, Nov. 6, 1924); *Věc Makropulos* (The Makropulos Affair; 1923–25; Brno, Dec. 18, 1926); *Z mrtvého domu* (From the House of the Dead; 1927–28; rev. and reorchestrated by O. Chlubna and B. Bakala, 1930; Brno, April 12, 1930). **FOLK BALLET:** *Rákos Rákoczy* (National Theater, Prague, July 24, 1891).

CHORAL: SACRED: *Fidelis servus* for Mixed Voices (c.1870); *Graduale in festo purificationis B.V.M.* for Mixed Voices (c.1870; rev. 1887); *Mass* (c.1870; not extant); *Graduale* (*Speciosus forma*) for Mixed Voices and Organ (1874); *Introitus* (*in festo Ss. Nominis Jesu*) for Mixed Voices and Organ (1874); *Benedictus* for Soprano, Mixed Voices, and Organ (1875); *Communio* for Mixed Voices (1875); *Exaudi Deus* for Mixed Voices (1875; rev. 1877); *Odpočin si* (Take Your Rest) for Male Voices (c.1875); *Regnum mundi* for Mixed Voices (1878); *Deset českých církevních zpěvů z Lehnerova mešího kancinonálu* (10 Czech Hymns from the Lehner Hymnbook for Mass) with Organ (1881); *Hospodine!* (Lord Have Mercy) for Soprano, Alto, Tenor, Bass, Double Chorus, Organ Harp, 4 Trombones, and Tuba (1896); *Slavnostní sbor* (Festival Chorus) for Male Voices (1897); *Svatý Václave!* (St. Wenceslas; 1902); *Constitues* for Male Voices and Organ (c.1902); *Zdráva Maria* for Tenor, Mixed Voices, and Organ (1904); [7] *Církevní zpěvy české vícelhlasné z příborského kancionálu* (Czech Hymns for Several Voices from the Příbor Hymnbook; c.1904); *Mass in E-flat major* for Voices and Organ (1907–8; left incomplete; finished and orchestrated by V. Petrželka; Brno, March 7, 1943); *Veni sancte spiritus* for Male Voices (1910). **SECULAR** (for Male Voices unless otherwise given): *Srbská lidová píseň* (Serbian Folk Song) for Mixed Voices (1873); *Oráni* (Ploughing; 1873); *Válečná* (War Song; 1873); *Nestálost lásky* (The Fickleness of Love; 1873); *Osámělábez techy* (Alone without Comfort; 1874; rev. 1898 and 1925); *Divím se milému* (I Wonder at My Beloved; 1875); *Vínek stonulý* (A Drowned Wreath; 1875); *Láska opravidá* (True Love; 1876); *Když mne nechceš coz je víc* (If You Don't Want Me, What Else Is There?; 1876); *Zpěvná duma* (Choral Elegy; 1876); *Slavnostní sbor* (Festival Chorus) for Soloists and Voices (1877); *Osudu neujdeš* (You Cannot Escape Your Fate; 1878); *Na košatej jedli dva holubi sedá* (On the Bushy Fir Tree 2 Pigeons Are Perched; c.1878); *Píseň v jeseni* (Autumn Song) for Mixed Voices (1880); *Na pripravo* (1883); *Mužskésbory* (Male Voice Choruses; 1885); *Kačena divoká* (The Wild Duck) for Mixed Voices (1885); *Tři mužskésbory* (3 Male Voice Choruses; 1888); *Naše píseň* (Our Song) for Mixed Voices and Orch. (1890); *Zelené sem sela* (I Have Sown Green) for Mixed Voices and Orch. (1892); *Což ta naše bříza* (Our Birch Tree; 1893); *Vínek* (The Garland; 1893); *Už je slúnko z tej hory ven* (The Sun Has Risen above That Hill) for Baritone, Mixed Voices, and Piano (1894); *Čtvero mužských sborů moravských* (4 Moravian Male Voice Choruses; 1904); *Kantor Halfar* (1906); *Maryčka Magdónova* (1906–7); *Sedmdesát tisíc* (The 70,000; 1909); *Perina* (The Eiderdown; 1914); *Vlčístopa* (The Wolf's Trail) for Soprano, Women's Voices, and Piano (1916); *Hradčansképisničky* (Songs of Hradčany) for Women's Voices (1916); *Kaspar Rucký's* for Soprano and Women's Voices (1916); *Českálegie* (The Czech Legion; 1918); *Potulnysílenec* (The Wandering Madman) for Soprano and Male Voices (1922); *Naše vlajka* (Our Flag) for 2 Sopranos and Male Voices (1925–26); *Sbor při kladenízakladního kamene Masarykovy university v Brne* (Chorus for Laying the Foundation Stone of Masaryk University in Brno; 1928). **CANTATAS:** *Amarus* for Soprano, Tenor, Baritone, Chorus, and Orch. (1897; Kroměříž, Dec. 2, 1900; rev. 1901 and 1906); *Otče náš* (Our Father) for Tenor, Chorus, and Piano or Harmonium (1901; Brno, June 15, 1901; rev. 1906); *Elegie na smrt dcery Olgy* (Elegy on the Death of My Daughter Olga) for Tenor, Chorus, and Piano (1903; rev. 1904; Brno Radio, Dec. 20, 1930); *Na Soláni Čarták* (Čarták on the Soláň) for Tenor, Male Voices, and Orch. (1911; Brno, March 13, 1912); *Věčné evangelium* (The Eternal Gospel) for Soprano, Tenor, Chorus, and Orch. (1914; Prague, Feb. 5, 1917; rev. 1924); *Glagolská mše* (Glagolitic Mass) for Soprano, Alto, Tenor, Bass, Chorus, Orch., and Organ (1926; Brno, Dec. 5, 1927). **CHAMBER VOCAL:** *Zapisnik zmizeleho* (The Diary of One Who Disappeared), song cycle for Tenor, Alto, 3 Women's Voices, and Piano (1917–19; Brno, April 18, 1921); *Říkadla* (Nursery Rhymes), 8 pieces for 3 Women's Voices, Clarinet, and Piano (Brno, Oct. 26, 1925; rev. version, 1927, as 18 pieces and an introduction for 2 Sopranos, 2 Altos, 3 Tenors, 2 Basses, 9 Instruments, and Children's Drum).

ORCH.: *Suite* for Strings (Brno, Dec. 2, 1877); *Idyll* for Strings (Brno, Dec. 15, 1878); *Suite* (*Serenade*), op. 3 (1891; Brno, Sept. 23, 1928); *Adagio* (1891); *Žárlivost* (Jealousy), overture (1894; 1st concert perf., Prague, Nov. 10, 1906); *Šumařovo dítě* (The Fiddler's Child), ballad (1912; Prague, Nov. 14, 1917); *Taras Bulba*, rhapsody after Gogol (1915–18; Brno, Oct. 9, 1921); *Balada blanická* (The Ballad of Blaník), symphonic poem (1920; Brno, March 21, 1920); *Sinfonietta* (Prague, June 29, 1926); *Dunaj* (The Danube), symphonic poem (1923–28; unfinished; completed by O. Chlubna, 1948); *Violin Concerto: Putovánídušičky* (Pilgrimage of the Soul; 1926; Brno, Sept. 29, 1988).

CHAMBER: *Znělka* (Fanfare) for 4 Violins (1875); *Zvuky ku památce Förchgotta-Tovačovského* (Sounds in Memory of Förchgotta-Tovačovského) for 3 Violins, Viola, Cello, and Double Bass (1875); *Romance* for Violin and Piano (1879); *Dumka* for Violin and Piano (1880); *Prohádka* (Fairy Tale) for Cello and Piano (1910; rev. 1923); *Presto* for Cello and Piano (c.1910); *Violin Sonata* (1914–21; Balada only); *String Quartet No. 1* (1923–24; Prague, Sept. 17, 1924; based on the lost Piano Trio of 1908–9); *Mládí* (Youth), suite for Wind Sextet (Brno, Oct. 21, 1924); *Pochod Modráčků* (March of the Blue Boys) for Piccolo and Piano (1924); *Concertino* for Piano, 2 Violins, Viola, Clarinet, Horn, and Bassoon (1925; Brno, Feb. 16, 1926); *Capriccio Vzdor* (Defiance) for Piano Left-hand and Chamber Ensemble (1926; Prague, March 2, 1928); *String Quartet No. 2, Listy důvěrné* (Intimate Letters; Brno, Sept. 11, 1928; rev. 1947, by O. Šourek).

PIANO: *Thema con variazioni* (*Zdenciny variace:* Zdenka Variations; 1880); *Na památku* (In Memoriam; c.1886); *Po zarostlém chodníčku* (On the Overgrown Path), 15 pieces (1901–8; 7 originally for Harmonium); *Sonata 1.X.1905 Z ulice* (From the Street; 1905; only 2 movements extant; inspired by the abortive but sanguine Russian revolt); *V mlhách* (In the Mists; 1912; rev. 1949, by B. Štědroň); *Vzpomínka* (Reminiscence; 1928).

Janáček made many arrangements of folk music and prepared the following eds. of folk songs: with F. Bartoš, *Kytice z národních písní moravských* (A Bouquet of Moravian Folk Songs; Telč, 1890; 3rd ed., rev., 1901; 4th ed., 1953, edited by A. Gregor and B. Štědroň); 53 songs (Telč, 1882–91; 2nd ed., 1908, as *Moravaskálidová poesie v písnich*; Moravian Folk Poetry in Songs; 4th ed., 1947, edited by B. Štědroň); with F. Bartoš, *Národní písne moravské v nově nasbírané* (Moravian Folk Songs Newly Collected; 1899); with P. Váša, *Moravské písně milostné* (Moravian Love Songs; 1928). A complete critical ed. of the works of Janáček began publication in Prague in 1978.

WRITINGS: J. Vysloužil, ed., *O lidovépísní a lidové hudbě*

(Folk Song and Folk Music; Prague, 1955); Z. Blažek, ed., *Hudebně teoretické dílo* (Music Theory Works; 2 vols., Prague, 1968, 1974).

BIBL.: SOURCE MATERIAL: His correspondence was ed. by A. Rektorys and J. Racek (9 vols., Prague, 1934–53); J. Racek, ed., *L. J.: Obraz života a díla* (L. J.: A Picture of His Life and Works; Brno, 1948); B. Štědroň, *L. J. v obrazech* (L. J. in Pictures; Prague, 1958); idem, *Dílo Leoše Janáčka: Abecední seznam Janáčkových skladeb a úprav* (L. J.'s Works: An Alphabetical Catalog of J.'s Compositions and Arrangements; Prague, 1959; Eng. tr., 1959, as *The Work of L. J.*); T. Strakova, ed., *Iconographia janáčkiana* (Brno, 1975). **BIOGRAPHICAL:** M. Brod, *L. J.: Život a dílo* (L. J.: Life and Works; Prague, 1924; German ed., 1925; 2nd ed., rev., 1956); D. Muller, *L. J.* (Paris, 1930); A. Vašek, *Po stopách dra Leoše Janáčka* (On the Track of Dr. L. J.; Brno, 1930); H. Kašlik, *L. J. dirigent* (Prague, 1936); O. Jeremiáš, *L. J.* (Prague, 1938); V. Helfert, *L. J.* (Brno, 1939); idem, *O Janáčkovi* (About J.; ed. by B. Štědroň, Prague, 1949); H. Richter, *L. J.* (Leipzig, 1958); J. Vogel, *L. J.: Leben und Werk* (Kassel, 1958; Eng. tr., 1962; 2nd ed., rev., 1980); J. Šeda, *L. J.* (Prague, 1961); J. Racek, *L. J.: Mensch und Künstler* (Leipzig, 1962; 2nd ed., 1971; Czech ed., 1963); H. Hollander, *L. J.* (London, 1963; German ed., 1964); M. Černohorská, *L. J.* (in Eng.; Prague, 1966); B. Štědroň, *L. J.: K jeho lidskému a uměleckému profilu* (L. J.'s Image as Man and Artist; Brno, 1976); J. Vysloužil, *L. J.* (Brno, 1978); I. Horsbrugh, *L. J.* (Newton Abbot, 1981); K. Honolka, *L. J.: Sein Leben, sein Werk, seine Zeit* (Stuttgart, 1982); S. Přibáňová, *L. J.* (Prague, 1984); C. Susskind, *J. and Brod* (London, 1986). **CRITICAL, ANALYTICAL:** L. Firkušný, *Odkaz Leoše Janáčka české opeře* (L. J.'s Legacy to Czech Opera; Brno, 1939); L. Kundera, *Janáčkova varhanická škola* (J.'s Organ School; Olomouc, 1948); J. Burghauser, "Janáčkova tvorba komorní a symfonická" (J.'s Chamber and Symphonic Works), *Musikologie*, III (1955); Č. Gardavský, "L. J., Chrámové a varhanní skladby Leoše Janáčka" (L. J.'s Stage Works), ibid.; L. Kundera, "Janáčkova tvorba klavírní" (J.'s Piano Works), ibid.; F. Pala, "Jevistni dílo Leoše Janáčka" (L. J.'s Stage Works), ibid.; T. Strakova, "Janáčkova opera Osud" (J.'s Opera *Fate*), *Časopis Moravského Musea*, XLI (1956); D. Shawe-Taylor, "The Operas of L. J.," *Proceedings of the Royal Musical Association*, LXXXV (1958–59); J. Vysloužil, "Janáčkova tvorba ve světle jeho hudebně folkloristické teorie" (J.'s Works in the Light of His Folk-Music Theories), *Sborník Janáčkovy akademie múzických umění*, II (1960); Z. Sádecký, "Celotónový charakter hudební řeči v Janáčkově 'Lišce Bystroušce'" (The Whole-Tone Character of the Musical Language of J.'s *Cunning Little Vixen*), *Živá hudba*, II (1962); J. Tyrrell, "The Musical Prehistory of J.'s *Počátek románu* and Its Importance in Shaping the Composer's Dramatic Style," *Časopis Moravského Musea*, LII (1967); Z. Sádecký, "Výstava dialogu a monologu v Janáčkově Její pastorkyni" (Dialogue and Monologue Structure in J.'s *Její pastorkyňa*), *Živá hudba*, IV (1968); B. Štědroň, *Zur Genesis von L. J.s Oper Jenůfa* (Brno, 1968; 2nd ed., 1971); A. Tučapský, *Mužské sbory Leoše Janáčka a jejich interpretační tradice* (L. J.'s Male Voice Choruses and Their Performance Tradition; Ostrava, 1968); J. Tyrrell, "Mr. Brouček's Excursion to the Moon," *Časopic Moravského Musea*, LIII–LIV (1968–69); J. Blatný, "J. učitel a teoretik" (J. as Teacher and Theorist), *Opus Musicum*, I (1969); J. Tyrrell, "J. and the Speech-Melody Myth," *Musical Times*, CXI (1970); E. Chisholm, *The Operas of L. J.* (Oxford, 1971); O. Chlubna, "O kompozicním myslení Leoše Janáčka" (L. J.'s Compositional Thought Processes), *Hudebni Rozhledy*, XXIV (1971); T. Kneif, *Die Bühnenwerke von L. J.* (Vienna, 1974); A. Geck, *Das Volksliedmaterial L. J.s: Analysen der Strukturen unter Einbeziehung von J.s Randbemerkungen und Volkstudien* (Regensburg, 1975); D. Ströbel, *Motiv und Figur in den Kompositionen der Jenufa-Werkgruppe* (Freiburg, 1975); M. Ewans, *J.'s Tragic Operas* (London, 1977); J. Vysloužil, "L. J. 1854–1928," *Acta Janáčkiana*, II (Brno, 1985); P. Wingfield, *J.'s 'Lost' Kreutzer Sonata*, *Journal of the Royal Musical Association*, 112/2 (1987); J. Vysloužil, "The Style and Musical Poetics of L. J.," *Acta Janáčkiana*, III (Brno, 1988).

Jander, Owen (Hughes), American musicologist; b. Mount Kisco, N.Y., June 4, 1930. He was educated at the Univ. of Virginia (B.A., 1951) and Harvard Univ. (M.A., 1952; Ph.D., 1962, with the diss. *The Works of Alessandro Stradella Related to the Cantata and the Opera*). In 1960 he joined the dept. of music at Wellesley College, where he later became the Catherine Mills Davis Prof. in Music History; was founder of its Collegium Musicum for the performance of early music and also initiated the project to construct the outstanding Fisk Organ there for the performance of the pre-Bach repertoire; also served as ed. of The Wellesley Edition and The Wellesley Edition Cantata Index Series (1962–74). In 1966–67 he held a Guggenheim fellowship, and in 1985 he received an N.E.H. Fellowship for Senior Scholars. He initially devoted himself to 17th-century Italian music, but later turned to Beethoven. He contributed numerous articles to *The New Grove Dictionary of Music and Musicians* (1980), and also served as co-ed. of *Charles Benton Fisk: Organ Builder* (2 vols., 1986).

Janeček, Karel, Czech composer and music theorist; b. Czestochowa, Poland, Feb. 20, 1903; d. Prague, Jan. 4, 1974. He spent his boyhood in Kiev. After completing his secondary education at an industrial school, he went to Prague, where he took courses in composition with Křička (1921–24) and Novák (1924–27). From 1929 to 1941 he taught at the Plzeň Music School; then was prof. of composition at the Prague Cons. (1941–46); subsequently helped to found the Prague Academy of Music (1947), where he taught; was a prof. there (from 1961). In his early works Janeček adopted a traditional national style; later he occasionally employed a personalized dodecaphonic scheme.

WORKS: *Overture* (1926–27); 2 syms. (1935–40, 1954–55); *Lenin*, symphonic triptych (1953); *Legend of Prague*, overture for String Orch. (1956); Fantasy for Orch. (1962–63); Sinfonietta (1967); *Large Symposium* for 15 Soloists (1967); 3 string quartets (1924, 1927, 1934); Divertimento for 8 Instruments (1925–26); String Trio (1930); Trio for Flute, Clarinet, and Bassoon (1931); Duo for Violin and Viola (1938); Violin Sonata (1939); Divertimento for Oboe, Clarinet, and Bassoon (1949); Cello Sonata (1958); *Little Symposium*, chamber suite for Flute, Clarinet, Bassoon, and Piano (1959); Duo for Violin and Cello (1960); *Chamber Overture* for Nonet (1960); Quartet for Flute, Oboe, Clarinet, and Bassoon (1966); *Trifles and Abbreviations* for Piano (1926); *Tema con variazioni* for Piano, inspired by the tragedy of the village of Lidice, destroyed by the Nazis (1942); several choral works, including *To the Fallen* (1950–51), *To the Living* (1951), and *My Dream* (1972); songs.

WRITINGS: *Otakar Šín* (Prague, 1944); *Hudební formy* (Musical Forms; Prague, 1955); *Melodika* (Prague, 1956); *Vyjádření souzvuku* (The Writing of Chords; Prague, 1958); *Harmonie rozborem* (Harmony Through Analysis; Prague, 1963); *Základy moderní harmonie* (The Basis of Modern Harmony; Prague, 1965); *Tektonika* (Structure; Prague, 1968); *Tvorba a tvůrci* (Creativity and Creations; Prague, 1968); *Skladatelská práce v oblasti klasické harmonie* (Composition Based on Classical Harmony; Prague, 1973).

Janequin (Jannequin), Clément, important French composer; b. Châtellerault, c.1485; d. Paris, 1558. He is 1st mentioned as a clerc in the service of Lancelot du Fau, a man of the court and church, in 1505; his patron became Bishop of Luçon in 1515, and he appears to have remained in the bishop's service until 1523, at which time he entered the service of Jean de Foix, bishop of Bordeaux. Having become a priest, he received several minor prebends there; became canon of St. Emilion in 1525, then procureur des âmes there in 1526. He was named curé of St. Michel de Rieufret in 1526; then of St. Jean de Mezos in 1530; also doyen of Garosse that same year. With the death of his patron in 1529, he lost his prebends. However, he had become known as a composer through Pierre Attaingnant's publication of some of his chansons. Janequin served as master of the choirboys at Auch Cathedral in 1531, then was made curé of Avrille in 1533; he was also maître de chapelle of Angers Cathedral (1534–37), and subsequently curé of Unverre. In 1549 he settled in Paris, being listed as a student at the Univ. He wrote a chanson on the siege of Metz, which brought him the honorary title of chapelain to the Duc de Guise; later was made chantre ordinaire du roi and then compositeur ordinaire du roi. Janequin was an outstanding composer of chansons and chansons spirituelles, of which more than 400 are extant. His mastery is evidenced both in his brief and witty settings and in those more lengthy and programmatic. Among his finest are *Le Chant des oiseaux, La Chasse, Les Cris de Paris,* and his most celebrated work, *La Bataille,* most likely written to commemorate the battle of Marignano. Pierre Attaingnant publ. several of his chansons between the 1520s and the 1530s; others appeared in various collections of the time.

WORKS: MASSES: *Missa super "L'Aveuglé Dieu," Missae duodecim* (Paris, 1554); *Missa super "La Bataille"* (1532). **MOTETS:** Attaingnant is believed to have publ. a vol. of his motets in Paris in 1533; however, no copy of the vol. has been found. The motet *Congregati sunt* (1538) is extant. **PSALMS AND CHANSONS SPIRITUELLES:** *Premier livre contenant XXVIII pseaulmes de David . . .* for 4 Voices (Paris, 1549); *Premier livre contenant plusieurs chansons spirituelles, avec les lamentations de Jeremie* (Paris, 1556); *Proverbes de Salomon . . .* for 4 Voices (Paris, 1558); *Octante deux pseaumes de David . . .* for 4 Voices (Paris, 1559). A. Merritt and F. Lesure ed. *Clément Janequin (c.1485–1558): Chansons polyphoniques* (Monaco, 1965–71).

BIBL.: M. Cauchie, "C. J.: Recherches sur sa famille et sur lui-même," *Revue de Musicologie,* IV (1923); idem, "C. J., chapelain du duc de Guise," *Le Ménestrel* (Jan. 21, 1927); J. Levron, *C. J., musicien de la renaissance: Essai sur sa vie et ses amis* (Grenoble and Paris, 1948); F. Lesure, "C. J.: Recherches sur sa vie et sur son œuvre," *Musica Disciplina,* V (1951); F. Lesure and P. Roudié, "C. J., chantre de François Ier (1531)," *Revue de Musicologie,* XXXIX–XL (1957); F. Lesure, "Les Chansons à trois voix de C. J.," ibid., XLIII–XLIV (1959); F. Lesure and P. Roudié, "La Jeunesse bordelaise de C. J.," ibid., XLIX (1963).

Janigro, Antonio, Italian cellist, conductor, and pedagogue; b. Milan, Jan. 21, 1918; d. there, May 1, 1989. He studied with Gilberto Crepax at the Milan Cons. and with Alexanian and Casals at the École Normale de Musique in Paris; pursued a successful career as a cellist but later turned mostly to conducting. From 1954 to 1964 he conducted the Zagreb Radio and Television Sym. Orch; in 1950 he founded the group I Solisti di Zagreb, with which he toured extensively until 1967; likewise was conductor of Milan's Angelicum Orch. (1965–67). In 1968 he became conductor of the Saarland Radio Chamber Orch. in Saarbrücken; continued to tour as a cellist as well, and also was made prof. of advanced cello at the Schumann Cons. in Düsseldorf (1965).

Janis (real name, **Yanks,** abbreviated from **Yankelevitch**), **Byron,** outstanding American pianist; b. McKeesport, Pa., March 24, 1928. He began to study piano with a local teacher; at the age of 7 he was taken to N.Y., where he became a pupil of Adele Marcus. Progressing rapidly, he made his professional debut in 1943, playing Rachmaninoff's 2nd Piano Concerto with the NBC Sym. Orch.; he played it again with the Pittsburgh Sym. Orch. on Feb. 20, 1944, with the 13-year-old Lorin Maazel on the podium; Vladimir Horowitz happened to be present at the concert and told Janis that he would be willing to take him as a private pupil; these private lessons continued for several years. In 1948 he toured South America; that same year he played in Carnegie Hall, N.Y., to critical acclaim. In 1952 he made a tour of Europe. In 1960 he made his 1st tour of Russia, under the auspices of the U.S. State Dept.; played there again in 1962. During a visit to France in 1967, he discovered the autograph MSS of 2 waltzes by Chopin, the G-flat major, op. 70, no. 1, and the E-flat major, op. 18; in 1973 he located 2 variants of these waltzes in the library of Yale Univ. In 1975 he made the film *Frédéric Chopin: A Voyage with Byron Janis,* which was produced by the Public Broadcasting Service. In 1953 he married June Dickinson

Wright; they were divorced in 1965; in 1966 he married Maria Veronica Cooper, the daughter of the movie star Gary Cooper. At the climax of his career, Janis was stricken with crippling psoriatic arthritis in his hands and wrists. In spite of the attendant physical and emotional distress, he persevered in his international career. On Feb. 25, 1985, he gave a special concert at the White House, at which time his illness was publicly disclosed. He was named Ambassador for the Arts of the National Arthritis Foundation, and subsequently gave concerts on its behalf.

BIBL.: B. Goldsmith, "To Conquer Fear: The Story of Concert Pianist B. J.," *Parade* (Oct. 13, 1985).

Janitsch, Johann Gottlieb, Silesian composer and bass viol player; b. Schweidnitz, June 19, 1708; d. Berlin, c.1763. He studied music in Breslau and law at the Univ. of Frankfurt an der Oder (1729–33). In 1733 he became secretary to Franz Wilhelm von Happe, a minister of state. In 1736 Crown Prince Friedrich (later Frederick the Great) made him a member of his personal orch. in Ruppin; he followed Friedrich to Rheinsberg, where he organized a series of famous concerts known as the "Friday Academies." In 1740 he was named "contraviolinist" in Frederick the Great's orch. in Berlin, and continued his "Friday Academies" there. His *Sonata da camera* for Flute, Oboe, Violin, Viola, Cello, and Harpsichord, entitled *Echo,* composed in 1757, is reprinted in *Collegium musicum,* LXVIII (Leipzig, 1938); another work in this genre was publ. in 1970. A collection of his compositions has been assembled from the available MSS by Josef Marx of the McGinnis & Marx firm of music publishers in N.Y.

Jankélévitch, Vladimir, French philosopher and writer on music; b. Bourges, Aug. 31, 1903; d. Paris, June 6, 1985. He was educated in Paris at the School of Oriental Languages and at the École Normale Supérieure; received a degree in philosophy in 1925 and the doctorat ès lettres in 1933. He was a prof. of philosophy at the Institut de Prague (1927–33); then at the Univs. of Lille (1933–39; 1945–52) and Toulouse (1939–45); was a prof. of ethics and moral philosophy at the Sorbonne (1952–78). His writings on music reflect his philosophical bent; these include *Gabriel Fauré et ses mélodies* (Paris, 1938; 2nd ed., augmented, 1951, as *Gabriel Fauré, Ses mélodies, son esthétique*); *Maurice Ravel* (Paris, 1939; 2nd ed., augmented, 1956, as *Ravel*); *Debussy et le mystère* (Neuchâtel, 1949); *La Rhapsodie, verve et improvisation musicale* (Paris, 1955); *Le Nocturne: Fauré: Chopin et la nuit: Satie et le matin* (Paris, 1957); *La Musique et l'ineffable* (Paris, 1961); *La Vie et la mort dans la musique de Debussy* (Neuchâtel, 1968); *Fauré et l'inexprimable* (Paris, 1974); *Debussy et le mystère de l'instant* (Paris, 1976).

BIBL.: L. Jerphagnon, *J.* (Paris, 1969).

Jankó, Paul von, Hungarian pianist and inventor; b. Totis, June 2, 1856; d. Constantinople, March 17, 1919. He studied at the Vienna Polytechnic and at the Vienna Cons. with Bruckner, Krenn, and H. Schmitt; then studied mathematics as well as piano with Ehrlich at the Univ. of Berlin (1881–82); settled in Constantinople. His keyboard, invented in 1882, is a new departure in piano mechanics, though standing in distant relationship to the older "chromatic" keyboard advocated by the Chroma society. It has 6 rows of keys; each pair of rows consists of 2 mutually exclusive whole-tone scales; the fingering of all diatonic scales is alike; chromatic scales are played by striking alternative keys in any 2 adjoining rows. A full description of the keyboard was publ. in pamphlet form by its inventor (1886). The "Jankó keyboard" was espoused by quite a few enthusiastic souls, but like many similar "inventions" it soon lapsed into innocuous desuetude.

BIBL.: F. Boyes, *Das J.-Klavier* (Vienna, 1904); H. Münnich, *Materialen für die J.-Klaviatur* (1905).

Jankŭ, Hana, Czech soprano; b. Brno, Oct. 25, 1940. She studied with Jaroslav Kvapil in Brno, making her debut in 1959; later sang with the Prague National Theater Opera. She made her 1st appearance at Milan's La Scala in 1967; appeared regularly at the Deutsche Oper am Rhein in Düsseldorf and the Deutsche Oper in West Berlin (from 1970). She also made guest appearances at the Vienna State Opera, the Bavarian State Opera in Munich, the Hamburg State Opera, the San Francisco Opera, and the Teatro Colón in Buenos Aires. In addition to the Czech repertory, she is also known for such roles as Gioconda, Elsa, Kundry, Desdemona, and Ariadne.

Jannaconi, Giuseppe, Italian composer; b. Rome, 1741; d. there, March 16, 1816. A pupil of S. Rinaldini and G. Carpani, he succeeded Zingarelli in 1811 as maestro di cappella at St. Peter's. He scored many of Palestrina's works, aided by his friend Pisari. His pupils included Baini and Abbé Santini. Some of his music is in MS in the Santini College in Münster; the collection once held 32 masses, 52 psalms, 70 motets, 57 offertories, antiphons, numerous canons for 4 to 64 Voices, 2 string quintets with Double Bass, etc.; other works are held in libraries and churches.

Janowitz, Gundula, esteemed German soprano; b. Berlin, Aug. 2, 1937. She studied with Herbert Thöny at the Graz Cons.; made her formal debut as Barbarina at the Vienna State Opera (1959), and later became one of its leading members. She sang at the Bayreuth Festivals (1960–63) and the Salzburg Festivals (from 1963); was a member of the Frankfurt Opera (1963–66); then joined the Deutsche Oper in West Berlin. She appeared at the Glyndebourne Festival (1964); sang at Karajan's Salzburg Easter Festivals (1967–68). She made her Metropolitan Opera debut in N.Y. as Sieglinde on Nov. 21, 1967. She was chosen to sing the role of Mozart's Countess at the reopening of the Paris Opéra in 1973; subsequently made her debut at London's Covent Garden as Donna Anna (1976). She was made an Austrian Kammersängerin in 1970. In 1990 she became director of the Graz Opera. Her notable roles included Fiordiligi, Agathe, Eva, Aida, Elisabeth, Desdemona, and Ariadne, as well as those already mentioned. She was also well known as a concert and lieder artist.

Janowka (Janovka), Thomas Balthasar (Tomáš Baltazar), Bohemian organist and musical lexicographer; b. Kuttenberg (baptized), Jan. 6, 1669; d. Prague (buried), June 13, 1741. He received a Jesuit education at the St. Wenceslas seminary in Prague; continued his studies at the Charles Univ. there (M.Phil., 1689); then was organist at Týn Church there from 1691 until his death. He compiled the *Clavis ad thesaurum magnae artis musicae* (Prague, 1701; 2nd ed., 1715, as *Clavis ad musicam*), which was the 2nd (after Tinctoris) dictionary of music ever publ. Only a few copies of the original ed. are extant, but it was reprinted in 1973.

Janowski, Marek, Polish-born German conductor; b. Warsaw, Feb. 18, 1939. He was taken to Germany while young; studied mathematics and music at the Univ. of Cologne; continued his musical studies in Vienna and at the Accademia Chigiana in Siena. He conducted sym. concerts in Italy, and then opera in Aachen and Cologne; subsequently held the post of 1st conductor at the Deutsche Oper am Rhein in Düsseldorf (1964–69) and at the Hamburg State Opera (1969–74); also made guest appearances in Stuttgart, Cologne, and Munich. In 1969 he made his English debut conducting the visiting Cologne Opera in the British premiere of Henze's *Der junge Lord*. From 1973 to 1975 he was chief conductor in Freiburg im Breisgau, and from 1975 to 1979 Generalmusikdirektor in Dortmund. He made his U.S. debut conducting *Lohengrin* at the Chicago Lyric Opera in 1980. He was principal guest conductor (1980–83) and artistic advisor (1983–86) of the Royal Liverpool Phil.; was also chief conductor of the Nouvel Orch. Philharmonique de Radio France in Paris (from 1984) and of the Gürzenich Orch. in Cologne (1986–91).

Jansa, Leopold, Bohemian violinist and composer; b. Wildenschwert, March 23, 1795; d. Vienna, Jan. 24, 1875. He studied with Jan Jahoda and Jan Zizius in Wildenschwert, then studied law in Vienna, where Voříšek encouraged him to resume his musical training; subsequently studied composition with Emanuel Alois Förster. He was in the service of

the Count of Braunschweig (1823–24), then was a violinist at the Vienna court chapel (1824); was made music director and prof. of violin at the Univ. of Vienna (1834); also played 1st violin in Schuppanzigh's quartet after its founder's death. He lost his Viennese positions in 1851 after he took part in a concert in London for the benefit of the Hungarian revolutionists. He remained in England until the amnesty of 1868, when he returned to Vienna and received a pension. He was greatly esteemed as a violinist; he composed 4 violin concertos, 36 violin duets, 8 string quartets, 3 string trios, and some sacred music.

Janson, Alfred, Norwegian composer; b. Oslo, March 10, 1937. His mother gave him piano lessons, but he soon turned to the accordion as his favorite musical instrument, and as a youth earned a living by playing in cafés and restaurants, mostly in jazz groups. He then took some composition lessons with Finn Mortensen. His music is a cross-section of a variety of modern techniques.

Works: Opera, *Fjeldeventyret* (A Mountain Adventure, 1970–73; Oslo, April 9, 1973); *Vuggesang* (Cradle Song) for 48 Strings and Piano (1963); *Konstruksjon og hymne* (Construction and Hymn) for Orch. (1963); *Canon* for Saxophone, Percussion, Piano, Hammond Organ, Double Bass, Voice, and Tape (1964); *Tema* for Chorus, Organ, Percussion, and Piano (1966); *Nocturne*, after Nietzsche, for 2 Choruses, 2 Cellos, 2 Percussion Groups, and Harp (1967); *Mot solen* (Toward the Sun), ballet with 2 Solo Saxophones, Chorus, and Orch. Ensemble (1968); *I dag død, imorgen rosenrød* (Candy and Balloons), ballet (1969); *Röster i mänskligt landskap* (Voices in Human Landscape), Mass for 3 Actors, Chorus, and 10 Instruments (1969); *Valse triste* for Jazz Quintet and Tape (1970); *Aberte*, music for a television play (1972); *Forspill* (Prelude), concerto for Violin and Orch. (1973–75); String Quartet (1978); *Vinger* (Wings) for Chorus and Jazz Orch. (1982–83); *Mellomspill* (Interlude) for Orch. (1985).

Jansons, Arvid. See **Yansons, Arvid.**

Jansons, Mariss, prominent Latvian conductor, son of **Arvid Yansons**; b. Riga, Jan. 14, 1943. He studied at the Leningrad Cons., where he took courses in violin, viola, piano, and conducting. He profited from initial conducting studies with his father; then studied with Swarowsky in Vienna, Karajan in Salzburg, and Mravinsky in Leningrad. In 1971 he won 2nd prize in the Karajan Competition in West Berlin; then made appearances with major orchs. and opera houses in the Soviet Union and Eastern Europe; also conducted in Western Europe and America. In 1979 he was named chief conductor of the Oslo Phil. Orch., with which he toured Europe; also toured the U.S. with it in 1987.

Bibl.: R. Plesner, "M. J. and the Oslo Philharmonic Orchestra," *Nordic Sounds* (March 1988).

Janssen, Herbert, noted German-born American baritone; b. Cologne, Sept. 22, 1892; d. N.Y., June 3, 1965. He studied in Cologne, and then with Oskar Daniel in Berlin, making his operatic debut in Schreker's *Der Schatzgräber* at the State Opera there (May 5, 1922), and remaining on its roster until 1938; he also made regular appearances at London's Covent Garden (1926–39) and at the Bayreuth Festivals (1930–37), where he excelled in such roles as Amfortas, the Dutchman, Gunther, Kurwenal, and Wolfram. He made his Metropolitan Opera debut as Wotan during the company's visit to Philadelphia (Jan. 24, 1939); his formal debut with the company followed in N.Y. as Wolfram (Jan. 28, 1939); he continued as a prominent member on its roster until 1952. He became an American citizen in 1946. In later years he was active as a voice teacher. He was also well known for his portrayal of Kothner.

Janssen, Werner, American composer and conductor; b. N.Y., June 1, 1899; d. Stony Brook, N.Y., Sept. 19, 1990. He studied with Clapp at Dartmouth College (B.Mus., 1921) and with Converse, Friedheim, and Chadwick at the New England Cons.

of Music in Boston; then studied conducting with Weingartner in Basel (1920–21) and Scherchen in Strasbourg (1921–25); won the Prix de Rome of the American Academy (1930) and made his debut as a conductor in Rome; he gave a concert of music by Sibelius in Helsinki in 1934 and was praised by Sibelius himself; received the Finnish Order of the White Rose. He made his American debut with the N.Y. Phil. on Nov. 8, 1934; served as conductor of the Baltimore Sym. Orch. (1937–39); then went to Hollywood, where he organized the Janssen Sym. (1940–52) and commissioned American composers to write special works. He was conductor of the Utah Sym. Orch. in Salt Lake City (1946–47), of the Portland (Ore.) Sym. (1947–49), and of the San Diego Phil. (1952–54). In 1937 he married the famous motion picture actress Ann Harding; they were divorced in 1963. As a composer, Janssen cultivated the art of literal pictorialism; his most successful work of this nature was *New Year's Eve in New York* (Rochester, N.Y., May 9, 1929), a symphonic poem for Large Orch. and Jazz Instruments; the orch. players were instructed to shout at the end "Happy New Year!" Other works were: *Obsequies of a Saxophone* for 6 Wind Instruments and a Snare Drum (Washington, D.C., Oct. 17, 1929); *Louisiana Suite* for Orch. (1930); *Dixie Fugue* (extracted from the *Louisiana Suite*; Rome, Nov. 27, 1932); *Foster Suite* for Orch., on Stephen Foster's tunes (1937); 2 string quartets.

Janssens, Jean-François-Joseph, Belgian composer; b. Antwerp, Jan. 29, 1801; d. there, Feb. 3, 1835. He studied with his father and later with Le Sueur in Paris. Returning to Antwerp, he practiced law until the siege of 1832; composed in his leisure hours. Going to Cologne, he lost his MSS and other possessions in a fire on the night of his arrival; this misfortune so affected him that he became insane. He wrote 4 operas, 2 cantatas, 2 syms., 5 masses; a number of motets, anthems, and hymns; songs.
Bibl.: Hendricks, *Simple histoire. Boutades biographiques à l'occasion du 25ᵉ anniversaire de la mort de J.-F.-J. J.* (Antwerp, 1860); E. van der Straeten, *J.-F.-J. J., Compositeur de musique* (Brussels, 1866; contains a list of his works).

Jaques-Dalcroze, Emile, Swiss music educator and composer, creator of "Eurhythmics"; b. Vienna (of French parents), July 6, 1865; d. Geneva, July 1, 1950. In 1873 his parents moved to Geneva; having completed his courses at the Univ. and at the Cons. there, he went to Vienna for further study under Fuchs and Bruckner; then to Paris, where he studied with Delibes and Fauré; he returned to Geneva as instructor of theory at the Cons. (1892). Since he laid special stress on rhythm, he insisted that all his pupils beat time with their hands, and this led him, step by step, to devise a series of movements affecting the entire body. Together with the French psychologist Edouard Claparide, he worked out a special terminology and reduced his practice to a regular system, which he called "Eurhythmics." When his application to have his method introduced as a regular course at the Cons. was refused, he resigned, and in 1910 established his own school at Hellerau, near Dresden. As a result of World War I, the school was closed in 1914; he then returned to Geneva and founded the Institut Jaques-Dalcroze. Interest in his system led to the opening of similar schools in London, Berlin, Vienna, Paris, N.Y., Chicago, and other cities. Aside from his rhythmical innovations, he also commanded respect as a composer of marked originality and fecundity of invention; many of his works show how thoroughly he was imbued with the spirit of Swiss folk music.
Writings: *Le Cœur chante: Impressions d'un musicien* (Geneva, 1900); *Méthode Jaques-Dalcroze* (Paris, 1906–17); *Le rhythme, la musique et l'education* (Paris, 1919; 2nd ed., 1965; Eng. tr., 1921; 2nd ed., 1967); *Souvenirs, notes et critiques* (Neuchâtel, 1942); *La Musique et nous: Notes de notre double vie* (Geneva, 1945).
Works: Operetta: *Riquet à la houppe* (1883). Opérascomiques: *Onkel Dazumal* (Cologne, 1905; as *Le Bonhomme Jadis*, Paris, 1906); *Les jumeaux de Bergame* (Brussels, 1908).

Comédie lyrique: *Sancho Pança* (Geneva, 1897). Various other dramatic works, as well as 2 violin concertos (1902, 1911), numerous orch. pieces, many choral works, chamber music, piano pieces, and songs.
Bibl.: P. Boepple, *Der Rhythmus als Erziehungsmittle für das Leben und die Kunst: Sechs Vorträge von E. J.-D. zur Begründung seiner Methode der rhythmischen Gymnastik* (Basel, 1907); W. Dohrn, *Die Bildungsanstalt E. J.-D.* (Dresden, 1912); M. Sadler, *The Eurhythmics of J.-D.* (London, 1912; 3rd ed., rev., 1920); K. Storck, *E. J.-D.: Seine Stellung und Aufgabe in unserer Zeit* (Stuttgart, 1912); H. Brunet-Lecomte, *J.-D., sa vie, son œuvre* (Geneva, 1950); F. Martin et al., *E. J.-D.: L'Homme, le compositeur, le créateur de la rhythmique* (Neuchâtel, 1965); M.-L. Bachmann, *Le Rhythmique J.-D.: Une éducation par la musique et pour la musique* (Neuchâtel, 1984); I. Spector, *Rhythm and Life: The Work of E. J.-D.* (Stuyvesant, N.Y., 1990).

Járdányi, Pál, Hungarian composer, ethnomusicologist, and music critic; b. Budapest, Jan. 30, 1920; d. there, July 27, 1966. He studied piano and violin as a child; in 1938, became a composition student of Kodály at the Budapest Academy of Music; concurrently studied at the Univ. of Budapest (Ph.D., 1943, with the diss. *A kidei magyarság világi zenéje*; The Secular Music of the Kide Magyars; pub. in Kolozsvar, 1943). He was active as a music critic (1943–49) and as a teacher at the Budapest Academy of Music (1946–59); then was a member of the folk music research commission of the Hungarian Academy. He was awarded the Erkel Prize in 1952 and in 1954 received the Kossuth Prize for his *Vörösmarty Symphony*. His works follow the style of modern Hungarian music, based on national folk songs. He publ. the vol. *Magyar népdaltípusok* (Budapest, 1961).
Works: Sinfonietta (1940); *Divertimento concertante* for Orch. (1942–49); *Dance Music* for Orch. (1950); *Tisza mentén* (Along the Tisza), symphonic poem (1951); *Vörösmarty Symphony* (1953); *Rhapsody from Borsod* for Orch. (1953); *Symphonic March* (1953); Harp Concerto (1959); *Vivente e moriente* for Orch. (1963); Concertino for Violin and String Orch. (1964); *Székely rapszódia* for Orch. (1965); violin duets (1934–37); Rondo for Piano (1939); Piano Sonata (1940); 2-piano Sonata (1942); 2 string quartets (1947, 1953–54); Flute Sonata (1952); *Fantasy and Variations on a Hungarian Folk Song* for Wind Quintet (1955); *Bulgarian Rhythm* for Piano Duet (1956); Quartet for 3 Violins and Cello (1958); String Trio (1959).

Jarecki, Henryk, Polish conductor and composer, father of **Tadeusz Jarecki**; b. Warsaw, Dec. 6, 1846; d. Lwow, Dec. 18, 1918. He studied composition with Moniuszko at the Warsaw Music Inst. After playing double bass in the orch. of the Wielki Theater there (1864–72), he served as conductor of the Polish Theater in Posen (1872–73); then was deputy conductor (1873–74) and chief conductor and director (1874–1900) of the Lemberg Opera. He wrote 9 operas, a Sym., masses, chamber music, and songs.

Jarecki, Tadeusz, Polish conductor and composer, son of **Henryk Jarecki**; b. Lemberg, Dec. 31, 1888; d. N.Y., April 29, 1955. He studied with his father, then with Niewiadomski in Lemberg; subsequently went to Moscow, where he studied with Taneyev at the Cons., graduating in 1913. During World War I he lived in N.Y.; then returned to Poland and conducted opera in Stanislawow (1932–37); after a sojourn in Paris and London, he returned to N.Y. in 1946, where he remained until his death. In 1921 he married the American soprano **Louise Llewellyn** (b. N.Y., Dec. 10, 1889; d. there, March 6, 1954). He publ. the book *The Most Polish of Polish Composers: Frédéric Chopin 1810–1849* (N.Y., 1949). Among his compositions are 5 syms., a symphonic suite, *Chimère* (1926), a *Sinfonia breve* (Lwow, Jan. 15, 1932), 3 string quartets, and numerous songs.

Jarnach, Philipp, German composer and pedagogue of Spanish descent; b. Noisy, France, July 26, 1892; d. Bornsen, near Bergedorf, Dec. 17, 1982. He was a son of a Catalonian sculptor and a Flemish mother. He studied with Risler (piano) and

Lavignac (theory) at the Paris Cons. (1912–14). At the outbreak of World War I he went to Zürich, where he met Busoni and taught at the Cons.; this meeting was a decisive influence on his musical development; he became an ardent disciple of Busoni, and after his death completed Busoni's last opera, *Doktor Faust*, which was produced in Jarnach's version in Dresden on May 21, 1925. During the years 1922–27 Jarnach wrote music criticism for Berlin's *Börsen-Kurier*. In 1931 he became a German citizen. From 1927 to 1949 he was prof. of composition at the Cologne Cons., and from 1949 to 1970 at the Hamburg Cons. Jarnach's music is determined by his devotion to Busoni's ideals; it is distinguished by impeccable craftsmanship, but it lacks individuality. He participated in the modern movement in Germany between the two world wars, and many of his works were performed at music festivals during that period. He wrote *Prolog zu einem Ritterspiel* for Orch. (1917); *Sinfonia brevis* (1923); *Musik mit Mozart* for Orch. (1935); String Quintet (1920); String Quartet (1924); *Musik zum Gedächtnis des Einsamen* for String Quartet (1952; also for Orch.); piano pieces; songs.

Bibl.: E. Klussmann, *Der Künstler P. J. und das Gesetz* (Hamburg, 1952).

Järnefelt, (Edvard) Armas, distinguished Finnish-born Swedish conductor and composer; b. Vyborg, Aug. 14, 1869; d. Stockholm, June 23, 1958. He studied with Wegelius and Busoni at the Helsinki Cons. (1887–90), with Becker in Berlin (1890), and with Massenet in Paris (1893–94); then was conductor of the Vyborg Municipal Orch. (1898–1903) and director of the Helsinki Music Inst. (1906–7). He became a conductor at the Royal Opera in Stockholm in 1907; was named court conductor in 1910, the same year he became a Swedish citizen; later was chief conductor of the Royal Opera (1923–32). He subsequently was chief conductor of the Finnish National Opera (1932–36) and the Helsinki Phil. Orch. (1942–43). He married the soprano **Maikki Pakarinen** (b. Joensuu, Aug. 26, 1871; d. Turku, July 4, 1929) in 1893; they were divorced in 1908; in 1910 he married the soprano **Liva Edström** (b. Vänersborg, March 18, 1876; d. Stockholm, June 24, 1971). Järnefelt was the brother-in-law of **Sibelius.** His compositions, which included the symphonic poem *Korsholma* (1894), a Symphonic Fantasy for Orch. (1895), and *Berceuse* for Small Orch. (1904), were written in the Finnish national style.

Jarno, Georg, Hungarian conductor and composer; b. Budapest, June 3, 1868; d. Breslau, May 20, 1920. He conducted opera in Breslau; produced his own operas there: *Die schwarze Kaschka* (May 12, 1895; his most successful opera), *Der Richter von Zalamea* (1899), and *Der Goldfisch* (1907); in Vienna he produced *Die Förster-Christel* (1907), *Das Musikantenmädel* (1910), and *Die Marine-Gustel* (1912), and in Berlin *Das Farmermädchen* (1913).

Jarnowick, Giovanni. See **Giornovichi, Giovanni Mare.**

Jarnowick, Pierre Louis Hus-Desforges. See **Hus-Desforges, Pierre Louis.**

Jaroch, Jiří, Czech composer; b. Smilkov, Sept. 23, 1920; d. Prague, Dec. 30, 1986. He studied composition with Řídký at the Prague Cons. (1940–46); was a manager and producer for Prague's Czech Radio (from 1947). As a composer, he took a median line in Central European music, within the pragmatic limits of modernistic permissiveness.

Works: *Scherzo* for Orch. (1947); *Burlesque* for Orch. (1951); *Symphonic Dance* (1953); *Smuteční fantasie* (Mourning Fantasy) for Orch. (1954); 4 syms.: No. 1 (1954–56), No. 2 (1958–60), No. 3, *Concertante,* for Violin and Orch. (1968–69), and No. 4 (1975); *Shakuntala,* suite for Orch. (1957); *Stařec a moře* (The Old Man and the Sea), symphonic poem based on the Hemingway novel (1961); *Summer Festival,* tarantella for Orch. (1964); *Fantasy* for Viola and Orch. (1966); 2 string quartets (1949–50; 1970); *Children's Suite* for Nonet (1952); Nonet No. 2 (1963); *Metamorphosis* for 12 Winds (1967–68); Sonata for Solo Violin (1973).

Jaroff, Sergei, Russian choral conductor; b. Moscow, March 20, 1896; d. Lakewood, N.J., Oct. 5, 1985. He studied at the Academy for Church Singing at the Imperial Synod; then became a Cossack officer. After the Revolution and the defeat of the White Army, he left Russia and established the Don Cossack Chorus, with which he made successful tours in Europe; eventually settled in America. The repertoire of his chorus included popular Russian songs in artful arrangements, emphasizing dynamic contrasts, and also sacred works by Russian composers.

Jarre, Maurice, French composer; b. Lyons, Sept. 13, 1924. He studied electrical engineering in Lyons, then attended courses in composition given by Honegger at the Paris Cons. He became best known as a film composer, winning an Academy Award for his emotional score to *Dr. Zhivago* (1965).

Works: *Mouvements en relief* for Orch.; *Polyphonies concertantes* for Piano, Trumpet, Percussion, and Orch.; *Passacaille,* in memory of Honegger (Strasbourg Festival, June 15, 1956); *Mobiles* for Violin and Orch. (Strasbourg Festival, June 20, 1961).

Jarreau, Al, black American singer of jazz and popular music; b. Milwaukee, March 12, 1940. He graduated with a psychology degree from the Univ. of Iowa, then went to San Francisco, where he worked as a rehabilitation counselor. He began singing in local clubs, quickly garnering a following with his flexible vocal technique and warm, sometimes even ecstatic performance style; he gained particular attention with his album *We Got By* (1975); he then toured Europe (1976), becoming one of the most popular jazz singers of the day. Other successful albums of this period include *Look to the Rainbow* (1977) and *All Fly Home* (1978). His audience changed substantially in the mid-1980s, when his songs and vocal style became less adventurous owing to an emphasized and often mundane disco beat. Albums dating from this later period include *High Crime* (1984) and *L Is for Lover* (1986).

Jarrett, Keith, versatile American pianist; b. Allentown, Pa., May 8, 1945. After studying at the Berklee School of Music in Boston, he plunged into the N.Y. jazz scene, coming to prominence as a member of the Charles Lloyd quartet (1966–70); he also worked with Miles Davis (1970–71) and toured with his own trio and as a solo artist. In 1975 he made a sensationally popular recording of solo improvisations, *The Köln Concert,* which established his reputation as a jazz virtuoso. From the early 1980s he made appearances as a Classical pianist, specializing in modern works and especially those of Béla Bartók; in 1987 he gave a particularly spirited performance in N.Y. of Lou Harrison's *Piano Concerto,* a performance he repeated in Tokyo which served as the basis for the critically acclaimed 1988 recording.

Bibl.: *Current Biography* (May 1985).

Järvi, Neeme, prominent Estonian conductor; b. Tallinn, June 7, 1937. He graduated with degrees in percussion and choral conducting from the Tallinn Music School, then studied conducting with Mravinsky and Rabinovich at the Leningrad Cons. (1955–60); he pursued postgraduate studies in 1968, and in 1971 captured 1st prize in the Accademia di Santa Cecilia conducting competition in Rome. He was active in Tallinn as music director of the Estonian State Sym. Orch. (1960–80) and of the Estonian Opera Theater (1964-77). He subsequently served as principal guest conductor of the City of Birmingham Sym. Orch. in England (1981–84). In 1982 he became music director of the Göteborg Sym. Orch. in Sweden; also was principal conductor of the Scottish National Orch. in Glasgow (1984-88). In 1990 he became music director of the Detroit Sym. Orch. His guest conducting engagements have taken him to most of the principal music centers of the world. He has won particular notice in concert settings and on recordings for his efforts in championing such rarely performed composers as Berwald, Gade, Svendsen, Stenhammar, and Tubin.

Jaubert, Maurice, French composer; b. Nice, Jan. 3, 1900; d. in battle in Azerailles, Meurthe-et-Moselle, June 19, 1940. He studied piano and composition at the Nice Cons., receiving 1st prize for piano in 1916; then studied harmony and counterpoint with Albert Groz in Paris (1923). He wrote the successful score for the film *Carnet de bal* (1937); other works included *Suite française* for Orch. (St. Louis, Nov. 10, 1933), a symphonic poem, *Jeanne d'Arc* (1937), and *Sonata a due* for Violin, Cello, and String Orch. (Boston, Dec. 27, 1946).

Jausions, Dom Paul, French writer on church music; b. Rennes, Nov. 15, 1834; d. Vincennes, Ind., Sept. 9, 1870. He entered the order of St. Benedict at Solesmes in 1856, and under the direction of Dom Guéranger began to study Gregorian chant; continued his investigations with Dom Pothier, whose *Mélodies grégoriennes* are the result of their joint labors. In 1869 he was sent to the U.S. to collect data for a biography of Bruté de Rémut, bishop of Vincennes (an uncle of Dom Guéranger). His interpretation of the Gregorian melodies according to the tonic accent has become one of the guiding principles in the publications of the Benedictines of Solesmes. A complete list of his writings is found in the *Bibliographie des Bénédictins de la congrégation de France* (1907).

Jean-Aubry, Georges, French writer on music; b. Le Havre, Aug. 13, 1882; d. Weldon, Northamptonshire, Nov. 14, 1949. He was a journalist; became interested in music; traveled in Europe and South America (1908–15); then lived in London, where he ed. the *Chesterian* (1919–30), house organ of the publishing firm J. & W. Chester; then returned to Paris. He publ. *La Musique française d'aujourd'hui* (1910; 2nd ed., 1916; in Eng., London, 1919) and *La Musique et les nations* (1922; in Eng., London, 1923).

Jeanneret, Albert, Swiss violinist, educator, and composer; b. La Chaux-de-Fonds, Feb. 7, 1886; d. Montreux, April 25, 1973. He studied violin with Andreas Moser at the Berlin Hochschule für Musik and with Henri Marteau at the Geneva Cons., graduating with the Premier Prix de Virtuosité (1909); then joined the staff of the Jaques-Dalcroze Inst. of Eurythmics in Hellerau, near Dresden. He went to Paris in 1919, where he founded a school of rhythmic gymnastics and a children's orch. In 1939 he returned to Switzerland and settled in Vevey, where he also led a children's orch. About the same time, he became a follower of the Moral Rearmament Movement. On July 21, 1968, he purportedly received (and subsequently publ.) a telepathic message from his brother, the architect Le Corbusier (Charles Édouard Jeanneret), who had died 3 years before, urging him to continue his pursuits of functional art. In accordance with these ideas, which he shared with his brother, Jeanneret wrote some 25 "symphonies enfantines" for children's orch., employing "bruits humanisés" produced by graduated bottles partially filled with water at different levels, metal pipes, wooden boxes, etc.; he also composed a *Suite pittoresque* for 3 Violins and a number of choruses for Moral Rearmament meetings.
Bibl.: P. Meylan, "A. J. et les 'bruits humanisés,'" *Revue Musicale de la Suisse Romande* (March 1971).

Jeannin, Dom Jules Cécilien, French musicologist; b. Marseilles, Feb. 6, 1866; d. Hautecombe, Feb. 15, 1933. He studied in Marseilles; later traveled extensively in Syria and Mesopotamia, gathering material for his collection *Mélodies liturgiques syriennes et chaldéennes* (Paris: Vol. I, 1925; Vol. II, 1928; III, not publ.); also publ. *Études sur le rythme grégorien* (Lyons, 1926), *Sur l'importance de la tierce dans l'accompagnement grégorien* (Paris, 1926), *Rythme grégorien: Réponse à Dom Mocquereau* (Lyons, 1927), *Accent bref ou accent long en chant grégorien?* (Paris, 1929), *Nuove osservazioni sulla ritmica gregoriana* (Turin, 1930), and *Rapport de l'accent latin et du rythme musical au moyen âge* (Paris, 1931).

Jedliczka, Ernst, Russian pianist and teacher; b. Poltava, June 5, 1855; d. Berlin, Aug. 3, 1904. He studied at the Moscow Cons. with Tchaikovsky and Nikolai Rubinstein; then taught

there (1881–88). In 1888 he settled in Berlin; was a prof. of the Klindworth Inst. (1888–97) and at the Stern Cons. (from 1897).

Jeep (Jepp), Johannes (Johann), German organist and composer; b. Dransfeld, near Göttingen, 1581 or 1582; d. Hanau, Nov. 19, 1644. In his youth he sang in the Celle Hofkapelle; then studied in Nuremberg and Altdorf, later traveling in France and Italy. He became Kapellmeister and organist of the court of the Count of Hohenlohe in Weikersheim (1613), deputy organist at the Frankfurt Cathedral (1635–36), and then municipal Kapellmeister of Frankfurt (1637–40). After working in Hanau schools, he served as Kapellmeister of the chapel of Count Ernst of Hanau-Münzenberg and organist of the St. Marien Church (1642–44). He was best known for his collection of 34 songs publ. in his *Studentengärtlein*; he also composed over 100 hymns and Psalm settings.
Works (all publ. in Nuremberg unless otherwise given): **SACRED:** [62] *Geistliche Psalmen und Kirchengesäng . . . D. Martini Lutheri und anderer frommen Christen, wie sie in christlichen Kirchen . . . zu singen gebräuchlich* for 4 Voices (1607; not extant; 2nd ed., 1609); [114] *Geistliche Psalmen und Kirchengesänge wie sie . . . auff alle Fest-, Sonn- und Feyertäge bevorab zu Weikersheimb . . . zu singen gebräuchlich* for 4 Voices (1629; 26th ed. in L. Schöberlein, *Schatz des Liturgischen Chor- und Gemeindegesang*, Göttingen, 1865–72); *Hymnus-hymenaeus, das ist Lieblich- und zierliches Hochzeit-Gesang . . . auss dem 2. Capitel dess Hohenlieds Salomonis . . . auff italiänische Madrigalen arth* for 5 Voices and Basso Continuo (Hanau, 1640); 6 lieder for 4 Voices publ. in L. Erhard's *Harmonisches Chor- und Figural Gesangbuch* (Frankfurt, 1659). **SECULAR:** *Studentengärtleins erster Theil* [17] *neuer . . . weltlicher Liedlein* for 3 to 5 Voices (1605; 7th ed., 1626); *Ander Theil* [17] . . . *Liedlein* for 4 and 5 Voices (1614; 3rd ed., 1622); both vols. ed. by R. Gerber in Das Erbe Deutscher Musik, 1st series, XXIX (1958); [24] *Schöne ausserlesene . . . Tricinia* (1610; 8th ed. in D. Kuchemann, *Zeitschrift für Spielmusik*, XLVI, Celle, 1936).
Bibl.: P. Bohm, *Christliche Leich-Predigt . . . dess . . . kunstreichen Herrn Johann Jeppen* (Hanua, 1645); G. Giesecke, "J. J., der 'Braunschweigische Orpheus,'" *Zeitschrift der Gesellschaft für Niedersächsische Kirchengeschichte*, XLI (1936); W. Jeep, *Die Familie J., 1540–1940* (Bremen, 1940); W. Brennecke, "Die Leichenpredigt auf Johann Jeep: Neues zur Biographie," *Archiv für Musikwissenschaft*, XV (1958); idem, "Das Hohenlohesche Gesangbuch von 1629 und J. J.," *Jahrbuch für Liturgik und Hymnologie*, IV (1958–59).

Jefferson, "Blind Lemon," black American blues singer and guitarist; b. near Wortham, Texas, July 1897; d. Chicago, Dec. ?, 1929. He was afflicted by poor eyesight from childhood; as a youth, he supported himself by singing in the streets of Texas towns and cities. He went to Dallas in 1917, where he formed a blues duo with Huddie Ledbetter; after touring the South, he settled in Chicago (1925). He made a series of historic blues recordings, many of which highlighted his own songs. His performances represented a Texas blues style akin to that of Leadbelly.
Bibl.: R. Groom, "The Legacy of B. L.," *Blues World*, nos. 18–40 (1968–71).

Jeffreys, George, English organist and composer; b. c.1610; d. Weldon, Northamptonshire, July 1, 1685. He was a member of the Chapel Royal; was made joint organist (with John Wilson) to King Charles I in Oxford (1643); from 1646, was steward to Sir Christopher (later Lord) Hatton at Kirkby, Northamptonshire. He composed both Latin and English sacred music, including about 70 Latin works and about 35 English anthems and devotional songs. He also wrote 6 string fantasias for 3 parts (1629); music for plays and masques (1631), dialogues, Italian songs, etc.
Bibl.: P. Aston, *G. J. and the English Baroque* (diss., Univ. of York, 1970; includes performing eds. of all of his instrumental pieces, theater music, and secular songs, as well as 30

sacred works); R. Thompson, "G. J. and the 'Stile Nuovo' in English Sacred Music: A New Date for his Autograph Score, British Library, Add. MS 10388," *Music & Letters* (Aug. 1989).

Jehan des Murs. See **Muris, Johannes de.**

Jehin-Prume (originally **Jehin**), **Frantz (François)**, celebrated Belgian-born Canadian violinist and composer; b. Spa, April 18, 1839; d. Montreal, May 29, 1899. As a child he studied with Servais and with his uncle, François Prume, whose name he added to his own; then took lessons with Bériot and Fétis at the Brussels Cons., winning 1st prizes in violin and theory; at the age of 16, after completing advanced studies with Vieuxtemps and Wieniawski, he undertook a European tour; appeared with Anton and Nikolai Rubinstein, Jenny Lind, and other celebrities; formed a famous trio with Kontski and Monsigny. In 1863 he traveled through Mexico, then in the U.S. and Canada (1865). He married the singer Rosita del Vecchio (1848–81) in 1866, and then divided his time between Europe and America; eventually settled in Montreal. His most famous pupil was Eugène Ysaÿe. He wrote 2 violin concertos and many effective pieces for solo violin. He also oversaw the publ. of his memoirs as *Une Vie d'artiste* (Montreal, 1899).

Jelich (Jeličić), Vincenz, Croatian composer; b. Fiume, 1596; d. Zabern, Alsace, c.1636. He was a choirboy in Graz (1606–9), where he studied music with Matthia Ferrabosco; then was at the Jesuit Univ. (1610–15). In 1618 he went to Zabern, where he took holy orders; then was active as vicar and then canon at Ste. Marie, as well as serving as a court musician. He publ. *Parnassia militia concertuum* for 1 to 4 Voices and Basso Continuo (organ) (Strasbourg, 1622), *Arion primus, sacrorum concertum* for 1, 2, and 4 Voices and Basso Continuo (organ) (Strasbourg, 1628), and *Arion secundus, psalmorum vespertinorum* for 4 Voices (Strasbourg, 1628); also a number of motets. **Bibl.:** H. Federhofer, "V. J.," *Archiv für Musikwissenschaft,* XII (1955).

Jelinek, Hanns, Austrian composer; b. Vienna, Dec. 5, 1901; d. there, Jan. 27, 1969. He studied harmony and counterpoint with Schoenberg (1918–19) and piano, harmony, and counterpoint with F. Schmidt (1920–22) at the Vienna Academy of Music. He made a living by playing piano in bars, leading his own band, and composing for films under the name Hanns Elin. He became a lecturer (1955) and a prof. (1965) at the Vienna Academy of Music. He publ. the manual *Anleitung zur Zwölftonkomposition* (2 vols., Vienna, 1952 and 1958; 2nd ed., 1967).

Works: Operetta, *Bubi Caligula* (1947; from this, the orch. pieces *Ballettmusik* and *Suite*). **orch.:** 6 syms.: No. 1 in D (1926–30; Breslau, June 13, 1932; rev., 1940 and 1945–46); No. 2, *Sinfonia ritmica,* for Jazz Band and Orch. (1929; Vienna, March 14, 1931; rev. 1949); No. 3, *Heitere Symphonie,* for Brass and Percussion (1930–31; Vienna Festival of the ISCM, June 20, 1932); No. 4, *Sinfonia concertante,* for String Quartet and Orch. (1931; rev. 1953; Vienna, May 2, 1958); No. 5, *Symphonie brevis* (1948–50; Vienna, Dec. 19, 1950); No. 6, *Sinfonia concertante* (Venice, Sept. 15, 1953; rev. 1957); *Praeludium, Passacaglia und Fuge* for Flute, Clarinet, Bassoon, Horn, and Strings (1922; Wuppertal, March 12, 1954); *Sonata ritmica* for Jazz Band and Orch. (1928; rev. 1960; Vienna, Nov. 26, 1960); *Rather Fast,* rondo for Jazz Band and Orch. (1929); Suite for String Orch. (1931); Concertino for String Quartet and String Orch. (1951); *Phantasie* for Clarinet, Piano, and Orch. (1951; Salzburg Festival of the ISCM, June 21, 1952); *Preludio solenne* for Orch. (1956); *Perergon* for Small Orch. (1957); *Rai buba,* étude for Piano and Orch. (1956–61). **vocal:** *Prometheus,* after Goethe, for Baritone and Orch. (1936); *Die Heimkehr,* radio cantata for Soloists, Chorus, Orch., and Tape (1954); *Unterwegs,* chamber cantata for Soprano, Vibraphone, and Double Bass (1957); *Begegnung,* dance scene for Chorus and Orch. (1965); songs. **chamber:** *6 Aphorismen* for 2 Clarinets and Bassoon (1923–30); Suite for Solo Cello (1930); 2 string quartets (1931, 1935); *Das Zwölftonwerk,* a

collection of 9 individually titled chamber pieces in 2 series: Series 1 of 6 works for Piano (1947–49) and Series 2 of 3 works for Various Instruments (1950–52); *3 Blue Sketches* for 9 Jazz Soloists (1956); Sonata for Solo Violin (1956); *Ollapotrida,* suite for Flute and Guitar (1957); *2 Blue O's* for 7 Jazz Performers (1959); *10 Zahme Xenien* for Violin and Piano (1960). **piano:** *4 Structuren* (1952); *Zwölftonfibel* (1953–54).

Jellinek, George, Hungarian-born American writer on music and broadcaster; b. Budapest, Dec. 22, 1919. He studied violin in Hungary (1925–37); in 1941 he went to the U.S.; was naturalized as an American citizen in 1943; served in the U.S. Army; was active in broadcasting; in 1968 was named music director of radio station WQXR in N.Y., where he produced such popular programs as "The Vocal Scene" and "Music at First Hearing." From 1958 he was a contributing ed. of *Stereo Review;* also wrote articles for the *Saturday Review, Opera News,* and other publications. In 1976 he became an adjunct assistant prof. of music at N.Y. Univ. He received an honorary doctorate from Long Island Univ. in 1984. He wrote librettos for Eugene Zador's operas *The Magic Chair* and *The Scarlett Mill.* His study of Maria Callas, *Portrait of a Prima Donna,* was publ. in 1960.

Jemnitz, Sándor (Alexander), Hungarian conductor, composer, and music critic; b. Budapest, Aug. 9, 1890; d. Balatonföldvár, Aug. 8, 1963. He studied with Koessler at the Budapest Royal Academy of Music (1906–8); then briefly with Nikisch (conducting), Reger (composition), Straube (organ), and Sitt (violin) at the Leipzig Cons. After conducting in various German opera houses (1911–13), he studied with Schoenberg in Berlin; returned to Budapest (1916) and was music critic of *Népszava* (1924–50); subsequently taught at the Budapest Cons. (from 1951). He publ. monographs on Mendelssohn (1958), Schumann (1958), Beethoven (1960), Chopin (1960), and Mozart (1961). As a composer, he followed the median line of Middle European modernism of the period between the 2 world wars, representing a curious compromise between the intricate contrapuntal idiom of Reger and the radical language of atonality modeled after Schoenberg's early works. He wrote mostly instrumental music.

Works: *Divertimento,* ballet (1921; Budapest, April 23, 1947); Concerto for Chamber Orch. (1931); *Prelude and Fugue* for Orch. (1933); *7 Miniatures* for Orch. (1948); *Overture for a Peace Festival* (1951); Concerto for String Orch. (1954); Fantasy for Orch. (1956); 3 violin sonatas (1921, 1923, 1925); Cello Sonata (1922); 3 solo violin sonatas (1922, 1932, 1938); Flute Trio (1924); 2 wind trios (1925); Trumpet Quartet (1925); 2 string trios (1925, 1929); Flute Sonata (1931); Partita for 2 Violins (1932); Guitar Trio (1932); Solo Cello Sonata (1933); Solo Harp Sonata (1933); *Duet Sonata* for Saxophone and Banjo (1934); Solo Double-bass Sonata (1935); Solo Trumpet Sonata (1938); Solo Flute Sonata (1941); Solo Viola Sonata (1941); String Quartet (1950); 2 suites for Violin and Piano (1952, 1953); Trio for Flute, Oboe, and Clarinet (1958); *3 Pieces* for Piano (1915); 2 piano sonatinas (1919); *17 Bagatelles* for Piano (1919); 5 piano sonatas (1914, 1927, 1929, 1933, 1954); *Recueil* for Piano (1938–45); Sonata for Pedal Organ (1941); *8 Pieces for Piano* (1951); 2 organ sonatas (1959); songs.

Jencks, Gardner, American pianist and composer; b. N.Y., Jan. 7, 1907. He studied piano with Heinrich Gebhard in Boston and with Josef and Rosina Lhévinne in N.Y.; later took courses at the Diller-Quaile School (1930–34); concurrently took private lessons in composition with Franklin Robinson, and then with Gustav Strube at the Peabody Cons. of Music (1934–40; artist's diploma, 1940). On Feb. 24, 1941, he made his debut in N.Y. as a pianist; while pursuing his career, he also studied composition with Goeb and Cowell at Columbia Univ. (1956). As a practicing musician, he set for himself a rigid regimen, with a minimum yearly output of 30 pieces, all of them for piano. His idiom of composition was derived from the considerations of relative sonorous masses in chordal structures and interactive rhythmic patterns; the general effect may be likened to neo-Classical concepts; indeed, most of his works bear formal designations, such as sonata; tonality and atonality are applied without prejudice in his melodic lines, as are concords and discords in contrapuntal combinations.

Jeney, Zoltán, Hungarian composer; b. Szolnok, March 4, 1943. He studied piano as a child; took courses in music theory with Zoltán Pongrácz at the Kodály Vocational Music School in Debrecen; then became a student of Farkas at the Budapest Academy of Music (1961–66) and of Goffredo Petrassi at Rome's Accademia di Santa Cecilia (1967–69). He subsequently founded the New Music Studio in Budapest (1970), which premiered many of his works. His music is constructivist, derived from the acoustical agglutination of kindred sounds.

WORKS: ORCH.: *Omaggio* for Soprano and Orch. (1966); *Alef—Hommage à Schoenberg* (1971–72); *Quemadmodum* for Strings (1975); *something round* for 25 String Players (1975); *Laude* (1967–77); *Sostenuto* (1979); *something like* for 25 String Players (1980). **CHAMBER ENSEMBLE:** *Coincidences: Movements of the Eye* No. 4 for 1 or 3 Chamber Ensembles (1973; also for 3 Pianos and 3 Chamber Ensembles, 1981); *for quartet* for 1 or More String Quartets (1973); *Orfeusz kertje* (Orpheus's Garden; 1974); 2 *Mushrooms: Amanita caesarea—Amenita muscaria* (1977); *Arupa* for 6 to 8 Chimes or Tuned Metal Percussion Instruments, Drum, and 1 Sustained Pitch (1981); *Cantos para todos,* 3 songs for Soprano and Chamber Ensemble (1983); *Spaziosa calma . . . ,* 3 songs for Female Voice and Chamber Ensemble (1984; rev. 1987); *Fantasia su una nota* for Optional Chamber Ensemble (1984). **CHAMBER:** *Öt dal* (5 Songs) for Soprano, Clarinet, Cello, and Harp (1963); *Az áramlás szobra* (Statue of Streaming) for Vocal Quintet (1965); *Aritmie—Ritmiche* for Flute, Viola, and Cello (1967); *Mandala* for 3 Electric Organs (1972); *A szem mozgásai II* (Movements of the Eye No. 2) for 2 Pianos (1973); *A szem mozgásai III* (Movements of the Eye No. 3) for 3 Pianos (1973); *Desert Plants* for 2 Prepared or Unprepared Pianos or 2 Pianos and Tape (1975); *a leaf falls—brackets to e.e. cummings* for Violin or Viola with Contact Microphone and Prepared Piano (1975); *Pontpoint,* sound ceremony for 6 Percussion Players (1978); *impho 102/6* for 6 Cymbales Antiques (1978); *OM* for 2 Electric Organs (1979); *Egy játszmavégződés* (The End of a Game)—*Epitaphium S. Altorjai* for 6 Instruments (1980); *Rondellus* for 6 Optional Instruments (1981); *Hérakleitosz-értelmezés* (Heraclitus-interpretation) for 5 or 6 Players (1984); *Hérakleitosz vizjele* (Heraclitus's Watermark) for 2 Players (1985); *El silencio* for Woman's Voice and String Quintet (1986); 8 Songs for Woman's Voice and Piano (1984–87); also choral works; works for solo instruments; electronic pieces of unspecified instrumentation; collaborative pieces; film music.

Jenkins, David, Welsh choral conductor, composer, and editor; b. Trecastell, Breconshire, Dec. 30, 1848; d. Aberystwyth, Dec. 10, 1915. He studied with Joseph Parry at Univ. College of Wales, Aberystwyth (1874–78); was awarded the Mus.B. externally by Cambridge Univ. (1878). He was made instructor (1882), lecturer (1899), and prof. (1910) at Univ. College of Wales; was ed. of the music periodical *Y Cerddor* (1889–1915). He was widely known as a choral conductor in Welsh communities in his homeland and in the U.S. He composed many choral works and hymn tunes.

Jenkins, Gordon, American pianist, composer, and arranger; b. Webster Groves, Mo., May 12, 1910; d. Malibu, Calif., April 24, 1984, of amyotrophic lateral sclerosis (Lou Gehrig's disease). He played "relief" organ at a Chicago movie theater, where his father was a regular organist; was a pianist at a St. Louis speakeasy during Prohibition; then was employed in various capacities at a St. Louis radio station. He was hired by Isham Jones as pianist and arranger in his band; in 1936 the band was taken over by Woody Herman, and Jenkins continued to arrange for him. He also wrote for Paul Whiteman, Benny Goodman, and André Kostelanetz. In 1938 he moved to California, where he took charge of the West Coast outlet of NBC. In 1945 he became conductor of Decca Records, and made records himself; his performing hits were *I Wanna Be*

Loved and *Bewitched;* the identifiable characteristic of his music was extreme sentimentality, with throbbing violins and sobbing female voices. In 1945 he composed the score for *Manhattan Tower,* and in 1949 wrote the Broadway musical *Along Fifth Avenue.* Among his hit songs were *P.S. I Love You* and *When a Woman Loves a Man.*

Jenkins, John, eminent English composer; b. Maidstone, 1592; d. Kimberley, Norfolk, Oct. 27, 1678. He most likely was the son of the carpenter Henry Jenkins, who at his death (1617) bequeathed his son a bandora. Jenkins was active as a music teacher and as a performer on the lute and lyra viol in various households. He spent the Commonwealth years at country estates; after the Restoration, he was made theorbo player in the King's Musick (1660), and during his last years, lived in the home of Sir Philip Wodehouse in Kimberley, Norfolk. Jenkins was the foremost master of consort music in his day. Among his more than 800 known instrumental pieces are fantasias, fantasia-suites, airs, and solo works; he also composed sacred and secular vocal music. See H. Sleeper, ed., *John Jenkins: Fancies and Ayres,* Wellesley Edition, I (1950); A. Dolmetsch, ed., *John Jenkins: 7 Fantasien,* Hortus Musicus, CXLIX (1957); R. Warner, ed., *John Jenkins: Three-part Fancy and Ayre Divisions,* Wellesley Edition, X (1966); A. Ashbee, ed., *John Jenkins: Consort Music of Four Parts,* Musica Britannica, XXVI (1969; 2nd ed., rev., 1975); R. Nicholson, ed., *John Jenkins: Consort Music in Five Parts* (London, 1971); R. Nicholson and A. Ashbee, eds., *John Jenkins: Consort Music in Six Parts* (London, 1976); D. Peart, ed., *John Jenkins: Consort Music of Six Parts,* Musica Britannica, XXXIX (1977).

BIBL.: H. Sleeper, "J. J. and the English Fantasia Suite," *Bulletin of the American Musicological Society,* IV (1940); R. Warner, *The Fantasia in the Work of J. J.* (diss., Univ. of Michigan, 1951); A. Ashbee, *The Four-part Instrumental Compositions of J. J.* (diss., Univ. of London, 1967); C. Coxon, "A Handlist of the Sources of J. J.' Vocal and Instrumental Music," *Royal Musical Association Research Chronicle,* IX (1971); A. Ashbee, "J. J., 1592–1678, and the Lyra Viol," *Musical Times,* CXIX (1978); idem, "J. J., 1592–1678: The Viol Consort Music in Four, Five and Six Parts," *Early Music,* VI (1978); P. Holman, "Suites by J. Rediscovered," ibid.

Jenkins, Leroy, black American jazz violinist and composer; b. Chicago, March 11, 1932. He was mainly autodidact in music, playing violin in a local Baptist church and picking up the rudiments of theory while teaching in a ghetto school in Chicago; then became affiliated with the Assoc. for the Advancement of Creative Musicians, and later studied on a scholarship with Bruce Hayden at Florida A. & M. Univ. He is best known for his atonal improvisations on violin and viola, in a bluesy, romantic style inspired by Charlie Parker. The groups he has led or co-led include the (Paris-based) Creative Construction Co., the Revolutionary Ensemble, the Leroy Jenkins Trio, the Leroy Jenkins Quintet, and Sting. Among his finest recordings, many of which include his own jazz compositions, are *Space Minds, New Worlds, Survival of America; The Legend of Al Glatson; Leroy Jenkins Solo Violin; For Players Only; Manhattan Cycles;* and *Urban Blues, Leroy Jenkins' Sting.*

BIBL.: L. Birnbaum, "L. J.," *Ear Magazine* (Nov. 1989).

Jenkins, Newell (Owen), American conductor and musicologist; b. New Haven, Conn., Feb. 8, 1915. He studied at the Orchesterschule der Sachsischen Staatskapelle in Dresden, and later in Freiburg at the Städtische Musikseminar; also took courses with Wilibald Gurlitt in Freiburg and with Carl Orff in Munich. Upon his return to the U.S., he worked with Leon Barzin at the National Orch. Assoc. in N.Y. Following army service in World War II, he received a Fulbright grant to study in Italy. In 1957 he founded the Clarion Music Soc. of N.Y.; with it he presented a stimulating series of annual concerts of rarely performed works of the Baroque period. He also appeared as a guest conductor in London, Hilversum, Milan, Naples, Turin, Florence, Stuttgart, and Stockholm. In 1975 he founded the Festival of Venetian Music of the 17th and 18th Centuries at Castelfranco Veneto. From 1964 to 1974 he taught at N.Y. Univ.; from 1971 to 1979 he was a lecturer at the Univ. of Calif. at Irvine. He ed. (with B. Churgin) *Thematic Catalogue of the Works of G.B. Sammartini* (1976); also ed. 9 syms. of Brunetti (1979).

Jenko, Davorin, Slovenian conductor and composer; b. Dvorje, Nov. 9, 1835; d. Ljubljana, Nov. 25, 1914. He studied in Ljubljana and Trieste; also studied law in Vienna, where he was conductor of the Slovene Choral Soc. (1858–62); then was conductor of the Serbian Church Choral Soc. in Pančevo (1863–65). He was conductor of the Belgrade Choral Soc. (1865–77); was also a conductor and composer of the National Theater there (1871–1902). He was a leading figure in the development of Serbian music; his *Vračara* (The Fortune Teller; Belgrade, May 3, 1882), was the 1st Serbian operetta; other works include 4 singspiels, incidental music to about 90 plays, orch. pieces, choral works, and songs. The melody of the royal Serbian national anthem was taken from one of his choruses.
    BIBL.: D. Cvetko, *D. J. i njeovo doba* (Belgrade, 1952); idem, *D. J.: doba, življenje, delo* (Ljubljana, 1955).

Jenks, Stephen, American composer and tunebook compiler; b. Glocester, R.I., March 17, 1772; d. Thompson, Ohio, June 5, 1856. He taught in New England and N.Y. State singing schools before settling in Ohio (1829), where he engaged in farming. A diligent advocate of American psalmody, he publ. 10 vols. of psalmody (1799–1818), which included 127 of his own works; was the leading composer of fuguing tunes of the 19th century.
    BIBL.: F. Metcalf, *American Writers and Compilers of Sacred Music* (N.Y., 1925); D. Steel, *S. J. (1772–1856): American Composer and Tunebook Compiler* (diss., Univ. of Michigan, 1982).

Jenner, Gustav, German composer; b. Keitum, Dec. 3, 1865; d. Marburg, Aug. 29, 1920. He studied with Mandyczewski, and also took some lessons with Brahms; in 1895, became music director at Marburg. He composed lieder, choral works, several violin sonatas, and a Trio for Piano, Clarinet, and Horn; publ. *Johannes Brahms als Mensch, Lehrer und Künstler* (1905; 2nd ed., 1930).
    BIBL.: W. Kohleick, *G. J.* (1943).

Jennings, Waylon (Arnold), American country-music singer, guitarist, and songwriter; b. Littlefield, Texas, June 15, 1937. Taking up the guitar in his youth, he dropped out of school at 14; then played bass in Buddy Holly's band (1958–59). He went to Nashville in 1965, where he turned out several albums and starred in the film *Nashville Rebel* (1966). Disdaining the "Nashville Sound," he became a leading figure in the promotion of "outlaw" country music, or "redneck rock," with his album *Ladies Love Outlaws* (1972). He subsequently won a wide following with such albums as *Lonesome, On'ry and Mean* (1973), *Honky Tonk Heroes* (1973), *This Time* (1974), *Waylon, the Ramblin' Man* (1974), *Dreamin' My Dreams* (1975), *Wanted: The Outlaws* (1976), and others.
    BIBL.: R. Serge Denisoff, *W.: A Biography* (Knoxville, Tenn., 1983); A. Cunniff, *W. J.* (N.Y., 1985).

Jensen, Adolf, German composer, brother of **Gustav Jensen;** b. Königsberg, Jan. 12, 1837; d. Baden-Baden, Jan. 23, 1879. He began his studies with E. Sobolewski, the Königsberg Kapellmeister; publ. a vol. of songs as his op.1 (1849; withdrawn and publ. as 6 songs, op.1, in 1859); continued his studies with Ehlert, Köhler, and F. Marpurg (1849–52). He went to Brest Litovsk as a music tutor (1856), then was a theater conductor in Posen, Bromberg, and Copenhagen (1857–58). He returned to Königsberg as assistant director of the Academy (1861); subsequently taught at Tausig's school in Berlin (1866–68). He ultimately settled in Baden-Baden, where he died of consumption. A great admirer of Schumann, he closely imitated him in his songs, of which about 160 were publ. He also wrote an opera, *Die Erbin von Montfort* (1864–65; rev. by Kienzl, to a new libretto by Jensen's daughter, as *Turandot*). P. Kuczynski ed. his letters (Berlin, 1879).

    BIBL.: A. Niggli, *A. J.* (Zürich, 1895); idem, *A. J.* (Berlin, 1900); G. Schweizer, *Das Liedschaffen A. J.s* (diss., Univ. of Giessen, 1932; publ. in Frankfurt, 1933).

Jensen, Gustav, German violinist and composer, brother of **Adolf Jensen;** b. Königsberg, Dec. 25, 1843; d. Cologne, Nov. 26, 1895. He studied with his brother; then with Dehn in Berlin (theory) and with Joachim (violin). In 1872 he became prof. of composition at the Cologne Cons., and held that position until his death. He wrote a Sym.; String Quartet; Violin Sonata; Cello Sonata; *Ländliche Serenade* for String Orch.; various violin pieces; publ. the series Klassische Violinmusik; tr. into German Cherubini's *Manual of Counterpoint.*

Jensen, Ludvig (Paul) Irgens. See **Irgens Jensen, Ludvig (Paul).**

Jensen, Niels Peter, Danish organist and composer; b. Copenhagen, July 23, 1802; d. there, Oct. 19, 1846. He was blind from childhood, but learned to play the flute and organ; was organist at St. Peter's Church in Copenhagen from 1828. He wrote 2 sonatas and other pieces for the flute.

Jensen, Thomas, admired Danish conductor; b. Copenhagen, Oct. 25, 1898; d. there, Nov. 13, 1963. He studied organ and cello at the Copenhagen Cons.; was a cellist in various Swedish and Danish orchs. (1917–27). After conducting studies in Paris and Dresden (1925–26), he went to Århus as conductor of the Phil. Soc. in 1927; founded that city's 1st permanent sym. orch. in 1935; also conducted the Tivoli summer concerts in Copenhagen (1936–48) and founded the Jutland Opera in Århus (1947); subsequently was conductor of the Danish Radio Sym. Orch. in Copenhagen (from 1957), with which he toured in Europe and the U.S. He was known especially as a champion of the music of Nielsen.

Jenson (Lockington), Dylana (Ruth), American violinist; b. Los Angeles, May 14, 1961. Her mother gave her early instruction in violin playing; also had lessons in childhood with Manuel Compinsky and, later, with Heifetz and Gingold. She made her formal debut as soloist in the Mendelssohn Concerto with Kostelanetz and the N.Y. Phil. at the age of 12; at 13 she made her European debut with Zürich's Tonhalle Orch. After further instruction in Milstein's master classes in Zürich (1973–76), she won 2nd prize in the Tchaikovsky Competition in Moscow; she played with the Philadelphia Orch., the Chicago Sym., the Cleveland Orch., the San Francisco Sym., the Minnesota Orch., and the Los Angeles Phil.; also toured in recital in Germany, the Soviet Union, and Latin America.

Jeppesen, Knud (Christian), eminent Danish musicologist and composer; b. Copenhagen, Aug. 15, 1892; d. Risskov, June 14, 1974. He began his career as an opera conductor, using the name Per Buch, in Elbing and Liegnitz (1912–14); then studied organ at the Royal Danish Cons. of Music (diploma, 1916) and musicology with Angul Hammerich at the Univ. of Copenhagen (M.A., 1918); he also received instruction from Carl Nielsen and Thomas Laub. He prepared his Ph.D. dissertation, *Die Dissonanzbehandlung bei Palestrina,* at the Univ. of Copenhagen; however, the retirement of Hammerich made it necessary for the dissertation to be approved by and completed under Guido Adler at the Univ. of Vienna (1922; publ., in an augmented ed., in Copenhagen in 1923 as *Palestrinastil med saerligt henblik paa dissonansbegandlingen*; Eng. tr. by M. Hamerik as *The Style of Palestrina and the Dissonance,* Copenhagen, 1927; 2nd ed., 1946). Jeppesen served as organist of Copenhagen's St. Stephen's (1917–32) and of the Holmens Church (1932–47); also taught theory at the Royal Danish Cons. of Music (1920–46). He became the 1st prof. of musicology at the Univ. of Århus (1946), where he founded its musicological inst. in 1950, retiring in 1957. He was ed. in chief of *Acta Musicologica* (1931–54) and president of the International Musicological Soc. (1949–52). Jeppesen was an authority on Palestrina and the music of the Italian Renaissance. As a composer, he demonstrates his erudition in his music: precise in its counterpoint, unfailingly lucid in its harmonic structure, and set in impeccable classical forms.

WRITINGS: *Kontrapunkt (vokalpolyfoni)* (Copenhagen, 1930; German tr., 1935; 5th ed., 1970; Eng. tr., 1939; 3rd Danish ed., 1962); *La frottola* (Copenhagen, 1968–70).

EDITIONS: With V. Brøndal, *Der Kopenhagener Chansonnier* (Copenhagen and Leipzig, 1927; 2nd ed., rev., 1965); *Vaerker af Mogens Pedersøn* (Copenhagen, 1933); with V. Brøndal, *Die mehrstimmige italienische Laude um 1500* (Copenhagen and Leipzig, 1935); *Die italienische Orgelmusik am Anfang des Cinquecento* (Copenhagen, 1943; 2nd ed., rev. and augmented, 1960); *La flora, arie & cantiche italiane* (Copenhagen, 1949); *Antichi balli veneziani per cembalo* (Copenhagen, 1962); *Italia sacra musica: Musiche corali italiane sconosciute della prima metà del cinquecento* (Copenhagen, 1962).

WORKS: *Rosaura, eller Kaerlighed besejrer alt*, opera (1946; Copenhagen, Sept. 20, 1950); *Sjaellandsfar*, sym. (1938–39); *Waldhorn Concerto* (1942); *Dronning Dagmar messe* (1945); *Te Deum danicum* for Soloists, 2 Choirs, Organ, and Orch. (1945); *Tvesang: Grundtvig-Kierkegaard* for Choir and Orch. (1965; Danish Radio, Copenhagen, Jan. 12, 1967); cantatas; motets; chamber music; songs; organ pieces.

BIBL.: B. Hjelmborg and S. Sørenson, eds., *Natalicia musicologica K. J. septuagenario collegis oblata* (Copenhagen, 1962).

Jepson, Helen, American soprano; b. Titusville, Pa., Nov. 28, 1904. Of a musical family, she sang in church choirs at 13 in Akron, Ohio, where she went to school; worked as a corset fitter and salesgirl; then was enabled to go to Philadelphia, where she studied with Queena Mario at the Curtis Inst. of Music (B.Mus., 1934); in 1936, went to Paris to study with Mary Garden. She sang with the Philadelphia Grand Opera (1928–30), then made her Metropolitan Opera debut in N.Y. as Helene in Seymour's *In the Pasha's Garden* on Jan. 24, 1935, remaining on its roster until 1943; also sang with the Chicago Opera (1935–42). Her roles of note included Eva in *Die Meistersinger von Nürnberg*, Marguerite in *Faust*, Desdemona in *Otello*, and Nedda in *Pagliacci*.

Jeremiáš, Bohuslav, Czech conductor, composer, and teacher, father of **Jaroslav** and **Otakar Jeremiáš;** b. Řestorky, Chrudim district, May 1, 1859; d. České Budějovice, Jan. 18, 1918. He studied with Skuherský at the Prague Organ School (1882–85), then was active as a conductor in Písek (1887–1906), where he promoted performances of works by Czech composers, including Smetana, Dvořák, Skuherský, and Foerster. He also organized a music school, and subsequently was founder-director of the Cons. in České Budějovice (1906–18). He composed a large output of sacred and secular music for choral forces; also wrote several vocal manuals.

Jeremiáš, Jaroslav, Czech pianist and composer, son of **Bohuslav** and brother of **Otakar Jeremiáš;** b. Písek, Aug. 14, 1889; d. České Budějovice, Jan. 16, 1919. He studied at his father's music school in Písek; then studied piano with A. Miks at the Prague Cons. and privately with Novák (1909–10). Although he died at the age of 29, he left several significant works: the opera *Starý král* (The Old King; 1911–12; Prague, April 13, 1919); the oratorio *Mistr Jan Hus* (1914–15; Prague, June 13, 1919); a Viola Sonata; songs.

BIBL.: B. Bělohlávek, *J. J.*(Prague, 1935).

Jeremiáš, Otakar, Czech conductor and composer, son of **Bohuslav** and brother of **Jaroslav Jeremiáš;** b. Písek, Oct. 17, 1892; d. Prague, March 5, 1962. He began his musical training with his parents; then studied composition at the Prague Cons. (1907) and privately with Novák (1909–10); also took cello lessons with Jan Burian. He was a cellist in the Czech Phil. (1911–13); took over his father's music school (1919). He then was conductor of the Prague Radio orch. (1929–45); subsequently was director of the Prague National Theater (1945–47); was also the 1st chairman of the Union of Czech Composers. He was made a National Artist (1950) and received the Order of the Republic (1960). His music continues the traditions of the Czech national school, with a pronounced affinity to the style of Smetana, Foerster, and Ostrčil.

WORKS: 2 operas: *Bratři Karamazovi* (The Brothers Karamazov, after Dostoyevsky, 1922–27; Prague, Oct. 8, 1928) and *Enšpígl* (Til Eulenspiegel, 1940–44; Prague, May 13, 1949); 2 cantatas: *Mohamedův zpěv* (1932) and *Písně o rodné zemi* (Song of the Native Land, 1940–41); *Písně jara* (Spring Song) for Orch. (1907–8); *Podzimní suita* (Autumn Suite) for Orch. (1907–8); 2 syms. (1910–11, 1914–15); *Jarní předehra* (Spring Overture, 1912); *Fantasie* for Orch. and 2 Mixed Choruses (1915; Prague Radio, Oct. 27, 1942); *Romance o Karlu IV*, melodrama with Orch. (1917); *Láska*, 5 songs with Orch. (1921); Piano Trio (1909–10); String Quartet (1910); Piano Quartet (1911); String Quintet (1911); *Fantasie na staročeské chorály* (Fantasy on Old Czech Chorales) for Nonet (1938); 2 piano sonatas (1909, 1913); songs; film music.

BIBL.: J. Plavec, *O. J.* (Prague, 1943); idem, *Národní umělec: O. J.* (National Artist: O. J.; Prague, 1964; includes list of works).

Jerger, Alfred, noted Austrian bass-baritone; b. Brünn, June 9, 1889; d. Vienna, Nov. 18, 1976. He studied at the Vienna Academy of Music, where his teachers included Fuchs, Grädener, and Gutheil; then became an operetta conductor at the Zürich Opera (1913). He began his vocal career in 1915, appearing as Lothario in *Mignon* at the Zürich Opera in 1917; then sang at the Bavarian State Opera in Munich (1919–21). He was a leading member of the Vienna State Opera (1921–53); also sang at the Salzburg Festivals, at London's Covent Garden, and other major music centers of Europe. In 1947 he joined the faculty of the Vienna Academy of Music; was also a producer at the Vienna Volksoper. He created the role of the Man in Schoenberg's *Die Glückliche Hand* (Vienna, Oct. 14, 1924) and the role of Mandryka in Strauss's *Arabella* (Dresden, July 1, 1933). His other outstanding Strauss roles included Baron Ochs, Orestes, John the Baptist, and Barak. He also was a fine Leporello, Don Giovanni, Pizzaro, Hans Sachs, Beckmesser, Grand Inquisitor, and King Philip.

Jeritza (real name, **Jedlitzková**), **Maria,** celebrated Moravian-born American soprano; b. Brünn, Oct. 6, 1887; d. Orange, N.J., July 10, 1982. She studied in Brünn and sang in the Stadttheater chorus there; after completing her training in Prague, she made her formal operatic debut as Elsa in *Lohengrin* in Olomouc (1910); then became a member of the Vienna Volksoper. In 1912 Emperor Franz Josef heard her sing in Bad Ischl, after which he decreed that she should be engaged at the Vienna Court Opera, where she made her 1st appearance as Oberleitner's Aphrodite. Strauss then chose her to create the title role in his opera *Ariadne auf Naxos* (Stuttgart, Oct. 25, 1912), and also in its revised version (Vienna, Oct. 4, 1916); she likewise created the role of the Empress in his *Die Frau ohne Schatten* (Vienna, Oct. 10, 1919). On Nov. 19, 1921, she made her U.S. debut at the Metropolitan Opera in N.Y. in the 1st U.S. production of Korngold's opera *Die tote Stadt*. Her compelling portrayals of Tosca and Turandot quickly secured her place as the prima donna assoluta there, and she remained on its roster until 1932. She made her debut at London's Covent Garden as Tosca on June 16, 1926. Throughout the years, she remained a leading singer in Vienna as well, continuing to appear there until 1935. In 1943 she became a naturalized U.S. citizen. She again sang in Vienna (1949–52); also appeared as Rosalinda in a Metropolitan Opera benefit performance of *Die Fledermaus* in N.Y. (Feb. 22, 1951). At the zenith of her career in the years between the 2 world wars, she won extraordinary acclaim in such roles as Sieglinde, Elisabeth, Santuzza, Fedora, Thais, Carmen, Salome, Octavian, Tosca, and Turandot. She led a colorful life, both on and off the operatic stage: she married 3 times, had many romantic affairs, and her spats with fellow artists became legendary. She publ. an autobiography, *Sunlight and Song* (N.Y., 1924).

BIBL.: E. Decsey, *M. J.* (Vienna, 1931); R. Werba, *M. J.: Primadonna des Verismo* (Vienna, 1981).

Jersild, Jørgen, Danish composer and teacher; b. Copenhagen, Sept. 17, 1913. He studied with Schierbeck in Copenhagen and then with Roussel in Paris (1936); subsequently studied musicology at the Univ. of Copenhagen (M.A., 1940). He taught music history and theory at the Copenhagen Cons. (from 1943). He publ. a book on solfege (Copenhagen, 1948; Eng. tr., N.Y., 1966). His works are written in an effective neo-Classical manner with an impressionistic flavor. He wrote mainly in small forms; among his works are *Pastorale* for Strings (1945); Serenade for Wind Instruments (1947); a group of *Quartetti piccoli* for String Quartet (1950); a ballet, *Lunefulde Lucinda* (1954); Harp Concerto (Aldeburgh, June 9, 1972).

Jerusalem, Siegfried, prominent German tenor; b. Oberhausen, April 17, 1940. He began his career as an orchestral bassoonist in 1961; was a member of the Stuttgart Radio Sym. Orch. (1972–77). He began vocal study in Stuttgart with Hertha Kalcher in 1972, appearing in minor roles at the Württemberg State Theater from 1975. He sang Lohengrin in Darmstadt and Aachen in 1976, and then at the Hamburg State Opera in 1977; that same year he made his debut at the Bayreuth Festival as Froh, returning in later seasons as Lohengrin, Walther, Parsifal, and Loge in the Solti-Hall mounting of the *Ring* cycle in 1983. After making his 1st appearance at the Berlin Deutsche Oper as Tamino in 1978, he became a leading member of the company. He made his U.S. debut with the Metropolitan Opera in N.Y. as Lohengrin on Jan. 10, 1980, his British debut at London's Coliseum as Parsifal on March 16, 1986, and his Covent Garden debut on March 18, 1986, singing Erik; he also appeared at the Vienna State Opera, Milan's La Scala, and the Paris Opéra.

Jesinghaus, Walter, Swiss violinist and composer; b. Genoa, July 13, 1902; d. Ticino, Sept. 17, 1966. He studied violin in Milan and Lugano; gave concerts as a child virtuoso. In 1918 he went to Zürich to study academic music subjects with Andreae and Jarnach; later at the Basel Cons. After working as a theater conductor in Germany (1921–25), he settled in Lugano. He wrote several operas (*Tartuffe, Sœur Béatrice, Belinda e il mostro, La luna e la città*); also a *Symphonia choralis* and much chamber music, including a number of pieces for viola d'amore.
BIBL.: D. Poli, *W. J.*(Bologna, 1929).

Jessel, Léon, German composer; b. Stettin, Jan. 22, 1871; d. Berlin, Jan. 4, 1942. He began his career as a theater conductor in Germany; then produced numerous operettas, some of which enjoyed considerable popular success, among them *Die beiden Husaren* (Berlin, 1913), *Schwarzwaldmädel* (1917), *Verliebte Frauen* (1920), *Die Postmeisterin* (1921), *Schwalbenhochzeit* (1921), *Des Königs Nachbarin* (1924), *Die Luxuskabine* (1929), *Junger Wein* (1933), and *Die goldene Mühle* (1940). His piano piece, *Die Parade der Zinnsoldaten* (1905), was a perennial favorite.

Ježek, Jaroslav, Czech composer; b. Prague, Sept. 25, 1906; d. N.Y., Jan. 1, 1942. He studied composition with Jirák and Josef Suk; also experimented with quarter-tone techniques under the direction of Alois Hába. In 1928 he became resident composer for the "Liberated Theater," a Prague satirical revue; produced the scenic music for 20 of its plays. In 1939, shortly before the occupation of Czechoslovakia by the Nazis, he emigrated to the U.S.
WORKS: ORCH.: Piano Concerto (Prague, June 23, 1927); *Nerves,* ballet (1928); Fantasy for Piano and Orch. (Prague, June 24, 1930); Concerto for Violin and Wind Orch. (Prague, Sept. 26, 1930); *Symphonic Poem* (Prague, March 25, 1936). **CHAMBER:** Wind Quartet (1929); Wind Quintet (1931); String Quartet No. 1 (1932); Violin Sonata (1933); Duo for 2 Violins (1934); String Quartet No. 2 (1941). **PIANO:** Suite for Quartertone Piano (1927); *Capriccio* (1932); *Bagatelles* (1933); *Rhapsody* (1938); *Toccata* (1939); Sonata (1941).

Jílek, František, Czech conductor; b. Brünn, May 22, 1913. He took courses with Balatka, Chalabala, and Kvapil at the

Brno Cons. and with Novák at the Prague Cons.; then was répétiteur and conductor at the Brno Opera (1936–39). After serving as assistant conductor at the Ostrava Opera (1939–48), he returned to Brno as conductor (1948–52) and chief conductor (1952–78) at the Opera; also taught at the Janáček Academy of Music there; was chief conductor of the Brno State Phil. (1978–83). He acquired a fine reputation through his championship of the music of his homeland, most notably of works by Smetana and Janáček.

Jiménez-Mabarak, Carlos, Mexican composer; b. Tacuba, Jan. 31, 1916. He studied piano with Jesús Castillo in Guatemala; attended classes in humanities in Santiago, Chile (1930–33); then studied musicology with Van den Borren in Brussels (1933–36); returned to Mexico in 1937 and studied conducting with Revueltas. He taught music theory at the National Cons. in Mexico City (1942–65) and at the Villahermosa School of Arts (1965–68). He drew his thematic materials from the folk songs of Mexico; he was one of the 1st to use electronic music and "musique concrète" in Mexico.
WORKS: Opera, *Misa de seis* (Mexico City, June 21, 1962); incidental music to *Calígula,* after Camus (1947); ballets: *Perifonema* (Mexico City, March 9, 1940); *El amor del agua* (Mexico City, 1950); *El Ratón Pérez* (1955); *El Paraíso de los Ahogados,* "música magnetofónica" (1960); *Pitágoras dijo . . .* for Small Ensemble (1966); several cantatas; Piano Concerto (1944); 2 syms. (1945, 1962); *Sinfonia Concertante* for Piano and Orch. (1966; Mexico City, March 11, 1977); *Concierto del abuelo* for Piano and String Quartet (1938); Concerto for Timpani, Bells, Xylophone, and Percussion (1961); *La ronda junto a la fuente* for Flute, Oboe, Violin, Viola, and Cello (1965); piano pieces; songs.

Jirák, K(arel) B(oleslav), distinguished Czech conductor and composer; b. Prague, Jan. 28, 1891; d. Chicago, Jan. 30, 1972. He studied privately with Novák (1909–11) and J.B. Foerster (1911–12). He was a répétiteur and conductor at the Hamburg Opera (1916–19); also conducted opera in Brno and Moravská Ostrava (1918–20). He then was conductor of Prague's Hlahol choir and 2nd conductor of the Czech Phil. (1920–21); was prof. of composition at the Prague Cons. (1920–30). From 1930 to 1945 he was music director of the Czech Radio. He was married to the mezzo-soprano **Marta Krásová** (1935–46). In 1947 he went to the U.S.; in 1948 became chairman of the theory dept. at Roosevelt College (later Univ.) in Chicago; held the same position also at Chicago Cons. College from 1967 to 1971. His music represents the finest traditions of Middle European 20th-century Romanticism. He publ. a textbook on musical form (Prague, 1922; 5th ed., 1946); also biographies of Fibich (Ostrava, 1947), Mozart (Ostrava, 1948), and Dvořák (N.Y., 1961).
WORKS: OPERA: *Žena a bůh* (The Woman and God; 1911–14; Brno, March 10, 1928). **ORCH.:** 6 syms.: No. 1 (1915–16); No. 2 (1924); No. 3 (1929–38; Prague, March 8, 1939); No. 4, *Episode from an Artist's Life* (1945; Prague, April 16, 1947); No. 5 (1949; Edinburgh Festival, Aug. 26, 1951; winner of the Edinburgh International Festival prize); No. 6 (1957–70; Prague, Feb. 17, 1972); *Overture to a Shakespearean Comedy* (1917–21; Prague, Feb. 24, 1927); Serenade for Strings (1939); *Symphonic Variations* (Prague, March 26, 1941); *Overture "The Youth"* (1940–41); Rhapsody for Violin and Orch. (1942); *Symphonietta* for Small Orch. (1943–44); Piano Concerto (1946; Prague, Dec. 12, 1968); *Symphonic Scherzo* for Band or Orch. (1950; orch. version, Chicago, April 25, 1953); Serenade for Small Orch. (1952; Santa Barbara, Calif., March 24, 1965); *Legend* for Small Orch. (1954; Chicago, March 20, 1962); Concertino for Violin and Chamber Orch. (1957; Chicago, May 18, 1963). **CHAMBER:** 7 string quartets (1915; 1927; 1937–40; 1949; 1951; 1957–58; 1960); String Sextet, with Alto Voice (1916–17); Cello Sonata (1918); Violin Sonata (1919); Viola Sonata (1925); Divertimento for String Trio (1925); Flute Sonata (1927); Wind Quintet (1928); *Variations, Scherzo and Finale,* nonet (1943); Serenade for Winds (1944); Piano Quintet (1945); *Mourning Music* for Viola and Organ (1946; also orches-

trated); Clarinet Sonata (1947); *Introduction and Rondo* for Horn and Piano (1951); *3 Pieces* for Cello and Piano (1952); Horn Sonata (1952); Oboe Sonata (1953); Trio for Oboe, Clarinet, and Bassoon (1956); Suite for Solo Violin (1964); Piano Trio (1966–67). VOCAL: Psalm 23 for Chorus and Orch. (1919); *Requiem* for Solo Quartet, Chorus, Organ, and Orch. (1952; Prague, Nov. 17, 1971); a cappella works for male chorus; song cycles (many with orch.): *Lyric Intermezzo* (1913); *Tragicomedy,* 5 songs (1913); *Fugitive Happiness,* 7 songs (1915–16); *13 Simple Songs* (1917); *3 Songs of the Homeland* (1919); *Evening and Soul* (1921); *Awakening* (1925); *The Rainbow* (1925–26); *The Year* (1941); *7 Songs of Loneliness* (1945–46); *Pilgrim's Songs* (1962–63); *The Spring* (1965). PIANO: *Summer Nights,* 4 pieces (1914); *Suite in Olden Style* (1920); *The Turning Point* (1923); 2 sonatas (1926, 1950); *Epigrams and Epitaphs* (1928–29); *4 Caprices in Polka Form* (1945); *5 Miniatures* (1954); *4 Pieces for the Right Hand* (1968–69). ORGAN: Suite (1958–64); Passacaglia and Fugue (1971); incidental music for plays.
BIBL.: M. Očadlík, *K.B. J.*(Prague, 1941); A. Tischler, *K.B. J.: A Catalog of his Works* (Detroit, 1975).

Jiránek, Josef, Bohemian violinist, pedagogue, and composer; b. Ledeč, March 24, 1855; d. Prague, Jan. 5, 1940. He studied music with Smetana, who legally adopted him; then took violin lessons with A. Hřímalý and harp lessons with Stanek; also became proficient as a pianist. He taught in Russia (1877–91) and at the Prague Cons. (1891–1923); publ. a number of useful piano manuals and composed *Scherzo fantastique* for Orch.; Piano Quintet; 2 piano sonatas; other pieces.

Jirásek, Ivo, Czech composer and conductor; b. Prague, July 16, 1920. He studied conducting with Dědeček and composition with Alois Hába, Řídký, M. Krejčí, and Šin at the Prague Cons. (1938–45); conducted opera in Opava (1946–55); then was engaged as a music ed. with the Copyright Union in Prague.
WORKS: 6 operas: *Pan Johanes* (Mr. Johanes, 1951–52; Opava, 1956); *Svítání nad vodami* (Daybreak over the Waters, 1960; Pilsen, 1963); *Medvěd* (The Bear, after Chekhov, 1964; Prague, 1965); *The Key* (1968); *And It Was Evening and It Was Morning* (on the theme of Bergman's film *The Seventh Seal,* 1971–72); *Mistr Jeroným* (1979–80); *Ciaconna* for Orch. (1944); *Concertant Symphony* for Violin and Orch. (1958); *Little Suite* for Orch. (1964); Variations for Orch. (Prague, April 15, 1965); *Festive Prelude* for Orch. (1971); Partita for Wind Orch. (Prague, June 2, 1973); Sym. for Baritone and Orch. (1973–74; Prague, March 16, 1974); *Mozartiana,* concertino for Chamber Orch. (1978); oratorio, *Stabat Mater,* for 4 Soloists, Children's and Mixed Choruses, Organ, Winds, and Percussion (1968; Prague, March 3, 1969); 3 cantatas: *Ballad from Hospital* (1944); *Love* (1960); *Zpěv o planetě Jménem země* (Song of the Planet Called Earth, 1976; Prague, April 2, 1977); *Riddles* for Children's Choir, Wind Quintet, and Percussion (1962); Violin Sonata (1946); *4 Studies* for String Quartet (1963–66); *Sonata da camera* for 13 Strings (1966); *Music for Soprano, Flute, and Harp* (1967); *Serenades* for Flute, Bass Clarinet, and Percussion (1967); *3 Pieces* for Flute, Violin, Viola, and Cello (1971); *Hudba k odpolední kávě* (Music for Afternoon Coffee) for 4 Clarinets (1972); Piano Sonata (1940); Suite for Piano (1943); choruses; songs.

Jirko, Ivan, Czech composer; b. Prague, Oct. 7, 1926; d. there, Aug. 20, 1978. He studied medicine at the Univ. of Prague (graduated, 1951), and also studied composition with K. Janeček (1944–49) and Bořkovec (1949–52) at the Prague Cons.; then pursued a dual career as a psychiatrist and a composer.
WORKS: 5 operas: *The Twelfth Night* (after Shakespeare, 1963–64; Liberec, Feb. 25, 1967); *The Strange Story of Arthur Rowe* (after Graham Greene's novel *Ministry of Fear,* 1967–68; Liberec, Oct. 25, 1969); *The Millionairess,* operatic divertimento (1969–72); *The Strumpet* (1970; Olomouc, June 23, 1974); *The Way Back* (1974); 4 piano concertos (1949, 1951, 1958, 1966); *Serenade* for Small Orch. (1951); Clarinet Concerto (1955); 3 syms.: No. 1 (1957); No. 2, *The Year 1945*

(1962, withdrawn); No. 3 (1977); *Macbeth,* symphonic fantasy (1962); *Elegy on the Death of a Friend* for Orch. (1965); *Divertimento* for Horn and Orch. (1965); *Symphonic Variations* (1966); *Serenata giocosa* for Chamber String Orch. (1967; alternate version for Violin and Guitar); Sonata for 14 Winds and Kettledrums (1967); *Capriccio all'antico* for Orch. (1971); *Prague Seconds,* symphonic sketches (1972); Trumpet Concerto (1972); Flute Concerto (1973); *Prague Annals,* symphonic triptych (1973); *At the Turning Point,* symphonic fantasy (1972–73; uses material from the 2nd sym.); *Double Concerto* for Violin, Piano, and Orch. (1976; Charleroi, Belgium, Nov. 18, 1976); *The Most Beautiful Land,* cantata (1950–51); *The Day,* cycle for Baritone and Orch. (1960–62); *Requiem* (1971); *Song of These Days,* 4 episodes for Baritone, Chorus, and Orch. (1973–74); *Štěstí* (Happiness), musical panorama for Narrator, Soprano, Baritone, and Orch. (1975–76); Wind Quintet (1947); 6 string quartets (1954, 1962, 1966, 1969, 1972, 1974); Cello Sonata (1954–55); Suite for Wind Quintet (1956); Violin Sonata (1959); *Kaleidoscope* for Violin and Piano (1965); *Serenata in due tempi* for Nonet or Oboe Quartet (1970); *Guiocchi per tre* for String Trio (1972); Partita for Solo Violin (1974); Piano Quintet (1977–78); 2 piano sonatas (1956; *Elégie disharmonique,* 1970); *Preludio, Canzone e Toccata* for Piano (1977).

Jírovec, Vojtěch Matyáš. See **Gyrowetz, Adalbert (Mathiás).**

Joachim, Amalie (née **Schneeweiss**), German soprano, later mezzo-soprano; b. Marburg, May 10, 1839; d. Berlin, Feb. 3, 1899. She began her career as a soprano, appearing in Vienna under the name Weiss (1854); later became a mezzo-soprano. She married **Joseph Joachim** in 1863, but after a bitter lawsuit, in which he accused her of infidelity with the publisher Fritz Simrock, they were divorced (1884). She was a fine lieder artist, excelling particularly in songs by Schumann.
BIBL.: O. Plaschke, *A. J.* (Berlin, 1899).

Joachim, Joseph, renowned Hungarian-born violinist, conductor, pedagogue, and composer; b. Kittsee, near Pressburg, June 28, 1831; d. Berlin, Aug. 15, 1907. His family moved to Pest in 1833 and he began to study violin with Szervaczinski in 1836, appearing with him in public at the age of 7. At the age of 10 he was sent to Vienna, where he studied with M. Hauser, G. Hellmesberger, Sr., and his major influence, J. Böhm. He went to Leipzig when he was 12 and was befriended by Mendelssohn; studied composition at the Cons. with Hauptmann and David. He 1st played in Leipzig on Aug. 19, 1843, in a concert with Pauline Viardot, Clara Schumann, and Mendelssohn, then appeared as soloist with Mendelssohn and the Gewandhaus Orch. (Nov. 16, 1843). In 1844 he made his London debut. His fame was assured with his remarkable performance of the Beethoven Violin Concerto at a Phil. Soc. concert there under Mendelssohn (May 27, 1844). During his years in Leipzig, he played in the Gewandhaus Orch., becoming its associate concertmaster under David. He was concertmaster of the Weimar Court Orch. (1850–53), but did not gain the favor of Liszt, who reigned supreme there. In 1853 he became Royal Music Director in Hannover, where he was active as both concertmaster and conductor. It was there that he met Brahms, who, with A. Dietrich and Schumann, wrote a Violin Sonata, F-A-E, on Joachim's motto, "Frei aber einsam" (Free but alone). His solitude ended in 1863 when he married the mezzo-soprano Amalie Weiss; they were divorced in 1884, following an acrimonious lawsuit brought by the overly jealous Joachim, charging him with infidelity with the publisher Fritz Simrock. A letter written by Brahms in support and defense of Mrs. Joachim was used in the trial, causing an estrangement between Joachim and Brahms, which was subsequently healed by the Double Concerto written by Brahms for Joachim, who gave its premiere (Cologne, Oct. 18, 1887). Joachim had previously assisted Brahms with the composition of the Violin Concerto, which they premiered (Leipzig, Jan. 1, 1879). In 1865 Joachim resigned from his Hannover duties in protest over anti-Jewish discrimination against J. Grün. He settled in Berlin in 1868 as director and prof. of violin at the Hochschule für

Ausübende Tonkunst, where aspiring violinists flocked from all over Europe to study with him; they included Auer, Hubay, and Huberman, who influenced subsequent generations of violinists in the Joachim tradition of excellence and faithful interpretation. From 1882 to 1887 he also was one of the principal conductors of the Berlin Phil. Joachim never abandoned his career as a virtuoso; he was particularly popular in England, which he visited annually from 1862; he received an honorary doctorate from Cambridge Univ. (1877), as well as from Oxford and Glasgow. He gave his farewell concert in Berlin on April 6, 1907.

Joachim's unswerving determination to interpret music in accordance with the intentions of the composer made him an outstanding exponent of the masterworks of the violin literature. Many composers, including Dvořák, Gade, Schumann, and Brahms, wrote large-scale concertos for him, consulting with him on the solo parts. As a player of chamber music, he was unexcelled in his day; in 1869 he organized the Joachim Quartet, which attained merited celebrity in Europe. His own compositions for the violin are virtuoso pieces that still attract performers; the most famous is the *Hungarian Concerto*. He also prepared cadenzas for violin concertos by Mozart (K. 218 and K. 219), Viotti (No. 22), Beethoven, and Brahms. With A. Moser, he publ. *Violinschule* (3 vols., Berlin, 1902–5; 2nd ed., rev., 1959 by M. Jacobsen).

WORKS: ORCH.: 5 overtures: *Hamlet*; *Demetrius*; *Henry IV*; overture inspired by 2 plays of Gozzi; "To the Memory of Kleist"; *Scena der Marfa* for Contralto. **VIOLIN AND ORCH.:** 3 concertos: No. 1 in G minor, op. 3, "in einem Satz" (c.1855); No. 2 in D minor, op. 11, "in ungarischer Weise" (1857; Hannover, March 24, 1860); No. 3 in G major (Hannover, Nov. 5, 1864; rev. 1889); *Andantino and Allegro scherzoso* (1850); *Notturno*; *Variations* in E minor (Berlin, Feb. 15, 1881). **VIOLIN AND PIANO:** *3 Stücke* (*Romanze, Fantasiestuck, Frühlingsfantasie*); *3 Stücke* (*Lindenrauschen, Abendglocken, Ballade*); *Romance*; *Hebrew Melodies*; also *Variations on an Original Theme* for Viola and Piano; 2 songs.

BIBL.: A. Moser, *J. J., Ein Lebensbild* (Berlin, 1898; 5th ed., rev., 1910; Eng. tr. from 2nd German ed., 1900); K. Storck, *J. J., Eine Studie* (Leipzig, 1902); J. Fuller Maitland, *J. J.* (London and N.Y., 1905); L. Brieger-Wasservogel, *J.-Gedenkbüchlein* (Dresden, 1907); H.J. Moser, "*J. J.,*" *Neujahrsblatt der Allgemeinen Musikgesellschaft in Zürich*, XCVI (1908); Johannes Joachim and A. Moser, eds., *Briefe von und an J. J.* (3 vols., Berlin, 1911–13; abridged Eng. tr., 1913); H. Kretzschmar, "*J. J.,*" *Archiv für Musikwissenschaft*, II (1920); A. Moser, *Geschichte des Violinspiels* (Berlin, 1923; 2nd ed., rev. and enl., 1966–67); S. Joachim-Chaigneau, "3 épisodes de la vie de J.," *Revue Musicale* (Jan. 1940); A. Holde, "Suppressed Passages in the Brahms-J. Correspondence, Published for the 1st Time," *Musical Quarterly* (July 1959); G. Maas, *The Instrumental Music of J. J.* (diss., Univ. of North Carolina, 1973); B. Schwarz, *Great Masters of the Violin* (N.Y., 1983).

Joachim, Otto, German-born Canadian composer, violinist, violist, and teacher; b. Düsseldorf, Oct. 13, 1910. He took violin lessons with his father, then later studied at the Buths-Neitzel Konservatorium in Düsseldorf (1916–28) and at the Rheinische Musik Schule in Cologne (1928–31). He fled Germany in 1934 and spent the succeeding 15 years in the Far East, mainly in Singapore and Shanghai; constructed electronic string instruments of the entire violin family (1944–45). In 1949 he emigrated to Canada, becoming a naturalized citizen in 1957. He was a member (1952–57) and later principal violist (1961–65) of the Montreal Sym. Orch.; also was a co-founder–member of the Montreal String Quartet (1957–58) and was associated with Glenn Gould. In 1956 he organized his own electronic music studio; was founder-director of the Montreal Consort of Ancient Instruments (1958–68). He taught at McGill Univ. (1956–64) and at the Cons. de Musique de Montréal et Québec (1956–76). His music is quaquaversal, but its favorite direction is asymptotic.

WORKS: *Asia*, symphonic poem (1928–39); *Music for Violin*

and *Viola* (1954); *L'Éclosion* for Piano (1954); Cello Sonata (1954); *Concertante No. 1* for Violin, String Orch., and Percussion (1955, rev. 1958; Paris, Sept. 9, 1958) and *No. 2* for String Quartet and String Orch. (1961; Montreal, March 12, 1962); String Quartet (1956); *12 12-Tone Pieces for Children* for Piano (1959); *Psalm* for Chorus (1960); *Interlude* for 4 Saxophones (1960); Nonet for Strings, Winds, and Piano (1960); Divertimento for Wind Quintet (1962); *Music for 4 Viols* (1962); *Illuminations I* and *II*—aleatory works of indeterminate duration, wherein performers are cued in by a light-triggering system operated by a "conductor": *I* for Live Narrator and 4 Instrumentalists (1965) and *II* for 10 Performers and 4-track Taped Reading of a Scientific Text (1969; Grand Prix Paul Gilson, 1969); *Contrastes* for Orch. (Montreal, May 6, 1967); *Katimavik* for Tape (1966–67); *Kinderspiel*, aleatory music for children, for Narrator, Violin, Cello, and Piano (1969; variable duration); *12 12-Tone Pieces for the Young* for Violin and Piano (1970); *5.9* for Tape (1971); *6 Pieces* for Guitar (1971); *Mankind*, multimedia work for 4 Synthesizers, Pianist, Timpanist, Slides, Burning Incense, and 4 Readers who are to be ordained clerics of 4 major world religions (1972); *Stimulus à goad* for Guitar, Synthesizer, and Electronic Peripherals (1973); *Night Music* for Flute, Bass Flute, and Guitar (1978); *Tribute to St. Romanus* for Organ, 4 Horns, and 4 Percussion (1980–81); *Mobile für Johann Sebastian Bach* for Oboe, Clarinet, Bassoon, String Quartet, Celesta, Organ, Tape, and Vocoder (1985).

João IV, King of Portugal; b. Villa-Vicosa, March 19, 1604; d. Lisbon, Nov. 6, 1656. As a prince he received a fine musical training at the court chapel. He began collecting church music, gradually accumulating a magnificent library, which was totally destroyed in the earthquake of 1755. However, a catalog of it was issued in Lisbon in 1649, and reprinted by Vasconcellos in 1873. João IV was a true music scholar, well acquainted with the flow of conflicting opinions regarding musical theory. He publ. (anonymously) the pamphlets *Defensa de la musica moderna contra la errada opinion del obispo Cyrillo Franco* (in Spanish; 1649) and *Respuesta a las dudas que se pusieron a la missa "Panis quem ego dabo" de Palestrina* (1654); Italian trs. were made of both. He composed a considerable quantity of church music; his motets *Crux fidelis* and *Adjuva nos* are reprinted in S. Lück's *Sammlung ausgezeichneter Kompositionen für die Kirche* (1884–85).

BIBL.: J. Freitas Branco, *D. J. IV, Músico* (Lisbon, 1956).

Jobert, Jean, French music publisher; b. Lyons, Oct. 11, 1883; d. Paris, Nov. 27, 1957. He was an employee of the publishing firm of Fromont in Paris; he purchased the business in 1922, including the valuable catalog of Debussy's early works (*L'Après-midi d'un faune, Clair de lune*, etc.). In 1945 he was elected president of the Syndicated Soc. of Music Publishers in France.

Jochum, Eugen, eminent German conductor, brother of **Georg Ludwig** and **Otto,** and father of **(Maria) Veronica Jochum;** b. Babenhausen, Bavaria, Nov. 1, 1902; d. Munich, March 26, 1987. He began playing the piano at 4 and the organ at 7; after attending the Augsburg Cons. (1914–22), he studied composition with Waltershausen and conducting with Hausegger at the Munich Academy of Music (1922–25). He commenced his career as a répétiteur at the Bavarian State Opera in Munich and in Mönchengladbach; appeared as a guest conductor with the Munich Phil. in 1926; then was a conductor at the Kiel Opera (1926–29) and conducted the Lübeck sym. concerts. After conducting at the Mannheim National Theater (1929–30), he served as Generalmusikdirektor in Duisburg (1930–32); then was music director of the Berlin Radio and a frequent guest conductor with the Berlin Phil. From 1934 to 1945 he was Generalmusikdirektor of the Hamburg State Opera. Although his tenure coincided with the Nazi era, Jochum successfully preserved his artistic independence; he avoided joining the Nazi party, assisted a number of his Jewish players, and programmed several works by officially unapproved composers. From 1934 to 1949 he also was Generalmusikdirektor of the Hamburg State Phil. In 1949 he was appointed chief conductor of the Bavarian Radio Sym. Orch. in Munich, a position he held with great distinction until 1960. He also appeared as a guest conductor throughout Europe. In 1953 he made his 1st appearance at the Bayreuth Festival, conducting *Tristan und Isolde*. He made his U.S. debut as a guest conductor with the Los Angeles Phil. in 1958. From 1961 to 1964 he was co–principal conductor of the Concertgebouw Orch. of Amsterdam, sharing his duties with Bernard Haitink. From 1969 to 1973 he was artistic director of the Bamberg Sym. Orch.; he also served as laureate conductor of the London Sym. Orch. (1977–79). His many honors included the Brahms Medal (1936), the Bruckner Medal (1954), the Bülow Medal of the Berlin Phil. (1978), and the Bruckner Ring of the Vienna Sym. Orch. (1980); he was also made an honorary prof. by the senate of the city of Hamburg (1949). Jochum became known as an outstanding interpreter of the music of Bruckner; he also gained renown for his performances of Bach, Haydn, Mozart, Beethoven, Schubert, Brahms, and Richard Strauss.

BIBL.: A. Orga, "E. J. (1902–87)," *Music and Musicians International* (Aug. 1987).

Jochum, Georg Ludwig, German conductor, brother of **Eugen** and **Otto Jochum;** b. Babenhausen, Dec. 10, 1909; d. Mülheim an der Ruhr, Nov. 1, 1970. He studied at the Augsburg Cons. and then with Haas and Hausegger at the Munich Academy of Music. He was music director in Münster (1932–34); then was a conductor at the Frankfurt Opera and Museumgesellschaft concerts (1934–37); subsequently was Generalmusikdirektor in Linz (1940–45) and Duisburg (1946–58); was also director of the Duisburg Cons. (1946–58). He appeared as a guest conductor in Europe, South America, and Japan.

Jochum, Otto, German composer, brother of **Eugen** and **Georg Ludwig Jochum;** b. Babenhausen, March 18, 1898; d. Bad Reichenhall, Oct. 24, 1969. He studied at the Augsburg Cons. and at the Munich Academy of Music with Heinrich Kasper Schmid, Gustav Geierhaas, and Joseph Haas (1922–31). From 1932 to 1951 he served as director of the Augsburg Municipal Singing School.

WORKS: *Goethe-Sinfonie* (1941); *Florianer-Sinfonie* (1946); 2 oratorios: *Der jüngste Tag* and *Ein Weihnachtssingen*; 12 masses; many choral works; arrangements of folk songs; songs.

Jochum, (Maria) Veronica, gifted German pianist, daughter of **Eugen Jochum;** b. Berlin, Dec. 6, 1932. She studied piano with Eliza Hansen and then with Maria Landes-Hindemith at the Munich Staatliche Hochschule für Musik (M.A., 1955; concert diploma, 1957); after additional studies with Edwin Fischer in Lucerne (1958–59), she completed her training with Rudolf Serkin in Philadelphia (1959–61). She commenced her career in Germany in 1954; made tours of Europe from 1961. Following her successful N.Y. debut as soloist in Beethoven's 1st Piano Concerto with Gerard Schwarz and the Y Chamber Sym. (March 21, 1981), she made appearances throughout the U.S. She maintained an intriguing repertoire, ranging from Mozart and Beethoven to Bartók and Schoenberg; she also championed lesser-known scores by such diverse composers as Clara Schumann and Ernst Krenek; likewise performed new works, including the premiere of Gunther Schuller's 2nd Piano Concerto (1982).

Jodál, Gábor, Rumanian composer of Hungarian parentage; b. Odorhei, April 25, 1913. He received a doctorate in jurisprudence at the Univ. of Cluj (1937), then studied composition with Kodály, Kósa, and J. Adám at the Budapest Academy of Music (1939–42). He was a répétiteur at the Cluj National Theater (1942–44); then was a lecturer at the Hungarian Inst. of Art (1948–50) and a lecturer (from 1950) and director (1965–73) of the Cons. As a composer, he continues an amiable but rhythmically incisive tradition of the ethnically variegated music of Transylvania.

WORKS: Sinfonietta (1957); *Divertimento* for Orch. (1964); *Nocturne* for Chamber Orch. (1976); *Scherzo* for Chamber

Orch. (1978); *Sinfonia brevis* (1981); ballet: *Meseorszag kapujaban* (At the Gate of the Land of Story; 1952); 2 cantatas: *Revoluţia* (1964) and *Treptele implinirii* (1977); 2 violin sonatas (1946, 1953); *3 Pieces* for Viola and Piano (1946); Suite for Flute and Piano (1955); String Quartet (1955); *3 Pieces* for Wind Quintet (1959); *Introduction and Scherzo* for Bassoon and Piano (1964); Suite for Wind Quintet (1966); *3 Nocturnes* for Flute, Clarinet, Viola, Cello, and Piano (1967); Viola Sonata (1974); Piano Sonata (1977); choruses; songs.

Jöde, (Wilhelm August Ferdinand) Fritz, prominent German music educator; b. Hamburg, Aug. 2, 1887; d. there, Oct. 19, 1970. He began his career as a provincial school teacher; after service in the German army during World War I, he studied musicology with Abert at the Univ. of Leipzig (1920–21). In 1923 he was made prof. of choral conducting and folk music education at Berlin's Staatliche Akademie für Kirchen- und Schulmusik. He organized societies for the propagation of folk music, and was very active in various youth movements in Germany until the Nazis removed him from his positions in 1935. He joined the faculty of the Salzburg Mozarteum in 1939, but was compelled to give up that position as well in 1943. After the fall of the 3rd Reich, he resumed his various activities; was made director of the youth music program of Hamburg's Hochschule für Musik (1947) and also director of the Internationales Institut für Jugend- und Volksmusik. He ed. several periodicals and many song collections.

WRITINGS: Ed. *Musikalische Jugendkultur* (Hamburg, 1918); *Musik und Erziehung* (Wolfenbüttel, 1919); *Pädagogik deines Wesens* (Hamburg, 1920); *Musikmanifest* (Rudolstadt, 1921); *Die Lebensfragen der neuen Schule* (Hamburg, 1921); *Unser Musikleben* (Wolfenbüttel, 1923; 2nd ed., 1925); *Musikschulen für Jugend und Volk* (Wolfenbüttel, 1924; 2nd ed., 1928); *Das schaffende Kind in der Musik* (Wolfenbüttel, 1928; 2nd ed., 1962); ed. *Musik in der Volksschule* (Berlin, 1928); *Kind und Musik* (Berlin, 1930; reprint, 1966); *Vom Wesen und Werden der Jugendmusik* (Mainz, 1954); *Die Herzberger Bachwochen* (Trossingen and Wolfenbüttel, 1959).

BIBL.: R. Stapelberg, *F. J.: Leben und Werk* (Trossingen and Wolfenbüttel, 1957); G. Trautner, *Die Musikerziehung bei F. J.: Quellen und Grundlagen* (Wolfenbüttel, 1968).

Joel, Billy (William Martin), top-seeded American pianist, singer, and songwriter of popular music; b. N.Y., May 9, 1949. Prematurely sophisticated, he joined the rock band The Echoes, which was later metamorphosed into a more belligerent group called The Hassles. When The Hassles disintegrated after internecine hassles, Joel teamed up with drummer Jon Small to form a duo named Attila after the murderous King of the Huns popularly known in Western Europe as "the scourge of God." They recorded an album, which did not sell. Joel then organized a band of his own and recorded his 1st original ballad, *Cold Spring Harbor* (1972), for the label Family Productions. It did not sell either, and after a family feud with Family Productions, Joel went over to Columbia Records, moved to Los Angeles, and thereafter marched on the gold-paved road to neon-lighted success. He composed a ballad called, autobiographically, *Piano Man* (1973), which made a hit. He soon progressed on the periodic table of elements from gold to platinum, and received a certified platinum award for his song *Just the Way You Are* from the album *The Stranger* in 1978. Other smash albums followed, including *52nd Street*, which captured a Grammy Award for best album of 1979 and also made him the Grammy Award male pop vocalist of the year. Other hit singles are numerous, including *My Life, Big Shot*, and *Honesty*; also *Say Goodbye to Hollywood* and *You May Be Right*. He signified his gratitude to his generating force in the top hit *It's Still Rock 'n' Roll to Me*. By 1984 he could demand, and get, million-dollar advances from royalty distributors. In the 1980s he was prolific; particularly notable albums of this decade include *The Nylon Curtain, An Innocent Man, The Bridge*, and *Kohupt*, a 2-record set of live concerts in Moscow and Leningrad in 1987.

Johannes Chrysorrhoas (John of Damascus), Christian saint; b. Damascus, c.700; d. at the monastery of St. Sabas, near Jerusalem, 754. He was canonized by both the Greek and Roman Church; was the earliest dogmatist of the Greek Church; wrote many examples of the *kanon,* a special type of Byzantine hymn that usually used a pre-existent melody. John is credited, by what may be a legend, with having arranged the Byzantine Oktoechos and having improved Byzantine notation.

Johannesen, Grant, eminent American pianist and pedagogue; b. Salt Lake City, July 30, 1921. He studied piano with Robert Casadesus at Princeton Univ. (1941–46) and with Egon Petri at Cornell Univ.; also took courses in composition with Roger Sessions and Nadia Boulanger. He made his concert debut in N.Y. in 1944. In 1949 he won 1st prize at the Ostend Concours Internationale, which was the beginning of his international career. He toured Europe with Mitropoulos and the N.Y. Phil. in 1956 and 1957; made another European tour with Szell and the Cleveland Orch. in 1968. From 1960 to 1966 he taught at the Aspen Music School; in 1973 he became music consultant and adviser of the Cleveland Inst. of Music; subsequently was its music director (1974–77), and finally its president (1977–85). He also taught at the Mannes College of Music in N.Y. and at the Salzburg Mozarteum. Johannesen acquired a reputation as a pianist of fine musicianly stature, subordinating his virtuoso technique to the higher considerations of intellectual fidelity to the composer's intentions; he was particularly esteemed for his performances of French and American music. He also composed some piano works. He was married to the Canadian cellist **Zara Nelsova** from 1963 to 1973.
BIBL.: L. Marum, "G. J. Champions the French," *Ovation* (July 1989).

Jóhannsson, Magnús Blöndal, Icelandic conductor and composer; b. Skálar, Sept. 8, 1925. He was taken to Reykjavík as an infant, and showed a precocious musical talent; at the age of 10, he was admitted to the Reykjavík School of Music, where he studied under F. Mixa and V. Urbantschitsch (1935–37 and 1939–45); then was sent to the U.S., where he took courses at the Juilliard School of Music in N.Y. (1947–53). He returned to Iceland in 1954 and became a staff member of the Iceland State Broadcasting Service (1956–76); was also a conductor at the National Theater in Reykjavík (1965–72). As a composer, he was attracted to the novel resources of electronic music; his *Study* for Magnetic Tape and Wind Quintet (1957) was the 1st Icelandic work employing electronic sound. His other works include *4 Abstractions* for Piano (1955); *Ionization* for Organ (1956); *Samstirni* for Tape (1960); *Punktar* (Points) for Tape and Small Orch. (1961); *15 Minigrams* for Flute, Oboe, Clarinet, and Double Bass (1961); *Dimensions* for Violin (1961); *Sonorities I–III* for Piano (1961–68); *Birth of an Island,* tape music for the film depicting the volcanic creation of an island near Iceland (1964); *Sequence,* ballet for Dancers, Instruments, and Lights (1968); *The Other Iceland,* music from the film (1973); *Adagio* for Percussion, Celesta, and Strings (1980); *Solitude* for Flute (1983).

Johanos, Donald, American conductor; b. Cedar Rapids, Iowa, Feb. 10, 1928. He studied violin and conducting at the Eastman School of Music in Rochester, N.Y. (Mus.B., 1950; Mus.M., 1952); received grants from the American Sym. Orch. League and the Rockefeller Foundation for conducting studies with Ormandy, Szell, Beecham, Beinum, Karajan, and Klemperer (1955–58). In 1957 he became associate conductor of the Dallas Sym. Orch., and then its resident conductor in 1961, and subsequently its music director in 1962, achieving estimable results. He was associate conductor of the Pittsburgh Sym. Orch. and director of its chamber orch. (1970–80); was music director of the Honolulu Sym. Orch. (from 1979) and artistic director of the Hawaii Opera Theatre (1979–83).

Johansen, David Monrad, Norwegian pianist, music critic, and composer, father of **(David) Johan Kvandal (Johansen);**
b. Vefsn, Nov. 8, 1888; d. Sandvika, Feb. 20, 1974. He studied piano with Winge and Johnson (1904–9); then theory with Elling and Holter, as well as piano with Nissen at the Christiania Cons. (1909–15); in 1915 he went to Berlin, where he took lessons with Humperdinck and Kahn; by this time in middle age, he continued his studies in composition in Paris (1927) and in Leipzig (1933, 1935), where he took a special course in counterpoint with Grabner. In the meantime he pursued an active career as a concert pianist and composer; made his debut in Christiania in 1910; was ed. of *Norsk musikerblad* (1917–18); was music critic of *Norske intelligenss edler* (1916–18) and of *Aftenposten* (1925–45). He wrote a monograph on Grieg (Oslo, 1934; 3rd ed., 1956; Eng. tr., 1938). His music continued the national Norwegian tradition, in the lyric manner of Grieg; as time went by, Johansen experienced a mild influence of Russian and French music, gradually forming an innocuous modern style with sporadic audacious incursions into the domain of sharp dissonance.
WORKS: *Symphonic Fantasy* (1936); symphonic poem, *Pan* (1939); Piano Concerto (1955); Violin Sonata (1912); Piano Quartet (1947); Quintet for Flute and String Quartet (1967); String Quartet (1969); oratorio, *Voluspa* (1926); *Sigvat Skald* for Baritone and Orch. (1928); several choruses and a group of songs; piano pieces.
BIBL.: O. Sandvik and O. Gaukstad, *D.M. J. i skrift og tate* (Oslo, 1968).

Johansen, Gunnar, remarkable Danish-American pianist, composer, and teacher; b. Copenhagen, Jan. 21, 1906; d. Blue Mounds, Wis., May 25, 1991. He made his public debut at the age of 12 in Copenhagen, where he studied with V. Schiøler; then went to Berlin when he was 14, becoming a member of the Busoni circle; after further piano studies with F. Lamond and E. Fischer, he completed his training with E. Petri at the Hochschule für Musik (1922–24). He toured Europe (1924–29) and then settled in the U.S., where he pursued an active concert career, gaining particular distinction for his series of 12 historical piano recitals encompassing works from Frescobaldi to Stravinsky, which he presented in San Francisco, Chicago, and N.Y. in the late 1930s; he held the specially created position of artist-in-residence at the Univ. of Wisconsin at Madison (1939–76). He produced a sensation when he substituted on short notice for a colleague as soloist in the piano version of Beethoven's Violin Concerto with Ormandy and the Philadelphia Orch. in N.Y. (Jan. 14, 1969). He excelled in works of transcendental difficulty; he played and recorded the complete solo piano works of Liszt and Busoni, including the latter's Bach transcriptions, as well as the complete solo clavier works of Bach. He was a composer of fantastic fecundity; among his compositions are 3 piano concertos (1930, 1970, 1981), 31 piano sonatas (1941–51), and 515 piano sonatas improvised directly on the keyboard and recorded on tape (1952–82).
BIBL.: A. Corleonis, "A Birthday Greeting to G. J. on His 80th," *Fanfare* (Feb. 1986).

Johanson, Sven-Eric (Emanuel), Swedish composer, organist, and pedagogue; b. Västervik, Dec. 10, 1919. He studied at the Ingesund School of Music (1938), then obtained diplomas as a music teacher (1943) and organist and choirmaster (1946) at the Stockholm Musikhögskolan; also studied composition with Melchers, and later with Valen (1951) and finally with Dallapiccola in Florence (1957). After serving as organist and choirmaster at the Uppsala Missionary Church (1944–50), he settled in Göteborg in 1952 and was organist at the Älvsborg Church (until 1977); was also active as a teacher. In 1971 he was made a member of the Royal Swedish Academy of Music in Stockholm. His output ranges from electro-acoustic compositions to popular scores.
WORKS: OPERAS: *Bortbytingarna* (1954–55); *Kunskapens vin* (Göteborg, May 21, 1959); *Sagan om ringen* (1972); *Reliken* (1974; Borås, Jan. 18, 1975); *Skandal, Ers Majestät* (Umeå, May 8, 1978); *Du människa* (1980); *Pojken med flöjten* (Göteborg, Dec. 3, 1980); *Tjuvens pekfinger,* opera-buffa (1968–82; Göteborg, Jan. 14, 1983); radio operas; incidental music; micro-

drama: *Rivalerna* (1967; Swedish Radio, March 16, 1969); mono-drama: *Kassandras omvändelse* (1977); ballet: *Slottet* (1983). **ORCH.:** Syms.: No. 1, *Sinfonia ostinata* (1949–54); No. 2, *Duinoelegi*, for Tenor, Chorus, and Orch. (1954; also for String Orch. as *Sinfonia elegiaca*, 1954–55; Göteborg, Feb. 8, 1956); No. 3 (1956; Göteborg, Sept. 23, 1959); No. 5, *Elementsymfonin* (1965–68); No. 6, *Sinfonietta pastorella* (1972; Abo, April 5, 1973); No. 7, *Spelmanssymfoni* for String Orch. (1974); No. 8, *En Frödingsymfoni* (1983–84; Swedish Radio, March 11, 1984); No. 9, *Sinfonia d'estate* (Malmö, May 6, 1987); Concerto for Organ and Strings (1946); *Sinfonietta concertante* for Violin, Balalaika, and Chamber Orch. (1951–81); *Concerto da camera* for Cello and Orch. (1958; Swedish Radio, June 25, 1959); *Maskarad-Divertissement* (1958); *Variations on a Värmland Folk Tune* (1963; Göteborg, March 8, 1964); *Vagues* (1965; Göteborg, Jan. 28, 1966); *Fotia* (Uppsala, Oct. 6, 1966); *Vientos* (1967; Swedish Radio, March 7, 1968); *Terra* for Orch. and Tape (Göteborg, Sept. 12, 1968); *Fantyr* (Göteborg, Aug. 31, 1969); *Concerto Götenburghese* for Piano and Orch. (1970; Göteborg, Aug. 19, 1971); Concerto for Nyckel Harp (keyed fiddle) and Strings (1971); *Astrofonia* for String Orch. (Uppsala, July 11, 1974); *Nalle Puh*, symphonic saga (1979; Göteborg, Jan. 3, 1980). **CHAMBER:** 8 string quartets (1947; 1948; 1950; 1961, *Séquences variables*; 1964; 1976; 1980; 1981); Sonata for Solo Violin (1948); 4 piano sonatas (1949; 1956; 1959; 1982–83, *Sonata flexa*); Wind Quintet (1964); Trio for Clarinet, Violin, and Cello (1974); *Slag i slag* for Percussion and Tape (1979). **VOCAL:** *Aff Sancto Christofforo*, chamber oratorio (1948); Sym. No. 4, *Sånger i Förvandlingens Natt* for a cappella Chorus (1958; Stockholm, April 3, 1959); *The Hazetrees* for Soprano, Clarinet, Violin, Cello, Piano, and Tape (1961); *Ave crax, ave crux* for Baritone, Chorus, Organ, and Tape (1967); *Det stora ljuset*, Advent cantata for Narrator, Soprano, Alto, Chorus, and Strings (1983); *Cantata concertante* for Chorus, Brass Quintet, and Organ (1984); various sacred works; choruses.

Johansson, Bengt (Viktor), Finnish composer; b. Helsinki, Oct. 2, 1914; d. Visuvesi, June 22, 1989. He studied composition with Sulho Ranta and Selim Palmgren; also cello at the Sibelius Academy in Helsinki, graduating in 1947; made study trips to Europe, Italy, and America; upon his return to Finland, he served as director of music broadcasting for the Finnish Radio (1952–74); was a teacher (from 1960) and a lecturer in music history (from 1965) at the Sibelius Academy. His music makes use of a wide variety of resources, including electronic sound.

Works: **OPERA:** *Linna* (1975). **ORCH.:** Serenade for Strings (1945); *Petite suite de ballet* (1948); *Aquarelles* (1948); Piano Concerto (1951); Suite for Violin, Strings, Piano, and Timpani (1952); *Festivo*, overture (1952); *Expressions* for Strings (1954); *Tema con 7 variazioni in modo antico* for Cello and Orch. (1954); *Dialogeja* for Cello and Orch. (1970). **VOCAL:** *Stabat Mater* for Chorus a cappella (1951); *It's Perfectly True*, "musical fairy tale" for Narrator, Solo Voices, Female Chorus, and Orch. (1957); *Missa Sacra* for Tenor, Chorus, and Orch. (1960); *12 Passages from the Bible* for Male Chorus and Organ (1960); *The Tomb at Akr Çaar*, to a text by Ezra Pound, for Baritone and Chamber Chorus (1964); *Triptych* for Soprano, Baritone, and Chorus (1965); *Requiem* for Baritone, 2 Choruses, 2 String Orchs., and Timpani (1966); *3 Classic Madrigals* for Chorus (1967); *Cantata humana*, to words of Dag Hammarskjöld, for Baritone, 4 Narrators on Tape, Chorus, and Orch. (Helsinki, April 9, 1970); *The Song of the Bride* for Soprano and Orch. (1972); *Venus and Adonis I–V* for Mixed Chorus (1972–74); *Songs of the Psyche* for Soprano and Piano (1978). **CHAMBER:** *Sonata piccola* for Cello and Piano (1945); *Dialogues* for Cello and String Quintet (1970); pieces for violin; also *3 Electronic Etudes* (1960).

John, Elton (real name, **Reginald Kenneth Dwight**), English rock pianist, singer, and songwriter; b. Pinner, Middlesex, March 25, 1947. He took up the piano in early childhood, then won a fellowship to the Royal Academy of Music in London at age 11; after dropping out of school when he was 17, he earned his keep as a jazz pianist in various London clubs and pubs; then joined a rock group bearing the pretentious appellation Bluesology, adopting the name Elton John by borrowing Elton from the sax player Elton Dean, of whom he was inordinately fond, and John from the 1st name of the leader of the band, John Baldry. For all his low aspirations, John is capable of forming lines of communication with kindred souls on a comparable level of intelligence among his audiences. He affects bizarre behavior, wearing multicolored attires and psychedelic eyeglasses of which he has collected several hundred. In 1971 he flew across the ocean and captivated American rock audiences with his strangulated voice and uninhibited conduct. He wrote most of his songs with lyricist Bernie Taupin. In May 1979 he gave 4 concerts in Leningrad and 4 in Moscow before thousands of young Soviet fans screaming with delight; as the 1st Western rock star to play in Moscow, his appearance was documented in the film *From Elton with Love*. Among his most successful albums are *Madman across the Water, Honky Chateau, Don't Shoot Me I'm Only the Piano Player*, and *Goodbye Yellow Brick Road*.

Johner, Dominicus (actually **Franz-Xaver Karl**), distinguished German music scholar; b. Waldsee, Dec. 1, 1874; d. Beuron, Jan. 4, 1955. He studied theology and music at the Benedictine abbeys in Prague, Seckau, and Beuron, his teachers at the latter being the cantor Ambrosius Kienle and the organist Raphael Molitor; after taking his vows in 1894, he studied theology at the Cucujães Monastery in Portugal (1896–1900), being ordained in 1898. In 1900 he returned to Beuron, where he was cantor of the abbey (1905–49); was also prior there (1913–33), and taught at the church music school of Gregoriushaus, near Beuron (1906–14). He was a lecturer at the Hochschule für Musik in Cologne (from 1925). He was a leading authority on ecclesiastical music. He also composed a cycle, *Neue Marienlieder* for Chorus in unison with Organ (2 books; 1916, 1918), and *Neue Kommunionslieder* (1916). **WRITINGS:** *Neue Schule des gregorianischen Choralgesanges* (Regensburg, 1906; 7th ed., 1937, as *Grosse Choralschule*; 8th ed., 1956, as *Choralschule*); *Der gregorianische Choral: Sein Wesen, Werden, Wert und Vortrag* (Stuttgart, 1924); *Die Sonn- und Festtagslieder des vatikanischen Graduale, nach Text und Melodie erklärt* (Regensburg, 1928; 2nd ed., 1933); *Erklärung des Kyriale nach Text und Melodie* (Regensburg, 1933); *Wort und Ton im Choral: Ein Beitrag zur Aesthetik des gregorianischen Gesanges* (Leipzig, 1940; 2nd ed., 1953). **BIBL.:** F. Tack, ed., *Der kultische Gesang der abendländischen Kirche: In gregorianisches Werkheftaus Anlass des 75. Geburtstages von D. J.* (Cologne, 1950).

Johns, Clayton, American pianist, teacher, and composer; b. New Castle, Del., Nov. 24, 1857; d. Boston, March 5, 1932. He studied composition with J.K. Paine (1879–81) and piano and W.H. Sherwood (1879–82) at Harvard Univ.; then composition with Kiel at the Berlin Hochschule für Musik (1882–83); also studied piano privately with Rummel in Berlin. He settled in Boston in 1884; taught at the New England Cons. of Music there (1912–16). His most popular work was the *Introduction and Fugue* for Piano (1899), which was often performed by Josef Hofmann; he also wrote other instrumental works and about 100 songs. He publ. an autobiography, *Reminiscences of a Musician* (1929) and the didactic *The Essentials of Pianoforte Playing* (1909); also ed. *From Bach to Chopin* (1911).

Johns, Paul Emile, Polish-born American pianist, music publisher, and composer; b. Krakow, c.1798; d. Paris, Aug. 10, 1860. He settled in New Orleans by 1818, where he was active as a pianist until 1830; had his own music store in New Orleans (1830–46). During a visit to Paris in 1832, he was befriended by Chopin, who dedicated his 5 mazurkas, op. 7, to him; with Pleyel, he publ. his *Album louisianais*, a vol. of piano pieces and songs. His other works, including a comic opera, *The Military Stay, A Warlike Symphony*, and *Grand Military March*, are not extant. In later years he was active as a cotton magnate; was Russian consul in New Orleans (1848–60).

BIBL.: J. Kendall, "The Friend of Chopin and Some Other New Orleans Musical Celebrities," *Louisiana Historical Quarterly* (Oct. 1948); J. Baron, "P.E. J. of New Orleans: Tycoon, Musician, and Friend of Chopin," in H. Glahn, S. Sørensen, and P. Ryom, eds., *International Musicological Society Congress Report*, XI, Copenhagen 1972.

Johnsen, Hallvard Olav, Norwegian flutist and composer; b. Hamburg (of Norwegian parents), June 27, 1916. He went to Norway as a youth; studied flute with Stenseth and Wang, conducting with Fjeldstad, harmony and counterpoint with Steenberg, and composition with Brustad at the Oslo Cons. (1930–41); then studied composition with Karl Andersen in Oslo (1942–45), and later with Holmboe in Copenhagen (1956). He was a flutist in the orch. of the National Theater in Oslo (1945–47) and also played in military bands.
WORKS: OPERAS: *The Legend of Svein and Maria* (1971; Oslo, Sept. 9, 1973); *Det Kjempende Menneske* (1982). **ORCH.:** Syms.: No. 1 (1949); No. 2, *Pastorale* (1954); No. 3 (1957); No. 4 (1959); No. 5 (1960); No. 6 (1961); No. 7 (1962); No. 8 (1964); No. 9 (1968); No. 10 (1973); No. 11 (1975); No. 12 (1976); No. 13 (1983); No. 14 (1985); No. 15 (1987); No. 16 (1989); 2 suites for Chamber Orch. (1939, 1947); *Fantasia (Serenade)* for Chamber Orch. (1947); *Ouverture Festivo* (1954); Concerto for Flute and String Orch. (1955); Concerto for Violin and Chamber Orch. (1959); Trumpet Concerto (1966); Violin Concerto (1968); *Ouverture Festoso* (1971); Cello Concerto (1977). **CHAMBER:** Trio for Flute, Violin, and Viola (1938); Quartet No. 1 for Flute and String Trio (1945); 3 string quartets (1962, 1966, 1972); *Serenade* for Wind Quintet (1962); Suite for Flute and Horn (1964); Wind Quintet with Vibraphone (1965); Sextet for Flute, Horn, Vibraphone, Violin, Viola, and Cello (1974); *Serenade* for Flute, Viola, and Cello (1974); Saxophone Quartet (1974); *Divertimento* for Brass Quintet (1974); Brass Quintet (1978); Trio for Trumpet, Trombone, and Vibraphone (1980); *Pastorale* for Flute, Violin, and Vibraphone (1981); Wind Quintet No. 3 (1985); Brass Quintet No. 3 (1986); piano pieces. **VOCAL:** *Norsk Natur* (Norwegian Nature) for Chorus and Orch. (1952); 2 Motets for Chorus (1959, 1965); *Krosspåske*, cantata for Baritone, Chorus, and Orch. (1963); *Der Ligger et Land*, cantata for Tenor, Men's Chorus, and Orch. (1966); *Logos*, oratorio for 8 Solo Voices, Chorus, Organ, and Orch. (1979); Cantata for Voice and Orch. (1984).

Johnson, A(rtemas) N(ixon), American organist, music educator, and composer; b. Middlebury, Vt., June 22, 1817; d. New Milford, Conn., Jan. 1, 1892. He studied with George Webb and Lowell Mason in Boston and later received instruction in theory from Schnyder von Wartensee in Frankfurt am Main (1842–43). He was active as a teacher in Boston for the Musical Education Soc. (1837–39), in the public schools (1839–c.1855), and at the Academy of Music (1840–49); was also organist and later director of music at the Park Street Church (1840–58); likewise was engaged in editorial and publishing affairs. He adopted his own "Johnson's System" (as opposed to Mason's "Pestalozzian" system) for vocal instruction in 1849, declaring that the student should learn his art by doing. He later produced the 1st formal choral method as the *Chorus Choir Instruction Book* (1877). At the close of the Civil War, he organized various music schools and conservatories from N.Y. to Indiana. He wrote 2 cantatas, 67 anthems and similar pieces, 279 hymn tunes, and 26 Sabbath school and gospel songs. He publ. 11 vols. of sacred music, 10 collections of choral music, 3 books of keyboard pieces, and 6 theory books.
BIBL.: J. Stopp, "A.N. J., Out of Oblivion," *American Music*, III (1985).

Johnson, Bengt-Emil, Swedish composer and poet; b. Ludvika, Dec. 12, 1936. He studied piano and composition with Knut Wiggen (1956–62), at the same time pursuing his abiding interest in modernistic poetry. In 1966 he joined the staff of the Swedish Radio in Stockholm, where he later was named director of the music dept. (1979) and program director (1984).

He publ. 14 collections of poetry (1963–86). Many of his compositions take the form of text-sound scores.
WORKS: *Disappearances* for Piano and Tape (1974); *Escaping (Memories 1961–1977)* (Swedish Radio, April 6, 1978); *Night Chants I*, radio piece (Swedish Radio, Aug. 19, 1981); *Night Chants II* for Voice and Tape (1985); *Döden sopran*, radio opera (Swedish Radio, Sept. 7, 1986); various text-sound scores.

Johnson, "Bunk" (William Geary), black American jazz trumpeter; b. New Orleans, Dec. 27, 1889?; d. New Iberia, La., July 7, 1949. As a youth he played trumpet with Dixieland bands; toured with minstrel shows, circus troupes, and numerous jazz aggregations. He lost all his teeth due to the ravages of pyorrhea and had to stop playing. After many years of musical inactivity he was "rediscovered" in 1937, working in sugarcane fields, by "hot jazz" aficionados; fitted with dentures, he resumed his career and enjoyed belated fame in a revival of Dixieland music. He made his 1st recording in 1942 and subsequently performed in N.Y., Boston, and Chicago.
BIBL.: A. Sonnier, *Willie Geary 'Bunk' J.: The New Iberia Years* (N.Y., 1977); C. Hillman, *B. J.: His Life & Times* (N.Y., 1988).

Johnson, Edward, distinguished Canadian-born American tenor and operatic administrator; b. Guelph, Ontario, Aug. 22, 1878; d. there, April 20, 1959. He sang in concert and oratorio performances before going to N.Y. in 1899 to study with Mme. von Feilitsch; after appearing in the U.S. premiere of Oscar Straus's *A Waltz Dream* in 1907, he continued his studies with Richard Barthélemy in Paris (1908) and Vincenzo Lombardi in Florence (1909); made his operatic debut as Andrea Chénier at the Teatro Verdi in Padua on Jan. 10, 1912, using the stage name of Edoardo Di Giovanni; he subsequently appeared in Milan at La Scala, where he sang the title role in *Parsifal* at its 1st complete stage production in Italy, on Jan. 4, 1914. He made his U.S. debut as Loris in *Fedora* at the Chicago Grand Opera on Nov. 20, 1919, remaining on its roster until 1922; then made his Metropolitan Opera debut in N.Y. as Avito in *L'amore dei tre Re* on Nov. 16, 1922, continuing to sing there until 1935, when he became its general manager, guiding its fortunes through the difficult years of World War II and the postwar era; he retired in 1950. Although he became an American citizen in 1922, he maintained a close connection with Canada; returned there after his retirement. He was particularly esteemed for such roles as Romeo, Tannhäuser, Don José, Siegfried, Canio, and Pelléas; he also created leading roles in Deems Taylor's *The King's Henchman* (1927) and *Peter Ibbetson* (1931) at the Metropolitan.
BIBL.: R. Mercer, *The Tenor of His Time: E. J. of the Met* (Toronto, 1976).

Johnson, Frank (Francis), black bandmaster and composer; b. probably on the island of Martinique, 1792; d. Philadelphia, April 6, 1844. He settled in Philadelphia (c.1809), where he organized his own band and dance orch. After touring England with his band in 1837, he led promenade concerts with his band throughout the U.S., highlighting his own works; in Philadelphia, his concerts were often graced by the presence of prominent white artists, an unheard-of practice in his era. Selected modern eds. of his works have been publ. by A. LaBrew (Detroit, 1977) and C. Jones and L. Greenwich, II (N.Y., 1983).
BIBL.: A. LaBrew, *Francis J. (1792–1844)* (Detroit, 1977); E. Southern, "F. J. and His Promenade Concerts," *Black Perspective in Music*, V (1977); R. Dudgeon, "America's Original Virtuoso: Francis J.," *Ovation* (Feb. 1989).

Johnson, (Francis) Hall, black American choral conductor, composer, and arranger; b. Athens, Ga., June 2, 1887; d. N.Y., April 30, 1970. He studied at the Univ. of Pa. (B.A., 1910), where he took a course in composition with Hugh A. Clark; later studied with Goetschius at the Inst. of Musical Art in N.Y. (1923–24). In 1925 he formed the Hall Johnson Choir, with which he gave numerous concerts; from 1938 to 1946 he conducted the Festival Choir of Los Angeles, and then settled in N.Y. as conductor of the Festival Negro Chorus, with which he toured Germany and Austria under the auspices of the U.S. State Dept. (1951). He composed a folk opera, *Run Littl' Chillun* (1933), a cantata, *Son of Man* (1946), choral music, songs, and arrangements for film and television.

Johnson, Horace, American composer; b. Waltham, Mass., Oct. 5, 1893; d. Tucson, Ariz., May 30, 1964. He studied with Bainbridge Crist. He wrote several popular pieces for orch., among them *Astarte* (Richmond, Jan. 2, 1936) and *Streets of Florence* (Mexico, July 9, 1937); also songs (*The Pirate, When Pierrot Sings, The Three Cherry Trees,* and *Thy Dark Hair*).

Johnson, Hunter, American composer; b. Benson, N.C., April 14, 1906. He studied at the Univ. of North Carolina (1924–26), and at the Eastman School of Music in Rochester, N.Y., graduating in 1929; subsequently taught at the Univ. of Michigan (1929–33), the Univ. of Manitoba (1944–47), Cornell Univ. (1948–53), the Univ. of Illinois (1959–65), and the Univ. of Texas (1966–71). **WORKS: STAGE:** 4 ballets: *In Time of Armament* (1939), *Letter to the World* (1940), *Deaths and Entrances* (1942), and *The Scarlet Letter* (1975). **ORCH.:** Sym. (1931); Concerto for Piano and Chamber Orch. (1935); *Elegy* for Clarinet and Strings (1937); *Music for Strings* (1939); Concerto for Orch. (1944); *North State,* to commemorate the tricentennial of Carolina Charter (1963); *Past the Evening Sun* (1964). **CHAMBER:** Piano Sonata (1934; rev., 1936 and 1947–48); Violin Sonatina (1937); Trio for Flute, Oboe, and Piano (1954).

Johnson, James P(rice), black American jazz pianist and composer; b. Brunswick, N.J., Feb. 1, 1891; d. N.Y., Nov. 17, 1955. He studied piano with his mother; began his career as a pianist in N.Y. and Atlantic City nightclubs; later led his own bands and appeared as soloist. He was the leading Harlem stride pianist of his day; he also was a gifted composer. **WORKS:** *De Organizer,* folk opera (n.d.); musical comedies: *Runnin Wild* (1923) and *Sugar Hill* (1948); operettas; ballets; film music; *Yamecraw* for Soloists, Chorus, and Orch. (1928); *Harlem Symphony* (1932); *Jasmine* (*Jazz-O-Mine*), concerto for Piano and Orch. (1935); piano pieces: *Caprice Rag* (1914); *Harlem Strut* (1917); *Carolina Shout* (1925); *Snowy Morning Blues* (1927); *You've Got to Be Modernistic* (1930); *Fascination* (1939); songs: *Old-Fashioned Love* (1923); *Charleston* (1923); *If I Could Be with You* (1926). **BIBL.:** F. Trolle, *J.P. J.: Father of the Stride Piano* (Alphen aan de Rijn, Netherlands, 1981; discography and rollography); S. Brown, *A Case of Mistaken Identity: The Life and Music of J.P. J.* (thesis, Yale Univ., 1982).

Johnson, James Weldon, black American man of letters, brother of **J(ohn) Rosamond Johnson;** b. Jacksonville, Fla., June 17, 1871; d. in an automobile accident in Wiscasset, Maine, June 26, 1938. He studied literature at Atlanta Univ. (B.A., 1894; M.A., 1904); also passed the Florida bar examination to practice law (1897). As a poet, he began writing texts to his brother's compositions; their song *Lift Every Voice and Sing* (1900) proved popular, becoming known as "the Negro National Anthem." The brothers settled in N.Y. in 1902, where they joined Bob Cole in the enormously successful songwriting team of Cole and Johnson Bros.; among their hit songs, mostly in black dialect, were *Under the Bamboo Tree* (1902), which was parodied by T.S. Eliot in "Fragment of the Agon," and *Congo Love Song* (1903). Under the pseudonym Will Handy, they produced *Oh, Didn't He Ramble* (1902), which became a jazz standard; the team's success was such that they became known as "Those Ebony Offenbachs." Johnson was then active as a diplomat (1906–14), serving as consul to Venezuela and, later, to Nicaragua. His tr. of Granados's *Goyescas* was used for the Metropolitan Opera's 1st performance of this work. He publ. anonymously the novel *The Autobiography of an Ex-Colored Man* (Boston, 1912), which includes vivid descriptions of the ragtime era in N.Y. He collaborated with his brother in compiling 2 books of American Negro spirituals (N.Y., 1926 and 1927); wrote *Black Manhattan* (N.Y., 1930), a history of

blacks in N.Y. which includes valuable information on black musical life; also publ. an autobiography, *Along This Way* (1931). His papers are on deposit at Yale Univ. **BIBL.:** E. Levy, *J.W. J.* (Chicago, 1973).

Johnson, "J. J." (James Louis), outstanding black American jazz trombonist and accomplished composer; b. Indianapolis, Jan. 22, 1924. He began to play the piano at the age of 9 and the trombone at 14; toured with Clarence Love and Isaac "Snookum" Russell (1941–42) before attracting attention as a member of Benny Carter's orch. (1942–45). After working with Count Basie in N.Y. (1945–46), he did stints with various artists there; also made a tour of Korea, Japan, and the South Pacific with a group led by Oscar Pettiford for the USO (1951). After a hiatus from the jazz scene, he resumed his career, touring with Kai Winding in a trombone duo known as Jay and Kai; then formed his own quintet (1956–60), with which he toured Europe. After working with Miles Davis (1961–62), he led his own quartet and sextet; gave increasing attention to composition, moving to Los Angeles as a composer for film and television in 1970; he returned to Indianapolis in 1988, at which time he was awarded an honorary doctorate by Indiana Univ. Johnson is acknowledged as one of the pioneer figures of the bop era. Among his works are *Poem* for Brass (also known as *Jazz Suite*), *El camino real, Sketch* for Trombone and Band, and *Perceptions,* all for large ensembles. **BIBL.:** D. Baker, *J.J. J.* (N.Y., 1979).

Johnson, John, distinguished English lutenist and composer, father of **Robert Johnson;** b. c.1540; d. c.1594. He was made 1 of the 3 lute musicians to Queen Elizabeth I in 1579. Johnson was one of the most significant composers of lute music of his time; he helped to develop the lute duet. Many of his works survive in various MS collections. **BIBL.:** L. Nordstrom, "The Lute Duets of J. J.," *Journal of the Lute Society of America,* IX (1976).

Johnson, J(ohn) Rosamond, black American composer and bass, brother of **James Weldon Johnson;** b. Jacksonville, Fla., Aug. 11, 1873; d. N.Y., Nov. 11, 1954. He studied at Atlanta Univ. and at the New England Cons. of Music in Boston; took voice lessons with David Bispham. He set his brother's poem *Lift Every Voice and Sing* (1900) to music, which later became known as "the Negro National Anthem." The brothers collaborated on many other songs, selling them to various musical reviews in N.Y.; in 1902 they formed, with Bob Cole, the songwriting team of Cole and Johnson Bros.; Johnson also wrote some songs that were accepted on the concert stage, among them *Li'l Gal* and *Since You Went Away.* In 1911–12 he was music director of Hammerstein's Opera House in London; also sang in opera, and later toured the U.S. and Europe in programs of Negro spirituals. With his brother, he compiled 2 vols. of Negro spirituals (1926, 1927), adding piano accompaniments; wrote a ballet, *African Drum Dance,* and many vocal works; also *Rolling Along in Song* (a history of black music with 85 song arrangements). He sang the role of Lawyer Frazier in the early performances of Gershwin's *Porgy and Bess.*

Johnson, Lockrem, American pianist, music publisher, and composer; b. Davenport, Iowa, March 15, 1924; d. Seattle, March 5, 1977. He studied at the Cornish School of Music in Seattle (1931–38) and at the Univ. of Washington (1938–42); subsequently was a member of its faculty (1947–49); concurrently served as music director of the Eleanor King Dance Co. (1947–50) and pianist in the Seattle Sym. Orch. (1948–51). In 1952 he held a Guggenheim fellowship; lived in N.Y., where he served as education director for Mercury Music (1951–54), head of the orch. dept. of C.F. Peters (1954–58), and president of Dow Publishers (1957–62); subsequently returned to Seattle as head of the music dept. at the Cornish School of Music (1962–69); also founded Puget Music Publications (1970), which was devoted to publishing works by composers of the Northwest. His works reveal a fine lyrical gift of expression.

WORKS: Chamber opera: *A Letter to Emily* (1951; N.Y., Jan. 25, 1955); *She*, ballet (1948; rev. 1950); *Lyric Prelude* for Orch. (1948; rev. 1949); Sym. No. 1 (Seattle, Dec. 2, 1966); *Suite of Noëls*, cantata for Chorus and Keyboard (1954); 3 violin sonatas (1942; 1948, rev. 1949; 1953); 2 cello sonatas (1949, 1953); Sonatina for Trumpet and Piano (1950); Guitar Sonata (n.d.); 3 piano sonatas (1947, 1949, 1954); various other piano pieces.

Johnson, Robert, eminent English lutenist and composer, son of **John Johnson;** b. probably in London, c.1583; d. there, before Nov. 26, 1633. He was indentured to Sir George Carey, the Lord Chamberlain, from 1596 to 1603, during which period he received instruction in music; then was made lutenist to King James I (1604), and remained in the service of the court until his death; was also composer for the lute and voices at the court from 1628. He composed songs for a number of plays, including Shakespeare's *Cymbeline* (1609–10), *The Winter's Tale* (1610–11), and *The Tempest* (1611). He also wrote music for works by Beaumont and Fletcher and by Ben Jonson. Of his instrumental music, some 20 lute works are extant. See I. Spink, ed., *Robert Johnson: Ayres, Songs and Dialogues,* The English Lute-Songs, 2nd series, XVII (1961; 2nd ed., rev., 1974), and A. Sundermann, *Robert Johnson: Complete Works for Solo Lute* (London, 1970).
BIBL.: J. Cutts, "R. J.: King's Musician in His Majesty's Public Entertainment," *Music & Letters,* XXXVI (1955); idem, "R. J. and the Court Masque," ibid., XLI (1960); B. Jeffrey, "The Lute Music of R. J.," *Early Music,* II (1974).

Johnson, Robert Sherlaw, English pianist and composer; b. Sunderland, May 21, 1932. He was educated at King's College, Univ. of Durham (1950–53), and at the Royal Academy of Music in London (1953–57); then studied piano with Février and composition with Boulanger in Paris (1957–58), where he also attended Messiaen's classes at the Cons.; returning to England, he gave piano recitals in programs of 20th-century music. He lectured at the Univs. of Leeds (1961–63) and York (1965–70). In 1970 he was appointed to the faculty of Oxford Univ.; was a visiting prof. at the Eastman School of Music in Rochester, N.Y. (1985). He wrote a study on Messiaen (1974). In his music he re-creates Renaissance forms and mannerisms in a modern modal idiom. He composes mainly for chamber ensembles and vocal groups.
WORKS: Opera, *The Lambton Worm* (1976); 2 string quartets (1966, 1969); *Triptych* for Flute, Clarinet, Violin, Cello, Piano, and Percussion (1973); Quintet for Clarinet, Violin, Viola, Cello, and Piano (1974); Sonata for Alto Flute and Cello (1976); *The Praises of Heaven and Earth* for Soprano, Electronic Tape, and Piano (1969); *Incarnatio* for Chorus a cappella (1970); *Green Whispers of Gold* for Voice, Electronic Tape, and Piano (1971); *Carmina vernalia* for Soprano and Instruments (1972); *Christus resurgens* for Chorus a cappella (1972); *Festival Mass of the Resurrection* for Choir and Chamber Orch. (1974); *Anglorum feriae* for Soprano, Tenor, Chorus, and Orch. (1976); *Veritas veritatus* for 6 Voices (1980); Piano Concerto (1983); 3 piano sonatas (1963, 1967, 1976); *Asterogenesis* for 8-octave Piano (manufactured by Bösendorfer of Vienna), extending the range to the C below the lowest C on an ordinary piano (1973); *Nymphaea* ("Projections") for Piano (1976).
BIBL.: R. Harris, "R.S. J. at 50," *Musical Times* (May 1982).

Johnson, Thor, American conductor; b. Wisconsin Rapids, Wis., June 10, 1913; d. Nashville, Tenn., Jan. 16, 1975. He studied at the Univ. of North Carolina and later at the Univ. of Michigan (M.A., 1935), where he was founder and conductor of its Little Sym. Orch. (1934–36; 1938–42); also took courses in conducting with Malko, Abendroth, Weingartner, and Bruno Walter in Europe, and with Koussevitzky at the Berkshire Music Center in Tanglewood. He was conductor of the Grand Rapids (Mich.) Sym. Orch. (1940–42); subsequently enlisted in the U.S. Army (1942), and conducted the 1st Army Sym. Orch. in Fort Myers, Va.; subsequently conducted the Juilliard School of Music orch. in N.Y. (1946–47). From 1947 to 1958

he was music director of the Cincinnati Sym. Orch., one of the 1st native-born Americans to hold such a position with a major U.S. orch. From 1958 to 1964 he was a prof. and director of orchestral activities at Northwestern Univ. in Chicago, and from 1964 to 1967 was director of the Interlochen Arts Academy. He was music director of the Nashville (Tenn.) Sym. Orch. from 1967 until his death.

Johnson, Tom, American composer and music critic; b. Greeley, Colo., Nov. 18, 1939. He studied at Yale Univ. (B.A., 1961; M.Mus., 1967) and with Morton Feldman in N.Y. In 1971 he became music critic of the radical Greenwich Village newspaper the *Village Voice,* for which he pugnaciously proceeded to preach the gospel of asymptotic modernity; after quitting his watch in 1982, he settled in Paris to devote himself fully to composing. A collection of his reviews was publ. as *The Voice of New Music: New York 1972–82* (Eindhoven, 1989).
WORKS: OPERAS: *The 4-Note Opera* (1972); *The Masque of Clouds* (1975); *5 Shaggy-dog Operas* (1978); *Sopranos Only* (1984); *Riemannoper* (1988); *200 ANS* (1989). **ORCH.:** *The Secret of the River* (1966); *Dragons in A* (1979); *Angst vor der Stille* for Baritone and String Orch. (1988). **INSTRUMENTAL:** *Transitory Circumlocutions* for Trombone (1973); *Verses* for Alto Flute, Horn, and Harp (1974); *Failing* for String Bass (1975); *60-note Fanfares* for Trumpet Quartet (1976); *Verses* for Viola (1976); *Monologue* for Tuba (1978); *8 Patterns* for 8 Instruments (1979); *9 Bells* (1979); *Mouvements* for Wind Quintet (1980); *Doublings* for Double Bass (1980); *Counting to 8* for Trombone and Tuba (1981); *Harpiano* for Harp and Piano (1982); *Self-Portrait* for 2 to 10 Musicians and Box Mover (1983); *Predictables* for Violin, Cello, and Piano (1984); *How to Count to 5, in 14 Easy Lessons* for Wind Quintet (1984); *Histoires à dormir debout* for Clarinet and Lecturer (1985); *Pouvoir du nombre* for Variable Ensemble (1987); *Fanfares à l'heure* for Trumpet Quartet (1988); *Respire* for Clarinet (1988); Flute Quartet (1989); *Les Vaches de Narayana* for Unspecified Ensemble and Narrator (1989); *Alexandrins* for Guitar (1989); *1789* for Variable Ensemble (1989); piano pieces.
BIBL.: G. Gronemeyer, "Lust am Zählen: T. J.—ein Porträt," *MusikTexte* (July–Aug. 1988).

Johnston, Ben(jamin Burwell), American composer and pedagogue; b. Macon, Ga., March 15, 1926. He studied at the College of William and Mary in Williamsburg, Va. (A.B., 1949), the Cincinnati Cons. of Music (M.Mus., 1950), and Mills College in Oakland, Calif. (M.A., 1953); held a Guggenheim fellowship (1959–60). He taught at the Univ. of Illinois in Urbana (1951–83).
WORKS: OPERAS: *Gertrude, or Would She Be Pleased to Receive It?* (1965); *Carmilla* (1970). **BALLETS:** *St. Joan* (1955); *Gambit* for Dancers and Orch. (1959; also concert version entitled *Ludes* for 12 Instruments). **ORCH.:** *Concerto for Brass* (1951); *Passacaglia and Epilogue* (1955–60); *Quintet for Groups* (1966); Sym. (Rocky Mount, N.C., Oct. 29, 1988); also 2 pieces for Jazz Band: *Ivesberg Revisited* and *Newcastle Troppo* (both 1960). **CHAMBER:** Septet for Wind Quintet, Cello, and Bass (1956–58); *9 Variations* for String Quartet (1959); *Knocking Piece* for 2 Percussionists and Piano (1962); Duo for Flute and String Bass (1963); string quartets (beginning with No. 2: 1964, 1966–73, 1973, 1980, 1980, 1985, 1986, 1988); Trio for Clarinet, Violin, and Cello (1982); *The Demon Lover's Double* for Trumpet and Microtonal Piano (1985); also a cantata, *Night* (1955); other choral music; songs; piano pieces.
BIBL.: H. Von Gunden, *The Music of B. J.* (Metuchen, N.J., and London, 1986).

Johnstone, Arthur Edward, English-American composer and teacher; b. London, May 13, 1860; d. Wilkes-Barre, Pa., Jan. 23, 1944. He was taken to N.Y. as a child and studied with Leopold Damrosch (composition), William Scharfenberg and William Mason (piano), and S.P. Warren (organ). He was a lecturer at Washington Univ. in St. Louis (summer sessions); composed an overture; piano works; songs; etc.; publ. a useful book, *Instruments of the Modern Symphony Orchestra and Band* (N.Y., 1917; rev. ed., 1948).

Jokinen, Erkki, Finnish composer; b. Janakkala, Oct. 16, 1941. He studied with Kokkonen and Bergman at the Sibelius Academy of Music in Helsinki (graduated, 1970); completed his studies with Ton de Leeuw in the Netherlands (1971); then was active as a teacher in his homeland, eventually becoming a lecturer in theory and composition at his alma mater.
Works: Cello Concerto (1969–70; Helsinki, Oct. 21, 1971); *Contrasts* for Flute, Clarinet, Violin, Cello, and Piano (1968); *Music* for 4 Brass Instruments (1968); 2 string quartets (1971–72; 1976); *Dô der Sumer komen was* for Clarinet, Horn, Flügelhorn, Piano, and Percussion (1978); *Songs* for Bass Clarinet, Trombone, Double Bass, Piano, and Percussion (1980); *Face* for Flute, Harp, Harpsichord, Violin, Viola, and Cello (1983); *Pillars* for Cello and Double Bass (1983); *Reflections* for 2 Accordions (1983); *Frieze* for Oboe, Horn, Trumpet, Violin, Double Bass, and Piano (1984); *CeGeda* for Cello (1969); *Air* for Bass Clarinet (1979); *Alone* for Accordion (1979); *Hommage à Marc Chagall* for Organ (1985); *Situation* for Harpsichord (1986); *Psalmus* for Choir (1971); *Tempora per omnia* for Men's Chorus (1980); *Oi, syntyös syömehen* for Choir (1985); *That Time of Year* for Choir, after Shakespeare (1986); *Uivat lehdet* (Floating Leaves), song cycle for Soprano and Piano (1982).

Jokl, Georg, Austrian composer, brother of **Otto Jokl;** b. Vienna, July 31, 1896; d. N.Y., July 29, 1954. He studied with Schreker; was active as an accompanist and teacher in Vienna; in 1938, settled in N.Y. Among his works are a Sym., a symphonic poem, *Heldensang* (Königsberg, 1923), and *Burletta piccola* for Wind Instruments (1952).

Jokl, Otto, Austrian composer, brother of **Georg Jokl;** b. Vienna, Jan. 18, 1891; d. N.Y., Nov. 13, 1963. He studied with Hermann Grädener and Alban Berg (1926–30). His Suite for Orch. (1934) won the Hertzka Prize in Vienna; other works are *Sinfonietta seria* (1935); 2 string quartets; etc. In 1940 he settled in N.Y.

Jolas, Betsy (real name, **Elizabeth Illouz**), American composer; b. Paris (of American parents), Aug. 5, 1926. She went to the U.S. (1940), where she studied with Boepple (composition), Helen Schnabel (piano), and Weinrich (organ) at Bennington College (B.A., 1946); then completed her studies with Milhaud (composition), Plé-Caussade (fugue), and Messiaen (analysis) at the Paris Cons.; taught the latter's course there (1971–74) until she was appointed to the faculty (1975); also taught widely in the U.S. She received numerous awards; was made a member of the American Inst. of Arts and Letters (1983). In her music she applies constructive methods in neo-Baroque forms and quasi-serial techniques.
Works: *Figures* for 9 Instruments (1956); *Mots* for 5 Voices and 8 Instruments (1963); *Quatuor* for Soprano, Violin, Viola, and Cello (1964); *J.D.E.* for 14 Instruments (1966); *D'un opéra de voyage* for 22 Instruments (1967); *Quatre plages* for String Orch. (1968); *États* for Violin and Percussion (1969); *Winter Music* for Organ and Chamber Orch. (1970); *Le Pavillon au bord de la rivière*, musical spectacle after a medieval Chinese play (Avignon, July 25, 1975); *O Wall*, a "mini-opera" as an instrumental counterpart to a line from Shakespeare's *A Midsummer Night's Dream*, for Woodwind Quintet (N.Y., Nov. 5, 1976); *Tales of a Summer Sea* for Orch. (1977); *Onze Lieder* for Trumpet and Chamber Orch. (1977); *Stances* for Piano and Orch. (1978); *Liring Ballade* for Baritone and Orch. (1980); *Cinq pièces pour Boulogne* for Small Orch. (1982); *Points d'or* for Saxophone and 15 Instruments (1982); *D'un opéra de poupée* for 11 Instruments (1982); *Préludes-Fanfares-Interludes-Sonneries* for Orch. and Percussion (1983; Paris, Jan. 28, 1984); works for solo instruments.

Jolivet, André, prominent French composer; b. Paris, Aug. 8, 1905; d. there, Dec. 20, 1974. A son of artistically inclined parents, he took an interest in the fine arts, wrote poetry, and improvised at the piano; studied cello with Louis Feuillard and theory with Aimé Théodas at Notre Dame de Clignancourt.

At the age of 15 he wrote a ballet and designed a set for it; then undertook a prolonged study of musical techniques with Paul Le Flem (1928–33). Of decisive importance to the maturation of his creative consciousness was his meeting in 1930 with Varèse, then living in Paris, who gave him a sense of direction in composition. In 1935 he organized in Paris the progressive group La Spirale. In 1936, in association with Yves Baudrier, Olivier Messiaen, and Daniel Lesur, he founded La Jeune France, dedicated to the promotion of new music in a national French style. He served as conductor and music director of the Comédie Française (1943–59); was technical adviser of the Direction Générale des Arts et des Lettres (1959–62), and president of the Concerts Lamoureux (1963–68); he also was prof. of composition at the Paris Cons. (1965–70). He toured throughout the world as a conductor of his own music. Jolivet injected an empiric spirit into his music, making free use of modernistic technical resources, including the electronic sounds of the Ondes Martenot. Despite these esoteric preoccupations, and even a peripheral deployment of serialism, his music was designed mainly to provide aural stimulation and esthetic satisfaction.
Works: Opera buffa, *Dolorès*, subtitled *Le Miracle de la femme laide* (1942; Paris Radio, May 4, 1947); 3 ballets: *Guignol et Pandore* for Piano or Orch. (1943; Paris, April 29, 1944); *L'Inconnue* (1950; Paris Opéra, April 19, 1950); *Ariadne* (1964; Paris, March 12, 1965); oratorio, *La Vérité de Jeanne* (1956; Domrémy Festival, May 20, 1956; 3 orch. interludes drawn from it are often played separately); 2 cantatas: *La Tentation dernière* (1941; Paris, May 16, 1941) and *Le Cœur de la matière* (1965; Paris, April 9, 1965); scenic music for radio legends and other productions such as *La Queste de Lancelot* (1943; Paris, Jan. 21, 1944); *Le Livre de Christophe Colomb* (1946; Paris, Feb. 21, 1947); *Hélène et Faust*, after Goethe (1949); 2 productions of *Antigone* (1951; 1960); *Empereur Jones* (1953); *L'Amour médecin* (1955); and *L'Eunuque* (1959); also *Andante* for String Orch. (1935); *Danse incantatoire* for Orch. with 2 Ondes Martenot (1936); 3 *chants des hommes* for Baritone and Orch. (1937); *Poèmes pour l'enfant* for Voice and 11 Instruments (1937; Paris, May 12, 1938); *Cosmogonie*, prelude for Orch. (1938; Paris, Nov. 17, 1947; also for Piano); 5 *danses rituelles* (1939; Paris, June 15, 1942); 3 *complaintes du soldat* for Voice, and Orch. or Piano (1940); *Symphonie de danses* (1940; Paris, Nov. 24, 1943); *Suite delphique* for Wind Instruments, Harp, Ondes Martenot, and Percussion (1943; Vienna, Oct. 22, 1948); *Psyché* for Orch. (1946; Paris, March 5, 1947); *Fanfares pour Britannicus* for Brass and Percussion (1946); Concerto for Ondes Martenot and Orch. (1947; Vienna, April 23, 1948); 2 trumpet concertos: Concertino (Concerto No. 1) for Trumpet, String Orch., and Piano (1948) and No. 2 (1954); 2 flute concertos: No. 1, with String Orch. (1949) and No. 2, *Suite en concert*, for Flute and Percussionists (1965); Piano Concerto (1949–50; Strasbourg Music Festival, June 19, 1951); Concerto for Harp and Chamber Orch. (1952); 3 numbered syms.: No. 1 (1953; ISCM Festival, Haifa, May 30, 1954), No. 2 (1959; Berlin Festival, Oct. 3, 1959), and No. 3 (1964; Mexico City, Aug. 7, 1964, composer conducting); Concerto for Bassoon, String Orch., Harp, and Piano (1954; Paris Radio, Nov. 30, 1954); *Suite transocéane* (1955; Louisville, Ky., Sept. 24, 1955); *Suite française* for Orch. (1957); Percussion Concerto (1958; Paris, Feb. 17, 1959); *Adagio* for Strings (1960); *Les Amants magnifiques* for Orch. (1961; Lyons, April 24, 1961); Sym. for Strings (1961; Paris, Jan. 9, 1962); 2 cello concertos: No. 1 (1962; Paris, Nov. 20, 1962) and No. 2, with String Orch. (1966; Moscow, Jan. 6, 1967); 12 *Inventions* for 12 Instruments (1966; Paris, Jan. 23, 1967); *Songe à nouveau rêvé* for Soprano and Orch. (1970); Violin Concerto (1972; Paris, Feb. 28, 1973); *La Flèche du temps* for 12 Solo Strings (1973); *Yin-Yang* for 11 Solo Strings (1974). His chamber and solo instrumental works include 3 *Temps* for Piano (1930); Suite for String Trio (1930); String Quartet (1934); *Mana* for Piano (1935); 3 *poèmes* for Ondes Martenot and Piano (1935); 5 *incantations* for Solo Flute (1936); *Messe pour le jour de la paix* for Voice, Organ, and Tambourine (1940); *Ballet des étoiles*

for 9 Instruments (1941); *Suite liturgique* for Voice, Oboe, Cello, and Harp (1942); Nocturne for Cello and Piano (1943); *Pastorales de Noël* for Flute or Violin, Bassoon or Viola, and Harp (1943); *Chant des Linos* for Flute and Piano, or Flute, Violin, Viola, Cello, and Harp (1944); *Sérénade* for Oboe and Piano, or Wind Quintet (1945); 2 piano sonatas (1945, 1957); *Hopi Snake Dance* for 2 Pianos (1948); *Epithalame* for 12-part Vocal "Orch." (1953; Venice, Sept. 16, 1956); *Sérénade* for 2 Guitars (1956); *Rhapsodie à 7* for Clarinet, Bassoon, Trumpet, Trombone, Percussion, Violin, and Double Bass (1957); Flute Sonata (1958); Sonatina for Flute and Clarinet (1961); *Hymne à l'univers* for Organ (1961); *Messe "Uxor tua"* for 5 Voices, and 5 Instruments or Organ (1962); Sonatina for Oboe and Bassoon (1963); *Madrigal* for 4 Voices and 4 Instruments (1963); *Alla rustica* for Flute and Harp (1963); *Suite rhapsodique* for Solo Violin (1965); *Suite en concert* for Solo Cello (1965); *5 églogues* for Solo Viola (1967); *Ascèses*, 5 pieces for Solo Flute or Clarinet (1967); *Cérémonial en hommage à Varèse* for 6 Percussionists (1968); *Controversia* for Oboe and Harp (1968); *Mandala* for Organ (1969); *Arioso barocco* for Trumpet and Organ (1969); *Patchinko* for 2 Pianos (1970); *Heptade* for Trumpet and Percussion (1971–72).

BIBL.: V. Fédorov and P. Guinard, compilers, *A. J.: Catalogue des œuvres* (Paris, 1969); H. Jolivet, *Avec A. J.* (Paris, 1978).

Jolson, Al (real name, **Asa Yoelson**), popular Lithuanian-born American singer and actor; b. Srednike, May 26, 1886; d. San Francisco, Oct. 23, 1950. His family emigrated about 1894 to the U.S., where he began his professional career as a performer in vaudeville, burlesque, and minstrel shows. He 1st attracted wide notice in N.Y. as a member of Lew Dockstader's Minstrels (1909); subsequently was engaged as a leading performer at the Winter Garden (1911), introducing his famous blackface character of Gus in *Whirl of Society* (1912); he continued to appear in popular shows there. He starred in the 1st feature sound film, *The Jazz Singer* (1927), winning immortality with his rendition in blackface of the song *My Mammy*; he appeared in several other films, and also returned to Broadway in *The Wonder Bar* (1931) and *Hold On to Your Hats* (1940). During the last few years of his life he appeared on radio and television; his voice was also used on the soundtracks for the films *The Jolson Story* (1946) and *Jolson Sings Again* (1949). He popularized many songs, including *Swanee*, *California, Here I Come*, *Toot, Toot, Tootsie!*, *April Showers*, *Rockaby Your Baby with a Dixie Melody*, *Let Me Sing and I'm Happy*, *There's a Rainbow 'round My Shoulder*, and *Sonny Boy*. He was married to Ruby Keeler (1928–39).

BIBL.: H. Jolson and A. Emley, *Mistah J.* (Hollywood, Calif., 1952); M. Freedland, *J.* (N.Y., 1972); L. Kiner, compiler, *The A. J. Discography* (Westport, Conn., 1983); H. Goldman, *J.: The Legend Comes to Life* (Oxford, 1988).

Jommelli, Niccolò, greatly significant Italian composer; b. Aversa, near Naples, Sept. 10, 1714; d. Naples, Aug. 25, 1774. He began his musical studies with Canon Muzzillo, the director of the Cathedral choir in Aversa; in 1725 he entered the Cons. S. Onofrio in Naples, where he studied with Prota and Feo; in 1728 he enrolled in the Cons. Pietà dei Turchini in Naples, where he continued his studies with Fago, Sarcuni, and Basso. In 1737 he composed a comic opera, *L'errore amoroso*, for Naples; this was followed by a 2nd comic opera, *Odoardo* (Naples, 1738). On Jan. 16, 1740, his 1st serious opera, *Ricimero rè de' Goti*, was produced in Rome. After composing *Astianatte* (Rome, Feb. 4, 1741), he went to Bologna for the premiere of his *Ezio* (April 29, 1741); there he studied with Padre Martini; was also elected to membership in the Accademia Filarmonica. He then proceeded to Venice, where his opera *Merope* was given on Dec. 26, 1741; in 1743 he became music director of the Ospedale degli Incurabili there; during this time he composed several notable sacred works, including the oratorios *Isacco figura del Redentore* and *La Betulia liberata*. In 1747 he left Venice for Rome; in 1749 he went to Vienna, where his opera *Achille in Sciro* was successfully staged on Aug. 30, 1749. Several of his operas had been performed in Stuttgart,

resulting in a commission for a new opera from Karl Eugen, the Duke of Württemberg. *Fetonte* was premiered in Stuttgart on the duke's birthday on Feb. 11, 1753. On Jan. 1, 1754, Jommelli became Ober-Kapellmeister in Stuttgart. Among the operas he composed for Stuttgart were *Pelope* (Feb. 11, 1755), *La Nitteti* (Feb. 11, 1759), and *L'Olimpiade* (Feb. 11, 1761); he also composed sacred music, including a *Miserere* and a *Te Deum*, both of which were widely performed. In 1768 Jommelli accepted an offer from King José of Portugal to compose operas and sacred music for the court of Lisbon. He left Stuttgart in 1769 and returned to Italy; for Naples he composed the operas *Armida abbandonata* (May 30, 1770) and *Ifigenia in Tauride* (May 30, 1771); also the serenata *Cerere placata* (Sept. 14, 1772). His opera *Il trionfo di Clelia* was produced in Lisbon with great success on June 6, 1774. His last work for Naples was a *Miserere* on Psalm 50, which was heard during Holy Week 1774.

The historical significance of Jommelli lies in his being a mediator between the German and Italian styles of composition, especially in opera. He introduced into Italian opera the German solidity of harmonic texture and also the expressive dynamics associated with the "Mannheim" school of composition; he also abandoned the formal Neapolitan convention of the da capo aria, thus contributing to a more progressive and realistic operatic form; this earned him the sobriquet "the Italian Gluck." On the other hand, he influenced the development, during his long stay in Stuttgart, of German opera in the direction of simple melodiousness and natural rhythmic flow without dependence on contrapuntal techniques. Thus his influence was beneficial both for his native art and for the most austere German operatic traditions.

WORKS: OPERAS: *L'errore amoroso*, comic opera (Naples, 1737; not extant); *Odoardo*, comic opera (Naples, 1738; not extant); *Ricimero rè de' Goti* (Rome, Jan. 16, 1740); *Astianatte* (Rome, Feb. 4, 1741; also known as *Andromaca*); *Ezio* (Bologna, April 29, 1741; 2nd ver., Naples, Nov. 4, 1748; 3rd ver., Stuttgart, Feb. 11, 1758, not extant; 4th ver., 1771; rev. by da Silva, Lisbon, April 20, 1772); *Merope* (Venice, Dec. 26, 1741); *Semiramide riconosiuta* (Turin, Dec. 26, 1741; 2nd ver., Piacenza, 1753; 3rd ver., Stuttgart, Feb. 11, 1762); *Don Chichibio*, intermezzi (Rome, 1742); *Eumene* (Bologna, May 5, 1742; 2nd ver., as *Artemisia*, Naples, May 30, 1747); *Semiramide* (Venice, Dec. 26, 1742); *Tito Manlio* (Turin, 1743; 2nd ver., Venice, 1746, not extant; 3rd ver., Stuttgart, Jan. 6, 1758, not extant); *Demofoonte* (Padua, June 13, 1743; 2nd ver., Milan, 1753; 3rd ver., Stuttgart, Feb. 11, 1764; rev., Ludwigsburg, Feb. 11, 1765; rev. by da Silva, Lisbon, June 6, 1775; 4th ver., Naples, Nov. 4, 1770); *Alessandro nell'Indie* (Ferrara, 1744, not extant; 2nd ver., Stuttgart, Feb. 11, 1760, not extant; rev. by da Silva, Lisbon, June 6, 1776); *Ciro riconosciuto* (Bologna, May 4, 1744; 2nd ver., Venice, 1749; 3rd ver., Venice, 1749; completely new ver., 1751 or 1758); *Sofonisba* (Venice, 1746; not extant; *Cajo Mario* (Rome, Feb. 6, 1746; 2nd ver., Bologna, 1751); *Antigono* (Lucca, Aug. 24, 1746); *Didone abbandonata* (Rome, Jan. 28, 1747; 2nd ver., Vienna, Dec. 8, 1749; 3rd ver., Stuttgart, Feb. 11, 1763); *L'amore in maschera*, comic opera (Naples, 1748; not extant); *La cantata e disfida di Don Trastullo*, intermezzi (Rome, 1749; 2nd ver., Lucca, 1762); *Artaserse* (Rome, Feb. 4, 1749; 2nd ver., Stuttgart, Aug. 30, 1756); *Demetrio* (Parma, 1749); *Achille in Sciro* (Vienna, Aug. 30, 1749; 2nd ver., Rome, Jan. 26, 1771); *Cesare in Egitto* (Rome, 1751; not extant); *La Villana nobile*, comic opera (Palermo, 1751; not extant); *Ifigenia in Aulide* (Rome, Feb. 9, 1751; rev. with arias by Traetta, Naples, Dec. 18, 1753); *L'Uccellatrice*, intermezzi (Venice, May 6, 1751; 2nd ver. as *Il paratajo* [*ovvero*] *La Pipée*, Paris, Sept. 25, 1753); *Ipermestra* (Spoleto, Oct. 1751); *Talestri* (Rome, Dec. 28, 1751); *I Rivali delusi*, intermezzi (Rome, 1752); *Attilio Regolo* (Rome, Jan. 8, 1753); *Fetonte* (Stuttgart, Feb. 11, 1753, not extant; 2nd ver., Ludwigsburg, Feb. 11, 1768); *La clemenza di Tito* (Stuttgart, Aug. 30, 1753, not extant; 2nd ver., Ludwigsburg, Jan. 6, 1765, not extant; rev. by da Silva, Lisbon, June 6, 1771); *Bajazette* (Turin, Dec. 26, 1753); *Don Falcone*, intermezzi (Bologna, Jan.

22, 1754); *Lucio Vero* (Milan, 1754); *Catone in Utica* (Stuttgart, Aug. 30, 1754; not extant); *Pelope* (Stuttgart, Feb. 11, 1755; rev. by da Silva, Salvaterra, 1768); *Enea nel Lazio* (Stuttgart, Aug. 30, 1755, not extant; rev. by da Silva, Salvaterra, 1767); *Creso* (Rome, Feb. 5, 1757); *Temistocle* (Naples, Dec. 18, 1757; 2nd ver., Ludwigsburg, Nov. 4, 1765); *La Nitteti* (Stuttgart, Feb. 11, 1759, not extant; rev. by da Silva, Lisbon, June 6, 1770); *Endimione ovvero Il trionfo d'amore*, pastorale (Stuttgart, 1759, not extant; 2nd ver., Queluz, June 29, 1780); *Cajo Fabrizio* (Mannheim, Nov. 4, 1760; includes arias by G. Cola); *L'Olimpiade* (Stuttgart, Feb. 11, 1761; rev. by da Silva, Lisbon, March 31, 1774); *L'isola disabitata*, pastorale (Ludwigsburg, Nov. 4, 1761, not extant; 2nd ver., Queluz, March 31, 1780); *Il trionfo d'amore*, pastorale (Ludwigsburg, Feb. 16, 1763; not extant); *La pastorella illustre*, pastorale (Stuttgart, Nov. 4, 1763, not extant; rev. by da Silva, Salvaterra, 1773); *Il Re pastore* (Ludwigsburg, Nov. 4, 1764, not extant; rev. by da Silva, Salvaterra, 1770); *Imeneo in Atene*, pastorale (Ludwigsburg, Nov. 4, 1765; rev. by da Silva, Lisbon, March 19, 1773); *La Critica*, comic opera (Ludwigsburg, 1766; rev. as *Il giuoco di picchetto*, Koblenz, 1772; rev. as *La conversazione [e] L'accademia di musica*, Salvaterra, 1775); *Vologeso* (Ludwigsburg, Feb. 11, 1766; rev. by da Silva, Salvaterra, 1769); *Il matrimonio per concorso*, comic opera (Ludwigsburg, Nov. 4, 1766, not extant; rev. by da Silva, Salvaterra, 1770); *Il Cacciatore deluso [ovvero] La Semiramide in bernesco*, serious-comic opera (Tübingen, Nov. 4, 1767; rev. by da Silva, Salvaterra, 1771); *La Schiava liberata*, serious-comic opera (Ludwigsburg, Dec. 18, 1768); rev. by da Silva, Lisbon, March 31, 1770); *Armida abbandonata* (Naples, May 30, 1770; rev. by da Silva, Lisbon, March 31, 1773); *L'amante cacciatore*, intermezzi (Rome, 1771; not extant); *Le avventure di Cleomede*, serious-comic opera (Naples, 1771?; rev. by da Silva, Lisbon, June 6, 1772); *Ifigenia in Tauride* (Naples, May 30, 1771; rev. by da Silva, Salvaterra, 1776); *Il trionfo di Clelia* (Naples, 1774?; rev. by da Silva, Lisbon, June 6, 1774); etc. His opera *Fetonte* was publ. in Denkmäler Deutscher Tonkunst, XXXII–XXXIII (1907).

OTHER STAGE WORKS: *Componimento drammatico* (Rome, Feb. 9, 1747; not extant); *Componimento drammatico* (Ronciglione, Feb. 28, 1751; not extant); *La reggia de' Fati* (with G.B. Sammartini; Milan, March 13, 1753); *La pastorale offerta* (with G.B. Sammartini; Milan, March 19, 1753); *Il giardino incanto* (Stuttgart, 1755; not extant); *L'asilo d'amore* (Stuttgart, Feb. 11, 1758; not extant); *Le Cinesi* (Ludwigsburg, 1765; not extant); *L'unione coronata* (Solitude, Sept. 22, 1768; not extant); *Cerere placata* (Naples, Sept. 14, 1772); etc.; also, serenatas, several secular cantatas and other vocal pieces; he also contributed to a number of pasticcios.

ORATORIOS, PASSIONS, AND SACRED CANTATAS: *Che impetuoso è questo torrente* for 2 Sopranos, Tenor, and Orch. (Naples, 1740); *Isacco figura del Redentore* for 2 Sopranos, Alto, Tenor, Bass, 4-part Chorus, and Orch. (Venice, 1742); *La Betulia liberata* for Soprano, Alto, Tenor, Bass, 4-part Chorus, and Orch. (Venice, 1743); *Gioas* for 3 Sopranos, 3 Altos, 4-part Chorus, and Strings (Venice, 1745); *Juda proditor* for 3 Sopranos, 3 Altos, and Chorus (Venice, 1746?; not extant); *Ove son? Chi mi guida?* for Soprano, Alto, Tenor, and Orch. (Naples, 1747); *La passione di Gesù Cristo* for Soprano, Alto, Tenor, Bass, 4-part Chorus, and Orch. (Rome, 1749); *Giuseppe glorificato in Egitto* for 2 Sopranos, Tenor, and Orch. (Rome, 1749); *Le Spose di Elcana* for 4-part Chorus (Palermo, 1750; not extant); *In questa incolte riva* for 2 Sopranos and Orch. (Rome, May 20, 1751); *Non più: L'atteso istante* for Soprano, Alto, Tenor, and Orch. (Rome, 1752); *Il sacrifizio di Gefte* for 4-part Chorus and Strings (Palermo, 1753; not extant); *La reconciliazione della Virtù e della Gloria* for 2-part Chorus (Pistoia, 1754; not extant); *Gerusalemme convertita* (Palermo, 1755; not extant); *Il sogno di Nabucco* (Palermo, 1755; not extant); etc. Additional sacred works include many masses, as well as graduals, offertories, antiphones, Psalms, motets, hymns, etc. His instrumental works include harpsichord concertos, quartets, divertimenti, and sonatas.

BIBL.: S. Mattei, *Elogio del J.* (Colle, 1785); P. Alfieri, *Notizie biografiche di N. J.* (Rome, 1845); H. Abert, *N. J. als Opernkomponist* (Halle, 1908); idem, "Die Stuttgarter Oper unter J.," *Neue Musikzeitung*, XLVI/24 (1925); F. Abbiati, "D'umor concettoso l'inedito J.," *La Scala*, no. 6 (1950); idem, "Qui buongustaio l'inedito J.," *La Scala*, no. 7 (1950); R. Pattengale, *The Cantatas of N. J.* (diss., Univ. of Michigan, 1973); H. Brofsky, "J. e Padre Martini," *Rivista Italiana di Musicologia*, VIII (1973); J. Carlson, *Selected Masses of N. J.* (diss., Univ. of Illinois, 1974); L. Tolkoff, *The Stuttgart Operas of N. J.* (diss., Yale Univ., 1974); M. McClymonds, *N. J.: The Last Years, 1769–1774* (Ann Arbor, Mich., 1980); W. Hochstein, *Die Kirchenmusik von N. J. (1714–1774): Unter besonderer Berücksichtigung der liturgisch gebundenen Kompositionen* (2 vols., Hildesheim, 1984).

Jonák, Zdeněk, Czech composer; b. Prague, Feb. 25, 1917. He studied composition with Řídký at the Prague Cons. (graduated, 1941), continuing his study with Řídký and Křička at its master school (graduated, 1947); subsequently devoted himself mainly to pragmatic musical tasks, such as making arrangements of folk songs and writing music for the theater.

WORKS: *Prelude* for Orch. (1939); *Passacaglia* for Orch. (1940); *Suite* for Orch. (1951); Chamber Sym. (1964); Trumpet Concerto (1972); *Epigrams*, song cycle for Chorus a cappella (1975); 3 string quartets (1941, 1947, 1980); Cello Sonata (1955).

Jonás, Alberto, Spanish-American pianist, teacher, and composer; b. Madrid, June 8, 1868; d. Philadelphia, Nov. 9, 1943. He received primary music training in Madrid; then studied piano and theory of composition at the Brussels Cons. In 1890 he went to St. Petersburg, where he had some lessons with A. Rubinstein. After a brief concert career in Europe, he went to the U.S., where he taught piano at the Univ. of Michigan (1894–98) and the Detroit Cons. (1898–1904). From 1904 to 1914 he taught in Berlin; after the outbreak of World War I, he settled in N.Y., where he established a fine reputation as a piano pedagogue. In collaboration with 16 pianists, he publ. *Master School of Modern Piano Playing and Virtuosity* (N.Y., 1922), which went through 5 eds., and he also brought out several books of piano exercises for beginners. He wrote a number of attractive piano pieces in a salon manner, among them *Northern Dances, Humoresque, Nocturne,* and *Evening Song.*

Jonas, Emile, French composer; b. Paris, March 5, 1827; d. St.-Germain-en-Laye, May 21, 1905. He studied at the Paris Cons. (1841–49), graduating with the 2nd Grand Prix de Rome for his cantata *Antonio*; was an instructor there (1847–66); also was music director at the Portuguese Synagogue, for which he publ. *Receuil de chants hébraïques* (1854).

WORKS: Light operas (all produced in Paris): *Le Duel de Benjamin* (1855); *La Parade* (Aug. 2, 1856); *Le Roi boit* (April 1857); *Les Petits Prodiges* (Nov. 19, 1857); *Job et son chien* (Feb. 6, 1863); *Le Manoir de La Renardière* (Sept. 29, 1864); *Avant la noce* (March 24, 1865); *Les Deux Arlequins* (Dec. 29, 1865); *Le Canard à trois becs* (Feb. 6, 1869); *Désiré, sire de Champigny* (April 11, 1869); operetta to an Eng. libretto, *Cinderella the Younger* (London, Sept. 25, 1871; in French as *Javotte*, Paris, Dec. 22, 1871).

Jonas, Maryla, Polish pianist; b. Warsaw, May 31, 1911; d. N.Y., July 3, 1959. She was a precocious child pianist, and appeared in public at the age of 8; took lessons with Turczynski and was commended by Paderewski. She began her professional career as a concert pianist at the age of 15; after the invasion of Poland in 1939, she made her way to Rio de Janeiro, and gave a series of concerts in South America; then went to N.Y., where she made an exceptionally successful debut in Carnegie Hall (Feb. 25, 1946); her auspicious career was thwarted by an irremediable illness.

Jonas, Oswald, Austrian-American musicologist; b. Vienna, Jan. 10, 1897; d. Riverside, Calif., March 19, 1978. He studied musicology with Schenker (1915–22); also studied law at the

Univ. of Vienna (Ph.D., 1921). He taught at Berlin's Stern Cons. (1930–34); then worked at the Schenker Inst. at the New Vienna Cons. (1935–38). After the annexation of Austria by the Nazis in 1938, he went to the U.S., where he taught at Roosevelt Univ. in Chicago and associated schools (1941–64); after a sojourn as a teacher at the Vienna Academy of Music (1964–65), he became a prof. at the Univ. of Calif. at Riverside (1966). He publ. *Das Wesen des musikalischen Kunstwerks* (Vienna, 1934; 2nd ed., rev., 1973 as *Einführung in die Lehre Heinrich Schenkers*); also wrote numerous articles on Schenker's theories and ed. several of his works.

Joncières, Victorin de (real name, **Felix Ludger Rossignol**), French composer; b. Paris, April 12, 1839; d. there, Oct. 26, 1903. He was first a student of painting; music was his avocation. At the age of 20 he produced a light opera for a student performance; encouraged by its success with the critics, he began to study music seriously, first with Elwart, then with Leborne at the Paris Cons. He was a great admirer of Wagner, and when Leborne expressed his opposition to Wagner, Joncières impulsively left his class.

WORKS: Operas (all produced in Paris): *Sardanapale* (Feb. 8, 1867); *Le Dernier Jour de Pompei* (Sept. 21, 1869); *Dimitri* (May 5, 1876; his most successful work); *La Reine Berthe* (Dec. 27, 1878); *Le Chevalier Jean* (March 11, 1885; successful in Germany under the title *Johann von Lothringen*); *Lancelot du lac* (Feb. 7, 1900); also music to *Hamlet* (Nantes, Sept. 21, 1867); *Symphonie romantique* (Paris, March 9, 1873); Violin Concerto (Paris, Dec. 12, 1869); symphonic ode, *La Mer*; etc.

Jones, remarkable family of black American jazz musicians, all brothers:
(1) Hank (Henry) Jones, pianist; b. Vicksburg, Miss., July 31, 1918. He was taken in early childhood to Pontiac, Mich., where he began his piano training; as a teenager, he performed with groups in Michigan and Ohio, then went to N.Y. (1944), where he worked with Hot Lips Page; then had stints with various jazz artists, including Coleman Hawkins and Billy Eckstine. He was an accompanist for Ella Fitzgerald (1948–53) and also worked with Charlie Parker; then was a staff musician with CBS (1959–76), during which period he also toured; later was a pianist and conductor for the Broadway musical *Ain't Misbehavin'*, based on the music of Fats Waller. He made innumerable recordings.
BIBL.: L. Feather, "Piano Giants of Jazz: H. J.," *Contemporary Keyboard,* IV/2 (1978).
(2) Thad(deus Joseph) Jones, trumpeter, cornetist, flügelhornist, bandleader, arranger, and composer; b. Pontiac, Mich., March 28, 1923; d. Copenhagen, Aug. 20, 1986. He taught himself to play trumpet when he was about 13; subsequently appeared professionally with his brother Hank at age 16, and also with Sonny Stitt; after working with various dance and show bands, he joined his brother Elvin as a member of Billy Mitchell's quintet in Detroit (1950–53). He worked with Charles Mingus (1954–55) and was a featured soloist and arranger with Count Basie's orch. (1954–63); also appeared with Thelonious Monk and Gerry Mulligan. With Mel Lewis, in 1965 he formed his own band, which subsequently gained fame through its tours of the U.S. and Europe, including a smashing visit to the Soviet Union in 1972. He left the band in 1979 and settled in Denmark, where he organized his own big band, the Thad Jones Eclipse; he was also active as an arranger and composer with Danish Radio. He returned to the U.S. to briefly take charge of Count Basie's orch. (1985). His best-known composition was *A Child Is Born,* which gained the status of a jazz classic.
(3) Elvin (Ray) Jones, drummer; b. Pontiac, Mich., Sept. 9, 1927. He performed with local groups in Pontiac and Detroit before playing in military bands during his service in the U.S. Army (1946–49); he performed in Michigan, then went to N.Y. (1956), where he played with J.J. Johnson's quintet and Donald Byrd's quintet, as well as with Bud Powell, Sonny Rollins, and Stan Getz. He then performed with John Coltrane's group (1960–66), acquiring renown for his imaginative drumming; subsequently led his own groups, touring widely in the U.S., Europe, South America, and the Orient.

Jones, Alton, American pianist and teacher; b. Fairfield, Nebr., Aug. 3, 1899; d. N.Y., Jan. 2, 1971. He studied at Drake Univ. (B.M., 1919) and at the Inst. of Musical Art in N.Y., where his teachers were Edwin Hughes and Richard Buhlig; he graduated in 1921; made his concert debut in N.Y. in 1924; was a soloist with the N.Y. Phil. in 1949; gave his last N.Y. recital in 1955. He taught at the Juilliard School of Music from 1921 until his death; his reputation as a pedagogue was high; many American pianists were his pupils.

Jones, Booker T., black American organist, founder of Booker T. and the MGs (Memphis Group), noted for its "Memphis sound"; b. Memphis, Sept. 12, 1944. The group lit the rock firmament in 1962 with their smash hit *Green Onions.* In 1965 he authored a blues song with the pseudo-astrological title *Born under a Bad Sign.* Seized by a peculiar yen for musical culture, he received a degree in applied music from the respectable Indiana Univ. Fortunately, this academic distinction did not kill off his natural gift for pleasing the public. His records sold well; among his greatest hits were *Soul Limbo* (1968) and *Time Is Tight* (1969).

Jones, Brian (real name, **Lewis Brian Hopkins-Jones**), English rock musician; b. Cheltenham, Feb. 28, 1942; d. (found inanimate in a swimming pool) San Francisco, July 3, 1969. He joined Mick Jagger and others to form The Rolling Stones in 1962; the group rapidly ascended the ladder of success on both sides of the Atlantic, finally graduating in the immensity of a cult. Brian Jones went through the customary drug period, but managed to learn to play the Hindu sitar and the plebeian dulcimer, making him the group's most versatile instrumentalist. In 1967 and again in 1968 he was busted for illicit drug possession; in 1969 he left The Rolling Stones and soon died an unnatural death.

Jones, Charles, American composer; b. Tamworth, Canada, June 21, 1910. He settled in the U.S. in 1928, where he studied violin at the Inst. of Musical Art in N.Y. (diploma, 1932) and composition with Wagenaar at the Juilliard School of Music (diploma, 1939). He taught at Mills College in Oakland, Calif. (1939–44); joined the faculty of the Juilliard School in 1954 and the Mannes College of Music in N.Y. in 1972; also taught at the Aspen School of Music (from 1951).
WORKS: BALLET: *Down with Drink* for Female Voices, Piano, and Percussion (1943). **ORCH.:** 4 syms.: No. 1 (1939); No. 2 (1957); No. 3 (1962); No. 4, in 5 short movements (1965); *Little Symphony for the New Year* (1953); Suite for Strings (1937); *Galop* (1940); *Pastorale* for Chamber Orch. (1940); *Cowboy Song* for Oboe and Strings (1941); *Overture* (1942); *5 Melodies* (1945); *Cassation* (1948); *Introduction and Rondo* for Strings (1957); *Suite after a Notebook of 1762* for Chamber Orch. (1957); Concerto for 4 Violins and Orch. (1963); *Allegory* (1970). **CHAMBER:** 9 string quartets (1936–89); Sonatina for Solo Violin (1938); Sonatina for Violin and Piano (1942); Suite for Violin and Piano (1945); Duo for Violin and Piano (1947); *Threnody* for Solo Viola (1947); *Lyric Waltz Suite* for Wind Quartet (1948); *Sonata a tre* for Piano Trio (1952); Duo for Violin and Viola (1956); Sonata for Violin and Piano (1958); *Sonata piccola* for Piccolo and Harpsichord (1961); Sonata for Oboe and Harpsichord (1965); *Music for 2 Violinists* (1966); String Trio (1968); *In Nomine* for Violin and Piano (1972); Serenade for Flute, Violin, Cello, and Harpsichord (1973); *Triptychon* for Violin, Viola, and Piano (1975); *Triptychon II* for Violin and Piano (1981); Trio for Violin, Cello, and Piano (1982); *Meditation* for Bass Clarinet and Piano (1982); *Capriccio* for Cello and Piano (1983); *Ballade* for Violin and Piano (1986); *Serena* for 9 Instruments (1986). **VOCAL:** *The Seasons,* cantata (1959); *I Am a Mynstrel* for Tenor, Violin, Harpsichord, Piano, and Percussion (1967); *Masque,* after

Pope's "Rape of the Lock," for Speaker and 12 Players (1968); 4 scenes for Voice and Piano, after Pope (1982); *Poemata* for Voice, Violin, and Cello (1987); songs. PIANO: 2 sonatas (1946, 1950); Sonata for 2 Pianos (1947); *Toccata* (1955); *Psalm* (1976); *Book of the Hours* (1979–81); Sonata for Piano, 4-hands (1983); also *Keyboard Book* for Harpsichord (1953); *Noël* for Organ (1983).

Jones, Daniel (Jenkyn), remarkable Welsh composer; b. Pembroke, Dec. 7, 1912. Both his parents were musicians, and he absorbed the natural rudiments of music instinctively at home. He studied English literature at Swansea Univ. College (B.A., 1934; M.A., 1939), then entered the Royal Academy of Music in London, where he studied a variety of theoretical and practical aspects of music: composition with Farjeon, conducting with Sir Henry Wood, viola with Lockyear, and horn with Aubrey Brain; later studied at the Univ. of Wales (D.Mus., 1951). He retained interest in literature; was ed. of the collected poems of Dylan Thomas (1971). He was made an Officer of the Order of the British Empire (1968). In 1936 he promulgated a system of "complex metres," in which the numerator in the time signature indicates the succession of changing meters in a clear numerical progression, e.g. 32-322-3222-322-32, followed by 332-3332-332, etc.; his other innovation is a category of "continuous modes," with the final note of the mode (nonoctaval) serving as the initial note of a transposed mode. He authored numerous articles expounding his philosophy of music, some of which were incorporated in the book *Music and Esthetic* (1954).
WORKS: Syms.: No. 1 (1944); No. 2 (1950); No. 3 (1951); No. 4 (1954); No. 5 (1958); No. 6 (1964); No. 7 (1971); No. 8 (1972); No. 9 (1974); operas: *The Knife* (London, Dec. 2, 1963) and *Orestes* (1967); oratorios and cantatas: *The Country beyond the Stars* (1958), *St. Peter* (1962), *The 3 Hermits* (1969), *The Ballad of the Standard-Bearer* (1969), and *The Witnesses* (1971); *Capriccio* for Flute, Harp, and Strings (1965); Violin Concerto (1966); Sinfonietta (1972); concert overtures and symphonic suites; 8 string quartets; 5 string trios; String Quintet; Sonata for Unaccompanied Cello (1946); Kettledrum Sonata (1947); 8 Pieces for Violin and Viola (1948); Wind Septet (1949); Wind Nonet (1950); Sonata for 4 Trombones (1955); Sonata for Cello and Piano (1972); piano pieces.

Jones, Edward, Welsh harper, historian, and composer, known as Barrd y Brenin; b. Llandderfel, Merionethshire (baptized), March 29, 1752; d. London, April 18, 1824. He was taught by his father; the family organized an ensemble consisting of harps and string instruments. In 1774 he went to London; described himself as Harper or Bard to the Prince of Wales from about 1788; was known as the King's Bard from 1820. He composed a number of songs, as well as pieces for harp and harpsichord; publ. several anthologies of Welsh music, the most important being *Musical and Poetical Relicks of the Welsh Bards . . .* (1784; 2nd ed., rev. and augmented, 1794), *The Bardic Museum . . .* (1802; 2nd ed., 1825), and *Hen Ganiadau Cymru: Cambro-British Melodies, or the National Songs and Airs of Wales* (1820); these vols. contain over 200 Welsh melodies; also publ. collections of melodies from other nations.
BIBL.: T. Ellis, *E. J., Barrd y Brenin* (Cardiff, 1957).

Jones, George, American country-music singer; b. Saratoga, Texas, Sept. 12, 1931. He began to play the guitar when he was 9; made some appearances locally before serving in the Korean War; then worked as a house painter. In 1955 he recorded his 1st hit song, *Why, Baby, Why*; subsequently gained fame with such songs as *Window Up Above* (1961), *She Thinks I Still Care* (1962), and *We Must Have Been Out of Our Minds* (1963). He was married to the country-music star Tammy Wynette (1969–75); after their divorce, he took to drink; his alcoholism did not prevent the Country Music Assoc., however, from naming him the male vocalist of the year in 1981.
BIBL.: B. Allen, *G. J.: The Saga of an American Singer* (Garden City, N.Y., 1984); D. Carlisle, *Ragged but Right: The Life and Times of G. J.* (Chicago, 1984).

Jones, Geraint (Iwan), Welsh organist, harpsichordist, and conductor; b. Porth, May 16, 1917. He studied at the Royal Academy of Music in London; made his debut as harpsichordist at the National Gallery in 1940; subsequently gave numerous recitals as an organist, often on historical instruments of Europe; in 1951 he founded the Geraint Jones Singers and Orch., which he led in many performances of Baroque music.

Jones, Grace, Jamaican soul and funk singer, songwriter, and actress; b. Spanishtown, May 19, 1952. After working as a model in Paris, she went to N.Y. and appeared as a singer in dance clubs during the disco craze; 1st gained success as a recording artist with her album *Warm Leatherette* (1980), which was followed by such albums as *Nightclubbing* (1981), *Living My Life* (1982), *Island Life* (1985), and *Slave to Rhythm* (1985); was also active as an actress in films.
BIBL.: *Current Biography* (Sept. 1987).

Jones, Dame Gwyneth, prominent Welsh soprano; b. Pontnewyndd, Nov. 7, 1936. She studied at the Royal College of Music in London, and in Siena, Geneva, and Zürich, where she made her operatic debut as Gluck's Orfeo (1962). In 1963 she 1st appeared at the Welsh National Opera in Cardiff and at London's Covent Garden; she also sang at the Vienna State Opera and at the Bayreuth Festivals from 1966. In 1966 she made her U.S. debut in N.Y. in a concert version of Cherubini's *Médée;* her Metropolitan Opera debut followed as Sieglinde in *Die Walküre* on Nov. 24, 1972. She also sang at the San Francisco Opera, Milan's La Scala, Munich's Bavarian State Opera, and the Rome Opera; appeared as Brünnhilde in the centenary performances of the *Ring* cycle at Bayreuth in 1976. In 1976 she was made a Commander of the Order of the British Empire and in 1986 a Dame Commander of the Order of the British Empire. In addition to her Wagner and Verdi roles, she has won praise for her portrayals of Donna Anna, Leonore, and the Marschallin. On Sept. 12, 1988, she celebrated the 25th anniversary of her Covent Garden debut by opening its season as Turandot.

Jones, Jo(nathan), black American jazz drummer, known as Kansas City Jo Jones and Papa Jo Jones; b. Chicago, Oct. 7, 1911; d. N.Y., Sept. 3, 1985. He was reared in Alabama; studied saxophone, trumpet, and piano before mastering the drums; joined Count Basie's band in 1934 and remained with his group, off and on, until 1948, establishing his own distinctive rhythmic style stressing all 4 beats of the bar and diversifying it with a wire-brush technique on the high-hat cymbal. In 1957 he traveled to Europe with Ella Fitzgerald and Oscar Peterson; then led his own groups. He appeared in several films, including *Jammin' the Blues* (1944), *Born to Swing* (1973), and *Last of the Blue Devils* (1979).

Jones, (Herbert) Kelsey, American-born Canadian composer; b. South Norwalk, Conn., June 17, 1922. He went to Canada in 1939; became a naturalized Canadian citizen in 1956. He studied with Harold Hamer at Mount Allison Univ. (B.Mus., 1945), then with Sir Ernest MacMillan, Healey Willan, and Leo Smith at the Univ. of Toronto (B.Mus., 1946; D.Mus., 1951), and with Nadia Boulanger in Paris (1949–50). Returning to Canada, he was appointed to the faculty of McGill Univ. in Montreal in 1954. In his compositions he follows traditional forms, with some use of electronics.
WORKS: Chamber opera, *Sam Slick* (Halifax, Sept. 5, 1967); *Miramichi Ballad,* suite for Orch. (1954); Suite for Flute and Strings (1954); *4 Pieces* for Recorder Quartet (1955); *Songs of Time* for Chorus and Piano, 4-hands (1955); *Sonata da camera* for Flute, Oboe, and Harpsichord (1957); *Introduction and Fugue* for Violin and Piano (1959); *Songs of Innocence,* after Blake, for Soprano and Chamber Orch. (1961); *Prelude, Fughetta, and Finale* for Violin, Cello, and Harpsichord (1963); *Rondo* for Solo Flute (1963); *Prophecy of Micah* for Chorus and Orch. (Montreal, Feb. 5, 1964); *Sonata da chiesa* for Flute, Oboe, and Harpsichord (1967); Wind Quintet (1968); *Hymn to Bacchus* for Chorus and Piano, 4-hands (1972); *Adagio, Presto, and Fugue* for String Quartet and String Orch. (1973);

Songs of Winter for Soprano, Contralto, and Piano (1973); *Passacaglia and Fugue* for Brass Quintet (1975).

Jones, Mason, American horn player, conductor, and teacher; b. Hamilton, N.Y., June 16, 1919. He was a pupil of Tabuteau and Reiner at the Curtis Inst. of Music in Philadelphia (1936–38). In 1938 he joined the Philadelphia Orch., where he was 1st horn (1940–78), personnel manager (1963–86), and conductor of the school concerts (1972–82); also was conductor of the Episcopal Academy Orch. (1958–60) and assistant conductor of the Philadelphia Chamber Orch. (1961–64). He was a founding member of the Philadelphia Woodwind Quintet (1950–80) and of the Philadelphia Brass Ensemble (from 1957); taught at the Curtis Inst. of Music (from 1946) and at Temple Univ. College of Music (1976–83); in 1986–87 he was president of the International Horn Soc. He ed. *Solos for the Horn Player* (1962) and *20th Century Orchestral Studies* (1971).

Jones, Parry, Welsh tenor; b. Blaina, Monmouthshire, Feb. 14, 1891; d. London, Dec. 26, 1963. He studied at the Royal College of Music in London; also with Colli in Italy, Scheidemantel in Dresden, and John Coates in England. He made his debut in London in 1914; then sang in the U.S. He survived the German submarine attack on the S.S. *Lusitania* on his return trip to England in 1915, and then sang with the Beecham and D'Oyly Carte opera companies. He was a leading member of the Carl Rosa Opera Co. (1919–22) and the British National Opera Co. (1922–28); made his Covent Garden debut in 1921 as Turiddu; sang there again (1925–26; 1930–32; 1935; 1937), serving as a principal tenor there from 1949 to 1955, the 1953–54 season excepted. He then taught voice at the Guildhall School of Music. In 1962 he was made an Officer of the Order of the British Empire. He sang in the 1st British performances of *Wozzeck, Mathis der Maler,* and *Doktor Faust* in concert broadcasts by the BBC; was also active as an oratorio singer.

Jones, Philip (Mark), outstanding English trumpeter; b. Bath, March 12, 1928. He studied at the Royal College of Music in London with Ernest Hall; then served as principal trumpet player in the Royal Phil. (1956–60), Philharmonia Orch. (1960–64), London Phil. (1964–65), New Philharmonia Orch. (1965–67), and BBC Sym. Orch. (1968–71). In 1951 he founded the Philip Jones Brass Ensemble, commissioning many composers to write works for his ensemble; remained its director until 1986. He was head of the wind and percussion dept. at the Royal Northern College of Music in Manchester (1975–77) and then at the Guildhall School of Music in London (from 1983). In 1988 he was appointed principal of Trinity College of Music in London. He was made an Officer of the Order of the British Empire in 1977 and in 1986 a Commander of the Order of the British Empire.

Jones, "Philly Joe" (Joseph Rudolph), American jazz drummer; b. Philadelphia, July 15, 1923; d. there, Aug. 30, 1985. He studied piano with his mother, saxophone with Jimmy Oliver, and drums with James Harris; then played with local groups. Making his way to N.Y., he played with Zoot Sims, Lee Konitz, and Miles Davis. In 1967 he went to Europe, remaining there until 1972; eventually formed the jazz-rock group Le Gran Prix (1975), with which he toured the U.S.; appeared at N.Y.'s Carnegie Hall (1980).

Jones, Quincy (Delight, Jr.), versatile black American pianist, trumpeter, bandleader, recording executive, composer, and film producer; b. Chicago, March 14, 1933. Taken to Seattle at the age of 10, he took up the trumpet at 14; later studied with Clark Terry (1950). He played in Lionel Hampton's band (1951–53), then was a performer-arranger in Dizzy Gillespie's touring band in the Near East (1956–57); subsequently worked in Europe (1957–60), which he toured with his own big band. After returning to the U.S., he was an artist and repertoire man for Mercury Records, becoming vice-president (1964); later founded his own record company. He composed such works as *Stockholm Sweetnin', Evening in Paris, Soundpiece* for String Quartet and Contralto, and *Soundpiece* for Jazz Orch.

He won a number of Grammy Awards, being honored in 1985 as producer of the recording and video productions of *We Are the World,* which helped raise millions of dollars for famine relief efforts in Africa. He also composed the score for and was co-producer of the film *The Color Purple* (1985).

Jones, Robert, English composer; b. c.1485; d. London, c.1536. He is believed to have been a chorister in Henry VII's Royal Household Chapel, a Gentleman of Henry VIII's Royal Household Chapel (1512), and a member of the chapel during its visit to France (1513). He is definitely known to have been a Gentleman of the Chapel Royal. His only extant works are the *Missa Spes nostra* for 5 Voices, a *Magnificat* for 5 Voices, and the song *Who Shall Have My Fayr Lady.*
Bibl.: W. Grattan Flood, *Early Tudor Composers* (London, 1925).

Jones, Robert, English lutenist and composer; b. c.1570; d. c.1615. He studied at Oxford Univ. (Mus.B., 1597); with several other musicians, he was granted a patent to form the "Children of the Revells of the Queene." He publ. 5 books of lute songs (1600, 1601, 1605, 1607, 1610; ed. by E.H. Fellowes in The English School of Lutenist Song Writers, 1920–32; rev., 1959, by T. Dart in The English Lute-Songs, 2nd series, IV) and a book of madrigals (1605; ed. by E.H. Fellowes in The English Madrigal School, 1913–24; rev., 1961, by T. Dart in The English Madrigalists).
Bibl.: E.H. Fellowes, *The English Madrigal Composers* (London, 1921; 2nd ed., 1948); idem, "The Text of the Song Book of R. J.," *Music & Letters,* VIII (1927).

Jones, (James) Sidney, English composer; b. London, June 17, 1861; d. there, Jan. 29, 1946. At an early age he became conductor of a military band; then toured the English provinces and Australia as conductor of various light opera companies; from 1905 to 1916 he was conductor at the London Empire Theatre. He owes his fame mainly to his enormously successful operetta *The Geisha* (London, April 25, 1896), which was for decades performed all over the world. His other operettas include *A Gaiety Girl* (London, 1893), *An Artist's Model* (London, 1895), *A Greek's Slave* (Vienna, 1899), *My Lady Molly* (London, 1903), *See* (London, 1906), *The King of Cadonia* (London, 1908), *A Persian Princess* (London, 1909), *The Girl from Utah* (London, 1913), and *The Happy Day* (London, 1916).

Jones, Sissieretta (born **Matilda Sissieretta Joyner**), noted black American soprano, known as the "Black Patti" (with reference to Adelina Patti); b. Portsmouth, Va., Jan. 5, 1868; d. Providence, R.I., June 24, 1933. She studied at the New England Cons. of Music in Boston; also with Louise Capianni and Mme. Scongia in London. She made her debut at a concert at N.Y.'s Steinway Hall on April 5, 1888, then began to tour from 1890, giving concerts in the West Indies, North America, and Europe. She gained prominence as a result of her appearances at the Grand Negro Jubilee at N.Y.'s Madison Square Garden and at the White House in a command performance for President Harrison (1892); then sang at the Pittsburgh Exposition and the Chicago World's Columbian Exposition (1893). N.Y.'s Metropolitan Opera considered her for African roles in *Aida* and *L'Africaine,* but racial attitudes and conservative management policies precluded such appearances. She was the principal soprano of the vaudeville troupe known as Black Patti's Troubadours (1896–1915), with which she toured throughout the world; she starred in its operatic "kaleidoscope," in which she sang a medley of arias from operas in staged scenes; she also sang art songs and popular ballads.
Bibl.: E. Southern and J. Wright, "S. J.," *Black Perspective in Music,* IV (1976).

Jones, "Spike" (Lindley Armstrong), American bandleader; b. Long Beach, Calif., Dec. 14, 1911; d. Los Angeles, May 1, 1965. He played drums as a boy; then led a school band. On July 30, 1942, he made a recording of a satirical song, *Der Führer's Face,* featuring a Bronx-cheer razzer; then toured the U.S. with his band, The City Slickers, which included a wash board, a Smith and Wesson pistol, anti-bug Flit guns in E-flat, doorbells, anvils, hammers to break glass, and a live goat trained to bleat rhythmically. Climactically, he introduced the Latrinophone (a toilet seat strung with catgut). With this ensemble, he launched a Musical Depreciation Revue. He retired in 1963, when the wave of extravaganza that had carried him to the crest of commercial success subsided. In his heyday he was known as the "King of Corn."

BIBL.: J. Young, *S. J. and His City Slickers: An Illustrated Biography* (Beverly Hills, Calif., 1984).

Jones, Tom (real name, **Thomas Jones Woodward**), Welsh singer and drummer; b. Pontypridd, June 7, 1940. He sang, as most Welshmen do, with a natural feeling for melody; dropped out of school at 16, and began to play drums and sing in British pubs; his big chance at success came when he was heard by Gordon Mills, a Welshman himself, who decided to propel him into fame; but first he had to abbreviate his name to plain Tom Jones. His greatest asset was lung power; he could outscream anyone in the rock field; he wore extremely tight "sexy" pants, whose protuberances excited middle-aged women; with these assets he successfully invaded the U.S. By the late 1980s his fame had largely dissipated, his performances relegated to the nostalgia circuit.

BIBL.: C. Macfarlane, *T. J.: The Boy from Nowhere* (N.Y., 1988).

Jones, William, English churchman, writer on music, and composer; b. Lowick, Northamptonshire (baptized), July 20, 1726; d. Nayland, Suffolk, Jan. 6, 1800. He studied at Oxford, and with James Oswald and Pepusch in London; subsequently was a vicar and curate. He publ. *A Treatise on the Art of Music; in which the Elements of Harmony and Air are practically considered* (Colchester, 1784; 2nd ed., 1827) and *The Nature and Excellence of Music: a Sermon* (London, 1787).

BIBL.: J. Kassler, "The Systematic Writings on Music of W. J. (1726–1800)," *Journal of the American Musicological Society,* XXVI (1973).

Jong, Marinus de, Dutch-born Belgian pianist and composer; b. Osterhout, Aug. 14, 1891; d. Ekeren, June 13, 1984. He studied composition with Mortelmans and piano with Bosquet at the Antwerp Cons. After several tours as pianist in Europe and America, he settled in Belgium in 1926, and became a prof. of piano (1931) and of counterpoint and fugue (1948) at the Antwerp Cons. He developed a neo-impressionistic style, with polytonal counterpoint as its mainstay.

WORKS: 3 operas: *Mitsanoboe* (1962); *Die häslichen Mädchen von Bagdad* (The Hateful Maidens of Baghdad; Antwerp, Jan. 7, 1967); *Esmoreit* (Antwerp, Sept. 11, 1970); 5 ballets: *De vrouwen van Zalongo* (1951); *De kleine haven* (1952); *De kringloop* (1955); *Carrefour* (1956); *De Reiskameraad* (1959); 4 oratorios: *Hiawatha's Lied* (1947); *Imitatio Christi* (1956); *Kerkhofblommen* (1957); *Proverbia Bruegeliana* (1961); the cantata *Summum bonum* (1955); *Ode aan Peter Benoit* for Baritone, Chorus, and Orch. (1946); *Hymnus "Civitas Dei"* for Soloists, Chorus, Children's Chorus, and Orch. (1957); *Hymne aan de Schoonheid* for Soprano, Baritone, Chorus, and Orch. (1961); 3 piano concertos (1924, 1952, 1956–57); concertos for Trumpet (1937), Cello (1946; rev. 1969), Violin (1954), Viola (1958), Oboe (1966–67), Horn (1966–67), Bassoon (1967), Flute (1967), Clarinet (1967), and Organ (1974); 3 syms. (1932, 1965–66, 1976); 3 *Flemish Rhapsodies:* No. 1 for Orch. (1955), No. 2 for Orch. (1971), and No. 3 for Piano and Orch. (1971); *Rhapsodie No. 4* for Wind Orch. (1974); *Heidestemmingen (Impressions de Bruyère)* for Orch. (1937); *Hiawatha,* symphonic poem (1945); *Aphoristische tryptiek* for Orch. or Wind Quintet (1952); *Boublitschky Suite* for Orch. (1956); *Ruimteraket, Atlas (Fusée interplanétaire),* symphonic poem (1964); 6 string quartets (1923, 1926, 1947, 1956, 1956, 1962); *Pacis, Doloris et Amoris,* violin sonata (1927); Quartet for 4 Cellos (1936); Nonet (1939); 3 wind quintets (1952, 1965, 1971); Suite for 4 Trombones (1958); Wind Quartet (1968); Fantasia for Saxophone and Piano (1968); Piano Quar-

tet (1971); Sextet for Piano and Wind Quintet (1972); 3 piano sonatas (1926, 1933, 1934); *12 Preludes* for Piano (1975); Concerto for Solo Organ (1964); organ pieces; choruses; songs.

Jongen, (Marie-Alphonse-Nicolas-) Joseph, eminent Belgian composer, brother of **Léon (Marie-Victor-Justin) Jongen;** b. Liège, Dec. 14, 1873; d. Sart-lez-Spa, July 12, 1953. He studied at the Liège Cons.; received a premier prix for each of the academic subjects and also for piano and organ. In 1891 he joined the faculty of the Liège Cons. as a teacher of harmony and counterpoint. In 1894 he gained attention as a composer when he won 2 national prizes; in 1897 he won the Belgian Prix de Rome. He then received advice from Strauss in Berlin and d'Indy in Paris. After returning to Brussels, he taught at a music academy; from 1898, also held the position of *professeur adjoint* at the Liège Cons., where he became a prof. in 1911. After the outbreak of World War I in 1914, he went to London; made appearances as a pianist and organist; with Defauw, Tertis, and Doehaerd, organized a piano quartet, which became known as the Belgian Quartet. In 1919 he returned to Belgium; in 1920 he became a prof. of counterpoint and fugue at the Brussels Cons.; from 1925 to 1939 he was its director; was succeeded by his brother, Léon. During World War II, he lived in France; then returned to his country estate at Sart-lez-Spa. He was a prolific composer and continued to write music to the end of his life; the total of his works aggregates to 137 opus numbers. While not pursuing extreme modern effects, Jongen succeeded in imparting an original touch to his harmonic style.

WORKS: ORCH.: Sym. (1899); Violin Concerto (1899); Cello Concerto (1900); *Fantasie sur deux Noëls populaires wallons* (1902); *Lalla-Roukh,* symphonic poem after Thomas Moore (1904); *Prélude et Danse* (1907); *2 Rondes wallones* (1912; also for Piano); Trumpet Concertino (1913); *Impressions d'Ardennes* (1913); Suite for Violin and Orch. (1915); *Épithalame et Scherzo* for 3 Violins, and Orch. or Piano (1917); *Tableaux pittoresques* (1917); *Poème héroïque* for Violin and Orch. (1919); *Prélude élégiaque et Scherzo* (1920); *Fantasie rhapsodique* for Cello and Orch. (1924); *Hymne* for Organ and Strings (1924); *Symphonie concertante* for Organ and Orch. (1926); *Pièce symphonique* for Piano and Orch. (1928); *Passacaille et Gigue* (1929); *Suite No. 3, dans le style ancien* (1930); *10 Pièces* (1932); *Triptyque* (1935); *Ouverture Fanfare* (1939); *Alleluia* for Organ and Orch. (1940); *Ouverture de fête* (1941); Piano Concerto (1943); *Bourrée* (1944); Harp Concerto (1944); Mass for Organ, Chorus, and Orch. (1946); *In memoriam* (1947); *Ballade, Hommage à Chopin* (1949); *3 Mouvements symphoniques* (1951). **CHAMBER:** 3 string quartets (1893, 1916, 1921); Piano Trio (1897); Piano Quartet (1901); 2 violin sonatas (1902, 1909); Trio for Piano, Violin, and Viola (1907); Cello Sonata (1912); 2 Serenades for String Quartet (1918); 2 *Pièces* for Flute, Cello, and Harp (1924); 2 *Pièces* for 4 Cellos (1929); *Sonata eroica* for Organ (1930); Wind Quintet (1933); Quintet for Harp, Flute, Violin, Viola, and Cello (1940); Concerto for Wind Quintet (1942); Quartet for 4 Saxophones (1942); String Trio (1948); a number of piano pieces, including 24 preludes in all keys (1941); solo pieces for various instruments with piano; many songs with instrumental accompaniment; choral works. A catalog of his works was publ. by the Centre Belge de Documentation Musicale (Brussels, 1954).

BIBL.: J. Whiteley, "J. and His Organ Music," *Musical Times* (March 1983; includes a biographical profile).

Jongen, Léon (Marie-Victor-Justin), important Belgian composer, brother of **(Marie-Alphonse-Nicolas-) Joseph Jongen;** b. Liège, March 2, 1884; d. Brussels, Nov. 18, 1969. He studied at the Liège Cons.; was organist at St. Jacques there (1898–1904). He received the Belgian Grand Prix de Rome for his cantata *Les Fiancés de Noël* (1913); was in the Belgian army during World War I; after the war, traveled to the Far East and served as conductor of the Tonkin Opera in Hanoi (1927–29). Returning to Belgium in 1934, he became an instructor at the Brussels Cons.; succeeded his brother as its director (1939–49).

WORKS: Operas: *L'Ardennaise* (1909) and *Thomas l'Agnelet* (1922–23; Brussels, Feb. 14, 1924); musical fairy tale, *Le Rêve d'une nuit de Noël* (1917; Paris, March 18, 1918); ballet, *Le Masque de la Mort rouge,* after Poe (1956). Also 2 lyric scenes for Chorus and Orch.: *Geneviève de Brabant* (1907) and *La Légende de St. Hubert* (1909; 1st public perf., St. Hubert, July 21, 1968); *Campéador* for Orch. (1932); *Malaisie,* suite for Orch. (1935); *In Memoriam Regis* for Orch. (1935); *Prélude, Divertissement et Final* for Piano and Orch. (1937); *Trilogie de Psaumes* for Chorus and Orch. (1937–39); *Rhapsodia belgica* for Violin and Orch. (1948); *Musique for a Ballet* (1954); *Divertissement en forme de variations sur un thème de Haydn* for Orch. (1956); Violin Concerto (1962; compulsory work for the 12 finalists of the 1963 Queen Elisabeth violin contest held in Brussels). He further wrote a String Quartet (1919); Fantasia for Piano (1930); *Divertissement* for 4 Saxophones (1937); Trio for Oboe, Clarinet, and Bassoon (1937); Trio for Flute, Violin, and Viola (1937); Piano Quartet (1955); Quintet for Piano, Flute, Clarinet, Horn, and Bassoon (1958); songs.

Jonsson, Josef Petrus, Swedish composer; b. Enköping, June 21, 1887; d. Norrköping, May 9, 1969. He studied piano, but soon turned to musical journalism. He wrote 3 syms. (*Nordland,* 1919–22; 1931; 1947); *Chamber Symphony* (1949); several orch. overtures and suites; Violin Concerto (Norrköping, April 10, 1960); *Festival Prelude* for Orch. (1961); *Korallrevet,* symphonic poem for Baritone, Chorus, and Orch. (1916); *Missa solemnis* for Chorus, Orch., and Organ (1934); Cantata for Speaking Chorus, Female Chorus, Soli, 2 Flutes, and Piano (Norrköping, May 5, 1962); chamber music; piano pieces; songs.

Joó, Arpád, Hungarian-born American conductor; b. Budapest, June 8, 1948. He pursued private musical instruction with Kodály (1954–65) and János Ferencsik (1954–68). From 1958 to 1964 he was a piano student at the Béla Bartók Cons. in Budapest; was a private pupil of Carlo Zecchi (piano and conducting, 1963–65) and of Nikita Magaloff (piano, 1964–65); studied piano with Joseph Gat and Pál Kadosa at the Franz Liszt Academy of Music in Budapest (1964–68). After further piano lessons with Irwin Freundlich at the Juilliard School in N.Y. (1968–69), he concentrated on conducting studies with Zoltán Rozsnyai in San Diego (1969), Wolfgang Vacano and Tibor Kozma at Indiana Univ. (1970–73), Igor Markevitch (1972–73), and Carlo Maria Giulini (1979). In 1975 he became a naturalized U.S. citizen. He was music director of the Knoxville (Tenn.) Sym. Orch. (1973–78) and the Calgary (Alberta) Phil. (1978–81), subsequently serving as music adviser and principal conductor of the latter (1981–83). In 1985 he was principal guest conductor of the European Community Chamber Orch.; from 1985 to 1987 he was music director of the Nyirbator Festival in Hungary. In 1986 he was appointed principal guest conductor of the Budapest Sym. Orch., and in 1987, music director of the sym. orch. and chorus of Spanish Radio and Television in Madrid, which position he held until 1991; also was prof. of conducting at the master classes in Assisi (from 1987) and music adviser and principal guest conductor of the Brabant Orch. (1989–91). He has won critical accolades for his idiomatic performances of Liszt, Bartók, and Kodály.

Joplin, Janis (Lyn), American rock and blues singer; b. Port Arthur, Texas, Jan. 19, 1943; d. of an overdose of heroin, Los Angeles, Oct. 4, 1970. She spent an unhappy childhood; ran away from home and delved into the bohemian life of San Francisco. After a brief stint in college, she joined the rock group Big Brother and the Holding Company as lead vocalist in 1966, winning acclaim for her rendition of *Love Is Like a Ball and Chain* when she appeared with the group at the Monterey International Pop Festival in 1967. Her passionate wailing in a raspy voice immediately established her as an uninhibited representative of the younger generation. After recording the album *Cheap Thrills* (1967), she left Big Brother and struck out on her own; formed her own backup group, the Full Tilt Boogie Band, in 1968 and then appeared in such esoteric emporia as the Psychedelic Supermarket in Boston, Kinetic Playground in Chicago, Whisky A-Go-Go in Los Angeles, and Fillmore East in N.Y. She produced the albums *I Got Dem Ol' Kozmic Blues Again Mama* and *Pearl* before her early demise. She was arrested in Tampa, Fla., in 1969 for having hurled porcine epithets at a policeman, which further endeared her to her public. On the more positive side, the Southern Comfort Distillery Co. presented her with a fur coat in recognition of the publicity she gave the firm by her habitual consumption of a quart of Southern Comfort at each of her appearances; she injected religious passion into a commercial theme in one of her own songs, *Oh Lord, Won't You Buy Me a Mercedes-Benz?*

BIBL.: D. Dalton, *Piece of My Heart: The Life, Times, and Legend of J. J.* (N.Y., 1985); G. Blumenstein, *J. J.: Biographie einer Rocksängerin* (Berlin, 1988).

Joplin, Scott, remarkable black American pianist and composer; b. probably near Marshall, Texas, Nov. 24, 1868; d. N.Y., April 1, 1917. He learned to play the piano at home in Texarkana, and later studied music seriously with a local German musician. He left home at 17 and went to St. Louis, earning his living by playing piano in local emporia. In 1893 he moved to Chicago (drawn by the prospect of music-making and other gaiety of the World's Fair), and in 1896 went to Sedalia, Mo., where he took music courses at George Smith College, a segregated school for blacks. His 1st music publications were in 1895, of genteel, maudlin songs and marches, typical of the period. His success as a ragtime composer came with the *Maple Leaf Rag* (1899; the most famous of all piano rags), which he named after a local dance hall, the Maple Leaf Club. The sheet-music ed. sold so well that Joplin was able to settle in St. Louis and devote himself exclusively to composition; he even tried to write a ragtime ballet (*The Ragtime Dance,* 1902) and a ragtime opera, *A Guest of Honor* (copyright 1903, but the music is lost; newspaper notices indicate it was probably perf. by the Scott Joplin Opera Co. in 1903). In 1907 he went to N.Y., where he continued his career as a composer and teacher. Still intent on ambitious plans, he wrote an opera, *Treemonisha,* to his own libretto (the title deals with a black baby girl found under a tree by a woman named Monisha); he completed the score in 1911 and produced it in concert form in 1915 without success. Interest in the opera was revived almost 60 years later; T.J. Anderson orchestrated it from the piano score, and it received its 1st complete performance in Atlanta on Jan. 28, 1972. Despite Joplin's ambitious attempts to make ragtime "respectable" by applying its principles to European forms, it was with the small, indigenous dance form of the piano rag that he achieved his greatest artistic success. As one noted historian phrased it, these pieces are "the precise American equivalent, in terms of a native dance music, of minuets by Mozart, mazurkas by Chopin, or waltzes by Brahms." Altogether, he wrote about 50 piano rags, in addition to the 2 operas, and a few songs, waltzes, and marches. The titles of some of these rags reflect his desire to transcend the trivial and create music on a more serious plane: *Sycamore,* "A Concert Rag" (1904); *Chrysanthemum,* "An Afro-American Intermezzo" (1904); *Sugar Cane,* "A Ragtime Classic 2 Step" (1908); *Fig Leaf Rag,* "A High Class Rag" (1908); *Reflection Rag,* "Syncopated Musings" (1917). In his last years he lamented at having failed to achieve the recognition he felt his music merited. Suffering from syphilis, he became insane and died shortly afterward in a state hospital. More than 50 years later, an extraordinary sequence of events— new recordings of his music and its use in an award-winning film, *The Sting* (1974)—brought Joplin unprecedented popularity and acclaim: among pop recordings, *The Entertainer* (1902) was one of the best-selling discs for 1974; among classical recordings, Joplin albums represented 74 percent of the best-sellers of the year. In 1976 he was awarded exceptional posthumous recognition by the Pulitzer Prize Committee. See V. Lawrence, ed., *The Collected Works of Scott Joplin* (2 vols., N.Y.,

1971; 2nd ed., rev., 1981 as *The Complete Works of Scott Joplin*).

BIBL.: R. Blesh and H. Janis, *They All Played Ragtime* (N.Y., 1950; 4th ed., 1971); A. Reed, "S. J., Pioneer," *Black Perspective in Music* (Spring 1975; Fall 1975); T. Waldo, *This Is Ragtime* (N.Y., 1976); K. Preston and N. Huggins, *S. J.* (N.Y., 1988).

Jora, Mihail, prominent Rumanian composer and pedagogue; b. Roman, Aug. 14, 1891; d. Bucharest, May 10, 1971. He studied piano privately in Iaşi (1901–12) and theory at the Cons. there (1909–11); then went to Germany, where he became a student of Krell and Reger at the Leipzig Cons. (1912–14); after World War I he went to Paris, where he studied with Florent Schmitt (1919–20). Returning to Rumania, he was music director of the Rumanian Radio (1928–33); also was prof. of composition at the Bucharest Cons. (1929–62). He was a founding member of the Soc. of Rumanian Composers in 1920, consultant to the Bucharest Opera (1931–45), and a music critic. He publ. the book *Momente muzicale* (Bucharest, 1968). Jora is regarded in Rumania as one of the finest composers of the Romantic national school, with a strongly pronounced lyric inspiration. Many composers of the younger generations were his students.

WORKS: 6 ballets: *La piaţă* (At the Market Place, 1928; Bucharest, 1931); *Demoazela Măriuţa* (Damoiselle Mariutza, 1940; Bucharest, 1942); *Curtea veche* (The Old Court, 1948); *Cînd strugurii se coc* (When the Grapes Ripen; Bucharest, 1954); *Întoarcerea din adîncuri* (Return to the Abyss, 1959; Bucharest, 1965); *Hanul Dulcinea* (The Inn Dulcinea; Bucharest, 1967); Suite for Orch. (1915); *Poveste indică* (Hindu Tale), symphonic poem with Vocalizing Tenor (1920); *Privelişti moldoveneşti* (Moldavian Landscapes), suite for Orch. (1924); *Şase cîntece şi-o rumbă* (6 Songs and a Rumba) for Orch. (1932); Sym. (1937); *Burlesca* for Orch. (1949); *Baladă* for Baritone, Chorus, and Orch. (1955); 2 string quartets (1926, 1966); Viola Sonata (1951); Violin Sonata (1962); choruses; song cycles; piano pieces, including *Joujoux pour ma dame* (1925); *Cortegiu* (Marche juive, 1925); Sonata (1942); *Variations on a Theme of Schumann* (1943); *Poze şi pozne* (Portraits and Jokes), miniatures in 3 sets (1948, 1959, 1963); *13 Preludes* (1960).

Jordá, Enrique, Spanish conductor; b. San Sebastian, March 24, 1911. He was a chorister in the parochial school and played organ at his parish church in Madrid; in 1929 he went to Paris as a medical student, but then turned decidedly to music, studying organ with Marcel Dupré, composition with Paul Le Flem, and conducting with Frans Rühlmann. He made his debut as an orch. conductor in Paris in 1938; conducted the Basque Ballet (1937–39), the Madrid Sym. Orch. (1940–45), and the Cape Town Sym. Orch. (1948–54). From 1954 to 1963 he was conductor of the San Francisco Sym. Orch.; from 1970 to 1976 he was conductor of the Antwerp Phil. and from 1982 to 1984 of the Euskadi Sym. Orch. He publ. *El director de orquesta ante la partitura* (Madrid, 1969).

Jordan, Armin, Swiss conductor; b. Lucerne, April 9, 1932. He received his musical training in Lucerne and Geneva. After holding the post of 1st conductor at the Zürich Opera (1963–68), he was conductor in St. Gallen (1968–71) and at the Basel Opera (1968–89). From 1973 to 1985 he was music director of the Lausanne Chamber Orch., with which he toured the U.S. in 1983. In 1985 he became chief conductor of l'Orch. de la Suisse Romande in Geneva, while concurrently serving as principal guest conductor of the Ensemble Orchestral de Paris from 1986. He conducted the soundtrack and also portrayed the role of Amfortas, with the vocal part dubbed in by Wolfgang Schöne, for the Syberberg film version of *Parsifal*. Jordan has appeared as a guest conductor with various opera houses and orchs., and has won particular distinction for his performances of the French repertoire.

Jordan, Irene, American soprano; b. Birmingham, Ala., April 25, 1919. Both her parents were professional music teachers, and she began playing piano at the age of 5; then studied voice at Judson College in Marion, Ala. (A.B., 1939); in 1939 she went to N.Y., where she continued vocal studies with Clytie Mundy; made her debut at the Metropolitan Opera in 1946, remaining on its roster until 1948 and singing there again in 1956–57. She sang opera in Chicago (1954) and also appeared with the N.Y. City Opera (1957); was a prof. of voice at Northwestern Univ. (from 1962). Possessing a diversified vocal technique, she was able to sing both dramatic and lyric soprano parts. Among her finest roles were Donna Elvira, the Queen of the Night, Beethoven's Leonore, Verdi's Lady Macbeth, and Aida.

Jordan, Jules, American singer, choral conductor, teacher, and composer; b. Willimantic, Conn., Nov. 10, 1850; d. Providence, R.I., March 5, 1927. He moved to Providence in 1870 and established himself as a singer, choral conductor, and teacher; conducted the 250-voice Arion Club (1880–1920). He was a successful composer of school operettas (*The Alphabet, Cloud and Sunshine*, etc.); wrote 6 light operas: *Star of the Sea; An Eventful Holiday; The Buccaneers; Princess of the Blood; Her Crown of Glory; A Leap Year Furlough*; the vaudeville sketches *Cobbler or King* and *Managerial Tactics*; etc.; also wrote a romantic comedy opera, *Rip Van Winkle* (Providence, May 25, 1897) and the opera *Nisiea* (not perf.).

Jordan, Louis, black American jazz alto saxophonist and singer; b. Brinkley, Ark., July 8, 1908; d. Los Angeles, Feb. 4, 1975. He took up the clarinet and the alto saxophone; from 1929, played with various bands; formed his own band in N.Y., the Tympany Five. As a soloist, he recorded with Louis Armstrong, Ella Fitzgerald, and other jazz luminaries; in later years he toured with his own combo, visiting England (1962) and Asia (1967 and 1968).

Jordan, Sverre, Norwegian pianist, conductor, and composer; b. Bergen, May 25, 1889; d. there, Jan. 10, 1972. He studied piano in Bergen; then took courses in piano and composition with Da Motta, Ansorge, Klatte, and Gortatowski in Berlin (1907–14). He made his debut as a pianist in Bergen (1911); was music critic of the *Morgenavisen* there (1917–31); also conducted the Bergen Harmonien choir (1922–32) and was director of Den Nasjonale Scene, Bergen's major theater (1931–57). In his works he made liberal use of national folk songs, which met the tastes of the general public. Typical of these nationally oriented works are *Suite in Old Style* for Small Orch. (1911); *Norvegiani* (1921); *Smeden* (The Smith) for Baritone, Chorus, and Orch. (1924); *Norge i vare hjerter*, cantata for the opening of the Bergen Exhibition (1928); *Suite on Norwegian Folk Tunes and Dances* for Orch. (1936); *Holbergsilhuetter* for Orch. (1938); *Norwegian Rhapsody* for Orch. (1950); *Suite in Old Style on Holberg Themes* for Orch. (1954); *Concerto romantico* for Horn and Orch. (1956); and *Kongen* (The King), orch. melodrama with narration and choral finale (1957). Other works are a Piano Concerto (1945); Cello Concerto (1947); *Concerto piccolo* for Piano and Orch. (1963); Violin Concerto (1966); 2 violin sonatas (1917, 1943); 2 piano trios (1958, 1963); Piano Sonata (1963); incidental music for plays; over 200 songs, often with orch. accompaniment.

Jørgensen, Erik, Danish composer; b. Copenhagen, May 10, 1912. He studied theory with Jeppesen, piano with Rachlew, organ with Rung-Keller, and composition with Høffding in Copenhagen (1928–31); then conducting with Scherchen in Geneva (1936). In 1947 he became a teacher of theory, analysis, and music history at the Copenhagen Inst. for the Blind. He evolved an individual idiom of composition, marked by an abundance of asymmetrical rhythmic configurations in the neo-Baroque manner; he later experimented with dodecaphony; eventually adopted a technique of "controlled coincidences."

WORKS: Concerto Grosso for Flute, Clarinet, Bassoon, and String Orch. (1933–34); *3 Antiphonies* for Soprano, Tenor, and Chamber Orch. (1934–35); Concerto for Solo Violin, String Orch., and Piano (1937); Concertino for Flute, Clarinet, Violin, and Piano (1938); *Rhapsodies* for Violin and Piano (1939–40); Sonatina for Clarinet and Bassoon (1942); *Modello per archi* for String Orch. or String Quartet (1957); *Figure in Tempo* for Cello and Piano (1960–61); Quintet for 2 Pianos, 2 Percussionists, and Double Bass (1962); *Modello 2* for 4 Vocal Soloists and 12 Instruments (1963); *Astrolabium*, chamber concerto for 11 Instruments (1964); String Quartet (1964–65); *Notturno* for 24 Solo Instruments (1965); Variations for Piano (1966); *Confrontations* for Orch. (1967–68); chamber opera, *The Shadow of a Dream* (1969); *Improvisations* for Wind Quintet (1971); *Moods and States*, quartet for Flute, Horn, Violin, and Cello (1973); madrigal comedy for children and grown-ups, *The Fairytale* (1973–77).

Jørgensen, Poul, Danish conductor; b. Copenhagen, Oct. 26, 1934. He was educated at the Univ. of Copenhagen and the Royal Academy of Music. In 1961 he became a conductor at the Royal Theater in Copenhagen; in 1966, was appointed Royal Conductor; was also active in Sweden as a conductor of the Radio Sym. Orch. in Stockholm. In his concert programs he steadfastly cultivated symphonic works by Danish, Norwegian, Swedish, and Finnish composers.

Jörn, Karl, Latvian tenor; b. Riga, Jan. 5, 1876; d. Denver, Dec. 19, 1947. He studied with Schütte-Harmsen, Jacobs, and Ress in Berlin; made his operatic debut as Lyonel in *Martha* in Freiburg im Breisgau (1896); then sang in Zürich (1898–99) and Hamburg (1899–1902). He was a member of Berlin's Royal Opera (1902–8). On Jan. 22, 1909, he made his Metropolitan Opera debut in N.Y. as Walther von Stolzing, remaining on its roster until 1914; after further appearances in Berlin (1914), he returned to the U.S.; toured with Gadski's German opera company (1929–31) and then taught voice in N.Y. and later in Denver, where he settled. He was best known for his Wagnerian roles.

Joseffy, Rafael, eminent Hungarian-American pianist and teacher; b. Hunfalu, July 3, 1852; d. N.Y., June 25, 1915. At the age of 8 he began to study piano with a local teacher at Miskolcz, and later at Budapest. In 1866 he entered the Leipzig Cons., where his principal teacher was E. Wenzel, although he also had some lessons with Moscheles. From 1868 to 1870 he studied with Tausig in Berlin, and the summers of 1870 and 1871 he spent with Liszt in Weimar. He made his debut at Berlin in 1870; his excellent technique and tonal variety elicited much praise; his career was then securely launched. He made his American debut in 1879, playing at a sym. concert of Leopold Damrosch in N.Y., where he settled; he taught at the National Cons. (1888–1906). He gained appreciation in the U.S. both as a virtuoso and as a musician of fine interpretative qualities; his programs featured many works of Brahms at a time when Brahms was not yet recognized in America as a great master. As a pedagogue, Joseffy was eminently successful; many American concert pianists were his pupils. He ed. a major edition of Chopin's works in 15 vols.; also publ. a *School of Advanced Piano Playing* (1902). He composed a number of piano pieces and made arrangements of works by Schumann, Bach, Boccherini, Gluck, and Delibes.

BIBL.: E. Hughes, "R. J.'s Contribution to Piano Technique," *Musical Quarterly* (July 1916).

Joselson, Tedd, talented American pianist; b. Antwerp (of American parents), Oct. 4, 1954. He studied piano with Adele Marcus at the Juilliard School of Music in N.Y.; in 1974 he was a soloist with the Philadelphia Orch.; then made a coast-to-coast recital tour of the U.S. in 1976–77; subsequently appeared as soloist with many of the major orchs. His forte is Russian music, but he also has a natural affinity with the masters of the Classical period.

Josephs, Wilfred, English composer; b. Newcastle upon Tyne, July 24, 1927. He studied harmony and dentistry; gained a degree in dental surgery in 1951, and was an orthodontist in the British army. In 1954 he entered the Guildhall School of Music in London, where he studied with Alfred Nieman until 1957; then went to Paris, where he took private lessons with Max Deutsch (1958–59). About that time he turned passionately toward the ideals of his ancestral Judaism; in memory of Jews who perished during World War II, he wrote a Requiem, to the text of the Hebrew prayer, Kaddish, which won 1st prize at the International Competition of La Scala in Milan in 1963. In his instrumental music he adopted the dodecaphonic method of composition without doctrinaire adherence to the idiom; he described his music as "atonal with tonal implications." A highly prolific composer, he wrote music of all genres.

WORKS: STAGE: Opera-entertainment, *Pathelin* (1963); television opera, *The Appointment* (1968); children's opera, *Through the Looking Glass and What Alice Found There* (1977–78); *Rebecca* (1982–83; Leeds, Oct. 15, 1983); 3 ballets: *The Magic Being* (1961); *La Répétition de Phèdre* (1964–65); *Equus* (1978; Baltimore, March 21, 1979); children's musical, *The King of the Coast* (1967); *A Child of the Universe* for Narrator, Soloists, Actors, Dancers, Mimes, Ballet, Choruses, Band, and Orch. (1971). **ORCH.:** *The Ants*, comedy overture (1955); 9 syms.: No. 1 (1955; rev. 1957–58 and 1974–75); No. 2 (1963–64); No. 3, *Philadelphia*, for Chamber Orch. (1967); No. 4 (1967–70); No. 5, *Pastoral* (1970–71); No. 6, with Solo Singer and Chorus (1972–74); No. 7, *Winter*, for Chamber Orch. (1976); No. 8, *The 4 Elements*, for Symphonic Band (1975–77); No. 9, *Sinfonia Concertante*, for Chamber Orch. (1979–80); *Elegy* for Strings (1957); *Concerto da Camera* for Solo Piano, Solo Violin, and Chamber Orch. (1959); *A Tyneside Overture* (1960); *Meditatio de Boernmundo* for Viola and Orch. (1960–61); *Cantus Natalis*, cello concerto (1961–62); *Aelian Dances*, 5 dances based on Newcastle tunes (1961); *Monkchester Dances*, 6 dances on Newcastle tunes (1961); Piano Concerto No. 1 (1965); *Canzonas on a Theme of Rameau* for Strings (1965); Concerto for Light Orch. (1966); *Polemic* for Strings (1967); *Rail*, symphonic picture (1967); Oboe Concerto (1967–68); *Serenade* for Chamber Orch. (1968); *Variations on a Theme of Beethoven* (1969); Double Violin Concerto (1969); Piano Concerto No. 2 (1971); *Saratoga Concerto*, triple concerto for Guitar, Harp, Harpsichord, and Chamber Orch. (1972); *The 4 Horsemen of the Apocalypse*, overture (1973–74); Concerto for Brass Band (1974); Clarinet Concerto (1975); *Eve (d'après Rodin)*, symphonic poem (1977–78); *Divertimento* for 2 Oboes, 2 Horns, and Strings (1979); *Concerto d'Amore* for 2 Violins and Orch. (1979); Double-bass Concerto (1980); *The Brontës*, overture (1981); *High Spirits*, overture (1981–82); Percussion Concerto (1982); Concerto for Viola and Chamber Orch. (1983); *Caen Wood* (1985); *Circadian Rhythms* (1985); *Fanfare Prelude* (1986). **CHAMBER:** 4 string quartets (1954, 1958, 1971, 1981); Sonata for Solo Violin (1957); *Requiescant pro defunctis iudaeis* for String Quintet, in memory of the Jews (1961); Octet (1964); 2 violin sonatas (1965, 1975); Trio for Flute, Violin, and Cello (1966); String Trio (1966); Sonata for Solo Cello (1970); Trio for Horn, Violin, and Piano (1971); Piano Quintet (1974–76); Sonata for Brass Quintet (1974; rev. 1981); Piano Trio (1974; rev. 1981); Flute Sonata (1976–77); Wind Quintet (1977); Concerto for 4 Pianos and 6 Percussionists (1978); Quartet for Oboe, Violin, Viola, and Cello (1979); Double-bass Sonata (1980); *8 Aphorisms* for 8 Trombones (1981); Clarinet Quinet (1985); *Northumbrian Dances* for Saxophone and Piano (1986). **VOCAL:** *12 Letters*, after Belloc, for Narrator, Clarinet, String Trio, and Piano (1957); *Requiem* (1962–63; Milan, Oct. 28, 1965); *Adam and Eve*, entertainment for Narrator and Ensemble (1967); *Mortales*, oratorio (1967–69; Cincinnati, May 23, 1970); *Nightmusic* for Voice and Orch. (1969–70); *Aeroplanes and Angels*, after 12 poems by Günter Grass, for Soloists and Piano Duo (1977–78); choruses, songs. **PIANO:** 29 *Preludes* (1969); *Doubles* for 2 Pianos (1970–73); *Sonata Duo* for 2 Pianos (1976); *Byrdsong* for Piano and Organ (1981). **ORGAN:** *Fantasia on 3 Notes* (1978); *Tombeau* (1980); *Testimony*, toccata in memoriam DSCH (1981; DSCH are Shostakovich's initials in German nomenclature).

Josephson, Jacob Axel, Swedish conductor, organist, teacher, and composer; b. Stockholm, March 27, 1818; d. Uppsala, March 29, 1880. He studied at the Univ. of Uppsala; in 1844 he went to Germany, where he studied with Hauptmann and Gade in Leipzig. After further study in Rome (1845–46), he returned to Uppsala as conductor of the Univ. orch.; was founder-conductor of the Filharmoniska Sallskäpet (1849) and also conducted the noted men's chorus Orphei Dränger (from 1854); was organist at the Cathedral (from 1864) and taught music history at the Univ. (from 1864). He composed a Sym., choral works, and songs; publ. 2 vols. of sacred songs (*Zion*, monthly issues, 1867–70, and *Sånger i Zion*, 1880).

BIBL.: K. Nyblom, *J.A. J.* (Stockholm, 1926).

Josif, Enriko, Serbian composer; b. Belgrade, May 1, 1924. He studied theory with Milenko Živković at the Belgrade Academy of Music (1947–54); then went to Italy and took a course in composition with Petrassi at the Accademia di Santa Cecilia in Rome (1961–62). He was a prof. of composition at the Belgrade Academy of Music from 1957.

WORKS: Ballet, *Ptico, ne sklapaj svoja krila* (Bird, Don't Break Your Wings, 1970; Belgrade, Oct. 7, 1970); Sinfonietta (1954); *Sonata antica* for Orch. (1955); *Lyrical Symphony* for 4 Flutes, Harp, and String Orch. (1956); Piano Concerto (1959); *Symphony in One Movement* (1964; Belgrade, Jan. 24, 1966); *Sinfonietta di tre re* (1968); *Oratorio profano da camera* for Narrator, Soprano, Celesta, Piano, and Percussion (1956); *Smrt Stefana Dečanskog* (The Death of Stefan of Decane), chamber motets for Narrator, Soloists, Chorus, and 16 Instruments (1956; enl. and orchestrated as a dramatic epic in 1970 under the title *Stefan Dečanski*; Belgrade, Oct. 7, 1970); *Rustikon,* cantata (1962); *Improvisations on a Folk Theme* for 14 Winds (1949); String Quartet (1953); *Snovidenja* (Dream Visions) for Flute, Harp, and Piano (1964); *Divertimento* for Wind Quintet (1964); *Epigram I* for Chamber Ensemble and *Epigram II* for Piano Trio (1967); *Zapisi* (Chronicles) for Wind Quintet (1971); *Vatrenja* for Piano Trio (1972); piano pieces.

Josquin des Prez. See **Des Prez, Josquin.**

Josten, Werner (Erich), German-born American conductor and composer; b. Elberfeld, June 12, 1885; d. N.Y., Feb. 6, 1963. He studied with Siegel in Munich; then with Jaques-Dalcroze in Geneva; later was made assistant conductor at the Bavarian State Opera in Munich (1918). In 1920 he went to the U.S.; became an American citizen in 1933. He taught at Smith College in Northampton, Mass. (1923–49); also conducted its orch. His compositions are couched in the lyrical manner of German Romantic music, with a strong undercurrent of euphonious counterpoint within the network of luscious harmonies. During his American period, he became interested in exotic art, and introduced impressionistic devices in his works.

WORKS: ORCH.: *Jungle,* symphonic movement, inspired by Henri Rousseau's painting *Forêt exotique* (Boston, Oct. 25, 1929); *Batouala,* choreographic poem (1931; symphonic suite as *Suite nègre,* Northampton, Mass., Nov. 10, 1963); *Concerto sacro I–II* for Piano and String Orch. (1925; N.Y., March 27, 1929); *Joseph and His Brethren,* ballet (1932; N.Y., March 9, 1936; as a symphonic suite, Philadelphia, May 15, 1939); *Endymion,* ballet (1933; as a symphonic suite, N.Y., Oct. 28, 1936); *Serenade for Small Orch.* (1934); Sym. in F (Boston, Nov. 13, 1936, composer conducting); *Symphony for Strings* (Saratoga Springs, N.Y., Sept. 3, 1946). **CHAMBER:** String Quartet (1934); Violin Sonata (1936); Cello Sonata (1938); Trio for Flute, Clarinet, and Bassoon (1941); Trio for Violin, Viola, and Cello (1942); Trio for Flute, Cello, and Piano (1943); Sonata for Horn and Piano (1944); *Canzona seria* for Flute, Oboe, Clarinet, Bassoon, and Piano (N.Y., Nov. 23, 1957). **VOCAL:** *Crucifixion* for Bass Solo and Mixed Chorus a cappella (1915); *Hymnus to the Quene of Paradys* for Women's Voices, Strings, and Organ (1921); *Indian Serenade* for Tenor with Orch. (1922); *Ode for St. Cecilia's Day* for Voices and Orch. (1925); *À une Madone* for Solo Tenor and Orch., after Baudelaire (1929); about 50 songs.

BIBL.: W. J., *1885–1963. A Summary of His Compositions with Press Reviews* (N.Y., 1964).

Joteyko, Tadeusz, Polish conductor and composer; b. Poczujki, near Kiev, April 1, 1872; d. Cieszyn, Silesia, Aug. 19, 1932. He studied at the Brussels Cons. with Jacobs (cello) and Gevaert (composition) and with Noskowski (composition) and Cinke (cello) at the Warsaw Cons.; conducted the Warsaw Phil. (1914–18) and taught at the Warsaw Cons. He wrote the operas *Grajek* (The Player; Warsaw, Nov. 23, 1919), *Zygmunt August* (Warsaw, Aug. 29, 1925), and *Królowa Jadwiga* (Queen Jadwiga; Warsaw, Sept. 7, 1928), but is best remembered for his choral music. He also composed a Sym. (1895), chamber music, songs, and piano pieces; publ. *Zasady muzyki* (Principles of Music; Warsaw, 1914) and *Historia muzyki polskiej i powszechnej w zarysie* (Warsaw, 1916).

Joubert, John (Pierre Herman), significant South African–born English composer; b. Cape Town, March 20, 1927. After preliminary studies in South Africa, he traveled to Great Britain on a Performing Right Scholarship in 1946 and studied with Ferguson and Holland at the Royal Academy of Music in London (1946–50). He was a lecturer in music at the Univ. of Hull (1950–62); then at the Univ. of Birmingham (1962–86). In his music he cultivates the pragmatic goal of pleasurability, wherein harmony and counterpoint serve the functional role of support for a flowing melody; in several works he makes use of primitive elements derived from Hottentot rites, transmuting the primitive vocalizations into modern polytonal and polyrhythmic formations. His carols *Torches* and *There Is No Rose* enjoy wide popularity.

WORKS: STAGE: *Antigone,* radio opera (BBC, London, July 21, 1954); *In the Drought,* chamber opera (Johannesburg, Oct. 20, 1956); *Silas Marner,* opera after the novel by George Eliot (Cape Town, May 20, 1961); *The Quarry,* opera for young people (Wembley, March 26, 1965); *Under Western Eyes,* opera after the novel by Joseph Conrad (Camden, England, May 29, 1969); *The Prisoner,* school opera (Barnet, March 14, 1973); *The Wayfarers,* school opera (1983; Huntington, April 4, 1984); *Legend of Princess Vlei,* ballet (Cape Town, Feb. 21, 1952). **CANTATAS:** *The Burghers of Calais* (1953); *Leaves of Life* (1962); *Urbs beata* (St. George's Cathedral, Cape Town, Nov. 26, 1963); *The Martyrdom of St. Alban* (1968; London, June 7, 1969). **ORCH.:** Overture (1951; Cheltenham, June 12, 1953); Symphonic Prelude (1953; Durban, May 15, 1954); Violin Concerto (York, June 17, 1954); 2 syms.: No. 1 (1955; Hull, April 12, 1956) and No. 2 (1970; London, March 24, 1971); Piano Concerto (1958; Manchester, Jan. 11, 1959); *A North Country Overture* (1958); Sinfonietta (1962); *In Memoriam 1820* (1962); *3 Interludes from Under Western Eyes* (1968); Bassoon Concerto (1974; Carlisle, March 12, 1975); *Threnos* for Harpsichord and 12 Solo Strings (London, March 30, 1974); *Déploration* (Birmingham, Dec. 28, 1978); *Temps Perdu* for String Orch. (London, Oct. 1, 1984). **VOCAL:** Oratorio, *The Raising of Lazarus* (1970; Birmingham, Sept. 30, 1971); 2 choral syms.: *The Choir Invisible* for Baritone, Chorus, and Orch. (Halifax, May 18, 1968) and *Gong-Tormented Sea* for Baritone, Chorus, and Orch. (1981; Birmingham, April 29, 1982); numerous other choral works, including *The Magus,* morality for Tenor, 2 Baritones, Chorus, and Orch. (1976; Sheffield, Oct. 29, 1977); *Herefordshire Canticles* for Soprano, Baritone, Chorus, Boys' Chorus, and Orch. (Hereford, Aug. 23, 1979); *South of the Line* for Soprano, Baritone, Chorus, 2 Pianos, Timpani, and Percussion (1985; Birmingham, March 1, 1986); other vocal works; also anthems, hymns, and carols. **CHAMBER:** 3 string quartets: No. 1 (1950); No. 2 (1977; Birmingham, Feb. 18, 1978); No. 3 (1986; Birmingham, March 13, 1987); Sonata for Viola and Piano (1951); Octet for Clarinet, Bassoon, Horn, String Quartet, and Double Bass (1961); *Chamber Music* for Brass Quintet (1985); Piano Trio (1986; Hereford, March 19, 1987); works for piano, including 2 sonatas (1957, 1972); organ music.

BIBL.: K. Birkin, "J. J. at 60," *Musical Times* (March 1987).

Jouret, Léon, Belgian composer; b. Ath, Oct. 17, 1828; d. Brussels, June 6, 1905. He studied at the Brussels Cons.; in 1874, was appointed prof. of singing there. His 2 operas, *Quen-*

tin Metsys and *Le Tricorne enchanté*, were produced semi-privately in Brussels (1865 and 1868); of more importance is his collection of folk melodies of his native region, *Chants populaires du pays d'Ath.*

Journet, Marcel, distinguished French bass; b. Grasse, Alpes Maritimes, July 25, 1867; d. Vittel, Sept. 5, 1933. He studied at the Paris Cons.; made his operatic debut in *La Favorite* in Montpellier (1891); then sang at the Théâtre Royal de la Monnaie in Brussels (1894–1900). On July 10, 1897, he made his debut at London's Covent Garden as the Duke of Mendoza in d'Erlanger's *Inez Mendo;* appeared there regularly until 1907, and returned in 1927–28. He made his Metropolitan Opera debut in N.Y. on Dec. 22, 1900, as Ramfis, and remained on its roster until 1908; then was a member of the Paris Opéra (1908–32); also sang at the Chicago Grand Opera (1915–17; 1918–19) and at Milan's La Scala (1917; 1922–27), where he created the role of Simon Mago in Boito's *Nerone* (May 1, 1924). Among his finest roles were Hans Sachs, Gurnemanz, Wotan, Méphistophélès, Golaud, and Scarpia.

Joy, Geneviève, French pianist; b. Bernaville, Oct. 4, 1919. She studied at the Paris Cons. with Yves Nat (piano) and Jean and Noël Gallon (theory); received the Premier Prix in piano in 1941. In 1945 she married the composer **Henri Dutilleux.** She specialized in modern music; gave numerous 1st performances of piano works by French composers, some of them written especially for her.

Juch, Emma (Antonia Joanna), noted American soprano; b. Vienna (of Austrian-born American parents), July 4, 1863; d. N.Y., March 6, 1939. She was taken at the age of 4 to the U.S., where she studied with her father and with Murio Celli in Detroit; she made her recital debut in N.Y.'s Chickering Hall (1881), then her stage debut as Philine in *Mignon* at London's Her Majesty's Theatre (1881); that same year she appeared at N.Y.'s Academy of Music. She was a leading member of the American (later National) Opera Co. (1884–89), subsequently touring the U.S., Canada, and Mexico with her own Emma Juch Grand Opera Co. (1889–91); she retired from the operatic stage upon her marriage (1894). She was a great advocate of opera in English. Her voice was admired for its extensive range, which enabled her to sing a wide repertoire.

Juchelka, Miroslav, Czech composer; b. Velká Polom, March 29, 1922. He studied composition with Řídký and Hlobil at the Prague Cons. (1939–43) and then with Albín Šíma at the Master School there (1943–47); was music director of the Czech Radio in Prague (1953–78).

WORKS: *Symphonic Fantasy* for Orch. (1952); Accordion Concerto (1954); *Burlesque* for Piano and Orch. (1958); Suite for String Orch. (1961); *Burlesque* for Clarinet and Promenade Orch. (1970); *From the Beskyds,* suite for Orch. (1972); Clarinet Concerto (1974); Piano Concerto (1979); *Tarantela festiva* for Orch. (1980); *Miniatures* for Cello and Piano (1951); Suite for Nonet (1962); Clarinet Sonatina (1964); *5 Compositions for Due Boemi* for Bass Clarinet and Piano (1972); Sonatina for Violin and Piano (1982).

Judd, James, English conductor; b. Hertford, Oct. 30, 1949. He studied piano with Alfred Kitchin and conducting with Bernard Keefe at Trinity College of Music in London (1967–71), then was active with the London Opera Centre; subsequently was assistant conductor of the Cleveland Orch. (1973–75). He was co-founder and conductor of the Chamber Orch. of Europe in 1981; toured with it in the U.S. (1984–85). He also appeared widely as a guest conductor in England, on the Continent, and in the U.S. In 1987 he became music director of the Phil. Orch. of Florida in Fort Lauderdale.

Judge, Jack, English composer of popular songs; b. 1878; d. West Bromwich, July 28, 1938. His song *It's a long, long way to Tipperary* (1912) attained enormous popularity in England and elsewhere as a wartime song during World War I.

Judson, Arthur (Leon), influential American concert manager; b. Dayton, Ohio, Feb. 17, 1881; d. Rye, N.Y., Jan. 28, 1975. He took violin lessons with Max Bendix and Leopold Lichtenberg in N.Y. He was dean of the music dept. at Denison Univ., Granville, Ohio (1900–1907); subsequently was manager of the Philadelphia Orch. (1915–35) and the N.Y. Phil. (1922–56); also devoted much time to artist representation, organizing the Judson Radio Program Corp. (1926) in order to showcase his artists; also organized Columbia Concerts Corp. (1932), which grew into one of the most powerful management agencies in the U.S.; it later became Columbia Artists Management, Inc. He later formed the Judson, O'Neill, Beall and Steinway (JOBS) Agency (1962), which was renamed Arthur Judson Management (1969); upon his retirement in 1972, it became Harry Beall Management, Inc.

Juhan, Alexander, American violinist, conductor, and composer, probably the son of **James Juhan;** b. Halifax, 1765; d. 1845. He was taken to Boston in 1768; was a violinist in Philadelphia in 1783; later went to Charleston, S.C., where he was active from 1790 to 1792; returned to Philadelphia in 1792. He composed 6 piano sonatas, of which 3 are accompanied by flute (or violin); also a book of 12 songs, with instrumental accompaniment.

Juhan, James, French musician, probably the father of **Alexander Juhan.** He was active in Boston (1768–70), Charleston, S.C. (1771), and Philadelphia, where he exhibited the "great North American Forte Piano" (1786).

BIBL.: O. Sonneck, *Early Concert Life in America* (1907).

Juilliard, Augustus D., American music patron; b. at sea during his parents' voyage from Burgundy to the U.S., April 19, 1836; d. N.Y., April 25, 1919. He was a prominent industrialist; left the residue of his estate for the creation of the Juilliard Musical Foundation (1920). The Juilliard Graduate School was founded in 1924 and the Juilliard School of Music was organized in 1926. The latter's board then took control of the Juilliard Graduate School and the Inst. of Musical Art, which had been founded by Frank Damrosch and James Loeb in 1905. The two schools were merged as the Juilliard School of Music in 1946. After the expansion of its activities to include dance and drama, it was renamed the Juilliard School in 1968.

Jullien, (Jean-Lucien-) Adolphe, French writer on music; b. Paris, June 1, 1845; d. Chaintreauville, Seine-et-Marne, Aug. 30, 1932. He studied piano, violin, and voice; then law in Paris, where he also studied harmony and counterpoint with Bienaimé. He became a music journalist; contributed to various magazines, and took a strong position in favor of the new music of Berlioz and Wagner.

WRITINGS: *L'Opéra en 1788* (1873); *La Musique et les philosophes au XVIIIe siècle* (1873); *La Comédie à la cour de Louis XVI, Le Théâtre de la reine à Trianon* (1873); *Histoire du théâtre de Mme. Pompadour, dit Théâtre des petits cabinets* (1874); *Les Spectateurs sur Le Théâtre* (1875); *Le Théâtre des demoiselles Verrières* (1875); *Les Grandes Nuits de Sceaux, Le Théâtre de la duchesse du Maine* (1876); *Un Potentat musical* (1876); *Weber à Paris* (1877); *Airs variés; Histoire, critique, biographie musicales et dramatiques* (1877); *La Cour et l'opéra sous Louis XVI; Marie-Antoinette et Sacchini; Salieri; Favart et Gluck* (1878); *Goethe et la musique* (1880); *L'Opéra secret au XVIIIe siècle* (1880); *Richard Wagner, sa vie et ses œuvres* (1886; Eng. tr., Boston, 1892); *Hector Berlioz* (1888); *Musiciens d'Aujourd'hui* (1st series, 1891; 2nd series, 1894); *Musique* (1895); *Le Romantisme et l'éditeur Renduel* (1897); *Amours d'opéra au XVIIIe siècle* (1908); *Ernest Reyer* (1909).

BIBL.: F. Delhasse, *A. J.* (Paris, 1884).

Jullien, Gilles, French organist; b. c.1650; d. Chartres, Sept. 14, 1703. He became organist at the Chartres Cathedral in 1667, and held this post until his death. His *Premier livre d'orgue* was publ. by Lesclop in Chartres (1680); a modern reprint, with annotations and an introduction by Norbert Dufourcq, was issued in Paris (1952).

Jullien, Louis (George Maurice Adolphe Roch Albert Abel Antonio Alexandre Noé Jean Lucien Daniel Eugène Joseph-le-brun Joseph-Barême Thomas Thomas

Thomas-Thomas Pierre Arbon Pierre-Maurel Barthé-lemi Artus Alphonse Bertrand Dieudonné Emanuel Jo-sué Vincent Luc Michel Jules-de-la-plane Jules-Bazin Julio César), famous eccentric French conductor and com-poser; b. Sisteron, April 23, 1812; d. Paris, March 14, 1860. The son of a bandmaster, he went to Paris in 1833 and studied composition with Le Carpentier and Halévy, but could not maintain the discipline of learning music, and began to com-pose light dances instead; of these, the waltz *Rosita* attained enormous, though transitory, popularity in Paris. He left the Cons. in 1836 without taking a degree, and became engaged as conductor of dance music at the Jardin Turc. He also at-tempted to launch a musical journal, but an accumulation of carelessly contracted debts compelled him to leave France (1838). He went to London, where he conducted summer con-certs at the Drury Lane Theatre (1840) and winter concerts with an enlarged ensemble of instrumentalists and singers (1841). He then opened a series of "society concerts," at which he presented large choral works, such as Rossini's *Stabat Mater,* as well as movements from Beethoven's syms. In 1847 he engaged Berlioz to conduct at the Drury Lane Theatre, which he had leased. He became insolvent in 1848, but attempted to recoup his fortune by organizing a "concert monstre" with 400 players, 3 choruses, and 3 military bands. He succeeded in giving 3 such concerts in London in 1849. He then essayed the composition of an opera, *Pietro il Grande,* which he pro-duced at his own expense at Covent Garden, on Aug. 17, 1852. He used the pseudonym Roch Albert for his spectacular pieces, such as *Destruction of Pompeii;* publ. some dance music (*Royal Irish Quadrille,* etc.) under his own name. In 1853 he was engaged by P.T. Barnum for a series of concerts in the U.S. For his exhibition at the Crystal Palace in N.Y. (June 15, 1854), attended by a great crowd, he staged a simulated conflagration for his *Fireman's Quadrille.* Despite his eccentricities, however, Jullien possessed a true interest in musical progress. At his American concerts he made a point of including several works by American composers: *Santa Claus Symphony* by William Henry Fry and some chamber music by George Frederick Bris-tow. In 1854 he returned to London; his managerial ventures resulted in another failure. In 1859 he went to Paris, but was promptly arrested for debt, and spent several weeks in prison. He died a few months later in an insane asylum to which he had been confined.

BIBL.: N. Slonimsky, *A Thing or Two about Music* (N.Y., 1948); A. Carse, *The Life of J.: Adventurer, Showman-Conductor and Establisher of the Promenade Concerts in England* (Cam-bridge, 1951); H. Schonberg, *The Great Conductors* (N.Y., 1967).

Jumilhac, Dom Pierre-Benoît de, Benedictine monk and writer on Gregorian chant; b. Château St. Jean-de-Ligourre, near Limoges, 1611; d. St. Germain-des-Prés, March 21, 1682. He studied in Bordeaux; became a novice of the Benedictine Order in the Congregation of St. Maur at St. Rémy in Rheims (1629); was professed there (1630). He was prior of St. Julien in Tours (1647–66), then retired to the Abbey in his birthplace. He publ. the erudite treatise *La Science et la pratique du plain-chant* (Paris, 1673; ed. by T. Nisard and A. Le Clerq, 1847).

Junck, Benedetto, Italian composer; b. Turin, Aug. 21, 1852; d. San Vigilio, near Bergamo, Oct. 3, 1903. He studied harmony and counterpoint with Alberto Mazzucato and Antonio Bazzini at the Milan Cons. He was best known for his songs, including the cycle *La Simona* (1878) and the album *8 romanze* (1880); also wrote a String Quartet (1886) and 2 violin sonatas (1884, 1885).

Jung, Manfred, German tenor; b. Oberhausen, July 9, 1945. He studied with Hilde Wesselmann at the Essen Folkwang-schule; then sang in the Bayreuth Festival chorus (1970–73); he made his operatic debut in Dortmund in 1974, and then sang in Kaiserslautern, Saarbrücken, and Karlsruhe. In 1977 he became a member of the Deutsche Oper am Rhein in Düssel-dorf; made his debut at the Bayreuth Festival as Siegfried in

Götterdämmerung (1977), and then appeared in the televised version of that role in the *Ring* cycle. He made his Metropolitan Opera debut in N.Y. in the title role of Siegfried on Sept. 24, 1981, and subsequently sang other Wagnerian roles there. He returned to the Bayreuth Festival in 1983 to sing Siegfried in the Solti-Hall production, commemorating the 100th anni-versary of Wagner's death; also appeared in concert throughout Europe, North America, and the Far East.

Jungwirth, Manfred, Austrian bass; b. St. Pölten, June 4, 1919. He studied voice in St. Pölten, Vienna, Bucharest, Mu-nich, and Berlin; entered the Univ. of Vienna to study medicine in 1937, but passed the examinations in voice, piano, and conducting instead (1940). He sang for German troops in Ru-mania and Bulgaria (1941–45); made his operatic debut as Gounod's Méphistophélès at the Bucharest Opera (1942). In 1948 he was awarded his Ph.D. in musicology in Vienna and also won 1st prize in the Geneva voice competition; then sang in Zürich, Berlin, Hamburg, and London; he made regular appearances at the Frankfurt Opera (1960–67) and the Vienna State Opera (from 1967). On Feb. 16, 1974, he made his debut at the Metropolitan Opera in N.Y. as Baron Ochs, which became his most famous role.

Juon, Paul (Pavel Fedorovich), Russian composer of Swiss and German descent; b. Moscow, March 6, 1872; d. Vevey, Aug. 21, 1940. He was a pupil of Hřimaly (violin) and of Ta-neyev and Arensky (composition) at the Moscow Cons.; then studied with Bargiel at the Berlin Hochschule für Musik (1894–95), where he won the Mendelssohn Prize; subsequently be-came a teacher (1906) and a prof. (1911) there. He was elected a member of the Prussian Academy of Arts in 1919; retired to Vevey in 1934. His works display pronounced Romantic inclinations.

WORKS: ORCH.: Sym. in A (1903); *Vaegtervise* (1906); *Psyche* for Tenor, Chorus, and Orch. (1906); *Aus einem Tage-buch,* suite (c.1906); Chamber Sym. (1907); *Eine Serenaden-musik* (1909); 3 violin concertos (1909, 1913, 1931); *Episodes concertantes* for Piano Trio and Orch. (1912); *Mysterien,* sym-phonic poem for Cello and Orch. (1928); Serenade for Strings (1929); *Little Symphony* for Strings (1930); *Divertimento* for Strings (1933); *Anmut und Würde,* suite (1937); *Rhapsodische Sinfonie* (1939); *Tanz-Capricen* (1941); *Burletta* for Violin and Orch. (1940); *Sinfonietta capricciosa* (1940). **CHAMBER:** 3 string quartets (1898, 1904, 1920); Piano Trios: No. 1 (1901), *Trio-Caprice* (1908), Trio (1915), *Litaniae* (1920; rev., 1929), *Legende* (1930), and *Suite* (1932); Sextet (1902); 2 piano quin-tets (1906, 1909); *Divertimento* for Wind Quintet and Piano (1913); Wind Quintet (1930); *Arabesken* for Oboe, Clarinet, and Bassoon (1941); various sonatas and piano pieces.

Juozapaitis, Jurgis, Lithuanian composer; b. near Šiauliai, June 29, 1942. He studied with Juzeliunas at the Lithuanian State Cons. in Vilnius, graduating in 1968. His music is rooted in native folk modes, which are enhanced by a modernistic harmonic investiture and a rich employment of polyrhythmic percussion.

WORKS: OPERA, *Sea Bird* (1976). **ORCH.:** Concerto for Organ, Strings, and Kettledrums (1970); *Vitrages,* symphonic poem (1971); *Rex,* sym. in memory of M.K. Čiurlionis (1973); *Festive Poem* (1976); *Zodiacus,* sym. (1977). **CHAMBER:** Wind Quintet (1970); *Music* for Flute, Percussion, Piano, Viola, and Cello (1970); Concerto for 4 Percussionists (1971); Sonata for Solo Violin (1972); *Jūrate and Kastytis,* chamber sym. for Flute, Oboe, Viola, Cello, Piano, Percussion, and Electronic Tape (1974); *Diptych* for Wind Quintet (1977); 2 string quartets (1978, 1980); organ pieces; songs; choruses.

Jupin, Charles-François, French violinist and composer; b. Chambéry, Nov. 30, 1805; d. Paris, June 12, 1839. He studied with Baillot at the Paris Cons., taking 1st prize in 1823; wrote an opera, *La Vengeance italienne* (1834); numerous pieces for violin.

Jürgens, Fritz, German composer; b. Düsseldorf, April 22, 1888; killed in action in Champagne, Sept. 25, 1915. He studied music largely by himself; wrote some fine lieder.

Jürgens, Jürgen, German conductor and teacher; b. Frankfurt am Main, Oct. 5, 1925. He studied with Kurt Thomas at the Frankfurt Musisches Gymnasium and with Konrad Lechner at the Freiberg Staatliche Hochschule für Musik. In 1955 he became conductor of the Hamburg Monteverdi Choir; toured with it throughout Europe, America, and the Far East. He became a lecturer (1960) and a prof. (1977) at the Univ. of Hamburg; was made its music director in 1966. He ed. works of Monteverdi and A. Scarlatti. As a conductor he cultivated works of the Baroque period, while not neglecting modern music of a polyphonic nature.

Jurgenson, Pyotr (Ivanovich), Russian music publisher; b. Reval, July 17, 1836; d. Moscow, Jan. 2, 1904. The youngest son of indigent parents, he learned the music trade with M. Bernard, owner of a music store in St. Petersburg; he served in 3 other music-selling houses there, before opening a business of his own in 1861, in Moscow. With a small investment, he gradually expanded his firm until it became one of the largest in Russia. Through N. Rubinstein he met the leading musicians of Russia, and had enough shrewdness of judgment to undertake the publication of works of Tchaikovsky, beginning with his op. 1. He became Tchaikovsky's close friend, and, while making a handsome profit out of his music, he demonstrated a generous regard for his welfare; he publ. full scores of Tchaikovsky's syms. and operas, as well as his songs and piano works. His voluminous correspondence with Tchaikovsky was pub. in a modern ed. (2 vols., Moscow, 1938 and 1952). He also publ. many works by other Russian composers; publ. the 1st Russian eds. of the collected works of Chopin, Schumann, and Mendelssohn, and the scores of Wagner's operas. His catalog contained some 20,000 numbers. After his death, his sons Boris and Grigory Jurgenson succeeded to the business; it was nationalized after the Russian Revolution.

Jurinac, Sena (actually, **Srebrenka**), famous Yugoslav soprano; b. Travnik, Oct. 24, 1921. She studied at the Zagreb Academy of Music, and also with Milka Kostrenčić, making her operatic debut as the 1st Flower Maiden at the Zagreb Opera (1942); her 1st major role there was Mimi that same year. In 1945 she made her Vienna State Opera debut as Cherubino, and soon established herself as one of its outstanding members; she accompanied it on its visit to London's Covent Garden in 1947, where she sang Dorabella; that same year she made her debut at the Salzburg Festival. She also appeared at the Glyndebourne Festivals (1949–56). She made her U.S. debut at the San Francisco Opera (1959); sang regularly at Covent Garden (1959–63; 1965; 1973). In 1953 she married the baritone **Sesto Bruscantini.** A distinguished interpreter of Mozart, she excelled as Fiordiligi, Cherubino, Pamina, and Donna Elvira, and later mastered the more demanding roles of Donna Anna and the Countess. She was also renowned for her portrayals of Octavian, the Composer, Elektra, and the Marschallin in the operas of Richard Strauss.
BIBL.: U. Tamussino, *S. J.* (Augsburg, 1971).

Jurjāns, Andrejs, Latvian composer; b. Erlaa, Sept. 30, 1856; d. Zehsis, Sept. 28, 1922. He studied organ with L. Homilius, horn with F. Homilius, and composition with Rimsky-Korsakov at the St. Petersburg Cons. (1875–82); was a prof. at the Kharkov Cons. (1882–1916). He was active as a folklorist and publ. *Latvju tautas mūzikas materiāli* (Materials of Latvian Folk Music; Riga, 1894–1926). He composed a symphonic poem, a Cello Concerto, cantatas, choral songs, and chamber music; also made orch. arrangements of Latvian folk melodies, which he employed in his original works.
BIBL.: O. Grāvitis, *Jurgānu Andrejs* (Riga, 1953).

Jurovský, Šimon, Slovak composer; b. Ulmanka, Feb. 8, 1912; d. Prague, Nov. 8, 1963. He attended the Bratislava Academy of Music (1931–36); then took courses in composition with

Josef Marx at the Vienna Academy of Music (1943–44). He was manager of the Bratislava Opera and director of the Slovak Folk Art Ensemble. In his music he followed the broad tenets of national Romanticism, with frequent references to folk themes.
WORKS: Opera, *Dcery Abelovy* (The Daughters of Abel, 1961); ballet, *Rytierska balada* (The Song of Chivalry; Bratislava, 1960); 2 orch. suites (1939; 1943); Serenade for String Orch. (1940); *Začatá cesta* (The Journey Begun), symphonic poem (1948); *Radostné súženie* (A Joyous Competition), symphonic scherzo (1949); 2 syms.: No. 1, *Mírová* (Peace), for Piano and Strings (1950), and No. 2, *Heroická* (Heroic), for Organ and Orch. (1960); Cello Concerto (1953); Concertino for Piano and String Orch. (1962); *3 uspávanky* (Lullabies) for Soprano, Piano, Harp, and Strings (1947); Quartet for Winds (1936); *Melodies and Dialogues,* string quartet (1944); String Trio (1948); *Concert Dance* for Piano (1960); much film music; choral pieces; songs (including arrangements of folk songs).
BIBL.: Z. Bokesová, *Š. J.* (Bratislava, 1955).

Juzeliūnas, Julius, Lithuanian composer; b. Čepole, Feb. 20, 1916. He studied with Gruodis at the Kaunas Cons. (graduated, 1948); then entered the Leningrad Cons., in the class of Voloshinov (graduated, 1952). Returning to Lithuania, he taught at the Vilnius Cons. (from 1952). His compositions follow the spirit of socialist realism, treating heroic themes in stage productions and romantic subjects in instrumental music; on occasion, he uses modern techniques, including dodecaphony.
WORKS: STAGE: 2 operas: *Sukiléliai* (The Rebels) (1957; Vilnius, 1960); *Žaidimas* (The Game; 1968). ORCH.: 5 syms.: No. 1 (1948); No. 2 (1949); No. 3, *Žmogaus lyra* (Man's Lyre) for Baritone, Chorus, and Orch. (1965); No. 4 (1974); No. 5, *Hymn of the Plains,* for Women's Chorus and String Orch. (1982); *Heroic Poem* (1950); *African Sketches,* suite (1961); *Poem-Concerto* for String Orch. (1961); *Passacaglia-Poem* (1962); Concerto for Organ, Violin, and String Orch. (1963); *Concerto Grosso* for String Orch., Wind Quintet, and Piano (1966); Concerto for Clarinet and String Orch. (1985; also for Clarinet and String Quartet). VOCAL: Concerto for Tenor and Orch. (1955); *Pelenu lopšine* (Lullaby to the Ashes), symphonic poem for Mezzo-soprano, Chorus, and Orch. (1963); *Melika,* sonata for Voice and Organ (1973); *Cantus magnificat,* sym.-oratorio for 2 Soloists, 2 Choruses, Organ, and Orch. (1979); *The Language of Flowers,* cantata for Soprano and String Orch. or Organ (1985). CHAMBER: 2 piano sonatas (1947, 1986); 4 string quartets (1962, 1966, 1969, 1980); Sonata for Oboe and Clarinet (1971); Violin Sonata (1972); Sonata for Horn Solo (1975); Sonata for Violin and Cello (1977); *Diptych* for Violin and Organ (1981); *Ragamalika* for Wind Quintet (1982); Sym. for Organ Solo (1984); *Flobo-Clavio,* quartet for Flute, Oboe, Harpsichord, and Cello (1987).

Jyrkiäinen, Reijo (Einari), Finnish composer; b. Suistamo, April 6, 1934. He studied composition with Nils-Eric Fougstedt and Joonas Kokkonen at the Sibelius Academy in Helsinki (1956–63), and theory at the Univ. of Helsinki (1958–63); attended modern music courses at Darmstadt (1962–63) and the electronic sessions at the Bilthoven Radio Studio in the Netherlands (1963). He taught at the Sibelius Academy (1966–67), then was managing director of the Helsinki Phil. (from 1972). In his works, he has pursued advanced experimentation, ranging from classical Schoenbergian dodecaphony to electronics.
WORKS: 5 Dodecaphonic Etudes for Piano (1961); *Frammenti per il septetto d'archi* for 3 Violins, 2 Violas, Cello, and Double Bass (1962); *Sounds I, II,* and *III,* concrete music on Tape (1963–66); *Mesto* for Flute, Clarinet, Guitar, and Percussion (1963); *For 4* for Violin, Clarinet, Guitar, and Percussion (1963); *Contradictions* for Flute, Clarinet, Piano, Guitar, and String Quartet (1965); 5 *Piano Pieces for Children* (1966); *Idiopostic I* and *II,* electronic music (1963, 1966); *Varianti* for Viola and Piano (1967).

K

Kàan-Albest, Heinrich (originally, **Jindřich z Albestů Kàan**), Bohemian pianist and composer; b. Tarnopol, May 29, 1852; d. Roudná, March 7, 1926. He studied in Prague with Blodek and Skuherský; from 1889, taught piano at the Prague Cons.; was its director from 1907 to 1918. He wrote 2 operas: *Escape* (1895) and *Germinal*, after Zola (1908); 2 ballets: *Bajaja* and *Olim*; a symphonic poem, *Sakuntala; Frühlings-Eklogen* for Orch.; piano pieces.

Bibl.: Vrkoćová, *J. K.* (diss., Univ. of Prague, 1960).

Kabaivanska, Raina (Yakimova), Bulgarian soprano; b. Burgas, Dec. 15, 1934. She studied at the Bulgarian State Cons. in Sofia; made her debut with the National Opera in Sofia in 1957. She went to Italy, where she studied with Zita Fumagalli-Riva in Milan and with Giulia Tess in Vercelli; then made her 1st appearance at La Scala as Agnese in *Beatrice di Tenda* (1961), and subsequently sang there regularly. In 1962 she made her debut at London's Covent Garden as Desdemona; made her American debut at the Metropolitan Opera in N.Y. as Nedda on Oct. 27, 1962; first sang at the Paris Opéra as Leonora in *La forza del destino* in 1975. She also made guest appearances in Chicago, San Francisco, Dallas, Vienna, and Buenos Aires. She is best known for her Verdi and Puccini roles.

Kabalevsky, Dmitri (Borisovich), noted Russian composer; b. St. Petersburg, Dec. 30, 1904; d. Moscow, Feb. 14, 1987. When he was 14 years old, his family moved to Moscow; he received his primary musical education at the Scriabin Music School (1919–25); also studied music theory privately with Gregory Catoire; in 1925 he entered the Moscow Cons. as a student of Miaskovsky in composition and Goldenweiser in piano; in 1932 he was appointed instructor in composition there; in 1939, became a full prof. As a pedagogue, he developed effective methods of musical education; in 1962, was elected head of the Commission of Musical Esthetic Education of Children; in 1969, became president of the Scientific Council of Educational Esthetics in the Academy of Pedagogical Sciences of the U.S.S.R.; in 1972, received the honorary degree of president of the International Soc. of Musical Education. As a pianist, composer, and conductor, he made guest appearances in Europe and the U.S. Kabalevsky's music represents a paradigm of the Russian school of composition in its Soviet period; his melodic writing is marked by broad diatonic lines invigorated by an energetic rhythmic pulse; while adhering to basic tonality, his harmony is apt to be rich in euphonious dissonances. A prolific composer, he wrote in all musical genres; in his operas he successfully reflected both the lyrical and the dramatic aspects of the librettos, several of which are based on Soviet subjects faithful to the tenets of socialist realism. His instrumental writing was functional, taking into consideration the idiomatic capacities of the instruments.

Works: operas: *Colas Breugnon,* after Romain Rolland (Leningrad, Feb. 22, 1938); *At Moscow* (Moscow, Nov. 28, 1943; rev. as *In the Fire,* Moscow, Nov. 7, 1947); *The Family of Taras* (Leningrad, Nov. 7, 1950); *Nikita Vershinin* (Moscow, Nov. 26, 1955); *The Sisters* (1969). **orch.:** 4 syms.: No. 1 (Moscow, Nov. 9, 1932); No. 2 (Moscow, Dec. 25, 1934); No. 3, *Requiem for Lenin* (Moscow, Jan. 21, 1934); No. 4 (Moscow, Oct. 17, 1956); *The Comedians,* orch. suite, from incidental music to a play (1940); *Spring,* symphonic poem (1960); *Pa-*

thetic Overture (1960); 3 piano concertos: No. 1 (Moscow, Dec. 11, 1931, composer soloist); No. 2 (Moscow, May 12, 1936); No. 3 (Moscow, Feb. 1, 1953, Ashkenazy soloist, composer conducting); Violin Concerto (Leningrad, Oct. 29, 1948); 2 cello concertos: No. 1 (Moscow, March 15, 1949) and No. 2 (1964). **CHAMBER:** 2 string quartets (1928, 1945); *20 Simple Pieces* for Violin and Piano (1965). **PIANO:** 3 piano sonatas (1928, 1945, 1946); 24 preludes (1943); many other piano pieces, including 30 children's pieces (1938); *24 Simple Pieces* for children (1944). **VOCAL:** *7 Merry Songs* for Voice and Piano (1945); numerous school songs and choruses; *Requiem* for Voices and Orch. (Moscow, Feb. 9, 1963); oratorio, *A Letter to the 30th Century* (1970); also incidental music for plays; film scores.
    BIBL.: L. Danilevich, *D. K.* (Moscow, 1954); G. Abramovsky, *D. K.* (Moscow, 1960); L. Danilevich, *Creative Work of D.B. K.* (Moscow, 1963); R. Glezer, *K.* (Moscow, 1969); Y. Korev, *K.* (Moscow, 1970).

Kabasta, Oswald, prominent Austrian conductor; b. Mistelbach, Dec. 29, 1896; d. (suicide) Kufstein, Feb. 6, 1946. He studied at the Vienna Academy of Music. After conducting in Wiener-Neustadt and Baden bei Wien, he was Generalmusikdirektor in Graz (1926–31). He became music director of the Vienna Radio (1931), and took its orch. on tours of Europe; concurrently taught at the Vienna Academy of Music; was also conductor of the Gesellschaft der Musikfreunde and the Vienna Sym. Orch. (from 1935); then was Generalmusikdirektor of the Munich Phil. (1938–45). Having compromised himself by a close association with the Austrian Nazis, he committed suicide a few months after the conclusion of World War II. He championed the music of the late Austro-German Romantic school; was particularly known for his performances of the works of Bruckner.

Kabeláč, Miloslav, Czech conductor and composer; b. Prague, Aug. 1, 1908; d. there, Sept. 17, 1979. He studied composition with K.B. Jirák and conducting with Pavel Dědeček (1928–31) and piano with Vilém Kurz (1931–34) at the Prague Cons. He served as conductor and music director at the Czech Radio in Prague (1932–39, 1945–54); taught composition at the Prague Cons. (1958–62) and lectured on electronic music at the Czech Radio in Plzeň (1968–70). In his music he followed a fairly advanced modern idiom, occasionally applying dodecaphonic devices, but hewing closely to the fundamentals of tonality.
    WORKS: ORCH. AND VOCAL: Sinfonietta (1931); *Fantasy* for Piano and Orch. (1934); *Little Christmas Cantata* for Soprano, Men's Chorus, and Chamber Ensemble (1937); resistance cantata, *Neustupujte* (Do Not Yield), for Men's Chorus, Band, and Percussion, to words urging Czechoslovakia to resist the Nazis (1939; Prague, Oct. 28, 1945); 2 overtures (1939, 1947); 8 syms.: No. 1, for Strings and Percussion (1941–42); No. 2 (1942–46); No. 3, for Organ, Brass, and Timpani (1948–57); No. 4, for Chamber Orch. (1954–58); No. 5, *Dramatica,* for Soprano and Orch. (1959–60); No. 6, *Concertante,* for Clarinet and Orch. (1961–62); No. 7, on Old Testament texts, for Narrator and Orch. (1967–68); No. 8, *Antiphonies,* for Soprano, Chorus, Percussion, and Organ (1970); *Moravian Lullabies* for Soprano and Chamber Orch. (1951); *Dětem* (For Children), suite for Orch. (1955); 6 lullabies for Alto, Women's Chorus, and Orch. (1955); *Mysterium času* (Mystery of Time) for Orch. (Prague, Oct. 23, 1957); *3 Melodramas* for Narrators and Orch. (1957); *Hamletovská improvizace* (Hamlet Improvisations), commemorating the Shakespeare quadricentennial (1962–63; Prague, May 26, 1964); *Zrcadlení* (Reflections), 9 miniatures (1963–64; Prague, Feb. 2, 1965); *Tajemství ticha* (Euphemias Mysterion) for Soprano and Chamber Orch. (1964–65; Warsaw Autumn Festival, Sept. 30, 1965); Variations on the chorale *Hospodine, pomiluj ny* (Our Lord, Forgive Us) *II* for Piano and Orch. (1978). **CHAMBER:** Wind Sextet (1940); *3 Pieces* for Cello and Piano (1941); *Ballade* for Violin and Piano (1956); *Suite* for Saxophone and Piano (1959); *8 Inventions* for Percussion (1963; in the form of a ballet, Strasbourg, April 22, 1965);

8 Ricercari for Percussion (1966–67; rev. 1971); *Laments and Smiles,* 8 bagatelles for Flute and Harp (1969; rev. 1976); *Fated Dramas of Man,* sonata for Narrator, Trumpet, Percussion, and Piano (1975–76); Variations on the chorale *Hospodine, pomiluj ny* (Our Lord, Forgive Us) *I* for Female Speaker, Baritone, Men's Chorus, and Mixed Chorus (1977). **PIANO:** *8 Preludes* (1955–56); *Motifs,* cycle (1959); *Small Suite* for Piano, 4-hands (1960). **ORGAN:** *Fantasy* (1957); *4 Preludes* (1963); also *E fontibus Bohemicis* (From Bohemian Sources, an anthology).

Kabós, Ilona, Hungarian pianist; b. Budapest, Dec. 7, 1893; d. London, May 28, 1973. She studied with Arpád Szendy, Zoltán Kodály, and Leo Weiner at the Budapest Academy of Music, winning the Liszt Prize when she was 15; then made her debut in Budapest at 16 and subsequently toured throughout Europe, eventually gaining a fine reputation as an interpreter of contemporary music. In later years she made her home in London, where she was active as a teacher; also gave master classes in Europe and North America, numbering among her outstanding students Peter Frankl, John Ogdon, and Joseph Kalichstein. She was married to the pianist **Louis Kentner** (1931; divorced, 1945).

Kačinskas, Jerome, Lithuanian-born American conductor and composer; b. Viduklé, April 17, 1907. He studied with his father, a church organist; then at the State Music School in Klaipeda and at the Prague Cons. with Jaroslav Křička and Alois Hába. Returning to Lithuania, he became conductor of the Klaipeda Sym. Orch. (1932–38); in 1938, was appointed music director for the Lithuanian Radio in Kaunas; during World War II, conducted the Vilnius Phil. In 1944 he left Lithuania, and from 1945 to 1949 lived in a displaced-persons camp in Augsburg; in 1949 he settled in the U.S., and in 1954 became a U.S. citizen. His music reflects the influences of Scriabin and French Impressionists. Among his works are a Trumpet Concerto; 2 string quartets; sacred choruses; piano pieces.

Kade, Otto, eminent German music scholar; b. Dresden, May 6, 1819; d. Bad Doberan, near Rostock, July 19, 1900. He studied at the Dresden Kreuzschule; then took courses with Julius Otto and Moritz Hauptmann (harmony and counterpoint) and Johann Schneider (piano and organ); also studied choral conducting. In 1848 he founded in Dresden the Cecilian Soc. for the promotion of early sacred music. In 1860 he became music director of the court of the Grand Duke of Mecklenburg-Schwerin; also taught at the Gymnasium there (1866–93). His important writings include *Der neu aufgefundene Lutherco-dez vom Jahre 1530* (Dresden, 1871), *Die älteren Musikalien der Stadt Freiberg in Sachsen* (Leipzig, 1888), and *Die Musikalien-Sammlung des grossherzoglich Mecklenburg-Schweriner Fürstenhauses aus den letzten zwei Jahrhunderten* (2 vols., Schwerin, 1893; supplement, *Der Musikalische Nachlass der Frau Erbgrossherzogin Auguste von Mecklenburg-Schwerin,* 1899). He also ed. the collections *Cantionale für die evangelisch-lutherischen Kirchen im Grossherzogtum Mecklenburg-Schwerin* (Schwerin, 1868–87) and *Vierstimmiges Choralbuch . . . zu dem . . . Mecklenburgischen Gesangbuch* (Schwerin, 1869).

Kadosa, Pál, talented Hungarian pianist, composer, and teacher; b. Léva, Sept. 6, 1903; d. Budapest, March 30, 1983. He studied piano with Arnold Székely and Kodály at the Budapest Academy of Music (1921–27); had a brief career as a concert pianist, then taught at Budapest's Fodor Music School (1927–43) and Goldmark Music School (1943–44); then at the Academy of Music (from 1945). He won the Kossuth Prize (1950) and the Erkel Prize (1955, 1962); was made a Merited Artist (1953) and an Honored Artist (1963) of the Hungarian People's Republic. In his music he combined the elements of the cosmopolitan modern idiom with strong Hungarian rhythms and folklike melodies; in his treatment of these materials, and particularly in the energetic asymmetrical passages, he was closer to the idiom of Bartók than to that of Kodály.

The lyrical element in modal interludes adds to the Hungarian charm of his music.

WORKS: Opera, *A huszti kaland* (The Adventure of Huszt; 1949–50; Budapest, Dec. 22, 1951); 5 cantatas: *De amore fatale* (1939–40); *Terjed a fény* (Light Is Spreading; 1949); *Sztálin esküje* (Stalin's Oath; 1949); *A béke katonai* (The Soldiers of Peace; 1950); *Március fia* (Son of March; 1950); Chamber Sym. (1926); 2 divertimentos for Orch. (1933; 1933–34, rev. 1960); 8 syms.: No. 1 (1941–42; Budapest, 1965); No. 2, *Capriccio* (Budapest, 1948); No. 3 (1953–55; Budapest, 1957); No. 4 for String Orch. (1958–59; Budapest, 1961); No. 5 (1960–61; Hungarian Radio, 1962); No. 6 (Hungarian Radio, Aug. 19, 1966); No. 7 (1967; Budapest, 1968); No. 8 (1968; Hungarian Radio, 1969); *Partita* for Orch. (1943–44); *Morning Ode* for Orch. (1945); *March,* overture (1945); *Honor and Glory,* suite (1951); Suite for Orch. (1954); *Pian e forte,* sonata for Orch. (1962); Suite for Small Orch. (1962); Sinfonietta (1974); 4 piano concertos: No. 1 (1931; Amsterdam ISCM Festival, June 9, 1933, composer soloist); No. 2, concertino (1938); No. 3 (1953); No. 4 (1966); 2 violin concertos (1932, rev. 1969–70; 1940–41, rev. 1956); Concerto for String Quartet and Chamber Orch. (1936); Viola Concertino (1937); 3 string quartets (1934–35; 1936; 1957); Serenade for 10 Instruments (1967); solo sonatinas for Violin (1923) and Cello (1924); Sonatina for Violin and Cello (1923); 2 violin sonatas (1925, rev. 1969–70; 1963); Suite for Violin and Piano (1926; rev. 1970); 2 string trios (1929–30; 1955); *Partita* for Violin and Piano (1931); Suite for Solo Violin (1931); Wind Quintet (1954); Piano Trio (1956); *Improvisation* for Cello and Piano (1957); Flute Sonatina (1961); Violin Sonatina (1962); 3 suites for Piano (1921; 1921–23; 1923, rev. 1970); piano cycles: 7 *Bagatelles* (1923), 8 *Epigrams* (1923–24), 5 *Sketches* (1931), 6 *Hungarian Folksongs* (1934–35), 6 *Little Preludes* (1944), 10 *Bagatelles* (1956–57), 4 *Caprichos* (1961), *Kaleidoscope* (8 pieces, 1966), *Snapshots* (1971); 4 piano sonatas (1926, rev. 1970; 1926–27; 1930; 1959–60); Piano Sonatina (1927); 2-piano Sonata (1947); Suite for Piano Duet (1955); 3 *Radnóti Songs* (1961); 7 *Attila József Songs* (1964); folk-song arrangements; piano albums for children.

BIBL.: F. Bónis, *K. P.* (Budapest, 1965).

Kaempfert, Bert(hold), German bandleader, composer, and arranger; b. Hamburg, Oct. 16, 1923; d. Majorca, June 22, 1980. He studied clarinet, saxophone, and accordion at the Hamburg Hochschule für Musik; was drafted into the German army as a member of a music corps and taken prisoner of war in 1945; conducted a band in the camp. After his release, he was active in Hamburg. He gained notice with his song *Wonderland by Night* (1961); other hits included *Spanish Eyes, Swinging Safari, African Night, Blue Midnight,* and *Strangers in the Night,* which was catapulted to the top of the charts by Frank Sinatra.

Kaempfert, Max, German violinist and composer; b. Berlin, Jan. 3, 1871; d. Solothurn, June 2, 1941. He studied violin in Paris and Munich; was a member of the Kaim Orch. in Munich (1893–98); settled in Frankfurt (1899). He wrote an opera in folk style, *Der Schatz des Sultans;* a grand opera, *Der tote Gast;* 3 rhapsodies for Orch.; chamber music and songs.

Kafenda, Frico, significant Slovak pedagogue and composer; b. Mošovce, Nov. 2, 1883; d. Bratislava, Sept. 3, 1963. He studied conducting with Nikisch and music theory with Jadassohn at the Leipzig Cons.; from 1922 to 1949 was director of the Bratislava Cons. As a teacher of composition, he had great influence upon Slovak music; among his students were R. Berger, M. Novák, and E. Suchoň. His wife, Anna Kafendová-Zochová, taught piano at the Cons. and the Academy in Bratislava. His compositions are permeated with the spirit of mid-European Romanticism; among them are a Sonata for Cello and Piano (1905), a String Quartet (1916), a Sonata for Violin and Piano (1918), choral music, and songs.

Kaffka (real name, **Engelmann**), **Johann Christoph,** German violinist, singer, and composer; b. Regensburg, 1754; d.

Riga, Jan. 29, 1815. He studied violin with his father and theory with Riepel; appeared on the stage as a singer and actor in various German cities (from 1777); settled in Riga as a bookseller (1803). He wrote singspiels, ballets, oratorios, masses, and songs, most of which are lost.

Kafka, Johann Nepomuk, Bohemian pianist, composer, and music collector; b. Neustadt an der Mettau, May 17, 1819; d. Vienna, Oct. 23, 1886. He publ. about 200 popular salon pieces for piano, many based on Austrian themes; collected a number of musical manuscripts, including early works by Beethoven.

Kagel, Mauricio (Maurizio Raúl), remarkable Argentine composer; b. Buenos Aires, Dec. 24, 1931. He studied in Buenos Aires with Juan Carlos Paz and Alfredo Schiuma; also attended courses in philosophy and literature at the Univ. of Buenos Aires. In 1949 he became associated with the Agrupación Nueva Música. From 1949 to 1956 he was choral director at the Teatro Colón. In 1957 he obtained a stipend of the Academic Cultural Exchange with West Germany and went to Cologne, which he made his permanent home. From 1960 to 1966 he was a guest lecturer at the International Festival Courses for New Music in Darmstadt; in 1961 and 1963 he gave lectures and demonstrations of modern music in the U.S., and in 1964–65 was Slee Prof. of composition at the State Univ. of N.Y. at Buffalo. In 1969 he became director of the Inst. of New Music at the Rheinische Musikschule in Cologne. In 1974 he was made prof. at the Cologne Hochschule für Musik. As a composer, Kagel evolved an extremely complex system in which a fantastically intricate and yet wholly rational serial organization of notes, intervals, and durations is supplemented by aleatory techniques; some of these techniques are derived from linguistic permutations, random patterns of lights and shadows on exposed photographic film, and other seemingly arcane processes. In his hyper-serial constructions, he endeavors to unite all elements of human expression, ultimately aiming at the creation of a universe of theatrical arts in their visual, aural, and societal aspects.

WORKS: *Palimpsestos* for Chorus a cappella (1950); String Sextet (1953); *Traummusik* for Instruments and Musique Concrète (1954); *Anagrama* for Speaking Chorus, 4 Vocalists, and Chamber Ensemble (1958); *Transición I* for Electronic Sounds (1958); *Transición II* for Piano, Percussion, and 2 Magnetic Tapes (1959); *Pandora's Box* for Magnetic Tape (1961); *Sonant* for Electric Guitar, Harp, Double Bass, and 20 Instruments (1961); *Sur scène* for 6 Participants in mixed media, with Musicians instructed to interfere with Actors and Singers (concert perf., Radio Bremen, May 6, 1962); *Heterophonie* for Optional Ensemble, in 5 sections, optionally played or unplayed, with the conductor given an option to regard all instructions in the score as binding or not binding (Cologne, May 22, 1962, optionally conducted by the composer with the oboe giving A-sharp for tuning); *Phonophonie,* 4 melodramas for 2 Voices and Sound Sources (1963); *Composition & Decomposition,* reading piece (1963); *Diaphonie* for Chorus, Orch., and Slide Projections (1964); *Music for Renaissance Instruments* for 23 Performers (1966); String Quartet (1967); *Montage* for different Sound Sources (1967); *Ornithologica multiplicata* for Exotic Birds (1968); *Ludwig van,* surrealistic film score bestrewed with thematic fragments from Beethoven's works (1970; a bicentennial homage to Beethoven); *Staatstheater,* "scenic composition" involving a ballet for "non-dancers" and orchestrated for a number of household objects, including a chamber pot and medical appurtenances such as a large clyster filled with water held in readiness to administer a rectal enema (Hamburg, April 25, 1971); *Variations ohne Fuge* for Orch. (1972); *Con voce* for 3 Mute Actors (1972); *Mare nostrum,* scenic play (1975); *Kantrimiusik* (phonetic rendition into German of "country music"; 1975); *Variété,* "concert-spectacle for Artists and Musicians" (Metz Festival, Fall 1977); opera, *Die Erschöpfung der Welt* (Stuttgart, Feb. 8, 1980); *Sankt-Bach-Passion* (1985).

BIBL.: D. Schnebel, *M. K.: Musik, Theater, Film* (Cologne, 1970); K. Zrius, *Staatstheater von M. K.* (Vienna, 1977).

Kagen, Sergius, Russian-born American pianist, teacher, and composer; b. St. Petersburg, Aug. 22, 1909; d. N.Y., March 1, 1964. He went to Berlin in 1921 and studied with Leonid Kreutzer and Paul Juon at the Hochschule für Musik; emigrated to the U.S. in 1925 and became a naturalized citizen in 1930; studied with Carl Friedberg, Rubin Goldmark, and Marcella Sembrich at the Juilliard School of Music in N.Y. (diploma, 1930); later joined its faculty (1940), and also taught at the Union Theological Seminary (1957–64). He wrote the books *Music for the Voice* (N.Y., 1949; 2nd ed., rev., 1968) and *On Studying Singing* (N.Y., 1950). He composed an opera, *Hamlet* (Baltimore, Nov. 9, 1962), more than 70 songs, and various piano pieces.

BIBL.: B. Woods, *S. K.: His Life and Works* (diss., George Peabody College for Teachers, 1969); idem, "The Songs of S. K.," *NATS Bulletin*, XXVII/3 (1971).

Kahane, Jeffrey (Alan), American pianist; b. Los Angeles, Sept. 12, 1956. He studied at the San Francisco Cons. and with Howard Wiesel, Jakob Gimpel, and John Perry at the Juilliard School in N.Y.; in 1978 he made his debut in San Francisco; won 2nd prize in the Clara Haskil Competition in 1977, 4th prize in the Van Cliburn Competition in 1981, and 1st prize in the Arthur Rubinstein Competition in 1983. He made his Carnegie Hall debut in N.Y. in 1983 and his London debut in 1985. In 1988 he joined the faculty of the Eastman School of Music in Rochester, N.Y.

Kahl, Willi, German musicologist; b. Zabern, Alsace, July 18, 1893; d. Cologne, Oct. 3, 1962. He first studied in Freiburg and Munich; received his Ph.D. in 1919 from the Univ. of Bonn with the dissertation *Das lyrische Klavierstück zu Beginn des 19. Jahrhunderts (1800 bis 1830) und seine Vorgeschichte im 17. und 18. Jahrhundert;* subsequently completed his Habilitation in 1923 at the Univ. of Cologne with his *Studien zur Geschichte der Klaviermusik des 18. Jahrhunderts.* In 1928 he became Bibliotheksrat of the Univ. of Cologne and of the city library; was also a reader at the Univ. from 1928; he retired in 1958. His writings include *Musik und Musikleben im Rheinland* (Cologne, 1923); *Herbart als Musiker* (Langensalza, 1936); *Verzeichnis des Schrifttums über Franz Schubert, 1828–1928* (Regensburg, 1938). He also ed. various works and compiled the important documentary vol. *Selbstbiographien deutscher Musiker des XVIII. Jahrhunderts* (Cologne, 1948).

Kähler, Willibald, German conductor and composer; b. Berlin, Jan. 2, 1866; d. Klein-Machnow, Oct. 17, 1938. He was a pupil of Kiel and Herzogenberg at Berlin's Hochschule für Musik. He was conductor in Mannheim (1891–1906) and Schwerin (1906–31). Among his compositions are music for Goethe's *Faust,* a symphonic prologue to Kleist's *Der Prinz von Homburg,* choral works, and piano pieces.

Kahn, Erich Itor, German-American pianist and composer; b. Rimbach, July 23, 1905; d. N.Y., March 5, 1956. He studied at the Hoch Cons. in Frankfurt; went to France in 1933; in 1938–39, toured as accompanist to Casals in France and North Africa. He emigrated in 1941 to the U.S., where he organized the Albeneri Trio (the name being derived from assorted syllables of the 1st names of the participants: Alexander Schneider, violin; Benar Heifetz, cello; and Erich Kahn, piano). In 1948 he was awarded the Coolidge Medal for eminent service to chamber music. He was held in high esteem as a composer of inventive intellect.

WORKS: Suite for Violin and Piano (1937); *Ciaccona dei tempi di guerra* for Piano (40 variations on a 12-tone theme in the bass; 1943); String Quartet (1953); 4 Nocturnes for Voice and Piano (1954); *Symphonies bretonnes* for Orch. (1955); *Actus tragicus* for 10 Instruments (Baden-Baden Festival, June 18, 1955).

BIBL.: D. Newlin, "In Memoriam: E.I. K., Retrospect and Prospect," *American Composers Alliance Bulletin,* 3 (1957); R. Leibowitz and K. Wolff, *E.I. K., un grand représentant de la musique contemporaine* (Paris, 1958).

Kahn, Otto Hermann, German-American patron of music; brother of **Robert Kahn;** b. Mannheim, Feb. 21, 1867; d.

N.Y., March 29, 1934. He was engaged in the banking profession in London (1888–93); settled in N.Y. in 1893; was a member of the firm Kahn, Loeb & Co.; became interested in the musical affairs of N.Y. City; from 1907 to his death, was on the board of the Metropolitan Opera Co.; was vice-president of the N.Y. Phil.

BIBL.: M. Matz, *The Many Lives of O. K.* (N.Y., 1963); J. Kobler, *O. the Magnificent: The Life of O. K.* (N.Y., 1989).

Kahn, Robert, German pianist and composer, brother of **Otto Hermann Kahn;** b. Mannheim, July 21, 1865; d. Biddenden, Kent, May 29, 1951. He studied music with Lachner in Mannheim and with Rheinberger in Munich. In 1885 he went to Berlin, and in 1890 moved to Leipzig, where he organized a Ladies' Choral Union, which he conducted; in 1893 he was appointed instructor of piano at the Berlin Hochschule für Musik, retiring in 1931. After the advent of the Nazi government in Germany, he went to England, where he remained until his death. He composed a considerable amount of respectable chamber music and many singable choruses.

BIBL.: E. Radecke, *R. K.* (Leipzig, 1894).

Kahnt, Christian Friedrich, German music publisher; b. Leipzig, May 10, 1823; d. there, June 5, 1897. He was founder and head of the music publishing firm of C.F. Kahnt in Leipzig and Zwickau (1856–86); was publisher (from 1857) and titular ed. (from 1868) of Schumann's *Neue Zeitschrift für Musik.* The firm and the magazine were acquired by Oscar Schwalm ("C.F. Kahnt Nachfolger") in 1886, by Paul Simon in 1888, and by Alfred Hoffmann in 1903. After Hoffmann's death in 1926, his wife, Maria, directed the business; when she died, in 1959, the firm was taken over by her son.

Kahowez, Günter, Austrian composer; b. Vöcklabruck, Dec. 4, 1940. He studied at the Bruckner Cons. in Linz and at the Vienna Academy of Music with Karl Schiske. With neo-Classical precepts as points of departure, he rapidly progressed in the direction of modern serialism.

WORKS: Wind Quintet (1959); String Quartet (1960); *Klangrhythmen* for Piano (1962); *Flächengitter* for Flute (1962); *Megalyse* for Electronic Instruments (1962); *Duale* for Clarinet and Guitar (1963); *Schichtungen* for Orch. (1963); *Ouverture & Pantomime* for Orch. (1964); *Elementalichemie* for Cello and Percussion (1975).

Kaim, Franz, German literary historian and patron of music; b. Kirchheim unter Tech, near Stuttgart, May 13, 1856; d. Munich, Nov. 17, 1935. After settling in Munich, he built a concert hall and organized the "Kaim-Konzerte" in 1891; then in 1893 organized an orch., which had such notable permanent conductors as Löwe (1897–98) and Weingartner (1898–1905). With the end of the Kaim Orch. in 1908, the Konzertverein was formed with Löwe as conductor (1908–14); later conductors included Pfitzner (1919–20) and Hausegger (from 1920); when the Konzertverein orch. officially became the Munich Phil. in 1928, Hausegger continued as conductor until 1938; his eminent successors included Rosbaud (1945–48), Kempe (1967–76), and Celibidache (from 1979).

BIBL.: E. Faehndrich and A. Ott, *Die Münchner Philharmoniker, 1893–1968: Ein Kapitel Kulturgeschichte* (Munich, 1968).

Kaipainen, Jouni (Ilari), Finnish composer; b. Helsinki, Nov. 24, 1956. He studied with Aulis Sallinen (1973–76) and Paavo Heininen (1976–82) at the Sibelius Academy in Helsinki. His style of composition is typical of the modern school of Finnish music, drawing away from the nationalistic trends of Sibelius and embracing the post-Impressionism of the French school.

WORKS: TELEVISION OPERA: *Konstanzin Ihme* (The Miracle of Konstanz; 1987). ORCH.: *Concerto grosso per orchestra di camera* (1974); *Apotheosis* for Chamber Orch. (1975); Sym. (1980–85). CHAMBER: 3 string quartets (1973, 1974, 1984); *". . . la chimère de l'humidité de la nuit?"* for Alto Saxophone (1978); *Ladders to Fire* for 2 Pianos (1979); *Je chante la chaleur désespérée* for Piano (1981); *Far from Home* for Flute, Alto

Saxophone, Guitar, and Percussion (1981); *Altaforte* for Electric Trumpet and Tape (1982); Trio No. 1 for Clarinet, Cello, and Piano (1983); *Piping Down the Valleys Wild* for Bass Clarinet and Piano (1984); *Conte* for Piano (1985); *Andamento: Trio No. 2* for Flute, Bassoon, and Piano (1986); Trio No. 3 for Violin, Cello, and Piano (1986–87). **VOCAL:** *Yölaujuja* (Nocturnal Songs) for Soprano and Chamber Ensemble (1978); *Cinq poèmes de René Char* for Soprano and Orch. (1978–80); *Pitkän kesän poikki iltaan* (Through the Long Summer to the Evening) for Soprano, Flute, Horn, Percussion, and Cello (1979); other songs.

Kaiser, Alfred, Belgian-born English composer; b. Brussels, Feb. 29, 1872; d. Bournemouth, Oct. 1, 1917. He studied composition with Bruckner in Vienna and with Foerster in Prague; went to London to live. During World War I, he changed his name to De Keyser to escape the odium attached to the Kaiser of Germany. Among his works are the operas *Le Billet de Joséphine* (Paris, 1902), *Die schwarze Nina* (Elberfeld, 1905), and *Stella Maris* (Düsseldorf, 1910). He also wrote a Sym., a Piano Concerto, and chamber music.

Kaiser, Henry, innovative American improvisational guitarist and keyboardist; b. Oakland, Calif., Sept. 19, 1952. He took up the guitar at 12; developed a unique and eclectic style that shows influences as varied as East Asian, classical North Indian, and Hawaiian music, free jazz and improvisation, and American steel-string guitar; he also draws freely from other abiding interests, which include information theory, experimental cinema and literature, mathematics, and scuba diving. He has performed extensively with such groups as Crazy-Backwards Alphabet, Invite the Spirit, the Henry Kaiser Band, the Obsequious Cheeselog, French-Frith-Kaiser-Thompson, and the Henry Kaiser Quartet. His list of collaborators is extensive; he also has assisted various composers and performers in their compositional and recording endeavors through his elaborate recording studio in Oakland, Calif. He is senior instructor in Underwater Scientific Research at the Univ. of Calif. at Berkeley. Among his solo recordings or recordings in which he is a featured artist are *Those Who Know History Are Doomed to Repeat It, Re-Marrying for Money,* and *Alternate Visions*; he also produced an instructional video, *Eclectric Electric, Exploring New Horizons of Guitar and Improvisation* (1990).

Kajanus, Robert, outstanding Finnish conductor; b. Helsinki, Dec. 2, 1856; d. there, July 6, 1933. He studied with R. Faltin and G. Niemann at the Helsinki Cons., and later at the Leipzig Cons. with Reinecke, Richter, and Jadassohn (1877–79); then went to Paris, where he studied with Svendsen (1879–80). After returning to Helsinki in 1882, he founded an orch. society that sponsored concerts by the newly organized Helsinki Phil., which he led until his death; from 1897 to 1926 he was music director at the Univ. of Helsinki. He was an early champion of the music of Sibelius; made the 1st recordings of the 1st and 2nd symphonic with the London Sym. Orch. He composed the symphonic poems *Kullervo* (1881) and *Aino* (1885); 2 Finnish rhapsodies (1882, 1889); an orch. suite, *Sommarminnen* (Summer Memories; 1896); piano pieces; songs. **BIBL.:** Y. Suomalainen, *R. K.: Hänen elämänsä ja toimintansa,* (R. K.: His Life and Work; Helsinki, 1952).

Kalabis, Viktor, Czech composer; b. Červený Kostelec, Feb. 27, 1923. He studied with Hlobil at the Prague Cons. (1945–48) and with Řídký at the Prague Academy of Music (1948–52); also took courses in philosophy and musicology at the Univ. of Prague. He was an ed. and music producer with the Czech Radio in Prague (1953–72); then devoted himself totally to composition. In 1967 he received the Czech Music Critics' Prize and in 1969 the Klement Gottwald State Prize; in 1983 he was made an Artist of Merit by the Czech government. In 1952 he married **Zuzana Růžičková.** His early works adhered to traditional methods, but he later adopted modified serial procedures. **WORKS: ORCH.:** Concerto for Chamber Orch., *Hommage à Stravinsky* (1948); Overture (1950); Cello Concerto (1951);

Piano Concerto (1954); 5 syms.: No. 1 (1957); No. 2, *Sinfonia Pacis* (1961); No. 3 (1971); No. 4 (1972); No. 5 (1976); 2 violin concertos (1959, 1978); *Chamber Music* for Strings (1963); *Symphonic Variations* (1964); *Concerto for Orchestra* (1966); Trumpet Concerto (1973); Concerto for Harpsichord and Strings (1975); *Fable* for Chamber Orch. (1983); Concertino for Bassoon and Wind Instruments (1983); Concerto No. 2 for Piano and Wind Instruments (1985); Diptych for Strings (1987); *Meantatioas* for 13 Wind Instruments (1988). **CHAMBER:** 6 string quartets (1949, 1962, 1977, 1984, 1984, 1987); Divertimento for Wind Quintet (1952); 2 nonets: *Classical* (1956) and *Homage to Nature* (1975); Sonata for Clarinet and Piano (1969); Variations for Horn and Piano (1969); Sonata for Trombone and Piano (1970); Trio for Violin, Cello, and Piano (1974); Sonata for Violin and Piano (1982); Duettino for Violin and Cello (1987); piano music, including 3 sonatas (1947, 1948, 1982); much vocal music.

Kalachevsky, Mikhail, Ukrainian composer; b. Polovka, near Elizavetgrad, Sept. 26, 1851; d. Kremenchug, c.1910. He studied piano with C. Reinecke and theory with E.F.E. Richter at the Leipzig Cons. (1872–76). Returning to Russia, he occupied provincial government positions. His music reflects the modalities of Ukrainian folk songs; his *Ukrainian Symphony* (1876) has some historical value. He also composed a Requiem for Chorus, String Quartet, and Organ; a String Quartet in E-flat major; a Piano Trio in A minor; and several works for solo piano, including 19 romances. **BIBL.:** N. Grinchenko, "Pervaya ukrainskaya simfoniya, M. K." (The 1st Ukrainian Symphony, M. K.), *Sovetskaya Muzyka,* 11 (1946); N. Gordeichuk, *M.N. K.* (Kiev, 1954); ibid., *Ukrainskaya simfoniya M. K.* (The Ukrainian Symphony of M. K.; Kiev, 1963).

Kalafati, Vasili (Pavlovich), Russian composer and pedagogue of Greek descent; b. Eupatoria, Feb. 10, 1869; d. Leningrad, Jan. 30, 1942. He studied at the St. Petersburg Cons. with Rimsky-Korsakov, graduating in 1899; subsequently was on its teaching staff (1907–29). A musician of thorough knowledge, he was held in great esteem by his colleagues and students; Rimsky-Korsakov sent Stravinsky to him for additional training in harmony. As a composer, Kalafati faithfully continued the traditions of the Russian national school; his works include an opera, *Zygany* (The Gypsies; 1939-41), a Sym., a Piano Quintet, 2 piano sonatas, piano pieces, and a number of songs, all set in impeccably euphonious harmonies.

Kalaš, Julius, Czech composer; b. Prague, Aug. 18, 1902; d. there, May 12, 1967. He studied composition with Foerster and Křička at the Prague Cons. (1921–24), then attended Suk's master classes there (1924–28). He was pianist and artistic director of the satirical male sextet the Teachers of Gotham (1925–53), for which he wrote numerous witty ballads and songs. He was a prof. in the film dept. of the Prague Academy of Musical Arts from 1948; was its dean (1949–50) and vice-dean (1955–57). He wrote 6 operas, the most notable being *Nepokoření* (The Proud Ones; 1960); 6 operettas, including the popular *Mlynářka z Granad* (The Miller's Wife of Granada; 1954); 2 ballets; Cello Concerto (1949); Viola Concerto (1950); cantatas; chamber music; film scores.

Kalbeck, Max, German writer on music; b. Breslau, Jan. 4, 1850; d. Vienna, May 4, 1921. He studied law and philosophy at the Univ. of Breslau, then music in Munich (1872–74). He returned to Breslau as music critic of the *Schlesische Zeitung* in 1875, and later wrote for the *Breslauer Zeitung;* then settled in Vienna in 1880, and wrote for the *Wiener Allgemeine Zeitung;* was music critic for the *Neue Freie Presse* (1883–86), the *Neues Wiener Tageblatt* (1886–90), and the *Wiener Montags-Revue* (from 1890). In addition to his monumental biography of Brahms, he also ed. Brahms's correspondence (Vols. I–II, Berlin, 1907; VIII, Berlin, 1915; IX–XII, Berlin, 1917–19). **WRITINGS:** *Richard Wagners Nibelungen* (Breslau, 1876; 2nd ed., 1883); *Das Bühnenfestspiel zu Bayreuth* (Breslau,

1877); *Richard Wagners Parsifal* (Breslau, 1883); *Gereimtes und Ungereimtes* (Berlin, 1885); *Wiener Opernabende* (Vienna, 1885); *Humoresken und Phantasien* (Berlin, 1896); *Opernabende* (2 vols., Berlin, 1898); *Johannes Brahms* (8 vols., Berlin, 1904–14).

BIBL.: A. Wurz, "M. K.," *Zeitschrift für Musik,* CXI (1950).

Kalhauge, Sophus Viggo Harald, Danish composer; b. Copenhagen, Aug. 12, 1840; d. there, Feb. 19, 1905. He studied with P. Heise, C. Rongsted, and J.C. Gebauer; also studied in Germany, Switzerland, and Italy; taught piano and singing in Copenhagen.

WORKS: 3 operas: *Zouavens Hjemkomst* (1868), *Paa Krigsfod* (1880), and *Mantillen* (1889); *An den Frühling* for Soloists, Chorus, and Orch.; piano pieces; songs.

Kalichstein, Joseph, Israeli-American pianist; b. Tel Aviv, Jan. 15, 1946. He studied at the Juilliard School of Music in N.Y. with Kabós and Steuermann (M.S., 1969); made his N.Y. recital debut and won the Young Concert Artists' Award (1967), then appeared as soloist in Beethoven's 4th Piano Concerto with Bernstein and the N.Y. Phil. on national television (1968). After winning 1st prize in the Leventritt Competition (1969), he pursued an active concert career; toured widely in a trio with the violinist Jaime Laredo and the cellist Sharon Robinson (from 1976).

Kálik, Václav, Czech pianist, conductor, and composer; b. Opava, Oct. 18, 1891; d. Prague, Nov. 18, 1951. He studied with V. Novák at the Univ. of Prague (1911–13); later attended Suk's master classes at the Prague Cons. (1924–26). He was mainly active as a pianist and conductor.

WORKS: 3 operas: *Jarní jitro* (A Spring Morning; 1933; Olomouc, 1943), *Lásky div* (Love's Miracle; 1942–43; Liberec, Nov. 20, 1950), and *Posvěcení mládí* (Consecration of Youth; 1946–48); *Fantazie* for Orch. (1915); *Moře* (The Sea), symphonic poem (1924); 2 syms.: No. 1, *Mírová* (Peace), for Soprano and Orch. (1927) and No. 2 (1941–43); Prelude for Orch. (1931); *Venezia* for String Orch. (1932); *Intermezzo* for Tenor, Violin, and Piano (1913); *Zlá láska* (Evil Love) for Soprano, Violin, and Piano (1919); Violin Sonata (1919); *Pražské obrazy* (Prague Pictures) for Male Chorus (1949–50); several piano pieces.

BIBL.: J. Vratislavský, *V. K.* (Ostrava, 1961).

Kalinnikov, Vasili (Sergeievich), Russian composer; b. Voin, near Mtzensk, Jan. 13, 1866; d. Yalta, Jan. 11, 1901. He studied in Orel; in 1884 he enrolled at the Moscow Cons., but had to leave it a year later because of inability to pay; he then studied the bassoon at the Music School of the Moscow Phil. Soc. which provided free tuition. He earned his living by playing bassoon in theater orchs.; also studied composition with A. Ilyinsky and Blaramberg. While still a student, he composed his 1st work, the symphonic poem *The Nymphs* (Moscow, Dec. 28, 1889); later wrote another symphonic poem, *The Cedar and the Palm* (1897–98), the incidental music for *Tsar Boris* (Moscow, Feb. 1, 1899), and the prelude to the unfinished opera *In the Year 1812* (1899–1900). In 1895 he completed his most successful work, the Sym. in G minor (Kiev, Feb. 20, 1897); a 2nd sym., in A major (Kiev, March 12, 1898), was not as successful; he also wrote a cantata, *John of Damascus* (1890; not extant), songs, and piano pieces.

BIBL.: V. Paskhalov, *V.S. K.: Life and Works* (Moscow and Leningrad, 1938; 2nd ed., augmented, 1951); V. Kiselyo, ed., *V. K.: Letters, Documents, Materials* (2 vols., Moscow, 1959).

Kalisch, Paul, German tenor; b. Berlin, Nov. 6, 1855; d. St. Lorenz am Mondsee, Austria, Jan. 27, 1946. He studied architecture; then went to Milan, where he took voice lessons with Leoni and Lamperti. He made his operatic debut under the name Paolo Alberti in Rome as Edgardo (1879); subsequently sang in Milan's La Scala (1882) and other Italian opera houses. After appearing in Munich (1883), he was a member of Berlin's Royal Opera (1884–87); made his 1st appearance in London at Her Majesty's Theatre (1887). In 1888 he married the soprano **Lilli Lehmann,** with whom he frequently appeared in operatic performances. On Jan. 30, 1889, he sang Tannhäuser in his Metropolitan Opera debut in N.Y.; sang there again in 1890 and 1892. He later separated from Lehmann, although they never legally divorced; after her death in 1929, he settled on her estate.

Kalischer, Alfred, German writer on music; b. Thorn, March 4, 1842; d. Berlin, Oct. 8, 1909. After obtaining his Ph.D. at the Univ. of Leipzig, he took music courses with Burgel and Bohmer in Berlin; he ed. the *Neue Berliner Musikzeitung* (from 1873). He was best known for his writings on Beethoven. He ed. *Neue Beethovenbriefe* (1902) and *Beethovens sämtliche Briefe* (5 vols., 1906–8; in Eng., 1909).

WRITINGS: *Lessing als Musikästhetiker* (1889); *Die "Unsterbliche Geliebte" Beethovens* (1891); *Die Macht Beethovens* (1903); *Beethoven und seine Zeitgenossen* (4 vols., 1908: I, *Beethoven und Berlin;* II and III, *Beethovens Frauenkreis;* IV, *Beethoven und Wien*).

Kalish, Gilbert, American pianist and teacher; b. N.Y., July 2, 1935. He studied at Columbia College (B.A., 1956) and the Columbia Univ. Graduate School of Arts and Sciences (1956–58). In addition, he took piano lessons with Isabelle Vengerova, Leonard Shure, and Julius Herford. He made his N.Y. recital debut in 1962; then was active with the Contemporary Chamber Ensemble and the Boston Sym. Chamber Players. He also was a regular accompanist to Jan DeGaetani. He was artist-in-residence at Rutgers, the State Univ. of New Jersey (1965–67), and Swarthmore (Pa.) College (1966–72); was head of keyboard activities at the Berkshire Music Center in Tanglewood, and also taught at the State Univ. of N.Y. at Stony Brook (from 1970).

Kalkbrenner, Christian, German composer and writer on music, father of **Frédéric (Friedrich Wilhelm Michael) Kalkbrenner;** b. Minden, Hannover, Sept. 22, 1755; d. Paris, Aug. 10, 1806. He studied piano with Becker and violin with Rodewald in Kassel; was choirmaster at the court of the Queen in Berlin (1788) and at the court of Prince Heinrich in Rheinsberg (1790–96); in 1798 he became choirmaster at the Paris Opéra, where he brought out the opera *Olimpie* (Dec. 18, 1798); also some pasticcios from music by Mozart and Haydn. He also wrote 2 syms., a Piano Concerto, and several piano sonatas. He publ. *Theorie der Tonkunst* (1789) and *Kurzer Abriss der Geschichte der Tonkunst* (1792).

Kalkbrenner, Frédéric (Friedrich Wilhelm Michael), celebrated French pianist, pedagogue, and composer of German descent, son of **Christian Kalkbrenner;** b. near Kassel, between Nov. 2 and 8, 1785; d. Enghien-les-Bains, June 10, 1849. He most likely began his musical training with his father, then in 1799 entered the Paris Cons., where he studied with Louis Adam and Nicodami (piano) and Catel (harmony), taking 1st prizes in 1801. From 1803 to 1804 he was in Vienna, where he profited from the advice of Haydn; then played in Munich, Stuttgart, and Frankfurt on his return to Paris in 1805; was in great demand as a teacher in Paris. He went to Bath (1814–15), and then enjoyed considerable success as a pianist in London (1815–23). In 1818 he took up Logier's newly invented Chiroplast, simplified it, and applied it practically. He returned to Paris in 1824, becoming a partner in the Pleyel piano factory (the future Mme. Camilla Pleyel was one of his pupils). He continued to tour as a virtuoso, acquiring great renown until ill health compelled him to curtail his travels in 1835. During the last years of his life, he made only sporadic appearances as a pianist. Kalkbrenner was inordinately vain of the success of his method of teaching, which aimed at the independent development of the fingers and wrist; his practical method of octave playing became a standard of piano teaching. He also developed left-hand technique, and a proper management of the pedals. As for his playing, his technique was smooth and well-rounded, his fingers supple and of equal strength, and his tone full and rich; his style, while fluent and graceful, lacked emotional power. His numerous études (among them several for left hand alone) are interesting and valuable. Chopin took some advice from him in Paris, but did not become his pupil, despite Kalkbrenner's urging. His most distinguished students were Hallé and Thalberg. He publ. the didactic works *Méthode pour apprendre le pianoforte à l'aide du guide-mains* (1830) and *Traité d'harmonie du pianiste* (1849).

WORKS: 4 piano concertos (1823, 1826, 1829, 1835); Concerto for 2 Pianos (1835); 13 piano sonatas (1807–45); many virtuoso pieces for Piano and Orch.; chamber music; numerous light pieces for Solo Piano.

BIBL.: "Memoir of Mr. Frederick K.," *Quarterly Music Magazine and Review* (1824); L. Boivin, *K.* (Paris, 1840).

Kallenberg, Siegfried Garibaldi, German composer; b. Bad Schachen, near Lindau, Nov. 3, 1867; d. Munich, Feb. 9, 1944. He studied with Faisst at the Stuttgart Cons. and at the Munich Academy of Music; became director of the Stettin Cons. (1892), and later taught in Königsberg, Hannover, and Munich (from 1910). He publ. *Musikalische Kompositionsformen* (Leipzig, 1913) and monographs on R. Strauss (Leipzig, 1926) and Reger (Leipzig, 1930). As a composer, he was inspired by neo-Romanticism; in some of his works there are touches of Impressionism; his absorption in symbolic subjects brought him into a kinship with the Expressionist school in Germany. Apart from works on exotic subjects, he wrote music in a traditional style; he was particularly strong in choral polyphony.

WORKS: 3 operas: *Sun Liao, Das goldene Tor,* and *Die lustigen Musikanten;* choral works: *90th Psalm, Germania an ihre Kinder,* Requiem, *Den Gefallenen, Eine kleine Passionsmusik, Eine Pfingstmusik;* 3 syms.; *Impressionen* for Orch.; *Konzertante Fantasie* for Piano and Orch.; about 10 chamber works; 3 piano sonatas; a set of *Miniaturen* for Piano; some 300 songs.

Kallir, Lilian, Czech-born American pianist and teacher; b. Prague, May 6, 1931. She was taken as a child to the U.S., where she studied with Isabelle Vengerova and Herman de Grab at the Mannes College of Music in N.Y. (1946–49); she won the National Music League Award and the American Artists Award of the Brooklyn Inst. of Arts and Sciences at 16; made her debut as soloist with the N.Y. Phil. at 17; then followed her recital debut at N.Y.'s Town Hall at 18; thereafter toured widely in the U.S., South America, Europe, and Israel, appearing as soloist with orchs. and as a recitalist. She married the pianist **Claude Frank** (1959), and subsequently appeared in duo recitals with him. In 1975 she joined the faculty of the Mannes College of Music.

Kalliwoda (Kalivoda), Johann Wenzel (Jan Křtitel Václav), Bohemian violinist, conductor, and composer, father of **Wilhelm Kalliwoda;** b. Prague, Feb. 21, 1801; d. Karlsruhe, Dec. 3, 1866. He studied at the Prague Cons. (1811–16) with Pixis (violin) and D. Weber (composition); played in the orch. of the Stavovské Theater in Prague (1816–21). In 1822 he became conductor of Prince Fürstenberg's orch. in Donaueschingen, where he remained for some 30 years; his duties were minimal after the orch. was dissolved in the wake of the 1848 Revolution and the destruction of the theater by fire (1856). After giving a farewell concert as a violinist in Prague (1858), he retired to Karlsruhe. His early success as a composer was not sustained in the later years of his career; some of his music was praised by Schumann.

WORKS: Operas: *Blanda, die silberne Birke* (Prague, Nov. 29, 1827) and *Prinzessin Christine von Wolfenburg* (Donaueschingen, 1828); 7 syms. (1826–41); 18 overtures; various works for Violin and Orch.; chamber music; piano pieces; songs; etc.

BIBL.: K. Strunz, *J.W. K.* (Vienna, 1910).

Kalliwoda, Wilhelm, German pianist, conductor, and composer, son of **Johann Wenzel (Jan Křtitel Václav) Kalliwoda (Kalivoda);** b. Donaueschingen, July 19, 1827; d. Karlsruhe, Sept. 8, 1893. He studied with Hauptmann in Leipzig; also took some lessons from Mendelssohn. He settled in Karlsruhe, where he was director of the Court Theater (from 1853); wrote piano pieces and songs.

Kallmann, Helmut (Max), German-born Canadian librarian, musicologist, and editor; b. Berlin, Aug. 7, 1922. He studied music with his father; left Germany in 1939 for London, where he was interned as a German citizen in 1940; then was interned in Canada (1940–43); after his release, he became a Canadian citizen (1946). He took music courses at the Univ. of Toronto (B.Mus., 1949); became a music librarian for the CBC in 1950; was supervisor of its music collection from 1962. From 1970 to 1987 he served as chief of the music division of the National Library of Canada in Ottawa. He publ. a number of useful books, including a *Catalogue of Canadian Composers* (Toronto, 1952) and *A History of Music in Canada 1534–1914* (Toronto, 1960); with G. Potvin and K. Winters, he ed. the authoritative *Encyclopedia of Music in Canada* (Toronto, 1981).

BIBL.: J. Beckwith and F. Hall, eds., *Musical Canada: Words and Music Honouring H. K.* (Toronto, 1988).

Kallstenius, Edvin, Swedish composer; b. Filipstad, Aug. 29, 1881; d. Danderyd, Nov. 22, 1967. He studied science at the Univ. of Lund (1898–1903) and music at the Leipzig Cons. (1903–7); then was active as a music critic in Stockholm. He also was a music librarian for the Swedish Radio (1928–46). In his early works he followed the Romantic traditions of Scandinavian music; later turned to advanced modern techniques, including explicit application of dodecaphonic configurations.

WORKS: ORCH.: *Scherzo fugato* for Small Orch. (1907; rev. 1923); *Sista Striden,* dramatic overture (1908); *En serenad i sommarnatten* (A Serenade in the Summer Night; 1918); *Sinfonia concertata* for Piano and Orch. (1922); 4 sinfoniettas (1923; 1946; *Dodicitonica,* 1956; *Semi-seriale,* 1958); 5 syms. (1926, rev. 1941; 1935; 1948; 1954; *Sinfonia su temi 12-tonici,* 1960); *Dalarapsodi* (1931); *Dalslandsrapsodi* (1936); *Romantico,* overture (1938); *Högtid och fest,* trilogy (1940); *Musica gioconda* for Strings (1942); *Cavatina* for Viola and Orch. (1943); *Passacaglia enarmonica* (1943); *Kraus-variationer* (1947); *Sonata concertate* for Cello and Orch. (1951); *Musica sinfonica* for Strings (1953; full orch. version, 1959); *Nytt vin i gamla läglar* (New Wine in Old Bottles) for Small Orch. (1954); *Choreographic Suite* (1957); *Prologo seriale* (1966). VOCAL: *När vi dö* (When Mankind Perishes), Requiem for Chorus and Orch. (1919); *Sångoffer* (Song Offering), cantata for Baritone and Orch. (1944); *Stjärntändningen* for Chorus and Orch. (1949); *Hymen, o, Hymenaios* for Soli, Chorus, and Orch. (1955). CHAMBER: 8 string quartets (1904; 1905; 1913; *Divertimento alla serenata,* 1925; 1945; 1953; *Dodecatonica,* 1957; 1961); Cello Sonata (1908); Violin Sonata (1909); Clarinet Quintet (1930); Suite for Winds and Percussion (1938); Wind Quintet (1943); *Trio divertente* for Flute, Violin, and Viola (1950); *Piccolo trio seriale* for Flute, English Horn, and Clarinet (1956); *Trio svagante* for Clarinet, Horn, and Cello (1959); solo sonatas for Cello (1961), Flute (1962), and Violin (1965); *Lyric Suite* for Flute, Saxophone, and Cello (1962); String Trio (1965).

Kálmán, Emmerich, Hungarian-born American composer; b. Siófok, Oct. 24, 1882; d. Paris, Oct. 30, 1953. He studied with Koessler at the Royal Academy of Music in Budapest; won the Franz Josef Prize (1907), then became a successful composer of operettas in Vienna. He went to Paris in 1939, then to the U.S. in 1940, becoming an American citizen in 1942; he returned to Europe in 1949.

WORKS: OPERETTAS: *Tatárjárás* (The Gay Hussars; Budapest, Feb. 22, 1908); *Der gute Kamerad* (Vienna, Oct. 10, 1911; rev. as *Gold gab ich für Eisen,* Vienna, Oct. 16, 1914); *Der kleine König* (Vienna, Nov. 27, 1912); *Zsuzsi kisasszony* (Miss Springtime; Budapest, Feb. 23, 1915); *Die Csárdásfürstin* (Vienna, Nov. 17, 1915); *Die Faschingsfee* (Vienna, Jan. 31, 1917); *Die Bajadere* (Vienna, Dec. 23, 1921); *Gräfin Mariza* (Vienna, Feb. 28, 1924); *Die Zirkusprinzessin* (Vienna, March 26, 1926); *Golden Dawn* (N.Y., Nov. 30, 1927); *Die Herzogin von Chicago* (Vienna, April 6, 1928); *Ronny* (Berlin, Dec. 22, 1931); *Kaiserin Josephine* (Zürich, Jan. 18, 1936); *Marinka* (N.Y., July 18, 1945); *Arizona Lady* (Bern, 1954).

BIBL.: J. Bistron, *E. K.* (Vienna, 1932); R. Oesterreicher,

E. K.: Der Weg eines Komponisten (Vienna, 1954); V. Kálmán, *Gruss' mir die süssen, die reizenden Frauen: Mein Leben mit E. K.* (Bayreuth, 1966); R. Oesterreicher, *E. K.: Das Leben eines Operettenfürsten* (Vienna, 1988).

Kalmár, László, Hungarian composer; b. Budapest, Oct. 19, 1931. He studied composition with Ervin Major at the Budapest Cons. and privately with Farkas. He was ed. in chief of Editio Musica Budapest (from 1970), becoming its head of music in 1987. **WORKS:** Cantata, *Soldiers Weep at Night,* after Quasimodo (1962); *Symmetriae* for String Orch. (1966); Trio for Flute, Marimba, and Guitar (1968); 3 *Monologos:* No. 1 for Guitar (1968), No. 2 for Violin (1973), and No. 3 for Flute (1973); *Toccata concertante* for Piano and String Orch. (1968–70); Flute Sonata (1970–71); *Triangoli* for Clarinet, Horn, Harp, Violin, and Cello (1970–71); *Cicli* for 18 Strings (1971); *Cantus* for 2 Contraltos, Clarinet, Cello, and Harp (1969–72); 2 *Duets* for 2 Trumpets (1972); Quartet for English Horn, Viola, Vibraphone, and Harpsichord (1972); String Trio (1972); *Sotto voce* for Harmonium, Vibraphone, and Harp (1973); *Sereno* for Cello and Harp (1974–75); *Morfeo* for String Quartet (1977); Trio Sonata for Clarinet, Horn, and Cello (1981); *Horae* for Orch. (1982); *Hermes* for Orch. (1983–84); Piano Concerto No. 2 (1984–85); Chamber Concerto for 10 Instruments (1986); 3 *Symphonic Pictures* for Orch. (1987–88); *At Janus's Gate* for Orch. (1988).

Kalninš, Alfreds, Latvian organist and composer, father of **Janis Kalninš;** b. Zehsis, Aug. 23, 1879; d. Riga, Dec. 23, 1951. He studied at the St. Petersburg Cons. with Homilius (organ) and Liadov (composition); then was organist in various Lutheran churches in Dorpat, Libau, and Riga; gave recitals in Russia, and was also active as a teacher in Riga. From 1927 to 1933 he lived in N.Y.; then returned to Riga, where he taught at the Latvian Cons.; was its rector (1944–48). He wrote the 1st national Latvian opera, *Banuta* (Riga, May 29, 1920); also the operas *Salinieki* (The Islanders; Riga, 1925) and *Dzimtenes atmoda* (The Nation's Awakening; Riga, Sept. 9, 1933); other works include a symphonic poem, *Latvia;* some 100 choruses; piano pieces; about 200 songs; arrangements of Latvian folk songs. **BIBL.:** J. Vitolinš, *A. K.* (Riga, 1968).

Kalninš, Imants, significant Latvian composer; b. Riga, May 26, 1941. He studied composition with A. Skulte at the Latvian Cons. in Riga, graduating in 1964. In 1959 he directed the choral organization Lachplesis in Lielvarde, then was pianist for a pantomime group in Riga (1962–64) and taught music in Liepaja and later at the Latvian Cons. (1973–80). About 1980 he turned his attention mostly to rock music. His output is innovative, fusing a diversity of styles; his 4th Sym. is scored for jazz ensemble and orch. **WORKS: STAGE: OPERAS:** *Is There Anyone Here?* (1971); *I Play, I Dance* (1977). **OPERETTA:** *Quo Vadis My Guitar?* (1971). **ORATORIOS:** *In October* (1967); *The Poet and the Mermaid* (1973); *Morning Drudgery* (1977). **ORCH.:** 4 syms. (1964, 1965, 1968, 1972); Cello Concerto (1963); Concerto (1966). **CHAMBER:** Toccata for Cello and Piano (1962); Viola Sonata (1962); Piano Sonata (1962); vocal pieces.

Kalninš, Janis, Latvian-born Canadian organist, conductor, pedagogue, and composer, son of **Alfreds Kalninš;** b. Pernu, Estonia (of Latvian parents), Nov. 3, 1904. He studied piano and organ with his father; then composition with Vitols at the Latvian State Cons. in Riga (1920–24); also studied conducting with Kleiber in Salzburg, Abendroth in Leipzig, and Blech in Berlin. Returning to Riga, he served as music director of the Latvian National Theater (1923–33) and the Latvian National Opera (1933–44). In 1948 he emigrated to Canada, becoming a naturalized citizen in 1954. From 1948 to 1989 he was organist and choirmaster at St. Paul's United Church in Fredericton, New Brunswick; he served as prof. of music at the Fredericton Teachers' College (1951–71), and was conductor of the Fredericton Civic Orch. (1951–58), the St. John

Sym. Orch. (1958–61), and the New Brunswick Sym. Orch. (1961–67). **WORKS: OPERAS:** *Lolita's Magic Bird* (1933); *Unguni* (1933); *In the Fire* (1934); *Hamlet* (1935; Riga, Feb. 17, 1936). **BALLETS:** *Autumn* (1936); *The Nightingale and the Rose* (1936). **ORCH.:** 5 syms.: No. 1 (1939–44); No. 2, *Symphony of the Beatitudes,* for Chorus and Orch. (1953); No. 3 (1972–73); No. 4 (1979); No. 5 (1990); 2 *Latvian Peasant Dances* (1936); Violin Concerto (1945–46); *Theme and Variations* for Clarinet, Horn, and Orch. (1963); *Music for String Orch.* (1965); *New Brunswick Rhapsody* (1967); *Latvian Rhapsody* (1975); Concerto for Piano and Chamber Orch. (1985). **CHAMBER:** String Quartet (1948); Sonata for Oboe and Piano (1963); Trio for Violin, Viola, and Cello (1979); Violin Sonata (1982); Piano Quartet (1987); 2 piano sonatas; organ music; choruses.

Kalomiris, Manolis, distinguished Greek composer and pedagogue; b. Smyrna, Dec. 26, 1883; d. Athens, April 3, 1962. He studied piano with Bauch and Sturm, composition with Grädener, and music history with Mandyczewski at the cons. of the Gesellschaft der Musikfreunde in Vienna (1901–6); then went to Russia, where he taught piano at a private school in Kharkov. He settled in Athens, where he taught at the Cons. (1911–19); was founder-director of the Hellenic Cons. (1919–26) and of the National Cons. (1926–48). He was greatly esteemed as a teacher; publ. several textbooks on harmony, counterpoint, and orchestration. Kalomiris was the protagonist of Greek nationalism in music; almost all his works are based on Greek folk-song patterns, and many are inspired by Hellenic subjects. In his harmonies and instrumentation he followed the Russian school of composition, with a considerable influx of lush Wagnerian sonorities. **WORKS: OPERAS:** *O Protomastoras* (The Master-Builder), to a libretto by Kazantzakis (Athens, March 24, 1916; rev. 1929 and 1940); *To dachtylidi tis manas* (The Mother's Ring; 1917; rev. 1939); *Anatoli* (Sunrise), musical fairy tale, to a libretto by Kalomiris, after Cambyssis (1945; rev. 1948); *Ta xotika nera* (The Shadowy Waters), after Yeats (1950; rev. 1952); *Constantinos o Palaeologus,* music legend after a story by Kazantzakis (Athens, Aug. 12, 1962). **ORCH.:** *Greek Suite* (1907); *The Olive Tree* for Women's Chorus and Orch. (1909); *Iambs and Anapests,* suite (1914); *Valor Symphony* for Chorus and Orch. (1920); *Greek Rhapsody* for Piano and Orch. (orchestrated by G. Pierné and conducted by him, Paris, April 3, 1926); *Island Pictures* for Violin and Orch. (1928); *Symphony of the Kind People* for Mezzo-soprano, Chorus, and Orch. (1931); 3 *Greek Dances* (1934); Piano Concerto (1935); *At the Ossios Loukas Monastery* for Narrator and Orch. (1937); *Triptych* (1940); *Minas the Rebel,* tone poem (1940); *The Death of the Courageous Woman,* tone poem (1945); Concertino for Violin and Orch. (1955); *Palamas Symphony* for Chorus and Orch., to texts by Palamas (Athens, Jan. 22, 1956). **CHAMBER:** Piano Quintet, with Soprano (1912); String Trio (1921); *Quartet quasi fantasia* for Harp, Flute, English Horn, and Viola (1921); Violin Sonata (1948). **PIANO:** *Sunrise* (1902); 3 *Ballads* (1906); *For Greek Children* (1910); 2 *Rhapsodies* (1921); 5 preludes (1939); choruses; songs.

Kalter (real name, **Aufrichtig**), **Sabine,** noted Hungarian mezzo-soprano; b. Jaroslaw, March 28, 1889; d. London, Sept. 1, 1957. She studied at the Vienna Academy of Music; made her debut at the Vienna Volksoper in 1911; then was a principal member of the Hamburg Opera (1915–35). After being compelled to leave Germany by the Nazis, she settled in London, where she sang at Covent Garden (1935–39); in later years she devoted herself to a concert career, making her last appearance with the Hamburg Radio in 1950. She was also active as a teacher. Her finest roles were Ortrud, Brangäne, and Fricka.

Kamensky, Alexander, Russian pianist; b. Geneva (of Russian parents), Dec. 12, 1900; d. Leningrad, Nov. 7, 1952. He studied piano at the Petrograd Cons. (graduated, 1923), then developed an energetic career as a concert pianist; did not interrupt his activities even during the siege of Leningrad in

1941–42, when he played almost 500 recitals under the most dangerous conditions. In his programs he featured many works by Soviet composers and also by modern Western music masters, including Schoenberg and Stravinsky. In 1934 he was appointed prof. of piano of the Leningrad Cons.

Kamieński, Lucian, Polish composer; b. Gniezno, Jan. 7, 1885; d. Thorn, July 27, 1964. He studied composition with Bruch and musicology with Kretzschmar and Johannes Wolf in Berlin (Ph.D., 1910, with the diss. *Die Oratorien von Johann Adolf Hasse;* publ. in Leipzig, 1912); then was a music critic in Königsberg (until 1919). He taught at the Poznan Academy of Music (1920–39); also taught musicology at the Univ. of Poznan. After World War II, he taught privately.

WORKS: 2 comic operas: *Tabu* (Königsberg, April 9, 1917) and *Dami i huzary* (Poznan, Oct. 2, 1938); *Sinfonia paschalis* (1928); *Silesia Sings,* symphonic sketch (1929); Violin Sonata; several piano suites on Polish themes; an album of 60 workers' songs to his own words (Berlin, 1905–10), which he issued under the name Dolega-Kamieński.

Kamieński, Maciej, significant Polish composer of Slovak descent; b. probably in Sopron or Magyar-Ovar, between Hungary and Slovakia, Oct. 13, 1734; d. Warsaw, Jan. 25, 1821. He studied composition in Vienna, then settled in Warsaw as a teacher, and brought out the 1st Polish opera to be premiered in a public theater, *Nędza uszczęśliwiona* (Poverty Made Happy; July 11, 1778); after its success, he wrote 7 more operas, only 2 of which are extant. He also composed a cantata for the unveiling of the Sobieski monument (Warsaw, Sept. 14, 1788); other works include masses, offertories, and piano pieces.

Kaminski, Heinrich, eminent German composer; b. Tiengen, Baden, July 4, 1886; d. Ried, Bavaria, June 21, 1946. He studied at Heidelberg Univ. with Wolfrum and in Berlin with Kaun, Klatte, and Juon; settled in Ried (1914); taught a master class at the Prussian Academy of the Arts in Berlin (1930–33) and then returned to Ried. His writing is strictly polyphonic and almost rigid in form; the religious and mystic character of his sacred music stems from his family origins (he was the son of a clergyman); the chief influences in his work were Bach and Bruckner. Interest in his music was enhanced after his death by posthumous eds. of his unpubl. works.

WORKS: STAGE: Opera, *Jürg Jenatsch* (Dresden, April 27, 1929); music drama for Narrator and Orch., *Das Spiel vom König Aphelius* (1946; Göttingen, Jan. 29, 1950); Passion, after an old French mystery play (1920). CHORAL: *69th Psalm* (1914); *Introitus und Hymnus* (1919); *Magnificat* (1925); *Der Mensch,* motet (1926); *Die Erde,* motet (1928); etc. ORCH.: Concerto Grosso for Double Orch. (1922); *Dorische Musik* (1933); Piano Concerto (Berlin, 1937); *In Memoriam Gabrielae* for Orch., Contralto, and Solo Violin (1940); *Tanzdrama* (1942). CHAMBER: Quartet for Clarinet, Viola, Cello, and Piano (1912); 2 string quartets (1913, 1916); Quintet for Clarinet, Horn, Violin, Viola, and Cello (1924); *Music for 2 Violins and Harpsichord* (1931); *Hauskonzert* (1941); *Ballade* for Horn and Piano (1943). ORGAN: Toccata (1923); *Chorale-Sonata* (1926); 3 chorale preludes (1928); Toccata and Fugue (1939). PIANO: *Klavierbuch* (1934); *10 kleine Übungen für das polyphone Klavierspiel* (1935). SONGS: *Brautlied* for Soprano and Organ (1911); *Cantiques bretons* (1923); *3 geistliche Lieder* for Soprano, Violin, and Clarinet (1924); *Triptychon* for Alto and Organ (1930); *Lied eines Gefangenen* (1936); *Weihnachtsspruch* (1938); *Hochzeitsspruch* for 2 Altos and Organ (1940); *Dem Gedächtnis eines verwundeten Soldaten* for 2 Sopranos and Piano (1941); folk-song arrangements.

BIBL.: K. Schleifer, *H. K.* (Kassel, 1945); K. Schleifer and R. Schwarz-Stilling, *H. K.: Werkverzeichnis* (Kassel, 1947); I. Samson, *Das Vokalschaffen von H. K., mit Ausnahme der Opern* (Frankfurt, 1956); A. Suder, ed., *H. K.* (Tutzing, 1986).

Kaminski, Joseph, Russian-born Israeli violinist and composer; b. Odessa, Nov. 17, 1903; d. Gedera, Oct. 14, 1972. He studied composition with Friedrich Koch in Berlin and

Hans Gál in Vienna; was concertmaster of the Warsaw Radio Orch., then emigrated to Tel Aviv, where he was concertmaster of the Palestine (later Israel Phil.) Orch. (1937–69).

WORKS: Trumpet Concertino (1940–41; Tel Aviv, May 5, 1941); *Ha'Alijah,* variations for Orch. (1942); *Comedy Overture* (1944); String Quartet (1945); *Ballade* for Harp and Chamber Orch. (Tel Aviv, Feb. 2, 1946); Violin Concerto (1947–49; Tel Aviv, 1954); *3 Israeli Sketches* for Orch. (1955); *Triptych* for Piano (1958); *Variations* for English Horn and String Orch. (1958); *Symphonic Overture* (1960).

Kamionsky, Oscar (Isaievich), Russian baritone; b. Kiev, 1869; d. Yalta, Aug. 15, 1917. He studied with Everard in St. Petersburg and Rossi in Naples; made his debut in Naples in 1891; sang in Kharkov (1893–94; 1898–99), Kiev (1894–95), and Tiflis (1896–98; 1899–1901); also appeared in St. Petersburg, Moscow, and other cities as a guest artist. He later sang in Moscow at the Zimin Theater (1905–8; 1913–14); retired from the stage in 1915. As a singer, he followed the precepts of the Italian school of *bel canto;* was famous for his roles as Valentin in *Faust,* Rigoletto, Wolfram in *Tannhäuser,* and other lyrico-dramatic parts.

Kämpf, Karl, German organist and composer; b. Berlin, Aug. 31, 1874; d. Mönchengladbach, Nov. 4, 1950. He was a pupil of F.E. Koch; became a professional performer on the harmonium; in 1925, was appointed conductor of the choral society Liedertafel in Mönchengladbach. He wrote several symphonic marches on literary subjects: *Hiawatha, Aus baltischen Landen, Andersens Märchen,* etc.; also a choral sym., *Die Macht des Liedes;* piano works; various pieces for the harmonium; etc.

BIBL.: J. Hagemann-Bonn, *K. K.* (Leipzig, 1907).

Kamu, Okko (Tapani), prominent Finnish conductor; b. Helsinki, March 7, 1946. He studied violin at the Sibelius Academy in Helsinki under Onni Suhonen (graduated, 1967). He played in the Helsinki Youth Orch.; founded the Suhonen Quartet (1964); was a member of the Helsinki Phil. (1965–66) and concertmaster of the orch. of the Finnish National Opera (1966–68); then was its 3rd conductor (1968–69). After winning 1st prize in the Karajan Competition for conductors (1969), he appeared as a guest conductor with the Royal Opera in Stockholm (1969–70); then was a conductor with the Finnish Radio Sym. Orch. (1970–71), and subsequently its chief conductor (1971–77). He was chief conductor of the Oslo Phil. (1975–79) and of the Helsinki Phil. (1979–90). In 1988 he became principal conductor of the Sjaelland Sym. Orch. in Copenhagen.

Kancheli, Giya (Alexandrovich), Russian composer; b. Tbilisi, Aug. 10, 1935. He studied composition at the Tbilisi Cons. (1959–63); in 1970, was appointed to its faculty. His sources of inspiration are nourished by Caucasian melos, with its quasi-oriental fiorituras and deflected chromatics which impart a peculiar aura of lyric introspection to the music; but his treatment of these materials is covertly modernistic and overtly optimistic, especially in sonoristic effects.

WORKS: Opera: *Music for the Living* (Moscow, 1984); 6 syms. (all 1st perf. in Tbilisi): No. 1 (May 12, 1968); No. 2 (Oct. 31, 1970); No. 3 (Oct. 11, 1973); No. 4 (Jan. 13, 1975); No. 5 (Feb. 27, 1978); No. 6 (April 7, 1980); Concerto for Orch. (Tbilisi, Feb. 2, 1963); *Largo and Allegro* for Strings, Piano, and Timpani (1963); *The Lucid Sorrow* for 2 Solo Children's Voices, Boys' Chorus, and Orch. (1985); musical comedy, *The Pranks of Hanum* (1973); film scores.

Kander, John (Harold), American composer of popular music; b. Kansas City, Mo., Mar. 18, 1927. He studied piano with Wiktor Labunski, then took courses with Beeson, Luening, and Douglas Moore at Columbia Univ. He tried his hand at a Broadway musical, *The Family Affair* (1962), but was unsuccessful; also in 1962 he teamed up with the lyricist Fred Ebb (b. N.Y., April 8, 1932), with whom he produced the hit songs *My Coloring Book* and *I Don't Care Much.* Encouraged by their success, they wrote the musical *Flora, the Red Menace* (1965) as a vehicle for Liza Minnelli; it was followed by their smash hit *Cabaret* (1966), which won the Tony and Drama Critics awards and later was made into a film (1972). Among their subsequent shows were *The Happy Time* (1968), *Zorba* (1968), *Chicago* (1975), *The Act* (1977), *Woman of the Year* (1981), and *The Rink* (1984).

Kang, Sukhi, Korean composer; b. Seoul, Oct. 22, 1934. He studied at the College of Music at the Seoul National Univ. (graduated, 1960), the Technische Universität in Berlin (graduated, 1965), and the Hochschule für Musik und Theater in Hannover (1971); subsequently taught at the Seoul National Univ. (1975–80; from 1982), and was named chairman of its composition dept. in 1987. Kang has actively promoted contemporary music in South Korea; he served as founding director of the annual Pan-Music-Festival in Seoul. In 1989 he was named Best Musician of the Year by the Assoc. of Korean Musicians. His compositions are meticulously crafted, utilizing densely stratified materials to create complex musical structures, including electronic sonorities. Many of these were presented in Berlin, securing for him international attention. His *The Feast of Id* (1966) was the 1st Korean composition to use electronically manipulated sounds. WORKS: STAGE: *Penthesilea*, music theater (1985; Berlin, March 2, 1986). ORCH.: *Generation '69* (Seoul, March 24, 1969); *Reflexionen* (Seoul, Sept. 9, 1975); *Dal-ha* (Seoul, Sept. 14, 1978); *Mega-Melos* (Berlin, Sept. 14, 1980); *Man-pa* for Solo Flute and Flute Orch. (Berlin, March 31, 1982); *Symphonic Requiem* (1983); *Successions* (Berlin, June 15, 1985); *Chuitahyang* for Traditional Korean Orch. (1987); *Prometheus kommt* (The Olympic Torch Music of the Seoul Olympiad; Seoul, Sept. 15, 1988). CHAMBER: *Nirmanakaya* for Cello, Piano, and Percussion (Seoul, Sept. 5, 1969); *Roundtone* for 7 Players (Seoul, Sept. 9, 1969); *Nong* for Flute and Piano (Berlin, March 1, 1973); *Banya* for 8 Players (Berlin, March 6, 1974); *Metamorphosen* for Flute and String Quartet (Tokyo, July 17, 1974); *Dialog* for Viola and Piano (Berlin, Feb. 23, 1977); *Myung* for 4 Huns, Taekum, Kayakum, and Tam-Tam (1978); *Thal* for Contrabass Flute (1982); String Quartet (1983; Saarbrücken, May 29, 1986). VOCAL: *Yong-Bi*, cantata (Seoul, April 21, 1978); *The Rite of Sun*, cantata (1984); also works utilizing tape, electronics, and computer-generated sounds, including *The Feast of Id* (Seoul, Dec. 9, 1966), *Klangspuren* (1981), and *Mosaico* (1981); film scores.

Kanitz, Ernest (actually, **Ernst**), Austrian-American composer; b. Vienna, April 9, 1894; d. Menlo Park, Calif., April 7, 1978. He changed his 1st name to Ernest in order to distinguish himself from a homonymous concert manager in Vienna. He studied with Richard Heuberger (1912–14) and Franz Schreker (1914–20) in Vienna; then taught at the Neues Konservatorium there (1922–38). After the Anschluss (1938), he emigrated to the U.S.; taught theory at various colleges, including the Univ. of Southern Calif. in Los Angeles (1945–59) and Marymount College in Palos Verdes, Calif. (1960–64). He publ. *A Counterpoint Manual: Fundamental Techniques of Polyphonic Music Writing* (Boston, 1948). WORKS: *Heitere Ouvertüre* (1918); oratorio, *Das Hohelied* (1921); radio cantata, *Zeitmusik* (1931); *Dance Sonata* for Flute, Clarinet, Trumpet, Bassoon, and Piano (1932); Concertino for Theremin and Orch. (1938); *Quintettino* for Piano and Wind Instruments (1945); Sonata for Violin and Cello (1947); *Intermezzo concertante* for Saxophone and Orch. (1948); *Divertimento* for Viola and Cello (1949); Concerto Grosso (1949); *Notturno* for Flute, Violin, and Viola (1950); String Trio (1951); *Sonata breve* for Violin, Cello, and Piano (1952); *Sonata californiana* for Alto Saxophone and Piano (1952); *Kumana*, opera (1953); Sonata for Unaccompanied Cello (1956); *Room No. 12* and *Royal Auction*, pair of 1-act operas (Los Angeles, Feb. 26, 1958); Sonatina for Viola and Piano (1958); *The Lucky Dollar*, opera (1959); Suite for Brass Quintet (1960); *Perpetual*, opera (Los Angeles, April 26, 1961); *Cantata 1961* for Mixed Chorus and 2 Pianos (1961); *Visions at Midnight*, opera-cantata (Los Angeles, Feb. 26, 1964); Bassoon Concerto (San Francisco, April 8, 1964); *Sinfonia seria*

(St. Louis, Oct. 17, 1964); Sym. No. 2 (1965; San Francisco, Dec. 11, 1968); *Little Concerto* for Unaccompanied Saxophone (Chicago, Dec. 15, 1970).

Kann, Hans, respected Austrian pianist, pedagogue, and composer; b. Vienna, Feb. 14, 1927. He studied piano with A. Bloch, A. Göllner, and F. Wührer, chamber music with O. Schulhoff, composition with J. Lechthaler, and analysis with J. Polnauer in Vienna, where he made his debut (1946). After winning the Silver Medal at the Geneva International Competition in 1948, he pursued an international career. Beginning in 1955, he made regular tours of Japan; he toured South America and Russia in 1966; gave concerts in China in 1980, 1982, and 1985; and played in the U.S. in 1981 and 1984. In 1987–88 he gave in Vienna the 1st complete performance of the Haydn sonatas; in 1988–89 he presented a "Biedermeier" cycle there, consisting of works by Beethoven and Schubert and their lesser-known contemporaries; in 1989–90 he performed the complete piano works of Mozart there, including Mozart's pieces for children and his didactic works. Among other places, Kann taught at the Vienna Academy of Music (1950–52), the Univ. of Arts in Tokyo (1955–58), and the Vienna Hochschule für Musik (from 1977). He also gave master classes at the Darmstadt Academy of Music (1961–67). He wrote a book on piano playing that was publ. in Japanese. His compositions include a ballet, theater and film scores, chamber music, lieder, works for synthesizer, and various pieces for solo piano, including a curious album entitled *10 Klavierstücke ohne Bassschlüssel*, and *12 Alt-Wiener Walzer*, as well as didactic pieces, exemplified by *33 Spezialstudien*, *Tägliche Fingerübungen*, and *Models*.

Kanner, Jerome Herbert, American violinist, conductor, composer, and arranger; b. N.Y., Nov. 17, 1903. He made his debut as a violinist in N.Y. at the age of 8; studied violin with Kneisel, Stoeving, and Auer; conducting with Walter Damrosch and Albert Stoessel; composition with Edward Kilenyi; also took some lessons with Ravel in Paris. After 1925 he gave up the violin and devoted himself mainly to composing and conducting for radio and motion pictures. He composed 2 syms.; a symphonic poem, *The Rubayat*; and songs in a light vein.

Kanner-Rosenthal, Hedwig, Hungarian-American pianist and pedagogue; b. Budapest, June 3, 1882; d. Asheville, N.C., Sept. 5, 1959. She studied with Leschetizky and **Moriz Rosenthal**, whom she married; appeared with him in duo recitals. She settled in N.Y. as a teacher (1939), numbering among her students Charles Rosen and Robert Goldsand.

Kantner, Paul, American pop musician and songwriter; b. San Francisco, March 12, 1942. He was a founding member of The Jefferson Airplane and contributed to its 1st album, *Jefferson Airplane Takes Off*. His own songs form a bridge between hippie ballads and psychedelic rock; later he was preoccupied with science fiction and expansion of consciousness, as expressed in *Wooden Ships* (co-authored with David Crosby and Stephen Stills) and *We Can Be Together*; he also was an eager participant in militant politics. In another avatar, he gave voice to the themes of unrequited love, as in his songs *Won't You Try* and *Saturday Afternoon*. He remained the constant member of the original Jefferson Airplane throughout its late psychedelic era.

Kapell, William, brilliant American pianist; b. N.Y., Sept. 20, 1922; d. in an airplane crash at King's Mountain, near San Francisco, Oct. 29, 1953. He studied with Olga Samaroff at the Philadelphia Cons. of Music and at the Juilliard School of Music in N.Y. After winning the Philadelphia Orch.'s youth competition and the Naumburg Award (1941), he made his N.Y. debut on Oct. 28, 1941; subsequently appeared as a soloist with the major American orchs. and in Europe, specializing in modern music. He died on a return flight from Australia, where he had been touring.

Kaper, Bronislaw, Polish-American composer; b. Warsaw, Feb. 5, 1902; d. Beverly Hills, Calif., April 26, 1983. He received his academic education in music at the Warsaw Cons.; left Poland in the 1920s, and proceeded to Hollywood via Berlin and Paris. He worked for MGM from 1940. An adept and intelligent musician who understood the requirements of the popular idiom, he composed background music for numerous films, among them *San Francisco*, *Gaslight*, 2 versions of *Mutiny on the Bounty* (with Clark Gable in 1935 and Marlon Brando in 1962), and *Lili* (for which he received an Academy Award in 1953).

Kaplan, Mark, American violinist; b. Cambridge, Mass., Dec. 30, 1953. He was brought up in Syracuse, N.Y.; began violin lessons as a small child; at the age of 8 he won a local violin competition, and enrolled as a student of Dorothy DeLay at the Juilliard School of Music in N.Y.; received its Fritz Kreisler Memorial Award. In 1973 he was awarded the prestigious Award of Special Distinction at the Leventritt Competition in N.Y.; subsequently was a soloist with many of the major orchs. of North America and Europe, meriting praise for his fine musicianship and virtuoso technique.

Kapp, Artur, significant Estonian composer, father of **Eugen (Arturovich)** and uncle of **Villem Kapp;** b. Suure-Jaani, Feb. 28, 1878; d. there, Jan. 14, 1952. He began his music training with his father, an organist and choral conductor; then continued his studies at the St. Petersburg Cons., where he received degrees in organ (1898) and composition (1900), studying the latter with Rimsky-Korsakov and Liadov. From 1903 to 1920 he was director of the Astrakhan Cons.; returning to Estonia, he was prof. of composition at the Tallinn Cons. (1924–43). He was the 1st Estonian composer to use native folk material, which he utilized in his 1st orch. suite (1906). His 4th Sym. was awarded the State Prize (1949) and the 1st Stalin Prize (1950).

WORKS: ORCH.: *Don Carlos*, symphonic poem (1900); 4 suites (1906, 1930, 1936, 1947); 5 syms. (1924–49); 5 concertos (1934–46). **CHAMBER:** Violin Sonata (1897); String Quintet (1918); Trio for Violin, Cello, and Organ (1936); String Sextet (1951). **VOCAL:** *Hiob*, oratorio (1929); 4 cantatas, including *For Peace* (1951); choral works; numerous songs.

Kapp, Eugen (Arturovich), important Estonian composer, son of **Artur Kapp;** b. Astrakhan, May 26, 1908. He graduated from his father's composition class at the Tallinn Cons. (1931), then became a teacher of composition there (1935); after serving as founder-director of the Estonian State Ensemble in Yaroslavl (1941–44), he became a prof. at the Estonian Cons. (1947) and was its director (1952–64). He received the Order of Lenin (1950) and was made a People's Artist of the Estonian S.S.R. (1950) and of the U.S.S.R. (1956). His operas *Tasuleegid* and *Vabaduse laulik* won Stalin Prizes in 1946 and 1950, respectively, as well as his ballet *Kalevipoeg* in 1952.

WORKS: STAGE: OPERAS: *Tasuleegid* (Flames of Vengeance; Tallinn, July 21, 1945); *Vabaduse laulik* (Freedom's Singer; Tallinn, July 20, 1950); *Talvemuinasjutt* (Winter Fairy Tale; 1958; Tartu, 1959); *Tabamatu* (Elusive Marta; 1960; Tartu, 1961); *Rembrandt* (Tartu, 1975); *An Unseen Wonder*, children's opera (1983). **OPERETTA:** *Assol* (1965). **BALLETS:** *Kalevipoeg* (1947); *Kullaketrajad* (Goldspinners; 1956); also oratorios and cantatas. **ORCH.:** 3 syms. (1942, 1954, 1964); 6 suites (1933–57); 4 overtures (1938–69); *The Avenger*, symphonic poem (1931); Piano Concerto (1969); Flute Concerto (1975); Concerto-Fantasy for Violin and Chamber Orch. (1978; also for Violin and Orch., 1980); *Theme and Variations on Ukrainian Folk Music* for String Orch. (1982). **CHAMBER:** Piano Trio (1930); 2 string quartets (1935, 1956); 2 violin sonatas (1936, 1943); Cello Sonata (1948); *Meditations for Cello* (1969); *4 Estonian Dances* for Violin and Piano (1973); *Starling's Song to the Sun* for Violin (1983); songs; film music. **BIBL.:** G. Polyanovsky, *E. K.* (Moscow, 1957); H. Kyrvits, *E. K.* (Tallinn, 1964); H. Olt, *Estonian Music* (Tallinn, 1980).

Kapp, Julius, German writer on music; b. Seelbach, Baden, Oct. 1, 1883; d. Sonthofen, March 18, 1962. He studied in Marburg, Munich, and Berlin (Ph.D. in chemistry, 1907). From 1904 to 1907 he ed. Berlin's *Literarischer Anzeiger*, which he founded; then was adviser on productions at the Berlin State Opera and ed. of its *Blätter der Staatsoper* (1921–45); subsequently was an adviser on productions at the Berlin Städtische Oper (1948–54). He wrote significant biographies of Liszt and Wagner.

WRITINGS: *Richard Wagner und Franz Liszt: Eine Freundschaft* (Berlin and Leipzig, 1908); *Arthur Schnitzler* (Berlin, 1909); *Franz Liszt: Eine Biographie* (Berlin and Leipzig, 1909; 20th ed., 1924); *Franz Liszt: Gesammelte Schriften (allgemeine Inhaltsübersicht)* (Leipzig, 1910); *Franz Liszt und die Frauen* (Leipzig, 1910); *Richard Wagner: Eine Biographie* (Berlin, 1910; 32nd ed., 1929); ed. *Der junge Wagner: Dichtungen, Aufsätze, Entwürfe, 1832–1849* (Berlin, 1910); ed. *Franz Liszt: Gesammelte Schriften* (Leipzig, 1910); *Richard Wagner und die Frauen: Eine erotische Biographie* (Berlin, 1912; 16th ed., 1929; rev. 1951; Eng. tr., 1951, as *The Loves of Richard Wagner*); *Niccolò Paganini: Eine Biographie* (Berlin and Leipzig, 1913; 18th ed., 1954); ed. *Richard Wagner: Gesammelte Schriften und Dichtungen* (Leipzig, 1914); ed. *Richard Wagners gesammelte Briefe*, I–II (Leipzig, 1914–33); ed. *Richard Wagner an Mathilde und Otto Wesendonk* (Leipzig, 1915; 2nd ed., 1936); *Berlioz: Eine Biographie* (Berlin and Leipzig, 1917; 2nd ed., rev., 1922); *Das Dreigestirn: Berlioz, Liszt, Wagner* (Berlin, 1920); *Giacomo Meyerbeer: Eine Biographie* (Berlin, 1920; 8th ed., rev., 1932); *Franz Schreker: Der Mann und sein Werk* (Munich, 1921); *Das Opernbuch* (Leipzig, 1922; 18th ed., 1928; rev. 1939); *Die Oper der Gegenwart* (Berlin, 1922); *Carl Maria von Weber* (Stuttgart and Berlin, 1922; 15th ed., 1944); ed. *Ludwig van Beethovens sämtliche Briefe* (Leipzig, 1923; rev. ed. of Kastner); ed. *Richard Strauss und die Berliner Oper* (Berlin, 1934); *Geschichte der Staatsoper Berlin* (Berlin, 1937).

Kapp, Richard, American conductor; b. Chicago, Oct. 9, 1936. He studied at Johns Hopkins Univ. (B.A., 1957); then took courses in conducting, composition, and piano at the Staatliche Hochschule für Musik in Stuttgart. Returning to the U.S., he studied jurisprudence at N.Y. Univ. (J.D., 1966) and had private lessons with Rosbaud and Halasz in conducting, with Simon in piano, and with Marlowe in harpsichord. He began his musical career as a répétiteur at the Basel Stadttheater (1960–62); then was music director of the Opera Theater of the Manhattan School of Music in N.Y. (1963–65). In 1968 he led a concert in N.Y. with a specially assembled group billed as the Philharmonia Virtuosi; later toured with it in programs of varied repertoire, from Baroque to jazz.

Kapp, Villem, Estonian composer, nephew of **Artur Kapp;** b. Suure-Jaani, Sept. 7, 1913; d. Tallinn, March 24, 1964. He began his training with his uncle, then studied with Eller at the Tallinn Cons. (1939–44); from 1945 to 1964, was a prof. of composition there. He wrote in an expansive Romantic style rooted in folk song; his opera, *Lembitu* (Tallinn, Aug. 23, 1961), glorifies Estes Lembitu, the leader of the Estonian struggle against the invading Teutonic crusaders in 1217. He also wrote 2 syms. (1947, 1955), 4 cantatas (1949–63), a Piano Sonata (1940), a Piano Trio (1946), a Wind Quintet (1957), and songs.

BIBL.: H. Tönson, *V. K.* (Tallinn, 1967).

Kappel, Gertrude, noted German soprano; b. Halle, Sept. 1, 1884; d. Pullach, April 3, 1971. She studied with Nikisch and Noe at the Leipzig Cons.; made her debut in 1903 at the Hannover Opera, where she was a regular member (until 1924); also sang at London's Covent Garden (1912–14; 1924–26) and the Vienna State Opera (1924–29). She was a principal member of the Bavarian State Opera in Munich (1927–31). She made her Metropolitan Opera debut in N.Y. as Isolde on Jan. 16, 1928, and remained a member until 1936; also sang with the San Francisco Opera Co.; she returned to Germany, retiring in 1937. Her finest roles were Isolde and Brünnhilde, but she also was admired for her Senta, Sieglinde, Marschallin, and Elektra.

Kapr, Jan, Czech composer; b. Prague, March 12, 1914; d. there, April 29, 1988. He studied with his father, a musician, then studied composition with Řídký and later with J. Křička at the Prague Cons. (1933–40). He was a music producer for the Czech Radio in Prague (1939–46), a music critic (1946–49), and an ed. in music publishing (1950–54); from 1961 to 1970 he taught at the Janáček Academy of Music and Dramatic Arts in Brno. His style of composition is derived from the Czech national school; in his later works he audaciously introduced modernistic serial procedures. He publ. a vol. on contemporary music entitled *Konstanty* (The Constants; Prague, 1967).

WORKS: Opera, *Muzikantská pohádka* (Musicians' Fairy Tale; 1962); 3 piano concertos (1938, 1953, 1986); *Marathon*, symphonic scherzo (1939); Sinfonietta for Small Orch. (1940); 10 syms.: No. 1 (1943); No. 2 (1946); No. 3 for Small Orch. (1946); No. 4 (1957); No. 5, *Olympijská* (Olympic; 1959); No. 6 (1960; rev. 1964); No. 7, *Krajina dětství* (Country of Childhood), for Children's Chorus and Orch. (1968); No. 8, *Campanae Pragenses* (The Bells of Prague), for Chorus, Orch., and Bell Sounds on Tape (1970); No. 9 (1982); No. 10, *Lanžhotská*, for 2 Vocal Soloists and Orch. (1985); 2 cantatas: *A Song to the Native Land* (1950) and *In the Soviet Land* (1950); *Harvested*, symphonic rhapsody (1950); *Zitra* (Tomorrow), symphonic picture (1953); *Léto* (Summer) for Chamber Orch. (1954); *Allegretto* for Violin and Orch. (1955); Violin Concerto (1955); Variations for Flute and String Orch. (1958); Concertino for Viola and Wind Orch. (1965); *Omaggio alla tromba* for 2 Solo Trumpets, Wind Orch., Piano, and Timpani (1967–68; Prague, March 6, 1970); *Anachron* for Chamber Orch. (1974); Concertino for Clarinet and Chamber Ensemble (1975); 8 string quartets (1937; 1941; 1954; 1957; 1961; with Solo Baritone, 1963; 1965; 1976); Nonet (1943); Fantasy for Violin and Piano (1958); *4 Moods* for Nonet (1959); *Šifry* (Ciphers) for Piano, Percussion, and Tape (1966); *Oscilace* (Oscillation) for Violin, Clarinet, Trumpet, Piano, Cello, and Percussion (1965); *Rotation 9* for Piano Quartet (1967); *Shadow Play and Dreambook* for Soprano, Flute, and Harp (1968); Sonata for Solo Cimbalom (1968); *Testimonies* for Cello, Bass Clarinet, Piano, and Light Source (1969); *Woodcuts* for 8 Brass (1973); *Colors of Silence* for 8 Instruments (1973); *Circuli* for Violin and Accordion (1974); Sonata for Flute, Horn, and Piano (1976); *Claricello* for Clarinet and Cello (1981); *Miniatures* for Winds and Cello (1985); 4 piano sonatas (1945, 1947, 1958, 1980); numerous piano works; choruses; film music.

Kaprál, Václav, Czech composer, father of **Vítězslava Kaprálová;** b. Určice u Prostějova, March 26, 1889; d. Brno, April 6, 1947. He studied with Janáček at the Brno Organ School (1908–10), Novák in Prague (1919–20), and Alfred Cortot in Paris (1923–24). He established his own music school in Brno in 1911; lectured at the Univ. of Brno (1927–36); then taught at the Brno Cons. from 1936 until his 3-year internment in a concentration camp in Svatobořice during World War II; in 1946 he became a prof. at the Janáček Academy of Music in Brno. In his works he shows a fine eclectic talent, enhanced by refulgent lyricism.

WORKS: *Uspávansky* (Lullabies) for Voice and Chamber Orch. (1932; ISCM Festival, Barcelona, April 20, 1936); 2 string quartets (1925; 1927, with Baritone); *Pro ni* (For Her) for Voice and Piano Quartet (1927); *Píseň podzimu* (Song of Autumn) for Voice and String Quartet (1929); 4 piano sonatas (1912, 1921, 1924, 1939); *Miniatury* (Miniatures) for Piano (1922); *Con duolo* for Piano, Left-Hand (1926); 3 piano sonatinas (1930, 1936, 1943); *Fantasie* for Piano (1934); *Ballad* for Cello and Piano (1946).

Kaprálová, Vítězslava, Czech composer, daughter of **Václav Kaprál;** b. Brünn, Jan. 24, 1915; d. Montpellier, June 16, 1940. She received her early education from her father, then studied with Petrželka (composition) and Chalabala (conducting) at the Brno Cons. (1930–35); subsequently took master classes with Novák (composition) and Talich (conducting) at the Prague Cons. (1935–37). In 1937 she received a scholarship to Paris, where she took lessons in conducting with Munch and composition with Martinů. She appeared as a guest conduc-

tor with the BBC Sym. Orch. at the ISCM Festival in London in 1938. She returned to France in 1939, her promising career being cut tragically short by miliary tuberculosis.

WORKS: *Suite en miniature* for Orch. (1932–35); Piano Concerto (Brno, June 17, 1935); *Military Sinfonietta* (Prague, Nov. 26, 1937); *Suita rustica* (Brno, April 16, 1939); *Partita* for String Orch. and Piano (Brno, Nov. 12, 1941); *Christmas Prelude* for Chamber Orch. (1939); Concertino for Violin, Clarinet, and Orch. (1940; unfinished); *Legenda a Burleska* for Violin and Piano (1932); *Sonata appassionata* for Piano (1933); String Quartet (1936); *6 Variations on the Bells of the Church of Saint Etienne in Paris* for Piano (1938); *2 Ritournelles* for Cello and Piano (1940).

BIBL.: J. Macek, *V. K.* (Prague, 1958).

Kapsberger, Johann Hieronymus, German instrumentalist and composer, known in Italy as **Giovanni Girolamo Tedesco della Tiorba** because of his virtuosity as a performer; b. Venice, c.1580; d. Rome, 1651. He lived in Venice until settling in Rome about 1604, becoming celebrated as a player on the theorbo, chitarrone, lute, etc.; also organized his own academy, which gave concerts in his home. He enjoyed the favor of Pope Urban VIII. He was a notable composer of instrumental music.

WORKS (all publ. in Rome unless otherwise given): SACRED VOCAL: *Libro I di* [20] *mottetti passeggiati* for Voice and Basso Continuo (1612); (21) *Cantiones sacrae* for 3 to 6 Voices and Basso Continuo (1628); *Modulatus sacri diminutis voculis concinnati* for Voice and Basso Continuo (1630); *I pastori di Bettelemme . . . dialogo recitativo* for 6 Voices and Basso Continuo (1630); (3) *Missae urbanae* for 4, 5, and 8 Voices and Basso Continuo (1631); (4) *Litaniae deiparae virginis* for 4, 6, and 8 Voices and Basso Continuo (1632). SECULAR VOCAL: *Libro I de madrigali* for 5 Voices and Basso Continuo (1609); *Libro I di* [20] *villanelle* for 1 to 3 Voices and Basso Continuo (1610); *Libro I di* [22] *arie passeggiate* for Voice and Basso Continuo (1612); *Maggio*, cantata (Florence, 1612; not extant); *Libro II di* [21] *villanelle* for 1 to 3 Voices and Basso Continuo (1619); *Libro III di* [20] *villanelle* for 1 to 3 Voices and Basso Continuo (1619); *Libro IV di* [23] *villanelle* for 1 to 3 Voices and Basso Continuo (1623); *Libro II di* [30] *arie* for 1 and 2 Voices and Basso Continuo (1623); (10) *Poematia et carmina . . . liber I* for Voice and Basso Continuo (1624); *Coro musicale*, wedding cantata for 1 to 5 Voices, Instruments, and Basso Continuo (1627); *Epitalamio . . . recitativo a più voci* (1628; not extant); *Libro V di villanelle* (1630; not extant); *Libro III d'arie passeggiate a una più voci* (1630; not extant); *Libro VI li firo di villanelle* (1632; not extant); *Poematia et carmina . . . liber II* (1633; not extant). INSTRUMENTAL: *Libro I d'intavolatura di chitarrone* (Venice, 1604); *Libro I d'intavolatura di lauto* (1611); *Libro I de* [8] *balli,* [6] *gagliarde et* [6] *correnti a 4* (1615); *Libro I di* [18] *sinfonie a 4* and Basso Continuo (1615); *Libro II d'intavolatura di chitarrone* (1616; not extant); *Capricci* for 2 Theorbos (1617; not extant); *Libro II d'intavolatura di lauto* (1623; not extant); *Libro III d'intavolatura di chitarrone* (1626); *Libro IV d'intavolatura di chitarrone* (1640).

BIBL.: P. Kast, "Biographische Notizen über J.H. K. aus den Vorreden zu seinen Werken," *Quellen und Forschungen aus italienischen Archiven und Bibliotheken,* XL (1960).

Karabits, Ivan, Russian composer; b. Yalta, Jan. 17, 1945. He studied at the Kiev Cons. with Boris Liatoshynsky, graduating in 1971.

WORKS: *Little Symphony* for String Orch. (1967); 2 piano concertos (1968, 1972); 2 syms. (1974, 1975); *Little Concerto* for Chamber Orch. (1970); *The Garden of Divine Songs* for Soloists, Chorus, and Orch. (1971); 2 cello sonatas (1968, 1972); String Quartet (1973); *Divertimento concertante* for 6 Performers (1975); *Impromptu* for Viola and Piano (1976); 24 Preludes for Piano (1976); numerous vocal cycles to Ukrainian words.

Karabtchewsky, Isaac, Brazilian conductor; b. São Paulo, Dec. 27, 1934. He studied in Brazil; then at the Hochschule für Musik in Freiburg im Breisgau. Upon his return to Brazil in 1969, he became music director of the Brazil Sym. Orch. in Rio de Janeiro; also was a guest conductor in the U.S. In 1987 he became chief conductor of the Vienna Niederösterreichisches Tonkünstler Orch. His conducting is marked by an expansively Romantic quality, much in the vein of the old Russian school of interpretation.

Karajan, Herbert von, preeminent Austrian conductor in the grand Germanic tradition, great-grandson of **Theodor Georg von Karajan;** b. Salzburg, April 5, 1908; d. Anif, near Salzburg, July 16, 1989. He was a scion of a cultured family of Greek-Macedonian extraction whose original name was Karajannis. His father was a medical officer who played the clarinet and his brother was a professional organist. Karajan himself began his musical training as a pianist; he took lessons with Franz Ledwinka at the Salzburg Mozarteum. He further attended the conducting classes of the Mozarteum's director, Bernhard Paumgartner. Eventually he went to Vienna, where he pursued academic training at a technical college and took piano lessons from one J. Hofmann; then entered the Vienna Academy of Music as a conducting student in the classes of Clemens Krauss and Alexander Wunderer. On Dec. 17, 1927, he made his conducting debut with a student orch. at the Vienna Academy of Music; shortly afterward, on Jan. 23, 1929, he made his professional conducting debut with the Salzburg Orch. He then received an engagement as conductor of the Ulm Stadttheater (1929–34). From Ulm he went to Aachen, where he was made conductor of the Stadttheater; he subsequently served as the Generalmusikdirektor there (1935–42). On April 9, 1938, he conducted his 1st performance with the Berlin Phil., the orch. that became the chosen medium of his art. On Sept. 30, 1938, he conducted *Fidelio* at his debut with the Berlin Staatsoper. After his performance of *Tristan und Isolde* there on Oct. 21, 1938, he was hailed by the *Berliner Tageblatt* as "das Wunder Karajan." His capacity of absorbing and interpreting the music at hand and transmitting its essence to the audience became his most signal characteristic; he also conducted all of his scores from memory, including the entire *Ring des Nibelungen*. His burgeoning fame as a master of both opera and sym. led to engagements elsewhere in Europe. In 1938 he conducted opera at La Scala in Milan and also made guest appearances in Belgium, the Netherlands, and Scandinavia. In 1939 he became conductor of the sym. concerts of the Berlin Staatsoper Orch.

There was a dark side to Karajan's character, revealing his lack of human sensitivity and even a failure to act in his own interests. He became fascinated by the ruthless organizing solidity of the National Socialist party; on April 8, 1933, he registered in the Salzburg office of the Austrian Nazi party, where his party number was 1 607 525; barely a month later he joined the German Nazi party in Ulm, as No. 3 430 914. He lived to regret these actions after the collapse of the Nazi empire, but he managed to obtain various posts, and in 1947 he was officially denazified by the Allies' army of occupation. His personal affairs also began to interfere with his career. He married the operetta singer Elmy Holgerloef in 1938, but divorced her in 1942 to marry Anita Gütermann. Trouble came when the suspicious Nazi genealogists discovered that she was one-quarter Jewish and suggested that he divorce her. But World War II was soon to end, and so was Nazi hegemony. He finally divorced Gütermann in 1958 to marry the French fashion model Eliette Mouret.

The irony of Karajan's racial pretensions was the physical inadequacy of his own stature. He stood only 5'8" tall, but he made up for his modest height by cultivating his rich chevelure of graying hair, which harmonized with his romantic podium manner. Greatly successful with the commercial world, he made about 800 sound and video recordings, which sold millions of copies. Karajan was also an avid skier and mountain-climbing enthusiast; he piloted his own plane and drove a fleet of flamboyant and expensive sports cars. He acquired considerable wealth, and kept homes in Switzerland and on the French Riviera. Supplementing his devotion to modern

technology, Karajan was also a devotee of assorted physical and spiritual fads. He practiced yoga and aerobics, and for a while embraced Zen Buddhism. Moreover, he was known to believe in the transmigration of souls, and expressed a hope of being reborn as an eagle soaring above the Alps, his favorite mountain range. As an alternative, he investigated the technique of cryogenics, hoping that his body could be thawed a century or so later to enable him to enjoy yet another physical incarnation. None of these endeavors prevented him from being overcome by a sudden heart attack in his home at Anif in the Austrian Alps. A helicopter with a medical staff was quickly summoned to fly him to a hospital, but it arrived too late.

Karajan was characteristically self-assertive and unflinching in his personal relationships and in his numerous conflicts with managers and players. Although he began a close relationship with the Vienna Sym. Orch. in 1948, he left it in 1958. His association as conductor of the Philharmonia Orch. of London from 1948 to 1954 did more than anything to re-establish his career after World War II, but in later years he disdained his relationship with that ensemble. When Wilhelm Furtwängler, the longtime conductor of the Berlin Phil., died in 1954, Karajan was chosen to lead the orch. on its 1st tour of the U.S. However, he insisted that he would lead the tour only on the condition that he be duly elected Furtwängler's successor. Protesters were in evidence for his appearance at N.Y.'s Carnegie Hall with the orch. on March 1, 1955, but his Nazi past did not prevent the musicians of the orch. from electing him their conductor during their visit to Pittsburgh on March 3. After their return to Germany, the West Berlin Senate ratified the musicians' vote on April 5, 1955.

Karajan soon came to dominate the musical life of Europe as no other conductor had ever done. In addition to his prestigious Berlin post, he served as artistic director of the Vienna Staatsoper from 1956 until he resigned in a bitter dispute with its general manager in 1964. He concurrently was artistic director of the Salzburg Festival (1957–60), and thereafter remained closely associated with it. From 1969 to 1971 he held the title of artistic adviser of the Orch. de Paris. In the meantime, he consolidated his positions in Berlin and Salzburg. On Oct. 15, 1963, he conducted the Berlin Phil. in a performance of Beethoven's 9th Sym. at the gala concert inaugurating the orch.'s magnificent new concert hall, the Philharmonie. In 1967 he organized his own Salzburg Easter Festival, which became one of the world's leading musical events. In 1967 he re-negotiated his contract and was named conductor-for-life of the Berlin Phil. He made a belated Metropolitan Opera debut in N.Y. on Nov. 21, 1967, conducting *Die Walküre.* He went on frequent tours of Europe and Japan with the Berlin Phil., and also took the orch. to the Soviet Union (1969) and China (1979).

In 1982 Karajan personally selected the 23-year-old clarinetist Sabine Meyer as a member of the Berlin Phil. (any romantic reasons for his insistence were not apparent). The musicians of the orch. rejected her because of their standing rule to exclude women, but also because the majority of the musicians had less appreciation of Fräulein Meyer as an artist than Karajan himself did. A compromise was reached, however, and in 1983 she was allowed to join the orch. on probation. She resigned in 1984 after a year of uneasy co-existence.

In 1985 Karajan celebrated his 30th anniversary as conductor of the Berlin Phil., and in 1988 his 60th anniversary as a conductor. In 1987 he conducted the New Year's Day Concert of the Vienna Phil., which was televised to millions on both sides of the Atlantic. In Feb. 1989 he made his last appearance in the U.S., conducting the Vienna Phil. at N.Y.'s Carnegie Hall. In April 1989 he announced his retirement from his Berlin post, citing failing health. Shortly before his death, he dictated an autobiographical book to Franz Endler; it was publ. in an English tr. in 1989.

BIBL.: E. Haeusserman, *H. v.K. Biographie* (Gütersloh, 1968; new ed., Vienna, 1978); C. Spiel, ed., *Anekdoten um H. v.K.* (Munich, 1968); P. Robinson, *K.* (Toronto, 1975); W. Stresemann, *The Berlin Philharmonic from Bülow to K.* (in German and Eng.; Berlin, 1979); R. Bachmann, *K.: Anmerkungen zu einer Karriere* (Düsseldorf, 1983); H. Kröber, *H. v.K.: Der Magier mit dem Takststock* (Munich, 1986); R. Vaughan, *H. v.K.: A Biographical Portrait* (N.Y. and London, 1986); H. Götze and W. Simon, eds., *Wo sprache aufhört . . . H. v.K. zum 5. April 1988* (Berlin, 1988); H. Goldsmith, "K.'s Early Years Reappraised," *Musical Times* (May 1989); R. Osborne, *Conversations with K.* (Oxford, 1989).

Karajan, Theodor Georg von, Austrian writer on music, great-grandfather of **Herbert von Karajan;** b. Vienna, Jan. 22, 1810; d. there, April 28, 1873. He studied history, philology, and law; after holding various minor posts, he was president of the Austrian Academy of Science (1866–69). His important monograph *J. Haydn in London, 1791 und 1792* (Vienna, 1861) contains Haydn's correspondence with Maria Anna von Genzinger; he also publ. *Aus Metastasios Hofleben* (Vienna, 1861).

Karasowski, Moritz (actually, **Maurycy**), Polish cellist and writer on music; b. Warsaw, Sept. 22, 1823; d. Dresden, April 20, 1892. He studied in Warsaw, Berlin, Vienna, and Paris. He was a cellist in the opera orch. in Warsaw from 1851, and later settled in Dresden as a member of the opera orch. (1864), being named a court musician in 1868.
WRITINGS: *Rys historyczny opery polskiej* (Historical Outline of Polish Opera; Warsaw, 1859); *Zycie Mozarta* (Life of Mozart; Warsaw, 1868); *Friedrich Chopin: Sein Leben, seine Werke und Briefe* (2 vols., Dresden, 1877; 4th ed., 1914; Eng. tr., London, 1879; 3rd ed., 1938).

Karastoyanov, Assen, Bulgarian composer; b. Samokov, June 3, 1893; d. Sofia, Sept. 8, 1976. He studied flute at the Sofia Music School (1914–18); subsequently took courses with Juon (harmony) at the Berlin Hochschule für Musik (1921–22), Dukas (composition) at the École Normale de Musique in Paris (1930–31), and Raphael (composition) at the Leipzig Cons. (1931–32). He taught at the Sofia State Academy of Music (1933–44), where he was a prof. (1944–58).
WORKS: 7 operettas, including *Michel Strogoff,* after Jules Verne (1937–40); 7 patriotic cantatas; *A Balkan Suite* for Orch. (1928); 4 syms.: No. 1, *Miner's Symphony* (1940); No. 2, *Danubian,* for Brass Orch. (1960); No. 3, *Rhodopean* (1973); No. 4, *Proto-Bulgarian* (1975); Flute Concerto (1959); *A Bogomil Legend* for String Orch. (1973); 2 string quartets (1937, 1970); 2 suites for Flute and Piano (1955, 1968); *Capriccio* for Violin and Piano (1970); *Scherzino* for Piano (1933); Piano Sonata (1938); songs.

Karatygin, Viacheslav (Gavrilovich), Russian writer on music; b. Pavlovsk, Sept. 17, 1875; d. Leningrad, Oct. 23, 1925. He learned to play the piano from his mother, who was a professional pianist, then took courses in physics and mathematics at the Univ. of St. Petersburg (graduated, 1897); subsequently was a chemist in the naval dept. (until 1907); also studied composition with Sokolov at the St. Petersburg Cons. (1897–1902). From 1907 to 1917 he was active as a music critic; also taught esthetics and music history at the Petrograd Cons. (from 1916), being made a prof. (1919). As a critic, he welcomed the music of Scriabin, Stravinsky, and Prokofiev at a time when most Russian critics regarded them as unacceptable, and he enunciated the idea of a "musical revolution." He publ. monographs on Mussorgsky, Chaliapin, and Scriabin, and also composed some piano pieces and songs.
BIBL.: A. Rimsky-Korsakov et al., eds., *V.G. K.: Zhizn, deyatelnost, stati i materiali* (V.G. K.: Life, Work, Articles, and Materials; Leningrad, 1927).

Karayev, Kara (Abulfazogli), Russian composer; b. Baku, Feb. 5, 1918; d. Moscow, May 13, 1982. He studied piano with Sharoyev at the Baku Music Technical School (1930–35) and then composition with Rudolf at the Azerbaijani Cons.; later took courses in composition with Alexandrov and Shostakovich and instrumentation with Vasilenko at the Moscow Cons. (graduated, 1946). He taught at the Azerbaijani Cons. (from 1946), serving as its director (1949–52). His music is derived mainly from his semi-oriental environment, compris-

ing not only the native Tartar motifs, but also other Asian resources; particularly effective are his theatrical spectacles featuring native dances and choral ensembles.
WORKS: STAGE: Opera, *Fatherland* (1945); ballets: *7 Beauties* (1952) and *On the Track of Thunder* (1958); cantatas: *The Song of the Heart* (1938) and *The Song of Happiness* (1947); oratorio, *Hymn of Friendship* (1972). **ORCH.:** 3 syms. (1944, 1946, 1965); *Leyly and Medzhnun,* symphonic poem (1947); *Albanian Rhapsody* (1952); *Don Quixote,* symphonic sketches (1960); *Poem of Joy* for Piano and Orch. (1937); Violin Concerto (1967); numerous pieces for folk instruments; 2 string quartets; a series of piano pieces, including 24 preludes; choruses; film music.
BIBL.: L. Karagicheva, *K. K.* (Baku, 1956).

Kardoš, Dezider, Slovak composer; b. Nadlice, Dec. 23, 1914. He studied composition with Alexander Moyzes at the Bratislava Academy of Music (graduated, 1937) and with Novák at the Prague Cons. (1937–39). He worked for the Czech Radio in Prešov (1939–45) and Košice (1945–51); then became a teacher at the Bratislava Academy of Music (1963), being made a prof. in 1968. The thematic sources of his musical inspiration are found in eastern Slovak folklore.
WORKS: *Peace Cantata* (1951); 7 syms.: No. 1 (1942); No. 2, *Of Native Land* (1955); No. 3 (1961); No. 4, *Piccola* (1962); No. 5 (1965); No. 6 (1974–75); No. 7, *Ballade vom Traum,* for Baritone, Chorus, and Orch. (1983–84); 3 overtures: *My Home* (1946); *East Slovak* (1950); *Res philharmonica* (1970); Concerto for Orch. (1957); *Heroic Ballad* for String Orch. (1959); Concerto for String Orch. (1963); Piano Concerto (1969); *Partita* for 12 Strings (1972); *Songs about Life,* cycle of 4 microdramas for Soprano, Tenor, and Orch. (1973–74); *Slovakophonia,* variations on a folk theme for Orch. (1975–76); Violin Concerto (1980); Symphonietta (1988); 4 string quartets (1935, 1966, 1978, 1985); 2 suites for Piano (1937); Wind Quintet (1938); *Preludium quasi una fantasia* for Organ (1940); *Bagatelles* for Piano (1948); *3 Compositions for Violin and Piano* (1966); *Elevazioni* for Organ (1967); choruses and songs.

Kardos, István, Hungarian conductor and composer; b. Debrecen, June 6, 1891; d. Budapest, Dec. 22, 1975. He studied composition with Herzfeld at the Budapest Academy of Music; then was a theater conductor in Hungary, Germany, and Switzerland (1917–46). From 1948 to 1959 he taught at the Budapest Academy of Music.
WORKS: *Dance* for Orch. (1918); 4 syms. (1919, 1958, 1967, 1968); *Hungarian Scherzo* for Orch. (1936); Violin Concertino (1947); *Áprilisi hajnal* (Dawn in April), cantata (1950); *Janus* for Orch. (1950); 2 piano concertos (1956, 1963); Concertino for Double Bass and Orch. (1959); Double Concerto for Viola, Double Bass, and Orch. (1964); *Alliage* for Violin and Chamber Orch. (1966); *Intrada* for Orch. (1968); *Visitation* for Orch. (1969); 6 string quartets (1917, 1925, 1951, 1960, 1967, 1971); Viola Sonata (1942); Double-bass Sonata (1949); Flute Sonata (1957); Wind Quintet (1959); String Trio (1960); *Bipartitum* for Bassoon and Piano (1963); Sonata for Solo Clarinet (1965); *Poem and Burlesque* for Double Bass and Piano (1969); 2 sextets for Clarinet, String Quartet, and Piano (1971); *Grotesque* for Octave Flute, Cello, and Double Bass (1971); *Notturno* for Horn, Flute, Violin, and Harp (1971); Piano Sonata (1916); piano pieces: *Dickens Suite* (1957); *Toccata* (1960); *Variations and Fugue* (1969); songs.

Karel, Rudolf, Czech composer; b. Plzeň, Nov. 9, 1880; d. in the Terezín concentration camp, March 6, 1945. He was the last student of Dvořák, with whom he studied in Prague for 1 year during his term at the Prague Cons. (1901–4). In 1914 he went to Russia as a teacher. After the Revolution, he made his way to Irkutsk, Siberia; during the Russian civil war, he became a member of the Czechoslovak Legion and conducted an orch. organized by the legionnaires. He returned to Prague in 1920; from 1923 to 1941, taught at the Prague Cons. As a member of the Czech resistance in World War II, he was arrested by the Nazis in March 1943; was transferred to Terezín in Feb. 1945, and died there of dysentery shortly before liberation. His music reflects Romantic concepts; he had a predilection for programmatic writing; the national element is manifested by his treatment of old modal progressions; his instrumental writing is rich in sonority; the polyphonic structure is equally strong.

Works: Lyric comedy, *Ilseino srdce* (Ilsea's Heart; 1906–9; Prague, Oct. 11, 1924); 2 musical fairy tales: *Smrt Kmotřička* (Godmother Death; 1928–33; Brno, Feb. 3, 1933) and *Tři vlasy děda Vševěda* (3 Hairs of the Wise Old Man; 1944–45; left as a draft only, arranged by his student Zbyněk Vostřák; Prague, Oct. 28, 1948); Suite for Orch. (1903–4); *Comedy Overture* (1904–5); Fantasy for Orch. (1905); *Ideály* (The Ideals), symphonic epic from an artist's life (1906–9); 2 syms.: *Renaissance* (1910–11) and *Spring* (1935–38) (2 other syms., of 1904 and 1917, are lost); *Vzkříšení* (Resurrection), sym. for Soli, Chorus, and Orch. (1923–27; Prague, April 9, 1928); *Capriccio* for Violin and Orch. (1924); *4 Slavonic Dance Moods* for Orch. (1912); *The Demon*, symphonic poem (1918–20); *Revolutionary Overture* (1938–41); *Sladká balada dětská* (Sweet Ballad for a Child) for Soprano, Chorus, and Orch. (1928–30); *Černoch* (A Negro), exotic ballad for Baritone, and Orch. or Piano (1934); 3 string quartets (1902–3; 1907–13; 1935–36); Piano Trio (1903–4); Violin Sonata (1912); Nonet for Wind Quintet and String Quartet (1945; left in draft form and completed by F. Hertl); Piano Sonata (1910); other piano pieces: *5 Pieces* (1902); *Notturno* (1906–7); *Thema con variazioni* (1910); *3 Waltzes* (1913); *Burlesques* (1913–14); also choruses; songs; incidental music.

Bibl.: O. Šourek, *R. K.* (Prague, 1947).

Karetnikov, Nikolai, significant Russian composer; b. Moscow, June 28, 1930. He graduated in composition from the class of Shebalin at the Moscow Cons. in 1953, and developed a highly fruitful career as a composer in various fields, employing modern systems of composition, including 12-tone techniques; his piano works and song cycles in particular attracted great attention in performances by Soviet artists in the U.S. and Europe. He has written several ballets for productions in Moscow, several syms., and an impressive assortment of chamber music. He also wrote the score for the film *Ten Days That Shook the World.*

Karg-Elert (real name, **Karg**), **Sigfrid,** distinguished German organist and composer; b. Oberndorf am Neckar, Nov. 21, 1877; d. Leipzig, April 9, 1933. (His real name, which means "avaricious," sounded unattractive to his audiences, so he changed it to Karg-Elert.) He studied with Homeyer, Jadassohn, Reinecke, and Teichmüller at the Leipzig Cons.; in 1919, joined its faculty. He gave organ recitals, becoming known as a great virtuoso; he also played the Kunstharmonium, for which he wrote many compositions. In 1931–32 he made a concert tour of the U.S. As a composer, he developed a brilliant style, inspired by the music of the Baroque, but he embellished this austere and ornamental idiom with impressionistic devices; the result was an ingratiating type of music with an aura of originality. He publ. *Akustische Ton-, Klang-, und Funktionsbestimmung* (1930) and *Polaristiche Klang- und Tonalitätslehre* (1931).

Works: KUNSTHARMONIUM: Sets of pieces: *Skizzen* (1903); *Aquarellen* (1906); *Miniaturen* (1908); *Intarsien* (1911); *Impressions* (1914); *Idyllen* (1915); *Innere Stimmen* (1918). FUNDAMENTAL TECHNICAL WORKS: *Die Kunst des Registrierens; Die ersten grundlegenden Studien; Hohe Schule des Legatospiels; Die Harmoniumtechnik* (*Gradus ad Parnassum*); *Theoretische-praktische Elementarschule.* ORGAN: 66 chorale improvisations (1908–10); 20 chorale preludes and postludes (1912); 10 *Poetic Tone Pictures; 3 Pastels, Cathedral Windows* (on Gregorian themes); also Wind Quintet; 2 clarinet sonatas; Sonata for Flute Unaccompanied; *Trio bucolico* for Violin, Flute, and Piano; a number of lieder.

Bibl.: A. Eaglefield Hull, "K.-E.," *Musical Times* (Feb.–March 1913); H. Gaul, "Bonnet, Bossi, K.-E.," *Musical Quarterly* (July 1918); P. Schenk, *S. K.-E.* (Berlin, 1927); H. Avril, *S. K.-E.: Kompositions-verzeichnis mit einer monographischen*

Skizze (Berlin, 1928); G. Sceats, *The Organ Works of K.-E.* (Orpington, 1940; rev. ed., London, 1950); W. Kwasnik, *S. K.-E.: Sein Leben und Werk in Heutiger Sicht* (1971); S. Gerlach, *S. K.-E.: Verzeichnis sämtlicher Werke* (Frankfurt, 1984); A. Hayden, "K.-E. and the Art of Registration," *Musical Times* (Nov. 1987).

Karjalainen, Ahti, Finnish conductor and composer; b. Oulu, March 20, 1907; d. Jyväskylä, Oct. 2, 1986. He studied composition at the Helsinki Cons., the Viipuri Inst., and the Sibelius Academy; played violin and trombone in various orchs.; later conducted the Jyväskylä City Orch.

Works: *Polonaise* for Trombone and Orch. (1935); *Scherzo* for Trumpet, Trombone, and Orch. (1940); Trombone Concerto (1942); *Summer Scenes* for Oboe and Orch. (1944); *Winter Scenes* for Orch. (1948); Sym. No. 1 (1948); Concert Suite for Bassoon and Orch. (1949); Duo for 2 Trumpets and Orch. (1950); Violin Concerto (1952); *Ostinato* for Cello and Orch. (1954); 2 cello concertos (1956, 1966); *The Eagle's Way* for Chorus and Orch. (1965); *Setting Out* for Narrator, Baritone, Mixed Chorus, Male Chorus, and Orch. (1968); *The Song of Wood*, cantata (1971); 6 partitas for various instrumental combinations (1936, 1940, 1945, 1961, 1964, 1965); Wind Sextet (1945); other chamber music; songs; solo pieces.

Karkoff, Maurice (Ingvar), prominent Swedish composer and teacher; b. Stockholm, March 17, 1927. He began his training in theory with Karl-Birger Blomdahl (1944–47), concurrently studying piano at the Stockholm Musikhögskolan (1945–51) and theory with Lars-Erik Larsson (1948–53); later pursued composition studies with Erland von Koch in Stockholm, Vagn Holmboe in Copenhagen, André Jolivet in Paris, and Wladimir Vogel in Switzerland. He was music critic of the Stockholm daily *Tidningen* (1962–66); in 1965 he became a teacher of theory and composition at the Stockholm Municipal Music Inst. In 1976 he was awarded the City of Stockholm Prize of Honor, and in 1977 was elected a member of the Royal Swedish Academy of Music in Stockholm. In his music he absorbed many cultures; these are reflected in his compositions, many of which may be described as romantically modernistic and thematically sensitive to exotic resources and coloristic instrumental timbres.

Works: ORCH.: Sinfonietta (1954); Saxophone Concertino (1955); syms.: No. 1 (Bergen, Oct. 22, 1956); No. 2 (1957; Swedish Radio, Jan. 5, 1959); No. 3, *Sinfonia breve* (1958–59; Gävle, Jan. 10, 1960); No. 4 (1963; Stockholm, April 4, 1964); No. 5, *Sinfonia da camera* (Gävle, Nov. 11, 1965); No. 6 (1972–73; Stockholm, Oct. 12, 1974); No. 7, *Sinfonia da camera* (1975); No. 8 (1979–80); *Short Symphony* for Symphonic Band (1980–81; Stockholm, Sept. 27, 1982); *Dolorous Symphony* for String Orch. (1981–82); *Sinfonia piccola* (1982–83); Sym. No. 10 (1984–85); Violin Concerto (1956); Piano Concerto (1957); Cello Concerto (1957–58); Trombone Concerto (1958); Horn Concerto (1959); *9 Aphoristic Variations* (1959); Clarinet Concerto (1959); Variations (1961); Serenata for Chamber Orch. (1961); Suite for Harpsichord and Strings (1962); *Concerto da camera* for Balalaika and Orch. (1962–63); Concerto for Orch. (1963); *Oriental Pictures* (1965–66; also for Piano); *Transfigurate mutate* (1965); *Tripartita* (1966–67); *Textum* for Strings (1967); *Metamorphoses* (1967); *Sinfonietta grave* (1968–69); *Epitaphium* for Small Chamber Orch. (1968; also for Nonet); *5 Summer Scenes* (1969); *Triptyk* (1970); *Partes caracteris* (1971); *Symphonic Reflexions* (1971); *Passacaglia* for Strings (1971); Trumpet Concerto (1977); *Texture* (1978). VOCAL: *6 Allvarliga Songs* for High Voice and Orch. (1955); *Det Svenska Landet*, festival cantata (1956); *Livet*, songs and recitation for Low Voice and Orch. (1959); *Gesang des Abgeschiedenen*, 5 songs for Baritone, High Voice, and Orch. or Piano (1959); *Himmel och Jord*, cantata (1960); *Sieben Rosen später*, cantata (1964); *Das ist sein Erlauten*, cantata (1965); *Landscape of Screams*, after Nelly Sachs, for Soprano, Narrator, and Instruments (1967); *The Boundary Kibbutz*, chamber opera (1972–73); *6 Chinese Impressions* for High Voice and Instrumental Ensemble (1973); songs. CHAMBER:

Flute Sonata (1953); Cello Sonata (1954–55); Violin Sonata (1956); Wind Quintet (1956–57); 2 string quartets (1957, 1984); Quartet for 2 Trumpets, Horn, and Trombone (1958); String Trio (1960); *Chamber Concerto* for 14 Winds, Timpani, Percussion, and String Basses (1961); *Metamorphoses* for 4 Horns (1966); *Terzetto* for Flute, Cello, and Piano (1967); *4 parte* for 13 Brasses and Percussion (1968); *Epitaphium* for Accordion, Electric Guitar, and Percussion (1970); *Ernst und Spass* for Saxophone Quartet (1984); *Profilen* for Alto and Baritone Saxophones (1984); *Reflexionen* for Saxophone Quartet (1986); *Ballata quasi una fantasia* for Baritone Saxophone and Piano (1988). PIANO: Sonata (1956); *Partita piccola* (1958); *Capriccio on Football* (1961; a musical report on a football game); *Monopartita* (1969); *3 Expressions* for 2 Pianos (1971); other pieces for piano.

Karkoschka, Erhard, German composer, conductor, and pedagogue; b. Moravská Ostrava, Czechoslovakia, March 6, 1923. He studied composition with Marx at the Stuttgart Hochschule für Musik (1946–53) and musicology with Gerstenberg and Reichert at the Univ. of Tübingen (Ph.D., 1959, with a diss. on Anton Webern's early compositional techniques). He was conductor of the orch. and choir at the Univ. of Hohenheim (1948–68), and in 1958 joined the faculty of the Stuttgart Hochschule für Musik, where he became a prof. in 1964 and director of its electronic music studio in 1973; he also founded its Ensemble for New Music (1962), which became an independent ensemble in 1976 under the name Contact-Ensemble. From 1974 to 1980 he was president of the Gesellschaft für Neue Musik. In 1987 he was elected a member of the Free Academy of the Arts in Mannheim. He adoped Webern's serial method of composition; often incorporated electronics and also occasionally resorted to graphic notation in order to achieve greater freedom of resulting sonorities; in his desire to unite the arts, he created various pieces of music sculpture.

WRITINGS: *Das Schriftbild der neuen Musik* (1965; Eng. tr., 1972, as *Notations of New Music*); *Analyse neuer Musik* (1976); *Neue Musik-Hören-Verstehen* (1978); with H. Haas, *Hörererziehung mit neuer Musik* (1982).

WORKS: ORCH.: Concertino for Chamber Orch. (1952); *Symphonische Evolution aus zwei eigenen Themen* (1953); *Streichersonate* (1954); Little Concerto for Violin and Chamber Orch. (1955); *Polphone Studie* for Orch. and Piano obbligato (1956); *Symphonia choralis über "Veni Sancte Spiritus"* for Wind Orch. (1957); *Undarum continuum* (1960); *vier stufen* (1965); *Variationen zu keinem Originalthema und aus diesem heraus* (1974); *Teleologies* (1978); *Entfalten* for Clarinet, Cello, Percussion, Piano, and Orch. (1982–83); *Kammermusik* (1983–84). CHAMBER: String Quartet (1952); Divertimento for Wind Quintet (1952); *Festmusik* for 6 Winds (1954); *quattrologe* for String Quartet (1966); *antinomie* for Wind Quintet (1969); *tempora mutantur* for String Quartet (1971); *kammerkitsch* for Soprano, Tenor, Bass, 3 Instruments, and Tape (1974); *CHRONOS II: Komposition-Improvisation* for 4 Instruments (1975); *im dreieck* for 3 Flutes or Flute and Stereo Sound System (1975); *links und rechts,* march for Flute, 2 Microphones, Amplifier, and Loudspeaker (1976); *Spiralend I and II* for 15 Flutes or 3 Flutes and Tape (1980); *Aus einer Figur* for 3 Flutes or 3 Flutes and Tape (1982); *Bläsergedichte* for Woodwind Quintet (1987); *Klangzeitspektakel* for String Quartet, Computer, and Performer (1988); a few vocal chamber pieces; keyboard music. ELECTRONIC: *Drei Bilder aus der Offenbarung des Johannes* (1960); *LSD* (1973); *Improvisation* (1974); *CHRONOS I* (1975) and *II* (1976); *Gag-Montagen* (1977); *Meditationsmühle I and II* (both 1982); *Zeitmosaik I* (1985); *Skulpturmusik* (1985); multimedia creations; *Geburtztaxtextelein,* word-music score (1989); etc.

Karl, Tom, Irish tenor; b. Dublin, Jan. 19, 1846; d. Rochester, N.Y., March 19, 1916. He studied in England with Henry Phillips, and in Italy with Sangiovanni. He sang in Italy for many years, then settled in N.Y. His remarkable success as Ralph in *Pinafore* (1879) encouraged him to pursue a career in light opera; with H. Barnabee and W. MacDonald, he formed the light opera company The Bostonians, which had a repertoire of about 150 operas and operettas. After his retirement in 1896, he taught voice in N.Y. and Rochester.

Karlins, M(artin) William, American composer and teacher; b. N.Y., Feb. 25, 1932. He studied composition in N.Y. with Frederick Piket (1954–57) and Stefan Wolpe (1960); then took courses with Vittorio Gianinni at the Manhattan School of Music (1958–61); later enrolled at the Univ. of Iowa (Ph.D., 1965). He taught at Western Illinois Univ. (1965–67); in 1967, joined the faculty at Northwestern Univ., where he became a prof. in 1973.

WORKS: LARGE ENSEMBLES: *Concert Music No. I* for Orch. (1959); *Concert Music No. II* for Chorus and Orch. (1960; Milwaukee, Feb. 14, 1971); *Concert Music No. III* for Woodwinds, Brass, Piano, and Percussion (Urbana, Ill., April 17, 1964); *Concert Music No. IV* for Orch. (1964; Evanston, Ill., May 14, 1965); *Lamentations—In Memoriam* for Speaker and Chamber Group (1968); *Passacaglia and Rounds* for Band (1970); *Reflux,* concerto for Amplified Double Bass and Wind Ensemble, Piano, and Percussion (Chicago, April 8, 1972); *Concert Music No. V* for Orch. (Chicago, Dec. 20, 1973); Sym. No. 1 (Chicago, May 10, 1980); *Catena I* for Little Orch. with Clarinet obbligato (1980–81); Concerto for Alto Saxophone and Orch. (Nuremberg, July 8, 1982); *Catena III,* concerto for Horn and Orch. (1983; Appleton, Wis., April 29, 1984). CHAMBER: *Concerto Grosso No. I* for 9 Instruments (1959–60); String Quartet with Soprano (1960); *Concerto Grosso No. II* for 7 Solo Instruments (1961); *Birthday Music No. I* for Flute, Bass Clarinet, and Double Bass (1962); String Trio (1962–63); *Birthday Music No. II* for Flute and Double Bass (1963); *Variations on "Obiter Dictum"* for Cello, Piano, and Percussion (1965); *Music* for Oboe, Bass Clarinet, and Piano (1966); Quartet for Saxophones (1966–67); *Graphic Mobile* for Any 3 or Multiples of 3 Instruments (1969); Woodwind Quintet (1970); Quintet for Alto Saxophone and String Quartet (1973–74); Quartet No. II for Saxophones: *Variations and Cadenzas* (1975); *Infinity* for Oboe d'Amore, Clarinet, Viola, and Female Voice (1978); *Fantasia* for Tenor Saxophone and Percussion (1978–79); *Fanfare with Fugato* for Cello, 2 Trumpets, and 2 Trombones (1981); *Catena II* for Soprano Saxophone and Brass Quintet (1982); *Returning the Scroll to the Arc* for Cantor and Organ (1985); *Impromptu* for Alto Saxophone and Organ (1985–86); many works for solo instruments, including 3 piano sonatas (1959, 1962, 1965); choral music.

Karlowicz, Mieczyslaw, Polish composer; b. Wiszniewe, Dec. 11, 1876; d. in an avalanche while mountain climbing in Zakopane, Feb. 8, 1909. He was the son of the music theorist **Jan Karlowicz** (b. Subortowicze, near Troki, May 28, 1836; d. Warsaw, June 14, 1903). He studied violin in Warsaw from 1887 with Jakowski and Barcewicz; also composition with Noskowski, Roguski, and Maszynski; continued his studies in Berlin with Urban (1895–1901). He was director of the Warsaw Music Soc. (1904–6); after a sojourn in Germany (where he studied conducting with Nikisch in Leipzig), he settled in Zakopane (1907). Essentially a Romanticist, he succeeded in blending the national elements of Polish folk music with the general European genre of mild modernism; there is an influence of Richard Strauss in his expansive tone painting. The appreciation of his music in Poland rose after his death; some of his piano pieces and songs have been established in the Polish repertoire.

WORKS: Serenade for String Orch. (1898); Sym. in E minor, *Odrodzenie* (Renaissance; 1902); Violin Concerto (1902); symphonic poems: *Powracające fale* (Returning Waves; 1904); *Odwieczne pieśni* (Eternal Songs; 1907); *Stanislaw i Anna Oświecimowie* (Stanislaw and Anna of Oświecim; 1908); *Smutna opowieśç* (Sad Story; 1908); *Epizod na maskaradzie* (Episode at the Masquerade; 1908–9; unfinished; completed by G. Fitelberg); *Rapsodia litewska* for Orch. (1908).

BIBL.: F. Kęcki, *M. K.: Szkic monograficzny* (Warsaw, 1934); A. Chybiński, *M. K. (1876–1909): Kronika życia artysty i tater-*

nika (M. K. [1876–1909]: Chronicle of the Life of an Artist; Krakow, 1949); E. Dziębowska, ed., *Z życia i twórczości M.a K.a* (From the Life and Works of M. K.; Krakow, 1970).

Karpath, Ludwig, Austrian singer and music critic; b. Budapest, April 27, 1866; d. Vienna, Sept. 8, 1936. He was a pupil at the Budapest Cons.; studied singing in Vienna; was a member of the National Opera Co. in the U.S. (singing minor bass roles; 1886–88). Returning to Vienna, he became an influential music critic; wrote for the *Neues Wiener Tageblatt* (1894–1921). He publ. *Siegfried Wagner als Mensch und Künstler* (1902), *R. Wagner, der Schuldenmacher* (1914), etc.

Kárpáti, János, Hungarian musicologist; b. Budapest, July 11, 1932. He studied musicology with Kodály, Szabolcsi, and Bartha at the Franz Liszt Academy of Music in Budapest; then was an ed. with the music dept. of the Hungarian Radio (1957–59) and music producer with the Hungaroton Record Co. (1959–61); in 1961 he was named chief librarian of the Liszt Academy; he obtained his degree of Candidate of Sciences in 1968 and his Ph.D. in 1969 with the dissertation *Bartók vonósnegyesei* (publ. in Budapest, 1967; Eng. tr., augmented, Budapest, 1975). His books include *Domenico Scarlatti* (Budapest, 1959); *Arnold Schönberg* (Budapest, 1963); *Bartók kamarazenéje* (Budapest, 1976); *Kelet zenéje* (Music of the Orient; Budapest, 1981). He compiled the 2nd and 4th vols. for an encyclopedic ed., *Muzsikáló zenetörténet* (History of Music). In 1981 he was guest lecturer at Harvard Univ.; in 1982 he was a delegate at the Bartók Memorial Conference in Bloomington, Ind., and in 1983 was a guest lecturer at the Univ. of Calif. at Los Angeles, at North Texas State Univ. in Denton, and at the Univ. of Texas in Austin.

Karpeles, Maud, English ethnomusicologist; b. London, Nov. 12, 1885; d. there, Oct. 1, 1976. She was educated in England and Germany. She was associated with Cecil Sharp in collecting and organizing English folk songs (from 1909); in 1914 she visited the U.S., where she assembled American songs of English origin. She founded the International Folk Music Council (1947), and ed. its journal (1949–63). She was made an Officer of the Order of the British Empire in 1961. With Sharp, she publ. the collections *English Folk Songs from the Southern Appalachians* (London, 1917; 3rd ed., 1960) and *The Country Dance Book*, V (London, 1918); her own collections included *The Lancashire Morris Dance Tunes* (London, 1930), *Folk Songs from Newfoundland* (London, 1934; 2nd ed., augmented, 1971), and *Cecil Sharp's Collection of English Folk Songs* (London, 1973). She also publ. *Cecil Sharp* (with A.H. Fox Strangways; London, 1932; 2nd ed., 1955; rev. ed., 1967, as *Cecil Sharp: His Life and Work*), *Folk Songs of Europe* (London, 1956), and *An Introduction to English Folk Song* (London, 1973).
BIBL.: W. Rhodes, "Memorial Obituary: M. K. 1885–1976," *Ethnomusicology* (May 1977).

Karpman, Laura, American composer; b. Los Angeles, March 1, 1959. She studied with William Bolcom and Leslie Bassett at the Univ. of Michigan (B.M., 1983), John Harbison at Tanglewood (1984), and Babbitt at the Juilliard School in N.Y. (M.M., 1983; D.M., 1985). She taught at the Manhattan School of Music (1985–87), the New School for Social Research (1986–87), and Whittier (Calif.) College (from 1989). Her compositions are vaguely surrealistic, and include *Matisse and Jazz* for Soprano, Piano, Percussion, and Saxophone (1987), *Portrait of Jaco* for Violin, Viola, Cello, Double Bass, and Piano (1988), and *Caprices* for String Trio (1990).

Karr, Gary (Michael), outstanding American double-bass player; b. Los Angeles, Nov. 20, 1941. He was born into a family of double-bass players, and thus turned to this mastodon of string instruments by natural selection. He gained experience by playing in local synagogues; subsequently took cello lessons with Gabor Rejto at the Univ. of Southern Calif. in Los Angeles and with Stuart Sankey at the Juilliard School of Music in N.Y. He founded the International Inst. for the String Bass in 1967 and subsequently taught in the U.S. and

Canada. His instrument, the 1611 Amati, was once owned by Koussevitzky and was given to Karr by Koussevitzky's widow. Karr's career was the subject of the BBC-TV documentary "Amazing Bass" (1985). In addition to performing the Classical repertoire, he has done much to enlarge the literature for his instrument by commissioning works from Henze, Schuller, Wilder, Arnold, and other composers; he also includes in his repertoire folk-inspired pieces, as well as modern rock and dance forms.
BIBL.: A. Angarano, "Romancing the Doublebass with G. K.," *MusicalAmerica* (Nov. 1987); H. Waleson, "Virtuoso Bassist G. K.," *Ovation* (March 1988).

Kars, Jean-Rodolphe, Austrian pianist; b. Calcutta, March 15, 1947. He studied with Jeanne Manchon-Theist and Julius Katchen at the Paris Cons. (1958–64); made his London recital debut in 1967, and subsequently pursued an international career as a soloist. He champions the music of Messiaen, and excels as an interpreter of Mozart, Schubert, Liszt, Debussy, and Ravel.

Kartsev, Alexander, Russian composer; b. Moscow, July 19, 1883; d. there, July 3, 1953. He was a pupil of Taneyev and Glière in Moscow, and later of Juon in Berlin. He wrote an opera, *Undine;* Sym.; Violin Concerto; chamber music; etc.

Karyotakis, Theodore, Greek composer; b. Argos, July 21, 1903; d. Athens, June 14, 1978. He studied with Mitropoulos (composition) and Varvoglis (counterpoint and orchestration) in Athens; concurrently was enrolled in the law dept. of the Univ. of Athens. He wrote music in a neo-Romantic vein, permeated with euphonious dissonances; several of his works are inspired by Greek folk modes.
WORKS: Opera, *Tou fengariou louloudi* (Flower of the Moon; 1953–55); *Rhapsody* for Violin and Orch. (1940); *Epic Song* for Orch. (1944); *Serenities*, 10 songs for Voice, Clarinet, Celesta, Strings, and Percussion (1962); Concerto for Orch. (1967); Sym. (1974); much chamber music, including 2 violin sonatas (1945, 1955); *6 Erotic Songs* for Voice, Flute, and Harp (1948); String Trio (1949); String Quartet, with Voice (1963); *11 Sketches* for Flute and Viola (1963); *9 Inventions* for Violin and Piano (1966); Trio for Clarinet, Viola, and Piano (1969); Duo for Flute and Clarinet (1969); *Music for Flute, Clarinet, Horn, and Bassoon* (1973); numerous piano pieces; also a dramatic scene from *The Iliad* (1964) and songs.

Kaschmann (Kašman), Giuseppe, Italian baritone; b. Lussimpiccolo, Istria, July 14, 1847; d. Rome, Feb. 7, 1925. He studied in Rome; made his operatic debut in Zagreb in 1869. He then sang the title role in Zajc's *Mislav* at the opening of the Zagreb Opera on Oct. 2, 1870; made his 1st appearance in Italy in Turin as Alfonso in *La Favorite* in 1876, and subsequently sang at Milan's La Scala in 1878. He made his Metropolitan Opera debut in N.Y. as Enrico in *Lucia di Lammermoor* on Oct. 24, 1883; returned for the 1895–96 season. He 1st appeared at the Bayreuth Festivals in 1892. In later years he took on buffo roles, making his farewell to the stage in Rome in 1921. His finest roles included Don Giovanni, Amfortas, Wotan, Telramund, Kurwenal, Dr. Bartolo, and Don Pasquale.

Kasemets, Udo, Estonian-born Canadian conductor, composer, and teacher; b. Tallinn, Nov. 16, 1919. He studied at the Tallinn Cons., the Stuttgart Staatliche Hochschule für Musik, and the Darmstadt Kranichstein Institut; also took conducting courses with Scherchen. He emigrated to Canada in 1951, becoming a Canadian citizen in 1957. In addition to his work as a conductor and composer, he was music critic for the *Toronto Daily Star* (1959–63); was on the faculty of the dept. of experimental art at the Ontario College of Art (1971–87). His early music is set in peaceful Romantic modalities with Estonian undertones, but soon he espoused serialism and the pantheatricalism of the most uninhibited avant-garde.
WORKS: *Estonian Suite* for Chamber Orch. (1950); *Sonata da camera* for Solo Cello (1955); Violin Concerto (1956); String Quartet (1957); *Logos* for Flute and Piano (1960); *Haiku* for Voice, Flute, Cello, and Piano (1961); *Squares* for Piano, 4-

hands (1962); $\sqrt{5}$ *for 2 Performers on 2 Pianos and Percussion (1962–63); Trigon* for 1, 3, 9, or 27 Performers, a multidimensional score in which thematic information is provided by a deoxyribonucleic matrix (1963; 11 subsequent versions, 1964–66); *Communications, a noncomposition to words by e.e. cummings*, a cybernetic manifestation for singular or plural Singers, Speakers, Instrumentalists, or Dancers, of an indeterminate duration (1963); *Cumulus* for Any Solo Instrument or Ensemble, and 2 Tape Recorders, the score consisting of 9 segments to be played in any order (1963–64; 2 later versions, 1966, 1968); *Calceolaria,* time/space variations on a floral theme, for any number of Performers (1966; version for 4-channel Tape, 1967); *Contactics,* choreography for Musicians and Audience (1966); *Variations on Variations on Variations* for Singers, Instrumentalists, and 4 Loudspeakers (1966); *Quartets of Quartets,* 4 separate works for varying ensembles of Readers, Tape, Calibrators, Wind-bells, Wind Generators, Opaque Projectors, and any other sound-producing media: *Music for Nothing, Music for Anything* (Wordmusic), *Music for Something* (Windmusic), and *Music for Everything* (all 1971–72); *Music(s) for John Cage*, incorporating *Guitarmusic for John Cage* for any number of Guitars, Projections, and Dimmers, *Voicemusic for John Cage* for any number of Voices, *Saladmusic for John Cage* for any number of Salad Makers, and *Walking/Talking* for any number of Walkers/Talkers (all 1972); *Time-Space Interface* for any number of Participants and any media, in both indoor and outdoor versions (1971–73); *Quadraphony* (Music of the Quarter of the Moon of the Lunar Year), an acoustical/architectural time/space exploration project (1972–73); *La Crasse du tympan* for Record/Tape Mix (1973); *WATEARTHUNDAIR: Music of the 10th Moon of the Year of the Dragon*, a nature-sound-mix with verbal and visual commentary (1976); *KANADANAK*, a "celebration of our land and its people . . ." for Readers, Drummers, and Audience participation (1976–77); *Counterbomb Renga*, spectacle by about 100 poets and musicians, protesting against the proliferation of nuclear weapons, conceived and coordinated by Kasemets (CBC, April 3, 1983); *Yi Jing Jitterbug: 50 Hz Octet* for 8 Winds and/or Bowed Strings (1984); *Vertical Music: In Remembrance of Morton Feldman* for Any 7 Instruments (1987); a series entitled *Portrait: Music of the 12 Moons of the I Ching* for Various Instruments (1988).

Kashin, Daniil Nikitich, Russian composer; b. Moscow, 1769; d. there, Dec. 22, 1841. He was a serf, the property of an aristocratic landowner, Gavril Bibikov, who engaged Sarti to teach him music; he demonstrated his ability by presenting a piano concerto and an overture of his composition in Moscow (March 17, 1790). Bibikov then sent him to Italy for further study; upon his return in 1798, he was given his liberty. On April 10, 1799, he gave in Moscow a monster concert with the participation of 200 executants, including an ensemble of Russian horns; he also presented several of his songs, which became popular. He wrote the operas *Natalya, boyarskaya doch* (Natalia, the Boyar's Daughter; Moscow, Oct. 21, 1801), *Selskiy prazdnik* (The Village Holiday; 1807), *Olga prekrasnaya* (Fair Olga; Moscow, Jan. 14, 1809), and *The 1-day Reign of Nourmahal,* after Thomas Moore's *Lalla Rookh* (1817; not perf.); also collections of patriotic songs as well as Russian folk songs (3 vols., Moscow, 1833–34). He publ. *Zhurnal octechestvennoy muziki* (Journal of National Music; 1806–9).
    Bibl.: R.A. Mooser, *Annales de la musique et des musiciens en Russie au XVIIIe siècle* (Vol. II, Geneva, 1950).

Kashkashian, Kim, American violist of Armenian descent; b. Detroit, Aug. 31, 1952. She studied with Walter Trampler (1969–70) and Karen Tuttle (1970–75) at the Peabody Cons. of Music in Baltimore; after winning several competitions, she was a soloist with major American and European orchs. She taught at the New School of Music in Philadelphia (1981–86), the Mannes College of Music in N.Y. (1983–86), and the Indiana Univ. School of Music in Bloomington (from 1985). She has done much to promote contemporary music, commissioning many works for viola.

Kashkin, Nikolai Dmitrievich, noted Russian music critic; b. Voronezh, Dec. 9, 1839; d. Kazan, March 15, 1920. After receiving rudimentary instruction in music from his father, an amateur, he went to Moscow (1860), where he studied piano with Dubuc. He commenced writing music criticism for the *Moskovskiye Vedomosti* (1862); that same year he became a teacher at the Moscow branch of the Russian Musical Soc.; remained there when it became the Moscow Cons. (1866), serving as prof. until 1896. He was also music critic for the *Russkiye Vedomosti* (1877–78; 1886–97). As a music critic, his opinions exercised considerable influence in the musical life of Moscow in the last quarter of the 19th century. He publ. a textbook on elementary music theory (Moscow, 1875); a close friend of Tchaikovsky, he publ. a pamphlet entitled *Reminiscences of Tchaikovsky* (Moscow, 1896), which is valuable for its authentic biographical and psychological data. A selection of his articles was publ. in Moscow (1953).
    Bibl.: V. Yakovlev, *N.D. K.* (Moscow and Leningrad, 1950); G. Glushchenko, *N.D. K.* (Moscow, 1974).

Kashperov, Vladimir (Nikitich), Russian composer; b. Tchufarovo, Simbirsk region, Sept. 6, 1826; d. Romantsevo, near Mozhaisk, July 8, 1894. He studied with Voigt and Henselt in St. Petersburg and with Dehn in Berlin (1856); went to Italy to study singing (1858), and remained there until 1864; he wrote several operas in the Italian style which were produced in Italy: *Maria Tudor* (Milan, 1859); *Rienzi* (Florence, 1863); *Consuelo* (Venice, 1865). In 1865 he returned to Russia and taught voice at the Moscow Cons. (1866–72); in 1872, opened his own school of singing. In Moscow he produced 2 operas with Russian librettos: *The Storm,* after Ostrovsky (1867), and *Taras Bulba,* after Gogol (1893). Even in his Russian works, Kashperov remained faithful to the Italian style of composition, taking Donizetti as a model.

Kasianov, Alexander, Russian composer; b. Bolobonovo, near Nizhny-Novgorod (Gorky), Aug. 29, 1891; d. Gorky, Feb. 13, 1982. He studied composition with Sokolov at the Petrograd Cons. (graduated, 1917); also studied piano with Liapunov. In 1918 he went to Nizhny-Novgorod, where he organized radio broadcasts; in 1951 he joined the faculty of the Cons. In his compositions he continued the tradition of old Russian music; his many choral works are quite effective.
    Works: operas: *Stepan Razin* (Gorky, Oct. 29, 1939; rev., Gorky, Nov. 14, 1953); *A Partisan Girl* (1941); *On Far North* (1947); *Ermak* (1957). **orch.:** *Overture on Russian Themes* (1943). **chamber:** 7 piano sonatas; 24 preludes for Piano; numerous choruses and songs.
    Bibl.: N. Ugrumov, *A. K.* (Moscow, 1957).

Kaskel, Karl von, German composer; b. Dresden, Oct. 10, 1866; d. Berlin, Nov. 22, 1943. While a law student at Leipzig, he studied music at the Cons. under Reinecke and Jadassohn (1886–87); later at Cologne under Wüllner and Jensen.
    Works: operas: *Hochzeitsmorgen* (Hamburg, 1893); *Sjula* (Cologne, 1895); *Die Bettlerin vom Pont des Arts* (Kassel, 1899); *Der Dusle und das Babeli* (Munich, 1903); *Der Gefangene der Zarin* (Dresden, 1910); *Die Nachtigall* (Stuttgart, 1910); *Die Schmiedin von Kent* (Dresden, 1916). **orch.:** *Lust-spielouvertüre; Humoresque; Ballade;* also piano pieces; songs.
    Bibl.: E. Schmitz, "K. v.K.," *Monographien moderner Musiker* (Leipzig, 1909).

Kašlík, Václav, Czech conductor, opera producer, and composer; b. Poličná, Sept. 28, 1917; d. Prague, June 4, 1989. He took courses in music theory and esthetics at the Charles Univ. in Prague (1936–39); received training in composition with Karel and A. Hába and in conducting with Doležil and Dědeček at the Prague Cons. (1936–40), completing his studies in conducting in Talich's master classes there (1940–42). He was principal conductor and opera producer in Brno (1944–45). Upon returning to Prague, he was conductor of the 5th of May Theater (1945–48); subsequently was an opera producer and conductor with the National Theater. In addition to his long association with the National Theater, he was a guest producer in Leningrad, Moscow, Milan, Vienna, London, Geneva, Verona, and Houston. In 1956 he was awarded the Klement Gottwald State Prize and in 1958 was made an Honored Artist by the Czech government. His productions were noteworthy for their use of film, experimental lighting, stereophonic sound, and other modern innovations.

WORKS: OPERAS: *Zbojnická balada* (1939; rev. 1963); *Křížova esta* (1944–45); *Krakatit* (1958); *La Strada* (1972); *Silnice* (1980); *Krysař* (1983). **BALLETS:** *Don Juan* (1940); *Jánošík* (1950); *Pražský karneval* (1954); film scores; *Vesnická symfonie* for Orch. (1955); *Slavnostic*, symphonic triptych (1981); String Quartet (1938); *Dramatic Cantata* (1944).

Kassern, Tadeusz (Zygfrid), Polish-born American composer; b. Lemberg, March 19, 1904; d. N.Y., May 2, 1957. He studied composition with Soltys and piano with Lalewicz at the Lwow Cons.; later with Opieński and Brzostowski at the Poznan Cons. (1922–26); also studied law. He went to Paris (1931), then was made cultural attaché at the Polish Consulate in N.Y. (1945). He broke with the Communist government in Poland, and remained in N.Y.; became an American citizen in 1956. As a composer, he pursued a cosmopolitan trend; although many of his works are inspired by Polish folk music, the idiom and the method are of a general European modern character.

WORKS: Operas: *The Anointed* (1949–51); *Sun-Up* (1952; N.Y., Nov. 10, 1954); *Comedy of the Dumb Wife* (1953); *Eros and Psyche* (1954; unfinished); Concerto for Soprano (1928); Flute Concerto (1934); *Dies irae*, symphonic poem in memory of Marshal Pilsudski (1935; not extant); Concerto for Double Bass and Orch. (1937); Concerto for String Orch. (1944); *Teen-Age Concerto* for Piano and Orch. (1952; N.Y., May 1956); choruses; chamber music; piano pieces; songs.

Kässmayer, Moritz, Austrian violinist, conductor, and composer; b. Vienna, March 20, 1831; d. there, Nov. 9, 1884. He studied with Sechter at the Vienna Cons.; then played violin in the orch. of the Vienna Court Opera; later became ballet conductor there. He wrote a comic opera, *Das Landhaus zu Meudon* (1869); syms.; masses and other church music; 5 string quartets; songs. His *Mesalliansen* for String Quartet, with Piano, 4-hands, and *Volksweisen und Lieder* for String Quartet "humoristisch und kontrapunktisch bearbeitet," are amusing specimens of old-fashioned humor.

Kastalsky, Alexander (Dmitrievich), Russian choral conductor and composer; b. Moscow, Nov. 28, 1856; d. there, Dec. 17, 1926. He was a pupil of Tchaikovsky, Taneyev, and Hubert at the Moscow Cons. (1875–81). In 1887 he joined the faculty of Moscow's Synodal School; in 1910 he was appointed director of the school and principal conductor of the choir. In 1911 he took the choir on an extended European tour. In 1918 the Synodal School became a choral academy; in 1923 it merged with the Moscow Cons. Kastalsky was also a teacher of conducting at the Moscow Phil. Inst. (1912–22); in 1923, was appointed prof. of choral singing at the Moscow Cons. He wrote *Peculiarities of the National Russian Musical System* (Moscow and Petrograd, 1923; 2nd ed., 1961); V. Belaiev ed. his *Foundations of National Polyphony* (Moscow and Leningrad, 1948). He also wrote the article "My Musical Career and My Thoughts on Church Music," *Musical Quarterly* (April 1925). He was a notable composer of Russian sacred music, into which he introduced modern elements, combining them with the ancient church modes.

WORKS: Opera, *Clara Militch*, after Turgenev (Moscow, 1916); oratorio, *The Furnace of Nabucho* (1909); Requiem (1916; in memory of Allied soldiers fallen in World War I; in 12 sections, based on the modes of the Greek Orthodox, Roman Catholic, and Anglican churches); *Rustic Symphony* (Moscow, Dec. 13, 1925); incidental music to *Stenka Rasin* (Moscow, 1918), to Shakespeare's *King Lear* (Moscow, 1919), and to Hauptmann's *Hannele* (Moscow, 1920); cantata, *1812*; symphonic suite, *Pictures of Russian Festivities* (1912); *A Marketplace in Ancient Russia* (completed 1924); 5 choruses on patri-

otic texts; about 80 sacred choruses a cappella; *In Georgia*, suite for Piano; *Ancient Times* (4 vols. of restorations of ancient music, for Piano: I. China, India, Egypt; II. Greece, Judea, Islam; III. Early Christianity; IV. Ancient Russia).

BIBL.: W. Pring, "K. and Russian Folk Polyphony," *Music & Letters*, X (1929).

Kastle, Leonard (Gregory), American composer and pianist; b. N.Y., Feb. 11, 1929. After attending the Juilliard School of Music in N.Y. (1938–40), he studied piano with Paul Wittgenstein and Isabelle Vengerova; also held scholarships in composition with Rosario Scalero, Gian Carlo Menotti, and Samuel Barber at the Curtis Inst. of Music in Philadelphia (1944–50; B.A., 1950); he further attended Columbia Univ. (1947–50), and was a student in conducting with Carl Bamberger in N.Y. (1950–52). He was a visiting prof. of humanities and fine arts at the State Univ. of N.Y. at Albany (1978–88).

WORKS: OPERAS: *The Swing* (1954; NBC-TV, June 11, 1956); *Deseret* (1960; NBC-TV, Jan. 1, 1961; rev. for Voices, Piano, and Organ, 1978); *The Pariahs* (1962–66); *The Calling of Mother Ann* (Hancock Shaker Village, Mass., June 21, 1985); *The Journey of Mother Ann* (1986–87; Albany, N.Y., Jan. 22, 1987). **ORCH.:** *From a Whitman Reader* for Voice and Orch. (1954); *Pontoosuc* for Baritone and Orch. (1974–75; Tanglewood, July 4, 1976); Piano Concerto (Albany, N.Y., Feb. 14, 1981, composer soloist). **VOCAL:** *3 Walt Whitman Songs* for Chorus (1956); *Acquainted with the Night*, song cycle, after Robert Frost (1957); *3 Songs from Moby Dick* for Chorus (1963); *Mass* for Chorus, Organ, and Piano (PBS, Dec. 25, 1977; rev. version, Albany, N.Y., May 30, 1978). **CHAMBER:** Piano Sonata (1950); Violin Sonata (1955; rev. version, Albany, N.Y., March 17, 1986); Piano Suite (1957).

Kastner, Alfred, Austrian harpist, composer, and teacher; b. Vienna, March 10, 1870; d. Los Angeles, May 24, 1948. He studied harp with Antonio Zamara at the Vienna Cons. (1882–88), then was 1st harp in the orchs. of the Warsaw Opera (1890) and the Budapest Opera (from 1893); was also active as a teacher. He was 1st harp in the Philadelphia Orch. (1901–2; 1903–4); also toured Europe as a soloist. After playing in the Queen's Hall Orch. (1904–14) and teaching at the Royal Academy of Music in London (1909–13), he joined the N.Y. Phil.; then was 1st harp in the Los Angeles Phil. (1919–36). He wrote several works for harp and made various arrangements.

BIBL.: M. Cambern, "A. K., Man, Musician, Pedagogue," *Harp News*, 1/10 (1954); A. Stockton, "A. K.," *American Harp Journal*, 1/4 (1968).

Kastner, Georges Frédéric Eugène (Georg Friedrich Eugen), Alsatian acoustician, son of **Jean-Georges (Johann Georg) Kastner;** b. Strasbourg, Aug. 10, 1852; d. Bonn, April 6, 1882. He followed his father's ideas of music as a science; at the age of 20, read a paper before the Académie des Sciences in Paris, *Pyrophone: Flammes chantantes*, which was subsequently publ. (Paris, 1875). He invented the Pyrophone, an organ of 3 octaves whose sound was produced by gas jets. A description and picture of the Pyrophone are in vol. 3 of H. Ludwig's biography of Kastner's father.

Kastner, Jean-Georges (Johann Georg), Alsatian music theorist and composer, father of **Georges Frédéric Eugène (Georg Friedrich Eugen) Kastner;** b. Strasbourg, March 9, 1810; d. Paris, Dec. 19, 1867. He studied organ as a child; later entered the Strasbourg Lutheran Seminary. After abandoning theology, he was granted a stipend by the Strasbourg town council to continue his music studies in Paris with Reicha and H.-M. Berton. An industrious writer on music, he acquired enormous erudition in various arts and sciences. He pursued the study of acoustics and formulated a theory of the cosmic unity of the arts. His great project, *Encyclopédie de la musique*, was left unfinished at his death. Among the grandiose projects that he carried out were several vols. of "Livres-Partitions," that is, sym.-cantatas illustrating musico-historical subjects, preceded by essays upon them. Of these the following were publ.: *Musik der Zigeuner* and *Les Romnitschels,* symphonie dramatique with Orch. (1849–50); *Les Danses des morts; dissertations et recherches historiques, philosophiques, littéraires et musicales sur les divers monuments de ce genre qui existent tant en France qu'à l'étranger* and *La Danse macabre, grande ronde vocale et instrumentale* (1852); *Recherches historiques sur le chant en chœur pour voix d'hommes* and *Les Chants de la vie* for 28 Choruses for 4 to 6 and 8 Voices Unaccompanied (1854); *Essai historique sur les chants militaires des français* and *Les Chants de l'armée française* for 22 Choruses for 4 Voices Unaccompanied (1855); *La Harpe d'Eole, et la musique cosmique* and *Stéphen, ou La Harpe d'Eole, grand monologue avec chœurs* (1856); *Les Voix de Paris* and *Les Cris de Paris,* symphonie dramatique with Orch. (1857); *Les Sirènes* and *Le Rêve d'Oswald ou Les Sirènes, grande symphonie dramatique vocale et instrumentale* (1858); *Parémiologie musicale de la langue française* and *La Saint-Julien de ménétriers, symphonie-cantate à grand orchestre, avec solos et chœurs* (1866); *Untersuchungen über die Beziehungen der Musik zum Mythus* and *La Fille d'Odin,* symphonie-cantate with Orch. (1866). He also composed the operas *Gustav Wasa* (1832); *Oskars Tod* (c.1833); *Der Sarazene* (1834); *Die Königin der Sarmaten* (Strasbourg, June 13, 1835); *Beatrice, die Braut von Messina* (1839); *Juana* (1840); *La maschera* (Opéra-Comique, Paris, June 17, 1841); *Le Dernier Roi de Juda* (concert perf., Paris, Dec. 1, 1844); Piano Concerto (1827); 10 serenades for Wind Band (1832–35); 3 syms. (1832–35); 5 overtures (1832–35); 2 festival overtures (1858–60); chamber music; piano pieces; choruses; etc.

WRITINGS: *Traité général d'instrumentation* (Paris, 1837; 2nd ed., augmented, 1844); *Tableaux analytiques et résumé général des principes élémentaires de musique* (Paris, 1838); *Cours d'instrumentation* (Paris, 1839; 2nd ed., 1844); *Mémoire sur l'état de la musique en Allemagne* (Paris, 1843); *Le Marseillaise et les autres chants nationaux de Rouget de Lisle* (Paris, 1848).

BIBL.: H. Ludwig, *Jean Georges K.: Ein elsässischer Tondichter, Theoretiker und Musikforscher* (2 vols., Leipzig, 1886); P. Spitta, "Johann George K.," *Musikgeschichtliche Aufsätze* (Berlin, 1894).

Kastner, (Macario) Santiago, distinguished English pianist, harpsichordist, and musicologist; b. London, Oct. 15, 1908. He studied in London and Amsterdam, then took courses with Hans Beltz (piano), Ramin (harpsichord), Hans Prüfner (musicology), and Friedrich Högner (theory) in Leipzig; completed his studies with Juan Gilbert Camins (harpsichord and clavichord) and Anglés (musicology) in Barcelona. He settled in Lisbon in 1933; taught at the Cons. there (from 1947). He was an authority on Hispanic keyboard music; in addition to writing several important books, he ed. works by Portuguese and Spanish composers.

WRITINGS: *Música hispânica: O estilo do P.M. Rodrigues Coelho: A interpretação de música hispânica para tecla desde 1450 ate 1650* (Lisbon, 1936); *Contribución al estudio de la música española y portuguesa* (Lisbon, 1941); *Carlos Seixas* (Coimbra, 1947); *Federico Mompou* (Madrid, 1947); *Antonio und Hernando de Cabezón: Eine Chronik dargestellt am Leben zweier Generationen von Organisten* (Tutzing, 1977); *The Interpretation of 16th- and 17th-century Iberian Keyboard Music* (Stuyvesant, N.Y., 1987).

Kastorsky, Vladimir (Ivanovich), Russian bass; b. Bolshive Soly, March 14, 1871; d. Leningrad, July 2, 1948. He studied with Cotogni and Gabel; made his debut with Champagner's touring opera company (1894); became a member of the Maryinsky Theater in St. Petersburg (1899) and later sang with Zimin's opera company in Moscow; also appeared in Diaghilev's Russian Seasons in Paris and London (1907–8); concurrently formed a vocal quartet specializing in Russian folk songs, with which he toured abroad. He remained on the operatic stage for nearly 45 years, and appeared in concerts to the end of his life.

Katchen, Julius, admired American pianist; b. Long Branch, N.J., Aug. 15, 1926; d. Paris, April 29, 1969. He studied in N.Y. with David Saperton; made his concert debut with the Philadelphia Orch. on Oct. 21, 1937. He studied academic subjects at Haverford College (graduated, 1945); after a period of study on a French scholarship, he settled in Paris. His career was entering its most promising phase when he was fatally stricken with cancer. He maintained a broad repertoire extending from the Classical era to contemporary music.

Kates, Stephen (Edward), American cellist and teacher; b. N.Y., May 7, 1943. He studied at the Meadowmount School of Music (1961–62), the Univ. of Southern Calif. in Los Angeles (1964–67), and the Juilliard School of Music in N.Y. (diploma, 1969). He made his N.Y. debut in 1963; after winning 2nd prize in the Tchaikovsky Competition in Moscow (1966), he appeared as soloist with leading orchs. in the U.S.; also was active as a chamber music artist and recitalist. He taught at Ohio State Univ. in Columbus (1969–72); then was a member of the cello and chamber music depts. of the Peabody Cons. in Baltimore (from 1974); also conducted master classes, and was president of the Violoncello Soc. (1983–87). His repertoire extends from Bach to contemporary music; he commissioned and gave the 1st performance of Claus Adam's Cello Concerto (1973).

Katims, Milton, American violist and conductor; b. N.Y., June 24, 1909. He attended Columbia Univ., studying violin with Herbert Dittler; also studied conducting with Leon Barzin. From 1935 to 1943 he was assistant conductor for WOR Radio in N.Y.; from 1943 to 1954, was 1st violist in the NBC Sym. Orch. in N.Y.; was its assistant conductor under Toscanini from 1947. From 1954 to 1976 he was music director of the Seattle Sym. Orch.; from 1976 to 1984, artistic director of the Univ. of Houston School of Music; then was a prof. at the Shanghai Cons. of Music (from 1985). He prepared various eds. of compositions for viola. In 1964 he received the Alice M. Ditson Award for conductors and in 1986 the Arturo Toscanini Artistic Achievement award.

Katin, Peter (Roy), English-born Canadian pianist; b. London, Nov. 14, 1930. He studied with Harold Craxton at the Royal Academy of Music in London (1943–48), making his debut at London's Wigmore Hall in 1948. He taught at the Royal Academy of Music (1956–69) and at the Univ. of Western Ontario in Canada (1978–84); became a naturalized Canadian citizen. He is best known for his performances of works from the Romantic and Impressionist periods, most especially of Chopin.

Katsaris, Cyprien, French pianist; b. Marseilles, May 5, 1951. He began piano lessons as a child; later pursued his studies with Aline von Barentzen, Monique de la Bruchollerie, and Jean Hubeau at the Paris Cons., where he won a premier prix for piano (1969) and for chamber music (1970). In 1970 he received the Albert Roussel Prize and in 1977 captured 1st prize in the Cziffra Competition; subsequently appeared as a soloist with the world's major orchs., and also gave recitals and played in chamber music concerts. On May 23, 1986, he made his N.Y. recital debut at Alice Tully Hall with notable success. He also was active as a composer. His repertoire is catholic, ranging from works of Bach to those of Boulez; he won particular acclaim for his virtuoso performances of Liszt's piano transcriptions of the 9 Beethoven syms.

Katwijk, Paul van, Dutch-American pianist, conductor, teacher, and composer; b. Delfshaters, Dec. 7, 1885; d. Dallas, Dec. 11, 1974. He studied at The Hague Cons., then in Berlin and Vienna with Klatte and Godowsky. In 1912 he settled in the U.S.; taught at Drake Univ. in Des Moines (1914–18), and also conducted the Des Moines Sym. Orch.; in 1918, he was appointed dean of music at Southern Methodist Univ. in Dallas; resigned in 1949, but continued to teach piano there until 1955. He was conductor of the Dallas Municipal Opera (1922–25) and the Dallas Sym. Orch. (1925–36). He composed several symphonic works, including the suite *Hollandia* (Dallas, March 15, 1931).

Katz, Israel J(oseph), American ethnomusicologist; b. N.Y., July 21, 1930. He studied at the Univ. of Calif. at Los Angeles with Klaus Wachsmann and Boris Kremenliev (B.A., 1956; Ph.D., 1967, with the diss. *Judeo-Spanish Traditional Ballads from Jerusalem: An Ethnomusicological Study*; publ. in 2 vols., N.Y., 1972, 1975). He taught at McGill Univ. in Montreal (1968–69) and at Columbia Univ. (1969–75); then at York College and the Graduate Center of the City Univ. of N.Y. (from 1977). He was ed. of *Ethnomusicology* (1971–72) and co-ed. of *Musica Judaica* (from 1975).

Katz, Mindru, Rumanian-born Israeli pianist; b. Bucharest, June 3, 1925; d. during a recital in Istanbul, Jan. 30, 1978. He studied with Floria Musicescu at the Royal Academy of Music in Bucharest; made his debut with the Bucharest Phil. in 1947, and then played throughout Eastern Europe. He made his Western European debut in Paris in 1957, then settled in Israel (1959). He joined the faculty of the Rubin Academy of Music in Tel Aviv in 1962, becoming a prof. of piano there in 1972.

Katzer, Georg, German composer; b. Habelschwerdt, Silesia, Jan. 10, 1935. He studied piano and composition with Rudolf Wagner-Régeny and Ruth Zechlin at the Hochschule für Musik in East Berlin (1954–59); then entered the classes of Hanns Eisler and Leo Spies at the Akademie der Künste there (1960–63), where he was elected to membership (1979) and became artistic director of its electronic music studio; served as president of the national section of the International Soc. for Electroacoustic Music (from 1989); in 1981 he received the National Prize for Art of the German Democratic Republic. In his music, Katzer is a universalist, applying constructivist principles with lapidary precision. Under the influence of Eisler, he adopted a broad variety of methods, including 12-tone techniques, using his materials for specific purposes accessible to mass audiences.

WORKS: STAGE: *Das Land Bum-Bum,* opera for children (1974); *Schwarze Vögel,* ballet (1975); *Ein neuer Sommernachtstraum,* ballet (1979–80); *Gastmahl,* opera (Berlin, April 30, 1988). ORCH.: 3 sonatas for Orch. (1968, 1969, 1970); *Baukasten* (1972); Concerto for Orch. (1973); *D-Dur Musikmaschine* (1973); Concerto for Jazz Group and Orch. (1975); *Empfindsame Musik* for 58 String Instruments and 3 Percussion Groups (1976); *Dramatische Musik* (1977); *Sound-Hous* for Orch., 3 Instrumental Groups, and Tape (1979); Piano Concerto (1980); Double Concerto for Cello, Harp, and Orch. (1980); Flute Concerto (Berlin, Feb. 25, 1986); Oboe Concerto (Leipzig, Sept. 21, 1989); Concerto for Orch. No. 3 (Berlin, Sept. 22, 1989); Cello Concerto (Karl-Marx-Stadt, Oct. 24, 1989). CHAMBER: String Quartet No. 1 (1966); String Quartet No. 2, with Soprano (1967); *Streichmusik I* for 14 Solo Strings (1971); *Streichmusik II* for 18 Solo Strings (1972); Piano Quintet (1972); *Scene* for Chamber Ensemble (1975); Concerto for Harpsichord and Wind Quintet (1977); Trio for Oboe, Cello, and Piano, with Tape (1979); choruses; songs.

Kauder, Hugo, Austrian-born American composer; b. Tobitschau, Moravia, June 9, 1888; d. Bussum, the Netherlands, July 22, 1972. He studied violin; was a member of the Konzertverein Orch. in Vienna (1910–19), then went to the U.S. (1938), where he became a naturalized U.S. citizen (1944). His music is contrapuntal, with canonic devices much used in free and often asymmetric rhythm, while the harmonies are conservative. He wrote 4 syms., a Cello Concerto, and a great number of works for chamber music combinations. He publ. *Entwurf einer neuen Melodie- und Harmonielehre* (Vienna, 1932) and *Counterpoint: An Introduction to Polyphonic Composition* (N.Y., 1960).

Kauer, Ferdinand, Moravian-born Austrian conductor and composer; b. Klein-Tajax (baptized), Jan. 18, 1751; d. Vienna, April 13, 1831. As a boy he played organ in a local Jesuit church; then was organist at the Jesuit seminary in Tyrnau, Hungary, where he took courses in philosophy and medicine. He went to Vienna about 1777; there he studied composition with Heidenreich and Zimmermann; then became a violinist in the orch. of the Theater in der Leopoldstadt about 1781;

was made director of the theater's music school (1789) and later 2nd Kapellmeister at the theater, scoring a success with his *Das Donauweibchen* (Jan. 11, 1798); it was subsequently performed all over Europe. After serving as Kapellmeister in Graz (1810–11), he returned to the Leopoldstadt theater; then was Kapellmeister at the Theater in der Josefstadt (1814–18); subsequently made a precarious living as a 2nd violinist in the Leopoldstadt theater orch. (1821–30). He lost almost all of his possessions, including his MSS, in the flood of 1830. He wrote about 200 works for the stage, as well as sacred music, syms., concertos, etc. He publ. *Singschule nach dem neuesten System der Tonkunst* (1790) and *Kurzgefasste Generalbass-Schule für Anfänger* (1800).

BIBL.: K. Manschinger, *F. K.: Ein Beitrag zur Geschichte des Wiener Singspiels um die Wende des 18. Jahrhunderts* (diss., Univ. of Vienna, 1929).

Kauffmann, Emil, German composer and writer on music, son of **Ernst Friedrich Kauffmann;** b. Ludwigsburg, Nov. 23, 1836; d. Tübingen, June 17, 1909. He studied at the Stuttgart Cons. with Keller, Faiszt, Jung, and Singer; joined the Court Orch. in 1863 as a violinist; was a teacher in the music school at Basel (1868–77) and music director at the Univ. of Tübingen (Ph.D., 1885). He wrote *Die Nacht;* over 60 lieder; male choruses; sonatas and other piano pieces; also *Entwickelung der Tonkunst von der Mitte des 18. Jahrhunderts bis zur Gegenwart* (1884) and *Justinus Heinrich Knecht: Ein schwäbischer Tonsetzer* (1892); contributed articles to the Leipzig *Musikalisches Wochenblatt.*

Kauffmann, Ernst Friedrich, German composer, father of **Emil Kauffmann;** b. Ludwigsburg, Nov. 27, 1803; d. Stuttgart, Feb. 11, 1856. He studied at the Univ. of Tübingen (1825–27); became principal of the Realschule at Ludwigsburg, but because of his connection with revolutionists he lost his position in 1835; was imprisoned in Asperg (1838–42), where he wrote 6 sets of songs, which became popular.

Kauffmann, Fritz, German choral conductor and composer; b. Berlin, June 17, 1855; d. Magdeburg, Sept. 29, 1934. He was an apothecary; began to study music seriously at 23, with Kiel in Berlin; 3 years later, won the Mendelssohn Prize for composition. After a sojourn in Vienna, he lived mostly in Berlin; in 1889, became choral conductor in Magdeburg; from 1897 till 1920 he conducted the Kirchengesangverein there. He wrote a comic opera, *Die Herzkrankheit;* Sym.; 2 violin concertos; Piano Concerto; Cello Concerto; 2 piano sonatas; *Tanz-Improvisationen* for Piano; choruses; songs.

Kauffmann, Leo Justinus, German composer; b. Dammerkirch, Sept. 20, 1901; d. in an air raid in Strasbourg, Sept. 25, 1944. He studied with Erb in Strasbourg and with Jarnach and Abendroth in Cologne; he taught at Cologne's Rheinische Musikschule (1929–32) and worked for the Cologne Radio (1932–33); later taught at the Strasbourg Cons., serving as its director until his death. He wrote the operas *Die Geschichte vom schönen Annerl* (Strasbourg, June 20, 1942) and *Das Perlenhem* (Strasbourg, 1944); a Sym.; a Mass; a Concertino for Double Bass and Chamber Orch.

Kaufman, Harry, American pianist; b. N.Y., Sept. 6, 1894; d. Beverly Hills, Calif., Aug. 22, 1961. He studied at the Inst. of Musical Art with Stokowski; later was a pupil of Josef Hofmann; in 1924 he was appointed teacher of the art of accompanying at the Curtis Inst. of Music in Philadelphia. Though principally known as an excellent accompanist, he also appeared as soloist with the N.Y. Phil., the Philadelphia Orch., etc., and as a member of several chamber music groups.

Kaufman, Louis, distinguished American violinist; b. Portland, Oreg., May 10, 1905. He studied with Kneisel; won the Loeb Prize in 1927 and the Naumburg Award in 1928; subsequently toured widely. He gave numerous 1st performances of works by contemporary composers, among them a violin concerto by Dag Wiren (Stockholm, Oct. 25, 1953), and 1st American performances of violin works by Milhaud, Knipper, Martinů, and others; also played American works in Europe;

gave the 1st performance in England of Walter Piston's Violin Concerto (London, April 6, 1956). He ed. 6 sonatas for Violin by G.P. Telemann and *Sonata concertante* by L. Spohr; publ. *Warming Up Scales and Arpeggios* (1957).

BIBL.: J. Yoell, "In Conversation with L. K.," *Fanfare* 9, no. 4 (March–April 1986).

Kaufmann, Armin, Rumanian-born Austrian composer; b. Itzkany, Bukovina, Oct. 30, 1902; d. Vienna, June 30, 1980. In 1914 his family settled in Vienna, where he enrolled at the Academy of Music, studying music theory with Joseph Marx. From 1938 to 1966 he played the viola in the Vienna Sym. Orch.

WORKS: 4 syms. (1929, 1962, 1966, 1968); Piano Concerto (1970); Concerto for Tárogató and Orch. (1967); Quintet for Piano, Violin, Viola, Cello, and Double Bass (1965); 7 string quartets; Trio for Violin, Zither, and Guitar (1962); Trio for Flute, Viola, and Harp (1967); Rhapsody for Solo Guitar (1970).

Kaufmann, Friedrich, German inventor; b. Dresden, Feb. 5, 1785; d. there, Dec. 1, 1866. He invented a trumpet automaton (1808), the Belloneon, the Klaviatur-Harmonichord, the Chordaulodion, and the Symphonion. In 1851 his son, **Friedrich Theodor Kaufmann** (b. Dresden, April 9, 1823; d. there, Feb. 5, 1872), made an Orchestrion from the Symphonion.

Kaufmann, Helen, American writer on music; b. N.Y., Feb. 2, 1887; d. there, Sept. 17, 1978. She was educated at Barnard College; upon graduation, devoted herself to educational work. She publ. a number of popular books on music appreciation, among them *Home Book of Music Appreciation* (1942); *Little Guide of Music Appreciation* (1948); *The Story of Music through the Ages* (1949); also concise biographies of Mozart, Prokofiev, and other composers.

Kaufmann, Walter, German-born American conductor, composer, and musicologist; b. Karlsbad, April 1, 1907; d. Bloomington, Ind., Sept. 9, 1984. He studied composition with Schreker in Berlin; also studied musicology in Prague. In 1935 he traveled to India, where he remained for 10 years; devoted much time to the study of the Hindu systems of composition; also appeared as conductor, serving as music director of the Bombay Radio. In 1947 he moved to Nova Scotia and taught piano at the Halifax Cons.; from 1948 to 1957 he was music director of the Winnipeg Sym. Orch. In 1957 he settled in the U.S., where he joined the faculty of the Indiana Univ. School of Music in Bloomington. He became an American citizen in 1964. He wrote *Musical Notations of the Orient* (Bloomington, 1967); *The Ragas of North India* (Bloomington, 1968); *Tibetan Buddhist Chant* (with tr. by T. Norbu; Bloomington, 1975); *Involvement with Music: The Music of India* (N.Y., 1976); *Musical References in the Chinese Classics* (Detroit, 1976); *The Ragas of South India* (Bloomington, 1976); *Altinden* (Leipzig, 1981); also valuable articles on Eastern music for American music journals.

WORKS: OPERAS: *Der grosse Dorin* (1932); *Der Hammel bringt es an den Tag* (1932); *Esther* (1931–32); *Die weisse Göttin* (1933); *Anasuya,* radio opera (Bombay, Oct. 1, 1938); *The Cloak,* after Gogol (1933–50); *A Parfait for Irene* (Bloomington, Feb. 21, 1952); *The Research* (1951); *The Golden Touch,* short opera for children (1953); *Christmas Slippers,* television opera (1955); *Sganarelle* (1955); *George from Paradise* (1958); *Paracelsus* (1958); *The Scarlet Letter,* after Hawthorne (Bloomington, May 6, 1961); *A Hoosier Tale* (Bloomington, July 30, 1966); *Rip van Winkle,* short opera for children (1966). **BALLETS:** *Visages* (1950); *The Rose and the Ring* (1950); *Wang* (1956). **ORCH.:** Sym. No. 1 for Strings (1931); *Prag,* suite (1932); Concerto No. 1 for Piano and Orch. (1934); Sym. No. 2 (1935); Sym. No. 3 (1936); Sym. No. 4 (1938); *2 Bohemian Dances* (1942); Concerto No. 1 for Violin and Orch. (1943); *6 Indian Miniatures* (1943); Concerto No. 2 for Violin and Orch. (1944); *Navaratnam,* suite for Piano and Chamber Orch. (1945); *Phantasmagoria* (1946); Variations for Strings (1947); Concertino for Piano and Strings (1947); *Dirge* (1947); *Madras Express* (Boston Pops, June 23, 1948); *Fleet Street Overture*

(1948); *Strange Town at Night* (1948); *Faces in the Dark* (1948); *Andhera* for Piano and Orch. (1942–49); Sinfonietta No. 1 (Sym. No. 5; 1949); Divertimento for Strings (1949); Concerto No. 2 for Piano and Orch. (1949); Concerto for Cello and Orch. (1950); *Chivaree Overture* (1950); *Main Street* for Strings (1950); *Kalif Storch,* fairy tale for Speaker and Orch. (1951); *Arabesques* for 2 Pianos and Orch. (1952); *Vaudeville Overture* (1952); *Sewanee River Variations* (1952); *Short Suite* for Small Orch. (1953); *Nocturne* (1953); *Pembina Highway* (1953); *4 Skies* (1953); *3 Dances to an Indian Play* (1956); Sym. No. 6 (1956); *4 Essays* for Small Orch. (1956); Sinfonietta No. 2 (1959); Concerto for Timpani and Orch. (1963); *Festival Overture* (1968); Concertino for Violin and Orch. (1977). **CHAMBER:** 10 string quartets (1935–46); 3 piano trios (1942–46); 6 Pieces for Piano Trio (1957); String Quartet (1961); Partita for Woodwind Quintet (1963); *Arabesques* for Flute, Oboe, Harpsichord, and Bass (1965); 8 Pieces for 12 Instruments (1967); *Passacaglia and Capriccio* for Brass Sextet (1967); Sonatina for Piccolo or Flute Solo (1968). **PIANO:** Concertino (1932); Sonatina No. 1 (1948); Sonata (1948–51); *Arabesques* for 2 Pianos (1952); Sonatina No. 2 (1956); Suite (1957); also the cantatas *Galizische Bäume* for Chorus and Orch. (1932), *Coronation Cantata* for Soloists, Chorus, and Orch. (1953), and *Rubayyat* for Soloist and Orch. (1954); songs.

BIBL.: T. Noblitt, ed., *Music East and West: Essays in Honor of W. K.* (N.Y., 1981).

Kaul, Oskar, German musicologist; b. Heufeld, Oct. 11, 1885; d. Unterwössen, July 17, 1968. He studied at the Cologne Cons., then took courses in musicology with Sandberger and Kroyer at the Univ. of Munich (Ph.D., 1911, with the diss. *Anton Rosetti: Sein Leben und seine Werke*). He joined the faculty of the Würzburg Cons. (1913); was its deputy director (1924–45); was also a Privatdozent (1922–28) and reader (1928–45) at the Univ. of Würzburg. He ed. 5 syms. and chamber music of Rosetti for the Denkmäler der Tonkunst in Bayern, XXII, Jg. XII/1 (1912; 2nd ed., rev., 1968) and XXXIII, Jg. XXV (1925). His writings include *Die Vokalwerke Anton Rosettis* (Cologne, 1911) and *Geschichte der Würzburger Hofmusik im 18. Jahrhundert* (Würzburg, 1924).

Kaun, Hugo, German composer; b. Berlin, March 21, 1863; d. there, April 2, 1932. He studied at the Berlin Hochschule für Musik (1879–80); then with Oskar Raif (piano) and at the Prussian Academy of Arts with Friedrich Kiel (composition); was active as a teacher and conductor of the Liederkranz in Milwaukee (1887–1901), then returned to Berlin, becoming a prof. at the Klindworth-Scharwenka Cons. (1922). He publ. *Harmonie- und Modulationslehre* (Leipzig, 1915; 2nd ed., 1921); also an autobiography, *Aus meinem Leben* (Berlin, 1932). A cultured composer, he incorporated in his well-crafted works elements of both Brahmsian and Wagnerian idioms.

WORKS: Operas: *Sappho* (Leipzig, Oct. 27, 1917); *Der Fremde* (Dresden, Feb. 23, 1920); *Menandra* (staged in Kiel and several other German opera houses simultaneously, Oct. 29, 1925). Orch.: 3 syms.; 2 piano concertos; *Der Sternenbanner,* a festival march on the *Star-Spangled Banner;* overture, *Der Maler von Antwerpen* (Chicago, Feb. 3, 1899); *Im Urwald,* 2 symphonic poems, after Longfellow's *Minnehaha* and *Hiawatha* (Chicago, Feb. 7, 1903); also chamber music, numerous choral works, many piano pieces, and songs.

BIBL.: W. Altmann, *H. K.* (Leipzig, 1906); G. Kruse, "H. K.," *Die Musik,* IX/24 (1909–10); R. Schaal, *H. K., 1863–1932, Leben und Werk: Ein Beitrag zur Musik der Jahrhundertwende* (Regensburg, 1946).

Kavafian, Ani, gifted Turkish-born American violinist of Armenian descent, sister of **Ida Kavafian;** b. Istanbul, May 10, 1948. In 1956 she went with her family to the U.S., where she took violin lessons with Ara Zerounian (1957–62) and Mischakoff (1962–66) in Detroit; then entered the Juilliard School of Music in N.Y., where she received instruction in violin from Galamian and in chamber music performance from Galimir and members of the Juilliard Quartet (M.A., 1972).

In 1969 she made her debut at Carnegie Recital Hall in N.Y.; her European debut followed in Paris in 1973. She appeared as soloist with the leading orchs.; also played chamber music concerts, serving as an artist-member of the Chamber Music Soc. of Lincoln Center (from 1980); likewise gave duo performances with her sister. She taught at the Mannes College of Music (from 1982), and at the Manhattan School of Music and Queens College of the City Univ. of N.Y. (from 1983).

Kavafian, Ida, talented Turkish-born American violinist of Armenian descent, sister of **Ani Kavafian**; b. Istanbul, Oct. 29, 1952. She went with her family to the U.S. (1956), where she took up violin studies with Ara Zerounian in Detroit at the age of 6, and later received instruction from Mischakoff there; entered the Juilliard School in N.Y. (1969), where she continued her training with Shumsky and Galamian (M.A., 1975); she won the Vianna da Motta International Violin Competition in Lisbon (1973) and the silver medal at the International Violin Competition of Indianapolis (1982). She helped to found the chamber group Tashi (1973), and subsequently toured with it; made her N.Y. recital debut (1978) and her European debut in London (1982); played in duo concerts with her sister.

Kay, Hershy, American composer, arranger, and orchestrator; b. Philadelphia, Nov. 17, 1919; d. Danbury, Conn., Dec. 2, 1981. He studied cello with Felix Salmond and orchestration with Randall Thompson at the Curtis Inst. of Music in Philadelphia (1936–40); then went to N.Y., and began a fruitful career as an arranger of Broadway musicals and ballets. He orchestrated a number of Leonard Bernstein's theater works: On the Town (1944), Peter Pan (incidental music; 1951), Candide (1956; revival, 1973), Mass (1971), and the Bicentennial pageant 1600 Pennsylvania Avenue (1976). His last arrangement for Bernstein was Olympic Hymn (Baden-Baden, Sept. 23, 1981). His other orchestrations for Broadway include Kurt Weill's A Flag Is Born (1947), Latouche's The Golden Apple (1954), Mary Rodgers's Once upon a Mattress (1958), Blitzstein's Juno (1958), Sand Hog (1958), Livin' the Life (1958), Milk and Honey (1961), The Happiest Girl in the World (1961), 110 in the Shade (1963), Coco (1969), A Chorus Line (1975), American Musical Jubilee (1976), Music Is (1976), On the Twentieth Century (1977), Evita (1979), Carmelina (1979), and Barnum (1980). He made numerous arrangements for the N.Y. City Ballet, among them Cakewalk (1951, after Gottschalk), Western Symphony (1954, after cowboy songs and fiddle tunes), The Concert (1956, after Chopin), Stars and Stripes (1958, after Sousa's marches), Who Cares? (1970, after Gershwin), and Union Jack (1976, after popular British music). His ballet arrangements for other companies include The Thief Who Loved a Ghost (1950, after Weber), L'Inconnue (1965), The Clowns (1968; a rare 12-tone arrangement), Meadowlark and Cortège Burlesque (1969), Grand Tour (1971, after Noel Coward), and Winter's Court (1972). He also orchestrated a Gottschalk piano piece, Grand Tarantella, for Piano and Orch. (1957) and completed the orchestration of Robert Kurka's opera The Good Soldier Schweik (N.Y., April 23, 1958).

Kay, Ulysses Simpson, eminent black American composer; b. Tucson, Ariz., Jan. 7, 1917. He received his early music training at home; on the advice of his uncle **"King" Oliver,** a leading jazz cornetist and bandleader, he studied piano. In 1934 he enrolled at the Univ. of Arizona at Tucson (Mus.B., 1938); he then went to study at the Eastman School of Music in Rochester, N.Y., where he was a student of Bernard Rogers and Howard Hanson (M.M., 1940); later attended the classes of Paul Hindemith at the Berkshire Music Center in Tanglewood (1941–42). He served in the U.S. Navy (1942–45); then studied composition with Otto Luening at Columbia Univ. (1946–49); went to Rome as winner of the American Rome Prize, and was attached there to the American Academy (1949–52). From 1953 to 1968 he was employed as a consultant by Broadcast Music Inc. in N.Y.; was on the faculty of Boston Univ. (1965) and of the Univ. of Calif., Los Angeles (1966–67); in 1968, was appointed prof. of music at the Herbert H.

Lehman College in N.Y.; was made Distinguished Prof. there in 1972, retiring in 1988. He received honorary doctorates from several American univs. His music follows a distinctly American idiom, particularly in its rhythmic intensity, while avoiding ostentatious ethnic elements; in harmony and counterpoint, he pursues a moderately advanced idiom, marked by prudentially euphonious dissonances; his instrumentation is masterly.

WORKS: OPERAS: The Boor, after Chekhov (1955; Lexington, Ky., April 3, 1968); The Juggler of Our Lady (1956; New Orleans, Feb. 3, 1962); The Capitoline Venus (1970; Urbana, Ill., March 12, 1971); Jubilee (Jackson, Miss., April 12, 1976); Frederick Douglass (1980–85; Newark, April 14, 1991). **BALLET:** Dance Calinda (Rochester, N.Y., April 23, 1941). **ORCH.:** Oboe Concerto (Rochester, N.Y., April 16, 1940); 5 Mosaics for Chamber Orch. (Cleveland, Dec. 28, 1940); Of New Horizons, overture (N.Y., July 29, 1944); Suite in 5 Movements (1945; N.Y., May 21, 1950); A Short Overture (N.Y., March 31, 1947); Portrait Suite (1948; Erie, Pa., April 21, 1964); Suite for Strings (Baltimore, April 8, 1949); Sinfonia in E major (Rochester, N.Y., May 2, 1951); 6 Dances for Strings (1954); Concerto for Orch. (N.Y., Feb. 1954); Serenade (Louisville, Sept. 18, 1954); Fantasy Variations (Portland, Maine, Nov. 19, 1963); Umbrian Scene (New Orleans, March 31, 1964); Markings, symphonic essay, dedicated to the memory of Dag Hammarskjöld (Rochester, Mich., Aug. 8, 1966); Sym. (1967; for the Illinois Sesquicentennial, Macomb, Ill., March 28, 1968); Theater Set (Atlanta, Sept. 26, 1968); Scherzi musicali for Chamber Orch. (Detroit, Feb. 13, 1969); Aulos for Flute and Chamber Orch. (Bloomington, Ind., Feb. 21, 1971); Quintet Concerto for 5 Brass Soli and Orch. (N.Y., March 14, 1975); Southern Harmony (Raleigh, N.C., Feb. 10, 1976); Chariots, rhapsody (Saratoga, N.Y., Aug. 8, 1979, composer conducting); String Triptych for String Orch. (1987). **VOCAL:** Song of Jeremiah, cantata (Nashville, Tenn., April 23, 1954); 3 Pieces after Blake for Soprano and Orch. (N.Y., March 27, 1955); The Western Paradise for Female Narrator and Orch. (Washington, D.C., Oct. 12, 1976). **CHAMBER:** 3 string quartets (1953, 1956, 1961); Piano Sonata (1940); Quintet for Flute and Strings (1947); Piano Quintet (1949); 5 Portraits for Violin and Piano (1972); 2 Nocturnes for Piano (1973); Guitarra, guitar suite (1973; rev. 1985); Tromba for Trumpet and Piano (1983); 5 Winds, divertimento for Woodwind Quintet (1984); Pantomime, fantasy for Clarinet (1986); 2 Impromptus for Piano (1986); Everett Suite for Bass Trombone (1988); film score for The Quiet One (1948); band music; many choral pieces; songs.

BIBL.: N. Slonimsky, "U. K.," American Composers Alliance Bulletin (Fall 1957); L. Hayes, The Music of U. K., 1939–1963 (diss., Univ. of Wisconsin, 1971); C. Dower, "U. K.: Distinguished American Composer," Musart (Jan.–Feb. 1972); R. Hadley, The Published Choral Music of U.S. K., 1943–1968 (diss., Univ. of Iowa, 1972); L. Wyatt, "U. K.'s Fantasy Variations: An Analysis," Black Perspective in Music (Spring 1977).

Kaye, Danny (real name, **David Daniel Kominsky**), American singer, dancer, and actor; b. N.Y., Jan. 18, 1913; d. Los Angeles, March 3, 1987. He began his career working in vaudeville; after appearances in nightclubs and comedic films, he attracted notice in the Broadway show Straw Hat Revue (1939); then went on to earn notable success in Lady in the Dark (1941) by Ira Gershwin and Kurt Weill and Let's Face It by Cole Porter (1941). He subsequently starred in a number of musical comedies for films and was active on radio and television; returned to the N.Y. stage as Noah in Richard Rodgers's Two by Two (1970). Although he never learned to read music, he made appearances as a conductor with major orchs. by dint of following the tunes.

BIBL.: K. Singer, The D. K. Story (N.Y., 1958).

Kaye, Sammy, American bandleader; b. Lakewood, Ohio, March 13, 1910; d. Ridgewood, N.J., June 2, 1987. He graduated from Ohio Univ.; having learned to play the clarinet and alto saxophone, he organized his own band, which gained notice in a coast-to-coast radio broadcast in 1935. He scored his 1st hit with a recording of the title song from the film *Rosalie* (1937); after appearing in N.Y. (1938), he became one of the most popular bandleaders of the swing era, as millions were enticed to "Swing and Sway with Sammy Kaye." He was host of the "Sunday Serenade" radio show, and later made appearances on television. During a career of some 50 years, he made more than 100 recordings; among the most popular were *The Old Lamp-Lighter, Harbor Lights, Remember Pearl Harbor, I Left My Heart at the Stage Door Canteen,* and *Walkin' to Missouri.*

Kayser, Heinrich Ernst, German violinist; b. Altona, April 16, 1815; d. Hamburg, Jan. 17, 1888. He was a theater violinist in Hamburg (1840–57); then became a violin teacher there; wrote numerous violin studies and a violin method.

Kayser, Leif, Danish composer, pianist, and organist; b. Copenhagen, June 13, 1919. He studied at the Copenhagen Cons., and later took courses with Rosenberg in Stockholm; then went to Rome, where he studied theology (1942–49), and was ordained a Catholic priest; later studied with Boulanger in Paris (1955). He served as chaplain at St. Ansgar church in Copenhagen (1949–64); in 1964, was appointed to the faculty of the Copenhagen Cons. He wrote 4 syms. (1939, 1940, 1956, 1963); *Christmas Oratorio* (1943); Sinfonietta for Amateur Orch. (1967); Divertimento for 4 Recorders (1968); Organ Sonata; sacred choruses; etc.

Kayser, Philipp Christoph, German composer; b. Frankfurt am Main, March 10, 1755; d. Oberstrass, near Zürich, Dec. 23, 1823. In 1775 he settled in Zürich as a teacher. He wrote music for Goethe's singspiel *Scherz, List und Rache* (1785–86) and incidental music for his drama *Egmont* (c.1786–88; not extant); he was best known for his songs, of which he wrote more than 100, a number of which were set to texts by Goethe.
    BIBL.: C. Burkhardt, *Goethe und der Komponist P.C. K.* (Leipzig, 1879); E. Refardt, *Der Goethe-K.* (Zürich, 1950).

Kazachenko, Grigori, Russian composer; b. St. Petersburg, May 3, 1858; d. there (Leningrad), May 18, 1938. He studied piano and composition at the St. Petersburg Cons.; then was chorus master at the Imperial Opera and appeared as conductor. In 1924 he became a prof. of choral singing at the Leningrad Cons. He wrote 2 operas, *Prince Serebryanny* (St. Petersburg, 1892) and *Pan Sotnik* (St. Petersburg, Sept. 17, 1902); Sym.; *An Armenian Overture; Fantasia on Russian Themes* for Viola and Orch.; choral works; songs; piano pieces.

Kazandjiev, Vasil, Bulgarian conductor and composer; b. Marten, near Ruse, Sept. 10, 1934. He studied composition with Vladigerov and conducting with Simeonov at the Sofia State Cons., graduating in 1957; in 1964, was appointed to its faculty. In 1979 he became principal conductor of the Bulgarian Radio and Television Sym. Orch. In his music he applies modern techniques, including modified serialism, to modalities of Bulgarian folk music.
    WORKS: ORCH.: Concerto for String Orch. (1951); Sinfonietta (1954); Trumpet Concerto (1955); *Divertimento* (1957); Concerto for Piano, Saxophone, and Orch. (1957–60); Violin Concerto (1961); *Complexi sonori* for Strings (1965); *Symphony of Timbres* (1968); *The Living Icons* for Chamber Orch. (1970; Sofia, Jan. 26, 1972); *Pictures from Bulgaria* for String Orch. and Percussion (1971); *Festive Music* (1972); *Capriccio* (1974); *Apocalypse* (1978); *Illuminations* (1980); Sym. No. 3 (1981). **CHAMBER:** Wind Quintet (1951); *Variations* for Oboe, Clarinet, Violin, Viola, Cello, and Piano (1954); Horn Sonata (1955); Clarinet Sonata (1956); Sonata for Solo Violin (1957); 2 string quartets (1965, 1970); *Concert Improvisations* for Flute, Viola, Harp, and Harpsichord (1974); *Poco a poco* for Percussion and Organ (1979); Piano Quintet (1981). **PIANO:** Sonata (1957); *The Triumph of the Bells* (1974); choruses; songs.

Kazanly, Nikolai (Ivanovich), Russian conductor and composer; b. Tiraspol, Dec. 17, 1869; d. Petrograd, Aug. 5, 1916. He studied in Odessa (1879–83); then went to St. Petersburg, where he entered the composition class of Rimsky-Korsakov

at the Cons. (1891–94); also studied with Balakirev. In 1897 he conducted in western Europe; returning to Russia, he supervised music education in military schools. He wrote an opera, *Miranda* (St. Petersburg, 1910); a Sym. (1897; St. Petersburg, March 8, 1910); several symphonic poems, among them *Noch Karnavala* (Carnival Night; 1914); cantatas; songs.

Kazuro, Stanislaw, Polish composer; b. Teklinapol, near Vilnius, Aug. 1, 1881; d. Warsaw, Nov. 30, 1961. He studied in Warsaw, Paris, and Rome; after his return to Warsaw, he was active mainly as a pedagogue and choral conductor; he also publ. several school manuals. His compositions, in an academic style, were chiefly designed for pedagogic purposes; among them are 2 folk operas, orch. music, choral works, piano pieces, etc.

Kazyński, Wiktor, Polish pianist, conductor, and composer; b. Vilnius, Dec. 30, 1812; d. St. Petersburg, March 18, 1867. He studied law at the Univ. of Vilnius; was mostly self-taught in music. From 1836 to 1840 he was organist at Vilnius's Cathedral of St. John; then went to Warsaw, where he took lessons with Chopin's teacher Elsner. In 1842 he settled in St. Petersburg, where he conducted the orch. of the Alexandrinsky Theater (1845–67). He was one of the 1st pianists to champion Chopin's works. His own compositions are of little importance, but they are of historical interest as early examples of Polish Romanticism; among them are a melodrama to a Polish libretto, *Zyd wieczny tulacz* (The Wandering Jew; Vilnius, 1842), and a melodrama to a French libretto, *Mąż i żona* (Man and Wife; St. Petersburg, 1848), as well as 7 other works in that genre; also 3 comic operas, including *Antoni i Antosia* (Vilnius, 1840), 4 operettas, 4 ballets, orch. music, and songs. He also publ. *History of Italian Opera* (St. Petersburg, 1851; in Polish and in a Russian tr.).

Keats, Donald (Howard), significant American composer; b. N.Y., May 27, 1929. He studied piano at the Manhattan School of Music; then enrolled in Yale Univ., where he attended classes with Quincy Porter and Paul Hindemith in composition (Mus.B., 1949) and musicology with Alfred Einstein and Leo Schrade; then attended classes in composition at Columbia Univ. with Otto Luening, Douglas Moore, and Henry Cowell (M.A., 1953), and took a course in musicology with Paul Henry Lang. Subsequently he entered the Graduate School of Music at the Univ. of Minnesota, where he studied composition with Paul Fetler and Dominick Argento and musicology with Johannes Riedel (Ph.D., 1962). In 1954 he received a Fulbright traveling grant and went to Germany, where he became a student of Philipp Jarnach at the Hochschule für Musik in Hamburg. In 1964–65 he received his 1st Guggenheim fellowship grant to continue his studies in Paris, Florence, and Vienna; in 1972–73 he obtained a 2nd Guggenheim grant and traveled to France and England. Other awards and prizes were from the National Endowment for the Arts, Yale Univ., the Rockefeller Foundation, and the Ford Foundation. In 1948–49 he served as a teaching fellow at the Yale Univ. School of Music; was then called to military service and was an instructor at the U.S. Naval School of Music in Washington, D.C. (1953–54); later was a member of the faculty of Antioch College in Yellow Springs, Ohio (1957–76); in 1969–70 he was visiting prof. of music at the School of Music, Univ. of Washington, in Seattle. In 1976 he was appointed prof. of music and composer-in-residence at the Univ. of Denver School of Music. In the meantime, he gave guest performances in various parts of the world as a pianist in his own works; he gave concerts of his own music in Tel Aviv and Jerusalem in 1973; performed at a concert of his music in N.Y. in 1975 under the auspices of the U.S. Dept. of the Interior; and accompanied singers in programs of American songs, including his own. In his own compositions, Keats appears as a classical lyricist; his music is sparse in texture but opulent in sonorous substance, frugal in diction but expansive in elaborate developments; its expressive power is a musical equivalent of "Occam's razor," a medieval law of parsimony which proclaims the principle of *multa paucis,* multitude by paucity, abundance in concision. The titles of his works often indicate this economic precision of design: *Musica instrumentalis; Polarities; Diptych; Branchings.* In his *Elegiac Symphony* he gives full expression to the lyric nature of his talent; it is an outgrowth of an orchestral *Elegy* inspired by the sadness upon the death of his infant son.

WORKS: ORCH.: Sym. No. 1 (1954); Sym. No. 2, *Elegiac Symphony* (Dayton, Ohio, Jan. 20, 1960); *The New Work,* ballet (1967); *Concert Piece* (Columbus, Ohio, Feb. 3, 1968); *Branchings* for Orch. (1976). **CHAMBER:** Sonata for Clarinet and Piano (1948); Piano Trio (1948); *Divertimento* for Wind and String Instruments (1949); 2 string quartets (1951, 1965); String Trio (1951); *Polarities* for Violin and Piano (1968); *Dialogue* for Piano and Wind Instruments (1973); *Diptych* for Cello and Piano (1973); *Epithalamium* for Violin, Cello, and Piano (1977); *Musica instrumentalis* for 9 Instruments (1980). **PIANO:** *Theme and Variations* (1954); Sonata (1966). **VOCAL:** *The Hollow Men* for Chorus, Clarinet, 3 Trombones, and Piano, to words by T.S. Eliot (Hamburg, July 12, 1955); *The Naming of Cats* for Vocal Quartet and Piano, to words by T.S. Eliot (1962); *A Love Triptych,* song cycle to poems by Yeats (1970); *Tierras del alma* for Soprano, Flute, and Guitar (Denver, May 23, 1979).

Kee, Cornelis, distinguished Dutch organist, pedagogue, and composer, father of **Piet(er Willem) Kee;** b. Zaandam, Nov. 24, 1900. He studied organ and piano with J. de Pauw, composition with S. Dresden, and voice with T. Denijs at the Amsterdam Cons.; then was active as a church and concert organist, becoming widely known as a master of improvisation. In 1951 he became a prof. at the Haarlem International Summer Academy. In 1976 he was made a Knight of the Order of Oranje-Nassau. He publ. 3 collections of Psalms for organ, which treat old Psalm tunes contrapuntally. In some of his own compositions (almost exclusively for organ) he applies polyphonic devices of the classical Flemish school in a modern way, including serial procedures.

WORKS: *Reeksveranderingen* (Serial Permutations; 1966); *Phases* for Organ (1966); *Phases* for Organ (1969); *Blijde incomste* (Joyful Entry), variations on a traditional song, for Brass, Percussion, and Piano (1969); *Sweelinck Variations* for Horn, 2 Trumpets, 2 Trombones, and Organ (1973); Suite for Harpsichord or Organ (1974); *Homopoly,* 4 pieces for Piano (1979); numerous teaching pieces for organ.

Kee, Piet(er Willem), noted Dutch organist, teacher, and composer, son of **Cornelis Kee;** b. Zaandam, Aug. 30, 1927. He studied organ with his father, and then with Anthon van de Horst at the Amsterdam Cons., graduating in 1948; won the International Organ Improvisation Competition for 3 consecutive years (1953–55); in 1956, became municipal organist at St. Bavo, Haarlem. From 1952 to 1987 he was organist at St. Laurens, Alkmar; from 1954 to 1987, prof. of organ at the Sweelinck Cons. in Amsterdam. In 1972 he was made a Knight of the Order of Oranje-Nassau; in 1987 he was elected an honorary fellow of the Royal College of Organists in London. Among his compositions are many organ pieces, including *Variations on a Carol* (1954), *Triptych on Psalm 86* (1960), *Music and Space* for 2 Organs, 3 Trumpets, and 2 Trombones (1969), *Confrontation* for 3 Street Organs and Church Organ (1979), and *Integration* for Choir, Flageolet, Mechanical Birds, Barrel Organs, and Church Organ (1980); chamber music; choral pieces; arrangements of hymns and folk songs.

Keene, Christopher, American conductor and music administrator; b. Berkeley, Calif., Dec. 21, 1946. He studied piano as a child, and during his high school years conducted several groups; then attended the Univ. of Calif. at Berkeley (1963–67). In 1965 he made his public debut conducting Britten's *The Rape of Lucretia* in Berkeley; in 1966 he became an assistant conductor at the San Francisco Opera, and in 1967 at the San Diego Opera. In 1968 he made his European debut conducting Menotti's *The Saint of Bleecker Street* at the Spoleto (Italy) Festival. He was music director of the American Ballet Co. (1969–70). On Oct. 18, 1970, he made his N.Y. City Opera

debut conducting Ginastera's *Don Ridrigo,* and, on Sept. 24, 1971, his Metropolitan Opera debut in N.Y. conducting *Cavalleria rusticana.* He served as co–music director (1971–73), general manager (1973–75), and music director (1975–76) of the Spoleto Festival; was music director (from 1974) and president (1975–89) of Artpark, the Lewiston, N.Y., summer festival. From 1975 to 1984 he was music director of the Syracuse (N.Y.) Sym. Orch.; also held that title with the Spoleto Festival U.S.A. in Charleston, S.C. (1977–80), and with the Long Island (N.Y.) Phil. (1979–90). He was artistic supervisor (1982–83) and music director (1983–86) of the N.Y. City Opera, returning there in 1989 as general director.

Keene, Constance, American pianist and pedagogue; b. N.Y., Feb. 9, 1921. She studied with **Abram Chasins** (1938–49), whom she married in 1949 and with whom she subsequently performed. She was an early teacher of Arthur Rubinstein's children; also taught at the Mannes School of Music in N.Y., numbering among her students Minoru Nojima, Peter Nero, and David Bar-Illan. Her 1964 recordings of the preludes of Rachmaninoff were critically acclaimed; in a letter dated Jan. 26, 1964, Rubinstein himself praised her for her "fantastic sweep, color, tone," and for her "incredible technique." As a soloist she appeared with major orchs. in the U.S. and abroad; also gave master classes.

Kéfer, Paul, French cellist and teacher; b. Rouen, Dec. 30, 1875; d. Rochester, N.Y., May 22, 1941. He studied cello at the Paris Cons. with Delsart; won 1st prize in 1900. After going to the U.S. in 1912, he formed, in N.Y., the Trio de Lutèce with Barrère (flute) and Salzedo (harp); was also founder and a member of the Franco-American Quartet. In 1923 he became a prof. of cello at the Eastman School of Music in Rochester, N.Y.

Kegel, Herbert, distinguished German conductor; b. Dresden, July 29, 1920; d. there, Nov. 20, 1990. He studied at the Dresden Staatskapelle's orch. school, where his mentors included Böhm and Blacher (1935–40). In 1946 he became conductor of the Rostock Opera; in 1949, was engaged as conductor of the Leipzig Radio Choir and Orch.; was made conductor (1953), Generalmusikdirektor (1958), and chief conductor (1960) of the Leipzig Radio Sym. Orch. From 1975 to 1978 he was a prof. at the Leipzig Hochschule für Musik, and in 1978 became a prof. at the Dresden Hochschule für Musik. From 1977 to 1985 he served as chief conductor of the Dresden Phil. He was regarded as one of the most competent conductors of East Germany, combining a thorough knowledge of his repertoire with a fine sense of effective presentation of the music.

Kehr, Günter, German violinist and conductor; b. Darmstadt, March 16, 1920; d. Mainz, Sept. 22, 1989. He studied violin in Frankfurt and Cologne; then took univ. courses in Berlin and Cologne, receiving a Ph.D. with the dissertation *Untersuchungen zur Violintechnik um die Wende des 18. Jahrhunderts* (1941). As a violinist, he gave the 1st German performances of the concertos of Hindemith and Bartók; also played in a string trio. He then pursued a career as a conductor; in 1955 he founded the Mainz Chamber Orch., with which he made numerous tours. From 1953 to 1961 he was director of the Peter-Cornelius-Konservatorium in Mainz; from 1959 he taught at the Hochschule für Musik in Cologne, becoming a prof. there in 1961; remained there until 1987. He ed. Urtext editions of the violin sonatas of Bach and Brahms; also supervised new editions of the orch. works of Albinoni, Rameau, Telemann, and other composers.

Keil, Alfredo, Portuguese composer and painter of German descent; b. Lisbon, July 3, 1850; d. Hamburg, Oct. 4, 1907. He studied music with António Soares, Oscar de la Cinna, and Ernesto Vieira in Lisbon; then went to Nuremberg (1868), where he studied music with Kaulbach and painting with Kremling. Returning to Portugal (1870), he pursued a dual career as composer and painter; devoted his energies to the furtherance of national music. His comic opera, *Susana* (Lisbon, 1883), is generally considered the 1st substantial work of the Portuguese stage; his song *A Portugueza* (1890) was adopted as the national anthem of Portugal in 1911. He also wrote the operas *Donna Bianca* (Lisbon, March 10, 1888), *Irene* (Turin, March 22, 1893), and *Serrana* (1st perf. in Italian at the Teatro San Carlos, Lisbon, March 13, 1899); other works include 3 symphonic suites, cantatas, piano pieces, and songs.

Keilberth, Joseph, distinguished German conductor; b. Karlsruhe, April 19, 1908; d. while conducting a performance of *Tristan und Isolde* at the Nationaltheater in Munich, July 20, 1968. He studied in Karlsruhe, where he became a répétiteur (1925), then Generalmusikdirektor (1935–40) at the State Opera. He was chief conductor of the German Phil. Orch. of Prague (1940–45), and then Generalmusikdirektor of the Dresden Staatskapelle (1945–50). He was chief conductor of the Bamberg Sym. Orch. (1949–68), with which he toured Europe in 1951 and the U.S. and Latin America in 1954; was also a conductor at the Bayreuth Festivals (1952–56) and concurrently Generalmusikdirektor of the Hamburg State Phil. Orch. (1950–59); then of the Bavarian State Opera in Munich (1959–68). He was particularly esteemed for his performances of works from the Classical and Romantic Austro-German repertoire.

BIBL.: W.-E. von Lewinski, *J. K.* (Berlin, 1968).

Keiser, Reinhard, important German opera composer; b. Teuchern, near Weissenfels, Jan. 9, 1674; d. Hamburg, Sept. 12, 1739. He received his early musical training from his father, Gottfried Keiser, an organist; was then sent to Leipzig, where he studied at the renowned Thomasschule directed by Johann Schelle. In 1693 he was in Braunschweig, where he began his career as a composer for the stage. His 1st opera-pastorale, *Der königliche Schäfer oder Basilius in Arcadien*, was performed shortly after his arrival in Braunschweig; in 1694 he produced a singspiel, *Procris und Cephalus*; there followed another pastorale, *Die wiedergefundenen Verliebten*, in 1695; it was revived in Hamburg in 1699 under the title *Die beständige und getreue Ismene*. In 1694 he was named Cammer-Componist in Braunschweig. In 1695 he went to Hamburg, which became his permanent residence. In 1696 he was engaged as Kapellmeister with the Hamburg Opera; in 1702 he became its co-director, retaining this position until 1707. Hamburg was then the main center of opera productions in Germany, and Keiser worked industriously producing not only his own operas there, but also the stage works of Handel and Mattheson. The number of Keiser's stage works was never calculated with credible precision; the best estimate is that he wrote in Hamburg at least 77 operas and 39 singspiels and theatrical intermezzi. The subjects of his operas are still predominantly taken from Greek and Roman mythology, as was customary in the Baroque era, but he introduced a decisive innovation by using the German language in his dramatic works; he further made use of popular local themes; he made a concession, however, in resorting to the Italian language in arias. Thus his last opera, *Circe,* produced in Hamburg on March 1, 1734, contains 21 German arias and 23 Italian arias. Keiser also continued the common tradition of having other composers contribute to the music. In his ballets he followed the French *style galant* and effectively used Rococo devices. In so doing he formed a German Baroque idiom national in essence and cosmopolitan in treatment; this aspect of his work influenced his younger contemporaries Bach and Handel. In 1718 Keiser became a guest Kapellmeister to the Duke of Württemberg in Stuttgart. In 1721 he went to Copenhagen to supervise the productions of his operas *Die unvergleichliche Psyche, Ulysses,* and *Der Armenier.* In 1723 he returned to Hamburg, and in 1725 composed 2 operas on subjects connected with Hamburg history and society: *Der Hamburger Jahrmarkt* and *Die Hamburger Schlachtzeit.* In 1728 he became Canonicus minor and Cantor of the Katharinenkirche in Hamburg. Apart from operas, he wrote many sacred works (oratorios, cantatas, Psalms, Passions), of which several were publ. in the collections *R. Keisers Gemüths-Ergötzung bestehend in einigen Sing-Gedichten mit einer*

Stimme und unterschiedlichen Instrumenten (1698); *Divertimenti serenissimi* (airs with harpsichord accompaniment, 1714); *Kaiserliche Friedenpost* (songs and duets with harpsichord, 1715); etc. Several excerpts from his operas were publ. in *Denkmäler Deutscher Tonkunst* and other collections.

WORKS: STAGE: *Der königliche Schäfer oder Basilius in Arcadien* (Braunschweig, 1693); *Procris und Cephalus,* singspiel (Braunschweig, 1694); *Die wiedergefundenen Verliebten,* Schäferspiel (Braunschweig, 1695; rev. as *Die beständige und getreue Ismene,* Hamburg, 1699); *Mahumet II,* Trauerspiel (Hamburg, 1696); *Der geliebte Adonis* (Hamburg, 1697); *Die durch Wilhelm den Grossen in Britannien wieder eingeführte Treue* (Hamburg, 1698); *Allerunterthäbigster Gehorsam,* Tantzspiel and singspiel (Hamburg, Nov. 15, 1698); *Der aus Hyperboreen nach Cymbrien überbrachte güldene Apfel zu Ehren Friedrichs und Hedwig Sophiens zu Holstein* (Hamburg, 1698); *Der bey dem allgemeinen Welt-Friede und dem Grossen Augustus geschlossene Tempel des Janus* (Hamburg, 1699); *Die wunderbahr-errettete Iphigenia* (Hamburg, 1699); *Die Verbindung des grossen Hercules mit der schönen Hebe,* singspiel (Hamburg, 1699); *Die Wiederkehr der güldnen Zeit* (Hamburg, 1699); *La forza della virtù, oder Die Macht der Tugend* (Hamburg, 1700); *Das höchstpreissliche Crönungsfest Ihrer Kgl. Majestät zu Preussen,* ballet opera (Hamburg, 1701); *Störtebecker und Jödge Michaels* (2 versions; Hamburg, 1701); *Die wunderschöne Psyche,* singspiel (Hamburg, Oct. 20, 1701); *Circe oder Des Ulisses erster Theil* (Hamburg, 1702); *Penelope oder Des Ulysses ander Theil* (Hamburg, 1702); *Sieg der fruchtbaren Pomona* (Hamburg, Oct. 18, 1702); *Die sterbende Eurydice oder Orpheus erster Theil* (Hamburg, 1702); *Orpheus ander Theil* (Hamburg, 1702); *Neues preussisches Ballet* (Hamburg, 1702); *Die verdammte Staat-Sucht, oder Der verführte Claudius* (Hamburg, 1703); *Die Geburt der Minerva* (Hamburg, 1703); *Die über die Liebe triumphierende Weissheit oder Salomon* (Hamburg, 1703); *Der gestürzte und wieder erhöhte Nebucadnezar, König zu Babylon* (Hamburg, 1704); *Die römische Unruhe oder Die edelmüthige Octavia* (Hamburg, Aug. 5, 1705); *Die kleinmüthige Selbstmörderinn Lucretia oder Die Staats-Thorheit des Brutus,* Trauerspiel (Hamburg, Nov. 29, 1705); *La fedeltà coronata oder Die gekrönte Treue* (Hamburg, 1706); *Masagniello furioso, oder Die Neapolitanische Fischer-Empörung* (Hamburg, June 1706); *La costanza sforzata, Die gezwungene Beständigkeit oder Die listige Rache des Sueno* (Hamburg, Oct. 11, 1706); *Il genio d'Holsatia* (Hamburg, 1706; used as prologue to succeeding work); *Der durchlauchtige Secretarius, oder Almira, Königin von Castilien* (Hamburg, 1706); *Der angenehme Betrug oder Der Carneval von Venedig* (Hamburg, 1707; includes arias by C. Graupner); *La forza dell'amore oder Die von Paris entführte Helena* (Hamburg, 1709); *Die blutdürstige Rache oder Heliates und Olympia* (Hamburg, 1709; with C. Graupner); *Desiderius, König der Langobarden* (Hamburg, July 26, 1709); *Die bis und nach dem Todt unerhörte Treue des Orpheus* (Hamburg, 1709; based on *Die sterbende Eurydice oder Orpheus erster Theil* and *Orpheus ander Theil*); *La grandezza d'animo oder Arsinoe* (Hamburg, 1710); *Le Bon Vivant oder Die Leipziger Messe* (Hamburg, 1710); *Der Morgen des europäischen Glückes oder Aurora,* Schäferspiel (Hamburg, July 26?, 1710); *Der durch den Fall des grossen Pompejus erhöhte Julius Caesar* (Hamburg, Nov. 1710); *Der hochmüthige, gestürtzte und wieder erhabene Croesus,* dramma musicale (Hamburg, 1710); *Die oesterreichische Grossmuth oder Carolus V* (Hamburg, June 1712); *Die entdeckte Verstellung oder Die geheime Liebe der Diana,* Schäferspiel (Hamburg, April 1712; rev. 1724); *Die wiederhergestellte Ruh oder Die gerönte Tapferkeit des Heraclius* (Hamburg, June 1712); *L'inganno fedele oder Der getreue Betrug* (Hamburg, Oct. 1714); *Die gerönte Tugend* (Hamburg, Nov. 15, 1714); *Triumph des Friedens,* serenata (Hamburg, March 1, 1715); *Fredegunda* (Hamburg, March 1715); *L'amore verso la patria oder Der sterbende Cato* (Hamburg, 1715); *Artemisia* (Hamburg, 1715); *Das römische Aprilfest,* Lust- und Tantz-spiel (Hamburg, June 1716); *Das vereinigte und triumphirende Ertz-Haus Oesterreich,* serenata (Hamburg, 1716); *Das zerstörte Troja oder Der durch den Tod*

Helenen versöhnte Achilles (Hamburg, Nov. 1716); *Die durch Verstellung und Grossmuth über die Grausamkeit siegende Liebe oder Julia* (Hamburg, Feb. 1717); *Die grossmüthige Tomyris* (Hamburg, Feb. 1717); *Der die Festung Siebenbürgisch-Weissenburg erobernde und über Dacier triumphirende Kayser Trajanus* (Hamburg, Nov. 1717); *Das bey seiner Ruh und Geburht eines Printzen frolockende Lycien unter der Regierung des Königs Jacobates und Bellerophon* (Hamburg, Dec. 28, 1717); *Die unvergleichliche Psyche* (Copenhagen, April 16, 1722); *Ulysses* (Copenhagen, Oct. 1722); *Der Armenier* (Copenhagen, Nov. 1722); *Die betrogene und nochmahls vergötterte Ariadne* (Hamburg, Nov. 25, 1722; based on the opera by Conradi of 1691); *Sancio oder Die siegende Grossmuth* (1723?); *Das wegen Verbannung der Laudplagen am Geburthstage Herrn Friedrich IV zu Dennemark jauchzende Cimbrien*, serenata (Copenhagen, 1724); *Das frohlockende Gross Britannien*, serenata (Hamburg, June 8, 1724); *Der sich rächende Cupido*, Schäferspiel (Hamburg, 1724; based on *Die entdeckte Verstellung oder Die geheime Liebe der Diana*); *Bretislaus oder Die siegende Beständigkeit* (Hamburg, Jan. 27, 1725); *Der Hamburger Jahrmarkt oder Der glückliche Betrug* (Hamburg, June 27, 1725); *Die Hamburger Schlachtzeit oder Der misslungene Betrug* (Hamburg, Oct. 22, 1725); *Prologus beim Geburths Feste Friderici Ludovici von Hannover*, serenata (Hamburg, Jan. 31, 1726); *Mistevojus König der Obotriten oder Wenden* (Hamburg, 1726); *Der lächerliche Printz Jodelet* (Hamburg, 1726); *Buchhofer der stumme Printz Atis*, intermezzo (Hamburg, 1726); *Barbacola*, intermezzo (Hamburg, 1726; includes music by Lully); *Lucius Verus oder Die siegende Treue* (Hamburg, Oct. 18, 1728; based on *Berenice* by Bronner of 1702); *Der hochmüthige, gestürzte und wieder erhabene Croesus*, singspiel (Hamburg, 1730; based on the dramma musicale of 1710); *Jauchzen der Kunste* (1733); *Circe* (Hamburg, March 1, 1734; with arias by other composers). Of these, *Die römische Unruhe oder Die edelmüthige Octavia* was ed. by M. Schneider in the supplement to the Handel *Gesamtausgabe* (Leipzig, 1902); *Der lächerliche Printz Jodelet* was ed. by F. Zelle in the *Publikationen der Gesellschaft für Musikforschung* (1892); the 1730 version of *Der hochmüthige, gesturtzte und wieder erhabene Croesus* was ed. by M. Schneider in the Denkmäler Deutscher Tonkunst, vol. 37 (1912).

SECULAR WORKS: *Gemüths-Ergötzung*, cantata (Hamburg, 1698); *Componimenti musicali, oder Teutsche und italiänische Arien, nebst unterschiedlichen Recitativen aus Almira und Octavia* (Hamburg, 1706); *Divertimenti serenissima delle cantate, duette ed arie diverse senza stromenti oder Durchlauchtige Ergötzung* (Hamburg, 1713); *Musikalische Land-Lust, bestehend in verschiedenen moralischen Cantaten* (Hamburg, 1714); *Kayserliche Friedenspost, nebst verschiedenen moralischen Singgedichten und Arien* (Hamburg, 1715).

SACRED WORKS: *Der blutige und sterbende Jesus* (Hamburg, Holy Week, 1704); *Der für die Sünde der Welt gemartete und sterbende Heiland Jesus* (Hamburg, 1712); *Der zum Tode verurtheilte und gecreutzigte Jesus* (Hamburg, 1715); *Passions Oratorium* (Hamburg, 1717?); *Die über den Triumph ihres Heylandes Jesu jubilirende gläubige Seele* (Hamburg, Nov. 2, 1717; not extant); *Die durch Grossmuth und Glauben triumphirende Unschuld oder Der siegende David* (Hamburg, Aug. 9, 1721); etc. The *Passions Oratorium* has been publ. in a modern ed. in the *Geistliche Chormusik*, vol. X (Stuttgart, 1963).

BIBL.: J. Mattheson, *Das neu-eröffnete Orchester . . .* (Hamburg, 1713); idem, *Grundlage einer Ehren-Pforte . . .* (Hamburg, 1740; new ed., by M. Schneider, Berlin, 1910); J. Sittard, "R. K. in Württemberg," *Monatshefte für Musikgeschichte*, XVIII (1886); F. Voigt, "R. K.," *Vierteljahrsschrift für Musikwissenschaft* (1890); H. Leichtentritt, *R. K. in seinen Opern* (diss., Univ. of Berlin, 1901); T. Krogh, "R. K. in Kopenhagen," *Musikwissenschaftliche Beiträge: Festschrift für Johannes Wolf* (Berlin, 1929); R. Petzold, *Die Kirchen-Kompositionen und weltliche Kantaten R. K.s* (Berlin, 1934); J. Rudolph, "R. K. und Masaniello," *Musik und Gesellschaft* (Oct. 1967); R. Brenner, *The Operas of R. K. in Their Relationship to the Affektenlehre* (diss., Brandeis Univ., 1968); D. Moe, *The St. Mark Passion of*

R. K. (diss., Univ. of Iowa, 1968); M. Peckham, "First Performances of R. K.'s *Croesus*," *Current Musicology*, 6 (1968); W. Paap, "De *Markus Passion* van R. K.," *Mens en Melodie* (March 1970); J. Rudolph, "Probleme der Hamburger deutschen Frühoper," *Händel-Jahrbuch 1969–70*; R. Brenner, "Emotional Expression in K.'s Operas," *Music Review* (Aug. 1972); B. Deane, "R. K.: An Interim Assessment," *Soundings*, IV (1974); K. Zelm, *Die Opern R. K.s* (Munich, 1975); J. Wenzel, *Geschichte der Hamburger Oper, 1678–1978* (Hamburg, 1978).

Kelberine, Alexander, Russian-American pianist; b. Kiev, Feb. 22, 1903; d. (suicide) N.Y., Jan. 30, 1940. He studied at the Kiev Cons., then at the Univ. of Vienna; took lessons from Busoni in Berlin; in 1923, went to America and studied at the Juilliard Graduate School in N.Y. with Siloti (piano) and Rubin Goldmark (composition); later also studied with Ernst Toch. A victim of acute depression, he programmed his last recital for pieces in minor keys and of funereal connotations, concluding with Liszt's *Todtentanz*; he then went home and took an overdose of sleeping pills. He was married to the pianist **Jeanne Behrend,** but was estranged from her.

Keldorfer, Robert, Austrian composer, son of **Viktor (Josef) Keldorfer;** b. Vienna, Aug. 10, 1901; d. Klagenfurt, Sept. 13, 1980. He received his early musical training from his father, then took courses at the Vienna Academy of Music with Carl Prohaska, Max Springer, and R. Stöhr (1917–19). From 1930 to 1939 he was director of the Linz Cons., and from 1941 to 1966 director of the Klagenfurt Cons. Among his works are an opera, *Verena* (1951); Oboe Concerto (1965); *Sonata ritmica* for Alto Recorder and Piano (1964); Viola Sonata (1964); Sonata for Recorder and Guitar (1967); choral works; songs.

Keldorfer, Viktor (Josef), Austrian conductor and composer, father of **Robert Keldorfer;** b. Salzburg, April 14, 1873; d. Vienna, Jan. 28, 1959. He was a student at the Salzburg Mozarteum. He was chief conductor of the Vienna Männergesang-Verein (1909–21). From 1922 to 1938, and again from 1945 to 1954, he was director of the Vienna Schubertbund; also conducted the Ostdeutscher Sängerbund, which became a model for many Austrian male choruses. His works include a *Missa solemnis*, 2 vols. of *Lieder für grosse und kleine Kinder*, many men's choruses, and arrangements of Strauss waltzes for men's chorus and orch. He also ed. a complete collection of Schubert's men's choruses.

BIBL.: O. Dobrowolny, *V. K.: Leben und Wirken eines österreichischen Künstlers* (Vienna, 1947).

Keldysh, Yuri, significant Russian musicologist; b. St. Petersburg, Aug. 29, 1907. He studied at the Moscow Cons. with M. Ivanov-Boretsky (Ph.D., 1947, with the diss. *The Artistic Outlook of V. Stasov*); was on its faculty from 1930 to 1950, and again from 1957; also taught at the Leningrad Cons. (1950–56) and was director of the Leningrad Inst. of Music and Theater (1955–57). He was ed. of the journal *Soviet Music* (1957–60) and of the valuable *Muzykalnaya Entsyklopediya* (6 vols., 1973–82). In 1976 he received the Glinka Prize. He has written many books on Russian music, the most notable being *The History of Russian Music* (3 vols., 1947–54), *Classical Russian Music* (1945; rev. ed., 1960), *Russian Music of the 19th Century* (1958), *Russian-Soviet Music* (1958), *Russian Music of the 18th Century* (1965), and *Rachmaninoff and His Time* (1973).

Kelemen, Milko, significant Croatian composer; b. Podrawska Slatina, March 30, 1924. He was taught to play piano by his grandmother; in 1945, entered the Zagreb Academy of Music, where he studied theory with Šulek; then went to Paris, where he took courses with Messiaen and Aubin at the Paris Cons. (1954–55); supplemented his studies at Freiburg with Fortner (1958–60); then worked on electronic music at the Siemens studio in Munich (1966–68). He taught composition at the Zagreb Cons. (1955–58; 1960–65), the Schumann Cons. in Düsseldorf (1969–73), and the Stuttgart Hochschule für Musik (from 1973). He publ. *Klanglabyrinthe: Reflexionen eines Komponisten über die Neue Musik* (Munich, 1981). As a composer, Kelemen began his career following the trend of European modernism well within academically acceptable lines, but changed his style radically about 1956 in the direction of the cosmopolitan avant-garde, adopting successively or concurrently the techniques of serialism, abstract expressionism, constructivism, and sonorism, making use of electronic sound; he also wrote alternatively valid versions for a single piece.

WORKS: STAGE: *Der Belagerungszustant,* opera, after Camus (Hamburg, Jan. 13, 1970); *Apocalyptica,* multimedia ballet-opera (concert perf., Graz, Oct. 10, 1979). **BALLETS:** *Der Spiegel* (Paris, Aug. 18, 1960); *Abbandonate* (Lübeck, Sept. 1, 1964); also *Der neue Mieter,* musical scene, after Ionesco (Münster, Sept. 15, 1964); *Yebell,* action for Soloists and Chamber Ensemble (Munich, Sept. 1, 1972). **ORCH.:** *Preludio, Aria e Finale* for Strings (Zagreb, May 20, 1948); Sinfonietta for Chamber Orch. (Zagreb, May 4, 1950); Sym. (Zagreb, Feb. 18, 1952); Piano Concerto (Zagreb, Feb. 22, 1953); Violin Concerto (Zagreb, June 20, 1957); *Koncertantne improvizacije* for Strings (Zagreb, Oct. 10, 1955); *Adagio ed Allegro* for Strings (Zagreb, Feb. 16, 1956); Concerto for Bassoon and Strings (Zagreb, May 13, 1957); *Concerto giocosa* for Chamber Orch. (Zagreb, Jan. 10, 1957); Concertino for Double Bass or Cello and Strings (Zagreb, April 20, 1957); *Skolion* (Cologne, June 12, 1960); *Transfigurationen* for Piano and Orch. (Hamburg, April 6, 1962); *Équilibres* for 2 Orchs. (Bonn, March 19, 1962); *Sub Rosa* (Zagreb, May 12, 1965); *Surprise* for Strings (Zagreb, May 12, 1967); *Composé* for 2 Pianos and Orch. Groups (Donaueschingen, Oct. 23, 1967); *Changeant* for Cello and Orch. (Cologne, Nov. 8, 1968); *Floreal* (Washington, D.C., Oct. 30, 1970); *Olifant* for 5 Winds and 2 Orch. Groups (Royan, April 8, 1971); *Mirabilia* for Piano, Ring Modulator, and 2 Orch. Groups (Paris, April 21, 1975); *Drammatico* for Cello and Orch. (Stuttgart, March 2, 1985); *Phantasmes* for Viola and Orch. (Stuttgart, Dec. 16, 1985); *Archetypon* (Hannover, Jan. 10, 1986); *Antiphony* for Organ and Orch. (1987). **VOCAL:** *Die Spiele,* song cycle for Baritone and Strings (Strasbourg, May 13, 1958); *Epitaph* for Mezzo-soprano, Viola, and Percussion (Darmstadt, Sept. 8, 1961); *Hommage à Heinrich Schütz* for Solo Voices and Chorus a cappella (1964); *O Primavera,* cantata for Tenor and Strings (Zagreb, May 19, 1965); *Die Wörter,* cantata for Mezzo-soprano and Orch. (Lübeck, May 9, 1966); *Musik für Heinssenbüttel* for Mezzo-soprano, Violin, Cello, and Clarinet (Rome, Feb. 24, 1968); *Gasho* for 4 Choral Groups (Tokyo, April 20, 1974); *Drei irische Volkslieder* (Cork, Ireland, May 10, 1980). **CHAMBER:** *Musika* for Solo Violin (Zagreb, April 4, 1958); *Études contrapuntiques* for Wind Quintet (Paris, Nov. 14, 1959); Oboe Sonata (Darmstadt, July 7, 1960); *Radiant* for Chamber Ensemble (Darmstadt, July 16, 1963); *Entrances* for Wind Quintet (Hanover, N.H., June 10, 1966); *Motion* for String Quartet (Madrid, March 4, 1969); *Varia melodia* for String Quartet (Düsseldorf, Sept. 21, 1972); *Tantana,* improvisations for 10 to 20 Performers (Opatija, Nov. 12, 1975); *Splintery* for String Quartet (Paris, Dec. 5, 1977); *Rontondo I* for Wind Trio (Cologne, April 27, 1977); *Rontondo II* for Harmonica and Wind Trio (Stuttgart, Oct. 3, 1980); piano pieces.

Kelemen, Zoltán, Hungarian bass; b. Budapest, March 12, 1926; d. Zürich, May 9, 1979. He was educated at the Budapest Academy of Music and at the Accademia di Santa Cecilia in Rome; made his debut in Augsburg (1959). After singing in Wuppertal, he joined the Cologne Opera (1961); also appeared at Bayreuth (from 1962) and Salzburg (from 1966). On Nov. 22, 1968, he made his Metropolitan Opera debut in N.Y. as Alberich in *Das Rheingold,* a role he repeated for his debut performance at London's Covent Garden (1970). He was at his best in portentous tragicomic roles; especially memorable were his interpretations of Falstaff and Leporello.

Kéler-Béla (real name, **Adalbert Paul [Albrecht Pál] von Kéler**), noted Hungarian violinist, conductor, and composer; b. Bartfeld, Feb. 13, 1820; d. Wiesbaden, Nov. 20, 1882. He was a law student; then became a farmer; finally took up music in 1845, studying under Sechter and Schlesinger in Vienna, and playing the violin at the Theater-an-der-Wien. He went to Berlin to conduct the Gungl Orch. (1854–55) and to Vienna

to conduct Janner's orch. (1855–56), then was bandmaster of the 10th Austrian Infantry Regiment (1856–63); from 1863 to 1873 he conducted the Wiesbaden Spa Orch. He wrote numerous dances and other light pieces, some of which attained enormous popularity, including the waltz *Hoffnungssterne,* the galop *Hurrah-Sturm,* and particularly the *Lustspiel Ouvertüre.*

BIBL.: Z. Sztehlo, *K. B.* (Budapest, 1930).

Kell, Reginald (Clifford), noted English clarinetist and pedagogue; b. York, June 8, 1906; d. Frankfort, Ky., Aug. 5, 1981. He studied violin at an early age, but later took up the clarinet, and earned a living by playing in silent-movie houses. He received a scholarship to the Royal Academy of Music in London (1929–32), where he studied with Haydn Draper. From 1931 he played in various London orchs., serving as principal clarinet in the London Phil. (1932–36), the London Sym. Orch. (1936–39), and the Philharmonia Orch. (1945–48); also with the Liverpool Phil. (1942–45). He taught at the Royal Academy of Music (1935–39; 1958–59) and at the Aspen Music School (1951–57).

Keller, Gottfried, German harpsichordist, teacher, and composer; place and date of birth unknown; d. London, Nov. 1704. He settled in London at the close of the 17th century as a performer and harpsichord teacher; was known as Godfrey or Godfrido Keller. He publ. *A Compleat Method for Attaining to Play a Thorough Bass upon either Organ, Harpsichord or Theorbo-lute* (London, 1705; 6th ed., 1717; also publ. as an appendix to the 1731 ed. of W. Holder's *A Treatise of the Natural Grounds, and Principles of Harmony).*

WORKS (all publ. in Amsterdam): *6 Sonates a 5* for 2 Recorders, 2 Oboes or 4 Violins, and Basso Continuo (1698; in collaboration with Finger); *8 sonates a trois instruments* for 2 Recorders or Violins, and Basso Continuo and Recorder or Violin, Oboe, and Basso Continuo (1699; 1 not by Keller); *6 Sonatas: 3 for Trumpet, Oboe or Violin, Bass, and Basso Continuo and 3 for 2 Recorders, Oboes or Violins, Bass, and Basso Continuo* (1700); *6 Sonatas for 2 Recorders and Basso Continuo,* op. posthumous (1706).

Keller, Hans (Heinrich), Austrian-born English writer on music; b. Vienna, March 11, 1919; d. London, Nov. 6, 1985. He emigrated to England in 1938 and became a naturalized British subject in 1948; studied violin and viola, and played in orchs. and string quartets; mastered the English language to an extraordinary degree, and soon began pointing out solecisms and other infractions on the purity of the tongue to native journalists; wrote articles on film music, and boldly invaded the sports columns in British newspapers, flaunting his mastery of the lingo. In 1947 he founded (with Donald Mitchell) the periodical *Music Survey* and was its co-ed. (1949–52); joined the music division of the BBC in 1959, retiring in 1979. He originated a system of functional analysis for radio, in which verbal communication was replaced solely by musical examples to demonstrate a composition's structure and thematic development. He publ. several articles expounding the virtues of his ratiocination, among them the fundamental essay "Functional Analysis: Its Pure Application," *Music Review* (1957).

WRITINGS (all publ. in London): *Albert Herring* (1947); *Benjamin Britten: The Rape of Lucretia* (1947); *The Need for Competent Film Music Criticism* (1947); ed. with D. Mitchell, *Benjamin Britten: A Commentary on His Works from a Group of Specialists* (1952); *1975 (1984 minus nine)* (1977); *The Great Haydn Quartets: Their Interpretation* (1986); *Criticism* (1987).

Keller, Hermann, German organist and musicologist; b. Stuttgart, Nov. 20, 1885; d. in an automobile accident, Freiburg im Breisgau, Aug. 17, 1967. He studied with Reger (composition), Straube (organ), and Teichmüller (piano), and musicology at the Univ. of Tübingen (Ph.D., 1924). He held various posts as organist; from 1919, taught at the Stuttgart Hochschule für Musik; was director of its church and school music dept. (from 1928) and then director (1946–52).

WRITINGS: *Reger und die Orgel* (Munich, 1923); *Schule des Klassichen Triospiels* (Kassel, 1928; 4th ed., 1955); *Schule des Generalbass-Spiels* (Kassel, 1931; 4th ed., rev., 1956; Eng. tr., 1965); *Schule der Choralimprovisation* (Leipzig, 1939); *Die Kunst des Orgelspiels* (Leipzig, 1941); *Die Orgelwerke Bachs* (Leipzig, 1948; Eng. tr., 1967); *Die Klavierwerke Bachs* (Leipzig, 1950); *Phrasierung und Artikulation* (Kassel, 1955; Eng. tr., 1965); *Domenico Scarlatti: Ein Meister des Klaviers* (Leipzig, 1957); *Das wohltemperierte Klavier von Johann Sebastian Bach* (Kassel, 1965).

Keller, Homer, American composer; b. Oxnard, Calif., Feb. 17, 1915. He studied at the Eastman School of Music in Rochester, N.Y., with Howard Hanson and Bernard Rogers (B.M., 1937; M.M., 1938), then in Paris, on a Fulbright grant, with Honegger and Boulanger (1950–51). He taught at the Univ. of Michigan (1947–54) and the Univ. of Oregon (1958–77).

WORKS: 3 syms.: No. 1 (N.Y. Nov. 2, 1940); No. 2 (Ann Arbor, Mich., April 1, 1948); No. 3 (Honolulu, Dec. 9, 1950); Concerto for Piano and Orch. (Ojai, Calif., May 29, 1949); *Sonorities* for Orch. (Eugene, Oreg., Feb. 23, 1971); many pieces of chamber music and works for voice.

Keller, Karl, German flutist and composer; b. Dessau, Oct. 16, 1784; d. Schaffhausen, July 19, 1855. He was a court musician in Berlin, Kassel (1806–14), Stuttgart (1814–16), and Donaueschingen (1817–49), where he later was chorus master. He married the singer Wilhelmine Meierhofer. He wrote 3 flute concertos; 4 polonaises, with Orch.; 2 divertissements, with Orch.; 6 part-songs for Male Chorus; duos and solos for flute; songs.

Keller, Matthias, German violinist and composer; b. Ulm, March 20, 1813; d. Boston, Oct. 12, 1875. He studied music in Stuttgart and Vienna, where he was 1st violin in the Royal Chapel (1829–34); then was an army bandmaster. He went to the U.S. in 1846; played in theater orchs. in Philadelphia; became interested in violin making and founded Keller's Patent Steam Violin Manufactory (1857). He then went to N.Y. and won a $500 prize for his *American Hymn* (*Speed our Republic, O Father on high*); composed over 100 songs, including some patriotic songs for the Civil War; also *Ravel Polka* (1846).

Keller, Otto, Austrian writer on music; b. Vienna, June 5, 1861; d. Salzburg, Oct. 25, 1928. He studied music history with Hanslick and theory with Bruckner; publ. biographies of Beethoven (1885), Goldmark (1900), von Suppé (1905), Tchaikovsky (1914), and Mozart (2 vols., 1926–27); also an illustrated history of music (5th ed., 1926) and *Die Operette* (1926); compiled a valuable collection of source material relating to music and the theater.

Keller, Walter, American organist and composer; b. Chicago, Feb. 23, 1873; d. there, July 7, 1940. He studied at the American Cons. of Music in Chicago (1891–94) and at the Leipzig Cons. (1894–96). Returning to America, he occupied various teaching posts; also was a church organist in Chicago from 1903. He wrote a comic opera, *The Crumpled Isle*; a melodrama, *Alaric's Death*; *Synchronous Prelude and Fugue* for Orch. (Chicago, 1924); also a number of works for organ; sacred choruses; songs.

Kellermann, Christian, Danish cellist; b. Randers, Jutland, Jan. 27, 1815; d. Copenhagen, Dec. 3, 1866. He studied with Merk in Vienna; made many concert tours; in 1847, was appointed soloist in the royal orch. at Copenhagen. He publ. solos for cello.

Kelley, Edgar Stillman, American composer and teacher; b. Sparta, Wis., April 14, 1857; d. N.Y., Nov. 12, 1944. He studied with F. Merriam (1870–74), then with Clarence Eddy and N. Ledochowsky in Chicago (1874–76); subsequently took courses at the Stuttgart Cons. with Seifritz (composition), Krüger and Speidel (piano), and Friedrich Finck (organ). Returning to the U.S., he served as an organist in San Francisco; conducted performances of light opera companies in N.Y.; taught piano and theory at various schools and at the N.Y. College of Music (1891–92); was music critic for the *San Francisco Examiner* (1893–95); lecturer on music for the Univ. Extension of N.Y. Univ. (1896–97); then acting prof. at Yale Univ. (1901–2). In 1902 he went to Berlin, where he taught piano and theory; from 1910 to 1934 he was dean of the composition dept. of the Cincinnati Cons. He publ. *Chopin the Composer* (N.Y., 1913) and *Musical Instruments* (Boston, 1925). With his wife, **Jessie Stillman Kelley,** he founded the Kelley Stillman Publishing Co., which brought out several of his scores. Although his stage and symphonic works were quite successful when first performed (some critics described him as a natural successor to MacDowell in American creative work), little of his music survived the test of time.

WORKS: Theme and Variations for String Quartet (c.1880); *Wedding Ode* for Tenor, Men's Chorus, and Orch. (c.1882); incidental music to *Macbeth*, for Orch. and Chorus (San Francisco, Feb. 12, 1885); comic opera, *Puritania* (Boston, June 9, 1892); *Aladdin*, Chinese suite for Orch. (San Francisco, April 1894); incidental music to *Ben Hur*, for Soli, Chorus, and Orch. (N.Y., Oct. 1, 1900); music to Fernald's play *The Cat and the Cherub* (N.Y., June 15, 1901); *Alice in Wonderland*, suite for Orch. (Norfolk [Conn.] Festival, June 5, 1919, composer conducting); 1st Sym., *Gulliver* (Cincinnati, April 9, 1937); 2nd Sym., *New England* (Norfolk Festival, June 3, 1913, composer conducting); *The Pilgrim's Progress*, musical miracle play for Soli, Chorus, Children's Chorus, Organ, and Orch. (Cincinnati May Festival, May 10, 1918); *A California Idyll* for Orch. (N.Y., Nov. 14, 1918); *The Pit and the Pendulum*, symphonic suite, after Poe (1925); *Israfel* and *Eldorado*, for Voice and Orch.; Piano Quintet; 2 piano quartets; many choral works, of which the best known are *My Captain*, after Whitman, and *The Sleeper*, after Poe; 3 pieces for Piano: *The Flower Seekers*; *Confluentia* (also arranged for String Orch., 1913); *The Headless Horseman*; a song, *The Lady Picking Mulberries* (1888); song cycle, *Phases of Love* (1890).

BIBL.: M. King, *E.S. K.: American Composer, Teacher, and Author* (diss., Florida State Univ., 1970).

Kelley, Jessie Stillman, American piano pedagogue; b. Chippewa Falls, Wis., 1866; d. Dallas, April 3, 1949. She studied piano with William Mason and X. Scharwenka, and theory with **Edgar Stillman Kelley** (whom she later married); received an L.H.D. from Western College in Oxford, Ohio, and a Litt.D. from Miami Univ. She taught piano in San Francisco, N.Y., and Berlin; from 1910 to 1934, was director of music at Western College.

Kellie, Lawrence, English tenor and composer; b. London, April 3, 1862; d. there, Aug. 20, 1932. He was apprenticed to a lawyer; began to study music in 1884 at the Royal Academy of Music in London; appeared in a minor operatic role at Covent Garden in 1886; made his American debut in a recital in N.Y. (May 23, 1887). His songs had a great vogue; the most popular were *Is It Too Late?, Sleeping Tide, All for Thee, This Heart of Mine*, and *Douglas Gordon*.

Kellogg, Clara (Louise), noted American soprano and operatic impresario; b. Sumterville, S.C., July 9, 1842; d. New Hartford, Conn., May 13, 1916. She received her vocal training in N.Y. from Manzocchi, Errani, and Muzio; made her professional debut there at the Academy of Music as Gilda in *Rigoletto* (Feb. 27, 1861); then sang in Boston. She sang Marguerite in the N.Y. premiere of *Faust* (Nov. 25, 1863); made her London debut in the same role on Nov. 2, 1867. In 1872 she organized an opera company with Pauline Lucca, but their rivalry precluded its success. In 1873 she launched an opera enterprise of her own, the English Opera Co., for which she herself sang 125 performances (1874–75). In 1887 she married her manager, Karl Strakosch, nephew of Maurice and Max Strakosch, and retired from the stage. She wrote *Memoirs of an American Prima Donna* (N.Y., 1913).

Kelly, Bryan, English composer; b. Oxford, Jan. 30, 1934. He studied with Jacob and Howells at the Royal College of

Music in London (1951–55); then with Nadia Boulanger in Paris. After teaching at the Royal Scottish Academy of Music in Glasgow, he was prof. of composition at his alma mater (1962–84).

WORKS: *Latin Quarter Overture* (1955); *Music for Ballet* for Orch. (1957); *The Tempest Suite* for Strings (1964); *Tenebrae nocturnes* for Tenor, Chorus, and Orch. (1965); *The Shell of Achilles* for Tenor and Orch. (1966); *Cookham Concertino* (1969); *Edinburgh Dances* for Brass Band (1973); *Andalucia* for Brass Band (1976); Guitar Concerto (1978); *Latin Magnificat* for Chorus and Wind Instruments (1979); 2 syms. (1983, 1984); *St. Francis of Assisi*, cantata for Soloists, Chorus, and Orch. (1983); *Suite parisienne* for Brass Quintet (1979); *Umbrian Variations* for 8 Cellos (1984); works for keyboard, including a Piano Sonata (1971) and organ pieces; the children's nativity opera *Herod, Do Your Worst* (1968) and the opera-pantomime *The Spider Monkey Uncle King* (1971).

Kelly, Michael, Irish tenor and composer; b. Dublin, Dec. 25, 1762; d. Margate, Oct. 9, 1826. He studied with Passerini and Rauzzini; sang in Dublin, then continued his studies with Fenarole and Aprile in Naples (1779). He then sang in Palermo, Livorno, Florence, Bologna, and Venice. He was a member of the Vienna Court Opera (1783–87); a friend of Mozart, he created the roles of Don Curzio and Don Basilio in *Le nozze di Figaro* (May 1, 1786). In 1787 he appeared for the 1st time at Drury Lane in London, and sang there until his retirement some 30 years later; also was stage manager at the King's Theatre, Haymarket (1793–1824). He wrote music for 62 stage pieces and many songs; had a music shop (1802–11), and then was active in the wine trade. As to the quality of his compositions and wines, Sheridan quipped that he was "a composer of wines and an importer of music." T. Hook prepared his amusing and valuable autobiography and publ. it as *Reminiscences of Michael Kelly, of the King's Theatre, and Theatre Royal, Drury Lane* (London, 1826; ed. by R. Fiske, London, 1975).

BIBL.: S. Ellis, *The Life of M. K., Musician, Actor and Bon Viveur* (London, 1930).

Kelly, Robert, American composer; b. Clarksburg, W.Va., Sept. 26, 1916. He studied composition with Scalero at the Curtis Inst. of Music in Philadelphia (B.M., 1942) and with Herbert Elwell at the Eastman School of Music in Rochester, N.Y. (M.M., 1952). After service in the U.S. Army, he joined the faculty of the Univ. of Illinois at Urbana (1946–76). His music, while experimental in nature, is skillfully written to utilize traditional forms and structures.

WORKS: STAGE: *Tod's Gal,* folk opera (1950; Norfolk, Va., Jan. 8, 1971); *The White Gods,* opera on the Aztec impression of the conquistadores (Urbana, Ill., July 3, 1966); *Paiyatuma,* ballet (1946). **ORCH.:** 3 syms.: No. 1, *A Miniature Symphony* (Austin, Texas, Oct. 15, 1950); No. 2 (1958; 1st perf. in a CRI recording, 1962); No. 3, *Emancipation Symphony* (Washington, D.C., Feb. 5, 1963); *Adirondack Suite* (Philadelphia, April 9, 1941); *An American Diptych* (Austin, Texas, April 26, 1963); *Colloquy* for Chamber Orch. (Chicago, April 17, 1965); Violin Concerto (Urbana, Ill., Oct. 17, 1968); Viola Concerto (1976; Urbana, Ill., Feb. 5, 1978); *The Celestial Trumpet,* "trinity" for Trumpet, Symphonic Brass Ensemble, and Percussion (1982); *Rural Songs* for Soprano and Orch. (1980; Urbana, Ill., Nov. 9, 1984). **CHAMBER:** 4 string quartets (1944, 1952, 1963, 1982); Viola Sonata (1950); Violin Sonata (1952); Sonata for Trombone and Piano (1952); Sonata for Oboe and Harp (1955); Quintet for Clarinet and Strings (1956); Cello Sonata (1958); *Triptych* for Cello and Piano (1962); *Fantasia* for Harp, Alto Flute, Oboe, and String Quartet (1984); band music; choruses; songs.

Kelterborn, Rudolf, prominent Swiss composer and pedagogue; b. Basel, Sept. 3, 1931. He studied at the Basel Academy of Music with Gustav Güldenstein and Walther Geiser (composition) and Alexander Krannhals (conducting); subsequently took lessons in conducting with Markevitch and in composition with Burkhard in Zürich (1952), Blacher in Salzburg (1953),

and Fortner and Bialas at the North-West German Music Academy in Detmold (1955). He taught at the Basel Academy of Music (1955–60) and at the North-West German Music Academy (1960–68); then was on the faculty of the Zürich Cons. and Musikhochschule (1968–75; 1980–83). He was ed. in chief of the *Schweizerische Musikzeitung* (1969–75); subsequently was a prof. at the Staatlichen Hochschule für Musik in Karlsruhe (1980–83) and director of the Basel Academy of Music from 1983. Kelterborn appeared as a guest conductor in performances of his own works; he also lectured in the U.S., England, and Japan. He was awarded the composer's prize of the Assoc. of Swiss Musicians and the Kunstpreis of the City of Basel in 1984. He publ. *Zum Beispiel Mozart: Ein Beitrag zur musikalischen Analyse* (Basel, 1980; Japanese tr., Tokyo, 1986). In his music, he applies a precisely coordinated serial organization wherein quantitative values of duration form a recurrent series; changes of tempo are also subjected to serialization. Both melody and harmony are derived from a tone row in which the dissonant intervals of the major seventh and minor second are the mainstays.

WORKS: OPERAS: *Die Errettung Thebens* (Zürich, June 23, 1963); *Kaiser Jovian* (1964–66; Karlsruhe, March 4, 1967); *Ein Engel kommt nach Babylon* (1975–76; Zürich, June 5, 1977); *Der Kirschgarten,* after Chekhov (1979–81; Zürich, Dec. 4, 1984); *Ophelia* (1982–83; Schwetzingen, May 2, 1984); *Die schwarze Spinne,* musical drama (1984). **BALLET:** *Relations* (Bern, Feb. 16, 1975). **ORCH.:** Suite for Woodwinds, Percussion, and Strings (1954); Sonata for 16 Solo Strings (1955); *Canto appassionato* (1959); *Metamorphosen* (1960); Cello Concerto (1962); *Phantasmen* (1966); Sym. No. 1 (Vienna, April 26, 1968); Sym. No. 2 (1969); *Musik* for Piano and 8 Wind Instruments (1970); *Traummusik* for Small Orch. (1971); *Kommunikationen* for 6 Instrumental Groups (1972); *Changements* (1973); *Tableaux en cadrés* (1974); Sym. No. 3, *Espansioni,* for Baritone, Orch., and Tape (1974–75; Basel, Sept. 29, 1976); *Gesänge zur Nacht* for Soprano and Small Orch. (1978); *Erinnerungen an Orpheus* (1978–79); *Chiaroscuro,* canzoni (Salzburg, Aug. 29, 1980); *Musica luminosa* (1983–84); Sym. No. 4 (Bamberg, Feb. 3, 1987). **CHAMBER:** 4 string quartets (1954, 1956, 1962, 1970); *5 Fantasien* for Wind Quintet (1958); *Meditationen* for 6 Wind Instruments (1962); *Kammersonate* for Flute, Oboe, String Trio, and Harpsichord (1963); *Fantasia a tre* for Piano, Violin, and Cello (1967); *Consort Music* for Singer and 7 Instruments (1976); *Visions sonores* for 6 Percussion Groups and 6 Instruments (1979); *Szene* for 12 Solo Cellos (Lucerne, Aug. 30, 1980); *Musik* for 6 Percussion (1983–84); Sonata for Cello and Piano (1984–85); Sonatas for Winds (1986). **VOCAL:** *Cantata profana* (1960); *Musica spei* for Soprano, Chorus, and Orch. (1968); *3 Fragmente* for Chorus and Orch. (1968); *Dies unus* for Voices and Orch. (1971); *3 Fragmente* for Chorus a cappella (1973); *5 Gesänge* for Chorus (1980–81); *Schlag an mit deiner Sichel: Madrigale zu einem imaginären Totentanz* for 4 Voices and Renaissance Instruments (1981–82).

BIBL.: D. Larese and F. Goebels, *R. K.* (Amriswiler, 1970); M. Weber, *Die Orchesterwerke R. K.s* (Regensburg, 1980); K. von Fischer, "R. K.," *Dissonanz,* no. 4 (1985).

Kemble, Adelaide, English soprano; b. London, 1814; d. Warsash House, Hampshire, Aug. 4, 1879. She first sang in concerts; then studied with Pasta in Italy; made her operatic debut as Norma in 1839 in Venice. In 1841 she appeared at Covent Garden in London. She retired from the stage following her marriage in 1843. Her life is recounted in *Record of a Girlhood* (London, 1878), written by her sister, the actress Fanny Kemble.

Kemp, Barbara, German soprano; b. Kochem an der Mosel, Dec. 12, 1881; d. Berlin, April 17, 1959. She studied at the Strasbourg Cons. (1902–5); in 1903 she made her operatic debut as the Priestess in *Aida* in Strasbourg. She then sang in Rostock (1906–8) and Breslau (1908–13) before being engaged as a member of the Berlin Royal (later State) Opera (1913–31); made her 1st appearance at the Bayreuth Festival as Senta (1914), and returned there as Kundry (1924–27). She made her Metropolitan Opera debut in N.Y. as Mona Fiordalisa and the Wife in **Max von Schilling**'s *Mona Lisa* (March 1, 1923), and married the composer that same year; sang there until 1924, and then continued her career in Europe. She later taught voice in Berlin.

Bibl.: O. Bie, *B. K.* (Berlin, 1921).

Kemp, "Father" (Robert J.), American showman; b. Wellfleet, Mass., June 6, 1820; d. Boston, May 14, 1897. He was a shoe merchant but loved music; as a leading proponent of the old-folks concerts revival (an attempt to restore the music and performance practices of the 18th-century New England singing schools), he organized the Old Folks Concert Troupe in Boston (1855), which gave regular concerts in N.Y., Philadelphia, and Washington, D.C., as well as in Boston (until 1866); also took it on a tour of the West (1858–59) and of England (1861). He publ. a collection of New England psalmody, with some popular songs and patriotic numbers, as *Father Kemp's Old Folks' Concert Tunes* (Boston, 1860); also wrote *Father Kemp and His Old Folks* (1868).

Bibl.: J. Steinberg, "Old Folks Concerts and the Revival of New England Psalmody," *Musical Quarterly*, LIX (1973).

Kemp, Joseph, English organist, teacher, and composer; b. Exeter, 1778; d. London, May 22, 1824. He studied organ with William Jackson at Exeter Cathedral; was organist of Bristol Cathedral (1802–7); then taught in London, and later in Exeter (1814–18; from 1821). As one of the earliest promoters of music instruction by classes, he publ. *The New System of Musical Education, Being a Self-instructor and Serviceable Companion to Music Masters* (London, c.1810–19). He composed *The Jubilee*, an entertainment (Haymarket, London, Oct. 25, 1809); *The Siege of Isca, or The Battles of the West*, a melodrama (London, May 10, 1810); *Musical Illustrations of The Lady of the Lake* (c.1810); *Musical Illustrations of the Beauties of Shakespeare* (c.1820); Psalms; anthems; songs; etc.

Kempe, Rudolf, eminent German conductor; b. Niederpoyritz, near Dresden, June 14, 1910; d. Zürich, May 11, 1976. He studied oboe at the Orchestral School of the Dresden Staatskapelle; in 1929, became 1st oboist of the Gewandhaus Orch. in Leipzig. He made his conducting debut at the Leipzig Opera in 1936. He served in the German army during World War II; then conducted in Chemnitz; was director of the Opera there (1945–48) and at the Weimar National Theater (1948–49). From 1949 to 1953 he was Generalmusikdirektor of the Dresden Staatskapelle; then served in an identical capacity with the Bavarian State Opera in Munich (1952–54); also made appearances in opera in Vienna, in London (Covent Garden), and at the Metropolitan in N.Y. In 1960 Sir Thomas Beecham named him associate conductor of the Royal Phil. Orch. of London; upon Beecham's death in 1961, he became its principal conductor; from 1963 till 1975, was artistic director as well. He was chief conductor of the Tonhalle Orch. in Zürich (1965–72) and of the Munich Phil. (from 1967); from 1975 he conducted the BBC Sym. Orch. He was a distinguished interpreter of Beethoven, Brahms, Wagner, Bruckner, and Richard Strauss; also conducted light opera.

Bibl.: C. Kempe-Oettinger, *R. K.: Pictures of a Life* (Munich, 1977; in Eng., London, 1979); a Kempe memorial issue was publ. in *Le Grand Baton* (March/June 1978).

Kempen, Paul van, prominent Dutch conductor; b. Zoeterwoude, near Leiden, May 16, 1893; d. Hilversum, Dec. 8, 1955. He studied violin in Amsterdam, then became concertmaster of the Concertgebouw Orch. when he was 17. In 1916 he went to Germany and served as concertmaster with several orchs. before embarking upon a conducting career, becoming music director in Oberhausen in 1932. From 1934 to 1942 he was chief conductor of the Dresden Phil.; although he was obliged to conduct concerts for the German army, he refused to join the Nazi party. After serving as Generalmusikdirektor in Aachen (1942–43), he returned to the Netherlands. Following World War II, he made guest conducting appearances

with the Rotterdam Phil. and the Residentie Orch. in The Hague; was chief conductor of the Radio Phil. in Hilversum (from 1949) and also taught conducting there and at the Accademia Chigiana in Siena. He proved himself a discriminating interpreter of the Austro-German repertoire.

Bibl.: N. Steffen, "P. v.K. in the Netherlands," *Le Grand Baton* (Sept./Dec. 1979).

Kempff, Wilhelm (Walter Friedrich), distinguished German pianist; b. Juterbog, Nov. 25, 1895; d. Positano, Italy, May 23, 1991. He studied piano with his father, also named Wilhelm Kempff; at the age of 9 he entered the Berlin Hochschule für Musik, where he studied composition with Robert Kahn and piano with Heinrich Barth; also attended the Univ. of Berlin. He began his concert career in 1916; in 1918 he made the 1st of many appearances with the Berlin Phil.; from that time he toured throughout Europe, South America, and Japan, featuring improvisation as part of his programs. From 1924 to 1929 he was director of the Stuttgart Hochschule für Musik; from 1957 he gave annual courses in Positano, Italy. He made his London debut in 1951 and his American debut in N.Y. in 1964. He continued to appear in concerts well past his octogenarian milestone; in 1979 he was a soloist with the Berlin Phil., after having had an association with it for more than 60 years. Kempff epitomized the classic tradition of German pianism; he eschewed flamboyance in his performances of Mozart, Beethoven, Schubert, and other masters. He publ. a book of memoirs, *Unter dem Zimbelstern* (Stuttgart, 1951).

Keneman, Feodor, Russian pianist and composer of German descent; b. Moscow, April 20, 1873; d. there, March 29, 1937. He studied with Safonov (piano; graduated, 1895) and Ippolitov-Ivanov (composition; graduated, 1897) at the Moscow Cons.; also with Taneyev (counterpoint) there. From 1899 to 1932 he taught music theory at the Moscow Cons. He gave recitals and was the favorite accompanist of Chaliapin, for whom he composed the popular Russian ballad *As the King Went to War* and arranged the folk song *Ei ukhnem!* He toured the U.S. with Chaliapin (1923–24). He also composed military marches and band pieces.

Kenessey, Jenö, Hungarian conductor and composer; b. Budapest, Sept. 23, 1905; d. there, Aug. 19, 1976. He studied with Lajtha and Siklós in Budapest and attended Franz Shalk's conducting course in Salzburg; was a conductor at the Budapest Opera (1932–65), where he conducted his opera *Arany meg az asszony* (Gold and the Woman; 1942; May 8, 1943) and his ballet *May Festival* (Nov. 29, 1948). His other works include the ballets *Montmartre* (1930), *Johnny in Boots* (1935), *Mine Is the Bridegroom* (1938), *Perhaps Tomorrow* (1938), *Miraggio* (1938), *The Kerchief* (1951), and *Bihari's Song* (1954); he also composed *Dance Impressions* for Orch. (1933); Divertimento for Orch. (1945); *Dances from Sárköz* for Orch. (1953); *Beams of Light*, cantata (1960); *Canzonetta* for Flute and Chamber Orch. (1970); *Dawn at Balaton*, symphonic poem, with Narrator and Female Voices (1972); Piano Quartet (1928–29); Sonata for Harp and Flute (1940); Sonata for Harp, Flute, and Viola (1940); Divertimento for Viola and Harp (1963); Trio for Violin, Viola, and Harp (1972); *Elegy and Scherzo* for Piano (1973); songs and choruses.

Kenins, Talivaldis, Latvian-born Canadian composer; b. Liepaja, April 23, 1919. He studied composition with Wihtol at the Riga State Cons., leaving his native land with the Soviet occupation during World War II. After the war, he studied with Aubin, Plé-Caussade, and Messiaen at the Paris Cons. (1945–50), winning a premier prix in composition. In 1951 he emigrated to Canada; settled in Toronto, where he served as music director of St. Andrew's Lutheran Church; from 1952 to 1984 he also taught at the Univ. of Toronto; in 1956, received Canadian citizenship. In his music, he maintains a rigorous formality of Classical design; his thematic material draws on folk-song resources of his native Latvia and the pentatonic Indian melos of his adoptive country; he also applies cosmopolitan modern techniques.

WORKS: Piano Concerto (1946); Duo for Piano and Orch. (1951); *Scherzo concertante* for Orch. (1953); 8 syms.: No. 1 for Chamber Orch. (1959); No. 2, *Sinfonia concertante,* for Flute, Oboe, Clarinet, and Orch. (1967); No. 3 (1970); No. 4 for Chamber Orch. (1972); No. 5 (1975); No. 6, *Sinfonia ad fugam* (1978); No. 7 (1980); No. 8, *Sinfonia concertata,* for Organ and Orch. (1986); *Nocturne and Dance* for String Orch. (1963); *Folk Dance, Variations and Fugue* for School Orch. (1964); Concerto for Violin, Cello, and String Orch. (1964); *Fantaisies concertantes* for Piano and Orch. (1971; Toronto, June 20, 1973); Violin Concerto (1974); *Naačnaača* (Trance), symphonic poem (1975); Sinfonietta (1976); *Beatae voces tenebrae* for Orch. (1977); *Concerto da camera* No. 1 for Piano, Flute, Clarinet, and Strings (1981); Concerto for 14 Instruments (1982); *Concerto da camera* No. 2 for Flute and Ensemble (1983); Concerto for 5 Percussionists and Orch. (1983); *Partita* for Strings on Lutheran Chorales (1983); Concerto for Flute, Guitar, Strings, and Percussion (1985); *Folk Dance and Fugue* No. 2 for Orch. (1986); *To a Soldier,* cantata for 2 Soloists, Chorus, and Organ (1953); *Daniel,* biblical scene after the 2nd Book of Daniel, for 2 Soloists, Chorus, and Organ (1956); *Lyrical Suite* for 2 Soloists, Chorus, and Organ (1962); *Gloria* (*Chants of Glory and Mercy*) for 4 Soloists, Chorus, and Orch. (Guelph, May 3, 1970); *Lagalai: Legend of the Stone,* chamber drama for Chorus, Flute, Horn, and Percussion (1970); *Sawan-Oong (The Spirit of the Winds)* for Narrator, Bass, Chorus, and Small Orch. (1973); *Baltica,* cantata for Bass or Alto, Chorus, 2 Trumpets, Timpani, and Organ (1974); a cappella choruses; String Quartet (1948); *Prelude and Scherzo* for Flute, Clarinet, and Bassoon (1947); Septet (1949); Cello Sonata (1950); Piano Trio (1952); Violin Sonata (1955); *Suite concertante* for Cello and Piano (1955); Concertino for 2 Pianos (1956); *Diversions on a Gypsy Song* for Cello and Piano (1958); Piano Quartet (1958); Divertimento for Clarinet and Piano (1960); *Little Suite* for String Quartet (1966); *Concertante* for Flute and Piano (1966); *Fantasy-Variations* for Flute and Viola (1967); *Concertino à cinque* for Flute, Oboe, Viola, Cello, and Piano (1968); 2 *Dialogues* for Cello and Piano (1968); *Partita brève* for Viola and Piano (1971); Serenade for Oboe and Cello (1973); *Concerto-Fantasy* for Organ and Percussion (1976); Violin Sonata No. 2 (1979); Piano Quartet No. 2 (1979); Quintet for Piano and Winds (1983); *Variations on a Theme by Schubert* for Woodwind Quintet (1984); *Concertino barocco* for 2 Violins (1985); keyboard pieces.

Kennan, Kent Wheeler, American composer and teacher; b. Milwaukee, April 18, 1913. He studied composition with Hunter Johnson at the Univ. of Michigan (1930–32); then with Hanson and Rogers at the Eastman School of Music in Rochester, N.Y. (M.B., 1934; M.M., 1936); won the American Prix de Rome, and took some lessons with Pizzetti in Rome. Returning to the U.S., he taught at Kent State Univ. (1939–40) and at the Univ. of Texas in Austin (1940–42); during World War II, served as bandleader in the U.S. Army (1942–45), then taught again at the Univ. of Texas (1945–46) and at Ohio State Univ. (1947–49). In 1949 he joined the staff of the Univ. of Texas on a permanent basis, retiring in 1983. He publ. *The Technique of Orchestration* (N.Y., 1952; rev. ed., 1970); *Counterpoint Based on 18th-Century Practice* (N.Y., 1959; 3rd ed., 1987); 2 workbooks on orchestration (1952, 1969); a counterpoint workbook (1959; 3rd ed., 1987). His music was so conducive to listening pleasure that Toscanini chose one of Kennan's innocent little symphonic pieces, *Night Soliloquy* for Flute and Orch., to conduct with the NBC Sym. Orch. (N.Y., Feb. 26, 1943), a rare distinction for an American composer. Kennan's other works are *Il campo dei fiori* for Trumpet and Orch. (1937); Nocturne for Viola and Orch. (1937); *Promenade* for Orch. (1938); Sym. (1938); *Blessed Are They That Mourn* for Chorus and Orch. (1939); *Andante* for Oboe and Orch. (Philadelphia, March 7, 1947); Trumpet Sonata (1956).

Kennedy-Fraser, Marjorie (née **Kennedy**), Scottish singer, pianist, and folk-song collector; b. Perth, Oct. 1, 1857; d. Edin-

burgh, Nov. 22, 1930. She was the daughter of the Scottish singer David Kennedy (1825–86), with whom she traveled as his accompanist from the age of 12. She then studied voice with Mathilde Marchesi in Milan and Paris; also took courses in piano with Matthay and in music history with Niecks. Inspired by the example of her father, she became a dedicated collector of folk songs. In 1905 she went to the Outer Hebrides, after which she made a specialty of research in Celtic music. She publ. the eds. *Songs of the Hebrides* (with K. Macleod; 3 vols., London, 1909, 1917, 1921); *From the Hebrides* (Glasgow and London, 1925); *More Songs of the Hebrides* (London and N.Y., 1929); also the handbook *Hebridean Song and the Laws of Interpretation* (Glasgow, 1922). She wrote the libretto and sang the title role in Bantock's opera *The Seal Woman* (1924). She publ. the autobiography *A Life of Song* (London, 1928).

Kennedy, (George) Michael (Sinclair), esteemed English writer on music; b. Manchester, Feb. 19, 1926. He was educated at the Berkhamstead School, then in 1941 joined the staff of the London *Daily Telegraph,* where he was its northern music critic (1950–60) and its northern ed. (1960–86). In 1981 he was made an Officer of the Order of the British Empire. **WRITINGS:** *The Halle Tradition: A Century of Music* (Manchester, 1960); *The Works of Ralph Vaughan Williams* (London, 1964; rev. 1980); *Portrait of Elgar* (London, 1968; rev. 1982; 3rd ed., 1987); *Elgar: Orchestral Music* (London, 1969); *Portrait of Manchester* (Manchester, 1970); *A History of the Royal Manchester College of Music* (Manchester, 1971); *Barbirolli: Conductor Laureate* (London, 1971); *Mahler* (London, 1974); ed. *The Autobiography of Charles Hallé, with Correspondence and Diaries* (London, 1976); *Richard Strauss* (London, 1976; rev. 1983); ed. *The Concise Oxford Dictionary of Music* (London, 3rd ed., rev., 1980; rev. and augmented as *The Oxford Dictionary of Music,* 1985); *Adrian Boult* (London, 1987); *Portrait of Walton* (London, 1989).

Kennedy, Nigel (Paul), versatile English violinist; b. Brighton, Dec. 28, 1956. He was born into a family of cellists; in 1972 he became a student of Dorothy DeLay at the Juilliard School in N.Y. In 1977 he made his London debut as soloist with the Philharmonia Orch., and subsequently performed throughout his homeland and on the Continent; in 1985 he made his 1st tour of the U.S. His interests range over the field of serious, jazz, rock, and pop music; he has been closely associated with jazz notable Stéphane Grappelli and has led his own rock group.

Kenny, Yvonne, Australian soprano; b. Sydney, Nov. 25, 1950. She studied at the New South Wales State Conservatorium in Sydney and at the opera school at La Scala in Milan (1973–74); made her debut in London as Donizetti's Rosamunda d'Inghilterra in a concert perf. in 1975; her Covent Garden debut followed there in 1976, when she sang in the premiere of Henze's *We Come to the River.* She was a member of the Victoria State Opera (from 1978). In 1989 she was made a Member of the Order of Australia. Among her admired roles are Pamina, Gilda, Ilia, Micaela, and Sophie.

Kent, James, English organist and composer; b. Winchester, March 13, 1700; d. there, May 6, 1776. He was a chorister at Winchester Cathedral and in the Chapel Royal; was organist of Trinity College, Cambridge (1731–37), then of Winchester Cathedral and College (1738–74). He publ. *Twelve Anthems* (1773); J. Corfe ed. *A Morning and Evening Service with Eight Anthems* (c.1777).

Kentner, Louis (actually, **Lajos Philip**), admired Hungarian-born English pianist; b. Karwin, July 19, 1905; d. London, Sept. 22, 1987. He studied piano with Arnold Székely and Leo Weiner and composition with Koessler and Kodály at the Royal Academy of Music in Budapest; made his formal debut in Budapest in 1920, then toured throughout Europe. In 1935 he settled in England, becoming a naturalized British citizen in 1946. On Nov. 28, 1956, he made his U.S. debut in N.Y. In 1978 he was made a Commander of the Order of the British Empire. In 1931 he married the pianist **Ilona Kabós;** they divorced in 1945. He was praised for his interpretations of works by Mozart, Beethoven, Schubert, Chopin, and Liszt, as well as those by Bartók and various contemporary English composers.

BIBL.: H. Taylor, ed., *K.: A Symposium* (N.Y., 1987).

Kenton (real name, **Kornstein**), **Egon,** Hungarian violinist, musicologist, and music librarian; b. Nagyszalonta, May 22, 1891; d. Paris, Dec. 3, 1987. He studied violin with Hubay at the Budapest Royal Academy of Music, graduating in 1911; was violist in the Hungarian String Quartet (1911–23); then emigrated to the U.S.; in 1947, received his M.A. in musicology from N.Y. Univ.; subsequently taught musicology at the Univ. of Conn. in Storrs (1950–61); from 1961 to 1971, served as librarian of the Mannes College of Music in N.Y. He wrote the 1st English-language study of the life and music of Giovanni Gabrieli (Rome, 1967).

Kenton, Stan(ley Newcomb), American jazz bandleader; b. Wichita, Kans., Dec. 15, 1911; d. Los Angeles, Aug. 25, 1979. He spent his youth in California; earned a living playing piano in local saloons and speakeasies and at the same time began experimenting with new sounds in jazz. He founded the 1st of many big ensembles of his own when he organized the Artistry in Rhythm Orch. (1941). His appearance at N.Y.'s Carnegie Hall with his Progressive Jazz orch. (1949) gave the name to that genre; after touring the country with his Innovations in Modern Music Orch. (1950–51), he led various big bands. He made many recordings, garnering Grammy awards with his albums *West Side Story* and *Adventures in Jazz* (both 1961). From 1959 he devoted much time to music education, founding jazz clinics at many institutions of higher learning. He kept discovering modernistic devices, such as already obsolescent progressions of whole-tone scales and consecutive major ninth-chords. He was ecstatic when he stumbled upon the Schillinger System of Composition, which professed to impart the power of creativity to untutored musicians. Although commercially successful, Kenton suffered mandatory nervous breakdowns, and at one time decided to abandon music and become a psychiatrist; he gave up the idea when he realized that he would have to learn Greek-derived words and unpronounceable German terms. He married frequently; one of his sons was indicted for conspiracy to commit murder (he put a snake in the mailbox of a bothersome attorney). He founded his own publishing and recording companies in 1970. A flamboyant and controversial musician, Kenton remained an influential figure in music until his death.

BIBL.: H. Dietzel and H. Lange, *S. K.* (Berlin, 1959); D. Schulz-Köhn, *S. K.* (Wetzlar, Germany, 1961); W. Lee, *S. K.: Artistry in Rhythm* (Los Angeles, 1980); L. Arganian, *S. K.: The Man and His Music* (East Lansing, Mich., 1989).

Kepler, Johannes, illustrious German astronomer; b. Weil der Stadt, Württemberg, Dec. 27, 1571; d. Regensburg, Nov. 15, 1630. He explored Pythagorean concepts of harmony and relationships among music, mathematics, and physics in books 3 and 5 of his *Harmonices mundi* (Linz, 1619).

BIBL.: D. Walker, "K.'s Celestial Music," *Journal of the Warburg and Courtauld Institutes,* XXX (1967); R. Haase, "K.s harmonikale Denkweise," *Musikerziehung* (Nov. 1969); idem, "J. K.s wahre Bedeutung," *Kunstjahrbuch der Stadt Linz 1970* (1971); R. Hannas, "J. K.'s Excursion into Political Proportions," *Diapason* (April 1972); M. Dickreiter, *Der Musiktheoretiker J. K.* (Bern and Munich, 1973).

Keppard, Freddie, black American jazz cornetist; b. New Orleans, Feb. 15, 1889; d. Chicago, July 15, 1933. He learned to play the mandolin, violin, and accordion before mastering the cornet; organized his own group, The Olympia Orch. (1906); later became co-leader of The Original Creole Orch. (1912), playing with it in Los Angeles, Chicago, and N.Y.; after moving to Chicago, he played with King Oliver, Jimmie Noone, and others. Although forgotten in the last years of his life, he was one of the pioneer jazz figures; he had few equals as a cornetist in his time.

Kerle, Jacobus de, eminent South Netherlandish organist and composer; b. Ypres, 1531 or 1532; d. Prague, Jan. 7, 1591. He is believed to have received his education at the monastery of St. Martin in Ypres; in 1555 was made magister capellae in Orvieto, where he most likely was active as a singer and master of the choristers; soon thereafter he became cathedral organist and town carillonist. After taking Holy Orders, he went to Venice in 1561 to prepare the publication of his *Liber psalmorum ad Vesperas.* The Bishop of Augsburg commissioned him to write his *Preces speciales pro salubri generalis Concilii successu* (1561–62) for the Council of Trent. He subsequently went to Rome in 1562 as director of the cardinal's private chapel; accompanied the cardinal on his travels throughout northern Italy to Barcelona and back (1563–64); then was in Dillingen until the cardinal disbanded his chapel in 1565. He became director of music at Ypres Cathedral in 1565, but lost that post in 1567 and was excommunicated following legal proceedings and a dispute with the cathedral chapter. He then went to Rome, where Cardinal Otto made him a member of the chapter of Augsburg Cathedral in 1568; that same year he was made vicar-choral and organist as well; he subsequently held a prebend in Cambrai (1575–87), and was made a member of the chapter of the Cathedral there (1579), but soon left owing to war. He served as Kapellmeister to Gebhard Truchess, the Archbishop and Elector of Cologne and Lord High Steward of Waldburg, in 1582; in Sept. 1582 he entered the Emperor's service in Augsburg, and in Oct. 1582 he became a member of the court chapel in Vienna. He settled in Prague in 1583; was made honorary precentor of the Mons choir in 1587, and was also canon of the collegiate foundation of the Heilige Kreuz in Breslau (1587–88). He was one of the last significant composers of the South Netherlandish tradition, excelling in sacred vocal music.

WORKS: SACRED VOCAL: *Motetti* for 4 and 5 Voices (Rome, 1557); [23] *Hymni totius anni . . . et Magnificat* for 4 and 5 Voices (Rome, 1558; 2nd ed., 1560); [16] *Magnificat octo tonorum* for 4 Voices (Venice, 1561); *Liber* [20] *Psalmorum ad Vesperas* for 4 Voices (Venice, 1561); 6 *missae* for 4 and 5 Voices (Venice, 1562); *Preces speciales pro salubri generalis Concilii successu* for 4 Voices (Venice, 1562; ed. in Denkmäler der Tonkunst in Bayern, XXXIV, Jg. XVI, 1926; 2nd ed., rev., 1974); [15] *Selectae quaedam cantiones* for 5 and 6 Voices (Nuremberg, 1571); *Liber modulorum* for 4 to 6 Voices (Paris, 1572); *Liber* [11] *modulorum sacrorum* for 5 and 6 Voices, *quibus addita est recens cantio de sacro foedere contra Turcas* for 8 Voices (Munich, 1572); *Liber* [16] *modulorum sacrorum* for 4 to 6 Voices (Munich, 1573); *Liber* [16] *mottetorum* for 4 and 5 Voices, *adiuncto in fine Te Deum laudamus* for 6 Voices (Munich, 1573); [9] *Sacrae cantiones, quas vulgo moteta vocant . . . ecclesiastici hymni de resurrectione et ascensione* for 5 and 6 Voices (Munich, 1575); 4 *missae* for 4 and 5 Voices (Antwerp, 1582); 4 *missae . . . adiuncto in fine Te Deum laudamus* for 4 and 5 Voices (Antwerp, 1583); [9] *Selectiorum aliquot modulorum* for 4, 5, and 8 Voices (Prague, 1585). SECULAR VOCAL: *Il primo libro capitolo del triumpho d'amore di Petrarca* for 5 Voices (Venice, 1570); *Madrigali, libro primo* (*Carmina italica musicis modulis ornata*) for 4 Voices (Venice, 1570); *Egregia cantio, in . . . honorem Melchioris Lincken Augustani* for 6 Voices (Nuremberg, 1574).

BIBL.: O. Ursprung, *J. d.K.* (1531/32–1591): *Sein Leben und seine Werke* (Munich, 1913); G. Haydon, "The Hymns of J. d.K." in J. LaRue, ed., *Aspects of Medieval and Renaissance Music: A Birthday Offering to Gustave Reese* (N.Y., 1966; 2nd ed., 1978).

Kerll (also **Kerl, Kherl, Cherl, Gherl,** etc.), **Johann Kaspar,** renowned German organist and composer; b. Adorf, Saxony, April 9, 1627; d. Munich, Feb. 13, 1693. He most likely began his musical studies with his father, Kaspar Kerll, an organist, before being called to Vienna by Archduke Leopold Wilhelm to serve as a youthful court organist; he concurrently studied with the imperial court Kapellmeister, Giovanni Valentini. The archduke then sent him to Rome to complete his studies with

Carissimi; he may have also studied with Frescobaldi. By 1650 he was in Brussels, where he was court organist to Archduke Leopold Wilhelm, who was serving as viceroy of the Spanish Netherlands. The Bavarian Elector Ferdinand Maria made him Vice-Kapellmeister of the Munich court on Feb. 27, 1656; he was promoted to Kapellmeister on Sept. 22, 1656. He wrote his 1st opera, *L'Oronte*, for the inauguration of Munich's opera house (Jan. 1657). For the coronation of Emperor Leopold I in Frankfurt am Main (July 22, 1658), he wrote a Mass and improvised on the organ with great success. He was ennobled in 1664. Although he was held in the highest regard at court, he found the Italian domination of the musical establishment not to his liking. He resigned his position in 1673 and went to Vienna, where he served as organist of St. Stephen's Cathedral (1674–77); he then (March 16, 1677) was appointed imperial court organist, a position he held until his death. He particularly distinguished himself as a composer of sacred music, and also wrote some fine keyboard pieces.

WORKS: 18 extant masses, several of which were publ. in *Missae sex, cum instrumentis concertantibus, e vocibus in ripieno, adjuncta una pro defunctis cum seq. Dies irae* for 4 to 6 Voices, Strings, Bassoon, and Basso Continuo (Munich, 1689); *Delectus* [26] *sacrarum cantionum* for 2 to 5 Voices, 2 Violins, and Basso Continuo, op. 1 (Munich, 1669); 16 Latin sacred works for 1, 3 to 6, 8, and 9 Voices, 3 Trombones, Strings, and Basso Continuo; 3 German sacred works for Voice, 2 Violins, and Basso Continuo; etc. His instrumental works include *Modulatio organica super Magnificat octo ecclesiasticis tonis respondens* for Keyboard (Munich, 1686; ed. by R. Walter, Altötting, 1956); 8 toccatas; 6 canzonas; many other keyboard pieces in MS; also a ricercata *a 4* in A. Kircher, *Musurgia universalis* (Rome, 1650). Many other works are lost, including 11 operas. For a selected edition of his works, see A. Sandberger, ed., Denkmäler der Tonkunst in Bayern, III, Jg. II/2 (1901).

BIBL.: H. Botstiber, "Ein Beitrag zu K.'s Biographie," *Sammelbände der Internationalen Musik-Gesellschaft,* VII (1905–6); A. Sandberger, "J.K. K.," *Ausgewählte Aufsätze zur Musikgeschichte,* I (Munich, 1921); A. Giebler, *The Masses of J.C. K.* (diss., Univ. of Michigan, 1956); R. Schall, *Quellen zu J.K. K.* (Vienna, 1962).

Kerman, Joseph (Wilfred), eminent American musicologist; b. London (of American parents), April 3, 1924. He studied at Univ. College School, London, then at N.Y. Univ. (A.B., 1943), subsequently taking courses with Strunk, Thompson, and Weinrich at Princeton Univ. (Ph.D., 1950, with the diss. *The Elizabethan Madrigal: A Comparative Study;* publ. in N.Y., 1962); also taught at Westminster Choir College in Princeton (1949–51). In 1951 he joined the faculty at the Univ. of Calif. at Berkeley, where he subsequently was chairman of its music dept. (1960–63). After serving as Heather Prof. of Music at Oxford Univ. (1971–74), he resumed his professorship at Berkeley. In 1977 he became a founding ed. of the journal *19th Century Music.* His various honors included his being made an Honorary Fellow of the Royal Academy of Music in London (1972) and a Fellow of the American Academy of Arts and Sciences (1973). An erudite scholar and provocative critic, he holds an influential position among American musicologists of his generation.

WRITINGS: *Opera as Drama* (N.Y., 1956; rev. 1988); *The Beethoven Quartets* (N.Y. and London, 1967); with H. Janson, *History of Art & Music* (N.Y. and Englewood Cliffs, N.J., 1968); ed. *L. van Beethoven: Autograph Miscellany* ("Kafka Sketchbook") (London, 1970); ed. *W.A. Mozart: Concerto in C, K. 503* (N.Y., 1970; Norton Critical Score); with V. Kerman, *Listen* (N.Y., 1972); *The Music of William Byrd:* Vol. I, *The Masses and Motets of William Byrd* (London, 1981); *Contemplating Music* (Cambridge, Mass., 1985; publ. in England as *Musicology,* London, 1985).

Kern, Adele, German soprano; b. Munich, Nov. 25, 1901; d. there, May 6, 1980. She studied in Munich, making her debut as Olympia in *Les Contes d'Hoffmann* at the Bavarian State Opera (1924); sang there until joining the Frankfurt

Opera in 1926. She toured South America; appeared at the Salzburg Festivals, in Munich, and with the Vienna State Opera and Berlin State Opera; made guest appearances at London's Covent Garden, Milan's La Scala, and the Rome Opera. She was best known for her soubrette roles in the operas of Mozart.

Kern, Jerome (David), famous American composer; b. N.Y., Jan. 27, 1885; d. there, Nov. 11, 1945. He was educated in N.Y. public schools; studied music with his mother, then with Paolo Gallico and Alexander Lambert (piano) and Austin Pearce and Albert von Doenhoff (theory) at the N.Y. College of Music (1902–3); subsequently theory and composition in Heidelberg (1903–4). He then returned to N.Y., where he became a pianist and salesman for a publishing firm in 1905; publ. his 1st song, *How'd You Like to Spoon with Me,* which became famous; in 1906 he was in London, where he was connected with a theatrical production. He obtained his 1st success as a composer for the stage with his musical comedy *The Red Petticoat* (Nov. 13, 1912). After that he produced musical comedies in rapid succession, bringing out more than 40 works; also wrote several film scores. Kern's greatest success was *Show Boat* (Washington, D.C., Nov. 15, 1927); a most remarkable score, and one of the finest of its kind in the genre, it contains the famous song *Ol' Man River.* On Jan. 23, 1985, Kern was immortalized in the 1st 22-cent American postage stamp, designed by James Sharpe of Westport, Conn. Among guests at the dedication ceremony, which took place in the main gallery of the Library of Performing Arts at Lincoln Center, were Hal David, president of ASCAP, as well as Kern's daughter, Betty Kern Miller, who traveled from her home in Danville, Ky.

WORKS (all perf. in N.Y. unless otherwise given): *La Belle Paree* (March 20, 1911; in collaboration with F. Tours); *Oh, I Say!* (Oct. 30, 1913); *90 in the Shade* (Jan. 15, 1915); *Nobody Home* (April 20, 1915); *Cousin Lucy* (Aug. 27, 1915); *Miss Information* (Oct. 5, 1915); *Very Good, Eddie* (Dec. 23, 1915); *Have a Heart* (Jan. 11, 1917); *Love o' Mike* (Jan. 15, 1917); *Oh Boy!* (Feb. 20, 1917); *Leave It to Jane* (Aug. 28, 1917); *Miss 1917* (revue; Nov. 5, 1917; in collaboration with V. Herbert); *Oh Lady! Lady!* (Feb. 1, 1918); *Toot, Toot* (March 11, 1918); *Head over Heels* (April 29, 1918); *Rock-a-bye-Baby* (May 22, 1918); *She's a Good Fellow* (May 5, 1919); *Night Boat* (Feb. 2, 1920); *Hitchy Koo of 1920* (revue; Oct. 19, 1920); *Sally* (Dec. 21, 1920; ballet music by V. Herbert; also a film, 1929); *Good Morning, Dearie* (Nov. 1, 1921); *The Cabaret Girl* (London, Sept. 19, 1922); *The Bunch and Judy* (Nov. 28, 1922); *The Beauty Prize* (London, Sept. 5, 1923); *Stepping Stones* (Nov. 6, 1923); *Sitting Pretty* (April 8, 1924); *Dear Sir* (Sept. 23, 1924); *Sunny* (Sept. 22, 1925; also films, 1930 and 1941); *The City Chap* (Oct. 26, 1925); *Criss Cross* (Oct. 12, 1926); *Lucky* (March 22, 1927); *Show Boat* (Washington, D.C., Nov. 15, 1927); *Blue Eyes* (London, April 27, 1928); *Sweet Adeline* (musical romance; Sept. 2, 1929; also a film, 1935); *The Cat and the Fiddle* (Oct. 15, 1931; also a film, 1933); *Music in the Air* (Nov. 8, 1932; also a film, 1934); *Roberta* (Nov. 18, 1933; also films, 1935 and 1952); *3 Sisters* (London, April 9, 1934); *Gentlemen Unafraid* (St. Louis, June 3, 1938); *Very Warm for May* (Nov. 17, 1939). *Show Boat* was also filmed in 1929, 1936, and 1951; his other films were *I Dream Too Much* (1935); *Swing Time* (1936); *High, Wide and Handsome* (1937); *When You're in Love* (1937); *Joy of Living* (1938); *One Night in the Tropics* (1940); *You Were Never Lovelier* (1942); *Can't Help Singing* (1944); *Cover Girl* (1944); *Centennial Summer* (1946); *Till the Clouds Roll By* (1946; a film biography after a song from *Oh Boy!*). He also wrote songs for various other musicals and films; among the most popular were *They Didn't Believe Me* for *The Girl from Utah* (1914) and *The Last Time I Saw Paris* for *Lady Be Good* (1941). His other works include *Scenario* for Orch. (based on themes from *Show Boat;* 1941) and *Mark Twain Suite* for Orch. (Cincinnati, May 14, 1942). For information on his songs, see *The Jerome Kern Song Book* (N.Y., 1955).

BIBL.: D. Ewen, *The Story of J. K.* (N.Y., 1953); idem, *The World of J. K.* (N.Y., 1960); H. Fordin, *J. K.: The Man and*

His Music (Santa Monica, Calif., 1975); A. Lamb, *J. K. in Edwardian London* (N.Y., 1981; 2nd ed., rev., 1985); G. Bordman, "J. K.: Innovator/Traditionalist," *Musical Quarterly*, no. 4 (1985).

Kern, Patricia, Welsh mezzo-soprano; b. Swansea, July 4, 1927. She studied with Parry Jones at the Guildhall School of Music in London; made her debut in London with the Opera for All group in 1952; then sang with the Welsh National Opera. In 1959 she joined the Sadler's Wells Opera in London; also sang at Covent Garden (1967–72). She made her U.S. debut in Washington, D.C., in 1969.

Kerr, Harrison, American composer; b. Cleveland, Oct. 13, 1897; d. Norman, Okla., Aug. 16, 1978. He completed his general studies with James H. Rogers and Claus Wolfram in Cleveland; in 1921 he went to France, where he took courses with Nadia Boulanger at the American Cons. in Fontainebleau and also had lessons with P. Vidal (composition) and A. Wolff (conducting). Upon returning to America, he became active mainly as a pedagogue; also organized musical exchange agencies in Europe and the Far East. He was dean of the College of Fine Arts at the Univ. of Oklahoma (1949–60), continuing there as composer-in-residence until 1968.
   WORKS: Opera, *The Tower of Kel* (1958–60); 3 syms.: No. 1 (1927–29; rev. 1938); No. 2 (1943–45); No. 3 (1953–54); Violin Concerto (1950–51; rev. 1956); *Sinfonietta da camera* (Norman, Okla., April 25, 1968); *Episodes from The Tower of Kel* for Orch. (1974); Trio for Clarinet, Cello, and Piano (1936); 3 string quartets (1935, 1937, 1973); Piano Trio (1938); *Overture, Arioso, and Finale* for Cello and Piano (1944–51; arranged for Cello and Orch., 1966–67); Solo Violin Sonata (1954); Sonata for Violin and Piano (1956); *Quasi Quodlibet* for 8 Trombones (1974); 2 piano sonatas (1929, 1943); *Dance Suite* for 2 Pianos and Percussion (1938); songs.
   BIBL.: A. Ringer, "H. K.: Composer and Educator," *American Composers Alliance Bulletin*, Vol. 8, No. 2 (1959).

Kersjes, Anton (Frans Jan), Dutch conductor; b. Arnhem, Aug. 17, 1923. He studied conducting with Felix Hupka in Amsterdam and Eugène Bigot in Paris. In 1953 he became co-founder and conductor of the Kunstmaand Chamber Orch. in Amsterdam, which became the Kunstmaand Orch. in 1955 and the Amsterdam Phil. in 1969; was its principal conductor until 1983. He took this orch. to the Soviet Union in 1972, making it the 1st Dutch ensemble to give concerts there. From 1969 to 1979 he led the conducting class at the Sweelinck Cons. in Amsterdam.

Kersters, Willem, Belgian composer; b. Antwerp, Feb. 9, 1929. He studied at the Brussels Cons. with Jean Louel, Jean Absil, Marcel Quinet, and Marcel Poot; then taught at the Antwerp Cons. (from 1962); was also a teacher at the Maastricht Cons. in the Netherlands (from 1968). His music reveals traits of the classical Flemish school of composition, with lucidly sonorous contrapuntal lines in which tonality is ingeniously intertwined with atonal melodic progressions.
   WORKS: STAGE: *Gansendonk,* opera (1979–82; Antwerp, 1984); 3 ballets: *Parwati* (1956), *Triomf van de Geest* (1959), and *Ulenspiegel de Geus* (1976). **ORCH.:** Sinfonietta (1955); *Sinfonia concertante* for Flute, Clarinet, Bassoon, and String Orch. (1957); *Sinfonia piccola* (1958); Divertimento for String Orch. (1958); 5 syms. (1962; 1963; 1967; 1979, *Gezelle;* 1987); *Suite in the Form of a French Overture* for 4 Clarinets and String Orch. (1964); Sinfonietta for Wind Orch. (1967); *Contrasts* for Percussion and Orch. or Piano (1969); *Anaglyphos* for 10 Percussion Players (1969); *Capriccio* (1972); *Laudes* for Brass and Percussion (1973); *Halewyn,* pas de deux (1973); *Serenade* for Chamber Orch. (1976); Piano Concerto (1977); *Incantations* for Brass Band (1983); *Ballade* for Alto Saxophone and String Orch. (1987). **CHAMBER AND INSTRUMENTAL:** Wind Quintet (1954); Viola Sonata (1954); *Berceuse and Humoresque* for Oboe, Clarinet, and Bassoon (1956); *Partita* for Violin and Piano (1956); 2 string quartets (1962, 1964); Solo Violin Sonata

(1965); *De drie tamboers,* septet for 4 Clarinets, Percussion, Timpani, and Piano (1966); *Variations on a Theme of Giles Farnaby* for 4 Clarinets (1967); *Notturno* for Guitar (1968); 3 *Rondos* for Brass Quintet (1969); Variations for Flute, Oboe, Clarinet, and Bassoon (1969); *Ballade* for Violin and Piano (1970); Piano Quartet (1970); Quartet for Clarinet, Violin, Viola, and Cello (1971); Oboe Sonatina (1974); *Coincidences* for 9 Percussion Players (1974); *Aveniana* for Oboe, Clarinet, and Bassoon (1984); Piano Sonata (1985); Nonetto for 9 Instruments (1985). **VOCAL:** *A Gospel Song* for Soloists, Choir, and Orch. (1965); *A Hymn of Praise,* oratorio for Soloists, Choirs, and Orch. (1966); *Het Zonnelied (Canticum Solis Fratris),* cantata for Choir, Trumpet, 2 Pianos, and Timpani (1986); *Kinderwereld* for Choir, Trumpet, 2 Pianos, and Timpani (1988); songs.

Kertész, István, noted Hungarian-born German conductor; b. Budapest, Aug. 28, 1929; d. (drowned while swimming in the Mediterranean) Kfar Saba, Israel, April 16, 1973. He studied violin and composition at the Franz Liszt Academy of Music in Budapest, where his principal teachers were Kodály and Weiner; also received instruction in conducting from Somogyi. He conducted in Györ (1953–55) and at the Budapest State Opera (1955–56); after the unsuccessful Hungarian revolution (1956), he settled in West Germany and became a naturalized citizen; he completed his conducting studies with Previtali at the Accademia di Santa Cecilia in Rome (1958). He was Generalmusikdirektor in Augsburg (1958–63); made his 1st appearances as a guest conductor in England in 1960 and in the U.S. in 1961. In 1964 he became Generalmusikdirektor of the Cologne Opera, a post he retained until his death; he was also principal conductor of the London Sym. Orch. (1965–68), which he led on a world tour (1965). His readings of the Romantic repertoire were especially admired for their warmth and lyricism.
   BIBL.: K. Richter, *I. K.* (1974).

Kes, Willem, Dutch conductor and composer; b. Dordrecht, Feb. 16, 1856; d. Munich, Feb. 21, 1934. He studied violin with various teachers in the Netherlands, then with Ferdinand David at the Leipzig Cons. (1871), Wieniawski in Brussels (1873), and Joachim in Berlin (1875); also composition with Reinecke, Bargiel, and Kiel in Berlin. In 1876 he was made 1st concertmaster of Amsterdam's Park-Orkest; was its conductor in 1883 and later conductor of Dordrecht's orch., choir, and music school (1877–88). He became the 1st conductor of Amsterdam's Concertgebouw Orch., leading its inaugural concert on Nov. 3, 1888, and remaining with it until 1895. In 1895 he succeeded Henschel as conductor of the Scottish Orch. in Glasgow. In 1898 he went to Russia, where he conducted the Moscow Phil. Soc. (1901–5); subsequently was conductor of the Koblenz Orch. and director of the music school there (1905–26). Among his works are a Sym.; overtures; Violin Concerto; Cello Concerto; *Der Taucher* for Chorus and Orch.; chamber music; piano pieces; songs.

Kessler (real name, **Kötzler**), **Joseph Christoph,** German pianist and pedagogue; b. Augsburg, Aug. 26, 1800; d. Vienna, Jan. 14, 1872. He studied with the organist Bilek in Feldsberg; then was tutor with the family of Count Potocki in Lemberg; from 1855, lived in Vienna. He publ. practical studies for piano, which Moscheles used in his teaching, and which Liszt recommended.

Kessler, Thomas, Swiss composer; b. Zürich, Sept. 25, 1937. He studied literature in Zürich and Paris, then took music courses with Blacher, Hartig, and Pepping at the Berlin Hochschule für Musik, graduating in 1968. From 1972 he taught at the Basel Academy of Music. His works include the ballets *Countdown for Orpheus* (1967) and *Revolutionsmusik* (1968); Trombone Concerto (1968); String Trio (1969); *Drumphony* for Percussion, Computer, and Orch. (Cologne, Sept. 19, 1981); several other pieces of chamber music.

Kessner, Daniel (Aaron), American composer; b. Los Angeles, June 3, 1946. He studied composition with Henri Lazarof at the Univ. of Calif. at Los Angeles (B.A., 1967; M.A., 1968; Ph.D., 1971). In 1970 he was appointed to the faculty of the Calif. State Univ. in Northridge, where he also conducted its New Music Ensemble; was prof. there from 1980. In 1970 and 1971 he received BMI awards; won the Queen Marie-José International Composition Prize in Geneva in 1972, and in 1974 and 1977 he received NEA grants.

WORKS: DRAMATIC: *The Telltale Heart*, monodrama for Tenor and Chamber Orch. (1975–78); *The Masque of the Red Death*, tale in music, dance, and light for Dancer, Conductor, and 7 Players (1979); *Texts for Nothing*, musical-literary-theatrical stream for Soprano, Flute, Trombone, Viol, Cello, and Conductor (1980–82). **ORCH.:** *Strata* (1971); *Mobile* (1973); *Romance: Orchestral Prelude No. 1* (1979); *Raging: Orchestral Prelude No. 2* (1981); Piano Concerto (1986). **SYMPHONIC BAND:** *Wind Sculptures* (1973); *Variations* (1977); *Sky Caves* (1984–85). **CHAMBER:** *Equali I–VI* for Various Groupings (1968–78); *Interactions* for Flute, Cello, Piano, and Tape (1971); *Array*, pieces for 2, 3, and 4 Guitars (1973); *Solennité* for Bass Flute, Viola, and Percussion (1975); Trio for Violin, Guitar, and Cello (1976); *Triform*, variations for Clarinet, Cello, and Piano (1976); *The Bells of Poe* for 4 Percussion (1978); *Ancient Song* for Alto Recorder, Viola, and Prepared Guitar (1980); *Arabesque* for Alto Saxophone and Vibraphone (1983); *Circle Music I* for Piano and Solo Instrument (1985) and *II* for Flute and Guitar (1985); Piano Sonata (1987); *2 Old English Songs* for Soprano, Flute, Viola, and Guitar (1988); also *Intercurrence I* for Harp and Tape (1972), *II* for Piano and Tape (1974), and *III* for Percussion and Tape (1975); *Continuum* for Marimba (1982).

Kestenberg, Leo, eminent Hungarian-born Israeli music educator; b. Rosenberg, Nov. 27, 1882; d. Tel Aviv, Jan. 14, 1962. He studied piano with Franz Kullak and Busoni and composition with Draeseke in Berlin; then taught at the Stern Cons. and at the Klindworth-Scharwenka Cons. He became music adviser to the Prussian Ministry of Science, Culture, and Education (1918); was made director of the Central Inst. for Education and Training (1922), and subsequently devoted himself to reorganizing the system of music education in Prussia. After the Nazis came to power (1933), he went to Prague; was founder-director of the International Soc. for Music Education; then settled in Tel Aviv, where he was general manager of the Palestine Sym. Orch. (1939–45); subsequently founded Israel's 1st training college for music teachers there. He publ. his memoirs as *Bewegte Zeiten: Musisch-musikantische Lebenserinnerungen* (Zürich, 1961).

WRITINGS: *Musikerziehung und Musikpflege* (Leipzig, 1921; 2nd ed., 1927); *Schulmusikunterricht in Preussen* (Berlin, 1927); ed. *Musik im Volk, Schule und Kirche* (Leipzig, 1927); ed. with W. Günther, *Der Musiklehrer* (Berlin, 3rd ed., 1928); ed. *Musikpädagogische Gegenswartsfragen* (Leipzig, 1928); *Musikpflege im Kindergarten* (Leipzig, 1928); *Schulmusik und Chorgesang* (Leipzig, 1930); *Jahrbuch der deutschen Musikorganisation 1931* (Berlin, 1931); *Der Privatunterricht in der Musik* (Berlin, 5th ed., 1932).

BIBL.: G. Braun, *Die Schulmusikerziehung in Preussen von den Falkschen Bestimmungen bis zur K.-Reform* (Kassel, 1957); U. Günther, *Die Schulmusikerziehung von der K.-Reform bis zum Ende des Dritten Reiches* (Neuwied, 1967).

Ketèlbey, Albert (William), English conductor and composer; b. Birmingham, Aug. 9, 1875; d. Cowes, Isle of Wight, Nov. 26, 1959. Precociously gifted in music, he wrote a piano sonata at the age of 11, and played it at the Worcester Town Hall; Elgar heard it and praised it. At the age of 13, he competed for a Trinity College scholarship, and was installed as Queen Victoria Scholar; at 16 he obtained the post of organist at St. John's Church at Wimbledon; at 20, began tours as the conductor of a musical comedy troupe, then was a theater conductor in London. He became best known for such light orch. pieces as *In a Monastery Garden* (1915), *In a Persian Market* (1920), *In a Chinese Temple Garden* (1923), *Sanctuary of the Heart* (1924), and *In the Mystic Land of Egypt* (1931); also wrote

many smaller pieces under various pseudonyms. His other works include the comic opera *The Wonder Worker* (1900) and chamber music.

Kettenus, Aloys, Belgian violinist and composer; b. Verviers, Feb. 22, 1823; d. London, Oct. 3, 1896. He studied at the Liège Cons. and in Germany; in 1845, became concertmaster of the Mannheim orch.; in 1855, a member of London's Royal Italian Opera Orch. He wrote an opera, *Stella Monti* (1862); Violin Concerto; Concertino for 4 Violins and Orch.; etc.

Ketterer, Eugène, French pianist and composer; b. Rouen, 1831; d. Paris, Dec. 18, 1870. He studied at the Paris Cons. He publ. 290 piano pieces in drawing-room style, many of which became popular (*Grand caprice hongrois, L'Argentine, La Châtelaine, Gaëtana, Rondo oriental*, etc.).

Ketting, Otto, Dutch composer, son of **Piet Ketting;** b. Amsterdam, Sept. 3, 1935. He studied composition at the Royal Cons. in The Hague (1952–58); played trumpet in the Residentie Orch., The Hague (1955–60); taught composition at the Rotterdam Cons. (1967–71) and at the Royal Cons. in The Hague (1971–74). His music represents a valiant effort to adapt Classical modalities to the esthetics of contemporary musical expression.

WORKS: 3 operas: *Dummies* (The Hague, Nov. 14, 1974), *O, Thou Rhinoceros* (Holland Festival, June 2, 1977), and *Ithaka* (Amsterdam, Sept. 23, 1986); 6 ballets: *Het laatste bericht* (The Last Message; 1962); *Intérieur* (1963); *Barrière* (1963); *The Golden Key* (1964); *Choreostruction* (1963); *Theater Piece* (1973); *Kerstliederen* (Christmas Songs) for Chorus and Small Orch. (1953); Sinfonietta (1954); *2 canzoni* for Orch. (1957); Passacaglia for Orch. (1957); Concertino for 2 Solo Trumpets, String Orch., 3 Horns, and Piano (1958); Sym. (1957–59); Concertino for Jazz Quintet and Orch. (1960); Variations for Wind Orch., Harp, and Percussion (1960); *Pas de deux*, choreographic commentary for Orch. (1961); a series of "collages," among which the most uninhibited is *Collage No. 9* for 22 Musicians (Conductor, 16 Brass, and 5 Percussionists; 1963; Amsterdam, Jan. 26, 1966; audience reaction, hopefully that of outrage, is part of the perf.: the conductor is instructed to treat his environment with disdain and contempt, to arrive late, leave early, and refuse to acknowledge social amenities); *In Memoriam Igor Stravinsky* for Orch. (1971); *Time Machine* for Winds and Percussion (Rotterdam, May 5, 1972); *For Moonlight Nights* for Flutist (alternating on Piccolo and Alto Flute) and 26 Players (1973; Hilversum, April 17, 1975); *Adagio* for Chamber Orch. (1977); *Symphony* for Saxophones and Orch. (1978); *The Light of the Sun* for Soprano and Orch., after poems of ancient Egypt (1978); *Monumentum* for Orch. (1983); Concerto for Solo Organ (1953); Sonata for Brass Quartet (1955); Piano Sonatina (1956); Serenade for Cello and Piano (1957); *A Set of Pieces* for Flute and Piano (1967); *A Set of Pieces* for Wind Quintet (1968); *Minimal Music* for 28 Toy Instruments (1970); *Musik zu einem Tonfilm* for Percussion and Various Instruments (1982); *Summer* for Piano, Flute, and Bass Clarinet (1985).

Ketting, Piet, Dutch pianist, conductor, and composer, father of **Otto Ketting;** b. Haarlem, Nov. 29, 1904; d. Rotterdam, May 25, 1984. He studied with Anton Averkamp in Utrecht, then took composition lessons with Willem Pijper (1926–32). As a pianist, he formed a duo with the flutist Johan Feltkamp (1927), and a unique trio with Feltkamp and oboist Jaap Stotijn (1935) that toured the Dutch East Indies in 1939. From 1949 to 1960 he conducted the Rotterdam Chamber Orch.; was also founder and conductor of the Rotterdam Chamber Choir (1937–60). From 1960 to 1974 he immersed himself in the numerical symbolism of J.S. Bach's works, with some startling, though unpubl., results. In his own music he pursued a modern Baroque system of composition, with a discreet application of euphonious dissonance.

WORKS: 2 syms. (1929, 1975); Sinfonia for Cello and Orch. (1963; radio perf., Dec. 1, 1965); *De minnedeuntjes* (The Love Songs) for Chorus and Orch. (1966–67; Dutch Radio, May 9,

1968); Bassoon Concertino (1968); Clarinet Concertino (1973); *Tema con 6 variazioni*, in modo cabalistico, for Flute and Orch. (1976); *Concertone 1980* for Viola, Winds, and Percussion (1980); String Trio (1925); 3 string quartets (1927–28); Cello Sonata (1928); Trio for Flute, Clarinet, and Bassoon (1929); Flute Sonata (1930); Sonata for Flute, Oboe, and Piano (1936); *Partita* for 2 Flutes (1936); *Fantasia No. 1* for Harpsichord, Descant, and Treble Recorders and Flute (1969); *Fantasia No. 2* for Harpsichord (1972); *Preludium e Fughetta* for Alto Flute and Piano (1969); 4 piano sonatinas (1926, 1926, 1927, 1929); *Prelude, Interlude and Postlude* for 2 Pianos (1971); *Jazon and Medea*, dramatic scene for Chorus, Piano, Flute, and Clarinet (1975).

Keuris, Tristan, Dutch composer; b. Amersfoort, Oct. 3, 1946. He studied theory with Jan van Vlijmen at the Amersfoort Music School, then composition with Ton de Leeuw at the Utrecht Cons. (1963–69), where he also studied piano. He subsequently taught at the Amsterdam Cons. His music is austerely structural. **WORKS: ORCH.:** *Quartet* for Orch. in 4 groups (1966–67); *Choral Music I* (1969); *Soundings* (1970); Saxophone Concerto (1971); Sinfonia (1972–74; Amsterdam, Jan. 31, 1976); Serenade for Oboe and Orch. (1974–76); Piano Concerto (1979–80); *Movements* (1981); *7 Pieces* for Bass Clarinet and Orch. (1983); Violin Concerto (1984). **CHAMBER:** Quartet for 4 Saxophones (1970); Piano Sonata (1970); Concertante Music for Clarinet, Oboe, Bassoon, Piano, and 5 Strings (1972–73); *Music for Violin, Clarinet, and Piano* (1973); *Fantasia* for Flute (1976); Concertino for Bass Clarinet and String Quartet (1977); Violin Sonata (1977); 2 string quartets (1982, 1985); Quartet for 3 Clarinets and Bass Clarinet (1983).

Keurvels, Edward (Hubertus Joannes), Belgian conductor and composer; b. Antwerp, March 8, 1853; d. Ekeren, near Antwerp, Jan. 29, 1916. He studied with Peter Benoit at the Vlaamse Music School in Antwerp; became conductor of the Nederslandse Schouwburg in 1882; helped to organize the Nederlands Lyrisch Toneel in 1890, which became the Vlaamse Opera in 1893; subsequently conducted there regularly, and also led sym. concerts at the Zoological Gardens (from 1896). He wrote an opera, *Parisina* (Antwerp, 1890), and numerous songs.

Keussler, Gerhard von, German conductor and composer; b. Schwanenburg, Livonia, July 5, 1874; d. Niederwartha bei Dresden, Aug. 21, 1949. He studied with Reinecke and Jadassohn at the Leipzig Cons., and musicology with Riemann and Kretzschmar at the Univ. of Leipzig (Ph.D., 1902, with the diss. *Die Grenzen der Aesthetik*). From 1906 to 1910 he was a choral conductor in Prague; then went to Hamburg, where he conducted the Phil. concerts until 1920 and led the Singakademie. In 1931 he toured in Australia as a conductor; returning to Germany, he taught at the Prussian Academy of Arts in Berlin (1934–41). He publ. the books *Das deutsche Volkslied und Herder* (Prague, 1915), *Händels Kulturdienst und unsere Zeit* (Hamburg, 1919), *Die Berufsehre des Musikers* (Leipzig, 1927), and *Paul Bucaenus* (Riga, 1931). He composed several symphonic dramas, including *Wandlungen* (1903), *Gefängnisse* (Prague, April 22, 1914), and *Die Gesselfahrt* (Hamburg, 1923); also 2 syms. (1925, 1928), the symphonic fantasy *Australia* (1935), and many songs.

Key, Francis Scott, American lawyer and author of the words of the U.S. national anthem, *The Star-Spangled Banner;* b. Carroll County, Md., Aug. 1, 1779; d. Baltimore, Jan. 11, 1843. He wrote the text of the anthem aboard a British ship (where he was taken as a civilian emissary to intercede for release of a Maryland physician) on the morning of Sept. 14, 1814, setting it to the tune of the popular British drinking song *To Anacreon in Heaven*, written by John Stafford Smith. The text and the tune did not become the official national anthem until March 3, 1931, when the bill establishing it as such was passed by Congress and signed by President Herbert Hoover. **BIBL.:** O. Sonneck, *Report on the Star Spangled Banner, Hail*

Columbia, Yankee Doodle (1909); idem, *The Star Spangled Banner* (1914); J. Muller, *The Star Spangled Banner* (N.Y., 1935); J. Kouwenhoven and L. Patten, "New Light on *The Star Spangled Banner,*" *Musical Quarterly* (April 1937); W. Lichtenwanger, "The Music of *The Star-Spangled Banner,*" *Quarterly Journal of the Library of Congress* (Washington, D.C., July 1977).

Key, Pierre van Rensselaer, American writer on music; b. Grand Haven, Mich., Aug. 28, 1872; d. N.Y., Nov. 28, 1945. He was educated at the Chicago Musical College; then held positions as music critic of the *Chicago Times-Herald, Chicago American, Chicago Examiner,* and *N.Y. World* (1907–19). He was the ed. of *Pierre Key's Musical Who's Who* (1931); *Pierre Key's Music Year Book; Pierre Key's Radio Annual;* the periodical *Music Digest;* publ. *John McCormack: His Own Life Story* (1919); *Enrico Caruso* (with B. Zirato; 1922); *This Business of Singing* (1936).

Khachaturian, Aram (Ilich), brilliant Russian composer of Armenian descent, uncle of **Karen (Surenovich) Khachaturian;** b. Tiflis, June 6, 1903; d. Moscow, May 1, 1978. His father was a bookbinder. Khachaturian played tuba in the school band, and also studied biology. He then went to Moscow and entered the Gnessin Music School (1922–25); later studied composition with Gnessin (1925–29). In 1929 he became a student at the Moscow Cons., graduating in 1934 in the class of Miaskovsky; finished his postgraduate studies there (1937). He commenced composing at the age of 21, and soon progressed to the 1st rank of Soviet composers of his generation. His music was in the tradition of Russian Orientalism; he applied the characteristic scale progressions of Caucasian melos, without quoting actual folk songs. His *Sabre Dance* from his ballet *Gayane* became popular all over the world. In 1948 he was severely criticized by the Central Committee of the Communist party, along with Prokofiev, Shostakovich, and others, for modernistic tendencies; although he admitted his deviations in this respect, he continued to compose essentially in his typical manner, not shunning highly dissonant harmonic combinations. He was made a People's Artist of the U.S.S.R. in 1954. He appeared as a conductor of his own works in Reykjavík in 1951; conducted in Bulgaria in 1952, in Finland in 1955, in London in 1955 and again in 1977, in Japan in 1963, and in Greece in 1965. He made his American debut in Washington, D.C., on Jan. 23, 1968, conducting the National Sym. Orch. in a program of his works; on Jan. 28, 1968, he conducted in N.Y. to a rousing audience reception. In 1933 he married the composer **Nina Makarova.** Khachaturian's name is properly pronounced Hachaturyán, with a stress on the palatalized last syllable, and with the initial consonant "H" ("Kh") pronounced as the German "ch." **WORKS: STAGE:** 3 ballets: *Shchastye* (Happiness; 1939; Erevan, 1939; Moscow, Oct. 24, 1939); *Gayane* (1940–42; Perm, Dec. 9, 1942; rev. 1952 and 1957; 3 symphonic suites, includes the immensely popular *Sabre Dance*); *Spartak* (Spartacus; 1950–56; Leningrad, Dec. 26, 1956; rev. 1957–58; 4 symphonic suites: Nos. 1–3, 1955, and No. 4, 1966). **ORCH.:** *Dance Suite* (1932–33); 3 syms.: No. 1 (1932–33; Moscow, April 23, 1935); No. 2 (Moscow, Dec. 30, 1943; rev., Moscow, March 6, 1944); No. 3 for 15 Solo Trumpets, Orch., and Organ (Leningrad, Dec. 13, 1947); Piano Concerto (1936; Leningrad, July 5, 1937); *The Widow of Valencia*, incidental music (1939–40; orch. suite, 1953); *Masquerade*, incidental music to Lermontov's play (1940; orch. suite, 1944); Violin Concerto (Moscow, Nov. 16, 1940; transcribed for Flute in 1968 by Jean-Pierre Rampal); 2 *Armenian Dances* for Cavalry Band (1943); *Solemn Overture* (1945); *Russian Fantasy* (1946); Cello Concerto (1945–46; Moscow, Oct. 30, 1946); *Ode in Memory of Lenin* (Moscow, Dec. 26, 1948); *Battle of Stalingrad*, music for film (screened in Moscow, Dec. 9, 1949); *Concerto-Rhapsody* for Piano and Orch. (1955–68); overture, *Salutation* (1958–59); *Concerto-Rhapsody* for Violin and Orch. (1961–62; Yaroslavl, Oct. 7, 1962; Moscow, Nov. 3, 1962); *Concerto-Rhapsody* for Cello and Orch. (1963; Gorky, Jan. 4, 1964). **CHAMBER:** *Song-Poem* for Violin and Piano (1929); Violin Sonata (1932); String

Quartet (1932); Trio for Clarinet, Violin, and Piano (1932); *Jazz Composition* for Solo Clarinet (1966; written for Benny Goodman); *Sonata-Monologue* for Solo Cello (1974); *Sonata-Fantasia* for Solo Violin (1975). VOCAL: *Poem about Stalin* for Orch., with choral ending (Moscow, Nov. 29, 1938); *3 Concert Arias* for Soprano and Orch. (1946); *Ode to Joy* for Mezzo-soprano, Chorus, 10 Harps, Unison Violins, Band, and Orch. (1955); *Ballade about the Fatherland* for Bass and Orch. (1961); *In Memory of the Heroes,* cantata for Soprano, Male Chorus, and Orch. (1976; a reworking of *Battle of Stalingrad*); songs. PIANO: 2 albums of children's pieces (1926–47; 1965); *Poem* (1927); *Suite* (1932); *Toccata* (1932); *Suite,* 3 pieces for 2 Pianos (1945); Sonatina (1952); Sonata (1961); *7 Fugues with Recitatives* (1928–66); music for films; numerous marches for band.

BIBL.: I. Martynov, *A. K.* (Moscow, 1956); G. Schneerson, *A. K.* (Moscow, 1959; in Eng.); G. Khubov, *A. K.* (Moscow, 1962; 2nd ed., 1966).

Khachaturian, Karen (Surenovich), Russian composer, nephew of **Aram (Ilich) Khachaturian;** b. Moscow, Sept. 19, 1920. He studied at the Moscow Cons. with Litinsky; during World War II, he served in the entertainment division of the Red Army. He resumed studies in 1945 at the Moscow Cons. with Shebalin, Shostakovich, and Miaskovsky, graduating in 1949; then joined its faculty in 1952. His music follows the general line of socialist realism, nationalist or ethnic in thematic resources and realistic in harmonic and contrapuntal treatment. He wrote a number of effective scores for films. His name, like the name of his uncle, is stressed on the last syllable.

WORKS: STAGE: Operetta, *An Ordinary Girl* (1959); ballet, *Cipollino,* after Rodari's fairy tale (Kiev, Nov. 8, 1974). ORCH.: 3 syms.: No. 1 (Moscow, March 12, 1955); No. 2 (Moscow, Nov. 27, 1968); No. 3 (Moscow, Oct. 15, 1982); Sinfonietta (1949); Overture (1949); *New-Year Tree,* suite (1951); *Youth Overture* (Moscow, Dec. 10, 1951); *In Mongolia,* suite (1951); *Oriental Suite* (1952); *Sports Suite* (1954); *Friendship Overture* (1959); *At the Circus,* suite (1968); Cello Concerto (1983). VOCAL: *Glory to Consomol* for Chorus and Orch. (Moscow, Oct. 29, 1948); *At the Lone Willow,* cantata (1950); *A Moment of History,* oratorio to documented texts of the Soviet Revolution of 1917 (Moscow, April 26, 1971); choruses; songs. CHAMBER: Violin Sonata (1947); Cello Sonata (1966); String Quartet (1969); Trio for Horn, Violin, and Piano (1981).

BIBL.: M. Uspenskaya, *K. K.* (Moscow, 1956); E. Dolinskaya, *K. K.* (Moscow, 1975).

Khadzhiev, Parashkev, Bulgarian composer; b. Sofia, April 14, 1912. He studied composition with Vladigerov and piano with Stoyanov at the Sofia Cons., graduating in 1936; then went to Vienna, where he studied composition with Joseph Marx (1937), and to Berlin, where he took a course in composition with Thiessen at the Hochschule für Musik (1938–40). Returning to Bulgaria, he occupied various teaching positions.

WORKS: 9 operas: *Imalo edno vreme* (Once upon a Time; Sofia, April 11, 1957); *Lud gidiya* (Madcap; Sofia, Nov. 15, 1959); *Albena* (Varna, Nov. 2, 1962); *Jukka nosht* (July Night; 1964; Plovdiv, Feb. 16, 1965); *The Millionaire* (1964; Sofia, March 14, 1965); *Master Woodcarvers* (Sofia, Oct. 9, 1966); *The Knight* (Varna, 1969); *The 3 Brothers and the Golden Apple* (1970; Sofia, Jan. 28, 1971); *The Year 893* (1972; Ruse, March 26, 1973); 4 operettas: *Delyana* (1952); *Aika* (1955); *Madame Sans-Gêne* (1958); *King Midas Has Ass's Ears* (1976); musical, *Job Hunters* (1972); ballet, *Srebarnite pantofki* (The Silver Slippers; 1961; Varna, March 20, 1962); *Skici* (Sketches) for Orch. (1940); Violin Concertino (1941); Flute Concertino (1945); *Capriccio* for Orch. (1951); *Small Dance Suite* for Orch. (1952); *Rondino* for Orch. (1969); 2 violin sonatas (1940, 1946); *3 Pieces* for Wind Quintet (1942); 2 string quartets (1948, 1953); piano pieces; choruses; arrangements of Bulgarian folk songs.

Khaikin, Boris (Emmanuilovich), prominent Russian conductor; b. Minsk, Oct. 26, 1904; d. Moscow, May 10, 1978. He studied piano with Goedicke and conducting with Sarad-

zhev and Malko at the Moscow Cons.; then was a conductor at the Stanislavsky Theater (1928–35). From 1936 to 1943 he served as principal conductor of the Maly Theater in Leningrad; from 1943 to 1954, at the Kirov Theater, and from 1954 to 1978, at Moscow's Bolshoi Theater. He taught at the Leningrad Cons. (1935–53); then was prof. of conducting at the Moscow Cons. (1954–78). His most famous student was Kirill Kondrashin. He was made a People's Artist of the U.S.S.R. in 1972. He conducted the premieres of a number of Soviet operas.

Khandoshkin, Ivan (Yevstafievich), Russian violinist and composer; b. 1747; d. St. Petersburg, March 28, 1804. He was a liberated serf; studied in St. Petersburg with an Italian musician, Tito Porta, then was sent to Italy, where he was a student at Tartini's school in Padua. Returning to Russia in 1765, he became a violinist at the St. Petersburg Imperial Chapel; then concertmaster of the Court Orch. (1773); also taught violin at the Academy of Arts there, and later in Moscow and Ekaterinoslav. His position in Russian musical life was highly unusual for a man of his origin. He was the 1st Russian violin virtuoso, and the 1st to write instrumental music on Russian folk themes. He publ. *6 sonates pour deux violons* (Amsterdam, 1781), *Chansons russes variées pour violon et basse* (Amsterdam, 1781), and *Nouvelles variations sur des chansons russes* for Violin (St. Petersburg, 1784).

BIBL.: G. Fesetchko, "I. K.," *Sovetskaya Muzica* (Dec. 1950); R. Aloys Mooser, *Annales de la musique et des musiciens en Russie au XVIIIe siècle* (Vol. II, Geneva, 1950); I. Yampolsky, *Russkoye skripichnoye iskusstvo* (The Art of the Violin in Russia; Vol. I, Moscow and Leningrad, 1951); A. Mischakoff, *K. and the Beginning of Russian String Music* (Ann Arbor, 1983).

Khodzha-Einatov, Leon, Russian composer; b. Tiflis, March 23, 1904; d. Leningrad, Nov. 1, 1954. He studied with Spendiarov; in 1927, went to Leningrad, where he wrote music for the stage. He wrote the opera *Rebellion* (Leningrad, May 16, 1938); 3 Armenian operas: *Arshak* (1945); *David Bek* (1951); *Namus* (1952); *Symphonic Dances* (16 numbers); Sym. (1953).

Khokhlov, Pavel (Akinfievich), noted Russian baritone; b. Spassky, Aug. 2, 1854; d. Moscow, Sept. 20, 1919. He studied in Moscow; made his debut with the Bolshoi Theater there as Valentin in *Faust* (March 3, 1879), and remained on its roster until he retired in 1900; also appeared at the Maryinsky Theater in St. Petersburg (1881; 1887–88). He sang the title role in *Eugene Onegin* at its 1st professional performance (Moscow, Jan. 23, 1881). His other outstanding roles included Rubinstein's Demon, Boris Godunov, Prince Igor, Don Giovanni, and Wolfram.

BIBL.: S. Durilin, *P.A. K. 1854–1919* (Moscow and Leningrad, 1947); B. Yakovlev, *P.A. K.* (Moscow and Leningrad, 1950).

Khrennikov, Tikhon (Nikolaievich), important Russian music administrator and composer; b. Elets, June 10, 1913. He was the 10th child in the family of a provincial clerk, but his parents, brothers, and sisters were musical, played the Russian guitar and the mandolin, and sang peasant songs. He took piano lessons with a local musician; in 1927 he went to Moscow, where he was introduced to Gnessin, who accepted him as a student in his newly founded musical Technicum; there he studied counterpoint with Litinsky and piano with Ephraim Hellman. After graduation, he entered the Moscow Cons., where he studied composition with Shebalin and piano with Neuhaus (1932–36); later continued postgraduate work with Shebalin. He developed a mildly modernistic, and technically idiomatic, type of composition which remained his recognizable style throughout his career as a composer. In 1961 he joined the faculty of the Moscow Cons., and was named a prof. in 1966. In the meantime he became engaged in the political life of the country. He was attached to the music corps of the Red Army and accompanied it during the last months of World War II; in 1947 he joined the Communist party, and also became a deputy of the Supreme Soviet. In

1948 he was named personally by Stalin as secretary-general of the Union of Soviet Composers, and in 1949 became president of the music section of the All-Union Soc. for Cultural Exchange with Europe and America. He further served as head of the organizing committee for the International Festivals and the Tchaikovsky Competitions in Moscow. He received numerous honors; was a member of the Soviet delegation to the U.S. in 1959, was named a Hero of Socialist Labor in 1973, and in 1974 received the Lenin Prize. Amid all this work he never slackened the tempo of his main preoccupation, that of composition. He wrote operas, ballets, syms., and concertos, and appeared as a piano soloist. During his entire career, he was a stout spokesman for Soviet musical policy along the lines of socialist realism. He compromised himself, however, by his vehement condemnation of "formalist" directions in modern music, specifically attacking Stravinsky, Prokofiev, Shostakovich, and, later, also Schnittke and Gubaidulina. But as Soviet esthetical directions underwent a liberal change, Khrennikov himself became the target of sharp criticism. He defended himself by claiming that he had protected a number of young musicians from attacks by entrenched functionaries of the Soviet musical establishment, and he succeeded in retaining his position as secretary-general of the Union of Soviet Composers for several years. His compositions express forcefully the desirable qualities of Soviet music, a flowing melody suggesting the broad modalities of Russian folk songs, a vibrant and expressive lyricism, and effective instrumental formation.

Works: STAGE: Operas: *Brothers* (later renamed *In the Storm;* Moscow, May 31, 1939); *Frol Skobeyev* (Moscow, Feb. 24, 1950; 2nd version renamed *Unrelated Son-in-Law*); *Mother,* after the novel by Gorky (Moscow, Oct. 26, 1957); fairy-tale opera for children, *Boy Giant* (1969); comic opera, *Much Ado about ... Hearts,* a parody on Shakespeare's *Much Ado about Nothing* (1976); operettas: *100 Devils and a Single Girl* (Moscow, May 16, 1963); *White Nights* (Moscow, Nov. 3, 1967); ballet, *Happy Childhood* (1970). ORCH.: 3 syms.: No. 1 (Moscow, Oct. 10, 1955); No. 2, expressing "the irresistible will to defeat the Fascist foe" (Moscow, Jan. 10, 1943); No. 3 (1973); 3 piano concertos (1933, 1970, 1982); 2 violin concertos (1959, 1975); Cello Concerto (Moscow, May 13, 1964). INCIDENTAL MUSIC: *A Soldier Returns from the Front* (1938); *Don Quixote* (1941). FILM MUSIC: *Shepherdess and Shepherd* (1941); *At Six o'Clock after the War* (1944); *The Balladeer Goes West* (1947); *Hussar's Ballad* (1962); *We Need Not a Password* (1964). Also chamber music; piano pieces; many songs; choruses.

BIBL.: L. Kaltat, *T. K.* (Moscow, 1946); V. Kukharsky, *T. K.* (Moscow, 1957); Y. Kremlev, *T. K.* (Moscow, 1963); I. Martinov, *T. K.* (Moscow, 1987).

Khubov, Georgi (Nikitich), Russian writer on music; b. Kars, Turkey, May 9, 1902; d. Moscow, Nov. 5, 1981. He studied piano at the Odessa Cons. (1920); later took courses in composition with Paliashvili at the Tiflis Cons. and in piano at the Moscow Cons. (1922–30). In Moscow he organized the 1st school of mass music; taught music history at the Moscow Cons. (1934–38), where he introduced the 1st special course in Soviet music; also ed. musical publications. During World War II (1941–45), he was in charge of the musical broadcasts over the Soviet Radio; in 1943 he joined the Communist party. He publ. informative monographs on Borodin (Moscow, 1933), Bach (Moscow, 1936; 4th ed., 1964), Khachaturian (Moscow, 1962; 2nd ed., 1966; Armenian tr., Erevan, 1977), and Mussorgsky (Moscow, 1969).

Kidson, Frank, English music scholar; b. Leeds, Nov. 15, 1855; d. there, Nov. 7, 1926. Originally a landscape painter, he became interested in historical studies and collected English, Scottish, and Irish folk songs and dance melodies; subsequently became one of the founders of the Folk-Song Soc. (1898); also studied the history of British music publishing. His most significant editions include *Old English Country Dances Gathered from Scarce Printed Collections and from Manuscripts* (London, 1890), *Songs of Britain* (London and N.Y., 1913), *A Garland of English Folk-songs* (London, 1926),

and *English Peasant Songs with Their Traditional Airs* (London, 1929). His writings include *English Folk-song and Dance* (Cambridge, 1915) and *The Beggar's Opera: Its Predecessors and Successors* (Cambridge, 1922).

Kiel, Friedrich, German violinist, pedagogue, and composer; b. Puderbach, near Siegen, Oct. 7, 1821; d. Berlin, Sept. 13, 1885. He studied the rudiments of music with his father, a schoolmaster. One of his youthful works, a set of variations (1832–34), attracted the attention of Prince Karl von Wittgenstein, who gave him violin lessons in 1835, and took him into his orch. Kiel further studied with Kaspar Kummer at Coburg, becoming concertmaster of the ducal orch. (1840); then moved to Berlin, and studied with Dehn (1842–44); received a stipend from King Friedrich Wilhelm IV; in 1865, was elected to the Prussian Academy of Fine Arts. From 1866 to 1870 he taught composition at the Stern Cons. He wrote the oratorios *Christus* and *Der Stern von Bethlehem; Stabat Mater; Requiem; Te Deum;* 4 piano sonatas. He was a prolific composer, but it was as a pedagogue that he gained distinction.

Kielland, Olav, noted Norwegian conductor and composer; b. Trondheim, Aug. 16, 1901; d. Bø, Telemark, Aug. 5, 1985. He studied music theory at the Leipzig Cons. (1921–23) and took Weingartner's conducting class in Basel (1929). He was conductor of the Oslo Phil. (1931–45) and the Bergen Phil. (1952–55); also appeared as a guest conductor abroad. His music followed the tradition of Norwegian national trends.

Works: 4 sinfonias: *I* (1935); *II* (1961); *III* (1966); *IV* (1976); Violin Concerto (1939–40); *Overtura tragica* (1941); *Mot blåsnøhøgdom* (The White-capped Mountains), symphonic suite for High Voice and Orch. (1945–46); *Concerto grosso norvegese* for 2 Horns and String Orch. (1952); *Tvileikar* for 4 Instruments (1954); String Quartet (1964); *Marcia del Coraggio* for Orch. (1968); *Ouverture solenne* (1974); Piano Concerto (1977).

Kienzl, Wilhelm, Austrian composer; b. Waizenkirchen, Jan. 17, 1857; d. Vienna, Oct. 3, 1941. He studied in Graz with Johann Buwart and Mortier de Fontaine (piano) and with Ignaz Uhl (violin); also with Mayer-Rémy (composition) at the Univ. there, and then with Krejči at the Univ. of Prague, at the Univ. of Leipzig, with Rheinberger in Munich, with Liszt in Weimar, and at the Univ. of Vienna (Ph.D., 1879, with the diss. *Die musikalische Deklamation;* publ. in Leipzig, 1880). He was director of Amsterdam's German Opera (1883); conducted in Krefeld before returning to Graz (1884); then was director of the Steiermärkischer Musikverein there until 1886. He held the post of 1st conductor of the Hamburg Opera (1890–92), then was court conductor in Munich (1892–94). His most successful work was the opera *Der Evangelimann* (Berlin, May 4, 1895). After World War I, he wrote the new national anthem of Austria (1918), replacing Haydn's; it was adopted on June 6, 1920, but was dropped on Dec. 13, 1929, in favor of Haydn's melody. He publ. several books, including an autobiography (1926).

Works: Operas: *Urvasi* (Dresden, Feb. 20, 1886; rewritten 1909); *Heilmar, der Narr* (Munich, March 8, 1892); *Der Evangelimann* (Berlin, May 4, 1895); *Don Quichote,* a "musical tragi-comedy" (Berlin, Nov. 18, 1898); *In Knecht Ruprechts Werkstatt,* a "Märchenspiel" (Graz, 1907); *Der Kuhreigen (Ranz des Vaches)* (Vienna, Nov. 23, 1911); *Das Testament* (Vienna, Dec. 6, 1916); *Hassan der Schwarmer* (Chemnitz, 1925); *Sanctissimum* (Vienna, 1925); *Hans Kipfel,* singspiel (Vienna, 1926); incidental music; choral works; songs; chamber music; piano pieces. He also completed Adolf Jensen's opera *Turandot.*

BIBL.: M. Morold, *W. K.* (Leipzig, 1909); H. Hagen, ed., *Festschrift zum 60. Geburtstag von W. K.* (Graz, 1917); *Festschrift zum 80. Geburtstag von W. K.* (Vienna, 1937); H. Sittner, *K.—Rosegger: Eine Künstlerfreundschaft* (Zürich, 1953).

Kiepura, Jan, Polish-American tenor; b. Sosnowiec, May 16, 1902; d. Rye, N.Y., Aug. 15, 1966. He studied in Warsaw and Milan; made his debut as Faust in Lwow (1924), then appeared in Vienna, Berlin, Milan, Paris, Buenos Aires, and other opera centers. He made his U.S. debut with the Chicago Opera in 1931; first appeared with the Metropolitan Opera in N.Y. as Rodolfo in *La Bohème* (Feb. 10, 1938); sang there until 1939 and again in 1942. He was admired for such roles as Des Grieux and Faust; also was successful as a film artist and as an operetta singer. He was married to the Austrian soprano Martha Eggerth.

Kiesewetter, Raphael Georg, Edler von Wiesenbrunn, Austrian government official and writer on music; b. Holleschau, Moravia, Aug. 29, 1773; d. Baden, near Vienna, Jan. 1, 1850. He studied piano and voice in his youth, and later flute, bassoon, and guitar; studied philosophy at the Univ. of Olmütz, took a course in counterpoint with Albrechtsberger, and studied law at the Univ. of Vienna before becoming an official in the chancellery of the Imperial Army in Schwetzingen. He was made a councillor in the War Office in Vienna (1807), where he served until his retirement (1845); was ennobled in 1843. A.W. Ambros was his nephew. **WRITINGS:** *Die Verdienste der Niederländer um die Tonkunst* (Vienna, 1828); *Geschichte der europäisch-abendländischen oder unserer heutigen Musik* (Leipzig, 1834; 2nd ed., 1846; Eng. tr., 1846); *Über die Musik der neuern Griechen, nebst freien Gedanken über altägyptische und altgriechische Musik* (Leipzig, 1838); *Guido von Arezzo: Sein Leben und Wirken* (Leipzig, 1840); *Schicksale und Beschaffenheit des weltlichen Gesangs vom frühen Mittelalter bis zur Erfindung des dramatischen Styles und den Anfängen der Oper* (Leipzig, 1841); *Die Musik der Araber nach Originalquellen* (Leipzig, 1842); *Der neuen Aristoxener zerstreute Aufsätze über das Irrige der musikalischen Arithmetik und das Eitle ihrer Temperaturrechnungen* (Leipzig, 1846; includes articles by Kiesewetter); *Catalog der Sammlung alter Musik des K. K. Hofrathes Raphael Georg Kiesewetter Edlen von Wiesenbrunn in Wien* (Vienna, 1847); *Gallerie der alten Contrapunctisten: Eine Auswahl aus ihren Werken in verständlichen Partituren* (Vienna, 1847); *Über die Octave des Pythagoras* (Vienna, 1848). **BIBL.:** H. Kier, *R.G. K.* (1773–1850): *Wegbereiter des musikalischen Historismus* (Regensburg, 1968).

Kiesewetter, Tomasz, Polish composer; b. Sosnowka, Sept. 8, 1911. He studied composition with Rytel and conducting with Bierdiajew at the Warsaw Cons.; during the German occupation in World War II, he was active in resistance groups; after the war, taught at the Lodz State College of Music. **WORKS:** Operetta, *The Lonely Ones* (1963); ballet, *King's Jester* (1954); *Polish Dances* for Orch. (1947, 1950); 3 syms. (1949, 1952, 1958); Viola Concerto (1950).

Kijima, Kiyohiko, Japanese composer; b. Tokyo, Feb. 19, 1917. He studied composition with Ikenouchi at Nihon Univ.; later joined its faculty. He received 2 prizes given by the Tokyo newspaper *Mainichi* (1938, 1948). His works include *Satsukino,* poem for Soprano and Small Orch. (1940); *Symphonic Overture* (1942); *Prelude and Fugue* for Orch. (1948); String Quartet (1950); Violin Sonata (1951); *5 Meditations* for Orch. (1956); *Trio* for Flute, Violin, and Piano (1958; rev. 1970); *Divertimento* for Orch. (1963); *Mi-Chi-No-Ku* for Chorus, Flute, Piano, and Percussion (1963); Piano Quintet (1965); 2 *Legends* for Piano (1969); songs.

Kiladze, Grigori, Russian composer; b. Batum, Oct. 25, 1902; d. Tbilisi, April 3, 1962. He studied at the Tiflis Cons. with Ippolitov-Ivanov (1924–27); then at the Leningrad Cons. with Shcherbachev (1927–29). He was an active proponent of ethnic Georgian music in a modern idiom derived thematically from folk melorhythms. He wrote operas on subjects from Caucasian revolutionary history: *Bakhtrioni* (1936) and *Lado Ketzkhoveli* (1941); a ballet, *Sinatle* (1947); *Poem about Stalin* for Chorus and Orch. (1935); *Heroic Symphony* (1944); oratorio, *Childhood and Adolescence of the Leader* (1951); overture, *Triumph* (1957).

Kilar, Wojciech, Polish composer; b. Lwow, July 17, 1932. He studied piano and composition with Woytowicza at the Katowice State College of Music (1950–55); later took courses

at the Krakow Cons. (1955–58); then went to Paris, where he took private lessons with Nadia Boulanger (1959–60). Returning to Poland, he became a teacher at the Katowice State College of Music. Of an experimental turn of mind, he makes use of a variety of modern techniques while retaining essential Classical forms. **WORKS:** *The Mask of the Red Death,* ballet after Poe (1962); 2 syms.: No. 1 for Strings (1955) and No. 2, *Sinfonia concertante,* for Piano and Orch. (1956); *Béla Bartók in Memoriam* for Violin, Winds, and 2 Percussion Groups (1957); Concerto for 2 Pianos and Percussion (1958); *Herbsttag,* after Rilke, for Soprano and String Quartet (1960); *Riff 62* for Orch. (1962); *Générique* for Orch. (1963); *Diphthongs* for Chorus, 6 Percussionists, 2 Pianos, and Strings (1964); *Springfield Sonnet* for Orch. (1965); *Solenne* for Soprano, Strings, and Brasses (1967); *Training 68* for Clarinet, Trombone, Cello, and Piano (1968); *Upstairs-Downstairs* for 2 Children's Choruses (without words) and Orch. (Warsaw, Sept. 25, 1971); *Prelude and a Carol* for 4 Oboes and String Orch. (1972); *Bogurodzica* (Mother of God) for Chorus and Orch. (1975); *Koscielec 1909,* symphonic poem (1976); *Exodus* for Chorus and Orch. (Warsaw, Sept. 19, 1981); *Angelus* for Soprano, Chorus, and Orch. (Katowice, Oct. 12, 1984); *Orawa* for 15 String Instruments (1986); incidental music for plays; film scores.

Kilenyi, Edward, Jr., American pianist and teacher, son of Edward Kilenyi, Sr.; b. Philadelphia, May 7, 1910. In 1927 he went to Budapest to study with Dohnányi at the Academy of Music; after graduating (1930), he gave concerts throughout Europe. He made his N.Y. recital debut on Oct. 21, 1940; was on the faculty of Florida State Univ. in Tallahassee (1953–83), and thereafter was adjunct prof. there.

Kilenyi, Edward, Sr., Hungarian-American composer, father of Edward Kilenyi, Jr.; b. Békésszentràndrás, Jan. 25, 1884; d. Tallahassee, Fla., Aug. 15, 1968. He studied in Budapest, in Szarvas, with Mascagni at Rome's Scuola Nazionale Musicale, and at the Cologne Cons.; then settled in the U.S. (1908), where he completed his training at Columbia Univ. with Rybner and Daniel Gregory Mason (M.A., 1915). He was a teacher of George Gershwin (1919–21). In 1930 he went to Hollywood, where he wrote film scores; he also wrote an opera, *The Cry of the Wolf* (1916), a String Quartet (1912), and other chamber music.

Killebrew, Gwendolyn, black American mezzo-soprano; b. Philadelphia, Aug. 26, 1939. She studied at Temple Univ. in Philadelphia; also at the Juilliard School of Music in N.Y. She won a Metropolitan Opera audition and made her debut with the company in N.Y. as Waltraute in *Die Walküre* on Nov. 21, 1967; made her 1st appearance at the N.Y. City Opera as Ulrica in *Un ballo in maschera* (Sept. 11, 1971). She was a member of the Deutsche Oper am Rhein in Düsseldorf (from 1976); also appeared in Munich, Geneva, Salzburg, Bayreuth, and other European opera centers. She made numerous concert, oratorio, and lieder appearances on both sides of the Atlantic. Among her notable operatic roles are Gluck's Orfeo, Azucena, Mistress Quickly, Amneris, Fricka, and Baba the Turk in *The Rake's Progress.*

Killmayer, Wilhelm, German composer; b. Munich, Aug. 21, 1927. He studied conducting and composition with Waltershausen (1945–50); then musicology with Ficker at the Univ. of Munich (1950–53), and later composition with Orff (1953). He taught at the Trapp Cons. in Frankfurt (1955–58); then was ballet conductor at the Bavarian State Opera in Munich (1961–64), and later a prof. at Munich's Staatliche Hochschule für Musik (from 1973). **WORKS:** STAGE: Operas: *La Buffonata* (ballet-opera; 1959–60; concert perf., South-German Radio, Stuttgart, Oct. 21, 1960; stage perf., Heidelberg, April 30, 1961); *La Tragedia di Orfeo* (Munich, June 9, 1961); *Yolimba oder Die Grenzen der Magie* (1962–63; Wiesbaden, March 15, 1964; rev. version, Munich, May 9, 1970); *Une leçon de français* (Die Französischstunde; 1964; concert perf., South-German Radio, Stuttgart, Oct. 20, 1964; stage perf., Stuttgart, Oct. 19, 1966). Ballets: *Pas de deux classique* (1964; Munich, May 12, 1965); *Encores*, 2 ballet pieces (Munich, May 9, 1970); *Paradies* (1974). ORCH.: Piano Concerto (1955; Munich, April 21, 1956); 3 syms.: No. 1, *Fogli* (1968; Hannover, Feb. 9, 1971); No. 2, *Ricordanze* (Berlin, May 14, 1969); No. 3, *Menschen-Los* (1972–73; Nuremberg, April 19, 1974); *Nachtgedanken* (Salzburg, Aug. 7, 1973); *The Broken Farewell* for Trumpet and Small Orch. (Braunschweig, Nov. 28, 1977); *Im Freien*, symphonic poem (1980; Munich, March 20, 1981); *Sostenuto* for Cello and Strings (Deutschlandsberg, Oct. 14, 1984). CHAMBER: *Kammermusik* for Jazz Instruments (1957; Munich, Feb. 28, 1958); 2 string quartets (1969, 1975); *The Woods so Wilde: Kammermusik No. 1* for Percussion, Flute, Viola, and Guitar (1970); *Schumann in Endenich: Kammermusik* No. 2 for Piano, Electric Organ or Harmonium, and Percussion (1972); *Kindertage: Kammermusik No. 3* for Flute, Viola, Electric Organ, Piano, Accordion, Zither, Guitar, and Percussion (1973); Trio for 2 Violins and Cello (1984); other chamber works; choral pieces; songs.

Kilpatrick, Jack (Frederick), American composer; b. Stillwater, Okla., Sept. 23, 1915; d. Muskogee, Okla., Feb. 22, 1967. He studied at the Univ. of Redlands, California, and at the Catholic Univ. of America in Washington, D.C. Of Cherokee origin, he derived virtually all of his music from Indian folklore, with the pentatonic scale as its foundation. He wrote more than 200 works.

Works: Music dramas: *Unto These Hills* (Cherokee, N.C., July 1, 1950); *The Golden Crucible* (Pittsburgh, 1959); *The Blessed Wilderness* (Dallas, April 18, 1959); 8 syms., of which No. 4 is scored for Voices and Orch. (Dallas, Jan. 17, 1951); No. 5 (Honolulu, Feb. 19, 1957); No. 6 (San Antonio, March 2, 1957); No. 7, "The Republic of Texas" (San Antonio, March 2, 1957); No. 8, "Oklahoma," for Narrator, Dancers, and Orch. (Oklahoma City, Nov. 17, 1957); numerous other instrumental works.

Kilpinen, Yrjö (Henrik), Finnish music critic and composer; b. Helsinki, Feb. 4, 1892; d. there, March 2, 1959. He studied with Furuhjelm at the Helsinki Music Inst. (1908–9; 1911–12; 1916–17), Hofmann and Heuberger in Vienna (1910–11), and Juon and Taubmann in Berlin (1913–14). He wrote music criticism in Helsinki (1919–31) and also taught at the Helsinki Cons.; he was elected a member of the Finnish Academy (1948). He was best known as a composer of songs, of which he wrote more than 750; many were popular in Germany as well as in Finland. He also wrote *Pastoral Suite* for Orch. (1944), *Totentanz* for Orch. (1945), more than 30 male choruses, chamber music, 6 piano sonatas and other piano pieces, etc.

BIBL.: W. Legge, *The Songs of Y. K.* (London, 1936); T. Karila, *Y. K.* (Borgå, 1964); F. Pullano, *A Study of the Published German Songs of Y. K.* (diss., Univ. of Illinois, 1970); M. Pulkinen, *Y. K.* (Helsinki, 1982).

Kim, Byong-kon, prominent Korean-born American composer, conductor, and teacher; b. Taegu, May 28, 1929. He studied with Bernhard Heiden, Tibor Kozma, Wolfgang Vacano, Willi Apel, and Walter Kaufmann at Indiana Univ. in Bloomington (M.M., 1964; D.M.A., 1968), then was on the faculty of Calif. State Univ., Los Angeles (from 1968). He was a guest conductor with the Seoul Phil. Orch. (1978–84), the Osaka Phil. Orch. (1980), the Korea Phil. Orch. (1984), and the Taegu Sym. Orch. (1981, 1985). In 1986 he founded and became the 1st director of the Pacific Contemporary Music Center; also served as adviser to the Hong Kong–based Asian Youth Sym. Orch. He became a U.S. citizen in 1974. His orch. compositions are boldly dramatic, making particularly effective use of brass and string instruments.

Works: ORCH.: *Symphonic Poem: Nak-Dong-Kang* (1964); *Symphony* (1967); *Sori* (1978); *Symphony of 3 Metaphors* (1983); *Festival Symphony* (1984); *Choyop* (1985). BAND: *Essay for Brass and Percussion* (1962); *Seoul Fanfare* (1986). CHAMBER: *Theme and Variations* for Violin and Viola (1962);

Suite for Clarinet, Flute, and Bassoon (1962); String Quartet (1964); *Concertino* for Percussion (1965); *Epitaph* for Flute, Cello, and Percussion (1985); *The 7 Last Words of Christ* for Organ and Percussion (1986); *Sinfonietta* for 15 Strings and Harpsichord (1987); also works for solo instruments. VOCAL: *Flower Seed*, song cycle for High Voice (1964); *A Sunday Hymn* for A Cappella Chorus (1965); *i am a little church* for Mixed Chorus and Organ (1970).

Kim, Earl (actually, **Eul**), American composer of Korean descent; b. Dinuba, Calif., Jan. 6, 1920. He commenced piano training at 9, and then studied with Homer Grun; subsequently studied with Schoenberg (composition and theory) at the Univ. of Calif. at Los Angeles (1939); then became a student of Bloch at the Univ. of Calif. at Berkeley (1940). His studies were interrupted by service in the U.S. Army Intelligence Service during World War II, after which he returned to Berkeley to study with Sessions (M.A., 1952). After serving as a prof. at Princeton Univ. (1952–67), he was James Edward Ditson Prof. of Music at Harvard Univ. (from 1967). In addition to his activities as a composer and teacher, he has made appearances as a pianist and conductor. Among his many honors are the Prix de Paris, a National Inst. of Arts and Letters award, the Brandeis Univ. Creative Arts Award, a Guggenheim fellowship, and an NEA fellowship.

Works: OPERA: *Footfalls* (1981). ORCH.: *Dialogues* for Piano and Orch. (1959); Violin Concerto (N.Y., Oct. 25, 1979). CHAMBER: 2 *Bagatelles* for Piano (1952); *12 Caprices* for Violin (1980); *Scenes from Childhood* for Brass Quintet (1984). VOCAL: *Letters Found near a Suicide*, song cycle (1954); *Exercises en Route* for Soprano, Flute, Oboe, Clarinet, Violin, Cello, and 2 Percussion (1961–71); *Narratives* for High Soprano, Woman's Voice, Actor, 2 Violins, Cello, 2 Trumpets, Trombone, Piano, Television, and Lights (1973–76); *Now and Then* for Soprano, Flute, Harp, and Viola (1981); *Where Grief Slumbers* for Soprano, Harp, and String Orch. (1982); *Cornet* for Narrator and Orch. (1983); *The 7th Dream* for Soprano, Baritone, Violin, Cello, and Piano (1986); *The 11th Dream* for Soprano, Baritone, Violin, Cello, and Piano (1988); *3 Poems in French* for Soprano and String Quartet (1989).

Kim, Jin Hi, talented Korean composer and komungo player; b. Inchon, Feb. 6, 1958. She studied in Seoul at the National Univ. (1976–80), then went to the U.S., where she studied composition with John Adams at the San Francisco Cons. of Music (1980–81) and electronic music at Mills College in Oakland, Calif. (M.F.A., 1985). Her compositions, which frequently utilize traditional Korean instruments, are often compared favorably to those of the eminent Japanese composer Toru Takemitsu; the precariously hovering and often luminous sonorities that emanate from juxtaposed atonal and microtonal structures blend the best of the East and the New West. Her solo and collaborative improvisations on the komungo (a Korean 6-string board zither) are spare, gestural, and formal, ever respectful of the meditative origins of the instrument.

Works: *The Spider's Web* for Kayagum, Yangkum, Daegum, Ajang, Piri, and Percussion (1978); *Yopo* for Flute, Ajang, Yangkum, and 2 Daegums (1980); *Kee Maek No. 1* for Bamboo Flutes and Percussion (1980), *No. 2* for Solo Violin (1986), *No. 3* for Violin and Cello (1986), and *No. 4* for Viola and Cello (1988); *Woon* for Chamber Ensemble (1981); *Movement and Resonance* for Dancer with 10 Asian Gongs (1985); *Su Qai Yong Yul* for Computer-generated Tape, Harpsichord, and Cello (1985; based on a 15th-century treatise on Korean music); *x5 for solo flute* for Pre-recorded Tape, Alto and Soprano Flutes, and Piccolo (1985); *x4 for solo violin* (1985); *Bamboo Permutations No. 1* for Pre-recorded Bamboo Flutes (Daegum and Hotchiku) and Digital Sampling Keyboard (1985); *Jinyang Delay* for Live and Taped Kayagum with Digital Delay (1986); *SuryongEum* for Pre-recorded Danso and Sho with Digital Delay (1986); *Linking* for String Quartet (1986); *Tehjoo Goong* for Komungo and Alto Flute (1986); *Komungo Permutations* for Sampled and Manipulated Komungo Sounds (1988); *Tchong* for Komungo and Alto Flute (1988).

Kim, Young-Uck, outstanding South Korean violinist; b. Seoul, Sept. 1, 1947. A typical child prodigy, he began to fiddle with astounding precocity on a minuscule violin. He was sent to the U.S. when he was 11 and accepted as a student of Ivan Galamian at the Curtis Inst. of Music in Philadelphia. On May 10, 1963, he made an auspicious appearance with Ormandy and the Philadelphia Orch. in a nationally televised concert; then toured with them in South America. He made a European tour as a soloist with the Berlin Phil., the Concertgebouw Orch. of Amsterdam, the Vienna Phil., and the London Sym. He also organized the Ax-Ma-Kim Trio in 1979, with the Polish-born American pianist Emanuel Ax and the Chinese cello virtuoso Yo-Yo Ma. He has applied his brilliant virtuoso technique and interpretive insights to many contemporary works.

Kimball, Jacob, Jr., American composer; b. Topsfield, Mass., Feb. 22, 1761; d. there, Feb. 6, 1826. In 1775 he was a drummer in the Massachusetts militia; then entered Harvard Univ. (graduated, 1780); subsequently studied law and was admitted to the bar, but soon gave up that profession for music, teaching in various New England towns. He died in an almshouse. He wrote hymns, Psalm tunes, and "fuguing pieces," in the style of Billings; he publ. 120 works, many of which appeared in the *Village Harmony* (Exeter, N.H., from 1800); he publ. the collections *Rural Harmony* (Boston, 1793) and *Essex Harmony* (Exeter, N.H., 1800).
BIBL.: F. Metcalf, *American Writers and Compilers of Sacred Music* (N.Y., 1925); G. Wilcox, *J. K., Jr. (1761–1826): His Life and Works* (diss., Univ. of Southern Calif., 1957).

Kincaid, Bradley, American folk-song collector and singer; b. Point Leavell, Ky., July 13, 1895; d. Springfield, Ohio, Sept. 23, 1989. He began to sing and play the guitar as a child; after serving in the U.S. Army in World War I, he went to Chicago and studied at the YMCA College. He made his 1st appearances as a singer on the "National Barn Dance" radio program; subsequently sang on the "Grand Ole Opry" in Nashville, Tenn.; he also owned his own radio station in Springfield, Ohio (1949–53). As a folk-song collector, he publ. 13 songbooks containing material from traditional sources, as well as some compositions of his own.
BIBL.: L. Jones, *Radio's Kentucky Mountain Boy, B. K.* (Berea, Ky., 1980).

Kincaid, William, outstanding American flutist and pedagogue; b. Minneapolis, April 26, 1895; d. Philadelphia, March 27, 1967. He studied flute with Georges Barrère at the Inst. of Musical Art in N.Y.; then played in the N.Y. Sym. Orch. (1914–18). In 1921 Stokowski engaged him as 1st flutist of the Philadelphia Orch., a position he held with great distinction until his retirement in 1960; he also was a distinguished teacher at the Curtis Inst. of Music, where he taught a number of noted flutists. He maintained a valuable collection of historic flutes; his own instrument was a specially made platinum flute.
BIBL.: J. Krell, *K.iana: A Flute Player's Notebook* (Culver City, Calif., 1973).

Kinder, Ralph, English-American organist and composer; b. Stalybridge, near Manchester, Jan. 27, 1876; d. Bala, suburb of Philadelphia, Nov. 14, 1952. He was taken to the U.S. at the age of 5; was a chorister in Bristol, R.I.; studied in America, and then in London with E.H. Lemare. He held various posts as a church organist in Bristol (1890–98), Providence (1898), and Philadelphia (from 1899). He wrote numerous organ pieces of considerable charm, including *Arietta, Berceuse, Caprice, Festival March, Jour de printemps, Moonlight, Souvenir,* and *In Springtime.*

Kindermann, August, German bass-baritone; b. Potsdam, Feb. 6, 1817; d. Munich, March 6, 1891. He sang in the chorus of the Berlin Royal Opera; then appeared at the Leipzig theater (1839–46); in 1846 he became a member of the Munich Court Opera, and remained on its roster until his death; he also

sang at Bayreuth, where he created the role of Titurel in *Parsifal* (1882).

Kindermann, Johann Erasmus, eminent German organist, composer, and teacher; b. Nuremberg, March 29, 1616; d. there, April 14, 1655. He was a student of J. Staden; completed his studies in Italy. He was recalled to Nuremberg in 1636 to become 2nd organist at the Frauenkirche; was organist in Schwäbisch-Hall in 1640; then returned to Nuremberg as organist of the Egidienkirche, where he served until his death. His students included Johann Agricola, Heinrich Schwemmer, and Georg Caspar Wecker. Kindermann excelled in both vocal and instrumental composition; his *Canzoni, sonatae* for violins is one of the earliest manifestations of scordatura in Germany. Among his other works are *Cantiones (pathētikai), hoc est Ad memoriam passionis . . . Jesu Christi* for 3 and 4 Voices and Basso Continuo (motets; 1639); *Friedens Clag* for 3 Voices and Basso Continuo (3 motets; 1640); *Concentus Salomonis, das ist Geistliche Concerten auss dem Hohen Lied dess hebraïschen Königes Salomonis* for 2 Voices, 2 Violins, and Basso Continuo (1642); *Opitianischer Orpheus, das ist* [13] *Musicalischer Ergetzligkeiten* for 1 and 2 Voices, 2 Violins, Violone or Bassoon, and Basso Continuo (1642); *Musica catechetica, das ist Musicalischer Catechismus* for 5 Voices and Basso Continuo (12 motets; 1643); *Deliciae studiosorum* a 3 to 5 and Basso Continuo (4 parts, 1640–43); *Harmonia organica, in tabulaturam germanicam* (1645); (27) *Canzoni,* [9] *Sonate* for 1 to 3 Violins, Cello, and Basso Continuo (1653); 30 suite movements for Keyboard (ed. in Hortus Musicus, LXI, 1950). See F. Schreiber, ed., *Ausgewählte Werke,* in Denkmäler der Tonkunst in Bayern, XXIV, Jg. XII and XXXII, Jg. XXI–XXIV (1913–24).
BIBL.: F. Schreiber, *Der Nürnberger Organist J.E. K. (1616–1655)* (Leipzig, 1913).

Kindler, Hans, Dutch-born American cellist and conductor; b. Rotterdam, Jan. 8, 1892; d. Watch Hill, R.I., Aug. 30, 1949. He studied at the Rotterdam Cons., receiving 1st prize for piano and cello in 1906. In 1911 he was appointed prof. at Berlin's Klindworth-Scharwenka Cons., and 1st cellist of Berlin's Deutsches Opernhaus. In 1912–13 he made a successful tour of Europe; from 1914 to 1920, was 1st cellist of the Philadelphia Orch. In 1927 he made his debut as a conductor in Philadelphia; organized the National Sym. Orch. in Washington, D.C., in 1931, and was permanent conductor until his resignation in 1948.

King, Alec (Alexander) Hyatt, esteemed English bibliographer and musicologist; b. Beckenham, Kent, July 18, 1911. He was educated at Dulwich College and King's College, Cambridge (B.A., 1933); in 1934 he joined the Dept. of Printed Books of the British Museum; became superintendent of its music room in 1944, retiring in 1976. He publ. a number of valuable textual and bibliographical studies.
WRITINGS (all publ. in London unless otherwise given): *Chamber Music* (1948); *Handel's Messiah* (the exhibition catalog of the British Museum; 1951); *Mozart in Retrospect: Studies in Criticism and Bibliography* (1955; 3rd ed., 1970); *Mozart in the British Museum* (1956; 2nd ed., 1966); *Henry Purcell 1659?–1695; George Frideric Handel 1685–1759* (the exhibition catalog of the British Museum; 1959); *Some British Collectors of Music c.1600–1960* (Cambridge, 1963); *Four Hundred Years of Music Printing* (1964; 2nd ed., 1968); *Handel and His Autographs* (1967); *Mozart Chamber Music* (1968; 2nd ed., 1969); *Mozart: A Biography, with a Survey of Books, Editions and Recordings* (1970); *Mozart Wind and String Concertos* (1978); *Printed Music in the British Museum: An Account of the Collections, the Catalogues, and Their Formation, up to 1920* (1979); *A Wealth of Music in the Collection of the British Library (Reference Section) and the British Museum* (1983); *A Mozart Legacy: Aspects of the British Library Collections* (1984); *Musical Pursuits: Selected Essays* (1987).
BIBL.: O. Neighbour, ed., *Music and Bibliography: Essays in Honour of A.H. K.* (London, 1980).

King, "B.B." (Riley B.), black American blues singer and guitarist; b. Itta Bena, Miss., Sept. 16, 1925. While working on a farm, he learned to play the guitar; then worked as a disc jockey for a Memphis radio station under the name "Blues Boy," which stuck as "B.B." In 1950 he scored his 1st hit with his recording of *3 O'Clock Blues;* in the late 1960s he assumed a prominent place among the great blues singers and guitarists; in 1968 he made his 1st tour of Europe, and then headed an all-blues concert at Carnegie Hall in N.Y. in 1970. He won a Grammy Award in 1981 for his album *There Must Be a Better World Somewhere.* Utilizing an electric guitar, he is regarded as one of the most innovative blues artists of his era.

BIBL.: C. Sawyer, *B.B. K.: The Authorized Biography* (Poole, England, 1980).

King (real name, **Klein**), **Carole,** American pop singer and songwriter; b. N.Y., Feb. 9, 1941. She took piano lessons as a child; an intellectually precocious teenager, she started a female vocal ensemble in school under a trigonometrical name, Co-Sines. At 17, she met the songwriter Gerry Goffin, whom she soon married. They produced a hit song, *Will You Love Me Tomorrow.* Several other hits followed, among them *Some Kind of Wonderful, When My Little Girl Is Smiling, Up on the Roof, Take Good Care of My Baby, The Loco-Motion,* and *It Might As Well Rain until September.* On her own, she produced the smash hits *You've Got a Friend, It's Too Late,* and *I Feel the Earth,* which had a direct appeal to folk-rockers of all ages. After two divorces, she married the songwriter Rick Evers; he died of a cocaine overdose in Los Angeles in 1978.

King, Harold Charles, Swiss-born Dutch composer; b. Winterthur, Dec. 30, 1895; d. Amsterdam, June 12, 1984. He went to the Netherlands to study engineering at the Delft Technical Univ.; served as a management consultant with a municipal corporation in Amsterdam; while thus occupied, he took composition lessons with Cornelis Dopper and Henk Badings.

WORKS: Serenade for String Orch. (1934); *Per Ardua,* symphonic suite (1946–49); *Concerto da camera* for Flute and Strings (1962); *Triptyque symphonique* (1964); Sinfonietta (1965); Organ Concerto (1966); *O Leben, Leben, wunderliche Zeit* for Middle Voice and Orch. (1983); Cello Sonata (1940); *Trio patetico* for Violin, Viola, and Cello (1942); *3 Impressions* for Solo Cello (1948); Wind Quintet (1949); 2 string quartets (1953, 1962); *A fleur d'eau* for Flute, Violin, Spinet, and Viola da Gamba (1964); Sonata for Solo Cello (1966); Duo for 2 Cellos (1966); *Piccolo quartetto* for String Quartet (1976); *Little Laddie,* piano sonatina (1966); *King David's Dance* for 4-octave Carillon (1975); *Cornet* for Choir and Instruments (1977); *3 chansons d'amour et une epigramme* for Voice and Instruments (1981); *Tres orationes* for Voice, Recorder, and Lute (1982).

King, James, American tenor; b. Dodge City, Kans., May 22, 1925. He studied at the Univ. of Kansas City; also received vocal training from Martial Singher and Max Lorenz. He then went to Europe and made his professional debut as Cavaradossi in Florence (1961); subsequently sang at the San Francisco Opera, the Berlin Deutsche Oper, the Salzburg Festival, the Bayreuth Festival, the Metropolitan Opera in N.Y. (debut as Florestan, Jan. 8, 1966), London's Covent Garden, and Milan's La Scala. He taught voice at the Indiana Univ. School of Music in Bloomington (from 1984). Among his prominent roles were Lohengrin, Walther von Stolzing, Parsifal, and Verdi's Otello.

King, Karl L(awrence), American bandmaster and composer of band music; b. Painterville, Ohio, Feb. 21, 1891; d. Fort Dodge, Iowa, March 31, 1971. After 8 grades of public schools in Cleveland and Canton, Ohio, during which he began to play brass instruments (primarily the baritone horn) under the tutelage of local musicians, he quit school to learn the printing trade, but soon began to play in and compose for local bands. In 1910 he initiated his short career as a circus bandsman, bandmaster, and composer, ending it in 1917–18 as bandmaster of the Barnum & Bailey Circus Band (for which he had already written what was to remain his most famous

march, *Barnum & Bailey's Favorite*). On Sept. 13, 1920, he conducted his 1st concert with the Fort Dodge Military Band, with which he was to be associated for half a century. It was a time when the small-town band in the U.S. was passing its heyday; but King took a group of only 18 bandsmen, added to them, and in a very few years had created a notable institution, not only in Iowa but in the whole Midwestern rural culture (and this over a period when most town bands were disappearing under the competition of radio, recordings, the school-band movement, and faster transportation and communications). In 1922 the band began to receive municipal tax support under the Iowa Band Law (for which one of King's marches is named), and its name was changed to the Fort Dodge Municipal Band, although it was known commonly as Karl L. King's Band. For 40 years it toured widely over its region, especially to play at county fairs, and King himself traveled even more widely to conduct or judge at band contests, conventions, massed band celebrations, and all manner of band events. He was one of the founders, in 1930, of the American Bandmasters Assoc.; he served as president of that group in 1939, and in 1967 was named honorary life president. Among his 260-odd works for band (most publ. by the firm of C.L. Barnhouse in Oskaloosa, Iowa) are concert works, novelties, waltzes, and all manner of dance forms; but marches predominate, from the circus marches of his early days to sophisticated marches for univ. bands (such as *Pride of the Illini* for Illinois and *Purple Pageant* for Northwestern) and especially to easy but tuneful and well-written marches for the less accomplished school bands. The musical *The Music Man* (1957) was inspired in part by King's music, according to its composer and fellow Iowan, Meredith Willson.

BIBL.: T. Hatton, *K.L. K., An American Bandmaster* (Evanston, Ill., 1975).

King, Matthew Peter, English composer and music theorist; b. London, c.1773; d. there, Jan. 1823. He composed a number of stage works, several of which became popular in their day. He also publ. *Thorough Bass Made Clear to every Capacity* (London, c.1810) and *A General Treatise on Music, Particularly Harmony or Thoroughbass* (London, 1812). Among his comic operas were *Matrimony* (London, Nov. 20, 1804), *Up All Night, or The Smuggler's Cave* (London, June 26, 1809), and *The Americans* (London, April 27, 1811; in collaboration with Braham). He also composed a grand Romantic opera, *1 o'Clock, or The Knight and the Wood Daemon* (London, Aug. 1, 1811; in collaboration with M. Kelly); several musical farces and melodramas; an oratorio, *The Intercession* (London, June 1, 1816); numerous instrumental pieces, as well as glees and songs.

King, Oliver A., English pianist, teacher, and composer; b. London, July 6, 1855; d. there, Aug. 23, 1923. He was a pupil of J. Barnby; later studied piano with Reinecke at the Leipzig Cons. (1874–77). From 1880 to 1883 he toured Canada. In 1893 he was appointed prof. of piano at the Royal Academy of Music in London.

WORKS: 3 cantatas: *The Romance of the Roses; Proserpina; The Naiades; 137th Psalm* (Chester Festival, 1888); symphonic poem, *Night;* 2 overtures; Piano Concerto; Violin Concerto; pieces for piano solo and for organ.

King, Pete, American composer, arranger, and conductor; b. Greenville, Ohio, Aug. 8, 1914; d. Newport Beach, Calif., Sept. 20, 1982. He attended a prep school in Newport, R.I., the Univ. of Michigan, and the Cincinnati Cons. of Music; then went to N.Y., where he began a successful career as conductor and arranger for Broadway productions. In 1952 he moved to Los Angeles, where he led popular ensembles advertised as the Pete King Chorale and the Pete King Orch. He became a favorite conductor-arranger for many Hollywood stars and television personalities, among them Bing Crosby, Frank Sinatra, and Lawrence Welk. He earned a credit line as music director for such famous motion pictures as *South Pacific* and *The Godfather.* Unhappily, he was stricken in 1974 with meningitis, which caused total deafness and forced him to retire.

King, Thea, English clarinetist and teacher; b. Hitchin, Hertfordshire, Dec. 26, 1925. She studied clarinet at the Royal College of Music in London (1943–47) with Frederick Thurston, whom she married in 1953. She played in the Sadler's Wells Orch. (1950–52), Portia Wind Ensemble (1955–68), London Mozart Players (1956–84), English Chamber Orch. (from 1964), Melos Ensemble (from 1974), and Robles Ensemble (from 1983); also made appearances as a soloist and recitalist. From 1961 to 1987 she was a prof. at the Royal College of Music in London, and from 1988 at the Guildhall School of Music. In 1985 she was made an Officer of the Order of the British Empire. She has performed many works by contemporary British composers and has also resuscitated numerous scores of the past.

Kinkel, Johanna (née **Mockel**), German composer; b. Bonn, July 8, 1810; d. London, Nov. 15, 1858. She studied music in Berlin with Karl Böhmer, and married Gottfried Kinkel, the poet, in 1843. She wrote *Die Vogel-Cantate;* the operetta *Otto der Schutz;* and the well-known song *The Soldier's Farewell;* also publ. *Acht Briefe an eine Freundin über Klavierunterricht* (1852).

Kinkeldey, Otto, eminent American musicologist; b. N.Y., Nov. 27, 1878; d. Orange, N.J., Sept. 19, 1966. He graduated from the College of the City of N.Y. in 1898 (B.A.) and from N.Y. Univ. in 1900 (M.A.); then took lessons with MacDowell at Columbia Univ. (until 1902). He went to Berlin (1902), where he undertook a course of study with Radecke, Egidi, and Thiel at the Königlisches Akademisches Institut für Kirchenmusik; then studied musicology at the Univ. of Berlin with Fleischer, Friedlaender, Kretzschmar, and J. Wolf (Ph.D., 1909, with the diss. *Orgel und Klavier in der Musik des 16. Jahrhunderts;* publ. in Leipzig, 1910). He taught at the Univ. of Breslau (1909–14); returning to the U.S., he was chief of the music division of the N.Y. Public Library (1915–23; 1927–30); was prof. of music at Cornell Univ. (1923–27), subsequently prof. of musicology and a librarian there (1930–46). He was a guest prof. at various American univs.; was president of the American Musicological Soc. (1934–36; 1940–42). He contributed numerous articles to scholarly journals; also publ. *What We Know about Music* (Ann Arbor, 1946).
Bibl.: E. Dent, "O. K.," *Musical Quarterly* (Oct. 1938); G. Dickinson, "O. K.: An Appreciation," ibid.; special issue of *Notes* (Dec. 1948); "A Musicological Offering to O. K. upon the Occasion of His 80th Birthday," *Journal of the American Musicological Society,* XIII (1960).

Kinsky, Georg Ludwig, distinguished German musicologist; b. Marienwerder, Sept. 29, 1882; d. Berlin, April 7, 1951. He was self-taught in music; after working under Klopfermann at the Prussian Royal Library in Berlin (1908–9), he was curator of the private museum of W. Heyer in Cologne from 1909 until it was closed in 1927; also was a lecturer in musicology at the Univ. of Cologne (1921–32), where he received his Ph.D. in 1925. In 1944 his home and his private library and collection were confiscated by the Nazi government; he then served a year at hard labor until the Allied victory in 1945. Although his health was shattered by this ordeal, he spent his last years in Berlin preparing a thematic catalog of Beethoven's works, a task completed by Hans Halm.
Writings: *Musikhistorisches Museum von Wilhelm Heyer in Cöln: Katalog* (Cologne, Vol. I, 1910; Vol. II, 1912, and Vol. IV, 1916; Vol. III not publ.; greater portion of the MS not extant); ed. *Glucks Briefe an Franz Kruthoffer* (Vienna, 1927); with R. Haas and H. Schnoor, *Geschichte der Musik in Bildern* (Leipzig, 1929; Eng. tr., 1930; 2nd ed., 1951); *Die Originalausgaben der Werke Johann Sebastian Bachs* (Vienna, 1937); *Manuskripte, Briefe, Dokumente von Scarlatti bis Stravinsky, Katalog der Musik-autographen-Sammlung Louis Koch* (Stuttgart, 1951; ed. by M.-A. Souchay); *Das Werk Beethovens: Thematisch-Bibliographisches Verzeichnis siner sämtlichen vollendeten Kompositionen* (Munich and Duisburg, 1955; completed by H. Halm).

Kipnis, Alexander, eminent Russian-born American bass, father of **Igor Kipnis;** b. Zhitomir, Feb. 13, 1891; d. Westport, Conn., May 14, 1978. He studied conducting at the Warsaw Cons. (graduated, 1912); later took voice lessons with Ernst Grenzebach at Berlin's Klindworth-Scharwenka Cons. In 1913 he sang at Monti's Operetten Theater and in 1914 at the Filmzauber operetta theater. At the outbreak of World War I, he was interned as an enemy alien, but was soon released and made his operatic debut as the hermit in *Der Freischütz* at the Hamburg Opera in 1915; sang there until 1917, then was a member of the Wiesbaden Opera (1917–22). He made his U.S. debut as Pogner in *Die Meistersinger von Nürnberg* with the visiting German Opera Co. in Baltimore on Jan. 31, 1923; he then was a member of the Chicago Civic Opera (1923–32). He also sang regularly at the Berlin Städtische Oper (1922–30), the Berlin State Opera (1932–35), and the Vienna State Opera (1935–38). He became an American citizen in 1931. During these years, he made guest appearances at the Bayreuth, Salzburg, and Glyndebourne festivals, as well as at Covent Garden in London and the Teatro Colón in Buenos Aires. On Jan. 5, 1940, he made his belated Metropolitan Opera debut in N.Y. as Gurnemanz in *Parsifal,* and continued to sing there until 1946; he then devoted himself mainly to teaching. Through the years he appeared as a soloist with Richard Strauss, Siegfried Wagner, and Toscanini.

Kipnis, Igor, distinguished American harpsichordist and fortepianist, son of **Alexander Kipnis;** b. Berlin, Sept. 27, 1930. In 1938 the family moved to the U.S., where he took piano lessons with his maternal grandfather, **Heniot Levy;** after attending the Westport (Conn.) School of Music, he studied with Randall Thompson and Thurston Dart at Harvard Univ. (B.A., 1952). He also took harpsichord lessons with Fernando Valenti. After graduation, Kipnis served abroad in the Signal Corps of the U.S. Army. Returning to the U.S., he eked out his living as a bookstore salesman in N.Y.; later was employed as an editorial adviser to Westminster Records Co. He made his concert debut as a harpsichordist in a N.Y. radio broadcast in 1959; his formal concert debut followed there in 1962. He taught at the Berkshire Music Center in Tanglewood (summers, 1964–67); in 1967 he made his 1st European tour, and subsequently toured throughout the world. He served as an associate prof. of fine arts (1971–75) and artist-in-residence (1975–77) at Fairfield Univ. in Conn.; also taught and played at the Festival Music Soc. concerts in Indianapolis and taught at its Early-Music Inst. In 1981 he made his debut as a fortepianist in Indianapolis. He did much to revive the fortepiano. He also promoted interest in modern music. Several contemporary composers, among them Ned Rorem, George Rochberg, Richard Rodney Bennett, Barbara Kolb, and John McCabe, have written works for him.

Király, Ernö, Hungarian composer and ethnomusicologist; b. Subotica, Yugoslavia, March 16, 1919. He studied trumpet at the Subotica School of Music (1939). In 1953 he became Hungarian folk music ed. for Novi Sad Broadcasting; in 1958, head of the folk music dept. at the Vojvodina Museum in Novi Sad. He publ. several books and articles on Hungarian folk music and instruments. As a composer, he was interested in folk music and experimented with new intonational and interpretive structures. Among his works are a children's opera, *A kis torkos* (The Little Glutton; 1962), *Vocalizzazioni* for Chorus (1969), and *Indications* for 3 Performers and Tape (1973).

Kirby, John, black American jazz string-bass player, combo leader, and arranger; b. Baltimore, Dec. 31, 1908; d. Los Angeles, June 14, 1952. He first played trombone, then tuba; subsequently was a string-bass player in Fletcher Henderson's band (1930–34; 1935–36); also played with Chick Webb (1934). He was a member of the Onyx Club band (1937–38); then took it over and toured as John Kirby and His Onyx Club Boys; later led his own sextet, which appeared at N.Y.'s Carnegie Hall (1950).

Kirby, Percival Robson, Scottish-born South African musicologist; b. Aberdeen, April 17, 1887; d. Grahamstown, South Africa, Feb. 7, 1970. He studied with Terry at the Univ. of Aberdeen (degree, 1910) and with Stanford at the Royal College of Music in London. In 1914 he emigrated to South Africa and became music organizer of the Natal Education Dept.; from 1921 to 1952, he was prof. of music at Univ. College in Johannesburg (later the Univ. of the Witwatersrand). He founded and conducted the Johannesburg Sym. Orch. (1927) and the Univ. Orch. (1930), for which he wrote numerous songs. He is best known for his scholarly work on South African music; much of his field research resulted in *The Musical Instruments of the Native Races of South Africa* (London, 1934). An expedition to the Kalahari Desert in 1936 led to important studies of Bushman music.

Kirbye, George, English composer; b. c.1565; d. Bury St. Edmunds (buried), Oct. 6, 1634. He served as a domestic musician at Rushbrooke Hall, near Bury St. Edmunds. He was a gifted madrigalist, as revealed in his *The first set of English madrigalls, to 4. 5. & 6. voyces* (London, 1597; ed. by E. Fellowes and rev. by T. Dart in The English Madrigalists, London, 2nd ed., 1961). He was also a fine composer of sacred music; contributed 19 pieces to East's *The Whole Booke of Psalmes* (London, 1592).
    BIBL.: C. Monson, "G. K. and the English Madrigal," *Music & Letters,* LIX (1978).

Kircher, Athanasius, significant German scholar; b. Geisa, near Fulda, May 2, 1601; d. Rome, Nov. 27, 1680. He attended a Jesuit school in Fulda (1612–18); became a novice at the Jesuit college in Paderborn in 1618. He subsequently studied physical sciences and philosophy in Cologne (1622), languages in Koblenz (1623), and theology in Mainz (ordained 1628); from 1629 to 1631 he taught mathematics, philosophy, and oriental languages at the Univ. of Würzburg; in 1631 he went to Avignon, and in 1633 to Vienna as court mathematician to Emperor Ferdinand II; that same year he went to Rome, where he taught at the Collegio Romano. His writings are a curious mixture of scientific speculation and puerile credulity. His *Oedipus aegiptiacus* (Rome, 1652–54) contains a curious chapter on hieroglyphic music; in his treatise *Magnes, sive De arte magnetica* (Rome, 1641; 2nd ed., rev., 1643) he gives examples of musical airs which were popularly regarded as a cure for tarantism (a nervous condition supposedly induced by the bite of a tarantula). His principal work is the Latin compendium *Musurgia universalis, sive Ars magna consoni et dissoni* (Rome, 1650; ed. by W. Goldhan, Leipzig, 1988).
    BIBL.: U. Scharlau, *A. K. (1601–1680) als Musikschriftsteller* (Marburg, 1969).

Kirchhoff, Walter, German tenor; b. Berlin, March 17, 1879; d. Wiesbaden, March 26, 1951. He studied in Berlin with Eugen Weiss and Lilli Lehmann; made his debut at the Berlin Royal Opera in 1906 as Faust; continued on its roster until 1920 after it became the Berlin State Opera in 1918; sang there again in 1923–24, 1928–29, and 1932; also appeared at the Bayreuth Festivals (1911–14) and at Covent Garden in London in 1913 and 1924. He made an acclaimed Metropolitan Opera debut in N.Y. as Loge in *Das Rheingold* on Jan. 28, 1927; remained on its roster until 1931. He was particularly successful in Wagnerian roles.

Kirchner, Leon, significant American composer; b. N.Y., Jan. 24, 1919. In 1928 the family went to Los Angeles, where he studied piano with Richard Buhlig; in 1938 he entered the Univ. of Calif., Berkeley, where he took courses in theory with Albert Elkus and Edward Strickland (B.A., 1940; M.M., 1949); he also took lessons with Ernest Bloch in San Francisco. In 1942 he went to N.Y., where he had fruitful private sessions with Sessions; in 1943 he entered military service in the U.S. Army; after demobilization in 1946, he was appointed to the faculty of the San Francisco Cons., concurrently teaching at the Univ. of Calif., Berkeley; in 1948 he received a Guggenheim fellowship; from 1950 to 1954, served as associate prof. at the Univ. of Southern Calif., Los Angeles; subsequently taught at Mills College in Oakland, Calif. (1954–61), and in 1961 was named prof. of music at Harvard Univ. He was elected a member of the National Inst. of Arts and Letters and the American Academy of Arts and Sciences in 1962; in 1967 he was awarded the Pulitzer Prize in Music for his 3rd String Quartet. In his music Kirchner takes the prudential median course, cultivating a distinct modern idiom without espousing any particular modernistic technique, but making ample and effective use of euphonious dissonance; the contrapuntal fabric in his works is tense but invariably coherent. Through his natural inclinations toward Classical order, he prefers formal types of composition, often following the established Baroque style.
    WORKS: OPERA: *Lily,* after Saul Bellow's *Henderson, the Rain King* (1973–76; N.Y., April 14, 1977; arranged for Soprano, Tape, and Chamber Ensemble, 1973). **ORCH.:** Sinfonia (1951; N.Y., Jan. 31, 1952); 2 piano concertos: No. 1 (1953; N.Y., Feb. 23, 1956); No. 2 (Seattle, Oct. 28, 1963); *Toccata* for Strings, Wind Instruments, and Percussion (1955; San Francisco, Feb. 16, 1956); Concerto for Violin, Cello, 10 Wind Instruments, and Percussion (1960); *Music for Orchestra* (N.Y., Oct. 16, 1969); *Music for Flute and Orchestra* (Indianapolis, Oct. 20, 1978). **CHAMBER:** Duo for Violin and Piano (1947); 3 string quartets: No. 1 (1949; N.Y., March 1950); No. 2 (1958); No. 3 (1966; N.Y., Jan. 27, 1967); awarded the Pulitzer Prize in Music); *Sonata concertante* for Violin and Piano (N.Y., Nov. 30, 1952); Trio for Violin, Cello, and Piano (Pasadena, Calif., Nov. 30, 1954); Fanfare for Brass Trio (1965); Fanfare for 7 Brass Instruments (1985); *Music for 12* (Boston, Feb. 17, 1985). **PIANO:** Sonata (1948; N.Y., March 1949); *Little Suite* (1949); *A Moment for Roger* (1978). **CHORAL:** *Dawn* for Chorus and Organ (1943–46; N.Y., Feb. 1949); *Words from Wordsworth* (1968); songs.

Kirchner, Theodor (Fürchtegott), German organist and composer; b. Neukirchen, near Chemnitz, Dec. 10, 1823; d. Hamburg, Sept. 18, 1903. On Mendelssohn's advice, he studied in Leipzig from 1838 to 1842 with C.F. Becker (theory) and J. Knorr (piano), and, in 1842–43, with Johann Schneider in Dresden. He was engaged as organist at Winterthur (1843–62); then went to Zürich, where he became director of the subscription concerts, choir conductor, and teacher at the music school. He was director of the Würzburg Cons. (1873–75); taught in Leipzig (1875); gave courses in chamber music at the Dresden Cons. (1883–90). As a youth he enjoyed the friendship of Mendelssohn and Schumann, who encouraged and aided him with advice. He wrote about 90 piano works; some of his miniatures are of very high quality; he also made numerous transcriptions for piano solo and piano duet; wrote chamber music.
    BIBL.: A. Niggli, *T. K.* (Leipzig, 1880); O. Klauwell, *T. K.* (Langensalza, 1909); P. Schneider, ed., *T. K.: Briefe aus den Jahren 1860–1868* (Zürich, 1949).

Kirckman (also **Kirchmann** or **Kirkman**), **Jacob,** German-born English organist, composer, and harpsichord maker; b. Bischweiler, near Strasbourg, March 4, 1710; d. Greenwich (buried), June 9, 1792. He settled about 1730 in London, where he was associated with a Flemish harpsichord maker, Hermann Tabel. After Tabel's death, he married his widow and acquired Tabel's tools. In 1755 he was naturalized as a British subject. About 1770 he formed a partnership with his nephew, Abraham Kirckman (1737–94), whose descendants continued the business until 1898, when the firm was merged with Collard; it was eventually absorbed by Chappell.
    BIBL.: D. Boalch, *Makers of the Harpsichord and Clavichord* (London, 1956; 2nd ed., rev., 1973).

Kiriac-Georgescu, Dumitru, Rumanian conductor, composer, and teacher; b. Bucharest, March 18, 1866; d. there, Jan. 8, 1928. He studied with Gheorghe Brătianu and Eduard Wachmann at the Bucharest Cons.; then with Dubois, Widor, and Bourgault-Ducoudray at the Paris Cons. (1892–99); also with d'Indy at the Schola Cantorum. He became a prof. at the Bucharest Cons. (1900); founded the Choral Soc. Carmen (1901); was active as a folklorist. He composed a large output of sacred choruses.

BIBL.: G. Breazul, *D. K.-G.* (Bucharest, 1973).

Kirigin, Ivo, Croatian conductor and composer; b. Zadar, Feb. 2, 1914; d. Zagreb, Oct. 21, 1964. He studied in Italy with Pizzetti; was active as a theater conductor in Zagreb; among his works are Concertino for Piano and Orch.; Sym. (1950); cantata, *Pjesma o zemlji* (Song of the Land; 1952); *Kameni horizonti* (Stone Horizons; Zagreb, March 16, 1955); 5 *Movements* for Strings (1958); numerous songs.

Kirk, "Andy" (Andrew Dewey), black American jazz saxophonist and bandleader; b. Newport, Ky., May 28, 1898. He studied piano, alto saxophone, and theory with Wilberforce Whiteman in Denver; then joined the George Morrison orch. in 1918; after moving to Dallas in 1925 he played in Terence Holder's Dark Clouds of Joy orch., becoming its conductor in 1929 and making a notable reputation in Kansas City; it was one of the leading big bands until its demise in 1948. His wife, **Mary Lou Williams,** was a composer-arranger for his band. With A. Lee, he publ. *Twenty Years on Wheels* (Ann Arbor, 1989), an account of his career.

Kirk, Rahsaan (originally, **Roland**), black American jazz instrumentalist and composer; b. Columbus, Ohio, Aug. 7, 1936; d. Bloomington, Ind., Dec. 5, 1977. He lost his sight in infancy and was brought up at the Ohio State School for the Blind; learned to play trumpet, tenor saxophone, flute, clarinet, manzello (a saxophone hybrid), strichophone (an abortion of a horn), and nose flute. He had an uncanny ability to play 2 or 3 wind instruments simultaneously. In 1963 he organized his own band, with which he toured Europe, Australia, and New Zealand. He composed many songs of the pop variety; typical titles are *Here Comes the Whistleman; I Talk with the Spirits; Rip, Rig and Panic; Funk Underneath.*

Kirkby, Emma, English soprano; b. Camberley, Feb. 26, 1949. She studied classics at Oxford; made her debut in London in 1974; specialized in early music; was a member of the Academy of Ancient Music, the London Baroque, and the Consort of Musicke. In 1978 she toured the U.S.; then gave concerts in the Middle East with the lutenist Anthony Rooley. Her repertoire ranges from the Italian quattrocento to arias by Handel, Mozart, and Haydn. The careful attention she pays to the purity of intonation free from intrusive vibrato has been praised.

Kirkby-Lunn, Louise, noted English mezzo-soprano; b. Manchester, Nov. 8, 1873; d. London, Feb. 17, 1930. She studied voice in Manchester and at the Royal College of Music in London; appeared as an opera singer at various London theaters, making her debut at Drury Lane in 1893; then sang with the Carl Rosa Opera Co. (until 1899). In 1901 she became a member of Covent Garden, where she became a popular favorite in such roles as Ortrud, Fricka, Carmen, and Massenet's Hérodiade. On Dec. 26, 1902, she sang for the 1st time at the Metropolitan Opera in N.Y. as Ortrud; was on its roster until 1903 and again during the 1906–8 seasons; sang with the British National Opera Co. (1919–22); then appeared as a concert singer.

Kirkpatrick, John, eminent American pianist and pedagogue; b. N.Y., March 18, 1905. He studied at Princeton Univ. (graduated, 1926), and in Paris with I. Philipp, C. Decreus, and Nadia Boulanger; returning to the U.S. in 1931, he became an energetic promoter of the cause of American music. His signal achievement was the 1st performance of the *Concord Sonata* by Charles Ives, which he gave in N.Y. on Jan. 20, 1939, playing it from memory, an extraordinary feat for the time; this performance, which earned enthusiastic reviews for both Ives and Kirkpatrick, played an important role in the public recognition of Ives. As a pedagogue, Kirkpatrick taught at Mount Holyoke College (1943–46) and at Cornell Univ. (1946–68); later was on the faculty of Yale Univ. (1968–73), where he was also curator of the Charles Ives Collection. His compendia *A Temporary Mimeographed Catalogue of the Music*

Manuscripts and Related Materials of Charles Edward Ives (New Haven, 1960; new ed., 1973) and *Charles E. Ives: Memos* (N.Y., 1972) are primary Ives sources.

Kirkpatrick, Ralph (Leonard), eminent American harpsichordist, clavichordist, pianist, music scholar, and pedagogue; b. Leominster, Mass., June 10, 1911; d. Guilford, Conn., April 13, 1984. He studied at Harvard Univ. (A.B., 1931); then went to Paris to study theory with Nadia Boulanger, and also took lessons in harpsichord playing with Wanda Landowska. He subsequently worked with Arnold Dolmetsch in Haslemere, in order to acquaint himself with the technical problems of performing on early keyboard instruments and on modern replicas. He also studied with Günther Ramin and Heinz Tiessen in Berlin. In 1937 he was awarded a Guggenheim fellowship for research in Baroque performing practices; he undertook an extensive tour of Europe, studying private collections of MSS. His research was particularly fruitful in Spain; he consulted the Madrid telephone book for descendants of Domenico Scarlatti (who spent his last years of life in Spain) and was fortunate enough to discover that several Scarlattis listed in the directory were indeed related to the family; the MSS he was able to find there became the foundation of his standard biography, *Domenico Scarlatti* (Princeton and London, 1953; 3rd ed., rev., 1968). In 1940 he joined the faculty of Yale Univ., becoming a prof. in 1965 and remaining on its staff until his retirement in 1976; he was also the 1st Ernest Bloch Prof. of Music at the Univ. of Calif. at Berkeley (1964). Kirkpatrick was highly selective in his evaluation of Baroque music; while emphasizing the importance of William Byrd, François Couperin, and Domenico Scarlatti, he regarded Vivaldi and Telemann as minor composers serving the temporary tastes of the general public. He ed. 60 sonatas by Scarlatti (N.Y., 1953) and recorded them, and produced a complete ed. of the keyboard works in facsimile (N.Y., 1971 and subsequent vols.). He also wrote *Interpreting Bach's "Well-tempered Clavier": A Performer's Discourse of Method* (New Haven and London, 1984) and *Early Years* (N.Y., 1984), a memoir. His interpretations as a harpsichordist were of the highest degree of fidelity to the Baroque style; he also gave brilliant performances of modern piano works, including those of Stravinsky, Milhaud, Cowell, Piston, and Carter.

Kirnberger, Johann Philipp, noted German music theorist and pedagogue; b. Saalfeld (baptized), April 24, 1721; d. Berlin, July 26 or 27, 1783. He studied violin and harpsichord at home, then took organ lessons with J.P. Kellner in Gräfenroda, and with H.N. Gerber in Sondershausen; also studied violin with Meil there; completed his studies with Bach in Leipzig (1739–41). He then traveled in Poland (1741–51) as a tutor in various noble Polish families; from 1751 to 1754 he was violinist to Frederick the Great in Berlin, and from 1754 to 1758 to Prince Heinrich of Prussia; from 1758 to 1783 he was Kapellmeister to Princess Anna Amalie. He was greatly renowned as a teacher; among his pupils were J.A.P. Schulz, C.P.E. Bach, the Graun brothers, and J.F. Agricola. As a theoretical writer, he was regarded as one of the greatest authorities of his time, even though his presentations were often disorganized to such an extent that he had to call upon others to edit or even rewrite his publications. In his compositions he displayed an amazing contrapuntal technique, and seriously strove to establish a scientific method of writing according to basic rules of combination and permutation; his *Der allezeit fertige Polonoisen- und Menuettencomponist* (1757) expounded the automatic method of composition. His other publs. include *Construction der gleichschwebenden Temperatur* (1760; reprint 1973), *Die Kunst des reinen Satzes in der Musik, aus sicheren Grundsätzen hergeleitet und mit deutlichen Beyspielen erläutert* (2 vols., Berlin and Königsberg, 1771 and 1776–79; 2nd ed., 1793; reprint 1973), *Grundsätze des Generalbasses als erste Linien zur Composition* (Berlin, 1781; reprint 1974), *Gedanken über die verschiedenen Lehrarten in der Komposition, als Vorbereitung zur Fugenkenntniss* (Berlin, 1782; 2nd ed., 1793; reprint 1974), and *Die wahren Grundsätze zum Gebrauch der Har-*

monie . . . als ein Zusatz zu der Kunst der reinen Satzes in der Musik (Berlin and Königsberg, 1773; 2nd ed., 1793; reprint 1974; written by J.A.P. Schulz under Kirnberger's supervision).

BIBL.: S. Borris- Zuckermann, *K.s Leben und Werk und seine Bedeutung für den Berliner Musikkreis um 1750* (Kassel, 1933); F. Bose, "Anna Amalie von Preussen und J.P. K.," *Die Musikforschung*, X (1957); H. Serwer, "Marpurg versus K.: Theories of Fugal Composition," *Journal of Music Theory*, XIV (1970).

Kirshbaum, Ralph (Henry), American cellist; b. Denton, Texas, March 4, 1946. He studied with Lev Aronson in Dallas; made his formal debut with the Dallas Sym. Orch. in 1959; subsequently studied with Parisot at Yale Univ. (B.A., 1968). He won the Cassadó Competition in Florence in 1969 and the Tchaikovsky Competition in Moscow in 1970; thereafter pursued a fine career as a soloist in the major music centers; also joined the pianist Peter Frankl and the violinist Gyorgy Pauk in organizing a trio in London in 1972, with which he appeared frequently.

Kirsten, Dorothy, noted American soprano; b. Montclair, N.J., July 6, 1915. She studied at the Juilliard School of Music in N.Y.; Grace Moore took an interest in her and enabled her to study with Astolfo Pescia in Rome. With the outbreak of World War II in 1939, she returned to the U.S. She became a member of the Chicago Opera Co. (debut as Pousette in *Manon*, Nov. 9, 1940); made her 1st appearance in N.Y. as Mimi with the San Carlo Opera Co. (May 10, 1942); appeared with the Metropolitan Opera in N.Y. in the same role on Dec. 1, 1945; sang there until 1952, from 1954 to 1957, and from 1960 until her farewell performance as Tosca (Dec. 31, 1975). Among her finest roles were Manon Lescaut, Cio-Cio-San, Marguerite, Louise (coached by the composer), and Nedda in *Pagliacci*; also sang in several films, including *The Great Caruso*. She publ. an autobiography, *A Time to Sing* (Garden City, N.Y., 1982).

Kishibe, Shigeo, Japanese ethnomusicologist; b. Tokyo, June 16, 1912. He studied at Tokyo Univ. (B.A. in oriental history, 1936; Ph.D. in literature, 1961), where he was a prof. (1949–73); also lectured (from 1952) at the Tokyo National Univ. of Fine Arts and Music and at various American univs., including the Univ. of Calif. at Los Angeles, Harvard Univ., and Stanford Univ. He is a founding member of the Soc. for Research in Asiatic Music. His research has focused particularly on the music of China and Japan, but he has also done fieldwork in Korea, India, Iran, and the Philippines. Among his numerous publications is *The Traditional Music of Japan* (Tokyo, 1966).

Kisielewski, Stefan, Polish composer, journalist, and novelist; b. Warsaw, March 7, 1911. He received training in philology at the Univ. of Warsaw; pursued studies in piano with Lefeld (diploma, 1934) and in theory and composition with Sikorski (diplomas in both, 1937) at the Warsaw Cons., completing his training in Paris (1938–39). In 1935 he began writing on music and politics; during the Nazi occupation of Poland, he was an official of the cultural dept. of the Underground. After the liberation in 1945, he was a prof. at the Krakow College of Music (until 1950); also served as ed. in chief of the music weekly *Puch Muzyczny* (1945–48) and was a columnist for the Catholic opposition weekly *Sygodnih Powysechny* (1945–83) in Krakow. In addition to his writings on music, he publ. novels and books on politics, some of which have appeared abroad in translations. For his musical efforts, he has received awards from the City of Krakow (1956) and the Union of Polish Composers (1982). His compositions generally follow along neo-Classical lines.

WORKS: 3 ballets: *Diably polski* (Polish Devils; 1957; Warsaw, 1958); *System doktora Smoly i doktora Pierza* (The System of Dr. Pitch and Dr. Feathers; 1962); *Wesole miasteczzko* (Amusement Grounds; 1966; Gdansk, 1967); scores for theater and films. ORCH.: 4 syms. (1939, 1951, 1961, 1978); Concerto for Chamber Orch. (1949); *Rustic Rhapsody* (1950); *Little Overture* (1953); *Divertimento* for Flute and Chamber Orch. (1964); *Journey in Time* for String Orch. (1965); *Sport Signals* (1966);

Cosmos (1973); *Voyage dans le temps* (1975). CHAMBER: *Intermezzo* for Clarinet and Piano (1942); Suite for Oboe and Piano (1957); *Capriccio energico* for Violin and Piano (1960); Clarinet Sonata (1972); *Capricious Impressions* for Woodwind Players (1982); many piano pieces, including 2 sonatas; choral music; songs.

Kiss, Janos, Hungarian-born American composer; b. Hosszupalyi, March 21, 1920. He studied at the Budapest Academy of Music (teaching diploma, 1954). In the wake of the Soviet invasion of Hungary (1956), he emigrated to the U.S., becoming a naturalized citizen in 1973. He took courses in music education at Case Western Reserve Univ. in Cleveland. He subsequently taught at the Cleveland Music School Settlement (1964–79), Western Reserve Academy in Hudson, Ohio (1967–72), Holy Family School in Parma, Ohio (1974–80), and other institutions. In 1982 he became choir director and composer-in-residence at Cleveland's West Side Hungarian Reformed Church. A prolific composer, he wrote numerous orch. and choral works which are distinguished by a facility of execution reflecting his experience as a teacher.

WORKS: *Spring at Last!* for Harp Ensemble (1970); Flute Concerto (1970); Trombone Concerto (1972); *Josepha* for 5 Alto Recorders, Violin, Viola, Cello, and Harp (1973); Cello Concerto (1975); Divertimento for Violin, Viola, Double Bass, Harp, and Chamber Ensemble (1977); *Suite in stilo antico* for Orch. (1978); *Episode* for Horn, Oboe, Bassoon, and Harp (1978); *Via Lactea*, symphonic fantasy (1978); *Sinfonia Atlantis* for Orch. (1979); *Las Vegas* for Cimbalom and Orch. (1980); *Benedictus Dominus* for Chorus and Orch. (1981); *Mount of Atlantis* for Clarinet, Synthesizer, and Orch. (1981); *Quo Vadis*, symphonic poem (1982); *Rainbow at the Sea* for Flute and Chamber Orch. (1982).

Kissin, Evgeny, amazingly precocious Russian pianist possessing interpretive capacity remarkable even for his proverbial wunderkindland; b. Moscow, Oct. 10, 1971. He enrolled at the Gnessin Music School for Gifted Children in Moscow at the incredible (but verified) age of 6 as a student of Anna Kantor, who remained his only teacher even after he began his rise toward the musical stratosphere. At the age of 12 he gave performances of both Chopin piano concertos with the Moscow Phil. International reputation came to him when he was engaged in 1987 to perform Tchaikovsky's 1st Piano Concerto with Karajan and the Berlin Phil. On Sept. 20, 1990, he made his U.S. debut playing Chopin's 1st Piano Concerto with the N.Y. Phil., conducted by Zubin Mehta. Ten days later there followed his appearance at Carnegie Hall on Sept. 30, which astonished audience and critics alike by a digital velocity and propulsive dexterity sensational enough to capture the imagination of the most seasoned and experienced listeners. Predictions are often false, but Kissin's concert successes, multiplied by the issuance of many recordings, make his accession to pianistic stardom a matter of certainty.

Kistler, Cyrill, German composer; b. Gross-Aitingen, near Augsburg, March 12, 1848; d. Bad Kissingen, Jan. 1, 1907. He was a schoolteacher (1867–76); then studied music in Munich under Wüllner, Rheinberger, and F. Lachner (1876–80). From 1883 to 1885 he taught music theory at the Fürstliche Konservatorium in Sondershausen; then was head of a music school in Bad Kissingen. He ed. the *Musikalische Tagesfragen* (1880–81; 1884–94; 1903–6). An enthusiastic admirer of Wagner, he unsuccessfully attempted to employ the master's forms and principles in his 10 operas, the most successful of which was his folk opera, *Röslein im Hag* (Elberfeld, 1903); other works include marches, choruses, songs, and organ pieces.

BIBL.: A. Eccarius-Sieber, *C. K.* (Leipzig, 1906).

Kistner, Carl Friedrich, German music publisher; b. Leipzig, March 3, 1797; d. there, Dec. 21, 1844. In 1831 he took over Probst's music publishing business, using his own name (from 1836); acquired many works by Mendelssohn, Schumann, and Chopin for his catalog. His brother, Julius Kistner (1805–68), succeeded him; he sold the business to Carl Friedrich Ludwig

Gurckhaus (1821–84) in 1866. In 1919 it was bought by Carl and Richard Linnemann, and in 1923 merged with C.F.W. Siegel, and operated under the name Fr. Kistner & C.F.W. Siegel. Damage sustained during World War II brought about the end of the firm in Leipzig, but it was reconstituted in Lippstadt as Fr. Kistner & C.F.W. Siegel and Co.; later operated in Porz.

Kitayenko, Dmitri, Russian conductor; b. Leningrad, Aug. 18, 1940. He studied choral conducting at the Leningrad Cons. and the Moscow Cons. He then went to Vienna to study conducting at the Academy of Music (1966–67). Upon his return to Moscow, he became a conductor at the Nemirovich-Danchenko Music Theater; in 1970, became chief conductor there. He also appeared as a guest conductor in Western Europe, usually in programs of Russian music; in 1975 he served as assistant conductor during the U.S. tour of the Moscow Phil. (1975). In 1976 he was appointed its chief conductor. In 1990 he was named chief conductor of the Frankfurt Radio Sym. Orch. and music director of the Bergen Phil. In 1991 he also assumed the post of music director of the Bern Sym. Orch.

Kitson, Charles Herbert, English organist and music theorist; b. Leyburn, Yorkshire, Nov. 13, 1874; d. London, May 13, 1944. He studied for an ecclesiastical career, but also took a D.Mus. degree at Oxford (1902). He was organist of Christ Church Cathedral in Dublin (1913–20); also taught at Univ. College in Dublin (1915–20) and at the Royal College of Music in London (from 1920); also held a non-resident post as prof. of music at Dublin's Trinity College (1920–35). He publ. a number of theoretical books.

Kitt, Eartha, black American singer of popular music and actress; b. North, S.C., Jan. 26, 1928. She was taken to N.Y. as a child; there she sang in church, received piano training, and studied dance at the High School for Performing Arts; won a scholarship to study dance with Katherine Dunham (1944), and then traveled with her troupe in South America and Europe until 1950; subsequently concentrated her career upon singing and acting, appearing in nightclubs, theaters, and films, and on recordings, radio, and television. She excelled particularly in earthy, passion-laden songs delivered in a low-key monotone. She publ. the autobiographical books *Thursday's Child* (1956; her birth indeed occurred on a Thursday) and *Alone with Me* (1975).

Kittel, Bruno, German violinist and conductor; b. Entenbruch, near Posen, May 26, 1870; d. Wasserberg, near Cologne, March 10, 1948. He studied in Berlin; played in theater orchs. there. From 1901 till 1907 he was conductor of the Royal Theater Orch. in Brandenburg; then was director of the Brandenburg Cons. (until 1914). In 1902 he established the Kittelsche Chor, which soon developed into one of the finest choral societies of Europe, and with which he made many tours. He was director of the Stern Cons. in Berlin (1935–45).

Kittel, Hermine, Austrian contralto; b. Vienna, Dec. 2, 1879; d. there, April 7, 1948. She began her career as an actress; then studied voice with Materna in Vienna; in 1900 she joined the Vienna Court (later State) Opera, and remained on its roster for 30 years; also sang at Bayreuth (1902, 1908) and Salzburg (1922, 1925); made guest appearances in Paris, Budapest, and other cities; following her retirement, she taught voice in Vienna.

Kittel, Johann Christian, noted German organist and composer; b. Erfurt, Feb. 18, 1732; d. there, April 17, 1809. He studied at the Thomasschule in Leipzig, and was one of Bach's last students there. After Bach's death, he became organist at Langensalza (1751–56); then at Erfurt's Barfüsserkirche (1756–62) and Predigerkirche (from 1762). Despite his meager remuneration, he remained in Erfurt almost all his life. Although he seldom made extensive tours, he acquired a fine reputation as a virtuoso; gave a series of recitals in Hamburg (1803). His most outstanding pupil was J.C.H. Rinck. He ed. *Vierstimmige Choräle mit Vorspielen* (2 vols., Altona, 1803); other works include *Der angehende praktische Organist* (3

books; Erfurt, 1801–8; 3rd ed., 1831) and *Grosse Präludien, Hymne an das Jahrhundert* (2 vols., 1801). Among his compositions are 6 sonatas and a Fantasia for Clavichord; also smaller organ pieces.

BIBL.: A. Dreetz, *J.C. K., der letzte Bach-Schüler* (Leipzig, 1932); G. Fock, "Zur Biographie des Bachschülers J.C. K.," *Bach-Jahrbuch,* XLIX (1962).

Kittl, Johann Friedrich (Jan Bedřich), prominent Bohemian composer; b. Castle Worlik, May 8, 1806; d. Lissa, German Poland, July 20, 1868. He studied law at the Univ. of Prague; took private lessons in piano with Zavora and in composition with Tomaschek. His *Jagdsinfonie* was premiered by Spohr (Kassel, 1839); it subsequently was performed widely in Germany. He was director of the Prague Cons. (1843–65). He was a friend of Liszt, Wagner, and Berlioz. As a symphonic composer, he pointed the way to Dvořák.

WORKS: Operas: *Daphnis' Grab* (Prague, 1825; not extant); *Die Franzosen vor Nizza* (Prague, Feb. 19, 1848; written to Wagner's libretto *Bianca und Giuseppe*); *Waldblume* (Prague, 1852); *Die Bilderstürmer* (Prague, 1854); 4 syms: No. 1 (1836); No. 2, *Jagdsinfonie* (1837; Kassel, 1839); No. 3 (1841–42); No. 4 (1857; Prague, July 7, 1858); 3 concert overtures; choral works; chamber music; piano pieces; songs.

BIBL.: W. Neumann, *J.F. K.* (Kassel, 1857); E. Rychnovsky, *J.F. K.* (2 vols., Prague, 1904–5); M. Tarantová, *J.F. K.* (Prague, 1948).

Kitzler, Otto, German conductor, teacher, and composer; b. Dresden, March 16, 1834; d. Graz, Sept. 6, 1915. He studied with Johann Schneider, J. Otto, and Kummer (cello); then at the Brussels Cons. with Servais and Fétis; was cellist in the opera orchs. at Strasbourg and Lyons; chorus master at theaters in Troyes, Linz, Königsberg, Temesvar, Hermannstadt, and Brünn. In 1868 he became director of the Brünn Music Soc. and Music School; also conductor of the Männergesangverein; retired in 1898. His reputation was very high; Bruckner, 10 years his senior, took orchestration lessons from him (1861–63). Kitzler wrote orch. music, piano pieces, songs, etc.; also *Musikalische Erinnerungen* (1904; containing letters from Wagner, Brahms, and Bruckner).

Kiurina, Berta, Austrian soprano; b. Linz, Feb. 19, 1882; d. Vienna, May 3, 1933. She studied voice with Geiringer at the Vienna Cons.; made her debut in Linz in 1904; then sang at the Vienna Court (later State) Opera (1905–22; 1926–27); made guest appearances in Salzburg, Berlin, and Buenos Aires. A fine coloratura, she excelled in such roles as the Queen of the Night, Desdemona, and Gilda.

Kiurkchiysky, Krasimir, Bulgarian composer; b. Troyan, June 22, 1936. He studied composition with Vladigerov at the Bulgarian State Cons. in Sofia (graduated, 1962); went to Moscow and took some lessons with Shostakovich. His music reflects Shostakovich's influence in its rhapsodic compactness.

WORKS: Opera, *Yula* (Zagora, 1969); Piano Concerto (1958); Trio for Violin, Clarinet, and Piano (1959); String Quartet (1959); *Adagio* for String Orch. (1959); Cello Sonata (1960); *Symphony Concertante* for Cello and Orch. (1960); Violin Sonata (1961); *Symphony-Requiem* (1966); *Diaphonous Study* for Orch. (1967); Concerto for Orch. (1975); choruses; incidental music.

Kivy, Peter, American musical philosopher; b. N.Y., Oct. 22, 1934. He studied philosophy at the Univ. of Michigan (B.A., 1956; M.A., 1958), music history at Yale Univ. (M.A., 1960), and philosophy at Columbia Univ. (Ph.D., 1966). He joined the faculty of Rutgers Univ. in 1967. His importance to the field of music is in his writings on esthetics, in which he has revitalized the complex and long-ignored problems of musical analysis as applied to external associations.

WRITINGS: *The Corded Shell: Reflections on Musical Expression* (Princeton, N.J., 1980); *Sound and Semblance: Reflections on Musical Representation* (Princeton, N.J., 1984); *Osmin's Rage: Philosophical Reflections on Opera, Drama and Text* (Princeton, N.J., 1988); *Sound Sentiment: An Essay on the Musical Emotions* (Philadelphia, 1989); *Music Alone: Philo-*

sophical Reflections on the Purely Musical Experience (Ithaca, N.Y., 1990).

Kiyose, Yasuji, Japanese composer; b. Yokkaichi, Jan. 13, 1900; d. Tokyo, Sept. 14, 1981. He studied with Yamada, Komatsu, Pringsheim, and A. Tcherepnin; was president of the Japanese section of the ISCM (1951–56).

WORKS: *Nihon sairei bukyoku* (Japanese Festival Dance) for Orch. (1940); Piano Concerto (Tokyo, March 10, 1955); *Nihon no sobyō* (A Sketch of Japan) for Orch. (1963); *Bokura wa umi ni yuku* (We Are Going on the Ocean, or Unknown Soldiers) for Soprano, Tenor, Chorus, and Orch. (1962); 2 piano trios (1938, 1955); 3 violin sonatas (1941, 1948, 1950); String Trio (1949); String Quartet (1951); Quintet for Harp and Woodwinds (1957); 2 *Movements* for Violin and Piano (1960); Quartet for 4 Recorders (1969); *Duet* for Flute and Clarinet (1970); 2 *Movements* for Cello (1973).

Kjellsby, Erling, Norwegian organist, choral conductor, and composer; b. Christiania, July 7, 1901; d. there (Oslo), Feb. 18, 1976. He studied composition with Brustad and Valen; lectured on music at Oslo's Teacher's College (1934–70) and was organist at Oslo's Uranienborg Church (1936–71). His early works, in a late Romantic style, eventually gave way to neo-Classical influences. He wrote *Norsk rapsodi* for Small Orch. (1937); choral works; 4 string quartets (1940–57); piano pieces.

Kjellström, Sven, Swedish violinist; b. Lulea, March 30, 1875; d. Stockholm, Dec. 5, 1950. He studied in Stockholm and later in Paris. Returning to Sweden in 1909, he was active in chamber music societies; was director of the Stockholm Cons. (1929–40). He also formed a string quartet, with which he traveled to remote communities in Scandinavia, including Lapland; he was an ardent collector of Swedish folk songs.

BIBL.: O. Ottelin, *S. K. och folkets musikliv* (1945).

Kjerulf, Halfdan, esteemed Norwegian composer; b. Christiania, Sept. 15, 1815; d. Grefsen, near Christiania, Aug. 11, 1868. He was a member of a family of artists and scholars; studied piano as a child; then took up law, subsequently working as a journalist. In 1848–49 he took lessons with Carl Arnold and in 1849–50 with Gade in Copenhagen; then with E.F. Richter at the Leipzig Cons. (1850–51). He taught piano in his homeland from 1851; was elected a member of the Swedish Royal Academy of Music in 1865. A monument was erected to him in Christiania in 1874. He limited himself to composition in small forms; although he followed the German model, he injected melodic and rhythmic elements of a national Norwegian character into his songs. Grieg was deeply influenced by his example and expressed admiration for his music; many celebrated singers (Jenny Lind, Christine Nilsson, and Henriette Sontag among them) included his songs in their programs. He wrote about 130 songs, utilizing Norwegian, Swedish, Danish, German, and French texts; some 40 works for male chorus, as well as over 50 arrangements for chorus; 10 albums of piano pieces and arrangements of Norwegian melodies for piano.

BIBL.: A. Grønvold, "H. K.," *Norske Musikere,* I (Christiania, 1883); K. Nyblom, *H. K.* (1926); D. Schjelderup-Erbe, "Modality in H. K.'s Music," *Music & Letters* (July 1957).

Klafsky, Anton Maria, Austrian musicologist and composer, nephew of **Katharina (Katalin) Klafsky;** b. Winden, Burgenland, July 8, 1877; d. Baden, near Vienna, Jan. 1, 1965. He studied at the Univ. of Vienna; took lessons in composition with Hermann Grädener. He composed much church music, 3 syms., piano pieces, and songs; ed. sacred choral works of Michael Haydn for Denkmäler der Tonkunst in Österreich, vols. 44 and 62 (22 and 32.i).

Klafsky, Katharina (Katalin), famous Hungarian soprano, aunt of **Anton Maria Klafsky;** b. St. Johann, Sept. 19, 1855; d. Hamburg, Sept. 22, 1896. She studied with Marchesi in Vienna and Hey in Berlin; began her career as a chorus singer in various opera houses. She appeared in minor roles in Salzburg (1875), then was a member of the Leipzig Opera

(1876–78); also studied with J. Sucher. In 1882 she attracted attention for her performance in the 1st London mounting of the *Ring* cycle; then toured with A. Neumann's Wagner company; was in Bremen (1884) and Vienna (1885). She was a leading member of the Hamburg Opera (1886–95), where she excelled as a Wagnerian; returned to London (1892, 1894). She married the conductor and composer **Otto Lohse** in 1893; they toured the U.S. with the Damrosch Opera Co. (1895–96); then were engaged for the 1896–97 season of the Metropolitan Opera in N.Y., but she died before her scheduled debut. As one of the outstanding sopranos of her day, she was widely mourned upon her early death.

BIBL.: L. Ordemann, *Aus dem Leben und Wirken von K. K.* (Hameln, 1903).

Klami, Uuno (Kalervo), Finnish composer; b. Virolahti, Sept. 20, 1900; d. Helsinki, May 29, 1961. He studied with Melartin at the Helsinki College of Music (1915–24), Ravel in Paris (1924–25), and Willner in Vienna (1928–29). He was music critic of the *Helsingin Sanomat* (1932–59); held a Finnish state pension (1938–59); was elected a member of the Finnish Academy (1959). His music was influenced by the folk modalities of the Karelian region, which was his birthplace; the impact of the profundities of the idiom of Sibelius was considerable, but Klami ornamented it with impressionistic detail.

WORKS: ORCH.: *Sérénades espagnoles* (1924; rev. 1944); *Karelian Rhapsody* (1927); *Rhapsody* (1927); *Merikuvia* (Sea Pictures; 1928–30); 3 syms.: *Symphonie enfantine* (1928); No. 1 (1937); No. 2 (1944); *Opernredoute* (1929); *Kuvia maalaiselämästä* (Rustic Scenes; 1930); *Helsinki March* (1930); *Fantaisie tschérémisse* for Cello and Orch. (1931); *Kalevala Suite* (1932; rev. 1943); *Sérénades joyeuses* (1933); *Lemminkäinen* (1934); *Karelian Dances* (1935); *Suomenlinna* (Fortress of Finland; 1940); *Revontulet* (Aurora Borealis; 1946); *Pyöräilijä* (The Cyclist), orch. rondo (1946); *Karjalainen tori* (Karelian Market Place; 1947); 2 piano concertos: No. 1, *Night in Montmartre* (1924), and No. 2 (1950); *4 Folk Songs* for Piano and Strings (1930); *Cheremissian Fantasy* for Cello and Orch. (1930); Violin Concerto (1942; rev. 1954); *Theme and Variations* for Cello and Orch. (1950). **VOCAL AND CHORAL:** *Psalmus* for Soloists, Chorus, and Orch. (1935–36); *Vipusessa käynti* (In the Belly of Vipunen) for Baritone, Male Chorus, and Orch. (1938); *Laulu Kuujärvestä* (The Song of Kuujarvi) for Baritone and Orch. (1956); *Kultasauvalliset* (The People with the Golden Staffs), festive cantata (1961). **CHAMBER:** String quartet, *Nain tragédie* (1920); Piano Quartet (1921); Piano Quintet (1923). At his death, Klami left over a thousand pages of an unfinished ballet score.

Klatte, Wilhelm, German conductor and writer on music; b. Bremen, Feb. 13, 1870; d. Berlin, Sept. 12, 1930. He studied music in Leipzig, and took lessons with Richard Strauss in Weimar; held various positions as a conductor and a music critic; from 1904 he taught at the Stern Cons. in Berlin; in 1925 he was appointed prof. at the Academy for Church and School Music in Berlin. He publ. (in collaboration with A. Seidl) *Richard Strauss, Eine Charakterskizze* (1895); "Zur Geschichte der Programm-Musik," *Die Musik* (1905); *Franz Schubert* (1907); *Grundlagen des mehrstimmigen Satzes* (1922; 3rd ed., 1930).

Klatzow, Peter (James Leonard), South African composer; b. Springs, Transvaal, July 14, 1945. He studied piano in his hometown (1951–57) and in Johannesburg (1958–62); then studied composition with Bernard Stevens and Gordon Jacob at the Royal College of Music in London (1964–65) and briefly with Nadia Boulanger in Paris (1966). He lectured in composition and piano at the Rhodesian College of Music in Salisbury (1966–68); then was a music producer at the South African Broadcasting Corp. (1968–73); subsequently lectured in composition at the Univ. of Cape Town (from 1973).

WORKS: *Variations* for Orch. (1965; London, Feb. 10, 1966); *Nagstuk* for Orch. (1966); Violin Sonata (1967); *Interactions I* for Piano, Percussion, and Chamber Orch. (1971) and *II* for Solo Piano (1972); *The Temptation of St. Anthony* for Cello and Orch. (1972; Barcelona, May 14, 1977); *The World of Paul Klee* for Flute, Viola, and Harp (1972); *Symphony 1972, Phoenix* (1972; 1st public perf., Cape Town, Oct. 21, 1975); *Time Structure I* for Piano (1973) and *II* for Orch. and Tape (1974; also for Orch. and Organ, 1976); *Still Life, with Moonbeams* for Orch. (Johannesburg, July 13, 1975); *The Garden of Memories and Discoveries* for Soprano, Ensemble, and Tape (1975); *Night Magic I* for Soprano and Chamber Orch. (1976) and *II*, trio for Violin, Horn, and Piano (1977); *Contours and Transformations* for Guitar and 5 Instrumentalists (1977); String Quartet (1977); Horn Concerto (Cape Town, June 16, 1978); Chamber Concerto (1978–79); Horn Sonata (1979).

Klaus, Kenneth Blanchard, American composer; b. Earlville, Iowa, Nov. 11, 1923; d. Baton Rouge, La., Aug. 4, 1980. He studied violin with Cecil Burleigh and Louis Krasner, and composition with Philip Greeley Clapp at the Univ. of Iowa (Ph.D., 1950); also studied meteorology at the Univ. of Chicago and served as a meteorologist in the Army Air Corps during World War II; in 1950, joined the faculty at Louisiana State Univ. In his works, he applied a sui generis synthesis of expanded tonality verging on serialism. In his vocal compositions, he modernized the medieval device of "sogetto cavato" by deriving a theme from the vowels of letter names. He publ. *The Romantic Period in Music* (Boston, 1970).

WORKS: Operas, *Tennis Anyone?* (1957) and *Crimson Stones; Moira* for Female Singer; *Deidra* for Female Singer; incidental music for *Death of a Salesman* (1954); 6 syms.; several symphonic poems; 2 violin concertos; Flute Concerto; Cello Concerto; Clarinet Concerto; *Concerto brevis* for Percussion and Orch. (1955); Concerto for Piano, right-hand, and Orch.; 4 string quartets (1947, 1951, 1957, 1963); Woodwind Quintet; Woodwind Sextet; sonatas for various instruments; vocal works.

Klauwell, Otto (Adolf), German writer on music and composer; b. Langensalza, April 7, 1851; d. Cologne, May 11, 1917. He studied with Reinecke and Richter at the Leipzig Cons.; also studied at the Univ. of Leipzig (Ph.D., 1874, with the diss. *Die historische Entwicklung des musikalische Canons*). He taught at the Cologne Cons. (from 1875); was made its deputy director (1905). He wrote the operas *Das Mädchen vom See* (Cologne, 1889) and *Die heimlichen Richter* (Elberfeld, 1902); overtures; chamber music; piano pieces; songs.

WRITINGS: *Musikalische Gesichtspunkte* (Leipzig, 1882; 2nd ed., 1892, as *Musikalische Bekenntnisse*); *Der Vortrag in der Musik* (Berlin and Leipzig, 1883; Eng. tr., N.Y., 1890); *Die Formen der Instrumentalmusik* (Leipzig and N.Y., 1894; 2nd ed., rev., 1918 by W. Niemann); *Geschichte der Sonate* (Cologne and Leipzig, 1899); *L. von Beethoven und die Variationenform* (Langensalza, 1901); *Theodor Gouvy* (Berlin, 1902); *Studien und Erinnerungen* (Langensalza, 1906); *Geschichte der Programm-Musik* (Leipzig, 1910).

Klebanov, Dmitri, outstanding Ukrainian composer; b. Kharkov, July 25, 1907. He studied with S. Bogatyrev at the Kharkov Inst. for Music and Drama, graduating in 1926; after playing viola in Leningrad (1927–28), he returned to Kharkov as director for several musical comedy theaters and as a teacher at the Cons. (1934–73; prof., 1960; emeritus, 1973). He wrote the Ukrainian State Hymn; was president of the local Composer's Union (1945–49).

WORKS: OPERAS: *Aistenok,* for children (1934); *Single Life* (1947); *Vasily Gubanov* (1966; rev. as *Communist,* 1967); *Red Cossacks* (1971). **BALLETS:** *Aistenok* (Moscow, 1936); *Svetlana* (Moscow, 1939). **ORCH.:** 5 syms. (1945, 1952, 1957, 1959, 1962); *Ukrainian Concertino* (1938); *Welcoming Overture* (1945); *Ukrainian Suite* (1946); 4 Preludes and Fugue (1975); 2 concertos for Violin (1940, 1951); 2 concertos for Cello (1950, 1973); Concerto for Domra (1953; rev. for Orch. of Native Instruments, 1973). **CHAMBER:** 6 string quartets (1925, 1926, 1933, 1946, 1966, 1968); String Quintet (1953); Woodwind Quartet (1957); Piano Trio (1958); many piano works; songs; choruses; musical comedies; film music.

BIBL.: M. Cherkashina, *D. K.* (1968).

Klebe, Giselher (Wolfgang), German composer; b. Mannheim, June 28, 1925. He studied at the Berlin Cons. with Kurt von Wolfurt (1941–43); later with Josef Rufer, and then with Boris Blacher (1946–51). He worked in the program division of the Berlin Radio (1946–49); taught at Detmold's Nordwestdeutsche Musik Akademie (from 1957). In 1963 he became a member of the Hamburg Academy of Fine Arts, in 1964 of the Berlin Academy of Fine Arts, and in 1978 of the Bavarian Academy of Fine Arts. An experimenter by nature, he writes music in widely ranging forms, from classically conceived instrumental pieces to highly modernistic inventions; his technique is basically dodecaphonic; coloristic and sonoristic schemes also play an important role.

WORKS: OPERAS: *Die Räuber,* after Schiller (1951–56; Düsseldorf, June 3, 1957; rev. 1962); *Die tödlichen Wünsche,* after Balzac (1957–59; Düsseldorf, June 14, 1959); *Die Ermordung Cäsars,* after Shakespeare (1958–59; Essen, Sept. 20, 1959); *Alkmene,* after Kleist (Berlin, Sept. 25, 1961); *Figaro lässt sich scheiden,* opera buffa after von Horváth (1962–63; Hamburg, June 28, 1963); *Jakobowsky und der Oberst,* comic opera after Werfel (Hamburg, Nov. 2, 1965); *Das Märchen von der schönen Lilie,* fairy-tale opera after Goethe (1967–68; Schwetzingen, May 15, 1969); *Ein wahrer Held,* after Synge's *Playboy of the Western World,* adapted by Böll (1972–73; Zürich Festival, Jan. 18, 1975); *Das Mädchen aus Domremy,* after Schiller (1975–76; Stuttgart, June 19, 1976); *Das Rendez-vous* (Hannover, Oct. 7, 1977); *Der jüngste Tag* (1980); *Die Fastnachtsbeichte* (1983). **BALLETS:** *Pas de trois* (Wiesbaden, 1951); *Signale* (Berlin, 1955); *Fleurenville* (Berlin, 1956); *Menagerie* (1958). **ORCH.:** *Con moto* (1948; Bremen, Feb. 23, 1953); *Divertissement joyeux* for Chamber Orch. (Darmstadt, July 8, 1949); *Die Zwitschermaschine,* metamorphosis on Klee's famous painting (Donaueschingen, Sept. 10, 1950); 2 *Nocturnes* (1951; Darmstadt, July 20, 1952); 5 syms.: No. 1 for 42 Strings (1951; Hamburg, Jan. 7, 1953); No. 2 (1953); No. 3 (1967); No. 4, *Das Testament,* ballet-sym. for Orch. and 2 Pianos tuned a quarter-tone apart (1970–71; Wiesbaden, April 30, 1971); No. 5 (1977); *Rhapsody* (1953); *Double Concerto* for Violin, Cello, and Orch. (Frankfurt, June 19, 1954); *Moments musicaux* (1955); Cello Concerto (1957); *Omaggio* (1960); *Adagio and Fugue,* on a motif from Wagner's *Die Walküre* (1962); *Herzschläge,* 3 symphonic scenes for Beat Band and Orch. (1969); Concerto for Electronically Altered Harpsichord and Small Orch. (1971–72); *Orpheus,* dramatic scenes (1976); *La Tomba di Igor Strawinsky* for Oboe and Chamber Orch. (1979); Organ Concerto (1980); Clarinet Concerto (1985); *Lied ohne Worte* (1986); *Notturno* (1988); Harp Concerto (1988). **VOCAL:** *Geschichte vom lustigen Musikanten* for Tenor, Chorus, and 5 Instruments (1946–47); 5 *Römische Elegien,* after Goethe, for Narrator, Piano, Harpsichord, and Double Bass (1952; Donaueschingen, Oct. 10, 1953); *Raskolnikows Traum,* dramatic scene after Dostoyevsky, for Soprano, Clarinet, and Orch. (1956); 5 *Lieder* for Alto and Orch. (1962); *Stabat Mater* for Soprano, Mezzo-soprano, Alto, Chorus, and Orch. (1964); *Gebet einer armen Seele,* dodecaphonic Mass for Chorus and Organ (1966); choruses; songs. **CHAMBER:** Wind Quintet (1948); 3 string quartets (1949, 1963, 1981); Viola Sonata (1949); 2 solo violin sonatas (1952, 1955); 2 violin sonatas (1953, 1972); *Elegia appassionata,* piano trio (1955); *Dithyrambe* for String Quartet (1957); *Missa "Miserere nobis"* for 18 Wind Instruments (1965); *Quasi una fantasia,* piano quintet (1967); *Scene and Aria* for 3 Trumpets, 3 Trombones, 2 Pianos, and 8 Cellos (1967–68); *Variations on a Theme of Berlioz* for Organ and 3 Drummers (1970); Double-bass Sonata (1971); *Nenia* for Violin (1975). **PIANO:** *Nocturnes* (1949); 2-piano Sonata (1949); 4 *Inventions* (1956).

Kleber, Leonhard, German organist; b. Göppingen, Württemberg, c.1490; d. Pforzheim, March 4, 1556. He studied at the Univ. of Heidelberg; was vicar-choral and organist in Horb (1516–17); then organist in Esslingen (1517–21). From 1521 he was organist at the collegiate and parish church in Pforzheim. Between 1521 and 1524 he oversaw the compilation

of a book of 112 pieces by Hofhaimer, Josquin, Obrecht, and others, arranged in keyboard tablature. Modern transcriptions of his books are to be found in: A. Ritter, *Zur Geschichte des Orgelspiels, vornemlich des deutschen, im 14. bis zum Anfang des 18. Jahrhunderts*, II (Leipzig, 1884); R. Eitner, *Monatshefte für Musikgeschichte*, XX (1888); H.J. Moser, *Paul Hofhaimer* (Stuttgart and Berlin, 1929); W. Apel, *Musik aus früher Zeit* (Mainz, 1934); W. Apel and A. Davison, *Historical Anthology of Music*, vol. I (Cambridge, Mass., 1946).
BIBL.: H. Löwenfeld, *L. K. und sein Orgeltabulaturbuch als Beitrag zur Geschichte der Orgelmusik im beginnenden XVI. Jahrhundert* (Berlin, 1897; reprint, Hilversum, 1968); K. Kotterba, *Die Orgeltabulatur des L. K.* (diss., Univ. of Freiburg, 1958).

Klecki, Pawel. See **Kletzki, Paul.**

Klee, Bernhard, respected German conductor: b. Schleiz, April 19, 1936. He studied piano and conducting at the Cologne Hochschule für Musik; then became répétiteur at the Cologne Opera (1957) and the Bern City Theater (1958); later was an assistant to Sawallisch and a conductor at the Cologne Opera. He was 1st conductor at the opera houses in Salzburg (1962–63), Oberhausen (1963–65), and Hannover (1965–66); then was Generalmusikdirektor in Lübeck (1966–77) and chief conductor of the Hannover Radio Orch. (1976–79). From 1977 to 1987 he was Generalmusikdirektor of the Düsseldorf Sym. Orch.; served as principal guest conductor of the BBC Phil. in Manchester (1985–89). In 1991 he returned to the Hannover Radio Orch. as chief conductor. Married to the Swiss soprano **Edith Mathis,** he served as her accompanist in recitals. As a conductor, he is admired for his insightful performances of the Austro-German repertoire.

Kleefeld, Wilhelm, German writer on music, teacher, and composer; b. Mainz, April 2, 1868; d. Berlin, April 2, 1933. He was a pupil of Spitta in Berlin; took his Ph.D. in 1898 at the Univ. there with the dissertation *Das Orchester der ersten deutschen Oper, Hamburg, 1678–1738* (publ., 1898). From 1898 to 1904 he taught at Berlin's Klindworth-Scharwenka Cons., and from 1904 at the Univ. of Berlin. He wrote numerous articles on opera; under the title *Opernrenaissance,* he ed. a number of early operas; publ. a monograph on Clara Schumann (1910). He wrote many songs and piano pieces (for 2 and 4 hands).

Kleffel, Arno, German composer and conductor; b. Pössneck, Sept. 4, 1840; d. Nikolassee, near Berlin, July 15, 1913. He studied with Hauptmann in Leipzig; then conducted theater orchs. and opera in Riga, Cologne, Amsterdam, Berlin, Augsburg, Magdeburg, etc. In 1904 he became conductor of Stern's Gesangverein in Berlin; in 1910, head of the operatic dept. at the Hochschule für Musik there. He wrote an opera, *Des Meermanns Harfe* (Riga, 1865); music to Goethe's *Faust;* many characteristic piano pieces; teaching pieces; songs.

Klega, Miroslav, Slovak composer; b. Ostrava, March 6, 1929. He studied composition with Křička at the Prague Cons. (1942–44) and with Suchoň and Cikker at the Bratislava Cons. (1946–50); taught at the Ostrava Cons. (1955–73); was its director (1967–73); then worked with the Czech Radio there.
WORKS: *Suite Bagatelle* for Piano (1948); *Černá země* (Black Soil), symphonic variations (1951); Sym. (1959); Concertino for 4 String Instruments (1961); *Pantomima,* suite for Orch. (1963); *Concerto-Partita* for Violin and Orch. (1965); *Výpověď osamělého pěšáka* (The Confession of a Lone Pedestrian) for Narrator and Orch. (1968); *Příběhy z zazraky,* sym.-ballet (1981).

Kleiber, Carlos, outstanding German-born Austrian conductor, son of **Erich Kleiber;** b. Berlin, July 3, 1930. He left Nazi Germany with his parents in 1935, eventually settling in South America in 1940. He evinced an early interest in music, but his father opposed it as a career; after studying chemistry in Zürich (1949–50), he turned decisively to music and completed his training in Buenos Aires. In 1952 he became a répétiteur and stage assistant at the Theater am Gärtnerplatz in Munich, making his conducting debut in 1954 with Millöcker's *Gasparone* in Potsdam, where he was active until becoming a répétiteur (1956) and conductor (1958) at the Deutsche Oper am Rhein in Düsseldorf. After conducting at the Zürich Opera (1964–66), he served as 1st conductor at the Württemberg State Theater in Stuttgart (1966–68). From 1968 to 1978 he conducted at the Bavarian State Opera in Munich. In 1966 he made his British debut conducting *Wozzeck* at the Edinburgh Festival; he led performances of *Tristan und Isolde* for his 1st appearances at the Vienna State Opera in 1973 and at the Bayreuth Festival in 1974, the year in which he made his 1st appearances at London's Covent Garden and Milan's La Scala with *Der Rosenkavalier.* On Sept. 8, 1977, he made his U.S. debut conducting *Otello* at the San Francisco Opera. His 1st appearance with a U.S. orch. came in 1978, when he conducted the Chicago Sym. Orch. In 1979 he conducted the Vienna Phil. and in 1982 the Berlin Phil. On Jan. 22, 1988, he made his Metropolitan Opera debut in N.Y. conducting *La Bohème,* and in 1989 he conducted the New Year's Day Concert of the Vienna Phil. He became a naturalized Austrian citizen in 1980. Kleiber has been accorded accolades from critics, audiences, and his fellow musicians. His brilliant performances reflect his unreserved commitment to the score at hand, his authority, and his mastery of technique. His infrequent appearances, combined with his passion for perfection, have made him a legendary figure among the world's contemporary podium celebrities.
BIBL.: W. Flowers, "C. K.—A Legend at 50," *Le Grand Baton* (March 1982); J. von Rhein, "The Unpredictable C. K.," *Ovation* (Sept. 1983).

Kleiber, Erich, eminent Austrian conductor, father of **Carlos Kleiber;** b. Vienna, Aug. 5, 1890; d. Zürich, Jan. 27, 1956. He studied at the Prague Cons. and the Univ. of Prague; made his debut at the Prague National Theater in 1911; then conducted opera in Darmstadt (1912–19), Barmen-Elberfeld (1919–21), Düsseldorf (1921–22), and Mannheim (1922–23). In 1923 he was appointed Generalmusikdirektor of the Berlin State Opera. His tenure was outstanding, both for the brilliant performances of the standard repertoire and for the exciting programming of contemporary works. He conducted the world premiere of Berg's *Wozzeck* (Dec. 14, 1925). In 1934, in protest against the German National Socialist government, he resigned his post and emigrated to South America. He conducted regularly at the Teatro Colón in Buenos Aires from 1936 to 1949. Having first conducted at London's Covent Garden in 1937, he returned there from 1950 to 1953. He then was appointed Generalmusikdirektor once more of the Berlin State Opera in 1954, but resigned in March 1955, before the opening of the season, because of difficulties with the Communist regime. He was renowned for his performances of the music of Mozart and Beethoven. He also composed; among his works are a Violin Concerto, a Piano Concerto, orch. variations, *Capriccio* for Orch., numerous chamber music works, piano pieces, and songs.
BIBL.: J. Russell, *E. K.: A Memoir* (London, 1957).

Klein, Bernhard (Joseph), German composer; b. Cologne, March 6, 1793; d. Berlin, Sept. 9, 1832. He went to Paris in 1812 and received some advice from Choron, but he was mainly self-taught; returning to Cologne, he was appointed music director of the Cathedral. In 1818 he settled in Berlin; from 1820, taught at the Royal Inst. for Church Music; also taught singing at the Univ. of Berlin, retiring in 1830. He was greatly praised by his Berlin contemporaries for his contrapuntal craftsmanship in sacred works and as a composer of lieder. His stepbrother, **Josef Klein** (b. Cologne, 1802; d. there, Feb. 10, 1862), was his pupil; he was one of the 1st composers to set Heine's texts to music.
WORKS: Operas: *Dido* (Berlin, Oct. 15, 1823) and *Ariadne* (Berlin, 1823); several oratorios, including *Jephtha* (Cologne, 1828) and *David* (Halle, 1830); several cantatas, including

Worte des Glaubens (1817) and *Hiob* (Leipzig, 1820); various other sacred vocal works; piano sonatas; songs.

BIBL.: C. Koch, *B. K.* (diss., Univ. of Rostock, 1902).

Klein, Bruno Oscar, German pianist, organist, teacher, and composer; b. Osnabrück, June 6, 1858; d. N.Y., June 22, 1911. He studied with his father, then with K. Bärmann (piano) at the Munich Cons. In 1878 he settled in the U.S., serving as head of the piano dept. at N.Y.'s Convent School of the Sacred Heart (1884–1911); also was a church organist. He wrote the opera *Kenilworth* (Hamburg, Feb. 13, 1895); Piano Concerto; Violin Concerto; *American Dances* for Orch.; choral works; chamber music; piano pieces; organ music.

Klein, Elisabeth, Hungarian-born Danish pianist; b. Trenčín, July 23, 1911. She studied at the Budapest Academy of Music (graduated, 1934); then had private lessons with Bartók. She settled in Denmark, becoming a Danish citizen; made her debut in Copenhagen (1946). She toured extensively and was also active as a teacher; championed the music of Bartók and contemporary Scandinavian composers.

Klein, Fritz Heinrich, Austrian music theorist and composer; b. Budapest, Feb. 2, 1892; d. Linz, July 11, 1977. He took piano lessons with his father; then went to Vienna, where he studied composition with Schoenberg and Berg, and became their devoted disciple. From 1932 to 1957 he taught theory at the Bruckner Cons. in Linz. His most ingenious composition was *Die Maschine* (1921; N.Y., Nov. 24, 1924), subtitled "Eine extonale Selbstsatire" and publ. under the pseudonym "Heautontimorumenos" (i.e., self-tormentor); this work features instances of all kinds of tonal combinations, including a "Mutterakkord," which consists of all 12 different chromatic tones and all 11 different intervals, the 1st time such an arrangement was proposed. He also publ. an important essay bearing on serial techniques then still in the process of formulation, "Die Grenze der Halbtonwelt," in *Die Musik* (Jan. 1925). He made the vocal score of Berg's opera *Wozzeck*. His other works include *Partita* for 6 Instruments (1953); Divertimento for String Orch. (1954); *Ein musikalisches Fliessband* for Orch. (1960); *Musikalisches Tagebuch* for Orch. (1970); also several stage works, among them the opera *Nostradamus*.

Klein, Herman, English writer on music; b. Norwich, July 23, 1856; d. London, March 10, 1934. He studied voice with Manuel Garcia; then taught singing and wrote music criticism; worked for the *Sunday Times* (1881–1901), the *N.Y. Herald* (1902–9), and London's *Saturday Review* (1917–21).

WRITINGS: *30 Years of Musical Life in London* (N.Y., 1903); *Unmusical New York* (London, 1910); *The Reign of Patti* (N.Y., 1920); *The Art of the Bel Canto* (London, 1923); *Musicians and Mummers* (London, 1925); *Great Women Singers of My Time* (London, 1931); *The Golden Age of Opera* (London, 1933).

Klein, Ivy Frances (née **Salaman**), English composer; b. London, Dec. 23, 1895. She wrote a number of songs to texts by English poets and appeared in concerts singing and accompanying herself. In 1924 she married Daryl Klein. Among her songs are *Ode on Solitude* (after Pope) and *Music When Soft Voices Die* (Shelley). Her choral work *She Walked in Beauty* (Byron) was performed at Queen Elizabeth II's coronation (1953).

Klein, John, American organist, pianist, and composer; b. Rahns, Pa., Feb. 21, 1915; d. there, April 30, 1981. He studied at the Philadelphia Musical Academy; then went to Salzburg, where he took courses at the Mozarteum, and later to Paris, where he had lessons with Nadia Boulanger in composition and with Marcel Dupré in organ. Returning to America, he was organist at the Presbyterian Church in Columbus, Ohio (1937–42); then was engaged in radio shows as a pianist (1944–57); played carillon in recitals and at carillon festivals in Cobb, Ireland, and at the World's Fair in Brussels. He publ. *The Art of Playing the Modern Carillon* and *The First 4 Centuries of Music;* composed a Violin Concerto and a number of songs and marches, including the U.S. Army radio show theme, *Sound Off.*

Klein, Kenneth, American conductor; b. Los Angeles, Sept. 5, 1939. He studied violin at the Univ. of Southern Calif. School of Music in Los Angeles with Eudice Shapiro, Vera Barstow, and Peter Meremblum; took piano lessons with Gerhard Albersheim; studied conducting with Fritz Zweig in Los Angeles, Izler Solomon at the Aspen School of Music, and Richard Lert in Asilomar, Calif. He was a violinist in the Pasadena Sym. Orch.; then was founder-conductor of the Westside Sym. Orch. in Los Angeles (1963–68). He was music director of the Guadalajara Sym. Orch. (1969–78), the Nassau (L.I.) Sym. Orch. (from 1980), the Santa Cruz (Calif.) Sym. Orch. (1981–85), the N.Y. Virtuosi (from 1982), and the South Dakota Sym. Orch. (1983–85). He also appeared widely as a guest conductor in Europe. He taught at the Univ. of Guadalajara (1968–69; 1973) and the Univ. of Calif. at Santa Cruz (1981–83).

Klein, Lothar, German-born Canadian composer; b. Hannover, Jan. 27, 1932. He went to England in 1939 and to the U.S. in 1941; studied composition with Paul Fetler at the Univ. of Minnesota (B.A., 1954); then composition with Petrassi at the Berkshire Music Center in Tanglewood (1956) and orchestration with Dorati in Minneapolis (1956–58). After winning a Fulbright fellowship, he went to Berlin to study composition with Josef Rufer at the Free Univ. and with Blacher at the Hochschule für Musik (1958–60); also with Nono in Darmstadt; subsequently completed his studies at the Univ. of Minnesota (Ph.D., 1961), serving on its faculty (1962–64). He later taught at the Univ. of Texas at Austin (1964–68); in 1968, joined the faculty of the Univ. of Toronto, where he was chairman of its graduate music dept. (1971–76). His early music is essentially tonal, esthetically derived from neo-Romantic procedures; he then experimented with various branches of serialism; also wrote collage pieces embodying elements of all historical periods through linkage of stylistic similarities.

WORKS: STAGE: Opera, *Tale of a Father and Son* (1983); *Lost Love,* ballet for Piano Solo (1950–56); *The Prodigal Son,* dance drama for Clarinet and Large Jazz Ensemble (1966); *Canadiana* (1980). **ORCH.:** 3 syms. (1955; 1966; 1972, *Symphonic Etudes*); Concerto for Winds, Timpani, and Strings (1956); *Symmetries* (1958); *Appassionato* (1958); *Trio concertante* for String Trio and Orch. (1961); *Epitaphs* (1963); *Le Trésor des dieux* for Guitar and Orch. (1969); *Janizary Music* for Military Orch. (1970); *Passacaglia of the Zodiac* for 14 Solo Strings (1971); *Music for Violin and Orch.* (1972); *Slices of Time* for Trumpet and Orch. (1973; also for Trumpet and String Quartet); *The Philosopher in the Kitchen,* "gastronomic meditations" for Contralto and Orch. (1974); *Invention, Blues, and Chase* for Free-bass Accordion and Strings (1975); *Musica antiqua,* allegory for Consort and Orch. (1975); *Boccherini Collage* for Cello and Orch. (1978); *Concerto sacro* for Viola and Orch. (1984). **CHAMBER:** Quintet for Winds (1952); Quintet for Piano and Strings (1954); *Trio Sonata* for Clarinet, Cello, Piano or Harpsichord, and Drum Set (1968); *Vaudeville,* "acrobatics" for Soprano Saxophone and Woodwind Quintet (1979); *Meditation* "for John Lennon, Dec. 9, 1980" for Violin and Piano (1980); *Partita II* for Trumpet, Tuba, and Piano (1980); *Choreagos* for Oboe and Percussion, with Optional Reciter (1982); also choruses; solo vocal music; piano pieces.

Klein, Peter, German tenor; b. Zündorf, near Cologne, Jan. 25, 1907. He studied at the Cologne Cons.; made appearances in Düsseldorf, Kaiserslautern, and Zürich; was a member of the Hamburg State Opera (1937–41), then at the Vienna State Opera; also appeared at Bayreuth (from 1964). He made his Metropolitan Opera debut in N.Y. on Nov. 21, 1949, as Valzacchi in *Der Rosenkavalier,* remaining on its roster until 1951. In 1956 he joined the faculty of the Vienna Cons.

Kleinheinz, Franz Xaver, German conductor and composer; b. Mindelheim (baptized), June 26, 1765; d. Budapest, Jan. 26, 1832. He played in the Munich Orch.; in 1803 he went to Vienna to study with Albrechtsberger; then was active in

Brünn; subsequently was a theater conductor in Budapest (1814–15; 1817–24). He wrote the operas *Harald* (Budapest, March 22, 1814) and *Der Käfig* (Budapest, 1816); Piano Concerto; chamber music; sacred choral works; also made transcriptions for string quartet of Beethoven's early piano sonatas.

BIBL.: E. Haraszti, "Les Compositions inconnues de F.X. K.," *Revue Musicale* (March 1930).

Kleinknecht, Jakob Friedrich, German flutist, violinist, and composer; b. Ulm (baptized), April 8, 1722; d. Ansbach, Aug. 14, 1794. He studied with his father; then joined his brother Johann Wolfgang at the Bayreuth court. He turned to the violin in 1747; was made assistant Kapellmeister in 1748, court composer in 1749, and Kapellmeister in 1761; remained with the court when it moved to Ansbach in 1769. His extant works include a Sinfonia concertante for 2 Flutes, 2 Oboes, Strings, and Keyboard obbligato; a Violin Concerto; a Concerto for 2 Flutes and Orch. (publ. in Paris, 1776); 6 *sonate da camera* for Flute and Harpsichord or Cello (publ. in Nuremberg, 1748); various keyboard sonatas; etc.

Kleinmichel, Richard, German pianist, conductor, and composer; b. Posen, Dec. 31, 1846; d. Charlottenburg, Aug. 18, 1901. He studied with his father, Friedrich Kleinmichel (1827–94), a bandmaster; then at the Leipzig Cons. (1863–66). He was music director of the Leipzig Theater (1882), and later held similar posts in Danzig and Magdeburg. He wrote the operas *Schloss de l'Orme,* after Prevost's *Manon Lescaut* (Hamburg, Oct. 8, 1883), and *Pfeifer von Dusenbach* (Hamburg, March 21, 1891); also 2 syms.; many piano pieces.

Kleinsinger, George, American composer; b. San Bernardino, Calif., Feb. 13, 1914; d. N.Y., July 28, 1982. He was apprenticed to study dentistry, then turned to music; studied with Philip James at N.Y. Univ. (B.A., 1937) and at the Juilliard Graduate School with Jacobi and Wagenaar (1938–40). From his earliest attempts at composition, he adopted a hedonistic regard toward music as a medium of education and entertainment. In this vein he wrote in 1942 a Broadway musical for children entitled *Tubby the Tuba,* which was highly successful; other works in a similarly whimsical manner were *Pee-Wee the Piccolo* (1946); *Street Corner Concerto* for Harmonica and Orch. (1946); and *Brooklyn Baseball Cantata* (1948). His crowning work was the chamber opera *Archy and Mehitabel,* based on the popular comic strip featuring a garrulous cockroach and an emotional cat; it was first performed in N.Y. on Dec. 6, 1954, and later metamorphosed into a Broadway musical under the title *Shinbone Alley.* Kleinsinger's private life reflected the eccentricity of his musical talents; he inhabited the famous bohemian Hotel Chelsea in N.Y., where he maintained a running waterfall, a turtle, a skunk, an iguana, 40 fish, a dog, a python, and a cat. He used to play the piano with a boa constrictor wrapped around him. How he maintained his menagerie in peace was his guarded secret.

Klementyev, Lev (Mikhailovich), Russian tenor; b. St. Petersburg, April 1, 1868; d. Tiflis, Oct. 26, 1910. He appeared in operetta in Kharkov and St. Petersburg; then was a member of the Kiev Opera (1888–89), the Tiflis Opera (1889–90), and Moscow's Bolshoi Theater (from 1892). He was noted for his faithful rendition of Russian operatic roles.

Klemetti, Heikki, Finnish composer and choral conductor; b. Kuortane, Feb. 14, 1876; d. Helsinki, Aug. 26, 1953. He studied philosophy; then music at the Stern Cons. in Berlin. In 1900 he founded the famous men's choir Suomen Laulu (became a mixed choir in 1907), with which he toured Scandinavia and Europe (1901–25); also the U.S. (1939); led it until 1942. He publ. a history of music (several vols. from 1916), a textbook of choral singing (1917), and a textbook of voice production (1920); composed numerous choruses, masses, and antiphons (collected and officially approved as the hymnal of the State Church of Finland in 1924); also arranged songs for school and home (3 vols., 1927–28) and some early church music.

Klemm, Johann Gottlob. See **Clemm, Johann Gottlob.**

Klemperer, Otto, celebrated German conductor; b. Breslau, May 14, 1885; d. Zürich, July 6, 1973. After early musical training from his mother, he entered the Hoch Cons. in Frankfurt (1901), where he studied piano with Kwast and theory with Knorr; he later received instruction in composition and conducting from Pfitzner in Berlin. He made his debut conducting Max Reinhardt's production of *Orpheus in the Underworld* in Berlin in 1906; on Mahler's recommendation, he then was appointed chorus master and subsequently conductor of the German Theater in Prague; he assisted Mahler in the latter's preparations for the Munich premiere of the *Symphony of a Thousand* in 1910. He became a conductor at the Hamburg Opera in 1910, but was obliged to leave in 1912 as the result of a scandalous liaison with the recently married soprano Elisabeth Schumann. After minor appointments at Barmen (1913–14) and Strasbourg (1914–17), where he was Pfitzner's deputy, he was appointed music director of the Cologne Opera in 1917. While in Cologne, he conducted the German premiere of Janá-ček's *Kát'a Kabanová.* In 1924 he was named music director of the Wiesbaden Opera. He made his U.S. debut as guest conductor with the N.Y. Sym. Orch. on Jan. 24, 1926. In 1927 he became music director of Berlin's Kroll Opera, where he was given a mandate to perform new works and present repertoire pieces in an enlightened manner. He conducted the world premiere of Hindemith's *Neues vom Tage* (June 8, 1929), as well as the 1st Berlin performances of Hindemith's *Cardillac,* Stravinsky's *Oedipus Rex,* and Schoenberg's *Die glückliche Hand;* he also conducted the premiere performance of Schoenberg's *Begleitungsmusik* as part of the Kroll concerts. When political and economic pressures forced the Kroll Opera to close in 1931, Klemperer became a conductor at the Berlin State Opera; when the Nazis came to power in 1933, he was compelled to emigrate to the U.S. That same year he became music director of the Los Angeles Phil.; he also appeared as a guest conductor in N.Y., Philadelphia, and Pittsburgh. His career was disrupted in 1939 when he underwent an operation for a brain tumor. In 1947 he was engaged as conductor at the Budapest State Opera, where he remained until 1950. He made his 1st appearance as a guest conductor with the Philharmonia Orch. of London in 1951; was appointed its principal conductor in 1959, and retained that position when the orch.'s manager, Walter Legge, unsuccessfully attempted to disband it in 1964.

Klemperer was accident-prone and a manic-depressive all his life; the 2 sides of his nature were reflected in his conducting styles on either side of World War II. He had earlier been noted for his energetic and hard-driven interpretations, but during his late London years he won great renown for his measured performances of the Viennese classics. He particularly distinguished himself by conducting a memorable series of the Beethoven syms. at the Royal Festival Hall. In the early 1960s he conducted new productions of *Fidelio, Die Zauberflöte,* and *Lohengrin* at Covent Garden. His serious and unsentimental readings of Mahler's syms. were largely responsible for the modern critical and popular interest shown in that composer's music. In 1970 he conducted in Jerusalem and accepted Israeli citizenship. He retired in 1972. He was also a composer; he studied with Schoenberg during the latter's American sojourn, but his compositional style had more in common with that of Pfitzner. He wrote an opera, *Das Ziel* (1915; rev. 1970), a *Missa sacra* (1916), 6 syms. (from 1960), 17 pieces for Voice and Orch. (1967–70), 9 string quartets (1968–70), and about 100 lieder. He publ. *Meine Erinnerungen an Gustav Mahler* (Zürich, 1960; in Eng. as *Minor Recollections,* London, 1964).

BIBL.: P. Heyworth, *Conversations with K.* (London, 1973); C. Osborne and K. Thomson, eds., *K. Stories: Anecdotes, Sayings and Impressions of O. K.* (London, 1980); P. Heyworth, *O. K.: His Life and Times,* vol. I, 1885–1933 (London, 1983); M. Anderson, ed., *K. on Music: Shavings from a Musician's Workbench* (London, 1986).

Klenau, Paul (August) von, Danish conductor and composer; b. Copenhagen, Feb. 11, 1883; d. there, Aug. 31, 1946. He studied violin with Hillmer and composition with Malling in Copenhagen; then took lessons in violin with Halíř and in composition with Max Bruch at the Berlin Hochschule für Musik (1902–4). In 1904 he went to Munich, where he studied composition privately with Thuille; in 1908, moved to Stuttgart, where he became a student of Max von Schillings. He began his conducting career at the Freiburg Opera during the season of 1907–8; from 1909 to 1912, was conductor at the Stuttgart Court Opera; in 1912 was conductor of the Bach Soc. in Frankfurt; then returned to the Freiburg Opera (1913). After World War I, he studied with Schoenberg. From 1920 to 1926 he was conductor of the Danish Phil. Soc.; concurrently conducted the Vienna Konzerthausgesellschaft (1922–30). He returned to Copenhagen in 1940.
WORKS: 6 operas: *Sulamith*, after the Song of Songs (Munich, Nov. 16, 1913); *Kjartan und Gudrun* (Mannheim, April 4, 1918; rev. as *Gudrun auf Island*, Hagen, Nov. 27, 1924); *Die Lästerschule*, after Sheridan (Frankfurt, Dec. 25, 1926); *Michael Kolhaas*, after Kleist (Stuttgart, Nov. 4, 1933; new version, Berlin, March 7, 1934); *Rembrandt van Rijn*, libretto by Klenau (Berlin and Stuttgart, Jan. 23, 1937); *Elisabeth von England* (Kassel, March 29, 1939; title changed to *Die Königin* after the outbreak of World War II to avoid mentioning England); ballets: *Kleine Idas Blumen*, after Hans Christian Andersen (Stuttgart, 1916), and *Marion* (Copenhagen, 1920); 7 syms. (1908, 1911, 1913, 1913, 1939, 1940, 1941); *Inferno*, 3 fantasies for Orch., after Dante; chamber music; piano pieces; songs.

Klengel, August (Stephan) Alexander, esteemed German pianist, organist, pedagogue, and composer; b. Dresden, June 29, 1783; d. there, Nov. 22, 1852. He studied with Milchmayer, and from 1803, with Clementi, with whom he traveled in Germany and later to St. Petersburg (1805), where he remained as a private tutor to aristocratic families until 1811. He then lived in Paris; visited London in 1815; returned to Dresden in 1816, and was appointed organist at the Hofkapelle in 1817. He was a fine organist and pianist, and a champion of the music of Bach. As a composer, he was a master of contrapuntal forms; his canons were so ingenious that he was known under the sobriquet "Kanon-Klengel." His major achievement was an outstanding set of 48 canons and fugues (publ. 1854), inspired by Bach's *Das wohltemperierte Clavier;* he also wrote various other keyboard works, including a vol. of piano canons as *Les Avantcoureurs* (Dresden, 1841), chamber music, songs, etc.
BIBL.: R. Jäger, *A.A. K., und seine Kanons und Fugen* (diss., Univ. of Leipzig, 1928).

Klengel, Julius, German cellist, pedagogue, and composer, brother of **Paul Klengel;** b. Leipzig, Sept. 24, 1859; d. there, Oct. 27, 1933. Brought up in a musical atmosphere (virtually all members of his family were professional or amateur musicians), he developed rapidly; studied cello with Emil Hegar and theory with Jadassohn. He joined the Leipzig Gewandhaus Orch. when he was 15; in 1881 he became 1st cellist, and remained in that post until his resignation in 1924. He was Royal Prof. at the Leipzig Cons. (from 1881); his most distinguished students were Suggia, Feuermann, and Piatigorsky. He composed 4 cello concertos and other works for cello; chamber music; etc.

Klengel, Paul, German conductor and composer, brother of **Julius Klengel;** b. Leipzig, May 13, 1854; d. there, April 24, 1935. He studied at the Leipzig Cons. and at the Univ. of Leipzig (Ph.D., 1876, with the diss. *Zur Ästhetik der Tonkunst*). From 1881 to 1886 he conducted the Leipzig Euterpe Concerts; from 1888 to 1893, was 2nd court conductor in Stuttgart. From 1898 to 1902 he conducted German choral societies in N.Y.; then returned to Leipzig, where he conducted the Arion Soc. (from 1902) and also taught at the Leipzig Cons. He wrote numerous works for violin, songs, and arrangements.

Klenovsky, Nikolai (Semyonovich), Russian conductor and composer; b. Odessa, 1853; d. Petrograd, July 6, 1915. He studied violin with Hřimalý and harmony with Tchaikovsky at the Moscow Cons. (graduated, 1879); conducted at Moscow's Bolshoi Theater (1883–93) and in Tiflis, where he also was made director of the Cons. (1893); then was deputy director of the Imperial Chapel in St. Petersburg (1902–6). He wrote 3 ballets: *Prelesti gashisha* (The Delights of Hashish; Moscow, 1885); *Svetlana* (Moscow, 1886); *Salanga* (St. Petersburg, 1900); also orch. works; 4 cantatas; songs.

Klenovsky, Paul. See **Wood, Sir Henry J(oseph).**

Klerk, Albert de, Dutch organist, choral conductor, and composer; b. Haarlem, Oct. 4, 1917. He served as assistant organist of Haarlem's St. Joseph Church as a boy; then studied at the Amsterdam Cons. with A. van der Horst (organ) and H. Andriessen (analysis) (graduated, 1939). In 1941 he was awarded the Prix d'Excellence. He was named city organist of Haarlem (1956); became a prof. of organ and improvisation at the Amsterdam Cons. in 1964.
WORKS: Concerto for Organ and Orch. (1941); *Jam lucis orto sidere* for High Voice and Orch. (1942–43); *Cantabile* for Orch. (1952); *Stabat Mater* for Alto, Tenor, Chorus, and Chamber Orch. (1952); *Super omnia,* sacred cantata for Alto, Chorus, and Organ (1960); *Adagium-Suite* for School Chorus and Orch. (1960); *5 noëls français* for Alto and 10 Wind Instruments (1963); Concerto for Organ-positive and String Orch. (1964); Concerto for Solo Organ, 2 Horns, 2 Trumpets, and 2 Trombones (1967); *Laudate Dominum* (Psalm 150) for Chorus and Orch. (1968); *Suite concertante* for Organ and String Orch. (1976); *Te Deum* for Choir and Orch. (1979); *In Honorem Sancti Bavonis* for Youth Choir and Orch. (1983); *Mater Sanctus Laelitiae* (Mother of Blessed Happiness) for Female Chorus, Flute, English Horn, and Bassoon (1957); *Aria met variaties* for Piano, 4-hands (1944); organ pieces, including Prelude and Fugue (1940); Sonata (1942); *6 Inventions* (1945); *Ricercare (Hommage à Sweelinck)* (1950); *8 Fantasies on a Gregorian Theme* (1954); *Fantasia, super "Te Deum laudamus"* for Carillon (1978).

Kletzki, Paul (originally, **Pawel Klecki**), distinguished Polish-born Swiss conductor; b. Lodz, March 21, 1900; d. while rehearsing the Royal Liverpool Phil. in Liverpool, March 5, 1973. He studied composition at the Warsaw Cons., where he also received instruction in violin from Mlynarski; after further studies at the Berlin Academy of Music, he played in the Lodz Phil. (1914–19). He was active as a conductor and composer in Berlin (1921–33); then taught composition at Milan's Scuola Superiora di Musica; at the outbreak of World War II (1939) he settled in Switzerland, becoming a naturalized citizen in 1947. After the war, he pursued a notable conducting career, appearing as a guest conductor with many of the major European orchs.; he also conducted in North and South America, and maintained a close association with the Israel Phil. He was music director of the Dallas Sym. Orch. (1958–62), the Bern Sym. Orch. (1964–66), and l'Orch. de la Suisse Romande in Geneva (1968–70). He was a fine interpreter of the Romantic orch. repertoire, excelling in both the Austro-German and the Slavic schools. He composed 4 syms., a Piano Concerto, a Violin Concerto, chamber music, and songs, but most of his works were destroyed by the havoc wreaked during World War II.

Kleven, Arvid, Norwegian composer; b. Drontheim, Nov. 29, 1899; d. Oslo, Nov. 23, 1929. He studied in Oslo, Paris, and Berlin; from 1919, played flute in the National Theater Orch. in Christiania, and in the Phil. Orch. there. His early neo-Romantic style developed along expressionist lines. Among his works are *Sinfonia libera in due parte* (1927); *Symfonisk fantasi* for Orch.; symphonic poems: *Lotusland* (1922) and *Skogens sovn* (The Sleeping Forest); songs with orch.; Violin Sonata; Cello Sonata; piano pieces.

Klička, Josef, Bohemian organist, choral conductor, and composer; b. Klattau, Dec. 15, 1855; d. there, March 28, 1937. He studied with Skuherský in Prague; then conducted various choral societies there; from 1906 to 1920 he was inspector of music in Bohemia. He was appointed prof. of organ at the Prague Cons. in 1885 and taught until his retirement in 1924. He wrote an opera, *Spanilá mylnářka* (Die Schöne Müllerin; Prague, 1886), 9 masses, 2 oratorios, chamber works, and many organ pieces.

BIBL.: K. Hoffmeister, *J. K.* (Prague, 1944).

Klien, Walter, Austrian pianist; b. Graz, Nov. 27, 1928; d. Vienna, Feb. 9, 1991. He studied at the Vienna Academy of Music with Josef Dichler, and with Arturo Benedetti Michelangeli and Hindemith. In 1951 and 1952 he won the Busoni prize. In 1963 he formed a duo-piano team with Wolfgang Schneiderhan. He was best known for his performances of Haydn, Mozart, Schubert, Schumann, and Brahms.

Klima, Alois, Czech conductor; b. Klatovy, Dec. 21, 1905; d. Prague, June 11, 1980. His father was a choral conductor who taught him to play different orch. instruments. Later Klima studied composition with Křička and Řídký and conducting with Dědeček and Doležil at the Prague Cons.; then conducted radio concerts in Košice and Ostrava. From 1950 to 1970 he was chief conductor of the Prague Radio Sym. Orch., with which he toured widely; also taught at the Prague Cons. and Academy of Music.

Klimov, Mikhail (Georgievich [originally, **Egorovich**]), Russian choral conductor and pedagogue; b. Moscow, Oct. 21, 1881; d. Zavidovo, near Tver, Feb. 20, 1937. He studied composition with Rimsky-Korsakov and conducting with Nikolai Tcherepnin at the St. Petersburg Cons., graduating in 1908. In 1919 he was called upon to reorganize the former Imperial Church Choir as a secular group, which he then conducted until 1935. In 1908 he joined the faculty of the St. Petersburg Cons., becoming a prof. in 1916 and artistic director of its opera studio in 1921.

BIBL.: V. Muzalevsky, *M.G. K.* (Leningrad, 1960).

Klimov, Valery (Alexandrovich), Russian violinist; b. Kiev, Oct. 16, 1931. His father was a professional conductor and a pedagogue. Klimov studied in Odessa and with D. Oistrakh at the Moscow Cons., graduating in 1956; won 1st prize in the Prague and Paris competitions (1956) and then at the Tchaikovsky Competition in Moscow (1958), which opened for him great opportunities for world tours; he played with much success in Europe, the U.S., and Australia.

Klindworth, Karl, eminent German pianist, conductor, pedagogue, and editor; b. Hannover, Sept. 25, 1830; d. Stolpe, near Potsdam, July 27, 1916. He learned to play violin and piano as a child; obtained work as conductor of a traveling opera company when he was only 17; also traveled in Germany as a concert pianist; then went to Weimar to study with Liszt (1852–53). In 1854 he went to London, where he remained until 1868, establishing himself as a popular piano teacher. When Wagner was in London in 1855, they became friends; as a result of his admiration for Wagner, Klindworth undertook the most important work of his life, the arrangement in vocal scores of Wagner's tetralogy *Der Ring des Nibelungen*. In 1868 he was engaged as a prof. at the newly founded Moscow Cons. at the invitation of its director, Nikolai Rubinstein; after Rubinstein's death in 1881, Klindworth returned to Germany; from 1882 to 1987, was one of the principal conductors of the Berlin Phil. In 1884 he established in Berlin his own Klavierschule; in 1893 it was merged with the Scharwenka Cons. in Berlin, as Konservatorium der Musik Klindworth-Scharwenka, which became one of the most famous music schools in Germany. Klindworth was an exceptionally competent arranger and music ed.; apart from his masterly transcriptions of Wagner's operas, he made an arrangement for 2 pianos of Schubert's C major Sym. He also wrote a number of virtuoso pieces for piano, of which the brilliant *Polonaise-Fantaisie* and 24 grand études in all keys enjoyed some vogue among pianists.

BIBL.: H. Leichtentritt, *Das Konservatorium der Musik K.-Scharwenka, 1881–1931* (Berlin, 1931).

Klingenberg, Friedrich Wilhelm, German pedagogue and composer; b. Sulau, June 6, 1809; d. Görlitz, April 2, 1888.

He was director of the Breslau Academy of Music (1830–37) and cantor of the Görlitz Peterskirche (1840–85). He wrote a Sym., overtures, piano pieces, vocal church music, and songs.

Klitzsch, Karl Emanuel, German conductor and composer; b. Schönhaide, Oct. 30, 1812; d. Zwickau, March 5, 1889. He lived most of his life in Zwickau; was co-founder and conductor of the Music Soc. there. Under the pen name of Emanuel Kronach, he composed the opera *Juana, oder Ein Tag auf St. Domingo*; the 96th Psalm for Soli, Chorus, and Orch.; songs.

Klobučar, Berislav, Yugoslav conductor; b. Zagreb, Aug. 28, 1924. He was educated at the Zagreb Academy of Music; studied conducting with Lovro von Matačić and Clemens Krauss. He was conductor at the Zagreb National Theater (1941–51); in 1953 he appeared at the Vienna State Opera; became a regular conductor there. He was chief conductor of the Graz Phil. and Opera (1961–72); after serving as principal conductor at Stockholm's Royal Theater (1972–81), he was music director of the Orch. Philharmonique de Nice (from 1982 to 1988). He also appeared as a guest conductor with the major European and U.S. opera houses.

Klose, Friedrich (Karl Wilhelm), Swiss composer; b. Karlsruhe (of Swiss parents), Nov. 29, 1862; d. Ruvigliana, near Lugano, Dec. 24, 1942. He studied with V. Lachner in Karlsruhe and Ruthardt in Geneva; then with Bruckner in Vienna (1886–91). He taught in Switzerland, Austria, and Germany before joining the faculty at Munich's Akademie der Tonkunst (1907–19). He publ. *Meine Lehrjahre bei Bruckner* (Regensburg, 1927) and *Bayreuth* (Regensburg, 1929).

WORKS: *Ilsebill*, dramatic sym. (Munich, Oct. 29, 1905); symphonic poems: *Elfenreigen* (1892); *Das Leben ein Traum* (1896); *Festzug* (1913); a Mass (1889); an oratorio, *Der Sonne-Geist* (Basel, 1918); String Quartet (1911); organ works; songs.

BIBL.: R. Louis, *F. K. und seine symphonische Dichtung "Das Leben ein Traum"* (Munich, 1905); H. Knappe, *F. K.: Eine Studie* (Munich, 1921); idem, ed., *F. K. zum 80. Geburtstag* (Lugano, 1942).

Klosé, Hyacinthe-Eléonore, noted French clarinetist and pedagogue; b. Corfu, Oct. 11, 1808; d. Paris, Aug. 29, 1880. He studied with Frédéric Berr at the Paris Cons.; then taught there (1838–68). With the instrument maker Louis-Auguste Buffet, he developed a clarinet utilizing the ring-key system of the Boehm flute; it was first shown in 1839 and patented in 1844. He publ. *Grande méthode pour la clarinette à anneaux mobiles* (1844) based on that system; did much to promote the then-novel saxophone, and wrote some music both for it and for the clarinet. He was made a Chevalier de la Légion d'Honneur in 1864.

BIBL.: P. Weston, *Clarinet Virtuosi of the Past* (London, 1971).

Klose, Margarete, esteemed German contralto; b. Berlin, Aug. 6, 1902; d. there, Dec. 14, 1968. She studied at the Klindworth-Scharwenka Cons. in Berlin; made her debut in Ulm in 1927, then sang in Kassel (1928–29) and Mannheim (1929–31). She was a leading member of the Berlin State Opera (1931–49; 1955–61); also sang at the Bayreuth Festivals (1936–42) and London's Covent Garden (1935, 1937), and was a member of the Berlin Städtische Oper (1949–58). She was particularly praised for her Wagner and Verdi portrayals.

Kloss, Erich, German writer on music; b. Görlitz, Feb. 19, 1863; d. in an automobile accident in Berlin, Nov. 1, 1910. He began his career as a teacher, but because of deafness he was obliged to give it up; directed his attention to writing.

WRITINGS: *20 Jahre Bayreuth* (1896); *Wagner, wie er war und ward* (1901); *Ein Wagner-Lesebuch* (1904); *Wagner-Anekdoten* (1908); *R. Wagner in seinen Briefen* (1908); ed. *Richard Wagner an Freunde und Zeitgenossen* (1909); *R. Wagner an siene Künstler* (1909); *R. Wagner im Liede* (1910); *R. Wagner über Die Meistersinger* (1910); *R. Wagner über den Ring des Nibelungen* (1913).

Klotz (originally **Kloz**), family of outstanding German violin makers. Their instruments were brought into repute by **Ma-**

thias **Klotz** (b. Mittenwald, June 11, 1653; d. there, Aug. 16, 1743); he served an apprenticeship with Giovanni Railich, a Paduan maker of lutes and other instruments; his violins date from late in his career, and are very rare. His son, **Sebastian Klotz** (b. Mittenwald, Jan. 18, 1696; d. there, Jan. 20, 1775), produced remarkable violins after Italian models. There followed, in the 18th century, several other violin makers named Klotz, but their relationship to the family cannot be established.

Klucevsek, Guy, American composer and accordionist; b. N.Y., Feb. 26, 1947. He grew up in a Slovenian community in Pennsylvania, where he learned to play polkas. He studied music theory and composition at the Indiana Univ. of Pennsylvania (B.A., 1969) and with Subotnick at the Univ. of Pittsburgh (M.A., 1971) and the Calif. Inst. of the Arts (1971–72). In 1980 he discovered the polkas of Cajun and Texan/Mexican origin, and in 1986 he invited a number of composers to contribute to his recording *Polkas from the Fringe* (1987). He also encouraged and created virtuoso accordion music in other styles, and premiered various works by composers including Henry Cowell, Lois Vierk, and John Zorn. Among his compositions are *Sea Chandeliers* for Gamelan (1985), *Scenes from a Mirage* for Accordion (1986), and *Flying Vegetables of the Apocalypse* for Violin, Cello, and Accordion (1988).

Klughardt, August (Friedrich Martin), German conductor and composer; b. Cöthen, Nov. 30, 1847; d. Rosslau, near Dresden, Aug. 3, 1902. He was a pupil of Blassmann and Reichel in Dresden. From 1867 to 1868 he was a theater conductor in Posen; held similar posts in Neustrelitz (1868–69) and Lübeck (1869). He served as court music director in Weimar (1869–73), where he became a friend of Liszt. He then was music director in Neustrelitz (1873–82) and Dessau (from 1882).

WORKS: 4 operas: *Mirjam* (Weimar, 1871); *Iwein* (Neustrelitz, 1879); *Gudrun* (Neustrelitz, 1882); *Die Hochzeit Mönchs* (Dessau, Nov. 10, 1886); 5 syms.; Cello Concerto (1894); Violin Concerto (1895); chamber music; piano pieces; songs.

BIBL.: L. Gerlach, *A. K.: Sein Leben und seine Werke* (Leipzig, 1902).

Klusák, Jan, Czech composer; b. Prague, April 18, 1934. He studied theory with Řídký and Bořkovec at the Prague Academy of Music (1953–57). He wrote a number of works in a neo-Baroque idiom, set in tolerably dissonant counterpoint; also paid tribute to the ethnic resources of Czech music. He soon succumbed, however, to the Circean lure of cosmopolitan formalism and total serialism, with a well-nigh monastic exercise of tonal egalitarianism.

WORKS: STAGE: Operas: *Proces* (The Trial), after Kafka (1966); *Viola* (1984–85). Ballet: *Stories from Tapestries* (1988). **ORCH.:** Concertino for Flute and Strings (1955); *Partita* for Strings (1955); 3 syms. (1956, 1959, 1960); Concerto Grosso for Wind Quintet and Strings (1957); *Inventions I, II, III, IV, VII, VIII* for Chamber Orch.: *I* (1961); *II* (1962); *III* (1962); *IV* (1964); *VII* (1973); *VIII, Quadratura orbis* (Squaring of the Circle; 1973); *Variations on a Theme of Mahler* (1960–62; based on a theme from Mahler's 5th Sym.); 2 *Czech Dances* for Wind Orch. (1964); *Lyric Fantasy, Hommage à Grieg* (1965); *Le Forgeron harmonieux,* after Handel's so-called *Harmonious Blacksmith* (1966); *Pasticcio olandese per orchestra, A Friesland Friday* (1969–70); *Hamburger Doppelinvention* (1974); *Kleine Farbenlehre, Hommage à Goethe* (1974–75); 6 *Small Preludes* (1984). **CHAMBER:** *Music to the Fountain* for Wind Quintet (1954); 4 string quartets (1956; 1961–62; 1975; 1990); *Přísloví* (Proverbs) for Low Voice and Wind Instruments (1959); *Obrazy* (Pictures) for 12 Wind Instruments (1960); *Monoinvention* for Cello (1962); *Risposte* for Violin (1963); Sonata for Violin and Wind Instruments (1964–65); *Invention V, Hra v šachy* (Game of Chess) for Wind Quintet (1965); *1-4-3-2-5-6-7-10-9-8-11* (invertible all-interval 12-tone series) for Flute (1965); *Invention VI* for Wind Quintet and String Quartet (1969); *Contrapunto fiorito* for 8 Instruments (1966); *Short John* for Cimbalom (1971); *Jupiter-Duo* for Clarinet and

Cello (1973); Sonata for Percussion (1974); *Solo* for Trumpet (1975–76); *Die heilige Zahl,* duo for Violin and Percussion (1975–76); *Tango-Polka* for Clarinet, Trumpet, Cello, and Piano (1980); *Variations* for 2 Harps (1982); *Diario* for Cello (1982); *Once There Were 3 Goddesses* for Brass Quintet and Harp (1983); *Fantasia on Adam Michna of Otradovice* for Brass Quintet and Harp (1983); piano pieces. **VOCAL:** *4 Small Vocal Exercises,* on texts by Kafka, for Narrator and 11 Wind Instruments (1960); *Radix nativitatis I. S.* (memorial for Igor Stravinsky) for Voice, Flute, Clarinet, Viola, and Piano (1972); *Bridal Cantata 1979* for Male Chorus and Orch. (1979); *The Moon in Zenith,* to words by Anna Akhmatova, for Mezzo-soprano, Clarinet, Viola, and Piano (1981).

Kmentt, Waldemar, Austrian tenor; b. Vienna, Feb. 2, 1929. He studied at the Vienna Academy of Music; made his concert debut in 1950 in Vienna, singing in Beethoven's 9th Sym.; in 1951, was engaged at the Vienna State Opera; sang regularly in Salzburg (from 1955) and Düsseldorf (from 1958). He made guest appearances in Milan, Paris, Rome, Bayreuth, Munich, and elsewhere; also sang in concerts and recitals. He was best known as an interpreter of the Austro-German repertoire.

Knab, Armin, German composer; b. Neu-Schleichach, Feb. 19, 1881; d. Bad Wörishofen, June 23, 1951. He studied piano in Würzburg; from 1934 to 1943, taught at the Hochschule für Musik-Erziehung in Berlin. He was particularly esteemed for his lieder. He followed the Romantic tradition, but tended toward a more severe modal style in his larger works.

WORKS: Sacred cantatas: *Mariae Geburt* (1928); *Vanitas mundi* (1946); *Engelsgruss* (1950); musical fairy tales: *Sneewittchen* and *Rumpelstilzchen;* folk-song cantatas: *Singt und klingt* (1934); *Grüss Gott, du schöner Maien* (1935); *Glück auf, ihr Bergleute* (1946); a great number of choral works; many instrumental pieces for school use.

BIBL.: O. Lang, *A. K., Ein Meister deutscher Liedkunst* (Munich, 1937).

Knabe, William (actually, **Valentine Wilhelm Ludwig**), German-born American piano manufacturer; b. Kreuzberg, near Oppeln, Prussia, June 3, 1803; d. Baltimore, May 21, 1864. He settled in the U.S. in 1833; formed a partnership to manufacture pianos with Henry Gaehle in Baltimore in 1839, which continued until the latter's death in 1855. The business was continued by Knabe's sons and grandsons until it was merged with the American Piano Co. in 1908; it became a part of the Aeolian American Corp. in 1932.

Knaifel, Alexander, Russian composer; b. Tashkent, Nov. 28, 1943. He studied cello with Rostropovich at the Moscow Cons.; took a course in composition with Arapov at the Leningrad Cons., graduating in 1967. He ed. the progressive publication *Soviet Composer* (1970–73). His music uses a variety of modern techniques, without venturing into unintelligibility.

WORKS: STAGE: Ballet, *Striving* (1964); chamber opera, *The Canterville Ghost,* after Oscar Wilde (1965–66); choreographic scene, *The Penitent Magdalene* (1967); ballet, *Medea* (1968). **ORCH.:** *Dream Fantasy* (1963); *Burlesque* for Trombone and Strings (1963); Concerto for Viola, Double Bass, and 23 Wind and Percussion Instruments (1964); *Vera,* variations and dedicatory strophe for Strings (1980); *Opposition,* suite (1984). **CHAMBER:** 2 *Pieces* for Flute, Viola, Piano, and Percussion (1962); *Ostinati* for Violin and Cello (1964); *Tournament Music* for Horn and Piano (1967); *Lamento* for Cello (1967); *Constanta* for Horn and 6 Percussion Groups (1969–71); *A prima vista* for 4 Players on 5 Percussion Sets (1972); *Anna Akhmatova: Midnight Poems,* commentary for 4 Performers (1973); *Joan of Arc,* choreography for 13 groups of Instruments (1970–78); *Da,* composition for Ensemble of Soloists (1980); *Nika,* 72 fragments for 17 Players (1984); Agnus Dei for 4 Instrumentalists (1985). **PIANO:** *Short Sonata* (1961); *Classic Suite* (1963); *Musique militaire* (1964). **VOCAL:** *150,000,000,* dithyramb after the poem of Mayakovsky, for Chorus, 6 Piccolos, 6 Trumpets, 6 Trombones, a few Violas and Double Basses, and Kettledrums (1966); *The Petrograd Sparrows,* phantasmagoria for Boys'

Chorus and Chamber Orch. (1967); *Funeral Music* for Soprano and Orch. (1967); *Monody* for Female Voice (1968); *Lenin: A Letter to the Central Committee Members* for Bass Voices in unison (1969); *Status nascendi* for 3 groups of Voices and Instruments (1973–75); *Ainana*, 17 variations for Chamber Choir, Percussion, and Electronic Tape (1978); *Stupid Horse*, 15 stories for Female Singer and Piano (1981); *Ordinary* for Chorus, Strings, Organ, and Female Soloist (1982); *Pagan Rock* for Chorus of Basses, Percussion, and Rock Group (1982); *God*, ode for 2 Choirs (1985).

Knap, Rolf, Dutch composer; b. Amsterdam, Oct. 17, 1937. He studied oboe at the Amsterdam Cons.; took private composition lessons with Karel Mengelberg; then studied electronic music at the Inst. of Sonology of the Univ. of Utrecht. He was an orch. oboist (1960–67); then taught oboe.
WORKS: *(Sym)phonic Piece* for Orch. (1971); *Le Couple(t)* for Voice, Piano, and Electronics (1971); *Dilemmaniana for Marrie* for Narrator, Cello, and Live Electronics (1972); *Zelomanniana* for Oboe and Piano (1974); 2 song cycles: *Liederen van Doofstommen* (Songs of Deaf-Mutes; 1974, 1976); *Harmonische reflecties* for Piano (1976; rev. 1984).

Knape, Walter, German musicologist, conductor, and composer; b. Bernburg, Jan. 14, 1906. He studied at the Univ. of Leipzig, receiving his Ph.D. in 1934 with the dissertation *Die Sinfonien von Karl Friedrich Abel;* then joined its faculty. From 1948 to 1957 he was conductor of the Leipzig Sing-Akademie and the Phil. Choir; he also taught at the Berlin Hochschule für Musik (1954–57), and subsequently at the Univs. of Hamburg, Hannover, and Cuxhaven. He devoted much time to the study of the life and works of Abel; ed. a complete edition of his works (16 vols., Cuxhaven, 1958–74) and a bibliographic-thematic catalog (Cuxhaven, 1971); also wrote *Karl Friedrich Abel: Leben und Werk eines frühklassischen Komponisten* (Bremen, 1973). He composed several symphonic and choral works, chamber music, and many piano pieces.

Knapp, Phebe (Phoebe) Palmer, American philanthropist and composer of gospel songs; b. N.Y., March 8, 1839; d. Poland Springs, Maine, July 10, 1908. She and her husband, Joseph F. Knapp, the founder of the Metropolitan Life Insurance Co. of N.Y., were actively engaged in philanthropic endeavors as members of the Methodist Episcopal Church. She wrote over 500 gospel songs and publ. the collections *Notes of Joy* (1869) and *Bible School Songs* (1873); a friend and benefactor of the poet Fanny Crosby, she wrote the music to her *Assurance* ("Blessed Assurance, Jesus is Mine"); it was publ. in 1873 and became one of the most popular works of its kind.
BIBL.: R. McCutchan, *Our Hymnody* (N.Y., 1937).

Knappertsbusch, Hans, eminent German conductor; b. Elberfeld, March 12, 1888; d. Munich, Oct. 25, 1965. He studied with Steinbach and Lohse at the Cologne Cons. (1908–12); served as assistant conductor at the Bayreuth Festivals (1910–12), then conducted in Bochum (1912–13). He was director of opera in Elberfeld (1913–18); subsequently conducted opera in Leipzig (1918–19) and Dessau (1919–22). In 1922 he became Generalmusikdirektor of the Bavarian State Opera in Munich, a post he held with great distinction until resigning in the face of Nazi pressure in 1936; then conducted at the Vienna State Opera (1936–45); was also a conductor with the Vienna Phil. (1937–44). After World War II, he returned to Germany and made his home in Munich. He conducted at the Salzburg Festivals (1947–50; 1954–55); was a regular guest conductor with the Vienna Phil. (1947–64) and at the Bayreuth Festivals (from 1951). He was one of the great interpreters of the operas of Wagner and Richard Strauss. The authority and spontaneity he brought to such masterworks as *Götterdämmerung* and *Parsifal* were extraordinary.
BIBL.: R. Betz and W. Panofsky, *K.* (Ingolstadt, 1958).

Knecht, Justin Heinrich, German organist, conductor, music theorist, and composer; b. Biberach, Sept. 30, 1752; d. there, Dec. 1, 1817. He was an organist and music director in Biberach from 1771 to the end of his life, traveling only

briefly to Stuttgart, where he was court conductor from 1806 till 1808. Despite his provincial field of activity, he attained considerable repute in Germany through his compositions and theoretical writings. He was a follower of the Vogler system of harmony; taught chord building by thirds up to chords of the eleventh on all degrees of the scale. He wrote 10 stage works, mostly singspiels; sacred works; the programmatic sym. *Le Portrait musical de la nature* (c.1784), to which he supplied a programmatic description, seemingly anticipating Beethoven's *Pastoral* Sym.
WRITINGS: *Erklärung einiger . . . missverstandenen Grundsätze aus der Vogler' schen Theorie* (Ulm, 1785); *Gemeinnützliches Elementarwerk der Harmonie und des Generalbasses* (4 parts, 1792–98); *Kleines alphabetisches Wörterbuch der vornehmsten und interessantesten Artikel aus der musikalischen Theorie* (1795); *Vollständige Orgelschule für Anfänger und Geübtere* (3 parts, 1795–98); *Allgemeiner musikalischer Katechismus* (Biberach, 1803); *Luthers Verdienst um Musik und Poesie* (1817).
BIBL.: E. Kauffmann, *J.H. K.* (Tübingen, 1892); A. Bopp, *J.H. K.* (Biberach, 1917); idem, *Das Musikleben der freien Reichsstadt Biberach* (Kassel, 1930).

Kneisel, Franz, German violinist and pedagogue; b. Bucharest (of German parents), Jan. 26, 1865; d. N.Y., March 26, 1926. He studied at the Bucharest Cons., graduating at the age of 14; in 1879 went to Vienna, where he became a pupil of Grün and Hellmesberger at the Cons.; made his debut on Dec. 31, 1882, then was concertmaster of the Bilse Orch. in Berlin (1884–85). From 1885 to 1903 he was concertmaster of the Boston Sym. Orch. In 1886 he organized the celebrated Kneisel Quartet (with Emmanuel Fiedler as 2nd violin; Louis Svecenski, viola; Fritz Giese, cello), which gave performances of high quality in Boston, N.Y., and other American cities, and also in Europe, obtaining world fame before dissolving in 1917. He taught at N.Y.'s Inst. of Musical Art (from 1905). Kneisel was admirable in ensemble playing; his service to the cause of chamber music in America was very great. He was made honorary Mus.Doc. by Yale Univ. (1911) and by Princeton Univ. (1915). He composed *Grand Concert Étude* for Violin; publ. *Advanced Exercises* for the violin (1900); ed. a collection of violin pieces (3 vols., 1900).

Kniese, Julius, German pianist, organist, conductor, composer, and teacher; b. Roda, near Jena, Dec. 21, 1848; d. Dresden, April 22, 1905. He studied with W. Stade in Altenburg, then in Leipzig with Brendel and C. Riedel (1868–70). From 1871 to 1876 he was director of the Glogau Singing Academy; then conducted the Rühl singing society and the Frankfurt Wagnerverein; was music director in Aix (1884–89); also was chorus master at Bayreuth (from 1882) and director of the Preparatory School for Stage Singers (from 1890). He wrote an opera, *Jery und Bätely* (Bayreuth, 1890); publ. 4 albums of songs.

Knight, Gladys, black American rhythm-and-blues singer; b. Atlanta, Ga., May 28, 1944. Her parents sang gospel hymns, and she herself joined a church choir as a mere tot; at 8 she won grand prize on Ted Mack's "Amateur Hour" television show; then began singing in a group with her siblings and cousins dubbed the Pips. Unusual for a family act, they continued to perform professionally for over 25 years. Their early repertoire reflected a religious background, but their greatest success came with a series of secular recordings. They first attracted attention with their recording of *Every Beat of My Heart* (1961). The group subsequently became notably successful as Gladys Knight and the Pips, turning out such hit recordings as *I Heard It through the Grapevine* (1967), *Neither One of Us* (1973), *Midnight Train to Georgia* (1973), *I've Got to Use My Imagination* (1974), and *On and On* (1975). Among the group's later recordings were *Landlord* (1980) and *You're Number One* (1983).
BIBL.: *Current Biography* (Feb. 1987).

Knight, Joseph Philip, English clergyman, organist, and composer; b. Bradford-on-Avon, July 26, 1812; d. Great Yarmouth, June 2, 1887. He studied organ with Corfe in Bristol. During a stay in the U.S. (1839–41), he wrote his most celebrated song, *Rocked in the Cradle of the Deep.* After 2 years as vicar and organist at St. Agnes in the Scilly Islands, he returned to England and continued to write songs. These included *Venice, Say What Shall My Song Be Tonight?, The Dream, All on the Summer Sea,* and *She Wore a Wreath of Roses.*

Knipper, Lev (Konstantinovich), important Russian composer; b. Tiflis, Dec. 3, 1898; d. Moscow, July 30, 1974. He studied piano and took lessons in composition with Glière and Zhilyaev at Moscow's Gnessin School; traveled to Germany and took private lessons with Jarnach in Berlin and Julius Weissmann in Freiburg. Under the influence of western European trends, he wrote music in a fairly advanced style of composition, but soon abandoned these experiments and devoted himself to the study of folk music of different nationalities of the Soviet Union.
WORKS: Operas: *Severniy veter* (The North Wind; 1929–30; Moscow, March 30, 1930); *Marya* (1936–38); *Aktrisa* (The Actress; 1942); *Na Baykale* (On the Baikal Lake; 1946–48); *Korenzhizni* (The Source of Life; 1948–49); 14 syms. (1929–54); several ballets and orch. suites on ethnic motifs; overtures; 3 violin concertos (1944, 1965, 1967); 2 cello concertos (1962, 1972); Clarinet Concerto (1966); Oboe Concerto (1967); Bassoon Concerto (1969); 3 string quartets and other chamber music; piano pieces; songs.

Knittl, Karel, Bohemian choral conductor and composer; b. Polna, Oct. 4, 1853; d. Prague, March 17, 1907. He was a pupil of Skuherský at the Prague Organ School; later of Pivoda (singing) and Smetana (conducting). From 1877 to 1890, and again from 1897 to 1901, he conducted the choral society Hlahol in Prague. He taught at the Prague Organ School (1882–89), and at the Prague Cons. (from 1889), serving as its administrative director (from 1901). He publ. a monograph on Skuherský (Prague, 1894); also composed orch. works, choruses, piano pieces, and songs.
BIBL.: J. Fiala, "K. K.," *Hudebni Rozhledy,* VI (1953).

Knorr, Ernst-Lothar von, German conductor and composer; b. Eitorf, near Cologne, Jan. 2, 1896; d. Heidelberg, Oct. 30, 1973. He studied at the Cologne Cons. with Bram Eldering (violin), Franz Bölsche (composition), and Fritz Steinbach (conducting). After graduation, he played violin in various provincial orchs.; in 1925 he moved to Berlin and taught violin at the Hochschule für Musik. He served as director of the Hannover Academy of Music (1952–61) and the Hochschule für Musik in Heidelberg (1961–69). Most of his MSS perished in an air raid on Frankfurt in 1944; his extant works include Concerto for 2 Orchs.; Chamber Concerto for Piano, Saxophone, Chorus, and Small Orch.; cantatas; choral works; chamber music. He was principally known for his educational work; his school cantatas are well adapted to performance.
BIBL.: O. Riemer, ed., *E.-L. v.K. zum 75. Geburtstag* (Cologne, 1971).

Knorr, Iwan (Otto Armand), German composer and teacher; b. Mewe, Jan. 3, 1853; d. Frankfurt am Main, Jan. 22, 1916. His family went to Russia when he was 3 years old, returning to Germany in 1868; he entered the Leipzig Cons., where he studied piano with Moscheles, theory with Richter, and composition with Reinecke. In 1874 he went back to Russia, where he taught in Kharkov; was made head of theoretical studies of the Kharkov division of the Russian Imperial Musical Soc. (1878). He settled in Frankfurt in 1883 as a teacher at the Hoch Cons.; in 1908, became its director. His most distinguished pupils were Cyril Scott, Pfitzner, and Ernst Toch. His works are conceived in a Romantic vein, several inspired by the Ukrainian folk songs which he had heard in Russia.
WRITINGS: (all publ. in Leipzig): *Aufgaben für den Unterricht in der Harmonielehre* (1903); *Lehrbuch der Fugenkomposition* (1911); *Die Fugen des Wohltemperieten Klaviers in bildlicher Darstellung* (1912; 2nd ed., 1926).

WORKS: Operas: *Dunja* (Koblenz, March 23, 1904); *Die Hochzeit* (Prague, 1907); *Durchs Fenster* (Karlsruhe, Oct. 4, 1908); *Ukrainische Liebeslieder* for Vocal Quartet and Piano, op. 6 (1890); *Variationen* (on a Ukrainian folk song), op. 7 (1891); Variations for Piano, Violin, and Cello, op. 1; Piano Quartet, op. 3; Variations for Piano and Cello, op. 4; etc.
BIBL.: M. Bauer, *I. K.: Ein Gedenkblatt* (Frankfurt, 1916).

Knorr, Julius, German pianist and pedagogue; b. Leipzig, Sept. 22, 1807; d. there, June 17, 1861. He made his debut at the Leipzig Gewandhaus (1831); was an intimate friend of Schumann; prepared a number of widely used technical exercises for piano.
WRITINGS: *Neue Pianoforteschule in 184 Übungen* (1835; 2nd ed., 1841, as *Die Pianoforteschule der neuesten Zeit; Ein Supplement zu den Werken von Cramer, Czerny, Herz, Hummel, Hünten, Kalkbrenner, Moscheles); Das Klavierspiel in 280 Übungen; Materialien für das mechanische Klavierspiel* (1844); *Methodischer Leitfaden für Klavierlehrer* (1849); *Ausführliche Klaviermethode,* in 2 parts: *Methode* (1859) and *Schule der Mechanik* (1860); *Erklärendes Verzeichniss der hauptsächlichsten Musikkunstwörter* (1854).

Knote, Heinrich, distinguished German tenor; b. Munich, Nov. 26, 1870; d. Garmisch, Jan. 12, 1953. He studied with Kirschner in Munich; was a principal member of the Munich Court Opera (from 1892), continuing on its roster when it became the Bavarian State Opera (1918); also sang at London's Covent Garden (1901; 1903; 1907–8; 1913); made his Metropolitan Opera debut in N.Y. as Walther von Stolzing in *Die Meistersinger von Nürnberg* (Dec. 3, 1904), singing there until 1906 and again in 1907–8; later toured the U.S. with the German Opera Co. (1923–24). His remarkable Munich career spanned almost half a century; made his farewell appearance there as Siegfried (Dec. 15, 1931); subsequently taught voice. He was a greatly esteemed Heldentenor, excelling in such roles as Tannhäuser, Lohengrin, and Tristan.
BIBL.: J. Wagenmann, *Der sechzigjährige deutsche Meistersinger H. K. in seiner stimmbildnerischen Bedeutung und im Vergleich mit anderen Sängern* (Munich, 1930).

Knüpfer, Paul, German bass; b. Halle, June 21, 1865; d. Berlin, Nov. 4, 1920. He studied in Sondershausen; made his debut there in 1885; then sang at the Leipzig Opera (1887–98). In 1898 he joined the Berlin Royal (later State) Opera, remaining on its roster until 6 months before his death; also sang at Bayreuth (1901–12) and London's Covent Garden (1904; 1907–14). His finest roles included Osmin, Baron Ochs, Gurnemanz, and King Marke.

Knüpfer, Sebastian, eminent German composer; b. Asch, Bavaria, Sept. 6, 1633; d. Leipzig, Oct. 10, 1676. He studied with his father, a Kantor and organist in Asch; after private musical studies, he took courses in organ as well as academic subjects at the Regensburg Gymnasium Poeticum (1646–54); he then settled in Leipzig, where he taught and was a bass singer in church choirs. On July 17, 1657, he was appointed Kantor of the Thomaskirche and director of music for the city; during his tenure, Leipzig resumed its preeminence as a center for music-making of the highest order. He composed sacred vocal works to both Latin and German texts, and also wrote some secular madrigals and canzonettas. Although few of his works are extant, those that have survived reveal him as a gifted musician.
BIBL.: O. Kandmann, *Das Werk S. K.s im Überblick* (diss., Univ. of Leipzig, 1960).

Knussen, (Stuart) Oliver, English composer; b. Glasgow, June 12, 1952. Remarkably precocious, he began playing piano as a small boy and showed unusual diligence also in his studies of music theory, mostly with John Lambert (1963–69) while attending the Central Tutorial School for Young Musicians (1964–67). On April 7, 1968, he made musical headlines when, at the age of 15, he conducted the London Sym. Orch. in the premiere performance of his own 1st Sym., written in an eclectic, but astoundingly effective, modern style. He was awarded fellowships for advanced study with Schuller at the Berkshire Music Center in Tanglewood (1970–73). He served as an artistic director of the Aldeburgh Festivals (from 1983) and as coordinator of contemporary music activities at Tanglewood (from 1986).

Works: Operas: *Where the Wild Things Are* (1979–81); *Max and the Maximonsters* (Brussels, Nov. 28, 1980); *Higglety Pigglety Pop!* (1983–84); 3 syms.: No. 1 (1966–67; London, April 7, 1968); No. 2 for Soprano and Orch. (1970–71; Tanglewood, Aug. 18, 1971); No. 3 (1973–76; rev. 1979; London, Sept. 6, 1979); *Pantomime* for Chamber Ensemble (1968; rev. 1971); Concerto for Orch. (1968–69; London, Feb. 1, 1970; rev. 1974); *Masks* for Flute (1969); *Fire-Capriccio* for Flute and String Trio (1969); *Tributum*, overture (1969); *Vocalise with Songs of Winnie-the-Pooh* for Soprano and 6 Instruments (1970; rev. without text, 1974–75); *Choral* for Wind Orch. (1970–72; Boston, Nov. 8, 1973); *Rosary Songs* for Soprano, Clarinet, Viola, and Piano (1972); *Océan de terre* for Soprano and Chamber Ensemble (1972–73; rev. 1975); *Puzzle Music*, 4 pieces after puzzle canons by John Lloyd, for Flute, Clarinet, 2 Percussionists, Harp, Guitar or Mandolin, and Celesta (1972–73); *Chiara* for Soprano, Female Chorus, and Small Orch. (1971–75); *Ophelia Dances*, Book I, for Ensemble (1975); *Coursing* for Chamber Ensemble (1979; rev. 1981); *Flourish with Fireworks*, overture (1988).

Knyvett, Charles, Jr., English singer and organist, son of **Charles Knyvett, Sr.,** and brother of **William Knyvett**; b. London, 1773; d. there, Nov. 2, 1859. He studied organ with Samuel Webbe; in 1801 he participated in the Vocal Concerts in London; in 1802 he became organist at St. George's; also was active as a teacher. He publ. a *Selection of Psalm Tunes* (1823).

Knyvett, Charles, Sr., English organist and tenor, father of **Charles Knyvett, Jr.,** and **William Knyvett;** b. probably in London, Feb. 22, 1752; d. there, Jan. 19, 1822. He was a chorister at Westminster Abbey; also studied at Westminster School. He became a member of the Royal Soc. of Musicians (1778); was a Gentleman of the Chapel Royal (1786–1808), serving as its organist (1796–1822); was also active with Samuel Harrison in various concert ventures (from 1789).

Knyvett, William, English singer, conductor, and composer, son of **Charles Knyvett, Sr.,** and brother of **Charles Knyvett, Jr.;** b. London, April 21, 1779; d. Ryde, Isle of Wight, Nov. 17, 1856. He was a pupil of his father and of Samuel Webbe. He became a treble singer at the Concerts of Ancient Music (1788); sang alto there from 1795; was its director (1832–40); also of the Birmingham Festivals (1834–43). He became a Gentleman of the Chapel Royal (1797), and later was made a composer there (1802). He composed a number of glees; his *When the Fair Rose* won a prize of the Harmonic Soc. in 1800.

Kobald, Karl, Austrian writer on music; b. Brünn, Aug. 28, 1876; d. Vienna, Oct. 12, 1957. He studied at the Univ. of Vienna with Adler, Hellmesberger, and Richter; also took lessons with Bruckner. In 1918 he became music adviser in the Austrian Ministry of Education; from 1932 to 1938, and again in 1945–46, was president of the Austrian State Academy.

Writings: *Alt-Wiener Musikstätten* (1919; 2nd ed., 1923); *Schubert und Schwind* (1920); *Franz Schubert* (1922); *In Memoriam Anton Bruckner* (1924); *Johann Strauss* (1925); *Beethoven* (1927; new eds., 1936, 1946, and 1952); *Franz Schubert und seine Zeit* (1927); *Klassische Musikstätten* (1929); *Joseph Haydn* (1929); *Wo unsterbliche Musik entstand* (1950).

Kobayashi, Ken-Ichiro, Japanese conductor; b. Iwaki, April 13, 1940. He studied composition with Mareo Ishiketa and piano with Atsuko Ohhori, then took courses in composition and conducting at the Tokyo Univ. of Fine Arts and Music, where his principal mentors were Akeo Watanabe and Kazuo Yamada. In 1970 he became assistant conductor of the Tokyo Sym. Orch.; after winning the Budapest conducting competition (1974), he appeared widely in Europe as well as in his homeland; was a conductor with the Amsterdam Phil. (from 1976), chief conductor of the Kyoto Sym. Orch. (from 1985), and principal conductor of the Hungarian State Orch. in Budapest (from 1987).

Kobbé, Gustav, American writer on music; b. N.Y., March 4, 1857; d. when his sailboat was struck by a Navy seaplane in the bay near Babylon, L.I., July 27, 1918. He studied piano and composition with Adolf Hagen in Wiesbaden (1867–72), and with Joseph Mosenthal in N.Y.; also attended Columbia College (1877–79). His most successful book was his *Complete Opera Book* (N.Y., 1919; rev. and augmented ed. by the Earl of Harewood, 1954, as *Kobbé's Complete Opera Book;* rev. ed., 1987, as *The Definitive Kobbé's Opera Book*). He also wrote *Wagner's Life and Works* (1890); *The Ring of the Nibelung* (1899; part of the preceding, printed separately); *Opera Singers* (1901); a novel, *Signora, A Child of the Opera House* (1902); *Loves of the Great Composers* (1905); *How to Appreciate Music* (1906); *Wagner and His Isolde* (1906); *Famous American Songs* (1906).

Koch, Caspar (Petrus), German-American organist, pedagogue, and composer; b. Karnap, Nov. 25, 1872; d. Pittsburgh, April 3, 1970. He was taken to the U.S. by his parents (1881); graduated from St. Francis College in Joliet, Ill., and later took courses with Heinrich Reimann and Franz Kullak in Berlin and at the Regensburg Kirchenmusikschule; was Pittsburgh city organist (1904–54) and also organist at the Holy Trinity Catholic Church there; taught at the Carnegie Inst. of Technology (1914–41). He wrote the valuable *Book of Scales for the Organ* (1918) and the *Organ Student's Gradus ad Parnassum* (1945); also composed organ music.

Koch, Eduard Emil, German clergyman and music scholar; b. Schloss Solitude, near Stuttgart, Jan. 20, 1809; d. Stuttgart, April 27, 1871. He became pastor in Gross-Anspach (1837), then at Heilbronn (1847); was superintendent there (1853–64). He was an authority on Lutheran church music; wrote *Geschichte des Kirchenliedes und Kirchengesanges, insbesondere der deutschen evangelischen Kirche* (1847; 3rd ed., 8 vols., 1866–77).

Koch, (Sigurd Christian) Erland von, Swedish composer, son of **(Richert) Sigurd (Valdemar) von Koch;** b. Stockholm, April 26, 1910. He studied music with his father, then at the Stockholm Cons. (1931–35); went to Germany, where he studied composition with Paul Höffer and conducting with Clemens Krauss and Gmeindl (1936–38); also had piano lessons with Arrau. He subsequently taught at Wohlfart's Music School in Stockholm (1939–53); was a sound technician with the Swedish Radio (1943–45); in 1953, joined the faculty of the Stockholm Musikhögskolan, becoming a prof. in 1968. In 1957 he became a member of the Royal Swedish Academy of Music in Stockholm. In some of his later works he endeavored to create a curious amalgam of folk motifs with 12-tone rows ("12-tone and folk-tone").

Works: stage: Children's opera, *Pelle svanslös* (Tailless Peter; 1948; Göteborg, Jan. 7, 1949; rev. 1966); 2 ballets: *Askungen* (Cinderella; 1942; also an orch. suite) and *Samson and Delila* (1963; orch. suite, 1964; rev. 1972); music for the radio play *Bjälbojarlen*, after Strindberg (Swedish Radio, Jan. 25, 1968). **orch.:** *Little Suite* for Chamber or String Orch. (1933); 3 piano concertos: No. 1 (1936); No. 2 (1962); No. 3, with Wind Orch. (1970; with Full Orch., 1972); 2 violin concertos (1937; 1979–80); 4 syms.: No. 1 (1938); No. 2, *Sinfonia Dalecarlia* (1944); No. 3 (1948); No. 4, *Sinfonia seria* (1952–53; rev. 1962); *Nordic Capriccio* (1943); *Rural Suite* for Strings (1945); Viola Concerto (1945; rev. 1966); *Sinfonietta* (1949); *Triptychon* for Violin and Orch. (1949); *Arkipelag* (1950); *Musica intima* for Strings (1950; rev. 1965); Cello Concerto (1951); *Musica malinconica* for Strings (1952); *Concert Music* (1955); Concerto for Small Orch. (1955); the Oxberg trilogy: *Oxberg Variations* (1956), *Lapland Metamorphoses* (1957), and *Dance-Rhapsody* (1957); Concerto for Saxophone and String Orch. (1958); *Concerto lirico* for Strings (1959; rev. of 4th String

Quartet); *Concerto piccolo* for Soprano and Alto Saxophones and Strings (1962); *Fantasia concertante* for Violin and Orch. (1964); the Impulsi trilogy: *Impulsi* (1964), *Echi* (1965), and *Ritmi* (1966); *Arioso e Furioso* for Strings (1967); *Polska svedese* (1968); *Musica concertante* for 8 Winds, Strings, and Percussion (1969); Double Concerto for Flute, Clarinet, and Strings (1971); *A Swede in New York* (1973); Concerto for Oboe and String Orch. (1978); Tuba Concerto (1978); *4 Symphonic Myths* (Stockholm, Oct. 9, 1982); Guitar Concerto (Göteborg, Feb. 3, 1983); *Svenska danser 1–6* (1982–83); *Romanza* for Violin and Orch. (1984); *Serenade* for Double Bass and String Orch. (1985); *Midvinterblot-Sommarsolstånd*, 2 Nordic frescoes (1986–87). CHAMBER: 6 string quartets: No. 1 (1934); No. 2 (1944); No. 3, *Musica intima* (1950); No. 4 (1956; rev. 1959); No. 5 (1961); No. 6, *Serenata espressiva* (1963); *Berceuse* for Violin and Piano (1953); *Varianti virtuosi II* for Violin and Piano (1968); *Quattro tempi* for Wind Quintet (1968); *Auda* for Brass Quintet (1981); *Tubania* for Tuba and Piano (1983); Sonata for Alto Saxophone and Piano (1985); solo piano pieces. VOCAL: *Midsommardalen* (Midsummer Valley) for Baritone, Chorus, and Orch. (1960–61); *Sångarkväll* (Evening Song) for Baritone, Male Chorus, and Wind Orch. (1972); songs.

BIBL.: B. Huldt, "A Portrait of E. v.K.," *Nordic Sounds* (Dec. 1988).

Koch, Friedrich E(rnst), German composer and teacher; b. Berlin, July 3, 1862; d. there, Jan. 30, 1927. He studied cello with Hausmann and composition with Bargiel at the Berlin Hochschule für Musik (1880–81; 1883–84); then with Radecke. He played cello in the Berlin Royal Orch. (1882–91); was Kapellmeister in Baden-Baden (1891–92), then taught privately in Berlin (1892–1918) and at the Hochschule für Musik there (from 1917), serving as head of theory and composition (from 1920). He was made a full member of the Royal Academy of the Arts (1901) and a member of the senate (1902). He publ. *Der Aufbau der Kadenz und anderes: Ein Beitrag zur Harmonielehre* (Leipzig, 1920). Among his compositions were the operas *Die Halliger* (Cologne, 1896) and *Die Hügelmühle* (Berlin, 1918), 2 syms. (1891, 1892), *Deutsche Rhapsodie* for Violin and Orch. (1907), choral works, and chamber music.

BIBL.: K. Kämpf, *F.E. K.* (Leipzig, 1907).

Koch, Heinrich Christoph, German music theorist; b. Rudolstadt, Oct. 10, 1749; d. there, March 19, 1816. He studied with Göpfert in Weimar; was made violinist in the Court Orch. in Rudolstadt (1768), then court musician (1772) and Konzertmeister (1777). He publ. the valuable *Versuch einer Anleitung zur Composition* (3 vols., Rudolstadt and Leipzig, 1782–93) and *Musikalisches Lexikon* (Frankfurt, 1802; 2nd ed., 1817); also *Handbuch bei dem Studium der Harmonie* (Leipzig, 1811) and a manual of enharmonic modulation (Rudolstadt, 1812). He launched the unsuccessful *Journal der Tonkunst* (Erfurt, 1795). He composed a *Choralbuch* for Wind Band and various choral works.

BIBL.: N. Baker, "The Aesthetic Theories of H.C. K.," *International Review of the Aesthetics and Sociology of Music*, VIII (1977).

Koch, Helmut, German conductor; b. Wuppertal-Barmen, April 5, 1908; d. Berlin, Jan. 26, 1975. He studied conducting with Fiedler, Lehmann, and Scherchen; led workers' choruses for many years; after World War II, was active in East Germany; was founder-conductor of the Berlin Chamber Orch. (1945), conductor of the Berlin Radio Choir (from 1948), and director of the Berlin Singakademie (from 1963); was also a guest conductor at the Berlin State Opera (from 1960). He was widely known in East Germany for his performances of the music of Handel. He made numerous arrangements of German folk songs.

Koch, Karl, Austrian organist, choral conductor, and composer; b. Biberwier, Tyrol, Jan. 29, 1887; d. Innsbruck, Sept. 20, 1971. He studied religion and music at a Brixen seminary (1905–9); took courses in conducting with Max Springer and composition with Joseph Marx at the Vienna Academy of Music (1920–21). In 1924 he settled in Innsbruck as a choral conductor, retiring in 1967. He publ. *Harmonielehre* (Vienna, 1948) and *Ergänzungsbuch zur Harmonielehre* (Vienna, 1957).

WORKS: *Jubilate Deo* for Chorus and Orch. (1916); *Festmesse zu Ehren der Geburt unseres Herren Jesu Christi* for Soloists, Chorus, and Orch. (1916; Bozen, Jan. 6, 1917); *Requiem* in C minor for Chorus and Organ (1916); *Missa "In medio vitae"* for Soloists, Chorus, and Orch. (1925); *Missa "Super flumina Babylonis"* for Soloists, Chorus, and Orch. (Innsbruck, Nov. 20, 1932); *Sinfonie "Aus den Bergen"* (1942; Innsbruck, Feb. 17, 1947); *Missa in honorem Papae Pii X*, in 2 versions (1953); *Psalm-kantate*, vocal sym. for Solo, Vocal Quartet, Female Chorus, Mixed Chorus, and Orch. (Wattens, Austria, Oct. 26, 1958); *Requiem* for Soloists, Chorus, and Orch. (1955–58; Innsbruck, Feb. 20, 1960); *Brixner Dom Messe* for Soloists, Boys' Chorus, Mixed Chorus, Organ, and Orch. (Brixen, Sept. 10, 1958); *Hubertus-Messe* for Unison Chorus and Wind Septet or Organ (1967); String Quartet (1948); 2 piano sonatas; sacred choruses; much organ music.

BIBL.: W. Isser, *K. K.: Das Bild eines zeitgenössischen Komponisten* (Innsbruck, 1969).

Koch, (Richert) Sigurd (Valdemar) von, Swedish composer, father of **(Sigurd Christian) Erland von Koch;** b. Ägnö, near Stockholm, June 24, 1879; d. Stockholm, March 16, 1919. He studied piano at the Richard Andersson School and composition with Lindegren; later studied piano in Berlin (1905, 1912) and Dresden (1905). He was active in Stockholm as an accompanist and music critic; was also a painter and poet. He wrote orch. works, much chamber music, and numerous songs in a late Romantic idiom.

BIBL.: F. Törnblom, "S. v.K.," *Ord och Bild*, XLV (1936).

Kochan, Günter, German composer; b. Luckau, Oct. 2, 1930. He studied composition with Blacher, Konrad Friedrich Noetel, and Hermann Wunsch at the (West) Berlin Hochschule für Musik (1946–50); then attended Eisler's master classes at the (East) Berlin Akademie der Künste of the German Democratic Republic (1950–53). From 1950 he taught at the (East) Berlin Hochschule für Musik; in 1965, was elected to the Akademie der Künste. His music is eminently functional, and in it the formal design is paramount; main subjects are stated repeatedly with utmost clarity; the rhythmic formulas are explicit; there is a distinct affinity with the symphonic processes used by Eisler; polymodal themes abound within starkly dissonant harmonies.

WORKS: STAGE: *Karin Lenz*, opera depicting the tragic conflict between enlightened socialist ideals and ingrained capitalistic habits in the life of a German woman (1968–70); *Luther*, melodrama (1981). ORCH.: Violin Concerto (1951–52); *Kleine Suite* (1956); Piano Concerto (1958); Sinfonietta (1960); *Fröhliche Ouvertüre* for Chamber Orch. (1960); Concerto for Orch. (1961–62); Flute Concertino (1964); 4 syms.: No. 1, with Chorus (1963–64); No. 2 (1968); No. 3, with Solo Soprano (1972); No. 4 (1983–84); *Divertimento*, variations on a theme of C.M. von Weber (1964); *Variationen über eine venezianische Canzonetta* for Piano and Chamber Orch. (1966); *4 Movements* for String Orch. (1966); 2 cello concertos (1967, 1976); *Mendelssohn-Variationen* for Piano and Orch. (1972); Viola Concerto (1974); Concerto for Wind Quintet and 2 String Groups (1975–77); *7 Orchesterstücke* (1976–77); *Passacaglia und Hymne* (1979); Violin Concerto (1980); *In Memoriam* (1982); *Präludium* (1985). VOCAL: *Die Welt ist jung*, cantata (1952); *Ernst Thälmann*, cantata in memory of the leader of the German Communist party who died in a concentration camp (1959); *3 Shakespeare-Lieder* for Alto, Flute, and Strings (1964); *Asche von Birkenau*, cantata for Alto and Orch. (1965); *Aurora* for Women's Voices, Chorus, and Orch. (1966; a tribute to the sailors of the Russian ship *Aurora*, which bombarded the Winter Palace in Petrograd on the day of the Soviet Revolution in 1917); *Wir, unaufhaltsam*, "symphonic demonstration" for Baritone, Speaker, Chorus, and Orch. (1970); *Das Testament von Ho Chi-Minh* for Speaker, Chamber Orch., and 9 Solo Instruments (1971); *Die Hände der Genossen*, cantata for Baritone and Orch. (1974); *3 Epitaphe* for Baritone and Instruments (1975); *Das Friedensfest oder Die Teilhabe*, oratorio (1978); choruses; songs. CHAMBER: Piano Trio (1953–54); *Divertimento* for Flute, Clarinet, and Bassoon (1956); Cello Sonata (1960); *5 Movements* for String Quartet (1961); *Short String Quartet* (1965); String Quartet (1973–74); *7 Miniaturen* for 4 Tubas (1977); String Trio (1979–80); Sonata for Violin and Piano (1984–85). PIANO: *Suite* (1952); *Präludien, Intermezzi und Fugen* (1954); *11 Short Pieces* for 4-hands (1958); *5 Piano Pieces* (1971); *7 Short Piano Pieces* (1971); Sonata (1981).

Kochánski, Paul (actually, **Pawel**), noted Polish violinist; b. Orel, Sept. 14, 1887; d. N.Y., Jan. 12, 1934. He studied with Mlynarski in Warsaw; in 1901, became concertmaster of the Warsaw Phil.; in 1903, went to Brussels to study with César Thomson; in 1907, was appointed prof. at the Warsaw Cons., and in 1913 at the St. Petersburg Cons. From 1917 to 1919 he taught at the Kiev Cons., then went to the U.S., making his debut with the N.Y. Sym. Orch. on Feb. 14, 1921. From 1924 he taught at the Juilliard School of Music in N.Y. He excelled in the performance of modern works; did a great service in promoting the violin music of Szymanowski, inspiring him to write his *Mity* (Myths; 1915) and 1st Violin Concerto (1916) for him. He made many transcriptions for violin and piano.

BIBL.: H. Roth, "Refined Colourist," *Strad* (Sept. 1987).

Köchel, Ludwig (Alois Ferdinand), Ritter von, Austrian botanist, mineralogist, and music bibliographer; b. Stein, near Krems, Jan. 14, 1800; d. Vienna, June 3, 1877. He studied law at the Univ. of Vienna (graduated, 1827), and attained distinction in botany and mineralogy; music was his hobby. His love for Mozart's art moved him to compile a Mozart catalog as methodically as he would a descriptive index of minerals; the result of this task of devotion was the monumental *Chronologisch-thematisches Verzeichnis sämtlicher Tonwerke Wolfgang Amade Mozarts* (Leipzig, 1862; 2nd ed., by Waldersee, 1905; 3rd ed., extensively rev. by A. Einstein, who supplemented the "K numbers" used to identify Mozart's works by secondary numbers, 1937; reprinted, with further alterations and corrections and supplement, Ann Arbor, 1947; 6th ed., a major rev., by F. Giegling, A. Weinmann, and G. Sievers, Wiesbaden, 1964; further supplementary material in the *Mozart-Jahrbuch 1971–72*, pp. 342–401, as prepared by P. van Reijen). Köchel publ. some supplementary matter in the *Allgemeine Musikalische Zeitung* (1864). He also publ. *Über den Umfang der musikalischen Produktivität W.A. Mozarts* (Salzburg, 1862); *Drei und achtzig neuaufgefundene Original-Briefe Ludwig van Beethovens an den Erzherzog Rudolf* (Vienna, 1865); *Die Pflege der Musik am österreichischen Hofe vom Schlusse das XV. bis zur Mitte des XVIII. Jahrhunderts* (privately publ., 1866); *Die Kaiserliche Hof-Musikkapelle in Wien von 1543–1867* (Vienna, 1869); *J.J. Fux Hofkompositor und Hofkapellmeister der Kaiser Leopold I, Joseph I, und Karl VI, von 1698–1740* (Vienna, 1872).

Kocher, Conrad, German composer; b. Ditzingen, near Stuttgart, Dec. 16, 1786; d. Stuttgart, March 12, 1872. In 1803 he went to St. Petersburg, where he studied piano with Klengel and Berger, and composition with J.H. Müller; traveled in Italy (1819). Returning to Germany in 1820, he settled in Stuttgart and devoted himself to composition; received an honorary Ph.D. from the Univ. of Tübingen in 1827. He wrote 2 operas, an oratorio, etc.; also publ. a piano method; a manual of composition, *Die Tonkunst in der Kirche* (1823); *Zionsharfe* (ancient and modern chorales).

Kocián, Jaroslav, noted Czech violinist and pedagogue; b. Ústí nad Orlicí, Feb. 22, 1883; d. Prague, March 9, 1950. He studied violin with Ševčík at the Prague Cons., and also took lessons in composition with Dvořák. After his graduation in 1901, he traveled widely as a concert violinist, almost rivaling the success of his famous compatriot Jan Kubelík. He made 4 American tours; also appeared in Asia and Africa. After 1920

he confined himself mainly to teaching; was a prof. at the Master School of the Prague Cons. (1924–43), and also its rector (1939–40). He composed several effective violin pieces, as well as choruses and songs.

BIBL.: C. Sychra, ed., *J. K.: Sborník statí a vzpomínek* (J. K.: Collections of Articles and Recollections; Prague, 1953); A. Slajs, *J. K.* (Pardubice, 1958).

Kocsár, Miklós, Hungarian composer; b. Debrecen, Dec. 21, 1933. He studied with Farkas at the Budapest Academy of Music (1954–59); taught at the Béla Bartók Cons. in Budapest (from 1972); was also on the staff of the music dept. of the Hungarian Radio (from 1974), serving as its deputy head (from 1983). He won the Erkel Prize in 1973 and again in 1980.

WORKS: Horn Concerto (1957); *Capriccio* for Orch. (1961); *Magányos ének* (Solitary Song) for Soprano and Chamber Ensemble (1969); *5 Movimenti* for Clarinet, Strings, and Harpsichord (1976); *Variations* for Orch. (1977); *Capricorn Concerto* for Flute and Chamber Ensemble (1978); *Metamorphoses* for Orch. (1979); *Sequenze* for Strings (1980); *Episodi* for Oboe and Strings (1982); *Concerto—In Memoriam ZH* for Horn and Chamber Orch. (1983); *Elegia* for Bassoon and Chamber Orch. (1985); *Formazioni* for Orch. (1986); *Hegyi legények* (Mountain Lads), cantata for Male Chorus, Brass Instruments, and Percussion (1957); *Magyar nyár* (Hungarian Summer) for Choir (1958); *Suhanj szerelem* (Glide Away, Love), cantata for Choir and Piano (1961); *Évszakok zenéje* (Music of the Seasons) for Female Chorus (1967); *Liliomdal* for Chorus (1971); *Csodafiu-Szarvas* for Chorus (1979); *Mégis mondom damion* (I Will Invoke You Demon) for Chorus (1985); Divertimento for Woodwind Trio (1956); Wind Quintet (1956; rev. 1959); Brass Trio (1958); *Dialoghi* for Bassoon and Piano (1964–65); *Variazioni* for Wind Quintet (1968); *Repliche* for Flute and Cimbalom or Harpsichord (1971); *Sestetto d'ottoni* (1972); *Hét változat* (7 Variations) for Viola (1983); *Echos* No. 1 for Horn (1984); Wind Quintet No. 3 (1984); *Quintetto d'ottoni* (1986); children's choruses; songs; piano pieces.

Kocsis, Zoltan (György), brilliant Hungarian pianist; b. Budapest, May 30, 1952. He began his studies at the Béla Bartók Cons. (1963–68), then trained with Pál Kadosa, Ferenc Rados, and György Kurtág at the Franz Liszt Academy of Music (graduated, 1973). In 1970 he won the Hungarian Radio Beethoven competition; after appearing as soloist with the Dresden Phil. in 1971, he made his 1st tour of the U.S. as soloist with the Hungarian Radio and Television Sym. Orch. In 1973 he won the Liszt Prize and soon launched an acclaimed international career. With the conductor Iván Fischer, he founded in 1983 the Budapest Festival Orch., with which he frequently appeared as a soloist and for which he served as artistic director. A performer of extraordinary versatility, he includes in his repertoire works ranging from Bach to the avant-garde. He has made numerous transcriptions for piano; has also composed orch. music, including the topical *Memento* (Chernobyl '86). In 1978 he was awarded the Kossuth Prize, and in 1984 he was named a Merited Artist by the Hungarian government.

BIBL.: H. Waleson, "Z. K.: Intensity, Originality and a Passion for Bartók," *Ovation* (Aug. 1988).

Koczalski, Raoul (actually, **Raul Armand Georg**), Polish pianist and composer; b. Warsaw, Jan. 3, 1884; d. Poznan, Nov. 24, 1948. He was trained by his parents; at the age of 4, he played at a charity concert in Warsaw and was at once proclaimed an "infant phenomenon." He studied with Mikuli in Lemberg, and then with Anton Rubinstein. He performed in Vienna (1892), Russia, Paris, and London (1893); made nearly 1,000 public appearances before he was 12. His sensational success diminished to some extent as he grew out of the prodigy age, but he was appreciated as a mature pianist, and particularly for his sensitive playing of Chopin. He lived mostly in France, Germany, and Sweden; after World War II, he returned to Poland and taught in Poznan and Warsaw. He publ. *Frédéric Chopin: Betrachtungen, Skizzen, Analysen* (Cologne, 1936). His precocity extended to composition as well; he wrote some 50 works before he was 10; he later wrote the operas *Rymond* (Elberfeld, Oct. 14, 1902) and *Die Sühne* (Mühlhausen, 1909), as well as many piano pieces.

BIBL.: B. Vogel, *R. K.* (Leipzig and Warsaw, 1896); M. Paruszewska, *Biographical Sketch and the Artistic Career of R. K.* (Poznan, 1936).

Koczirz, Adolf, Austrian musicologist; b. Wierowan, Moravia, April 2, 1870; d. Vienna, Feb. 22, 1941. He studied law, and also musicology with Adler, at the Univ. of Vienna (Ph.D., 1903); was employed in the Ministry of Finance (1891–1935). He distinguished himself as an authority on the lute and guitar; ed. 2 vols. of 16th- and 17th-century lute music in Denkmäler der Tonkunst in Österreich, XXXVII, Jg. XVIII/2 (1911) and I, Jg. XXV/2 (1918).

BIBL.: R. Haas and J. Zuth, eds., *Festschrift A. K. zum 60. Geburtstag* (Vienna, 1930).

Koczwara, František, Bohemian composer; b. probably in Prague, c.1750; d. (by hanging) London, Sept. 2, 1791. He traveled in Europe, then settled in London toward the end of the 18th century. In 1790 he went to Dublin as a viola player in the orch. at the King's Theatre; returning to London the same year, he played in the orch. at the Handel Commemoration in May. He is remembered solely for his horripilating piece *The Battle of Prague* for Piano or Harpsichord, Violin, Cello, and Drum ad libitum (publ. in Dublin, c.1788), purporting to depict in appropriately loud banging chords the effect on the ear of the defeat inflicted by the Austrian armies upon the Prussians at the crucial encounter on May 6, 1757, during the 7 Years' War. A person of curious sexual diversions, he convinced a prostitute to enhance their encounter by strangling him through repeated hangings. This peculiar event became the subject of a court trial of the prostitute in question, held on Sept. 9, 1791, in which she was acquitted. An account of the legal proceedings was publ. in London on Sept. 16, 1791, under the title "The Trial of Susannah Hill for the Murder of F. Kotzwarra."

Kodalli, Nevit, Turkish conductor and composer; b. Mersin, Jan. 12, 1924. He studied with Necil Kazim Akses at the Ankara Cons., graduating in 1947; then went to Paris, where he took lessons with Honegger and Boulanger (1948–53). He was a composer at the Ankara State Theater (from 1962). His music preserves the traits of Turkish folk melos, but the harmonic and contrapuntal treatment is in the manner of the French modern school. Among his works are 2 operas (1955, 1963), a Sym. (Ankara, May 20, 1950), an oratorio, *Ataturk* (Ankara, Nov. 9, 1953), and 2 string quartets (1947, 1966).

Kodály, Zoltán, renowned Hungarian composer, ethnomusicologist, and music educator; b. Kecskemét, Dec. 16, 1882; d. Budapest, March 6, 1967. He was brought up in a musical family; received general education at the Archiepiscopal Grammar School in Nagyszombat; at the same time, he took lessons in piano, violin, viola, and cello. He soon began to compose, producing an overture when he was 15; it was performed in Nagyszombat in 1898. He then went to Budapest (1900), where he entered the Univ. as a student of Hungarian and German; also studied composition with Koessler at the Royal Academy of Music (diplomas in composition, 1904, and teaching, 1905; Ph.D., 1906, with a diss. on the stanzaic structure of Hungarian folk song). He became associated with Bartók, collecting, organizing, and editing the vast wealth of national folk songs; he made use of these melodies in his own compositions. In 1906 he went to Berlin, and in 1907 proceeded to Paris, where he took some lessons with Widor, but it was the music of Debussy which most profoundly influenced him in his subsequent development as a composer. He was appointed a prof. at the Royal Academy of Music in Budapest in 1907. In collaboration with Bartók, he prepared the detailed paper "Az uj egyetemes népdalgyüjtemény tervezete" (A Project for a New Universal Collection of Folk Songs) in 1913. They continued their collecting expeditions until World War I intervened. Kodály wrote music criticism for several newspapers in Budapest (1917–19); in 1919, was appointed deputy director of the Budapest Academy of Music, but lost his position that same year for political reasons; however, he resumed his teaching there in 1922. In 1923 he was commissioned to write a commemorative work in celebration of the half-century anniversary of the union of Buda, Pest, and Obuda into Budapest. The resulting work, the oratorio *Psalmus hungaricus* (1923), brought him wide recognition. The initial performance in Budapest was followed by numerous productions all over Europe, and also in America. Another major success was his opera *Háry János* (1926); an orch. suite from this work became highly popular in Hungary and throughout the world. His orch. works *Marosszéki táncok* (Dances of Marosszék; 1930; based on a piano work) and *Galántai táncok* (Dances of Galánta; for the 80th anniversary of the Budapest Phil. Soc., 1933) were also very successful. His reputation as one of the most significant national composers was firmly established with the repeated performances of these works. Among his most important subsequent works were the orch. pieces *Variations on a Hungarian Folk Song* "Felszállott a páva," the *Peacock Variations* (for the 50th anniversary of the Amsterdam Concertgebouw Orch., 1939), and the Concerto for Orch. (for the 50th anniversary of the Chicago Sym. Orch., 1941). His great interest in music education is reflected in his numerous choral works, which he wrote for both adults and children during the last 30 years of his life. He also pursued his ethnomusicological studies; from 1940 he was associated with the Hungarian Academy of Sciences, serving as its president (1946–49). He continued to teach at the Academy of Music until 1940, and then gave instruction in Hungarian folk music until 1942; even after his retirement, he taught the latter course there. He toured as a conductor of his own music in England, the U.S., and the Soviet Union (1946–47); then throughout Western Europe. In succeeding years, he held a foremost place in the musical life of his country, receiving many honors; was awarded 3 Kossuth Prizes (1948, 1952, 1957). He also received foreign honors, being made an honorary member of the Moscow Cons. (1963) and the American Academy of Arts and Sciences (1963); was also awarded the Gold Medal of the Royal Phil. Soc. of London (1967). An International Kodály Soc. was organized in Budapest in 1975. As a composer, Kodály's musical style was not as radical as that of Bartók; he never departed from basic tonality, nor did his experiments in rhythm reach the primitivistic power of Bartók's percussive idiom. He preferred a Romantic treatment of his melodic and harmonic materials, with an infusion of Impressionistic elements. All the same, he succeeded in producing a substantial body of music of notable distinction. He was married twice; his 1st wife, Emma, whom he married in 1910, died in 1958; on Dec. 18, 1959, he married Sarolta Péczely, a student (b. 1940).

WRITINGS: With B. Bartók, *Erdelyi magyarsag: Nepdalok* (The Hungarians of Transylvania: Folk Songs; Budapest, 1923); *A magyar népzene* (Hungarian Folk Music; Budapest, 1937; 2nd ed., augmented, 1943; 3rd ed., augmented, 1952 by L. Vargyas; Eng. tr., 1960); with A. Gyulai, *Arany János népdalgyüjteménye* (The Folk Song Collection of János Arany; Budapest, 1953); A. Szöllöy, ed., *A zene mindenkie* (Budapest, 1954; 2nd ed., 1975); F. Bónis, ed., *The Selected Writings of Zoltán Kodály* (Budapest, 1974).

WORKS: STAGE: *Notre Dame de Paris*, incidental music for a parody (Budapest, Feb. 1902); *Le Cid*, incidental music for a parody (Budapest, Feb. 1903); *A nagybácsi* (The Uncle), incidental music (Budapest, Feb. 1904); *Pacsirtaszó* (Lark Song), incidental music for Voice and Small Orch. (Budapest, Sept. 14, 1917); *Háry János*, singspiel (Budapest, Oct. 16, 1926); *Székely fonó* (The Transylvanian Spinning Room), lyrical play (1924–32; Budapest, April 24, 1932); *Czinka Panna*, singspiel (1946–48; Budapest, March 15, 1948).

ORCH.: Overture in D minor (1897; Nagyszombat, Feb. 1898); *Nyári este* (Summer Evening; Budapest, Oct. 22, 1906; rev. 1929–30; N.Y., April 3, 1930); *Régi magyar katonadalok* (Old Hungarian Soldiers' Songs; 1917; Vienna, Jan. 12, 1918; also arranged for Cello and Piano as *Magyar Rondo*); *Ballet Music* (1925; Budapest, Oct. 16, 1926; originally for *Háry Já-*

nos); *Háry János Suite* (version for Brass Band, not by Kodály, Barcelona, March 24, 1927; version for Orch., N.Y., Dec. 15, 1927); *Szinházi nyitány* (Theater Overture; 1927; Budapest, Jan. 10, 1928; originally for *Háry János*); *Marosszéki táncok* (Dances of Marosszék; Dresden, Nov. 28, 1930; based on a piano work; also arranged as a ballet); *Galántai táncok* (Dances of Galánta; Budapest, Oct. 23, 1933); *Variations on a Hungarian Folk Song* "Felszállott a páva," the *Peacock Variations* (Amsterdam, Nov. 23, 1939); Concerto for Orch. (1939–40; Chicago, Feb. 6, 1941); *Honvéd Parad March* for Brass Band (1948; from *Háry János*); *Minuetto serio* (1948–53; augmented from *Czinka Panna*); Sym. in C major (begun in the 1930s and completed 1961; Lucerne, Aug. 16, 1961).

CHAMBER: *Romance lyrique* for Cello and Piano (1898); Trio in E-flat major for 2 Violins and Viola (1899); *Adagio* for Violin, Viola or Cello, and Piano (1905); 2 string quartets (1908–9; 1916–18); Cello Sonata (1909–10); *Duo* for Violin and Cello (1914); Sonata for Solo Cello (1915); *Capriccio* for Cello (1915); *Magyar Rondo* for Cello and Piano (1917); *Serenade* for 2 Violins and Viola (1919–20); *Sonatina* for Cello and Piano (1921–22); *Hivogató tábortüzhöz* (Calling to Camp Fire) for Clarinet (1930); Exercise for Violin (1942); *Feigin* for Violin and Piano (1958; arrangement of *Kállai kettös*); Wind Quartet (c.1960).

VOCAL: *CHORAL MUSIC WITH ORCH.:* *Offertorium* (*Assumpta est*) for Baritone, Chorus, and Orch. (1901); *Psalmus hungaricus* for Tenor, Chorus, Organ, Orch., and Children's Chorus ad libitum (Budapest, Nov. 19, 1923); *Budavári Te Deum* for 4 Soloists, Chorus, Organ, and Orch. (Budapest Cathedral, Sept. 12, 1936); *Missa brevis* for Chorus and Organ or 3 Sopranos, Alto, Tenor, Bass, Chorus, Orch., and Organ ad libitum (1942–44; Budapest, Feb. 11, 1945); *Vértanúk sírjánál* (At the Martyr's Grave) for Chorus and Orch. (1945); *Kállai kettös* (Kallo Double Dance) for Chorus and Small Orch. (1950; Budapest, April 4, 1951); *The Music Makers: An Ode* for Chorus and Orch., after A. O'Shaughnessy (1964). *CHORAL MUSIC WITH INSTRUMENTAL ACCOMPANIMENT:* Mass for Chorus and Organ (c.1896; unfinished); *Ave Maria* for Chorus and Organ (c.1899); 5 *Tantum ergo* for Children's Chorus and Organ (1928); *Pange lingua* for Chorus or Children's Chorus and Organ (1929); *Kantonadal* (Soldier's Song) for Male Chorus, Trumpet, and Side Drum (1934); *Karácsonyi pásztortánc* (Shepherds' Christmas Dance) for Children's Chorus and Recorder (1935); *Ének Szent István királyhoz* (Hymn to St. Stephen) for Chorus and Organ (1938); *Vejnemöjnen muzsikál* (Vejnemojnen Makes Music) for High Voices and Harp or Piano (1944); *A 114. genfi zsoltár* (Geneva Psalm CXIV) for Chorus and Organ (1952); *Intermezzo* for Chorus and Piano (1956; from *Háry János*); *Magyar mise* (Hungarian Mass) for Unison Chorus and Organ (1966); *Laudes organi* for Chorus and Organ (1966). Kodály also composed many choral works for mixed voices a cappella; also children's choruses; songs.

PIANO: *Valsette* (1907); *Méditation sur un motif de Claude Debussy* (1907); *Zongoramuzsika* (Piano Music; 9 pieces; 1909); 7 pieces (1910–18); *Ballet Music* (1925; arrangement of orch. work); *Marosszéki táncok* (Dances of Marosszék; 1927; also arranged for orch. and as a ballet); *Gyermektancok* (Children's Dances; 1945). He also wrote some organ music, numerous educational works, and several Bach arrangements.

BIBL.: B. Bartók, "K. Z.," *Nyugat*, XIV (1921); M.D. Calvocoressi, "Choral Music of K.," *Listener*, XV (1936); A. Molnár, *K. Z.* (Budapest, 1936); B. Szabolcsi and D. Bartha, eds., *Emlékkönyv K. Z. 70. születésnapjára* (Budapest, 1953); L. Eösze, *K. Z. élete és munkássága* (Z. K.'s Life and Work; Budapest, 1956); P. Young, *K.: A Hungarian Musician* (London, 1964); H. Stevens, "The Choral Music of Z. K.," *Musical Quarterly* (April 1968); L. Eösze, *Z. K.: His Life in Pictures* (Budapest, 1971); E. Hegyi, *Solfege According to the K. Concept* (Kecskemét, 1975); L. Eösze, *K. Z. életének krónikája* (Z. K.: Chronicle of His Life; Budapest, 1977); E. Lendvai, *The Workshop of Bartók and K.* (Budapest, 1983); E. Szönyi, *K. nevelési eszméi* (Budapest, 1984); I. Kecskeméti, *K., the Composer; Brief Studies on the First Half of K.'s Œuvre* (Kecskemét, 1986); G. Ránki, *Bartók and K. Revisited* (Budapest, 1987).

Koeberg, Frits Ehrhardt Adriaan, Dutch composer; b. The Hague, July 15, 1876; d. there, Nov. 9, 1961. He studied with H. Viotta in the Netherlands and with Xaver Scharwenka in Berlin; returned to The Hague in 1902; taught at the Cons. and conducted the Musica orch. there.

WORKS: Opera, *Bloemenkind* (1917); 3 syms.; symphonic poems: *Zeelandia* (1920) and *Chimères* (1941); *Suite de Lage Landen* for Orch. (1946); *Dances in the Village* for Orch. (1948); *Hollandia* for Band (1933); chamber music; songs.

Koechlin, Charles (Louis Eugène), noted French composer, pedagogue, and writer on music; b. Paris, Nov. 27, 1867; d. Le Canadel, Var, Dec. 31, 1950. He studied for a military career, but was compelled to change his plans when stricken with tuberculosis; while recuperating in Algeria, he took up serious music studies; then entered the Paris Cons. (1890), where he studied with Gédalge, Massenet, and Fauré, graduating in 1897. He lived mostly in Paris, where he was active as a composer, teacher, and lecturer; with Ravel and Schmitt, he organized the Société Musicale Indépendante (1909) to advance the cause of contemporary music; with Satie, Roussel, Milhaud, and others, he was a member of the group Les Nouveaux Jeunes (1918–20), a precursor to Les Six. Although he composed prolifically in all genres, he became best known as a writer on music and as a lecturer. He made 3 lecture tours of the U.S. (1918, 1928, 1937). He became president of the Fédération Musicale Populaire (1937). His pro-Communist leanings caused him to promote music for the proletariat during the 1930s; wrote a number of works "for the people" and also film scores. In spite of the fact that such works as his *Symphonie d'hymnes* (Prix Cressent, 1936) and Sym. No. 1 (Prix Halphan, 1937) won honors, his music made no real impact. Taking Fauré as his model, he strove to preserve the best elements in the French Classical tradition. A skillful craftsman, he produced works of clarity and taste, marked by advanced harmonic and polyphonic attributes.

WRITINGS: *Étude sur les notes de passage* (Paris, 1922); *Précis des règles du contrepoint* (Paris, 1926; Eng. tr., 1927); *Gabriel Fauré* (Paris, 1927; Eng. tr., 1946); *Claude Debussy* (Paris, 1927); *Traité de l'harmonie* (3 vols., Paris, 1927–30); *Étude sur le choral d'école* (Paris, 1929); *Théorie de la musique* (Paris, 1934); *Étude sur l'écriture de la fugue d'école* (Paris, 1934); *Pierre Maurice, musicien* (Geneva, 1938); *Les instruments à vent* (Paris, 1948); *Traité de l'orchestration* (4 vols., Paris, 1954–59).

WORKS (Koechlin orchestrated many of his works well after their original completion. Dates given are those of original, often unorchestrated, versions): **STAGE:** *Jacob chez Laban*, pastorale biblique for Soprano, Tenor, Chorus, and Orch. (1896–1908; Paris, May 19, 1925); ballets: *La Forêt païenne* (1911–16; Paris, June 17, 1925); *La Divine Vesprée* (1917); *L'Âme heureuse* (1945–47); *Voyages: Film danse* (1947). **ORCH.:** Sym. in A major (1895–1900; unfinished); *La Forêt*, symphonic poem in 2 parts: No. 1, *Le Jour* (1897–1904); No. 2, *La Nuit* (1896–1907); *En mer, la nuit*, symphonic poem after Heine (1899–1904); *L'Automne*, symphonic suite (1896–1906); *Nuit de walpurgis classique* (*Ronde nocturne*), symphonic poem after Verlaine (1901–7; rev. 1915–16); 2 symphonic poems: *Soleil et danses dans la forêt* and *Vers la plage lointaine* (1898–1909); *Études antiques* (*Suite païenne; Poèmes antiques*), symphonic suite (1908–14); 2 symphonic poems: *Le Printemps* and *L'Hiver* (1908–16); 2 symphonic poems: (*L'Été*): *Nuit de juin* and *Midi en août* (1908–11); *Ballade* for Piano and Orch. (1911–15); *Suite légendaire* (*La Nuit féerique*) (1901–15); Sym. No. 1 (1911–16; arranged from the String Quartet No. 2); *Rapsodie sur des chansons françaises* (1911–16); *La Course de printemps*, symphonic poem after Kipling (1908–25); *The Bride of a God*, symphonic poem (1929; in collaboration with C. Urner); *Symphonic Fugue* (1932); *Choral fugué* in C major (1933); *Choral fugué du style modal* for Organ and Orch. (1933); *Sur les flots lointaines*, symphonic poem (1933); *Hymne à la jeunesse*, after Gide (1934); *Symphonie d'hymnes* (1936; arranged from several other works); *La Méditation de Purun Bhagat*, symphonic poem after Kipling (1936); *La Cité nouvelle, rêve d'avenir*, symphonic poem after Wells (1938); *Le Buisson ardent*, symphonic poem after Rolland (1938); *La Loi de la jungle*, symphonic poem after Kipling (1939); *Les Bandar-log*, symphonic poem after Kipling (1939); *Offrande musical sur le nom de BACH* (1942); *Silhouettes de comédie* for Bassoon and Orch. (1942–43); Sym. No. 2 (1943–44; arranged from several other works); *Le Docteur Fabricius*, symphonic poem after C. Dollfus (1941–44); *Partita* for Chamber Orch. (1945); *Introduction et 4 interludes de style atonal-sériel* (1947). CHAMBER: 3 string quartets (1911–13; 1911–16; 1917–21); Flute Sonata (1911–13); Viola Sonata (1902–15); *Suite en quatuor* for Flute, Violin, Viola, and Piano (1911–15); Oboe Sonata (1911–16); Violin Sonata (1915–16); Cello Sonata (1917); Horn Sonata (1918–25); Bassoon Sonata (1918–19; also for Horn and Piano); Sonata for 2 Flutes (1918–20); Piano Quintet (1908; 1911; 1917–21); 2 clarinet sonatas (1923, 1923); Trio for Strings or Woodwinds (1924); Quintet *Primavera* for Flute, Harp, Violin, Viola, and Cello (1936); Wind Septet (1937); Trio for Oboe, Clarinet, and Bassoon (1945); Quintet for Flute, Harp, Violin, Viola, and Cello (1949); also many works for piano, including *Paysages et marines* (12 pieces; 1915–16); *Les Heures persanes* (16 pieces; 1916–19); *L'Ancienne Maison de campagne* (12 pieces; 1932–33); also choral works, music for band, film scores, organ music, and songs.

BIBL.: M.D. Calvocoressi, "C. K.'s Instrumental Works," *Music & Letters*, V (1924); W. Mellers, "A Plea for K.," *Music Review*, III (1942); R. Myers, "C. K.: Some Recollections," *Music & Letters*, XLVI (1965); R. Orledge, "C. K. and the Early Sound Film 1933–38," *Proceedings of the Royal Musical Association*, XCVIII (1971–72); idem, *A Study of the Composer C. K.* (*1867–1950*) (diss., Cambridge Univ., 1973); J. Woodward, *The Theoretical Writings of C. K.* (diss., Univ. of Rochester, 1974); H. Sauget, ed., *Oeuvres de C. K.* (Paris, 1975; a catalog); E. Kirk, *The Chamber Music of C. K.* (diss., Catholic Univ. of America, Washington, D.C., 1977); R. Orledge, "Satie, K. and the Ballet 'Uspud,'" *Music & Letters* (Jan. 1987); idem, *C. K.* (*1867–1950*): *His Life and Works* (Vol. I, N.Y., 1989).

Koellreutter, Hans Joachim, German conductor, composer, and teacher; b. Freiburg im Breisgau, Sept. 2, 1915. He studied in Berlin and Geneva; in 1937, went to Rio de Janeiro, where he taught at the Brazilian Cons. (1937–52) and at the São Paulo Inst. of Music (1942–44). He was director of the São Paulo Free Academy of Music (1952–55) and the music dept. of Bahia Univ. (1952–62); was also chief conductor of the Bahia Sym. Orch. (1952–62). He then was in charge of the music programs of the Goethe Inst. in Munich (1963–65); was its regional representative in New Delhi (1965–69), where he also was head of the Delhi School of Music (1966–69). From 1970 to 1975 he was director of the Goethe Inst. in Tokyo; then returned to Brazil (1975) and taught at the Goethe Inst. in Rio de Janeiro (until 1980). After serving as director of the Tatui Cons. (1983–84), he was a prof. at the São Paulo Cons. and at the Univ. in Minas Gerais. His music follows Classical forms, while the thematic materials are modeled after the 12-tone method of composition; in several of his works he makes use of exotic motifs of South America, India, and Japan.

WRITINGS: *Attitudes of Consciousness in Indian and Western Music* (New Delhi, 1966); *Three Lectures on Music* (Mysore, 1968); *Jazz Harmonia* (São Paulo, 1969); *Ten Lectures on Music* (New Delhi, 1969); *History of Western Music* (New Delhi, 1970).

WORKS: ORCH.: 4 Pieces (1937); Variations (1945); *Música* (1947); *Sinfonia de camara* for 11 Instruments (1948); *Mutacoes* (1953); *Concretion* for Orch. or Chamber Orch. (1960); *Constructio ad synesin* for Chamber Orch. (1962); *Advaita* for Sitar and Orch. or Chamber Orch. (1968); *Sunyata* for Flute, Chamber Orch. of Western and Indian Instruments, and Tape (1968). VOCAL: *Noturnos de Oneyda Alvarenga* for Mezzo-soprano and String Quartet (1945); *O cafe*, choral drama (1956); *8 Haikai de Pedro Xisto* for Baritone, Flute, Electric Guitar, Piano, and Percussion (1963); *Cantos de Kulka* for Soprano and Orch. (1964); *Indian Report*, cantata for Soprano, Speaker, Chamber Chorus, Speaking Chorus, and Chamber Orch. of Western and Indian Instruments (1967); *Yū* for Soprano and Japanese Instruments (1970); *Mu-dai* for Voice (1972); *O cafe* for Chorus (1975). CHAMBER: 2 sonatas for Flute and Piano (1937, 1939); Violin Sonata (1939); *Inventions* for Oboe, Clarinet, and Bassoon (1940); *Variations* for Flute, English Horn, Clarinet, and Bassoon (1941); *Música 1947* for String Quartet (1947); *Diaton 8* for Flute, English Horn, Bassoon, Harp, and Xylophone (1955); *Tanka I* for Speaker and Koto (1971); *Tanka II* for Speaker and Piano (1973).

Koenemann, Theodore. See **Keneman, Feodor.**

Koenen, Friedrich, German composer; b. Rheinbach, near Bonn, April 30, 1829; d. Cologne, July 6, 1887. He studied piano and organ with his father, and cello with Biermann; in 1854, was ordained priest; from 1862 to 1863, studied church music in Regensburg with Haberl, Schrems, and Witt; went to Cologne, where he was choirmaster of the Cathedral; also taught music at the seminary for priests. In 1869 he founded the Cäcilienverein. Among his works are 7 masses, 2 church cantatas, a Te Deum, motets, Psalms, organ preludes, and songs.

Koenen, Tilly (actually, **Mathilde Caroline**), Dutch mezzo-soprano; b. Salatiga, Java, Dec. 25, 1873; d. The Hague, Jan. 4, 1941. She studied piano, on which she became a proficient performer, then voice with Cornelia van Zanten. She toured Germany and Austria from 1900 with excellent success; visited the U.S. in 1909–10 and 1915–16. She was particularly impressive in her interpretations of German Romantic songs; also performed some songs by her compatriots.

Koenig, Gottfried Michael, German composer; b. Magdeburg, Oct. 5, 1926. He studied at the Braunschweig Staatsmusikschule, the Nordwestdeutsche Musikakademie in Detmold, the Hochschule für Musik in Cologne, and the Univ. of Bonn. He was active at the electronic music studios of the West German Radio in Cologne (1954–64); also taught electronic music in various German music centers. He became artistic and scientific director of the Instituut voor Sonologie at the Univ. of Utrecht in 1964; he remained there until 1987. His philosophical attitude toward music is that it should represent the past, present, and future; accordingly he is apt to give abstract and scientific titles to his works. His electronic compositions include *Terminus I* (1963); *Terminus II* (1967); *Funktion Grün* (1968); *Funktion Gelb* (1968); *Funktion Orange* (1968); *Funktion Rot* (1968); *Output* (1979). He also wrote 2 quintets for Wind Instruments (1959, 1965); String Quartet (1962); *Beitrag* for Orch. (1986); piano pieces.

Koering, René, French composer; b. Andlau, Alsace, May 27, 1940. He studied piano; in 1960, went to Darmstadt, where he absorbed some modernistic notions through his attendance at courses given by Boulez, Stockhausen, and Maderna; subsequently taught at the École des Beaux Arts in Paris (from 1969). He composed experimentally in every conceivable classical and popular genre. His denouement came with his decision to write understandable music with a minimum of feasible modernities.

WORKS: *Triple et trajectoires* for Piano and 2 Orchs. (1963); *Combat T 3 N* for Piano and Orch. (1970); Sym. No. 1 (Royan, March 23, 1974).

Koessler (Kössler), Hans, German organist, composer, and pedagogue; b. Waldeck, Jan. 1, 1853; d. Ansbach, May 23, 1926. He studied with Rheinberger and Wüllner at the Munich Königliche Musikschule; then taught at the Dresden Cons. (1877–81) and conducted the Dresden Liedertafel (1879–82). He taught at the Royal Academy of Music in Budapest (1882–1925). Among his outstanding pupils were Bartók, Kodály, and Dohnányi. In his music he followed the tradition of Brahms; although his technical achievements inspire respect, his works lack any durable quality that would distinguish them from the mass of other competent compositions by German composers of his generation. He was best known for his choral works.

WORKS: Opera, *Der Münzenfranz* (Strasbourg, 1903); oratorio, *Triumph der Liebe* (1897); *Silvesterglocken* for Chorus and Orch. (1912); 2 syms.; Symphonic Variations for Orch. (1909); Violin Concerto (1914); Cello Concerto; chamber music; songs.

Koetsier, Jan, Dutch conductor and composer; b. Amsterdam, Aug. 14, 1911. He studied in Berlin at the Stern Cons. (1924–26) and at the Hochschule für Musik (1927–34); was a conductor in Lübeck and Berlin, and then in The Hague (1941–42); was 2nd conductor of the Concertgebouw Orch. in Amsterdam (1942–49), then again conducted in The Hague (1949–50). He thereafter was a conductor with the Bavarian Radio Sym. Orch. in Munich (1950–66); subsequently he was a prof. at the Munich Staatliche Hochschule für Musik (1966–76). In his music he explores the modern applications of Baroque techniques.

WORKS: THEATER: *Frans Hals*, opera (1949); *Demeter*, ballet (1943). ORCH.: 3 syms. (1945, 1946, 1954); *Variations on a Children's Song* (1932; rev. 1967); *Concerto capriccioso* for Piano and Orch. (1935; rev. 1975); Concertino for Oboe and Orch. (1936; rev. 1953); *Serenata Serna* for Strings (1937; rev. 1953); *Duo concertante* for Flute, Violin, and Orch. (1937; rev. 1956); *Vision pastorale* for English Horn and Strings (1937; rev. 1954); *Sinphonische Musik* (1939); *Valerius Overture* (1942; rev. 1966); *Music* for 2 String Orchs., 3 Trumpets, 3 Trombones, and Timpani (1943); Sinfonietta (1943; rev. 1960); *Divertimento* (1943); *Music* for 4 Orchs. (1944); *Music* for Small Orch. (1948); *Kreisleriana* for 2 Pianos and Orch. (1965); Sinfonietta Concertante for Oboe, Clarinet, Horn, Bassoon, and Strings (1968); *Concertino lirico* for Violin, Cello, and Strings (1968); *Homage to Gershwin* (1969); *Intrada classica* for Wind Instruments, Timpani, and Harp (1971); *Hymnus monaciensis* (1971); *Concertino drammatico* for Violin, Viola, and Strings (1981); Concertino for Trombone and Strings (1983); Concerto for 4 Horns and Orch. (1983); *Französisches Concerto*, suite for 2 Flutes and Strings (1984); *Dance Suite* (1985); *Burg-Serenade* (1987). CHAMBER: Numerous works, including Quintet for Flute, Oboe, Violin, Viola, and Cello (1932; rev. 1965); Septet (1932; rev. 1959); 2 divertimentos for Wind Quintet (1937, 1947); Octet for 2 Oboes, 2 Clarinets, 2 Horns, and 2 Bassoons (1968); sonatinas: for Trumpet, for Trombone, and for Tuba (all 1970); Trio for Alto Flute, Viola da Gamba, and Harpsichord (1971); Sonata for Cello and Harp (1972); Serenade for String Trio (1977); *Fantasie*, trio for Cello, Bassoon, and Piano (1981); Quartet for 4 Cellos (1981); String Quartet (1985); *Petit Concert pour Violin et Contrebasse* for Violin, Double Bass, Clarinet, Bassoon, Cornet, Trombone, and Percussion (1987). CHORAL: *Von Gottes und des Menschen Wesen*, 7 madrigals for Chorus and 7 Instruments (1940; rev. 1969); *Gesang der Geister über Wassern* for Chorus and 7 Instruments (1940; rev. 1973); *Der Mann Lot* for Baritone, Speaker, Men's Chorus, and Orch. (1940; rev. 1962); *Antonius Mass* (1984). Other works include songs, organ music, and piano pieces.

BIBL.: H. Beermann et al., *J. K.* (Tutzing, 1988).

Koffler, Józef, Polish composer; b. Stryj, Nov. 28, 1896; d. (killed, with his wife and child, during a street roundup of Jews) Wieliczka, near Krakow, 1943. He was a pupil of Schoenberg and Guido Adler; graduated from the Univ. of Vienna (Ph.D., 1925); then went to Lwow, where he taught at the Cons. (1929–41) and ed. the periodicals *Orkiestra* (1930–38) and *Echo* (1936–37). He was the 1st Polish composer to use the method of composition with 12 tones according to Schoenberg's principles; his *15 Variations* for String Orch. (Amsterdam, June 9, 1933) were derived from a 12-tone row. He also composed 3 syms. (No. 3, London, June 17, 1938); *Miłość* (Love) Cantata; String Trio (Oxford, July 23, 1931); Divertimento for Oboe, Clarinet, and Bassoon; String Quartet; *40 polskich pieśni ludowych* (40 Polish Folk Songs) for Piano; other piano pieces.

Kogan, Leonid (Borisovich), outstanding Russian violinist; b. Dnepropetrovsk, Nov. 14, 1924; d. on the train at the Mytishcha railroad station, Dec. 17, 1982. His father was a photographer who played the violin; when Kogan was 10 years old the family moved to Moscow, where he became a pupil of Abram Yampolsky, first at the Central Music School and later at the Cons. (1943–48). He was obviously a *wunderkind*, but was prudently spared harmful exploitation. In 1947 he was a co-winner of the 1st prize at the World Festival of Democratic Youth in Prague; then won 1st prize in the Queen Elisabeth of Belgium Competition in 1951. His career was instantly assured; he played recitals in Europe to unanimous acclaim. He made an auspicious American debut, playing the Brahms Violin Concerto with Monteux and the Boston Sym. Orch. on Jan. 10, 1958. In 1952 he joined the faculty of the Moscow Cons.; was named prof. in 1963 and head of the violin dept. in 1969; in 1965 he received the Lenin Prize. His playing exemplified the finest qualities of the Russian School: an emotionally romantic élan and melodious filigree of technical detail. In addition to the standard repertoire, in which he excelled, he also played modern violin works, particularly those by Soviet composers. He was married to **Elizabeth Gilels.** Following the violinistic genetic code, their 2 children were also musical: a girl played the piano, and a boy, **Pavel Kogan** (b. Moscow, June 6, 1952), was so good on the violin that in 1970 he won the Sibelius contest in Finland. On Oct. 16, 1975, Pavel was soloist with the Philadelphia Orch. Pavel later was active as a conductor at Moscow's Bolshoi Theater (from 1988), the Zagreb Phil. (from 1988), and the Moscow Sym. Orch. (from 1989). The family shunned politics, and Leonid resolutely declined to participate in any protests, domestic or foreign, against the presumed anti-Semitism in Russian politics, even though he himself was patently Jewish.

BIBL.: M. Zazovsky, *L. K.* (Moscow, 1956); B. Schwarz, *Great Masters of the Violin* (N.Y., 1983).

Kogel, Gustav Friedrich, German conductor; b. Leipzig, Jan. 16, 1849; d. Frankfurt am Main, Nov. 13, 1921. He studied at the Leipzig Cons.; was ed. for C.F. Peters (1870–74); then was active as a conductor in various provincial theaters; was conductor of the Museum Concerts in Frankfurt (1891–1903); also filled engagements as a guest conductor in Europe and with the N.Y. Phil. (1906).

Köhler, Ernesto, Italian flutist and composer; b. Modena, Dec. 4, 1849; d. St. Petersburg, May 17, 1907. He studied flute with his father; became 1st flutist of the Court Orch. at Modena, then at the Karltheater in Vienna, and, in 1871, of the Imperial Orch. in St. Petersburg. He wrote numerous compositions for the flute; also an opera, *Ben Achmed*, and several ballets.

Köhler, Ernst, German organist, pianist, and composer; b. Langenbielau, May 28, 1799; d. Breslau, May 26, 1847. He was 1st organist of the Elisabethkirche in Breslau from 1827 until his death. He wrote 2 syms., 9 overtures, 12 church cantatas, 12 large vocal works with orch., organ works, and piano pieces.

Köhler, Louis, German pianist, pedagogue, and composer; b. Braunschweig, Sept. 5, 1820; d. Königsberg, Feb. 16, 1886. He studied piano in Braunschweig with Sonnemann; then took courses in composition in Vienna (1839–43) with Sechter and Seyfried; also studied piano there with Bocklet. He settled in Königsberg (1847), where he established a successful piano school; in 1880, was granted the title Royal Prof. He wrote 3 operas, a ballet, a Sym., overtures, cantatas, and other works, but he is best remembered for his albums of piano studies, which were adopted in music schools all over the world; next to Czerny's, they were the most popular didactic piano works of their time. It must be observed that while his studies are of great instructive value, they are also worthwhile from a purely musical standpoint. His major work, in which he laid the foundation of methodical piano pedagogy, is *Systematische Lehrmethode für Klavierspiel und Musik: I, Die Mechanik als*

Grundlage der Technik (1856; 3rd ed., rev. by Riemann, 1888), and *II, Tonschriftwesen, Harmonik, Metrik* (1858).

Köhler, Siegfried, German conductor; b. Freiburg im Breisgau, July 30, 1923. He studied at the local Hochschule für Musik; after conducting opera in provincial German cities, he conducted in Cologne; in 1964 he was named Generalmusikdirektor in Saarbrücken, and in 1974 in Wiesbaden. In 1990 he became chief conductor of the Royal Opera in Stockholm.

Kohn, Karl (Georg), Austrian-born American pianist, conductor, teacher, and composer; b. Vienna, Aug. 1, 1926. After the Anschluss in 1938, he emigrated with his family to the U.S., becoming a naturalized citizen in 1945. He studied piano with C. Werschinger and conducting with Prüwer at the N.Y. College of Music (graduated, 1944), then studied composition with Piston, Ballantine, Fine, and Thompson at Harvard Univ. (B.A., 1950; M.A., 1955), where he was a teaching fellow (1954–55); also taught at the Berkshire Music Center in Tanglewood, Mass. (summers, 1954, 1955, 1957). In 1950 he joined the music faculty at Pomona College in Claremont, Calif., where from 1985 he served as William M. Keck Distinguished Service Prof. With his wife, Margaret, he performed the contemporary 2-piano repertoire in the U.S. and Europe; he also made appearances as a conductor. He held a Fulbright scholarship for study in Finland (1955–56), a Guggenheim fellowship (1961–62), and 4 grants from the NEA (1975, 1976, 1979, 1986). In his compositions he tends toward prudent serialism but also explores diatonic modalities, applying the power of pervicacious iteration of pandiatonic chordal complexes; he successfully adapts to contemporary usages medieval polyphonic devices such as the integration of precomposed thematic fragments, a technique anciently known as "centone" (literally, "patchwork quilt"). He makes use of topological rearrangements of Classical pieces, as in *Son of Prophet Bird,* dislocated and paraphrased from Schumann's *Bird as a Prophet.*
Works: orch.: *Sinfonia concertante* for Piano and Orch. (1951); *Overture* for String Orch. (Helsinki, April 17, 1956); *Castles and Kings,* symphonic suite for children (1958); *Concerto mutabile* for Piano and Orch. (1962); *Episodes* for Piano and Orch. (1966); *Intermezzo I* for Flute and String Orch. (1969); *Centone per orchestra* (Claremont Music Festival, June 27, 1973); *Concerto* for Horn and Small Orch. (1974); *Innocent Psaltery,* "colonial music" (1976); *The Prophet Bird I* (a metamorphosis of Schumann's *Bird as a Prophet;* 1976); *The Prophet Bird II* for Piano and Chamber Orch. (Los Angeles, March 9, 1982); *Time Irretrievable,* 3 movements for Orch. (1983); *An Amiable Piece* for 2 Pianos, Winds, and Percussion (1987); *Lions on a Banner,* 7 Sufi Texts for Soprano, Chorus, and Orch. (1988). **chamber:** *Motets* for 8 Horns (1953); *Concert Music* for 12 Wind Instruments (1956); *Serenade* for Wind Quintet and Piano (1962); *Kaleidoscope* for String Quartet (1964); *Rhapsodies* for Marimba, Vibraphone, and Percussion (1968); *Impromptu* for 8 Wind Instruments (1969); *Concerto* for Horn and Piano (1974); *Quintet for Brass* (1976); *Son of Prophet Bird* for Harp (1977); *San Gabriel Set* for Clarinet, Violin, Viola, Cello, and Piano (1984); *Entr'acte* for String Quartet (1985); *Cantilena II* for Violin and Marimba (1985); *Choice Wood, Precious Metals,* music for Flute, Trumpet, Marimba, and Glockenspiel (1986); *For 4 Flutes* (1989); *Concert Music IV* for Wind Quintet (1990); other chamber works and many choral works.

Kohoutek, Ctirad, prominent Czech composer, pedagogue, music theorist, and administrator; b. Zábřeh na Moravě, March 18, 1929. He studied at the Brno Cons. with Vilém Petrželka, and with Jaroslav Kvapil at the Janáček Academy of Music there (1949–53); later attended Lutoslawski's lectures at the Dartington Summer School of Music (1963) and sessions given by Boulez and Ligeti at the Darmstadt summer courses in new music; obtained his Ph.D. from Palacky Univ. in Olomouc (1973) and his C.Sc. from J.E. Purkyne Univ. in Brno (1980). In 1953 he joined the faculty of the Janáček Academy of Music in Brno (associate prof., 1965–80). In 1980 he became associate prof. of composition at the Prague Academy of Music, and

later that year prof. of composition; also served as artistic director of the Czech Phil. (1980–87). In 1988 he was made an Artist of Merit by the Czech government. His music follows the traditions of Central European modernism, well contained within Classical forms but diversified by serial procedures and glamorized by electronic sounds.
Works: opera: *O Kohoutkovi a Slepičce* (About the Cock and Hen; 1988–89). **orch.:** *Mnichov* (Munich), symphonic poem (1952–53); *Festivalová předehra* (Festival Overture; 1955–56); Violin Concerto (1958); *Velký přelom* (Great Turning Point; 1960–62); *Symfonické tance* (Symphonic Dances; 1961); Symfonieta (1962–63); Concertino for Cello and Chamber Orch. (1964); *Preludia* for Chamber Orch. (1965); *Teatro del mondo,* symphonic rotation in 4 scenes (1968–69); *Panteon,* sound image (1970); *Slavonstní prolog* (Ceremonial Prologue; 1971); *Slavností světla* (Feast of Light), cycle of symphonic pictures (1975); *Symfonické aktuality* (Symphonic Newsreel), concert frescoes (1976–78); *Pocta životu* (Homage to Life; 1988–89). **chamber:** Suite for Wind Quintet (1958–59); String Quartet (1959); *Memento 1967,* concerto for Percussion and Winds (1966); *Panychida: Hudba o dvou zvukových vrstvách* (Prayer for the Dead: Music in 2 Sound Layers) for 2 Violas, 2 Pianos, Percussion, and Tape (1968); *Tkaniny doby* (Fabrics of Time), sound fantasies for Bass Clarinet or Cello, Piano, and Percussion (1977); *Minuty jara* (Minutes of Spring), impressions for Wind Quintet (1980); 3 Variations of Folk Dances for 2 Accordions or Accordion Ensemble (1986). **vocal:** *Za všechny děti: Ukolébavka černošské mámy* (For All Children: Black Mama's Lullaby), cantata for Contralto, Choir, and Orch. (1951–52); *Balady z povstání* (Ballads from the Uprising), 2 cantatas (1960); *Pátý živel* (The 5th Element), melodrama for Reciter and Small Orch. (1964); *The Birth of Man,* monologues for Male and Female Voice and Orch. or Piano (1981); various choruses.

Kohs, Ellis Bonoff, noted American composer; b. Chicago, May 12, 1916. His mother was a good violinist, and when Kohs learned to play the piano he often accompanied her at home. In 1928 the family moved from San Francisco (following his early musical studies there at the Cons.) to N.Y., where he studied with Adelaide Belser at the Inst. of Musical Art. In 1933 he returned to Chicago and enrolled at the Univ. of Chicago as a student in composition with Carl Bricken (M.A., 1938). Upon graduation, he proceeded to N.Y., where he entered the Juilliard School of Music, studying composition with Bernard Wagenaar and musical pedagogy with Olga Samaroff. He continued his musical studies at Harvard Univ., with Walter Piston in composition and Hugo Leichtentritt and Willi Apel in musicology (1939–41); also attended a seminar given by Stravinsky at Harvard Univ. in 1940–41. During the summer of 1940, he was a lecturer in music at the Univ. of Wisconsin in Madison. From 1941 to 1946 he served in the U.S. Army as a chaplain's assistant and organist, and in the U.S. Air Force as a bandleader. After his discharge from service, he engaged in pedagogical work and in active composition; his teaching posts included Wesleyan Univ. (1946–48), the Kansas City Cons. of Music (1946–47), the College of the Pacific, Stockton, Calif. (1948–50), Stanford Univ. (1950), and the Univ. of Southern Calif., Los Angeles (1950–85). In his music he pursues the aim of classical clarity; he is particularly adept in variation structures; the rhythmic patterns in his works are often asymmetrical, and the contrapuntal fabric highly dissonant; in some of his works he makes use of a unifying 12-tone row, subjecting it to ingenious metamorphoses, as revealed in his opera *Amerika,* after the novel by Franz Kafka. A humorous streak is shown in his choral piece *The Automatic Pistol,* to words from the U.S. Army weapons manual, which he composed during his military service. He publ. the useful manuals *Music Theory, a Syllabus for Teacher and Student* (2 vols., N.Y., 1961); *Musical Form: Studies in Analysis and Synthesis* (Boston, 1976); and *Musical Composition: Projects in Ways and Means* (Metuchen, N.J., 1980).
Works: stage: Opera, *Amerika,* after Kafka (1969;

abridged concert version, Los Angeles, May 19, 1970; 2 orch. suites, 1986, 1987); *Lohiau and Hiiaka*, Hawaiian legend for Narrators, Flute, Cello, Percussion, and Dancers (1987; also as a suite for Flute, Cello, and Percussion, 1988); incidental music to Shakespeare's *Macbeth* (1947). ORCH.: Concerto for Orch. (Berkeley, Calif., Aug. 9, 1942); *Passacaglia* for Organ and String Orch. (1946); *Legend* for Oboe and String Orch. (Columbus, Ohio, Feb. 27, 1947); Cello Concerto (1947); Chamber Concerto for Viola and String Nonet (1949); Sym. No. 1 (1950); Sym. No. 2, with Chorus (Urbana, Ill., April 13, 1957); Violin Concerto (1980; Los Angeles, April 24, 1981). CHAMBER: String Quartet (1942); *Night Watch* for Flute, Horn, and Timpani (1943); Sonatina for Bassoon and Piano (1944); *Short Concert* for String Quartet (1948); Clarinet Sonata (1951); *Variations* for Recorder (1956); Brass Trio (1957); *Studies in Variation* in 4 parts: for Woodwind Quintet, for Piano Quartet, for Piano Solo, for Violin Solo (1962); Sonata for Snare Drum and Piano (1966); *Duo* for Violin and Cello, after Kafka's *Amerika* (1971); Concerto for Percussion Quartet (1979); Trio for Strings (1983); Concerto for String Quartet: String Quartet No. 3 (1984); *Fantasies, Intermezzi, and Canonic Etudes on the Name EuDiCe SHApiro* for Violin (1985). VOCAL: *The Automatic Pistol* for Male Voices a cappella (Washington, D.C., Sept. 5, 1943); *25th Psalm* (1947); *Fatal Interview*, song cycle (text by Edna St. Vincent Millay; 1951); *Lord of the Ascendant* (based on the Gilgamesh legend) for Chorus, Soloists, Dancers, and Orch. (1956); *3 Songs* from the Navajo for Mixed Chorus (1957); *3 Greek Choruses* for Women's Chorus (1957); *23rd Psalm* for Soloists and Chorus a cappella (1957); *Men* for Narrator and 3 Percussionists (1982; Los Angeles, March 15, 1984); *Subject Cases* for Narrator and Percussionist, text by Gertrude Stein (Los Angeles, Feb. 14, 1983). PIANO: *Etude in Memory of Bartók* (1946); *Variations* (1946); *Variations on L'Homme armé* (1947); *Toccata* for Harpsichord or Piano (1948); *Fantasy on La, Sol, Fa, Re, Mi* (1949); *10 Inventions* (1950). ORGAN: *Capriccio* (1948); *3 Chorale-Variations on Hebrew Hymns* (1952).

Koizumi, Fumio, Japanese ethnomusicologist; b. Tokyo, April 4, 1927. He studied esthetics at Tokyo Univ. (degree, 1951); also took courses in music with Eishi Kikkawa. In 1960 he was appointed to the faculty of the Tokyo National Univ. of Fine Arts and Music; in 1969 and 1970 he lectured at Wesleyan Univ. in the U.S. His primary field of study is Japanese music, but he has also worked on the problems of national music in India, Iran, the Near East, Eastern Europe, and Spain. Among his publications is *Nihon dentō ongaku no kenkyū* (Study of Japanese Traditional Music; Tokyo, 1958).

Koizumi, Kazuhiro, Japanese conductor; b. Kyoto, Oct. 16, 1949. He studied at the Tokyo Univ. of the Arts, and later at the Berlin Hochschule für Musik; also worked with Seiji Ozawa. In 1970 he won 1st prize in the Min-Ono conducting competition in Japan, and in 1972, 1st prize in the Karajan Competition in Berlin. After serving as assistant conductor of the Japan Phil. in Tokyo (1970–72), he was music director of the New Japan Phil. there (1975–80) and of the Winnipeg Sym. Orch. (1983–89); also was chief conductor of the Tokyo Metropolitan Orch. (1984–87).

Kojian, Varujan (Haig), Armenian-born American conductor; b. Beirut (of Armenian parents), March 12, 1935. He studied violin at the Paris Cons. (1953–56), winning a premier prix, with Galamian at the Curtis Inst. of Music in Philadelphia, and with Heifetz in Los Angeles (1960). He subsequently became assistant concertmaster of the Los Angeles Phil. (1965); then went to Vienna for additional conducting studies with Swarowsky (1971), taking 1st prize in the Sorrento competition (1972). From 1973 to 1976 he was assistant conductor of the Seattle Sym. Orch., and from 1973 to 1980, principal guest conductor of the Royal Opera in Stockholm; then was music director of the Utah Sym. Orch. in Salt Lake City (1980–83), the Chautauqua (N.Y.) Sym. Orch. (1981–86), and Ballet West in Salt Lake City (from 1984). In 1967 he became a naturalized U.S. citizen.

Kókai, Rezső, Hungarian composer; b. Budapest, Jan. 15, 1906; d. there, March 6, 1962. He studied composition with János Koessler (1920); took courses in composition and piano at the Budapest Academy of Music (1925–26); he completed his studies at the Univ. of Freiburg (Ph.D., 1933, with a diss. on Liszt's early piano music). From 1929 to 1962 he was a prof. at the Budapest Academy of Music.

WORKS: Oratorio, *István király* (King Stephen; 1942); ballet, *A rossz feleség* (The Bad Wife; 1946); 2 *Rondos* for Small Orch. (1947); *Verbunko szvit* (Recruiting Suite) for Orch. (1950); Violin Concerto (1952); *Dances from Szék* for Orch. (1952); *Concerto all'Ungherese* for Orch. (1957); *Hungarian Dance* for Youth Orch. (1960); *Toccata* for Piano (1927); Serenade for String Trio (1949–50); 2-piano Sonata (1949); 4 *Improvisations* for Piano (1949–50); Quartet for Clarinet and String Trio (1952); *Capriccio* for Violin and Piano (1952); music for radio plays and films; songs. He wrote 2 books, *Methodical Aesthetics of Music* (Budapest, 1938) and *The Music of Our Century* (Budapest, 1961).

Kokkonen, Joonas, prominent Finnish composer; b. Iisalmi, Nov. 13, 1921. He studied with Palmgren, Ranta, and Hannikainen at the Sibelius Academy in Helsinki (diploma, 1949); also studied musicology with Krohn at the Univ. of Helsinki (M.A., 1948). He taught at the Sibelius Academy (from 1950); was prof. of composition (1959–63) and chairman of the dept. (1965–70). In 1963 he was elected to membership in the Finnish Academy; in 1973 he was awarded the Sibelius Prize. Like all composers of his generation in Finland, he experienced the inevitable influence of Sibelius, but he soon abandoned the characteristic diatonic modalities of Finnish folk music and formed an individual style of composition marked by a curiously anfractuous chromaticism and involuted counterpoint, freely dissonant but hewing to clearly identifiable tonal centers. For a period he dabbled in dodecaphonic writing, but found its doctrinaire discipline uncongenial. He derives his techniques from the contrapuntal procedures of Bach and, among the moderns, from Bartók. Thematically, he adopts an objective method of formal structure, in which a free succession of formative motifs determines the content.

WORKS: Opera, *Viimeiset Kiusaukset* (The Last Temptations), on the subject of the life of a 19th-century Finnish evangelist (1973–75; Helsinki, Sept. 2, 1975). ORCH.: 5 syms.: No. 1 (1958–60); No. 2 (1961); No. 3 (Helsinki, Sept. 12, 1967); No. 4 (1970; Helsinki, Nov. 7, 1971); No. 5 (1982; Helsinki, Jan. 12, 1983); *Sinfonia da camera* for 12 Strings (1962); *Opus sonorum* (1964); Cello Concerto (1969); *Inauguratio* (1971); "*. . . durch einen Spiegel . . .*" for 12 Strings and Harpsichord (1976–77); *Il Paesaggio* for Chamber Orch. (1986–87). CHAMBER: Trio for Violin, Cello, and Piano (1948); Quintet for Piano and String Quartet (1953); Duo for Violin and Piano (1955); 3 string quartets (1958–59; 1964–66; 1976); Wind Quintet (1973); Sonata for Cello and Piano (1976); *Improvvisazione* for Violin and Piano (Indianapolis, Sept. 12, 1982); also piano pieces and organ works. VOCAL: *Lintujen Tuonela* (The Hades of the Birds) for Voice and Orch. (1958–59); *Erekhteion*, cantata for Soloists, Mixed Chorus, and Orch. (1969–70); *Requiem* for Soprano, Baritone, Mixed Chorus, and Orch. (1981); also choral pieces and solo songs.

Kolachevsky, Mikhail. See Kalachevsky, Mikhail.

Kolar, Victor, Bohemian-American violinist, conductor, and composer; b. Budapest (of Bohemian parents), Feb. 12, 1888; d. Detroit, June 16, 1957. He studied violin with Ševčik and composition with Dvořák at the Prague Cons. (graduated, 1904). He then settled in the U.S.; was a violinist in the Chicago Sym. Orch. (1904–5), the Pittsburgh Sym. Orch. (1905–8), and the N.Y. Sym. Orch. (1908–20), serving the latter as assistant conductor as well (1914–20). He subsequently became a violinist in the Detroit Sym. Orch., and also held various conducting posts with it until 1942. After teaching at the Arthur Jordan Cons. of Music in Indianapolis, he returned to Detroit to conduct its Scandinavian Sym. Orch. (1950–53) and Women's Sym. Orch. (1950–57); also taught at the Inst. of

Musical Arts (1950–56). He wrote a Sym. (N.Y., Jan. 28, 1916); *Hiawatha*, symphonic poem (Pittsburgh, Jan. 31, 1908); *Americana*, symphonic suite (1912); *Slovakia*, rhapsody for Orch. (1922); many songs.

Kolb, Barbara, talented American composer; b. Hartford, Conn., Feb. 10, 1939. She was of a musical family; her father was a song composer. She studied the visual arts; also took up clarinet. She enrolled at the Hartt College of Music in Hartford, where she studied composition with Arnold Franchetti (B.A., 1961; M.M., 1964). During the summers of 1960, 1964, and 1968, she attended the classes of Lukas Foss and Gunther Schuller at the Berkshire Music Center in Tanglewood. In 1969 she became the 1st American woman to win the U.S. Prix de Rome in composition. She held 2 Guggenheim fellowships (1971, 1976); also received grants from the NEA (1972, 1974, 1977, 1979). She taught at Brooklyn College (1973–75). In her music she builds a sui generis melodic, harmonic, and rhythmic environment, making use of variegated techniques; a factor in several of her works is a persistent iteration and emphatic reiteration of thematic materials, creating an aura of quaquaversal melorhythmic rotation invariably reverting to the thematic exordium, while constantly changing the timbres. The most remarkable of her compositions in this manner of flowing recurrence is *Soundings*.

WORKS: *Rebuttal* for 2 Clarinets (1964); *Chansons bas* for Voice, Harp, and Percussion (1965); *Fragments* for Flute and Piano (1966); *3 Place Settings* for Narrator, Clarinet, Violin, Double Bass, and Percussion (1968); *Trobar clus* for 13 Instruments, representing wordlessly the ancient Provençal verse form of the rondeau type (Tanglewood, Aug. 29, 1970); *Soundings* for 11 Instruments and Electronic Tape (N.Y., Oct. 27, 1972; rev. for Full Orch., N.Y., Dec. 11, 1975; 2nd rev., 1977, Boston, Feb. 16, 1978); *Frailties* for Tenor, 4-channel Electronic Tape, and Orch. (1972); *Spring, River, Flowers, Moon, Night* for 2 Pianos and Electronic Tape (1974); *Looking for Claudio* for Guitar and Electronic Tape (1975); *Appello* for Piano (1976); *Musique pour un vernissage* for Flute, Violin, Viola, and Guitar, originally intended as "furniture music" or "music to walk by" à la Satie, to be played at the opening of a Paris art exhibition (1977; 1st perf. as such in Paris, composer conducting, then as a formal concert piece, Washington, D.C., Feb. 3, 1979); *Songs before an Adieu* for Flute, Guitar, and Voice (1977–79); *Chromatic Fantasy* for Narrator and Chamber Ensemble (1979); *3 Lullabies* for Guitar (1980); *Related Characters* for Viola and Piano (1980); *The Point That Divides the Wind* for Organ and 4 Percussionists (1981).

Kolbe, Oskar, German music theorist and composer; b. Berlin, Aug. 10, 1836; d. there, Jan. 2, 1878. He studied with Grell and Löschhorn in Berlin; taught theory at the Stern Cons. (1859–75). He publ. a *Kurzgefasstes Handbuch der Generalbasslehre* (1862) and a *Handbuch der Harmonielehre* (1873); also wrote an oratorio, *Johannes der Täufer;* an overture to *Wallensteins Tod;* piano music; songs.

Kolberg, (Henryk) Oskar, Polish music scholar and composer; b. Przysucha, near Radom, Feb. 22, 1814; d. Krakow, June 3, 1890. He studied at the Warsaw Cons. with Elsner and Dobržyski, then with Girschner and Rungenhagen in Berlin (1835–36). He devoted a major part of his life to traveling and collecting folk songs; his major achievement was the publication of a series of monographs on the various regions of his homeland (33 vols., 1861–90). His collected works began to appear under the auspices of the Polish Academy of Sciences in 1960. He composed a number of popular dances and songs; also an entertainment, *Krol Pasterzy* (The Shepherd's Inn; Warsaw, March 2, 1859).

BIBL.: I. Kopernicki, *O. K.* (Krakow, 1889); S. Lam, *O. K.: Żywot i praca* (O. K.: Life and Works; Lemberg, 1914); special issue of *Lud*, XIII (1956).

Kolessa, Filaret (Mikhailovich), significant Ukrainian ethnomusicologist; b. Chodowitschi, July 17, 1871; d. Lwow, March 3, 1947. He studied in Lemberg (Lwow); later took a course in musicology with Adler at the Univ. of Vienna (Ph.D., 1918). He taught at the state high school in Lemberg (from 1898); became a prof. at the Univ. of Lwow and director of the Ethnographic Museum there (1939). He laid the foundation for the comparative study of Slavonic and East European folk music.

WRITINGS: *Rytmika ukrayinskykh narodnykh pisen* (Rhythm in Ukrainian Folk Songs; Lemberg, 1906–7); "Pro muzychnu formu dum" (On the Musical Form of Historical Chants), *Melodiyi ukrayinskykh narodnykh dum* (Lemberg, 1910; 2nd ed., rev., 1969); *Varianty melodiy ukrainskykh narodnykh dum, ikh kharakterystyka i grupovannya* (Variations in Melody of Ukrainian Folk Historical Chants, Their Characteristics and Classification; Lemberg, 1913); *Pro genezu ukrayinskykh narodnykh dum (ukrainksi narodni dumy u vidnoshenni do pisen, virshiv i pokhoronnykh holosin)* (On the Origin of Ukrainian Folk Historical Chants in Relation to Songs, Religious Songs, and Folk Laments; Lwow, 1920–22). He also publ. a number of collections, including *Melodii haivok, skhopleni na fonograf Y. Rozdolskym* (Easter Song Melodies Recorded by Rozdolsky; Lemberg, 1909); *Melodiyi ukrayinskykh narodnykh dum* (Tunes of Ukrainian Historical Chants; Lemberg, 1910–13; 2nd ed., rev., 1969); "Narodni pisni z pivdennoho Pidkarpattya" (Folk Songs from Southern Subcarpathia), *Naukoviy zbirnyk tovarystva "Prosvita" v Uzhhorodi* (1923); *Narodni pisni z halytskoyi Lemkivshchyny: Teksty i melodiyi* (Folk Songs from West Galicia, Lemky Country: Texts and Melodies; Lwow, 1929); "Narodni pisni z pidkarpatskoy Rusi, melodii i teksty" (Folk Songs from Subcarpathian Ruthenia, Melodies and Texts), *Naukovyy zbirnyk tovarystva "Prosvita" v Uzhhorodi*, XIII–XIV (1938).

BIBL.: K. Kvitka, "F. K.," *Muzyka*, 11–12 (Kiev, 1925); S. Hrytsa, *F.M. K.* (Kiev, 1962).

Kolff, J. van Santen, Dutch-born German writer on music; b. Rotterdam, April 19, 1848; d. Berlin, Nov. 29, 1896. A polyglot, he contributed hundreds of articles and essays on music to publications in German, French, and Dutch; was the 1st to use the term "reminiscence motif" in reference to Wagner's works.

Kolinski, Mieczyslaw, Polish-born Canadian ethnomusicologist, music theorist, and composer; b. Warsaw, Sept. 5, 1901; d. Toronto, May 7, 1981. He studied piano and composition at the Berlin Hochschule für Musik; took courses in musicology, psychology, and anthropology at the Univ. of Berlin (Ph.D., 1930); concurrently assisted Hornbostel at the Berlin Staatliches Phonogramm-Archiv (1926–33); then moved to Prague, where he remained until 1938, when he went to Belgium to avoid the Nazis; during much of the German occupation, he was in hiding. He settled in N.Y. in 1951; was co-founder (1955) and president (1958–59) of the Soc. for Ethnomusicology; taught at the Univ. of Toronto (1966–76); became a Canadian citizen in 1974. He transcribed more than 2,000 works from all over the world; publ. *Konsonanz als Grundlage einer neuen Akkordlehre* (Prague, 1936).

WORKS: 3 ballets, including *Expresszug-Phantasie* (Salzburg, 1935); 2 piano sonatas (1919; 1946, rev. 1966); Violin Sonata (1924); Cello Sonata (1926); *Lyric Sextet* for Soprano, Flute, and String Quartet (1929); 4 piano suites (1929–46); String Quartet (1931); *Dahomey Suite* for Flute or Oboe and Piano or String Orch. (1951); *Hatikvah Variations* for String Quartet (1960); *Dance Fantasy* for String Orch. (1969); *Encounterpoint* for Organ and String Quartet (1973); music for recorder ensemble; songs; folk-song arrangements.

BIBL.: R. Kennedy, "A Bibliography of the Writings of M. K.," *Current Musicology*, 3 (1966).

Kolisch, Rudolf, Austrian-born American violinist; b. Klamm am Semmering, July 20, 1896; d. Watertown, Mass., Aug. 1, 1978. He began training in childhood; after sustaining an injury to his left hand, he learned to hold his violin with his right hand and the bow with his left. He continued his studies at the Vienna Academy of Music and the Univ. of Vienna (graduated, 1913); took courses with Ševčik (violin) and Schreker and Schoenberg (theory and composition). In 1922 he organized the Kolisch Quartet, which systematically presented works by modern composers. It was the 1st string quartet to perform works from the standard repertoire from memory. In 1935 he went to the U.S.; after his quartet disbanded (1939), he became 1st violin of the Pro Arte Quartet (1942). He taught at the Univ. of Wisconsin (1944–67), and served as artist-in-residence and head of the chamber music dept. of the New England Cons. of Music in Boston.

Kollmann, Augustus Frederic Christopher (actually, **August Friedrich Christoph**), German-born English organist, music theorist, and composer; b. Engelbostel, March 21, 1756; d. London, April 19, 1829. He studied with Böttner, the Hannover organist. He was made organist and schoolmaster of Kloster Lüne, near Lüneburg (1781); soon after, he went to London, where he served as organist and schoolmaster of the Royal German Chapel in St. James's (1782–1829); was also chapel-keeper (1784–1829). Among his practical works are 4 Sonatas for Harpsichord or Piano and Violin (1788), *The Shipwreck* for Piano, Violin, and Cello (1796), Piano Concerto (1804), and *The Praise of God*, oratorio (1817). He also composed a number of theoretico-practical works, including *A Symphony* [for Piano, Violin, and Cello] *with Analytical Explanations*, "Analyzed Sym." (1798), *The Melody of the Hundredth Psalm, with Examples and Directions for an Hundred Different Harmonies* for 4 Voices (1809), and *An Introduction to Extemporary Modulation, in Six General Lessons* for Piano, Harp, Violin, or Cello (1820).

WRITINGS: *An Essay on Musical Harmony* (1796; 2nd ed., 1817); *An Essay on Practical Musical Composition* (1799; 2nd ed., rev., 1812; reprint, 1973; *A Practical Guide to Thorough-Bass* (1801); *A New Theory of Musical Harmony* (1806; 2nd ed., rev., 1823); *A Second Practical Guide to Thorough-Bass* (1807).

Kollo (Kollodzieyski), René, esteemed German tenor, grandson of **(Elimar) Walter Kollo (Kollodzieyski);** b. Berlin, Nov. 20, 1937. He studied with Elsa Varena in Berlin; made his operatic debut as Oedipus Rex in Braunschweig (1965). He sang in Düsseldorf (1967–71); then with the Vienna State Opera. In 1969 he first appeared at Bayreuth as the Steersman; sang in the centenary *Ring* performances there (1976); made his Covent Garden debut in London that same year as Siegmund. He made his Metropolitan Opera debut in N.Y. as Lohengrin on Nov. 4, 1976. Among his other roles were Walther von Stolzing, Parsifal, Tamino, and Lensky.

Kollo (Kollodzieyski), (Elimar) Walter, German composer, grandfather of **René Kollo (Kollodzieyski);** b. Neidenburg, Jan. 28, 1878; d. Berlin, Sept. 30, 1940. He studied in Sondershausen, then was a theater conductor in Königsberg; subsequently was a composer for the Berliner Theater (1908–18), where he produced his most popular operetta, *Wie unst im Mai* (Oct. 4, 1913; in collaboration with W. Bredschneider; perf. in the U.S. as *Maytime*, 1917); also wrote many successful songs, the most famous being *Solang noch Untern Linden.*

Kolman, Petr, Slovak composer; b. Bratislava, May 29, 1937. He studied in Bratislava with Očenáš and Cikker (theory) at the Cons. (1951–56) and with Alexander Moyzes (advanced composition) at the College of Music (1956–60); was made music adviser (1961) and head of the experimental studio (1965) of the Bratislava Radio. He adopted the serial method of composition, according to Schoenberg's practice.

WORKS: *Romeo and Juliet*, symphonic poem (1956); String Trio (1957); Violin Concerto (1959–60); *3 Piano Pieces in Memory of Schoenberg* (1960); *Participazioni* for 12 Instruments (1962); *Sonata canonica* for Clarinet and Bass Clarinet (1963); *Panegyrikos* for 16 Instruments (1964); *Homage to Kandinsky* for String Quartet (1964); *Monumento per 6,000,000* for Orch. (1964); *Mollisation mobile* for Flute and Vibraphone (1965).

Kolneder, Walter, noted Austrian musicologist; b. Wels, July 1, 1910. He studied composition privately with Johann Nepomuk David (1927–29); also studied with Paumgartner (conducting) and Strub (viola) at the Salzburg Mozarteum (1925–35); took courses in musicology at the Univ. of Vienna (1934–35) and with W. Fischer at the Univ. of Innsbruck (Ph.D., 1949, with the diss. *Die vokale Mehrstimmigkeit in der Volksmusik der österreichischen Alpenländer*); completed his Habilitation at the Univ. of Saarbrücken with his *Antonio Vivaldi: Neue Studien zur Biographie und Stilistik seiner Werke* (extracts in *Aufführungspraxis bei Vivaldi*, Leipzig, 1955; 2nd ed., 1973). He taught at the Graz Cons. (1936–39) and the Staatliche Hochschule für Musikerziehung in Graz-Eggenberg (1936–45); was director of the Luxembourg Cons. (1953–59); also was a Privatdozent at the Univ. of Saarbrücken (from 1956). He was director of the Darmstadt Academy from 1959 to 1965 and of the Karlsruhe Hochschule für Musik from 1966 to 1972; was made Ausserplanmässiger Professor of musicology at the Univ. of Karlsruhe (1966). His writings include *Anton Webern: Einführung in Werk und Stil* (Rodenkirchen, 1961; Eng. tr. as *Anton Webern: An Introduction to His Works*, Los Angeles, 1968); *Geschichte der Musik: Ein Studien- und Prüfungshelfer* (Heidelberg, 1961; 5th ed., 1973); *Musikinstrumentenkunde: Ein Studien- und Prüfungshelfer* (Heidelberg, 1963; 3rd ed., 1972); *Singen, Hören, Schreiben: Eine praktische Musiklehre in vier Lehr- und vier Übungsheften* (Mainz, 1963–67); *Antonio Vivaldi: Leben und Werk* (Wiesbaden, 1965; Eng. tr., 1970); *Das Buch der Violine* (Zürich, 1972); *Anton Webern: Genesis und Metamorphosen eines Stils* (Vienna, 1973); *Melodietypen bei Vivaldi* (Zürich, 1973); *Schule des Generalbassspiels* (7 vols., Wilhelmshaven, 1983–).

Kolodin, Irving, prominent American music critic and writer on music; b. N.Y., Feb. 22, 1908; d. there, April 29, 1988. He studied at the Inst. of Musical Art in N.Y. (1930–31); was music critic for the *N.Y. Sun* (1932–50) and the *Saturday Review* (1947–82); served as program annotator for the N.Y. Phil. (1953–58); also taught at N.Y.'s Juilliard School (from 1968).

WRITINGS: (all publ. in N.Y. unless otherwise given): *The Metropolitan Opera* . . . (1936; 4th ed., rev., 1966); with Benny Goodman, *The Kingdom of Swing* (1939); ed. *The Critical Composer* (1940); *A Guide to Recorded Music* (Garden City, N.Y., 1941; 2nd ed., rev., 1946 as *New Guide to Recorded Music*; 3rd ed., rev., 1950); *Mozart on Records* (1942); with C. Burke and E. Canby, *The Saturday Review Home Book of Recorded Music and Sound Reproduction* (1952; 2nd ed., 1956); *Orchestral Music* (1955); *The Musical Life* (1958); ed. *The Composer as Listener: A Guide to Music* (1958); *The Continuity of Music: A History of Influence* (1969); *The Interior Beethoven: A Biography of the Music* (1975); *The Opera Omnibus: Four Centuries of Critical Give and Take* (1976); *In Quest of Music* (1980).

Komitas (real name, **Sogomonian**), Armenian ethnomusicologist and composer; b. Kutina, Turkey, Oct. 8, 1869; d. Paris, Oct. 22, 1935. He studied at the Gevorkian Theological Seminary in Vagharshapat; was made a vardapet (archimandrite) in 1894, taking the name Komitas, after a 7th-century Armenian hymn writer. In 1895 he went to Tiflis, where he studied music theory; then lived in Berlin (1896–99), where he took courses at Richard Schmidt's private cons. and with Bellermann, Fleischer, and Friedlaender at the Univ. He studiously collected materials on Armenian folk music, publishing articles on the subject and also composing works utilizing Armenian motifs. In 1910 he moved to Constantinople; the Armenian massacre of 1915 so affected him that he became incurably psychotic, and lived from 1919 in a Paris hospital. His body was reburied in the Pantheon of Armenian Artists in Erevan in 1936. His collected compositions were ed. by R. Atayan (3 vols., Erevan, 1960–69).

BIBL.: A. Shaverdian, *K. i armyanskaya musikalmaya kultura* (K. and Armenian Music; Erevan, 1956); H. Begian, *Gomidas Vartabed: His Life and Importance to Armenian Music* (diss., Univ. of Michigan, 1964); G. Geodakian, *K.* (Erevan, 1969).

Komorous, Rudolf, Czech composer; b. Prague, Dec. 8, 1931. He studied at the Prague Cons. (1946–52); then with Pavel Bořkovec at the Prague Academy of Music (1952–56); was a bassoonist in the Smetana theater orch. He taught chamber music at the Peking Cons. (1959–61); returning to Prague, he took an active part in the modern music movement; in 1961 he was one of the organizers of the progressive group Musica Viva Pragensis. After the Soviet occupation of Czechoslovakia in 1968, Komoros went to Canada. In 1971 he was appointed prof. of composition at the Univ. of Victoria in British Columbia. In his works he explores the ultramodern potentialities of composition, often resorting to graphic music notation.

Works: *Lady Whiterose*, chamber opera for Voices a cappella (1964–66); *Chamber Music* for Bassoon and Small Orch. (1959); *The Green Twig* for Basset Horn, Triangle, Harmonium, Piano, Viola, and Cello (1960); *Still Life with Florets* for 2 Clarinets, Bassoon, Cymbal, and 3 Violas (1961); *The Sweet Queen* for Mouth Harmonica, Bass Drum, and Piano (1962–63); *Venus* for Strings and Percussion (1963); *Olympia* for Flexatone, Harmonica, Nightingale, Acolyte Bells, Sleigh Bells, and Rattle (1964); *Piccolomini* for 4 Piccolos (1964); *The Devil's Trills* for Piano (1964); *Mignon* for 4 Four-string Instruments (1965); *Chanson* for Guitar, Spirale, and Viola (1965); *York* for Flute, Oboe or Trumpet, Bassoon, Triangle, Piano, Mandolin, and Double Bass (1967); *The Gloomy Grace* for 11 Instruments and Nightingale (1968); *Bare and Dainty* for Orch. (1970); *Lethe* for Orch. and Tape (1971); *Dingy Yellow* for Soprano Saxophone, Piano, and Tape (1972); *Untitled 1* for Tape (1973), *2* for Trumpet (1973), *3* for 10 Instruments (1974), *4* for 4 Oboes, 2 Trumpets, and Violin (1974), and *5* for Flute, Horn, Viola, and Double Bass (1974); *Preludes* for 13 Early Instruments (1974); *The Grand Chopper* for Tape (1974); *Anatomy of Melancholy* for Tape (1974); *Rossi* for Small Orch. (1975); *At Your Memory the Transparent Tears Are Like Molten Lead* for Viola da Gamba and Harpsichord (1976); *The Gentle Touch (In Answer to Assistant Magistrate Chang)* for 5 Flutes, 4 Violas, 3 Cellos, and Piano (1977).

Komorzynski, Egon, Austrian musicologist; b. Vienna, May 7, 1878; d. there, March 16, 1963. He took courses at various univs., including those of Berlin, Leipzig, Munich, and Vienna (graduated, 1900). He was a prof. of German language studies and literature at Vienna's Handelsakademie (1904–34); was also music critic of the *Österreichische Volkszeitung* for 40 years.

Writings: *Emanuel Schikaneder: Ein Beitrag zur Geschichte des deutschen Theaters* (Berlin, 1901; 2nd ed., rev., 1951); *Mozarts Kunst der Instrumentation* (Stuttgart, 1906); *Mozart: Sendung und Schicksal eines deutschen Künstlers* (Berlin, 1941; 2nd ed., rev., 1955); *Der Vater der Zauberflöte: Emanuel Schikaneders Leben* (Vienna, 1948).

Kondorossy, Leslie, Hungarian-American composer; b. Pressburg, June 25, 1915. He studied at the Academy of Music in Budapest; after World War II, he settled in Cleveland; continued his studies at Western Reserve Univ., and later studied Japanese music and theater at Tokyo's Sophia Univ.; was active as a teacher, conductor, and composer. He was especially proficient in producing short operas.

Works: OPERAS: *Night in the Puszta* (Cleveland, June 28, 1953); *The Voice* (Cleveland, May 15, 1954); *The Pumpkin* (Cleveland, May 15, 1954); *The Midnight Duel*, radio opera (Cleveland, March 20, 1955); *The String Quartet*, radio opera (Cleveland, May 8, 1955); *Unexpected Visitor* (Cleveland, Oct. 21, 1956); *The 2 Imposters* (Cleveland, Oct. 21, 1956); *The Fox* (Cleveland, Jan. 28, 1961); *The Baksis* (1964); *Nathan the Wise* (1964); *The Poorest Suitor*, children's opera (Cleveland, May 24, 1967); *Shizuka's Dance*, children's opera (Cleveland, April 22, 1969); *Kalamona and the 4 Winds*, children's opera (Cleveland, Sept. 12, 1971); *Ruth and Naomi*, church opera (Cleveland, April 28, 1974). BALLETS: *Magic Dance* (1948); *The Ideal* (1950); *King Solomon*, with Tenor Solo and Chorus (1952). ORCH.: Serenade for English Horn and Chamber Orch. or Piano (Bavarian Radio, Munich, Feb. 2, 1948); Trombone Concerto (1958); Trumpet Concerto (1959); Harp Concerto (1961); Harpsichord Concerto (1972); *Music for Orchestra* (1973). CHAMBER: 2 piano sonatas (No. 1, Cleveland, May 17, 1966; No. 2, 1955); Harpsichord Sonata (1958); Trio

for Violin, Viola, and Cello (1958); String Quartet No. 1 (Cleveland, Dec. 9, 1960); Harpsichord Trio (Cleveland, Dec. 8, 1972); Suite for Brass Sextet (Cleveland, July 9, 1977); other works include *Kossuth Cantata* (Cleveland, March 16, 1952); *David, A Son of Jesse*, oratorio (Cleveland, June 4, 1967); *Jazz Mass* for Voices and Jazz Band (1968); other vocal and choral works; numerous organ pieces.

Kondracki, Michal, Russian-American composer; b. Poltava, Oct. 5, 1902. He studied with Statkowski, Melcer, and Szymanowski at the Warsaw Cons. (graduated, 1926); then with Dukas and Boulanger at the Paris École Normale de Musique (until 1931). He was a music critic in Warsaw (1933–39); with the outbreak of World War II (1939), he went to Brazil; then settled in the U.S. in 1943

Works: Opera, *Popiliny* (Warsaw, May 3, 1934; not extant); ballet, *Metropolis* (1929; not extant); Concerto for Orch. (1936); *Cantata ecclesiastica* (1937); Sym. (1942); a set of Brazilian dances for Orch. (1944); *Pastorale* for Orch. (1953); *Afrodite* for Strings (1957).

Kondrashin, Kirill (Petrovich), noted Russian conductor; b. Moscow, March 6, 1914; d. Amsterdam, March 7, 1981. He studied piano and music theory at the Musical Technicum in Moscow; then took a course in conducting with Khaikin at the Moscow Cons. (1932–36). While still a student, he conducted light opera (1934–37); then conducted at the Malyi Opera Theater in Leningrad (1937–41). In 1943 he received the prestigious appointment to the staff of the Bolshoi Theater in Moscow, where he conducted a wide repertoire emphasizing Russian operas (until 1956). He received Stalin prizes in 1948 and 1949. In 1969 he was named People's Artist of the U.S.S.R. Kondrashin was the 1st Soviet conductor to appear in the U.S. (1958), and held numerous subsequent engagements in America, the last being a concert he conducted at the Hollywood Bowl in Feb. 1981. In 1960 he was appointed chief conductor of the Moscow Phil., with which he performed numerous new Soviet works, including Shostakovich's controversial 13th Sym. He also taught at the Moscow Cons. (1950–53, 1972–75). After 1975 he increased his guest engagements outside Russia, and in 1978 decided to emigrate; in 1979 he assumed the post of permanent conductor of the Concertgebouw Orch. in Amsterdam. His conducting style was marked by an effective blend of lyrical melodiousness and dramatic romanticism, without deviating from the prevalent Russian traditions. He publ. a book, *On the Art of Conducting* (Leningrad, 1970).

Bibl.: D. McIntire, "K. K. (1914–1981)," *Le Grand Baton* (Sept./Dec. 1981).

Konetzni, Anny, esteemed Austrian soprano, sister of **Hilde Konetzni**; b. Ungarisch-Weisskirchen, Feb. 12, 1902; d. Vienna, Sept. 6, 1968. She studied with Erik Schmedes at the Vienna Cons. and later in Berlin with Jacques Stuckgold; made her operatic debut as a contralto at the Vienna Volksoper in 1925; soon turned to soprano roles. She sang in Augsburg, Elberfeld, and Chemnitz; sang with the Berlin State Opera (1931–34) and also appeared with the Vienna State Opera, La Scala in Milan, the Paris Opéra, and London's Covent Garden. She made her Metropolitan Opera debut in N.Y. as Brünnhilde in *Die Walküre* on Dec. 26, 1934; remained on its roster until the close of the season. After World War II, she taught voice in Vienna. She was particularly notable in Wagner and Strauss roles.

Konetzni, Hilde, famous Austrian soprano, sister of **Anny Konetzni**; b. Vienna, March 21, 1905; d. there, April 20, 1980. She studied at the Vienna Cons., and later in Prague with Prochaska-Neumann; made her debut as Sieglinde in *Die Walküre* in Chemnitz in 1929; then sang at the German Theater in Prague (1932–36). In 1936 she became a member of the Vienna State Opera; also appeared at Salzburg, La Scala in Milan, Covent Garden in London, South America, and the U.S. In 1954 she joined the faculty of the Vienna Academy of Music. She was an outstanding interpreter of Wagner and Strauss.

Königslöw, Johann Wilhelm Cornelius von, German organist and composer; b. Hamburg, March 16, 1745; d. Lübeck, May 14, 1833. He studied piano and voice with his father; at 13 he became a boy soprano in Lübeck's Abendmusiken under A. Kenzen at the Marienkirche. Kenzen taught him organ, violin, and composition; he became his assistant (1772) and successor (1781); also took over the direction of his Abendmusiken (1773), and soon established himself as a leading figure in the musical life of Hamburg. He wrote a number of oratorios, most of which are lost; also composed cantatas, orch. works, and keyboard music.

Königslöw, Otto Friedrich von, German violinist and conductor; b. Hamburg, Nov. 13, 1824; d. Bonn, Oct. 6, 1898. He studied at the Leipzig Cons. with David (violin) and Hauptmann (theory); following 12 years of concert tours, he was conductor of the Gürzenich Orch. at Cologne (1858–81); also was a member of the staff of the Cologne Cons.

Koning, David, Dutch pianist, choral conductor, and composer; b. Rotterdam, March 19, 1820; d. Amsterdam, Oct. 6, 1876. He studied with Aloys Schmitt in Frankfurt; from 1840, was conductor of the choral society Felix Meritis in Amsterdam; was active mainly as a piano teacher. He wrote a comic opera, *The Fishermaiden; Elegy on the Death of an Artist* for Soli, Chorus, and Orch.; much vocal music; many piano pieces and studies.

Konitz, Lee, American jazz alto saxophonist; b. Chicago, Oct. 13, 1927. He took up the clarinet at 11, but eventually made the saxophone his chosen instrument. He gained early experience with the Gay Claridge band in Chicago; then appeared with Claude Thornhill (1947–48), Charlie "Bird" Parker, and Lennie Tristano, and recorded with Miles Davis (1948–50). After working with Stan Kenton (1952–53), he was involved mainly with his own combos; made a major tour of Europe (1965–66); appeared at N.Y.'s Carnegie Hall (1980). He developed a sui generis variations style related to bebop, with the melody notes patterned after the available ingredients in piano harmonies.
BIBL.: M. Frohne, *Subconscious L.: 35 Years of Records and Tapes: The L. K. Discography 1947–82* (Freiburg, 1983).

Konius, Georgi. See **Conus, Georgi.**

Konjović, Petar, Serbian composer; b. Sombor, May 6, 1882; d. Belgrade, Oct. 1, 1970. He studied at the Prague Cons. with Novák and Stecker. He was director of the Zagreb Opera (1921–26), the national theaters in Osijek, Split, and Novi Sad (1927–33), and again at the Zagreb Opera (1933–39); then was prof. at the Belgrade Academy of Music (1939–50), where he also served twice as rector.
WORKS: Operas: *Vilin Veo* or *Ženidba Miloševa* (The Wedding of Milos; Zagreb, April 25, 1917); *Knez od Zete* (The Duke of Zeta; Belgrade, May 25, 1929); *Koštana* (Zagreb, April 16, 1931); *Sel jaci* (The Peasants; Belgrade, March 3, 1952); *Otadžbina* (Homeland; 1960); *Serbia liberata*, symphonic poem (1906); Sym. (1907; rev. by D. Jakšić, 1955); *Na selu* (In the Country), symphonic variations (1915; rev. 1935); *Jadranski capriccio* (Adriatic Capriccio) for Violin and Orch. (1920); *Makar Čudra*, symphonic poem (1944); 3 string quartets; solo pieces for violin, cello, and piano; songs; *Moja zemlja* (My Country), 100 Yugoslav folk songs, of which 25 are arranged for Voice and Small Orch.

Kono, Kristo, Albanian composer; b. Tirana, July 17, 1907. He studied at the Milan Cons.; wrote the 1st national Albanian operetta, *The Dawn* (1954); also an opera, *Flowers of Memories* (1959), and many choruses.

Konoye, Hidemarō, Japanese conductor and composer; b. Tokyo, Nov. 18, 1898; d. there, June 2, 1973. A member of an aristocratic Japanese family, he received his education in Japan and in Europe; attended classes in composition of d'Indy at the Schola Cantorum in Paris; then took courses with Franz Schreker and Georg Schumann at the Berlin Cons. He made his European debut as a conductor with the Berlin Phil. on Jan. 18, 1924. Returning to Japan, he was principal conductor of the New Sym. Orch. in Tokyo (1926–34), specializing in new works of Japanese, European, and American composers. He conducted in the U.S. in 1937 and 1957. He was the composer of several orch. pieces based on Japanese subjects; also orchestrated early Japanese court music for the modern Western orch.; arranged the music of *Madama Butterfly* for the films (inserting many Japanese folk melodies).
BIBL.: B. Flowers, "Viscount H. K. 1898–1973," *Le Grand Baton* (Dec. 1984).

Kont, Paul, Austrian composer and teacher; b. Vienna, Aug. 19, 1920. He studied violin with Vittorio Borri and piano with Hans Nast at the Vienna Cons. (1939–40), then took a course in conducting with Josef Krips and Hans Swarowsky (diploma, 1947) and in composition with Josef Lechthaler (diploma, 1948) at the Vienna Academy of Music; also studied analysis with Josef Polnauer. After attending Fortner's class in Darmstadt (1951), he completed his training with Messiaen, Milhaud, and Honegger in Paris (1952). In 1969 he joined the faculty of the Vienna Academy of Music, where he was a prof. of composition (from 1980). His honors have included the Austrian State Prize (1964), the prize of the City of Vienna (1975), the Gold Medal of the City of Vienna (1986), and the Great Honorary Citation of the Austrian Republic (1987). He adopted a serial method applying the statistical principles of valid recurrences of all musical parameters, including pitch, rhythm, and dynamics. He publ. *Antianorganikum* (Vienna, 1967).
WORKS: STAGE: OPERAS: *Indische Legende* (1950); *Peter und Susanne* (Vienna, June 26, 1959); *Lysistrate* (1957–60); *Inzwischen* (1953–66; Vienna, Jan. 5, 1967); *Plutos* (1975–76; Klagenfurt, Feb. 7, 1977); *Die Paare* (1985–86); *Traumleben*, musical fairy tale (1958; Salzburg, Dec. 22, 1963); *Celestina*, musical play (1966); other dramatic stage pieces. **BALLETS:** *Italia passata* (1967); *Komödie der Unart* (Vienna, Dec. 12, 1978); *Il ballo del mondo* (1980–82); *Arkadien* (1984); *K* (1984; Klagenfurt, Feb. 2, 1985). **ORCH.:** *Drei Tanzskizzen* (1946–51); *Komplex E* (1956; Vienna, Sept. 12, 1957); *Concerto des Infants* for Piano and Small Orch. (1956); Cello Concerto (1960; Vienna, May 2, 1966); Concerto for Winds and Strings (1964; Vienna, Nov. 27, 1970); *Konzertantes Triptychon* (1950–69); Suite (1971; Vienna, Aug. 14, 1980); Partita for String Orch. (1971–72; Vienna, April 8, 1973); Divertimento for Trumpet and Small Orch. (1966–73; Vienna, Feb. 1, 1976); *Kurzkonzert* for Clarinet and Orch. (1973; Vienna, Jan. 25, 1974); *Der Raucher* for Cello and String Orch. (1973; Vienna, Jan. 22, 1975); *Mediterrane Harmonien* for Double Bass and Orch. (1976–77; Vienna, Feb. 28, 1983); *Konzert 1977* for Piano and Orch. (1977; Bregenz, Aug. 13, 1979); *Vivaldi-Monument* (1978; Vienna, Feb. 10, 1980); 5 syms.: No. 1 (1979); No. 2, *Den Toten*, for Soprano, Chorus, and Orch. (1983); No. 3 (1981); No. 4, *Den Liebenden*, for Tenor, Women's Chorus, and Orch. (1983); No. 5 (1980; Vienna, March 11, 1982); Concerto for Percussion and Orch. (1983; Vienna, May 11, 1986); Concerto (1984); *Sache für Musikanten* (1985); *Regeriana* (1987); *Miss Lyss Nausick* (1988); *Serenade* for String Orch. (1989). **CHAMBER:** Quartet for Oboe, Clarinet, Bass Clarinet, and Bassoon (1947); *Meditationes Beatae Virginis Mariae* for 7 Instruments (1956–61); Piano Trio (1964); *Blechmusik I*: 1, Trio for Trumpet, Horn, and Trombone (1966), 2, Quartettino for Trumpet, 2 Horns, and Trombone (1966), and 3, Quartet for Trumpet, Horn, Trombone, and Tuba (1968); *Blechmusik II*: 1, *Blechmusik* for 2 Trumpets, Horn, Trombone, and Tuba (1971), and 2, *Harmonien* for 2 Trumpets, 2 Horns, 2 Trombones, and Tuba (1973); *Finis austriae* for String Quartet (1973–76); *Musica marina* for 2 Violins, Viola, and Cello (1978); *Sonate und Sonatine* for String Quartet (1944–81); *Holzmusik I* for Oboe, Clarinet, Bassoon, and Flute (1956–82); *Holzmusik II* for 6 Instruments (1980–82); *Übung für Streicher* (3 sets, 1956–83); *Kammertanz Suite* for Saxophone Quartet (1988); 5 *Sketches* for Saxophone Quartet (1989); *En rose et noir* for Piano Trio (1989); keyboard pieces; choral works; lieder.

Kontarsky, Alfons, German pianist, brother of **Aloys** and **Bernhard Kontarsky;** b. Iserlohn, Westphalia, Oct. 9, 1932. He studied piano with Else Schmitz-Gohr and Maurits Frank at the Cologne Hochschule für Musik (1953–55) and with Eduard Erdmann in Hamburg (1955–57); with his brother Aloys, won 1st prize for duo-piano playing in the Bavarian Radio Competition in Munich (1955); they subsequently toured throughout the world, giving performances of many modern scores. He taught at the Cologne Hochschule für Musik (from 1967). He publ. *Pro musica nova: Studien zum Spielen neuer Musik für Klavier* (Cologne, 1973).

Kontarsky, Aloys, German pianist, brother of **Alfons** and **Bernhard Kontarsky;** b. Iserlohn, Westphalia, May 14, 1931. He studied piano with Else Schmitz-Gohr and Maurits Frank at the Cologne Hochschule für Musik (1952–55) and with Eduard Erdmann in Hamburg (1955–57); with his brother Alfons, won 1st prize for duo-piano playing at the Bavarian Radio Competition in Munich (1955); thereafter they made tours throughout the world, specializing in contemporary music. He taught master classes at the Cologne Hochschule für Musik (from 1969).

Kontarsky, Bernhard, German pianist and conductor, brother of **Alfons** and **Aloys Kontarsky;** b. Iserlohn, Westphalia, April 26, 1937. He studied at the Cologne Hochschule für Musik and at the Univ. of Cologne. In 1964 he received the Mendelssohn Prize in Chamber Music. He was a conductor at the Württemberg State Theater in Stuttgart; also appeared as a pianist, both as a soloist and in ensemble with his brothers.

Kontski, Antoine de, famous Polish pianist, brother of **Apollinaire** and **Charles de Kontski;** b. Krakow, Oct. 27, 1817; d. Ivanichi, near Okulova, Russia, Dec. 7, 1899. He studied with John Field in Moscow (1830), then toured widely; also taught in Paris (1851–53), Berlin (1853–54), St. Petersburg (1854–67), and subsequently in London. He toured the U.S. (1883, 1885); made a world tour when he was nearly 80 (1896–98). He composed 2 piano concertos and various virtuoso and salon pieces for piano; his picturesque *Réveil du lion* was enormously successful for many years; it was an epitome of Romantic exuberance to the point of being ludicrous. He also composed the light operas *Les Deux Distraits* (London, 1872) and *Le Sultan de Zanzibar* (N.Y., May 8, 1886).

Kontski, Apollinaire de, Polish violinist and pedagogue, brother of **Antoine** and **Charles de Kontski;** b. Krakow, Oct. 23, 1825; d. Warsaw, June 29, 1879. He studied with his elder brother Charles; he appeared with his brothers as a small child in Russia and later in Germany, frankly exploited by his family for sensational publicity and gain. In 1837 he played for Paganini in Paris; in 1861 he became director of the Warsaw Cons., of which he was a founder, and remained in that post until his death. He publ. some violin music.

Kontski, Charles de, Polish pianist and teacher, brother of **Antoine** and **Apollinaire de Kontski;** b. Krakow, Sept. 6, 1815; d. Paris, Aug. 27, 1867. Like his brothers, he was a child prodigy, and made appearances with them at various public exhibitions and concerts. He studied in Warsaw and in Paris, eventually settling in Paris as a private piano teacher, enjoying considerable success in society.

Konwitschny, Franz, esteemed German conductor; b. Fulnek, northern Moravia, Aug. 14, 1901; d. Belgrade, July 28, 1962. He studied violin at the German Musikverein School in Brünn and at the Leipzig Cons. (1923–25); while a student, he played viola and violin in the theater orch. and the Gewandhaus Orch. in Leipzig, subsequently becoming a violist in the Fitzner Quartet in Vienna (1925), and also a teacher at the Volkskonservatorium there. He became répétiteur at the Stuttgart Opera in 1927, rising to chief conductor in 1930; after serving as Generalmusikdirektor in Freiburg im Breisgau (1933–38), he assumed that position with the Frankfurt Opera and Museumgesellschaft concerts in 1938, and then with the Hannover Opera in 1945. He was appointed chief conductor of the Gewandhaus Orch. in 1949; was also Generalmusik-direktor of the Dresden State Opera (1953–55) and the (East) Berlin State Opera (1955–62). Although he held posts under both the Nazi and Communist regimes, he successfully avoided political encounters. He died while on tour and was given a state funeral by the German Democratic Republic; his request for a Requiem Mass was honored, much to the chagrin of the authorities.

BIBL.: H. Sanders, ed., *Vermächtnis und Verpflichtung: Festschrift für F. K.* (Leipzig, 1961).

Konya, Sándor, Hungarian tenor; b. Sarkad, Sept. 23, 1923. He was educated at the Budapest Academy of Music; also studied in Detmold, Rome, and Milan. He made his 1st professional appearance as Turiddu in Bielefeld in 1951, singing there until 1954; in 1958, sang for the 1st time at the Bayreuth Festival as Lohengrin. On Oct. 28, 1961, he made his Metropolitan Opera debut in N.Y. as Lohengrin; sang there regularly until 1973. He first appeared at London's Covent Garden in the same role (1963). His most notable roles included Walther von Stolzing, Parsifal, Max, and Don Carlos.

Koole, Arend (Johannes Christiaan), Dutch musicologist; b. Amsterdam, April 22, 1908. He studied at the Amsterdam Cons. (1925–30) and later at the Univ. of Utrecht (Ph.D., 1949, with the diss. *Leven en werken van Pietro Antonio Locatelli da Bergamo*; publ. in Amsterdam, 1949; 2nd ed., rev., 1970). He taught at the Cons. in Rotterdam (1938–41), Utrecht (1941–44), and Amsterdam (1946–49); also made appearances as a pianist and conductor. In 1949 he went to South Africa, where he served as senior lecturer in musicology at the Univ. of Bloemfontein; from 1964 to 1973 he was a prof. of music history at the Univ. of Southern Calif. in Los Angeles; in 1974 he returned to South Africa. He publ. a monograph on Mendelssohn (Haarlem, 1953; 2nd ed., 1958).

Kooper, Al, American rock musician and producer; b. N.Y., Feb. 5, 1944. In 1968, together with Steve Katz (b. N.Y., May 9, 1945) and Bobby Colomby (b. N.Y., Dec. 20, 1944), he founded a synthetic group of rock, pop, and jazz music known as Blood, Sweat, and Tears, with the name patently derived from Winston Churchill's famous wartime speech promising his people nothing but hemorrhage, perspiration, and copious discharge from lachrymal glands. The individual songs hurled by the group at the defenseless populace expressed similar sentiments, as in *My Days Are Numbered.* However, that same year, Kooper left the group for the more lucrative role of a producer. Without Kooper, the group fell into desuetude; hopeful zombies dropping in and out did not stop the deterioration. On Jan. 31, 1971, one such extraterrestrial, Gregory Herbert, a member of BST, justified the title by being found dead in a dingy hotel room in Amsterdam during the group's European tour. The group finally expired in 1977.

Koopman, Ton, remarkable Dutch organist, harpsichordist, and conductor; b. Zwolle, Oct. 12, 1944. He studied organ with Simon Jansen and harpsichord with Gustav Leonhardt in Amsterdam, and also took courses in musicology; obtained doctorates in all 3 (1968–70), then won the Prix d'excellence for organ (1972) and harpsichord (1974). After serving as director of Musica Antiqua and as a teacher at the Sweelinck Cons. in Amsterdam, he founded the Amsterdam Baroque Orch. (1979). He toured widely in subsequent years as a conductor, organist, and harpsichordist, excelling in early music performances.

Kopecký, Pavel, Czech composer; b. Prague, April 5, 1949. He studied with Dobiáš at the Prague Academy of Arts and Music (1972–77) and with Donatoni in Siena (1976); after pursuing postgraduate studies with Sidelnikov at the Moscow Cons. (1977–79), he joined the faculty of the film academy at the Prague Academy of Arts. His music explores the dynamics of modern compositional trends.

WORKS: *3 Studies* for 2 Cellos (1974); 2 piano sonatas (1975, 1979); *Cesty* (The Roads), variations for String Orch. (1976); *Syntéza* for Piano and Tape (1976); Piano Concerto (1977);

Quartet for Flute and Strings (1978); *4 Symphonic Preludes—Moscow* (1979); *Bláznovy zápisky* (Madman's Diary), piano suite, after Gogol (1980); Piano Trio (1981); *On a oni* (He and They), concerto for Clarinet and Strings (1982).

Kopelent, Marek, Czech composer; b. Prague, April 28, 1932. He studied composition with Řídký at the Prague Academy of Musical Arts (1951–55); then was a music ed. for Supraphon, the state music publishing house (1956–71). In his music he experiments with a wide variety of musical resources of the multimedia avant-garde.
WORKS: 5 string quartets (1954, 1955, 1963, 1967, 1980); *3 Movements* for String Orch. (1958); *Nénie s flétnou* (Nenie with Flute) for Flute, 9 Female Voices, and Chamber Ensemble (1961); *Small Pantomime* for Wind Quintet (1961); Trio for Flute, Clarinet, and Bassoon (1962); *Reflexe* for Flute, Violin, Viola, and Cello (1962); *Chléb a ptáci* (Bread and Birds), oratorio (1957–62); *Canto intimo* for Flute and Vibraphone (1963); *Matka* (The Mother), fresco for Chorus and Flute (1964); *Hudba pro pět* (Music for 5) for Oboe, Clarinet, Bassoon, Viola, and Piano (1964); *Modlitba kamene* (Prayer of Stones) for Narrator, 2 Small Choruses, 3 Gongs, and Tam-tam (1965); *Rozjímání* (Contemplation) for Chamber Orch. (1966); *Game*, "happening" for String Quartet (1965–66); *Snehah* (Sanskrit for "love") for Soprano and Chamber Ensemble (1967); *Sváry* (Quarrels) for 12 Solo Instruments and Orch. (1967–68; Prague, March 7, 1969); *Zátiší* (Seclusion) for Viola and Chamber Orch. (1968); *Žaloby* (Complaints) for 2 Choruses, Trumpet, Percussion, and ad libitum Tape (1969); *Bludný hlas* (The Wandering Voice) for Actress, Chamber Ensemble, Tape, and ad libitum Film and Light Projection (1969–70); *Appassionato* for Piano and Orch. (1970–71); *Intimissimo* for Chamber Ensemble (1971); *Musique piquante* for Violin and Cimbalom (1971); *A Few Minutes with an Oboist* for Oboe and Chamber Orch. (1972); Wind Quintet (1972); *Black and White Tears* for Solo Voices (1972); *Syllabes mouvementées* for Vocal Soloists (1972); *Veroničina rouška* (Veronika's Veil), sonata for 11 Strings (1972–73); *Rondo* for 5 Percussionists (1973); *T'ukáta* (Taps) for Harp, Harpsichord, Cimbalom, and Guitar (1974); *Hrátky* (A Cozy Chat) for Saxophone and Orch. (1974–75); *Il Canto degli Augei*, aria for Soprano and Orch. (1978); *Lament of Woman*, melodrama-monologue for Actress, 7 Brass, 4 Women's Voices, and Children's Choir (1980); Sym. (Basel, Feb. 17, 1983); *Cantus supplex* for Chorus (1986); *Messaggio della povertà* for Soprano, Baritone, Children's Chorus, Chorus, and Orch. (1988).

Koppel, Herman D(avid), Danish pianist and composer of Polish parentage, father of **Thomas Herman Koppel;** b. Copenhagen, Oct. 1, 1908. He studied piano and composition at the Copenhagen Cons. (1926–29); made his debut in 1930 as a concert pianist; toured widely in Europe. He taught at the Royal Inst. of Music for the Blind in Copenhagen (1940–43; 1945–49); lived in Örebro, Sweden (1943–45), to avoid the Nazi occupation. In 1949 he joined the faculty of the Royal Danish Cons. of Music in Copenhagen; was a prof. there (from 1955). As a pianist, he performed the music of Nielsen and other 20th-century Danish composers. His early compositions were influenced by Nielsen, Stravinsky, and Bartók, but he eventually developed an individualistic style, marked by rhythmic intensity and melodic expressivity.
WORKS: Opera: *Macbeth,* after Shakespeare (1968; Copenhagen, 1970); 7 syms.: No. 1 (1930); No. 2 (1943); No. 3 (1944–45); No. 4 (1946); No. 5 (1955); No. 6, *Sinfonia breve* (1957); No. 7 (1960–61; Copenhagen, May 16, 1961); Violin Concerto (1929); *Music for Strings* (1930); 4 piano concertos (1931–32; 1936–37; 1948; 1960–63); *Music for Jazz Orchestra* (1932); *Capriccio* for Violin and Orch. (1934); Variations for Small Orch. (1935); 2 concertinos for Strings (1937–38; 1957); Clarinet Concerto (1941); Sinfonietta (1945); Concerto for Violin, Viola, and Orch. (1947); *3 Psalms of David* for Tenor, Chorus, and Orch. (1949); Cello Concerto (1952); *Immortalis mortalium* for Baritone, Boys' Chorus, and Orch. (1954); *2 Biblical Songs* for Soprano and Orch. or Piano (1955); *The*

Song of the Sun for Children's Chorus, Strings, and Piano (1958); *Moses,* oratorio (1963–64; Copenhagen, Oct. 21, 1965); *Requiem* (1965–66); Oboe Concerto (1970); Chamber Concerto for Violin and Strings (1970); Flute Concerto (1971); *Hymns of Thanksgiving* for Soli, Chorus, and Orch. (1974); Concerto for Orch. (1977–78); *Intrada* for Orch. (1979); Concerto for Violin, Viola, Cello, and Small Orch. (1984); 6 string quartets (1928–29; 1939; 1944–45; 1964; 1975; 1979); Trio for Clarinet, Violin, and Piano (1931); Sextet for Winds and Piano (1942); *Fantasy* for Clarinet (1947); Piano Sonata (1950); *Ternio I* for Cello or Violin and Piano (1951); Piano Quintet (1953); Cello Sonata (1956); Variations for Clarinet and Piano (1961); *9 Variations* for Piano Trio (1969); Suite for Cello (1971); Piano Trio (1971); *8 Variations and Epilogue* for Piano and 13 Players (1972); Divertimento for String Trio (1972); *Ternio II* for Saxophone (1973); *Pastorale Variations* for Flute, Violin, Viola, and Cello (1975); Piano Quartet (1985); Trio for Clarinet, Cello, and Piano (1986); incidental music for plays; music to 29 films; songs.

Koppel, Thomas Herman, Danish composer, son of **Herman D(avid) Koppel;** b. Örebro, Sweden, April 27, 1944. He studied piano and theory with his father at the Royal Danish Cons. of Music in Copenhagen (1963–67). In 1968 he organized in Copenhagen the pop group Savage Rose, and joined the Danish avant-garde in other venturesome activities.
WORKS: Operas: *Historien om en moder* (The Story of a Mother), after H.C. Andersen (Copenhagen, Oct. 17, 1965), and *Bérénice* (1968); 3 string quartets (1963, 1964, 1966); *Cloches* for Voice, Clarinet, Horn, Celesta, Piano, Cello, and Percussion (1964); *Phrases,* cantata for 2 Sopranos, 12 Mezzo-sopranos, 4 Solo Instruments, and Orch. (Danish Radio, April 6, 1967); *Visions fugitives* for Piano and Orch. (1965); *Concert héroïque* for 3 Pianos, Orch., Chorus, and Wind Machine (Copenhagen, Jan. 9, 1967); *Petit air* for Soprano and 4 Instruments (1966); *Ouverture solennelle* (1967); *Impressions lyriques* for Percussion (1968); music for the ballet *Dødens triumf* (Triumph of Death; Danish Radio, May 23, 1971); *Nocturne fra den lange grå gade* (Nocturne from a Long Gray Street) for Mezzo-soprano and String Trio (1983); *Skipper Klement* for 2 Violins, Viola, Guitar, and Double Bass (1984); *The Emperor's New Clothes* (1985–86), music for ice ballet.

Kopylov, Alexander (Alexandrovich), Russian composer; b. St. Petersburg, July 14, 1854; d. Strelna, near St. Petersburg, March 5, 1911. He studied violin and piano at the court chapel (1862–72); upon graduation, took lessons in composition with Rimsky-Korsakov and Liadov. From 1872 to 1896 he taught singing to the court chapel choir. He was an epigone of the Romantic school of minor Russian composers. He wrote a Sym.; an overture; 5 string quartets; many piano pieces.

Kopytman, Mark, Russian-born Israeli composer, b. Kamenets-Podolski, Dec. 6, 1929. He studied with Simovitz at the Lwow Academy of Music (M.A., 1955) and with Bogatirev at the Moscow Cons. (Ph.D., 1958); taught in various Russian music institutes (1955–72), then emigrated to Israel, where he joined the faculty of the Rubin Academy of Music in Jerusalem in 1974. He also was a guest prof. at the Hebrew Univ. in Jerusalem (from 1979) and the Univ. of Pa. (1985).
WORKS: **OPERAS:** *Casa mare* (1966); *Chamber Scenes from the Life of Susskind von Trinberg* (1983). **ORCH.:** Sym. (1955); *6 Moldavian Tunes* (1965); Piano Concerto (1971); Concerto (1976); *Rotations for Vocalise* (1979); *Kaddish* for Cello and Strings (1982). **CHAMBER:** *2 Miniatures on Kazakh Folk Tunes* for String Quartet (1961); String Quartet No. 2 (1965); String Quartet No. 3 (1969); *Monodrama* for Sextet (1975); *For Harpsichord* (1976); *About an Old Tune* for Piano Quartet (1977); *For Organ* (1978); *And a Time for Every Purpose* for Flute, Trumpet, Trombone, and Percussion (1979). **VOCAL:** *Songs of Kodr,* oratorio (1966); *Unfinished Lines* for Baritone and Orch. (1970); *October Sun* for Mezzo-soprano, Flute, Violin, Cello, Piano, and Percussion (1974); *Voices* for Voice, Flute, Trombones, Percussion, and Strings (1975); *Day and Night Will Rise to Heaven* for Soprano, Mime, Flute, Trumpet, Trombone,

and Percussion (1977); *Memory* for Voice and Orch. (1981); *Life of the World to Come* for Voice and Chamber Orch. (1986); *Letters of Creation* for Voice and Strings (1986); songs; also piano pieces.

Korbay, Francis Alexander, Hungarian tenor, pianist, teacher, and composer; b. Budapest, May 8, 1846; d. London, March 9, 1913. He was a pupil of Gustave Roger; sang at the Hungarian Opera in Budapest (1865–68); at the same time he pursued piano study, profiting by advice from Liszt, who was his godfather; made a rather successful tour as a pianist in Europe (1869–71), and then went to N.Y. as a teacher of voice and piano; was a prof. of singing at the Royal Academy of Music in London (1894–1903). He wrote an orch. work, *Nuptiale; Hungarian Overture; Le Matin* for Solo Voice and Piano, which was arranged by Liszt for Orch.; also numerous lieder and piano pieces.

Korchmarev, Klimenti (Arkadievich), Russian composer; b. Verkhnedneprovsk, July 3, 1899; d. Moscow, April 7, 1958. He studied at the Odessa Cons. with Maliszewski and Biber (graduated with the gold medal, 1919); then went to Moscow (1923), where he became one of the 1st Soviet composers to embrace revolutionary themes; he wrote *Leviy marsh* (March on the Left; to words by Mayakovsky) for Chorus and Piano (1923); then composed the operas *Ivan-Soldat* (Ivan the Soldier; 1925–27) and *Desyat dney, kotoriye potryasili mir* (10 Days That Shook the World; 1929–31) and the ballet *Krepostnaya balerina* (The Serf Ballerina; Leningrad, Dec. 11, 1927). His other works in this vein included the choral syms. *Oktyabr* (October; 1931) and *Narodi sovetskoy strani* (The Peoples of the Soviet Land; 1935). From 1939 to 1947 he was in Turkmenistan, where he collected native songs; also composed the 1st native ballet, *Vesyoliy obmanschchik* (The Merry Deceiver). In 1950 he wrote a cantata, *Svobodniy Kitay* (Free China), for which he received a Stalin Prize.

Kord, Kazimierz, Polish conductor; b. Pogórze, Nov. 18, 1930. He studied piano at the Leningrad Cons.; then took courses in composition and conducting at the Krakow Academy of Music. He conducted at the Warsaw Opera (1960–62); from 1962 to 1970, was artistic director of the Krakow Opera; from 1968 to 1973, was chief conductor of the Polish Radio and Television Sym. Orch. in Katowice. He was chief conductor with the National Phil. in Warsaw (from 1977); was also principal guest conductor of the Cincinnati Sym. Orch. (1980–82), chief conductor of the South-West Radio Sym. Orch. in Baden-Baden (1980–86), and principal guest conductor and music adviser of the Pacific Sym. Orch. in California (1989–91).

Koreshchenko, Arseni, Russian composer; b. Moscow, Dec. 18, 1870; d. Kharkov, Jan. 6, 1921. He studied piano with Taneyev and composition with Arensky at the Moscow Cons.; later was an instructor in music theory there; from 1906 to 1919 he taught composition at the Moscow Phil. Inst.; then went to Kharkov, where he taught piano and composition at the Academy until his death. He wrote music imitative of Tchaikovsky and Arensky; his songs have a certain obsolete charm. He composed 3 operas: *Belshazzar's Feast* (Moscow, 1892); *The Angel of Death* (1893); *The House of Ice* (Moscow, Nov. 19, 1900); ballet, *The Magic Mirror* (Moscow, 1902); several orch. pieces, including *Armenian Suite* for Orch. and *Concerto Fantasy* for Piano and Orch.; String Quartet; choruses; piano pieces; songs.

Korganov, Genari, Armenian pianist and composer; b. Kvarely, May 12, 1858; d. Rostov-on-the-Don, March 7, 1890. He studied with Reinecke at the Leipzig Cons. and with L. Brassin in St. Petersburg. In 1879 he settled in Tiflis. He often used authentic Caucasian motifs, while his harmonic treatment was modeled after Rimsky-Korsakov's oriental pieces. His fantasia for piano on Caucasian themes, *Bayati,* presents a certain interest.

Kořínek, Miroslav, Slovak composer; b. Brno, Jan. 29, 1925. He studied composition with Alexander Moyzes at the Bratislava Cons.; joined its faculty (1950).

WORKS: Concertino for Viola and Orch. (1951); Accordion

Concerto (1956); *Divertimento concertato* for String Orch. (1962); Flute Concerto (1964); *Chamber Concerto* for Clarinet and Orch. (1966); Horn Concerto (1968); *Atlantide,* cantata (1972); 2 string quartets (1951, 1963); Trio for 2 Oboes and English Horn (1961); Piano Quintet (1967); Wind Quintet (1970); 2 Capriccios for Trombone and Piano (1973); *Concertante Fantasy* for Flute and Guitar (1974).

Korn, Clara Anna, German-American composer and teacher; b. Berlin, Jan. 30, 1866; d. N.Y., July 14, 1940. She was taken to America at an early age; studied with Horatio Parker and Bruno Oscar Klein; taught at the National Cons. in N.Y. (1893–98); then was a private teacher. She wrote an opera, *Their Last War;* Sym.; symphonic poem, *Morpheus;* orch. suite, *Rural Snapshots;* Piano Concerto; Violin Concerto; piano pieces; songs.

Korn, Peter Jona, German composer; b. Berlin, March 30, 1922. He studied at the Berlin Hochschule für Musik (1932–33), with Rubbra in London (1934–36), Wolpe at the Jerusalem Cons. (1936–38), Schoenberg at the Univ. of Calif. at Los Angeles (1941–42), and Eisler and Toch at the Univ. of Southern Calif. in Los Angeles (1946–47); also studied the technique of film composition with Dahl and Rózsa. He was founder-conductor of the New Orch. of Los Angeles (1948–56); then taught at the Univ. of Calif. at Los Angeles (1964–65). Returning to Germany, he was director of Munich's Richard Strauss Konservatorium (from 1967). He publ. a book of essays, *Musikalische Unwelt Verschmutzung* (Wiesbaden, 1975). His compositional style is a pragmatic Romanticism marked by polycentric tonality in the framework of strong rhythmic counterpoint.

WORKS: Opera, *Heidi in Frankfurt (Das fremde Haus),* after Johanna Spyri (1961–63; Saarbrücken, Nov. 28, 1978); 3 syms.: No. 1 (1941–46; rev. 1956, 1977); No. 2 (1950–51); No. 3 (1956; new version, 1969); *Tom Paine Overture* (1949–50); *Rhapsody* for Oboe and Strings (1951); *In medias res,* overture (1953); *Variations on a Theme from The Beggar's Opera* for Orch. (Louisville, Oct. 1, 1955); Saxophone Concerto (1956; new version, 1982); Violin Concerto (1964–65); *Toccata* for Orch. (1966); Serenade for 12 Strings (1968); *Eine Kleine Popmusik* for Orch. (1972); *Beckmesser Variations* for Orch. (1977); Trumpet Concerto (1979); *Eine Kleine Deutsche Stadt,* cantata for Tenor, Harpsichord, and Orch. (1980–81); *Psalm of Courage,* cantata for Baritone, Chorus, and Orch. (1983); *Romanza concertante* for Oboe and Small Orch. (1987); *Concerto classico* for Harpsichord and Orch. (1988); Cello Sonata (1948–49); Oboe Sonata (1949); Horn Sonata (1952); 2 string quartets (1949–50; 1963); *Serenade* for 4 Horns (1957); *Quintettino* for Flute, Clarinet, Bassoon, Cello, and Piano (1964); Wind Quintet (1966); Wind Octet (1976); *Fantasia* for Oboe and Organ (1981); piano pieces; numerous organ works; songs.

BIBL.: N. Düchtel et al., *P.J. K.* (Tutzing, 1989).

Kornauth, Egon, Austrian pianist and composer; b. Olmütz, May 14, 1891; d. Vienna, Oct. 28, 1959. He studied with Fuchs at the Vienna Academy of Music, winning the Austrian State Prize for his Viola Sonata (1912); then studied musicology with Adler at the Univ. of Vienna (Ph.D., 1915). He toured widely with his Vienna Trio (1928–29); then received Vienna's Music Prize (1930). He became a teacher of theory at the Vienna Hochschule für Musik (1940) and a prof. at the Salzburg Mozarteum (1945). His music generally followed along Romantic lines, demonstrating considerable contrapuntal skill.

WORKS: 4 symphonic suites (1913–39); Symphonic Overture (1914; rev. 1925); *Ballade* for Orch., with Cello obbligato (Vienna, Feb. 20, 1919); *Romantische Suite* for Orch. (1932–36; rev. 1940); Suite for Orch. (1937–38); Viola Sonata (1912); Clarinet Sonata (1912–13); Violin Sonata (1913–14); 2 string quartets (1920, 1920); Cello Sonata (1922); 2 string quintets (1923; 1938, rev. 1947); Piano Quintet (1931); Clarinet Quintet (1931); various choral works and song cycles; piano pieces.

BIBL.: E. Müller von Asow, *E. K.* (Vienna, 1941); T. Leibnitz, *Österreichische Spätromantiker: Studien zu Emil Nikolaus von Reznicek, Joseph Marx, Franz Schmidt, und E. K.* (Tutzing, 1986).

Korndorf, Nikolai, Russian composer; b. Moscow, Jan. 23, 1947. He studied composition with Balasanian at the Moscow Cons., graduating in 1970. In 1973 he was appointed to the staff of the Moscow Cons.

WORKS: Opera, *Feast during the Plague* (1973); *Cantata of Lenin* (1970; on Lenin's centennial); Concerto for Organ, Piano, and Strings (1969); Viola Concerto (1970); *Concerto-Pastorale* for Bassoon and Orch. (1972); Concerto for Double Bass and 12 Wind Instruments (1973); Concerto for Harp and 10 Brass Instruments (1974); 2 syms. (1975, 1980); *Confessions,* chamber sym. (1979); *Yarilo* (old Slavic name for "Sun"), chamber sym. (1979); Concerto for Violin, Cello, Piano, and Orch. (1980); Piano Trio (1971); Sonata for 3 Violins and Piano, in memory of Stravinsky (1971); *Polyphonic Suite* for Saxophone and Piano (1972); 6 Songs for Voice and Wind Quintet, to words by Alexander Blok (1968).

Körner, Christian Gottfried, German music theorist; b. Leipzig, July 2, 1756; d. Berlin, May 13, 1831. He was the father of Theodor Körner, the poet. He publ. an essay, "Über den Charakter der Töne oder über Charakterdarstellung in der Musik," in the *Horen* (1775); also composed songs, etc.

BIBL.: W. Seifert, *C.G. K.: Ein Musikästhetiker der deutschen Klassik* (Regensburg, 1960).

Korngold, Erich Wolfgang, remarkable Austrian-born American composer, son of **Julius Korngold;** b. Brünn, May 29, 1897; d. Los Angeles, Nov. 29, 1957. He received his earliest musical education from his father, then studied with Fuchs, Zemlinsky, and Grädener in Vienna. His progress was astounding; at the age of 12 he composed a Piano Trio, which was soon publ., revealing a competent technique and an ability to write in a style strongly influenced by Richard Strauss. About the same time he wrote (in piano score) a pantomime, *Der Schneemann;* it was orchestrated by Zemlinsky and performed at the Vienna Court Opera (Oct. 4, 1910), creating a sensation. In 1911 Nikisch conducted Korngold's *Schauspiel-Ouvertüre* with the Leipzig Gewandhaus Orch.; that same year the youthful composer gave a concert of his works in Berlin, appearing also as a pianist; his Sinfonietta was conducted by Weingartner and the Vienna Phil. in 1913. Korngold was not quite 19 when his 2 short operas, *Der Ring des Polykrates* and *Violanta,* were produced in Munich. His 1st lasting success came with the simultaneous premiere in Hamburg and Cologne of his opera *Die tote Stadt* (Dec. 4, 1920). In 1929 he began a fruitful collaboration with the director Max Reinhardt; in 1934 he went to Hollywood to arrange Mendelssohn's music for Reinhardt's film version of *A Midsummer Night's Dream.* He taught at the Vienna Academy of Music (1930–34) before settling in Hollywood. He became a naturalized U.S. citizen in 1943.

Korngold's music represents the last breath of the Romantic spirit of Vienna; it is marvelously consistent with the melodic, rhythmic, and harmonic style of the judicious modernity of the nascent 20th century. When Mahler heard him play some of his music as a young boy, he kept repeating: "Ein Genie! Ein Genie!" Korngold never altered his established idiom of composition, and was never tempted to borrow modernistic devices, except for some transitory passages in major seconds or an occasional whole-tone scale. After the early outbursts of incautious enthusiasms on the part of some otherwise circumspect critics nominating Korngold as a new Mozart, his star, its erupting nova, began to sink rapidly, until it became a melancholy consensus to dismiss his operas at their tardy revivals as derivative products of an era that had itself little to exhibit that was worthwhile. Ironically, his film scores, in the form of orchestral suites, experienced long after his death a spontaneous renascence, particularly on records, and especially among the unprejudiced and unopinionated American musical youth, who found in Korngold's music the stuff of their own new dreams.

WORKS: OPERAS: *Der Ring des Polykrates* and *Violanta* (Munich, March 28, 1916); *Die tote Stadt* (simultaneous premiere,

Hamburg and Cologne, Dec. 4, 1920); *Das Wunder der Heliane* (Hamburg, Oct. 7, 1927); *Die Kathrin* (Stockholm, Oct. 7, 1939); *Die stumme Serenade* (Dortmund, Dec. 5, 1954); pantomime, *Der Schneemann* (Vienna, Oct. 4, 1910). **ORCH.:** *Schauspiel-Ouvertüre* (Leipzig, 1911); Sinfonietta (Vienna, Nov. 28, 1913); Suite from the music to Shakespeare's *Much Ado about Nothing,* for Chamber Orch. (Vienna, 1919); *Sursum Corda,* symphonic overture (1919); Piano Concerto for Left Hand Alone (1923; written for Paul Wittgenstein); Cello Concerto (1946); Violin Concerto (St. Louis, Feb. 15, 1947, Heifetz soloist); *Symphonic Serenade* for String Orch. (1949); Sym. in F-sharp (1950; Munich, Nov. 27, 1972); *Theme and Variations* (1953). **CHAMBER:** Piano Trio (1910); Violin Sonata; String Sextet; Piano Quintet; 3 string quartets (1922, 1935, 1945); 3 piano sonatas (1908, 1910, 1932).

BIBL.: R. Hoffmann, *E.W. K.* (Vienna, 1923); L. Korngold, *E.W. K.. Ein Lebensbild* (Vienna, 1967); B. Carroll, "K.'s 'Violanta,' " *Musical Times* (Nov. 1980); idem, *E.W. K. 1897–1957: His Life and Works* (Paisley, 1984).

Korngold, Julius, noted Austrian music critic, father of **Erich Wolfgang Korngold;** b. Brünn, Dec. 24, 1860; d. Los Angeles, Sept. 25, 1945. He was a law student; at the same time he studied music with Franz Krenn at the Vienna Cons. In 1902 he became music critic of the influential *Neue Freie Presse,* which position he retained until 1934. He was much in the limelight when his son began his spectacular career at the age of 13 as a child composer, and an unfounded suspicion was voiced that Korngold was using his position to further his son's career. He publ. a book on contemporary German opera, *Deutsches Opernschaffen der Gegenwart* (1922). In 1938 he joined his son in the U.S., settling in Hollywood.

Kornmüller, Otto, German writer on music and composer; b. Straubing, Jan. 5, 1824; d. Metten, Feb. 13, 1907. He was ordained a priest in 1847; became choirmaster at Metten's Benedictine monastery (1858). He wrote masses and motets. He publ. *Lexikon der kirchlichen Tonkunst* (1870); *Der katholische Kirchenchor* (1868); *Die Musik beim liturgischen Hochamt* (1871).

Kórodi, András, Hungarian conductor; b. Budapest, May 24, 1922; d. Treviso, Sept. 17, 1986. He studied with Ferencsik (conducting) and Lajtha (composition) at the Budapest Academy of Music, where he later taught conducting (1957–82); was a conductor (1946–63) and principal conductor (1963–86) of the Hungarian State Opera in Budapest, where he led the premieres of many contemporary scores; was also conductor of the Budapest Phil. (1967–86).

Korte, Karl (Richard), American composer; b. Ossining, N.Y., Aug. 25, 1928. He studied at Illinois Wesleyan Univ. (1948–49); then took composition courses with Mennin and Bergsma at the Juilliard School of Music in N.Y. (B.S., 1953); in 1953 he went to Italy on a Fulbright grant and studied with Petrassi at the Accademia di Santa Cecilia in Rome. From 1954 to 1956 he was again a student at Juilliard, in the composition class of Persichetti (M.S., 1956); later took private lessons with Luening (1956–59), and also attended seminars given by Copland at the Berkshire Music Center in Tanglewood (1960, 1961). He was awarded Guggenheim fellowships (1960, 1970). He taught at Arizona State Univ. (1963–64), the State Univ. of N.Y. at Binghamton (1964–71), and the Univ. of Texas in Austin (from 1971), where he was co-director of its electronic music studio (from 1984). In 1985 he was a Fulbright lecturer on music in New Zealand. His music is quaquaversal in an attractively scientific manner, with the stylistic spectrum ranging from infrared, so to speak, in his archaically impressed works through the mandatory neo-Baroque essays to the ultraviolet rarefaction of mathematical conceits, abstractions, serialism, and electronics.

WORKS: ORCH.: Concertato on a Choral Theme (1955); *For a Young Audience* (1959); Sym. No. 2 (1961); *Southwest,* dance overture (1963); Sym. No. 3 (1968); Concerto for Piano and Wind Instruments (1976). **BAND:** *Ceremonial Prelude and Pas-*

sacaglia (1962); *Nocturne and March* (1962); *Prairie Song* for Trumpet and Band (1963); *Gestures* for Wind Ensemble, Amplified Double Bass, Percussion, and Piano (1970); *I Think You Would Have Understood* for Trumpet, Tape, and Band (1971); *Fibers* (1977). **CHAMBER:** 2 string quartets (1948, 1965); *Fantasy* for Violin and Piano (1959); Quintet for Oboe and Strings (1960); *Matrix* (1968); *Facets* (1969); *Remembrances* for Flute and Tape (1971); *Symmetrics* (1974); Trio for Piano, Violin, and Cello (1977; rev. 1982); Double Concerto for Flute, Double Bass, and Tape (1984); *Vochi*, trio for Clarinet, Violin, and Piano (1984); *Colloquy* for Flute and Tape (1987); *Evocation and Dance* for Trombone and Tape (1988). **VOCAL:** *Mass for Youth* for Women's Voices and Orch. (1963); *Aspects of Love* for Chorus (1968); *May the Sun Bless Us* for Men's Voices, Brass, and Percussion (1968); *Pale Is This Good Prince*, oratorio for Solo Voices, Chorus, 2 Pianos, and 4 Percussion (1973); *Of Time and Season* for Piano, Marimba, Solo Voices, and Chorus (1975); *Sappho Says* for Women's Voices, Solo Voice, Flute, and Piano (1980); *The Whistling Wind* for Mezzo-soprano and Tape (1983); *5 New Zealand Songs* for Voice and Piano (1989).

Korte, Oldřich František, Czech composer; b. Šala, Slovakia, April 26, 1926. During World War II, he was held in a concentration camp; after his release, he studied with Pícha, and later at the Prague Cons. He toured as a pianist and actor with the modernistic group Laterna Magica; he also worked as a photographer. His music is similarly quaquaversal and quite uninhibited in its methods and resources.

WORKS: *Iniuria* for Piano (1942–44); *The Drinker's Transformations*, variations for Piano (1945); Sinfonietta (1945–47); *In Praise of Death* for Piccolo and Glockenspiel (1948); *Příběh fléten* (The Story of the Flutes) for Orch. (1949–51; Prague Radio, Oct. 23, 1953); *Concerto grosso* for Strings, Trumpets, and Piano (1954–62; rev. 1968); *Philosophical Dialogues* for Violin and Piano (1964–68); 2-act musical, *The Pirates of the Fortune* (Vienna, April 15, 1974); *Kouzelný cirkus*, suite for Orch. (1977); *Canzona a Ritornel* for Orch. (1979); *Zrcadlení* for Orch. (1981–82).

Korte, Werner, German musicologist; b. Münster, May 29, 1906; d. there, Nov. 26, 1982. He studied mathematics, natural sciences, and musicology at the Univs. of Freiburg and Münster (1924–26); then took courses in musicology, art history, and philosophy at the Univ. of Berlin (1926–28), where his principal mentor was J. Wolf (Ph.D., 1928, with the diss. *Die Harmonik des frühen 15. Jahrhunderts in ihrem Zusammenhang mit der Formtechnik*; publ. in Münster, 1929). He completed his Habilitation in 1932 at the Univ. of Münster with his *Studien zur Geschichte der Musik in Italien im ersten Viertel des 15. Jahrhunderts* (publ. in Kassel, 1933). He was an assistant lecturer in musicology at the Univ. of Heidelberg (1928–31), then became director of the musicology dept. at the Univ. of Münster (1932), where he was made reader (1937) and prof. (1946).

WRITINGS: *Deutsche Musikerziehung in Vergangenheit und Gegenwart* (Danzig, 1932); *J.S. Bach* (Berlin, 1935); *Ludwig van Beethoven* (Berlin, 1936); *Robert Schumann* (Potsdam, 1937); *Musik und Weltbild* (Leipzig, 1940); *Händel und der deutsche Geist* (Leipzig, 1942); *Bruckner und Brahms: Die spätromantische Lösung der autonomen Konzeption* (Tutzing, 1963); *De musica: Monolog über die heutige Situation der Musik* (Tutzing, 1966).

Kortekangas, Olli, Finnish composer; b. Turku, May 16, 1955. He studied composition and theory with Einojuhani Rautavaara and Eero Hämeenniemi at the Sibelius Academy in Helsinki, and attended courses led by Dieter Schnebel in Berlin (1981–82). Returning to Helsinki, he taught at the Academy of Dramatic Art (1983–86), then joined the faculty of the Sibelius Academy.

WORKS: **STAGE:** *Short Story*, chamber opera (1979–80); *Grand Hotel*, opera (1984–85); incidental music. **ORCH.:** *Arr* for Strings (1980); *Fanfares* for 3 Instrumental Groups (1980); *Ökologie I: Vorspiel* (1983); *Ökologie 2: Konzert* (1986–87).

CHAMBER: *Threnody* for Horn and Piano (1977); *Emotion* for Brass Quintet (1982); *Konsequenz* for Violin and Piano (1982–83); *Sehr schnell* for Violin (1984). **VOCAL:** *Vihreä madonna* (The Green Madonna) for Choir (1975); *Stanzas* for Women's Choir, after C. Rossetti and D.H. Lawrence (1976); *Psalmi* for Soprano and Choir (1977); *Ave Maria . . . virgo serena* for Choir (1978); *Viideksän chorusta vaimolleni* (Choruses for My Wife) for 32 Solo Voices (1981); *Paraabeli* (Parable) for 5 Solo Men's Voices (1983); *Metamatiikkaa* for Soprano and Alto with Instruments ad libitum (1983); *Lumen valo* (The Glow of Snow) for Men's Choir (1984); *MAA* (Earth) for Children's Choir and Instruments (1984–85); *Kolme Waltarin tekstiä* (3 Texts of Waltari) for Choir (1985); keyboard works.

Kortschak, Hugo, Austrian-American violinist, conductor, and teacher; b. Graz, Feb. 24, 1884; d. Honolulu, Sept. 20, 1957. He studied violin with Ševčik at the Prague Cons.; went to America and in 1913 organized in Chicago the Kortschak Quartet, later renamed Berkshire String Quartet. He was head of the violin dept. at Yale Univ. (1924–52); then was a member of the Honolulu Sym. Orch.; was awarded the Coolidge Medal (1938).

Kortsen, Bjarne, Norwegian musicologist; b. Haugesund, July 4, 1930. He studied music and electrical engineering; was employed by the Norwegian railways while studying musicology at the Univ. of Oslo (M.A., 1962); later studied at the Univ. of Glasgow (Ph.D., 1964). He publ. *Fartein Valen, Life and Music* (3 vols., Oslo, 1965); *Modern Norwegian Chamber Music* (Haugesund, 1965); *Contemporary Norwegian Orchestral Music* (Berlin, 1969); *Chamber Music Works by Johan Svendsen* (Bergen, 1971).

Kósa, György, Hungarian pianist and composer; b. Budapest, April 24, 1897; d. there, Aug. 16, 1984. He exhibited a precocious talent for music, and when he was 10 years old studied piano privately with Bartók and then later with him at the Royal Academy of Music in Budapest (1908–15); also studied composition with Herzfeld and Kodály (1908–12) and piano with Dohnányi (1915–16) there. He was co-répétiteur at the Royal Opera House in Budapest (1916–17); then toured Europe and North Africa as a pianist (1917–20); subsequently was a theater conductor in Tripoli (1920–21). He then returned to Budapest as an accompanist (1921); from 1927 to 1960 he was prof. of piano at the Budapest Academy of Music, with the exception of a period during World War II when he was compelled to work as a manual laborer in a war camp. He was actively engaged in the promotion of modern Hungarian music; played both traditional and contemporary scores. He was awarded the Erkel Prize (1955); was made a Merited Artist (1963) and an Honored Artist (1972) of his homeland. As a composer he was initially influenced by Bartók, but he later developed an individualistic style of expressionism.

WORKS: **OPERAS:** *A király palástja* (The King's Robe; 1926); *Az két lovagok* (2 Knights), comic opera (1934; Budapest, 1936); *Cenodoxus*, mystery opera (1942); *Anselmus diák* (Student Anselmus; 1945); *Tartuffe*, comic opera (1951); *Pázmán lovag* (Knight Pázmán), comic opera (1962–63); *Kocsonya Mihály házassága* (The Marriage of Mihály Kocsonya), comic opera (1971); *Kiálts város* (City, Shout!; 1980–81). **BALLETS:** *Fehér Pierrot* (White Pierrot; 1916; Budapest, 1920); *Phaedra* (1918); *Dávid király* (King David; 1936); *Ének az örök bánatról* (Song about the Everlasting Sorrow; 1955). **PANTOMIMES:** *Mese a királykisasszonyról* (A Tale of a Princess; 1919); *Laterna Magica* (1922; Budapest, Feb. 23, 1927); *Árva Józsi három csodája* (The 3 Miracles of Józsi Árva; 1932; Budapest, Feb. 26, 1933). **ORCH.:** 9 syms. (1920, 1927, 1933, 1936, 1937, 1946, 1957, 1959, 1969); Suite (1915); Suite, *Ironic Portraits* (1924); Concerto for Piano, Violin, Cymbals, Percussion, and Orch. (1973). **CHORAL: ORATORIOS:** *Jonah* (1931); *Easter Oratorio* (1932); *Saulus* (1935); *Joseph*, chamber oratorio (1939); *Elijah*, chamber oratorio (1940); *Christus*, chamber oratorio (1943); *Hajnóczy* (1954); *Villon* (1960). **CANTATAS:** *Laodomeia* (1924); *Job* (1933); *Küldetés* (Mission; 1948); *Szól az úr* (The Lord Is Saying; 1957); *Amor sanctus* (1958); 2 cantatas (1964); *Cantata* *humana* (1967); *Johannes* (1972); 2 cantatas (1973–74); Cantata (1974). *OTHER WORKS: Dies irae* (1937); 2 masses (1946, 1949); *Requiem* (1949); *Te Deum* (1949); *De profundis* (1970). **CHAMBER:** 8 string quartets (1920, 1929, 1933, 1936, 1956, 1959, 1963, 1965); Quintet for Harp and Winds (1938); Trio for Flute, Viola, and Cello (1946); Trio for Soprano, Clarinet, and Violin (1947); Wind Quintet (1960); *Duo* for Violin and Cello (1964); Sonata for Cello and Piano (1965); 6 *Intermezzos* for String Trio (1969); *Dialogus* for Bass Tuba and Marimba (1975). He also wrote 3 piano sonatas (1941, 1947, 1956) and other piano music, as well as some 500 songs.

BIBL.: M. Pandi, *K. G.* (Budapest, 1966).

Kosakoff, Reuven, American pianist and composer; b. New Haven, Conn., Jan. 8, 1898; d. N.Y., May 6, 1987. He studied at Yale Univ. and at the Juilliard School of Music in N.Y.; then went to Berlin as a private piano student of Artur Schnabel. He wrote several biblical cantatas; 2 Sabbath services; Piano Concerto on Hebrew themes (Pittsburgh, March 24, 1941); *Jack and the Beanstalk* for Narrator and Orch. (New Haven, April 22, 1944).

Koschat, Thomas, Austrian bass and composer; b. Viktring, near Klagenfurt, Aug. 8, 1845; d. Vienna, May 19, 1914. He sang in church choirs. He publ. his 1st vocal quartets in the Carinthian dialect in 1871; they became so successful that he publ. some 100 more. In 1875 he organized the famous Kärntner Quintett with 4 other singers; their performances were exceedingly popular. His "Liederspiel" *Am Wörthersee* (Vienna, March 22, 1880), containing many of his favorite vocal numbers, had great vogue; he also produced a 4-act "Volksstück mit Gesang," *Die Rosenthaler Nachtigall*, and the singspiel *Der Bürgermeister von St. Anna* (Vienna, May 1, 1884; given in Italian as *Un colpo di fuoco*).

BIBL.: K. Krobath, *T. K., der Sänger Kärnthners* (Leipzig, 1912).

Köselitz, Johann Heinrich, German writer and composer; b. Annaberg, Jan. 10, 1854; d. there, Aug. 15, 1918. He studied with Richter at the Leipzig Cons. While in Basel, he formed a close friendship with Nietzsche, from whom he also took lessons in composition; after Nietzsche's death, Köselitz became his literary executor; ed. Nietzsche's letters. As a composer, he elaborated the Wagnerian system of *Leitmotive;* he used the pen name of Peter Gast for his musical productions, among them the operas *Wilbraum und Siegeheer* (1879); *Scherz, List und Rache* (1881); *Die heimliche Ehe* (Danzig, 1891; publ. in 1901 as *Der Löwe von Venedig*); *König Wenzel* (not produced); and *Orpheus und Dionysos* (not produced); a festival play, *Walpurgisnacht* (1903); a symphonic poem, *Helle Nächte;* choruses; songs.

BIBL.: L. Brieger-Wasservogel, *Peter Gast* (Leipzig, 1906); F. Götz, *Peter Gast* (Annaberg, 1934); F. Tutenberg, "Peter Gasts Löwe von Venedig," *Zeitschrift für Musik* (Feb. 1940).

Koshetz, Nina (Pavlovna), Russian-American soprano; b. Kiev, Dec. 30, 1894; d. Santa Ana, Calif., May 14, 1965. Her father, Paul Koshetz, was a tenor; she began piano study when she was 4 and gave her 1st recital at 9; then enrolled at the Moscow Cons. at 11, studying piano with Konstantin Igumnov and Vasili Safonov and singing with Enzo Masetti; later studied with Félia Litvinne. She toured Russia with Rachmaninoff, of whose songs she was a congenial interpreter; also toured with Koussevitzky and his orch.; made her operatic debut as Donna Anna at the Imperial Opera in St. Petersburg (1913); toured the U.S. with the Ukrainian National Chorus, under the conductorship of her brother (1920); then settled there. She sang the role of Fata Morgana in the 1st performance of Prokofiev's *The Love for 3 Oranges* (Chicago, Dec. 30, 1921); subsequently devoted herself mainly to concert appearances; later taught voice.

BIBL.: J. Dennis, "N.P. K.," *Record Collector*, XVII (1967–68; with discography).

Kosleck, Julius, German trumpeter, cornetist, and pedagogue; b. Neugard, Dec. 3, 1825; d. Berlin, Nov. 5, 1904. He

was a trumpeter in the Berlin Königliche Kapelle (1853–93); also taught trumpet and trombone at the Berlin Hochschule für Musik (1872–1903); was founder of the Kaiser-Kornettquartett (c.1885), which became the Kosleck'sche Bläserbund (1890). He promoted the so-called Bach Trumpet, and played it in a performance of the Bach Mass in B minor in London (1885). He publ. the method *Grosse Schule für Cornet à piston und Trompete* (Leipzig, 1872; Eng. tr., c.1907, by W. Morrow).

Košler, Zdeněk, prominent Czech conductor; b. Prague, March 25, 1928. He studied in Prague with Grünfeldová (piano), Jeremiáš and Řídký (theory and composition), and Dědeček (conducting); then took conducting courses with Ančerl, Brock, and Doležil at the Academy of Music (1948–52). He made his conducting debut at the National Theater of Prague with *Il barbiere di Siviglia* (1951), and conducted there until 1958; then conducted the Olomouc (1958–62) and Ostrava (1962–66) operas. He was chief conductor of the Prague Sym. Orch. (1966–67); also served as Generalmusikdirektor of the Komische Oper in East Berlin (1966–68); then was chief conductor of the Slovak National Theater in Bratislava (1971–79). He was chief conductor of the Prague National Theater from 1980 to 1985; in 1989 he resumed that position there. In 1974 he was made an Artist of Merit and in 1984 a National Artist by the Czech government. He is especially noted for his idiomatic performances of the Czech operatic and symphonic repertoire.

Kosma, Joseph, Hungarian-French composer; b. Budapest, Oct. 22, 1905; d. La Roche-Guyon, near Paris, Aug. 7, 1969. He studied at the Budapest Academy of Music; then with Eisler in Berlin (1929); settled in Paris (1933).

WORKS: Ballets: *Le Rendez-vous* (Paris, June 15, 1945); *Baptiste* (1946); *L'Ecuyère* (1948); *Le Pierrot de Montmartre* (1952); film scores to *La Grande Illusion, Les Enfants du paradis*, etc.; comic operas: *Les Chansons de Bilitis* (1954); *Un Amour électronique* (Paris, 1962); *La Révolte des canuts* (Lyons, 1964); *Les Hussards* (Lyons, Oct. 21, 1969); an oratorio, *Les Ponts de Paris* (1947); piano pieces; songs.

Kössler, Hans. See **Koessler, Hans.**

Kossmaly, Carl, German conductor, composer, and writer on music; b. Breslau, July 27, 1812; d. Stettin, Dec. 1, 1893. He studied in Berlin with Berger, Zelter, and Klein; eventually settled in Stettin as a conductor and teacher. He wrote syms., overtures, songs, etc. He publ. *Schlesisches Tonkünstler-Lexikon* (1846–47); *Mozarts Opern* (1848); *Über die Anwendung des Programmes zur Erklärung musikalischer Compositionen* (1858); *Über Richard Wagner* (1873).

Kostelanetz, André, highly successful Russian-born American conductor, uncle of **Richard Kostelanetz;** b. St. Petersburg, Dec. 22, 1901; d. Port-au-Prince, Haiti, Jan. 13, 1980. He studied at the St. Petersburg Cons. In 1922 he left Russia and went to the U.S., becoming a naturalized American citizen (1928). He was employed as a rehearsal accompanist at the Metropolitan Opera in N.Y.; then came to prominence as a conductor on the radio; appeared regularly with the CBS Sym. Orch. (from 1930); enjoyed tremendous success with his own orch. on radio and recordings, making the lush "Kostelanetz sound" and arrangements his trademark. He married the soprano **Lily Pons** in 1938, but they subsequently were divorced. During World War II, he conducted many concerts for the U.S. armed forces. He later appeared as a guest conductor with leading orchs. in North America, Europe, Israel, and Japan. He also conducted popular concerts in America and in Europe; made successful arrangements of light music, his technique of massive concentration of instrumental sonorities and of harmonic saturation by means of filling in harmonies with inner thirds and sixths having influence upon film music. An intelligent musician, he commissioned special works from American composers, of which the most successful was Copland's *Lincoln Portrait*. With G. Hammond, he wrote *Echoes: Memoirs of André Kostelanetz* (N.Y., 1981).

Kostelanetz, Richard, versatile American music critic, writer on contemporary music and the arts, and composer, nephew of **André Kostelanetz**; b. N.Y., May 14, 1940. He studied American civilization and history at Brown Univ. (A.B., 1962) and Columbia Univ. (M.A., 1966); was a Fulbright scholar at King's College, Univ. of London (1964–65), and also attended classes at London's Morley College and the New School in N.Y. He lectured at Harvard Univ., Wellesley College, Carnegie-Mellon Univ., and the Univ. of Calif. at Santa Cruz, among other institutions. His extensive list of publications includes articles, books, poetry, fiction, plays, and experimental prose; among his numerous anthologies on contemporary American arts are several with emphasis on music, including *The Theatre of Mixed Means* (N.Y., 1968), *Master Minds* (N.Y., 1969), *Conversing with Cage* (N.Y., 1988), and *On Innovative Musicians* (N.Y., 1989). Included in his compositional output are audiotapes and videotapes as well as a number of films and holograms, many of which have been exhibited and broadcast around the world. He was a visiting artist at Syracuse Univ. (1975), the Electronic Music Studio of Stockholm (1981–88), and the Experimental Television Center in Oswego, N.Y. (1985–90). He wrote numerous theatrical (*Epiphanies*, 1980) and performance (*Central Park*, 1980) texts; also composed choreographic works (*Invocations*, 1985). He prepared extended features for radio, and his work has appeared in both solo and group exhibitions. Among his awards are a Pulitzer fellowship for critical writing (1965), a Guggenheim fellowship (1967), and annual ASCAP stipends (from 1983). His compositions include audiocassette eds. (*The 8 Nights of Hanukah/ Praying to the Lord*, 1983; *Onomatopoeia*, 1988; *Carnival of the Animals/Karneval der Tiere*, 1988) and hörspiels (*Die Evangelien*, 1982; *Invocations*, 1983; *New York City*, 1984; *The Gospels Abridged*, 1986; *Kaddish*, 1990), many of which were commissioned by the West German Radio; also *Lovings* (1990). His videotapes, for which he customarily provides the visuals, include *3 Prose Pieces* (1975), *Epiphanies* (1980), *Seductions/ Relationships* (1987), and *Kinetic Writings* (1989). He describes his critical writings and his art as both "avant-garde" and "anarchist libertarian."

Kostić, Dušan, Croatian composer; b. Zagreb, Jan. 23, 1925. He studied at the Belgrade Academy of Music (1947–55); later took a course in conducting with Scherchen in Bayreuth (1955). He was music ed. for Radio Belgrade (1957–59); then taught at his alma mater (from 1964). He incorporated neo-Classical, impressionistic, and serial techniques in his music; also wrote occasional pieces on national folk themes.

WORKS: 2 syms. (1957, 1961); symphonic poem, *Contrasts* (1954); *Crnogorska suita* for Orch. (1957); *Sonata amorosa* for Violin and Piano (1957); opera buffa, *Majstori su prvi ljudi* (Belgrade, April 23, 1962); *Kragujevac*, symphonic poem for Voices and Orch., commemorating the execution of the schoolboys at Kragujevac in 1941 by the Nazi occupation forces (Belgrade, Feb. 5, 1962); choruses; songs; piano pieces.

Kostić, Vojislav, Serbian composer; b. Belgrade, Sept. 21, 1931. He studied in his native city; adopted a sophisticated style of utilitarian music. His *Karakteri* for Clarinet, Piano, and 18 Percussion Instruments (1958) had numerous performances in Yugoslavia. He also wrote a Divertimento for Wind Quintet; Suite for Bassoon and Piano; *Cíganska pri-ča* (Gypsy Tale) for Male Chorus and Chamber Orch., to Gypsy texts (1964).

Köstlin, Heinrich Adolf, German theologian and choral conductor; b. Tübingen, Oct. 4, 1846; d. Cannstadt, June 4, 1907. He was the son of **Josephine Lang-Köstlin** (1815–80), the song composer. In 1875 he united the choirs of 3 towns (Sulz, Kalw, Nagold) for church music performances, which became the nucleus of the Württemberg Evangelical "Kirchengesangverein" (1877); with L. Hallwachs, he organized a similar society for all of Germany (1883). He publ. *Geschichte der Musik im Umriss* (1873; 6th ed., rev. by W. Nagel, 1910); *Die Tonkunst: Einführung in die Ästhetik der Musik* (1878); *Luther als Vater des evangelischen Kirchenliedes* (1882); *Geschichte des christlichen Gottesdienstes* (1886); also a biographical sketch of his mother (Leipzig, 1881).

Kostov, Georgi, Bulgarian composer; b. Sofia, Jan. 21, 1941. He studied composition with Vladigerov and Stoyanov at the Bulgarian State Cons. in Sofia, graduating in 1966; pursued his studies at the Moscow Cons. (1972); then taught at his alma mater.

WORKS: Ballet, *The Broadside of "Avrora"* (1967); 2 oratorios: *Glorious Days* (1969) and *Alive He Is* (1976); 2 cantatas: *The Communist Man* (1964) and *We Are Proud of You, Our Party* (1975); Clarinet Concerto (1958); Viola Concertino (1965); Concerto for Horn, String Orch., and Timpani (1966); *Youth Overture* (1967); *3 Diaphonous Dances* for Orch. (1972); *Poem* for Trumpet, Percussion, and String Orch. (1973); *Prelude, Chorale, and Fugue* for Orch. (1974); *Rhythmic Movements* for Orch. (1974); *Antiphonous Dialogues* for Orch. (1974); *September Ballad* for Orch. (1974); chamber music; choral songs; popular music.

Kosugi, Takehisa, inventive Japanese composer and violinist; b. Tokyo, March 24, 1938. He studied at the Tokyo Univ. of Fine Arts and Music, then founded the group Ongaku, which introduced mixed-media improvisational performance in Japan. In 1969 he founded the Taj Mahal Travelers ("TMT"), with which he toured in India, the Near East, and Europe; upon returning to Japan, the group frequently participated in rock and jazz festivals. In 1976 Kosugi was invited to compose for the Merce Cunningham Dance Co., and, after moving to the U.S. in 1977, appeared in performances with John Cage and David Tudor. Kosugi regularly creates installations in which he employs acoustic and self-designed electronic instruments; his esthetic premise is that a performance must make the invisible aspects of a given situation perceptible, audible, and tangible, revealing what is hidden and enabling sounds to be seen as well as heard. In this original capacity he has performed since 1978 in Paris, Rome, Berlin, Bremen, Cologne, and London. Among his commissioned works for the Merce Cunningham Dance Co. are *S.E. Wave/E.W. Song* (1976), *Interspersion* (1979), *Cycles* (1981), *Spacings* (1984), *Assemblage* (1986), *Rhapsody* (1987), and *Spectra* (1989). His major installations include *Interspersions* for 54 Sounds (1980), *Spacings* (audiovisual version; 1985), and *Loops* (1988). As a violinist, he made a remarkable recording, entitled simply *Violin Improvisations*, issued in 1990 by Lovely Music in N.Y.

Kotek, (Eduard) Joseph (actually, **Yosif Yosifovich**), Russian violinist and composer; b. Kamenets-Podolsk, Nov. 11, 1855; d. Davos, Switzerland, Jan. 4, 1885. He studied violin with Ferdinand Laub and composition with Tchaikovsky at the Moscow Cons.; later took violin lessons with Joachim in Berlin. He was a close friend of Tchaikovsky, and often served as mediator in financial matters between him and Nadezhda von Meck; also worked over the solo part of Tchaikovsky's Violin Concerto, and played it with the composer at the piano, privately, in Clarens, Switzerland (April 3, 1878); however, he was reluctant to try it out in public performance despite Tchaikovsky's urgings. He taught violin at the Berlin Hochschule für Musik (1878–82). He was stricken with tuberculosis at the age of 29; Tchaikovsky made a special trip to Davos to see him before Kotek's death.

Köth, Erika, German soprano; b. Darmstadt, Sept. 15, 1925; d. Speyer, Feb. 20, 1989. She studied with Elsa Blank in Darmstadt; after winning 1st prize in a Hessische Radio competition (1947), she made her debut as Adele in a radio broadcast in Darmstadt; made her stage debut as Philine in *Mignon* in Kaiserslautern (1948); then sang in Karlsruhe (1950–53). She then appeared with the Bavarian State Opera in Munich, the Vienna State Opera, and in Berlin; taught at the Cologne Hochschule für Musik (from 1973).

Kothe, Aloys, German teacher and composer, brother of **Bernhard** and **Wilhelm Kothe**; b. Gröbnig, Oct. 3, 1828; d. Breslau, Nov. 13, 1868. He studied with Grell in Berlin; taught at the Breslau Teachers' Seminary. He wrote a Mass for Men's Voices, songs, piano pieces, etc.

Kothe, Bernhard, German teacher and composer, brother of **Aloys** and **Wilhelm Kothe**; b. Gröbnig, May 12, 1821; d.

Breslau, July 25, 1897. He studied with A.B. Marx in Berlin; became church music director and teacher in Oppeln (1851); then a teacher at the Breslau Teachers' Seminary (1868). He wrote motets and organ pieces.

Kothe, Wilhelm, German teacher and composer, brother of **Aloys** and **Bernhard Kothe;** b. Gröbnig, Jan. 8, 1831; d. Habelschwerdt, Dec. 31, 1897. He studied organ in Berlin; taught at the Habelschwerdt Teachers' Seminary (1871–97). He wrote songs and piano pieces.

Kothen, Karl Axel, Finnish singer and composer; b. Frederikshamm, Aug. 15, 1871; d. Helsinki, July 7, 1927. He studied in Helsinki, Rome, St. Petersburg, Vienna, Paris, and Munich; was prof. of singing at the Helsinki Cons. (from 1908). He wrote several choral works, among them *Vagorna sjunga* and *Finlands namn* (both for the Finland Jubilee of 1920); also a cantata for the festival of the tercentenary of Vasa; incidental music to *Kristina Vasa;* piano pieces and songs.

Kotík, Petr, Czech-born American flutist and composer; b. Prague, Jan. 27, 1942. He studied flute with Frantisek Cech at the Prague Cons. (B.A., 1962) and at the Prague Academy of Music (M.A., 1969); also had lessons in composition with Jan Rychlik in Prague, and in flute with Hans Resnicek (M.A., 1966) at the Vienna Academy of Music; studied composition at the Vienna Academy of Music with Karl Schiske, Hans Jelinek, and Friedrich Cerha (B.A., 1966). In 1961 he founded Musica Viva Pragensis, and in 1966 the Prague experimental music ensemble QUAX. He went to the U.S. in 1969; became a naturalized citizen in 1977. From 1969 to 1974 he was a member of the Center of the Creative and Performing Arts at the State Univ. of N.Y. in Buffalo. In 1970 he founded the S.E.M. Ensemble, with which he toured in the U.S. and abroad; also toured as a solo flutist. He taught flute (1971–77) and composition (1976–77) at the State Univ. of N.Y. in Buffalo; also taught composition at York Univ. in Toronto (1975–76). In 1983 he settled in N.Y.; continued to tour with the S.E.M. Ensemble and as a soloist. **WORKS:** *Congo* for Flute, Oboe, Clarinet, Bassoon, Viola, Cello, and Double Bass (1962; Prague, Jan. 18, 1963); *Spontano* for Piano and 10 Wind Instruments (1964; Buffalo, May 22, 1973); *6 Plums* for Orch. (1965–68); *Contraband* for Live Electronics and 2 to 6 Performers (Cologne, April 28, 1967); *Aria,* tape or theater piece (1969; Buffalo, May 27, 1971); *There Is Singularly Nothing,* 21 solos for Ensemble (1971–73); *John Mary* for 2 Voices, 3 Melodic Instruments, and Percussionist (Witten, April 27, 1974); *Many Many Women* for 2, 4, or 6 Singers and 2, 4, or 6 Instruments (1975–78); *Drums* for Percussion Ensemble (1977–81); *Explorations in the Geometry of Thinking* for Vocal Ensemble (1978–82); *August/October* for Viola or Cello and Ensemble (1981; rev. as *Apparent Orbit,* 1981–85); *Integrated Solo* for Flute, Tambourine, Trumpet, and Keyboard (1986–88); *Wilsie Bridge* for Winds, Keyboards, and Percussion (N.Y., Jan. 13, 1987); *Letters to Olga* for 5 Voices, Flute, Trumpet, and 3 Guitars (1989).

Kotilainen, Otto, Finnish composer; b. Heinävesi, Feb. 5, 1868; d. Helsinki, Aug. 9, 1936. He studied with Wegelius and Sibelius at the Helsinki Cons.; then in Berlin. He wrote an orch. suite; *Legend* for String Orch.; incidental music; choral works; chamber music; songs.

Kotoński, Wlodzimierz, Polish composer; b. Warsaw, Aug. 23, 1925. He studied theory with Piotr Rytel at the Warsaw Cons. (1945–51); also privately with Tadeusz Szeligowski in Poznan (1950–51); later took courses in Darmstadt (1957–60). In the meantime, he began experimenting with alteration of sound by electronic means; produced an *Étude concrète* in which a single stroke of cymbals was electronically metamorphosed and expanded into a work of considerable length (1949). He did research in Polish folk music at the State Inst. of Art (1951–59); then studied the problems of musique concrète with Pierre Schaeffer in Paris. He subsequently worked at the Electronic Music Studio of the West German Radio in Cologne (1966–67); taught electronic music at the Warsaw

Cons. (from 1967) and also lectured at the State Univ. of N.Y. at Buffalo (1978). In 1983 he became president of the Polish Soc. for Contemporary Music. He publ. *Instrumenty perkusyjne we wspólczesnej orkiestrze* (Percussion Instruments in the Modern Orchestra; Krakow, 1963). **WORKS:** *Étude concrète* for a single stroke of Cymbals electronically metamorphosed (1949; Darmstadt, July 9, 1960); *Poème* for Orch. (1949); *Danses montagnardes* for Orch. (1950); *Prelude and Passacaglia* for Orch. (1953); *6 Miniatures* for Clarinet and Piano (1957); *Chamber Music* for 21 Instruments and Percussion (Warsaw, Oct. 2, 1958); *Musique en relief,* cycle of 5 miniatures for 6 Orch. Groups (Darmstadt, Sept. 5, 1959); *Concerto per quattro* for Harp, Harpsichord, Guitar, Piano, and Chamber Orch. (1960); *Canto* for 18 Instruments (1961); *Selection I* for 4 Jazz Players (1962); 2 wind quintets (1964, 1967); *Monochromie* for Oboe (1964); *A battere* for Guitar, Viola, Cello, Harpsichord, and Percussion (1966); *Pour quatre* for Clarinet, Trombone, Cello, and Piano (1968); *Music for 16 Cymbals and Strings* (Warsaw, Sept. 20, 1969); *Multiplay,* instrumental theater for Brass Quintet (1971); Oboe Concerto (1972); *Promenade* for Clarinet, Trombone, and Cello, all electronically amplified, and 2 Synthesizers (1973); *Wind Rose* for Orch. (1976); *Spring Music* for Flute, Oboe, Violin, and Synthesizer (1978); *Bora* for Orch. (1979); *Sirocco* for Orch. (1981); *Terra incognita* for Orch. (1984); *Textures* for Computer (1984); *Lyric Scenes* for 9 Performers (1986); *Tialoc,* duo for Harpsichord and Percussion (1987); *Birds,* 8 pieces for Clarinet, Cello, and Piano (1988).

Kotter, Hans (Johannes), Alsatian organist and composer; b. Strasbourg, c.1485; d. Bern, 1541. He studied organ with Paul Hofhaimer; was organist at the electoral court in Torgau; then of the collegiate church of St. Nikolaus in Fribourg from 1514 until being banished in 1530 for espousing the doctrines of Zwingli. In 1534 Kotter was able to return to Switzerland; became a Bern schoolmaster. He compiled a collection of keyboard pieces in tablature (1513), including preambles, fantasies, dances, transcriptions of vocal music, and settings of plainchant; his setting of a *Nobis post hoc* was interpolated in a *Salve Regina* by Hofhaimer. See H. Marx, ed., *Tabulaturen des XVI. Jahrhunderts,* I: *Die Tabulaturen aus dem Besitz des Basler Humanisten Bonifacius Amerbach,* Schweizerische Musikdenkmäler, VI (1967). **BIBL.:** W. Merian, *Die Tabulaturen des Organisten H. K.* (Leipzig, 1916); W. Gurlitt, "J. K. und sein Freiburger Tabulaturbuch von 1513," *Elsass-Lothringisches Jahrbuch,* XIX (1941); M. Schuler, "Ein Beitrag zur Biographie H. K.s," *Die Musikforschung,* XXII (1969).

Kottlitz, Adolf, German violinist; b. Trier, Sept. 27, 1820; killed while hunting in Uralsk, Russia, Oct. 26, 1860. He began his career as a child prodigy; gave public concerts at the age of 10; spent 3 years in Paris, where he was a protégé of Liszt; then played violin in the orch. of the Königsberg Opera (1848–56). In 1856 he made a tour of Russia; settled in Uralsk as a violin teacher. He publ. 2 string quartets. His wife, Clothilde (née Ellendt; 1822–67), was a singing teacher in Königsberg.

Kotzolt, Heinrich, German vocal teacher and composer; b. Schnellewalde, Aug. 26, 1814; d. Berlin, July 2, 1881. He first studied philology in Breslau, but turned to music, studying in Berlin with Dehn and Rungenhagen (1836–38); then sang at the Danzig Opera (1838–42). Returning to Berlin, he founded a singing society in 1849. He publ. a method for a cappella singing; also composed a setting of the 54th Psalm for Double Chorus a cappella; *Lobet den Herrn alle Heiden* for 8-part Chorus; etc.

Kotzschmar, Hermann, German-American organist, conductor, teacher, and composer; b. Finsterwalde, July 4, 1829; d. Portland, Maine, April 12, 1909. He studied piano, organ, and violin with his father and then in Dresden. In 1848 he went to the U.S. as a member of the Saxonia Band; after its demise, he went to Portland, Maine, as a conductor of the 4-man band at the Union Street Theater (1849); was organist of the 1st Unitarian Church (1851–98) and conductor of the Haydn Soc. (from 1869). He was also active as a teacher; J.K. Paine was one of his students. He wrote sacred music, vocal quartets, songs, piano pieces, etc.

BIBL.: G. Edwards, *Music and Musicians of Maine* (Portland, Maine, 1928).

Kouguell, Arkadie, Russian-American pianist and composer; b. Simferopol, Dec. 25, 1898; d. Glen Head, L.I., N.Y., Nov. 20, 1985. He studied at the St. Petersburg Cons.; lived in Beirut (1928–48) and Paris (1948–52), then settled in N.Y. as a piano teacher.

WORKS: *Impressions of Damascus* for Orch. (1930); Piano Concerto (1930); *Bédouin Dance* for 60 Cellos (1932); Piano Concerto for Left Hand (1934); *Rapsodi tartare* for Orch. (1947); Cello Concerto (1950); Concertino for Trombone and Piano (1956); suites for various chamber groups; chamber music; etc.

Koukouzeles, Joannes, famous singer and composer of Byzantine chant; b. Dyrrachium, c.1280; d. probably in Great Laura, Mount Athos, between 1360 and 1375. Although his surname has been given as Papadopoulos in some sources, there is no reason to believe that he was of Greek origin; he most likely was of Slavonic descent. While still a boy, he was sent to the imperial school in Constantinople by the Byzantine emperor; following his studies, he established himself as a celebrated singer at the Constantinople court, becoming renowned as the angelophonos (angel voice) of the age; he eventually turned his back on the secular world to pursue a monastic life in the Great Laura, on the southern slopes of Mount Athos. In his epoch he was the foremost composer of chants, many of which appeared in various anthologies from the middle of the 14th century on.

BIBL.: E. Williams, *John K.'s Reform of Byzantine Chanting for Great Vespers in the Fourteenth Century* (diss., Yale Univ., 1968).

Kounadis, Arghyris, Greek composer; b. Constantinople, Feb. 14, 1924. He was taken to Athens in his infancy; studied piano at home and then with S. Farandatos at the Athens Cons. (graduated, 1952); also studied law at the Univ. of Athens. After studying composition with Yannis Papaioannou at Athens's Hellenic Cons. (graduated, 1956), he continued his studies with Fortner in Freiburg (1958–61). In 1963 he joined the faculty of the Freiburg Hochschule für Musik, becoming a prof. there in 1972.

WORKS: THEATER: *Der Gummisarg* (1968); *Die verhexten Notenständer* (1971); *Der Ausbruch* (1975); *Die Bassgeige* (1979; rev. 1987); *Lysistrata,* after Aristophanes (1983); *Der Sandmann* (1986). **ORCH:** *Chorikon I* (1958) and *II* (1960); *Triptychon* (1964); *Heterophonika Idiomela* (1967). **VOCAL:** *Quattro pezzi per trio et soprano* (1968); *Die Nachtigall* for Soprano and 10 or More Double Basses (1975); *9 Gedichte des M. Sochtouris* for Bass, Chorus, and Instrumental Ensemble (1980).

Koussevitzky, Serge (Alexandrovich), celebrated Russian-born American conductor; b. Vishny-Volochok, July 26, 1874; d. Boston, June 4, 1951. His father and his 3 brothers were all amateur musicians. Koussevitzky learned to play the trumpet and took part, with his brothers, in a small wind ensemble, numbering 8 members in all; they earned their living by playing at balls and weddings and occasionally at village fairs. At the age of 14 he went to Moscow; since Jews were not allowed to live there, he became baptized. He then received a fellowship with free tuition at the Musico-Dramatic Inst. of the Moscow Phil. Soc., where he studied double bass with Ramboušek; he also studied music theory with Blaramberg and Kruglikov. In 1894 he joined the orch. of the Bolshoi Theater, succeeding Ramboušek as principal double-bass player in 1901, retaining that post until 1905. In the meantime, he became known as a soloist of the 1st magnitude; made his public debut in Moscow on March 25, 1901. He garnered great attention with a double-bass recital in Berlin on March 27, 1903. To supplement the meager repertoire for his instrument, he arranged various

works; also wrote several pieces. With some aid from Glière, he wrote a Double-bass Concerto, which he performed for the 1st time in Moscow on Feb. 25, 1905. On Sept. 8, 1905, he married Natalie Ushkov, daughter of a wealthy tea-merchant family. He soon resigned from the orch. of the Bolshoi Theater; in an open letter to the Russian publication *Musical Gazette,* he explained the reason for his resignation as the economic and artistic difficulties in the orch. He then went to Germany, where he continued to give double-bass recitals; played the 1st Cello Concerto by Saint-Saëns on the double bass. In 1907 he conducted a student orch. at the Berlin Hochschule für Musik; his 1st public appearance as a conductor took place on Jan. 23, 1908, with the Berlin Phil. In 1909 he established a publishing house, Editions Russes de Musique; in 1915 he purchased the catalog of the Gutheil Co.; among composers with whom he signed contracts were Scriabin, Stravinsky, Prokofiev, Medtner, and Rachmaninoff; the association with Scriabin was particularly fruitful, and in subsequent years Koussevitzky became the greatest champion of Scriabin's music. In 1909 he organized his own sym. orch. in Moscow, featuring works by Russian composers, but also including classical masterpieces; played many Russian works for the 1st time, among them Scriabin's *Prometheus.* In the summer of 1910 he took his orch. to the towns along the Volga River in a specially chartered steamboat. He repeated the Volga tour in 1912 and 1914. The outbreak of World War I in 1914 made it necessary to curtail his activities; however, he continued to give his concerts in Moscow; in 1915 he presented a memorial Scriabin program. After the Revolution of 1917, he was offered the directorship of the State Sym. Orch. (former Court Orch.) in Petrograd; he conducted it until 1920; also presented concerts in Moscow, despite the hardships of the revolutionary times. In 1920 he left Russia; went first to Berlin, then to Rome, and finally to Paris, where he organized the Concerts Koussevitzky with a specially assembled orch.; presented many new scores by French and Russian composers, among them Ravel's orchestration of Mussorgsky's *Pictures at an Exhibition,* Honegger's *Pacific 231,* and several works by Prokofiev and Stravinsky. In 1924 Koussevitzky was appointed the conductor of the Boston Sym. Orch., a position he held with great eminence until 1949. Just as in Russia he championed Russian composers, in France the French, so in the U.S. he encouraged American composers to write works for him. Symphonic compositions by Copland, Harris, Piston, Barber, Hanson, Schuman, and others were performed by Koussevitzky for the 1st time. For the 50th anniversary of the Boston Sym. Orch. (1931), he commissioned works from Stravinsky (*Symphony of Psalms*), Hindemith, Honegger, Prokofiev, Roussel, Ravel (piano concerto), Copland, Gershwin, and others. A highly important development in Koussevitzky's American career was the establishment of the Berkshire Music Center at Tanglewood, Mass. This was an outgrowth of the Berkshire Sym. Festival, organized in 1934 by Henry Hadley; Koussevitzky and the Boston Sym. Orch. presented summer concerts at the Berkshire Festival in 1935 for the 1st time; since then, the concerts have become an annual institution. The Berkshire Music Center was opened on July 8, 1940, with Koussevitzky as director and Copland as assistant director; among the distinguished guest instructors were Hindemith, Honegger, and Messiaen; Koussevitzky himself taught conducting; he was succeeded after his death by his former student Leonard Bernstein.

Koussevitzky held many honorary degrees: Mus.Doc. from Brown Univ. (1926), Rutgers Univ. (1937), Yale Univ. (1938), Univ. of Rochester (1940), Williams College (1943), and Boston Univ. (1945); LL.D. from Harvard Univ. (1929) and Princeton Univ. (1947). He was a member of the French Legion of Honor and held the Cross of Commander of the Finnish Order of the White Rose. He became a naturalized American citizen on April 16, 1941. His wife died in 1942; he established the Koussevitzky Foundation as a memorial to her, the funds to be used for commissioning works by composers of all nationalities. He married Olga Naoumoff (1901–78), a niece of Natalie Koussevitzky, on Aug. 15, 1947.

As a conductor, Koussevitzky possessed an extraordinary emotional power; in Russian music, and particularly in Tchaikovsky's syms., he was unexcelled; he was capable of achieving the subtlest nuances in the works of the French school; his interpretations of Debussy were notable. As a champion of modern music, he had few equals in his time; his ardor in projecting unfamiliar music before new audiences in different countries served to carry conviction among the listeners and the professional music critics. He was often criticized for the liberties he allowed himself in the treatment of classical masterpieces; undoubtedly his performances of Bach, Beethoven, Brahms, and Schubert were untraditional; but they were nonetheless musicianly in the sincere artistry that animated his interpretations.

BIBL.: M. DeWolfe Howe, *The Boston Symphony Orchestra 1881–1931* (Boston, 1931); A. Lourié, *S.A. K. and His Epoch* (N.Y., 1931); M. DeWolfe Howe, *The Tale of Tanglewood* (Boston, 1946); H. Leichtentritt, *S. K., The Boston Symphony Orchestra and the New American Music* (Cambridge, Mass., 1946); M. Smith, *K.* (N.Y., 1947; a controversial biography; Koussevitzky instituted a suit against the author and publisher for invasion of his right of privacy, but lost his case in court); K. DeKay, "K.—Review and Commentary," *Le Grand Baton* (Dec. 1983); idem, "K. and His Biographers," *Koussevitzky Recordings Society*, newsletter, II/1 (1988).

Koutzen, Boris, Russian-American violinist and composer; b. Uman, near Kiev, April 1, 1901; d. Mount Kisco, N.Y., Dec. 10, 1966. He studied violin with Leo Zetlin and composition with Glière at the Moscow Cons. (1918–22). In 1922 he went to the U.S. and joined the violin section of the Philadelphia Orch. (until 1927); later played in the NBC Sym. Orch. in N.Y. (1937–45). He was head of the violin dept. at the Philadelphia Cons. (1925–62) and a teacher at Vassar College in Poughkeepsie, N.Y. (1944–66). His music possesses an attractive Romantic flavor in an old Russian manner. He composed a number of orch. pieces, among them *Solitude* (Philadelphia, April 1, 1927, composer conducting); *Valley Forge*, symphonic poem (N.Y., Feb. 19, 1940); Concerto for 5 Solo Instruments (Boston, Feb. 23, 1940); Violin Concerto (Philadelphia, Feb. 22, 1952, Nadia Koutzen, composer's daughter, soloist); *Concertante* for 2 Flutes and Orch. (1965); also an opera, *You Never Know* (1962).

Kovačević, Krešimir, significant Croatian musicologist; b. Zagreb, Sept. 16, 1913. He studied at the Univ. of Leipzig (Ph.D., 1943, with a diss. on folk music from the Meotimurje region of Croatia); taught music in Osijek and Dubrovnik (1940–50) and then at the Zagreb Academy of Music (prof., 1950; vice-dean, 1961–71; dean, from 1971). He was also a répétiteur in Zagreb and Belgrade (1936–39), conductor of the Dubrovnik Orch. (1946–50), and a music critic for several publications. He wrote primarily on Croatian contemporary music; publ. the valuable *Hrvatski kompozitori i njihova djela* (Croatian Composers and Their Works; Zagreb, 1960) and *The History of Croatian Music of the Twentieth Century* (in Eng.; Zagreb, 1967). He also edited the 2nd ed. of the *Muzička enciklopedija* (3 vols., 1971–77) and contributed the Croatian entries to the Slovene reference work *Jugoslovanska glasbena dela* (1980).

Koval, Marian (Viktorovich), Russian composer; b. Pristan Voznesenya, Olonets district, Aug. 17, 1907; d. Moscow, Feb. 15, 1971. He studied composition with Gnessin and Miaskovsky at the Moscow Cons. (1925–30). Inspired by the revolutionary ideas of a new collective society, he organized with others a group named Procoll ("Productive Collective"), dedicated to the propaganda of music in its sociological aspects; was also a member of the Russian Assoc. of Proletarian Musicians from 1929 until it was disbanded by the Soviet government in 1931 as being counterproductive. He became known mainly through his choruses and songs on socialist subjects; all of his music is derived from modalities of Russian folk songs and those of the ethnic group of the Urals, to which he belonged. He wrote the operas *Emelian Pugatchev* (Moscow, Nov. 25,

1939) and *Sevastopoltzy* (Perm, Nov. 28, 1946); cantatas: *The People's Sacred War* (1941); *Valery Tchkalov* (1942); *The Kremlin Stars* (1947); children's opera, *The Wolf and 7 Little Goats* (1939); 2 cycles of songs about Lenin; etc.

BIBL.: G. Polyanovsky, *M. K.* (Moscow, 1968).

Kovalev, Pavel, Russian composer; b. Nikolayev, Jan. 6, 1890; d. Paris, Nov. 16, 1951. He studied at the Odessa Cons. and with Teichmüller and Reger at the Leipzig Cons.; then taught at the Odessa Cons. (1919–22). In 1927 he left Russia via China and Japan and settled in Paris. He wrote an opera, *Ariane et Barbe-bleue*; ballet scores; chamber music; songs.

Kovaříček, František, Czech composer; b. Liteniny, May 17, 1924. He studied with Hlobil at the Prague Cons. and with Řidký at the Prague Academy of Music, graduating in 1952; was music director of the Czech Radio in Prague (1953–58). From 1966 to 1985 he taught at the Prague Cons.

WORKS: Comic opera, *Ukradený mesíc* (The Stolen Moon; 1966; Czech Radio, July 1, 1970); Cello Sonata (1958); *Serenade* for 9 Instruments (1958); *Divertimento* for Strings (1960); *Larghetto* for Clarinet and Piano (1963); Clarinet Concerto (1964); *Capriccio* for Chamber Orch. (1970–71); *Music for Chamber Orch.* (1982; Prague, March 23, 1984); 2 piano sonatas; songs.

Kovařovic, Karel, noted Czech conductor and composer; b. Prague, Dec. 9, 1862; d. there, Dec. 6, 1920. He studied clarinet, harp, and piano at the Prague Cons. (1873–79); also studied composition privately with Fibich (1878–80). He was harpist in the orch. of Prague's National Theater (1879–85); also was director of Pivoda's Vocal School (1880–1900). In 1900 he was appointed opera director of the National Theater in Prague, a position he held until his death; he also led sym. concerts in Prague. As a conductor, he demonstrated great craftsmanship and established a high standard of excellence in his operatic productions; his interpretations of Dvořák and Smetana were particularly notable; an ardent believer in the cause of Czech music, he promoted national compositions. In his own music, he also made use of national materials, but his treatment was mostly imitative of the French models; the influences of Gounod and Massenet are particularly noticeable. He publ. some of his lighter works under a series of humorously misspelled names of French composers (C. Biset, J. Héral, etc.).

WORKS: Operas (all 1st perf. in Prague): *Ženichové* (The Bridegrooms; May 13, 1884); *Cesta oknem* (Through the Window; Feb. 11, 1886); *Noc Šimona a Judy* (The Night of Simon and Jude; original title, *Frasquita*; Nov. 5, 1892); *Psohlavci* (The Dog-Heads; April 24, 1898; his most famous opera); *Na starém bélidle* (At the Old Bleaching-House; Nov. 22, 1901); ballets: *Hashish* (June 19, 1884); *Pohádka o nalezeném štěstí* (A Tale of Found Happiness; Dec. 21, 1886); *Na zaletech* (Flirtation; Oct. 24, 1909); symphonic works; Piano Concerto (1887); 3 string quartets (1878, 1887, 1894).

BIBL.: J. Němeček, *Opera Národního divadla za Karla Kovařovice* (Prague, 1968–69).

Koven, Reginald de. See **De Koven, Reginald.**

Kowalski, Henri, French pianist and composer of Polish and Irish descent; b. Paris, 1841; d. Bordeaux, July 8, 1916. He studied piano with Marmontel, Prudent, and Anatole Petit and composition with Carafa and Samuel David at the Paris Cons.; toured extensively (1858–82), relating his visit to the U.S. as *À travers l'Amérique: Impressions d'un musicien* (Paris, 1872), which contains a list of his compositions; these include characteristic piano pieces.

Kowalski, Július, Slovak composer; b. Ostrava, Feb. 24, 1912. He studied composition with Rudolf Karel and Alois Hába at the Prague Cons. (1929–33); subsequently composition with Suk and conducting with Talich at the Master School there (1933–34); then went to Vienna, where he studied conducting with Clemens Krauss (1939). After World War II, he held administrative and managerial positions in Bratislava. He wrote some microtonal pieces, e.g., Suite for Violin and Viola in the sixth-tone system (1936) and Duo for Violin and Cello in the quarter-tone system (1937), but later composed in a more or less traditional style.

WORKS: Chamber opera, *Lampionová slávnost* (The Chinese Lantern Celebration; 1961; Ostrava, 1963); *Russian Rhapsody* for Orch. (1933–34); *Serbian Fantasy* for Orch. (1934); 7 syms. (1954; 1957; 1959; 1970; 1974; 1980; *Peace*, 1981); Concertino for Violin and Chamber Orch. (1955); *Impressions* for Orch. (1965); Concerto for Cello and String Orch. (1970); Concerto for String Quartet and Orch. (1973–74; Bratislava, Nov. 14, 1974); *Concertante Symphonietta* for Wind Quintet and Orch. (1976; Bratislava, Feb. 7, 1977); 2 piano trios (1931, 1975); 6 string quartets (1932, 1954, 1965, 1975, 1977, 1979); *Divertimento* for Flute, Oboe, and Bassoon (1966); Violin Sonatina (1966); *Little Fantasy* for Flute and Piano (1969); *Grimaces* for Flute, Clarinet, Trombone, and Tuba (1970).

Kowalski, Max, Polish-born German composer; b. Kowal, Aug. 10, 1882; d. London, June 4, 1956. He was taken to Frankfurt as an infant, and received his primary education there; studied voice with Heinemann in Berlin and composition with Sekles in Frankfurt; also obtained a law degree from the Univ. of Marburg. He wrote a song cycle to Guiraud's *Pierrot Lunaire* (1912), and during the following 20 years composed a number of lieder, which found favor in Germany. After the Nazis came to power (1933), he was sent to the Buchenwald concentration camp; after his release (1939), he settled in London and eked out a living as a teacher, synagogue cantor, and piano tuner.

Kox, Hans, Dutch composer; b. Arnhem, May 19, 1930. He studied at the Utrecht Cons., then became a private student of Henk Badings; subsequently taught at the Doetinchem Music School (1956–70); then was appointed prof. of composition at the Utrecht Cons. He became fascinated with mathematical properties of music, both in formal structure and in the intervallic divisions; in some of his works he applies a scale of 31 equal intervals, invented by the Dutch physicist Adriaan Fokker. In his series of *Cyclophonies* (*Sound Cycles*), he experimented with "open-end" forms.

WORKS: Operas: *Dorian Gray*, after Wilde (1972–73; Scheveningen, March 30, 1974; rev. 1976); *Lord Rochester* (1978); *Little Lethe Symphony* (1956); *Concertante Music* for Horn, Trumpet, Trombone, and Orch. (1956); Flute Concerto (1957); *Macbeth*, overture (1958); Concerto for Orch. (1959); 3 syms.: No. 1 for String Orch. (1959); No. 2 (1960–66; incorporates the orch. pieces *Ballade* and *Paraklesis*); No. 3, after Isaiah I (1985); *Ballet "Spleen"* for Orch. (1960); Piano Concerto (1961); *De Kantate van St. Juttemis* for Baritone, Tenor, Chorus, and Piano (1962); 2 violin concertos (1963; 1978, rev. 1981); 2-violin Concerto (1964); 12 *Cyclophonies*: No. 1 for Cello and Small Orch. (1964); No. 2 for 3 Orch. Groups (1964); No. 3 for Piano and Tape (1964); No. 4 for Treble Recorder and 9 Strings (1965); No. 5 for Oboe, Clarinet, Bassoon, and 19 Strings (1966); No. 6 for Violin, Trumpet, Piano, Vibraphone, and 16 Strings (1967); No. 7 for Violin, Piano, and 6 Percussionists (1971); No. 8 for Wind Quintet, Violin, Viola, Cello, and Double Bass (1971; rev. 1982); No. 9 for Solo Percussion and Small Orch. (1974); No. 10 for Mixed Choir and Strings (1975); No. 11 for Big Band (1978); No. 12 for 8 Cellos (1979); *Zoo*, cantata (1964); *Litania* for Female Chorus, Percussion, and Strings (1965); *Music for Status Seekers* for Orch. (1966); *L'Allegria* for Soprano and Orch. (1967); Cello Concerto (1969); *Phobos* for Orch. (1970); 6 *One-act Plays* for 29 Musicians (1971); *Gedächtnislieder* for Voice and Orch. (1972); *Concerto bandistico* for Orch. (1973); *Gothic Concerto* for Harp and Chamber Orch. (1975); *Sinfonia concertante* for Violin, Cello, and Orch. (1976); *Vangoghiana* for Brass Band, Strings, and Percussion (1977); Concerto for Alto Saxophone and Orch. (1978); Concertino for Chamber Ensemble (1982); *Notturno e Danza* for Violin, Viola or Clarinet, Cello, Piano, and Strings (1983); *Le Songe du Vergier* for Cello and Orch. (1986); *Musica reservata* for 2 Wind Orchs. (1986); 4 violin sonatas (1952, 1955, 1961, 1966); 2 trios for 2 Violins and Viola (1952, 1954);

4 sextets of varying instrumental combinations (1957, 1957, 1959, 1961); String Quartet (1955); Trio No. 3A for Violin, Viola, and Cello (1955); String Quintet (1957); 3 *Pieces* for Violin, in the 31-tone system (1958); 2 piano quartets (1959, 1968); Sonata for Solo Cello (1959); 4 *Pieces* for String Quartet, in the 31-tone system (1961); the 31-tone 4 *Pieces* for 2 Trumpets and Trombone (1964); Serenade for 3 Violins (1968); *Préludes* for Violin (1971); *De Vierde Kraai oftewel De Kraaiende Vier* for Male Chorus, Brass Quartet, and Percussion (1972); *The Jealous Guy Plays His Tune* for Violin and Piano (1975); Piano Trio (1976); *Suite* for Cello (1976); *Suite* for Guitar Trio (1977); Sonata for Saxophone and Piano (1983); 2 piano sonatas (1954, 1955); 3 *Études* for Piano (1961); *Melancholies* for Piano (1975); Prelude and Fugue for Organ (1954); the 31-tone Passacaglia and Chorale for Organ (1960).

Koyama, Kiyoshige, Japanese composer; b. Nagano, Jan. 15, 1914. He studied composition with Komei Abe; wrote a number of works in a Japanese national style, among them *Shina no Bayashi* for Orch. (Tokyo, June 3, 1946); *Kobiki-Uta* for Orch. (Tokyo, Oct. 3, 1957); symphonic suite, *Nomen*, for a Noh play (Tokyo, Dec. 5, 1959); *Ubusuna* for Koto and other Japanese Instruments (1962); *Ainu no Uta* for String Orch. (Tokyo, May 23, 1964); opera, *Sansho Dayū* (Tokyo, March 29, 1972); several pieces for Japanese instruments.

Koželuh (Kozeluch, Koscheluch), Johann Antonín (Jan Evangelista Antonín Tomáš), Bohemian composer, cousin of **Leopold (Jan Antonín) Koželuh (Kozeluch, Kotzeluch);** b. Welwarn, Dec. 14, 1738; d. Prague, Feb. 3, 1814. He began music studies at school in Welwarn; was then a chorister at the Jesuit College in Breznice; subsequently, studied with J.F.N. Seger in Prague; then went to Vienna, where he had instruction from Gluck, Gassmann, and Hasse. Upon his return to Prague, he became Kapellmeister at St. Vitus's Metropolitan Cathedral (1784–1814). His cousin was one of his pupils. He composed 2 operas: *Alessandro nell'Indie* (Prague, 1769) and *Il Demofoonte* (Prague, 1771); much sacred music, including 2 oratorios, about 45 masses, 5 Requiems, etc.; 4 syms.; an Oboe Concerto; 2 bassoon concertos; and many other instrumental works.

BIBL.: R. Fikrle, *Jan Evangelista Antonín K.: Život, dilo a osobnost svatovitsheho kapelnika* (a study of his life and music with a list of works; Prague, 1946).

Koželuh (Kozeluch, Kotzeluch), Leopold (Jan Antonín), Bohemian pianist, teacher, and composer, cousin of **Johann Antonín (Jan Evangelista Antonín Tomáš) Koželuh (Kozeluch, Koscheluch);** b. Welwarn, June 26, 1747; d. Vienna, May 7, 1818. He began his musical studies in Welwarn; then had instruction with his cousin and with F.X. Dušek in Prague. He also studied law but turned to a career in music after the success he attained with his ballets and pantomimes. In 1778 he went to Vienna, where he established himself as a pianist, teacher, and composer; also was active as a music publisher. In 1792 he was appointed Kammer Kapellmeister and Hofmusik Compositor, succeeding Mozart; he held this position until his death. Although Beethoven referred to him contemptuously in a letter of 1812 as "miserabilis," Koželuh was an excellent pianist; he composed about 50 solo sonatas, 22 piano concertos, 28 syms., about 80 piano trios, and other pieces of chamber music. His stage works included operas, ballets, and pantomimes, but little of this music is extant; his only extant opera is *Gustav Wasa* (c.1792).

BIBL.: G. Löbl, *Die Klaviersonate bei L. Kozeluch* (diss., Univ. of Vienna, 1937); O. Deutsch, "Kozeluch ritrovato," *Music & Letters*, XXVI (1945); M. Poštolka, *Leopold Koželuh: Život a dilo* (a study of his life and music with summary in Eng. and Ger.; Prague, 1964); C. Flamm, *L. Koželuch: Biographie und stilkritische Untersuchung der Sonaten für Klavier, Violine und Violoncello* (diss., Univ. of Vienna, 1968).

Kozina, Marjan, Slovenian composer; b. Novo Mesto, June 4, 1907; d. there, June 19, 1966. He studied at the Ljubljana Cons. (1925–27); later took courses with Joseph Marx at the

Vienna Academy of Music and with Josef Suk at the Prague Cons. During the Nazi occupation, he took part in the armed resistance movement; after the liberation, he was director of the Slovene Phil. (1947–50) and then taught composition at the Ljubljana Academy of Music (1950–60). He wrote music in a fine, unaffected manner, making circumspect use of modern harmonies, while deriving his melorhythmic essence from native Slovene folk-song patterns. His most important work was the opera *Ekvinokoij* (Equinox; Ljubljana, May 2, 1946), which had numerous revivals in Yugoslavia and was also performed in Prague and Moscow. Other works include the ballet *Diptihon* (1952), a cantata, *Lepa Vida* (Beautiful Vida; 1939), choral pieces, and songs.

Kozlovsky, Ivan (Semyonovich), Russian tenor; b. Maryanovka, near Kiev, March 24, 1900. He studied at the Kiev Cons. with Lysenko and Muravyova; made his debut as Faust in Poltava in 1918; then sang in Kharkov (1924) and Sverdlovsk (1925); in 1926 he joined the Bolshoi Theater in Moscow, where he was one of the leading singers until 1954. An artist of imaginative power, Kozlovsky expanded his activities into stage direction, striving to synthesize dramatic action with its musical realization. Apart from operatic performances, he gave recitals in programs of the classical repertoire as well as Russian and Ukrainian songs.
BIBL.: G. Polinovsky, *I. K.* (Moscow, 1945); V. Sletov, *I. K.* (Moscow, 1951); A. Kuznetzova, *I. K.* (Moscow, 1964).

Kozma, Matei, Rumanian organist and composer; b. Tîrgu-Mureş, July 23, 1929. He acquired the rudiments of music from his father, Géza Kozma, a composer and cellist; then studied at the Cluj Cons. (1947–54), where his teachers were Jodal and Demian. He was organist (1955–57) and director (1959–66) of the Tîrgu-Mureş Phil.; then taught at the Music Inst. there.
WORKS: *Rondo* for Piano (1954); 2 ballets: *Balada lacului Sf. Ana* (1957) and *Balada celui care cînta in cătuşe* (1963); Organ Concerto (1961; rev. 1965); *Trandafirii roşii,* poem for Chorus and Orch. (1962); *Theme and Variations* for Organ (1963); Trio for Solo Clarinet (1965); *Omagiu eroilor,* overture (1967); *Toccata, Trio, and Ricercari* for Organ (1968); choruses; songs.

Krader, Barbara (née **Lattimer**), American ethnomusicologist; b. Columbus, Ohio, Jan. 15, 1922. She studied music with Krenek at Vassar College (A.B., 1942); later took courses in Russian and Slavonic languages, and in literature with Roman Jakobson at Columbia Univ. (A.M., 1948). After a brief period at the Univ. of Prague (1948–49), she completed her education with Jakobson at Radcliffe College (Ph.D., 1955, with the diss. *Serbian Peasant Wedding Ritual Songs: A Formal, Semantic and Functional Analysis*). She worked as a reference librarian in the Slavonic division of the Library of Congress (1959–63) and as a lecturer in Slavonic at Ohio State Univ. (1963–64); in 1965–66 she was executive secretary of the International Folk Music Council in London. On returning to the U.S., she taught at Columbia Univ. (1969) and also served as president of the Soc. for Ethnomusicology (1972–73). She made valuable field recordings in Czechoslovakia, Yugoslavia, Greece, and Rumania.

Kraft, Anton, Austrian cellist and composer, father of **Nikolaus Kraft**; b. Rokitzán, near Plzeň, Dec. 30, 1749; d. Vienna, Aug. 28, 1820. He began to study at an early age with his father, an amateur cellist; then went to Prague, where he studied with one Werner, cellist of the Kreuzherren Church; also studied law and philosophy at the Univ. of Prague. He then was a cellist in the chapel of Prince Esterházy (1778–90); also studied composition with Haydn (c.1780). He subsequently was a cellist in the orch. of Prince Grassalkowicz de Gyarak in Pressburg (1790–96), and then of Prince Joseph Lobkowitz in Vienna. He toured widely as a virtuoso with his son (from 1789); became a teacher of cello at the Cons. of the Gesellschaft der Musikfreunde in Vienna (1820). Haydn wrote his Cello Concerto in D major, H VIIb:2, for him, and

Beethoven wrote his Triple Concerto with Kraft in mind. Kraft's own works include a Cello Concerto (publ. in Leipzig, 1792?; ed. in Musica Viva Historica, II, 1961), 6 sonatas for Cello (3 as op. 2, Amsterdam and Berlin, 1790; 3 as op. 2, Offenbach, 1790?), and 3 grands duos concertantes for Violin and Cello, op. 3 (Leipzig, 1792?).

Kraft, Leo (Abraham), American composer and pedagogue; b. N.Y., July 24, 1922. He studied composition with Karol Rathaus at Queens College of the City Univ. of N.Y. (B.A., 1945), Randall Thompson at Princeton Univ. (M.F.A., 1947), and Nadia Boulanger in Paris on a Fulbright fellowship (1954–55). He taught at Queens College (1947–89); then was Distinguished Composer-in-Residence at N.Y. Univ. (from 1989). He received various ASCAP awards (from 1961); in 1975 and 1978 he held NEA fellowships. Kraft's craftsmanship preserves formal ties with the revered past, along with a salute to the turbulent present and a wink at an ominous future.
WRITINGS: With S. Berkowitz and G. Frontrier, *A New Approach to Sight Singing* (N.Y., 1960; 3rd ed., 1986); *Gradus: An Integrated Approach to Harmony, Counterpoint, and Analysis* (N.Y., 1976; 2nd ed., 1987); *A New Approach to Ear Training (Melody)* (N.Y., 1967); with others, *A New Approach to Keyboard Harmony* (N.Y., 1978).
WORKS: ORCH.: Concerto No. 1 for Flute, Clarinet, Trumpet, and Strings (1951); *Variations* (1958); *3 Pieces* (1963); *Toccata* for Band (1968); Concerto No. 3 for Cello, Wind Quintet, and Percussion (1968); Concerto No. 2 for 12 Instruments (1966–72); *Music* (1975); Concerto No. 4 for Piano and 14 Instruments (1978); Chamber Sym. for 12 Instruments (1980); *Symphony in 1 Movement* (1985); *A New Ricercar* for String Orch. (1985); Concerto No. 5 for Oboe and Strings (1986); Concerto No. 6 for Clarinet and Orch. (1986); *Pacific Bridges* for String Orch. and Clarinet obbligato (1989); *Tableaux* for 10 Winds and Piano (1989). CHAMBER: 2 string quartets (1951, 1959); Sextet for Clarinet, Piano, and String Quartet (1952); Cello Sonata (1954); *Partita No. 2* for Violin and Viola (1962); *Partita No. 3* for Wind Quintet (1964); *Trios and Interludes* for Flute, Viola, and Piano (1965); *Dualities* for 2 Trumpets (1971); *Partita No. 4* for Flute, Clarinet, Violin, Bass, and Piano (1975); *Dialectica* for Flute, Clarinet, Violin, Cello, and Tape (1976); *Conductus novus* for 4 Trombones (1979); *Arietta da capo* for Soprano Saxophone (1982); *O Primavera* for Flute, Oboe, and Clarinet (1983); *Inventions and Airs* for Clarinet, Violin, and Piano (1984); *Hallelujah: A Joyous Fanfare* for Brass Quintet (1987); *Statements and Commentaries No. 2* for 2 Cellos (1988); piano pieces; choruses; songs.

Kraft, Nikolaus, renowned Hungarian cellist, son of **Anton Kraft**; b. Esterház, Dec. 14, 1778; d. Eger, May 18, 1853. He studied with his father, and toured with him while quite young; during a visit to the Dresden court, they performed with Mozart (April 14, 1789). He joined the orch. of Prince Joseph Lobkowitz in Vienna (1796); also was a member of the Schuppanzigh Quartet. After further study with Jean-Pierre Duport in Berlin (1801–2), he toured widely; returned to Vienna as principal cellist of the orch. of the Kärnthnertortheater (1809); also continued to serve Prince Lobkowitz as a chamber virtuoso. He subsequently was a chamber musician in Stuttgart from 1814 until an accident to his hand compelled him to retire in 1834. He wrote 4 cello concertos (1810?, 1813, 1819, 1820) and various salon pieces for the instrument. His son, **Friedrich Anton Kraft** (b. Vienna, Feb. 13, 1807; d. Stuttgart, Dec. 4, 1874), was a cellist in the Stuttgart Court Orch. from 1824.

Kraft, Walter, noted German organist; b. Cologne, June 9, 1905; d. in a hotel fire in Antwerp, May 9, 1977. He studied piano with Rebbert and organ with Hannemann in Hamburg, and composition with Hindemith in Berlin. From 1924 to 1927 he was organist of the Markuskirche in Hamburg, and from 1927 to 1929 of the Lutherkirche in Altona-Bahrenfeld. From 1929 he was organist of the Marienkirche in Lübeck; the church was destroyed in 1942, but he resumed his post there after the church was restored. He was also a prof. of organ at the Freiburg music college (from 1947); in addition, served as director of the Schleswig-Holstein Academy of Music (1950–55). He composed the oratorios *Christus* (1942–43), *Die Bürger von Calais* (1953–54), *Lübecker Totentanz* (1954), and *Die Gemeinschaft der Heiligen* (1956–57). As an organist, he gained wide distinction as an interpreter of Baroque music and as an improviser.

Kraft, William, American percussionist, composer, and conductor; b. Chicago, Sept. 6, 1923. His parental name was Kashareftsky, which his parents Americanized to Kraft. The family moved to California and Kraft began to study piano. He took music courses at San Diego State College and at the Univ. of Calif. at Los Angeles, where he also had professional percussion instruction with Murray Spivack. In 1943 he was called to arms, and served in the U.S. forces as pianist, arranger, and drummer in military bands; while in Europe with the army, he took time to attend music courses at Cambridge Univ. Returning to the U.S. after discharge from military duty, he earned a living as percussionist in jazz bands. In the summer of 1948 he enrolled in the Berkshire Music Center in Tanglewood, where he studied composition with Irving Fine and conducting with Leonard Bernstein. In 1949 he entered Columbia Univ., where his instructors in composition were Jack Beeson, Otto Luening, Seth Bingham, Vladimir Ussachevsky, and Henry Cowell; he also attended classes in musicology with Erich Hertzmann and Paul Henry Lang (B.S., 1951; M.A., 1954). He continued to perfect his technique as a percussionist, and took lessons with Morris Goldenberg and Saul Goodman; he attained a high degree of virtuosity as a percussion player, both in the classical tradition and in jazz. In 1955 he became a percussionist with the Los Angeles Phil., retaining this position until 1981. In the meantime he developed his natural gift for conducting; from 1969 to 1972 he served as assistant conductor of the Los Angeles Phil.; in a parallel development, he composed assiduously and successfully. From 1981 to 1985 he was composer-in-residence of the Los Angeles Phil.; also founded the Los Angeles Phil. New Music Group, presenting programs of modern works for chamber orch. combinations. From 1988 to 1990 he was a visiting prof. at the Univ. of Calif. at Los Angeles. He held 2 Guggenheim fellowships (1967, 1972). As a composer, he explores without prejudice a variety of quaquaversal techniques, including serial procedures; naturally, his music coruscates with a rainbow spectrum of asymmetrical rhythms. There is a tendency in the very titles of his works toward textured constructivism, e.g., *Momentum, Configurations, Collage, Encounters, Translucences, Triangles,* and *Mobiles;* but there are also concrete representations of contemporary events, as in *Contextures: Riots–Decade '60.*

WORKS: Music for Samuel Beckett's radio drama *Cascando* (1988); film scores. **ORCH.:** *A Simple Introduction to the Orchestra* (1958); *Variations on a Folksong* (Los Angeles, March 26, 1960); Sym. for Strings and Percussion (N.Y., Aug. 21, 1961); *Concerto grosso* for Violin, Flute, Cello, Bassoon, and Orch. (1961; San Diego, March 22, 1963); *American Carnival Overture* (1962); Concerto for 4 Percussionists and Orch. (Los Angeles, March 10, 1966); *Configurations,* concerto for 4 Percussionists and Jazz Orch. (Los Angeles, Nov. 13, 1966); *Contextures: Riots–Decade '60* (1967; Los Angeles, April 4, 1968); Piano Concerto (Los Angeles, Nov. 21, 1973); *Tintinnabulations: Collage No. 3* (Anaheim, March 22, 1974); *Dream Tunnel* for Narrator and Orch. (Los Angeles, May 12, 1976); *Andirivieni* for Tuba and Orch. (1977; Los Angeles, Jan. 26, 1978; rev. as Concerto for Tuba, 3 Chamber Groups, and Orch., 1979); *Settlers Suite* (Merced, Calif., March 10, 1981); *Double Play* for Violin, Piano, and Chamber Orch. (1982; St. Paul, Minn., Jan. 7, 1983); Timpani Concerto (1983; Indianapolis, March 9, 1984); *Contextures II: The Final Beast* for Soprano, Tenor, and Chamber Orch. (Los Angeles, April 2, 1984; also for Soprano, Tenor, Boys' Choir, and Orch., 1986; Los Angeles, April 2, 1987); *Interplay* (Los Angeles, Nov. 1, 1984); *Of Ceremonies, Pageants, and Celebrations* (Costa Mesa, Calif., Sept. 19, 1986; rev. 1987); *A Kennedy Portrait* for Narrator and Orch., in com-

memoration of the 25th anniversary of the assassination of President John F. Kennedy (Boston, Nov. 19, 1988); *Veils and Variations* for Horn and Orch. (1988; Berkeley, Calif., Jan. 27, 1989); *Vintage Renaissance* (Boston, June 10, 1989); *Vintage 1990–91* (Costa Mesa, Calif., Oct. 9, 1990); also works for wind ensemble. **CHAMBER:** Nonet for 2 Trumpets, Horn, Trombone, Tuba, and 4 Percussion (Los Angeles, Oct. 13, 1958); *Triangles,* concerto for Percussion and 10 Instruments (1965–68; Los Angeles, Dec. 8, 1969); *Mobiles* for 3 Instrumental Groups (1970); *Cadenze* for Flute, Oboe, Clarinet, Bassoon, Horn, Violin, and Viola (1971; Los Angeles, March 20, 1972); *In Memoriam Igor Stravinsky* for Violin and Piano (1972–74); *Des Imagistes* for 6 Percussion and Reciter(s) (Los Angeles, March 12, 1974); *Encounters V: In the Morning of the Winter Sea* for Cello and Percussion (1975; N.Y., Jan. 6, 1976); *Encounters IX* for Saxophone and Percussion (Nuremberg, July 9, 1982); *Melange* for Flute, Clarinet, Violin, Cello, Piano, and Percussion (1985; Dallas, March 10, 1986); *Quartet for the Love of Time* for Clarinet, Violin, Cello, and Piano (Portland, Oreg., July 6, 1987); Quartet for Percussion (Sacramento, Calif., Nov. 7, 1988); also many vocal works. **PERCUSSION:** *Theme and Variations* for Percussion Quartet (1956); *Suite* for 4 Percussion (1958; Los Angeles, Nov. 6, 1961); *Soliloquy: Encounters I* for Percussion and Tape (1975); *Encounters VI,* concertino for Roto-toms and Percussion Quartet (Atlantic City, N.J., March 10, 1976); *Encounters VII* for 2 Percussion (1977; Boston, Jan. 22, 1978); *Variations for King George* for Timpani (1980); *Weavings* for String Quartet and Percussion (San Francisco, Nov. 30, 1984); various other works.

Krainev, Vladimir (Vsevolodovich), Russian pianist; b. Krasnoyarsk, April 1, 1944. He studied with Anaida Sumbatian at Moscow's Central Music School (graduated, 1962), then with Heinrich Neuhaus (1962–64) and Stanislav Neuhaus (1964–67) at the Moscow Cons., where he completed his postgraduate studies (1969). He won 2nd prize in the Leeds Competition (1963); then 1st prize in the Vianna da Motta Competition in Lisbon (1964) and the Tchaikovsky Competition in Moscow (1970). He subsequently made tours of Europe and the U.S.

Kramer, A(rthur) Walter, American music critic, publishing executive, and composer; b. N.Y., Sept. 23, 1890; d. there, April 8, 1969. He studied music with his father; took violin lessons with Carl Hauser and Richard Arnold. After graduating from the College of the City of N.Y. in 1910, he joined the staff of *Musical America* (1910–22) and served as its ed. in chief (1929–36); then was managing director of the Galaxy Music Corp. (1936–56). He publ. over 300 compositions, including orch. pieces, choral works, chamber music, piano pieces, and songs.

BIBL.: J. Howard, *A.W. K.* (N.Y., 1926).

Kramer, Jonathan, American composer, music theorist, teacher, and writer on music; b. Hartford, Conn., Dec. 7, 1942. He studied at Harvard Univ. (A.B., 1965) and the Univ. of Calif. at Berkeley (M.A., 1967; Ph.D., 1969); also received training in computer music at Stanford Univ. (1967–68) and was a postdoctoral fellow in criticism and theory at the Univ. of Calif. at Irvine (1976). He taught at the Univ. of Calif. at Berkeley (1969–70), the Oberlin Cons. (1970–71), and Yale Univ. (1971–78); in 1978 he joined the faculty of the Univ. of Cincinnati College-Cons. of Music, where he later was prof. of composition and theory (1983–90); from 1988 he was a prof. of music at Columbia Univ. In 1980 he became program annotator of the Cincinnati Sym. Orch., and in 1988 its composer-in-residence. He publ. *The Time of Music* (N.Y., 1988) and *Listen to the Music* (N.Y., 1988).

WORKS: THEATER AND MULTIMEDIA: *For Broken Piano, Truck, Shaving Cream, Fruit Salad, Toilet, Wife, San Francisco, Color TV, Tape, and Slide Projections* (1969–70; Santa Cruz, Calif., April 3, 1970); *Blue Music* for Tape and Actor (1970–72); *An Imaginary Dance* for Tape and Slide Projections (1970–73); *Fanfare* for Actors and Tape (1973–76); *En noir et blanc* for 2 Actor-Pianists and Actor-Dancer (1988). **ORCH.:** *Funeral March* (1957–61); *Rhapsody* (1958); *Prelude and Fugue* (1964);

Clarinet Concerto (1965; Sacramento, March 30, 1967); *Requiem for the Innocent* (1970); *Moments in and out of Time* (1981–83; Cincinnati, Feb. 10, 1984); *No Beginning, No End* for Chorus and Orch. (1982–83; Cincinnati, Oct. 30, 1983); *Musica pro musica* (1986–87; Columbus, Ohio, Nov. 14, 1987); *About Face* (1988–89; Cincinnati, Nov. 10, 1989); also band music. **CHAMBER:** Suite for 10 Instruments (1958); *3 Inventions* for 2 Clarinets and Cello (1960); Trio for Violin, Viola, and Cello (1962–65); *3 Pieces* for Clarinet (1965–66); *Obstacles* for Trumpet, Trombone, and Piano (1967); Septet (1968); *Renaissance Motet* for 2 Flutes and Bassoon (1970); *1 for 5 in 7, Mostly* for Woodwind Quintet (1971); *1 More Piece for Solo Clarinet* (1972); *Moving Music* for Solo Clarinet and 12 Clarinets (1975–76); *Atlanta Licks* for Flute, Clarinet, Violin, Viola, Cello, and Piano (1984); also keyboard and tape pieces.

Kranich & Bach, well-known firm of American piano makers founded in N.Y. in 1864 by Helmuth Kranich, Sr. (b. Grossbreitenbach, Germany, Aug. 22, 1833; d. N.Y., Jan. 29, 1902), and Jacques Bach (b. Lorentzen, Alsace, June 22, 1833; d. N.Y., Oct. 29, 1894). The business was incorporated in 1890 and remained in the hands of the founders' descendants for several generations.

Krantz, Eugen, German pianist, teacher, music critic, and composer; b. Dresden, Sept. 13, 1844; d. Gohrisch, near Königstein, May 26, 1898. He studied at the Dresden Cons.; was chorus master at the Court Opera there (1869–84); taught at the Dresden Cons. (from 1877), becoming director in 1890, when he bought the institution; was also music critic for the Dresden *Presse* and the *Nachrichten*. He publ. some songs and a *Lehrgang im Klavierunterricht* (1882).

Krapf, Gerhard, German-American organist and composer; b. Meissenheim-bei-Lahr, Dec. 12, 1924. He studied piano and organ in Karlsruhe; was church organist in Offenburg (1939–42); was drafted into the German army and taken prisoner of war in Russia; upon his release, he returned to Karlsruhe, where he studied organ, choral conducting, and composition (1950). In 1951 he went to the U.S., where he studied organ at the Univ. of Redlands in California, and took a course in composition with Paul Pisk. He then taught music at Albion, Mich. (1953–54), at the Northwest Missouri State College in Maryville (1954–58), and at the Univs. of Wyoming (1958–61) and Iowa (1961–77). He joined the faculty of the Univ. of Alberta in Edmonton (1977), where he became chairman of the division of keyboard studies. He composed a great number of organ pieces and sacred choral works. He publ. *Liturgical Organ Playing* (Minneapolis, 1964), *Organ Improvisation: A Practical Approach to Chorale Elaborations for the Service* (Minneapolis, 1967), and *Bach: Improvised Ornamentation and Keyboard Cadenzas: An Approach to Creative Performance* (Dayton, Ohio, 1983). He also tr. H. Klotz's *The Organ Handbook* (St. Louis, 1969) and Werckmeister's 1698 *Orgelprobe* (Raleigh, N.C., 1976).

Krapp, Edgar, distinguished German organist and pedagogue; b. Bamberg, June 3, 1947. He studied the organ at the Hochschule für Musik in Munich, where he was a pupil of Franz Lehrndorfer; subsequently took organ lessons with Marie-Claire Alain in Paris. In 1970 he won 1st prize in the Competition of the German Academies in Munich, and in 1971 the prize of the Mendelssohn Competition in Berlin. In 1974 he was named successor to Helmut Walcha as prof. of organ at the Hochschule für Musik in Frankfurt; from 1982, was a visiting prof. at the Salzburg Mozarteum. He is particularly noted for his performance of the organ music of Bach.

Krása, Hans, Czech composer; b. Prague, Nov. 30, 1899; d. in the concentration camp in Auschwitz, Oct. 16, 1944. He studied with Zemlinsky and Keussler in Prague, at the Berlin Cons., and with Roussel in Paris. He conducted at Berlin's Kroll Opera; then was active in Prague from 1928 until his internment in the Theresienstadt concentration camp in 1942; nevertheless he continued to compose, producing his opera, *Brundibár*, which was performed by an opera group of the

Jewish inmates. On Oct. 16, 1944, he was transported to the concentration camp in Auschwitz and put to death. He composed some interesting works in a "hedonistic" manner, aiming at sophisticated entertainment; his idiom was mildly atonal. Among his works are *Grotesques* for Orch. (Prague, May 20, 1921); *Pastorale* and *March* (originally the 1st and 2nd movements of a sym.; Paris, April 24, 1923); incidental music to *Lysistrata*; the cantata *Die Erde ist des Herrn; Theme with Variations* for String Quartet (1942); String Trio (Aspen, Oct. 22, 1951); songs to words by Rimbaud; piano pieces.

Krasnapolsky, Yuri, American conductor; b. N.Y., Nov. 24, 1934. He studied piano with Isabelle Vengerova at the Curtis Inst. of Music in Philadelphia; subsequently took courses in conducting with Leonard Bernstein, and also with Jean Morel at the Juilliard School of Music in N.Y. He began his career as an assistant conductor to Bernstein at the N.Y. Phil. (1962–63); then was guest conductor-in-residence of the Florida Sym. Orch. and music director of the Omaha Sym. Orch. (1969–75). From 1974 to 1987 he was music director of the Des Moines Sym. Orch.

Krasner, Louis, Russian-born American violinist; b. Cherkassy, June 21, 1903. He was taken to the U.S. as a small child; studied violin with Eugene Gruenberg and composition with Converse at the New England Cons. of Music in Boston, graduating in 1923; then went abroad, where he studied violin with Carl Flesch, Lucien Capet, and Ševčik. From 1944 to 1949 he was concertmaster of the Minneapolis Sym. Orch.; then was prof. of violin and chamber music at Syracuse Univ. (1949–71); subsequently taught at the New England Cons. of Music (from 1974). He commissioned and gave the 1st performance of Berg's Violin Concerto (Barcelona, April 19, 1936); also gave the world premiere of Schoenberg's Violin Concerto (Philadelphia, Dec. 6, 1940, Stokowski conducting).

Krásová, Marta, prominent Czech mezzo-soprano; b. Protivín, March 16, 1901; d. Vráž u Berouna, Feb. 20, 1970. She studied with Olga Borová-Valoušková and Růžena Maturová in Prague; then with Ullanovsky in Vienna. She began her career as a soprano (1922), but soon turned to mezzo-soprano roles. She made her debut at the Prague National Theater as Azucena (1926), then was one of its principal singers (1928–66); also made successful guest appearances in Hamburg, Dresden, Madrid, Paris, Moscow, and Warsaw; toured the U.S. in 1937. In 1935 she married the composer **Karel Boleslav Jirák;** they divorced in 1946. In 1958 she was made a National Artist. She achieved distinction for her roles in Czech operas; was also noted as a Wagnerian singer.

BIBL.: V. Šolín, *M. K.* (Prague, 1960).

Kraus (Trujillo), Alfredo, distinguished Spanish tenor of Austrian descent; b. Las Palmas, Canary Islands, Sept. 24, 1927. He had vocal training with Gali Markoff in Barcelona and Francisco Andrés in Valencia, then completed his studies with Mercedes Llopart in Milan (1955). In 1956 he won 1st prize in the Geneva Competition and made his operatic debut as the Duke of Mantua in Cairo; he also made his European debut in Venice as Alfredo Germont, a role he repeated for his British debut at London's Stoll Theatre in 1957. After he scored a remarkable success in the same role at Lisbon's Teatro São Carlo on March 27, 1958, an international career beckoned. On July 10, 1959, he appeared at London's Covent Garden for the 1st time, as Edgardo in *Lucia di Lammermoor*. His U.S. debut followed at the Chicago Lyric Opera, as Nemorino in *L'elisir d'amore* on Oct. 31, 1962. He made his Metropolitan Opera debut in N.Y. as the Duke of Mantua on Feb. 16, 1966. A consummate artist with a voice of remarkable beauty, he was particularly noted for his portrayals of Rossini's Count Almaviva, Don Ottavio, Ernesto in *Don Pasquale*, Des Grieux, Nadir in *Les Pêcheurs de perles*, and Massenet's Werther.

BIBL.: *Current Biography* (June 1987).

Kraus, Detlef, distinguished German pianist; b. Hamburg, Nov. 30, 1919. He made a notable debut at the age of 16, performing the complete *Well-tempered Clavier* in 2 successive recitals in Hamburg; then continued his studies with Edwin Fischer and later with Wilhelm Kempff in Berlin and Potsdam. In 1958 he performed a cycle of Beethoven piano sonatas in London; in 1970 he gave Beethoven cycles in Tokyo, Valencia, and Pittsburgh; in 1980 he played all of the solo piano works of Brahms in N.Y. He also taught classes at the Folkwang Hochschule für Musik in Essen. His playing is remarkable for its freedom from pedantry; his interpretations are notable for their spontaneity. He publ. *Johannes Brahms als Klavierkomponist: Wege und Hinweise zu seiner Klaviermusik* (Wilhelmshaven, 1986).

Kraus, Ernst, outstanding German tenor: b. Erlangen, June 8, 1863; d. Wörthsee, Sept. 6, 1941. He studied in Milan with Cesare Galliera and in Munich with Schimon-Regan; made his concert debut at a Kaim Concert in Munich (Jan. 18, 1893), and then his operatic debut in Mannheim on March 26, 1893, as Tamino in *Die Zauberflöte;* remained on its roster until 1896, and thereafter was a leading member of the Berlin Royal (later State) Opera until 1924. He also was a leading singer with the Damrosch Opera Co. in N.Y. (1896–99) and at the Bayreuth Festivals (1899–1909); appeared at London's Covent Garden (1900, 1907, 1910). He made his Metropolitan Opera debut in N.Y. on Nov. 25, 1903, as Siegmund in *Die Walküre,* remaining on its roster for a season. After retiring from the Berlin State Opera in 1924, he returned to Munich as a singing teacher. He was one of the foremost Wagnerians of his day, excelling in such roles as Siegfried, Siegmund, and Walther von Stolzing.

Kraus, Felix von, noted Austrian bass; b. Vienna, Oct. 3, 1870; d. Munich, Oct. 30, 1937. He studied music theory at the Univ. of Vienna (Ph.D., 1894); also received vocal instruction from C. Van Zanten in Amsterdam and from Stockhausen in Frankfurt. He made his debut in a Vienna concert (1896); made his operatic debut as Hagen at the Bayreuth Festival (1899), and continued to appear there until 1909, excelling as Gurnemanz, the Landgrave, and King Marke; sang at London's Covent Garden (1907). In 1908 he became a prof. at the Munich Academy of Music. He married the American contralto **Adrienne Osborne** (1899).

Kraus, Joseph Martin, important German-born Swedish composer; b. Miltenberg-am-Main, June 20, 1756; d. Stockholm, Dec. 15, 1792. He attended the Jesuit School in Mannheim; subsequently studied law at the Univs. of Mainz (1773–74), Erfurt (1775–76), and Göttingen (1777–78). In 1778 he went to Sweden, making his home in Stockholm; in 1780, was elected a member of the Swedish Academy of Music; in 1781 was appointed deputy conductor of the Court Orch. His great interest in Swedish culture prompted King Gustavus III to send him to Germany, Austria, Italy, France, and England for study purposes between the years 1782 and 1787. During his travels, he met Gluck and Haydn, both of whom warmly praised his music. In 1788 he was appointed Hovkapellmästare in Stockholm, holding this position until his untimely death from tuberculosis. During his short life (he was almost an exact contemporary of Mozart), he composed several distinguished works for the stage; his operas (to Swedish texts) are estimable achievements, especially *Aeneas i Carthago* (*Dido och Aeneas*), which was premiered posthumously in Stockholm on Nov. 18, 1799. He also composed a *Symphonie funèbre* and *Begravingskantata* for the assassinated Gustavus III. After Kraus's death, his MSS and letters were deposited in the library of the Univ. of Uppsala. In recent years, a number of his works have been publ. His writings include *Versuch von Schäfergedichten* (Mainz, 1773) and *Etwas von und über Musik fürs Jahr 1777* (Frankfurt, 1778).

WORKS: STAGE: *Azire,* opera (1778; only fragments extant); *Proserpina,* opera (Ulriksdal Castle, June 1781); *Fintbergs Bröllop* (Fintberg's Wedding), comic play with music (Stockholm, Jan. 1788); *Soliman II, eller De tre sultaninnorna,* comic opera (Stockholm, Sept. 22, 1789); *Afventyraren* (The Adventurer), comic play with music (Stockholm, Jan. 30, 1791); *Aeneas i Carthago* (*Dido och Aeneas*), opera (Stockholm, Nov. 18, 1799);

etc. VOCAL: *Cantata for the King's Birthday* (1782–83); *Begravningskantata* (1792); songs; sacred music. ORCH.: *Wiener Sinfonie* (1783); *Pariser Sinfonie* (1784); *Symphonie funèbre* (1792); Violin Concerto (1777); Sinfonia Concertante (1780); overtures, etc. CHAMBER: 9 string quartets, 4 violin sonatas, pieces for solo piano.

BIBL.: F. Silverstolpe, *Biographie af K.* (Stockholm, 1833); B. Anrep-Nordin, "Studier över J.M. K.," *Svensk Tidskrift för Musikforskning,* V (1923) and VI (1924); K. Schreiber, "Verzeichnis der musikalischen Werke von J. K.," *Archiv für Musikwissenschaft,* VII (1925; not complete); K. Schreiber, *Biographie über den Odenwälder Komponisten J.M. K.* (Buchen, 1928); R. Engländer, *J.M. K. und die Gustavianische Oper* (Uppsala and Leipzig, 1943); H.C. Robbins Landon, "J.M. K.," *Musical Times,* CIII (1972); V. Bungardt, *J.M. K. . . . ein Meister des klassischen Klavierliedes* (Regensburg, 1973); I. Leux-Henschen, *J.M. K. in seinen Briefen* (Stockholm, 1978); F. Riedel, ed., *J.M. K. und Italien: Beiträge zur Rezeption italienischer Kultur, Kunst und Musik im späten 18. Jahrhundert* (Munich, 1987); B. Van Boer, *Die Werke von J.M. K.: Systematisch-thematisches Werkverzeichnis* (Stockholm, 1988).

Kraus, Lili, noted Hungarian-born English pianist; b. Budapest, March 4, 1903; d. Asheville, N.C., Nov. 6, 1986. She studied piano, and was accepted as a student of Bartók and Kodály at the Budapest Academy of Music, at the age of 17. She then went to Vienna, where she studied piano with Steuermann at the Cons.; then attended Schnabel's master classes in Berlin (1930–34). She became known in Europe as a congenial Chopin player, but after a series of concerts and duo recitals with the violinist Szymon Goldberg in Beethoven programs, she was hailed as a true Beethovenian; then she played Mozart and was extolled as an authentic Mozartian. She also gave performances of piano works by Bartók. Thus equipped, she toured Europe, Japan, Australia, and South Africa. She married the German philosopher Otto Mandl and settled in London. Recklessly, she engaged in a world tour through the Orient in 1942, only to be interned by the Japanese when they captured the island of Java; fortunately she was helped by a Japanese conductor with whom she played in Tokyo, and he made her life tolerable. After World War II, she resumed her career with appearances in most of the leading music centers; was artist-in-residence at Texas Christian Univ. in Fort Worth (1967–83). She became a British subject in 1948. On March 4, 1978, she was awarded by her native Austria the Cross of Honor for Science and Art.

Kraus, Otakar, Czech-born English baritone; b. Prague, Dec. 10, 1909; d. London, July 28, 1980. He was educated in Prague and Milan; made his debut as Amonasro in Brno (1935); then sang in Bratislava. At the outbreak of World War II, he went to England, where he sang with the Carl Rosa Opera Co. (1940); then joined the English Opera Group (1946), creating Tarquinius in Britten's *The Rape of Lucretia.* He sang with the Netherlands Opera (1950–51); created Nick Shadow in Stravinsky's *The Rake's Progress* (Venice, 1951); subsequently appeared at London's Covent Garden (1951–73), where he created Diomede in Walton's *Troilus and Cressida* (1954) and King Fisher in Tippett's *The Midsummer Marriage* (1955); also appeared as Alberich at the Bayreuth Festivals (1960–62). After his retirement, he devoted himself to teaching. He was made an Officer of the Order of the British Empire (1973).

Krause, Anton, German pianist, conductor, and composer; b. Geithain, Nov. 9, 1834; d. Dresden, Jan. 31, 1907. He began to study piano at an early age; then studied at Dresden; studied at the Leipzig Cons. with Wenzel, Moscheles, Hauptmann, Richter, Rietz, and David (1850–53); taught music and also conducted in Leipzig. From 1859 to 1897 he was director of the Singverein and the Konzertgesellschaft in Barmen. He wrote *Prinzessin Ilse* for Soli, Female Chorus, Piano, and Declamation; choral works; songs; also instructive piano pieces. He publ. a collection of classical sonatinas and *Library for Two Pianofortes* (18 vols.).

Krause, Emil, German pianist, teacher, music critic, and composer; b. Hamburg, July 30, 1840; d. there, Sept. 5, 1916. He was a pupil of Hauptmann, Richter, Rietz, Moscheles, and Plaidy at the Leipzig Cons. In 1860 he went to Hamburg, where he taught at the Cons.; also wrote music criticism for the *Fremdenblatt* (1864–1907). He publ. several pedagogical works; also *Johannes Brahms in seinen Werken* (Hamburg, 1892). He composed an oratorio, *Den Heimgegangenen*; chamber music; songs; piano pieces.

Krause, Martin, German pianist and pedagogue; b. Lobstadt, near Leipzig, June 17, 1853; d. Plattling, Bavaria, Aug. 2, 1918. He was a pupil of his father, a cantor, and of Wenzel and Reinecke at the Leipzig Cons. After successful tours in the Netherlands and Germany (1878–80), he was prostrated by nervous exhaustion for 2 years. He played before Liszt in 1883, and remained closely associated with him until the latter's death in 1886. In 1885 he helped organize the Leipzig Lisztverein with 2 grand concerts, and remained its leading figure until its demise in 1900. He subsequently taught in Leipzig and Dresden and at Berlin's Stern Cons.

Krause, Theodor, German choral conductor, teacher, music critic, and composer; b. Halle, May 1, 1833; d. Berlin, Dec. 12, 1910. He was a theological student; studied music with Hentschel, Hauptmann, and Grell. He organized church choirs in Berlin; was conductor of the Seiffert a cappella society; taught sight-singing by use of the "Wandernote" (movable "do"). He also was active as a music critic; publ. *Die Wandernote* (1888) and *Deutsche Singschule* (1888). He composed church music, part-songs, and songs.

Krause, Tom, Finnish baritone; b. Helsinki, July 5, 1934. He studied in Helsinki, Vienna, and Hamburg; made his concert debut in Helsinki in 1957; his operatic debut at the Berlin Städtische Oper was as Escamillo in 1958. In 1962 he joined the Hamburg State Opera; also sang at Bayreuth, Covent Garden in London, Glyndebourne, and the Vienna State Opera. On Oct. 11, 1967, he made his American debut at the Metropolitan Opera in N.Y. as Count Almaviva in *Le nozze di Figaro*.

Krauss, Clemens (Heinrich), eminent Austrian conductor, great-nephew of **(Marie) Gabrielle Krauss**; b. Vienna, March 31, 1893; d. Mexico City, May 16, 1954. His father was a court figure, and his mother a dancer; of illegitimate birth, he took his mother's maiden name. He was a chorister in the Imperial Choir; then studied piano with Reinhold, composition with Grädener, and theory with Heuberger at the Vienna Cons. (graduated, 1912). He was a chorus master at the Brünn Theater (1912–13), making his conducting debut there with a performance of *Zar und Zimmermann* (Jan. 13, 1913); then was 2nd conductor at Riga's German Theater (1913–14) and in Nuremberg (1915–16); after serving as 1st conductor in Stettin (1916–21), he conducted in Graz (1921–22). In 1922 he became Schalk's assistant at the Vienna State Opera; he also taught conducting at the Vienna Academy of Music (1922–24) and was conductor of the Vienna Tonkünstlerkonzerte (1923–27). He was director of the Frankfurt Opera and its Museumgesellschaft concerts (1924–29), and then of the Vienna State Opera (1929–34); was also conductor of the Vienna Phil. (1930–33). In 1926 he made his 1st appearance at the Salzburg Festivals, and returned there regularly (1929–34); he also conducted in South America (1927) and was a guest conductor with the N.Y. Phil. and the Philadelphia Orch. (1929); he also made his debut at London's Covent Garden in 1934. He was director of the Berlin State Opera (1934–37) and Generalmusikdirektor of the Bavarian State Opera in Munich (1937–44); also conducted at the Salzburg Mozarteum (1939–45) and appeared with the Vienna Phil. (1944–45). Having been a friend of Hitler and Göring, and a prominent figure in the musical life of the 3rd Reich, Krauss was held accountable for his actions by the Allied authorities after the end of World War II. There was a strain of humanity in Krauss, however, for he had assisted Jews to escape the clutches of the barbarous Führer's fury. In 1947 he was permitted to resume his career

with appearances at the Vienna State Opera; he took it to London that same year. He was a conductor with the Vienna Phil. from 1947, and also served as conductor of its famous New Year's Day Concerts. From 1951 to 1953 he conducted at London's Covent Garden, and in 1953–54 at the Bayreuth Festivals. He died during a visit to Mexico. He was married to the soprano **Viorica Ursuleac,** who often appeared in operas under his direction; he also accompanied her in recitals. He was a close friend and collaborator of Richard Strauss, who considered him one of the finest interpreters of his works; he conducted the premieres of *Arabella, Friedenstag, Capriccio* (for which he wrote the libretto), and *Die Liebe der Danae*. Krauss was renowned as a conductor of works by Mozart, Wagner, and Verdi, as well as those by the Viennese waltz composers.
    Bibl.: A. Berger, *C. K.* (Graz, 1924; 3rd ed., 1929); O. van Pander, *C. K. in München* (Munich, 1955); B. Flowers, "*C. K.* (1893–1954): An Evolution," *Le Grand Baton* (Nov. 1986; with discography); G. Kende and S. Scanzoni, *Der Prinzipal. C. K.: Fakten, Vergleiche, Rückschlüsse* (Tutzing, 1988).

Krauss, (Marie) Gabrielle, esteemed Austrian soprano, great-aunt of **Clemens (Heinrich) Krauss;** b. Vienna, March 24, 1842; d. Paris, Jan. 6, 1906. She studied with Mathilde Marchesi at the Vienna Cons.; made her concert debut in Schumann's *Das Paradies und die Peri* in Berlin (1858). She then joined the Vienna Court Opera, where she made her 1st important appearance as Mathilde in *Wilhelm Tell* (July 20, 1860); remained on its roster until 1867. She made her debut at the Théâtre-Italien in Paris as Leonora in *Il Trovatore* (April 6, 1867), becoming a great favorite. The Franco-Prussian War of 1870 compelled her to leave France; she sang in Italy and in Russia. When the new building of the Paris Grand Opéra was opened, she sang Rachel in *La Juive* (Jan. 5, 1875); remained with the Opéra until 1888, with the exception of the 1885–86 season. She subsequently gave concerts and was active as a teacher. She was greatly admired for her Donna Anna, Leonora, Aida, and roles in Meyerbeer's operas; she also created Catharine of Aragon in Saint-Saëns's *Henry VIII* (1883).

Krauze, Zygmunt, Polish pianist and composer; b. Warsaw, Sept. 19, 1938. He studied composition with Sikorski and piano with Maria Wilkomirska at the Warsaw Cons. (M.A., 1964); completed his studies with Nadia Boulanger in Paris (1966–67). As a pianist, he specialized in contemporary music. In 1982 he settled in Paris; in 1987, became president of the ISCM. He is an inventive composer, cultivating with equal devotion primitive rustic instruments and electronic sounds.
    Works: *3 Malay Pantuns*, to Indonesian texts, for 3 Flutes and Contralto (1961); *Voices* for 5 to 15 Optional Instruments (1968); *Polychrony* for Clarinet, Trombone, Cello, and Piano (1968); 3 string quartets (1960, 1969, 1982); *Piece for Orchestra No. 1* (1969); *Piece for Orchestra No. 2* (1970); *Folk Music* for Orch. (1971–72); *Aus aller Welt stammende* for 10 Strings (1973); *Song* for Flute, Clarinet, Bassoon, Violin, Cello, Double Bass, and 3 Automatophones (1974); *Automatophone* for 15 Musical Boxes and 15 Plucked Instruments (1974); *Fête galante et pastorale*, space music for a castle, for 13 Tapes and 6 Instrumental Groups (Graz, Oct. 12, 1974); *Idyll* for Tape, 4 Hurdy-gurdies, 4 Bagpipes, 4 Zlobcoki, 8 Fifes, 16 Bells, and 4 Whistles (1974); Piano Concerto (1974–76); *Die Kleider*, chamber opera (1981; Mannheim, March 26, 1982); *Piece for Orchestra No. 3* (Metz, Oct. 22, 1982); *Arabesque* for Piano and Chamber Orch. (1983); Double Concerto for Violin, Piano, and Orch. (1985); *Symphonie parisienne* (Paris, June 4, 1986); *La Rivière souterraine* for 7 Instrumentalists and Conductor (1987); numerous piano pieces.

Krebs, family of German musicians:
    (1) Johann Tobias Krebs, organist and composer; b. Heichelheim, Weimar, July 7, 1690; d. Buttelstädt, Weimar, Feb. 11, 1762. He became organist in Buttelstädt (1710); concurrently studied with J.G. Walther and later with Bach in Weimar; then was made organist of the Michaeliskirche in Buttelstädt

(1721). His sacred music is not extant; several choral settings for organ have survived.

(2) Johann Ludwig Krebs, organist and composer, son of the preceding; b. Buttelstädt, Weimar (baptized), Oct. 12, 1713; d. Altenburg, Jan. 1, 1780. He received methodical training in music from his father; subsequently studied keyboard playing, lute, and violin at the Leipzig Thomasschule (1726–35), receiving valuable training from Bach. He then studied at the Univ. of Leipzig (1735–37), but continued to be active at the Thomaskirche and also performed as a harpsichordist in Bach's Collegium Musicum. Later he was organist at Zwickau, Zeitz, and Altenburg. He was a talented composer whose works reveal the combined influences of Bach and the galant style.

WORKS: ORGAN: 8 preludes and fugues; 2 toccatas and fugues; 2 fantasias and fugues; 10 free preludes or fantasias; 16 fugues, including 1 on the name of B-A-C-H; 14 trios; many chorale settings; also a number of works for organ and other instruments. See C. Geissler, ed., *J.L. Krebs: Gesamt-Ausgabe der Tonstücke für die Orgel* (Magdeburg, 1847–49); K. Tittel, ed., *J.L. Krebs: Ausgewählte Orgelwerke,* Die Orgel, 2nd series, XVIII, XX, XXI, XXVI (Lippstadt, 1963–75); and G. Weinberger, ed., *J.L. Krebs: Sämtliche Orgelwerke* (1985–86). OTHER KEYBOARD: *Erste Piece, bestehend in 6 leichten . . . Praembulis* (Nuremberg, 1740); *Andere Piece, bestehend in einer leichten . . . Suite* (Nuremberg, 1741); *Dritte Piece, bestehend in einer . . . Ouverture* (Nuremberg, 1741); *Vierte Piece, bestehend in einem . . . Concerto* (Nuremberg, 1743); *Clavier Ubung, bestehend in verschiedenen Vorspielen und Veranderungen einiger Kirchen Gesänge* (Nuremberg, n.d.); *Clavier-Ubung bestehend in einer . . . Suite . . . zweyter Theil* (Nuremberg, n.d.); *Clavier-Ubung bestehend in sechs Sonatinen . . . IIIer Theil* (Nuremberg, n.d.); *Exercice sur le clavessin consistant en VI suites,* op. 4 (Nuremberg, n.d.); Concerto for 2 Harpsichords (ed. by B. Klein, Leipzig, 1966). INSTRUMENTAL: 2 sinfonias for 2 Violins, Viola, and Basso Continuo; 2 concertos for Lute and Strings (ed. by R. Chiesa, Milan, 1970–71); Concerto for Harpsichord, Oboe, and Strings (ed. by K. Jametzky, Heidelberg, 1976); 6 trios for 2 Flutes or Violins and Basso Continuo (Nuremberg, n.d.); 6 *Sonata da camera* for Harpsichord and Flute or Violin (Leipzig, 1762; ed. by B. Klein as *Sechs Kammersonaten,* Leipzig, 1963); *Musikalischer und angenehmer Zeitvertreib bestehet in 2 Sonaten* for Harpsichord and Flute or Violin (Nuremberg, n.d.). He also wrote a number of sacred vocal works.

BIBL.: H. Löffler, "J.L. K.: Mitteilungen über sein Leben und Wirken," *Bach-Jahrbuch,* XXVII (1930); J. Horstmann, *The Instrumental Music of J.L. K.* (diss., Boston Univ., 1959; with thematic catalog); D. Mulberry, "Bach's Favorite Pupil: J.L. K.," *Music/The A.G.O. Magazine,* ii (1968).

(3) Johann Gottfried Krebs, organist and composer, son of the preceding; b. Zwickau (baptized), May 29, 1741; d. Altenburg, Jan. 5, 1814. He served as Mittelorganist in Altenburg (1758–81); then was Stadtkantor there until his death. He wrote much sacred music, including some 70 cantatas and an oratorio; he also wrote a musical drama and keyboard pieces. His 2 brothers were also musicians: Carl Heinrich Gottlieb Krebs (1747–93) was court organist in Esenberg from 1774; Ehrenfried Christian Traugott Krebs (1753–1804) was his father's successor as Altenburg court organist (1780); he publ. 6 organ chorale-preludes (Leipzig, 1787).

Krebs (real name, **Miedcke**), **Carl August,** German conductor and composer; b. Nuremberg, Jan. 16, 1804; d. Dresden, May 16, 1880. He studied with the tenor and composer Johann Baptist Krebs (1774–1851), who legally adopted him. He made his debut as a pianist at 6, and then commenced composing at 7. After studies with Schelble, he continued his training with Seyfried in Vienna (1825); then was 3rd Kapellmeister at the Kärntnertortheater there. He subsequently was Kapellmeister in Hamburg (1827–50), where he brought out the operas *Sylvia* (Feb. 4, 1830) and *Agnes* (Oct. 8, 1833; rev. as *Agnes Bernauer,* Dresden, 1858). He succeeded Wagner as Kapellmeister of the Dresden Court Opera (1850), where he

remained until 1872; then was director of music of the city's Roman Catholic church. Krebs championed the works of Spontini, Meyerbeer, and the young Wagner. He wrote sacred music, piano pieces, and numerous songs, several of which became well known in his day. He married the mezzo-soprano **Aloysia Michalesi** (b. Prague, Aug. 29, 1826; d. Dresden, Aug. 5, 1904) in 1850; she made her debut in Brünn in 1843, then sang in Hamburg and Dresden; retired from opera (1870) and subsequently appeared in concerts and taught. Their daughter **Marie Krebs** (b. Dresden, Dec. 5, 1851; d. there, June 27, 1900) was a talented pianist; made her debut in Meissen when she was 11; later toured throughout Europe, becoming quite popular in England; accompanied Vieuxtemps on a concert tour of the U.S. in 1870.

Krebs, Helmut, German tenor; b. Dortmund, Oct. 8, 1913. He studied at the Berlin Hochschule für Musik; made his debut at the Berlin Städtische Oper (1938); then sang with the Düsseldorf Opera (1945–47) and again with the Berlin Städtische Oper. He also sang opera in Hamburg, Munich, Milan, London, Glyndebourne, Edinburgh, and Salzburg; likewise appeared as an oratorio and concert artist. In 1963 he was made a Berlin Kammersänger. He taught at the Frankfurt Hochschule für Musik (1963–75).

Krehbiel, Henry (Edward), noted American music critic; b. Ann Arbor, Mich., March 10, 1854; d. N.Y., March 20, 1923. He was music critic of the *Cincinnati Gazette* (1874–80), and subsequently of the *N.Y. Tribune* until his death. He also wrote the program notes for the N.Y. Phil., was American ed. of the 2nd edition of *Grove's Dictionary of Music and Musicians* (1904–10), and brought out the rev. and completed ed. of the Eng. version of Thayer's *Life of Beethoven* (3 vols., 1921). He was a brilliant writer of music criticism, able to project his opinions (and prejudices) in vivid prose. He was an ardent champion of Wagner, and also wrote with warm admiration for the late Romantic composers; however, he deprecated the modern school of composition, hurling invectives on Stravinsky, Prokofiev, and Schoenberg (whose music he described as excrement).

WRITINGS: (all publ. in N.Y.): *Notes on the Cultivation of Choral Music, and the Oratorio Society of New York* (1884); *Review of the New York Musical Season* (5 vols., 1886–90); *Studies in the Wagnerian Drama* (1891); *The Philharmonic Society of New York: A Memorial Published on the Occasion of the Fiftieth Anniversary of the Founding of the Philharmonic Society* (1892); *How to Listen to Music* (1896); *Annotated Biography of Fine Art* (with R. Sturgis; 1897); *Music and Manners in the Classical Period* (1898); *Chapters of Opera* (1908; 2nd ed., 1911); *A Book of Operas* (1909); *The Pianoforte, and Its Music* (1911); *Afro-American Folksongs* (1914); *A Second Book of Operas* (1917); *More Chapters of Opera* (1919).

Krehl, Stephan, German music theorist and composer; b. Leipzig, July 5, 1864; d. there, April 7, 1924. He studied at the Leipzig and Dresden Cons. He taught piano and theory at the Karlsruhe Cons. (1889–1902); then at the Leipzig Cons. (1902–24), where he was made prof. (1910) and director (1921). He wrote a cantata, *Tröstung;* choral works; chamber music; songs; piano pieces.

WRITINGS: *Musikalische Formenlehre* (Leipzig, 1902–5; 2nd ed., augmented, 1917–20); *Allgemeine Musiklehre* (Leipzig, 1906; 3rd ed., 1933, by R. Hernried); *Fuge, Erläuterung und Anleitung für Komposition derselben* (Leipzig, 1908); *Kontrapunkt* (Leipzig, 1908); *Theorie der Tonkunst und Kompositionslehre* (Berlin and Leipzig, 1920–22); *Harmonielehre* (Leipzig, 1921; 2nd ed., 1928).

BIBL.: F. Reuter, *S. K.* (Leipzig, 1921).

Krein, Alexander (Abramovich), Russian composer, brother of **Grigori (Abramovich) Krein** and uncle of **Julian (Grigorievich) Krein;** b. Nizhny-Novgorod, Oct. 20, 1883; d. Staraya Ruza, near Moscow, April 21, 1951. At the age of 13 he entered the Moscow Cons. and studied cello; also studied composition privately with Nikolayev and Yavorsky. He taught at the People's Cons. in Moscow (1912–17); after the Revolution, he worked in the music division of the Commissariat of Education and in the Ethnographic Dept. From 1923 he was associated with the productions of the Jewish Drama Theater in Moscow, and wrote music for many Jewish plays. Together with Gnessin, he was a leader of the National Jewish movement in Russia. In general, his style was influenced by Scriabin and Debussy, but he made considerable use of authentic Hebrew material.

WORKS: Operas: *Zagmuk,* on a revolutionary subject based on an ancient Babylonian tale (Moscow, May 29, 1930), and *Daughter of the People* (1946); ballet after Lope de Vega, *Laurencie* (1938); incidental music to the Jewish plays *The Eternal One* (1923), *Sabbati Zewi* (1924), *Ghetto* (1924), *The People* (1925), and *The Doctor* (1925); *Salome* for Orch. (1923); *Elegy* for String Orch. (1914); *The Rose and the Cross,* symphonic fragments (1917–21); *Kaddish,* symphonic cantata for Tenor, Mixed Choir, and Orch. (1921); 2 syms. (1922–25; 1946); *U.S.S.R., Shock Brigade of the World Proletariat,* symphonic dithyramb for Narrator, Chorus, and Orch. (1925); *Threnody in Memory of Lenin* for Chorus and Orch. (1925); various symphonic suites on Hebrew themes; String Quartet; *Jewish Sketches* for Clarinet and String Quartet; *Elegiac Trio* for Violin, Cello, and Piano; *Jewish Capriccio* for Violin and Piano; Piano Sonata; *3 Poems* for Piano; *Jewish Songs* (to Russian words); vocalises.

BIBL.: L. Sabaneyev, *A. K.* (Moscow, 1928; in Russian and German); J. Krein and N. Rogozhina, *A. K.* (Moscow, 1964).

Krein, Grigori (Abramovich), Russian composer, brother of **Alexander (Abramovich) Krein** and father of **Julian (Grigorievich) Krein;** b. Nizhny-Novgorod, March 18, 1879; d. Komarovo, near Leningrad, Jan. 6, 1955. He studied with Juon and Glière. His music underwent the influence of Jewish culture, and he wrote many works on Jewish themes; however, he also cultivated strict classical forms, adapting them to his needs. He wrote a descriptive symphonic cycle on Lenin's life (1937); Violin Concerto; *Hebrew Rhapsody* for Clarinet and Orch.; String Quartet; piano pieces.

Krein, Julian (Grigorievich), Russian composer and musicologist, son of **Grigori (Abramovich) Krein;** b. Moscow, March 5, 1913. He studied with his father; wrote his 1st compositions at the age of 13. In 1927 he went to Paris, where he completed his studies with Dukas at the École Normale (graduated, 1932). In 1934 he returned to Moscow. He publ. several monographs (all in Moscow), including ones on Falla (1960), Debussy (1962), Ravel (1962), and his uncle **Alexander (Abramovich) Krein** (with N. Rogozhina; 1964). His music was inspired by both Russian and French models, resulting in works of notable lyricism and harmonic inventiveness.

WORKS: *Razrusheniye* (Destruction), symphonic prelude (1929); Cello Concerto (1929); 3 piano concertos (1929, 1942, 1943); *Vesennyaya simfoniya* (Spring Symphony; 1935–59); *Serenade* for Orch. (1943); *Arkticheskaya poema,* sym. (1943); *Poemasimfoniya* (1954); *Poema* for Violin and Orch. (1956); Violin Concerto (1959); *Rembrandt,* vocal-symphonic picture (1962–69); 4 string quartets (1925, 1927, 1936, 1943); 2 violin sonatas (1948, 1971); Flute Sonata (1957); Piano Trio (1958); Clarinet Sonata (1961); *Sonata-Poema* for Cello and Piano (1972); 2 piano sonatas (1924, 1955); other piano pieces; songs.

BIBL.: Y. Tyulin, *J. K.: Ocherk zhizni i tvorchestva* (J. K.: Sketch of His Life and Work; Moscow, 1971).

Kreisler, Fritz (actually, **Friedrich**), great Austrian-born American violinist; b. Vienna, Feb. 2, 1875; d. N.Y., Jan. 29, 1962. His extraordinary talent manifested itself when he was only 4, and it was carefully fostered by his father, under whose instruction he made such progress that at age 6 he was accepted as a pupil of Jacob Dont; he also studied with Jacques Auber until, at 7, he entered the Vienna Cons., where his principal teachers were Hellmesberger, Jr. (violin), and Bruckner (theory); he gave his 1st performance there when he was 9 and

was awarded its gold medal at 10. He subsequently studied with Massart (violin) and Delibes (composition) at the Paris Cons., sharing the premier prix in violin with 4 other students (1887). He made his U.S. debut in Boston on Nov. 9, 1888; then toured the country during the 1889–90 season with the pianist Moriz Rosenthal, but had only moderate success. Returning to Europe, he abandoned music to study medicine in Vienna and art in Rome and Paris; then served as an officer in the Austrian army (1895–96). Resuming his concert career, he appeared as a soloist with Richter and the Vienna Phil. on Jan. 23, 1898. His subsequent appearance as a soloist with Nikisch and the Berlin Phil. on Dec. 1, 1899, launched his international career. Not only had he regained his virtuosity during his respite, but he had also developed into a master interpreter. On his 2nd tour of the U.S. (1900–1901), both as a soloist and as a recitalist with Hofmann and Gerardy, he carried his audiences by storm. On May 12, 1902, he made his London debut as a soloist with Richter and the Phil. Soc. orch.; was awarded its Gold Medal in 1904. Elgar composed his Violin Concerto for him, and Kreisler gave its premiere under the composer's direction in London on Nov. 10, 1910. At the outbreak of World War I in 1914, Kreisler joined his former regiment, but upon being quickly wounded he was discharged. He then returned to the U.S. to pursue his career; after the U.S. entered the war in 1917, he withdrew from public appearances. With the war over, he reappeared in N.Y. on Oct. 27, 1919, and once again resumed his tours. From 1924 to 1934 he made his home in Berlin, but in 1938 he went to France, and became a naturalized citizen. In 1939 he settled in the U.S., becoming a naturalized citizen (1943). In 1941 he suffered a near-fatal accident when he was struck by a truck in N.Y.; however, he recovered and continued to give concerts until 1950.

Kreisler was one of the greatest masters of the violin. His brilliant technique was ably matched by his remarkable tone, both of which he always placed in the service of the composer. He was the owner of the great Guarneri "del Gesu" violin of 1733 and of instruments by other masters. He gathered a rich collection of invaluable MSS; in 1949 he donated the original scores of Brahms's Violin Concerto and Chausson's *Poème* for Violin and Orch. to the Library of Congress. He wrote some of the most popular violin pieces in the world, among them *Caprice viennois, Tambourin chinois, Schön Rosmarin,* and *Liebesfreud.* He also publ. a number of pieces in the classical vein, which he ascribed to various composers (Vivaldi, Pugnani, Couperin, Padre Martini, Dittersdorf, Francœur, Stamitz, and others). In 1935 he reluctantly admitted that these pieces were his own, with the exception of the 1st 8 bars from the "Couperin" *Chanson Louis XIII,* taken from a traditional melody; he explained his motive in doing so as the necessity of building up well-rounded programs for his concerts that would contain virtuoso pieces by established composers, rather than a series of compositions under his own, as yet unknown name. He also wrote the operettas *Apple Blossoms* (N.Y., Oct. 7, 1919) and *Sissy* (Vienna, Dec. 23, 1932), publ. numerous arrangements of early and modern music (Corelli's *La Folia,* Tartini's *The Devil's Trill,* Dvořák's *Slavonic Dances, Spanish Dance* by Granados, *Tango* by Albeniz, etc.), and prepared cadenzas for the Beethoven and Brahms violin concertos. He publ. a book of reminiscences of World War I, *Four Weeks in the Trenches: The War Story of a Violinist* (Boston, 1915).

BIBL.: O. Downes, "K.'s Delectable Musical Hoax," N.Y. *Times* (March 3, 1935); L. Lochner, *F. K.* (N.Y., 1950; 3rd ed., rev., 1981); B. Schwarz, *Great Masters of the Violin* (N.Y., 1983).

Kreissle von Hellborn, Heinrich, Austrian writer on music; b. Vienna, Jan. 19, 1822; d. there, April 6, 1869. He studied law; was a Dr.Juris, and secretary in the Ministry of Finance in Vienna. A passionate admirer of Schubert, he publ. *Franz Schubert, Eine biographische Skizze* (1861), followed in 1865 by the exhaustive biography *Franz Schubert* (condensed Eng. tr. by Wilberforce, 1866; full tr. by A.D. Coleridge, 1869).

Krejčí, Iša (František), prominent Czech composer and conductor; b. Prague, July 10, 1904; d. there, March 6, 1968. He studied composition with Jirák and Novák and conducting with Talich at the Prague Cons. (graduated, 1929). He conducted at the Bratislava Opera (1928–32), then at the Prague National Theater (1933–34) and at the Prague Radio (1934–45). From 1945 to 1958 he was chief conductor of the Olomouc Opera; then was artistic director of the Prague National Theater (1958–68). His music, in a neo-Classical idiom, is distinguished by vivacious rhythms and freely flowing melody; the national Czech element is not ostentatious, but its presence is well marked.

Works: 2 operas: *Antigone,* after Sophocles (1934), and *Pozdviženi v Efesu* (The Revolt at Ephesus), after Shakespeare's *Comedy of Errors* (1939–43; Prague, Sept. 8, 1946); Sinfonietta (1929); *Malý balet* (Small Ballet) for Chamber Orch. (1927–30); Concertino for Piano and Wind Instruments (1935); Concertino for Violin and Wind Instruments (1936); *Antické motivy* (Antique Motifs) for Low Male Voice and Orch. or Piano (1936); Suite for Orch. (1939); *Sinfonietta-Divertimento* for Orch. (1939); Cello Concertino (1939–40); *20 Variations on an Original Theme* for Orch. (1946–47); Serenade for Orch. (1947–50); *14 Variations* on the folk song *Goodnight, My Beloved* for Orch. (1951–52); 4 syms. (1954–55; 1956–57; 1961–63; 1961–66); *Vivat Rossini,* overture (1967); *Divertimento-Cassation* for Flute, Clarinet, Bassoon, and Trumpet (1925); 5 string quartets (1928, rev. 1935; 1953; 1960; 1962; 1965); Viola Sonatina (1928–29); Clarinet Sonatina (1929–30); Trio for Oboe, Clarinet, and Bassoon (1935); Trio for Clarinet, Double Bass, and Piano (1936); Nonet (1937); *Sonatina concertante* for Cello and Piano (1939); Wind Quintet (1964); *4 Pieces* for Violin and Piano (1967); *A Little Mourning Music* for Alto, Violin, Cello, Double Bass, and Piano (1936); *Ohlasy* (Night Sounds) for Voice and Wind Quintet (1936); Piano Trio, with Female Voice, to words of a Psalm (1967); Piano Sonatina (1934); *3 Scherzinos* for Piano (1945); songs.

Krejčí, Josef, Bohemian organist and composer; b. Milostin, Dec. 17, 1821; d. Prague, Oct. 19, 1881. He studied with Josef Proksch in Prague; was active as a church organist; in 1858 he became director of the Organ School in Prague, and in 1865 of the Prague Cons. He wrote mainly sacred choruses and organ pieces.

Krejčí, Miroslav, Czech composer; b. Rychnov nad Kněžnou, Nov. 4, 1891; d. Prague, Dec. 29, 1964. He studied piano, organ, and theory at home; subsequently took courses in natural history, geography, and music at the Univ. of Prague (1910–14); also studied composition privately with Novák (1911–13). He then taught in Prague and Litoměřice (1915–53); was a prof. at the Prague Cons. (1943–53).

Works: 2 operas: *Léto* (Summer; 1937; Prague, Dec. 4, 1940) and *Poslední Hejtman* (The Last Captain; 1944; Prague, March 18, 1948); cantatas: *The Wedding Song* (1926); *Smrt Kristova* (The Death of Christ; 1937–40); *Better Love* (1954); *Rodné Zemi* (Homeland; 1958); *Mír* (Peace; 1959); Vocal Sym. (1930); 3 numbered syms.: No. 1 (1944–46); No. 2 (1952–54); No. 3 (1955); *King Lávra,* symphonic poem (1917); *Life and Time* for String Orch. and Horn (1927); Viola Concerto (1947); Clarinet Concerto (1949); *Capriccio* for Viola, Winds, and Percussion (1950); *Dance Suite* for Orch. (1950); Violin Concerto (1953); *Funeral Music* for Wind Orch. (1960); 7 string quartets (1913, 1918, 1926, 1941, 1943, 1953, 1955); Clarinet Quintet (1920); 3 string quintets (1926, 1952, 1957); Divertimento for Flute, Clarinet, Horn, and Bassoon (1926); 2 violin sonatas (1926, 1952); Viola Sonata (1942); Cello Sonata (1943); Sonatina for Bassoon or Oboe or Horn and Piano (1950); Septet (1950); Nonet (1953); Organ Sonata (1954); Quartet for Oboe, Clarinet, Bassoon, and Piano (1955); Wind Octet (1956); Suite for Horn (1956); *3 Pieces* for 3 Violas and Piano (1957); Flute Sonata (1958); Divertimento for 10 Winds (1958); Horn Sonata (1959); choruses; songs.

Krek, Uroš, Slovene composer; b. Ljubljana, May 21, 1922. He studied composition with Škerjanc at the Ljubljana Academy of Music, graduating in 1947. He worked for the Ljubljana Radio (1950–58); then did research for the Ljubljana Ethnomusicological Inst. (1958–67); subsequently taught at his alma mater (1967–86). He was made a member of the Yugoslav Academy of Science and Art (1977) and the Slovene Academy of Science and Art (1979). His style of composition is classical in form, but contains some elements of folk modalities.

Works: Violin Concerto (1949); Bassoon Concerto (1954); *Mouvements concertants* for String Orch. (1956); Horn Concerto (1960); *Inventiones ferales* for Violin and Orch. (1962); Concerto for Piccolo and Orch. (1966); *Old Egyptian Stanzas* for Tenor and Orch. (1967); *Capriccio* for Viola and 10 Instruments (1971); Sinfonia for Strings (1973); Cello Concerto (1984); choral music; film scores; Violin Sonata (1946); Sonata for 2 Violins (1971); *La Journée d'un bouffon* for Brass Quintet (1973); Clarinet Sonata (1976); Trio for Violin, Viola, and Cello (1977); String Quartet (1979); Cello Sonata (1984); *Espressivo* for Flute and Piano (1985); *Jeux pour quatre* (1986).

Kremenliev, Boris, Bulgarian-American musicologist and composer; b. Razlog, May 23, 1911; d. Los Angeles, April 25, 1988. He went to the U.S. in 1929; studied composition with La Violette at De Paul Univ. in Chicago (B.M., 1936; M.M., 1938) and with Hanson at the Eastman School of Music in Rochester, N.Y. (Ph.D., 1942). He was a member of the Psychological Warfare Branch of the U.S. Army in Europe during World War II. In 1947 he was appointed to the faculty of the Univ. of Calif. at Los Angeles. He publ. *Bulgarian-Macedonian Folk Music* (Los Angeles, 1952). Several of his compositions were imbued with Bulgarian melorhythms; of these, the most interesting are *Pravo Horo* for Orch. (Rochester, N.Y., April 18, 1940) and *Bulgarian Rhapsody* for Orch. (1952); he also composed various other orch. works, including *Crucifixion* (1952), *Elegy: June 5, 1968* (1968–69), and *Peasant Dance* (1984); among his chamber works are 2 string quartets (1954, 1965), 2 piano sonatas (1954, 1959), Double-bass Sonata (1966–67), and *Overtones* for Brass (1983–84).

Kremer, Gidon, brilliant Latvian violinist; b. Riga, Feb. 27, 1947. His parents were violinists in the Riga Sym. Orch. He obtained the elements of violin study from his father and grandfather, then continued professional studies with David Oistrakh at the Moscow Cons. He took part in several competitions, culminating in 1st prizes at the Paganini Competition in Genoa in 1968 and the Tchaikovsky Competition in Moscow in 1970. He made an auspicious N.Y. debut at Avery Fisher Hall on Jan. 14, 1977. In subsequent years he appeared as a soloist with many of the major orchs. of the world, gave recitals, and performed in chamber music settings. He has won special commendation for his efforts to broaden the repertoire for his instrument; his great contribution to modern music has been the consistent presentation of new violin works, particularly those of Soviet composers, among them Alfred Schnittke and Sofia Gubaidulina. He has also given notable performances of the works of the Estonian composer Arvo Pärt.

Bibl.: *Current Biography* (March 1985).

Kremer, Isa, Russian-born Jewish folksinger; b. Beltzi, Bessarabia, 1885; d. Cordoba, Argentina, July 7, 1956. She acquired early fame as a singer of Russian, Yiddish, Polish, and German ballads; made many tours in Russia and eastern Europe before going to the U.S. in 1923; she appeared in vaudeville in N.Y.; gave her final U.S. concert at N.Y.'s Carnegie Hall on Dec. 3, 1950. She married Dr. Gregorio Bermann, an Argentine psychiatrist, in 1940.

Kremlev, Yuli (Anatolyevich), Russian musicologist and composer; b. Essentuki, June 19, 1908; d. Leningrad, Feb. 19, 1971. He studied at the Leningrad Cons.; devoted himself mainly to musical biography. From 1957 he was head of the music dept. of the Leningrad Inst. of the Theater, Music, and Cinematography. His most significant monographs (all publ. in Moscow) were those on Chopin (1949; 3rd ed., 1971), Grieg (1958), Debussy (1964), Massenet (1969), and Saint-Saëns (1970). He wrote a Sym., 14 piano sonatas, and songs.

Krempelsetzer, Georg, German composer; b. Vilsbiburg, April 20, 1827; d. there, June 9, 1871. He was by trade a cloth weaver; studied music in Munich with Franz Lachner; became chorus master at theaters in Munich (1865), Görlitz (1868), and Königsberg (1870). He wrote the opera *Der Onkel aus der Lombardei* (1861) and the operettas *Die Franzosen in Gotha; Der Vetter auf Besuch* (1863); *Die Kreuzfahrer* (1865); *Das Orakel in Delphi* (1867); *Die Geister des Weins* (1867); *Aschenbrödel; Rotmantel* (1868).

Kremser, Eduard, Austrian composer; b. Vienna, April 10, 1838; d. there, Nov. 27, 1914. He studied in Vienna; in 1869, became chorus master of the Männergesangverein there; also conducted various other choral societies. He wrote light operas: *Der Botschafter* (Vienna, Feb. 25, 1886); *Der kritische Tag* (Vienna, Dec. 6, 1891); etc.; several symphonic sketches with Voices: *Balkanbilder; Prinz Eugen; Das Leben ein Tanz*; etc.; many part-songs (his settings of *6 altniederländische Volkslieder* are especially fine; of these the most celebrated is the Dutch *Prayer of Thanksgiving*); *Das Herzklopfen, Erinnerungen*, and *Fröhliche Armuth*, for Men's Chorus and Orch.; songs (*Jagdlied*, with accompaniment of 4 Horns; 2 songs from *Der Trompeter von Säkkingen*, with Solo Cornet); piano music; also ed. *Wiener Lieder und Tänze* (2 vols., 1912, 1913).
    BIBL.: H. von Paumgarten, *E. K.* (Vienna, 1915).

Krenek (originally, **Křenek**), **Ernst,** remarkable Austrian-born American composer, whose intellect responds equally to his musical philosophy and his imaginative technique of composition; b. Vienna, Aug. 23, 1900. He studied with Franz Schreker in Vienna (from 1916), and at the Berlin Academy of Music (1920–23). He then was a conductor and composer at the operas in Kassel and Wiesbaden (1925–27). He returned to Vienna in 1928; was a writer for the *Frankfurter Zeitung* (1930–33); also traveled widely in Europe as a lecturer and an accompanist in programs of his own songs. With the Anschluss of 1938, he settled in the U.S.; became a naturalized American citizen in 1945 and thereafter rendered his name without the diacritical sign over the *r*. He was a prof. of music at Vassar College (1939–42); then head of the music dept. at Hamline Univ. in St. Paul, Minn. (1942–47). He subsequently made his home in California. He married Gustav Mahler's daughter, Anna, in 1923; they were divorced in 1925, and he married Berta Hermann; later married Gladys Nordenstrom (1950).
    Krenek's evolution as a composer mirrors the development of modern music in general. The tradition of Mahler, strengthened by the domestic ties of Krenek's 1st marriage, was the dominant influence of his early life in music; he then became associated with the modern groups in Vienna, particularly Schoenberg, Berg, and Webern. In Germany he was associated with Hindemith as a creator of modern opera in a satiric manner. He achieved a masterly technique of composition in his earliest works, and developed his melodic and harmonic idiom in the direction of atonality and polytonality. His 1st international success came to him at the age of 26, with the production of his opera *Jonny spielt auf* (Leipzig, Feb. 10, 1927). Although it is described as a "jazz opera," no such designation appears in the score. It deals with a jazz fiddler whose fame sweeps the world; in the apotheosis, Jonny sits atop a gigantic globe. In the years following its premiere, the work was produced all over the world; it was translated into 18 languages; a brand of Austrian cigarettes was named after it; it was staged at the Metropolitan Opera in N.Y. (Jan. 19, 1929) with the hero as a black-faced musician rather than a Negro as in the original. In 1933 Krenek adopted an integral 12-tone method of composition; his historical opera *Karl V* was written in this idiom. In his treatment of 12-tone composition, however, he introduced numerous textual and textural indulgences, such as division of the basis 12-tone theme into fractional groups, permutation of thematic elements, and shifting the initial notes of the basic dodecaphonic system.
    The accession of the Nazi governments in Germany and Austria forced the exclusion of performances of Krenek's works from Europe where the Hitlerites held sway; the scheduled production of *Karl V* in Vienna was canceled after Austria was occupied by the Nazis. Even though Krenek was of unimpeachable Aryan origin, his music was banned from performance by the Nazi authorities because of his adherence to an advanced musical idiom which was proscribed by the Nazis. His viciously retouched photograph was featured, along with those of Mahler, Schoenberg, and others, in the infamous collection of Entartete Musik (Degenerate Music). Deprived of all means of subsistence, he went to the U.S.; friends and admirers secured for him a modest engagement as teacher of composition at the Malkin Cons. in Boston, and a few performances of his works by American orchs. followed. Still, his modernistic idiom upset some American music-lovers. (A Boston Sym. Orch. dowager was heard to say after a performance of Krenek's Piano Concerto, "Conditions must be terrible in Europe!")
    Strangely enough, there have been fewer performances of Krenek's works in the U.S., where he has made his home, than in Europe. Stravinsky, who admired him as an intellectual and as a composer, predicted in 1963 that Krenek will one day be honored in both America and Europe. Krenek himself wrote, in his 1950 autobiography, *Selbstdarstellung:* "It is quite possible that the unusual variety of my output has baffled observers accustomed to more homogeneous phenomena. It is my impression that this confusion has surrounded my work with an unusual obscurity—almost anonymity." Stravinsky's prediction came at least partially true when the liberated Austrian government awarded Krenek the Grand State Prize of 1963. A number of festivals and other celebrations, timed for Krenek's 90th birthday in 1990, included the world premiere of his oratorio, *Opus sine nomine* (op. 238; Vienna, May 8, 1990); 3 short operas, *Der Diktator, Das geheime Königreich*, and *Schwergewicht oder Die Ehre der Nation* (Vienna, June 4–6, 1990); the Salzburg Festival presenting Krenek's orch. music (Salzburg, Aug. 22, 1990); a revival of *Jonny spielt auf* at the Leipzig Opera (Sept. 30, 1990); and concluded with the Stuttgart Krenek Festival (Nov. 16–23, 1990). Krenek's voluminous autobiography, completed in 1950 and deposited at the Library of Congress, is not to be opened until 15 years after his death. Excerpts were publ. under the title "Self-Analysis."

WORKS: OPERAS AND DRAMAS WITH MUSIC: *Zwingburg* (Berlin, Oct. 16, 1924); *Der Sprung über den Schatten* (Frankfurt, June 9, 1924); *Orpheus und Eurydike* (Kassel, Nov. 27, 1926); *Jonny spielt auf* (Leipzig, Feb. 10, 1927); *Leben des Orest* (Leipzig, Jan. 19, 1930); *Kehraus um St. Stephan* (1930); *Cefalo e Procri* (Venice, Sept. 15, 1934); *Karl V* (Prague, June 15, 1938); *Tarquin* (Vassar College, May 13, 1941; Cologne, July 16, 1950); *What Price Confidence?* (1946; Saarbrücken, May 22, 1962); *Dark Waters* (1951; Los Angeles, Feb. 5, 1952); *Pallas Athene weint* (Hamburg, Oct. 17, 1955); *The Bell Tower* (Urbana, Ill., March 17, 1957); 3 short operas: *Der Diktator; Das geheime Königreich; Schwergewicht oder Die Ehre der Nation* (Wiesbaden, May 6, 1928); *Ausgerechnet und verspielt*, comic opera (Vienna, June 27, 1962); *Der goldene Bock*, fantastic chamber opera (Hamburg, June 16, 1964, composer conducting); *Der Zauberspiegel*, television opera (1966; Bavarian Television, Sept. 6, 1967); *Das kommt davon, oder Wenn Sardakai auf Reisen geht* (Hamburg, June 27, 1970, composer conducting).
    BALLETS: *Der vertauschte Cupido*, after Rameau (Kassel, Oct. 25, 1925); *Mammon* (Munich, Oct. 1, 1927); *8-column Line* (Hartford, Conn., 1939); *Spass mit Karten* (1957).
    ORCH.: 5 syms.: No. 1 (1921); No. 2 (1922); No. 3 (1922); No. 4 (N.Y., Nov. 27, 1947); No. 5 (Albuquerque, March 16, 1950); 2 *concerti grossi* (1921); *Symphonische Musik* for 9 Solo Instruments (Donaueschingen, July 30, 1922); Piano Concerto No. 1 (1923); Concertino for Flute, Violin, Harpsichord, and String Orch. (1924); Violin Concerto (Dessau, Jan. 5, 1925); *Symphonie* for Brass and Percussion (1924–25); *3 Military Marches* (Donaueschingen, 1926); *Potpourri* (Cologne, Nov. 15, 1927); *Kleine Symphonie* (Berlin, Nov. 1, 1928);

Theme and Variations (1931); Music for Wind Orchestra (1931); Piano Concerto No. 2 (Amsterdam, March 17, 1938); Symphonic Piece for String Orch. (Ann Arbor, Mich., Aug. 1, 1939); Little Concerto for Piano and Organ, with Chamber Orch. (1940); I Wonder as I Wander, variations on a North Carolina folk song (1942); Tricks and Trifles, orch. version of the Hurricane Variations (1945); Symphonic Elegy for Strings, on the death of Webern (1946); Piano Concerto No. 3 (Minneapolis, Nov. 22, 1946, Mitropoulos pianist-conductor; the 12-tone system consistently used by Krenek after 1936 is not applied in this concerto); Piano Concerto No. 4 (1950); Double Concerto for Violin, Piano, and Chamber Orch. (Donaueschingen, Oct. 6, 1951); Concerto for Harp and Chamber Orch. (Philadelphia, Dec. 12, 1952); Concerto for 2 Pianos and Orch. (N.Y., Oct. 24, 1953); Medea for Contralto and Orch. (Philadelphia, March 13, 1953); 11 Transparencies (Louisville, Feb. 12, 1955); Kette, Kreis und Spiegel, symphonic poem (1957); Spiritus Intelligentiae, Sanctus for Voices and Electronic Sounds (1957); Hexaeder, 6 pieces for Chamber Ensemble (1958); Missa duodecim tonorum for Mixed Chorus and Organ (1958); Sestina for Soprano and Small Ensemble (1958); Quaestio temporis for Chamber Orch. (Hamburg, Sept. 30, 1960); La Corona, cantata (1959); From 3 Make 7 for Chamber Orch. (1961); 5 + 1 (Alpbach Quintet; 1962); Exercises of a Late Hour (1967); 6 Profiles (1968); Statisch und Ekstatisch (1972); Von vorn herein (1974); Auf- und Ablehnung (1974); Dream Sequence for Concert Band (1975); Concerto for Organ and String Orch. (1979); Im Tal der Zeit, symphonic sketch (1979); Concerto for Organ and Orch. (1982); Cello Concerto No. 2 (1982).

CHAMBER: Violin Sonata (1919); Serenade for Quartet (1919); 8 string quartets: No. 1 (1921); No. 2 (1921); No. 3 (1923); No. 4 (1923–24); No. 5 (1930); No. 6 (1937); No. 7 (1943); No. 8 (1952); Suite for Clarinet and Piano (1924); Solo Violin Sonata (1924–25); Suite for Cello (1939); Sonatina for Flute and Viola (1942); Sonata for Violin Solo (1942); Sonata for Viola and Piano (1948); String Trio (1948); Parvula corona Musicalis ad honorem J.S. Bach for String Trio (1950); Fibonacci-Mobile for String Quartet, 2 Pianos, and Coordinator (Hanover, N.H., July 7, 1965); String Trio (1987).

PIANO: Double Fugue for Piano, 2-hands (1918); Dance Studies, in Grotesken-Album (ed. by K. Seeling, 1922); 6 sonatas: No. 1 (1919); No. 2 (1928); No. 3 (1943); No. 4 (1948); No. 5 (1950); No. 6 (1951); 5 sonatinas (1920); Toccata and Chaconne on the chorale Ja, ich glaub' an Jesum Christum (1922; also a suite of pieces on the chorale); 2 suites (1924); 5 pieces (1925); 12 Short Piano Pieces (1938); Hurricane Variations (1944); 8 Piano Pieces (1946); George Washington Variations (1950); also an Organ Sonata (1941).

CHORAL: Concert Aria, to text from Goethe's Stella (1928); Von der Vergänglichkeit des Irdischen, cantata (1932); Reisebuch aus den Österreichischen Alpen (1935); Symeon, der Stylit, oratorio (1935–87); 2 a cappella choruses for Women's Voices, on Elizabethan poems (1939); Proprium Missae in Festo SS. Innocentium for Women's Voices (1940); Lamentatio Jeremiae Prophetae, Secundum Brevarium Sacrosanctae Ecclesiae Romanae (1941); Cantata for Wartime (1943); 5 Prayers for Women's Voices, from the Litanie by John Donne (1944); The Santa Fe Time Table for Chorus a cappella, to the text of names of railroad stops between Albuquerque and Los Angeles (1945); In Paradisum, motet for Women's Voices a cappella (1946); Opus sine nomine (oratorio; Vienna, May 8, 1990).

WRITINGS: Über neue Musik: Sechs Vorlesungen zur Einführung in die theoretischen Grundlagen (Vienna, 1937; rev. ed., N.Y., 1939, as Music Here and Now); Studies in Counterpoint (N.Y., 1940; German tr., Mainz, 1952, as Zwölfton-Kontrapunkt Studien); ed. Hamline Studies in Musicology (St. Paul, Minn., 1945, 1947); Selbstdarstellung (Zürich, 1948; rev. and enl. as "Self-Analysis," University of New Mexico Quarterly, XXIII, 1953); Musik im goldenen Westen (Vienna, 1949); Johannes Okeghem (N.Y., 1953); De rebus prius factis (Frankfurt, 1956); Zur Sprache gebracht (Munich, 1958; essays); Tonal Counterpoint (N.Y., 1958); Gedanken unterwegs (Munich, 1959; es-

says); Modal Counterpoint (N.Y., 1959); Komponist und Hörer (Kassel, 1964); Prosa, Drama, Verse (Munich, 1965); Exploring Music (London, 1966; essays); Horizons Circled: Reflections on My Music (Berkeley, 1974); Im Zweifelsfalle: Aufsätze über Musik (Vienna, 1984); Franz Schubert: Ein Porträt (Tutzing, 1990).

BIBL.: A. Weissmann, "E. K.," Modern Music (Dec. 1928); J. Schneider, "E. K.," Revue Musicale (Aug. 1930); F. Saathen, E. K., Ein Essay (Munich, 1959); L. Knessl, E. K. (Vienna, 1967); W. Rogge, E. K.s Opern—Spiegel der zwanziger Jahre (Wolfenbüttel, 1970); O. Kolleritsch, ed., E. K. (Vienna, 1982); E. K.: Katalog zur Ausstellung (Vienna, 1982); C. Zenck, "The Ship Loaded with Faith and Hope: K.'s Karl V and the Viennese Politics of the Theatres," Musical Quarterly, 2 (1985); S. Cook, Opera during the Weimar Republic: The Zeitopern of E. K., Kurt Weill, and Paul Hindemith (Ann Arbor, 1987); G. Bowles, E. K.: A Bio-Bibliography (London, 1989); J. Stewart, E. K.: The Man and His Music (Berkeley, 1991).

Krenn, Franz, Austrian organist, composer, and pedagogue; b. Dross, Feb. 26, 1816; d. St. Andrä, June 18, 1897. He studied music with his father; was a church organist in Vienna; from 1869 to 1893, was a prof. of harmony and counterpoint at the Vienna Cons. Gustav Mahler was his pupil. He wrote 29 masses, a Sym., chamber music, and a manual, Musik- und Harmonielehre (1890).

Krenn, Fritz, Austrian bass; b. Vienna, Dec. 11, 1897; d. there, July 17, 1964. He studied at the Vienna Academy of Music; made his debut as the Herald in Lohengrin in Trieste in 1917; then sang in Vienna at the Volksoper (1917–18) and in Bratislava (1918–19); subsequently at the Vienna State Opera (1919–25; 1934–42; 1946–59); also sang with the Berlin State Opera (1927–43) and with Covent Garden in London (1935). He made his Metropolitan Opera debut in N.Y. on Jan. 5, 1951, as Baron Ochs in Der Rosenkavalier; then continued his career in Europe. He was highly successful in buffo roles.

Krenn, Werner, Austrian tenor; b. Vienna, Sept. 21, 1943. He sang in the Vienna Boys' Choir; then studied bassoon, and played in the Vienna Sym. Orch. (1962–66); took voice lessons with Elisabeth Rado in Vienna. In 1966 he made his operatic debut in Purcell's The Fairy Queen at the Berlin Deutsche Oper; then sang regularly at the Vienna State Opera. He made his English debut as Jaquino with the Scottish Opera (1970). He also appeared frequently as a concert and oratorio singer. He was married to the soprano **Helga Dernesch.**

Krentzlin, Richard, German piano pedagogue and composer; b. Magdeburg, Nov. 27, 1864; d. Oldendorf, Hesse, Nov. 27, 1956. He studied at Berlin's Kullak Academy; became a successful piano teacher; publ. numerous character pieces and 8 books of piano studies, Der gute Pädagoge.

Krenz, Jan, noted Polish conductor and composer; b. Wloclawek, July 14, 1926. He managed to take music lessons as a boy in Warsaw during the German occupation; after the liberation, he studied composition with Sikorski, conducting with Wilkomirski and Górzyński, and piano with Drzewiecki at the Lodz Academy of Music. In 1948 he became conductor of the Poznan Phil. and Opera; was made 2nd conductor (1950) and conductor (1953) of the Polish Radio National Sym. Orch. in Katowice, which he led on tours of Europe and the Far East; was its regular conductor until 1956, and then again from 1958 to 1967. From 1967 to 1973 he served as artistic director of the Warsaw Opera; then was Generalmusikdirektor in Bonn (1979–82). His music is audaciously modernistic in its orientation, while preserving a classical form.

WORKS: Toccata for Piano and Orch. (1943); Sym. No. 1 (1947–49); Nocturnes for Orch. (1950); Classical Serenade for Orch. (1950); Rozmowa dwóch miast (Conversation of 2 Towns) for 2 Choruses and Orch. (1950); Rustic Serenade for Orch. (1951); Piano Concertino (1952); Rhapsody for Xylophone, Tam-tam, Timpani, Celesta, and Strings (1952); Capriccio for 24 Instruments (1962); Antisymphony (1962).

Kresánek, Jozef, Slovak musicologist and composer; b. Čičmany, Dec. 20, 1913; d. Bratislava, March 14, 1986. He studied composition with Karel at the Prague Cons. (1932–37) and with Novák at the Master School there (1937–39); taught in Prešov, and in 1944 was appointed a lecturer at the Bratislava Univ., becoming a full prof. of musical science in 1963. As a music scholar, he dedicated himself mainly to the stylistic analysis and codification of Slovak folk songs, and publ. numerous treatises on the subject. He also publ. a monograph on Eugen Suchoň (Bratislava, 1961), as well as other musical studies. His compositions include a String Quartet (1935), Piano Trio (1939), 2 suites for Violin and Piano (1947, 1951), 2 suites for Orch. (1951, rev. 1961; 1953), *Prelude and Toccata* for Orch. (1957), and a Piano Quintet (1975).

Kretschmer, Edmund, German organist and composer; b. Ostritz, Aug. 31, 1830; d. Dresden, Sept. 13, 1908. He studied with Julius Otto (composition) and Johann Schneider (organ) in Dresden; was its court organist (1863–1901). He was a successful composer; his choral work *Geisterschlacht* won a prize at the Dresden singing festival (1865); his 3-part Mass for Men's Chorus won the Brussels Academy's prize in 1868. He wrote several operas to his own librettos in a Wagnerian manner; at least 2 of them were successful: *Die Folkunger* (Dresden, March 21, 1874) and *Heinrich der Löwe* (Leipzig, Dec. 8, 1877); he also produced 2 light operas: *Der Flüchtling* (Ulm, 1881) and *Schön Rotraut* (Dresden, 1887); several choral works for festive occasions; church music; etc.
BIBL.: O. Schmid, *E. K.* (Dresden, 1890).

Kretzschmar, (August Ferdinand) Hermann, eminent German musicologist; b. Olbernhau, Jan. 19, 1848; d. Nikolassee, near Berlin, May 10, 1924. He was a chorister and a pupil of Julius Otto at the Dresden Kreuzschule (1862–67); then studied with Paul, Ritschl, and Voigt at the Univ. of Leipzig (Ph.D., 1871, with the diss. *De signis musicis*; publ. in Leipzig, 1871); also took courses with Paul, E.F. Richter, and Reinecke at the Leipzig Cons. (1869–70), where he then taught organ and harmony (1871–76); was also active as a choral conductor. In 1876 he was a theater conductor in Metz; in 1877, was made music director at the Univ. of Rostock; in 1880, municipal music director there. He returned to Leipzig as music director of the Univ. (1887); was conductor of the Riedelverein (1888–97) and founder-conductor of the Akademische Orchesterkonzerte (1890–95); was also a founder of the Neue Bach-Gesellschaft (1900). In 1904 he went to Berlin as a prof. at the Univ.; from 1909 to 1920, was director of the Berlin Hochschule für Musik; served as general ed. of the Denkmäler Deutscher Tonkunst (1911–19). He was a thoroughly educated musician, a good organist as well as choral conductor, and composer of some secular and sacred vocal music. But his importance in musicology lies in his establishment of certain musical and esthetic concepts that elucidate the historical process. He introduced the term "Hermeneutik" (taken from theology), applying it to the explanation of musical melodies and intervallic progressions as expressive of human emotions.
WRITINGS (all publ. in Leipzig): *Peter Cornelius* (1880); *Führer durch den Konzertsaal* (3 vols.; I, 1887, 7th ed., 1932; II, 1888, 5th ed., 1921; III, 1890, 5th ed., 1939); *Musikalische Zeitfragen* (1903); *Gesammelte Aufsätze über Musik und anderes aus den Grenzboten* (1910); *Aus den Jahrbüchern der Musikbibliothek Peters* (1911); *Geschichte des neuen deutschen Liedes* (1912); *Geschichte der Oper* (1919); *Einführung in die Musikgeschichte* (1920); *Bach-Kolleg* (1922).
BIBL.: *Festschrift zu K.s 70. Geburtstag* (Leipzig, 1918); H. Abert, "Zum Gedächtnis H. K.s," *Jahrbuch der Musikbibliothek Peters* (1924); A. Einstein, "H. K.," *Zeitschrift für Musikwissenschaft,* VI (1924).

Kreubé, Charles Frédéric, French conductor and composer; b. Luneville, Nov. 5, 1777; d. near St.-Denis, 1846. He studied violin in Paris with R. Kreutzer (1800); joined the orch. of the Paris Opéra-Comique as violinist; from 1816 to 1828, was

1st conductor. He wrote 16 operas; also violin pieces.

Kreuder, Peter Paul, German composer; b. Aachen, Aug. 18, 1905; d. Salzburg, June 28, 1981. He studied in Munich and in Hamburg; then became active as music director of the Reinhardt theaters in Berlin (1928–30) and at the drama theater in Munich (1930–33). In 1936 he was appointed state music director in Munich. In 1945 he went to Argentina, where he occupied educational posts under the regime of Juan Perón. He wrote an opera, *Der Zerrissene* (Stockholm, 1940), and several operettas. His song *Schön war die Zeit* became extremely popular in Germany. It also served as the title of his autobiography (Munich, 1955).

Kreutz, Arthur, American composer; b. La Crosse, Wis., July 25, 1906; d. Oxford, Miss., March 11, 1991. He studied music at the Univ. of Wisconsin and at Columbia Univ. in N.Y.; then was lecturer at the latter (1946–52); in 1952 he was appointed to the staff of the music dept. of the Univ. of Mississippi, where he remained until 1964. His works include a "ballad opera," *Acres of Sky* (Fayetteville, Ark., Nov. 16, 1951); symphonic poem, *Winter of the Blue Snow* (1942); 2 syms. (1945, 1946); opera, *The University Greys* (Clinton, Miss., March 15, 1954); folk opera, *Sourwood Mountain* (Clinton, Jan. 8, 1959); also *Dance Concerto* for Clarinet and Orch. (1958); Violin Concerto (1965); 2 "jazz sonatas" for Violin and Piano, and other pieces in a jazz vein; also *New England Folksing* for Chorus and Orch. (N.Y., Feb. 17, 1948) and *Mosquito Serenade* for Orch. (N.Y., Feb. 21, 1948).

Kreutzer, Conradin (originally, **Conrad**), German conductor and composer; b. Messkirch, Baden, Nov. 22, 1780; d. Riga, Dec. 14, 1849. He was a pupil of Johann Baptist Rieger; then entered the Zwiefalten monastery (1789), where he studied organ and theory with Ernst Weinrauch (1792–97). He then studied law at the Univ. of Freiburg (1799–1800) before devoting himself to music. He changed his 1st name to Conradin in 1799. About 1800 he brought out his 1st operetta, *Die lächerliche Werbung,* in Freiburg. After a sojourn in Switzerland, he went to Vienna (1804), where met Haydn and most likely studied with Albrechtsberger. His Singspiel *Jery und Bätely,* after Goethe (May 19, 1810), met with considerable success. He then scored major successes in Stuttgart with the premieres of his operas *Konradin von Schwaben* (March 30, 1812) and *Feodora* (1812). He subsequently served as Kapellmeister there (1812–16), and then held that title in the service of Prince Carl Egon of Fürstenberg in Donaueschingen (1818–22). After the success of his opera *Libussa* at Vienna's Kärntnertortheater (Dec. 4, 1822), he served as its Kapellmeister (1822–27, 1829–32); was also active in Paris. He was Kapellmeister of Vienna's Theater in der Josefstadt (1833–35), where he achieved his greatest success with *Das Nachtlager von Granada* (Jan. 13, 1834) and *Der Verschwender* (Feb. 20, 1834). After another period as Kapellmeister at the Kärnthnertortheater (1835–40), he served as municipal music director in Cologne (1840–42). He spent much time touring with his daughters Cäcilie and Marie, both of whom were singers. He accompanied the latter to Riga (1848). The success Kreutzer achieved during his lifetime was not sustained after his death. Only *Der Verschwender* is retained in the Austrian repertoire. He was an effective composer of songs, several of which are still sung in Austria and Germany. He also composed several oratorios, masses, cantatas, 3 piano concertos (1819?, 1822?, 1825?), much chamber music, and numerous piano pieces.
BIBL.: A. Prümers, "Aus K.s Briefwechsel," *Neue Musikzeitung,* XXXIII (1912); R. Rossmayer, *Konradin K. als dramatischer Komponist* (diss., Univ. of Vienna, 1928); A. Landau, *Das einstimmige Kunstlied C. K.s und seine Stellung zum zeitgenossischen Lied in Schwaben* (Leipzig, 1930); idem, "Die Klavier-Musik C. K.s," *Zeitschrift für Musikwissenschaft,* XIII (1930–31); H. Leister, *C. K.s Lieder für Männerchor* (diss., Univ. of Mainz, 1963).

Kreutzer, Jean Nicolas Auguste, French violinist and composer, brother of **Rodolphe Kreutzer** and father of **Léon**

Charles François Kreutzer; b. Versailles, Sept. 3, 1778; d. Paris, Aug. 31, 1832. He studied with his brother at the Paris Cons. (premier prix, 1801); played in the orch. of the Théâtre Favart (from 1798) and of the Opéra (from 1800); also played in the imperial chapel orch. (1804–30). He taught at the Paris Cons., later taking over his brother's class there (1826). He publ. a number of works for violin, including 2 concertos, 3 sonatas, duos, etc.

Kreutzer, Léon Charles François, French music critic and composer, son of **Jean Nicolas Auguste Kreutzer;** b. Paris, Sept. 23, 1817; d. Vichy, Oct. 6, 1868. He studied piano with Fleche and composition with Benoist; wrote for the *Revue et Gazette Musicale, Revue Contemporaine, La Quotidienne, L'Union,* etc.; composed 2 operas, 2 syms., 4 string quartets, a Piano Trio, 3 piano sonatas and other works for piano, some 50 songs, and organ pieces.

Kreutzer, Leonid, Russian pianist and pedagogue; b. St. Petersburg, March 13, 1884; d. Tokyo, Oct. 30, 1953. He studied piano with Anna Essipova and composition with Glazunov at the St. Petersburg Cons. In 1906 he went to Germany; from 1921 to 1932, taught at the Berlin Hochschule für Musik. After the advent of the Nazi regime in 1933, he went to the U.S., and in 1938 traveled to Japan, where he became a prof. of piano at the Tokyo Cons. He publ. *Das Wesen der Klaviertechnik* (Berlin, 1923).

Kreutzer, Rodolphe, famous French violinist, pedagogue, and composer, brother of **Jean Nicolas Auguste Kreutzer;** b. Versailles, Nov. 16, 1766; d. Geneva, Jan. 6, 1831. His father, a wind player, gave him early instruction in music; he began studying violin and composition with Anton Stamitz in 1778. On May 25, 1780, he played a Stamitz violin concerto at the Paris Concert Spirituel, and returned there in May 1784 to play his own 1st Violin Concerto. In 1785 he became a member of the king's music, and soon established a notable reputation as a virtuoso. In 1789 he settled in Paris, where he 1st gained success as a composer for the theater with his opéra-comique *Paul et Virginie* (Jan. 15, 1791). His opéra-comique *Lodoiska* (Aug. 1, 1791) was also a success, being accorded an even warmer reception than Cherubini's score of the same name. In 1793 Kreutzer became a prof. at the Inst. National de Musique; when it became the Paris Cons. in 1795, he remained on its faculty, retiring in 1826. Beginning in 1798 he made a number of outstanding concert appearances at the Théâtre Feydeau and the Opéra in Paris, being made solo violin at the latter in 1801; he also became a member of Napoleon's chapel orch. (1802) and of his private orch. (1806). His ballet-pantomime *Paul et Virginie* (June 12, 1806) found favor with Paris audiences, as did his ballet *Les Amours d'Antoine et Cléopatre* (March 8, 1808) and his comédie lyrique *Aristippe* (May 24, 1808). In 1810 Kreutzer suffered a broken arm in a carriage accident, which effectively put an end to his career. However, he continued to hold his various positions as a violinist. In 1815 he was made maître de la chapelle du roi. In 1816 he was appointed 2nd conductor, and in 1817 1st conductor at the Opéra, retaining this post until 1824, at which time he became director (1824–26). His last opera, *Matilde* (c.1826–27), was refused by the Opéra management. By then in declining health, he spent his remaining years in retirement. Kreutzer was one of the foremost violinists of his era. With Baillot and Rode, he stands as one of the founders of the French violin school. Beethoven greatly admired his playing, and was moved to dedicate his Violin Sonata, op. 47 (the *Kreutzer*), to him. Kreutzer's most celebrated publication remains the brilliant *42 études ou caprices* (originally 40) for Unaccompanied Violin. He also composed a number of fine violin concertos. His renown as a teacher brought him many students, including his brother Jean Nicolas Auguste Kreutzer, C. Lafont, and Massart. With Rode and Baillot, he publ. *Méthode de violon* (Paris, 1803).

WORKS: STAGE (all 1st perf. in Paris unless otherwise given): *Jeanne d'Arc,* drame historique mêlé d'ariettes (1790); *Paul et Virginie,* opéra-comique (1791); *Le Franc breton,* opéra-comique (1791; in collaboration with Solié); *Lodoiska,* opéra-comique (1791); *Charlotte et Werther,* opéra-comique (1792); *Le Siège de Lille,* opéra-comique (1792); *Le Déserteur ou La Montagne de Ham,* opera (1793); *Le Congrès des rois,* opéra-comique (1793; in collaboration with 11 other composers); *On respire,* comédie mêlée d'ariettes (1795); *Le Brigand,* drame mêlé d'ariettes (1795); *La Journée du 10 août 1792,* opera (1795); *Imogène ou La Gageure indiscrète,* comédie mêlée d'ariettes (1796); *Le Petit Page,* comédie mêlée d'ariettes (1800; in collaboration with N. Isouard); *Flaminius à Corinthe,* opera (1801; in collaboration with N. Isouard); *Astyanax,* opera (1801); *Le Baiser et la quittance,* opéra-comique (1803; in collaboration with Boieldieu, Isouard, and Méhul); *Les Surprises ou L'Étourdi en voyage,* opera (1806); *Paul et Virginie,* ballet-pantomime (St. Cloud, 1806); *François I ou La Fête mystérieuse,* comédie mêlée d'ariettes (1807); *Les Amours d'Antoine et Cléopatre,* ballet (1808); *Aristippe,* comédie lyrique (1808); *Jadis et aujourd'hui,* opéra-comique (1808); *La Fête de Mars,* divertissement-pantomime (1809); *Abel,* tragédie lyrique (1810; rev. as *La Mort d'Abel,* 1823); *Le Triomphe du mois de Mars,* ceremonial drama for the King of Rome's birth (1811); *L'Homme sans façon,* opéra-comique (1812); *Le Camp de Sobieski,* opéra-comique (1813); *Constance et Théodore,* opéra-comique (1813); *L'Oriflamme,* opera (1814; in collaboration with Berton, Méhul, and Paer); *Les Béarnais ou Henri IV en voyage,* opéra-comique (1814; in collaboration with Boieldieu); *La Perruque et la redingote,* opéra-comique (1815; in collaboration with Kreubé); *La Princesse de Babylone,* opera (1815); *L'Heureux Retour,* ballet (1815; in collaboration with Berton and Persuis); *Le Carnaval de Venise,* ballet (1816; in collaboration with Persuis); *Les Dieux rivaux,* opera-ballet (1816; in collaboration with Berton, Persuis, and Spontini); *Le Maître et le valet,* opéra-comique (1816); *La Servante justifiée ou La Fête de Mathurine,* ballet villageois (1818); *Clari ou La Promesse de mariage,* ballet-pantomime (1820); *Blanche de Provence ou La Cour des fées,* opera (1821; in collaboration with Berton, Boieldieu, Cherubini, and Paer); *Le Négociant de Hambourg,* opéra-comique (1821); *Le Paradis de Mahomet,* opéra-comique (1822; in collaboration with Kreubé); *Ipsiboe,* opera (1824); *Pharamond,* opera (1825; in collaboration with Berton and Boieldieu); *Matilde,* opera (c.1826–27; not perf.). **ORCH.:** Violin Concertos: No. 1, op. 1 (1783–84); No. 2, op. 2 (1784–85); No. 3, op. 3 (1785); No. 4, op. 4 (1786); No. 5, op. 5 (1787); No. 6, op. 6 (c.1788); No. 7, op. 7 (c.1790); No. 8, op. 8 (c.1795); No. 9, op. 9 (c.1802); No. 10, op. 10 (c.1802); No. 11, op. 11 (c.1802); No. 12, op. 12 (1802–3); No. 13, op. A (1803); No. 14, op. B (1803–4); No. 15, op. C (1804); No. 16, op. D (1804); No. 17, op. E (1805); No. 18, op. F (1805–9); No. 19, op. G (1805–10). **SINFONIAS CONCERTANTES:** No. 1 for 2 Violins (c.1793); No. 2 for 2 Violins and Cello (c.1794); No. 3 for 2 Violins (1803); No. 4 for 2 Violins (n.d.); *Ouverture de la journée de marathon* for Woodwind and Brass (1794). **CHAMBER:** Quintet for Oboe or Clarinet and String Quartet (c.1795); **STRING QUARTETS:** *6 quatuors concertans* (c.1790); 3 quartets, op. 2 (c.1795); 2 quartets (c.1795); *6 nouveaux quatuors,* op. 2, part 1 (c.1798); **TRIOS:** *Premier pot-pourri* for Violin Solo, Violin, and Bass (c.1800); Trio for Oboe or Clarinet, Bassoon, and Viola (c.1803); *3 trios brillans* for 2 Violins and Bass (c.1803); **DUETS:** Duos for Violin and Viola (1783); 3 violin duos, op. 11, part 2 (c.1800); 3 violin duos, op. 3 (c.1805); *3 duos concertans* for 2 Violins, op. B (c.1820); *6 nocturnes concertans* for Harp and Violin (c.1822; in collaboration with C. Bochsa); **SONATAS:** 3 sonatas for Violin and Bass, op. 1 (c.1795); 3 sonatas for Violin and Bass, op. B (c.1795); *Grande sonate* for Violin and Piano (1799); *3 sonates faciles* for Violin and Bass (c.1803); 3 sonatas for Violin and Bass, op. 2 (c.1805); also *42 études ou caprices* for Unaccompanied Violin (originally 40; 1796; 1st extant ed., c.1807) and *18 nouveaux caprices ou études* for Unaccompanied Violin (c.1825).

BIBL.: J. Massart, *L'Art de travailler les études de K.* (Paris, n.d.; Eng. tr., 1926); H. Kling, *R. K.* (Brussels, 1898); J. Hardy, *R. K.* (Paris, 1910); A. Moser, *Geschichte des Violinspiels* (Berlin, 1923; 2nd ed., rev. and enl., 1966–67); H.-J. Nösselt,

"R. K., der klassische Violinist," *Das Orchester*, XIV (1966); M. Williams, *The Violin Concertos of R. K.* (diss., Indiana Univ., 1973); B. Schwarz, *Great Masters of the Violin* (N.Y., 1983).

Křička, Jaroslav, eminent Czech composer and pedagogue; b. Kelc, Moravia, Aug. 27, 1882; d. Prague, Jan. 23, 1969. He studied law in Prague (1900–1902); then studied music at the Prague Cons. (1902–5) and in Berlin (1905–6). He was in Ekaterinoslav (1906–9), where he was active as a teacher and conductor; then returned to Prague as a choirmaster; later was prof. of composition at the Prague Cons. (1918–45), where he also served as rector. His music was influenced by Dvořák and native folk songs.

WORKS: OPERAS: *Hypolita* (1910–16; Prague, Oct. 10, 1917); *Bílý pán* (The White Gentleman), after Oscar Wilde's *The Canterville Ghost* (1927–29; Brno, 1929; rev. 1930; Breslau, Nov. 14, 1931); *Kral Lavra* (King Lawrence; 1936–37; rev. 1938–39; Prague, June 7, 1940); *České jesličky* (The Czech Christmas Manger; 1936–37; rev. 1948; Prague, Jan. 15, 1949); *Jáchym a Juliána* (Joachim and Julia; 1945–48; Opava, 1951); *Serenáda*, opera buffa (Plzeň, 1950); *Kolébka* (The Cradle), musical comedy (1950; Opava, 1951); *Zahořanský hon* (The Zahořany Hunt; Opava, 1955). **CHILDREN'S OPERAS:** *Ogaři* (Country Lads; 1918; Nové Město, Sept. 7, 1919); *Dobře to dopadlo* or *Tlustý pradědeček* (It Turned Out Well or The Fat Great-Grandfather; 1932) and *Lupici a detekotyvove* (Robbers and Detectives; 1932; both operas, Prague, Dec. 29, 1932); several small operas for children's theater; television opera, *Kalhoty* (A Pair of Trousers; Czech television, 1962). **ORCH.:** Sym., *Jarní* (Spring; 1905–6; rev. 1942); *Nostalgie* for String Orch. and Harp (1905); *Faith*, symphonic poem (1907); *A Children's Suite* (1907); *Scherzo Idyllic* (1908; Prague, Nov. 13, 1910; 3rd movement of an uncompleted Sym. No. 2); *Modrý pták* (A Blue Bird), overture after a Maeterlinck fairy tale (1911; Prague, March 3, 1912, composer conducting); *Adventus*, symphonic poem (1920–21; Prague, Nov. 6, 1921); *Matěj Kopecký*, overture (1928); *Horácká suita* (Suite montagnarde; Prague, Sept. 8, 1935); Sinfonietta for String Orch. and Timpani (1940–41); *Majales*, overture (1942); Violin Concerto (1944); Concertino for Horn and String Quartet or String Orch. (1951); *Variations on a Theme of Boccherini* for Bassoon and String Quartet or String Orch. (1952); Sinfonietta semplice (1962). **CANTATAS:** *Pokušeni na poušti* (Temptation in the Desert; 1921–22); *Jenny, the Thief* (1927–28); *Tyrolese Elegies* (1930–31); *A Eulogy to a Woman* (1933); *Recollections of Student Years* (1934); *Moravian Cantata* (1935–36); *The Golden Spinning Wheel* (1943); *To Prague* (1960). **CHAMBER:** *Small Suite in Old Style* for 2 Violins and Piano (1907); 3 string quartets (1907; 1938–39; *Wallachian*, 1949); *Doma* (At Home), piano trio (1924–25); Violin Sonata (1925); Sonatina for 2 Violins (1926–27; rev. for Violin and Viola); Concertino (septet) for Violin, Wind Quintet, and Piano (1940); *Partita* for Solo Violin (1941); Divertimento for Wind Quintet (1950); Flute Sonatina (1951); Variations for Solo Violin (1956); Violin Sonatina (1962); several albums of piano pieces; a number of songs; arrangements of folk songs.

BIBL.: J. Dostál, *J. K.* (Prague, 1944).

Krieger, Adam, esteemed German organist and composer; b. Driesen, Neumark, Jan. 7, 1634; d. Dresden, June 30, 1666. He studied organ with Samuel Scheidt in Halle; from 1655 to 1657 he was organist at the Nikolaikirche in Leipzig; then went to Dresden (1657), where he was made keyboard teacher to the Elector of Saxony's daughter; in 1658 was made chamber and court organist there. He was one of the most important of the early composers of German lieder, which he called his "Arien," ranging from the risqué to the sublime; for most of them he wrote the words as well as the music.

WORKS: (50) *Arien* for 1 to 3 Voices, 2 Violins, Violone, and Basso Continuo (Leipzig, 1657; excerpts ed. by H. Osthoff and N. Schiørring in *Det 16. og 17. Århundredes Verdslige Danske Visesang*, Copenhagen, 1950); (50) *Neue Arien in 6 Zehen eingetheilet* for 2, 3, and 5 Voices, 2 Violins, 2 Violas, and Basso Continuo (Dresden, 1667; 2nd ed., augmented, 1676, with 10 more songs, and with ritornellos by J. Furchheim; selections in Denkmäler Deutscher Tonkunst, XIX, 1905). He also composed 5 sacred cantatas and 4 funeral songs, as well as an aria.

BIBL.: H. Osthoff, *A. K.* (Leipzig, 1929).

Krieger, Armando, Argentine pianist, conductor, and composer; b. Buenos Aires, May 7, 1940. He studied piano with John Montés and Robert Kinsky and composition with Ginastera, later with Copland, Dallapiccola, Maderna, R. Malipiero, and Messiaen at the Di Tella Inst. (1963–64); continued his piano training with Loriod at the Mozarteum Argentino (1964). He became widely known in his native country as a pianist and conductor, often giving performances of avant-garde music; also conducted his own chamber orch. and was active as a teacher. In his works he adopted a serial technique in which rhythmic, melodic, and harmonic elements follow a predetermined formula of contrasts.

WORKS: Sym. for Strings (1959); Concerto for 2 Pianos and Orch. (1963); *Métamorfosis d'après une lecture de Kafka* for Piano and 15 Instruments (1968); *Angst* for Orch. (1970); several cantatas and various solo vocal works; 2 string quartets (1960, 1961); other chamber music; keyboard pieces.

Krieger, Edino, Brazilian composer; b. Brusque, Santa Catarina, March 17, 1928. He studied music with his father, a conductor, composer, and founder of the local Cons.; later studied violin with Edith Reis (1943) and composition with Koellreutter (1944–48) at the Rio de Janeiro Cons.; subsequently had lessons with Copland at the Berkshire Music Center in Tanglewood and with Mennin at the Juilliard School of Music in N.Y.; also violin with Nowinsky at N.Y.'s Henry Street Settlement School; completed his studies with Krenek in Brazil (1952) and Berkeley at London's Royal Academy of Music (1955). He was active as a broadcaster, music critic, conductor, and teacher in his homeland; was director of the art and music dept. of the Radio Jornal do Brasil in Rio de Janeiro (1963–73); was also president of the Brazilian Soc. of Contemporary Music (1971–73). His early works were in a late Romantic and Impressionist style; after a brief dodecaphonic period (1947–53), he turned toward neo-Classicism with national allusions; he fused the latter 2 styles from 1966.

WORKS: ORCH.: *Movimento misto* (1947); *Contrasts* (1949); *Musica 1952* for Strings (1952); *Chôro* for Flute and Strings (1952); *Suite* for Strings (1954); *Abertura sinfônica* (1955); *Concertante* for Piano and Orch. (1955); *Andante* for Strings (1956); *Divertimento* for Strings (1959); *Brasiliana* for Viola or Alto Saxophone and Strings (1960); *Variações elementares* for Strings (1964); *Ludus symphonicus* (1966); Toccata for Piano and Orch. (1967); *Canticum naturale* (1972); several choral works. **CHAMBER:** Trio for Oboe, Clarinet, and Bassoon (1945); *Peça lenta* for Flute and String Trio (1946); *Música 1947* for String Quartet (1947); *Música de cámara* for Flute, Trumpet, Timpani, and Violin (1948); *Melopéia* for Soprano, Tenor Saxophone, Trombone, and Viola (1949); String Quartet No. 1 (1955); piano pieces; songs.

Krieger, Johann, distinguished German organist and composer, brother of **Johann Philipp Krieger;** b. Nuremberg, Dec. 28, 1651; d. Zittau, July 18, 1735. He received keyboard training from G.C. Wecker (1661–68) and then studied composition with his brother in Zeitz (1671), and became his successor as court organist at Bayreuth (1673–77). He was subsequently Kapellmeister to Count Heinrich I in Greiz (1678–80), then held that post at the court of Duke Christian in Eisenberg (1680–82). He subsequently went to Zittau, where he was active as organist of St. Johannis and director choris musici, a position he held for 53 years, playing for the last time on the day before he died. His music was appreciated by Handel; some of his organ compositions are regarded as presaging the grand style of Bach.

WORKS: INSTRUMENTAL: *6 musicalische Partien* (Nuremberg, 1697); *Anmuthige Clavier-Ubung* (Nuremberg, 1698); *Allein Gott in der Höh sei Ehr, a 4*; other pieces in MS. **ARIAS AND LIEDER:** *Neue musicalische Ergetzligkeit, das ist Unter-*

schiedene Erfindungen welche Herr Christian Weise, in Zittau von geistlichen Andachten, Politischen Tugend-Liedern und Theatralischen Sachen bishero gesetzet hat (Frankfurt und Leipzig, 1684); 19 occasional songs for weddings or funerals (publ. separately, 1684–97). Of some 235 known sacred vocal works, only 33 are extant: 12 German cantatas, 2 Latin cantatas, 5 settings of the Sanctus, 2 settings of the Magnificat, motets, and solo and choral concertos. He also wrote 10 operas, but only a few arias are extant. Some of his works are found in the following: M. Seiffert, ed., Nuremberger Meister der zweiten Hälfte des 17. Jahrhunderts, Denkmäler der Tonkunst in Bayern, X, Jg. VI/I (1906); idem, ed., J. Krieger: Gesammelte Werke für Klavier und Orgel, ibid., XXX, Jg. XVIII (1917); and F. Riedel, ed., Johann Krieger: Präludiem und Fugen, Die Orgel, II/3 (Leipzig, 1957). BIBL.: R. Eitner, "J. K.," Monatshefte für Musikgeschichte, XXVII (1895).

Krieger, Johann Philipp, eminent German organist, keyboard player, and composer; brother of **Johann Krieger;** b. Nuremberg, Feb. 25, 1649; d. Weissenfels, Feb. 6, 1725. He was a pupil of Johann Dretzel and Gabriel Schütz in Nuremberg; went to Copenhagen, where he studied organ with the royal organist Johann Schröder and composition with Kaspar Förster. He went to Italy in 1673, continuing his studies in Rome. Krieger was subsequently court musician in Halle (from 1677); when the court moved to Weissenfels in 1680, he went with it as Kapellmeister, retaining that post for the rest of his life. He was particularly important as a composer of sacred cantatas; by introducing madrigal verse for his texts, he came to be regarded as the "father of the new cantata." He wrote more than 2,000 such works, only 74 of which are extant. He also composed some 18 operas, but only arias are extant, along with several librettos. His extant publ. instrumental works are Lustige Feld-Music (Nuremberg, 1704; 6 suites for Wind Instruments), 12 suonate for 2 Violins (Nuremberg, 1688), and 12 suonate for Violin and Viola da Gamba (Nuremberg, 1693). For eds. of his extant works, see the following: M. Seiffert, ed., J.P. Krieger: 21 ausgewählte Kirchencomposition, Denkmäler Deutscher Tonkunst, LIII–LIV (1916); idem, ed., J.P. Krieger: Gesammelte Werke für Orgel und Klavier, Denkmäler der Tonkunst in Bayern, XXX, Jg. XVIII (1917); idem, ed., J.P. Krieger: Partie, Sonate, Organum, III/9, 11 (Leipzig, 1925–26; 2nd ed., 1951–52); H.J. Moser, ed., J.P. Krieger: 24 Lieder und Arien, Nagels Musikarchiv, CLXXXIV–CLXXV (1930); H. Osthoff, ed., J.P. Krieger: Triosonate, ibid., CXXXV (1937); and C. Crussard, ed., J.P. Krieger: Sonate à trois, Flores Musicae, VII (1958). BIBL.: R. Eitner, "J.P. K.," Monatshefte für Musikgeschichte, XXIX (1897); R. Wagner, "Beiträge zur Lebensgeschichte J.P. K.s und seines Schülers Nikolaus Deinl," Zeitschrift für Musikwissenschaft, VIII (1925–26); D. Stout, Four Cantatas by J.P. K. (diss., Indiana Univ., 1966).

Kriens, Christian, Dutch-American pianist, violinist, and composer; b. Brussels, April 29, 1881; d. (suicide) Hartford, Conn., Dec. 17, 1934. He was taken to the Netherlands as a child; studied with his father, a clarinetist, and later at The Hague Cons. At 14 he made his debut in Amsterdam, playing the Emperor Concerto and conducting his own 2nd Sym. From 1896 to 1899 he toured Europe as a violinist; then taught at The Hague Cons. He went to the U.S. as conductor of the French Opera Co. (1906); then was a violinist in the N.Y. Sym., and N.Y. Phil., and at the Metropolitan Opera. He then became director of WTIC Radio in Hartford, Conn.

Krips, Henry (Joseph), Austrian-born Australian conductor, brother of **Josef Krips;** b. Vienna, Feb. 10, 1912; d. Adelaide, Jan. 25, 1987. He studied at the Vienna Cons. and the Univ. of Vienna; made his conducting debut at Vienna's Burgtheater in 1932; subsequently was conductor in Innsbruck (1933–34), Salzburg (1934–35), and Vienna (1935–38). In 1938 he emigrated to Australia and became a citizen in 1944; conducted ballet and opera. He was principal conductor of the West Australia Sym. Orch. in Perth (1948–72) and the South Australia Sym. Orch. in Adelaide (1949–72); also made guest appearances in Europe. He was best known for his performances of light Viennese music.

Krips, Josef, eminent Austrian conductor, brother of **Henry (Joseph) Krips;** b. Vienna, April 8, 1902; d. Geneva, Oct. 13, 1974. He studied with Mandyczewski and Weingartner in Vienna; was 1st violinist in the Volksoper orch. there (1918–21); then became répétiteur and chorus master there, making his conducting debut with Un ballo in maschera (1921). In 1924–25 he conducted opera in Aussig an der Elbe; in 1925–26, in Dortmund; from 1926 to 1933 he was was Generalmusikdirektor in Karlsruhe. In 1933 he became a conductor at the Vienna State Opera; also was made a prof. at the Vienna Academy of Music. In 1938 he lost these positions, after the annexation of Austria to Germany; conducted a season of opera in Belgrade (1938–39). In 1945 he rejoined the Vienna State Opera as principal conductor; later that year he conducted the 1st post-war subscription concert of the Vienna Phil., and quickly moved to reestablish the musical life of his native city. In 1947 he appeared with the Vienna State Opera at London's Covent Garden. After leaving the Vienna State Opera in 1950, he served as principal conductor of the London Sym. Orch. until 1954. In 1953 he made his U.S. debut as a guest conductor with the Buffalo Phil., and subsequently was its music director (1954–63); from 1963 to 1970 he was music director of the San Francisco Sym. Orch. He also was a guest conductor of the major opera houses and orchs. of Europe and the U.S.; he conducted at Chicago's Lyric Opera (1960, 1964), at Covent Garden (1963; 1971–74), and at N.Y.'s Metropolitan Opera (1966–67; 1969–70). He excelled in works of the Austro-German repertoire, his interpretations being notable for their authority, insight, warmth, and lyricism.

Kristofferson (Carson), Kris, American country-music singer, songwriter, and actor; b. Brownsville, Texas, June 22, 1936. Of an intellectual bent, he studied at Pomona College, winning such high grades that he was given a Rhodes scholarship to Oxford Univ. (B.A., 1960). Upon returning to the U.S., he served in the U.S. Army as a helicopter pilot stationed in Germany. He found his true vocation when he moved to Nashville in 1965; he produced the song Me and Bobby McGee, which had the right countrified twang to it; his subsequent songs For the Good Times and Sunday Mornin' Comin' Down made the top of the charts. He then recorded Full Moon with his fiancée, Rita Coolidge, whom he married in 1973. The song was successful, the marriage was not (divorced in 1979). Overflowing with quaquaversal talents, Kristofferson turned to movies, and made a hit in the screen epic A Star Is Born opposite Barbra Streisand; also co-starred in Blume in Love.

Kriukov, Nikolai, Russian composer, brother of **Vladimir Kriukov;** b. Moscow, Feb. 2, 1908; d. there (suicide), April 5, 1961. He studied with Vasilenko; devoted himself chiefly to folk-song arrangements and film music. He wrote orch. suites on folk themes gathered in various republics of the Soviet Union, sometimes including native instruments. He received 2 Stalin prizes for his film scores.

Kriukov, Vladimir, Russian composer, brother of **Nikolai Kriukov;** b. Moscow, July 22, 1902; d. Staraya Rusa, near Moscow, June 14, 1960. He studied composition with Miaskovsky at the Moscow Cons., graduating in 1925. In 1949–50 he was director of the Moscow Phil. Inst.; from 1957 to 1959, taught composition at the Gnessin Inst. in Moscow. His music is harmoniously and melodiously eclectic, while adhering to an effective Russian style. WORKS: Operas: Railroad Stationmaster, after Pushkin's tale (Moscow, Oct. 30, 1940), and Dmitri Donskoy (1947); October Cantata (1947); Russian Rhapsody for Orch. (1944); symphonic poems: January 9, commemorating the march on the Winter Palace in St. Petersburg in 1905 (1931), and Dreadnought Potemkin (1955); Piano Concerto (1959); chamber music; piano pieces; songs.

Krivine, Emmanuel, French conductor; b. Grenoble, May 7, 1947. He studied violin at the Paris Cons., winning a premier prix at age 16; after further studies at Brussel's Chapelle Musicale Reine Elisabeth, he completed his training with Szeryng and Menuhin. While pursuing his career as a violinist, he also launched a 2nd career as a conductor in 1976; received instruction in conducting from Böhm; following an automobile accident in 1981, he was compelled to give up violin playing and devote himself to conducting. Having conducted regularly for the ORTF in Paris, he then was principal conductor of the Orch. Philharmonique in Lorraine (1981–83). On Jan. 30, 1987, he made his U.S. debut as a guest conductor with the Indianapolis Sym. Orch. He was music director of the Orch. de Lyon (from 1987). In addition to appearances with leading French orchs., he appeared widely in Europe and North America.

Křivinka, Gustav, Czech composer; b. Doubravice nad Svitavou, April 24, 1928. He studied with Kapral and Petrželka at the Brno Cons. (1946–50); then with Kvapil at the Brno Academy of Music (graduated, 1954). He wrote 2 syms. (1951, 1955), 2 violin concertos (1950, 1952), 2 piano concertos, song cycles, and chamber music.

Křížkovský, Pavel (baptized **Karel**), Bohemian choral conductor and composer; b. Kreuzendorf, Jan. 9, 1820; d. Brünn, May 8, 1885. He was a chorister at the Troppau monastery church, and was a student at the German Gymnasium there. In 1845 he joined the Old Brno Augustinian monastery, taking the name Pavel; was a theology student (1846–50), and also took holy orders (1848). He was greatly interested in Moravian folk songs and collected many of them in the field. At the same time, he began to compose choruses in the national manner; one of his earliest works, *Utonulá* (The Girl Who Drowned), became popular; other favorites were *Žaloba* (The Plaint) and *Odvedeného prosba* (The Recruit's Prayer). He also wrote much sacred music (Roman Catholic) for the Olmütz Cathedral, where he was music director from 1873. Among his pupils was Janáček. A complete ed. of his works was prepared by V. Steinman and J. Racek (Prague, 1949).
Bibl.: J. Geisler, *P. K.* (Prague, 1886); E. Eichler, *P. K.* (Brünn, 1904); J. Racek, *P. K.: Prameny, literatura a ikonografie* (P. K.: Sources, Bibliography, and Iconography; Olomouc, 1946).

Kroeger, Ernest Richard, American organist, teacher, and composer; b. St. Louis, Aug. 10, 1862; d. there, April 7, 1934. He studied piano with his father and Charles Kunkel; was organist at various St. Louis churches; taught at a number of schools throughout the country; was elected to the National Inst. of Arts and Letters (1915). He wrote the symphonic poem *Mississippi, Father of Waters* (Feb. 19, 1926), several overtures, chamber music, many piano pieces, organ music, and songs.

Kroeger, Karl, American musicologist, teacher, and composer; b. Louisville, Ky., April 4, 1932. He studied at the Univ. of Louisville (B.M., 1954; M.M., 1959) and the Univ. of Illinois (M.S., 1962); completed his education with Janet Knapp at Brown Univ. (Ph.D., 1971). He was curator of the Americana Collection in the Music Division of the N.Y. Public Library (1962–64); was composer-in-residence of the Eugene (Oreg.) public schools (1964–67). He taught at Wake Forest Univ. in Winston-Salem, N.C., where he was also director of the Moravian Music Foundation (1972–80); subsequently he taught at the Univ. of Keele in England (1980–81) and then became associate prof. and music librarian at the Univ. of Colorado at Boulder in 1982. With H. Nathan, he ed. *The Complete Works of William Billings* (4 vols., Charlottesville, Va., 1977–90).
Works: 2 sinfoniettas (1958, 1965); Chamber Concerto for Oboe and Strings (1961); *Dramatic Overture* (1964); 4 suites for Orch. (1965, 1966, 1967, 1968); Concerto for Alto Saxophone and Winds (1982); band music; 2 string quartets (1960, 1966); 3 *Canzonas* for Brass Sextet (1961, 1966, 1967); *Partita* for Brass Quintet (1963); *Toccata* for Clarinet, Trombone, and Percussion (1968); *Fantasy* for Brass Quartet (1969); Sonata

for Trombone Quartet (1978); Suite for Oboe and Harp (1979); also choral works; anthems; songs; piano pieces; organ music.

Krohn, Ernst C(hristopher), American musicologist; b. N.Y., Dec. 23, 1888; d. Santa Fe, N.Mex., March 21, 1975. He settled in St. Louis in 1898; studied piano with his father and with Ottmar Moll, attaining a modicum of virtuosity; gave recitals and taught piano in various schools in St. Louis; also taught music history at Washington Univ. (1938–53) and was director of music at St. Louis Univ. (1953–63).
Writings: *A Century of Missouri Music* (St. Louis, 1924; reprint, with additions, 1965, as *Missouri Music*); *The History of Music: An Index to the Literature Available in a Selected Group of Musicological Publications* (St. Louis, 1952); *Music Publishing in the Middle Western States before the Civil War* (Detroit, 1972).

Krohn, Felix (Julius Theofil), Finnish conductor and composer; b. Tampere, May 20, 1898; d. Lahti, Nov. 11, 1963. He studied with his father; later at the Helsinki School of Music and the Hochschule für Musik in Berlin. Returning to Finland in 1922, he was active as a conductor and teacher.
Works: *Sotarukous* (War Prayer) for Orch. (1918); sinfonia brevis, *Vuodenajat* (The Seasons; 1921); *Kyllikki*, cantata (1923); *Odalisque* for Orch. (1924); 4 suites for Orch.: *Sysmäläinen* (The Man from Sysma; 1938); *Vihreä kulta* (Green Gold; 1939); *Anu and Mikko* (1940); *Linnaisten kartanon vihreä kamari* (The Green Room at Linnainen Manor; 1944); *Uskollinen sisar* (The Faithful Sister), opera for children (1945); chamber music.

Krohn, Ilmari (Henrik Reinhold), eminent Finnish musicologist; b. Helsinki, Nov. 8, 1867; d. there, April 25, 1960. After studying with Richard Faltin in Helsinki, he took courses at the Leipzig Cons. with Papperitz and Reinecke (1886–90); obtained his Ph.D. from the Univ. of Helsinki in 1900 with the dissertation *Über die Art und Enstehung der geistlichen Volksmelodien in Finnland* (publ. in Helsinki, 1899). He lectured at the Univ. of Helsinki (1900–18); then was its 1st prof. of musicology (1918–35); also taught at the Church Music Inst. (1923–30; 1933–44). He was active in folk music research from 1886, resulting in his valuable compilation of some 7,000 Finnish folk songs in *Suomen kansan sävelmiä* (1898–1933). He founded the Finnish section of the IMS (1910); was founder (1916) and chairman (1917–39) of the Finnish Musicological Soc. Krohn was also a composer; wrote an opera, *Tuhotulva* (Deluge; 1918; Helsinki, Oct. 25, 1928); 2 oratorios: *Ikiaartehet* (Eternal Treasures; 1912) and *Voittajat* (Victors; 1935); *St. John Passion* (1940); cantatas; Psalms; songs.
Writings: *Musiikin teorian oppijakso* (Principles of Music Theory; 5 vols., Porvoo: I, *Rytmioppi* [Rhythm; 1911–14; rev. ed., 1958]; II, *Säveloppi* [Melody; 1917]; III, *Harmoniaoppi* [Harmony; 1923]; IV, *Polyfoniaoppi* [Polyphony; 1929]; V, *Muoto-oppi* [Form; 1937]); *Puhdasvireisen säveltapailun opas* (Guide to Solfège in Natural Tuning; Helsinki, 1911); *Die Sammlung und Erforschung der Volksmusik in Finnland* (Helsinki, 1933); *Die finnische Volksmusik* (Griefswald, 1935); *Liturgisen sävellystyylin opas* (The Liturgical Style of Composition; Porvoo, 1940); *Der Formenbau in den Symphonien von Jean Sibelius* (Helsinki, 1942); *Der lutherische Choral in Finnland* (Åbo, 1944); *Der Stimmungsgehalt in den Symphonien von Jean Sibelius* (2 vols., Helsinki, 1945–46); *Sävelmuistoja elämäni varrelta* (Porvoo, 1951; memoirs); *Anton Bruckners Symphonien: Untersuchung über Formenbau und Stimmungsgehalt* (3 vols., Helsinki, 1955–57).

Kroll, Erwin, German musicologist; b. Deutsch-Eylau, Feb. 3, 1886; d. Berlin, March 7, 1976. He studied in Königsberg; later took a course in music theory with Sandberger in Munich and also in composition with Pfitzner and Braunfels. From 1919 to 1924 he served as répétiteur at the Bavarian State Opera in Munich; was active as a music journalist in Königsberg (1925–33) and then in Berlin (from 1934); later was director of the Berlin studios of the Northwest German Radio (1946–53). He also composed chamber music and songs.
Writings: *E.T.A. Hoffmanns musikalische Anschauungen*

(Königsberg, 1909); *E.T.A. Hoffmann* (Leipzig, 1923); *Hans Pfitzner* (Munich, 1924); *Aus den Werdejahren der neudeutschen Musik* (Königsberg, 1933); *Carl Maria von Weber* (Potsdam, 1934); *Carl Maria von Weber: Sein Leben in Bildern* (Leipzig, 1936); *Musikstadt Königsberg: Geschichte und Erinnerung* (Freiburg, 1966).

Kroll, William, American violinist and teacher; b. N.Y., Jan. 30, 1901; d. Boston, March 10, 1980. He studied at the Berlin Hochschule für Musik (1911–14); made his debut in N.Y. in 1915, then continued his studies at the Inst. of Musical Art there (1917–22). He played in the Elshuco Trio (1922–29), then was 1st violinist of the Coolidge Quartet (1936–44) and subsequently of his own Kroll Quartet (1944–69); toured with these ensembles, and also made solo appearances. He taught at the Inst. of Musical Art (1922–38), the Mannes College of Music in N.Y. (from 1943), the Peabody Cons. of Music in Baltimore (1947–65), and the Cleveland Inst. of Music (1964–67); was made prof. of violin at Queens College of the City Univ. of N.Y. (1969). He composed some chamber orch. works, chamber music, and violin pieces.

Krombholc, Jaroslav, esteemed Czech conductor; b. Prague, Jan. 30, 1918; d. there, July 16, 1983. He studied composition with Novák (1937–40) and conducting with Dědeček, Ostrčil, and Talich (1940–41) at the Prague Cons. and its Master School; also studied quarter-tone music with A. Hába and attended V. Nejedlý's classes at the Univ. of Prague. He 1st gained attention as a composer, winning 1st prize in a Czech Phil. competition with his Suite for Piano and Orch. (1939). He then made his conducting debut at the Prague National Theater (1940); after serving as chief conductor of the Ostrava Opera (1944–45), he rejoined the roster of the Prague National Theater; later was its chief conductor (1968–75), and chief conductor of the Prague Radio Sym. Orch. (1973–78). He also appeared as a guest conductor with leading European opera houses. He was especially renowned for his idiomatic performances of works by Smetana, Dvořák, Janáček, Martinů, and other Czech composers, as well as for his distinguished interpretations of the music of Prokofiev and Shostakovich.

Krombholc, Karlo, Hungarian-Serbian pianist and composer; b. Budapest, Dec. 20, 1905. He studied at the Vienna Academy of Music; was active as a pianist (1927–39); after World War II, settled in Novi Sad as a piano teacher. His works are influenced mainly by Bartók, with ethnic modalities gadrooned by atonal extrapolations. Typical of these is his extensive piano work *Sazvezda* (Constellations; 1969). He also wrote orch. works based on Hungarian and Balkan folk tunes.

Krommer (Kramář), Franz Vincez (František Vincenc), Moravian violinist, conductor, and composer; b. Kamenitz, Nov. 27, 1759; d. Vienna, Jan. 8, 1831. He studied with his uncle, Anton Matthias Krommer, a choirmaster and composer in Turăn (1773–76); was self-taught in composition. He became a violinist in the orch. of the Duke of Styrum in Simontornya (1786), becoming his music director (1788). He was made Kapellmeister of Pecs Cathedral (1790), then Kapellmeister and composer to Duke Károlyi (1793) and Prince Grassalkovich de Gyarak; became Kapellmeister to Duke Ignaz Fuchs (1798). He returned to Vienna, and was made Ballett-Kapellmeister at the Hofkapelle (1810); then Kammertürhüter to the Emperor (1815); was the last official director of chamber music and court composer to the Habsburg monarchy (from 1818). He wrote a number of accomplished solo concertos for wind instruments; also syms., sacred works, much chamber music, and piano pieces.

BIBL.: K. Padrta, *František K. a jeho orchestrální skladby* (F. K. and His Orchestral Compositions; diss., Univ. of Brno, 1949); idem, *František Vincenc Kramář-Krommer: Studie k životopismým a slohovým otázkám* (F.V. K.-K.: Bibliographical and Stylistic Questions; Brno, 1966).

Kromolicki, Joseph, Polish-born German choral conductor, musicologist, and composer; b. Posen, Jan. 16, 1882; d. Berlin, Oct. 11, 1961. He studied with Haberl and Haller in Regensburg and with Pfitzner, Kretzschmar, and Wolf in Berlin, where he took his Ph.D. at the Univ. in 1909 with the dissertation *Die Practica artis musicae des Amerus.* He was active as a choral conductor in Berlin; ed. *Musica Sacra* from 1908 and vols. 45, 48, and 57 of Denkmäler Deutscher Tonkunst; composed 5 masses, a Te Deum, organ preludes, sacred songs, etc.

Kronke, Emil, German pianist and composer; b. Danzig, Nov. 29, 1865; d. Dresden, Dec. 16, 1938. He was a pupil of Reinecke in Leipzig and of Nicodé and Kirchner in Dresden; won 1st prize for piano at the Dresden Cons. (1886). He was an ardent admirer of Liszt, and wrote several virtuoso pieces for piano; also publ. several manuals and ed. more than 200 of Chopin's works.

Kronold, Hans, Polish-American cellist and composer, brother of **Selma Kronold;** b. Krakow, July 3, 1872; d. N.Y., Jan. 10, 1922. He studied in Leipzig and Berlin; went to the U.S. at the age of 14, where he joined the orch. of the Metropolitan Opera. He then played in the N.Y. Sym. Orch.; taught at the N.Y. College of Music. He publ. cello pieces and songs.

Kronold, Selma, Polish-American soprano, sister of **Hans Kronold;** b. Krakow, Aug. 18, 1861; d. N.Y., Oct. 9, 1920. She made her debut as Agathe in *Der Freischütz* in Leipzig when she was 16; then was engaged to sing Wagnerian roles in various European cities. In 1888 she went to the U.S.; sang leading roles in the American premieres of *Cavalleria rusticana* (Philadelphia, Sept. 9, 1891) and *Pagliacci* (N.Y., June 15, 1893). She first appeared at the Metropolitan Opera in N.Y. as Helmwige in *Die Walküre* (Feb. 6, 1891); was again on its roster (1898–99; 1903–4); then founded the Catholic Oratorio Soc.

Kroó, György, Hungarian musicologist; b. Budapest, Aug. 26, 1926. He studied violin at the National Cons. and at the Academy of Music in Budapest; also attended classes in musicology there with Szabolcsi and Bartha. In 1957 he was named head of music education of the Hungarian Radio; in 1960, became a guest lecturer at the Academy of Music, joining its permanent faculty in 1967; was chairman of its musicology dept. from 1973; was a prof. of musicology (from 1975). His writings include *Robert Schumann* (Budapest, 1958); *Hector Berlioz* (Budapest, 1960); *Bartók Béla szinpadi müvei* (Bartók's Stage Works; Budapest, 1962); *Wenn Schumann ein Tagebuch geführt hätte* (Budapest, 1962); *A "szabadito" opera* (The "Rescue" Opera; Budapest, 1966); *Richard Wagner* (Budapest, 1968); *Bartók kalauz* (A Guide to Bartók; Budapest, 1971; in Eng., 1974); *A magyar zeneszerzés harminc éve* (30 Years of Hungarian Composition; Budapest, 1975); *Rácz Aladár* (Budapest, 1979); *Heilawâc. Négy tanulmány Wagner a Nibelung gyürüjéröl* (4 Studies on Wagner's *Ring des Nibelungen*; Budapest, 1983); *Az albumtól a szvitig* (From the Album to the Suite; Budapest, 1986).

Krow, Josef Theodor, Bohemian singer and composer; b. Nové Strašeci, Dec. 19, 1797; d. Draguignan, near Nice, March 1, 1859. He studied at the Piarist Gymnasium in Prague. He sang minor operatic roles in Hungary, Poland, and the Netherlands; was a singing teacher in London (1835–40), then went to Nice (1858). His claim to a small niche in music history rests upon his publication of a drinking song to the words "Těšme se blahou nadějí" (Blissfully Hoping We Will Enjoy) in 1825, claiming it to be an authentic melody of the Bohemian religious reformer, martyr, and saint Ján Hus. His claim was widely believed; Liszt wrote a piano paraphrase of the song as *Hussittenlied aus dem 15. Jahrhundert;* Balfe made use of it in his opera *The Bohemian Girl,* and Angelo Tessaro in his opera *Giovanni Huss.* Even more spectacular was Krow's success in setting the same tune to his own German words, "Polen wird für ewig Polen," publ. under the pseudo-Polish pseudonym Workinski ("Work" is the crab form of "Krow") in 1831; caught in the wave of universal sympathy for Poland after the unsuccessful rebellion, the song achieved tremendous popularity all over Europe.

Kroyer, Theodor, eminent German musicologist; b. Munich, Sept. 9, 1873; d. Wiesbaden, Jan. 12, 1945. He studied piano with Lang, counterpoint with Rheinberger, and musicology with Sandberger; took his Ph.D. from the Univ. of Munich with the dissertation *Die Anfange der Chromatik im italienischen Madrigal des XVI. Jahrhunderts* (publ. in Leipzig, 1902); completed his Habilitation there in 1902 with his *Ludwig Senfl und sein Motettenstil* (publ. in Munich, 1902). He was music critic of the *Münchener Allgemeine Zeitung* (1897–1910). He taught at the Univs. of Munich (1902–20), Heidelberg (1920–23), Leipzig (1923–33), and Cologne (1932–38). In 1925 he purchased for the Univ. of Leipzig the rich collection of instruments, MSS, and portraits from the famous Heyer Museum in Cologne; also in 1925 he began issuing the valuable series *Publikationen Älterer Musik*. He ed. a vol. (motets and Magnificat) of the complete works of Senfl in Denkmäler der Tonkunst in Bayern, V, Jg. III/2 (1903); also ed. a selection from the works of G. Aichinger for the same series (XVIII, Jg. X/I, 1909).

BIBL.: H. Zenck et al., eds., *T. K.: Festschrift zum 60. Geburtstage am 9. September 1933 überreicht von Freunden und Schülern* (Regensburg, 1933); O. Ursprung, "*T. K.*," *Zeitschrift für Musikwissenschaft* (Nov. 1933); H. Zenck, "*T. K.*," *Die Musikforschung*, I (1948).

Krstič, Petar, Serbian composer; b. Belgrade, March 2, 1877; d. there, Jan. 21, 1957. He studied with R. Fuchs at the Vienna Cons. He conducted opera at Belgrade's National Theater; in 1930, became inspector of music schools. His works, based on Serbian national tunes, included the opera *Zulumćar* (Belgrade, Nov. 23, 1927); cantata, *Jutro Slobode* (1919); several orch. suites of national dances; choruses and songs. He ed. a Serbian music dictionary.

Krückl, Franz, Moravian baritone; b. Edlspitz, Nov. 10, 1841; d. Strasbourg, Jan. 13, 1899. He studied with Dessoff; made his debut in 1868 in Brünn; then sang in Kassel, Augsburg, Hamburg, and Cologne (1874–86); taught at the Hoch Cons. in Frankfurt; in 1892, became director of the Strasbourg Municipal Theater. He publ. *Der Vertrag zwischen Direktor und Mitglied der deutschen Bühne* (1899).

Krueger, Karl (Adalbert), American conductor; b. Atchison, Kans., Jan. 19, 1894; d. Elgin, Ill., July 21, 1979. He learned to play the cello and organ in his early youth; then studied at Midland College in his hometown (B.A. 1913), with Chadwick (composition) and Goodrich (organ) at the New England Cons. of Music in Boston (1914–15), and at the Univ. of Kansas (M.A., 1916). He was an organist at St. Ann's Episcopal Church in N.Y. (1916–20). In 1920 he made a concert tour of Brazil as an organist; then went to Vienna, where he studied music theory with Robert Fuchs and conducting with Franz Schalk. He also attended classes in economics at the Univ. of Vienna and the Univ. of Heidelberg. Returning to the U.S. in 1922, he married the heiress Emma McCormick Jewett, of Chicago. He was conductor of the Seattle Sym. Orch. (1926–32), the Kansas City Phil. (1933–43), and the Detroit Sym. Orch. (1943–49). In 1958 he founded the Soc. for the Preservation of the American Musical Heritage and made numerous recordings of American works. He wrote *The Way of the Conductor: His Origins, Purpose and Procedures* (N.Y., 1958).

Krug, Friedrich, German baritone and composer; b. Kassel, July 5, 1812; d. Karlsruhe, Nov. 3, 1892. He was court music director at Karlsruhe. He wrote the operas *Die Marquise* (Kassel, 1843); *Meister Martin der Kufer und seine Gesellen* (Karlsruhe, 1845); *Der Nachtwächter* (Mannheim, 1846).

Krug, (Wenzel) Joseph, German composer and conductor, known as **Krug-Waldsee;** b. Waldsee, Nov. 8, 1858; d. Magdeburg, Oct. 8, 1915. He developed precociously; entered the Stuttgart Cons. at 14, studying violin, piano, singing, and theory; graduated in 1880 and went to Switzerland, where he was active as a teacher in Hofwyl; then conducted a choral society in Stuttgart (1882–89); was subsequently chorus master in Hamburg (1889–92) and in Nuremberg and Augsburg (from 1894); then lived in Magdeburg. He wrote several cantatas in a grand manner; 4 operas; chamber music; songs.

Krüger, Eduard, German writer on music; b. Lüneburg, Dec. 9, 1807; d. Göttingen, Nov. 8, 1885. He studied philology, history, and music at the Univs. of Berlin and Göttingen (Ph.D. from the latter, 1830); then taught at the Emden Gymnasium (1833–51) and also conducted the local choral society. He was chief inspector for East Friesland (1851–59); then was made a prof. at the Univ. of Göttingen (1861).

WRITINGS: *Grundriss der Metrik antiker und moderner Sprachen* (Emden, 1838); *Beiträge für Leben und Wissenschaft der Tonkunst* (Leipzig, 1847); *System der Tonkunst* (Leipzig, 1866); *Musikalische Briefe aus der neuesten Zeit* (Münster, 1870).

BIBL.: K. Hoppenrath, *E. K.: Leben und Wirken eines Musikgelehrten zwischen Schumannscher Tradition und Neudeutscher Schule* (diss., Univ. of Göttingen, 1964).

Krüger, Wilhelm, German pianist, teacher, and composer; b. Stuttgart, Aug. 5, 1820; d. there, June 16, 1883. He studied piano with Ziegele and composition with Lindpaintner. In 1845 he settled in Paris, where he enjoyed an excellent reputation as a pianist and teacher; in 1870, the outbreak of the Franco-Prussian War compelled him to return to Germany; he was then active as a pedagogue. He publ. a number of brilliant salon pieces for piano (168 opus numbers in all), which included caprices, nocturnes, genre pieces (*Harpe éolienne, Guitare*), a *Polonaise-Boléro*, études (*Les Six Jours de la semaine*, etc.), and transcriptions, fantasias, etc., of and on operatic airs.

Kruis, M.H. van't, Dutch organist and composer; b. Oudewater, March 8, 1861; d. Lausanne, Feb. 14, 1919. He studied in The Hague; then filled various posts as organist and teacher; in 1886 he founded the musical monthly *Het Orgel*. He publ. *Beknopt overzicht der muziekgeschiedenis* (1892); also wrote an opera, *De bloem van Island*; 3 syms.; 8 overtures; organ music; piano pieces; etc.

Krul, Eli, Polish-American composer; b. Pabianice, Jan. 1, 1926; d. N.Y., June 28, 1971. He studied at the Hochschule für Musik in Munich (1945–49); in 1950 he settled in N.Y. His works include String Quartet (1958); *O Come, Let Us Sing* for Chorus and Organ (1960); *Alleluia* for Chorus a cappella (1962); etc.

Krumpholtz, Anne-Marie (née **Steckler**), celebrated German harpist; b. Metz, c.1755; d. London, after 1824. She studied with **Jean-Baptiste Krumpholtz** in Metz, becoming his 2nd wife about 1778; she appeared at a Paris Concert Spirituel in 1779, and subsequently performed many of her husband's compositions there. After having taken a lover by 1788, she went to London. She made her 1st London appearance on June 2 of that year, and thereafter gave many concerts; also appeared under Salomon's auspices (1791–93). She retired in 1803. She was greatly renowned as a master of her instrument, being considered the equal and often the superior of her husband as a virtuoso.

BIBL.: H. Tribout de Morembert, *A.-M. Steckler: Une Virtuose de la harpe au XVIIIe siècle* (Metz, 1962).

Krumpholtz, Jean-Baptiste (Johann Baptist or **Jan Křtitel),** famous Bohemian harpist and composer; b. Budenice, near Zlonice, May 3, 1742; d. (suicide) Paris, Feb. 19, 1790. He received his 1st instruction from his father, a bandmaster in the service of Count Kinský; later studied and gave concerts in Vienna (1773); also studied composition with Haydn and was harp soloist in the service of Count Esterházy. He made an extensive tour of Europe in 1776; during his stay in Metz, **Anne-Marie** (née **Steckler**) **Krumpholtz** became his pupil and then his 2nd wife (c.1778); however, she took a lover by 1788 and eloped to England. Krumpholtz, in despair, drowned himself in the Seine. Krumpholtz added to his fame as a harpist by inventing a harp with 2 pedals, loud and soft; he also stimulated Erard to make experiments that led to the invention of the modern pedal mechanism. He was a distinguished composer for the instrument as well, producing several concertos, many sonatas, and various other works. His brother, **Wenzel (Václav) Krumpholtz** (b. probably in Budenice, c.1750; d. Vienna, May 2, 1817), was a violinist and composer; he was a member of Prince Esterházy's orch. before joing the orch. of the Vienna Hofoper (1796). He is best remembered as a close friend of Beethoven, and as one of his early champions; upon his death, Beethoven wrote the *Gesang der Mönche* for 3 Men's Voices after Schiller, Wo 0104. Krumpholtz wrote several violin pieces.

Krupa, Gene, American jazz drummer; b. Chicago, Jan. 15, 1909; d. Yonkers, N.Y., Oct. 16, 1973. He joined a jazz band when still in his adolescence; studied percussion with Al Silverman, Ed Straight, and Roy Knapp (1925); worked with local musicians. He then went to N.Y. (1929), where he performed in bands led by Red Nichols and Irving Aaronson; after working with others (1932–34), he became a featured member of Benny Goodman's band (1934), winning acclaim for his brilliant playing in the recording of *Sing, Sing, Sing.* He left Goodman in 1938, forming his own band; he toured Europe and the Orient and became internationally famous. He was again a member of Goodman's band (1943), and then of Tommy Dorsey's band (1943–44). He subsequently led his own band (until 1951); later toured with Jazz at the Phil., and with his own trios and quartets. Possessed with a phenomenal technique and a penchant for showmanship, Krupa "popularized" the drums with extended, virtuosic solos. He recorded the soundtrack for the largely fictional film *The Gene Krupa Story* (1959).
BIBL.: G. Hall and S. Kramer, *G. K. and His Orchestra* (Laurel, Md., 1975); K. Stratemann, *Buddy Rich and G. K.: A Filmodiscography* (Lübeck, Germany, 1980); B. Crowther, *G. K.: His Life and Times* (Tunbridge Wells and N.Y., 1987).

Krushelnitskaya, Salomea (Ambrosivna), noted Russian soprano; b. Belavyntsy, near Tarnopol, Sept. 23, 1872; d. Lwow, Nov. 16, 1952. As a child she sang in a village choir; after studying voice with Wysocki in Lemberg, made her debut there in *La Favorite* in 1892; then went to Milan, where she took lessons with Crespi. From 1898 to 1902 she was a member of the Warsaw Opera; then scored a remarkable success as Cio-Cio-San in Brescia (1904). After singing at La Scala in Milan (from 1906) and in Buenos Aires (1906–13), she made her operatic farewell in Naples in 1920; subsequently devoted herself to concert appearances. She taught at the Lwow Cons. (from 1939). Her voice was of particular beauty, spanning fully 3 octaves. Among her most notable roles were Brünnhilde, Isolde, Elisabeth in *Tannhäuser*, Elsa in *Lohengrin*, Aida, Desdemona, and Elektra. In her concert programs she promoted songs by Ukrainian composers. A collection of articles about her career was publ. in Ukrainian (Lwow, 1956).

Kruyf, Ton de, Dutch composer; b. Leerdam, Oct. 3, 1937. He studied violin; attended seminars in Darmstadt led by Maderna, Boulez, Stockhausen, and Ligeti; then studied with Fortner in Heidelberg. In his music he pursues the goal of maximum effect with a minimum of means; he makes use of serialism when it is structurally justified.
WORKS: DRAMATIC: Opera, *Spinoza* (Amsterdam, June 15, 1971); radio opera, *Quauhquauhtinchan in den vreemde* (Quauhquauhtinchan in Foreign Parts; Hilversum, June 3, 1972); ballet, *Chronologie II* (The Hague, 1968). **ORCH.:** *Mouvements symphoniques* (1955; rev. 1966); *Sinfonietta,* 3 dances for Strings (1956; rev. 1965); *5 Impromptus* for Small Orch. (1958); *Einst dem Grau der Nacht enttäuscht,* after poems by the painter Paul Klee, for Mezzo-soprano and Chamber Ensemble (Hilversum, Sept. 15, 1964); *Pour faire le portrait d'un oiseau,* after Jacques Prévert, for Mezzo-soprano and Chamber Ensemble (Hilversum, Sept. 17, 1965); *De blinde zwemmers,* 3 fragments for Youth Chorus and 2 Instrumental Groups (1966); *Töne aus der Ferne,* after a poem by Paul Klee, for Alto and Chamber Orch. (Amsterdam, Sept. 11, 1968); *Sinfonia II* (Hilversum, May 14, 1969; developed from an orch. interlude in the opera *Spinoza*); *4 pas de deux* for Flute and Orch. (1972); *Echoi* for Oboe and String Orch. (1973); *Twee uur* (2 Hours) for Speaker and Orch. (1973); *Meditations* for Baritone and Orch., after poems by Dylan Thomas (1976); *Cantate* (1978); *Ode to the West Wind* for Chorus and Orch., after Shelley (1978); *Spring-time fantasietta* for 13 Solo Strings (1978).

CHAMBER AND INSTRUMENTAL: Quartet for Flute, Violin, Trumpet, and Bassoon (1959); *Sgrafitti* for Piano (1960); *Music* for String Quartet (1962); Solo Cello Sonata (1964); *Aubade* for Horn, 2 Trumpets, Trombone, and Tuba (1965); *Serenata per complesso da camera* for Flute, Clarinet, Harp, and String Quintet (1968); *Mosaico* for Oboe and String Trio (1969); *Echoi* for Oboe (1973); *Arioso* for Piano, 4-hands (1975); *Musica portuensis* for 4 Saxophones (1983).

Krygell, Johan Adam, Danish organist and composer; b. Næstved, Sept. 18, 1835; d. Copenhagen, July 27, 1915. He began his career as a painter, but turned his attention to music; entered the Copenhagen Cons. in 1867, studying organ under G. Matthison-Hansen; won the Ancker stipend, and spent 1874–75 studying in Germany; returning to Copenhagen in 1880, he became organist at St. Matthew's Church; also taught. He wrote an opera, *Saul* (not produced); an oratorio; a Mass; 24 string quartets; a Septet; syms.; overtures; organ works.

Krylov, Pavel, Russian composer; b. Tver, March 3, 1885; d. Moscow, April 21, 1935. He studied at the Phil. Inst. in Moscow; graduated in 1910 with honors. In 1920 he joined the staff of the Moscow Cons. Among his works are an opera, *The Fountain of Bakhtchissaray;* Sym.; symphonic poem, *The Spring;* symphonic suite, *Volga;* Concerto for Clarinet and Orch.; 3 piano sonatas; songs.

Kryzhanovsky, Ivan, Russian music theorist and composer; b. Kiev, March 8, 1867; d. Leningrad, Dec. 9, 1924. He studied medicine and music; took lessons with Rimsky-Korsakov at the St. Petersburg Cons.; worked in Pavlov's laboratory of conditioned reflexes; served in the medical corps in the Russian army during World War I, and was taken prisoner. After his release, he lectured on the physiology of piano technique. He wrote several symphonic works, chamber music, and a Piano Concerto. His *Biological Bases of the Evolution of Music* was publ. in an Eng. tr. (London, 1928).

Kubelík, Jan, famous Czech-born Hungarian violinist, father of **(Jeroným) Rafael Kubelík;** b. Michle, near Prague, July 5, 1880; d. Prague, Dec. 5, 1940. He began violin training with his father, then studied with Ševčik (violin) and Foerster (composition) at the Prague Cons. (1892–98); continued his studies in Vienna, where he performed for the 1st time on Nov. 26, 1898. In 1900 he made his London debut, and thereafter made a series of triumphant tours of Europe and the U.S. He was awarded the Gold Medal of the Phil. Soc. of London in 1902. In 1903 he married a Hungarian countess and became a naturalized Hungarian citizen. He continued his active career for over 4 decades, giving a series of farewell concerts in 1939–40. On May 8, 1940, he gave his last concert in Prague, after his beloved homeland had been dismembered by the Nazis. Kubelík was one of the foremost virtuosos of his day. He also composed; wrote 6 violin concertos, as well as a Sym. and some chamber music; likewise prepared cadenzas for the Beethoven, Brahms, and Tchaikovsky violin concertos.
BIBL.: J. Celeda, *J. K.* (Prague, 1930); B. Voldan, *Skladby J.a K.a* (J. K.'s Compositions; Prague, 1933); H. Doležil, *Mistr houslí J. K.* (The Master of the Violin J. K.; Prague, 1941); K. Hoffmiester, *J. K.* (Prague, 1941); J. Dostal, ed., *J. K.* (Prague, 1942); B. Schwarz, *Great Masters of the Violin* (N.Y., 1983).

Kubelík, (Jeroným) Rafael, eminent Czech-born Swiss conductor, son of **Jan Kubelík;** b. Býchory, near Kolín, June 29, 1914. He studied violin with his father, and then continued his musical training at the Prague Cons.; he made his conducting debut with the Czech Phil. in Prague on Jan. 24, 1934, then was conductor at the National Theater in Brno (1939–41). He was chief conductor of the Czech Phil. from 1942 to 1948, one of the most difficult periods in the history of the orch. and the Czech nation. He refused to collaborate with the Nazi occupation authorities; when the Communists took control of the government in 1948, he left the country for the West, vowing not to return until the political situation changed. He appeared as a guest conductor in England and

Western Europe, then made his U.S. debut with the Chicago Sym. Orch. on Nov. 17, 1949; his success led to his appointment as the orch.'s music director in 1950; however, his inclusion of many contemporary works in his programs and his insistence on painstaking rehearsals antagonized some of his auditors, including members of the Chicago press, causing him to resign his post in 1953. He subsequently was music director at the Royal Opera House at Covent Garden in London (1955–58); his tenure was notable for important productions of *Les Troyens, Boris Godunov* (in the original version), and *Jenůfa*. He then was chief conductor of the Bavarian Radio Sym. Orch. in Munich (1961–79). He made his Metropolitan Opera debut in N.Y. as its 1st music director on Oct. 22, 1973, conducting *Les Troyens;* however, he again became an epicenter of controversy, and soon submitted his resignation. In spite of the contretemps, his artistic integrity remained intact; he continued to appear widely as a guest conductor in Western Europe and the U.S. In light of his controversial tenure in Chicago, it was ironic that he became an honored guest conductor with that orch. in later years. He retired in 1985, although he returned to Czechoslovakia in 1990 after an absence of 42 years to conduct the Czech Phil. in 2 performances of Smetana's symphonic cycle *Má Vlast* during the opening of the Prague Spring Festival. Kubelík was the foremost Czech conductor of his generation; in addition to his idiomatic and authoritative performances of the music of his native country, he was greatly esteemed for his distinguished interpretations of the standard repertoire, which were marked by a pristine musicianship, unfettered by self-indulgence. Kubelík became a Swiss citizen in 1966. His 2nd wife was the Australian soprano **Elsie Morison.** He also composed several operas, including *Veronika* (Brno, April 19, 1947) and *Cornelia Faroli* (Augsburg, 1972); a Sym. for Chorus and Orch. (1941); a Sym. in 1 Movement (Westdeutscher Rundfunk, Cologne, 1974); *Sequences* for Orch. (Lucerne Festival, 1976); a Sym., *Orphikon* (N.Y., April 2, 1981); *Symphonic Peripeteia* for Organ and Orch. (Chicago Sym. Orch., March 14, 1985); a number of choral works; 6 string quartets and other chamber music works; and songs.

Kubiak, Teresa (originally, **Tersa Wojtaszek**), Polish soprano; b. Ldzan, Dec. 26, 1937. She was educated at the Academy of Music in Lodz; made her debut with the Lodz Opera in 1965; then appeared with the Warsaw Opera. She made her U.S. debut in a concert performance of Goldmark's *Die Königen von Saba* in N.Y. (1970); then appeared with the San Francisco Opera, with the Chicago Lyric Opera, and at the Glyndebourne Festival (1971). She made her Metropolitan Opera debut in N.Y. as Liza in *The Queen of Spades* on Jan. 18, 1973; that same year she appeared at the Vienna State Opera as Elsa. Among her other roles were Senta, Aida, Tosca, Jenůfa, and many from the 20th-century repertoire.

Kubik, Gail (Thompson), American composer; b. South Coffeyville, Okla., Sept. 5, 1914; d. (of the side effects of kalaazar, a visceral protozoan infection he contracted on a trip to Africa) Covina, Calif., July 20, 1984. He studied the rudiments of music with his mother, who had been trained as a concert singer; then enrolled at the Eastman School of Music in Rochester, N.Y., where he studied violin with Samuel Belov, composition with Bernard Rogers and Edward Royce, and theory with Irving McHose; in 1934 he received his B.M. degree. He continued his studies in composition with Leo Sowerby at the American Cons. of Music in Chicago (M.M., 1936); subsequently studied with Piston at Harvard Univ., and with Nadia Boulanger in Paris. He taught at Monmouth College in Illinois (1934), Dakota Wesleyan Univ. in Mitchell, S. Dak. (1936–37), and Teachers College at Columbia Univ. (1938–40). He was also active as a violinist; was soloist in the premiere of his 1st Violin Concerto in Chicago (Jan. 2, 1938). He was a staff composer and music program adviser for NBC (1940–42); then was director of music for the Bureau of Motion Pictures of the U.S. Office of War Information and served in the U.S. Air Force during World War II. He received 2 Guggenheim fellowships (1944, 1956); won the American Prix de Rome

(1950, 1951), and then worked at the American Academy in Rome. He was awarded the Pulitzer Prize in Music in 1952 for his *Symphonie concertante* for Piano, Viola, Trumpet, and Orch. In 1970 he was appointed composer-in-residence at Scripps College in Claremont, Calif.; when he was asked to retire at the age of 65 (1980), he brought an unsuccessful suit against the school, claiming that productivity and not age should determine the time of retirement. His gift of musical humor was expressed at its best in the music he wrote for the animated film cartoon *Gerald McBoing-Boing* (1950), which received both a Motion Picture Academy Award and the British Film Inst. Award, and which incidentally launched a vogue of twangy rhinogenic tunes in popular music. In his symphonic and other scores he cultivated a manner that was expressively modern, without abandoning the basic tenets of tonality; the rhythmic patterns of his music were apt to be stimulatingly asymmetric.

WORKS: STAGE: *A Mirror for the Sky,* folk opera on the life of Audubon (Eugene, Oreg., May 23, 1939); *Boston Baked Beans,* "opera piccola" (N.Y., March 9, 1952); *Frankie and Johnnie,* ballet for Dance Band and Folk Singer (1946). **ORCH.:** *American Caprice* for Piano and Orch. (1936); *Scherzo* (1940); 2 violin concertos: No. 1 (1934; rev. 1936; Chicago, Jan. 2, 1938, composer soloist); No. 2 (1940; rev. 1941; won 1st prize in the Jascha Heifetz competition); *Spring Valley Overture* (1947); 3 syms.: No. 1 (1949); No. 2 (Louisville, Ky., April 7, 1956); No. 3 (N.Y., Feb. 28, 1957); *Symphonie concertante* for Piano, Viola, Trumpet, and Orch. (N.Y., Jan. 27, 1952; received the Pulitzer Prize in Music in 1952); *Thunderbolt Overture* (1953); *Scenario* (1957). **CHAMBER:** *Trivialities* for Flute, Horn, and String Quartet (1934); Piano Trio (1934); Wind Quintet (1937); *Suite* for 3 Recorders (1941); Sonatina for Violin and Piano (1944); *Toccata* for Organ and Strings (1946); *Little Suite* for Flute and 2 Clarinets (1947); *Soliloquy and Dance* for Violin and Piano (1948); Divertimento No. 1 for 13 Players (1959); Divertimento No. 2 for 8 Players (1959); *Prayer and Toccata* for Organ and Chamber Orch. (1968); Divertimento No. 3 for Piano Trio (1970–71); *5 Birthday Pieces* for 2 Recorders (1974). **VOCAL:** *In Praise of Johnny Appleseed* for Bass-baritone, Chorus, and Orch. (1938; rev. 1961); *Choral Profiles, Folk Song Sketches* for Chorus (1938); *Puck: A Legend of Bethlehem,* radio music (NBC, Dec. 29, 1940); *Litany and Prayer* for Men's Chorus, Brass, and Percussion (1943–45); *Fables and Song* for Voice and Piano (1950–59); *A Christmas Set* for Chorus and Chamber Orch. (1968); *A Record of Our Time,* "protest piece" for Chorus, Narrator, Soloist, and Orch. (Manhattan, Kans., Nov. 11, 1970); *Scholastics* for a cappella Chorus (1972); *Magic, Magic, Magic* for Chorus and Chamber Orch. (San Antonio, April 25, 1976). **FILM SCORES:** *The World at War* (1942); *Memphis Belle* (1943); *Gerald McBoing-Boing* (1950); *The Miner's Daughter* (1950); *Two Gals and a Guy* (1951); *Translantic* (1952); *The Desperate Hours* (1955); *Down to Earth* (1959); also piano pieces.

Kubín, Rudolf, Czech composer; b. Moravská, Ostrava, Jan. 10, 1909; d. there, Jan. 11, 1973. He studied cello with Junek and composition with A. Hába at the Prague Cons. (1924–29). He became a cellist in the Prague Radio Orch. (1929); also was active as music director of the Ostrava and Brno depts. of the Czech Radio. He helped organize the Ostrava Higher Music Teaching College, serving as its director (1953–54); after it became a cons., he was its director (1958–60). He wrote music in disparate styles, some extremely modern, others designed for utilitarian purposes (mass songs, military marches, patriotic cantatas, etc.).

WORKS: 3 operas: *Letní noc* (A Summer Night; 1930–31; Czech Radio, 1931; 1st Czech radio opera); *Naši furianti* (Our Wild Ones; 1942–45; Ostrava, Sept. 18, 1949); *Koleje mládí* (The Rails of Youth; 1948–49; radio opera); numerous operettas, including *Heva* (1955–57); *Prolog* for Orch. (1929); *Czech Overture* (1932); Sinfonietta for Orch. and Organ (1935–36); Overture to the unfinished opera *Zpěv uhlí* (Song of Coal; 1936); Trombone Concerto (1936); *Symphony concertante* for

4 Horns and String Orch. (1937); Clarinet Concerto (1939); 2 violin concertos (1940, 1960); *Moravian Rhapsody* for Orch. (1942); overture, *Květen* (May; 1945); Accordion Concerto (1950); symphonic cycle, *Ostrava* (1950–51), consisting of 5 separate works: *Vítězství* (Victory), *Maryčka Magdónova*, *Ostrava*, *V Beskydách* (In the Beskid Mountains), and *Ocelové srdce* (Heart of Steel); symphonic poem, *Geroj, In Memoriam K. Gottwalda* (1953); dramatic overture, *Julius Fučík* (1954); Cello Concerto (1960); *Salutation to Frenštát*, melodrama for Orch. (Ostrava, Jan. 9, 1969); *Reminiscence*, sym. (Ostrava, Jan. 9, 1969); String Quartet (1925–26); *Scherzo* for 2 Clarinets and Piano (1933); *Jazzety* for Piano (1940); *Scherzo* for Violin and Piano (1942); *Ballade* for 4 Cellos (1942); Nonet (1946); Suite for Cello (1970); songs; choruses; numerous quarter-tone pieces written during his studies with Hába: 2 suites for Piano (1926, 1927); 2 fantasies for Piano (1926, 1927); Fantasy for Clarinet and Piano (1926); 5 *Pieces* for Cello and Piano (1926); *Piano Piece* (1927).

Kučera, Václav, Czech composer; b. Prague, April 29, 1929. He studied at the Univ. of Prague (1948–51); then went to Russia, where he took a course in composition with Shebalin at the Moscow Cons. (1951–56). Upon returning to Prague, he served as head of foreign music at the Czech Radio (1956–59). He worked in the Inst. for Musicology of the Czech Academy of Sciences (1962–69); was head of contemporary music (1959–69) and general secretary (1969–89) of the Union of Czech Composers. He taught composition at the Prague Academy of Arts (from 1975). In his music he follows the precepts of socialist realism, often using historical subjects in his radio productions, with the application of electronic sounds; but he is also a prolific composer of chamber music in purely structural techniques. He also publ. a number of monographs on Czech and Russian composers.

WORKS: BALLETS: *The Brigands' Fire* (1958); *Festival Fairy Tale* (1959); *Kinetic Ballet* (1968); *Heart and Dream* (1973); *Life without Fault* (1979); 2 dramatic radio sketches: *Lidice* for Narrator, 2 Reporters, Announcer, Soprano, Chorus, Instrumental Ensemble, and Electronic Sounds, commemorating the destruction of the Czech village by the Nazis (1972); *Spartacus* for Chorus and Electronic Sound (1976). **ORCH.:** Sym. (1962); *Krysař* (The Pied Piper), stereophonic concertino for Flute and 2 Chamber Orchs. (1964); *Obraz* (Picture) for Piano and Orch. (1966–70); *Salut*, symphonic mosaic (1975); *Operand* for Chamber Orch. (1979); *Fortunata* (*Omaggio a Vivaldi*) for Chamber Orch. (1979); *Avanti*, symphonic movement (1981). **CHAMBER:** *Dramas* for 9 Instruments (1961); *Protests*, chamber cycle for Violin, Piano, and Kettledrums (1963); *Hic sunt homines* for Piano Quartet (1965); *Spectra* for Dulcimer (1965); *Diptychon* for Flute, Bass Clarinet, Piano, and Percussion (1966); *Duodrama* for Bass Clarinet and Piano (1967); *To Be*, an affirmative optimistic reply to Hamlet's question, for Percussion Quartet (1968); *Panta Rhei* (All Flows, according to the Greek philosopher Heraclitus) for Flute, Vibraphone, and Percussion (1969); *Invariant* for Bass Clarinet, Piano, and Electronic Tape (1969); *Argot* for Brass Quintet (1970); *Diario* (Homage to Ché Guevara), concert cycle for Guitar (1971); *Taboo a due boemi* for Bass Clarinet, Piano, and Percussion (1972); *Manifesto of Spring* (In Memory of Prague, May, 1945) for 4 Players (1974); *Imaginable Connections* for String Quartet (1976); *Horizons* for 5 Players (1978); *Science Fiction* for Jazz Ensemble (1980); *Boiling Point* for 4 Brass Instruments (1981); *Wagnerian Improvisations* for Flute (1982); other chamber works. **VOCAL:** *Orbis pictus* for Mixed Chorus and Old Instruments (1975); *Gallant Songs* for Mezzo-soprano, Flute, Clarinet, and Viola (1978); *Catharsis*, concert monologue for Soprano and Chamber Ensemble (1979); *Ecce Homo*, 5 Greek and Latin sentences for Bass, Violin, Viola, Cello, Harp, and Percussion (1980); *Listening Time*, concert monodrama for Voice and Percussion (1981).

Kucharz (Kuchař), Johann Baptist (Jan Křtitel), Bohemian organist and composer; b. Chotec, March 5, 1751; d. Prague, Feb. 18, 1829. He studied at the Jesuit colleges in Königsgratz and Gitschin, then with Seger in Prague; was organist at Prague's Heinrichskirche (1772–90), then at the Premonstratensian Abbey (1790–1829); he was also maestro di cappella of Prague's Italian Opera (1791–97). He made the 1st piano scores of Mozart's operas. His works include organ and sacred pieces.

Kücken, Friedrich Wilhelm, German conductor and composer; b. Bleckede, Nov. 16, 1810; d. Schwerin, April 3, 1882. He studied thoroughbass with his brother-in-law, the organist Friedrich Lührss, and piano with Aron and Rettberg in Schwerin; in 1832, went to Berlin, where he studied counterpoint with Birnbach; from 1841 to 1843, studied with Sechter in Vienna, and later took courses in orchestration with Halevy and composition with Bordogni. He was Kapellmeister in Stuttgart (1851–61). He wrote the operas *Die Flucht nach der Schweiz* (Berlin, Feb. 26, 1839) and *Der Prätendent* (Stuttgart, April 21, 1847); also sonatas for violin and for cello; etc. He is most noted for his songs (*Ach, wie wär's möglich dann; Das Sternelein; O weine nicht; Trab, trab; Das Mädchen von Juda; The Swallows;* etc.).

Kuckertz, Josef, German ethnomusicologist; b. Würseln, near Aachen, Nov. 24, 1930. After initial schooling at the Rheinische Musikschule in Cologne, he studied musicology with Marius Schneider at the Univ. of Cologne (Ph.D., 1962, with the diss. *Gestaltvariation in den von Bartók gesammelten rumänischen Colinden*). He then taught at the Univ. of Cologne, completing his Habilitation with a study of South Indian music (1967). His research focuses on the music and theory of the more developed oriental cultures and the relationship between oriental and European music, with particular emphasis on South India.

Kuczinski, Paul, German composer; b. Berlin, Nov. 10, 1846; d. there, Oct. 21, 1897. He was a banker by profession; also an excellent musician (studied with Bülow and Kiel). He was a friend of Adolf Jensen, whose letters he publ. in part as *Aus Briefen Adolf Jensens* (1879); also publ. *Erlebnisse und Gedanken, Dichtungen zu Musikwerken* (1898), showing his admiration for Wagner. He wrote the poems for his own numerous vocal scores; also wrote piano pieces.

Kudelski, Karl Matthias, German violinist and composer; b. Berlin, Nov. 17, 1805; d. Baden-Baden, Oct. 3, 1877. He studied with Lafont; played 1st violin in the orch. of the City Theater in Berlin; played in a quartet in Dorpat (1830); was Kapellmeister to a Russian Prince (1839); from 1841 to 1851, was concertmaster and director of the Imperial Theater in Moscow. He publ. *Kurzgefasste Harmonielehre* (1865); also violin concertos; cello concertos; violin sonatas; piano trios; fantasies for violin and piano; etc.

Kuerti, Anton (Emil), esteemed Austrian-born pianist; b. Vienna, July 21, 1938. He was taken by his parents to the U.S. as a child and was naturalized in 1944; began his piano studies with Edward Goldman in Boston and made his debut as soloist in the Grieg Piano Concerto with the Boston Pops Orch. at age 9; he also received training in piano from Erwin Bodky and Gregory Tucker and in composition from Arthur Shepherd at the Longy School in Cambridge, Mass. (1948–52), in piano from Erno Balogh and in composition from Henry Cowell at the Peabody Inst. in Baltimore (1952–53), in piano from Arthur Loesser and Beryl Rubinstein and in composition from Marcel Dick at the Cleveland Inst. of Music (B.Mus., 1955), and in piano from Rudolf Serkin and Mieczyslaw Horszowski at the Curtis Inst. of Music in Philadelphia (diploma, 1959). After winning the Levintritt Competition in N.Y. in 1957 he toured widely, settling in 1965 in Toronto, where he later became a naturalized citizen (1984). He was pianist-in-residence (1965–68) and an associate prof. (1968–72) at the Univ. of Toronto; in later years he gave occasional master classes, but he devoted himself mainly to concertizing. In 1988 he exercised his Canadian citizenship by running as a candidate for Parliament. He was awarded honorary doctorates in 1987 by York Univ. in Toronto and Laurentian Univ. in Sud-bury. While Kuerti has won accolades for his fine performances of the Viennese classics, he has also played various works by contemporary composers. Among his compositions are 2 string quartets (1954, 1972), *Linden Suite* for Piano (1970), *Magog* for Cello and Piano (1972), *Symphony "Epomeo"* (1973), a Violin Sonata (1973), *6 Arrows* for Piano (1973), *Piano Man Suite* (1985), and a Piano Concerto (1985).

Kufferath, Hubert Ferdinand, German violinist, pianist, conductor, and composer, brother of **Johann Hermann** and **Louis Kufferath,** and father of **Maurice Kufferath;** b. Mülheim an der Ruhr, June 11, 1818; d. St. Josse-ten-Noode, near Brussels, June 23, 1896. He studied first with his brothers; then with Hartmann (violin) in Cologne and Schneider in Dessau (1833–36); subsequently studied violin with David at the Leipzig Cons., where he also took courses with Mendelssohn and Hauptmann. He conducted the Cologne Männergesangverein (1841); then settled in Brussels (1844), where he ultimately served as prof. of counterpoint and fugue at the Cons. (1872–96). He wrote syms., piano concertos, and piano pieces.

Kufferath, Johann Hermann, German violinist, conductor, and composer, brother of **Hubert Ferdinand** and **Louis Kufferath;** b. Mülheim an der Ruhr, May 12, 1797; d. Wiesbaden, July 28, 1864. He studied with his father, then violin with Spohr and composition with Hauptmann; in 1823, became music director in Bielefeld, and, in 1830, in Utrecht, of the Collegium Musicum and Gesangverein (until 1862). His works include overtures, cantatas, and motets.

Kufferath, Louis, German pianist, conductor, and composer, brother of **Hubert Ferdinand** and **Johann Hermann Kufferath;** b. Mülheim an der Ruhr, Nov. 10, 1811; d. St. Josse-ten-Noode, near Brussels, March 2, 1882. He studied with his brother Johann Hermann, and with Schneider in Dessau. He toured as a pianist in Holland and Germany; was director of the Leeuwarden Cons. (1836–50); then was in Ghent, and later in Brussels. He wrote a Mass, a cantata, 250 canons, many piano pieces in salon style, and songs.

Kufferath, Maurice, Belgian cellist, conductor, and writer on music of German descent, son of **Hubert Ferdinand Kufferath;** b. St. Josse-ten-Noode, near Brussels, Jan. 8, 1852; d. Uccle, near Brussels, Dec. 8, 1919. He studied with his father, then cello with the Servais (père and fils); also studied law and art history in Brussels and Leipzig. He wrote on politics for *L'Indépendance Belge* (from 1874); was ed. of *Le Guide Musical* (1875–90), subsequently being its main proprietor (until 1914). With G. Guidé, he was co-director of the Théâtre Royal de la Monnaie (1900–1914). An ardent Wagnerian, he publ. *Le Théâtre de Wagner de Tannhäuser à Parsifal* (6 vols., Brussels, 1891–98). Under the pen name Maurice Reymont, he tr. Wagner's librettos and texts of songs by Brahms into French.
BIBL.: L. Solvay, *Notice sur M. K.* (Brussels, 1923).

Küffner, Joseph, German composer; b. Würzburg, March 31, 1776; d. there, Sept. 8, 1856. He wrote 2 operas: *Sporn und Schärpe* and *Der Cornett;* 7 syms.; 10 overtures; music for military band and wind instruments; Fantasy for Violin, with Orch.; Quintet for Flute and Strings; string quartets; trios and duets for flutes; duets for clarinet; violin sonatas; guitar music; etc.
BIBL.: M. Henke, *J. K.: Leben und Werk des Würzburger Musikers im Spiegel der Geschichte* (Tutzing, 1985).

Kuhač, Franz Xaver (Franjo Zaver), Croatian music theorist; b. Osijek, Nov. 20, 1834; d. Agram, June 18, 1911. He studied with Thern in Leipzig and Liszt in Weimar (1856); then with Czerny and Hanslick in Vienna. He taught piano in Osijek (1858–71); then was a music critic in Zagreb (1871–74); subsequently taught at the Croatian Music Inst. (1872–76). He publ. 4 books of folk songs (1878–81; remaining songs publ. in 1941).
WRITINGS: *Katekizam glazbe: Prva hrvatska glazena teorija po J. Ch. Lobeu* (A Musical Catechism: The 1st Croatian Music

Theory after Lobe; Zagreb, 1875; 2nd ed., enl., 1890); *Vatroslav Lisinski i njegovo doba* (V. L. and His Time; Zagreb, 1887; 2nd ed., enl., 1904); *Ilirski glazenici* (The Musicians of the Illyrian Movement; Zagreb, 1893); *Prva hrvatska uputa u glaso-viranje* (The 1st Croatian School of Piano Playing; Zagreb, 1896–97); *Moj rad* (My Work; Zagreb, 1904).

Kuhe, Wilhelm, Bohemian pianist and composer; b. Prague, Dec. 10, 1823; d. London, Oct. 9, 1912. He studied with Proksch, Tomaschek, and Thalberg. He went to London with the singer Pischek, settling there (1847). He was founder-director of his own festival in Brighton (1871–82); then was a prof. at the Royal Academy of Music in London (1886–1904). He publ. *My Musical Recollections* (London, 1896); also wrote much piano music.

Kuhlau, (Daniel) Friedrich (Rudolph), German-born Danish pianist and composer; b. Ülzen, near Hannover, Sept. 11, 1786; d. Copenhagen, March 12, 1832. He lost an eye in a childhood accident, and studied piano during his recovery; later studied theory and composition with C.F.G. Schwenke, Kantor of Hamburg's Catherinenkirche. He went to Copenhagen in 1810 to avoid conscription into Napoleon's army; he prospered there, being made court chamber musician (1813). He appeared often in concerts, championing the music of Beethoven.
WORKS: Stage (all 1st perf. in Copenhagen): *Røverborgen* (The Robber's Castle), singspiel (May 26, 1814); *Trylleharpen* (The Magic Harp), opera (Jan. 30, 1817); *Elisa*, opera (April 17, 1820); *Lulu*, opera (Oct. 29, 1824); *William Shakespeare*, drama (March 28, 1826); *Hugo og Adelheid*, opera (Oct. 29, 1827); *Elverhøj* (The Fairies' Mound), incidental music (Nov. 6, 1828); *Trillingbrødrene, fra Damask* (The Triplet Brothers from Damascus), incidental music (Sept. 1, 1830); Piano Concerto (1810); Concertino for 2 Horns and Orch. (1821); numerous chamber music pieces with flute; keyboard works, including pieces for piano 2- and 4-hands; songs; etc. D. Fog ed. a thematic and bibliographic catalog (Copenhagen, 1977).
BIBL.: C. Thrane, *F. K.: Zur 100-jährigen Wiederkehr seines Geburtstages* (Leipzig, 1886); K. Graupner, *F. K.* (Leipzig, 1930).

Kuhlmann, Kathleen, American mezzo-soprano; b. San Francisco, Dec. 7, 1950. She studied in San Francisco and at the Chicago Lyric Opera School, making her debut as Maddalena in *Rigoletto* with that company in 1979. She made her European debut in 1980 as Preziosilla in *La forza del destino* at the Cologne Opera; subsequently appeared at Milan's La Scala (as Meg Page in *Falstaff,* Dec. 7, 1980) and at London's Covent Garden (as Ino and Juno in Handel's *Semele*; Nov. 25, 1982). She sang the leading role in *La Cenerentola* at the Glyndebourne Festival in 1983. In 1987 she scored a major success as Falliero in Rossini's *Bianca e Falliero* in its U.S. premiere at the Greater Miami Opera. Among her other notable roles are Charlotte in *Werther*, Isabella in *L'Italiana in Algeri*, Dorabella, and Rosina.

Kühmstedt, Friedrich Karl, German music theorist and composer; b. Oldisleben, near Weimar, Dec. 20, 1809; d. Eisenach, Jan. 8, 1858. He studied with Hummel in Weimar and Rinck in Darmstadt; then taught music there (1831–36); settled in Eisenach, where he taught at the Gymnasium (from 1836); was also active as a church music director. He publ. a *Theoretisch-praktische Harmonien- und Ausweichungs-Lehre* (Eisenach, 1838); also many pedagogical compositions. He wrote 3 syms., sacred music, choral songs, organ music, and lieder.

Kuhn, Gustav, Austrian conductor; b. Turrach, Aug. 28, 1947. He studied conducting at the Salzburg Mozarteum and with Swarowsky at the Vienna Hochschule für Musik; later had instruction from Maderna and Karajan, completing his education at the Univ. of Salzburg (Ph.D., 1970). He then served as conductor at the Istanbul Opera (1970–73) and 1st conductor at the Dortmund Stadttheater (1975–77). In 1978 he was named a conductor at the Vienna State Opera; also was chief conductor of the Bern Sym. Orch. and Opera (1979–81); conducted at the Glyndebourne and Salzburg festivals (1980) and made his U.S. debut at the Chicago Lyric Opera (1981). In 1983 he became Generalmusikdirektor of Bonn, a post he held until being dismissed in 1985 after he physically assaulted the director of the Stadttheater during a dispute. He then served as chief conductor of the Rome Opera (from 1987).

Kuhnau (real name, **Kuhn**), **Johann,** erudite German organist, writer on music, and composer; b. Geising, April 6, 1660; d. Leipzig, June 5, 1722. He studied at the Kreuzschule in Dresden with Krügner and Kittel; became a chorister at the Kreuzkirche (1671), where he studied organ with Heringk; also received instruction from Albrici, and then from Edelmann at the Zittau Gymnasium (1680–82), where he was acting Kantor (1681–82). He attended the Univ. of Leipzig from 1682 to 1688, studying law; meanwhile, in 1684, he succeeded Kühnel as organist at the Thomaskirche; in 1688 he organized a Collegium Musicum and also began to practice law. He was appointed Thomaskantor (1701); was also active as a teacher at the Thomasschule, was a conductor of church music at the Thomaskirche and Nikolaikirche, and later was named music director at the Peterskirche (1711); likewise served as music director of the Univ. His last years became increasingly difficult owing to poor health. He also had to contend with the efforts of others to encroach upon his duties. For example, Telemann organized his own Collegium Musicum (1701), and was also successful in obtaining the right to compose for the Thomaskirche. Kuhnau remains best known for his keyboard music, especially the 6 program sonatas found in his *Musicalische Vorstellung eininiger biblischer Historien* (Leipzig, 1700). His Sonata in B-flat major from the *Neue Clavier-Übung* (Leipzig, 1692) is of historical significance as the earliest known example of the genre in Germany. He also composed many sacred cantatas. His secular vocal music is not extant.

WRITINGS: *Divini numinis assistentia, illustrique jure consultorum in florentissima academia Lipsiensi* (Leipzig, 1688); *Fundamenta compositionis* (MS, 1703); 2 other works not extant.

WORKS: *Neue Clavier-Übung, erster Theil* (Leipzig, 1689; 7 suites; ed. in Denkmäler Deutscher Tonkunst, IV, 1901); *Neue Clavier-Übung, anderer Theil* (Leipzig, 1692; 7 suites and 1 sonata; ed. in ibid.); *Frische Clavier Früchte* (Leipzig; 1696; 7 sonatas; ed. in ibid.); *Musicalische Vorstellung eininiger biblischer Historien* (Leipzig, 1700; reprint, 1973; 6 program sonatas; ed. in ibid.).

BIBL.: R. Münnich, "K.s Leben," *Sammelbände der Internationalen Musik-Gesellschaft,* III (1901–2); J. Martin, *Die Kirchenkantaten J. K.s* (Leipzig, 1928); H. Menck, "J. K.s 'Musickalische Quacksalber,'" *Der Musiker im Roman* (Heidelberg, 1931); R. Gutmann, "J. K. (1660–1722)," *Zeitschrift für Hausmusik,* VII (1939); E. Rimbach, *The Church Cantatas of J. K.* (diss., Univ. of Rochester, 1966); J. Arbogast, *Stilkritische Untersuchungen zum Klavierwerk des Thomaskantors J. K. (1660–1722)* (Regensburg, 1983).

Kühnau, Johann Christoph, German conductor and composer; b. Volkstadt, near Eisleben, Feb. 10, 1735; d. Berlin, Oct. 13, 1805. He studied piano and organ with Martin Grosse in Klosterbergen, then became a schoolteacher at Berlin's Realschule in 1763; was founder-director of a choir there, which he led until his death, and a teacher (from 1783) and Kantor and music director (from 1788) of Berlin's Dreifaltigkeitskirche. He compiled several collections of vocal and instrumental works by his eminent contemporaries, the best known being the *Vierstimmige alte, und neue Choralgesänge* (2 vols., Berlin, 1786–90; 10th ed., 1885). His son, **Johann Friedrich Wilhelm Kühnau** (b. Berlin, June 29, 1780; d. there, Jan. 1, 1848), was an organist at the Dreifaltigkeitskirche from 1814.

Kühner, Basil, German pedagogue and composer; b. Stuttgart, April 1, 1840; d. Vilnius, Aug. 1911. He studied at the Stuttgart Cons. with Faiszt and Lebert; then studied violin with Massart in Paris, and piano with Henselt in St. Petersburg; was director of the Tiflis Cons. (1870–76). In 1878 he settled in St. Peters-

burg, where he established his own music school (1892). He wrote the opera *Taras Bulba* (after Gogol; St. Petersburg, Dec. 24, 1880); a sym. subtitled *Liberation of the Serfs in Russia* (St. Petersburg, 1866); String Quintet; 2 string quartets; Suite for Cello and Piano; *Snowflakes,* suite for Piano; other piano pieces.

Kuhse, Hanne-Lore, German soprano; b. Schwaan, March 28, 1925. She was educated at the Rostock Cons. and the Stern Cons. in Berlin; later studied in Potsdam. She made her debut in Gera in 1951 as Leonore in *Fidelio;* from 1952 to 1959 she was a member of the Schwerin Opera; then sang at the Leipzig Opera (1959–64). In 1964 she joined the East Berlin State Opera. In 1974 she was appointed prof. at the Hochschule für Musik in East Berlin. In 1954 she was named a Kammersängerin. A versatile artist, she was as stylistically faithful to her roles in Mozart's operas as to the heroic and lyric Wagnerian parts.

Kuijken, prominent family of Belgian musicians, all brothers: **(1) Wieland Kuijken,** cellist and viola da gambist; b. Dilbeek, near Brussels, Aug. 31, 1938. He studied piano and cello at the Bruges Cons. and the Brussels Cons. (1957), graduating with the prix d'excellence in 1962; was self-taught as a violist. He played in the Baroque group known as the Alarius Ensemble (1959–72) and in the avant-garde Musiques Nouvelles from 1962; later appeared in concerts with his brothers, and also toured extensively as a soloist; likewise taught master classes. **(2) Sigiswald Kuijken,** violinist, violist, and conductor; b. Dilbeek, near Brussels, Feb. 16, 1944. He enrolled at the Bruges Cons. at age 8 as a student of violin, then entered the Brussels Cons. in 1960, winning the premier prix in 1964; was autodidact as a Baroque violinist, beginning his career on the instrument in 1970. He played in the Alarius Ensemble and the Musiques Nouvelles before gaining wide recognition with his own Baroque orch., La Petite Bande (founded 1972); subsequently led it on many tours and in numerous recordings; was also active as a teacher. **(3) Barthold Kuijken,** flutist and recorder player; b. Dilbeek, near Brussels, March 8, 1949. He studied at the conservatories in Bruges, Brussels, and The Hague, his principal teachers being Franz Vester (flute) and Frans Brüggen (recorder); he was self-taught as a Baroque flutist. He performed in concerts with his brothers and with others; also toured widely and was active as a teacher.

Kuivila, Ron, American composer and instrument designer; b. Boston, Dec. 19, 1955. He studied music and mathematics at Wesleyan Univ. (B.A., 1977) and electronic music and studio recording techniques at Mills College in Oakland, Calif. (M.F.A., 1979); then was artist-in-residence at Media Study in Buffalo (1979–80) and at Wesleyan Univ. (from 1981). His work includes sound installations and electronic instruments of his own design; he pioneered ultrasound (*In Appreciation,* 1979) and sound sampling (*Alphabet,* 1982) in live performance. His installations have appeared throughout the U.S. and Europe. He has also designed commercial music software and exhibited at visual art galleries. His music involves complex, often unpitched, electronic timbres; some of his compositions utilize existing recordings as source material. Among his works are *Minute Differences/Closely Observed* (1984), *Loose Canons* (1986–87), and *Pythagorean Puppet Theatre* (1989).

Kulenkampff, Georg, eminent German violinist and pedagogue; b. Bremen, Jan. 23, 1898; d. Schaffhausen, Oct. 4, 1948. He studied violin with Willy Hess in Berlin; in 1916, became concertmaster of the Bremen Phil. From 1923 to 1926 he taught at the Berlin Hochschule für Musik; then toured throughout Europe as a soloist; in 1943, went to Switzerland and taught at the Lucerne Cons. He was regarded as one of the most brilliant German violinists of his generation; his book *Geigerische Betrachtungen,* partly didactic, partly autobiographical in content, was ed. by G. Meyer-Stichtung (Regensburg, 1952).

Kulenkampff, Gustav, German pianist and composer; b. Bremen, Aug. 11, 1849; d. Berlin, Feb. 10, 1921. He studied with Barth (piano) and Bargiel (composition) in Berlin; then taught in music schools and appeared as a pianist there. He wrote the operas *Der Page* (Bremen, 1890); *Der Mohrenfürst* (Magdeburg, 1892); *Die Braut von Cypern* (Schwerin, 1897); *König Drosselbart* (Berlin, 1899); *Ammarei* (1903); *Anneliese* (Kassel, 1904); women's choruses; Piano Sonata; songs; etc.

Kulesha, Gary, Canadian composer, conductor, and pianist; b. Toronto, Aug. 22, 1954. He studied composition with Samuel Dolin and piano at the Royal Cons. of Music of Toronto, receiving degrees in piano performance (1973) and composition (1978); continued private studies in England with John McCabe and in N.Y. with John Corigliano. He returned to Canada in 1982, and in 1983 became principal conductor of the Stratford Shakespearean Festival Theatre in Stratford, Ontario, for which he provided incidental music; he also served as music producer for the CBC and as artistic director of the Canadian Contemporary Music Workshop in Toronto. In 1989 he was named composer-in-residence with the Kitchener-Waterloo Sym. Orch. His music makes eclectic use of influences as diverse as Prokofiev, Messiaen, musique concrète, jazz, and rock.

WORKS: ORCH.: *Variations* for Winds (1975); *Divertimento* for Strings (1975); *1st Essay* (1977); Concerto for Tuba and Full Orch. or Winds (1978–81); *Ensembles* for Winds (1979); *1st Chamber Concerto* for Winds and Percussion (Kitchener, Ontario, Nov. 28, 1981); *2nd Chamber Concerto* for Trumpet, Piano, and Winds (Toronto, March 28, 1982); *3rd Chamber Concerto* for Bass Clarinet and Winds (1982–83; Toronto, Jan. 31, 1984); *2nd Essay* (1984; Kitchener, Jan. 18, 1985); *Celebration Overture* (1985); *Lifesongs* for Contralto and String Orch. (Markham, Ontario, Nov. 18, 1985); *Nocturne* for Chamber Orch. (1985); *4th Chamber Concerto* for 10 Winds, String Quintet, and Percussion (Kitchener, April 13, 1988). **CHAMBER:** String Trio (1971); Sonata for Horn, Tuba, and Piano (1975); Sonata for Tuba and Organ (1976); *Concertante Music* for Soprano Saxophone and Wind Quintet (1979); *Mysterium coniunctionis* for Clarinet, Bass Clarinet, and Piano (1980); *Passacaglia, Cadenzas, and Finale* for Trumpet, Tuba, and Piano (1981); *Canticles* for Brass Quintet and Organ (1982); *Angels* for Marimba and Tape (1983); *Jazz Music* for Brass Quintet, Marimba, and Piano (1985); *Complex* for Electric Bass Guitar and Tape (1986); Cello Sonata (1986–87); *Demons* for Tuba and Tape (1988); *Political Implications* for Clarinet Quartet (1988); songs; incidental music. **PIANO:** 3 sonatas (1970; 1980, rev. 1984; 1986); Sonata for 2 Pianos (1970–72); *Aphorisms* (1978); *Monument* for Piano, 4-hands (1978); *Mythologies* for 2 Pianos (1987).

Kulka, János, Hungarian conductor; b. Budapest, Dec. 11, 1929. He studied conducting with Ferencsik and Somogyi; also composition with Kodály. He became a répétiteur and choirmaster at the Budapest State Opera (1950); was a conductor there (1953–57). He conducted at the Bavarian State Opera in Munich (1957–59); was 1st conductor at the Württemberg State Theater in Stuttgart (1959–61) and the Hamburg State Opera (1961–64). He subsequently was Generalmusikdirektor in Wuppertal (1964–76) and of the North-West German Phil. in Herford (1975–87).

Kullak, Adolf, German music theorist, critic, and composer; brother of **Theodor Kullak;** b. Meseritz, Feb. 23, 1823; d. Berlin, Dec. 25, 1862. He studied at the Univ. of Berlin, then music with A.B. Marx in Berlin; subsequently taught at his brother's academy there and wrote music criticism for various periodicals. He publ. *Das Musikalisch-Schöne* (Leipzig, 1858) and *Die Ästhetik des Klavierspiels* (Berlin, 1861; 4th ed., 1906, by W. Niemann; 5th ed., 1916; Eng. tr., N.Y., 1892); also composed piano pieces and songs. His son, **Ernst Kullak** (b. Berlin, Jan. 22, 1855; d. there, 1914), was a pianist and composer.

Kullak, Franz, German pianist, teacher, and composer, son of **Theodor Kullak;** b. Berlin, April 12, 1844; d. there, Dec. 9, 1913. He studied with his father and briefly with Liszt; later with Wehle and Litolff in Paris. He was a piano teacher at his father's academy in Berlin (1867–82); served as director (1882–1890); then was director of his own Akademie für Höheres Klavierspiel (1891–1900). He prepared a valuable ed. of the Beethoven piano concertos; also several piano methods. He composed an opera, *Ines de Castro* (Berlin, 1877); also orch. works; piano pieces; songs.

Kullak, Theodor, famous German pianist and pedagogue, brother of **Adolf** and father of **Franz Kullak;** b. Krotoschin, Sept. 12, 1818; d. Berlin, March 1, 1882. He studied piano with local teachers; in 1837 he went to Berlin at his father's behest to study medicine; also studied there with Dehn (theory); then went to Vienna, where he took lessons with Czerny, Sechter, and Nicolai (1842–43). Returning to Berlin in 1846, he became court pianist to the King of Prussia. In 1850 he founded a cons. in Berlin in partnership with Julius Stern and A.B. Marx; however, dissension soon arose among them, and in 1855 Kullak established his own school, the Neue Akademie der Tonkunst, which greatly prospered and became famous as Kullak's Academy, turning out such students as Moszkowski, N. Rubinstein, and the Scharwenka brothers. He publ. the methods *Schule des Oktavenspiel,* op. 48 (Berlin, 1848; 3rd ed., 1877), *Schule der Fingerübungen,* op. 61 (Berlin, c.1850), *Ratschläge und Studien,* op. 74 (Berlin, c.1852), and *Materialien für den Elementar-Klavierunterricht* (Berlin, c.1859); also composed pieces for piano.

BIBL.: O. Reinsdorf, *T. K. und seine Neue Akademie der Tonkunst in Berlin* (Neusalz, 1870); H. Bischoff, *Zur Erinnerung an T. K.* (Berlin, 1883).

Kullman, Charles, American tenor; b. New Haven, Conn., Jan. 13, 1903; d. there, Feb. 8, 1983. He entered Yale Univ., and sang at the Yale Glee Club; then took courses at the Juilliard School of Music in N.Y. After singing with the American Opera Co. in Rochester, N.Y., he went to Berlin, where he made his European debut on Feb. 24, 1931, as Pinkerton in *Madama Butterfly,* at the Kroll Opera. He sang at the Berlin State Opera (1932–35); also appeared at the Vienna State Opera, at the Salzburg Festivals, and at Covent Garden in London (1934–36). On Dec. 19, 1935, he made his debut at the Metropolitan Opera in N.Y. as Gounod's Faust. He remained on the roster of the Metropolitan until 1960. His repertoire comprised over 30 roles. He scored a signal success in the role of Eisenstein in *Die Fledermaus.* He joined the faculty of Indiana Univ. in 1956; he was prof. of music there until his retirement in 1971.

Kumer, Zmaga, Yugoslav ethnomusicologist; b. Ribnica, April 24, 1924. She studied Slovene literature at the Univ. of Ljubljana (degree, 1948) and musicology at the Ljubljana Academy of Music (degree, 1952); then returned to the Univ., where she received her Ph.D. (1955, with a diss. on Slovene variants of the song *Puer natus in Bethlehem*) and subsequently taught (from 1966). Her studies focus on the texts of Slovene folk songs as well as on the migration and transformation of these songs among other Alpine cultures.

Kummer, Friedrich August, noted German cellist, oboist, teacher, and composer; b. Meiningen, Aug. 5, 1797; d. Dresden, Aug. 22, 1879. His father, also named Friedrich August Kummer (1770–1849), was oboist at the courts in Meiningen and then Dresden (from 1805). The young Kummer went with his family to Dresden, where he studied cello with Dotzauer; also studied oboe, and joined the electoral Court Orch. as an oboist (1814); after further cello studies, he became a cellist there, eventually succeeding Dotzauer as principal (1852–64). He made tours as a virtuoso in Germany and Italy, but was content to remain at his Dresden post. He taught at the Dresden Cons. and privately. He composed over 400 works, about half of which were publ. His output included virtuoso pieces for cello and orch., as well as chamber music and many didactic pieces; also some 200 entr'actes for the Dresden Court Theater. He publ. the *Violoncello-Schule,* op. 60 (Leipzig, 1839).

Kummer, Kaspar, German flutist and composer; b. Erlau, Dec. 10, 1795; d. Coburg, May 21, 1870. He was a member of the Court Orch. at Coburg; then music director there. He wrote quintets and quartets for flute and strings; flute concertos, trios, duos, etc.; and a method for flute.

Kümmerle, Salomon, German organist, teacher, and editor; b. Malmsheim, near Stuttgart, Feb. 8, 1838; d. Samaden, Aug. 28, 1896. He was an organist and teacher in various German towns before taking positions in Nice (1861–66) and Samaden (1874–90). He ed. the valuable *Encyklopädie der evangelischen Kirchenmusik* (4 vols., 1888–95); also ed. the vocal collections *Grabgesänge* (1869), *Musica sacra* (1869–70), *Zionsharfe* (1870–71), and *Choralbuch für evangelische Kirchenchöre* (1887–89).

Kunad, Rainer, German composer; b. Chemnitz, Oct. 24, 1936. He studied in Chemnitz, at the Dresden Cons. (1955–56), and with Finke, Gerster, and Schenk at the Leipzig Hochschule für Musik; then worked at the Dresden State Opera (1960–75). After serving as a prof. of composition at the Dresden Hochschule für Musik (1978–84), he settled in West Germany.
WORKS: OPERAS: *Bill Brook!/Old Fritz* (1965); *Maître Pathelin oder Die Hammelkomödie* (Dresden, 1969); *Sabellicus* (Berlin, 1974); *Litauische Klaviere* (Dresden, 1977); *Vincent* (Dresden, 1979); *Amphytrion* (Berlin, May 26, 1984); *Der Meister und Margarita* (Karlsruhe, 1986). **SCENIC MYSTERY PLAY:** *Die Menschen von Babel* (1986). **ORCH.:** *Aphorismen* (1956); *Sinfonia variatione* (1959); *Sinfonie* (1964); *Sinfonietta* (1969); *Concerto per archi* (1967); Piano Concerto (1969); also choral works, chamber music, and piano pieces.

Kunc, Božidar, Croatian-American pianist and composer; b. Zagreb, July 18, 1903; d. Detroit, April 1, 1964. He received his academic training at the Zagreb Academy of Music, graduating in 1927; taught there from 1929 to 1951, when he emigrated to the U.S. His sister was the soprano **Zinka Milanov.** His music is impressionistic in its harmonic palette.
WORKS: 2 violin concertos (1928, 1955); *Dramatic Prologue* for Orch. (1929); *Symphonic Intermezzo* (1934); 2 piano concertos: No. 1 (Zagreb, April 27, 1934, composer soloist) and No. 2 (1962); *Marcia funebre* for Orch. (1936); *Triptihon* for Cello and Orch. (1940); *3 Episodes* for Piano and String Orch. (1955); syms.; several chamber works, including Cello Sonata (1927); *Cycle* for Piano and Percussion (1956); *Pieces* for Double Bass (1959); 4 piano sonatas (1930–43); several cycles and pieces; songs.

Kunc, Jan, Czech composer; b. Doubravice, Moravia, March 27, 1883; d. Brno, Sept. 11, 1976. He studied with Janáček in Brno and with Novák in Prague. He wrote music criticism in Brno (1909–18); then became an instructor at the Brno Cons. (1919); from 1923 to 1945, was its director; lectured at the Masaryk Univ. in Brno (1947–52). He was best known as a composer of choral music and songs.
WORKS: Unfinished opera, *The Lady from the Seashore* (begun 1919); *Píseň mládí* (Song of Youth), symphonic poem (1915–16); *Stála Kačenka u Dunaja* (Catherine Stood by the Danube), ballad for Alto and Orch. (1918–19); Piano Sonata (1903); Piano Trio (1905); String Quartet (1909); *4 Compositions* for Piano (1917); *Chronicle,* 20 variations on a Slovak folk song for Piano (1926); Violin Sonata (1931); Serenade for Violin and Piano (1952); *Miniatures* for Piano (1954–57; also Piano Quintet, 1958); *Sedmdesát tisíc* (70,000) for Chorus (1907); *Ostrava* for Male Chorus (1912); *35 Folk Songs of Moravian Slovakia* for Female Chorus (1960); many folksong arrangements.

Kundera, Ludvík, Czech pianist and musicologist; b. Brünn, Aug. 17, 1891; d. there (Brno), May 12, 1971. He studied voice and piano in Vienna and also took courses at the Univ. of Prague. He made his debut in a Prague recital in 1912; later attended Cortot's master classes in piano in Paris (1925) and studied musicology at the Univ. of Brno (Ph.D., 1925). He toured widely in Europe as a soloist and chamber music player, doing much to promote the music of Czech composers. He was prof. of piano and esthetics at the Brno Cons. from

1922 until his removal by the Nazi occupation authorities in 1941. After the liberation of his homeland, he was director of the Brno Cons. (1945–46), prof. of piano and deputy dean of the Brno branch of the Prague Academy of Music (1946–47), and prof. of piano at the Brno Academy, serving as dean of its music faculty (1948–50) and as rector (1949–62).
WRITINGS: *Omuzike chekhoslovatskovo naroda* (Music of the Czechoslovak Nation; Ekaterinburg, 1919); *Jaroslav Kvapil* (Prague, 1944); *Jak organizovati hudební výchovu v obnoveném státě* (How to Organize Music Education in the Renewed State; Brno, 1945); *Janáček a Klub přátel uměni* (Janáček and the Club of the Friends of Art; Olomouc, 1948); *Janáčkova varhanická škola* (Janáček's Organ School; Olomouc, 1948); *Ludvík van Beethoven* (Prague, 1952); *Beethovenovy klavírní sonáty,* I (Prague, 1964); *V. Kaprál: Kapitola z historie české meziválečné hudby* (A Chapter in the History of Czech Music between the Wars; Brno, 1968).
BIBL.: J. Vysloužil, *L. K.* (Brno, 1962).

Kunits, Luigi von (actually, **Ludwig Paul Maria**), Austrian violinist and conductor; b. Vienna, July 20, 1870; d. Toronto, Oct. 8, 1931. He studied composition with Bruckner, music history with Hanslick, and violin with Grün and Ševčik in Vienna. In 1893 he went to the U.S., where he played at the Chicago World's Columbian Exposition with an Austrian orch.; then taught violin at the Pittsburgh Cons. (1896–1910). He was also concertmaster of the Pittsburgh Sym. Orch. (1897–1910). He toured widely as a soloist in Europe before settling in Toronto; was a teacher at the Canadian Academy of Music, where he was a founder-member of the Academy String Quartet (1912–23); also founded the *Canadian Journal of Music* (1915–19). He was founder-conductor of the New Sym. Orch. (1922), which became the Toronto Sym. Orch. (1927); he remained with the orch. until his death. He wrote an unpubl. book on Beethoven, *The Hero as Musician* (1913). His compositions include 2 violin concertos; *Lullaby* for Violin and Orch. (1916); String Quartet (1890); Viola Sonata (1917); pieces for Violin and Piano; songs.
BIBL.: A. Bridle, *L. v. K.* (Toronto, 1931).

Kunkel, Charles, German-American pianist, teacher, music publisher, and composer, brother of **Jacob Kunkel;** b. Sipperfeld, Rheinpfalz, July 22, 1840; d. St. Louis, Dec. 3, 1923. He was taken to America in 1848 by his father, who gave him elementary musical training. In 1868 he and his brother went to St. Louis, where he established a music publishing business and started a music periodical, *Kunkel's Musical Review,* which included sheet music and articles; with his brother he also opened a music store selling pianos and other instruments; in 1872 he founded the St. Louis Cons. of Music, which continued in business for several years; furthermore, he presented an annual series of concerts in St. Louis known as Kunkel's Popular Concerts (1884–1900). He taught piano to the last years of his life; also publ. a method of piano playing, which was commended favorably by Liszt; Anton Rubinstein praised him as a pianist during his visit to St. Louis in 1873. Kunkel was reputed to be quite formidable as a sight reader. Altogether, he was certainly a shining light in the German musical colony in middle America in the 2nd half of the 19th century. With his brother he gave, to tumultuous applause, a series of concerts playing piano duets. His publishing business put out a cornucopia of his own piano solos with such titles as *Nonpareil, Galop Brilliant, Philomel Polka, Snowdrops Waltz,* and *Southern Jollification,* most of these highly perishable; however, one piece, *Alpine Storm,* deserves retrieval, if for no other reason than its dedication: "To my son, Ludwig van Beethoven Kunkel." (This piece also contains "tone clusters" played with the palm of the hand in the bass to imitate thunder.)

Kunkel, Jacob, German-American pianist, teacher, music publisher, and composer, brother of **Charles Kunkel;** b. Kleiniedesheim, Oct. 22, 1846; d. St. Louis, Oct. 16, 1882. He studied with his brother, and was also a nominal pupil of Tausig, who, according to the Kunkel family report, refused to teach him because he thought that the younger man was equal to the master. He was taken to America with his brother, and participated in most of the latter's enterprises. He composed piano pieces in a salon manner.

Künneke, Eduard, German composer; b. Emmerich, Jan. 27, 1885; d. Berlin, Oct. 27, 1953. He studied with Bruch at the Berlin Hochschule für Musik. After bringing out the operas *Robins Ende* (Mannheim, 1909) and *Coeur As* (Dresden, Nov. 1913), with little success, he turned to producing operettas; his 1st success in this genre was *Das Dorf ohne Glocke* (Berlin, April 5, 1919); then followed such successful scores as *Der Vetter aus Dingsda* (Berlin, April 15, 1921), *Lady Hamilton* (Berlin, Sept. 25, 1926), *Glückliche Reise* (Berlin, Nov. 23, 1932), *Die lockende Flamme* (Berlin, Dec. 25, 1933), *Herz über Bord* (Zürich and Düsseldorf, March 30, 1935), and *Der grosse Sünderin* (Berlin, Dec. 31, 1935). He also wrote 2 piano concertos, various orch. pieces, and many film scores.

Kunsemüller, Ernst, German conductor and composer; b. Rehme, June 24, 1885; d. as a result of war wounds, Düsseldorf, April 25, 1918. He studied at the Univs. of Berlin and Bonn (Ph.D., 1909), then at the Cologne Cons. with Friedberg, Wölsche, and Steinbach; in 1912 he became conductor of the Kiel Verein der Musikfreunde and Gesangverein and in 1914 music director of the Univ. there. He wrote a Serenade for Small Orch.; 2 piano sonatas; choruses; songs; etc.

Kunst, Jaap (Jakob), noted Dutch ethnomusicologist; b. Groningen, Aug. 12, 1891; d. Amsterdam, Dec. 7, 1960. He began playing the violin at an early age; soon became interested in Dutch folk songs. He received a degree in law at the Univ. of Groningen (1917), then toured with a string trio in the Dutch East Indies (1919). He remained in Java, where he worked in a government post in Bandung while pursuing his interest in indigenous Javanese music. He subsequently founded an archive there for folk instruments, field recordings, books, and photographs for the Batavia museum. He returned to the Netherlands in 1934; in 1936, became curator of the Royal Tropical Inst. in Amsterdam, which developed into one of the most important organizations of its kind in Europe. He gave lectures at the Univ. of Amsterdam (1953), becoming a member of its faculty (1958). Kunst is credited with having coined the word "ethnomusicology" as a more accurate term than "comparative musicology."

WRITINGS: With C. Kunst Van-Wely, *De Toonkunst van Bali* (Weltevreden, 1924; part 2 in *Tijdschrift voor Indische taal-, land- en volkenkunde,* LXV, Batavia, 1925); with R. Goris, *Hindoe-Javaansche muziekinstrumenten* (Batavia, 1927; 2nd ed., rev., 1968, as *Hindu-Javanese Musical Instruments*); *A Study on Papuan Music* (Weltevreden, 1931); *Musicologisch onderzoek 1930* (Batavia, 1931); *Over zeldzame fluiten en veelstemmige muziek in het Ngada- en Nagehgebied, West-Flores* (Batavia, 1931); *De toonkunst van Java* (The Hague, 1934; Eng. tr., 1949, as *Music in Java*; 3rd ed., augmented, 1973); *Verslagen van den ambtenaar voor het systematisch musicologisch onderzoek in den Indischen archipel omtrent de door hem verrichte werkzaamheden* (Bandung, 1934); *Een en ander over den Javaanschen gamelan* (Amsterdam, 1940; 4th ed., 1945); *De waardering van exotische muziek in den loop der eeuwen* (The Hague, 1942); *Music in Flores: A Study of the Vocal and Instrumental Music among the Tribes Living in Flores* (Leiden, 1942); *Music in Nias* (Leiden, 1942); *Een en ander over de muziek en den dans op de Kei-eilanden* (Amsterdam, 1945); *Muziek en dans in de buitengewesten* (Amsterdam, 1946); *De inheemsche muziek en de zending* (Amsterdam, 1947); *Around von Hornbostel's Theory of the Cycle of Blown Fifths* (Amsterdam, 1948); *The Cultural Background of Indonesian Music* (Amsterdam, 1949); *Begdja, het gamelanjongetje* (Amsterdam, 1950); *De inheemsche muziek in Westelijk Nieuw-Guinea* (Amsterdam, 1950); *Metre, Rhythm and Multipart Music* (Leiden, 1950); *Musicologica: A Study of the Nature of Ethno-musicology, Its Problems, Methods and Representative Personalities* (Amsterdam, 1950; 2nd ed., augmented, 1955, as *Ethnomusicology;* 3rd ed., 1959; supplement, 1960); *Kultur-*

historische Beziehungen zwischen dem Balkan und Indonesien (Amsterdam, 1953; Eng. tr., 1954); *Sociologische bindingen in der muziek* (The Hague, 1953); ed. collections of folk songs of the Netherlands and Northern New Guinea, including *Terschellinger volksleven* (Uithuizen, 1916; 3rd ed., 1951); *Noord-Nederlandsche volksliederen en -dansern* (Groningen, 1916–18; 2nd ed., 1918–19); *Het levende lied van Nederland* (Amsterdam, 1918–19; 4th ed., 1947); *Songs of North New Guinea* (Weltevreden, 1931); *Oude westersche liederen uit oostestersche landen* (Bandung, 1934).

Kunst, Jos, Dutch composer; b. Roermond, Jan. 3, 1936. He studied composition with Ton de Leeuw at the Amsterdam Cons. (1965–70); also studied electronic music at the Inst. for Sonology at the Univ. of Utrecht. He taught at the Amsterdam Cons. (from 1971). In his music he utilizes a great variety of modernistic techniques, especially metamorphoses of given thematic material.

WORKS: *Stenen eten* (The Stone Eaters) for 2 Pianos (1965); *Ijzer* (Iron) for Violin and Piano (1965); *Insecten* for 13 Strings (1966); *Glass Music* for Piano (1966); *Extérieur* for 2-track Tape (1967); *Arboreal* for Orch. (Rotterdam, Sept. 11, 1969); *Expulsion* for 2-track Tape (1969); *Trajectoire* for 16 Voices and 11 Instruments (1970); *XVII One Way* for Small Orch. (Amsterdam, March 13, 1971); *XVIII Outward Bound* for Harp (1971); *Solo Identity I* for Bass Clarinet (1972); *Solo Identity II* for Piano (1973); *Elements of Logic* for Wind Orch. (in collaboration with Jan Vriend; 1972; Scheveningen, Feb. 25, 1973); *No Time at All* for Bass Clarinet and Piano (1973; a fusion of *Solo Identity I* and *II*); *No Time* for 3 Clarinets, Bass Clarinet, Piano, and 3 Percussionists (1974; an amplified version of *No Time at All*); *XXII: Any 2* for Woodwinds (1975).

Kuntze, Karl, German organist and composer; b. Trier, May 17, 1817; d. Delitzsch, Sept. 7, 1883. He studied in Berlin with A.W. Bach, Marx, and Rungenhagen; was cantor and organist in Pritzwalk, then organist in Aschersleben (1858–73); in 1873, settled in Delitzsch, where he taught at the seminary. He was best known for his humorous male choruses (*Adam und Eva, Der Hecht im Karpfenteich, Weingalopp, Der neue Bürgermeister,* and *Die Schweigermutter*); also wrote an operetta, *Im Gebirge* (Dessau, 1875); motets and songs for mixed chorus; organ pieces; etc.

Kunwald, Ernst, Austrian conductor; b. Vienna, April 14, 1868; d. there, Dec. 12, 1939. He studied law at the Univ. of Vienna (Dr.Juris, 1891); at the same time, studied piano with Leschetizky and J. Epstein, and composition with H. Grädener; then at the Leipzig Cons. with Jadassohn. He conducted opera in Rostock (1895–97), Sondershausen (1897–98), Essen (1898–1900), Halle (1900–1901), Madrid (1901–2), and Frankfurt (1902–5), and at Kroll's Theater in Berlin (1905–6); served as 2nd conductor of the Berlin Phil. (1907–12). In 1906 he was guest conductor of the N.Y. Phil.; in 1912, became conductor of the Cincinnati Sym. Orch., and, from 1914, also of the May Festival. He was arrested as an enemy alien on Dec. 8, 1917, but was released on bail and allowed to continue to conduct until his internment. After his release, he conducted in Königsberg (1920–27); then conducted the Berlin Sym. Orch. (1928–31).

Kunz, Alfred, Canadian composer; b. Neudorf, Saskatchewan, May 26, 1929. He studied with Delamont and Weinzweig in Toronto (1949–55); then attended Stockhausen's classes in Darmstadt and Cologne; subsequently taught in Canada.

WORKS: Operetta for high school, *The Watchful Gods* (1962); 7 ballets, including *Moses* (1965); 2 sinfoniettas (1957, 1961); Violin Sonata (1959); *The Song of the Clarinet* for Narrator, Flute, Oboe, Clarinet, Bassoon, and String Quintet (1961); *Behold the Beauty of the Sky* for High School Chorus and Orch. (1961); *Excursion* for Orch. (1964); *Emanation No. 1* for Violin, Horn, and Piano (1962); *Emanation No. 2* for Flute, Clarinet, Horn, and Bassoon (1964); *Fun for 2* for 2 Bassoons or 2 Bass Clarinets (1964); *Love, Death, and Full Moonnights* for Baritone and Instrumental Ensemble (1964); Wind Quintet (1964); *The*

Big Land, oratorio (1967); *In the Park of October Colour,* "song of love" for Piano, Chorus, and Orch. (1969); 5 *Night Scenes* for Orch. (1971); *The Creation* for Narrator, 3 Sopranos, Alto, Chorus, and Orch. (1972); Concerto for 8 Percussion Players and Orch. (1973); Piano Concerto (1975).

Kunz, Erich, Austrian bass-baritone; b. Vienna, May 20, 1909. He was educated at the Vienna Academy of Music. He first sang in several provincial opera houses; then was on the roster of the Vienna State Opera (from 1940); later sang in London and in Tokyo. He made his Metropolitan Opera debut in N.Y. on Nov. 26, 1952, as Leporello in *Don Giovanni;* remained on its roster until 1954. He was chiefly known for his buffo roles, and also acquired popularity as an operetta singer.

Kunz, Ernst, Swiss conductor and composer; b. Bern, June 2, 1891; d. Olten, Feb. 7, 1980. He studied at the Univ. of Munich and at the Munich Academy of Music; from 1916 to 1918, was a conductor of the Bavarian Court Opera in Munich; returning to Switzerland, he was active mainly as a theater conductor. His music is neo-Romantic in essence; the influences of Richard Strauss and Pfitzner are especially pronounced. He wrote operas: *Der Fächer* (1924; Zürich, 1929); *Vreneli ab em Guggisberg* (in Swiss dialect; 1935); *Die Bremer Stadtmusikanten* (1937); *Der Traum ein Leben* (1968); singspiel, *Die Hochzeitsreise* (1960); oratorios: *Vom irdischen Leben* (1931–49); *Christmas Oratorio* (1936); *Weisheit des Herzens* (1946); *Einkehr* (1951); *Psalter und Harfe* (1956); 5 syms. (1917, 1921, 1942, 1965, 1966); symphonic triptych, *Drei Lebensalter* (1964); *Serenata strana* for Orch. (1971); Viola Concerto (1952); Chamber Concerto for Strings, Solo Flute, and Piano (1971); 3 string quartets; Piano Quartet; piano pieces; about 500 choruses; several song cycles.

Kunzel, Erich, American conductor; b. N.Y., March 21, 1935. He was educated at Dartmouth College (B.Mus., 1957); took postgraduate courses at Harvard Univ. and Brown Univ. He also studied conducting with Monteux, serving as his assistant (1963–64); likewise was assistant conductor of the Rhode Island Phil. (1960–65). He was assistant conductor (1965–67), associate conductor (1967–69), and resident conductor (1969–74) of the Cincinnati Sym. Orch.; also taught at the Univ. of Cincinnati College-Cons. of Music (1965–71); was music director of the New Haven (Conn.) Sym. Orch. (1974–77); subsequently conducted his own Cincinnati Pops Orch. (from 1977). He also toured widely as a guest conductor, leading the pops series of many U.S. orchs.

Kunzen, family of German musicians:
(1) Johann Paul Kunzen, organist and composer; b. Leisnig, Saxony, Aug. 31, 1696; d. Lübeck, March 20, 1757. He studied organ at an early age; deputized for the Leisnig organist by the age of 9. He later studied various keyboard instruments and violin; subsequently studied with Kuhnau in Leipzig (1716–18). He played and sang at the Leipzig Opera; also deputized as organist at the Nikolaikirche; then was made Kapellmeister in Zerbst (1718). He served as director of the Hamburg Opera (1723–25); became organist of Lübeck's Marienkirche in 1732. He achieved distinction as a composer and conductor, presenting a noteworthy series of Abendmusiken. Only a few of his compositions are extant.
(2) Adolph Carl Kunzen, organist and composer, son of the preceding; b. Wittenberg, Sept. 22, 1720; d. Lübeck (buried), July 11, 1781. He studied with his father and with W. Lustig in Hamburg; toured in England with his father (1728–29). He was made Konzertmeister at the Mecklenburg-Schwerin court in 1749; was its Kapellmeister (1752–53). In 1757 he settled in Lübeck as his father's successor as organist of the Marienkirche; was also active as a composer and conductor, following in his father's footsteps with a distinguished series of Abendmusiken. He wrote 21 oratorios, but only 2 are extant; however, many of his fine songs exist. He also wrote syms., several concertos, and chamber music.
(3) Friedrich Ludwig Aemilius Kunzen, composer, son of the preceding; b. Lübeck, Sept. 24, 1761; d. Copenhagen,

Jan. 28, 1817. He studied music with his father, then law at the Univ. of Kiel (1781–84). He was active as a keyboard player, concert organizer, and composer in Copenhagen (1784–89), then went to Berlin, where he set up a music shop with Reichert and ed. the journal *Musikalisches Wochenblatt* (1791); subsequently was made Kapellmeister at the theaters in Frankfurt (1792) and Prague (1794); finally settled in Copenhagen as Royal Kapellmeister (1795), and also served as director of the oratorio society Det Harmoniske Selskab. He composed a number of fine stage works, as well as cantatas and oratorios.
WORKS: STAGE (all 1st perf. in Copenhagen unless otherwise given): *Holger Danske* (opera; March 31, 1789); *Das Fest der Winzer, oder Die Weinlese* (singspiel; Frankfurt, May 3, 1793; as *Viinhøsten,* Copenhagen, Dec. 1796); *Festen i Valhal* (Festival in Valhalla; prologue; 1796); *Hemmeligheden* (The Secret; singspiel; Nov. 22, 1796); *Dragedukken* (The Dragon Doll; singspiel; March 14, 1797); *Erik Ejegod* (opera; Jan. 30, 1798); *Naturens røst* (The Cry of Nature; singspiel; Nov. 22, 1799); *Min bedste moder* (My Grandmother; May 15, 1800); *Hjemkomsten* (The Homecoming; singspiel; 1802); *Gyrithe* (1807); *Kaerlighed paa landet* (Love in the Country; March 23, 1810); incidental music; various choral works; Sym.; several overtures; songs; keyboard music.
BIBL.: B. Friis, *F.A. K.: Sein Leben und Werk I. Bis zur Oper "Holger Danske" (1761–1789)* (diss., Univ. of Berlin, 1943).
(4) Louise Friederica Ulrica Kunzen, singer, daughter of **Adolph Carl Kunzen;** b. Lübeck, Feb. 15, 1765; d. Ludwigslust, May 4, 1839. She began singing in private concerts in Lübeck when she was 16; joined the Ludwigslust Court Theater (1787), where she enjoyed a remarkable career until her retirement (1837).

Kupferberg, Herbert, American journalist and music critic; b. N.Y., Jan. 20, 1918. He was educated at Cornell Univ. (B.A., 1939) and Columbia Univ. (M.A., 1940; M.S., 1941). From 1942 to 1966 he was on the staff of the *N.Y. Herald Tribune;* was also music critic of the *Atlantic Monthly* (1962–69) and of the *National Observer* (1967–77). He served as rapporteur for the Twentieth Century Fund's N.Y. task force on cultural exchange with the Soviet Union, which led to the publication of the report *The Raised Curtain* in 1977.
WRITINGS: *Those Fabulous Philadelphians: The Life and Times of a Great Orchestra* (N.Y., 1969); *The Mendelssohns: Three Generations of Genius* (N.Y., 1972); *Opera* (N.Y., 1975); *Tanglewood* (N.Y., 1976); *The Book of Classical Music Lists* (N.Y., 1985); *Basically Bach* (N.Y., 1986); *Amadeus: A Mozart Mosaic* (N.Y., 1986); also 2 books for young readers, *Felix Mendelssohn: His Life, His Family, His Music* (N.Y., 1972) and *A Rainbow of Sound: The Instruments of the Orchestra and Their Music* (N.Y., 1973).

Kupferman, Meyer, American composer, clarinetist, and teacher; b. N.Y., July 3, 1926. He attended N.Y.'s High School of Music and Art and then Queens College of the City Univ. of N.Y. (1943–45); was active as a clarinetist and taught at Sarah Lawrence College (from 1951); was also composer-in-residence at the Calif. Music Center in Palo Alto (from 1977). With John Yannelli, he founded the recording and publishing company Soundspells Productions in 1986. In 1975 he received a Guggenheim fellowship and in 1981 an award from the American Academy and Inst. of Arts and Letters. While he has principally applied serial procedures in his music since 1948, his vast catalog of works is nevertheless highly eclectic, displaying significant examples of neo-Classicism, electronic music, and jazz.
WORKS: STAGE: OPERAS: *In a Garden,* after Gertrude Stein (N.Y., Dec. 29, 1949); *Doctor Faustus Lights the Lights,* after Stein (1952; rev. 1963); *The Curious Fern* and *Voices for a Mirror* (both perf. in N.Y., June 5, 1957); *Draagenfut Girl,* children's opera (N.Y., May 8, 1958); *The Judgement (Infinities No. 18a)* for A Cappella Voices and Tape Chorus (1966–67); *Prometheus* (1975–77). **BALLETS:** *Persephone* (1968); *The Possessed* for Tape (1974); *O Thou Desire Who Art About to Sing*

(1977); *Icarus* (1980). ORCH.: 2 piano concertos (1948, 1978); *Divertimento* (1948); 11 numbered syms.: No. 1 (1950); No. 2, *Chamber Symphony* (1950); No. 3, *Little Symphony* (1952; rev. 1983); No. 4 (1955; Louisville, Jan. 28, 1956); No. 5, *Lyric Symphony* (1956); No. 6, *Symphony of the Yin-Yang* (1972); No. 7 (1974); No. 8, *Steps* (1975); No. 9 (1979); No. 10, *F.D.R.* (1981; for the 100th anniversary of the birth of President Franklin D. Roosevelt); No. 11 (1983); *Jazz Symphony* for Mezzo-soprano, Jazz Saxophonist, and Orch. (Middletown, N.Y., Oct. 14, 1988); *Ostinato Burlesque* (1954; orchestration of a 1948 piano piece); *Variations* (1958); Concerto for Cello and Jazz Band (*Infinities No. 5*; 1962; rev. 1982); *Infinities No. 14* for Trumpet and Chamber Orch. (1965); *Schemata* (*Infinities No. 20*; 1967); *Infinities No. 24* for String Orch. (1968); Concerto for Cello, Tape, and Orch. (1974); *Prometheus profundis* for Chorus, Brass, and Percussion (1975); *Passage* for String Orch. (1976); Violin Concerto (1976); *Atto* (1977); Concerto for 6 Solo Instruments and Orch. (1978); *Sound Objects No. 10* for Small Orch. (1979); *Phantom Rhapsody* for Guitar and Small Orch. (1980); *Sound Phantoms No. 8* (1980); Tuba Concerto (1983); Clarinet Concerto (1984); *Wings of the Highest Tower* (1988); *Overture for Double Orch.* (1988); *Savage Landscape* (1989). CHAMBER: 5 numbered string quartets, including Nos. 4 (1958) and 5 (1959); Concerto for 11 Brass (1948); Wind Quintet (1958); *Infinities*, cycle of 34 pieces on the same tone row, mostly for Chamber Groupings, including No. 8 for Jazz String Quartet (1964), No. 12 for Chamber Ensemble (1964), and No. 29 for Wind Quintet (1978); *Moonchild and the Doomsday Trombone* for Oboe, Voice, and Jazz Band (1968); *Fantasy Concerto* for Cello, Piano, and Tape (1974); *Abracadabra Quartet* for Piano and String Trio (1976); *Masada*, chamber sym. for Flute, Clarinet, Cello, Double Bass, Piano, and Violin (1977); *Sound Objects*, cycle of 10 pieces, mostly for Chamber Groupings, including Nos. 1 and 3 for Trumpet, Tuba, and Piano (1978); *Sound Phantoms*, cycle of 10 pieces, mostly for Chamber Groupings, including No. 2, *Concerto grosso*, for Flute, Viola, Double Bass, and 8 Guitars (1979), No. 6 for String Quartet (1980), and No. 10 for 14 Brass (1981); *Jazz Essay* for Saxophone Quartet (1982); *Symphony for 6* for Clarinet, Bassoon, Horn, Violin, Cello, and Bass (1984); Quintet for Piano and Strings (1985); *And 5 Quartets* for 5 String Quartets (1986); *Rock Shadows* for Brass Quintet (1986); *Summer Music* for 2 Guitars, Flute, and Cello (1987); *Top Brass 5* for 5 Trumpets (1989); *Moontrek Fantasy* for Trumpet, Flute, Cello, and Piano (1989); *Triple Suite* for 3 Flutes Doubling Piccolo (1989); piano pieces. VOCAL: *Ode to Shreveport*, cantata for 4 Soloists, Chorus, and Orch. (1985); *A Crucible for the Moon* for Soprano, Alto Saxophone, and Percussion Orch. (1986); *Wicked Combinations*, song cycle for Mezzo-soprano and Piano (1989).

Kupkovič, Ladislav, Slovak conductor and composer; b. Bratislava, March 17, 1936. He studied violin in Bratislava at the Cons. (1950–55) and at the Academy of Music (1955–61); played violin in the Slovak Phil. (1960–63). In 1963 he organized the chamber ensemble Hudba Dneška (Music of Today). He left Czechoslovakia after the Soviet invasion in 1968 and went to Germany; was a stipendiary at Berlin's Deutscher Akademischer Austauschdienst (1969–71); was made a lecturer (1973) and a prof. (1976) of composition at the Hannover Hochschule für Musik. His music utilizes the cosmopolitan resources of ultramodern music. He initiated "walking concerts," in which a group of musicians walk in the streets playing segments of familiar pieces ad nauseam. **WORKS:** *Maso kríža* (Flesh of the Cross), an impression of a surrealist painting of the crucifix, for Trombone and 10 Percussion Players (1961–62); *Psalm* for 4 Horns (1962); *Výkřiky* (Exclamations) for Flute, Bass Clarinet, Piano, and Percussion (1964); *Rozhovor času s hmotou* (A Conversation between Time and Matter) for Bassoon and 3 Percussion Players (1965); *Ozveny* (Echoes) for 31 Players (1966); *Pred s za* (Before and After) for Chamber Ensemble (1967); *Dioe* for Orch., with Conductor (1968); *Oktoedr* (Octohedron) for Chamber Ensemble (1968); *Ad libitum*, a "happening" for a random group of Performers (1969); *Klanginvasion auf Bonn*, a spectacle of indeterminate duration, representing the invasion of noise on the population of Bonn (1970); *Notausgang* for Orch. and Microphones (1970); *Erinnerungen* for Orch. and Tape (1970); *Monolith* for 48 Strings (1971); *Ein Gespräch mit Gott* for Orch. (1972); *Das Gebet* for String Orch. and Percussion (1972–73); *Concours* for the "orchestra of the future" (1973); *Čarovné sláčiky* (Magic Bows) for 30 Violins and Low Strings (1974); *312-SL/723* for 2 Accordions (1975); *Serenata* for Orch. (1976); *Postillon-Cornet* for Trumpet and Orch. (1977); *K.-u. K. Musik* for Orch. (1978); 3 string quartets (1978, 1978, 1984); String Quintet for 2 Violins, Viola, and 2 Cellos (1978); Cassation for Orch. (1979); *Missa Papae Ioannis Pauli Secundi* for Choir and Orch. (1979); 2 violin sonatas (1979, 1980); Quartet for Flute, Violin, Viola, and Cello (1980); 3 violin concertos (1980, 1981, 1985); Cello Concerto (1980); Accordion Concerto (1980); Piano Concerto (1980); Wind Serenade (1981); 2 piano sonatas (1981, 1981); Sym. (1981); 2 *Rococo Symphonies* (1982, 1982); Cello Sonata (1984); Trio for Violin, Cello, and Piano (1985); Octet for Clarinet, Bassoon, Horn, 2 Violins, Viola, Cello, and Double Bass (1986); 2 quartets for Violin, Viola, Cello, and Piano (1986, 1986); many other chamber works; piano pieces.

Kupper, Annelies (Gabriele), German soprano; b. Glatz, July 21, 1906; d. Haar, near Munich, Dec. 8, 1987. She studied at the Univ. of Breslau, and then taught in that city (1929–35); made her debut at the Breslau Opera (1935), remaining there until 1937. She then sang in Schwerin (1937–38) and Weimar (1938–39); was a principal member of the Hamburg State Opera (1940–46) and the Bavarian State Opera in Munich (1946–61); also sang at Bayreuth, Salzburg, and London's Covent Garden (Chrysothemis, 1953); appeared as Danae in the 1st public performance of Richard Strauss's *Die Liebe der Danae* (Salzburg, 1952). She became a teacher at the Munich Academy of Music (1956). In addition to her Mozart and Strauss roles, she became known for her performances of works by contemporary German composers.

Kurath, Gertrude Prokosch (Tula), American ethnomusicologist; b. Chicago, Aug. 19, 1903. She studied at Bryn Mawr College (B.A., 1922; M.A. in art history, 1928), concurrently studying music and dance in Berlin, Philadelphia, N.Y., and Providence, R.I.; she then attended the Yale School of Drama (1929–30). She conducted field research for the Wenner-Gren Foundation (1949–73), the American Philosophical Soc. (1951–65), and the National Museum of Canada (1962–65; 1969–70); also taught dance, lectured on dance history, and was dance ed. for *Ethnomusicology* (1958–72). She made substantial contributions to the study of American Indian dance and to dance theory and notation.

WRITINGS: *Iroquois Music and Dance: Ceremonial Arts of Two Seneca Longhouses* (Washington, D.C., 1964); *Michigan Indian Festivals* (Ann Arbor, 1966); *Dance and Song Rituals of Six Nations Reserve, Ontario* (Ottawa, 1968).

Kuri-Aldana, Mario, Mexican composer; b. Tampico, Aug. 15, 1931. He studied piano with Carlos del Castillo at the Academia Juan Sebastián Bach in Mexico City (1948–51) and composition with Tercero, Vazquez, and Michaca at the Escuela Nacional de Música of the Autonomous Univ. of Mexico (1952–60); took conducting courses from Markevitch and Giardino at the National Inst. of Fine Arts (1957–58); then privately studied advanced techniques of composition with Rodolfo Halffter and Luis Herrera de la Fuente (1961–62); took lessons with Ginastera, R. Malipiero, Messiaen, Maderna, Dallapiccola, Copland, and Chase in various venues (1963–64), and with Stockhausen at the Mexico City Cons. (1965). Returning to Mexico, he devoted himself to teaching.

WORKS: 3 syms.: No. 1, *Sacrificio* (1959); No. 2 for String Orch. (1966); No. 3, *Ce Actal-1521* (1976); *Los cuatro Bacabs*, suite for Double Wind Orch. and optional Narrator (1960); *Máscaras*, concerto for Marimba and Wind Orch. (1962); *Pasos* for Piano and Orch. (1963); *Bacab de las plegarias* for 2 Flutes,

2 Clarinets, Trumpet, Harp, and Strings (1966); *Formas de otros tiempos* for String Orch. and Harp (1971); *Concierto de Santiago* for Flute, String Orch., and 2 Percussion Players (1973); *Concertino mexicano* for Violin and String Orch. (1974); numerous songs accompanied by various instrumental combinations, among them *Cantares para una niña muerta* for Mezzo-soprano, Flute, and Guitar (1961); *Este, ese y aquel* (This, That and the Other) for Mezzo-soprano, Flute, Violin, Viola, Cello, and Vibraphone (1964); *Amarillo era el color de la Esperanza* (Yellow Was the Color of Hope), secular cantata for Narrator, Mezzo-soprano, and Jazz Band (1966); *Noche de verano* for Narrator, Soprano, and Small Orch (1975); *A mi hermano* for Baritone, Chorus, and Orch. (1977); *Canto de 5-Flor* for Cello and Piano (1957); *Sonatina mexicana* for Violin and Piano (1959); *Xilofonías* for Piccolo, Oboe, Bass Clarinet, Double Bassoon, and Percussion (1963); *Puentes* for String Quartet (1965; rev. 1977); *Candelaria*, suite for Wind Quintet (1965); *3-Silvestre*, concerto for 9 Instruments (1966); *Fuga para metales* (1968); also piano works, including *Suite ingenua* (1953); *Villancico, Canción y Jarabe* (1965); Sonata (1972).

Kurka, Robert (Frank), American composer; b. Cicero, Ill., Dec. 22, 1921; d. N.Y., Dec. 12, 1957. He studied violin with Kathleen Parlow and Hans Letz, and composition with Luening and Milhaud, but considered himself autodidact; received a Guggenheim fellowship (1951–52), and taught at the City College of N.Y., Queens College, and Dartmouth College. His satirical opera, *The Good Soldier Schweik*, the composition of which was delayed for years due to problems in clearing rights for the libretto and which existed only as an orchestral suite until 1956, was completed shortly before his untimely death from leukemia and was orchestrated by Hershy Kay; it was premiered with extraordinary success at the N.Y. City Center on April 23, 1958, and has since been widely performed in the U.S. and in Europe. Kurka's music, though quite melodic, makes use of harmonious dissonance, imbuing neo-Classical forms with a rhythmic and harmonic intuition reminiscent of Prokofiev and Shostakovich.

WORKS: OPERA: *The Good Soldier Schweik*, after J. Hašek (1952–57; N.Y., April 23, 1958; European premiere, Dresden, Nov. 10, 1959; premiered as a chamber orch. suite, N.Y., Nov. 24, 1952). **ORCH.:** Chamber Sym. (1946; N.Y., March 7, 1948); Sym. for Brass and Strings (1948; N.Y., March 13, 1950); Violin Concerto (1948); *Music for Orchestra* (1949); *3 Pieces* (1951); 2 numbered syms.: No. 1 (1951) and No. 2 (1953; San Diego, July 8, 1958); *Serenade*, after lines of Whitman, for Small Orch. (La Jolla, Calif., June 13, 1954); *John Henry*, portrait (1954); *Julius Caesar*, symphonic epilogue after Shakespeare (San Diego, July 12, 1955); Concertino for 2 Pianos, String Orch., and Trumpet (1955); Marimba Concerto (1956; N.Y., Nov. 11, 1959); *Ballad* for Horn and Strings (1956); *Chamber Sinfonietta* (1957). **CHAMBER:** 5 string quartets (1945, 1947, 1949, 1950, 1954); 4 violin sonatas (1946, 1949, 1953, 1955); Sonata for Solo Violin (1947); *Music* for Violin, Trumpet, Clarinet, Horn, and Double Bass (1951); Piano Trio (1951); 7 *Moravian Folksongs* for Wind Quintet (1951); piano pieces, including a Sonata (1952). **VOCAL:** *Who Shall Speak for the People*, after Sandburg, for Male Chorus and Orch. (1956); *Song of the Broad-Axe* for Male Chorus (1956); songs.

Kurpiński, Karol (Kazimierz), prominent Polish conductor and composer; b. Wloszakowice, March 6, 1785; d. Warsaw, Sept. 18, 1857. He studied with his father, Marcian Kurpiński, an organist; in 1797, became organist in Sarnów; then was a violinist in the private orch. of Feliks Polanowski at his Moszków estate (1800–1808); subsequently was music master to the Rastawiecki family in Lemberg (1808–10). He settled in Warsaw, where he became a theater violinist; then was made deputy conductor of the Opera, and also Kapellmeister of the Polish royal court (1819); was principal conductor of the Opera (1824–40). He also taught music at the schools of drama (1812, 1817) and voice (1835–40), which he founded. He was founder-ed. of the 1st Polish music journal, *Tygodnik Muzyczny* (Music

Weekly; 1820–21). As one of the leading Polish composers of his day, he helped to establish the national Polish school. He wrote 24 stage works, including the operas *Jadwiga królowa Polska* (Jadwiga, Queen of Poland; Warsaw, Dec. 23, 1814) and *Zamek na Czorsztynce, czyli Bojomic i Wanda* (The Castle of Czorsztyn, or Bojomic and Wanda; Warsaw, March 5, 1819); also sacred works, polonaises for orch., chamber music, and piano pieces.

BIBL.: T. Przybylski, *K. K., 1785–1857* (Warsaw, 1975).

Kürsteiner, Jean Paul, American pianist, pedagogue, and composer; b. Catskill, N.Y. (of a French-Swiss father and an American mother), July 8, 1864; d. Los Angeles, March 19, 1943. He studied in Leipzig with Jadassohn and R. Hofmann; piano with Weidenbach and Teichmüller. Returning to America in 1893, he taught piano and theory at the Ogontz School in Philadelphia, holding this position until 1930. In 1938 he moved to Los Angeles. He wrote a number of piano pieces, of which *Invocation to Eros* became fairly well known. He publ. *Essays on Expert Aid to Artistic Piano Playing.*

Kurt, Melanie, Austrian soprano; b. Vienna, Jan. 8, 1880; d. N.Y., March 11, 1941. She studied piano at the Vienna Cons. (1887–94), winning the gold medal and Liszt prize; then took lessons from Fannie Mütter in Vienna, and made a successful operatic debut as Elisabeth in *Tannhäuser* (Lübeck, 1902); then sang in Leipzig (1903–4). She then completed her vocal training with Lilli and Marie Lehmann in Berlin. From 1905 to 1908 she sang in Braunschweig; then (1908–12) at the Berlin Royal Opera. She became an outstanding Wagner interpreter and appeared in London, Brussels, Milan, Budapest, etc. When the Deutsches Opernhaus in Charlottenburg was opened in 1912, she was engaged as chief soprano for heroic roles. On Feb. 1, 1915, she made her debut at the Metropolitan Opera in N.Y. as Isolde; remained on its roster until her contract was terminated with the U.S. entry into World War I in 1917. After returning to Germany, she appeared at the Berlin Volksoper (1920–25); also taught there, and later in Vienna. In 1938 she settled in N.Y. Her roles included Pamina, Beethoven's Leonore, Sieglinde, Brünnhilde, Kundry, and the Marschallin.

Kurtág, György, Rumanian-born Hungarian composer; b. Lugoj, Feb. 19, 1926. He studied piano with Magda Kardos and composition with Max Eisikovits in Timişoara; then settled in Hungary (1946), becoming a citizen (1948); studied piano with Kadosa, composition with Veress and Farkas, and chamber music with Leo Weiner at the Budapest Academy of Music (1946–55), graduating with diplomas in all 3. He then went to Paris and took lessons with Milhaud and Messiaen at the Paris Cons. (1957–58), and studied with Marianne Stein. He subsequently was a prof. of piano at the Budapest Academy of Music, being made a prof. of chamber music in 1967. In his music he sometimes applies serial principles to classical melodic configurations and forms.

WORKS: ORCH.: Viola Concerto (1954); *Quasi una fantasia* for Chamber Orch. (Berlin, Oct. 16, 1988). **CHORAL:** *Omaggio a Luigi Nono* (1979; London, Feb. 3, 1981); 8 Choruses to poems by Dezső Tandori (1981–82; 1984). **CHAMBER:** String Quartet (1959); Wind Quintet (1959); 8 *Duos* for Violin and Cimbalom (1961); *Hommage a Mihály András*, 12 microludes for String Quartet (1977); *The Little Predicament* for Piccolo, Trombone, and Guitar (1979). **SOLO PIECES:** 8 Piano Pieces (1960); *Signs* for Viola (1961); *Splinters* for Cimbalom (1973); *Guitar Pieces* (1975); *Games* for Piano (4 vols., 1973–76). **VOCAL:** *The Sayings of Péter Bornemisza*, concerto for Soprano and Piano (1963–68); *In Memory of a Winter Sunset*, 4 fragments for Soprano, Violin, and Cimbalom (1969); 4 *Capriccios* for Soprano and Chamber Ensemble (1972); 4 *Songs* for Bass or Bass-baritone and 9 Instruments (1975); *Herdecker Eurythmie* for Lyre with Flute, Violin, and Speaking Voice (1978); *Messages of the Late Miss R.V. Troussova* for Soprano and Chamber Ensemble (1976–80; Paris, Jan. 14, 1981); *Scenes from a Novel*, 15 songs for Soprano, Violin, Double Bass, and Cimbalom (1981–82); *Kafka-Fragmente* for Soprano and Violin

(1985–86); *3 Old Inscriptions* for Soprano and Piano (1986; Berlin, Oct. 16, 1988); *Requiem po drugu* for Soprano and Piano (1986–87; London, Oct. 31, 1989).

Kurth, Ernst, eminent Austrian-born Swiss musicologist; b. Vienna, June 1, 1886; d. Bern, Aug. 2, 1946. He studied with Guido Adler at the Univ. of Vienna (Ph.D., 1908, with the diss. *Der Stil der opera seria von Gluck bis zum Orfeo;* publ. in *Studien zur Musikwissenschaft,* I, 1913); completed his Habilitation at the Univ. of Bern (1912). He was made a reader (1920) and a prof. of musicology (1927) there. His principal work, *Grundlagen des linearen Kontrapunkts: Bachs melodische Polyphonie* (Bern, 1917; 5th ed., 1956), profoundly influenced musicology and practical composition, and also introduced the term "linear counterpoint." A companion vol., *Romantische Harmonik und ihre Krise in Wagners Tristan* (Bern, 1920; 3rd ed., 1923), is a psychological analysis of Romantic music. His *Musikpsychologie* (Berlin, 1931; 2nd ed., 1947) represents a synthesis of his theoretical ideas on musical perception. He also publ. *Anton Bruckner* (2 vols., Berlin, 1925).

BIBL.: E. Bücken, "K. als Musiktheoretiker," *Melos,* IV (1924–25); K. von Fischer, "In memoriam E. K.," *Der Musikalmanach,* VIII (1948); D. Menstell Hsu, "E. K. and His Concept of Music as Motion," *Journal of Music Theory,* X (1966); L. Rothfarb, *E. K. as Theorist and Analyst* (Philadelphia, 1988).

Kurtz, Edward Frampton, American violinist and composer; b. New Castle, Pa., July 31, 1881; d. Cedar Falls, Iowa, June 8, 1965. He studied at the Univ. of Iowa, the Detroit Cons., and the Cincinnati Cons.; took violin lessons with Ysaÿe in Cincinnati and composition with Clapp, Goetschius, and E.S. Kelley. After teaching at various Midwestern colleges, he became head of the music dept. of Iowa State Teachers College (1940). He wrote 5 syms. (1932, 1939, 1940, 1943, 1944); several symphonic poems; a Suite for String Quartet, subtitled *From the West;* violin pieces.

Kurtz, Efrem, Russian-born American conductor; b. St. Petersburg, Nov. 7, 1900. He studied with N. Tcherepnin, Glazunov, and Wihtol at the St. Petersburg Cons.; then at the Univ. of Riga (1918–20); then took music courses at the Stern Cons. in Berlin, graduating in 1922. He made his conducting debut in Berlin in 1921; then was a guest conductor with the Berlin Phil.; subsequently was conductor of the Stuttgart Phil. (1924–33). He was conductor of the Ballets Russes de Monte Carlo (1933–42), with which he toured throughout Europe and the U.S.; then went to the U.S., becoming a naturalized citizen in 1944. He was conductor of the Kansas City Phil. (1943–48) and the Houston Sym. Orch. (1948–54); then was joint conductor of the Liverpool Phil. (1955–57). In subsequent years he appeared as a guest conductor in Europe, the U.S., and Japan. He married the flutist Elaine Shaffer in 1955.

Kurz, Selma, noted Austrian soprano; b. Bielitz, Silesia, Nov. 15, 1874; d. Vienna, May 10, 1933. She studied with Johannes Ress in Vienna and Mathilde Marchesi in Paris; made her 1st appearance as a mezzo-soprano as Mignon at the Hamburg Opera (May 12, 1895); then sang in Frankfurt (1896–99). She made her 1st appearance at the Vienna Court Opera as Mignon (Sept. 3, 1899); after singing lyric-dramatic soprano roles, she turned to coloratura roles; continued on its roster when it became the State Opera (1918), singing there until her retirement (1927). She made her London debut at Covent Garden as Gilda (June 7, 1904), creating a profound impression; sang there again in subsequent seasons. She appeared as a concert singer in the U.S. She was esteemed for such roles as Elizabeth, Eva, Sieglinde, Lucia, and Mimi; also created Zerbinetta in the rev. version of Richard Strauss's *Ariadne auf Naxos* (1916). She married the famous Viennese gynecologist Josef Halban in 1910; their daughter was the soprano **Desi Halban-Kurz** (b. Vienna, April 10, 1912).

BIBL.: H. Goldmann, *S. K.* (Bielitz, 1933).

Kurz, Siegfried, German conductor and composer; b. Dresden, July 18, 1930. He studied conducting with Ernst Hintze, composition with Fidelio Finke, and trumpet with Gerd Seifert at the Staatlichen Akademie für Musik und Theater in Dresden (1945–50); from 1949 to 1960 he was conductor of music for dramatic productions at the Dresden State Theater. In 1960 he became a conductor at the Dresden State Opera; in 1975 he was named its music director; in 1979 he also became a prof. of composition at the Dresden Hochschule für Musik. He toured with the Dresden State Orch. to Austria, Japan, and the U.S. As a conductor, he was honored with the titles of Staatskapellmeister (1965) and Generalmusikdirektor (1971); as a composer, he received the Kunstpreis and the Nationalpreis of the German Democratic Republic. His compositions combine the principles of Classical lucidity with the dissonant counterpoint of the modern era.

WORKS: 2 syms. (1958, 1959); *Sinfonia piccola* (1953); Trumpet Concerto (1953); Chamber Concerto for Wind Quintet and String Orch. (1962); Piano Concerto (Dresden, Oct. 2, 1964); Variations for Orch. (1968); *Sonatine* for Orch. (1969); Music for Winds, Percussion, and Strings (1969); Horn Concerto (Dresden, Dec. 20, 1973); Wind Quintet (1950); Sonatine for 7 Brass Instruments (1952).

Kürzinger, Ignaz Franz Xaver, German composer; b. Rosenheim, Upper Bavaria, Jan. 30, 1724; d. Würzburg, Aug. 12, 1797. He studied for the priesthood in Innsbruck, but became a trumpeter in a Hungarian cuirassier regiment; was taken prisoner during the 1st Silesian War, and was sent to Berlin, where he studied composition with C.H. Graun. He was later taken to Italy by the Elector Clemens August of Cologne, who made him grand master of the Teutonic Knights; he was active at its chapel in Mergentheim, Württemberg, where he later served as Kapellmeister (1751–63); he then went to Würzburg as a violinist in the Court Orch. of the Prince-Bishop; subsequently became music director of the orphanage at the Julius Hospital. He wrote sacred and secular vocal music, orch. works, and piano pieces; much of his work was destroyed during World War II. He publ. the useful manual *Getreuer Unterricht zum Singen mit Manieren, und die Violin zu spielen* (Augsburg, 1763; 5th ed., 1821). His son, **Paul Ignaz Kürzinger** (b. Mergentheim, Württemberg, April 28, 1750; d. Vienna, after 1820), was also a composer; after studying with his father, he played violin in the Munich electoral Court Orch. (1775–77); then in the orch. of the Prince of Thurn and Taxis in Regensburg (1777–80), where he was director of the Court Theater (1780–83); he subsequently settled as a theater composer and director of a private school in Vienna. He wrote the operas *La Contessina* (Munich, 1775); *Robert und Kalliste* (Regensburg, 1780); *Der Bergknappen* (Regensburg, 1782); and *Die Illumination* (Vienna, 1787; not extant); 4 ballets; a cantata; piano pieces; songs.

Kusche, Benno, German bass-baritone; b. Freiburg im Breisgau, Jan. 30, 1916. He studied in Karlsruhe; made his operatic debut in Koblenz in 1938; then sang in Augsburg (1939–44); subsequently became a leading member of the Bavarian State Opera in Munich (1946). He made his debut at London's Covent Garden as Beckmesser (1952); chose that same role for his Metropolitan Opera debut in N.Y. on Dec. 27, 1971. He was made a Bavarian Kammersänger in 1955. His notable roles included Papageno, Figaro, Leporello, Don Alfonso, and Alberich.

Kusevitsky, Moshe, Polish cantor; b. Smorgon, June 9, 1899; d. Kings Point, N.Y., Aug. 23, 1966. He studied in Vilnius; became a cantor in Warsaw in 1926, and also pursued a concert career; made his Paris debut as a concert singer in 1930; then appeared several times in England; in 1934, gave concerts in Palestine; in 1938, sang in the U.S. He returned to Warsaw before the outbreak of World War II; escaped to Russia, where he remained from 1939 until 1946, and gave concerts in Leningrad, Moscow, Odessa, etc.; in 1946–47, toured in England; then settled in N.Y. Although his last name is identical (in Russian characters) with that of Serge Koussevitzky, the 2 were not related.

Kusser (or **Cousser**), **Johann Sigismund,** noted German conductor and composer of Hungarian parentage; b. Pressburg (baptized), Feb. 13, 1660; d. Dublin, Nov. 1727. He received his early musical training from his father, Johann Kusser (1626–75), a minister and organist. He lived in Stuttgart as a boy; then spent 8 years in Paris (1674–82), where he became a pupil of Lully. He subsequently was a violin teacher at the Ansbach court (1682–83); then became opera Kapellmeister in Braunschweig (1690). In 1695 he became co-director of the Hamburg Opera, but left the next year and was active in Nuremberg and Augsburg as an opera composer. He was again in Stuttgart from 1700 to 1704 as Ober-Kapellmeister. In 1705 he appeared in London, and in 1709 settled in Dublin, where he was made Chappel-Master of Trinity College in 1717 and Master of the Musick "attending his Majesty's State in Ireland" in 1717. He was greatly esteemed as an operatic conductor; Mattheson, in his *Volkommener Capellmeister*, holds him up as a model of efficiency. Kusser is historically significant for being the mediator between the French and the German styles of composition, and the 1st to use Lully's methods and forms in German instrumental music. Lully's influence is shown in Kusser's set of 6 suites for Strings, *Composition de musique suivant la méthode française* (Stuttgart, 1682).

WORKS: Operas: *Julia* (Braunschweig, 1690); *Cleopatra* (Braunschweig, 1691); *La Grotta di Salzdahl*, divertimento (Braunschweig, 1691); *Ariadne* (Braunschweig, Feb. 15, 1692); *Andromeda* (Braunschweig, Feb. 20, 1692); *Jason* (Braunschweig, Sept. 1, 1692); *Narcissus* (Braunschweig, Oct. 14, 1692); *Porus* (Braunschweig, 1693); *Erindo, oder Dir unsträfliche Liebe* (pastorale play; Hamburg, 1694); *Der grossmüthige Scipio Africanus* (Hamburg, 1694); *Gensericus, als Rom und Karthagens Überwinder* (Hamburg, 1694?; may be by Conradi); *Pyramus und Thisbe getreu und festverbundene Liebe* (Hamburg, 1694?); *Der verliebte Wald* (Stuttgart, 1698); *Erminia* (Stuttgart, Oct. 11, 1698); *The Man of Mode* (London, Feb. 9, 1705); 18 ouvertures or suites, 6 publ. as *Composition de musique suivant la méthode française* (Stuttgart, 1682), 6 as *Apollon enjoué* (Stuttgart, 1700), and 6 as *Festin des muses* (Stuttgart, 1700).

BIBL.: F. Chrysander, "Die Hamburger Oper unter der Direktion von J.S. K.," *Allgemeine Musikalische Zeitung* (1879); H. Scholz, *J.S. K.: Sein Leben und seine Werke* (Leipzig, 1911).

Kussevitsky, Serge (Alexandrovich). See **Koussevitzky, Serge (Alexandrovich).**

Küster, Hermann, German organist, composer, and writer on music; b. Templin, July 14, 1817; d. Herford, March 17, 1878. He studied with A.W. Bach, L. Berger, A.B. Marx, and Rungenhagen in Berlin; was music director in Saarbrücken (1845–52); then became a music teacher in Berlin, and later court and Cathedral organist (1857). He composed sacred music, orch. pieces, songs, etc. He publ. *Über Händels Israel in Ägypten* (1854); *Populäre Vorträge über Bildung und Begründung eines musikalischen Urteils* (4 vols., 1870–77); *Methode für den Unterricht im Gesang auf höheren Schulanstalten* (1872); *Über die Formen in der Musik* (1872); etc.

Kutavičius, Bronislovas, Lithuanian composer; b. Molainiai, near Panevežys, Sept. 13, 1932. He studied composition with Antanas Račiunas at the Vilnius Cons., graduating in 1964. In 1975 he was appointed to the music faculty at the Arts School in Vilnius. In his music he evolves a complex system of varied techniques, impressionistic pointillism, intervallic serialism, and aleatory sonorism, all this intertwined with Lithuanian melorhythms.

WORKS: STAGE: Opera-ballet for children, *Doddering Old Man on Iron Mountain* (1976); opera-poem, *The Green Bird* (1981). **ORCH.:** *Sinfonietta* (1964); *Divertimento* for Piano and String Orch. (1967); Sym. with Male Chorus (1973); *Dzukija Variations* for String Orch. (1974). **VOCAL:** *Pantheistic Oratorio* for Soprano, Narrator, 4 Male Voices, and 12 Instruments (1970); *On the Shore* for High Voice and 4 Violas (1972); *Little Performance* for Actress, 2 Pianos, and 2 Violins (1975); *2 Birds in the Thick of the Woods*, cantata for Soprano, Oboe, Prepared Piano, and Electronic Tape (1978); *The Last Pagan Rites*, oratorio for Soprano, Girls' Chorus, Horns, and Organ

(1978). **CHAMBER:** Violin Sonata (1962); *Prelude and Fugue* for 4 Violins (1966); *Poem* for Cello, Piano, and Wind Quintet (1967); Viola Sonata (1968); *From Madrigal to Aleatory*, suite for children, for Violin and Piano (1972); 2 string quartets: No. 1 (1972); No. 2, *Anno cum tettigonia* (Year with a Cicada; 1980); *Prutiena* (Buried Village) for Violin, Organ, and Chimes (1977); String Quintet (1978); *Clocks of the Past* for String Quartet and Guitar (1978); *Perpetuum mobile* for Cello and Piano (1978). **PIANO:** *3 Metamorphoses* (1966); *Collages* for 2 Pianos (1970); Piano Sonata (1975); *A Disputation with a Stranger*, concerto for 2 Pianos and Tape (1982).

Kutev, Filip, Bulgarian bandmaster, choral conductor, and composer; b. Aytos, June 26, 1903; d. Sofia, Nov. 27, 1982. He studied at the Sofia Academy of Music (graduated, 1929); was a bandmaster in Burgas, and then in Sofia; in 1951 he organized an ensemble of largely untutored folksingers, musicians, and dancers; he brought it to a high point of virtuosity and toured in Europe (1958) and the U.S. (1963), eliciting great praise. Virtually all of his compositions are derived from Bulgarian melorhythms; among these are *Bulgarian Rhapsody* for Orch. (1937); cantata, *September the 9th*, in honor of the entry of the Soviet army into Bulgaria in 1944; *Stalin Cantata* (1949); Sym. (1950).

BIBL.: S. Stoyanov, *F. K.* (Sofia, 1962).

Kuula, Toivo (Timoteus), Finnish conductor and composer; b. Vasa, July 7, 1883; d. (shot to death during a street fight in the aftermath of the Finnish Civil War) Viipuri, May 18, 1918. He studied at the Helsinki Music Inst. with Sibelius, Wegelius, Nováček, and Järnefelt (1900–1908); then with Bossi in Bologna, in Leipzig, and with Labey in Paris (1908–10); finally in Berlin (1911–12). He taught and conducted in Vasa (1903–5); was conductor of the Oulu Orch. (1910–11), vice-conductor of the Native Orch. (1912–14), and assistant conductor of the Helsinki Municipal Orch. (1914–16); then conducted the orch. of the Viipuri Friends of Music (1916–18). His music, rooted in Finnish folk song, is occasionally touched with Impressionism.

WORKS: *Eteläpohjalainen sarja* (South Ostrobothnians Suites) for Orch. (1906–9; 1912–14); *Prelude and Fugue* for Orch. (1909); *Prelude and Intermezzo* for Strings and Organ (1909); *Orjanpoika* (The Son of a Slave), symphonic legend (1910); *Kuolemattomuuden toivo* (Hope of Immortality) for Baritone, Chorus, and Orch. (1910); *Merenkylpijäneidot* (Maids on the Seashore) for Soprano and Orch. (1910); *Impi ja pajarinpoika* (The Maid and the Boyar's Son) for Soprano and Orch. (1911); *Bothnic Poem* for Orch. (Petrograd, Oct. 26, 1918); Violin Sonata; music for plays; piano pieces; songs. He left unfinished a *Jupiter Symphony;* also a *Stabat Mater* for Chorus, Organ, and Orch. (1914–18; completed by Madetoja and 1st perf. in Helsinki in 1919).

BIBL.: T. Elmgreen-Heinonen and E. Roiha, *T. K.: A Finnish Composer of Genius* (Helsinki, 1952).

Kuusisto, Ilkka Taneli, Finnish composer, conductor, and operatic administrator, son of **Taneli Kuusisto;** b. Helsinki, April 26, 1933. He studied organ at the Sibelius Academy in Helsinki; also composition with Arre Merikanto and Nils-Eric Fougstedt. In 1958 he went to N.Y. to study organ with Seth Bingham; later continued his studies in Germany and Vienna. Returning to Helsinki, he was a conductor at the City Theater (1965–68; 1971–75); also was head of the Klemetti Inst. (1969–71); after serving as artistic director of Fazer Music (1981–84), he was director of the Finnish National Opera (from 1984).

WORKS: 3 *Introductions* for Brass, Percussion, and Organ (1956); 3 *Chinese Songs* for Soprano, Flute, and Piano (1956); Duo for Flute and Cello (1957); *Valkeneva päivä* (Daybreak), cantata for Solo Voices, Youth Chorus, and Organ (1957); *Coelestis aulae nuntius* for Trombone and Organ (1959); *Crucifixus* for Baritone and String Quartet (1959); *Cassazione* for 2 Clarinets and 2 Horns (1961); *Jazzationes*, suite for Jazz Quartet and String Quartet (1965); *Ritornells* for Viola and Marimba (1970); *The Pain* and *Alfhid*, 2 songs for Baritone, 2 Clarinets, and Strings (1972); music for Brecht's play *Saint*

Joan of the Stockyards (1972); operas: *Muumiooppera* (1974); *Miehen kylkiluu* (1977); *Sota valosta* (1980; Helsinki, April 2, 1981); *Jääkäri Stahl* (1981); *Pierrot tai yön salaisuudet* (1991); musicals: *Lumikuningatar* (1979); *Robin Hood* (1987); film music; organ pieces; song cycles.

Kuusisto, Taneli, Finnish organist and composer, father of **Ilkka Taneli Kuusisto;** b. Helsinki, June 19, 1905. He studied at the Helsinki Inst. of Church Music, in Paris, and in Leipzig with J.N. David. He centered his career on Helsinki; was assistant conductor of the Finnish Radio (1936–42) and chorus director of the Finnish National Opera (1942–46); was organist of Töölö (1942–63). He taught at the Sibelius Academy (1948–57), serving as head of its church music dept. (1955–57); was vice-director (1956–59) and director (1959–71) there. He was a member of the Swedish Royal Academy of Music.

WORKS: Sonatina for String Quartet (1927); *Pastorale* for Orch. (1934); Nocturne for Cello and Orch. (1936); *Sonatina di Natale* for Flute, Cello, and Piano (1936); *Psalm 40* for Baritone, Chorus, Organ, and Strings (1939); *Jouluyö* (Christmas Night) for Chorus, Organ, and Orch. (1941); *Laatokka* (Lake Ladoga), symphonic legend (1944); *Kangastuksia* (Mirages) for Mezzo-soprano and Orch. (1945); Trio for Flute, Viola, and Piano (1945); *Saimoon helmi* (The Pearl of Saimaa), cantata (1949); *Toccata* for Orch. (1953); piano pieces; organ pieces; sacred music.

Kuyper, Elisabeth, Dutch conductor and composer; b. Amsterdam, Sept. 13, 1877; d. Lugano, Feb. 26, 1953. She studied with Max Bruch in Berlin. From 1908 to 1920 she taught theory at the Hochschule für Musik there; was founder (1908) and conductor of the Berlin Tonkünstlerinnen Orch.; in 1922 she led concerts of the London Women's Sym. Orch., and in 1923 conducted the N.Y. Women's Sym. Orch.; she settled in Lago Maggiore in Brissago. She composed a Sym.; Violin Concerto; several violin sonatas; Ballade for Cello and Piano; Piano Trio; songs.

Küzdö, Victor, Hungarian-American violinist, teacher, and composer; b. Budapest, Sept. 18, 1859; d. Glendale, Calif., Feb. 24, 1966, at the age of 106. He studied at the Budapest Cons. with Karl Huber; made his debut there in 1882; toured in Europe, and visited the U.S. in 1884 and 1887. In 1894 he settled in N.Y.; from 1918 to 1931, taught at the summer school of the Chicago Musical College; in 1932, settled in Glendale. He became totally blind in 1950. He publ. several violin pieces, among them a Serenade and *Witches' Dance.*

Kuznetsova, Maria (Nikolaievna), prominent Russian soprano; b. Odessa, 1880; d. Paris, April 25, 1966. She studied in St. Petersburg with Tartakov; made her debut in an operatic production at the Cons. there (1904); then was a member of the Maryinsky Theater (1905–13), where she distinguished herself in Russian roles and as Juliette, Elsa, Carmen, and Madama Butterfly. She made guest appearances in Berlin, Paris, and London. After the Russian Revolution (1918), she fled to Sweden; made appearances in Stockholm and Copenhagen, and then toured with her own opera company; later was artistic adviser of Barcelona's Teatro Liceo.

Kuznetzov, Konstantin (Alexeievich), Russian musicologist; b. Novocherkassk, Sept. 21, 1883; d. Moscow, May 25, 1953. He studied at the Univ. of Heidelberg and at the Univ. of Moscow; later studied music history with Wolfram and composition with Reger in Germany. He taught at the Univ. of Moscow (1912–14) and the Univ. of Odessa (1914–20). He worked at Moscow's State Inst. for Music Research (from 1921); taught at the Moscow Cons. (1923–31; 1934–38; 1941–49), where he intermittently served as a prof., head of the music history dept., and head of the dept. of Russian music; was named senior research fellow at Moscow's Inst. of Fine Arts (1946). An erudite scholar, he wrote on music history from a broad sociological standpoint; publ. *Studies in Music* (Odessa, 1919), *Introduction to the History of Music* (Moscow and Petrograd, 1923), and *Glinka and His Epoch* (Moscow, 1926).

Kvam, Oddvar S(chirmer), Norwegian composer; b. Oslo, Sept. 9, 1927. He studied at the Oslo Cons. (1943–52), where he took a degree in harmony and counterpoint (1950) and received training in piano and theory; also obtained a law degree from the Univ. of Oslo (1949); he later studied conducting with Odd Grüner-Hegge (1955–57) and composition with David Monrad Johansen (1964–66) in Oslo, completing his training in composition with Herman Koppel in Copenhagen (1969). He practiced law while devoting much time to composition; was the 1st composer to hold the influential post of chairman of the Norwegian Arts Council (1985–88). Two of his orch. works, *Prologue* (1967) and *Opening* (1974), received awards at the inauguration of the Oslo Concert Hall in 1977. Kvam's compositions tend to be free of tonally based strictures, yet they preserve a feeling of tonality.

WORKS: OPERAS: *The Dream of the 13th Hour* (1986); *The Cabinet,* chamber opera (1989). **ORCH.:** 2 syms.: No. 1, *3 Contrasts* (1972); No. 2, *Communication* (1981); *Prologue* (1967); *Afterwards Everything Is Too Late* (1967; rev. for Narrator and Orch., 1977); *Concert Overture* (1969); *Dialogues* for Oboe and Strings (1973; also for Oboe and Clarinet Quintet); *Opening* (1974); *Suffragette* for Piano and Orch. (1975); *Legend* for String Orch. (1975); *Trim* for School Orch. (1976); *Ostinato festoso* (1976); *Vibrations* (1976–82); *From the Young People's World* for Orch., Percussion, and Electric Guitar (1978); *Phoenix* for Cello and Orch. (1988); *Colors* for Harmonica and String Orch. (1989); *Towards the End* (1989). **SYMPHONIC BAND:** *Concert March* (1977); *Flight 77* (1977); *Blow Out!* (1978); *Vacation* (1982); *Apollonia* (1983); *Homecoming* (1984); *Sightseeing* (1987); *Downwards and Upwards* (1987). **CHAMBER:** 3 string quartets (1973, 1976, 1985); *3 Centrifuges* for Wind Quintet (1975); *5 Monophonies,* 1 for Each of the Woodwind Quintet Instruments (1977); Trio for Piano, Violin, and Cello (1979); *Ave Maria* for Violin or Cello and Piano or Guitar (1981); *Trio ostinato* for Flute, Viola, and Guitar (1982); *Andando e tornando* for 2 Violins (1984); *Changes* for Violin, Viola, and Cello (1988). **PIANO:** *A Rather Ordinary Week* (1960–68); *Encyclopedia* (1976); *Plastic Arts* (1979); *Hommage à Prokofiev* (1983); *4 Hands across the Sea* for Piano, 4-hands (1984). **VOCAL:** *Festival Cantata* for Men's Chorus and Orch. (1966); *Epinikion* for Chorus and Orch. (1971–75); *Clarina the Clarinet,* fairy tale for Narrator and Clarinet (1975); *The Great Language* for Chorus (1977); *Psalmus XVIII* for Chorus and Organ (1979); *Come!* for Chorus and Piano (1982); *Querela pacis* for 2 Choruses and Piano (1983); *Born Anew* for Chorus (1988); songs.

Kvandal (real name, **Johansen**), **(David) Johan,** Norwegian composer, organist, and music critic, son of **David Monrad Johansen;** b. Christiania, Sept. 8, 1919. He studied organ and conducting at the Oslo Cons.; also received training in theory and composition from Geirr Tveitt, in theory from Per Steenberg, and in organ from Arild Sandvold; pursued his studies in composition with Joseph Marx in Vienna and with Nadia Boulanger in Paris. He was organist at Oslo's Valerengen Church (1959–74) and a member of the governing board of the Soc. of Norwegian Composers (1960–75); also wrote music criticism.

WORKS: String Trio (1951); *Song of Stella* for Soprano and String Orch. (1952); 3 solo cantatas: No. 1 for Soprano or Tenor and Orch. (1953); No. 2, *O Domine Deus,* for Soprano and Organ (1966); No. 3 for Baritone and Organ (1970); 3 string quartets (1954, 1966, 1983); *Variations and Fugue* for Orch. (1954); *Norwegian Overture* (1959); Sym. No. 1 (1959); Duo for Violin and Cello (1959); *Symphonic Epos* for Orch. (1961–62); Concerto for Flute and Strings (1963); orch. suite from incidental music to the play *Skipper Worse* (1967); *Sinfonia concertante* (1968); *Introduction and Allegro* for Horn and Piano (1969); *3 Fantasy Country Dances* for Piano (1969); Wind Quintet (1971); *Nature,* chamber cantata for Baritone, Violin, and Piano (1972); *Antagonia,* concerto for 2 String Orchs. and Percussion (1972); *Duo concertante* for 2 Pianos (1974); Quartet for Flute, Violin, Viola, and Cello (1975); Concerto for Oboe and String Orch. (1977); Violin Concerto (1979); *Triptychon* for Orch. (1979); Concerto for Chamber Orch.

(1980); *Night Music*, nonet (1981); *Overture Fantasy* for 8 Winds and Double Bass (1982); Sonata for Solo Harp (1984); Sonata for Solo Guitar (1984); *Poem* for Violin and Piano, or Organ, or String Orch. (1985); *Visions norvégiennes* for Orch. (1985); *The Miracle* for Chorus (1986); Sonata for Solo Accordion (1987); Horn Quartet (1988); songs.

Kvapil, Jaroslav, significant Czech composer; b. Fryšták, April 21, 1892; d. Brno, Feb. 18, 1958. He studied with Nešvera in Olmütz (1902–6), Janáček at the Brno Organ School (1906–9), and Reger at the Leipzig Cons. (1911–13). He was in the Austrian army during World War I; then was conductor of the Brno Beseda (1919–47); then taught at the Janáček Academy of Music there (1947–57). His works show the double influence of Janáček's national and rhapsodic style and Reger's strong polyphonic idiom.

WORKS: Opera, *Pohádka máje* (A Romance in May; 1940–43; Prague, May 12, 1950; rev., Brno, 1955); oratorio, *Lví srdce* (The Lion's Heart; 1928–31; Brno, Dec. 7, 1931); 2 cantatas: *A Song on Time That Is Passing* (1924) and *Small Italian Cantata* (1950); 4 syms.: No. 1 (1913–14); No. 2 (1921); No. 3 (1936–37); No. 4, *Vítězná* (Victory; 1943); *Thema con variazioni e fuga* for Orch. (1912); 2 violin concertos (1927–28; 1952); *Z těžkých dob* (From Anxious Times), symphonic variations (1939); *Slavonic (Jubilee) Overture* (1944); *Burlesque* for Flute and Orch. (1945); *Svítání* (Daybreak), symphonic poem (1948–49); Oboe Concerto (1951); Piano Concerto (1954); 3 violin sonatas (1910, 1914, 1931); Sonata for Violin and Organ (1931); Piano Trio (1912); Cello Sonata (1913); 6 string quartets (1914, 1926, 1931, 1935, 1949, 1951); Piano Quintet (1914–15); Brass Quintet (1925); Variations for Trumpet and Piano (1929); Suite for Trombone and Piano (1930); *Intimate Pictures* for Violin and Piano (1934); Wind Quintet (1935); Violin Sonatina (1941); *Fantasy* for Cello and Piano (1942); Nonet (1944); Quartet for Flute, Violin, Viola, and Cello (1948); Duo for Violin and Viola (1949); Suite for Viola and Piano (1955); also 3 piano sonatas (1912, 1925, 1946); Variations for Piano (1914); *Fantasy in the Form of Variations* for Piano (1952); *10 Pieces* for Piano (1957); Fantasy for Organ (1935); several song cycles; many transcriptions of folk songs; a piano album of 100 folk songs from Moravian Slovakia (1914).

BIBL.: L. Kundera, *J. K.* (Prague, 1944).

Kvernadze, Bidzina (actually, **Alexander Alexandrovich**), Russian composer; b. Signahi, Georgia, July 29, 1928. He studied with Andrey Balanchivadze at the Tbilisi Cons. (graduated, 1953). Among his works are 2 piano concertos (1950, 1965); Violin Concerto (1956); *Dance-Fantasy* for Orch. (1959); Sym. (1961); violin pieces; film music.

Kvitka, Klyment, Ukrainian ethnomusicologist; b. Kiev, Feb. 4, 1880; d. Moscow, Sept. 19, 1953. During his early career, he was a lawyer and a judge; it was not until after 1920 that he devoted himself to music. He was director of the Ethnomusicology Bureau at the Ukrainian Academy of Sciences (1922–33); during the 1920s he conducted fieldwork on ritual song, the music of minorities (Bulgarians, Albanians, and Greeks in the Ukraine), and that of professional folk musicians. In 1933 he moved to Moscow, where he founded the Folk Music Bureau at the Moscow Cons.; he also studied organology and the geographical dispersal of songs and instruments. His song collections (1917–18; 1922), noted for their scholarship and erudition, are landmarks in Ukrainian ethnomusicology.

Kwalwasser, Helen, American violinist and teacher, daughter of **Jacob Kwalwasser;** b. Syracuse, N.Y., Oct. 11, 1927. She studied with Louis Persinger (1936–39), with Zimbalist at the Curtis Inst. of Music in Philadelphia (1939–41), and with Galamian (1941–48); made her debut in N.Y. on March 25, 1947; then toured Europe (1949); then was active in N.Y. as a performer and teacher.

Kwalwasser, Jacob, American music psychologist and educator, father of **Helen Kwalwasser;** b. N.Y., Feb. 27, 1894; d. Pittsburgh, Aug. 7, 1977. He received his education at the Univs. of Pittsburgh and Iowa (Ph.D., 1926). He taught in the public schools in Pittsburgh (1918–23); was head of the dept. of public school music at the Univ. of Iowa (1923–26); from 1926 to 1954 he was a prof. and head of the dept. of music education at Syracuse Univ. He was co-author of the Kwalwasser-Dykema Music Tests; publ. a manual on the subject in 1913; also collaborated in establishing the Kwalwasser-Ruch Musical Accomplishment Test, and various other melodic, harmonic, and instrumental tests; publ. numerous magazine articles on music education.

WRITINGS: *Tests and Measurements in Music* (1927); *Problems in Public School Music* (1932; rev. 1941); *Exploring the Musical Mind* (N.Y., 1955).

Kwast, James, famous German pianist and teacher; b. Nijkerk, the Netherlands, Nov. 23, 1852; d. Berlin, Oct. 31, 1927. He studied with his father and Ferdinand Böhme; later with Reinecke and Richter at the Leipzig Cons., Theodor Kullak and Würst in Berlin, and Brassin and Gevaert in Brussels. He taught at the Cologne Cons. (1874–83) and the Frankfurt Hoch Cons. (1883–1903); then went to Berlin as a prof. at the Klindworth-Scharwenka Cons. (1903–6) and the Stern Cons. (from 1906). He was greatly esteemed by his colleagues and students; among the latter were Grainger and Pfitzner. He wrote a Piano Concerto and other piano music. His 1st wife, Antonia (d. Stuttgart, Feb. 10, 1931), was a daughter of Ferdinand Hiller; his 2nd wife, **Frieda Hodapp-Kwast** (b. Bargen, Aug. 13, 1880; d. Bad Wiessee, Sept. 14, 1949), was a pianist.

Kwiatkowski, Ryszard, Polish composer; b. Jaranowo Kujawy, June 27, 1931. He studied composition with T. Szeligowski and W. Rudziński at the Warsaw State College of Music (1958–63); then took private lessons with Petrassi in Rome. His style of composition is free from repressive modernism, but is imbued with impressionistic metaphors, even when he wanders into the forbidding fields of dodecaphony.

WORKS: *Serenade* for Trombone and Orch. (1957); 4 syms.: No. 1 (1958); No. 2 (1964); No. 3 (1969); No. 4 (1970); *Pictures* for Chamber Orch. (1963); *Colors* for Orch. (1963); *Shapes* for Orch. (1963); 3 string quartets (1963, 1966, 1970); *Lights* for Orch. (1964); *Polyphonic Music* for Orch. (1967); Piano Quintet, with Metronome (1968); *Music* for Winds, Percussion, and Piano (1968); 2 percussion quartets (1968, 1971); *Pulsations* for Orch. (1969; Szczecin, Sept. 10, 1976); *Lyrical Music* for Violin and Double Bass (1969); *7 Photographs from the Moon* for Piano (1970); *Apotheosis of October* for Orch. (1972); *Marine Impressions* for String Quartet (1973); *Legend* for Viola and Piano (1975); *Seascapes* for Piano Trio (1975); Piano Sonata (1975); *Baltic Pictures* for Mezzo-soprano, 2 Violins, Cello, and Piano (1975); Violin Sonata (1976); Tuba Concerto (1977); *Lyrics of Torún* for Chamber Orch. (1980); Sonata No. 2 for Piano (1983); *Sea Stories* for String Orch. (1984).

Kyllönen, Timo-Juhani, Finnish composer; b. Saloinen, Dec. 1, 1955. He was reared in Sweden, where he commenced playing the accordion when he was 9; in 1976 he entered the Gnessin Inst. in Moscow as an accordion student of Friedrich Lips, and also took courses in composition and conducting before graduating in 1982; he then studied composition, orchestration, and counterpoint with Alexei Nikolaiev, Yuri Fortunatov, and Georgi Tchugaiev at the Moscow Cons., graduating in 1986; then taught theory and composition at the Sibelius Academy in Helsinki.

WORKS: ORCH.: Sym. No. 1 (Novosibirsk, June 17, 1986); *Passio secularis* for Soprano, Men's Chorus, and Orch. (1988–89; Helsinki, Dec. 8, 1989). CHAMBER: 2 string quartets (1985, 1989); Trio No. 1 for Violin, Cello, and Accordion (1986); Trio No. 2 for Piano, Violin, and Cello (1988); *Elegia "quasi una sonata"* for Violin and Piano (1987); *Desolazione* for Organ and Oboe (1987); *Contrasts* for 5 Percussionists (1988); several pieces for solo instruments; various choral and vocal pieces with instrumental accompaniment; scores for stage, television, and films.

Kyriakou, Rena, Greek pianist; b. Iraklion, Feb. 25, 1918. She was a proverbial child prodigy who made her public debut in Athens at 6; later studied in Vienna with Paul Weingarten and Richard Stöhr; then joined the piano class of Isidor Philipp at the Paris Cons.; she also studied composition there with Henri Busser; received its premier prix at the age of 15. She then embarked on a concert career in programs of neglected piano pieces by 18th- and 19th-century composers.

Kyser, Kay (James King Kern), American bandleader; b. Rocky Mount, N.C., June 18, 1906; d. Chapel Hill, N.C., July 23, 1985. He studied at the Univ. of North Carolina (graduated, 1928); although he never learned to read music or play an instrument, he led his own college band while still a student; he gained success as a bandleader when he began appearing at Chicago's Blackhawk Restaurant (1934); it was at that locale that he commenced his radio show "Kay Kyser's Kampus Klass" (1937), which then became a favorite network radio show as "Kay Kyser's Kollege of Musical Knowledge" (from 1938). As the "old professor," he presided over a program consisting of music, comedy skits, and quizzes for contestants; a version for network television ran from 1949 until his retirement in 1951. His most celebrated recording was of Loesser's *Praise the Lord and Pass the Ammunition* (1942), which became a hit during his appearances before Allied troops during World War II. He also appeared in 8 films (1939–44).

L

La Barbara, Joan (Linda, née Lotz), American composer and experimental vocalist; b. Philadelphia, June 8, 1947. She learned piano from her grandfather; later sang in church and school choirs, and joined a folk music group. She studied voice with Helen Boatwright at the Syracuse Univ. School of Music (1965–68) and music education at N.Y. Univ. (B.S., 1970); also studied voice with Phyllis Curtin at the Berkshire Music Center at Tanglewood (1967–68) and with Marion Szekely-Freschl at the Juilliard School in N.Y. In 1971 she made her debut as a vocalist at N.Y.'s Town Hall with Steve Reich and Musicians, with whom she continued to perform until 1974; also worked with Philip Glass (1973–76). She toured in the U.S. and Europe; in 1979 she was composer-in-residence in West Berlin under the aegis of the Deutscher Akademischer Austauschdienst; taught voice and composition at the Calif. Inst. of the Arts in Valencia (from 1981). In 1979 she married **Morton Subotnick.** A champion of contemporary music, she developed her performing talents to a high degree; her vocal techniques include multiphonics and circular breathing, with unique throat clicks and a high flutter to match. Her compositions effectively exploit her vocal abilities.

WORKS: LARGE ENSEMBLE: *Chandra* for Amplified Solo Voice, Men's Voices, and Chamber Orch. (1978; rev. 1983); *The Solar Wind III* for Voice and Chamber Orch. (1984). **AMPLIFIED VOICE(S):** *Hear What I Feel* for Voice (1974); *Vocal Extensions* for Voice and Live Electronics (1975); *Space Testing* for Acoustic Voice (1976); *Cathing* for Voice and Tape (1977); *12 for 5 in 8* for 5 or More Voices (1979); *October Music: Star Showers and Extraterrestrials* for Voice and Tape (1980); *Winds of the Canyon* for Voice and Tape (1982); *Time(d) Trials and Unscheduled Events* for Tape (1984; rev. for 8 Solo Voices, 1987); *Loose Tongues* for 8 Solo Voices and Tape (1985). **AMPLIFIED VOICE(S) AND INSTRUMENTS:** *Thunder* for Voice, 6 Timpani, and Electronics (1975); *Ides of March I to VIII* for Voice and Instruments (1975–77); *Chords and Gongs* for Voice, Cimbalom, and Gongs (1976); *Silent Scroll* for Voice, Flute, Cello or Double Bass, Percussion, Gong, and Zoomoozophone (1982); *The Solar Wind I* for 1 Solo Voice and 10 Instruments (1983) and *II* for 16 Solo Voices, 2 Percussion, Flute, and Electric Keyboard (1983); also tape and video pieces.

Labarre, Théodore (François-Joseph), eminent French harpist, conductor, and composer; b. Paris, March 5, 1805; d. there, March 9, 1870. He studied privately with Cousineau, Bochsa, and Nadermann; then at the Paris Cons. with Dourlen, Eler, Fétis, and Boieldieu. From 1824 to 1847 he lived alternately in London and Paris; was a conductor at the Paris Opéra-Comique (1847–49); was made director of the imperial chapel in 1852, and in 1867 a prof. at the Paris Cons. He publ. a *Méthode complète pour la harpe* (Paris, 1844). He wrote operas, ballets, numerous pieces for harp, and songs.

Labatt, Leonard, Swedish tenor; b. Stockholm, Dec. 4, 1838; d. there, March 7, 1897. He studied with J. Günther; then with Masset in Paris; made his debut in Stockholm as Tamino in *Die Zauberflöte* (1866); in 1868–69, was at the Dresden Court Opera; from 1869 to 1883, at the Vienna Court Opera; he sang in London in 1881; made an American tour in 1888–89. He was especially fine in Wagnerian roles.

L'Abbé (real name, **Saint-Sévin**), family of French musicians: **(1) Pierre-Philippe Saint-Sévin,** cellist, known as **L'Abbé**

l'aîné; b. probably in Agen, c.1700; d. Paris, May 15, 1768. He was maître de musique at the church of St. Caprais in Agen, where he took Holy Orders and the name L'Abbé. After settling in Paris, he became a cellist in the orch. of the Opéra (1727); he was soon made 1st cellist, a post he held until his retirement in 1767; he also played in the orch. of the Concert Spirituel from the 1740s to 1762, and likewise was a member of the musique de la chambre of the French court from about 1753 until his death. He was greatly esteemed as a virtuoso on his instrument.

(2) Pierre Saint-Sévin, cellist, brother of the preceding, known as **L'Abbé le cadet;** b. probably in Agen, c.1710; d. Paris, March 1777. He took minor orders at the church of St. Caprais in Agen; then settled in Paris, where he became a cellist in the orch. of the Opéra (1730). He was a member of the basses du Petit Chœur there until 1767, and then leader of the basses du Grand Chœur until his retirement in 1776; also played at the Sainte-Chapelle (1764–77).

(3) Joseph-Barnabé Saint-Sévin, violinist and composer, son of **L'Abbé l'aîné,** known as **L'Abbé le fils;** b. Agen, June 11, 1727; d. Paris, July 20, 1803. A precocious child, he began his musical training with his father; secured a position in the orch. of the Paris Comédie-Française through winning a competition when he was only 11; then continued his studies with Leclair (1740–42). He was a member of the orch. of the Opéra from 1742 until his retirement in 1762; however, he was denied a pension on the ground that he was too young, although he had served the requisite number of years. He also appeared as a soloist; made his solo debut at the Concert Spirituel in 1741, and continued to appear there until 1754. In later years he devoted himself mainly to teaching. With the coming of the Revolution, he was forced to eke out a living as a member of the orch. of the Théâtre de la République and des Arts. He eventually was granted a minuscule pension and lived out his last days in obscurity. He was one of the most important French musicians of his day. A distinguished performer, he publ. the valuable treatise *Principes du violon pour apprendre le doigté de cet instrument, et les differens agremens dont il est susceptibles* (Paris, 1761; 2nd ed., 1772). He was also a fine composer, producing a number of notable syms. and sonatas. He was one of the 1st composers to write out cadenzas in full in several of his sonatas.

WORKS: ORCH.: *Premier simphonie en concert* for Strings and Basso Continuo (c.1751); *Second simphonie* (c.1752); 6 Syms. for Strings and Basso Continuo, op. 2 (1753); *Menuet[s] de MM. Exaudet et Granier, mis en grand symphonie avec des variations* for 2 Violins, Oboes or Flutes, Viola, 2 Horns, and Cello or Bassoon (1764). **CHAMBER:** 6 Sonates for Violin and Basso Continuo, op. 1 (1748); Symphonie for 2 Horns (1750); *Suite d'airs* for 2 Oboes, Viola d'Amore, and Viola (1754); *Premier [-Troisième] recueil d'airs français et italiens avec des variations,* op. 3 (1756), op. 4 (1757), op. 5 (1758); *Recueil d'airs* for Violin, op. 6 (c.1759); *Jolis airs ajustés et variés* for Violin, op. 7 (1763); 6 Sonates for Violin and Basso Continuo, op. 8 (1763); *Recueil quatrième de duos d'Opéra-Comique* for 2 Violins (1772).

LaBelle, Patti (real name, **Patricia Louise Holte**), black American singer of popular music and actress; b. Philadelphia, Oct. 4, 1944. She sang in a local Baptist church choir, then teamed up with 3 other youthful singers to form the Bluebelles Quartet, achieving gold status in 1962 with their 1st recording, *I Sold My Heart to the Junkman.* As Patti LaBelle and the Bluebelles, they toured regularly and made recordings. The quartet became a trio in 1967, assumed the name Labelle in 1970, and then proved successful as a funk rock outfit. After recording several successful albums, they struck gold with their recording *Night Birds* (1974). Affecting an outrageous stage persona, the trio embarked on a major tour of the U.S. during the 1974–75 season; they became the 1st pop group ever to appear at N.Y.'s Metropolitan Opera House. When the trio broke up in 1976, Patti launched a solo career, bringing out the particularly fine album *Released* in 1980. She first

appeared as an actress on television in 1981 and then sang numbers for the sound track and acted in the film *Beverly Hills Cop* (1985). Although her music remains lively and interesting through its rock, disco, and pop incarnations, her most striking contributions have been through her lesser-known but nonetheless extraordinarily flexible and expressive jazz vocalizations. Her album *Winner in You* (1986) proved a particularly popular success.

BIBL.: *Current Biography* (July 1986).

Labèque, Katia (b. Hendaye, March 3, 1950) and **Marielle** (b. Hendaye, March 6, 1952), extraordinarily gifted French sisters, duo-pianists. They began to study piano in early childhood with their mother, a pupil of Marguerite Long, making their formal debut in Bayonne in 1961. After completing their studies with Jean-Bernard Pommier at the Paris Cons., they were awarded 1st prize at their graduation in 1968. They subsequently embarked upon a remarkable career as duo-pianists, touring widely in Europe, North America, the Middle East, and the Far East. In addition to giving numerous recitals, they also appeared with the leading orchs. of the world. Their repertoire is catholic, ranging from the masterworks of the past to contemporary scores by Messiaen, Boulez, Berio, and others; they play popular works as well, from Scott Joplin to Gershwin; they championed the latter's duo-piano versions of *Rhapsody in Blue,* Piano Concerto in F, and *An American in Paris.*

BIBL.: D. Hendricks, "K. and M. L.: A Dynamic Duo," *Ovation* (Aug. 1986).

Labey, Marcel, French conductor and composer; b. Le Vésinet, Seine-et-Oise, Aug. 6, 1875; d. Nancy, Nov. 25, 1968. He studied law in Paris, receiving his degree in 1898; then turned his attention to music, studying piano with Delaborde, harmony with Lenormand, and composition with d'Indy at the Paris Schola Cantorum; taught piano there, and at d'Indy's death (1931), became director; was also director of the César Franck School (from 1935). He wrote music in a late Romantic style.

WORKS: Opera, *Bérengère* (1912; Le Havre, April 12, 1929); 3 syms. (1903, 1908, 1934); *Ouverture pour un drame* (Paris, Jan. 22, 1921); *Suite champêtre* for Orch. (1923); Piano Sonata; Viola Sonata; 2 violin sonatas; String Quartet; Piano Trio; Piano Quartet; Piano Quintet; songs; etc.

Labia, Fausta, Italian soprano, sister of **Maria Labia;** b. Verona, April 3, 1870; d. Rome, Oct. 6, 1935. She studied with her mother and with Aldighieri; made her debut as Alice in *Robert le Diable* in Verona (1892). She sang in Stockholm (1893–95) and Lisbon (1895–96); then appeared in various Italian opera centers, including Milan's La Scala and Rome's Teatro Costanzi (1901). She sang in Barcelona (1904–5); made her last stage appearance in Buenos Airea (1912); subsequently taught in Rome. In 1907 she married the tenor Emilia Perea. She wrote the method *L'arte del respiro nella recitazione e nel canto* (1936).

Labia, Maria, noted Italian soprano, sister of **Fausta Labia;** b. Verona, Feb. 14, 1880; d. Malcesine del Garda, Feb. 10, 1953. She received her musical education from her mother, an excellent amateur singer; made her operatic debut as Mimi in Stockholm on May 19, 1905. She scored a remarkable success as Tosca at Berlin's Komische Oper (1907), continuing to sing there until 1911. She appeared as Tosca in her debut with the Manhattan Opera on Nov. 9, 1908. After a season there, she continued her career in Europe with engagements in Paris, Vienna, and Milan. She was arrested as a German agent by the Italian authorities in 1916 and spent a year in prison in Ancona. After the close of World War I, she resumed her career in Rome (1919); subsequently became closely associated with the role of Felice in Wolf-Ferrari's *I quatro rusteghi,* which she sang many times from 1922 until 1936. After teaching at the Warsaw Cons. (1930–34), she gave instruction in Rome and Siena. She wrote *Guardare indietro: che fatica* (1950).

Labitzky, August, German violinist, conductor, and composer, son of **Joseph Labitzky;** b. Petschau, Oct. 22, 1832; d. Reichenhall, Aug. 28, 1903. He studied at the Prague Cons., and with Ferdinand David and Hauptmann in Leipzig. He became a violinist in his father's Karlsbad spa orch. in 1853, and then its conductor in 1868; composed some 50 dances.

Labitzky, Joseph, Bohemian-born German violinist, conductor, and composer, father of **August Labitzky;** b. Schönfeld, Eger, July 5, 1802; d. Karlsbad, Aug. 19, 1881. He studied with Veit in Petschau; in 1820, joined the spa orch. in Marienbad as 1st violinist; then occupied a similar post in Karlsbad. He studied with Winter in Munich (1823–24); then toured southern Germany before founding his own orch in 1825; returning to Karlsbad in 1835, he was made conductor of the spa orch., which became successful; when he stepped down from his Karlsbad post (1868), he was succeeded by his son August. He wrote over 300 dances, many of which enjoyed a great vogue until the rise of Gungl and Johann Strauss, Jr.
BIBL.: E. Rychnovsky, "J. L., der Walzerkönig Böhmens," *Keilberg-Jahrbuch 1909* (St. Joachimsthal, 1909); M. Kaufmann, *J. L.* (Reichenberg, 1930).

Lablache, Luigi, famous Italian bass of French and Irish descent; b. Naples, Dec. 6, 1794; d. there, Jan. 23, 1858. He was admitted at 12 to the Conservatorio della Pietà dei Turchini in Naples, where he studied with Valesi; commenced his operatic career as a buffo napoletano in Fioravanti's *La Molinara* at the Teatro San Carlino there (1812), then studied in Messina, where he appeared as a buffo; was made primo basso cantante in Palermo (1813). He gained acclaim at his La Scala debut in Milan as Dandini in Rossini's *La Cenerentola* (1817), and continued to sing there until 1823; also sang in Rome, Turin, and Venice. He then became a principal member of Barbaja's Vienna opera enterprise (1824); Ferdinand I of Naples made him a member of the royal chapel and the Teatro San Carlo in Naples. He scored a triumphant London debut at the King's Theatre as Geronimo in Cimarosa's *Il matrimonio segreto* (March 30, 1830), and continued to appear there every year until 1852 (1833–34 excepted). He made his Paris debut as Geronimo at the Théâtre-Italien (Nov. 4, 1830), where he was a great favorite until 1851; created the roles of Sir George Walton in Bellini's *I Puritani* (Jan. 25, 1835), and Marino Faliero (March 12, 1835) and Don Pasquale (Jan. 3, 1843) in Donizetti's operas, ensuring his success with Paris audiences. During one of his stays in England (1836–37), he served as singing teacher to Princess Victoria. He was a principal singer of Gye's company at Covent Garden (1854) until his retirement from the stage owing to ill health (1856). Although he was best known for his buffo roles, he was capable of remarkable serious portrayals as well.
BIBL.: F. Castil-Blaze, *Biographie de L.* (Paris, 1850); G. Widén, *L. L.* (Göteborg, 1897).

Labor, Josef, Austrian pianist, organist, and composer; b. Horowitz, June 29, 1842; d. Vienna, April 26, 1924. He lost his sight as a youth; studied with Sechter at the Vienna Cons.; in 1863, was tutor to the princesses of Hannover, who were then living in exile with their family in Vienna. He played in London (1865), Paris, and Russia; in 1868, returned to Vienna, where he settled as a teacher; among his students were Bittner and Schoenberg. He wrote a Konzertstück for Piano and Orch.; church music; chamber music; pieces for organ and for piano; songs.
BIBL.: P. Kundi, *J. L., Sein Leben und Wirken* (Vienna, 1963; contains a thematic catalogue).

La Borde (Laborde), Jean-Benjamin (-François) de, French violinist, composer, and writer on music; b. Paris, Sept. 5, 1734; d. there (guillotined), July 22, 1794. He studied violin with Dauvergne and composition with Rameau; was chamberlain to Louis XV, and a member of the Compagnie des Fermiers-Généraux; then withdrew from the court and devoted himself to composition. He wrote about 30 stage pieces, mostly opéras comiques, and many chansons; also an *Essai sur la musique*

ancienne et moderne (Paris, 1780); *Mémoires historiques sur Raoul de Coucy* [with] *recueil de ses chansons en vieux langage, avec la traduction et l'ancienne musique* (Paris, 1781); *Mémoires sur les proportions musicales, le genre énarmonique . . . avec une lettre de l'auteur de l'Essai à M. l'Abbé Roussier* (Paris, 1781).
BIBL.: J. de Visme, *Un Favori des dieux* (Paris, 1935); E. Haraszti, "J.-B. d.L.B. et la musique hongroise," *Revue de Musicologie*, XIX (1935).

Labroca, Mario, Italian composer; b. Rome, Nov. 22, 1896; d. there, July 1, 1973. He studied composition with Malipiero and Respighi, and graduated from the Parma Cons. in 1921. He held numerous administrative and teaching posts; was music director of the Teatro La Fenice in Venice (from 1959); lectured at the Univ. of Perugia (from 1960). He was closely connected with the theater and the cinema in Italy and composed many scores for plays and films.
WORKS: Operas: *La Principessa di Perepepè* (Rome, Dec. 11, 1927) and *Le tre figliole di Babbo Pallino* (Rome, Jan. 27, 1928); *Sinfonia* (1927); Sym. (1935); *Stabat Mater* for Soprano, Chorus, and Orch. (Rome, Dec. 15, 1935); *3 cantate sulla Passione di Cristo* for Baritone, Chorus, and Orch. (1950); *8 madrigali di Tomaso Campanella* for Baritone and Orch. (1958); 3 string quartets (1923, 1932, 1939); Piano Trio (1925); Suite for Viola and Piano (1923).

Labunski, Felix (actually, **Feliks Roderyk**), Polish-born American composer, brother of **Wiktor Labunski;** b. Ksawerynów, Dec. 27, 1892; d. Cincinnati, April 28, 1979. Brought up in a musical environment (his father, a civil engineer, was an amateur singer; his mother played the piano), he began studying piano as a child; then entered the Warsaw Cons., where he was a student of Marczewski and Maliszewski (1922–24). He met Paderewski, who arranged for him a stipend at the École Normale de Musique in Paris, where he studied with Boulanger and Dukas (1924–34). In 1927 he formed, with Czapski, Perkowski, and Wiechowicz, the Assoc. of Young Polish Composers in Paris. Returning to Poland, he held the post of director of the dept. of classical music of the Polish Radio in Warsaw (1934–36). In 1936 he emigrated to America; became a naturalized citizen in 1941. He lived in N.Y. until 1945, when he joined the staff of the Cincinnati College of Music, continuing in this position when it merged with the Cincinnati Cons. of Music in 1955; he retired in 1964 as prof. emeritus in composition. In his music, he remained faithful to the legacy of Romanticism as cultivated in Poland and Russia.
WORKS: *Danse fantastique* for Orch. (1926); *Triptyque champêtre* for Orch. (1931); *Polish Cantata* (1932); *Ptaki* (The Birds) for Soprano and Orch. (1934); String Quartet No. 1 (1935); *Divertimento* for Flute and Piano (1936); Sym. No. 1, in G minor (1937); *In Memoriam*, symphonic poem in memory of Paderewski (1941); *Suite* for String Orch. (1941; Berkeley, Calif., Aug. 2, 1942); *Song without Words* for Soprano and Strings (1946); *There Is No Death*, cantata (1950); Variations for Orch. (1951); Sym. No. 2, in D (1954); *Elegy* for Orch. (Cincinnati, Dec. 11, 1955); *Images of Youth*, cantata (Cincinnati May Festival, May 11, 1956); *Xaveriana*, fantasy for 2 Pianos and Orch., commissioned for the 125th anniversary of Xavier Univ. (1956); *Divertimento* for Flute, Oboe, Clarinet, and Bassoon (1956); *Diptych* for Oboe and Piano (1958); *Symphonic Dialogues* (Cincinnati, Feb. 9, 1961); String Quartet No. 2 (1962); *Canto di aspirazione* for Orch. (1963; revision of the slow movement of his Sym. No. 2); *Polish Renaissance Suite* for Orch. (1967); *Intrada festiva* for Brass Choir (1968); *Salut à Paris*, ballet suite for Orch. (1968); *Music for Piano and Orch.* (1968); *Primavera* for Orch. (Cincinnati, April 19, 1974).

Labunski, Wiktor, Polish-born American pianist and composer, brother of **Felix (Feliks Roderyk) Labunski;** b. St. Petersburg, April 14, 1895; d. Kansas City, Mo., Jan. 26, 1974. He studied at the St. Petersburg Cons. with Nikolayev (piano), and Kalafati and Wihtol (composition); later studied piano with

Felix Blumenfeld and Safonov, and conducting with Emil Mlynarski. From 1919 to 1928 he was head of the piano dept. at the Krakow Cons.; then went to the U.S.; made his debut in 1928 as a pianist at Carnegie Hall in N.Y.; was an instructor at the Nashville (Tenn.) Cons. (1928–31), then prof. and director of the Memphis (Tenn.) College of Music (1931–37); in 1937, was appointed prof. and director of the Kansas City Cons. of Music. In 1920 he married Wanda Mlynarska, daughter of his teacher.

Works: Sym. in G minor (1936); Piano Concerto (Kansas City, Feb. 16, 1939, composer soloist); Concerto for 2 Pianos and Orch. (Kansas City, May 31, 1957); many piano pieces.

Bibl.: J. Belanger, *W. L.: Polish-American Musician in Kansas City, 1937–1974* (diss., Columbia Univ., 1982).

Laburda, Jiří, Czech composer; b. Soběslav, April 3, 1931. He received private training in composition from Karel Hába and Zdeněk Hůla and in musicology from Eduard Herzog; took courses in music education and philology at the Charles Univ. in Prague (1952–55); after studies at the Prague Teacher Training College (1957–61), he returned to the Charles Univ., where he took his Ph.D. (1970, with a diss. on Shostakovich's syms.) and subsequently taught. His works follow along traditional paths with infusions of aleatory and dodecaphonic writing; his vocal and chamber pieces are particularly effective.

Works: BALLET: *Les Petits Riens* (1967; Liberec, March 15, 1986). ORCH.: *Burlesca* for Horn and Orch. (Košice, April 11, 1963); Piano Concerto (1969; Prague, Feb. 5, 1973); *Sinfonia* (1975); Concerto for Accordion and String Orch. (Kralupy, April 21, 1980); Concertino for Trumpet and String Orch. (Mariánskié Lázné, July 17, 1981); *Pastorale* for Flute and String Orch. (1981; Joschkar-Ola, Russia, March 2, 1987); *Overture solenne* (1983; Prague, June 18, 1985); *Divertimento in RE* for String Orch. (1983; České Budějovice, March 22, 1984); *Concerto da camera* for Violin and Orch. (1986). CHAMBER: *Kasace I* for Flute, Clarinet, Horn, Trumpet, and Trombone (1978), *II* for Violin, Clarinet or Oboe d'Amore, Percussion, and Piano (1979), and *III* for Bass Clarinet and Percussion (1979); Partita for Violin (1978); Brass Quintet No. 2 (1980); Sonata for Trombone and Piano (1981); Sonata for Solo Marimba (1983); *Rondo* for 3 Violins (1984); Sonata for 2 Marimbas (1986); Sonata for Clarinet and Piano (1987); Sonata for Tuba and Piano (1987); Trio for Oboe, Clarinet, and Bassoon (1989); piano pieces. VOCAL: *Glagolitica* for Soloists, Chorus, Organ, Brass, and Percussion (1964; Freiburg im Breisgau, Jan. 11, 1990); *Metamorphoses* for Soloists, Chorus, and Orch. (1966; Wolfsburg, May 18, 1969); *Marriage* for Soloists, Women's Chorus, and Piano (1980; Prague, Nov. 12, 1989); choruses; songs.

Laccetti, Guido, Italian singer and composer; b. Naples, Oct. 1, 1879; d. Cava dei Tirreni, Oct. 8, 1943. He studied at the Naples Cons.; from 1925, taught at the Palermo Cons. His works include the operas *La Contessa di San Remo* (1904); *Hoffmann* (Naples, 1912); *Il miracolo* (Naples, 1915); *Carnasciali* (Rome, 1925); *La favola dei gobbi* (1935).

Lacerda, Francisco (Inácio da Silveira de Sousa Pereira Forjaz) de, Portuguese conductor, musicologist, and composer; b. Ribeira Seca, S. Jorge, Azores, May 11, 1869; d. Lisbon, July 18, 1934. He studied at the Lisbon Cons.; received a government stipend for study in Paris, where he took a course with d'Indy at the Schola Cantorum. In Paris he associated himself with Bourgault-Ducoudray and worked with him in the International Folklore Assoc.; also conducted concerts. At the outbreak of World War I (1914), he returned to Portugal; later founded the Orquesta Filarmonica in Lisbon (1923). He ed. the important *Cancioneiro musical português* (Lisbon, 1935–36), a collection of some 500 folk songs. Among his compositions are the symphonic poems *Adamastor* (1902) and *Almourol* 1926), several ballets, incidental music, and piano pieces.

Bibl.: F. de Sousa, *F. d.L.: Exposição commemorativa do primeiro centenario do nascimento* (Lisbon, 1969).

Lach, Robert, eminent Austrian musicologist and composer; b. Vienna, Jan. 29, 1874; d. Salzburg, Sept. 11, 1958. He was a pupil of R. Fuchs at the Cons. of the Gesellschaft der Musikfreunde in Vienna (1893–99); also studied philosophy and musicology at the Univ. there with Wallaschek and Adler (1896–99); completed his study of musicology with Rietsch at the German Univ. in Prague (Ph.D., 1902, with the diss. *Studien zur Entwicklungsgeschichte der ornamentalen Melopöie*; publ. in Leipzig, 1913). From 1913 to 1918 he was director of the music collection of Vienna's Hofbibliothek; remained in that post when it became the Staatsbibliothek (1918–20). From 1915 he lectured at the Univ. of Vienna; was prof. of musicology and chairman of its Musicological Inst. (1927–39); was also prof. at the Vienna Academy of Music (from 1924). He recorded for the Phonogram Archives of Vienna the songs of Russian prisoners of World War I (with particular emphasis on Asian and Caucasian nationalities), and publ. numerous papers on these melodies. He was pensioned in 1939, and lived in Vienna in retirement, devoting his time to the compilation of oriental glossaries (Babylonian, Sumerian, Egyptian, etc.). In 1954 he became general ed. of the new Denkmäler der Tonkunst in Österreich. In addition to his books, he contributed articles to various music journals; also wrote philosophical poems and mystical plays. Among his compositions are 10 syms., 25 string quartets, 14 string quintets, 8 string sextets, other chamber music, 8 masses, cantatas, etc.

Writings: *W.A. Mozart als Theoretiker* (Vienna, 1918); *Zur Geschichte des Gesellschaftstanzes im 18. Jahrhundert* (Vienna, 1920); *Zur Geschichte des musikalischen Zunftwesens* (Vienna, 1923); *Die vergleichende Musikwissenschaft: Ihre Methoden und Probleme* (Vienna, 1924); *Das Konstruktionsprinzip der Wiederholung in Musik, Sprache und Literatur* (Vienna, 1925); *Vergleichende Kunst- und Musikwissenschaft* (Vienna, 1925); *Geschichte der Staatsakademie und Hochschule für Musik und darstellende Kunst in Wien* (Vienna, 1927); *Das Ethos in der Musik Franz Schuberts* (Vienna, 1928).

Bibl.: W. Graf, ed., *R. L.: Persönlichkeit und Werk* (Vienna, 1954).

Lachenmann, Helmut Friedrich, German composer; b. Stuttgart, Nov. 27, 1935. He studied with Jürgen Uhde (piano) and J.N. David (theory and counterpoint) at the Stuttgart Hochschule für Musik (1955–58); also took courses in Darmstadt (1957), and then with Nono in Venice (1958–60) and Stockhausen in Cologne (1963–64); pursued research in the electronic music studio at the Univ. of Ghent (1965). He taught theory at the Stuttgart Hochschule für Musik (1966–70); then was an instructor at the Ludwigsburg Pädagogische Hochschule (1970–76); also taught a master class in composition at the Univ. of Basel (1972–73); subsequently taught at the Hannover Hochschule für Musik (from 1976). He was elected a member of Berlin's Akademie der Künste (1984).

Works: ORCH.: *Souvenir* for 41 Instruments (1959); *Notturno (Musik für Julia)* for Cello and Small Orch. (1966–68; Brussels, April 25, 1969); *Air* for Percussion and Orch. (1968–69; Frankfurt, Sept. 1, 1969); *Kontrakadenz* (Stuttgart, April 23, 1971); *Klangschatten—mein Saitenspiel* (Hamburg, Dec. 20, 1972); *Fassade* for Tape and Orch. (Bonn, Sept. 22, 1973); *Schwankungen am Rand* for Brass and Strings (1974–75; Donaueschingen, Oct. 17, 1975); *Accanto* for Clarinet and Orch. (Saarbrücken, May 30, 1976); *Tanzsuite mit Deutschlandlied* for String Quartet and Orch. (1979–80; Donaueschingen, Oct. 18, 1980); *Harmonica* for Tuba and Orch. (1981–83; Saarbrücken, May 15, 1983); *Mouvement (vor der Erstarrung)* for Chamber Ensemble (1982–84; Paris, Nov. 12, 1984); *Ausklang* for Piano and Orch. (1984–85; Cologne, April 18, 1986); *Staub* (1986); *Tableau* (1987). CHAMBER: 5 *Strophen* for 9 Instruments (1961); *Introversion I* for 6 Instruments (1963) and *II* for 6 Instruments (1964); *Szenario*, electronic music (1965); String Trio (1965); *Intérieur I* for Percussion (1966); *Trio fluido* for Clarinet, Viola, and Percussion (1966); *temA* for Flute, Mezzo-soprano, and Cello (1968); *Pression* for Cello (1969); *Dal niente (Intérieur III)* for Clarinet (1970); *Gran torso* for

String Quartet (1971–72); *Salut für Caudwell* for 2 Guitars (1977); *Studie* for Violin (1986); also several vocal works, including *Les Consolations* for 16 Voices and Orch. (1967–68; 1977–78; Darmstadt, Aug. 10, 1978); piano music; etc.

Lachmann, Robert, noted German musicologist; b. Berlin, Nov. 28, 1892; d. Jerusalem, May 8, 1939. He studied languages in Berlin and London; served in the German army during World War I, when he began to collect folk melodies from African and Indian war prisoners; later studied musicology with Stumpf and Johannes Wolf, and Arabic with Mittwoch at the Univ. of Berlin; received his Ph.D. there (1922) with the dissertation *Die Musik in den tunesischen Städten*, publ. in the *Archiv für Musikwissenschaft*, V (1923). He worked at the Berlin State Library (1924–26); after a period in Kiel, he resumed his work at the Berlin State Library (1927), serving under Wolf; was ousted by the Nazis as a Jew in 1933. He went to Palestine (1935) and became a member of the faculty of the Univ. of Jerusalem.

WRITINGS: *Musik des Orients* (Breslau, 1929); *Die Musik der aussereuropäischen Natur- und Kulturvölker* in Bücken's Handbuch der Musikwissenschaft series (1929); E. Gerson-Kiwi, ed., *Robert Lachmann: Posthumous Works*, I (Jerusalem, 1974).

BIBL.: E. Gerson-Kiwi, "R. L.: His Achievement and His Legacy," *Yuval*, III (1974).

Lachmund, Carl (Valentine), American pianist, conductor, teacher, and composer; b. Booneville, Mo., March 27, 1857; d. Yonkers, N.Y., Feb. 20, 1928. He studied at the Cologne Cons. with Hiller (graduated, 1875), with Moszkowski in Berlin, and later with Liszt in Weimar (1881–84); taught at the Scharwenka Cons. in Berlin, and appeared as a pianist, touring America with August Wilhelmj in 1880. Settling in N.Y. in 1891, he conducted the Women's String Orch. (from 1896); then founded his own cons. (1905). He publ. a vol. relating to his period of study with Liszt (issued in a German tr. as *Mein Leben mit Liszt*, 1970); also composed 2 concert overtures, an "Italian" Suite for Orch., chamber music, and piano pieces.

Lachner, family of German musicians, all brothers:
(1) Theodor Lachner, organist and composer; b. Rain-am-Lech, 1788; d. Munich, May 23, 1877. He served as Munich court organist throughout most of his career; was known as a composer of choral music and lieder.
(2) Franz Paul Lachner, conductor and composer; b. Rain-am-Lech, April 2, 1803; d. Munich, Jan. 20, 1890. He studied piano and organ with his father, Anton Lachner, the town organist. He then went to Vienna, where he studied with Sechter and Stadler; became a close friend of Schubert, and also came to know Beethoven; was made organist of the Lutheran Church (1823); then was assistant conductor (1827–29) and principal conductor (1829–34) of the Kärnthnertortheater. He was conductor of the Mannheim National Theater (1834–36); then was court conductor (1836–52) and Generalmusikdirektor (1852–65) in Munich.

WORKS: Operas: *Die Bürgschaft* (Pest, Oct. 30, 1828); *Alidia* (Munich, April 12, 1839); *Catarina Cornaro* (Munich, Dec. 3, 1841); *Benvenuto Cellini* (Munich, Oct. 7, 1849); 8 syms. (1828–51); 7 suites for Orch. (1861–81); 2 harp concertos (1828, 1833); Flute Concerto (1832); *Die vier Menschenalter*, cantata (1829); *Moses*, oratorio (1833); 8 masses; *Stabat Mater*; choral works; much chamber music; piano pieces; songs.

BIBL.: G. Wagner, *F. L. als Liederkomponist, nebst einem biographischen Teil und dem thematischen Verzeichnis sämtlicher Lieder* (diss., Univ. of Mainz, 1969).

(3) Ignaz Lachner, organist, conductor, and composer; b. Rain-am-Lech, Sept. 11, 1807; d. Hannover, Feb. 24, 1895. He studied with his father and then in Vienna (1824) with his brother Franz, whom he succeeded as organist of the Lutheran Church; was assistant conductor of the Kärnthnertortheater (1825–28) and the Court Opera (1828–31) there. He was court conductor in Stuttgart (1831–36) and Munich (1836–53), conductor of the Hamburg Opera (1853–58), then court

conductor in Stockholm (1858–61); subsequently was principal conductor in Frankfurt (1861–75).

WORKS: Operas: *Der Geisterturm* (Stuttgart, 1837); *Die Regenbrüder* (Stuttgart, May 20, 1839); *Loreley* (Munich, 1846); also singspiels and other dramatic works; ballets; syms.; masses; chamber music; piano pieces.

BIBL.: H. Müller, *I. L.: Versuch einer Würdigung, mit Werkverzeichnis* (Celle, 1974).

(4) Vincenz Lachner, organist, conductor, and composer; b. Rain-am-Lech, July 19, 1811; d. Karlsruhe, Jan. 22, 1893. He studied with his father and then with his brothers in Vienna, succeeding Ignaz as organist of the Kärnthnertortheater (1834) and at the Mannheim National Theater (1836). He conducted the German Opera in London (1842), then became conductor of the Frankfurt Opera (1848); he was pensioned in 1872. From 1884 he taught at the Karlsruhe Cons. He wrote syms., overtures, chamber music, and numerous songs, but was best known for his 4-part male choruses.

Lachnith, Ludwig Wenzel, Bohemian horn player and composer; b. Prague, July 7, 1746; d. Paris, Oct. 3, 1820. He studied violin, harpsichord, and horn; then joined the orch. in Pfalz-Zweibrücken; about 1780 he went to Paris and studied with Rodolphe (horn) and F.A. Philidor (composition). He is known chiefly for his pasticcios; an instance is his oratorio *Saul* (April 6, 1803), with music taken from scores by Mozart, Haydn, Cimarosa, Paisiello, Gossec, and Philidor. He also arranged the music of Mozart's *Die Zauberflöte*, to a libretto reworked by Étienne Morel de Chefdeville, and produced it under the title *Les Mystères d'Isis* (Aug. 20, 1801), justly parodied as *Les Misères d'ici*. In several of his ventures he had the older Kalkbrenner as his collaborator. Among his original works were the operas *L'Heureuse Réconciliation* (June 25, 1785) and *Eugénie et Linval* (1798); syms.; 6 concertos for Harpsichord or Piano; chamber music.

Lacombe, Louis (Trouillon), French pianist and composer; b. Bourges, Nov. 26, 1818; d. Saint-Vaast-la-Hougue, Sept. 30, 1884. He studied piano at the Paris Cons. with Zimmerman, winning the premier prix at the age of 13. After touring through France, Belgium, and Germany, he took courses with Czerny, Sechter, and Seyfried in Vienna. Following another concert tour, he settled in Paris (1839), concentrating on composition. His essay *Philosophie et musique* was publ. posth. (Paris, 1895).

WORKS: STAGE: *L'Amour*, melodrama (Paris, Dec. 2, 1859); *La Madone*, opera (Paris, Jan. 16, 1861); *Le Tonnelier de Nuremberg*, comic opera (perf. as *Meister Martin und seine Gesellen*, Koblenz, March 7, 1897); *Winkelried*, opera (Geneva, Feb. 17, 1892); *La Reine des eaux* (perf. as *Die Korrigane*, Sondershausen, March 12?, 1901); *Der Kreuzritter*, comic opera (Sondershausen, March 21, 1902); 2 dramatic syms. with Soli and Chorus: *Manfred* (1847) and *Arva ou Les Hongrois* (1850); *Lassan et Friss*, Hungarian fantasy for Orch. (1890); *Sapho*, cantata (1878); choruses; chamber music; piano pieces.

BIBL.: E. Bourdin, *La Musique et les musiciens: L. L.* (Paris, 1882); H. Boyer, *L. L. et son œuvre* (Paris, 1888); L. Gallet, *Conférence sur L. L. et son œuvre* (Paris, 1891); E. Jongleux, *Un Grand Musicien méconnu: L. L.* (Bourges, 1935).

Lacombe, Paul, French composer; b. Carcassonne, Aude, July 11, 1837; d. there, June 5, 1927. He studied in Carcassonne with François Teysserre, an organist. He was a prolific composer; his works total more than 150, including *Ouverture symphonique* (1876); 3 syms. (No. 3 won the prize of the Société des Compositeurs de Musique, 1886); *Suite pastorale* for Orch.; *Marche dernière* for Orch.; *Scène au camp* for Orch.; 3 violin sonatas; Cello Sonata; 3 trios; String Quartet; Mass; Requiem; songs; characteristic piano pieces.

BIBL.: L. Moulin, *P. L. et son œuvre* (Paris, 1924).

Lacome (actually, **Lacôme d'Estalenx**), **Paul (-Jean-Jacques),** French composer; b. Le Houga, Gers, March 4, 1838; d. there, Dec. 12, 1920. He studied with José Puig y Absubide, organist in Aire-sur-Adour (1857–60); then went to Paris, where he became known as a composer of operettas, including *Jeanne, Jeannette et Jeannot* (Paris, Oct. 27, 1876) and *Ma Mie Rosette* (Paris, Feb. 4, 1890); he also wrote orch. suites, chamber music, piano pieces, and over 200 songs.

Laderman, Ezra, noted American composer; b. N.Y., June 29, 1924. He studied at the High School of Music and Art in N.Y., where he appeared as soloist in the premiere of his 1st Piano Concerto with the school orch. in 1939; then studied composition with Wolpe in N.Y. (1946–49) and with Miriam Gideon at Brooklyn College of the City Univ. of N.Y. (B.A., 1949); took courses with Luening and Moore (composition) and Lang (musicology) at Columbia Univ. (M.A., 1952). He held 3 Guggenheim fellowships (1955, 1958, 1964). He taught at Sarah Lawrence College (1960–61; 1965–66); was composer-in-residence and prof. at the State Univ. of N.Y. in Binghamton (1971–82); served as director of the music program of the N.E.A. (1979–82) and was active at the American Academy in Rome (1982–83). In 1989 he became dean of the Yale Univ. School of Music. Laderman's works are marked by an effective utilization of contemporary techniques with a patina of traditional lyricism.

WORKS: STAGE: OPERAS: *Jacob and the Indians* (1954; Woodstock, N.Y., July 24, 1957); *Goodbye to the Clowns* (1956; N.Y., May 22, 1960); *The Hunting of the Snark*, opera-cantata after Lewis Carroll (1958; N.Y., March 26, 1961; 1st stage perf., N.Y., April 13, 1978); *Sarah* (CBS-TV, Nov. 30, 1958); *Air Raid* (1965); *Shadows among Us* (1967); *And David Wept*, opera-cantata (1970; CBS-TV, April 11, 1971; 1st stage perf., May 31, 1980); *The Questions of Abraham*, opera-cantata (CBS-TV, Sept. 30, 1973); *Galileo Galilei* (1978; Binghamton, N.Y., Feb. 3, 1979; based on the oratorio *The Trials of Galileo*). MUSICAL COMEDY: *Dominique* (1962). OTHER DRAMATIC: *Duet for Flute and Dancer* (1956); *Dance Quartet* for Flute, Clarinet, Cello, and Dancer (1957); *Esther*, dance score for Narrator, Oboe, and String Orch. (1960); *Song of Songs*, dance score for Soprano and Piano (1960); *Solos and Chorale*, dance score for 4 Mixed Voices (1960). INCIDENTAL MUSIC: *Machinal* (N.Y., April 7, 1960); *The Lincoln Mask* (N.Y., Oct. 30, 1972); also numerous film and television scores. ORCH.: *Leipzig Symphony* (Wiesbaden, May 1945); 7 numbered syms.: No. 1 (Rome, July 2, 1964); No. 2, *Luther* (1969); No. 3, *Jerusalem* (1973; Jerusalem, Nov. 7, 1976); No. 4 (1980; Los Angeles, Oct. 22, 1981); No. 5 for Soprano and Orch., *Isaiah* (1982; Washington, D.C., March 15, 1983); No. 6 (1983; Houston, Sept. 28, 1985); No. 7 (1984); 2 unnumbered piano concertos (N.Y., June 1939; 1957); Piano Concerto No. 1 (1978; Washington, D.C., May 12, 1979); Concerto for Bassoon and Strings (1948); Concerto for Violin and Chamber Orch. (1951; rev. 1960; CBS-TV, Nov. 10, 1963); *Organization No. 1* (1952); *Sinfonia* (1956); *Identity* (1959); *Stanzas* for 21 Solo Instruments (1959); *Magic Prison* for 2 Narrators and Orch. (N.Y., June 12, 1967); *Concerto for Orchestra* (Minneapolis, Oct. 24, 1968); Flute Concerto: *Celestial Bodies* for Flute and Strings (1968); *Priorities* for Jazz Band, Rock Band, and String Quartet (1969); Concerto for Viola and Chamber Orch. (1977; St. Paul, April 13, 1978); Violin Concerto (1978; Philadelphia, Dec. 11, 1980); *Summer Solstice* (Philadelphia, Aug. 5, 1980); Concerto for String Quartet and Orch. (Pittsburgh, Feb. 6, 1981); Concerto for Flute, Bassoon, and Orch. (1982; Philadelphia, Jan. 27, 1983); *Sonore* (Denver, Nov. 10, 1983); Cello Concerto (1984; Chicago, Feb. 22, 1990); Flute Concerto (1985; Detroit, Jan. 22, 1986); *Pentimento* (Albany, N.Y., May 16, 1986); Concerto for Violin, Cello, and Orch. (1987; Binghamton, N.Y., Feb. 25, 1988). ORATORIOS: *The Eagle Stirred* for Soloists, Chorus, and Orch. (1961); *The Trials of Galileo* for Soloists, Chorus, and Orch. (1967; later reworked into the opera *Galileo Galilei*); *A Mass for Cain* for Soloists, Chorus, and Orch. (1983); also cantatas and other vocal works. CHAMBER: String Quartet (1953); 8 numbered string quartets (1959, 1962, 1966, 1974, 1976, 1980, 1983, 1985); Cello Sonata (1948); 2 flute sonatas (1951, 1957); Piano Quintet (1951); Woodwind Quintet (1954); Piano Trio (1955; rev. 1959); Violin Sonata (1956); Wind Octet (1957); Clarinet

Sonata (1958); *Double Helix* for Flute, Oboe, and String Quartet (1968); *Concerto (Echoes in Anticipation)* for Oboe and 7 Instruments (1975); *Cadence* for 2 Flutes and 9 Strings (1978); Double String Quartet (1983); several keyboard works, including 2 piano sonatas (1952, 1955); 25 *Preludes for Organ in Different Forms* (1975); etc.

Ladmirault, Paul (-Émile), French composer; b. Nantes, Dec. 8, 1877; d. Kerbili en Kamoel, St. Nazaire, Oct. 30, 1944. As a child, he studied piano, organ, and violin; entered the Nantes Cons. in 1892, winning 1st prize in 1893; he was only 15 when his 3-act opera *Gilles de Retz* was staged in Nantes (May 18, 1893); he entered the Paris Cons. in 1895, studying with Gédalge and Fauré; subsequently returned to Nantes, where he taught at the Cons. His *Suite bretonne* (1902–3) and symphonic prelude *Brocéliande au matin* (Paris, Nov. 28, 1909) were extracts from a 2nd opera, *Myrdhin* (1902–9), which was never performed; the ballet *La Prêtresse de Koridwen* was produced at the Paris Opéra (Dec. 17, 1926). Other works include the operetta *Glycère* (Paris, 1928); Sym. (1910); *La Brière* for Orch. (Paris, Nov. 20, 1926); *En forêt*, symphonic poem (1932); incidental music to *Tristan et Iseult* (1929); *Valse triste* for Piano and Orch.; *Airs anciens* for Tenor, String Quartet, and Piano (1897); *Ballet bohémien* for Flute, Oboe, Double String Quartet, and Piano (1898); *Fantaisie* for Violin and Piano (1899); *Chanson grecque* for Flute and Piano (1900); Violin Sonata (1901); *De l'ombre à la clarté* for Violin and Piano (1936); piano pieces; songs; many arrangements of Breton folk songs.

BIBL.: C. Debussy, "P.-É. L.," *Gil Blas* (March 9, 1903).

Ladnier, Tommy (Thomas), black American jazz trumpeter; b. Mandeville, La., May 28, 1900; d. N.Y., June 4, 1939. He studied trumpet with "Bunk" Johnson; after working in Chicago with King Oliver, he played in Europe with Sam Wooding's band (1925–26), with Fletcher Henderson (1926–27), and again with Wooding in Europe (1928–29). He continued to make appearances in Europe until his return to the U.S. in 1931; then played with Sidney Bechet, and later led his own quintet.

Ladunka, Naum, Russian composer; b. Dec. 13, 1730; d. St. Petersburg, Aug. 2, 1782. One of the few secular Russian composers of the 18th century, he is chiefly known for his arrangements of many Russian folk songs.

Ladurner, Ignace Antoine (François Xavier) (actually, **Ignaz Anton Franz Xaver Joseph**), Austrian pianist, teacher, and composer of Tirolean descent; b. Aldein, near Bolzano, Aug. 1, 1766; d. Villain, near Massy, March 4, 1839. He studied with his uncle at the Benediktbeuren monastery, and succeeded his father as organist in Algund; then studied at the Lyceum Gregorianum in Munich; subsequently became a pianist in the service of Countess Heimhausen in Longeville. In 1788 he settled in Paris, where he became active as a teacher; taught piano at the Paris Cons. (1797–1802); settled in Villain (1836). He wrote the operas *Wenzel, ou Le Magistrat du peuple* (Paris, April 10, 1793) and *Les Vieux Fous, ou Plus de peur que de mal* (Paris, Jan. 15 or 16, 1796); 15 piano sonatas; 6 violin sonatas; variations; divertissements; etc.

BIBL.: G. de Saint-Foix, "Les Premiers Pianistes parisiens (VIII): I.-A. L. (1766–1839)," *La Revue Musicale*, VIII/1 (1926).

La Fage, (Juste-) Adrien (-Lenoir) de, French writer on music and composer; b. Paris, March 28, 1801; d. Charenton, March 8, 1862. He studied in Paris with Perne and Choron, and in Rome with Baini. Returning to Paris, he devoted himself to scholarly analysis of music theory. He ended his life at the Charenton Insane Asylum. He was a prolific composer of sacred music; also produced much chamber music.

WRITINGS: *Manuel complet de musique vocale et instrumentale* (6 vols., 1836–38; elaborated from Choron's sketches and notes); *Séméiologie musicale* (1837; an epitome was also publ. in 1837 as *Principes élémentaires de musique*); *De la chanson considérée sous le rapport musical* (1840); *Histoire générale de la musique et de la danse* (2 vols., 1844; incomplete); *De l'unité tonique et de la fixation d'un diapason universel* (1859); *Essais de diphthérographie musicale* (1864); many works on plainsong: *De la réproduction des livres de plain-chant romain* (1853); *Cours complet de plain-chant* (2 vols., 1855–56); *Nouveau traité de plain-chant* (1859; supplement to the former); *Routine pour accompagner le plain-chant;* etc.

BIBL.: R. Denne-Baron, *A. d.L.F.* (Paris, 1863).

L'Affilard, Michel, French singer, music theorist, and composer; b. c.1656; d. probably in Versailles, 1708. He was made chantre clerc at the Sainte-Chapelle in Paris (1679); was a member of the Versailles royal chapel (1683–1708). His major work is a treatise on sight singing, *Principes très faciles pour bien apprendre la musique* (Paris, 1694; 11th ed., 1747), which is notable because the tempo of the airs is indicated according to a pendulum, thus anticipating the use of the metronome.

BIBL.: E. Schwandt, "L. on the French Court Dances," *Musical Quarterly*, LX (1974); idem, "L.'s Published Sketchbooks," ibid., LXIII (1977).

Lafont, Charles-Philippe, noted French violinist; b. Paris, Dec. 1, 1781; d. in a carriage accident near Tarbes, Aug. 14, 1839. He received violin instruction first from his mother, and then with his uncle; then studied in Paris with Kreutzer and Rode. From 1801 to 1808 he toured Europe; then became solo violinist at the Russian court in St. Petersburg (1808); returned to Paris in 1815 as solo violinist to Louis XVIII. He engaged in a violin contest of skills with Paganini in Milan (1816). He made an extended tour with the pianist Henri Herz beginning in 1831, losing his life in southern France. He was also a composer; wrote an opera, *La Rivalité villageoise* (1799); 7 violin concertos; many other violin pieces with various instrumental groups; about 200 romances for voice. These works have no intrinsic value.

La Forge, Frank, American pianist, vocal teacher, and composer; b. Rockford, Ill., Oct. 22, 1879; d. while playing the piano at a dinner given by the Musicians' Club in N.Y., May 5, 1953. He studied piano with Leschetizky in Vienna; toured Germany, France, Russia, and the U.S. as accompanist to Marcella Sembrich (1908–18) and to Schumann-Heink (1919). In 1920 he settled in N.Y. as a voice teacher; among his students were Lawrence Tibbett, Marian Anderson, Lucrezia Bori, and Richard Crooks. He wrote many effective songs, including *To a Violet, Retreat, Come Unto These Yellow Sands, My Love and I, To a Messenger, I Came with a Song, Before the Crucifix,* and *Like a Rosebud,* and piano pieces.

Lagger, Peter, Swiss bass; b. Buchs, Sept. 7, 1930; d. Berlin, Sept. 17, 1979. He studied at the Zürich Cons. and at the Vienna Academy of Music; made his debut in Graz in 1953; then sang in Zürich (1955–57), Wiesbaden (1957–59), and Frankfurt (1959–63); from 1963 he was a leading member of the Berlin Deutsche Oper. He made appearances in Hamburg, Vienna, Paris, and Geneva, and also at the Salzburg, Aix-en-Provence, and Glyndebourne festivals. He won acclaim in lieder recitals as well.

Lagoanère, Oscar de, French conductor and composer; b. Bordeaux, Aug. 25, 1853; d. Paris, May 23, 1918. He studied at the Paris Cons. with Marmontel, Duprato, and Savard. From 1876 to 1908 he conducted operettas at various theaters in Paris; from 1908 to 1914, was administrator and director of music at the Théâtre de la Gaîté. He was a prolific composer of operettas, the most successful of which were *Le Cadeau d'Alain* (Paris, Sept. 14, 1902); *L'Habit de César* (Paris, May 14, 1906); *Amour et sport* (Paris, July 28, 1907); *Un Ménage au violon;* also piano pieces and songs.

La Grange, Henry-Louis de, eminent French writer on music; b. Paris, May 26, 1924. He was a scion of a distinguished family, his father being French and his mother an American. After studying belles lettres in Aix-en-Provence and at the Sorbonne in Paris, he took courses at the Yale Univ. School of Music (1945–53); then completed his musical training with Y. Lefébure (piano) and Boulanger (harmony, counterpoint, and analysis) in Paris. He wrote music criticism for various American and French periodicals. In 1960 he commenced exhaustive research on the life and works of Gustav Mahler, resulting in his monumental biography *Gustav Mahler: Chronique d'une vie* (3 vols., 1973–84; also in Eng.). He was a guest lecturer at Columbia Univ., N.Y. Univ., Stanford Univ., and Indiana Univ. (1974–81); in Geneva (1982), Brussels (1983–84), and Leipzig (1985); and at the Juilliard School, the Univ. of Southern Calif. in Los Angeles, and Johns Hopkins Univ. (1986). In Paris in 1986 he founded the Bibliothèque Musicale Gustav Mahler, a vast repository for researchers. He received many awards and honors, including his being made a Chevalier de la Légion d'honneur.

La Guerre, Élisabeth Jacquet de, French composer, organist, and clavecinist; b. Paris, 1659; d. there, June 27, 1729. A member of a family of professional musicians, she evinced talent at an exceptionally early age; was favored by the court of Louis XIV, completing her education under the patronage of Mme. de Montespan. She married Marin de La Guerre, organist of several Paris churches. Her works include an opera, *Céphale et Procris* (Paris, March 15, 1694); a ballet (1691); keyboard suites; a Violin Sonata; cantatas, mostly sacred; etc.

La Guerre, Michel de, French organist and composer; b. Paris, 1605 or 1606; d. there (buried), Nov. 13, 1679. He became organist at St. Leu when he was about 14; then was organist at Sainte-Chapelle from 1633 until his death; also was active at the court. His historical importance rests upon his being the composer of the 1st French comédie en musique, the pastorale *Le Triomphe de l'Amour sur bergers et bergères* (Louvre, Paris, Jan. 22, 1655), to a libretto by the court poet Charles de Beys; only the text is extant.

BIBL.: H. Quittard, "La Première Comédie française en musique," *Bulletin Français de la Société Internationale de Musique*, IV (1908).

La Hèle, George de, Netherlandish composer; b. Antwerp, 1547; d. Madrid, Aug. 27, 1586. After early training as a chorister, he was sent to Madrid to join the royal chapel of Philip II in 1560, remaining in Spain for 10 years. In 1571 he entered the Univ. of Louvain; in 1572, became choirmaster at the church of Saint-Rombaud in Malines, remaining there until 1574, when he accepted a similar post at the Tournai Cathedral; he returned to Madrid in 1582 to take charge of music in the royal chapel. In 1576 he won prizes in the competition at Évreux for his motet *Nonne Deo subjecta* and his chanson *Mais voyez mon cher esmoy.* His 8 masses (Antwerp, 1578), dedicated to Philip II, are all parody masses and are modeled on works by Josquin, Lassus, Rore, and Crecquillon; he also wrote other sacred works. L. Wagner ed. *Collected Works of George de la Hèle,* Corpus Mensurabilis Musicae, LVI (1972).

BIBL.: G. van Doorslaer, *G. d.l.H., Maître de chapelle-compositeur* (Antwerp, 1924).

La Houssaye, Pierre (-Nicolas), French violinist and composer; b. Paris, April 11, 1735; d. there, 1818. He studied violin with Pagin; later in Padua with Tartini. He played in the court Orch. of Parma; in 1768, went to London with Guglielmi; returning to Paris, was concertmaster and conductor of the Concert Spirituel (1777–81), of the Comédie-Italienne (1781–90), then at the Théâtre de Monsieur (1790–1801); he also taught at the Paris Cons. (1795–1802). He publ. an accomplished vol. of *Sei sonate* for Violin and Bass (Paris, c.1774); also wrote the comic opera *Les Amours de Courcy* (Théâtre de Monsieur, Aug. 22, 1790); his other works are not extant.

Laidlaw, Anna Robena, English pianist; b. Bretton, Yorkshire, April 30, 1819; d. London, May 29, 1901. She studied in Edinburgh with Robert Müller, in Königsberg, and in London with Henry Herz. In 1837 she played with the Gewandhaus Orch. in Leipzig; continued her successful career as a concert pianist until her marriage in 1855. She was an acquaintance of Schumann, whose *Fantasiestücke* are inscribed to her.

Laine, Cleo (real name, **Clementina Dinah Campbell**), remarkably gifted and versatile English singer and actress; b.

Southall, Middlesex, Oct. 28, 1927. Her father was a Jamaican street entertainer; in spite of the family's poverty, her mother succeeded in finding the means to pay for her singing, dancing, and piano lessons; after performing locally, she quit school when she was 14 to help support her family. In 1951 she became vocalist with **John Dankworth**'s jazz group, making her mark under the name Cleo Laine; they were married in 1958. Her career advanced as she became popular as a singer in cabarets, concerts, and recordings, and on television; she also appeared in stage and film roles as both a singer and an actress. As a concert artist, she made her recitals memorable by encompassing the repertoire from Schumann to Sondheim. She made her U.S. debut at N.Y.'s Alice Tully Hall in 1972, followed by a sensational appearance at Carnegie Hall in 1973. Thereafter she toured throughout the U.S., appearing with her husband and his group and also with the major sym. orchs. In 1985 she appeared on Broadway in Rupert Holmes's musical *The Mystery of Edwin Drood*. With a vocal range of nearly 4 octaves, she failed to be intimidated by any period or genre of the repertoire. She was made an Officer of the Order of the British Empire in 1979.

BIBL.: G. Collier, *C. and John: A Biography of the Dankworths* (London, 1976); *Current Biography* (Feb. 1986).

Lajarte, Théodore (-Édouard Dufaure de), French writer on music and composer; b. Bordeaux, July 10, 1826; d. Paris, June 20, 1890. He studied at the Paris Cons. with Leborne; was archivist of the Paris Grand Opéra (1873–90). He wrote some 10 opéras comiques, the most successful being *Le Secret de l'oncle Vincent* (1855); 2 ballets; choral works; music for military band. However, he is best known for his writings; also prepared *Airs à danser de Lully à Méhul* (Paris, 1876), *Chefs-d'œuvre classiques de l'opéra français* (Paris, 1880), and various vocal scores for the Michaelis collection (1880–82).

WRITINGS: *Bibliothèque musicale du théâtre de l'opéra: Catalogue historique, chronologique, anecdotique* (2 vols., Paris, 1876–78; reprint, Geneva, 1969); *Instruments Sax et fanfares civiles* (Paris, 1867); with A. Bisson, *Grammaire de la musique* (Paris, 1880; 3rd ed., 1913); idem, *Petit traité de composition musicale* (Paris, 1881); idem, *Petite encyclopédie musicale* (Paris, 1881–84); *Les Curiosités de l'Opéra* (Paris, 1883).

Lajeunesse, Marie Louise Cecilia Emma. See **Albani, Dame Emma.**

Lajtha, László, eminent Hungarian ethnomusicologist and composer; b. Budapest, June 30, 1892; d. there, Feb. 16, 1963. He studied piano with Árpád Szendy and theory with Victor von Herzfeld at the Budapest Academy of Music; traveled to Leipzig, Geneva, and Paris; returned to Budapest in 1913 to become an associate of the Ethnographical Dept. of the Hungarian National Museum. From 1919 to 1949 he was a prof. at the National Cons., and from 1952 was a teacher of musical folklore at the Academy of Music. In 1951 he was awarded the Kossuth Prize for his work on Hungarian folk music. He was a brilliant symphonist; his instrumental music is distinguished by consummate mastery of contrapuntal writing.

WORKS: 3 ballets: *Lysistrata* (1933; Budapest, Feb. 25, 1937); *Le Bosquet des quatre dieux* (1943); *Capriccio* (1944); 10 syms.: No. 1 (1936); No. 2 (1938); *Les Soli*, sym. for String Orch., Harp, and Percussion (1941); No. 3 (1947–48); No. 4, *Le Printemps* (The Spring; 1951); No. 5 (1952; Paris, Oct. 23, 1954); No. 6 (1955; Brussels, Dec. 12, 1960); No. 7 (1957; Paris, April 26, 1958); No. 8 (1959; Budapest, May 21, 1960); No. 9 (1961; Paris, May 2, 1963); *Hortobágy Suite* for Orch. (1935); 2 divertissements for Orch. (1936, 1939); 3 *Nocturnes* for Chorus and Orch. (1941); *In Memoriam* for Orch. (1941); 2 sinfoniettas for String Orch. (1946, 1956); 11 *Variations* for Orch. (1947); *Missa in tono phrygio* for Chorus and Orch. (1949–50); *Dramma per musica*, piano quintet (1922); 10 string quartets (1923; 1926; 1929; 1930; 5 *études*, 1934; 4 *études*, 1942; 1950; 1951; 1953; *Suite Transylvaine*, 1953); Piano Quartet (1925); 3 string trios (1927, 1932, 1945); Piano Trio (1928); Violin Sonatina (1930); Cello Sonata (1932); 2 trios for Harp, Flute, and Cello (1935, 1949); 2 quintets for Flute,

Violin, Viola, Cello, and Harp (*Marionettes*, 1937; 1948); *Sonata en concert* for Cello and Piano (1940); *Sonata en concert* for Flute and Piano (1958); *Sonata en concert* for Violin and Piano (1962); *Des esquisses d'un musicien* for Piano (1913); *Contes I* for Piano (1913); Piano Sonata (1914); *Scherzo and Toccata* for Piano (1930); Mass for Chorus and Organ (1951–52).

BIBL.: *L. L.* (Paris, 1954); *L. L.: Quelques œuvres* (Paris, 1961); J. Weissmann, "L. L.: The Symphonist," *Music Review*, XXXVI (1975).

Lakner, Yehoshua, Czech-born Swiss composer; b. Bratislava, April 24, 1924. He went to Palestine in 1941; studied there with Partos, Boscovich, and Pelleg in Haifa, Jerusalem, and Tel Aviv; in 1952, attended Copland's classes in composition at the Berkshire Music Center in Tanglewood; in 1959–60, was in West Germany, where he worked with Stockhausen and Kagel in the electronic studio of the West German Radio and with Bernd Alois Zimmermann in Cologne. He went to Switzerland (1963), becoming a naturalized Swiss citizen (1980); taught at the Zürich Cons. and Hochschule für Musik (from 1974). He was active as a composer for the theater. His music follows the tenets of the modern Central European school of Abstract Expressionism and its concomitant atonality, with an application of serial techniques; later took up computer music as well.

WORKS: Flute Sonata (1948); Sextet for Piano and Woodwinds (1951); *Toccata* for Orch. (1953); *Improvisations* for Viola (1958); *Hexachords* for Orch. (1960); *The Dream of Muhammed* for Choir and Electronic Music (1968); *Kaninchen* for Speaker, Percussion, and Tape (1973); *Umläufe* for Flute, Bass Clarinet, Piano, and 2 Tapes (1976); *Aus Fermaten* for Piano and 2 Tapes (1980–81); *Theater an der Winkelwiese* for Tape (1965–81); *Einwürfe* for Viola (1984); *Kreise und Signale* for 2 Pianos (1985).

Laks, Simon (actually, **Szymon**), Polish-born French composer; b. Warsaw, Nov. 1, 1901; d. Paris, Dec. 11, 1983. He studied at the Warsaw Cons. with Melcer (conducting) and Statkowski (composition); went to Paris in 1925, continuing his musical studies under Rabaud and Vidal at the Cons. He was interned by the Nazis in the Auschwitz and Dachau concentration camps (1941–44), where he was active as a performer and music director; after his liberation, he returned to Paris. He publ. his experiences of his internment as *La Musique d'un autre monde* (Paris, 1948; Eng. tr., 1989, as *Music of Another World*).

WORKS: *L'Hirondelle inattendue*, opera buffa (1965); *Farys*, symphonic poem (1924); *Symphonic Blues*, jazz fantasy (1928); *Suite polonaise* (1936); Sinfonietta for Strings (1936); *Suite on Silesian Tunes* for Small Orch. (1945); *Songs of the Polish Earth* for Orch. (1946); 3 *Warsaw Polonaises* for Chamber Orch. (1947); Sym. for Strings (1964); 5 string quartets (1928–64); Piano Trio (1950); *Concerto da camera* for Piano, 9 Wind Instruments, and Percussion (1963); Concertino for Wind Trio (1965); *Piano Quintet on Polish Themes* (1967); songs; keyboard pieces.

Lalande, Michel-Richard. See **Delalande, Michel-Richard.**

La Laurencie, Lionel de, important French musicologist; b. Nantes, July 24, 1861; d. Paris, Nov. 21, 1933. After studying law and science, he became a pupil of Léon Reynier (violin) and Alphonse Weingartner (harmony), and of Bourgault-Ducoudray at the Paris Cons. In 1898 he became a lecturer at the École des Hautes Études Sociales. He contributed regularly to several music journals. In 1916 he became ed. of Lavignac's *Encyclopédie de la musique et dictionnaire du Conservatoire*, to which he contributed articles on French music of the 17th and 18th centuries. The *Catalogue des livres de musiciens de la bibliothèque de l'Arsénal à Paris*, ed. by La Laurencie and A. Gastoué, was publ. in 1936.

WRITINGS: *La Légende de Parsifal et le drame musical de R. Wagner* (1888–94); *España* (1890); *Le Goût musical en France* (1905); *L'Académie de musique et le concert de Nantes*

(1906); "Rameau," in *Musiciens célèbres* (1908); "Lully," in *Les Maîtres de la Musique* (1911); "Contribution à l'histoire de la symphonie française vers 1750," *L'Année Musicale* (with G. de Saint-Foix; 1911); *Les Créateurs de l'opéra français* (1920; 2nd ed., 1930); *L'École française de violon, de Lully à Viotti* (3 vols., 1922–24); *Les Luthistes*, in *Musiciens célèbres* (1928); *La Chanson royale en France* (1928); *Inventaire critique du fonds Blancheton à la Bibliothèque du Conservatoire* (2 vols., 1930–31); *Chansons au luth et airs du XVIᵉ siècle* (with Thibault and Mairy; 1931); *Orfée de Gluck* (1934).

BIBL.: *Mélanges de musicologie offerts à M. L. d.l.L.* (Paris, 1933); B. Brook, "L. d.l.L.'s *L'École française de violon*," *Notes* (Sept. 1969).

Laliberté, (Joseph François) Alfred, Canadian pianist and composer; b. St. Jean, Quebec, Feb. 10, 1882; d. Montreal, May 7, 1952. He studied in Berlin (1900–1905) with Lutzenko (piano) and Klatte (theory); later took lessons with Carreño. In 1906 he formed a friendship with Scriabin and ardently championed his music. He wrote an opera, *Sœur Béatrice* (after Maeterlinck), 2 string quartets, several piano pieces (some on Canadian themes); also made arrangements of some 800 Canadian songs. Most of his music remains in MS; a few original songs have been publ.

Lalo, Charles, French esthetician; b. Périgueux, Feb. 24, 1877; d. Paris, April 1, 1953. He studied esthetics and philosophy in Bayonne, and then at the Univ. of Paris (Ph.D., 1908, with 2 dissertations: *Esquisse d'une esthétique musicale scientifique*; publ. in Paris, 1908; 2nd ed., augmented, 1939 as *Éléments d'une esthétique*; and *L'Esthétique expérimentale contemporaine*; publ. in Paris, 1908). He lectured at the Univ. of Bordeaux, then taught esthetics and art history at the Sorbonne in Paris (1933–53); was also president of the Société Française d'Esthétique.

WRITINGS (all publ. in Paris): *Les Sentiments esthétiques* (1910); *Introduction à l'esthétique* (1912; 4th ed., rev., 1952 as *Notions de philosophie, notions d'esthétique*); *L'Art et la vie sociale* (1921); *La Beauté et l'instinct sexuel* (1922); *L'Art et la morale* (1922); *L'Expression de la vie dans l'art* (1933); *L'Art loin de la vie* (1939); *L'Économie des passions* (1947); *Les Grandes Évasions esthétiques* (1947).

BIBL.: Special issue of *Revue d'esthétique*, VI/2 (1953).

Lalo, Édouard (-Victoire-Antoine), distinguished French composer of Spanish descent, father of **Pierre Lalo;** b. Lille, Jan. 27, 1823; d. Paris, April 22, 1892. He studied violin and cello at the Lille Cons.; after his father objected to his pursuing a career as a professional musician, he left home at age 16 to study violin with Habeneck at the Paris Cons.; he also studied composition privately with Schulhoff and Crèvecœur. He then made a precarious living as a violinist and teacher; also began to compose, producing some songs and chamber music between 1848 and 1860. In the meantime, he became a founding member of the Armingaud Quartet (1855), serving first as a violist and subsequently as 2nd violinist. Since his own works met with indifference, he was discouraged to the point of abandoning composition after 1860. However, his marriage to the contralto Bernier de Maligny (1865), who sang many of his songs, prompted him to resume composition. He wrote an opera, *Fiesque*, and sent it to a competition sponsored by the Théâtre-Lyrique in Paris in 1867. It was refused a production, a rebuke that left him deeply embittered. He was so convinced of the intrinsic worth of the score that he subsequently reworked parts of it into various other works, including the 1st *Aubade* for Small Orch., the *Divertissement*, and the Sym. in G minor. Indeed, the *Divertissement* proved a remarkable success when it was introduced at the Concert Populaire (Paris, Dec. 8, 1872). Sarasate then gave the premiere performance of his Violin Concerto (Paris, Jan. 18, 1874), and subsequently of his *Symphonie espagnole* for Violin and Orch. (Paris, Feb. 7, 1875). The latter work, a brilliant virtuoso piece with vibrant Spanish rhythms, brought Lalo international fame. It remains his best-known composition outside his native country. While continuing to produce orch. works, he had not given up his intention

to write for the stage. In 1875 he began work on the opera *Le Roi d'Ys*. The major portion of the score was finished by 1881, which allowed extracts to be performed in concerts. However, no theater was interested in mounting a production. While pursuing his work on several orch. pieces, he accepted a commission from the Opéra to write a ballet. Although the resulting work, *Namouna* (Paris, March 6, 1882), failed to make an impression, he drew a series of orch. suites from it, which became quite popular. He finally succeeded in persuading the Paris Opéra-Comique to produce *Le Roi d'Ys*. Its premiere on May 7, 1888, was an enormous success. Lalo was rewarded by being made an Officer of the Legion of Honor (1888). While *Le Roi d'Ys* is considered his masterpiece by his countrymen, his instrumental music is of particular importance in assessing his achievement as a composer. His craftsmanship, combined with his originality, places him among the most important French composers of his time.

WORKS: STAGE: *Fiesque*, opera (1866–67; not perf.; parts of the score subsequently used in various other works); *Namouna*, ballet (1881–82; Opéra, Paris, March 6, 1882; also made into a series of orch. suites); *Le Roi d'Ys*, opera (1875–88; Opéra-Comique, Paris, May 7, 1888); *Néron*, pantomime with Chorus (1891; Hippodrome, Paris, March 28, 1891; based on *Fiesque* and other works); *La Jacquerie*, opera (1891–92; Monte Carlo, March 9, 1895; Act 1 only; finished by A. Coquard). **ORCH.:** 2 syms. (n.d.; destroyed by the composer); 2 *Aubades* for 10 Instruments or Small Orch. (1872; based on *Fiesque*); *Divertissement* (Paris, Dec. 8, 1872; ballet music from *Fiesque* with the 2 aubades); Violin Concerto in F major, op. 20 (1873; Paris, Jan. 18, 1874); *Symphonie espagnole* for Violin and Orch., op. 21 (1874; Paris, Feb. 7, 1875); Cello Concerto in D minor (Paris, Dec. 9, 1877); *Fantaisie norvégienne* for Violin and Orch. (1878); *Rapsodie norvégienne* (Paris, Oct. 26, 1879; partly based on the *Fantaisie norvégienne*); *Romance-sérénade* for Violin and Orch. (1879); *Concerto russe* for Violin and Orch., op. 29 (1879); *Fantaisie-ballet* for Violin and Orch. (1885; from *Namouna*); *Andantino* for Violin and Orch. (from *Namouna*); *Sérénade* for Strings (from *Namouna*); Sym. in G minor (1886; Paris, 1887); Piano Concerto in F minor (1888–89). **CHAMBER:** *Fantaisie originale* for Violin and Piano, op. 1 (c.1848); *Allegro maestoso* for Violin and Piano, op. 2 (c.1848); *Deux impromptus* for Violin and Piano, op. 4: *Espérance* and *Insouciance* (c.1848); *Arlequin, esquisse-caractéristique* for Violin and Piano (c.1848; also orchestrated); Piano Trio No. 1, in C minor, op. 7 (c.1850); *Pastorale* and *Scherzo alla Pulcinella* for Violin and Piano, op. 8 (c.1850); Piano Trio No. 2, in B minor (c.1852); Violin Sonata, op. 12 (1853; orig. *Grand duo concertant*); *Chanson villageoise*, *Sérénade* for Violin or Cello and Piano, op. 14 (1854); *Allegro* for Cello and Piano, op. 16 (c.1856; also for Cello and Orch., op. 27, and as *Allegro symphonique*); *Soirées parisiennes* for Violin and Piano, op. 18 (1856; in collaboration with C. Wehle); Cello Sonata (1856); String Quartet in E-flat major, op. 19 (1859; rev. as op. 45, 1880); Piano Trio No. 3, in A minor, op. 26 (1880; Scherzo orchestrated, 1884); *Guitare* for Violin and Piano, op. 28 (1882); *Valse* for Cello and Piano (n.d.); Piano Quintet in A-flat major (n.d.); *Adagio*, 2nd fantaisie-quintette for Piano and String Quartet (n.d.). **VOCAL: COLLECTIONS:** 6 *romances populaires* (1849); 6 *mélodies*, op. 17 (1856); 3 *mélodies* (c.1870); 5 *Lieder* (1870); 3 *mélodies* (1887). **SONGS:** *Adieux au désert* (1848); *L'Ombre de Dieu* (c.1848); *Le Novice*, op. 5 (1849); *Ballade à la lune* (1860); *Humoresque* (c.1867); *Aubade* (1872); *Chant breton* (1884); *Marine*, op. 33 (1884); *Dansons*, op. 35 (1884; from *Namouna*); *Au fond des halliers* (1887; from *Fiesque*); *Le Rouge-gorge* (1887); *Veni, Creator, d'après un thème bohème* (n.d.). **CHORAL:** *Litanies de la sainte Vierge* (1876); *O salutaris* for Women's Voices, op. 34 (1884). **PIANO:** *Sérénade* (1864); *La Mère et l'enfant* for Piano, 4-hands, op. 32 (1873).

BIBL.: A. Pougin, "É. L.," *Le Ménestrel*, LVIII (1892); M. Dufour, *É. L.* (Lille, 1908); G. Servières, "La Musique de chambre d'É. L.," *Guide Musical*, LVI (1910); H. Malherbe, *É. L., conférence prononcée . . . 23 décembre, 1920* (Paris, 1921); P. Dukas, "É. L.," *Revue Musicale*, IV/5 (1923); A. Jullien,

"Quelques lettres inédites de L.," ibid.; P. Lalo, "La Vie d'É. L.," ibid.; G. Servières, *É. L.* (Paris, 1925); K. Brachtel, "É. L. zum 75. Todestag am 22 April," *Musica*, XXI (1967).

Lalo, Pierre, French music critic, son of **Édouard (-Victoire-Antoine) Lalo;** b. Puteaux, Sept. 6, 1866; d. Paris, June 9, 1943. He studied literature and philosophy; also took courses in modern languages at the École de Chartes and the École Polytechnique. He began writing music criticism for the *Journal des débats* (1896), then was music critic of *Le Temps* (1898–1914). He became known as a caustic critic of Debussy.
WRITINGS: *La Musique* (Paris, 1898–99; a selection of his articles); *Richard Wagner ou le Nibelung* (Paris, 1933); *De Rameau à Ravel: Portraits et souvenirs* (Paris, 1947).

Laloy, Louis, French musicologist and music critic; b. Grey, Haute-Saône, Feb. 18, 1874; d. Dôle, March 3, 1944. He settled in Paris, where he studied at the École Normale Supérieure (1893; agrégé des lettres, 1896; docteur ès lettres, 1904, with the diss. *Aristoxène de Tarente et la musique de l'antiquité*); also studied with Bordes, Breéille, and d'Indy at the Schola Cantorum (1899–1905). He was co-founder (1901) of the *Revue d'Histoire et de Critique Musicale*; in 1905 he founded, with J. Marnold, the *Mercure Musical*; contributed articles to *Revue de Paris, Grande Revue, Mercure de France,* and *Gazette des Beaux-Arts.* He was prof. of music history at the Paris Cons. (1936–41).
WRITINGS: *Jean Philippe Rameau* (Paris, 1908; 3rd ed., 1919); *Claude Debussy* (Paris, 1909; 2nd ed., 1944); *La Musique chinoise* (Paris, 1910); *The Future of Music* (London, 1910); *La Musique retrouvée, 1902–1927* (Paris, 1928); *Une Heure de musique avec Beethoven* (Paris, 1930); *Comment écouter la musique* (Paris, 1942).

La Mara. See **Lipsius, Marie.**

La Marre (Lamare), Jacques-Michel-Hurel de, French cellist; b. Paris, May 1, 1772; d. Caen, March 27, 1823. He toured Europe, including Russia, with great success; Clementi called him "the Rode of the violoncello." Four cello concertos and an *air varié* publ. under La Marre's name are actually by Auber.

Lamb, Joseph F(rancis), remarkable American ragtime pianist and composer; b. Montclair, N.J., Dec. 6, 1887; d. N.Y., Sept. 3, 1960. Although he had no formal musical training and spent most of his life in the textile import business, he was one of the most important composers of piano rags during the heyday of ragtime; also wrote a number of songs for Tin Pan Alley. After almost 30 years, he was rediscovered in 1949 and began composing rags again; also appeared as a ragtime pianist. His most notable piano rags were *Sensation* (1908), *Ethiopia Rag* (1909), *Excelsior Rag* (1909), *Champagne Rag* (1910), *American Beauty Rag* (1913), *Cleopatra Rag* (1915), *Contentment Rag* (1915), *The Ragtime Nightingale* (1915), *Reindeer* (1915), *Patricia Rag* (1916), *Top Liner Rag* (1916), and *Bohemia Rag* (1919). An anthology of his works appeared in N.Y. in 1964.
BIBL.: R. Cassidy, "J. L.: Last of the Ragtime Composers," *Jazz Report*, I (Jan.–Aug. 1961); M. Montgomery, "J.F. L.: A Ragtime Paradox, 1887–1960," *Sound Line*, XII/3–4 (1961); M. Den, *J.F. L., a Ragtime Composer Recalled* (thesis, Brooklyn College, City Univ. of N.Y., 1975); J. Scotti, *Joe L.: A Study of Ragtime's Paradox* (diss., Univ. of Cincinnati, 1977; with list of works); idem, "The Musical Legacy of J. L.," in J. Hasse, ed., *Ragtime: Its History, Composers, and Music* (N.Y., 1985).

Lamb, Walter, English composer; b. c.1450; d. 1499. He became a clerk of the choir of St. George's Chapel (1479), serving as Informator there (1479–85?); resumed his post as clerk (1492). He distinguished himself as a composer of polyphonic choral music; contributed many works to *The Eton Choirbook* (ed. by F. Harrison, Musica Britannica, X–XII, 1956–61; 2nd ed., 1969–73).

Lambardi, Camillo, Italian tenor, organist, and composer, father of **Francesco Lambardi;** b. Naples, c.1560; d. there, Nov. 1634. He sang at the Santa Casa dell'Annunziata at Naples as a treble (from 1569) and as a tenor (from 1579); studied there with Gian Domenico da Nola, whom he succeeded as a maestro di cappella in 1592; retired in 1631. He publ. music for Holy Week for 2 Choirs (1592); 2 books of motets (1613, 1628); 2 books of madrigals (1600, 1609); etc.

Lambardi, Francesco, Italian tenor, organist, and composer, son of **Camillo Lambardi;** b. Naples, c.1587; d. there, July 25, 1642. He became a treble (1599) and an alto (1600) at the Santa Casa dell'Annunziata in Naples; was made a tenor at the royal chapel (1607), and then served as its organist (1615–42); was also maestro di cappella of the Pièta dei Turchini Cons. (1626–30) and S. Maria della Nova (1628); founded a singing school (1623). He publ. 2 sets of *villanelle* for 3 to 5 Voices (Naples, 1607, 1614) and a book of canzonette for 1 and 3 to 5 Voices (Naples, 1616).

Lambelet, George, Greek composer and musicologist; b. Corfu, Dec. 24, 1875; d. Athens, Oct. 30, 1945. He studied in Naples; returned to Greece in 1901; co-ed. *Critique* with Axiotis, and *Musical Chronicles* with J. Papadopoulos; publ. a number of studies on Greek folk music, including *Nationalism in Art and Greek Folk Music* (Athens, 1928). He is noted for *La Musique populaire grecque* (Athens, 1934), a collection of 60 Greek folk songs and dances, together with harmonizations and a critical study. His musical compositions have a strong national flavor. He wrote choral works: *The Hymn to Peace; Balkan Hymn; Hymn to Greece;* etc.; *The Feast,* symphonic poem; *Elegy* for Orch.; *Dirge* for Orch.; songs.

Lambert, (Leonard) Constant, remarkable English conductor, composer, and writer on music; b. London, Aug. 23, 1905; d. there, Aug. 21, 1951. He won a scholarship to the Royal College of Music in London, where he studied with R.O. Morris and Vaughan Williams (1915–22). His 1st major score, the ballet *Romeo and Juliet* (Monte Carlo, May 4, 1926), was commissioned by Diaghilev. This early association with the dance proved decisive, for he spent most of his life as a conductor and composer of ballets. His interest in jazz resulted in such fine scores as *Elegiac Blues* for Orch. (1927), *The Rio Grande* for Piano, Chorus, and Orch. (1927; to a text by S. Sitwell), and the Concerto for Piano and 9 Performers (1930–31). Of his many ballets, the most striking in craftsmanship was his *Horoscope* (1937). In the meantime, he became conductor of the Camargo Soc. for the presentation of ballet productions (1930). He was made music director of the Vic-Wells Ballet (1931), and remained in that capacity after it became the Sadler's Wells Ballet and the Royal Ballet, until resigning in 1947; he then was made one of its artistic directors (1948), and subsequently conducted it on its 1st visit to the U.S. (1949). He also appeared at London's Covent Garden (1937; 1939; 1946–47); was associate conductor of the London Promenade Concerts (1945–46), and then frequently conducted broadcast performances over the BBC. He contributed articles on music to the *Nation and Athenaeum* (from 1930) and to the *Sunday Referee* (from 1931). He also penned the provocative book *Music Ho! A Study of Music in Decline* (London, 1934). Lambert was one of the most gifted musicians of his generation. However, his demanding work as a conductor and his excessive consumption of alcohol prevented him from fully asserting himself as a composer in his later years.
WORKS: BALLETS: *Romeo and Juliet* (1924–25; Monte Carlo, May 4, 1926); *Pomona* (1926; Teatro Colón, Buenos Aires, Sept. 9, 1927); *Horoscope* (1937; Sadler's Wells, London, Jan. 27, 1938, composer conducting); *Tiresias* (1950–51; Covent Garden, London, July 9, 1951, composer conducting); also various arrangements. ORCH.: *The Bird Actors,* overture (1925; reorchestrated, 1927; London, July 5, 1931, composer conducting; orig. for Piano, 4-hands); *Champêtre* for Chamber Orch. (London, Oct. 27, 1926); *Elegiac Blues* (1927; also for Piano); *Music for Orchestra* (1927; BBC, June 4, 1929); *The Rio Grande* for Piano, Chorus, and Orch., after S. Sitwell (1927; BBC, Feb. 27, 1928, composer conducting); Concerto for Piano, Flute, 2 Clarinets, Bass Clarinet, Trumpet, Trombone, Percus-

sion, Cello, and Double Bass (London, Dec. 18, 1931, composer conducting); *Summer's Last Will and Testament* for Baritone, Chorus, and Orch., after T. Nashe (1932–35; London, Jan. 29, 1936, composer conducting); *Dirge from Cymbeline* for Tenor, Baritone, Male Chorus, and Strings or Piano, after Shakespeare (with Piano, Cambridge, Nov. 1940; with Strings, BBC, March 23, 1947, composer conducting); *Aubade héroïque* (1942; London, Feb. 21, 1943, composer conducting). PIANO: *Pastorale* (1926); *Elegiac Blues* (1927; also for Orch.); Sonata (1928–29; London, Oct. 30, 1929); *Elegy* (1938); *Trois pièces nègres pour les touches blanches* (4-hands; 1949). SONGS: *8 Poems of Li-Po* for Voice, and Piano or 8 Instruments (1926–29; with Instruments, London, Oct. 30, 1929); also film scores, incidental music, and arrangements or eds. of works by Boyce, Handel, and Purcell.

BIBL.: H. Foss, "C. L.," *Musical Times,* XCII (1951); D. Webster, "C. L.—an Appreciation," *Opera,* II (1951); R. McGrady, "The Music of C. L.," *Music & Letters,* LI (1970); C. Palmer, "C. L.—a Postscript," ibid., LII (1971); R. Shead, *C. L.* (London, 1973; 2nd ed., rev., 1987); K. DeKay, "C. L.: Genius and Tragedy," *Le Grand Baton* (Sept. 1982; with discography by N. Brown).

Lambert, Juan Bautista, Catalan composer; b. Barcelona, 1884; d. there, May 4, 1945. He studied with Pedrell and Morera (composition) and Pellicer and Malats (piano) at Barcelona's municipal music school, then was active as an organist and conductor. He was a leading composer of Catalan sacred music, producing 3 masses, motets, hymns, and organ works; also wrote 3 operas, 5 zarzuelas, orch. works, chamber music, and piano pieces.

Lambert, Lucien, French composer and pianist; b. Paris, Jan. 5, 1858; d. Oporto, Portugal, Jan. 21, 1945. He studied first with his father; after a tour of America and Europe, returned to Paris to study at the Cons. with Dubois and Massenet, taking the Prix Rossini in 1885 with his cantata *Prométhée enchaîné.* He settled in Portugal in 1914; was a prof. of composition at the Oporto Cons. (1922–37).

WORKS: Operas: *Brocéliande* (Rouen, Feb. 25, 1893); *Le Spahi* (Paris, Oct. 18, 1897); *La Marseillaise* (Paris, July 14, 1900); *La Flamenca* (Paris, Oct. 31, 1903); *Harald* (1937); *Penticosa; La Sorcière;* ballets: *La Roussalka* (Paris, Dec. 8, 1911) and *Les Cloches de Porto* (1937); *Florette,* lyric comedy (1921); *Légende roumaine,* symphonic poem; *Fantaisie mono-thématique* for Orch., on an oriental theme (Paris, March 19, 1933); *Tanger le soir,* Moorish rhapsody for Orch.; *Esquisses créoles,* orch. suite, on themes by Gottschalk; *Andante et fantaisie tzigane* for Piano and Orch.; String Quartet; String Sextet; Mass; piano pieces; songs.

Lambert, Michel, eminent French composer; b. Champigny-sur-Veude, near Chinon, Indre-et-Loire, 1610; d. Paris, June 29, 1696. He was a page in the Paris chapel of Gaston of Orléans, brother of Louis XIII; then was a singer, member, and subsequently director of Mlle. de Montpensier's 6 "violons"; also appeared as a singer and dancer in the court ballets. He was maître de musique de la chambre du Roi (1661–96). His daughter married Lully (1662). Lambert was greatly esteemed as a composer, and also renowned as a singing teacher. Only some 300 of his airs are extant.

WORKS: *Les Airs de Monsieur Lambert* (Paris, 1660); (60) *Airs à 1–4* and Basso Continuo (Paris, 1689); *Airs de Monsieur Lambert non imprimez* (c.1710); also airs in various collections; other works include dialogues and récrits for the stage and a few pieces of sacred music.

Lambillotte, Louis, French organist, composer, and writer on music; b. Charleroi, Hainaut, March 27, 1796; d. Vaugirard, Feb. 27, 1855. He was an organist at Charleroi, then at Dinant; in 1822, became maître de chapelle at the Jesuit Seminary at St.-Acheul, joining the order in 1825; subsequently settled in Vaugirard. He wrote 4 masses (one in the Lydian mode), other sacred music, organ pieces, fugues, etc.

WRITINGS: *Antiphonaire de Saint-Grégoire, Facsimile du manuscrit de Saint-Gall* (1851); *Clef des mélodies grégoriennes* (1851); *Quelques mots sur la restauration du chant liturgique* (1855); *Esthétique, théorie et pratique du chant grégorien* (1855); other essays.

BIBL.: J. Dufour, *Mémoire sur les chants liturgiques restaurés par L.* (Paris, 1857); T. Nisard, *Le Père L. et Dom A. Schubiger* (Paris, 1857); M. de Monter, *L. et ses frères* (Paris, 1871).

Lambord, Benjamin, American organist and composer; b. Portland, Maine, June 10, 1879; d. Lake Hopatcong, N.J., June 6, 1915. He studied in Boston with A. Whiting, at Columbia Univ. with MacDowell, and in Paris with Vidal. He was organist and choirmaster in various churches in N.Y.; organized the Lambord Choral Soc. (1912) and the Modern Music Soc. (1914). He wrote *Introduction and Variations on an English Dance Theme* for Orch.; *Clytie* for Soprano and Orch.; *Verses from Omar Khayyam* for Mixed Chorus and Orch.; *10 Lyric Studies for Piano;* piano pieces; part-songs; songs.

Lambro, Philip, American composer and conductor; b. Wellesley, Mass., Sept. 2, 1935. His father, of Italian origin, emigrated from Albania and settled in the U.S. Lambro studied piano with György Sándor. He learned the art of composition mainly by analyzing the music of Classical composers and that of modern composers whose works he admired. As he himself stated, he had "an abundant and unique talent as a composer," which was unfortunately obstructed by the "vicissitudes of life." Still, the list of his works is impressive. A fair selection includes *Miraflores* for String Orch. (1955); *Dance Barbaro* for Percussion (1958–60); *2 Pictures* for Percussion and Orch. (1965–66); *Parallelograms* for Flute Quartet and Jazz Ensemble (1969–75); *Obelick* for Oboe and Percussion (1970); *Biospheres* for 6 Percussion (1973); *8 Little Trigrams* for Piano (1979). He believes in the existence of extraterrestrials, "who created mankind in a laboratory." To maintain his physical health, he practices the Japanese macrobiotic diet.

Lammers, Gerda, esteemed German soprano; b. Berlin, Sept. 25, 1915. She studied with L. Mysz-Gmeiner and M. Schwedler-Lohmann at the Berlin Hochschule für Musik; then appeared as a concert and lieder artist (1940–55). She made her stage debut as Ortlinde at the Bayreuth Festival (1955); that same year she made her 1st appearance at the Kassel State Theater as Marie in *Wozzeck,* remaining there for some 15 years. She made an acclaimed debut as Elektra at London's Covent Garden (1957), substituting on short notice for an indisposed Christel Goltz; she returned there as Kundry in 1959. She made her Metropolitan Opera debut in N.Y. as Elektra on March 16, 1962. Her other distinguished roles included Alceste, Medea, Senta, Isolde, and Brünnhilde.

Lammers, Julius, German composer; b. Leipzig, April 20, 1829; d. there, Sept. 20, 1888. He taught at the Leipzig Cons.; composed numerous works and some piano pieces.

Lamond, Frederic(k Archibald), distinguished Scottish pianist; b. Glasgow, Jan. 28, 1868; d. Stirling, Feb. 21, 1948. He played organ as a boy in a local church; also studied oboe and violin; in 1882, entered the Raff Cons. in Frankfurt, studying with Heermann (violin), Max Schwarz (piano), and Urspruch (composition); then piano with Hans von Bülow, Clara Schumann, and Liszt. He made his debut in Berlin (Nov. 17, 1885); then appeared in Vienna and Glasgow, and later in London, N.Y., and Russia. He married the German actress Irene Triesch (1904), making Berlin his center of activities until the coming of World War II, when he went to England. While continuing to make tours, he also was engaged as a pedagogue. He became renowned for his performances of Beethoven and Liszt; publ. an ed. of the Beethoven piano sonatas and the book *Beethoven: Notes on the Sonatas* (Glasgow, 1944); his reminiscences appeared as *The Memoirs of Frederic Lamond* (Glasgow, 1949). He was also a composer; wrote a Sym. (Glasgow, Dec. 23, 1889), some chamber music, and numerous piano pieces.

La Montaine, John, American composer and pianist; b. Oak Park, Ill., March 17, 1920. He studied piano with Muriel Parker and Margaret Farr Wilson, then received training in theory in Chicago from Stella Roberts (1935–38); subsequently took courses in piano with Max Landow and in composition with Howard Hanson and Bernard Rogers at the Eastman School of Music in Rochester, N.Y. (B.Mus., 1942); after further training from Rudolph Ganz at the Chicago Musical College (1945), he completed his studies in composition with Bernard Wagenaar at the Juilliard School of Music in N.Y. and with Nadia Boulanger at the American Cons. in Fontainebleau. He received a Guggenheim fellowship (1959–60); in 1961 he was a visiting prof. of composition at the Eastman School of Music; in 1962, served as composer-in-residence at the American Academy in Rome. He received the Pulitzer Prize in Music for his 1st Piano Concerto in 1959. In 1977 he was a Nixon Distinguished Scholar at Nixon's alma mater, Whittier College, in California.

WORKS: OPERAS: Christmas trilogy on medieval miracle plays: *Novellis, Novellis* (Washington, D.C., Dec. 24, 1961), *The Shephardes Playe* (Washington, D.C., Dec. 27, 1967), and *Erode the Great* (Washington, D.C., Dec. 31, 1969); Bicentennial opera, *Be Glad, Then, America: A Decent Entertainment from the 13 Colonies* (Univ. Park, Pa., Feb. 6, 1976). **ORCH.:** *Songs of the Rose of Sharon*, biblical cycle for Soprano and Orch. (Washington, D.C., May 31, 1956); piano concertos: No. 1 (Washington, D.C., Nov. 25, 1958; won the Pulitzer Prize in Music in 1959); No. 2, *Transformations* (1987); No. 3, *Children's Games* (1987); *Fragments from the Song of Songs*, biblical cycle for Soprano and Orch. (New Haven, Conn., April 14, 1959); *From Sea to Shining Sea* (for the inaugural concert of President John F. Kennedy, Washington, D.C., Jan. 19, 1961); *Birds of Paradise* for Piano and Orch. (Rochester, N.Y., April 29, 1964, composer soloist; also perf. as the ballet *Nightwings*, N.Y., Sept. 7, 1966); *Wilderness Journal*, sym. for Bass-baritone, Organ, and Orch., after Thoreau (Washington, D.C., Oct. 10, 1972); Flute Concerto (Washington, D.C., April 12, 1981); Concerto for String Orch. (Vancouver Radio, March 17, 1981); *Symphonic Variations* for Piano and Orch. (Peninsula Music Festival, Wis., Aug. 20, 1982, composer soloist). **CHORAL:** *Te Deum* for Chorus, Winds, and Percussion (Washington, D.C., May 7, 1964); *Mass of Nature* (*Missa Naturae*) for Chorus and Orch. (Washington, D.C., May 26, 1976); *The Whittier Service*, 9 hymn-anthems for Chorus, Incidental Solos, Guitar, Brass Quintet, Strings, and Optional Organ and Timpani (Washington, D.C., May 20, 1979); *The Lessons of Advent* for Chorus, Incidental Solos, Narrator, Trumpet, Drums, Handbell Choir, Harp, Oboe, Guitar, and Organ (San Francisco, Dec. 4, 1983); *The Marshes of Glynn* for Bass, Chorus, and Orch. (Rochester, N.Y., Nov. 11, 1984). Other works include some chamber music, organ works, and piano pieces.

Lamote de Grignon, Juan, Catalan conductor and composer, father of **Ricardo Lamote de Grignon y Ribas;** b. Barcelona, July 7, 1872; d. there, March 11, 1949. He studied at the Barcelona Cons., and upon graduation, became prof. (1890) and director (1917) there; made his debut as a conductor in Barcelona (April 26, 1902). In 1910 he founded the Orquesta Sinfónica of Barcelona, which carried on its activity until 1924; also was founder-conductor of the Valencia Municipal Orch. (1943–49). He publ. *Musique et musiciens français à Barcelone: Musique et musiciens catalans à Paris* (Barcelona, 1935). He wrote an opera, *Hesperia* (Barcelona, Jan. 25, 1907); orch. works; an oratorio, *La Nit de Nadal;* numerous songs.

Lamote de Grignon y Ribas, Ricardo, Catalan cellist, conductor, and composer, son of **Juan Lamote de Grignon;** b. Barcelona, Sept. 23, 1899; d. there, Feb. 5, 1962. He studied cello and composition at the Barcelona Cons.; played cello in the Orquesta Sinfónica of Barcelona, conducted by his father; then conducted provincial orchs.; became assistant conductor of the municipal band of Barcelona. He publ. a manual, *Síntesis de técnica musical* (Barcelona, 1948).

WORKS: Opera, *La caperucita verde;* children's opera, *La flor;* symphonic legend, *Joan de Os* (Barcelona, April 19, 1936, composer conducting); symphonic poem, *Boires; Tríptico de* *Rabindranath Tagore* for Soprano and Orch.; *Enigmas* for Orch. (won the Barcelona Municipal Prize, 1951); Piano Trio; songs.

Lamothe, Georges, French composer; b. 1837; d. Courbevoie, Oct. 15, 1894. He was a prolific composer of dance music; wrote more than 1,000 opus numbers.

Lamoureux, Charles, noted French conductor and violinist; b. Bordeaux, Sept. 28, 1834; d. Paris, Dec. 21, 1899. He studied at the Paris Cons. with Girard (violin; premier prix, 1852, 1854), Tolbecque (harmony), Leborne (counterpoint and fugue), and Chauvet (composition). In 1850 he became solo violinist in the Théâtre du Gymnase orch.; then became a member of the Paris Opéra orch. In 1860 he helped to organize the Séances Populaires de Musique de Chambre; in 1874 he organized the Société Française de l'Harmonie Sacrée; he became known as assistant conductor of the Cons. Concerts (1872–73); was a conductor of the Paris Opéra (1877–79). He founded the celebrated Concerts Lamoureux (Nouveaux Concerts) on Oct. 23, 1881; retired as its conductor in 1897, and was succeeded by his son-in-law, Chevillard; he also served as music director of the Opéra (1891–92). More than any other French musician, Lamoureux educated Parisians to appreciate Wagner; he was responsible not only for highly competent performances of Classical masterpieces, but also for presentation of compositions of his contemporaries. However, as a conductor, he had a reputation as an abusive and dictatorial taskmaster; he was so loathed by some of the musicians who performed under him that he carried a pistol for protection.

BIBL.: R. Rolland, *Musiciens d'aujourd'hui* (Paris, 1908; 8th ed., 1947; Eng. tr., 1914).

Lamperti, Francesco, eminent Italian singing teacher, father of **Giovanni Battista Lamperti;** b. Savona, March 11, 1811; d. Cernobbio, May 1, 1892. He studied at the Milan Cons.; was director at the Teatro Filodrammatico in Lodi; tutored many distinguished singers, including Albani, Artôt, both Cruvelis, Campanini, Collini, and Lagrange; taught at the Milan Cons. (1850–75). He publ. *Guida teorico-pratico-elementare per lo studi del canto; Studi di bravura per soprano; Esercizi giornalieri per soprano o mezzo-soprano; L'arte del canto; Osservazioni e consigli sul trillo; Solfeggi;* etc. His methods and studies in voice production have also appeared in Eng. tr.: *Studies in Bravura Singing for the Soprano Voice* (N.Y., 1875); *A Treatise on the Art of Singing* (London, 1877; rev. ed., N.Y., 1890).

Lamperti, Giovanni Battista, Italian singing teacher, son of **Francesco Lamperti;** b. Milan, June 24, 1839; d. Berlin, March 18, 1910. At the age of 9 he was a choirboy at the Milan Cathedral; studied piano and voice at the Milan Cons.; served as accompanist in his father's class there. He taught first in Milan; subsequently in Dresden for 20 years; then in Berlin. Among his pupils were Sembrich, Schumann-Heink, Bispham, and Stagno. He publ. *Die Technik des Bel Canto* (1905; Eng. tr. by T. Baker, N.Y., 1905); *Scuola di canto* (8 vols. of solfeggi and vocalises); other technical exercises. His pupil W.E. Brown publ. *Vocal Wisdom; Maxims of G.B. Lamperti* (N.Y., 1931; new ed., 1957).

Lampugnani, Giovanni Battista, Italian teacher and composer; b. Milan, 1706; d. probably there, after 1786. From 1743 to 1745 he was active at the King's Theatre in London; later was maestro al cembalo at La Scala in Milan. Over the period of 1732–69, he wrote 28 operas in the style of Hasse, which were presented in London, Venice, Milan, and other cities; publ. some trio sonatas; also wrote syms. and concertos.

Lancen, Serge Jean Mathieu, French composer and pianist; b. Paris, Nov. 5, 1922. He studied at the Paris Cons. with Aubin, Büsser, and Noël Gallon. During World War II, he went to Switzerland; returning to Paris, he continued his studies; obtained the Premier Prix de Rome for composition in 1949.

WORKS: *La Mauvaise Conscience*, chamber opera (Paris, Jan. 4, 1964); *Les Prix*, ballet (Bordeaux, March 13, 1954); Piano Concerto (1947); Concerto for Mouth Harmonica, written for

Larry Adler (1955); Concerto for Double Bass and Orch. (1960); *Manhattan Symphony* (1962); *Concert à 6* for 6 Clarinets (1962); light pieces for radio; etc.

Lanchbery, John (Arthur), English conductor; b. London, May 15, 1923. He studied at the Royal Academy of Music in London; was then music director of the Metropolitan Ballet (1948–50) and the Sadler's Wells Royal Ballet (1951–60); subsequently occupied a similar post with the Royal Ballet at Covent Garden (1960–72). In 1972 he was named music director of the Australian Ballet.

Lancie, John (Sherwood) de. See **de Lancie, John (Sherwood).**

Land, Jan Pieter Nicholaas, Dutch orientalist and musicologist; b. Delft, April 23, 1834; d. Arnhem, April 30, 1897. He was prof. of classical and oriental languages and of philosophy at the Amsterdam Academy (1864–72); then was prof. of philosophy at the Univ. of Leiden (1872–94). He was an accomplished linguist, specializing in Semitic philology; was deeply interested in musico-historical research, to which he made valuable contributions.

WRITINGS: *Noord Nederlands muziekgeschiedenis* (1874–81); *Over de toonladders der arabische muziek* (1880); *Musique et musiciens au XVIIᵉ siècle. Correspondance et œuvres musicales de Constantijn Huygens* (with Jonckbloet; Leyden, 1882); *Recherches sur l'histoire de la gamme arabe* (Leyden, 1884); *Essai de notation musicale chez les arabes et les persans* (1885); *Over onze kennis der javaansche muziek* (Amsterdam, 1891).

Landau, Siegfried, German-born American conductor and composer; b. Berlin, Sept. 4, 1921. He studied at the Stern Cons. and at the Klindworth-Scharwenka Cons. in Berlin. He continued his studies at the Guildhall School of Music and Drama and at Trinity College of Music in London (1939–40); he pursued conducting studies at the Mannes College of Music in N.Y. (diploma, 1942); also received conducting lessons from Monteux. In 1946 he became a naturalized U.S. citizen. In 1955 he organized the Brooklyn Philharmonia, which he conducted until 1971; concurrently was conductor of the Chattanooga Opera Assoc. (1960–73) and of the Music for Westchester (later White Plains) Sym. Orch. (1961–81); likewise served as Generalmusikdirektor of the Westphalian Sym. Orch. (1973–75). He wrote an opera, *The Sons of Aaron* (Scarsdale, N.Y., Feb. 28, 1959), ballet music, orch. pieces, chamber music, and film scores.

Landi, Stefano, significant Italian composer; b. Rome, 1586 or 1587; d. there, Oct. 28, 1639. He became a boy soprano at Rome's Collegio Germanico (1595), taking minor orders there (1599); then studied rhetoric and philosophy at the Seminario Romano (1602–7); subsequently was organist of S. Maria in Trastevere (1610) and a singer at the Oratorio del SS. Crocifisso (1611). He served as maestro di cappella to Marco Cornaro, Bishop of Padua (1618–20); then returned to Rome, where he was made a clericus beneficiatus of St. Peter's and maestro di cappella of the church of the Madonna ai Monti (1624); was also active as a teacher, and was in the service of Cardinal Maurizio of Savoy and the Barberini family. He became an alto in the papal choir (1629). His opera *Il Sant' Alessio* is important in the history of opera as the 1st such work to treat the inner life of a human subject and to include true overtures in the form of sinfonias. His sacred music ranges from the stile antico of his 2 masses to the new concertato style of his Vespers Psalms and his Magnificats.

WORKS: OPERAS: *La morte d'Orfeo*, tragicommedia pastorale (Rome?, 1619; publ. in Venice, 1619; libretto ed. by A. Solerti in *Gli albori del melodramma*, III, Milan, 1904; reprint, 1969); *Il Sant' Alessio*, dramma musicale (Rome, 1631?; publ. in Rome, 1634; reprint, 1970; libretto ed. by A. della Corte in *Drammi per musica dal Rinuccini allo Zeno*, I, Turin, 1958). **SACRED:** *Psalmi integri* for 4 Voices and Basso Continuo (Rome, 1624; ed. by S. Leopold, Hamburg, 1976); *Missa in benedictione nuptiarum* for 6 Voices (Rome, 1628; ed. by S. Leopold, Hamburg, 1976); *Messa* for 5 Voices and Basso Continuo (ed. by S. Leo-

pold, Hamburg, 1976); motets. **SECULAR:** (18) *Madrigali . . . libro primo* for 5 Voices and Basso Continuo (Venice, 1619); *Arie* for Voice and Basso Continuo (Venice, 1620); *Il secondo libro d'arie musicali* for Voice and Basso Continuo (Rome, 1627); *Il quinto libro d'arie* for Voice and Basso Continuo (Venice, 1637); *Il sesto libro d'arie* for Voice and Basso Continuo (Venice, 1638); Dialogues for Soprano and Basso Continuo; Cantata for Tenor and Basso Continuo (ed. by S. Leopold, Hamburg, 1976); etc.

BIBL.: R. Rolland, "La Première Représentation du *San Alessio* de S. L. en 1632, à Rome, d'après le journal manuscrit de Jean Jacques Bouchard," *La Revue Musicale,* II (1902); G. Pavan, "Un dramma musicale a Roma nel 1634: Il S. Alessio di S. L.," *Musica d'Oggi,* III (1921); S. Carfagno, *The Life and Dramatic Music of S. L. with a Transliteration and Orchestration of the Opera Sant' Alessio* (diss., Univ. of Calif., Los Angeles, 1960); E. Barassi, "Il 'S. Alessio' di S. L.," *Musica Università,* II (Rome, 1964); S. Leopold, *S. L.: Beiträge zur Biographie: Untersuchungen zur weltlichen und geistlichen Vokalmusik* (Hamburg, 1976).

Landini, Benedetto, Italian organist and composer; b. Calenzano, Jan. 31, 1858; d. Florence, July 11, 1938. He studied at the Florence Cons., graduating in 1886; became a teacher of organ there in 1888; also was organist of the Church of Santissima Annunziata and choirmaster at S. Lorenzo and S. Trinità; from 1891, was active in church music reforms in Tuscany. He wrote a Mass, a Requiem, *De profundis, Hymnus,* Psalms, and other sacred works; also a children's opera, *L'Arancia di Codino* (1913); ed. works of Frescobaldi, Marco da Gagliano, and Corteccia, and numerous early Tuscan folk songs.

Landini, Francesco (also known as **Franciscus Landino, Francesco degli orghany, Magister Franciscus de Florentia, Magister Franciscus Cecus Horghanista de Florentia,** and **Cechus de Florentia**), important Italian composer; b. probably in Florence, c.1325; d. there, Sept. 2, 1397. His father was the painter Jacopo Del Casentino, co-founder of Florence's guild of painters (1339). After being blinded by smallpox as a child, Francesco turned to music; he learned to play the organ and other instruments and also sang. He became well known as an organist, organ builder, organ tuner, and instrument maker; was also active as a poet. He was organist at the monastery of S. Trinità (1361); was cappellanus at the church of S. Lorenzo from 1365 until his death. His output is particularly significant, for it represents about a quarter of extant Italian 14th-century music. Some 154 works have been identified as his; these include 90 ballate for 2 Voices, 42 for 3 Voices, and 8 in both 2- and 3-part versions; 9 madrigals for 2 or 3 Voices; 1 French virelai; 1 caccia. See L. Ellinwood, ed., *The Works of Francesco Landini* (Cambridge, Mass., 1939; 2nd ed., 1945); J. Wolf, ed., *Der Squarcialupi-Codex Pal. 87 der Biblioteca medicea laurenziana zu Florenz* (Lippstadt, 1955); and L. Schrade, ed., *The Works of Francesco Landini,* Polyphonic Music of the Fourteenth Century, IV (1958).

BIBL.: G. Galletti, ed., *Philippi Villani liber de civitatis Florentiae famosis civibus* (written c.1400; Florence, 1847); E. Li Gotti and N. Pirrotta, *Il Sacchetti e la tecnica musicale del trecento italiano* (Florence, 1935); M. Johnson, "A Study of Conflicting Key-signatures in F. L.'s Music," *Hamline Studies in Musicology,* II (1947); H. Nolthenius, *Renaissance in Mei: Florentijns leven rond F. Landino* (Utrecht, 1956); T. Göllner, "L.'s 'Questa fanciulla' bei Oswald von Wolkenstein," *Die Musikforschung,* XVII (1964); C. Schachter, "L.'s Treatment of Consonance and Dissonance," *Music Forum,* II (N.Y., 1970); D. Baumann, *Die dreistimmige Satztechnik bei F. L.* (Baden-Baden, 1978); M. Long, "L.'s Musical Patrimony: A Reassessment of Some Compositional Conventions in Trecento Polyphony," *Journal of the American Musicological Society* (Spring 1987).

Landon, H(arold) C(handler) Robbins, eminent American musicologist; b. Boston, March 6, 1926. He studied music history and theory with Alfred J. Swan at Swarthmore College, and composition there with Harl McDonald; he also took a course in English literature with W.H. Auden (1943–45); then enrolled in the musicology class of Karl Geiringer at Boston Univ. (B.Mus., 1947). In 1948 he traveled to Europe and settled in Vienna; in 1949 he founded the Haydn Soc., with a view to preparing a complete ed. of Haydn's works. He also instituted an energetic campaign to locate music MSS which had disappeared or been removed; thus, he succeeded in finding the MS of Haydn's Mass No. 13; also found the MS of the so-called Jena Sym., erroneously ascribed to Beethoven, and proved that it had actually been composed by Friedrich Witt. In *The Symphonies of Joseph Haydn* (London, 1955; supplement, 1961), he analyzes each sym. and suggests solutions for numerous problems of authenticity; in his new ed. of the syms. (12 vols., Vienna, 1965–68), he carefully establishes the version nearest to the original authentic text. He subsequently publ. his massive study *Haydn: Chronicle and Works* in 5 vols. (Bloomington, Ind., and London): vol. I, *Haydn: The Early Years, 1732–1765* (1980); vol. II, *Haydn at Esterháza, 1766–1790* (1978); vol. III, *Haydn in England, 1791–1795* (1976); vol. IV, *Haydn: The Years of "The Creation," 1796–1800* (1977); vol. V, *Haydn: The Late Years, 1801–1809* (1977). His other publications include *The Mozart Companion* (ed. with D. Mitchell; London, 1956; 2nd ed., rev., 1965); *The Collected Correspondence and London Notebooks of Joseph Haydn* (London, 1959); a foreword with many emendations to C.S. Terry's *John Christian Bach* (London, 1929; 2nd ed., rev., 1967); *Beethoven: A Documentary Study* (London, 1970); *Essays on the Viennese Classical Style: Gluck, Haydn, Mozart, Beethoven* (London and N.Y., 1970); *Haydn: A Documentary Study* (London, 1981); *Mozart and the Masons* (London, 1983); *1791: Mozart's Last Year* (London, 1988); with D. Jones, *Haydn: His Life and Music* (London, 1988); *Mozart: The Golden Years* (N.Y., 1989); ed. *The Mozart Compendium* (N.Y., 1990); *Mozart and Vienna* (N.Y., 1991). He was named Distinguished Prof. of the Humanities at Middlebury (Vt.) College (1983). During his early years in Europe, his wife, **Christa Landon** (b. Berlin, Sept. 23, 1921; d. Funchal, Madeira, Nov. 19, 1977), joined him as a research partner in the search for rare MSS in libraries, churches, and monasteries. She publ. eds. of works by Haydn, Mozart, and Bach; her ed. of Haydn's piano sonatas (3 vols., Vienna, 1963–66) supersedes the one by Hoboken.

Landormy, Paul (Charles-René), French musicologist and music critic; b. Issy-les-Moulineaux, Jan. 3, 1869; d. Paris, Nov. 17, 1943. He was an agrégé des lettres of the École Normale in Paris; studied voice with Sbriglia and Plançon. With Rolland, he organized a series of lectures on music history at the École des Hautes Études Sociales (1902) and was founder-director of its acoustic laboratory (1904–7); became music critic of *La Victoire* (1918), and contributed articles to other publications.

WRITINGS (all publ. in Paris): *Histoire de la musique* (1910; 3rd ed., 1923); *Brahms* (1920; rev. ed., 1948); *Bizet* (1924); *La Vie de Schubert* (1928); *Albert Roussel* (1938); *Gluck* (1941); *Gounod* (1942); *La Musique française* (3 vols., 1943–44).

Landowska, Wanda (Alexandra), celebrated Polish-born French harpsichordist, pianist, and pedagogue; b. Warsaw, July 5, 1879; d. Lakeville, Conn., Aug. 16, 1959. She studied piano at the Warsaw Cons. with Michalowski and in Berlin with Moszkowski. In 1900, she went to Paris, where she married Henry Lew, a writer. She traveled widely in Europe as a pianist, and as a harpsichordist from 1903; in 1909 made a tour of Russia, and played for Tolstoy, who showed great interest in her ideas on classical music. Subsequently, she devoted her efforts principally to reviving the art of playing upon the harpsichord. In 1912 she commissioned the Pleyel firm of Paris to construct a harpsichord for her; this was the 1st of the many keyboard instruments built for her in subsequent years. In 1913 she was invited by Kretzschmar to give a special course in harpsichord playing at the Berlin Hochschule für Musik. The outbreak of World War I in 1914 found her in Germany, and she was interned there until the Armistice; in 1918 her husband was killed in an automobile accident in Berlin. In 1919 she gave master classes in harpsichord playing

at the Basel Cons.; then returned to Paris. In 1925 she bought a villa in St.-Leu-la-Forêt, near Paris, and established there a school for the study of early music. A concert hall was built there in 1927; she presented regular concerts of early music, and gave lessons on the subject; also assembled a large collection of harpsichords. Her school attracted students from all over the world; she also taught at the Fontainebleau Cons., and frequently appeared at concerts in Paris, both as a pianist and as a harpsichordist. She commissioned Manuel de Falla to compose a Chamber Concerto for Harpsichord, and played the solo part in its 1st performance in Barcelona (Nov. 5, 1926); another commission was Poulenc's *Concert champêtre* for Harpsichord and Small Orch. (Paris, May 3, 1929). She appeared for the 1st time in America on Nov. 20, 1923, as soloist with the Philadelphia Orch., under Stokowski; then returned to France. When the Germans invaded France in 1940, Landowska fled to Switzerland, abandoning her villa, her library, and her instruments. In 1941 she made N.Y.; presented a concert of harpsichord music there on Feb. 21, 1942; then devoted herself mainly to teaching; also made recordings; settled in her new home at Lakeville, Conn. She was acknowledged as one of the greatest performers on the harpsichord; her interpretations of Baroque music were notable in their balance between Classical precision and freedom from rigidity, particularly in the treatment of ornamentation. She wrote *Bach et ses interprètes* (Paris, 1906) and *Musique ancienne* (Paris, 1909; 7th ed., 1921; Eng. tr., N.Y., 1924). A collection of her articles was publ. posth. under the title *Landowska on Music*, ed. and tr. by D. Restout and R. Hawkins (N.Y., 1964). She also wrote cadenzas for Mozart's concertos.

BIBL.: B. Gavoty and R. Hauert, *W. L.* (Geneva, 1957); H. Schott, "*W. L.*," *Early Music*, VII (1979); D. Alfano, "Remembering W. L. (1879–1959)," *Music and Musicians International* (March 1989).

Landowski, Marcel (François Paul), significant French composer; b. Prêt L'Abbé (Finistère), Feb. 18, 1915. His father, Paul Landowski, was a famous sculptor and his great-grandfather was **Henri Vieuxtemps**. He studied at the Paris Cons. (1933–37) with Gallon (fugue), Gaubert (conducting), and Busser (composition); also had conducting lessons with Monteux (1935), who later performed 2 of his works in one of his concerts with the Paris Sym. Orch. (Oct. 24, 1937). Landowski was director of the Boulogne-sur-Seine Cons. (1959–62) and director of music at the Comédie-Française (1962); also was inspector general for the Ministry of Cultural Affairs (1964–74), which, because of his conservative position, caused a serious rift in the French musical establishment; Boulez voiced his opposition to Landowski's appointment in an acerbic article publ. in *Le Nouvel Observateur*. Landowski's music is decidedly conservative, redolent of an earlier Romantic era, with lush melodies and symmetric rhythmic patterns. His stage work *Le Rire de Nils Halerius* (1948) divides into 3 acts, sequentially an opera, a ballet, and an oratorio. Many of his piano works were written for his wife, Jacqueline Potier, whom he married in 1941, and some later works for Galina Vishnevskaya and her husband, Mstislav Rostropovich. He publ. *L'Orchestre* (with L. Aubert; Paris, 1951), *Honegger* (Paris, 1957), and *Louis Aubert: Musicien français* (with G. Morançon; Paris, 1967).

WORKS (all 1st perf. in Paris unless otherwise given): **STAGE:** *Le Tour d'une Aile de Pigeon*, operetta (April 1, 1938); *Le Rire de Nils Halerius*, lyric legend (1948; Mulhouse, Jan. 19, 1951); *Le Fou*, lyric drama (1948–55; Nancy, Feb. 1, 1956); *Le Ventriloque*, lyric comedy (1955–56; Feb. 8, 1957); *Les Adieux*, lyric drama (Oct. 8, 1960); *L'Opéra de Poussière*, lyric drama (Avignon, Oct. 25, 1962); *La Sorcière du Placard aux Balais*, mini-opera for children (Sèvres, May 2, 1983); *Montségur*, opera (1980–84; Jan. 1, 1985). **BALLETS:** *Les Fleurs de la petite Ida* (June 19, 1938); *Après-midi champêtres* (Versailles, March 30, 1941); *Les Djinns* (March 11, 1944); *Rabelais, François de France*, opera-ballet (Tours, July 26, 1953); *Abîmes* (Essen, Feb. 12, 1959); *La Leçon d'anatomie* (based on music from Sym. No. 1; The Hague, 1964); *Le Fantôme de l'Opéra*

(1979; Feb. 22, 1980); *Les Hauts de Hurlement* for Orch. and Live Electronics (1981; Dec. 28, 1982). **ORCH.:** *Clairs-obscurs*, symphonic poem (Nov. 1938); 2 piano concertos: No. 1, *Poème pour piano* (1938–40; March 1, 1942), and No. 2 (1963; Feb. 28, 1964); *Brumes*, symphonic poem (March 5, 1944); Cello Concerto (1944–46; Nov. 25, 1946); *Edina*, symphonic poem (Dec. 17, 1946); *Le Petit Poucet*, suite (Cannes, Feb. 1947); *Ballet des jeux du monde* (1948); 4 syms.: No. 1, *Jean de la Peur* (1948; April 3, 1949); No. 2 (1963; Strasbourg, June 24, 1965); No. 3, *Des Espaces* (1965–65); No. 4 (Oct. 15, 1988); *3 histoires de la prairie*, suite (1951); Ondes Martenot Concerto (1954; Vichy, Sept. 16, 1955); Bassoon Concerto (June 1958); *La Passante*, suite (1958); *L'Orage*, symphonic poem (1961); *Mouvement* (1960); *Les Notes de nuit*, symphonic tale with Narrator (Boulogne-sur-Seine, Dec. 16, 1961); *Paysage*, symphonic movement (1961); Flute Concerto (1967; Dec. 13, 1968); Trumpet Concerto, *Au bout de chagrin, une fenêtre ouverte* (1976; June 24, 1977); *Un Enfant appelle*, concerto for Soprano, Cello, and Orch., after poems of Marie-Noel (1978; Washington, D.C., Jan. 9, 1979); *L'Horloge*, symphonic poem (May 6, 1982); *Improvisation* for Trombone (Toulon, May 1983). **VOCAL WITH ORCH.:** *Les Sept Loups* and *Les Sorcières*, ballades for Female Chorus (Oct. 24, 1937); 3 Melodies for Soprano (1938; Cannes, Sept. 1942); *Rhythmes de monde*, oratorio (April 26, 1941); *Desbat du Cœur et du Corps*, melody for 2 Voices (Jan. 20, 1944); *La Quête sans fin*, oratorio (March 1945); 7 cantatas, including No. 1, *Jésus, là es-tu?* (April 1948), and No. 6, *Aux mendiants du Ciel* (Fontevrault Abbey, June 11, 1966); *Espoir*, hymn for Chorus and Narrator (1959); *Messe de l'Aurore* (Nov. 14, 1977); *Le Pont de l'Espérance*, oratorio (Aug. 8, 1980); *La Prison* for Soprano and Cello (1981; Aix-en-Provence, July 18, 1983); *Cantate à la Paix* (July 1985). **CHAMBER:** Trio for Horn, Trumpet, and Piano (1954); *4 Préludes* for Percussion and Piano (1963); *Étude de sonorité* for Violin and Piano (1974); Concerto in Trio for Ondes Martenot, Percussion, and Piano (1975); *Cahier pour quatre jours* for Trumpet and Organ (1977); *Souvenir d'un jardin d'enfance* for Oboe and Piano (1977); also piano pieces; vocal works; 89 film scores, incidental music, spectacles with lights, and television scores.

BIBL.: A. Golea, *M. L.: L'Homme et son œuvre* (Paris, 1969); *M. L.: Le Musicien de l'espérance* (Paris, 1984).

Landowski, W.-L. (actually, **Alice-Wanda**), French writer on music; b. Paris, Nov. 28, 1899; d. there, April 18, 1959. She studied piano in Paris at the Marguerite Long School; also theory with Gustave Bret. She taught music history at the Clermont Cons.; in 1945, became a prof. at the Rouen Cons.; also was engaged as music critic of *Le Parisien*. She adopted the initials W.-L. (L. for Ladislas, her father's name) to avoid confusion with Wanda Landowska, who was not a relation.

WRITINGS: *L'Année Musicale* (Paris, 1936–39; annual reports of musical events); *La Musique à travers les âges* (1937); *Maurice Ravel* (1938); *Les Grands Musiciens* (1938); *Histoire universelle de la musique moderne* (1941); *Histoire générale de la musique* (1945); *L'Œuvre de Claude Delvincourt* (1947); *Chopin et Fauré* (1946); *Le Travail en musique* (1949); *La Musique américaine* (1952); *Paul Paray* (1956).

Landré, Guillaume (Louis Frédéric), important Dutch composer, son of **Willem (Guillaume Louis Frédéric) Landré;** b. The Hague, Feb. 24, 1905; d. Amsterdam, Nov. 6, 1968. He took music lessons from Zagwijn and Pijper (1924–29); studied jurisprudence at Utrecht Univ., receiving a master's degree in 1929; then was a teacher of economics in Amsterdam (1930–47). He was chairman of the Dutch Music Copyright Council (1947–58) and president of the Soc. of Netherlands Composers (1950–62). As a composer, he endeavored to revive the spirit and the polyphonic technique of the national Flemish School of the Renaissance in a 20th-century guise, with euphonious dissonances and impressionistic dynamics creating a modern aura. In his later works he experimented with serial devices.

WORKS: 3 operas: *De Snoek* (The Pike), comic opera (1934; Amsterdam, March 24, 1938); *Jean Lévecq*, after Maupassant (1962–63; Holland Festival, Amsterdam, June 16, 1965); *La Symphonie pastorale*, after André Gide (1965–67; Rouen, March 31, 1968); 4 syms.: No. 1 (1932; Amsterdam ISCM Festival, June 9, 1933); No. 2 (1942; The Hague, March 6, 1946); No. 3 (Amsterdam, June 16, 1951); No. 4, *Symphonie concertante* (1954–55; Stockholm ISCM Festival, June 5, 1956); Suite for String Orch. and Piano (1936); *4 Pieces* for Orch. (1937); *Concert Piece* for Orch. (1938); Cello Concerto (1940); *Sinfonietta* for Violin and Orch. (1941); *Piae memoriae pro patria mortuorum* for Chorus and Orch. (1942); *Groet der martelaren* (Salute to the Martyrs) for Baritone and Orch. (1943–44); *Symphonic Music* for Flute and Orch. (1947–48); *Sinfonia sacra in memoriam patris* (1948; Rotterdam, Nov. 7, 1948; uses motifs from his father's *Requiem*); *4 mouvements symphoniques* (1948–49; The Hague, Jan. 17, 1950); *Berceuse voor moede mensen* for Soloists, Chorus, and Orch. (1952); Chamber Sym. for 13 Instruments (1952; Amsterdam, Feb. 24, 1953); *Sonata festiva* for Chamber Orch. (1953); *Kaleidoscope*, symphonic variations (1956); *Symphonic Permutations* (1957); Clarinet Concerto (Amsterdam, June 25, 1959); *Concertante* for Contrabass Clarinet and Orch. (1959); *Anagrams* for Orch. (1960); *Variazioni senza tema* for Orch. (Amsterdam, Dec. 11, 1968); Violin Sonata (1927); 4 string quartets (1927; 1942–43; 1949; 1965); Piano Trio (1929); 2 wind quintets (1930, 1960); *4 Miniatures* for Clarinet, and String Quartet or String Orch. (1950); Sextet for Flute, Clarinet, and String Quartet (1959); *Quartetto piccolo* for 2 Trumpets, Horn, and Trombone (1961); incidental music to the play *Cortez*.

Landré, Willem (actually, **Guillaume Louis Frédéric**), Dutch writer on music and composer, father of **Guillaume (Louis Frédéric) Landré;** b. Amsterdam, June 12, 1874; d. Eindhoven, Jan. 1, 1948. He was a pupil of Bernard Zweers. In 1901 he became music critic of the *Oprechte Haarlemsche Courant* in Haarlem; was music ed. of the *Nieuwe Courant* in The Hague (1901–5), then of the *Nieuwe Rotterdamsche Courant* in Rotterdam (1905–37); taught theory, composition, and the history of music at the Rotterdam Cons.; was ed. of *Caecilia, Het Muziekcollege*.

WORKS: Operas: *De Roos van Dekama* (Haarlem, 1897) and *Beatrijs* (The Hague, 1925); Orch.: *In memoriam matris; 3 Mood Pictures; Le Jardin de Marguerite; Requiem in memoriam uxoris; Fragments from the Book of Baruch* for Chorus; Piano Concerto; Piano Trio; numerous part-songs and songs.

Lane, Burton (real name, **Morris Hyman Kushner**), American composer of popular music; b. N.Y., Feb. 2, 1912. He studied with Simon Bucharoff; began to compose for musicals on Broadway; composed the musical *On a Clear Day You Can See Forever* (1965); wrote for the films *St. Louis Blues* and *Ship Ahoy*. Among the lyricists who worked with him were Ira Gershwin, Frank Loesser, E.Y. Harburg, and Alan Jay Lerner.

Lane, Eastwood, American composer; b. Brewerton, N.Y., May 22, 1879; d. Central Square, N.Y., Jan. 22, 1951. He attended Syracuse Univ.; then devoted himself to composition. He wrote mostly piano pieces in a light, descriptive vein: *In Sleepy Hollow*, 4 tone pictures (1913); *5 American Dances* (1919); *Adirondack Sketches* (1922); *Mongoliana*, suite (1922); *Eastern Seas*, suite (1925; includes *Sea Burial*, orchestrated by Grofé); *Persimmon Pucker* (1926; orchestrated by Grofé); *Sold Down the River*, ballet suite (1928); *Pantomimes* (c.1933); *4th of July* (1935; orchestrated by Grofé); *Here Are Ladies*, 5 pieces (1944); etc.

BIBL.: J. Howard, "E. L.," *Contemporary American Composers* (N.Y., 1925); N. Gentieu, "E. L.," *Journal of Jazz Studies*, III/2 (1976).

Lane, Louis, American conductor; b. Eagle Pass, Texas, Dec. 25, 1923. He studied composition with Kent Kennan at the Univ. of Texas (B.Mus., 1943), Bohuslav Martinů at the Berkshire Music Center in Tanglewood (1946), and Bernard Rogers at the Eastman School of Music in Rochester, N.Y. (M.Mus., 1947); also took a course in opera with Sarah Caldwell (1950). In 1947 he became apprentice conductor to George Szell and the Cleveland Orch.; subsequently was assistant conductor (1956–60), associate conductor (1960–70), and resident conductor (1970–73) there; also was co-director of the Blossom Festival School (1969–73). He served as music director of the Akron (Ohio) Sym. Orch. (1959–83) and of the Lake Erie Opera Theatre (1964–72). In 1973 he became principal guest conductor of the Dallas Sym. Orch., and later held various positions with it until 1978. From 1977 to 1983 he was co-conductor of the Atlanta Sym. Orch.; then was its principal guest conductor (1983–88); also was principal guest conductor (1982–83) and principal conductor (1984–85) of the National Sym. Orch. of the South African Broadcasting Corp. in Johannesburg. As a guest conductor, he appeared with major orchs. on both sides of the Atlantic; also was adjunct prof. at the Univ. of Akron (1969–83), visiting prof. at the Univ. of Cincinnati (1973–75), and artistic adviser and conductor at the Cleveland Inst. of Music (from 1982). In 1971 he received the Mahler Medal and in 1972 the Alice M. Ditson Award; in 1979 he was named a Chevalier of the Order of Arts and Letters of France.

Lang, Benjamin (Johnson), American pianist, organist, conductor, teacher, and composer, father of **Margaret Ruthven Lang;** b. Salem, Mass., Dec. 28, 1837; d. Boston, April 3, 1909. He studied with his father and with Alfred Jaëll. In 1855 he went to Berlin for advanced studies; for a time, took piano lessons with Liszt. Returning to America, he was engaged as a church organist; was also organist of the Handel and Haydn Soc. in Boston (1859–95); then was its conductor (1895–97); directed the Apollo Club and the Cecilia Soc. from their foundation (1868 and 1874, respectively); gave numerous concerts of orch., choral, and chamber music on his own account. As a pianist, teacher, conductor, and organizer, he was in the 1st rank of Boston musicians for a third of a century, and brought out a long list of important works by European and American composers. Among his pupils were Arthur Foote and Ethelbert Nevin. He wrote an oratorio, *David,* and a great many sacred works; also songs and piano pieces.

Lang, David, American composer; b. Los Angeles, Jan. 8, 1957. He studied with Lou Harrison, Martin Bresnick, and Leland Smith at Stanford Univ. (A.B., 1978), with Richard Hervig, Donald Jenni, and William Hibbard at the Univ. of Iowa (M.M., 1980), and with Bresnick, Druckman, Reynolds, and Subotnick at the Yale Univ. School of Music (D.M.A., 1989); also trained at the Aspen Music Festival (1977–81) and the Tanglewood Music Center (1983). Among his awards were an N.E.A. grant (1986) and the Rome Prize (1990); also BMI awards (1980, 1981). In 1987, with Michael Gordon and Julia Wolfe, he founded the international N.Y. festival BANG ON A CAN. His compositions are starkly dissonant.

WORKS: STAGE: *Judith and Holofernes* (1989; Munich, April 27, 1990). ORCH.: *Hammer Amour* for Piano and Chamber Orch. (1979, rev. 1989; Sept. 25, 1989; Alan Feinberg, soloist); *Eating Live Monkeys* (Cleveland, April 19, 1985, Hans Werner Henze conducting); *Spud* for Chamber Orch. (St. Paul, Minn., March 6, 1986); *Are You Experienced?* for Chamber Orch. (Pittsburgh, May 27, 1988); *Dance/Drop* for Chamber Orch. (Toronto, Feb. 10, 1989, composer conducting); *International Business Machine* (Boston, Aug. 25, 1990, Leonard Slatkin conducting); *Bonehead* (N.Y., 1990). CHAMBER: *Illumination Rounds* for Violin and Piano (N.Y., April 23, 1982); *Frag* for Flute, Oboe, and Cello (Philadelphia, Oct. 1, 1985); *Burn Notice* for Flute, Cello, and Piano (N.Y., Nov. 7, 1988); *Orpheus Over and Under* for 2 Pianos (N.Y., March 27, 1989); *The Anvil Chorus* for Percussion (1990); also *By Fire* for Chorus (1984; London, June 30, 1986).

Lang, Eddie (real name, **Salvatore Massaro**), American jazz guitarist; b. Philadelphia, Oct. 25, 1902; d. N.Y., March 26, 1933. He studied the violin; then took up the banjo and the guitar. He made many appearances throughout the U.S., playing with Joe Venuti, Red Nichols, Paul Whiteman, and Bing Crosby. He was a pioneer among jazz guitarists; his early death was widely lamented in jazz circles.

Lang, Hans, Austrian composer; b. Vienna, July 15, 1908. He studied at the Vienna Cons.; wrote popular songs; composed a number of operettas, the most successful being *Lisa, benimm dich!* (Vienna, March 21, 1939).

Láng, István, Hungarian composer; b. Budapest, March 1, 1933. He studied with Viski (1951–56) and Ferenc Szabó (1956–58) at the Budapest Academy of Music; joined its faculty (1973). His music is rooted in euphonious dissonance, without venturing into fashionable ugliness.

WORKS: STAGE: 3 operas: *Pathelin mester* (Master Pathelin; Budapest, 1958); *The Great Dramatist,* television opera (1960; rev. 1974; Budapest, Feb. 14, 1975); *A gyáva* (The Coward; Budapest, 1968); *A Dream about the Theater* (1979–81; Budapest, March 25, 1984); 4 ballets: *Mario és a varázsló* (Mario and the Magician, after Thomas Mann; 1962); *Hiperbola* (1963; suite, 1968); *Lebukott* (Nabbed; 1968); ballet-cantata, *Csillagra-török* (Starfighters; 1972; rev. 1977). ORCH.: Viola Concerto (1957); Concerto for String Orch. (1960); Concertino for Xylophone and Orch. (1961; rev. 1967); *Variazioni ed Allegro* (1965; revision of a discarded sym.); *Gyászzene* (Funeral Music; 1969); *Impulsioni* for Oboe and Instrumental Groups (1969); *3 Sentences from Romeo and Juliet* for Strings (1969–70); *Concerto bucolico* for Horn and Orch. (1970–71); *Tüzoszlop* (Firepillar; 1972); Sym. No. 2 (1972–74); *Egloga* (1976); Violin Concerto (1976–77; Budapest, May 1, 1980); Double Concerto for Clarinet, Harp, and Orch. (1979–80; Budapest, April 7, 1981); Sym. No. 3 (Szombathely, June 7, 1982); Sym. No. 4 (1983; Budapest, Nov. 28, 1984); 3 Songs for Bass and Orch. (1985); *Pezzo lirico* for Oboe and Orch. (1985); Organ Concerto (1987). CHAMBER: *Chamber Cantata* for Soprano, Clarinet, Cello, Piano, and Percussion (1962); Solo Cello Sonata (1960); 3 string quartets (1961, 1966, 1978); 3 wind quintets (1964; *Transfigurazioni,* 1965; 1975); *Pezzi* for Soprano, Flute, Clarinet, Viola, and 2 Percussionists (1964); *Monodia* for Clarinet (1965); *Dramma breve* for Flute (1970); *Cassazione* for Brass Septet (1971); *Töredékek* (Fragments) for Female Voice, Oboe, Bassoon, and Harp (1971–72); *Rhymes* for Flute, Clarinet, Viola, Cello, and Piano (1972); *Villanások* (Flashes) for Violin (1973); *Improvisazioni* for Cimbalom (1973); *Constellations* for Oboe, Violin, Viola, and Clarinet (1974–75); *Surface Metamorphosis* for Tape (1975); *Waves I* for Soprano and Vibraphone (1975); *Constellations* for Oboe and String Trio (1975–76); *Waves II* for Flute, Guitar, and Harpsichord (1976); 2 *Preludes for a Postlude* for Bass and String Trio (1977); *Music 2-4-3* for Ensemble (1979); *Iocaste,* chamber cantata (1979); *Prelude, 3 Mobils and Postlude* for Brass Quintet (1980); *Chagall Flies Away over His Sleeping Vitebsk* for Percussion Quartet (1985; Budapest, May 18, 1986); *Interpolations* for Bassoon (1988).

Lang, Josephine (Caroline), German composer; b. Munich, March 14, 1815; d. Tübingen, Dec. 2, 1880. She was the granddaughter of the soprano Sabina (née Renk) Hitzelberger and the daughter of the soprano **Regina Hitzelberger-Lang** (b. Würzburg, Feb. 15, 1788; d. Munich, May 10, 1827) and the court music director **Theobald Lang** (1783–1839). She studied with her mother and also took lessons in theory with Mendelssohn; composed and publ. a considerable number of competent lieder in an amiably songful, Germanically Romantic vein, in addition to some very playable piano pieces. She was married to the lawyer and music theorist Christian R. Köstlin (1813–56), who sometimes wrote under the nom de plume C. Reinhold.

lang, k.d. (real name, **Kathy Dawn Lang**), Canadian-American pop vocalist; b. Consort, near Edmonton, Nov. 2, 1961. She was reared in a farming community (pop. 650) and began playing piano at age 7; by 10 she had switched to guitar, and within 3 years was writing original songs and performing. In the early 1980s she formed "the reclines" (already showing a predilection for a cummings-like lowercase); the group's local success led to their debut single, *Friday Dance Promenade*, which was soon followed by an independently released album, *A Truly Western Experience* (1984). Lang then signed with Sire Records; her critically acclaimed debut album, *Angel with a Lariat* (1987), established her "torch and twang" style; subsequent albums include *Shadowland* (1988; with guest performances by Loretta Lynn and Brenda Lee) and *Absolute Torch and Twang* (1989). Lang's boyish face and hair, representing a radical departure of style from that of most female country singers, are seen increasingly on television and at all-star concerts. Her remarkable voice and highly flexible approach to country traditions mixes cabaret and pop styles. A child of the '80s, she transforms both the image and the sound of country music into something thoroughly contemporary that has won numerous listeners outside traditional boundaries. A devout vegetarian, she found her songs temporarily banned from airplay on numerous Midwest radio stations for her outspoken views on the evils of eating meat.

Lang, Margaret Ruthven, American composer, daughter of **Benjamin J(ohnson) Lang;** b. Boston, Nov. 27, 1867; d. there, May 29, 1972, at the age of 104(!). She studied in Boston with her father and later in Munich; also with Chadwick and MacDowell. She was the 1st woman composer in the U.S. to have a work performed by a major orch. when Nikisch conducted the premiere of her *Dramatic Overture* with the Boston Sym. Orch. (April 7, 1893). She stopped composing in 1917. She attended the Boston Sym. Orch. concerts from their inception in 1881; was present at a concert 3 days before her 100th birthday, at which Leinsdorf included in the program the psalm tune *Old Hundredth* in her honor.

Works: *Witichis,* overture (1893); *Dramatic Overture* (Boston, April 7, 1893); *Sappho's Prayer to Aphrodite* for Mezzo-soprano and Orch. (1895); *Phoebus' Denunciation of the Furies at the Delphian Shrine* for Bass and Orch.; *Totila,* overture (1895); *Ballade* for Orch. (1901); *Te Deum* for Chorus (1899); *The Lonely Rose,* cantata (1906); *The Night of the Star,* cantata (1913); *The Heavenly Noël* (1916); etc.; about 150 songs, including the popular *An Irish Love Song* (1895); piano pieces.

Lang, Paul Henry, eminent Hungarian-born American musicologist, editor, and teacher; b. Budapest, Aug. 28, 1901. He studied bassoon with Wieschendorf, chamber music with L. Weiner, composition with Kodály, and counterpoint with Koessler at the Budapest Academy of Music (graduated, 1922); then studied musicology with Kroyer and comparative literature with Ernst Curtius and Friedrich Gundorff at the Univ. of Heidelberg (1924); subsequently studied musicology with Pirro, art history with Henri Focillon, literature with Fernand Baldensperger and Félix Gaiffe, and esthetics with Victor Basch at the Sorbonne in Paris (degree in literature, 1928). He settled in the U.S. in 1928, becoming a naturalized citizen in 1934; studied musicology with Kinkeldey and French literature and philosophy with James Frederick Mason at Cornell Univ. (Ph.D., 1934, with the diss. *A Literary History of French Opera*). He was an assistant prof. at Vassar College (1930–31); associate prof., Wells College (1931–33); visiting lecturer, Wellesley College (1934–35); associate prof. of musicology, Columbia Univ. (1933–39; full prof., 1939; prof. emeritus, 1970). He was vice-president of the American Musicological Soc. (1947–49) and president of the International Musicological Soc. (1955–58). From 1945 to 1973 he was ed. of the *Musical Quarterly;* from 1954 to 1963, music ed. of the *N.Y. Herald Tribune.* He publ. the valuable and very popular book *Music in Western Civilization* (N.Y., 1941; many subsequent reprints) and the important and comprehensive study *George Frideric Handel* (N.Y., 1966); also ed. several vols. of articles reprinted from the *Musical Quarterly,* and the anthologies *The Concerto 1800–1900* (N.Y., 1969) and *Symphony 1800–1900* (N.Y., 1969).

Bibl.: E. Strainchamps and M. Maniates, eds., *Music and Civilization: Essays in Honor of P.H. L.* (N.Y., 1984).

Lang, Walter, Swiss pianist and composer; b. Basel, Aug. 19, 1896; d. Baden, Aargau canton, March 17, 1966. He was a pupil of Jaques-Dalcroze; taught at the Dalcroze School in Geneva; then studied in Munich with Klose, and in Zürich with Andreae and W. Frey; appeared as a concert pianist and as an accompanist; was a prof. of piano at the Zürich Cons. (1922–41) and Academy of Music (1949–64). He was married to the soprano Mimi Lang-Seiber.

Works: *Scherzo fugato* for Strings (1929); Piano Concerto (1940); Sym. (1946); *Jour de Fête,* overture (1947); Cello Concerto (1951); Suite for 2 Pianos and Strings (1954); Divertimento for Strings (1957); String Quartet (1919); 2 violin sonatas (1920, 1939); Piano Trio (1925); Flute Sonata (1956); numerous piano pieces.

Langdon, Michael, English bass; b. Wolverhampton, Nov. 12, 1920; d. Hove, Sussex, March 12, 1991. He studied at the Guildhall School of Music in London; subsequently took voice lessons with Alfred Jerger in Vienna, Maria Carpi in Geneva, and Otakar Kraus in London. In 1948 he joined the chorus at the Royal Opera House, Covent Garden; made his operatic debut there in 1950. In subsequent years he sang with many of the major opera houses of the world. On Nov. 2, 1964, he made his Metropolitan Opera debut in N.Y. as Baron Ochs. He created several bass roles in operas by Benjamin Britten; was also noted for his command of the standard operatic repertoire. After his retirement from the stage in 1977, he was director of the National Opera Studio (1978–86). In 1973 he was made a Commander of the Order of the British Empire. He publ. *Notes from a Low Singer* (with R. Fawkes; London, 1982).

Langdon, Richard, English composer and organist; b. Exeter, c.1729; d. there, Sept. 8, 1803. He studied at Oxford (Mus.Bac., 1761); was organist of Exeter Cathedral (1753–77), Ely Cathedral (1777–78), Bristol Cathedral (1778–82), and Armagh Cathedral (1782–94). He publ. *Divine Harmony . . . by the Most Eminent Masters,* op. 5 (1774; Psalms, anthems, etc.); also *12 Glees* for 3 to 4 Voices (c.1780); cantatas; songs.

Lange, prominent family of Dutch musicians:

(1) Samuel de Lange, organist and composer; b. Rotterdam, June 9, 1811; d. there, May 15, 1884. He studied organ and piano with Pruys and van Bree. He was organist of the Lutherse Kerk (1827–33), the Waalse Kerk (1833–54), the Zuider-Kerk (1854–64), and the St. Laurenskerk (1864–84); established a famous recital series at the latter. He also taught at the school of the Rotterdam Maatschappij tot Bevordering der Toonkunst from 1844 and was municipal carillonist. He wrote many works for the organ, including sonatas, fantasias, and various transcriptions; also composed some chamber music and songs. His 2 sons were also distinguished musicians:

(2) Samuel de Lange, organist, conductor, and composer; b. Rotterdam, Feb. 22, 1840; d. Stuttgart, July 7, 1911. He studied with his father and with J.F. Dupont and Verhulst; while on a concert tour with his brother, he studied with Winterberger in Vienna (1859) and then with Mikuli in Lemberg. He became a teacher at the school of the Rotterdam Maatschappij tot Bevordering der Toonkunst in 1862; was also made director of the society's choir and organist of the Waalse Kerk; conducted concerts of Bach's orch. works. After a period in Basel (1874–76) and Paris (1876–77), he taught organ at the Cologne Cons. (1877–84); was also active as a choral conductor. He became director of the (Toonkunst) Maatschappij music school at The Hague in 1885; then joined the faculty of the Stuttgart Cons. in 1893, serving as its director (1900–1908). He wrote 3 syms.; a Piano Concerto; an oratorio, *Mozes;* cantatas; choruses; chamber music; organ pieces; songs; piano pieces.

(3) Daniël de Lange, cellist, conductor, and composer; b. Rotterdam, July 11, 1841; d. Point Loma, Calif., Jan. 31, 1918. He studied with his father and with J.F. Dupont and Verhulst; then studied cello with Ganz in Rotterdam and with Servais at the Brussels Cons., where he also had lessons in composition with Damcke. After concert tours with his brother, he taught cello at the school of the Rotterdam Maatschappij tot Bevordering der Toonkunst (1863–64); was an organist and choral conductor in Paris (1864–70); then taught at the (Toonkunst)

Maatschappij music school in Amsterdam, later serving as director of the Cons. (1895–1913); was also active as a conductor, gaining distinction through his performances of early music and contemporary compositions. He then went to the U.S., where he became director of the music dept. of the Isis Cons. of Art, Music, and Drama in Point Loma, Calif., in 1914. He wrote an opera, *De val van Kuilenberg;* 2 syms.; a Cello Concerto; cantatas; chamber music; piano pieces.

BIBL.: A. Averkamp, *Levensbericht van D. d.L.* (Leiden, 1918).

Lange, Francisco Curt (actually, **Franz Kurt**), German musicologist; b. Eilenburg, Dec. 12, 1903. He studied with Abert, Bekker, Bücken, and Sandberger. He received his Ph.D. in 1929 from the Univ. of Bonn with the dissertation *Über die Mehrstimmigkeit der Niederländischen Motetten.* In 1930 he went to Uruguay; established the Instituto Interamericano de Musicología, and Editorial Cooperativo Interamericano de Compositores, which publ. a long series of works by Latin American composers (1941–56). Beginning in 1935, he ed. the Boletín Latino-Americano de Música, a series containing documentary data on Latin American music and composers. He also publ. numerous essays and pamphlets dealing with literature, philosophy, pedagogy, and sociology (all in Spanish); brought out an anthology, *Latin-American Art Music for the Piano* (N.Y., 1942), with biographical sketches of 12 composers; also publ. a collection of Brazilian church music of the 18th century. In 1948 he founded the musicology dept. of the National Univ. of Cuyo in Mendoza, Argentina.

Lange, Gustav, German pianist and composer; b. Schwerstedt, near Erfurt, Aug. 13, 1830; d. Wernigerode, July 19, 1889. He studied with A.W. Bach, Grell, and Löschhorn; wrote more than 400 piano pieces, generally facile, elegant, and effective, many of which gained great vogue.

Lange-Müller, Peter Erasmus, Danish composer; b. Frederiksberg, Dec. 1, 1850; d. Copenhagen, Feb. 26, 1926. He studied at the Copenhagen Cons. His early compositions show the influence of J.P.E. Hartmann; those of his later period exhibit distinct individuality.

WORKS: Operas (all 1st perf in Copenhagen): *Tove* (Jan. 19, 1878); *Spanske studenter* (Oct. 21, 1883); *Fru Jeanna* (Feb. 4, 1891); *Vikingeblod* (April 29, 1900); incidental music; 2 syms. (1879–81; 1889; rev. 1915) orch. suites *Alhambra* (1875) and *Weyerburg* (1894); Violin Concerto (1904); Trio for Violin, Cello, and Piano; piano pieces; etc.; some 200 songs, many of which gained great popularity.

BIBL.: J. Clausen, *P.E. L.-M.* (Copenhagen, 1938); H. Bonnen, *P.E. L.-M.* (Copenhagen, 1946).

Langendorff, Frieda, German contralto; b. Breslau, March 24, 1868; d. N.Y., June 11, 1947. She studied with Mathilde Mallinger; made her debut in Strasbourg (1901); sang at the Metropolitan Opera in N.Y. (debut, Dec. 7, 1907, as Ortrud in *Lohengrin*) in 1907–8 and 1910–11. She then made an extensive concert tour throughout the U.S. (1912–13). From 1914 to 1916 she was engaged by the Dresden Court Opera; also sang at Bayreuth, Berlin, Helsinki, Brussels, and Amsterdam. She returned to N.Y. after World War II. Among the 76 operatic roles (which included mezzo-soprano parts) in her repertoire were Fricka, Amneris, Azucena, and Dalila.

Langenus, Gustave, Belgian-American clarinetist; b. Mechelen, Aug. 6, 1883; d. N.Y., Jan. 30, 1957. He studied at the Brussels Cons. As a youth of 18, he traveled with Sousa's band in Europe; then lived in England; in 1910, settled in the U.S.; was a clarinetist with the N.Y. Sym. Orch. (1910–20); was one of the founders of the Chamber Music Soc. in N.Y. (1914); then a member of the N.Y. Phil. (1920–23); taught at the Juilliard School of Music and the Dalcroze School of Music. He publ. *Fingered Scale Studies for the Boehm Clarinet* (N.Y., 1911); *Modern Clarinet Playing* (N.Y., 1913); *Virtuoso Studies and Duos for Clarinet* (N.Y., 1915); *Complete Method for the Boehm Clarinet* (8 vols., N.Y., 1916).

Langer, Suzanne K(atherina), important American philosopher of musical esthetics; b. N.Y., Dec. 20, 1895; d. Old Lyme,

Conn., July 17, 1985. She studied philosophy at Radcliffe College (Ph.D., 1926) and at the Univ. of Vienna, her principal teachers being Whitehead and Cassirer. She held teaching positions at Radcliffe and Columbia Univ., then became a prof. at Conn. College, retiring in 1962. Her publications center on a philosophy of art derived from a theory of musical meaning, which in turn exemplify a general philosophy of mind. According to her theory, modes of understanding are forms of symbolic transformation, i.e., one understands any phenomenon by constructing an object analogous to it or referring to it. She extended this theory to argue that the patterns of musical form are structurally similar to those of human feelings. She later expanded this into a general theory of the fine arts, her final work suggesting that art criticism might form the basis of a new structure for the behavioral sciences. Her lucid, strongminded writings are widely considered crucial in understanding musical esthetics.

WRITINGS: *The Practice of Philosophy* (N.Y., 1930); *Philosophy in a New Key* (Cambridge, Mass., 1942); *Feeling and Form* (N.Y., 1953); *Problems of Art* (N.Y., 1957); *Mind: An Essay in Human Feeling* (3 vols., Baltimore, 1967–72).

Langer, Victor, Hungarian composer; b. Budapest, Oct. 14, 1842; d. there, March 19, 1902. He studied in Budapest with R. Volkmann, and later at the Leipzig Cons. Returning to Budapest, he was active as a teacher, theater conductor, and ed. of a Hungarian music journal. His songs, Hungarian dances, arrangements, etc., publ. under the pen name of **Aladar Tisza,** are in the genuine national vein; they enjoyed great popularity.

Langert, Johann August Adolf, German conductor and composer; b. Coburg, Nov. 26, 1836; d. there, Dec. 27, 1920. He was a theater conductor in Coburg, Mannheim, and Basel; in 1873, became court conductor at Gotha, retiring in 1897 to his native town. He composed several operas: *Die Jungfrau von Orleans* (Coburg, 1861); *Des Sängers Fluch* (Coburg, 1863); *Dona Maria* (Darmstadt, 1866); *Die Fabier* (Coburg, 1866); *Dornröschen* (Leipzig, 1871); *Jean Cavallier* (Coburg, 1880; rewritten as *Die Camisarden,* 1887).

Langgaard, Rued (Immanuel), distinguished Danish composer and organist; b. Copenhagen, July 28, 1893; d. Ribe, July 10, 1952. His father, **Siegfried Langgaard** (1852–1914), a student of Liszt, pursued a career as a pianist, composer, and teacher at the Royal Academy of Music in Copenhagen; his mother, Emma Foss, was a pianist. He began his musical training with his parents, then studied organ with G. Helsted, violin with C. Petersen, and theory with V. Rosenberg in Copenhagen. He made his debut as an organist at age 11; subsequently was intermittently active as a church organist until becoming organist of Ribe Cathedral (1940). His early works were influenced by Liszt, Gade, Wagner, and Bruckner; following a period in which he was at times highly experimental (1916–24), he returned to his Romantic heritage; however, even in his last period of production, he produced some works with bizarre and polemical overtones. During his lifetime, he was almost totally neglected in official Danish music circles and failed to obtain an important post. A quarter century after he died, his unperformed works were heard for the 1st time.

WORKS: STAGE: *Antikrist,* biblical opera (1921–39; Danish Radio, June 28, 1980). ORCH.: 16 syms.: No. 1, *Klippepastoraler* (Rock Pastorals; 1908–11; Berlin, April 10, 1913); No. 2, *Vaarbrud* (Awakening of Spring), with Soprano Solo (1912–14; Copenhagen, Nov. 17, 1914; rev. 1926–33; Danish Radio, May 21, 1948); No. 3, *Ungdomsbrus* (Youthfulness), with Piano and Chorus ad libitum (1915–16; April 9, 1918; rev. 1925?–29; Danish Radio, May 4, 1934); No. 4, *Løvfald* (Falling Leaves; 1916; Copenhagen, Dec. 7, 1917); No. 5, *Steppenatur* (1917–18, 1920, 1931; 1st version, rev. 1926; Copenhagen, April 11, 1927; 2nd version, Copenhagen, July 8, 1937); No. 6, *Det himmelrivende* (Tearing the Heavens; 1920; Karlsruhe, Jan. 15, 1923; rev. c.1926–30; Danish Radio, May 29, 1935); No. 7, *Ved Tordenskjold i Holmens Kirke* (By Tordenskjold's Tomb in Holmen's Church; 1925–26; Copenhagen, March 8, 1926; rev. 1930–32; Danish Radio, Dec. 10, 1955); No. 8,

Minder om Amalienborg (Memories at Amalienborg), with Tenor Solo and Chorus (1926–28; rev. 1932–34; not perf.); No. 9, *Fra Dronning Dagmars By* (From the Town of Queen Dagmar; 1942; Copenhagen, May 31, 1943); No. 10, *Hin Tordenbolig* (Yon Dwelling of Thunder; 1944–45; Danish Radio, July 22, 1947); No. 11, *Ixion* (1944–45; Odense, July 29, 1968); No. 12, *Hélsingeborg* (1946; Danish Radio, July 22, 1977); No. 13, *Undertro* (Belief in Miracles; 1947; Danish Radio, Oct. 21, 1970); No. 14, *Morgenen* (The Morning), with Chorus (1948; Copenhagen, May 24, 1979); No. 15, *Søstormen* (The Gale at Sea), with Baritone Solo and Male Chorus (1937–49; Danish Radio, Nov. 23, 1976); No. 16, *Syndflod af sol* (Flood of Sun; 1950–51; Danish Radio, March 17, 1966); *Heltedød* (Death of a Hero) for Orch. (1907); *Drapa* for Orch. (1907); *Sfinx*, tone picture for Orch. (1909–10); *Saga blot* (A Thing of the Past) for Orch. (1917–18); Violin Concerto (1943–44; Danish Radio, July 29, 1968). **VOICES WITH ORCH.:** *Musae triumphantes*, cantata for Soloists, Male Chorus, and Orch. (1906); *Drømmen* (The Dream) for Soloists, Chorus, and Orch. (1915–16; rev. 1945); *Angelus* (The Gold Legend) for Soloists, Chorus, and Orch. (1915–37); *Sfaerernes musik* (Music of the Spheres) for Soprano, Chorus, and Orch. (1916–18; Karlsruhe, Nov. 26, 1921); *Endens tid* (The Time of the End; 1921–44); *Fra Højsangen* (From the Song of Solomon), 6 works for Solo Voice, and Orch. or Ensemble (1949; Danish Radio, Feb. 24, 1969); *Fra Dybet* (From the Deep) for Chorus and Orch. (1950–52). **CHAMBER:** 8 string quartets (1914–31); 5 violin sonatas (1915–49); Septet for Wind Instruments (1915); *Humoreske* for 5 Wind Instruments and Drum (1923); *Dies irae* for Tuba and Piano (1948); Quartet for Brass Instruments (1949); about 50 works for piano, including 6 sonatas; organ music, including *Messis* (*Høstens tid*) (Messis [The Time of Harvest]), drama in 3 "evenings" (1932–39), and some 100 organ preludes; also about 25 motets and 150 songs.—**BIBL.:** B. Nielsen, "Pettersson and L.," *Nordic Sounds* (March 1988).

Langhans, (Friedrich) Wilhelm, German composer and violinist; b. Hamburg, Sept. 21, 1832; d. Berlin, June 9, 1892. He studied at the Leipzig Cons. with David (violin) and Hauptmann and Richter (composition); then in Paris with Alard (violin). From 1852 to 1856 he played violin in the Gewandhaus Orch. at Leipzig; from 1857 to 1860 he was concertmaster at Düsseldorf; then was a teacher and violinist in Hamburg, Paris, and Heidelberg; received his Ph.D. at Heidelberg (1871). He taught music history at Kullak's Neue Akademie der Tonkunst in Berlin (1874–81); in 1881, joined the faculty of the Scharwenka Cons. there. In 1858 he married the pianist Louise Japha (divorced in 1874). He wrote a Sym.; String Quartet; Violin Sonata; violin studies.—**WRITINGS:** *Das musikalische Urtheil und seine Ausbildung durch die Erziehung* (Berlin, 1872; 2nd ed., 1886); *Die königliche Hochschule für Musik in Berlin* (Leipzig, 1873); *Die Musikgeschichte in zwölf Vorlesungen* (Leipzig, 1878; 2nd ed., 1879; Eng. tr., 1886); *Die Geschichte der Musik des 17., 18. und 19. Jahrhunderts in chronologischem anschlusse an die Musikgeschichte von A.W. Ambros* (Leipzig, 1881–87).

Langlais, Jean, French organist and composer; b. La Fontenelle, Feb. 15, 1907; d. Paris, May 8, 1991. He was blind from infancy; studied organ with Dupré at the Paris Cons., winning 1st prize in 1930; also studied composition with Dukas and Tournemire there. He became organist at Montrouge in 1932; from 1945 to 1988, was organist at Ste.-Clotilde in Paris; also taught organ at the School for the Blind. His works are mainly for organ (2 *offertoires pour tous les temps, 3 paraphrases grégoriennes*, etc.); he also wrote a symphonic poem, *Cloches*; Suite for Cello and Orch.; numerous choral works; Trio for Flute, Violin, and Viola.—**BIBL.:** K. Thomerson, *J. L.: A Bio-Bibliography* (Westport, Conn., 1988).

Langlé, Honoré (François Marie), French music theorist and composer; b. Monaco, 1741; d. Villiers-le-Bel, near Paris, Sept. 20, 1807. He studied in Naples at the Conservatorio della Pietà dei Turchini with Cafaro. In 1768 he went to Paris, becoming a singing teacher at the École Royale de Chant et de Déclamation in 1784; then was a prof. of harmony and librarian at the Paris Cons. (1795–1802). He composed a number of operas, including *Antiochus et Stratonice* (Versailles, 1786) and *Corisandre, ou Les Fous par enchantement* (Paris, March 8, 1791); also other vocal works. He ed. Mengozzi's *Méthode de chant du Conservatoire* (1804; 2nd ed., c.1815) and collaborated with Cherubini on his *Méthode de chant*.—**WRITINGS** (all publ. in Paris): *Traité d'harmonie et de modulation* (1793; 2nd ed., 1797); *Traité de la basse sous le chant précédé de toutes les règles de la composition* (c.1798); *Nouvelle méthode pour chiffrer les accords* (1801); *Traité de la fugue* (1805).

Langridge, Philip (Gordon), esteemed English tenor; b. Hawkhurst, Kent, Dec. 16, 1939. He studied violin at the Royal Academy of Music in London; took voice lessons with Bruce Boyce and Celia Bizony; was active as a violinist but also began to make appearances as a singer from 1962. He first sang at the Glyndebourne Festival in 1964, and made regular appearances there from 1970; also sang at the Edinburgh Festivals from 1970. He appeared at Milan's La Scala in 1979; then sang for the 1st time at London's Covent Garden as the Fisherman in Stravinsky's *The Nightingale* in 1983. He made his Metropolitan Opera debut in N.Y. as Ferrando in *Così fan tutte* on Jan. 5, 1985. He was chosen to create the role of Orpheus in Birtwistle's opera *The Mask of Orpheus* at London's English National Opera in 1986. Admired as both an operatic and a concert singer, he maintains an extensive repertoire ranging from the Baroque masters to contemporary works. He is married to **Ann Murray.**

Lanier, Nicholas, English lutenist, singer, composer, and painter; b. London (baptized), Sept. 10, 1588; d. there (buried), Feb. 24, 1666. He was made lutenist in the King's Musick (1616); then Master of the Musick to Prince Charles, and subsequently Master of the King's Musick upon the latter's accession (1625), although no formal appointment as such was made. A large portion of his music is not extant. He was a significant composer of songs. He may have introduced the stylo recitativo to England in his music to Ben Jonson's masque *Lovers Made Men* (London, Feb. 22, 1617; music not extant); he sang in the production, and also painted the scenery. His other stage works were *Marke . . . at the Marriage of . . . the Earle of Somerset*, to a text by T. Campion (London, 1613; in collaboration with G. Coprario); *The Vision of Delight*, to a text by B. Jonson (London, 1621; in collaboration with R. Johnson); and *The Masque of Augurs* (London, 1622). He also set to music (1630) Herrick's poem on the birth of Prince Charles and wrote the extended recitative *Nor can'st thou yet* for *Hero and Leander*. His song MSS are found in various British libraries; many of them appeared in various collections of his time. See I. Spink, ed., *English Songs 1625–1660*, Musica Britannica, XXXIII (1971), and E. Huws Jones, ed., *Nicholas Lanier: Six Songs* (London, 1976).—**BIBL.:** M. Emslie, "N. L.'s Innovations in English Song," *Music & Letters*, XLI (1960); F. Graham, *The Earlier Life and Work of N. L. . . . Collector of Paintings and Drawings* (diss., Columbia Univ., 1967).

Lanier, Sidney (Clopton), American poet and musician; b. Macon, Ga., Feb. 3, 1842; d. Lynn, N.C., Sept. 7, 1881. Best known for his poetry, Lanier learned as a child to play the piano, flute, guitar, violin, and organ. After serving in the Civil War, he was organist and choirmaster for a short period at a church in Montgomery, Ala. In 1873 he became 1st flutist of the Peabody Sym. Orch. in Baltimore; also lectured on literature at the Peabody Inst. and was lecturer in English literature at Johns Hopkins Univ. (from 1879). He discussed aspects of music in such books as *The Science of English Verse* (N.Y., 1880) and *Music and Poetry* (N.Y., 1899); see C. Anderson, ed., *The Centennial Edition of the Works of Sidney Lanier* (10 vols., Baltimore, 1945). He composed songs and flute pieces.

BIBL.: H. Thorpe, "S. L.: A Poet for Musicians," *Musical Quarterly* (July 1925); A. Starke, "S. L. as a Musician," ibid. (Oct. 1934).

Lankester, Michael (John), English conductor; b. London, Nov. 12, 1944. He studied at the Royal College of Music in London (1962–67), and after making his formal conducting debut with the English Chamber Orch. in London (1967), he was a conductor (1969–80) and head of the opera dept. (1975–80) at the Royal College of Music; also was founder-conductor of Contrapuncti (1967–79) and music director of the National Theatre of Great Britain (1969–74) and of the Surrey Phil. (1974–79). He was assistant conductor (1980–82), associate conductor (1982–84), and conductor-in-residence (1984–88) of the Pittsburgh Sym. Orch.; was also music director of the Hartford (Conn.) Sym. Orch. (from 1986).

Lankow, Anna, noted German contralto and singing teacher; b. Bonn, Jan. 13, 1850; d. there, March 19, 1908. She studied singing in Cologne, Leipzig, and Dresden; began her career as a concert singer; then was engaged as a contralto in the Weimar Opera; however, because she had been lame since childhood, she was forced to abandon the stage. In 1883 she married the sculptor Paul Pietsch of Berlin; after his death in 1885, she went to in N.Y. as a singing teacher; subsequently returned to Germany. She publ. a treatise, *Die Wissenschaft des Kunstgesangs* (1899; in German and Eng.).

Lanner, August (Joseph), Austrian violinist, conductor, and composer, son of **Joseph (Franz Karl) Lanner;** b. Vienna, Jan. 23, 1834; d. there, Sept. 27, 1855. A talented violinist, dance composer, and conductor, he died in his 22nd year.

Lanner, Joseph (Franz Karl), historically significant Austrian violinist, conductor, and composer, father of **August (Joseph) Lanner;** b. Vienna, April 12, 1801; d. Oberdöbling, near Vienna, April 14, 1843. A self-taught violinist and composer, he joined Pamer's dance orch. when he was 12. In 1818 he formed a trio; Johann Strauss, Sr., joined it in 1819, making it a quartet. The group grew in size, and by 1824 it was a full-sized classical orch. which became famous and performed in coffeehouses, taverns, at balls, etc. The orch. was subsequently divided into 2 ensembles, with Lanner leading one, and Strauss the other. Strauss went his own way in 1825. With Strauss, Lanner is acknowledged as the creator of the mid-19th-century Viennese waltz. Lanner's output totals 209 popular pieces, including 112 waltzes, 25 Ländler, 10 quadrilles, 3 polkas, 28 galops, and 6 marches; overture to *Der Preis einer Lebensstunde; Banquet-Polonaise; Tarantella;* and *Bolero.* His complete works in 8 vols., ed. by E. Kremser, were publ. between 1889 and 1891 (reprint, N.Y., 1971); selections were brought out by O. Bie (Munich, 1920) and A. Orel in Denkmäler der Tonkunst in Österreich, LXV, Jg. XXXIII/2 (1926).

BIBL.: H. Sachs, *J. L.* (Vienna, 1889); F. Rebay and O. Keller, *J. L.* (Vienna, 1901); F. Lange, *J. L. und Johann Strauss: Ihre Zeit, ihr Leben, und ihre Werke* (Vienna, 1904; 2nd ed., 1919); A. Weinmann, *Verzeichnis der im Druck erschienen Werke von J. L.* (Vienna, 1948); M. Schönherr, *L., Strauss, Zuhrer: Synoptic Handbook of the Dances and Marches* (1982).

Lantins, Arnold de, Franco-Flemish composer; b. probably in Lantin, near Liège, c.1400; place and date of death unknown. He may have been related to **Hugo de Lantins.** He was in Venice in 1428; was a singer in the Papal Chapel in Rome between Nov. 1431 and July 1432. He wrote several sacred works, as well as ballades and rondeaux. His employment of carefully connected chords suggesting purely harmonic procedures is of historical interest. For his works, see C. Van den Borren, *Polyphonia Sacra: A Continental Miscellany of the 15th Century* (Burnham Wood, 1932; 2nd ed., rev., 1962) and *Pièces polyphoniques profanes de provenance liégeoise (XVᵉ siècle)* (vol. I, Brussels, 1950).

BIBL.: C. Van den Borren, "Hugo et A. d.L.," *Annales de la Fédération archéologique et historique de Belgique,* XXIX (1932).

Lantins, Hugo de, Franco-Flemish composer; b. probably in Lantin, near Liège, c.1399; place and date of death unknown. He may have been related to **Arnold de Lantins.** He spent his early career in Italy, where he wrote the ballata *Tra quante regione* (1421); in addition to other ballate, he composed rondeaux and sacred music. For his works, see C. Van den Borren, *Polyphonia Sacra: A Continental Miscellany of the 15th Century* (Burnham Wood, 1932; 2nd ed., rev., 1962) and *Pièces polyphoniques profanes de provenance liégeoise (XVᵉ siècle)* (vol. I, Brussels, 1950).

BIBL.: C. Van den Borren, "H. et Arnold d.L.," *Annales de la Fédération archéologique et historique de Belgique,* XXIX (1932).

Lanza, Mario (real name, **Alfredo Arnold Cocozza**), American tenor and actor; b. Philadelphia, Jan. 31, 1921; d. Rome, Oct. 7, 1959. He studied singing with Enrico Rosati; appeared in recitals and opera. In 1951 he starred in the title role of a highly successful film, *The Great Caruso;* also appeared in 6 other films, including *The Toast of New Orleans,* in which he sang his most popular song, *Be My Love.* His career quickly unraveled shortly thereafter as obesity overtook him, which led to his early death.

Lanzetti, Salvatore, noted Italian cellist and composer; b. Naples, c.1710; d. Turin, c.1760. He publ. a method, *Principes ou l'application de violoncelle par tous les tons* (Amsterdam, c.1769). His works include 12 sonatas for Cello and Basso Continuo (Amsterdam, 1736); 6 *Solos* for 2 Cellos and Basso Continuo (Harpsichord) (London, 1740); 6 *solos* for 2 Cellos or Flutes, and Bass (London, c.1745); 6 *Solos after an Early & Elegant Taste* for Cello and Basso Continuo (Harpsichord) (London, c.1760).

Laparra, Raoul, French composer; b. Bordeaux, May 13, 1876; d. in an air raid in Suresnes, near Paris, April 4, 1943. He studied at the Paris Cons. with Gédalge, Massenet, and Fauré; won the Grand Prix de Rome with his cantata *Ulysse* (June 27, 1903). He was music critic of *Le Matin,* resigning in 1937 to dedicate himself entirely to composition. He was at his best in music inspired by Spanish subjects.

WORKS: Operas: *Peau d'âne* (Bordeaux, 1899); *La Habanera* (Paris, Feb. 26, 1908; his best-known work); *La Jota* (Paris, April 26, 1911); *Le Joueur de viole* (Paris, Dec. 24, 1925); *Las toreras* (Lille, Feb. 1929); *L'Illustre Fregona* (Paris, Feb. 16, 1931); incidental music to *El Conquistador; Un Dimanche basque,* suite for Orch. and Piano; etc.

Laplante, (Joseph) André (Roger), Canadian pianist; b. Rimouski, Quebec, Nov. 12, 1949. He commenced piano studies at 7, then continued his training with Nathalie Pépin and Yvonne Hubert at the École Vincent-d'Indy in Montreal (B.Mus., 1968; M.Mus., 1970); then pursued further studies with Gorodnitzki at the Juilliard School in N.Y. (1970–71; 1976–78) and with Lefébure in Paris (1971–74). He won 3rd prizes in the Long-Thibaud (Paris, 1973) and Sydney (1977) competitions, and then shared 2nd prize at the Tchaikovsky Competition in Moscow (1978); made his N.Y. recital debut (Oct. 21, 1978), and subsequently toured throughout North America, Europe, and the Far East. He won accolades for his performances of the Romantic repertoire.

Laporte, André, Belgian composer; b. Oplinter, July 12, 1931. He studied musicology and philosophy at the Catholic Univ. of Louvain, graduating in 1956; studied organ with Flor Peeters and counterpoint with Marinus De Jong at the Lemmens Inst. in Mechelen (1956–58); also attended the summer courses in Darmstadt and Cologne (1960–65). In 1963 he was engaged as a producer for the Belgian Radio; in 1968 he was appointed to the faculty of the Brussels Cons.

WORKS: Piano Sonata (1954); *Psalm* for 6 Voices and Brass (1956); *Introduction and Fughetta* for Guitar (1956); *Sequenza I* for Clarinet (1964); *Sequenza II* for Bass Clarinet and 3 Clarinets (1965); *Jubilius* for 12 Brasses and 3 Percussionists (1966); *Ludus fragilis* for Oboe (1967); *Story* for 3 Viole de

Gamba and Harpsichord (1967); *Ascension* for Piano (1967); *Inclinations* for Flute (1968); *Alliances* for Cello and Piano (1968); *De profundis* for Mixed Choir (1968); *Le morte chitarre* for Tenor, Flute, and 14 String Soloists (1969); *Reflection* for Clarinet (1970); *Night Music* for Orch. (1970; Brussels, March 15, 1971); *La vita non è sogno*, oratorio for Narrator, Tenor, Baritone, Chorus, and Orch. (Ghent, Sept. 13, 1972); *Péripétie* for Brass Sextet (1973); *Arboreal*, film music for Piano and Tape (1974); *Chamber Music* for Soprano, Flute, Clarinet, Violin, and Piano (1975); *Transit* for 48 Strings (1978–79); *Das Schloss*, opera (1981–85); *Fantasia-Rondino con tema reale* for Violin and Orch. (1989).

Laporte, Joseph de, French writer on the theater and music; b. Belfort, 1713; d. Paris, Dec. 19, 1779. He was a Jesuit abbé. **WRITINGS:** *Almanach historique et chronologique de tous les spectacles de Paris,* I (1752); *Calendrier historique de théâtre de l'Opéra et des Comédies Française et Italienne et des Foires,* II (1753); *Les Spectacles de Paris, ou Suite du Calendrier historique et chronologique et des théâtres,* III–XXVII (1754–78; continued by Duchesne and others); with J. Suard, *Nouveaux choix de pièces tirées des anciens Mercures et des autres journeaux,* LX–CVIII (Paris, 1762–64); *L'Esprit de l' "Encyclopédie" ou Choix des articles les plus curieux* (Geneva and Paris, 1768); with J. Clement, *Anecdotes dramatique contenant toutes les pièces de théâtres . . . jusqu'en 1775* (Paris, 1775); with S. Chamfort, *Dictionnaire dramatique contenant l'histoire des théâtres et les règles du genre dramatique* (Paris, 1776).

La Pouplinière, Alexandre-Jean-Joseph Le Riche de, French musical amateur; b. Chinon, July 26, 1693; d. there, Dec. 5, 1762. A wealthy member of the nobility and a statesman, he was a patron of music and a pupil of Rameau. The musical soirées he sponsored in his Paris home and Passy country estate became famous; his directors were Rameau, J. Stamitz, and Gossec; upon Stamitz's advice, he added horns, clarinets, and a harp to his orch., instruments seldom heard in a concert orch. before that time. La Pouplinière wrote a number of arias, some of which Rameau incorporated into his own works. **BIBL.:** G. Cucuel, *L. P. et la musique de chambre au XVIIIᵉ siècle* (Paris, 1913).

La Prade, Ernest, American violinist and composer; b. Memphis, Tenn., Dec. 20, 1889; d. Sherman, Conn., April 20, 1969. He studied violin at the Cincinnati College of Music, at the Royal Cons. in Brussels with César Thomson, and in London with J. Jongen (composition). He subsequently taught at the Cincinnati College of Music; was a member of the Cincinnati Sym. Orch. (1909–12), the Belgian and Holbrook Quartets in London (1914–17), and the N.Y. Sym. Orch. (1919–28); in 1929, he joined the staff of NBC; in 1950, became supervisor of music research there. He wrote a comic opera, *Xantha* (London, 1917), and songs; publ. *Alice in Orchestralia* (1925); *Marching Notes* (1929); *Broadcasting Music* (1947).

La Presle, Jacques de, French composer; b. Versailles, July 5, 1888; d. Paris, May 6, 1969. He studied at the Paris Cons.; received the Grand Prix de Rome in 1921; in 1937, was appointed prof. of harmony at the Paris Cons. His works include *Apocalypse de St.-Jean* (1928); *Album d'images,* suite for Orch. (1935); Piano Concerto (1949); chamber music; songs.

Laquai, Reinhold, Swiss composer; b. Zürich, May 1, 1894; d. Oberrieden, Oct. 3, 1957. He studied at the Zürich Cons.; later with Busoni in Berlin. In 1920 he became a teacher at the Zürich Cons. **WORKS:** Operas: *Der Schleier der Tanit* and *Die Revisionsreise;* many orch. works (3 syms., 5 overtures, 2 serenades, a concert piece for Piano and Orch., etc.); chamber music (trios; sonatas for violin, flute, cello, bassoon, and horn, clarinet, etc.; Piano Quintet); piano pieces; and more than 200 songs.

Lara, Augustín, phenomenally successful Mexican composer of popular songs; b. Mexico City, Oct. 30, 1897; d. there, Nov. 5, 1970. He began his career playing in bordellos until his father sent him to a military academy, which he soon fled, taking a job on a railroad line in Durango. He eventually re-

turned to music, selling his 1st song, *Imposible,* for 50 pesos. Like Irving Berlin, to whom he is often compared, Lara was self-taught as a musician; nonetheless, his style was broad and adaptable, his output ranging from romantic ballads, pasodobles, and rancheras to tangos and marches. In 1930 he had his own radio program, and in 1931 he produced the score for *Santa,* one of Mexico's earliest talking pictures, and the 1st of what would be his more than 30 film scores. Among his most popular songs among U.S. audiences were *Granada, The Nearness of You, Be Mine Tonight,* and *You Belong to My Heart,* all written between 1932 and 1934 and popularized by such artists as Bing Crosby, Frank Sinatra, and the Ames Brothers. Among his most popular songs in Mexico were *Noche criolla, La clave azul, Palmera,* and *La Cumbancha,* which were performed by such leading South American artists as Ortiz Tirado, Pedro Vargas, and Marco Antonio Muñiz. Several of his songs, including *Noche de ronda* and *Novillero,* were publ. under his sister's name (María Teresa Lara) to avoid prosecution for having sold them to firms other than RCA Victor, with which he had signed an exclusive contract.

Among Lara's several wives was the film star María Félix, for whom he wrote many songs, including *Maria Bonita,* which subsequently became the name of a street in Mexico City; it has been performed by such disparate song stylists as Pedro Vargas, Josephine Baker (in French), Julio Iglesias, and Plácido Domingo. In 1953 Lara was honored with a special 2-hour program at the Palace of Fine Arts commemorating the 25th anniversary of his career; in 1958 he became the subject of Alejandro Galindo's biographical film *La vida de Augustín Lara.* In 1965 the City of Granada gave him a house in recognition of his musical genius, and in 1966, Generalissimo Franco accorded him honorary Spanish citizenship for his songs named for Spanish cities, among them *Granada* (recorded by Mario Lanza), *Madrid,* and *Toledo.* He was also honored by every president in his native Mexico beginning with Ávila Camacho; not to be outdone, Veracruz gave him a house complete with a piano-shaped swimming pool. Lara retired in 1967 to his home in Mexico City, where he died of a stroke at the Hospital Inglés; he was buried at the Rotonda de los Hombres Illustres by order of President Luis Echeverría. One year later, a postage stamp was issued in his honor. Two statues have been erected in his memory, one in Veracruz and one in Madrid, both the work of Humberto Peraza Ojeda. The statue in Madrid, erected on May 13, 1975, carries the dedication: "Descansa en paz, Flaco de Oro." **BIBL.:** D. Castañeda, *Balance de A. L.* (Mexico City, 1941); P. Taibo, *La música de A. L. en el cine* (Mexico City, 1984); idem, *A. L.* (Mexico City, 1985).

Lara, Isidore de. See **De Lara, Isidore.**

Lara-Bareiro, Carlos, Paraguayan composer; b. Capiatá, March 6, 1914. He played in the boy scout band conducted by his father; then studied violin in Asunción and Rio de Janeiro; during his stay in Brazil he also took lessons in composition and conducting. Returning to Paraguay in 1951, he organized in Asunción the Sym. Orch. of the Assoc. of Musicians of Paraguay. Eventually he moved to Buenos Aires. His works reflect the modes and moods of Paraguayan folk music. He wrote several symphonic suites on Paraguayan themes and a Piano Concerto.

Laredo (y Unzueta), Jaime (Eduardo), Bolivian violinist; b. Cochabamba, June 7, 1941. He was taken to the U.S. as a child; studied violin with Antonio de Grassi and Frank Houser in San Francisco, Josef Gingold in Cleveland, and Ivan Galamian at the Curtis Inst. of Music in Philadelphia. In 1959, a week before his 18th birthday, he won the Queen Elisabeth of Belgium Competition in Brussels, and subsequently appeared with great success in America and Europe as a soloist with leading orchs. The proud Bolivian government issued a series of airmail stamps with Laredo's picture and a musical example with the notes A, D, C in the treble clef, spelling his name in Latin notation (La-Re-Do). In 1960 he married the pianist **Ruth** (née **Meckler**) **Laredo** (divorced in 1974);

his 2nd wife, **Sharon Robinson,** was a cellist. With her and the pianist Joseph Kalichstein, he formed a trio which gave successful concerts. He appeared regularly as a soloist and conductor with the Scottish Chamber Orch. in Glasgow from 1977, and led it on tours of the U.S.; taught at the St. Louis Cons. from 1983; was appointed co-artistic director of the Philadelphia Chamber Orch. in 1985.

Laredo, Ruth (née **Meckler**), American pianist; b. Detroit, Nov. 20, 1937. She studied with Rudolf Serkin at the Curtis Inst. of Music in Philadelphia (B.M., 1960); in 1962, made her debut with Leopold Stokowski and the American Sym. Orch. in N.Y. In 1965 she played in Europe with Rudolf Serkin and his son Peter Serkin; in 1977 she toured Japan. In 1960 she married the Bolivian violinist **Jaime Laredo,** with whom she played numerous recitals; but they were divorced in 1974. She is particularly fond of Russian music, and plays piano works of Rachmaninoff and Scriabin with passionate devotion.

La Rocca, Nick (Dominick James), American jazz cornetist, trumpeter, bandleader, and composer; b. New Orleans, April 11, 1889; d. there, Feb. 22, 1961. After graduating from high school, he became a cornetist and local bandleader. He formed the Original Dixieland Jass (later Jazz) Band (1916), which gained wide popularity and brought attention to the New Orleans style of jazz; it played at Reisenweber's in N.Y. in 1917 and toured throughout the U.S. and Europe; the group is most noted for having made, in 1917, the 1st jazz recordings, these becoming a major influence on the next generation (the "Chicago School") of white jazz musicians. He led various groups in N.Y. (1920–25; 1936–38) before returning to New Orleans.
  BIBL.: H. Brunn, *The Story of the Original Dixieland Jazz Band* (Baton Rouge, 1960).

Laroche, Hermann, Russian music critic; b. St. Petersburg, May 25, 1845; d. there, Oct. 18, 1904. He studied with Rubinstein and Zaremba at the St. Petersburg Cons., and with Tchaikovsky in Moscow. He was a prof. at the Moscow Cons. (1867–70), then at the St. Petersburg Cons. (1872–79); contributed numerous articles to Russian journals; collected his essays and criticisms and publ. them in 1894. His most important work is *M.I. Glinka and His Place in Russian Music* (1867; new ed., 1953); with N. Kashkin he wrote *Reminiscences of Tchaikovsky* (1894).

La Rosa Parodi, Armando, Italian conductor and composer; b. Genoa, March 14, 1904; d. Rome, Jan. 21, 1977. He studied in Genoa and Milan; began his career as a conductor in 1929. He was active as a guest conductor in Genoa, Milan, Turin, and Rome; in 1963 he was named chief conductor of the RAI Orch. of Rome, a post he held until his death. He composed the operas *Il Mercante e l'avvocato* (1934) and *Cleopatra* (1938), and several symphonic works.

La Rotella, Pasquale, Italian composer and conductor; b. Bitonto, Feb. 26, 1880; d. Bari, March 20, 1963. He studied in Naples; was choirmaster at Bari Cathedral (1902–13); taught at the Liceo Musicale there (1934–49); toured Italy as an opera conductor. His works include the operas *Ivan* (Bari, Jan. 20, 1900), *Dea* (Bari, April 11, 1903), *Fasma* (Milan, Nov. 28, 1908), *Corsaresca* (Rome, Nov. 13, 1933), and *Manuela* (Nice, March 4, 1948); much sacred music.

Larrivée, Henri, French bass-baritone; b. Lyons, Jan. 9, 1737; d. Vincennes, Aug. 7, 1802. He sang in the chorus of the Paris Opéra; made his debut there in Rameau's *Castor et Pollux* in 1755; he subsequently distinguished himself in the operas of Gluck, creating the roles of Agamemnon in *Iphigénie en Aulide* (1774), Ubalde in *Armide* (1777), and Orestes in *Iphigénie en Tauride* (1779). Gossec wrote the title role of his opera *Sabinus* (1773) for him. His wife, **Marie Jeanne** (née **Le Miere**) **Larrivée** (b. Sedan, Nov. 29, 1733; d. Paris, Oct. 1786), was a soprano at the Paris Opéra (1750–77); she created the title role of Ernelinde in Philidor's opera of 1767, and also the role of Éponine in *Sabinus*.

Larrocha (y de la Calle), Alicia de, brilliant Spanish pianist; b. Barcelona, May 23, 1923. She studied piano with Frank

Marshall and theory with Ricardo Lamote de Grignon. She made her 1st public appearance at the age of 5; was soloist with the Orquesta Sinfónica of Madrid at the age of 11. In 1940 she launched her career in earnest; she began making major tours of Europe in 1947; made her 1st visit to the U.S. in 1955 and thereafter toured throughout the world to great acclaim. She also served as director of the Marshall Academy in Barcelona from 1959. Her interpretations of Spanish music have evoked universal admiration for their authentic quality, but she has also been exuberantly praised by sober-minded critics for her impeccable taste and exquisitely polished technique in classical works.

L'Arronge, Adolf, German composer and conductor; b. Hamburg, March 8, 1838; d. Berlin, May 25, 1908. He studied at the Leipzig Cons. with R. Genée; was a theater conductor in Cologne, Danzig, Königsberg, Würzburg, Stuttgart, Budapest, etc.; became director of the Kroll Opera in Berlin in 1866; then of the Lobetheater in Breslau (1874–78). Returning to Berlin, he bought the Friedrich-Wilhelmstädtisches Theater in 1881, and managed it until 1894 as the Deutsches Theater. He brought out many musical farces, singspiels, etc. at the Wallnertheater, including his comic operas *Das Gespenst* and *Der zweite Jakob,* the "Volksstücke" *Das grosse Los* (1868) and *Mein Leopold,* etc.; also wrote many songs.

Larsen, Jens Peter, distinguished Danish musicologist; b. Copenhagen, June 14, 1902; d. there, Aug. 22, 1988. He studied mathematics and musicology at the Univ. of Copenhagen (M.A., 1928); then joined its staff; later obtained his Ph.D. there in 1939; retired in 1970. A leading authority on the music of Haydn, he served as general ed. of the critical edition sponsored by the Joseph Haydn Inst. of Cologne from 1955 to 1960; his studies on the music of Handel are also of value.
  WRITINGS: *Drei Haydn-Kataloge in Faksimile: Mit Einleitung und ergänzenden Themenverzeichnissen* (Copenhagen, 1941; 2nd ed., rev., 1979); *Weyses sange: Deres betydning for sangen i hjem, skole og kirke* (Copenhagen, 1942); *Handel's "Messiah": Origins, Composition, Sources* (Copenhagen, 1957; 2nd ed., rev., 1972); *Essays on Handel, Haydn, and the Viennese Classical Style* (tr. by U. Krämer; Ann Arbor, 1988).

Larsen, Libby (actually, **Elizabeth Brown**), American composer; b. Wilmington, Del., Dec. 24, 1950. She was a pupil of Argento, Fetler, and Eric Stokes at the Univ. of Minnesota (B.A., 1971; M.A., 1975; Ph.D., 1978). With Stephen Paulus, she founded the Minnesota Composers Forum in Minneapolis in 1973, serving as its managing composer until 1985; she also was composer-in-residence of the Minnesota Orch. (1983–87). Her works have been widely performed in the U.S. and abroad. One of her most impressive scores, the choral sym. *Coming Forth into Day* (1986), utilizes a text by Jehan Sadat, the widow of the slain leader of Egypt.
  WORKS: OPERAS: *The Words upon the Windowpane* (1978); *The Silver Fox,* children's opera (1979); *Tumbledown Dick* (1980); *Clair de lune* (1984); *Frankenstein: The Modern Prometheus* (1989; St. Paul, Minn., May 25, 1990). **ORCH.:** *Tom Twist* for Narrator and Orch. (1975); *Weaver's Song and Jig* for String Band and Chamber Orch. (1978); *Pinions* for Violin and Chamber Orch. (1981); *Deep Summer Music* (1983); *Parachute Dancing,* overture (1983); *Water Music,* sym. (1984; N.Y., Jan. 30, 1985); *Coming Forth into Day,* choral sym. (St. Paul, Minn., April 14, 1986); *Coriolis* (1986); *What the Monster Saw* (1987); Trumpet Concerto (1988); *Collage Boogie* (1988); *3 Summer Scenes* (1989); *Cold, Silent Snow,* concerto for Chamber Orch. (1989); Piano Concerto (1989). **CHAMBER:** *Bronze Veils* for Trombone and Percussion (1979); *Ulloa's Ring* for Flute and Piano (1980); *Scudding* for Cello (1980); *Triage* for Harp (1981); *Aubade* for Flute (1982); also vocal music, including choral pieces and songs.

Larsen, Nils, Norwegian pianist, teacher, and composer; b. Christiania, June 7, 1888; d. there (Oslo), Nov. 7, 1937. He studied in Christiania with M. Knutzen and in Vienna with Ganz and da Motta. He made tours of Scandinavia and taught in the Norwegian capital; wrote a number of piano pieces and songs.

Larsén-Todsen, Nanny, Swedish soprano; b. Hagby, Aug. 2, 1884; d. Stockholm, May 26, 1982. She studied at the Stockholm Cons. and in Germany and Italy. In 1906 she made her debut at the Royal Theater in Stockholm as Agathe in *Der Freischütz;* was a member of the Royal Theater (1907–22), specializing in Wagnerian roles; sang at La Scala in Milan (1923–24), at the Metropolitan Opera in N.Y. (1925–27; debut Jan. 31, 1925, as Brünnhilde in *Götterdämmerung*), and at Bayreuth (1927–28; 1930–31); made guest appearances at most of the European opera houses. Her principal roles were the 3 Brünnhildes, Isolde, Fricka, and Leonore. She married H. Todsen in 1916; following her retirement from the stage, she became a teacher in Stockholm.

Larsson, Lars-Erik (Vilner), important Swedish composer and pedagogue; b. Åkarp, near Lund, May 15, 1908; d. Hälsingborg, Dec. 27, 1986. He studied composition and conducting at the Stockholm Cons. (1924–29); then completed his training with Alban Berg in Vienna (1929–30) and with Fritz Reuter in Leipzig (1930–31). Returning to Sweden, he was active with the Swedish Radio (1937–53). He was prof. of composition at the Stockholm Musikhögskolan (1947–59) and director of music at the Univ. of Uppsala (1961–65). His early compositions were in a classical spirit, but with time his idiom became increasingly complex; there are some instances of dodecaphonic procedures in his later compositions. The importance of his works lies in the freedom of application of various techniques without adhering to any current fashion.

WORKS: STAGE: Opera, *Prinsessan av Cypern* (The Princess of Cyprus; 1935–36; Stockholm, April 29, 1937); opera buffa, *Arresten på Bohus* (The Arrest at Bohus; 1938–39); ballet, *Linden* (1958). ORCH.: 3 syms. (1927–28; 1936–37; 1945); 3 concert overtures (1929, 1934, 1945); *Symphonic Sketch* (1930); *Sinfonietta* for Strings (1932); *Little Serenade* for Strings (1934); Saxophone Concerto (1934); *Divertimento* for Chamber Orch. (1935); *Little March* (1936); *Ostinato* (Stockholm, Nov. 24, 1937); *En vintersaga* (A Winter Tale), suite (1937); *Pastoral Suite* (1938); *The Earth Sings,* symphonic poem (1940); *The Land of Sweden,* suite (1941); *Gustavian Suite* for Flute, Harpsichord, and Strings (1943); Cello Concerto (1947); *Music for Orchestra* (1948–49); Violin Concerto (1952); 12 concertinos, with String Orch., for solo instruments: Flute, Oboe, Clarinet, Bassoon, Horn, Trumpet, Trombone, Violin, Viola, Cello, Double Bass, and Piano (1953–57); *Adagio* for Strings (1960); *3 Pieces* (1960); *Orchestral Variations* (1962); *Lyric Fantasy* for Small Orch. (1967); *2 auguri* (1971); *Barococo,* suite (1973); *Musica permutatio* (1980; Swedish Radio, Feb. 27, 1982). VOCAL: *Förklädd gud* (The Disguised God), lyric suite for Narrator, Soprano, Baritone, Chorus, and Orch. (1940); *Väktarsånger* (Watchman's Songs) for Narrator, Baritone, Male Chorus, and Orch. (1940); *Missa brevis* for a cappella Chorus (1954); *Intrada Solemnis* for 2 Choruses, Boys' Chorus, Winds, and Organ (1964); *Soluret och urnan* (The Sundial and the Urn), cantata (1965–66). CHAMBER: *Intimate Miniatures* for String Quartet (1938); 3 string quartets (1944, 1955, 1975); *4 tempi,* divertimento for Wind Quintet (1968); Cello Sonatina (1969); *Aubade* for Oboe, Violin, and Cello (1972). PIANO: 3 sonatinas (1936, 1947, 1950); *Croquiser* (1947); 7 *Little Preludes and Fugues* (1969).

La Rue, (Adrian) Jan (Pieters), eminent American musicologist; b. Kisaran, Sumatra (of American parents), July 31, 1918. (His ancestor was a French Huguenot who fled first to the Palatinate and then to America, landing in Massachusetts in 1670; La Rue's parents spent 3 years in Indonesia, where his father served as a botanist and developed a basic budding process used on rubber trees.) He studied at Princeton Univ. (M.F.A., 1942) and at Harvard Univ. (Ph.D., 1952); taught at Wellesley College (1942–43; 1946–57); then was a prof. at N.Y. Univ. (from 1957), serving as chairman of its music dept. (1970–71; 1972–73). From 1966 to 1968 he was president of the American Musicological Soc. He specialized in 18th-cen-

tury music and style analysis. He prepared a thematic catalogue of about 10,000 entries on syms. and instrumental concertos of the Classical period; contributed to various publications a number of original articles bringing informing light on obscure subjects. His most important papers include: "Native Music in Okinawa," *Musical Quarterly* (April 1946); "The Okinawan Notation System," *Journal of the American Musicological Society* (1951); "Die Datierung von Wasserzeichen im 18. Jahrhundert," *Kongress-Bericht,* Mozart-Jahr, 1956 (also in Eng., "Watermarks and Musicology," *Acta Musicologica,* 1961). He publ. *Guidelines for Style Analysis* (N.Y., 1970); was ed. of the *Report of the Eighth Congress of the International Musicological Society, New York 1961* (Kassel, 1961); co-ed. of the Festschrift for Otto Erich Deutsch (Kassel, 1963) and of the Festschrift for Gustave Reese (N.Y., 1965).

La Rue, Pierre de (Petrus Platensis, Pierchon, Pierson, Pierzon, Perisone, Pierazon de la Ruellien), eminent Flemish composer; b. probably in Tournai, c.1460; d. Courtrai, Nov. 20, 1518. The 1st record of his activities is as a tenor at Siena Cathedral (1482; 1483–85); he then was at 's-Hertogenbosch Cathedral (1489–92); subsequently became a member of the Marian Brotherhood; he most likely was also a singer in Archduke Maximilian's Hofkapelle in Burgundy. He was canon at the court of Philippe le Beau in Mechelen (1501); prebend at Courtrai, Namur, and Termonde (from 1501); *cantor principis* at Courtrai (1502). He returned to the Netherlands about 1508; was a singer at the court of Margaret of Austria at Mechelen; then served Archduke Karl (1514–16). He wrote 47 masses, several of which have been publ. in modern eds.; 7 Mass sections; 7 Magnificats; a Lamentation; motets; etc. For his works, see A. Tirabassi, ed., *Pierre de La Rue: Liber missarum* (Kassel, 1941), and M. Picker, *The Chanson Albums of Marguerite of Austria* (Berkeley and Los Angeles, 1965).

BIBL.: A. Ambros, *Geschichte der Musik* (vol. 3, Breslau, 1868); P. Wagner, *Geschichte der Messe* (vol. I, Leipzig, 1913); K. Roediger, *Die geistlichen Musikhandschriften der Universitäts-Bibliothek Jena* (1935); J. Robyns, *P. d.l.R. (circa 1460–1518): een bio-bibliographische studie* (Brussels, 1954); M. Staehelin, "P. d.l.R. in Italien," *Archiv für Musikwissenschaft* (1970).

La Salette, Joubert de, French music theorist; b. Grenoble, Sept. 4, 1743; d. there, Feb. 4, 1833. He wrote *Sténographie musicale* (1805; an unsuccessful invention on the lines of German tablature); *Considérations sur les divers systèmes de la musique ancienne et moderne* (1810; his best work); *De la notation musicale en général, et en particulier de celle du système grec* (1817); *De la fixité et de l'invariabilité des sons musicaux* (1824); and other essays.

Lasalle, Jean-Louis. See **Lassalle, Jean (Louis).**

Laserna, Blas de, Spanish conductor and composer; b. Corella, Navarre (baptized), Feb. 4, 1751; d. Madrid, Aug. 8, 1816. He was official composer for several theaters; was also conductor of the Teatro de la Cruz (1790–1818). He composed the music for Ramón de la Cruz's comedy *El café de Barcelona* (Barcelona, Nov. 4, 1788); also the operas *La gitanilla por amor* (Madrid, 1791; successful) and *Idomeneo* (Madrid, Dec. 9, 1792); incidental music to plays of Calderón, Lope de Vega, Moreto, etc.; many *tonadillas, sainetes,* etc.

BIBL.: J. Gómez, J. de Arrese, and E. Aunós, *El músico B. d.L.* (Corella, 1952).

Las Infantas, Fernando de. See **Infantas, Fernando de las.**

Láska, Gustav, Bohemian composer and double-bass player; b. Prague, Aug. 23, 1847; d. Schwerin, Oct. 16, 1928. He studied at the Prague Cons. with Hrabe, Kittl, and Krejči. Following a year of giving double-bass concerts, he joined the Court Orch. in Kassel (1868–72), then in Sondershausen (1872–75); was a theater conductor in Göttingen, Eisleben, and Halberstadt; played double bass in Berlin; in 1878, became double-bass player in the Court Orch. in Schwerin.

WORKS: Opera, *Der Kaisersoldat;* cantata, *Deutsches Aufge-*

bot; 2 syms.; 2 overtures; Double-bass Concerto; 3 masses; several works for Double Bass and Piano (*3 Romanzen, Rhapsodie, Erotik, Ballade und Polonaise, Schlummerlied, Karneval von Venedig,* etc.); piano pieces; songs.

Laskine, Lily, noted French harpist and teacher; b. Paris, Aug. 31, 1893; d. there, Jan. 4, 1988. She studied at the Paris Cons. with Alphonse Hasselmans and Georges Marty; won a premier prix there in 1905; was then a member of the orch. of the Paris Opéra (1909–26); from 1934, made numerous tours as a soloist; was a prof. of harp at the Paris Cons. (1948–58).

Lasner, Ignaz, Bohemian cellist and composer; b. Drosau, Aug. 8, 1815; d. Vienna, Aug. 18, 1883. He studied with Goltermann in Prague, and Merk and Servais in Vienna. He was an orch. player in Vienna; composed cello pieces.

Lassalle, Jean (-Louis), French baritone; b. Lyons, Dec. 14, 1847; d. Paris, Sept. 7, 1909. After training in industrial design and painting, he entered the Paris Cons. to study voice; also studied privately with Novelli; made his debut as St. Bris in *Les Huguenots* in Liège (1868); then he sang in Lille, Toulouse, The Hague, and Brussels. He made his 1st appearance at the Paris Opéra in the title role of Rossini's *Guillaume Tell* (June 7, 1872); remained there for more than 20 years, with extended leaves of absence, during which he toured throughout Europe, Russia, and the U.S. (debut, Metropolitan Opera, N.Y., Jan. 15, 1892, as Nelusko in *L'Africaine*); was again on the Metropolitan Opera roster in 1893–94 and 1896–97. He returned to Paris in 1901 and settled there as a singing teacher; in 1903, became a prof. at the Paris Cons. His repertoire comprised about 60 operas, ranging from Donizetti to Wagner.

Lassen, Eduard, Danish conductor and composer; b. Copenhagen, April 13, 1830; d. Weimar, Jan. 15, 1904. His family moved to Brussels when he was a child; he entered the Brussels Cons., taking the Belgian Prix de Rome (1851). Following a tour through Germany and Italy, he went to Weimar, where Liszt fostered the presentation of his 5-act opera *Landgraf Ludwigs Brautfahrt* (1857). He was court music director in Weimar (1858–95); led the world premiere of Saint-Saëns's opera *Samson et Dalila* (Weimar, Dec. 2, 1877). He also wrote the operas *Frauenlob* (Weimar, 1860) and *Der Gefangene* (given in Brussels as *Le Captif,* April 24, 1865); a ballet, *Diana;* 2 syms.; *Fest-Cantate;* 2 overtures; *Te Deum;* a set of *Biblische Bilder* for Chorus and Orch.; songs; incidental music.

Lasso, Orlando di, great Franco-Flemish composer, also known in Latin as **Orlandus Lassus,** and in French as **Roland de Lassus,** father of **Ferdinand** and **Rudolph de Lassus;** b. Mons, 1532; d. Munich, June 14, 1594. He entered the service of Ferrante Gonzaga when he was about 12 years old, and subsequently traveled with him; then was placed in the service of Constantino Castrioto of Naples at the age of 18. He later proceeded to Rome and entered the service of Antonio Altoviti, the Archbishop of Florence; then was maestro di cappella at St. John Lateran (1553–54). He went to Antwerp (1555), where he enjoyed a fine reputation both socially and artistically; his 1st works were publ. that year in Venice, containing 22 madrigals set to poems of Petrarch; also that year he brought out a collection of madrigals and motets set to texts in Italian, French, and Latin in Antwerp. In 1556 he became a singer at the Munich court chapel of Duke Albrecht of Bavaria. He took Regina Wechinger (Wäckinger), an aristocratic woman, in marriage in 1558. In 1563 he was made maestro di cappella of the Munich court chapel, a position he held with great eminence until his death. He made occasional trips, including to Flanders to recruit singers (1560), to Frankfurt for the coronation of Emperor Maximilian II (1562), to Italy (1567), to the French court (1571; 1573–74), again to Italy (1574–79), and to Regensburg (1593). On Dec. 7, 1570, he received from the Emperor Maximilian a hereditary rank of nobility. Lasso represents the culmination of the great era of Franco-Flemish polyphony; his superlative mastery in sacred as well as secular music renders him one of the most versatile composers of his time; he was equally capable of writing in the most elevated style and in the popular idiom; his art was supranational; he wrote Italian madrigals, German lieder, French chansons, and Latin motets. Musicians of his time described him variously as the "Belgian Orpheus" and the "Prince of Music." The sheer scope of his production is amazing: he left more than 2,000 works in various genres. The Patrocinium Musices (1573–98), a 12-vol. series publ. in Munich by Adam Berg, under ducal patronage, contains 7 vols. of Lasso's works: vol. I, 21 motets; vol. II, 5 masses; vol. III, Offices; vol. IV, a Passion, vigils, etc.; vol. V, 10 Magnificats; vol. VI, 13 Magnificats; vol. VII, 6 masses. Lasso's sons publ. 516 of his motets under the title *Magnum opus musicum* (1604). Eitner publ. *Chronologisches Verzeichnis der Druckwerke des Orlando di Lassus* (Berlin, 1874). His collected works (21 vols., 1894–1926) were issued by Breitkopf & Härtel of Leipzig under the editorship of Haberl and Sandberger; a new series was begun in 1956 by the Bärenreiter Verlag of Kassel under the editorship of S. Hermelink and others. W. Boetticher publ. a complete catalogue of his works (Berlin, 1956).

BIBL.: H. Delmotte, *Notice biographique sur Roland Delattre connu sous le nom d'Orland de Lassus* (Valenciennes, 1836); A. Mathieu, *Biographie de Roland de Lattre* (Mons, 1851); D. Mettenleiter, ed., *Register für die Geschichte der Musik in Bayern* (Brixen, 1868); W. Bäumker, *Orlandus de Lassus, der letzte grosse Meister der niederländischen Tonschule* (Freiburg, 1878); E. Destouches, *O. d.L.: Ein Lebensbild* (Munich, 1894); J. Declève, *Roland de Lassus: Sa vie et ses œuvres* (Mons, 1894); F. Haberl, "Synchronistische Tabelle über den Lebensgang von Giovanni Pierluigi da Palestrina und O. d.L.," *Kirchenmusikalisches Jahrbuch,* 9 (1894); A. Sandberger, *Beiträge zur Geschichte der bayrischen Hofkapelle* (vols. I and III; Leipzig, 1894); E. Schmitz, *O. d.L.* (Leipzig, 1915); E. Closson, *Roland de Lassus* (1919); R. Casimiri, *O. d.L., maestro di cappella al Laterano nel 1553* (Rome, 1920); C. Van den Borren, *Orlande de Lassus* (Paris, 1920); A. Sandberger, *Ausgewählte Aufsätze zur Musikgeschichte* (Munich, 1921); idem, *O. d.L. und die geistigen Strömungen seiner Zeit* (Munich, 1926); C. Van den Borren, *En quelle année Roland de Lassus est-il né?* (The Hague, 1926); E. Lowinsky, *Der Motettenstil O. d.L.s* (Heidelberg, 1933); L. Behr, *Die deutschen Gesänge O. d.L.s* (Erlangen, 1935); E. Lowinsky, *Das Antwerpener Motettenbuch O. d.L.s und seine Beziehungen zum Motettenschaffen der niederländischen Zeitgenossen* (The Hague, 1937); L. Balmer, *O. d.L.s Motetten* (Berne, 1938); J. Huschke, *O. d.L.s Messen* (Leipzig, 1941); F. Blume, "Lasso und Palestrina," *Deutsche Musikkultur,* 9 (1944); C. Van den Borren, *Roland de Lassus* (1944); A. Einstein, *The Italian Madrigal* (Princeton, 1949); W. Boetticher, *O. d.L. und seine Zeit, 1532–1594* (2 vols., Kassel and Basel, 1958); H. Leuchtmann, *Die musikalischen Wortausdeutungen in den Motetten des Magnum opus musicum von O. d.L.* (Strasbourg, 1959); idem, *O. d.L.: Sein Leben; Briefe* (2 vols., Wiesbaden, 1976–77); F. Messmer, *O. d.L.: Ein Leben in der Renaissance* (Munich, 1982); J. Roche, *Lassus* (London, 1982); idem, "Lassus Yesterday and Today," *Musical Times* (May 1982); R. Orlich, *Die Parodiemessen von O. d.L.* (Munich, 1985); D. Zager, *The Polyphonic Latin Hymns of O. d.L.: A Liturgical and Repertorial Study* (diss., Univ. of Minnesota, 1985); J. Erb, *O. d.L.: A Guide to Research* (N.Y., 1990).

Lassus, Ferdinand de, German singer and composer, son of **Orlando di Lasso** and brother of **Rudolph de Lassus;** b. Munich, c.1560; d. there, Aug. 27, 1609. He became a member of the Bavarian court chapel in Munich (1584); then entered the service of Friedrich von Hohenzollern-Sigmaringen (1585); subsequently returned to Munich and Landshut (1590), becoming Kapellmeister (1602). His son, also named **Ferdinand de Lassus** (1592–1630), was also a musician; studied in Rome and then was Kapellmeister in Munich (1616–29).

WORKS: *Cantiones sacrae* for 6 Voices (Graz, 1587); *Apparatus musicus* for 8 Voices and Basso Continuo (organ) (Munich, 1622); various other works in contemporary collections.

Lassus, Rudolph de, German organist and composer, son of **Orlando di Lasso** and brother of **Ferdinand de Lassus;** b. Munich, c.1563; d. there, 1625. He was made a member of the Bavarian court chapel (1585); was its 1st organist (1589–1625); was also court composer to the Duke (from 1609). With his brother, he compiled and publ. the *Magnum opus musicum* (1604), a comprehensive survey of his father's motets. In some of his settings of the Magnificat, he parodied pieces by his father.

WORKS: *Teutsche Psalmen: Geistliche psalmen* for 3 Voices (Munich, 1588; ed. by W. Lipphardt, Kassel, 1928); *Cantiones sacrae* for 6 Voices (Munich, 1601); *Selectae aliquot cantiones* for 4 Voices (Munich, 1606); *Circus symphoniacus commissi in arenam Phonomachi* for 9, 11, and 12 Voices (Munich, 1607); *Triga musica qua missae odaeque Marianae triplice fugantur: in Viadanae modo* for 4 to 6 Voices (Munich, 1612); *Virginalia Eucharistica* for 2 to 8 Voices (Munich, 1615); *Ad sacrum convivium modi sacri* for 2 to 6 Voices (Munich, 1617); *Alphabetum Marianum triplici cantionum* for 2 to 4 Voices and Basso Continuo (organ) (Munich, 1621); *Cygnaeum melos* for 2 to 4 Voices, *una cum litaneis* for 4 Voices (Munich, 1626); *Missae* (Ingolstadt, n.d.; not extant); also works in *Pantheon musicum* (Paris, 1600).

Lászlo, Alexander, Hungarian-American composer; b. Budapest, Nov. 22, 1895; d. Los Angeles, Nov. 17, 1970. He studied piano and composition at the Budapest Academy of Music. In 1915 he went to Berlin, where he was active as a pianist and arranger of radio and film scores. In 1938 he emigrated to the U.S., and in 1945 settled in Hollywood. He cultivated the notion of uniting tones with colors, and for that purpose introduced a specially constructed "color pianoforte" (*Farblichtklavier*), which he demonstrated at the Kiel music festival (June 14, 1925). To establish a correspondence between the proportional wavelengths in both acoustic elements and light waves, he invented an instrument he called the Sonchromatoscope and a new system of notation he called Sonchromatography. His book *Die Farblichtmusik* (1925) discusses this new technique. His works include, besides special compositions for color lights, the pantomimes *Marionetten* (Budapest, 1916); *Die schöne O-sang* (Hamburg, 1919); *Panoptikum*; etc.; for Piano: *News of the Day*, *Hungarian Dance Suite*, and *Fantasy of Colors*; *Mechanized Forces* for Orch.; *Hollywood Concerto* and *The Ghost Train of Marshall Pass* for Piano and Orch.; arrangements for piano of various works by classical composers; film music. His sophisticated ideas about music and color found a fertile ground in Hollywood, where he supplied many musical scores to television; also wrote a musical, *Wanted: Sexperts and Serpents for Our Garden of Maidens* (1968); *Pacific Triptych* for Orch. (1962); symphonic fantasy, *Roulette hématologique* (1969).

Lateiner, Jacob, American pianist of Austrian-Polish descent; b. Havana, May 31, 1928. He studied piano with Jascha Fischermann in Havana, and with Isabelle Vengerova at the Curtis Inst. of Music in Philadelphia; also attended the chamber music classes given by Piatigorsky and Primrose there. Having won the Philadelphia Youth Competition, he made his debut as soloist in Tchaikovsky's 1st Piano Concerto at a youth concert of the Philadelphia Orch. (Dec. 6, 1944); subsequently performed throughout America and in Europe. He appeared regularly in chamber music recitals with Heifetz and Piatigorsky. From 1963 to 1970 he taught at the Mannes College of Music in N.Y.; in 1966, was appointed to the faculty of the Juilliard School of Music in N.Y. In addition to the standard repertoire, he has played a number of contemporary scores; was soloist in the premiere of Elliott Carter's Piano Concerto (1967).

Latham, William P(eters), American composer and educator; b. Shreveport, La., Jan. 4, 1917. He studied trumpet at the Cincinnati Cons. of Music (1936–38); received his B.S. degree in music education from the Univ. of Cincinnati (1938) and continued his studies at the College of Music in Cincinnati (B.M., 1940; M.M., 1941); subsequently studied composition

with Howard Hanson and Herbert Elwell at the Eastman School of Music in Rochester, N.Y. (Ph.D., 1951). During World War II, he served in the U.S. Army as a cavalry bandsman and later as an infantry platoon leader in active combat in Germany in 1945. After the war, he taught at Iowa State Teacher's College in Cedars Falls (1946–65); became a prof. at North Texas State Univ. in Denton in 1965, director of graduate studies in music in 1969, and Distinguished Prof. in 1978; he retired in 1984. He excelled as a composer of sacred choruses and band music; in the latter, he boldly experimented with modern techniques, as exemplified by his *Dodecaphonic Set* and, most spectacularly, in *Fusion*, in which he endeavored to translate the process of atomic fusion into musical terms through an ingenious application of asymmetrical rhythms.

WORKS: STAGE: *Orpheus in Pecan Springs*, opera (Denton, Dec. 4, 1980); *A Modern Trilogy*, ballet (Cincinnati, April 2, 1941). **ORCH.:** *The Lady of Shalott* (1939; Cincinnati, March 7, 1941); *Fantasy Concerto* for Flute, String Orch., and Harp (NBC radio broadcast, Cincinnati, May 5, 1941); *River to the Sea* for Baritone and Orch. (Cincinnati, Dec. 11, 1942); *Fantasy* for Violin and Orch. (1946; Minneapolis, May 23, 1948); *And Thou America* (1947; Rochester, Oct. 18, 1948); Sym. No. 1 (Rochester, April 25, 1950); Suite for Trumpet and String Orch. (Rochester, May 4, 1951); Sym. No. 2, *Sinfonietta* (1953; Fish Creek, Wis., Aug. 20, 1955); Concerto Grosso for 2 Saxophones and Symphonic Wind Ensemble (Chicago, Dec. 16, 1960; rev. 1962, for 2 Saxophones and Chamber Orch.); Concertino for Saxophone and Symphonic Wind Ensemble (1968; rev. 1969, for Saxophone and Orch.); *American Youth Performs* (Fort Worth, Aug. 1, 1969); *A Lenten Letter* for Soprano, String Orch., and Percussion, to a text by Alexander Solzhenitsyn (Denton, Oct. 9, 1974); *Jubilee 13/50* (Sherman, Texas, Nov. 4, 1978); *Supernovae* (1983). **BAND:** *Brighton Beach*, march (1954); *Proud Heritage*, march (1955); *3 Chorale Preludes* (1956); *Court Festival* (1957); *Passacaglia and Fugue* (1959); *Plymouth Variations* (1962); *Escapades* (1965); *Dionysian Festival* (1965); *Dodecaphonic Set* (Colorado Springs, Colo., March 11, 1966); *Prayers in Space* (1971); *The Music Makers*, with Chorus, Rock Group, Tape, and Guru (1972); *Dilemmae* (1973); *Prolegomena* (1974); *Revolution!* (1975); *Fusion* (1975; New Orleans, April 12, 1976); *March 6* (Dallas, Feb. 23, 1979); *Drones, Airs, and Games* (1983). **CHAMBER:** 3 string quartets (1938–40); 3 string trios (1938–39); Sonata for Oboe and Piano (1947); Sonata for Violin and Piano (1949); *Suite in Baroque Style* for Flute and Piano (1954); Sonata for Recorder and Harpsichord (1959); *Sisyphus 1971* for Alto Saxophone and Piano (1971); *Preludes before Silence*, 9 pieces for Flute and Piccolo (1974); *Eidólons* for Euphonium and Piano (1977); *Ex Tempore* for Alto Saxophone and Piano (1978); *Ion, the Rhapsode* for Clarinet and Piano (1984). **CHORAL:** *Peace* for Chorus and Orch., to a text by Rupert Brook (1943); *Prayer after World War* (1945); *Prophecy of Peace*, with Organ, Piano, and Cymbals (1951; also versions with Orch., 1952, and Small Wind Ensemble, 1961); *Music for 7 Poems*, to texts by James Hearst, for Chorus and Orch. (1958); *Blind with Rainbows*, cantata (1962); *Te Deum*, with Wind Ensemble and Organ (1964); *Epigrammata* (1978); *My Heart Sings*, anthem, with Organ (1987); *Missa Novella* for Young Choirs (1988); also *Te Deum Tejas*, 8 songs for Soprano, Flute, and Percussion, to texts by the composer (1981); *Metaphors*, 3 songs for Soprano and Piano (1988); *A Green Voice*, cantata for Soprano, Tenor, and Piano (1989).

Latilla, Gaetano, Italian composer; b. Bari, Jan. 21, 1711; d. Naples, Jan. 15, 1788. As a child, he sang in the choir of the Cathedral in Bari; then studied at the Conservatorio di S. Onofrio in Naples. He was 2nd maestro di cappella at S. Maria Maggiore in Rome (1738–41); then was in Venice as maestro di coro at the Conservatorio della Pietà (1753–66) and as 2nd maestro di cappella at S. Marco (1762–70?); subsequently returned to Naples about 1774. He wrote 46 operas, but the music to most is not extant; his works include *Li Mariti a forza* (Naples, 1732); *Angelica ed Orlando* (Naples, 1735); *Gismòndo* (Naples, 1737; also known as *La finta giardi-*

niera; perf. as *Don Colascione* in London, 1749); *Madama Ciana* (Rome, 1738; perf. as *Gli Artigiani arrichiti* in London, 1750, and in Paris, 1753); *I Sposi incogniti* (Naples, 1779); also the oratorio *L'onnipotenza e la misericordia divina*; 3 sinfonias; 6 string quartets; church music; etc.

La Tombelle, (Antoine Louis Joseph Gueyrand) Fernand (Fouant) de, French organist and composer; b. Paris, Aug. 3, 1854; d. Château de Fayrac, Dordogne, Aug. 13, 1928. He first studied with his mother; then at the Paris Cons. with Guilmant (organ) and Dubois (composition); also with Saint-Saëns. From 1885 to 1898 he was assistant organist at the Madeleine; from 1896 to 1904, prof. of theory at the Schola Cantorum. He publ. the book *L'Oratorio et la cantate* (Paris, 1911). He wrote the operettas *Un Bon Numéro* (1892) and *Un Rêve au pays du bleu* (1892); 2 ballets; orch. music; incidental music, oratorios, masses, and motets; chamber music; organ works; songs.

Lattuada, Felice, Italian composer; b. Caselle di Morimondo, Milan, Feb. 5, 1882; d. Milan, Nov. 2, 1962. He studied at the Milan Cons. with Ferroni, graduating in 1911; then was director of the Milan Civic School of Music (1935–62). He wrote an autobiography, *La passione dominate* (Bologna, 1951).

WORKS: Operas: *La tempestà* (Milan, Nov. 23, 1922); *Sandha* (Genoa, Feb. 21, 1924); *Le Preziose ridicole* (Milan, Feb. 9, 1929); *Don Giovanni* (Naples, May 18, 1929); *La caverna di Salamanca* (Genoa, March 1, 1938); *Caino* (Milan, Jan. 10, 1957); *Canto augurale per la Nazione Eletta* for Tenor, Chorus, and Orch.; orch. works: *Sinfonia romantica* (1911); *Cimitero di guerra*; *Il mistero della Passione di Cristo*; *Incanti della notte*; *Divertimento rustico*; *Prelude and Fugue*; other choral, orch., and chamber works; film music.

Laub, Ferdinand, eminent Czech violinist and composer; b. Prague, Jan. 19, 1832; d. Gries, near Bozen, Tirol, March 18, 1875. A child of great precocity, he studied violin with his father; made his 1st public appearance when he was 6, then studied with Mořic Mildner at the Prague Cons. (1843–46). He toured Austria and Germany (from 1846), then studied counterpoint with Sechter in Vienna, where he was soloist in the orch. of the Theater an der Wien (1848–50). He subsequently performed in London, Berlin, Paris, and St. Petersburg before serving as Konzertmeister in Weimar (1853–55); then was prof. of violin at Berlin's Stern Cons. (1855–57); also was chamber virtuoso to the Prussian court (1856–58). He founded a series of chamber music concerts in Berlin (1858–62) and Vienna (1862–66); then went to Russia, where he attained great distinction as a performer and teacher; was made a prof. of violin at the Moscow Cons. (1866). Ill health compelled him to return in 1874 to his homeland, where he made his last appearance that same year. He was held in great esteem by his contemporaries; his repertoire extended from Bach to the masters of his own day. He composed several brilliant virtuoso pieces for his instrument, and also some vocal music. His son, **Váša (Václav) Laub** (b. Berlin, Dec. 31, 1857; d. Khabarovsk, Nov. 23, 1911), was a choirmaster, piano teacher, and composer; he studied with his father in Moscow and later in Prague with Karel Bendl (1875); he wrote orch. music, choruses, piano pieces, and songs.

BIBL.: L. Ginzburg, *F. L.* (Moscow and Leningrad, 1951); B. Šich, *F. L.* (Prague, 1951).

Laub, Thomas (Linnemann), significant Danish organist and composer; b. Langaa, Fyn, Dec. 5, 1852; d. Gentofte, near Copenhagen, Feb. 4, 1927. He studied with Gebauer at the Copenhagen Cons. (1873–76); subsequently was organist at Copenhagen's Hellingåndskirken (1884–91) and Holmens Kirke (1891–1925). He devoted his life to reforming ecclesiastical music in Denmark, restoring the melody, rhythm, and harmony of hymns to their primordial form and composing music reflecting that tradition. The Danish Hymn Soc. was organized in 1922 to propagate his ideas. He publ. the books *Vor musikundervisning og den musikalske dannelse* (Copenhagen, 1884), *Om kirkesangen* (Copenhagen, 1887), and *Musik og kirke* (Copenhagen, 1920; 2nd ed., 1938).

WORKS (all publ. in Copenhagen unless otherwise given): SACRED: *80 rytmiske koraler* (1888); *Kirkemelodier, firstemmig udsatte* (1888–90); *Salmemelodier i kirkestil* (1896–1902); *Forspil og melodier: Forsøg i kirkestil* (1890); *Dansk kirkesang: Gamle og nye melodier* (1918; supplement, 1930); *Aandelige sange* (1925); *24 salmer og 12 folkeviser* (ed. by M. Wöldike; 1928); *Liturgisk musik* (ed. by Wöldike; 1937). SECULAR: *10 gamle danske folkeviser* (1890); *Danske folkeviser med gamle melodier* (1899–1904; 2nd ed., 1930); with C. Nielsen, *En snes danske viser* (1915–17); *Ti Aarestrupske ritorneller* (1920); *Tolv viser og sange af danske digtere* (Kolding, 1920; 2nd ed., 1938); with Nielsen, O. Ring, and T. Aagaard, *Folkehøjskolens melodibog* (1922; supplement, 1927); *30 danske sange for 3 og 4 lige stemmer* (1922); *Faerøske og danske folkevisemelodier udsatte for mandskor af Henrik Rung og Thomas Laub* (ed. by K. Clausen; 1942); *Danske folkeviser* (ed. by Wöldike and A. Arnholtz; 1948); *Sange med klaver* (ed. by H. Glahn and Wöldike; 1957).

BIBL.: P. Hamburger, *Bibliografisk fortegnelse over T. L.s litteraere og musikalske arbejder* (Copenhagen, 1932); idem, *T. L.: Hans liv og gerning* (Copenhagen, 1942); M. Wöldike, "Erindringer om L. og Carl Nielsen," *Dansk Kirkesange Årsskrift*, XX (1967–68); J. Jensen, "Musikalisk isolation og gudstjenstligt faellesskab i T. L.s to tidlige skrifter," ibid., XXII (1971–72).

Laubenthal (originally, **Neumann**), **Horst (Rüdiger),** German tenor; b. Duderstadt, March 8, 1939. He was legally adopted by the German tenor **Rudolf Laubenthal**, with whom he studied. He made his debut in Würzburg in 1967 as Don Ottavio; then was a member of the Württemberg State Theater in Stuttgart (until 1973); subsequently sang at Berlin's Deutsche Oper (from 1973). He also made guest appearances in Vienna, Munich, Hamburg, and Berlin and toured as a concert artist.

Laubenthal, Rudolf, German tenor; b. Düsseldorf, March 18, 1886; d. Pöcking, Starnberger See, Oct. 2, 1971. At first he studied medicine in Munich and Berlin; simultaneously took vocal lessons with Lilli Lehmann; in 1913 he made his debut in Berlin at the Deutsches Opernhaus, and sang there regularly; from 1919 to 1923 he was engaged by the Bavarian State Opera in Munich. He made his Metropolitan Opera debut in N.Y. as Walther von Stolzing in *Die Meistersinger von Nürnberg* on Nov. 9, 1923; continued on the company's roster until 1933; he also sang with the Covent Garden Opera in London (1926–30) and made guest appearances in Chicago and San Francisco. He was primarily noted as a Wagnerian singer.

Lauber, Joseph, Swiss composer; b. Ruswil, Lucerne canton, Dec. 27, 1864; d. Geneva, May 28, 1952. He studied in Zürich with Hegar, in Munich with Rheinberger, and in Paris with Massenet and Diémer. Returning to Switzerland, he taught at the Zürich Cons.; then conducted a theater orch. in Geneva (1905–7). He wrote more than 200 compositions, including the opera *Die Hexe*; an oratorio, *Ad gloriam Dei*; 6 syms. and other orch. works; 5 concertos (including one for Double Bass); chamber works; choral music; piano pieces; songs; etc.

Launis (real name, **Lindberg**), **Armas (Emanuel),** Finnish composer; b. Hämeenlinna, April 22, 1884; d. Nice, Aug. 7, 1959. He studied composition with Sibelius in Helsinki; took courses at the Univ. of Helsinki with Ilmari Krohn; earned his doctorate there with the dissertation *Über Art, Entstehung und Verbreitung der Estnisch-Finnischen Runenmelodien* (publ. in Helsinki, 1913). In 1930 he settled in Nice.

WORKS: Operas: *Seitsemän veljestäf* (The 7 Brothers; Helsinki, April 11, 1913); *Kullervo* (Helsinki, Feb. 28, 1917); *Aslak Hetta* (Helsinki, 1922); *Noidan laulu* (The Sorcerer's Song; 1932); *Lumottu silkkihuivi* (The Magic Silk Kerchief; 1937); *Jehudith* (1940); 2 cantatas (1906, 1910); *Andante religioso* for Violin and Orch. (1932); *Northern Suite* for Violin and Orch. (1950); *Karelian Suite* for Orch. (1952); Piano Quintet and other chamber music; piano pieces; songs.

Lauper, Cyndi (Cynthia), colorful American rock singer and songwriter; b. N.Y., June 20, 1953. She set out on her own at age 17; held various odd jobs until breaking into the music business as a singer with a Long Island disco band in 1974. She first attracted notice as both a singer and a songwriter with the Blue Angel band in 1978; scored a major success with her 1st album, *She's So Unusual*, in 1983; that same year she became a rock superstar sensation via her video production of *Girls Just Want to Have Fun*. Her album *True Colors* followed in 1986; its title song became associated with the 1986 Olympics and was also used extensively in advertising by the Eastman Kodak Co. She also made a stab at acting and starred in the comic film *Vibes* (1988). Her propensity for uninhibited expression in Queens-accented salvos, multi-colored dyed hair, and outlandish sartorial display made her a natural as a rock and feminist idol. She has a powerful and idiosyncratic voice and a provocative approach to lyrics; her adaptations and subtle parodies are among her best projections.

BIBL.: K. Willis, Jr., *C. L.* (N.Y., 1984); *Current Biography* (Aug. 1985).

Laurencie, Lionel de la. See **La Laurencie, Lionel de.**

Laurens, Edmond, French composer; b. Bergerac, Nov. 10, 1852; d. Paris, Nov. 27, 1925. He studied with Guiraud at the Paris Cons.; later became a teacher of harmony and composition there.

WORKS: *La Harpe et le glaive,* grand opera; *Les Amours d'un soldat de plomb,* pantomime; *La Neuvaine,* lyric play; other works for the stage: *Irlande, Conte d'amour, Roses d'automne; Suite japonaise* for Orch.; *Silhouettes* for Piano and Orch.; piano pieces; numerous songs. He also was the author of the manuals *Cours d'enseignement musical pianistique* and *L'Art du correcteur.*

Laurenti, Bartolomeo Girolamo, Italian violinist and composer; b. Bologna, c.1644; d. there, Jan. 18, 1726. He played violin at the Basilica San Petronio; was one of the earliest members of the Accademia Filarmonica in Bologna. He wrote *12 Suonate per camera a violino e violoncello* (1691); *Sei concerti a tre, cioè violino, violoncello ed organo* (1720); Sonata for Violin and Continuo; etc.

Lauri-Volpi, Giacomo, famous Italian tenor; b. Lanuvio, near Rome, Dec. 11, 1892; d. Valencia, Spain, March 17, 1979. He studied law before receiving vocal instruction from Antonio Cotogni at Rome's Accademia di Santa Cecilia, and subsequently from Enrico Rosati. He made his debut under the name Giacomo Rubini as Arturo in *I Puritani* in Viterbo in 1919; then sang in various Italian opera centers before appearing at La Scala in Milan in 1922. He made his 1st American appearance at the Metropolitan Opera in N.Y. on Jan. 26, 1923, as the Duke of Mantua in *Rigoletto;* remained a member of the Metropolitan until 1933, while filling guest engagements at Covent Garden in London, at the Paris Opéra, and at the Teatro Colón in Buenos Aires. In 1934 he returned to Europe, and lived mostly in Burjasot, near Valencia. After World War II, he continued to sing in Spain and Italy in concert and in opera, and in a remarkable demonstration of his tenorial vim and vigor, he sang an aria of Calaf from Puccini's *Turandot* at the Teatro Liceo in Barcelona in 1972, at the age of 80. He publ. several books of reminiscences, among them *L'equivoco* (Milan, 1938); *Cristalli viventi* (Rome, 1948); *A visa aperto* (Milan, 1953); 2 books on voices of the present and past, *Voci paralele* (Milan, 1955) and *Misteri della voce umana* (Milan, 1957).

BIBL.: A. Gustarelli, *Chi è G. L.-V.?* (Milan, 1932).

Lauro, Antonio, Venezuelan guitarist and composer; b. Ciudad Bolívar, Aug. 3, 1909; d. Caracas, April 17, 1986. He studied in Caracas; wrote much guitar music, including a Guitar Concerto (Caracas, July 25, 1956, composer soloist); a choral symphonic poem, *Cantacharo;* several symphonic suites; choruses; songs.

Lauska, Franz (Seraphinus Ignatius), Bohemian pianist, teacher, and composer; b. Brünn, Jan. 13, 1764; d. Berlin, April 18, 1825. He studied in Vienna with Albrechtsberger;

was a chamber musician in Munich; from 1794 to 1798, taught in Copenhagen; settled in Berlin in 1798; became a teacher at the court; among his pupils was Meyerbeer. He wrote 24 sonatas (*Grande sonate, Sonate pathétique,* etc.); Cello Sonata; pieces for Piano, 4-hands (*6 Easy and Agreeable Pieces, Polonaise,* etc.); variations for 2-hands; rondos; etc.

Lautenbacher, Susanne, German violinist; b. Augsburg, April 19, 1932. She studied at the Munich Hochschule für Musik; took private lessons with Szeryng; then appeared in Europe as a soloist and chamber music player; also taught violin. She was praised for her sensitive performances of the classical violin repertoire.

Laux, Karl, German writer on music; b. Ludwigshafen, Aug. 26, 1896; d. Dresden, June 27, 1978. He studied at the Univ. of Heidelberg (Ph.D., 1926); later was rector of the Dresden Hochschule für Musik (1951–63). He was a music critic (1945–51).

WRITINGS: *Anton Bruckner* (Leipzig, 1940; 2nd ed., rev., 1947); *Musik und Musiker der Gegenwart* (Essen, 1949); *Die Musik in Russland und in der Sowjetunion* (Berlin, 1958); *Carl Maria von Weber* (Leipzig, 1966); *Robert Schumann* (Leipzig, 1972).

Lavagne, André, French composer; b. Paris, July 12, 1913. He studied at the Paris Cons.; won 1st prize in piano (1933) and Premier 2nd Grand Prix de Rome (1938); in 1941, was appointed inspector of music in Paris schools.

WORKS: Operas: *Comme ils s'aiment* (Paris, 1941) and *Corinne* (Enghiens-les-Bains, 1956); *Concert dans un parc* for Piano and Orch., inspired by Watteau's painting (1941); *Concerto romantique* for Cello and Orch. (1941); *Nox,* symphonic poem for Voice and Orch.; *Spectacle rassurant* for Voice and Orch.; several ballets (*Le Pauvre Jongleur, Kermesse,* etc.).

Lavagnino, Angelo Francesco, Italian composer; b. Genoa, Feb. 22, 1909; d. Gavi, Aug. 21, 1987. He studied with Renzo Rossi and Vito Frazzi at the Milan Cons., graduating in 1933; from 1948 to 1962 he was a prof. of film music at the Accademia Musicale in Siena.

WORKS: Opera, *Malafonte* (Antwerp, 1952); for Orch.: *Volo d'api* (1932) and *Tempo alto* (1938); Violin Concerto (1941); Piano Quintet (1942); Violin Sonata (1943); *Pocket Symphony* (title in Eng.; 1949).

Lavallée, Calixa, Canadian pianist and composer; b. Verchères, Quebec, Dec. 28, 1842; d. Boston, Jan. 21, 1891. He first studied with his father; then at the Paris Cons. with Marmontel (piano), and Bazin and Boieldieu *fils* (composition). Returning to Canada, he made tours of his native country and the U.S.; took part in the American Civil War; in 1881, became soloist in the company of Etelka Gerster. He wrote the music to the Canadian national song *O Canada* (Montreal, June 24, 1880; poem by Judge Adolphe B. Routhier). He subsequently settled in Boston, where he became an instructor at the Petersilea Academy. He wrote a comic opera, *The Widow* (Springfield, Ill., March 25, 1882); orch. works; chamber music; songs; piano pieces.

BIBL.: S. Salter, "Early Encouragement to American Composers," *Musical Quarterly* (Jan. 1932); E. Lapierre, *C. L., Musicien national du Canada* (Montreal, 1936).

Lavalle-García, Armando, Mexican composer; b. Ocotlán, Jalisco, Nov. 23, 1924. He studied violin at the National Cons. of Music in Mexico City and took courses in composition with Bernal Jiménez, Revueltas, and Rodolfo Halffter; subsequently played the viola with the National Sym. Orch. of Mexico City and conducted the Xalapa Sym. Orch. His music is permeated with the essence of Mexican folklore, even in pieces of ostensibly abstract connotations.

WORKS: 3 ballets: *La canción de los Buenos Principios* (1957); *3 tiempos de amor* (1958); *Corrido* (1959); *Mi viaje,* symphonic poem (1950); *Estructuras geométricas* for String Orch. and Percussion (1960); Concerto for Viola and String Orch. (1965); Concerto for Violin, String Orch., and Percussion (1966); *Divertimento* for Wind Quintet (1953); Violin Sonata

(1966); Oboe Sonata (1967); *Potencial* for Spanish Guitar, Psaltery, Harp, and Percussion (1967); *Trígonos* for Flute, Clarinet, and Bassoon (1968); Trio for Oboe, Bassoon, and Cello, with Percussion accompaniment (1969).

Lavigna, Vincenzo, Italian composer and teacher; b. Altamura, Feb. 21, 1776; d. Milan, Sept. 14, 1836. He studied at the Conservatorio di S. Maria di Loreto in Naples; subsequently went to Milan, where he was maestro al cembalo at La Scala (1802–32); also was prof. of solfeggio at the Milan Cons. (from 1823); he was a teacher of Verdi. He wrote 10 operas, of which his 1st, *La muta per amore, ossia Il Medico per forza* (Milan, 1803), was his best; also 2 ballets.
    Bibl.: G. De Napoli, *La triade melodrammatica altamurana: Giacamo Tritto, V. L., Saverio Mercadante* (Milan, 1931).

Lavignac, (Alexandre Jean) Albert, eminent French musicologist and pedagogue; b. Paris, Jan. 21, 1846; d. there, May 28, 1916. He studied at the Paris Cons. with Marmontel (piano), Bazin and Benoist (harmony), and A. Thomas (composition), winning 1st prize for *solfège* in 1857, for piano in 1861, for harmony and accompaniment in 1863, and for counterpoint and fugue in 1864; he won 2nd prize for organ in 1865; was appointed assistant prof. of *solfège* (1871), prof. of *solfège* (1875), and then prof. of harmony (1891) there. His *Cours complet théorique et pratique de dictée musicale* (6 vols., Paris and Brussels, 1882) attracted considerable attention and led to the introduction of musical dictation as a regular subject in all the important European conservatories; it was followed by *Dictées musicales* (additional exercises) in 1900. His magnum opus was the famous *Encyclopédie de la musique et Dictionnaire du Conservatoire* (Paris, 3 vols., 1920–31), which he ed. from 1913 until his death. Other writings include *École de la pédale du piano* (Paris, 1889); *La Musique et les musiciens* (Paris, 1895; 8th ed., 1910; entirely rev., 1950; Eng. tr. by H. Krehbiel, 1899); *Le Voyage artistique à Bayreuth* (Paris, 1897; rev. ed. by H. Busser, 1951; Eng. tr. as *The Music Dramas of Richard Wagner,* 1898; 2nd Eng. ed., 1904); *Les Gaîtés du Conservatoire* (Paris, 1900); *L'Éducation musicale* (Paris, 1902; 4th ed., 1908; Eng. tr., 1903); *Notions scolaires de musique* (Paris and Brussels, 1905); *Théorie complète des principes fondamentaux de la musique moderne* (Paris and Brussels, 1909).

La Violette, Wesley, American composer; b. St. James, Minn., Jan. 4, 1894; d. Escondido, Calif., July 29, 1978. He studied at Northwestern Univ. and at the Chicago Musical College (M.M.; Mus.Doc., 1925); taught at the latter (1923–33), then at De Paul Univ. (1933–40), and later at the Los Angeles Cons. (from 1946). He was the author of books on philosophy and religion: *The Creative Light* (N.Y., 1947); *The Wayfarer* (Los Angeles, 1956); *The Crown of Wisdom* (Bombay, 1960); etc.
    Works: Opera, *Shylock* (1927; awarded the David Bispham Memorial Medal, 1930; excerpts perf., Chicago, Feb. 9, 1930); opera on the life of Buddha, *The Enlightened One* (1955); Sym. No. 1 (Rochester, N.Y., Oct. 19, 1938); Sym. No. 2, *Miniature,* or *Tom Thumb Symphony* (Chicago, May 25, 1942); *The Song of the Angels,* choral sym. (1952); *Penetrella* for Divided Strings, 18 parts (Chicago, Nov. 30, 1928); 2 violin concertos (1929, 1938); *Osiris,* Egyptian tone poem (1929); *Chorale* for Large Orch. (Chicago, July 31, 1936); Piano Concerto (1937); *Music from the High Sierras* (San Francisco, March 4, 1941); Sym. No. 4 for Band (1942); Concertino for Flute and Orch. (1943); *The Road to Calvary,* cantata (1952); 3 string quartets; Piano Quintet (1927); Octet (1937); Sextet for Piano, Flute, Oboe, Clarinet, Bassoon, and Horn (1940); Flute Quintet (1943); Flute Sonata; 2 violin sonatas; Viola Sonata; Piano Sonata; etc.

Lavista, Mario, Mexican composer of the extreme avantgarde; b. Mexico City, April 3, 1943. He studied harmony with Rodolfo Halffter and composition with Héctor Quintanar; then attended classes and seminars of Stockhausen, Pousseur, Xenakis, and Ligeti in Darmstadt and Cologne. Returning to Mexico in 1970, he founded Quanta, an improvisational music group. In his music he explores all resources of sound, and all idiomatic textures, from deliberate homophony to horrendous explosions of ear-splitting dissonance.
    Works: *Monologue,* after Gogol's *Diary of a Madman,* for Baritone, Flute, Vibraphone, and Double Bass (1966); *5 Pieces* for String Quartet (1967); *Divertimento* for Wind Quintet, 5 Woodblocks, and 3 Shortwave Radios (1968); *Homage to Samuel Beckett* for 3 Amplified Choruses (1968); *Diacronia* for String Quartet (1969); *Kronos* for a minimum of 15 Alarm Clocks, and Loudspeakers and Tapes, with an indeterminate chronometric duration of 5 to 1,440 minutes (1969); *Piece for 1 Pianist and 1 Piano* (1970; also a version called *Piece for 2 Pianists and 2 Pianos,* in which a 2nd pianist maintains an absolute silence that must be "communicated" to the listeners); *Game* for Flute (1970); *Continuo* for Brass, Percussion, 2 Prepared Pianos, and Strings (1970); Trio for 2 String Instruments and Ring Modulator (1972); *Diafonia* for 1 Performer on 2 Pianos and Percussion (1973); *Cluster* for Piano (1973); *Antinomia* for Tape (1973); *Antifonia* for Flute, 2 Bassoons, and Percussion (1974); *Dialogos* for Violin and Piano (1974); *Espejos* (Mirrors) for Piano, 4-hands (1975); *Quotations* for Cello and Piano (1975); *Lyhannh* for Orch. (1976; the title is Swift's word for the "swallow" in Part 4 of *Gulliver's Travels*); Piano Trio (1976); *Jaula* for any number of Prepared Pianos and Pianists (1976).

Lavoix, Henri-Marie-François, French writer on music; b. Paris, April 26, 1846; d. there, Dec. 27, 1897. He was graduated from the Sorbonne; then studied harmony and counterpoint with H. Cohen; in 1865, became librarian of the Bibliothèque Nationale (1865); contributed articles to the *Revue et Gazette Musicale.*
    Writings: *Les Traducteurs de Shakespeare en musique* (1869); *La Musique dans l'imagerie du moyen-âge* (1875); *La Musique dans la nature* (1873); *Histoire de l'instrumentation* (1878); *Le Chant, ses principes et son histoire,* in collaboration with T. Lemaire (1881); *Histoire de la musique* (Paris, 1884); *La Musique du siècle de Saint-Louis* (1884); *La Musique française* (1891).

Lavrangas, Dionyssios, Greek conductor, composer, and pedagogue; b. Argostólion, Cephalonia, Oct. 17, 1860?; d. Razata, Cephalonia, July 18, 1941. He studied first in Argostólion with N. Serao (violin) and N. Metaxas-Tzanis (harmony); then at the Cons. of S. Pietro a Majella in Naples, privately with Dubois in Paris, and at the Paris Cons. with Delibes and Massenet. He conducted a French touring opera company; then conducted in Italy. After serving as artistic director of the Athens Phil. Soc. (1894–96), he served as founder-conductor of the Greek Opera Co. (1900–1935).
    Works: STAGE: OPERAS: *Elda di Vorn* (Naples, 1890); *Tadyo adelfia* (The 2 Brothers; Athens, April 24, 1900); *Mayissa* (The Sorceress; Athens, Oct. 8, 1901); *O lytrotis* (The Redeemer; c.1902; Corfu, Feb. 24, 1934); *Dido* (c.1906; Athens, April 10, 1909); *Mavri petalouda* (Black Butterfly; 1923; Athens, Jan. 25, 1929); *Fakanapas* (1935; Athens, Dec. 2, 1950). OPERETTAS: *Iaspri tricha* (The White Hair; Athens, March 22, 1917); *Sporting Club* (Athens, Aug. 4, 1917); *Dipli fotia* (Double Flame; Athens, Jan. 10, 1918); several ballets; orch. works; choral music; piano pieces; songs.

Lavrovskaya, Elizaveta Andreievna, Russian mezzo-soprano; b. Kashin, Tver district, Oct. 13, 1845; d. Petrograd, Nov. 4, 1919. She studied at the Elizabeth Inst. and the St. Petersburg Cons.; made her debut in Gluck's *Orfeo* (1867), then studied with P. Viardot in Paris. She sang opera in St. Petersburg (1868–72; 1879–80) and at the Bolshoi Theater in Moscow (1890); also appeared as a recitalist. She taught at the Moscow Cons. (from 1888). Tchaikovsky admired her vocal abilities and wrote his 6 songs of op. 27 for her.

Lavry, Marc, significant Latvian-born Israeli conductor and composer; b. Riga, Dec. 22, 1903; d. Haifa, March 20, 1967. He studied with Teichmüller at the Leipzig Cons.; then was active as a conductor in Germany and in Sweden. In 1935 he went to Palestine; was conductor of the Palestine Folk Opera (1941–47) and then director of the music dept. of the short-wave radio station Kol Zion La Gola (1950–58). In 1952 he visited the U.S. His music is imbued with intense feeling for Jewish folk motifs. Among his works prior to his going to Palestine, the most notable is *Fantastische Suite* for Orch. (1932). He was the composer of the 1st Palestinian opera in Hebrew to receive a stage performance, *Dan Hashomer* (Dan the Guard; Tel Aviv, Feb. 17, 1945, composer conducting); also wrote an opera in the form of a series of cantillations with homophonic instrumental accompaniment entitled *Tamar and Judah* (1958; concert perf., N.Y., March 22, 1970); other works include 5 syms., among them the *Tragic* (1945), the *Liberation* (1951), and No. 4 (1957); the symphonic poems *Stalingrad* (c.1943) and *Negev* (c.1954); 2 piano concertos (1945, 1947); Flute Concerto (1965); Harp Concerto; Viola Concerto; the oratorio *Esther ha'malka* (Queen Esther; 1960); many songs.

Law, Andrew, American singing teacher and composer; b. Milford, Conn., March 21, 1749; d. Cheshire, Conn., July 13, 1821. He graduated from Rhode Island College, receiving his M.A. in 1778; then studied theology and was ordained in Hartford (1787); subsequently he was active as a preacher in Philadelphia and Baltimore, later as a pioneer singing teacher in New England. He invented a new system of notation, patented in 1802, which employed 4 (later increased to 7) different shapes of notes without the staff; it was not successful and was used in only a few of his own books. A 2nd innovation (at least as far as American usages were concerned) was his setting of the melody in the soprano instead of in the tenor. In 1786 he received an honorary M.A. degree from Yale Univ.; in 1821, an LL.D. from Allegheny College in Meadville, Pa. He compiled *A Select Number of Plain Tunes Adapted to Congregational Worship* (1775); *Select Harmony* (Cheshire, 1778); *A Collection of Hymns for Social Worship* (Cheshire, 1782); *The Rudiments of Music* (Cheshire, 1783); *The Art of Singing,* in 3 parts, each separately paged: I. *The Musical Primer;* II. *The Christian Harmony;* III. *The Musical Magazine* (Cheshire, 1792–93; 4th ed., Windsor, Vt., 1803; part III contains 6 books of tunes); *Harmonic Companion, and Guide to Social Worship: Being a Choice Selection of Tunes Adapted to the Various Psalms and Hymns* (Philadelphia, 1807); *The Art of Playing the Organ and Pianoforte* (Philadelphia, 1809); *Essays on Music* (Philadelphia, 1814). Only one of his hymn tunes, *Archdale,* acquired some popularity; but his teaching books, quaintly but clearly written, contributed considerably to early music education in America. **Bibl.:** F. Metcalf, *American Psalmody* (N.Y., 1917); idem, *American Writers and Compilers of Sacred Music* (N.Y., 1925); R. Crawford, *A. L., American Psalmodist* (Evanston, Ill., 1968).

Lawes, Henry, English composer, brother of **William Lawes;** b. Dinton, Wiltshire, Jan. 5, 1596; d. London, Oct. 21, 1662. He studied in London; in 1626, became "pistoler" and Gentleman of the Chapel Royal, then clerk; in 1631 became one of the King's musicians for the lutes and voices; also was music master to the Earl of Bridgewater; lost these appointments during the Protectorate, but was reinstated in 1660. He is interred in the cloisters of Westminster Abbey. Lawes is historically important because his infinite care in setting texts with proper note and accent marked a step in the development of vocal composition which culminated in Purcell. **Works** (all publ. in London unless otherwise given): SACRED VOCAL: *A Paraphrase upon the Psalmes of David by G*[eorge] *S*[andys] *set to New Tunes for Private Devotion* for Voice and Basso Continuo (1638); *Choice Psalmes put into Musick* for 3 Voices and Basso Continuo (1648; includes 30 full anthems); 3 other full anthems; 6 verse anthems; 11 anthems (only text extant). SECULAR VOCAL: *Ayres and Dialogues…* for 1 to 3 Voices (3 vols., 1653, 1655, 1658); in all, his songs number 434; also the masques *Comus* (Sept. 29, 1634) and *The Triumphs of Peace.* **Bibl.:** W. McClung Evans, *H. L., Musician and Friend of*

Poets (N.Y., 1941); E. Hart, "Introduction to H. L.," *Music & Letters,* XXXII (1951); A. Davidson, "Milton on the Music of H. L.," *Milton Newsletter* (May 1968); R. McGrady, "H. L. and the Concept of Just Note and Accent," *Music & Letters* (Jan. 1969); P. Willett, *The H. L. Manuscript* (London, 1969); N. Carpenter, "Milton and Music: H. L., Dante, and Casella," *English Literary Renaissance* (1972).

Lawes, William, important English composer, brother of **Henry Lawes;** b. Salisbury (baptized), May 1, 1602; d. in battle at the siege of Chester, Sept. 24, 1645. He most likely commenced his musical studies with his father, then found a patron in Edward Seymour, Earl of Hertford, who enabled him to study with Coperario in London. He became active at the court, being made "musician in ordinary for the lutes and voices" to Charles I in 1635; he joined his monarch's army in 1642, losing his life during the Civil War. He excelled as a composer of both vocal and instrumental music. Of historical significance is the music he wrote for the court masques, occasionally in collaboration with his brother or others. **Works:** Over 200 songs; also music to Jonson's *Entertainment at Welbeck* (1633); Fletcher's play *The Faithful Shepherdess* (1633); Shirley's masque *The Triumph of Peace* (1634); Davenant's play *Love and Honour* (1634); Davenant's masque *The Triumphs of the Prince d'Amour* (1636); Jonson's play *Epicoene, or The Silent Woman* (1636); W. Cartwright's play *The Royal Slave* (1636); Shirley's play *The Duke's Mistress* (1636); W. Berkeley's play *The Lost Lady* (1637); J. Mayne's play *The City March* (1637); J. Suckling's play *Aglaura* (1637); Beaumont and Fletcher's play *Cupid's Revenge* (1637); Davenant's masque *Britannia triumphans* (1638); Ford's play *The Lady's Trial* (1638); Davenant's play *The Unfortunate Lovers* (1638); Suckling's play *The Goblins* (1638); Suckling's play *The Tragedy of Brennoralt* (1639); H. Glapthorne's play *Argalus and Parthenia* (1639); Cavendish's play *The Country Captain* (1640); Shirley's play *The Cardinal* (1641); J. Denham's play *The Sophy* (1641); R. Brome's play *The Jovial Crew* (1641); etc.; sacred vocal music, including some 48 anthems and 10 canons; instrumental music, including consort suites; sonatas or fantasia-suites; numerous aires, almans, corants, sarabands, and other dances; various pieces for virginals or harpsichord; etc. For modern editions of his works, see the following: A. Sabol, ed., *Songs and Dances for the Stuart Masque* (Providence, R.I., 1959; 2nd ed., rev. and augmented, 1978); M. Lefkowitz, ed., *William Lawes: Select Consort Music,* Musica Britannica, XXI (1963; 2nd ed., 1971); idem, ed., *Trois masques à la cour de Charles Ier d'Angleterre* (Paris, 1970); I. Spink, ed., *English Songs, 1625–1660,* Musica Britannica, XXXIII (1971); D. Pinot, ed., *William Lawes: Consort Sets in Five and Six Parts* (London, 1979). **Bibl.:** M. Lefkowitz, *W. L.* (London, 1960); H. Poulos, *Giovanni Coperario and W. L.: The Beginnings of Pre-Commonwealth Violin Music* (diss., Indiana Univ., 1971); D. Pinto, "W. L.'s Music for Viol Consort," *Early Music,* VI (1978); idem, "W. L. at the Siege of York," *Musical Times* (Oct. 1986).

Lawrence, Dorothea Dix, American soprano and folk-song collector; b. N.Y., Sept. 22, 1899; d. Plainfield, N.J., May 23, 1979. She studied with Cesare Stunai, Henry Russell, and Katherine Opdycke in N.Y.; made her debut as Gounod's Marguerite with the Quebec Opera in Montreal in 1929, then appeared in opera in N.Y., Philadelphia, and elsewhere. She became active as a folk-song collector, presenting recitals in which she sang American Indian songs in their original languages as well as other folk songs and art songs by established composers; toured Europe as a recitalist (1952–54). She publ. the book *Folklore Songs of the United States* (1959).

Lawrence, Gertrude (real name, **Gertrud Alexandra Dagmar Lawrence Klasen**), English actress, singer, and dancer; b. London, July 4, 1898; d. N.Y., Sept. 6, 1952. She began her career with appearances in British revues (from 1910); starred in *André Charlot's Revue* in London, with which she made her N.Y. debut (1924). George and Ira Gershwin wrote for her the musicals *Oh, Kay!* (1926) and *Treasure Girl* (1928);

after working mainly as an actress in England and the U.S., she won great critical acclaim as Liza Elliot in the Kurt Weill and Moss Hart musical play *Lady in the Dark* (1941); her last role was as Anna in the Rodgers and Hammerstein musical *The King and I* (1951). She publ. her autobiography as *A Star Danced* (1945).

BIBL.: R. Aldrich, *G. L. as Mrs. A.* (N.Y., 1954).

Lawrence, Lucile, American harpist and teacher; b. New Orleans, Feb. 7, 1907. She studied with Carlos Salzedo and was 1st harpist in his harp ensemble; organized her own Lawrence Harp Quintet and appeared as a soloist with major orchs., a chamber music artist, and a recitalist. She taught at the Curtis Inst. of Music in Philadelphia (1927–30), then founded the harp dept. at the Philadelphia Musical Academy; also taught at the Mannes College of Music in N.Y. (from 1945), Boston Univ. (from 1966), the Manhattan School of Music in N.Y. (from 1967), and the Berkshire Music Center in Tanglewood (from 1968).

Lawrence, Marjorie (Florence), noted Australian soprano; b. Dean's Marsh, Victoria, Feb. 17, 1907; d. Little Rock, Ark., Jan. 13, 1979. She studied in Melbourne with Ivor Boustead; then in Paris with Cécile Gilly. She made her debut as Elisabeth in *Tannhäuser* in Monte Carlo (1932); then sang at the Paris Opéra (1933–36). She made her American debut at the Metropolitan Opera in N.Y. on Dec. 18, 1935, as Brünnhilde in *Die Walküre;* remained on its roster until 1941; made guest appearances with the Chicago, San Francisco, St. Louis, and Cincinnati operas. An attack of poliomyelitis while she was in Mexico (1941) interrupted her career. While she never walked again unaided, her determination to return to the operatic stage led to numerous subsequent performances; her 1st appearance at the Metropolitan Opera following her illness came on Dec. 27, 1942, when she sang the Venusberg duet in a concert with Melchior, reclining upon a couch. Her last appearance there took place when she sang Venus on April 6, 1944. She continued to make occasional appearances until her retirement in 1952, then devoted herself to teaching. She was a prof. of voice at Tulane Univ. (1956–60) and prof. of voice and director of the opera workshop at Southern Illinois Univ. (from 1960). She publ. an autobiography, *Interrupted Melody, The Story of My Life* (N.Y., 1949), which was made into a motion picture in 1955.

Lawrence, Steve (real name, **Sidney Leibowitz**), American singer of popular music and actor; b. N.Y., July 8, 1935. He dropped out of high school to pursue a career as a singer; in 1953 he joined the "Steve Allen Show" on NBC-TV in N.Y., which became the nationally televised "Tonight" show in 1954; there he met the singer **Eydie Gorme,** whom he married in 1957; they subsequently appeared successfully in numerous nightclub engagements; he also acted in Broadway musicals, among them *What Makes Sammy Run?* in 1964, and co-starred with his wife in *Golden Rainbow* (1967).

Lawrence, Vera Brodsky, American pianist and music editor; b. Norfolk, Va., July 1, 1909. She studied piano with Josef and Rosina Lhévinne and theory with Goldmark and Wagenaar at the Juilliard School of Music in N.Y. (1929–32); gave duo-piano concerts with Harold Triggs, and appeared as a soloist with American orchs. In a radical change of direction, she abandoned her concert career in 1965 to become a historian of American music. In 1967 she was appointed administrator of publications for the Contemporary Music Project, and supervised the publication of numerous works by American composers. In 1969 she brought out the collected piano works of Louis Moreau Gottschalk, in 5 vols.; in 1970 she compiled, ed., and produced the collected works of Scott Joplin, in 2 vols., and in 1975 publ. the valuable vol. *Music for Patriots, Politicians, and Presidents,* tracing American history as reflected in popular music, profusely illustrated with title pages and musical excerpts from publ. songs and dances celebrating historical events, and campaign ballads written during presidential elections; this work received the ASCAP–Deems Taylor award in 1976. She also publ. *Strong on Music: The New York Music Scene in the Days of George Templeton Strong, 1836–1875: Vol. I: Resonances, 1836–1850* (Oxford and N.Y., 1988).

Laws, Hubert, black American flutist; b. Houston, Nov. 10, 1939. He learned to play saxophone, piano, and guitar as well as flute; played saxophone with the Jazz Crusaders (1954–60) while pursuing classical music studies, then was a member of several popular orchs. before joining the Metropolitan Opera orch. in N.Y. as a flutist. He also appeared as a soloist with the N.Y. Phil.; also continued to appear in jazz settings.

Layton, Billy Jim, American composer and musicologist; b. Corsicana, Texas, Nov. 14, 1924. He studied at the New England Cons. of Music in Boston with Carl McKinley (B.Mus., 1948); then at Yale Univ. with Quincy Porter (M.Mus., 1950), and at Harvard Univ. with Walter Piston (composition) and Gombosi and Pirrotta (musicology); obtained his Ph.D. at Harvard with the dissertation *Italian Music for the Ordinary of the Mass* (1960), then was on its faculty (1960–66); in 1966, was appointed a prof. of music at the State Univ. of N.Y. at Stony Brook.

WORKS: *An American Portrait,* symphonic overture (1957); *Dante Fantasy* for Orch. (1964); *3 Dylan Thomas Poems* for Chorus and Brass Sextet (1954–56); chamber music of various descriptions.

Layton, Robert, noted English musicologist; b. London, May 2, 1930. He was educated at Worcester College, Oxford (B.A., 1953); then went to Sweden, learned the language, and took courses at the Univs. of Uppsala and Stockholm (1953–55); in 1959 he joined the staff of the BBC in London, where he prepared music seminars. He became an authority on Scandinavian music. He contributed the majority of the articles on Scandinavian composers to *The New Grove Dictionary of Music and Musicians* (1980), and in a spirit of mischievous fun also inserted a biography of a nonexistent Danish composer, making up his name from the stations of the Copenhagen subway. The editor was not amused, and the phony entry had to be painfully gouged in the galleys for the new printing.

WRITINGS: *Franz Berwald* (in Swedish, Stockholm, 1956; in Eng., London, 1959); *Sibelius* (London, 1965; 3rd ed., rev., 1983); *Sibelius and His World* (London, 1970); ed. *A Companion to the Concerto* (London, 1988).

Lazăr, Filip, Rumanian composer; b. Craiova, May 18, 1894; d. Paris, Nov. 3, 1936. He studied with Kiriac and Castaldi at the Bucharest Cons. (1907–12) and with Teichmüller and Krehl at the Leipzig Cons. (1913–14). In 1915 he went to Paris; was a founding member of the modern music society Triton (1928). His music is brilliantly hedonistic, with the ethnic Rumanian element furnishing an exotic element *à la moderne.*

WORKS: *Prelude* for Orch. (1919); *Suita română* for Orch. (1921); *Divertissement* for Orch. (1924); *Suite valaque* for Small Orch. (1925); *Tziganes,* scherzo for Orch. (Boston, Oct. 29, 1926); *Music for an Orchestra* (Boston, March 23, 1928); *Le Ring: Un Round de 4 minutes* (Paris, Jan. 10, 1930); 4 concertos: No. 1, *Concerto Grosso in the Old Style* (Boston, Feb. 21, 1930); No. 2 for Piano and Small Orch. (1931); No. 3 for Piano and Orch. (Paris, Nov. 4, 1934); No. 4, *Concerto da camera,* for Percussion and 12 Instruments (Paris, Dec. 11, 1935); *Musică pentru radio* (Music for Radio), overture for Small Orch. (Paris, Feb. 26, 1931); 2 piano sonatas (1913, 1929); Violin Sonata (1919); 2 suites for Piano (1924, 1925); *Bagatelles* for Cello and Piano (1925); *3 Dances* for Violin and Piano (1927); *Bagatelles* for Piano (1927); Trio for Oboe, Clarinet, and Bassoon (1934); String Trio (1935); *Petite suite* for Oboe, Clarinet, and Bassoon (1936); choruses; songs.

BIBL.: V. Tomescu, *F. L.* (Bucharest, 1963).

Lazare, Martin, Belgian pianist and composer; b. Brussels, Oct. 27, 1829; d. there, Aug. 6, 1897. He studied in The Hague with van der Does, and at the Paris Cons. with Zimmerman; traveled to London, Germany, the U.S., and Canada.

WORKS: Opera, *Le Roi de Bohème* (The Hague, 1852); operetta, *Les Deux Mandarins* (Brussels, 1878); chamber music; piano works.

Lazaro, Hippolito, Spanish tenor; b. Barcelona, Aug. 13, 1887; d. Madrid, May 14, 1974. He studied in Milan; then sang operetta in Barcelona; went to London in 1912, singing at the Coliseum under the name of **Antonio Manuele;** in 1913 returned to Italy, where Mascagni chose him to create the role of Ugo in *Parisina* at La Scala in Milan. He made his Metropolitan Opera debut in N.Y. on Jan. 31, 1918, as the Duke of Mantua in *Rigoletto;* remained on its roster until 1920. In 1921 he created the role of Piccolo Marat in Mascagni's opera in Rome; also the role of Giannetto in *La cena delle beffe* by Giordano at La Scala in 1924. He made guest appearances with the Vienna State Opera, the Budapest Opera, and the Teatro Colón in Buenos Aires. He retired in 1950.

Lazarof, Henri, brilliant Bulgarian-born American composer and pedagogue; b. Sofia, April 12, 1932. He left Bulgaria in 1946 for Palestine, and studied composition with Paul Ben-Haim in Jerusalem (1949–52); then took courses with Goffredo Petrassi at the Accademia di Santa Cecilia in Rome (1955–57). He completed his studies with Arthur Berger and Harold Shapiro on a fellowship at Brandeis Univ. (M.F.A., 1959). In 1959 he became a naturalized U.S. citzen; that same year he became a teacher of French language and literature at the Univ. of Calif., Los Angeles; in 1962 he joined its music faculty; in 1970–71 he was artist-in-residence in West Berlin; then returned to U.C.L.A., retiring in 1987 as prof. emeritus. His music is marked by inventive originality in its thematic structure and subtle "sonorism" in instrumentation, without imperiling the pragmatic quality of the basic design; instances of serial procedures are unobtrusive.

Works: Piano Concerto (1957); *Piccola serenata* for Orch. (Boston, June 14, 1959); Viola Concerto (Monaco, Feb. 20, 1962; 1st prize at the International Competition of Monaco); Concerto for Piano and 20 Instruments (Milan Radio, May 28, 1963); *Odes* for Orch. (1963); *Concertino da camera* for Woodwind Quintet (1959); *Tempi concertati*, double concerto for Violin, Viola, and Chamber Orch. (1964); 2 string quartets (1956, 1962); String Trio (1957); Sonata for Violin Solo (1958); *Inventions* for Viola and Piano (1962); *Asymptotes* for Flute and Vibraphone (1963); *Quantetti* (a telescoped title for "Quattro canti per quartetto di pianoforte") for 4 Pianos (1964); *Structures sonores* for Orch. (1966; received 1st International Prize of the City of Milan, La Scala Award); *Rhapsody* for Violin and Piano (1966); *Espaces* for 10 Instruments (1966); Octet for Wind Instruments (1967); *Mutazione* for Orch. (1967); Cello Concerto (1968; Oslo, Sept. 12, 1969); *Omaggio*, chamber concerto for 19 Players (1968); *Divertimenti* for 5 Players (1969); *Textures* for Piano and 5 Ensembles (1970); *Continuum* for Strings (1970); *Events*, ballet (1973); *Partita* for Brass Quintet (1973); *Concertazioni* for Orch. (1973); Chamber Concerto No. 3 (1974); *Spectrum* for Trumpet, Orch., and Tape (Salt Lake City, Jan. 17, 1975); *Volo* for Viola and 2 String Ensembles (1976); *Chamber Symphony* (1977); Concerto for Orch. (1977); *Canti*, ballet (1980); *Mirrors, Mirrors*, ballet (1981); *Icarus*, 2nd concerto for Orch. (1984; Houston, April 12, 1986); *Celebration* for 4 Brass Choirs (1984); *Poema* for Orch. (1985; Seattle, May 10, 1986); Violin Concerto (1985); Concertante for 16 Strings and 2 Horns (1988); Concertante II, octet for Flute, Oboe, Clarinet, Violin, Cello, Double Bass, Percussion, and Piano (1988); Clarinet Concerto (1989).

Lazarus, Daniel, French conductor and composer; b. Paris, Dec. 13, 1898; d. there, June 27, 1964. He studied at the Paris Cons., taking 1st prize in composition (1915). He was conductor of the Théâtre du Vieux Colombier (1921–25), then artistic director of the Paris Opéra-Comique (1936–39); later was chorus master of the Paris Opéra (1946–56), then prof. at the Schola Cantorum in Paris (from 1956). He publ. *Accès à la musique* (Paris, 1960). His works include the operas *L'Illustre Magicien* (1924), *La Véritable Histoire de Wilhelm Meister* (1927), *Trumpeldor* (1935), and *La Chambre bleue* (1938);

also 3 ballets; incidental music; 2 syms. (1933, 1934); Piano Concerto (1929); chamber music; piano pieces; songs.

Lazarus, Gustav, German pianist and composer; b. Cologne, July 19, 1861; d. Berlin, May 24, 1920. He studied with I. Seiss, G. Jensen, and F. Wüllner; was a prof. of piano at the Scharwenka Cons. in Berlin (1887–99); in 1899, became director of the Breslaur Cons. and Seminary in Berlin; appeared with success as a pianist in Germany, France, and England. He wrote 170 opus numbers, including the operas *Mandanika* (Elberfeld, 1899) and *Das Nest der Zaunkönige;* choral works, with Orch.; an Orch. Suite; chamber music; choruses; piano works; songs.

Lazzari, Sylvio, Austrian-born French composer; b. Bozen, Dec. 30, 1857; d. Paris, June 18, 1944. He entered the Paris Cons. in 1883, studying with Franck and Guiraud; became a naturalized French citizen, settling in Paris. Up to 1894 he was an active propagandist for the works of Wagner, contributing essays to various journals; then devoted himself entirely to composition, adopting the principles of Impressionism. He visited the U.S. to conduct the world premiere of his opera *Le Sautériot* (Chicago, Jan. 19, 1918). He also wrote the operas *Armor* (Prague, Nov. 7, 1898), *La Lépreuse* (Paris, Feb. 7, 1912), *Melaenis* (Mulhouse, 1927), and *La Tour de feu* (Paris, Jan. 16, 1928); a pantomime, *Lulu* (1887); orch. works: Sym.; *Rapsodie espagnole; Ophélie*, symphonic poem; *Impressions d'Adriatique; Effet de nuit*, symphonic poem (1904); *Marche pour une fête joyeuse; Tableau symphonique d'après Verlaine; Chanson de Moulin; Au bois de Misène; Cortège nocturne; Fête bretonne; Et la jeune fille parla; Perdu en mer; Rapsodie* for Violin and Orch.; *Le Nouveau Christ* for Baritone and Orch.; *Des choses des choses* for Soprano and Orch.; *Apparitions* for Soprano and Orch.; incidental music to *Faust;* Piano Trio; String Quartet; Octet for Wind Instruments; Violin Sonata; piano works; songs; etc.

Lazzari, Virgilio, Italian-born American bass; b. Assisi, April 20, 1887; d. Castel Gandolfo, Oct. 4, 1953. He studied in Rome with Antonio Cotogni; made his debut in 1908 with the Vitale Light Opera Co.; then sang in South America. In 1916 he made his U.S. debut as Ramfis in St. Louis. He settled in the U.S. and became a naturalized citizen. From 1918 to 1933 he was a member of the Chicago Opera. On Dec. 28, 1933, he made his Metropolitan Opera debut in N.Y. as Pedro in *L'Africaine;* remained on the roster until 1940; then returned for the 1943–51 seasons. He also sang at the Salzburg Festivals (1934–39); appeared as Leporello at London's Covent Garden (1939). He became celebrated for his portrayal of Archibaldo in Montemezzi's *L'amore dei tre re*.

Lear, Evelyn (née **Shulman**), outstanding American soprano; b. N.Y., Jan. 8, 1926. Her grandfather Zavel Kwartin was a synagogue cantor; her mother was a professional singer; her father, a lawyer, was an amateur musician. She studied piano; also practiced on the horn, and played it in a student orch. at the Berkshire Music Center in Tanglewood. She married Dr. Walter Lear at 17, and assumed his name in her professional career, keeping it after her divorce. She began to take voice lessons in Washington, D.C., with the baritone John Yard and sang in musicals. Realizing her inadequacies in vocal technique, she enrolled in the class of Sergius Kagen at the Juilliard School of Music in N.Y. There she met the baritone **Thomas Stewart,** who in 1955 became her 2nd husband. They obtained Fulbright grants and went to Berlin for further study; she took voice with Maria Ivogün at the Hochschule für Musik. Soon both she and Stewart received a contract to sing at the Städtische Oper in Berlin. She made her debut there in 1959. An extraordinary opportunity to show her expertise was presented to her when she was asked to sing the challenging title role in a concert performance of Berg's opera *Lulu* in Vienna on May 24, 1960. She acquitted herself brilliantly, and was engaged to sing Lulu in the stage performance in Vienna in 1962. She was then invited to sing parts in other modern operas; she also gave fine performances in standard operas. She made her debut at the Metropolitan Opera in N.Y.

on March 17, 1967, as Lavinia in Levy's opera *Mourning Becomes Electra*. She sang regularly at the Metropolitan until her farewell performance as the Marschallin on Oct. 15, 1985. Among her memorable roles were the Countess, Marie in *Wozzeck*, Fiordiligi, Octavian, Pamina, and Tosca, as well as those already mentioned; also created the role of Irma Arkadina in Pasatieri's *The Seagull* in Houston (1974) and the role of Magda in Ward's *Minutes to Midnight* in Miami (1982). She often appeared in opera and concerts with her husband.

Le Bé, Guillaume, French type-founder; b. Troyes, 1525; d. Paris, 1598. He was trained in Rome and Venice; in 1550 he settled in Paris. He followed the method of Petrucci, printing notes and staff lines separately, thus necessitating 2 impressions. He also made tablature type. His punches and other equipment were acquired by Ballard, and were in use for another couple of centuries.

BIBL.: S. Morison, *L'Inventaire de la fonderie L.B.* (Paris, 1957).

Lebègue, Nicolas-Antoine, French organist, harpsichordist, and composer; b. Laon, c.1631; d. Paris, July 6, 1702. From 1664 until his death he was organist at St. Merry in Paris; from 1678, was also one of the court organists. He publ. 3 books of organ music (I, 1676; II and III, after 1678); 2 vols. of *Pièces de clavessin* (1677, 1687); and *Airs* for 2–3 Voices, with Continuo. An ed. of his complete keyboard works was edited by N. Dufourcq in *Œuvres de clavecin* (Monaco, 1956).

BIBL.: N. Dufourcq, *N.-A. L. . . .* (Paris, 1954).

Lebert (real name, **Levi**), **Sigmund,** German pianist and pedagogue; b. Ludwigsburg, near Stuttgart, Dec. 12, 1821; d. Stuttgart, Dec. 8, 1884. He was a pupil of Tomaschek in Prague. In 1856 he founded, with Faiszt, Stark, Brachmann, and Speidel, the Stuttgart Cons. His *Grosse Klavierschule* (which included numerous studies of his own composition), publ. in cooperation with Stark, ran through many eds. (rev. by M. Pauer, 1904), and appeared also in Eng., French, Italian, and Russian trs. He also publ. an *Instructive Edition* of classical piano works and ed. Clementi's *Gradus ad Parnassum*.

Lebeuf, Abbé Jean, French music scholar; b. Auxerre, March 6, 1687; d. Paris, April 10, 1760. In 1740 he succeeded to Lancelot's chair in the Académie. He wrote about 180 essays on all manner of subjects, including a series publ. in the *Mercure de France* (1725–28) dealing with plainchant, in strong opposition to Motz's newly invented style of notation; he also wrote *Traité historique et pratique sur le chant ecclésiastique précédé d'une nouvelle méthode pour l'enseigner et l'apprendre facilement* (1741).

Leborne, Aimé-Ambroise-Simon, French composer; b. Brussels, Dec. 29, 1797; d. Paris, April 2, 1866. He went to France as a child; studied at the Paris Cons. with Berton and Cherubini; won the 2nd Prix de Rome (1818) and then the 1st Prix de Rome (1820); subsequently was on its faculty, later serving as prof. of counterpoint and fugue (1836–40), then of composition (1840–66); also was made librarian of the Paris Opéra (1829) and of the Royal Chapel (1834). In 1853 he became a chevalier of the Legion of Honor. He ed. a new edition of Catel's *Traité d'harmonie* (Paris, 1848; with numerous additions). He wrote the operas *Les Deux Figaro* (Paris, Aug. 22, 1827; in collaboration with Carafa); *Le Camp du drap d'or* (Paris, Feb. 23, 1828; in collaboration with Baton and Rifaut); *Cinq ans d'entr'acte* and *Lequel* (Paris, March 21, 1838); also songs.

Leborne, Fernand, French music critic and composer; b. Charleroi, March 10, 1862; d. Paris, Jan. 15, 1929. He was a pupil at the Paris Cons. of Massenet, Saint-Saëns, and Franck. He lived mostly in Paris; was music critic for *Le Monde Artiste*, later for the *Petit Parisien*; as a composer, he won the Prix Chartier in 1901.

WORKS: OPERAS: *Daphnis et Chloé* (Brussels, May 10, 1885); *Hedda* (Milan, 1898); *Mudarra* (Berlin, April 19, 1899); *Les Girondins* (Lyons, March 25, 1905); *La Catalane* (Paris, May 24, 1907); *Cléopâtre* (Rouen, 1914); *Néréa* (Marseilles,

Jan. 12, 1926). ORCH.: *Suite intime, Symphonie dramatique, Aquarelles, Temps de guerre, Fête bretonne, Marche solennelle, Ouverture guerrière, Ouverture symphonique; Symphonie-Concerto* for Violin and Piano, with Orch.; incidental music to *L'Absent* (Paris, 1903); String Quartet; Piano Trio; Violin Sonata; Mass; motets; piano pieces; songs.

Lebouc, Charles-Joseph, French cellist and composer; b. Besançon, Dec. 22, 1822; d. Hyères, March 6, 1893. He studied at the Paris Cons. with Franchomme, Halévy, and Colet (composition), winning 1st prize for cello (1842) and for harmony (1844). He played in the Paris Opéra orch. (1844–48); was a member of the Société des Concerts from 1852; was founder of the Soirées de Musique Classique. He wrote *Trio de concert* for Piano, Violin, and Cello; *Ave verum* for Voice, with Piano and Cello; duos for cello, with piano; cello pieces; also a method for cello.

Lebrun, Franziska (Dorothea) (née **Danzi**), renowned German soprano; b. Mannheim (baptized), March 24, 1756; d. Berlin, May 14, 1791. She made her debut as Sandrina in Sacchini's *La Contadina in corte* in Schwetzingen (Aug. 9, 1772), then became a prominent member of the Mannheim Court Opera, where she created the countess in Holzbauer's *Günther von Schwarzburg* (Jan. 5, 1777). She made her 1st appearance in London at the King's Theatre as Ariene in Sacchini's *Creso* (Nov. 8, 1777); then was chosen to sing in Salieri's *Europa riconosciuta* at the opening of Milan's Teatro alla Scala (Aug. 3, 1778). She appeared at the Paris Concert Spirituel (1779) and again in London (1779–81); also continued to sing with the Court Opera in Mannheim, and later when the court went to Munich; likewise made guest appearances in Vienna and Verona, and later in Naples (1786–87) and Berlin (1789–90). She also composed; publ. 36 sonatas for Violin and Piano. She married the oboist and composer **Ludwig August Lebrun** (1778), with whom she appeared in concerts.

Lebrun, Jean, famous French horn-player; b. Lyons, April 6, 1759; d. Paris, c.1809. He went to Paris about 1780 to study with Punto; then made his debut at the Concert Spirituel in 1781. He was 1st horn in the Paris Opéra orch. (1786–92) and in the Berlin Prussian Court Orch. (from 1792); also toured in a celebrated duo with Türschmidt until the latter's death in 1797. He wrote a number of concertos, but they are lost.

Lebrun, Louis-Sébastien, French tenor and composer; b. Paris, Dec. 10, 1764; d. there, June 27, 1829. He studied at the maîtrise of Notre Dame in Paris (1771–83). Unsuccessful as a singer at the Paris Opéra and Opéra-Comique, he became one of the 4 "maîtres de chant" at the Opéra; in 1807, became a tenor in Napoleon's chapelle, and in 1810, "chef du chant" there. He wrote 15 operas, the most successful being *Marcelin* (Paris, March 22, 1800) and *Le Rossignol* (Paris, April 23, 1816); also a Te Deum (1809); *Missa solemnis* (1815); and a collection of *romances*.

Lebrun, Ludwig August (actually, **Ludwig Karl Maria**), celebrated German oboist and composer; b. Mannheim (baptized), May 2, 1752; d. Berlin, Dec. 16, 1790. He studied with his father, Jakob Alexander Lebrun, an oboist and répétiteur at the Mannheim court (1747–71). A precocious talent, he was admitted to the Mannheim Court Orch. as a scholar at the age of 12; at 15 became a full member, a position he held until his death. He also toured as a virtuoso from about 1772, increasing his appearances after his marriage to the soprano **Franziska (Dorothea)** (née **Danzi**) **Lebrun** in 1778. He visited Milan (1778), Paris (1779), London (1779–81), Vienna (1785), Prague (1785), Naples (1786–87), and Berlin (1789–90). In addition to solo appearances, he often appeared with his wife. He composed several fine oboe concertos, and also wrote ballets, chamber music, and duos for flute.

Lebrun, Paul Henri Joseph, Belgian conductor, teacher, and composer; b. Ghent, April 21, 1863; d. Louvain, Nov. 4, 1920. He was a pupil at the Ghent Cons.; won the Belgian Prix de Rome in 1891 with his cantata *Andromeda*, and 1st prize of the Belgian Académie for a sym.; in 1890, became prof. of theory at the Ghent Cons. and conductor of the Orphéon at Cambrai; in 1895, became conductor of the Cercle Artistique at Ghent; was director of the music school in Louvain (1913–20). He wrote an opera, *La Fiancée d'Abydos* (Ghent, 1897); orch. and choral works; chamber music; etc.

Leça, Armando Lopes, Portuguese conductor, folk-song collector, and composer; b. Leça da Palmeira, Aug. 9, 1893; d. Vila Nova de Gaia, Sept. 7, 1977. He studied with Oscar da Silva; was active as a choral conductor and a collector of native folk songs; publ. an authoritative ed. of popular Portuguese music (1922; expanded ed. in 2 vols., 1947). He wrote several dance suites for Orch., of which the *Dansa de Don Pedro* attained considerable popularity; 2 operettas: *Maio florido* (1918) and *Bruxa* (1919); many piano pieces of pictorial character; songs.

Le Caine, Hugh, Canadian, physicist, acoustician, and innovative creator of prototypical electronic musical instruments; b. Port Arthur, Ontario, May 27, 1914; d. Ottawa, July 3, 1977, of a stroke suffered 364 days after a motorcycle accident en route to Montreal. Although his childhood training combined music and science, he chose to emphasize science in his formal studies; he received a B.S. degree from Queen's Univ. in Kingston, Ontario, in 1938 and an M.S. in 1939, and obtained his Ph.D. in nuclear physics from the Univ. of Birmingham in 1952; he also studied piano briefly at the Royal Cons. of Music of Toronto and privately with Viggo Kihl. His childhood dream was to one day apply scientific techniques to the development and invention of new musical instruments, and he went on to develop ground-breaking electronic musical instruments which ultimately formed the basis of pioneering electronic music studios at the Univ. of Toronto (1959) and McGill Univ. in Montreal (1964). He exhibited electronic-music instruments at Expo '67 in Montreal; contributed numerous articles on his findings in various scholarly journals. While he saw himself as a designer of instruments which assisted others in creative work, he himself realized a number of striking electronic compositions in the course of his development, among them the now-classic *Dripsody* (1959), which used only the sound of a single drop of water falling; other compositions were *Alchemy* (1964) and *Perpetual Motion* for Data Systems Computer (1970). His instruments revolutionized musical composition; his Sackbut synthesizer (1945–48; 1954–60; 1969–73) is today recognized as the 1st voltage-controlled synthesizer; among his other instruments are The Spectrogram (1959–62; designed to facilitate the use of complex sine tones in composition), The Alleatone (c.1962; "a controlled chance device selecting one of 16 channels with weighted probabilities"), Sonde (1968–70; which can generate 200 sine waves simultaneously), and Polyphone (1970; a polyphonic synthesizer operated by a keyboard with touch-sensitive keys).
BIBL.: G. Young, *The Sackbut Blues: H. L.C.: Pioneer in Electronic Music* (1989).

Le Carpentier, Adolphe-Clair, French pianist and composer; b. Paris, Feb. 17, 1809; d. there, July 14, 1869. He was a pupil of Le Sueur and Fétis at the Paris Cons. (1818), winning several prizes. He publ. an excellent *Méthode de piano pour les enfants*; also 25 *Études élémentaires* (op. 59), and a collection of 24 études, *Le Progrès*; also nearly 300 fantasias on operatic and national airs, well arranged and of moderate difficulty.

Lechner, Leonhard (Leonardus Lechner Atheses or **Athesinus),** outstanding Austrian-born German composer; b. in the Adige valley, Tirol, c.1550; d. Stuttgart, Sept. 9, 1606. He was a chorister under Orlando di Lasso at the Munich Hofkapelle (1564?–68) and under Ivo de Vento and Antonius Gosswin at the Landshut Hofkapelle (1570). After serving as an assistant teacher at the St. Lorenz school in Nuremberg (1575–84), he obtained the position of Kapellmeister to Count Eitelfriedrich IV von Hohenzollern-Hechingen. However, being an adherent to Lutheranism, he found his position unten-

able at the Catholic Hofkapelle. In 1585 he secretly made his way to Tübingen. The Count sent Lechner a letter in which he promised to release him without prejudice. Lechner's reply was one of uncompromising defiance, prompting the angry Count to order his bodily return forthwith. Lechner then took refuge in Stuttgart in 1585 at the court of Duke Ludwig of Württemberg, who successfully mediated his dispute with his former patron and the Nuremberg town council. Lechner began his service in Stuttgart as a tenor, but soon was named composer in 1586. He served as assistant Hofkapellmeister until 1594; was formally installed as Hofkapellmeister in 1595, and proceeded to upgrade the Kapelle to a high level. Lechner's innovative genius is most strikingly revealed in his lieder. He was the 1st composer to set a complete cycle of German poems to music.
WORKS (all publ. in Nuremberg): SACRED VOCAL: *Motectae sacrae* for 4 to 6 Voices, . . . *addita esta in fine motecta* for 8 Voices (2 Choirs) (1575); *Sanctissimae virginis Mariae canticum, quod vulgo Magnificat inscribitur, secundum octo vulgares tonos* for 4 Voices (1578); *Sacrarum cantionum, liber secundus* for 5 to 6 Voices (1581); *Liber missarum . . . adjunctis aliquot introitibus in praecipua festa, ab Adventu Domini usque ad festum Sanctissimae Trinitatis* for 5 to 6 Voices (1584); *Septum psalmi poenitentiales . . . additis aliis quibusdam piis cantionibus* for 6 and More Voices (1587); also *Historia der Passion und Leidens Christi* for 4 Voices (perf. in Stuttgart, 1593).
LIEDER: *Neu teutsche Lieder, nach art der welschen Villanellen gantz kurtzweilig zu singen, auch auff allerley Seytenspil zu gebrauchen* for 3 Voices (1576; 3rd ed., 1586); *Der ander Theyl neuer teutscher Lieder, nach art der welschen Villanellen* for 3 Voices (1577; 2nd ed., 1586); *Neue teutsche Lieder* for 4 to 5 Voices (1577; includes sacred lieder); *Neue teutsche Lieder, erstlich durch . . . Jacobum Regnart . . . componirt mit drey Stimmen, nach art der welschen Villanellen, jetzund aber . . . mit fünff Stimmen gesetzet . . . con alchuni madrigali in lingua Italiana* for 5 Voices (1579); *Neue teutsche Lieder* for 4 to 5 Voices (1582; includes sacred lieder); *Neue lustige teutsche Lieder nach art der welschen Canzonen* for 4 Voices (1586); *Neue geistliche und weltliche teutsche Lieder* for 4 to 5 Voices (1589); also several works for special occasions. A complete ed. of his works commenced publication in Kassel in 1954 under the editorship of K. Ameln et al.
BIBL.: U. Martin, *Historische und stilkritische Studien zu L. L.s Strophenliedern* (diss., Univ. of Göttingen, 1957); K. Ameln, "L. L., ein eigenwüchsiger Meister der deutschen Chormusik," *Württembergische Blätter für Kirchenmusik,* XXVII (1960); W. Blankenburg, "Zu den Johannes-Passionen von Ludwig Daser (1578) und L. L. (1593)," *Musa—Mens—Musici: Im Gedenken an Walther Vetter* (Leipzig, 1969).

Lechthaler, Josef, Austrian composer and teacher; b. Rattenberg, Dec. 31, 1891; d. Vienna, Aug. 21, 1948. He studied philology in Innsbruck, and musicology with Guido Adler at the Univ. of Vienna; obtained his Ph.D. there in 1919; from 1925, taught theory at the Vienna Academy of Music; was director of the church music school there from 1933 until 1938, and again from 1945 to his death. He wrote "Der katholische Organist als Baumeister des Gesamtkunstwerks," in *Kongress-Bericht für Kirchenmusik* (Berlin, 1927); composed cantatas: *Der lichte Tag* and *Lieder der Wanderschaft;* a cappella choruses; 2 string quartets; Trio for Violin, Viola da Gamba, and Harpsichord; song cycle, *Conjunx conjugi;* Piano Sonata; choruses; much guitar music; various songs and pieces for children.
BIBL.: E. Tittel, *J. L.* (Vienna, 1966).

Leclair, family of notable French musicians, which included the following 3 brothers:
(1) Jean-Marie Leclair (l'aîné), celebrated violinist and composer; b. Lyons, May 10, 1697; d. (murdered) Paris, Oct. 22, 1764. His father was the master lacemaker and cellist Antoine Leclair. Jean-Marie studied violin, dancing, and lace-making in his youth, excelling in all 3. He then began his career as a dancer at the Lyons Opera, where he met Marie-

Rose Casthagnié; they were married in 1716. About 1722 he went to Turin, where he was active as a ballet master. During a visit to Paris in 1723 to arrange for the publication of his op. 1, a distinguished set of sonatas, he acquired a wealthy patron in Joseph Bonnier. Returning to Turin, he wrote ballets for the Teatro Regio Ducale; also received instruction from Somis. He then made a series of appearances at the Concert Spirituel in Paris in 1728. He also visited London, and then made a great impression when he played at the Kassel court with Pietro Locatelli. He subsequently received additional instruction from André Chéron in Paris. After the death of his 1st wife, Leclair married Louise Roussel in 1730; she engraved all of his works from op. 2 forward. From 1733 to 1737 he served as ordinaire de la musique du roi to Louis XV. He then entered the service of Princess Anne at the Orange court in the Netherlands in 1738, and was honored with the Croix Néerlandaise du Lion. He was active 3 months of the year at the court, and, from 1740, spent the remaining months as maestro di cappella to the commoner François du Liz at The Hague. He returned to Paris in 1743. With the exception of a brief period of service with the Spanish Prince Don Philippe in Chambéry in 1744, he remained in Paris for the rest of his life. From 1748 until his death, he was music director and composer to his former student, the Duke of Gramont, who maintained a private theater in the Parisian suburb of Puteaux. Leclair separated from his wife about 1758. He was murdered as he was entering his home. The Paris police report listed 3 suspects: his gardener (who discovered his body), his estranged wife, and his nephew, the violinist Guillaume-François Vial, with whom he was on poor terms. The evidence clearly pointed to the nephew, but he was never charged with the deed. Leclair was the founder of the French violin school. He was also a distinguished composer who successfully combined the finest elements of the Italian and French styles of his day. Among his works, all publ. in Paris, are *Premier livre de sonates* for Violin and Basso Continuo (1723; 12 sonatas; 2 also for Flute; ed. as op. 3, 1905, by A. Guilmant and J. Debroux); *Second livre de sonates* for Violin and Basso Continuo (c.1728; 12 sonatas; 5 also for Flute; ed. in Publikationen Älterer Praktischer und Theoretischer Musikwerke, XXVII, 1903); *Troisième livre de sonates* for Violin and Basso Continuo, op. 5 (1734; 12 sonatas; ed. in Recent Researches in the Music of the Baroque Era, IV–V, 1968–69); 6 Concertos for Violin, Strings, and Basso Continuo, op. 7 (1737; No. 3 for Flute or Oboe, Strings, and Basso Continuo); *Quatrième livre de sonates* for Violin and Basso Continuo, op. 9 (1743; 12 sonatas; 2 also for Flute; 6 publ. as op. 1, London, c.1755; ed. in Recent Researches in the Music of the Baroque Era, X–XI, 1969–72); also *Première recréation de musique d'une exécution facile* for 2 Violins and Basso Continuo, op. 6 (1736; suite with overture; ed. by H. Ruf, Kassel, 1976), and *Scylla et Glaucus*, opéra tragédie, op. 11 (perf. at the Académie Royale de Musique, Paris, Oct. 4, 1746; publ. 1746; rev. version, Lyons, c.1755).

BIBL.: E. Appia, "The Violin Sonatas of L.," *Score*, no. 3 (1950); G. Nutting, "J.-M. L., 1697–1764," *Musical Quarterly* (Oct. 1964); J.-F. Paillard, "Les Concertos de J.-M. L.," *Chigiana*, XXI (1964); G. Sadler and N. Zaslaw, "Notes on L.'s Theatre Music," *Music & Letters*, LXI (1980); A. Borowitz, "Finale Marked Presto: The Killing of L.," *Musical Quarterly*, no. 2 (1986).

(2) Jean-Marie Leclair (le second or **le cadet),** violinist and composer; b. Lyons, Sept. 23, 1703; d. there, Nov. 30, 1777. After serving as director of Besançon's Académie de Musique (1732–33), he returned to his native town to serve as director of its Académie des Beaux-Arts; he also was active as a teacher, and became widely known as a violinist. His works include *Premier livre de sonates* for Violin and Basso Continuo, op. 1 (Paris, 1739; 12 sonatas); Sonates for 2 Violins, op. 2 (Paris, c.1750; 6 sonatas); also a Sym. (1768), Cantata, Divertissement, and other works, all of which are lost.

BIBL.: L. Vallas, "Une Famille de violinistes lyonnais, les L.," *Bulletin de la Société Française de Musicologie* (July 1921).

(3) Jean-Benoît Leclair, violinist and composer; b. Lyons,

Sept. 25, 1714; d. after 1759. He was director of the Moulins Académie de Musique (1736–37); later was director of his own touring company of actors, dancers, and musicians (from c.1747). He wrote a ballet héroïque, *Le Retour de la paix dans les Pays-Bas* (Brussels, April 27, 1749; only libretto extant).

BIBL.: N. Zaslaw, "Some Notes on J.-B. L.," *Revue Belge de Musicologie*, XIX (1965).

Lecoq, (Alexandre) Charles, noted French composer; b. Paris, June 3, 1832; d. there, Oct. 24, 1918. He learned to play the flageolet and piano as a youth, and later studied harmony with Crèvecœur; then was admitted to the Paris Cons. (1849), where he took courses with Bazin, Halévy, and Benoist; won 2nd prize in counterpoint and was primus accessit in the organ class, but was compelled to leave the Cons. to assist his family (1854). He first gained notice as a composer when he shared a prize with Bizet sponsored by Offenbach for the Théâtre des Bouffes-Parisiens, for the operetta *Le Docteur Miracle* (April 8, 1857). Although he brought out 7 more works for the stage during the next decade, it was only with his *Fleur-de-thé* (Paris, April 11, 1868) that he attained success. After going to Brussels (1870), he scored notable successes with his operettas *Les Cent Vierges* (March 16, 1872), *La Fille de Madame Angot* (Dec. 4, 1872), and *Giroflé-Girofla* (March 24, 1874); they subsequently were performed in Paris with great success, making Lecoq the leading Parisian operetta composer of his day after Offenbach. After returning to Paris, he brought out such popular favorites as *La Petite Mariée* (Dec. 21, 1875), *Le Petit Duc* (Jan. 25, 1878), *Janot* (Jan. 21, 1881), *Le Jour et la nuit* (Nov. 5, 1881), and *Le Cœur et la main* (Oct. 19, 1882). In subsequent years he continued to write works for the stage, but he failed to equal his previous successes. He also tried his hand at more serious compositional efforts, for example his opera *Plutus* (Paris, March 31, 1886), but was unsuccessful. He was made a Chevalier (1900) and an Officer (1910) of the Légion d'honneur. His music was distinguished by melodic grace, instrumental finish, and dramatic acumen. Among his other operettas, all 1st perf. in Paris, were *Huis-clos* (Jan. 28, 1859), *Le Baiser à la porte* (March 26, 1864), *Le Barbier de Trouville* (Nov. 19, 1871), *La Marjolaine* (Feb. 3, 1877), *Le Grand Casimir* (Jan. 11, 1879), and *La Princesse des Canaries* (Feb. 9, 1883); also composed the opéras comiques *L'Égyptienne* (Paris, Nov. 8, 1890), *Yetta* (Brussels, March 7, 1903), and *Le Trahison de Pan* (Aix-les-Bains, 1911), and the ballet *Le Cygne* (Paris, April 20, 1899). He also wrote several orch. works, more than 100 songs, dances, and piano pieces.

BIBL.: L. Schneider, *Les Maîtres de l'opérette française: Hervé, C. L.* (Paris, 1924); idem, *Une Heure de musique avec C. L.* (Paris, 1930).

Le Couppey, Félix, French pianist, teacher, and composer; b. Paris, April 14, 1811; d. there, July 5, 1887. He was a pupil at the Paris Cons.; from 1843, taught piano and harmony there. He publ. several successful piano methods: *École du mécanisme du piano, 24 études primaires; Cours de piano élémentaire et progressif; L'Art du piano* (50 études with annotations); a pamphlet, *De l'enseignement du piano: Conseils aux femmes professeurs* (1865); piano character pieces and songs.

Lecuna, Juan Vicente, Venezuelan composer; b. Valencia, Nov. 20, 1891; d. Rome, April 15, 1954. He studied at the Escuela Normal, graduating in 1906; then went to Caracas and studied music theory with Juan Vicente and piano with Salvador Llamozas at the Cons.; later took a course in composition with Jaime Pahissa in Buenos Aires (1937–41), where he also received instruction from Falla; likewise studied orchestration with Strube in Baltimore (1941). In the meantime, he entered the diplomatic service. In 1936 he was appointed a civil employee at the Venezuelan embassy in Washington, D.C. In 1943 he was sent by the Venezuelan dept. of education to study musical education in Brazil, Uruguay, Argentina, and Chile. In 1947 he was named Secretary of the Legation of Venezuela in Rome, and later was appointed a member of the Venezuelan legation at the Vatican. He composed a Piano

Concerto; *Suite venezolana* for 4 Guitars; a String Quartet; a Harp Sonata; songs; and a suite of 4 Venezuelan dances for Piano.

BIBL.: W. Guido, "Ficha biográfica y catálogo de la obra musical de J.V. L.," *Revista Musical de Venezuela* (Jan.–April 1981).

Lecuona, Ernesto, Cuban composer of popular music; b. Havana, Aug. 7, 1896; d. Santa Cruz de Tenerife, Canary Islands, Nov. 29, 1963. He played piano as a child, and wrote his 1st song when he was 11 years old. He graduated from the National Cons. of Havana (1911); then continued his training with Joaquín Nin; subsequently toured South America, Europe, and the U.S. as leader of his own dance band known as Lecuona's Cuban Boys. Among his most popular songs were *Malagueña, Andalucía,* and *Siboney.* He also wrote several zarzuelas, orch. pieces, dances for piano, etc.

BIBL.: G. Jacobson, *The Life and Music of E. L.* (diss., Univ. of Florida, 1982).

Ledbetter, Huddie "Leadbelly," black American folksinger, guitarist, and composer; b. Mooringsport, La., Jan. 21, 1885; d. N.Y., Dec. 6, 1949. He never had an education in music but possessed a genuine talent for folk-song singing. After mastering the 12-string guitar, he worked as accompanist to Blind Lemon Jefferson in Dallas. While in Texas, he was jailed for murder (1918–25); served another term for attempted homicide at the Louisiana State Penitentiary (1930–34), where he was discovered by folk researchers John and Alan Lomax, who recorded him in prison and helped obtain his release. He then settled in N.Y., where he made a series of historically significant recordings for the Library of Congress (1935–40). He served another term for assault (1939–40). He spent his last years playing in nightclubs. A cult arose around his name after his death; the "hootenanny" movement was much influenced by his style. He wrote the song *Good Night, Irene,* but it did not become popular until after his death. His career was made the subject of the film *Leadbelly* (1975). M. Asch and A. Lomax ed. *The Leadbelly Songbook* (N.Y., 1962).

BIBL.: M. Jones and A. McCarthy, *A Tribute to H. L.* (London, 1946).

Ledenev, Roman (Semyonovich), Russian composer; b. Moscow, Dec. 4, 1930. He studied composition at the Moscow Cons. with Rakov and Anatoly Alexandrov; later was an instructor there. His music is marked by a typically Russian lyric quality touched with permissible dissonances in harmonic treatment.

WORKS: Oratorio, *The Chronicle of the Campaign of Igor* (1954); *The Song of Freedom* for Chorus, to words by Asian and African poets (1961); Violin Concerto (1964); Viola Concerto (1964); Sonata in memory of Prokofiev (1956); numerous songs.

Ledent, Félix-Étienne, Belgian pianist and composer; b. Liège, Nov. 20, 1816; d. there, Aug. 23, 1886. He studied at the Liège Cons. with J. Jalheau, and in Paris with Daussoigne-Méhul, taking the 2nd Prix de Rome (1843); in 1844, became prof. of piano at the Liège Cons. He publ. *Adagio et Rondo* for Piano and Orch.; piano pieces and songs.

Ledger, Philip (Stevens), noted English conductor, organist, harpsichordist, pianist, editor, and arranger; b. Bexhill-on-Sea, Sussex, Dec. 12, 1937. He was educated at King's College, Cambridge, and at the Royal College of Music, London. He served as Master of the Music at Chelmsford Cathedral (1962–65) and as director of music at the Univ. of East Anglia (1965–73), where he served as dean of the School of Fine Arts and Music (1968–71). In 1968 he was named an artistic director of the Aldeburgh Festival; subsequently was engaged as conductor of the Cambridge Univ. Musical Soc. (1973) and director of music and organist at King's College (1974). In 1982 he was appointed principal of the Royal Scottish Academy of Music and Drama in Glasgow. He ed. *The Oxford Book of English Madrigals* (1978) and works of Byrd, Purcell, and Handel. A versatile musician, he is renowned as an elegant performer

of early English music. In 1985 he was made a Commander of the Order of the British Empire.

Leduc, Alphonse, French music publisher and composer; b. Nantes, March 9, 1804; d. Paris, June 17, 1868. He studied harmony with Reicha at the Paris Cons.; also mastered the bassoon, flute, and guitar; composed over 1,000 works, mainly piano pieces. In 1841 he founded a music publishing business in Paris; after his death, his son **Alphonse Leduc II** (b. probably in Paris, May 29, 1844; d. there, June 4, 1892) inherited the business; at the death of the latter, his widow directed the firm until 1904, when their son **Émile-Alphonse Leduc III** (b. Nov. 14, 1878; d. Paris, May 24, 1951) became its director; his sons **Claude-Alphonse** and **Gilbert-Alphonse Leduc** (partners with their father from 1938) continued the business. From 1860 to 1895 the firm publ. *L'Art Musical,* which was then assimilated with the *Guide Musical.*

BIBL.: C. Hopkinson, *A Dictionary of Parisian Music Publishers, 1700–1950* (London, 1954).

Leduc, Jacques, Belgian composer; b. Jette, near Brussels, March 1, 1932. He studied music at the Royal Cons. in Brussels and privately with Jean Absil. He was director of the Uccle Academy of Music (1962–83); was made a prof. of harmony (1968), of counterpoint (1972), and of fugue (1979) at the Royal Cons. in Brussels; was also director of the Chapelle Musicale Reine Elisabeth (from 1976). He was made a member of the Royal Academy of Sciences, Letters, and Fine Arts of Belgium in 1983.

WORKS: STAGE: Lyric comedy, *Nous attendons Sémiramis* (Belgian Television, Feb. 6, 1973); cantata, *L'Aventure* (1961). **ORCH.:** *Antigone,* symphonic poem (1960); Concertino for Oboe and String Orch. (1962); *Divertissement* for Flute and String Orch. (1962); *Fantaisie sur le thème de "La Folia"* for Clarinet, and Chamber Orch. or Piano (1964); *4 Études* for Chamber Orch. (1966); *Le Printemps,* symphonic sketch (1967); *Ouverture d'été* (1968); Sym. (1969); Piano Concerto (1970); *5 croquis* (1971); *Dialogue* for Clarinet, and Chamber Orch. or Piano (1972); *Instantanés,* 5 pieces for String Ensemble (1972); *Suite de danses* (1976); *3 Esquisses concertantes* (1978). **CHAMBER:** Wind Quintet (1960); *3 petites pièces en quatuor* for 4 Flutes or Clarinets (1963); String Trio (1963); *Suite en quatuor* for 4 Saxophones (1964); *Sortilèges africains,* sequence for Voice, Saxophone, Percussion, and Piano (1966); Flute Sonata (1966); Violin Sonata (1967); *Capriccio* for Wind Quartet (1969); *Sérénade* for Wind Quintet (1977); *Trois pièces* for 5 Brass Instruments (1980); *Lamento* for Viola (1986). **PIANO:** *4 pièces brèves* (1965); *Prelude, Variations, and Fugato* (1965); *Contrastes* (1967); *Apostrophes* (1971); also organ music; choruses; songs.

Leduc (Le Duc), Simon (l'aîné), French violinist and composer; b. Jan. 15, 1742; d. Paris, Jan. 20, 1777. He studied violin with Gaviniès; was 2nd violin in the Concert Spirituel (1759–63), making his solo debut there on Sept. 8, 1763; then was 1st violin there, but also made appearances as a soloist; with Gaviniès and Gossec, he became a director there (1773). He was a talented composer of orch. and chamber music; was active as a publisher exclusively of his own works.

BIBL.: B. Brook, "S. Le Duc l'aîné, a French Symphonist at the Time of Mozart," *Musical Quarterly* (Oct. 1962).

Lee, Brenda (real name, **Brenda Mae Tarpley**), American singer of popular music; b. Lithonia, Ga., Dec. 11, 1944. She abbreviated her last name to a monosyllable evocative of her southern heritage. She won a local television prize as a babbling babe, and at the age of 13 made a hit with a recording of *1 Step at a Time.* She never joined a band, and thus owed all her successes to herself; was dubbed "Little Miss Dynamite" for her ability to sing soft-rock, country, and pop numbers with equal ease. Among her most popular singles were *Dynamite* (1957), *I'm Sorry* (1960), and *Rockin' around the Christmas Tree* (1960). She recorded several autobiographical discs, such as *The Brenda Lee Story, Sincerely, Brenda Lee,* and *Let It Be Me.*

Lee, Dai-Keong, Hawaiian composer of Chinese descent; b. Honolulu, Sept. 2, 1915. He studied with Sessions and Jacobi at the Juilliard Graduate School in N.Y. (1938–41), with Copland at the Berkshire Music Center in Tanglewood (1941), and with Luening at Columbia Univ. (M.A., 1951); held 2 Guggenheim fellowships (1945, 1951).

WORKS: OPERAS: *The Poet's Dilemma* (N.Y., April 12, 1940); *Open the Gates* (1951); *Phineas and the Nightingale* (1952); *Speakeasy* (N.Y., Feb. 8, 1957); *2 Knickerbocker Tales* (1957); *Ballad of Kitty the Barkeep* (1979; based on *Speakeasy*). MUSICAL PLAYS: *Noa Noa* (1972); *Jenny Lind* (1981; based on *Phineas and the Nightingale*). INCIDENTAL MUSIC: *Teahouse of the August Moon* (1953; orch. suite, 1954). BALLET: *Waltzing Matilda* (1951). ORCH.: *Hawaiian Festival Overture* (1940); Sym. No. 1 (1941–42; rev. 1946); *Pacific Prayer* (1943; rev. as *Canticle of the Pacific* for Chorus and Orch., 1968); Violin Concerto (1947; rev. 1955); Sym. No. 2 (San Francisco, March 14, 1952); *Polynesian Suite* (1958); *Mele olili* (Joyful Songs) for Soloists, Chorus, and Orch. (1960); Concerto Grosso for String Orch. (1985); also chamber music; film scores; songs.

Lee, Ernest Markham, English organist, composer, and writer on music; b. Cambridge, June 8, 1874; d. Eastbourne, Nov. 13, 1956. While a student at Emanuel College, he acted as organist at All Saints', Woodford Green; in 1917 he was appointed prof. of organ at the Guildhall School of Music and examiner at the Univs. of London, Oxford, and Cambridge.

WORKS: Services, anthems, sacred and secular songs, piano pieces (*Hesperis, Serapis, Modern Suite*).

WRITINGS: *Edvard Grieg* (1908); *The Story of Opera* (1909); *Brahms: The Man and His Music* (1915); *The Story of Symphony* (1916); *On Listening to Music* (1918); *Musical Theory and Knowledge* (1923); *Brahms' Orchestral Works* (1931).

Lee, Louis, German cellist, pianist, conductor, and composer, brother of **Maurice** and **Sebastian Lee;** b. Hamburg, Oct. 19, 1819; d. Lübeck, Aug. 26, 1896. He studied cello with J.N. Prell; gave concerts at the age of 12 in German cities and in Copenhagen. He organized chamber music soirées (with Hafner, then with Boie) in Hamburg; taught at the Hamburg Cons. (1873–84). He publ. a Piano Quartet; Piano Trio; Cello Sonata; Cello Sonatina; pieces for piano and cello; piano pieces; music to Schiller's *Die Jungfrau von Orleans* and *Wilhelm Tell*; etc.

Lee, Maurice, German pianist, teacher, and composer, brother of **Louis** and **Sebastian Lee;** b. Hamburg, Feb. 1821; d. London, June 23, 1895. He spent many years in London as a piano teacher and composer of popular salon music.

Lee, Peggy (real name, **Norma Dolores Egstrom**), American singer of popular music, songwriter, and actress; b. Jamestown, N.Dak., May 26, 1920. After graduating from high school, she sang on a radio station in Fargo; in 1941 Benny Goodman chose her as vocalist with his band; she gained her 1st success with *Why Don't You Do Right?* She soon launched a solo career; with her 1st husband, Dave Barbour, she collaborated on writing such hits as *Mañana, Golden Earrings,* and *I Don't Know Enough about You,* which she interpreted with great acumen; she was equally successful with her sophisticated renditions of *Lover, Fever,* and particularly *Is That All There Is?,* which became her theme song. With the composer Paul Horner and the playwright William Luce, she wrote the autobiographical musical *Peg* (1983). She also penned an autobiography (N.Y., 1989).

BIBL.: R. Towe, *Here's to You: The Complete Bio-discography of Miss P. L.* (1986).

Lee, Sebastian, German cellist and composer, brother of **Louis** and **Maurice Lee;** b. Hamburg, Dec. 24, 1805; d. there, Jan. 4, 1887. He studied with J.N. Prell; from 1837 to 1868, was solo cellist of the Opéra Orch. in Paris; returned to Hamburg in 1868. The method for cello he publ. under his own name was actually the work of others. He composed variations, divertissements, and fantasies for cello, with orch.; variations for cello with string quartet; cello duos.

Leedy, Douglas, American composer, pianist, and conductor; b. Portland, Oreg., March 3, 1938. He studied at Pomona College (B.A., 1959) and at the Univ. of Calif. at Berkeley (M.A., 1962). He played the horn in the Oakland (Calif.) Sym. Orch. and in the San Francisco Opera and Ballet orchs. (1960–65); in 1965–66 he held a joint U.S.-Polish government grant for study in Poland; from 1967 to 1970 was on the faculty of the Univ. of Calif., Los Angeles; from 1973 to 1978 taught at Reed College in Portland, Oreg. He was conductor of the Oregon Telemann Ensemble, later known as the Harmonie Universelle. From 1984 to 1985 he was music director of the Portland Baroque Orch. His early works cultivated avant-garde methods of electronic application to mixed media, but later he sought to overcome the restrictions of Western music and its equal temperament; for this purpose, he began in 1979 to work with the Carnatic vocalist K.V. Narāyanaswāmy in Madras, India. Parallel to that, he evinced an interest in early Western music; ed. *Chansons from Petrucci in Original Notation . . .* in the *Musica Sacra et Profana* series (1983).

WORKS: *Exhibition Music* (1965; continued indefinitely); *Decay,* theater piece for Piano, Wagner Tuba, and Tape (1965); *Antifonia* for Brass Quartet (1965); *Usable Music I for Very Small Instruments with Holes* (1966); *Usable Music II* for Brass Instruments (1966); *Teddy Bear's Picnic,* audio-tactile electronic theater piece (1968); *Ave Maris Stella* for Soprano, Instrumental Trio, Organ, and Electronic Sound (1968); *88 Is Great,* theater piece for many-handed Piano (1968); *The Electric Zodiac,* electronic music (1969); *Entropical Paradise: 6 Sonic Environments* for Electronic Recordings (1970); *Gloria* for Soprano, Chorus, and Instruments (1970); *The 24th Psalm* for 6 Solo Soprano Voices, Chorus, and Orch. (1972); *Sebastian,* chamber opera based on documents of J.S. Bach, for Soprano, Baritone, Chamber Ensemble, and Tape (1971–74); chorale fantasia, *Wie schön leuchtet der Morgenstern,* for Organ and unseen Soprano (1972); String Quartet, in just tuning (1965–75); *Canti: Music for Contrabass and Chamber Ensemble* (1975); *Symphoniae sacrae* for Soprano, Bass, Viola da Gamba, and Harpsichord (1976); *Sur la couche de miettes* for Flute, Oboe, Violin, Viola, Cello, Guitar, Piano, equal-temperament Harpsichord, and just-intonation Harpsichord (1981); *Harpsichord Book, Parts I–II,* in traditional mean-tone temperament (1974, 1982); *Harpsichord Book, Part III,* in just tuning (1982); *4 Hymns from the Rigveda* for Chorus, and Javanese or American Gamelan (1982–83); *5 Organ Chorales* (1983); *Music for Meantone Organ* (1983–84); *Canto orphea* for Voice and Harp (1987); *Pastorale* for Solo Voices, Chorus, and Retuned Piano (1987).

Lees (real name, **Lysniansky**), **Benjamin,** outstanding American composer of Russian parentage; b. Harbin, Manchuria, Jan. 8, 1924. He was taken to the U.S. in infancy; studied piano in San Francisco and Los Angeles; served in the U.S. Army (1942–45); then enrolled at the Univ. of Southern Calif., Los Angeles, as a student in theory with Halsey Stevens, Ingolf Dahl, and Ernst Kanitz (1945–48); subsequently took private lessons with George Antheil. He held 2 Guggenheim fellowships (1955, 1966). In 1956 he went to Europe on a Fulbright fellowship, returning to America in 1962; in 1967 he visited Russia under the auspices of the State Dept. He taught at the Peabody Cons. of Music in Baltimore (1962–64; 1966–68), Queens College, N.Y. (1964–66), the Manhattan School of Music (1972–74), and the Juilliard School (1976–77). He writes mostly for instruments; his music possesses an ingratiating quality, modern but not arrogantly so; his harmonies are lucid and are couched in euphonious dissonances; he favors rhythmic asymmetry; the formal design of his works is classical in its clarity. An interesting idiosyncrasy is the use of introductory instrumental solos in most of his syms. and concertos. The accessibility of his musical expression makes his music attractive to conductors and soloists.

WORKS: 4 piano sonatas (1949, 1950, 1951, 1963); Sonata for 2 Pianos (1951); *Profile* for Orch. (1952; N.Y., April 18, 1954); String Quartet No. 1 (1952); Sonata for Horn and Piano (1952); *Declamations* for String Orch. and Piano (1953; Oklahoma City, Feb. 15, 1956); Sym. No. 1 (1953); Violin Sonata

No. 1 (1954); *3 Variables* for Wind Quartet and Piano (1955); *The Oracle*, music drama, libretto by the composer (1955); String Quartet No. 2 (1955); Piano Concerto No. 1 (1955; Vienna, April 26, 1956); *Divertimento burlesca* for Orch. (1957); Sym. No. 2 (Louisville, Dec. 3, 1958); Violin Concerto (1958; Boston, Feb. 8, 1963); *Concertante breve* for Oboe, 2 Horns, Piano, and Strings (1959); *Prologue, Capriccio, and Epilogue* (Portland, April 9, 1959); Concerto for Orchestra No. 1 (1959; Rochester, N.Y., Feb. 22, 1962); *Visions of Poets*, dramatic cantata after Whitman (1961; Seattle, May 15, 1962); Concerto for Oboe and Orch. (1963); *Spectrum* for Orch. (1964); *The Gilded Cage*, opera (N.Y., 1964); Concerto for String Quartet and Orch. (Kansas City, Mo., Jan. 19, 1965); Concerto for Chamber Orch. (1966); Piano Concerto No. 2 (1966; Boston, March 15, 1968); *Silhouettes* for Wind Instruments and Percussion (1967); Sym. No. 3 (1968; Detroit, Jan. 16, 1969); *Medea of Corinth* for Vocal Soloists, Wind Quintet, and Timpani (1970; London, Jan. 10, 1971); *The Trumpet of the Swan* for Narrator and Orch. (Philadelphia, May 13, 1972); *Collage* for String Quartet, Woodwind Quintet, and Percussion (Milwaukee, May 8, 1973); Violin Sonata No. 2 (1972); *Etudes* for Piano and Orch. (Houston, Oct. 28, 1974); *Labyrinths* for Wind Ensemble (Bloomington, Ind., Nov. 18, 1975); Variations for Piano and Orch. (Dallas, March 31, 1976); *Passacaglia* for Orch. (Washington, D.C., April 13, 1976); Concerto for Woodwind Quintet and Orch. (Detroit, Oct. 7, 1976); *Scarlatti Portfolio*, ballet (1978; San Francisco, March 15, 1979); *Mobiles* for Orch. (N.Y., April 13, 1979); String Quartet No. 3 (1980); Cello Sonata (1981); Double Concerto for Piano, Cello, and Orch. (N.Y., Nov. 7, 1982); Concerto for Brass and Orch. (Dallas, March 18, 1983); *Portrait of Rodin* (1984; Portland, Oreg., April 5, 1987); Sym. No. 4, *Memorial Candles* (Dallas, Oct. 10, 1985); Sym. No. 5 (1988); piano pieces.

BIBL.: D. Cooke, "The Music of B. L.," *Tempo* (Summer 1959); idem, "The Recent Music of B. L.," ibid. (Spring 1963); N. Slonimsky, "B. L. in Excelsis," ibid. (June 1975).

Leeuw, Reinbert de, Dutch composer; b. Amsterdam, Sept. 8, 1938. He studied at the Amsterdam Cons.; in 1963, was appointed to the faculty of the Royal Cons. of The Hague. A political activist, he collaborated with Louis Andriessen, Mischa Mengelberg, Peter Schat, and Jan van Vlijmen on the anti-American multimedia spectacle *Reconstructie*, produced during the Holland Festival in Amsterdam on June 29, 1969. He further wrote an opera, *Axel* (with Vlijmen; 1977); *Solo I* for Cello (1961); *3 Positions* for Violin (1963); String Quartet (1963); *Interplay* for Orch. (1965); *Hymns and Chorals* for 15 Winds, 2 Electric Guitars, and Electric Organ (Amsterdam, July 5, 1970); *Duets* for Recorder (1971); *Abschied*, symphonic poem (1971–73; Rotterdam, May 11, 1974). He publ. a book about Ives (with J. Bemlef; Amsterdam, 1969) and a collection of 17 articles, *Muzikale anarchie* (Amsterdam, 1973).

Leeuw, Ton (actually, **Antonius Wilhelmus Adrianus**) de, Dutch composer; b. Rotterdam, Nov. 16, 1926. He studied piano and theory with Louis Toebosch in Breda, and composition with Badings in Amsterdam (1947–49) and with Messiaen and Thomas de Hartmann in Paris (1949–50); then took courses in ethnomusicology with Jaap Kunst in Amsterdam (1950–54). He was director of sound for the Dutch Radio Union in Hilversum (1954–60); then taught composition at the Amsterdam Cons., where he served as director (1971–73); also taught musicology at the Univ. of Amsterdam. In his works he explores all thinkable, and some unthinkable but conceptually plausible, ways, pathways, and byways of musical techniques. A government grant in 1961 enabled him to make a tour of Iran and India, where he studied non-European systems of composition. He publ. the book *Muziek van de twintigste eeuw* (Music of the 20th Century; Utrecht, 1964).

WORKS: STAGE: *Alceste*, television opera (Dutch Television, March 13, 1963); *De droom* (The Dream), opera based on 14 haiku (Holland Festival, June 16, 1965); *Hiob* (Job), radio oratorio for Soloists, Chorus, Orch., and Tape (1956); *Litany of Our Time*, television play for Soprano, Chorus, Instruments,

and Electronic Sound (1969; Dutch Television, Jan. 1, 1971); 2 ballets: *De bijen* (The Bees; Arnhem, Sept. 15, 1965) and *Krishna and Radha* for Flute, Harp, and Percussion (1964). **ORCH.:** Concerto Grosso for String Orch. (1946); *Treurmuziek in memoriam Willem Pijper* for Chamber Orch. (1948); Sym. for Strings and Percussion (1950); Sym. for String Orch. (1951); *Plutos-Suite* for Chamber Orch. (1952); 2 violin concertos (1953, 1961); *Suite* for Youth Orch. (1954); *10 mouvements rétrogrades* (1957); *Brabant*, symphonic song for Middle Voice and Orch. (1959); *Nritta*, orch. dance (1961); *Ombres* (1961); *Symphonies for Winds*, an homage to Stravinsky, for 29 Winds (1962–63); *Haiku II* for Soprano and Orch. (Rotterdam, July 5, 1968); *Spatial Music III* for Orch. in 4 groups (1967); *Syntaxis II* (1966; Utrecht, May 16, 1966); *Gending* for Javanese Gamelan Orch. (Hilversum, Oct. 11, 1975); *Alba*, concerto da camera (1982); *Résonances* (1985); Concerto for 2 Guitars and String Orch. (1988). **CHAMBER:** String Trio (1948); Flute Sonata (1949); Violin Sonata (1951); Trio for Flute, Clarinet, and Piano (1952); *5 Sketches* for Oboe, Clarinet, Bassoon, Violin, Viola, and Cello (1952); 2 string quartets (1958; with Tape, 1964); *Antiphony* for Wind Quintet and 4 Electronic Tracks (1960); *Schelp* for Flute, Viola, and Guitar (1964); *The 4 Seasons* for Harp (1964); *Night Music* for 1 Performer on 3 different Flutes (1966); *Music for 1 or 2 Violins* (1967); *Music* for Oboe (1969); *Reversed Night* for Flute (1971); *Midare* for Marimba (1972); *Music* for Trombone (1973–74); *Canzone* for 4 Horns, 3 Trumpets, and 3 Trombones (1973–74); *Rime* for Flute and Harp (1974); *Mo-Do* for Amplified Harpsichord (1974); *Modal Music* for Accordion (1978–79); *Apparences I* for Cello (1986–87). **KEYBOARD:** Piano Sonatina (1949); *Introduzione e Passacaglia* for Organ (1949); 2-piano Sonata (1950); *5 Études* for Piano (1951); *4 Rhythmic Études* for Piano (1952); *Lydische Suite* for Piano (1954); *3 African Studies* for Piano (1954); *Men Go Their Ways* for Piano (1964); *Sweelinck Variations* for Organ (1972–73). **VOCAL:** *De Toverfluit*, 4 songs for Soprano, Flute, Cello, and Piano (1954); *Car nos vignes sont en fleur* for 12 Mixed Voices (1981); *And They Shall Reign Forever* for Mezzo-soprano, Clarinet, Horn, Piano, and Percussion (1981); *Les Chants de Kabir* for Solo Voices (1985); *Transparence* for Chorus, 3 Trumpets, and 3 Trombones (1986); also tape pieces, including *Electronic Suite* (1958) and *Clair-Obscur* (1982).

BIBL.: W. Markus, "Music and Time: Observations on Arnold Schoenberg and T. d.L.," *Key Notes*, no. 23 (1986); R. de Groot, "Aspects of T. d.L.'s Musical Universe," ibid.

LeFanu, Nicola (Frances), English composer; b. Wickham Bishops, Essex, April 28, 1947. She was the daughter of William LeFanu, a British literary figure, and **Elizabeth Maconchy,** the composer. Although she scrutinized her mother's works with great care and interest, she never engaged in a course of formal instruction with her. Instead, she studied music at St. Hilda's College, Oxford (B.A., 1968); also took private lessons with Jeremy Dale Roberts, Wellesz, Musgrave, and Maxwell Davies in England and with Petrassi in Italy. She taught at Morley College (1970–75) and served as director of music at Francis Holland School (1975–77); then taught at King's College, London Univ. (from 1977). In 1979 she married **David Lumsdaine.** Her style of composition represents a median line of modernism which she developed *sine ira et studio*, without discrimination even against such obsolescent resources as major triads. As a result, her music pleased the public and appealed to unprejudiced judges of musical competitions. Thus, in 1971, she won 1st prize at the BBC National Competition for her Variations for Oboe Quartet (1968).

WORKS: STAGE: *Anti-World* for Dancer, Soprano, Baritone, and Ensemble (1972); *The Last Laugh*, ballet for Soprano, Tape, and Instrumental Ensemble (1972); *Dawnpath*, chamber opera (London, Sept. 29, 1977); *The Story of Mary O'Neill*, radiophonic opera (1986). **ORCH.:** *Preludio I* for Strings (1967; rev. 1976, as *Preludio II* for Strings); *The Hidden Landscape* (London, Aug. 7, 1973); *Columbia Falls* for Percussion, Harp, and Strings (Birmingham, Nov. 20, 1975); *Farne* (Bradford,

March 28, 1980); *Variations* for Piano and Orch. (London, Dec. 31, 1982). CHAMBER: *Variations* for Oboe Quartet (1968); *Abstracts and a Frame* for Violin and Piano (1971); *Collana* for Solo Percussion and 5 Players (Boston, April 25, 1976); *Deva* for Solo Cello and 7 Players (London, March 23, 1979); Trio for Flute, Cello, and Percussion (1980; London, June 15, 1981); *Moon over Western Ridge Mootwingee*: Quartet for Saxophones (Stuttgart, Nov. 6, 1985); *Invisible Places*: Clarinet Quintet (Southampton, June 4, 1986); *Lament 1988* for Oboe, Clarinet, Viola, and Cello (London, March 30, 1988); String Quartet (London, Oct. 3, 1988). VOCAL: *Christ Calls Man Home* for 2 Sopranos and 3 Choirs (Cheltenham, July 4, 1971); *The Valleys Shall Sing* for Choir and 7 Instruments (1973); *The Same Day Dawns* for Soprano and 5 Players (Boston, Nov. 4, 1974); *For We Are the Stars* for 16 Solo Voices (1978); *Like a Wave of the Sea* for Choir and Early Instruments (Nottingham, March 1, 1981); *The Old Woman of Beare* for Soprano and 13 Players (London, Nov. 3, 1981); *Stranded on My Heart* for Tenor, Chorus, and String Orch. (St. Alban's, June 16, 1984); *Wind Among the Pines* for Soprano and Orch. (Aldeburgh, July 31, 1987).

Lefébure, Louis-François Henri, French composer and writer on music; b. Paris, Feb. 18, 1754; d. there, Nov. 1840. He was a government official until 1814; publ. several instructive books on singing: *Nouveau Solfège*, a 23-page pamphlet (1780), containing ideas put into practice by Gossec in the *École royale de chant*; a polemical brochure, *Bévues, erreurs et méprises de différents auteurs célèbres en matières musicales* (1789); etc. He also composed 2 oratorios and other choral works.

Lefébure, Yvonne, French pianist and teacher; b. Ermont, Seine-et-Oise, June 29, 1898; d. Paris, Jan. 23, 1986. She began piano studies at an early age and won the "prix de petits prodiges" of the Paris Cons., where she took courses with M. Emmanuel, Georges Caussade, and C. Widor; won 6 premiers prix in all; also studied privately with A. Cortot. She taught at the École Normale de Musique in Paris (from 1924); was also on the faculty of the Paris Cons. (1952–67). She toured widely as a soloist and recitalist.

Lefébure-Wély, Louis James Alfred, French organist and composer; b. Paris, Nov. 13, 1817; d. there, Dec. 31, 1869. A pupil of his father, he took, at the age of 8, the latter's place as organist of the church of St.-Roch, becoming its regular organist at 14. Entering the Paris Cons. in 1832, he was taught by Benoist (organ), Laurent and Zimmerman (piano), and Berton and Halévy (composition). From 1847 to 1858 he was organist at the Madeleine; then at St. Sulpice. WORKS: Opera, *Les Recruteurs* (1861); cantata, *Après la victoire* (1863); 3 masses; 3 syms.; String Quintet; String Quartet; much elegant salon music for piano (his most celebrated piece is *The Monastery Bells*); 50 piano études; harmonium music.

Lefebvre, Charles Édouard, French composer; b. Paris, June 19, 1843; d. Aix-les-Bains, Sept. 8, 1917. He studied at the Paris Cons.; won the Premier Grand Prix de Rome in 1870 for his cantata *Le Jugement de Dieu*; joined the faculty of the Paris Cons. in 1895. WORKS: Operas: *Lucrèce* (1877–78); *Le Trésor* (Angers, 1883); *Zaïre* (Lille, 1887); *Djelma* (Paris, May 25, 1894); *Judith*, biblical drama (Paris, 1879); Sym. (1879); *Ouverture dramatique* (1875); *Dalila*, symphonic poem (1875); *Melka*, legend for Orch. (1880); *Une sérénade* for Orch. (1884); *Eloâ*, poème lyrique for Orch. (1888); *Sainte Cécile* for Voice, Chorus, and Orch. (1896); *La Fille de Jephté*, lyric poem for Orch. (1908); chamber music; works for organ; piano pieces.

Lefeld, Jerzy Albert, Polish pianist, composer, and pedagogue; b. Warsaw, Jan. 17, 1898; d. there, Feb. 22, 1980. He studied piano with Michalowski and composition with Statkowski at the Warsaw Cons.; in 1918 he joined its faculty. He became known principally as a fine piano accompanist. His own compositions include 2 syms., a String Sextet, piano pieces, and songs.

Lefèvre, (Jean) Xavier, Swiss-born French clarinetist and composer; b. Lausanne, March 6, 1763; d. Paris, Nov. 9, 1829. He studied with Michel Yost in Paris; first appeared as a soloist at the Concert Spirituel (1783). He played in the Paris Opéra orch. (1791–1817); was also principal cellist in the imperial (later royal) chapel from 1807; was a prof. at the Cons. (1795–1824). He wrote a clarinet method (1802); composed 7 clarinet concertos, as well as trios, duos, sonatas, and other works for his instrument. He popularized the 6th key of the clarinet, although he did not invent it.

BIBL.: L. Youngs, *J.X. L., His Contributions to the Clarinet and Clarinet Playing* (diss., Catholic Univ. of America, 1970).

Leffler-Burckard, Martha, German soprano; b. Berlin, June 16, 1865; d. Wiesbaden, May 14, 1954. She studied with Anna von Meichsner in Dresden and Pauline Viardot-Garcia in Paris; made her debut in Strasbourg (1888); then sang at Breslau, Cologne, and Bremen; from 1898 to 1900, was at the Court Theater in Weimar; from 1900 to 1912, was at Wiesbaden; after that, was at the principal German opera houses; from 1906 to 1908, at Bayreuth. She made her Metropolitan Opera debut in N.Y. as Brünnhilde in *Die Walküre* on March 4, 1908; was a member of the Berlin Royal Opera (1913–18), then sang at the Deutsches Opernhaus there (1918–19); subsequently was active as a teacher. Her finest roles were Fidelio, Isolde, and the 3 Brünnhildes.

Le Flem, Paul, French composer and music critic; b. Lézardrieux, Côtes-du-Nord, March 18, 1881; d. Trégastel, Côtes-du-Nord, July 31, 1984. He studied philosophy at the Sorbonne in Paris and harmony with Lavignac at the Paris Cons. (1899); in 1901 traveled to Russia; then studied with d'Indy and Roussel at the Paris Schola Cantorum (1904). He subsequently taught a course in counterpoint at the Schola Cantorum; was engaged as a chorus master at the Paris Opéra-Comique in 1924; then devoted himself mainly to music criticism; was for 17 years principal music critic of *Comœdia*; was one of the founders of the modern concert series "La Spirale" in Paris in 1935. He received the Grand Prix Musical of the City of Paris in 1951 in appreciation of his work as a writer, scholar, and composer. In his writings he energetically promoted the cause of modern music. His own compositions followed the musical methods of the French neo-Classical school; in several of his works he employed the melodic patterns of his native Brittany.

WORKS: STAGE: *Endymion et Séléné*, opera (1903); *Aucassin et Nicolette*, fairy tale (Paris, July 20, 1923); *Le Rossignol de St. Malo* (Paris, May 5, 1942); *La Clairière des fées*, lyric fantasy (1943; Paris Radio, Nov. 29, 1968); *La Magicienne de la mer*, lyric opera (Paris, Oct. 29, 1954). ORCH.: 4 syms. (1908; 1958; 1967; 1977–78); *Konzertstück* for Violin and Orch. (1965); *La Maudite*, dramatic legend for Voices and Orch. (1967; new version, 1971); also chamber music; piano pieces; choruses; songs.

Le Fleming, Christopher (Kaye), English composer; b. Wimborne, Feb. 26, 1908; d. Woodbury, Devon, June 19, 1985. He studied at the Brighton School of Music and at the Royal School of Church Music in London; then held many teaching posts. He wrote several orch. works, incidental music to plays, choral music, piano pieces, and songs.

Le Gallienne, Dorian, Australian composer; b. Melbourne, April 19, 1915; d. there, July 27, 1963. He graduated from Melbourne Univ. in 1938; then studied with Arthur Benjamin and Howells at the Royal College of Music in London; during World War II, he worked with the Dept. of Information and the Australian Broadcasting Commission. On another trip to England, he took private lessons in composition with Gordon Jacob; in 1953, returned to Melbourne. His music is marked by clear linear procedures, often in dissonant counterpoint.

WORKS: 2 ballets: *Contes heraldiques* (1947) and *Voyageur* (1954); *3 Psalms* for Chorus and Orch. (1948); *Overture* (1952); Sym. in E (1952–53); Sinfonietta (1951–56); *Symphonic Study* for Orch. (1962–63; a posthumous work derived from material intended as a 2nd Sym.); Flute Sonata (1943); Violin Sonata (1945); Duo for Violin and Viola (1956); Trio for Oboe, Violin, and Viola (1957); 2 *Pieces*: No. 1 for Violin, Cello, Clarinet, Percussion, and Harp, and No. 2 for 2 Clarinets and String Quartet (both 1959); piano pieces; numerous songs, including *3 Sonnets of Shakespeare* (1946) and *4 Divine Poems of John Donne* (1947–50); incidental and film music.

Legge, Walter, influential English recording executive, orchestral manager, and writer on music; b. London, June 1, 1906; d. St. Jean, Cap Ferrat, March 22, 1979. Although not a professional musician by education or training, he became an ardent promoter of high-grade recordings of classical music with the Gramophone Co. of London from 1926; artists who worked in recording sessions with him described him as a rigorous taskmaster who was willing to work endless hours until satisfactory results were achieved. Among the singers who recorded for him was **Elisabeth Schwarzkopf,** whom he married in 1953. He also supervised records by Artur Schnabel and Wanda Landowska. He founded a subscription society for the purpose of recording unrecorded works in 1931, which eventually encompassed composers from Bach to Delius. In 1945 he founded the Philharmonia Orch. of London, primarily for recording purposes; it helped to further the careers of such notable masters of the baton as Karajan, Klemperer, and Giulini; he continued to manage its affairs until he unsuccessfully attempted to disband it in 1964. An important contribution to the auditory preservation of great performances was Legge's recordings of the piano performances by the brilliant Rumanian pianist Dinu Lipatti. His wife ed. the book *On and Off the Record: A Memoir of Walter Legge* (N.Y., 1982; 2nd ed., 1988). See also A. Sanders, compiler, *Walter Legge: A Discography* (London, 1985). Incidentally, Legge pronounced his name "leg," as in a leg of lamb.

Leginska (real name, **Liggins**), **Ethel,** English pianist, teacher, and composer; b. Hull, April 13, 1886; d. Los Angeles, Feb. 26, 1970. She showed a natural talent for music at an early age; the pseudonym Leginska was given to her by Lady Maud Warrender, under the illusion that a Polish-looking name might help her artistic career. She studied piano at the Hoch Cons. in Frankfurt, and later in Vienna with Leschetizky. After making her London debut (1907), she toured Europe; on Jan. 20, 1913, she appeared for the 1st time in America, at a recital in N.Y. Her playing was described as having masculine vigor, dashing brilliance, and great variety of tonal color; however, criticism was voiced against an individualistic treatment of classical works. In the midst of her career as a pianist, she developed a great interest in conducting; she organized the Boston Phil. Orch. (100 players), later the Women's Sym. Orch. of Boston; appeared as a guest conductor with various orchs. in America and in Europe. In this field of activity she also elicited interest, leading to a discussion in the press of a woman's capability of conducting an orch. While in the U.S., she took courses in composition with Rubin Goldmark and Ernest Bloch; wrote music in various genres, distinguished by rhythmic display and a certain measure of modernism. She married the composer **Emerson Whithorne** in 1907 (divorced in 1916). In 1939 she settled in Los Angeles as a piano teacher.

WORKS: Operas: *Gale* (Chicago, Nov. 23, 1935, composer conducting) and *The Rose and the Ring* (1932; Los Angeles, Feb. 23, 1957, composer conducting); *From a Life* for 13 Instruments (N.Y., Jan. 9, 1922); *Beyond the Fields We Know,* symphonic poem (N.Y., Feb. 12, 1922); 2 *Short Pieces* for Orch. (Boston, Feb. 29, 1924, Monteux conducting); *Quatre sujets barbares,* suite for Orch. (Munich, Dec. 13, 1924, composer conducting); *Fantasy* for Orch. and Piano (N.Y., Jan. 3, 1926); *Triptych* for 11 Instruments (Chicago, April 29, 1928); String Quartet, after 4 poems by Tagore (Boston, April 25, 1921); 6 *Nursery Rhymes* for Soprano and Chamber Orch.; piano pieces; songs.

Legley, Victor, outstanding Belgian composer; b. Hazebrouck, French Flanders, June 18, 1915. He studied viola, chamber music, counterpoint, and fugue at the Brussels Cons. (from 1934); then took private lessons in composition with Jean Absil (1941), subsequently winning the Belgian 2nd Prix de Rome (1943). He was a violist in the Belgian Radio Sym. Orch. (1936–48); then was a music producer for the Flemish dept. of the Belgian Radio, and later was made head of its serious music broadcasts on its 3rd program (1962). He taught at the Brussels Cons. (1949–80). He became a member of the Belgian Royal Academy (1965); was its president (1972); was made president of the Belgian copyright society and of the Union of Belgian Composers (1981). In his works, he adheres to the pragmatic tenets of modern music, structurally diversified and unconstricted by inhibitions against dissonance.

WORKS: STAGE: *La Farce des deux nus,* opera (Antwerp, Dec. 10, 1966); *Le Bal des halles,* ballet (1954). **ORCH.:** 6 syms. (1942, 1947, 1953, 1964, 1965, 1976); *Concert à 13,* chamber sym. (1944); *Suite* (1944); *Music for a Greek Tragedy* (1946); *Symphonie miniature* for Chamber Orch. (1946); 2 violin concertos: No. 1 (1947) and No. 2 (1966; Brussels, May 22, 1967; mandatory work of the 1967 Queen Elisabeth violin competition finals); *The Golden River,* symphonic sketch (1948); Piano Concerto (1952); *Serenade* for String Orch. (1957); *La Cathédrale d'acier* (The Steel Cathedral), symphonic sketch after a painting by Fernand Steven (1958); *Overture to a Comedy by Goldoni* (1958); *3 Pieces* for Chamber Orch. (1960); *Dyptiek* (1964); *Harp Concerto* (1966); *Paradise Regained* (1967); *Prélude for a Ballet* (1969); *3 Movements* for Brass and Percussion (1969); *Espaces* for String Orch. (1970); Viola Concerto (1971); *Before Endeavors Fade* for Strings (1977); *Festival Overture* for Sym. Orch. and Jazz Band (1978); Cello Concerto (1984); Concerto Grosso for Violin, Alto Saxophone, and Chamber Orch. (1985). **CHAMBER:** 5 string quartets (1941; 1947; 1956; 1963; *Esquisses,* 1970); Quartet for 4 Flutes (1943); Violin Sonata (1943); Viola Sonata (1943); Sextet for Piano and Wind Quintet (1945); Cello Sonata (1945); *Musique de midi,* nonet (1948); Clarinet Sonata (1952); Trumpet Sonata (1953); *Serenade* for Flute, Violin, and Cello (1957); *5 Miniatures* for 4 Saxophones (1958); Trio for Flute, Viola, and Guitar (1959); Wind Quintet (1961); *4 Pieces* for Guitar (1964); Piano Quartet (1973); Piano Trio (1973); String Trio (1973); 3 works entitled *Parades: I* for 4 Clarinets (1977); *II* for 6 Saxophones (1978); *III* for 4 Horns (1981); *Suite en ré* for Harpsichord (1986); 2 pieces for Accordion (1986); also works for Piano, including 4 sonatas (1946–85), 4 *Portraits* (1954–55), *Music* for 2 Pianos (1966), 3 *Marches* (1968), and *Brindilles* (1974); vocal works.

BIBL.: R. Wangermée, *V. L.* (Brussels, 1953).

Legnani, (Rinaldo) Luigi, outstanding Italian guitarist and instrument maker; b. Ferrara, Nov. 7, 1790; d. Ravenna, Aug. 5, 1877. After making appearances as a tenor, he launched a remarkable career as a guitar virtuoso, creating a minor sensation in Milan in 1819; subsequently toured widely in Europe, including concert appearances with Paganini (1836–38). He later settled in Ravenna and established a workshop as a maker of guitars and violins. He also composed duos for violin or flute and guitar.

BIBL.: R. Verrari, "L. L.," *Der Gitarrenfreund,* XXVII (1926).

Legrand, Michel, French composer of popular music; b. Paris, Feb. 24, 1932. He entered the Paris Cons. at the age of 11; while still a student, he began making professional jazz arrangements; wrote for radio, television, and the cinema. His inventive score for the motion picture *Les Parapluies de Cherbourg* (1965), written throughout in singsong fashion, received merited praise.

Legrenzi, Giovanni, celebrated Italian composer; b. Clusone, near Bergamo (baptized), Aug. 12, 1626; d. Venice, May 27, 1690. He was the son of a violinist and composer named Giovanni Maria Legrenzi. In 1645 he became organist at S. Maria Maggiore in Bergamo; in 1651 he was ordained and made resident chaplain there; in 1653 became 1st organist. In 1656 he was named maestro di cappella of the Accademia dello Spirito Santo in Ferrara; his 1st opera, *Nino il giusto,* was given in Ferrara in 1662. He left Ferrara in 1665; in 1671 he settled in Venice, where he served as an instructor at the Conservatorio dei Mendicanti; in 1683 was its maestro di coro. In 1677 he was maestro of the Oratorio at S. Maria della Fava. In 1681 he became vice-maestro of S. Marco; in 1685 was elected maestro there; under his regimen the orch. was increased to 34 instrumental parts (8 violins, 11 violettas, 2 viole da braccio, 3 violones, 4 theorbos, 2 cornets, 1 bassoon, and 3 trombones). Legrenzi was a noted teacher; among his pupils were Gasparini, Lotti, and Caldara, as well as his own nephew, **Giovanni Varischino**. Legrenzi's sonatas are noteworthy, since they served as models of Baroque forms as later practiced by Vivaldi and Bach. His operas and oratorios were marked by a development of the *da capo* form in arias, and his carefully wrought orch. support of the vocal parts was of historic significance as presaging the development of opera.

WORKS: OPERAS: *Nino il giusto* (Ferrara, 1662; not extant); *L'Achille in Sciro* (Ferrara, 1663; not extant); *Zenobia e Radamisto* (Ferrara, 1665); *Tiridate* (based upon the preceding; Venice, 1668; not extant); *Eteocle e Polinice* (Venice, 1675); *La divisione del mondo* (Venice, 1675); *Adone in Cipro* (Venice, 1676; not extant); *Germanico sul Reno* (Venice, 1676); *Totila* (Venice, 1677); *Il Creso* (Venice, 1681); *Antioco il grande* (Venice, 1681); *Il Pausania* (Venice, 1682); *Lisimaco riamato* (Venice, 1682); *L'Ottaviano Cesare Augusto* (Mantua, 1682; not extant); *Giustino* (Venice, 1683); *I due Cesari* (Venice, 1683); *L'anarchia dell'imperio* (Venice, 1684; not extant); *Publio Elio Pertinace* (Venice, 1684; not extant); *Ifianassa e Melampo* (Pratolino, 1685; not extant). **ORATORIOS:** *Oratorio del giuditio* (Vienna, 1665; not extant); *Gli sponsali d'Ester* (Modena, 1676; not extant); *Il Sedicia* (Ferrara, 1676); *La vendita del core humano* (Ferrara, 1676); *Il Sisara* (Ferrara, 1678; not extant); *Decollatione di S. Giovanni* (Ferrara, 1678; not extant); *La morte del cor penitente* (Vienna, 1705; also the following publ. sacred works: *Concerti musicali per uso di chiesa* (Venice, 1654); *Harmonia d'affeti devoti* for 2–4 Voices (Venice, 1655); *13 Salmi a 5* (Venice, 1657); *Sentimenti devoti* for 2–3 Voices (Venice, 1660); *Compiete con le lettanie & antifone della BV a 5* (Venice, 1662); *Sacri e festivi concenti, messa e psalmi a due chori* (Venice, 1667); *Acclamationi divoti* for 1 Voice (Bologna, 1670); *Sacri musicali concerti* for 2–3 Voices (Venice, 1689); *Motetti sacri* for 1 Voice (G. Varischino, ed.; Venice, 1692); additional sacred works include Psalms, motets, etc. His secular vocal works include *Cantate e canzonette* for 1 Voice (Bologna, 1676; modern ed. in *Recent Researches in the Music of the Baroque Era*, XIV–XV, 1972); *Idee armoniche* for 2–3 Voices (Venice, 1678); *Echi di riverenza di cantate e canzoni* (Bologna, 1678); cantatas; etc. **INSTRUMENTAL:** *18 Sonate a 2–3* (Venice, 1655); *30 Sonate da chiesa e da camera . . . a 3* (Venice, 1656); *16 Sonate a 2, 3, 5, & 6* (Venice, 1663); *La cetra, sonate a 2–4* (Venice, 1673); *Balletti e correnti a 5* (G. Varischino, ed.; Venice, 1691); *Sonate, 2–7 insts. con trombe e senza, overo flauti* (Venice, c.1695; not extant); several of the sonatas have been publ. in Hortus Musicus, XXXI (1949) and LXXXIII and LXXXIV (1951), and in Le Pupitre, IV (Paris, 1968).

BIBL.: H. Nüssle, *G. L. als Instrumentalkomponist* (diss., Univ. of Munich, 1917); G. Tebaldini, "G. L.," *Musica d'Oggi* (April 1937); P. Fogaccia, *G. L.* (Bergamo, 1954); S. Bonta, *The Church Sonatas of G. L.* (diss., Harvard Univ., 1964); J. MacDonald, *The Sacred Vocal Music of G. L.* (diss., Univ. of Michigan, 1964); C. Sartori, "Due L. ricuperati," *Acta Musicologica*, XLVI (1974); J. Swale, *A Thematic Catalogue of the Music of G. L.* (diss., Univ. of Adelaide, 1983).

Legros, Joseph, French tenor; b. Monampteuil, Sept. 7, 1739; d. La Rochelle, Dec. 20, 1793. He was a choirboy in Laon; made his debut at the Paris Opéra in 1764 as Titon in Mondonville's *Titon et l'Aurore*; subsequently created several roles in operas by Gluck, including Achilles in *Iphigénie en Aulide* (1774) and Pylades in *Iphigénie en Tauride* (1779); also sang in operas by Piccinni, Grétry, and others; retired from the stage in 1783. He served as director of the Concert Spirituel

(1777–90). He also was a composer; wrote several operas and a number of songs.

Lehár, Franz (actually, **Ferenc**), celebrated Austrian operetta composer of Hungarian descent; b. Komorn, Hungary, April 30, 1870; d. Bad Ischl, Oct. 24, 1948. He began his music training with his father, **Franz Lehár** (1838–98), a military bandmaster. He then entered the Prague Cons. at 12 and studied violin with A. Bennewitz and theory with J. Foerster. In 1885 he was brought to the attention of Fibich, who gave him lessons in composition independently from his studies at the Cons. In 1887 Lehár submitted 2 piano sonatas to Dvořák, who encouraged him in his musical career. In 1888 he became a violinist in a theater orch. in Elberfeld; in 1889, entered his father's band (50th Infantry) in Vienna, and assisted him as conductor. From 1890 to 1902 Lehár led military bands in Pola, Trieste, Budapest, and Vienna. Although his early stage works were unsuccessful, he gained some success with his marches and waltzes. With *Der Rastelbinder* (Vienna, Dec. 20, 1902), he established himself as a composer for the theater. His most celebrated operetta, *Die lustige Witwe*, was first performed in Vienna on Dec. 30, 1905; it subsequently received innumerable performances throughout the world. From then on Vienna played host to most of his finest scores, including *Der Graf von Luxemburg* (Nov. 12, 1909), *Zigeunerliebe* (Jan. 8, 1910), and *Paganini* (Oct. 30, 1925). For Berlin, he wrote *Der Zarewitsch* (Feb. 21, 1927), *Friederike* (Oct. 4, 1928), and *Das Land des Lächelns* (Oct. 10, 1929; rev. version of *Die gelbe Jacke*). Lehár's last years were made difficult by his marriage to a Jewish woman, which made him suspect to the Nazis. Ironically, *Die lustige Witwe* was one of Hitler's favorite stage works. After World War II, Lehár went to Zürich (1946); then returned to Bad Ischl shortly before his death. Lehár's music exemplifies the spirit of gaiety and frivolity that was the mark of Vienna early in the 20th century; his superlative gift for facile melody and infectious rhythms is combined with genuine wit and irony; a blend of nostalgia and sophisticated humor, undiminished by the upheavals of wars and revolutions, made a lasting appeal to audiences.

WORKS: STAGE (all 1st perf. in Vienna unless otherwise given): **OPERETTAS:** *Fräulein Leutnant* (1901); *Arabella, die Kubamerin* (1901; unfinished); *Das Club-Baby* (1901; unfinished); *Wiener Frauen* (*Der Klavierstimmer*) (Nov. 21, 1902; rev. as *Der Schlüssel zum Paradies*, Leipzig, Oct. 1906); *Der Rastelbinder* (Dec. 20, 1902); *Der Göttergatte* (Jan. 20, 1904; rev. as *Die ideale Gattin*, Vienna, Oct. 11, 1913; rev. as *Die Tangokönigin*, Vienna, Sept. 9, 1921); *Die Juxheirat* (Dec. 22, 1904); *Die lustige Witwe* (Dec. 30, 1905); *Peter und Paul reisen im Schlaraffenland* (*Max und Moritz reisen ins Schlaraffenland*) (Dec. 1, 1906); *Mstislaw der Moderne* (Jan. 5, 1907); *Der Mann mit den drei Frauen* (Jan. 21, 1908); *Das Fürstenkind* (Oct. 7, 1909; rev. as *Der Fürst der Berge*, Berlin, Sept. 23, 1932); *Der Graf von Luxemburg* (Nov. 12, 1909); *Zigeunerliebe* (Jan. 8, 1910; rev. as the opera *Garabonciás diák*, Budapest, Feb. 20, 1943); *Die Spieluhr* (Jan. 7, 1911); *Eva* (Nov. 24, 1911); *Rosenstock und Edelweiss* (Dec. 1, 1912); *Endlich allein* (Feb. 10, 1914; rev. as *Schön ist die Welt*, Berlin, Dec. 3, 1930); *Der Sterngucker* (Jan. 14, 1916; rev. as *La danza delle libellule*, Milan, May 3, 1922; rev. as *Gigolette*, Milan, Oct. 30, 1926); *A Pacsirta* (*Wo die Lerche singt*) (Budapest, Jan. 1, 1918); *Die blaue Mazur* (May 28, 1920); *Frühling* (Jan. 20, 1922; rev. as *Frühlingsmädel*, Berlin, May 29, 1930); *Frasquita* (May 12, 1922); *Die gelbe Jacke* (Feb. 9, 1923; rev. as *Das Land des Lächelns*, Berlin, Oct. 10, 1929); *Cloclo* (March 8, 1924); *Paganini* (Oct. 30, 1925); *Der Zarewitsch* (Berlin, Feb. 21, 1927); *Friederike* (Berlin, Oct. 4, 1928); *Giuditta* (Jan. 20, 1934). **OPERAS:** *Der Kurassier* (1891–92; unfinished); *Rodrigo* (1893; unfinished); *Kukuška* (Leipzig, Nov. 27, 1896; rev. as *Tatjana*, Brünn, Feb. 21, 1905). **FILM SCORES:** *Die grosse Attraktion* (1931); *Es war einmal ein Walzer* (1932); *Grossfürstin Alexandra* (1934); *Die ganze Welt dreht sich um Liebe* (1936); *Une Nuit à Vienne* (1937). He also wrote a number of orch. pieces, including several symphonic poems; 2 violin concertos; about 65 waltzes, the most famous being his *Gold und Silber* (1899); more than 50 marches; various works for piano, including sonatas; over 90 songs; etc. S. Rourke ed. a thematic index of his works (London, 1985).

BIBL.: E. Decsey, *F. L.* (Munich, 1924; 2nd ed., 1930); S. Czech, *F. L.: Sein Weg und sein Werk* (Lindau, 1948); M. von Peteani, *F. L.: Seine Musik, sein Leben* (Vienna, 1950); W. Macqueen-Pope and D. Murray, *Fortune's Favourite: The Life and Times of F. L.* (London, 1953); B. Grun, *Gold and Silver: The Life and Times of F. L.* (London, 1970); M. Schönherr, *F. L.: Bibliographie zu Leben und Werk* (Vienna, 1970); O. Schneidereit, *F. L.: Eine Biographie in Zitaten* (Innsbruck, 1984).

Lehel, György, Hungarian conductor; b. Budapest, Feb. 10, 1926; d. there, Sept. 26, 1989. He was educated at the Budapest Academy of Music; made his conducting debut in 1946. In 1950 he began a long and successful association with the Hungarian Radio; was named chief conductor of the Radio-Television Sym. Orch. in 1962. In addition to performing traditional Hungarian music, Lehel was also a determined champion of contemporary music.

Lehmann, Fritz, esteemed German conductor; b. Mannheim, May 17, 1904; d. Munich, March 30, 1956. He studied at the Univs. of Heidelberg and Göttingen; was a conductor in Göttingen (1923–27), Hildesheim (1927–38), and Hannover (1929–38). In 1934 he became conductor of the Handel Festival in Göttingen; was also Generalmusikdirektor in Bad Pyrmont (1934–38), Wuppertal (1938–47), and Göttingen (1946–50); subsequently was a teacher at the Hochschule für Musik in Munich (from 1953). A consummate conductor, he led notable performances in both the operatic and symphonic literature, ranging from the Baroque period to the 20th century.

BIBL.: J. Herrmann and F. Hamel, "Abschied von F. L.," *Musica,* X (1956).

Lehmann, Hans Ulrich, Swiss composer; b. Biel, May 4, 1937. He studied with Paul Müller (theory) and Rudolf Looser (cello); then attended the advanced seminars in composition given by Boulez and Stockhausen at the Basel Academy of Music (1960–63); also studied musicology with Kurt von Fischer at the Univ. of Zürich. He taught theory and cello at the Basel Academy of Music (1964–72); also taught in the musicology dept. of the Univ. of Zürich (from 1969). In 1972 he joined the theory and composition faculty at the Zürich Cons. and Musikhochschule; was its director from 1976. After an early period as a composer of orthodox serialism, he developed an individual style with serial connotations.

WORKS: ORCH.: *Quanti* for Flute and Chamber Ensemble (1962); *Komposition für 19* for Chamber Ensemble (1964–65); *Rondo* for Soprano and Orch. (1967); *Positionen* (1971); Concerto for Flute, Clarinet, and Strings (1969); *Dis-Cantus I* for Oboe and Strings (1971); *Streuungen* for Choir and Orch. (1975–76); *Kammermusik I, Hommage à Mozart* for Small Orch. (1978–79); *Kammermusik II* for Small Orch. (1979); *Canticum I* and *II* for Soprano and Instruments (1981); *Gottes panarchische nacht,* cantata for Soprano, Trumpet, Women's Chorus, and Orch. (1981–82); *Kammermusik III* for 12 Solo Strings (1983); *Aphorismus* for Chamber Orch. (1985). **CHAMBER:** *Episoden* for Wind Quintet (1963–64); *Regions III* for Clarinet, Trombone, and Cello (1970); *Sonata da chiesa* for Violin and Organ (1971); *Faces* for Harpsichord or Piano, and Flute, Oboe, Clarinet, Violin, and Cello (1972); *gegen- (bei-) spiele* for 5 Wind Instruments (1973); *. . . zu streichen* for 2 Cellos, 2 Violins, and 2 Violas (1974); *flautando* for 3 Flutes (1981); *battuto a tre—tratto* for 3 Percussion (1983); *Triplum* for 3 Horns (1984); *sich fragend nach frühster erinnerung* for Flute Quartet (1985); *Alleluja I* for Soprano, Clarinet, Japanese Temple Bell, and Organ (1985).

Lehmann, Lilli, celebrated German soprano, sister of **Marie Lehmann;** b. Würzburg, Nov. 24, 1848; d. Berlin, May 16, 1929. Her father, August Lehmann, was a singer. Her mother, **Marie Loew** (1807–83), who had sung leading soprano roles and had also appeared as a harpist at the Kassel Opera under Spohr, became harpist at the National Theater in Prague in 1853, and there Lehmann spent her girlhood. At the age of 6 she began to study piano with Cölestin Müller, and at 12 progressed so far that she was able to act as accompanist to her mother, who was her only singing teacher. She made her professional debut in Prague on Oct. 20, 1865, as the 1st Page in *Die Zauberflöte;* then sang in Danzig (1868) and Leipzig (1869–70). In the meantime, she made her 1st appearance at the Berlin Royal Opera as Marguerite de Valois in *Les Huguenots* (Aug. 31, 1869); then joined its roster (1870) and established herself as a brilliant coloratura. During the summer of 1875 she was in Bayreuth, and was coached by Wagner himself in the parts of Woglinde (*Das Rheingold* and *Götterdämmerung*), Helmwige, and the Forest Bird; these roles she created at the Bayreuth Festival the following summer. She then returned to Berlin under a life contract with the Royal Opera; she was given limited leaves of absence, which enabled her to appear in the principal German cities, in Stockholm (1878), in London (debut as Violetta, June 3, 1880), and in Vienna (1882). She made her American debut at the Metropolitan Opera in N.Y. on Nov. 25, 1885, as Carmen; 5 days later she sang Brünnhilde in *Die Walküre;* then sang virtually all the Wagner roles through subsequent seasons until 1890; her last season there was 1898–99; she also appeared as Norma, Aida, Donna Anna, Fidelio, etc. She sang Isolde at the American premiere of *Tristan und Isolde* (Dec. 1, 1886), and appeared in Italian opera with the De Reszkes and Lassalle during the season of 1891–92. In the meantime, her contract with the Berlin Royal Opera was canceled (1889), owing to her protracted absence, and it required the intervention of Kaiser Wilhelm II to reinstate her (1891). In 1896 she sang the 3 Brünnhildes at the Bayreuth Festival. Her great admiration for Mozart caused her to take an active part in the annual Festivals held at Salzburg (1901–10), where she was artistic director. Her operatic repertoire comprised 170 roles in 114 operas (German, Italian, and French). She possessed in the highest degree all the requisite qualities of a great interpreter; she had a boundless capacity for work, a glorious voice, and impeccable technique; she knew how to subordinate her fiery temperament to artistic taste; on the stage she had plasticity of pose, grace of movement, and regal presence; her ability to project her interpretation with conviction to audiences in different countries was not the least factor in her universal success. Although she was celebrated chiefly as an opera singer, she was equally fine as an interpreter of German lieder; she gave recitals concurrently with her operatic appearances, and continued them until her retirement in 1920; her repertoire of songs exceeded 600. She was also a successful teacher; among her pupils were Geraldine Farrar and Olive Fremstad. On Feb. 24, 1888, in N.Y. she married the tenor **Paul Kalisch,** with whom she often sang in opera in subsequent years. They later separated, but never divorced. After her death, Kalisch inherited her manor at Salzkammergut, and remained there until his death in 1946, at the age of 90. Lehmann authored *Meine Gesangskunst* (Berlin, 1902; Eng. tr., 1914, as *How to Sing;* 3rd ed., rev. and supplemented, 1924 by C. Willenbücher); *Studie zu Fidelio* (1904); *Mein Weg,* an autobiography (Leipzig, 1913; 2nd ed., 1920; Eng. tr., 1914, as *My Path through Life*).

BIBL.: J. Wagenmann, *L. L.s Geheimnis der Stimmbänder* (Berlin, 1905; 2nd ed., 1926); L. Andro, *L. L.* (Berlin, 1907).

Lehmann, Liza (actually, **Elizabetha Nina Mary Frederica**), English soprano and composer; b. London, July 11, 1862; d. Pinner, Middlesex, Sept. 19, 1918. She was of German-Scottish parentage; grew up in an intellectual and artistic atmosphere: her grandfather was a publisher, her father a painter, her mother a singer. From her childhood she lived in Germany, France, and Italy; among the guests at her house in Rome was Liszt. She studied voice with Randegger and Lind in London, and composition with Raunkilde in Rome, Freudenberg in Wiesbaden, and MacCunn in London. She made her professional debut as a singer at a Monday Popular Concert in London

(Nov. 23, 1885), and subsequently appeared at various festivals in England. On Oct. 10, 1894, she married the English painter and composer **Herbert Bedford,** and retired from the stage; she then applied herself with great earnestness to composition, with remarkable results, for she was able to produce a number of works (mostly vocal) of undeniable merit, and was the 1st English woman composer to enjoy success with a large public in England and in America. Her best-known work is *In a Persian Garden*, to words from Omar Khayyám's *Rubaiyát*, in Fitzgerald's version; it is a song cycle, with recitatives, scored for 4 voices, with piano accompaniment; while the music itself is entirely conventional, the vocal parts are eminently effective, both in dramatic and in lyrical passages. In 1910 Lehmann made a tour in the U.S., presenting concerts of her songs, with herself at the piano. Her memoirs, *The Life of Liza Lehmann, by Herself*, were publ. shortly after her death (London, 1919).

WORKS: *Sergeant Brue*, musical farce (London, June 14, 1904); *The Vicar of Wakefield*, "romantic light opera" (Manchester, Nov. 12, 1906); *Everyman*, 1-act opera (London, Dec. 28, 1915); *Once upon a Time*, "fairy cantata" (London, Feb. 22, 1903); *Young Lochinvar* for Baritone, Chorus, and Orch.; *Endymion* for Soprano and Orch.; *Romantic Suite* for Violin and Piano; *In a Persian Garden* for Vocal Quartet and Piano (London, Jan. 10, 1897); song cycles (several of a humorous nature): *The Daisy Chain* (12 songs of childhood); *More Daisies; Prairie Pictures; In Memoriam* (after Tennyson); *Nonsense Songs* (from *Alice in Wonderland*); *The Cautionary Tales and a Moral* (after Hilaire Belloc); also piano pieces.

Lehmann, Lotte, celebrated German-born American soprano; b. Perleberg, Feb. 27, 1888; d. Santa Barbara, Calif., Aug. 26, 1976. She studied in Berlin with Erna Tiedka, Eva Reinhold, and Mathilde Mallinger. She made her debut on Sept. 2, 1910, as the 2nd Boy in *Die Zauberflöte* at the Hamburg Opera, but soon was given important parts in Wagner's operas, establishing herself as one of the finest Wagnerian singers. In 1914 she made her 1st appearance in London, as Sophie at Drury Lane. In 1916 she was engaged at the Vienna Opera. Richard Strauss selected her to sing the Young Composer in the revised version of *Ariadne auf Naxos* when it was first performed in Vienna (Oct. 4, 1916); then she appeared as Octavian in *Der Rosenkavalier*, and later as the Marschallin, which became one of her most famous roles. In 1922 she toured in South America. In 1924 she made her 1st appearance at London's Covent Garden as the Marschallin, and continued to sing there regularly with great success until 1935; appeared there again in 1938. On Oct. 28, 1930, she made her U.S. debut as Sieglinde with the Chicago Opera, and on Jan. 11, 1934, sang Sieglinde at her Metropolitan Opera debut in N.Y. She continued to appear at the Metropolitan, with mounting success, in the roles of Elisabeth in *Tannhäuser*, Tosca, and the Marschallin, until her farewell performance as the Marschallin on Feb. 23, 1945. In 1946 she appeared as the Marschallin for the last time in San Francisco. In 1945 she became a naturalized American citizen; gave her last recital in Santa Barbara, Calif., on Aug. 7, 1951, and thereafter devoted herself to teaching. Lehmann was universally recognized as one of the greatest singers of the century. The beauty of her voice, combined with her rare musicianship, made her a compelling artist of the highest order. In addition to her unforgettable Strauss roles, she excelled as Mozart's Countess and Donna Elvira, Beethoven's Leonore, and Wagner's Elisabeth, Elsa, and Eva, among others. She publ. a novel, *Orplid mein Land* (1937; Eng. tr., 1938, as *Eternal Flight*); an autobiography, *Anfang und Aufstieg* (Vienna, 1937; in London as *Wings of Song*, 1938; in N.Y. as *Midway in My Song*, 1938); *More Than Singing* (N.Y., 1945); *My Many Lives* (N.Y., 1948); *Five Operas and Richard Strauss* (N.Y., 1964; in London as *Singing with Richard Strauss*, 1964); *Eighteen Song Cycles* (London and N.Y., 1971).

BIBL.: B. Wessling, *L. L. . . . mehr als eine Sängerin* (Salzburg, 1969); B. Glass, *L. L., A Life in Opera & Song* (Santa

Barbara, Calif., 1988); A. Jefferson, *L. L.: 1888–1976: A Centenary Biography* (London, 1988); D. Shawe-Taylor, "L. L. and Elisabeth Schumann: A Centenary Tribute," *Musical Times* (Oct. 1988).

Lehmann, Marie, esteemed German soprano, sister of **Lilli Lehmann;** b. Hamburg, May 15, 1851; d. Berlin, Dec. 9, 1931. She was a pupil of her mother, and later of her sister; made her debut in Leipzig (May 1, 1867); in 1876 she created the parts of Wellgunde (*Das Rheingold* and *Götterdämmerung*) and Ortlinde (*Walküre*) at Bayreuth; from 1882 to 1896 she was a prominent member of the Vienna Court Opera; then lived in Berlin as a teacher.

Lehrman, Leonard J(ordan), American composer, pianist, and choral conductor; b. Ft. Riley, Kans., Aug. 20, 1949. He studied at Harvard Univ. with Kim, Del Tredici, Kirchner, and Foss (graduated, 1971); received a Fulbright grant for study with Boulanger in Paris (1972); completed his education with Karel Husa and Robert Palmer at Cornell Univ. (D.M.A., 1977), where he was also piano assistant to Malcolm Bilson. In 1973 he completed Marc Blitzstein's opera *Idiots First*; composed a companion work, *Karla*, also to a Malamud text, with which Blitzstein's work was presented as *Tales of Malamud* (Bloomington, Ind., March 7, 1976). He served as assistant chorus master at the Metropolitan Opera in N.Y.; made a number of trs. for N.Y.'s Bel Canto Opera, including *Rusalka* (Pushkin-Dargomyzhsky), *L'Étoile* (Chabrier), and *A Life for the Czar* (Glinka). In 1983 he founded the Jewish Music Theatre of (West) Berlin.

WORKS: STAGE: Operas: *Tales of Malamud*, 2 1-act operas after Malamud: *Idiots First* (completion of Blitzstein's unfinished opera; 1973) and *Karla* (1974; Bloomington, Ind., March 7, 1976); *Beowulf or The Great Dane*, parodic musical fantasy (1970); *Sima* (1976); *Hannah* (1980); *The Family Man* (1984); *The Birthday of the Bank* (1988); also musicals, including *E. G.: A Musical Portrait of Emma Goldman* (1987), incidental music, and cabarets, including *The Blitzstein Cabaret* (N.Y., 1988). **ORCH.:** *Bloody Kansas*, prelude (1975); Concerto for Violin and Orch. (1975); Concerto for Flute and Orch. (1982). **CHAMBER:** Sonata for Flute and Piano (1963–64); *String Trio* (1968); Piano Trio (1969–70); *Sonatina for Tuba Alone* (1980); *Reinecke Fuchs*, piano suite (1982); numerous vocal works, including *We Are Innocent*, cantata on the letters of Julius and Ethel Rosenberg for Soloists, Optional Chorus, and Piano or Orch. (1988), and *The Universal Declaration of Human Rights* for Chorus and Piano, or Winds and Percussion (1988); solo songs and song cycles.

Leibowitz, René, noted Polish-born French conductor, composer, writer on music, music theorist, and pedagogue; b. Warsaw, Feb. 17, 1913; d. Paris, Aug. 28, 1972. His family settled in Paris in 1926; from 1930 to 1933 he studied in Berlin with Schoenberg and in Vienna with Webern; also studied orchestration with Ravel in Paris (1933). He was active as a conductor from 1937. As a composer, he adopted the 12-tone method of composition, becoming its foremost exponent in France; he had numerous private students, among them Boulez. He publ. the influential books *Schoenberg et son école* (Paris, 1946; Eng. tr., N.Y., 1949) and *Introduction à la musique de douze sons* (Paris, 1949). He also wrote *L'Artiste et sa conscience* (Paris, 1950); *L'Évolution de la musique de Bach à Schönberg* (Paris, 1952); *Histoire de l'Opéra* (Paris, 1957); with J. Maguire, *Thinking for Orchestra* (N.Y., 1958); with K. Wolff, *Erich Itor Kahn, Un Grand Représentant de la musique contemporaine* (Paris, 1958; Eng. tr., N.Y., 1958); *Schönberg* (Paris, 1969); *Le Compositeur et son double* (Paris, 1971); *Les Fantômes de l'opéra* (Paris, 1973).

WORKS: OPERAS: *La Nuit close* (1949); *La Rumeur de l'espace* (1950); *Ricardo Gonfolano* (1953); *Les Espagnols à Venise*, opera buffa (1963; Grenoble, Jan. 27, 1970); *Labyrinthe*, after Baudelaire (1969); *Todos caerán* (1970–72). **ORCH.:** Sym. (1941); 2 chamber concertos (1942, 1944); Chamber Sym. (1948); Piano Concerto (1954); Viola Concerto (1954); *Fantaisie symphonique* (1956); Violin Concerto (1959); *3 Bagatelles* for String Orch. (1959); Concertino for Trombone (1960); Cello Concerto (1962); *Rapsodie symphonique* (1964–65). CHAMBER: *Marijuana* for Violin, Trombone, Vibraphone, and Piano (1960); *Sinfonietta da camera* (1961); *Capriccio* for Flute and Strings (1967); *Suite* for 9 Instruments (1967); Saxophone Quartet (1969); *Petite suite* for Clarinet Sextet (1970); 8 string quartets (1940, 1950, 1952, 1958, 1963, 1965, 1966, 1968); VOCAL: *Tourist Death* for Soprano and Chamber Orch. (1943); *L'Explication des métaphores* for Speaker, 2 Pianos, Harp, and Percussion (1947); *Chanson Dada* for Children's Chorus and Instruments (1968); *Laboratoire central* for Speaker and Chorus (1970); numerous songs.

BIBL.: J. Maguire, "R. L.," *Tempo* (Feb. and March 1980).

Leich, Roland (Jacobi), American composer; b. Evansville, Ind., March 6, 1911. He studied composition with Borowski and Sowerby in Chicago, Webern in Vienna (1933–34), Scalero at the Curtis Inst. of Music in Philadelphia (B.M., 1934), and Rogers at the Eastman School of Music in Rochester, N.Y. (M.M., 1942); also studied at Dartmouth College (B.A., 1935), where he served on the faculty (1935–41). In 1946 he became a teacher at the Carnegie Inst. of Technology (later Carnegie-Mellon Univ.) in Pittsburgh, remaining on its faculty until 1976. He was particularly successful as a composer of songs, of which he wrote more than 150.

WORKS: ORCH.: *Rondo* (1942); *Concert Piece* for Oboe and Strings (1952); *Prelude and Fugue* (1954). CHAMBER: String Quartet (1936); Flute Sonata (1953); *A Musical Christmas Wreath* for Woodwind Quintet and Harp (1980); piano pieces; organ music. VOCAL: *Housman Songs* (1932); 5 songs, after Housman (1939–78); 40 songs, after Milne (1940); 47 songs, after Dickinson (1950–65); 17 songs, after S. Hay (1956–84); also cantatas and other choral works, hymn tunes, and arrangements of folk melodies and hymns.

Leichtentritt, Hugo, eminent German-American music scholar; b. Pleschen, Posen, Jan. 1, 1874; d. Cambridge, Mass., Nov. 13, 1951. He studied with J. K. Paine at Harvard Univ. (B.A., 1894); continued his studies in Paris (1894–95) and at the Berlin Hochschule für Musik (1895–98); obtained his Ph.D. at the Univ. of Berlin in 1901 with the dissertation *Reinhard Keiser in seinen Opern: Ein Beitrag zur Geschichte der frühen deutschen Oper* (publ. in Berlin, 1901); he subsequently taught at the Klindworth-Scharwenka Cons. in Berlin (1901–24) and wrote music criticism for German and American publications. In 1933 he left Germany and became a lecturer on music at Harvard Univ. (until 1940); then taught at Radcliffe College and N.Y. Univ. (1940–44). Although known chiefly as a scholar, he also composed; he wrote a Sym.; Violin Concerto; Cello Concerto; Piano Concerto; much chamber music; several song cycles; numerous piano pieces. He also wrote a comic opera, *Der Sizilianer* (Freiburg, May 28, 1920). His MSS are in the Library of Congress in Washington, D.C.

WRITINGS: *Frédéric Chopin* (Berlin, 1905; 3rd ed., 1949); *Geschichte der Musik* (Berlin, 1905; Eng. tr., N.Y., 1938 as *Everybody's Little History of Music*); *Geschichte der Motette* (Leipzig, 1908); *Musikalische Formenlehre* (Leipzig, 1911; 5th ed., 1952; Eng. tr., Cambridge, Mass., 1951 as *Musical Form*); *Erwin Lendvai* (Berlin, 1912); *Ferruccio Busoni* (Leipzig, 1916); *Analyse der Chopin'schen Klavierwerke* (2 vols., Berlin, 1921–22); *Händel* (Berlin and Stuttgart, 1924); *Music, History, and Ideas* (Cambridge, Mass., 1938); *Serge Koussevitzky, the Boston Symphony Orchestra and the New American Music* (Cambridge, Mass., 1946); *Music of the Western Nations* (ed. and amplified by N. Slonimsky; Cambridge, Mass., 1956).

Leider, Frida, outstanding German soprano; b. Berlin, April 18, 1888; d. there, June 4, 1975. She was employed as a bank clerk in Berlin, and studied voice with Otto Schwarz there on the side. She made her debut in Halle in 1915 as Venus in *Tannhäuser;* then sang at Rostock (1916–18), Königsberg (1918–19), and Hamburg (1919–23). She was engaged by the Berlin State Opera in 1923, and remained on its roster until 1940; was also highly successful in Wagnerian roles at London's Covent Garden (1924–38) and at the Bayreuth Festivals

(1928–38). In 1928 she made her American debut at the Chicago Civic Opera Co. as Brünnhilde in *Die Walküre;* then made her debut at the Metropolitan Opera in N.Y. on Jan. 16, 1933, as Isolde. In 1934 she returned to Germany; she encountered difficulties because her husband, a violinist named Rudolf Deman, was Jewish. She was confronted by the Nazis with the demand to divorce him, but refused; he succeeded in going to Switzerland. After the war and the collapse of the Nazi regime (1945), she maintained a vocal studio at the (East) Berlin State Opera until 1952; also taught at the (West) Berlin Hochschule für Musik from 1948 to 1958. She publ. a memoir, *Das war mein Teil, Erinnerungen einer Opernsängerin* (Berlin, 1959; Eng. tr., N.Y., 1966 as *Playing My Part*).

Leifs, Jón, eminent Icelandic conductor and composer; b. Sólheimar, May 1, 1899; d. Reykjavík, July 30, 1968. After completing his primary education at Reykjavík, he studied at the Leipzig Cons. with Teichmüller, Szendrei, Scherchen, Lohse, and Graener (1916–22); then conducted concerts in various German towns; in 1926, led the Hamburg Phil. when it visited Iceland. He was adviser to the Icelandic Radio (1934–37), and also founder of the Union of Icelandic Artists (1928), the Icelandic Composers' Soc. (1945), and the Icelandic Performing Rights Soc. (1948). He publ. a manual on musical forms (in Icelandic), wrote the book *Islands künstlerische Anregung* (Reykjavík, 1951), and contributed articles on Icelandic music to various publications. His music is technically derived from the German Romantic tradition; but in several of his works he makes use of Icelandic melodies and rhythms; often he abandons opulent harmonic accoutrements to portray Arctic nature in bleak, organum-like diaphony.

WORKS: Wordless music dramas: *Loftr* (Copenhagen, Sept. 3, 1938) and *Baldr* (1950); *Hljomkvida,* symphonic trilogy (Karlsbad, 1925); *Icelandic Overture* (Oslo, 1926; his most successful work); *Kyrie on Icelandic Themes* for a cappella Chorus; *Island-Kantate* (Greifswald, 1930); *Saga-symfoni* (Helsinki, Sept. 18, 1950); 2 string quartets; several piano cycles based on Icelandic dance tunes; songs.

BIBL.: Special issue of *Tonfallet* (Autumn 1989).

Leigh, Mitch (real name, **Irwin Mitchnick**), American composer, arranger, and conductor of popular music; b. N.Y., Jan. 30, 1928. He studied with Hindemith at Yale Univ.; upon graduation, entered the field of commercial music productions; founded Music Makers, Inc. His most successful work was the musical *Man of La Mancha* (1965), which included the hit song *The Impossible Dream.*

Leigh, Walter, English composer; b. London, June 22, 1905; killed in action near Tobruk, Libya, June 12, 1942. He was an organ scholar at Christ's College, Cambridge (1922–26), where he studied with Dent; also took lessons with Harold Darke and later with Paul Hindemith at the Hochschule für Musik in Berlin (1927–29). He was particularly adept in his writing for the theater.

WORKS: 2 light operas: *The Pride of the Regiment, or Cashiered for His Country* (Midhurst, England, Sept. 19, 1931) and *The Jolly Roger, or The Admiral's Daughter* (Manchester, Feb. 13, 1933); musical revue, *9 Sharp* (London, 1938); incidental music; several pieces designated for amateur orch.; Sonatina for Viola and Piano (ISCM Festival, Vienna, June 17, 1932); Trio for 3 Pianos (1934); Trio for Flute, Oboe, and Piano (1935); songs; piano pieces.

Leighton, Kenneth, English composer; b. Wakefield, Yorkshire, Oct. 2, 1929; d. Edinburgh, Aug. 24, 1988. He studied classics (1947–50) and composition with Rose (B.Mus., 1951) at Queen's College, Oxford, where he later earned his doctorate in music; also won the Mendelssohn Scholarship (1951), which enabled him to study with Petrassi in Rome. He was a lecturer at the Univ. of Edinburgh (1956–68); after serving as a lecturer at Worcester College, Oxford (1968–70), he returned to the Univ. of Edinburgh as Reid Prof. of Music (from 1970).

WORKS: OPERA: *Columba* (1980; Glasgow, June 16, 1981).

ORCH.: *Veris gratia*, suite for Oboe, Cello, and String Orch. (1950); 3 piano concertos: No. 1 (1951; BBC, Glasgow, March 7, 1958; rev. 1959); No. 2 (1960; BBC, Manchester, Jan. 18, 1962); No. 3 (1969; Birmingham, March 11, 1970); Violin Concerto (1952; BBC, London, May 5, 1953); Concerto for Viola, Harp, Timpani, and String Orch. (1952; BBC, London, Sept. 5, 1954); *Burlesque* (1956; London, May 3, 1959); Cello Concerto (Cheltenham, July 20, 1956); *Passacaglia, Chorale, and Fugue* (1957; BBC, London, May 23, 1959); Concerto for String Orch. (1961; London, June 19, 1962); *Festive Overture* (1962); 3 syms.: No. 1 (1964; Trieste, May 31, 1966); No. 2, *Sinfonia mistica*, for Soprano and Chorus (1974; Edinburgh, March 4, 1977); No. 3, *Laudes musicae*, with Tenor Solo (1983; Glasgow, March 15, 1985); 3 dance suites: No. 1 (Glasgow, July 10, 1968); No. 2 (1970; Farnham, May 12, 1971); No. 3, *Scottish Dances* (1983; Edinburgh, Feb. 25, 1984); Organ Concerto (1970; Cambridge, Aug. 4, 1971); Concerto for Harpsichord, Recorder, and String Orch. (1982; Warrington, Feb. 14, 1983). CHAMBER: 2 violin sonatas (1951, 1956); 2 string quartets (1956, 1957); Piano Quintet (1959); *7 Variations* for String Quartet (1964); Sonata for Solo Cello (1967); *Quartet in 1 Movement: Contrasts and Variants* (London, Oct. 13, 1972); *Fantasy on an American Hymn Tune: The Shining River* for Clarinet, Cello, and Piano (1974; Cheltenham, July 8, 1975); *Fantasy-Octet: Homage to Percy Grainger* for 4 Violins, 2 Violas, and 2 Cellos (Edinburgh, Aug. 29, 1982); vocal works, including *Animal Heaven*, diptych for Soprano, Recorder, Cello, and Harpsichord (Manchester, July 24, 1980); piano pieces; organ music.

Leighton, Sir William, English poet and composer; b. probably in Plash, Shropshire, c.1565; d. London (buried), July 31, 1622. He publ. *The Teares or Lamentacions of a Sorrowfull Soule Composed with Musicall Ayres and Songs both for Voyces and Divers Instruments* (1613), containing 18 consort songs for 4 Voices (the 1st 8 are by Leighton), 12 unaccompanied songs for 4 Voices, and 25 unaccompanied songs for 5 Voices; see C. Hill, ed., Early English Church Music, XI (London, 1970).

Leimer, Kurt, German-born Austrian pianist and composer; b. Wiesbaden, Sept. 7, 1920; d. Vaduz, Liechtenstein, Nov. 20, 1974. He studied piano with his great-uncle Karl Leimer (1858–1944), who was the teacher of Gieseking. After a brief concert career, he took lessons in composition with Kurt von Wolfurt; made rapid progress as a composer, and produced 4 piano concertos (1 for left hand), all very effective in their high-flown Romantic style; he was soloist in his 4th Piano Concerto in N.Y., on Oct. 14, 1956, with Stokowski conducting. He became an Austrian citizen in 1956, but lived in Vaduz.

Leinsdorf (real name, **Landauer**), **Erich,** eminent Austrian-born American conductor; b. Vienna, Feb. 4, 1912. He entered a local music school when he was 5; began piano studies with the wife of Paul Pisk at age 8; then continued his piano studies with Paul Emerich (1923–28), and subsequently studied theory and composition with Pisk. In 1930 he took a master class in conducting at the Mozarteum in Salzburg, and then studied for a short time in the music dept. of the Univ. of Vienna; from 1931 to 1933 he took courses at the Vienna Academy of Music, making his debut as a conductor at the Musikvereinsaal upon his graduation. In 1933 he served as assistant conductor of the Workers' Chorus in Vienna; in 1934 he went to Salzburg, where he had a successful audition with Bruno Walter and Toscanini at the Salzburg Festivals, and was appointed their assistant. In 1937 he was engaged as a conductor of the Metropolitan Opera in N.Y.; he made his American debut there conducting *Die Walküre* on Jan. 21, 1938, with notable success; he then conducted other Wagnerian operas, ultimately succeeding Bodanzky as head of the German repertoire there in 1939. In 1942 he became an American citizen. In 1943 he was appointed music director of the Cleveland Orch.; however, his induction into the U.S. Army in Dec. 1943 interrupted his term there. After his discharge in 1944, he once again conducted at the Metropolitan in 1944–

45; also conducted several concerts with the Cleveland Orch. in 1945 and 1946, and made appearances in Europe. From 1947 to 1955 he was music director of the Rochester (N.Y.) Phil. Orch. In the fall of 1956 he was briefly music director of the N.Y. City Opera; then returned to the Metropolitan as a conductor and musical consultant in 1957. He also appeared as a guest conductor in the U.S. and Europe. In 1962 he received the prestigious appointment of music director of the Boston Sym. Orch., a post he retained until 1969; then he conducted opera and sym. concerts in many of the major music centers of America and in Europe; from 1978 to 1980 he held the post of principal conductor of the (West) Berlin Radio Sym. Orch. He publ. a semi-autobiographical and rather candid book of sharp comments, *Cadenza: A Musical Career* (Boston, 1976); also *The Composer's Advocate: A Radical Orthodoxy for Musicians* (New Haven, 1981).

Leisner, David, American guitarist and composer; b. Los Angeles, Dec. 22, 1953. He was educated at Wesleyan Univ. (B.A., 1976); received instruction in guitar from John Duarte, David Starobin, and Angelo Gilardino, in interpretation from John Kirkpatrick and Karen Tuttle, and in composition from Richard Winslow; won 2nd prize at the Toronto International Guitar Competition (1975) and a silver medal at the Geneva International Guitar Competition (1981). He made his N.Y. debut in 1979, then toured extensively. He taught guitar at Amherst College (1976–78) and at the New England Cons. of Music in Boston (from 1980). He became well known for his programming of contemporary American music at his concerts. His own compositions include pieces for solo guitar and duos for guitar and viola, cello, or voice.

Leitch, Donovan. See **Donovan.**

Leite, Antonio (Joaquim) da Silva, Portuguese organist, guitarist, teacher, and composer; b. Oporto, May 23, 1759; d. there, Jan. 10, 1833. He studied in Oporto; was mestre de capela at the Cathedral there by 1808. He publ. *Rezumo de todas as regras e preceitos de cantoria assim da musica metrica como da cantochão* (Oporto, 1787) and *Estudo de guitarra* (Oporto, 1796). He wrote the operas *Puntigli per equivico* (Oporto, 1807) and *L'astuzie delle donne* (Oporto, 1807); *Restoration* Sym. (1808); *Os génios premiados*, cantata (Oporto, 1807); 6 masses; 23 motets; 6 sonatas for Guitar, Violin, and 2 Horns ad libitum (publ. in Oporto, 1792).

Leitner, Ferdinand, noted German conductor; b. Berlin, March 4, 1912. He studied composition with Schreker and conducting with Prüwer at the Berlin Hochschule für Musik; also studied piano with Schnabel and conducting with Muck. He then was active as a pianist until making his debut as a theater conductor in Berlin in 1943. He became conductor of the Württemberg State Theater in Stuttgart in 1947; was its Generalmusikdirektor (1950–69). He subsequently was chief conductor of the Zürich Opera (1969–84); also of the Residentie Orch. at The Hague (1976–80). From 1986 to 1990 he served as principal conductor of the RAI Orch. in Turin. He was known for his musicianly readings of works by Mozart, Wagner, Bruckner, and Richard Strauss; also conducted a number of modern scores, including premieres of works by Orff and Egk.

Leitzmann, Albert, German musicologist; b. Magdeburg, Aug. 3, 1867; d. Jena, April 16, 1950. He studied chiefly literature and esthetics; established himself as Privatdozent for German language and literature at the Univ. of Jena. Besides numerous books dealing with literature and philology, he publ. *Mozarts Persönlichkeit* (1914); *Beethovens Persönlichkeit* (2 vols., 1914); *Beethovens persönliche Aufzeichnungen* (1918); *Ludwig van Beethoven. Berichte der Zeitgenossen* (2 vols., 1921); *W.A. Mozart. Berichte der Zeitgenossen* (1926).

Leiviskä, Helvi (Lemmikki), Finnish composer; b. Helsinki, May 25, 1902; d. there, Aug. 12, 1982. She studied under Erkki Melartin at the Helsinki Music Inst. (graduated, 1927) and with Arthur Willner in Vienna; then studied privately with Funtek and Madetoja. She was a librarian at the Helsinki Academy of Music (1933–66).

Works: *Folk Dance Suite* for Orch. (1929; rev. 1971); Piano Concerto (1935); 2 orch. suites (1934, 1938); *Triple Fugue* for Orch. (1935); *Pimeän peikko* (Goblin of Darkness) for Chorus and Orch. (1942); 3 syms. (1947, 1954, 1971); *Mennyt manner* (The Lost Continent) for Solo Voices, Chorus, and Orch. (1957); *Sinfonia brevis* (1962; rev. 1972); Piano Quartet (1926); String Quartet (1926); Violin Sonata (1945).

Le Jeune, Claude (or **Claudin**), important French composer; b. Valenciennes, c.1528; d. Paris, Sept. 25, 1600. He most likely studied in or near Valenciennes; was in Paris by 1564. After Baïf and Courville founded the Académie de Poésie et de Musique in 1570, he became a major figure in promoting the new style of composition known as "musique mesurée à l'antique," in which the music is made to follow the metrical rhythm of the text in conformity with the rules of classical prosody. The type of poetry set to music in this manner was called "vers mesurez," and 33 examples of such settings by Le Jeune are to be found in the work entitled *Le Printemps,* publ. posth. in Paris in 1603 by his sister Cécile Le Jeune. The metrical scanning is given at the head of each song. In the preface to this work Le Jeune is given credit for having been the 1st to achieve the "mating of ancient rhythm and modern harmony"; if not the 1st, he was at least, together with his contemporary and friend Jacques Mauduit, one of the earliest and most notable cultivators of this new and significant style. Having espoused the Huguenot cause during the wars of the Catholic League, he was compelled to flee Paris during the siege of 1588; his MSS were saved by the intervention of his Catholic colleague Mauduit. After a period of refuge in La Rochelle, he eventually returned to Paris. He served as maistre compositeur ordinaire de la musique de nostre chambre to Henri IV in 1596. Le Jeune cultivated every variety of vocal music known in his time, such as French chansons in "vers rimez," Italian madrigals, Latin motets, etc. Special mention must be made of his settings of the Psalms, of which 8 collections appeared between 1564 and 1612. So great was his renown even during his lifetime that a wood engraving dated 1598 bore the legend: "Le Phénix des Musiciens." His best-known work is his setting of the Genevan Psalter *a* 4 and 5, publ. by Cécile Le Jeune in 1613. This simple contrapuntal setting of the Psalms was widely used in the Reformed churches of France and the Netherlands, and it was also publ. in a German tr. Some of these harmonizations even found their way into early New England psalmbooks, such as *The Ainsworth Psalter* (see C. Smith, *Early Psalmody in America*, N.Y., 1939). A more elaborate setting of some Psalms, *12 psaumes de David,* in motet style for 2 to 7 voices, was contained in the work entitled *Dodecacorde,* publ. at La Rochelle in 1598. In all, Le Jeune composed 347 Psalms, 146 airs (143 are mesurés), 66 secular chansons, 43 Italian madrigals, 38 sacred chansons, 11 motets, a Mass, and 3 instrumental fantasies. Some of his works are found in the following modern eds.: O. Douen, ed., *Clément Marot et le psautier huguenot,* II (Paris, 1879); D. Walker, ed., *Claude Le Jeune: Airs of 1608,* AIM Miscellanea, I (1951–59); F. Lesure, ed., *Anthologie de la chanson Parisienne au XVIe siècle* (Monaco, 1953); M. Honegger, ed., *Chorals de la Réforme* (Paris, 1953). **Bibl.:** E. Bouton, *Esquisse biographique et bibliographique sur C. L.J.* (Valenciennes, 1845); M. Cauchie, "La Mort de C. L.J.," *Revue de Musicologie,* XI (1927); D. Walker and F. Lesure, "C. L.J. and Musique mesurée," *Musica Disciplina,* III (1949); D. Walker, "The Rhythm and Notation of Musique Mesurée," ibid., IV (1950).

Lekeu, Guillaume (Jean Joseph Nicolas), talented Belgian composer; b. Heusy, near Verviers, Jan. 20, 1870; d. Angers, Jan. 21, 1894. He went to school in Poitiers; after graduation, followed his family to Paris, where he studied with Gaston Vallin; he also received some advice from César Franck and took a course with Vincent d'Indy. He subsequently went to Brussels to compete for the Belgian Prix de Rome; won 2nd prize with his cantata *Andromède* (1891). Returning to Paris, he wrote several works of excellent quality, but death (of ty-

phoid fever) intervened when he was barely 24 years old. His style of composition was influenced mainly by Franck; his most durable work, a Violin Sonata with modal inflections and chromatic progressions, closely follows the procedures of Franck's Violin Sonata. **Works:** String Quartet (1887); *Meditation* and *Minuet* for String Quartet (1887); Cello Sonata (1888; completed by d'Indy); *Adagio* for 2 Violins and Piano (1888); Piano Quartet (1888; completed by d'Indy); *Noël* for 2 Sopranos, String Quartet, and Piano (1888); *Barberine* (fragments of an opera, 1889); *Chant de triomphale délivrance* for Orch. (1889); *Hamlet* for Orch. (1890); *Fantaisie contrapunctique* for Orch. (1890); *Chant lyrique* for Chorus and Orch. (1891); *Adagio* for String Quartet and String Orch. (1981); Piano Trio (1891); Piano Sonata (1891); Violin Sonata (1892); *Fantaisie sur deux airs populaires angevins* for Orch. (1892); *Suite* for Voice and Orch. (1892); piano pieces; songs. **Bibl.:** A. Tissier, *G. L.* (Verviers, 1906); M. Lorrain, *G. L.: Sa correspondance, sa vie et son œuvre* (Liège, 1923); R. Stengel, *L.* (Brussels, 1944); P. Prist, *G. L.* (Brussels, 1946).

Lemacher, Heinrich, German composer, pedagogue, and writer on music; b. Solingen, June 26, 1891; d. Munich, March 15, 1966. He studied at the Cologne Cons.; in 1925, he became a teacher at the Cologne Hochschule für Musik; was a prof. there (1928–56). A disciple of the German Romantic school, he elaborated its principles in a number of choral and instrumental works; the chief influences are Bruckner and Reger; he wrote several symphonic suites; chamber music; piano pieces. More important than these are his compositions for the Catholic service: several masses, offertories, motets, cantatas with organ accompaniment, etc., in which he succeeded in establishing a practical style of modern polyphony. He publ. books on music theory: *Lehrbuch des Kontrapunktes* (Mainz, 1950; 4th ed., 1962); *Harmonielehre* (Cologne, 1958; 5th ed., 1967); *Formenlehre der Musik* (with H. Schroeder, Cologne, 1962; in Eng. as *Musical Form,* 1967). **Bibl.:** W. Hammerschlag and A. Schneider, *Musikalisches Brauchtum: Festschrift H. L.* (Cologne, 1956).

Lemaire (or **Le Maire**), **Jean,** French musician; b. Chaumont-en-Bassigny, Haute-Marne, c.1581; d. c.1650. He is said to have proposed the adoption of a 7th solmisation syllable *si* (so asserted by Rousseau in his *Dictionnaire de musique; za,* according to Mersenne's *Harmonie universalle*). However, the designation *si* seems to have been proposed even earlier, so the question of priority remains moot. Lemaire constructed a lute which he called the "Alméric" (anagram of Lemaire). **Bibl.:** A. Cohen, "J. Le Maire and La Musique Almérique," *Acta Musicologica* (1963); J. Knowlson, "J. Le Maire, the Almérie, and the 'Musique Almérique': A Set of Unpublished Documents," ibid. (1968).

Lemaire, Jean Eugène Gaston, French composer; b. Château d'Amblainvilliers, Seine-et-Oise, Sept. 9, 1854; d. (suicide; body found in the Seine) Paris, Jan. 9, 1928. He studied at the École Niedermeyer; was a prolific composer of light music. **Works:** *Pierrette et le pot au lait,* pantomime (Paris, Feb. 11, 1891); *Conte de printemps,* pantomime (Paris, May 18, 1892); *La Belle Tunisienne,* opera in 1 act (Paris, Aug. 26, 1892); operettas: *Les Maris de Juanita, Le Supplice de Jeannot, Le Rêve de Manette; Rose,* lyric fairy tale (Paris, March 14, 1895); ballets: *Feminissima* (1902) and *Pierrot venge son rival* (1917). He also wrote a number of fox-trots, one of which, *La Grenouille,* became popular; and songs, of which *Vous dansez, marquise,* was a great favorite.

Le Maistre (or **Le Maître**), **Mattheus,** Franco-Flemish composer; b. near Liège, c.1505; d. Dresden, April 1577. In 1554 he succeeded J. Walter as Kapellmeister at the court in Dresden; retired on a pension, Feb. 12, 1568. Fétis and Otto Kade wrongly identified him with Hermann Matthias Werrekoren, choirmaster in Milan. **Works:** *Magnificat octo tonorum* (1577); *Catechesis numeris musicis inclusa* (1563; for the choirboys of the Dresden

Chapel); *Geistliche und weltliche teutsche Gesänge* for 4–5 Voices (1566); motets for 5 Voices (1570); *Officia de nativitate et Ascensione Christi* for 5 Voices (1574); *Schöne und auserlesene teutsche und lateinische geistliche Lieder* (1577). A motet for 4 Voices, *Estote prudentes*, is in Commer's *Collectio* (vol. 8); 2 lieder for 4 Voices are in Ambros's *Geschichte der Musik* (vol. 5, *Beispielband*, ed. by O. Kade, 1882).

BIBL.: D. Gresch, *M.L. M., a Netherlander at the Dresden Court* (diss., Univ. of Michigan, 1970).

Lemare, Edwin (Henry), English-American organist and composer; b. Ventnor, Isle of Wight, Sept. 9, 1865; d. Los Angeles, Sept. 24, 1934. He received his early training from his father, an organist; then studied at the Royal Academy of Music in London; at the age of 17 he played at the Inventions Exhibition in London; in 1892 he began a series of weekly organ recitals at Holy Trinity Church in London; from 1897 to 1902 he was organist at St. Margaret's, Westminster. In 1900–1901 he made a concert tour through the U.S. and Canada; from 1902 to 1905 he was organist at the Carnegie Inst. in Pittsburgh; then held the post of municipal organist in San Francisco (1917–21), Portland, Maine (1921–23), and Chattanooga, Tenn. (1924–29). He wrote about 200 organ works, an Easter cantata, anthems, settings of sacred texts, and songs; his *Andantino* acquired wide popularity when it was used for the American ballad *Moonlight and Roses*; he also prepared innumerable transcriptions for the organ. His reminiscences appeared as *Organs I Have Met: The Autobiography of Edwin H. Lemare, 1866–1934, Together With Reminiscences by His Wife and Friends* (Los Angeles, 1956).

Lemeshev, Sergei (Yakovlevich), prominent Russian tenor; b. Knyazevo, near Tver, July 10, 1902; d. Moscow, June 26, 1977. In his youth he worked at a cobbler's shop in Petrograd; then went to Moscow, where he studied at the Cons. with Raysky, graduating in 1925. He made his operatic debut at Sverdlovsk in 1926; then was a member of the Kharbin Opera in Manchuria (1927–29) and at the Tiflis Opera (1929–31). In 1931 he joined the Bolshoi Theater in Moscow, and gradually created an enthusiastic following; he was particularly admired for his performance of the role of Lensky in *Eugene Onegin;* in 1972, on his 70th birthday, he sang it again at the Bolshoi Theater. Other roles in which he shone, apart from the Russian repertoire, included Faust, Romeo, and Werther. He also made numerous appearances in solo recitals; was the 1st to present an entire cycle of Tchaikovsky's songs in 5 concerts. His autobiography was publ. in Moscow in 1968.

BIBL.: M. Lvov, *S. L.* (Moscow, 1947); E. Grosheva, *S. L.* (Moscow, 1960).

Lemmens, Jacques Nicolas (Jaak Nikolaas), eminent Belgian organist, pedagogue, and composer; b. Zoerle-Parwijs, Antwerp, Jan. 3, 1823; d. Zemst, near Mechelen, Jan. 30, 1881. He was first trained in music by his father, an organist; then attended the Brussels Cons., where he studied piano, organ (with Christian Girschner), and composition (with Fétis); subsequently studied with Adolf Hesse in Breslau (1846–47). He became prof. of organ at the Brussels Cons. in 1849. In 1857 he married **Helen Lemmens-Sherrington.** His distinguished students included Guilmant and Widor. He publ. *École d'orgue basée sur le plainchant romain* (Brussels, 1862); his *Du chant grégorien, sa mélodie, son rhythme, son harmonisation* was publ. posth. (Ghent, 1884). A collection of his masses, motets, organ music, and other works appeared as *Œuvres inédites* (4 vols., Leipzig, 1883–87).

Lemmens-Sherrington (originally, **Sherrington**), **Helen,** noted English soprano; b. Preston, Oct. 4, 1834; d. Brussels, May 9, 1906. When she was 4 her family took her to Rotterdam, where she had vocal training with Verhulst; then entered the Brussels Cons. (1852). She made her London debut as a concert singer (April 7, 1856); later sang with the English Opera (1860–65) and at Covent Garden (1866), where she appeared as Donna Elvira, Adalgisa, Isabella in *Robert le Diable*, and Elisabeth de Valois; however, it was as a concert and oratorio singer

that she gained her greatest distinction. She married **Jacques Nicolas (Jaak Nikolaas) Lemmens** in 1857. After his death, she made her home in Brussels; continued to make appearances as a singer until 1894, but devoted herself mainly to teaching at the Brussels Cons.; also taught at the Royal Manchester College of Music (1893–97).

Lemnitz, Tiana (Luise), remarkable German soprano; b. Metz, Oct. 26, 1897. She studied with Hoch in Metz and Kohmann in Frankfurt; made her debut in Lortzing's *Undine* in Heilbronn (1920), then sang in Aachen (1922–28). She subsequently pursued a distinguished career as a member of the Hannover Opera (1928–33), the Dresden State Opera (1933–34), and the Berlin State Opera (1934–57). She also made guest appearances in Vienna, Munich, London's Covent Garden (1936, 1938), and Buenos Aires's Teatro Colón (1936, 1950). Her repertoire included many leading roles in German, Italian, French, and Russian operas.

Lemoine, Antoine-Marcel, French violist, conductor, and music publisher, father of **Henry Lemoine;** b. Paris, Nov. 3, 1753; d. there, April 10, 1816. A self-taught musician, he played viola at the Théâtre de Monsieur, conducted at minor Parisian theaters, and finally founded a music publishing firm.

Lemoine, Henry, French music publisher and composer, son of **Antoine-Marcel Lemoine;** b. Paris, Oct. 21, 1786; d. there, May 18, 1854. He studied at the Paris Cons. (1798–1809); in 1821 he also had harmony lessons from Reicha; taught piano; at his father's death, succeeded to the latter's music publishing business. He publ. methods for harmony, piano, and solfeggio; *Tablettes du pianiste: Memento du professeur de piano;* sonatas, variations, dances, etc., for piano.

Lemont, Cedric Wilmont, Canadian-American organist and composer; b. Fredericton, New Brunswick, Dec. 15, 1879; d. N.Y., April 27, 1954. He studied with Carl Faelten (piano) and Dunham (organ) in Boston; filled various positions as organist and choirmaster in Canada; in 1907, settled in the U.S.; taught in Chicago and N.Y. He publ. over 600 compositions, including piano pieces, anthems, etc.; also publ. 3 vols. of the *American History and Encyclopedia of Music.*

Lemoyne, Jean-Baptiste, French conductor and composer; b. Eymet, Périgord, April 3, 1751; d. Paris, Dec. 30, 1796. He studied with J. G. Graun, Kirnberger, and J. A. P. Schulz at Berlin; also held a minor post in the service of the Prussian Crown Prince; then went to Waraw, where he brought out his opera *Le Bouquet de Colette* (1775). Returning to Paris, he brought out an opera, *Électre* (July 2, 1782), pretending to be a pupil of Gluck, an imposture that Gluck did not see fit to expose until the failure of Lemoyne's piece. In his next operas, Lemoyne abandoned Gluck's ideas, copied the style of Piccinni and Sacchini, and produced several successful works, including *Phèdre* (Fontainebleau, Oct. 26, 1786), *Les Prétendus* (Paris, June 2, 1789), and *Nephté* (Paris, Dec. 15, 1789). His son, **Gabriel Lemoyne** (b. Berlin, Oct, 14, 1772; d. Paris, July 2, 1815), was a pianist and composer; studied piano with C.-F. Clément and J.F. Edelmann. He wrote 3 opéras comiques, 2 piano concertos, chamber music, vocal romances, and piano pieces.

Lenaerts, René Bernard (Maria), distinguished Belgian musicologist; b. Bornem, Oct. 26, 1902. He studied at the Mechelen theological seminary and at the Lemmens Inst., being ordained a priest (1927); continued his education at the Univ. of Louvain (Ph.D., 1929, with the diss. *Het Nederlands polifonies lied in de zestiende eeuw;* publ. in Mechelen and Amsterdam, 1933); after additional studies with Pirro in Paris (1931–32), he taught in secondary schools in Geel and Antwerp; then was a junior lecturer (1944–46), lecturer (1946–49), and full prof. (1949–73) in musicology at the Catholic Univ. of Louvain; was also a reader in Renaissance music history at the Univ. of Utrecht (1958–71); was made ed. of *Monumenta Musicae Belgicae* (1959); became a canon (1955). He publ. *Oude Nederlandse muziek* (Brussels, 1937), *Johann Sebastian Bach* (Diest, 1943), *Belangrijke verzamelingen Neder-*

landse muziek uit de zestiende eeuw in Spanje (Brussels, 1957), and *De Nederlandse muziek uit de vijftiende eeuw* (Louvain, 1959).

BIBL.: J. Robijns, ed., *Renaissance-Muziek 1400–1600: Donum natalicium R.B. L.* (Louvain, 1969).

Lendvai, Ernő, Hungarian musicologist; b. Kaposvár, Feb. 6, 1925. He studied at the Budapest Academy of Music (1945–49); was made director of the Szombathely Music School (1949) and the Győr Cons. (1954); was also prof. at the Szeged Cons. (from 1957) and a teacher at the Budapest Academy of Music (1954–56; from 1973). He distinguished himself as a writer on the life and works of Bartók.

WRITINGS: *Bartók stilusa* (Bartók's Style; Budapest, 1955); *Bartók's Dramaturgy: Stage Works and Cantata Profana* (Budapest, 1964); *Toscanini és Beethoven* (Budapest, 1967; in Eng. in *Studia musicologica Academiae scientiarum hungaricae,* VIII, 1966); *Bartók költoi vilaga* (The Poetic World of Bartók; Budapest, 1971); *Béla Bartók: An Analysis of His Music* (London, 1971); *Bartók és Kodály harmóniavilága* (The Harmonic World of Bartók and Kodály; Budapest, 1975); *The Workshop of Bartók and Kodály* (Budapest, 1983); *Verdi és a 20. szazad: A Falstaffhangzás-dramaturgiája* (Budapest, 1984).

Lendvai, Erwin, Hungarian conductor and composer; b. Budapest, June 4, 1882; d. Epsom, Surrey, March 31, 1949. He studied with Koessler in Budapest; later went to Milan, where he had some lessons with Puccini; taught at Jaques Dalcroze's School of Eurhythmics (1913–14); then was an instructor of dramatic composition at the Hoch Cons. in Frankfurt (1914–19); later at the Klindworth-Scharwenka Cons. in Berlin (1919–22); was a teacher at the Hamburg Volksmusikschule (1923–25); a choral conductor in Koblenz (1926–27), then in Munich and in Erfurt; in 1938 he went to Switzerland, and later to London. He composed a Sym. (1909); *Archaische Tänze* for Small Orch.; *Masken,* orch. scherzo; *Nippon,* choral suite for Women's Voices; String Quartet; several piano trios and other chamber music; an opera, *Elga* (Mannheim, Dec. 6, 1916). He publ. a method, *Chorschule.*

BIBL.: H. Leichtentritt, *E. L.* (Berlin, 1912).

Lendvay, Kamilló, Hungarian conductor and composer; b. Budapest, Dec. 28, 1928. He studied composition with Viski at the Budapest Academy of Music (graduated, 1959). He conducted at the Szeged Opera (1956–57), then was music director of the Budapest State Puppet Theater (1960–66) and the Army Art Ensemble (1966–68); subsequently was conductor (1970–72) and music director (1972–74) of the Budapest Operetta Theater. He was a prof. at the Budapest Academy of Music (from 1973); was head of its music theory dept. (from 1978).

WORKS: OPERAS: *The Magic Chair* (Hungarian Television, 1972); *The Respectful Prostitute* (1976–78; Hungarian Television, 1979). **ORCH.:** *Concertino* for Piano, Wind Instruments, Percussion, and Harp (1959); 2 violin concertos (1962, 1986); *4 Invocations* (1965); *Concerto da camera* for 13 Players (1969); *Expressions* for 11 Strings or String Orch. (1974); *Pezzo concertato* for Cello and Orch. (1975); *The Harmony of Silence* (1980); *Festspiel Ouverture* for Wind Band (1984); *Concertino semplice* for Cimbalom and String Orch. (1986). **VOCAL:** *Orogenesis,* oratorio (1969–70); *Ride at Night,* song cycle for Contralto and 7 Performers (1970); *Scenes,* cantata for Soprano, Bass-baritone, and Orch., after Thomas Mann's tetralogy *Joseph and His Brothers* (1978–81). **CHAMBER:** *Disposizioni* for Cimbalom (1975); *5th Music* for Cello (1978–79); *5 Arrogant Ideas* for Brass Sextet (1979); *5 Movements in Quotation Marks* for Horn, Trombone, and Tuba (1980); *As You Like It* for 2 Pianos (1982–83); *24 Duos* for 2 Violins (1985); *8 More Arrogant Ideas* for Brass Quintet (1986).

Lenepveu, Charles (Ferdinand), French composer and pedagogue; b. Rouen, Oct. 4, 1840; d. Paris, Aug. 16, 1910. While a law student, he took music lessons from Servais; won 1st prize at Caen in 1861 for a cantata; entered Ambroise Thomas's class at the Paris Cons. in 1863, and in 1865 took the Grand Prix de Rome with the cantata *Renaud dans les*

jardins d'Armide (Paris, Jan. 3, 1866). His comic opera *Le Florentin* also won a prize, offered by the Ministry of Fine Arts (1867), and was performed at the Opéra-Comique (Feb. 26, 1874). The grand opera *Velléda* was produced at Covent Garden in London (July 4, 1882), with Adelina Patti in the title role. In 1891 Lenepveu succeeded Guiraud as prof. of harmony at the Cons., and in 1893 again succeeded him as prof. of composition, taking an advanced class in 1894. In 1896 he was elected to Ambroise Thomas's chair in the Académie des Beaux-Arts; was a Chevalier of the Legion of Honor, and an Officer of Public Instruction.

BIBL.: R. de Saint-Arroman, *C. L.* (Paris, 1898).

Léner, Jenö, Hungarian violinist; b. Szabadka, April 7, 1894; d. N.Y., Nov. 4, 1948. He studied at the Royal Academy of Music in Budapest; worked as a violinist in theater orchs.; in 1918, organized the Léner String Quartet (with Joseph Smilovits, Sándor Roth, and Imre Hartmann), which appeared regularly in London (1922–39). It became one of the most renowned string quartets of modern times, being particularly noted for its performances of Beethoven's quartets. It made its U.S. debut in 1929; it was disbanded in 1942, but reorganized, with a partly new membership, in 1945. The fame enjoyed by the Léner quartet can be judged by Aldous Huxley's discussion of its performance of Beethoven's last quartets in his novel *Point Counterpoint* (1928).

BIBL.: A. Molnár, *The L. Quartet* (Budapest, 1969).

Leng, Alfonso, Chilean composer; b. Santiago, Feb. 11, 1884; d. there, Nov. 7, 1974. He was of mixed German and English descent; studied dentistry, and became a professional dentist in Santiago; also took music lessons with Enrique Soro at the Santiago Cons. (1905–6). In his leisure time, he composed short symphonic sketches in a Romantic vein, songs, and evocative piano pieces.

WORKS: *5 dolores* for Orch. (1920); *La muerte de Alsino,* symphonic poem (1920; Santiago, May 30, 1931); *Canto de Invierno* for Orch. (1932); *Fantasia* for Piano and Orch. (Santiago, Aug. 28, 1936); *Psalm 77* for Soloists, Chorus, and Orch. (1941); *Fantasia quasi Sonata* for Piano (1909); *10 Preludes* for Piano (1919–32); *Andante* for Piano and String Quartet (1922); *2 Otoñales* for Piano (1932); 2 piano sonatas (1927, 1950); many songs.

BIBL.: Special issue of the *Revista Musical Chilena* (Aug./Sept. 1957).

Lennon, John (Winston), English rock singer, guitarist, poet, and songwriter, member of the celebrated group The Beatles; b. Liverpool, Oct. 9, 1940, during a German air raid on the city; d. N.Y., Dec. 8, 1980, gunned down by a wacko in front of his apartment building. He was educated by an aunt after his parents separated; played the mouth organ as a child; later learned the guitar; was encouraged to become a musician by the conductor of a Liverpool-Edinburgh bus. Emotionally rocked over by Elvis Presley's animal magnetism, he became infatuated with American popular music; formed his 1st pop group, the Quarry Men, in 1957. He was soon joined by 3 other rock-crazed Liverpudlians, **Paul McCartney, George Harrison,** and Stuart Sutcliffe, in a group he first dubbed the Silver Beatles, later to become simply The Beatles. (Inspired by the success of a local group, The Crickets, Lennon hit upon the name The Beatles, which possessed the acoustical ring of the coleopterous insect *beetle* and the rock-associated *beat.*) The Beatles opened at the pseudo-exotic Casbah Club in Liverpool in 1959; soon moved to the more prestigious Cavern Club (1961), where they co-opted Pete Best as drummer. In 1960 they played in Hamburg, scoring a gratifyingly vulgar success with the beer-sodden customers by their loud, electrically amplified sound. Back in England, The Beatles crept on to fame. In 1961 they were taken up by the perspicacious promoter Brian Epstein, who launched an extensive publicity campaign to put them over the footlights. Sutcliffe died of a brain hemorrhage in 1962. Best left the group and was replaced by Richard Starkey, whose "nom-de-beatle" became **Ringo Starr.** The quartet opened at the London Palladium in 1963 and drove the youthful audience to a frenzy, a scene that was to be repeated elsewhere in Europe, in America, in Japan, and in Australia. After a period of shocked recoil, the British establishment acknowledged the beneficial contribution of The Beatles to British art and the Exchequer. In 1965 each Beatle was made a Member of the Order of the British Empire. Although American in origin, the type of popular music plied by Lennon and The Beatles as a group had an indefinably British lilt. The meter was square; the main beat was accentuated; syncopation was at a minimum; the harmony was modal, with a lowered submediant in major keys as a constantly present feature; a propensity for plagal cadences and a proclivity for consecutive triadic progressions created at times a curiously hymnal mood. But professional arrangers employed by The Beatles invested their bland melodies in raucous dissonance; electronic amplification made the music of The Beatles the loudest in the world for their time. The lyrics, most of them written by Lennon and McCartney, were distinguished by suggestive allusions, sensuous but not flagrantly erotic, anarchistic but not destructive, cynical but also humane. There were covert references to psychedelic drugs. The Beatles produced the highly original films *A Hard Day's Night, Help!, Yellow Submarine,* and *Let It Be.* The most successful individual songs in The Beatles' repertoire were *Love Me Do, I Want to Hold Your Hand, Can't Buy Me Love, Ticket to Ride, Day Tripper, All My Loving, I Wanna Be Your Man, And I Love Her, 8 Days a Week, Yesterday, Michelle, Eleanor Rigby, With a Little Help from My Friends, Sergeant Pepper's Lonely Hearts Club Band, Magical Mystery Tour, Lady Madonna, You're Gonna Lose That Girl, Norwegian Wood, Good Day Sunshine, Hey Jude;* also title songs of the films. The Beatles were legally dissolved in 1970. By then Lennon's career had taken a new turn as a result of his relationship with the Japanese-American avant-garde film producer and artist **Yoko Ono;** through her, Lennon's social consciousness was raised, and he subsequently became an outspoken activist for peace. They appeared nude on the cover of their album *2 Virgins* and celebrated their honeymoon with a "bed-in" for peace. Lennon withdrew from public life in 1975. He and Ono brought out the album *Imagine* (1971), which contained what would become his best-known song of the period, *Imagine;* they also collaborated on his last album, *Double Fantasy* (1980), which achieved great popularity. The shock waves produced by Lennon's senseless murder reverberated throughout the world; crowds in deep mourning marched in N.Y., Liverpool, and Tokyo; Ono issued a number of declarations urging Lennon's fans not to give way to despair. Not even the death of Elvis Presley generated such outbursts of grief. A photograph taken on the afternoon before his murder, of John in the nude, embracing a fully dressed Ono, was featured on the cover of a special issue of *Rolling Stone* magazine (Jan. 22, 1981). His life was the subject of a touching documentary film, *Imagine,* in 1988.

BIBL.: H. Davies, *The Beatles* (N.Y., 1968); N. Rorem, "The Beatles," *N.Y. Review of Books* (Jan. 18, 1968); E. Davies, "The Psychological Characteristics of Beatle Mania," *Journal of the History of Ideas* (April–June 1969); P. McCabe and R. Schonfeld, *Apple to the Core: The Unmaking of the Beatles* (N.Y., 1972); W. Mellers, *Twilight of the Gods: The Music of the Beatles* (N.Y., 1973); T. O'Grady, *The Beatles: A Musical Evolution* (Boston, 1983); R. Coleman, *L.* (N.Y., 1984); J. Wiener, *Come Together: J. L. in His Time* (N.Y., 1984); A. Goldman, *The Lives of J. L.* (N.Y., 1988); E. Thomson and D. Gutman, eds., *The L. Companion: Twenty Five Years of Comment* (N.Y., 1988).

Lennox, Annie, Scottish pop vocalist; b. Aberdeen, Dec. 25, 1954. With **David (Allan) Stewart** (b. Sunderland, England, Sept. 9, 1952), she formed the pop duo Eurhythmics; their recording debut came with *In the Garden* (1981), which met with mixed critical success. Their 1st hit album was *Sweet Dreams (Are Made of This)* (1982), which includes the song *Love Is a Stranger;* later albums featured *Who's That Girl, Here Comes the Rain Again (Touch,* 1983), and the explosively

satiric *I Need a Man (Savage,* 1987). They made a sound track for the movie *1984* that was not used but was released as an album that included the song *Sexcrime.* Stewart's cool, sometimes bloodless accompaniments were usually performed on keyboards and guitars, sometimes via computer, while the striking androgynous looks of Lennox and her intense voice made impressive experimental videos. Their work is imbued with a sharp-edged tension supported by intensely ironic and often bitter lyrics. Other successful albums include *Be Yourself Tonight* (1985), *Revenge* (1986), and *We Too Are One* (1989).

Lenormand, René, French composer; b. Elbeuf, Aug. 5, 1846; d. Paris, Dec. 3, 1932. He received his musical training from his mother, who was an excellent pianist; in 1868 he went to Paris, where he studied with Damcke. Lenormand's main interest was in the creation of an international type of the German lied, and for that purpose he organized in Paris a society which he called Le Lied en Tous Pays. Besides his songs, he wrote an opera, *Le Cachet rouge* (Le Havre, 1925); Piano Concerto; *Le Lahn de Mabed* (on an old Arabian theme) for Violin and Orch.; *Le Voyage imaginaire,* symphonic tableaux after Loti; *2 esquisses sur des thèmes malais* for Orch.; piano pieces (*Une Journée à la campagne, Le Nuage vivant, Valses sérieuses, Pièces exotiques,* etc.); for 4-hands: *Divertissement américain, La Nouba Medjenneba,* etc.); also publ. a valuable manual on harmony, *Étude sur l'harmonie moderne* (Paris, 1912; Eng. tr. as *A Study of Modern Harmony,* London, 1915).

BIBL.: H. Woollett, *Un Mélodiste français: R. L.* (Paris, 1930).

Lentz, Daniel (Kirkland), American composer; b. Latrobe, Pa., March 10, 1941. He studied music and philosophy at St. Vincent College (B.A., 1962), music history and composition at Ohio State Univ. (M.A., 1965), and composition with Arthur Berger, Alvin Lucier, and Harold Shapero at Brandeis Univ. (1965–67) and with Roger Sessions and George Rochberg at the Berkshire Music Center at Tanglewood (1966). He went to Stockholm on a Fulbright grant to study electronic music and musicology (1967–68); then was a visiting lecturer at the Univ. of Calif. at Santa Barbara (1968–70) and at Antioch College in Yellow Springs, Ohio (1973). He formed the performing groups California Time Machine (1969–73) and San Andreas Fault (1974, 1976); later was active with the Los Angeles–based ensemble LENTZ (from 1982), featuring the agile vocalist Jessica Lowe (actually Lynn Mary Karraker; b. St. Louis, Mo., Sept. 4, 1953; conceived and born in the St. Louis City Hospital), other vocalists, multiple keyboardists, and occasional percussion. He held grants from various organizations, including the N.E.A. (1973, 1975, 1977, 1979) and the Deutscher Akademischer Austauschdienst in Berlin (1979). Lentz is a proponent of the avant-garde; one of his most interesting early works was *Love and Conception* (1968–69), in which 2 young people, a male pianist and his female page-turner, are ultimately directed to crawl under the lid of a grand piano and engage in sexual intercourse. Their performance, which is at first accompanied by 2 tandem AM radio broadcasts of fictional reviews of the piece, is finally replaced by a live, synchronous FM broadcast of the piece itself, which frees them to waltz about the stage, fall into each other's arms, and, overcome with passion, fall into the piano. (It might be mentioned that in all realizations of this piece to date, the final act of intercourse has only been simulated.) It was performed at the Univ. of Calif. at Santa Barbara on Feb. 26, 1969; as a result of this and later performances, Lentz was dismissed from his lectureship position there. He thereafter abandoned full-time teaching and devoted himself to composing, with increasing reliance on computer and synthesizer technologies. Many of his works, such as the orchestral *An American in L.A.* (1989), are pure sensuality, with less attention given by Lentz to formal procedures than to rhythmic vibrancy and sonorous effect. His text settings can challenge the ear; frequently phonemes are introduced in the beginning of a piece, which, through a gradual interlocking of parts, form audible words (and occasional truncated sentences) only at the very finish. While retaining its freshness and, at times, almost exquisite beauty, Lentz's music throughout the 1980s has been heavily equipment-reliant, demanding much not only from the vocalists and instrumentalists in his ensemble, but from Lentz himself, who must function as composer, producer, editor, sound mixer, and recording engineer during live performances. Much of his work dating from 1989 has been for acoustic media.

WORKS: THEATER AND MIXED MEDIA: *A Piano: Piece* (1965); *Ecumenical Council* (1965); *Gospel Meeting* (1965); *Paul and Judy Meet the Time Tunnel* (1966); *Paul and Judy Meet Startrek* (1966); *Hi-yo Paint* (1968); *Air Meal Spatial Delivery* (1969); *Work of Crow* (1970). **PERFORMERS AND ECHO DELAY:** *Canon and Fugue (Canon and Fugle)* (1971); *King Speech Songs* (1972); *You Can't See the Forest . . . Music* (1972); *Missa umbrarum* (1973); *Song(s) of the Sirens (Les Sirènes)* (1973); *3 Pretty Madrigals* (1976); *Dancing on the Sun* (1980); *Music by Candlelight (Love and Death)* (1980); *Uitoto* (1980). **PERFORMERS WITH MULTI-TRACKING:** *Is It Love* (Santa Barbara, Calif., Aug. 1984); *On the Leopard Altar* (1983; Santa Barbara, Calif., 1984); *Time Is a Trick* (Rouen, Dec. 1985); *Bacchus with Wineglasses* (Los Angeles, Nov. 1985); *Wild Turkeys* for 3 Keyboard Synthesizers (N.Y., Dec. 1985); *La Tache* with Wineglasses (Boston, June 5, 1987); *Night Breaker* for 4 Pianos (Los Angeles, March 30, 1990). **VOCAL:** *I*, a Double Concerto *(Senescence sonorum)* for Amplified Body Sounds, Chorus, and Orch. (1970); *Fermentation Notebooks: 1, Kissing Song; 2, Rising Song; 3, Drinking Song* for 28 to 48 Unaccompanied Voices, with Wineglasses in No. 3 (1972); *O-Ke-Wa (North American Eclipse)* for 12 Solo Voices, Bells, Rasps, and Drums (1974); *Sun Tropes* for 7 Solo Voices, Recorders, and Kalimbas (1975); *Composition in Contrary and Parallel Motion* for 16 Solo Voices, Percussion, and 4 Keyboards (1977); *The Elysian Nymph* for 8 Solo Voices and 8 Marimbas (1978); *Wolf Is Dead* for Solo Voices and Percussion (1979; rev. for 6 Solo Voices and 8 Keyboards, 1982); *Wail Song* for Vocal Soloist, 5 Voices, and 8 Keyboards (1983); *Wolf Mass* for Vocalist, Keyboards, and Percussion (1988). **INSTRUMENTAL:** *Piano Piece for Little Kids with Big Hands* (1962); *3 Episodes from Exodus* for Organ and Percussion (1962); *3 Haiku in 4 Movements* for String Quartet (1963); *8 Dialectics 8* for 18 Instruments (1964); *Fünke* for Flute, Vibraphone, Drums, Double Bass, and Piano (1964); *Sermon: Saying Something with Music* for String Quartet and Electronics (1966); *The Last Concert, in 3: Love and Conception, Birth and Death, Fate and Death* for Piano and Electronics (1968); *Pastime* for String Instruments and Electronics (1969); *10 Minus 30 Minutes* for String Orch. (1970); *Point Conception* for 9 Pianos (1981); *Lascaux (Chumash Tombs)* for Wineglasses (1984); *Topanga Tango* for Chamber Ensemble (Pittsburgh, Oct. 1985); *A Crack in the Bell* for Vocal Soloist, 3 Keyboards, and Optional Chamber Orch. (Los Angeles, Nov. 10, 1986); *An American in L.A.* for Orch. and Synthesizer (Los Angeles, March 30, 1989); *A California Family (Group Portrait)*, trio for Violin, Piano, and Percussion (N.Y., Nov. 1989); *Apache Wine* for Chamber Orch. (1989; Tucson, Feb. 16, 1990). **TAPE:** *Montage Shift* (1963); *No Exit* (1963); *Eleison* (1965); *Medeighnia's* (1965).

Lenya, Lotte (real name, **Karoline Wilhelmine Blamauer**), Austrian-American singer and actress; b. Vienna, Oct. 18, 1898; d. N.Y., Nov. 27, 1981. She began her stage career as a dancer in Zürich, where she went at the outbreak of World War I in 1914; in 1920 she went to Berlin. There she met **Kurt Weill,** whom she married in 1926; in 1927 she made her debut as a singer in the Brecht-Weill scenic cantata *Mahagonny* in Baden-Baden; in 1928 she created the role of Jenny in the premiere of the Brecht-Weill *Die Dreigroschenoper* in Berlin; from then on she identified herself with practically all of Weill's musicals. She and Weill fled Nazified Berlin in 1933, and after a couple of years in Paris and London, went to America. Although not a singer of a professional caliber, Lenya adapted herself to the peculiar type of half-spoken, half-sung roles in Weill's works with total dedication. She created the roles of Miriam in his *The Eternal Road* (N.Y., 1937) and the Duchess in his *The Firebrand of Florence* (N.Y., 1945). After his death

in 1950, she devoted herself to reviving his works for the American stage.

BIBL.: H. Marx, ed., *Weill-L.* (N.Y., 1976).

Lenz, Wilhelm von, Russian government official and writer on music of German descent; b. Riga, June 1, 1809; d. St. Petersburg, Jan. 31, 1883. He studied in Riga; then with Liszt in Paris (1828) and Moscheles in London (1829); became a government councillor in St. Petersburg (1842). Although Fétis first suggested the division of Beethoven's output into 3 stylistic periods, it was Lenz who fully explored the idea in his study *Beethoven et ses trois styles: Analyses des sonates de piano suivies de l'essai d'un catalogue critique chronologique et anecdotique de l'œuvre de Beethoven* (2 vols., St. Petersburg, 1852; 3rd ed., 1855; new ed. by M.D. Calvocoressi, Paris, 1909). This arbitrary division held sway for many decades until it was tempered by modern critical analysis. He also wrote *Beethoven: Eine Kunststudie*, I–II (Kassel, 1855); III/1–2, IV–V: *Kritische Katalog sämtlicher Werke Ludwig van Beethovens mit Analysen derselben* (Hamburg, 1860; ed. by A. Kalischer, Berlin, 1908; 3rd ed., 1921); *Die grossen Pianoforte-Virtuosen unserer Zeit aus persönlicher Bekanntschaft: Liszt, Chopin, Tausig, Henselt* (Berlin, 1872; Eng. tr., N.Y., 1899).

Leo, Leonardo (actually, **Lionardo Ortensio Salvatore de**), important Italian composer; b. San Vito degli Schiavi, near Brindisi, Aug. 5, 1694; d. Naples, Oct. 31, 1744. In 1709 he went to Naples, where he studied with Fago at the Conservatorio S. Maria della Pietà dei Turchini; his sacred drama *S. Chiara, o L'infedeltà abbattuta* was given there in 1712. In 1713 he was made supernumerary organist in the Viceroy's Chapel; also served as maestro di cappella to the Marchese Stella. His 1st opera, *Il Pisistrato,* was performed in Naples on May 13, 1714. His 1st comic opera, *La 'mpeca scoperta,* in the Neapolitan dialect, was given in Naples on Dec. 13, 1723. In all, he wrote some 50 operas, most of them for Naples. Following Alessandro Scarlatti's death in 1725, he was elevated to the position of 1st organist at the viceregal chapel. In 1730 he became provicemaestro of the Royal Chapel; in 1737 vicemaestro. He taught as vicemaestro at the Conservatorio S. Maria della Pietà dei Turchini from 1734 to 1737; from 1741 was primo maestro in succession to his teacher, Fago; also was primo maestro at the Conservatorio S. Onofrio from 1739. In Jan. 1744 he became maestro di cappella of the Royal Chapel, but died that same year. Among his famous pupils were Piccinni and Jommelli. Leo's music for the theater (especially his comic operas) is noteworthy; of no less significance were his theoretical works, *Istituzioni o regole del contrappunto* and *Lezione di canto fermo.*

WORKS: OPERAS (all premiered in Naples unless otherwise given): *Il Pisistrato* (May 13, 1714); *Sofonisba* (Jan. 22, 1718); *Caio Gracco* (April 19, 1720); *Arianna e Teseo* (Nov. 26, 1721); *Baiazete, imperator dei Turchi* (Aug. 28, 1722); *Timocrate* (Venice, 1723); *La 'mpeca scoperta,* comic opera (Dec. 13, 1723); *Il Turno Aricino* (with L. Vinci; 1724); *L'amore fedele,* comic opera (April 25, 1724); *Lo pazzo apposta,* comic opera (Aug. 26, 1724); *Zenobia in Palmira* (May 13, 1725); *Il trionfo di Camilla, regina dei Volsci* (Rome, Jan. 8, 1726); *Orismene, ovvero Dalli sdegni l'amore,* comic opera (Jan. 19, 1726); *La semmeglianza de chi l'ha fatta,* comic opera (Fall 1726); *Lo matrimonio annascuso,* comic opera (1727); *Il Cid* (Rome, Feb. 10, 1727); *La pastorella commattuta,* comic opera (Fall 1727); *Argene* (Venice, Jan. 17, 1728); *Catone in Utica* (Venice, 1729); *La schiava per amore,* comic opera (1729); *Semiramide* (Feb. 2, 1730); *Rosmene,* comic opera (Summer 1730); *Evergete* (Rome, 1731); *Demetrio* (Oct. 1, 1732); *Amor da' senno,* comic opera (1733); *Nitocri, regina d'Egitto* (Nov. 4, 1733); *Il castello d'Atlante* (July 4, 1734); *Demofoonte* (Jan. 20, 1735; Act 1 by D. Sarro, Act 2 by F. Mancini, Act 3 by Leo, and intermezzos by G. Sellitti); *La clemenza di Tito* (Venice, 1735); *Emira* (July 12, 1735; intermezzos by I. Prota); *Demetrio* (Dec. 10, 1735; different setting from earlier opera of 1732); *Onore vince amore,* comic opera (1736); *Farnace* (Dec. 19, 1736); *L'amico traditore,* comic opera (1737); *Siface* (Bologna, May 11, 1737; rev. version as *Viriate*, Pistoia, 1740); *La simpatia del sangue*, comic opera (Fall 1737); *Olimpiade* (Dec. 19, 1737); *Il conte*, comic opera (1738); *Il Ciro riconosciuto* (Turin, 1739); *Amor vuol sofferenze*, comic opera (Fall 1739; rev. version as *La finta frascatana*, Nov. 1744); *Achille in Sciro* (Turin, 1740); *Scipione nelle Spagne* (Milan, 1740); *L'Alidoro*, comic opera (Summer 1740); *Demetrio* (Dec. 19, 1741; different setting from the earlier operas of 1732 and 1735); *L'ambizione delusa*, comic opera (1742); *Andromaca* (Nov. 4, 1742); *Il fantastico, od Il nuovo Chisciotte*, comic opera (1743; rev. version, Fall 1748); *Vologeso, re dei Parti* (Turin, 1744); *La fedeltà odiata*, comic opera (1744); he also contributed to a pasticcio setting of *Demetrio* (June 30, 1738); he likewise composed prologues, arias, etc., to operas by other composers. A number of operas long attributed to Leo are now considered doubtful.

Leo also composed serenatas, feste teatrali, chamber cantatas, etc. He wrote the following sacred dramas and oratorios: *S. Chiara, o L'infedeltà abbattuta* (Naples, 1712); *Il trionfo della castità di S. Alessio* (Naples, Jan. 4, 1713); *Dalla morte alla vita di S. Maria Maddalena* (Atrani, July 22, 1722); *Oratorio per la Ss. vergine del rosario* (Naples, Oct. 1, 1730); *S. Elena al Calvario* (Bologna, 1734); *La morte di Abele* (Bologna, 1738); *S. Francesco di Paola nel deserto* (Lecce, 1738); *Il verbo eterno e la religione* (Florence, 1741); he also composed 6 Neapolitan masses, various Mass movements, 2 Magnificats, offertories, antiphons, motets, etc.; most notable is his *Miserere* for Double Choir and Organ (1739), publ. in a modern ed. by H. Wiley Hitchcock (St. Louis, 1961). His instrumental works include 6 concerti for Cello, String Orch., and Basso Continuo (1737–38); of these, 1 in D major has been ed. by F. Cilea (Milan, 1934), 1 in A major by E. Rapp (Mainz, 1938), and 3 in the Series of Early Music, VII (1973); he also wrote Concerto in D major for 4 Violins and Basso Continuo (publ. in *Musikschätze der Vergangenheit*, XXIV, Berlin, 1952); works for harpsichord; etc.

BIBL.: C. Leo, *L. L. e sua epoca musicale* (Brindisi, 1894); G. Leo, *L. L., musicista del secola XVIII e le sue opere musicali* (Naples, 1905); E. Dent, "L. L.," *Sammelbände der Internationalen Musik-Gesellschaft*, VIII (1906–7); F. Piovano, "À propos d'une récente biographie de L. L.," ibid.; K. Geiringer, "Eine Geburtstagskantate von P. Metastasio und L. L.," *Zeitschrift für Musikwissenschaft* (1927); E. Faustini-Fasini, "L. L. e la sua famiglia," *Note d'Archivio per la Storia Musicale*, XIV (1937); F. Walker, "Cav. Giacomo Leo and His Famous 'Ancestor,'" *Music Review* (Nov. 1948); F. Schlitzer, ed., *Tommaso Traetta, L. L., Vincenzo Bellini: Noti e documenti raccolti da F. Schlitzer* (Siena, 1952); G. Pastore, *L. L.* (Galatina, 1957); R. Krause, *Die Kirchenmusik von L. L. (1694–1744): Ein Beitrag zur Musikgeschichte Neapels im 18. Jahrhundert* (Regensburg, 1987).

León, Tania (Justina), Cuban-born American composer, conductor, pianist, and teacher; b. Havana, May 14, 1943. She studied in Havana at the Carlos Alfredo Peyrellade Cons. (B.A., 1963; M.A. in music education, 1964). She went in 1967 to the U.S., where she enrolled at N.Y. Univ. (M.S., 1973) and had conducting lessons with Laszlo Halasz and at the Berkshire Music Center at Tanglewood with Bernstein and Ozawa. In 1968 she joined the Dance Theatre of Harlem as its 1st music director, a position she held until 1980; also organized the Brooklyn Phil. Community Concert Series (1977). She was a guest conductor with several U.S. and European orchs., including the Genoa Sym. Orch., the BBC Sym. Orch., the Hallé Orch., the Brooklyn Phil., and the Metropolitan Opera Orch. Among her many awards were the Young Composer's Prize from the National Council of the Arts, Havana (1966), the Alvin John Award from the Council for Émigrés in the Professions (1971), and the Cintas Award (1974–75); she also was an N.E.A. Fellow (1975). In 1978 she was music director for Broadway's smash musical *The Wiz*, and in 1985 served as resident composer for the Lincoln Center Inst. in N.Y.; also joined the composition faculty of Brooklyn College; later was artistic director of the Composers' Forum in N.Y. Her composi-

tions are written in an accessible style, rhythmically vibrant, with some novel piano and percussion effects. Her *Kabiosile* for Piano and Orch. (1988) brings together the rich and disparate elements of her own cultural heritage, combining Afro-Cuban, Hispanic, and Latin jazz elements within a classical Western concerto format. Her ballet *Dougla* (with Geoffrey Holder; 1974) was heard in the Soviet Union during the Dance Theatre of Harlem's 1988 tour.

WORKS: STAGE: *Tones*, ballet (with Arthur Mitchell; 1970); *The Beloved*, ballet (1972); *Dougla*, ballet (with Geoffrey Holder; 1974); *Maggie Magalita*, theater piece (with Wendy Kesselman; 1980); *The Golden Windows*, theater piece (with Robert Wilson; 1982). **ORCH.:** *Concerto criollo* for Piano, 8 Timpani, and Orch. (1980); *Batá* (1985); *Kabiosile* (1988). **CHAMBER:** *Haiku* for Flute, Bassoon, and Percussion (1973); *Pet's Suite* for Flute and Piano (1980); *Ascend* for 4 Horns, 4 Trumpets, 3 Trombones, Tuba, and Percussion (1983); *A la par* for Piano and Percussion Duet (1986); *Parajota delaté* for Flute, Clarinet, Violin, Cello, and Piano (1988); also various works for solo instruments. **VOCAL:** *De-Orishas* for 2 Sopranos, Countertenor, 2 Tenors, and Bass (1982); *Pueblo mulato*, 3 songs on poems by Nicolás Guillén for Soprano, Oboe, Guitar, Double Bass, Percussion, and Piano (1987); *Heart of Ours—A Piece* for Men's Chorus, Flute, 4 Trumpets, and Percussion (1988); *Batéy* for 2 Sopranos, Countertenor, 2 Tenors, Bass, and Percussion (1989); *To and Fro* for Mezzo-soprano and Piano (1990); *Journey* for Soprano, Flute, and Harp (1990).

Léonard, Hubert, Belgian violinist, pedagogue, and composer; b. Bellaire, near Liège, April 7, 1819; d. Paris, May 6, 1890. He studied violin with Rouma in Liège, where he made his debut (March 13, 1832); then studied with Prume at the Brussels Cons. (1832), and later with Habeneck at the Paris Cons. (1836–39). He toured Europe (1845–48); was a teacher at the Brussels Cons. (1853–66); then was active in Paris. He was especially esteemed as a chamber music artist and as a teacher. He publ. *Petite gymnastique du jeune violiniste; 24 études classiques; Études harmoniques;* a method for violin, *École Léonard; L'Ancienne École italienne*, a collection of special studies in double stopping, including examples from Corelli, Tartini, Geminiani, and Nardini; *Le Violon au point de vue de l'orchestration;* also 5 violin concertos; 6 concert pieces, with Piano; Serenade for 3 Violins; Concert Duo for 2 Violins; fantasias and character pieces.

BIBL.: G. Weiss, ed., *Der Lehrer und Wegbereiter von Henri Marteau, H. L.* (Tutzing, 1987).

Leoncavallo, Ruggero, noted Italian composer; b. Naples, April 23, 1857; d. Montecatini, Aug. 9, 1919. He attended the Naples Cons. (1866–76), where his teachers were B. Cesi (piano) and M. Ruta and L. Rossi (composition), and at 16 made a pianistic tour. His 1st opera, *Tommaso Chatterton*, was about to be produced in Bologna (1878) when the manager disappeared, and the production was called off. Leoncavallo earned his living as a young man by playing piano in cafés; this life he continued for many years, traveling through Egypt, Greece, Turkey, Germany, Belgium, and the Netherlands before settling in Paris. There he found congenial company; composed chansonettes and other popular songs; wrote an opera, *Songe d'une nuit d'été* (after Shakespeare's *Midsummer Night's Dream*), which was privately sung in a salon. He began to study Wagner's scores, and became an ardent Wagnerian; he resolved to emulate the master by producing a trilogy, *Crepusculum*, depicting in epical traits the Italian Renaissance; the separate parts were to be *I Medici, Girolamo Savonarola*, and *Cesare Borgia*. He spent 6 years on the basic historical research; having completed the 1st part, and with the scenario of the entire trilogy sketched, he returned in 1887 to Italy, where the publisher Ricordi became interested in the project, but kept delaying the publication and production of the work. Annoyed, Leoncavallo turned to Sonzogno, the publisher of Mascagni, whose opera *Cavalleria rusticana* had just obtained a tremendous vogue. Leoncavallo submitted a short opera in a similarly realistic vein; he wrote his own libretto based on a factual story of passion and murder in a Calabrian village, and named it *Pagliacci*. The opera was given with sensational success at the Teatro dal Verme in Milan under the direction of Toscanini (May 21, 1892), and rapidly took possession of operatic stages throughout the world; it is often played on the same evening with Mascagni's opera, both works being of brief duration. Historically, these 2 operas signalized the important development of Italian operatic *verismo*, which influenced composers of other countries as well.

The enormous success of *Pagliacci* did not deter Leoncavallo from carrying on his more ambitious projects. The 1st part of his unfinished trilogy, *I Medici*, was finally brought out at the Teatro dal Verme in Milan on Nov. 9, 1893, but the reception was so indifferent that he turned to other subjects; the same fate befell his youthful *Tommaso Chatterton* at its production in Rome (March 10, 1896). His next opera, *La Bohème* (Venice, May 6, 1897), won considerable success, but had the ill fortune of coming a year after Puccini's masterpiece on the same story, and was dwarfed by comparison. There followed a light opera, *Zazà* (Milan, Nov. 10, 1900), which was fairly successful, and was produced repeatedly on world stages. In 1894 he was commissioned by the German Emperor Wilhelm II to write an opera for Berlin; this was *Der Roland von Berlin*, on a German historic theme; it was produced in Berlin on Dec. 13, 1904, but despite the high patronage it proved a fiasco. In 1906 Leoncavallo made a tour of the U.S. and Canada, conducting his *Pagliacci* and a new operetta, *La Jeunesse de Figaro*, specially written for his American tour; it was so unsuccessful that he never attempted to stage it in Europe. Back in Italy he resumed his industrious production; the opera *Maia* (Rome, Jan. 15, 1910) and the operetta *Malbrouck* (Rome, Jan. 19, 1910) were produced within the same week; another operetta, *La Reginetta delle rose*, was staged simultaneously in Rome and in Naples (June 24, 1912). In the autumn of that year, Leoncavallo visited London, where he presented the premiere of his *Gli Zingari* (Sept. 16, 1912); a year later, he revisited the U.S., conducting in San Francisco. He wrote several more operettas, but they made no impression; 3 of them were produced during his lifetime: *La Candidata* (Rome, Feb. 6, 1915), *Goffredo Mameli* (Genoa, April 27, 1916), and *Prestami tua moglie* (Montecatini, Sept. 2, 1916); posthumous premieres were accorded the operetta *A chi la giarettiera?* (Rome, Oct. 16, 1919), the opera *Edipo re* (Chicago, Dec. 13, 1920), and the operetta *Il primo bacio* (Montecatini, April 29, 1923). Another score, *Tormenta*, remained unfinished. Salvatore Allegra collected various sketches by Leoncavallo and arranged from them a 3-act operetta, *La maschera nuda*, which was produced in Naples on June 26, 1925.

BIBL.: C. Trevor, "R. L.," *Musical Monthly Record*, XLIX (1919); R. de Rensis, *Per Umberto Giordano e R. L.* (Siena, 1949); J. Klein, "R. L. (1858–1919)," *Opera*, IX (1958); M. Sansone, "The 'Verismo' of R. L.: A Source Study of 'Pagliacci,'" *Music & Letters* (Aug. 1989).

Leonhardt, Gustav (Maria), eminent Dutch organist, harpsichordist, conductor, and pedagogue; b. 's Graveland, May 30, 1928. He studied organ and harpsichord with Eduard Müller at the Schola Cantorum in Basel (1947–50), then made his debut as a harpsichordist in Vienna (1950); after studying musicology there, he served as prof. of harpsichord at the Academy of Music (1952–55); was prof. of harpsichord at the Amsterdam Cons. (from 1954); was also active as a church organist there. He made numerous tours of Europe and North America, mainly appearing as a harpsichordist; also led his own Leonhardt Consort on tours from 1955. He ed. Bach's *Die Kunst der Fuge*, pieces by Sweelinck, and other works.

Leoni, Franco, Italian composer; b. Milan, Oct. 24, 1864; d. London, Feb. 8, 1949. He studied at the Milan Cons. with Dominiceti and Ponchielli; in 1892, went to London, where he remained until 1917; then lived in France and Italy, eventually returning to England.

WORKS: OPERAS: *Raggio di luna* (Milan, June 5, 1890); *Rip van Winkle* (London, Sept. 4, 1897); *Ib and Little Christina,*

"a picture in 3 panels" (London, Nov. 14, 1901); *L'oracolo* (London, June 28, 1905); *Tzigana* (Genoa, Feb. 3, 1910); *Le baruffe chiozzotte* (Milan, Jan. 2, 1920); *La terra del sogno* (Milan, Jan. 10, 1920); *Falene* (Milan, 1920). **ORATORIOS:** *Sardanapalus* (London, 1891); *The Gate of Life* (London, 1891); *Golgotha* (London, 1909); songs.

Leoni, Leone, distinguished Italian composer; b. Verona, c.1560; d. Vicenza, June 24, 1627. He studied at the "academy" maintained by Count Mario Bevilacqua in Verona; was maestro di cappella in Vicenza from Oct. 4, 1588, until his death. He was a disciple of the Venetian school; his works are characteristic for their application of chromatic devices in harmony, and antiphonal choral usages. He wrote about 130 madrigals (41 not extant) and around 185 motets (about 40 not extant). He was an important composer of motets.

WORKS (all publ. in Venice): **SACRED:** *Penitenza: primo libro de* [21] *madrigali spirituali* for 5 Voices (1596); *Sacri fiori:* [20] *motetti* [and 1 Magnificat] for 2 to 4 Voices and Organ, *libro primo* (1606); [20] *Sacrarum cantionum liber primus* for 8 Voices and 2 Organs (1608); *Sacri fiori: secondo libro de* [31] *motetti* for 1 to 3 Voices and Organ . . . *con una messa* for 4 Voices (1612); *Omnium solemnitatum psalmodia* for 8 Voices (1613); *Aurea corona ingemmata d'armonici, concerto a 10* for 4 Voices and 6 Instruments (1615); *Sacri fiori: quarto libro de* [25] *motetti* for 1 to 4 Voices and Organ (1622). **SECULAR:** *Il primo libro de* [21] *madrigali* for 5 Voices (1588); *Bella Clori: secondo libro de* [22] *madrigali* for 5 Voices (1591); *Il terzo libro de* [21] *madrigali* for 5 Voices (1595); *Il quarto libro de* [20] *madrigali* (1598; not extant); *Bell'Alba: quinto libro de* [21] *madrigali* for 5 Voices (1602).

BIBL.: H. Wing, *The Polychoral Motets of L. L.* (diss., Boston Univ., 1966).

Leoninus (Magister Leoninus, Magister Leonini, Magister Leo, Magister Leonis), celebrated French composer and poet; b. Paris, c.1135; d. there, c.1201. He most likely received his initial education at the Notre Dame Cathedral schools in Paris; was active at the collegiate church of St. Benoît in Paris by the mid-1150s, eventually serving as a canon there for some 20 years. He was also a member of the clergy of Notre Dame by reason of his position at St. Benoît. He had earned the academic degree of master by 1179, probably in Paris; later became a canon at Notre Dame, where he was a priest by 1192; was also a member of the congregation of St. Victor by 1187. His great achievement was the creation of organa to augment the divine service; this has come down to us as the *Magnus liber organi de graduali et antiphonario pro servitio divino multiplicando*. It is also possible that he prepared many of the revisions and variant versions of the organi, preceding the work of revision by Pérotin. The original form of the work is not extant, but there are 3 extant later versions dating from the 13th and 14th centuries: Florence, Biblioteca Medicea-Laurenziana, MS Pluteus 29.1; Wolfenbüttel, Herzog August Bibliothek, Cod. Guelf. 628 Helmst.; Wolfenbüttel, Cod. Guelf. 1099 Helmst. As a poet, he wrote the extensive *Hystorie sacre gestas ab origine mundi*.

BIBL.: H. Tischler, "New Historical Aspects of the Parisian Organa," *Speculum*, XXV (1950); N. Smith, "Interrelationships among the Alleluias of the *Magnus liber organi*," *Journal of the American Musicological Society*, XXV (1972); E. Roesner, "The Problem of Chronology in the Transmission of Organum Duplum," in I. Fenlon, ed., *Music in Medieval and Early Modern Europe* (Cambridge, 1981); C. Wright, "Leoninus, Poet and Musician," *Journal of the American Musicological Society*, XXXIX (1986).

Leonova, Darya (Mikhailovna), Russian contralto; b. Vyshny-Volochok, March 9, 1829; d. St. Petersburg, Feb. 6, 1896. She studied singing in St. Petersburg; in 1852, sang the part of Vanya in Glinka's *A Life for the Czar*, and was greatly praised by Glinka himself; then sang regularly in St. Petersburg and Moscow (until 1874). In 1875 she went on a concert tour around the world, through Siberia, China, Japan, and America. In 1879 she traveled in southern Russia and the Crimea with Mussorgsky as accompanist; sang arias from Mussorgsky's operas and his songs; in 1880, opened a singing school in St. Petersburg, with Mussorgsky acting as coach. She also taught at the Moscow drama school (1888–92). Her memoirs were publ. in *Istorichesky vestnik*, nos. 1–4 (1891). She devoted much of her career to promoting Russian music; created the roles of the Princess in Dargomyzhsky's *Rusalka* (1856) and the Hostess in Mussorgsky's *Boris Godunov* (1874); her non-Russian roles included Orfeo, Azucena, and Ortrud.

BIBL.: V. Yakovlev, *D.M. L.* (Moscow, 1950).

Leopold I, Holy Roman Emperor (1658–1705), patron of music, and composer; b. Vienna, June 9, 1640; d. there, May 5, 1705. In addition to his general education, he received instruction on various instruments and in composition. During his reign, Vienna's musical life flourished; over 400 dramatic works were produced, as well as much sacred and instrumental music. In addition to being an enlightened patron, he was also a diligent composer of sacred music, producing about 10 oratorios, masses, motets, etc. He likewise worte some 12 stage works, although a number are not extant. See G. Brosche, "Die musikalischen Werke Kaiser Leopold I: Ein systematisch-thematisches Verzeichnis der erhaltenen Kompositionen," *Beiträge zur Musikdokumentation: Franz Grasberger zum 60. Geburtstag* (Tutzing, 1975).

L'Epine, (Francesca) Margherita de, famous Italian soprano; b. c.1683; d. London, Aug. 8, 1746. She began her career at the court in Mantua, then appeared in Venice (1700). She sang in the works of the German composer Jakob Greber at Lincoln's Inn Fields in London; was also his mistress (from 1702). She joined London's Drury Lane Theatre in 1704; made her 1st appearance in an opera there in Haym's pasticcio *Camillo* in 1706, replacing her archrival, the English soprano Catherine Tofts. When the opera company moved to the Queen's Theatre in 1708, she continued as a leading member with it until 1714. She sang in several works by Handel, creating the roles of Eurilla in his *Il Pastor fido* (Nov. 22, 1712) and Agilea in his *Teseo* (Jan. 10, 1713). She also became associated with the composer **Pepusch;** she appeared in his works at Drury Lane (1715–17) and at Lincoln's Inn Fields (1718–19); married him about 1718. In later years she was active mainly as a teacher; made her last appearance at Drury Lane in 1733. She was the most celebrated soprano on the London stage of her time. Contemporary accounts praise her musical gifts highly but describe her as physically unattractive; indeed, Pepusch dubbed her "Hecate."

BIBL.: E. Moor, "Some Notes on the Life of François Marguerite de L'E.," *Music & Letters*, XXVIII (1947).

Leplin, Emanuel, American composer; b. San Francisco, Oct. 3, 1917; d. Martinez, Calif., Dec. 1, 1972. He studied violin with Enesco, conducting with Monteux, and composition with Sessions.

WORKS: *Galaxy* for 2 Cellos and Orch. (1942); *Cosmos* for Violin and Orch. (1949); 2 symphonic poems: *Landscapes* and *Skyscrapers* (San Francisco, May 5, 1960); Sym. (San Francisco, Jan. 3, 1962); 3 string quartets; chamber music for various instrumental combinations; piano pieces.

Leppard, Raymond (John), eminent English conductor; b. London, Aug. 11, 1927. He studied harpsichord and viola at Trinity College, Cambridge (M.A., 1952), where he also was active as a choral conductor and served as music director of the Cambridge Phil. Soc. In 1952 he made his London debut as a conductor, and then conducted his own Leppard Ensemble. He became closely associated with the Goldsbrough Orch., which became the English Chamber Orch. in 1960. He also gave recitals as a harpsichordist, and was a Fellow of Trinity College and a lecturer on music at his alma mater (1958–68). His interest in early music prompted him to prepare several realizations of scores from that period; while his eds. provoked controversy, they had great value in introducing early operatic masterpieces to the general public. His 1st realization, Monteverdi's *L'incoronazione di Poppea*, was presented at the Glyndebourne Festival under his direction in 1962. He subsequently prepared performing eds. of Monteverdi's *Orfeo* (1965) and *Il ritorno d'Ulisse in patria* (1972), and of Cavalli's *Messa concertata* (1966), *L'Ormindo* (1967), *La Calisto* (1969), *L'Egisto* (1974), and *L'Orione* (1980). During this period he made appearances as a guest conductor with leading European opera houses, orchs., and festivals. On Nov. 4, 1969, he made his U.S. debut conducting the Westminster Choir and N.Y. Phil., at which occasion he also appeared as soloist in the Haydn D-major Harpsichord Concerto. In 1973 he became principal conductor of the BBC Northern Sym. Orch. in Manchester, a position he retained until 1980. He made his U.S. debut as an opera conductor leading a performance of his ed. of *L'Egisto* at the Santa Fe Opera in 1974. Settling in the U.S. in 1976, he subsequently appeared as a guest conductor with the major U.S. orchs. and opera houses. On Sept. 19, 1978, he made his Metropolitan Opera debut in N.Y. conducting *Billy Budd*. He was principal guest conductor of the St. Louis Sym. Orch. (1984–90). In 1987 he became music director of the Indianapolis Sym. Orch. At the invitation of the Prince of Wales, he conducted his ed. of Purcell's *Dido and Aeneas* at London's Buckingham Palace in 1988. He returned there in 1990 to conduct the 90th-birthday concert of the Queen Mother. On Jan. 27, 1991, he conducted a special concert of Mozart's works with members of the N.Y. Phil. and the Juilliard Orch. at N.Y.'s Avery Fisher Hall in Lincoln Center; telecast live to millions via PBS, it re-created a concert given by Mozart in Vienna on March 23, 1783, and celebrated his 235th birthday and the launching of Lincoln Center's commemoration of the 200th anniversary of his death. Leppard was made a Commander of the Order of the British Empire in 1983. As a composer, he produced film scores for *Lord of the Flies* (1963), *Alfred the Great* (1969), *Laughter in the Dark* (1969), *Perfect Friday* (1970), and *Hotel New Hampshire* (1985). He also orchestrated Schubert's "Grand Duo" Sonata and conducted its 1st performance with the Indianapolis Sym. Orch. (Nov. 8, 1990). Although long associated with early music, Leppard has acquired mastery of a truly catholic repertoire, ranging from Mozart to Britten. His thoughtful views on performance practice are set forth in his book *The Real Authenticity* (London, 1988).

BIBL.: T. Aldridge, "R. L. and the Indianapolis Symphony Orchestra," *Ovation* (Sept. 1989).

Leps, Wassili, Russian-American conductor and composer; b. St. Petersburg, May 12, 1870; d. Toronto, Dec. 22, 1942. He studied at the Dresden Cons. with Draeseke, Wüllner, and Theodor Kirchner. In 1894 he settled in America; taught at the Philadelphia Musical Academy; then became conductor of the Philadelphia Operatic Soc., which he led until 1923. In 1932 he organized the Providence (R.I.) Sym. Orch.; was its conductor until 1941, when he retired and went to Toronto to reside with a daughter. He wrote an opera on a Japanese subject, *Hoshi-San*, which he conducted with the Philadelphia Operatic Soc. on May 21, 1909; a cantata, *Yo-Nennen;* and some symphonic music.

Lerdahl, (Al)Fred (Whitford), American composer and music theorist; b. Madison, Wis., March 10, 1943. He studied at Lawrence Univ. (B.M., 1965) and Princeton Univ. (M.F.A., 1968), where his teachers included Milton Babbitt, Edward Cone, and Earl Kim; then studied with Wolfgang Fortner at the Freiburg Hochschule für Musik on a Fulbright grant (1968–69); was composer-in-residence at IRCAM (1981–82) and at the American Academy in Rome (1987). He held teaching appointments at the Univ. of Calif. at Berkeley (1969–71), Harvard Univ. (1970–79), Columbia Univ. (1979–85), and the Univ. of Michigan (from 1985). From 1974, he collaborated with linguist Ray Jackendoff on a theory of tonal music based on generative linguistics; several articles along these lines culminated in the innovative *A Generative Theory of Tonal Music* (Cambridge, Mass., 1983). Lerdahl's studies include music cognition and computer-assisted composition. As a composer, he features in his works the dismantling of texts and a technique of "expanding variation" wherein each variation is longer than the preceding by a predetermined ratio.

WORKS: *Piano Fantasy* (1964); String Trio (1965–66); *Wake* for Mezzo-soprano, Violin, Viola, Cello, Harp, and Percussion Ensemble (1968); *Chromorhythmos* for Orch. (1972); *Aftermath*, cantata for Soprano, Mezzo-soprano, Baritone, and Chamber Ensemble (1973); *Chords* for Orch. (1974; rev. 1983); *Eros: Variations* for Mezzo-soprano, Alto Flute, Viola, Harp, Piano, Electric Guitar, Electric Bass, and Percussion (1975); 6 *Études* for Flute, Viola, and Harp (1977); 2 string quartets (1978, 1982); *Beyond the Realm of Bird* for Soprano and Chamber Orch. (1981–84); *Episodes and Refrains* for Wind Quintet (1982); *Fantasy Études* for Chamber Ensemble (1985); *Crosscurrents* for Orch. (1987); *Waves* for Chamber Orch. (1988).

Lerner, Alan Jay, distinguished American lyricist and playwright; b. N.Y., Aug. 31, 1918; d. there, June 14, 1986. He was educated at Harvard Univ. (graduated, 1940); also attended the Juilliard School of Music in N.Y. (summers 1936, 1937). He met the composer Frederick Loewe in 1942, resulting in their collaboration on the musical *What's Up?* (1943). It proved a failure, but they obtained better luck with their next work, *The Day before Spring* (1945). Their collaborative efforts paid off when they produced the outstanding score of *Brigadoon* (1947). Following the popular *Paint Your Wagon* (1951), they wrote the smashing success *My Fair Lady* (1956), after George Bernard Shaw's play *Pygmalion*. There followed their film score *Gigi* (1958; after Colette's story), which garnered 9 Academy Awards. They returned to the Broadway stage with the enormously successful musical *Camelot* (1960). After Loewe's retirement, Lerner continued to write musicals, but he failed to equal his previous successes. His most popular later score was *On a Clear Day You Can See Forever* (1965), written in collaboration with Burton Lane; a film version appeared in 1970. He wrote an autobiography entitled *The Street Where I Live* (1978); also (with D. Shapiro) *We Danced All Night: My Life behind the Scenes* (N.Y., 1990). See A. Sirmay, ed., *The Lerner and Loewe Songbook* (N.Y., 1962) and B. Green, ed., *A Hymn to Him: The Lyrics of Alan Jay Lerner* (N.Y., 1987).

Lerner, Bennett, American pianist; b. Cambridge, Mass., March 21, 1944. He was a piano student of Claudio Arrau, Rafael de Silva, German Diez, Sascha Gorodnitski, and Robert Helps; attended Columbia Univ. and the Manhattan School of Music (B.Mus., 1973; M.Mus., 1975); also profited from a close association with Aaron Copland, Virgil Thomson, and Paul Bowles, whose music he came to champion. He taught at the Manhattan School of Music (1972–82), the Greenwich House Music School (from 1979), Sarah Lawrence College (1983–84), and Brooklyn College's Cons. of Music (from 1987). He appeared as a soloist with the Boston Pops Orch. (1966–68); in 1976 he made his Carnegie Recital Hall debut. On Nov. 14, 1985, he gained national recognition when he appeared as soloist in Copland's Piano Concerto with Mehta and the N.Y. Phil.; the concert, marking Copland's 85th birthday, was telecast live to the nation by PBS. In 1987 Lerner gave a 4-hour marathon recital at N.Y.'s 92nd St. Y in which he performed premieres of works by Virgil Thomson, Roy Harris, Samuel Barber, David Diamond et al. On Feb. 4, 1988, he was the featured performer at Vittorio Rieti's 90th-birthday concert in N.Y., where he was soloist in Rieti's *Enharmonic Variations* for Piano and Orch., a score written especially for him. While Lerner has played much contemporary music, he has also programmed a number of neglected works from the past.

Le Roux, Maurice, French composer and conductor; b. Paris, Feb. 6, 1923. He studied with Messiaen at the Paris Cons.; then worked at the electronic studios of Radiodiffusion Française. In 1952 he embarked on a conductor's career. He was conductor of the Orch. National de l'ORTF (1959–67), then was artistic adviser of the Paris Opéra (1969–73); subsequently served as Inspecteur Général de la Musique. In his music he adopts serial procedures. He publ. *Introduction à la musique contemporaine* (Paris, 1947) and *Claudio Monteverdi* (Paris, 1951).

WORKS: 2 ballets: *Le Petit Prince* (1950) and *Sables* (1956); *Le Cercle des métamorphoses* for Orch. (1953); *Un koan* for Orch. (1973); Piano Sonata (1946); other works for piano; songs; film scores.

Leroux, Xavier (Henry Napoléon), French composer; b. Velletri, Papal States, Oct. 11, 1863; d. Paris, Feb. 2, 1919. He was a pupil of Dubois and Massenet at the Paris Cons.; won 1st Grand Prix de Rome in 1885; was appointed a prof. at the Cons. in 1896.

WORKS: THEATER: *Evangeline* (Brussels, Dec. 18, 1885); *Astarté* (Paris, Feb. 15, 1901); *La Reine Fiammette* (Paris, Dec. 23, 1903); *Vénus et Adonis* (Paris, 1897); *William Ratcliff* (Nice, Jan. 26, 1906); *Théodora* (Monte Carlo, March 19, 1907); *Le Chemineau* (Paris, Nov. 6, 1907; *Le Carillonneur* (Paris, March 20, 1913); *La Fille de Figaro* (Paris, March 11, 1914); *Les Cadeaux de Noël* (Paris, Dec. 25, 1915); *1814* (Monte Carlo, April 6, 1918); *Nausithoé* (Nice, April 9, 1920); *La Plus Forte* (Paris, Jan. 11, 1924); *L'Ingénu* (Bordeaux, Feb. 13, 1931); songs; piano pieces.

Le Roy, René, French flutist; b. Maisons-Lafitte, near Paris, March 4, 1898; d. Paris, Jan. 3, 1985. He studied at the Paris Cons. with Hennebains, Lafleurance, and Gaubert. In 1918 he won 1st prize for flute playing; in 1919, succeeded Gaubert as director of the Société des Instruments à Vent; in 1922 he founded the Quintette Instrumental de Paris, with which he gave numerous concerts in Europe and America. He subsequently occupied various teaching positions; was prof. of chamber music for wind instruments at the Paris Cons. (1955–64). He compiled (with C. Dorgeuille) the manual *Traité de la flûte, historique, technique et pédagogique* (Paris, 1966).

Lert, Ernst (Josef Maria), Austrian operatic Intendant, brother of **Richard (Johanes) Lert;** b. Vienna, May 12, 1883; d. Baltimore, Jan. 30, 1955. He studied at the Univ. of Vienna with G. Adler (Ph.D., 1908); was producer and dramaturge in Breslau (1909) and Leipzig (1912–19); then was director of the operas in Basel (1919–20) and in Frankfurt (1919–23), where he also taught at the Hoch Cons.; from 1923 to 1929 was producer at La Scala in Milan, and from 1929 to 1931, at the Metropolitan Opera in N.Y.; from 1936 to 1938 was head of the opera dept. of the Curtis Inst. of Music in Philadelphia. From 1938 to 1953 he was head of the opera dept. of the Peabody Cons. in Baltimore. He wrote *Mozart auf dem Theater* (Berlin, 1918; 4th ed., 1922) and *Otto Lohse* (Leipzig, 1918).

Lert, Richard (Johanes), Austrian conductor and teacher, brother of **Ernst (Josef Maria) Lert;** b. Vienna, Sept. 19, 1885; d. Los Angeles, April 25, 1980. He studied with Heuberger in Vienna; then served as a conductor in Düsseldorf, Darmstadt, Frankfurt, Hannover, and Mannheim; later was guest conductor with the Berlin State Opera. He emigrated to the U.S. in 1934 and settled in Pasadena, Calif., as a conductor and teacher. In 1916 he married the novelist Vicki Baum. He celebrated his 90th birthday in 1975, but continued to be active, conducting summer concerts at Orkney Springs, Va.; also gave courses in conducting.

Leschetizky, Theodor (Teodor), renowned Polish pianist and pedagogue; b. Lancut, June 22, 1830; d. Dresden, Nov. 14, 1915. He first studied with his father, who took him to Vienna, where he became a pupil of Czerny (piano) and Sechter (composition). He acquired a mastery of the piano in an amazingly short time, and was only 14 when he himself began to teach. He also attended the Univ. of Vienna as a student of philosophy, until its closure in the wake of the 1848 revolution. In 1852 he went to Russia; his initial concerts in St. Petersburg were extremely successful, and gradually he attracted many pupils. He was also active as music director to the Grand Duchess Helen. In 1862 Anton Rubinstein, director of the newly opened St. Petersburg Cons., engaged him as a teacher. After 16 years in Russia, Leschetizky returned to Vienna; there he married his former pupil **Anna Essipoff** (1880), with whom he appeared in duo recitals; they were divorced in 1892; Leschetizky contracted 2 more marriages after that. He continued to make occasional concert tours, but concentrated mainly on teaching; his fame grew, and pupils flocked from all over the world to his studio in Vienna. His most celebrated pupil was Paderewski; other pupils were Gabrilowitsch, Schnabel, and Isabelle Vengerova, as well as his 3rd and 4th wives, Dominirska Benislavska and Marie Rozborska. His method of playing with the "Kugelhand" (arched hand) was to secure fullness of tone and finger dexterity, with the flexible wrist reserved for octave playing and chord passages. A Leschetizky Soc. was organized after his death; a branch was established in the U.S. He was also a composer; he wrote 2 operas, *Die Brüder von Marco* (not perf.) and *Die erste Falte* (Prague, Oct. 9, 1867), some chamber music, and 49 pieces for piano, a number of which proved quite effective.

BIBL.: M. Brée, *Die Grundlage der Methode L.* (Vienna, 1902; 4th ed., 1914; Eng. tr., 1902); Countess A. Potocka, *T. L.* (London, 1903); A. Hullah, *T. L.* (London, 1906); E. Newcomb, *L. as I Knew Him* (London, 1921); G. Woodhouse, "How L. Taught," *Music & Letters*, XXXV (1954).

Leslie, Henry (David), English conductor and composer; b. London, June 18, 1822; d. Llansaintfraid, near Oswestry, Feb. 4, 1896. He was a pupil of Charles Lucas; was cellist in the Sacred Harmonic Soc., and its conductor from 1853 to 1861. In 1855 he organized (with Heming) an a cappella singing society, which won 1st prize at Paris in 1878. He was also conductor of the Herefordshire Phil. Soc. (1863–89) and principal of the National College of Music (1864–66). He composed the operas *Romance, or Bold Dick Turpin* (1857) and *Ida* (1864); oratorios: *Immanuel* (1853) and *Judith* (1858); cantatas: *Holyrood* (1860); and *Daughter of the Isles* (1861); a "biblical pastoral," *The 1st Christian Morn* (1880); Sym.; overture, *The Templar*.

Lessard, John (Ayres), American composer and teacher; b. San Francisco, July 3, 1920. He commenced piano lessons when he was 5 and trumpet lessons at 9; became a member of the San Francisco Civic Sym. Orch. at age 11. He received instruction in piano and theory from Elsie Belenky; after brief studies with Henry Cowell, he continued his training with Nadia Boulanger, Georges Dandelot, Alfred Cortot, and Ernst Lévy at the École Normale de Musique in Paris (1937–40); completed his studies with Boulanger at the Longy School of Music in Cambridge, Mass. In 1946–47 and 1953–54 he held Guggenheim fellowships; received a National Inst. of Arts and Letters award in 1952 and an N.E.A. grant in 1976. From 1962 to 1990 he taught at the State Univ. of N.Y. at Stony Brook. His works follow along neo-classical lines with occasional adherence to serial procedures.

WORKS: ORCH.: Violin Concerto (1942); *Box Hill Overture* (1946); *Cantilena* for Oboe and String Orch. (1947); *Little Concert* (1947); Concerto for Wind Instruments (1949); Concerto for Flute, Clarinet, Bassoon, String Quartet, and String Orch. (1952); *Don Quixote and the Sheep* for Bass-baritone and Orch. (1955); Sinfonietta Concertante (1961); Harp Concerto (1963–83); *Pastimes and an Alleluia* (1974). **CHAMBER:** Partita for Woodwind Quintet (1952); Wind Octet (1952); Sonata for Cello and Piano (1956); Trio for Flute, Violin, and Piano (1959); String Trio (1963); *Trio in sei parti* for Violin, Cello, and Piano (1966); *Quodlibets I–III* for 2 Trumpets and Trombone (1967); Woodwind Quintet No. 2 (1970); Brass Quintet (1971); *Trios of Consanguinity* for 8 Combinations of Winds and Strings (1973); *Movements: I* for Trumpet and Vibraphone (1976), *II* for Trumpet and Viola (1976), *III* for Trumpet and Violin (1976), *IV* for Trumpet and Percussion (1976), *V* for Trumpet, Violin, and Cello (1977), *VI* for Trumpet, Viola, Cello, and Percussion (1978), *VII* for Trumpet and Cello (1978), and *VIII* for Trumpet, Marimba, and Vibraphone (1984); Divertimento for Guitar (1981–83); *Music* for Guitar and Percussion: *I* for Guitar and Xylophone (1982), *II* for Guitar and Xylophone (1983), and *III* for Guitar, Vibraphone, and

Bongos (1983); *Weatherscenes* for Violin, Guitar, and Cello (1987); *Drift, Follow, Persist* for Horn, Piano, and Percussion (1988). **PIANO:** Sonata (1940); *Mask* (1946); *New Worlds* (2 vols., 1965); *Threads of Sound Recalled* (1980); *For Aaron* (1981); 2 bagatelles (1986, 1988). **HARPSICHORD:** Toccata in 4 Movements (1951); *Perpetual Motion* (1952). **VOCAL:** 12 Songs from Mother Goose for Voice and String Trio (1964); *Fragments from the Cantos of Ezra Pound* for Baritone and 9 Instruments (1969); *The Pond in a Bowl* for Soprano, Piano, Marimba, and Vibraphone (1984); etc.

Lessel, Franz (actually, **Franciszek**), Polish pianist and composer; b. probably in Pulawy, c.1780; d. Petrikow, Dec. 26, 1838. He went to Vienna in 1797 to study medicine, but became a pupil of Haydn and one of his few close friends; returned to Poland upon Haydn's death, continuing to compose. He was a talented composer; wrote 5 syms., a Piano Concerto, sacred music, 8 string quartets, a Piano Trio, 3 piano sonatas, various piano pieces, and songs.

Le Sueur or **Lesueur, Jean François,** eminent French composer and writer on music; b. Drucat-Plessiel, near Abbeville, Feb. 15, 1760; d. Paris, Oct. 6, 1837. At 7 he was a choirboy at Abbeville; at 14, in Amiens, where he took a course of studies; interrupting his academic education, he became maître de musique at the Cathedral of Séez; then served as assistant choirmaster at the Church of the Holy Innocents in Paris; during this time, he studied harmony and composition with Abbé Roze. He subsequently was maître de musique at the cathedrals of Dijon (1781), Le Mans (1783), and Tours (1784). He then returned to Paris, serving (upon the recommendation of Grétry) as maître de chapelle at the Holy Innocents. When the competition for the post of maître de chapelle at Notre Dame was announced in 1786, Le Sueur entered it, and won. He organized an orch. for the chief festive days, and brought out masses, motets, services, etc., using a full orch., thus completely transforming the character of the services; he was greatly successful with the congregation, but the conservative clergy strongly objected to his innovations; other critics called his type of musical productions "opéra des gueux" (beggars' opera). He expounded his ideas of effective and descriptive music in a pamphlet, *Essai de musique sacrée ou musique motivée et méthodique, pour la fête de Noël, à la messe de jour* (1787); this evoked an anonymous attack, to which he replied with another publication, *Exposé d'une musique unie, imitative, et particulière à chaque solennité* (1787), reasserting his aim of making church music dramatic and descriptive. He left Notre Dame in 1788. After a sojourn in the country, he returned to Paris and produced 3 successful operas at the Théâtre Feydeau: *La Caverne* (Feb. 16, 1793), which had a popular success, *Paul et Virginie* (Jan. 13, 1794), and *Télémaque* (May 11, 1796). He also composed 10 hymns, written for various revolutionary festivals, which proved popular. He joined the Inst. National de Musique in 1793, the predecessor of the Paris Cons., which was organized in 1795; he subsequently served there as an inspector and a member of the Committee on Instruction; with Méhul, Langlé, Gossec, and Catel, he wrote the *Principes élémentaires de la musique* and the *Solfèges du Conservatoire*. Le Sueur was dismissed in 1802 because of an altercation that occurred following the rejection, by the Opéra, of 2 of his operas in favor of Catel's *Sémiramis*. For 2 years he lived in poverty and suffering, until Napoleon, in 1804, raised him to the highest position attainable by a musician in Paris by appointing him as his maître de chapelle, succeeding Paisiello. His rejected opera, *Ossian ou Les Bardes*, was then produced (Paris, July 10, 1804) with great applause; his other rejected opera, *La Mort d'Adam* (Paris, March 21, 1809), was a failure. After the restoration of the monarchy, and despite Le Sueur's avowed veneration of Napoleon, the government of Louis XVIII appointed him superintendent and composer to the Chapelle du Roi; he retained his post until 1830; he was also prof. of composition at the Paris Cons. from 1818 until his death, his celebrated pupils numbering Berlioz, Gounod, and Ambroise Thomas. He was made a member of the Institut (1813). His last operas, *Tyrtée* (1794), *Artaxerse* (1797), and *Alexandre à Babylone* (1815), were accepted for performance, but were not produced. His other works include the intermède *L'Inauguration du temple de la Victoire* (Paris, Jan. 20, 1807; in collaboration with L. Loiseau de Persuis) and the opera *Le Triomphe de Trajan* (Paris, Oct. 23, 1807; in collaboration with Persuis); several sacred oratorios (*Debora, Rachel, Ruth et Noémi, Ruth et Booz*); Solemn Mass for 4 Voices, Chorus, and Orch.; cantata, *L'Ombre de Sacchini;* 3 Te Deums; 2 Passions; *Stabat Mater;* these, and some other works, were publ.; he left many more (over 30 masses, etc.) in MS. His major theoretical and historical work was his *Exposé d'une musique unie, imitative et particulière à chaque solennité* (4 vols., Paris, 1787). J. Mongrédien ed. *Jean-François Le Sueur: A Thematic Catalogue of His Complete Works* (N.Y., 1980).

BIBL.: C. Ducanel, *Mémoire pour J.F. Lesueur* (Paris, 1802); Raoul-Rochette, *Notice historique sur la vie et les œuvres de J.-F. L.S.* (Paris, 1837); S. de la Madeleine, *Biographie de J.-F. L.S.* (Paris, 1841); P. Fouque, "L.S. comme prédécesseur de Berlioz," in *Les Révolutionnaires de la musique* (Paris, 1882); H. Berlioz, *Les Musiciens et la musique* (Paris, 1903); C. Pierre, *Hymnes et chants de la Révolution* (Paris, 1904); W. Buschkötter, *J.F. L.S.* (Halle, 1912); F. Lamy, *J.F. L.S. (1760–1837)* (Paris, 1912); G. Servières, "Les Oratoires de J.-F. L.S.," *Épisodes d'histoire musicale* (Paris, 1912); M. Herman, *The Sacred Music of J.-F. L.S.: A Musical and Biographical Source Study* (diss., Univ. of Michigan, 1964); J. Mongrédien, "La Musique du sacre de Napoléon Ier," in *Revue de Musicologie* (1967); W. Dean, "Opera under the French Revolution," *Proceedings of the Royal Musical Association* (1967–68); M. Herman, "The Turbulent Career of J.-F. L.S.," *Recherches sur la musique française classique* (1969); O. Saloman, "The Orchestra in L.S.'s Musical Aesthetics," *Musical Quarterly,* LX (1974).

Lesur, Daniel (Jean Yves), French pianist, organist, pedagogue, and composer; b. Paris, Nov. 19, 1908. He studied harmony and fugue with Jean Gallon and Georges Caussade, piano with Armand Ferté, and organ and composition with Charles Tournemire at the Paris Cons. (1919–29). He was assistant organist of St. Clotilde in Paris (1927–37); then was organist of the Benedictine Abbey (1937–44). In 1936 he organized the Groupe Jeune France with Messiaen, Baudrier, and Jolivet. He taught counterpoint at the Paris Schola Cantorum (1935–64), where he also was director (1957–64); also was active with the French Radio (from 1939) and Television (from 1968); served as principal inspector of music of the Ministry of Culture (from 1969) and as administrator of the Paris Réunion des Théâtres Lyriques Nationaux (1971–73). He was made a Commandeur de la Légion d'honneur and a Commandeur de l'Ordre National du Mérite et Commandeur des Arts et Lettres; in 1982 he was elected to membership in the Inst. of the Académie des Beaux-Arts.

WORKS: STAGE: OPERAS: *Andrea del Sarto* (Marseilles, Jan. 24, 1969); *Ondine* (Paris, April 26, 1982); *La Reine morte* (1987). **BALLETS:** *L'Infante du monstre* (1938; with A. Jolivet); *Bal du destin* (1965); film scores. **ORCH.:** *Suite française* (1935); *Passacaille* for Piano and Orch. (1937); *Pastorale* for Chamber Orch. (1938); *Ricercare* (1939); *L'Étoile de Séville,* suite for Chamber Orch. (1941); *Variations* for Piano and String Orch. (1943); *Andrea del Sarto,* symphonic poem (Paris, June 21, 1949); *Ouverture pour un festival* (1951); *Concerto da camera* for Piano and Chamber Orch. (1953); *Serenade* for String Orch. (1954); *Symphonie de danses* (1958); *Symphonie d'ombre et de lumière* (1964). **CHAMBER:** String Quartet (1941); Suite for Piano and String Trio (1943); *Suite médiévale* for Flute, Harp, and String Trio (1944); *Élégie* for 2 Guitars (1956); piano pieces; organ music. **VOCAL:** *Quatre lieder* for Voice and Orch. (1933–39); *Chansons cambodgiennes* for Voice and Chamber Orch. (1947); *L'Annonciation,* cantata (1952); *Cantique des cantiques* for 12 Voices (1953); *Cantique des colonnes* for Women's Voices and Orch. (1954); *Messe du jubile* for Choir, Orch., and Organ (1960); *Chanson du mariage* for Women's Voices (1964).

Lesure, François (-Marie), distinguished French music librarian, musicologist, and writer; b. Paris, May 23, 1923. He studied at the École des Chartres, the École Pratique des Hautes Études, and the Sorbonne, and musicology at the Paris Cons. A member of the music dept. at the Bibliothèque Nationale (from 1950), he was made its chief curator in 1970. He retired in 1988. From 1953 to 1967 he headed the Paris office (responsible for Series B) of the Répertoire International des Sources Musicales (RISM), for which he himself ed. *Recueils imprimés: XVIe–XVIIe siècles* (Munich, 1960); *Recueils imprimés: XVIIIe siècle* (Munich, 1964; supplement in *Notes,* March 1972, vol. XXVIII, pp. 397–418, and the 2 vols. of *Écrits imprimés concernant la musique* (Munich, 1971). He also was a prof. at the Free Univ. of Brussels, ed. of the early music series known as Le Pupitre (from 1967), president of the Société Française de Musicologie (1971–74), and prof. at the École Pratique des Hautes Études (from 1973). He ed. such nonserial works as *Anthologie de la chanson parisienne au XVIe siècle* (Monaco, 1953); the report of the 1954 Arras Conference, *La Renaissance dans les provinces du Nord* (Paris, 1956); P. Trichet's *Traité des instruments de musique (vers 1640)* (Neuilly, 1957); 6 vols. of *Chansons polyphoniques* (with A.T. Merrit, Monaco, 1967–72; the 1st 5 vols. constitute the collected works of C. Janequin); a collected ed. of Debussy's writings on music, *Monsieur Croche et autres écrits* (Paris, 1971; in Eng., N.Y., 1977); ed. the letters of Debussy for the period 1884–1918 (Paris, 1980); was ed.-in-chief of the complete works of Debussy (from 1986). His own publications include a *Bibliographie des éditions d'Adrian Le Roy et Robert Ballard, 1551–1598* (with G. Thibault, Paris, 1955; supplement in *Revue de Musicologie,* 1957); *Musicians and Poets of the French Renaissance* (N.Y., 1955); *Mozart en France* (Paris, 1956); *Collection musicale A. Meyer* (with N. Bridgman, Abbeville, 1961); *Musica e società* (Milan, 1966; German version as *Musik und Gesellschaft im Bild: Zeugnisse der Malerei aus sechs Jahrhunderten,* Kassel, 1966; in Eng. as *Music and Art in Society,* Univ. Park, Pa., 1968); *Bibliographie des éditions musicales publiées par Estienne Roger et Michel-Charles Le Cene, Amsterdam, 1696–1743* (Paris, 1969); *Musique et musiciens français du XVIe siècle* (Geneva, 1976, a reprinting in book form of 24 articles orig. publ. 1950–69). He contributed *L'Opéra classique français: 17e et 18e siècles* (Geneva, 1972) and *Claude Debussy* (Geneva, 1975) to the series Iconographie Musicale. For the Bibliothèque Nationale, he prepared a series of exhibition catalogs, most notably one on Berlioz (Paris, 1969). He prepared a *Catalogue de l'œuvre de Claude Debussy* (Geneva, 1977).

BIBL.: J.-M. Fauquet, ed., *Musiques, Signes, Images: Liber amicorum F. L.* (Geneva, 1988).

Letelier (-Llonas), Alfonso, Chilean composer and teacher; b. Santiago, Oct. 4, 1912. He studied with Allende at the Conservatorio Nacional in Santiago, where he became a prof. of harmony (1946); was also dean of the faculty of fine arts (1951–62) and vice-rector (1958–62) of the Univ. of Chile. He was made a member of the Chilean Academy of Fine Arts (1967); was awarded the Chilean National Arts Prize (1968). His compositions include *La vida del campo,* symphonic poem for Piano and Orch. (1937); *Los sonetos de la muerte* for Female Voice and Orch. (1948); *Aculeo,* suite for Orch. (Louisville, Jan. 30, 1957); Guitar Concerto (1961); Concerto for Strings (1972); choral works; chamber music; piano pieces.

Letorey, Omer, French composer; b. Châlon-sur-Saône, May 4, 1873; d. Paris, March 21, 1938. He studied at the École Niedermeyer, and with Pessard at the Paris Cons.; in 1895, won the Prix de Rome with his scena *Clarisse Harlowe.* He later wrote the operas *Cléopâtre* (1918); *L'Œillet blanc* (1930); *Le Sicilien ou L'Amour peintre* (Paris, Opéra-Comique, March 19, 1930).

Lettvin, Theodore, American pianist and teacher; b. Chicago, Oct. 29, 1926. He studied with Howard Wells, making his 1st public appearance at the age of 5 in Chicago; was invited to perform at a young people's concert with the Chicago Sym.

Orch. when he was 13; then continued his studies at the Curtis Inst. of Music in Philadelphia with Serkin and Horszowski (Mus.B., 1949); also took courses at the Univ. of Pa. (1947–48). He made his European debut in Paris in 1952. He was a visiting lecturer at the Univ. of Colorado (1956–57), then head of the piano dept. at the Cleveland Music School Settlement (1956–68); subsequently was prof. of piano at the New England Cons. of Music in Boston (1968–77), the Univ. of Michigan (1977–87), and Rutgers, the State Univ. of New Jersey (from 1987).

Leuckart, F. Ernst Christoph, German music publisher; b. Halberstadt, March 21, 1748; d. Breslau, Feb. 2, 1817. He established a music business at Breslau in 1782; it was acquired in 1856 by Constantin Sander, who removed it to Leipzig in 1870, and added to it by buying out the firms of Weinhold & Förster (Breslau), Damköhler (Berlin), and Witzendorf (Vienna). The new firm, Constantin Sander, vormals F.E.C. Leuckart, publ. many books and compositions. Sander's son, Martin (b. Breslau, Nov. 11, 1859; d. Leipzig, March 14, 1930), was head of the firm until his death.

Leutgeb, Joseph (Ignaz), Austrian horn player; b. probably in Salzburg, c.1745; d. Vienna, Feb. 27, 1811. He became 1st horn in the orch. of the Salzburg archbishop in 1770; also made appearances in Paris, Vienna, Milan, and other music centers. After settling in Vienna, he became a cheesemonger but continued to play the horn until 1792. He was a close friend of Mozart, who wrote a number of works for him, including the horn concertos K. 417, 447, and 495. Although Mozart's autographs of many of the horn parts make Leutgeb appear an incompetent from the humorous asides he made (e.g., "Thank Heaven, that's enough" and "You ass"), independent reports of Leutgeb's playing praise him highly.

Bibl.: K. Pisarowitz, "Mozarts Schnorrer L.," *Mitteilungen der Internationale Stiftung Mozarteum,* XVIII (1970).

Lev, Ray, Russian-American pianist; b. Rostov, May 8, 1912; d. N.Y., May 20, 1968. Her father was a synagogue cantor, and her mother a singer. The family went to the U.S. in 1913; she sang in her father's synagogue choirs in N.Y.; studied piano with Walter Ruel Cowles in New Haven and with Gaston Déthier. She also took lessons with Tobias Matthay in London (1930–33); then returned to N.Y. and appeared in recitals.

Leva, Enrico de, Italian composer of popular music; b. Naples, Jan. 19, 1867; d. there, July 28, 1955. He studied with d'Arienzo; early in life, began writing popular ballads that proved of wide appeal (*Non mi guarda, E spingole frangese, Triste aprile, Ultima serenata,* etc.) and earned him great financial returns. He also wrote an opera, *La Camargo* (Turin, March 2, 1898).

Levadé, Charles (Gaston), French composer; b. Paris, Jan. 3, 1869; d. there, Oct. 27, 1948. He was a pupil of Massenet at the Paris Cons.; won the Grand Prix de Rome in 1899.

Works: Opera, *Les Hérétiques* (Béziers, Aug. 27, 1905); lyric comedies: *La Rôtisserie de la reine Pédauque,* after Anatole France (Paris, Jan. 12, 1920) and *La Peau de chagrin,* after Balzac (Paris, April 24, 1929); orch. suites; chamber music; piano pieces; songs.

Levant, Oscar, American pianist and composer; b. Pittsburgh, Dec. 27, 1906; d. Beverly Hills, Aug. 14, 1972. He studied piano with Stojowski; also took a few composition lessons with Schoenberg and Schillinger. As a pianist, he established himself by his authentic performances of Gershwin's music; also emerged as a professional wit on the radio; publ. a brilliant book, *A Smattering of Ignorance* (1940), and *The Memoirs of an Amnesiac* (1965). He wrote music of considerable complexity, in the modern vein; was soloist in his Piano Concerto (NBC Sym. Orch., Feb. 17, 1942); other works were *Nocturne for Orch.* (Los Angeles, April 14, 1937); String Quartet (1937); piano pieces; film scores.

Levarie, Siegmund, Austrian-born American musicologist and conductor; b. Lemberg, Galicia, July 24, 1914. He studied

conducting with Joseph Mertin at the New Vienna Cons. (diploma, 1935) and musicology with Robert Haas at the Univ. of Vienna (Ph.D., 1938); concurrently, took private lessons in composition with Hugo Kauder. He emigrated to the U.S. in 1938; became a naturalized U.S. citizen in 1943. He was director of concerts at the Univ. of Chicago (1938–52); conducted the Collegium Musicum there, mostly in programs of medieval and Renaissance music; he also taught there; was dean of the Chicago Musical College (1952–54). From 1954 to 1962 he served as prof. of music and head of the music dept. at Brooklyn College.

Writings: *Fugue and Form* (Chicago, 1941); *Mozart's "Le Nozze di Figaro": A Critical Analysis* (Chicago, 1952; reprint, N.Y., 1977); *Fundamentals of Harmony* (N.Y., 1954; reprint, N.Y., 1962); *Guillaume de Machaut* (N.Y., 1954; reprint, N.Y., 1970); *Musical Italy Revisited* (N.Y., 1963; reprint 1973); *Tone: A Study in Musical Acoustics* (with E. Lévy; Kent, Ohio, 1968; 2nd ed., rev., 1980); *Musical Morphology: A Discourse and a Dictionary* (with Lévy; Kent, Ohio, 1983).

Levasseur, Jean-Henri, French cellist and composer; b. Beaumont-sur-Oise, May 29, 1764; d. Paris, c.1826. He studied with J. Cupis and J.L. Duport; was a member of the Paris Opéra orch. (1782–1820) and prof. of cello at the Paris Cons. (1795–1826); belonged to the Imperial Chapel. He publ. sonatas, études, and duets for cello; was co-ed. of the cello method used at the Paris Cons. (Paris, 1804).

Levasseur, Nicolas (-Prosper), prominent French bass; b. Bresles, March 9, 1791; d. Paris, Dec. 6, 1871. In 1807 he entered the Paris Cons., where he studied in Garat's singing class in 1811; made his debut as Osman Pacha in Grétry's *La Caravane du Caire* at the Paris Opéra (Oct. 14, 1813). He made his London debut in Mayr's *Adeasia ed Alderano* at the King's Theatre (Jan. 10, 1815), and then returned to the Paris Opéra as an understudy until he made his debut at the Théâtre-Italien as Almaviva (Oct. 5, 1819). He appeared in the premiere of Meyerbeer's *Margherita d'Anjou* at Milan's La Scala (Nov. 14, 1820), and then returned to the Théâtre-Italien. In 1828 he rejoined the Paris Opéra, establishing himself as its principal bass; among the roles he created there were Bertram in *Robert le diable* (1831), Brogni in *La Juive* (1835), Marcel in *Les Huguenots* (1836), and Balthazar in *La Favorite* (1840). He left the Opéra in 1845, but was recalled by Meyerbeer to sing the role of Zacharie in the premiere of *Le Prophète* (1849); he retired from the stage in 1853. He was a prof. at the Paris Cons. (1841–69). He was made a Chevalier de la Légion d'honneur in 1869.

Levasseur, Rosalie (actually, **Marie-Rose-Claude-Josèphe**), esteemed French soprano; b. Valenciennes, Oct. 8, 1749; d. Neuwied am Rhein, May 6, 1826. She was the illegitimate daughter of Jean-Baptiste Levasseur and Marie-Catherine Tournay; the parents married when she was 11. She made her debut under the name Mlle. Rosalie in the role of Zaide in Campra's *L'Europe galante* at the Paris Opéra (1766), and continued to appear in minor roles there until 1776; taking the name Levasseur, she took on major roles there, gaining success as Eurydice and Iphigenia. She then was chosen over her rival, Sophie Arnould, to create the title role in the 1st Paris staging of Gluck's *Alceste* (1776). She was greatly admired by Gluck, who chose her to create the title roles in his *Armide* (1777) and *Iphigénie en Tauride* (1779); she likewise created roles in works by Philidor, Piccinni, and Sacchini, remaining at the Opéra until 1788. She was the mistress of Count Mercy-Argentau, the Austrian ambassador in Paris, who used his influence to promote her career.

Bibl.: J.-G. Prod'homme, "R. L.: Ambassadress of the Opéra," *Musical Quarterly* (April 1916).

Levens, Charles, French music theorist and organist; b. Marseilles, 1689; d. Bordeaux, March 11, 1764. He received his musical training at the St.-Sauveur Cathedral in Aix-en-Provence; subsequently was maître de chapelle at the Cathedral St.-Pierre in Vannes; then went to Bordeaux, where he was maître de musique at the St.-André church. He publ. in 1743 an elaborate book on harmony, *Abrégé des règles de l'Harmonie, pour apprendre la composition, avec un nouveau projet sur un système de musique sans tempérament ni cordes mobiles*, in which he attempted to correlate the ascending harmonic progression, in natural overtones, with the descending arithmetical progression in undertones, thereby obtaining a dual harmonic basis; his elucubrations proved futile in practice.

Levenson, Boris, Russian-American composer and conductor; b. Ackerman, Bessarabia, March 10, 1884; d. N.Y., March 11, 1947. He studied at the St. Petersburg Cons. with Glazunov and Rimsky-Korsakov, graduating in 1907; in 1920, emigrated to America; lived mostly in N.Y. He wrote a Sym.; *Palestine,* orch. suite (N.Y., 1927); *Night in Bagdad*, oriental tone poem (N.Y. Phil., Aug. 17, 1938); *Volga*, tone poem; *Hebrew Suite* for 8 Instruments; 2 string quartets; songs.

Leveridge, Richard, noted English bass and composer; b. London, c.1670; d. there, March 22, 1758. He first gained notice in London in 1695; after a sojourn in Dublin (1699–1702), he returned to London; was a member of Handel's company (1712–13), appearing in the premieres of his *Il Pastor fido* and *Teseo*; then sang at Lincoln's Inn Fields (1714–20). He ran a coffeehouse from about 1716. He returned to the stage in 1723; was principal bass at Lincoln's Inn Fields, and subsequently at Covent Garden; retired in 1751. He publ. 5 collections of songs (London, 1697–1730). His most popular and enduring song was *The Roast Beef of Old England*, which he introduced at his Covent Garden benefit on April 15, 1735. He also wrote works for the stage, including incidental music to *Macbeth* (London, Nov. 21, 1702) and a number of masques.

BIBL.: O. Baldwin and T. Wilson, "250 Years of Roast Beef," *Musical Times* (April 1985).

Levey (real name, **O'Shaughnessy**), **Richard Michael**, Irish violinist, conductor, teacher, and composer, father of **Richard C.** and **William Charles Levey;** b. Dublin, Oct. 25, 1811; d. there, June 28, 1899. He received a practical musical education playing in various orchs. in Dublin and writing incidental music for productions of plays. About 1835 he became a theater conductor; wrote some 50 overtures and a number of ballad scores. He publ. a *Collection of the Dance Music of Ireland* (1858) and the *Annals of the Theatre Royal, Dublin* (with J. O'Rorke; 1880).

Levey, Richard C., Irish violinist, son of **Richard Michael** and brother of **William Charles Levey;** b. Dublin, 1833; d. c.1904. He became known as a touring violinist via an act dubbed as Paganini Redivivus.

Levey, William Charles, Irish conductor and composer, son of **Richard Michael** and brother of **Richard C. Levey;** b. Dublin, April 25, 1837; d. London, Aug. 18, 1894. He studied with his father, and then with Auber, Thalberg, and Prudent in Paris; then was a conductor at London's Drury Lane Theatre (1868–74), Covent Garden, and other theaters. He wrote the operettas *Fanchette* (London, Jan. 4, 1864), *Punchinello* (London, Dec. 28, 1864), and *The Girls of the Period* (London, Feb. 25, 1869); incidental music; pantomimes; *The Man of War*, fantasia for Chorus, Military Band, and Orch. (1874); 3 cantatas; many songs; piano pieces.

Levi, Hermann, eminent German conductor; b. Giessen, Nov. 7, 1839; d. Munich, May 13, 1900. He was a pupil of Vincenz Lachner in Mannheim (1852–55) and of Hauptmann and Rietz at the Leipzig Cons. (1855–58). He was music director in Saarbrücken (1859–61); after serving as assistant Kapellmeister of the Mannheim National Theater (1861), he was Kapellmeister of the German Opera in Rotterdam (1861–64). He became Hofkapellmeister in Karlsruhe in 1864, and in 1872 was named Hofkapellmeister of the Bavarian Court Opera in Munich; was made Generalmusikdirektor of the city in 1894, but was compelled by ill health to give up his duties in 1896. He enjoyed great respect among German musicians, and was influential in spreading the Wagnerian gospel. He conducted the 1st performance of *Parsifal* at Bayreuth (July 26, 1882),

and his interpretation received complete approval from Wagner himself, who, for the nonce, repressed his opposition to Jews. Levi conducted the musical program at Wagner's funeral. He was also a friend of Brahms until his championship of Wagner led to an estrangement. He wrote *Gedanken aus Goethes Werken* (1901; 3rd ed., 1911).

BIBL.: E. von Possart, *Erinnerungen an H. L.* (Munich, 1901).

Levi, Yoel, Rumanian-born American conductor; b. Sotmar, Aug. 16, 1950. He was taken in infancy to Israel, where he received instruction in violin, percussion, cello, and piano; then pursued training in violin and percussion at the Univ. of Tel Aviv (M.A., 1975); concurrently studied conducting with Mendi Rodan at the Jerusalem Academy of Music (graduate degree, 1976); subsequently took instruction in conducting with Franco Ferrara in Siena, at the Accademia di Santa Cecilia in Rome, at the Guildhall School of Music and Drama in London (diploma, 1978), and with Kirill Kondrashin in Hilversum. In 1975 he became a percussionist in the Israel Phil.; after winning 1st prize in the Besançon conducting competition in 1978, he was made a conducting assistant with the Cleveland Orch.; was its resident conductor (1980–84). In 1979 he made his European debut as a guest conductor with the (West) Berlin Radio Sym. Orch. He became a naturalized U.S. citizen in 1987. In 1988 he assumed the position of music director of the Atlanta Sym. Orch.

Levidis, Dimitri (Dimitrios), Greek-born French composer; b. Athens, April 8, 1885?; d. Palaeon Phaleron, near Athens, May 29, 1951. He studied at the Lottner Cons. in Athens, then with Boemer, Choisy, Lavrangas, and Mancini at the Athens Cons. (1898–1905). He subsequently studied with Denéréaz at the Lausanne Cons. (1906–7) and with Klose (fugue), Mottl (orchestration), and Strauss (composition) at the Munich Academy of Music (1907–8). He went to France (1910); served in the French Army during World War I; became a naturalized French citizen in 1929. He returned to Greece about 1932, and was active as a teacher; in 1934 founded the Phaleron Cons., which became a part of the Hellenic Cons. He was the 1st to write works for the Martenot "Ondes Musicales," including *Poème symphonique pour solo d'Ondes Musicales et Orchestre* (Paris, Dec. 23, 1928) and *De profundis* for Voice and 2 Soli of Ondes Musicales (Paris, Jan. 5, 1930). Other works include a ballet, *Le Pâtre et la nymphe* (Paris, April 24, 1924); *Divertissement* for English Horn, Harps, Strings, Celesta, and Percussion (Paris, April 9, 1927); oratorio, *The Iliad; Poem* for Violin and Orch. (1927); *Chant payen* for Oboe and Strings; compositions for the "Dixtuor æolien d'orchestre"; pieces for chamber ensembles; song cycles; piano pieces.

Levina, Zara, Russian pianist and composer; b. Simferopol, Crimea, Feb. 5, 1906; d. Moscow, June 27, 1976. She studied piano at the Odessa Cons., graduating in 1923; then entered the Moscow Cons., where she was a student of Felix Blumenfeld in piano and of Miaskovsky in composition, graduating in 1931. She subsequently gave piano recitals. She distinguished herself primarily as a composer of children's songs, which achieved great popularity; also set to music some 100 texts by Russian poets; wrote 2 piano concertos (1945, 1975); 2 violin sonatas (1928, 1948); piano pieces.

BIBL.: N. Mikhailovskaya, *Z. L.* (Moscow, 1960).

Levine, Gilbert, American conductor; b. N.Y., Jan. 22, 1948. He attended Reed College (1965–67) and the Juilliard School of Music in N.Y. (1967–68); then studied music history with Arthur Mendel and Louis Lockwood, conducting with Jacques-Louis Monod, and music theory with Milton Babbitt and J.K. Randall at Princeton Univ. (A.B., 1971), completing his study of music theory at Yale Univ. (M.A., 1972); also received instruction in conducting from Franco Ferrara in Siena. In 1973 he made his professional debut as a guest conductor with the Nouvel Orch. Philharmonique de Radio France in Paris; then toured widely as a guest conductor, appearing with the North German Radio Sym. Orch. in Hamburg (1977), the Royal

Phil. in London (1978), the (West) Berlin Radio Sym. Orch. (1980), the Minnesota Orch. (1984), and the Toronto Sym., the N.Y. Phil., the Dresden State Orch., the San Francisco Sym., and the Philadelphia Orch. (1986). In 1987 he became music director of the Krakow Phil., the 1st American conductor ever to hold such a position with a major Eastern European orch.

Levine, James (Lawrence), brilliant American pianist and conductor; b. Cincinnati, June 23, 1943. His maternal grandfather was a cantor in a synagogue; his father was a violinist who led a dance band; his mother was an actress. He absorbed music by osmosis and began playing the piano as a small child. At the age of 10 he was soloist in Mendelssohn's 2nd Piano Concerto at a youth concert of the Cincinnati Sym. Orch.; he then studied music theory with Walter Levin, 1st violinist in the La Salle Quartet; in 1956 he took piano lessons with Rudolf Serkin at the Marlboro School of Music; in 1957 he began piano studies with Rosina Lhévinne at the Aspen Music School. In 1961 he entered the Juilliard School of Music in N.Y., and took courses in conducting with Jean Morel; he also had conducting sessions with Wolfgang Vacano in Aspen. In 1964 he graduated from the Juilliard School and joined the American Conductors Project connected with the Baltimore Sym. Orch., where he had occasion to practice conducting with Alfred Wallenstein, Max Rudolf, and Fausto Cleva. In 1964–65 he served as an apprentice to George Szell with the Cleveland Orch.; then became a regular assistant conductor with it (1965–70). In 1966 he organized the Univ. Circle Orch. of the Cleveland Inst. of Music; also led the student orch. of the summer music inst. of Oakland Univ. in Meadow Brook, Mich. (1967–69). In 1970 he made a successful appearance as guest conductor with the Philadelphia Orch. at its summer home at Robin Hood Dell; subsequently appeared with other American orchs. In 1970 he also conducted the Welsh National Opera and the San Francisco Opera. He made his Metropolitan Opera debut in N.Y. on June 5, 1971, in a festival performance of *Tosca*; his success led to further appearances and to his appointment as its principal conductor in 1973; he then was its music director from 1975 until becoming its artistic director in 1986. In 1973 he also became music director of the Ravinia Festival, the summer home of the Chicago Sym. Orch., and served in that capacity with the Cincinnati May Festival (1974–78). In 1975 he began to conduct at the Salzburg Festivals; in 1982 he conducted at the Bayreuth Festival for the 1st time. He continued to make appearances as a pianist, playing chamber music with impeccable technical precision. But it is as a conductor and an indefatigable planner of the seasons at the Metropolitan Opera that he inspired respect. Unconcerned with egotistical projections of his own personality, he presided over the singers and the orch. with concentrated efficiency.

Levitzki, Mischa, outstanding American pianist; b. Kremenchug (of naturalized Russian-born American parents), May 25, 1898; d. Avon-by-the-Sea, N.J., Jan. 2, 1941. He began his studies with Michalowski in Warsaw at the age of 7; then his parents returned to their adopted country and he continued his training at the Inst. of Musical Art in N.Y. with Stojowski (1906–11). In 1911 he went to Germany, where he studied with Dohnányi at the Hochschule für Musik in Berlin; won the Mendelssohn Prize. In 1915 he returned to America; appeared in a N.Y. recital on Oct. 17, 1916; subsequently made numerous tours in the U.S. and in the Orient. He wrote a number of attractive piano pieces, a Piano Concerto, and a cadenza for Beethoven's 3rd Piano Concerto.

Lévy, Alexandre, Brazilian composer of French descent; b. São Paulo, Nov. 10, 1864; d. there, Jan. 17, 1892. He studied harmony with Émile Durand at the Paris Cons. His compositions include a Sym., which received a Columbus Celebration prize in 1892; *Comala*, symphonic poem; *Suite brasileira* for Orch.; chamber music and piano works (*Schumanniana*, suite; *Allegro appassionato*; etc.). Although his music is steeped in the European Romantic tradition and his technique is limited, he appears an important figure in Brazilian music because of his contribution to the nationalist movement in music; he was one of the earliest Brazilian composers to use native folk material in instrumental works.

BIBL.: G. Pimenta, *A. L.* (São Paulo, 1911).

Levy, Burt (Jerome), American composer; b. N.Y., Aug. 5, 1936. He studied with Keith Robinson in N.Y. (1953–57), Homer Keller at the Univ. of Oregon (1958–60), and Kenneth Gaburo, Herbert Brun, Ben Johnston, and Salvatore Martirano at the Univ. of Illinois (D.M.A., 1967); was a teacher at Western Illinois Univ. (1967–68), the Univ. of Wisconsin (1968–71), the State Univ. of N.Y. at Albany (1973–77), and at the Wisconsin Cons. in Milwaukee (from 1977). Among his works are *Tryonym* for Orch. (1972), *Orbs with Flute* (N.Y., Feb. 5, 1973), *6 Moments* for Piano (1976), and a String Quartet (1978).

Lévy, Ernst, distinguished Swiss pianist and composer, father of **Frank Levy**; b. Basel, Nov. 18, 1895; d. Morges, April 19, 1981. He studied in Basel with Huber and Petri, and in Paris with Pugno; was head of the piano master class at the Basel Cons. (1917–21); then was founder-conductor of the Chœur Philharmonique in Paris (1928). In 1941 he went to the U.S.; taught at the New England Cons. of Music in Boston (1941–45), Bennington (Vt.) College (1946–51), the Univ. of Chicago (1951–54), the Mass. Inst. of Technology (1954–59), and Brooklyn College of the City Univ. of N.Y. (1959–66). In 1966 he returned to Switzerland. A man of profound culture, he was also a virtuoso pianist. Besides his musical accomplishments, he was an alpinist and a master carpenter; his writings on philosophical subjects remain unpubl. He composed 15 syms. (1920–67); many choral works; chamber music; various pieces for solo instruments; etc. Among his publications are *Tone: A Study in Musical Acoustics* (with S. Levarie; Kent, Ohio, 1968; 2nd ed., rev., 1980), *Musical Morphology: A Discourse and a Dictionary* (with Levarie; Kent, Ohio, 1983), and *A Theory of Harmony* (Albany, N.Y., 1985).

Levy (originally, **Lévy**), **Frank,** Swiss-American cellist and composer, son of **Ernst Lévy**; b. Paris, Oct. 15, 1930. He went to America with his father; studied at the Juilliard School of Music in N.Y. (B.S., 1951) and at the Univ. of Chicago (M.A., 1954); studied cello with Leonard Rose and Janos Starker in N.Y.; was a cellist in various orchs.

WORKS: *Ricercar* for 4 Cellos (1958); Sonata for Unaccompanied Cello (1959); Quintet for Flute and Strings (1959); Bassoon Concerto (1961); Trio for Clarinet, Horn, and Bassoon (1961); Sonata for Bassoon and Piano (1963); *Fantasy* for Tuba, Harp, Timpani, and Strings (1965); choruses and solo songs.

Lévy, Heniot, Polish-American pianist, teacher, and composer; b. Warsaw, July 19, 1879; d. Chicago, June 16, 1946. He was a pupil at the Hochschule für Musik in Berlin, and of Max Bruch (composition); made his debut as a pianist with the Berlin Phil. (1899); in 1900 he emigrated to America, and became a piano teacher at the American Cons. in Chicago. Among his works are 24 *Variations on an Original Theme* for Orch. (Chicago, April 9, 1942); Piano Concerto; String Sextet; String Quintet; 2 piano quintets; 4 string quartets; 2 piano trios; Cello Sonata; numerous piano pieces; songs.

Levy, Jules, Bulgarian conductor and composer; b. Salonika, June 19, 1930. He studied in Sofia with Stoyanov at the Cons., graduating in 1957; then was active as a theater conductor.

WORKS: STAGE: 3 musicals: *The Girl I Was in Love With* (1963), *The World Is Small* (1970), and *The Phone Which . . .* (1975); ballet, *Fair in Sofia* (1968); choreographic oratorio, *Onward to the Rising World* (1973). ORCH.: *Youth Concerto* for Violin and Orch. (1953); 3 syms.: No. 1, *Life and Death* (1958); No. 2 (1970); No. 3 (1976); *Divertimento-Concertante No. 1* for Trumpet and Pop Orch. (1961) and *No. 2* for Flute and Orch. (1971); *Overture-Poem* (1962); *The Blacksmith*, symphonic fantasy (1964); *Pirin Mountain Rhapsody* for Jazz and Sym. Orchs. (1972); also a string quartet, *Masks* (1974), and other chamber pieces; choral songs; popular music.

Lévy, Lazare, distinguished French pianist and pedagogue; b. Brussels (of French parents), Jan. 18, 1882; d. Paris, Sept.

20, 1964. He studied piano with Diémer at the Paris Cons. (1894–98), where he was awarded 1st prize for piano; also studied harmony with Lavignac and composition with Gédalge there. He gave concerts with the principal orchs. of Europe; in 1920, succeeded Alfred Cortot as a prof. at the Paris Cons. He publ. numerous piano pieces.

Levy, Marvin David, American composer; b. Passaic, N.J., Aug. 2, 1932. He studied composition with Philip James at N.Y. Univ., and with Otto Luening at Columbia Univ.; was awarded 2 Guggenheim fellowships (1960, 1964) and 2 American Prix de Rome fellowships (1962–63; 1965). Levy showed a particular disposition toward the musical theater. In his vocal and instrumental writing he adopted an expressionistic mode along atonal lines, in an ambience of cautiously dissonant harmonies vivified by a nervously asymmetric rhythmic pulse.

WORKS: OPERAS: *Sotoba Komachi* (N.Y., April 7, 1957); *The Tower* (Santa Fe, Aug. 2, 1957); *Escorial* (N.Y., May 4, 1958); *Mourning Becomes Electra,* after O'Neill (Metropolitan Opera, N.Y., March 17, 1967). **MUSICAL:** *The Balcony* (1981–87). **ORCH.:** *Caramoor Festival Overture* (1959); Sym. (Los Angeles, Dec. 15, 1960); *Kryos,* dance poem for Chamber Orch. (1961); Piano Concerto (Chicago, Dec. 3, 1970); *Trialogues I* and *II* (1972); *In memoriam W.H. Auden* (1974); *Canto de los Marranos* for Soprano and Orch. (1977); *Arrows of Time* (Orlando, Fla., Oct. 3, 1988). **CHAMBER:** String Quartet (1955); *Rhapsody* for Violin, Clarinet, and Harp (1956); *Chassidic Suite* for Horn and Piano (1956). **VOCAL:** *For the Time Being,* Christmas oratorio (1959); *Sacred Service* for the Park Avenue Synagogue in N.Y. (1964); *Masada,* oratorio for Narrator, Tenor, Chorus, and Orch. (1973; rev. version, Chicago, Oct. 15, 1987).

Lévy, Michel-Maurice, French composer; b. Ville-d'Avray, June 28, 1883; d. Paris, Jan. 24, 1965. He studied at the Paris Cons. with Lavignac and Leroux. From 1920 to 1932 he was popular as a musical parodist in vaudeville under the name of **Bétove** (i.e., Beethoven); wrote operettas under that name: *Pom-Pom* (1928); *Les Exploits galants du Baron de Crac* (1932); *D'Artagnan* (1945). Under his own name he wrote the operas *Le Cloître* (Lyons, 1932) and *Dolorés* (Paris, 1952); operettas: *Lydia* (Brussels, 1936) and *La Demoiselle de Carentan* (Paris, 1951); *Les Trois Pantins de bois,* ballet suite for Orch.; *Le Chant de la terre,* symphonic poem (1945); *Moïse,* "fresque lyrique" (Mulhouse, 1955); film music; choral works; songs.

Lewandowski, Louis, eminent German Jewish scholar; b. Wreschen, near Posen, April 3, 1821; d. Berlin, Feb. 3, 1894. He studied at the Academy of Music in Berlin; was music director of the Berlin Synagogue from 1840; established himself as a voice teacher. His greatest accomplishment was the compilation of the Jewish service music for use by Berlin's Jewish community; in his arrangements of the traditional tunes, Lewandowski applied the technique of German Romantic music, and often reduced the exotic and asymmetrical pattern of the Jewish cantilena to simple song meters; his compositions for organ also employed ordinary 19th-century harmonies. This treatment contributed to the popularity of Lewandowski's service music, but at the same time traduced the true spirit of Jewish cantillation, so that the more nationalistic Jewish scholars refused to accept it.

Lewenthal, Raymond, American pianist; b. San Antonio, Texas, Aug. 29, 1926; d. Hudson, N.Y., Nov. 21, 1988. He was taken to Hollywood as a child; studied piano with local teachers. He then enrolled at the Juilliard School of Music in N.Y., as a student of Olga Samaroff; continued his studies in Europe with Alfred Cortot; spent a year in Rio de Janeiro as a piano teacher. Returning to the U.S., he devoted himself to promoting the piano music of neglected Romantic composers, among them Thalberg, Hummel, and Henselt, whose works he performed at his recitals. Particularly meritorious was his redemption from undeserved oblivion of the voluminous output of Charles-Valentin Alkan. He ed. a collection of Alkan's piano works for G. Schirmer, Inc.

Lewin, David (Benjamin), American music theorist, teacher, and composer; b. N.Y., July 2, 1933. He studied piano, har-

mony, and composition with Steuermann (1945–50), mathematics at Harvard Univ. (B.A., 1954), and theory and composition with Sessions, Babbitt, Kim, and Cone at Princeton Univ. (M.F.A., 1958); also undertook further graduate work at Yale Univ. (M.A., 1980). He taught at the Univ. of Calif. at Berkeley (1961–67), the State Univ. of N.Y. at Stony Brook (1967–80), and Yale Univ. (1979–85); then was a prof. at Harvard Univ. (from 1985). He held a Guggenheim fellowship (1983–84); was president of the Soc. for Music Theory (1985–88); wrote numerous articles for various learned journals.

WORKS: 4 Short Pieces for String Quartet (1956; rev. 1969); Viola Sonata (1957–58); *Essay on a Subject by Webern* for Chamber Orch. (1958); *Classical Variations on a Theme by Schoenberg* for Cello and Piano (1960); 2 Studies for Computer (1961); Fantasia for Organ (1962); 5 *Characteristic Pieces* for 2 Pianos (1964); *Fantasy-Adagio* for Violin and Orch. (1963–66); *Quartet Piece* for String Quartet (1969); Woodwind Trio (1969); *Computer Music* for Computer (1970–71); *Just a Minute, Roger* for Piano (1978); *Fanfare* for Bass Clarinet, Cello, and Piano (1980); *For Piano* for Piano (1982); songs.

Lewinger, Max, Polish violinist and composer; b. Sulkow, near Krakow, March 17, 1870; d. Dresden, Aug. 31, 1908. He studied at the conservatories of Krakow, Lemberg, and Vienna; in 1893, became a teacher of violin at the Bucharest Cons.; then played in the Gewandhaus Orch. in Leipzig (1897) and in Dresden (from 1898). He publ. *Legende* for Violin and Orch., and a number of pieces for Violin and Piano (*Tarantella, Polonaise, Capriccio, Dumka, Serenade,* etc.).

Lewis, Sir Anthony (Carey), eminent English conductor, musicologist, composer, and teacher; b. Bermuda, March 2, 1915; d. Haslemere, June 5, 1983. He became an organ scholar at Peterhouse, Cambridge (1932); continued his studies with Dent at Cambridge (B.A. and Mus.B., 1935); also took courses with Boulanger in Paris (1934). He joined the music staff of the BBC (1935); then was the creator of its Third Programme (1946). From 1947 to 1968 he was a prof. of music at the Univ. of Birmingham; also was dean of the faculty of fine arts there (1961–64). From 1968 to 1982 he served as principal of the Royal Academy of Music in London. In 1967 he was made a Commander of the Order of the British Empire. He was knighted in 1972. His specialty was the music of the Baroque period; he ed., conducted, and recorded works by Purcell, Rameau, and Handel. He publ. *The Language of Purcell* (Hull, 1968); was a founder and ed. of the prestigious series *Musica Britannica* (1951). His compositions include *Choral Overture* (1938), *Elegy and Capriccio* for Trumpet and Orch. (1947), a Trumpet Concerto (1950), *A Tribute of Praise* for Voices a cappella (1951), and a Horn Concerto (1956).

Lewis, Daniel, American conductor; b. Flagstaff, Ariz., May 10, 1925. He studied composition with Nino Marcelli in San Diego (1939–41); also took violin lessons in Boston; graduated from San Diego State College (B.M., 1949); attended the Claremont (Calif.) Graduate School (M.A., 1950). In 1959 he went to Germany, where he attended the Munich Hochschule für Musik and studied conducting with Eugen Jochum; also participated in a conducting seminar with Herbert von Karajan in Salzburg (1959–60). Returning to the U.S., he was conductor of the La Jolla (Calif.) Sym. Orch. (1961–69) and the Orange County (Calif.) Sym. Orch. (1966–70); was music director of the Pasadena Sym. Orch. (1972–84), which he brought to a high degree of excellence; made numerous appearances as a guest conductor with several major American orchs. He was also active as a teacher, serving on the faculties of Calif. State Univ. at Fullerton (1963–70) and the Univ. of Southern Calif. at Los Angeles (from 1970).

Lewis, Henry, black American conductor; b. Los Angeles, Oct. 16, 1932. He learned to play piano and string instruments as a child; at the age of 16, was engaged as a double-bass player in the Los Angeles Phil.; from 1955 to 1959, played double bass in the 7th Army Sym. Orch. overseas, and also conducted it in Germany and the Netherlands. Returning to the U.S., he founded the Los Angeles Chamber Orch.; in 1963, traveled with it in Europe under the auspices of the State Dept. From 1968 to 1976 he was music director of the New Jersey Sym. Orch. in Newark; subsequently conducted opera and orch. guest engagements. In 1989 he became chief conductor of the Radio Sym. Orch. in Hilversum. He married **Marilyn Horne** in 1960, but they were separated in 1976.

Lewis, Jerry Lee, gyrating American rock 'n' roll and country-music pianist and singer; b. Ferriday, La., Sept. 29, 1935. He assaulted the piano keys with unusual ferocity as if seeking the rock bottom of the sound, and whenever he had a chance also vocalized in a frenetic seizure of the larynx. He tried every style, including rock, folk, western, and rhythm-and-blues, always hitting hard on mental torment. He never wrote his own songs, but he sure could metamorphosize and transmogrify ready-made tunes such as *Great Balls of Fire* (1957). His rendition of *Whole Lotta Shakin' Going On* (1957) became a rock-'n'-roll classic. His career came to a halt in 1958 during his English tour after it was revealed in lurid headlines that he was traveling with a 13-year-old girl, who he said was his 1st cousin and child wife. Even his records were put on the shelf at radio stations, and he was reduced to playing at village fairs and roadhouses. It was not until 1968 that he was able to return to public favor, with records such as *Another Place, Another Time* and *What's Made Milwaukee Famous (Has Made a Loser Out of Me)*. In 1977 he recorded an autobiographical single, *Middle-Age Crazy*. With his sister Linda Gail Lewis, he brought out the album *Together* (1969); his later albums included *The Session* (1973), *Southern Roots* (1973), *Jerry Lee Lewis Keeps Rockin'* (1978), and *Killer Country* (1980).

BIBL.: R. Cain, *Whole Lotta Shakin' Going On* (N.Y., 1981); R. Palmer, *J.L. L. Rocks* (N.Y., 1981); N. Tosches, *Hellfire: The J.L. L. Story* (N.Y., 1982).

Lewis, John (Aaron), esteemed black American jazz pianist and composer; b. La Grange, Ill., May 3, 1920. He studied anthropology and music at the Univ. of New Mexico; completed his studies at the Manhattan School of Music (M.A., 1953). In 1952 he founded the Modern Jazz Quartet (piano, vibraphone, drums, double bass), a group that for 22 years was one of the focal points of both "cool" jazz and "classical" jazz, a merger known as Third Stream. To this end he composed and arranged works that, while leaving room for jazz improvisation, also included such formal devices as fugal counterpoint; he also composed extended compositions requiring the additional forces of string quartet or orch., several movie scores (*Odds against Tomorrow, No Sun in Venice, A Milanese Story*), and a ballet, *Original Sin* (San Francisco Ballet, March 1961). Significantly, the Modern Jazz Quartet (known as MJQ) abandoned the usual nightclub habitat of jazz in favor of formal, tuxedoed performances in concert halls. The Modern Jazz Quartet disbanded in 1974, but in later years its members reunited for occasional tours; he also led his own sextet.

BIBL.: N. Hentoff, *J. L.* (N.Y., 1960); L. Feather, "Piano Giants of Jazz: J. L.," *Contemporary Keyboard*, III/7 (1977).

Lewis, Meade (Anderson) "Lux," black American jazz pianist; b. Chicago, Sept. 4, 1905; d. in an automobile accident in Minneapolis, June 7, 1964. He was nicknamed "The Duke of Luxembourg" as a child, hence the contraction "Lux." He studied violin and piano; played in nightclubs and bars in Chicago; then went to N.Y., where he played with Pete Johnson and Albert Ammons; then appeared as a soloist in N.Y. and California nightclubs. He was a leading exponent of the boogie-woogie style; his recording of *Honky Tonk Train Blues* (1927) was a landmark of the era.

Lewis, Ramsey, black American jazz pianist; b. Chicago, May 27, 1935. He studied at the Chicago Musical College (1947–54), the Univ. of Illinois at Urbana (1953–54), and DePaul Univ. (1954–55). He began his career as a member of a local jazz group; in 1956 he formed his own Ramsey Lewis Trio, and filled engagements at nightclubs, college campuses, and jazz festivals; he also wrote music for his group.

Lewis, Richard (real name, **Thomas Thomas**), noted English tenor; b. Manchester, May 10, 1914; d. Eastbourne, Nov.

13, 1990. He studied with T.W. Evans, then with Norman Allin at the Royal Manchester College of Music (1939–41) and at the Royal Academy of Music in London (1945); made his operatic debut with the Carl Rosa Opera Co. in 1939; from 1947 he sang at the Glyndebourne Festivals and at London's Covent Garden. He sang with the San Francisco Opera (1955–60); then appeared there as a guest artist (1962–68). He toured extensively as a concert and oratorio singer. In 1963 he was named a Commander of the Order of the British Empire. His repertoire was extensive, including roles in operas ranging from Monteverdi and Mozart to Schoenberg, Britten, and Tippett.

Lewis, Robert Hall, American composer and teacher; b. Portland, Oreg., April 22, 1926. He studied with Rogers and Hanson at the Eastman School of Music in Rochester, N.Y. (B.M., 1949; M.M., 1951; Ph.D., 1964), Boulanger and Bigot in Paris (1952–53), and Apostel, Krenek, and Schiske in Vienna (1955–57); also received instruction in conducting from Monteux in Hancock, Maine (1954). He taught at Goucher College and the Peabody Cons. of Music in Baltimore (from 1958); also was on the faculty of Johns Hopkins Univ. (1969–80). He held 2 Fulbright scholarships (1955–57) and 2 Guggenheim fellowships (1966, 1980).

WORKS: ORCH.: 4 syms. (1964; 1971; 1982–85; 1990); *Poem for Strings* (1949); *Concert Overture* (1951); *Sinfonia, Expression for Orchestra* (1955); *Prelude and Finale* (1959); *Designs* (1963); *Music for 12 Players* (1965); *3 Pieces* (1965; rev. 1966); Concerto for Chamber Orch. (1967; rev. 1972); *Intermezzi* (1972); *Nuances II* (1975); *Osservazioni II* for Winds, Keyboard, Harpsichord, and Percussion (1978); *Moto* (1980); *Atto* for Strings (1981); Concerto for Strings, 4 Trumpets, Harps, and Piano (1984); *Destini* for Strings and Winds (1985); *Invenzione* (1988); *3 Movements on Scenes of Hieronymous Bosch* (1989). CHAMBER: 3 string quartets (1956, 1962, 1981); Trio for Clarinet, Violin, and Piano (1966); *Monophonies I–IX* for Winds (1966–77); *Tangents* for Double Brass Quartet (1968); Violin Sonata (1968); *Inflections I* for Double Bass (1969) and *II* for Piano Trio (1970); *Serenades I* for Piano (1970), *II* for Flute, Piccolo, Cello, and Piano (1976), and *III* for Brass Quintet (1982); *Combinazioni I* for Clarinet, Violin, Cello, and Piano (1974), *II* for 8 Percussion and Piano (1974), *III* for Narrator, Oboe, English Horn, and Percussion (1977), *IV* for Cello and Piano (1977), and *V* for 4 Violas (1982); *Osservazioni I* for Flutes, Piano, and Percussion (1975); *A due I* for Flute, Piccolo, Alto Flute, and Harp (1981), *II* for Oboe, English Horn, and Percussion (1981), *III* for Bassoon and Harp (1985), and *IV* for Soprano and Piano (1986); Quintet for Winds (1983); *Dimensioni* for Clarinet, Violin, Viola, Cello, and Piano (1988). VOCAL: *Acquainted with the Night* for Soprano and Chamber Orch. (1951); 5 Songs for Soprano, Clarinet, Horn, Cello, and Piano (1957); 2 madrigals for Chorus (1972); *3 Prayers of Jane Austen* for Small Chorus, Piano, and Percussion (1977); *Kantaten* for Chorus and Piano (1980); *Monophony X* for Soprano (1983).

Lewisohn, Adolph, German-American businessman and philanthropist; b. Hamburg, May 27, 1849; d. Saranac Lake, N.Y., Aug. 17, 1938. The principal services to music and education performed by this prominent industrialist were the erection in 1914 of the Lewisohn Stadium, which he donated to the College of the City of N.Y., and the inauguration of summer concerts by the N.Y. Phil. there (1918). He also founded the Lewisohn chamber music foundation at Hunter College in N.Y. (1932).

Lewkowitch, Bernhard, Danish organist and composer; b. Copenhagen (of Polish parents), May 28, 1927. He studied organ, theory, and music history at the Royal Danish Cons. of Music in Copenhagen (graduated in theory, 1948; organ degree, 1949); completed his studies of composition and orchestration there with Jersild and Schierbeck (1950). He was organist and choirmaster at Copenhagen's St. Ansgar Catholic Church (1947–63); also founded the Schola Cantorum choral society (1953), with which he performed medieval and Renaissance music. He served as director of music at Copenhagen's Church of the Holy Sacrament (1973–85). In 1963 he was awarded the Carl Nielsen Prize; in 1966 he was given a lifetime Danish government pension. His music is primarily choral, to Latin texts, and is derived essentially from the Renaissance paradigms of modal counterpoint; it has an affinity with sacred works of Stravinsky, but is otherwise sui generis in its stylized archaisms; several of these works have become repertoire pieces in Denmark, and were also performed at various international festivals.

WORKS: *Mariavise* for Chorus (1947); *Tres orationes* for Tenor, Oboe, and Bassoon (1958); *Il cantico delle creature* for 8 Voices, after St. Francis of Assisi (1962–63); *Laudi a nostra Signora* for Chorus (1969); *De Lamentatione Jeremiae Prophetae* for Chorus and Orch. (1977); *Vesper in Advent* for Tenor, Chorus, and Organ (1979); *Requiem* for Baritone, Chorus, and Orch. (1981); *Tenebrae-Responsoria* for Chorus (1983); *Deprecations* for Tenor, Horn, and Trombone (1984); *Songs of Solomon* for Tenor, Clarinet, Horn, and Trombone (1985); *Via Stenonis* for Chorus and Brass Quintet (1987); 6 partitas for Brass (1986–88).

BIBL.: M. Chestnut, "Cantio sacra: The Music of B. L.," *Nordic Sounds* (Dec. 1987).

Ley, Salvador, Guatemalan pianist and composer; b. Guatemala City, Jan. 2, 1907; d. there, March 21, 1985. He studied at the Berlin Hochschule für Musik (1922–30); concurrently studied piano with Georg Bertram (1922–30) and theory and composition with Klatte (1923–25) and Leichtentritt (1928–29). He was director of the National Cons. in Guatemala City (1934–37; 1944–53); then went to the U.S., where he taught at the Westchester (N.Y.) Cons. (1963–70).

WORKS: *Lera*, opera (1959); *Danza exotica* for Piano (1959); Suite for Flute and Piano (1962); *Concertante* for Viola and String Orch. (1962); *Toccatina* for Piano (1965); *Introduction and Movement* for Unaccompanied Cello (1965); other piano pieces; songs.

Leybach, Ignace (Xavier Joseph), Alsatian pianist, organist, and composer; b. Gambsheim, July 17, 1817; d. Toulouse, May 23, 1891. He studied in Paris with Pixis, Kalkbrenner, and Chopin; in 1844, became organist at the Toulouse Cathedral. He publ. some 225 piano pieces, in a facile and pleasing manner. His 5th Nocturne, op. 52, became famous, and its popularity continued among succeeding generations of piano students; it was reprinted in countless anthologies of piano music. Other piano compositions are: *Boléro brillant; Ballade; Valse poétique; Les Batelières de Naples;* etc.; he also publ. an extensive organ method (3 vols.; 350 pieces).

Leyden, Norman, American conductor; b. Springfield, Mass., Oct. 17, 1917. He studied at Yale Univ. (B.A., 1938; Mus.B., 1939) and at Teachers College of Columbia Univ. (M.A., 1965; Ed.D., 1968). He organized the Westchester Youth Sym. Orch. in White Plains, N.Y., in 1957; led it until 1968. In 1974 he became associate conductor of the Oregon Sym. Orch. in Portland; also pursued a successful career as a guest conductor with leading U.S. orchs. in concerts of popular fare.

Leygraf, Hans, Swedish pianist, teacher, and composer; b. Stockholm, Sept. 7, 1920. He appeared as a soloist with the Stockholm Orch. at the age of 10; then studied at the Stockholm Cons., in Munich, and in Vienna; acquired a fine reputation as a concert pianist; was particularly noted as a Mozart interpreter. In 1944 he married the Austrian pianist **Margarete Stehle** (b. Vienna, April 26, 1921). In 1956 he joined the faculty of the Salzburg Mozarteum. He wrote a Piano Concerto, chamber music, and piano pieces.

Lhéritier, Jean, French composer; b. c.1480; d. after 1552. He studied with Josquin Des Prez. He was active at the Estense court in Ferrara (1506–8); later was capellanus and maestro di cappella at Rome's St.-Louis-des-Français (1521–22). Cardinal François de Clermont, the papal legate in Avignon, was his major patron; he received several benefices. He was a particularly notable composer of motets. L. Perkins ed. his *Opera omnia* in Corpus Mensurabilis Musicae, XLVIII/1–2 (1969).

BIBL.: F. Lesure, "Notes pour une biographie de J. L.," *Revue de Musicologie*, XLII (1958); L. Perkins, *The Motets of J. L.* (diss., Yale Univ., 1965).

Lhévinne, Josef, celebrated Russian pianist and pedagogue, husband of **Rosina** (née **Bessie**) **Lhévinne;** b. Orel, Dec. 13, 1874; d. N.Y., Dec. 2, 1944. After some preliminary study in his native town, he was taken to Moscow, and entered Safonov's piano class at the Cons. (1885); at the age of 15, he played the *Emperor Concerto*, with Anton Rubinstein conducting; he graduated in 1891; won the Rubinstein Prize in 1895. In 1900 he traveled to the Caucasus; taught piano at the Tiflis Cons.: from 1902 to 1906, taught at the Moscow Cons. In 1906 he went to the U.S.; made his American debut in N.Y. with the Russian Sym. Orch., conducted by Safonov (Jan. 27, 1906); afterward he made numerous concert tours in America. He lived mostly in Berlin from 1907 to 1919; was interned during World War I, but was able to continue his professional activities. In 1919 he returned to the U.S.; appeared in recitals, and with major American orchs.; also in duo recitals with his wife, whom he married in 1898. They established a music studio, where they taught numerous pupils; also taught at the Juilliard Graduate School in N.Y. (from 1922). He publ. *Basic Principles in Pianoforte Playing* (Philadelphia, 1924). Lhévinne's playing was distinguished not only by its virtuoso quality, but by an intimate understanding of the music, impeccable phrasing, and fine gradations of singing tone. He was at his best in the works of the Romantic school; his performances of the concertos of Chopin and Tchaikovsky were particularly notable.

BIBL.: R. Wallace, *A Century of Music-Making: The Lives of J. and Rosina L.* (Bloomington, Ind., 1976).

Lhévinne, Rosina (née **Bessie**), distinguished Russian pianist and pedagogue, wife of **Josef Lhévinne;** b. Kiev, March 28, 1880; d. Glendale, Calif., Nov. 9, 1976. She graduated from the Moscow Cons. in 1898, winning the gold medal; that same year she married Josef Lhévinne. She appeared as a soloist in Vienna (1910), St. Petersburg (1911), and Berlin (1912); remained in Berlin with her husband through World War I; in 1919, they went to the U.S., where they opened a music studio; also taught at the Juilliard Graduate School in N.Y. (from 1922); later taught privately. Among her famous students were Van Cliburn, Mischa Dichter, John Browning, and Garrick Ohlsson.

BIBL.: R. Wallace, *A Century of Music-Making: The Lives of Josef and R. L.* (Bloomington, Ind., 1976).

Lhotka-Kalinski, Ivo, Yugoslav composer, son of **Fran Lhotka;** b. Zagreb, July 30, 1913; d. there, Jan. 29, 1987. He studied composition with his father and also voice at the Zagreb Academy of Music; after further composition lessons with Pizzetti in Rome (1937–39), he was active as a teacher; then was prof. of singing at the Zagreb Academy of Music (from 1951), becoming its regional director in 1967. He had a natural flair for stage composition in the folk style; he wrote several brilliant musical burlesques, among them *Analfabeta* (The Illiterate; Belgrade, Dec. 19, 1954); *Putovanje* (The Journey), 1st television opera in Yugoslavia (Zagreb, June 10, 1957); *Dugme* (The Button; Zagreb, April 21, 1958); *Vlast* (Authority; Zagreb Television, Oct. 18, 1959); *Svjetleći grad* (The Town of Light; Zagreb, Dec. 26, 1967); also a children's opera, *Velika coprarija* (The Great Sorcerer; 1952); Sym. (1937); *Jutro* (Morning), symphonic poem (1941–42); *Misli* (Thoughts) for Clarinet and Strings (1965); chamber music; choral works; songs; piano pieces.

Lhotka, Fran, Yugoslav composer and teacher of Czech descent, father of **Ivo Lhotka-Kalinski;** b. Wožice, Dec. 25, 1883; d. Zagreb, Jan. 26, 1962. He took lessons with Dvořák in Prague, and with Janáček and Klička (1899–1905). After teaching in Ekaterinoslav (1908–9), he settled in Zagreb; was a prof. at the Academy of Music (1920–61), where he also served as rector (1923–40; 1948–52). He publ. a harmony manual (Zagreb, 1948). His music followed in the late Romantic style.

WORKS: Operas: *Minka* (Zagreb, 1918) and *The Sea* (Zagreb, 1920); ballets: *The Devil of the Village* (Zürich, Feb. 18, 1935); *Ballad of Medieval Love* (Zürich, Feb. 6, 1937); *Luk* (Munich, Nov. 13, 1939); Sym.; Violin Concerto (1913); Concerto for String Quartet (1924); chamber music; choral works; songs.

Liadov, Anatoli (Konstantinovich), prominent Russian conductor, teacher, and composer, son of **Konstantin (Nikolaievich) Liadov;** b. St. Petersburg, May 11, 1855; d. Polynovka, Novgorod district, Aug. 28, 1914. He began his musical training with his father, then entered the St. Petersburg Cons. (1870), where he took courses in piano and violin; then studied counterpoint and fugue with J. Johannsen and composition with Rimsky-Korsakov; he was expelled for failing to attend classes (1876), but after his readmission, obtained his diploma with a highly successful graduation piece, the final scene from Schiller's *Die Braut von Messina* (1878). He became an instructor of theory (1878), advanced counterpoint (1901), and composition (1906) at the Cons.; also taught theory at the Court Chapel (from 1885). He was active as a conductor. With Balakirev and Liapunov, he collected folk songs for the Imperial Geographic Soc. (publ. in 1897). He was a teacher of Prokofiev and Miaskovsky. As a composer, Liadov was fascinated by variation techniques and canonic writing; many of his works possess the imaginative quality of Russian fairy tales. Among his most popular works were the orch. pieces *Baba Yaga, The Enchanted Lake,* and *Kikimora.*

WORKS: ORCH.: *Scherzo* (1879–86); *Village Scene by the Inn,* mazurka (1887); *Polonaise* (1899); *Polonaise* in D major (1902); *Baba Yaga* (1891–1904; St. Petersburg, March 18, 1904); *8 Russian Folk Songs* (1906); *The Enchanted Lake* (St. Petersburg, March 18, 1909); *Kikimora* (St. Petersburg, Dec. 8, 1912); *Danse de l'Amazone* (1910); *From the Apocalypse* (1910–12; St. Petersburg, Dec. 8, 1912); *Nenie* (1914); also numerous piano pieces, including études, preludes, intermezzos, mazurkas, bagatelles, etc.; choral works; songs; numerous arrangements of folk songs.

BIBL.: V. Vasina-Grossman, *A.K. L.* (Moscow and Leningrad, 1945); N. Zaporozhets, *A.K. L.: Zhizn i tvorchestvo* (Life and Works; Moscow, 1954); M. Mikhailov, *A.K. L.: Ocherk zhizni i tvorchestva* (Life and Works; Leningrad, 1961).

Liadov, Konstantin (Nikolaievich), Russian conductor, father of **Anatoli (Konstantinovich) Liadov;** b. St. Petersburg, May 10, 1820; d. there, Dec. 19, 1868. He studied at the St. Petersburg Theatrical School; in 1850, became conductor of the St. Petersburg Imperial Opera; resigned shortly before his death, and was succeeded by Nápravník. He was an efficient drillmaster, and did much to raise the standard of performance; premiered several Russian operas, and was instrumental in encouraging Russian music; he was greatly appreciated by his co-workers; Glinka often sought his advice on details of production of his operas.

Liapunov, Sergei (Mikhailovich), noted Russian pianist, conductor, teacher, and composer; b. Yaroslavl, Nov. 30, 1859; d. Paris, Nov. 8, 1924. He began piano studies with his mother, a talented pianist, then took courses at the Russian Musical Soc. in Nizhny-Novgorod; later studied piano with Klindworth, Pabst, and Wilborg and composition with Hubert, Tchaikovsky, and Taneyev at the Moscow Cons. (1878–83). He went in 1884 to St. Petersburg, where he entered the Balakirev circle; was assistant director of the Imperial Chapel (1894–1902), inspector of music at St. Helen's Inst. (1902–10), and director of the Free Music School (1905–11); was prof. of piano and music theory at the Cons. (1910–17) and a lecturer at the State Inst. of Art (1919). Liapunov toured widely as a pianist in Europe, and also appeared as a conductor; he spent his last years in Paris. He wrote a number of virtuoso pieces for piano, including the *12 études d'exécution transcendante* in sharp keys, written in emulation of Liszt's similarly titled works in flat keys. He also wrote some attractive character pieces for piano and songs. With Balakirev and Liadov, he was commissioned by the Imperial Geographic Soc. in 1893 to collect folk songs from the regions of Vologda, Viatka, and Kostroma;

30 of his arrangements of them for voice and piano were publ. by the society in 1897. He also utilized original folk songs in several of his works.

WORKS: 2 syms.: No. 1 (1887; St. Petersburg, April 23, 1888); No. 2 (1910–17; Leningrad, Dec. 28, 1950); *Ballada,* overture (1883; rev. 1894–96); 2 piano concertos (1890, 1909); *Solemn Overture on Russian Themes* (St. Petersburg, May 6, 1896); *Polonaise* for Orch. (1902); *Rhapsody on Ukrainian Themes* for Piano and Orch. (1907; Berlin, March 23, 1908); *Zelazowa Wola,* symphonic poem named after Chopin's birthplace, commemorating his centennial (1909); *Hashish,* symphonic poem (1913); Violin Concerto (1915; rev. 1921); numerous piano pieces, including *12 études d'exécution transcendante* (1900–1905) and a Sonata (1906–8); many songs.

BIBL.: A. Liapunova, "S.M. L.," *Sovetskaya Muzyka,* no. 9 (1950); M. Shifman, *S.M. L.: Zhizn i tvorchestvo* (Life and Works; Moscow, 1960); R. Davis, "S. L. (1859–1924): The Piano Works—A Short Appreciation," *Music Review,* XXI (1960).

Liatoshinsky, Boris (Nikolaievich), significant Ukrainian composer; b. Zhitomir, Jan. 3, 1895; d. Kiev, April 15, 1968. He studied jurisprudence at the Univ. of Kiev, simultaneously taking lessons in composition at the Kiev Cons. with Glière, graduating in 1919. He was an instructor (1919–35) and then a prof. (1935–68) at the Kiev Cons.; also taught at the Moscow Cons. (1936–37; 1941–43). His style of composition follows the broad outlines of national music, with numerous thematic allusions to folk songs.

WORKS: OPERAS: *The Golden Hoop* (1929; Odessa, March 26, 1930); *Shchors* (1937; Kiev, Sept. 1, 1938; rev., Kiev, Feb. 18, 1970). **ORCH.:** 5 syms. (1918–66); *Poem of Reunification* (1949–50); *Slavonic Concerto* for Piano and Orch. (1953); *Grazina,* ballad (Kiev, Nov. 26, 1955); *On the Banks of the Vistula,* symphonic poem (1958); *Solemn Overture* (1967). **CHAMBER:** 4 string quartets (1915–43); 2 piano trios (1922, rev. 1925; 1942); *Ukrainian Quintet* for Piano (1942; rev. 1945); *Suite on Ukrainian Folk Themes* for String Quartet (1944); piano pieces; also choral works; songs; many folk-song arrangements.

BIBL.: I. Boelza, *B.M. L.* (Moscow, 1947); V. Samokhvalov, *B. L.* (Kiev, 1970; 2nd ed., 1974).

Liberace (in full, **Wladziu Valentino Liberace**), popular American pianist of Italian-Polish parentage; b. West Allis, Wis., May 16, 1919; d. Palm Springs, Calif., Feb. 4, 1987. He received musical training from his father, a horn player; then studied piano, exhibiting so natural a talent that no less a master than Paderewski encouraged him to try for a concert career. However, he was sidetracked from serious music by jobs at silent-movie houses and nightclubs, where he was billed as Walter Busterkeys. In 1940 he moved to N.Y. and soon evolved a facile repertoire of semiclassical works, such as a synthetic arrangement of the 1st movement of Beethoven's *Moonlight* Sonata and Rachmaninoff's Prelude in C-sharp minor, taking advantage of the fact that both works are in the same key. He prospered and made lucrative inroads into television (1951–55; 1958–59); also made numerous recordings and toured extensively overseas. He built himself a house in California, complete with a piano-shaped swimming pool. Inspired by a popular movie on Chopin, he placed a candelabrum on the piano at his public appearances; this decorative object identified him as a Romantic musician, an impression enhanced by his dress suit of white silk mohair and a wardrobe of glittering cloaks, which he removed with theatrical flair before performing. In 1959 he won a lawsuit for defamation of character against the London *Daily Mirror* and its columnist "Cassandra" (William Neil Connor) for suggesting in print that he was a practitioner of the inverted mode of love. But then in 1982 his former chauffeur-bodyguard-companion sued him for $380 million for services rendered in "an exclusive non-marital relationship." In 1984 most of the suit was quashed, and in 1986 Liberace settled out of court for $95,000. When he died of AIDS in 1987, his multimillion-dollar estate containing valuable curiosa was sold at auction. A large percentage of the sale price was bequeathed to charities, for Liberace was a generous man. In spite of his critics, he once said, he cried all the way to the bank. His autobiography was publ. in 1973.

BIBL.: *Current Biography* (March 1986); B. Thomas, *L.* (N.Y., 1988); S. Thorson, with A. Thorleifson, *Behind the Candelabra: My Life with L.* (N.Y., 1988).

Libert, Henri, French organist, teacher, and composer; b. Paris, Dec. 15, 1869; d. there, Jan. 14, 1937. He studied at the Paris Cons. with Marmontel and Diémer (piano), Franck and Widor (organ), and Massenet and Godard (composition); took 1st organ prize (1894); was titular organist at the Basilica of St. Denis in Paris, and a prof. of organ at the American Cons. in Fontainebleau. He wrote many organ works, including *Variations symphoniques, Chorals, Préludes et fugues;* piano pieces; motets; songs; also publ. didactic works.

Libon, Philippe, French violinist and composer; b. Cadiz (of French parents), Aug. 17, 1775; d. Paris, Feb. 5, 1838. He studied in London with Viotti; in 1796, became a chamber violinist in Lisbon; in 1798, a member of the Court Orch. in Madrid. In 1800 he settled in Paris as a member of the Court Orch. He publ. 6 violin concertos; 6 string trios; duets; 2 vols. of *Airs variés;* 30 caprices for Violin Solo.

Licad, Cecile, Filipino pianist; b. Manila, May 11, 1961. She studied piano with Rosario Picazo; made her public concert debut at the age of 7; then went to the U.S.; enrolled at the Curtis Inst. of Music in Philadelphia in the classes of Rudolf Serkin, Seymour Lipkin, and Mieczyslaw Horszowski. In 1979 she was soloist with the Boston Sym. Orch. at the Berkshire Music Center in Tanglewood; in 1981 she won the Leventritt Gold Medal, which launched her on a fine career; subsequently appeared with major orchs. on both sides of the Atlantic. She married **António Meneses.**

Lichard, Milan, Slovak authority on folk songs; b. Uhorská Skalica, Feb. 24, 1853; d. Užhorod, April 21, 1935. He studied music in Budapest; also worked for the railway administration. He devoted his entire life to collecting and editing Slovak songs; contributed numerous articles on the subject to various scholarly magazines. From 1921 he lived in Užhorod, where he was also active as a choral conductor.

Lichey, Reinhold, German organist and composer; b. Pohlsdorf, near Liegnitz, March 26, 1879; d. Plaue, Dec. 5, 1957. He studied music in Breslau; then went to Berlin, where he took lessons with Max Bruch. He subsequently held numerous positions as a church organist and a choirmaster in Aachen, Königsberg, Naumburg, Pforta, and finally Plaue, near Arnstadt. He was a voluminous composer; wrote mostly for organ and chorus; also composed the *Goethe-Symphonie* (1948) and *Deutsches Friedens-Quartett.*

Lichnowsky, Prince Karl (actually, **Carl Alois Johann Nepomuk Vinzenz Leonhard**) **von,** Austrian patron of music of Polish descent; b. Vienna, June 21, 1761; d. there, April 15, 1814. He received the title of nobility from the Russian government in 1773, but spent most of his life in Vienna. He was a pupil of Mozart, who accompanied him on a visit to Prague, Dresden, Leipzig, and Berlin in 1789. Beethoven's opp. 1, 13, 26, and 36 are dedicated to Lichnowsky. In his home, Lichnowsky presented regular chamber music concerts with a quartet composed of Schuppanzigh, Sina, Weiss, and Kraft. His brother, **Count Moritz (Josef Cajetan Gallus) von Lichnowsky** (b. Vienna, Oct. 17, 1771; d. there, March 17, 1837), was a pianist and composer; he was also a patron and friend of Beethoven and Chopin. Beethoven dedicated his opp. 35, 51, and 90 to the Count and his wife.

Lichtenstein, Karl August, Freiherr von, German theater manager, conductor, and composer; b. Lahm, Franconia, Sept. 8, 1767; d. Berlin, Sept. 10, 1845. He studied in Gotha and then in Göttingen with Forkel. He gained attention as composer of the opera *Glück und Zufall* (Hannover, 1793) and the singspiel *Knall und Fall* (Bamberg, 1795); then was made manager

of the Dessau Opera, where his opera *Bathmendi* opened its new theater (Dec. 26, 1798); then followed his popular singspiel *Die steinerne Braut* (1799). He was made conductor and artistic director of the Vienna Court Theater (1800); after a period in the diplomatic service, he resumed his musical career as director of the Bamberg theater (1813–14); was music director in Strasbourg (1814–17), then went to Berlin (1823), where he was music director of the Royal Opera (1825–32). He wrote 17 works for the stage.

Lichtenthal, Peter, Austrian composer and writer on music; b. Pressburg, May 10, 1780; d. Milan, Aug. 18, 1853. He was a doctor by profession, and composed music as an avocation; settled in Milan in 1810 as a government censor; produced 3 operas and 7 ballets at La Scala; publ. a String Quartet, 2 piano trios, and piano pieces. His chief writings are: *Cenni biografici intorno al celebre maestro Wolfgang Amadeus Mozart* (1814); *Dizionario e bibliografia della musica* (4 vols., 1826); *Estetica, ossia Dottrina del bello e delle belle arti* (1831); *Mozart e le sue creazioni* (1842).

Lichtenwanger, William (John), learned American librarian; b. Asheville, N.C., Feb. 28, 1915. He studied at the Univ. of Michigan at Ann Arbor (B.Mus., 1937; M.Mus., 1940); played double bass, oboe, and other instruments in the band and orch.; wrote pieces with whimsical titles, e.g., *Phrygidair* (in Phrygian mode, naturally). He served as assistant reference librarian of the Music Division at the Library of Congress in Washington, D.C. (1940–53, except for service in the U.S. Army, 1941–45), then assistant head (1953–60) and head (1960–74) of the music reference section there; was associate ed. of *Notes* of the Music Library Assoc. (1946–60), then its ed. (1960–63); in 1975 he was made a member emeritus of the Music Library Assoc. In addition, he was music ed. of *Collier's Encyclopedia* (1947–50) and consultant for the biographical dictionary *Notable American Women* (1971); also was a contributor to supplements II and III of the *Dictionary of American Biography;* was chairman and compiler of *A Survey of Musical Instrument Collections in the U.S. and Canada* (1974). A polyglot and a polymath, he is fluent in German, French, and Turkish; nearly fluent in Japanese, and fairly fluent in personalized Russian. With his excellent wife, Carolyn, he ed. an analytic index to *Modern Music* (N.Y., 1976). Among his scholarly achievements, perhaps the highest is his incandescent essay "The Music of *The Star-Spangled Banner*— From Ludgate Hill to Capitol Hill," in the *Quarterly Journal of the Library of Congress* (July 1977), in which he furnishes documentary proof that the tune of the American national anthem was indeed composed by John Stafford Smith, all demurrings by various estimable historians to the contrary notwithstanding. To the 6th ed. of *Baker's Biographical Dictionary of Musicians* he contributed incalculably precious verifications, clarifications, rectifications, and refutations of previous inadvertent and/or ignorant fabrications and unintentional prevarications; he also ed. *Oscar Sonneck and American Music* (Urbana, Ill., 1984) and compiled *The Music of Henry Cowell: A Descriptive Catalog* (Brooklyn, 1986).

Lichtveld, Lou (actually, **Lodewijk Alphonsus Maria**), Dutch composer; b. Paramaribo, Surinam, Nov. 7, 1903. He went to Amsterdam in 1922 and was active as an organist and music critic. In 1936 he joined the International Brigade on the Loyalist side in the Spanish Civil War. During the Nazi occupation of the Netherlands, he served in the resistance movement, and became its representative in the emergency parliament of 1945. He returned to Surinam in 1949, and served as Minister of Education and Public Health and later President of the Exchequer; organized the facilities for musical education. From 1961 to 1969 he was in the diplomatic service of the Netherlands, stationed in Washington, D.C., and at the United Nations; then retired and lived mostly on the island of Tobago in the West Indies. He wrote about 2 dozen novels and essays under the pen name of **Albert Helman.** His musical works include an oratorio, *Canciones* (1934; MS lost in the Spanish Civil War); Piano Concertino (1932); Flute Sonata

(1930); Violin Sonata (1931); *Triptych* for Piano (1925); Piano Sonata (1927); also experimental pieces employing oriental scales. He used a 24-tone scale for 2 Dutch documentary films produced by Joris Ivens: *Regen* (1929; musical score added in 1932) and *Philips-Radio* (1930; also known as *Industrial Symphony*). He also composed several choruses a cappella.

Lickl, Johann Georg, Austrian conductor and composer; b. Korneuburg, Lower Austria, April 11, 1769; d. Fünfkirchen, May 12, 1843. He studied music with the Korneuburg church organist Witzig, then went to Vienna (1785), where he continued his studies with Albrechtsberger and Haydn; subsequently was active as a teacher and as organist at the Carmelite Church in the Leopoldstadt. He became associated around 1789 with Schikaneder's Freihaus-Theater auf der Wieden, where he contributed numbers to popular singspiels or wrote entire scores for them. His *Der Brigitten-Kirchtag* (1802) was composed for the new Theater an der Wien, and his comic opera *Slawina von Pommern* (1812) for the Leopoldstadt Theater. He served as regens chori at Fünfkirchen Cathedral (from 1805), producing much sacred music. He publ. arrangements for piano and harmonium of popular classics in *Wiener Salon-Musik*. He had 2 sons: **Karl Georg Lickl** (b. Vienna, Oct. 28, 1801; d. there, Aug. 8, 1877), a civil servant who became well known as a physharmonica player and composer for the instrument, and **Aegidius (Ferdinand) Karl Lickl** (b. Vienna, Sept. 1, 1803; d. Trieste, July 22, 1864), who studied with his father, appeared as a pianist, and then settled in Trieste as a teacher, conductor, and composer; he wrote the opera *La disfida Berletta* (1848) and sacred music.

Lidholm, Ingvar (Natanael), Swedish composer; b. Jönköping, Feb. 24, 1921. He studied violin with Hermann Gramms and orchestration with Natanael Berg in Södertälje; then received violin training from Alex Ruunqvist and conducting lessons from Tor Mann at the Stockholm Musikhögskolan (1940–45); also studied composition with Hilding Rosenberg (1943–45). He was a violinist in the orch. of the Royal Theater in Stockholm (1943–47); received a Jenny Lind fellowship and pursued his studies in France, Switzerland, and Italy (1947); later studied in Darmstadt (summer 1949) and with Mátyás Seiber in England (1954). He served as director of music in Örebro (1947–56); was director of chamber music for the Swedish Radio (1956–65); after holding the position of prof. of composition at the Stockholm Musikhögskolan (1965–75), he returned to the Swedish Radio as director of planning in its music dept. (1975). In 1960 he was elected a member of the Royal Swedish Academy of Music in Stockholm. He became active in Swedish avant-garde circles, contributing greatly to the formulation of methods and aims of contemporary music. In his works, he applies constructivist methods with various serial algorithms.
Works: *Toccata e canto* for Chamber Orch. (1944); Concerto for String Orch. (1945); Solo Flute Sonata (1945); *Laudi* for a cappella Chorus (1947); Piano Sonata (1947); *Music for String Orch.* (1952); Concertino for Flute, Oboe, English Horn, and Cello (1954); *Ritornell* for Orch. (Stockholm, Feb. 17, 1956); *4 Pieces* for Cello and Piano (1955); *Canto LXXXI* for a cappella Chorus, after Ezra Pound (1956); *Skaldens Natt* (The Night of the Poet) for Soprano, Chorus, and Orch. (Hamburg, April 6, 1959); *Mutanza* for Orch. (Örebro, Nov. 15, 1959); ballet, *Riter* (Rites; Stockholm, March 26, 1960); *Motus Colores* for Orch. (Cologne Festival, June 13, 1960); *Poesis* for Orch. (Stockholm, Jan. 14, 1964); *Nausikaa ensam* (Nausikaa Alone), lyrical scene, based on a section of Eyvind Johnson's novel *Return to Ithaca*, for Soprano, Chorus, and Orch. (Ingesund, June 2, 1963); *Holländarn* (The Dutchman), opera, after Strindberg (Swedish Television, Dec. 10, 1967); *Stamp Music,* an improvisatory piece in graphic notation for Variable Performers (1970; composed for a Swedish postage stamp; version for Soprano and Tam-tam, 1971); *Inga träd skall väcka dig,* dramatic music for television (1974); *Greetings (from an old world)* for Orch. (N.Y., Nov. 10, 1976); *Kontakion,* hymn for

Orch. (1978); *De profundis* for Chorus (1983); *Tre elegier-Epilog* for String Quartet (1982–86).

Lídl, Václav, Czech composer; b. Brno, Nov. 5, 1922. He studied with Kvapil at the Brno Cons., graduating in 1948. In addition to writing numerous film scores, he also composed 4 syms. (1965, 1974, 1975, 1979), *Radostná predehra* for Orch. (1981), *Balada o červnovém ránu* (*Lidice 1942*) for Orch. (1982), *Serenade* for Orch. (1982); chamber music, and choral works.

Lidón, José, Spanish organist and composer; b. Béjar, June 2, 1748; d. Madrid, Feb. 11, 1827. He studied at Madrid's Réal Colegio di Niños Cantores; was organist at Orense Cathedral, then was made 4th organist (1768) and 1st organist (1787) of Madrid's royal chapel; was master there and rector of the Réal Colegio (1805–27). He wrote an opera, *Glauca y Coriolano* (Madrid, 1791), about 60 sacred vocal works, chamber music, and organ pieces; also wrote several theoretical works.

Lie, Erika. See **Lie-Nissen, Erika.**

Lie, Harald, Norwegian composer; b. Christiania, Nov. 21, 1902; d. there (Oslo), May 23, 1942. He studied piano at the Christiania Cons.; went to the U.S. (1923), where he earned his living as a piano tuner; then studied piano manufacturing in Leipzig. Returning to Norway in 1929, he took lessons in composition with Fartein Valen. He was stricken with tuberculosis in 1932. His works were written in a late Romantic style. He withdrew a number of his scores: among those acknowledged are 2 syms. (1934, 1937), a *Symphonic Dance,* the scherzo from his unfinished 3rd Sym. (1942), several fine songs with orch., and choral pieces.

Lie, Sigurd, Norwegian composer; b. Drammen, May 23, 1871; d. there, Sept. 29, 1904. He was a pupil of Lindeman and Holter; then studied at the Leipzig Cons. (1891–93) and with Urban in Berlin (1894–95); was appointed conductor of the Handelsstand Sangforening in Christiania (1902).
Works: Sym. in A minor (Christiania, Feb. 28, 1903); *Oriental Suite* for Orch. (Christiania, Oct. 28, 1899); Violin Concerto (Bergen, Feb. 13, 1896); *Erling Skjalgson* for Baritone Solo, Men's Chorus, and Orch. (Christiania, Oct. 28, 1899); *Norske dans* for Violin and Piano; men's choruses; a song cycle, *Wartburg;* about 80 separate songs, including the well-known *Sne* (Snow); piano pieces.

Liebe, Eduard Ludwig, German composer; b. Magdeburg, Nov. 19, 1819; d. Chur, Feb. 4, 1900. He studied in Kassel with Spohr and Baldewein; then was a music director at Koblenz, Mainz, and Worms; went to Strasbourg as a teacher; later taught in London. He wrote an opera, *Die Braut von Azola* (Karlsruhe, 1868); also publ. popular songs and piano pieces.

Liebermann, Rolf, esteemed Swiss operatic administrator and composer; b. Zürich, Sept. 14, 1910. He studied law at the Univ. of Zürich and received private instruction in music from José Berr (1929–33); took a conducting course with H. Scherchen in Budapest (1936), and served as his assistant in Vienna (1937–38); also had composition studies with W. Vogel (1940). He was a producer at Radio Zürich (1945–50); then was director of the orch. section of the Schweizerische Rundspruchgesellschaft in Zürich (1950–57); subsequently was director of music of the North German Radio in Hamburg (1957–59). He was Intendant of the Hamburg State Opera (1959–73), where he pursued a policy of staging numerous 20th-century operas, including specially commissioned works from leading contemporary composers; then was general administrator of the Paris Opéra (1973–80), bringing enlightened leadership to bear on its artistic policies; subsequently was recalled to his former post at the Hamburg State Opera in 1985, remaining there until 1988. He was made a Commandeur de la Légion d'honneur in 1975. His autobiography was publ. in English as *Opera Years* (1987). As a composer, he worked mostly in an experimental idiom, sharing the influence of hedonistic eclecticism, French neo-Classicism, and Viennese dodecaphony; he became particularly attracted to theatrical applications of modernistic procedures.

WORKS: OPERAS: *Leonore 40/45* (Basel, March 25, 1952); *Penelope* (Salzburg, Aug. 17, 1954); *The School for Wives* (Louisville, Dec. 3, 1955; rev. as *Die Schule der Frauen*, Salzburg, 1957); *La Forêt* (1986). **ORCH.:** *Furioso* (1947; Dallas, Dec. 9, 1950); *Schweizerische Volksliedersuite* (BBC, Jan. 10, 1947); Music for Orch. and Speaker (1949); Sym. No. 1 (1949); Concerto for Jazz Band and Orch. (Donaueschingen Festival, Oct. 17, 1954); *Geigy Festival Concerto* (1958); *Concert des échanges* for 52 Industrial Machines recorded on tape (Lausanne, April 24, 1964); also chamber pieces, including *Essay 81* for Cello and Piano (1981); choral works; songs; piano pieces.

BIBL.: I. Scharberth and H. Paris, eds., *R. L. zum 60. Geburtstag* (Hamburg, 1970); C. Riess, *R. L., "Nennen Sie mich einfach Musiker"* (Hamburg, 1977).

Lieberson, Goddard, English-American recording executive and composer, father of **Peter Lieberson;** b. Hanley, Staffordshire, April 5, 1911; d. N.Y., May 29, 1977. He was taken to the U.S. as a child; studied composition with George Frederick McKay at the Univ. of Washington in Seattle and with Bernard Rogers at the Eastman School of Music in Rochester, N.Y. In 1939 he joined the Masterworks division of Columbia Records in N.Y.; was its president (1955–66; 1973–75), during which period he recorded many contemporary works as well as those of the standard repertoire. In 1964 he was named president of the Record Industry Assoc. of America; in 1978 the American Academy and Inst. of Arts and Letters set up the Lieberson fellowships to assist young composers. He composed a Sym., a ballet, *Yellow Poodle*, chamber music, choral works, and piano pieces.

Lieberson, Peter, American composer, son of **Goddard Lieberson;** b. N.Y., Oct. 25, 1946. He took a degree in English literature at N.Y. Univ. (1972); after studies with Milton Babbitt, he trained with Charles Wuorinen at Columbia Univ. (M.A. in composition, 1974), then studied Vajrayana Buddhism with Chögyam Trungpa of the Shambhala tradition. After completing his doctoral studies with Donald Martino and Martin Boykan at Brandeis Univ., he taught at Harvard Univ. (1984–88). He then settled in Halifax, Nova Scotia, as international director of Shambhala training, while continuing to pursue his career as a composer. His compositions are written in a well-crafted 12-tone system.

WORKS: *Motetti di Eugenio Montali* for Soprano, Alto, and 4 Instruments (1971–72); Concerto for 4 Groups of Instruments (1972–73); Concerto for Cello and 4 Trios (1974); *Piano Fantasy* (1975); *Accordance* for 9 Instruments (1975–76); *Tashi Quartet* for Clarinet, Violin, Cello, and Piano (1978–79); Piano Concerto (1980–83; Boston, April 21, 1983); 3 *Songs for Soprano and Chamber Orch.* (1981); *Lalita (Chamber Variations)* for 10 Instruments (1983–84); *Feast Day* for Flute, Oboe, Cello, and Piano or Harpsichord (Washington, D.C., Sept. 21, 1985); *Drala* for Orch. (Boston, Oct. 9, 1986); *Ziji* for Clarinet, Horn, Violin, Viola, Cello, and Piano (1987; N.Y., Jan. 17, 1988); *Gesar Legend* for Orch. (Boston, June 12, 1988); *Raising the Gaze* for 7 Instrumentalists (San Francisco, March 28, 1988); *Wind Messengers* for 13 Instruments (1990).

Liebig, Karl, German conductor; b. Schwedt, July 25, 1808; d. Berlin, Oct. 6, 1872. He was oboist in the Alexander Grenadier Regiment in Berlin; in 1843 he organized the Berlin Symphoniekapelle, which under his leadership attained a very high standard of performance; in 1867 the orch. elected another conductor; his attempts to form a rival organization proved futile.

Liebling, Emil, German-American pianist and composer, brother of **Georg Liebling;** b. Pless, Silesia, April 12, 1851; d. Chicago, Jan. 20, 1914. He studied piano with Theodor Kullak in Berlin, Dachs in Vienna, and Liszt in Weimar; also composition with Dorn in Berlin. In 1867 he went to America and lived in Chicago from 1872, actively engaged as a concert pianist and teacher. He wrote a number of effective piano pieces in a light vein (*Florence Valse, Feu follet, Albumblatt,*

2 Romances, Cradle Song, Canzonetta, Menuetto scherzoso, Mazurka de concert, Spring Song). He ed. *The American History and Encyclopedia of Music* and co-ed. a *Dictionary of Musical Terms.*

Liebling, Estelle, American soprano and pedagogue, sister of **Leonard** and niece of **Emil** and **Georg Liebling;** b. N.Y., April 21, 1880; d. there, Sept. 25, 1970. She studied with Mathilde Marchesi in Paris and S. Nicklass-Kempner in Berlin; made her debut as Lucia at the Dresden Court Opera; also appeared at the Stuttgart Opera, the Opéra-Comique in Paris, and the Metropolitan Opera in N.Y. (debut Feb. 24, 1902, as Marguerite in *Les Huguenots*); was again on the Metropolitan's roster in 1903–4; was a soloist with leading orchs. in the U.S., France, and Germany; also with Sousa; from 1936 to 1938, was a prof. at the Curtis Inst. of Music in Philadelphia; then settled in N.Y. as a vocal teacher. Her most famous pupil was Beverly Sills. She publ. *The Estelle Liebling Coloratura Digest* (N.Y., 1943).

Liebling, Georg, German-American pianist and composer, brother of **Emil Liebling;** b. Berlin, Jan. 22, 1865; d. N.Y., Feb. 7, 1946. He studied piano with Theodor and Franz Kullak and Liszt, composition with Urban and Dorn; toured Europe (1885–89); was court pianist to the Duke of Coburg (1890). From 1894 to 1897 he directed his own music school in Berlin; from 1898 to 1908, was a prof. at the Guildhall School of Music in London. He settled in the U.S. in 1924, making his N.Y. debut that same year. He used the pseudonym **André Myrot.**

WORKS: *Great Mass* for Soli, Chorus, Orch., and Organ (Los Angeles, 1931); *Concerto eroico* for Piano and Orch. (1925); 2 violin concertos; 2 violin sonatas; 3 Preludes for Violin and Piano; *Aria e Tarantella* for Cello and Piano; *Légende* for Violin and Piano; etc.; piano pieces; songs.

BIBL.: G. Braun, *Hofpianist G. L.* (Berlin, 1896).

Liebling, Leonard, American pianist, music critic, and editor, nephew of **Georg** and **Emil** and brother of **Estelle Liebling;** b. N.Y., Feb. 7, 1874; d. there, Oct. 28, 1945. He studied at City College in N.Y., and privately with Leopold Godowsky (piano); then in Berlin with Kullak and Barth (piano) and Urban (composition); toured Europe and America as a pianist. In 1902 he joined the staff of the *Musical Courier* in N.Y., and in 1911 became its ed.-in-chief; his weekly columns on topical subjects were both entertaining and instructive. He also served as music critic of the *N.Y. American* (1923–34; 1936–37). He wrote some chamber music, piano pieces, and songs, as well as librettos of several light operas, including Sousa's *The American Maid.*

Lienau, Emil Robert, German music publisher; b. Neustadt, Holstein, Dec. 28, 1838; d. there, July 22, 1920. He studied music with Moscheles and Rietz; joined Schlesinger's firm in Berlin (1863), purchasing it (1864); also acquired Haslinger's firm in Vienna (1875). His son, **Robert Heinrich Lienau** (b. Neustadt, July 27, 1866; d. Berlin, Nov. 8, 1949), took over the direction of the firm in 1898; another son, **Friedrich Wilhelm Lienau** (b. Berlin, Jan. 6, 1876; d. Vienna, Nov. 15, 1973), was active with the firm from 1907 to 1938. After the elder brother's death, his children assumed control.

BIBL.: R. Elvers, *A.M. Schlesinger—R. L.: 150 Jahre Musik-Verlag* (Berlin, 1960).

Lie-Nissen (originally, **Lie**), **Erika,** Norwegian pianist; b. Kongsvinger, Jan. 17, 1845; d. Christiania, Oct. 27, 1903. She studied with Kjerulf in Christiania, T. Kullak in Berlin, and Tellefsen in Paris; taught at Kullak's Academy in Berlin; toured throughout Europe, becoming noted for her performances of Chopin. She was prof. of piano at the Copenhagen Cons. (1870–74); then married Dr. Oscar Nissen and settled in Christiania.

Liepe, Emil, German singer, teacher, and composer; b. Potsdam, Jan. 16, 1860; d. Berlin, Feb. 18, 1940. He studied in Leipzig and Vienna; from 1884 to 1890, sang in various German opera theaters; in 1891–92 he appeared at the Bayreuth Festival; then retired from the stage, and taught voice at the Sondershausen Cons. (1903–7) and then in Berlin. He wrote an opera, *Colomba* (Danzig, 1894); symphonic poems: *Fatum* and *Rückblick*; Sym.; a number of songs.

Lier, Bertus van. See **Van Lier, Bertus.**

Lier, Jacques van. See **Van Lier, Jacques.**

Lierhammer, Theodor, Austrian baritone and teacher; b. Lemberg, Nov. 18, 1866; d. Vienna, Jan. 6, 1937. He was a practicing physician when he began to study singing with Ress in Vienna, Carafa in Milan, and Stockhausen in Frankfurt; made his debut at Vienna in 1894 in a concert with Fritz Kreisler; toured Austria and Hungary (1896), Germany (1898), Russia (1899), France and England (1900), and the U.S. (1904). From 1904 to 1914 he was a prof. of singing at the Royal Academy of Music in London; served as an army physician during World War I; from 1922 to 1924 he was in London as a singer and teacher; in 1924, was named prof. of singing at the Academy of Music in Vienna; from 1932 to 1935, taught at the Austro-American Summer Cons., in Mondsee (Salzburg). One of his American pupils was Roland Hayes.

Lieurance, Thurlow (Weed), American composer; b. Oskaloosa, Iowa, March 21, 1878; d. Boulder, Colo., Oct. 9, 1963. He studied at the Cincinnati College of Music; served as an army bandmaster during the Spanish-American War. He became interested in American Indian music, and lived on various reservations, studying the culture of Indian tribes; this research resulted in the composition of music showing the influence of Indian melodies; one of his songs, *By the Waters of Minnetonka* (also known as *Moon Deer*), achieved tremendous popularity; he also publ. *9 Indian Songs* (1919); *Songs of the North American Indian* (1921); *8 Songs from the Green Timber* (1922); *Forgotten Trails* (1923); wrote several symphonic pieces: *Medicine Dance, Colonial Exposition Sketches, Scenes Southwest, Prairie Sketches, Water Moon Maiden,* etc. In 1940 he was appointed dean of the music dept. of Municipal Univ. of Wichita, Kans.; in 1957, was named dean emeritus.

Ligendza, Catarina (real name, **Katarina Beyron**), Swedish soprano; b. Stockholm, Oct. 18, 1937. Her parents sang at Stockholm's Royal Theater; she studied at the Würzburg Cons., in Vienna, and with Greindl in Saarbrücken. She made her debut as Countess Almaviva in Linz (1965); then sang in Braunschweig and Saarbrücken (1966–69); subsequently became a member of the Deutsche Oper in West Berlin and of the Württemberg State Theater in Stuttgart. She made her Metropolitan Opera debut in N.Y. as Leonore in *Fidelio* on Feb. 25, 1971; her Covent Garden debut in London followed as Senta in 1972. Her other roles included Agathe, Isolde, Brünnhilde, Desdemona, Chrysothemis, and Ariadne.

Ligeti, György (Sándor), eminent Hungarian-born Austrian composer and pedagogue; b. Dicsöszentmárton, Transylvania, May 28, 1923. The original surname of the family was Auer; his great-uncle was **Leopold Auer.** He studied composition with Ferenc Farkas at the Kolozsvar Cons. (1941–43) and privately with Pál Kadosa in Budapest (1942–43); then continued his training with Sándor Veress, Pál Járdányi, Farkas, and Lajos Bárdos at the Budapest Academy of Music (1945–49), where he subsequently was a prof. of harmony, counterpoint, and analysis (from 1950). After the Hungarian revolution was crushed by the Soviet Union in 1956, he fled his homeland for the West; in 1967 he became a naturalized Austrian citizen. He worked at the electronic music studio of the West German Radio in Cologne (1957–58); from 1959 to 1972 he lectured at the Darmstadt summer courses in new music; from 1961 to 1971 he also was a visiting prof. at the Stockholm Musikhögskolan. In 1972 he served as composer-in-residence at Stanford Univ., and in 1973 he taught at the Berkshire Music Center at Tanglewood. In 1973 he became a prof. of composition at the Hamburg Hochschule für Musik. He has received numerous honors and awards. In 1964 he was made a member of the Royal Swedish Academy of Music in Stockholm, in 1968 a member of the Akademie der Künste in Berlin, and in 1984 an honorary member of the American Academy and Inst. of

Arts and Letters; in 1986 he received the Grawemeyer Award of the Univ. of Louisville; in 1988 he was made a Commandeur in the Ordre National des Arts et Lettres in Paris. In his bold and imaginative experimentation with musical materials and parameters, Ligeti endeavors to bring together all aural and visual elements in a synthetic entity, making use of all conceivable effects and alternating tremendous sonorous upheavals with static chordal masses and shifting dynamic colors. He describes his orch. style as micropolyphony.

WORKS: OPERA: *Le Grand Macabre* (1974–77; Stockholm, April 12, 1978). **ORCH.:** *Alte ungarische Tänze* for Flute or Clarinet and String Orch. (1949); *Apparitions* (1958–59; Cologne, June 19, 1960); *Atmosphères* (Donaueschingen, Oct. 22, 1961); *Poème symphonique* for 100 Metronomes (1962; Hilversum, Sept. 13, 1963); *Requiem* for Soprano, Mezzo-soprano, 2 Choruses, and Orch. (1963–65; Stockholm, March 14, 1965; the *Kyrie* was used in the film score for *2001: A Space Odyssey*); Cello Concerto (1966; Berlin, April 19, 1967); *Lontano* (Donaueschingen, Oct. 22, 1967); *Ramifications* for String Orch. or 12 Solo Strings (1968–69; 1st version, Berlin, April 23, 1969; 2nd version, Saarbrücken, Oct. 10, 1969); Chamber Concerto for 13 Instruments (Ottawa, April 2, 1970); *Melodien* (Nuremberg, Dec. 10, 1971); Double Concerto for Flute, Oboe, and Orch. (Berlin, Sept. 16, 1972); *Clocks and Clouds* for Women's Chorus and Orch. (Graz, Oct. 15, 1973); *San Francisco Polyphony* (1973–74; San Francisco, Jan. 8, 1975); Piano Concerto (1985–88; N.Y., Jan. 17, 1990; Anthony de Bonaventura, soloist). **VOCAL:** *Ifúsági kantáta* (Cantata for Youth) for Soprano, Contralto, Tenor, Baritone, Chorus, and Orch. (1949); *Pápainé* for Chorus (1953); *Éjszaka* (Night) and *Reggel* (Morning) for Chorus (1955); *Aventures* for 3 Singers and 7 Instruments (1962; Hamburg, April 4, 1963); *Nouvelles aventures* for Aventures Ensemble (1962–65; Hamburg, May 26, 1966); *Aventures & Nouvelles aventures*, theater piece based on the 2 preceding works (Stuttgart, Oct. 19, 1966); *Lux aeterna* for 16 Voices (Stuttgart, Nov. 2, 1966); *Drei Phantasien* for 16 Voices (Stockholm, Sept. 26, 1983); *Magyar etüdök* (Hungarian Studies) for 16 Voices (1983). **CHAMBER:** Cello Sonata (1948–53); 2 string quartets: No. 1, *Métamorphoses nocturnes* (1953–54; Vienna, May 8, 1958); No. 2 (1968; Baden-Baden, Dec. 14, 1969); 10 Pieces for Wind Quintet (1968; Malmö, Jan. 20, 1969); Trio for Violin, Horn, and Piano (Hamburg-Bergedorf, Aug. 7, 1982). **PIANO:** *Musica ricercata* (1951–53); *Trois bagatelles* (1961); *Monument, Selbstportrait, Bewegung* for 2 Pianos (1976); *Études* (1985). **ORGAN:** *Volumina* (1961–62); 2 studies: No. 1, *Harmonies* (1967); No. 2, *Coulée* (1969). **HARPSICHORD:** *Continuum* (1968); *Hungarian Rock* (Chaconne) (1978); *Passacaglia ungherese* (1978). **ELECTRONIC:** *Glissandi* (1957); *Artikulation* (1958); *Pièce électronique* No. 3 (1957–58).

BIBL.: E. Salmenhaara, *Das musikalische Material und seine Behandlung in den Werken "Apparitions," "Atmosphères," "Aventures" und "Requiem" von G. L.* (Helsinki and Regensburg, 1969); O. Nordwall, *G. L.: Eine Monographie* (Mainz, 1971); P. Griffiths, *G. L.* (London, 1983); E. Restagno, ed., *L.* (Turin, 1985); H. Sabbe, *G. L.: Studien zur kompositorischen Phänomenologie* (1987); D. Soria, "G. L.: Distinguished and Unpredictable," *Musical America* (Sept. 1987); S. Rourke, "L.'s Early Years in the West," *Musical Times* (Sept. 1989).

Lightfoot, Gordon, Canadian singer, guitarist, and composer in the popular-music genres; b. Orillia, Ontario, Nov. 17, 1938. He learned to play folk guitar; then enrolled in Westlake College of Music in Los Angeles to acquire the rudiments of music theory. After working in Canada and England, he met Bob Dylan, who impressed him with the importance of social concerns in songs. In 1966 he brought out an album, *Lightfoot*, in which he demonstrated his facile talents as singer, composer, and guitarist.

BIBL.: M. Collins, *L.: If You Could Read His Mind: A Biography* (Toronto, 1988).

Lilburn, Douglas (Gordon), New Zealand composer; b. Wanganui, Nov. 2, 1915. He studied with J.C. Bradshaw at Canterbury Univ. College (1934–36), then won the Grainger Competition with his tone poem *Forest* (1936); subsequently studied with Edward Mitchell (piano) and Vaughan Williams (composition) at the Royal College of Music in London (1937–40), where he received the Cobbett Prize for his *Phantasy* for String Quartet (1939). He began teaching at Victoria Univ. in Wellington (1947); was made prof. and director of the electronic music studio (1970), positions he held until his retirement in 1979. He publ. *A Search for a Language* (Wellington, 1985).

Works: orch.: 3 syms.: No. 1 (1949; Wellington, May 12, 1951); No. 2 (1951; rev. 1974); No. 3 (1961); *Forest*, tone poem (1936); *Aotearoa Overture* (1940); *A Song of Islands* (1946); *Diversions* for String Orch. (1947); *A Birthday Offering* (1956); 4 Canzonas for Strings (1980). **chamber:** String Quartet (1946); Sonata for Violin and Piano (1950); Quartet for Brass Instruments (1957); Wind Quintet (1957); piano pieces; also vocal works; tape pieces.

Bibl.: V. Harris and P. Norman, eds., *D. L.: A Festschrift* (Wellington, 1980).

Liliencron, Rochus (Traugott Ferdinand), Freiherr von, eminent German music scholar; b. Plön, Dec. 8, 1820; d. Koblenz, March 5, 1912. He studied theology, law, and philology at the Univs. of Kiel and Berlin (Ph.D., 1846); took a course in Nordic philology in Copenhagen. In 1850 he became a teacher of Old Norse language and literature at the Univ. of Kiel; in 1852, was made prof. of philology at the Univ. of Jena; then was privy councillor at Saxe-Meiningen (1855–68); in 1869, went to Munich; there he ed. the *Allgemeine deutsche Biographie* (with F. von Wegele; 1875–1907); collected and annotated German folk songs of the Middle Ages, publ. as *Die Historische Volkslieder der Deutschen vom 13.–16. Jahrhundert* (4 vols. and an appendix, Leipzig, 1865–69); from 1876 he lived in Schleswig as provost of St. John's Monastery; in 1894, was appointed ed. of Denkmäler Deutscher Tonkunst. He wrote an autobiography, *Frohe Jugendtage* (1902). H. Kretzschmar ed. a Festschrift in honor of his 90th birthday (1910).

Writings: *Die historischen Lieder und Sprüche aus der letzten Zeit des Minnesangs* (with W. Stade; Weimar, 1854); *Über den Chorgesang in der evangelischen Kirche* (1881); *Deutsches Leben im Volkslied um 1530* (Berlin and Stuttgart, 1885; 2nd ed., 1925); *Die horazischen Metren in deutschen Kompositionen des XVI. Jahrhunderts* (Leipzig, 1887); *Liturgisch-musikalische Geschichte der evangelischen Gottesdienste von 1523 bis 1700* (Schleswig, 1893); *Die Aufgaben des Chorgesanges im heutigen evangelischen Gottesdienste* (Oppeln, 1895); *Chorordnung für die Sonn- und Festtage des evangelischen Kirchenjahres* (Gütersloh, 1900; 2nd ed., 1929, by H.J. Moser).

Bibl.: A. Bettelheim, *Leben und Wirken des Freiherrn R. v. L.* (Berlin, 1917).

Lili'uokalani (Lydia Kamaka'eha Paki), Hawaiian queen and composer; b. Honolulu, Sept. 2, 1838; d. there, Nov. 11, 1917. She entered the Chief's Children's School to study music when she was 4; became a skillful pianist, organist, and choral director; composed a number of attractive songs, including the popular *Aloha 'oe* (1878); also wrote the Hawaiian national anthem, *He mele lahui Hawaii*. Her reign as queen was brief (1891–93); she was removed by American interests.

Liljeblad, Ingeborg, Finnish soprano; b. Helsinki, Oct. 17, 1887; d. there, Feb. 28, 1942. She studied in Berlin with Etelka Gerster, and in Paris with Félia Litvinne; was engaged at the Mannheim Opera (1911–13) and the Hamburg Opera (1913–14). Returning to Helsinki in 1927, she taught at the Sibelius Academy. She was married to the conductor Leo Funtek.

Liljefors, Ingemar (Kristian), Swedish pianist and composer, son of **Ruben (Mattias) Liljefors;** b. Göteborg, Dec. 13, 1906; d. Stockholm, Oct. 14, 1981. He studied at the Royal Academy of Music in Stockholm (1923–27; 1929–31) and in Munich (1927–29); in 1938, was appointed to the staff of the Stockholm Musikhögskolan. From 1947 to 1963 he was chairman of the Assoc. of Swedish Composers. He publ. a manual on harmony from the functional point of view (1937) and one on harmonic analysis along similar lines (1951). His compositions frequently employed elements of Swedish folk music with a later infusion of some modernistic techniques.

Works: Opera, *Hyrkusken* (The Coachman; 1951); *Rhapsody* for Piano and Orch. (1936); Piano Concerto (1940); Sym. (1943); Piano Concertino (1949); Violin Concerto (1956); *En Tijdh-Spegel* (A Mirror of the Times) for Soli, Chorus, and Orch. (1959; Swedish Radio, April 16, 1961); Sinfonietta (1961); 2 *Intermezzi* for Strings (1966); *Divertimento* for Strings (1968); 2 piano trios (1940, 1961); Violin Sonatina (1954); 3 piano sonatinas (1954, 1964, 1965); Cello Sonatina (1958); String Quartet (1963); Sonatina for Solo Violin (1968).

Liljefors, Ruben (Mattias), Swedish composer and conductor, father of **Ingemar (Kristian) Liljefors;** b. Uppsala, Sept. 30, 1871; d. there, March 4, 1936. He studied in Uppsala; then with Jadassohn at the Leipzig Cons.; later in Dresden with Draeseke and with Reger in Leipzig. Returning to Sweden, he was conductor of the Göteborg Phil. (1902–11) and the Gavleborg Orch. Soc. (1912–31). His works followed in the Romantic tradition.

Works: Piano Concerto (1899; rewritten 1922); Sym. (1906); *Sommer-Suite* for Orch. (1920); choral works; chamber music; piano pieces; songs.

Lill, John (Richard), English pianist; b. London, March 17, 1944. He studied at the Royal College of Music in London; also with Wilhelm Kempff in Positano. He made his debut at a concert in the Royal Festival Hall in London in 1963; was joint 1st prizewinner at the Tchaikovsky Competition in Moscow (1970), which was the beginning of his successful international career. In 1978 he received the Order of the British Empire.

Lillo, Giuseppe, Italian composer; b. Galatina, Lecce, Feb. 26, 1814; d. Naples, Feb. 4, 1863. He studied at the Naples Reale Collegio di Musica (later the Conservatorio di S. Pietro a Majella) with Furno, Lanza, and Zingarelli; in 1846, became a teacher of harmony there; later (1859), a teacher of counterpoint and composition there. He had to retire from active life in 1861 because of mental illness.

Works: Operas: *La moglie per 24 ore ossia L'ammalato di buona salute* (Naples, 1834) and *L'osteria d'Andujar* (Naples, 1840); syms.; sacred choral works; chamber music; piano pieces.

Limnander de Nieuwenhove, Armand Marie Ghislain, Belgian composer; b. Ghent, May 22, 1814; d. Moignanville, near Paris, Aug. 15, 1892. He studied in Freiburg with Lambillotte and in Brussels with Fétis; in 1835, became a choral director in Mechelen; settled in Paris (1845).

Works: Grand opera, *Le Maître-chanteur* (Paris, 1853); comic operas: *Les Monténégrins* (Paris, 1849); *Le Château de la Barbe-Bleue* (1851); *Yvonne* (1859); sym., *La Fin des Moisson*; *Scènes druidiques* for Orch.; String Quartet; Cello Sonata; church music; songs; etc.

Lin, Cho-Liang, outstanding Chinese-born American violinist; b. Hsin-Chu, Taiwan, Jan. 29, 1960. He began to study the violin as a child and won the Taiwan National Youth Violin Competition at age 10; when he was 12 he became a pupil of Robert Pikler at the New South Wales State Conservatorium of Music in Sydney; at 15 he went to the U.S., where he enrolled at the Juilliard School in N.Y. as a scholarship student of Dorothy DeLay (graduated, 1981). He won wide notice when he was chosen to play at the inaugural concert for President Jimmy Carter in 1977; that same year he won 1st prize in the Queen Sofia International Competition in Madrid. In subsequent years he pursued a highly rewarding career as a virtuoso, touring throughout the world; he appeared as a soloist with virtually every major orch., and also was active as a recitalist and chamber music player. In 1988 he became a naturalized U.S. citizen. His extensive repertoire ranges from the standard literature to specially commissioned works. In his performances, he combines effortless technique with a beguiling luminosity of tone.

Bibl.: H. Kupferberg, "C.-L. L.," *Musical America* (July 1987); B. Jepson, "C.-L. L.," *Ovation* (Jan. 1988).

Lincke, Joseph, Silesian cellist and composer; b. Trachenberg, June 8, 1783; d. Vienna, March 26, 1837. He studied violin with his father and cello with Oswald. He settled in Vienna, where he was cellist in Schuppanzigh's quartet (1808–16); after serving as chamber musician to Countess Erdődy in Pancovecz, near Zagreb (1816–18), he returned to Vienna as 1st cellist of the orch. at the Theater an der Wien. He composed concertos, variations, capriccios, etc.

Lincke, (Carl Emil) Paul, German conductor and composer; b. Berlin, Nov. 7, 1866; d. Klausthal-Zellerfelde, near Göttingen, Sept. 3, 1946. He studied with Rudolf Kleinow in Wittenberge (1880–84); was active in many fields; played violin and bassoon; conducted theater orchs.; engaged in music publishing. His chief fame comes from his operettas; he is generally credited as being the progenitor of a special type of "Berlin operetta," as distinguished from the Vienna genre. The best known of these are *Venus auf Erden* (Berlin, June 6, 1897); *Im Reiche des Indra* (Berlin, Dec. 17, 1899); *Frau Luna* (Berlin, Dec. 31, 1899); *Fräulein Loreley* (Berlin, Oct. 15, 1900); *Lysistrata* (Berlin, April 1, 1902; contains the famous tune *Glühwürmchen-Idyll* [Glowworm]); *Grigri* (Cologne, March 25, 1911); *Casanova* (Chemnitz, Nov. 5, 1913); *Ein Liebestraum* (Berlin Radio, July 20, 1940). A postage stamp in Lincke's honor, with a musical example showing the melody *Berliner Luft* from *Frau Luna*, was issued by the West German government in 1957.
Bibl.: E. Nick, *P. L.* (Hamburg, 1953); O. Schneidereit, *P. L. und die Entstehung der Berliner Operette* (Berlin, 1974).

Lind, Jenny (actually, **Johanna Maria**), famous Swedish soprano, called the "Swedish Nightingale"; b. Stockholm, Oct. 6, 1820; d. Wynds Point, Herefordshire, Nov. 2, 1887. She made her 1st stage appearance in Stockholm at the age of 10 (Nov. 29, 1830); that same year she entered the Royal Opera School there, where she studied with C. Craelius and I. Berg; during this period, she also sang in many comedies and melodramas; continued her studies with A. Lindblad and J. Josephson at the school, and then made her formal operatic debut as Agathe in *Der Freischütz* at the Royal Opera in Stockholm (March 7, 1838); later that year appeared as Pamina and Euryanthe there, and then as Donna Anna (1839) and Norina (1841). In 1840 she was appointed a regular member of the Royal Swedish Academy of Music, and was also given the rank of court singer. However, she felt the necessity of improving her voice, and went to Paris to study with Manuel García (1841–42). Upon her return to Stockholm, she sang Norma (Oct. 10, 1842); later appeared there as the Countess in *Le nozze di Figaro*, Anna in *La Sonnambula*, Valentine in *Les Huguenots*, and Anna Bolena. Although Meyerbeer wrote the role of Vielka in his opera *Ein Feldlager in Schlesien* for her, the role was first sung by Tuczec in Berlin (Dec. 7, 1844); Lind first essayed it there on Jan. 4, 1845. She also sang in Hannover, Hamburg, Cologne, Koblenz, Frankfurt, Darmstadt, and Copenhagen. She appeared at the Leipzig Gewandhaus (Dec. 4, 1845) and made her Vienna debut as Norma at the Theater an der Wien (April 22, 1846); subsequently sang throughout Germany, returning to Vienna as Marie in 1847 and creating a sensation. Lind made a phenomenally successful London debut as Alice in *Robert le Diable* at Her Majesty's Theatre in London (May 4, 1847); her appearances in *La Sonnambula* (May 13, 1847) and *La Fille du régiment* (May 27, 1847) were acclaimed; she then created the role of Amalia in Verdi's *I Masnadieri* there (July 22, 1847).

After touring the English provinces, Lind decided to retire from the operatic stage, making her farewell appearance as Norma in Stockholm (April 12, 1848) and as Alice at London's Her Majesty's Theatre (May 10, 1849). If her success in Europe was great, her U.S. concert tour exceeded all expectations in public agitation and monetary reward. Sponsored by P.T. Barnum, she was seen as a natural phenomenon rather than an artist; nonetheless, her outstanding musicality made a deep impression upon the musical public. She made her N.Y. debut on Sept. 11, 1850, subsequently giving 93 concerts in all, her final one in Philadelphia (1851). On Feb. 5, 1852, she married her accompanist, Otto Goldschmidt, in Boston; they returned to Europe, settling permanently in England in 1858. She continued to appear in concert and oratorio performances until her retirement in 1883, when she became prof. of singing at London's Royal College of Music. She also devoted much time to charitable causes. Lind possessed an extraordinary coloratura voice, with a compass reaching high G. She was, without question, one of the greatest vocal artists of her era.
Bibl.: J. Lyser, *G. Meyerbeer and J. L* (Vienna, 1847); C. Rosenberg, *J. L. in America* (N.Y., 1851); C. Wilkens, *J. L.: Ein Cäcilienbild aus der evangelischen Kirche* (Gütersloh, 1854; 5th ed., 1926); H. Holland and W. Rockstro, *Memoir of Mme. J. L.-Goldschmidt* (2 vols., 1893); W. Rockstro and O. Goldschmidt, *J. L.-Goldschmidt: A Record and Analysis of the Method of the Late J. L.-Goldschmidt* (London, 1894); "J. L.'s Singing Method" (a letter written by her), *Musical Quarterly* (July 1917); T. Norlind, *J. L.* (Stockholm, 1919); R. Maude, *The Life of J. L.* (London, 1926); G. Humphrey, *J. L.* (Philadelphia, 1928); E. Wagenknecht, *J. L.-Goldschmidt* (Boston, 1931); L. Benet, *Enchanting J. L.* (N.Y., 1939); H. Headland, *The Swedish Nightingale: A Biography of J. L.* (Rock Island, Ill., 1940); M. Pergament, *J. L.* (Stockholm, 1945); K. Rotzen and T. Meyer, *J. L.* (Stockholm, 1945); J. Bulman, *J. L.* (London, 1956); G. Schultz, *J. L.: The Swedish Nightingale* (Philadelphia, 1962); A. Dunlop, *The Swedish Nightingale* (N.Y., 1965); W. Ware and T. Lockard, Jr., translators and eds., *The Lost Letters of J. L.* (London, 1966); E. Myers, *J. L.: Songbird from Sweden* (Champaign, Ill., 1968).

Lindberg, Magnus, Finnish pianist and composer; b. Helsinki, June 27, 1958. He began playing the piano at age 11, then at 15 entered the Sibelius Academy in Helsinki, where he studied composition with Einojuhani Rautavaara and Paavo Heininen (graduated, 1981); also received instruction in electronic music there with Osmo Lindemann and took courses with Gérard Grisey and Vinko Globokar in Paris, Franco Donatoni in Siena, and Brian Ferneyhough in Darmstadt. His works are cast in a decisive contemporary idiom. He won the Prix Italia for his *Faust* in 1986 and the Nordic Music Prize for his *Kraft* in 1987.

Works: orch.: *Drama* (Helsinki, Feb. 8, 1981); *Sculpture II* (1981; Helsinki, Oct. 13, 1982); *Tendenza* (1982; Paris, Jan. 27, 1983); *Ritratto* (1979–83; Milan, Feb. 27, 1983); *Kraft* (1983–85; Helsinki, Sept. 4, 1985); *Trois sculptures* (1988; Finnish Radio, March 13, 1989). **chamber:** *Tre stycken* (3 Pieces) for Horn, Violin, Viola, and Cello (1976; Helsinki, May 25, 1977); *Arabesques* for Wind Quintet (1978; Helsinki, Oct. 5, 1980); *Quintetto dell'estate* for Flute, Clarinet, Violin, Cello, and Piano (1979; Helsinki, May 24, 1980); *Layers* for Unspecified Ensemble (1979–); *. . . de Tartuffe, je crois* for String Quartet and Piano (Kuhmo, July 27, 1981); *Linea d'ombra* for Flute, Saxophone, Guitar, and Percussion (1981; Milan, March 17, 1983); *Action-situation-signification* for Horn or Clarinets, Piano, Percussion, Cello, and Tape (Jyväskylä, July 6, 1982); *Zona* for Cello, Alto Flute, Bass Clarinet, Percussion, Harp, Piano, Violin, and Double Bass (Hilversum, Dec. 2, 1983); *Metal Work* for Accordion and Percussion (1984; Joensuu, June 18, 1985); *UR* for 5 Players and Live Electronics (Paris, Oct. 11, 1986); *Twine* for Piano (Bremen, May 19, 1988). **tape:** *Etwas zarter* (1977); *Ohne Ausdruck* (1978; Helsinki, April 15, 1983); *Faust*, radiophonic score (1985–86; Finnish Radio, Aug. 17, 1986); also vocal works.

Lindberg, Oskar (Fredrik), Swedish composer and organist; b. Gagnef, Feb. 23, 1887; d. Stockholm, April 10, 1955. He studied at the Stockholm Cons. with Andreas Hallén and Ernst Ellberg; was a church organist in Stockholm (1906–55); in 1919, was appointed a teacher of harmony at the Stockholm Cons., becoming a prof. there in 1936.

Works: Opera, *Fredlös* (1936–42; Stockholm, Nov. 25, 1943); Sym. (1909); *Dalmålningar* (Pictures from Dalarna;

1908); symphonic poems: *Florez och Blanzeflor, Från de stora skogarna, Hemifrån, Vildmark, Gesunda*; overtures; orch. suites; Piano Quartet; Piano Quintet; Requiem; choral works; piano pieces; songs.

Lindblad, Adolf Fredrik, esteemed Swedish composer; b. Skännige, near Stockholm, Feb. 1, 1801; d. Löfvingsborg, near Linköping, Aug. 23, 1878. In his youth he learned to play the flute and the piano, as well as to compose; after studying music formally in Uppsala (1823–25), he completed his training under Zelter in Berlin. He was director of his own music school in Stockholm (1827–61); his pupils included Jenny Lind and members of the royal family. He became a member of the Royal Swedish Academy of Music (1831). Lindblad was a gifted composer of songs; Lind introduced many of them at her concerts, earning him the title of the "Schubert of the North." He wrote some 215 songs (9 vols., Stockholm, 1878–90), including such notable examples as *I dalen* (In the Valley), *En sommardag* (A Summer's Day), and *Aftonen* (Evening). He also wrote a fine Sym. in C major, which was a great success when performed by the Leipzig Gewandhaus Orch. (1839). His other works include an opera, *Frondörerna* (The Frondists; Stockholm, May 11, 1835), 7 string quartets, and a Piano Trio.
BIBL.: F. Törnblon, "A.F. L. och Jenny Lind," *Svensk tidskrift för musikforskning,* XXIII (1941); K. Linder, *Den unge A.F. L. (1801–27)* (diss., Univ. of Uppsala, 1973).

Lindblad, Otto (Jonas), Swedish choral conductor and composer; b. Karlstorp, March 31, 1809; d. Norra Mellby, Jan. 26, 1864. He studied music in Lund with Mathias Lundholm (1832–36) and with K.-A. Krebs in Hamburg (1841); subsequently graduated from Lund Univ. (1844). He devoted himself to choral conducting; was at his finest as a composer of male songs a cappella. His works include 66 vocal quartets, 14 vocal trios, 3 duets, 36 solo songs, and 5 choruses with solos.
BIBL.: T. Nerman, *O. L.: Ett sångaröde* (Uppsala, 1930).

Linde, (Anders) Bo (Leif), Swedish composer; b. Gävle, Jan. 1, 1933; d. there, Oct. 2, 1970. He studied composition with Lars-Erik Larsson at the Stockholm Musikhögskolan; then took courses in conducting in Vienna (1953–54). In 1960 he returned to Gävle. In his music he followed a healthy Scandinavian style of composition, liberally diversified with cosmopolitan neo-Classical techniques, bordering on polytonality.
WORKS: *Sinfonia fantasia* (1951); *6 Character Studies* for Piano (1952); *Ballet blanc* (1953; Gävle, May 11, 1969); 2 piano trios (1953, 1969); String Quartet (1953); Violin Sonata (1953); 2 piano concertos (1954, 1956); *Suite in an Old Style* for Orch. (1954); 2 piano sonatinas (1955, 1962); *Preludium and Final* for Strings (1955); Violin Concerto (1957); *Suite* for Orch. (1959); *Slotts-skoj* (Fun in the Castle), children's opera for radio (1959); *Sinfonia* (1960); Concerto for Orch. (1961–62); *6 Pieces* for Piano (1962); *Concert Music* for Small Orch. (1963); *Vårbilder* (Spring Scenes) for Soli, Chorus, and Orch. (1963); Cello Concerto (1964); *Serenata nostalgica* for 11 Strings (1965); *Quartet in Miniature* for Clarinets (1965); *Suite Boulogne* for Orch. (1966); *Little Concerto* for Wind Quintet and Strings (1966); *Pensieri sopra un cantico vecchio* for Orch. (Gävle, Jan. 1, 1968); String Trio (1968); *Pezzo concertante,* concertino for Bass Clarinet and Strings (Gävle, Sept. 9, 1970); *6 Italian Songs* for Baritone, Violin, Cello, and Piano (1970).

Linde, Hans-Martin, noted German-born Swiss recorder player, flutist, and teacher; b. Werne, May 24, 1930. He studied at the Freiburg Staatliche Hochschule für Musik (1947–51); gave recitals throughout Europe; made his 1st American tour in 1967. In 1957 he became a lecturer at the Basel Academy of Music; also taught at the Schola Cantorum Basiliensis; led his own Linde Consort. He is particularly noted for his performances of Baroque music.

Lindegren, Johan, Swedish organist, teacher, and composer; b. Ullared, Jan. 7, 1842; d. Stockholm, June 8, 1908. He studied at the Stockholm Cons., where he became a teacher of counter-

point in 1876; from 1884, was organist and cantor of the Storkyrkan. Among his pupils were Alfvén, Melchers, Bäck, Håkanson, and Wiklund. He ed. *Tidning för Kyrkomusik* (1881–82); also publ. a *Koralbok* (1905). He excelled as a composer of piano music.

Lindeman, family of Norwegian musicians:
(1) Ole Andreas Lindeman, organist, teacher, and composer; b. Surnadal, Jan. 17, 1769; d. Trondheim, Feb. 26, 1857. He was a student at the Trondheim cathedral school; after studying law in Copenhagen, he received music instruction from I. Wernicke; then was organist of the church of Our Lady in Trondheim (1799–1857). He ed. the 1st book of Norwegian chorales (1835), which was given official sanction (1838); also wrote some piano pieces and songs. He had 3 sons:
(2) Fredrik Christian Lindeman, organist; b. Trondheim, Dec. 4, 1803; d. there, July 29, 1868. He studied in Christiania and was organist of the church of Our Savior there; then was organist of the church of Our Lady in Trondheim (1857–68).
(3) Ludvig Mathias Lindeman, organist, folk-song collector, teacher, and composer; b. Trondheim, Nov. 28, 1812; d. Christiania, May 23, 1887. He studied with his father in Trondheim, becoming his deputy organist at the church of Our Lady when he was 12; then went to Christiania to study theology (1833), but subsequently resumed his interest in music. He was organist at the church of Our Savior in Christiania (1839–87); also made tours as a concert artist. He taught at the Christiania theological seminary (1849–87). With his son **Peter Brynie Lindeman,** he founded an organ school in Christiania (1883), which became the Cons. (1894). He also spent much time collecting folk songs and editing church music. He prepared a chorale book for the Norwegian church that was officially sanctioned in 1877 and was used until being superseded in 1926. It contained his harmonizations of earlier hymn tunes and a number of his own. He also composed other sacred music, works for organ, and piano pieces.
EDITIONS (all publ. in Christiania): FOLK MUSIC: *Norske fjeldmelodier harmonisk bearbeidede* (1841); *Norske folkeviser udsatte for fire mandstemmer* (1850); *Aeldre og nyere norske fjeldmelodier: Samlede og bearbeidede for pianoforte* (1853–67); *Halvhundrede norske fjeldmelodier harmoniserede for mandsstemmer* (1862); *30 norske kjaempevise-melodier harmoniserede for 3 lige stemmer* (1863); *Norske kjaempevise-melodier harmoniserede for blandede stemmer* (1885); O. Sandvik, ed., *Kingo-Tona: Fra Vang, Valdres* (Oslo, 1939–40). CHURCH MUSIC: *Melodier til W.A. Wexels christelige psalmer* (1840); *Martin Luthers aandelige sange* (1859); *Norsk messebog* (1870; 2nd ed., 1885); *Melodier til Landstads Salmebog* (1873); *Koralbog: Indeholdende de i Landstads salmebog forekommende melodier* (1878).
BIBL.: O. Sandvik, *L.M. L. og folkemelodien* (Oslo, 1950).
(4) Just Riddervold Lindeman, organist and composer; b. Trondheim, Sept. 26, 1822; d. there, Jan. 21, 1894. He was organist of Trondheim Cathedral (1858–94); wrote works for organ, piano pieces, and songs.
(5) Peter Brynie Lindeman, organist, teacher, and composer, son of **Ludvig Mathias Lindeman;** b. Christiania, Feb. 1, 1858; d. there (Oslo), Jan. 1, 1930. He studied with his father and at the Stockholm Cons. He was organist in Christiania (1880–1923); with his father, he founded an organ school there (1883), which became the Cons. (1894); he was its director for many years. He ed. the periodical *Musikbladet* (1908–21). He wrote sacred music, chamber music, organ works, and piano pieces. His son, **Kristian Theodor Madsen Lindeman** (b. Christiania, March 8, 1870; d. Trondheim, Nov. 15, 1934), was an organist and composer; was Trondheim Cathedral organist (1894–1934); wrote numerous choral works.

Lindeman, Osmo (Uolevi), Finnish composer; b. Helsinki, May 16, 1929; d. there, Feb. 15, 1987. He studied with Eino Linnala and Nils-Eric Fougstedt at the Sibelius Academy in Helsinki. In 1959 he was awarded a UNESCO grant to the Hochschule für Musik in Munich, where he studied for a year with Carl Orff; upon returning to Finland, he taught at the Sibelius Academy (1961–84). In his works he at first adopted a traditional Romantic manner, but after 1968 devoted himself to electronic music.

WORKS: ORCH.: Sym. No. 1, *Sinfonia inornata* (1959); Piano Concerto No. 1 (1963); Sym. No. 2 (1964); Piano Concerto No. 2 (1965); *Music* for Chamber Orch. (1966); Concerto for Chamber Orch. (1966); *Huutokauppa* (Auction), ballet with 6 Reciters, Chorus, 2 Pianos, and Orch. (1967); *Variabile* for Orch. (1967). **CHAMBER:** String Trio (1958); *Partita* for Percussion (1962); 2 *Expressions* for Vibraphone and Marimba (1965); String Quartet (1966). **TAPE:** *Kinetic Forms* (1969); *Mechanical Music* (1969); *Tropicana* (1970); *Midas* (1970); *Ritual* (1972); also much film music.

Lindholm, Berit (real name, **Berit Maria Jonsson**), Swedish soprano; b. Stockholm, Oct. 18, 1934. She studied with Britta von Vegesack and Käthe Sundström in Stockholm; made her debut as Mozart's Countess at the Royal Opera there in 1963. She first appeared at London's Covent Garden as Chrysothemis in *Elektra* (1966); sang at the Bayreuth Festivals (1967–74). She made her U.S. debut as Brünnhilde with the San Francisco Opera (1972); her Metropolitan Opera debut followed in N.Y. in the same role on Feb. 20, 1975. She became best known for her Wagnerian roles.

Lindley, Robert, English cellist; b. Rotherham, Yorkshire, March 4, 1776; d. London, June 13, 1855. He studied cello with Cervetto; from 1794 to 1851, was 1st cellist at the Royal Opera in London; in 1822, became prof. of cello at the Royal Academy of Music there. He wrote pieces for the cello.

Lindpaintner, Peter Joseph von, German conductor and composer; b. Koblenz, Dec. 9, 1791; d. Nonnenhorn, Lake Constance, Aug. 21, 1856. He studied violin and piano in Augsburg, theory in Munich with Winter and Joseph Grätz; in 1812, became music director of the Isarthor Theater in Munich; from 1819 until his death, was conductor of the Court Orch. at Stuttgart, where his ability made the orch. famous.

WORKS: 28 operas, including *Der Bergkönig* (Stuttgart, Jan. 30, 1825); *Der Vampyr* (Stuttgart, Nov. 21, 1828); *Die Genueserin* (Vienna, Feb. 8, 1839); *Lichtenstein* (Stuttgart, Aug. 26, 1846); 3 ballets (*Joko*, etc.); 5 melodramas; 5 oratorios; syms.; overture to *Faust*; incidental music to *Lied von der Glocke*; 6 masses; *Stabat Mater*; songs.

BIBL.: R. Hänsler, *P. L. als Opernkomponist* (diss., Univ. of Munich, 1928).

Lineva, Evgenia (née **Papritz**), Russian folk-song collector; b. Brest-Litovsk, Jan. 9, 1854; d. Moscow, Jan. 24, 1919. She studied voice with her mother, a pupil of Glinka; then took lessons with Marchesi in Vienna; later sang opera in Paris, London, and Moscow. In 1889 she married the engineer A.L. Linev (1840–1916); because of his revolutionary activities, he served a prison term, and was then forced to emigrate. They were in London (1891–92) and the U.S. (1892–94). They then returned to Russia, where she undertook a series of trips in the Volga region, using a phonograph constructed by her husband to record folk songs. She publ. her findings in 2 vols. in a Russian ed. (St. Petersburg, 1904–9; in Eng., 1905–12, as *The Peasant Songs of Great Russia*); her *Folk Songs of the Ukraine* appeared posth. (Godfrey, Ill., 1958).

BIBL.: E. Kann-Novikova, *E. L.* (Moscow, 1952).

Linjama, Jouko (Sakari), Finnish organist and composer; b. Kirvu, Feb. 4, 1934. He studied composition with Merikanto and Kokkonen at the Sibelius Academy in Helsinki (1954–60) and musicology and literature at the Univ. of Helsinki; continued his composition training with Zimmermann and Koenig at the Cologne Staatliche Hochschule für Musik (1962–64) and also worked with Stockhausen in the Cologne course for new music (1963). He was organist at St. Henrik's Catholic Church (1958–60) and then in the Tuusula parish (from 1964); also taught at the Sibelius Academy (1964–68). A prominent composer of sacred music, he was awarded the composition prize of the Finnish church in 1979. In his works he attempts to fuse Burgundian strict counterpoint with serial techniques.

WORKS: ORCH.: *La Migration d'oiseaux sauvages* (1977). **CHAMBER:** 5 *Metamorphosen für 5 Instrumente über 5 Canons Op. 16 von Anton Webern* for Celesta, Vibraphone, Guitar, Harpsichord, and Piano (1963); . . . *lehtiä* . . . (. . . leaves . . .) for Cello and Piano (1974); *Hommage à Dandrieau* for 2 Cellos or 2 Men's Voices, and Organ (1977); 2 string quartets: No. 1, *Cantiones* (1978); No. 2, *Variazioni* (1979); Concerto for Organ, Marimba, Vibraphone, and 2 Wind Quartets (1981). **ORGAN:** *Sonatina supra b-a-c-h* (1961); *Partita-sonata Veni Creator Spiritus* (1968); *Intrada* (1969); *Magnificat* (1970); Concerto (1971); *Triptychon* for 2 Organs (1971); *Partita* (1973); *Piae cantiones per organo piccolo* (1976); *Missa cum jubilo* (1977); *Consolation pour l'orgue* (1978); *Toccatina, danza e contradanza per organo piccolo* (1981); also various choral works and songs.

Linko, Ernst, Finnish composer and pianist; b. Helsinki, July 14, 1889; d. there, Jan. 28, 1960. He studied piano at the Helsinki School of Music (1909–11); then in Berlin, St. Petersburg, and Paris. He was director of the Sibelius Academy in Helsinki (1939–59); for many years, was active as a concert pianist. He wrote 4 piano concertos (1916, 1920, 1931, 1957); *Symphonie chevaleresque* (1949); *Ariette* for Wind Ensemble; *Rigaudon* for Strings; Piano Trio; String Quartet; numerous piano pieces.

Linley, George, English composer; b. Leeds, 1798; d. London, Sept. 10, 1865. He settled in London, where he wrote words and music of songs, many of which acquired great vogue (*Ever of thee; I cannot mind my wheel, mother; Thou art gone from my gaze;* etc.); he also wrote the cantata *The Jolly Beggars;* the operas *Francesca Doria* (1849), *La Poupée de Nuremberg* (London, 1861), *The Toy Makers* (1861), and *Law versus Love* (1862); part-songs, trios, duets, hymns; ed. the collections *Scottish Melodies, Songs of the Camp, Original Hymn Tunes,* etc.; publ. *The Musical Cynics of London* (1862), a satirical poem aimed at the critic Chorley, and *Modern Hudibras* (1864).

Linley, Thomas, Sr., English harpsichordist, concert director, singing teacher, and composer; b. Badminton, Gloucestershire, Jan. 17, 1733; d. London, Nov. 19, 1795. He began his studies with the Bath Abbey organist Thomas Chilcot; later studied with William Boyce in London. From the mid-1750s he was active as a concert director and singing teacher in Bath, and also wrote for the London stage from 1767. He was made joint director (with John Stanley) of London's Drury Lane Theatre in 1774; then continued in that capacity (with Samuel Arnold) from 1786; was also its joint manager (with his son-in-law, the dramatist Richard Brinsley Sheridan) from 1776. With his son Thomas Linley, Jr., he composed the music for Sheridan's comic opera *The Duenna, or The Double Elopement* (1775). He was made a member of the Royal Soc. of Musicians in 1777. Of his 12 children, the following should be noted: **Elizabeth Ann Linley** (b. Bath, Sept. 5, 1754; d. Bristol, June 28, 1792), soprano; **Thomas Linley, Jr.** (b. Bath, May 5, 1756; d. [drowned] Grimsthorpe, Aug. 5, 1778), violinist and composer; **Mary Linley** (b. Bath, Jan. 4, 1758; d. Clifton, Bristol, July 27, 1787), soprano; **Ozias Thurston Linley** (b. Bath, Aug. 1765; d. London, March 6, 1831), organist and clergyman; **William Linley** (b. Bath, Feb. 1771; d. London, May 6, 1835), composer.

WORKS: STAGE (all 1st perf. in London): *The Royal Merchant,* opera (Dec. 14, 1767); *The Duenna, or The Double Elopement,* comic opera (Nov. 21, 1775; in collaboration with his son Thomas, Jr.); *Selima and Azor,* comic opera (Dec. 5, 1776); *The Beggar's Opera,* ballad opera (Jan. 29, 1777); *The Camp,* musical entertainment (Oct. 15, 1778); *Zoraida,* tragedy (Dec. 13, 1779); *The Generous Imposter,* comedy (Nov. 22, 1780); *The Gentle Shepherd,* pastoral (Oct. 29, 1781); *The Carnival of Venice,* comic opera (Dec. 13, 1781); *The Spanish Rivals,* musical farce (Nov. 4, 1784); *The Strangers at Home,* comic opera (Dec. 8, 1785); *Love in the East, or Adventures of 12 Hours* (Feb. 25, 1788). He also publ. *6 Elegies* (London, 1770) and *12 Ballads* (London, 1780); 14 pieces appeared in *The*

Posthumous Vocal Works of Mr. Linley and Mr. T. Linley (London, c.1798).

BIBL.: E. Green, *T. L., Richard Brinsley Sheridan, and Thomas Matthews: Their Connection with Bath* (Bath, 1903); C. Black, *The L.s of Bath* (London, 1911; 3rd ed., augmented, 1971).

Linn, Robert, American composer; b. San Francisco, Aug. 11, 1925. He studied with Milhaud at Mills College in Oakland, Calif. (1947–49), and with Sessions, Stevens, and Dahl at the Univ. of Southern Calif. in Los Angeles (M.M., 1951); taught there (from 1958) and served as chairman of the music theory and composition dept. (from 1973).

WORKS: ORCH.: *Overture for Symphony Orchestra* (1952); Sym. in 1 Movement (1956; rev. 1961); *Hexameron* for Piano and Orch. (1963; reconstruction of Liszt's orchestration of *Hexaméron*, variations on a theme by Bellini); Sinfonia for String Orch. (1967; rev. 1972); Concertino for Oboe, Horn, Percussion, and String Orch. (1972); Fantasia for Cello and String Orch. (1975–76); Concertino for Woodwind Quintet and String Orch. (1981–82). **WOODWIND ORCH.:** *Elevations* (1964); *Propagula* (1970); Concerto for Flute and Woodwind Orch. (1980); Partita (1980); Concerto for Piano and Woodwind Orch. (1984). **CHAMBER:** Clarinet Sonata (1949); String Quartet No. 1 (1951); Quartet for 4 Saxophones (1953); 2 piano sonatas (1955, 1964); Quartet for 4 Horns (1957); *Prelude and Dance* for 4 Saxophones (1960); Brass Quintet (1963); Woodwind Quintet (1963); *Dithyramb* for 8 Cellos (1965); Concertino for Violin and Wind Octet (1965); *12 for Chamber Ensemble* (1976–77); *Diversions* for 6 Bassoons (1979); *Trombosis* for 12 Trombones (1979); *Serenade* for Flute, Clarinet, Cello, and Guitar (1982); also several choral works; pieces for bands.

Linnala, Eino (Mauno Aleksanteri), Finnish composer; b. Helsinki, Aug. 19, 1896; d. there, June 8, 1973. He studied composition with Melartin, at the Univ. of Helsinki, in Berlin, and with Willner in Vienna; subsequently taught theory and analysis at the Univ. of Helsinki (1927–66); was also chairman of the Finnish Composers' Copyright Bureau (1960–68). He publ. several textbooks on theory. His compositions, all composed in the Romantic tradition, included 2 syms. (1927, 1935); *Dance Suite* for Orch. (1931); *Suomalainen rapsodia* for Orch. (1932); *Overture* (1933); *Elegia* for Orch. (1945); 4 cantatas (1932–40); more than 100 choral songs; chamber music; about 50 songs.

Linstead, George (Frederick), Scottish organist, choirmaster, music critic, teacher, and composer; b. Melrose, Jan. 24, 1908; d. Sheffield, Dec. 29, 1974. He wrote an oratorio at the age of 13 and an opera, *Agamemnon*, at 16; studied with F. Shera in Sheffield; also with E. Bairstow (composition) and James Ching (piano); was awarded a D.Mus. degree from the Univ. of Durham (1946). He was active as a church organist and choirmaster, as well as a music critic, in Sheffield; was also a part-time lecturer at the Univ. there (1947–74). Among his compositions were an opera, *Eastward in Eden* (1937); a ballet, *Hylas*; Sym.; Sinfonietta; *Moto perpetuo* for Orch.; Overture "In the French Style"; *Anglican Overture*; 2 concertinos for Piano and Orch.; choral music; 2 string quartets and other chamber works; band music; piano pieces; songs.

Lioncourt, Guy de, French composer; b. Caen, Dec. 1, 1885; d. Paris, Dec. 24, 1961. He studied with his uncle (by marriage) d'Indy and with Gastoué and Roussel at the Paris Schola Cantorum (graduated, 1916); in 1918 he won the Grand Prix Lasserre with his *La Belle au bois dormant* (1912–15). He became prof. of counterpoint (1914) at the Schola Cantorum; at d'Indy's death in 1931, he became subdirector and prof. of composition. He helped to found the École César Franck in Paris (1935), and then was its director. He publ. an autobiography, *Un Témoignage sur la musique et sur la vie au XXᵉ siècle* (Paris, 1956).

WORKS: DRAMA: *Jan de la lune* (1915–21). **LITURGICAL DRAMAS:** *Le Mystère de l'Emmanuel* (1924); *Le Mystère de l'Alléluia* (1925–26); *Le Mystère de l'Esprit* (1939–40). **SOLOISTS, CHO-**

RUS, AND ORCH.: *Hyalis, le petit faune aux yeux bleus* (1909–11); *La Belle au bois dormant* (1912–15); *Le Réniement de St.-Pierre* (1928); *Le Navrement de Notre Dame* (1943); also *Les Dix Lépreux* for Voice, Women's Chorus, and Orch. (1918–19); *Le Dict de Mme. Sante Barbe* for Soloists, Chorus, Harp, and Strings (1937); 3 masses; motets; Piano Quintet (1908); String Quartet (1933); organ works; many songs; piano pieces.

Lipatti, Dinu (actually, **Constantin**), outstanding Rumanian pianist and composer; b. Bucharest, April 1, 1917; d. Chêne-Bourg, near Geneva, Dec. 2, 1950. His father was a violinist who had studied with Sarasate, and his mother, a pianist; his godfather was Enesco. He received his early training from his parents; then studied with Florica Musicescu at the Bucharest Cons. (1928–32). He received a 2nd prize at the International Competition at Vienna in 1934, a judgment which prompted Cortot to quit the jury in protest; Lipatti then studied piano with Cortot, conducting with Munch, and composition with Dukas and Boulanger in Paris (1934–39). He gave concerts in Germany and Italy, returning to Rumania at the outbreak of World War II. In 1943 he settled in Geneva as a teacher of piano at the Cons. After the war, he resumed his career; played in England 4 times (1946–48). His remarkable career was tragically cut short by lymphogranulomatosis, which led to his early death. He was generally regarded as one of the most sensitive interpreters of Chopin, and was also praised for his deep understanding of the Baroque masters; was also a fine composer. Lipatti was married to the pianist and teacher Madeleine Cantacuzene.

WORKS: Piano Sonata (1932); Violin Sonatina (1933); *Sătrarii*, symphonic poem (1933); *Concertino in the Classic Style* for Piano and String Orch. (1936; Bucharest, Oct. 5, 1939); *Fantasy* for Piano Trio (1936); *Nocturne* for Piano (1937); *Suite* for 2 Pianos (1938); *Symphonie concertante* for 2 Pianos and Orch. (1938); *Improvisation* for Piano Trio (1939); *3 Nocturnes* for Piano (1939); *Fantasy* for Piano (1940); Piano Sonatina for the Left Hand (1941); *3 Rumanian Dances* for 2 Pianos (1943), or Piano and Orch. (1945; Geneva, Oct. 11, 1945); *Aubade* for Wind Quartet (1949); songs.

BIBL.: M. Lipatti, ed., *Hommage à D. L.* (Geneva, 1952); A. Lipatti, *La Vie du pianiste D. L., écrite par sa mère* (Paris, 1954); T. Dragos, *L.* (Bucharest, 1965); C. Păsculescu-Florian, *Vocaţie Şi destin, D. L.* (Bucharest, 1986); D. Tanasescu and G. Bargauanu, *L.* (London, 1988).

Lipawsky (Lipavský), Joseph (Josef), Bohemian pianist and composer; b. Hohenmauth, Feb. 22, 1769; d. Vienna, Jan. 7, 1810. He studied organ and philosophy in Prague and law in Vienna, where he ultimately settled and enjoyed the friendship of Mozart, who may have given him some instruction; was house musician for Count Adam Teleky; also gave public piano concerts. He wrote singspiels, orch. works, chamber music, and songs, but achieved popular favor primarily as a composer of piano music.

Lipínsky, Carl (actually, **Karol Józef**), Polish violinist, teacher, and composer; b. Radzyn, Oct. 30, 1790; d. Urlów, near Lemberg, Dec. 16, 1861. His father was a professional musician and gave him his primary education. He met Paganini, who agreed to teach him the violin; in 1835 he visited Leipzig; Schumann was greatly impressed by his playing and dedicated *Carnaval* to him. Lipínsky appeared in London on April 25, 1836, as soloist in his *Military Concerto* for Violin and Orch.; in 1839 he settled in Dresden as concertmaster of the Court Orch.; Liszt once played at the same concert with him. Among his renowned students were Joachim and Wieniawski. He wrote a comic opera, *Klótnia przez zaklad* (Lemberg, May 27, 1814), and other stage pieces; also 3 syms., concertos, various pieces for violin and piano, and numerous technical violin studies.

Lipkin, Malcolm (Leyland), English composer, pianist, and teacher; b. Liverpool, May 2, 1932. He studied piano with Gordon Green in Liverpool; following further piano training from Kendall Taylor at the Royal College of Music in London

(1949–53), he studied composition privately with Mátyás Seiber (1954–57); received his doctorate from the Univ. of London (1972). In 1951 he made his debut as a pianist performing his 3rd Piano Sonata at the Gaudeamus Foundation Music Week in the Netherlands; in 1952 he made his London debut playing the same score. He served as a tutor for the external dept. of Oxford Univ. (1965–75) and for the School of Continuing Education at the Univ. of Kent (from 1975).

WORKS: ORCH.: 3 syms.: No. 1, *Sinfonia di Roma* (1958–65; Liverpool, Jan. 18, 1966); No. 2, *The Pursuit* (1975–79; Manchester, Feb. 9, 1983); No. 3, *Sun* (1979–86); 2 violin concertos (1952; 1960–62; Bournemouth, Oct. 17, 1963); *Movement* for Strings (1956–57; rev. 1960); Piano Concerto (1957; Cheltenham, July 16, 1959); *Mosaics* for Chamber Orch. (London, Oct. 23, 1966; rev. 1969); Concerto for Flute and Strings (1974); Oboe Concerto (London, June 20, 1989). **CHAMBER:** 5 piano sonatas, including Nos. 3 (Bilthoven, Sept. 6, 1951; rev. 1979), 4 (Cheltenham, July 17, 1955; rev. 1987), and 5 (1986; Kent, July 21, 1989); String Quartet (1951); Violin Sonata (1957); String Trio (1963–64); *Capriccio* for Piano and String Quartet (1966); *Interplay* for Treble Recorder, Viola da Gamba, Harpsichord, and Percussion (London, March 5, 1976); Wind Quintet (1985; London, July 14, 1986); Piano Trio (1988; London, March 22, 1989); also vocal works.

Lipkin, Seymour, American pianist, conductor, and teacher; b. Detroit, May 14, 1927. He studied piano as a child and appeared as soloist in Beethoven's 1st Piano Concerto with the Detroit Civic Orch. (1938); then studied formally at the Curtis Inst. of Music in Philadelphia with D. Saperton (1938–41) and with R. Serkin and M. Horszowski (B.Mus., 1947); also studied conducting with Koussevitzky at the Berkshire Music Center in Tanglewood (1946; 1948–49) and was apprentice conductor to Szell and the Cleveland Orch. (1947–48). After winning 1st prize in the Rachmaninoff Piano Competition (1948), he played the Tchaikovsky 1st Piano Concerto with Koussevitzky and the Boston Sym. Orch. that same year and subsequently appeared as a soloist with major U.S. orchs. He made his formal conducting debut with the N.Y. City Opera leading Bernstein's *Trouble in Tahiti* (1958); then was an assistant conductor of the N.Y. Phil. (1959–60) and music director of the Long Island Sym. Orch. (1963–79). He was also music director of N.Y.'s Joffrey Ballet (1966–68), then its principal guest conductor (1968–72), and once again its music director (1972–79). He taught at Marymount College in Tarrytown, N.Y. (1963–72; chairman of the music dept., 1968–71), the Curtis Inst. of Music (from 1969), the Manhattan School of Music (1972–87), the New England Cons. of Music in Boston (1984–86), and the Juilliard School in N.Y. (from 1986); also served as artistic director of the Univ. of Maryland International Piano Festival and William Kapell Piano Competition (from 1988).

Lipkovska, Lydia (Yakovlevna), Russian soprano; b. Babino, Khotin district, Bessarabia, May 10, 1882; d. Beirut, Jan. 22, 1955. She studied with Iretzkaya in St. Petersburg and Vanzo in Milan; made her debut as Gilda at the St. Petersburg Imperial Opera (1907), singing there until 1908 and again from 1911 to 1913. She appeared in Diaghilev's season in Paris (1909), as well as at the Opéra and the Opéra-Comique. Her American debut took place with the Boston Opera on Nov. 12, 1909, when she sang Lakmé; on Nov. 18, 1909, she made her Metropolitan Opera debut in N.Y. as Violetta opposite Caruso. She was reengaged for the following season in the U.S.; also appeared at London's Covent Garden as Mimi (July 11, 1911). During World War I, she was in Russia; after the Revolution, she went to France; in 1919 she married Pierre Bodin, a lieutenant in the French army; toured the U.S. again, appearing at the Chicago Grand Opera (1921–22). She then lived in France and Bessarabia; during the Rumanian occupation of Odessa (1941–44), she appeared at the Odessa Opera in her favorite role of Violetta; also acted in drama. In 1944 she went to Paris; then accepted a teaching position in Beirut; during her last years of life, she was supported by the Tolstoy Foundation of America.

Lipman, Samuel, American pianist, teacher, and music critic; b. Los Gatos, Calif., June 7, 1934. He commenced piano studies in his youth, making his debut at age 9; attended L'École Monteux in Hancock, Maine (summers, 1951–57), and the Aspen Music School (summers, 1959–61); completed his piano training with Rosina Lhévinne at the Juilliard School of Music in N.Y. (1959–62). He also took courses in government at San Francisco State College (B.A., 1956) and pursued graduate work in political science at the Univ. of Calif. at Berkeley (M.A., 1958). His tours as a pianist took him all over the U.S. and Europe; he also served as music critic of *Commentary* (from 1976) and publ. the *New Criterion* (from 1982); taught at the Aspen Music School (from 1971) and at the Waterloo Music Festival in Stanhope, N.J. (from 1976), where he was artistic director (from 1985). In 1977 he won the ASCAP–Deems Taylor Award for music criticism, and in 1980 for his vol. of essays *Music after Modernism* (1979). He also wrote *The House of Music: Art in an Era of Institutions* (1982).

Lipowsky, Felix Joseph, German music lexicographer and composer, son of **Thaddäus Ferdinand Lipowsky;** b. Wiensteig, Jan. 25, 1764; d. Munich, March 21, 1842. He was engaged in many scholarly pursuits, as a legal scientist, politician, art historian, etc. He was active as a church organist and choir leader; in 1787 he obtained his Dr.Jur. degree from the Univ. of Ingolstadt; then served as a municipal officer in Bavaria. He publ. *Baierische Musik-Lexikon* (Munich, 1811), which contains valuable material despite many faults of commission and omission. He wrote several sacred choral works and some instrumental music, but his only extant work is a Mass.

Lipowsky, Thaddäus Ferdinand, German composer, father of **Felix Joseph Lipowsky;** b. St. Martin, Bavaria, Dec. 28, 1738; d. Wiesensteig, March 18, 1767. He studied with Leopold Mozart in Salzburg; obtained a law degree in Wiesensteig (1763); composed many violin pieces. A lengthy account of his career is found in the *Baierisches Musik-Lexikon* compiled by his son.

Lipp, Wilma, Austrian soprano; b. Vienna, April 26, 1925. She studied at the Vienna Cons. and with Toti Dal Monte in Milan; made her debut as Rosina in Vienna (1943), then joined the Vienna State Opera (1945). She also sang opera in Milan, London, Hamburg, Paris, Munich, and Berlin; took part in the music festivals in Salzburg, Bayreuth, and Edinburgh. She was equally distinguished as a coloratura and as a lyric soprano.

Lipphardt, Walther, German musicologist; b. Wiescherhöfen bei Hamm, Oct. 14, 1906; d. Frankfurt am Main, Jan. 17, 1981. He studied musicology with Moser at the Univ. of Heidelberg and with Gurlitt at the Univ. of Freiburg im Breisgau; then took additional courses at the Univ. of Heidelberg with Besseler, graduating with a Ph.D. in 1931 with a dissertation on medieval German Marian litanies. He subsequently was on the faculty of the Hochschule für Musik in Frankfurt (1946–70). He publ. numerous valuable papers on liturgical music and ed. works of Renaissance composers.

WRITINGS: *Die Weisen der lateinischen Osterspiele des 12. und 13. Jahrhunderts* (Kassel, 1948); *Die Geschichte des mehrstimmigen Proprium Missae* (Heidelberg, 1950); *Der karolingische Tonar von Metz* (Münster, 1965); *Gesangbuchdrucke in Frankfurt am Main vor 1569* (Frankfurt am Main, 1974).

Lippman, Edward A(rthur), American musicologist; b. N.Y., May 24, 1920. He was educated at the City College of N.Y. (B.S., 1942), N.Y. Univ. (M.A., 1945), and Columbia Univ. (Ph.D., 1952, with the diss. *Music and Space: A Study in the Philosophy of Music*); held a Guggenheim fellowship (1958–59). He taught at Columbia Univ. (from 1954), where he was a prof. (from 1969).

WRITINGS: *Musical Thought in Ancient Greece* (N.Y., 1964); *A Humanistic Philosophy of Music* (N.Y., 1977); *Musical Aesthetics: A Historical Reader* (3 vols., N.Y., 1986 et seq.).

Lipps, Theodor, German writer on music; b. Wallhalben, July 28, 1851; d. Munich, Oct. 17, 1914. He occupied the chair of philosophy at the Univs. of Bonn (1889), Breslau (1890–94), and Munich (from 1894). Besides the musical sections of his *Ästhetik* (2 vols., 1903–6), his writings on music comprise *Zur Theorie der Melodie* (1901) and *Psychologische Studien* (vol. 2: *Das Wesen der musikalischen Harmonie und Disharmonie*; 1885; 2nd ed., 1905).

BIBL.: P. Moos, *T. L. als Musikästhetiker* (1907); F. Liuzzi, *Essenza dell' arte e valore estetico nel pensiero di T. L.* (Bologna, 1924).

Lipsius, Marie (pen name, **La Mara**), German writer on music; b. Leipzig, Dec. 30, 1837; d. Schmölen, near Wurzen, March 2, 1927. She received her academic training from her father, Adalbert Lipsius, rector of the Thomasschule in Leipzig; also studied music with Richard Müller in Leipzig. Through R. Pohl, she was introduced to Liszt (1856); in Liszt's circle at Weimar she had the happy fortune of meeting the foremost musicians of the time. Her writings on Liszt and Wagner, and on other German composers of the Romantic school, possess a stamp of authority and intimate understanding. In addition to a number of popular biographies of composers, she wrote *Musikalische Studienköpfe* (5 vols., Leipzig, 1868; 2nd ed., augmented, 1875–82), *Musikerbriefe aus fünf Jahrhunderten* (2 vols., Leipzig, 1886), *Beethovens Unsterbliche Geliebte: Das Geheimnis der Gräfin Brunsvik und ihre Memoiren* (Leipzig, 1909), *Liszt und die Frauen* (Leipzig, 1911; 2nd ed., 1919), *An der Schwelle des Jenseits: Letzte Erinnerungen an die Fürstin Carolyne Sayn-Wittgenstein* (Leipzig, 1925), and her autobiography, *Durch Musik and Leben im Dienst des Ideals* (2 vols., Leipzig, 1917; 2nd ed., 1925).

Lipton, Martha, American mezzo-soprano; b. N.Y., April 6, 1913. She was educated at the Juilliard School of Music in N.Y.; made her debut in a recital. In 1944 she appeared with the Metropolitan Opera in N.Y. and remained on its roster until 1960; also sang with the N.Y. City Opera (1944, 1958, 1961) and at the Chicago Lyric Opera (1956). In Europe she sang in Amsterdam and The Hague, and at the Holland and Edinburgh festivals, the Vienna State Opera, and the Paris Opéra; also made appearances in South America. In 1960 she became a prof. of voice at the Indiana Univ. School of Music.

Lirou, Jean François Espic, Chevalier de, French composer and music theorist; b. Paris, 1740; d. there, 1806. He was an officer in the "Mousquetaires du roi," for whom he wrote *Marche des Mousquetaires,* which was performed until the Revolution. He publ. *Explication du système de l'harmonie* (1785), the 1st French theory of harmony that opposed Rameau's system and sought to establish the laws of chord progressions from the inherent affinities of tonality.

Lishin, Grigori, Russian composer; b. St. Petersburg, May 5, 1854; d. there, June 27, 1888. He studied piano with his mother; became a proficient accompanist; also wrote music criticism. He composed 2 operas, *Don Caesar* (Kiev, 1888) and *Count Nulin* (after Pushkin), to his own librettos. His sentimental ballad *She Laughed* was extremely popular with Russian singers.

Lisinski, Vatroslav (real name, **Ignacije Fuchs**), important Croatian composer; b. Zagreb, July 8, 1819; d. there, May 31, 1854. He was a student of Sojka and Wiesner von Morgenstern in Zagreb; as late as 1847, he went to Prague to study with Pitsch and Kittl. Although he never acquired a solid technique of composition, he was notable in that he tried to establish a national style in dramatic writing. He was the composer of the 1st Croatian opera, *Ljubav i zloba* (Love and Malice), for which he wrote only the vocal score; it was orchestrated by Wiesner von Morgenstern, and performed in Zagreb on March 28, 1846. His 2nd opera, *Porin* (1848–51), also in Croatian, was given many years after his death, in Zagreb, on Oct. 2, 1897. He further wrote 7 overtures, a number of choruses and songs, and piano pieces.

BIBL.: V. Novak, *V. L.* (Belgrade, 1925); L. Zupanović,

V. L. (*1819–1854*), *život—djelo—znacenje* (V. L. [1819–1854], Life—Work—Significance; Zagreb, 1969).

Lisitsyan, Pavel (Gerasimovich) (actually, **Pogos Karapetovich**), Armenian baritone; b. Vladikavkaz, Nov. 6, 1911. He studied in Leningrad; sang at the Maly Theater there (1935–37); then was a member of the Armenian Opera Theater in Erevan (1937–40); in 1940 he joined the Bolshoi Theater in Moscow, remaining on its roster until 1966, but in the interim filled engagements all over Europe, in India, and in Japan. From 1967 to 1973 he was on the faculty of the Erevan Cons. On March 3, 1960, he made his Metropolitan Opera debut in N.Y. as Amonasro in *Aida*. He was best known for his roles in Russian operas.

Liška, Zdeněk, Czech composer; b. Smečno, March 16, 1922; d. Prague, July 13, 1983. He studied at the Prague Cons.; beginning in 1945 he was active as a composer for the State Studios of Documentary Films. For the Czech spectacle *Laterna Magica,* he wrote a modernistic violin concerto in which actors and musicians alternate with their screen images without loss of continuity. This work, first performed in Leningrad on Dec. 5, 1960, was featured in the presentation of *Laterna Magica* in N.Y. in the summer of 1964.

Lissa, Zofia, distinguished Polish musicologist; b. Lemberg, Oct. 19, 1908; d. Warsaw, March 26, 1980. She studied with Chybiński at the Univ. of Lemberg (1925–29), where she also took courses in philosophy, psychology, and art history (Ph.D., 1930); subsequently completed her Habilitation at the Univ. of Poznan (1947); later took a 2nd Ph.D. there in 1954. She taught at the Lwow Cons. (1931–41); later was reader (1948–51), prof. (1951–57), and director (from 1957) of the musicological inst. of the Univ. of Warsaw. She was a voluminous writer; was a leading proponent of socialist realism as a critical method of musical evaluation.

WRITINGS: *Zarys nauki o muzyce* (A Short Music Textbook; Lwow, 1934; 4th ed., augmented, 1966); *Muzykologia polska na przelomie* (A Turning Point in Polish Musicology; Krakow, 1952); with J. Chomiński, *Muzyka polskiego odrodzenia* (Music of the Polish Renaissance; Warsaw, 1953; 3rd ed., rev., 1958, in *Odrodzenie w Polsce,* V); *Historia muzyki rosyjskiej* (History of Russian Music; Krakow, 1955); *Estetyka muzyki filmowej* (Krakow, 1964); *Skice z estetyki muzycznej* (A Sketch of Musical Esthetics; Krakow, 1965); *Polonica Beethovenowskie* (Krakow, 1970); *Studia nad twórczościg Fryderyka Chopina* (Studies of Frédéric Chopin's Works; Krakow, 1970).

BIBL.: *Studia musicologica aesthetica, theoretica, historica: Z. L. w 70. roku urodzin* (Krakow, 1979).

Lissenko, Nikolai (Vitalievich), significant Ukrainian composer; b. Grinki, near Kremenchug, March 22, 1842; d. Kiev, Nov. 6, 1912. He was the son of a landowner; grew up in a musical atmosphere; the singing of Ukrainian songs by local peasants produced a lasting impression on him, and determined his future as a national composer. He studied natural sciences at the Univ. of Kiev, graduating in 1864; was a justice of the peace in the Kiev district (1864–66); then abandoned his nonmusical pursuits and went to Leipzig, where he entered the Cons., and took courses with Richter (theory), Reinecke (piano), and Papperitz (organ). Returning to Russia in 1868, he taught piano at the Kiev Inst. of the Daughters of Nobility; from 1874 to 1876 he studied orchestration with Rimsky-Korsakov in St. Petersburg. As early as 1868 he publ. his 1st collection of Ukrainian songs (printed in Leipzig); subsequent issues comprised 240 songs in 5 books, arranged according to their categories (Spring Songs, Midsummer Night Songs, Christmas Songs, etc.); he set to music a great number of poems from *Kobzar* by the Ukrainian poet Shevchenko (5 albums for 2, 3, and 4 Voices; publ. in Kiev, 1870–97). In 1903, on the occasion of the 35th anniversary of the publication of his 1st collection of Ukrainian songs, Lissenko received a gift of 5,000 rubles from his admirers.

In his pamphlet *The Characteristics of the Ukrainian Dumki* (1874), Lissenko presents a theory that Ukrainian modes are derived from Greek music, and that antiphonal construction is one of the main features of Ukrainian songs, while the persistence of symmetrical rhythms distinguishes them from Russian songs. In his original compositions, he asserted himself as an ardent Ukrainian nationalist.

WORKS: OPERAS: *Chernomortsy* (Sailors of the Black Sea Fleet; 1870); *Nich pid Rizdvo,* after Gogol's *Christmas Eve Night* (1874; rev. 1877–82; Kharkov, 1883); *Utoplennitsa* (The Drowned Woman), after Gogol's *May Night* (1871–83; Kharkov, 1885); *Koza-Dereza* (The Goat), children's opera (1888; Kiev, April 20, 1901); *Natalka-Poltavka* (Natalie from Poltava), after Kotlarevsky's play (1889; orig. incidental music); *Taras Bulba,* after Gogol (1880–90; Kiev, Dec. 20, 1903; rev. by Liatoshinsky, Kiev, 1937); *Pan Kotsky* (Puss-in-Boots), children's opera (1891); *Zima i vesna, ili Snezhnaya krasavitsa* (Winter and Spring, or The Snow Maiden), children's opera (1892); *Sappho* (1896–1900); *Aeneid* (1910; Kiev, 1911); also orch. works, cantatas, choruses, chamber music, songs, and piano pieces. A complete ed. of his works was publ. in Kiev (20 vols., 1950–59).

BIBL.: V. Chagovets, *N.V. L.* (Kiev, 1949); L. Arkimova and N. Hordiychuk, *N.V. L.: Life and Works* (Kiev, 1952); Z. Vasylenko, *N.V. L.'s Works as a Folklorist* (Kiev, 1972).

List (real name, **Fleissig**), **Emanuel,** noted Austrian-born American bass; b. Vienna, March 22, 1888; d. there, June 21, 1967. He was a chorister at the Theater-an-der-Wien; studied voice in Vienna, and made his debut at the Volksoper there in 1922 as Méphistophélès in *Faust;* then sang at Berlin's Städtische Opera (1923–25) and State Opera (1925–33); also appeared at London's Covent Garden (1925; 1934–36), the Salzburg Festival (1931–35), and the Bayreuth Festival (1933). On Dec. 27, 1933, he made his 1st American appearance at the Metropolitan Opera in N.Y., as the Landgrave in *Tannhäuser;* in subsequent seasons, sang almost all Wagnerian bass roles; remained with the company until 1948, returning in 1949–50. He also appeared as a lieder artist.

List, Eugene, American pianist; b. Philadelphia, July 6, 1918; d. N.Y., Feb. 28, 1985. He was taken to Los Angeles when a year old; studied there at the Sutro-Seyler Studios and made his debut with the Los Angeles Phil. at the age of 12; later studied in Philadelphia with Olga Samaroff, and at the Juilliard Graduate School in N.Y.; played the solo part in the American premiere of Shostakovich's Piano Concerto No. 1 with the Philadelphia Orch. (Dec. 12, 1934). As a sergeant in the U.S. Army, he was called upon to play the piano at the Potsdam Conference in July 1945, in the presence of Truman, Churchill, and Stalin. In 1964 he was appointed a prof. of piano at the Eastman School of Music in Rochester, N.Y.; left there in 1975; then joined the faculty of N.Y. Univ. His repertoire ranged from Mozart to contemporary composers. He championed the cause of Gottschalk, and in later years oversaw a series of "monster concerts" à la Gottschalk in which 10 or more pianos and various pianists were involved.

List, Garrett, American composer; b. Phoenix, Sept. 10, 1943. He studied with Bertram McGarrity at Calif. State Univ. in Long Beach, and in N.Y. with Hall Overton and at the Juilliard School (B.M., 1968; M.M., 1969). He became proficient as a trombonist and was active with various new-music groups, both as performer and as composer; was music director of N.Y.'s Kitchen (1975–77); taught at the Liège Cons. (from 1980).

WORKS: *Orchestral Études* (1972–79); *9 Sets of 7* for Chamber Orch. (1975); *Songs* for Chamber Orch. (1975); *I Am Electric* for Jazz Band (1976); *The Girls* for Narrator and Small Orch. (1977); *Escape Story* for Soloists and Orch. (1979); *Fear and Understanding* for Jazz Band (1981); *2 Wind Studies* for 9 to 16 Winds (1971); *Songs* for 7 to 12 Instruments (1972); *Your Own Self* for Any Instrument(s) (1972); *Elegy: To the People of Chile* for Any Instrument(s) (1973); *Requiem for Helen Lopez* for Piano and 4 to 6 Instruments (1981); *Flesh and Steel* for Piano, Guitar(s), and Instrument(s) (1982); *Baudelaire* for Instrument(s) (1983); *Hôtel des étrangers* for 5 to 21 Instruments (1983); pieces for Trombone; *American Images,* cantata

for Voice and Instrument(s) (1972); *Standard Existence* for Voice and Instrument(s) (1977); many songs.

List, Kurt, Austrian musicologist, music critic, conductor, record producer, and composer; b. Vienna, June 21, 1913; d. Milan, Nov. 16, 1970. He studied at the Vienna Academy of Music (M.A., 1936) and at the Univ. of Vienna (Ph.D., 1938); also took private lessons with Alban Berg (1932–35) and Anton Webern (1935–38). He went to the U.S. in 1939; became active in the field of recording; wrote music criticism. After World War II he returned to Europe and lived mostly in Italy. His String Quartet and a Wind Quintet were performed in N.Y.; he also wrote 2 unperformed operas, *Der Triumph des Todes* and *Mayerling,* stylistically influenced by Richard Strauss.

Listemann, Bernhard, German-American violinist, conductor, and composer, brother of **Fritz** and father of **Franz** and **Paul Listemann;** b. Schlotheim, Aug. 28, 1841; d. Chicago, Feb. 11, 1917. He studied with Ferdinand David in Leipzig, with Vieuxtemps in Brussels, and with Joachim in Hannover; was chamber virtuoso in Rudolstadt (1859–67); then went with his brother Fritz to America; from 1871 to 1874, was concertmaster of the Thomas Orch. in N.Y.; in 1874 he went to Boston, where he founded the Phil. Club, and later the Phil. Orch., which he conducted until 1881, when he became concertmaster of the newly established Boston Sym. Orch. (until 1885); meanwhile, he started the Listemann Quartet; also was director of the Listemann Concert Co. (1885–93). In 1893 he went to Chicago, where he taught violin at the College of Music.

Listemann, Franz, American cellist, son of **Bernhard** and brother of **Paul Listemann;** b. N.Y., Dec. 17, 1873; d. Chicago, March 11, 1930. He studied with Fries in Boston, with Julius Klengel in Leipzig, and with Haussmann in Berlin. After a year as 1st cellist in the Pittsburgh Orch., he settled in N.Y.; he was soloist at the American premiere of Dvořák's Cello Concerto (1896).

Listemann, Fritz, German violinist, brother of **Bernhard Listemann;** b. Schlotheim, March 25, 1839; d. Boston, Dec. 28, 1909. He studied with Ferdinand David at the Leipzig Cons.; was a member of the Court Orch. at Rudolstadt (1858–67); he went with his brother to America; played violin in the Thomas Orch. in N.Y. (1871–74); then was in Boston, where he played in various chamber music organizations, and (from 1878) in his brother's Phil. Orch.; from 1881 to 1885, was a violinist in the Boston Sym. Orch.; then played in the Listemann Concert Co. directed by his brother. He wrote 2 violin concertos; violin pieces.

Listemann, Paul, American violinist, son of **Bernhard** and brother of **Franz Listemann;** b. Boston, Oct. 24, 1871; d. Chicago, Sept. 20, 1950. He was taught by his uncle **Fritz Listemann,** and also by his father; as a boy, participated in the various organizations directed by his father; then studied in Leipzig with Brodsky and in Berlin with Joachim; he was subsequently engaged as an orch. violinist in Pittsburgh, N.Y., etc.; was a member of the Metropolitan Opera Orch. in N.Y. from 1903 to 1920. In 1930 he moved to Chicago.

Listov, Konstantin, Russian composer; b. Odessa, Sept. 19, 1900; d. Moscow, Sept. 6, 1983. He learned music by ear; then studied piano in Tsaritsin and in Saratov. In 1923 he went to Moscow and began to write music for the theater. His Red Army song *Tachanka* became immensely popular. He also wrote a Sym. in commemoration of the centennial of Lenin (1970).

BIBL.: A. Tishchenko, *K. L.* (Moscow, 1962).

Liszt, Franz (Ferenc; baptized **Franciscus),** greatly celebrated Hungarian pianist and composer, creator of the modern form of the symphonic poem, and innovating genius of modern piano technique; b. Raiding, near Odenburg, Oct. 22, 1811; d. Bayreuth, July 31, 1886. His father was an amateur musician who devoted his energies to the education of his son; at the age of 9, young Liszt was able to play a difficult piano concerto by Ries. A group of Hungarian music-lovers provided sufficient funds to finance Liszt's musical education. In 1822 the family traveled to Vienna. Beethoven was still living, and Liszt's father bent every effort to persuade Beethoven to come to young Liszt's Vienna concert on April 13, 1823. Legend has it that Beethoven did come and was so impressed that he ascended the podium and kissed the boy on the brow. There is even in existence a lithograph that portrays the scene, but it was made many years after the event by an unknown lithographer and its documentary value is dubious. Liszt himself perpetuated the legend, and often showed the spot on his forehead where Beethoven was supposed to have implanted the famous kiss. However that might be, Liszt's appearance in Vienna created a sensation; he was hailed by the press as "child Hercules." The link with Beethoven was maintained through Liszt's own teachers: Czerny, who was Beethoven's student and friend and with whom Liszt took piano lessons, and the great Salieri, who was Beethoven's early teacher and who at the end of his life became Liszt's teacher in composition.

On May 1, 1823, Liszt gave a concert in Pest. The announcement of the concert was made in the florid manner characteristic of the period: "Esteemed Gentlemen! High born nobility, valorous army officers, dear audience! I am a Hungarian, and before traveling to France and England, I am happy now to present to my dear Fatherland the first fruits of my training and education." Salieri appealed to Prince Esterházy for financial help so as to enable Liszt to move to Vienna, where Salieri made his residence. "I recently heard a young boy, Francesco Liszt, improvise on the piano," Salieri wrote, "and it produced such a profound impression on me that I thought it was a dream." Apparently Esterházy was sufficiently impressed with Salieri's plea to contribute support.

Under the guidance of his ambitious father (a parallel with Mozart's childhood suggests itself), Liszt applied for an entrance examination at the Paris Cons., but its powerful director, Cherubini, declined to accept him, ostensibly because he was a foreigner (Cherubini himself was a foreigner, but was naturalized). Liszt then settled for private lessons in counterpoint from Antoine Reicha, a Parisianized Czech musician who instilled in Liszt the importance of folklore. Liszt's father died in 1837; Liszt remained in Paris, where he soon joined the brilliant company of men and women of the arts. Paganini's spectacular performances of the violin in particular inspired Liszt to emulate him in creating a piano technique of transcendental difficulty and brilliance, utilizing all possible sonorities of the instrument. To emphasize the narrative Romantic quality of his musical ideas, he accepted the suggestion of his London manager, Frederick Beale, to use the word "recital" to describe his concerts, and in time the term was widely accepted by other pianists.

In his own compositions, Liszt was a convinced propagandist of program music. He liked to attach descriptive titles to his works, such as *Fantasy, Reminiscence,* and *Illustrations.* The musical form of *Rhapsody* was also made popular by Liszt, but he was not its originator; it was used for the 1st time in piano pieces by Tomaschek. A true Romantic, Liszt conceived himself as an actor playing the part of his own life, in which he was a child of the Muses. Traveling in Switzerland, he signed his hotel register as follows: "Place of birth—Parnasse. Arriving from—Dante. Proceeding to—Truth. Profession—Musician-philosopher." He was fascinated by a popular contemporary novel that depicted a fictional traveler named Oberman, and he wrote a suite of piano compositions under the general title *Années de pèlerinage,* in which he followed in music the imaginary progressions of Oberman.

Handsome, artistic, a brilliant conversationalist, Liszt was sought after in society. His 1st lasting attachment was with an aristocratic married woman, the Comtesse Marie d'Agoult; they had 3 daughters, one of whom, Cosima, married Liszt's friend Hans von Bülow before abandoning him for Richard Wagner. D'Agoult was fluent in several European languages and had considerable literary talents, which she exercised under the nom de plume of Daniel Stern. Liszt was 22 when he entered his concubinage with her; she was 28. She confided her impressions of Liszt in her diary: "He was tall and rather slender with a pale visage and green eyes, the color of seawater, which suddenly came to life with sparks of excitement. He talked very fast, exposing his ideas with a strange passion. The spark of his looks, his gesticulation, his conversational manner, his smile, all these traits were full of depth and infinite tenderness." The growing intimacy between Liszt and d'Agoult soon became the gossip of Paris. Berlioz warned Liszt not to let himself become too deeply involved with her. "She possesses a calculated attraction," he told Liszt. "She has a lively spirit, but she lacks true friendship." D'Agoult rapidly established herself as a salon hostess in Paris; she was a constant intermediary between Liszt and his close contemporary Chopin. Indeed, the book on Chopin publ. under Liszt's name after Chopin's early death was largely written by d'Agoult, whose literary French was much superior to Liszt's. His 2nd and final attachment was with another married woman, Carolyne von Sayn-Wittgenstein, who was separated from her husband. Her devotion to Liszt exceeded all limits, even in a Romantic age. "I am at your feet, beloved," she wrote him. "I prostrate myself under your footprints."

Liszt held a clerical title of Abbé, conferred upon him by Pope Pius IX, but his religious affiliations were not limited to the Catholic church. He was also a member of the order of Freemasons and served as a tertiary of the Order of St. Francis. In 1879 he received the tonsure and 4 minor orders (ostuary, lector, exorcist, and acolyte) and an honorary canonry. But he was never ordained a priest, and thus was free to marry if he so wished. When he met an attractive woman in Rome, he said to her, "Under this priestly cloak there beats the passionate heart of a man."

Liszt fully intended to marry Sayn-Wittgenstein, but he encountered resistance from the Catholic church, to which they both belonged and which forbade marriage to a divorced woman. His own position as a secular cleric further militated against it. Thus, Liszt, the great lover of women, never married.

The legend of Liszt as a man of fantastic sexual powers persisted even after his death. It found its most repellent expression in a motion picture directed by Ken Russell under the title *Lisztomania.* In it, Liszt was portrayed with a grotesquely extended male organ on which a bevy of scantily dressed maidens obscenely disported themselves.

Liszt's romantic infatuations did not interfere with his brilliant virtuoso career. One of his greatest successes was his triumphant tour in Russia in 1842. Russian musicians and music critics exhausted their flowery vocabulary to praise Liszt as the miracle of the age. "How fortunate we are that we live in the year 1842 and so are able to witness the living appearance in our own country of such a great genius!" wrote the music critic Stasov. His Majesty Czar Nicholas I himself attended a concert given by Liszt in St. Petersburg, and expressed his appreciation by sending him a pair of trained Russian bears. Liszt acknowledged the imperial honor, but did not venture to take the animals with him on his European tour; they remained in Russia.

Liszt was a consummate showman. In Russia, as elsewhere, he had 2 grand pianos installed on the stage at right angles, so that the keyboards were visible from the right and the left respectively and he could alternate his playing on both. He appeared on the stage wearing a long cloak and white gloves, discarding both with a spectacular gesture. Normally he needed eyeglasses, but he was too vain to wear them in public.

It is not clear why, after all his triumphs in Russia and elsewhere in Europe, Liszt decided to abandon his career as a piano virtuoso and devote his entire efforts to composition. He became associated with Wagner, his son-in-law, as a prophet of "music of the future." Indeed, Liszt anticipated Wagner's chromatic harmony in his works. A remarkable instance of such anticipation is illustrated in his song *Ich möchte hingehen,* which prefigures, note for note, Wagner's theme from the prelude to *Tristan und Isolde.* Inevitably, Liszt and Wagner became objects of derision on the part of conservative music critics. A pictorial example of such an attack was an extraordinary caricature entitled "Music of the Future," distributed by G. Schirmer in N.Y. in 1867. It represented Liszt with arms and legs flailing symmetrically over a huge orch. that comprised not only human players but also goats, donkeys, and a cat placed in a cage with an operator pulling its tail. At Liszt's feet there was placed a score marked "Wagner, not to be played much till 1995."

In 1848 Liszt accepted the position of Court Kapellmeister in Weimar. When Wagner was exiled from Saxony, Liszt arranged for the production of Wagner's opera *Lohengrin* in Weimar on Aug. 28, 1850; he was also instrumental in supervising performances in Weimar of Wagner's operas *Der fliegende Holländer* and *Tannhäuser*, as well as music by Berlioz and a number of operas by other composers.

In Weimar, Liszt established a teaching series at his home. A vivid description of these classes was compiled by one of his students, August Göllerich. Liszt was invariably kind to his students; occasionally he would doze off, but would always wake up when a student completed his or her playing and say "Schön." When one of his American students called to his attention that the date was July 4, Liszt asked if someone would play variations on *Yankee Doodle* for him, for as he said, "Today we are all Americans."

Apparently Liszt gave instruction gratis. He was also generous to colleagues and often lent them money; Wagner, who constantly had financial difficulties, often asked Liszt for loans (which were seldom, if ever, returned), and Liszt invariably obliged. He was also hospitable to his colleagues; during his Weimar years, for instance, young Brahms stayed in his home for 3 weeks.

Liszt was very much interested in the progress of Russian music. In Weimar he received young Glazunov, who brought with him his 1st sym. He played host to Borodin and Cui, who came to Weimar to pay their respects, and was lavish in his appreciation of their works; he also expressed admiration for Rimsky-Korsakov and Mussorgsky, although they never came to see him personally. When Rimsky-Korsakov asked him to contribute a variation to a Russian collection based on the popular *Chopsticks* waltz, known in Europe as the *Cutlet Waltz*, Liszt obliged with his own contribution, adding, "There is nothing wittier than your variations. Here you have at last a condensed manual of harmony and counterpoint. I would gladly recommend this album to conservatory professors as an aid to teaching composition."

Liszt never wrote a full-fledged opera, but he composed several sacred oratorios that were operatic in substance. In his secular works he was deeply conscious of his Hungarian heritage, but he gathered his material mainly from Gypsy dances that he heard in public places in Budapest. In a strange show of negligence, he borrowed a theme for one of the most famous of his Hungarian Rhapsodies from an unpubl. work by an obscure Austrian musician named Heinrich Ehrlich, who had sent him a MS for possible inclusion in one of Liszt's recitals. He explained this faux pas as an oversight.

As a composer, Liszt made every effort to expand the technical possibilities of piano technique; in his 2 piano concertos, and particularly in his *Études d'exécution transcendante*, he made use of the grand piano, which expanded the keyboard in both the bass and the extreme treble. He also extended the field of piano literature with his brilliant transcriptions of operas, among them those by Mozart, Verdi, Wagner, Donizetti, Gounod, Rossini, and Beethoven. These transcriptions were particularly useful at the time when the piano was the basic musical instrument at home.

Although Liszt is universally acknowledged to be a great Hungarian composer, he was actually brought up in the atmosphere of German culture. He spoke German at home, with French as a 2nd language. His women companions conversed with him in French, and most of Liszt's own correspondence was in that language. It was not until his middle age that he decided to take lessons in Hungarian, but he never acquired fluency. His knowledge of Hungarian folk songs came through the medium of the popular Gypsy dance bands that played in Budapest. He used to refer to himself jocularly as "half Gypsy and half Franciscan monk." This self-identification pursued him through his life, and beyond; when the question was raised after his death in Bayreuth regarding the transfer of his body to Budapest, the prime minister of Hungary voiced objection, since Liszt never regarded himself as a purely Hungarian musician.

In his Weimar years, Liszt aged rapidly. Gone were the classical features that had so fascinated his contemporaries, especially women, during his virtuoso career. Photographs taken in Weimar show him with snow-white hair descending upon his shoulders. He walked with difficulty, dragging his feet. He suffered attacks of phlebitis in his legs and had constant intestinal difficulties. He neglected his physical state, and finally developed double pneumonia and died during his sojourn in Bayreuth at the age of 74.

Liszt was an eager correspondent; his letters, written in longhand, in French and in German, passed upon his death into the possession of Sayn-Wittgenstein; after her death in 1887, they were inherited by her daughter, Marie Hohenlohe-Schillingsfürst. She, in turn, left these materials to the Weimar court; eventually they became part of the Liszt Museum in Weimar.

Liszt was a great musical technician. He organized his compositions with deliberate intent to create music that is essentially new. Thus he abandons the traditional succession of 2 principal themes in sonata form. In his symphonic poem *Les Préludes*, the governing melody dominates the entire work. In his popular 3rd *Liebestraum* for Piano, the passionate melody modulates by thirds rather than by Classically anointed fifths and fourths. The great *Faust* sym. is more of a literary essay on Goethe's great poem than a didactic composition. His 2 piano concertos are free from the dialectical contrasts of the established Classical school. The chromatic opening of the 1st Concerto led Hans von Bülow to improvise an insulting line to accompany the theme, "Sie sind alle ganz verrückt!," and the introduction of the triangle solo aroused derisive whoops from the press. Liszt was indifferent to such outbursts. He was the master of his musical fate in the ocean of sounds.

WORKS: OPERA: *Don Sanche, ou Le Château d'amour* (1824–25; Paris, Oct. 17, 1825; in collaboration with Paër).

ORCH.: 2 syms.: *Eine Faust-Symphonie in drei Charakterbildern* for Tenor, Men's Voices, and Orch. (1854–57; Weimar, Sept. 5, 1857); *Eine Symphonie zu Dantes Divina commedia* (1855–56; Dresden, Nov. 7, 1857); 13 symphonic poems: *Ce qu'on entend sur la montagne* or *Bergsymphonie* (1848–49; orchestrated by Raff; Weimar, Feb. 1850; rev. 1850 and 1854); *Tasso: Lamento e trionfo* (1841–45; orchestrated by Conradi; Weimar, Aug. 28, 1849; rev. 1850–51 and 1854); *Les Préludes* (1848; Weimar, Feb. 23, 1854); *Orpheus* (1853–54; Weimar, Feb. 16, 1854); *Prometheus* (1850; orchestrated by Raff; Weimar, Aug. 24, 1850; rev. 1855); *Mazeppa* (1851; orchestrated by Raff; Weimar, April 16, 1854); *Festklänge* (1853; Weimar, Nov. 9, 1854); *Héroïde funèbre* (1849–50; orchestrated by Raff; rev. c.1854; Breslau, Nov. 10, 1857); *Hungaria* (1854; Budapest, Sept. 8, 1856); *Hamlet* (1858; Sondershausen, July 2, 1876); *Hunnenschlacht* (1857; Weimar, Dec. 29, 1857); *Die Ideale* (1857; Weimar, Sept. 5, 1857); *Von der Wiege bis zum Grabe—Du berceau jusqu'à la tombe* (1881–82); 4 piano concertos: No. 1, in E-flat major (1832; rev. 1849 and 1853; Weimar, Feb. 17, 1855; rev. 1856); No. 2, in A major (1839; various revisions; Weimar, Jan. 7, 1857); E-flat major (c.1839; Chicago, May 3, 1990); *Piano Concerto in the Hungarian Style* (1885); *Malédiction* for Piano and Strings (1833); *Grande fantaisie symphonique* on themes from Berlioz's *Lélio* for Piano and Orch. (1834; Paris, April 1835); *Fantasie über Motive aus Beethovens Ruinen von Athen* for Piano and Orch. (c.1837; rev. 1849; Budapest, June 1, 1853); *Totentanz* for Piano and Orch. (1849; rev. 1853 and 1859; The Hague, April 15, 1865); *Festmarsch zur Goethejubiläumsfeier* (1849; orchestrated by Conradi; Weimar, Nov. 8, 1860); *Fantasie über ungarische Volksmelodien* for Piano and Orch. (Budapest, June 1, 1853);

Künstlerfestzug zur Schillerfeier 1859 (1857; Weimar, Nov. 8, 1860); *Festmarsch nach Motiven von E.H. zu S.-C.-G.* on themes from Duke Ernst of Saxe-Coburg-Gotha's *Diana von Solange* (c.1860); 2 episodes from Lenau's *Faust* (1860–61; No. 2, Weimar, March 8, 1861); *Salve Polonia* (1863; Weimar, 1884); *Rákóczy March* (1865; rev. 1867; Budapest, Aug. 17, 1875); *Trois odes funebrès:* No. 1 (1860–66; Weimar, May 21, 1912); No. 2 (1863–64; Weimar, Dec. 6, 1912); No. 3 (1866; N.Y., March 1877); *Ungarischer Marsch zur Krönungsfeier in Ofen-Pest am 8. Juni 1867* (1870); *Ungarischer Sturmmarsch* (1875); 2nd *Mephisto Waltz* (1880–81; Budapest, March 9, 1881).

PIANO: *Variation über einen Walzer von Diabelli* (1822); *Huit variations* (c.1824); *Sept variations brillantes sur un thème de Rossini* (c.1824); *Impromptu brillant sur des thèmes de Rossini et Spontini* (1824); *Allegro di bravura* (1824); *Rondo di bravura* (1824); *Étude en douze exercices* (1826); *Scherzo* in G minor (1827); *Grandes études de Paganini* (1831); *Harmonies poétiques et religieuses* (1833; rev. 1835); *Apparitions* (1834); *Fantaisie romantique sur deux mélodies suisses* (1836); *Vingt-quatre grandes études* (1837); *Album d'un voyageur* (3 vols., 1835–38); *Études d'exécution transcendante d'après Paganini* (1838–39); *Mazeppa* (1840); *Morceau de salon, étude de perfectionnement* (1840); *Venezia e Napoli* (c.1840; rev. 1859); *Albumblatt* in E major (c.1841); *Feuilles d'album* in A-flat major (1841); *Albumblatt in Walzerform* in A major (1841); *Feuille d'album* in A minor (1842); *Élégie sur des motifs du Prince Louis Ferdinand de Prusse* (1842; rev. c.1851); *Madrigal* (1844); *Tre sonetti del Petrarca* (1844–45); 19 Hungarian Rhapsodies: No. 1, in C-sharp minor (1846); No. 2, in C-sharp minor (1847); No. 3, in B-flat major (1853); No. 4, in E-flat major (1853); No. 5, in E minor (1853); No. 6, in D-flat major (1853); No. 7, in D minor (1853); No. 8, in F-sharp minor (1853); No. 9, in E-flat major (1848); No. 10, in E major (1853); No. 11, in A minor (1853); No. 12, in C-sharp minor (1853); No. 13, in A minor (1853); No. 14, in F minor (1853); No. 15, in A minor, *Rákóczy March* (1851; rev. 1871); No. 16, in A minor (1882); No. 17, in D minor (1886); No. 18, in C-sharp minor (1885); No. 19, in D minor (1885); 6 *Consolations* (1844–48); *Ballade* No. 1, in D-flat major (1845; rev. 1848); *Hymne de la nuit; Hymne du matin* (1847); *Trois études de concert* (c.1848); *Romance* (1848); *Années de pèlerinage: Deuxième année, Italie* (1837–49); *Grosses Konzertsolo* (c.1849); *Études d'exécution transcendante* (1851); *Scherzo und Marsch* (1851); *Harmonies poétiques et religieuses* (1840–52); *Ab irato* (1852); *Ballade* No. 2, in B minor (1853); Sonata in B minor (1851–53); *Années de pèlerinage: Première année, Suisse* (1848–52); *Berceuse* (1854; rev. 1862); *Weinen, Klagen, Sorgen, Zagen, Präludium* (1859); *Klavierstück* in F-sharp minor (c.1861); *Zwei Konzertetüden:* No. 1, *Waldersrauschen,* and No. 2, *Gnomenreigen* (1862–63); *Variationen über das Motiv von Bach* (1862); *Ave Maria* (1862); *Alleluja et Ave Maria* (1862); *Légendes* (1863); *Urbi et orbi, bénédiction papale* (1864); *Vexilla regis prodeunt* (1864); *Weihnachtsbaum—Arbre de Noël* (1866; rev. 1876); *La Marquise de Blocqueville, portrait en musique* (1868); *Mosonyi gyázmenete—Mosonyis Grabgeleit* (1870); *Impromptu* (1872); *Élégie* (1874); *Années de pèlerinage, troisième année* (1867–77); *Sancta Dorothea* (1877); *Resignazione* (1877); *Petofi szellemenek—Dem Andenken Petofis* (1877); *Zweite Elegie* (1877); *Fünf kleine Klavierstücke* (1865–79); *Technische Studien* (12 vols., 1868–80); *In festo transfigurationis Domini nostri Jesu Christi* (1880); *Wiegenlied—Chant du berceau* (1880); *Toccata* (1879–81); *Nuages gris* (1881); *La Lugubre gondola* (1882; rev. 1885); *R.W.—Venezia* (1883); *Am Grabe Richard Wagners* (1883); *Schlaflos, Frage und Antwort* (1883); *Historische ungarische Bildnisse—Magyar történelmi arcképek* (1870–85); *Trauervorspiel und Trauermarsch* (1885); *En rêve* (1885); *Ruhig* (1883–86); *Recueillement* (1887); also numerous arrangements and transcriptions.

CHORAL: SACRED: *Pater noster* for Men's Voices (1846; also for 4 Equal Voices and Organ, c.1848); *Ave Maria* for Chorus and Organ (1846; also for 4 Voices and Organ, c.1852); *Hymne de l'enfant à son réveil* for Women's Voices, Harmonium or Piano, and Harp ad libitum (1847; rev. 1862, 1865, and 1874;

Weimar, June 17, 1875); *Mass* for 4 Men's Voices and Organ (1848; Weimar, Aug. 15, 1852; rev. 1859; 2nd version, 1869; Jena, June 1872); *Pater noster* for Mixed Voices and Organ (1850); *Te Deum* for Men's Voices and Organ (c.1853); *Domine salvum fac regem* for Tenor, Men's Voices, and Organ or Orch. (1853; orchestrated by Raff); *Missa solemnis zur Einweihung der Basilika in Gran* for Soprano, Alto, Tenor, Bass, Chorus, and Orch. (1855; Gran, Aug. 31, 1856; rev. 1857–58); *Psalm XIII* for Tenor, Chorus, and Orch. (Berlin, Dec. 6, 1855; rev. 1858 and 1862); *Festgesang zur Eröffnung der zehnten allgemeinen deutschen Lehrerversammlung* for Men's Voices and Organ (Weimar, May 27, 1858); *Die Seligkeiten* for Baritone, Mixed Voices, and Organ (1855–59; Weimar, Oct. 2, 1859); *Christus,* oratorio for Soprano, Alto, Tenor, Baritone, Bass, Chorus, Organ, and Orch. (1855; 1859; rev. 1862–66; Weimar, May 29, 1873); *Psalm XXIII* for Tenor or Soprano, Men's Voices, and Instrumental Accompaniment (1859; rev. 1862); *Psalm CXXXVII* for Soprano, Women's Voices, Violin, Harp, and Organ (1859; rev. 1862); *An den heiligen Franziskus von Paula* for Solo Men's Voices, Men's Chorus, Harmonium or Organ, 3 Trombones, and Timpani ad libitum (c.1860; rev. c.1874); *Pater noster* for 4 Voices and Organ (c.1860; Dessau, May 25, 1865); *Psalm XVIII* for Men's Voices and Instrumental Accompaniment (1860; Weimar, June 25, 1861); Responses and antiphons for 4 Voices (1860); *Cantico del sol di S. Francesco d'Assisi* for Baritone, Men's Chorus, Orch., and Organ (1862; rev. 1880–81); *Die Legende von der heiligen Elisabeth,* oratorio for Soprano, Alto, 3 Baritones, Bass, Chorus, Orch., and Organ (1857–62; Budapest, Aug. 15, 1865); *Christus ist geboren* (5 versions, c.1863); *Slavimo slavno slaveni!* for Men's Voices and Organ (Rome, July 3, 1863; rev. 1866); *Missa choralis* for Chorus and Organ (1865; Lemberg, 1869); *Crux!* for Men's Voices Unaccompanied, or Women's or Children's Voices and Piano (1865); *Ave maris stella* for Mixed Voices and Organ (1865–66; also for Men's Voices and Organ or Harmonium, 1868); *Dall'alma Roma* for 2 Voices and Organ (1866); *Hungarian Coronation Mass* for Soprano, Alto, Tenor, Bass, Chorus, and Orch. (Budapest, June 8, 1867); *Te Deum* for Mixed Voices, Organ, Brass, and Drums ad libitum (1867); *Mihi autem adhaerere* for Men's Voices and Organ (1868); *Requiem* for 2 Tenors, 2 Basses, Men's Voices, Organ, and Brass ad libitum (1867–68; Lemberg, 1869); *Psalm CXVI* for Men's Voices and Piano (1869); *Ave Maria* for Mixed Voices and Organ (1869); *Inno a Maria Vergine* for Mixed Voices, Harp, and Organ (1869); *O salutaris hostia* for Women's Voices and Organ (1869); *Pater noster* for Mixed Voices, and Organ or Piano (1869; also for Men's Voices and Organ); *Tantum ergo* for Men's Voices and Organ (1869; also for Women's Voices and Organ); *O salutaris hostia* for Mixed Voices and Organ (c.1870); *Libera me* for Men's Voices and Organ (1870); *Ave verum corpus* for Mixed Voices and Organ ad libitum (1871); *Anima Christi sanctifica me* for Men's Voices and Organ (1874); *Die heilige Cäcilia,* legend for Mezzo-soprano, Chorus ad libitum, and Orch. or Piano (1874; Wiemar, June 17, 1875); *Die Glocken des Strassburger Münsters* for Mezzo-soprano, Baritone, Chorus, and Orch. (1874; Budapest, March 10, 1875); *Der Herr bewahret die Seelen seiner Heiligen, Festgesang zur Enthüllung des Carl-August-Denkmals in Weimar* (Weimar, Sept. 3, 1875); *O heilige Nacht,* Christmas carol for Tenor, Women's Chorus, and Organ or Harmonium (c.1877; Rome, Dec. 25, 1881); *Septum sacramenta,* responsories for Mezzo-soprano, Baritone, Mixed Voices, and Organ (1878); *Gott sei uns gnädig und barmherzig* for Mixed Voices and Organ (1878); *O Roma nobilis* for Mixed Voices and Organ ad libitum (1879); *Ossa arida* for Unison Men's Voices and Organ, 4-hands, or Piano, 4-hands (1879); *Rosario* (1879); *Cantantibus organis,* antiphon for the feast of St. Cecilia for Solo Voices, Chorus, and Orch. (1879); *Zwölf alte deutsche geistliche Weisen* (1878–79); *Via Crucis, Les 14 Stations de la croix* for Solo Voices, Chorus, and Organ or Piano (1878–79); *Psalm CXXIX* for Baritone, Men's Voices, and Organ, or Baritone or Alto and Piano or Organ (1880–81); *Sankt Christoph,* legend for Baritone, Women's Voices, Piano, Harmonium, and Harp ad libitum

(1881); *In domum Domini ibimus* for Mixed Voices, Organ, Brass, and Drums (c.1881); *O sacrum convivium* for Alto, Women's Voices ad libitum, and Organ or Harmonium (c.1881); *Pro Papa* (c.1881); *Nun danket alle Gott* (1883); *Mariengarten* for Chorus and Organ (c.1884); *Qui seminant in lacrimis* for Mixed Voices and Organ (1884); *Pax vobiscum!* for Men's Voices and Organ (1885); *Qui Mariam absolvisti* for Baritone, Unison Mixed Voices, and Organ or Harmonium (1885); *Salve regina* for Mixed Voices (1885). SECULAR: *Das deutsche Vaterland* for 4 Men's Voices (1839; Leipzig, Dec. 1841); *Vierstimmige Männergesänge* (1841–42); *Das düstre Meer umrauscht mich* for Men's Voices and Piano (1842); *Über allen gipfeln ist Ruh* for Men's Voices (1842; also for Men's Voices and 2 Horns, 1849); *Titan* for Baritone, Men's Voices, and Piano (1842; rev. 1845 and 1847); *Trinkspruch* for Men's Voices and Piano (1843); *Festkantate zur Enthüllung des Beethoven-Denkmals in Bonn* for 2 Sopranos, 2 Tenors, 2 Basses, Chorus, and Orch. (Bonn, Aug. 13, 1845); *Le Forgeron* for Men's Voices, and Piano or Orch. (1845); *Les Quatre Élémens* for Men's Voices, and Piano or Orch. (1839–45); *Die lustige Legion* for Men's Voices and Piano ad libitum (1846); *A patakhoz* (To the Brook) for Men's Voices (1846); *Arbeiterchor* for Bass, 4 Men's Voices, Men's Chorus, and Piano (c.1848); *Hungaria 1848*, cantata for Soprano, Tenor, Bass, Men's Voices, and Piano or Orch. (1848; orch. version, Weimar, May 21, 1912); *Es war einmal ein König* for Bass, Men's Voices, and Piano (1849); *Licht, mehr Licht* for Men's Voices and Brass (1849); *Chor der Engel* for Mixed Voices, and Harp or Piano (1849); *Festchor zur Enthüllungs des Herder-Denkmals in Weimar* for Men's Voices, and Piano or Orch. (orchestrated by Raff; Weimar, Aug. 25, 1850); *Chöre zu Herders Entfesseltem Prometheus* for Soprano, Alto, 2 Tenors, 2 Basses, Double Chorus, and Orch. (orchestrated by Raff; Weimar, Aug. 24, 1850; rev. 1855); *An die Künstler* for 2 Tenors, 2 Basses, Men's Chorus, and Orch. (1853; orchestrated by Raff; Karlsruhe, June 1853; rev. 1856); *Weimars Volkslied* (Weimar, Sept. 3, 1857); *Morgenlied* for Women's Voices (1859); *Mit klingendem Spiel* for Children's Voices (c.1859); *Für Männergesang* (1842–49); *Gaudeamus igitur* for Solo Voices ad libitum, Men's or Mixed Voices, and Orch. (1869); *Zur Säkularfeier Beethovens*, cantata for Soprano, Alto, Tenor, Bass, Double Chorus, and Orch. (1869–70; Weimar, May 29, 1870); *A lelkesedés dala—Das Lied der Bergeisterung* (1871; rev. 1874); *Carl August weilt mit uns, Festgesang zur Enthüllung des Carl-August-Denkmals in Weimar* for Men's Voices, Brass, Drums, and Organ ad libitum (Weimar, Sept. 3, 1875); *Magyar király-dal—Ungarisches Königslied* (1883); *Grüss* for Men's Voices (c.1885). He also wrote numerous solo songs and some chamber music. For his works, see F. Busoni, P. Raabe et al., eds., *Franz Liszt: Musikalische Werke* (Leipzig, 1907–36), the *Liszt Society Publications* (London, 1950–), and *Franz Liszt: Neue Ausgabe sämtlicher Werke/New Edition of the Complete Works* (Kassel and Budapest, 1970–).

WRITINGS: *De la fondation Goethe à Weimar* (Leipzig, 1851); *Lohengrin et Tannhäuser de R. Wagner* (Leipzig, 1851); *F. Chopin* (Paris, 1852); *Des bohémiens et de leur musique en Hongrie* (Paris, 1859); *Über John Fields Nocturne* (Leipzig, 1859); *R. Schumanns musikalische Haus- und Lebensregeln* (Leipzig, 1860). L. Ramann edited his *Gesammelte Schriften* (Leipzig, 1880–83); a new critical ed. of his writings, under the general editorship of D. Altenburg, began to appear in 1987.

BIBL.: SOURCE MATERIAL: F. Liszt, *Thematisches Verzeichnis der Werke von F. L.* (Leipzig, 1855); idem, *Thematisches Verzeichnis der Werke, Bearbeitungen und Transkriptionen von F. L.* (Leipzig, 1877); L. Friwitzer, "Chronologisch-systematisches Verzeichnis sämtlicher Tonwerke F. L.s," *Musikalische Chronik*, V (Vienna, 1887); C. Suttoni, "F. L.'s Published Correspondence: An Annotated Bibliography," *Fontes Artis Musicae*, XXVI (1979); E. Waters, *L. Holographs in the Library of Congress* (Washington, D.C., 1979); M. Saffe, *F. L.: A Guide to Research* (N.Y., 1990).

ICONOGRAPHIES: D. Bartha, *F. L., 1811–1886: Sein Leben in Bildern* (Leipzig, 1936); R. Bory, *La vie de L. par l'image*

(Paris, 1936); W. Füssmann and B. Mátéka, *F. L.: Ein Künstlerleben in Wort und Bild* (Langensalza, 1936); Z. László and B. Mátéka, *F. L.: Sein Leben in zeitgenossischen Bildern* (Budapest, 1967; Eng. tr., 1968).

BIOGRAPHICAL: J. Christern, *F. L., nach seinem Leben und Werke, aus authentischen Berichten dargestellt* (Hamburg, 1841); L. Rellstab, *F. L.: Beurteilungen-Bericht-Lebensskizze* (Berlin, 1842; 2nd ed., 1861); G. Schilling, *F. L.: Sein Leben und Werken aus nächster Beschauung* (Stuttgart, 1844); R. de Beaufort, *F. L.: The Story of His Life* (Boston and London, 1866; 2nd ed., 1910); J. Schubert, *F. L.s Biographie* (Leipzig, 1871); L. Ramann, *F. L. als Künstler und Mensch* (3 vols., Leipzig, 1880–94; Eng. tr. of vol. I, 1882); O. Lessmann, *F. L.: Eine Charakterstudie* (Berlin, 1881); L. Nohl, *F. L.* (Leipzig, 1882–88); R. Pohl, *F. L.* (Leipzig, 1883); B. Vogel, *F. L.: Abriss seines Lebens und Würdigung seiner Werke* (Leipzig, 1898); O. Lüning, *F. L., ein Apostel der Ideale* (Zürich, 1896); E. Reuss, *F. L.* (Dresden, 1898); R. Louis, *F. L.* (Berlin, 1900); A. von Pozsony, *L. und Hans von Bülow* (Munich, 1900); M.-D. Calvocoressi, *F. L.* (Paris, 1905; Eng. tr. in the *Musical Observer*, N.Y., 1910–11); A. Göllerich, *F. L.* (Berlin, 1908); J. Kapp, *F. L.* (Berlin, 1909; 20th ed., 1924); idem, *L.-Brevier* (Leipzig, 1910); idem, *R. Wagner und F. L.: Eine Freundschaft* (Berlin, 1910); J. Chantavoine, *L.* (Paris, 1911; 6th ed., 1950); A. Hervey, *F. L. and His Music* (London, 1911); J. Huneker, *F. L.* (N.Y. and London, 1911); J. Kapp, *F. L. und die Frauen* (Leipzig, 1911); La Mara, *L. und die Frauen* (Leipzig, 1911; 2nd ed., 1919); H. Thode, *F. L.* (Heidelberg, 1911); P. Bekker, *F. L.* (Bielefeld, 1912); B. Schrade, *F. L.* (Berlin, 1914); P. Raabe, *Grossherzog Karl Alexander und L.* (Leipzig, 1918); R. Bory, *Une Retraite romantique en Suisse: L. et la Comtesse d'Agoult* (Geneva, 1923; 2nd ed., 1930); K. Grunsky, *F. L.* (Leipzig, 1924); F. Corder, *L.* (London, 1925; 2nd ed., 1933); R. Wetz, *F. L.* (Leipzig, 1925); G. de Pourtalès, *La Vie de F. L.* (Paris, 1926; 2nd ed., 1950; Eng. tr., 1926); W. Wallace, *L., Wagner and the Princess* (London, 1927); C. van Wessem, *F. L.* (The Hague, 1927); M. d'Agoult, *Erinnerungen an F. L.* (ed. by S. Wagner; 1928); G. de Pourtalès, *L. et Chopin* (Paris, 1929); M. Herwegh, *Au banquet des dieux: F. L., Richard Wagner et leurs amis* (Paris, 1931); R. Raabe, *F. L.* (Stuttgart, 1931; 2nd ed., rev., 1968); E. Newman, *The Man L.* (London, 1934; 2nd ed., 1970); S. Sitwell, *L.* (London, 1934; 3rd ed., rev., 1966); R. Bory, *L. et ses enfants: Blandine, Cosima et Daniel* (Paris, 1936); H. Engel, *F. L.* (Potsdam, 1936); Z. Harsányi, *Magyar Rapszódia* (Budapest, 1936; Eng. tr., London, 1936, as *Hungarian Melody* and N.Y., 1937, as *Immortal Franz*); A. Hevesy, *L., ou Le Roi Lear de la musique* (Paris, 1936); R. Hill, *L.* (London, 1936; 2nd ed., 1949); L. Nowak, *F. L.* (Innsbruck, 1936); B. Ollivier, *L., le musicien passionné* (Paris, 1936); E. von Liszt, *F. L.* (Vienna, 1937); M. Tibaldi Chiesa, *Vita romantica di L.* (Milan, 1937; 2nd ed., 1941); P. Raabe, *Wege zu L.* (Regensburg, 1944); A. Pols, *F. L.* (Bloemendaal, 1951); J. Vier, *La Comtesse d'Agoult et son temps* (Paris, 1955–63); B. Voelcker, *F. L., der grosse Mensch* (Weimar, 1955); W. Beckett, *L.* (London, 1956; 2nd ed., 1963); Y. Milstein, *F. L.* (Moscow, 1956; 2nd ed., rev., 1971); B. Szabolcsi, *L. F. estéje* (The Twilight of F. L.; Budapest, 1956; Eng. tr., 1959); C. Rostand, *L.* (Paris, 1960; Eng. tr., 1972); J. Rousselot, *F. L.* (London, 1960); W. Armando, *F. L.: Eine Biographie* (Hamburg, 1961); M. Bagby, *L.'s Weimar* (N.Y., 1961); J. Hankiss, *Wenn L. ein Tagebuch geführt hätte* (Budapest, 1961); P. Rehberg and G. Nestler, *F. L.* (Zürich, 1961); K. Hamburger, *L. F.* (Budapest, 1966); E. Haraszti, *F. L.* (Paris, 1967); A. Leroy, *F. L.* (Lausanne, 1967); A. Walker, ed., *F. L.: The Man and His Music* (London, 1970; 2nd ed., 1976); idem, *L.* (London, 1971); E. Perényi, *L.: The Artist as Romantic Hero* (Boston, 1974); K. Hamburger, ed., *F. L.: Beiträge von ungarischen Autoren* (Leipzig, 1978); E. Horvath, *F. L.:* vol. I, *Kindheit, 1811–27* (Eisenstadt, 1978), and vol. II, *Jugend* (Eisenstadt, 1982); R. Rehberg, *L.: Die Geschichte seines Lebens, Schaffens und Wirkens* (Munich, 1978); B. Gavoty, *L.: Le Virtuose, 1811–1848* (Paris, 1980); D. Legány, *L. and His Country 1869–1873* (Budapest, 1983); L. Rabes, "F. L.: The Freemason," *Ars Qua-*

tuor Coronatorum, 96, Transactions of Quatuor Coronati Lodge No. 2076, London (Masonic Lodge of Research; 1983); A. Walker, *F. L.: Vol. I, The Virtuoso Years, 1811–1847* (London, 1983; rev. ed., 1987); idem, *F. L.: Vol. II, The Weimar Years, 1848–1861* (London, 1989); W. Dömling, *F. L. und seine Zeit* (Laaber, 1986); N. Cook, "L.—100 Years On," *Musical Times* (July 1986); R. Taylor, *F. L.: The Man and the Musician* (London, 1986); K. Hamburger, *L.* (Budapest, 1987); S. Gut, *F. L.* (1989); D. Watson, *L.* (London, 1989); A. Williams, *Portrait of L.: By Himself and His Contemporaries* (Oxford, 1990). CRITICAL, ANALYTICAL: R. Wagner, *Ein Brief über L.s symphonische Dichtungen* (Leipzig, 1857); E. Segnitz, *F. L.s Kirchenmusik* (Langensalza, 1911); P. Roberts, *Études sur Boieldieu, Chopin et L.* (Rouen, 1913); P. Raabe, *Die Entstehungsgeschichte der ersten Orchesterwerke F. L.s* (diss., Univ. of Jena, 1916); J. Wenz, *F. L. als Liederkomponist* (diss., Univ. of Frankfurt am Main, 1921); G. Galston, *Studienbuch: F. L.* (Munich, 1926); J. Weber, *Die symphonischen Dichtungen F. L.s* (diss., Univ. of Vienna, 1928); H. Arminski, *Die ungarischen Phantasien von F. L.s* (diss., Univ. of Vienna, 1929); J. Heinrichs, *Über den Sinn der L.schen Programmusik* (diss., Univ. of Bonn, 1929); J. Bergfeld, *Die formale Struktur der "Symphonischen Dichtungen" F. L.s* (diss., Univ. of Berlin, 1931); Z. Gárdonyi, *Die ungarischen Stileigentümlichkeiten in den musikalischen Werken F. L.s* (diss., Univ. of Berlin, 1931); H. Dobiey, *Die Klaviertechnik des jungen F. L.s* (diss., Univ. of Berlin, 1932); I. Philipp, *La Technique de L.* (Paris, 1932); B. Bartók, *L. problémák* (Budapest, 1936); Z. Gárdonyi, *L. F. magyar stilusa/Le Style hongrois de F. L.* (Budapest, 1936); M. Cooper, "L. as a Song Writer," *Music & Letters*, XIX (1938); D. Presser, *Studien zu den Opern- und Liedbearbeitungen F. L.s* (diss., Univ. of Cologne, 1953); H. Searle, *The Music of L.* (London, 1954; 2nd ed., rev., 1966); B. Hansen, *Variationen und Varianten in den musikalischen Werken F. L.s* (diss., Univ. of Hamburg, 1959); L. Bárdos, *L. F. a jövö zenésze* (F. L. the Innovator; Budapest, 1976); E. Heinemann, *F. L.s Auseinandersetzung mit der geistlichen Musik* (Munich, 1978); B. Ott, *L. et la pédagogie du piano* (Issy-les-Moulineaux, 1978); D. Torkewitz, *Harmonisches Denken im Frühwerk F. L.s* (Munich, 1978); S. Winklhofer, *L.'s Sonata in B Minor: A Study of Autograph Sources and Documents* (diss., Univ. of Michigan, 1980); R. Kaplan, "Sonata Form in the Orchestral Works of L.: The Revolutionary Reconsidered," *19th Century Music* (Fall 1984); A. Bonner, "L.'s *Les Préludes* and *Les Quatre Élémens*: A Reinvestigation," ibid. (Fall 1986); J. Williamson, "The Revision of L.'s 'Prometheus,' " *Music & Letters* (Oct. 1986); P. Merrick, *Revolution and Religion in the Music of L.* (Cambridge and N.Y., 1987). CORRESPONDENCE: F. Hueffer, ed., *Briefwechsel zwischen Wagner und L.* (Leipzig, 1887; 4th ed., 1919; Eng. tr., 1888); La Mara, ed., *F. L.'s Briefe* (Leipzig, 1893–1902); C. Bache, ed., *Letters of F. L.* (London, 1894); La Mara, ed., *Briefe hervorragender Zeitgenossen an F. L.* (Leipzig, 1895–1904); idem, ed., *Briefwechsel zwischen F. L. und Hans von Bülow* (Leipzig, 1898); A. Stern, ed., *L.s Briefe an Carl Gille* (Leipzig, 1903); La Mara, ed., *Briefwechsel zwischen F. L. und Carl Alexander, Grossherzog von Sachsen* (Leipzig, 1909); V. Csapó, ed., *L. F. levelei baró Augusz A.* (F. L.'s Letters to the Baron Augusz; Budapest, 1911; German tr., 1911); N. de Gutmansthal, *Souvenirs de F. L.: Lettres inédites* (Paris, 1913); La Mara, ed., *F. L.: Briefe an seine Mutter* (Leipzig, 1918); D. Ollivier, ed., *Correspondance de L. et de la comtesse d'Agoult 1833–1840* (Paris, 1933–34); idem, ed., *Correspondance de L. et de sa fille Mme. Émile Ollivier* (Paris, 1936); H. Hugo, ed., *The Letters of F. L. to Marie zu Sayn-Wittgenstein* (Cambridge, Mass., 1953); M. Prahacs, ed., *F. L.: Briefe aus ungarischen Sammlungen 1835–1886* (Kassel, 1969); W. Tyler and E. Waters, eds., *Letters of F. L. to Olga von Meyendorff* (Washington, D.C., 1979); D. Legány, *F. L.: Unbekannte Presse und Briefe aus Wien (1822–1886)* (Budapest, 1984).

Litaize, Gaston (Gilbert), French composer and organist; b. Ménil-sur-Belvitte, Aug. 11, 1909. He was blind from in-

fancy; studied at the National Inst. of the Blind; also at the Paris Cons.; in 1938 won the 2nd Prix de Rome (unprecedented for a blind person); was appointed organist at the church of St.-François Xavier in Paris in 1946; also was on the staff of the National Inst. of the Blind. In the autumn of 1957 he made his 1st American tour as a concert organist. He composed a number of organ pieces and several sacred choruses, among them *Messe solennelle en français* (1966).

Literes Carrión, Antonio, Spanish composer; b. Artá, Majorca, June 18, 1673?; d. Madrid, Jan. 18, 1747. He was a composer and bass-viol player at the Royal Choir School in Madrid under Charles II, Philip V, and Ferdinand VI. In 1693 he was appointed to the royal chapel as bassist. After the fire at the old Alcazar in Madrid on Christmas Eve of 1734, Literes and Nebra were charged with the reconstruction of musical MSS that were damaged or completely burned. They also wrote new music for church services to replace the material destroyed. He wrote an opera, *Los elementos*, and several zarzuelas, including *Accis y Galatea* (Madrid, Dec. 19, 1708); also various sacred works. His son, **Antonio Literes Montalbo** (d. Madrid, Dec. 2, 1768), was a composer and organist under Ferdinand VI.
BIBL.: N. Solar Quintes, "A. L.C. y sus hijos (nuevos documentos para su biografia)," *Anuario Musical*, 5 (1950); A. Martín Moreno, "El compositor mallorquin A. L. (1673–1747)," *Tesoro sacro musical*, no. 648 (1978).

Litinsky, Genrik, distinguished Russian composer; b. Lipovetz, March 17, 1901; d. Moscow, July 26, 1985. He studied composition with Glière at the Moscow Cons., graduating in 1928; subsequently taught there (1928–43); among his students were Khrennikov, Zhiganov, Arutiunian, and other Soviet composers. In 1945 he went to Yakutsk as an ethnomusicologist; in collaboration with native Siberian composers he produced the 1st national Yakut operas, based on authentic folk melorhythms and arranged in contemporary harmonies according to the precepts of socialist realism: *Nurgun Botur* (Yakutsk, June 29, 1947); *Sygy Kyrynastyr* (Yakutsk, July 4, 1947); *Red Shaman* (Yakutsk, Dec. 9, 1967). He wrote 3 Yakut ballets: *Altan's Joy* (Yakutsk, June 19, 1963); *Field Flower* (Yakutsk, July 2, 1947); *Crimson Kerchief* (Yakutsk, Jan. 9, 1968). Other works include: Sym. (1928); *Dagestan Suite* for Orch. (1931); Trumpet Concerto (1934); *Festive Rhapsody* for Orch. (1966); 12 string quartets (1923–61); String Octet (1944); 12 concert studies for Cello (1967); 12 concert studies for Trumpet and Piano (1968); 15 concert studies for Oboe and Piano (1969). He publ. the valuable manuals *Problems of Polyphony* (3 vols., 1965, 1966, 1967), ranging from pentatonic to dodecaphonic patterns and from elementary harmonization to polytonality; also *Formation of Imitation in the Strict Style* (1970). He also collected, transcribed, and organized the basic materials of several Soviet Republics; altogether he compiled musical samples from as many as 23 distinct ethnic divisions of folkloric elements. He was in time duly praised by the Soviet authorities on esthetics, but not until the policy of the Soviet Union itself had changed. In the meantime, Litinsky became the target of unconscionable attacks by reactionary groups within Soviet musical organizations who denounced him as a formalist contaminated by Western bourgeois culture. In one instance, his personal library was ransacked in search of alleged propaganda. In 1964 he was named a People's Artist of the Yakut Soviet Socialist Republic and of the Tatar Autonomous Soviet Socialist Republic.

Litolff, Henry Charles, French pianist, conductor, music publisher, and composer; b. London (of an Alsatian father and English mother), Feb. 6, 1818; d. Bois-Colombes, near Paris, Aug. 6, 1891. A precocious pianist, he studied with Moscheles; made his professional debut in London on July 24, 1832, at the age of 14. An early marriage (at 17) forced him to seek his livelihood in Paris, where he attracted attention with his brilliant concerts; then he became an itinerant musician, traveling in Poland, Germany, and the Netherlands; was in Vienna during the Revolution of 1848; he became involved, and was compelled to flee. He then settled in Braunschweig; after the termination of his 1st marriage, he married Julie Meyer (1851), widow of the music publisher Meyer, acquiring the business. Litolff was one of the pioneers in the publication of cheap eds. of classical music. He was made Kapellmeister at the court of Saxe-Coburg-Gotha (1855). After divorcing his 2nd wife (1858), he became active as a conductor in Paris. In 1860 he married his 3rd wife, Comtesse de Larochefoucauld, and also turned his firm over to his adopted son, **Theodor Litolff** (1839–1912). Following the death of his wife (1870), he married a 15-year-old girl. Besides his business pursuits, he was a prolific composer; 115 of his works were publ.; of these, the most famous is the overture *Robespierre* (1856; Paris, Feb. 2, 1870), which carries the idea of programmatic music to its utmost limit, with a vivid description of Robespierre's execution (drumbeats, etc.); operas: *Die Braut von Kynast* (Braunschweig, 1847); *Héloïse et Abélard* (Paris, Oct. 17, 1872); *Les Templiers* (Brussels, Jan. 25, 1886); oratorio, *Ruth et Boaz* (1869); *Szenen aus Goethes Faust* for Soli, Chorus, and Orch.; 5 *Concertos-Symphonies* for Piano and Orch., of which the 4th contains a brilliant scherzo which became a perennial favorite; *Eroica*, violin concerto; a funeral march for Meyerbeer; 3 piano trios; 6 *études de concert* for Piano; many character pieces for piano, of which *Chant de la fileuse* became popular.

BIBL.: P. Magnette, "H. L.: Seine Laufbahn in Deutschland," *Die Musik*, XIII (1914); T. Blair, *H.C. L. (1818–1891): His Life and Piano Music* (diss., Univ. of Iowa, 1968).

Litta, Giulio, Italian composer; b. Milan, 1822; d. Vedano, near Monza, May 29, 1891. A composer of precocious talent and excellent training, he produced an opera at 20, *Bianca di Santafiora* (Milan, Jan. 2, 1843), followed by 6 more: *Sardanapalo* (Milan, Sept. 2, 1844); *Maria Giovanna* (Turin, Oct. 28, 1851); *Edita di Lorno* (Genoa, June 1, 1853); *Il Viandante* (Milan, April 17, 1873); *Raggio d'amore* (Milan, April 6, 1879); *Il violino di Cremona* (Milan, April 18, 1882). He also wrote an oratorio, *La Passione*; church music; songs.

Little Richard. See **Penniman, Richard Wayne.**

Little Walter. See **Jacobs, Marion Walter.**

Little Willie John. See **Woods, William.**

Litton, Andrew, American conductor; b. N.Y., May 16, 1959. He studied piano with Nadia Reisenberg and conducting with Sixten Ehrling at the Juilliard School in N.Y.; also received lessons in conducting from Walter Weller at the Salzburg Mozarteum, Neeme Järvi in Hilversum, and Edoardo Müller in Milan. In 1982 he won the BBC/Rupert Foundation International Conductors' Competition; then was the Exxon–Arts Endowment assistant conductor of the National Sym. Orch. in Washington, D.C. (1982–85), where he subsequently was associate conductor (1985–86); also appeared as a guest conductor in North America and Europe. In 1988 he assumed the position of principal conductor and artistic adviser of the Bournemouth Sym. Orch.

Litvinne, Félia (real name, **Françoise-Jeanne Schütz**), noted Russian soprano; b. St. Petersburg, Aug. 31, 1860?; d. Paris, Oct. 12, 1936. She studied in Paris with Barth-Banderoli, Viardot, and Maurel; made her debut there in 1882 at the Théâtre-Italien as Maria Boccanegra; then sang throughout Europe. In 1885 she made her 1st appearance in the U.S. with Mapleson's company at N.Y.'s Academy of Music; after singing at the Théâtre Royal de la Monnaie in Brussels (1886–88), at the Paris Opéra (1889), and at Milan's La Scala, Rome, and Venice (1890), she appeared at the imperial theaters in St. Petersburg and Moscow (from 1890). She made her Metropolitan Opera debut in N.Y. as Valentine in *Les Huguenots* on Nov. 26, 1896, but remained on the roster for only that season. In 1899 she first appeared at London's Covent Garden as Isolde, and made several further appearances there until 1910. She made her farewell to the operatic stage in Vichy in 1919, but continued to give concerts until 1924. In 1927 she became prof. of voice at the American Cons. in Fontainebleau. Her pupils included Nina Koshetz and Germain Lubin.

She publ. her memoirs as *Ma vie et mon art* (Paris, 1933). Her most outstanding roles included Gluck's Alceste, Donna Anna, Aida, Kundry, Brünnhilde, and Selika.

Litzau, Johannes Barend, Dutch organist and composer; b. Rotterdam, Sept. 9, 1822; d. there, July 18, 1893. He studied with J.B. Bremer and B. Tours; in 1855 became organist of the Lutheran church in Rotterdam. He founded an organ school and wrote a number of organ works, including 3 sonatas; also a cantata, *Sneeuw-vermaak*.

Litzmann, Berthold, German writer on music; b. Kiel, April 18, 1857; d. Munich, Oct. 13, 1926. He wrote a biography, *Clara Schumann, Ein Künstlerleben, nach Tagebüchern und Briefen* (3 vols., Leipzig, 1902–10; Eng. tr., 1913); also ed. the correspondence between Brahms and Clara Schumann (2 vols., Leipzig, 1927; Eng. tr., N.Y., 1927).

Liuzzi, Fernando, Italian composer and musicologist; b. Senigallia, Dec. 19, 1884; d. Florence, Oct. 6, 1940. He studied in Bologna with Fano, and at the Liceo di Santa Cecilia in Rome; then went to Munich, where he studied with Mottl and Reger. He taught at the Parma Cons. (1910–17), the Conservatorio "Luigi Cherubini" in Florence (1917–23), the Univ. of Florence (1923–27), and the Royal Univ. in Rome (1927–38). In 1939 he went to Belgium; returned to Italy in 1940.

WORKS: Puppet opera, *L'Augellin bel verde* (Rome, 1917); *Le Vergini savie e le vergini folli*, liturgical drama transcribed and rearranged for Soli, Chorus, and Orch. from a French MS of the 12th century (Florence, 1930); *La Passione* for Soli, Chorus, and Orch., based on religious melodies of the 13th century (1930); *Hyla*, symphonic poem; *Gaiola e Marechiaro*, Neapolitan rhapsody for Orch.; Violin Sonata; *Sonata-fantasia* for Violin and Organ; songs; etc.

WRITINGS: *Estetica della musica* (Florence, 1924); *Essenza dell'arte e valore estetico nel pensiero di T. Lipps* (Bologna, 1924); *La Lauda e i primordi della melodia italiana* (2 vols. of facsimiles and transcriptions of medieval Italian music; Rome, 1935); *Musicista italiani in Francia* (Rome, 1946).

BIBL.: E. Ferand, "In Memoriam: F. L.," *Musical Quarterly* (Oct. 1942).

Liverati, Giovanni, Italian tenor, conductor, teacher, and composer; b. Bologna, March 27, 1772; d. Florence, Feb. 18, 1846. He studied voice with Giuseppe and Ferdinando Tibaldi in Bologna; then voice with Lorenzo Gibelli and composition with Stanislao Mattei there (1786–90). He was made 1st tenor of the Italian theaters in Barcelona and Madrid (1792), and then Kapellmeister of the Italian Opera in Potsdam (1796) and the Prague National Theater (1799). After teaching voice in Vienna (1805–11), he was music director and composer of the King's Theatre in London (1815–17); later taught at the Royal Academy of Music there. He returned to Italy about 1835, becoming a prof. at Florence's Accademia di Belle Arti.

WORKS: OPERAS: *Il divertimento in campagna* (Bologna, 1790); *Enea in Cartagine* (Potsdam?, 1796); *La prova generale al teatro* (Vienna?, 1799); *Il convito degli dei* (Vienna, c.1800); *La presa d'Egea* (Vienna, 1809); *Il tempio d'eternità* (Vienna, 1810); *David, oder Goliaths Tod* (Vienna, 1813); *I Selvaggi* (London, 1815); *Gli amanti fanatica* (London, 1816); *Gastone e Bajardo* (London, 1820); *The Nymph of the Grotto* (London, 1829); *Amore e Psiche* (London, 1831); also sacred and secular vocal music.

Liviabella, Lino, Italian composer; b. Macerata, April 7, 1902; d. Bologna, Oct. 21, 1964. He studied with Respighi at the Accademia di Santa Cecilia in Rome; was director of the Pesaro Cons. from 1953 to 1959; then taught at Parma.

WORKS: *L'usignola e la Rosa* for Chamber Orch. (1926); *I canti dell' amore*, triptych for String Orch. (1929); *Suite per una fiaba* for Orch. (1933); *Il Vincitore*, written for the Berlin Olympiad (1936); *Il Poeta e sua moglia* for Orch. (1938); *La mia terra* for Orch. (1942); oratorios: *Sorella Chiara* (1947); *Caterina da Siena* (1949); *O Crux Ave* (1953); *Conchiglia*, dramatic musical play (1955); 3 violin sonatas; String Quartet; songs.

Ljungberg, Göta (Albertina), Swedish soprano; b. Sundsval, Oct. 4, 1893; d. Lidingö, near Stockholm, June 28, 1955. She studied at the Royal Academy of Music and the Royal Opera School in Stockholm; also studied privately in London, Milan, and Berlin; in 1918, made her debut (as Elsa) at the Royal Stockholm Opera, remaining there until 1926; was a member of the Berlin State Opera (1926–32); also appeared at London's Covent Garden (1924–29), creating the title role there of Goossens's *Judith* (1929). She made her Metropolitan Opera debut in N.Y. as Sieglinde in *Die Walküre* on Jan. 20, 1932; she remained on the roster until 1935; created the role of Lady Marigold Sandys in Hanson's *Merry Mount.* After World War II, she lived in N.Y. as a voice teacher; then returned to Sweden.

Llobet, Miguel, Catalan guitar virtuoso; b. Barcelona, Oct. 18, 1875; d. there, Feb. 22, 1938. He began his career as a painter; then turned to music and studied with Alegre and Tarrega; lived in Paris (1900–1914); toured in Argentina (1910), Chile (1912), the U.S. (1915–17), and throughout Europe. Manuel de Falla composed his *Homenaje* (for the *Tombeau de Debussy*) for him, and Llobet himself made many arrangements for the guitar.

Llongueras y Badía, Juan, Catalan composer; b. Barcelona, June 6, 1880; d. there, Oct. 13, 1953. He studied in Barcelona with Morera, Millet, and Granados, and with Jaques-Dalcroze in Dresden and Geneva; founded the Inst. Catala de Rítmica i Plástica in Barcelona for the exposition in Spain of the Dalcroze methods; was also a music critic, writer, and prof. of music education in Barcelona. His compositions include piano pieces (*La vida sencilla, L'estiu efimer,* etc.), a quantity of *Canciones y juegos infantiles,* and other songs; he also wrote *Les cançuons de Nadal* (Catalan Christmas songs); publ. a book of reminiscences, *Evocaciones y recuerdos de mi primera vida musical en Barcelona* (Barcelona, 1944).

Lloyd, A(lbert) L(ancaster), noted English ethnomusicologist and folksinger; b. London, Feb. 29, 1908; d. Greenwich, Sept. 29, 1982. His early commitment to the Socialist cause contributed to his interest in folk-song research; he collected folk songs in Australia, and in later years in Eastern Europe; he lectured widely in England and the U.S., and also produced radio programs and documentary films. He publ. the valuable books *Come All Ye Bold Miners: Songs and Ballads of the Coalfields* (1952), *The Penguin Book of English Folk Song* (with Vaughan Williams; 1959), and the standard text *Folk Song in England* (1967).

Lloyd, Charles Harford, English organist, conductor, and composer; b. Thornbury, Gloucestershire, Oct. 16, 1849; d. Slough, Oct. 16, 1919. He attended Magdalen Hall, Oxford (Mus.Bac., 1871; B.A., 1872; M.A., 1875; Mus.Doc., 1892); from 1887 to 1892, was a teacher of organ and composition at the Royal College of Music in London; from 1892, at Eton College; from 1914 until his death, organist at the Chapel Royal, St. James's.

WORKS: Cantatas: *Hero and Leander* (Worcester, 1884); *The Song of Balder* (Hereford, 1885); *Andromeda* (Gloucester, 1886); *A Song of Judgment* (Hereford, 1891); *Sir Ogie and Lady Elsie* (Hereford, 1894); 7 services; Organ Concerto (1895) and other organ works; piano pieces.

Lloyd, David, American tenor; b. Minneapolis, Feb. 29, 1920. He studied at the Minneapolis College of Music (B.A., 1941), and later at the Curtis Inst. of Music in Philadelphia and the Berkshire Music Center in Tanglewood. After singing with the N.Y. City Opera (debut as David in *Die Meistersinger von Nürnberg,* Oct. 13, 1950) and the New England Opera Co., he made appearances at the Festival of Athens and the Glyndebourne Festival. He later served as director of the opera program at Hunter College in N.Y. while continuing his career as a concert singer. From 1971 he taught at the Univ. of Illinois in Urbana.

Lloyd, George (Walter Selwyn), English composer and conductor; b. St. Ives, Cornwall, June 28, 1913. He learned to play violin at home before taking composition lessons with Harry Farjeon. He was in the Royal Marines during World War II; served in the Arctic on convoys to Russia, and nearly lost his life when his ship was torpedoed. After his recuperation, he resumed composing; in later years he was active as a conductor; in 1989 he became principal guest conductor and music adviser of the Albany (N.Y.) Sym. Orch. He composed avidly for the stage and concert hall. Among his operas are *Iernin* (Penzance, Nov. 6, 1934), *The Serf* (London, Oct. 20, 1938), and *John Socman* (Bristol, May 15, 1951). He also wrote 12 syms. (1932–89), which were praised by knowledgeable English critics as a perfect model for modern neoclassicism. Other works include 4 piano concertos (1962–70), 2 violin concertos (1970, 1977), and chamber music. His productivity appears to be matched by the ascertainable goodness of his music. It must be said, however, that appreciation of him is largely an English phenomenon; little of his music is heard in the world at large, except through radio broadcasts and recordings.

Lloyd, Jonathan, English composer; b. London, Sept. 30, 1948. He took composition lessons in London with Emile Spira (1963–65), and with Edwin Roxburgh (1965–69) and John Lambert (1966–69) at the Royal College of Music; also worked with Tristram Cary at the electronic music studio there and then completed his training with György Ligeti at the Berkshire Music Center in Tanglewood (1973). He was composer-in-residence at the Dartington College Theatre Dept. (1978–79). He has produced a number of compositions of considerable and lasting value, distinguished by a variety of forms and styles.

WORKS: DRAMATIC: *Scattered Ruins,* music theater piece for Ensemble with Solo Soprano (Tanglewood, Aug. 1973; won the Koussevitzky Composition Prize); *Musices genus,* masque for Ensemble and Piano (1974); *The Adjudicator,* "community opera" (1985; Blewbury, April 15, 1986). **ORCH.:** *Cantique* for Small Orch. (1968; rev. 1970); *Time Caught by the Tail* for Strings and Percussion (1969); Concerto for Viola and Small Orch. (1979–80; London, Nov. 10, 1981); *Fantasy* for Violin and Orch. (1980); *Rhapsody* for Cello and Orch. (1982); 4 syms.: No. 1 (1983; Birmingham, Jan. 19, 1989); No. 2 (1983–84; Baden-Baden, Feb. 12, 1988); No. 3 for Chamber Orch. (Wilde Festival, June 27, 1987); No. 4 (London, July 26, 1988). **ENSEMBLE:** *Won't It Ever Be Morning* (1980); *Waiting for Gozo* (1981; London, Jan. 15, 1982); *3 Dances* (Reykjavík, June 18, 1982); *Don't Mention the War* (1982; Montepulciano, Aug. 2, 1983); *The Shorelines of Certainty* (Aldeburgh Festival, June 17, 1984; incorporated in *Songs from the Other Shore,* 1984–86; London, May 11, 1986); *Time between Trains* (Wilde Festival, June 30, 1984); *The New Ear* (Colchester, Sept. 28, 1985); *Almeida Dances* (London, June 25, 1986). **VOCAL:** *Coming into Gone* for Chanters and Orch. (1974); *The Other Shore* for Chorus and Orch. (1975); *Everything Returns* for Wordless Soprano and Orch. (1977–78; BBC, Oct. 4, 1979); *3 Songs* for Voice, Viola, and Piano (1980); *Toward the Whitening Dawn* for Chorus and Chamber Orch. (1980; London, March 4, 1981); *If I Could Turn You On* for High Soprano and Chamber Orch. (1981); *No Man's Land* for Chorus and Orch. (1982); *Mass for 6 Solo Voices* (1983; London, April 10, 1984). **CHAMBER:** 2 string quintets: No. 1 for 2 Violins, 2 Violas, and Cello (1982); No. 2 for Mandolin, Lute, Guitar, Harp, and Double Bass (1982); Brass Quintet for 2 Trumpets, 2 Trombones, and Tuba (1982); Wind Quintet for Flute, Oboe, Clarinet, Bassoon, and Horn (1982; London, Jan. 5, 1984); String Quartet No. 1, "Of Time and Motion" (1984; London, June 25, 1986); Sonata for Oboe and Piano (1985); *1 Step More* for Flute, Oboe, Cello, and Harpsichord (1986); *Airs and Graces* for Violin (1987).

Lloyd, Norman, American composer and music theorist; b. Pottsville, Pa., Nov. 8, 1909; d. Greenwich, Conn., July 31, 1980. He studied at N.Y. Univ.; received a D.Mus. from the Philadelphia Cons. in 1963, and was engaged as a teacher there and at other music schools. He served as director of education at the Juilliard School of Music in N.Y. (1946–49) and remained on its faculty until 1963; served as dean of the Oberlin College Cons. of Music (1963–65). He became greatly interested in rural and urban folk music, including ragtime; also worked with choreographers on musical arrangements for modern dances. In 1947 he publ. *The Fireside Book of Favorite American Songs;* also ed. *The Fireside Book of Love Songs* (1954) and *The Golden Encyclopedia of Music* (1968). With his wife, the pianist Ruth Dorothy Lloyd, he compiled *The Complete Sight Singer.*

Lloyd, Robert (Andrew), esteemed English bass-baritone; b. Southend-on-Sea, March 2, 1940. He studied history at Keble College, Oxford, then studied voice at the London Opera Centre (1968–69), making his debut at London's Collegiate Theatre (1969). He was a member of Sadler's Wells (1969–72) and the Royal Opera at Covent Garden (1972–81) in London; also made guest appearances in Berlin, Paris, Hamburg, Milan, Munich, San Francisco, and Salzburg. Among his best roles are Sarastro, the Commendatore, Oroveso, Banquo, Boris Godunov, King Philip, and Gurnemanz (he appeared as the latter in the Syberberg film version of *Parsifal* in 1981).

Lloyd-Jones, David (Mathias), English conductor; b. London, Nov. 19, 1934. He studied at Magdalen College, Oxford; then appeared as a guest conductor with the leading British opera houses, including Covent Garden, the English National Opera, the Scottish Opera, and the Welsh National Opera; in 1978 was named music director of the newly organized English National Opera North in Leeds, which was renamed Opera North in 1981; he retained this post until 1990; in 1989 he became artistic adviser of the Guildhall School of Music and Drama in London. He conducted the English premieres of works from the traditional and modern operatic repertoire; also ed. the full score of Mussorgsky's *Boris Godunov* (1975) and Borodin's *Prince Igor* (1982).

Lloyd Webber, Andrew, tremendously successful English composer, brother of **Julian Lloyd Webber;** b. London, March 22, 1948. His father, William Southcombe Lloyd Webber, was the director of the London College of Music and his mother was a piano teacher; inspired and conditioned by such an environment, Lloyd Webber learned to play piano, violin, and horn, and soon began to improvise music, mostly in the style of American musicals. He attended Westminster School in London, then went to Magdalen College, Oxford, the Guildhall School of Music, and the Royal College of Music in London. In college he wrote his 1st musical, *The Likes of Us,* dealing with a philanthropist. In 1967, at the age of 19, he composed the theatrical show *Joseph and the Amazing Technicolor Dreamcoat,* which was performed at St. Paul's Junior School in London in 1968; it was later expanded to a full-scale production, and achieved considerable success for its amalgam of a biblical subject with rock music, French chansonnettes, and country-western songs. In 1970 it was produced in America and in 1972 was shown on television. He achieved his 1st commercial success with *Jesus Christ Superstar,* an audacious treatment of the religious theme in terms of jazz and rock. It was produced in London on Aug. 9, 1972, and ran for 3,357 performances; it was as successful in America. Interestingly enough, the "rock opera," as it was called, was first released as a record album, which eventually sold 3 million copies. *Jesus Christ Superstar* opened on Broadway on Oct. 12, 1971, even before the London production. There were protests by religious groups against the irreverent treatment of a sacred subject; particularly offensive was the suggestion in the play of a carnal relationship between Jesus and Mary Magdalen; Jewish organizations, on the other hand, protested against the implied portrayal of the Jews as guilty of the death of Christ. The musical closed on Broadway on June 30, 1973, after 720 performances; it received 7 Tony awards. In 1981 the recording of *Jesus Christ Superstar* was given the Grammy award for best cast show album of the year. The great hullabaloo about the musical made a certainty of his further successes. His early musical *Joseph and the Amazing Technicolor Dreamcoat* was revived at the off-Broadway Entermedia Theatre in N.Y.'s East Village on Nov. 18, 1981, and from there moved to the Royale Theater on Broadway. In the meantime, he produced a musical with a totally different chief character, *Evita,* a semi-fictional account of the career of the 1st wife of Argentine dictator Juan Perón; it was staged in London on June 21, 1978; a N.Y. performance soon followed, with splendid success. But perhaps his most spectacular production was *Cats,* inspired by T.S. Eliot's *Old Possum's Book of Practical Cats;* it was produced in London on May 11, 1981, and was brought out in N.Y. in Oct. 1982 with fantastic success; *Evita* and *Joseph and the Amazing Technicolor Dreamcoat* were still playing on Broadway, so that Lloyd Webber had the satisfaction of having 3 of his shows running at the same time. Subsequent successful productions were his *Song and Dance* (1983) and *Starlight Express* (London, March 27, 1984). His series of commercial successes reached a lucrative apex with the production of *The Phantom of the Opera* (London, Oct. 19, 1986; N.Y., Jan. 26, 1988), a gothically oriented melodramatic tale of contrived suspense. On April 17, 1989, his musical *Aspects of Love* opened in London. Apart from popular shows, Lloyd Webber wrote a mini-opera, *Tell Me on a Sunday,* about an English girl living in N.Y., which was produced by BBC Television in 1980. Quite different in style and intent were his *Variations* for Cello and Jazz Ensemble (1978), written for his brother; and his *Requiem Mass* (N.Y., Feb. 4, 1985). **BIBL.:** G. McKnight, *A. L.W.* (London and N.Y., 1984); M. Walsh, *A. L.W.: His Life and Works* (N.Y., 1989).

Lloyd Webber, Julian, talented English cellist, brother of **Andrew Lloyd Webber;** b. London, April 14, 1951. He studied with Douglas Cameron (1964–67) and then at the Royal College of Music in London (1967–71); he also studied with Pierre Fournier in Geneva. He made his concert debut at London's Queen Elizabeth Hall in 1972; subsequently played many engagements as a soloist with English orchs. He made his American debut in N.Y. in 1980. In 1978 he became prof. of cello at the Guildhall School of Music in London. He publ. an account of his career, *Travels with My Cello* (1984), and also ed. *Song of the Birds: Sayings, Stories and Impressions of Pablo Casals* (London, 1985).

Lobaczewska (Gérard de Festenburg), Stefania, Polish musicologist; b. Lemberg, July 31, 1888; d. Krakow, Jan. 16, 1963. She studied piano with V. Kurc at the Lemberg Cons., then musicology with Adler at the Univ. of Vienna and with Chybiński at the Univ. of Lemberg (1914–18; Ph.D., 1929, with the diss. *O harmonice Klaudiusza Achillesa Debussy'ego w pierwszym okresie jego twórczosci* [Claude Achille Debussy's Harmony in His 1st Creative Period]; publ. in *Kwartalnik Muzyczny,* II/5, 1929–30); completed her Habilitation at the Univ. of Poznan in 1949, with *Karol Szymanowski: Zycie i twórczość (1882–1937)* (Karol Szymanowski: Life and Works [1882–1937]; publ. in Krakow, 1950). She taught at the Szymanowski School of Music in Lwow (1931–39) and at the Lwow Cons. (1940–41), then went to Krakow (1945), where she became a prof. at the State College of Music; later served as its rector until 1955; was also head of the musicology dept. at the Univ. of Krakow (1952–63). **WRITINGS:** *Zarys estetyki muzycznej* (Outline of Music Esthetics; Lwow, 1937); *Tablice do historii muzyki* (Krakow, 1949); *Zarys historii form muzycznych: Próba ujecia socjologicznego* (Outline of the History of Musical Form: Attempt at a Sociological Approach; Krakow, 1950); *Ludwik van Beethoven* (Krakow, 1953; 2nd ed., 1955); *Wklad Chopina do romantyzmu europejskiego* (Chopin's Contribution to European Romanticism; Warsaw, 1955); *Style muzyczne* (Krakow, 1960–62).

Lobe, Johann Christian, German flutist, writer on music, and composer; b. Weimar, May 30, 1797; d. Leipzig, July 27, 1881. He studied with A.E. Müller; was a flutist (from 1808), later a viola player, in the Weimar Court Orch. until 1842; founded a music school; from 1846 to 1848, was in Leipzig as ed. of the *Allgemeine musikalische Zeitung,* and from 1855 to 1857 of the *Fliegende Blätter für Musik;* was music ed. of *Illustrierte Zeitung.* He championed the cause of Weimar classicism and the German Romantic movement. **WORKS:** Operas (all 1st perf. in Weimar): *Wittekind*

(1819); *Die Flibustier* (1829); *Die Fürstin von Granada* (Sept. 28, 1833); *Der rote Domino* (1835); *König und Pächter* (1844); also 2 syms.; overtures; concertos; piano quartets; variations and solos for flute.

WRITINGS: *Compositionslehre* (1844); *Lehrbuch der musikalischen Komposition* (vol. I, *Harmony*, 1850; rev. by Kretzschmar, 5th ed., 1884; vol. II, *Instrumentation*, 3rd ed., 1879; vol. III, *Canon, Fugue, etc.*, 1860; vol. IV, *Opera*, 1867; rev. by Kretzschmar, 1884–87); *Katechismus der Musik* (1851; ed. by W. Neumann, 1949; 7th ed., 1968; Eng. tr., N.Y., 1886); *Musikalische Briefe eines Wohlbekannten* (1852; 2nd ed., 1860); *Aus dem Leben eines Musikers* (1859); *Vereinfachte Harmonielehre* (1861); *Consonanzen und Dissonanzen* (1869); *Katechismus der Compositionslehre* (1872; 7th ed., 1902; Eng. tr., 1891); *Handbuch der Musik* (n.d.; ed. by R. Hofmann, 1926).

BIBL.: W. Bode, ed., *Goethes Schauspieler und Musiker, Erinnerungen von Eberwein und L.* (Berlin, 1912).

Lobkowitz, Bohemian family of the nobility and patrons of music:

(1) Philipp Hyacinth (Filipp Hyacint) Lobkowitz, lutenist and composer; b. Neustadt an der Waldnab, Feb. 25, 1680; d. Vienna, Dec. 21, 1734. In 1729 he settled in Vienna, where he sponsored private concerts at the Lobkowitz-Althan palace; Gluck commenced his career as a composer at these concerts (c.1735–36). Lobkowitz's only extant work is a Suite in B-flat major.

(2) Ferdinand Philipp Joseph (Ferdinand Filipp Josef) Lobkowitz, composer, son of the preceding; b. Prague, April 27, 1724; d. Vienna, Jan. 11, 1784. He became the ruling prince of the family in Vienna in 1743. He was a patron of Gluck; the latter accompanied him to London in 1745. He was later made a member of the Berlin Academy of Sciences; studied violin there with F. Benda. All of his music is lost.

(3) Joseph Franz Maximilian (Josef František Maximilián) Lobkowitz, singer, violinist, and cellist, son of the preceding; b. Roudnice nad Labem, Dec. 7, 1772; d. Třeboň, Dec. 15, 1816. He was active in the administration of the Vienna court theaters (1807–14); was also founder of the Gesellschaft der Musikfreunde there. He was a patron of Haydn and Beethoven. Haydn dedicated his String Quartet, op. 77, to him. Beethoven dedicated his 3rd, 5th, and 6th syms., the Triple Concerto, the string quartets, opp. 18 and 74, and the song cycle *An die ferne Geliebte* to him.

(4) Ferdinand Joseph Johann (Ferdinand Josef Jan) Lobkowitz, music patron, son of the preceding; b. Oberhollabrunn, Lower Austria, April 13, 1797; d. Vienna, Dec. 18, 1868. He had a private orch. in Vienna; also founded a private music school in Eisenberg (1831). He was the patron of Gyrowetz. Beethoven wrote the *Lobkowitz Cantata* for his birthday in 1823.

BIBL.: A. Thayer, "The L. Family," *Musical World* (1879); S. Ley, "Beethoven and Fürst L.," *Atlantis*, IX (1937); T. Volek and J. Macek, "Beethoven's Rehearsals at the L.'s," *Musical Times* (Feb. 1986).

Lobo, Alonso, Spanish composer; b. Osuna, c.1555; d. Seville, April 5, 1617. He was a choirboy at Seville Cathedral; obtained the degree of licenciado at Osuna Univ. He was canon of the collegiate church in Osuna by 1591; was assistant to the maestro de capilla at Seville Cathedral (1591–93); then was maestro de capilla at Toledo Cathedral (1593–1604) and subsequently at Seville Cathedral. He publ. *Liber primus missarum* for 4 to 8 Voices (Madrid, 1602), containing 6 masses and 7 motets; his other works include *Credo romano* (his most famous piece), 3 Passions, Lamentations, Psalms, and hymns.

Lobo, Duarte (Latinized as **Eduardus Lupus**), noted Portuguese composer; b. Alcáçovas, c.1565; d. Lisbon, Sept. 24, 1646. He was a pupil of Manuel Mendes at Évora; served as choirmaster there before moving to Lisbon; in 1594, became master of the chapel at the Cathedral. As a composer of church music, he enjoyed considerable renown; his mastery of polyphony inspired respect.

WORKS: *Natalitiae noctis responsoria* for 4 to 8 Voices, *missa*

eiusdem noctis for 8 Voices, *Beatae Mariae Virginis antiphonae* for 8 Voices . . . *virginis Salve* for 3 Choirs and 11 Voices (Antwerp, 1602); *Cantica Beatae Mariae Virginis, vulgo Magnificat* for 4 Voices (Antwerp, 1605); 2 books of masses (Antwerp, 1621, 1639). See M. Joaquim, ed., *Duarte Lobo: Composições polifónicas* (Lisbon, 1945–).

BIBL.: A. Borges, *D. L.* (156?–1646): *Studien zum Leben und Schaffen des portugesischen Komponisten* (Regensburg, 1986).

Locatelli, Pietro Antonio, important Italian violinist and composer; b. Bergamo, Sept. 3, 1695; d. Amsterdam, March 30, 1764. As a youth, he played violin at S. Maria Maggiore in Bergamo; then went to Rome, where he performed in the basilica of S. Lorenzo in Damaso (1717–23). After serving as virtuoso da camera at the Mantuan court, he traveled in Italy; then played at the Bavarian court in Munich and at the Prussian court in Berlin (1727) and in Kassel (1728). He settled in Amsterdam, where he devoted himself principally to leading an amateur ensemble and teaching; also made occasional tours abroad. As a virtuoso, he amazed his auditors with his technical feats, particularly in double stops; by changing the tuning of his violin, he produced marvelous effects; Paganini is said to have profited by his innovations. Among his works were *XII concerti grossi a 4 e a 5 con 12 fughe* for 2 Violins, 1 or 2 Violas, and Basso, op. 1 (1721; corrected ed., 1729); *XII sonate* for Flute and Basso, op. 2 (1732); *L'arte del violino: XII concerti . . . con XXIV capricci ad libitum* for Violin, 2 Violins, Viola, Cello, and Bass, op. 3 (1733); *Parte I°: VI introduttioni teatrali; Parte II°: VI concerti* for 2 Violins, Viola, and Cello, and for 2 Violins, Viola, and Bass, op. 4 (1735); *VI sonate a 3* for 2 Violins, or Flute and Basso Continuo, op. 5 (1736); *XII sonate de camera* for Violin and Basso Continuo, op. 6 (1737); *VI concerti* for 4 Violins, 2 Violas, and Bass, op. 7 (1741); and *X sonate*, op. 8 (1744; 2nd ed., 1752; 6 for Violin and Basso Continuo and 4 for 2 Violins and Basso Continuo). See A. Koole, ed., *Pietro Antonio Locatelli: Gesamtausgabe*, Monumenta Musicae Neerlandicae, IV (1961).

BIBL.: A. Koole, *Leven en werken van P.A. L. da Bergamo* (Amsterdam, 1949); idem, "P.A. L.," *Chigiana*, XXI (1964); idem, "P.A. L.," *Conferenza tenuta al Lions Club: Bergamo 1969*; A. Meli, *Gli esodi in patria di P.A. L.* (Bergamo, 1971).

Locke (also **Lock**), **Matthew,** English composer; b. Exeter, c.1621; d. London, Aug. 1677. He was a chorister at Exeter Cathedral, where he studied with Edward Gibbons, William Wake, and John Lugge; was in the Netherlands (c.1646–51); at the Restoration, he was made private composer-in-ordinary to the King, composer for the wind music, and composer for the band of violins (1660); was also made organist to the Queen (c.1662).

WORKS: Operas: *The Siege of Rhodes* (London, 1656; in collaboration with other composers; music not extant); *The Tempest*, after Shakespeare as adapted by Davenant and Dryden (London, 1674; in collaboration with other composers); *Psyche* (London, March 9, 1675); various other works for the theater, including music to Shirley's masque *Cupid and Death* (March 26, 1653; in collaboration with C. Gibbons; not extant; rev. 1659) and to Shakespeare's *Macbeth* (c.1663–74). His instrumental music includes many dances and suites for strings, wind music (most notable being the music for "His Majesty's Sagbutts and Cornetts"), and keyboard pieces. He also wrote over 35 English anthems, some 15 Latin motets, several services, 6 sacred canons, 4 sacred songs, and over 25 secular songs. See T. Dart, ed., *Matthew Locke: Keyboard Suites* (London, 1959; 2nd ed., rev., 1964); M. Tilmouth, ed., *Matthew Locke: Chamber Music: I, II*, Musica Britannica, XXXI–XXXII (1971–72); P. le Huray, *Matthew Locke: Anthems and Motets*, ibid., XXXVIII (1976).

WRITINGS: *Observations upon a Late Book, Entitled, An Essay to the Advancement of Musick, etc., written by Thomas Salmon, M.A. of Trinity College in Oxford: by Matthew Locke* (London, 1672); *The Present Practice of Musick Vindicated against the Exceptions; and New Way of Attaining Musick* *lately published by Thomas Salmon M.A. etc. by Matthew Locke . . . to which is added Duellum Musicum by John Phillips . . . together with a Letter from John Playford to Mr. T. Salmon by way of Confutation of his Essay* (London, 1673); *Melothesia, or, Certain General Rules for Playing upon a Continued-Bass, with a Choice Collection of Lessons for the Harpsichord and Organ of all Sorts: Never before published* (London, 1673).

BIBL.: W. Cummings, "M. L., Composer for the Church and Theatre," *International Musical Society Congress Report: London, 1911*; E. Fairley, *Studies in the Music of M. L.* (diss., Univ. of Rochester, N.Y., 1941); idem, "The String Fantasias of M. L.," *Bulletin of the American Musicological Society*, VII (Oct. 1943); W. Sleeper, *The Harmonic Style of the Four-part Viol Music of Jenkins, L. and Purcell* (diss., Univ. of Rochester, N.Y., 1964); A. Kooiker, *L's "Melothesia": Its Place in the History of Keyboard Music in Restoration England* (diss., Univ. of Rochester, N.Y., 1965); R. Harding, *A Thematic Catalogue of the Works of M. L. with a Calendar of the Main Events of His Life* (Oxford, 1971); M. Tilmouth, "Revisions in the Chamber Music of M. L.," *Proceedings of the Royal Musical Association*, XCVIII (1971–72).

Lockhart, James (Lawrence), Scottish conductor; b. Edinburgh, Oct. 16, 1930. He studied at Edinburgh Univ. and at the Royal College of Music in London. He served as apprentice conductor of the Yorkshire Sym. Orch. (1954–55), assistant conductor at Münster (1955–56), Munich (1956–57), Glyndebourne (1957–59), and Covent Garden in London (1959–68). Intercalatorily, he was music director of the Opera Workshop of the Univ. of Texas in Austin (1957–59), and conductor of the BBC Scottish Sym. Orch. in Glasgow (1960–61). From 1968 to 1973 he was music director of the Welsh National Opera; from 1972 to 1980 he served as Generalmusikdirektor of the State Theater in Kassel. In addition, he appeared as a guest conductor with several orchs. in England; in 1981 he became Generalmusikdirektor of the Rheinische Phil. in Koblenz and at the Koblenz Opera. He was made head of the opera school at the Royal College of Music (1986).

Lockspeiser, Edward, English writer on music; b. London, May 21, 1905; d. Alfriston, Sussex, Feb. 3, 1973. He studied in Paris with Alexandre Tansman and Nadia Boulanger; then attended the classes of C. Kitson and Malcolm Sargent at the Royal College of Music in London. He dedicated himself to musical journalism, particularly to the cause of French music; publ. valuable monographs on Debussy (London, 1936; 5th ed., rev., 1980), Berlioz (London, 1939), and Bizet (London, 1951), and an exhaustive biography, *Debussy: His Life and Mind* (2 vols., London, 1962, 1965; 2nd ed., rev., 1978). He also publ. *Music and Painting: A Study in Comparative Ideas from Turner to Schoenberg* (London, 1973); also ed. *Lettres inédites de Claude Debussy à André Caplet, 1908–1914* (Monaco, 1957).

Lockwood, Annea (actually, **Anna Ferguson**), New Zealand composer and instrument builder; b. Christchurch, July 29, 1939. She studied at Canterbury Univ. in New Zealand (B.Mus., 1961); then went to London, where she took courses with Peter Racine Fricker and Gottfried M. Koenig at the Royal College of Music (diplomas in piano and composition, 1963); also attended courses in new music in Darmstadt (1961–62), had lessons with Koenig at the Hochschule für Musik in Cologne (1963–64), and studied at the Bilthoven (Netherlands) Electronic Music Center (1963–64); also worked in computer composition at the Electronic Music Studio in Putney, England (1970), and undertook research at the Univ. of Southampton's Inst. for Sound and Vibration Research (1969–72). In 1968 she gave non-lectures at the Anti-Univ. of London; later taught at Hunter College of the City Univ. of N.Y. (1973–78) and Vassar College (1973–83). In 1968, with her then husband, Harvey Matusow, she undertook a series of experiments in total art, including aural, oral, visual, tactile, gustatory, and olfactory demonstrations and sporadic transcendental manifestations; of these, the most remarkable was the summoning (in German) of Beethoven's ghost at a séance held

in London on Oct. 3, 1968, with sound recorded on magnetic tape, which in playback revealed some surprisingly dissonant music of apparently metapsychic origin, tending to indicate that Beethoven was a posthumous avant-garde composer. The séance was preceded by the burning of a combustible piano and of an inflammable microphone. Not content with setting the piano afire, she also demonstrated the drowning of an upright piano in a lake in Amarillo, Texas (Dec. 27, 1972). Since the mid-1970s, her concerns have been with aural perception and the utilization of sounds found in nature and the environment in participatory, on-site installations.

WORKS (descriptive materials provided by the composer): Violin Concerto (1962); *À Abélard, Héloïse,* chamber cantata for Mezzo-soprano and 10 Instruments (1963); *Glass Concert* for 2 Performers and Amplified Glass Instruments (1966); *River Archives,* recordings of select world rivers and streams (1966–); *Tiger Balm,* tape collage of sensual and erotic sounds including sonic images of a woman and a tiger making love (1972); *Malaman,* solo chant using very old words for sound from many languages, based upon the belief that these words contain and can release specific, useful acoustic energy (1974); *World Rhythms,* 10-channel live mix of the sounds of such natural phenomena as earthquakes, radio waves from a pulsar star, fire, human breathing, tree frogs, geysers, etc., together with a biorhythm produced by a gong player (1975); *Spirit Songs Unfolding* for Tape and Slides (1977); *Delta Run,* mixed-media work for Tape, Slide Projection, and Movement centered around a dying sculptor's reflections on death (1982); *A Sound Map of the Hudson River,* illustration work tracing the course of the Hudson, by means of recordings of water and ambient sounds made over the course of a year along its banks, from source to ocean (1982–83); *Night and Fog,* settings of texts by Osip Mandelstam and Carolyn Forche for Baritone, Baritone Saxophone, Percussion, and Tape (1987); *The Secret Life* for Amplified Double Bass, using a form of improvisatory ventriloquism with the player initially talking about his or her relationship with the bass, then the point of view shifting to the bass itself, which talks back to the player, all spoken material being transduced through the bass itself (1989); *Amazonia Dreaming* for Snare Drum (1989); *Nautilus* for Didjeridu, Conch Shells, and Percussion (1989).

Lockwood, Lewis (Henry), distinguished American musicologist; b. N.Y., Dec. 16, 1930. He studied musicology with Lowinsky at Queens College in N.Y. (B.A., 1952) and with Strunk and Mendel at Princeton Univ. (M.F.A., 1955; Ph.D., 1960, with the diss. *The Counter-Reformation and the Sacred Music of Vincenzo Ruffo,* publ. in Venice, 1970). In 1958 he joined the faculty of Princeton Univ. In 1980 he was appointed prof. at Harvard Univ. Since about 1970 Lockwood has contributed substantially to current Beethoven scholarship; his article on the autograph of Beethoven's Violoncello Sonata in A major, op. 69, which appeared in *The Music Forum,* II (1970), won the Alfred Einstein Award of the American Musicological Soc. for 1970. He publ. a valuable book, *Music in Renaissance Ferrara, 1400–1505* (London, 1984). He was a senior consulting ed. of *The New Grove Dictionary of Music and Musicians* (1980) and served as president of the American Musicological Soc. (1987–88).

Lockwood, Normand, American composer; b. N.Y., March 19, 1906. He studied at the Univ. of Michigan; in 1925, went to Europe and took lessons with Respighi in Rome and Boulanger in Paris; he was a Fellow at the American Academy in Rome (1929–31); upon his return to America, he was an instructor in music at the Oberlin (Ohio) Cons. (1932–43); from 1945 to 1953, was a lecturer at Columbia Univ., then at Trinity Univ. in San Antonio (1953–55); later taught at the Univ. of Hawaii and at the Univ. of Oregon (1955–61). In 1961 he was appointed a member of the faculty of the Univ. of Denver; became prof. emeritus in 1974.

WORKS: OPERAS: *The Scarecrow* (N.Y., May 19, 1945); *Early Dawn* (Denver, Aug. 7, 1961); *The Wizards of Balizar* (Denver, Aug. 1, 1962); *The Hanging Judge* (Denver, March 1964); *Re-*

quiem for a Rich Young Man (Denver, Nov. 24, 1964). ORCH.: 2 syms. (1935; 1978–79); *Moby Dick* for Chamber Orch. (1946); Oboe Concerto (1966); *Symphonic Sequences* (1966); *From an Opening to a Close* for Wind Instruments and Percussion (1967); 2 concertos for Organ and Brass (1950, 1970); *Panegyric* for Horn and Strings (1978–79); Concerto for 2 Harps and Strings (1981); *Prayers and Fanfares* for Brass, Strings, and Percussion (1982). CHAMBER: 7 string quartets (1933–50); Piano Quintet (1940); *6 Serenades* for String Quartet (1945); Clarinet Quintet (1960); *Excursions* for 4 String Basses (1976); Piano Trio (1985). VOCAL: *4 Songs from James Joyce's "Chamber Music"* for Medium Voice and String Quartet (N.Y., March 28, 1948); 2 oratorios: *Light out of Darkness* (1956) and *Children of God* (Cincinnati, Feb. 1, 1957); numerous other sacred works.

Loeb, John Jacob, American composer of popular songs; b. Chicago, Feb. 18, 1910; d. Valley Stream, Long Island, N.Y., March 2, 1970. He began writing songs for Broadway shows and jazz bands at the age of 18. Among his best-known songs are *Sweetie Pie, Masquerade,* and *Reflections in the Water.* In collaboration with Carmen Lombardo, he wrote the tune of *Boo Hoo.*

Loeffler, Charles Martin (Tornow), outstanding Alsatian-born American composer; b. Mulhouse, Jan. 30, 1861; d. Medfield, Mass., May 19, 1935. His father was a writer who sometimes used the nom de plume Tornow, which Loeffler later added to his name. When he was a child, the family moved to Russia, where his father was engaged in government work in the Kiev district; later they lived in Debrecen, and in Switzerland. In 1875 Loeffler began taking violin lessons in Berlin with Rappoldi, who prepared him for study with Joachim; he studied theory with Kiel; also took lessons with Bargiel at the Berlin Hochschule für Musik (1874–77). He then went to Paris, where he continued his musical education with Massart (violin) and Guiraud (counterpoint and composition). He was engaged briefly as a violinist in the Pasdeloup Orch.; then was a member of the private orch. of the Russian Baron Paul von Derwies at his sumptuous residences near Lugano and in Nice (1879–81). When Derwies died in 1881, Loeffler went to the U.S., with letters of recommendation from Joachim; he became a naturalized citizen in 1887. He played in the orch. of Leopold Damrosch in N.Y. in 1881–82. In 1882 he became 2nd concertmaster of the newly organized Boston Sym. Orch., but was able to accept other engagements during late spring and summer months; in the spring of 1883, he traveled with the Thomas Orch. on a transcontinental tour; the summers of 1883 and 1884 he spent in Paris, where he took violin lessons with Hubert Léonard. He resigned from the Boston Sym. Orch. in 1903, and devoted himself to composition and farming in Medfield. He was married to Elise Burnett Fay (1910). After his death, she donated to the Library of Congress in Washington, D.C., all of his MSS, correspondence, etc.; by his will, he left the material assets of his not inconsiderable estate to the French Academy and the Paris Cons. He was an officer of the French Academy (1906); a Chevalier in the French Legion of Honor (1919); a member of the American Academy of Arts and Letters; Mus. Doc. (*honoris causa*), Yale Univ. (1926).

Loeffler's position in American music is unique, brought up as he was under many different national influences, Alsatian, French, German, Russian, and Ukrainian. One of his most vivid scores, *Memories of My Childhood,* written as late as 1924, reflects the modal feeling of Russian and Ukrainian folk songs. But his esthetic code was entirely French, with definite leanings toward Impressionism; the archaic constructions that he sometimes affected, and the stylized evocations of "ars antiqua," are also in keeping with the French manner. His most enduring work, *A Pagan Poem,* is cast in such a neo-archaic vein. He was a master of colorful orchestration; his harmonies are opulent without saturation; his rhapsodic forms are peculiarly suited to the evocative moods of his music. His only excursion into the American idiom was the employment of jazz rhythms in a few of his lesser pieces.

WORKS: OPERAS: *The Passion of Hilarion* (1912–13); *Les Amants jaloux* (1918); *The Peony Lantern* (c.1919). INCIDENTAL MUSIC: *Ouverture pour le T.C. Minstrel Entertainment* (Boston, 1906?); *The Countess Cathleen* (Concord, Mass., May 8, 1924; not extant); *The Reveller* (Boston, Dec. 22, 1925). ORCH.: *Les Veillées de l'Ukraine* for Violin and Orch. (1890; Boston, Nov. 20, 1891); *Morceau fantastique: Fantastic Concerto* for Cello and Orch. (1893; Boston, Feb. 2, 1894); *Divertissement* for Violin and Orch. (1894; Boston, Jan. 4, 1895); *La Mort de Tintagiles* for 2 Violas d'Amore and Orch. (1897; Boston, Jan. 7, 1898; rev. for Viola d'Amore and Orch., 1900); *Divertissement espagnol* for Saxophone and Orch. (1900; Boston, Jan. 29, 1901); *Poem* (*La Bonne Chanson; Avant que tu ne t'en ailles;* 1901; Boston, April 11, 1902; rev. 1915; Boston, Nov. 1, 1918); *La Villanelle du diable* (1901; Boston, April 11, 1902; revision of his 3rd song in the set *Rapsodies,* 1898); *A Pagan Poem* (1906; Boston, Oct. 29, 1907; revision of *Poème païen* for 13 Instruments, 1902); *Hora mystica* for Men's Chorus and Orch. (1915; Norfolk, Conn., June 6, 1916); *5 Irish Fantasies* for Voice and Orch. (1920; 3 numbers, Boston, March 10, 1922); *Memories of My Childhood* (*Life in a Russian Village*) (Evanston, Ill., May 30, 1924); *Canticum fratris solis* (*Canticle of the Sun*) for Voice and Chamber Orch. (Washington, D.C., Oct. 28, 1925); *Evocation* for Women's Voices and Orch. (1930; for the opening of Severance Hall, Cleveland, Feb. 5, 1931). CHAMBER: Violin Sonata (1886); String Quartet (1889); String Sextet (1891?); Quintet (*Lyrisches Kammermusikstück; Eine Frühlingsmusik*) for 3 Violins, Viola, and Cello (1894); Octet for 2 Clarinets, Harp, 2 Violins, Viola, Cello, and Double Bass (1896?); *Poème païen* (*Poème antique*) for 2 Flutes, Oboe, Clarinet, English Horn, 3 Trumpets, 2 Horns, Viola, Double Bass, and Piano (1902; rev. for Orch., 1906); *Ballade carnavalesque* for Flute, Oboe, Saxophone, Bassoon, and Piano (1902); *Music for 4 Stringed Instruments* for String Quartet (1917–19); *Historiettes* for String Quartet and Harp (1922); *Paraphrase on 2 Western Cowboy Songs* for Saxophone, Viola d'Amore, and Piano (unfinished); *Mescolanza "Olla Podrida"* for Viola d'Amore and Piano; also many works for violin and piano. CHORAL: *L'Archet* for Soprano, Women's Chorus, Viola d'Amore, and Piano (1900?); *The Sermon on the Mount* for Women's Chorus, 2 Violas d'Amore, Viola da Gamba, Harp, and Organ (unfinished); *Psalm 137* (*By the Rivers of Babylon*) for Women's Chorus, 2 Flutes, Cello, Harp, and Organ (1901?); *For One Who Fell in Battle* for 8-voice Chorus a cappella (1906; rev. as *Ode for One Who Fell in Battle,* 1911); *Beat! Beat! Drums!* for Men's Chorus in Unison and Pianos (1917; also 2 other versions); over 40 songs. E. Knight prepared *Charles Martin Loeffler: Catalog of Works* (MS, 1985).

BIBL.: C. Engel, "C.M. L.," *Musical Quarterly* (July 1925); idem, "C.M. L.," *Chesterian,* VI (1928); E.B. Hill, "C.M. L," *Modern Music* (Nov.–Dec. 1935); W. Damrosch, *C.M. L.* (N.Y., 1936); E. Waters, "New L.iana," *Library of Congress Quarterly Journal* (April–June 1945); H. Colvin, *C.M. L.: His Life and Works* (diss., Univ. of Rochester, 1959); E. Henry, *Impressionism in the Arts and Its Influence on Selected Works of C.M. L. and Charles Tomlinson Griffes* (diss., Univ. of Cincinnati, 1976); E. Knight, "C.M. L. and George Gershwin: A Forgotten Friendship," *American Music,* III (1985).

Loeillet (also spelled **L'Oeillet, Luly, Lulli, Lullie, Lully**), noted family of Flemish musicians:

(1) Jean Baptiste Loeillet, oboist, flutist, harpsichordist, and composer, known as **John Loeillet of London;** b. Ghent (baptized), Nov. 18, 1680; d. London, July 19, 1730. He studied in Ghent and Paris, then went about 1705 to London, where he joined the orch. at Drury Lane (1707); was principal oboe and flute in the orch. at the Queen's Theatre, Haymarket (1709). He popularized the German transverse flute in England. His compositions follow Italian models, showing thorough understanding of the virtuoso possibilities of his instruments.

WORKS: *Lessons* for Harpsichord or Spinet (London, c.1712); ed. in *Monumenta Musicae Belgicae,* I, 1932); (6) *Sonatas* *for Variety of Instruments,* op. 1 (London, 1722); *6 Suits of Lessons* for Harpsichord or Spinet (London, 1723; ed. in Monumenta Musicae Belgicae, I, 1932); *12 Sonatas in 3 Parts,* op. 2 (London, c.1725); *12 Solos,* op. 3 (London, 1729).

BIBL.: P. Bergmans, "Une famille de musiciens belges du XVIIIᵉ siècle: Les L.," *Académie Royale de Belgique: Bulletin de la Classe des Beaux Arts,* IX (1927); B. Priestman, "Catalogue thématique des œuvres de J.-B., John et Jacques L.," *Revue de Musicologie* (Oct.–Dec. 1952); idem, "The Keyboard Works of John L.," *Music Review* (May 1955).

(2) Jacques (Jacob) Loeillet, oboist and composer, brother of the preceding; b. Ghent (baptized), July 7, 1685; d. there, Nov. 28, 1748. He was an oboist in the service of the Elector of Bavaria in the Netherlands and at his court in Munich (1726); later was hautbois de la chambre du roi in Versailles; returned to Ghent in 1726. He publ. 6 Sonates for 2 Flutes or Violin, op. 4 (Paris, 1728), and 6 Sonates for Flute or Violin and Basso Continuo (Paris, 1728).

(3) Jean Baptiste Loeillet, composer, cousin of the 2 preceding, known as **Loeillet de Gant;** b. Ghent (baptized), July 6, 1688; d. Lyons, c.1720. He was in the service of the archbishop of Lyons. He publ. 3 books of 12 sonatas each for Recorder and Basso Continuo, opp. 1, 2, and 4 (Amsterdam, c.1710, 1714, 1716); also 2 books of 6 Sonates each for Flute, Oboe or Violin, and Basso Continuo, op. 5 (1717).

Loeillet, John. See **Loeillet, Jean Baptiste (1).**

Loeschhorn, Albert. See **Löschhorn, (Carl) Albert.**

Loesser, Arthur, esteemed American pianist, teacher, and writer on music, half-brother of **Frank (Henry) Loesser;** b. N.Y., Aug. 26, 1894; d. Cleveland, Jan. 4, 1969. He studied with Stojowski and Goetschius at the Inst. of Musical Art in N.Y.; made his debut in Berlin (1913). He first played in N.Y. in 1916; after touring the Orient and Australia (1920–21), he appeared widely in the U.S. In 1926 he was appointed a prof. of piano at the Cleveland Inst. of Music. In 1943 he was commissioned in the U.S. Army as an officer in the Japanese intelligence dept.; mastered the language and, after the war, gave lectures in Japanese in Tokyo; was the 1st American musician in uniform to play for a Japanese audience (1946). He publ. *Humor in American Song* (N.Y., 1943) and an entertaining vol., *Men, Women and Pianos: A Social History* (N.Y., 1954).

Loesser, Frank (Henry), talented American composer and lyricist, half-brother of **Arthur Loesser;** b. N.Y., June 29, 1910; d. there, July 28, 1969. He was educated at City College in N.Y., where he began writing songs for college activities; he subsequently was active as a reporter, singer, and vaudeville performer. In 1931 he settled in Hollywood and devoted himself mainly to writing musical comedies. During World War II he was in the U.S. Army, and wrote several Army songs, including *Praise the Lord and Pass the Ammunition* (1942) and *Roger Young* (1945). Although he continued to compose successful songs, he found his greatest reward in producing shows for Broadway; these included *Where's Charley?* (Oct. 11, 1948), *Guys and Dolls* (Nov. 24, 1950), *The Most Happy Fella* (May 3, 1956), and *How to Succeed in Business Without Really Trying* (Oct. 14, 1961), which won a Pulitzer Prize and ran for 1,416 performances. His last musical was *Pleasures and Palaces* (Detroit, 1965).

BIBL.: A. Loesser, "My Brother F.," *Notes* (March 1950); M. Mann, *The Musicals of F. L.* (diss., City Univ. of N.Y., 1974); *F. L. Remembered* (N.Y., 1977).

Loevendie, Theo, Dutch composer; b. Amsterdam, Sept. 17, 1930. He studied composition and clarinet at the Amsterdam Cons. (1956–61); taught clarinet at the Toonkunst Music School in Haarlem (1960–65); in 1968, was appointed instructor in improvisation at the Rotterdam Cons. In 1973 he organized STAMP concerts with the purpose of presenting contemporary music of various styles (jazz, folk music, avant-garde, etc.).

WORKS: Opera for young people, *Esperanza* (Holland Festival, Amsterdam, July 1971); *Confluxus* for Jazz and Sym. Orchs. (1966); *3 Pieces* for 3 different Clarinets (1968); *Scaramuccia* for Clarinet and Orch. (Utrecht, April 14, 1971); *Music for Bass Clarinet and Piano* (1971); *Music for Double Bass and Piano* (1971); *Aulos* for Winds and/or Strings (1972; rev. 1975); *2 Trios* for 3 Percussionists (1973); *Timbo* for 6 Percussionists (1974); *Prelude* for 6 Percussionists (1974; rev. 1980); *De nachtegaal,* musical theater piece (1974); *Incantations* for Bass Clarinet and Orch. (The Hague, Oct. 25, 1975); *Orbits* for Solo Horn, 4 Obbligato Horns, and Orch. (Rotterdam, Feb. 28, 1976); *Strides* for Piano (1976); *6 Turkish Folk Poems* for Female Voice and 7 Instruments (Holland Festival, The Hague, June 21, 1977); *Flexio* for Orch. (1979; rev. 1981); *Voor Jan, Piet en Klass* for 2 Pianos (1979); *Music for Flute and Piano* (1979); *Nonet* (1980); *Venus and Adonis Suite* for Clarinet, Violin, Mandolin, Guitar, and Percussion (1981); *Dance* for Violin (1986).

Loewe, (Johann) Carl (Gottfried), outstanding German composer of lieder; b. Löbejün, near Halle, Nov. 30, 1796; d. Kiel, April 20, 1869. His father, a schoolmaster and cantor, taught him the rudiments of music; when he was 12 he was sent to the Francke Inst. in Halle, where his attractive manner, excellent high voice, and early ability to improvise brought him to the attention of Jerome Bonaparte, who granted him a stipend of 300 thalers annually until 1813. His teacher was Türk, the head of the Francke Inst.; after Türk's death in 1813, Loewe joined the Singakademie founded by Naue. He also studied theology at the Univ. of Halle, but soon devoted himself entirely to music. He had begun to compose as a boy; under the influence of Zelter, he wrote German ballades, and developed an individual style of great dramatic force and lyrical inspiration; he perfected the genre, and was regarded by many musicians as the greatest song composer after Schubert and before Brahms. His setting of Goethe's poem *Erlkönig* (1818), which came before the publication of Schubert's great song to the same poem, is one of Loewe's finest creations; other songs that rank among his best are *Edward, Der Wirthin Töchterlein, Der Nöck, Archibald Douglas, Tom der Reimer, Heinrich der Vogler, Oluf,* and *Die verfallene Mühle.* Loewe was personally acquainted with Goethe, and also met Weber. In 1820 he became a schoolmaster at Stettin, and in 1821 music director there and organist at St. Jacobus Cathedral. He lived in Stettin, except for frequent travels, until 1866, when he settled in Kiel. He visited Vienna (1844), London (1847), Sweden and Norway (1851), and Paris (1857), among other places. Loewe was an excellent vocalist, and was able to perform his ballades in public. He publ. the pedagogic works *Gesang-Lehre, theoretisch und practisch für Gymnasien, Seminarien und Bürgerschulen* (Stettin, 1826; 5th ed., 1854); *Musikalischer Gottesdienst; Methodische Anweisung zum Kirchengesang und Orgelspiel* (Stettin, 1851, and subsequent eds.); *Klavier- und Generalbass-Schule* (Stettin, 2nd ed., 1851).

WORKS: 6 operas: *Die Alpenhütte* (1816); *Rudolf der deutsche Herr* (1825); *Malekadhel* (1832); *Neckereien* (1833); *Die drei Wünsche* (Berlin, Feb. 18, 1834); *Emmy* (1842); several cantatas; 2 syms.; 2 piano concertos; 4 string quartets; Piano Trio; piano sonatas; 368 ballades for Voice and Piano. M. Runze ed. a *Gesamtausgabe der Balladen, Legenden, Lieder und Gesänge* (17 vols., Leipzig, 1899–1905).

BIBL.: C. Bitter, ed., *Dr. C. L.'s Selbstbiographie* (Berlin, 1870); K. König, *K. L.: Eine aesthetische Beurteilung* (Leipzig, 1884); A. Wellmer, *K. L.: Ein deutscher Komponist* (Leipzig, 1887); M. Runze, *L. redivivus* (Berlin, 1888); A. Bach, *The Art-Ballad: L. and Schubert* (London, 1890; 3rd ed., 1891); M. Runze, *Ludwig Giesebrecht und C. L.* (Berlin, 1894); W. Wossidlo, *C. L. als Balladenkomponist* (Berlin, 1894); A. Niggli, *C. L.* (Zürich, 1897); H. Bulthaupt, *C. L., Deutschlands Balladenkomponist* (Berlin, 1898); H. Draheim, *Goethes Balladen in L.s Komposition* (Langensalza, 1905); K. Anton, *Beiträge zur Biographie C. L.s* (Halle, 1912); idem, "C. L. als Lehrer Walter von Goethes," *Goethe Jahrbuch* 23 (1913); H. Kleemann, *Beiträge zur Ästhetik und Geschichte der L.schen Ballade* (diss.,

Univ. of Halle, 1913); L. Hirschberg, *C. L.s Instrumentalwerke* (Hildburghausen, 1919); O. Altenburg, *C. L.* (Stettin, 1924); H. Engel, *C. L.: Überblick und Würdigung seines Schaffens* (Greifswald, 1934); W. Serauky, "Zu *C. L.s* Biographie und musikalischen Schaffen," *Festschrift A. Schering* (Berlin, 1937); R. Sietz, *C. L.: Ein Gedenkbuch zum 150. Geburtstag* (Cologne, 1948); M. Brown, "C. L., 1796–1869," *Musical Times*, CX (1969); B. Baselt, "C. L. (30.11.1796–20.4.1869): Zur Konzeption eines zeitgenössischen L.-Bildes," *Musik und Gesellschaft*, XIX (1969); J. Elson, "C. L. and the Nineteenth Century German Ballad," *NATS Bulletin*, XXV (1971).

Loewe, Ferdinand. See **Löwe, Ferdinand.**

Loewe, Frederick, remarkable Austrian-American composer of popular music; b. Vienna, June 10, 1901; d. Palm Springs, Calif., Feb. 14, 1988. He studied piano in Berlin with Busoni and d'Albert and composition with Reznicek; emigrated to the U.S. in 1924, and after a period as a concert pianist, devoted himself to composing popular music. Adapting himself adroitly to the American idiom, he became one of the most successful writers of musical comedies. His 1st musical comedies were *Salute to Spring* (St. Louis, June 12, 1937), *Great Lady* (N.Y., Dec. 1, 1938), and *The Life of the Party* (Detroit, Oct. 8, 1942). He met the lyricist and playwright Alan Jay Lerner in 1942, which led to their collaboration on the unsuccessful musical *What's Up?* (N.Y., Nov. 11, 1943). Their next effort, *The Day before Spring* (N.Y., Nov. 22, 1945), received a respectable hearing, but it was with *Brigadoon* (N.Y., March 13, 1947) that they achieved success. After *Paint Your Wagon* (N.Y., Nov. 12, 1951), they took Broadway by storm with *My Fair Lady* (N.Y., March 15, 1956; with 2,717 subsequent perfs.), based on George Bernard Shaw's *Pygmalion*. They then brought out the film score *Gigi* (1958), after a story by Colette, which won 9 Academy Awards. Their final collaboration was the highly acclaimed musical *Camelot* (N.Y., Dec. 3, 1960). See A. Sirmay, ed., *The Lerner and Loewe Songbook* (N.Y., 1962).

Loewe, Sophie (Johanna), German soprano; b. Oldenburg, March 24, 1815; d. Budapest, Nov. 28, 1866. She studied in Vienna with Ciccimarra and in Milan with Lamperti; made her debut as Elisabetta in *Otto mesi in due ore* at Vienna's Kärnthnertortheater in 1832; sang in London in 1841; also in 1841, appeared at La Scala in Milan, where she created Donizetti's Maria Padilla; also created Verdi's Elvira in *Ernani* (1844) and Odabella in *Attila* (1846) at the Teatro La Fenice in Venice. She retired from the stage in 1848.

Loewenberg, Alfred, German-born English musicologist; b. Berlin, May 14, 1902; d. London, Dec. 29, 1949. He studied at the Univs. of Berlin and Jena (Ph.D., 1925); settled in London in 1934. His unique achievement is the compilation of *Annals of Opera: 1597–1940* (Cambridge, 1943; new ed., Geneva, 1955; rev. and corrected, 1978), tabulating in chronological order the exact dates of 1st performances and important revivals of some 4,000 operas, with illuminating comments of a bibliographical nature. He also publ. *Early Dutch Librettos and Plays with Music in the British Museum* (London, 1947) and *The Theatre of the British Isles, Excluding London: A Bibliography* (London, 1950).

Loewengard, Max Julius, German writer on music, teacher, and composer; b. Frankfurt am Main, Oct. 2, 1860; d. Hamburg, Nov. 19, 1915. He was a pupil of Raff in Frankfurt; from 1891 to 1904 he was on the faculty of the Scharwenka Cons. in Berlin, and wrote music criticism for the *Börsen-Zeitung*; from 1904 to 1908, taught at the Hamburg Cons.; founded the Inst. für Musikwissenschaft there. His compositions include an opera, *Die vierzehn Nothelfer* (Berlin, 1896); Serenade for Orch.; many songs.

WRITINGS: *Lehrbuch der Harmonie* (1892; 6th ed., 1906; Eng. tr. by H. Peacock, 1905; F. Liebing, 1907; T. Baker, 1910); *Lehrbuch des Kontrapunkts* (1902; Eng. tr. by F. Liebing, 1907); *Aufgabenbuch zur Harmonielehre* (1903); *Lehrbuch des Kanons und der Fuge* (1903); *Lehrbuch der musikalischen For-

men* (1904); *Praktische Anleitung zum Generalbassspiel, Harmonisieren, Transponieren und Modulieren* (1913).

Logan, Frederick Knight, American composer of popular songs; b. Oskaloosa, Iowa, Oct. 15, 1871; d. June 11, 1928. He wrote a number of sentimental ballads in collaboration with his mother, Virginia Logan. He was the composer of the celebrated *Missouri Waltz*, which he publ. as a piano solo in 1914 with his name on the cover of the sheet music as an "arranger," for he was reluctant to admit the authorship of the tune that seemed beneath his estimate of himself as a composer. When the words were added in 1916, the thing became a sensational hit. The state of Missouri accepted it as its official song. Harry Truman loved to play it on the piano and, for better or for worse, the *Missouri Waltz* became associated with his (Truman's) political deeds and misdeeds.

Logar, Mihovil, Croatian composer; b. Rijieka, Oct. 6, 1902. He studied in Prague with K.B. Jirák and J. Suk. In 1927 he returned to Belgrade and was a prof. of composition at the Academy of Music (1945–72). A highly prolific composer, he writes in all genres, employing a restrained modern idiom.

WORKS: Operas: *Sablazan u dolini šentflorijansko* (Blasphemy in the Valley of St. Florian; 1937); *Pokondirena tikva* (Middle-class Noblewoman; Belgrade, Oct. 20, 1956); *Četrdesetprva* (The Year of 1941; Sarajevo, Feb. 10, 1961); ballet, *Zlatna ribica* (The Golden Fish), after Pushkin's tale (Belgrade, Nov. 11, 1953); *4 Scenes from Shakespeare*, incidental music for Orch. (1954); *Rondo rustico* for Orch. (1945); Violin Concerto (1954); Clarinet Concerto (1956); *Vatra* (Fire), cantata (Belgrade, Sept. 27, 1960); *Kosmonauti*, concert overture in honor of the Soviet cosmonauts (Belgrade, June 8, 1962); *Sinfonia italiana* (Belgrade, Nov. 24, 1964); *Doppio Concerto* for Clarinet and Horn (Belgrade, April 5, 1968); piano pieces.

Loggins, Kenny, American pop vocalist and songwriter; b. Everett, Wash., Jan. 7, 1948. He formed the soft-rock duo Loggins & Messina with **Jim Messina** (b. Maywood, Calif., Dec. 5, 1947). Messina was a veteran of the groups Buffalo Springfield and Poco; his 1st major project as a producer for Columbia Records was Loggins. Loggins had worked with groups of no interest (e.g., the Electric Prunes), and created the song *The House at Pooh Corner* for the Nitty Gritty Dirt Band (1971). His 1st album with Messina was *Kenny Loggins with Jim Messina Sittin' In* (1971); they subsequently produced 7 more albums, featuring such songs as *Your Mama Don't Dance* and *Thinking of You* (Loggins & Messina, 1972), before parting company in 1977. Loggins continued alone with such successful songs as *Whenever I Call You Friend* (with Stevie Nicks, *Nightwatch*, 1978). His gentle, imaginative music and enthusiastic delivery have made him a beloved figure in pop music circles. Among his most successful albums are *Celebrate Me Home* (1977), *High Adventure* (1982), and *Vox Humana* (1985).

Logier, Johann Bernhard, German pianist, teacher, and composer; b. Kassel, Feb. 9, 1777; d. Dublin, July 27, 1846. He received his early musical training at home; as a youth he went to England and played the flute in a regimental band; he was employed as an organist in Westport, Ireland, where he perfected his invention of the "chiroplast," for holding the hands in the most convenient positions during piano practice; he patented it in 1814 and promoted it with fanatic persistence. Amazingly enough, it obtained great vogue in England, and was equally successful in Germany; in 1821 he was invited to Berlin, where he taught his method from 1822 to 1826; settled in Dublin in 1829. In reply to numerous polemical attacks on his invention, Logier publ. equally bitter assaults on his detractors, among them the pamphlets *An Explanation and Description of the Royal Patent Chiroplast, or Hand-Director for Pianoforte* (London, 1816?; 2nd ed., 1816) and *An Authentic Account of the Examination of Pupils Instructed on the New System of Musical Education, by J.B. Logier* (London, 1818). He further publ. *A Companion to the Royal Patent Chiroplast* (London, c.1815), *Sequel to the Chiroplast Companion* (c.1815), and *Logier's Theoretical and Practical Studies for the Pianoforte* (London, 1816). He also introduced a method of simultaneous practice on different pianos, which for a time was adopted even in such a bastion of traditional music instruction as the Paris Cons. In the end, Logier's "chiroplast" joined a number of other equally futile pseudo-scientific inventions in the repository of musical curiosities.

BIBL.: G. Pügner, *J.B. L., Ein Musikerzieher des 19. Jahrhunderts* (diss., Univ. of Leipzig, 1959).

Logothetis, Anestis, Bulgarian-born Austrian composer of Greek parentage; b. Burgas, Oct. 27, 1921. He went to Vienna in 1942 and studied at the Technischen Hochschule until 1944; then received training in theory and composition from Ratz and Uhl and in piano and conducting from Swarowsky at the Academy of Music, graduating in 1951. In 1952 he became a naturalized Austrian citizen. He worked with Gottfried Michael König at the electronic music studio of the West German Radio in Cologne (1957). In 1960 and 1963 he was awarded the Theodor Körner Prize; in 1986 he received the honorary gold medal of the city of Vienna. He exhibited in Vienna galleries a series of polymorphic graphs capable of being performed as music by optional instrumental groups. He employs a highly personalized "integrating" musical notation, making use of symbols, signs, and suggestive images, playing on a performer's psychological associations.

WORKS: *Integration* for Violin, Cello, and Piano (1953); *Peritonon* for Horn and Piano (1954); *Polynom* for Orch. in 5 groups (1958); *2 Textures* for 2 Piano Groups (1959); *Kompression* for Any Instrument (1959); *Textur—Struktur—Spiegel—Spiel* (1959); *Fantasmata and Meditation*, tape ballet music (1959); *Agglomeration* for Violin (1960); *5 Portraits of Love*, ballet (1960); *Koordination* for 5 Orch. Groups (1960); *Himmelsmechanik*, ballet (1960); *Katalysator* for Horns (1960). The following "polymorphic" pieces are for variable Chamber Instrumental Groups: *Kulmination I + II + III* (1961); *Meditation* for Any Instruments or Voices (1961); *Impulse* (1961); *Vibration* (1962); *Mäandros* (1963); *Odyssee* (1963); *Dynapolis* (1963); *Dispersion* (1963); *Kentra* (1964); *Seismographie I* and *II* (1964); *Osculations* (1964); *Ichnologia* (1964); *Labyrinthos* (1965); *Reversible Bijunktion* (1965); *1.65AL* (1965); *Orbitals* (1965); *Enòsis* (1965); *Diffusion* (1965); *Integration* (1966); *Enclaves* (1966); *Diptychon* for Piano (1966); *Desmotropie* for Orch. (1967); *Karmadharmadrama*, musical theater (1967; Graz, Oct. 12, 1972); *Polychron* (1967); *Syrroi* (1967); *Konvektionsströme* for Orch. (1968); *Styx* for Orch. of Plucked Strings (1968); *Evektion* (1968); *Anastasis*, stage piece for Voices, Tape Film, Television, and Instruments (1969); *Kollisionen* (1970); *Komplementäres* (1970); *Pyrifleghethon—Acheron—Kokkytos* for 3 Choirs and Optional Instruments (Athens, Sept. 26, 1971; refers to the 3 rivers of the Greek netherworld); *Klangraum I* and *II* for Orch. (1972); *Musik-Fontane für Robert Moran* (1972); *Emanationen* for Clarinet and Tape (1973); *Ghia tin ora* for Orch. (1975–78); *Daidalia oder Das Leben einer Theorie*, music theater (1976–78); *Rondo* for Orch. (1979); *Wellenformen 1981*, computer piece (1981–82); *Brunnenburg-Hochzeit-Symphionetten* for Chamber Ensemble (1981–87); *Meridiane I und Bretiengrade* for Soli and Orch. (1981–88).

Logroscino, Nicola Bonifacio, Italian composer; b. Bitonto (baptized), Oct. 22, 1698; d. Palermo, after 1765. He was a pupil of Veneziano and Perugino (1714–27) at the Conservatorio di S. Maria di Loreto in Naples; from 1728 to 1731, was organist at Conza (Avellino); then was active in Naples to about 1756. He subsequently went to Palermo, where he taught at the Ospedale dei Figliuoli Dispersi (c.1758–64). Of his many works, the comic opera *Il Governatore* (Naples, Carnival 1747) and the heroic opera *Giunio Bruto* (Rome, Jan. 1748) are the only 2 in which the music is extant in full.

BIBL.: H. Kretzschmar, "Zwei Opern N. L.s," *Jahrbuch Peters* (1908); E. Morello, *A Scarlatti e N. L.* (1927); U. Prota-Giurleo, *N. L.: "il dio dell'opera buffa"* (Naples, 1927). M. Belluci La Salandra, *Triade musicale Bitontina, Brevi cenni biografici di N.B. L., 1698–1760* (Bitonto, 1936).

Löhlein, Georg Simon, German music theorist and composer; b. Neustadt an der Heide, near Coburg (baptized), July 16, 1725; d. Danzig, Dec. 16, 1781. On account of his tall stature (6 feet, 2 inches), he was seized on a journey and forced into the Prussian Guard when he was 16; he was stationed at Potsdam and served at the palace of Frederick the Great. He was severely wounded at the battle of Collin (1757) during the Seven Years' War, but recovered. He then studied at the Univ. of Jena (1760), where he was made director of its Academy Concerts and principal of the Collegium Musicum (1761); subsequently studied philosophy, ethics, and poetry at the Univ. of Leipzig (1763); also received instruction in music from J.A. Hiller; served as music director of the Grosses Konzert there. He became Kapellmeister at Danzig's Marienkirche (1781), but suffered from the rigors of the climate, and died a few months after his arrival. Löhlein wrote a singspiel, *Zemire und Azor* (Leipzig, 1775); several instrumental concertos; chamber music; etc. He became known mainly through his pedagogical work, *Clavier-Schule* (2 vols., Leipzig and Züllichau, 1765 and 1781; many subsequent eds.); he also publ. *Anweisung zum Violinspielen . . . mit 24 kleinen Duetten erläutert* (Leipzig and Züllichau, 1774; 3rd ed., augmented, 1797 by J. Reichardt).

BIBL.: F. von Glasenapp, *G.S. L.* (Halle, 1937).

Löhse, Otto, German conductor and composer; b. Dresden, Sept. 21, 1858; d. Baden-Baden, May 5, 1925. He was a pupil at the Dresden Cons. of Richter (piano), Grützmacher (cello), Draeseke, Kretschmer, and Rischbieter (theory), and Wüllner (conducting). He began his conducting career in Riga (1882); was 1st conductor there (1889–93); in 1893 he was in Hamburg; there he married **Katharina Klafsky,** and in 1895–96 both artists were members of the Damrosch Opera Co. in N.Y., with Löhse as conductor. From 1897 to 1904, Löhse conducted opera in Strasbourg; from 1904 to 1911, in Cologne; from 1911 to 1912, at the Théâtre Royal de la Monnaie in Brussels; from 1912 to 1923, at the Leipzig Stadttheater; from 1923 to 1925, in Baden-Baden. He composed an opera, *Der Prinz wider Willen* (Riga, 1890), and songs.

BIBL.: E. Lert, *O. L.* (Leipzig, 1918).

Lokshin, Alexander, Russian composer; b. Biisk, Altai Region, Sept. 19, 1920. He studied with Miaskovsky at the Moscow Cons. (graduated, 1941). The major portion of his output is devoted to his 11 syms., 10 of them vocal, which promote their often poetic and profound expressions through a unique blend of lyricism and contemporary compositional techniques.

WORKS: ORCH.: 11 syms.: No. 1, *Requiem,* for Chorus and Orch. (1958); No. 2, *Greek Epigrams,* for Voices and Orch., to words by ancient Greek poets (1963); No. 3 for Baritone, Men's Chorus, and Orch., after Kipling (1966); No. 4, *Sinfonia stretta* (1967); No. 5, *Sonnets for Shakespeare,* for Baritone, String Orch., and Harp (1969); No. 6 for Baritone, Chorus, and Orch., after Alexander Blok (1971); No. 7 for Contralto and Chamber Orch., after Japanese poets of the 7th to the 13th century (1972); No. 8 for Tenor and Orch., after Pushkin (1973); No. 9 for Baritone and String Orch., after Martynow (1975); No. 10 for Contralto, Organ, and Orch., after Zabolotsky (1976); No. 11 for Soprano and Chamber Orch., after Camoëns (1977). OTHER: *Wait for Me,* symphonic poem for Voice and Orch. (1943); *Hungarian Fantasia* for Violin and Orch. (1952); *The Giant Cockroach,* comic oratorio (1962); *Speaking Out Loud,* symphonic poem for Bass, Organ, and Orch., after Mayakovsky (1968); *Songs of Margaret* for Soprano and Chamber Orch., after Goethe's *Faust* (1973); *Mater dolorosa,* cantata (1977); *Variations* for Piano (1953); Clarinet Quintet (1955); String Quintet (1978).

Lolli, Antonio, noted Italian violinist and composer; b. Bergamo, c.1725; d. Palermo, Aug. 10, 1802. Little is known of his early life; he was in Stuttgart at the court of the Duke of Württemberg from 1758 to 1772; asked for a leave of absence, but did not return to Stuttgart; however, he drew his salary until 1774. He gave violin concerts in Hamburg, Lübeck, and Stettin in 1773–74; then proceeded to St. Petersburg, where he became a special favorite of Catherine II, and also ingratiated himself with Potemkin. He received 4,000 rubles annually as violinist to the Empress and chapel master of the court. In Dec. 1777 he visited Stockholm, and then went to Germany. An incorrigible gambler, he dissipated the fortune of 10,000 florins he had accumulated from the Russian emoluments, and in 1780, after protracted journeys through Europe, went back to St. Petersburg; there he was able to regain his social and artistic position; gave concerts at Potemkin's palace in St. Petersburg, and also played in Moscow. Despite his frequent derelictions of duty, he was retained at the court until 1783, when his contract was canceled and he was succeeded by his former pupil G.M. Giornovichi. However, he continued to give some public concerts, and also lessons, before leaving Russia in 1784. In 1785 he appeared in London; then was in Paris and in Naples, finally settling in Palermo, where he died in poverty. Contemporary accounts indicate that Lolli was a violinist of great ability, but also addicted to eccentricities in playing technical passages. He also composed and publ. several sets of violin works. **WORKS: VIOLIN CONCERTOS:** *Deux concerto*, op. 2 (Paris, 1764); (2) Concerto, op. 4 (Paris, 1766); (2) Concerto, op. 5 (Paris, 1768); *Septième concerto* (Paris, 1775); *Huitième concerto* (Paris, 1776); etc. **CHAMBER:** *Sei sonate* for Violin and Bass, op. 1 (Amsterdam, 1760?); *Sei sonate* for Violin and Bass, op. 2 (Amsterdam, 1769); *Sei sonate* for Violin and Bass, op. 3 (Paris, c.1767); *Cinq sonates & un divertissement* for Violin and Bass, op. 3 (Berlin, 1776); Six Sonatas for 2 Violins, op. 9 (Paris, c.1785). **BIBL.:** A. Moser, "Arcangelo Corelli und A. L.: Zwei künstlerische Ehrenrettungen," *Zeitschrift für Musikwissenschaft* (April 1921); R.-A. Mooser, *Annales de la Musique et des Musiciens en Russie au XVIIIᵉ siècle* (vol. II, Geneva, 1951); N. Nunamaker, *The Virtuoso Violin Concerto Before Paganini: The Concertos of L., Giornovicchi and Waldemar* (diss., Indiana Univ., 1968).

Lomakin, Gavriil Yakimovich, Russian singer, choral conductor, and composer; b. Borisovka, Kursk district, April 6, 1812; d. Gatchina, May 21, 1885. He studied theory with Sapienza in St. Petersburg; in 1830, became choirmaster and singing master at several institutions in St. Petersburg, and later conductor of the court chapel (1848–59). Together with Balakirev, he established in 1862 the Free School for Music, and had charge of the singing classes until 1870. He wrote 10 *Cherubim Songs*; 14 *Penitential Songs*; a Liturgy; etc.; publ. a *Treatise on Choral Singing*; arrangements for chorus of early Russian hymns.

Lomax, Alan, American ethnomusicologist, son of **John Avery Lomax;** b. Austin, Texas, Jan. 31, 1915. He acquired his métier from his father; then studied at the Univ. of Texas in Austin (B.A., 1936) and at Columbia Univ. (1939). He joined his father as a researcher in 1933; collected folk songs in the Southwestern and Midwestern regions of the U.S.; they supervised field recordings of rural and prison songs, discovering Leadbelly; they also "discovered" Jelly Roll Morton and recorded interviews with him at the Library of Congress in Washington, D.C. (1938). He also collected folk songs in Europe. In 1963 he was made director of the Bureau of Applied Social Research; also of the cantometrics project at Columbia Univ. (1963). Among his eds., compiled with his father, are *American Ballads and Folksongs* (N.Y., 1934); *Negro Folk Songs as Sung by Leadbelly* (N.Y., 1936); *Our Singing Country* (N.Y., 1941); *Folk Song: U.S.A.* (N.Y., 1947; 4th ed., 1954); *Leadbelly: A Collection of World Famous Songs* (N.Y., 1959; 2nd ed., augmented, 1965 as *The Leadbelly Legend*); he also prepared *The Folk Songs of North America in the English Language* (N.Y., 1960); *The Penguin Book of American Folk Songs* (Harmondsworth, 1966); *Hard-Hitting Songs for Hard-Hit People* (N.Y., 1967); *Folk Song Style and Culture* (Washington, D.C., 1968). **WRITINGS:** With S. Cowell, *American Folk Song and Folk Lore: A Regional Bibliography* (N.Y., 1942); *Mr. Jelly Roll* (N.Y., 1950; 2nd ed., 1973); *Harriett and Her Harmonium* (London,

1955); *The Rainbow Sign* (N.Y., 1959); *Cantometrics: A Handbook and Training Method* (Berkeley, 1976); *Index of World Song* (N.Y., 1977).

Lomax, John Avery, American ethnomusicologist, father of **Alan Lomax;** b. Goodman, Miss., Sept. 23, 1867; d. Greenville, Miss., Jan. 26, 1948. He began collecting and notating American folk songs in his early youth; studied music at the Univ. of Texas in Austin; founded the Texas Folklore Soc. In 1933 his son joined him in his research; for the eds. they publ., see the entry on his son. He publ. an autobiography, *Adventures of a Ballad Hunter* (N.Y., 1947).

Lombard, Alain, French conductor; b. Paris, Oct. 4, 1940. He studied with Gaston Poulet at the Paris Cons. at age 9, making his debut with the Pasdeloup Orch. when he was 11; later studied with F. Fricsay. He conducted at the Lyons Opera (1960–64); won the gold medal at the Mitropoulos Competition in N.Y. (1966); then was music director of the Miami Phil. (1966–74). He made his Metropolitan Opera debut in N.Y. conducting *Faust* on Dec. 24, 1966, and continued to appear there until 1973. He was chief conductor of the Strasbourg Phil. (1972–83), artistic director of the Opéra du Rhin (1974–80), and music director of the Paris Opéra (1981–83). In 1988 he became artistic director of the Orch. National Bordeaux Aquitaine.

Lombardi, Luca, Italian composer; b. Rome, Dec. 24, 1945. He studied in Vienna and Rome; took composition lessons with Globokar at the Cologne Hochschule für Musik (1968–72); also attended the Cologne new music courses led by Stockhausen, Schnebel, and others; studied electronic music with Eimert, and with G.M. Koenig at the Univ. of Utrecht (1970–71). He taught at the Pesaro Cons. (1973–80) and at the Verdi Cons. in Milan (from 1980). **WORKS:** *Elegia* for Violin and Piano (1965); *Albumblätter* for Piano (1967–68); *Proporzioni* for 4 Trombones (1968–69); *Wiederkehr* for Piano (1971); *Non Requiescat: Musica in memoria di Hanns Eisler* for Chamber Orch. (1973); *Canzone* for Chamber Orch. (1974–75); Sym. No. 1 (1974–75); *Essay* for Double Bass (1975); *Essay No. 2* for Clarinet (1979); *Gespräch über Bäume* for 9 Players (1976); *Hasta que Caigan las Puertas del Odio* for 16 Voices a cappella (1976–77); *Variazioni* for Orch. (1977); *Tui-Gesänge* for Soprano and 5 Instrumentalists (1977; Paris, March 18, 1978); *Klavierduo* for 2 Pianos (1978–79); *Majakowski*, cantata for Bass, Chorus, and 7 Instruments (1979–80); *Sisifo felice* for 8 Instruments (1984); *Celan-Lieder* for Soprano and 6 Instruments (1985).

Lombardini-Sirmen, Maddalena Laura, Italian violinist and composer; b. Venice, 1735; d. after 1785. She studied at the Mendicanti Cons. and then took private lessons with Giuseppe Tartini in Padua. (A letter Tartini sent to Lombardini after her return to Venice about technique was tr. and publ. widely in Europe as a valuable treatise on the violin.) In 1760 she married Luigi de Sirmen, also a violinist and choirmaster in Bergamo, with whom she gave concerts throughout Europe (1760–68). She enjoyed a brilliant success in her own right in England (1771–72). Tartini considered her a talent of the 1st rank. By 1774 she turned inexplicably to singing. Although she was principal singer at the court of Dresden in 1782, contemporary critics lamented the exchange of her brilliant career as a violinist for that of a singer of no particular distinction. Her last public appearance was again as a violinist at the Concert Spirituel in Paris (1785). Her compositions include 6 violin concertos (Amsterdam, 1770), 6 concertos for Harpsichord (London, 1773), 6 trios for Cello and 2 Violins, 6 sonatas for 2 Violins, 6 duets for Violin (Amsterdam, 1770), and 6 violin quartets written in collaboration with her husband.

Lombardo, Guy (actually, **Gaetano Alberto**), popular Canadian-American bandleader; b. London, Ontario (of Italian parents), June 19, 1902; d. Houston, Nov. 5, 1977. With his brother Carmen Lombardo, the saxophone player, he organized a dance band, The Royal Canadians, and took it to the U.S. in 1924;

2 other brothers, Lebert and Victor, were also members of the band. The band rapidly rose to success on the commercial wave of pervasive sentimentality; in 1928 it was publicized as the purveyor of "the sweetest music this side of Heaven"; in 1929 they began playing at the Roosevelt Grill, where they held sway for some 33 years; thereafter they performed at the Waldorf-Astoria Hotel; the band's rendition of *Auld Lang Syne* was a nostalgic feature at each New Year's Eve celebration from 1929, being broadcast live on radio and later on television. In his arrangements, Lombardo cultivated unabashed emotionalism; in his orchestrations, all intervallic interstices were well filled and saxophones were tremulous with vibrato. The result was a velvety, creamy, but not necessarily oleaginous harmoniousness, which possessed an irresistible appeal to the obsolescent members of the superannuated generation of the 1920s. His preferred dynamic was *mezzo-forte*, and his favorite tempo, *andante moderato;* he never allowed the sound of his band to rise to a disturbing *forte* or to descend to a squeaking *pianissimo.* He was a wizard of the golden mean, and his public loved it. With J. Altshul, he publ. the autobiography *Auld Acquaintance* (N.Y., 1975).
BIBL.: B. Herndon, *The Sweetest Music This Side of Heaven* (N.Y., 1964); B. Cline, *The L. Story* (Don Mills, Ontario, 1979); S. Richman, *G.: The Life and Times of G. L.* (N.Y., 1980).

Lomon, Ruth, Canadian-born American composer, pianist, and teacher; b. Montreal, Nov. 8, 1930. She studied at McGill Univ. in Montreal; in 1960 she went to the U.S. and continued her training with Frances Judd Cooke and Miklos Schwalb at the New England Cons. of Music in Boston; in 1964 she took a course with Lutoslawski at the Dartington Summer School of Music in England; she also attended the Darmstadt summer courses in new music. In 1965 she became a naturalized U.S. citizen. From 1971 to 1983 she was half of the duopiano team of Lomon and Wenglin, specializing in the performance of works by women composers. Several of her most important works have been inspired by Native American ceremonials.
WORKS: CHAMBER OPERA: *The Fisherman and His Soul* (1963). **ORCH.:** Bassoon Concerto (1979). **CHAMBER:** Trio for Horn, Cello, and Piano (1961); *Dartington Quintet* for Soprano, Flute, Clarinet, Violin, and Piano (1964); *Shapes* for Violin, Cello, Guitar, and Piano (1964); *Soundings* for Piano, 4-hands (1975); *The Furies: Erinnyes* for Oboe, Oboe d'Amore, and English Horn (1977); *Equinox* for Brass (1978); *Solstice* for Brass Quartet (1978); *Celebrations* for 2 Harps (1978); *Triptych* for 2 Pianos (1978); 5 *Ceremonial Masks* for Piano (1980); *Vitruvian Scroll* for String Quartet (1981); 7 *Portals of Vision* for Organ (1982); *Diptych* for Woodwind Quintet (1983); *Iatiku: "bringing to life . . ."* for Bass Clarinet, Marimba, Vibes, Harp, Harpsichord, and Piano (1983); *Janus* for String Quartet (1984); *Desiderata* for Oboe, Marimba, and Optional Bow Chime (1984); *Spells* for Piano, Woodwind Quintet, String Quartet, Trumpet, and Percussion (1985); *Imprints,* concerto for Piano and 4 Percussion (1987; Columbus, Ohio, May 15, 1989); *The Talisman* for B-flat and Bass Clarinets, Violin, Viola, Cello, and Synthesizer (1988; Boston, Feb. 12, 1989). **VOCAL:** *Requiem* for Soprano, Chorus, and Instruments (1977); *Songs from a Requiem* for Soprano and Piano (1982); *Winnowing Song* for Chorus, Cello, and Piano (1982); *Symbiosis* for Mezzosoprano, Percussion, and Piano (1983); *A Fantasy Journey into the Mind of a Machine* for Soprano and Saxophone (1985).

Lonati, Carlo Ambrogio (real name, **Giovanni Ambrogio Leinati**), famous Italian violinist and composer, known as "Il Gobbo della Regina" ("the Queen's hunchback"); b. probably in Milan, c.1645; d. probably there, c.1710. He was a violinist in the Naples royal chapel (1665–67). He went in 1668 to Rome, where he entered the service of Queen Christina of Sweden; although a hunchback, he was greatly admired as a violinist, hence his sobriquet. He also appeared as a singer; likewise was principal violinist at S. Luigi dei Francesi (1673–74), and was concertino violinist at the Oratorio della Stimmate at S. Francesco and the Oratorio del Crocifisso at S. Marcello

(1674–75), and at the Oratorio della Pietà at S. Giovanni dei Fiorentini (1675). Having become a close friend of Stradella, he was compelled to leave Rome in 1677 after his friend's notorious conduct became general knowledge. They went to Genoa, but Lonati left the city after Stradella's murder in 1682. He then was in the service of the Mantuan court. He spent his last years in Milan. He was a distinguished composer of operas, cantatas, and instrumental music.
WORKS: OPERAS: *Amor per destino* (Genoa, 1678); *Ariberto e Flavio, regi di Longobardi* (Venice, 1684?); *Enea in Italia* (Milan, 1686; in collaboration with others); *I due germani (fratelli) rivali* (Modena, 1686); *Antico, principe della Siria* (Genoa, 1690); *Scipione africano* (Milan, 1692); *L'Aiace* (Milan, 1694; in collaboration with Magni and Ballarotti); *Aetna festivo* (Milan, 1696; in collaboration with others); also cantatas and 12 sonates for Violin and Basso Continuo (1701).

London, Edwin, American composer; b. Philadelphia, March 16, 1929. He studied horn at the Oberlin College Cons. of Music (B.M., 1952) and composition at the Univ. of Iowa (Ph.D., 1961); also took courses with Schuller, Dallapiccola, and Milhaud and received instruction in conducting from Solomon. He taught at Smith College (1960–68), the Univ. of Calif. at San Diego (1972–73), and the Univ. of Illinois (1973–83), where he was also founder-conductor of its new-music choral group, Ineluctable Modality; was chairman of the music dept. at Cleveland State Univ. (from 1978), and founder-conductor of the Cleveland Chamber Orch.
WORKS: *Santa Claus,* mime opera (1960); *The Death of Lincoln,* opera (1976); *Metaphysical Vegas,* musical (1981); *The Iron Hand,* oratorio (1975); Trio for Flute, Clarinet, and Piano (1956); Woodwind Quintet (1958); Brass Quintet (1965).

London (real name, **Burnstein**), **George,** esteemed Canadian-born American bass-baritone; b. Montreal (of Russian parents), May 5, 1919; d. Armonk, N.Y., March 23, 1985. The family moved to Los Angeles in 1935; there he took lessons in operatic interpretation with Richard Lert; also studied voice with Hugo Strelitzer and Nathan Stewart; made his public debut in the opera *Gainsborough's Duchess* by Albert Coates in a concert performance in Los Angeles on April 20, 1941. He appeared as Dr. Grenvil in Verdi's *La Traviata* on Aug. 5, 1941, at the Hollywood Bowl; also sang with the San Francisco Opera on Oct. 24, 1943, in the role of Monterone in *Rigoletto.* He took further vocal lessons with Enrico Rosati and Paola Novikova in N.Y.; then, anticipating a serious professional career, he changed his name from the supposedly plebeian and ethnically confining Burnstein to a resounding and patrician London. In 1947 he toured the U.S. and Europe as a member of the Bel Canto Trio, with Frances Yeend, soprano, and Mario Lanza, tenor. His European operatic debut took place, as Amonasro, at the Vienna State Opera on Sept. 3, 1949; he made his Metropolitan Opera debut in N.Y. in the same role on Nov. 13, 1951; this was also the role he sang at his last Metropolitan appearance on March 10, 1966. Altogether he sang with the Metropolitan 249 times in N.Y. and 54 times on tour. On Sept. 16, 1960, he became the 1st American to sing Boris Godunov (in Russian) at the Bolshoi Theater in Moscow. He also appeared at the Bayreuth Festivals (1951–64). In 1967 he was stricken with a partial paralysis of the larynx, but recovered sufficiently to be able to perform administrative duties. From 1968 to 1971 he was artistic administrator of the John F. Kennedy Center for the Performing Arts in Washington, D.C.; was also executive director of the National Opera Inst. from 1971 to 1977. He was general director of the Opera Soc. of Washington, D.C., from 1975 to 1977, when he suffered a cardiac arrest that precluded any further public activities. For several years before his death he suffered from a grave neurological disease. Among his best roles were Wotan, Don Giovanni, Scarpia, Escamillo, and Boris Godunov.
BIBL.: J. Wechsberg, "The Vocal Mission," *New Yorker* (Oct. 26 and Nov. 2, 1957).

Long, Marguerite (Marie Charlotte), notable French pianist and pedagogue; b. Nîmes, Nov. 13, 1874; d. Paris, Feb.

13, 1966. She studied piano with Marmontel at the Paris Cons.; was appointed an instructor there in 1906, her tenure running until 1940; in 1920 she founded her own music school; in 1940 Jacques Thibaud, the violinist, joined her; with him she gave numerous recitals and established the Long-Thibaud competitions (1943). She played an important role in promoting French music; she was esteemed for her performances of works by Fauré, Debussy, and Ravel, all of whom she knew personally. In 1932 she was soloist in the 1st performance of Ravel's Piano Concerto in G major, with the composer conducting; the work is dedicated to her. She was married to the writer on music **Joseph de Marliave.** She publ. *Le Piano* (Paris, 1959), *Au piano avec Claude Debussy* (Paris, 1960; Eng. tr., 1972), *Au piano avec Gabriel Fauré* (Paris, 1963), and *Au piano avec Maurice Ravel* (Paris, 1971; Eng. tr., 1973).

BIBL.: J. Weill, *M. L.: Une Vie fascinante* (Paris, 1969).

Longas, Federico, Spanish pianist and composer; b. Barcelona, July 18, 1893; d. Santiago, Chile, June 17, 1968. He was a pupil of Granados and Malats; toured widely in the U.S., South America, and Europe as accompanist to Tito Schipa and as a soloist. He founded a piano school, the Longas Academy, in Barcelona; later he went to Paris; then to the U.S., settling in N.Y. His works include effective piano pieces (*Jota, Aragon,* etc.) and over 100 songs (*Castilian Moonlight, La guinda, Muñequita,* etc.).

Longo, Achille, Italian composer, son of **Alessandro Longo;** b. Naples, March 28, 1900; d. there, May 28, 1954. He studied with his father and with A. Savasta; then at the Naples Cons. (diplomas in piano, 1918, and composition, 1920); he taught harmony there (1926–30); then at the Parma Cons. (1930–34); subsequently taught composition at the Naples Cons. (1934–54).

WORKS: *Scenetta pastorale* for Orch. (1924); Piano Concerto (Venice, 1932); *La burla del Pievano Arlotto* for Orch. (1933); *Missa di requiem* (1933); Violin Concerto (1937); *Notturno* and *Corte* for Orch. (1942); *Serenata in do* for Orch. (1950); Suite for Flute, Oboe, Clarinet, Bassoon, and Piano (1926; won the Bellini Prize); Piano Quintet (1934).

Longo, Alessandro, Italian pianist, teacher, editor, and composer, father of **Achille Longo;** b. Amantea, Dec. 30, 1864; d. Naples, Nov. 3, 1945. He began his studies with his father, **Achille Longo** (b. Melicuccà, Feb. 27, 1832; d. Naples, May 11, 1919), a pianist and composer; then entered the Naples Cons. (1878), where he studied piano with Cesi, composition with Serrao, and organ (diplomas in all 3, 1885). He was appointed prof. of piano there in 1897, retiring in 1934; later returned as its interim director (1944). In 1892 he founded the Circolo Scarlatti to promote the works of Domenico Scarlatti; ed. the *Opere complete per clavicembalo di Domenico Scarlatti* (11 vols., Milan, 1906–8); also became ed. of the periodical *L'Arte Pianistica* (1914), which became the *Vita Musicale Italiana;* it discontinued publication in 1926. He publ. the study *Domenico Scarlatti e la sua figura nella storia della musica* (Naples, 1913). He also was the composer of over 300 works, including numerous pieces for piano solo and piano, 4-hands; chamber music; and songs.

BIBL.: M. Limoncelli, *A. L.* (Naples, 1956).

Longy, (Gustave-) Georges (-Léopold), French oboist, conductor, music educator, and composer; b. Abbeville, Aug. 28, 1868; d. Moreuil, March 29, 1930. He studied at the Paris Cons. (1st prize, 1886); was a member of the Lamoureux Orch. (1886–88) and of the Colonne Orch. (1888–98). In 1898 he was engaged as 1st oboe player of the Boston Sym. Orch., and remained there until 1925. From 1899 to 1913 he conducted the Boston Orchestral Club. In 1900 he founded the Longy Club for chamber music; in 1916 he established his own music school in Boston (later the Longy School of Music in Cambridge, Mass.).

Lonque, Georges, Belgian composer; b. Ghent, Nov. 8, 1900; d. Brussels, March 3, 1967. He studied with Moeremans, Mathieu, and Lunssens at the Ghent Cons.; was awarded the

2nd Prix de Rome for his cantatas *Le Rossignol* (1927) and *Antigone* (1929). He joined the faculty of his alma mater (1926); was a lecturer in harmony there (1932–65); was also director of the Renaix music academy (1938–64). His music was influenced mainly by Franck, Debussy, Fauré, and Ravel.

WORKS: *Impressions d'Hemelrijk* for Orch. (1925); *Vieux quai* for Violin or Cello, and Orch. (1928); *Aura,* symphonic poem and ballet (1930); *Wiener Walzer* for Small Orch. (1933); *Poème de la mer* for Cello and Orch. (1935); *Images d'Orient* for Saxophone or Viola, and Orch. (1935); *Porcelaines de Saxe* for Small Orch. (1939); *Prélude et Aria* for Cello and Orch. (1943); *Estrelle* for Violin and Orch. (1944); Violin Concerto (1948); *Afgoden* (Idoles) for Clarinet and Orch. (1950); Violin Sonata (1925); *Caprice* for Violin and Piano (1930); String Quartet (1937); piano pieces, including *Nuit d'automne* (1929), 2 sonatinas (1939, 1944), *Voilier* (1952), *Tableaux d'une chambre bleue* (1952), and *Nocturne* (1955); *Missa pro pace* for Male Chorus and Organ (1941); numerous songs, including *Faune* (1933), *Why Don't You Come?* (1944), *La Question* (1957), and *Portrait* (1957).

Loomis, Clarence, American pianist, teacher, and composer; b. Sioux Falls, S.Dak., Dec. 13, 1889; d. Aptos, Calif., July 3, 1965. He studied at the American Cons. of Chicago with Heniot Lévy (piano) and Adolph Weidig (composition); subsequently took lessons with Leopold Godowsky in Vienna. Returning to the U.S., he held various positions as a music teacher; taught piano and organ at Highland Univ. in New Mexico (1945–55); in 1960 he settled in Aptos, Calif. As a composer, he was mainly successful in writing light operas in a Romantic vein; among them are *Yolanda of Cyprus* (London, Ontario, Sept. 25, 1929); *A Night in Avignon* (Indianapolis, July 1932); *The White Cloud* (1935); *The Fall of the House of Usher* (Indianapolis, Jan. 11, 1941); *Revival* (1943); *The Captive Woman* (1953); he further wrote a comic ballet, *The Flapper and the Quarterback,* which was first performed in Kyoto, Japan, at the coronation of Emperor Hirohito, Nov. 10, 1928. Among his orch. works were *Gargoyles,* symphonic prelude (1936); *Gaelic Suite* for Strings (1953); *Fantasy* for Piano and Orch. (1954); *Macbeth* (1954); *The Passion Play* for Chorus and Orch.; 2 string quartets (1953, 1963); cantata, *Song of the White Earth* (1956); numerous sacred choruses; *Susanna Don't You Cry,* a stage extravaganza (1939); piano suites; songs; organ pieces.

Loomis, Harvey Worthington, American composer; b. Brooklyn, Feb. 5, 1865; d. Boston, Dec. 25, 1930. He was a pupil in composition of Dvořák at the National Cons. in N.Y. (1891–93); later lived mostly in Boston; became interested in American Indian music, and publ. many arrangements of American Indian melodies; also original works in that style (*Lyrics of the Red Man,* etc.).

WORKS: Grand opera, *The Traitor Mandolin;* 2 melodramas: *The Song of the Pear* and *The Story of a Faithful Soul;* 4 comic operas: *The Maid of Athens, The Burglar's Bride, Going Up?, The Bey of Baba;* musical pantomimes: *Put to the Test, Her Revenge, In Old New Amsterdam, The Enchanted Fountain, Love and Witchcraft, Blanc et Noir;* incidental music to *The Tragedy of Death* and *The Coming of the Prince; Fairy Hill; Song Flowers for Children to Gather; Toy Tunes.*

Loose, Emmy, Austrian soprano; b. Karbitz, Bohemia, Jan. 22, 1914; d. Vienna, Oct. 14, 1987. She was educated at the Prague Cons.; then made her debut as Blondchen in *Die Entführung aus dem Serail* in Hannover (1939). From 1941 she sang with the Vienna State Opera; also appeared at the festivals in Salzburg, Glyndebourne, and Aix-en-Provence, at Milan's La Scala, London's Covent Garden, and in South America. From 1970 she taught at the Vienna Academy of Music.

Looser, Rolf, Swiss cellist and composer; b. Niederscherli, near Bern, May 3, 1920. He studied cello with Richard Sturzenegger at the Bern Cons. and theory with Moeschinger; received his concert diploma in 1944 and subsequently took additional cello lessons with Pierre Fournier in Paris; also continued his composition study with Willy Burkhardt in Zürich and with Frank Martin in Geneva. In 1953 he joined the staff of the Bern Cons. as a cello instructor; in 1963 he took up residence in Biel. Among his works are a *Fantasie* for Cello and Orch. (1958); *Rhapsodie* for Cello and Chamber Orch. (1961); *Fantasia a quattro* (1966); *Alyssos*, 5 pieces for String Orch. and Percussion (1968).

Lopatnikoff, Nicolai (Nikolai Lvovich), outstanding Russian-born American composer; b. Tallinn, Estonia, March 16, 1903; d. Pittsburgh, Oct. 7, 1976. He studied at the St. Petersburg Cons. (1914–17); after the Revolution, continued his musical training at the Helsinki Cons. with Furuhjelm (1918–20); then studied with Hermann Grabner in Heidelberg (1920) and Ernst Toch and Willy Rehberg in Mannheim (1921); concurrently took civil engineering at the Technological College in Karlsruhe (1921–27). He lived in Berlin (1929–33) and London (1933–39) before settling in the U.S., becoming a naturalized citizen in 1944. He was head of theory and composition at the Hartt College of Music in Hartford, Conn., and of the Westchester Cons. in White Plains, N.Y. (1939–45); then was a prof. of composition at the Carnegie Inst. of Technology (later Carnegie-Mellon Univ.) in Pittsburgh (1945–69). In 1951 he married the poet Sara Henderson Hay. He was elected to the National Inst. of Arts and Letters in 1963. His music is cast in a neo-Classical manner, distinguished by a vigorous rhythmic pulse, a clear melodic line, and a wholesome harmonic investment. A prolific composer, he wrote music in all genres; being a professional pianist, he often performed his own piano concertos with orchs.
WORKS: STAGE: Opera, *Danton* (1930–32, not perf.; *Danton Suite* for Orch., Pittsburgh, March 25, 1967); ballet, *Melting Pot* (1975; Indianapolis, March 26, 1976). **ORCH.:** *Prelude to a Drama* (1920; lost); 2 piano concertos: No. 1 (1921; Cologne, Nov. 3, 1925); No. 2 (1930; Düsseldorf, Oct. 16, 1930); *Introduction and Scherzo* (1927–29; 1st complete perf., N.Y., Oct. 23, 1930); 4 syms.: No. 1 (1928; Karlsruhe, Jan. 9, 1929); No. 2 (1938–39; 4-movement version, Boston, Dec. 22, 1939; withdrawn and rev. in 3 movements); No. 3 (1953–54; Pittsburgh, Dec. 10, 1954); No. 4 (1970–71; Pittsburgh, Jan. 21, 1972); *Short Overture* (1932; lost); *Opus Sinfonicum* (1933; rev. 1942; Cleveland, Dec. 9, 1943); *2 Russian Nocturnes* (1939; orig. the 2 middle movements of the 2nd Sym.); Violin Concerto (1941; Boston, April 17, 1942); Sinfonietta (1942; ISCM Festival, Berkeley, Calif., Aug. 2, 1942); Concertino for Orch. (1944; Boston, March 2, 1945); Concerto for 2 Pianos and Orch. (Pittsburgh, Dec. 7, 1951); Divertimento (La Jolla, Calif., Aug. 19, 1951); *Variazioni concertanti* (Pittsburgh, Nov. 7, 1958); *Music for Orchestra* (1958; Louisville, Ky., Jan. 14, 1959); *Festival Overture* (Detroit, Oct. 12, 1960); Concerto for Orch. (Pittsburgh, April 3, 1964; orch. version of Concerto for Wind Orch.); *Partita concertante* for Chamber Orch. (1966); *Variations and Epilogue* for Cello and Orch. (Pittsburgh, Dec. 14, 1973; orchestration of 1946 chamber piece). **WIND ORCH.:** Concerto for Wind Orch. (Pittsburgh, June 23, 1963); *Music for Band* (1963; transcribed by William Schaefer from *Music for Orchestra*). **CHAMBER:** 2 piano trios (1918, lost; 1935); 3 string quartets (1920; 1924, rev. 1928; 1955); Sonata for Violin, Piano, and Snare Drum (1927; rev. in 1967 as Sonata for Violin, Piano, and Percussion); Cello Sonata (1929); *Arabesque* for Cello or Bassoon, and Piano (1931); *Variations and Epilogue* for Cello and Piano (1946; orchestration, 1973); Violin Sonata No. 2 (1948); *Fantasia concertante* for Violin and Piano (1962); *Divertimento da camera* for 10 Instruments (1965). **PIANO:** *4 Small Piano Pieces* (1920); Prelude and Fugue (1920); Sonatina (1926; rev. 1967); *2 Pieces* for Mechanical Piano (1927; lost); *2 danses ironiques* (1928; rev. 1967); *5 Contrasts* (1930); *Dialogues* (1932); *Variations* (1933); Sonata (1943); *Intervals*, 7 studies (1957); also songs.
BIBL.: W. Critser, compiler, *The Compositions of N. L.: A Catalogue* (privately publ., Pittsburgh, 1979).

Lopes-Graça, Fernando, eminent Portuguese composer, musicologist, pianist, and pedagogue; b. Tomar, Dec. 17, 1906.

He took piano lessons at home, then studied with Merea and da Motta (piano), Borba (composition), and de Freitas Branco (theory and musicology) at the Lisbon Cons. (1923–31); also studied at the Univ. of Lisbon (1932–36). He taught at the Coimbra music inst. (1932–36). In 1937 he left his homeland for political reasons; went to Paris, where he studied composition and orchestration with Koechlin, and musicology with Masson at the Sorbonne. After the outbreak of World War II (1939), he returned to Lisbon, where he served as a prof. at the Academia de Amadores de Música (1941–54); from 1950 was director of its chorus, a position he held for 40 years; also made appearances as a pianist. His music is inspired by nationalistic themes, and is inherently lyrical. He publ. some 25 books, including *Música e músicos modernos (Aspectos, obras, personalidades)* (Oporto, 1943; 2nd ed., 1985); with T. Borba, *Dicionário de música* (Lisbon, 1956–58); *Escritos musicológicos* (Lisbon, 1977); also biographies of Mozart, Chopin, and Bartók. With M. Giacometti, he publ. the 1st vol. of the *Antologia da Música Regional Portuguesa*, the 1st attempt to collect, in a systematic way, the regional songs of Portugal.
WORKS: STAGE: *La Fièvre du temps*, revue-ballet (1938); *D. Duardos e Flérida*, cantata-melodrama (1964–69; Lisbon, Nov. 28, 1970); *Dançares*, choreographic suite (1984). **ORCH.:** *Poemeto* for Strings (1928); *Prelúdio, Pastoral e Dança* (1929); 2 piano concertos (1940, 1942); *3 Portuguese Dances* (1941); Sinfonia (1944); *5 estelas funerárias* (1948); *Scherzo heróico* (1949); *Suite rústica No. 1* (1950–51); *Marcha festiva* (1954); Concertino for Piano, Strings, Brass, and Percussion (1954); *5 Old Portuguese Romances* (1951–55); *Divertimento* for Winds, Kettledrums, Percussion, Cellos, and Double Basses (1957); *Poema de Dezembro* (1961); Viola Concertino (1962); *4 bosquejos* (4 Sketches) for Strings (1965); *Concerto da camera*, with Cello obbligato (Moscow, Oct. 6, 1967; Rostropovich, soloist); *Viagens na minha terra* (1969–70); *Fantasia* for Piano and Orch., on a religious song from Beira-Baixa (1974); *Homenagem a Haydn*, sinfonietta (1980); *Em louvor da paz* (1986). **CHAMBER:** *Estudo-Humoresca* for Flute, Oboe, Clarinet, 2 Violins, Viola, and Cello (1930); Piano Quartet (1939; rev. 1963); *Prelúdio, Capricho e Galope* for Violin and Piano (1941; rev. 1951); *Página esquecida* for Cello and Piano (1955); *Canto de Amor e de Morte* for Piano Quintet (1961); String Quartet (1964); *Suite rústica No. 2* for String Quartet (1965); *14 anotações* for String Quartet (1966); *7 souvenirs for Vieira da Silva* for Wind Quintet (1966); *The Tomb of Villa-Lobos* for Wind Quintet (1970); *3 capriccetti* for Flute and Guitar (1975); *Quatro peças em suite* for Viola and Piano (1978); *Sete Apotegmas* for Oboe, Viola, Double Bass, and Piano (1981); *Homenagem a Beethoven—Três Equali* for Double-bass Quartet (1986); *Geórgicas* for Oboe, Viola, Double Bass, and Piano (1989). **PIANO:** 6 sonatas (1934; 1939, rev. 1956; 1952; 1961; 1977; 1981); *8 Bagatelles* (1939–48; No. 4, 1950); *Glosas* (Glosses, 1950); *24 Preludes* (1950–55); *Album do jovem pianista* (1953–63); *In Memoriam Béla Bartók*, 8 progressive suites (1960–75); *4 Impromptus* (1961); *Piano Music for Children* (1968–76); *Melodias rústicas portuguesas* No. 3 for Piano, 4-hands (1979); *Deploração na morte trágica de Samora Machel* (1986); *Pranto à memória de Francisco Miguel, uma vida heróica* (1988). **GUITAR:** *Prelúdio e Baileto* (1968); *Partita* (1970–71); Sonatina (1974); *Quatro peças* (1979). **VOCAL:** *Pequeno cancioneiro do Menino Jesus* for Women's Chorus, 2 Flutes, String Quartet, Celesta, and Harp (1936–59); *História trágicomarítima* for Baritone, Contralto, Chorus, and Orch. (1942–59); *9 Portuguese Folk Songs* for Voice and Orch. (1948–49); *4 Songs of Federico García Lorca* for Baritone, 2 Clarinets, Violin, Viola, Cello, Harp, and Percussion (1953–54); *Cantos do Nata* for Female Voices and Instrumental Ensemble (1958); *9 cantigas de amigo* for Voice and Chamber Ensemble (1964); *6 cantos sefardins* for Voice and Orch. (1971); *. . . meu país de marinheiros . . .* for Narrator, 4 Women's Voices, 4 Men's Voices, Flute, and Guitars (1981); many choruses; songs.
BIBL.: M. Henriques, *F. L.G. na música portuguesa contemporanea* (Sacavém, 1956).

Lopez, Vincent (Joseph), American pianist, bandleader, and composer; b. Brooklyn, Dec. 30, 1894; d. North Miami Beach, Fla., Sept. 20, 1975. His father, of Portuguese ancestry, a bandmaster in the U.S. Navy, taught Lopez the rudiments of music. However, he sent him to St. Mary's Passionist Monastery in the hope that he would become a Roman Catholic priest. But Lopez turned to music, and as a teenager played in the beer halls of Brooklyn. Later he led restaurant orchs. in N.Y. In 1927 he inaugurated a regular broadcasting hour of dance band music over the radio station WJX in Newark, on which he popularized the song *Nola*, using it as a signature, opening with a greeting, "Hello, everybody . . . Lopez speaking." He had the 1st sustaining television show, "Dinner Date with Lopez," which featured show-business personalities. Among his song hits were *Rockin' Chair Swing; Knock, Knock, Who's There?;* and *The World Stands Still.* He also gave lectures on numerology and related pseudo-sciences.

López-Buchardo, Carlos, Argentine composer; b. Buenos Aires, Oct. 12, 1881; d. there, April 21, 1948. He studied piano and harmony in Buenos Aires and composition with Albert Roussel in Paris. He was founder-director of the National Cons. in Buenos Aires (1924–48); also founded the school of fine arts at the Univ. of La Plata, where he was a prof. of harmony. His music is set in a vivid style, rooted in national folk song; particularly successful in this respect is his symphonic suite *Escenas argentinas* (Buenos Aires, Aug. 12, 1922). His other works are the opera *El sueño de alma* (Buenos Aires, Aug. 4, 1914; won the Municipal Prize); lyric comedies: *Madama Lynch* (1932); *La perichona* (1933); *Amalia* (1935); several piano pieces in an Argentine folk manner; songs.

López-Calo, José, Spanish Jesuit priest and music scholar; b. Nebra, La Coruña, Feb. 4, 1922. After graduating with degrees in philosophy and theology from the Univs. of Comillas and Granada, he studied church music at the Madrid High School of Sacred Music and musicology with Anglés at the Rome Pontifical Inst. for Sacred Music (Ph.D., 1962, with the diss. *La música en la catedral de Granada;* publ. in Granada, 1963). He served as assistant to Anglés (1964–65), then was prof. of musicology at the Pontifical Inst. for Sacred Music (1965–70); also was musical adviser for the Vatican Radio (1962–70) and general secretary of the International Soc. for Church Music (1964–70). In 1970 he returned to Spain to pursue research in Spanish cathedral archives; in 1973 he became prof. of music history at the Univ. of Santiago de Compostela, and was made prof. emeritus upon his retirement in 1988. His valuable research is reflected in his cataloging of musical archives and in the gathering of an immense collection of firsthand documentation on music history.
Writings: *Canti sacri per la Santa Messa* (Rome, 1965; 2nd ed., 1967); *Presente y futuro de la música sagrada* (Madrid, 1967; Italian tr., Rome, 1968); *Catálogo musical del archivo de la santa iglesia catedral de Santiago* (Cuenca, 1972); *Hygini Anglés Scripta musicologica* (3 vols., Rome, 1976); *Catálogo del archivo de música de la catedral de Ávila* (Santiago de Compostela, 1978); *Francisco Valls: Missa Scala Aretina* (London, 1978); *Esencia de la música sagrada* (La Coruña, 1980); *La música en la catedral de Palencia* (2 vols., Palencia, 1981); *La música medieval en Galicia* (La Coruña, 1982); *Indices de la revista Tesoro Sacro Musical* (Madrid, 1983); *Historia de la música española en el siglo XVII* (Madrid, 1983); *The Symphony in Spain: 3 Symphonies by José Pons* (N.Y., 1983); *La música en la catedral de Zamora* (Zamora, 1985); *Las sonatas de Beethoven para piano* (Santiago de Compostela, 1985); *Melchor López: Misa de Requiem* (Santiago de Compostela, 1987); *La música en la catedral de Segovia* (Segovia, 1988); *Catálogo del archivo de música de la catedral de Santo Domingo de La Calzada* (Logroño, 1988).

López-Cobos, Jesús, distinguished Spanish conductor; b. Toro, Feb. 25, 1940. He took a doctorate in philosophy at the Univ. of Madrid; also courses in conducting with Ferrara in Venice, Swarowsky at the Vienna Academy of Music, Maag at the Accademia Chigiana in Siena, and Morel at the Juilliard School of Music in N.Y. In 1969 he won 1st prize at the Besançon Competition; that same year he conducted at the Prague Spring Festival and at the Teatro La Fenice in Venice; subsequently was a regular conductor at the Deutsche Oper in West Berlin (1970–75). In 1972 he made his American debut with the San Francisco Opera, and thereafter appeared as a guest conductor throughout the U.S. He was Generalmusikdirektor of the Deutsche Oper in West Berlin (1980–90), chief conductor of the Orquesta Nacional de España in Madrid (1984–89), and music director of the Cincinnati Sym. Orch. (from 1986) and of the Lausanne Chamber Orch. (from 1990).

Lo Presti, Ronald, American composer; b. Williamstown, Mass., Oct. 28, 1933. He studied composition with Louis Mennini and Bernard Rogers at the Eastman School of Music in Rochester, N.Y. (M.M., 1956); subsequently was engaged as a clarinet teacher in public schools; in 1964 was appointed an instructor in music theory at Arizona State Univ. at Tempe. He obtained popular success with his score *The Masks,* which was commissioned for the space exhibit at the aerospace building at the Smithsonian Inst.
Works: stage: *The Birthday,* opera (1962; Winfield, May 1962); *Playback,* children's opera (Tucson, Ariz., Dec. 18, 1970). orch.: *The Masks* (Rochester, May 8, 1955); *Nocturne* for Small Orch. (1955–56); *Nocturne* for Viola and String Orch. (1959); *Kansas Overture* (1960); *Kanza Suite* (1961); *Llano estacado* (The Staked Plain; 1961); *Port Triumphant* (1962); 2 syms. (1966, 1968); *From the Southwest* (1967); *Rhapsody* for Marimba, Vibraphone, and Orch. (1975). vocal: *Alleluia* for Chorus, Brass, and Timpani (1960); *Kanza* for 4 Narrators, Chorus, and Orch. (1961); *Tribute* for Chorus, and Orch. and/or Band (1962); *Scarecrow* for Children's Ballet Co., Mixed Voices, and Cello Orch. (1973); *Ode to Independence* for Baritone, Chorus, and Band (1974); *Requiem* for Chorus and Orch. (1975); *Memorials* for Chorus and Orch. (1975); choruses; songs. symphonic band: *Pageant* (1956); *Prelude* (1959); *Introduction, Chorale and Jubilee* (1961); *Tundra* (1967); *A Festive Music* (1968). chamber: *Suite* for 8 Horns (1952); *Sketch* for Percussion (1956); *Suite* for 4 Horns (1958); *5 Pieces* for Violin and Piano (1960); *Scherzo* for Violin Quartet (1960); *Chorale* for 3 Tubas (1960); *Fanfare* for 38 Brasses (1960); *Requiescat* for Brass Ensemble (1961); *Suite* for 5 Trumpets (1961); *Miniature* for Brass Quartet (1962); *Rondo* for Timpani and Piano (1969); Trio for 3 Percussionists (1971); String Quartet (1970); *Suite* for 6 Bassoons (1971); Fantasy for 5 Horns (1972); *Cantalena* for Cello Orch. (1972); Wind Quintet (1975).

Lorengar, Pilar (real name, **Pilar Lorenza Garcia**), prominent Spanish soprano; b. Saragossa, Jan. 16, 1928. She studied in with Angeles Ottein in Madrid, where she made her debut as a mezzo-soprano in zarzuela (1949); after becoming a soprano in 1951, she made her operatic debut as Cherubino at the Aix-en-Provence Festival. Her 1st appearance in the U.S. took place that same year as Rosario in a concert perf. of *Goyescas* in N.Y. She made her debut at London's Covent Garden as Violetta in 1955, making frequent appearances there from 1964; also sang at the Glyndebourne Festivals (1956–60) and the Berlin Deutsche Oper (from 1958). On Feb. 11, 1966, she made her Metropolitan Opera debut in N.Y. as Donna Elvira. She was named a Kammersängerin of the Berlin Deutsche Oper in 1963, and in 1984 Lifetime Member of the company on the occasion of her 25th anniversary with them. On Sept. 29, 1989, she received the San Francisco Opera Medal in an on-stage ceremony after their final performance of *Falstaff* in that season. She also received the Medallo d'Oro de Zaragoza of Saragossa and the Order of Isabella de Catolica (1965). Among her finest roles are Donna Anna, Fiordiligi, Countess Almaviva, Alice Ford, Eva, and Mélisande.
Bibl.: W. Elsner and M. Busch, *P. L.: ein Portrait* (Berlin, 1985).

Lorentz, Alfred, German composer and conductor; b. Strasbourg, March 7, 1872; d. Karlsruhe, April 23, 1931. He studied with Rheinberger in Munich (composition), and with Mottl at Karlsruhe (conducting). He was chorus master, and later conductor, at the Municipal Theater in Strasbourg; from 1899 to 1925, was court conductor in Karlsruhe. He wrote the operas *Der Mönch von Sendomir* (Karlsruhe, 1907), *Die beiden Automaten* (Karlsruhe, 1913), *Liebesmacht* (Karlsruhe, 1922), and *Schneider Fips* (Coburg, 1928); an operetta, *Die Mondscheindame* (Karlsruhe, 1919); some orch. works.

Lorentzen, Bent, Danish composer; b. Stenvad, Feb. 11, 1935. He studied with Knud Jeppesen at the Univ. of Århus and with Vagn Holmboe, Jørgen Jersild, and Finn Høffding at the Royal Danish Cons. of Music in Copenhagen (graduated, 1960); worked at the Stockholm electronic music studio (1967–68); after teaching at the Århus Cons. (1962–71), he settled in Copenhagen and devoted himself to composition; in 1982 he was awarded a State Grant for Life. Among his honors are the Prix Italia (1970) and 1st prizes in the "Homage to Kazimierz Serocki" International Competition (1984) and the Spittal International Composition Competition (1987). In his music he employs a variety of quaquaversal techniques, often utilizing highly sonorous effects.

WORKS: OPERAS: *Stalten Mette* (Århus, Nov. 17, 1963; rev. 1980); *Die Schlange* (1964; rev. 1974); *Eurydike* (1965; Danish Radio, Dec. 16, 1969); *Die Musik kommt mir äusserst bekannt vor* (Kiel, May 3, 1974); *Eine wundersame Liebesgeschichte* (Munich, Dec. 2, 1979); *Klovnen Toto* (1982); *Fackeltanz* (1986). **INSTRUMENTAL THEATER:** *Studies for 2* for Cello or Guitar, and Percussion (1967); *Studies for 3* for Soprano, Cello or Guitar, and Percussion (1968); *The End* for Cello (1969); *Friisholm,* film (1971); *3 Mobiles* for 3 Different Instruments (1979; rev. 1988). **ORCH.:** *Deep* (1967; rev. 1981); *Tide* (Copenhagen, March 31, 1971); *Partita popolare* for String Orch. (1976); Oboe Concerto (1980; Danish Radio, Feb. 18, 1982); Cello Concerto (Danish Radio, May 11, 1984); Piano Concerto (1984; Odense, Jan. 11, 1985); *Latin Suite I* (1984; also for Symphonic Band); Saxophone Concerto (1986; Danish Radio, March 6, 1987); *Latin Suite II* for Symphonic or Brass Band (1987). **CHAMBER:** *Quadrata* for String Quartet (1963); *Cyclus I* for Viola, Cello, and Double Bass (1966; rev. 1986), *II* for 2 Percussion and Harp (1966; rev. 1987), and *III* for Cello and Tape (1966; rev. 1981); *Syncretism* for Clarinet, Trombone, Cello, and Piano (1970); *Quartetto rustico* for String Quartet (1972); *Contorni* for Violin, Cello, and Piano (1978); *Samba* for Clarinet, Trombone, Cello, and Piano (1980); *Wunderblumen* for 12 Musicians (1982); *Mambo* for Clarinet, Cello, and Piano (1982); *Paradiesvogel* for Flute, Clarinet, Violin, Cello, Guitar, Percussion, and Piano (1983; Warsaw, July 7, 1984); *Dunkelblau* for Flute, Viola, and Harp (1985); also piano pieces; organ music; choral and other vocal works; tape pieces.

Lorenz, Alfred (Ottokar), Austrian musicologist, composer, and conductor; b. Vienna, July 11, 1868; d. Munich, Nov. 20, 1939. He studied with Radecke (conducting) and Spitta (musicology) in Berlin. He was a conductor in Königsberg, Elberfeld, and Munich (1894–97), then became a conductor (1898) and later chief conductor (1904) in Coburg; was made director of its Opera (1917); was also director of the Musikverein in Gotha (1901–18) and Coburg (1907–20). He then gave up his conducting career and studied musicology with Moritz Bauer at the Univ. of Frankfurt (graduated, 1922); lectured at the Univ. of Munich from 1923. He made a specialty of Wagnerian research; publ. the comprehensive work *Das Geheimnis der Form bei Richard Wagner* (4 vols., Berlin, 1924–33; 2nd ed., 1966); also publ. *Alessandro Scarlattis Jugendoper* (Augsburg, 1927) and *Abendländische Musikgeschichte im Rhythmus der Generationen* (Berlin, 1928). He composed an opera, *Helges Erwachen* (Schwerin, 1896); incidental music to various plays; symphonic poems: *Bergfahrt* and *Columbus;* chamber music; songs.

Lorenz, Max, greatly admired German tenor; b. Düsseldorf, May 17, 1901; d. Salzburg, Jan. 11, 1975. He studied with Grenzebach in Berlin; made his debut as Walther von der Vogelweide in *Tannhäuser* at the Dresden State Opera (1927); sang at the Berlin State Opera (1929–44) and the Vienna State Opera (1929–33; 1936–44; 1954). He made his Metropolitan Opera debut in N.Y. as Walther von Stolzing in *Die Meistersinger von Nürnberg* on Nov. 12, 1931; was again on its roster in 1933–34 and from 1947 to 1950; was also on the roster of the Chicago Opera (1939–40). He also sang at London's Covent Garden (1934, 1937), the Bayreuth Festivals (1933–39; 1952), and the Salzburg Festivals (1953–55; 1961). Lorenz was particularly esteemed as a Wagnerian; was also a noted Florestan, Othello, and Bacchus.

BIBL.: W. Hermann, *M. L.* (1976).

Lorenzani, Paolo, Italian composer; b. Rome, 1640; d. there, Oct. 28, 1713. He was a pupil of Orazio Benevoli at the Vatican; having failed to obtain Benevoli's position after the latter's death in 1672, he was given the post of maestro di cappella at the Jesuit church, the Gesù, and at the Seminario Romano in Rome in 1675; from 1675 to 1678, held a similar position at the Messina Cathedral; when Sicily was captured by the French, the Duc de Vivonne, who was the French viceroy, induced Lorenzani to go to Paris (1678); he found favor with Louis XIV, with whose financial support he purchased the post of Surintendant de la musique de la Reyne (1679); held that post until the Queen's death (1683), then was maître de chapelle to the Italian Théatine religious order (1685–87). He produced the Italian pastoral *Nicandro e Fileno* (Fontainebleau, Sept. 1681); having won the support of the Paris faction opposed to Lully, he produced an opera with a French libretto, *Orontée* (Paris, Aug. 23, 1687). This having failed, Lorenzani turned to the composition of motets, which proved his best works; the famous Paris publisher Ballard brought them out in an impressively printed ed.; Ballard also publ. a book of Italian airs by Lorenzani. In 1694 Lorenzani returned to Italy, and was appointed maestro di cappella of the Cappella Giulia at the Vatican.

WORKS: SACRED: Motet for 2 Voices and Basso Continuo (1675); Motet for 3 Voices and Basso Continuo (1675); (25) *Motets à I, II, III, IV, et V parties* (Paris, 1693); Mass for 2 Choirs and Basso Continuo; Magnificat for 2 Choirs and Basso Continuo. **SECULAR:** 4 airs and cantatas for Voice and Basso Continuo (publ. in the *Mercure Galant,* May 1680); (6) *Airs italiens de M. Lorenzani* (Paris, 1695); other airs, arias, and cantatas.

BIBL.: W. Gürtelschmied, "P. L. (1640–1713): Seine Tätigkeiten in Paris und Rom," *Internationaler musikwissen schaftlicher Kongress: Berlin 1974;* idem, *P. L. (1640–1713): Leben, Werk, thematischer Katalog* (diss., Univ. of Vienna, 1975).

Lorenzi-Fabris, Ausonio de, Italian composer; b. Montebelluna, Jan. 18, 1861; d. Venice, July 30, 1935. He studied at the Liceo Benedetto Marcello in Venice. He composed the operas *Gli Adorati del fuoco* (Venice, Jan. 27, 1891); *Maometto II* (Venice, July 9, 1892; rev., Florence, May 9, 1903); *Il Re si annoia* (Trieste, Dec. 19, 1904); a religious play, *Refugium peccatorum* (Venice, March 24, 1897).

Lorenzo, Leonardo de, Italian-American flutist, teacher, and composer; b. Viggiano, Aug. 29, 1875; d. Santa Barbara, Calif., July 27, 1962. He studied at the Naples Cons.; from 1897 to 1907, was a flutist in various traveling orchs. In 1910 he emigrated to the U.S.; was 1st flutist of the N.Y. Phil. (1910–12); later with the Minneapolis Sym. Orch., the Los Angeles Phil., and the Rochester Phil.; taught flute at the Eastman School of Music in Rochester, N.Y.; in 1935, settled in California. He publ. several books of flute studies and some solo pieces, and an informative book on flute playing and flute players, *My Complete Story of the Flute* (N.Y., 1951).

Loriod, Yvonne, distinguished French pianist and teacher; b. Houilles, Seine-et-Oise, Jan. 20, 1924. She studied at the Paris Cons., winning no less than 7 premiers prix; among her mentors were Nelly Eminger-Sivade, L. Lévy, I. Philipp, and Marcel Ciampi for piano, C. Estyle for piano accompaniment, Joseph Calvet for chamber music, S. Plé-Caussade for fugue, and Messiaen and Milhaud for composition. After World War II, she toured extensively; made her U.S. debut in the premiere of Messiaen's *Turangalila-Symphonie* with the Boston Sym. Orch. (Dec. 2, 1949). She taught at the Paris Cons. A foremost champion of the music of Messiaen, she married him in 1961. She also excelled in performances of the music of Bartók, Schoenberg, and Boulez.

Lortzing, (Gustav) Albert, celebrated German opera composer; b. Berlin, Oct. 23, 1801; d. there, Jan. 21, 1851. His parents were actors, and the wandering life led by the family did not allow him to pursue a methodical course of study. He learned acting from his father, and music from his mother at an early age. After some lessons in piano with Griebel and in theory with Rungenhagen in Berlin, he continued his own studies, and soon began to compose. On Jan. 30, 1823, he married the actress Rosina Regina Ahles in Cologne; they had 11 children. In 1824 he wrote his stage work, the singspiel *Ali Pascha von Janina, oder Die Franzosen in Albanien,* which, however, was not produced until 4 years later (Münster, Feb. 1, 1828). He then brought out the liederspiel *Der Pole und sein Kind, oder Der Feldwebel vom IV. Regiment* (1832) and the singspiel *Szenen aus Mozarts Leben* (Osnabrück, Oct. 11, 1832), which were well received on several German stages. From 1833 to 1844 he was engaged at the Municipal Theater of Leipzig as a tenor; there he launched a light opera, *Die beiden Schützen* (Feb. 20, 1837), which became instantly popular; on the same stage he produced, on Dec. 22, 1837, his undoubted masterpiece, *Czaar und Zimmermann, oder Die zwei Peter.* It was performed with enormous success in Berlin (1839), and then in other European music centers. His next opera, *Caramo, oder Das Fischerstechen* (Leipzig, Sept. 20, 1839), was a failure; there followed *Hans Sachs* (Leipzig, June 23, 1840) and *Casanova* (Leipzig, Dec. 31, 1841), which passed without much notice; subsequent comparisons showed some similarities between *Hans Sachs* and *Die Meistersinger von Nürnberg,* not only in subject matter, which was derived from the same source, but also in some melodic patterns; however, no one seriously suggested that Wagner was influenced by Lortzing's inferior work. There followed a comic opera, *Der Wildschütz, oder Die Stimme der Natur* (Leipzig, Dec. 31, 1842), which was in many respects the best that Lortzing wrote, but its success, although impressive, never equaled that of *Czaar und Zimmermann.* At about the same time, Lortzing attempted still another career, that of opera impresario, but it was short-lived; his brief conductorship at the Leipzig Opera (1844–45) was similarly ephemeral. Composing remained his chief occupation; he produced *Undine* in Magdeburg (April 21, 1845) and *Der Waffenschmied* in Vienna (May 30, 1846). He then went to Vienna as conductor at the Theater an der Wien, but soon returned to Leipzig, where he produced the light opera *Zum Grossadmiral* (Dec. 13, 1847). The revolutionary events of 1848 seriously affected his position in both Leipzig and Vienna; after the political situation became settled, he produced in Leipzig an opera of a Romantic nature, *Rolands Knappen, oder Das ersehnte Gluck* (May 25, 1849). Although at least 4 of his operas were played at various German theaters, Lortzing received no honorarium, owing to a flaw in the regulations protecting the rights of composers. He was compelled to travel again as an actor, but could not earn enough money to support his large family, left behind in Vienna. In the spring of 1850 he obtained the post of conductor at Berlin's nondescript Friedrich-Wilhelmstadt Theater. His last score, the comic opera *Die Opernprobe, oder Die vornehmen Dilettanten,* was produced in Frankfurt am Main on Jan. 20, 1851, while he was on his deathbed in Berlin; he died the next day. His opera *Regina,* written in 1848, was ed. by Richard Kleinmichel, with the composer's libretto revised by Adolf L'Arronge, and performed in Berlin as *Regina, oder Die Marodeure* on March 21, 1899; his singspiel *Der Weihnachtsabend* was produced in Münster on Dec. 21, 1832. Lortzing also wrote an oratorio, *Die Himmelfahrt Jesu Christi* (Münster, Nov. 15, 1828); some incidental music to various plays; choral works; and songs. But it is as a composer of characteristically German Romantic operas that Lortzing holds a distinguished, if minor, place in the history of dramatic music. He was a follower of Weber, without Weber's imaginative projection; in his lighter works,

he approached the type of French operetta; in his best creations he exhibited a fine sense of facile melody, and infectious rhythm; his harmonies, though unassuming, were always proper and pleasing; his orchestration, competent and effective.

BIBL.: P. Düringer, *A. L., Sein Leben und Wirken* (Leipzig, 1851); H. Wittmann, *L.* (Leipzig, 1890; 2nd ed., 1902); G. Kruse, *A. L.* (Berlin, 1899); R. Bürner, *A. L. in Detmold, Pyrmont, Münster und Osnabrück* (Detmold, 2nd ed., 1900); G. Kruse, ed., *A. L.: Gesammelte Briefe* (Leipzig, 1902; 2nd ed., augmented, 1913; 3rd ed., 1947); idem, *A. L.: Leben und Werk* (Leipzig, 1914; 2nd ed., 1947); H. Laue, *Die Operndichtung L.s* (Würzburg, 1932); H. Killer, *A. L.* (Potsdam, 1938); O. Schumann, *A. L. 1801–1851: Sein Leben in Bildern* (Leipzig, 1941); G. Dippel, *A. L.: Ein Leben für das deutsche Musiktheater* (Berlin, 1951); H. Burgmüller, *Die Musen darben: Ein Lebensbild A. L.s* (Berlin, 1955); M. Hoffmann, *G.A. L., der Meister der deutschen Volksoper* (Leipzig, 1956); E. Lotzing, *A. L.: Zur Familienchronik L.-L.* (Starnberg, 1963); H. Schirmag, *A. L.: Ein Lebens- und Zeitbild* (Berlin, 1982).

Löschhorn, (Carl) Albert, German pianist, composer, and pedagogue; b. Berlin, June 27, 1819; d. there, June 4, 1905. He studied at the Royal Inst. for Church Music with L. Berger, Killitschgy, Grell, and A.W. Bach; became a piano teacher there in 1851. He publ. a series of excellent piano studies, including *Melodious Studies, La Vélocité, Universal Studies, Le Trille,* and *School of Octaves,* which became standard pedagogical works; also wrote attractive piano solos: *La Belle Amazone,* 4 *pièces élégantes, Tarentelle;* 2 *valses,* the barcarolle *A Venise,* and 3 *mazurkas;* suites, sonatas, sonatinas, etc. With J. Weiss he publ. a *Wegweiser in die Pianoforte-Literatur* (1862; 2nd ed., 1885, as *Führer durch die Klavierliteratur*).

Lott, Felicity (Ann), English soprano; b. Cheltenham, May 8, 1947. She studied in London at Royal Holloway College, Univ. of London, and at the Royal Academy of Music; in 1976 she sang at Covent Garden in the world premiere of Henze's *We Come to the River;* she also appeared there as Anne Trulove in Stravinsky's *The Rake's Progress,* as Octavian in *Der Rosenkavalier,* and in various other roles. She appeared in Paris for the 1st time in 1976; made her Vienna debut in 1982 singing the 4 *Letze Lieder* of Strauss; in 1984 was engaged as soloist with the Chicago Sym. Orch. In 1986 she sang at the wedding of the Duke and the Duchess of York at Westminster Abbey. In 1990 she was made a Commander of the Order of the British Empire. On Sept. 4, 1990, she made her Metropolitan Opera debut in N.Y. as the Marschallin. Among her finest roles are Pamina, Countess Almaviva, Donna Elvira, Oktavian, Arabella, and Anne Trulove.

Lotti, Antonio, eminent Italian organist, pedagogue, and composer; b. probably in Venice, c.1667; d. there, Jan. 5, 1740. He was a student of Legrenzi in Venice by 1683, then became an extra (1687) and regular (1689) singer at S. Marco; was made assistant to the 2nd organist (1690), 2nd organist (1692), 1st organist (1704), and primo maestro di cappella (1736). He visited Novara (1711) and later was in Dresden at the Crown Prince's invitation (1717–19). Lotti was one of the most important composers of the late Baroque and early Classical eras in Italy; his sacred music and madrigals are particularly notable. He was held in great esteem as a pedagogue, numbering among his students Domenico Alberti, Baldassari Galuppi, Michelangelo Gasparini, and Benedetto Marcello. His *Duetti, terzetti e madrigali a più voci,* op. 1 (Venice, 1705), dedicated to Emperor Joseph I, includes the madrigal *In una siepe ombrosa;* it was arranged by Bononcini and presented as his own work in London in 1731, but Lotti successfully defended his authorship in 1732. Much of his music is not extant.

WORKS: OPERAS (all 1st perf. in Venice unless otherwise given): *Il trionfo dell'innocenza* (1692); *Tirsi,* dramma pastorale (1696; Act 1 by Lotti); *Sidonio* (1706); *Achille placato,* tragedia per musica (1707); *Le rovine de Troja,* intermezzo (1707); *Dragontana e Policrone,* intermezzo (1707); *Teuzzone* (1707; rev. by G. Vignola as *L'inganno vinto dalla ragione,* Naples, Nov. 19, 1708); *Cortulla e Lardone,* intermezzo (1707);

Il Vincitor generoso (Jan. 10, 1708); *Il comando non inteso et ubbidito* (Feb. 6, 1709); *La Ninfa Apollo*, scherzo comico pastorale (Feb. 12, 1709; in collaboration with F. Gasparini); *Ama più chi men si crede*, melodramma pastorale (Nov. 20, 1709); *Isacio tiranno* (1710); *Il tradimento traditor di se stesso* (Jan. 17, 1711; rev. by F. Mancini as *Artaserse, re di Persia*, Naples, Oct. 1, 1713); *La forza del sangue* (Nov. 14, 1711); *Porsenna* (1712; rev. by A. Scarlatti, Naples, Nov. 19, 1713); *L'infedeltà punita* (Nov. 12, 1712; in collaboration with C. Pollarolo); *Irene augusta* (1713); *Polidoro*, tragedia per musica (1714); *Ciro in Babilonia* (Reggio Emilia, April 1716); *Costantino* (Vienna, Nov. 19, 1716; in collaboration with others); *Foca superbo* (Dec. 1716); *Alessandro Severo* (Dec. 26, 1716); *Giove in Argo*, melodramma pastorale (Dresden, Oct. 25, 1717); *Ascanio, ovvero Gli odi delusi dal sangue* (Dresden, Feb. 1718); *Teofane* (Dresden, Sept. 13, 1719); *Li quattro elementi*, carosello teatrale (Dresden, Sept. 15, 1719); *Griletta e Serpillo*, intermezzo (n.d.). **ORATORIOS:** *La Giuditta* (1701); *Il voto crudele* (Vienna, 1712); *Triumphus fidei* (Venice, 1712); *L'umiltà coronata in Esther* (Vienna, c.1714); *Il ritorno di Tobia* (Bologna, 1723); *Gioas, re di Giuda* (Venice, n.d.); *Judith* (Venice, n.d.); other sacred music including masses and choral works. **INSTRUMENTAL:** Concerto for Oboe d'Amore and Strings; 6 sinfonie; 6 trios for Various Instruments; 6 sonatas for Violin and Basso Continuo; also numerous secular cantatas, [12] *Duetti*, [4] *terzetti e* [2] *madrigali a più voce* for Voices and Basso Continuo, op. 1 (Venice, 1705), and *Spirito di Dio ch'essendo il mondo* for 4 Voices and Basso Continuo (Ascension Day, 1736).

BIBL.: H. Bishop, ed., *Lettres from the Academy of Ancient Music of London to Signor A. L. of Venice with his Answers and Testimonies* (London, 1732); O. Chilesotti, *Sulla letteracritica di B. Marcello contro A. L.* (Bassano, 1885); C. Spitz, *A. L. in seiner Bedeutung als Opernkomponist* (diss., Univ. of Munich, 1918); R. Holden, *6 Extant Operas of A. L. (1667–1740)* (diss., Univ. of Conn., 1967); K. O'Donnell, *The Secular Solo Cantatas of A. L.* (diss., Iowa State Univ., 1975).

Lotze, Rudolf Hermann, German writer on music; b. Bautzen, May 21, 1817; d. Berlin, July 1, 1881. He became a prof. of philosophy at Leipzig Univ. in 1842; in 1844, prof. in ordinary, and court councillor at Göttingen; he settled in Berlin shortly before his death. He publ. *Geschichte der Ästhetik in Deutschland* (1868), which contains criticism of Helmholtz, Hauptmann, and others; also interesting ideas on musical esthetics.

Loucheur, Raymond, French composer; b. Tourcoing, Jan. 1, 1899; d. Nogent-sur-Marne, Sept. 14, 1979. He studied music with Henry Woollett at Le Havre (1915–18) and with Nadia Boulanger, Gédalge, d'Indy, Fauchet, and Paul Vidal at the Paris Cons. (1920–23). In 1928 he won the Premier Grand Prix de Rome for his cantata *Héracles à Delphe*. From 1925 to 1940 he was a teacher in Paris; in 1941, became the principal inspector of musical education in the Paris city schools and later was director of the Paris Cons. (1956–62). His music is chromatically lyrical and displays rhythmic spontaneity.

WORKS: Ballet, *Hop-Frog*, after Poe (1935–48; Paris, June 17, 1953). **ORCH.:** 2 symphonic suites, Paris, June 30, 1949; cantata, *Héracles à Delphe* (Le Havre, June 12, 1929); 3 syms.: No. 1 (1929–33; Paris, Dec. 15, 1936; rev. 1969); No. 2 (1944; Paris, Feb. 15, 1945); No. 3 (1971; Paris, Oct. 17, 1972); *En famille* for Chamber Orch. or Clarinet Sextet (1932; orchestrated 1940); 3 *Duos* for Soprano, Chorus, and Orch. (1934); *Défilé* for Orch. (1936); *L'Apothéose de la Seine* for Narrator, Mezzo-soprano, Chorus, Ondes Martenot, and Orch. (1937; Paris, July 7, 1937); *Pastorale* for Orch. (1939); *Rapsodie malgache* for Orch. (1945; Paris, Oct. 10, 1945); *Divertissement* for Orch. (1951); Concertino for Trumpet, and Orch. or Clarinet Sextet (1954; orchestrated 1956); Violin Concerto (1960–63; Paris, Feb. 28, 1965); Percussion Concertino (1963; Paris, Jan. 9, 1966); *Cortège, Interlude, et Danse* for Winds, Harp, and Percussion (1964–65); Cello Concerto (1967–68; Radio Luxembourg, July 11, 1968); *Thrène* for String Orch. and Flute (1971); *Hommage à Raoul Dufy* for Orch. (1973; Paris, Oct. 27, 1974); *Évocations* for Wind Orch. (1974; Paris, March 7,

1976). **CHAMBER:** String Quartet (1930); *En famille* for Clarinet Sextet (1932; orchestrated 1940); *La Ballade des petites filles qui n'ont pas de poupée* for 4 Soli, Chorus, and Piano (1936); *Portraits* for Clarinet, Oboe, and Bassoon (1947); *4 pièces en quintette* for Harp, Flute, Violin, Viola, and Cello (1953); Concertino for Trumpet and Clarinet Sextet (1954; orchestrated 1956); *5 poèmes de R.-M. Rilke* for Mezzo-soprano and String Quartet (1952–57); Solo Violin Sonata (1959); *Dialogues* for Flute and Harp; *Rencontres* for Oboe and Cello (1972); *Divertissement sur les flûtes* for 4 Flutes (1975); *Reflets* for Brass Quintet (1976); songs.

BIBL.: *Courrier Musical de France*, no. 68 (1979).

Loudová, Ivana, Czech composer; b. Chlumec nad Cidlinou, March 8, 1941. She studied composition with Kabeláč at the Prague Cons. (1958–61) and with Hlobil at the Prague Academy of Arts (1961–66); in 1971 she went to Paris, where she took lessons with Messiaen and Jolivet. Her music is richly dissonant and impressionistically colorful.

WORKS: ORCH.: *Fantasy* (1961); Concerto for Chamber Orch. (1962); Sym. No. 1 (1964); Sym. No. 2 for Contralto, Chorus, and Orch. (1965); *Spleen* (*Hommage à Charles Baudelaire*) (1971); *Chorale* for Wind Orch., Percussion, and Organ (1971); *Hymnos* for Wind Orch. and Percussion (1972); Concerto (1974); *Magic Concerto* (1976); *Dramatic Concerto* (1979); *Luminous Voice*, concerto for English Horn and Wind Orch. (1986); Double Concerto for Violin, Percussion, and Strings (1989). **CHAMBER:** Violin Sonata (1960–61); Clarinet Sonata (1963); 2 string quartets (1964; 1974–76); *Per tromba*, 5 studies for Trumpet (1969); *Agamemnon* for Percussion (1973); *Romeo and Juliet*, suite for Flute, 2 Violins, Cello, and Harp (1973); *Meditations* for Flute, Bass Clarinet, Piano, and Percussion (1977); *Hukvaldy Suite* for String Quartet (1984); *Trio Italiano* for Clarinet, Bassoon, and Piano (1988); *Don Giovanni's Dream*, fantasy for Wind Octet (1989); also various choral pieces.

Louël, Jean (Hippolyte Oscar), Belgian composer and conductor; b. Ostend, Jan. 3, 1914. He studied at the Ghent Cons. with Joseph Ryelandt (composition), and at the Brussels Cons. with Joseph Jongen (theory) and Désiré Defauw (conducting); then studied conducting with Eugène Bigot and Paul Paray at the Paris Cons. (diploma, 1943); won the Belgian Prix de Rome in 1943 for his cantata *La Navigation d'Ulysse*. He became a teacher at the Brussels Cons. (1943); was director of music academies in Alost (1945–49) and Anderlecht (1949–56). He was founder-conductor of the chamber orch. of the Concerts di Midi in Brussels (1949–70). In 1956 he became inspector of music schools in Flemish Belgium; in 1959, became a teacher of composition at the Chapelle Musicale Reine Elisabeth, retiring in 1984.

WORKS: ORCH.: *Fantaisie sur 2 chansons de trouvères* (1942); *Suite* for Chamber Orch. or Piano (1942); *Burlesque* for Bassoon and Orch. (1943); *March funèbre* and *Triomfmarch* (1945); 2 piano concertos (1945, 1949); *Concerto da camera* for Flute and Orch. (1946–47); 2 violin concertos (1950, 1971); Sym. No. 2 for String Orch. (1968; Sym. No. 1 withdrawn); *Toccata and Fugue* for Winds (1974); *Rhapsody* (1975); Horn Concerto (1981); Sym. No. 3 (1984–85); *Funeral Music* (1984); Cello Concerto (1986). **CHAMBER:** Clarinet Sonata (1935); Brass Trio (1951); Wind Quintet (1958); Violin Sonata (1960); *Suite* for Flute, Cello, Vibraphone, and Harp (1967); *L'Art d'être Grand'père*, 10 pieces for Piano (1978); Saxophone Quartet (1983); Sonata for Solo Violin (1985); Clarinet Quartet (1986).

Loughran, James, Scottish conductor; b. Glasgow, June 30, 1931. He studied with Peter Maag in Bonn, where he was a répétiteur at the City Theater; also studied in Amsterdam and Milan. From 1962 to 1965 he was associate conductor of the Bournemouth Sym. Orch.; then was principal conductor of the BBC Scottish Sym. Orch in Glasgow (1965–71). He served as principal conductor of the Hallé Orch. in Manchester (1971–83), and chief conductor of the Bamberg Sym. Orch. (1979–83); served as chief guest conductor of the BBC Welsh Sym. Orch. in Cardiff (from 1986).

Louis, Rudolf, German writer on music and composer; b. Schwetzingen, Jan. 30, 1870; d. Munich, Nov. 15, 1914. He studied philosophy at the Univs. of Geneva and Vienna (Ph.D., 1893); then had instruction from Klose (composition) and Mottl (conducting) in Karlsruhe; was conductor at the theaters in Landshut (1895–96) and in Lübeck (1896–97); in 1897, settled in Munich, where he became critic for the influential periodical *Neueste Nachrichten* (from 1900). He wrote a symphonic fantasy, *Proteus* (1903), as well as pieces for piano, 4-hands, and songs.

WRITINGS: *Die Weltanschauung Richard Wagners* (Leipzig, 1898); *Franz Liszt* (Berlin, 1900); *Hector Berlioz* (Leipzig, 1904); *Anton Bruckner* (Munich and Leipzig, 1904); with L. Thuille, *Harmonielehre* (1907; 10th ed., 1933; abridged as *Grundriss der Harmonielehre*, 1908); *Die deutsche Musik der Gegenwart* (Munich, 1909; 3rd ed., 1912); *Aufgaben für den Unterricht in der Harmonielehre* (Stuttgart, 1911); *Schlüssel für Harmonielehre* (Stuttgart, 1912).

Louis Ferdinand (actually, **Friedrich Christian Ludwig**), Prince of Prussia, German pianist and composer, nephew of **Frederick (Friedrich II) the Great;** b. Friedrichsfelde, near Berlin, Nov. 18, 1772; d. in battle in Saalfeld, Oct. 10, 1806. He showed remarkable talent as a pianist in childhood; was educated for a military career, entering the army in 1789; however, he continued his interest in music and later studied composition with Dussek in Hamburg, who subsequently entered his entourage (1804); that same year he met Beethoven, expressing great admiration for his music; in return, Beethoven dedicated his 3rd Piano Concerto to him.

WORKS (all publ. in Leipzig unless otherwise given): 2 piano quintets (Paris, 1803, 1806); 2 piano quartets (1806); 3 piano trios (Berlin, 1806); *Andante with Variations* for Violin, Viola, Cello, and Piano (1806); *Larghetto with Variations* for Violin, Viola, Cello, Double Bass, and Piano (Berlin, 1806); Fugue for Piano (1807); 2 Rondos for Piano and Orch. (1808, 1823); Octet (1808); *Nocturne* for Flute, Violin, Cello, and Piano (1808). H. Kretzschmar ed. his collected works (Leipzig, 1915–17).

BIBL.: E. Wintzer, *Prinz L. F. von Preussen als Mensch und Musiker* (Leipzig, 1915); R. Hahn, *L. F. von Preussen als Musiker* (diss., Univ. of Breslau, 1935); B. McMurty, *The Music of Prince L. F.* (diss., Univ. of Illinois, 1972).

Louis XIII, King of France from 1610 to 1643; b. Paris, Sept. 27, 1601; d. there, May 14, 1643. He was an amateur musician; among his works are a couple of airs de cour and some motets; he also wrote the words and music for *Le Ballet de la Merlaison* (Chantilly, March 15, 1635). The well-known *Amaryllis,* arranged by Henri Ghis and widely publ. as *Air of Louis XIII,* is a misattribution; the melody first appears in print as *La Clochette* in the *Ballet-Comique de la Reine* by Balthazar de Beaujoyeux, produced in 1582. A gavotte, also entitled *Amaryllis,* with a melody totally different from the apocryphal *Air of Louis XIII* and dated 1620, may be an authentic composition of Louis XIII.

BIBL.: R. Cotte, "L. XIII musicien," *La Vie musicale,* IV (1952).

Loulié, Étienne, French writer on music and inventor; b. probably in Paris, c.1655; d. there, c.1707. He studied with Gehenault and Ouvrard under the patronage of Mlle. de Guise; was at the Sainte-Chapelle in Paris from 1663 to 1673. He publ. *Éléments ou principes de musique dans un nouvel ordre . . . avec l'estampe et l'usage du chronomètre* (Paris, 1696; Eng. tr., 1965), which describes and illustrates his invention, the chronomètre, an unwieldy device 6 feet tall that was the precursor of the metronome; also publ. *Nouveau système de musique . . .* (Paris, 1698), describing his "sonomètre," a monochord to aid in tuning.

BIBL.: A. Cohen, "E. L. as a Music Theorist," *Journal of the American Musicological Society,* XVIII (1965).

Lourié, Arthur (Vincent), Russian-born American composer; b. St. Petersburg, May 14, 1892; d. Princeton, N.J.,

Oct. 13, 1966. He studied at the St. Petersburg Cons.; participated in various modernistic groups, and wrote piano music, much influenced by Scriabin (*Préludes fragiles, Synthèses,* etc.); experimented in futuristic composition (e.g., *Formes en l'air,* dedicated to Picasso, and graphically imitating a Cubist design by omitting the staves instead of using rests); also composed religious music (*Lamentations de la Vierge,* etc.). After the Soviet Revolution, he was appointed chief of the music dept. of the Commissariat for Public Instruction in 1918; in 1921 he went to Berlin, then lived in Paris from 1924; in 1941, emigrated to the U.S., and became a naturalized U.S. citizen in 1947. In his music written after 1920, he followed mainly Stravinsky's practice of stylizing early forms, secular and sacred. A vol. of essays and memoirs appeared as *Profanation et sanctification du temps* (Paris, 1966).

WORKS: *Nash marsh* (Our March), to a poem by Mayakovsky, for Declamation with Piano (1918); *La Naissance de la beauté,* cantata for a Chorus of 6 Sopranos, Soprano Solo, and Piano (1922); *Dithyrambes* for Flute (1923); *Liturgical Sonata* for Piano, Chorus, and Orch. (1928); *Concerto spirituale* for Piano, Chorus, and Double Basses (N.Y., March 26, 1930); *Sinfonia dialectica,* Sym. No. 1 (Philadelphia, April 17, 1931); *Kormtschaya,* Sym. No. 2 (Boston, Nov. 7, 1941); *The Feast during the Plague,* opera-ballet after Pushkin (1935; arranged for Soprano Solo, Chorus, and Orch.; Boston, Jan. 5, 1945); *De ordinatione angelorum* for Chorus (1948); *Piano Gosse* (1917; republ. in N.Y., 1944, under the title *8 Scenes of Russian Childhood*); 2 pieces for Piano: *Berceuse de la chevrette* (1936) and *A Phoenix Park Nocturne* (1938); *The Mime* for Clarinet (1956); *Concerto da camera* for Violin Solo and String Orch. (1957); *The Blackamoor of Peter the Great,* opera (1961).

BIBL.: G. Camajani, "The Music of A. L.," *Ramparts* (Menlo Park, Calif., Jan. 1965); D. Gojowy, "Zwölftontechnik in Russland," *Melos* (May–June 1972).

Love, Shirley, American mezzo-soprano; b. Detroit, Jan. 6, 1940. She studied voice in Detroit with Avery Crew and in N.Y. with Marinka Gurewich and Margaret Harshaw; then sang with the Baltimore Opera (1962). She first appeared in a minor role at the Metropolitan Opera in N.Y. on Nov. 30, 1963; subsequently gained experience as a singer with other American opera companies; returned to the Metropolitan in 1970. Her operatic repertoire includes more than 100 roles.

Løveberg, Aase (née **Nordmo**), Norwegian soprano; b. Målselv, June 10, 1923. She was born into a peasant family; spent her childhood on a farm near the Arctic Circle. When she was 19 she went to Oslo, where she studied voice with Haldis Ingebjart; made her operatic debut in Oslo on Dec. 3, 1948; then sang in Stockholm, Vienna, Paris, and London. She made her 1st American appearance as a soloist with the Philadelphia Orch. (Dec. 6, 1957); pursued her career mainly in Norway, later serving as manager of the Oslo Opera (1978–81).

Løvenskjold, Herman Severin, Norwegian organist and composer; b. Holdensjärnbruk, July 30, 1815; d. Copenhagen, Dec. 5, 1870. At the age of 13 his parents took him to Copenhagen, where he studied music; in 1836 he brought out his ballet *Sylphiden* there with much success. After the premiere of his 2nd ballet, *Sara,* in 1839, he went to Vienna, where he took some lessons with Seyfried; returned to Denmark in 1851; was appointed organist at the Slottskyrka in Christiansborg. He wrote an opera, *Turandot* (Copenhagen, Dec. 3, 1854); *Festouvertüre* (for the coronation of Christian VIII); *Ouverture de concert idyllique;* the overture *Fra Skoven ved Furesø;* Piano Trio; Piano Quartet; piano pieces for 2- and 4-hands.

Lover, Samuel, Irish novelist, poet, painter, and composer; b. Dublin, Feb. 24, 1797; d. St. Helier, Jersey, July 6, 1868. He wrote music to several Irish plays, and to many songs; publ. *Songs and Ballads* (London, 1859). Among his most popular songs (some of which are set to old Irish tunes) are *The Angel's Whisper, Molly Bawn,* and *The Low-Backed Car.* He wrote an opera, *Grana Uile, or The Island Queen* (Dublin, Feb. 9, 1832). He devised a very successful musical entertainment, *Irish Evenings* (1844), with which he toured the British Isles and the U.S. (1846). He was **Victor Herbert**'s grandfather.

BIBL.: B. Bernard, *Life of S. L., R.H.A., Artistic, Literary, and Musical* (London, 1874); A. Symington, *S. L. A Biographical Sketch* (London, 1880).

Löw, Joseph, Bohemian pianist and composer; b. Prague, Jan. 23, 1834; d. there, Oct. 5, 1886. In 1854 he toured through Moravia, Silesia, Galicia, and the Bukovina; returning to Prague in 1856, he was active as a concert pianist and composer. He publ. over 450 numbers of light piano music, including *Jugend-Album; 2 impromptus romantiques; Allegro brillant* for 2 Pianos; *Soir de printemps; Maiengruss;* etc.

Löwe, (Johann) Carl Gottfried. See **Loewe, (Johann) Carl (Gottfried).**

Löwe, Ferdinand, noted Austrian conductor; b. Vienna, Feb. 19, 1865; d. there, Jan. 6, 1925. He studied with Dachs, Krenn, and Bruckner at the Vienna Cons.; then taught piano and choral singing there (1883–96). In 1897 he became conductor of the Kaim Orch. in Munich; then of the Court Opera in Vienna (1898–1900) and of the Vienna Gesellschaftskonzerte (1900–1904); in 1904 he became conductor of the newly organized Vienna Konzertverein Orch., which he made one of the finest instrumental bodies in Europe; he returned to Munich as conductor of the Konzertverein Orch. (1908–14), which comprised members of the former Kaim Orch.; also conducted in Budapest and Berlin; from 1918 to 1922, was head of the Vienna Academy of Music. He was a friend and trusted disciple of Bruckner; ed. (somewhat liberally) several of Bruckner's works, including his 4th Sym., preparing a new Finale (1887–88); he also made a recomposed version of his unfinished 9th Sym., which he conducted in Vienna with Bruckner's *Te Deum* in lieu of the unfinished Finale (Feb. 11, 1903).

Lowens, Irving, eminent American musicologist, music critic, and librarian; b. N.Y., Aug. 19, 1916; d. Baltimore, Nov. 14, 1983. He studied at Teachers College, Columbia Univ. (B.S. in Music, 1939). During World War II he served as an air-traffic controller for the Civil Aeronautics Administration; continued in this capacity at the National Airport in Washington, D.C.; then took special courses in American civilization at the Univ. of Maryland (M.A., 1957; Ph.D., 1965). In 1953 he began to write music criticism for the *Washington Star;* from 1960 to 1978 he was its chief music critic; received the ASCAP–Deems Taylor Award for the best articles on music in 1972 and 1977. From 1960 to 1966 he was a librarian in the Music Division of the Library of Congress in Washington, D.C. From 1978 to 1981 he was dean of the Peabody Inst. of the Johns Hopkins Univ. in Baltimore; also wrote music criticism for the *Baltimore News American.* A linguist, he traveled widely on numerous research grants in Europe. He was a founding member of the Music Critics' Assoc., and from 1971 to 1975 served as its president.

WRITINGS: *The Hartford Harmony: A Selection of American Hymns from the Late 18th and Early 19th Centuries* (Hartford, 1953); *Music and Musicians of Early America* (N.Y., 1964); *Source Readings in American Music History* (N.Y., 1966); *Lectures on the History and Art of Music at the Library of Congress, 1946–63* (N.Y., 1968); *A Bibliography of American Songsters Published before 1821* (Worcester, Mass., 1976); *Haydn in America* (Washington, D.C., 1977).

Lowenthal, Jerome (Nathaniel), American pianist; b. Philadelphia, Feb. 11, 1932. He studied piano at an early age; made his debut with the Philadelphia Orch. at the age of 13; then took lessons with Samaroff at the Philadelphia Cons. (1947–50); while taking courses at the Univ. of Pa. (B.A., 1953), he received private piano instruction from Kapell; continued his studies with Steuermann at the Juilliard School of Music in N.Y. (M.S., 1956) and with Cortot at the École Normale de Musique (licence de concert, 1958). He then traveled to Israel, where he gave concerts and taught at the Jerusalem Academy of Music; returned to the U.S. in 1961. He made his professional

debut as soloist with the N.Y. Phil. in 1963, and subsequently toured throughout North and South America, the Middle East, and the Far East. His repertoire embraces the standard piano literature as well as contemporary works; among composers who wrote special works for him were George Rochberg and Ned Rorem.

Lowinsky, Edward E(lias), eminent German-born American musicologist; b. Stuttgart, Jan. 12, 1908; d. Chicago, Oct. 12, 1985. He studied at the Hochschule für Musik in Stuttgart (1923–28); took his Ph.D. at the Univ. of Heidelberg in 1933 with the dissertation *Das Antwerpener Motettenbuch Orlando di Lassos und seine Beziehungen zum Motettenschaffen der niederländischen Zeitgenössen* (publ. in The Hague, 1937). When the Nazis came to power in Germany in 1933, he fled to the Netherlands; when the dark cloud of anti-Semitism reached the Netherlands, he emigrated to the U.S. (1940), becoming a naturalized U.S. citizen in 1947. He was assistant prof. of music at Black Mountain College (1942–47); associate prof. of music at Queens College, N.Y. (1948–56); prof. of music at the Univ. of Calif., Berkeley (1956–61); and prof. of music at the Univ. of Chicago (1961–76), where he also held a post-retirement professorship until 1978. He held Guggenheim fellowships in 1947–48 and 1976–77; was a Fellow at the Inst. for Advanced Study at Princeton Univ. from 1952 to 1954; was made a Fellow of the American Academy of Arts and Sciences in 1973; was named Albert A. Bauman Distinguished Research Fellow of the Newberry Library in 1982. He was general ed. of the Monuments of Renaissance Music series; publ. the valuable studies *Secret Chromatic Art in the Netherlands Motet* (N.Y., 1946) and *Tonality and Atonality in Sixteenth-Century Music* (Berkeley and Los Angeles, 1961; rev. printing, 1962). He also prepared the vol. *Josquin des Prez. Proceedings of the International Josquin Festival-Conference* (London, 1976) and wrote the study *Cipriano de Rore's Venus Motet: Its Poetic and Pictorial Sources* (Provo, 1986). He was married to the musicologist **Bonnie Blackburn.** She ed. his *Music in the Culture of the Renaissance and Other Essays* (Chicago, 1989).

Lowry, Robert, American hymn writer; b. Philadelphia, March 12, 1826; d. Plainfield, N.J., Nov. 25, 1899. He was a Baptist preacher and studied music in his middle age. He wrote the tunes for such popular hymns as *I Need Thee Every Hour* (1872) and *All the Way My Savior Leads Me* (1875); he wrote both texts and tunes for the successful hymns *Shall We Gather at the River?* (1865), *Low in the Grave He Lay* (1875), and *Where Is My Wandering Boy Tonight?* (1877).

BIBL.: J. Zellner, III, "R. L.: Early American Hymn Writer," *Hymn,* XXVI (1975) and XXVII (1976).

Lowtzky, Hermann, Russian composer; b. Kamenetz-Podolsk, June 20, 1871; d. Zürich, Dec. 8, 1957. He studied law, philosophy, and music; went to St. Petersburg in 1899 and enrolled in Rimsky-Korsakov's class at the Cons. He moved to Switzerland in 1910. His music preserves the Russian elements of style and idiom. Among his publ. works are the opera *Lucretia,* to his own libretto (Kiev, Dec. 18, 1912); Piano Trio (1905); cantata, *Paradies und Peri.* In MS are an opera, *Mozart,* and *Kol Nidre* for Cello and Orch.

Lualdi, Adriano, Italian composer, writer on music, and conductor; b. Larino, Campobasso, March 22, 1885; d. Milan, Jan. 8, 1971. He studied composition with Falchi in Rome and Wolf-Ferrari in Venice; began his musical career as an opera conductor; in 1918 he went to Milan, where he was active as a music critic and government administrator on musical affairs; from 1936 to 1944 he was director of the Cons. of San Pietro a Majella in Naples; then was director of the Florence Cons. (1947–56). He was a voluminous composer, excelling particularly in opera. His *Le nozze di Haura,* written in 1908, had its concert premiere by the Italian Radio on Oct. 15, 1939, and its 1st stage production in Rome on April 17, 1943. His subsequent operas were *La Figlia del re,* after the *Antigone* of Sophocles (1914–17; Turin, March 18, 1922); *Le furie d'Arlecchino* (Milan, May 10, 1915; rev. 1925); *Il Diavolo nel* *campanile* (1919–23; Milan, April 22, 1925; rev. 1954); *La granceola* (Venice, Sept. 10, 1932); *La luna dei Caraibi*, after O'Neill (1944; Rome, Jan. 29, 1953); mimodrama, *Lumawig e la saetta* (1936; Rome, Jan. 23, 1937; rev. 1956); *Euridikes diatheke* or *Il testamento di Euridice*, lyric tragedy (1939–52); satiric radio comedy, *Tre alla radarstratotropojonosferaphono-theca del Luna Park* (1953–58); cantata, *La rosa di Saron* (1915; also titled *Il cantico;* Milan, May 10, 1915); symphonic poems: *La leggenda del vecchio marinaio* (1910) and *L'interludio del sogno* (1917); *Suite adriatica* for Orch. (1932); *Africa*, rhapsody for Orch. (1936); *Divertimento* for Orch. (1941); numerous choruses and minor pieces for various instruments.

WRITINGS: *Viaggio musicale in Italia* (Milan, 1927); *Viaggio musicale in Europa* (Milan, 1928); *Viaggio musicale nel Sud-America* (Milan, 1934); *L'arte di dirigere l'orchestra* (Milan, 1940; 3rd ed., 1958); *Viaggio musicale nell'URSS* (Milan, 1941); *Tutti vivi* (Milan, 1955).

BIBL.: G. Confalonieri, *L'opera di A. L.* (Milan, 1932).

Lübeck, Ernst, Dutch pianist and composer, son of **Johann Heinrich** and brother of **Louis Lübeck;** b. The Hague, Aug. 24, 1829; d. Paris, Sept. 17, 1876. He was trained as a pianist by his father; as a youth, he made a voyage to America, playing concerts in the U.S., Mexico, and Peru (1849–54); then settled in Paris, where he acquired the reputation of a virtuoso; Berlioz wrote enthusiastically about his playing. He became mentally unbalanced following the events of the Paris Commune of 1871. He wrote some pleasing salon pieces for Piano, among them *Berceuse; Tarentelle; Polonaise; Trilby the Sprite; Rêverie caractéristique.*

Lübeck, Johann Heinrich, Dutch violinist, conductor, and composer, father of **Ernst** and **Louis Lübeck;** b. Alphen, Feb. 11, 1799; d. The Hague, Feb. 7, 1865. He was a Prussian regimental musician (1813–15); studied music in Potsdam; then was a player in theater orchs. in Riga and Stettin; in 1823, settled in the Netherlands, giving violin concerts. From 1827 until his death he was director of The Hague Cons.; was also conductor of the "Diligentia" concerts there, and in 1829, became court conductor.

Lübeck, Louis, Dutch cellist and composer, son of **Johann Heinrich** and brother of **Ernst Lübeck;** b. The Hague, Feb. 14, 1838; d. Berlin, March 8, 1904. He studied with Jacquard in Paris; from 1863 to 1868, taught cello at the Leipzig Cons.; toured Germany, the Netherlands, England, and the U.S. (1875–81); in 1881 he settled in Berlin as a cellist in the Court Orch. He wrote 2 cello concertos, and solo pieces.

Lübeck, Vincent or **Vincenz,** eminent German organist and composer; b. Padingbüttel, Sept. 1654; d. Hamburg, Feb. 9, 1740. He studied with his father; from 1675 to 1702, was an organist at Stade; in 1702, became organist at the Nicolaikirche in Hamburg, remaining in that post until his death. Lübeck's works, including 3 cantatas, chorale preludes for organ, etc., were publ. by G. Harms (Klecken, 1921). An ed. of the complete organ works was publ. by K. Beckmann (Wiesbaden, 1973).

Lubin, Germaine (Léontine Angélique), noted French soprano; b. Paris, Feb. 1, 1890; d. there, Oct. 27, 1979. She studied at the Paris Cons. (1909–12) and with F. Litvinne and Lilli Lehmann; made her debut at the Paris Opéra-Comique in 1912 as Antonio in *Les Contes d'Hoffmann.* In 1914 she joined the Paris Opéra, remaining on its roster until 1944; also appeared at London's Covent Garden (1937, 1939); in 1938 she became the 1st French singer to appear at Bayreuth, gaining considerable acclaim for her Wagnerian roles. She continued her career in Paris during the German occupation and was briefly under arrest after the liberation of Paris, charged with collaboration with the enemy; she was imprisoned for 3 years. After her release, she taught voice, dying in her 90th year. Her most distinguished roles included Alceste, Ariane, Isolde, Kundry, Donna Anna, Leonore, Brünnhilde, Sieglinde, and the Marschallin.

BIBL.: N. Casanov, *Isolde 39—G. L.* (Paris, 1974).

Lubin, Steven, esteemed American pianist and fortepianist; b. N.Y., Feb. 22, 1942. After initial piano training, he studied

philosophy at Harvard Univ. (B.A., 1963); he then continued his piano studies at the Juilliard School of Music in N.Y. (M.A., 1965), where his mentors included Rosina Lhévinne and Beveridge Webster, and studied musicology at N.Y. Univ. (Ph.D., 1974). He made his N.Y. debut in 1977. In 1978 he organized the Mozartean Players, a chamber ensemble devoted to presenting period instrument performances; subsequently he toured with them throughout the U.S. He was equally adept in projecting discriminating interpretations of the Classical and Romantic keyboard repertoire, using the keyboard of the fortepiano modeled after the 1800 type of instrument.

Luboff, Norman, American conductor, composer, and arranger; b. Chicago, May 14, 1917; d. Bynum, N.C., Sept. 22, 1987. He received his training in Chicago, where he attended the American Cons. of Music, in the class of Leo Sowerby. After graduation, he went to Hollywood as an arranger for films and television. He founded the Norman Luboff Choir in 1963, and subsequently conducted it on numerous tours, maintaining a vast repertoire of works ranging from classical to popular genres. As a composer, he devoted himself mainly to choral music.

Luboshutz (real name, **Luboshitz**), **Léa,** Russian-American violinist and teacher, sister of **Pierre Luboshutz;** b. Odessa, Feb. 22, 1885; d. Philadelphia, March 18, 1965. She studied violin with her father; played in public at the age of 7; after study at the Odessa Music School, she went to the Moscow Cons., graduating with a gold medal (1903); gave concerts in Germany and France, and also took additional lessons from Eugène Ysaÿe in Belgium; returned to Russia, and organized a trio with her brother and her sister Anna (cello); left Russia after the Revolution and lived in Berlin and Paris (1921–25). In 1925 she settled in N.Y.; played the American premiere of Prokofiev's 1st Violin Concerto (Nov. 14, 1925); made several appearances in joint recitals with her son, the pianist **Boris Goldovsky.** From 1927, she was on the faculty of the Curtis Inst. of Music in Philadelphia.

Luboshutz (real name, **Luboshitz**), **Pierre,** Russian-American pianist, brother of **Léa Luboshutz;** b. Odessa, June 17, 1891; d. Rockport, Maine, April 17, 1971. He studied violin with his father; then turned to the piano, and entered the Moscow Cons. as a pupil of Igumnov, graduating in 1912; also studied in Paris with Edouard Risler; returning to Russia, he played in a trio with his 2 sisters, Léa (violin) and Anna (cello); in 1926, went to America as accompanist to Zimbalist, Piatigorsky, and others. In 1931 he married **Genia Nemenoff** (b. Paris, Oct. 23, 1905; d. N.Y., Sept. 19, 1989); with her he formed a piano duo (N.Y. debut, Jan. 18, 1937); as Luboshutz-Nemenoff, they gave annual concerts with considerable success. From 1962 to 1968, they headed the piano dept. at Michigan State Univ.; then returned to N.Y.

Lubotsky, Mark (Davidovich), Russian violinist; b. Leningrad, May 18, 1931. He began his training at the Moscow Cons., and later was a student of David Oistrakh; then gave concerts throughout the Soviet Union. In 1970 he made his British debut as soloist in Britten's Violin Concerto at a London Promenade Concert, and subsequently pursued an international career. From 1967 he taught at the Gnessin Inst. in Moscow.

Luca, Sergiu, noted Rumanian-born American violinist and teacher; b. Bucharest, April 4, 1943. He began to study violin as a child; in 1950 his parents took him to Israel, where he made his debut as a soloist with the Haifa Sym. Orch. (1952); later continued his studies with Max Rostal in London, at the Bern Cons. (1958–61), and with Galamian at the Curtis Inst. of Music in Philadelphia (1961–65). He made his U.S. debut as soloist with the Philadelphia Orch. in 1965; subsequently appeared with many American and European orchs. with considerable success. In 1966 he became a naturalized U.S. citizen. He was founder-director of the Chamber Music Northwest Festival in Portland, Oreg. (1971–80); then was prof. of violin at the Univ. of Illinois (1980–83); subsequently was prof. of violin and violinist-in-residence at the Shepherd School of Music at Rice Univ. in Houston (from 1983) and also served as music director of the Texas Chamber Orch. He distinguished himself in a broad repertoire, ranging from the Baroque to the contemporary eras. His performances of early music are notable for their stylistic propriety.

Lucantoni, Giovanni, Italian composer and singing teacher; b. Rieti, Jan. 18, 1825; d. Paris, May 30, 1902. He studied with his parents, who were both good amateur musicians; then with Giovanni Pacini in Lucca and Nicola Vaccaj in Milan. In 1857 he settled in Paris as a singing teacher; also lived in London. His vocal compositions were very popular for a time; particularly well known was the vocal duet *Una notte a Venezia;* he also wrote an opera, *Elisa* (Milan, June 20, 1850); a 4-part Mass; a cantata; a Sym.; various "ballabili" for piano.

Lucas, Leighton, English conductor and composer; b. London, Jan. 5, 1903; d. there, Nov. 1, 1982. He was trained to be a dancer, and was a member of Diaghilev's Ballets Russes in Paris and in London (1918–21). Then he learned conducting and traveled with various ballet companies. From 1946 he conducted his own orch. He made arrangements of classical pieces for ballet and composed his own ballets, *The Wolf's Ride* (1935), *Death in Adagio,* after Scarlatti (1936), *The Horses* (1945–46), and *Tam O'Shanter* (1972–73). He also wrote *Divertissement* for Harp and 8 Instruments (1955); Cello Concerto (1956); Clarinet Concerto (1957); *Disquisition* for 2 Cellos and Piano, 4-hands (1967); String Trio (1969); etc.

Lucas, Mary Anderson, English composer; b. London, May 24, 1882; d. there, Jan. 14, 1952. She studied piano at the Dresden Cons. and at the Royal Academy of Music in London; then had composition lessons from R.O. Morris, H. Howells, and M. Jacobson. She adopted an advanced harmonic style of composition; her works include a ballet, *Sawdust* (1941), which had considerable success; 6 string quartets; Trio for Clarinet, Viola, and Piano; *Rhapsody* for Flute, Cello, and Piano; many songs.

Lucca, Pauline, famous Austrian soprano of Italian-German parentage; b. Vienna, April 25, 1841; d. there, Feb. 28, 1908. She studied singing in Vienna and sang in the chorus of the Vienna Court Opera. Her professional debut took place in Olmütz as Elvira in *Ernani* on Sept. 4, 1859. Her appearances in Prague as Valentine and Norma (1860) attracted the attention of Meyerbeer, who arranged for her to become a member of Berlin's Royal Opera (1861–72). She made her 1st appearance at London's Covent Garden as Valentine (July 18, 1863), and sang there until 1867, returning from 1870 to 1872 and in 1882. After singing in the U.S. (1872–74), she was a leading member of the Vienna Court Opera until retiring from the stage in 1889. In her prime she was regarded as "prima donna assoluta," and her private life and recurring marriages and divorces were favorite subjects of sensational press stories; a curious promotional pamphlet, *Bellicose Adventures of a Peaceable Prima Donna,* was publ. in N.Y. in 1872, presumably to whip up interest in her public appearances, but it concerned itself mainly with a melodramatic account of her supposed experiences during the Franco-Prussian War. Among her finest roles were Cherubino, Selika, Carmen, and Marguerite.
    BIBL.: A. Jansen-Mara and D. Weisse-Zehrer, *Die Wiener Nachtigall: Der Lebensweg der P. L.* (Berlin, 1935).

Lucchesi, Andrea, Italian composer; b. Motta di Livenza, near Treviso, May 23, 1741; d. Bonn, March 21, 1801. He studied in Venice, then settled in Bonn as director of a traveling opera troupe (1771). He was made court Kapellmeister and Kurfürstlicher Rat (1774), and then Titularrat (1787); however, after the court left Bonn and the French occupied the city (1794), he was deprived of his positions.
    WORKS: STAGE: *L'isola della fortuna* (Venice, 1765); *Le Donne sempre donne* (Venice, Feb. 27, 1767); *Il matrimonio per astuzia* (Venice, Oct. 1771); *Il Giocatore amoroso,* intermezzo (Bonn, 1772); *L'inganno scoperto* (Bonn, 1773); *L'improvisota, ossia La galanteria disturbata* (Bonn, 1773–74); *Ademira*

(Venice, May 2, 1784); *L'amore e la misericordia guadagnano il giuoco* (Passua, 1794); also sacred works; chamber music.

Lucchesini, Andrea, Italian pianist; b. Montecatini, July 8, 1965. He began studies at the age of 7 with Maria Tipo, continuing his training at the Istituto Musicale Giuseppe Verdi. After winning the Dino Ciani Competition in Milan in 1983, he embarked upon a tour of Italy, giving a particularly noteworthy recital at Milan's La Scala; also toured in Germany, France, and Switzerland. He made his U.S. debut at the Newport (R.I.) Music Festival in 1984; also appeared elsewhere in the U.S. and throughout Europe.

Lucier, Alvin (Augustus, Jr.), American composer; b. Nashua, N.H., May 14, 1931. He studied with H. Boatwright, Richard Donovan, David Kraehenbuhl, and Quincy Porter at Yale Univ. (1950–54); continued his training with A. Berger, I. Fine, and H. Shapero at Brandeis Univ. (1958–60); also studied with Lukas Foss (composition) and Copland (orchestration) at the Berkshire Music Center in Tanglewood (1958, 1959); then went to Rome on a Fulbright scholarship (1960–62). He was on the faculty of Brandeis Univ. (1962–70), where he served as choral director. With Robert Ashley, David Behrman, and Gordon Mumma, he founded the Sonic Arts Union (1966), an electronic music performing group with which he toured the U.S. and Europe. He joined the faculty of Wesleyan Univ. (1970); was music director of the Viola Farber Dance Co. (1972–77). He contributed many articles to music journals and other publications; with D. Simon, he publ. *Chambers* (Middletown, Conn., 1980). In 1990 he was in Berlin on a Deutscher Akademischer Austauschdienst fellowship. His works exploit virtually all known musical and non-musical resources available to the creative artist.
    WORKS: *Action Music* for Piano (1962); *Music for Solo Performer* for Amplified Brain Waves and Percussion (1965); *North American Time Capsule* for Voices and Vocoder (1967); *Chambers,* realized by moving large and small resonant environments (1968); *Vespers,* acoustic orientation by means of echolocation (1969); *"I am sitting in a room"* for Voice and Electromagnetic Tape (1970); *The Queen of the South* for Players, Responsive Surfaces, Strewn Material, and Closed-circuit Television System (1972); *Still and Moving Lines of Silence in Families of Hyperbolas* for Singers, Players, Dancers, and Unattended Percussion (Paris, Oct. 18, 1974); *Outlines* of persons and things for Microphones, Loudspeakers, and Electronic Sounds (1975); *Bird and Person Dyning* for Performer with Microphones, Amplifiers, Loudspeakers, and Sound-producing Object (1975); *Music on a Long Thin Wire* for Audio Oscillators and Electronic Monochord (1977); *Directions of Sounds from the Bridge* for Stringed Instrument, Audio Oscillator, and Sound-sensitive Lights (N.Y., Feb. 11, 1978); *Solar Sounder I,* electronic music system powered and controlled by sunlight (1979; in collaboration with John Fullemann); *Shapes of the Sounds from the Board* for Piano (1979); *Lullaby* for Unamplified or Amplified Voice (1979); *Music for Pure Waves, Bass Drums, and Acoustic Pendulums* (1980); *Reflections of Sounds from the Wall* (1981); *Crossings* for Small Orch. with Pure Wave Oscillator (Chicago, July 6, 1982); *Seesaw,* sound installation (1983); *Still and Moving Lines of Silence in Families of Hyperbolas,* Part II, Nos. 1–12 (Oakland, Calif., Feb. 16, 1984); *Spinner,* sound installation (1984); *In Memoriam Jon Higgins* for Clarinet and Slow-sweep, Pure Wave Oscillator (Hartford, Conn., Dec. 8, 1984); *Serenade* for 13 Winds and Pure Wave Oscillator (Aspen, Colo., Aug. 8, 1985); *Sound on Paper,* sound installation (1985); *Septet* for 3 Strings, 4 Winds, and Pure Wave Oscillator (Middletown, Conn., Sept. 20, 1985); *Music for Men, Women, and Reflecting Walls* for Pure Wave Oscillators (N.Y., June 11, 1986); *Salmon River Valley Songs* for Soprano, English Horn, Xylophone, and Pure Wave Oscillators (Hartford, Conn., Sept. 27, 1986); *Kettles* for 5 Timpani and 2 Pure Wave Oscillators (1987); *Fideliotrio* for Viola, Cello, and Piano (1988); *Clocker* for Amplified Clock, Galvanic Skin Response Sensor, and Digital Delay System (1978–88); *Silver Streetcar for the Orchestra* for Triangle (1988); *Carbon Copies* for Piano, Saxophone, and Percussion

(1988); *Amplifier and Reflector I* for Open Umbrella, Ticking Clock, and Glass Oven Dish (1991); *Navigations* for String Quartet (Frankfurt am Main, Oct. 11, 1991).

Luciuk, Juliusz (Mieczyslaw), Polish composer; b. Brzeźnica, Jan. 1, 1927. He studied musicology with Jachimecki at the Jagiellonian Univ. in Krakow (1947–52), concurrently taking courses in composition with Wiechowicz at the State College of Music in Krakow (1947–56); then had lessons with Nadia Boulanger and Max Deutsch in Paris (1958–59). He evolved a sui generis technique according to the pragmatic purposes of each specific composition.

WORKS: Ballets: *Niobe* (1962); *Battleship Potemkin* (1967); *Orpheus* (1973); *Medea* (1975); *So Pass 5 Years* for Prepared Piano and Chamber Ensemble (Amsterdam, Oct. 9, 1972); oratorio, *Francis of Assisi* (Krakow, Oct. 3, 1976); cantata, *Dzikie wino* (Virginia Creeper; 1955); *Pour un ensemble* for Narrator and 24 Strings (1961); *Melorythmes* for Orch. (1962); *Lirica di timbri,* 5 pieces for Prepared Piano (1963); *Metamorphoses* for Orch. (1963); *Pacem in terris* for Vocalizing Soprano and Prepared Piano (1964); *Variété* for Trumpet and Orch. (1965); *Poème de Loire,* 5 songs for Soprano and Orch. (1968); *Speranza sinfonica* (1969); *Lamentazioni in memoriam Grazyna Bacewicz* for Orch. (1970); *Mini-Opus* for Piano, 4-hands (1971); *Concertino* for Piano and Chamber Orch. (1973); *Portraits lyriques* for Mezzo-soprano, 2 Violins, Cello, and Piano (1974); *Image* for Organ (1977); *Willows,* 5 pieces for Chamber String Orch. (1979); *Polish Litany* for Soloists, Chorus, and String Orch. (1984); *Apocalypsis* for Soloists and Chorus (1985; Poznan, April 28, 1987); Double Bass Concerto (1986).

Lucký, Štěpán, Czech composer; b. Žilina, Jan. 20, 1919. He studied with O. Šín and Řídký and received instruction in quarter-tone composition with Alois Hába at the Prague Cons. (1936–39). During the occupation of Czechoslovakia by the Nazis, he was interned in concentration camps at Bucharest, Auschwitz, and Buchenwald; after his release, he enrolled in the Prague Cons., where he again studied with Řídký, graduating in 1947. His music is couched in a pragmatic modernistic manner without circumscription by any particular doctrine or technique.

WORKS: STAGE: *Půlnoční překvapení* (Midnight Surprise), opera (1958; Prague, 1959). **ORCH.:** *Divertimento* for 3 Trombones and String Ensemble (1946); Cello Concerto (1946); Piano Concerto (1947); Violin Concerto (1963–65); Octet for Strings (1970); *Double Concerto* for Violin, Piano, and Orch. (1971); *Nénie* for Violin, Cello, and Orch. (1976); Concerto (1976); Concerto for Clarinet, Piano, and String Orch. (1979–83). **CHAMBER:** 2 wind quintets (1946, 1982); Brass Quartet (1949); Sonata for Solo Violin (1967–69); *Sonata doppia* for 2 Violins (1971); Flute Sonata (1973); *Divertimento* for Wind Quintet (1974); *Invence* for Flute, Oboe, Piano, and Percussion (1977); *Musica collegialis* for Various Instruments (1980); String Quartet (1984); Wind Quartet (1985); Sonatina for 2 Guitars (1986); also piano pieces, including Sonata (1940); Sonatina (1945); *3 Etudes* for Quarter-tone Piano (1946); *Little Suite* (1971); songs.

Ludford, Nicholas, English composer; b. c.1485; d. c.1557. He was one of the musicians at the Royal Free Chapel of St. Stephen's, Westminster, until it was dissolved in 1547; in 1521 he was admitted to the Fraternity of St. Nicholas, a guild of musicians. His surviving works (all in MS) include masses, motets, and a Magnificat. His *Collected Works,* ed. by J. Bergsagel, were issued in Corpus Mensurabilis Musicae, XXVI (1965).

BIBL.: H. Baillie, "N. L. (c.1485–c.1557)," *Musical Quarterly* (April 1958); J. Milsom, "The Date of L.'s Lady Masses: A Cautionary Note," *Music & Letters* (Oct. 1985).

Ludgin, Chester (Hall), American baritone; b. N.Y., May 20, 1925. After service in the U.S. Army (1943–46), he was a student of the American Theatre Wing Professional Training Program (1948–50); studied voice with Armen Boyajian. He began his career by singing in nightclubs; made his operatic debut in 1956 as Scarpia with the New Orleans Experimental

Opera Theatre of America; in 1957 became a member of the N.Y. City Opera; sang leading roles with the San Francisco Opera from 1964; made his European debut with the Netherlands Opera in 1977. He created major roles in Ward's *The Crucible* (N.Y., 1961), Imbrie's *Angle of Repose* (San Francisco, 1967), and Bernstein's *A Quiet Place* (Houston, 1983); also made successful appearances in productions of Broadway musicals.

Ludikar (real name, **Vyskočil**), **Pavel,** Czech bass-baritone; b. Prague, March 3, 1882; d. Vienna, Feb. 19, 1970. He studied law in Prague; then took piano lessons, acquiring sufficient proficiency to accompany singers; then finally devoted himself to his real profession, that of opera singing; studied with Lassalle in Paris. He made his operatic debut as Sarastro at the Prague National Theater (1904); then appeared in Vienna, Dresden, and Milan; was a member of the Boston Civic Opera (1913–14). He made his Metropolitan Opera debut in N.Y. as Timur in *Turandot* on Nov. 16, 1926; remained on its roster until 1932; also sang with Hinshaw's touring opera company. He essayed the role of Figaro in *Il Barbiere di Siviglia* more than 100 times in the U.S. He created the title role in Krenek's opera *Karl V* (Prague, June 22, 1938).

Ludkewycz, Stanislaus, significant Polish composer; b. Jaroslav, Galicia, Jan. 24, 1879; d. Lwow, Sept. 10, 1979, at the age of 100. He studied philosophy at the Univ. of Lemberg, graduating in 1901; then went to Vienna, where he studied composition with Grädener and Zemlinsky at the Cons. (Ph.D., 1908). He then settled in Lemberg. From 1910 to 1914 he served as director of the Inst. of Music there; then was recruited in the Austrian army, and was taken prisoner by the Russians (1915). After the Russian Revolution, he was evacuated to Tashkent; liberated in 1918, he returned to Lemberg; from 1939 to 1972, until the age of 93, he was a prof. of composition at the Cons. there. When the city was incorporated in the Ukrainian Soviet Republic after World War II, Ludkewycz was awarded the Order of the Red Banner by the Soviet government (1949). On the occasion of his 100th birthday in 1979, he received the Order of Hero of Socialist Labor. His music followed the precepts of European Romanticism, with the representational, geographic, and folkloric aspects in evidence. Stylistically, the influence of Tchaikovsky was paramount in his vocal and instrumental compositions.

WORKS: DRAMATIC: *Dovbush,* opera (1955); *Caucasus,* symphonic ode for Chorus and Orch. (1905–13); *The Testament,* cantata (1934; rev. 1955). **ORCH.:** *Carpathian Symphony* (1952); symphonic poems: *Stone Carvers* (1926); *Valse mélancolique* (1920); *Dnieper* (1947); *Moses* (1956); 2 piano concertos (1920, 1957); Violin Concerto (1945). **CHAMBER:** Piano Trio (1919); *Variations on a Ukrainian Theme* for Violin and Piano (1949). **CHORAL, WITH ORCH.:** *Eternal Revolutionary* (1898); *Conquistadores* (1941); *A Testament for the Pioneers* (1967); also numerous piano pieces, songs, and arrangements of popular melodies.

BIBL.: M. Zagaikevycz, *S. L.* (Kiev, 1957); S. Pavlishin, *S. L.* (Kiev, 1974).

Ludwig, August, German composer and musical journalist; b. Waldheim, Jan. 15, 1865; d. Dresden, April 9, 1946. He studied at the Cologne Cons., and later in Munich; brought out a number of orch. compositions, notably the overtures *Ad astra* and *Luther-Ouvertüre;* also a comic opera, *Kunst und Schein* (1906). From 1894 to 1903 he was ed. of the *Neue Berliner Musikzeitung.* He publ. *Geharnischte Aufsätze über Musik* (collection of essays); *Der Konzertagent* (1894); *Stachel und Lorbeer* (1897); *Zur Wertschätzung der Musik* (1898); *Tannhäuser redivivus* (1908). He attracted unfavorable attention by his abortive attempt to "complete" Schubert's "Unfinished" Sym., adding 2 movements, a *Philosophen-Scherzo,* and a *Schicksalsmarsch.*

Ludwig, Christa, remarkable German soprano; b. Berlin, March 16, 1924. She was reared in a musical family; her father managed an opera; her mother sang. Ludwig studied at the

Hochschule für Musik in Frankfurt; in 1946 she made her operatic debut in Frankfurt in the role of Orlofsky in *Die Fledermaus*, singing there until 1952. In 1954 she sang the roles of Cherubino and Octavian at the Salzburg Festival; in 1955, was engaged by the Vienna State Opera; made her Metropolitan Opera debut in N.Y. as Cherubino on Dec. 10, 1959. In subsequent years she made considerable impact as a Wagnerian singer, being equally successful in such disparate roles as Kundry in *Parsifal*, Fricka in *Das Rheingold*, Venus in *Tannhäuser*, and Magdalene in *Die Meistersinger von Nürnberg*. She also obtained brilliant success as the Marschallin in *Der Rosenkavalier*, and in other operas by Richard Strauss. In the Italian repertoire she gave fine interpretations of the roles of Amneris in *Aida*, Rosina in *Il Barbiere di Siviglia*, and Lady Macbeth in Verdi's opera. Her career took her to opera theaters all over the world; she sang at La Scala in Milan, Covent Garden in London, the Teatro Colón in Buenos Aires, and the Nissei Theater in Tokyo. Sober-minded, skeptical music critics in Europe and America exerted their vocabularies to extol Ludwig as a superb singer not only in opera but also in the art of German lieder; some even praised her physical attributes. In 1962 she was named a Kammersängerin of Austria, and in 1969 she received the Cross of Merit, First Class, of the Republic of Austria. In 1980 she received the Golden Ring and in 1981 was made an honorary member of the Vienna State Opera; in 1980 she was awarded the Silver Rose of the Vienna Phil. On Sept. 29, 1957, she married **Walter Berry**, the Austrian baritone; they frequently appeared in the same opera together; they separated and in 1970 were divorced; in 1972 she married the French actor Paul-Émile Deiber.

BIBL.: P. Lorenz, *C. L.*; *Walter Berry* (Vienna, 1968).

Ludwig, Franz, Bohemian composer and musicologist; b. Graslitz, July 7, 1889; d. Münster, June 15, 1955. He studied first with his father, director of the Graslitz Music School; then with Pembaur, Reger, and Krehl at the Leipzig Cons., and with Riemann (musicology) at Leipzig Univ. He publ. a *Kurzgefasste Musikgeschichte des Erzgebirges* (1924); composed an opera, *Schlag zwölf* (Münster, 1928); a scenic oratorio, *Das Lambertusspiel* (Bremerhaven, 1933); *Lustspielouvertüre* for Orch.; Piano Concerto; Horn Concerto; *Serenade* for 8 Wind Instruments; sonatas and other pieces for piano; men's choruses; songs.

Ludwig, Friedrich, eminent German musicologist; b. Potsdam, May 8, 1872; d. Göttingen, Oct. 3, 1930. He studied history at the Univs. of Marburg and Strasbourg (Ph.D., 1896); then musicology with G. Jacobsthal. He was a reader (1905–10) and a prof. (1910–20) at the Univ. of Göttingen. He was an authority on medieval music. His most valuable work was *Repertorium organorum recentioris et motetorum vetustissimi stili*, I: *Catalogue raisonné der Quellen*, part 1: *Handschriften in Quadrat-Notation* (Halle, 1910); part 2: *Handschriften in Mensural-Notation* (ed. by F. Gennrich in Summa Musicae Medii Aevi, VII, 1961); II: *Musikalisches Anfangs Verzeichnis des nach Tenores geordneten Repertorium* (ed. by Gennrich in ibid., VIII, 1962). He also ed. an incomplete collection of the works of Guillaume de Machaut (1926–34).

BIBL.: J. Müller-Blattau, *Dem Andenken F. L.s* (Kassel, 1931).

Ludwig, Leopold, Austrian conductor; b. Witkowitz, Jan. 12, 1908; d. Lüneburg, April 25, 1979. He studied piano at the Vienna Cons.; then conducted in provincial opera houses. He was made Generalmusikdirektor of the Oldenburg State Theater (1936); then was a conductor at the Vienna State Opera (1939–43), the Berlin Städtische Oper (1943–51), and the Berlin State Opera (1945–51). From 1951 to 1970 he was Generalmusikdirektor of the Hamburg State Opera; also conducted at the Edinburgh Festivals (1952, 1956), the San Francisco Opera (1958–68), and the Glyndebourne Festival (1959). On Nov. 14, 1970, he made his Metropolitan Opera debut in N.Y. conducting *Parsifal*, and remained on its roster until 1972. He was known as an unostentatious but thoroughly competent interpreter of the Austro-German operatic and symphonic repertoire.

BIBL.: B. Wessling, *L. L.* (Bremen, 1968).

Ludwig, Walther, German tenor; b. Bad Oeynhausen, March 17, 1902; d. Lahr, May 15, 1981. He studied jurisprudence and medicine before deciding on a singing career; studied voice in Königsberg, where he made his debut in 1928. After singing in Schwerin (1929–32), he was a member of the Berlin Städtische Oper (1932–45). He also made appearances at the Glyndebourne Festival, Milan's La Scala, London's Covent Garden, the Salzburg Festival, and the Vienna State Opera; likewise toured as a concert artist. From 1952 to 1969 he was a prof. at the (West) Berlin Hochschule für Musik. He also completed his medical studies in Berlin (M.D., 1971). He was best known for his Mozart roles.

Ludwig II, King of Bavaria and patron of Wagner; b. Munich, Aug. 25, 1845; d. (suicide) in the Starnberg Lake, June 13, 1886. As crown prince, he conceived an extreme adulation for Wagner, and when he became King, at 19, he declared his intention to sponsor all of Wagner's productions, an event that came at the most difficult time of Wagner's life, beset as he was by personal and financial problems. In sincere gratitude, Wagner spoke of his future plans of composition as "a program for the King." In his total devotion to Wagner, Ludwig converted his castle Neuschwanstein into a "worthy temple for my divine friend," installing in it architectural representations of scenes from Wagner's operas. His bizarre behavior caused the government of Bavaria to order a psychiatric examination, and he was eventually committed to an asylum near the Starnberg Lake. During a walk, he overpowered the psychiatrist escorting him, and apparently dragged him to his death in the lake, and drowned himself, too. Much material on Ludwig II is found in Wagner's bibliography; see also W. Blunt, *The Dream King, Ludwig II of Bavaria* (London, 1970), and C. McIntosh, *The Swan King: Ludwig II of Bavaria* (London, 1982).

Luening, Otto (Clarence), multifaceted American composer, teacher, flutist, and conductor; b. Milwaukee, June 15, 1900. He was of deeply rooted German ancestry, traceable to one Manfried von Lüninck, who flourished in 1350; one of Luening's maternal ancestors was said to be a descendant of Martin Luther's sister. Luening's great-grandfather emigrated to the U.S. in 1839 and settled in Wisconsin; he made the 1st barley beer in Milwaukee. Luening's paternal grandfather was American-born; he became active in bilingual culture in Wisconsin and was an organizer of the German-English Academy. Luening's father was an educated musician who received his training at the Leipzig Cons.; he had met Wagner and sung in performances of Beethoven's 9th Sym., with Wagner conducting; returning to Milwaukee, he became active in German-American music; he kept his cultural associations with Germany, and in 1912 took his family to Munich. There Luening enrolled in the Akademie der Tonkunst, where he studied flute with Alois Schellhorn, piano with Josif Becht, and composition with A. Beer-Walbrunn. He gave his 1st concert as a flutist in Munich on March 27, 1916. When America entered World War I in 1917, Luening went to Switzerland, where he studied with Philip Jarnach and Volkmar Andreae at the Zürich Cons. (until 1920); he also had an opportunity to take private lessons with Busoni; pursuing his scientific interests, he attended a seminar in abnormal psychology at the Univ. of Zürich, and also appeared as an actor in the English Players Co. in Switzerland. It was during this period he began to compose; his 1st Violin Sonata and a Sextet were performed at the Zürich Cons. Luening returned to the U.S. in 1920; he earned a living as a flutist and conductor in theater orchs. In 1925 he moved to Rochester, N.Y., where he served as coach and executive director of the opera dept. at the Eastman School of Music; in 1928 he went to Cologne; from 1932 to 1934 he was on the faculty of the Univ. of Arizona in Tucson. In 1934 he became chairman of the music dept. at Bennington College in Vermont, keeping this position until 1944. After teaching at Barnard College in N.Y. (1944–47), he was on the philosophy faculty at Columbia Univ. (1949–68), where he also was co-director of the Columbia-Princeton Electronic Music Center (1959–80) and music chairman of the School of the Arts (1966–70); likewise taught composition at the Juilliard School (1971–73).

An important development in Luening's career as a composer took place in 1952, when he began to experiment with the resources of the magnetic tape; he composed a strikingly novel piece, *Fantasy in Space*, in which he played the flute with its accompaniment electronically transmuted on tape; Stokowski featured it on his program in N.Y. on Oct. 28, 1952, along with Luening's 2 other electronic pieces, *Low Speed* and *Invention*. He found a partner in Vladimir Ussachevsky, who was also interested in musical electronics. Together, they produced the 1st work that combined real sounds superinduced on an electronic background, *Rhapsodic Variations* for Tape Recorder and Orch., performed by the Louisville Orch. on March 20, 1954; its performance anticipated by a few months the production of Varèse's similarly constructed work, *Déserts*. Another electronic work by Luening and Ussachevsky, *A Poem in Cycles and Bells* for Tape Recorder and Orch., was played by the Los Angeles Phil. on Nov. 18, 1954. Bernstein conducted the 1st performance of still another collaborative composition by Luening and Ussachevsky, *Concerted Piece* for Tape Recorder and Orch., with the N.Y. Phil. on March 31, 1960. Thenceforth, Luening devoted a major part of his creative effort to an integration of electronic sound into the fabric of a traditional orch., without abondoning the fundamental scales and intervals; most, but not all, of these works were in collaboration with Ussachevsky. Unaided, he produced *Synthesis* for Electronic Tape and Orch. (1960) and *Sonority Canon* (1962). He also wrote straightforward pieces without electronics; of these the most important is *A Wisconsin Symphony*, a sort of musical memoir of a Wisconsin-born composer; it was performed in Milwaukee, Luening's birthplace, on Jan. 3, 1976. His native state reciprocated proudly, awarding Luening an hononary doctorate from the Univ. of Wisconsin in Madison, a medal from the Wisconsin Academy of Sciences, Arts, and Letters, and a citation from the Wisconsin State Assembly. In addition to many other honors, he also held Guggenheim fellowships in 1930–31 and 1974–75. He described his career, with its triumphs and disappointments, in an autobiography, *The Odyssey of an American Composer*, publ. in 1980.

WORKS: STAGE: *Evangeline*, opera, after Longfellow (1930–32; rev. 1947–48; N.Y., May 5, 1948, composer conducting); incidental music to Maeterlinck's *Sister Beatrice* (Rochester, N.Y., Jan. 15, 1926) and to García Lorca's *Blood Wedding* (Bennington, Vt., Dec. 1, 1940). **ORCH.:** Concertino for Flute and Chamber Orch. (1923; Philadelphia, Jan. 30, 1935, composer conducting); *Music for Orchestra* (1923; N.Y., May 26, 1978); *Symphonic Fantasia I* (1924; Rochester, N.Y., Nov. 25, 1925); *Serenade* for 3 Horns and String Orch. (1927; Rochester, N.Y., Jan. 12, 1928); *2 Symphonic Interludes* (1935; N.Y., April 11, 1936); *Prelude to a Hymn Tune by William Billings* for Chamber Orch. (N.Y., Feb. 1, 1937, composer conducting); *Suite* for String Orch. (Saratoga Springs, N.Y., Sept. 12, 1937); *Symphonic Fantasia II* (1939–49; N.Y., Oct. 13, 1957); *Pilgrim's Hymn* for Chamber Orch. (Saratoga Springs, N.Y., Sept. 14, 1946, composer conducting); *Prelude* for Chamber Orch. (Saratoga Springs, N.Y., Sept. 14, 1946, composer conducting); *Legend* for Oboe and String Orch. (WNYC Radio, N.Y., July 1, 1951); *Louisville Concerto*, later renamed *Kentucky Concerto* (Louisville, March 5, 1951, composer conducting); *Wisconsin Suite: Of Childhood Tunes Remembered* (N.Y., March 28, 1954); *Serenade* for Flute and String Orch. (N.Y., Oct. 19, 1956); *Lyric Scene* for Flute and String Orch. (1958; Arlington, Va., Oct. 25, 1964); *Fantasia* for String Quartet and Orch. (N.Y., April 18, 1959); *Broekman Fantasia* for String Orch. (1966); *Symphonic Fantasia III* (1969–82; N.Y., Jan. 26, 1982); *Symphonic Fantasia IV* (1969–82; N.Y., May 14, 1984); *Sonority Forms No. 1* (North Bennington, Vt., Oct. 14, 1973, composer conducting); *Wisconsin Symphony* (1975; Milwaukee, Jan. 3, 1976); *Symphonic Interlude* No. 3 (1975; Lenox, Mass., Aug.

13, 1980); *Short Symphony* for Chamber Orch. (1979; Milwaukee, Feb. 28, 1982); *Symphonic Fantasia V* (1979–85); *Potawatomi Legends* for Chamber Orch. (Parkside, Wis., April 13, 1980, composer conducting); *Sonority Forms II* (Bennington, Vt., June 4, 1983, composer conducting); *Symphonic Fantasia VI* (1985); *Symphonic Interlude No. 4* (1985); *Symphonic Fantasia VII* (1987); *Symphonic Fantasia VIII* (1987); *Symphonic Interlude No. 5* (1987); *Symphonic Fantasia IX* (1988). **CHAMBER:** Violin Sonata No. 1 (1917); Sextet for Flute, Clarinet, Horn, Violin, Viola, and Cello (1918); String Quartet No. 1 (1919–20); Piano Trio (1921); Violin Sonata No. 2 (1922); String Quartet No. 2 (1923); Cello Sonata (1924); String Quartet No. 3 (1928); *Fantasia brevis* for Violin, Viola, and Cello (1936); *Fuguing Tune* for Woodwind Quintet (1938); *The Bass with the Delicate Air* for Flute, Oboe, Clarinet, and Bassoon (1940); *Andante and Variations:* Violin Sonata No. 3 (1943–51); Suite for Cello or Viola, and Piano (1946); Suite for Flute No. 1 (1947); Trio for Flute, Violin, and Piano (1952); Sonata for Bassoon or Cello, and Piano (1952); Suite for Flute No. 2 (1953); Sonata for Trombone and Piano (1953); Viola Sonata (1958); Sonata No. 1 for Violin (1958); *3 Fantasias* for Guitar (1960); Suite for Flute No. 3 (1961); Trio for Flute, Cello, and Piano (1962); *Sonority Canon* for 2 to 37 Flutes (1962); Suite for Flute No. 4 (1963); 2 Pieces: *Short Sonata* for Flute and Piano No. 3 (1966); *Fantasia* for Cello (1966); Trio for 3 Flutists (1966); Sonata No. 2 for Violin (1968); Suite for Flute No. 5 (1969); Trio for Trumpet, Horn, and Trombone (1969); Sonata No. 3 for Violin (1970); *8 Tone Poems* for 2 Violas (1971); *Short Sonata* No. 2 for Flute and Piano (1971); *Elegy for the Lonesome Ones* for 2 Clarinets and Strings (1974); *Prelude and Fugue* for Flute, Clarinet, and Bassoon (1974); *Mexican Serenades* for Wind Instruments, Double Bass, and Percussion (1974); Suite for 2 Flutes and Piano (1976); *Potawatomi Legends No. 2: Fantasias on Indian Motives* for Flute (1979); *Fantasia* for Violin, Cello, and Piano (1981); *Serenade* for Violin, Cello, and Piano (1983); *3 Fantasias* for Baroque Flute (1987); *Bells on the River* for Carillon (1988); *Divertimento* for Oboe, Violin, Viola, and Cello (1988); *Divertimento* for 2 Trumpets, Horn, Trombone, and Tuba (1988); *Green Mountain Evening* for 6 Instruments (1988); pieces for piano, organ, and harpsichord. **ELECTRONIC:** *Fantasy in Space* for Tape (N.Y., Oct. 28, 1952); *Low Speed* for Tape (N.Y., Oct. 28, 1952); *Theatre Piece No. 2*, ballet for Voice, Instruments, and Tape (N.Y., April 20, 1956, composer conducting); *Gargoyles* for Violin and Tape (1960); *Synthesis* for Orch. and Tape (1962; Erie, Pa., Oct. 22, 1963); *Moonflight* for Tape (1968); *In the Beginning* (1970); *Variations on "Fugue and Chorale Fantasy"* for Organ and Electronic Doubles (1973). The following were produced in collaboration with V. Ussachevsky: *Rhapsodic Variations* for Orch. and Tape (Louisville, March 20, 1954); *A Poem in Cycles and Bells* for Orch. and Tape (Los Angeles, Nov. 18, 1954); *Of Identity*, ballet (1954; N.Y., Feb. 9, 1955); *Carlsbad Caverns*, television score (1955); *King Lear*, incidental music to Shakespeare's play (1956); *Back to Methuselah*, incidental music to Shaw's play (1960); *Concerted Piece* for Orch. and Tape (N.Y., March 31, 1960); *Incredible Voyage*, television score (1968). The following were produced in collaboration with H. El-Dabh: *Diffusion of Bells* (1962–65); *Electronic Fanfare* (1962–65). Also much vocal music, including choral pieces and songs.

Lugert, Josef, Bohemian music educator and composer; b. Frohnau, Oct. 30, 1841; d. Prague, July 24, 1936. He studied organ in Prague; in 1868, was appointed to the faculty of the Prague Cons.; later organized schools for instrumentalists in the provinces. He wrote a Sym. and several pieces of chamber music; publ. various manuals.

Luigini, Alexandre (-Clément-Léon-Joseph), French violinist, conductor, and composer of Italian descent; b. Lyons, March 9, 1850; d. Paris, July 29, 1906. He was the son of Giuseppe Luigini (1820–98), who conducted at the Théâtre-Italien in Paris. He studied at the Paris Cons. with Massart (violin) and Massenet (composition); then became concertmaster at the Grand Théâtre in Lyons (1869), and began his very successful career as a ballet composer with the production of his 1st stage work, *Le Rêve de Nicette* (Lyons, 1870); in 1877 he became conductor at the Grand Théâtre at Lyons and a prof. of harmony at the Lyons Cons.; after 20 years there, went to Paris as conductor at the Opéra-Comique, where he remained until his death, except during 1903, when he conducted the orch. at the Théâtre-Lyrique. His greatest success as a composer came with the production of the *Ballet égyptien* (Lyons, Jan. 13, 1875); it was inserted, with Verdi's permission, in the 2nd act of *Aida* at its performance in Lyons in 1886. In addition to a number of other ballets, he composed the comic operas *Les Caprices de Margot* (Lyons, April 13, 1877) and *Faublas* (Paris, Oct. 25, 1881); *Romance symphonique* for Orch.; marches for Orch.; 3 string quartets; many piano pieces.

Lukačić, (Marko) Ivan, Croatian organist and composer; b. Šibenik (baptized), April 17, 1587; d. Split, Sept. 20, 1648. He studied music in Italy, and in 1597 entered the Franciscan order. In 1620 he became prior of the Franciscan monastery and music master at the Split Cathedral. His book of *Sacrae cantiones* (Venice, 1620; destroyed in World War II) includes 27 motets; they reflect the influence of the early Baroque style and employ instrumental accompaniment. Modern eds. of his works appear in D. Plamenac, ed., *Odabarani moteti* (Zagreb, 1935) and J. Andreis, ed., *Šesnaesi moteta* (Zagreb, 1970).
Bibl.: N. O'Loughlin, "A Note on L.," *Musical Times,* CXIV (1973).

Lukács, Miklós, Hungarian conductor; b. Gyula, Feb. 4, 1905; d. Budapest, Nov. 1, 1986. He took courses with A. Schnabel and Hindemith at the Berlin Hochschule für Musik; conducted in various German theaters (1930–43), then at the Hungarian State Opera in Budapest (1943–78), where he also served as its director (1944; 1966–78).

Lukáš, Zdeněk, Czech composer; b. Prague, Aug, 21, 1928. He studied at the Prague teachers' inst.; also had lessons with Řídký (composition) and Modr (theory); was active with the Czech Radio in Plzeň (1953–64) and received instruction from Kabeláč in Prague (1961–70). In his works he explores various compositional forms.
Works: operas: *At žije mrtvý* (Long Live the Deceased; Prague, Dec. 11, 1968); *Domácí karneval* (Domestic Carnival; Prague, March 29, 1969); *Planeta a tiše fialovou září* (Planet with Soft Violet Glow; 1978). **orch.:** 5 syms. (1960, 1961, 1965, 1965, 1972); Piano Concerto (1955); Violin Concerto (1956); Cello Concerto (1957); Concerto for Soprano Saxophone and Orch. (1962); *Concerto grosso* for String Quartet and String Orch. (1964); *Symphonietta solemnis* (1965); *Sonata concertata* for Piano, Winds, and Percussion (1966); *Musica ritmica* for Percussion and Winds (1966); Concerto for Violin, Viola, and Orch. (Prague, March 7, 1969); Variations for Piano and Orch. (1970); *Postludium* (1971); *Concerto grosso* No. 2 for Flute, Violin, Orch., and Tape (1972); Bassoon Concerto (1976); Clarinet Concerto (1976); *Concerto grosso* No. 3 for Chamber Orch. (1977); *Transformations* for Piano and Orch. (1978); *Musica Boema,* 2 symphonic movements for Winds, Percussion, and Harp (1978); Flute Concerto (1981); Viola Concerto (1983); *Concert Music* for Violin and Strings (1986).
vocal: *Adam a Eva,* oratorio (1969); *Nezabiješ* (Thou Shalt Not Kill), oratorio (1971); 2 cantatas (1977; *To Prague,* 1982); also many choral works; songs. **chamber:** 3 string quartets (1960, 1965, 1973); Trio for Violin, Piano, and Side Drum (1962); *Partita semplice* for 4 Violins and Piano (1964); Wind Quintet (1968); *Amoroso* for Clarinet, Bagpipes, and Double Bass (1970); Trio for Violin, Cello, and Piano (1974); *Meditations* for Viola and Harpsichord (1976); *Cathedrals* for Brass Instruments and Organ (1976); *Intarsia* for Violin, Viola, and Cello (1977).

Luke, Ray, American composer and conductor; b. Fort Worth, Texas, May 30, 1926. He studied at Texas Christian Univ. in Fort Worth (B.M., 1949; M.M., 1950) and at the Eastman School of Music in Rochester, N.Y., with Bernard Rogers (Ph.D., 1960). In 1969 he received the gold medal at the Queen Elisabeth of Belgium International Competition for his Piano Concerto. He taught at East Texas State College from 1951 to 1962; in 1962, was appointed to the faculty of Oklahoma City Univ. He served as associate conductor of the Oklahoma City Sym. (1968–73), then as principal guest conductor (1974–78).
Works: stage: *Medea,* opera (Boston, May 3, 1979); *Tapestry,* ballet (Oklahoma City, May 8, 1975). **orch.:** 4 syms.: No. 1 (Rochester, N.Y., March 26, 1959); No. 2 (Oklahoma City, Feb. 3, 1963); No. 3 (Oklahoma City, Feb. 21, 1964); No. 4 (Oklahoma City, March 30, 1970); 2 suites: No. 1 (Rochester, N.Y., April 15, 1958); No. 2 (1967); *Miniatures* (1957); *Epilogue* (1958); Bassoon Concerto (1965); *Symphonic Dialogues* for Violin, Oboe, and Orch. (1965); *Incantation* for Cello, Harp, and Strings (1968); Piano Concerto (Brussels, Nov. 26, 1970); *Compressions* No. 1 (Oklahoma City, Jan. 9, 1973); *Compressions* No. 2 (Fort Worth, Nov. 9, 1973). **chamber:** Trio for Flute, Clarinet, and Piano (1974); 2 *Odes* for Mezzo-soprano, Flute, and Piano (1965); String Quartet (1966); Septet (1979).

Lully, Jean-Baptiste (originally, **Giovanni Battista Lulli**), celebrated Italian-born French composer; b. Florence, Nov. 28, 1632; d. Paris, March 22, 1687. The son of a poor Florentine miller, he learned to play the guitar at an early age. His talent for singing brought him to the attention of Roger de Lorraine, Chevalier de Guise, and he was taken to Paris in 1646 as a page to Mlle. d'Orléans, a young cousin of Louis XIV. He quickly adapted to the manner of the French court; although he mastered the language, he never lost his Italian accent. There is no truth in the report that he worked in the kitchens, but he did keep company with the domestic servants, and it was while he was serving in Mlle. d'Orléans's court in the Tuileries that he perfected his violin technique. He also had the opportunity to hear the 24 Violons du Roi and was present at performances of Luigi Rossi's *Orfeo* at the Louvre in 1647. When Mlle. d'Orléans suffered political disgrace in 1652 and was forced to leave Paris, Lully was released from her service, and early in 1653 he danced with the young Louis XIV in the ballet *La Nuit.* Shortly thereafter, he was made compositeur de la musique instrumentale du Roi, with joint responsibility for the instrumental music in court ballets. At some time before 1656 he became conductor of Les Petits Violons du Roi, a smaller offshoot of the grand bande. This ensemble was heard for the 1st time in 1656 in *La Galanterie du temps.* Thanks to Lully's strict discipline with regard to organization and interpretation, Les Petits Violons soon came to rival the parent ensemble. The 2 groups were combined in 1664.

Lully became a naturalized French citizen in 1661, the same year in which he was appointed surintendant de la musique et compositeur de la musique de la chambre; he also became maître de la musique de la famille royale in 1662. His association with Molière commenced in 1664; he provided Molière with the music for a series of comédies-ballets, culminating with *Le Bourgeois Gentilhomme* in 1670. Lully acquired the sole right to form an Académie Royale de Musique in 1672, and thus gained the power to forbid performances of stage works by any other composer. From then until his death he produced a series of tragédies lyriques, most of which were composed to texts by the librettist Philippe Quinault. The subject matter for several of these works was suggested by the King, who was extravagantly praised and idealized in their prologues. Lully took great pains in perfecting these texts, but was often content to leave the writing of the inner voices of the music to his pupils. His monopoly of French musical life created much enmity. In 1674 Henri Guichard attempted to establish an Académie Royale des Spectacles, and their ensuing rivalry resulted in Lully accusing Guichard of trying to murder him by mixing arsenic with his snuff. Lully won the court case that followed, but the decision was reversed on appeal. A further setback occurred when Quinault was thought to have slandered the King's mistress in his text of *Isis* (1677) and was compelled to end his partnership with Lully in disgrace for some time. The King continued to support Lully, however, in spite of the fact that the composer's homosexuality had become a public scandal (homosexuality at the time was a capital offense). Lully's acquisition of titles culminated in 1681, when noble rank was conferred upon him with the title Secré-taire du Roi. In his last years he turned increasingly to sacred music. It was while he was conducting his *Te Deum* on Jan. 8, 1687, that he suffered a symbolic accident, striking his foot with a pointed cane used to pound out the beat. Gangrene set in, and he died of blood poisoning 2 months later. Lully's historical importance rests primarily upon his music for the theater. He developed what became known as the French over-ture, with its 3 contrasting slow-fast-slow movements. He fur-ther replaced the Italian recitativo secco style with accompa-nied French recitative. Thus, through the Italian-born Lully, French opera came of age.

WORKS: OPERAS (all are tragédies lyriques unless otherwise given): *Les Fêtes de l'Amour et de Bacchus*, pastorale-pastiche (Opéra, Paris, Nov. 15, 1672); *Cadmus et Hermione* (Opéra, Paris, April 27, 1673); *Alceste, ou Le Triomphe d'Alcide* (Opéra, Paris, Jan. 19, 1674); *Thésée* (Saint-Germain, Jan. 12, 1675); *Atys* (Saint-Germain, Jan. 10, 1676); *Isis* (Saint-Germain, Jan. 5, 1677); *Psyché* (Opéra, Paris, April 19, 1678); *Bellérophon* (Opéra, Paris, Jan. 31, 1679); *Proserpine* (Saint-Germain, Feb. 3, 1680); *Persée* (Opéra, Paris, April 18, 1682); *Phaëton* (Ver-sailles, Jan. 9, 1683); *Amadis* (Opéra, Paris, Jan. 18, 1684); *Roland* (Versailles, Jan. 8, 1685); *Armide* (Opéra, Paris, Feb. 15, 1686); *Acis et Galatée*, pastorale héroïque (Anet, Sept. 6, 1686); *Achille et Polyxène* (Opéra, Paris, Nov. 7, 1687; Overture and Act 1 by Lully; Prologue and Acts 2 to 5 by Collasse).

BALLETS (all or most music by Lully): *Alcidiane* (Feb. 14, 1658); *La Raillerie* (Louvre, Paris, Feb. 19, 1659); *Xerxes* (Lou-vre, Paris, Nov. 22, 1660); *Ballet de Toulouze "au mariage du Roy"* (1660); *L'Impatience* (Tuileries, Paris, Feb. 14, 1661); *Les Saisons* (Fontainebleau, July 23, 1661); *Hercule amoureux* (Tuileries, Paris, Feb. 7, 1662); *Les Arts* (Palais Royal, Paris, Jan. 8, 1663); *Les Noces de village* (Vincennes, Oct. 3, 1663); *Les Amours déguisés* (Palais Royal, Paris, Feb. 13, 1664); 5 entrées for *Œdipe* (Fontainebleau, July 21, 1664); *La Naissance de Vénus* (Palais Royal, Paris, Jan. 26, 1665); *Les Gardes* (June 1665); *Ballet de Créqui ou Le Triomphe de Bacchus dans les Indes* (Hôtel de Créqui, Paris, Jan. 9, 1666); *Les Muses* (Saint-Germain, Dec. 2, 1666); *Le Carnaval ou Mascarade de Versailles* (Tuileries, Paris, Jan. 18, 1668); *Flore* (Tuileries, Paris, Feb. 13, 1669); *La Jeunesse* (1669); *Les Jeux pythiens* (Saint-Germain, Feb. 7, 1670); *Ballet des ballets* (Saint-Germain, Dec. 2, 1671); *Le Carnaval* (Opéra, Paris, Oct. 17, 1675); *Le Triomphe de l'amour* (Saint-Germain, Jan. 21, 1681); *Le Temple de la paix* (Fontainebleau, Oct. 20, 1685). **BALLETS** (music by Lully and others): *La Nuit* (Petit Bourbon, Paris, Feb. 23, 1653); *Les Proverbes* (Louvre, Paris, Feb. 17, 1654; music not extant); *Les Noces de Pelée et de Thétis* (Petit Bourbon, Paris, April 14, 1654); *Le Temps* (Louvre, Paris, Dec. 3, 1654); *Les Plaisirs* (Louvre, Paris, Feb. 4, 1655); *Les Bienvenus* (Com-piègne, May 30, 1655; music not extant); *La Révente des habits de ballet* (1655?); *Psyché et la puissance de l'amour* (Louvre, Paris, Jan. 16, 1656; music not extant); *La Galanterie du temps* (Paris, Feb. 19, 1656); *L'Amour malade* (Louvre, Paris, Jan. 17, 1657); *Les Plaisirs troublés* (Louvre, Paris, Feb. 11 or 12, 1657; music not extant); *Mascarade du capitaine* (Palais Royal, Paris, 1664; music not extant).

OTHER WORKS FOR STAGE: *L'Impromptu de Versailles*, com-edy (Versailles, Oct. 14, 1663); *Le Mariage forcé*, comedy (Lou-vre, Paris, Jan. 29, 1664); *Les Plaisirs de l'île enchantée*, comé-die-ballet (Versailles, May 7, 1664); *La Princesse d'Élide*, comédie-ballet (Versailles, May 8, 1664); *L'Amour médecin*, comedy (Versailles, Sept. 16, 1665); *La Pastorale comique*, pas-torale (Saint-Germain, Jan. 5, 1667); *Le Sicilien, ou L'Amour peintre*, comedy (Saint-Germain, Feb. 10, 1667); *Georges Dan-din*, with *Grand divertissement royal de Versailles*, comedy (Versailles, July 18, 1668); *La Grotte de Versailles*, divertisse-ment (Versailles, Aug. 1668); *Monsieur de Pourceaugnac*, com-edy (Chambord, Oct. 6, 1669); *Les Amants magnifiques*, comé-die-ballet (Saint-Germain, Feb. 7, 1670); *Le Bourgeois Gentil-homme*, comédie-ballet (Chambord, Oct. 14, 1670); *Psyché*, tragédie-ballet (Tuileries, Paris, Jan. 17, 1671); *Idylle sur la paix*, divertissement (Sceaux, July 16, 1685).

CHORAL: *Te Deum* (1677); *De profundis* (1683); *Motets à deux pour la chapelle du Roi* (Paris, 1684); 6 grands motets for 2 Choirs and Orch. (1685); 14 petits motets.

INSTRUMENTAL: Overtures; suites; dances; organ pieces; etc. A complete edition of Lully's works was ed. by H. Prunières (9 vols., Paris, 1930–39). A complete catalog of his works was ed. by H. Schneider (Tutzing, 1981).

BIBL.: H. Guichard, *Requête servant de factums contre B. L.* (Paris, 1673); C. Perrault, "Éloge de J.-B. L.," *Les Hommes illustres qui ont paru en France*, I (Paris, 1696); T. Lajarte, *L.* (Paris, 1878); E. Radet, *L., homme d'affaires, propriétaire et musicien* (Paris, 1891); J. Écorcheville, *De L. à Rameau, 1690–1730* (Paris, 1906); H. Prunières, *L.* (Paris, 1909; 2nd ed., 1927); L. de La Laurencie, *L.* (Paris, 1911; 2nd ed., 1919); H. Prunières, *La Vie illustre et libertine de J.-B. L.* (Paris, 1929); E. Borrel, *J.-B. L.* (Paris, 1949); N. Slonimsky, "L'Acte de nais-sance de L.," *Guide du Concert* (Feb. 1, 1952); T. Valensi, *Louis XIV et L.* (Nice, 1952); E. Eppelsheim, *Das Orchester in den Werken J.-B. L.s* (Tutzing, 1961); M.-F. Christout, *Le Ballet de cour de Louis XIV, 1643–1673* (Paris, 1967); W. Cole, *The Motets of J.B. L.* (diss., Univ. of Michigan, 1967); H. Ellis, *The Dances of J.B. L. (1632–1687)* (diss., Stanford Univ., 1967); L. Auld, *The Unity of Molière's Comedy-ballets* (diss., Bryn Mawr College, 1968); H. Ellis, "The Sources of J.-B. L.'s Secular Music," *Recherches sur la Musique Française Classique*, VIII (1968); A. Ducrot, "Les Représentations de l'Académie Royale de Musique à Paris au temps de Louis XIV, 1617–1753," ibid., X (1970); M. Benoit, *Musiques de cour: Chapelle, chambre, écurie, 1661–1733* (Paris, 1971); idem, *Versailles et les musi-ciens du Roi, 1661–1733* (Paris, 1971); G. Mongrédien, "Molière et L.," *XXVIIe Siècle*, no. 98–99 (1973); P. Howard, *The Operas of L.* (diss., Univ. of Surrey, 1974); idem, "The Académie Royale and the Performances of L.'s Opera," *Consort*, XXXI (1975); H. Schneider, *Der Rezeption der L.-Oper im 17. und 18. Jahr-hundert in Frankreich* (diss., Univ. of Mainz, 1976); J. New-man, *J.-B. de L. and His Tragédies lyriques* (Ann Arbor, 1979); H. Schneider, "Die Uberlieferung der Frühen Bühnenwerke von J.-B. L.," *Die Musikforschung*, XXXIV (1981); C. Wood, *J.-B. L. and His Successors: Music and Drama in the "Tragédie en musique," 1673–1715* (diss., Univ. of Hull, 1981); H. Schneider, *Die Rezeption der Opern L.s im Frankreich des An-cien Régime* (Tutzing, 1982); J. Hajdu, "Recent Findings in the Sources of L.'s Motets: The Traditions of Philidor and Foucault," *Le Grand Motet français (1663–1792): CNRS Paris 1984*; J. Anthony, "L.'s airs—French or Italian?," *Musical Times* (March 1987); idem, "Towards a principal source for L.'s court ballets: Foucault vs Philidor," *Recherches sur la Musi-que Française Classique*, XXV (1987); A. Cohen, "The L. Ar-chive at Stanford University," *Notes* (Sept. 1987); B. Gustafson, "The L. Labyrinth: Cross References and Misattributions in the L.-Werke-Verzeichnis," ibid.; C. Schmidt, "Newly Identi-fied Manuscript Sources for the Music of J.-B. L.," ibid.; J. Heyer, ed., *J.-B. L. and the Music of the French Baroque: Essays in Honour of James R. Anthony* (Cambridge, 1988).

Lumbye, Hans Christian, famous Danish conductor and composer; b. Copenhagen, May 2, 1810; d. there, March 20, 1874. He played in military bands as a youth; in 1839, formed his own orch. in Copenhagen, soon achieving fame as music director of the Tivoli Gardens there (1843–72). He composed about 400 pieces of dance music, including waltzes, galops, polkas, marches, etc., which earned him the sobriquet of "the Johann Strauss of the North." His 2 sons were also musicians; the elder, **Carl (Christian) Lumbye** (b. Copenhagen, July 9, 1841; d. there, Aug. 10, 1911), was a violinist, conductor, and composer of dance music; the younger son, **Georg (Au-gust) Lumbye** (b. Copenhagen, Aug. 26, 1843; d. there, Oct. 29, 1922), was a conductor and composer; studied at the Paris Cons., then conducted in Copenhagen; wrote operettas, including *Heksefløtjen* (The Witch's Flute; 1869), incidental music, songs, etc.

BIBL.: G. Skjerne, *H.C. L. og hans Samtid* (Copenhagen, 1912; 2nd ed., 1946).

Lummis, Charles F(letcher), American ethnomusicologist; b. Lynn, Mass., March 1, 1859; d. Los Angeles, Nov. 25, 1928. He received instruction in Hebrew, Greek, and Latin from his father; later took courses at Harvard Univ. (1877–80). During a cross-country hike from Ohio to California, he became interested in the cultures of the American Indians and of Mexican-Americans; he made pioneering recordings of American Indian music and folk songs. He was city ed. of the *Los Angeles Times* (1885–87) and also ed. of *Land of Sunshine* (1894–1901) and *Out West* (1902–9); he also wrote novels and poetry. He founded the Landmarks Club (1895) and the Sequoia Club (1902), which espoused Indian causes. In 1907 he founded the Southwest Museum in Los Angeles, which serves as the depository of his valuable collection. With A. Farwell, he publ. *Spanish Songs of Old California* (1923).

BIBL.: M. Newmark, "C.F. L.," *Historical Society of Southern California Quarterly,* XXXII/1 (1950); E. Bingham, *C.F. L.: Editor of the Southwest* (San Marino, Calif., 1955); M. Simmons, *Two Southwesterners: C. L. and Amando Chaves* (Cerillos, N.Mex., 1968); D. Gordon, *C.F. L.: Crusador in Corduroy* (Los Angeles, 1972); T. Fiske and K. Lummis, *C.F. L.: The Man and His West* (Norman, Okla., 1975); R. Fleming, *C.F. L.* (Boise, Idaho, 1981).

Lumsdaine, David (Newton), Australian composer; b. Sydney, Oct. 31, 1931. He studied piano, viola, and composition at the Sydney Cons. and at the Univ. of Sydney (B.A., 1953); then studied in London at the Royal Academy of Music and took private composition lessons with M. Seiber. He was a lecturer on music at the Univ. of Durham (1970–81), where he founded an electronic music studio; then held a senior lectureship at King's College, London (from 1981). In 1979 he married **Nicola LeFanu.** His works display a highly complex idiom of composition.

WORKS: *Variations for Orchestra* (1957); *Short Symphony* (1959); *Annotations from Auschwitz,* chamber cantata (1964; rev. 1970); Cantata No. 2 (1964); *Missa brevis* (1964); *Bach Music* for Large Orch., based on material from Bach's *The Art of the Fugue,* transformed into a complex continuum of metric elements (1965); Cantata No. 3, *Story from a Time of Disturbance,* for Baritone and Chamber Ensemble (1965); *Easter Frescoes* for Soprano and Chamber Orch., after the *New Testament* (1966; rev. 1971); *Flights* for 2 Pianos (1967); *Mandala I* for Wind Quintet (1968); *Bourbon* for Computer and Tape (1968); *Babel* for Tape (1968); *Episodes* for Orch. (1969); *Mandala II* for Flute, Clarinet, Viola, Cello, and Percussion (1969); *Looking Glass Music* for Brass Quintet and Magnetic Tape (1971); *Kangaroo Hunt* for Piano and Percussion (1971); *Caliban Impromptu* for Piano Trio and Electronic Instruments, after Shakespeare's play *The Tempest* (1972); *Salvation Creek with Eagle* for Chamber Orch. (1974); *Sunflower* for Chamber Orch. (1975); *Evensong* for Brass Ensemble (1975); *Hagoromo* for Orch. (1975); *Mandala III* for Piano and Ensemble (1978); *Wild Ride to Heaven* for Tape (1980); *Mandala IV* for String Quartet (1983); *Empty Sky, Mootwingee* for Flute, Trombone or Horn, Cello, Pitched Percussion, and 2 Pianos (1986); *Mandala V* for Orch. (1988); *Round Dance* for Sitar, Tabla, Flute, Cello, and Keyboard (1989).

BIBL.: R. Cooke, "D. L.," *Music and Musicians,* 21 (1972–73); N. LeFanu, "D. L.," *Musical Times,* CXVII (1976).

Lumsden, Sir David (James), noted English organist, harpsichordist, choirmaster, and music editor; b. Newcastle upon Tyne, March 19, 1928. He studied with Ord and Dart at Cambridge Univ. (Mus.B., 1951; Ph.D., 1955) and at Oxford Univ. (Ph.D., 1959). He was organist of the Univ. of Nottingham (1954–56); also founder-conductor of the Nottingham Bach Soc.; served as rector chori at Southwell Minster and director of music at the Univ. College of North Staffordshire, Keele (1956–59). He then was organist at New College, Oxford

(1959–78); also taught at the Royal Academy of Music in London (1960–62). He was principal of the Royal Scottish Academy of Music in Glasgow (1978–82) and of the Royal Academy of Music in London (from 1982). He was knighted in 1985.

Lunceford, Jimmie (James Melvin), black American jazz instrumentalist, bandleader, and arranger; b. Fulton, Mo., June 6, 1902; d. Seaside, Oreg., July 12, 1947. He studied music with Wilberforce Whiteman, the father of Paul Whiteman; he mastered the saxophone, guitar, trombone, and flute; then went to Fisk Univ. in Nashville, Tenn. (B.M., 1926). In 1929 he formed his own band, with which he made numerous tours of the U.S., becoming one of the most popular figures of the big-band period.

Lund, Signe, Norwegian composer; b. Christiania, April 15, 1868; d. there (Oslo), April 6, 1950. She studied in Berlin, Copenhagen, and Paris; spent several years in America. As a composer, she was completely under the lyrical domination of Grieg's music, and her works are eminently perishable. She wrote a ceremonial overture, *The Road to France,* on the occasion of America's entry into World War I in 1917; also various instrumental pieces and songs. She publ. an autobiography, *Sol gjennem skyer* (Oslo, 1944).

Lundquist, Torbjörn (Iwan), Swedish composer and conductor; b. Stockholm, Sept. 30, 1920. He studied composition with Dag Wirén; then conducting with Otmar Suitner in Salzburg and Vienna; was active as a conductor in Stockholm; appeared as a guest conductor throughout Europe; in 1978 he was awarded a government income to pursue composition. In his output he utilized various styles and techniques, ranging from the traditional to the avant-garde and incorporating elements from jazz to Eastern music. He also experimented with techniques referred to as "organized spontaneity."

WORKS: *Divertimento* for Chamber Orch. (1951); 8 syms.: No. 1, *Kammarsymfoni* (1952–56; rev. 1971); No. 2, *For Freedom* (1956–70); No. 3, *Sinfonia dolorosa* (1971–75); No. 4, *Sinfonia ecologica* (1985); No. 5, *Vienna Symphony* (1987); No. 6, *Sarek* (1988); No. 7, *Humanity* for Soprano, Baritone, Chorus, and Orch. (1988); No. 8, *Kroumata Symphony* (1989); *Elegies from Bergen* for Tenor, Male Chorus, and Orch. (1958); *Via tomheten* (Via the Emptiness), "visions" for Soli, Chorus, and Chamber Orch. (1959); *Anrop* (Call) for Soprano and Orch. (1963–64); works for Solo Concert Accordion: *Partita piccola* (1964); *Metamorphoses* (1965); *9 2-part Inventions* (1966); *Plasticity* (1966); *Sonatina piccola* (1967); *Botany Play* (1968); *Microscope* (1971); *Concerto da camera* for Accordion and Orch. (1965; Gävle, Feb. 20, 1966); *Movements* for Accordion and String Quartet (1966); *Duell* for Accordion and Percussion (1966); *Combinazione* for Violin and Percussion (1966); 2 string quartets (1966, 1969); *Férvor* for Violino Grande and Orch. (1967); *Hangarmusik,* "concerto sinfonico" for Piano and Orch. (1967); *Teamwork* for Wind Quintet (1967); *Confrontation* for Orch. (Stockholm, Oct. 5, 1968); *Evoluzione* for Strings (1968); *Intarzia* for Accordion and Strings (1968); *Sogno* for Oboe and Strings (1968); *Sound on Sound* for Audience, Speaker, Composer, and Stereo Orch. (Stockholm, Jan. 25, 1969); *Stereogram III* for Xylorimba, Electric Guitar, and Accordion (1969); *4 rondeaux* for Wind Quartet and Piano (1969); *Tempera* for 6 Brass Instruments (1969); *Galax* for Orch. (1971); Marimba Concerto (1972); opera, *Moment of Eternity* (1973; Stockholm, May 27, 1974); *Concerto grosso* for Violin, Cello, and String Orch. (1974); *Trio fiorente* for Piano Trio (1975); *Suite* for 6 Percussionists (1976); Violin Concerto (1978); *Arktis* for Symphonic Band (1984); *Integration* for 5 Percussionists and String Quartet (1984); opera, *Jason and Medea* (1985–89).

Lundsten, Ralph, Swedish composer, film creator, and artist; b. Ersnäs, Oct. 6, 1936. He was basically autodidact; settled in the wooden fairy-tale mansion of Castle Frankenburg (built 1878) in Saltsjö-Boo, where he founded Andromedia (1959), Sweden's best-known private electronic music studio and film center. A pioneer in electronic music in Sweden, he has gone on to secure an international following via the popularity of the "New Age" movement. In 1982 the Andromedia Fan Soc. was organized to promote his activities as a composer, artist, and "New Age" visionary. In 1984 Radio Sweden International adopted "Out in the Wide World" from his *Nordic Nature Symphony No. 4* as its theme signature for its international broadcasts. Much of his output has been recorded and performed throughout the world.

WORKS: *Aloha Arita* (1966); *Kaleidoscope* (1966); *Mums: EMS No. 1* (1967); *3 Electronic "Pop" Pieces* (1967); *Visions of Flying Saucers* (1967); *Happy Music* (1968); *Winter Music* (1968); *Mizar* (1968); *Tellus* (1969); *Blue Bird* (1969); *Suite for Electronic Accordion* (1969); *Energy for Biological Computer* (1969); *Erik XIV* (1969); *Carvings* (1969); *Ölskog: Through a Landscape of Mirrors* (1970); *Cosmic Love—Trial and Discussion* (1970); *Gustav III* (1971); *Nightmare* (1971); *Ourfather* (1972); *Nordic Nature Sympony No. 1, The Water Sprite* (1972–73); *The Midnight Hour* (1973); *Ode to a Lost Soul* (1973); *On Tottering Toes* (1973); *Feel It* (1973); *Gunnar of Lidarände* (1973); *Shangri-la* (1975); *Winter Music* (1975); *Heaven by Night* (1975); *Raped Planet* (1975); *Icelandic Dancing Pictures* (1975); *Nordic Symphony No. 2, Johannes and the Lady of the Woods* (1975); *Universe* (1977); *Discophrenia* (1978); *Alpha Ralpha Boulevard* (1979); *Paradise Symphony* (1980); *Nordic Nature Symphony No. 3, A Midwinter Saga* (1981); *A New Age* (1982); *Aspects of Nature* (1982); *Nordic Nature Symphony No. 4, A Summer Saga* (1983); *Strangers in Paradise* (1984); *Nordic Nature Symphony No. 5, Bewitched* (1984); *Dreamscape* (1984); *Welcome* (1985); *Fantasia by Starlight* (1986); *The Dream Master* (1986); *Suite amoroso* (1986); *The Gate of Time* (1988).

Lunn, Louise Kirkby. See **Kirkby-Lunn, Louise.**

Lunssens, Martin, Belgian conductor and composer; b. Molenbeek-Saint-Jean, April 16, 1871; d. Etterbeek, Feb. 1, 1944. He studied with Gevaert, Jehin, and Kufferath at the Brussels Cons., gaining the 1st Belgian Prix de Rome in 1895 with the cantata *Callirhoé;* then became a prof. at the Brussels Cons.; subsequently was director of the Music Academy at Courtrai (1905–16); at Charleroi (1916–21); at the Louvain Cons. (1921–24); and finally at the Ghent Cons. (from 1924). He was also known as an excellent conductor; was in charge of the Flemish Opera in Antwerp, where he conducted many Wagner operas.

WORKS: 4 syms., the 1st 3 with the programmatic titles *Symphonie romaine, Symphonie florentine,* and *Symphonie française;* symphonic poems (*Roméo et Juliette; Phèdre; Le Cid; Timon d'Athènes*); 3 violin concertos; Viola Concerto; Cello Concerto; much chamber music; songs.

Lupi, Johannes, distinguished Franco-Flemish composer; b. c.1506; d. Cambrai, Dec. 20, 1539. He was a choirboy at Notre Dame Cathedral in Cambrai (1514–21), then studied philosophy at the Univ. of Louvain (1522). After returning to Cambrai Cathedral as a parvus vicarius (1526), he was made master of the choristers (1527); then was magnus vicarius and subdeacon (from 1530, except for a period of ill health [1535–37]). He excelled as a composer of motets; also wrote many chansons. Attaingnant and Jullet publ. a book of his motets in 1542, which helped to spread his fame.

BIBL.: H. Albrecht, "Lupus Hellinck und J. L.," *Acta Musicologica,* VI (1934); B. Blackburn, *The Lupus Problem* (diss., Univ. of Chicago, 1970); idem, "J. L. and Lupus Hellinck: A Double Portrait," *Musical Quarterly,* LIX (1973).

Lupi, Roberto, Italian conductor and composer; b. Milan, Nov. 28, 1908; d. Dornach, Switzerland, April 17, 1971. He studied at the Milan Cons.; then was a prof. of harmony and counterpoint at the Cherubini Cons. in Florence (1941–71). Among his works are the cantata *Orfeo; Sacra sinfonia;* Cello Sonata; songs. He publ. a treatise, *Armonia di gravitazione* (Rome, 1946), emphasizing the importance of the focal tone in composition rather than key. He ed. several works by Galuppi, Caldara, Stradella, and other Italian composers.

Luporini, Gaetano, Italian composer; b. Lucca, Dec. 12, 1865; d. there, May 12, 1948. He was a pupil of Primo Quilici,

and a protégé of Ricordi, the publisher. After graduating from the Pacini Music Inst. in Lucca, he studied at the Milan Cons. with Carlo Angeloni and Catalani; returning to Lucca in 1902, he became director of the Pacini Music Inst.; also choirmaster of the Cathedral.

WORKS: OPERAS: *I dispetti amorosi* (Turin, Feb. 27, 1894); *La collana di Pasqua* (Naples, Nov. 1, 1896; renamed *Nora,* and perf. under that title in Lucca, Sept. 7, 1908); *L'aquila e le colombe* (Rome, Feb. 17, 1914); *Chiaro di luna* (Bologna, Nov. 20, 1925); also orch. pieces; songs.

Lupu, Radu, outstanding Rumanian pianist; b. Galaţi, Nov. 30, 1945. He began his piano studies at the age of 6, making his recital debut when he was 12; then studied with Florica Muzicescu and on scholarship at the Moscow Cons. (1963), where he studied with Heinrich and Stanislau Neuhaus until 1969. In quick succession he won 1st prize in the Van Cliburn (1966), Enesco (1967), and Leeds (1969) competitions. In 1972 he made his American debut as soloist with the Cleveland Orch., and subsequently played with the Chicago, Los Angeles, N.Y., and Boston orchs. In Europe he made successful appearances in Berlin, Paris, Amsterdam, London, Vienna, and other cities in varied programs ranging from Classical to modern works.

Lupus, Eduardus. See **Lobo, Duarte.**

Lussan, Zélie de, American soprano; b. Brooklyn, Dec. 21, 1862; d. London, Dec. 18, 1949. She was trained in singing by her mother, and made her 1st public appearance at Chickering Hall in N.Y. (April 2, 1878); in 1885, joined the Boston Ideal Opera Co., and in 1888 went to London, where she made her debut as Carmen with A. Harris's Italian Opera Co. at Covent Garden (July 7, 1888); subsequently sang with the Carl Rosa Opera Co. and Mapleson's company. She sang Carmen again for her Metropolitan Opera debut in N.Y. on Nov. 26, 1894; after that season, was on its roster again from 1898 to 1900. She was particularly successful at Covent Garden (1890–93; 1895–1900; 1902–3; 1910). She was called upon to sing Carmen more than 1,000 times during her career; she was also a noted Cherubino, Zerlina, Mignon, and Nedda. She was married to the pianist Angelo Fronani.

Lussy, Mathis, Swiss writer on music and piano teacher; b. Stans, April 8, 1828; d. Montreux, Jan. 21, 1910. He studied with Businger and Nägeli; went to Paris in 1846 to study medicine but soon resumed his music studies; subsequently taught piano in Kloster Piepus for 40 years before settling in Montreux (1902). He wrote *Exercices de mécanisme* (1863); *Traité de l'expression musicale* (1873; partial reprint as *Le Rythme musical,* 1883); with E. David, *Histoire de la notation musicale* (1882); *L'Anacrouse dans la musique moderne* (1903); *La "Sonate pathétique" de Beethoven* (ed. by A. Dechevrens; 1912).

BIBL.: E. Monod, *M. L. et le Rythme Musical* (Neuchâtel, 1912).

Lütgendorff, Willibald Leo, German art historian; b. Augsburg, July 8, 1856; d. Weimar, Dec. 31, 1937. He studied at the Kunstakademie in Munich; in 1889, became director of the Kunstschule and curator of the Art Gallery in Lübeck. Besides writings on the plastic arts, he publ. *Die Geigen- und Lautenmacher vom Mittelalter bis zur Gegenwart* (1904; 2nd ed., enl., 1913; new ed., 1990, by T. Drescher).

Luther, Martin, great German religious reformer; b. Eisleben, Nov. 10, 1483; d. there, Feb. 18, 1546. His reform of the church extended to the musical services, in which he took the deepest interest. After leaving the Wartburg, near Eisenach (March 22, 1522), he gave his ideas practical shape; his *Formula missae* (1523) and *Deutsche Messe* (1526; facsimile ed. by J. Wolf, Kassel, 1934) established the new service. He changed the order of the Mass; a German Psalm took the place of the introit; the German Creed was substituted for the Latin Credo. The German Mass was sung for the 1st time in the Parish Church at Wittenberg on Christmas Day, 1524. Kapellmeister Conrad Rupsch and cantor Johann Walter aided Luther in organizing the musical part of the Mass. Walter states that Luther invented chorale melodies on the flute (he was an excellent flutist), and that these were noted down by Walter and Rupsch. It is impossible to establish with certainty which hymn tunes ascribed to Luther are really his; *Jesaia dem Propheten das geschah* is definitely Luther's; the celebrated hymn tune *Ein' feste Burg ist unser Gott* is most probably authentic. Most important, the words of many chorales were written, arranged, or tr. from Latin by Luther.

BIBL.: A. Rambach, *Über L.s Verdienst um den Kirchengesang* (Hamburg, 1813); K. von Winterfeld, *L.s deutsche geistliche Lieder* (Leipzig, 1840); K. Loewe, *L.studien* (1846; publ. in Wittenberg, 1918); M. Rade, *M. L.s Leben, Taten und Meinungen* (3 vols., Tübingen, 1883; 2nd ed., 1901); H. von Stephen, *L. als Musiker* (Bielefeld, 1899); F. Zelle, *Das älteste lutherische Haus-Gesangbuch* (Göttingen, 1903; with commentary); J. Lyra, *L.s Deutsche Messe* (1904); idem, *Die Lieder L.s in ihrer Bedeutung für das evangelische Kirchenlied* (Göttingen, 1905); idem, *Studien zu L.s Liedern* (Göttingen, 1907); H. Lehmann, *L. im deutschen Lied* (Halle, 1910); H. Kretzschmar, "L. und die Musik," in *Jahrbuch Peters* (1917); K. Anton, *Luther und die Musik* (1918); H. Preuss, *L. der Künstler* (1931); H. Moser, *Die Melodien der L.lieder* (Leipzig, 1935); G. Wolfram, "Ein' feste Burg ist unser Gott" (Berlin, 1936); C. Mahrenholz, *L. und die Kirchenmusik* (Kassel, 1937); C. Schneider, *L. poète et musicien et les Enchiridiens de 1524* (Geneva, 1942); W. Buszin, "L. on Music," *Musical Quarterly* (Jan. 1946); F. Smend, *L. und Bach* (Berlin, 1947); P. Nettl, *L. and Music* (Philadelphia, 1948); W. Stapel, *L.s Lieder und Gedichte* (Stuttgart, 1950); C. Schalk, *L. on Music: Paradigms of Praise* (St. Louis, 1987).

Lutkin, Peter Christian, American organist, choral conductor, music educator, and composer; b. Thompsonville, Wis., March 27, 1858; d. Evanston, Ill., Dec. 27, 1931. He studied music in Chicago; then took lessons with A. Haupt (organ) and W. Bargiel (composition) in Berlin; had further instruction in piano from Moszkowski in Paris and Leschetizky in Vienna. Returning to America, he filled various posts as an organist in Chicago; taught theory at the American Cons. of Music there. In 1883 he became an instructor in piano and organ at Northwestern Univ. in Evanston, Ill.; from 1895 to 1928, was dean of the School of Music there; also taught church music at the Garrett Biblical Inst. at Evanston (1915–28); was choral conductor at the Chicago North Shore Festival (1909–30); publ. church music and pedagogical works for piano; ed. the *Methodist Sunday School Hymnal;* was co-ed. of the *Episcopal Church Hymnal.*

Lutoslawski, Witold, outstanding Polish composer; b. Warsaw, Jan. 25, 1913. He learned to play the piano as a child; then studied violin with Lidia Kmitowa (1926–32) and theory and composition with Witold Maliszewski (from 1927); also studied mathematics at the Univ. of Warsaw (1931–33). He entered the Warsaw Cons. (1932), where he continued composition studies with Maliszewski and also studied piano with Jerzy Lefeld (graduated as a pianist, 1936, and as a composer, 1937). He served in the Polish Army (1937–38); was mobilized in the summer of 1939 and was taken prisoner of war by the invading Nazi armies at the outbreak of World War II; he managed to escape to Warsaw, where he earned a living by playing piano in cafes (1939–44); also participated in clandestine concerts in private homes. After the war, he worked briefly for the Polish Radio (1945), then devoted himself to composition; when his renommée reached the outside world, he obtained prestigious engagements as a lecturer and instructor in England, West Germany, Denmark, and Sweden; he also appeared as a conductor of his own works from 1963. As his reputation grew, he received numerous awards: the City of Warsaw Prize (1948), the State Music Prize, 1st class (1955, 1964, 1978), the prize of the Union of Polish Composers (1959, 1973), the Maurice Ravel Prize of Paris (1971), the Sibelius de Wihuri Prize of Helsinki (1973), the "Solidarity" Award of Poland (1984), the 1st Grawemeyer Award of $150,000 from

the Univ. of Louisville (1985), the Gold Medal of the Royal Phil. Soc. of London (1985), etc. He was made an honorary member of Hamburg's Freie Akademie der Kunste (1966), extraordinary member of West Berlin's Akademie der Kunste (1968), honorary member of the ISCM (1969), corresponding member of East Berlin's Deutsche Akademie der Kunste (1970), corresponding member of the American Academy of Arts and Letters (1975), honorary member of London's Royal Academy of Music (1976), etc. He also received honorary D.Mus. degrees from the Cleveland Inst. of Music (1971) and the Univ. of Warsaw (1973), and an honorary degree of D.F.A. from Northwestern Univ. (1974). His early works are marked by a neo-Classical tendency, with an influx of national Polish motifs; gradually he turned to a more structural type of composition in which melodic and rhythmic elements are organized into a strong unifying network, with occasional incursions of dodecaphonic and aleatory practices. He was also extraordinarily open-minded; he was attracted by the music of John Cage, finding useful applications in the operations of chance. The influence of Béla Bartók is felt in the constantly changing colors, angular intervallic progressions, and asymmetrical rhythms. In this respect, Lutoslawski's *Musique funèbre* for String Orch., dedicated to the memory of Bartók, thematically built on a concatenation of upward tritones and downward semitones, is stylistically significant. He freely applied sonorism in building orchestral colors. Although possessing a masterful technique of composition, he allowed himself plenty of time for revisions; willing to make any number of successive changes to attain his goal, it took him fully 10 years to achieve the desired balance of structural contents to complete his 3rd Sym. His list of works is therefore not exceptionally large, but each composition, whatever its length, is an accomplished masterpiece.

WORKS: ORCH.: *Symphonic Variations* (1936–38; Krakow, June 17, 1939); 3 syms.: No. 1 (1941–47; Katowice, April 6, 1948); No. 2 (1966–67; Katowice, June 9, 1967); No. 3 (1972–83; Chicago, Sept. 29, 1983); *Overture for Strings* (Prague, Nov. 9, 1949); *Little Suite* for Chamber Orch. (1950; Warsaw, April 20, 1951); Concerto for Orch. (1950–54; Warsaw, Nov. 26, 1954); 5 *Dance Preludes* for Clarinet, Harp, Piano, Percussion, and Strings (1955; a version for Nonet, 1959); *Musique funèbre* for String Orch., in memory of Béla Bartók (Katowice, March 26, 1958); *3 Postludes:* No. 1 for the centennial of the International Red Cross (1958); No. 2 (1960); No. 3 (1960); *Jeux vénitiens* (Venice, April 24, 1961); *Livre* (The Hague, Nov. 18, 1968; individual movements are called Chapters); Cello Concerto (London, Oct. 14, 1970; Rostropovich, soloist); *Mi-parti* (Rotterdam, Oct. 22, 1976); *Novelette* for Orch. (1979; Washington, D.C., Jan. 29, 1980); Double Concerto for Oboe, Harp, and Chamber Orch. (Lucerne Festival, Aug. 24, 1980); *Partita* for Violin, Piano, and Orch. (St. Paul, Minn., Jan. 18, 1985); Piano Concerto (N.Y., Dec. 1, 1988). **CHAMBER:** Trio for Oboe, Clarinet, and Bassoon (1945); *Recitativo e Arioso* for Violin and Piano (1951); 5 *Folk Melodies* for Strings (1952); *Bucoliche,* 5 pieces for Viola and Piano (1952); *Preludia taneczne* for Clarinet and Piano (1954); String Quartet (1964); *Preludes and Fugue* for 13 Solo Strings (1971; ISCM Festival, Graz, Oct. 22, 1972). **VOCAL:** *Belated Nightingale* and *Mr. Tralala,* 2 songs for Voice and Orch. (1947); *A Straw Chain* for Soprano, Mezzo-soprano, Flute, Oboe, 2 Clarinets, and Bassoon (1951); *Silesian Triptych* for Soprano and Orch. (Warsaw, Dec. 2, 1951); 5 *Songs* for Female Voice and 30 Solo Instruments (1958); *3 poèmes d'Henri Michaux* for Choir, Wind Instruments, Percussion, 2 Pianos, and Harp (Zagreb, May 9, 1963; perf. requires 2 conductors reading from separate scores); *Paroles tissées* for Tenor, String Ensemble, Harp, Piano, and Percussion (Aldeburgh [England] Festival, June 20, 1965); *Les Espaces du sommeil* for Baritone and Orch. (1975; Berlin, March 12, 1978); piano pieces.

BIBL.: S. Jarociński, "W. L.," *Polish Music* (Warsaw, 1965); O. Nordwall, *L.* (Stockholm, 1968); B. Varga, *L. Profile: W. L. in Conversation with Bálint András Varga* (London, 1976); J.-P. Couchod, *La Musique polonaise et W. L.* (1981); S. Stucky,

L. and His Music (Cambridge, 1981); T. Kaczynski, *Conversations with W. L.* (London, 1984); C. Rae, "L.'s Golden Year," *Musical Times* (Oct. 1986).

Lütschg, Karl, Russian pianist, pedagogue, and composer; b. St. Petersburg, Oct. 15, 1839; d. Blankenburg, Germany, June 6, 1899. He studied piano with Henselt in St. Petersburg and Moscheles in Leipzig, and composition with Richter and Kiel. Returning to St. Petersburg, he became a prof. at the Cons. there; then publ. a number of valuable piano studies and instructive eds. of classical works: *École d'études* (12 books), *Bibliothèque des œuvres classiques et modernes* (420 nos.); etc. His son, **Waldemar Lütschg** (b. St. Petersburg, May 16, 1877; d. Berlin, Aug. 29, 1948), was also a pianist and teacher; he studied with his father at the St. Petersburg Cons.; was in Berlin (1899–1905); taught piano at the Chicago Musical College (1905–6).

Lutyens, (Agnes) Elisabeth, important English composer; b. London, July 9, 1906; d. there, April 14, 1983. She was a daughter of the noted architect Sir Edwin Lutyens, and was brought up in an atmosphere of cultural enlightenment. She studied at the École Normale de Musique in Paris (1922–23) and with H. Darke at the Royal College of Music in London (1926–30). In her vivid autobiography, *A Goldfish Bowl* (London, 1972), she recounted her search for a congenial idiom of musical expression, beginning with the erstwhile fashionable Romantic manner and progressing toward a more individual, psychologically tense writing in an atonal technique using a sui generis dodecaphonic method of composition. In 1969 she was made a Commander of the Order of the British Empire. She was married to the conductor **Edward Clark.**

WORKS: STAGE: *The Pit,* dramatic scene for Tenor, Bass, Women's Chorus, and Orch. (Palermo, April 24, 1949); *Penelope,* radio opera (1950); *Infidelio,* chamber opera (1956; London, April 17, 1973); *The Numbered,* an opera (1965–67); "a charade in 4 acts and 3 interruptions," *Time Off? Not a Ghost of a Chance* (1967–68; Sadler's Wells, London, March 1, 1972); *Isis and Osiris,* lyric drama for 8 Voices and Chamber Orch. (1969); *The Linnet from the Leaf,* musical theater for 5 Singers and 2 Instrumental Groups (1972); *The Waiting Game,* 5 scenes for Mezzo-soprano, Baritone, and Chamber Orch. (1973); *One and the Same,* scena for Soprano, Speaker, and Mimes (1973); *The Goldfish Bowl,* ballad opera (1975); *Like a Window,* extracts from letters of van Gogh (1976); ballet, *The Birthday of the Infanta* (London, 1932).

ORCH.: *3 Pieces* (1939); 6 chamber concertos, some with Solo Instruments (1939–48); *3 Symphonic Preludes* (1942); Viola Concerto (1947); *Music I* (1954); *Music II* (1962); *Music III* (1964); *Quincunx* (1960); *En voyage,* symphonic suite (London, July 2, 1960); *Symphonies* for Piano, Wind Instruments, Harps, and Percussion (London, July 28, 1961); *Music for Piano and Orch.* (1964); *Novenaria* (1967); *Plenum II* for Oboe and Chamber Orch. (London, June 14, 1974); *The Winter of the World* for Cello and Chamber Ensemble (London, May 5, 1974); *Eos* for Chamber Orch. (1975); *Rondel* (1976); *6 Bagatelles* for Chamber Orch. (1976); *Nox* for Piano and 2 Chamber Orchs. (1977); *Wild Decembers* (1980); *Music for Orchestra IV* (1981).

CHAMBER: Solo Viola Sonata (1938); 13 string quartets (1938–82); String Trio (1939); *9 Bagatelles* for Cello and Piano (1942); *Aptote* for Violin (1948); *Valediction* for Clarinet and Piano (1954); *Nocturnes* for Violin, Cello, and Guitar (1956); *Capricci* for 2 Harps and Percussion (1956); *6 Tempi* for 10 Instruments (1957); Wind Quintet (1960); String Quintet (1963); Trio for Flute, Clarinet, and Bassoon (1963); *Scena* for Violin, Cello, and Percussion (1964); *Music for Wind* for Double Wind Quintet (1964); *Music for 3* for Flute, Oboe, and Piano (1964); *The Fall of the Leafe* for Oboe and String Quartet (1967); *Horai* for Violin, Horn, and Piano (1968); *The Tides of Time* for Double Bass and Piano (1969); *Driving Out the Death* for Oboe and String Trio (1971); *Rape of the Moone* for Wind Octet (1973); *Plenum II* for Oboe and 13 Instruments

(1973); *Plenum III* for String Quartet (1974); *Kareniana* for Viola and Instrumental Group (1974); *Go, Said the Bird* for Electric Guitar and String Quartet (1975); *Mare et Minutiae* for String Quartet (1976); *Fantasia* for Alto Saxophone and 3 Instrumental Groups (1977); *O Absalom* for Oboe and String Trio (1977); *Constants* for Cello and Piano (1977); *Doubles* for String Quartet (1978); *Footfalls* for Flute and Piano (1978); *Prelude* for Violin (1979); Trio for Clarinet, Cello, and Piano (1979); *Morning Sea* for Oboe and Piano (1979); *Rapprochement* for Horn, Harp, Wind Quartet, String Quartet, Piano, and Percussion (1980); *6* for an ensemble of 6 Instruments and Percussion (1980); *Soli* for Clarinet, interchangeable with Bass Clarinet, and Double Bass (1980); *Branches of the Night and of the Day* for Horn and String Quartet (1981); *The Living Night* for Percussion (1981); *Echo of the Wind* for Viola (1981); *Triolet I* for Clarinet, Mandolin, and Cello (1982); *Triolet II* for Cello, Marimba, and Harp (1982).

PIANO: 5 *Intermezzi* (1942); *Piano e Forte* (1958); *Plenum I* (1973); *The Ring of Bone* (1975); 5 impromptus (1977); *3 Books of Bagatelles* (1979); *La natura dell'acqua* (1981).

ORGAN: *Sinfonia* (1956); *Plenum IV* (1975).

VOCAL: *O Saisons, O Châteaux,* cantata for Soprano, Mandolin, Guitar, Harp, and Strings (1946); *Requiem for the Living* for Soloists, Chorus, and Orch. (1948); *Bienfaits de la lune* for Soprano, Tenor, Chorus, Strings, and Percussion (1952); *De Amore,* cantata (1957; London, Sept. 7, 1973); *Catena* for Soprano, Tenor, and 21 Instruments (1961–62); *Encomion* for Chorus, Brass, and Percussion (1963); *The Valley of Haisu-Se* for Soprano and Instrumental Ensemble (1965); *Akapotik Rose* for Soprano and Instrumental Ensemble (1966); *And Suddenly It's Evening* for Tenor and 11 Instruments (1967); *Essence of Our Happiness,* cantata (1968; London, Sept. 8, 1970); *Phoenix* for Soprano, Violin, Clarinet, and Piano (1968); *Anerca* for Women's Speaking Chorus, 10 Guitars, and Percussion (1970); *Vision of Youth* for Soprano, 3 Clarinets, Piano, and Percussion (1970); *Islands* for Soprano, Tenor, Narrator, and Instrumental Ensemble (London, June 7, 1971); *The Tears of Night* for Countertenor, 6 Sopranos, and 3 Instrumental Ensembles (1971); *Requiescat,* in memoriam Igor Stravinsky, for Soprano and String Trio (1971); *Dirge for the Proud World* for Soprano, Countertenor, Harpsichord, and Cello (1971); *Counting Your Steps* for Chorus, 4 Flutes, and 4 Percussion Players (1972); *Chimes and Cantos* for Baritone and Instrumental Ensemble (1972); *Voice of Quiet Waters* for Chorus and Orch. (1972; Huddersfield, April 14, 1973); *Laudi* for Soprano, 3 Clarinets, Piano, and Percussion (1973); *Chorale Prelude and Paraphrase,* to text from a letter of Keats, for Tenor, String Quintet, and Percussion (1977); *Cascando* for Contralto, Violin, and Strings (1977); *Elegy of the Flowers* for Tenor and 3 Instrumental Groups (1978); *Echoi* for Mezzo-soprano and Orch. (1979); Cantata for Dramatic Soprano and Instruments (1979); Cantata, to text by Baudelaire, for 3 Soloists and Instrumental Ensemble (1979); *The Roots of the World,* to text by Yeats, for Chorus and Cello obbligato (1979); *Echoes* for Contralto, Alto Flute, English Horn, and String Quartet (1979); *Mine Eyes, My Bread, My Spade* for Baritone and String Quartet (1980); *Fleur du silence,* to words by Rémi de Gourmont, for Tenor, Flute, Oboe, Horn, Harp, Violin, Viola, and Percussion (1980); *The Singing Birds* for Actress and Viola (1980).

BIBL.: M. and S. Harries, *A Pilgrim Soul: The Life and Work of E. L.* (London, 1989).

Lutz, (Wilhelm) Meyer, German-born English organist, conductor, and composer; b. Männerstadt, near Kissingen, 1822; d. London, Jan. 31, 1903. He studied music with his father, an organist, and later at Würzburg. In 1848 he settled in England; played organ in various churches in Birmingham, Leeds, and London; conducted theater music in London from 1851; in 1869, was appointed music director at the Gaiety Theatre, for which he wrote numerous light operas; the following were successful: *Faust and Marguerite* (May 16, 1855); *Blonde or Brunette* (May 19, 1862); *Zaida* (1868); *The Miller of Milburg* (April 13, 1872); *Legend of the Lys* (1873). His popular dance

Pas de quatre is from the burlesque *Faust Up to Date* (Oct. 30, 1888).

Luvisi, Lee, American pianist and teacher; b. Louisville, Dec. 12, 1937. He first studied at the Curtis Inst. of Music in Philadelphia with Rudolf Serkin and Mieczyslaw Horszowski; upon graduation in 1957, he joined its faculty. In 1963 he was named artist-in-residence at the Univ. of Louisville School of Music; later became chairman of its piano dept. He appeared as soloist with many of the major American and European orchs.; gave numerous recitals.

Lux, Friedrich, German conductor and composer; b. Ruhla, Nov. 24, 1820; d. Mainz, July 9, 1895. He studied with his father, a cantor at Ruhla; at 12, he gave an organ concert at Gotha; then studied with F. Schneider at Dessau, where he remained as music director at the Court Theater (1841–50). From 1851 to 1877 he was conductor at the City Theater in Mainz; from 1867, also conducted the Oratorio Soc. there.
WORKS: Operas: *Das Käthchen von Heilbronn* (Dessau, March 23, 1846); *Der Schmied von Ruhla* (Mainz, March 28, 1882); *Die Fürstin von Athen* (Frankfurt, 1890); 4 syms. (No. 3 subtitled *Die vier Menschenalter*; No. 4, *Durch Nacht zum Licht*, with Chorus); 3 string quartets; Piano Trio; many choral works and songs. He publ. transcriptions of Beethoven's syms. (except the 9th) for piano, 4-hands.
BIBL.: A. Reissmann, *F. L.: Sein Leben und seine Werke* (Leipzig, 1888).

Luxon, Benjamin, esteemed English baritone; b. Redruth, March 24, 1937. He studied with Walter Brünner at the Guildhall School of Music in London, then joined the English Opera Group, with which he sang Sid in *Albert Herring* and Tarquinius in *The Rape of Lucretia* on its tour of the Soviet Union (1963). He was chosen by Britten to create the title role in the opera *Owen Wingrave* (BBC-TV, May 16, 1971); then made his debut at London's Covent Garden as Monteverdi's Ulysses (1972), and subsequently sang there regularly; also appeared at the festivals in Aldeburgh, Edinburgh, and Glyndebourne, and with the English National Opera in London. On Feb. 2, 1980, he made his Metropolitan Opera debut in N.Y. as Eugene Onegin. His other roles include Count Almaviva, Don Giovanni, Papageno, Wolfram, Eisenstein, and Wozzeck. He also distinguished himself as a concert artist, his repertoire ranging from the standard literature to folk songs. In 1986 he was made a Commander of the Order of the British Empire.

Luython, Charles, Flemish composer; b. Antwerp, c.1556; d. Prague, Aug. 1620. After receiving elementary training as a chorister, he was sent at the age of 10 to the Imperial Chapel in Vienna, where he remained until he was 15. He composed 2 masses for Emperor Maximilian II. Following studies in Italy, he was back in Vienna by 1576 as a member of the Kammermusik of the court; was made a chamber organist in 1577 by Rudolf II, whose court was moved to Prague; he composed a book of madrigals for his patron. He was made court organist in 1582, and then assumed the duties of 1st organist in 1593, being officially named to that post in 1596; that same year he became court composer, succeeding Philippe de Monte. With the death of the Emperor in 1612, Luython lost his positions and attendant financial security. He died in poverty. Apart from his book of madrigals (Venice, 1582), he publ. *Popularis anni jubilus* for 6 Voices (Prague, 1587); *Selectissimarum sacrarum cantionum . . .* for 6 Voices (Prague, 1603); *Opus musicum in Lamentationes Hieremiae prophetae* for 6 Voices (Prague, 1604); and *Liber primus missarum* for 3 to 7 Voices (Prague, 1609). Among his extant instrumental music is a *Fuga suavissima* (publ. in Woltz's *Tabulatur-Buch*, 1617). Luython was a composer of extraordinary ingenuity; Michael Praetorius recounts in his *Syntagma musicum* that Luython owned a keyboard instrument with 3 manuals, representing the diatonic, chromatic, and enharmonic intervals (18 notes to the octave), thus securing theoretically correct modulations through sharps or flats.
BIBL.: L. de Burbure, *C. L.* (Brussels, 1880); A. Smijers,

Karl L. als Motettenkomponist (Amsterdam, 1923); C. Saas, *C. L.: Ses madrigaux et œuvres instrumentales* (diss., Univ. of Louvain, 1958).

Luzzaschi, Luzzasco, eminent Italian organist, pedagogue, and composer; b. Ferrara, 1545?; d. there, Sept. 10, 1607. He began studies as a child with Cipriano de Rore, remaining under his tutelage until 1558; became a singer at the Este court (1561); was 1st organist there from 1564 until the court's demise in 1597, and also directed one of its orchs.; likewise was organist at Ferrara Cathedral and at the Accademia della Morte; also became director of Duke Alfonso's private musica da camera about 1569. He was one of the finest madrigalists of his day. He was also highly esteemed as a teacher, and was the mentor of Frescobaldi. Among his secular vocal works are 7 books of madrigals for 5 Voices (1571–1604), *Madrigali . . . per cantare, et sonare a uno, e doi, e tre soprani* (Rome, 1601; ed. in Monumenti di Musica Italiana, II/2, 1965), and others in contemporary anthologies; he also composed the sacred *Sacrarum cantionum liber primus* for 5 Voices (Venice, 1598). Included in his instrumental works are Canzona for Organ in A. Raverii, *Canzoni per sonar* (Venice, 1608), a number of ricercari, a toccata, and a dance.
BIBL.: O. Kinkeldey, "L. L.'s Solo-Madrigale mit Klavierbegleitung," *Sammelbände der Internationalen Musik-Gesellschaft,* IX (1907–8); J. Orbaan, "Notizie su L. L.," *Bollettino bibliografico musicale,* IV/1 (1929); J. Racek, "Les Madrigaux à voix seule de L. L.," *La Revue Musicale,* no. 123 (1932); E. Strainchamps, *L. L. and His Five-part Madrigals* (diss., Columbia Univ., 1960); A. Spiro, *The Five-part Madrigals of L. L.* (diss., Boston Univ., 1961).

Luzzi, Luigi, Italian composer; b. Olevano di Lomellina, March 28, 1828; d. Stradella, Feb. 23, 1876. He studied medicine at Turin, but later entered the musical profession; wrote successful songs (*Mia madre,* etc.); an opera, *Tripilla* (Novara, Feb. 7, 1874); Sym.; hymns for chorus and orch.; piano pieces.

Lvov, Alexei Feodorovich, Russian violinist and composer; b. Reval, June 5, 1798; d. Romano, near Kovno, Dec. 28, 1870. He was the son of the director of the Imperial Court Chapel Choir in St. Petersburg; received his primary education at home; attended the Inst. of Road Engineering (graduated in 1818); at the same time, studied violin. In 1827 he was sent to the Turkish front in Bulgaria; then was attached to the court. He wrote the national anthem *God Save the Czar* in 1833, and it was 1st performed in Moscow on the name day of Czar Nicholas I, on Dec. 6 (O.S.; 18 N.S.), 1833; it remained the official anthem until the Revolution of 1917. In 1837 he succeeded his father as director of the St. Petersburg Imperial Court Chapel Choir, remaining there until 1861; in 1839 he organized instrumental classes there; ed. a collection of services for the entire ecclesiastical year of the Greek Orthodox Church. In 1840 he traveled in Europe; played his Violin Concerto with the Gewandhaus Orch. in Leipzig (Nov. 8, 1840); Schumann greatly praised his playing. Returning to Russia, he established a series of orch. concerts in St. Petersburg, presenting classical programs. Growing deafness forced him to abandon his activities in 1867. As a composer, he slavishly followed the Italian school.
WORKS: Operas: *Bianca und Gaultiero* (Dresden, Oct. 13, 1844); *Ondine* (in Russian; St. Petersburg, Sept. 20, 1847); *Starosta Boris, or The Russian Muzhik and the French Marauders* (on the 1812 war; in Russian; St. Petersburg, May 1, 1854); also several violin works, including a concerto; many sacred choral works; Stabat Mater for Soloists and Orch. (1851).
BIBL.: I. Yampolsky, *Russkoye skripichnoye iskusstvo* (Russian Violin Art, Vol. I; Moscow, 1951).

Lybbert, Donald, American composer; b. Cresco, Iowa, Feb. 19, 1923; d. Norwalk, Conn., July 26, 1981. He studied at the Univ. of Iowa (B.M., 1946), at the Juilliard School of Music with Robert Ward and Bernard Wagenaar (1946–48), at Columbia Univ. with Elliott Carter and Otto Luening (M.A., 1950), and with Nadia Boulanger at Fontainebleau, France (1961). He was on the music faculty at Hunter College (1967–80) while continuing to compose. His music was evolved from Classical foundations, but he refrained from using key signatures and often applied quasi-serial procedures in his melodic patterns; in his rhythmic textures he often resorted to asymmetrical beat formations.

WORKS: Opera, *The Scarlet Letter* (1964–67); operetta, *Monica* (Amsterdam, Nov. 2, 1952); 2 piano sonatas (1947, 1954); Octet for Wind Instruments (1947); *Concert Overture* (1952); *From Harmonium*, song cycle (1954); *Introduction and Toccata* for Brass Instruments and Piano (1955); Trio for Clarinet, Horn, and Bassoon (1956); *Chamber Sonata* for Viola, Horn, and Piano (1957); *Leopardi Canti*, song cycle for Soprano, Flute, Viola, and Bass Clarinet to poems by Giacomo Leopardi (1959); *Movement* for Piano, 4-hands (1960); *Sonorities* for 11 Instruments (1960); *Sonata brevis* for Piano (1962); *Praeludium* for Brass and Percussion (1962); *Lines for the Fallen* for Soprano and 2 Pianos tuned a quarter-tone apart (1967); *Zap*, after a text from Ecclesiastes, for Multiantiphonal Chorus, Instruments, and Rock Group, composed for the centennial of Hunter College (1970); *Variants* for 5 Wind Instruments (1971); *Octagon* for Soprano and 7 Chamber Players, to text of Molly Bloom's erotic monologue in the conclusion of James Joyce's *Ulysses* (1975); choral pieces; songs.

Lyford, Ralph, American conductor and composer; b. Worcester, Mass., Feb. 22, 1882; d. Cincinnati, Sept. 3, 1927. He began to study piano and violin as a child; entered the New England Cons. of Music in Boston at 12, studying piano with Helen Hopekirk, organ with Goodrich, and composition with Chadwick; then went to Leipzig to study conducting with Arthur Nikisch (1906). Returning to America, he became assistant conductor of the San Carlo Opera Co. (1907–8); then was with the Boston Opera Co. (1908–14). In 1916 he settled in Cincinnati, where he taught at the Cons., and also conducted the summer seasons of opera at the Zoölogical Gardens; from 1925 to 1927 he was associate conductor of the Cincinnati Sym. Orch. He wrote an opera, *Castle Agrazant* (Cincinnati, April 29, 1926; won the David Bispham Medal); Piano Concerto (1917); chamber music; songs.

Lympany, Moura (actually, **Mary Johnstone**), esteemed English pianist; b. Saltash, Aug. 18, 1916. She studied in Liège; then was a scholarship student of Coviello at London's Royal Academy of Music; also studied in Vienna with Paul Weingarten; then returned to England for further training with Mathilda Verne and Tobias Matthay. In 1938 she won 2nd prize in the Ysaÿe Competition in Brussels; subsequently she developed an international career; made her American debut in 1948. In her programs she championed works by British composers; in 1969 she performed the Piano Concerto by Cyril Scott on the occasion of his 90th birthday, with the composer himself present and joining in appreciative applause. In 1979 she was made a Commander of the Order of the British Empire.

Lyne, Felice, American soprano; b. Slater, Mo., March 28, 1887; d. Allentown, Pa., Sept. 1, 1935. Her family moved to Allentown when she was a child; she studied there with F.S. Hardman; then in Paris with Marchesi, J. de Reszke, and L. d'Aubigne. She made a successful debut as Gilda in *Rigoletto* at Hammerstein's London Opera (Nov. 25, 1911), and appeared there 36 times that season, creating the principal soprano parts in the English premieres of Massenet's *Don Quichotte* and *Jongleur de Notre-Dame*, and Holbrooke's *Children of Don;* toured with the Quinlan Opera Co. Returning to the U.S., she became a member of the Boston Opera Co.; also appeared in concerts.

Lynes, Frank, American composer and organist; b. Cambridge, Mass., May 16, 1858; d. Bristol, N.H., June 24, 1913. He was a student at the New England Cons. of Music in Boston; later studied piano and organ with B.J. Lang and harmony with J.K. Paine. He then went to Germany and enrolled in the Leipzig Cons. (1883–85), where his teachers were Reinecke (piano) and Jadassohn (theory). Returning to America, he settled in Boston. He held various positions as a church organist. He wrote mainly for piano.

WORKS: PIANO: *Analytical Sonatinas* (a set of 4, so named to emphasize the formal element); *10 Bagatelles; 12 Recreations; 8 Fairy Tales for Musical Children; Woodland Notes* (6 pieces); *Scenes from Alice in Wonderland* (10 pieces); *Independence* (16 studies); also pedagogical works: *Key Circle Exercises; 10 Special Studies*; pieces for piano, 4-hands and 6-hands; pieces for 2 pianos, 8-hands; many songs; anthems.

BIBL.: O. Downes, *F. L.* (Boston, 1914).

Lynn, George, American choral conductor and composer; b. Edwardsville, Pa., Oct. 5, 1915; d. Colorado Springs, March 16, 1989. He studied at Westminster Choir College (B.Mus., 1938); after military service in World War II, had composition lessons with Randall Thompson at Princeton Univ. (M.F.A., 1947). He was prof. of choral arts at Westminster Choir College (1946–50) and at the Univ. of Colorado (1950–52); after serving as music director of the Westminster Choir (1963–69), he was a visiting composer-in-residence at the Univ. of New Mexico (1971) and prof. of choral arts at the Colorado School of Mines (1971–80), Loretto Heights College (1971–86), and Rice Univ. (1986–87). He composed a Piano Concerto; a choral work, *Gettysburg Address;* 5 syms. (3 with Chorus); some chamber music; organ pieces; songs.

Lynn, Loretta (née **Webb**), American country-music singer, guitarist, and songwriter, sister of **Crystal Gayle;** b. Butcher Hollow, Ky., April 14, 1932. A coal miner's daughter, she taught herself the rudiments of guitar playing; making her way to Nashville, Tenn., she joined the Grand Ole Opry; later organized her own group, The Blue Kentuckians, with which she toured widely. Unable to read music, she nevertheless scored enormous success with such songs as *Don't Come Home A-Drinkin' (with Lovin' on Your Mind), You Ain't Woman Enough (to Take My Man),* and *Coal Miner's Daughter.* She publ. an autobiography in 1976, aptly named *Coal Miner's Daughter;* it was made into a motion picture in 1980.

Lyon, James, American composer; b. Newark, N.J., July 1, 1735; d. Machias, Maine, Oct. 12, 1794. He graduated from the College of New Jersey at Princeton in 1759; in 1764, accepted a pastorate in Nova Scotia; then in Machias, Maine (1772 until his death). The *N.Y. Mercury* of Oct. 1, 1759, speaks of an ode composed by Lyon, a member of the graduating class of Princeton, and mentions its performance at the graduation exercises on Sept. 26; but the music of this work, written in the same year that Hopkinson wrote his 1st songs, is lost. The 1st known compositions of Lyon are 6 Psalm tunes publ. by him in the collection *Urania* (Philadelphia, 1761; facsimile ed. by R. Crawford, N.Y., 1973); he also wrote settings of 2 poems by Watts, *A Marriage Hymn* and *Friendship,* and of Psalms 8, 17, 19, 23, 95, 104, and 150.

BIBL.: O. Sonneck, *Francis Hopkinson and J. L.: Two Studies in Early American Music* (Washington, D.C., 1905; reprint, with new introduction by R. Crawford, N.Y., 1969); F. Metcalf, *American Writers and Compilers of Sacred Music* (N.Y., 1925); G. Edwards, *Music and Musicians of Maine* (Portland, 1928).

Lyon & Healy, American manufacturers of musical instruments. The firm was founded in Chicago in 1864 by **George Washburn Lyon** (b. 1820) and **Patrick Joseph Healy** (b. March 17, 1840; d. Chicago, April 3, 1905). They began orig. as dealers in sheet music, books, and the smaller musical instruments; in 1871 they took over the piano business of Smith & Dixon, and gradually began also to manufacture other instruments. After the retirement of Lyon in 1889, Healy became the sole head and general manager; he expanded the manufacturing dept. and erected larger factories. Among the firm's instruments, the Lyon & Healy harp, put on the market in 1899, has become universally known; its collection of old violins once rivaled those of the world's most famous dealers.

Lyons, James, American music critic and editor; b. Peabody, Mass., Nov. 24, 1925; d. N.Y., Nov. 13, 1973. He studied musicology with Karl Geiringer at Boston Univ. and music history with Warren Storey Smith at the New England Cons.

of Music. He was a music critic for the *N.Y. Herald Tribune* (1953–62); in 1957, became ed. and publisher of the *American Record Guide;* with J. Howard, he publ. *Modern Music* (N.Y. 1957).

Lyra, Justus Wilhelm, German clergyman, writer on music, and composer; b. Osnabrück, March 23, 1822; d. Gehrden, Dec. 30, 1882. He studied philosophy and theology in Berlin; filled various church offices, eventually becoming "pastor primarious" at Gehrden and Hannover. As a student, he wrote many scholastic songs, which became very popular in German univs. (e.g., *Der Mai ist gekommen, Durch Feld und Buchenhallen, Zwischen Frankreich und dem Böhmerwald, Meine Mus'*

ist gegangen); he also wrote church music (Christmas cantata, 1872); publ. 5 books of songs, ranging from one voice to mixed chorus; *Die liturgischen Altarweisen des lutherischen Hauptgottesdienstes* (1873); *Andreas Ornithoparchus und dessen Lehre von den Kirchenakzenten* (Gütersloh, 1877); *Luthers Deutsche Messe* (publ. posth., 1904).
     BIBL.: Bär and Ziller, *J.W. L.*(Leipzig, 1901); I. Lindemann, *J.W. L.: Ein Leben zwischen Biedermeier und Kaiserreich* (Osnabrück, 1987).

Lysberg, Charles-Samuel. See **Bovy-Lysberg, Charles-Samuel.**

M

Ma, Yo-Yo, brilliant Chinese cellist; b. Paris, Oct. 7, 1955. He was born into a musical family active in Paris; his father was a violinist, his mother a mezzo-soprano. He began to study violin as a small child, then graduated to the viola and finally the cello; was taken to N.Y. when he was 7, and enrolled at the Juilliard School of Music when he was 9; his principal teachers were Leonard Rose and János Scholz; he subsequently received additional musical training at Harvard Univ. He quickly established a formidable reputation as a master of the cello in his appearances with the great orchs. of the world, as a recitalist, and as a chamber music player, being deservedly acclaimed for his unostentatious musicianship, his superlative technical resources, and the remarkable tone of his melodious lyricism. In order to extend his repertoire, he made a number of effective transcriptions for his instrument. He was awarded the Avery Fisher Prize in 1978.

Maag, (Ernst) Peter (Johannes), distinguished Swiss conductor; b. St. Gallen, May 10, 1919. His father was the Lutheran minister and educated musician Otto Maag; his mother played violin in the Capet Quartet. After studying music at home, he went to the Univs. of Zürich, Basel, and Geneva; among his teachers were Karl Barth in theology and Karl Jaspers in philosophy. He studied piano and music theory with Czeslaw Marek in Zürich; then went to Paris, where he had private lessons with Cortot; he studied conducting with Franz von Hoesslin and Ernest Ansermet in Geneva. He began his professional career as répétiteur and chorus master at the town theater in Biel-Solothurn. In 1952 he was appointed 1st conductor of the Düsseldorf Opera; from 1955 to 1959 he was Generalmu-

sikdirektor of the Bonn Opera; from 1964 to 1968, chief conductor of the Vienna Volksoper; from 1972 to 1974, artistic director of the Teatro Regio in Parma; held a similar post with the Teatro Regio in Turin from 1974 to 1976. He conducted at Covent Garden in London in 1958. He made his U.S. debut in 1959 as a guest conductor of the Cincinnati Sym. Orch.; in 1961 conducted at the Chicago Lyric Opera. On Sept. 23, 1972, he made his Metropolitan Opera debut in N.Y. conducting *Don Giovanni;* was guest conductor with the Boston Sym. Orch., Detroit Sym. Orch., and National Sym. Orch. of Washington, D.C. He also toured South America and Japan. He was music director of the Bern Sym. Orch. from 1984 to 1991.

BIBL.: D. McIntire, "P. M.: Switzerland's Musical Ambassador," *Northern Light* (Jan. 1979).

Maas, Louis (Philipp Otto), German-American pianist and composer; b. Wiesbaden, June 21, 1852; d. Boston, Sept. 17, 1889. He studied with Reinecke and Papperitz at the Leipzig Cons. (1867–71), and for 3 summers with Liszt. From 1875 to 1880 he taught at the Leipzig Cons.; in 1880 he emigrated to the U.S., settling in Boston; conducted the Boston Phil. Concerts (1881–82). As a token of gratitude to his adoptive country, he wrote an "American Symphony," *On the Prairies,* dedicated to President Chester A. Arthur, which he conducted in Boston, Dec. 14, 1882. This sym., Germanic in form and harmonic language, contained some Indian themes. He also wrote overtures, suites, marches, fantasias, etc., for orch.; Piano Concerto; String Quartet; violin sonatas; piano pieces; songs.

Maasalo, Armas (Toivo Valdemar), Finnish composer; b. Rautavaara, Aug. 28, 1885; d. Helsinki, Sept. 9, 1960. He studied at the Helsinki Music Inst. (1907–10), serving as its director (1923–51); then was director of the church music dept. of the Sibelius Academy in Helsinki (1951–55). He wrote much sacred music.

WORKS: *Ricordanza* for Cello, Piano, and Orch. (1919); Piano Concerto (1919); *Karelian Scenes* for Orch. (1920); *The Path of Man*, cantata (1926); *2 Stars* for Alto, Chorus, and Orch. (1929); *Partita seria* for Strings (1934); *Christmas Oratorio* (1945); Suite for Organ and Orch. (1945); organ pieces; religious songs for chorus and solo voice.

Ma'ayani, Ami, Israeli composer; b. Ramat-Gan, Jan. 13, 1936. He studied composition privately with Ben-Haim (1956–60); concurrently attended courses in architecture at the Technion School in Haifa, receiving a diploma in 1960; then worked on electronic music with Ussachevsky at Columbia Univ. in N.Y. (1961–62; 1964–65); also studied philosophy at the Univ. of Tel Aviv (M.A., 1973).

WORKS: STAGE: *The War of the Sons of Light*, opera-oratorio for 4 Soloists, Chorus, Ballet, and Orch. (1970–72); *A Legend of 3s and 4s*, ballet (1978). **ORCH.:** *Divertimento concertante* for Chamber Orch. (1957); 2 harp concertos (1960, 1966); *Mizorim* (Psalms) for Soprano, Flute, Bass Clarinet, Harp, Percussion, and Strings (1965); Concerto for 8 Wind Instruments and Percussion (1966); *Regalim* (Festivals) for Soprano or Tenor, and Orch. (1966); Violin Concerto (1967); Cello Concerto (1967); 2-piano Concerto (1969); *Qumran*, symphonic metaphor (1970); *Symphony Concertante* for Wind Quintet and Orch. (1972); Sym. No. 2 (1975); Viola Concerto (1975); Guitar Concerto (1976); Sym. No. 3, *Hebrew Requiem*, for Mezzo-soprano, Chorus, and Orch. (1977); Concertino for Harp and Strings (1980); Sinfonietta No. 1 for Chamber Orch. (1980); *Ouverture solonelle* (1982); Sym. No. 4, *Sinfonietta on Popular Hebraic Themes*, for Chamber Orch. (1982); *Scherzo Mediterranean* (1983). **CHAMBER:** *Poème* for Flute and String Trio (1965); *Improvisation variée* for Flute, Viola or Violin, and Harp (1966); *4 Preludes* for 4 Percussionists and Piano (1968); *2 Madrigals* for Harp and Wind Quintet (1969); 2 pieces for Harp Solo: *Magamat* (1960) and *Toccata* (1962); Sonatina for Clarinet, Cello, and Piano (1985); piano pieces.

Maazel, Lorin (Varencove), brilliant American conductor; b. Neuilly, France (of American parents), March 6, 1930. His parents took him to Los Angeles when he was an infant. At a very early age he showed innate musical ability; he had perfect pitch and could assimilate music osmotically; he began to study violin at age 5 with Karl Moldrem, and then piano at age 7 with Fanchon Armitage. Fascinated by the art of conducting, he went to sym. concerts and soon began to take lessons in conducting with Vladimir Bakaleinikov, who was an associate conductor of the Los Angeles Phil.; on July 13, 1938, at the age of 8, he was given a chance to conduct a performance of Schubert's *Unfinished Symphony* with the visiting Univ. of Idaho orch. In 1938 Bakaleinikov was appointed assistant conductor of the Pittsburgh Sym. Orch., and the Maazel family followed him to Pittsburgh. From Bakaleinikov, Maazel quickly learned to speak Russian. On Aug. 18, 1939, he made a sensational appearance in N.Y. conducting the National Music Camp Orch. of Interlochen at the World's Fair, eliciting the inevitable jocular comments (he was compared to a trained seal). Maazel was only 11 when he conducted the NBC Sym. Orch. (1941) and 12 when he led an entire program with the N.Y. Phil. (1942). He survived these traumatic exhibitions, and took academic courses at the Univ. of Pittsburgh; in 1948 he joined the Pittsburgh Sym. Orch. as a violinist, and at the same time was appointed its apprentice conductor. In 1951 he received a Fulbright fellowship for travel in Italy, where he undertook a serious study of Baroque music; he also made his adult debut as a conductor in Catania on Dec. 23, 1953. In 1955 he conducted at the Florence May Festival, in 1957 at the Vienna Festival, and in 1958 at the Edinburgh Festival. In 1960 he became the 1st American to conduct at the Bayreuth Festival, where he led performances of *Lohengrin*. In 1962 he toured the U.S. with the Orch. National de France; on Nov. 1, 1962, he made his Metropolitan Opera debut in N.Y. conducting *Don Giovanni*. In the summer of 1963 he made a tour of Russia, conducting concerts in Moscow and Leningrad. From 1965 to 1971 he was artistic director of the Deutsche Oper in West Berlin; from 1965 to 1975 also served as chief conductor of the (West) Berlin Radio Sym. Orch. He was associate principal conductor of the New Philharmonia Orch. of London from 1970 to 1972, and its principal guest conductor from 1976 to 1980. In 1972 he became music director of the Cleveland Orch., a position he held with great distinction until 1982; was then made conductor emeritus. He led the Cleveland Orch. on 10 major tours abroad, including Australia and New Zealand (1973), Japan (1974), twice in Latin America, and twice in Europe, and maintained its stature as one of the world's foremost orchs. He was also chief conductor of the Orch. National de France from 1977 to 1982; then was its principal guest conductor until 1988, and then its music director until 1991. In 1980 he became conductor of the famous Vienna Phil. New Year's Day Concerts, a position he retained until 1986. In 1982 he assumed the positions of artistic director and general manager of the Vienna State Opera, the 1st American to be so honored; however, he resigned these positions in the middle of his 4-year contract in 1984 after a conflict over artistic policies with the Ministry of Culture. He then served as music consultant to the Pittsburgh Sym. Orch. (1984–86); was its music adviser and principal guest conductor in 1986, becoming its music director that same year.

Maazel is equally adept as an interpreter of operatic and symphonic scores; he is blessed with a phenomenal memory, and possesses an extraordinary baton technique. He also maintains an avid interest in nonmusical pursuits; a polyglot, he is fluent in French, German, Italian, Spanish, Portuguese, and Russian. He was married twice; 1st in 1952, to the Brazilian-American pianist Miriam Sandbank, and, after their divorce in 1969, to the Israeli pianist Israela Margalit (also later divorced). Maazel was the recipient of many awards; he received an honorary doctorate from the Univ. of Pittsburgh in 1965, the Sibelius Prize in Finland, the Commander's Cross of the Order of Merit from West Germany, and, for his numerous recordings, the Grand Prix de Disque in Paris and the Edison Prize in the Netherlands.

Mabellini, Teodulo, Italian conductor and composer; b. Pistoia, April 2, 1817; d. Florence, March 10, 1897. He studied with Pillotti and Gherardeschi in Pistoia; then was a student at Florence's Istituto Reale Musicale (1833–36); at the age of 19, he produced there an opera, *Matilda a Toledo* (Aug. 27, 1836), which made so favorable an impression that Grand Duke Leopold II gave him a stipend to study with Mercadante at Novara. His 2nd opera, *Rolla* (Turin, Nov. 12, 1840), was no less successful; thereupon he wrote many more operas, among them *Ginevra degli Almieri* (Turin, Nov. 13, 1841), *Il Conte di Lavagna* (Florence, June 4, 1843), *I Veneziani a Costantinopoli* (Rome, 1844), *Maria di Francia* (Florence, March 14, 1846), *Il venturiero* (Livorno, Carnival 1851; in collaboration with L. Gordigiani), *Il convito di Baldassare* (Florence, Nov. 1852), and *Fiammetta* (Florence, Feb. 12, 1857). He also wrote several effective oratorios and cantatas: *Eudossia e Paolo* (Florence, 1845), *Etruria* (Florence, Aug. 5, 1849), *Lo spirito di Dante* (Florence, May 15, 1865), and a patriotic hymn, *Italia risorta* (Florence, Sept. 12, 1847); *Grande fantasia* for Flute, Clarinet, Horn, Trumpet, and Trombone; sacred works for chorus and orch. He lived in Florence from 1843 until his death; conducted the concerts of the Società Filarmonica (1843–59); taught composition at the Istituto Reale Musicale (1859–87).

BIBL.: M. Giannini, *M. e la musica* (Pistoia, 1899); A. Simonatti, *T. M.* (Pistoia, 1923).

Macák, Ivan, Slovak ethnomusicologist; b. Gbelce, near Nové Zámky, Aug. 26, 1935. He studied ethnomusicology at Bratislava Univ., where he received his Ph.D. (1969) with the dissertation *Štúdie k typológii a histórii slovenských l'udo-*

vych nástrojov (Studies in the Classification and History of Slovak Folk Instruments). He was ed. of *L'udová tvorivost'* (1959–65), and research fellow in music at the Slovak National Museum in Bratislava (from 1967), where he subsequently built its collection to include over 900 folk instruments and 7,000 pictorial records. He lectured in ethnomusicology at the Bratislava Academy (1962–73) and co-ed. the *Annual Bibliography of European Ethnomusicology* (Bratislava, 1967–). His chief contribution is in the area of organology, particularly the earliest history of instruments and their methodology.

Mácal, Zdeněk, prominent Czech conductor; b. Brno, Jan. 8, 1936. He studied with Břetislav Bakala, František Jílek, and Josef Veselka at the Brno Cons. (1951–56), then at Brno's Janáček Academy of Music. He was conductor of the Moravian Phil. in Olomouc (1963–67); won the Besançon (1965) and Mitropoulos (1966) competitions; in 1966 made his 1st appearance as a guest conductor with the Czech Phil., with which he then toured Europe. In 1968 he left his homeland in the wake of the Soviet-led invasion; served as chief conductor of the Cologne Radio Sym. Orch. (1970–74) and the Hannover Radio Orch. (1980–83); also appeared as a guest conductor throughout Europe and the U.S. He was principal guest conductor (1985–86) and music director (from 1986) of the Milwaukee Sym. Orch.; also chief conductor of the Sydney Sym. Orch. (1986), and principal guest conductor (1986–88) and artistic director and principal conductor (1988–92) of the San Antonio Sym. Orch.

BIBL.: C. Passy, "Z. M. & the Milwaukee Symphony," *Ovation* (Nov. 1988).

MacArdle, Donald Wales, American musicologist; b. Quincy, Mass., July 3, 1897; d. Littleton, Colo., Dec. 23, 1964. He studied science at the Mass. Inst. of Technology, obtaining an M.S. in chemical engineering; he also took courses at the Juilliard School of Music in N.Y., and studied musicology at N.Y. Univ. Although he earned his living as an engineer, he devoted much time to scholarly research, mainly to the minutiae of Beethoven's biography; he contributed a number of valuable articles on the subject to the *Musical Quarterly* and other journals. He ed., with L. Misch, *New Beethoven Letters* (Norman, Okla., 1957); ed. and tr. Schindler's *Biographie von Ludwig van Beethoven*, 3rd ed., 1860, as *Beethoven as I Knew Him* (London and Chapel Hill, 1966); he also prepared *An Index to Beethoven's Conversation Books* (Detroit, 1962) and, with S. Pogodda, *Beethoven Abstracts* (Detroit, 1973).

Macbeth, Allan, Scottish organist and composer; b. Greenock, March 13, 1856; d. Glasgow, Aug. 25, 1910. He studied at the Leipzig Cons. with Richter, Reinecke, and Jadassohn (1875–76). His subsequent musical activities were largely confined to playing the organ in Glasgow churches and directing choral groups; from 1890 he was principal of the School of Music at the Glasgow Athenaeum. He wrote an operetta, *The Duke's Doctor*; 2 cantatas: *The Land of Glory* (1890) and *Silver Bells*; *Jubilee Chorus* (1896); *Intermezzo* for Strings; *Danze pizzicate* for Orch.; also chamber music and songs.

Macbeth, Florence, American soprano; b. Mankato, Minn., Jan. 12, 1891; d. Hyattsville, Md., May 5, 1966. She studied in N.Y. and Paris; in 1913, made her operatic debut as Rosina in *Il Barbiere di Siviglia* in Braunschweig. On Jan. 14, 1914, she made her American debut with the Chicago Opera Co. and remained on its staff as prima coloratura soprano until 1930; for a season she undertook an American tour with the Commonwealth Opera Co., singing in Gilbert and Sullivan operettas. So melodious and mellifluous were her fiorituras that she was dubbed the "Minnesota Nightingale." In 1947 she married the novelist James M. Cain and settled in Maryland.

MacCunn, Hamish, Scottish composer and conductor; b. Greenock, March 22, 1868; d. London, Aug. 2, 1916. He went to London and studied with Parry, Stanford, and Franklin Taylor at the Royal College of Music (1883–86); then taught at the Royal Academy of Music (1888–94); subsequently taught composition at the Guildhall School of Music (1912–16). He also pursued a conducting career; in 1898, became conductor of the Carl Rosa Opera Co.; from 1900 to 1905, conducted at the Savoy Theatre; later he toured with various troupes, conducting light opera.

WORKS: STAGE: Operas: *Jeanie Deans*, after Scott's *The Heart of Midlothian* (Edinburgh, Nov. 15, 1894); *Diarmid* (London, Oct. 23, 1897); *The Masque of War and Peace* (London, Feb. 13, 1900); *The Golden Girl*, musical comedy (Birmingham, Aug. 5, 1905). **CANTATAS:** *Lord Ullin's Daughter*, after Walter Scott (London, Feb. 18, 1888); *Bonny Kilmeny* (Edinburgh, Dec. 15, 1888); *The Lay of the Last Minstrel* (Glasgow, Dec. 18, 1888); *The Cameronian's Dream* (Edinburgh, Jan. 27, 1890); *Queen Hynde of Caledon* (Glasgow, Jan. 28, 1892); *The Wreck of the Hesperus*, after Longfellow (London, Aug. 28, 1905). **ORCH.:** Overtures: *Cior Mhor* (London, Oct. 27, 1885) and *The Land of the Mountain and the Flood*, after Scott (London, Nov. 5, 1887); ballades: *The Ship o' the Fiend* (London, Feb. 21, 1888) and *The Dowie Dens o' Yarrow* (London, Oct. 13, 1888); and *Highland Memories*, suite (London, March 13, 1897); also *Scotch Dances* for Piano; songs; etc.

Macdonald, Hugh (John), distinguished English musicologist; b. Newbury, Berkshire, Jan. 31, 1940. He was educated at Pembroke College, Cambridge (B.A., 1961; M.A., 1965; Ph.D., 1969); in 1966 he became a lecturer at Cambridge Univ., then at Oxford Univ. in 1971; in 1979 he was a visiting prof. at Indiana Univ. in Bloomington; in 1980 he was named Gardiner Prof. of Music at Glasgow Univ.; then was a prof. at Washington Univ. in St. Louis (from 1987). His special field of interest is 19th-century music; he is particularly noted for his studies in French music, and is a leading authority on the life and works of Berlioz; in 1965 he became general ed. of the *New Berlioz Edition*. He publ. *Berlioz: Orchestral Music* (London, 1969), *Skryabin* (London, 1978), and *Berlioz* (London, 1982).

MacDonald, Jeanette (Anna), notoriously propelled American soprano; b. Philadelphia, June 18, 1903; d. Houston, Jan. 14, 1965. She started a career as a chorus girl and model in N.Y. (1920) and unexpectedly won encomia for her starring role in the musical *The Magic Ring* (1923). She then attained wide recognition as a singing actress via 29 films, especially those in which she paired with Nelson Eddy: *Naughty Marietta* (1935), *Rose Marie* (1936), *Maytime* (1937), *The Girl of the Golden West* (1938), *Sweethearts* (1939), *New Moon* (1940), *Bittersweet* (1940), and *I Married an Angel* (1942). She made a belated operatic debut as Juliette in Montreal (May 1944); she also sang in Chicago, but her voice was too small to meet the demands of the large opera halls.

BIBL.: S. Rich, *J. M.: A Pictorial Biography* (Los Angeles, 1973); E. Knowles, *Films of J. M. and Nelson Eddy* (1975); J. Parish, *The J. M. Story* (N.Y., 1976); L. Stern, *J. M.* (N.Y., 1977).

MacDowell, Edward (Alexander), greatly significant American composer; b. N.Y., Dec. 18, 1860; d. there, Jan. 23, 1908. His father was a Scotch-Irish tradesman; his mother, an artistically inclined woman who encouraged his musical studies. He took piano lessons with Juan Buitrago and Paul Desvernine; also had supplementary sessions with Teresa Carreño, who later championed his works. In 1876, after traveling in Europe with his mother, MacDowell enrolled as an auditor in Augustin Savard's elementary class at the Paris Cons.; on Feb. 8, 1877, he was admitted as a regular student; he also studied piano with Antoine-François Marmontel and solfège with Marmontel's son, Antonin. Somewhat disappointed with his progress, he withdrew from the Cons. on Sept. 30, 1878, and went to Wiesbaden for further study with Louis Ehlert; in 1879 he enrolled at the newly founded but already prestigious Hoch Cons. in Frankfurt as a student of Carl Heymann in piano, of Joachim Raff (the Cons. director) in composition, and of Franz Böhme in counterpoint and fugue. During MacDowell's stay there, Raff's class had a visit from Liszt, and MacDowell performed the piano part in Schumann's Quintet, op. 44, in

Liszt's presence. At another visit, MacDowell played Liszt's *Hungarian Rhapsody* No. 14 for him; 2 years later he visited Liszt in Weimar, and played his own 1st Piano Concerto for him, accompanied by Eugène d'Albert at the 2nd piano. Encouraged by Liszt's interest, MacDowell sent him the MS of his *Modern Suite*, op. 10, for piano solo; Liszt recommended the piece for performance at the meeting of the Allgemeiner Deutscher Musikverein (Zürich, July 11, 1882); he also recommended MacDowell to the publishers Breitkopf & Härtel, who subsequently brought out the 1st works of MacDowell to appear in print, the *Modern Suites* for piano, opp. 10 and 14.

Despite his youth, MacDowell was given a teaching position at the Darmstadt Cons.; he also accepted private pupils, among them Marian Nevins of Connecticut; they were secretly married on July 9, 1884, in N.Y., followed by a public ceremony in Waterford, Conn., on July 21. During the early years of their marriage, the MacDowells made their 2nd home in Wiesbaden, where MacDowell composed industriously; his works were performed in neighboring communities; Carreño put several of his piano pieces on her concert programs. There were also performances in America. However, the MacDowells were beset by financial difficulties; his mother proposed that he and his wife live on the family property, but MacDowell declined. He also declined an offer to teach at the National Cons. in N.Y. at the munificent fee of $5 an hour. Similarly, he rejected an offer to take a clerical position at the American Consulate in Krefeld, Germany. In 1888 he finally returned to the U.S., where he was welcomed in artistic circles as a famous composer and pianist; musical America at the time was virtually a German colony, and MacDowell's German training was a certificate of his worth. The Boston Sym. Orch. conductors Gericke, Nikisch, and Paur, all Austro-Germans, played his works. On Nov. 19, 1888, MacDowell made his American debut as a composer and pianist at a Boston concert of the Kneisel String Quartet, featuring his *Modern Suite*, op. 10. On March 5, 1889, he was the soloist in the premiere performance of his 2nd Piano Concerto with the N.Y. Phil., under the direction of Theodore Thomas. Frank van der Stucken invited MacDowell to play his concerto at the spectacular Paris Exposition on July 12, 1889. MacDowell had no difficulty having his works publ., although for some reason he preferred that his early piano pieces, opp. 1–7, be printed under the pseudonym Edgar Thorn.

In 1896 Columbia Univ. invited MacDowell to become its 1st prof. of music, "to elevate the standard of musical instruction in the U.S., and to afford the most favorable opportunity for acquiring instruction of the highest order." MacDowell interpreted this statement to its fullest; by 1899, 2 assistants had been employed, Leonard McWhood and Gustav Hinrichs, but students received no credit for his courses. At the same time, he continued to compose and to teach piano privately; he also conducted the Mendelssohn Glee Club (1896–98) and served as president of the Soc. of American Musicians and Composers (1899–1900). In the academic year 1902–3, he took a sabbatical; played concerts throughout the U.S. and in Europe; played his 2nd Piano Concerto in London (May 14, 1903). During his sabbatical, Columbia Univ. replaced its president, Seth Low, with Nicholas Murray Butler, whose ideas about the role of music in the univ. were diametrically opposed to the ideals of MacDowell. MacDowell resigned in 1904 and subsequently became a "cause célèbre," resulting in much acrimony on both sides. It was not until some time later that the Robert Center Chair that MacDowell had held at Columbia Univ. was renamed the Edward MacDowell Chair of Music to honor its 1st recipient.

Through the combination of the trauma resulting from this episode, an accident with a hansom, and the development of what appears to have been tertiary syphilis, MacDowell rapidly deteriorated mentally; he showed signs of depression, extreme irritability, and a gradual loss of vital functions; he eventually lapsed into total insanity, and spent the last 2 years of his life in a childlike state, unaware of his surroundings. In 1906 a public appeal was launched to raise funds for his care; among the signers were Horatio Parker, Victor Herbert, Arthur Foote,

George Chadwick, Frederick Converse, Andrew Carnegie, J. Pierpont Morgan, and former President Grover Cleveland. MacDowell was only 47 years old when he died. The sum of $50,000 was raised for the organization of the MacDowell Memorial Assoc. Mrs. MacDowell, who outlived her husband by nearly half a century (she died at the age of 98, in Los Angeles, on Aug. 23, 1956), deeded to the association her husband's summer residence at Peterborough, N.H. This property became a pastoral retreat, under the name of the MacDowell Colony, for American composers and writers, who could spend summers working undisturbed in separate cottages, paying a minimum rent for lodging and food. During the summer of 1910, Mrs. MacDowell arranged an elaborate pageant with music from MacDowell's works; the success of this project led to the establishment of a series of MacDowell Festivals at Peterborough.

MacDowell received several awards during his lifetime, including 2 honorary doctorates (Princeton Univ., 1896; Univ. of Pa., 1902) and election into the American Academy of Arts and Letters (1904); in 1940 a 5-cent U.S. postage stamp with his likeness was issued; in 1960 he was the 2nd composer elected to the Hall of Fame at N.Y. Univ., where, in 1964, a bust was unveiled.

Among American composers, MacDowell occupies a historically important place as the 1st American whose works were accepted as comparable in quality and technique with those of the average German composers of his time. His music adhered to the prevalent representative Romantic art. Virtually all of his works bear titles borrowed from mythical history, literature, or painting; even his piano sonatas, set in Classical forms, carry descriptive titles, indicative of the mood of melodic resources, or as an ethnic reference. Since he lived in Germany during his formative years, German musical culture was decisive in shaping his musical development; even the American rhythms and melodies in his music seem to be European reflections of an exotic art. A parallel with Grieg is plausible, for Grieg was also a regional composer trained in Germany. But Grieg possessed a much more vigorous personality, and he succeeded in communicating the true spirit of Norwegian song modalities in his works. Lack of musical strength and originality accounts for MacDowell's gradual decline in the estimation of succeeding generations; his romanticism was apt to lapse into salon sentimentality. The frequency of performance of his works in concert (he never wrote for the stage) declined in the decades following his death, and his influence on succeeding generations of American composers receded to a faint recognition of an evanescent artistic period.

Works: Orch.: *Hamlet* and *Ophelia*, 2 tone poems, op. 22 (1885; *Ophelia*, N.Y., Nov. 4, 1886; *Hamlet*, N.Y., Nov. 15, 1887; together, Chicago, March 26, 1890); *Lancelot and Elaine*, symphonic poem, op. 25 (Boston, Jan. 10, 1890); *Lamia*, symphonic poem, op. 29 (1889; Boston, Oct. 23, 1908); *The Saracens* and *The Lovely Alda*, 2 fragments after the Song of Roland, op. 30 (Boston, Nov. 5, 1891); Suite No. 1, op. 42 (Worcester Festival, Sept. 24, 1891; 3rd movement, "In October," op. 42a, added in 1894; complete work 1st perf., Boston, 1896); Suite No. 2, *Indian*, op. 48 (N.Y., Jan. 23, 1896); Piano Concerto No. 1, in A minor, op. 15 (movements 2 and 3, N.Y., March 30, 1885, Adele Margulies soloist; complete version, Chicago, July 5, 1888, Teresa Carreño soloist); Piano Concerto No. 2, in D minor, op. 23 (N.Y., March 5, 1889, composer soloist); *Romance* for Cello and Orch., op. 35 (1888).

choral: 2 choruses for Men's Voices, op. 3: *Love and Time* and *The Rose and the Gardener* (1897); *The Witch* for Men's Chorus, op. 5 (1898); *War Song* for Men's Chorus, op. 6 (1898); 3 songs for Men's Chorus, op. 27 (1887); 2 songs for Men's Chorus, op. 41 (1890); 2 *Northern Songs* for Mixed Voices, op. 43 (1891); 3 choruses for Men's Voices, op. 52 (1897); 2 *Songs from the 13th Century* for Men's Chorus (1897); 2 choruses for Men's Voices, op. 53 (1898); 2 choruses for Men's Voices, op. 54 (1898); *College Songs* for Men's Voices (1901); *Summer Wind* for Women's Chorus (1902).

voice and piano: 2 *Old Songs*, op. 9 (1894); 3 songs, op.

11 (1883); 2 songs, op. 12 (1883); *From an Old Garden* (6 songs), op. 26 (1887); 3 songs, op. 33 (1888; rev. 1894); 2 songs, op. 34 (1884); *6 Love Songs*, op. 40 (1890); 8 songs, op. 47 (1893); 4 songs, op. 56 (1898); 3 songs, op. 58 (1899); 3 songs, op. 60 (1902).

PIANO: *Amourette*, op. 1 (1896); *In Lilting Rhythm*, op. 2 (1897); *Forgotten Fairy Tales* (*Sung outside the Prince's Door, Of a Tailor and a Bear, Beauty in the Rose Garden, From Dwarfland*), op. 4 (1898); *6 Fancies* (*A Tin Soldier's Love, To a Humming Bird, Summer Song, Across Fields, Bluette, An Elfin Round*), op. 7 (1898); *Waltz*, op. 8 (1895); *1st Modern Suite*, op. 10 (1880); *Prelude and Fugue*, op. 13 (1883); *2nd Modern Suite*, op. 14 (1881); *Serenata*, op. 16 (1883); *2 Fantastic Pieces* (*Legend, Witches' Dance*), op. 17 (1884); *2 Pieces* (*Barcarolle, Humoresque*), op. 18 (1884); *Forest Idyls* (*Forest Stillness, Play of the Nymphs, Reverie, Dance of the Dryads*), op. 19 (1884); *4 Pieces* (*Humoresque, March, Cradle Song, Czardas*), op. 24 (1887); *6 Idyls after Goethe* (*In the Woods, Siesta, To the Moonlight, Silver Clouds, Flute Idyl, The Bluebell*), op. 28 (1887); *6 Poems after Heine* (*From a Fisherman's Hut, Scotch Poem, From Long Ago, The Post Wagon, The Shepherd Boy, Monologue*), op. 31 (1887); *4 Little Poems* (*The Eagle, The Brook, Moonshine, Winter*), op. 32 (1888); *Étude de concert* in F-sharp, op. 36 (1889); *Les Orientales*, after Victor Hugo (*Clair de lune, Danse le Hamac, Danse Andalouse*), op. 37 (1889); *Marionnettes, 8 Little Pieces* (*Prologue, Soubrette, Lover, Witch, Clown, Villain, Sweetheart, Epilogue*), op. 38 (1888; originally only 6 pieces; *Prologue* and *Epilogue* were added in 1901); *12 Studies, Book I* (*Hunting Song, Alla Tarantella, Romance, Arabesque, In the Forest, Dance of the Gnomes*); *Book II* (*Idyl, Shadow Dance, Intermezzo, Melody, Scherzino, Hungarian*), op. 39 (1890); *Sonata No. 1, Tragica*, op. 45 (1893); *12 Virtuoso Studies* (*Novelette, Moto perpetuo, Wild Chase, Improvisation, Elfin Dance, Valse triste, Burleske, Bluette, Träumerei, March Wind, Impromptu, Polonaise*), op. 46 (1894); *Air* and *Rigaudon*, op. 49 (1894); *Sonata No. 2, Eroica*, op. 50 (1895); *Woodland Sketches*, 10 pieces (*To a Wild Rose, Will o' the Wisp, At an Old Trysting Place, In Autumn, From an Indian Lodge, To a Water Lily, From Uncle Remus, A Desert Farm, By a Meadow Brook, Told at Sunset*), op. 51 (1896); *Sea Pieces* (*To the Sea, From a Wandering Iceberg, A.D. 1620, Star-light, Song, From the Depths, Nautilus, In Mid-Ocean*), op. 55 (1898); *Sonata No. 3, Norse*, op. 57 (1900); *Sonata No. 4, Keltic*, op. 59 (1901); *Fireside Tales* (*An Old Love Story, Of Br'er Rabbit, From a German Forest, Of Salamanders, A Haunted House, By Smouldering Embers*), op. 61 (1902); *New England Idyls*, 10 pieces (*An Old Garden, Midsummer, Midwinter, With Sweet Lavender, In Deep Woods, Indian Idyl, To an Old White Pine, From Puritan Days, From a Log Cabin, The Joy of Autumn*), op. 62 (1902); *6 Little Pieces on Sketches by J.S. Bach* (1890); *Technical Exercises*, 2 Books (1893, 1895). MacDowell's writings were collected by W. Baltzell and publ. as *Critical and Historical Essays* (1912; reprinted, with new introduction by I. Lowens, N.Y., 1969).

BIBL.: L. Gilman, *E. M.: A Study* (N.Y., 1908; corrected reprint, N.Y., 1969); E. Page, *E. M.: His Works and Ideals* (N.Y., 1910); J. Adams, *What the Piano Writings of M. Mean to the Piano Student* (Chicago, 1913); T. Currier, "M. as I Knew Him," *Musical Quarterly* (Jan. 1915); O. Sonneck, *Suum cuique: Essays in Music* (N.Y., 1916); idem, *Catalogue of First Editions of E. M.* (Washington, D.C., 1917; reprint, N.Y., 1973); W. Humiston, *M.* (N.Y., 1921); J. Matthews, *Commemorative Tributes to M.* (N.Y., 1922); J. Porte, *A Great American Tone Poet: E. M.* (London, 1922); A. Brown, *The Boyhood of E. M.* (N.Y., 1924); U. Sinclair, "M.," *American Mercury* (1926); J. Cooke, *E. M., A Short Biography* (Philadelphia, 1928); R. Brown, "A Listener to the Winds, E. M.," in *Lonely Americans* (N.Y., 1929); A. Brown, *A Mosaic of Muses of the M. Club of New York* (N.Y., 1930); *Catalogue of an Exhibition Illustrating the Life and Work of E. M.* (N.Y., 1938); M. MacDowell, "M.'s Peterborough Idea," *Musical Quarterly* (Jan. 1932); idem, *Random Notes on E. M. and His Music* (Boston, 1950); I. Lowens, "E. M.," *Hi-Fi Stereo Review* (Nov. 1967); A. Schwab, "E. M.'s

Birthdate: A Correction," *Musical Quarterly* (April 1975); C. Kefferstan, *The Piano Concertos of E. M.* (diss., Univ. of Cincinnati, 1984); D. Pesce, "New Light on the Programmatic Aesthetic of M.'s Symphonic Poems," *American Music* (Winter 1986); F. Brancaleone, "E. M. and Indian Motives," *American Music* (Winter 1989).

Maceda, José, Filipino ethnomusicologist and composer; b. Manila, Jan. 31, 1917. He studied at the Manila Academy of Music and the École Normale de Musique in Paris (1937–41), where his teachers included Boulanger (analysis) and Cortot (piano); he also studied piano with Schmitz in San Francisco (1946–50), musicology with Lowinsky at Queens College, N.Y., and Lang at Columbia Univ. (1950–52), and ethnomusicology at the Univ. of Calif. at Los Angeles (Ph.D., 1963, with the diss. *The Music of the Magindanao*). As a pianist, he gave concerts in Paris, the U.S., and Manila in programs of new French music; worked in the electronic music studios of the French Radio (1958), in association with Boulez, Xenakis, and others. In 1960 he became prof. of ethnomusicology at the Univ. of the Philippines. His field research focused on music of the Philippines and Southeast Asia, with studies in Africa and Brazil (1968). His compositions combine modernistic and ethnic elements; from 1963 he appeared as a conductor of avant-garde and Asian ethnic music.

WORKS: *Ugma-ugma* (Structures) for Voice and Asian Instruments (1963); *Agungan* (Gong Sounds) for 6 Gong Families (1966); *Kubing* (Music) for Male Voices and Bamboo Percussion (1966); *Pagsamba* (Ritual Music) for 241 Performers (1968); *Cassettes 100* for 100 Cassette Recordings played by the Audience (1971); *Agnayan* for 20 Radio Stations (1973).

Macfarren, Sir George (Alexander), eminent English composer and pedagogue, brother of **Walter (Cecil) Macfarren;** b. London, March 2, 1813; d. there, Oct. 31, 1887. He began his studies with his father, George Macfarren, who was a dancing-master and dramatist, and with Charles Lucas; then studied composition with C. Potter at the Royal Academy of Music in London (1829–36); was a tutor there (1834–37); then a prof. (1837–47; 1851–75); subsequently was its principal (1875–87). He was also a prof. of music at Cambridge Univ. (1875–87). He was knighted in 1883. He suffered from eye problems from the age of 10; became totally blind in 1860, but continued to compose by dictating to an amanuensis. He had the great satisfaction of having his early overture *Chevy Chace* performed by Mendelssohn in Leipzig (1843) and by Wagner in London (1855). Macfarren's greatest ambition was to write an opera that would reflect the spirit of England, as the operas of Weber were redolent of the mythical lyricism of German folklore, but he signally failed in this endeavor. His 9 syms. enjoyed transient favor, but attempts at their revival foundered in time. His wife, **Natalia Macfarren** (née **Clarina Thalia Andrae;** b. Lübeck, Dec. 14, 1826; d. Bakewell, April 9, 1916), was a singer; she studied with Macfarren and dutifully sang in his operas. She publ. a *Vocal Method* and an *Elementary Course of Vocalising and Pronouncing the English Language.*

WORKS: OPERAS: *The Prince of Modena* (1833); *El Malhechor* (1837–38); *The Devil's Opera* (London, Aug. 13, 1838); *An Adventure of Don Quixote* (London, Feb. 3, 1846); *King Charles II* (London, Oct. 27, 1849); *Allan of Aberfeldy* (c.1850); *Robin Hood* (London, Oct. 11, 1860); *Jessy Lea*, opera di camera (London, Nov. 2, 1863); *She Stoops to Conquer* (London, Feb. 11, 1864); *The Soldier's Legacy*, opera di camera (London, July 10, 1864); *Helvellyn* (London, Nov. 3, 1864); *Kenilworth* (1880); other stage works. ORCH.: 9 syms. (1828; 1831; 1832; 1833; 1833; 1836; 1839–40; 1845; 1874); Overture (1831); Piano Concerto (1835); Flute Concerto (1863); Violin Concerto (1871–74); overtures: *The Merchant of Venice* (1834); *Romeo and Juliet* (1836); *Chevy Chace* (1836); *Don Carlos* (1842); *Hamlet* (1856); *Festival Overture* (1874). VOCAL: Oratorios and cantatas: *The Sleeper Awakened* (London, Nov. 15, 1850); *Lenora* (London, April 25, 1853); *Christmas* (London, May 9, 1860); *St. John the Baptist* (Bristol, Oct. 23, 1873); *The Resurrection* (Birmingham, 1876); *Joseph* (Leeds, 1877); *King David*

(Leeds, 1883); numerous sacred and secular vocal works; choral works; part-songs; trios; duets; some 160 solo songs. **CHAMBER:** 5 string quartets (1834, 1842, 1846, 1849, 1878); Quintet for Violin, Viola, Cello, Double Bass, and Piano (1844); Violin Sonata (1887); 3 piano sonatas (1842, 1845, 1880); various piano and organ pieces. **ARRANGEMENTS:** *Popular Music of the Olden Time* (1859); *Popular Songs of Scotland* (1874).

BIBL.: H. Banister, *G.A. M.: His Life, Works and Influence* (London, 1891); W. Macfarren, "G.A. M.," *RAM Magazine*, 1 (1900); A. Jacobs, "Cradled among the Reeds: Two Victorian Operettas," *Musical Times* (May 1988).

Macfarren, Walter (Cecil), English pianist and composer, brother of **Sir George (Alexander) Macfarren;** b. London, Aug. 28, 1826; d. there, Sept. 2, 1905. He was a chorister at Westminster Abbey (1836–41); then studied at the Royal Academy of Music in London (1842–46), with Holmes (piano) and his brother (composition); from 1846 to 1903 he was a prof. of piano there; also conducted its concerts (1873–80). He composed a number of overtures on Shakespearean subjects; a Piano Concerto; many piano pieces; ed. Beethoven's sonatas, and several albums of piano pieces under the title *Popular Classics.* He publ. *Memories; An Autobiography* (London, 1905).

Mach, Ernst, eminent German physicist and philosopher; b. Turas, Moravia, Feb. 18, 1838; d. Vaterstetten, near Munich, Feb. 19, 1916. He was prof. of mathematics at the Univ. of Graz (1864–67), of physics at the Univ. of Prague (1867–95), and of inductive philosophy at the Univ. of Vienna (1895–1901). Besides his scientific works of far-reaching importance, he publ. studies dealing with musical acoustics: *Zwei populäre Vorträge über musikalische Akustik* (1865); *Einleitung in die Helmholtz'sche Musiktheorie* (1866); *Zur Theorie des Gehörorgans* (1872); *Beitrag zur Geschichte der Musik* (1892); *Die Analyse der Empfindungen und das Verhältnis des Physischen zum Psychischen* (5th ed., 1906); "Zur Geschichte der Theorie der Konsonanz," in *Populärwissenschaftliche Vorträge* (3rd ed., 1903). The unit of velocity of sound ("Mach") is named after him.

Mácha, Otmar, Czech composer; b. Ostrava, Oct. 2, 1922. He studied with Hradil (1941–42); then at the Prague Cons. (1943–45), where he subsequently attended Řídký's master class (1945–48); was active with the Czech Radio (1945–62); then devoted himself to composing; was awarded the State Prize in 1967 and was made a Merited Artist by the Czech government in 1982.

WORKS: STAGE: Operas: *Polapená nevěra* (Entrapped Faithlessness; 1956–57; Prague, Nov. 21, 1958); *Jezero Ukereve* (Lake Ukereve; 1960–63; Prague, May 27, 1966); comic opera, *Svatba na oko* (Feigned Wedding; 1974–76); musical comedy, *Kolébka pro hříšné panny* (Cradle for Sinful Maidens; 1975–76); oratorio, *Odkaz J.A. Komenského* (J.A. Comenius's Legacy; 1952–55). **ORCH.:** Sym. (1947–48); *Slovak Rhapsody* (1951); *Symphonic Intermezzo* (1958); *Noc a naděje* (Night and Hope), symphonic poem (1959); *Variace na téma a smrt Jana Rychlíka* (Variations on a Theme by Jan Rychlík; 1964; Prague, March 15, 1966); *4 Monologues* for Soprano, Baritone, and Orch. (1965–66); *Variants,* short studies (1968); *Janinka zpívá* (Janinka Sings), suite for Soprano and Orch. (1969); 2 sinfoniettas (1970–71; 1978–80); *Double Concerto* for Violin, Piano, and Orch. (1976); Concerto grosso for Vocal Soloists and Orch. (1980). **CHAMBER:** 2 string quartets (1943; 1981–82); 2 violin sonatas (1948, 1987); Cello Sonata (1949); Bassoon Sonata (1963); *Saxophone Cries* for Saxophone and Piano (1963–68); Small Triptych, 3 songs for Soprano, Flute, and Tam-tam (1971); *Oči a ruce* (Eyes and Hands), dramatic song for Mezzo-soprano, Clarinet, Viola, and Piano (1975); *Elegy* for Violin and Piano (1982); organ music; piano pieces; also choruses; songs; film scores.

Machabey, Armand, French musicologist; b. Pont-de-Roide, Doubs, May 7, 1886; d. Paris, Aug. 31, 1966. He studied with d'Indy and Pirro; received his doctorat ès lettres from the Univ.

of Paris in 1928 with the dissertation *Essai sur les formules usuelles de la musique occidentale (des origines à la fin du XVᵉ siècle);* publ. in a rev. ed., Paris, 1955, as *Genèse de la tonalité musicale classique.* He was subsequently active as a music historian and essayist; also was one of the eds. of *Larousse de la musique* (Paris, 1957).

WRITINGS (all publ. in Paris unless otherwise given): *Sommaire de la méthode en musicologie* (1930); *Précis-manuel d'histoire de la musique* (1942; 2nd ed., 1947); *La Vie et l'œuvre d'Anton Bruckner* (1945); *Maurice Ravel* (1947); *Traité de la critique musicale* (1947); *Le "bel canto"* (1948); *Portraits de trente compositeurs français* (1950); *Gerolamo Frescobaldi Ferrarensis (1583–1643)* (1952); *La Musique et la médicine* (1952); *La Notation musicale* (1952; 3rd ed., rev., 1971 by M. Huglo); *Guillaume de Machaut: La Vie et l'œuvre musicale* (1955); *Problèmes de notation musicale* (1958); *La Musicologie* (1962; 2nd ed., 1969); *Embryologie de la musique occidentale* (1963); *La Musique de danse* (1966).

Machado, Augusto (de Oliveira), Portuguese composer; b. Lisbon, Dec. 27, 1845; d. there, March 26, 1924. He was a pupil of Junior, Lami, and D'Almeide in Lisbon, and of Lavignac and Danhauser in Paris; from 1892 to 1908, was director of the San Carlos Theater in Lisbon; also taught singing at the Cons. (from 1893), serving as its director (1901–10). Besides numerous operettas, he wrote the operas *A Cruz de oiro* (Lisbon, 1873); *A Maria da Fonte* (Lisbon, 1879); *Lauriane* (Marseilles, Jan. 9, 1883; his most successful work); *Os Dorias* (Lisbon, 1887); *Mario Wetter* (Lisbon, 1898); *Venere* (Lisbon, 1905); *La Borghesina* (Lisbon, 1909). For the 3rd centenary of the death of Camoëns he wrote the symphonic ode *Camões es os Luziadas* (1880); also wrote organ and piano pieces.

Machaut (also **Machault, Machau, Mauchault**), **Guillaume de (Guillelmus de Mascaudio),** important French composer and poet; b. probably in Machaut, Champagne, c.1300; d. probably in Rheims, April 13?, 1377. He entered the service of John of Luxembourg, King of Bohemia, about 1323; was his secretary until the King's death (1346). He was granted a canonry in Verdun (1330), a 2nd in Arras (1332), and a 3rd in Rheims (1333), retaining the 1st 2 until 1335. He settled in Rheims permanently about 1340; from 1346 was in the service of the French nobility, including the future King Charles V. His *Messe de Nostre Dame* for 4 Voices is one of the earliest polyphonic settings of the Mass. He also wrote 42 ballades, 33 virelais, 23 motets, 22 rondeaux, 19 lais, a double hocket, a complainte, and a chanson royal. An ed. of his works was prepared by F. Ludwig for the Publikationen Älterer Musik (1926–34; continued by H. Besseler, 1954) and by L. Schrade in Polyphonic Music of the Fourteenth Century (Vols. 2 and 3, Monaco, 1956).

BIBL.: H. Quittard, "Notes sur G. d.M. et son œuvre," *Bulletin de la Société Française de Musicologie* (1918); A. Machabey, "G. d.M., La Vie et l'homme," *Revue Musicale* (May 1930; April–May 1931); A. Douce, *G. d.M., Musicien et poète rémois* (Rheims, 1948); G. Perle, "Integrative Devices in the Music of M.," *Musical Quarterly* (April 1948); O. Gombosi, "M.'s Messe Notre-Dame," *Musical Quarterly* (April 1950); S. Levarie, *G. d.M.* (N.Y., 1954); A. Machabey, *G. d.M.: La Vie et l'œuvre musicale* (2 vols., Paris, 1955); G. Reaney, "Notes on the Harmonic Technique of G. d.M.," in H. Tischler, *Essays in Musicology* (Apel Festschrift, Bloomington, Ind., 1968); H. Eggebrecht, "M.s Motette Nr. 9," *Archiv für Musikwissenschaft* (Aug. 1968); S. Williams, "Vocal Scoring in the Chansons of M.," *Journal of the American Musicological Society* (Fall 1968); W. Dömling, *Die mehrstimmigen Balladen, Rondeaux und Virelais von G. d.M.* (Tutzing, 1970); M. Hasselman and T. Walker, "More Hidden Polyphony in a M. Manuscript," *Musica Disciplina* (1970); G. Reaney, *G. d.M.* (London, 1971); B. Harden, *Sharps, Flats, and Scribes: Musica ficta in the M. Manuscripts* (diss., Cornell Univ., 1983); L. Earp, "M.'s Role in the Production of Manuscripts of His Works," *Journal of the American Musicological Society* (Fall 1989).

Machavariani, Alexei (Davidovich), Russian composer; b. Gory, Sept. 23, 1913. He studied at the Tbilisi Cons., graduating in 1936; then was on its faculty as a teacher of theory (1940–63) and as a prof. of composition (from 1963). He was made a People's Artist of the U.S.S.R. in 1958. His music is profoundly infused with Caucasian melorhythms.
WORKS: STAGE: Operas: *Deda da shvili* (Mother and Son; 1944; Tbilisi, May 1, 1945); *Hamlet* (1964); ballets: *Otello* (1957); *Knight in a Tiger's Skin* (1965). **ORCH.:** 2 syms. (1947, 1973); 3 symphonic poems: *Mumly Muhasa* (1939), *Satchidao* (1940), and *On the Death of a Hero* (1948); overture, *The People's Choice* (1950); Piano Concerto (1944); Violin Concerto (1949). **VOCAL:** cantata, *For Peace, for Fatherland* (1951); oratorio, *The Day of My Fatherland* (1954); many songs, of which *Blue Light* (1949) achieved great popularity in Russia; *Khorumy*, Georgian military dance, for Piano (1941; very popular).

Mâche, François-Bernard, remarkable French composer and classical scholar; b. Clermont-Ferrand, April 4, 1935. Of a musical family, he studied piano locally; in 1955 entered L'École Normale Supérieure in Paris, studying classical languages and literature; received his diploma in 1958; then enrolled at the Paris Cons., in the composition class of Messiaen; continued his classical studies, and in 1962 was given a professorship in classical literature. He also learned modern Greek, and tr. contemporary Greek poetry and prose into English; several of his works are inspired by Greek mythology. In musical composition, he became an adherent of experimental methods; in 1980 he received a national doctorate for his thesis on models of new music. He adopted the ideal of "organized sound" as enunciated by Varèse; but he also annexed sounds of nature; for resources he studied ornithology, but rather than translate the intonations of bird songs into human melorhythms performable on instruments, as Messiaen professed to do, he transmuted the natural material into suggestive images of sound; in one of his works, *Amorgos*, named after an island in the Aegean Sea, he used as a background the actual sound of the sea waves recorded on magnetic tape. In another score, *Naluan*, he used recorded animal sounds. He publ. an essay, *Musique, mythe, nature ou Les Dauphins d'Arion* (1982).
WORKS: *La Peau du silence* for Orch. (1962); *Rituel d'Oubli* for Orch. and Concert Band (1969); *Danae* for 12 Solo Voices and Percussion (1970); *Naluan* for 8 Instruments and Animal Sounds (1974); *Marae* for 6 Percussionists and Sounds of Nature (1974); *Kassandra* for 14 Instruments and Band (Paris Radio, Oct. 16, 1977); *Andromède* for Orch., Double Chorus, and 3 Pianos (1979); *Amorgos* for 12 Instruments and Recorded Sea Waves (Metz Festival, Nov. 16, 1979); *Sopiana* for Flute, Piano, and Magnetic Tape (Pecs, Hungary, July 12, 1980); *Temboctou*, musical spectacle (1982); *Eridan* for String Quartet (1986; Paris, Jan. 17, 1987).

Machl, Tadeusz, Polish organist, composer, and pedagogue; b. Lwow, Oct. 22, 1922. He studied composition with Malawski and organ with Rutkowski at the State College of Music in Krakow (1949–52); subsequently occupied various teaching and administrative positions in Krakow.
WORKS: *3 miniatury symfoniczne* (1946); 5 syms.: No. 1, with Chorus (1947); No. 2 (1948); No. 3, *Tatry* (1949); No. 4 (1954); No. 5 for Soprano, Female Chorus, and Orch. (1963); many concertos, including 6 for Organ (1950, 1952, 1953, 1958, 1978, 1983) and 1 each for Soprano (1958), Violin (1960), Harpsichord (1962), Piano (1965), and Harp (1967); *Double Concerto* for Piano, Harpsichord, and Orch. (1967); 2 triple concertos: No. 1 for 3 Organs (1969) and No. 2 for 2 Pianos, Organ, and Orch. (1971); *Lyrical Suite* for Orch. (1956); *Jubilee Overture* (1971); *Dzień pracy* (Labor Day) for Chorus and Small Orch. (1948); 4 string quartets (1952, 1957, 1962, 1972); Piano Sonata (1940); pieces for organ solo and for piano; choruses; songs.

Machlis, Joseph, Latvian-born American writer on music and pedagogy; b. Riga, Aug. 11, 1906. He was taken to the U.S. as an infant. He studied at the College of the City Univ. of N.Y. (B.A., 1927), and at the Inst. of Musical Art (teacher's diploma, 1927); also took an M.A. in English literature from Columbia Univ. (1938). He was on the music faculty of Queens College of the City Univ. of N.Y. (1938–74); then on the graduate faculty at the Juilliard School (from 1976). He made English trs. of a number of opera librettos; publ. several well-written texts: the immensely popular *The Enjoyment of Music* (N.Y., 1955; 5th ed., rev., 1984); *Introduction to Contemporary Music* (N.Y., 1961; 2nd ed., 1979); *American Composers of Our Time* for young people (N.Y., 1963); *Getting to Know Music* for high school students (N.Y., 1966). He also publ. 2 novels: *57th Street*, about the "concert industry" (N.Y., 1970), and *Lisa's Boy* (N.Y., 1982), publ. under the phonetically palindromic pseudonym George Selcamm.

Machover, Tod, American cellist, conductor, and composer; b. N.Y., Nov. 24, 1953. He studied composition at the Univ. of Calif. at Santa Cruz (1971–73), Columbia Univ. (1973–74), and the Juilliard School in N.Y. (B.M., 1975; M.M., 1977); among his mentors were Dallapiccola (1973), Sessions (1973–75), and Carter (1975–78); also studied computer music at the Mass. Inst. of Technology and at Stanford Univ. He was 1st cellist in the orch. of the National Opera of Canada in Toronto (1975–76), guest composer (1978–79) and director of musical research (1980–84) at I.R.C.A.M. in Paris, and a teacher at the Mass. Inst. of Technology (from 1985). Among his honors were the Koussevitzky Prize (1984) and the Friedheim Award (1987).
WORKS: OPERA: *Valis* (Paris, Dec. 2, 1987). **ORCH.:** *Nature's Breach* for Chamber Orch. (1984–85); *Desires* (1985–89). **CHAMBER:** Concerto for Amplified Guitar and Ensemble (1978); *Fresh Spring* for Baritone and 10 Instruments (1977); *Ye Gentle Birds* for Soprano, Mezzo-soprano, and 6 Instruments (1977); *Yoku Mireba* for Flute, Cello, and Piano (1977); *With Dadaji in Paradise* for Cello (1978; rev. 1983); *Light* for 15 Instruments (1979); *Winter Variations* for 9 Instruments (1981); String Quartet No. 1 (1981); *Hidden Sparks* for Violin (1984). **ELECTRONIC:** *Deplacements* for Guitar and Computer Electronics (1979); *Soft Morning, City!* for Soprano, Double Bass, and Tape (1980); *Fusione Fugace* for Live Computer Electronics (1981); *Electric Études* for Cello and Computer Electronics (1983); *Spectres parisiens* for Flute, Horn, Cello, Synthesizer, 18 Instruments, and Computer (1984); *Flora* for Computer Tape (1989); *Bug-Mudra* for 2 Guitars, Percussion, Conductor with Gesture-tracking "Dataglove," and Live Computer (1989–90); *Epithalamion* for Vocal Soloists, 25 Players, and Live and Recorded Computer Electronics (1990); various solo works; piano pieces.

Maciejewski, Roman, Polish pianist, organist, choral conductor, and composer; b. Berlin (of Polish parents), Feb. 28, 1910. His mother taught him to play piano at an early age; he then took regular piano lessons with Goldenweiser at the Berlin Cons. (1916–19) and with Zeleski at the Poznan Cons. (diploma, 1922); also studied composition with Wiechowicz in Poznan and with Sikorski at the Warsaw Cons. He went to Paris in 1934, and studied with Boulanger; then lived in Sweden (1939–51). In 1952 he emigrated to the U.S., settling in Redondo Beach, Calif., as a church organist and director of the Roman Choir. He excelled in writing lush, resonant, protracted choruses in self-confident tonal harmonies.
WORKS: Requiem for Soloists, Chorus, and Orch. (part I, 1944–60, Warsaw Autumn Festival, Sept. 1960); *Allegro concertante* for Piano and Orch. (1944; Göteborg, Jan. 11, 1945); *Song of Bilitis* for Soprano and Orch. (1932); Brass Quartet (1937); String Quartet (1938); Violin Sonata (1940); String Trio (1948); *Nocturne* for Flute, Celesta, and Guitar (1951); *Variations* for Wind Quintet (1971); *Bajka* (Fairy Tale), ballet for children for 2 Pianos (1931); Concerto for 2 Solo Pianos (1935); 2 piano sonatas (1926, 1932); 25 *Mazurkas* for Piano (1928–38); several masses with organ; a cappella songs.

Mackenzie, Sir Alexander (Campbell), distinguished Scottish conductor, educator, and composer; b. Edinburgh, Aug. 22, 1847; d. London, April 28, 1935. A scion of a musical family (there were 4 generations of musicians in his paternal line), he showed musical aptitude as a child; was sent to Germany, where he studied violin with K.W. Ulrich and theory with Eduard Stein at the Schwarzburg-Sondershausen Realschule (1857–62); returning to England, he studied violin with Sainton, piano with Jewson, and music theory with Charles Lucas at the Royal Academy of Music in London; subsequently was active in Edinburgh as a violinist and teacher (1865–79). Between 1879 and 1885 he lived in Florence. In 1888 he was elected principal of the Royal Academy of Music in London, holding this post until 1924. From 1892 to 1899 he conducted the concerts of the Phil. Soc. of London. His reputation as an educator and composer was very high among musicians. He was knighted in 1895. As a composer, he was a staunch believer in programmatic music; he introduced national Scottish elements in many of his works; his *Pibroch Suite* for Violin and Orch., 1st introduced by Sarasate at the Leeds Festival (1889), acquired considerable popularity; Paderewski gave the 1st performance of his *Scottish Concerto* with the Phil. Soc. of London (1897). In 1922 he was made a Knight Commander of the Royal Victorian Order.

Works (all 1st perf. in London unless otherwise given): **OPERAS:** *Colomba* (April 9, 1883; rev. version, Dec. 3, 1912); *The Troubadour* (June 8, 1886); *Phoebe*, comic opera (n.d.; not perf.); *His Majesty, or The Court of Vingolia*, comic opera (Feb. 20, 1897); *The Cricket on the Hearth* (1900; June 6, 1914); *The Knights of the Road*, operetta (Feb. 27, 1905); incidental music to plays. **CANTATAS:** *The Bride* (Worcester Festival, 1881); *Jason* (Bristol Festival, 1882); *The Story of Sayid* (Leeds Festival, 1886); *The Dream of Jubal* (Liverpool, 1889); *The Witches' Daughter* (Leeds Festival, 1904); *The Sun-God's Return* (Cardiff Festival, 1910). **ORATORIOS:** *The Rose of Sharon* (Norwich Festival, Oct. 16, 1884; rev. 1910); *Bethlehem* (1894; also known as *The Holy Babe*); *The Temptation* (1914). **ORCH.:** *Larghetto and Allegretto* for Cello and Orch. (1875); *Overture to a Comedy* (Düsseldorf, 1876); *Cervantes*, overture (Sondershausen, 1877); *Scherzo* (Glasgow, 1878); *Rhapsodie écossaise: Scottish Rhapsody* No. 1 (1880); *Tempo di ballo*, overture (c.1880); *Burns: Scottish Rhapsody* No. 2 (1880); *La Belle Dame sans merci*, ballad (1883); Violin Concerto (Birmingham Festival, 1885); *12th Night*, overture (1888); *Pibroch*, suite for Violin and Orch. (Leeds Festival, Oct. 10, 1880; also for Violin and Piano); *Highland Ballad* for Violin and Orch. (1893); *Britannia*, overture (1894); *Scottish Concerto* for Piano and Orch. (March 24, 1897); *Processional March* (1899); *Coronation March* (1902); *London Day by Day*, suite (Norwich Festival, 1902); *Canadian Rhapsody* (1905); *Tam o' Shanter: Scottish Rhapsody* No. 3 (1911); *Youth, Sport and Loyalty*, overture (1922). **CHAMBER:** Piano Trio (1874); String Quartet (1875); Piano Quartet (1875); *From the North*, 9 pieces for Violin and Piano (1895); *4 Dance Measures* for Violin and Piano (1915); *Distant Chimes* for Violin and Piano (1921); *2 Pieces* for Cello and Piano (1928); several piano works, including *Rustic Suite* (1876?), *In the Scottish Highlands*, 3 scenes (1880), *Odds and Ends, par ci, par là* (1916), (6) *Jottings* (1916), and *In Varying Moods* (1921); many songs; arrangements of Scottish melodies and airs.

Mackerras, Sir (Alan) Charles (MacLaurin), eminent American-born Australian conductor; b. Schenectady, N.Y. (of Australian parents), Nov. 17, 1925. He was taken to Sydney, Australia, as an infant; studied oboe, piano, and composition at the New South Wales Conservatorium there; then was principal oboist in the Sydney Sym. Orch. (1943–46). He subsequently went to London, where he joined the orch. at Sadler's Wells and studied conducting with Michael Mudie; he won a British Council Scholarship in 1947, which enabled him to study conducting with Václav Talich at the Prague Academy of Music. Returning to London in 1948, he joined the conducting staff at the Sadler's Wells Opera; then was engaged as principal conductor of the BBC Concert Orch. (1954–56); subsequently appeared as a guest conductor with British orchs.; also had engagements on the Continent. From 1966 to 1970 he held the post of 1st conductor at the Hamburg State Opera. In 1970 he became music director at the Sadler's Wells Opera

(it was renamed the English National Opera in 1974), a position he held until 1978. On Oct. 31, 1972, he made his Metropolitan Opera debut in N.Y. conducting Gluck's *Orfeo et Euridice.* After serving as chief conductor of the Sydney (Australia) Sym. Orch. (1982–85), he was artistic director of the Welsh National Opera in Cardiff (1987–92). He was made a Commander of the Order of the British Empire in 1974, and was knighted in 1979. He has distinguished himself as an opera conductor by championing the works of Janáček; has also conducted operas by Handel, Gluck, and J.C. Bach; also is a discriminating interpreter of the orch. repertoire.

BIBL.: N. Phelan, *C. M.: A Musicians' Musician* (London, 1987).

Maclean, Alick (actually, **Alexander Morvaren**), English composer and conductor, son of **Charles (Donald) Maclean;** b. Eton, near Windsor, July 20, 1872; d. London, May 18, 1936. He studied with Joseph Barnby; later conducted the Spa Orch. at Scarborough (from 1911) and Ballard Concerts at the Queen's Hall (1915–23).

Works: Operas: *Quentin Durward* (1892; Newcastle upon Tyne, Jan. 13, 1920); *Petruccio* (London, June 29, 1895); *The King's Price* (London, April 29, 1904); *Die Liebesgeige* (Mainz, April 15, 1906); *Maître Seiler* (London, Aug. 20, 1909); *Waldidyll* (Mainz, March 23, 1913); also an oratorio, *The Annunciation* (London, 1909); *Rapsodie monégasque* for Orch. (1935); choral works.

Maclean, Charles (Donald), English organist, editor, and composer, father of **Alick (Alexander Morvaren) Maclean;** b. Cambridge, March 27, 1843; d. London, June 23, 1916. He studied theory with Ferdinand Hiller in Cologne; later at Oxford Univ. (D.Mus., 1865). He was music director at Eton College (1871–75); then entered the Indian Civil Service, returning to London in 1898. He was the English ed. of the publications of the I.M.S. He composed a large output of orch. music.

Maclean, Quentin (Stuart Morvaren), English-Canadian organist and composer; b. London, May 14, 1896; d. Toronto, July 9, 1962. He studied organ with Karl Straube and composition with Max Reger in Leipzig (1912–14); was interned as an enemy alien in Germany during World War I. Upon his return to London, he was active as an organist; in 1939 he emigrated to Canada.

Works: *Concert Piece* for Organ and Orch. (1932); *Rhapsody on 2 English Folk Tunes* for Harp and Small Orch. (1938); *Stabat Mater* for Tenor, Chorus, Organ, and Strings (1941); *Concerto Grosso in Popular Style* for 4 Electric Instruments (Solovox, Electric Organ, Electric Guitar, Theremin) and Small Orch. (1942); *Concerto* for Electric Organ and Dance Orch. (1945); *The Well-tempered Orchestra*, prelude and fugue on a tuning formula, for Orch. (1950); *Concerto romantico* for Piano and Orch. (1953); *Rustic Rhapsody* for Orch. (1954); *Theme and Variations* for Harpsichord and Orch. (1954); *Concerto rococo* for Violin and Orch. (1957); String Quartet (1937); Piano Trio (1937); Trio for Flute, Viola, and Guitar (1937); organ pieces; choruses; songs.

Maclennan, Francis, American tenor; b. Bay City, Mich., Jan. 7, 1879; d. Port Westminster, N.Y., July 17, 1935. He studied voice in N.Y., and later with Henschel in London and Franz Emerich in Berlin; made his debut as Faust at London's Covent Garden (1902); in 1904 he sang Parsifal in Savage's Opera Co. on a tour of the U.S.; from 1907 to 1913 he was a member of the Berlin Royal Opera, where he had the distinction of being the 1st foreigner to sing Tristan in Germany; also performed Wagnerian roles in England; was a member of the Hamburg Opera (1913–16); sang with the Chicago Opera (1915–17); then taught voice. He was best known as a Wagnerian. He was married for several years to the soprano **Florence Easton,** with whom he appeared in duo recitals.

Mac Low, Jackson, American poet, composer, painter, and multimedia performance artist; b. Chicago, Sept. 12, 1922. He studied piano, violin, and harmony at Chicago Musical

College (1927–32) and Northwestern Univ. Music School (1932–36); then took courses in philosophy, poetics, and English at the Univ. of Chicago (A.A., 1941); also studied Greek at Brooklyn College of the City Univ. of N.Y. (B.A., 1958); had piano lessons with Shirley Gablis (1943–44), Grete Sultan (1953–55), and Franz Kamin (1976–79), composition with Erich Katz (1948–49), recorder with Tui St. George Tucker (1948–53), experimental music with John Cage at the New School for Social Research in N.Y. (1957–60), and voice with Pandit Pran Nath (1975–76). He taught at N.Y. Univ. (1966–73), the Mannes College of Music in N.Y. (1966), the State Univ. of N.Y. at Albany (1984), Binghamton (1989), and Buffalo (1990), and Temple Univ. (1989); in 1990 was Regents Lecturer at the Univ. of Calif. at San Diego. Among his 25 books, many—e.g., *Stanzas for Iris Lezak* (1972), *21 Matched Asymmetries* (1978), *Asymmetries 1–260* (1980), "*Is That Wool Hat My Hat?*" (1982), *Bloomsday* (1984), *Representative Works: 1938–1985* (1986), and *Words nd Ends from Ez* (1989)—comprise or include works realizable as musical-verbal performances. He wrote several chance-generated plays, including *The Marrying Maiden* (1958; unpubl.), *Verdurous Sanguinaria* (1961; publ. in anthology, 1980), and *The Twin Plays: Port-au-Prince and Adams County Illinois* (1963, 1966). *The Pronouns* (1964, 1971, 1979) are both poems and dance instructions, realized in the U.S., England, and Australia; he also wrote, directed, and performed in several Hörspiele. Mac Low adopted chance operations, indeterminacy, and related methods in 1954. His many "simultaneities" include musical, verbal, and visual elements; these and other compositions are for live voices, instruments (often variable), and/or tape multitracking, and usually involve guided improvisation and indeterminacy. He has performed extensively throughout North America, Western Europe, and New Zealand, often with the painter, multimedia performance artist, composer, and writer Anne Tardos. An 8-hour retrospective concert on the occasion of his 60th birthday was given at Washington Square Church in N.Y. (1982). His awards include fellowships from N.Y. State's Creative Artists Public Service Program (1973–74; 1976–77), the NEA (1979), the Guggenheim Memorial Foundation (1985), and the N.Y. Foundation for the Arts (1988); he also received a Fulbright grant for travel in New Zealand and a composer's grant from New Zealand's Queen Elizabeth II Art Council (both 1986).

Works: Overture to Paul Goodman's *Faustina* (1949); Overture, Songs, and Incidental Music for Paul Goodman's *Jonah* (1950); *Hear, O Israel!*, choral canon (1950); *5 biblical poems* (1954–55); Songs and Incidental Music for W.H. Auden's *The Age of Anxiety* (1955); *Rush Hour* (1955); *4 Pianissimo Pieces* (1955); *Peaks & Lamas* (1958–59); *Sade Suit* (1959); *Headline Glass Material Buildings* (1959); *Stanzas for Iris Lezak* (1960); *A Piece for Sari Dienes* (1960); *Asymmetries 1–501* (1960–61); *Thanks, a simultaneity for people* (1960–61); *Nembutsu Gathas* (1961); *1st Aum Gatha* (1961); *Aum Field* (1961); *1st Mani Gatha* (1961); *An Asymmetry for La Monte Young* (1961); *A Piece for Recorder, Right Hand Moving* (1961); *F# for Simone Forti* (1961); *Pitches* (1961); *A Word Event for George Brecht* (1961); "*The text on the opposite page . . .*" (1961; various realizations, 1965–70); *Gate Gate Gathas* (1961–66); *Jesus Gathas* (1961–66); *Chamber Music for Barney Childs* (1963); *Jail Break* (1963–66); *Hare Krna Gathas* (1967); *The 10 Bluebird Asymmetries* (1967); *The 6 Asymmetries for Dr. Howard Levy* (1967); *The 5 Young Turtle Asymmetries* (1967); *A Vocabulary for Carl Fernbach-Glarsheim* (1968); *LETT* (1969; quarter-tone guitar realization, 1976); *Word Event(s) for Bici Forbes* (1971–72); *A Word Event for Bici Forbes on the Book Title "Lucy Church Amiably"* (1971); *A Word Event for Bici Forbes on the Word "Environmentally"* (1971); *The Black Tarantula Crossword Gathas* (1973; 8-voice multitrack tape realization, 1973); *Gutu Gathas* (1973); *A Vocabulary for Michael Wiater* (1973); *A Vocabulary for Sharon Belle Mattlin* (1973); *The Tennyson Asymmetries* (1973); *Phoneme Dance for/from John Cage* (1974); *Govinda Gathas* (1974); *A Vocabulary for Vera Regina Lachmann* (1974); *A Vocabulary for Charlotte Moorman* (1974);

Counterpoint for Candy Cohen (multitrack tapes, 1974, 1978); *A Vocabulary for Peter Innisfree Moore* (1974–75); *Heavens* (1974–75); *Mani-Mani Gatha* (1975); *Guru-Guru Gatha* (1975); *Tara Gathas* (1975); *Kaddish Gatha* (1975); *1st Sharon Belle Mattlin Vocabulary Crossword Gatha* (1976); *1st Milarepa Gatha* (1976, 1979); *A Word Event for Bici Forbes on the Word "Bicentennial"* (1976); *Homage to Leona Bleiweiss* (1976); *Stephanie Vevers Vocabulary Gatha* (1977); *Albuquerque Antiphones* (1977); *Musicwords (for Phill Niblock)* (1977–78); *Free Gatha 1* (1978); *A Notated Vocabulary for Eve Rosenthal* (1978); *A Vocabulary Gatha for Pete Rose* (1978); *A Vocabulary for Custer LaRue* (1978–79); *A Vocabulary for Annie Brigitte Gilles Tardos* (1979; rev. 1980–82); *A Vocabulary Gatha for Anne Tardos* (1980); "*Is That Wool Hat My Hat?*" (1980); *Winds/Instruments* (1980); *Dream Meditation* (1980–82); *Words nd Ends from Ez* (text, 1981–83; used in radio work, 1981; arranged as multitrack tape, 1985; music, "*Ezra Pound*" and *99 Anagrams for Instrument(s)*, 1989–90); *Dialog unter Dichten/Dialog among Poets*, radio work (1981); *Canon for the Summer Solstice* (1981); *Free Gatha 2* (1981); *Transverse Flute Mime Piece* (1981); *2nd Aum Gatha* (1982); *Milarepa Quartet for 4 Like Instruments* (1982); *Thanks/Danke*, radio work (1983); *Heterophonies from "Hereford Bosons 1 and 2"* (1984); *Phonemicon from "Hereford Bosons 1"* (1984); *A Bean Phonemicon for Alison Knowles* (1984); *Reisen*, radio work (1984); *Locks*, radio work (1984); *Für Stimmen, etc.*, radio work (1985); *Definitive Revised Instructions for Performing Gathas* (1985); *Wörter nd Enden aus Goethe/Words and Ends from Goethe* (arranged as radio work, 1986); *Phoneme Dance for John Cage/Phonemtanz für John Cage*, radio work (with A. Tardos; 1986); *The Birds of New Zealand* for Multitrack Tape (1986); *Iran-Contra Hearings* (1987–90); *Westron Winde 2* (1987–88); *22nd Merzgedicht in Memoriam Kurt Schwitters* (1988); *Westron Winde 4* (1988–89); *Definitive Revised Performance Instructions* for each of the *Vocabularies* (1989–90); *Lucas 1–29* (1990); *There Is No Way to Peace. Peace Is the Way*, motet (1990–91).

Bibl.: J. Cage, "Music and Particularly Silence in the Work of J. M.L.," *Paper Air*, II/3 (1980); H. Smith, "Image, Text, and Performance: Inter-artistic Relationships in Contemporary Poetry," in D. Murray, ed., *Literary Theory and Poetry: Extending the Canon* (1989).

MacMillan, Sir Ernest (Alexander Campbell), eminent Canadian conductor and composer; b. Mimico, Aug. 18, 1893; d. Toronto, May 6, 1973. He began organ studies with Arthur Blakeley in Toronto at age 8, making his public debut at 10; continued organ studies with A. Hollins in Edinburgh (1905–8), where he was also admitted to the classes of F. Niecks and W.B. Ross at the Univ. He was made an associate (1907) and a fellow (1911) of London's Royal College of Organists, and received the extramural B.Mus. degree from Oxford Univ. (1911). He studied modern history at the Univ. of Toronto (1911–14) before receiving piano instruction from Therese Chaigneau in Paris (1914). In 1914 he attended the Bayreuth Festival, only to be interned as an enemy alien at the outbreak of World War I; while being held at the Ruhleben camp, he gained experience as a conductor; was awarded the B.A. degree in absentia by the Univ. of Toronto (1915); his ode, *England*, submitted through the Prisoners of War Education Committee to Oxford Univ., won him his D.Mus. degree (1918). After his release, he returned to Toronto as organist and choirmaster of Timothy Eaton Memorial Church (1919–25). He joined the staff of the Canadian Academy of Music (1920) and remained with it when it became the Toronto Cons. of Music, serving as its principal (1926–42); was also dean of the music faculty at the Univ. of Toronto (1927–52). He was conductor of the Toronto Sym. Orch. (1931–56) and of the Mendelssohn Choir there (1942–57); also appeared as guest conductor in North and South America, Europe, and Australia. He served as president of the Canadian Music Council (1947–66) and of the Canadian Music Centre (1959–70). In 1935 he was the 1st Canadian musician to be knighted, an honor conferred upon him by King George V; also received honorary doctorates from

Canadian and U.S. institutions. He conducted many works new to his homeland, both traditional and contemporary.

WORKS: *England*, ode after Swinburne, for Soprano, Baritone, Chorus, and Orch. (1914–18; Sheffield, England, March 17, 1921); *Overture* (1924); 2 *Sketches* on French-Canadian airs for String Orch. (1927); *Prince Charming*, ballad opera (1933); *A Song of Deliverance* for Chorus and Orch. (1944); *Fantasy on Scottish Melodies* for Orch. (1946); 6 *Bergerettes du Bas Canada* for Soprano, Alto, Tenor, Oboe, Viola, Cello, and Harp; 3 *Indian Songs of the West Coast* for Voice and Piano; many other songs and choruses; etc.

BIBL.: "Sir E. M., 1893–1973," *Canadian Composer*, 82 (1973).

Macmillen, Francis, American violinist; b. Marietta, Ohio, Oct. 14, 1885; d. Lausanne, July 14, 1973. A precocious child, he was sent to Germany at the age of 10 and was accepted by Joachim as a pupil; later studied with César Thomson at the Brussels Cons., winning 1st prize in 1901; continued his studies with Carl Flesch in Berlin and Leopold Auer in St. Petersburg. He made his professional debut as a concert violinist at the age of 17 in Brussels (March 30, 1903); appeared with the N.Y. Sym. Orch. (Dec. 7, 1906); then embarked on a concert tour of Europe; after the outbreak of World War I in 1914, he returned to the U.S. and taught violin in Ithaca, N.Y.; resumed his European tours in 1929; then lived in N.Y., Florence, Italy, and lastly, Switzerland.

MacNeil, Cornell, American baritone; b. Minneapolis, Sept. 24, 1922. He began to earn his living as a machinist, and simultaneously made appearances as a radio actor and operetta singer; then was a scholarship student of Friedrich Schorr at the Hartt College of Music in Hartford. He made his professional operatic debut as Sorel in the premiere of Menotti's *The Consul* in Philadelphia on March 1, 1950. He joined the N.Y. City Opera in 1953; also made guest appearances in San Francisco, Chicago, and Mexico City. On March 5, 1959, he sang the role of Charles V in *Ernani* at his La Scala debut in Milan. On March 21, 1959, he sang Rigoletto at his Metropolitan Opera debut in N.Y. and became a regular member of the company; also sang in Europe. He attracted unexpected notoriety when he walked off the stage during the 3rd act of Verdi's *Un ballo in maschera* on Dec. 27, 1964, in Parma, in protest against the offensive attitude of the audience, and engaged in a fistfight with the opera manager. Pacified, he resumed his career in America, but also became active in labor union affairs.

Maconchy, Dame Elizabeth, significant English composer of Irish parentage, mother of **Nicola LeFanu**; b. Broxbourne, Hertfordshire, March 19, 1907. She studied with Vaughan Williams and Charles Wood at the Royal College of Music in London (1923–29); then studied in Prague with Jirák, where she absorbed the styles and techniques of Expressionism; upon returning to England, she composed prolifically in all genres; developed a style peculiarly her own: tonally tense, contrapuntally dissonant, and coloristically sharp in instrumentation. In 1977 she was made a Commander of the Order of the British Empire. In 1987 she was made a Dame Commander of the Order of the British Empire.

WORKS: STAGE: 3 one-act operas: *The Sofa*, to a libretto by Ursula Vaughan Williams (London, Dec. 13, 1959); *The Departure* (London, Dec. 16, 1962); *The 3 Strangers*, after Thomas Hardy (London, June 5, 1968); *The Birds*, operatic extravaganza, after Aristophanes (London, June 5, 1968, on the same day with *The 3 Strangers*); church masque, *The Jesse Tree* (Dorchester Abbey, Oct. 7, 1970); *The King of the Golden River* (1975); ballets: *Great Agrippa* (1933); *The Little Red Shoes* (1935); *Puck Fair* (1940). **ORCH.:** *The Land*, symphonic suite (1929); Piano Concerto (1930); *Theme and Variations* for Strings (1942); Sym. (1945–48); Viola Concerto (1937); *Dialogue* for Piano and Orch. (1940); Concertino for Clarinet and Strings (ISCM Festival, Copenhagen, June 2, 1947); Sym. for Double String Orch. (1953); *Proud Thames*, overture (1953); *Serenata concertante* for Violin and Orch. (1962); *An Essex*

Overture (1966); 3 *Cloudscapes* for Orch. (1968); *Sinfonietta* (1975–76); *Epyllion* for Cello and 14 Strings (1975); *Romanza* for Viola and Chamber Orch. (London, March 12, 1979); Little Sym. (1980; Norwich, July 28, 1981); *Music for Strings* (London, July 26, 1983); Clarinet Concertino (Glasgow, Dec. 6, 1985). **CHAMBER:** 12 string quartets (1933, 1936, 1938, 1943, 1948, 1951, 1956, 1966, 1967, 1970, 1978, 1979); Quintet for Oboe and Strings (1932); *Prelude, Interlude and Fugue* for 2 Violins (ISCM Festival, Prague, Sept. 4, 1935); Viola Sonata (1938); Violin Sonata (1944); Concertino for Piano and Strings (1951); Concertino for Bassoon and Strings (1954); String Trio (1957); Double Concerto for Oboe, Clarinet, Viola, and Harp (1960); Clarinet Quintet (1963); *Music* for Double Bass and Piano (1970); 3 *Bagatelles* for Oboe and Harp (1972); *Contemplation* for Cello and Piano (1978); *Colloquy* for Flute and Piano (1979); *Fantasia* for Clarinet and Piano (1979); *Piccola musica* for String Trio (Cheltenham, July 13, 1981); *Trittico* for 2 Oboes, Bassoon, and Harpsichord (1981); Wind Quintet (1982); *Tribute* for Violin and 8 Wind Instruments (1983). **VOCAL:** *Samson at the Gates of Gaza* for Chorus and Orch. (1963); *The Starlight Night and Peace* for Soprano and Chamber Orch. (1964); *Witnesses* for 2 Sopranos, Flute, Oboe, Clarinet, Horn, Cello, Percussion, and Ukelele (1966); 3 *Donne Songs* for Tenor and Piano (1966); *The Leaden Echo and the Golden Echo* for Chorus, Flute, Viola, and Harp (1978); *Creatures* for Chorus (1979); 3 settings of poems by Gerard Manley Hopkins for Soprano and Orch. (1964–70); *Ariadne* for Soprano and Orch. (1970); *Heloise and Abelard*, cantata for Soloists, Chorus, and Orch. (1978); *My Dark Heart*, after Petrarch, for Soprano and Instrumental Ensemble (1982); *L'Horloge* for Soprano, Clarinet, and Piano (1983); also piano pieces.

BIBL.: F. Howes, "E. M.," *Monthly Musical Record* (July–Aug. 1938); E. Maconchy, "A Composer Speaks," *Composer* (1971–72).

Maconie, Robin (John), New Zealand composer and writer on music; b. Auckland, Oct. 22, 1942. He studied at Victoria Univ., Wellington (B.A., 1962; M.A., 1963), and later with Messiaen at the Paris Cons. (1963–64) and with Zimmermann and Eimert at the Cologne Hochschule für Musik (1964–65); attended Stockhausen's lectures at the Darmstadt summer courses. He returned to New Zealand as a composer for film and theater; also lectured at Auckland Univ. (1967–68). In 1969 he settled in England, where he engaged in music criticism and research in musical phenomenology. He publ. *The Works of Karlheinz Stockhausen* (London, 1975; 2nd ed., 1991) and ed. *Stockhausen on Music: Lectures and Interviews* (London, 1989).

WORKS: Sonata for Clarinet and Piano (1961); *Music for a Masque* for String Orch. (1962); *Basia Memoranda*, song cycle for Low Voice and String Quartet (1962); *Canzona* for Chamber Orch. (1962); *A:B:A:* for Harp (1964); *Ex evangelio Sancti Marci* for Chorus (1964); *A:D:C:* for Piano (1965); Sonata for String Quartet (1964); String Quartet (1970); *Māui*, television ballet for Speaker, Dancers, and Orch. (1967–72); *Limina*, modified sound track (1975).

Macque, Giovanni (Jean) de, eminent Flemish organist, teacher, and composer; b. Valenciennes, c.1548; d. Naples, Sept. 1614. He was a boy chorister at Vienna's imperial chapel, then studied at a Jesuit college before receiving instruction from Philippe de Monte. He was in Rome by 1574; was organist at S. Luigi dei Francesi (1580–81); was a member of the Compagnia dei Musici di Roma when it was sanctioned by the Pope (1584). He went to Naples about 1585 and became active in the affairs of the academy of Don Fabrizio Gesualdo da Venosa, father of the composer Carlo Gesualdo; became 2nd organist at the Santa Casa dell'Annunziata (1590); was made organist (1594) and then maestro di cappella (1595) of the Spanish viceregal chapel. He was a distinguished composer of both vocal and instrumental music. He was also highly esteemed as a teacher, his pupils including Mayone, Trabaci, Luigi Rossi, Falconieri, Francesco Lambardi, G.D. Montella, and Spano.

WORKS: VOCAL: *Primo libro de madrigali* for 6 Voices (Venice, 1576); *Madrigali* for 4 to 6 Voices (Venice, 1579); *Madrigaletti e napolitane* for 6 Voices (Venice, 1581); *Secondo libro de madrigaletti e napolitane* for 6 Voices (Venice, 1582); *Madrigali* for 5 Voices (Venice, 1583; not extant); *Primo libro de madrigali* for 4 Voices (Venice, 1587); *Secondo libro de madrigali* for 5 Voices (Venice, 1587); *Secondo libro de madrigali* for 6 Voices (Venice, 1589); *Motectorum* for 5 to 6 and 8 Voices, *liber primus* (Rome, 1596); *Terzo libro de madrigali* for 5 Voices (Ferrara, 1597); *Quarto libro de madrigali* for 5 Voices (Naples, 1599); *Terzo libro de madrigali* for 4 Voices (Naples, 1610); *Sesto libro de madrigali* for 5 Voices (Venice, 1613); various other pieces in contemporary collections. **INSTRUMENTAL:** *Ricercate e canzone francesi, a 4* (Rome, 1586); *Secondo libro de ricercari, a 4* (not extant); other pieces in MS collections.
BIBL.: L. Anderson, *G. d.M. of Valenciennes and the Evolution of Polyphonic Music in Naples at the End of the Sixteenth Century* (diss., Univ. of Liège, 1970); W. Shindle, *The Madrigals of G. d.M.* (diss., Indiana Univ., 1970); F. Lippmann, "G. d.M. tra Roma e Napoli: Nuovi documenti," *Rivista Musicale Italiana*, XIII (1978).

MacRae, Gordon, American singer of popular music and actor; b. East Orange, N.J., March 12, 1921; d. Lincoln, Nebr., Jan. 24, 1986. He learned to play piano and clarinet in his youth; when he was 19, made his way to N.Y., where he won an amateur singing contest at the World's Fair; after appearing with the bands of Harry James and Horace Heidt, he made his Broadway debut in a revue in 1946. He subsequently gained distinction as a star in films, including the musicals *The Desert Song* (1953), *Oklahoma!* (1955), and *Carousel* (1956). He then toured the U.S. in musicals; also performed as a vocalist in nightclubs and on television; his wife, **Sheila MacRae** (b. London, Sept. 24, 1924), appeared with him regularly until their divorce in 1967. He made a successful return to Broadway in 1967 when he starred in the musical *I Do! I Do!* A victim of alcoholism, he made frequent appearances on behalf of the National Council on Alcoholism in later years.

Macurdy, John, American bass; b. Detroit, March 18, 1929. He was educated at Wayne State Univ.; then began vocal studies with Avery Crew and studied dramatic interpretation with Boris Goldovsky; made his operatic debut in *Samson et Dalila* with the New Orleans Opera in 1952. He joined the N.Y. City Opera in 1959; on Dec. 8, 1962, made his Metropolitan Opera debut in N.Y. as Samuele in *Un ballo in maschera*; thereafter sang there regularly. In addition, he sang opera in Baltimore, Houston, San Francisco, Philadelphia, Glasgow, Milan, and Salzburg.

Maddy, Joe (Joseph Edgar), American educator and conductor; b. Wellington, Kans., Oct. 14, 1891; d. Traverse City, Mich., April 18, 1966. He studied at Bethany College, Wichita College, and the Columbia School of Music in Chicago; played the viola and clarinet; was a member of the Minneapolis Sym. Orch. (1909–14) and St. Paul Sym. Orch. (1914–18); was supervisor of instrumental music in the public schools of Rochester, N.Y. (1918–20), and Richmond, Ind. (1920–24), and instructor of public school methods at Earlham College (1922–24); in 1924, was appointed to the faculty of the Univ. of Michigan as a prof. of music education; in 1926 founded and conducted the National High School Orch., for which he established, with T.P. Giddings, the National Music Camp at Interlochen, Mich., in 1928.
BIBL.: N. Browning, *J. M. of Interlochen* (Chicago, 1963).

Madeira, Francis, American pianist, composer, and conductor; b. Jenkintown, Pa., Feb. 21, 1917. He studied piano and conducting at the Juilliard School of Music in N.Y. (1937–43). He was appointed to the faculty of Brown Univ. in 1943. In 1945 he organized the Rhode Island Phil. Orch. in Providence; resigned in 1980. He was also active as a concert pianist in the U.S. and in Europe; composed a number of symphonic and other works. He married **Jean** (née **Browning**) **Madeira** in 1957.

Madeira, Jean (née **Browning**), American mezzo-soprano; b. Centralia, Ill., Nov. 14, 1918; d. Providence, R.I., July 10, 1972. She studied piano with her mother, and was regarded as a child prodigy; at the age of 12, she was piano soloist with the St. Louis Sym. Orch.; took vocal lessons in St. Louis; then studied both piano and voice at the Juilliard School of Music in N.Y. Subsequently she became a member of the Chautauqua Opera Co. and the San Carlo Opera Co.; in 1948 joined the Metropolitan Opera in N.Y., where she sang minor roles. She went to Europe, where she 1st gained notice as Carmen in Vienna, Aix-en-Provence, and Munich in 1955; also sang Erda at her Covent Garden debut in London that same year. She then returned to the Metropolitan, where she appeared as Carmen on March 17, 1956; she remained on the Metropolitan's roster until 1971. Her European tours included appearances at the Vienna State Opera, the Bavarian State Opera in Munich, Milan's La Scala, the Paris Opéra, and Bayreuth. She married **Francis Madeira** in 1957.

Maderna, Bruno, outstanding Italian-born German conductor and composer; b. Venice, April 21, 1920; d. Darmstadt, Nov. 13, 1973. He commenced musical studies at 4, and soon took violin lessons; began touring as a violinist and conductor when he was only 7, appearing under the name Brunetto in Italy and abroad. He studied at the Verdi Cons. in Milan, with Bustini at the Rome Cons. (diploma in composition, 1940), and with Malipiero at the Venice Cons.; also took a conducting course with Guarnieri at the Accademia Chigiana in Siena (1941). He then served in the Italian army during World War II, eventually joining the partisan forces against the Fascists. After the war, he studied conducting with Scherchen in Darmstadt; taught composition at the Venice Cons. (1947–50); then made his formal conducting debut in Munich (1950). He subsequently became a great champion of the avant-garde; with Luciano Berio, he helped to form the Studio di Fonologia in Milan (1954); also with Berio, he was conductor of the RAI's Incontri Musicali (1956–60). He taught conducting and composition in various venues, including Darmstadt (from 1954), the Salzburg Mozarteum (1967–70), the Rotterdam Cons. (from 1967), and the Berkshire Music Center in Tanglewood (1971–72). He was chief conductor of the RAI in Milan from 1971. In 1963 he became a naturalized German citizen. Stricken with cancer, he continued to conduct concerts as long as it was physically possible. He was held in great esteem by composers of the international avant-garde, several of whom wrote special works for him.
WORKS: STAGE: *Don Perlimplin*, radio opera after Lorca (1961; RAI, Aug. 12, 1962); *Hyperion*, "lirica in forma di spettacolo" (Venice Festival, Sept. 6, 1964; a composite of *Dimensioni III*, *Aria de Hyperion*, and tape); *Von A bis Z*, opera (1969; Darmstadt, Feb. 22, 1970); *Oedipe-Roi*, electronic ballet (Monte Carlo, Dec. 31, 1970); *Satyrikon*, opera after Petronius (1972; Scheveningen, the Netherlands, March 16, 1973).
ORCH.: *Introduzione e Passacaglia* (1947); Concerto for 2 Pianos, Percussion, and 2 Harps (Venice, Sept. 17, 1948); *Composizioni No. 1* (1949); *Composizioni No. 2* for Chamber Orch. (1950); *Improvvisazione I* and *II* (1951, 1952); *Composizioni in 3 tempi* (Hamburg Radio, Dec. 8, 1954); Flute Concerto (1954); *Dark Rapture Crawl* (1957); Piano Concerto (Darmstadt, Sept. 2, 1959); 3 oboe concertos: No. 1, with 23 Instruments (1962; rev. 1965); No. 2 (Cologne Radio, Nov. 10, 1967); No. 3 (Amsterdam, July 6, 1973); *Dimensioni III* for Flute and Orch. (Paris Radio, Dec. 12, 1963); *Stele per Diotima* for Orch., with cadenzas for Violin, Clarinet, Bass Clarinet, and Horn (1965; Cologne Radio, Jan. 19, 1966); *Dimensioni IV* (combination of *Dimensioni III* and *Stele per Diotima*); *Amanda* for Chamber Orch. (Naples, Nov. 22, 1966); *Quadrivium* for 4 Percussionists and 4 Orch. Groups (1969); Violin Concerto (Venice, Sept. 12, 1969); *Grande aulodia* for Flute, Oboe, and Orch. (1969; Rome, Feb. 7, 1970); *Juilliard Serenade* (*Free Time I*) for Chamber Orch. and Tape Sounds (1970; N.Y., Jan. 31, 1971); *Music of Gaiety* for Solo Violin, Oboe, and Chamber Orch., based on pieces in the "Fitzwilliam Virginal

Book" (1970); *Aura* (1971; Chicago, March 23, 1972); *Biogramma* (1972); *Giardino religioso* for Chamber Ensemble (Tanglewood, Aug. 8, 1972).

VOCAL: *3 Greek Lyrics* for Soprano, Chorus, and Instruments (1948); *Studi per "Il Processo" di Kafka* for Narrator, Soprano, and Small Orch. (1949); *4 Briefe* for Soprano, Bass, and Chamber Orch. (1953); *Aria da "Hyperion"* for Soprano, Flute, and Orch. (1964); *Hyperion II* (combination of *Dimensioni III, Cadenza* for Flute, and *Aria da "Hyperion"*); *Hyperion III* (combination of *Hyperion* and *Stele per Diotima*); *Ausstrahlung* for Soprano, Chorus, and Orch. (1971); *Boswell's Journal* for Tenor and Chamber Orch. (N.Y., March 12, 1972).

CHAMBER: *Serenata* for 11 Instruments (1946; rev. 1954); *Musica su 2 dimensioni* for Flute and Tape (1952; rev. 1958); String Quartet (1955); *Serenata No. 2* for 11 Instruments (1957); *Serenata No. 4* for 20 Instruments and Tape (1961); *Honey rêves* for Flute and Piano (1961); *Aulodia per Lothar* for Oboe d'Amore and Guitar ad libitum (1965); *Widmung* for Violin (1967); *Serenata per un satellite* for 7 Instruments (1969).

ELECTRONIC: *Notturno* (1955); *Syntaxis* for 4 different but unspecified timbres produced electronically (1956); *Continuo* (1958); *Dimensioni II*, "invenzioni sue una voce" (1960); *Serenata No. 3* (1962); *Le Rire* (1964); *Ages* (with G. Pressburger, 1972).

PIANO: *B-A-C-H Variations* for 2 Pianos (1949).

BIBL.: K. Jansen, "B. M. and Dutch Concert Life," containing an intimate account of Maderna's private life, *Keynote* (1980); M. Baroni and R. Dalmonte, eds., *B. M.: Documenti* (Milan, 1985).

Madetoja, Leevi (Antti), outstanding Finnish composer; b. Oulu, Feb. 17, 1887; d. Helsinki, Oct. 6, 1947. He was educated at the Univ. of Helsinki (M.A., 1910) and studied composition with Sibelius at the Helsinki Music Inst. (diploma, 1910); then took courses with d'Indy in Paris (1910–11) and R. Fuchs in Vienna (1911–12) and in Berlin. After serving as deputy conductor of the Helsinki Phil. (1912–14) and as conductor of the Vyborg Music Soc. Orch. (1914–16), he taught at the Helsinki Music Inst. (1916–38); was also music critic of the *Helsingen Sanomat* (1916–32); became a lecturer in music at the Univ. of Helsinki (1928). In 1917 he founded the Finnish Musicians' Assoc., with which he remained involved until his death. He was awarded a state composer's pension in 1919. He was one of Finland's leading composers; his music for the stage and his symphonic works are particularly notable.

WORKS: OPERAS: *Pohjalaisia* (The Bothnians; 1923; Helsinki, Oct. 25, 1924); *Juha* (1934; Helsinki, Feb. 17, 1935). **ORCH.:** 3 syms.: No. 1 (Helsinki, Feb. 10, 1916); No. 2 (Helsinki, Dec. 17, 1918); No. 3 (Helsinki, April 8, 1926); *Symphonic Suite* (Helsinki, Sept. 26, 1910); *Concert Overture* (1911); *Tanssinäky* (Dance Vision; 1911–19); *Kullervo*, symphonic poem (Helsinki, Oct. 14, 1913); *Huvinäytelmäalkusoitto* (Comedy Overture; Helsinki, April 12, 1923); *Okon-Fuoko*, ballet-pantomime (Helsinki, Feb. 12, 1930); Trio for Violin, Cello, and Piano (1910); Sonatina for Violin and Piano (1913); *Lyric Suite* for Cello and Piano (1922); much choral music; many songs; piano pieces, including the suite *Kuoleman puutarha* (Garden of Death; 1919).

BIBL.: K. Tuukkahen, *L. M.* (Helsinki, 1947); *L. M.: Teokset—Works* (1982).

Madey, Boguslaw, Polish conductor and composer; b. Sosnowiec, May 31, 1932. He received diplomas in composition, piano, and conducting from the Academy of Music in Poznan; then went to England, where he took a course in conducting with Norman del Mar at the Guildhall School of Music in London (1959–60). Returning to Poland, he was a conductor at the Warsaw Opera (1960–72); later was music director at the Grand Theater of Opera and Ballet in Lodz (1972–77); in 1982 he became artistic director of the Baltic Phil. in Gdańsk. He composed a Piano Concerto (1957); Flute Concerto (1960); a concerto for Voice and Instruments entitled *Transfiguration* (1965); some short piano pieces.

Madge, Geoffrey Douglas, extraordinary Australian pianist; b. Adelaide, Oct. 3, 1941. He studied piano with Clemens Leski at the Elder Cons. of the Univ. of Adelaide, graduating in 1959; toured Australia in a piano trio (1959–63). In 1963 he went to Europe; studied piano with Géza Anda in Switzerland (1964) and with Peter Solymos in Hungary (1967). In 1971 he was appointed senior lecturer of classical and contemporary piano repertoire at the Royal Cons. of The Hague. As a pianist, he became known chiefly by his propaganda of ultramodern music; his repertoire includes works by Ives, Sorabji, Xenakis, Boulez, Cage, Stockhausen, Wolpe, Barraqué, and Bussotti; a specialty is rarely played music of the Russian modernists, Mossolov, Obouhov, Roslavetz, Lourié, Alexandrov, and Wyschnegradsky. On June 11, 1982, at Utrecht, during the Holland Festival, he gave the 2nd complete performance (after 50 years) of Kaikhosru Sorabji's mammoth *Opus clavicembalisticum;* he began it at 8:16 P.M. and finished at 12:47 the next morning. On April 24, 1983, he gave another performance of the work at the Univ. of Chicago; then repeated the feat at Bonn on May 10, 1983. On Sept. 19, 1979, as part of that year's ISCM Festival in Athens, he gave the 1st complete performance of Nikos Skalkottas's 2-hour set of *32 Piano Pieces*, as well as his *4 Études*. His technical powers as a pianist are astonishing, and possibly without equal; certainly no other pianist has assembled such a repertoire of formidable modern works. Madge is a self-taught composer; he wrote a Viola Sonata (1963); a String Quartet (1965); a Violin Sonatina (1966); *Monkeys in a Cage*, a ballet for 12 Instruments (1976; Sydney, 1977); *Tendrils of the Rock*, 3 movements for Piano (1979); and a Piano Concerto (1979; Amsterdam, 1980).

Madonna (born **Madonna Louise Veronica Ciccone**), fantastically popular and audacious American rock singer, improviser, and actress; b. Bay City, Mich., Aug. 16, 1958. She took up acting and dancing while attending junior high school in Pontiac, Mich.; after private dance lessons with Christopher Flynn (1972–76), she studied on a scholarship at the Univ. of Michigan (1976–78). Making her way to N.Y., she eked out a living by modeling and acting in an underground softcore film; aboveground, she worked with Alvin Ailey's dance group, and studied choreography with Pearl Lang; then studied drums and guitar with Dan Gilroy. After working with the disco star Patrick Hernandez in Paris, she returned to N.Y., appearing as a drummer and singer with Gilroy's Breakfast Club rock outfit. In 1982 she organized her own band, and in 1983 brought out her 1st album, *Madonna*; with her album *Like a Virgin* (1984), she captured the imagination of America's youth, which led to her 1st coast-to-coast tour. In 1985 Madonna pursued her thespian bent by appearing in the critically acclaimed film *Desperately Seeking Susan;* also acted in *Who's That Girl?* (1987). The popular movie *Dick Tracy* (1990) featured Madonna as a slinky, sequined, torch-singer gun moll. Her album *True Blue* (1986) proved a popular success. In 1987 she made a smashingly successful tour of Europe. In 1989, the year of her album *Like a Prayer*, she was listed among *People Magazine's* "20 Who Defined the Decade"; she also was awarded *Musician Magazine's* highest editorial distinction, "Artist of the Decade." Her athletic "Blond Ambition" tour of 1990 was criticized for its use of more than 50% canned music. That same year she brought out the sizzling video *Justify My Love*.

BIBL.: M. McKenzie, *M.: Lucky Star* (Chicago, 1985); *Current Biography* (May 1986).

Madriguera, Enric, Catalan-American composer; b. Barcelona, Feb. 17, 1904; d. Danbury, Conn., Sept. 7, 1973. He studied violin at the Barcelona Liceo Musical; in 1916 emigrated to the U.S., where he took a master course with Leopold Auer. He then devoted himself to the composition of tunes in the Latin American vein; of these the most popular were *Take It Away* and *Adios*. He organized a Latin American orch., and was named "Music Ambassador of the Americas" by the U.S. Congress.

Maegaard, Jan (Carl Christian), Danish musicologist and composer; b. Copenhagen, April 14, 1926. He studied music theory with Poul Schierbeck and B. Hjelbmorg, and counterpoint with Knud Jeppesen and orchestration with J. Jersild at the Royal Danish Cons. of Music in Copenhagen (teacher's diploma, 1953), and at the Univ. of Copenhagen, where he took a course in musicology with Jens Peter Larsen (M.A., 1957). He then went to the U.S., where he studied musicography with Robert Nelson at the Univ. of Calif., Los Angeles (1958–59). Returning to Denmark, he taught at Copenhagen's Royal Cons.; also taught at the Univ. of Copenhagen (from 1959), where he became a prof. of music (1971) and obtained his Ph.D. (1972) with the dissertation *Studien zur Entwicklung des dodekaphonen Satzes bei Arnold Schoenberg* (publ. in Copenhagen, 1972); likewise was a visiting prof. at the State Univ. of N.Y. at Stony Brook (1974) and a prof. of music at the Univ. of Calif. at Los Angeles (1978–81). He publ. *Musikalsk modernisme 1945–62* (Copenhagen, 1964; 2nd ed., 1971), *Praeludier til musik af Schönberg* (Copenhagen, 1976), and *Indføring i romantisk harmonik* (2 vols., Copenhagen, 1981, 1986; Vol. I with T. Larsen).
WORKS: ORCH.: *Chamber Concerto No. 1* (1949); *Chamber Concerto No. 2* (1961–62); *Gaa udenom sletterne* (Avoid the Plains) for Chorus and Orch. (1953; Copenhagen, March 21, 1957); *Due tempi* (Copenhagen, Aug. 31, 1961); music for a television production of *Antigone* for Chorus, Orch., and Tape (1966); March for Military Band (1980); *Triptykon* for Violin and String Orch. (1984); Sinfonietta for String Orch. (1985). **CHAMBER:** *Suite* for Violin and Piano (1949); Trio for Oboe, Clarinet, and Bassoon (1950); Wind Quintet (1951); *Suite* for 2 Violins (1951); *Den gyldne harpe* (The Golden Harp) for Mezzo-soprano, Oboe, Cello, and Piano (1951); *Quasi una sonata* for Viola and Piano (1952); Bassoon Sonata (1952); *Variations impromptus* for Violin, Viola, Cello, and Piano (1953); *Jaevndøgnselegi* (Equinox Elegy) for Soprano, Cello, and Organ (1955); *Alter Duft aus Märchenzeit* for Piano Trio (1960); *Movimento* for Clarinet, Horn, Hammond Organ, String Quartet, and Percussion (1967); *Musica riservata No. 1* for String Quartet (1970); *Musica riservata No. 2* for Oboe, Clarinet, Saxophone, and Bassoon (1976); *Pastorale* for 2 Clarinets (1976); Canon for 3 Flutes (1981); *Musica riservata No. 3* for Flute, Oboe, Cello, and Harpsichord (1982); *Labirinto* for Viola (1986); also a Piano Sonata (1955); choruses; songs; organ pieces; cadenzas; transcriptions of Bach, Mozart, and Schoenberg.

Maelzel, Johannes Nepomuk, German inventor; b. Regensburg, Aug. 15, 1772; d. on board the brig *Otis* in the harbor of La Guiara, Venezuela, en route to Philadelphia, July 21, 1838. He studied music with his father, an organ manufacturer. In 1792 he went to Vienna, where he began constructing mechanical instruments, which attracted great attention there and subsequently in other European cities; of these, the Panharmonicon, exhibited in Vienna in 1804, was particularly effective. He then purchased the "automatic chess player," which he claimed was his invention; in fact it was designed and built by Wolfgang von Kempelen. He was able to impress the public by his "scientific" miracle, but it was soon exposed by skeptical observers, among them Edgar Allan Poe, as an ingenious mechanical contrivance concealing a diminutive chess master behind its gears. He subsequently invented the automatic trumpeter, displaying it and a new version of the Panharmonicon in his Kunstabinet in 1812. In 1816 he constructed the metronome, the idea for which he obtained from Winkel of Amsterdam, who had exhibited similar instruments, but without the scale divisions indicating the number of beats per minute. Maelzel put the metronome on the market, despite a lawsuit brought by Winkel, and the initial of his last name was thenceforth added to the indication of tempo in musical compositions (M.M., Maelzel's metronome). Beethoven wrote a piece for the Panharmonicon, which he subsequently orchestrated and publ. as *Wellington's Victory*. After Maelzel declared that the composition was his property, Beethoven sued him in the Viennese courts, but nothing ever came from his legal action.
BIBL.: P. Stadlen, "Beethoven and the Metronome," *Music & Letters*, XLVIII (1967); C. Carroll, *The Great Chess Automaton* (N.Y., 1975).

Maes, Jef, Belgian composer; b. Antwerp, April 5, 1905. He studied with N. Distelmans (viola), L. Mortelmans (chamber music), and Karl Candael (harmony, counterpoint, and fugue) at Antwerp's Royal Flemish Cons.; was a violist in several orchs. in Antwerp; became a teacher of viola (1932) and director (1952) of the Boom Academy of Music; from 1942 to 1970 he was on the faculty of the Royal Flemish Cons. In his compositions, he continues the traditions of the Belgian national school.
WORKS: DRAMATIC: Opera buffa, *Marise* (1946); television opera, *De antikwaar* (The Antique Dealer; 1959; Antwerp Television, March 1963); ballet, *Tu auras nom . . . Tristan* (1960; Geneva, June 1963; orch. suite, 1963–64). **ORCH.:** *3 rythmen in dansvorm* (1931); *Légende* for Violin and Orch. (1933); Viola Concerto (1937); *Concertstück* (1938); *Ouvertura buffa* (1939); *Concertstück* for Trombone and Orch. (1944); Piano Concerto (1948); Violin Concerto (1951); 3 syms. (1953, 1965, 1975); Concerto for Harpsichord and String Orch. (1955); *Burlesque* for Bassoon and Orch. (1957); *Rosa mystica* for Soprano and Orch. or Piano (1959); *Kempische Suite* for Orch. or Wind Orch. (1960); *Concertante ouverture* (1961); *Arabesque en scherzo* for Flute and Orch. (1963); *Praeludium, Pantomime, Scherzo,* suite (1966); *Partita* for String Orch. (1966); *Ouverture op een Belcanto Thema van Verdi* for Orch. or Wind Orch. (1967); *De verloofden* (1969); *Mei 1871* for Narrator and Orch. (1971); *Music pour le podium* for Wind Orch. (1971); *Dialogue* for Violin and Orch. (1972); *Intrada* (1980). **CHAMBER:** Sonatina for Flute and Viola (1934); Violin Sonata (1934); *Concertstück* for Trumpet and Piano (1957); *Prelude and Allegro* for 2 Trumpets, Horn, Trombone, and Tuba (1959); *Fantasia* for 2 Pianos (1960); Duo for Violin and Piano (1962); Trio for Violin, Viola, and Percussion (1964); *4 contrastes* for 4 Clarinets (1965); *Suite* for Percussion and Piano (1968); Piano Quartet (1970); *Studie* for Violin (1978); *Saxo-scope* for Saxophone Quartet (1979); *Adagio en allegretto* for Violin and Piano (1985); also choruses and songs.

Magalhaes, Filipe, important Portuguese composer; b. Azeitão, near Évora, c.1571; d. Lisbon, Dec. 17, 1652. He studied with Manuel Mendes at the Évora Cathedral cloister school, where he became a singer; then joined Lisbon's royal chapel choir (1602), serving as its master from 1623 until 1641. He was one of the foremost masters of Portuguese music of his era.
WORKS: *Cantus ecclesiasticus commendandi animas corporaque* for 3 to 5 Voices (Lisbon, 1614; 3rd ed., 1691, as *Cantum ecclesiasticum*); *Missarum liber cum antiphonis domincalibus in principio, et motetto pro defunctis* for 4 to 6 Voices (Lisbon, 1636); *Cantica beatissimae virginis* (Lisbon, 1636); *Domine, probasti me* for Voices (n.d.).
BIBL.: M. De Sampayo Ribeiro, "A data da morte do Padremestre F.d. M.," *Olisipo*, XXIV/93 (1961).

Magaloff, Nikita, Russian-born Swiss pianist; b. St. Petersburg, Feb. 21, 1912. His family left Russia after the Revolution; he enrolled in the Paris Cons. as a student of Isidor Philipp; graduated with a premier prix at the age of 17; also studied composition with Prokofiev in Paris. In 1939 he settled in Switzerland; in 1947 he made his 1st American tour; also toured Europe, South America, South Africa, etc. From 1949 to 1960 he taught piano at the Geneva Cons.; then gave summer courses at Taormina, Sicily, and at the Accademia Musicale Chigiana in Siena. In 1956 he became a Swiss citizen. He is renowned for his lyrico-dramatic interpretations of Chopin, with lapidary attention to detail. He was also a composer; wrote a Piano Toccata; Sonatina for Violin and Piano; songs; cadenzas for Mozart's piano concertos. He was the son-in-law of **Joseph Szigeti.**

Maganini, Quinto, American flutist, conductor, arranger, and composer; b. Fairfield, Calif., Nov. 30, 1897; d. Greenwich, Conn., March 10, 1974. He played flute in the San Francisco Sym. (1917–19) and in the N.Y. Sym. (1919–28); studied flute with Barrère in N.Y. and composition with Boulanger at the American Cons. in Fontainebleau; in 1927, won a Pulitzer scholarship; in 1928–29, was awarded a Guggenheim fellowship; in 1930, became conductor of the N.Y. Sinfonietta; in 1932 he organized his own orch., the Maganini Chamber Sym., with which he toured widely. From 1939 to 1970 he was conductor of the Norwalk (Conn.) Sym. Orch.

WORKS: *Toulumne,* "a Californian Rhapsody," for Orch., with Trumpet obbligato (N.Y., Aug. 9, 1924); *South Wind,* orch. fantasy (N.Y., April 7, 1931); *Sylvan Symphony* (N.Y., Nov. 30, 1932); *Napoleon,* an orch. portrait (N.Y., Nov. 10, 1935); *The Royal Ladies,* orch. suite on airs ascribed to Marie Antoinette (Greenwich, Conn., Feb. 3, 1940); opera, *Tennessee's Partner* (WOR Radio, N.Y., May 28, 1942); numerous arrangements for small orch. of classical and modern works.

Mager, Jörg, German music theorist and pioneer in electronic music; b. Eichstätt, Nov. 6, 1880; d. Aschaffenburg, April 5, 1939. After completing his univ. studies, he became interested in electronic reproduction of sounds; constructed several instruments capable of producing microtonal intervals by electronic means, which he named Sphärophon, Elektrophon, and Partiturophon; he was also active in visual music for film. He publ. *Vierteltonmusik* (Aschaffenburg, 1916) and *Eine neue Epoche der Musik durch Radio* (Berlin, 1924).

Maggini, Gio(vanni) Paolo, important Italian instrument maker; b. Brescia (baptized), Nov. 29, 1579; d. there, c.1630. He worked in the shop of Gasparo da Salò; after his marriage in 1615, he set up his own workshop and became prosperous, thanks to the excellence of his manufacture. His instruments are highly prized; among his extant instruments are violins, violas, cellos, basses, various examples of the viol family, and citterns. His label reads: Gio. Paolo Maggini, Brescia.

BIBL.: M. Huggins, *Gio P. M., His Life and Work* (London, 1892); A. Berenzi, *Di Gio P. M.* (Cremona, 1907).

Maggioni, Aurelio Antonio, Italian composer; b. Milan, April 8, 1908. He studied at the Milan Cons.; graduated as a pianist (1926) and composer (1933). He subsequently taught music theory in Parma (1938); Florence (1939–51); Milan (1952–54); Lima, Peru (1954–59); and again in Milan (from 1959). He wrote the opera *Il gioco di Soleima* (Bergamo, 1955); during his stay in Peru he composed a *Suite incaici* for Orch., making use of indigenous themes; he also wrote chamber music and minor pieces, all set in a competent Italianate style.

Magnard, (Lucien-Denis-Gabriel-) Albéric, distinguished French composer; b. Paris, June 9, 1865; d. (killed by German soldiers at his home) Baron, Oise, Sept. 3, 1914. He was reared in an intellectual family of means; his father was ed. of *Le Figaro.* He studied with Dubois and Massenet at the Paris Cons. (1886–88; premier prix in harmony, 1888) and with d'Indy (1888–92); subsequently taught counterpoint at the Schola Cantorum. He was killed while defending his property during the early days of World War I. He was a composer of high attainments; his mastery of orchestration is incontestable, and the rhapsodic sweep of his 3rd and 4th syms. is impressive. Despite these qualities, none of his music found a permanent place in the repertoire.

WORKS: OPERAS: *Yolande* (1888–91; Brussels, Dec. 27, 1892); *Guercoeur* (1897–1900; rev. by Guy-Ropartz; Paris, April 24, 1931); *Bérénice* (1905–9; Paris, Dec. 15, 1911). **ORCH.:** 4 syms.: No. 1 (1889–90; Paris, April 18, 1891); No. 2 (1892–93; rev. 1896; Nancy, Feb. 9, 1896); No. 3 (1895–96; Paris, May 18, 1899); No. 4 (1911–13; Paris, May 16, 1914); *Suite d'orchestre dans le style ancien* (1888; rev. 1889); *Chant funèbre* (1895); *Ouverture* (1894–95); *Hymne à la justice* (1902); *Hymne à Vénus* (1903–4). **CHAMBER:** Piano Quintet (1894); Violin Sonata (1901); String Quartet (1902–3); Piano Trio (1904–5); Cello Sonata (1909–10). **PIANO:** 3 Pieces (1887–88);

Promenades (1893); *Pièces, En Dieu mon Espérance et mon Espée pour ma Défense* (1889). **VOCAL:** 6 Poems (1887–90); *À Henriette* (1890 or 1891); 4 Poems (1902); 12 Poems (1913–14; lost in fire at his death).

BIBL.: M. Boucher, *A. M.* (Lyons, 1919); G. Carrauld, *La Vie, l'œuvre et la mort d'A. M.* (Paris, 1921); F. Schmitt, "Les Symphonies de M.," *Le Temps* (Nov. 16, 1929); B. Bardet, *A. M., 1865–1914* (Paris, 1966).

Magne, Michel, French composer; b. Lisieux, March 20, 1930; d. (suicide) Cergy-Pontase, Val d'Oise, Dec. 19, 1984. He was mainly self-taught, beginning to compose as a very young man in an ultramodern style; later took lessons with S. Plé-Caussade. His film score *Le Pain vivant* (1955) received critical acclaim; he also experimented with electronic music; on May 26, 1955, he conducted in Paris his *Symphonie humaine* for 150 Performers, making use of inaudible "infrasounds" to produce a physiological reaction by powerful low frequencies. He wrote the musical score for Françoise Sagan's ballet *Le Rendez-vous manqué* (1957).

Magomayev, (Abdul) Muslim, Azerbaijani conductor and composer; b. Shusha, Sept. 18, 1885; d. Baku, July 28, 1937. He studied at the Gori teachers' seminary (1899–1904); learned to play violin and clarinet, and taught at Lenkoran College (1905–11). He then settled in Baku as an orch. player, conductor, and teacher at the Azerbaijani Theater; later was associated with the National Commissariat of Enlightenment, becoming artistic director and conductor of the musical theater (1924); was music director of the Azerbaijani Radio (from 1929). The 1st version of his opera *Shah Ismail* (1916; Baku, 1919) was mainly made up of improvised songs and dialogue; he later revised it with notated improvisatory sections and added recitatives (1920–23; 1930–32). His 2nd opera, *Nergiz* (1934; Baku, Jan. 1, 1936), was fully notated. He also wrote orch. pieces, incidental music, film scores, and numerous arrangements of folk songs and dances.

BIBL.: G. Ismailova, *M. M.* (Baku, 1975).

Mahillon, Charles (-Borromée), Belgian manufacturer of wind instruments; b. Brussels, Nov. 4, 1814; d. Molenbeek-St.-Jean, Sept. 4, 1887. He received his training as an instrument maker in England; then organized his own firm in Brussels (1836), where he became esteemed as a manufacturer of clarinets. His son **Victor-Charles Mahillon** (b. Brussels, March 10, 1841; d. St. Jean, Cap Ferrat, June 17, 1924) worked in his father's shop as a youth; pursued a diligent study of acoustics; publ. the periodical *L'Echo Musical* (1869–87). Upon his father's death, he took charge of the firm; also served as curator of the Brussels Cons. Instrument Museum (from 1876), enlarging its collection from his own holdings. He publ. *Les Éléments d'acoustique musicale et instrumentale* (Brussels, 1874); *Catalogue descriptif et analytique du Musée instrumental du Conservatoire royal de musique de Bruxelles* (Ghent, 1880–1922); *Le Matériel sonore des orchestres de symphonie, d'harmonie et de fanfares, ou Vade mecum du compositeur* (Brussels, 1897; 5th ed., 1920); *Instruments à vent* (Brussels, 1906–7); *Notes théoriques et pratiques sur la résonance des colonnes d'air dans les tuyaux de la facture instrumentale* (St. Jean, Cap Ferrat, 1921); etc. His brother, **Fernand Mahillon** (b. Brussels, March 3, 1866; d. there, March 6, 1948), ran the London branch of the firm for some 30 years; upon Victor-Charles's death, he took control of the firm, turning it over to J.A. Smits in 1936; it ceased making wind instruments in 1935.

Mahler, Fritz, Austrian-born American conductor and composer, 2nd cousin of **Gustav Mahler;** b. Vienna, July 16, 1901; d. Winston-Salem, N.C., June 18, 1973. He studied composition in Vienna with Schoenberg, Webern, and Berg; musicology with Guido Adler at the Univ. of Vienna (1920–24); conducting with Leopold Reichwein. He conducted summer orchs. in Bad Hall (1924–26) and light opera at the Volksoper in Vienna; from 1931 to 1935, was a conductor of the radio orch. in Copenhagen; in 1936, emigrated to America, becoming a naturalized citizen in 1939; taught at the Juilliard Summer School (1938–53); was conductor of the Erie (Pa.) Phil. (1947–53); from 1953 to 1964, conductor of the Hartford (Conn.) Sym. Orch. He wrote a symphonic poem, some chamber music, and songs.

Mahler, Gustav, great Austrian composer and conductor; b. Kalischt, Bohemia, July 7, 1860; d. Vienna, May 18, 1911. He attended school in Iglau; in 1875 entered the Vienna Cons., where he studied piano with Julius Epstein, harmony with Robert Fuchs, and composition with Franz Krenn. He also took academic courses in history and philosophy at the Univ. of Vienna (1877–80). In the summer of 1880 he received his 1st engagement as a conductor, at the operetta theater in the town of Hall in Upper Austria; subsequently he held posts as theater conductor at Ljubljana (1881), Olmütz (1882), Vienna (1883), and Kassel (1883–85). In 1885 he served as 2nd Kapellmeister to Anton Seidl at the Prague Opera, where he gave several performances of Wagner's operas. From 1886 to 1888 he was assistant to Arthur Nikisch in Leipzig; in 1888 he received the important appointment of music director of the Royal Opera in Budapest. In 1891 he was engaged as conductor at the Hamburg Opera; during his tenure there, he developed a consummate technique for conducting. In 1897 he received a tentative offer as music director of the Vienna Court Opera, but there was an obstacle to overcome. Mahler was Jewish, and although there was no overt anti-Semitism in the Austrian government, an imperial appointment could not be given to a Jew. Mahler was never orthodox in his religion, and had no difficulty in converting to Catholicism, which was the prevailing faith in Austria. He held this position at the Vienna Court Opera for 10 years; under his guidance, it reached the highest standards of artistic excellence. In 1898 Mahler was engaged to succeed Hans Richter as conductor of the Vienna Phil. Here, as in his direction of opera, he proved a great interpreter, but he also allowed himself considerable freedom in rearranging the orchestration of classical scores when he felt it would redound to greater effect. He also aroused antagonism among the players by his autocratic behavior toward them. He resigned from the Vienna Phil. in 1901; in 1907 he also resigned from the Vienna Court Opera. In the meantime, he became immersed in strenuous work as a composer; he confined himself exclusively to composition of symphonic music, sometimes with vocal parts; because of his busy schedule as conductor, he could compose only in the summer months, in a villa on the Wörthersee in Carinthia. In 1902 he married Alma Schindler; they had 2 daughters. The younger daughter, Anna Mahler, was briefly married to Ernst Krenek; the elder daughter died in infancy. Alma Mahler studied music with Zemlinsky, who was the brother-in-law of Arnold Schoenberg.

Having exhausted his opportunities in Vienna, Mahler accepted the post of principal conductor of the Metropolitan Opera in N.Y. in 1907. He made his American debut there on Jan. 1, 1908, conducting *Tristan und Isolde.* In 1909 he was appointed conductor of the N.Y. Phil. His performances both at the Metropolitan and with the N.Y. Phil. were enormously successful with the audiences and the N.Y. music critics, but inevitably he had conflicts with the board of trustees in both organizations, which were mostly commanded by rich women. He resigned from the Metropolitan Opera; on Feb. 21, 1911, he conducted his last concert with the N.Y. Phil. and then returned to Vienna; he died there of pneumonia on May 18, 1911, at the age of 50. The N.Y. newspapers publ. lurid accounts of his struggle for artistic command with the regimen of the women of the governing committee. Alma Mahler was quoted as saying that although in Vienna even the Emperor did not dare to order Mahler about, in N.Y. he had to submit to the whims of 10 ignorant women. The newspaper editorials mourned Mahler's death, but sadly noted that his N.Y. tenure was a failure. As to Mahler's own compositions, the *N.Y. Tribune* said bluntly, "We cannot see how any of his music can long survive him." His syms. were sharply condemned in the press as being too long, too loud, and too discordant. It was

not until the 2nd half of the 20th century that Mahler became fully recognized as a composer, the last great Romantic symphonist. Mahler's syms. were drawn on the grandest scale, and the technical means employed for the realization of his ideas were correspondingly elaborate. The sources of his inspiration were twofold: the lofty concepts of universal art, akin to those of Bruckner, and ultimately stemming from Wagner; and the simple folk melos of the Austrian countryside, in pastoral moods recalling the intimate episodes in Beethoven's syms. True to his Romantic nature, Mahler attached descriptive titles to his syms.; the 1st was named the *Titan;* the 2nd, *Resurrection;* the 3rd, *Ein Sommermorgentraum;* and the 5th, *The Giant.* The great 8th became known as "sym. of a thousand" because it required about 1,000 instrumentalists, vocalists, and soloists for performance; however, this sobriquet was the inspiration of Mahler's agent, not of Mahler himself. Later in life Mahler tried to disassociate his works from their programmatic titles; he even claimed that he never used them in the 1st place, contradicting the evidence of the MSS, in which the titles appear in Mahler's own handwriting. Mahler was not an innovator in his harmonic writing; rather, he brought the Romantic era to a culmination by virtue of the expansiveness of his emotional expression and the grandiose design of his musical structures. Morbid by nature, he brooded upon the inevitability of death; one of his most poignant compositions was the cycle for voice and orch. *Kindertotenlieder;* he wrote it shortly before the death of his little daughter, and somehow he blamed himself for this seeming anticipation of his personal tragedy. In 1910 he consulted Sigmund Freud in Leiden, Holland, but the treatment was brief and apparently did not help Mahler to resolve his psychological problems. Unquestionably, he suffered from an irrational feeling of guilt. In the 3rd movement of his unfinished 10th Sym., significantly titled *Purgatorio,* he wrote on the margin, "Madness seizes me, annihilates me," and appealed to the Devil to take possession of his soul. But he never was clinically insane. He died of a heart attack brought on by a bacterial infection.

Mahler's importance to the evolution of modern music is very great; the early works of Schoenberg and Berg show the influence of Mahler's concepts. A society was formed in the U.S. in 1941 "to develop in the public an appreciation of the music of Bruckner, Mahler and other moderns." An International Gustav Mahler Soc. was formed in Vienna in 1955, with Bruno Walter as honorary president. On Mahler's centennial, July 7, 1960, the government of Austria issued a memorial postage stamp of 1½ shillings, with Mahler's portrait.

WORKS: SYMS.: No. 1, in D, *Titan* (1883–88; Budapest, Nov. 20, 1889, composer conducting; U.S. premiere, N.Y., Dec. 16, 1909, composer conducting; a rejected movement, entitled *Blumine,* was reincorporated and perf. at the Aldeburgh Festival, June 18, 1967); No. 2, in C minor, *Resurrection,* with Soprano, Contralto, and Chorus (1887–94; Berlin, Dec. 13, 1895, composer conducting; U.S. premiere, N.Y., Dec. 8, 1908, composer conducting); No. 3, in D minor, *Ein Sommermorgentraum* (1893–96; Krefeld, June 9, 1902, composer conducting; U.S. premiere, N.Y., Feb. 8, 1922, Mengelberg conducting); No. 4, in G (1899–1901; Munich, Nov. 25, 1901, composer conducting; U.S. premiere, N.Y., Nov. 6, 1904); No. 5, in C-sharp minor, *The Giant* (1901–2; Cologne, Oct. 18, 1904, composer conducting; U.S. premiere, Cincinnati, March 24, 1905); No. 6, in A minor (1903–5; Essen, May 27, 1906, composer conducting; U.S. premiere, N.Y., Dec. 11, 1946, Mitropoulos conducting); No. 7, in E minor (1904–6; Prague, Sept. 19, 1908, composer conducting; U.S. premiere, Chicago, April 15, 1921); No. 8, in E-flat, "Symphony of a Thousand," with 8 Solo Voices, Adult and Children's Choruses (1906–7; Munich, Sept. 12, 1910, composer conducting; U.S. premiere, Philadelphia, March 2, 1916, Stokowski conducting); No. 9, in D (1909–10; Vienna, June 26, 1912, Bruno Walter conducting; U.S. premiere, Boston, Oct. 16, 1931, Koussevitzky conducting); No. 10, in F-sharp minor (sketched 1909–10, unfinished; 2 movements, *Adagio* and *Purgatorio,* perf. in Vienna, Oct. 12, 1924, Franz Schalk conducting; publ. in facsimile, 1924, by

Alma Mahler; a performing version of the 10th Sym., using the sketches then available and leaving the 2 scherzo movements in fragmentary form, was made by Deryck Cooke; it was broadcast by the BBC, London, Dec. 19, 1960; Alma Mahler approved of Cooke's realization; further sketches were made available, and a full performing version was premiered in London, Aug. 13, 1964; a final revision of the score was made in 1972).

VOCAL: *Das klagende Lied* for Soprano, Contralto, Tenor, Chorus, and Orch. (1878–80; rev. 1896–98; Vienna, Feb. 17, 1901, composer conducting); *Lieder und Gesänge aus der Jugendzeit*, 14 songs for Voice and Piano (1880–91); *Lieder eines fahrenden Gesellen*, 4 songs with Orch. (1883–85; Berlin, March 16, 1896, composer conducting); 14 Lieder from *Das Knaben Wunderhorn* for Voice and Orch. (1892–1901); 5 songs, to poems by Rückert (1901–3); *Kindertotenlieder*, 5 songs, with Piano or Orch., to poems by Rückert (1901–4; Vienna, Jan. 29, 1905, composer conducting); *Das Lied von der Erde*, sym. for Contralto or Baritone, Tenor, and Orch. (1907–9; Munich, Nov. 20, 1911, Bruno Walter conducting).

Mahler destroyed the MSS of several of his early works, among them a piano quintet (perf. in Vienna, July 11, 1878, with the composer at the piano) and 3 unfinished operas: *Herzog Ernst von Schwaben*, to a drama by Uhland; *Die Argonauten*, from a trilogy by Grillparzer; and *Rübezahl*, after Grimm's fairy tales. He also made an arrangement of Weber's *Die drei Pintos* (Leipzig, Jan. 20, 1888, composer conducting) and *Oberon* (c.1907); also arranged Bruckner's 3rd Sym. for 2 Pianos (1878). Mahler made controversial reorchestrations of syms. by Beethoven, Schumann, and Bruckner, and a version for String Orch. of Beethoven's String Quartet in C-sharp minor, op. 131.

BIBL.: L. Schiedermair, *G. M.* (Leipzig, 1901); P. Stefan, *G. M.: Eine Studie über Persönlichkeit und Werk* (Munich, 1910; 4th ed., 1921; Eng. tr., N.Y., 1913); R. Specht, *G. M.* (Berlin, 1913); G. Adler, *G. M.* (Vienna, 1916); A. Neisser, "G. M.," *Reclams Universal-Bibliothek* (Berlin, 1918); H. Redlich, *G. M.: Eine Erkenntnis* (Nuremberg, 1919); P. Bekker, *M.s Sinfonien* (Berlin, 1921); A. Roller, *Die Bildnisse G. M.s* (Leipzig, 1922); N. Bauer-Lechner, *Erinnerungen an G. M.* (Vienna, 1923); A. Mahler, *Briefe G. M.s* (Berlin, 1924); W. Hutschenruyter, *G. M.* (The Hague, 1927); H. Holländer, "G. M.," *Musical Quarterly* (Oct. 1931); G. Engel, *G. M.* (Vienna, 1936; Eng. tr., N.Y., 1957); A. Mahler, *G. M.: Erinnerungen und Briefe* (Amsterdam, 1940; Eng. tr., *Memories and Letters*, London, 1946); E. Wellesz, "The Symphonies of G. M.," *Music Review* (Jan.–April 1940); B. Walter (with E. Krenek), *G. M.* (N.Y., 1941); D. Newlin, *Bruckner-M.-Schoenberg* (N.Y., 1947; 2nd ed., rev., 1978); N. Loeser, *G. M.* (Haarlem, 1950); H. Tischler, "M.'s Impact on the Crisis of Tonality," *Music Review* (April 1951); T. Reik, *The Haunting Melody* (N.Y., 1953); E. Stein, *Orpheus in New Guises* (London, 1953); D. Mitchell, "Some Notes on M.'s Tenth Symphony," *Musical Times* (Dec. 1955); H. Redlich, *Bruckner and M.* (London, 1955; 2nd ed., rev., 1963); D. Mitchell, *G. M.: I: The Early Years* (London, 1958; rev. 1980), *G. M.: II: The Wunderhorn Years* (Boulder, Colo., 1976), and *G. M.: III: Songs and Symphonies of Life and Death* (London, 1985); W. Reich, ed., *G. M.: Im eigenen Wort, im Wort der Freunde* (Zürich, 1958); T. Adorno, *M.: Eine musikalische Physiognomik* (Frankfurt, 1960); S. Vestdijk, *G. M.* (The Hague, 1960); N. Cardus, *G. M.: His Mind and His Music, vol. I* (London, 1965); H. Kralik, *G. M.* (Vienna, 1968); K. Blaukopf, *G. M., oder Zeitgenosse der Zukunft* (Vienna, 1969); J. Diether, "Notes on Some M. Juvenilia," *Chord and Discord*, III/1 (1969); H.-L. de La Grange, *G. M.: Chronique d'une vie* (3 vols., Paris, 1973–84; also in Eng.); D. Holbrook, *G. M. and the Courage to Be* (London, 1975); K. Blaukopf, ed., *M.: A Documentary Study* (N.Y., 1976); A. Shelley, ed., *G. M. in Vienna* (N.Y., 1976); C. Floros, *G. M.* (3 vols., Wiesbaden, 1977–85); P. Ruzicka, *M.: Eine Herausforderung* (Wiesbaden, 1977); E. Gartenberg, *M.: The Man and His Music* (N.Y., 1978); E. Reilly, *G. M. und Guido Adler: Zur Geschichte einer Freundschaft* (Vienna, 1978; Eng. tr.,

Cambridge, 1982); B. and E. Vondenhoff, *G. M. Dokumentation* (Tutzing, 1978); D. Cooke, *G. M.: An Introduction to His Music* (London, 1980); H. Eggebrecht, *Die Musik G. M.s* (Munich, 1982); E. Seckerson, *M.: His Life and Times* (N.Y., 1982); H. Blaukopf, ed., and E. Jephcott, tr., *G. M.—Richard Strauss: Correspondence 1888–1911* (London, 1984); D. Greene, *M.: Consciousness and Temporality* (N.Y., 1984); C. Lewis, *Tonal Coherence in M.'s Ninth Symphony* (Ann Arbor, 1984); H. Lea, *G. M.: Man on the Margin* (Bonn, 1985); H. Danuser, *G. M.: Das Lied von der Erde* (Munich, 1986); H.-P. Jülg, *G. M.s Sechste Symphonie* (Munich, 1986); H. Blaukopf, ed., *M.'s Unknown Letters* (Boston, 1987); S. Namenwirth, *G. M.: A Critical Bibliography* (3 vols., Wiesbaden, 1987); K.-J. Müller, *M.: Leben, Werke, Dokumente* (Mainz, 1988); M. Oltmanns, *Strophische Strukturen im Werk G. M.s: Untersuchungen zum Liedwerk und zur Symphonik* (Pfaffenweiler, 1988); S. Filler, *G. and Alma M.: A Guide to Research* (N.Y., 1989); Z. Roman, *G. M.'s American Years: A Documentary History* (Stuyvesant, N.Y., 1989).

Mahrenholz, Christhard (actually, **Christian Reinhard**), prominent German musicologist; b. Adelebsen, near Göttingen, Aug. 11, 1900; d. Hannover, March 15, 1980. He studied musicology with A. Schering at the Leipzig Cons., H. Abert at the Univ. of Leipzig, and F. Ludwig and F. Spitta at the Univ. of Göttingen (Ph.D., 1923, with the diss. *Samuel Scheidt: Sein Leben und sein Werk*; publ. in Leipzig, 1924). He served as a pastor in Göttingen; then taught at the Univ. there, being made honorary prof. of church music (1946). He was a member of the Hannover Landes Kirchenamt (1930–65), president of the Assoc. of Protestant Church Choirs in Germany (1934–73), and chairman of the Neue Bach-Gesellschaft (1949–74); was co-ed. of *Musik und Kirche* (from 1929), the *Handbuch der deutschen evangelischen Kirchenmusik* (from 1935), the *Jahrbuch für Liturgik und Hymnologie* (from 1955), and the *Handbuch zum Evangelischen Kirchengesangbuch* (from 1956); was the general ed. of the complete works of Samuel Scheidt (from 1932). He was made abbot of the Amelungsborn Cloister in 1960; retired from active work in 1967. His books include *Die Orgelregister: Ihre Geschichte und ihr Bau* (Kassel, 1930; 2nd ed., 1944); *Luther und die Kirchenmusik* (Kassel, 1937); *Die Berechnung der Orgelpfeifen-Mensuren vom Mittelalter bis zur Mitte des 19. Jahrhunderts* (Kassel, 1938); *Glockenkunde* (Kassel, 1949); with R. Untermöhlen, *Choralbuch zum evangelischen Kirchengesangbuch* (Kassel, 1950); *Das evangelische Kirchengesangbuch: Vorgeschichte, Werden und Grundsätze seiner Gestaltung* (Kassel, 1950); *Das Schicksal der deutschen Kirchenglocken* (Hamburg, 1952); *Kompendium der Liturgik des Hauptgottesdienstes* (Kassel, 1963). K. Müller ed. a collection of his articles as *Musicologica et liturgica: Aufsätze von Christhard Mahrenholz* (Kassel, 1960). His 70th birthday was honored by the Festschrift *Kerygma und Melos* (Kassel and Berlin, 1970).

Maiboroda, Georgi, Ukrainian composer; b. Pelekhovshchina, near Poltava, Dec. 1, 1913. He studied at the Kiev Cons. with Revutsky, graduating in 1941; from 1952 he taught there. His music tends toward heroically patriotic themes according to the precepts of socialist realism.

WORKS: OPERAS: *Milana* (1957); *The Arsenal* (1960); *Taras Shevchenko* (1964); *Yaroslav the Wise* (1975). ORCH.: 4 syms. (1940; 1952; 1976; 1988, *Autumn*); Concerto for Voice and Orch. (1969); Violin Concerto (1977); Cello Concerto (1984); *Joyful Overture* (1985); also numerous vocal pieces, including a cantata, *Friendship of Peoples* (1948).

BIBL.: O. Zinkevich, *G. M.* (Kiev, 1973; in Ukrainian).

Maichelbeck, Franz Anton, German organist and composer; b. Reichenau, July 6, 1702; d. Freiburg im Breisgau, June 14, 1750. He studied theology in Freiburg, then went to Rome to study music; returned to Freiburg and became organist at the Cathedral and a prof. of Italian at the Univ. in 1730. He publ. *Die auf dem Clavier spielende . . . Caecilia . . .* (1736; contains 8 sonatas), *Die auf dem Clavier lehrende Caecilia* (1738; a book of studies), and *VI . . . Missen* (1739).

Maier, Guy, American pianist and teacher; b. Buffalo, Aug. 15, 1891; d. Santa Monica, Calif., Sept. 24, 1956. He studied at the New England Cons. of Music in Boston (graduated, 1913) and with A. Schnabel in Berlin (1913–14); made his U.S. debut in Boston (1914); in addition to solo appearances, he also toured as a duo-pianist with Lee Pattison (1916–31); taught at the Univ. of Michigan (1924–31), the Juilliard School of Music in N.Y. (1935–42), and the Univ. of Calif. at Los Angeles (1946–56).

Maillart, Aimé (actually, **Louis**), French composer; b. Montepellier, March 24, 1817; d. Moulins-sur-Allier, May 26, 1871. He studied at the Paris Cons. with Halévy and Leborne (composition) and with Guérin (violin); won the Grand Prix de Rome in 1841.
    Works: Operas: (all 1st perf. in Paris): *Gastibelza ou Le Fou de Tolède* (Nov. 15, 1847); *Le Moulin des tilleuls* (1849); *La Croix de Marie* (1852); *Les Dragons de Villars* (Sept. 19, 1856; his most successful opera; perf. also in Germany under the title *Das Glöckchen des Eremiten*); *Les Pêcheurs de Catane* (Dec. 19, 1860); *Lara* (March 21, 1864); also several cantatas and other sacred works.

Maillart, Pierre, Franco-Flemish music theorist; b. Valenciennes, 1551; d. Tournai, July 16, 1622. He was a chorister at the Flemish chapel in Madrid (1563–70), where he studied with its director, Jean Bonmarché; then entered the Univ. of Louvain (1572); was later in Antwerp (1574) and Tournai (1581), where he became phonascus (singing master) in 1581, and later canon (1589) and chantre (1606) at the Cathedral. He publ. *Les tons, ou discours, sur les modes de musique, et les tons de l'église, et la distinction entre iceux* (Tournai, 1610; reprint, 1972).

Mailly, Alphonse-Jean-Ernest, Belgian organist and composer; b. Brussels, Nov. 27, 1833; d. there, Jan. 10, 1918. He studied at the Brussels Cons.; taught piano and organ there; gave numerous and successful organ concerts in France and England; wrote various pieces for piano and organ.

Mailman, Martin, American composer, conductor, and teacher; b. N.Y., June 30, 1932. He studied composition with Mennini, Barlow, Rogers, and Hanson at the Eastman School of Music in Rochester, N.Y. (B.M., 1954; M.M., 1955; Ph.D., 1960); taught at the U.S. Naval School of Music during his naval service (1955–57); after teaching at the Eastman School of Music (1958–59), he was composer-in-residence of Jacksonville, Fla., under a Ford Foundation grant (1959–61). During the summers of 1960–61 and 1983, he taught at the Brevard Music Center; from 1961 to 1966 he was composer-in-residence and prof. of music at East Carolina College; also taught at West Virginia Univ. (summer 1963). In 1966 he joined the faculty of North Texas State Univ. (later the Univ. of North Texas) in Denton, where he served as Regents Prof. of Music (from 1987). He was active as a guest conductor, composer, and lecturer at more than 80 colleges and univs. In 1982 he won the Queen Marie-Jose Prize for Composition for his Violin Concerto and an NEA grant; in 1983 he received the American Bandmasters Assoc./NABIM Award for his *Exaltations*; in 1989 he won the National Band Assoc./Band Mans Award and the American Bandmasters Assoc./Ostwald Award for his *For Precious Friends Hid in Death's Dateless Night*.
    Works: STAGE: *The Hunted*, opera (Rochester, N.Y., April 27, 1959); *Mirrors*, multimedia theater piece (1986). ORCH.: 3 syms. (1969; 1979; 1983, *Fantasies*); *Dance in 2 Moods* (1952); *Autumn Landscape* (1954); *Jubilate* (1955); *Elegy* (1955); *Cantiones* (1957); Prelude and Fugue No. 1 (1959); *Partita* for String Orch. (1960); *Gateway City Overture* (1960); *Suite in 3 Movements* (1961); Prelude and Fugue No. 2 (1963); Sinfonietta (1964); *Generations 2* for 3 String Orchs. and Percussion (1969); Violin Concerto (1982); *Elegy* for String Orch. (1985); *Mirror Music* (1987). BAND: *Partita* (1958); *Commencement March* (1960); *4 Miniatures* (1960); *Geometrics* No. 1 (1961); *Geometrics in Sound* No. 2 (1962); *Alarums* (1962); Concertino for Trumpet and Band (1963); *Liturgical Music*

(1964); *Geometrics* No. 3 (1965); *Geometrics* No. 4 (1968); *Associations No. 1* (1968–69); *In Memoriam Frankie Newton* (1970); *Shouts, Hymns and Praises* (1972); *Geometrics* No. 5 (1976); *Night Vigil* (1980); *Exaltations* (1981); *Toward the 2nd Century* (1989). VOCAL: *Alleluia* for Chorus and Band (1960); *Leaves of Grass* for Narrator, Chorus, and Band (1963); *Shakespearean Serenade* for Chorus and 9 Instruments (1968); *Requiem, Requiem* for Chorus, Soloists, and Orch. (1970); *Let Us Now Praise Famous Men* for Solo Voice, Narrators, and Band (1975); *Generations 3: Messengers* for Children's Choirs, Solo Voice, and Stage Band (1977); *Soft Sounds for a Wordless Night* for Chorus (1979); *Secular Hours* for Chorus (1982); Cantata for Soloists, Jazz Choir, and Large Jazz Ensemble (1984); songs. CHAMBER: *Promenade* for Brass and Percussion (1953); *Brevard Fanfare* for Brass (1961); String Quartet (1962); *4 Divisions* for Percussion Ensemble (1966); *Partita No. 4* for 9 Players (1967); *2 Fanfares* for Brass (1970); *Clastics: Formations* for Cello (1977); *Clastics 2* for Euphonium and Percussion (1979); *Nocturne* for Trumpet Choir (1985); Trio for Violin, Cello, and Piano (1985); *For Precious Friends Hid in Death's Dateless Night* for Wind Ensemble (1988). PIANO: *Petite Partita* (1961); *Variations on a Short Theme* (1966); *Martha's Vineyard* (1969); *In Memoriam Sylvia Scionti* (1974); *Clastics 3* for 2 Pianos (1980); *6 Brief Obituaries* (1988).

Mainardi, Enrico, Italian cellist, teacher, and composer; b. Milan, May 19, 1897; d. Munich, April 10, 1976. He studied cello and composition at the Milan Cons., graduating in 1920; then went to Berlin, where he was a student of Hugo Becker, and to Venice, where he studied with Malipiero. He became a teacher of cello and chamber music at Rome's Accademia di Santa Cecilia (1930); also taught in Berlin, Salzburg, and Lucerne; gave master classes in various locales.
    Works: ORCH.: 3 cello concertos: No. 1 (1943; Rome, May 13, 1947; composer soloist); No. 2 (1960); No. 3, with String Orch. (1966); *Musica per archi*; *Elegie* for Cello and String Orch. (1957); Concerto for 2 Cellos and Orch. (1969; Freiburg, Oct. 12, 1970); *Divertimento* for Cello and String Orch. (1972). CHAMBER: 2 unnumbered string trios (1939, 1954); *Suite* for Cello and Piano (1940); Cello Sonatina (1943); *Notturno* for Piano Trio (1947); String Quartet (1951); Cello Sonata (1955); Sonata and *Sonata breve* for Solo Cello; 7 *studi brevi* for Cello (1961); *Sonata quasi fantasia* for Cello and Piano (1962); Violin Sonata; Piano Quartet (1968); Viola Sonata (1968); *Burattini*, suite of 12 pieces for Cello and Piano (1968); Trio for Clarinet, Cello, and Piano (1969); String Quintet (1970); Piano Sonatina (1941); other piano pieces.
    Bibl.: E. M.: *Bekenntnisse eines Künstlers* (Wiesbaden, 1977).

Maine, Basil (Stephen), English writer on music and composer; b. Norwich, March 4, 1894; d. Sheringham, Norfolk, Oct. 13, 1972. He studied with Stanford, Rootham, and Dent at Queen's College, Cambridge; was active after graduation as a schoolteacher and occasionally an actor; was music critic for London's *Daily Telegraph* (1921–26) and *Morning Post* (1926–37); was ordained a priest in the Church of England in 1939. He composed orch. works, choral music, and organ pieces. His writings include *Elgar, His Life and Works* (2 vols., 1933), *Chopin* (1933; 2nd ed., 1948), *The Glory of English Music* (1937), *The Best of Me: A Study in Autobiography* (1937), *Basil Maine on Music* (1945), and *Twang with Our Music, Being a Set of Variants to Mark the Completion of Thirty Years' Practice in the Uncertain Science of Music Criticism* (London, 1957).

Mainwaring, John, English churchman and writer on music; b. Drayton Manor, Staffordshire, c.1724; d. Church Stretton, April 15, 1807. He was educated at St. John's College, Cambridge; was ordained in 1748; in 1749 he became rector of Church Stretton, Shropshire; was a Fellow of St. John's College, 1748–88; then became Lady Margaret Prof. of Divinity at Cambridge Univ. His biography of Handel, which utilized material provided by John Christopher Smith, appeared under the title *Memoirs of the Life of the Late George Frederic Handel* (London,

1760); a portion of the biography was written by Robert Price; it was tr. into German by J. Mattheson (Hamburg, 1761).

Mainzer, Joseph, German singing teacher and musical journalist; b. Trier, Oct. 21, 1801; d. Salford, Lancashire, Nov. 10, 1851. He was a chorister at the Trier Cathedral; then studied music in Darmstadt, Munich, and Vienna; returning to Trier, he was ordained a priest (1826); taught at the seminary there, and publ. a sight-singing method, *Singschule* (1831). He then abandoned the priesthood; moved to Brussels (1833), and then to Paris (1834), where he started the short-lived *Chronique Musicale de Paris* (1838). In 1841 he went to London. In 1844 he began publication of the monthly *Mainzer's Musical Times and Singing Circular*, which in 1846 became the *Musical Times* (publ. without interruption through nearly 1½ centuries). In 1847 he settled in Manchester as a singing teacher. He mastered the English language to such an extent that he was able to engage in aggressive musical journalism. His methods of self-advertising were quite uninhibited; he arranged singing courses in open-air gatherings, and had pamphlets printed with flamboyant accounts of receptions tendered him.
WRITINGS: *Singschule* (Trier, 1831); *Méthode de chant pour les enfants* (Paris, 1835); *Méthode de chant pour voix d'hommes* (Paris, 1836); *Bibliothèque élémentaire de chant* (Paris, 1836); *Méthode pratique de piano pour enfants* (Paris, 1837); *Abécédaire de chant* (Paris, 1837); *École chorale* (Paris, 1838); *Esquisses musicales, ou Souvenirs de voyage* (Paris, 1838–39); *Cent mélodies enfantines* (Paris, 1840); *Singing for the Million* (London, 1841); *The Musical Athenaeum* (London, 1841); *Music and Education* (London and Edinburgh, 1848).
BIBL.: P. Scholes, "The M. Movement," *The Mirror of Music* (vol. I, London, 1947).

Mair, Franz, Austrian conductor and composer; b. Weikersdorf, March 15, 1821; d. Vienna, Nov. 14, 1893. He was founder-conductor of the Vienna Schubertbund (1883); composed music to *Die Jungfrau von Orleans* and other theatrical productions; wrote a number of male choruses and a cycle of 15 folk songs of various nations, arranged for Men's Chorus and Orch., as *Die Völker und ihre Lieder*. His reminiscences were publ. as *Aus meinem Leben* (Vienna, 1897).

Maisky, Mischa, Russian-born Israeli cellist; b. Riga, Jan. 10, 1948. He was a pupil of Rostropovich at the Moscow Cons. In 1965 he won 1st prize in the All Russian Competition and made his formal debut as a soloist with the Leningrad Phil.; in 1966 he was a laureate at the Tchaikovsky Competition in Moscow. Despite his successful career, he got into trouble with the Soviet authorities when he bought a tape recorder without proper permission; he was duly arrested and spent a few months in jail. Determined to leave Russia, he approached a liberal-minded psychiatrist, who, like Maisky, was of the Jewish faith, and was committed to an asylum. He was finally permitted to emigrate to Israel, where he settled and became an Israeli citizen. In 1973 he captured 1st prize at the Gaspar Cassadó Competition in Florence. He also pursued further studies with Piatigorsky in the U.S. From 1975 he toured throughout the world; made his Paris debut in 1976, and by 1983 had established himself as a concert cellist with engagements throughout the world.

Maison, René, Belgian tenor; b. Frameries, Nov. 24, 1895; d. Mont-Dore, France, July 15, 1962. He studied at the Brussels and Paris conservatories; made his debut as Rodolfo in *La Bohème* in Geneva (1920); was on the roster of the Monte Carlo Opera (1922), then of the Opéra and Opéra-Comique in Paris (from 1925), and of Covent Garden in London. He was a member of the Chicago Opera (1927–32) and the Teatro Colón in Buenos Aires (1934–37). He made his Metropolitan Opera debut in N.Y. as Walther von Stolzing in *Die Meistersinger von Nürnberg* on Feb. 3, 1936, remaining there until 1943. He later taught voice in N.Y. and Boston.

Maitland, J(ohn) A(lexander) Fuller. See **Fuller Maitland, J(ohn) A(lexander).**

Maizel, Boris, significant Russian composer; b. St. Petersburg, July 17, 1907; d. Moscow, July 9, 1986. He graduated from the Leningrad Cons. in 1936 in the composition class of Riazanov; during the siege of Leningrad by the Germans in 1942, he was evacuated to Sverdlovsk; in 1944 he settled in Moscow.
WORKS: ORCH.: 9 syms.: No. 1 (1940); No. 2, *Ural Symphony* (1944); No. 3, *Victoriously Triumphant*, written in celebration of the victory over Germany (1945); No. 4 (1947); No. 5 (1962); No. 6 (1967); No. 7 (1970); No. 8 (1973); No. 9 (1976); Double Concerto for Violin, Piano, and Orch. (1949); Double Concerto for Flute, Horn, Strings, and Percussion (1971); Concerto for 10 Instruments (1977); Concerto for 2 Pianos and String Orch. (1978); 3 symphonic poems: *Distant Planet* (1961; also as a ballet, 1962); *Leningrad Novella* (1969); *Along Old Russian Towns* (1975). **STAGE:** *The Shadow of the Past,* opera (1964); *Snow Queen,* ballet (1940; also a symphonic suite, 1944); *Sombrero,* children's ballet (1959). **CHAMBER:** Cello Sonata (1936); Piano Trio (1951); 2 string quartets (1937, 1974); also song cycles; piano pieces; various theatrical compositions based on the themes of the Buryat Soviet Republic; film music.

Majo, Gian Francesco (de), Italian organist and composer, son of **Giuseppe de Majo,** known as **Ciccio di Majo;** b. Naples, March 24, 1732; d. there, Nov. 17, 1770. He received his primary training from his father; also studied with his uncle Gennaro Manno and his great-uncle Francesco Feo; was his father's assistant as organista soprannumerario at the royal chapel, being made its 2nd organist by 1758. His 1st opera, *Ricimero re dei Goti* (Parma, 1758), scored a great success in Rome in 1759; his next opera, *Astrea placata* (Naples, June 29, 1760), established his reputation as a composer for the theater. After further studies with Padre Martini (1761–63), he went to Vienna to produce his opera *Alcide negli orti Esperidi* (June 7, 1764) for the coronation of the emperor of the Holy Roman Empire, Joseph II. He then toured widely, returning to his birthplace the year of his death.
WORKS: Operas: *Ricimero re dei Goti* (Parma, 1758); *Astrea placata* (Naples, June 29, 1760); *Cajo Fabricio* (Naples, Nov. 29, 1760); *L'Almeria* (Livorno, 1761); *Artaserse* (Venice, Jan. 30, 1762); *Catone in Utica* (Turin, Dec. 26, 1762); *Demofoonte* (Rome, Carnival 1764); *Alcide negli orti Esperidi* (Vienna, June 7, 1764); *Ifigenia in Tauride* (Mannheim, Nov. 4, 1764); *Montezuma* (Turin, Carnival 1765); *La constancia dichosa* (Madrid, 1765); *Alessandro nell'Indie* (Mannheim, 1766); *Antigono* (Venice, Dec. 26, 1767); *Antigona* (Rome, Carnival 1768); *Ipermestra* (Naples, Aug. 13, 1768); *Adriano in Siria* (Rome, Carnival 1769); *Didone abbandonata* (Venice, Dec. 26, 1769); *Eumene* (Naples, Jan. 21, 1771; finished by Insanguine and Errichelli); also arias for 3 London pasticcios: *Ezio* (1764); *Solimano* (1765); *The Golden Pippin* (Feb. 6, 1773). He also wrote many oratorios, cantatas, and other sacred works.
BIBL.: D. DiChiera, *The Life and Operas of G.F. d.M.* (diss., Univ. of Calif., Los Angeles, 1962).

Majo, Giuseppe de, Italian organist and composer, father of **Gian Francesco (de) Majo;** b. Naples, Dec. 5, 1697; d. there, Nov. 18, 1771. He studied with Nicola Fago and Andrea Basso at the Cons. della Pietà dei Turchini in Naples (1706–18); was organista soprannumerario (1736–37), provicemaestro (1737–44), vicemaestro (1744–45), and maestro (1745–71) at the royal chapel. His most successful stage work was the serenata *Il sogno d'Olimpia* (Naples, Nov. 6, 1747), written to celebrate the birth of the heir apparent.
WORKS: Stage: *Lo vecchio avaro,* opera buffa (Naples, Carnival 1727); *La Milorda,* opera buffa (Naples, 1728); *La Baronessa, overo Gli equivoci,* opera buffa (Naples, 1729); *Arianna e Teseo,* opera seria (Naples, Jan. 20, 1747); *Il sogno d'Olimpia,* serenata (Naples, Nov. 6, 1747); *Semiramide riconosciuta,* opera seria (Naples, Jan. 20, 1751); *Il Napolitano nelli fiorentini,* farsa (n.d.); also a Concerto for 2 Violins and Orch. (1726); cantatas; various sacred works.

Majone or **Mayone, Ascanio,** Italian organist and composer; b. Naples, c.1565; d. there, March 9, 1627. He was a pupil of Giovanni de Macque in Naples; was organist (from 1593) and maestro di cappella (from 1621) at the Santa Casa dell'Annunziata there. Existing musical publications by Majone are: *Primo libro di diversi capricci per sonare* (Naples, 1603); *Il primo libro di madrigali a 5 voci* (Naples, 1604); *Secondo libro di diversi capricci per sonare* (Naples, 1609; reprinted in *Orgue et Liturgie,* 63 and 65; Paris, 1964). Two of his madrigals are included in the collection *Teatro di madrigali a 5 v. de div. excell. musici Napolitani, posti in luce da Scipione Ricci, Libraro* (Naples, 1609). Majone is mentioned in Scipione Cerreto's *Della prattica musica vocale e strumentale* (Naples, 1601) as an outstanding performer on the organ and harp. Majone's keyboard toccatas are among the earliest examples of the affective Baroque style found later in Frescobaldi.
Bibl.: W. Apel, "Neapolitan Links between Cabezón and Frescobaldi," *Musical Quarterly* (Oct. 1938).

Major, Ervin, Hungarian musicologist and composer, son of **(Jakab) Gyula Major;** b. Budapest, Jan. 26, 1901; d. there, Oct. 10, 1967. He studied with his father, then with Kodály at the Budapest Academy of Music (1917–21); also studied philosophy at the Budapest Scientific Univ. (1920–24) and musicology at the Univ. of Szeged (Ph.D., 1930). He was ed. of the journal *Zenei Szemle* (1926–28); taught composition, theory, and music history and was librarian at the Budapest Cons. (later the Béla Bartók Music School; 1928–44; 1945–63); also taught Hungarian music history at the Budapest Academy of Music (1935–41; 1945–46). He wrote some choral works, chamber music, piano pieces, organ music, and arrangements of Hungarian melodies, but he is best known for his studies of 18th- and 19th-century Hungarian music.

Major (real name, **Mayer**), **(Jakab) Gyula,** Hungarian pianist, choral conductor, and composer, father of **Ervin Major;** b. Kassa, Dec. 13, 1858; d. Budapest, Jan. 30, 1925. He studied at the Buda Cons.; then with Erkel and Liszt (piano) and Robert Volkmann (composition) at the Academy of Music there (1877–81); subsequently taught in music schools and teacher-training colleges; toured in Europe as a pianist; then returned to Budapest. His music follows the German Romantic tradition with some infusion of original Hungarian folk melos.
Works: operas: *Erzsike* (Budapest, Sept. 24, 1901); *Széchy Mária* (1906); *Mila* (1913). **orch.:** 6 syms. (1883–c.1918); 2 piano concertos (1882; n.d.); Violin Concerto (n.d.); Cello Concerto (n.d.); also 4 string quartets (1882–1905); 3 piano trios (1881–1907); 2 violin sonatas (both 1907); etc.

Makarov, Nikolai, Russian guitarist; b. Chukhloma, Feb. 16, 1810; d. Funtikovo-Rozhestvino, near Tula, Dec. 17, 1890. He appeared as a soloist in Tula in 1841; in 1852 he went abroad; in 1856 he organized in Brussels an international competition for the best works for the guitar. In his leisure time, he wrote unsuccessful novels and compiled a French dictionary. He publ. an autobiography, *My Septuagenarian Reminiscences* (1881).

Makarova, Nina, Russian composer; b. Yurino, Aug. 12, 1908; d. Moscow, Jan. 15, 1976. She studied with Miaskovsky at the Moscow Cons., graduating in 1936. Her early works show a Romantic flair, not without some coloristic touches of French Impressionism. She wrote an opera, *Zoya* (1955); a Sym. (1938), which she conducted herself in Moscow on June 12, 1947; a number of violin pieces; a Sonatina and 6 études for piano; several song cycles; a cantata, *The Saga of Lenin* (1970). She was married to **Aram Khachaturian.**
Bibl.: I. Martinov, *N. M.* (Moscow, 1973).

Makeba, Miriam, black South African singer; b. Prospect, near Johannesburg, March 4, 1932. She sang in a mission choir in Pretoria; then joined an itinerant minstrel show. She 1st attracted attention when she sang the leading part in the African opera *King Kong* (Johannesburg, Feb. 2, 1959). In 1959 she went to the U.S.; appeared in N.Y. nightclubs and on television; testified at the United Nations on the racist policies of South Africa; made a successful tour of Europe;

also traveled to Ethiopia and Kenya as a representative of Negro art. She was married to the black American activist Stokely Carmichael from 1968 to 1978. With J. Hall, she publ. *Makeba: My Story* in 1988.

Makedonski, Kiril, Macedonian composer; b. Bitol, Jan. 19, 1925; d. Skopje, June 2, 1984. After completing his academic schooling in Skopje, he studied with Krsto Odak at the Zagreb Academy of Music; later continued his composition studies with Brkanović in Sarajevo, and in Ljubljana with Škerjanc. He was the composer of the 1st national Macedonian opera, *Goce* (Skopje, May 24, 1954); his 2nd opera was *Tsar Samuil* (Skopje, Nov. 5, 1968). He also wrote 4 syms., chamber music, and a number of choruses. His idiom follows the fundamental vocal and harmonic usages of the Russian national school.

Maklakiewicz, Jan Adam, Polish composer; b. Chojnata, Mazuria, Nov. 24, 1899; d. Warsaw, Feb. 7, 1954. He studied with Statkowski at the Warsaw Cons. and with Dukas in Paris. Returning to Poland, he was a prof. at the Lodz Cons. (1927–29) and at the Warsaw Cons. (from 1929); was director of the Krakow Cons. (from 1947); also was director of the Krakow Phil. (1945–47) and the Warsaw Phil. (1947–48). After writing a number of works in an advanced style, including a Cello Concerto and his 2nd Sym., he developed a highly simplified idiom.
Works: ballets: *Cagliostro w Warsawie* (Cagliostro in Warsaw; 1938; Poznan, Oct. 1, 1946); *Zlota kaczka* (1950). **orch.:** *Wariacje symfoniczne* (1922); Sym. No. 2, *Święty Boze* (O Holy Lord), for Baritone, Chorus, and Orch. (1928); *Pieśni japoński* (Japanese Songs) for Soprano and Orch. (1930); ISCM Festival, Oxford, July 23, 1931); Cello Concerto (1932); Violin Concerto (1933); *Grundwald,* symphonic poem (1939–44; Krakow, Sept. 1, 1945); *Uwertura praska* (Prague Overture; Prague, May 8, 1947); also much sacred music; incidental music; film scores; chamber music; many arrangements of Polish folk songs.

Maksimović, Rajko, Serbian composer; b. Belgrade, July 27, 1935. He studied with Predrag Milošević at the Belgrade Academy of Music (graduated, 1961; M.A., 1965); continued his training at Princeton Univ. (1965–66), devoting himself mainly to electronic music; taught at the Belgrade Academy of Music (from 1963). In his works, he utilizes resources ranging from the Ars Nova to the contemporary period.
Works: orch.: Piano Concerto (1961; Belgrade, Jan. 28, 1964); *Musique de devenir* (1965; Belgrade, Dec. 15, 1967); *Partita concertante* for Violin and Strings (1965); *Not to Be or to Be?* and *Eppur si muove,* diptych (1969–70); *Concerto non grosso* for Student String Orch. (1970); *Nežno* (Tenderly?) for Chamber Ensemble (1979). **vocal:** *Kad su živi zavideli mrtvima* (When the Living Envied the Dead), epic partita for Choir and Orch. (1963; Belgrade, Feb. 2, 1967); *2 Basho's Haiku* for Voice, Ensemble, and Tape (1966); *3 Haiku* for Female Choir and 24 Instruments (Zagreb, May 16, 1967); *Iz tmine pojanje* (Chants out of Darkness), book of madrigals to ancient Serbian texts for Choir (1975); *Buna protiv dahija* (Uprising against Dakhias), dramatic oratorio for 4 Actors, Choirs, Orch., and Tape (1978; Belgrade, March 20, 1979); *Palabras en piedra,* madrigal suite to pre-Columbian Mexican Indian texts in Spanish for Choir and Optional Percussion (1980); *After the Scent of the Blossomed Cherry,* 5 haiku for Voice and Ensemble (1981); *Veče na školju* (An Evening on the Reef) for Choir (1982); *Les Proverbes de Fenis,* choral suite to ancient French texts (1983; also for 4 Voices and Ancient Instruments, 1984, and for Female Choir and Orch., 1986); *Prometheus* for Choir (1985); *Testament of the Bishop of Montenegro Peter Petrovich Nyegosh* for Choir (1984; also for Bass, Choir, Orch., and Tape, 1986). **chamber:** Piano Suite (1957); *Ab aqua terraque* for Piano (1966); *Trialogue* for Clarinet, String Trio, and Piano (1968); *Jeu à quatre* for 2 Pianos, 8-hands (1977).

Maksymiuk, Jerzy, Polish conductor and composer; b. Grodno, April 9, 1936. He studied piano with Kirjacka and Lefeld, composition with Perkowski, and conducting with Madey at the Warsaw Cons.; won several composition prizes. He conducted at Warsaw's Wielki Theater (1970–72); then in 1972 founded the Polish Chamber Orch. in Warsaw, which he led as music director; was also conductor of the Polish Radio National Sym. Orch. in Katowice (1976–77) and principal conductor of the BBC Scottish Sym. Orch. in Glasgow (from 1983). He appeared as a guest conductor in North and South America. He wrote several ballets, orch. music, and choral pieces.

Malanotte (-Montresor), Adelaide, Italian contralto; b. Verona, 1785; d. Salò, Dec. 31, 1832. She made her debut in 1806 in Verona; created the title role in Rossini's opera *Tancredi* in Venice at the Teatro La Fenice in 1813. She retired from the stage in 1821.

Malas, Spiro, American bass-baritone; b. Baltimore, Jan. 28, 1933. He studied voice with Nagy at the Peabody Cons. of Music in Baltimore and with Elsa Baklor and Daniel Ferro in N.Y.; was also coached by Ivor Chichagov. In 1959 he made his operatic debut as Marco in *Gianni Schicchi* in Baltimore, and in 1961 won the Metropolitan Opera Auditions. On Oct. 5, 1961, he made his 1st appearance at the N.Y. City Opera as Spinellocchio in *Gianni Schicchi*, and continued to sing there regularly. In 1965 he toured Australia with the Sutherland-Williamson International Grand Opera Co., and in 1966 made his debut at London's Covent Garden as Sulpice in *La Fille du régiment;* sang Assur in *Semiramide* for his 1st appearance at the Chicago Lyric Opera in 1971. On Oct. 8, 1983, he made his Metropolitan Opera debut in N.Y. as Sulpice, and later appeared as Zuniga in *Carmen,* as Mozart's Bartolo, as Frank in *Die Fledermaus,* and as the sacristan in *Tosca.* He also toured widely as a concert artist.

Malashkin, Leonid, Russian composer; b. 1842; d. Moscow, Feb. 11, 1902. He was an ardent song collector; his anthology *50 Ukrainian Folksongs* is valuable. His original compositions were not successful; he wrote an opera, *Ilya Murometz* (Kiev, 1879), a *Russian Symphony on Folk Themes* (Moscow, March 27, 1873), and a great deal of church music.

Malawski, Artur, Polish violinist, conductor, teacher, and composer; b. Przemyśl, July 4, 1904; d. Krakow, Dec. 26, 1957. He graduated as a violinist from the Krakow Cons. in 1928; then studied composition with Sikorski and conducting with Bierdiajew at the Warsaw Cons. (1936–39). He taught conducting and composition in Krakow (1945–57) and conducting in Katowice (1950–54). His noted pupils included Penderecki and Schäffer. He developed an individual compositional voice, drawing on Romantic elements treated in a general modern idiom.
Works: *Allegro capriccioso* for Small Orch. (1929); *Sinfonietta* (1936); *Symphonic Variations* (1937); cantata, *Wyspa Gorgon* (Gorgons' Island; 1939); 2 syms. (1938–43; 1953–56); ballet-pantomime, *Wierchy* (The Peaks; 1942; rev. 1950–52); *6 Symphonic Études* for Piano and Orch. (Sopot, April 30, 1948); *Tryptyk góralski* (Highland Triptych) for Small Orch. or Piano (1949); *Toccata and Fugue* for Piano and Orch. (1949); cantata, *Stara baśń* (The Old Tale; 1950); *Suite popularna* for Orch. (1952); *Hungaria 1956* for Orch. (1957; Warsaw, Feb. 14, 1958; descriptive of the Hungarian insurrection of 1956); 2 string quartets (1926, 1943); String Sextet (1932); *Ziabia Ballad* (Ballad of the Frogs), 2 recitations for Voice and Wind Ensemble (1934); *Burlesque* for Violin and Piano (1940); *Miniatures* for Piano (1947); Violin Sonata (1951); Piano Trio (1953).
Bibl.: B. Schäffer, ed., *A. M.: Życie i twórczość* (Krakow, 1969).

Malcolm, George (John), esteemed English harpsichordist, pianist, conductor, and teacher; b. London, Feb. 28, 1917. He studied at Balliol College, Oxford, and at the Royal College of Music in London. Following military service in the Royal Air Force during World War II, he took up a distinguished career as a harpsichord virtuoso, chamber music pianist, and conductor; was also active as a teacher. He was Master of Music at Westminster Cathedral (1947–59) and artistic director

of the Philomusica of London (1962–66). He was particularly associated with the Baroque revival. In 1965 he was made a Commander of the Order of the British Empire.

Malcuzynski, Witold, outstanding Polish pianist; b. Koziczyn, near Vilnius, Aug. 10, 1914; d. Palma, Majorca, July 17, 1977. He studied with Turczyński at the Warsaw Cons. (graduated, 1936); then took lessons with Paderewski in Switzerland. After his marriage to the French pianist **Colette Gaveau,** he went to Paris (1939); then toured in South America (1940–42); made his U.S. debut at N.Y.'s Carnegie Hall (1942); gave concerts in Australia in 1950. He made in all 14 U.S. tours, 9 South American tours, and 2 world tours (1949, 1956). He was particularly distinguished as an interpreter of Chopin.
Bibl.: B. Gavoty, *W. M.* (London, 1957).

Maldeghem, Robert Julien van, Belgian organist, music editor, and composer; b. Denterghem, Oct. 9, 1806; d. Ixelles, near Brussels, Nov. 13, 1893. He studied with Fétis at the Brussels Cons., winning the Belgian Prix de Rome; obtained a post as church organist; undertook a thorough research of early Flemish music, and publ. an anthology of choral works, *Trésor musical . . .* (29 vols., Brussels, 1865–93; reprint, 1965), an ed. of great documentary and historical importance, despite many errors of transcription; comments and rectifications were made by G. Reese, "Maldeghem and His Buried Treasure: A Bibliographical Study," in *Notes* (Dec. 1948).

Maldere, Pierre van, noted South Netherlands violinist, conductor, and composer; b. Brussels, Oct. 16, 1729; d. there, Nov. 1, 1768. In 1746 he became a member of the ensemble of the Royal Chapel of Brussels; was also in the service of Prince Charles of Lorraine, the governor-general of the Netherlands. From 1751 to 1753 he was in Dublin as a violinist, conductor, and composer. He then traveled to Paris (1754); returning to Brussels, he became director of concerts to Prince Charles (1754); then was made his valet de chambre (1758); also conducted at the Brussels Opera, and later was director of the Grand Théâtre there (1762–67). He excelled as a composer of syms., in which he anticipated the masterpieces of Haydn and Mozart.
Works: Operas: *Le Déguisement pastoral* (Vienna, July 12, 1756); *Les Amours champêtres* (Vienna, Nov. 5, 1758; not extant); *Les Précautions inutiles* (1760); *Les Sœurs rivals* (1762); *La Bagarre* (Paris, Feb. 10, 1763; not extant); *Le Médecin de l'amour* (Brussels, 1766; not extant); *Le Soldat par amour* (Brussels, Nov. 4, 1766; not extant); numerous syms., many of which were publ.; other extant works include overtures and chamber music.
Bibl.: S. Clercx, *P. v.M.: Virtuose et maître des concerts de Charles de Lorraine (1729–1786)* (Brussels, 1948).

Malec, Ivo, Yugoslav-born French composer, conductor, and teacher; b. Zagreb, March 30, 1925. He studied at the Univ. and at the Academy of Music in Zagreb (1945–51); was director of the Rijeka (Fiume) Opera (1952–53); in 1955 he traveled to Paris, where he met Pierre Schaeffer (1957) and participated in his Groupe de Musique Concrète; in 1959 he settled in Paris and joined the Service de la Recherche de l'ORTF in 1960. He also worked with the Groupe de Recherche Musicale and taught at the Paris Cons. (from 1972). From 1956 his music has explored the extremes of timbre and complexity.
Works: STAGE: *Opérabus,* 2 scenes from the collective opera, to a libretto by Schaeffer (1965); *Le Roi Lear,* theater score (1967); *Victor Hugo—Un contre tous,* "musical poster" for 2 Actors, Chorus, Orch., and Tape, after Hugo's political texts (Avignon, Aug. 1, 1971); incidental music. ORCH.: Sym. (1951); *Maquettes* for 17 Instruments (1957); *Mouvements en couleur* (1959); *Séquences* for Vibraphone and Strings (1960); *Tutti,* with Tape (1962); *Sigma* (Zagreb, May 16, 1963); *Vocatif* (1968); *Lied* for 39 Strings and 18 Voices (Dubrovnik, July 30, 1969); *Gam(m)es* (Strasbourg, June 10, 1971); *Tehrana* (1975); *Arco-22* for 22 Strings (1976); *Ottava bassa* for Double Bass and Orch. (1983; Paris, April 10, 1984); *Exemples* (1988). VOCAL: *Poèmes de Radovan* for Voice and Orch. (1956); *Cantate*

pour elle for Soprano, Harp, and Tape (Paris, May 25, 1966); *Oral* for Actor and Orch. (Zagreb, May 19, 1967); *Dodecameron* for 12 Solo Voices (1970; Bologna, Feb. 22, 1971); *Vox, vocis, f.* for 3 Women's Voices and 9 Instruments (Metz, Nov. 16, 1979). CHAMBER: Piano Trio (1950); *Trois stèles* for Instruments (1963); *Miniatures pour Lewis Carroll* for Violin, Flute, Harp, and Percussion (1964); *Échos* for 10 Musicians (1965); *Planètes* for Instruments (1966); *Lumina* for 12 Strings and Tape (Lucerne, Sept. 7, 1968); *Kitica* for Violin, Flute, Clarinet, and Trombone (1972); *Actuor* for 6 Percussionists (Strasbourg, April 1, 1973); *Arco-11* for 11 Strings (Paris, June 12, 1975); *Pieris* for 2 Harps (1985); *Attacca*, concerto for Solo Percussion and Tape (Metz, Nov. 20, 1986); *Arco 1* for Violin (1987). PIANO: Sonata (1949); *Dialogues* (1961; also for Harpsichord). TAPE: *Mavena* (1956); *Reflets* (1960); *Dahovi I* (1961) and *II* (1962); *Luminétudes* (1968); *Bizarra* (1972); *Triola* (Metz, Nov. 18, 1978); *Recitativo* (1980); *Carillon Choral* (1981); *Weekend* for 3 Synthesizers and Tape (Paris, May 3, 1982).

Maleingreau (or **Malengreau**), **Paul (Eugène) de,** Belgian organist, pedagogue, and composer; b. Trélon-en-Thiérache, Nov. 23, 1887; d. Brussels, Jan. 9, 1956. He studied with Gilson and Tinel at the Brussels Cons. (1905–12); in 1913, became a prof. of harmony there; in 1919 was appointed instructor of organ, and from 1929 to 1953 was prof. of organ. He was elected president of the Froissart Academy in 1946. His performances of Bach organ works were highly regarded in Belgium.
WORKS: 2 syms.: *Symphonie de Noë; Symphonie de la Passion;* oratorio, *Légende de St. Augustin* for Solo Voices, Chorus, and Orch. (1934); masses; motets; chamber music; songs; organ works, including 3 organ syms.; piano pieces.

Maler, Wilhelm, German composer and music educator; b. Heidelberg, June 21, 1902; d. Hamburg, April 29, 1976. He studied music history with Kroyer and composition with Grabner in Heidelberg; then took courses with Haas in Munich and Jarnach in Berlin. He subsequently occupied several teaching positions in Cologne, Bonn, Detmold, and Hamburg; also was active in theatrical organizations. He publ. *Beitrag zur Harmonielehre* (Leipzig, 1931; 2nd ed., rev., 1950, as *Beitrag zur durmolltonalen Harmonielehre;* 3rd ed., rev., 1957). His music reveals the influence of Reger and Busoni, with an infusion of Impressionism and folk melos.
WORKS: Concerto for Harpsichord and Chamber Orch. (1927); *Orchesterspiel* (1930); Violin Concerto (1932); *Flämisches Rondo* for Orch. (1937); 2 string quartets; String Trio; 6 piano sonatas; various minor pieces.

Malfitano, Catherine, American soprano; b. N.Y., April 18, 1948. She received her early training at home from her father, a violinist in the Metropolitan Opera orch., then continued her studies at the Manhattan School of Music (B.A., 1971); made her professional debut as Nannetta in *Falstaff* at Denver's Central City Opera (1972). She appeared with the Minnesota Opera (1972–73); on Sept. 7, 1974, she made her debut at the N.Y. City Opera as Mimi, remaining on the company's roster until 1979; made her European debut as Susanna in *Le nozze di Figaro* at the Holland Festival (1974); later sang in various European opera centers. She made her Metropolitan Opera debut in N.Y. as Gretel on Dec. 24, 1979; also pursued a career as a concert artist. Her other roles include Rosina, Servilia, Violetta, Julietta, Micaela, and Massenet's Manon; she also created leading roles in Susa's *Transformations* (1973), Floyd's *Bilby's Doll* (1976), and Pasatieri's *Washington Square* (1976).

Malgoire, Jean-Claude, French oboist, conductor, and musicologist; b. Avignon, Nov. 25, 1940. He studied from 1957 to 1960 at the Paris Cons., where he won 1st prizes in the categories of oboe and chamber music; in 1968 he won the International Prize of Geneva for his performances as an oboist. In 1974 he founded La Grande Ecurie et La Chambre du Roy, with the avowed purpose of presenting early French music in historically authentic instrumentation; he toured with this ensemble in Europe, South America, Australia, and the U.S. He also appeared as a guest conductor, leading performances of rarely heard operas in Copenhagen, Stockholm, and London.

Malherbe, Charles (-Théodore), French writer on music and composer; b. Paris, April 21, 1853; d. Cormeilles, Eure, Oct. 5, 1911. First he studied law, and was admitted to the bar; but then took up music under A. Danhauser, A. Wormser, and J. Massenet. After a tour (as Danhauser's secretary) through Belgium, the Netherlands, and Switzerland in 1880–81 to inspect the music in the public schools, he settled in Paris; in 1896, was appointed assistant archivist to the Grand Opéra, succeeding Nuitter as archivist in 1899. He ed. *Le Ménestrel* and contributed to many leading reviews and musical journals. His collection of musical autographs, which he left to the Paris Cons., was one of the finest private collections in the world. With Saint-Saëns, he ed. an edition of the work of Rameau; also was ed., with Weingartner, of a complete edition of Berlioz's works. He composed 4 opéras-comiques; a ballet-pantomime, *Cendrillon;* chamber music; and piano pieces.
WRITINGS (all publ. in Paris): *L'Œuvre dramatique de Richard Wagner* (with A. Soubies; 1886); *Précis d'histoire de l'Opéra-Comique* (with A. Soubies; 1887); *Mélanges sur Richard Wagner* (with A. Soubies; 1891); *Histoire de l'Opéra-Comique: La seconde Salle Favart* (with A. Soubies; 2 vols., 1892–93); *Programmes et concerts* (1898); *Auber* (1911).

Malherbe, Edmond Paul Henri, French composer; b. Paris, Aug. 21, 1870; d. Corbeil-Essonnes, Seine-et-Oise, March 7, 1963. He studied at the Paris Cons. with Massenet and Fauré; in 1898, won the Premier Second Prix de Rome, and in 1899, the Deuxième Premier Grand Prix; won the Prix Trémont of the Académie des Beaux-Arts (1907, 1913, 1921); in 1950 he received the Grand Prix Musical of the City of Paris for the total of his works. A productive composer, he continued to write music in his 80s, but very few of his larger compositions were performed, and virtually none publ. He publ. *L'Harmonie du système musical actuel à demi-tons* (1920) and *Le Tiers-de-ton: Deux Systèmes: Tempéré et non-tempéré* (1900, 1950).
WORKS: Operas: *Madame Pierre* (1903; Paris, 1912); *L'Avare* (1907); *L'Emeute* (1911; Paris, 1912); *Cléanthis* (1912); *Anna Karénine* (1914); *Le Mariage forcé* (1924); *Néron* (1945); *L'Amour et Psyché,* lyric tragedy with ballet (1948; State Prize, 1950); *Monsieur de Pourceaugnac,* pantomime with Chorus (1930); a series of "tableaux symphoniques" after great paintings; 3 syms. (1948, 1956, 1957); Violin Concerto; Nonet; Sextet; many choruses, songs, and piano pieces.

Malibran, María (Felicità) (née **García**), famous Spanish mezzo-soprano, daughter of **Manuel (del Popolo Vicente Rodriguez) García;** b. Paris, March 24, 1808; d. Manchester, Sept. 23, 1836. She was taken to Naples, where she sang a child's part in Paër's *Agnese* (1814); studied voice with her father from the age of 15; also studied solfeggio with Panseron. She made her debut as Rosina in *Il Barbiere di Siviglia* at the King's Theatre in London (June 7, 1825); then went to N.Y., where she sang in the same opera in her family's season at the Park Theatre, which commenced on Nov. 29, 1825. She became a popular favorite, singing in *Otello, Tancredi, La Cenerentola, Don Giovanni,* and the 2 operas written for her by her father, *L'Amante astuto* and *La Figlia dell'aria.* She married the French merchant François Eugène Malibran, but he soon became bankrupt, and she returned to Europe without him in 1827. Malibran made her Paris debut as Semiramide at the Théâtre-Italien (April 8, 1828); then alternated her appearances in Paris and London during the 1829–32 seasons. She subsequently went to Italy, singing in Bologna (1832) and Naples (1833); made her debut at Milan's La Scala as Norma (March 29, 1836). She met the violinist Charles de Bériot in 1829; they lived together until her marriage to Malibran was annulled in 1836, and then were married that same year. Malibran suffered serious injuries when thrown from her horse in 1836; since she was pregnant, complications developed and she lost her life. Her voice was of extraordinary compass, but the medium register had several "dead" tones. She was also a good pianist, and composed numerous nocturnes, romances, and chansonnettes, publ. in album form as *Dernières pensées*.

BIBL.: I. Nathan, *The Life of Mme. M. M. de Bériot* (London, 1836); Comtesse Merlin, *Loisirs d'une femme de monde* (Paris, 1838; Eng. tr., London, 1844; more romantic than trustworthy); E. Legouvé, "M. M.," *Études et souvenirs de théâtre* (Paris, 1880); E. Heron-Allen, "A Contribution towards an Accurate Biography of Ch. de Bériot and M. M.," *De fidiculis opuscula*, 6 (1894); A. Pougin, *M. M.: Histoire d'une cantatrice* (Paris, 1911; Eng. tr., London, 1911); J.-G. Prod'homme, "La Fayette and M. M.," *Chesterian* (Sept. 1919); L. Héritte-Viardot, *Une Famille de grands musiciens* (1923); C. Engel, "Again La Fayette and M. M.," *Chesterian* (Jan.–Feb. 1925); "6 Unpublished Letters from La Fayette to M. M.," ibid. (March–April 1925); A. Flament, *Une Étoile en 1830: La M.* (Paris, 1928); P. Crump, *Musset and M.* (Cambridge, 1932); P. Larionoff, *M. M. e i suoi tempi* (Florence, 1935); D. Bielli, *M. M.* (1936); A. Flament, *L'Enchanteresse errante, La M.* (Paris, 1937); S. Desternes and H. Chandet, *La M. et Pauline Viardot* (Paris, 1969); C. de Reparaz, *M. M.* (Madrid, 1976); H. Bushnell, *M. M.: A Biography of the Singer* (University Park, 1979); R. Giazotto, *M. M. (1808–1836): Una vita nei nomi di Rossini e Bellini* (Turin, 1986); A. Fitzlyon, *M. M.: Diva of the Romantic Age* (London, 1987).

Malipiero, Francesco, Italian composer, grandfather of **Gian Francesco Malipiero;** b. Rovigio, Jan. 9, 1824; d. Venice, May 12, 1887. He studied with Melchiore Balbi at the Liceo Musicale in Venice. At the age of 18 he wrote an opera, *Giovanna di Napoli*, which was produced with signal success; Rossini praised it. Other operas were *Attila* (Venice, Nov. 15, 1845; renamed *Ildegonda di Borgogna*); *Alberigo da Romano* (Venice, Dec. 26, 1846; his best); *Fernando Cortez* (Venice, Feb. 18, 1851).

Malipiero, Gian Francesco, eminent Italian composer and teacher, grandson of **Francesco** and uncle of **Riccardo Malipiero;** b. Venice, March 18, 1882; d. Treviso, near Venice, Aug. 1, 1973. His father, Luigi Malipiero, was a pianist and conductor. In 1898 Malipiero enrolled at the Vienna Cons. as a violin student; in 1899 he returned to Venice, where he studied at the Liceo Musicale Benedetto Marcello with Marco Bossi, whom he followed to Bologna in 1904, and took a diploma in composition at the Liceo Musicale G.B. Martini that same year; subsequently worked as amanuensis to Smareglia, gaining valuable experience in orchestration. He studied briefly with Bruch in Berlin (1908); later went to Paris (1913), where he absorbed the techniques of musical Impressionism, cultivating parallel chord formations and amplified tonal harmonies with characteristic added sixths, ninths, and elevenths. However, his own style of composition was determined by the polyphonic practices of the Italian Baroque. In 1921 Malipiero returned to Italy; was a prof. of composition at the Parma Cons. (1921–23); afterwards lived mostly in Asolo, near Venice. He was made prof. of composition at the Liceo Musicale Benedetto Marcello in Venice (1932), continuing there when it became the Cons. (1940); was its director (1939–52). He ed. a complete edition of the works of Monteverdi (16 vols., Bologna and Vienna, 1926–42) and many works by Vivaldi, as well as works by other Italian composers. He was made a member of the National Inst. of Arts and Letters in N.Y. in 1949, the Royal Flemish Academy in Brussels in 1952, the Institut de France in 1954, and the Akademie der Künste in West Berlin in 1967.

WORKS: OPERAS: *Canossa* (1911–12; Rome, Jan. 24, 1914; destroyed); *Sogno d'un tramonto d'autunno* (1913; concert perf., RAI, Milan, Oct. 4, 1963); *L'Orfeide*, in 3 parts: *La morte delle maschere, 7 canzoni,* and *Orfeo* (1918–22; 1st complete perf., Düsseldorf, Nov. 5, 1925; *7 canzoni* [Paris, July 10, 1920] is often perf. separately); *3 commedie goldoniane: La bottega da caffè, Sior Todaro Brontolon,* and *Le baruffe chiozzotte* (1920–22; 1st complete perf., Darmstadt, March 24, 1926); *Filomela*

e l'Infatuato (1924–25; Prague, March 31, 1928); *Merlino, Maestro d'organi* (1926–27; Rome Radio, Aug. 1, 1934); *Il mistero di Venezia*, in 3 parts: *Le aquile di aquileia, Il finto Arlecchino,* and *I corvi di San Marco* (1925–28; 1st complete perf., Coburg, Dec. 15, 1932); *Torneo notturno* (1929; Munich, May 15, 1931); *Il festino* (1930; Turin Radio, Nov. 6, 1937); *La favola del figlio cambiato* (1932–33; in German, Braunschweig, Jan. 13, 1934); *Giulio Cesare* (1934–35; Genoa, Feb. 8, 1936); *Antonio e Cleopatra* (1936–37; Florence, May 4, 1938); *Ecuba* (1939; Rome, Jan. 11, 1941); *La vita è sogno* (1940; Breslau, June 30, 1943); *I capricci di Callot* (Rome, Oct. 24, 1942); *L'allegra brigata* (1943; Milan, May 4, 1950); *Mondi celesti e infernali* (1948–49; RAI, Turin, Jan. 12, 1950; 1st stage perf., Venice, Feb. 2, 1961); *Il Figliuol prodigo* (1952; RAI, Jan. 25, 1953; 1st stage perf., Florence May Festival, May 14, 1957); *Donna Urraca* (Bergamo, Oct. 2, 1954); *Il capitan Spavento* (1954–55; Naples, March 16, 1963); *Venere prigioniera* (1955; Florence May Festival, May 14, 1957); *Rappresentazione e festa del Carnasciale e della Quaresima* (1961; concert perf., Venice, April 20, 1962; 1st stage perf., Venice, Jan. 20, 1970); *Don Giovanni*, after Pushkin (1962; Naples, Oct. 22, 1963); *Le metamorfosi di Bonaventura* (1963–65; Venice, Sept. 4, 1966); *Don Tartufo bacchettone* (1966; Venice, Jan. 20, 1970); *Il marescalco* (1960–68; Treviso, Oct. 22, 1969); *Gli Eroi di Bonaventura* (1968; Milan, Feb. 7, 1969); *L'Iscariota* (1970; Siena, Aug. 28, 1971); *Uno dei dieci* (1970; Siena, Aug. 28, 1971).

BALLETS: *Pantea* (1917–19; Venice, Sept. 6, 1932); *La mascherata delle principesse prigioniere* (1919; Brussels, Oct. 19, 1924); *Stradivario* (1947–48; Florence, June 20, 1949); *Il mondo novo* (Rome, Dec. 16, 1951; rev. as *La lanterna magica*, 1955).

DIALOGHI: No. 1, *con M. de Falla,* for Orch.; No. 2 for 2 Pianos; No. 3, *con Jacopone da Todi,* for Voice and 2 Pianos; No. 4 for Wind Quintet; No. 5 for Viola and Orch.; No. 6 for Harpsichord and Orch.; No. 7 for 2 Pianos and Orch.; No. 8, *La morte di Socrate,* for Baritone and Small Orch. (all 1956–57).

OTHER WORKS FOR ORCH.: *Sinfonia degli eroi* (1905; lost); *Sinfonia del mare* (1906); *Sinfonie del silenzio e della morte* (1908); *Impressioni dal vero* in 3 parts (1st part, Milan, May 15, 1913; 2nd part, Rome, March 11, 1917; 3rd part, Amsterdam, Oct. 25, 1923); *Armenia*, on Armenian folk songs (1917); *Ditirambo tragico* (1917; London, Oct. 11, 1919); *Pause del silenzio* in 2 parts (1st part, 1917; Rome, Jan. 27, 1918; 2nd part, 1925–26; Philadelphia, April 1, 1927); *Per una favola cavalleresca* (1920; Rome, Feb. 13, 1921); *Oriente immaginario* for Chamber Orch. (Paris, Dec. 23, 1920); *Variazioni senza tema* for Piano and Orch. (1923; Prague, May 19, 1925); *L'esilio dell'eroe*, symphonic suite (1930); *Concerti per orchestra* (1931; Philadelphia, Jan. 29, 1932); *Inni* (Rome, April 6, 1933); 2 violin concertos: No. 1 (1932; Amsterdam, March 5, 1933) and No. 2 (1963; Venice, Sept. 14, 1965); *7 invenzioni* (1932; Rome, Dec. 24, 1933); *4 invenzioni* (1932; Dresden, Nov. 11, 1936); 11 numbered syms.: No. 1 (1933; Florence, April 2, 1934); No. 2, *Elegiaca* (1936; Seattle, Jan. 25, 1937); No. 3, *Delle campane* (Florence, Nov. 4, 1945); No. 4, *In Memoriam* (1946; Boston, Feb. 27, 1948; dedicated to the memory of Natalie Koussevitzky); No. 5, *Concertante, in eco,* for 2 Pianos and Orch. (London, Nov. 3, 1947); No. 6, *Degli archi,* for Strings (1947; Basel, Feb. 11, 1949); No. 7, *Delle canzoni* (1948; Milan, Nov. 3, 1949); No. 8, *Symphonia brevis* (1964); No. 9, *Dell'ahimè* (Warsaw, Sept. 21, 1966); No. 10, *Atropo* (1967); No. 11, *Delle cornamuse* (1969); 6 piano concertos: No. 1 (1934; Rome, April 3, 1935); No. 2 (1937; Duisburg, March 6, 1939); No. 3 (1948; Louisville, Ky., March 8, 1949); No. 4 (1950; RAI, Turin, Jan. 28, 1951); No. 5 (1958); No. 6, *Delle macchine* (1964; Rome, Feb. 5, 1966); Cello Concerto (1937; Belgrade, Jan. 31, 1939); *Concerto a 3* for Violin, Cello, Piano, and Orch. (1938; Florence, April 9, 1939); *Sinfonia in un tempo* (1950; Rome, March 21, 1951); *Sinfonia dello zodiaco* (1951; Lausanne, Jan. 23, 1952); *Passacaglie* (1952); *Fantasie di ogni giorni* (Fantasies of Every Day; 1953; Louisville, Nov.

17, 1954); *Elegy-Capriccio* (1953); 4 *Fantasie concertanti* (all 1954): No. 1 for String Orch.; No. 2 for Violin and Orch.; No. 3 for Cello and Orch.; No. 4 for Piano and Orch.; Concerto for 2 Pianos and Orch. (Besançon Festival, Sept. 11, 1957); *Notturno di canti e ballo* (1957); *Serenissima* for Saxophone and Orch. (1961); *Sinfonia per Antigenida* (1962); Flute Concerto (1968).

OTHER VOCAL: *San Francesco d'Assisi,* mystery for Soli, Chorus, and Orch. (1920; N.Y., March 29, 1922); *La Principessa Ulalia,* cantata (1924; N.Y., Feb. 19, 1927); *La cena* for Soli, Chorus, and Orch. (1927; Rochester, N.Y., April 25, 1929); *Il commiato* for Baritone and Orch. (1934); *La Passione* for Soli, Chorus, and Orch. (Rome, Dec. 15, 1935); *De Profundis* for Solo Voice, Viola, Bass Drum, and Piano (1937); *Missa pro mortuis* for Solo Baritone, Chorus, and Orch. (Rome, Dec. 18, 1938); 4 *vecchie canzoni* for Solo Voice and 7 Instruments (1940; Washington, D.C., April 12, 1941); *Santa Eufrosina,* mystery for Soli, Chorus, and Orch. (Rome, Dec. 6, 1942); *Universa Universis* for Male Chorus and Chamber Orch. (1942; Liviano, April 11, 1943); *Vergilii Aeneis,* heroic sym. for 7 Soli, Chorus, and Orch. (1943–44; Turin, June 21, 1946; scenic version, Venice, Jan. 6, 1958); *Le 7 allegrezze d'amore* for Solo Voice and 14 Instruments (Milan, Dec. 4, 1945); *La Terra* for Chorus and Orch. (1946; Cambridge, Mass., May 2, 1947, with Organ); *I 7 peccati mortali* for Chorus and Orch. (1946; Monteceneri, Nov. 20, 1949); *Mondi celesti* for Solo Voice and 10 Instruments (1948; Capri, Feb. 3, 1949); *La festa de la Sensa* for Baritone, Chorus, and Orch. (1948; Brussels Radio, July 2, 1954); 5 *favole* for Solo Voice and Small Orch. (Washington, D.C., Oct. 30, 1950); *Passer mortuus est* for a cappella Chorus (Pittsburgh, Nov. 24, 1952); *Magister Josephus* for 4 Voices and Small Orch. (1957); *Preludio e Morte di Macbeth* for Baritone and Orch. (1958); *L'asino d'oro* for Baritone and Orch., after Apuleius (1959); *Concerto di concerti ovvero Dell'uom malcontento* for Baritone, Concertante Violin, and Orch. (1960); *Abracadabra* for Baritone and Orch. (1962); *Ave Phoebe, dum queror* for Chorus and 20 Instruments (1964); *L'Aredodese* for Reciter, Chorus, and Orch. (1967).

OTHER CHAMBER: 8 string quartets: No. 1, *Rispetti e Strombotti* (1920); No. 2, *Stornelli e Ballate* (1923); No. 3, *Cantari alla madrigalesca* (1930; also for String Orch.); No. 4 (1934); No. 5, *Dei capricci* (1940); No. 6, *L'arca di Noè* (1947); No. 7 (1950); No. 8, *Per Elisabetta* (1964); *Ricercari* for 11 Instruments (Washington, D.C., Oct. 7, 1926); *Ritrovari* for 11 Instruments (1926; Gardone, Oct. 26, 1929); *Sonata a 3* for Piano Trio (1927); *Epodi e giambi* for Violin, Viola, Oboe, and Bassoon (1932); *Sonata a 5* for Flute, Violin, Viola, Cello, and Harp (1934); Cello Sonatina (1942); *Sonata a 4* for 4 Winds (1954); *Serenata mattutini* for 10 Instruments (1959); *Serenata* for Bassoon and 10 Instruments (1961); *Macchine* for 14 Instruments (1963); *Endecatode,* chamber sym. for 14 Instruments and Percussion (1966; Hanover, N.H., July 2, 1967).

OTHER WORKS FOR PIANO: 6 *morceaux* (1905); *Bizzarrie luminose dell'alba, del meriggio e della notte* (1908); *Poemetti lunari* (1910); *Preludi autunnali* (1914); *Poemi asolani* (1916); *Barlumi* (1917); *Risonanze* (1918); *Maschere che passano* (1918); 3 *omaggi* (1920); *Omaggio a Claude Debussy* (1920); *Cavalcate* (1921); *La siesta* (1921); *Il tarlo* (1922); *Pasqua di Risurrezione* (1924); *Preludi a una fuga* (1926); *Epitaffio* (1931); *Omaggio a Bach* (1932); *Preludi, ritmi e canti gregoriani* (1937); *Preludio e fuga* (1941); *Hortus conclusus* (1946); 5 *studi per domani* (1959).

WRITINGS: *L'orchestra* (Bologna, 1920; Eng. tr., 1920); *Teatro* (Bologna, 1920; 2nd ed., 1927); *Oreste e Pilade, ovvero "Le sorprese dell'amicizia"* (Parma, 1922); *I profeti di Babilonia* (Milan, 1924); *Claudio Monteverdi* (Milan, 1930); *La pietra del bando* (Venice, 1945); *Strawinsky* (Venice, 1945); *Anton Francesco Doni, musico* (Venice, 1946); *Così va lo mondo* (Milan, 1946); *L'armonioso labirinto (da Zarlino a Padre Martini, 1558–1774)* (Milan, 1946); *Antonio Vivaldi, il prete rosso* (Milan, 1958); *Il filo d'Arianna (saggi e fantasie)* (Turin, 1966); *Ti co mi e mi co ti (soliloqui di un veneziano)* (Milan, 1966); *Così parlò Claudio Monteverdi* (Milan, 1967); *Di palo in frasca*

(Milan, 1967); *Da Venezia lontan* (Milan, 1968); *Maschere della commedia d'arte* (Bologna, 1969).

BIBL.: F. Alfano, A. Casella, M. Castelnuovo-Tedesco et al., *M. e le sue "Sette canzoni"* (Rome, 1929); special issue of *La Rassegna Musicale,* XV (1942); F. Ballo, *"I 'Capricci' di Callot" di G.F. M.* (Milan, 1942); M. Bontempelli and R. Cumar, *G.F. M.* (Milan, 1942); F. D'Amico, *"G.F. M.," Melos,* XVII (1950); G. Scarpa, ed., *L'opera di G.F. M.* (Treviso, 1952); M. Labroca, *M., musicista veneziano* (Venice, 1957; 2nd ed., 1967); special issue of *Approdo Musicale,* 9 (Rome and Turin, 1960); special issue of *Musica d'Oggi,* new series, IV (Milan, 1961); F. Degrada, *"G.F. M. e la tradizione musicale italiana," Quadrivium,* XIV (1973); A. Gianuario, *G.F. M. e l'arte monteverdiana* (Florence, 1973); M. Messinis, ed., *Omaggio a M.* (Florence, 1977); M. Muraro, ed., *M.: Scittura e critica* (Florence, 1984).

Malipiero, Riccardo, Italian composer, nephew of **Gian Francesco Malipiero;** b. Milan, July 24, 1914. He studied piano and composition at the Milan and Turin conservatories (1930–37); completed studies with his uncle at the Liceo Musicale Benedetto Marcello in Venice (1937–39); traveled as a lecturer and pianist in Europe, South America, and the U.S.; was director of the Varese Liceo Musicale (1969–84). He adopted 12-tone composition in 1945.

WRITINGS: *La dannazione di Faust di Berlioz* (with B. dal Fabbro; Milan, 1946); *G.S. Bach* (Brescia, 1948); *C. Debussy* (Brescia, 1948; 2nd ed., 1958); *L'Enfant et les sortilèges, La Valse, Daphnis et Chloé de Ravel* (Milan, 1948); *Pelléas et Mélisande di Debussy* (Milan, 1949); *Le Martyre de Saint Sébastien* (Milan, 1951); *Guida alla dodecafonia* (Milan, 1961); *Musica ieri oggi* (with G. Severi; 6 vols., Rome, 1970).

WORKS: OPERAS: *Minnie la Candida* (Parma, Nov. 19, 1942); *La Donna è mobile,* opera buffa (1954; Milan, Feb. 22, 1957); television opera, *Battono alla Porta* (Italian Television, Feb. 12, 1962; stage version, Genoa, May 24, 1963). ORCH.: Piano Concerto (1937); 3 *Dances* (1937); 2 cello concertos (1938, 1957); *Balleto* (1939); *Piccolo concerto* for Piano and Orch. (1945); *Antico sole* for Soprano and Orch. (1947); *Cantata sacra* for Soprano, Chorus, and Orch. (1947); 3 syms.: No. 1 (1949); No. 2, *Sinfonia cantata,* for Baritone and Orch. (1956; N.Y., March 19, 1957); No. 3 (1959; Univ. of Florida, Miami, April 10, 1960); Violin Concerto (1952; Milan, Jan. 31, 1953); *Studi* (Venice Festival, Sept. 11, 1953); *Ouverture-Divertimento "del Ritorno"* (1953); Concerto for Piano and Chamber Orch. (1955); *Concerto breve* for Ballerina and Chamber Orch. (Venice Festival, Sept. 11, 1956); *Cantata di natale* for Soprano, Chorus, and Orch. (Milan, Dec. 21, 1959); Sonata for Oboe and Strings (1960); *Concerto per Dimitri* for Piano and Orch. (Venice Festival, April 27, 1961); *Nyktghersia* (1962); *Cadencias* (1964; Geneva Radio, Jan. 13, 1965); *Muttermusik* (Milan, Feb. 28, 1966); *Mirages* (1966; Milan, Feb. 6, 1970); *Carnet de notes* for Chamber Orch. (1967); *Rapsodia* for Violin and Orch. (1967); *Serenata per Alice Tully* for Chamber Orch. (1969; N.Y., March 10, 1970); *Monologo* for Female Voice and Strings (1969); Concerto for Piano Trio and Orch. (1971; Milan, Jan. 16, 1976); *Requiem 1975* (Florence, Nov. 6, 1976); *Go Placidly* for Baritone and Chamber Orch. (N.Y., Nov. 10, 1976); *Due pezzi sacri* (1976–77); *Canti* for Viola and Orch. (1978; Milan, May 17, 1982); *Divertimento* for Oboe, Bassoon, and Strings (1978; Milan, Jan. 14, 1979); *Preludio e rondò* (1979); *Composizione concertata* for English Horn, Oboe, Oboe d'Amore, and Strings (Turin, Oct. 9, 1982); *Notturno* for Cello and Chamber Orch. (1983; Milan, Jan. 29, 1984); *Racconto* (1985); *Ombre* for Chamber Orch. (1986). CHAMBER: *Musik I* for Cello and 9 Instruments (1938); 3 string quartets (1941, 1954, 1960); Violin Sonata (1956); Piano Quintet (1957); *Musica da camera* for Wind Quintet (1959); Oboe Sonata (1959); 6 *poesie di Dylan Thomas* for Soprano and 10 Instruments (1959); *Mosaico* for Wind and String Quintets (1961); *Preludio Adagio e Finale* for Soprano, 5 Percussionists, and Piano (1963); *In Time of Daffodils,* to poems by e.e. cummings, for Soprano, Baritone, and 7 Instrumentalists (Washington, D.C., Oct. 30,

1964); *Nuclei* for 2 Pianos and Percussion (1966); *Cassazione* for String Sextet (1967); Piano Trio (1968); *Giber Folia* for Clarinet and Piano (1973); *Winter Quintet* for Clarinet and String Quartet (1976); *Musica* for 4 Cellos (1979); *Diario* for Oboe and String Trio (1981); *Diario D'Agosto* for Piano, Clarinet, and Cello (1985); *Rinelcarlido*, duo for Oboe and Piano (1986). PIANO: *14 Inventions* (1938); *Musik* for 2 Pianos (1939); *Piccolo musica* (1941); *Invenzioni* (1949); *Costellazioni* (1965); *Le Rondini de Alessandro* (1971); *Diario secondo* (1985).

BIBL.: C. Sartori, *R. M.* (in Eng.; Milan, 1957); P. Franci et al., *Piccolo omaggio a R. M.* (Milan, 1964); C. Sartori and P. Santi, *Due tempi di R. M.* (Milan, 1964).

Maliponte, Adriana, Italian soprano; b. Brescia, Dec. 26, 1938. Her family moved to Mulhouse, and she studied at the Cons. there. She made her operatic debut as Mimi in *La Bohème* at the Teatro Nuovo, Milan, in 1958; also sang minor roles at La Scala; subsequently had engagements at the Paris Opéra and the Opéra-Comique. She made her American debut in Philadelphia in 1963; then sang in Chicago and Cincinnati. On March 19, 1971, she made her Metropolitan Opera debut in N.Y. as Mimi; returned there in 1985 to sing the role of Alice Ford.

Maliszewski, Witold, Polish composer and teacher; b. Mohylev-Podolsk, July 20, 1873; d. Zalesie, July 18, 1939. He studied piano in Warsaw and violin in Tiflis; then enrolled in the St. Petersburg Cons. in the class of Rimsky-Korsakov. He became director of the Odessa Cons. in 1908. He then went to Warsaw in 1921, where he later was director of the Chopin Music School (1925–27), head of the music dept. of the Ministry of Culture (1927–34), and prof. at the Cons. (1931–39); was also a founder of Warsaw's Chopin Inst. (1933). His most distinguished student was W. Lutoslawski. After following the Russian Romantic tradition in his works, he made use of Polish folk music in his compositions from 1921. He wrote 5 syms., ballets, sacred works, chamber music, piano pieces, and songs.

BIBL.: E. Wrocki, "W. M.: Rys życia i działalności artystycznej," *Śpiewak*, XI (1931).

Malkin, Jacques, Russian-American violinist and teacher, brother of **Joseph** and **Manfred Malkin;** b. Slobodka, near Odessa, Dec. 16, 1875; d. N.Y., Dec. 8, 1964. He studied in Odessa, and later enrolled at the Paris Cons.; from 1893 he played the viola d'amore in the Société des Instruments Anciens in Paris. In 1918 he went to America and settled in N.Y. as a violin teacher; played in a trio with his brothers.

Malkin, Joseph, Russian-American cellist and teacher, brother of **Jacques** and **Manfred Malkin;** b. Propoisk, near Odessa, Sept. 24, 1879; d. N.Y., Sept. 1, 1969. After studying in Odessa, he went to Paris and studied cello at the Cons., graduating in 1902; then was 1st cellist of the Berlin Phil. (1902–8); toured America as a member of the Brussels Quartet. He remained in the U.S.; was 1st cellist of the Boston Sym. Orch. (1914–19) and of the Chicago Sym. Orch. (1919–22); played in a trio with his brothers; was founder-director of Boston's Malkin Cons. (1933–43). He publ. arrangements and studies for cello.

Malkin, Manfred, Russian-American pianist and teacher, brother of **Jacques** and **Joseph Malkin;** b. Odessa, Aug. 11, 1884; d. N.Y., Jan. 8, 1966. He studied at the Paris Cons.; in 1905 he went to the U.S.; established his own music school in N.Y. (1914–31); played in a trio with his brothers.

Malko, Nicolai (Nikolai Andreievich), eminent Russianborn American conductor; b. Brailov, May 4, 1883; d. Sydney, Australia, June 23, 1961. He studied philology at the Univ. of St. Petersburg, graduating in 1906; also studied composition and orchestration with Rimsky-Korsakov, Liadov, and Glazunov and conducting with N. Tcherepnin at the St. Petersburg Cons.; completed his studies with Mottl at Munich. Returning to Russia, he conducted opera in St. Petersburg; was conductor of the Leningrad Phil. (1926–28), with which he performed many new works by Soviet composers, including the premiere of Shostakovich's 1st Sym. In 1928 he left Russia; conducted

orchs. in Vienna, Buenos Aires, Prague, etc.; was particularly successful in Denmark, where he made frequent appearances, and established a conducting class; many Danish musicians became his pupils, including the King of Denmark, who was a talented amateur. In 1938 he visited the U.S. as a lecturer; also appeared as guest conductor with several American orchs.; became an American citizen on May 7, 1946. He subsequently conducted the Yorkshire Sym. Orch. in England (1954–55). In 1956 he was appointed resident conductor of the Sydney Sym. Orch. in Australia, where he established a fine tradition of orch. performance, striving above all for clarity and balance of sonorities. He publ. a manual, *The Conductor and His Baton* (Copenhagen, 1950), and a memoir, *A Certain Art* (N.Y., 1966); also composed various works, among them a Clarinet Concerto (Copenhagen, Sept. 27, 1952). The Danish Radio inaugurated in his honor a triennial Malko international competition for conductors.

Malling, Jørgen (Henrik), Danish organist, teacher, and composer; b. Copenhagen, Oct. 31, 1836; d. there, July 12, 1905. He studied with Gade; was 1st winner of the Ancher stipend in 1861; went to Paris and became enthusiastic over Chevé's system of vocal notation, which he tried (unsuccessfully) to introduce in various cities in Scandinavia and Russia; was an organist in Svendborg (1869–72); lived in Vienna (1879–82) and Munich (1882–95); returned to Copenhagen in 1901; was active there as a teacher and composer. He wrote the operas *Lisenka* and *Frithjof*; a cantata, *Küvala*; String Quartet; Piano Trio; numerous piano pieces and songs.

Malling, Otto (Valdemar), Danish organist, conductor, and composer; b. Copenhagen, June 1, 1848; d. there, Oct. 5, 1915. He studied with Gade, J.P.E. Hartmann, and Matthison-Hansen at the Copenhagen Cons. (1869–71); conducted the Student's Choral Soc. (1875–84); was an organist at various churches in Copenhagen (1878–1901); also conductor of the Concert Soc. there (1874–93); in 1885, was appointed instructor of music theory at the Copenhagen Cons.; in 1899, became its director. He wrote a treatise on instrumentation (1894).

WORKS: Sym. (1884); Piano Concerto (1890); ballet, *Askepot* (Cinderella; 1908; Copenhagen, Sept. 25, 1910); Piano Trio (1889); Piano Quintet (1889); String Octet (1893); Violin Sonata (1894); Piano Quartet (1903); choral works; pieces for organ and for piano; songs.

Mallinger, Mathilde (née **Lichtenegger**), noted Croatian soprano and teacher; b. Agram, Feb. 17, 1847; d. Berlin, April 19, 1920. She studied in Prague and Vienna; made her debut in Munich as Norma (Oct. 4, 1866), and created the role of Eva in *Die Meistersinger von Nürnberg* there (June 21, 1868); made her 1st appearance at the Berlin Royal Opera as Elsa in *Lohengrin* (April 6, 1869), remaining there until her retirement in 1882; sang in the U.S. (1873) and in Russia; taught voice in Prague (1890–95) and then in Berlin. She was the teacher of Lotte Lehmann. She was married to Baron von Schimmelpfennig of Berlin.

Malm, William P(aul), distinguished American ethnomusicologist; b. La Grange, Ill., March 6, 1928. He studied composition at Northwestern Univ. (B.M., 1949; M.M., 1950) and ethnomusicology at the Univ. of Calif. at Los Angeles (Ph.D., 1959, with the diss. *Japanese Nagauta Music*). He taught at the Univ. of Illinois (1950), the U.S. Naval School of Music in Washington, D.C. (1951–53), and at the Univ. of Calif. at Los Angeles (1958–60); was assistant prof. (1960–63), associate prof. (1963–66), and prof. (from 1966) at the Univ. of Michigan. He was president of the Soc. for Ethnomusicology (1978–80). He received many honors and awards for his research on Asian studies; lectured widely in the U.S. and abroad; was a Distinguished Visiting Prof. at Baylor Univ. (1977), the Ernst Bloch Prof. of Music at the Univ. of Calif. at Berkeley (1981), a Distinguished Visiting Prof. at the Univ. of Iowa (1982), and a research fellow at the National Univ. of Australia (1987). He contributed many articles to learned journals and reference books.

WRITINGS: *Japanese Music and Musical Instruments* (Tokyo,

1959); *Nagauta: The Heart of Kabuki Music* (Tokyo, 1963); *Music Cultures of the Pacific, the Near East and Asia* (Englewood Cliffs, N.J., 1967; 2nd ed., 1977); ed., with J. Crump, *Chinese and Japanese Music Drama* (Ann Arbor, 1975); with J. Brandon and D. Shively, *Studies in Kabuki* (Honolulu, 1977); *Six Hidden Views of Japanese Music* (Berkeley, 1985).

Malotte, Albert Hay, American organist and composer; b. Philadelphia, May 19, 1895; d. Los Angeles, Nov. 16, 1964. He was a chorister at St. James Episcopal Church; studied with W.S. Stansfield, and later in Paris with Georges Jacob; then moved to Hollywood, where he became a member of the music staff of the Walt Disney Studios; composed the scores for some of Disney's "Silly Symphonies" and "Ferdinand, the Bull." He was the composer of the enormously popular setting *The Lord's Prayer* (1935); he also set to music the 23rd Psalm and other religious texts.

Malovec, Jozef, Slovak composer; b. Hurbanovo, March 24, 1933. He studied with A. Moyzes at the High School of Musical Arts in Bratislava (1951–53) and with Sommer and Řídký at the Prague Academy of Music (1953–57); subsequently was active with the Bratislava Radio.
    WORKS: *Scherzo* for Orch. (1956); *3 Studies* for String Quartet (1962); *Little Chamber Music* for Flute, Clarinet, Trumpet, Vibraphone, Viola, Cello, and Percussion (1964); *Kryptogram* for Piano, Bass Clarinet, and Percussion (1965); *Suite* for Strings and Harpsichord (1974); *5 National Songs* for Alto and Orch. (1975); *Prelude and Burlesque* for Wind Quintet (1976); electronic pieces: *Orthogenesis* (1967); *Punctum Alpha* (1968); *Theorem* (1971).

Malten (real name, **Müller**), **Therese,** German soprano; b. Insterburg, June 21, 1855; d. Neuzschieren, near Dresden, Jan. 2, 1930. She studied with Gustav Engel in Berlin; made her operatic debut as Pamina at the Dresden Court Opera in 1873, and remained for some 30 years a principal singer on its roster; also sang in Berlin, Vienna, and London. Wagner heard her and engaged her as Kundry at the premiere of *Parsifal* at Bayreuth in 1882; she continued to sing there until 1894. She was particularly renowned as a Wagnerian, excelling as Elsa, Elisabeth, Eva, Kundry, and Isolde.

Malvezzi, Cristofano, Italian composer and organist; b. Lucca (baptized), June 28, 1547; d. Florence, Jan. 22, 1599. In 1551 he settled in Florence, where he became canonico supernumerario at S. Lorenzo in 1562; after serving as organist at S. Trinità (1565–70), and as maestro di cappella at the Cathedral and at S. Giovanni Battista there (1573–74), he returned to S. Lorenzo as organist in succession to his father. Among his pupils was Peri. He wrote music for Florentine intermedi, instrumental ricercares (1577), and 3 vols. of madrigals (1583–90). His brother, **Alberigo Malvezzi** (b. probably in Lucca, c.1550; d. Florence, Dec. 29, 1615), was also a composer and organist.

Mamangakis, Nikos, Greek composer; b. Rethymnon, Crete, March 3, 1929. He studied at the Hellikon Cons. in Athens (1947–53); then composition with Carl Orff and Harald Genzmer at the Hochschule für Musik in Munich (1957–61) and electronic music at the Siemens Studio in Munich (1961–64). His works reflect modern quasi-mathematical procedures, with numerical transformations determining pitch, rhythm, and form.
    WORKS: *Music for 4 Protagonists* for 4 Voices and 10 Instrumentalists, on a text by Kazantzakis (1959–60); *Constructions* for Flute and Percussion (1959–60); *Combinations* for Solo Percussionist and Orch. (1961); *Speech Symbols* for Soprano, Bass, and Orch. (1961–62); "Cycle of Numbers": No. 1, *Monologue,* for Cello (1962); No. 2, *Antagonisms,* for Cello and 1 Percussionist moving in an arc along the stage (1963); No. 3, *Trittys* (Triad), for Guitar, 2 Double Basses, Santouri, and Percussion (1966); and No. 4, *Tetraktys,* for String Quartet (1963–66); *Kassandra* for Soprano and 6 Performers (1963); *Erotokritos,* ballad for 3 Voices and 5 Instruments in an old style (1964); *Ploutos,* popular opera after Aristophanes (1966);

Theama-Akroama, visual-auditive event (happening) for Actor, Dancer, Painter, Singer, and 8 Instruments (Athens, April 3, 1967); *Scenario for 2 Improvised Art Critics* for Voice, Instruments, and Tape (1968); *Antinomies* for Solo Voice, Flute, Electric Double Bass, 2 Harps, 4 Cellos, 2 Percussionists, Hammond Organ, 4 Basses, and 4 Sopranos (Athens, Dec. 18, 1968); *Bolivar,* folk cantata in pop-art style (1968); *The Bacchants,* electronic ballet (1969); *Parastasis* for various Flutes, Voice, and Tape (1969); *Askesis* for Cello (1969–70); *Perilepsis* for Flute (1970); *Erophili,* popular opera (1970); *Anarchia* for Solo Percussion and Orch. (Donaueschingen, Oct. 16, 1971); *Penthima,* in memory of Jani Christou, for Guitar (1970–71); *Monologue II* for Violin and Tape (1971); *Kykeon* for several Solo Instruments (1972); *Olophyrmos* for Magnetic Tape (1973).

Mamiya, Michio, Japanese composer; b. Asahikawa, Hokkaido, June 29, 1929. He studied with Ikenouchi at the Music School in Tokyo; upon graduation, he devoted himself mainly to the cultivation of national Japanese music in modern forms, with inventive uses of dissonant counterpoint and coloristic instrumentation.
    WORKS: STAGE: *Mukashi banashi hitokai Tarobê* (A Fable from Olden Times about Tarobê, the Slave Dealer), opera (1959); *Narukami,* opera (1974); oratorio, *15 June 1960,* homage to an activist Japanese student killed during the demonstration against the renewal of the Japanese-American defense treaty (1961); musical, *Elmer's Adventure* (Tokyo Radio, Aug. 28, 1967). ORCH.: 2 piano concertos (1954, 1970); Sym. (1955); Violin Concerto (Tokyo, June 24, 1959); Cello Concerto (1975); Concerto (1978); chamber music, including Quartet for Japanese Instruments (1962); Sonata for Violin Solo (1971); and Nonet (1972); choral works.

Mamlok, Ursula, German-born American composer and teacher; b. Berlin, Feb. 1, 1928. She studied piano and composition in childhood in Berlin; after her family went to Ecuador, she continued her training there and then emigrated to the U.S., settling in N.Y. in 1941. In 1945 she became a naturalized U.S. citizen. She studied with Szell at the Mannes College of Music (1942–46) and with Giannini at the Manhattan School of Music (M.M., 1958); also took instruction from Wolpe, Sessions, Steuermann, and Shapey. She taught at N.Y. Univ. (1967–76), Kingsborough Community College (1972–75), and the Manhattan School of Music (from 1974). In 1989 she received the Walter Hinrichsen Award of the American Academy and Inst. of Arts and Letters. Her works reveal a fine craftsmanship, lyricism, and wit; in a number of her works she utilizes serial techniques.
    WORKS: ORCH.: Concerto for Strings (1950); *Grasshoppers: 6 Humoresques* (1957); Oboe Concerto (1974; also for Oboe, 2 Pianos, and Percussion); Concertino for Wind Quintet, 2 Percussion, and String Orch. (1987). CHAMBER: Woodwind Quintet (1956); *Variations* for Flute (1961); String Quartet (1962) *Concert Piece for 4* for Flute, Oboe, Percussion, and Viola (1964); *Capriccios* for Oboe and Piano (1968); *Variations and Interludes* for Percussion Quartet (1971); Sextet for Flute, Clarinet, Bass Clarinet, Piano, Cello, and Double Bass (1978); *Festive Sounds* for Woodwind Quintet (1978); *When Summer Sang* for Flute, Clarinet, Piano, Violin, and Cello (1980); String Quintet (1981); *From My Garden* for Violin or Viola (1983); *Alarina* for Recorder or Flute, Clarinet, Bassoon, Violin, and Cello (1985); *Bagatelles* for Clarinet, Violin, and Cello (1988); *Rhapsody,* trio for Clarinet, Viola, and Piano (1989). VOCAL: *Stray Birds* for Soprano, Flute, and Cello (1963); *Haiku Settings* for Soprano and Flute (1967); *Der Andreas Garten* for Mezzo-soprano, Flute, Alto Flute, and Harp (N.Y., Oct. 5, 1987). TAPE: *Sonar Trajectory* (1966). PIANO: Various didactic pieces, including *6 Recital Pieces for Children* (1983) and *4 Recital Pieces for Young Pianists* (1983).

Mamoulian, Rouben, Russian-born director of operas, musicals, and films; b. Tiflis, Oct. 8, 1897; d. Los Angeles, Dec. 4, 1987. He showed an early interest in theater, founding a drama studio in his native city in 1918; in 1920 he toured England with the Russian Repertory Theater. Later he directed several hit plays in London during a 3-year span. In 1923 he emigrated to the U.S. to become director of operas and operettas at the George Eastman Theater in Rochester, N.Y. He was an innovator of both stage and screen, using an imaginative and bold blend of all the components of film with the new dimension of sound. He directed the noted early "talkie" *Applause* in 1929, as well as the film version of Gershwin's *Porgy and Bess* in 1935. He was the 1st director to use a mobile camera in a sound movie, and among the 1st to use a multiple-channel sound track. He directed the film of the Rodgers and Hammerstein musical *Oklahoma!* (1955), which was the 1st musical to utilize songs and dance as an integral part of the dramatic flow of the plot.

Mana-Zucca (real name, **Gizella Augusta Zuckermann**), American pianist, singer, and composer; b. N.Y., Dec. 25, 1887; d. Miami Beach, March 8, 1981. She studied piano with Alexander Lambert in N.Y.; then went to Europe, where she took some lessons with Leopold Godowsky and Busoni in Berlin. Upon her return to the U.S., she was exhibited as a piano prodigy. In 1916 she changed her name by juggling around the syllables of her real last name and dropping her 1st name altogether. She was soloist in her own Piano Concerto in N.Y. on Aug. 20, 1919; her Violin Concerto, op. 224, was performed in N.Y. on Dec. 9, 1955. She further wrote 2 operas, *Hypatia* and *The Queue of Ki-Lu*; a ballet, *The Wedding of the Butterflies*; and a number of unpretentious orch. pieces, such as *Frolic for Strings, Fugato Humoresque, Bickerings*, and *Havana Nights*. She publ., under the title *My Musical Calendar*, a collection of 366 piano pieces, one to be played every day, with the supernumerary opus to account for leap years. But she attained real success with her lyrically soaring songs, most of them to her own words, with such appealing titles as *I Love Life* and *There's Joy in My Heart*. In 1940 she settled in Florida.

Manchester, Melissa (Toni), American songwriter and singer of popular music; b. N.Y., Feb. 15, 1951. She studied at the High School of Performing Arts in N.Y.; then launched a career as a pop vocalist; made numerous appearances on television. Her record albums brought her a number of awards and citations, including a Grammy Award as best female pop vocalist in 1982 for her *You Should See How She Talks about You*.

Manchicourt, Pierre de, Franco-Flemish composer; b. Bethune, c.1510; d. Madrid, Oct. 5, 1564. He was a choirboy at Arras Cathedral (1525); after serving as director of the choir at Tours Cathedral (1539) and as master of the choirboys and maître de chapelle at Tournai Cathedral (1545), he was made a canon of Arras Cathedral in 1556; from 1559 he was master of Philip II's Flemish chapel in Madrid. He composed many fine masses, motets, and Parisian chansons.

Mancinelli, Luigi, distinguished Italian conductor and composer; b. Orvieto, Feb. 5, 1848; d. Rome, Feb. 2, 1921. He studied organ and cello with his brother, Marino; then was a cellist in the Orvieto cappella and the orch. of the Teatro della Pergola in Florence; also studied cello with Sbolà and composition with Mabellini in Florence; then was 1st cellist and maestro concertatore at the Teatro Morlacchi in Perugia; in 1874 he made his conducting debut there in *Aida* after the regular conductor was unable to lead the performance owing to a temporarily inebriated condition. He then was called to Rome, where he was conductor of the Teatro Apollo from 1874 to 1881; subsequently he served as director of the Bologna Cons. On June 18, 1886, he made his London debut conducting a concert performance; in 1887 he conducted at Drury Lane; from 1888 to 1905 he was chief conductor at Covent Garden; from 1887 to 1893 he conducted opera in Madrid. He joined the roster of the Metropolitan Opera in N.Y. in 1893, and continued to conduct there until 1903. On May 25, 1908, he led the 1st performance at the newly opened Teatro Colón in Buenos Aires; returned there in 1909, 1910, and 1913. He enjoyed a fine reputation as a competent, dependable, and

resourceful opera conductor; naturally, he excelled in the Italian repertoire, but he also conducted Wagner's operas, albeit in dubious Italian translation. From his experience as an opera conductor, he learned the art of composing for the theater; his operas are indeed most effective; of these, *Ero e Leandro* became a favorite.

Works: operas: *Isora de Provenza* (Bologna, Oct. 2, 1884); *Tizianello* (Rome, June 20, 1895); *Ero e Leandro* (Norwich Festival, Oct. 8, 1896); *Paolo e Francesca* (Bologna, Nov. 11, 1907); *Sogno di una notte d'estate*, after Shakespeare's *Midsummer Night's Dream* (not produced). **oratorios:** *Isaia* (Norwich, Oct. 13, 1887); *Santa Agnese* (Norwich, Oct. 27, 1905); cinematic cantata, *Giuliano l'Apostata* (Rome, 1920); also *Intermezzi sinfonici* for *Cleopatra* by Cossa, a symphonic suite.
Bibl.: L. Arnedo, *L. M. y su opera Hero y Leandro* (Madrid, 1898); G. Orefice, *L. M.* (Rome, 1921); L. Silvestri, *L. M.; Direttore e compositore* (Milan, 1966).

Mancini, Francesco, Italian composer and teacher; b. Naples, Jan. 16, 1672; d. there, Sept. 22, 1737. He became an organ student at the Cons. della Pietà dei Turchini in Naples (1688), where he later was organist (c.1694–1702). He held the post of 1st organist at the royal chapel in Naples (1704–7); subsequently was its director (1707–8), assistant director (1708–25), and again director (1725–37). He was also director of the Cons. di S. Maria di Loreto in Naples from 1720 until he suffered a stroke in 1735. He was held in high regard as a composer of operas and cantatas, and as a teacher.
Works (all 1st perf. in Naples unless otherwise given): **operas:** *Ariovisto* (Nov. 15, 1702); *Lucio Silla* (Jan. 1703); *La constanza nell'honore* (June 1704); *Gli amanti generosi* (1705); *La Serva favorita* (1705); *Alessandro il Grande in Sidone* (1706); *Turno Aricino* (1708); *Engelberta o sia La forza dell'innocenza* (Nov. 4, 1709; in collaboration with A. Orefici); *Hydaspe (Idaspe) fedele* (London, April 3, 1710); *Mario fuggitivo* (1710); *Selim re d'Ormuz* (Feb. 26, 1712); *Artaserse re di Persia* (Oct. 18, 1713); *Il Gran Mogol* (Dec. 26, 1713); *Il Vincislao* (Dec. 26, 1714); *Alessandro Severo* (Rome, Carnival 1718); *La fortezza al cimento* (1721); *Il Trajano* (Jan. 1723); *Orontea* (Carnival 1729); *Alessandro nelle Indie* (1732); *Don Aspremo* (1733); *Il Demofoonte* (1735; Act 1 by D. Sarro, Act 2 by Mancini, Act 3 by L. Leo); also several intermezzos, serenatas, and over 200 secular cantatas. His sacred music includes oratorios, masses, motets, cantatas, a Magnificat, and Psalms for Vespers. He also publ. *XII Solos* for Violin or Flute and Basso Continuo, *which Solos are Proper Lessons for the Harpsichord* (London, 1724; 2nd rev. ed., 1727, by F. Geminiani).
Bibl.: J. Wright, *The Secular Cantatas of F. M. (1672–1737)* (diss., N.Y. Univ., 1975).

Mancini, Henry, highly successful American composer, arranger, pianist, and conductor of popular music; b. Cleveland, April 16, 1924. He studied flute and piano in childhood; later received training from Max Adkins in Pittsburgh and attended the Juilliard Graduate School in N.Y. (1942). He worked as a pianist and arranger with Tex Beneke's orch. (1945–47); also studied composition with M. Castelnuovo-Tedesco, E. Krenek, and A. Sendrey in Los Angeles. He then was on the music staff of Universal-International film studios (1952–58), for which he wrote many scores. He also wrote for television, gaining success with his music for the "Peter Gunn" series (1958). His scores for the films *Breakfast at Tiffany's* (1961), which included the hit song *Moon River*, and *The Days of Wine and Roses* (1962) both won him Academy and Grammy awards. In later years he appeared widely as a guest conductor in concerts of popular fare with American orchs. He publ. *Sounds and Scores* (1962), a guide to orchestration. With G. Lees, he publ. his autobiography as *Did They Mention the Music?* (Chicago, 1989).
Works: orch.: *Beaver Valley '37*, suite (1978); over 70 film scores, including *Touch of Evil* (1958), *Breakfast at Tiffany's* (1961), *The Days of Wine and Roses* (1962), *Charade* (1963), *The Pink Panther* (1964), *Two for the Road* (1967), *The Molly Maguires* (1970), *The Night Visitor* (1971), *The White Dawn*

(1974), *10* (1979), *Victor-Victoria* (1982), and *Sunset* (1988); television scores: *Peter Gunn* (1958); *Mr. Lucky* (1960); *The Thorn Birds* (1983). See M. Okun, ed., *Henry Mancini Songbook* (1981).

Mandac, Evelyn (Lorenzana), Filipino soprano; b. Malaybalay, Mindanao, Aug. 16, 1945. She studied voice at the Univ. of the Philippines; then went to the U.S. and enrolled at Oberlin College and later at the Juilliard School of Music. She began her career in 1968 with a concert debut in Mobile, Ala.; then sang with opera companies in Washington, D.C., and San Francisco. On Dec. 19, 1975, she made her debut as Lauretta in *Gianni Schicchi* at the Metropolitan Opera in N.Y.

Mandel, Alan (Roger), gifted American pianist; b. N.Y., July 17, 1935. He began taking piano lessons with Hedy Spielter at the incredible underage of 3½, and continued under her pianistic care until he was 17. In 1953 he entered the class of Rosina Lhévinne at the Juilliard School of Music in N.Y. (B.S., 1956; M.S., 1957); later took private lessons with Leonard Shure (1957–60). In 1961 he obtained a Fulbright fellowship; went to Salzburg, where he studied advanced composition with Henze (diplomas in composition and piano, 1962); completed his training at the Accademia Monteverdi in Bolzano (diploma, 1963). He made his debut at N.Y.'s Town Hall in 1948. He taught piano at Pa. State Univ. (1963–66); then was head of the piano dept. at the American Univ. in Washington, D.C. (from 1966); also founded the Washington (D.C.) Music Ensemble (1980) with the aim of presenting modern music of different nations. As a pianist, he made numerous tours all over the globe. One of Mandel's chief accomplishments was the recording of the complete piano works of Charles Ives; he also recorded 40 piano works of Gottschalk and all the piano sonatas of Elie Siegmeister. Mandel's own compositions include a Piano Concerto (1950), a Sym. (1961), and a number of pieces for piano solo.

Mandelbaum, (Mayer) Joel, American composer; b. N.Y., Oct. 12, 1932. He studied with Piston at Harvard Univ. (B.A., 1953), with Irving Fine and Shapero at Brandeis Univ. (M.F.A., 1955), and at Indiana Univ. (Ph.D., 1961, with the diss. *Multiple Division of the Octave and the Tonal Resources of 19-tone Temperament*); also studied with Dallapiccola at the Berkshire Music Center at Tanglewood and with Blacher at the Berlin Hochschule für Musik. He held a Fulbright fellowship (1957) and was a fellow at the MacDowell Colony (1968); also taught at Queens College of the City Univ. of N.Y. (from 1961), where he served as director of its Aaron Copland School of Music. Many of his compositions reflect his study of microtonal music and the utilization of the Scalatron, an instrument with a color-coordinated keyboard that can be rearranged into divisions of the octave up to and including 31 tones. **WORKS: OPERAS:** *The Man in the Man-made Moon* (1955); *The 4 Chaplains* (1956); *The Dybbuk* (1971; rev. 1978). **ORCH.:** *Convocation Overture* (1951); Piano Concerto (1953); *Sursum corda* (1960); Sinfonia Concertante for Oboe, Horn, Violin, Cello, and Small Orch. (1962); *Memorial* for String Orch. (1965); Trumpet Concerto (1970). **CHAMBER:** Flute Sonata (1950); Wind Quintet (1957); 2 string quartets (1959, 1979); *Moderato* for 2 Pianos (1965); *Xenophony No. 1* for 3 Horns and Trombone (1966); *Romance* for String Trio (1973); *Fanfare* for Brass (1974); *Allegro agitato* for 2 Pianos (1979); *3 Tonal Studies* for Large Chamber Ensemble (1979); *Xenophony No. 2* for Violin, Cello, Double Bass, Woodwind Quintet, and Organ (1979); Oboe Sonata (1981); Clarinet Sonata (1983). **KEYBOARD:** Piano Sonata (1958); 9 Preludes in 19-tone temperament for 2 Specially Tuned Pianos (1961); 10 Studies for Fokker Organ based on the Conora Suler (1964); 4 Miniatures in 31-tone temperament for Architone or Scalatron (1979). **VOCAL:** Mass for Men's Voices and Organ (1954); choruses; songs; light operas; musicals; incidental music; film scores.

Mandić, Josip, Croatian composer; b. Trieste, April 4, 1883; d. Prague, Oct. 5, 1959. He studied music in Trieste, Zagreb, and Vienna; composed 4 syms. (1929, 1930, 1953, 1954); a

Croatian Mass; several cantatas and other vocal music; a Nonet and String Quartet; also the operas *Mirjana* (Olomouc, Feb. 20, 1937) and *Kapetan Niko* (1944).

Mandl, Richard, Austrian composer; b. Prossnitz, May 9, 1859; d. Vienna, April 1, 1918. He studied at the Vienna Cons. and with Delibes at the Paris Cons. He wrote a 1-act comic opera, *Nächtliche Werbung* (Prague, 1888); cantata, *Griselidis*; symphonic poem, *Stimme des Orients*; symphonic rhapsody, *Algier*; dance suite, *Viennensia*; several violin pieces; String Quintet; songs. He was married to Camilla Barda (1872–1922), who publ. a pedagogical work, *Kompendium der gesamten Klaviertechnik* (3 vols.).

Mandrell, Barbara (Ann), American country-music singer and instrumentalist; b. Houston, Dec. 25, 1948. She learned to play the accordion; then took up the steel guitar and performed at local entertainment places; later went to Nashville, where she joined the "Grand Ole Opry." She quickly gained a wide following with her performances of such songs as *I've Been Loving You Too Long, Standing Room Only, Woman to Woman, Midnight Angel, Midnight Oil,* and *Best of Strangers.* In 1980 she starred in her own television show, which proved to be quite successful.

Mandyczewski, Eusebius, eminent Rumanian musicologist; b. Czernowitz, Aug. 17, 1857; d. Vienna, July 13, 1929. He entered the Univ. of Vienna (1875), where his teachers included Hanslick (music history) and Nottebohm (music theory); he also studied harmony with R. Fuchs at the Vienna Cons. In 1880 he became conductor of the Vienna Singakademie and archivist of the Gesellschaft der Musikfreunde; was made a prof. of music history and composition at the Cons. (1892). He oversaw the 1st complete critical ed. of Schubert's works (40 vols. in 21 series, Leipzig, 1884–97), for which he received an honorary Ph.D. from the Univ. of Leipzig (1897). In 1879 he met Brahms, and they subsequently became good friends; with H. Gál, he ed. selected works by other composers. He composed some songs and piano pieces.
BIBL.: K. Geiringer, "Brahms in Briefwechsel mit E. M.," *Zeitschrift für Musikwissenschaft,* XV (1933).

Manelli, Francesco, Italian composer; b. Tivoli, Sept. 1594; d. Parma, July 1667. He served as a chorister at the Cathedral of Tivoli from c.1605, and continued his service there as chapel singer (1609–24); he then was maestro di cappella there (1627–29). He produced an opera, *Gelia,* in Bologna (1630); in 1636 he went to Venice, where he was chapel singer at San Marco (from 1638); from 1645 to his death, he was in the service of the Duke of Parma. In 1637 the Teatro San Cassiano in Venice, the 1st public opera house in Europe, was opened with Manelli's opera *L'Andromeda;* he wrote several other operas, which enjoyed considerable popularity. All the musical scores of Manelli are lost, but some librettos are preserved. His op. 4, *Musiche varie* (Venice, 1626), a collection of cantatas, arias, *canzonette,* and *ciacone,* shows that he had adopted the "parlando" recitative.
BIBL.: P. Petrobelli, "F. M.: Documenti e osservasioni," *Chigiana,* XXIV (1967).

Manén, Juan, Catalan composer; b. Barcelona, March 14, 1883; d. there, June 26, 1971. He studied both piano and violin, and was exhibited as a piano prodigy in public; then decided to switch to the violin, and went on a European tour; was particularly welcome in Germany, where he resided most of the time from 1908 on. His music is redolent of Spanish, and more specifically Catalan, melorhythms. He wrote an autobiography in 2 vols., titled, with a wistful retrospection, *El niño prodigioso* and *El jóven artista* (Barcelona, 1944, 1964).
WORKS: STAGE: Operas: *Juana de Nápoles* (Barcelona, 1902); *Acté* (Barcelona, 1903; rev. as *Nero und Akté,* Karlsruhe, Jan. 28, 1928); *Der Fak-keltanz* (Frankfurt, 1909); *Soledad* (Barcelona, 1952); "theater sym.," *Camino del sol* (Braunschweig, May 2, 1926); theater triptych, *Don Juan* (unperf.); ballet, *Triana* (1952). **ORCH.:** Concertino for Violin and Orch. (1965); *Sinfonía ibérica* (1966); *Festividad,* overture (1966);

Rapsodia catalana for Piano and Orch. (1968); *Nova Catalonia, Romanza mistica,* and *Romanza amorosa* for Violin and String Orch.; also Fantasia-Sonata for Guitar; pieces for violin.

Manfredini, Francesco Onofrio, Italian violinist and composer, father of **Vincenzo Manfredini;** b. Pistoia (baptized), June 22, 1684; d. there, Oct. 6, 1762. He studied violin with Torelli and counterpoint with Perti in Bologna; went to Ferrara (c.1699), where he was made 1st violinist at the Church of the Holy Spirit; then entered the orch. of S. Petronio in Bologna (1704), and also became a member of the Accademia Filarmonica in that city; subsequently was maestro di cappella at St. Philip's Cathedral in Pistoia (1727–62).

WORKS: (12) *Concertini per camera* for Violin, and Cello or Theorbo, op. 1 (Bologna, 1704); (12) *Sinfonie da chiesa* for 2 Violins, Basso Continuo (Organ), and Viola ad libitum, op. 2 (Bologna, 1709); (12) *Concerti* for 2 Violins and Basso Continuo obbligato and 2 Violins, Viola, and Bass, op. 3 (Bologna, 1718); 6 Sonatas for 2 Violins, Cello, and Basso Continuo (Harpsichord) (London, c.1764); 6 oratorios.

BIBL.: U. Pineschi, "Precisazioni biografiche su F. M.," *Bolletino Storico Pistoiese,* 3rd series, III (1968).

Manfredini, Vincenzo, Italian composer, son of **Francesco Onofrio Manfredini;** b. Pistoia, Oct. 22, 1737; d. St. Petersburg, Aug. 16, 1799. He was a pupil of his father; later studied with Perti in Bologna and with Fioroni in Milan. In 1758 he went to Russia, where he was attached to the court (until 1769); then returned to Italy; lived in Bologna and Venice; his former pupil, now Czar Paul I, recalled him to Russia (1798). He publ. *Regole armoniche, o sieno Precetti ragionati* (Venice, 1775; 2nd ed., rev. and augmented, 1797).

WORKS (all 1st perf. in St. Petersburg unless otherwise given): **OPERAS:** *Semiramide* (1760); *L'Olimpiade* (Moscow, Nov. 24, 1762); *La pupilla* (1763); *La finta ammalata* (1763); *Carlo Magno* (Nov. 24, 1763); *Armida* (Bologna, May 1770); *Artaserse* (Venice, Jan. 1772). **BALLETS:** *Amour et Psyché* (Moscow, Oct. 20, 1762); *Pygmalion* (Sept. 26, 1763); *Les Amants réchappés du naufrage* (1766); *Le Sculpteur de Carthage* (1766); *La Constance récompensée* (Moscow, 1767); also several cantatas; sacred vocal works; Harpsichord Concerto (The Hague and Amsterdam, 1769?); 6 syms. (Venice, 1776); 6 string quartets (Florence, 1781?); 6 Harpsichord Sonatas (St. Petersburg, 1765).

Mangione, "Chuck" (Charles Frank), American jazz flügelhornist, pianist, and composer; b. Rochester, N.Y., Nov. 29, 1940. He studied at the Eastman School of Music in Rochester, where he earned his bachelor's degree (1963); gained practical experience as a member of a jazz combo with his brothers. He also began to compose, producing *Friends and Love* for his appearance as guest conductor with the Rochester Phil. in 1970; subsequently made numerous tours with his own band. His record album *Bellavia* (1976) was a major success, winning a Grammy Award; it was followed by *Feels So Good* (1977), an instrumental number of his own composition which found acclaim among jazz and pop-music lovers and attained double-gold-album status.

Mangold, Carl (Ludwig Amand), German conductor and composer, brother of **(Johann) Wilhelm Mangold;** b. Darmstadt, Oct. 8, 1813; d. Oberstdorf im Allgäu, Aug. 5, 1889. He studied at the Paris Cons. with Berton and Bordogni; returning to Darmstadt, became a violinist in the Court Orch.; from 1848 to 1869, was court music director; also conducted various choral societies there. He wrote an opera, *Tannhäuser,* which was produced in Darmstadt on May 17, 1846, only a few months after the premiere of Wagner's great work; in order to escape disastrous comparisons, the title was changed to *Der getreue Eckart,* and the libretto revised; the new version was produced posthumously in Darmstadt on Jan. 17, 1892. Mangold also wrote 4 more operas, *Das Köhlermädchen, oder Das Tournier zu Linz* (1843), *Die Fischerin* (1845), *Dornröschen* (1848), and *Gudrun* (1851); 8 syms.; concertos; several oratorios; masses; cantatas; various choral works, many of which were

popular in his day, particularly the "concert drama" *Die Hermannsschlacht* (Mainz, 1845); chamber music; some 375 songs; piano pieces.

Mangold, (Johann) Wilhelm, German violinist, conductor, and composer, brother of **Carl (Ludwig Amand) Mangold;** b. Darmstadt, Nov. 19, 1796; d. there, May 23, 1875. He studied with Rinck and Abbé Vogler; then went to Paris for lessons with Cherubini, Méhul, and Kreutzer at the Cons. (1815–18); in 1825, became a court conductor at Darmstadt; was pensioned in 1857. He wrote 3 operas, chamber music, and melodies for clarinet with piano, which were popular for a time.

Manilow, Barry, American singer, arranger, and composer of popular music; b. N.Y., June 17, 1946. He played the accordion and piano in his youth; then worked as a successful arranger and composer of radio and television commercials; scored enormous success with his pop hits *Mandy, It's a Miracle, Could It Be Magic?, I Write the Songs, Looks Like We Made It, Can't Smile without You,* and others. He publ. the autobiographical book *Sweet Life: Adventures on the Way to Paradise* (N.Y., 1987).

Mankell, (Ivar) Henning, Swedish composer; b. Härnösand, June 3, 1868; d. Stockholm, May 8, 1930. He studied piano and composition in Stockholm; composed a number of works, mostly for piano; in his style, he followed some models of French impressionist music. Among his works are a Piano Concerto (1917); 3 piano sonatas; 8 ballads for Piano; 3 string quartets; Piano Quintet; Piano Trio; songs.

Mann, Alfred, German-born American musicologist and choral conductor; b. Hamburg, April 28, 1917. He was a pupil of Kurt Thomas, Hans Mahlke, and Max Seiffert at the Berlin Hochschule für Musik (certificate, 1937); after teaching at the Berlin Hochschule für Kirchen- und Schulmusik (1937–38), he continued his training at the Milan Cons. (1938); taught at the Scuola Musicale di Milano (1938–39). In 1939 he emigrated to the U.S., and became a naturalized citizen in 1943; studied at the Curtis Inst. of Music in Philadelphia (diploma, 1942), where he also taught (1939–42); completed his education with Paul Henry Lang, William J. Mitchell, and Erich Hertzmann at Columbia Univ. (M.A., 1950; Ph.D., 1955, with the diss. *The Theory of Fugue*). He was on the faculty of Rutgers Univ. from 1947 to 1980; in 1978 he was a visiting prof. at Columbia Univ.; was on the faculty of the Eastman School of Music in Rochester, N.Y. (1980–87). From 1952 to 1959 he was conductor of the Cantata Singers in N.Y. and later of the Bach Choir in Bethlehem, Pa. (1970–80). He ed. works for the critical editions of Mozart, Fux, Handel, and Schubert; was editor of the Rutgers Documents of Music series (1951–88) and the *American Choral Review* (from 1962); contributed many articles to scholarly journals.

WRITINGS: Ed. J. Fux's *Gradus ad Parnassum* (*Die Lehre vom Kontrapunkt,* Celle, 1938; 2nd ed., 1951; partial Eng. tr., N.Y., 1943, as *Steps to Parnassus;* 2nd ed., N.Y. and Toronto, 1965, as *The Study of Counterpoint*); *The Study of Fugue* (New Brunswick, N.J., 1958; 3rd ed., 1987); *Bethlehem Bach Studies* (N.Y., 1985); *Theory and Practice: The Great Composer as Student and Teacher* (N.Y. and London, 1987); ed. *Modern Music Librarianship* (Stuyvesant, N.Y., and Kassel, 1988).

Mann, Herbie, American jazz flutist; b. N.Y., April 16, 1930. He studied at the Manhattan School of Music, and became a successful jazz flutist. He made extensive solo tours and played in pop concerts with the leading American orchs.

Mann, Leslie (Douglas), Canadian composer and clarinetist; b. Edmonton, Alberta, Aug. 13, 1923; d. Balmoral, Manitoba, Dec. 7, 1977. He studied music in Toronto; was 1st clarinetist of the CBC Winnipeg Orch. (1958) and of the Winnipeg Sym. Orch. (1960–71). His music follows tradition, and contributes to listening pleasure without straining.

WORKS: OPERA: *The Donkey's Tale,* chamber opera (1971). **ORCH.:** *Concertino in the Old Style* for String Orch. (1955); Flute Concerto (1964); Clarinet Concerto (1970); *Sinfonia concertante* for Bassoon and Chamber Orch. (1971); *Concerto* grosso No. 1 for Chamber Orch. (1972); 3 syms. (1973; 1974; 1976, *Typhoon*); *Weep You No More Sad Fountains*, 7 songs to Elizabethan poems, for Voice and Chamber Orch. (1974). CHAMBER: 5 *Bagatelles* for Clarinet or Viola, and Piano (1951); Trio for Flute, Clarinet, and Cello (1952); Cello Sonata (1953); 5 *Improvisations* for Flute and Piano (1954); *Toccata alla Barocco* for Flute, Clarinet, and Cello (1956); Wind Quintet (1961); Clarinet Sonata (1962); *Suite* for Clarinet Solo (1963); *Suite* for Flute Solo (1963); Trio for Clarinet, Cello, and Piano (1967); 4 *Studies in the Blues Idiom* for Wind Quintet (1969); *Music* for Clarinet, Viola, and Piano (1971); *Partita* for Violin and Bassoon (1972); Sonata for Solo Violin (1974); *Vocalise* for Oboe or Clarinet, and Piano (1974); String Quartet (1975); Suite for Solo Saxophone (1976); Flute Sonata (1977); songs.

Mann, Robert (Nathaniel), American violinist, conductor, teacher, and composer; b. Portland, Oreg., July 19, 1920. He studied violin with Edouard Déthier at the Juilliard Graduate School in N.Y., and had instruction in chamber music with Adolfo Betti, Felix Salmond, and Hans Letz; also took courses with Edgar Schenkman in conducting, and Bernard Wagenaar and Stefan Wolpe in composition. In 1941 he won the Naumburg Competition, and made his N.Y. debut as a violinist. From 1943 to 1946 he was in the U.S. Army; then joined the faculty of the Juilliard School and in 1948 founded the Juilliard String Quartet, in which he played 1st violin, and which was to become one of the most highly regarded chamber music groups; in 1962 it was established as the quartet-in-residence under the Whittall Foundation at the Library of Congress in Washington, D.C., without suspending its concert tours in America and abroad. As a conductor, Mann specialized in contemporary music; was associated as a performer and lecturer with the Music Festival and Inst. at Aspen, Colo., and also served with the NEA; in 1971 he was appointed president of the Walter W. Naumburg Foundation. He has composed a String Quartet (1952); *Suite* for String Orch. (1965); several "lyric trios" for Violin, Piano, and Narrator.

Mann, William (Somervell), English music critic, writer on music, and translator; b. Madras, Feb. 14, 1924; d. Bath, Sept. 5, 1989. He studied piano with Ilona Kabós and composition with Mátyás Seiber; also studied at Magdalene College, Cambridge, with Patrick Hadley, Hubert Middleton, and Robin Orr. He was on the music staff of the *Times* of London (1948–60); was its chief music critic (1960–82). He made many serviceable Eng. trs. of opera librettos and lieder texts. He publ. *Introduction to the Music of Johann Sebastian Bach* (London, 1950), *Richard Strauss: A Critical Study of the Operas* (London, 1964), and *The Operas of Mozart* (London, 1977).

Manne, Shelly (Sheldon), American jazz drummer; b. N.Y., June 11, 1920; d. Los Angeles, Sept. 26, 1984. He 1st learned to play the saxophone, and then took up the drums when he was 18; appeared on Coleman Hawkins's recording of *The Man I Love* (1943) and worked with Dizzy Gillespie (1945). He was engaged by Stan Kenton (1946–52) and subsequently settled in Los Angeles, where he became a prominent figure in the West Coast jazz movement; led his own groups, and also worked with André Previn's trio. He operated his own club, Shelly's Mann Hole in Hollywood (1960–74), and was a founding member of the L.A. Four.

Manneke, Daan, Dutch composer; b. Kruiningen, Nov. 7, 1939. He studied organ with Houet and Toebosch and composition with Van Dijk at the Brabant Cons. (1960–66); then organ with D'Hooge and composition with de Leeuw in Amsterdam (1967–73); in 1972 he was appointed lecturer on analysis of modern music at the Amsterdam Cons.

WORKS: Opera, *De passie van Johannes Mattheus Lanckohr* (1977); *Walking in Fog Patches* for Wind Quintet (1971); *Jeu* for Flute (1971); *Plein jeu* for Brass Quintet (1972); 4 *Sonatas* for Youth Orch. (1972); *Stages* for Variable Ensemble (1972); *Music about Poor and Bad People* for a cappella Chorus (1972); *Sine nomine* for 3 Instrumental Groups (1972); 3 *Times* for Chorus and Small Orch. (1974); *Ordre* for 4 Recorders (1975);

Sinfonia for 13 String Instruments (1975); *Job* for Male Chorus, 4 Brasses, and 3 Percussionists (1976); *En passant (Touching in Passing)* for Small Orch. (1977); *Ruimten* for Strings (1978); *Ramificazioni* for Piano Trio (1979); Rondeau for Percussion (1979); Concerto for Carillon (1980); *Gestures* for Clarinet, Marimba, and Percussion (1981); Sinfonia for 11 Instruments (1982); *Babel* for 6 Orchs. (1985); *Archipel II* for Viola, Cello, and Double Bass (1985); *Messe de Notre Dame* for Chorus (1986); *Archipel III* for Guitar (1987).

Manners, Charles (real name, **Southcote Mansergh**), Irish bass and operatic impresario; b. London, Dec. 27, 1857; d. Dundrum, County Dublin, May 3, 1935. He studied in Dublin; then at the Royal Academy of Music in London and in Florence. In 1882 he made his stage debut with the D'Oyly Carte company in London, creating the role of Private Willis in Gilbert and Sullivan's *Iolanthe*. In 1890 he married the soprano **Fanny Moody,** with whom he organized the Moody-Manners Opera Co. (1898); it toured widely until its demise in 1916; he retired from active management of its affairs in 1913.

Mannes, Clara Damrosch, German-born American pianist and teacher, daughter of **Leopold Damrosch;** b. Breslau, Dec. 12, 1869; d. N.Y., March 16, 1948. At the age of 6, she began to study piano in N.Y.; then went to Dresden, where she took lessons with H. Scholtz; later was a pupil of Busoni in Berlin (1897). On June 4, 1898, she married the violinist **David Mannes,** with whom she toured the U.S. and England for 20 years in joint recitals; was co-director of the Mannes School in N.Y.

Mannes, David, American violinist, conductor, and teacher; b. N.Y., Feb. 16, 1866; d. there, April 25, 1959. He studied violin in Berlin, and was briefly a student of Ysaÿe in Brussels (1903). He was a member of the N.Y. Sym. Orch. beginning in 1891, and was its concertmaster from 1898 to 1912; married **Clara Damrosch Mannes,** June 4, 1898. In 1912 he founded in N.Y. the Music School Settlement for Colored Children; conducted a series of free sym. concerts at the Metropolitan Museum of Art in N.Y. (1918–47). In 1916 he opened his own music school in N.Y., known as the Mannes School of Music; continued to be active until a very advanced age; on his 90th birthday, in 1956, a special concert was organized in his honor at the Metropolitan Museum of Art. He publ. an autobiography, *Music Is My Faith* (N.Y., 1938).

Mannes, Leopold (Damrosch), American pianist, teacher, composer, and inventor; son of **David** and **Clara Damrosch Mannes;** b. N.Y., Dec. 26, 1899; d. Martha's Vineyard, Mass., Aug. 11, 1964. He studied at Harvard Univ. (B.A., 1920) and took courses at the Mannes School of Music and the Inst. of Musical Arts in N.Y.; among his teachers were E. Quaile, G. Maier, Berthe Bert, and A. Cortot in piano, and Johannes Schreyer, Goetschius, and Scalero in composition. He won a Pulitzer scholarship (1925) and a Guggenheim fellowship (1927). In 1922 he made his debut in N.Y. as a pianist; taught theory and composition at the Mannes School (1927–31), then worked for the Eastman Kodak Co. in Rochester, N.Y., where he invented the Kodachrome process of color photography with Loepold Godowsky, son of the pianist, in 1935. He subsequently was director (1940–48) and a teacher of theory and composition (1946–48) at the Mannes School; was its co-director (1948–52) and president (1950–64); was also active with his own Mannes Trio (1948–55). He wrote 3 *Short Pieces* for Orch. (1926); incidental music to Shakespeare's *Tempest* (1930); String Quartet (1928); Suite for 2 Pianos (1924); songs.

Manning, Jane (Marian), English soprano; b. Norwich, Sept. 20, 1938. She studied at the Royal Academy of Music in London; in 1964 she made her debut in London in a program of contemporary music, and subsequently established herself as a leading interpreter of modern music in England. She married the composer **Anthony Payne** in 1966. She publ. the vol. *New Vocal Repertory: An Introduction* (Basingstoke and London, 1986). In 1990 she was made a member of the Order of the British Empire.

Manning, Kathleen Lockhart, American composer; b. Hollywood, Oct. 24, 1890; d. Los Angeles, March 20, 1951. She played as a child pianist in public concerts; took lessons with Moszkowski in Paris; also appeared as an opera singer with the Hammerstein Opera Co. in London (1911–12). She wrote 2 operas (*Mr. Wu* and *For the Soul of Rafael*); several song cycles: *Sketches of Paris* (which includes *In the Luxemburg Gardens*), *Sketches of London, Songs of Egypt, Sketches of New York*, etc.; also piano pieces.

Mannino, Franco, Italian pianist, conductor, and composer; b. Palermo, April 25, 1924. He studied piano with R. Silvestri and composition with V. Mortari at the Accademia di Santa Cecilia in Rome; made his debut as a pianist at the age of 16; subsequently toured as a pianist in Europe and America. In 1957 he conducted the orch. of the Maggio Musicale of Florence on a tour of the U.S. He subsequently conducted in Europe, South America, and the Far East; was a frequent guest conductor in the Soviet Union, where he regularly appeared with the Leningrad Phil. In 1969 he became artistic director of the Teatro San Carlo in Naples; from 1974 was its artistic adviser. In 1982 he was appointed principal conductor and artistic adviser of the National Arts Centre Orch. in Ottawa, which posts he held until 1986. He is a prolific composer; his operas and other works are written in traditional melodramatic Italian style, diversified by occasional modernistic procedures.

WORKS: OPERAS: *Mario e il mago* (1952; Milan, Feb. 23, 1956); *Vivì* (1955; Naples, March 28, 1957); *La speranza* (1956; Trieste, Feb. 14, 1970); *La stirpe di davide* (1958; Rome, April 19, 1962); *Le notti della paura* (1960; RAI, Rome, May 24, 1963); *Il Diavolo in giardino* (1962; Palermo, Feb. 28, 1963); *Il quadro delle meraviglie* (Rome, April 24, 1963); *Luisella* (Palermo, Feb. 28, 1969); *Il ritratto di Dorian Gray* (1973; Catania, Jan. 12, 1982); *Il Principe Felice* (1981). ORCH.: Piano Concerto (Remsched, Dec. 1, 1954); *Sinfonia americana* (1954; Florence, Nov. 11, 1956); *Sinfonia* (1958); *Demoniaca*, overture (1963); Concerto for 3 Violins (1965; Moscow, March 21, 1966); *Laocoonte* for Orch. (1966; Trieste, May 8, 1968); Concerto for Piano, 3 Violins, and Orch. (1969); *Notturno napoletano* (1969; Naples, March 13, 1970); *Concerto grosso* (1970); Violin Concerto (1970; Milan, May 14, 1971); Concerto No. 2 for Piano (1974; Cagliari, April 22, 1980); Cello Concerto (1974; Naples, July 14, 1975); *Supreme Love*, cantata for Solo Voices, Chorus, and Orch. (1977; Naples, Sept. 30, 1978); *Settecento* (1979); *Olympic Concert* for 6 Violins, 2 Pianos, and Orch. (1979); *Nirvana*, poem (Cagliari, April 22, 1980); Concerto for 6 Violins, 2 Pianos, and Orch. (1980); Sym. No. 4, *Leningrad* (1981; Lecce, May 11, 1982); Sym. No. 5, *Rideau Lake* (1985; Ottawa, Feb. 12, 1986); *Tropical Dances* for 20 Cellos (1984); *Piccolo concerto grosso* for Flute, Oboe, and String Orch. (1985).

Manns, Sir August (Friedrich), prominent German-born English conductor; b. Stolzenberg, near Stettin, March 12, 1825; d. London, March 1, 1907. He learned to play the violin, clarinet, and flute; was a member of various bands in Danzig and Berlin; then conducted bands in Königsberg and Cologne. In 1854 he went to London, where he became a conductor at the Crystal Palace; in 1856 he inaugurated the famous Saturday Concerts there, which he conducted until 1901, presenting about 14,000 concerts. In 1894 he became a naturalized British subject. He became a celebrated musical and social figure in London, and was knighted in 1903. He also conducted the orch. concerts of the Glasgow Choral Union (1879–87) and 6 Triennial Handel Festivals (1883–1900).

BIBL.: H. Wyndham, *A. M. and the Saturday Concerts* (London, 1909).

Manojlović, Kosta, Serbian composer; b. Krnjevo, Dec. 3, 1890; d. Belgrade, Oct. 2, 1949. He studied in Munich and at Oxford Univ. (B.A., 1919). He wrote a Serbian liturgy, and a cantata, *By the Waters of Babylon*; characteristic piano pieces (*Danse fantastique*, etc.) and songs. He publ. several studies

on Serbian folk music; his collection of 337 songs of east Serbia was publ. posthumously (Belgrade, 1953).

Manowarda, Josef von, esteemed Austrian bass; b. Krakow, July 3, 1890; d. Berlin, Dec. 24, 1942. He studied in Graz, making his debut there (1911); sang at the Vienna Volksoper (1915–18) and in Wiesbaden (1918–19); then was a principal member of the Vienna State Opera (1919–42); also appeared at the Salzburg Festivals (from 1922), the Bayreuth Festivals (1931, 1934, 1939, 1942), and the Berlin State Opera (1934–42); in addition, he taught at the Vienna Academy of Music (1932–35). Among his notable roles were Osmin, King Mark, Gurnemanz, and King Philip; created the role of the Messenger in Strauss's *Die Frau ohne Schatten* (1919). He also pursued a fine concert career.

Manrique de Lara (y Berry), Manuel, Spanish music critic, folklorist, and composer; b. Cartagena, Oct. 24, 1863; d. St. Blasien, Germany, Feb. 27, 1929. He entered the Spanish army and rose to the rank of brigadier general; studied music with Chapí; became a leading authority on early Spanish ballads, including those sung by Jewish communities in the Near East. He wrote an opera, *Rodrigo de Vivar* (*El Cid*) (1906); a zarzuela, *El ciudadano Simon* (1900); a Sym. (1890); *La Orestiada*, symphonic trilogy (1900); and chamber music.

Manschinger, Kurt, Austrian conductor and composer; b. Zeil-Wieselburg, July 25, 1902; d. N.Y., Feb. 23, 1968. He studied musicology at the Univ. of Vienna, and at the same time took private lessons with Anton von Webern (1919–26). After graduation, he was mainly active as a theatrical conductor in Austria and Germany. His practical acquaintance with operatic production led to his decision to write operas, for which his wife, the singer Greta Hartwig, wrote librettos. Of these his 1st opera, *Madame Dorette*, was to be performed by the Vienna State Opera, but the Anschluss in 1938 made this impossible. He and his wife fled to London, where they organized an émigré theater, The Lantern. In 1940 they emigrated to America; Manschinger changed his name to Ashley Vernon and continued to compose; earned his living as a musical autographer by producing calligraphic copies of music scores for publishers.

WORKS: Operas: *The Barber of New York* (N.Y., May 26, 1953); *Grand Slam* (Stamford, Conn., June 25, 1955); *Cupid and Psyche* (Woodstock, N.Y., July 27, 1956); *The Triumph of Punch* (N.Y., Jan. 25, 1969); *Der Talisman* for Voices, Violin, Viola, Cello, and Piano (London, Feb. 24, 1940); Sinfonietta (1964); Sym. (1967); chamber music.

Manski, Dorothée, German-American soprano and teacher; b. Berlin, March 11, 1891; d. Atlanta, Feb. 24, 1967. She studied in Berlin, where she made her debut at the Komische Oper (1911); then sang in Mannheim (1914–20) and Stuttgart (1920–24). She was a member of the Berlin State Opera (1924–27); also sang in Max Reinhardt's productions; then appeared as Isolde at the Salzburg Festival (1933) and the Vienna State Opera (1934). She made her Metropolitan Opera debut in N.Y. as the Witch in *Hänsel und Gretel* on Nov. 5, 1927, and remained on the company's roster until 1941; also sang opera in Philadelphia, Chicago, and San Francisco, and appeared as a concert singer with leading European and U.S. orchs. She was prof. of voice at the Indiana Univ. School of Music in Bloomington (1941–65). Among her other roles were Sieglinde, Venus, Gutrune, Brünnhilde, Freia, and Elsa.

Mansurian, Tigran, Lebanese-born Armenian composer; b. Beirut, Jan. 27, 1939. His family moved to Soviet Armenia when Mansurian was 8 years old. He studied with Sarian at the Erevan Cons. (1960–65). In 1968 he was appointed to the faculty of his alma mater. His early works were substantially neo-Classical in form and ethnic Armenian in their thematic and rhythmic material; he later adopted 12-tone and serial techniques.

WORKS: ORCH.: Concerto for String Orch. (1962); Concerto for Organ and Chamber Orch. (1964); *Partita* (1965); *Preludes* (1975); Cello Concerto, to the memory of Shostakovich (1976);

Concerto for Violin, Cello, and Orch. (1979); *Praeludium* (1980). **CHAMBER:** Solo Cello Sonata (1960); 2 string quartets (1960, 1963); Viola Sonata (1961); *Suite* for Wind Instruments and Piano (1961); Flute Sonata (1962); *Scherzo* for Violin and Piano (1962); *Allegro barbaro* for Cello and Piano (1963); Violin Sonatina (1964); 2 violin sonatas (1964, 1965); Piano Trio (1965); *Psalm* for 2 Flutes and Violin (1966); *Music* for 12 Instruments (1966); *Arabesques I* and *II* for Chamber Ensemble (1969, 1970); *Bird's Silhouette I, II,* and *III* for Harpsichord and Percussion (1971, 1972, 1973); 2 *Elegies* for Violin and Piano (1972); *Interior* for String Quartet (1972); 2 cello sonatas (1973, 1974). **VOCAL:** *Ariens,* after the 15th-century Armenian poet Naapet Kuchack, for Soprano and Chamber Orch. (1967); *Intermezzo* for Vocal and Instrumental Ensemble (1972); 2 *Maidens,* madrigal after Kostan Sarian, for Soprano and Chamber Ensemble (1981); choruses; songs. **PIANO:** Sonatina (1963); 3 *Preludes* (1965); Sonata (1965); 4 *Miniatures* (1969); 3 *Pieces* (1971).

Mantelli, Eugenia, Italian mezzo-soprano; b. c.1860; d. Lisbon, March 3, 1926. She made her debut in Treviso in 1883 as Kalad in *Le Roi de Lahore*; subsequently sang in Germany, South America, England, and Russia. On Nov. 23, 1894, she made her Metropolitan Opera debut in N.Y. as Amneris; she continued to make appearances there until 1903. She retired in 1910.

Mantovani (, Annunzio Paolo), enormously successful Italian-born English conductor of popular music; b. Venice, Nov. 15, 1905; d. Tunbridge Wells, March 29, 1980. He was taken to London as a youth; studied at Trinity College of Music there; became a British subject in 1933. He formed an orch. of his own in Birmingham at the age of 18; then led bands in hotels and in theaters. His ingratiatingly harmonious orch. arrangements made his name famous; the "Mantovani sound" became a byword with sedentary music-lovers seeking relaxation and listening pleasure as an antidote to the dramatic enervation of hazardous modern living and raucous popular music.

Mantuani, Josef, Austrian music scholar; b. Laibach, March 28, 1860; d. there (Ljubljana), March 18, 1933. He studied composition with Bruckner and others at the Vienna Cons. and musicology at the Univ. of Vienna (Ph.D., 1894, with a diss. on art history); was a librarian (1893–98) and director of the music division (1898–1909) at the Vienna Hofbibliothek; then returned to his birthplace as director of the Museal Verein für Krain. He ed. several vols. of Denkmäler der Tonkunst in Österreich; publ. *Codicum musicorum pars I–II, Tabulae codicum manuscriptorum . . . asservatorum,* IX–X (Vienna, 1897–99; a complete catalog of the MSS in the Vienna Hofbibliothek) and *Geschichte der Musik in Wien. I. Teil: Von den Römerzeiten bis zum Tode des Kaisers Max I.* (Vienna, 1904).

Manuel, Roland. See **Roland-Manuel, Alexis.**

Manziarly, Marcelle de, Russian-born French conductor, pianist, and composer; b. Kharkov, Sept. 13, 1899; d. Ojai, Calif., May 12, 1989. She studied in Paris with Boulanger, in Basel with Weingartner (1930–31), and in N.Y. with Vengerova (1943); appeared as a pianist and conductor in the U.S. and taught privately in Paris and N.Y. Her works extend the boundaries of tonality through such resources and procedures as polytonality, serialism, and atonality. **WORKS: OPERA:** *La Femme en flèche* (1954). **ORCH.:** Piano Concerto (1932); *Sonate pour Notre-Dame de Paris* (1944–45); *Musique pour orchestre* for Small Orch. (1950); *Incidences* for Piano and Orch. (1964). **CHAMBER:** String Quartet (1943); Trio for Flute, Cello, and Piano (1952); *Trilogue* for Flute, Viola da Gamba, and Harpsichord (1957); *Dialogue* for Cello and Piano (1970); *Périple* for Oboe and Piano (1972). **VOCAL:** 3 *fables de La Fontaine* (1935); *Chœurs pour enfants* (1938); *Poèmes en trio* for 3 Female Voices and Piano (1940); Duos for 2 Sopranos or 2 Tenors, and Piano (1952); Duos for Soprano and Clarinet (1953); 3 chants for Soprano and Piano (1954); 2 *odes de Grégoire de Marek* for Alto and Piano (1955); 3 *sonnets*

de Pétrarque for Baritone and Piano (1958); *Le Cygne et le cuisinier* for 4 Solo Voices and Piano (1959). **PIANO:** *Mouvement* (1935); *Arabesque* (1937); *Toccata* (1939); *Bagatelle* (1940); Sonata for 2 Pianos (1946); 6 *études* (1949); *Stances* (1967).

Manzoni, Giacomo, Italian composer, teacher, and writer on music; b. Milan, Sept. 26, 1932. He studied composition with Contilli at the Messina Liceo Musicale (1948–50); then pursued training at the Milan Cons., where he received diplomas in piano (1954) and composition (1956); also obtained a degree in foreign languages and literature at the Bocconi Univ. in Milan (1955). He was ed. of *Il Diapason* (1956), music critic of the newspaper *L'Unità* (1958–66), and music ed. of the review *Prisma* (1968); later was on the editorial staff of the review *Musica/Realtà.* He taught harmony and counterpoint at the Milan Cons. (1962–64; 1968–69; from 1974) and composition at the Bologna Cons. (1965–68; 1969–74). In 1982 he was a guest of the Deutscher Akademischer Austauschdienst in Berlin. He contributed articles to Italian and other journals and publications; tr. works of Schoenberg and Adorno into Italian; publ. the books *Guida all'ascolto della musica sinfonica* (Milan, 1967) and *Arnold Schönberg: L'uomo, l'opera, i testi musicati* (Milan, 1975).

WORKS: OPERAS: *La sentenza* (1959–60; Bergamo, Oct. 13, 1960); *Atomtod* (1963–64; Milan, March 27, 1965); *Per Massimiliano Robespierre* (1974; Bologna, April 17, 1975); *Doktor Faustus,* after Thomas Mann (1985–88; Milan, May 16, 1989). **ORCH.:** *Fantasia-Recitativo-Finale* for Chamber Orch. (1956; Milan, Jan. 21, 1957); *Studio per 24* for Chamber Orch. (Venice, April 13, 1962); *Studio No. 2* for Chamber Orch. (1962–63; Milan, April 20, 1963); *Insiemi* (1966–67; Milan, Sept. 30, 1969); *Multipli* for Chamber Orch. (1972; Washington, D.C., Feb. 23, 1973); *Variabili* for Chamber Orch. (1972–73; Bolzano, March 8, 1973); *Masse: Omaggio a Edgar Varèse* for Piano and Orch. (1976–77; Berlin, Oct. 6, 1977); *Lessico* for String Orch. (Piacenza, March 23, 1978); *Modulor* (1978–79; Venice, Oct. 7, 1979); *Ode* (1982; Milan, March 11, 1983); *Nuovo incontro* for Violin and Strings (Florence, June 5, 1984). **VOCAL:** *Preludio: Grave: di Waring Cuney—Finale* for Female Voice, Clarinet, Violin, Viola, and Cello (1956; Rome, June 30, 1958); *Cinque Vicariote* for Chorus and Orch. (1958; Turin, Nov. 29, 1968); *Tre liriche di Paul Éluard* for Female Voice, Flute, Clarinet, Trumpet, Violin, and Cello (Rome, May 14, 1958); *Don Chisciotte* for Soprano, Small Chorus, and Chamber Orch. (1961; Venice, Sept. 14, 1964); *Quattro poesie spagnole* for Baritone, Clarinet, Viola, and Guitar (Florence, March 21, 1962); *Ombre (alla memoria di Che Guevara)* for Chorus and Orch. (1967–68; Bologna, May 10, 1968); *Parole da Beckett* for 2 Choruses, 3 Instrumental Groups, and Tape (1970–71; Rome, May 21, 1971); *Hölderlin (frammento)* for Chorus and Orch. (Venice, Sept. 17, 1972); *Omaggio a Josquin* for Soprano, Chorus, 2 Violas, and Cello (1985; Rome, Feb. 24, 1987); *Dedica* for Bass, Flute, and Orch. (1985; Parma, May 9, 1986); *Dieci versi di Emily Dickinson* for Soprano, String Quartet, 10 Strings, and 2 Harps (1988). **CHAMBER:** 2 *Piccola suites* for Violin and Piano (1952–55; 1956); *Improvvisazione* for Viola and Piano (1958); *Musica notturna* for 7 Instrumentalists (1966; Venice, Sept. 12, 1967); *Quadruplum* for 2 Trumpets and 2 Trombones (1968); *Spiel* for 11 Strings (1968–69; London, April 26, 1969); *Parafrasi con finale* for 10 Instrumentalists (Bavarian Radio, Munich, June 6, 1969); Quartet for Violin, Viola, and Cello (1971); *Percorso a otto* for Double Woodwind Quartet (1975); *Percorso C2* for Bassoon and 11 Strings (1976; Graz, Oct. 15, 1977); *Epodo* for Flute, Oboe, Clarinet, Horn, and Bassoon (1976); *Sigla* for 2 Trumpets and 2 Trombones (1976); *Hölderlin: Epilogo* for 10 Instrumentalists (1980); *Incontro* for Violin and String Quartet (Naples, Nov. 22, 1983); *Opus 50 (Daunium)* for 11 Instrumentalists (Foggia, Nov. 14, 1984); *Die Strahlen der Sonne . . .* for 9 Instrumentalists (Milan, April 21, 1985); *To Planets and to Flowers* for Saxophone Quartet (1989).

BIBL.: M. Romito, *Le composizioni sinfonico-corali di G. M.*

(Bologna, 1982); J. Noller, *Engagement und Form: G. M.s Werk in kulturtheoretischen und musikhistorischen Zusammenhängen* (Frankfurt am Main, 1987); F. Dorsi, *G. M.* (Milan, 1989).

Mapleson, James Henry, English operatic impresario, known as **Colonel Mapleson;** b. London, May 4, 1830; d. there, Nov. 14, 1901. He studied at the Royal Academy of Music in London; subsequently was engaged as a singer and a viola player; sang in Italy under the name of Enrico Mariani. In 1861 he became the manager of the Italian Opera at the Lyceum Theatre in London; then of Her Majesty's Theatre (1862–67); at Drury Lane (1868); in partnership with Gye at Covent Garden (1869–70); again at Drury Lane (1871–76); at the reconstructed (after the fire of 1868) Her Majesty's Theatre (1877–81); returned to Covent Garden (1885, 1887) and to Her Majesty's Theatre (1887, 1889); also presented opera at N.Y.'s Academy of Music (1878–97) and in other U.S. cities, his ventures fluctuating between success and disaster. On March 17, 1890, he married the American singer Laura Schirmer. An exuberant personality, he dominated the operatic news in both England and America by his recurrent professional troubles and his conflicts with, and attachments to, prima donnas. He publ. a lively account of his life as *The Mapleson Memoirs* (2 vols., London, 1888; 2nd ed., rev., 1966, by H. Rosenthal). His nephew, **Lionel S. Mapleson** (b. London, Oct. 23, 1865; d. N.Y., Dec. 21, 1937), joined the orch. of the Metropolitan Opera as a violinist (1889); then was its librarian for 50 years; left his own valuable library to the Metropolitan Opera, including the 1st recordings, made by himself, ever taken of actual performances by de Reszke, Calvé, and others.

Mara, Gertrud (Elisabeth) (née **Schmeling**), famous German soprano; b. Kassel, Feb. 23, 1749; d. Reval, Russia, Jan. 20, 1833. A neglected child, she suffered from disfiguring rickets; her father exhibited her as a violin prodigy in Vienna (1755), and she later played before the Queen (1759); then studied voice with Paradisi. In 1765 she returned to Germany and became a principal singer at Hiller's concerts in Leipzig (1766); then made her operatic debut in Dresden (1767), but soon returned to Leipzig. She subsequently entered the service of Frederick the Great (1771), singing at the Berlin Royal Opera; her marriage to the cellist Johann Baptist Mara (1746–1808) brought her grief, for Frederick opposed their union; when the couple tried to leave Leipzig, Frederick had them arrested; however, he eventually consented to their marriage after Gertrud agreed to remain at the Berlin Royal Opera; during this period, she also received instruction in harmony from Kirnberger. In 1779 she finally escaped Berlin, and subsequently sang in other German cities, in the Low Countries, and in Vienna (1780–81); appeared at the Concert Spirituel in Paris (1782), and again as a rival to Todi (1783). In 1784 she went to London, where she gained renown as a result of her participation in the Handel Commemoration performances; subsequently appeared at the King's Theatre there (1786–91); also sang in Turin (1788) and Venice (1789–90; 1792); thereafter mainly in concerts and oratorios in London until 1802, when she and her lover, the flutist and composer Charles Florio, left to tour France, Germany, and Austria; they finally landed in Moscow, but soon separated. Stricken with poverty, she was forced to eke out a meager existence as a teacher; after losing everything in the French destruction of Moscow (1812), she went to Reval as a teacher. In 1819 she made a brief and unsuccessful return to London's King's Theatre; then returned to Reval. During the glory days of her career, her voice ranged from g' to e'''.

BIBL.: G. Grosheim, *Das Leben der Künstlerin M.* (Kassel, 1823; reprint, 1972); G. Bürkli, *G.E. M.* (Zürich, 1835); O. von Riesemann, ed., "Eine Selbstbiographie der Sängerin G.E. M.," *Allgemeine Musikalische Zeitung,* new series, X (1875); A. Niggli, "G.E. M.," in Waldersee's *Sammlung musikalischer Vorträge* (Leipzig, 1881; after the autobiography); E. Wolff, *Mignon* (Munich, 1909); R. Kaulitz-Niedeck, *Die M.: Das Leben einer berühmten Sängerin* (Heilbronn, 1929); O. Anwand, *Die Prima Donna Friedrichs des Grossen* (Berlin,

1930); V. Huber, *Flirt und Flitter; Lebensbilder aus der Bühnenwelt* (Düsseldorf, 1970).

Maragno, Virtú, Argentine composer; b. Santa Fe, March 18, 1928. He studied in Buenos Aires and later in Rome with Goffredo Petrassi. Returning to Argentina, he became active as a choral conductor and teacher. He writes in a distinctly modernistic vein, leaning toward serial techniques.

WORKS: *Triste y Danza* for Small Orch. (1947); *Divertimento* for Wind Quintet (1952); *Scherzo sinfónico* (Buenos Aires, June 16, 1953); Concertino for Piano and 14 Instruments (1954); 2 string quartets (1958, 1961); *Expresión* for Double Orch. and Percussion (Rome, June 23, 1961); *Intensidad y Espacio* for Orch. (1962); *Composición I* for Voices, Instruments, and Magnetic Tape (Buenos Aires, Oct. 5, 1962); music for the theater; film scores; choruses; songs.

Marais, Josef, South African–born American folksinger and composer; b. Sir Lowry Pass, Nov. 17, 1905; d. Los Angeles, April 27, 1978. He studied at the South African College of Music and at the Royal Academy of Music in London; then took violin lessons with Otakar Sevčik in Prague. He emigrated to the U.S. in 1939; worked at the Office of War Information in N.Y. and broadcast songs from the South African *veld*; in 1947 married Roosje Baruch de la Bardo, a Dutch immigrant *chanteuse*, who took on the professional name Miranda. Together they publ. a number of song collections; Marais wrote the music for several stage productions, including Alan Paton's *Too Late the Phalarope*; he composed the orch. work *Paul Gauguin Suite* and other descriptive pieces.

Marais, Marin, great French viola da gambist and composer; b. Paris, May 31, 1656; d. there, Aug. 15, 1728. He studied bass viol with Sainte-Colombe and composition with Lully (whom he addresses as teacher in a letter publ. in his 1st book of pieces for his instrument); became a member of the royal orch. (1676); was made Ordinaire de la chambre du Roi (1679); retired (1725). Marais possessed matchless skill as a virtuoso on the viola da gamba, and set a new standard of excellence by enhancing the sonority of the instrument. He also established a new method of fingering, which had a decisive influence on the technique of performance. As a composer, he was an outstanding master of bass viol music, producing 5 extensive collections between 1686 and 1725, numbering some 550 works in all. In his dramatic music, he followed Lully's French manner; his recitatives comport with the rhythm of French verse and the inflection of the rhyme. The purely instrumental parts in his operas were quite extensive; in *Alcione* (Paris, Feb. 18, 1706) he introduced a "tempeste," which is one of the earliest attempts at stage realism in operatic music. His other operas are *Alcide* (Paris, 1693), *Ariane et Bacchus* (Paris, 1696), and *Sémélé* (Paris, 1709). He also publ. 5 books of pieces for viola da gamba (1686–1725); trios (or "symphonies") for violin, flute, and viola da gamba (1692); a book of trios for violin, viola da gamba, and harpsichord under the title *La Gamme* (1723). An edition of his instrumental works, ed. by J. Hsu, began publication in N.Y. in 1980. He was married in 1676 and had 19 children; his son Roland Marais was also a talented viola da gambist who publ. 2 books of pieces for his instrument with basso continuo (Paris, 1735, 1738) and a *Nouvelle méthode de musique pour servir d'introduction aux acteurs modernes* (Paris, 1711; not extant).

BIBL.: R. Newton, "Hommage à M. M.," *Consort,* IX (1952); M. Barthélemy, "Les Opéras de M. M.," *Revue Belge de Musicologie,* VII (1953); F. Lesure, "M. M., Sa carrière, sa famille," ibid.; R. Newton, "More about M. M.," *Consort,* X (1953); L. Boulay, "La Musique instrumentale de M. M.," *La Revue Musicale,* 226 (1955); C. Thompson, *M. M., 1656–1728* (diss., Univ. of Michigan, 1956); M. Urquhart, *Style and Technique in the "Pièces de violes" of M. M.* (diss., Univ. of Edinburgh, 1970); B. McDowell, *M. and Forqueray: A Historical and Analytical Study of Their Music for Solo Basse de Viole* (diss., Columbia Univ., 1974); J. Vertrees Sadie, "M. M. and His Contemporaries," *Musical Times,* CXIX (1978); D. Teplow, *Performance*

Practice and Technique in M. M.'s "Pièces de viole" (Ann Arbor, 1986).

Mařák, Otakar, prominent Czech tenor; b. Esztergom, Hungary, Jan. 5, 1872; d. Prague, July 2, 1939. He studied with Paršova-Zikešová at the Prague Cons.; made his debut as Faust in 1899 in Brünn; then sang with the Prague National Theater Opera (1901–7; 1914–34), in Vienna, Berlin, London, Paris, and Chicago. He died in poverty after the failure of a business venture.

Marazzoli, Marco, significant Italian composer; b. Parma, between 1602 and 1608; d. Rome, Jan. 26, 1662. In 1631 he gained the patronage of Cardinal Antonio Barberini in Rome; in 1637 he settled in Rome in the cardinal's service and became a tenor in the Papal Chapel, a position he held until his death; he also was engaged by Cardinal Mazarin in Paris in 1643; returned to Rome in 1645; in 1656 he became virtuoso di camera to Queen Christina of Sweden, who held her court in Rome at the time. Marazzoli was a prolific composer of choral music; about 375 of his cantatas and oratorios are extant. His name is also associated with that of Virgilio Mazzocchi; they collaborated on the 1st comic opera, *Chi soffre, speri* (Rome, Feb. 27, 1639), which was a revision of *Il facone* (Rome, Feb. 1637). His other operas include *L'amore trionfante dello sdegno* (also known as *L'Armida*; Ferrara, Feb. 1641); *Gli amori di Giasone e d' Issifile* (Venice, 1642; not extant); *Le pretensioni del Tebro e del Po* (Ferrara, March 4, 1642); *Il capriccio* or *Il giudizio della ragione fra la Beltà e l'Affetto* (Rome, 1643); *Dal male il bene* (with A.M. Abbatini; Rome, 1653); *Le armi e gli amori* (Rome, 1654); *La vita humana, ovvero Il trionfo della pietà* (Rome, Jan. 31, 1656). **BIBL.:** M. Grace, *M. M. and the Development of the Latin Oratorio* (diss., Yale Univ., 1974).

Marbé, Myriam, Rumanian composer; b. Bucharest, April 9, 1931. She began her musical training with her mother, Angela Marbé, a piano pedagogue; continued her studies with Ioan Chirescu (theory), Martian Negrea and Ion Dumitrescu (harmony), Mihail Jora and Leon Klepper (counterpoint and composition), Theodor Rogalski (orchestration), Zeno Vancea and Vasile Popovici (music history), Sabin Drăgoi and Emilia Comisel (folk music), and Florica Musicescu and Silvia Căpătînă (piano) at the Bucharest Cons. (1944–54); later attended courses in new music in Darmstadt (1968, 1969, 1972). She taught at the Bucharest Cons. (from 1954). She was awarded prizes by the Union of Rumanian Composers (1970–71; 1973–74; 1980; 1982), the Bernier Prize of the Académie des Beaux-Arts of Paris (1972), and the prize of the Rumanian Academy (1977). **WORKS: DRAMATIC:** *Noapte țărănească,* cantata for Choir and Orch. (1958). **ORCH.:** *In Memoriam—Pièce lyrique* for Oboe, String Orch., 2 Horns, Piano, Celesta, and Percussion (1959); *Musica festiva,* divertissement for String Orch., Brass, and Percussion (1961); *Clime* for Mezzo-soprano, Choir, and Chamber Orch. (1966); *. . . De aducere aminte (. . . En souvenir)* for Choir and Orch. (1967); *Temps et espace* (1972); *Evocări* for String Orch. and Percussion (1976); Concerto for Viola and Orch. (1977); *Trium* (1978); Concerto for Viola da Gamba or Cello, and Orch. (1982); Concerto for Saxophone(s) and Orch. (1986). **CHAMBER:** Sonata for Viola and Piano (1955); Sonata for Clarinet and Piano (1961); *Incantatio,* sonata for Solo Clarinet (1964); Sonata for 2 Violas (1965); *Jocus secundus* for Violin, Clarinet, Viola, Cello, Piano, Percussion, Small Vocal Group, and Tape ad libitum (1969); *Cyclus* for Flute, Guitar, and Percussion (1974); *Vocabulaire—I, Chanson* for Soprano, Clarinet, Piano, and Bells (1974); *La Parabole du Grenier I* for Piano and Harpsichord, with Celesta, Glockenspiel, and Bells ad libitum (1975–76; rev. 1979); *Narratio* for Flute, Violin, Viola, and Percussion (1979); *Les Oiseaux artificiels* for Clarinet, Violin, Viola, Cello, Harpsichord, Celesta, and Reciter (1979); 2 string quartets (1981, 1985); *An die Musik* for Mezzo-soprano, Organ, and Flute (1983); *Trommelbass* for String Trio (1985); *Des-Cantec* for Wind Quintet (1985); *An die Sonne* for Mezzo-soprano and Wind Quintet (1986); various works

for piano, including a Sonata (1956), *Le Temps inévitable I and II* (1968; also for Piano and Orch., 1971), and *Cluster Studien I and II* (1970); *Accents* (1971); also choruses; songs. **BIBL.:** L. Danceanu, "Portrait M. M.," *Muzica,* 7 (Bucharest, 1983).

Marbeck or **Marbecke, John,** English organist, composer, and writer on theology; b. probably in Windsor, c.1505; d. 1585. He became a clerk and organist at St. George's Chapel, Windsor (1531). His interest in religion prompted him to prepare a concordance of the English Bible, as well as various theological tracts. However, he was arrested for heresy in 1543 and sentenced to die at the stake. After being saved by the intercession of Henry VIII, he resumed his duties at St. George's Chapel and returned to his theological pursuits. He brought out the 1st publ. concordance of the English Bible (1550). After the Act of Uniformity (1549) made the use of English services in the 1st Book of Common Prayer mandatory throughout the realm, he was commissioned to prepare a musical setting for liturgical use, which was publ. as *The Booke of Common Praier Noted* (London, 1550; facsimile ed., 1939). **BIBL.:** R. Terry, "J. Marbecke: 1523?–1585," *Proceedings of the Musical Association,* XLV (1918–19); R. Stevenson, "J. Marbeck's 'Noted Book' of 1550," *Musical Quarterly,* XXXVII (1951); R. Leaver, *The Work of J. Marbeck* (Oxford, 1978).

Marcel (real name, **Wasself**), **Lucille,** American soprano; b. N.Y., 1885; d. Vienna, June 22, 1921. She studied in N.Y., Berlin, and with J. de Reszke in Paris, where she made her debut as Mallika in *Lakmé* at the Opéra-Comique (1903). After marrying the conductor **Felix Weingartner** (1907), she sang the title role in *Elektra* at its 1st Viennese staging under his direction (March 24, 1908); continued to sing at the Court Opera until 1911, then was a member of the Hamburg Opera (1912–14). She made her U.S. debut as Tosca with the Boston Opera Co. (Feb. 14, 1912), and remained on its roster until 1914. After a period in Darmstadt, she settled in Vienna. Her other roles included Eva, Marguerite, Desdemona, and Aida.

Marcello, Alessandro, Italian violinist, composer, poet, and painter, brother of **Benedetto Marcello;** b. Venice, Aug. 24, 1669; d. Padua, June 19, 1747. He studied violin with his father. He publ. his compositions under the name of Eterio Stinfalico. He was the composer of the Oboe Concerto in D minor transcribed by Bach (BWV 974), formerly attributed to Vivaldi and later to Benedetto Marcello. Other extant works are *La cetra,* [6] *concerti di Eterio Stinfalico* for 2 Flutes or Oboes, Bassoon, Strings, and Basso Continuo (Augsburg, c.1740) and Concerto No. 2 in *Concerti a cinque* for Oboe, Strings, and Basso Continuo (Amsterdam, c.1717); also other concertos, solo cantatas, arias, and canzonets. **BIBL.:** F. Walker, "A Little Bach Discovery," *Music & Letters* (April 1950); E. Selfridge-Field, *The Works of Benedetto and A. M.: A Thematic Catalogue* (Oxford, 1990).

Marcello, Benedetto, famous Italian composer and teacher, brother of **Alessandro Marcello;** b. Venice, July 24 or Aug. 1, 1686; d. Brescia, July 24 or 25, 1739. He studied violin with his father; later took courses in singing and counterpoint with F. Gasparini. Having prepared for a legal career, he accepted a number of distinguished positions in public life: was made a member of the Grand Council of the Republic (1707); served on the Council of Forty for 14 years; was governor of Pola (1730–37); subsequently camarlingo (chamberlain) of Brescia (1738–39); was also active as an advocate and magistrate. Adopting the pseudonym Driante Sacreo, he became a member of Rome's Arcadian Academy; was also elected a member of Bologna's Accademia Filarmonica (1712). His distinguished students included the singer Faustina Bordoni and the composer Baldassare Galuppi. He most likely was the author of *Lettera famigliare d'un accademico filarmonico ed arcade discorsiva sopra un libro di duetti, terzetti e madrigali a più voci* (Venice, 1705), an anonymous and rather captious critique of Lotti. He publ. a famous satire on Vivaldi and his contemporaries as *Il teatro alla moda, o sia Metodo sicuro e facile per il ben comporre ed eseguire l'opere italiane in musica all'usu* *moderno* (Venice, c.1720; Eng. tr. by R. Paul, *Musical Quarterly,* July 1948 and Jan. 1949). Marcello was one of the most gifted Italian composers of his time, his mastery ranging from sacred and secular vocal works to instrumental works.

WORKS: **ORATORIOS:** *Il sepolcro* (Venice?, 1705); *Giuditta* (Rome, 1709); *Gioàz* (Vienna, 1726); *Il pianto e il riso delle quattro stagioni* (Venice?, 1731); *Il trionfo della poesia e della musica* (Venice?, 1733); other sacred vocal works include *Estro poetico-armonico, parafrasi sopra li primi [secondi] 25 salmi* (Venice, 1724–26; reprint, 1967); 10 masses; 15 motets; etc. **STAGE:** 2 serenatas: *Serenata da cantarsi ad uso di scena* (Vienna, 1725) and *La morte di Adone* (Rome, 1729); the *intreccio scenico musicale Arianna* (Florence, 1727); a cantata; etc. **SECULAR VOCAL:** (12) *Canzoni madrigalesche e* [6] *arie per camera* for 2 to 4 Voices, op. 4 (Bologna, 1717); over 500 cantatas; about 85 duets; etc. **INSTRUMENTAL:** (12) *Concerti a cinque,* with Violin and Cello obbligato, op. 1 (Venice, 1708); (12) *Suonate* for Recorder and Basso Continuo, op. 2 (Amsterdam, before 1717; as op. 1 for Flute or Violin, and Basso Continuo, London, 1732); 6 sonatas for Cello and Basso Continuo, op. 1 (Amsterdam, c.1732; as op. 2, London, 1732; as op. 1, Paris, c.1735); 6 sonatas for 2 Cellos or 2 Bass Viols, and Basso Continuo or Cello, as op. 2 (Amsterdam, c.1734); Concerto for Violin and Strings; Concerto for 2 Violins and Strings; 7 sinfonias for Strings; various harpsichord sonatas (12 ed. in Le Pupitre, XXVIII, Paris, 1971); etc.

BIBL.: F. Fontana, *Vita di B. M., patrizio Veneto* (Venice, 1788); F. Caffi, *Della vita e della opera di B. M.* (Venice, 1830); L. Busi, *B. M.* (Bologna, 1884); O. Chilesotti, *Sulla lettera critica di B. M. contro A. Lotti* (Bassano, 1885); E. Fondi, *La vita e l'opera letteraria del musicista B. M.* (Rome, 1909); A. d'Angeli, *B. M.: Vita e opere* (Milan, 1940); G. Tinctori, *L'Arianna di B. M.* (Milan, 1951); C. Sites, *B. M.'s Chamber Cantatas* (diss., Univ. of North Carolina, 1959); E. Selfridge-Field, *The Works of B. and Alessandro M.: A Thematic Catalogue* (Oxford, 1990).

Marchal, André (-Louis), distinguished blind French organist and pedagogue; b. Paris, Feb. 6, 1894; d. St. Jean-de-Luz, Aug. 27, 1980. He was blind from birth; studied at the Institution Nationale des Jeunes Aveugles; later entered the Paris Cons. in the class of Gigout. In 1915 he became organist at St. Germain-des-Près in Paris; then served at St. Eustache from 1945 to 1963. He began a concert career in 1923; was greatly admired for his exhaustive repertoire and brilliance as an improviser. He was also esteemed as a teacher.

Marchand, Louis, French organist, harpsichordist, and composer; b. Lyons, Feb. 2, 1669; d. Paris, Feb. 17, 1732. He went to Paris in 1689; in 1691 he received the post of organist of the Jesuit church in the rue St. Jacques; he was also organist at other Parisian churches; in 1708 he was named an organiste du roi, in which capacity he earned a considerable reputation; in 1713 he made a major tour of Germany. Marchand's name is historically connected with that of Bach because both were scheduled to meet in open competition in Dresden in 1717; however, Marchand failed to appear and Bach was deemed the superior virtuoso by default. He subsequently was organist at the Cordeliers in Paris.

WORKS: *Pièces de clavecin, livres 1–2* (Paris, 1702); (12) *Pièces choisies pour l'orgue* (Paris, after 1732); also 42 organ pieces in 4 books in MS and vocal works, including various airs in anthologies (1706–43). See T. Dart, ed., *Louis Marchand: Pièces de clavecin* (Paris, 1960) and J. Bonfils, ed., *Louis Marchand: L'Œuvre d'orgue édition intégrale* (Paris, 1970–   ).

BIBL.: G. Sharp, "L. M., 1669–1732: A Forgotten Virtuoso," *Musical Times,* CX (1969).

Marchant, Sir Stanley (Robert), English organist, teacher, and composer; b. London, May 15, 1883; d. there, Feb. 28, 1949. He studied organ at the Royal Academy of Music in London; completed his studies at Oxford (D.Mus., 1914). He occupied various posts as organist in London churches from 1899; was made prof. (1913) and principal (1936) at the Royal Academy of Music; was named King Edward VII Prof. of Music at London Univ. (1937); was knighted (1943). He wrote sacred music, secular choral works, songs, and organ pieces.

Marchesi, Blanche, French soprano and teacher, daughter of **Salvatore** and **Mathilde Marchesi de Castrone;** b. Paris, April 4, 1863; d. London, Dec. 15, 1940. She was 1st trained as a violinist; took lessons with Nikisch in Germany and with Colonne in Paris. In 1881 she began to study singing with her mother, and, until her marriage to Baron Caccamisi, acted as her mother's assistant. She made her concert debut in Berlin (1895); when she sang in London (1896), the reception was so enthusiastic that she made England her home; her operatic debut followed in Prague in 1900 as Brünnhilde in *Die Walküre;* then sang with the Moody-Manners company in London; from 1902, sang Wagner roles at Covent Garden in London; made tours of Russia and Central Europe; also made 2 concert tours of the U.S. (1899, 1909); gave her farewell concert in 1938. In her last years, she established herself as a highly esteemed teacher in London. She publ. her memoirs under the title *A Singer's Pilgrimage* (London, 1923); also publ. *The Singer's Catechism* (London, 1932).

Marchesi, Luigi (Lodovico), celebrated Italian castrato soprano, known as "Marchesini"; b. Milan, Aug. 8, 1754; d. Inzago, Dec. 14, 1829. He studied horn with his father; after having himself castrated, he pursued vocal training with Alluzzi and Caironi; at age 11, he joined the choir at the Milan Cathedral, where he studied composition with its director Fioroni. He made his debut as Giannetta in Anfossi's *L'Incognita perseguitata* in Rome (1773); sang in Treviso (1775), and then was a member of the Munich court (1776–78); subsequently gained renown as a member of the Teatro San Carlo in Naples (1778–79); appeared in Florence (1780) and then again in Naples (1780–81). He sang in Milan and also in Turin, where he held the title of musico di corte (1782–98). In 1785 he was engaged by the court of Catherine the Great; on his way to St. Petersburg, he appeared in Sarti's *Giulio Sabino* in Vienna before Emperor Joseph II (Aug. 4, 1785), who ordered a medal be struck in his honor. He made his Russian debut as Rinaldo in Sarti's *Armida e Rinaldo* at the inaugural performance of the Hermitage Theater in St. Petersburg (Jan. 15, 1786). The soprano Luiza-Rosa Todi intrigued against him, however, and despite his successes, he left Russia before the expiration of his contract. He then appeared in Berlin on March 9, 1787, and subsequently scored a London triumph in *Giulio Sabino* on April 5, 1788; made his last appearance in London on July 17, 1790, and then pursued his career mainly in Italy; also sang in Vienna again (1798, 1801). He sang in the premiere of Mayr's *Ginevra di Scozia* at the dedicatory performance of the Teatro Nuovo in Trieste on April 21, 1801; made his farewell stage appearance in Mayr's *Lodoiska* in Milan in May 1805, but sang in public as late as 1820 in Naples. Blessed with a range of 2½ octaves, Marchesi was unsurpassed in the opera seria genre of his era.

Marchesi de Castrone, Mathilde (née **Graumann**), famous German mezzo-soprano and pedagogue, mother of **Blanche Marchesi;** b. Frankfurt am Main, March 24, 1821; d. London, Nov. 17, 1913. She studied in Frankfurt with Felice Ronconi, in Vienna with Nicolai, in Paris with Manuel García, and in London; made her concert debut in Frankfurt on Aug. 31, 1844. In 1849 she went to London; in 1852 she married the Italian baritone **Salvatore Marchesi de Castrone.** Later in life she devoted herself mainly to teaching; had classes at the Vienna Cons. (1854–61; 1868–78); also taught privately in Paris. Among her famous pupils were Murska, Gerster, Melba, Eames, Calvé, and Sanderson. She wrote an autobiography, *Erinnerungen aus meinem Leben* (Vienna, 1877), which was publ. in a revised and amplified ed. under the title *Marchesi and Music: Passages from the Life of a Famous Singing Teacher* (N.Y., 1897). She further publ. a vocal manual, *10 Singing Lessons* (N.Y., 1910), which was reprinted under a new title, *Theoretical and Practical Vocal Method* (N.Y., 1970, with an introduction by P. Miller).

Marchesi de Castrone, Salvatore (full name and title, **Salvatore Marchesi, Cavaliere de Castrone, Marchese della Rajata**), distinguished Italian baritone and teacher, father of **Blanche Marchesi;** b. Palermo, Jan. 15, 1822; d. Paris, Feb. 20, 1908. Of a noble family, he was destined for a government career and studied law in Palermo; however, he turned to music, and took lessons in singing and theory with Raimondi in Palermo, and with Lamperti in Milan. He was involved in the revolutionary events of 1848, and was compelled to leave Italy; went to N.Y., where he made his operatic debut as Carlos in *Ernani.* He then studied with García in London; married **Mathilde Marchesi de Castrone** (née **Graumann**) in 1852, and sang with her in opera on the Continent. From 1854 to 1861, they both taught at the Vienna Cons.; later at the Cologne Cons. (1865–68), and again in Vienna (1868–78); after that they resided in Paris.

Marchetti, Filippo, Italian composer; b. Bolognola, near Camerino, Feb. 26, 1831; d. Rome, Jan. 18, 1902. He was a pupil of Lillo and Conti at the Royal Cons. in Naples. His 1st opera, *Gentile da Varano* (Turin, Feb. 1856), was extremely well received, and he repeated his success with another opera, *La Demente,* for Turin (Nov. 27, 1856); however, his next opera, *Il Paria,* never reached the stage. He was not discouraged by this and wrote his *Romeo e Giulietta* (Trieste, Oct. 25, 1865), which made little impression until it was mounted at Milan's Teatro Carcano in 1867. He achieved his greatest success with *Ruy-Blas* (La Scala, Milan, April 3, 1869), which was produced also in Germany and England; his remaining operas were *Gustavo Wasa* (La Scala, Feb. 7, 1875) and *Don Giovanni d'Austria* (Turin, March 11, 1880). In 1881 he was appointed president of the Accademia di Santa Cecilia in Rome; then was director of the Liceo Musicale there (1886–1901). He also wrote some orch. pieces, choral works, and sacred music.

Marchetto da Padua (Marchettus de Padua, Marcus de Padua, Marcus Paduanus), Italian music theorist and composer; b. Padua, c.1274; d. after 1326. He was maestro di canto at Padua Cathedral (1305–7). He is known for the treatises *Lucidarium in arte musicae planae* (on plainsong, early 14th century) and *Pomerium artis musicae mensurabilis* (on mensural music, 1318); the latter is included (in part) in O. Strunk's *Source Readings in Music History* (N.Y., 1950); a modern ed. is found in Corpus Scriptorum de Musica, VI (1961). He also wrote *Brevis compilatio in arte musicae mensuratae,* which has been ed. by G. Vecchi, "Su la composizione del *Pomerium* di Marchetto de Padova e la *Brevis compilatio,*" in *Quadrivium,* I (1956). Three motets have been ascribed to him.

BIBL.: O. Strunk, "Intorno a M. da Padova," *Rassegna Musicale* (Oct. 1950); N. Pirotta, "Marchettus de Padova and the Italian Ars Nova," *Musica Disciplina,* IX (1955); M. Martinez-Göllner, "Marchettus of Padua and Chromaticism," *L'ars nova italiana del tracento II: Certaldo 1969;* F. Gallo, "Marchettus in Padua und die Franco-venetische' Musik des frühen Trecentos," *Archiv für Musikwissenschaft,* XXXI (1974); K. Berger, *Musica Ficta: Theories of Accidental Inflections in Vocal Polyphony from M. da Padova to Gioseffo Zarlino* (Cambridge, 1987).

Marchisio, Barbara, Italian contralto and teacher; b. Turin, Dec. 6, 1833; d. Mira, April 19, 1919. She studied with her brother, the composer Antonino Marchisio (1817–1875), and with L. Fabbrica in Turin; made her debut as Adalgisa in *Norma* in Vicenza (1856), and sang Rosina in Madrid that same year. Her sister, **Carlotta Marchisio** (b. Turin, Dec. 8, 1835; d. there, June 28, 1872), also studied with her brother and with Fabbrica in Turin; made her debut as Norma in Madrid (1856). The 2 sisters 1st appeared together in Turin in 1858; after singing in Trieste, they made their joint debut at Milan's La Scala in *Semiramide* (Dec. 29, 1858); this opera continued as their vehicle for their joint debut at the Paris Opéra (in French, July 9, 1860) and at Her Majesty's Theatre in London (May 1, 1862). They last appeared together in Rome in 1871. After Carlotta died in childbirth, Barbara continued

her career for several more years, appearing in Milan (1872) and Venice (1876). She then devoted herself to teaching, numbering Raisa and dal Monte among her students. Rossini held the Marchisio sisters in the highest esteem.

Marco, Tomás, Spanish composer; b. Madrid, Sept. 12, 1942. He studied violin and composition at the Univ. of Madrid (1959–64); also attended the Darmstadt summer course in new music (1967). An ardent modernist, he founded in 1967 the magazine *Sonda,* dedicated to new music. His compositions are of an experimental, almost exhibitionistic, theatrical nature.

WORKS: *Los caprichos* for Orch. (1959–67); *Trivium* for Piano, Tuba, and Percussion (1963); *Roulis-Tangage* for Trumpet, Cello, Guitar, Piano, Vibraphone, and 2 Percussionists (1962–63); *Glasperlenspiel* for Chamber Orch. (1963–64); *Car en effet* for 3 Clarinets and 3 Saxophones (1965); *Piraña* for Piano (1965); *Jabberwocky* for Actors, Tenor, Saxophone, Piano, 4 Percussionists, Tape, 6 Radios, Lights, and Slides (1966); *Schwan* for Trumpet, Trombone, Viola, Cello, and 2 Percussionists (1966); *Cantos del pozo artesiano* for Actress, 3 Chamber Ensembles, and Lights (1967); *Vitral (Música celestial No. 1)* for Organ and String Orch. (1968); *Maya* for Cello and Piano (1968–69); *Anábasis* for Orch. (1968–70); *Rosa-Rosae,* quartet for Flute, Clarinet, Violin, and Cello (1969); *Tea Party* for 4 Vocal Soloists, Clarinet, Trombone, Cello, and Vibraphone (1969); *Floreal* for a Percussionist (1969); *Kukulcan* for Wind Quintet (1969–72); *Mysteria* for Chamber Orch. (1970–71); *Albor* for Flute, Clarinet, Violin, Cello, and Piano (1970); *Evos* for Piano (1970); *Necronomicon,* choreography for 6 Percussionists (1971); *L'Invitation au voyage* for Soprano, optional Narrator, 3 Clarinets, Piano, and Percussion (1971); *Angelus novus (Hommage à Mahler)* for Orch. (1971); *Jetztzeit* for Clarinet and Piano (1971); Violin Concerto, subtitled *Les Mécanismes de la mémoire* (1971–72; Royan Festival, April 19, 1973); *Nuba* for Flute, Oboe, Clarinet, Violin, Cello, and Percussion (1973); *Ultramarina* for Soprano, Clarinet, Piano, and Percussion (1975); *Concerto austral* for Oboe and Orch. (1982); *Espacio sagrado* for Piano, 2 Choruses, and Orch. (1982); Sym. No. 3 (1986).

Marcoux, Vanni (actually, **Jean Émile Diogène**), noted French bass-baritone; b. Turin (of French parents), June 12, 1877; d. Paris, Oct. 21, 1962. He was a law student at the Univ. of Turin; then enrolled at the Paris Cons. He made his debut in Turin in 1894 as Sparafucile; subsequently obtained considerable success at his debut at the Paris Opéra as Colonna in the premiere of Février's *Monna Vanna* (Jan. 13, 1909). Massenet entrusted to him the part of Don Quichotte in the Paris premiere of his opera of that name (Dec. 29, 1910). In 1912 he sang with the Boston Opera Co., and later with the Chicago Grand Opera Co. (1913–14). His repertoire included more than 200 roles in several languages. He eventually returned to Paris, where he taught at the Cons. (1938–43); sang at the Paris Opéra for nearly 40 years; was also director of the Grand Théâtre in Bordeaux (1948–51). In professional appearances, he used the hyphenated name Vanni-Marcoux.

Marcovici, Silvia, Rumanian violinist; b. Bacau, Jan. 30, 1952. She studied in Bacau and at the Bucharest Cons.; her principal teacher was S. Gheorghiu. She made her professional debut in The Hague in 1967; in 1969 she won the Long-Thibaud Competition in Paris and in 1970 the Enescu Competition in Bucharest. She appeared for the 1st time in London in 1970; in 1977, performed in N.Y.; subsequently appeared with many of the world's major orchs.

Marcuse, Sibyl, German-born American musicologist; b. Frankfurt am Main (of Swiss-English parents), Feb. 13, 1911. After studies in Europe, she lived in China (1932–35); emigrated to the U.S. with the coming of World War II, becoming a naturalized citizen in 1945; studied at a N.Y. school for piano technicians and then worked as a keyboard technician. She was curator of the Yale Univ. Collection of Musical Instruments (1953–60); publ. *Musical Instruments, A Comprehensive*

Dictionary (1964; 2nd ed., rev., 1975) and *A Survey of Musical Instruments* (1975).

Maréchal, Adolphe, Belgian tenor; b. Liège, Sept. 26, 1867; d. Brussels, Feb. 1, 1935. He studied at the Liège Cons.; made his debut in Tournai in 1891; then sang in Rheims, Bordeaux, and Nice; in 1895 he became a member of the Opéra-Comique in Paris, where he remained until 1907; during that time, he created the roles of Julien in *Louise*, Alain in *Grisélidis*, and Danielo in *La Reine fiammette*; also Jean in *Le Jongleur de Notre-Dame* at Monte Carlo. He retired in 1907 after the loss of his singing voice.

Maréchal, (Charles-) Henri, French composer; b. Paris, Jan. 22, 1842; d. there, May 12, 1924. He studied with Chauvet (counterpoint and fugue), Benoist (organ), and Massé (composition) at the Paris Cons.; won the Grand Prix de Rome (1870) with the cantata *Le Jugement de Dieu*. After his return from Rome, he produced an oratorio, *La Nativité* (1875), and operas: *Les Amoureux de Catherine* (Paris, May 8, 1876), *L'Étoile* (Paris, March 12, 1881), *La Taverne des Trabans* (Paris, Dec. 31, 1881), *Déidamie* (Paris, Sept. 15, 1893), *Calendal* (Rouen, Dec. 21, 1894), and *Ping-Sin* (1895; Paris, Jan. 25, 1918); also wrote several orch. suites, choral works, etc. He publ. 2 vols. of reminiscences: *Rome: Souvenirs d'un musicien* (Paris, 1904; 2nd ed., 1913) and *Paris: Souvenirs d'un musicien* (Paris, 1907).

Marek, Czeslaw (Josef), Polish-born Swiss pianist, teacher, and composer; b. Przemysl, Sept. 16, 1891; d. Zürich, July 17, 1985. He studied with Loewenhoff (piano) and Niewiadomsky (harmony) at the Lemberg Music Inst., Leschetizky (piano) and Weigl (composition) in Vienna, and Pfitzner (composition) in Strasbourg. He made his debut in Lemberg (1909), where he taught at the Music Inst. until 1915; then settled in Zürich as a pianist, teacher, and composer, becoming a Swiss citizen (1932); was also prof. of composition at the Poznan Cons. (1929–30). He publ. the manual *Lehre des Klavierspiels* (Zürich, 1972).

WORKS: ORCH.: *Méditations* (1911–13); *Scherzo symfoniczne* (1914); Sinfonietta (1914–16); Serenade for Violin and Orch. (1916–18); Suite (1925); Sinfonia (1927); also Sonata for Violin and Piano (1914); piano pieces; songs.

Marenco, Romualdo, Italian composer; b. Novi Ligure, March 1, 1841; d. Milan, Oct. 9, 1907. He played the violin, then the bassoon at the Doria Theater in Genoa, for which he wrote his 1st ballet, *Lo sbarco di Garibaldi a Marsala*. He studied counterpoint and composition with Taddei, but was mainly self-taught via the manuals of Fenaroli and Mattei; was director of ballet music at Milan's La Scala (1873–86). He composed some 15 ballets, the most popular being *Sieba* (1878), *Excelsior* (1881), *Amor* (1886), and *Sport* (1897). He also wrote the operas *Lorenzio de' Medici* (Lodi, 1874), *I Moncada* (Milan, 1880), *Le Diablo au corps* (Paris, 1884), and *Strategia d'amore* (Milan, 1896). A posthumous opera, *Federico Struensea*, was produced in Milan in 1908. He also composed 2 syms. and piano pieces.

BIBL.: S. Cavazza, *R. M.* (Novi Ligure, 1957).

Marenzio, Luca, important Italian composer; b. Coccaglio, near Brescia, 1553 or 1554; d. Rome, Aug. 22, 1599. Little is known of his early life; he may have studied with Giovanni Contino in Brescia; about 1574 he entered the service of Cardinal Cristoforo Madruzzo in Rome; following Madruzzo's death in 1578, he entered the service of Cardinal Luigi d'Este; he made an extended visit with the cardinal to the court of Duke Alfonso II d'Este in Ferrara, where he spent the months of Nov. 1580 to May 1581; he dedicated 2 vols. of madrigals to the duke and his sister Lucrezia. After the death of the cardinal in 1586, he entered the service of Ferdinando de' Medici, the grand duke of Florence (1588); in 1589 he returned to Rome, where he apparently received the patronage of several cardinals; about 1593 he entered the service of Cardinal Cinzio Aldobrandini; he subsequently served at the court of Sigismund III of Poland (1596–98); he then returned to Rome, where

he died the following year. Marenzio was one of the foremost madrigalists of his time; his later works in the genre are historically significant for their advanced harmonic procedures. He also composed about 75 motets. He was called by his contemporaries "il più dolce cigno d'Italia" and "divino compositore."

WORKS: SECULAR: *Il primo libro di madrigali* for 5 Voices (Venice, 1580); *Il primo libro de madrigali* for 6 Voices (Venice, 1581); *Il secondo libro de madrigali* for 5 Voices (Venice, 1581); *Il terzo libro de madrigali* for 5 Voices (Venice, 1582); *Il secondo libro de madrigali* for 6 Voices (Venice, 1584); *Madrigali spirituali* for 5 Voices (Rome, 1584; enl. ed., 1610); *Il quarto libro de madrigali* for 5 Voices (Venice, 1584); *Il primo libro delle villanelle* for 3 Voices (Venice, 1584); *Il quinto libro de madrigali* for 5 Voices (Venice, 1585); *Il terzo libro de madrigali* for 6 Voices (Venice, 1585); *Il secondo libro delle canzonette alla napolitana* for 3 Voices (Venice, 1585); *Madrigali . . . libro primo* for 4 Voices (Rome, 1585); *Il terzo libro delle villanelle* for 3 Voices (Venice, 1585; 4th ed., enl., 1600); *Il quarto libro de madrigali* for 6 Voices (Venice, 1587; 3rd ed., rev., 1593); *Il quarto libro delle villanelle* for 3 Voices (Venice, 1587; 4th ed., rev., 1600); *Il quinto libro delle villanelle* for 3 Voices (Venice, 1587); *Madrigali . . . libro primo* for 4, 5, and 6 Voices (Venice, 1588); *Il quinto libro de madrigali* for 6 Voices (Venice, 1591); *Il sesto libro de madrigali* for 5 Voices (Venice, 1594); *Il sesto libro de madrigali* for 6 Voices (Venice, 1595); *Il settimo libro de madrigali* for 5 Voices (Venice, 1595); *L'ottavo libro de madrigali* for 5 Voices (Venice, 1598); *Il nono libro de madrigali* for 5 Voices (Venice, 1599); also *Il secondo libro de madrigali* for 4 Voices, which is not extant. **SACRED:** *Motectorum pro festis totius anni cum Communi Sanctorum* for 4 Voices (Venice, 1585); *Completorium et antiphonae* for 6 Voices (Venice, 1595; not extant); *Motetti* for 12 Voices (Venice, 1614); *Sacrae cantiones* for 5, 6, and 7 Voices (Venice, 1616). B. Meier and R. Jackson ed. the *Opera omnia* in Corpus Mensurabilis Musicae (1976); S. Ledbetter and P. Myers are also editing *The Secular Works* (N.Y., 1977–).

BIBL.: F. Haberl, "L. M.: Eine bio-bibliographische Skizze," *Kirchenmusikalisches Jahrbuch*, XV (1900); J. Orbaan, "Notizie inedite su L. M.," *Bolletino Bibliografico Musicale*, III/3 (1928); A. Einstein, *The Italian Madrigal* (Princeton, 1949); P. Guerrini, *L. M.: il più dolce cigno d'Italia nel centenario della nascita* (Brescia, 1953); H. Engel, *L. M.* (Florence, 1956); D. Arnold, *M.* (London, 1965); J. Steele, "The Later Madrigals of L. M.," *Studies in Music* (1969); R. Jackson, "Two Newly-Found Motets by M. (?)," *Journal of the American Musicological Society*, XXIV (1971); S. Ledbetter, *L. M.: New Biographical Findings* (diss., N.Y. Univ., 1971); W. Kirkendale, "Franceschina, Girometta, and Their Companions in a Madrigal 'A diversi linguaggi' by L. M. and Orazio Vecchi," *Acta Musicologica*, XLIV (1972); N. Pirrotta, "Note su M. e il Tasso," *Scritti in onore di Luigi Ronga* (Milan and Naples, 1973); J. Chater, "Fonti poetichi dei madrigali di L. M.," *Rivista Italiana di Musicologia*, XIII (1978); S. Ledbetter, "M.'s Early Career," *Journal of the American Musicological Society*, XXXII (1979); J. Chater, *L. M. and the Italian Madrigal 1577–1593* (2 vols., Ann Arbor, 1981); idem, "L. M.: New Documents, New Observations," *Music & Letters* (Jan.–April 1983).

Maresch (Mareš), Johann Anton (Jan Antonín), Bohemian horn player, cellist, and composer; b. Chotěboř, 1719; d. St. Petersburg, June 10, 1794. He studied horn with Hampel and cello with Zyka in Dresden. After teaching music in Berlin, he was engaged by the Russian Grand Chancellor A.P. Bestuzhev-Ryumin as horn player in his private orch. in St. Petersburg (1748); later was horn player (1752–74) and 2nd cellist (1774–92) in the imperial Court Orch. In 1751 he was commissioned to organize an ensemble of hunting horns for the court; he formed a group comprising 2 complete octaves tuned chromatically, adding large drums with church bells suspended within them; also constructed wooden horns for soft accompaniment to operas. The vogue of horn orchs. in Russia continued for about 50 years after Maresch's death; the players were recruited usually from among serfs. After the emancipation of serfs in Russia in 1861, the horn orchs. gradually disappeared.

BIBL.: J. Hinrichs, *Entstehung, Fortgang und jetzige Beschaffenheit der russischen Jagdmusik* (St. Petersburg, 1796); K. Vertkov, *Russian Horn Music* (Moscow, 1948); R.-A. Mooser, *Annales de la musique et des musiciens en Russie au XVIIIe siècle* (3 vols., Geneva, 1948–51); R. Ricks, "Russian Horn Bands," *Musical Quarterly*, LV (1969).

Mareschall, Samuel, Swiss organist, writer on music, and composer of South Netherlands descent; b. Tournai, May 22?, 1554; d. Basel, Dec. 1640?. He studied at the Univ. of Basel. In 1577 he became a prof. of music there and organist at the Basel Cathedral. His collection of 4-part vocal settings of the Psalms (1606) became a traditional Lutheran hymnbook; another book of Psalms (including hymns by Luther) appeared in 1606. He also compiled *Melodiae suaves* (1622); publ. a teaching manual, *Porta musices, das ist Eynführung zu der edlen Kunst Musica, mit einem kurtzen Bericht und Anleitung zu den Violen, auch wie ein jeder Gesang leichtlich anzustimmen seye* (Basel, 1589).

BIBL.: W. Kendall, "The Life and Works of S. M.," *Musical Quarterly* (Jan. 1944).

Marescotti, André-François, Swiss composer; b. Carouge, near Geneva, April 30, 1902. He studied with A. Mottu (piano), J. Lauber (instrumentation), and C. Chaix (composition) at the Geneva Cons. and with Roger-Ducasse (composition) in Paris. He was made choirmaster of the boys' choir at Sacré-Coeur (1924) and at the St.-Joseph Church in Geneva (1940); also taught at the Geneva Cons. (1931–73). He publ. the valuable folio vol. *Les Instruments d'orchestre, Leurs caractères, leurs possibilités et leur utilisation dans l'orchestre moderne* (with 900 musical examples; Paris, 1950). After composing works in the French Impressionist manner, he turned to serial procedures.

WORKS: ORCH.: *Aubade* (1936; Geneva, Jan. 27, 1938); *Concert carougeois:* I (1941), II (1958), III (1966), and IV (1985); *Giboulées* for Bassoon and Orch. (1949); Piano Concerto (1956); *Festa,* overture (1961); *Insomnies* for Mezzo-soprano and Orch. (1951–61); *Hymnes* (1963); *Rondeau capriccioso* (1972); Cello Concerto (1979); *Nuage sur la vigne,* suite (1984); also *Les Anges du Greco,* ballet (Zürich, June 1, 1947); *La Lampe d'argile,* dramatic legend (Strasbourg, April 1951); choral works; piano pieces.

BIBL.: A. Golea, *A.-F. M.* (Paris, 1963); C. Tappolet, *A.-F. M.* (Geneva, 1986).

Maretzek (Mareček), Max, Czech-born American conductor, operatic impresario, and composer; b. Brünn, June 28, 1821; d. Staten Island, N.Y., May 14, 1897. He studied medicine and law at the Univ. of Vienna; music with Ignaz von Seyfried. He progressed rapidly, and at the age of 22 conducted his 1st opera, *Hamlet* (Brünn, 1843). He then traveled in Germany, France, and England as a theater conductor and composer of ballet music. In 1848 he settled in N.Y. as conductor and manager of the Italian Opera Co. He presented Adelina Patti for the 1st time in opera (as Lucia, 1859); in 1876 he staged his own play with music, *Baba;* conducted his pastoral opera *Sleepy Hollow; or, The Headless Horseman,* after Washington Irving (N.Y., Sept. 25, 1879). As a worldly impresario, he was extremely successful; traveled to Mexico and Cuba, but lived mostly in N.Y., and became an American citizen. He publ. a book of reminiscences, *Crotchets and Quavers, or Revelations of an Opera Manager in America* (N.Y., 1855); and a sequel, *Sharps and Flats* (N.Y., 1870).

Marez Oyens, Tera de, Dutch composer; b. Velzen, Aug. 5, 1932. She studied piano, violin, composition, and conducting at the Amsterdam Cons., graduating in 1953; attended a course in electronic music given by Koenig in Utrecht (1964–65); was subsequently associated with the Inst. of Sonology there and as a teacher.

WORKS: 2-Piano Sonatina (1961); *Der Chinesche Spiegel,* 3 songs for Tenor and Orch. (1962); *2 Sketches* for Wind Quintet

(1963); *Deducties* for Oboe and Harpsichord (1964); *Photophonie I* for Tape (1969); *Introduzione* for Orch. (1969); *Communication* for Chorus and Dancers (1970); *Ryoanji Temple* for Contralto, Oboe, Violin, Viola, and Cello (1972); *Transformation* for Orch. (1972); Wind Octet (1972); *Canzone per Sonar* for variable instrumentation (1972); *Delta Ballet* for Tape (1973); *Mixed Feelings* for 4-track Tape and Percussion (1973); *3 Modi* for 3 Violins, Cello, and Recorder Quartet (1973); *From Death to Birth* for Chorus (1974); *Starmobile* for variable instrumentation (1974); Trio for Cello, Percussion, and Tape (1974); *Human* for Orch. and Tape (1975); *Ode to Kelesh* for Chorus and Instruments (1975); *Shoshadre,* in 2 parts, for Strings (1976); *Episodes* for Orch. and variable Ensemble (1976; rev. 1981); *Inter-Times* for Oboe, Bassoon, Piano, and Harpsichord (1977); *Mosaic* for Oboe, Clarinet, Horn, Bassoon, and Piano (1979); Concerto for Horn and Tape (1980); *Polskie miasta* (Polish Cities) for Flute, Oboe, Violin, Viola, Cello, and Piano (1981); *Contrafactus* for 2 Violins, Viola, and Cello (1982); *Trajectory* for 4 Saxophones (1985); Cello Concerto for Cello and Tape (1986); *Structures and Dance,* concerto for Violin and Orch. (1987); *Sinfonia testimonial* for Chorus, Orch., and Tape (1987); choral works; songs; music for radio broadcasts of poetry, plays, and various "verbosonic" compositions.

Margola, Franco, Italian composer; b. Orzinuovi, near Brescia, Oct. 30, 1908. He studied violin and composition at the Parma Cons.; then took a course in advanced music theory with Casella at the Accademia di Santa Cecilia in Rome. He then taught at the conservatories in Cagliari, Bologna, Milan, Rome, and Parma. He publ. a manual, *Guida pratica per lo studio della composizione* (Milan, 1954).

WORKS: OPERA: *Il mito di Caino* (Bergamo, 1940). **ORCH.:** Piano Concerto (1943; Florence, Feb. 12, 1944); 2 syms. (1950, 1961); Cello Concerto (1949); Children's Concerto for Piano and Small Orch. (1954); Concerto for Violin, Piano, and Strings (1960); Horn Concerto (1960); Double Concerto for Violin, Piano, and String Orch. (1960); Concerto for Oboe and Strings (1962); Passacaglia for Strings, Piano, and Percussion (1970). **CHAMBER:** 4 violin sonatas (1932–44); 2 piano quintets (1933, 1946); 8 string quartets (1936–50); *4 Episodi* for Flute and Guitar (1970); piano pieces.

Marguste, Anti, Estonian composer and teacher; b. Are, Aug. 5, 1931. He studied with M. Saar and A. Garshnek at the Tallinn Cons. (graduated, 1960), then taught at the Tallinn Music School from 1962. His output is marked by the use of folk elements.

WORKS: 6 syms. (1960, 1963, 1966, 1967, 1970, 1981); *Pieces* for Reed-pipe, Flutes, and Strings (1967); *Symphonic Runes* (1974); *Organ Tunes* for Organ and Orch. (1974); *Concertino piccolo* No. 1 for Woodwind Quintet (1967) and No. 2 for 12 Flutes and Percussion (1979); piano pieces; choral music, including *Old Proverb—Old Silver,* cycle for Children's Chorus, Women's Chorus, and Mixed Chorus (1974), and *Red Data Book* for Soprano, Mezzo-soprano, Tenor, Bass, Chorus, Trumpet, Trombone, Horn, Tuba, and Piano (1980); songs; pedagogical pieces.

Maria Antonia Walpurgis, electress of Saxony, daughter of the elector of Bavaria, later Holy Roman Emperor Charles VII; b. Munich, July 18, 1724; d. Dresden, April 23, 1780. She was not only a generous patroness of the fine arts, but a trained musician, pupil of Hasse and Porpora (1747–52); under the pseudonym E.T.P.A. (Ermelinda Talea Pastorella Arcada, her name as member of the Academy of Arcadians) she produced and publ. 2 Italian operas to her own librettos, and sang in their premieres: *Il trionfo della Fedeltà* (Dresden, 1754) and *Talestri, regina delle Amazoni* (Nymphenburg, near Munich, Feb. 6, 1760); she also wrote texts of oratorios and cantatas for Hasse and Ristori.

BIBL.: C. von Weber, *M.A. W., Churfürstin zu Sachsen* (2 vols., Dresden, 1857); H. Drewes, *M.A. W. als Komponistin* (Leipzig, 1934); A. Yorke-Long, *Music at Court: 4 Eighteenth-Century Studies* (London, 1954).

Mariani, Angelo (Maurizio Gaspare), eminent Italian conductor; b. Ravenna, Oct. 11, 1821; d. Genoa, June 13, 1873. He studied violin with P. Casalini and counterpoint with G. Roberti at the Ravenna Phil. Academy's music school; also learned to play other instruments. He began his career as bandmaster of the city of Sant' Agata Feltria (1842); became a violinist and violist in the orch. in Rimini (1843). That same year he brought out a concerto and 2 overtures in Macerata, gaining the admiration and friendship of Rossini. He was 1st violinist and maestro concertatore in Messina (1844–45); then made his 1st appearance in Milan at the Teatro Re conducting Verdi's *I due Foscari* (July 1, 1846), winning the praise of the composer; subsequently conducted at the Teatro Carcano there; then conducted at the Copenhagen Court Theater (1847–48). After taking part in the Italian war of independence in 1848, he was compelled to leave his homeland and went to Constantinople; was conductor at the Pera theater there until 1850. He returned to Italy in 1851, conducting in Messina; then was appointed director and conductor of the Teatro Carlo Felice in Genoa, making his debut conducting *Robert le diable* on May 15, 1852; led many fine performances there of operas by Rossini, Bellini, Donizetti, Meyerbeer, and Verdi, becoming a close friend of the latter; also assumed the directorship of the Teatro Comunale in Bologna, making his debut leading *Un ballo in maschera* on Oct. 4, 1860. He conducted the 1st Italian performances of *Lohengrin* (Nov. 1, 1871) and *Tannhäuser* (Nov. 11, 1872) in Bologna. Stricken with intestinal cancer, he was unable to accede to Verdi's request that he conduct the premiere of *Aida* in Cairo. In spite of his grave illness, he carried out his duties in both Genoa and Bologna until his death. Mariani was one of the foremost Italian operatic conductors of his era, especially esteemed for his authoritative performances of the great masterpieces of the Italian stage. He wrote several cantatas, chamber music, songs, and piano pieces.
BIBL.: A. Ghislanzoni, "A. M.," *Gazzetta Musicale di Milano,* XXIII (1868); S. Busmanti, *Cenni su A. M.* (Ravenna, 1887); T. Mantovani, *A. M.* (Rome, 1921); U. Zoppi, *A. M., Giuseppe Verdi e Teresa Stolz in un carteggio inedito* (Milan, 1947); S. Martinotti, "A. M., direttore e musicista, nel suo tempo," *Studi Musicali,* II (1973).

Marić, Ljubica, remarkable Serbian composer; b. Kragujevac, March 18, 1909. She studied with Josip Slavenski in Belgrade; then went to Prague, where she took composition courses with J. Suk and Alois Hába; also studied conducting with Malko in Prague (1929–32) and with Scherchen in Strasbourg (1933); she returned to Prague for more study with Hába in his special quarter-tone classes (1936–37). She subsequently taught at a music school in Belgrade. During the period of Nazi occupation of Serbia, she was an active participant in the resistance. After the liberation, she was a member of the teaching staff of the Belgrade Academy of Music (1945–67). In her music she adopted a global type of modern technique, utilizing variable tonal configurations, atonal melodic progressions, and microtonal structures while adhering to traditional forms of composition.
WORKS: String Quartet (1931); Wind Quintet (1932); Trio for Clarinet, Trombone, and Double Bass in quarter-tones (1937); Violin Sonata (1948); *Passacaglia* for Orch. (Belgrade, April 21, 1958); cantatas: *Pesme prostora* (Songs of Space), based on inscriptions on the graves of Bogomils, a heretical religious sect of the Middle Ages (Belgrade, Dec. 8, 1956; her most acclaimed work); *Slovo svetlosti* (Sound of Light), oratorio to texts from medieval Serbian poetry (1966); *Prag sna* (Threshold of Dream), chamber cantata for Narrator, Soprano, Alto, and Instrumental Ensemble (1961; Opatija, Oct. 30, 1965); numerous piano pieces and songs; also wrote modern realizations of the Serbian Octoichos: *Muzika oktoiha No. 1* for Orch. (Belgrade, Feb. 28, 1959); *Vizantijski koncert* (Byzantine Concerto) for Piano and Orch. (Belgrade, June 4, 1963); *Ostinato super thema octoicha* for String Quintet, Harp, and

Piano (Warsaw, Sept. 27, 1963); and *Simfonija oktoiha,* begun in 1964.

Marie, Gabriel, French conductor and composer; b. Paris, Jan. 8, 1852; d. Puigcerdá, Catalonia, Aug. 29, 1928. He studied at the Paris Cons.; was chorus master of the Lamoureux Concerts (1881–87); conductor of the orch. concerts of the Société Nationale de Musique (1887–94), of Ste.-Cécile in Bordeaux, at Marseilles, and (during the summer months) at the Casino in Vichy. He wrote a number of melodious pieces for orch., of which *La Cinquantaine* (in arrangements for violin or cello, with piano) became immensely popular. He also wrote music criticism, collected in *Pour la musique* (Paris, 1930).

Marini, Biagio, distinguished Italian violinist and composer; b. Brescia, c.1587; d. Venice, March 20, 1665. He was a violinist under Monteverdi at San Marco in Venice (1615–18); then was music director of the Accademia degli Erranti in Brescia (1620–21); subsequently was a violinist in the Farnese court in Parma (1621–23); then served at the court in Neuberg an die Donau (1623–49). In 1649 he was appointed maestro di cappella at S. Maria della Scala in Milan; in 1652–53 he was director of the Accademia della Morte in Ferrara. He was an accomplished composer of both instrumental and vocal music. His op. 1, *Affetti musicali* (Venice, 1617), contains the earliest example of the Italian solo sonata with basso continuo.
BIBL.: A. Einstein, "Italienische Musiker am Hofe der Neuberger Wittelsbacher (1614 bis 1716)," *Sammelbände der Internationalen Musik-Gesellschaft,* IX (1907–8); A. Schering, "Zur Geschichte der Solosonate in der ersten Hälfte des 17. Jahrhunderts," *Riemann-Festschrift* (Leipzig, 1909); A. Moser, *Geschichte des Violinspiels* (Berlin, 1923; 2nd ed., rev., 1966–67); D. Iselin, *B. M.: Sein Leben und seine Instrumentalwerke* (Hildburghausen, 1930); W. Clark, *The Vocal Music of B. M.* (c1598–1665) (diss., Yale Univ., 1966); T. Dunn, *The Instrumental Music of B. M.* (diss., Yale Univ., 1969); idem, "The Sonatas of B. M.: Structure and Style," *Music Review,* XXXVI (1975).

Marini, Ignazio, noted Italian bass; b. Tagliuno (Bergamo), Nov. 28, 1811; d. Milan, April 29, 1873. In 1833 he joined La Scala in Milan, where he sang until 1847; then appeared in London (1847–49) and N.Y. (1850–52); in 1856 he went to St. Petersburg, where he remained until 1863. He was one of the leading bass singers of his day; created the title roles in Verdi's *Oberto* and *Attila;* was a distinguished interpreter of bass parts in Rossini's operas.

Marinkoví, Josef, Serbian choral conductor, teacher, and composer; b. Vranjevo, Sept. 15, 1851; d. Belgrade, May 13, 1931. He studied composition with F. Skuherský at the Prague Organ School, then was active as a choral conductor in Belgrade (1881–1924). He was the father of the Serbian lied, and the last champion of the Serbian national Romantic movement. In addition to his songs, he wrote incidental music, choral works, sacred music, and piano pieces.
BIBL.: M. Milojeví, "J. M. kao kompositor solo-pesme" (J. M. as Composer of Solo Songs), *Srpski Knjizevni Glasnik,* VIII (1936); B. Dragutinovic, "Licnost i delo J. a M.a" (J. M.'s Personality and Work), *Dvadeseti Vek,* III (1938); V. Pericic, *J. M.: Zivot i dela* (J. M.: Life and Works; Belgrade, 1967).

Marino, Amerigo, American conductor; b. Chicago, Feb. 5, 1925; d. Nashville, Tenn., April 26, 1988. He studied violin in Chicago, then conducting with Malko, Szell, Rudolf, and Wallenstein; was music director of the Birmingham (Ala.) Sym. Orch. (1964–85); then was associate conductor of the Nashville (Tenn.) Sym. Orch. (1985–88).

Marinov, Ivan, Bulgarian composer and conductor; b. Sofia, Oct. 17, 1928. He studied conducting with Goleminov and composition with V. Stoyanov and P. Khadziev at the Sofia State Cons., graduating in 1955.
WORKS: *Dvuboj* (Duel), poem for Tenor and Orch. (1953); *Suite on 4 Folk Songs* for Orch. (1955); *Ilinden,* symphonic poem (1956); *Paraphrases* for Orch. (1957); *Fantastic Scenes* for Orch. (1959); *Divertimento* for Orch. (1961); *Pentagram* for Bass, String Orch., Piano, and Timpani (1965–66); Sym.

No. 1 for Bass and Orch. (1967); *Festive Suite* for Orch. (1968); *Ode on Liberty* for Orch. (1969); chamber music; songs.

Marinuzzi, Gino (actually, **Giuseppe**), Italian conductor and composer, father of **Gino Marinuzzi**; b. Palermo, March 24, 1882; d. Milan, Aug. 17, 1945. He studied with Zuelli at the Palermo Cons.; began his career as a conductor in Catania; conducted in Italy and Spain; went to South America on tour with the Teatral Opera Co.; then was director of the Liceo Musicale in Bologna (1915–18); in 1919 he conducted in Rome; went to the U.S. as artistic director of the Chicago Grand Opera Co. (1919–21); in 1921 returned to Italy, where he served as chief conductor of the Rome Opera (1928–34) and of Milan's La Scala (1934–44), serving as its superintendent (1944). False dispatches about his assassination at the hands of the Italian anti-Fascists found their way into periodicals and eventually into reputable reference works, but he died peacefully in a hospital, a victim not of a bullet but of hepatic anemia. He wrote 3 operas: *Barberina* (Palermo, 1903); *Jacquerie* (Buenos Aires, Aug. 11, 1918); *Palla de' Mozzi* (La Scala, Milan, April 5, 1932); a Sym.; chamber music.
BIBL.: A. Garbelotto, *G. M.* (Ancona, 1965).

Marinuzzi, Gino, Italian conductor and composer, son of **Gino (Giuseppe) Marinuzzi**; b. N.Y., April 7, 1920. He studied at the Milan Cons. with Renzo Bossi, graduating as a pianist and composer in 1941; was assistant conductor at the Rome Opera (1946–51). He was one of the 1st Italian composers to explore the potentialities of electronic music; in collaboration with Ketoff, he developed an electronic synthesizer, the "Fonosynth," and was a founder of an electronic studio in Rome. His compositions include a radio opera, *La Signora Paulatim* (Naples, 1966); Violin Concerto; Piano Concerto; chamber music; piano pieces; film scores; pieces for electronic tape.

Mario, Giovanni Matteo, Cavaliere de Candia, celebrated Italian tenor, known professionally as **Mario**; b. Cagliari, Sardinia, Oct. 17, 1810; d. Rome, Dec. 11, 1883. Born into a noble family, he studied at the Turin military academy and then joined the regiment of which his father was colonel. He eloped with a ballerina to Paris (1836), where he studied voice with Bordogni and Poncharde at the Cons.; made his debut as Robert le Diable at the Paris Opéra (Dec. 5, 1838). He made his 1st London appearance as Gennaro in *Lucrezia Borgia* opposite Giulia Grisi's Lucrezia at Her Majesty's Theatre (June 6, 1839); the 2 singers remained intimate, without benefit of marriage, for 22 years. He made his debut at the Théâtre-Italien in Paris as Nemorino (Oct. 17, 1839), and soon became one of its principal members; created the role of Ernesto in *Don Pasquale* there (Jan. 3, 1843); continued to sing in London at Her Majesty's Theatre until 1846, and then was a leading artist at the Royal Italian Opera at Covent Garden until 1871; also sang in St. Petersburg (1849–53; 1868–70), N.Y. (1854), and Madrid (1859, 1864). He retired from the stage in 1871, giving farewell appearances in Paris, London, and the U.S. Mario's beautiful voice, matched by an exquisite vocal style, handsome figure, and effective acting gifts, made him one of the most renowned operatic singers of his day; he also was greatly esteemed as a concert singer. Among his other roles were the Duke of Mantua, Faust, John of Leyden, Almaviva, Raoul, and Roméo.
BIBL.: L. Engel, *From Mozart to M.* (London, 1886); Mrs. Godfrey Pearce (M.'s daughter) and F. Hird, *The Romance of a Great Singer* (London, 1910); E. Forbes, *M. and Grisi* (London, 1985).

Mario (real name, **Tillotson**), **Queena,** American soprano; b. Akron, Ohio, Aug. 21, 1896; d. N.Y., May 28, 1951. She was a practicing journalist in N.Y. before she began to study music; took voice lessons with Oscar Saenger and Marcella Sembrich; made her debut with the San Carlo Opera in N.Y. (Sept. 4, 1918); made her Metropolitan Opera debut in N.Y. as Micaela in *Carmen* (Nov. 30, 1922); remained on its roster until 1939; taught at the Curtis Inst. of Music in Philadelphia (from 1931). She married **Wilfred Pelletier** in 1925; they

divorced in 1936. She was the author of several mystery novels, including *Murder in the Opera House.*

Mariotte, Antoine, French composer; b. Avignon, Dec. 22, 1875; d. Izieux, Loire, Nov. 30, 1944. He was trained at the Naval Academy; in 1897 he became a pupil of d'Indy at the Schola Cantorum in Paris; in 1899, was appointed conductor of the sym. concerts at St.-Etienne, Loire; from 1902 until 1919 he taught at the Orléans Cons.; in 1920, was appointed its director; from 1936 to 1938 he was director of the Paris Opéra-Comique.
WORKS: Operas: *Salomé* (Lyons, Oct. 30, 1908); *Le Vieux Roi* (Lyons, 1911); *Léontine Sœurs* (Paris, May 21, 1924); *Esther, Princesse d'Israël* (Paris, May 5, 1925); *Gargantua* (1924; Paris, Feb. 13, 1935); *Nele Dooryn* (1940); also a symphonic suite, *Impressions urbaines* (1921); songs; numerous teaching pieces for piano.

Mariz, Vasco, Brazilian bass, musicologist, and diplomat; b. Rio de Janeiro, Jan. 22, 1921. He studied composition with Oscar Lorenzo Fernandez and voice with Vera Janacopoulos; also took courses in law at the Univ. of Rio de Janeiro, obtaining his D.J. degree in 1943. He sang minor roles in opera in Rio de Janeiro, São Paulo, and Porto Alegre, and also gave lieder recitals; recorded Brazilian songs. In 1945 he entered the diplomatic service; was vice-consul at Oporto, Portugal (1948–49); attaché in Belgrade (1950–51); consul in Rosario, Argentina (1952–53); consul in Naples (1956–58); counselor of the Brazilian embassy in Washington, D.C. (1959–60); counselor of the Brazilian mission to the U.N. (1961–62); envoy to the Organization of American States in Washington, D.C. (1967–69); head of the Cultural Dept. of the Brazilian Ministry of Foreign Affairs (1970); ambassador to Ecuador (1971–74); assistant secretary of state for legislative affairs in Brasília (1975–76); ambassador to Israel (1977–82); ambassador to Peru (1983–84).
WRITINGS: *A canção brasileira* (Oporto, 1948; 2nd ed., 1959); *Figuras da música brasileira contemporánea* (Oporto, 1948; 2nd ed., Brasília, 1970); *Dicionário bio-bibliográfico musical* (Rio de Janeiro, 1948; 2nd ed., 1984); *Heitor Villa-Lobos, Compositor brasileiro* (Rio de Janeiro, 1949; 6th ed., 1983); *Alberto Ginastera* (Rosario, 1954); *Vida musical I* (Oporto, 1950); *Vida musical II* (Rio de Janeiro, 1970); *Historia de musica no Brasil* (Rio de Janeiro, 1981; 2nd ed., 1983); *Tres musicologos brasileiros* (Rio de Janeiro, 1983).

Markert, Russell, innovative American choreographer; b. Jersey City, N.J., Aug. 8, 1899; d. Waterbury, Conn., Dec. 8, 1990. He served in the Army Quartermaster Corps in France, where he performed in military shows in his free time. His professional career began on Broadway, where he danced in and later directed the annual revue *Earl Carroll's Vanities.* In 1925 in St. Louis he founded a women's precision dance troupe called the Missouri Rockets; the group was seen and immediately signed to perform by the owner of N.Y.'s Roxy Theater. When Radio City Music Hall opened in 1932, the troupe was invited to be resident there and became the Rockettes. A Rockettes routine usually had its inception in an evocative piece of music; applicants were required to have a background in modern jazz in addition to "exceptionally limber kicks." In the heyday of the Music Hall, Markert trained and rehearsed some 2,500 young women for performances to capacity audiences every day of the year. He retired in 1971. The Juilliard School in N.Y. offers a Russell Markert Dance Scholarship.

Markevitch, Igor, greatly talented Russian-born composer and conductor; b. Kiev, July 27, 1912; d. Antibes, France, March 7, 1983. He was taken to Paris in his infancy; in 1916 the family settled in Vevey, Switzerland, which remained Markevitch's home for the next decade. He began to study piano with his father, and subsequently took piano lessons with Paul Loyonnet; he also took academic courses at the Collège de Vevey. In 1925 he joined the piano class of Alfred Cortot in Paris at the École Normale de Musique, and studied harmony, counterpoint, and composition with Nadia Boulanger. He attracted the attention of Serge Diaghilev, who commissioned him to write a piano concerto and also to collaborate with Boris Kochno on a ballet. Markevitch was soloist in his Piano Concerto at Covent Garden in London on July 15, 1929. Diaghilev died on Aug. 19, 1929, and Markevitch interrupted his work on the ballet for him; he used the musical materials from it in his *Cantate*, which achieved an extraordinary success at its Paris premiere on June 4, 1930. On Dec. 8, 1930, his Concerto Grosso was performed for the 1st time in Paris with even greater acclaim. Finally, his ballet, *Rébus*, was produced in Paris on Dec. 15, 1931, to enthusiastic press reviews. Markevitch was hailed, only half-facetiously, as "Igor II" (the 1st Igor being, of course, Stravinsky). His ballet *L'Envol d'Icare* was premiered in Paris on June 26, 1933, prompting Milhaud to opine that the occasion would probably "mark a date in the evolution of music." But swift as was Markevitch's Icaruslike ascent as a composer, even more precipitous was his decline. He began to be sharply criticized for his penchant toward unrelieved dissonance. When he conducted the premiere of his oratorio *Le Paradis perdu* (London, Dec. 20, 1935), it was roundly condemned for sins of dissonance. Although he continued to compose, Markevitch turned his attention more and more to conducting. He made his professional conducting debut with the Concertgebouw Orch. of Amsterdam in 1930. In 1934–35 he took conducting lessons in Switzerland with Hermann Scherchen. During World War II he was in Italy; after the war, he devoted himself to conducting. He conducted in Stockholm (1952–55); made his U.S. debut as a guest conductor with the Boston Sym. Orch. (1955); then conducted the Montreal Sym. Orch. (1957–61), the Havana Phil. (1957–58), and the Lamoureux Orch. in Paris (1957–62). He was founder-conductor of the Spanish Radio and Television Sym. Orch. (1965); then conducted the U.S.S.R. State Sym. Orch. in Moscow (1965), the Monte Carlo Orch. (1967–72), and the orch. of the Accademia di Santa Cecilia in Rome (1973–75). He also gave master classes in conducting in various European music centers. Markevitch wrote *Introduction à la musique* (Paris, 1940), *Made in Italy* (London, 1949), and *Point d'orgue* (Paris, 1959). In addition to the Russian repertoire, he exhibited special affinity for the works of Stravinsky, Bartók, and other 20th-century composers.

Works: *Noces*, suite for Piano (1925); *À la foire* (1926); *Sinfonietta in F* (Brussels, Nov. 30, 1929); Piano Concerto (London, July 15, 1929, composer soloist); *Cantate*, to a text by Jean Cocteau (Paris, June 4, 1930); Concerto Grosso (Paris, Dec. 8, 1930); *Serenade* for Violin, Clarinet, and Bassoon (Wiesbaden, Aug. 5, 1931); *Ouverture symphonique* (1931); *Rébus*, ballet, dedicated to the memory of Serge Diaghilev (Paris, Dec. 15, 1931); *Partita* (Paris, May 13, 1932); *Galop* for 8 Players (1932); *L'Envol d'Icare*, ballet (Paris, June 26, 1933; also arranged for Piano under the title *La Mort d'Icare*); *Hymnes* for Orch. (Paris, June 26, 1933, composer conducting); *Petite suite d'après Schumann* for Orch. (1933); *Psaume* for Soprano and Chamber Orch. (Amsterdam, Dec. 3, 1933, composer conducting); *Le Paradis perdu*, oratorio after Milton (London, Dec. 20, 1935, composer conducting); *3 poèmes* for Voice and Piano (1935); *Hymne à la mort* for Chamber Orch. (1936); *Cantique d'amour* for Chamber Orch. (Rome, May 14, 1937); *Le Nouvel Age*, sinfonia concertante for Orch. (Warsaw, Jan. 21, 1938, composer conducting); *La Taille de l'homme* for Soprano and 12 Instruments (1939; unfinished; 1st perf. as *Oraison musicale*, Maastricht, Feb. 7, 1982); *Duo* for Flute and Bassoon (1939); *Stefan le poète* for Piano (1939–40); *Lorenzo il magnifico*, sinfonia concertante for Soprano and Orch. (Florence, Jan. 12, 1941); *Variations, Fugue and Envoi on a Theme of Handel* for Piano (Rome, Dec. 14, 1941); *Inno della liberazione nazionale*, songs for the Italian underground resistance (1943–44); *Le Bleu Danube* for Chamber Orch. (Florence, May 24, 1946, composer conducting).

Bibl.: B. Gavoty, *I. M.* (Geneva, 1954); special issue of *Tempo* (Sept. 1980); J. Heinzelmann, *I. M.* (Bonn, 1982).

Markova, Juliana, gifted Bulgarian pianist; b. Sofia, July 8, 1945. She studied at the Sofia Cons. and then with Ilonka

Deckers at the Milan Cons., graduating with the highest honors in 1969. She won prizes in the Enesco Competition in Bucharest (1964) and the Long-Thibaud Competition in Paris (1965). She appeared as soloist with the leading orchs. of Europe and the U.S., including the London Sym., Philharmonia Orch., Royal Phil., Los Angeles Phil., Chicago Sym., Cleveland Orch., and Philadelphia Orch.; also toured in solo recitals. She settled in London; married the English pianist Michael Roll. A technically brilliant pianist, she excels in the Romantic and the early modern repertoire.

Markowski, Andrzej, Polish conductor and composer; b. Lublin, Aug. 22, 1924; d. Warsaw, Oct. 30, 1986. He studied theory and composition with Malawski in Lublin (1939–41); after studies in composition with Rowley at Trinity College of Music in London (1946–47), he completed his training as a composer with Rytel and Szeligowski and studied conducting with Rowicki at the Warsaw State High School of Music (1947–55). He conducted the Szczecin Theater (1949–50), the Poznan Phil. (1954–55), the Silesian Phil. in Katowice (1955–59), and the Krakow Phil. (1959–64), with which he toured the U.S. (1961). After conducting the Wroclaw Phil. (1965–69), he was one of the conductors of the National Phil. in Warsaw (1971–78); toured with it in Europe and Japan; then was conductor of the Artur Rubinstein Phil. in Lodz (1982–86), touring Italy with this orch. in 1984. He was best known as an interpreter of contemporary music. He wrote instrumental works, chamber music, film and theater scores, and electronic pieces.

Marks, Alan, talented American pianist; b. Chicago, May 14, 1949. His family moved to St. Louis when he was a child; he studied piano with Shirley Parnas Adams. In 1965 he won a prize in Interlochen; gave his 1st piano recital in St. Louis in 1966. In 1967 he went to N.Y., where he studied at the Juilliard School of Music with Irwin Freundlich (B.M., 1971); then with Leon Fleisher at the Peabody Cons. in Baltimore (1971–72). Subsequently he gave successful recitals in Boston, Washington, Philadelphia, Los Angeles, San Francisco, and other cities. In 1976 he played the 1st performance of *Caprichos* for Piano by Carlos Chávez; also participated in numerous concerts of chamber music. He possesses an innate virtuoso technique, and is able to interpret with perfect stylistic fidelity piano works by classical as well as modern composers.

Marks, Edward B(ennett), American music publisher; b. Troy, N.Y., Nov. 28, 1865; d. Mineola, N.Y., Dec. 17, 1945. With Joseph Stern, he organized the music publishing concern of Joseph Stern and Co. (1894); they composed the popular song *The Little Lost Child*, which became their 1st great publishing success. Marks bought out Stern in 1920, and the company became the Edward B. Marks Music Co.; it became the Edward B. Marks Music Corp. in 1932 and subsequently brought out a considerable body of serious music by contemporary composers; it took over the catalog of the George M. Cohan Music Publishing Co. in 1967. Belwin-Mills became its distributor in 1973.

Marks, Johnny, American songwriter; b. Mount Vernon, N.Y., Nov. 10, 1909; d. N.Y., Sept. 3, 1985. He began songwriting at age 13, then studied at Colgate Univ. (B.A., 1935) and later in Paris. Although he publ. over 175 songs, he gained enduring fame and royalties with the perennial favorite *Rudolph the Red-nosed Reindeer* (1949), 1st made popular by Gene Autry; it eventually sold over 150 million recordings and 8 million copies of sheet music. His other holiday numbers included *I Heard the Bells on Christmas Day* (1956), *Rockin' around the Christmas Tree* (1960), and *A Holly, Jolly Christmas* (1963).

Markull, Friedrich Wilhelm, German organist, pianist, and composer; b. Reichenbach, near Elbing, Prussia, Feb. 17, 1816; d. Danzig, April 30, 1887. He studied organ and composition with F. Schneider in Dessau; became a church organist in Danzig (1836), and also conductor of the Gesangverein there; likewise appeared as a pianist. He wrote 3 operas for Danzig: *Maja und Alpino, oder Die bezauberte Rose* (Dec. 23, 1843);

Der König von Zion (March 22, 1850); *Das Walpurgisfest* (Jan. 14, 1855); also syms.; 2 oratorios (1845, 1856); organ pieces; piano music; many songs.

BIBL.: W. Neumann, *F.W. M.* (Kassel, 1857).

Markwort, Johann Christian, German tenor and voice teacher; b. Reisling, near Braunschweig, Dec. 13, 1778; d. Bessungen, near Darmstadt, Jan. 13, 1866. He took courses in theology in Leipzig; then went to Vienna to study voice; sang opera in Munich and in Liechtenstein; in 1810 he was engaged as choirmaster in Darmstadt. In 1830 he dedicated himself entirely to teaching; he publ. pedagogical books: *Umriss einer Gesammt-Tonwissenschaft überhaupt wie auch einer Sprach- und Tonsatzlehre* (Darmstadt, 1826); *Gesang-, Ton- und Rede-Vortraglehre* (Mainz, 1827); *Über Klangveredelung der Stimme* (Mainz, 1847); also a piano method.

Marley, Bob (Robert Nesta), Jamaican reggae singer and composer; b. Rhoden Hall, Feb. 6, 1945; d. Miami, May 11, 1981. He was taken to Kingston as a child and worked as an electrical welder. He picked up popular tunes in the streets and from the radio, opened a small recording shop of his own, and then began making records of some of his own tunes, a mixture of calypso and "soul" music. He joined the Rastafarian religious group, followers of Haile Selassie of Ethiopia (whose original name was Ras Tafari). In 1976 he became embroiled in politics, supporting the People's National Party; as he was preparing to sing at a band concert on Dec. 3, 1976, he was shot and wounded. After that episode, he went to Europe, scoring an unusual popular success, particularly in England, Sweden, the Netherlands, and West Germany. In 1977 he made a tour of the U.S., where his fame had preceded him via his record albums. His songs, in Jamaican dialect, preached revolution; typical of them were *Rebel Music, Everywhere Be War,* and *Death to the Downpressors.*

BIBL.: M. Whitney and D. Hussey, *B. M.: Reggae King of the World* (Kingston, Jamaica, 1984); S. Davis, *B. M.* (Garden City, N.J., 1985); C. May, *B. M.* (London, 1985).

Marliani, Count Marco Aurelio, Italian composer; b. Milan, Aug. 1805; d. Bologna, May 8, 1849. He studied philosophy; took some lessons with Rossini in Paris, where he went in 1830; under Rossini's influence, he wrote several operas, which reached the stage in Paris: *Il Bravo* (Feb. 1, 1834); *Ildegonda* (March 7, 1837); *La Xacarilla* (Oct. 28, 1839); a ballet, *La Gypsy* (with A. Thomas; Jan. 28, 1839). He returned to Italy in 1847; produced another opera in Bologna, *Gusmano il Buono* (Nov. 7, 1847). He was involved in the revolutionary struggle of 1848; was wounded in a skirmish near Bologna, and died as a result of his injuries.

Marliave, Joseph de, French writer on music; b. Toulouse, Nov. 16, 1873; d. (killed in battle) Verdun, Aug. 24, 1914. He wrote a valuable monograph, *Les Quatuors de Beethoven* (Paris, 1917; reprint, 1925; Eng. tr., London, 1928). He was the husband of the pianist **Marguerite Long.**

Marlowe (real name, **Sapira**), **Sylvia,** American harpsichordist; b. N.Y., Sept. 26, 1908; d. there, Dec. 11, 1981. She studied piano; went to Paris to take courses with Nadia Boulanger at the École Normale de Musique; later became a student of Wanda Landowska in harpsichord playing. In 1953 she joined the faculty of the Mannes School of Music in N.Y. In 1957 she founded the Harpsichord Music Soc., which commissioned works by Elliott Carter, Ned Rorem, Vittorio Rieti, Henri Sauguet, and others. Although her primary devotion was to the Baroque style of composition, she adventurously espoused the cause of popular American music; she was a member of the pop group called Chamber Music Soc. of Lower Basin Street and even performed in nightclubs, ostentatiously proclaiming her belief in music as an art in flux. She was married to a landscape painter named Leonid Berman, who died in 1976.

Marmontel, Antoine-François, celebrated French pedagogue and pianist, father of **Antonin Émile Louis Corbaz Marmontel;** b. Clermont-Ferrand, July 16, 1816; d. Paris,

Jan. 17, 1898. He studied at the Paris Cons. with Zimmerman (piano), Dourlen (harmony), Halévy (fugue), and Le Sueur (composition); won the premier prix for piano in 1832. In 1837 he became instructor in solfeggio at the Cons.; in 1848 he succeeded Zimmerman as head of its piano class, and won enduring fame as an imaginative and efficient teacher; among his pupils were Albéniz, Bizet, Debussy, Diemer, d'Indy, Dubois, Pierné, and Planté. He continued to teach until 1887. He wrote numerous didactic works for piano; also sonatas, serenades, characteristic pieces, salon music, dances, etc.

WRITINGS (all publ. in Paris): *L'art classique et moderne du piano* (1876); *Les Pianistes célèbres* (1878); *Symphonistes et virtuoses* (1880); *Virtuoses contemporains* (1882); *Elements d'esthétique musicale, et considérations sur le beau dans les arts* (1884); *Histoire du piano et de ses origines* (1885).

Marmontel, Antonin Émile Louis Corbaz, French piano teacher, son of **Antoine-François Marmontel;** b. Paris, Nov. 22, 1850; d. there, July 23, 1907. He studied at the Paris Cons. (premier prix, 1867); was 2nd chorus master at the Paris Opéra (1878–89); taught at the Paris Cons. (1901–7).

Maros, Miklós, Hungarian-born Swedish composer, son of **Rudolf Maros;** b. Pécs, Nov. 14, 1943. He studied composition in Budapest with Rezsö Sugár at the Béla Bartók Cons. (1958–63) and with Ferenc Szabó at the Franz Liszt Academy of Music (1963–67); settled in Stockholm, where he continued his training with Ingvar Lidholm and Ligeti at the Musikhögskolan (1968–72); in 1975 became a naturalized Swedish citizen. He taught electronic music at the Stockholm Electronic Music Studio (1971–78) and at the Musikhögskolan (1976–80); also taught privately. In 1972, with his wife, the singer Ilona Maros, he founded the Maros Ensemble, which championed contemporary music. In 1980–81 he held a Deutscher Akademischer Austauschdienst fellowship in West Berlin; in 1982–83 he was composer-in-residence of the Swedish Inst. for National Concerts. In his music, Maros utilizes both traditional and experimental techniques, including electronics.

WORKS: DRAMATIC: *Jag önkar jag vore* (I Wish I Could Be), opera (1971); *Stora grusharpan* (The Huge Gravel-sifter), radio opera (1982); *Att i denna natt . . .* (In This Night . . .), church opera (1986). **ORCH.:** *Pezzo* for Chamber Orch. (1967); *Denique* for Soprano and Orch. (1967); *Mutazioni* for Wind Orch. (1971); Concertino for Double Bass or Tuba, and 6 to 24 Instruments (1971); *Confluentia* for Strings (1972); *Proportio* for Wind Orch. (1973); 2 syms.: No. 1 (1974); No. 2 for Wind and Percussion Orch. (1979); Concerto for Harpsichord and Chamber Orch. (1978); *Circulation* for Strings (1980); Concerto for Wind Quintet and Orch. (1980); *Coalottino II* for Bass Clarinet and Strings (1981); *Konzertsatz* for Accordion and Strings (1982); *Fantasi* (1983); Trombone Concerto (1983); Sinfonietta for Chamber Orch. (1985); Sinfonia Concertante for Strings (1986); *Introduzione e Marcia* for Wind Orch. (1986); *Concerto grosso* for Saxophone Quartet and Orch. (1988). **CHAMBER:** *Fúvósötös:* Wind Quintet No. 1 (1962); *Spel* (Game) for Clarinet, Trombone, Cello, and Percussion (1969); *Anenaika* for Soprano, Chamber Ensemble, and Tape (1970); *Diversion* for Soprano, Contralto, Alto Flute, Viola, Guitar, and 3 Percussionists (1971); *Festeggiamento* for Recorder, Violin, and Harp (1971); *Xylographia* for Soprano, Violin, Bassoon, Harp, Harpsichord, and Vibraphone (1972); *Oolit* for 10 Instruments (1974); Divertimento for Wind Quintet, Violin, and Piano (1976); String Quartet No. 1 (1977); *Psalm 98* for Soprano, Flute, Clarinet, Bassoon, Violin, Cello, and Percussion (1978); *Åtbörder* (Gestures) for Flute, Clarinet, Violin, Viola, Cello, Piano, and Percussion (1979); Wind Quintet No. 2 (1980); *Clusters for Clusters* for Flute, Soprano Saxophone, Guitar, and Percussion (1981); *Spelingar* (Reflections) for Winds, Guitars, Pianos, and Strings (1983); Saxophone Quartet (1984); *Picchiettato* for 5 Percussionists (1986); *Aulos,* trio for Oboe, Cello, and Harpsichord (1987); *Goboj* for Oboe and Guitar (1987). **VOCAL:** *Prelude* for Mezzo-soprano and Orch. (1967); *Inversioni* for Soprano and Chamber Ensemble (1968); *Erotikon* for Mezzo-soprano and Orch. (1968); *Laus Pannoniae* for Soprano, Chorus, and Chamber Ensemble (1972); *Lunovis* for Soprano, Violin, Bassoon, Harp, and Celesta (1973); *Fabula* for Alto, Cello, 2 Pianos, and Percussion (1974); *Elementen* for Soprano, Reciter, Women's Trio, and Youth Orch. (1975); *4 sänger ur Gitanjali* (4 Songs from Gitanjali) for Soprano, Flute, Clarinet, and 2 Percussionists (1979); *Drehlieder* for Tenor, Hurdy-gurdy, Cello, and Harpsichord (1984); choruses; songs; also live electronic pieces; electro-acoustic works.

Maros, Rudolf, Hungarian composer, father of **Miklós Maros;** b. Stachy, Jan. 19, 1917; d. Budapest, Aug. 2, 1982. He studied composition with Kodály and Siklós and viola at the Budapest Academy of Music (1938–42); later attended A. Hába's master class there (1949). He played viola in the Budapest Concert Orch. (1942–49); from 1949 to 1978 he was on the faculty of the Budapest Academy of Music. The early period of his music is marked by nationalistic tendencies; later he adopted serial techniques and began to explore the field of "sonorism," or sound for sound's sake, making use of all available sonorous resources, such as tone clusters and microtones.
WORKS: BALLETS: *The Wedding at Ecser* (1950); *Bányászballada* (Miner's Ballad; 1961); *Cinque studi* (1967; after the orch. set of the same title); *Quadros soltos (Musica da ballo)* (1968); *Reflexionen* (1970); *Dance Pictures* (1971); *Metropolis* (1972); *The Poltroon* (1972). **ORCH.:** *Puppet Show Overture* (1944); 2 sinfoniettas (1944, 1948); Bassoon Concertino (1954); *Symphony for Strings* (1956); *Ricercare* (1959); *Musica da ballo,* suite (1962; based on the ballet *Miner's Ballad*); *Cinque studi* (1960; as a ballet, 1967); *3 Eufonias: I* for Strings, 2 Harps, and Percussion (1963); *II* for 24 Winds, 2 Harps, and Percussion (1964); *III* for Orch. (1965); *Gemma (In Memoriam Kodály)* (1968); *Monumentum* (1969); *Notices* for Strings (1972); *Landscapes* for Strings (1974); *Fragment* (1977). **CHAMBER:** String Quartet (1948); *Serenade* for Oboe, Clarinet, and Bassoon (1952); *Musica leggiera* for Wind Quintet (1956); String Trio (1957); *Musica da camera per 11* (1966; Hanover, N.H., July 12, 1967); Trio for Violin, Viola, and Harp (1967); *Consort* for Wind Quintet (1970); *Albumblätter* for Double Bass (1973); *Kaleidoscope* for 15 Instruments (1976); *4 Studies* for 4 Percussionists (1977); *Contrasts* for Chamber Ensemble (1979). **VOCAL:** *2 Laments* for Soprano, Alto Flute, Harp, Piano, and Percussion (1962); *Lament* for Soprano and Chamber Ensemble (1967); *Messzeségek* (Remoteness) for Chorus a cappella (1975); *Strophen* for Soprano, Harp, and Percussion (1975); *Nyúlfarkkantáta* (Tiny Cantata) for Voices, Strings, and Piano (1976); *Cheremiss Folksongs* for Chorus a cappella (1977).
BIBL.: P. Várnai, *M. R.* (Budapest, 1967).

Marpurg, Friedrich, German conductor and composer, great-grandson of **Friedrich Wilhelm Marpurg;** b. Paderborn, April 4, 1825; d. Wiesbaden, Dec. 2, 1884. He played the violin and piano as a child; studied composition later with Mendelssohn and Hauptmann at Leipzig. He became conductor at the Königsberg Theater, then at Sondershausen (1864); succeeded Mangold as court music director at Darmstadt (1868); then was at Freiburg (1873), Laibach (1875), and Wiesbaden, where he became conductor of the Cäcilienverein.
WORKS: Operas: *Musa, der letzte Maurenkönig* (Königsberg, 1855); *Agnes von Hohenstaufen* (Freiburg, 1874); *Die Lichtensteiner* (not perf.).

Marpurg, Friedrich Wilhelm, German music theorist and composer, great-grandfather of **Friedrich Marpurg;** b. Seehof bei Seehausen, Brandenburg, Nov. 21, 1718; d. Berlin, May 22, 1795. While secretary to Generallieutenant Friedrich Rudolph Graf von Rothenburg in Paris (1746–49), he became acquainted with Rameau and his theories; after a short stay in Berlin and a prolonged sojourn in Hamburg, he joined the Prussian lottery at Berlin (1763), and was its director from 1766 until his death. In addition to editing collections of songs and keyboard works, he also composed sonatas, other pieces for keyboard, and songs.
WRITINGS: *Die Kunst das Clavier zu spielen, durch den Verfasser des critischen Musicus an der Spree* (Berlin, 1750; 4th

ed., rev. and augmented, 1762); *Abhandlung von der Fuge nach dem Grundsätzen der besten deutschen und ausländischen Meister* (2 vols., Berlin, 1753–54; 2nd ed., 1858); *Historisch-kritische Beyträge zur Aufnahme der Musik* (5 vols., Berlin, 1754–78); *Anleitung zum Clavierspielen der schönen Ausübung der heutigen Zeit gemäss* (Berlin, 1755; 2nd ed., 1765); *Handbuch bey dem Generalbasse und der Composition mit zwey - drey - vier - fünf - sechs - sieben - acht und mehreren Stimmen* (3 vols., Berlin, 1755–58; 2nd ed., 1762); *Kritische Einleitung in die Geschichte und Lehrsätze der alten und neuen Musik* (Berlin, 1759); *Kritische Briefe über die Tonkunst, mit kleinen Clavierstücken und Singoden begleitet, von einer musikalischen Gesellschaft in Berlin* (weekly publication; Berlin, 1760–64); *Anleitung zur Musik überhaupt und zur Singkunst besonders mit Uebungsexampeln erläutert* (Berlin, 1763); *Neue Methode allerley Arten von Temperaturen dem Claviere aufs Bequemste mitzutheilen* (Berlin, 1790); etc.
BIBL.: E. Bieder, *Ueber F.W. M.s System der Harmonie, des Kontrapunkts und der Temperatur* (diss., Univ. of Berlin, 1923); J. Mekeel, "The Harmonic Theories of Kirnberger and M.," *Journal of Music Theory,* IV (1960); H. Serwer, *F.W. M.* (1718–1795): *Music Critic in a Galant Age* (diss., Yale Univ., 1969).

Marqués y García, Pedro Miguel, Spanish composer; b. Palma de Mallorca, May 20, 1843; d. there, Feb. 25, 1918. He studied in Paris with Alard and Armingaud, then at the Paris Cons. with Massart (violin) and Bazin (composition); also studied privately with Berlioz, and in 1867 in Madrid with Monasterio. From 1870 to 1896 he was one of the most successful of the zarzuela composers, his most popular works being *El anillo de hierro* (1878) and *El monaguillo* (1891); also wrote 4 syms.; orch. variations; etc.

Marriner, Sir Neville, outstanding English conductor; b. Lincoln, April 15, 1924. He studied violin with his father, and then with Frederick Mountney; subsequently entered the Royal College of Music in London when he was 13, but his studies were interrupted by military service during World War II; after resuming his training at the Royal College of Music, he completed his violin studies in Paris with René Benedetti and took courses at the Cons. He was active as a violinist in chamber music ensembles; was a prof. of violin at the Royal College of Music (1949–59); joined the Philharmonia Orch. of London as a violinist (1952), and then was principal 2nd violinist of the London Sym. Orch. (1956–58). His interest in conducting was encouraged by Pierre Monteux, who gave him lessons at his summer school in Hancock, Maine (1959). In 1958 he founded the Academy of St.-Martin-in-the-Fields; served as its director until 1978, establishing an international reputation through recordings and tours. From 1968 to 1978 he also served as music director of the Los Angeles Chamber Orch.; then was music director of the Minnesota Orch. in Minneapolis (1978–86). In 1981 he became principal guest conductor of the Stuttgart Radio Sym. Orch.; was its chief conductor from 1983 to 1989. He appeared as a guest conductor with many of the world's leading orchs. In 1979 he was made a Commander of the Order of the British Empire. He was knighted in 1985. Marriner has proved himself one of the most remarkable conductors of his day. His extensive activities as a chamber music player, orch. musician, and chamber orch. violinist-conductor served as an invaluable foundation for his career as a sym. conductor of the 1st rank. His enormous repertoire encompasses works from the Baroque era to the great masterworks of the 20th century. In all of his performances, he demonstrates authority, mastery of detail, and impeccable taste.

Marrocco, W(illiam) Thomas, American violinist and musicologist; b. West New York, N.J., Dec. 5, 1909. After initial music studies in the U.S., he went to Italy and entered the Cons. di Musica S. Pietro a Majella in Naples, receiving his diploma di Magistero in 1930; then studied violin and musicology at the Eastman School of Music in Rochester, N.Y. (B.M., 1934; M.A., 1940); earned his Ph.D. at the Univ. of Calif. at Los Angeles with the dissertation *Jacopo da Bologna and His*

Works (1952; publ. as *The Music of Jacopo da Bologna*, Berkeley, 1954); was on the music faculty of the Univ. of Kans. in Lawrence (1946–49); was prof. of music at the Univ. of Calif. at Los Angeles (1950–77); also played in the Roth String Quartet. He publ. numerous informative essays dealing with early Italian and American music; ed. Vols. VI–IX of Polyphonic Music of the Fourteenth Century: Italian Secular Music (Monaco, 1967–78); also publ. *Fourteenth Century Italian Cacce* (Cambridge, Mass., 1942; 2nd ed., rev. and augmented, 1961); *Music in America: An Anthology* (with H. Gleason; N.Y., 1964); *Medieval Music* (with N. Sandon; London, 1977); *Inventory of Fifteenth Century Bassedanze, Balli and Balletti in Italian Dance Manuals* (N.Y., 1981); *Memoirs of a Stradivarius* (N.Y., 1988).

Marsalis, Wynton, outstanding black American trumpet virtuoso; b. New Orleans, Oct. 18, 1961. He was born into a cultured musical family; his father, Ellis Marsalis, was a trained pianist and active as a jazz musician; he insisted that his sons receive professional training. In 1974 the elder Marsalis founded the jazz program for the nascent New Orleans Center for the Creative Arts, which nurtured important new talent. Wynton took up the trumpet at age 6; later studied with John Longo, and also received instruction at his father's school. He appeared as soloist in the Haydn Trumpet Concerto with the New Orleans Phil. when he was 14; also performed with local groups in classical, jazz, and rock settings. He won the Harvey Shapiro Award as the most gifted brass player at the Berkshire Music Center at Tanglewood at age 17; then attended the Juilliard School in N.Y. (1979–81). He joined Art Blakey's Jazz Messengers (1980–81); played with them at the jazz festival at Montreux, Switzerland (1980); then toured with his own quintet, which included his brother Branford, a fine saxophonist; he also worked with Miles Davis. In 1984 he achieved unprecedented success when he won Grammy awards in both the jazz and classical categories for his recordings. As of 1990 he had released 12 jazz and 5 classical recordings, for which he garnered a grand total of 8 Grammy awards. He is credited with leading a jazz revival which has brought forward many young musicians of great talent. On Oct. 30, 1990, Marsalis hosted a benefit concert for Graham-Windham (a private childcare agency), the Autism Soc. of America, and the Immunohematology Research Foundation at Alice Tully Hall in N.Y.; featured were the musical members of his family: patriarch Ellis on piano, youngest brother Jason, making his debut on drums, Branford on saxophone, and Wynton on trumpet; absent was Delfeayo, a trombonist. The Marsalis clan was joined by the members of Wynton's jazz septet in an evening of critically acclaimed hard-bop.

BIBL.: T. Sancton, "Horn of Plenty," *Time* (Oct. 22, 1990).

Marschalk, Max, German music critic and composer; b. Berlin, April 7, 1863; d. Poberow-on-the-Ostsee, Aug. 24, 1940. He was a pupil of H. Urban; from 1894 until its dissolution in 1933, was music critic of the *Vossische Zeitung*; from 1934, music director of the Dreililien publishing company in Berlin. He composed a short opera, *In Flammen* (Gotha, 1896); a "Liederspiel," *Aucassin und Nicolette* (Stuttgart, 1907); incidental music to Hauptmann's *Hanneles Himmelfahrt* (1894), *Die versunkene Glocke* (1898), and *Und Pippa tanzt* (1906); also to Maeterlinck's *Sœur Béatrice*, etc.

Marschner, Franz, Bohemian pianist, pedagogue, writer on music, and composer; b. Leitmeritz, March 1855; d. Weissphyra, Aug. 22, 1932. He studied with Skuherský at the Prague Cons. and with Bruckner in Vienna. He publ. essays on the techniques of piano playing, among them *Entwurf einer Neugestaltung der Theorie und Praxis des kunstgemässen Anschlags* (on piano touch; Vienna, 1888); also wrote essays on musical esthetics; composed choral pieces, some chamber music, and songs.

Marschner, Heinrich (August), important German opera composer; b. Zittau, Saxony, Aug. 16, 1795; d. Hannover, Dec. 14, 1861. He sang in the school choir at the Zittau Gymnasium, and also studied music with Karl Hering. In 1813 he went to Leipzig, where he studied jurisprudence at the Univ.; encouraged by the cantor of the Thomasschule, J.C. Schicht, he turned to music as his main vocation. In 1816 he became a music tutor in Count Zichy's household in Pressburg, and also served as Kapellmeister to Prince Krasatkowitz. In his leisure hours he began to compose light operas; his 1st opera, *Titus* (1816), did not achieve a performance, but soon he had 2 more operas and a singspiel produced in Dresden. His 1st signal success was the historical opera *Heinrich IV und d'Aubigné*, which was accepted by Weber, who was then music director at the Dresden Court Opera, and was produced there on July 19, 1820. In 1817 he was in Vienna, where he was fortunate enough to meet Beethoven. In 1821 Marschner moved to Dresden and had his singspiel *Der Holzdieb* staged at the Court Opera (Feb. 22, 1825). He expected to succeed Weber as music director at the Court Opera after Weber died in London, but failed to obtain the post. He went to Leipzig, where he became Kapellmeister of the Stadttheater, and wrote for it 2 Romantic operas, in the manner of Weber: *Der Vampyr* (March 29, 1828) and *Der Templer und die Jüdin,* after the famous novel *Ivanhoe* by Sir Walter Scott (Dec. 22, 1829). In 1830 he received the position of Kapellmeister of the Hannover Hoftheater. His most successful opera, *Hans Heiling* (Berlin, May 24, 1833), exhibited the most attractive Romantic traits of his music: a flowing melody, sonorous harmony, and nervous rhythmic pulse; the opera formed a natural transition to the exotic melodrama of Meyerbeer's great stage epics and to Wagner's early lyrical music dramas. Historically important was his bold projection of a continuous dramatic development, without the conventional type of distinct arias separated by recitative. In this respect he was the heir of Weber and a precursor of Wagner.

WORKS: *Titus,* opera (1816; not perf.); *Der Kyffhäuserberg,* singspiel (1816; Zittau, Jan. 2, 1822); *Heinrich IV und d'Aubigné,* opera (1817–18; Dresden, July 19, 1820); *Saidar und Zulima,* romantic opera (Pressburg, Nov. 26, 1818); *Der Holzdieb,* singspiel (1823; Dresden, Feb. 22, 1825; rev. 1853 as *Geborgt*); *Lukretia,* opera (1820–26; Danzig, Jan 17, 1827); *Der Vampyr,* romantic opera (1827; Leipzig, March 29, 1828); *Der Templer und die Jüdin,* romantic opera (Leipzig, Dec. 22, 1829); *Des Falkners Braut,* comic opera (1830; Leipzig, March 10, 1832); *Hans Heiling,* romantic opera (1831–32; Berlin, May 24, 1833); *Das Schloss am Ätna,* romantic opera (1830–35; Leipzig, Jan. 29, 1836); *Der Bäbu,* comic opera (1836–37; Hannover, Feb. 19, 1838); *Kaiser Adolf von Nassau,* romantic opera (Dresden, Jan 5, 1845); *Austin,* romantic opera (1850–51; Hannover, Jan. 25, 1852); *Sangeskönig Hiarne, oder Das Tyringsschwert,* romantic opera (1857–58; Frankfurt, Sept. 13, 1863); ballet, *Die stolze Bäuerin* (Zittau, 1810); incidental music; also 2 unfinished syms.; choral works.

BIBL.: W. Neumann, *H. M.* (Kassel, 1854); H. Borges, "H. M.s Oper 'Hiarne,'" *Neue Zeitschrift für Musik,* LXXIX (1883); E. Danzig, *H. M. in seinen minderbekannten Opern und Liedern* (Leipzig, 1890); M. Wittmann, *H. M.* (Leipzig, 1897); G. Münzer, *H. M.* (Berlin, 1901); L. Hirschberg, "M. als Balladenkomponist," *Musikwelt,* XXXVII (1905); C. Preiss, *Templer und Jüdin* (Graz, 1911); L. Hirschberg, "H. M.s Balladen," *Die Musik,* XI (1911–12); H. Gaartz, *Die Opern H. M.s* (Leipzig, 1912); L. Hirschberg, "H. M.s Chöre," *Neue Musik-Zeitung,* XXXIII (1912); H. Wetzel, "H. M.s Balladen," *Musikpädagogische Blätter* (1914); G. Fischer, *M. Erinnerungen* (Hannover, 1918); H. Pfitzner, "M.s Vampyr," *Neue Musik-Zeitung,* XLV (1924); A. Bickel, *H. M. in seinen Opern* (diss., Univ. of Erlangen, 1929); A. Gnirs, *Hans Heiling* (Karlsbad, 1931); G. Hausswald, *H. M.* (Dresden, 1938); V. Köhler, *H. M.s Bühnenwerke* (diss., Univ. of Göttingen, 1956); idem, "H. M.," *Hannoversche Geschichtsblätter,* new series, XVI (1962); idem, "Rezitativ, Szene und Melodram in H. M.s Opern," *Gesellschaft für Musikforschung Kongressbericht* (Bonn, 1970); A. Dean Palmer, *H.A. M., 1795–1861: His Life and Stage Works* (1980).

Marsh, Robert C(harles), noted American music critic; b. Columbus, Ohio, Aug. 5, 1924. At Northwestern Univ. he stud-

ied journalism (B.S., 1945) and philosophy (A.M., 1946); earned a doctorate in education at Harvard Univ. (1951); synchronously he took courses in music theory with Robert Palmer at Cornell Univ. (1946–47) and attended lectures of Hindemith at Harvard Univ. (1949–50); studied musicology with Thurston Dart and theory of criticism with H.S. Middleton at Cambridge Univ. (1953–56). He held teaching positions at the Univ. of Illinois (1947–49), Chicago City Junior College (1950–51), Univ. of Kansas (1951–52), State Univ. of N.Y. (1953–54), and Univ. of Chicago (1956–58). He became music critic of the *Chicago Sun Times* in 1956; contributed articles on music to various literary publications and philosophical journals; ed. *Logic and Knowledge of Bertrand Russell* (1956); publ. *Toscanini and the Art of Orchestral Performance* (Philadelphia, 1956; rev. as *Toscanini and the Art of Conducting*, 1962); also a book on the Cleveland Orch. (1967).

Marsh, Roger, English composer and teacher; b. Bournemouth, Dec. 10, 1949. He studied with Ian Kellam at the London College of Music and privately (1966–68); continued his training at the Univ. of York (B.A., 1971), where he became a composition student of Bernard Rands (Ph.D., 1975); received a Harkness fellowship to study at the Univ. of Calif. at San Diego (1976–78). Returning to England, he was a lecturer at the Univ. of Keele (1978–88), where he was founder-director of the Keele New Music Ensemble (1979–88) and head of the music dept. (1985–88); then accepted a position as lecturer at the Univ. of York (from 1988).

WORKS: MUSIC THEATER: *Cass* (1970); *PS* (1971); *Calypso* (1973); *Scènes de ballet* (London, Feb. 17, 1974); *Dum* (1973; rev. version, San Diego, April 29, 1977; also for Orch. as *Dum's Dream*, 1973); *Time Before* (1977; London, Jan. 19, 1979); *Bits and Scraps* (London, May 6, 1979); *Spit and Blow* (1981; Birmingham, Feb. 27, 1983); *Samson* (London, Oct. 20, 1984); *Love on the Rocks* (1989); *The Big Bang* (part 1, 1989). ORCH.: *Dum's Dream* (1973; also a music theater version); *Still* (Birmingham, Nov. 13, 1981; rev. 1987). CHAMBER: *Jesters (for sicks)* for 2 Oboes, 2 Clarinets, and 2 Bassoons (1972); *Serenade* for Amplified Double Bass and 15 Strings (London, July 16, 1974); *Variations for [4] Trombones* (1977; Los Angeles, Feb. 5, 1979); *Point to Point* for 2 Oboes, 2 Clarinets, 2 Horns, and 2 Bassoons (1979); *2 Movements* for 2 Flutes, 2 Clarinets, Harp, and String Quartet (London, Oct. 9, 1979); *Heaven Haven* for Harp (1982); *Music* for Piano and Wind Instruments (York, March 17, 1986); *Dying for it* for 9 Instruments (1988); Trio for Piano, Clarinet, and Cello (1988). VOCAL: *Streim* for Soprano, Flute, Clarinet, Trumpet, and Double Bass (1972); *The Lover's Ghost*, folk song for Soprano, 2 Flutes, 2 Clarinets, and Cello (1972; also for High Voice and Harp, 1976); *On and On*, folk song for Soprano, 2 Clarinets, and Bass Clarinet (1975); *3 Hale Mairies* for 3 Sopranos, Flute, Clarinet, Trumpet, Harp, Piano, 2 Percussion, Viola, and Cello (San Diego, March 17, 1977); *Another Silly Love Song* for Soprano, Clarinet, and Piano (1976); *Not a Soul but Ourselves . . .* for 2 Female and 2 Male Voices with independent amplification (San Diego, Nov. 29, 1977); *A Psalm and a Silly Love Song* for Soprano, Mezzo-soprano, Flute, Clarinet, Trumpet, Harp, Viola, and Cello (London, April 25, 1979); *The Wormwood and the Gall* for Mezzo-soprano, Flute, Clarinet, Percussion, Harp, Viola, and Cello (London, July 6, 1981); *Words of Love* for Baritone, 2 Oboes, Bassoon, and Harpsichord (1982); *Songs of Devotion* for Soprano, Clarinet, and Guitar (York, March 10, 1984); *3 Biblical Songs* for Soprano, Baritone, Small Female Chorus, and Orch. (1985); *The Song of Abigail* for Soprano and Orch. (London, March 7, 1986).

Marshall, Ingram D(ouglass), American composer; b. Mount Vernon, N.Y., May 10, 1942. He studied at Lake Forest (Ill.) College (B.A., 1964); after studies in musicology with Lang and in electronic music with Ussachevsky at Columbia Univ. (1964–66), he pursued training with Subotnick at N.Y.'s School of the Arts (1969–70); continued his studies with Subotnick and with K.R.T. Wasitodipura (traditional Indonesian music) at the Calif. Inst. of the Arts in Valencia (M.F.A., 1971),

where he subsequently taught (until 1974). He was active as both a composer and a music critic; was awarded various grants and commissions. His compositions reflect his extensive travels, as well as an artful incorporation of non-traditional instruments, live electronics, and improvisation. His highly successful *Fog Tropes* (1982) makes use of electronically manipulated taped sounds gathered around the San Francisco Bay that include not only foghorns but the falsetto keenings of seagulls and the lowing of a gambuh (a Balinese flute).

WORKS: *Transmogrification* for Tape (1966); *3 Buchla Studies* for Synthesizer (1968–69); *Cortez*, text-sound piece (1973); *Vibrosuperball* for 4 Amplified Percussion (1975); *Non confundar* for String Sextet, Alto Flute, Clarinet, and Electronics (1977); *Adendum: In aeternum* for Clarinet, Flute, and String Sextet (1979); *Spiritus* for 6 Strings, 4 Flutes, Harpsichord, and Vibraphone (1981; rev. for String Orch., 1983); *Fog Tropes* for Brass Sextet and Tape (1982); string quartet, *Voces resonae* (1984).

Marshall, Lois (Catherine), prominent Canadian soprano, later mezzo-soprano; b. Toronto, Jan. 29, 1924. She began her vocal training at age 12 with Weldon Kilburn, whom she married in 1968; also studied lieder interpretation with Emmy Heim (1947–50). She 1st gained notice as a soloist in Bach's *St. Matthew Passion* with Sir Ernest MacMillan and the Toronto Sym. Orch. (1947). In 1952 she made her operatic stage debut as the Queen of the Night in Toronto, won the Naumburg Award, and made her N.Y. recital debut. She appeared as a soloist in Beethoven's *Missa solemnis* with Toscanini and the NBC Sym. Orch. in 1953, and subsequently sang with many other important American orchs. She made her London debut in 1956 with Beecham and the Royal Phil. Orch., and began a series of world concert tours in 1960; began singing as a mezzo-soprano in the mid-1970s. She was made a Companion of the Order of Canada (1968).

Marshall, Margaret (Anne), Scottish soprano; b. Stirling, Jan. 4, 1949. She studied at the Royal Scottish Academy of Music in Glasgow; also took voice lessons with Edna Mitchell and Peter Pears in England and with Hans Hotter in Munich. In 1974 she won 1st prize at the International Competition in Munich; made her London concert debut in 1975; in 1978 she made her operatic debut in Florence as Euridice in *Orfeo*; she then sang the role of the Countess in the 1979 Florence production of *Le nozze di Figaro*, and made her Covent Garden debut in London in the same role in 1980. In 1982 she appeared in Milan and at the Salzburg Festival. She made her 1st appearances in the U.S. in 1980 as a soloist with the Boston Sym. Orch. and N.Y. Phil.; subsequently made several American tours as a concert artist.

Marshall, Mike, American mandolinist and guitarist; b. Newcastle, Pa., July 17, 1957. He studied with James Hilligoss in Lakeland, Fla.; performed in various ensembles, including the Sunshine Bluegrass Boys (1972–76), the David Grisman Quintet (1979–84), and Montreux (1984–89); in 1986 he formed, with mandolinist Dana (William) Rath (b. West Bend, Wis., May 21, 1956), The Modern Mandolin Quartet, the 1st mandolin quartet, comprising mandolins, mandola, and mando-cello, corresponding to the string quartet; other members are Paul Binkley (b. Minneapolis, May 9, 1954) and John Eric Imholz (b. San Francisco, June 9, 1953). Marshall helped to spearhead the New Acoustic movement with the David Grisman Quintet and New Age music as a recording artist for Windham Hill; an accomplished international performer, he performs in bluegrass, jazz, classical, and New Acoustic Music styles. His goal as a composer and performer is to "fuse musical styles such as jazz, bluegrass, world music, and classical to form new styles reflective of a less-structured, freer world." Among his compositions are *Gator Strut, Dolphins,* and *Free D;* also songs.

Marshall, Robert L(ewis), distinguished American musicologist; b. N.Y., Oct. 12, 1939. He studied at Columbia Univ.

(A.B., 1960) and with Babbitt, Lockwood, Mendel, and Strunk at Princeton Univ. (M.F.A., 1962; Ph.D., 1968, with the diss. *The Compositional Process of J.S. Bach: A Study of the Autograph Scores of the Vocal Works*; publ. in Princeton, 1972). He was chairman of the music dept. of the Univ. of Chicago (1972–77) and served as a prof. on its faculty from 1977 to 1983. He then was appointed to the faculty of Brandeis Univ., teaching there from 1983. He was general ed. of the series Recent Researches in the Music of the Baroque Era (1977–87); publ. the book *The Music of Johann Sebastian Bach: The Sources, the Style, the Significance* (N.Y., 1989).

Marsick, Armand (Louis Joseph), Belgian conductor, teacher, and composer, nephew of **Martin (-Pierre-Joseph) Marsick;** b. Liège, Sept. 20, 1877; d. Haine-St.-Paul, April 30, 1959. He studied with his father, Louis Marsick; then took a course in composition with Sylvain Dupuis at the Liège Cons., with Guy Ropartz at the Nancy Cons., and d'Indy in Paris. After playing 1st violin in the Municipal Théâtre in Nancy, he became concertmaster at the Concerts Colonne in Paris (1898); in 1908 he obtained the position of instructor at the Athens Cons., where he remained until 1921; was appointed director at the Bilbao Cons. in 1922. He returned to Belgium in 1927; was a prof. at the Liège Cons. (1927–42) and conductor of the Société des Concerts Symphoniques (1927–39).

WORKS: DRAMATIC: 3 operas: *La Jane* (1903; 1st perf. as *Vendetta corsa*, Rome, 1913; Liège, March 29, 1921); *Lara* (1913; Antwerp, Dec. 3, 1929); *L'Anneau nuptial* (1920; Brussels, March 3, 1928); radio play, *Le Visage de la Wallonie* (1937). **ORCH.:** 2 symphonic poems: *Stèle funéraire* (1902) and *La Source* (1908); *Improvisation et Final* for Cello and Orch. (1904); 2 suites: *Scènes de montagnes* (1910) and *Tableaux grecs* (1912); *Tableaux de voyage* for Small Orch. (1939); *Loustics en fête* for Small Orch. (1939); *3 morceaux symphoniques* (1950). **CHAMBER:** Violin Sonata (1900); Quartet for 4 Horns (1950); *4 pièces* for Piano (1912); songs; choruses.

Marsick, Martin (-Pierre-Joseph), distinguished Belgian violinist, uncle of **Armand (Louis Joseph) Marsick;** b. Jupille-sur-Neuse, near Liège, March 9, 1848; d. Paris, Oct. 21, 1924. He studied at the Liège Cons.; at the age of 12, played the organ at the Cathedral; then studied violin with Léonard at the Brussels Cons. and with Massart at the Paris Cons., taking 1st prize there (1869). In 1870 he became a pupil of Joachim in Berlin. After a brilliant debut in Paris in the Concerts Populaires (1873), he undertook long tours in Europe; also played in the U.S. (1895–96). He was a prof. of violin at the Paris Cons. (1892–1900). Among his pupils were Carl Flesch and Jacques Thibaud. He wrote 3 violin concertos, chamber music, numerous pieces for solo violin, and songs.

Marteau, Henri, greatly esteemed French-born Swedish violinist and pedagogue; b. Rheims, March 31, 1874; d. Lichtenberg, Bavaria, Oct. 3, 1934. He studied violin with Léonard and Garcin at the Paris Cons. (premier prix, 1892) and began his concert career as a youth; played in Vienna when he was 10 and in London when he was 14. In 1892, 1893, 1894, 1898, and 1906 he also toured the U.S.; gave concerts in Scandinavia, Russia, France, and Germany. In 1900 he was appointed prof. of violin at the Geneva Cons., and in 1908 succeeded Joachim as violin teacher at the Hochschule für Musik in Berlin; conducted the Göteborg orch. (1915–20) and became a Swedish citizen (1920); then taught at the German Academy of Music in Prague (1921–24), the Leipzig Cons. (1926–27), and the Dresden Cons. (from 1928). He was greatly appreciated by musicians of Europe; Reger, who was a personal friend, wrote a violin concerto for him, as did Massenet; his teacher Léonard bequeathed to him his magnificent Maggini violin, once owned by the Empress Maria Theresa. He championed the music of Bach and Mozart. Marteau was also a competent composer; he wrote an opera, *Meister Schwable* (Plauen, 1921); *Sinfonia gloria naturae* for Orch. (Stockholm, 1918); 2 violin concertos; Cello Concerto; much chamber music; many choral works; numerous violin pieces and arrangements of classical works.

BIBL.: B. Marteau, *H. M., Siegeszug einer Geige* (Tutzing, 1971); G. Weiss, ed., *Der Lehrer und Wegbereiter von H. M., Hubert Léonard* (Tutzing, 1987).

Martelli, Henri, French composer; b. Santa Fe, Argentina, Feb. 25, 1895; d. Paris, July 15, 1980. He studied law at the Univ. of Paris; simultaneously took courses in composition with Widor and Caussade. He was secretary of the Société Nationale de Musique (1945–67) and director of programs there from 1968; from 1953 to 1973, was president of the French section of the ISCM. In his compositions he attempted to re-create the spirit of early French music using modern techniques.

WORKS: STAGE: Opera, *La Chanson de Roland* (1921–23; rev. 1962–64; Paris, April 13, 1967); opera buffa, *Le Major Cravachon* (1958; French Radio, June 14, 1959); 2 ballets: *La Bouteille de Panurge* (1930; Paris, Feb. 24, 1937) and *Les Hommes de sable* (1951). **ORCH.:** *Rondo* (1921); *Sarabande, Scherzo et Final* (1922); *Divertimento sarrasin* (1922); *Sur la vie de Jeanne d'Arc* (1923); *Scherzo* for Violin and Orch. (1925); *Mors et Juventas* (1927); *Bas-reliefs assyriens* (1928; Boston, March 14, 1930); *Passacaille sur un thème russe* (1928); Concerto (1931; Boston, April 22, 1932); 3 suites: No. 1, *Suite sur un thème corse* (1936); No. 2 (1950); No. 3 (1971); Concerto No. 1 for Violin and Chamber Orch. (1938); *Ouverture pour un conte de Boccace* (1942); *Suite concertante* for Wind Quintet and Orch. (1943); *Divertimento* for Wind Orch. (1945); *Fantaisie* for Piano and Orch. (1945); Sinfonietta (1948); 3 syms.: No. 1 for Strings (1953; French Radio, March 13, 1955); No. 2 for Strings (1956; Paris, July 17, 1958); No. 3 (1957; Paris, March 8, 1960); Concertino No. 2 for Violin and Chamber Orch. (1954); Concertino for Oboe, Clarinet, Horn, Bassoon, and String Orch. (1955); Double Concerto for Clarinet, Bassoon, and Orch. (1956); *Le Radeau de la Méduse*, symphonic poem (1957); *Variations* for String Orch. (1959); *Scènes à danser* (1963); *Rapsodie* for Cello and Orch. (1966); Oboe Concerto (1971). **VOCAL:** *Le Temps*, cantata for Voice and 8 Instruments (1945); *Chrestomathie* for a cappella Chorus (1949). **CHAMBER:** *Invention* for Cello and Piano (1925); Duo for Oboe and English Horn (1925); 2 string quartets (1932–33; 1944); Piano Trio (1935); Violin Sonata (1936); *Suite* for 4 Clarinets (1936); *Introduction et Final* for Violin and Piano (1937); Wind Octet (1941); *Scherzetto, Berceuse et Final* for Cello and Piano (1941); Bassoon Sonata (1941); Cello Sonatina (1941); Flute Sonata (1942); *3 esquisses* for Saxophone and Piano (1943); *Préambule et Scherzo* for Clarinet and Piano (1944); *7 Duos* for Violin and Harp (1946); *Fantaisiestück* for Flute and Piano (1946); Wind Quintet (1974); Cornet Sonatina (1948); *Adagio, Cadence et Final* for Oboe and Piano (1949); 2 quintets for Flute, Harp, and String Trio (1950, 1952); Trio for Flute, Cello, and Piano (1951); *Cadence, Interlude et Rondo* for Saxophone and Piano (1952); *15 études* for Bassoon (1953); Bass Trombone Sonata (1956); Viola Sonata (1959); *Suite* for Solo Guitar (1960); *Concertstück* for Viola and Piano (1962); Concertino for Cornet and Piano (1964); *Dialogue* for Trombone, Tuba or Bass Saxophone, and Piano (1966); Oboe Sonata (1972); String Trio (1973–74); Trio for Flute, Cello, and Harp (1976). **PIANO:** *Suite galante* (1924); *Guitare* (1931); *3 Petites suites* (1935, 1943, 1950); *Suite* (1939); 2-piano Sonata (1946); *Sonorités* for Piano, left-hand (1974); also 17 radiophonic works (1940–62); songs.

Martenot, Maurice (Louis Eugène), French inventor of the electronic instrument "Ondes musicales," a.k.a. "Ondes Martenot"; b. Paris, Oct. 14, 1898; d. there, Oct. 10, 1980, as a result of a velocipede accident. He studied composition at the Paris Cons. with Gédalge; began to work on the construction of an electronic musical instrument with a keyboard, which he called Ondes musicales. He gave its 1st demonstration in Paris on April 20, 1928, and, on Dec. 23, 1928, the 1st musical work for the instrument, *Poème symphonique pour solo d'Ondes musicales et orchestre*, by Dimitri Levidis, was presented in

Paris. Martenot publ. *Méthode pour l'enseignement des Ondes musicales* (Paris, 1931). The instrument became popular, especially among French composers: it is included in the score of Honegger's *Jeanne d'Arc au bûcher* (1935); Koechlin's *Le Buisson ardent*, part 1 (1938); Martinon's 2nd Sym., *Hymne à la vie* (1944); and Messiaen's *Turangalîla-Symphonie* (1946–48). It was used as a solo instrument in Koechlin's *Hymne* (1929), Jolivet's *Concerto* (1947), Landowski's *Concerto* (1954), Bondon's *Kaleidoscope* (1957), and Charpentier's *Concertino "alla francese"* (1961). Many other composers were attracted to it as well. Of all the early electronic instruments—Ondes Martenot, Trautonium, and Theremin—only Martenot's has proved a viable musical instrument. When Varèse's *Ecuatorial*, written in 1934 for a brass ensemble and including a Theremin, was publ. in 1961, the score substituted an Ondes Martenot for the obsolescent Theremin. Martenot's sister, Ginette Martenot, became the chief exponent of the Ondes Martenot in concert performances in Europe and the U.S.

Martienssen, Carl Adolf, German musicologist and pedagogue; b. Güstrow, Dec. 6, 1881; d. Berlin, March 1, 1955. He studied piano with Klindworth and Wilhelm Berger in Berlin and musicology with Kretzschmar at the Univ. there. In 1914 he was appointed instructor of piano at the Leipzig Cons.; in 1932 he became prof. at the Musical Inst. for Foreigners in Berlin. He taught at the Hochschule für Musik in Berlin from 1934 to 1945; then at the Hochschule für Musik in Rostock (1945–50); subsequently at the Hochschule für Musik in East Berlin (1950–52). He prepared Urtexts of the Haydn, Mozart, and Beethoven piano sonatas.

WRITINGS (all publ. in Leipzig): *Die individuelle Klaviertechnik auf der Grundlage des schöpferischen Klangwillens* (1930); *Die Methodik des individuellen Klavierunterrichts* (1934); *Grundlage einer deutschen Klavierlehre* (1942); *Das Klavierkunstwerk* (1950).

Martín, Edgardo, Cuban composer and writer on music; b. Cienfuegos, Oct. 6, 1915. He studied with his maternal grandmother, the pianist Aurea Suárez; later took piano lessons in Havana with Jascha Fischermann and studied composition with José Ardévol. He taught music history at the Cons. Municipal (1945–68) and music analysis in the Escuela Nacional de Arte (1969–73) in Havana. From 1962 to 1971 he served as executive secretary of the National Committee of Music for UNESCO. As a Castro partisan, he was a leading figure in the reform of music teaching under the Communist regime. As a composer, he pursued the plausible genre of pleasurable modern music. He publ. *Catálogo biográfico de compositores de Cuba* (Havana, 1970) and *Panorama histórico de la música en Cuba* (Havana, 1971).

WORKS: Ballet, *El Caballo de coral* (Havana, 1960); 2 syms. (1947, 1948); Concerto for 9 Wind Instruments (1944); Trio for Oboe, Clarinet, and Bassoon (1963); 2 string quartets (1967, 1968); *Recitativo y Aria* for Viola and Piano (1979); *Los 2 abuelos* for Chorus and Instrumental Ensemble (1949); *Canto de héroes* for Voices, with Orch. (1967); *La carta del soldado* for Narrator, Tenor, Chorus, Speaking Chorus, and Orch. (1970); *Granma* for Chorus and Instruments (1976); songs: *4 cantos de la Revolución* (1962); *7 cantos del Amor Imposible* (1964); *Antiquas comuniones* (1972); *Cantos de Martí* (1976); piano pieces, including Sonata (1943); *2 Preludios* (1950); *Soneras:* No. 1 (1950); No. 2 (1971); No. 3 (1975); also pieces for guitar.

Martin, François, significant French cellist and composer; b. 1727; d. Paris, 1757. He became well known as a cellist and composer in Paris; appeared at the Concert Spirituel (1747); was an ordinaire de l'Académie Royale de Musique (1746–48); also taught. He was granted several royal privileges to publ. his music. His place in French music rests primarily upon his syms. and overtures, which were some of the finest works of their kind written in the pre-Classical period. They were featured at the Concert Spirituel (1751–55). His motets were also performed there, including his notable *Cantate Domino*. His early death was greatly lamented.

WORKS: INSTRUMENTAL (all publ. in Paris): 6 *sonates* for Cello, with duo for Violin and Cello, op. 2 (1746); 6 *trios ou Conversations à 3* for 2 Violins, or Flute and Cello, op. 3 (1746); *Sonate da camera* for Cello and Basso Continuo, op. 1 (1748); (6) *Symphonies et ouvertures* for 2 Violins, Viola, and Bass, op. 4 (1751); *Symphonie à cors de chasse* (Concert Spirituel, June 10, 1751); various other works, including a Cello Concerto (Concert Spirituel, April 1747). **SECULAR VOCAL:** *Le Bouquet de Thémire*, cantatille (La Planchette, July 28, 1745); *Le Soupçon amoureux*, cantatille (1747); *Le Suisse amoureux*, cantatille (1747); several other works. **SACRED VOCAL: *GRANDS MOTETS FOR CHORUS AND INSTRUMENTS*** (all perf. at the Concert Spirituel): *Laetatus sum* (April 3, 1747); *In exitu* (April 19, 1748); *Cantate Domino* (May 7, 1750); *Jubilate Deo* (April 24, 1753). ***PETITS MOTETS*** (all 1st perf. at the Concert Spirituel): *Laetentur coeli* (Feb. 2, 1751); *Inclina Domine* (Nov. 1, 1751). **MOTETS:** *Notum fecit dominus* (1752); *Super flumina Babilonis* (n.d.).

BIBL.: M. Cyr, " 'Inclina Domine': A M. Motet Wrongly Attributed to Rameau," *Music & Letters*, LVIII (1977).

Martin, Frank, greatly renowned Swiss composer; b. Geneva, Sept. 15, 1890; d. Naarden, the Netherlands, Nov. 21, 1974. He was the last of 10 children of a Calvinist minister, a descendant of the Huguenots. He studied privately with Joseph Lauber in Geneva (1906–14), who instructed him in the basics of the conservative idiom of Swiss music of the fin de siècle; then had lessons with Hans Huber and Frederic Klose, who continued to emphasize the conservative foundations of the religious and cultural traditions of the Swiss establishment. However, Martin soon removed himself from the strict confines of Swiss scholasticism, encouraged in this development by Ernest Ansermet, then conductor of the Orch. de la Suisse Romande in Geneva. In 1918 Martin went to Zürich and, in 1921, to Rome; finally settled in Paris in 1923, then the center of modern music. He returned to Geneva in 1926 as a pianist and harpsichordist; taught at the Inst. Jaques-Dalcroze (1927–38), was founder and director of the Technicum Moderne de Musique (1933–39), and served as president of the Assoc. of Swiss Musicians (1942–46). He moved to the Netherlands in 1946; also taught composition at the Cologne Hochschule für Musik (1950–57). His early music showed the influence of Franck and French impressionists, but soon he succeeded in creating a distinctive style supported by a consummate mastery of contrapuntal and harmonic writing, and a profound feeling for emotional consistency and continuity. Still later he became fascinated by the logic and self-consistency of Schoenberg's method of composition with 12 tones, and adopted it in a modified form in several of his works. He also demonstrated an ability to stylize folk-song materials in modern techniques. In his music, Martin followed the religious and moral precepts of his faith in selecting several subjects of his compositions. In 1944 the director of Radio Geneva asked him to compose an oratorio to be broadcast immediately upon the conclusion of World War II. He responded with *In terra pax* for 5 Soli, Double Chorus, and Orch., which was given its broadcast premiere from Geneva at the end of the war in Europe, May 7, 1945; a public performance followed in Geneva 24 days later. He publ. *Responsabilité du compositeur* (Geneva, 1966); M. Martin ed. his *Un compositeur médite sur son art* (Neuchâtel, 1977).

WORKS: STAGE: Operas: *Der Sturm* (The Tempest), after Shakespeare (1952–54; Vienna, June 17, 1956); *Monsieur de Pourceaugnac*, after Molière (1960–62; Geneva, April 23, 1963); ballets: *Das Märchen vom Aschenbrödel*, after the Cinderella legend (1941; Basel, March 12, 1942); *Ein Totentanz zu Basel im Jahre 1943* (Basel, May 27, 1943); also a play with music, *La Nique à Satan*, for Baritone, Male, Female, and Children's Choruses, Winds, Percussion, 2 Pianos, and Double Bass (1930–31; Geneva, Feb. 25, 1933); incidental music to *Oedipus Rex* (1923), *Oedipus Coloneus* (1924), *Le Divorce* (1928), *Romeo and Juliet* (1929), and *Athalic* (1946).

VOCAL: *3 poèmes païens* for Baritone and Orch. (1910); *Les Dithyrambes* for 4 Soli, Mixed Chorus, Children's Chorus, and

Orch. (1918); *4 sonnets à Cassandre* for Mezzo-soprano, Flute, Viola, and Cello (1921); *Messe* for Double Chorus a cappella (1922); *Musique pour les Fêtes du Rhône* for Chorus and Winds (1929); *Cantate sur la Nativité* for Soli, Chorus, String Orch., and Piano (1929; unfinished); *Chanson en canon* for Chorus a cappella (1930); *Le Vin herbé*, oratorio after the Tristan legend, for 12 Solo Voices, 7 Strings, and Piano (1938–41; 1st complete perf., Zürich, March 26, 1942); *Cantate pour le 1er août* for Chorus, and Organ or Piano (1941); *Der Cornet* or *Die Weise von Liebe und Tod des Cornets Christoph Rilke*, after Rilke, cycle for Alto and Orch. (1942–43; Basel, Feb. 9, 1945); *Sechs Monologe aus "Jedermann,"* after Hofmannsthal, for Baritone or Alto and Piano (1943; orchestrated 1949); *In terra pax*, oratorio for 5 Soli, Double Chorus, and Orch. (Radio Geneva, May 7, 1945); *Dédicace* for Tenor and Piano (1945); *3 Chants de Noël* for Soprano, Flute and Piano (1947); *Golgotha*, oratorio for 5 Soli, Chorus, Orch., and Organ (1945–48; Geneva, April 29, 1949); *5 chansons d'Ariel* for Small Chorus a cappella (1950); *Psaumes de Genève*, Psalm cantata for Chorus, Children's Chorus, Orch., and Organ (1958); *Le Mystère de la Nativité*, oratorio (1957–59; Geneva, Dec. 24, 1959); *3 Minnelieder* for Soprano and Piano (1960); *Ode à la musique* for Chorus, Trumpet, 2 Horns, 3 Trombones, Double Bass, and Piano (1961); *Verse à boire* for Chorus a cappella (1961); *Pilate*, short oratorio (Rome, Nov. 14, 1964); *Maria Triptychon* for Soprano, Violin, and Orch. (consists of the separate works *Ave Maria*, *Magnificat*, and *Stabat Mater*, 1967–69; Rotterdam, Nov. 13, 1969); *Poèmes de la Mort* for 3 Male Voices and 3 Electric Guitars (1969–71); *Requiem* (1971–72; Lausanne, May 4, 1973); *Et la vie l'emporta*, chamber cantata for Small Vocal and Instrumental Ensembles (1974; his last work; orchestrated by B. Reichel, 1975). INSTRUMENTAL: Suite for Orch. (1913); 2 violin sonatas (1913; 1931–32); *Symphonie pour orchestre burlesque sur des thèmes savoyards*, with Children's Instruments (1915); Piano Quintet (1919); *Esquisses* for Small Orch. (1920); *Pavane couleur de temps* for String Quintet or String Orch. or Small Orch. (1920); *Foxtrot*, overture for 2 Pianos (1924; also for Orch.); Piano Trio on popular Irish themes (1924); *Rythmes*, 3 symphonic movements (1926; ISCM Festival, Geneva, April 6, 1929); *Guitare*, 4 small pieces for Guitar (1933; versions for Piano and Orch.); 2 piano concertos: No. 1 (1933–34; Geneva, Jan. 22, 1936) and No. 2 (1968–69; The Hague, June 27, 1970); *Rhapsodie* for String Quintet (1935); *Danse de la peur* for 2 Pianos and Small Orch. (1936; music from an uncompleted ballet, *Die blaue Blume*); String Trio (1936); Sym. with Jazz Instruments (1937; Geneva, March 10, 1938); *Ballade* for Saxophone, Strings, Piano, and Percussion (1938); *Sonata da chiesa* for Viola d'Amore or Flute, and Organ or Orch. or String Orch. (1938); *Ballade* for Flute, and Orch. or String Orch. (1939); *Ballade* for Piano and Orch. (1939); *Ballade* for Trombone or Saxophone, and Piano or Orch. (1940); *Passacaille* for Organ (1944; versions for String Orch., 1952, and for Full Orch., 1962); *Petite symphonie concertante* for Harp, Harpsichord, Piano, and Double String Orch. (1944–45; Zürich, May 17, 1946; an alternate version, *Symphonie concertante*, was created in 1946 for Full Orch., eliminating the solo instruments); *8 Preludes* for Piano (1947–48); Concerto for 7 Winds, Strings, and Percussion (Bern, Oct. 25, 1949); *Ballade* for Cello, and Piano or Small Orch. (1949); Violin Concerto (1950–51; Basel, Jan. 24, 1952); Concerto for Harpsichord and Small Orch. (Venice, Sept. 14, 1952); *Clair de lune* for Piano (1953); *Études* for String Orch. or 2 Pianos (1955–56); *Ouverture en hommage à Mozart* (1956); *Pièce brève* for Flute, Oboe, and Harp (1957); *Ouverture en rondeau* (1958); *Inter arma caritas* for Orch. (1963); *Les Quatre Éléments* for Orch. (1963–64; Geneva, Oct. 7, 1964); *Étude rythmique* and *Étude de déchiffrage* for Piano (both 1965); Cello Concerto (1965–66; Basel, Jan. 26, 1967); String Quartet (1966–67); *Erasmi monumentum* for Orch. and Organ (Rotterdam, Sept. 24, 1969); *3 danses* for Oboe, Harp, and String Orch. (Zürich, Oct. 9, 1970); *Ballade* for Viola, Winds, Harp, and Harpsichord (1972); *Polyptyque*, 6 images of the Passion of Christ, for Violin and 2 String

Orchs. (Lausanne, Sept. 9, 1973); *Fantaisie sur des rythmes flamenco* for Piano (1973).

BIBL.: R. Klein, *F. M.: Sein Leben und Werk* (Vienna, 1960); A. Koelliker, *F. M.: Biographie, les œuvres* (Lausanne, 1963); B. Billeter, *F. M.: Ein Aussenseiter der neuen Musik* (Frauenfeld, 1970); B. Martin, *F. M. ou la réalité du rêve* (Neuchâtel, 1973); special issue of *Schweizerische Musikzeitung*, CXVI (1976); W. Misteli, ed., *F. M.: Né le 15 septembre 1890, décédé le 21 novembre 1974: Liste des œuvres: Werkverzeichnis* (Zürich, 1981); M. Martin, ed., *Apropos de . . . commentaires de F. M. sur ses œuvres* (Neuchâtel, 1984); C. King, *F. M.: A Bio-Bibliography* (Westport, Conn., 1990).

Martin, Janis, American mezzo-soprano, later soprano; b. Sacramento, Aug. 16, 1939. She studied in San Francisco and N.Y., making her operatic debut as Teresa in *La Sonnambula* at the San Francisco Opera in 1960; subsequently sang Marina, Venus, and Meg Page there. On March 25, 1962, she made her 1st appearance at the N.Y. City Opera as Mrs. Grose in Britten's *The Turn of the Screw*. She won the Metropolitan Opera Auditions, making her debut as Flora in *La Traviata* on Dec. 19, 1962, in N.Y. After singing for 3 seasons as a mezzo-soprano, she returned to the Metropolitan Opera in 1973 as a soprano and sang such roles as Kundry, Sieglinde, and Berg's Marie in *Wozzeck*. In 1968 she appeared as Magdalene and as Fricka at the Bayreuth Festival; she sang Tosca at the Chicago Lyric Opera in 1971; made her Covent Garden debut in London as Marie in *Wozzeck* in 1973. Among her other roles are Ortrud, Brangäne, Senta, Elisabeth in *Tannhäuser*, Ariadne, Judith in *Duke Bluebeard's Castle*, and the Woman in *Erwartung*.

Martin, (Nicolas-) Jean-Blaise, famous French baritone; b. Paris, Feb. 24, 1768; d. Ronzières, Rhône, Oct. 28, 1837. He made his debut at Paris's Théâtre de Monsieur in 1789 in *Le Marquis de Tulipano*; sang at the Théâtre Feydeau and the Théâtre Favart from 1794 until they were united as the Opéra-Comique in 1801, remaining there until 1823; sang there again in 1826 and 1833. He was also a member of the Imperial (later Royal) Chapel from its founding until 1830. He was a prof. at the Paris Cons. (1816–18; 1832–37). He wrote an opéra-comique, *Les Oiseaux de mer* (Paris, 1796). His voice, while essentially baritone in quality, had the extraordinary range of 2½ octaves, E flat to a'.

Martin, Mary (Virginia), American singer, dancer, and actress; b. Weatherford, Texas, Dec. 1, 1913; d. Rancho Mirage, Calif., Nov. 3, 1990. The daughter of a lawyer and a violinist, she 1st established a dance school in Weatherford. She studied at the Ward-Belmont School in Nashville, Tenn.; then went to N.Y., where, although totally unknown to the general public, she stopped the show with her rendition of the song *My Heart Belongs to Daddy* in Cole Porter's musical comedy *Leave It to Me* (1938). Her N.Y. success brought her a film contract with Paramount studios in Hollywood, which was short-lived, as she preferred the theater. On the stage she scored a series of hits, beginning with a starring role in the Rodgers and Hammerstein musical *South Pacific* (1949) and later in *The Sound of Music* (1959), 2 of the longest-running musicals in Broadway history. She became best known for her 1954 creation of the lead character in the musical *Peter Pan*, in which she seemed to fly through the air; her career was once interrupted when she suffered an accident during levitation. In 1969 she retired to Brazil with her husband; after his death, she resumed her career (1979). In 1989 Martin was honored by the Kennedy Center of the Performing Arts in Washington, D.C., for her achievements in the theater. Her autobiography, *My Heart Belongs*, was publ. in 1976. Her son, Larry Hagman, is a veteran television actor whose fame was assured when he was cast as the villainous J.R. Ewing in the nighttime soap series *Dallas*.

Martin, Riccardo (real name, **Hugh Whitfield Martin**). American tenor; b. Hopkinsville, Ky., Nov. 18, 1874; d. N.Y., Aug. 11, 1952. He studied violin in Nashville and singing in N.Y.; was a pupil in composition of MacDowell at Columbia Univ.; in 1901 he went to Paris, where he took singing lessons with Sbriglia; made his debut as Faust in Nantes (1904) and his American debut as Canio in *Pagliacci* with the San Carlo Opera Co. in New Orleans (1906); was a member of the Metropolitan Opera in N.Y. (1907–15); then was with the Boston Grand Opera Co. (1916–17); again with the Metropolitan (1917–18); then with the Chicago Grand Opera Co. (1920–22); subsequently settled in N.Y. and taught singing.

Martin, Sallie, black American gospel singer; b. Pittfield, Ga., Nov. 20, 1896; d. Chicago, June 18, 1988. She became a member of Thomas A. Dorsey's Ebenezer Baptist Church gospel choir in Chicago (1932); then helped him to found the National Convention of Gospel Choirs and Choruses that same year, remaining active with it until 1940; subsequently toured extensively in the U.S. and Europe with her own Sallie Martin Singers; with Kenneth Morris, she also was co-founder and co-director of the Martin and Morris Music Co. in Chicago (1940–75).

Martinelli, Giovanni, famous Italian tenor; b. Montagnana, near Padua, Oct. 22, 1885; d. N.Y., Feb. 2, 1969. One of the 14 children of a fertile Italian family, he played clarinet in the town band; then went to Milan and studied voice with Mandolini. On Dec. 3, 1910, he made his debut in Milan in Rossini's *Stabat Mater;* made his operatic debut at the Teatro del Varme in Milan as Ernani on Dec. 29, 1910; Puccini heard him and invited him to sing in the European premiere of *La Fanciulla del West* (Rome, June 12, 1911); he sang for the 1st time at London's Covent Garden on April 22, 1912, as Cavaradossi in *Tosca;* sang there again in 1913, 1914, 1919, and 1937. He made his American debut on Nov. 3, 1913, in Philadelphia as Cavaradossi. On Nov. 20, 1913, he appeared at the Metropolitan Opera in N.Y. as Rodolfo in *La Bohème,* scoring an immediate success; he remained with the Metropolitan for 30 years, until 1943; then returned in 1944, giving his farewell on March 8, 1945, as Pollione in *Norma;* during his final season there (1945–46), he appeared as a concert artist. He then taught voice in N.Y. while making occasional appearances as a singer; he made his last appearance in a production of *Turandot* in Seattle in 1967 in his 82nd year. At the Metropolitan, he sang Radames in *Aida* 126 times, Don José in *Carmen* 75 times, Canio in *Pagliacci* 68 times, and Manrico in *Il Trovatore* 70 times; other parts in his rich repertoire were the title roles in *Faust, Samson et Delila, Andrea Chénier,* and *Otello.* However, he shunned the Wagnerian characters in opera.

Martinet, Jean-Louis, French composer; b. Ste.-Bazeille, Nov. 8, 1912. He studied music theory with Charles Koechlin, Roger-Ducasse, and Messiaen; also took lessons in conducting with Charles Munch and Roger Desormière. He naturally absorbed the harmonic essence of French Impressionism and the contrapuntal rigor of the neo-Classical style as practiced by Stravinsky and Bartók; in later works he succumbed to the fashionable temptation of dodecaphony *à la française.* Among his works are a symphonic poem, *Orphée* (1945–46); several works entitled *Mouvement symphonique* (1953–63); 2 *Images* for Orch. (1953–54); Sym., *In memoriam* (1962–63); *Divertissement pastoral* for Piano and Orch. (1966); *La Triomphe de la Mort,* dramatic sym. (1967–73); *Variations* for String Quartet (1946, in dodecaphonic technique); cantatas: *Episodes* (1950); *Elsa* (1959); *Les Amours* for Chorus a cappella (1960); *Les Douze* for Narrator, Chorus, and Orch., after a revolutionary poem by Alexander Blok (1961).

Martinez, José Daniel, Puerto Rican composer and pianist; b. San Juan, Sept. 8, 1956. He studied with Luis Antonio Ramírez and Luz N. Hutchinson at the Cons. of Music in Puerto Rico (certificate of diploma, 1975) and at the Eastman School of Music in Rochester, N.Y., where he earned advanced degrees in composition and piano (1980). He taught piano and music theory at the Hochstein School of Music in Rochester (1977–80) and at the Cons. of Music in Puerto Rico (1981–82); in 1982–83 he worked as an accompanist in N.Y. In 1985 he made a recording of Puerto Rican "Danzas" for the Cir-

culo de Recreo de San Germán, where he subsequently taught at the Interamerican Univ. of Puerto Rico.

WORKS: *Dos preludios* for Piano (1971); *Fantasía* for Violin and Piano (1973); *Tema y variaciones* for Piano (1974); *Tiempo sinfónico* for Chamber Orch. (1976); *Impromptu* for Chamber Ensemble (1983); *Música para la Interamericana* for Organ and Baroque Orch. (1984); *Concierto para aulos . . . Reflexiones sobre el retorno de un cometa* for Flute, Piccolo, Oboe, Horn, and Piano (1986); Cello Sonata (1987).

Martínez, Marianne (actually, **Anna Katharina**) **von,** Austrian singer, pianist, and composer; b. Vienna, May 4, 1744; d. there, Dec. 13, 1812. She was the daughter of Nicoló Martínez, who went to Vienna as "gentiluomo" to the papal nuncio. Thanks to his privileged social position in the diplomatic circles in Vienna, her father was able to engage the best instructors for her; Metastasio was put in charge of her education, and he saw that she received lessons in singing, piano, and composition from Porpora and Haydn; she also studied counterpoint with G. Bonno. She appeared as a singer and pianist at the court while still a child; later performed in aristocratic salons. She composed several oratorios and cantatas, a Sym., 2 piano concertos, and a group of minor instrumental pieces. None of these was in any way remarkable, but her works are of historical interest as examples of musical composition by a woman of high society who contributed to the artistic life of the Austrian capital during its greatest ascendance on the international scene. Manuscripts of some of her works are preserved in the archives of the Gesellschaft der Musikfreunde in Vienna.

Martínez, Miguel Angel Gomez. See **Gomez Martínez, Miguel Angel.**

Martinez, Odaline de la, Cuban-born American conductor and composer; b. Matanzas, Oct. 31, 1949. She emigrated to the U.S. in 1961 and became a naturalized citizen in 1971; studied composition with Paul Patterson at the Royal Academy of Music in London (1972–76) and with Reginald Smith Brindle at the Univ. of Surrey (M.M., 1977). In 1976 she founded the London chamber ensemble Lontano, which she conducted in programs of contemporary music; was also founder-conductor of the Contemporary Chamber Orch. (1982). While thus preoccupied, she found time to compose successful stage works as well as orch. and chamber pieces.

WORKS: OPERA: *Sister Aimee,* on the life of the American evangelist Aimee Semple McPherson (1978–83). **ORCH.:** *Phasing* for Chamber Orch. (1975). **CHAMBER:** *A Moment's Madness* for Flute and Piano (1977); *Litanies* for Flutes, Harp, and String Trio (1981); Suite for English Horn and Cello (1982); String Quartet (1985); *Improvisations* for Violin (1977); *Colour Studies* for Piano (1978); *Asonancias* for Piano (1982). **VOCAL:** 5 *Imagist Songs* for Soprano, Clarinet, and Piano (1974); *Absalom* for Countertenor, 2 Tenors, Baritone, and Bass (1977); *Canciones* for Soprano, Percussion, and Piano (1983); *Cantos de amor* for Soprano, Piano, and String Trio (1985). **TAPE:** *Hallucination* (1975); *Visions and Dreams* (1978); *Lamento* for Amplified Vocal Quartet and Tape (1978); 3 *Studies* for Percussion and Electronics (1980).

Martini, Giovanni Battista, famous Italian pedagogue, writer on music, and composer, known as **Padre Martini;** b. Bologna, April 24, 1706; d. there, Aug. 3, 1784. He received the rudiments of musical knowledge from his father, a violinist; then took courses with Angelo Predieri, Giovanni Antonio Ricieri, and Francesco Antonio Pistocchi. A man of unquenchable intellectual curiosity, he studied mathematics with Zanotti, and took a seminar in ecclesiastical music with Giacomo Perti. In 1721 he entered the Franciscan conventual monastery in Lugo di Romagna, but abandoned monastic aspirations and returned to Bologna in 1722; there he became organist, and later maestro di cappella, at S. Francesco in 1725, and was ordained a priest in 1729. He was a prolific composer and a learned scholar; his *Storia della musica* (3 vols., Bologna, 1757, 1770, and 1781; reprinted 1967) gives an extensive survey of music in ancient Greece. But it is as a pedagogue that

Padre Martini achieved lasting fame. His magnum opus in music theory was *Esemplare ossia Saggio fondamentale practico di contrappunto* (2 vols., Bologna, 1774 and 1775). J.C. Bach, Jommelli, Grétry, and Mozart were his students. A by-product of his various activities was the accumulation of a magnificent library, which Burney estimated at nearly 17,000 vols.; after Martini's death, it became the foundation of the collection in the library of the Liceo Musicale (later the Civico Museo Bibliografico Musicale). He received many honors during his long life; in 1758 he became a member of the Accademia dell' Istituto delle Scienze di Bologna and of the Accademia dei Filarmonici di Bologna. In 1776 he was elected to membership in the Arcadi di Roma, where his Arcadian title was "Aristosseno Anfioneo" ("Aristoxenos Amphion"). He conducted a voluminous correspondence; about 6,000 letters are extant; it included communications with scholars, kings, and popes.

Works: Oratorio, *L'assunzione di Salomone al tronto d'Israello* (1734); masses, introits, graduals, offertories, vespers, hymns; *Litaniae atque antiphonae finales B. Virginis Mariae* for 4 Voices, Organ, and Instruments, publ. in Bologna in 1734; secular vocal works: 24 sinfonias, numerous concertos for various instruments, about 100 keyboard sonatas. **Writings:** *Regola agli organisti per accompagnare il canto fermo* (Bologna, 1756); *Compendio della teoria de' numeri per uso del musico* (Bologna, 1769). Correspondence: A selection of his letters was ed. by F. Parisini as *Carteggio inedito del G. Martini, coi più celebri musicisti del suo tempo* (Bologna, 1888). A. Schnoebelen ed. *Padre Martini's Collection of Letters in the Civico Museo Bibliografico Musicale in Bologna: An Annotated Index* (N.Y., 1979). **Bibl.:** A. Eximeno, *Dubbio sopra il saggio fondamentale pratico di contrappunto del P. G.B. M.* (Rome, 1775); G. Della Valle, *Memorie storiche del p. m. Giambattista M.* (Naples, 1785); G. Gandolfi, *Elogio di G.B. M.* (Bologna, 1813); F. Parisini, *Della vita e delle opere del P. G.B. M.* (Bologna, 1887); L. Busi, *Il P. G.B. M.* (Bologna, 1891); F. Haberl, "P. G.B. M. als Musiker und Componist," *Kirchenmusikalisches Jahrbuch,* VII (1892); W. Reich, *P. M. als Theoretiker und Lehrer* (diss., Univ. of Vienna, 1934); G. Tebaldini, "La scolastica del P. M.," *Rivista Musicale Italiana,* XLIII (1939) and XLIV (1940); P. Pauchard, *Ein italienischer Musiktheoretiker: Pater Giambattista M.* (Lugano, 1941); N. Gallini, "Le dimissioni di P. M.," *La Scala* (Sept. 1953); P. Zaccaria, *P. M. compositore* (diss., Pontificio Istituto di Musica Sacra, Rome, 1959); H. Brofsky, *The Instrumental Music of P. M.* (diss., N.Y. Univ., 1963); idem, "The Symphonies of P. M.," *Musical Quarterly,* LI (1965); idem, "The Keyboard Sonatas of P. M.," *Quadrivium,* VIII (1967); P. Wiechens, *Die Kompositionstheorie und das kirchenmusikalische Schaffen P. M.s* (Regensburg, 1968); P. Zaccaria, *P. Giambattista M.: Compositore musicologo e maestro* (Padua, 1969); H. Brofsky, "J.C. Bach, G.B. Sammartini, and P. M.: A *Concorso* in Milan in 1762," in *A Musical Offering: Essays in Honor of Martin Bernstein* (N.Y., 1977).

Martini, Jean Paul Egide (real name, **Johann Paul Ágid Schwarzendorf**), German organist, teacher, and composer; b. Freystadt, Upper Palatinate (baptized), Aug. 31, 1741; d. Paris, Feb. 10, 1816. At the age of 10 he enrolled in the Jesuit Seminary in Neuburg an der Donau, becoming organist there. He began to tour as an organist in 1758; went to Nancy in 1760, and was known as Martini il Tedesco; was in the service of the former king of Poland, Prince Stanislaus Leszcynski, duke of Lorraine, in Lunéville (1761–64). He then went to Paris, where he won a prize for a military march for the Swiss Guard; this introduced him into army circles in France; he enlisted as an officer of a Hussar regiment, and wrote more band music; also composed an opera, *L'Amoureux de quinze ans, ou Le Double Fête,* which was produced with extraordinary success at the Italian Opera in Paris (April 18, 1771). Leaving the army, he became music director to the Prince of Condé, and later to the Comte d'Artois. He purchased the reversion of the office of 1st Intendant of the King's Music, a speculation brought to naught by the Revolution, which caused him to

resign in haste his position as conductor at the Théâtre Feydeau, and flee to Lyons in 1792. He then returned to Paris, winning acclaim with the production of his opera *Sappho* (1794). He became Inspector at the Paris Cons. in 1798; also taught composition there (1800–1802). In appreciation of his royalist record, he was given the post of Royal Intendant at the Restoration in 1814, serving as chief director of the Royal Court Orch. until his death. He wrote 13 operas, a Requiem for Louis XVI, Psalms, and other church music, but he is chiefly remembered as the composer of the popular air *Plaisir d'amour,* which was arranged by Berlioz for Voice and Orch.

Bibl.: A Pougin, *J.P.E. M.* (Paris, 1864); G. Widenbauer, "J.P.Á. M., ein vergessener Oberpfälzer Tondichter," *Unser Bayern,* III/10 (1954).

Martino, Donald (James), American composer; b. Plainfield, N.J., May 16, 1931. He learned to play the clarinet, oboe, and saxophone in his youth; then studied composition with Ernst Bacon at Syracuse Univ. (B.M., 1952), Milton Babbitt and Roger Sessions at Princeton Univ. (M.F.A., 1954), and Luigi Dallapiccola in Florence on a Fulbright scholarship (1954–56). In 1958–59 he was an instructor at Princeton Univ.; from 1959 to 1969, taught theory and composition at Yale Univ.; then was a prof. of composition at the New England Cons. of Music in Boston (1970–80), where he served as chairman of the composition dept. He was Irving Fine Prof. of Music at Brandeis Univ. (1980–83); in 1983, became a prof. of music at Harvard Univ., serving as Walter Bigelow Rosen Prof. of Music (from 1989). He held 3 Guggenheim fellowships (1967, 1973, 1982); was awarded the Pulitzer Prize in Music in 1974 for his chamber piece *Notturno;* in 1981, was made a member of the American Academy and Inst. of Arts and Letters, and in 1987 a fellow of the American Academy of Arts and Sciences. In his music, he adopts a quasi-mathematical method of composition based on arithmetical permutations of tonal and rhythmic ingredients.

Works: orch.: *Contemplations* (1956; Lenox, Mass., Aug. 13, 1964; originally entitled *Composition*); Piano Concerto (1965; New Haven, March 1, 1966); *Mosaic for Grand Orchestra* (Chicago, May 26, 1967); Cello Concerto (1972; Cincinnati, Oct. 16, 1973); *Ritorno* (1975; Plainfield, N.J., Dec. 12, 1976); Triple Concerto for Clarinet, Bass Clarinet, Contrabass Clarinet, and Chamber Orch. (1977; N.Y., Dec. 18, 1978); *Divertissements* for Youth Orch. (1981); Concerto for Alto Saxophone and Chamber Orch. (1987). **chamber:** 4 string quartets (n.d., withdrawn; 1952, withdrawn; 1954, withdrawn; 1983); Clarinet Sonata (1950–51); *A Set* for Clarinet (1954; rev. 1974); *Quodlibets* for Flute (1954); *Sette canoni enigmatici,* puzzle canons with various solutions for 2 Violas and 2 Cellos or 2 Bassoons, or for String Quartet, or for 4 Clarinets (1955–56); Quartet for Clarinet and String Trio (1957); *Cinque frammenti* for Oboe and Double Bass (1961); *Fantasy-Variations* for Violin (1962); Concerto for Wind Quintet (1964); *Parisonatina al'dodecafonia* for Cello (1964); *B,A,B,B,IT,T* for Clarinet with Extensions (1966); *Strata* for Bass Clarinet (1966); *Notturno* for Piccolo, Flute, Alto Flute, Clarinet, Bass Clarinet, Violin, Viola, Cello, Piano, and Percussion (1973); *Quodlibets II* for Flute (1980); *Canzone e Tarantella sul nome Petrassi* for Clarinet and Cello (1984); *From the Other Side,* divertimento for Flute, Cello, Percussion, and Piano (1988). **vocal:** *Portraits: A Secular Cantata* for Mezzo-soprano, Bass, Chorus, and Orch., to texts by Walt Whitman, Edna St. Vincent Millay, and e.e. cummings (1954); *7 Pious Pieces* for Chorus and Optional Piano or Organ, to a text by Robert Herrick (1972); *Augenmusik: A Mixed Mediacritique* for "actress, danseuse or uninhibited female percussionist and electronic tape" (1972); *Paradiso Choruses,* oratorio for 12 Soloists, Chorus, Children's Chorus ad libitum, Tape, and Orch., after Dante's *Divine Comedy* (1974; Boston, May 7, 1975); *The White Island* for Chorus and Chamber Orch., after Robert Herrick (1985); songs. **piano:** *Fantasy* (1958); *Pianississimo,* sonata (1970); *Fantasies and Impromptus* (1978); *Suite in Old Form: Parody Suite* (1982).

Martinon, Jean, significant French conductor and composer; b. Lyons, Jan. 10, 1910; d. Paris, March 1, 1976. He studied violin at the Lyons Cons. (1924–25) and at the Paris Cons. (1926–29), winning the premier prix; then took lessons in composition with Roussel and d'Indy and in conducting with Munch and Desormière; obtained his M.A. degree in arts from the Sorbonne (1932). He was in the French army during World War II; was taken prisoner in 1940 and spent 2 years in a German prison camp (Stalag IX); during imprisonment he wrote several works of a religious nature, among them *Psalm 136, Musique d'exil ou Stalag IX,* and *Absolve Domine,* in memory of French musicians killed in the war. After his release, he appeared as a conductor with the Pasdeloup Orch. in Paris (1943); then was conductor of the Bordeaux Sym. Orch. (1943–45), assistant conductor of the Paris Cons. Orch. (1944–46), and associate conductor of the London Phil. (1947–49). He made his American debut with the Boston Sym. Orch. on March 29, 1957, conducting the U.S. premiere of his 2nd Sym. Martinon was artistic director of the Israel Phil. (1958–60) and Generalmusikdirektor of the Düsseldorf Sym. Orch. (1960–66). In 1963 he was appointed music director of the Chicago Sym. Orch.; during the 5 years of his tenure, he conducted about 60 works by American and European composers of the modern school; this progressive policy met opposition from some influential people in Chicago society and in the press, and he resigned in 1968. He returned to France and led the Orch. National de la Radio Television Française in Paris (from 1968) and the Residente Orch. in The Hague (from 1974). As a conductor, he became best known for his idiomatic performances of the French repertoire. His own compositions follow the spirit of French neo-Classicism, euphonious in their modernity and expansive in their Romantic élan.

WORKS: STAGE: Opera, *Hécube,* after Euripides (1949–54; 1st scenic perf., Strasbourg, Nov. 10, 1956); ballet, *Ambohimanga ou La Cité bleue,* with Soloists and Chorus (1946; Paris, 1947). **ORCH.:** 4 syms.: No. 1 (1934–36; Paris, March 1940); No. 2, *Hymne à la vie* (1942–44; Paris, Feb. 13, 1944); No. 3, *Irlandaise* (Radio Eirean, Dublin, 1949); No. 4, *Altitudes* (Chicago, Dec. 30, 1965); *Symphoniette* for Strings, Piano, Harp, and Percussion (1935; Paris, May 30, 1938); 2 violin concertos: No. 1, *Concerto giocoso* (1937–42); No. 2 (1958; Selle, Bavaria, May 28, 1961); *Musique d'exil ou Stalag IX,* musical reminiscence of imprisonment (1941; Paris, Jan. 11, 1942); *Divertissement* (1941); *Obsession* for Chamber Orch. (1942); *Romance bleue,* rhapsody for Violin and Orch. (1942); *Concerto lyrique* for String Quartet and Chamber Orch. (1944; transcribed as Concerto for 4 Saxophones and Chamber Orch. in 1974); *Overture for a Greek Tragedy* (1949; prelude to the 2nd act of *Hécube*); *Symphonies de voyages* (1957); *Introduction and Toccata* (1959; orch. of the piano piece *Prelude and Toccata*); Cello Concerto (1963; Hamburg, Jan. 25, 1965); *Le Cène* (The Last Supper; 1962–63); *Hymne, Variations et Rondo* (1967; Paris, Feb. 15, 1969); Flute Concerto (1970–71); *Sonata movimento perpetuo* (1973). **CHAMBER:** 7 sonatinas: No. 1 for Violin and Piano (1935); No. 2 for Violin and Piano (1936); No. 3 for Piano (1940); No. 4 for Wind Trio (1940); No. 5 for Solo Violin (1942); No. 6 for Solo Violin (1958); No. 7 for Flute and Piano (1958); *Domenon* for Wind Quintet (1939); String Trio (1943) *Suite nocturne* for Violin and Piano (1944); Piano Trio (1945); *Scherzo* for Violin and Piano (1945); 2 string quartets (1946; 1963–66); *Prelude and Toccata* for Piano (1947); *Duo* for Violin and Piano (1953); *Introduzione, Adagio et Passacaille* for 13 Instruments (1967); *Vigentuor* for 20 Instruments (1969); Octet (1969). **VOCAL:** *Absolve Domine* for Male Chorus and Orch. (1940; perf. at Stalag IX prison camp, Nov. 2, 1940); *Appel de parfums* for Narrator, Male Chorus or Mixed Chorus, and Orch. (1940); *Psalm 136 (Chant de captifs)* for Narrator, Soloists, Chorus, and Orch. (1942); *Ode au Soleil né de la Mort* for Narrator, Chorus, and Orch. (1945); *Le Lis de Sharon,* oratorio (1951; Tel Aviv, 1952); songs.

BIBL.: A. Machabey, *Portraits de trente musiciens français* (Paris, 1950); *Le Courrier Musical de France,* 26 (1969) and 40 (1973).

Martins, João Carlos, Brazilian pianist; b. São Paulo, June 25, 1940. He studied piano with José Kliass; made his professional debut at Teresopolis in 1954; other concerts followed in Brazilian cities; in 1960 he made his American debut at Carnegie Hall in N.Y., evoking superlatives for his "passionate subjectivity" from the critics; later he made a specialty of performing all of Bach's 48 preludes and fugues in 2 consecutive concerts; he also appeared as a soloist with orchs. in N.Y., Philadelphia, and Boston. But at the height of his successes, in 1969, he was knocked down during a soccer match, and hurt his arm to the point of a painful neuralgia, so that he had to stop playing piano. But in a surprising change of direction, he went into banking, managed a champion prizefighter, started a construction company, and became a multimillionaire in devalued Brazilian currency. An even more surprising development followed when, in 1981, he was appointed to the post of the Brazilian state secretary of culture; in this capacity he exhibited an extraordinary knack for urban recovery in the direction of futuristic Americanization. In the meantime, his neurological ailment subsided, and he returned to his career as a virtuoso pianist.

Martinů, Bohuslav (Jan), remarkable Czech composer; b. Polička, Dec. 8, 1890; d. Liestal, near Basel, Aug. 28, 1959. He was born in the bell tower of a church in the village where his father was a watchman. He studied violin with the local tailor when he was 7; from 1906 to 1909 he was enrolled at the Prague Cons.; then entered the Prague Organ School (1909), where he studied organ and theory, but was expelled in 1910 for lack of application; played in the 2nd violin section in the Czech Phil. in Prague (1913–14), returning to Polička (1914–18) to avoid service in the Austrian army; after World War I, he reentered the Prague Cons. as a pupil of Suk, but again failed to graduate; also played again in the Czech Phil. (1918–23). In 1923 he went to Paris and participated in progressive musical circles; took private lessons with Albert Roussel. In a relatively short time his name became known in Europe through increasingly frequent performances of his chamber works, ballets, and symphonic pieces; several of his works were performed at the festivals of the ISCM In 1932 his String Sextet won the Elizabeth Sprague Coolidge Award. He remained in Paris until June 1940, when he fled the German invasion and went to Portugal; finally reached the U.S. in 1941 and settled in N.Y.; personal difficulties prevented him from accepting an offer to teach at the Prague Cons. after the liberation of Czechoslovakia in 1945; later was a visiting prof. of music at Princeton Univ. (1948–51). Although Martinů spent most of his life away from his homeland, he remained spiritually and musically faithful to his native country. He composed a poignant tribute to the martyred village of Lidice when, in 1943, the Nazi authorities ordered the execution of all men and boys over the age of 16 to avenge the assassination of the local Gauleiter. Martinů immortalized the victims in a heartfelt lyric work entitled *Memorial to Lidice.* In 1953 he returned to Europe, spending the last 2 years of his life in Switzerland. On Aug. 27, 1979, his remains were taken from Schönenberg, Switzerland, to Polička, Czechoslovakia, where they were placed in the family mausoleum. Martinů's centennial was celebrated in 1990 all over Czechoslovakia. As a musician and stylist, he belonged to the European tradition of musical nationalism. He avoided literal exploitation of Czech or Slovak musical materials, but his music is nonetheless characterized by a strong feeling for Bohemian melorhythms; his stylizations of Czech dances are set in a modern idiom without losing their authenticity or simplicity. In his large works he followed the neo-Classical trend, with some impressionistic undertones; his mastery of modern counterpoint was extraordinary. In his music for the stage, his predilections were for chamber forms; his sense of operatic comedy was very strong, but he was also capable of sensitive lyricism.

WORKS: OPERAS: *Voják a tanečnice* (The Soldier and the Dancer; 1926–27; Brno, May 5, 1928); *Les Larmes du couteau* (The Knife's Tears; 1928); *Trois souhaits, ou Les Vicissitudes* de la vie (3 Wishes, or The Fickleness of Life), "opera-film in 3 acts" (1929; Brno, June 16, 1971; the normal orch. is augmented by a Jazz Flute, Saxophones, Flexatone, Banjo, and Accordion); La Semaine de bonté (1929; unfinished); Hry o Marii (The Miracle of Our Lady; 1933–34; Brno, Feb. 23, 1935); Hlas lesa (The Voice of the Forest), radio opera (Czech Radio, Oct. 6, 1935); Divadlo za bránou (The Suburban Theater), opera buffa (1935–36; Brno, Sept. 20, 1936); Veselohra na mostě (Comedy on a Bridge), radio opera (1935; rev. 1950; Czech Radio, March 18, 1937); Julietta, or The Key to Dreams, lyric opera (1936–37; Prague, March 16, 1938); Alexandre bis, opera buffa (1937; Mannheim, Feb. 18, 1964); What Men Live By (Čím člověk žije), pastoral opera after Tolstoy (1951–52; N.Y., May 20, 1955); The Marriage (Ženitba), television opera after Gogol (1952; NBC television, N.Y., Feb. 7, 1953); La Plainte contre inconnu (1953; unfinished); Mirandolina, comic opera (1954; Prague, May 17, 1959); Ariadne, lyric opera (1958; Gelsenkirchen, March 2, 1961); Greek Passion (Řecké pašije), musical drama after Kazantzakis (1955–59; Zürich, June 9, 1961).

BALLETS: Noc (Night), "meloplastic scene" (1913–14); Stín (The Shadow; 1916); Istar; (1918–22; Prague, Sept. 11, 1924); Who Is the Most Powerful in the World? (Kdo je na světě nejmocnější), ballet comedy, after an English fairy tale (1922; Brno, Jan. 31, 1925); The Revolt (Vzpoura), ballet sketch (1922–23; Brno, Feb. 11, 1928); The Butterfly That Stamped (Motýl, ktery dupal), after Kipling (1926); La Revue de cuisine (Prague, 1927); On tourne (Natáčí se), for a cartoon and puppet film (1927); Le Raid merveilleux (Báječný let), "ballet mécanique" for 2 Clarinets, Trumpet, and Strings (1927); Echec au roi, jazz ballet (1930); Špalíček (The Chapbook), with Vocal Soloists and Chorus (1931; Prague, Sept. 19, 1933; rev. 1940; Prague, April 2, 1949); Le Jugement de Paris (1935); The Strangler (Uškreovač), for 3 Dancers (New London, Conn., Aug. 15, 1948).

ORCH.: 6 syms.: No. 1 (Boston, Nov. 13, 1942); No. 2 (Cleveland, Oct. 28, 1943); No. 3 (1944; Boston, Oct. 12, 1945); No. 4 (Philadelphia, Nov. 30, 1945); No. 5 (1946; Prague, May 27, 1947); No. 6, Fantaisies symphoniques (1951–53; Boston, Jan. 7, 1955); Concertino for Cello, Wind Instruments, and Piano (1924); 5 piano concertos: No. 1 (1925; Prague, Nov. 21, 1926); No. 2 (1934; rescored 1944; Prague, 1935); No. 3 (1947–48; Dallas, Nov. 20, 1949); No. 4, Incantation (N.Y., Oct. 4, 1956); No. 5, Fantasia concertante (1957; Berlin, Jan. 31, 1959); Concertino for Piano, left-hand, and Chamber Orch. (1926; Prague, Feb. 26, 1947; originally titled Divertimento); 2 cello concertos: No. 1 for Cello and Chamber Orch. (1930; rev. for Full Orch., 1939, and rescored in 1955) and No. 2 (1944–45); Concerto for String Quartet and Orch. (1931; also known as String Quartet with Orch.); 2 violin concertos: No. 1 (1931–32; Chicago, Oct. 25, 1973) and No. 2 (Boston, Dec. 31, 1943); Divertimento (Serenade No. 4) for Violin, Viola, Oboe, Piano, and String Orch. (1932); Concertino for Piano Trio and Orch. (1933; Basel, Oct. 16, 1936); Concerto for Harpsichord and Chamber Orch. (1935); Concerto for Flute, Violin, and Chamber Orch. (1936); Duo concertante for 2 Violins and Orch. (1937); Suite concertante for Violin and Orch. (1937; rev. for Piano Concertino (1938; London, Aug. 5, 1948); Sonata da camera for Cello and Chamber Orch. (1940); Sinfonietta giocosa for Piano and Chamber Orch. (1940; rev. 1941; N.Y., March 16, 1942); Concerto da camera for Violin, String Orch., Piano, and Timpani (1941; Basel, Jan. 23, 1942); 2-Piano Concerto (Philadelphia, Nov. 5, 1943); Sinfonia concertante for Oboe, Bassoon, Violin, Cello, and Small Orch. (1949; Basel, Dec. 8, 1950); 2-Violin Concerto (1950; Dallas, Jan. 8, 1951); Rhapsody-Concerto for Viola and Orch. (1952; Cleveland, Feb. 19, 1953); Concerto for Violin, Piano, and Orch. (1953); Oboe Concerto (1955); Smrt Tintagilova (The Death of Tintagile), music for the Maeterlinck drama (1910; also for Piano); Anděl smrti (Angel of Death), symphonic poem (1910; also for Piano); Nocturno No. 1 (1914); Ballada (1915); Míjející půlnoc (Vanishing Midnight; 1921–22); Half-Time, rondo (Prague, Dec. 7, 1924); La Bagarre (The Tumult), rondo (1926; Boston, Nov.

18, 1927); Jazz Suite (1928); La Rhapsodie (Boston, Dec. 14, 1928); Praeludium, in the form of a scherzo (1930); Serenade for Chamber Orch. (1930); Sinfonia concertante for 2 Orchs. (1932); Partita (Suite No. 1) (1932); Invence (Inventions; 1934); Concerto Grosso for Small Orch. (1938; Boston, Nov. 14, 1941); 3 ricercari for Chamber Orch. (Venice, 1938); Double Concerto for 2 String Orchs., Piano, and Timpani (1938; Basel, Feb. 9, 1940); Memorial to Lidice (N.Y., Oct. 28, 1943); Thunderbolt P-47, scherzo (Washington, D.C., Dec. 19, 1945); Toccata e due canzone for Small Orch. (1946; Basel, Jan. 21, 1947); Sinfonietta La Jolla for Chamber Orch. and Piano (1950); Intermezzo (N.Y., Dec. 29, 1950); Les Fresques de Piero della Francesca, impressions of 3 frescoes (1955; Salzburg Festival, Aug. 28, 1956); The Rock, symphonic prelude (1957; Cleveland, April 17, 1958); Parables (1957–58; Boston, Feb. 13, 1959); Estampes, symphonic suite (1958; Louisville, Feb. 4, 1959).

VOCAL: Nipponari, 7 songs for Female Voice and Chamber Ensemble (1912); cantata, Česká rapsódie (1918; Prague, Jan. 12, 1919); Kouzelné noci (Magic Nights), 3 songs for Soprano and Orch. (1918); Le Jazz, movement for Voice and Orch. (1928); cantata on Czech folk poetry, Kytice (Bouquet of Flowers; 1937; Czech Radio, May 1938); Polní mše (Field Mass) for Male Chorus, Baritone, and Orch. (1939; Prague, Feb. 28, 1946); Hora tři světel (The Hill of 3 Lights), small oratorio for Soloists, Chorus, and Organ (1954; Bern, Oct. 3, 1955); Hymnus k sv. Jakubu (Hymn to St. James) for Narrator, Soloists, Chorus, Organ, and Orch. (1954; Polička, July 31, 1955); Gilgameš (The Epic of Gilgamesh) for Narrator, Soloists, Chorus, and Orch. (1954–55; Basel, Jan. 24, 1958); Otvírání studánek (The Opening of the Wells) for Narrator, Soloists, Female Chorus, 2 Violins, Viola, and Piano (1955); Legend from the Smoke of Potato Fires for Soloists, Chorus, and Chamber Ensemble (1957); Mikeš z hor (Mikesh from the Mountains) for Soloists, Chorus, 2 Violins, Viola, and Piano (1959); The Prophecy of Isaiah (Proroctví Izaiášovo) for Male Chorus, Soloists, Viola, Trumpet, Piano, and Timpani (1959; Jerusalem, April 2, 1963); numerous part-songs and a cappella choruses.

CHAMBER: 7 string quartets: No. 1 (1918; reconstructed, with the addition of a newly discovered 4th movement, by Jan Hanuš in 1972); No. 2 (1925); No. 3 (1929); No. 4 (1937); No. 5 (1938); No. 6 (1946); No. 7, Concerto da camera (1947); 5 violin sonatas: in C major (1919); in D minor (1926); No. 1 (1929); No. 2 (1931); No. 3 (1944); 2 string trios (1923, 1934); Quartet for Clarinet, Horn, Cello, and Drum (1924); 2 unnumbered nonets: for Violin, Viola, Cello, Flute, Clarinet, Oboe, Horn, Bassoon, and Piano (1924–25), and for Violin, Viola, Cello, Double Bass, Flute, Clarinet, Oboe, Horn, and Bassoon (1959); 2 duos for Violin and Cello (1927, 1957); Impromptu for Violin and Piano (1927); String Quintet (1927); Sextet for Winds and Piano (1929); 5 Short Pieces for Violin and Piano (1929); Wind Quintet (1930); Les Rondes, 6 pieces for 7 Instruments (1930); 3 piano trios (5 Brief Pieces, 1930; 1950; 1951); Sonatina for 2 Violins and Piano (1930); Études rythmiques for Violin and Piano (1931); Pastorales and Nocturnes for Cello and Piano (both 1931); Arabesques for Violin or Cello, and Piano (1931); String Sextet (1932); Sonata for 2 Violins and Piano (1932); Serenade No. 1 for 6 Instruments; No. 2 for 2 Violins and Viola; No. 3 for 7 Instruments (all 1932; No. 4 is the Divertimento for Violin, Viola, Oboe, Piano, and String Orch.); 2 piano quintets (1933, 1944); Sonata for Flute, Violin, and Piano (1936); 4 Madrigals for Oboe, Clarinet, and Bassoon (1937); Violin Sonatina (1937); Intermezzo, 4 pieces for Violin and Piano (1937); Trio for Flute, Violin, and Bassoon (1937); 3 cello sonatas (1939, 1944, 1952); Bergerettes for Piano Trio (1940); Promenades for Flute, Violin, and Harpsichord (1940); Piano Quartet (1942); Madrigal Sonata for Flute, Violin, and Piano (1942); Variations on a Theme of Rossini for Cello and Piano (1942); Madrigal Stanzas, 5 pieces for Violin and Piano (1943); Trio for Flute, Cello, and Piano (1944); Flute Sonata (1945); Czech Rhapsody for Violin and Piano (1945); Fantasia for Theremin, Oboe, String Quartet, and Piano (1945); 2 duos for Violin and Viola (3 Madrigals, 1947; 1950); Quartet for Oboe, Violin, Cello, and Piano (1947); Mazurka-

Nocturne for Oboe, 2 Violins, and Cello (1949); *Serenade* for Violin, Viola, Cello, and 2 Clarinets (1951); Viola Sonata (1955); Clarinet Sonatina (1956); Trumpet Sonatina (1956); *Divertimento* for 2 Flutes-à-bec (1957); *Les Fêtes nocturnes* for Violin, Viola, Cello, Clarinet, Harp, and Piano (1959); *Variations on a Slovak Theme* for Cello and Piano (1959). **PIANO:** *Puppets*, small pieces for children (in 3 sets, 1914–24); *Scherzo* (1924; discovered 1971); *Fables* (1924); *Film en miniature* (1925); *3 Czech Dances* (1926); *Le Noël* (1927); *4 Movements* (1928); *Borová*, 7 Czech dances (1929; also for Orch.); *Préludes (en forme de . . .)* (1929); *Fantaisie* for 2 Pianos (1929); *À trois mains* (1930); *Esquisses de danse*, 5 pieces (1932); *Les Ritournelles* (1932); *Dumka* (1936); *Fenêtre sur le jardin* (Window in the Garden), 4 pieces (1938); *Fantasia and Toccata* (1940); *Mazurka* (1941); *Etudes and Polkas* (in 3 books, 1945); *The 5th Day of the 5th Moon* (1948); *3 Czech Dances* for 2 Pianos (1949); Sonata (1954); *Reminiscences* (1957). **HARPSICHORD:** *2 Pieces* (1935); Sonata (1958); *Impromptus* (1959). **ORGAN:** *Vigilie* (1959).

BIBL.: M. Šafránek, "B. M.," *Musical Quarterly* (July 1943); idem, *B. M.: The Man and His Music* (N.Y., 1944); J. Löwenbach, *M. pozdravuje domov* (Prague, 1947); M. Šafránek, *B. M.: His Life and Works* (London, 1962); H. Halbreich, *B. M.* (Zürich, 1968); C. Martinů, *Můj život s B. M.* (My Life with B. M.; Prague, 1971); B. Large, *M.* (N.Y., 1975).

Martín y Soler, (Atanasio Martín Ignacio) Vicente (Tadeo Francisco Pellegrin), distinguished Spanish composer; b. Valencia, May 2, 1754; d. St. Petersburg, Jan. 30, 1806. He was a choirboy in Valencia and a church organist in Alicante before going to Madrid; there he brought out his 1st work for the stage, the zarzuela *La Madrileña, o Tutor burlado*, most likely in 1776. He then went to Italy, where he became known as Martini lo Spagnuolo; wrote operas for several theaters there; entered the service of the Infante, the future King Charles IV of Spain, about 1780. With Da Ponte as his librettist, he wrote the opera buffa *Il Burbero di buon cuore*, which was premiered in Vienna to much acclaim on Jan. 4, 1786. It was revived there on Nov. 9, 1789, and included 2 additional arias written expressly for the occasion by Mozart. Martín y Soler and Da Ponte then collaborated on the opera buffa *Una cosa rara, o sia Bellezza ed onestà*, a masterful stage work 1st given in Vienna on Nov. 17, 1786, and subsequently performed throughout Europe. Mozart used a theme from this popular work in the supper scene of his *Don Giovanni*. Martín y Soler and Da Ponte subsequently collaborated on the successful opera buffa *L'arbore di Diana* (Vienna, Oct. 1, 1787). The composer was then called to St. Petersburg to serve as court composer to Catherine II the Great, who wrote the libretto for his comic opera *Gore bogatyr Kosometovich* (St. Petersburg, Feb. 9, 1789). He then went to London, collaborating again with Da Ponte on the highly successful *La scuola dei maritati* (Jan. 27, 1795) and *L'isola del piacere* (May 26, 1795), both engaging opere buffe. He returned to St. Petersburg in 1796 and was made Imperial Russian Privy Councillor by Paul I in 1798; was inspector of the Italian Court Theater there (1800–1804).

WORKS: STAGE: *La Madrileña, o Tutor burlado*, zarzuela (Madrid, 1776?); *Ifigenia in Aulide*, opera seria (Naples, Jan. 12, 1779); *Ipermestra*, opera seria (Naples, Jan. 12, 1780); *Andromaca*, opera seria (Turin, Dec. 26, 1780); *Astartea*, opera seria (Lucca, Carnival 1781); *Partenope*, componimento drammatico (Naples, 1782); *L'amor geloso*, azione teatrale comica (Naples, Carnival 1782); *In amor ci vuol destrezza*, opera buffa (Venice, 1782); *Vologeso*, opera seria (Turin, Carnival 1783); *Le burle per amore*, opera buffa (Venice, Carnival 1784); *La Vedova spiritosa*, opera buffa (Parma, Carnival 1785); *Il Burbero di buon cuore*, opera buffa (Vienna, Jan. 4, 1786); *Una cosa rara, o sia Bellezza ed onestà*, opera buffa (Vienna, Nov. 17, 1786); *L'arbore di Diana*, opera buffa (Vienna, Oct. 1, 1787); *Gore bogatyr Kosometovich* (The Unfortunate Hero Kosometovich), comic opera (St. Petersburg, Feb. 9, 1789); *Pesnolyubie* (Beloved Songs), comic opera (St. Petersburg, Jan. 18, 1790);

Il castello d'Atlante, opera buffa (Desenzano, Carnival 1791); *La scuola dei maritati*, opera buffa (London, Jan. 27, 1795); *L'isola del piacere*, opera buffa (London, May 26, 1795); *Le nozze de' contadini spagnuoli*, intermezzo (London, May 28, 1795); *La festa del villagio*, opera buffa (St. Petersburg, Jan. 26 or 30, 1798). **BALLETS:** *La bella Arsene* (Naples, 1779 or 1780); *I Ratti Sabini* (Naples, 1779 or 1780); *La Regina di Golconda* (Lucca, 1781); *Cristiano II, rè di Danimarca* (Venice, 1782); *Aci e Galatea* (Parma, 1784); *Didon abandonée* (St. Petersburg, 1792); *L'Oracle* (St. Petersburg, 1793); *Amour et Psyché* (St. Petersburg, 1793); *Tancrède* (St. Petersburg, 1799); *Le Retour de Poliorcete* (St. Petersburg, 1799 or 1800); other works include a Salve Regina, cantatas, many canzonets, ariettas, duets, and canons.

BIBL.: F.-J. Fétis, "Noticias biográficas de D.V. M.," *Gaceta Musical de Madrid*, I (1855); B. Saldoni, "Apunte biográfico del célebre maestro español Don V. M. conocido . . . por Martini lo Spagnuolo," *Heraldo de les Artes, de las Letras y de los Espectáculos* (Madrid, Dec. 14, 1871); R. G(enée), " 'Una cosa rara' in Mozart's 'Don Juan,' " *Mitteilungen für die Mozart-Gemeinde Berlin*, I (1900); "Vinzenz M., der Komponist von 'Una cosa rara,' " ibid., II (1906); E. Walter, "V. M.," *Der Auftakt*, V (1925); I. Salvat, "Vicenc M. i S. i la seva òpera 'Una cosa rara o sia Bellezza ed onestà,' " *Revista Musical Catalana*, XXXIII (1936); R.-A. Mooser, "Un Musicien espagnol en Russie," *Rivista Musicale Italiana*, XL (1936); U. Prota-Giurleo, "Del compositore spagnuolo Vincente M. y S.," *Archivi*, XXVII (1960); R. Jesson, "Una cosa rara," *Musical Times*, CIX (1968); idem, "M. y S.'s 'L'arbore di Diana,' " ibid., CXIII (1972).

Martirano, Salvatore, American composer; b. Yonkers, N.Y., Jan. 12, 1927. He studied piano and composition at the Oberlin Cons. of Music (B.M., 1951); then composition at the Eastman School of Music in Rochester, N.Y., with Bernard Rogers (M.M., 1952); later went to Italy, where he took courses with Luigi Dallapiccola at the Cherubini Cons. in Florence (1952–54). He served in the U.S. Marine Corps; played clarinet and cornet with the Parris Island Marine Band; from 1956 to 59 he held a fellowship to the American Academy in Rome, and in 1960 received a Guggenheim fellowship and the American Academy of Arts and Letters Award. In 1963 he joined the faculty of the Univ. of Illinois at Urbana. He writes in a progressive avant-garde idiom, applying the quaquaversal techniques of unmitigated radical modernism, free from any inhibitions.

WORKS: Sextet for Wind Instruments (1949); Prelude for Orch. (1950); Variations for Flute and Piano (1950); String Quartet No. 1 (1951); *The Magic Stones*, chamber opera after the *Decameron* (Oberlin Cons., April 24, 1952); *Piece for Orchestra* (1952); Violin Sonata (1952); *Contrasto* for Orch. (1954); *Chansons innocentes* for Soprano and Piano (1957); *O, O, O, O, That Shakespeherian Rag* for Mixed Chorus and Instrumental Ensemble (1958); *Cocktail Music* for Piano (1962); *Octet* (1963); *Underworld* for 4 Actors, 4 Percussion Instruments, 2 Double Basses, Tenor Saxophone, and Tape (1965; video version, 1982); *Ballad* for amplified Nightclub Singer and Instrumental Ensemble (1966); *L's.G.A.* for a gas-masked Politico, Helium Bomb, 3 16mm Movie Projectors, and Tape (1968); *The Proposal* for Tapes and Slides (1968); *Action Analysis* for 12 People, Bunny, and Controller (1968); *Selections* for Alto Flute, Bass Clarinet, Viola, and Cello (1970); *Sal-Mar Construction I–VII* for Tape (1971–75); *Fast Forward* for Tape (1977); *Fifty One* for Tape (1978); *In Memoriam Luigi Dallapiccola* for Tape (1978); *Thrown*, sextet for Wind and Percussion (1984); *Look at the Back of My Head for Awhile*, video piece (1984); *Sampler: Everything Goes When the Whistle Blows* for Violin and Synthetic Orch. (1985; rev. 1988); *Dance/Players I* and *II*, video pieces (1986); *3 not 2*, variable-forms piece (1987); *Phleu* for Amplified Flute and Synthetic Orch. (1988); *LON/dons* for Chamber Orch. (1989).

Marton, Eva, outstanding Hungarian soprano; b. Budapest, June 18, 1943. She studied with Endre Rösler and Jenöd Sipos at the Franz Liszt Academy of Music in Budapest; made her formal operatic debut as the Queen of Shemakha in *Le Coq* *d'or* at the Hungarian State Opera there in 1968, remaining on its roster until joining the Frankfurt Opera in 1971; then became a member of the Hamburg State Opera in 1977. On Feb. 23, 1975, she made her U.S. debut in N.Y. as a soloist in the world premiere of Hovhaness's folk oratorio *The Way of Jesus;* then made her 1st appearance at the Metropolitan Opera there as Eva in *Die Meistersinger von Nürnberg* on Nov. 3, 1976. After singing at the Bayreuth Festivals (1977–78) and at Milan's La Scala (1978), she scored a notable success as the Empress in *Die Frau ohne Schatten* at the Metropolitan Opera in 1981; thereafter she was one of its most important artists, appearing as Elisabeth in *Tannhäuser* (1982), Leonore in *Fidelio* (1983), Ortrud in *Lohengrin* (1984), Tosca (1986), and Lady Macbeth (1988). She 1st sang Turandot at the Vienna State Opera in 1983; appeared as Elektra there in 1989. Her appearances as an oratorio and lieder artist were also well received.

BIBL.: C. Wilkens, *E. M.* (Hamburg, 1982); H. Waleson, "E. M.," *Ovation* (Oct. 1987).

Martopangrawit, R.L., significant Indonesian composer, teacher, performer, and music theorist; b. Surakarta, Central Java, April 4, 1914; d. there, April 17, 1986. He was a descendant of many generations of royal musicians and became a member of the royal gamelan at the Kraton [palace] Surakarta at 13. In 1948 he joined the offices of the Central Javanese Ministry of Education and Culture; also taught in Surakarta at the Konservatori Karawitan (K.O.K.A.R., 1951–64) and Akademi Seni Karawiten Indonesia (A.S.K.I., from 1964; later Sekolah Tinggi Seni Indonesia [S.T.S.I.]). Considered among the finest of traditional musicians, Martopangrawit garnered fame for his inventive and stylistically diverse compositions, which numbered over 100; his earliest dated work was *Ladrang Biwadhapraja* (1939), and his last was *Ra Ngandel* (1986); others included *Ladrang Cikar Bobrok* (1943), *Ketawang ASKI, Ladrang Asri* (1946), *Ladrang Gandasuli* (1946), *Ladrang Lo Kowe Nang* (1954), *Lancaran Kebat* (1961), *Lancaran Uyal-uyel* (1962), *Ketawang Pamegatsih* (1966), *Nglara Ati* (1970), *Mijil Anglir Medung* (1981), and *Gending Parisuka* (1982). He was also active in the preservation and development of many classical music and dance forms, particularly those associated with the Kraton Surakarta, where he was promoted to "Bupati Anonanon" and given the honorary title Raden Tumenggung Martodipura (1984). He also publ. many books on the Central Javanese gamelan; some of these comprise collections of music notation, including those of this own pieces—*Gending-gending Martopangrawit* (1968) and *Lagu Dolanan Anggitan Martopangrawit* (children's songs). Among his theoretical works is his landmark treatise *Pengetahuan Karawitan* (The Theory of Classical Javanese Music; Surakarta, 1972; Eng. tr. by M. Hatch, in J. Becker and A. Feinstein, eds., *Karawitan: Source Readings in Javanese Gamelan and Vocal Music,* vol. I, Ann Arbor, 1984). Other publications include a book of drumming notation, *Titilaras Kendangan;* a compendium of melodic patterns used by the gender (an important instrument in the Javanese gamelan), *Titilaras Cengkok-cengkok Genderan Dengan Wiledannya* (2 vols.); and a collection of children's songs, *Lagu Dolanan Larelare.*

Marttinen, Tauno, Finnish conductor, teacher, and composer; b. Helsinki, Sept. 27, 1912. He studied piano, composition, and conducting at the Viipuri Inst. of Music and composition with Palmgren at the Sibelius Academy in Helsinki (1935–37); concurrently received private lessons from Vogel in Switzerland. He was conductor of the Hämeenlinna City Orch. (1949–59) and director of the Inst. of Music there (1950–75). He began writing music in a traditional "Scandinavian" manner; about 1955 he adopted a serial technique. His adventurous style, marked by a sense of enlightened eclecticism and drawing its inspiration from national sources, caused some enthusiastic Finnish commentators to compare him to Charles Ives.

WORKS: STAGE: OPERAS: *Neiti Gamardin talo* (The House of Lady Gamard; 1960–71); *Päällysviitta* (The Cloak; 1962–63); *Kihlaus* (The Engagement; 1964); *Apotti ja ikäneito* (The Abbot and the Old Maid; 1965); *Tulitikkuja lainaamassa* (Borrowing Matches; 1965–69); *Lea* (1967); *Poltettu oranssi* (Burnt Orange; 1968); *Mestari Patelin* (Master Patelin; 1968–72); *Noitarumpu* (Shaman's Drum; 1974–76); *Psykiatri* (The Psychiatrist; 1974); *Meedio* (The Medium; 1975–76); *Jaarlin sisar* (The Earl's Sister; 1977); *Faaraon kirje* (The Pharaoh's Letter; 1978–80); *Suuren joen laulu* (Song of the Great River; 1982–84). **MUSICAL:** *Kullanmuru* (Golden Treasure; 1980). **BALLETS:** *Tikkaat* (The Ladder; 1955); *Dorian Grayn muotokuva* (Portrait of Dorian Gray; 1969); *Lumikuningatar* (Snow Queen; 1970); *Beatrice* (1970); *Päivänpäästö* (The Sun out of the Moon; 1975–77); *Ruma ankanpoikanen* (The Ugly Duckling; 1976–83). **ORCH.:** 7 syms. (1958–77); *Linnunrata* (The Milky Way; 1960–61); *Rembrandt* for Cello and Orch. (1962); Violin Concerto (1962); 3 piano concertos (1963, 1972, 1981); *Manalan linnut* (Birds of the Underworld; 1964); *Fauni* (1965); *Panu, tulen jumala* (Panu, the God of Fire; 1966); Cello Concerto, *Dalai Lama* (1966; rev. 1979); *Maailman synty* (Birth of the Earth; 1966); *Mont Saint Michel* (1968); *Pentalia* (1969); *Pohjola* (The North; 1970–71); Bassoon Concerto (1971; rev. 1983–84); Flute Concerto (1972); clarinet concerto, *Hirvenhiihto* (On the Tracks of the Winter Moose; 1974); *Concerto espagnole* for Flute and Orch. (1978); *Yö linnakkeessa* (Night on the Fortress; 1978); *Elegia* for Harp and Strings (1979); *Voces Polaris* (1979); *Sirius* (1980); *Väinämöisen synty* (The Birth of Väinämöinen; 1981); *Väinämöisen lähtö Pohjolaan* (Väinämöinen's Departure for Pohjola; 1982); *Pohjolan neiti* (The Maid of Pohjola; 1982); Concerto Grosso (1983). **CHAMBER:** *Loitsu* (The Conjuration) for 3 Percussionists (1963); *Alfa* for Flute and 7 Cymbals (1963); 3 nonets (1963, 1968, 1973); *Vipusessa käynti* (Visit to the Giant Sage Vipunen) for 7 Double Basses (1969); 3 string quartets (1969, 1971, 1983); *Septemalia* for 7 Double Basses (1975); Trio for Piano, Violin, and Cello (1978); *Le Commencement* for Flute, Oboe, and Piano (1978); *Quo vadis* for Flute, Oboe, Bassoon, and Harpsichord (1979); Trio for Violin, Viola, and Cello (1982); various solo pieces for piano, organ, and other instruments; vocal works, including choruses and solo songs.

Martucci, Giuseppe, esteemed Italian pianist, conductor, teacher, and composer, father of **Paolo Martucci;** b. Capua, Jan. 6, 1856; d. Naples, June 1, 1909. A pupil of his father (a bandmaster), he made his debut as a child pianist at the age of 7; at 11 he was admitted to the Cons. di San Pietro a Majella in Naples; there he studied piano with B. Cesi and composition with P. Serrao, but left in 1871. Subsequently he traveled as a pianist in Italy, France, Germany, and England; in 1880 he became a prof. of piano at the Naples Cons.; conducted sym. concerts established by Prince d'Ardore, and was the director of the Neapolitan Società del Quartetto. From 1886 until 1902 he was director of the Bologna Cons.; in 1902 he returned to Naples, and became director of the Cons., a post he held until his death. His activities as a fine sym. conductor contributed much to Italian musical culture, and he was greatly esteemed by his colleagues and the public; an ardent admirer of Wagner, he conducted the Italian premiere of *Tristan und Isolde* (Bologna, June 2, 1888); also led performances of other operas by Wagner. In his own works, he followed the ideals of the German school; the influences of Wagner and Liszt are particularly pronounced. As a composer, he was greatly admired by Toscanini, who repeatedly performed his orch. music.

WORKS: 2 syms. (1888–95; 1904); 2 piano concertos (1878; 1884–85); *Messa di Gloria* for Voices and Orch. (1871); *Samuel,* oratorio for Soloists, Chorus, and Orch. (1881; rev. 1905); Piano Quintet (1878); 2 piano trios (1882–83); Violin Sonata (1874); numerous songs; piano pieces, including the popular *Notturno,* op. 70, no. 1 (1891), and *Noveletta,* op. 82, no. 2 (1905).

BIBL.: R. Prati, *G. M.* (Turin, 1914); G. Tebaldini, ed., *Capua a G. M.* (Capua, 1915); L. Perrachio, "L'opera pianistica di M.," *Il Pianoforte* (March 1922); M. Limoncelli, *G. M.* (Naples, 1939); F. Fano, *G. M.* (Milan, 1950); *Comitato nazionale per la celebrazione del centenario della nascita di G. M.: Nostra* di autografi, cimeli e documenti (Naples, 1956); J. Waterhouse, "M. Reconsidered," *Ricordiana,* X/4 (London, 1965).

Martucci, Paolo, Italian pianist, son of **Giuseppe Martucci;** b. Naples, Oct. 8, 1881; d. N.Y., Oct. 18, 1980. He studied with his father; made his concert debut in Bologna with Tchaikovsky's 1st Piano Concerto on June 27, 1902; from 1904 to 1911 he lived in England; then went to the U.S.; taught at the Cincinnati Cons. (1911–13); in 1913, moved to N.Y. and taught piano.

Marty, Georges-Eugène, French composer and conductor; b. Paris, May 16, 1860; d. there, Oct. 11, 1908. He attended the Paris Cons. (1872–82), winning the Grand Prix de Rome with the cantata *Edith;* in 1894 was appointed instructor at the Paris Cons.; in 1903, became conductor of the Société des Concerts du Conservatoire. He wrote 3 operas (*Le Duc de Ferrare, Daria,* and *La Grande Mademoiselle*); symphonic poem, *Merlin enchanté; Suite romantique* for Orch.; choruses; songs; much piano music.

Martzy, Johanna, Hungarian violinist; b. Timişoara, Oct. 26, 1924; d. Glarus, Switzerland, Aug. 13, 1979. She received instruction from J. Hubay before entering the Budapest Academy of Music at age 10; made her debut in Budapest when she was 13, and graduated from the Academy (1942). After winning 1st prize in the Geneva Competition (1947), she toured widely; 1st played in England in 1953 and in the U.S. in 1957. She acquired a fine reputation as a soloist and chamber music artist.

Marvin, Frederick, American pianist and musicologist; b. Los Angeles, June 11, 1923. He studied with Maurice Zam (1935–39) and Milan Blanchet (1940–41; 1945–48) in Los Angeles, with Rudolf Serkin at the Curtis Inst. of Music in Philadelphia (1939–40), and with Claudio Arrau (1950–54); made his N.Y. debut in 1948; subsequently toured widely in North America, Europe, and India; was a prof. and artist-in-residence at Syracuse Univ. (from 1968). As a pianist, he made it a practice to include rarely heard works on his programs; he particularly championed the music of Antonio Soler; ed. a number of Soler's works, and developed a numbering system (Marvin Verzeichnis) that was widely adopted.

Marx, Adolf Bernhard, eminent German music theorist and writer on music; b. Halle, May 15, 1795; d. Berlin, May 17, 1866. Intended for the law, he matriculated at the Univ. of Halle, but also studied music with Türk, and gave up a subsequent legal appointment at Naumburg to gratify his love for art. He continued the study of composition in Berlin with Zelter; in 1824 he founded the *Berliner Allgemeine Musikalische Zeitung* (with the publisher Schlesinger); he ed. this publication with ability, and proved himself a conspicuous advocate of German music; however, the publication ceased in 1830. After taking the degree of Ph.D. at the Univ. of Marburg (1827), Marx lectured on music at the Univ. of Berlin; was appointed a prof. in 1830; became music director of the scholastic choir there in 1832. He was co-founder (with Kullak and Stern) of the Berliner Musikschule (1850), retiring in 1856 to devote himself to literary and univ. work. He was a close friend of the Mendelssohn family, and advised young Mendelssohn in musical matters. While Marx was greatly esteemed as a music theorist, his own compositions were unsuccessful; he wrote a singspiel, *Jery und Bätely,* after Goethe (1824); an oratorio, *Mose* (1841); instrumental works; songs; choral works; etc.
Writings: *Die Lehre von der musikalischen Komposition, praktisch-theoretisch* (4 vols., Leipzig, 1837–47; several times reprinted; new eds. by H. Riemann, 1887–90); *Allgemeine Musiklehre* (Leipzig, 1839; 10th ed., 1884); *Die alte Musiklehre im Streit mit unserer Zeit* (Leipzig, 1841); *Die Musik des neunzehnten Jahrhunderts und ihre Pflege: Methode der Musik* (Leipzig, 1855; 2nd ed., 1873; Eng. tr., 1855); *Ludwig van Beethoven: Leben und Schaffen* (Berlin, 1859; 7th ed., 1907–10); *Gluck und die Oper* (Berlin, 1863; 2nd ed., 1866, as *Gluck's Leben und Schaffen*); *Anleitung zum Vortrag Beethovenscher Klavier-*

werke (Berlin, 1863; 5th ed., 1912; Eng. tr., 1895); *Erinnerungen: Aus meinem Leben* (Berlin, 1865); *Das Ideal und die Gegenwart* (Jena, 1867); L. Hirschberg, ed., *Musikalische Schriften über Tondichter und Tonkunst* (Hildburghausen, 1912–22; a collection of most of his major articles from the *Berliner Allgemeine Musikalische Zeitung*).
Bibl.: G. Selle, *Aus A.B. M.'s literarischen Nachlass* (Berlin, 1898); L. Hirschberg, "Der Tondichter A.B. M.," *Sammelbände der Internationalen Musik-Gesellschaft,* X (1908–9); B. Moyer, *Concepts of Musical Form in the Nineteenth Century with Special Reference to A.B. M. and Sonata Form* (diss., Stanford Univ., 1969).

Marx, Josef, German-American oboist, musicologist, and music publisher; b. Berlin, Sept. 9, 1913; d. N.Y., Dec. 21, 1978. He emigrated to America in his early youth; studied oboe with Marcel Dandois at the Cincinnati Cons. and with Leon Goossens in London; then took lessons in music theory with Stefan Wolpe. He was an oboist in the Palestine Orch. (1936–37) and the Pittsburgh Sym. Orch. (1942–43); also played English horn in the orch. of the Metropolitan Opera in N.Y. (1943–51); in addition, he appeared as an oboe soloist; several contemporary composers wrote special works for him. In 1945 he founded the McGinnis-Marx Edition in N.Y., which publ. works by Wolpe, Wuorinen, Sydeman, Schuller, and other contemporary composers. From 1956 to 1960 he taught oboe at the Hartt College of Music in Hartford.

Marx, Joseph, Austrian composer, pedagogue, and music critic; b. Graz, May 11, 1882; d. there, Sept. 3, 1964. He studied musicology with Degner at the Univ. of Graz, being awarded the degree of Ph.D. in 1909 with the dissertation *Über die Funktionen von Intervallen, Harmonie und Melodie beim Erfassen von Tonkomplexen.* In 1914 he went to Vienna, where he taught at the Academy of Music; was its director (1922–24); then rector of the Hochschule für Musik in Vienna (1924–27); then was an adviser to the Turkish government, traveling to Ankara in that capacity (1932–33). He was music critic of the *Neues Wiener Journal* (1931–38); after World War II, he wrote for the *Wiener Zeitung;* was also active as a teacher in Vienna and later at the Univ. of Graz (1947–57). As a composer, he styled himself a "Romantic realist"; excelled particularly as a composer of songs.
Writings: *Harmonielehre* (Vienna, 1934; 3rd ed., 1948); *Kontrapunkt-Lehre* (Vienna, 1935); *Betrachtungen eines romantischen Realisten* (Vienna, 1947); *Weltsprache Musik* (Vienna, 1964).
Works: *Herbstchor an Pan* for Chorus, Children's Chorus, Orch., and Organ (1911); a *Ballade,* a *Scherzo,* and a *Quartett in Form einer Rhapsodie,* all for Piano Quartet (1911); *Italienisches Liederbuch* (3 vols., 1912); *Frühlingssonate* for Violin and Piano (1913); *Trio Phantasie* for Piano Trio (1913); *Lieder und Gesänge* (3 vols., 1910–17); *Romantische Klavierkonzert* (1919–20); *Eine Herbstsymphonie* (1920–21; Vienna, Feb. 5, 1922; its final movement, *Ein Herbstpoem,* is often played as a separate piece); 5 *Lieder* for Voice and Orch. (1921); *Naturtrilogie* for Orch., consisting of the separate pieces *Eine symphonische Nachtmusik, Idylle,* and *Eine Frühlingsmusik* (1922–25); *Nordlands-Rhapsodie* for Orch. (1928–29); *Castelli Romani,* 3 pieces for Piano and Orch. (1930); *Verklärtes Jahr,* 5 songs for Middle Voice and Orch. (1930–32); *Verklärtes Jahr,* song cycle for Mezzo-soprano or Baritone and Orch. (1935–36); 3 string quartets: No. 1, *Quartetto in modo chromatico* (1937; rev. 1948); No. 2, *in modo antico* (1938); No. 3, *in modo classico* (1941); *AltWiener Serenaden* for Orch. (1941–42; Vienna, April 14, 1942); *Sinfonische Rhapsodie* (1943); *Sinfonietta in modo classico* for Strings (1944; arrangement of the 3rd string quartet); *Sinfonia in modo antico* for Strings (1947; arrangement of the 2nd string quartet).
Bibl.: A. Lies, *J. M.: Leben und Werk* (Graz, 1943); T. Leibnitz, *Österreichische Spätromantiker: Studien zu Emil Nikolaus von Reznicek, J. M., Franz Schmidt, und Egon Kornauth* (Tutzing, 1986).

Marx, Karl, German composer and pedagogue; b. Munich, Nov. 12, 1897; d. Stuttgart, May 8, 1985. He served in the German army during World War I and was a prisoner of war in England; after the Armistice, studied with Orff, Hausegger, Beer-Walbrunn, and Schwickerath in Munich. In 1924 he was appointed to the faculty of the Akademie der Tonkunst in Munich; in 1928 he became the conductor of the Bach Soc. Chorus in Munich; from 1939 to 1946 he was instructor at the Hochschule für Musikerziehung in Graz; subsequently taught at the Hochschule für Musik in Stuttgart (1946–66). A master of German polyphony, Marx distinguished himself as a composer of both sacred and secular choral music.

WORKS: ORCH.: Concerto for 2 Violins and Orch. (1926); Piano Concerto (1929; rev. 1959); Viola Concerto (1929); *Passacaglia* (1932); Violin Concerto (1935); Concerto for Flute and Strings (1937); *15 Variations on a German Folk Song* (1938); *Musik nach alpenländischen Volksliedern* for Strings (1940); *Festival Prelude* (1956); Concerto for String Orch. (1964; a reworking of his 1932 *Passacaglia*); *Fantasia sinfonica* (1967; rev. 1969); *Fantasia concertante* for Violin, Cello, and Orch. (1972). **VOCAL:** Several large cantatas, including *Die heiligen drei Könige* (1936); *Rilke-Kantate* (1942); *Und endet doch alles mit Frieden* (1952); *Raube das Licht aus dem Rachen der Schlange* (1957); *Auftrag und Besinnung* (1961); chamber cantatas, including *Die unendliche Woge* (1930); also cantatas for special seasons, children's cantatas, and the like; a cappella pieces; songs, many with Orch., including *Rilke-Kreis* for Voice and Piano (1927; version for Mezzo-soprano and Chamber Orch., 1952) and *3 Songs*, to texts by Stefan George, for Baritone and Chamber Orch. (1934). **CHAMBER:** *Fantasy and Fugue* for String Quartet (1927); *Variations* for Organ (1933); *Divertimento* for 16 Winds (1934); *Turmmusik* for 3 Trumpets and 3 Trombones (1938); *Divertimento* for Flute, Violin, Viola, Cello, and Piano (1942); 6 sonatinas for various instrumental combinations (1948–51); *Kammermusik* for 7 Instruments (1955); Trio for Piano, Flute, and Cello (1962); Cello Sonata (1964); *Fantasy* for Violin (1966); *Partita über "Ein' feste Burg"* for String Quartet or String Orch. (1967); Wind Quintet (1973).

BIBL.: R. von Saalfeld, "K. M.," *Zeitschrift für Musik*, XXI (1931); F. Oberborbeck, "K. M.," *Hausmusik*, XXI (1957); E. Karkoschka, "Über späte Instrumentalwerke von K. M.," *Musica*, XXVI (1972).

Marxsen, Eduard, German pianist, organist, teacher, and composer; b. Nienstädten, near Altona, July 23, 1806; d. Altona, Nov. 18, 1887. He studied with his father, an organist, in Altona, then with J.H. Clasing in Hamburg; went to Vienna (1830) to continue his training with Bocklet (piano) and I. Seyfried (composition); settled as a teacher in Hamburg (1834), where Brahms later became his pupil. He wrote orch. music, piano pieces, songs, and other works.

BIBL.: G. Jenner, "War M. der rechte Lehrer für Brahms?," *Die Musik*, XII (1912–13).

Maryon (-d'Aulby), (John) Edward, English composer; b. London, April 3, 1867; d. there, Jan. 31, 1954. He began to compose early in life; went to Paris, where his 1st opera, *L'Odalisque*, won the Gold Medal at the Exposition of 1889; however, he regarded the work as immature and destroyed the score. In 1891 he studied with Max Pauer in Dresden; later took lessons with Wüllner in Cologne; then lived in France; from 1914 to 1919 he was in Montclair, N.J., where he established a cons. with a fund for exchange of music students between England and America; in 1933 he returned to London. He wrote the operas *Paolo and Francesca; La Robe de plume; The Smelting Pot; The Prodigal Son; Werewolf; Rembrandt; Greater Love;* and *Abelard and Heloise.* In his *Werewolf* he applied a curious system of musical symbolism, in which the human part was characterized by the diatonic scale and the lupine self by the whole-tone scale; Maryon made a claim of priority in using the whole-tone scale consistently as a leading motive in an opera. His magnum opus was a grandiose operatic heptalogy under the title *The Cycle of Life*, comprising 7 mystical dramas: *Lucifer, Cain, Krishna, Magdalen, Sangraal, Psyche,*

and *Nirvana.* He also wrote a symphonic poem, *The Feather Robe,* subtitled *A Legend of Fujiyama* (1905), which he dedicated to the Emperor of Japan; and *Armageddon Requiem* (1916), dedicated to the dead of World War I. After Maryon's death, his complete MSS were donated to the Boston Public Library. Maryon developed a theory of universal art, in which colors were associated with sounds; an outline of this theory was publ. in his *Marcotone* (N.Y., 1915).

Märzendorfer, Ernst, Austrian conductor; b. Oberndorf, May 26, 1921. He studied in Graz and with C. Krauss at the Salzburg Mozarteum; then conducted at the Landestheater in Graz (1945–51). After conducting at the Teatro Colón in Buenos Aires (1952–53), he was conductor of the Mozarteum Orch. (1953–58); subsequently conducted at the Berlin Städtische Oper (from 1958), the Vienna State Opera (from 1961), and the Vienna Volksoper (from 1971). He made his Metropolitan Opera debut in N.Y. in 1965.

Marzo, Eduardo, Italian-American pianist, organist, and composer; b. Naples, Nov. 29, 1852; d. N.Y., June 7, 1929. As a boy of 15, he settled in N.Y., and appeared in concerts as a pianist; was accompanist to many celebrated artists, among them Carlotta Patti, Mario, and Sarasate on their American tours. From 1878 he played the organ in various N.Y. churches. He held numerous honorary orders, conferred on him by the King of Italy. He wrote many masses and other sacred choral works; cantatas; operettas; songs; piano pieces.

Mascagni, Pietro, famous Italian opera composer; b. Livorno, Dec. 7, 1863; d. Rome, Aug. 2, 1945. His father was a baker who wished him to continue in that trade, but yielded to his son's determination to study music. He took lessons with Alfredo Soffredini in his native town until he was enabled, by the aid of an uncle, to attend the Milan Cons., where he studied with Ponchielli and Saladino (1882). However, he became impatient with school discipline, and was dismissed from the Cons. in 1884. Ht then conducted operetta troupes and taught music in Cerignola. He composed industriously, and in 1888 he sent the MS of his 1-act opera *Cavalleria rusticana* to the music publisher Sonzogno for a competition, and won 1st prize. The opera was performed at the Teatro Costanzi in Rome on May 17, 1890, with sensational success; the dramatic story of village passion, and Mascagni's emotional score, laden with luscious music, combined to produce an extraordinary appeal to opera lovers. The short opera made the tour of the world stages with amazing rapidity, productions being staged all over Europe and America with never-failing success; the opera was usually presented in 2 parts, separated by an "intermezzo sinfonico" (which became a popular orch. number performed separately). *Cavalleria rusticana* marked the advent of the operatic style known as *verismo,* in which stark realism was the chief aim and the dramatic development was condensed to enhance the impressions. When, 2 years later, another "veristic" opera, Leoncavallo's *Pagliacci,* was taken by Sonzogno, the 2 operas became twin attractions on a single bill. Ironically, Mascagni could never duplicate or even remotely approach the success of his 1st production, although he continued to compose industriously and opera houses all over the world were only too eager to stage his successive operas. Thus, his opera *Le Maschere* was produced on Jan. 17, 1901, at 6 of the most important Italian opera houses simultaneously (Rome, Milan, Turin, Genoa, Venice, Verona); it was produced 2 days later in Naples. Mascagni himself conducted the premiere in Rome. But the opera failed to fire the imagination of the public; it was produced in a revised form in Turin 15 years later (June 7, 1916), but was not established in the repertoire even in Italy. In 1902 he made a tour of the U.S., conducting his *Cavalleria rusticana* and other operas, but, owing to mismanagement, the visit proved a fiasco; a South American tour in 1911 was more successful. He also appeared frequently as a conductor of sym. concerts. In 1890 he was made a Knight of the Crown of Italy; in 1929 he was elected a member of the Academy. At various times he also was engaged in teaching; from 1895 to 1902 he was director of the Rossini Cons. in Pesaro. His last years were darkened by the inglorious role that he had played as an ardent supporter of the Fascist regime, so that he was rejected by many of his old friends. It was only after his death that his errors of moral judgment were forgiven; his centennial was widely celebrated in Italy in 1963.

WORKS: Operas: *Pinotta* (c.1880; San Remo, March 23, 1932); *Guglielmo Ratcliff* (c.1885; Milan, Feb. 16, 1895); *Cavalleria rusticana* (Rome, May 17, 1890); *L'Amico Fritz* (Rome, Oct. 31, 1891); *I Rantzau* (Florence, Nov. 10, 1892); *Silvano* (Milan, March 25, 1895); *Zanetto* (Pesaro, March 2, 1896); *Iris* (Rome, Nov. 22, 1898; rev. version, Milan, Jan. 19, 1899); *Le Maschere* (simultaneous premiere in Rome, Milan, Turin, Genoa, Venice, and Verona, Jan. 17, 1901); *Amica* (Monte Carlo, March 16, 1905); *Isabeau* (Buenos Aires, June 2, 1911); *Parisina* (Milan, Dec. 15, 1913); *Lodoletta* (Rome, April 30, 1917); *Scampolo* (1921); *Il piccolo Marat* (Rome, May 2, 1921); *Nerone* (Milan, Jan. 16, 1935); *I Bianchi ed i Neri* (1940); also the operettas *Il re a Napoli* (n.d.) and *Sì* (Rome, Dec. 13, 1919). Other works include 2 syms.: No. 1 (1879) and No. 2 (1881); *Poema leopardiano* (for the centenary of G. Leopardi, 1898); Hymn in honor of Admiral Dewey (July 1899); *Rapsodia satanica* (music for a film, Rome, July 2, 1917); *Davanti Santa Teresa* (Rome, Aug. 1923); chamber music; choral works; songs; piano pieces.

BIBL.: G. Monaldi, *P. M.: L'Uomo e l'artista* (Rome, 1899); G. Marvin, *P. M.: Biografia aneddotica* (Palermo, 1904); G. Bastianelli, *P. M., con nota delle opere* (Naples, 1910); E. Pompei, *P. M., nella vita e nell'arte* (Rome, 1912); G. Orsini, *L'arte di P. M.* (Milan, 1912); G. Scuderi, *Iris* (1923); T. Mantovani, *Iris* (1930); A. Donno, *Modernità di P. M.* (1931); G. Cogo, *Il nostro M.* (1931); "Bibliografia delle opere di P. M.," *Bolletino Bibliografico Musicale* (Milan, 1932); A. Donno, *M. nel 900 musicale* (Rome, 1935); A. Jeri, *M., 15 Opere, 1000 Episodi* (Milan, 1940); D. Cellamare, *M. e la "Cavalleria" visti da Cerignola* (Rome, 1941); *M. parla* (Rome, 1945); *Comitato nazionale delle onoranze a P. M. nel primo centenario della nascità* (Livorno, 1963); M. Morini, ed., *P. M.* (2 vols., Milan, 1964); G. Gavazzeni, *Discorso per M. nel centenario della nascità* (Rome, 1964); D. Cellamare, *P. M.* (Rome, 1965); D. Stivender, ed. and tr., *The Autobiography of P. M.* (N.Y., 1975); H. Goetz, "Die Beziehungen zwischen P. M. und Benito Mussolini," *Analecta Musicologica*, 17 (1976); R. Iovino, *M: L'avventuroso dell'opera* (Milan, 1987).

Maschera, Florentio or **Florenzo,** Italian organist, string player, and composer; b. probably in Brescia, c.1540; d. there, c.1584. He 1st studied with his father; then was a pupil of Merulo; served as organist at Santo Spirito in Venice; on Aug. 22, 1557, he succeded Merulo as organist at the Brescia Cathedral. He publ. *Libro primo de canzoni da sonare a quattro voci* (Brescia, 1584), which was ed. by W. McKee in *The Music of Florentio Maschera (1540–1584)*– (diss., North Texas State Univ., 1958).

Mascheroni, Edoardo, distinguished Italian conductor; b. Milan, Sept. 4, 1852; d. Ghirla, near Varese, March 4, 1941. As a boy, he showed special interest in mathematics and literature; wrote literary essays for the journal *La Vita Nuova* before he decided to study music seriously; took lessons with Boucheron in Milan, and composed various pieces. In 1880 he began a career in Brescia as a conductor, and it was in that capacity that he distinguished himself. He was 1st a theater conductor in Livorno; then went to Rome, where he established his reputation as an opera conductor (1884). Upon Verdi's explicit request, he was selected to conduct the premiere of *Falstaff* at La Scala in Milan (1893); he remained on the staff of La Scala until 1897; then conducted in Germany, Spain, and South America. He wrote 2 operas, *Lorenza* (Rome, April 13, 1901) and *La Perugina* (Naples, April 24, 1909), 2 Requiems, and chamber music.

Mašek, Vincenz, Bohemian pianist and organist; b. Zwikovecz, April 5, 1755; d. Prague, Nov. 15, 1831. He was a pupil of Seeger and F.X. Dussek; became an accomplished player of the piano and harmonica; after long tours, he settled in

Prague as an organist and music dealer. His brother Paul Mašek (1761–1826) was a pianist and a teacher in Vienna.

Masetti, Enzo, Italian composer; b. Bologna, Aug. 19, 1893; d. Rome, Feb. 11, 1961. He studied with Franco Alfano at the Liceo Musicale in Bologna; devoted his life mainly to film music; from 1942 until his death he was connected with the Centro Sperimentale di Cinematografia in Rome; publ. *La musica nel film* (Rome, 1950) and composed about 60 film scores. He also wrote several dramatic fables, among them *La fola delle tre ochette* (Bologna, 1928), *La mosca mora* (Bologna, 1930), and *La bella non può dormire* (Bologna, 1957); *Contrasti* for Orch. (1921); *Il gioco del cucù* for Piano and Orch. (1928); a number of piano pieces and songs.

Masini, Angelo, Italian tenor; b. Terra del Sole, near Forlì, Nov. 28, 1844; d. Forlì, Sept. 26, 1926. He studied with Gilda Minguzzi; made his debut as Pollione in *Norma* in Finale Emilia (1867); then sang throughout Italy, Spain, and Russia; was chosen by Verdi to sing in the *Requiem*, appearing under Verdi's direction in London, Paris, and Vienna in 1875. He gave his farewell stage performance in Paris in 1905. Among his finest roles were Count Almaviva, Don Ottavio, Faust, and Radames.

BIBL.: C. Rivalta, *Il tenore A. M. e Faenza* (Faenza, 1927).

Masley, Michael, American instrumentalist and composer; b. Trenton, Mich., Sept. 22, 1952. He studied creative writing at Northwestern Michigan College (1970–72); in 1973 began working with hammer dulcimer player Bob Spinner, who became a mentor. He played using traditional 2-hammer technique until 1979; during months at a fishing lodge in northern Michigan, he developed a 10-fingered "finger-hammer" technique. In 1982 he engaged the dulcimer maker William Webster of Detroit to make him a cymbalom (a large chromatic concert dulcimer); he added violin bows to the finger hammers in 1983, creating his unique "bowhammers." In 1982 he moved to Palo Alto, Calif., where he met guitarist Barry Cleveland (1983); they performed as the duo Thin Ice, releasing the recordings *Thin Ice Live* (1984) and *1st Frost* (1985); he also played on Cleveland's later albums, *Mythos* (1986) and *Voluntary Dreaming* (1990); moved to Berkeley, Calif., in 1985. His own recordings include the cymbalom solos *The Moment's River* (1987), *Bells & Shadows* (1989), and *Mystery Loves Company* (1990). His innovative cymbalom technique enables the player to strike, bow, or pluck notes with all 10 fingers in any combination. The resulting timbral distinctions are used to create unusually complex contrapuntal textures for a solo instrument, to which he often adds pitched and tunable percussion instruments.

Mason, Daniel Gregory, eminent American composer and educator; b. Brookline, Mass., Nov. 20, 1873; d. Greenwich, Conn., Dec. 4, 1953. He was a scion of a famous family of American musicians; grandson of **Lowell Mason** and nephew of **William Mason;** his father, Henry Mason, was a co-founder of the piano manufacturing firm Mason & Hamlin. He entered Harvard Univ., where he studied with J.K. Paine (B.A., 1895); after graduation, he continued his studies with Arthur Whiting (piano), Goetschius (theory), and Chadwick (orchestration). Still feeling the necessity for improvement of his technique as a composer, he went to Paris, where he took courses with d'Indy. Returning to America, he became active as a teacher and composer. In 1905 he became a member of the faculty of Columbia Univ.; in 1929, was appointed MacDowell Professor of Music; he was chairman of the music dept. until 1940, and continued to teach there until 1942, when he retired. As a teacher, he developed a high degree of technical ability in his students; as a composer, he represented a conservative trend in American music; while an adherent to the idea of an American national style, his conception was racially and regionally narrow, accepting only the music of Anglo-Saxon New England and the "old South"; he was an outspoken opponent of the "corrupting" and "foreign" influences of 20th-century Afro-American and Jewish-American music. His ideals were the German masters of the Romantic school; but there is an admixture of impressionistic colors in his orchestration; his harmonies are full and opulent, his melodic writing expressive and songful. The lack of strong individuality, however, has resulted in the virtual disappearance of his music from the active repertoire, with the exception of the overture *Chanticleer* and the Clarinet Sonata.

WORKS: ORCH.: 3 syms.: No. 1 (1913–14; Philadelphia, Feb. 18, 1916; radically rev., N.Y., Dec. 1, 1922); No. 2 (Cincinnati, Nov. 23, 1928); No. 3, *Lincoln* (1935–36; N.Y., Nov. 17, 1937); *Prelude and Fugue* for Piano and Orch. (1914; Chicago, March 4, 1921); *Scherzo-Caprice* for Chamber Orch. (N.Y., Jan. 2, 1917); *Chanticleer*, festival overture (1926; Cincinnati, Nov. 23, 1928); *Suite* (1933–34); *Prelude and Fugue* for Strings (1939). **CHAMBER:** Quartet for Piano and Strings (1909–11); *Pastorale* for Violin, Clarinet or Viola, and Piano (1909–12); Sonata for Violin and Piano (1907–8); 3 pieces for Flute, Harp, and String Quartet (1911–12); Sonata for Clarinet or Violin and Piano (1912–15); *Intermezzo* for String Quartet (1916); *String Quartet on Negro Themes* (1918–19); *Variations on a Theme of John Powell* for String Quartet (1924–25); *Divertimento* for Flute, Oboe, Clarinet, Horn, and Bassoon (1926); *Fanny Blair*, folk-song fantasy for String Quartet (1929); *Serenade* for String Quartet (1931); *Sentimental Sketches*, 4 short pieces for Violin, Cello, and Piano (1935); *Variations on a Quiet Theme* (1939). **VOCAL:** *Russians* for Voice and Piano (1915–17; also for Baritone and Orch.); *Songs of the Countryside* for Chorus and Orch. (1923); *Soldiers* for Baritone and Piano (1948–49).

WRITINGS (all publ. in N.Y.): *From Grieg to Brahms* (1902; rev. 1930); *Beethoven and His Forerunners* (1904; 2nd ed., 1930); *The Romantic Composers* (1906); *The Appreciation of Music* (1907; with T.W. Surette); *The Orchestral Instruments and What They Do* (1909); *A Guide to Music* (1909); *A Neglected Sense in Piano Playing* (1912); *Great Modern Composers* (with M. Mason; 1916; 2nd ed., 1968); *Short Studies of Great Masterpieces* (1917); *Contemporary Composers* (1918); *Music as a Humanity: And Other Essays* (1921); *From Song to Symphony* (1924); *Artistic Ideals* (1925); *The Dilemma of American Music* (1928); *Tune In, America!* (1931); *The Chamber Music of Brahms* (1933); *Music in My Time and Other Reminiscences* (1938); *The Quartets of Beethoven* (1947).

BIBL.: B. Tuthill, "D.G. M.," *Musical Quarterly* (Jan. 1948); M. Klein, *The Contribution of D.G. M. to American Music* (diss., Catholic Univ. of America, 1957); R. Lewis, *The Life and Music of D.G. M.* (diss., Univ. of Rochester, 1959); D. Kapec, *The Three Symphonies of D.G. M.: Style-Critical and Theoretical Analyses* (diss., Univ. of Florida, 1982).

Mason, Lowell, distinguished American organist, conductor, music educator, and composer, father of **William Mason;** b. Medfield, Mass., Jan. 8, 1792; d. Orange, N.J., Aug. 11, 1872. As a youth he studied singing with Amos Albee and Oliver Shaw; at 16 he directed the church choir at Medfield; in 1812 he went to Savannah, Ga.; studied harmony and composition with Frederick Abel; taught singing in schools (1813–24) and became principal of the singers (1815) and organist (1820) of the Independent Presbyterian Church. In 1827 he went to Boston and was president of the Handel and Haydn Soc. (until 1832); established classes on Pestalozzi's system, teaching it privately from 1829 and in the public schools from 1837. He founded the Boston Academy of Music in 1833 with George J. Webb; was superintendent of music in the Boston public schools (1837–45), remaining active as a teacher until 1851; made 2 sojourns in Europe to study pedagogic methods (1837; 1851–53). In 1854 he settled in Orange, N.J. He received an honorary doctorate in music from N.Y. Univ. (1855), only the 2nd such conferring of that degree in the U.S. He publ. *Musical Letters from Abroad* (N.Y., 1853). M. Broyles ed. *A Yankee Musician in Europe: The 1837 Journals of Lowell Mason* (Ann Arbor, 1990). Mason became wealthy through the sale of his many collections of music: *Handel and Haydn Society's Collection of Church Music* (1822; 16 later eds.); *Juvenile Psalmist* (1829); *Juvenile Lyre* (1830); *Lyra Sacra* (1832); *Sabbath School*

Songs (1836); *Boston Academy Collection of Church Music* (1836); *Boston Anthem Book* (1839); *The Psaltery* (1845); *Cantica Laudis* (1850); *New Carmina Sacra* (1852); *Normal Singer* (1856); *Song Garden* (3 parts; 1864–65); etc. Many of his own hymn tunes, including *Missionary Hymn* (*From Greenland's Icy Mountains*), *Olivet*, *Boylston*, *Bethany*, *Hebron*, and *Olmutz*, are still found in hymnals. His valuable library, including 830 MSS and 700 vols. of hymnology, was given to Yale College after his death.

BIBL.: T. Seward, *The Educational Work of Dr. L. M.* (Boston, 1885); F. Metcalf, *American Writers and Compilers of Sacred Music* (N.Y., 1925); H. Mason, *Hymn Tunes of L. M., A Bibliography* (Cambridge, Mass., 1944); idem, *L. M.: An Appreciation of His Life and Work* (N.Y., 1944); A. Rich, *L. M.: The Father of Singing among the Children* (Chapel Hill, N.C., 1946); J. Higginson, "Notes on L. M.'s Hymn Tunes," *Hymn* (April 1967); E. O'Meara, "The L. M. Library," *Notes* (Dec. 1971); C. Pemberton, *L. M.: His Life and Work* (Ann Arbor, 1985); idem, *L. M.: A Bio-Bibliography* (Westport, Conn., 1988).

Mason, Luther Whiting, American music educator; b. Turner, Maine, April 3, 1828; d. Buckfield, Maine, July 4, 1896. He studied with Lowell Mason at the Boston Academy of Music; in 1853, became a music teacher in Louisville schools, then in 1856 in Cincinnati, where he invented the "National System" of music charts and books, which had instant success and made him famous. He settled in Boston in 1864, and reformed music instruction in the primary schools; in 1880 he was invited by the Japanese government to supervise music in the schools of Japan, where he labored 3 years with notable results (school music in Japan was termed "Masonsong"). He spent some time in Germany perfecting his principal work, *The National Music-Course*.

BIBL.: K. Hartley, *A Study of the Life and Works of L.W.M.* (diss., Florida State Univ., 1960); B. Hall, "The American Education of L.W.M.," *American Music* (Spring 1988).

Mason, Marilyn (May), American organist and pedagogue; b. Alva, Okla., June 29, 1925. She studied at Oklahoma State Univ. and the Univ. of Michigan; also took lessons with Boulanger and Schoenberg, completing her studies at the Union Theological Seminary in N.Y. (D.S.M., 1954). She became a teacher at the Univ. of Michigan in Ann Arbor (1946); was made chairman of its organ dept. in 1962 and a prof. in 1965. She made many tours as a recitalist in North America, Europe, South America, and the Far East, performing commissioned works from such composers as Henry Cowell, Ross Lee Finney, Ulysses Kay, Ernst Krenek, and Leo Sowerby.

Mason, William, esteemed American pianist, pedagogue, and composer, son of **Lowell Mason;** b. Boston, Jan. 24, 1829; d. N.Y., July 14, 1908. He studied with his father and Henry Schmidt in Boston; made his debut at an Academy of Music concert there (March 7, 1846); then went to Leipzig (1849), where he continued his studies with Moscheles, Hauptmann, and Richter; after further instruction from Dreyschock in Prague, he completed his training with Liszt in Weimar (1853–54). After appearances in Weimar, Prague, Frankfurt, and other continental cities, as well as in London (1853), he toured in the U.S. (1854–55). He then settled in N.Y., where he founded the Mason and Thomas Soirées of Chamber Music with Theodore Thomas in 1855; after they were discontinued in 1868, he devoted himself mainly to teaching. In 1872 he was awarded an honorary doctorate in music from Yale College. He publ. *Memories of a Musical Life* (N.Y., 1901). Mason composed a *Serenata* for Cello and Piano and some 40 piano pieces. His pedagogical works include *A Method for the Piano-forte* (with E. Hoadley; N.Y., 1867); *A System for Beginners* (with E. Hoadley; Boston, 1871); *A System of Technical Exercises for the Piano-forte* (Boston, 1878); *Touch and Technique*, op.44 (Philadelphia, 1889); *A Primer of Music* (with W. Mathews; N.Y., 1894).

BIBL.: K. Graber, *W. M. (1829–1908): An Annotated Bibliography and Catalog of Works* (Warren, Mich., 1987).

Mason & Hamlin Co., celebrated firm of piano manufacturers. The firm was founded as the M. & H. Organ Co. in Boston in 1854 by Henry Mason, a son of **Lowell** and the father of **Daniel Gregory Mason,** and Emmons Hamlin. The latter, a brilliant mechanic, turned his attention to improving the quality of the reeds and obtaining great variety of tonal color, with the result that in 1861 the firm introduced the American Cabinet Organ. The firm became internationally famous when at the Paris Exposition of 1867 its organs were awarded 1st prize over numerous European competitors. In 1882 it began the construction of pianos, introducing a new system of stringing which found immediate favor; of several improvements patented by Mason & Hamlin, the most important was the Tension-Resonator (1900; described in *Scientific American,* Oct. 11, 1902), a device for preserving the tension of the sounding board. The firm subsequently became a subsidiary of the Aeolian American Corp. and eventually of the American Piano Corp. Henry Lowell Mason, son of the founder, was president of the firm until 1929.

Massa, Juan Bautista, Argentine composer; b. Buenos Aires, Oct. 29, 1885; d. Rosario, March 7, 1938. He studied violin and composition; became a choral conductor; moved to Rosario, where he was active as a teacher.
WORKS: Operas: *Zoraide* (Buenos Aires, May 15, 1909); *L'Evaso* (Rosario, June 23, 1922); *La Magdalena* (Buenos Aires, Nov. 9, 1929); 3 operettas: *Esmeralda* (1903); *Triunfo del corazón* (1910); *La eterna historia* (1911); ballet, *El cometa* (Buenos Aires, Nov. 8, 1932); symphonic poem, *La muerte del Inca* (Buenos Aires, Oct. 15, 1932); 2 Argentine suites for Orch.; other pieces on native themes.
BIBL.: F. Lange, "J.B. M.," *Boletín Latino-Americano de Música* (Dec. 1938).

Massa, Nicolò, Italian composer; b. Calice Ligure, Oct. 26, 1854; d. Genoa, Jan. 24, 1894. He studied at the Milan Cons. with Bazzini; wrote the operas *Aldo e Clarenza* (Milan, April 11, 1878); *Il Conte di Chatillon* (Reggio Emilia, Feb. 11, 1882); *Salammbò* (Milan, April 15, 1886; his most successful opera); *Eros* (Florence, May 21, 1895); also composed *Inno al lavoro* (1892).

Massaino (Massaini), Tiburtio, Italian composer; b. Cremona, c.1549; d. Piacenza or Lodi, c.1609. He was a member of the Augustinian order, in charge of music at the church of S. Maria de Populo, Salo, from 1571; in 1587 became maestro di cappella at Salo Cathedral and, later, chaplain and singer at the court chapel of Archduke Ferdinand II in Innsbruck (c.1589). He then entered the service of Archbishop Wolf Dietrich von Raitenau in Salzburg, where he remained until his arrest as a suspected homosexual (1591). Despite this lapse, he was highly esteemed as a composer, and later was active in Prague, Cremona, and Piacenza; was maestro di cappella in Lodi (1608) and at Piacenza Cathedral (1609).
WORKS: (all publ. in Venice unless otherwise given): **SACRED VOCAL:** *Concentus in universos psalmos . . . in vesperis omnium festorum per totum annum frequentatos, cum 3 Magnificat* for 5 and 9 Voices (1576; 2nd ed., 1588); *Motectorum liber primus* for 5 to 6 Voices (1576); *Missae, liber primus* for 5 to 6 Voices (1578); *Sacri cantus . . . liber secundus* for 5 Voices (1580); *Psalmi omnes ad vesperas per totum annum decantandi, una cum 4 Magnificat* for 8 Voices (1587); *Secundus liber missarum* for 5 Voices (1587); *Motectorum . . . liber tertius* for 5 Voices (1590); *Liber primus cantionum ecclesiasticarum* for 4 Voices (Prague, 1592; ed. in Denkmäler der Tonkunst in Österreich, CX, 1964); *Sacrae cantiones . . . liber primus* for 6 Voices (1592); *Sacri modulorum concentus* for 6 to 10 and 12 Voices (1592); *Primus liber missarum* for 6 Voices (1595); *Sacrae cantiones . . . liber secundus* for 6 Voices (1596); *Tertius liber missarum* for 5 Voices (1598); *Motectorum liber quartus* for 5 Voices (1599); *Musica super Threnos Ieremiae prophete in maiori hebdomada decantandas* for 5 Voices (1599); *Missarum liber primus* for 8 Voices (1600); *Sacrae cantiones . . . liber tertius* for 6 Voices (1601); *Sacri modulorum concentus* for 8 to 10 and 12, 15, and 16 Voices, op. 31 (1606); *Musica*

per cantare con l'organo for 1 to 3 Voices and Organ, op. 32 (1607); *Sacrarum cantionum liber primus* for 7 Voices and Basso Continuo (organ), op. 33 (1607); *Quaerimoniae cum responsoriis infra hebdomadam sanctam concinendae, et passiones pro Dominica Palmarum, et feria sexta* for 5 Voices, op. 34 (1609); various other works in contemporary collections.
SECULAR VOCAL: *Il primo libro de madrigali* for 4 Voices (1569); *Il primo libro de madrigali* for 5 Voices (1571); *Il secundo libro de madrigali* for 4 Voices (1573); *Il secundo libro de madrigali* for 5 Voices (1578); *Trionfo di musica . . . libro primo* for 6 Voices (1579); *Il terzo libro de madrigali* for 5 Voices (1587); *Il quarto libro de madrigali* for 5 Voices (1594); *Madrigali . . . libro primo* for 6 Voices (1604); *Il secondo libro de madrigali* for 6 Voices (1604).

Massarani, Renzo, Italian-born Brazilian composer; b. Mantua, March 26, 1898; d. Rio de Janeiro, March 28, 1975. He studied with Respighi at Rome's Accademia di Santa Cecilia (diploma, 1921), then was active as music director of Vittorio Podrecca's puppet theater Il Teatro dei Piccoli and as a music critic. He left Fascist Italy and settled in Rio de Janeiro in 1935, becoming a naturalized Brazilian citizen in 1945; was active as a music critic. Through the banning of his works during the Mussolini dictatorship, the havoc of World War II, and his own destruction of many scores, much of his output is not extant. His surviving music reveals a composer of considerable talent.
WORKS: **OPERAS:** *Noi due* (c.1921); *La Donna nel pozzo* (1930); *Eliduc* (1938; unfinished). **OPERINAS:** *Bianco e nero* (Rome, 1921); *Le nozze di Takiù* (Rome, 1927); *Gilbetto e Gherminella* (Rome, 1929); *I dolori della principessa Susina* (Rome, 1929). **BALLETS:** *Guerin detto il meschino* (1928); *Boè* (Bergamo, 1937); also orch. works, including a Sinfonietta (1924); *Introduzione, tema e 7 variazioni* for Small Orch. (1934); *Il molinaro* for Violin and Orch. (1935); *Squilli e danze per il 18BL* for Orch. (1937); chamber music; songs; piano pieces.
BIBL.: G. Rossi-Doria, "Laborca—M.—Rieti," *Il Pianoforte,* V (1924); A. Casella, "Jeunes et indépendants: R. M.," *La Revue Musicale,* VIII/3 (1927).

Massart, (Joseph) Lambert, eminent Belgian violinist and pedagogue; b. Liège, July 19, 1811; d. Paris, Feb. 13, 1892. He studied music with his father and brother, then violin with Ambroise Delaveux; following his debut at the Liège Theater (March 26, 1822), he received financial assistance from the King for further studies at the Paris Cons.; when Cherubini refused him admission because he was a foreigner, he found a mentor in R. Kreutzer. In 1829 he was allowed to enter the Cons., where he studied theory with P. Zimmerman and counterpoint and fugue with F.-J. Fétis. He gave many successful concerts in Paris; was prof. of violin at the Cons. (1843–90), and was also active as a chamber music artist of great distinction. He married the pianist and teacher **Louise Anglaë Masson** (b. Paris, June 10, 1827; d. there, July 26, 1887), with whom he performed regularly in chamber music settings; she succeeded Farrenc as a teacher at the Cons. in 1875. Among Massart's foremost pupils were Wieniawski, Marsick, Sarasate, and Kreisler.

Massart, Nestor-Henri-Joseph, Belgian tenor; b. Ciney, Oct. 20, 1849; d. Ostend, Dec. 19, 1899. He was an officer in the Belgian army when his remarkable voice attracted the attention of the royal family, through whose influence he was granted a leave of absence for study. He then sang with success in Brussels, Lyons, Cairo, New Orleans, San Francisco, and Mexico.

Massé, Victor (real name, **Félix-Marie**), French opera composer; b. Lorient, Morbihan, March 7, 1822; d. Paris, July 5, 1884. He was a child prodigy; was accepted at the Paris Cons. at the age of 12, and studied with Zimmerman (piano) and Halévy (composition); in 1844 he won the Grand Prix de Rome with the cantata *Le Renégat de Tanger.* While in Rome he wrote an Italian opera, *La Favorita e la schiava* (c.1845; Venice,

1855). After his return, his *romances* had great vogue, and his 1st French opera, *La Chambre gothique* (Paris, 1849), was fairly successful. In 1866 he succeeded Leborne as prof. of counterpoint at the Paris Cons.; in 1872 he was elected a member of the Institut de France, as successor to Auber. His most successful light opera was *Les Noces de Jeannette* (Paris, Feb. 4, 1853); his other operas, performed in Paris, include *La Chanteuse voilée* (Nov. 26, 1850); *Galathée* (April 14, 1852); *La Fiancée du Diable* (June 3, 1854); *Miss Fauvette* (Feb. 13, 1855); *Les Saisons* (Dec. 22, 1855); *La Reine Topaze* (Dec. 27, 1856); *Fior d'Aliza* (Feb. 5, 1866); *Le Fils du Brigadier* (Feb. 25, 1867); and *Paul et Virginie* (Nov. 15, 1876); his last opera, *Une Nuit de Cléopatre*, was performed posthumously (April 25, 1885).

BIBL.: L. Delibes, *Notice sur V. M.* (Paris, 1885); J. Ropartz, *V. M.* (Paris, 1887); H. Delaborde, *Notice sur la vie et les ouvrages de V. M.* (Paris, 1888).

Masselos, William, American pianist; b. Niagara Falls, N.Y., Aug. 11, 1920. He studied piano with Carl Friedberg at the Juilliard School of Music in N.Y. (1932–42) and ensemble playing with Felix Salmond and Louis Persinger; also music theory with Bernard Wagenaar. He made his professional debut in N.Y. in 1939; was a soloist with the N.Y. Phil. in 1952 under Mitropoulos; then played with Monteux in 1959 and with Bernstein in 1973. He served as pianist-in-residence at Indiana Univ. (1955–57); at Catholic Univ. of America in Washington, D.C. (1965–71); and at Georgia State Univ. in Atlanta (1972–75); in 1976 he was appointed to the piano faculty at Juilliard.

Massenet, Jules (-Emile-Frédéric), illustrious French composer; b. Montaud, near St.-Etienne, Loire, May 12, 1842; d. Paris, Aug. 13, 1912. At the age of 9 he was admitted to the Paris Cons.; studied with Laurent (piano), Reber (harmony), and Savard and Thomas (composition); after taking 1st prize for piano (1859), he carried off the Grand Prix de Rome with the cantata *David Rizzio* (1863). In 1878 he was appointed prof. of composition at the Cons., and at the same time was elected a member of the Académie des Beaux-Arts; he continued to teach at the Paris Cons. until 1896; among his students were Alfred Bruneau, Gabriel Pierné, and Gustave Charpentier. As a pedagogue, he exercised a profound influence on French opera. After Gounod, Massenet was the most popular French opera composer; he possessed a natural sense of graceful melody in a distinctive French style; his best operas, *Manon*, *Werther*, and *Thaïs*, enjoy tremendous popularity in France; the celebrated *Meditation* for Violin and Orch. from *Thaïs* was a regular repertoire number among violinists. He wrote an autobiography, *Mes souvenirs* (completed by X. Leroux; Paris, 1912; Eng. tr., as *My Recollections*, by H. Barnett; Boston, 1919).

WORKS: OPERAS: *La Coupe du roi de Thulé* (1866); *La Grand'tante* (Paris, April 3, 1867); *Don César de Bazan* (Paris, Nov. 30, 1872); *Bérangère et Anatole* (Paris, Feb. 1876); *Le Roi de Lahore* (Paris, April 27, 1877); *Hérodiade* (Brussels, Dec. 19, 1881); *Manon* (Paris, Jan. 19, 1884); *Le Cid* (Paris, Nov. 30, 1885); *Esclarmonde* (Paris, May 14, 1889); *Le Mage* (Paris, March 16, 1891); *Werther* (Vienna, Feb. 16, 1892); *Thaïs* (Paris, March 16, 1894); *Le Portrait de Manon* (Paris, May 8, 1894); *La Navarraise* (London, June 20, 1894); *Sapho* (Paris, Nov. 27, 1897; rev. 1909); *Cendrillon* (Paris, May 24, 1899); *Grisélidis* (Paris, Nov. 20, 1901); *Le Jongleur de Notre Dame* (Monte Carlo, Feb. 18, 1902); *Chérubin* (Monte Carlo, Feb. 14, 1905); *Ariane* (Paris, Oct. 31, 1906); *Thérèse* (Monte Carlo, Feb. 7, 1907); *Bacchus* (Paris, May 5, 1909); *Don Quichotte* (Monte Carlo, Feb. 19, 1910); *Roma* (Monte Carlo, Feb. 7, 1912); *Panurge* (Paris, April 25, 1913); *Cléopatre* (Monte Carlo, Feb. 23, 1914); *Amadis* (Monte Carlo, April 1, 1922). **INCIDENTAL MUSIC:** *Les Érinnyes* (1873); *Un drame sous Philippe II* (1875); *La Vie de Bohème* (1876); *L'Hetman* (1877); *Notré-Dame de Paris* (1879); *Michel Strogoff* (1880); *Nana-Sahib* (1883); *Théodora* (1884); *Le Crocodile* (1886); *Phèdre* (1900); *Le Grillon du foyer* (1904); *Le Manteau du Roi* (1907);

Perce-Neige et les sept gnomes (1909); *Jérusalem* (1914). **BALLETS:** *Le Carillon* (Vienna, Feb. 21, 1892); *Cigale* (Paris, Feb. 4, 1904); *Espada* (Monte Carlo, Feb. 13, 1908). **ORATORIOS:** *Marie-Magdeleine* (1873); *Eve* (1875); *La Vierge* (1880); *La Terre promise* (1900); also the choral works *Narcisse* (1877) and *Biblis* (1886); secular cantatas, including *David Rizzio* (1863); part songs; about 200 songs. **ORCH.:** 7 suites: No. 1 (1865); No. 2, *Scènes hongroises* (1871); No. 3, *Scènes dramatiques* (1873); No. 4, *Scènes pittoresques* (1874); No. 5, *Scènes napolitaines* (1876); No. 6, *Scènes de féerie* (1879); No. 7, *Scènes alsaciennes* (1881); 3 overtures: *Ouverture de concert* (1863); *Phèdre* (1873); *Brumaire* (1899); symphonic poem, *Visions* (1890); *Parade militaire* (1887); *Devant la Madone* (1897); *Marche solennelle* (1897); *Les Rosati* (1902); *Fantasie* for Cello and Orch. (1897); Concerto for Piano and Orch. (1903). He also wrote a number of works for piano, both for 2- and 4-hands. He completed and orchestrated Delibes's opera *Kassya* (Paris, March 24, 1893).

BIBL.: E. de Solenière, *M.: Étude critique et documentaire* (Paris, 1897); C. Fournier, *Étude sur le style de M.* (Amiens, 1905); L. Schneider, *M.: L'Homme, le musicien* (Paris, 1908; 2nd ed., 1926); H. Finck, *M. and His Operas* (London and N.Y., 1910); O. Séré, *M.* (Paris, 1911); special issue of *Musica* (Sept. 1912); A. Soubies, *M. historien* (Paris, 1913); A. Pougin, *M.* (Paris, 1914); C. Widor, *Notice sur la vie et les travaux de M.* (Paris, 1915); G. Jean-Aubry, "Un Mot sur M.," *La Musique française d'aujourd'hui* (Paris, 1916); H. Twitchell, "M. as a Teacher," *Musician*, XXV (1920); J. Loisel, *Manon de M.: Étude historique et critique* (Paris, 1922); C. Bouvet, *M.* (Paris, 1929); J. d'Udine, *L'Art du lied et les mélos de M.* (Paris, 1931); M. Delmas, *M., Sa vie, ses oeuvres* (Paris, 1932); A. Bruneau, *M.* (Paris, 1935); A. Morin, *J. M. et ses opéras* (Montreal, 1944); N. Boyer, *Trois musiciens français: Gounod, M., Debussy* (Paris, 1946); J. Bruyr, *M.* (Geneva, 1948); idem, *M., musicien de la belle époque* (Lyons, 1964); A. Coquis, *J. M.: L'Homme et son oeuvre* (Paris, 1965); E. Bouihol, *M.: Son rôle dans l'évolution du théâtre musical* (St.-Etienne, 1969); J. Harding, *M.* (London, 1970); O. Salzer, *The M. Compendium* (Fort Lee, N.J., 1984); G. Marschall, *M. et la fixation de la forme mélodique française* (Saarbrücken, 1988).

Masséus, Jan, Dutch composer; b. Rotterdam, Jan. 28, 1913. He studied at the Rotterdam Cons.; was a music critic in Rotterdam from 1956 to 1960; then moved to Leeuwarden, where he was director of the Music School from 1961 to 1972.

WORKS: ORCH.: Sinfonietta for Chamber Orch. (1952); Concerto for Violin and Chamber Orch. (1953); Concerto for 2 Flutes and Orch. (1956); *Cassazione*, 4 dances for Small Orch. (1960); Piano Concerto (1966); *Schermutselingen* (Skirmishes) for Chorus and Orch. (Leeuwarden, Dec. 17, 1975); *Iowa Serenade* (1981); *Skriabinade*, symphonic suite (1983); *Homo Ludens* (1986). **VOCAL:** *Gezelle liederen* for Soprano, Alto, Piano, 4-hands, and Percussion (1955); *Camphuysen-liederen* for Chorus, 3 Trumpets, 3 Trombones, and Tuba (1967); *4 Songs* for Chorus, 9 Brasses, Double Bass, and Percussion (1970); *The 7 Tile Tableaux* for Baritone, Brass Instruments, Double Bass, and Percussion (1973); *Schermutselingen* for Choir and Orch. (1975); *Het meezennestje* for Choir and Piano (1979); *Triptyque maçonnique* for Bass, Flute, and Organ (1981). **CHAMBER:** 2 violin sonatas (1946, 1950); Trio for Flute, Violin, and Piano (1948); *Quintetto* for Piano and String Quartet (1952); *Introduction and Allegro* for Oboe, Clarinet, and Piano (1952); *Partita* for Violin and Piano (1956); Flute Sonata (1957); *Serenade* for Oboe, Bassoon, Violin, and Viola (1958); *7 Minutes of Organized Sound* for 3 Winds, Guitar, and Percussion (1968). **PIANO:** *Symphonic Fantasy* for 2 Pianos (1947); *Helicon Suite* for Piano, 4-hands (1952); *Zoological Impressions* for Piano, 4-hands (1954); *Balletto piccola* for 2 Pianos (1955); *Confetti* for Piano, 4-hands (1969); *Pentatude*, 5 studies (1974).

Masson, Gérard, French composer; b. Paris, Aug. 12, 1936. He took courses in advanced techniques with Stockhausen, Pousseur, and Earle Brown in Cologne (1965–66), working along the lines of serial methods and acoustical coordination of sonorous blocs; experienced profound influence of the theory and practice of Varèse's "organized sound." His music is marked by strict constructivism, enlivened by lyric exoticism. Stravinsky, who had opportunity to examine some of Masson's scores, commended him in one of his last publ. interviews.

Works: *Pièce* for 14 Instruments and Percussion (1964); *Dans le deuil des vagues I* for 14 Instruments (Royan Festival, April 1, 1967); *Ouest I* for 10 Instruments (Vienna, April 25, 1968); *Dans le deuil des vagues II* for Orch. (London, Nov. 20, 1968); *Bleu loin* for 12 Strings (1970); *Ouest II* for Voice and Instruments (Paris, April 26, 1971); *Ici c'est la tyrannie* for Orch. (1973); String Quartet (1973); *Hymnopsie* for Orch. (1974); Piano Concerto (1977); *Pas seulement des moments, des moyens d'amour* for 2 Pianos and Orch. (1980); *Gymnastique de l'éponge* for Piano and 10 Instrumentalists (1985); *Offs* for Orch. (1988).

Masson, Paul-Marie, eminent French musicologist; b. Sète, Hérault, Sept. 19, 1882; d. Paris, Jan. 27, 1954. He studied music history with Romain Rolland at the Sorbonne in Paris; received his degree with the dissertation. *La Musique mesurée à l'Antique au XVIe siècle* (1907); subsequently enrolled in the Schola Cantorum as a pupil of d'Indy and Koechlin; was made docteur ès lettres by the Univ. of Paris in 1930 for his dissertation. *L'Opéra de Rameau* (publ. in Paris, 1930). In 1910 he was appointed prof. of the history of music at the Univ. of Grenoble, and entrusted with the organization of the Inst. Français de Florence, with the aim of publishing complete eds. of works of the early Italian masters. He taught music history at the Sorbonne (1931–52); in 1937 he was elected vice-president of the Société Française de Musicologie, and in 1949 its president. He publ. *Lullistes et Ramistes* (1912); *Musique italienne et musique française* (1912); *Berlioz* (1923); *L'Opéra de Rameau* (1930); ed. *Chants de carnaval florentins* (vol. I); contributed numerous articles to European music magazines; etc. He was also a competent composer; his works include a cantata to his own words, *Chant des peuples unis;* *Suite pastorale* for Wind Quintet; songs and piano pieces. A 2-vol. offering, *Mélanges d'histoire et d'esthétique musicale offertes à Paul-Marie Masson* (containing a brief biographical sketch and bibliography), was presented to him by his colleagues, friends, and pupils on his retirement from the Sorbonne in 1952; it was publ. posthumously (Paris, 1955).

Massonneau, Louis, German violinist and composer; b. Kassel, Jan. 10, 1766; d. Ludwigslust, Oct. 4, 1848. He was the son of a Frenchman engaged as head chef at the Kassel court. Musically gifted, he had an opportunity to study the violin and eventually received a position in the court chapel there. He subsequently held positions as Kapellmeister in various German courts. He was a prolific composer of instrumental music, including full-fledged syms. His 3rd Sym., *La Tempête et le calme* (1794), is of significance because of the seeming anticipation of Beethoven's *Pastoral* Sym. in imitating birdcalls and a storm followed by a calm. However, the score itself is merely an imitation of program music as it was practiced late in the 18th century.

Masterson, Valerie, English soprano; b. Birkenhead, June 3, 1937. She studied at the Matthay School of Music in Liverpool and the Royal College of Music in London; also in Milan. She made her debut as Frasquita in *Carmen* at the Salzburg Landestheater in 1963; then sang with the D'Oyly Carte Opera Co. in London (1966–70); became a member of the Sadler's Wells Opera in London in 1970; from 1974, sang at Covent Garden. She made her debut at the Paris Opéra as Marguerite (1978); made her U.S. debut as Violetta with the San Francisco Opera (1980). In 1988 she was made a Commander of the Order of the British Empire.

Mastilović, Danica, Yugoslav soprano; b. Negotin, Nov. 7, 1933. She was a pupil of Nikola Cvejić in Belgrade; while still a student, she sang with the Belgrade Operetta Theater (1955–59); in 1959 made her formal operatic debut as Tosca at the Frankfurt Opera, where she sang until 1969. Her guest appearances took her to Hamburg, Vienna, Munich, Bayreuth, Paris, and London. In 1963 she made her 1st U.S. appearance at the Chicago Lyric Opera as Abigaille, and on Nov. 25, 1975, her Metropolitan Opera debut in N.Y. as Elektra. She became principally known for her roles in operas by Verdi, Wagner, and Strauss.

Masur, Kurt, eminent German conductor; b. Brieg, Silesia, July 18, 1927. He received training in piano and cello at the Breslau Music School (1942–44); then studied conducting with H. Bongartz and took courses in piano and composition at the Leipzig Hochschule für Musik (1946–48). In 1948 he commenced his career with appointments as répétiteur and conductor at the Halle Landestheater; held the title of 1st conductor at the Erfurt City Theater (1951–53) and at the Leipzig City Theater (1953–55). He was conductor of the Dresden Phil. (1955–58), Generalmusikdirektor of the Mecklenburg State Theater in Schwerin (1958–60), and senior director of music at the Komische Oper in East Berlin (1960–64). In 1967 he returned to the Dresden Phil. as its music director, a position he retained until 1972. In 1970 he assumed the time-honored position of Gewandhauskapellmeister of Leipzig, where he served as music director of the Gewandhaus Orch. with notable distinction. He also made extensive tours with his orch. in Europe and abroad. In 1973 he made his British debut as a guest conductor with the New Philharmonia Orch. of London; his U.S. debut followed in 1974 as a guest conductor with the Cleveland Orch. On Oct. 9, 1981, he conducted the Beethoven 9th Sym. at the gala opening of the new Gewandhaus in Leipzig. In 1988 he was named principal guest conductor of the London Phil. In the autumn of 1989, during the period of political upheaval in East Germany, Masur played a major role as peacemaker in Leipzig. In 1990 he was appointed music director of the N.Y. Phil., to commence with the 1991–92 season. While he has earned a reputation as a faithful guardian of the hallowed Austro-German repertoire, he frequently programs contemporary scores as well.

Bibl.: D. Härtwig, *K. M.* (Leipzig, 1975); A. Fritzsch and M. Simon, *Der Gewandhauskapellmeister K. M.* (Leipzig, 1987).

Masurok, Yuri (Antonovich), Polish-born Russian baritone; b. Krasnik, July 18, 1931. He studied at the Lwow Inst. and the Moscow Cons.; won prizes in singing competitions in Prague (1960), Bucharest (1961), and Montreal (1967); in 1964 he made his debut as Eugene Onegin at the Bolshoi Theater in Moscow, where he later sang Prince Andrei in Prokofiev's *War and Peace.* He made his London debut at Covent Garden in 1975 as Anckarström, the same role he chose for his U.S. debut with the San Francisco Opera in 1977. In 1979 he sang Escamillo in Zeffirelli's production of *Carmen* at the Vienna State Opera, and also appeared there as Scarpia and Luna. His other roles include Rossini's Figaro, Giorgio Germont, and Rodrigo in *Don Carlos.*

Mata, Eduardo, Mexican conductor and composer; b. Mexico City, Sept. 5, 1942. He studied composition with Rodolfo Halffter at the National Cons. of Mexico City (1954–60); then took lessons in composition and conducting with Carlos Chávez (1960–65) and Julian Orbón (1960–63); there in 1964 he went to the Berkshire Music Center at Tanglewood, where he attended conducting seminars led by Max Rudolf, Gunther Schuller, and Erich Leinsdorf. He was conductor of the Mexican Ballet Co. (1963–64), the Guadalajara Sym. Orch. (1964–66), and the Phil. Orch. of the National Univ. of Mexico (1966–76); from 1970 to 1978 he was principal conductor of the Phoenix (Ariz.) Sym. Orch.; in 1977 he was appointed music director of the Dallas Sym. Orch.; also appeared as a guest conductor with leading orchs. throughout North America and Europe. In 1990 he became principal guest conductor of the Pittsburgh Sym. Orch. At the beginning of his career, he was active as a composer; however, he virtually abandoned composition after 1970. Among his works are 3 syms. (1962; 1963; 1966–67), the ballet music *Débora* (1963), and chamber music.

Matačić, Lovro von, noted Yugoslav conductor; b. Sušak, Feb. 14, 1899; d. Zagreb, Jan. 4, 1985. He studied with Herbst and Nedbal at the Vienna Cons.; later worked under Brechner at the Cologne Opera, where he made his debut in 1919; then conducted in Ljubljana (1924–26), Belgrade (1926–32), and Zagreb (1932–38). He was chief conductor of the Belgrade Opera (1938–42); then conducted at the Vienna Volksoper (1942–45); subsequently was Generalmusikdirektor of the Dresden State Opera (1956–58); also conducted at the (East) Berlin State Opera. He was chief conductor of the Frankfurt Opera (1961–65), the Zagreb Phil. (1970–80), and the Monte Carlo Opera (1974–78). His guest conducting engagements included appearances in Europe, the U.S., and South America.

Matěj, Josef, Czech composer; b. Brušperk, Feb. 19, 1922. He learned to play the trombone from his father; studied composition with Emil Hlobil at the Prague Cons. (1942–47) and Jaroslav Řídký at the Prague Academy of Musical Arts (1947–51). His early works are characterized by folk-song inflections of the Lachian region of his birth; after 1960 he introduced into his works some coloristic oriental elements; also made discreet use of dodecaphonic techniques.

WORKS: OPERA: *Čtyřicet dní hory Musa Dagh* (40 Days of Musa Dagh Mountain; 1979–82). ORCH.: 5 syms.: No. 1 for Soloists, Chorus, and Orch. (1953–55); No. 2 (1959–60); No. 3, *Sinfonia dramatica* (1969–70); No. 4 (1974); No. 5 (1977); 2 trombone concertos (1947–51; 1952); *Sonata da camera* for Oboe and Chamber Orch. (1955); Violin Concerto (1961); *Rhapsody* for Viola and Orch. (1962); Trumpet Concerto (1963; Prague, April 15, 1965); Concerto for Flute, Strings, and Harpsichord (1967); Concerto for Clarinet, Strings, and Piano (1970); Cello Concerto (1972; Prague, March 7, 1973); *Triple Concerto* for Trumpet, Horn, Trombone, and Chamber Orch. (1974). CHAMBER: 2 string quartets (1947–48; 1966); *Invocation* for 4 Trombones (1950); Wind Quintet (1955–56); Sonata for Trombone and Strings (1965); Sonata for Violin and Piano (1971); Music for 5 Brass Instruments, *Omaggio à Leoš Janáček* (1978); *Canzona* for Trumpet and Piano (1980); *Fantasia* for Organ (1981); *Inventions* for Flute and Piano (1982–83); also choral works; songs.

Materna, Amalie, remarkable Austrian soprano; b. St. Georgen, Styria, July 10, 1844; d. Vienna, Jan. 18, 1918. She was 1st a church singer; married the actor Karl Friedrich; together they sang in light opera. She made her debut in Graz in 1865; in 1869 she 1st sang at the Vienna Court Opera as Selika, and remained on its staff until 1894. Her dramatic talent, powerful voice, and beauteous features attracted the notice of Wagner, who selected her for the role of Brünnhilde in the 1st Bayreuth Festival of 1876; the following year she sang at the Wagner festival in London, under the composer's own direction, and also sang in Wagner festivals in N.Y., Chicago, and Cincinnati. From 1882 to 1891 she sang regularly at Bayreuth. Her American opera debut took place on Jan. 5, 1885, as Elisabeth in *Tannhäuser* during the 1st season of German opera at the Metropolitan Opera in N.Y.; in 1894 she became a member of Walter Damrosch's German company in N.Y. In 1902 she returned to Vienna and opened a singing studio there.

Mather, Bruce, Canadian pianist, teacher, and composer; b. Toronto, May 9, 1939. He studied composition with Ridout, Morawetz, and Weinzweig at the Royal Cons. of Music of Toronto (B.Mus., 1959); also had training in piano from Alberto Guerrero; attended the Aspen (Colo.) Music School as a piano student of Alexandre Uninsky (summers 1957–58); then went to Paris and studied at the Cons. with Simone Plé-Caussade, Messiaen, and Milhaud (1959–61); also studied composition with Roy Harris and conducting with Pierre Boulez in Paris; continued his musical education with Leland Smith at Stanford Univ. (M.A., 1964) and at the Univ. of Toronto (Ph.D., 1967). In 1966 he joined the faculty of McGill Univ. in Montreal. He also pursued a career as a pianist, winning approbation as an interpreter of contemporary scores; appeared in duo-piano concerts with his wife, Pierrette LePage. In 1979 he won the Jules Léger Prize for his *Musique pour Champigny.* His music follows the path of unprejudiced modernism, extend-

ing from neo-Classicism to Expressionism and comprising elements of serialism and microtonality.

WORKS: Violin Sonata (1956); 2 *Songs,* after Thomas Hardy, for Bass-baritone and Small Orch. (1956); *Venice,* after Byron, for Soprano, Clarinet, Cello, and Piano (1957); 3 *Songs,* to poems of Robert Graves, for Soprano and String Orch. (1957–58); Concerto for Piano and Chamber Orch. of Wind Quintet and String Quartet (Aspen, Aug. 20, 1958, composer soloist); *Elegy* for Saxophone and Strings (1959); *Cycle Rilke* for Voice and Guitar (1959–60); *Étude* for Clarinet (1962); *Orphée* for Soprano, Piano, and Percussion (1963); *Symphonic Ode* for Orch. (Toronto, March 28, 1965); *Orchestra Piece 1967* (Toronto, Jan. 11, 1967); *Ombres* for Orch. (Montreal, May 1, 1968); 5 *Madrigals: I* for Soprano, Alto, Flute, Mandolin, Harp, Violin, and Cello (1967); *II* for Soprano, Alto, Flute, Harp, Violin, Viola, and Cello (1968); *III* for Alto, Marimba, Harp, and Piano (1971); *IV* for Soprano, Flute, Piano, and Tape (1972); *V* for Soprano, Alto, and 17 Instrumentalists (1972–73; rev. 1980); *Music for Vancouver* for Small Orch. (1969; rev. 1980); 2-Piano Sonata (1970); *Musique pour Rouen* for String Orch. (1970–71); *Mandola* for Mandolin and Piano (1971); *Music for Organ, Horn and Gongs* (1973); *In memoriam Alexandre Uninsky* for Piano (1974); *Eine kleine Bläsermusik* for Wind Quintet 1975); *Au Château de Pompairain* for Mezzo-soprano and Orch. (1976; Ottawa, May 4, 1977); *Musique pour Champigny* for Soprano, Mezzo-soprano, Contralto, Clarinet, Horn, Harp, Piano, and Percussion (1976); *Clos de Vougeot* for 4 Percussionists (1977); *Ausone* for 11 Instruments (1979); *Musigny* for Orch. (1980); *Barbaresco* for Viola, Cello, and Double Bass (Metz, Oct. 7, 1984); *Scherzo* for Orch. (1987); *Dialogue pour trio basso et orchestre* (1988); songs.

Mathews, Max (Vernon), American computer scientist and composer; b. Columbus, Nebr., Nov. 13, 1926. He studied electrical engineering at the Calif. Inst. of Technology (B.S., 1950) and at the Mass. Inst. of Technology (M.S., 1952; D.Sc., 1954). He joined the Bell Telephone Laboratories in Murray Hill, N.J. (1955), and developed its MUSIC programs, the 1st computer sound-synthesis languages; with other scientists, he developed its GROOVE (Generated Real-time Operations on Voltage-controlled Equipment) system; he also developed electronic violins. He wrote the book *The Technology of Computer Music* (1969). His compositions for computer include *May Carol II* (1960); *Numerology* (1960); *The 2nd Law* (1961); *Masquerades* (1963); *Slider* (1965); *International Lullaby* (1966; in collaboration with O. Fujimura); *Swansong* (1966).

Mathews, W(illiam) S(mythe) B(abcock), American organist, teacher, editor, and writer on music; b. London, N.H., May 8, 1837; d. Denver, April 1, 1912. He studied music in Boston; occupied various teaching posts in Georgia, North Carolina, Alabama, Chicago, and Denver; was organist in Chicago churches; ed. the *Musical Independent* (1868–71); was music critic of the *Chicago Tribune* (1878–86); in 1891, founded and ed. the monthly magazine *Music* (until 1902).

WRITINGS: *An Outline of Musical Form* (Boston, 1868); *How to Understand Music* (Philadelphia, 1888); ed. *A Hundred Years of Music in America* (Chicago, 1889); *A Popular History of the Art of Music* (Philadelphia, 1891); with E. Liebling, *Pronouncing and Defining Dictionary of Music* (Cincinnati, 1896); *Music, Its Ideals and Methods* (Philadelphia, 1897); *The Masters and Their Music* (Philadelphia, 1898); *The Great in Music* (Chicago, 1900–1902); also several other pedagogical works.

BIBL.: R. Groves, *The Life and Works of W.S.B. M.* (diss., Univ. of Iowa, 1981); J. Clarke, *Prof. W.S.B. M. (1837–1912): Self-made Musician of the Gilded Age (Illinois)* (diss., Univ. of Minnesota, 1983).

Mathias, Franz Xaver, Alsatian organist and composer; b. Dinsheim, July 16, 1871; d. Strasbourg, Feb. 2, 1939. He studied in Germany with Hugo Riemann; was organist at the Strasbourg Cathedral (1898–1908); then a prof. of sacred music at the Univ. of Strasbourg. Among his works, the best known is the oratorio *Mystère de Joseph,* containing an instrumental *Ballet égyptien.* He also wrote an oratorio of gigantic dimensions, *Urbem Virgo tuam serva* for 2 Choruses (with the assistance of a "crowd" of many voices); 28 cantatas; several masses; Psalms; motets; many organ pieces; publ. a manual of accompaniment of Gregorian chant.

Mathias, Georges (-Amédée-Saint-Clair), French pianist, teacher, and composer; b. Paris, Oct. 14, 1826; d. there, Oct. 14, 1910. As a youth he had the privilege of taking piano lessons with Chopin; studied composition with Halévy and others at the Paris Cons.; in 1862 he was appointed prof. of piano there, and taught until 1893. He composed 2 piano concertos; 6 piano trios; 5 *morceaux symphoniques* for Piano and Strings; a number of studies, under the promising titles *Études de style et de mécanisme* and *Études de genre;* also attractive piano pieces for 2- and 4-hands; his overtures and other symphonic works are less interesting.

Mathias, William (James), Welsh composer; b. Whitland, Carmarthenshire, Nov. 1, 1934. He studied at the Univ. College of Wales, Aberystwyth (B.Mus., 1956); then at the Royal Academy of Music in London with Lennox Berkeley (composition) and Peter Katin (piano). In 1965 he was elected a Fellow of the Royal Academy of Music; was awarded the D.Mus. degree by the Univ. of Wales in 1966; in 1968 he received the Bax Soc. Prize for composition. He was a lecturer in music at the Univ. College of North Wales, Bangor (1959–68); then senior lecturer in composition at the Univ. of Edinburgh (1968–69); subsequently prof. of music at the Univ. College of North Wales, Bangor (from 1970). In 1985 he was made a Commander of the Order of the British Empire. His style of composition may be described as civilized modernism, sophisticated but free of exhibitionistic affectation, optimistically tonal but occasionally somber, brilliantly idiomatic in instrumentation, and unequivocally populist in its euphonious appeal. **Works: opera:** *The Servants* (Cardiff, Sept. 15, 1980). **orch.:** 3 piano concertos: No. 1 (1955); No. 2 (1960); No. 3 (Swansea, Oct. 15, 1968); *Divertimento* for String Orch. (London, March 1958); *Music for Strings* (London, Dec. 3, 1961); *Dance Overture* (Wales, Aug. 10, 1962); *Invocation and Dance* (Cardiff, March 1, 1962); *Serenade* for Small Orch. (Carmarthen, June 5, 1962); Concerto (Liverpool, March 29, 1966); 2 syms.: No. 1 (Llandaff Festival, June 23, 1966); No. 2, *Summer Music* (Liverpool, May 14, 1983); Sinfonietta (Leicester, May 1, 1967); *Litanies* (BBC, Feb. 28, 1968); *Festival Overture* (Caernarvon, June 1970); Harp Concerto (Llandaff Festival, June 1, 1970); *Intrada* (Aberystwyth, April 8, 1971); Concerto for Harpsichord, Strings, and Percussion (Fishguard Festival, Aug. 26, 1971); *Holiday Overture* (Llandudno, Sept. 30, 1971); *Celtic Dances* (1972); *Laudi* (Llandaff Festival, June 11, 1973); Clarinet Concerto (North Wales Music Festival, Sept. 22, 1975); *Vistas* (Swansea Festival, Oct. 25, 1975); *Dance Variations* (London, July 1, 1977); *Melos* (Abbotsholme, April 24, 1977); *Helios* (Llandaff Festival, June 16, 1977); *Requiescat* (Portmadoc, Feb. 9, 1978); *Reflections on a Theme of Tomkins* (1981); Organ Concerto (London, Sept. 12, 1984); Horn Concerto (Llandaff Festival, June 9, 1984); *Anniversary Dances* (Bangor, Feb. 16, 1985); *Carnival of Wales* (Cardiff, July 24, 1987); Violin Concerto (1989). **chamber:** 2 violin sonatas (1962, 1984); Quintet for Flute, Oboe, Clarinet, Horn, and Bassoon (1963); Divertimento for Flute, Oboe, and Piano (1964); 3 string quartets (1968, 1981, 1986); Concertino for Flute or Recorder, Oboe, Bassoon, and Harpsichord or Piano (1974); *Zodiac Trio* for Flute, Viola, and Harp (1976); Sonatina for Flute and Piano (1986); *Soundings* for Brass Quintet (1988); piano pieces, including 2 sonatas (1964, 1970); organ pieces; also choruses; songs; anthems; canticles; carols.

Mathieu, Émile (-Louis-Victor), Belgian composer and pedagogue; b. Lille (of Belgian parents), Oct. 18, 1844; d. Ghent, Aug. 20, 1932. He studied at the Brussels Cons. with Fétis and Auguste Dupont; in 1869, 1871, and 1873, he won the 2nd Grand Prix de Rome in Brussels. He taught at Louvain (1867–73); then was in Paris as a theater conductor; returning to Louvain, he became director of the music school there (1881–

98); in 1898 was appointed director of the Ghent Cons. He retired in 1924. **Works:** Cantatas: *Torquato Tasso's dood* (1869); *La Dernière Nuit de Faust* (1870); *Le Songe de Colomb* (1872); *Debout, Peuple* (1894); *Les Bois* (1894); comic operas: *L'Échange* (Liège, 1863); *Georges Dandin* (Brussels, 1877); *La Bernoise* (Brussels, 1880); grand operas: *Richilde* (Brussels, 1888) and *L'Enfance de Roland* (1895); also Violin Concerto (1899); other instrumental works; symphonic poems: *Noces féodales* (1873); *Le Lac* (1874); etc.

Mathieu, Rodolphe, Canadian composer; b. Grondines, Portneuf, Quebec, July 10, 1890; d. Montreal, June 29, 1962. He moved to Montreal at the age of 16; had composition lessons from Alexis Contant; then went to Paris, where he took courses with d'Indy and Aubert at the Schola Cantorum (1920–27); in 1927 he returned to Montreal. His music is cast in a modern French manner. **Works:** *Les Yeux noirs* for Tenor and Piano (1911); *Chevauchée* for Piano (1911); *3 Preludes* for Piano (1912–15); *Un Peu d'ombre* for Tenor and Chamber Orch. (1913); String Quartet (1920); Piano Trio (1921); *12 études modernes* for Violin (1920–23); *Harmonie du soir* for High Voice, Violin, and Orch. (1924); Piano Sonata (1927); Violin Sonata (1928); *2 poèmes* for Voice and String Quartet (1928); *Lève-toi, Canadien* for Chorus and Orch. (Montreal, Oct. 25, 1934); Piano Quintet (1942).

Mathis, Edith, admired Swiss soprano; b. Lucerne, Feb. 11, 1938. She studied in Zürich and Lucerne, where she made her operatic debut at the age of 18 in *Die Zauberflöte;* was subsequently engaged at the Cologne Opera (1959–62), the Salzburg Festival (1960), and Glyndebourne (1962). In 1963 she joined the staff of the Deutsche Oper in Berlin; from 1960 to 1975, was a member of the Hamburg State Opera. She made her debut at the Metropolitan Opera in N.Y. on Jan. 19, 1970, as Pamina. Although best known for her Mozart roles, she also is a fine Mélisande and Sophie; also appears in contemporary operas and is widely respected as a concert singer. She is married to **Bernhard Klee.**

Mathis, Johnny (John Royce), black American singer of popular music; b. San Francisco, Sept. 30, 1935. He received classical vocal training before deciding upon a singing career as a popular vocalist; appeared as a nightclub singer; subsequently made tours of the U.S., Europe, Africa, and the Far East. He was particularly adept in renditions of pseudoromantic ballads such as *Misty, Chances Are, The 12th of Never,* and *Wonderful, Wonderful.*

Mátray (real name, **Róthkrepf**), **Gábor,** Hungarian music scholar, teacher, and composer; b. Nágykáta, Nov. 23, 1797; d. Budapest, July 17, 1875. He studied law and at the same time learned to compose. In 1812, at the age of 15, he wrote the earliest surviving Hungarian piece of stage music, *Cserni György;* also publ. a general history of music (1828–32), the 1st such history in the Hungarian language; wrote treatises on folk music and Gypsy music, and made arrangements of Hungarian folk songs. His own works (for piano, guitar, and chorus) are mostly salon music, but some of them are historically important because of the use of native rhythms.

Matsudaira, Yoriaki, Japanese composer of the avant-garde, son of **Yoritsuné Matsudaira;** b. Tokyo, March 27, 1931. He studied science at the Tokyo Metropolitan Univ., completing his graduate studies in 1958; then taught physics and biology at Rikkyo Univ. in Tokyo. He was self-taught as a composer; was active with "Group 20.5," a composing collective he founded. **Works:** *Variations* for Piano Trio (1957); *Speed Coefficient* for Flute, Piano, and Keyboard Percussion (1958); *Variation on the Theme of Noh* for Flute, Clarinet, 3 Percussionists, Piano, Violin, Viola, and Cello (1960); *Orbits I–III* for Flute, Clarinet, and Piano (1960); *Instruction* for Piano (1961); *Configuration* for Chamber Orch. (1961–63; Tokyo, March 29, 1967); *Co-Action I & II* for Cello and Piano (1962); *Parallax* for Flute, Oboe, Clarinet, Bassoon, and Saxophone (1963); *Tangent '64* for Tape (1964); *Rhymes for Gazelloni* for Flute (1965–66); *Distribution* for String Quartet and Ring Modular (1966–67); *What's Next!* for Soprano and 2 Noisemakers (1967; rev. 1971); *Alternation for Combo* for Trumpet, Percussion, Piano, Double Bass, and Ring Modulator (1967); *Assemblage* for Tape (1968); *Assemblage* for Female Voice and Ring Modulator (1968); *Wand Waves* for Narrator and Tape (1970); *Allotropy* for Piano (1970); *Why Not?* for 4–5 Operators with Live Electronics (1970); *"The Symphony"* for 14 Players (1971); *Gradation* for Violin, Viola, and Oscillator (1971); *Substitution* for Soprano and Piano (1972); *Messages* for Wind Orch. and Tape (1972); *Trichromantic Form* for Harp (1973); *Where Now?* for 3 Dancers and Ensemble (1973); *Transient '74* for Guitar, Organ, Harp, and Percussion (1974); *Shift* for Tape and Dance (1976); *Coherency for Ark* for Flute, Clarinet, Percussion, Harp, and Keyboard (1976); *Brilliancy* for Flute and Piano (1978).

Matsudaira, Yoritsuné, Japanese composer, father of **Yoriaki Matsudaira;** b. Tokyo, May 5, 1907. He studied composition privately with Kōsuke Komatsu; also received instruction from A. Tcherepnin during the latter's sojourn in Japan (1935); won the Weingartner Prize in 1936 and the International Composition Competition Prize in Rome in 1962. His music amalgamates old Japanese modalities with modern harmonies.

WORKS: ORCH.: *Theme and Variations* on popular Japanese songs (Tokyo, Dec. 17, 1939); *Ancient Japanese Dance* (Berlin, Oct. 9, 1953); *Negative and Positive Figures* (Tokyo, May 28, 1954); *Figures sonores* (1956; Zürich Festival, June 1, 1957); *U-Mai,* ancient dance (Darmstadt, Sept. 11, 1958); *Samai* for Chamber Orch. (Rome Festival, June 15, 1959); *Dance Suite* for 3 Orchs. (Donaueschingen, Oct. 18, 1959); *Bugaku* for Chamber Orch. (Palermo, Oct. 6, 1962); *3 Movements* for Piano and Orch. (Stockholm, March 20, 1964); *Ritual Dance and Finale* (1963); *Piano Concerto* (Madrid Festival, May 20, 1965); *Dialogo coreografico* for 2 Pianos and Chamber Ensemble (1966; Royan, April 3, 1967); *Mouvements circulatoires* for 2 Chamber Orchs. (Graz Festival, Oct. 10, 1972); *Prelude, Interlude and Aprèslude* (1973); *Rhapsody on a Gagaku Theme* for Chamber Ensemble (Washington, D.C., Oct. 30, 1983). **VOCAL:** *Metamorphoses on "Saibara"* (an old Japanese melody) for Soprano and 18 Instruments (Haifa Festival, June 3, 1954); *Koromogae* (Love Song) for Soprano and 19 Instruments (1954; Venice, Dec. 11, 1968); *Katsura* for Soprano, Harp, Harpsichord, Guitar, and Percussion (1957; rev. 1967); *Roei "Jisei"* (2 Stars in Vega) for Voice and Instrumental Ensemble (1967). **CHAMBER:** Sonatina for Flute and Clarinet (1940); Cello Sonata (1942); Concerto for 2 Solo Pianos (1946); Piano Trio (1948); 2 string quartets (1948, 1951); 2 violin sonatas (1948, 1952); Suite for Flute, Bassoon, and Piano (1950); Piano Sonata (1953); *Somaksah* for Flute (1961); *Serenata* for Flute and 10 Instruments (1963); *Concerto da camera* for Harpsichord, Harp, and Instrumental Ensemble (1964); *Music* for 17 Instruments (1967); *Portrait B* for 2 Pianos and 2 Percussionists (1967–68); *12 pezzi facili* for Piano (1968–69).

Matsumura, Teizo, Japanese composer; b. Kyoto, Jan. 15, 1929. He studied with Tsuneharu Takahashi (piano) and Toshio Nagahiro (harmony) in Kyoto; then went to Tokyo, where he had lessons in harmony, counterpoint, and composition with Tomojiro Ikenouchi and in composition with Akira Ifukube; subsequently taught at the Tokyo Geijutsu Daigaku (from 1970). He rebelled early on against dodecaphonism, the then-prevailing musical ideology in Japan, turning instead for his inspiration to the rich historical inheritance of Asian culture; several of his works, i.e., his Sym. (1965) and *Prélude pour orchestre* (1968), commingle traditional music of India, Tibet, and Bali. Orphaned at a young age and later battling with life-threatening tuberculosis (1950–55), Matsumura developed a deep-seated spirituality, which permeates his work.

WORKS: *Introduction and Allegro Concertante* for Orch. (1955); *Achime* for Soprano, Percussion, and 11 Players (1957);

Crytogam for Chamber Ensemble (1958); *Music for String Quartet and Piano* (1962); Sym. (1965); *Flute of Evil Passions,* mono opera for Baritone, Men's Chorus, and Orch. (1965); *Prélude pour orchestre* (1968); *Deux Berceuses à la Grèce* for Piano (1969); *Totem Ritual* for Soprano, Chorus, and Orch. (1969); *Apsaras* for Women's Voices and Small Orch. (1969); *Poem I* for Shakuhachi and Koto (1969) and *II* for Shakuhachi (1972); *Courtyard of Apsaras* for Flute, Violin, and Piano (1971); *2 Poems by the Prince of Karu* for Soprano and Piano (1973); 2 piano concertos (1973, 1978); *Hymn to Aurora* for Chorus and Chamber Ensemble (1978); *The Drifting Reed,* musical fantasy (1979); *Poème pour shinobue et biwa* (1979); *Fantasy* for Koto (1980); *Poème pour alto saxophone et biwa* (1980); Cello Concerto (1984); *Air of Prayer* for Koto (1984) and for Cello (1985); *The Patient Waters (A Lyric Tragedy),* musical fantasy (1985); *Spelmatica* for Violin (1985); *Pneuma* for Strings (1987); Piano Trio (1987); *Hommage à Akira Ifukube* for Orch. (1988); *Offrande orchestrale* (1989).

Matsushita, Shin-ichi, Japanese composer; b. Osaka, Oct. 1, 1922. He graduated in mathematics from the Kyushu Univ. in Fukuoka in 1947; concurrently studied music. In 1958 he went to work in an electronic music studio in Osaka; taught both mathematics and music at the Univ. of Osaka City. In his music he follows cosmopolitan modernistic techniques, mostly of a functional, pragmatic nature.

WORKS: *Ouvrage symphonique* for Piano and Orch. (1957); *Correlazioni per 3 gruppi* for 12 Players (1958); *Composizione da camera per 8* (1958); *Isomorfismi* for Orch. (1958); *5 tempi per undici* for 11 Instruments (1958–59); *Le Croître noir* for Chorus, Electronic, and Musique Concrète Sounds, Piano, Harp, and Percussion (Osaka, Nov. 14, 1959); *Faisceaux* for Flute, Cello, and Piano (1959); *Jet Pilot* for Narrator, Orch., String Quartet, and Female Chorus (1960); 2 radio operas: *Comparing Notes on a Rainy Night* and *Amayo* (both 1960); *Sinfonia "Le Dimensioni"* (1961); *Cube for 3 Players* for Flute, Celesta, and Viola (1961); *Successioni* for Chamber Orch. (Radio Palermo, Oct. 1, 1962); *Meta-Musique* No. 1 for Piano, Horn, and Percussion (1962); *Uro* for Chamber Ensemble (1962); *Sinfonia "Vita"* (1963); *Musique* for Soprano and Chamber Ensemble (Osaka, Sept. 14, 1964); *Fresque sonore* for 7 Instruments (1964); *Hexahedra A, B* and *C* for Piano and Percussion (1964–65); *Spectra 1–4* for Piano (1964; 1967; for 2 Players, 1971; 1971); *Kristalle* for Piano Quartet (1966); *Alleluja in der Einsamkeit* for Guitar, Piccolo, and 2 Percussionists (1967); *Serenade* for Flute and Orch. (1967); *Subject 17* for Piano, Percussion, Horn, Trumpet, and Trombone (San Francisco, Oct. 31, 1967); *Sinfonie Pol* for Orch., Harp, and Piano (1968); *Haleines astrales* for Chamber Ensemble (1968); *Astrate Atem* for Orch., Harp, and Piano (1969–70); *Requiem on the Place of Execution* for 4 Soloists, Chorus, Orch., and Tape (1970); *Musik von der Liebe* for Flute, Vibraphone, Harp, Piano, Electone, and Tape (1970); *Musik der Steinzeit* for Violin, Ondes Martenot, Tape, and the sound of Cracking Stone (1970); *Ostinato obbligato* for Piano (1972).

Mattei, Tito, Italian pianist, conductor, and composer; b. Campobasso, near Naples, May 24, 1841; d. London, March 30, 1914. He studied with Parisi, Conti, and Thalberg; made rapid progress, so that at the age of 11 he obtained a nominal appointment as "professore" of the Accademia di Santa Cecilia in Rome; received a gold medal for playing before Pope Pius XI, and was appointed pianist to the King of Italy. About 1865 he settled in London, where he was active principally as an opera conductor. He composed the operas *Maria di Gand* (London, 1880); *The Grand Duke* (London, 1889); *La Prima Donna* (London, 1889); a ballet, *The Spider and the Fly* (London, 1893); songs; piano pieces.

Matteis, Nicola, Italian violinist and composer, who settled in London in 1672, and publ. there 4 books of violin pieces (airs, preludes, fugues, allemandes, sarabands, etc.) under varying Italian and English titles; also *The False Consonances of Musick, or, Instructions for playing a true Base upon the Guitarre, with Choice Examples and Clear Directions to enable* *any man in a short time to play all Musicall Ayres,* etc. In addition, he wrote *A Collection of New Songs* (2 vols., London, 1696). His son, also named Nicola (d. 1749), lived in Vienna and in Shrewsbury, England. He was Burney's teacher.

BIBL.: P. Nettl, "An English Musician at the Court of Charles VI in Vienna," *Musical Quarterly* (April 1942).

Matteo da Perugia, outstanding Italian composer; b. Perugia, date unknown; d. before Jan. 13, 1418. A *musicus,* he was the 1st *magister capellae* and the only *cantor* at Milan Cathedral (1402–7; 1414–16); was also in the service of Petros Cardinal Filargo di Candia of Pavia, later the Antipope Alexander V. His extant works include 5 Glorias, a motet, 4 ballades, 7 virelais, 10 rondeaux, a canon, and 2 ballate. See F. Fano, ed., *La cappella musicale del duomo di Milano,* I: *Le origini e il primo maestro di cappella: Matteo da Perugia,* Istituzioni e Monumenti dell'Arte Musicale Italiana, new series, I (1956), and W. Apel, ed., *French Secular Compositions of the Fourteenth Century,* Corpus Mensurabilis Musicae, LIII/1–3 (1970–72).

BIBL.: H. Bessler, "Hat Matheus de Perusio Epoche gemacht?," *Die Musikforschung,* VIII (1955); C. Sartori, "M. de P. e Bertrand Feragut," *Acta Musicologica,* XXVIII (1956).

Mattfeld, Julius, American librarian, organist, and musicographer; b. N.Y., Aug. 8, 1893; d. there, July 31, 1968. He studied at the N.Y. German Cons. In 1910 he joined the staff of the N.Y. Public Library; resigned in 1926 to become music librarian of NBC (until 1929); then was librarian of CBS; was also organist of the Fordham Lutheran Church in N.Y. (1915–32). He publ. *The Folk Music of the Western Hemisphere* (1925); *A Hundred Years of Grand Opera in New York, 1825–1925* (1927); *Variety Music Cavalcade, 1620–1950* (N.Y., 1952; rev. 1962); *A Handbook of American Operatic Premieres, 1731–1962* (Detroit, 1963).

Mattfeld, Victor Henry, American organist, conductor, music editor, and teacher; b. Bunceton, Mo., Sept. 1, 1917. He studied at the Univ. of Chicago (B.A. in psychology, 1942), the American Cons. of Music, Chicago (B.Mus., 1944; M.Mus., 1946, both in organ), and Yale Univ. (Ph.D. in music history, 1960); also studied orch. conducting privately with Malko (1945–47) and choral conducting at the Berkshire Music Center at Tanglewood (1946). He was active as a church organist and music director in Chicago, N.Y., New Haven, and Boston (1938–63); was ed. in chief of E.C. Schirmer Music Co. (1956–58) and the Ione Press (1963–68); taught at the American Cons. of Music (1945–47), Yale Univ. (1952–55), and the Mass. Inst. of Technology (1957–66) before becoming associated with N.Y.'s Richmond College (1967–76) and College of Staten Island (1976–82). He publ. *Georg Rhaw's Publications for Vespers* (1966). He married the musicologist **Jacquelyn Mattfeld** (b. Baltimore, Oct. 5, 1925; she studied at Goucher College (B.A., 1948) and Yale Univ. (Ph.D., 1959); taught at the Mass. Inst. of Technology (1963–65), Sarah Lawrence College (1965–71), and Brown Univ. (from 1971).

Matthaei, Karl, Swiss organist and musicologist; b. Olten, April 23, 1897; d. Winterthur, Feb. 8, 1960. He studied piano and organ at the Basel Cons.; also took courses in musicology there with Karl Nef; then went to Leipzig, where he pursued his organ studies with Straube (1920–23); subsequently was organist in Wadenswil; from 1925, was organist and director of the Winterthur music school; from 1938 served also as organist of the city church. He ed. *J. Pachelbel: Ausgewählte Orgelwerke* (4 vols., Kassel, 1928–36), *M. Praetorius: Sämtliche Orgelwerke* (Wolfenbüttel, 1930), and *J.J. Froberger: Ausgewählte Orgelwerke* (Kassel, 1932). He also ed. a *Bach-Gedenkschrift* (Zürich, 1950); publ. the books *Vom Orgelspiel* (Leipzig, 1936) and *Die Baugeschichte der Stadtkirchenorgel in Winterthur* (Winterthur, 1941).

BIBL.: *K. M.: Gedenkschrift* (Winterthur, 1960).

Matthay, Tobias (Augustus), eminent English pianist and pedagogue; b. London, Feb. 19, 1858; d. High Marley, near Haslemere, Surrey, Dec. 14, 1945. He began to play the piano at the age of 6; was taught by private teachers; in 1871 he entered the Royal Academy of Music in London as a pupil of Dorrell (piano); won the Sterndale Bennett scholarship, and continued to study piano (with Macfarren); took courses with Sterndale Bennett, and after the latter's death (1875) completed his studies with Ebenezer Prout and Arthur Sullivan. He subsequently was on the faculty of the Royal Academy of Music as a sub-prof. (1876–80) and full prof. (1880–1925); in 1900 he established his own piano school in London. The Matthay System, as his teaching method was known, stressed mastery of both the psychological and physiological aspects of piano performance; it became famous not only in England but on the Continent and in America. Students flocked to him and carried his method abroad. Matthay also composed *In May,* an overture; Piano Quartet; numerous piano pieces; songs.

WORKS (all publ. in London unless otherwise given): *The Art of Touch in All Its Diversity* (1903); *The First Principles of Pianoforte Playing* (1905; 2nd ed., rev., 1906); *Relaxation Studies . . . in Pianoforte Playing* (Leipzig, 1908); *Some Commentaries on the Teaching of Pianoforte Technique* (1911); *The Child's First Steps in Pianoforte Playing* (1912); *The Forearm Rotation Principle in Pianoforte Playing* (1912); *Musical Interpretation* (1913); *On Method in Teaching* (1921); *An Epitome of the Laws of Pianoforte Technique* (1931); *The Visible and Invisible in Pianoforte Technique* (1932; 2nd ed., rev., 1947); etc.

BIBL.: J. Henderson Matthay, *The Life and Work of T. M.* (London, 1945); A. Coviello, *What M. Meant* (London, 1948); R. Hoare, "What Did M. Mean?," *Piano Teacher,* IV (1962).

Mattheson, Johann, famous German composer, music theorist, and lexicographer; b. Hamburg, Sept. 28, 1681; d. there, April 17, 1764. He received a thorough education in the liberal arts at the Johanneum; acquired proficiency in English, Italian, and French; studied music there with the Kantor, Joachim Gerstenbüttel. He received private musical instruction studying keyboard music and composition with J.N. Hanff; also took singing lessons and learned to play the violin, gamba, oboe, flute, and lute. At a very early age he began to perform as an organist in the churches of Hamburg; also sang in the chorus at the Hamburg Opera. He graduated from the Johanneum in 1693; concurrently took courses in jurisprudence. He then served as a page at the Hamburg court of Graf von Güldenlöw, who held the title of Vice-König of Norway. He made his debut as a singer in a female role with the Hamburg Opera during its visit to Kiel in 1696; from 1697 to 1705 he was a tenor with the Hamburg Opera, conducted rehearsals, and also composed works for it. He befriended Handel in 1703; together they journeyed to Lübeck to visit Buxtehude, who was about to retire as organist, and to apply for his post. The unwritten requirement for the job was marriage to one of Buxtehude's five daughters, whose attractions seemed dubious; both Mattheson and Handel declined the opportunity. In 1704 a violent quarrel broke out between Mattheson and Handel during a performance of Mattheson's opera *Cleopatra* at the Hamburg Opera. Mattheson sang the principal male role of Antonius while Handel acted as conductor from the keyboard in the capacity of maestro al cembalo. Upon the conclusion of his role on stage, Mattheson asked Handel to let him assume the position at the keyboard, since he was the composer. Handel refused and an altercation ensued. The dispute was finally decided by a duel, during which Mattheson broke his sword on a metal button of Handel's coat, or so at least the most credible report of the episode went. They were, however, soon reconciled and remained friends. In 1704 Mattheson became the tutor of Cyrill Wich, the son of Sir John Wich, British envoy at Hamburg. In 1706 he became secretary to Sir John; when the younger Wich became ambassador in 1715, he retained Mattheson as secretary, a position he held for most of his life. During this period Mattheson diligently studied English politics, law, and economics, thereby adding to his many other accomplishments. In 1715 he assumed the post of music director of the Hamburg Cathedral. He composed much sacred music for performance there, including many oratorios. In

1719 he also became Kapellmeister to the court of the duke of Holstein. Growing deafness compelled him to resign his post at the Cathedral in 1728. In 1741 he was given the title of legation secretary to the duke of Holstein, and was made counsel in 1744. Mattheson's output as a composer was substantial, but little of his music has survived. Of his major compositions, only the MSS of one of his operas, *Cleopatra* (modern ed., by G. Buelow in *Das Erbe deutscher Musik*, LXIX, 1975), and one of his oratorios, *Das Lied des Lammes* (modern ed. by B. Cannon, Madison, Wis., 1971), are extant; the bulk of his MSS kept in the Hamburg Stadtbibliothek were destroyed during the hideous "fire-storm" bombing of Hamburg during World War II. However, most of his numerous literary writings are preserved. Outstanding among his books is *Der vollkommene Capellmeister* (1739), an original theoretical treatise on the state of music in his era. Also valuable are his *Grosse General-Bass-Schule* (1731; based on his earlier work *Exemplarische Organisten-Probe*, 1719) and *Kleine General-Bass-Schule* (1735). Of great historical value is his biographical dictionary, *Grundlage einer Ehren-Pforte . . .* (1740), which contains 149 entries. Many of the entries on musicians of his own time were compiled from information provided by the subjects themselves, and several prepared complete autobiographical accounts for his lexicon.

WRITINGS (all publ. in Hamburg): *Das neu-eröffnete Orchestre, oder gründliche Anleitung, wie ein "galant homme" einen vollkommenen Begriff von der Hoheit und Würde der edlen Musik erlangen möge* (1713); *Das beschützte Orchestre* (1717); *Exemplarische Organisten-Probe im Artikel vom General-Bass* (1719; publ. in an enl. ed. as *Grosse-General-Bass-Schule, oder: Der exemplarischen Organisten-Probe zweite, verbesserte und vermehrte Auflage*, 1731; reprint, 1968); *Réflexions sur l'éclaircissement d'un problème de musique pratique* (1720); *Das forschende Orchester* (1721; reprint, 1976); *Melotheta, das ist der grundrichtige, nach jetziger neuesten Manier angeführte Componiste* (1721–22); *Critica musica* (1722–25; reprint, 1964); *Der neue gottingische, aber viel schlechter, als die alten lacedämonischen urtheilende Ephorus* (1727); *Der musicalische Patriot* (1728; reprint, 1975); *De eruditione musica, ad virum plurimum reverendum, amplissimum atque doctissimum, Joannes Christophorum Krüsike* (1732); *Kleine General-Bass-Schule* (1735); *Kern melodischer Wissenschaft* (1737; reprint, 1976); *Gültige Zeugnisse über die jüngste Matthesonisch-Musicalische Kern-Schrift* (1738); *Der vollkommene Capellmeister, das ist gründliche Anzeige aller derjenigen Sachen, die einer wissen, können und vollkommen inne haben muss, der eine Capelle mit Ehren und Nützen verstehen will*, Mattheson's fundamental publication, which served a generation of musicians of the time (1739; facsimile reprint, Kassel, 1954; rev. Eng. tr. by E. Harriss, 1980); this was followed by the biographical compilation, the "honor gate" of composers and performing artists, *Grundlage einer Ehren-Pforte, woran die tüchtigsten Capellmeister, Componisten, Musikgelehrten, Tonkünstler, etc. Leben, Werke, Verdienste, etc., erscheinen sollen* (1740; new ed., with addenda, by M. Schneider, Berlin, 1910; reprint, 1969); *Die neuste Untersuchung der Singspiele, nebst beygefügter musicalischen Geschmacksprobe* (1744; reprint, 1975); *Das erläuterte Selah, nebst einigen anderen nützlichen Anmerkungen und erbaulichen Gedanken über Lob und Liebe* (1745); *Behauptung der himmlischen Musik aus den Gründen der Vernunft, Kirchen-Lehre und heiligen Schrift* (1747); *Matthesons Mithridat wider den Gift einer welschen Satyre, genannt: La Musica* (by S. Rosa) 1749); *Matthesons bewährte Panacea, als eine Zugabe zu seinem musicalischen Mithridat, erste Dosis* (1750); *Wahrer Begriff des harmonischen Lebens. Der Panacea zwote Dosis* (1750); *Sieben Gespräche der Weisheit und Musik samt zwo Beylagen: Als die dritte Dosis der Panacea* (1751); *Philologisches Tresespiel, als ein kleiner Beytrag zur kritischen Geschichte der deutschen Sprache* (1752; reprint, 1975); *Plus ultra, ein Stückwerk von neuer und mancherley Art* (4 vols., 1754, 1755, 1755, 1756); *Georg Friederich Händels Lebensbeschreibung* (German tr. of J. Mainwaring's biography; 1761; reprint, 1976); etc.

WORKS (all 1st perf. in Hamburg unless otherwise given): **OPERAS:** *Die Plejades oder Das Sieben-Gestirne* (1699); *Der edelmüthige Porsenna* (1702); *Victor, Hertzog der Normannen* (pasticcio; Act 1 by Schiefferdecker; Act 2 by Mattheson; Act 3 by Bronner; 1702); *Die unglückselige Cleopatra* (1704); *Le Retour du siècle d'or* (Holstein, 1705); *Boris Goudenow* (1710); *Die geheimen Begebenheiten Henrico IV* (1711); he also prepared a German version of Orlandini's *Nero* (1723), with additions.

ORATORIOS: *Die heylsame Geburth und Menschwerdung unsers Herrn und Heylandes Jesu Christi* (1715); *Die gnädige Sendung Gottes des Heiligen Geistes* (1716); *Chera, oder Die Leidtragende und getröstete Wittwe zu Nain* (1716); *Der verlangte und erlangte Heiland* (1716); *Der Altonaische Hirten-Segen, nebst einer Passions-Andacht über den verlassenen Jesum* (1717); *Der reformirende Johannes* (1717); *Der für die Sünde der Welt gemartete und sterbende Jesus* (1718); *Der aller-erfreulichste Triumph oder Der überwindende Immanuel* (1718); *Die glücklich-streitende Kirche* (1718); *Die göttliche Vorsorge über alle Creaturen* (1718); *Die Frucht des Geistes* (1719); *Christi Wunder-Wercke bey den Schwachgläubigen* (1719); *Die durch Christi Auferstehung bestägte Auferstehung aller Todten* (1720); *Das gröste Kind* (1720); *Der Blut-rünstige Kelter-Treter und von der Erden erhöhete Menschen-Sohn* (1721); *Das irrende und wieder zu recht gebrachte Sünde-Schaaf* (1721); *Die Freudenreiche Geburt und Menschwerdung unsers Herrn und Heilandes Jesu Christi* (1721); *Der unter den Todten gesuchte, und unter den lebendigen gefundene Sieges-Fürst* (1722); *Das Grosse in dem Kleinen, oder Gott in dem Herzen eines gläubigen Christen* (1722); *Das Lied des Lammes* (1723); *Der liebreiche und gedultige David* (1723); *Der aus dem Löwen-Graben befreyte, himmlische Daniel* (1725); *Das gottseelige Geheimnis* (1725); *Der undanckbare Jerobeam* (1726); *Der gegen seine Brüder barmherzige Joseph* (1727); *Das durch die Fleischwerdung des ewigen Wortes erfüllte Wort der Verheissung* (1727). Additional vocal works include many secular wedding cantatas, 18 Italian secular cantatas, serenades, etc. He also composed his own funeral oratorio, *Das fröhliche Sterbelied*.

INSTRUMENTAL: *Sonate à due cembali per il Signore Cyrillo Wich gran virtuoso* (1705; ed. by B. Cannon, London, 1960); *Suite für 2 Cembali* (1705; ed. by B. Cannon, London, 1960); *XII sonates à deux et trois flûtes sans basse* (publ. in Amsterdam, 1708); Sonate for Harpsichord (1713); *Pièces de clavecin en deux volumes* (publ. in London, 1714; German ed. as *Matthesons Harmonisches Denkmahl, aus zwölff-erwählten Clavier-Suiten* (publ. in London, 1714; reprint, 1965); *Der brauchbare Virtuoso, welcher sich . . . mit zwölff neuen Kammer-Sonaten* for Flute, Violin, and Harpsichord (1720); *Die wol-klingende Finger-Sprache, in zwölff Fugen, mit zwey bis drey Subjecten* (1st part, 1735; 2nd part, 1737; ed. by L. Hoffmann-Erbrecht, Leipzig, 1954).

BIBL.: L. Meinardus, *M. und seine Verdienste um die deutsche Tonkunst*, in Waldersee's *Sammlung musikalischer Vorträge* (Leipzig, 1879); H. Schmidt, *J. M., ein Förderer der deutschen Tonkunst, im Lichte seiner Werke* (diss., Univ. of Munich, 1897); F. Stege, "J. M. und die Musikkritik des 18. Jahrhunderts," *Zeitschrift für Musik*, CVI (1939); B. Cannon, *J. M., Spectator in Music* (New Haven, 1947); H. Becker, "J. M. handschriftliche Einzeichnungen im 'Musikalischen Lexicon' Johann Gottfried Walthers," *Die Musikforschung*, V (1952); W. Braun, *J. M. und die Aufklärung* (diss., Univ. of Halle, 1952); F. Feldmann, "M. und die Rhetorik," *Gesellschaft für Musikforschung Kongressbericht* (Hamburg, 1956); H. Reddick, *J. M.'s Forty-eight Thorough-bass Test-Pieces: Translation and Commentary* (diss., Univ. of Michigan, 1956); H. Lenneberg, "J. M. on Affect and Rhetoric in Music," *Journal of Music Theory*, II (1958); F. Feldmann, "Der Hamburger J. M. und die Musik Mittel- und Ostdeutschlands," *Hamburger Mittel- und Ostdeutsche Forschungen*, V (1966); G. Buelow, "J. M., the Composer, An Evaluation of His Opera *Cleopatra* (Hamburg, 1704)," in *Studies in Eighteenth Century Music: A Tribute to Karl Geiringer* (London and N.Y., 1970); J. Wenzel, *Geschichte der Hamburger Oper, 1678–1978* (Hamburg, 1978);

H. Marx, J. M. (Hamburg, 1982); G. Buelow and H. Marx, eds., *New M. Studies* (Cambridge, 1984).

Matthews, Artie, black American ragtime composer; b. Braidwood, Ill., Nov. 15, 1888; d. Cincinnati, Oct. 25, 1958. He spent his formative years in Springfield, Ill.; learned ragtime from the pianists Banty Morgan and Art Dillingham. After working in the tenderloin district of St. Louis (c.1908), he took lessons in piano, organ, and theory; was active as a composer and arranger for local theaters. In 1915 he went to Chicago as a church organist, and after World War I settled in Cincinnati; obtained a degree from the Metropolitan College of Music and Dramatic Arts (1918). Together with his wife, Anna Matthews, he founded the Cosmopolitan School of Music for classical training of black musicians in 1921. He was an outstanding composer of piano rags, producing 5 *Pastime* rags (1913, 1913, 1916, 1918, 1920); also wrote a jazz classic for piano, *Weary Blues* (1915), and several songs.

Matthews, Colin, English composer, writer on music, and broadcaster, brother of **David Matthews;** b. London, Feb. 13, 1946. He studied classics (B.A., 1967) and received instruction in composition from Arnold Whittal (M.Phil., 1969) at the Univ. of Nottingham; also had lessons in composition from Nicholas Maw; completed his education at the Univ. of Sussex (Ph.D., 1977, with the diss. *Mahler at Work: A Study of the Creative Process*). With his brother, he collaborated with Deryck Cooke on a performing ed. of Mahler's 10th Sym. (1964–74); was associated with Benjamin Britten (1971–76) and later edited many of Britten's early and unpubl. scores; worked with Imogen Holst on eds. of her father's scores (1972–84); subsequently was director of the Holst Estate and the Holst Foundation; also contributed articles to various journals and was active as a broadcaster.

WORKS: ORCH.: *Night Music* for Small Orch. (1977); *Divertimento* for Double String Orch. (1983); *Canonic Overture: Arms Racing* (1983); Cello Concerto (1984); *Toccata meccanica* (1984); *Monody: Cano-Ostinato-Threnody* (1987); *Variation on "Sumer is Icumen In"* (1987); *2 Part Invention* for 19 Players (1988); *Cortège* (1988; London, Feb. 17, 1989). CHAMBER: *Ceres* for 9 Instruments (1972); *Specula* for 4 Instruments (1976); *Rainbow Studies* for Piano and Wind Quartet (1977); 2 string quartets (1979, 1985); Oboe Quartet (1981); *Divertimento* for Double String Quartet (1982); *Triptych* for Piano Quintet (1984); *Sun's Dance* for 10 Players (1985; arranged as the ballet *Pursuit*, 1986); *4 out of 5 Untitled Pieces* for Flute or Piccolo (1986); *(Chiar)oscuro* for Viola (1987); *Chaconne with Chorale and Moto Perpetuo* for Violin and Piano (1988). PIANO: 5 *Studies* (1974–76); 11 *Studies in Velocity* (1987). VOCAL: *2nd Hand Flames* for Choir (1982); *Night's Mask* for Soprano and 7 Instruments (1984); also arrangements of works by other composers, including Holst's *The Dream-City* (1983).

Matthews, David, English composer and writer on music, brother of **Colin Matthews;** b. London, March 9, 1943. He studied classics at the Univ. of Nottingham (1962–65) and then took lessons in composition from Anthony Milner. He was associated with Benjamin Britten and the Aldeburgh Festival (1966–69). With his brother, he collaborated with Deryck Cooke on a performing ed. of Mahler's 10th Sym.; wrote articles on music and publ. the book *Michael Tippett: An Introductory Study* (London, 1980); served as artistic adviser of the English Chamber Orch. and as music director of the Deal Festival (from 1988).

WORKS: ORCH.: *Little Concerto* for Chamber Orch. (1971; rev. 1985); 3 syms.: No. 1 (Stroud Festival, Oct. 8, 1975; rev. 1978); No. 2 (1976–79; London, May 13, 1982); No. 3 (Sheffield, Sept. 27, 1985); *Sonata canonica* (1979; BBC, Glasgow, Jan. 10, 1982); *September Music* (BBC, Glasgow, April 28, 1980; rev. 1982); *White Nights,* fantasia for Violin and Small Orch. (1980; rev. 1988); *Introit* for 2 Trumpets and Strings (Windsor, Nov. 13, 1981); *Serenade* for Chamber Orch. (Jerusalem, May 17, 1982); Violin Concerto (1980–82; BBC, Manchester, Nov. 2, 1983); *In the Dark Time,* symphonic poem (London,

Dec. 11, 1985); *Variations* for Strings on Bach's chorale *Die Nacht ist kommen* (1986; Uppingham, March 23, 1987); *Chaconne* (1986–87; Manchester, Oct. 7, 1988); *Monody: Sonata No. 6* (1987); *Cortège* (1988); *Chiaroscuro* (London, Aug. 3, 1990). CHAMBER: 5 string quartets (1970, rev. 1980; 1976, rev. 1979; 1978, rev. 1981; 1981; 1984, rev. 1985); *Music of Evening* for Flute, Guitar, Marimba, Harpsichord, and Bass (1976); *Toccatas and Pastorals* for Oboe d'Amore, English Horn, Bassoon, and Harpsichord (1976; rev. 1979); *Duet Variations* for Flute and Piano (1982); *Winter Journey* for Violin (1983); Piano Trio (1983); Clarinet Quartet (1984); 3 *Studies* for Violin (1985); *Aria* for Violin and Piano (1986); Concertino for Oboe and String Quartet (1987); *Quatrain* for Wind, Brass, and Percussion (1989); 2nd Oboe Quartet (1989); 5 Concertinos for Wind Quintet (1990); solo piano pieces. VOCAL: *Christ Is Born of Maiden Fair,* carol for Chorus (1968); 3 *Songs* for Soprano and Orch., after Hugo, Baudelaire, and Éluard (1968–71); *Stars,* cantata for Chorus and Orch. (1970); *Eclogue* for Soprano, Flute, Clarinet, Piano, Percussion, Violin, Viola, and Cello, after Henry Vaughan (1975–79); *4 Hymns* for Chorus (1972–78); *A Cloud Sequence,* incidental music for Reciter, 2 Oboes, Bassoon, and Harpsichord, after Shelley, Wordsworth, Hopkins, James Thomson, and Rupert Brooke (1979); *The Company of Lovers,* 5 songs for Chorus, after Judith Wright and David Campbell (1980); *The Rose Carol* for Chorus (1986); *Marina* for Baritone, Basset Horn, Viola, and Piano (1988); *Cantiga* for Soprano and Chamber Orch., after Maggie Hemingway (1988); *Cantata on the Death of Anthony* for Soprano and 5 Instrumentalists (1990); songs.

Matthews, Denis (James), English pianist, teacher, and writer on music; b. Coventry, Feb. 27, 1919; d. (suicide) Birmingham, Dec. 24, 1988. He studied with Harold Craxton (piano) and W. Alwyn (composition) at the Royal Academy of Music in London (1935–40); made his London debut in 1939. During World War II, he served in the Royal Air Force while continuing to make appearances as a pianist; after the war, he toured throughout the world; was the 1st prof. of music at the Univ. of Newcastle upon Tyne (1971–84); was made a Commander of the Order of the British Empire (1975).

WRITINGS: *In Pursuit of Music* (autobiography; London, 1966); *Beethoven's Piano Sonatas* (London, 1967); *Arturo Toscanini* (Tunbridge Wells and N.Y., 1982); *Beethoven* (London, 1985).

Matthews, Michael Gough, English pianist and music educator; b. Wanstead, Essex, July 12, 1931. He studied at the Royal College of Music in London, where he received the Hopkinson Gold Medal (1953); then took a course at the Accademia di Santa Cecilia in Rome, and subsequently toured as pianist in Europe and the Far East. From 1964 to 1971 he was on the staff of the Royal Scottish Academy of Music and Drama in Glasgow; then was prof. of piano at the Royal College of Music (1972–75), where he was vice-director (1978–84) and director (from 1985).

Matthison-Hansen, (Johan) Gottfred, Danish organist and composer, son of **Hans Matthison-Hansen;** b. Roskilde, Nov. 1, 1832; d. Copenhagen, Oct. 14, 1909. He studied piano with his father; later took lessons in piano and theory with W.H. Barth; then enrolled at the Univ. of Copenhagen as a law student. Although mainly self-taught, he trained himself so as to hold church positions as an organist at the Fredericks Church (1859), St. John's (1871), and the Trinity Church (1881) in Copenhagen; also made tours in organ recitals in Denmark and Germany. In 1867 he began teaching organ at the Copenhagen Cons.; in 1884 he also assumed the position of piano teacher there. He composed a number of works for organ which he included in his recitals; in addition to the Classical repertoire, he championed the Romantic works of the time.

Matthison-Hansen (originally, **Matthias Hansen**), **Hans,** esteemed Danish organist and composer, father of **(Johan) Gottfred Matthison-Hansen;** b. Adelby, near Flensburg,

Feb. 6, 1807; d. Roskilde, Jan. 7, 1890. He learned to play the violin, viola, and cello at the Copenhagen Academy of Art; then took general music courses with C.E.F. Weyse. In 1832 he was appointed organist of Roskilde Cathedral, a position he retained until his death. He gave solo recitals in Denmark, Norway, Sweden, and Germany (1861–62); visited London in 1864. He wrote a Sym. (1848); 2 oratorios; 2 Easter cantatas; numerous organ works. His surname was legally changed in 1859.

Matthus, Siegfried, German composer; b. Mallenuppen, East Prussia, April 13, 1934. He studied composition with Wagner-Régeny at the Deutsche Hochschule für Musik (1952–58) and with Eisler at the Deutsche Akademie der Künste (1958–60) in East Berlin; in 1964 he was appointed a composer and dramatist at the (East) Berlin Komische Oper; in 1972 he became a member of the presidium of the Deutsche Akademie der Künste.

Works: operas: *Lazarillo vom Tormes* (1960–63; Karl-Marx-Stadt, May 26, 1964); *Der letzte Schuss* (1966–67; Berlin, Nov. 5, 1967); *Noch ein Löffel Gift, Liebling?* (1971–72; Berlin, April 16, 1972); *Omphale* (1972–73; Weimar, Aug. 29, 1976); *Judith* (Berlin, Sept. 28, 1985); *Eine Opernvision* (1985); *Mirabeau* (1989). **orch.:** *Concerto for Orchestra* for 2 Flutes, 3 Trombones, Harp, Piano, Percussion, and Strings (1963); *Inventions* (1964); *Tua res agitur* for 15 Instruments and Percussion (1965); *Violin Concerto* (1968; Berlin, Feb. 24, 1969); 2 syms.: No. 1, *Dresdener Sinfonie* (1969), and No. 2 (1976); *Piano Concerto* (1970; Berlin, Feb. 18, 1971); *Orchesterserenade* (1974); *Cello Concerto* (1975); *Werther*, "musical metaphor" (1976); *Responso*, concerto for Orch. (1977); *Visions* for Strings (1978); *Flute Concerto* (1978); *Kammerkonzert* for Flute, Harpsichord, and Strings (1980–81); *Der Wald*, concerto for Kettledrum and Orch. (Dresden, June 6, 1985); *Oboe Concerto* (1985); *Die Windsbraut*, concerto (1985); *Das Triangelkonzert*, divertimento (1985); *Nächtliche Szenen im Park* (1987); *Concerto for 3 Trumpets and Strings, Ornamenlose Freude* (1989). **vocal:** *Es wird ein grosser Stern in meinen Schoss fallen*, 5 love songs for Soprano and Orch. (1961–62; East Berlin, Oct. 5, 1962); *Das Manifest*, cantata (1965); *Kammermusik* for Alto, 3 Female Voices, and 10 Instruments (1965); *Galileo* for Voice, 5 Instruments, and Tape (1966); *Vokalsinfonie* for Soprano, Baritone, 2 Choruses, and Orch. (1967; from the opera *Der letzte Schuss*); *Kantate von den Beiden* for Narrator, Soprano, Baritone, and Orch. (1968); *Vokalisen* for Soprano, Flute, Double Bass, and Percussion (1969); *Laudate pacem*, oratorio (1974); *Unter dem Holunderstrauch*, scene after Kleist for Soprano, Tenor, and Orch. (1976); *Holofernes-Portrait* for Baritone and Orch. (1981); *Nachtlieder* for Baritone, String Quartet, and Harp (1987); choruses; songs. **chamber:** Sonatina for Piano and Percussion (1960); Sonata for Brasses, Piano, and Kettledrums (1968); Music for 4 Oboes and Piano (1968); Octet (1970); String Quartet (1971); Harp Trio for Flute, Viola, and Harp (1971). **piano:** *Variations* (1958); *Konzertstück* (1958).

Mattila, Karita, Finnish soprano; b. Somero, Sept. 5, 1960. She was a pupil of Liisa Linko-Malmio and Kim Borg at the Sibelius Academy in Helsinki and of Vera Rozsa in London. In 1982 she made her operatic debut as Mozart's Countess at the Finnish National Opera in Helsinki; after winning the Singer of the World Competition in Cardiff in 1983, she appeared as a soloist with many of the world's major orchs. In 1983 she sang Fiordiligi at the Munich Festival and also made her U.S. debut as Donna Elvira in Washington, D.C.; in 1986 she made her 1st appearance at London's Covent Garden as Fiordiligi. Her other operatic engagements include the Hamburg State Opera, the Chicago Lyric Opera, the Vienna State Opera, and N.Y.'s Metropolitan Opera. In addition to her Mozart roles, she also became well known as a Wagnerian.

Matton, Roger, Canadian composer; b. Granby, Quebec, May 18, 1929. He studied at the Montreal Cons. (1943–50); was a composition student of Claude Champagne. He then went to Paris and studied with Boulanger and others. From 1956 to 1976 he was a researcher and ethnomusicologist at the Archives de Folklore at the Laval Univ. in Quebec City. In 1984 he was made an Officer of the Order of Canada. His music is marked by dramatic lyricism enlivened by propulsive rhythms.

Works: *Danse brésilienne* for 2 Pianos (1946; rev. 1971); *Étude* for Clarinet and Piano (1946); *Danse lente* (*Gymnopédie*) for Small Orch. (1947); Concerto for Saxophone and Strings (1948); 3 *Préludes* for Piano (1947–49); *Esquisse* for String Quartet (1949); *Pax*, symphonic suite (1950); *Suite on Gregorian Themes* for Organ (1952); Concerto for 2 Pianos and Percussion (1954–55); *L'Escaouette*, suite of folk songs for 4 Soloists, Chorus, and Orch. (1957); *L'Horoscope*, choreographic suite (Toronto, Oct. 12, 1958); 4 *Mouvements symphoniques*: No. 1 (Quebec City, Nov. 14, 1960); No. 2, *Music for a Drama* (Montreal, April 17, 1962); No. 3 (Quebec City, May 7, 1974); No. 4 (1977); Concerto for 2 Pianos and Orch. (Quebec City, Nov. 30, 1964); *Te Deum* for Baritone, Chorus, and Orch., with Electronic Sound (Quebec City, Nov. 27, 1967); *Tu es petrus* for Orch. (1984).

Mattox, Janis, American composer; b. St. Paul, Minn., March 18, 1949. She studied at the Univ. of Minnesota (B.A., 1972) and Northwestern Univ. in Evanston, Ill. (M.A., 1974); in 1978 began composing and producing works involving computer music technologies and live performers at Stanford Univ.'s Center for Computer Research in Music and Acoustics (CCRMA); among the virtuoso performers she has collaborated with are jazz bassist Mel Graves (*Voice of the Ancestors*, 1983), actor Bob Ernst (*Spirits Rising*, 1984), flutist (Moroccan ney) Richard Horowitz (*Night Flyer*, 1985), and drummer George Marsh (*Adowa*, 1987); works for dance include *Song from the Center of the Earth* for belly dancer Rachel Dutton (1982) and *Beehive Suite* (1985) for Jim Self and Beehive. Mattox taught and gave lecture demonstrations on computer music at CCRMA; also lectured in Los Angeles and Venice. She is project consultant for Good Sound Foundation and a performing member (piano) of The Good Sound Band. Her other works include *Dragon's View* for Computer-generated Quadraphonic Tape (1980); *Shaman*, music theater piece for Percussionist, Belly Dancer, Bassist, Actor/Vocalist, Live Digital Processing, and Computer-generated Tape (1984); *Adowa* for Percussionist and Dancer (1987); *Book of Shadows, Part I*, for Film, 2 Pianos in just intonation, Soprano, Violin, Garden Hose, Ney, Didjeridu, Contrabass, Saxophone, Accordion in just intonation, and Live Digital Processing (1989); and *Pulse* for 2 Drummers (1990). She is married to **Loren Rush.**

Bibl.: A. Rich, "A Composer Whose Music Has a Magical Twist," *Smithsonian* (Dec. 1984).

Matys, Jiří, Czech composer; b. Bakov, Oct. 27, 1927. He studied organ with František Michálek at the Brno Cons., graduating in 1947; then took a course in composition with Kvapil at the Janáček Academy of Music in Brno; joined its faculty after graduation (1953–57); was then headmaster of the School of Music at Králové Pole in Brno (1957–60). In 1960 he moved to Ostrava, where he was active as a music administrator.

Works: Horn Sonata (1948); *Fantasy* for String Orch. (1949); Partita for Piano Trio (1949); *To Those Fallen in May 1945*, symphonic poem (1949); Piano Sonata (1950); Wind Quartet (1951); Sym. (1951); Viola Sonata (1954); *The Bells of Velice*, chamber cantata (1954); *Impromptus* for Violin and Piano (1955); 4 string quartets (1957; 1961; 1962–63; 1973); *Lyrical Melodramas* for Narrator and Piano (1957); *Children's Ballets* for Wind Quintet (1959); *Variace na smrt* (Variations on Death) for Narrator, Horn, and String Quartet (1959); Quartet for 4 Violins (1960); *Inventions* for 3 Violins (1960); *Jitřní hudba* (Mourning Music) for String Orch., 2 Trumpets, and Percussion (1961–62); *Pictures of Winter* for Piano (1962); Solo Viola Sonata (1963); Duet for Violin and Viola (1963); Violin Sonata (1964–65); *Sonata balladica* for Piano (1966); 5 *Bagatelles* for Accordion (1966); *Inventions* for Flute and Cello (1969); 3 *Movements* for Wind Quintet (1969); *Suite* for Trumpet and Piano (1969); *Music* for Wind Quintet (1970);

Pictures, 3 pieces for Cello and Piano (1970); *Allusions*, 3 compositions for 4 Flutes (1971); *Music* for String Quartet and Orch. (1971); *Written by Grief into Silence* for Medium Voice and Orch. (1972); *Suite* for Viola and Bass Clarinet (1972–73); *Symphonic Overture* (1973–74); *Partita* for Oboe (1974); *Poetic Movements*, 3 compositions for Flute, Violin, and Piano (1975); *Dialogue* for Cello and Piano (1976); Suite for Flute and Guitar (1981); *Music for Strings* (1982).

Matz, Rudolf, Croatian cellist and composer; b. Zagreb, Sept. 19, 1901. He studied cello and composition at the Zagreb Academy of Music; in 1950 he was appointed instructor in cello there; then taught chamber music at the Ljubljana Academy of Music. He publ. a manual for cello playing (Zagreb, 1951).
　　WORKS: *Classical Concert* for Cello and Orch. (1949); *Lyric Sketches* for Cello Solo and String Orch. (1959); Flute Concerto (1963); 4 string quartets (1924, 1932, 1935, 1944); *Baroque Concerto* for 3 Cellos and Piano (1952); *12 Pieces* for 3 Cellos and Piano (1960); Violin Sonata (1941); 2 cello sonatas (1941, 1942); *11 Caprices* in 12-tone technique for Cello (1964); *24 Songs on Croatian Folk Poems* and other pieces based on native themes.

Matzenauer, Margarete, celebrated Hungarian soprano and contralto; b. Temesvár, June 1, 1881; d. Van Nuys, Calif., May 19, 1963. Her father was a conductor and her mother a soprano; she grew up in favorable musical surroundings, and began to study singing at an early age, 1st in Graz, then in Berlin, and finally in Munich. In 1901 she joined the staff of the Strasbourg Opera; then sang contralto roles at the Munich Court Opera (1904–11); also sang at Bayreuth in 1911. She made her American debut as Amneris in *Aida* at the Metropolitan Opera in N.Y. (Nov. 13, 1911) and remained one of its leading members until 1930; in the interim, she sang in opera in Germany and South America. She gave her farewell concert recital in Carnegie Hall, N.Y., in 1938; settled in California. She had one of the most remarkable singing careers of her day; she sang both soprano and contralto roles until 1914, and thereafter concentrated on contralto roles. Among her many outstanding roles were Brünnhilde, Venus, Isolde, Fricka, Ortrud, Eboli, Azucena, Leonora, and Laura in *La Gioconda*.

Mauceri, John (Francis), American conductor; b. N.Y., Sept. 12, 1945. He studied with Gustav Meier at Yale Univ. (B.A., 1967; M.Phil., 1972) and with Maderna, Colin Davis, Ozawa, and Bernstein at the Berkshire Music Center at Tanglewood (1971). He conducted the Yale Univ. Sym. Orch. (1968–74); subsequently appeared widely as a guest conductor of opera, musical theater, and sym. orchs. He was music director of the Washington (D.C.) Opera (1980–82), the American Sym. Orch. in N.Y. (1984–87), the Scottish Opera in Glasgow (from 1987), and the Hollywood Bowl Orch. (from 1990).

Mauduit, Jacques, noted French composer; b. Paris, Sept. 16, 1557; d. there, Aug. 21, 1627. He studied humanities and philosophy, but was self-taught in music. He served as royal secretary and registrar in the judiciary. His gifts as a composer were recognized when he won the St. Cecilia's Day Competition in Evreux in 1581 for his motet *Afferte Domine* for 5 Voices. He became associated with Baïf's Académie de Poésie et de Musique in Paris, and made several settings of Baïf's poems. During the siege of Paris, he saved Baïf's unpubl. MSS and helped Le Jeune escape the city, saving the MS of his *Dodecacorde.* Many of his own works are lost.
　　WORKS: (23) *Chansonettes mesurées de Jean-Antoine de Baïf* for 4 Voices (Paris, 1586; ed. by H. Expert in Les Maîtres Musiciens de la Renaissance Française, X, 1899); *Psaumes mesurées à l'antique, 1 prière* for 4 and 5 Voices (publ. in M. Mersenne's *Quaestiones celeberrimae in Genesim,* 1623); *Requiem aeternum* for 5 Voices, for the funeral of Rosnard (1585; publ. by M. Mersenne, 1636–37).
　　BIBL.: M. Brenet, "J. M.," *Musique et musiciens de la vieille France* (Paris, 1911).

Mauersberger, Rudolf, German organist, choral conductor, teacher, and composer; b. Mauersberg, Erzgebirge, Jan. 29, 1889; d. Dresden, Feb. 22, 1971. He studied piano, organ, and composition at the Leipzig Cons. (1912–14; 1918–19); won the Nikisch Prize for composition in 1914; served as organist and choirmaster in Aachen (1919–25); then was in charge of church music in Thuringia (1925–30), directing the choir at Eisenach's Georgenkirche. In 1930 he became choirmaster of the Kreuzkirche in Dresden; directed its famous boys' choir, taking it on numerous tours in Europe and abroad. He composed a number of choral works, including the *Dresdner Requiem* (1948), written in memory of those who lost their lives during the barbarous bombing of the beautiful porcelaneous city just a few weeks before the end of World War II.
　　BIBL.: M. Grun, *R. M.: Studien zu Leben und Werk* (Regensburg, 1986).

Mauke, Wilhelm, German music critic and composer; b. Hamburg, Feb. 25, 1867; d. Wiesbaden, Aug. 24, 1930. He 1st studied medicine; then turned to music; was a pupil of Huber in Basel. He then established himself as a music critic in Munich; wrote the operas *Der Taugenichts* (1905), *Fanfreluche* (1912), *Die letzte Maske* (1917), *Das Fest des Lebens* (1926); other stage works: *Romantische Sinfonie*; an oratorio, *Die Vertreibung aus dem Paradies*; a symphonic poem, *Einsamkeit*, after Nietzsche; a Piano Concerto; 160 songs.
　　BIBL.: W. Nagel, *W. M.* (Vienna and Leipzig, 1919).

Maunder, John Henry, English organist and composer; b. London, Feb. 21, 1858; d. Brighton, Jan 25, 1920. He studied at the Royal Academy of Music in London; served as organist in several London churches. He began his career as a theater composer; wrote an operetta, *Daisy Dingle* (1885); later devoted himself exclusively to sacred music; his oratorio *The Martyrs* (Oxford, May 25, 1894) became a perennial favorite; even more successful was his oratorio *From Olivet to Calvary;* he also wrote sacred works for chorus a cappella (*Praise the Lord, Blessed Be Thy Name, Christ Awake, Conquering Kings, This Is the Day, Worship the King, Sing of Heaven*); other choral works are *Bethlehem, Song of Thanksgiving,* and *Christ Is Risen* for Voice, with Orch. Accompaniment.

Maurel, Victor, famous French baritone; b. Marseilles, June 17, 1848; d. N.Y., Oct. 22, 1923. He studied singing at the Paris Cons.; made his debut in *Guillaume Tell* in Marseilles (1867); made his 1st appearance at the Paris Opéra as De Nevers in *Les Huguenots* in 1868; then sang in Italy, Spain, England, and Russia; in 1873 he made an American tour. Returning to Paris, he was on the staff of the Opéra (1879–94). He made his debut at the Metropolitan Opera in N.Y. on Dec. 3, 1894, as Iago in *Otello;* sang there until 1896, then returned in 1898–99; was a member of the Opéra-Comique in Paris until 1904. In 1909 he emigrated to the U.S., where he remained until his death; in his last years he was active as a stage designer in N.Y. He created the role of Iago in Verdi's *Otello* (Milan, Feb. 5, 1887) and the title role in *Falstaff* (Milan, Feb. 9, 1893); also distinguished himself in Wagnerian roles. He publ., in Paris, several monographs on the esthetics of singing and also autobiographical reminiscences, among them *Le Chant remové par la science* (1892); *Un Problème d'art* (1893); *L'Art du chant* (1897); *Dix ans de carrière* (1897).
　　BIBL.: F. Rogers, "V. M.: His Career and His Art," *Musical Quarterly* (Oct. 1926).

Maurer, Ludwig (Wilhelm), German violinist and composer; b. Potsdam, Feb. 8, 1789; d. St. Petersburg, Oct. 25, 1878. He studied with K. Haack. A precocious child musician, he appeared in concerts at the age of 13; at 17 he went to Russia, remaining there for 10 years, giving concerts and serving as house musician to Russian aristocrats. From 1817 until 1832 he traveled in Europe, and was successful as a violinist in Berlin and in Paris. He was in Russia again (1832–45), then lived in Dresden, eventually returning to St. Petersburg. He produced 2 operas in Hannover, *Der neue Paris* (Jan. 27, 1826) and *Aloise* (Jan. 16, 1828); also wrote many stage pieces in Russia; with Aliabiev and Verstovsky, he contributed the music to Chmelnitsky's comedy *A Novel Prank, or Theatrical Combat* (1822). In addition, he wrote a curious quadruple concerto, *Symphonie concertante*, for 4 Violins with Orch. (1838); 10 violin concertos; 6 string quartets; and other chamber music. His 2 sons Vsevolod (1819–92), a violinist, and Alexis, a cellist, remained in Russia.

Maurice, Alphons, German composer; b. Hamburg, April 14, 1862; d. Dresden, Jan. 27, 1905. He studied with Dessoff, Krenn, and Grädener at the Vienna Cons.; wrote the operas *Josepha, Schatz,* and *Der Wundersteg; Waldestraum* for Orch.; *Spanische Serenade* for Violin and Orch.; choruses; piano pieces; songs.

Maurice, Pierre, Baron de, Swiss composer; b. Allaman, Nov. 13, 1868; d. Geneva, Dec. 25, 1936. He attended the Geneva Cons., then for a short time studied at Stuttgart, finishing his musical education with Lavignac and Massenet at the Paris Cons. He lived many years in Munich; composed the operas *Die weisse Flagge* (Kassel, 1903), *Misé brun* (Stuttgart, 1908), *Lanval* (Weimar, 1912), *Kalif Storch* (not perf.), *Andromède* (1923), *Le Mystère de la Nativité* (1933), etc.; a biblical drama, *La Fille de Jephthé* (Geneva, 1899); a symphonic suite, *Die Islandfischer* (after Loti); *Chanson des quatre saisons* for Piano, and other piano pieces; songs.
BIBL.: M. Maurice, *P. M.* (Geneva, 1938).

Mauricio, José, Portuguese organist, music theorist, and composer; b. Coimbra, March 19, 1752; d. Figueira da Foz, Sept. 12, 1815. He studied theology at Coimbra Univ.; was mestre de capela at Guarda Cathedral from about 1784 to 1786; then served as organist at the Santa Cruz monastery in Coimbra. In 1791 he became director of the music school in the bishop's palace and mestre de capela of Coimbra Cathedral; in 1802 he was appointed prof. of music at Coimbra Univ. He wrote a great deal of church music and some instrumental works revealing the influence of Haydn. He also publ. a *Metodo de musica* (Coimbra, 1806).

Mauro, Ermanno, Italian-born Canadian tenor; b. Trieste, Jan. 20, 1939. He emigrated to Canada in 1958 and became a naturalized citizen in 1963; after vocal training with Jean Létourneau in Edmonton, he entered the Royal Cons. Opera School in Toronto in 1964 and studied with George Lambert, Herman Geiger-Torel, and Ernesto Barbini. In 1962 he made his operatic debut as Manrico in Edmonton; after appearances in opera productions at the Royal Cons. in Toronto and with the Canadian Opera Co., he sang at London's Covent Garden (1967–72). On Feb. 3, 1975, Mauro made his debut at the N.Y. City Opera, remaining with the company until 1979; on Jan. 6, 1978, he made his Metropolitan Opera debut in N.Y. as Canio, and continued to sing there in subsequent seasons. Among his other roles are Ernani, Des Grieux, Alfredo, Faust, Pinkerton, and Rodolfo.

Maury, Lowndes, American composer; b. Butte, Mont., July 7, 1911; d. Encino, Calif., Dec. 11, 1975. He earned his B.A. degree in music at the Univ. of Montana in 1931; went to Los Angeles, where he studied composition with Wesley La Violette and Schoenberg; became active in Hollywood as a pianist, arranger, and teacher. He publ. *Magic Lines and Spaces,* a series of piano instruction books in correlated notation, a system employing a 3-line staff (1974).
WORKS: *In Memory of the Korean War Dead* for Violin and Piano (1952); *Proud Music of the Storm,* cantata to words by Walt Whitman (1953); *Passacaglia* for String Orch. (1959); *Springtime Digressions* for Piano, Flute, and String Quintet (1961); *Speculations* for Piano and 3 String Instruments (1964); *Summer of Green,* rhapsody for Alto Flute and String Orch. (1964); *Scène de ballet* for Piccolo and String Quartet (1965); 11 *Sketches* for Piano Trio (1968); *The Imprisoned Cellist,* suite for Solo Cello (1973).

Maus, Octave, Belgian journalist and musician; b. Brussels, June 12, 1856; d. Lausanne, Nov. 26, 1919. He studied music with Louis Brassin. An ardent admirer of Wagner, he went to Bayreuth to attend the 1st Wagner Festival in 1876; in 1881 he was co-founder of the weekly magazine *L'Art Moderne,* in Brussels, which promoted Wagnerian ideas; then participated in the musical society "XX," the title of which symbolized the future 20th century; it was active from 1884 to 1893. From 1894 to the outbreak of World War I in 1914 he led in Brussels a concert group, Libre Esthétique. He spent the last years of his life in Switzerland.
BIBL.: M. Maus (his wife), *Trente années de lutte pour art* (n.d.); A. Van Der Linden, *O. M. et la vie musicale belge* (Brussels, 1950).

Maw, (John) Nicholas, remarkable English composer; b. Grantham, Lincolnshire, Nov. 5, 1935. He played clarinet and piano; studied composition with Lennox Berkeley and Paul Steinitz at the Royal Academy of Music in London (1955–58) and with Nadia Boulanger and Max Deutsch in Paris (1958–59). From 1966 to 1970 he was fellow-commoner in creative arts at Trinity College, Cambridge. In his music he makes use of serial methods of composition without abandoning the principle of tonality.
WORKS: STAGE: *1 Man Show,* comic opera (London, Nov. 12, 1964; rev. 1966); *The Rising of the Moon,* opera (1967–70; Glyndebourne, July 19, 1970). **ORCH.:** *Scenes and Arias* for Solo Voices and Orch. (London, Aug. 31, 1962); *Sinfonia* for Chamber Orch. (Newcastle upon Tyne, May 30, 1966); *Severn Bridge Variations* (1967); *Sonata* for String Orch. and 2 Horns (Bath, June 7, 1967); *Serenade* (Singapore, March 31, 1973); *Summer Dances* for Youth Orch. (Aldeburgh, July 27, 1981); *Toccata* (Norwich, Oct. 15, 1982); *Morning Music* (1982; rev. as *Spring Music,* 1984); *Sonata notturna* for Cello and String Orch. (1985); *Odyssey* (1973–87; partial perf., London, Aug. 10, 1987; 1st complete perf., London, April 8, 1989). **VOCAL:** *Nocturne* for Mezzo-soprano and Chamber Orch. (1957–58); 5 *Epigrams* for Mixed Voices a cappella (1960); *Our Lady's Song* for Mixed Voices a cappella (1961); *The Angel Gabriel* for Mixed Chorus (1963); *Round* for Children's Chorus, Mixed Chorus, and Piano (1963); 6 *Interiors* for High Voice and Guitar (1966); *The Voice of Love* for Mezzo-soprano and Piano (1966); 5 *Irish Songs* for Mixed Chorus (Cork, May 4, 1973); *Reverdie,* 5 songs for Male Voices (Glasgow, Oct. 29, 1975); *Te Deum* for Soprano, Tenor, Mixed Chorus, and Organ (Bruton, May 29, 1975); 20 *Nonsense Rhymes* for Voices and Piano (1976); *Annes!* for Mixed Chorus (1976); *La vita nuova* for Soprano and Chamber Ensemble (London, Sept. 2, 1979); *The Ruin* for Double Chorus and Horn (Edinburgh, Aug. 27, 1980). **CHAMBER:** *Sonatina* for Flute and Piano (1957); *Essays* for Organ (1961); *Chamber Music* for Oboe, Clarinet, Horn, Bassoon, and Piano (1962); 2 string quartets (1965, 1982); *Personae* for Piano (1973); *Life Studies* for 15 Solo Strings (1973); *Quartet* for Flute and Strings (1981); *Night Thoughts* for Flute (1982).
BIBL.: B. Northcott, "N. M.: The Second Phase," *Musical Times* (Aug. 1987).

Maxfield, Richard (Vance), American avant-garde composer; b. Seattle, Wash., Feb. 2, 1927; d. (suicide) Los Angeles, June 27, 1969. He studied at the Univ. of Calif., Berkeley, with Sessions, and at Princeton Univ. with Babbitt (M.F.A., 1955); also took courses with Krenek; held a Fulbright fellowship (1955–57), which enabled him to continue his training with Dallapiccola in Florence and Maderna in Milan. He became deeply engaged in acoustical electronics; taught experimental music at the New School for Social Research in N.Y. (1959–62) and then at San Francisco State College; contributed essays to avant-garde publications; 2 of them, in free verse, were publ. in *Contemporary Composers on Contemporary Music,* ed. by E. Schwartz and B. Childs (N.Y., 1967). He acquired an excellent technique of composition in the traditional idiom before adopting an extreme avant-garde style. He took his own life by self-defenestration from a hotel room.
WORKS: *Classical Overture* (1942); Trio for Clarinet, Cello, and Piano (1943); Septet for 2 Flutes, 3 Clarinets, French Horn, and Bassoon (1947); Sonata for Unaccompanied Violin (1949); Violin Sonata (1950); String Trio (1951); Sonata for

Unaccompanied Flute (1951); *Structures* for 10 Wind Instruments (1951); *11 Variations* for String Quartet (1952); *5 Movements* for Orch. (1956); Chamber Concerto for 7 Instruments (1957); *Structures* for Orch. (1958); *Sine Music* (1959); *Stacked Deck*, opera for Tape, Actors, and Lighting (1959); *Perspectives* for Violin and Tape (1960); *Peripeteia* for Violin, Saxophone, Piano, and Tape (1960); *Clarinet Music* for 5 Clarinets and Tape (1961); *Cough Music*, with sonic materials obtained from coughs and other bronchial sound effects recorded during a modern dance recital and electronically arranged in a piece of tussive polyphony (N.Y., Jan. 13, 1961); *Toy Symphony* for Flute, Violin, Wooden Boxes, Ceramic Vase, and Tape (1962); *African Symphony* (1964); *Venus Impulses* for Electronic Sound (1967).

Maxwell Davies, Peter. See **Davies, Peter Maxwell.**

May, Edward Collett, English organist and singing teacher, father of **Florence May;** b. Greenwich, Oct. 29, 1806; d. London, Jan. 2, 1887. He studied with C. Potter and Crivelli; was organist of Greenwich Hospital (1837–69); prof. of vocal music at Queen's College, London (1879–83). He did much to popularize singing among the masses; publ. *Progressive Vocal Exercises for Daily Practice* (1853); songs.

May, Florence, English pianist and writer on music, daughter of **Edward Collett May;** b. London, Feb. 6, 1845; d. there, June 29, 1923. She studied music with her father and with an uncle, Oliver May; began a promising career as a pianist in London; in 1871 she took lessons with Clara Schumann in Baden-Baden; there she made the acquaintance of Brahms, who gave her some lessons. She became his enthusiastic admirer; upon her return to England, she started a vigorous campaign for performances of the music of Brahms; she gave many 1st performances of his works in London. The important result of her dedication to Brahms was her comprehensive work *The Life of Johannes Brahms* (2 vols., London, 1905; 2nd ed., 1948); she also publ. *The Girlhood of Clara Schumann* (London, 1912).

Mayall, John, English rhythm-and-blues singer; b. Manchester, Nov. 29, 1933. An ardent promoter of black American blues, he formed a group called The Bluesbreakers, serving as a laboratory for instrumentalists, which included Eric Clapton, Peter Green, John McVie, Mick Taylor, Aynsley Dunbar, and Mick Fleetwood. The Bluesbreakers released a number of successful albums, among them *A Hard Road* and *The Turning Point*, and the 1st classic of British blues, under the title *Bluesbreakers with Eric Clapton*. Another album, *U.S.A. Union*, produced a workable amalgam of jazz and blues. Eventually Mayall emigrated to America.

Maybrick, Michael (pseudonym, Stephen Adams), English baritone and composer; b. Liverpool, Jan. 31, 1844; d. Buxton, Aug. 25, 1913. He studied at the Leipzig Cons. with Plaidy, Moscheles, and E. Richter (1866–68), and was a vocal pupil of Nava in Milan. He sang at the principal concerts in London and the provinces, and toured the U.S. and Canada in 1884. Many of his songs (sung by himself) had great vogue (e.g., *Nancy Lee*). His sacred solo *The Holy City* was sung in churches in England and America.

Mayer, Charles, German pianist, teacher, and composer; b. Königsberg, March 21, 1799; d. Dresden, July 2, 1862. He was taken to Russia as a child; was taught by John Field in Moscow; lived in Moscow until Napoleon's invasion in 1812; then went to St. Petersburg, and in 1814 to Paris. He returned to Russia in 1819 and formed a large class of pupils in St. Petersburg; in 1845 he made a tour of Scandinavia and Germany; in 1850 he settled in Dresden. He publ. an enormous number of piano pieces in salon style; one of his mazurkas was once misattributed to Chopin.

Mayer, Joseph Anton, German composer; b. Pfullendorf, Baden, Dec. 5, 1855; d. Stuttgart, Dec. 3, 1936. He studied at the Stuttgart Cons. and with Bargiel in Berlin; then taught at the Stuttgart Cons. He wrote the operas *Der Stern von Bethle-*

hem and *Magdelenenbrunnen;* also choral works; piano pieces; songs.

Mayer, Sir Robert, industrious German-born English patron of music who completed his earthly round at the age of 105; b. Mannheim, June 5, 1879; d. London, Jan. 9, 1985. His love for music was established early when he entered the Mannheim Cons. as a piano student; there he also met Brahms. His father sent him at age 17 to relatives in England to establish himself, since business opportunities were limited for Jews in Germany. So totally immersed did he become in English life that his family asserted he even spoke his native German with a British accent. He was an entrepreneur in the grand manner of the Victorian age. He never wrote music, but he promoted the art with youthful enthusiasm. In 1923, inspired by Walter Damrosch's concerts for children in N.Y., Mayer and his wife, the singer Dorothy Moulton-Mayer, began a series of children's concerts, whose 1st regular conductor was Adrian Boult. The tremendous success of making serious classical music available to young children everywhere in England, from slums to suburbs, encouraged a new enterprise in 1954, Youth and Music, which was specifically offered to adolescents, with the view to creating lifetime participants in musical culture. Mayer's business acumen launched this program successfully as well. In 1939 he was knighted, and in 1973 made a Companion of Honour. His centennial was gloriously celebrated, with himself as the center of festivities, at the Royal Festival Hall in London, and he was elevated to Knight Commander of the Royal Victorian Order. His autobiography was publ. as *My First Hundred Years* (London, 1979). He had the wit to proclaim that music exercised a curative power over the human body and mind, and he adjusted his entire life accordingly.

Mayer-Serra, Otto, eminent Spanish musicologist; b. Barcelona (of German-Catalan parents), July 12, 1904; d. Mexico City, March 19, 1968. He studied in Germany with H. Abert, Curt Sachs, J. Wolf, and E. von Hornbostel; received his Ph.D. in 1929 with the dissertation *Die romantische Klaviersonaten* from the Univ. of Greifswald. He returned to Spain in 1933, and was music critic of the Catalan weekly *Mirador.* In 1936, at the outbreak of the Spanish Civil War, he was appointed head of the music division of the propaganda ministry of the Catalan government; served in the Loyalist army in 1938–39; after its defeat, he fled to France. In 1940 he reached Mexico, where he became active as a writer, editor, lecturer, and manager.

WRITINGS (all publ. in Mexico City): *El romanticismo musical* (1940); *Panorama de la música mexicana desde la independencia hasta la actualidad* (1941); *Música y músicos de Latino-América* (2 vols., 1947); *Breve diccionario de la música* (1948); *La música contemporánea* (1954).

Mayer, (Benjamin) Wilhelm, Austrian pianist, pedagogue, and composer who used the pseudonym W.A. Rémy; b. Prague, June 10, 1831; d. Graz, Jan. 22, 1898. He studied with C. Pietsch; also took a degree in law (1856). In 1862 he became conductor of the Graz Musical Soc. resigning in 1870 to apply himself to pedagogy; he taught both piano and composition, and achieved great renown; among his pupils were Busoni, Rezniček, and Weingartner. He wrote a concert opera, *Das Waldfräulein* (Graz, 1876), a number of syms. and other orch. works, and numerous songs.

BIBL.: W. Suppan, "W. M. (W.A. Rémy)," *Neue Chronik zur Geschichte und Volkskunde der innerösterreichischen Alpenländer,* X (Graz, 1961).

Mayer, William (Robert), American composer; b. N.Y., Nov. 18, 1925. He studied with Richard Donovan and Herbert Baumgartner at Yale Univ. (B.A., 1949), Sessions at the Juilliard School of Music in N.Y. (summer 1949), and Salzer at the Mannes College of Music there (1949–52); later studied conducting with Izler Solomon at the Aspen Music School (1960); held a Guggenheim fellowship in 1966.

WORKS: STAGE: *The Greatest Sound Around,* short children's opera (1954); *Hello World!,* "a musical trip around the world," children's opera for Narrator, Orch., and Audience Participation (N.Y., Nov. 10, 1956); *One Christmas Long Ago,* 1-act opera (Philadelphia, Dec. 12, 1964); *Brief Candle,* "micro-opera" (1964); *A Death in the Family,* opera based on James Agee's eponymous novel and Tad Mosel's play *All the Way Home* (Minneapolis, March 11, 1983); *The Snow Queen,* ballet (1963). ORCH.: *Andante for Strings* (1955); *Hebraic Portrait* (1957); *Overture for an American* (1958); *2 Pastels* (1960); *Octagon* for Piano and Orch. (N.Y., March 21, 1971); *Inner and Outer Strings* for String Quartet and String Orch. (1982); *Of Rivers and Trains* (Albany, N.Y., Nov. 4, 1988); also many choruses; String Quartet and other chamber music; Piano Sonata; children's piano pieces; songs.

Mayfield, Curtis, black American rhythm-and-blues and soul singer, guitarist, and songwriter; b. Chicago, June 3, 1942. Extremely precocious, he produced a song, *For Your Precious Love,* then joined Jerry Butler's band The Impressions as a guitarist, and co-authored with him the hit solo *He Will Break Your Heart.* In 1961 he practically took over Butler's band and led it until 1970, scoring hits with *Hey Little Girl, Gypsy Woman,* and *This Is My Country.* Self-confident to the point of arrogance, he put out a solo album egotistically named *Curtis,* and followed it up with *Curtis Live!* They were successful. But a greater success came with his soundtrack to the film *Superfly.* In 1990 he was struck in the head by a lighting tower in N.Y. and was left paralyzed from the neck down.

Maykapar, Samuil, Russian pianist, composer, and teacher; b. Kherson, Dec. 18, 1867; d. Leningrad, May 8, 1938. He studied at the St. Petersburg Cons. with B. Cesi (piano) and Soloviev (theory); then in Vienna with Leschetizky; gave concerts in Germany (1903–10). From 1910 to 1930 he was a prof. at the St. Petersburg (later Leningrad) Cons. He composed almost exclusively for piano; was particularly successful in miniature forms. His piano works include *Biriulki* (suite of 26 pieces); *24 Miniatures; The Marionette Theater* (7 pieces); *2 sonatinas;* etc.; also piano studies and special exercises. He publ. *The Musical Ear* (Moscow, 1900) and *The Years of Study and of Musical Activity* (partly autobiographical; Moscow, 1938).

Maylath, Heinrich, Austrian-American pianist, teacher, and composer; b. Vienna, Dec. 4, 1827; d. N.Y., Dec. 31, 1883. He was a pupil of his father; traveled as a concert pianist in Europe, including Russia. In 1867 he settled in America, and became a teacher in N.Y. He publ. some excellent, instructive piano music, as well as concert pieces; made numerous transcriptions of various works for piano.

Maynor (Mainor), Dorothy (Leigh), noted black American soprano; b. Norfolk, Va., Sept. 3, 1910. She was educated at the Hampton Inst. (B.S., 1933); began her career singing in various choirs, and later toured with the inst.'s famous chorus in Europe; subsequently studied at Westminster Choir College and with William Kamroth and John Alan Haughton in N.Y. After a successful appearance at the Berkshire Music Festival at Tanglewood in 1939, she made her Town Hall debut in N.Y. on Nov. 19, 1939. In subsequent years she toured widely in the U.S. and Europe as a concert singer, appearing with leading orchs. She founded the Harlem School of the Arts in 1963 to provide music education for underprivileged children, and served as its executive director until her retirement in 1979.

Mayr, Richard, renowned Austrian bass-baritone; b. Henndorf, near Salzburg, Nov. 18, 1877; d. Vienna, Dec. 1, 1935. He studied medicine in Vienna before being persuaded by Mahler to take up music; after training at the Vienna Cons., he made his operatic debut as Hagen at the Bayreuth Festival (1902); then was engaged by Mahler for the Vienna Opera, where he made his 1st appearance as Don Gomez in *Ernani* that same year; remained on the company's roster until his death; was also a principal singer at the Salzburg Festivals (1921–34). He made his 1st appearance at London's Covent Garden as Baron Ochs, his most celebrated role, on May 23,

1924, and continued to appear there until 1931; made his Metropolitan Opera debut in N.Y. as Pogner on Nov. 2, 1927; remained on the company's roster until 1930. Mayr possessed a rich and powerful voice, equally suited for serious and buffo roles. In addition to his remarkable portrayal of Baron Ochs, he also excelled as Figaro, Leporello, Sarastro, Wotan, Gurnemanz, and Rocco; was chosen by Strauss to create the role of Barak in his *Die Frau ohne Schatten* (Vienna, Oct. 10, 1919).
BIBL.: H. Holz, *R. M.* (Vienna, 1923); O. Kunz, *R. M.* (Vienna, 1933).

Mayr (Mayer), (Johannes) Simon (actually, **Giovanni Simone**), outstanding German opera composer; b. Mendorf, Bavaria (of Italian parents), June 14, 1763; d. Bergamo, Dec. 2, 1845. He 1st studied music with his father, a schoolteacher and organist; he sang in a church choir and played organ. In 1774 he entered the Jesuit college in Ingolstadt; in 1781 he began a study of theology at the Univ. of Ingolstadt. In 1787 a Swiss Freiherr, Thomas von Bassus, took him to Italy to further his musical education; in 1789 he commenced studies with Carlo Lenzi in Bergamo; he then was sent to Ferdinando Bertoni in Venice. He began his career as a composer of sacred music; his oratorios were performed in Venice. After the death of his patron, Count Presenti, in 1793, he was encouraged by Piccinni and Peter von Winter to compose operas. His 1st opera, *Saffo o sia I riti d'Apollo Leucadio,* was performed in Venice in 1794. He gained renown with his opera *Ginevra di Scozia* (Trieste, April 21, 1801), and it remained a favorite with audiences; also successful were his operas *La rosa bianca e la rosa rossa* (Genoa, Feb. 21, 1813) and *Medea in Corinto* (Naples, Nov. 28, 1813). In 1802 he became maestro di cappella at S. Maria Maggiore in Bergamo; in 1805 he reorganized the choir school of the Cathedral as the Lezioni Caritatevoli di Musica and assumed its directorship; intractable cataracts, which led to total blindness in 1826, forced him to limit his activities to organ playing. In 1822 he founded the Società Filarmonica of Bergamo. Mayr's operas, while reflecting the late Neapolitan school, are noteworthy for their harmonization and orchestration, which are derived from the German tradition. After 1815 he devoted most of his time to composing sacred music, which totals some 600 works in all. He was also an eminent pedagogue. Donizetti was his pupil.
WORKS: OPERAS: *Saffo o sia I riti d'Apollo Leucadio,* dramma per musica (Venice, Feb. 17, 1794); *La Lodoiska,* dramma per musica (Venice, Jan. 26, 1796; rev. for Milan, Dec. 26, 1799); *Un pazzo ne fa cento [I Rivali delusi; La Contessa immaginaria],* dramma giocoso (Venice, Oct. 8, 1796); *Telemaco nell'isola di Calipso,* dramma per musica (Venice, Jan. 16, 1797); *Il segreto,* farsa (Venice, Sept. 24, 1797); *L'intrigo della lettera [Il pittore astratto],* farsa (Venice, fall 1797); *Avviso ai maritati,* dramma giocoso (Venice, Jan. 15, 1798); *Lauso e Lidia,* dramma per musica (Venice, Feb. 14, 1798); *Adriano in Siria,* dramma per musica (Venice, April 23, 1798); *Che originali [Il trionfo della musica; Il fanatico per la musica: La musicomania],* farsa (Venice, Oct. 18, 1798); *Amor ingegnoso,* farsa (Venice, Dec. 27, 1798); *L'ubbidienza per astuzia,* farsa (Venice, Dec. 27, 1798); *Adelaide di Gueselino,* dramma per musica (Venice, May 1, 1799); *Labino e Carlotta,* farsa (Venice, Oct. 9, 1799); *L'Avaro,* farsa (Venice, Nov. 1799); *L'accademia di musica,* farsa (Venice, fall 1799); *Gli sciti,* dramma per musica (Venice, Feb. 1800); *La Locandiera,* farsa (Vicenza, spring 1800); *Il caretto del venditore d'aceto,* farsa (Venice, June 28, 1800); *L'Imbroglione e il castiga-matti,* farsa (Venice, fall 1800); *L'equivoco, ovvero Le bizzarie dell'amore,* dramma giocoso (Milan, Nov. 5, 1800); *Ginevra di Scozia [Ariodante],* dramma serio eroico per musica (Trieste, April 21, 1801; inaugural perf. at the Teatro Nuovo there); *Le due giornate [Il Portatore d'acqua],* dramma eroicomico per musica (Milan, Aug. 18, 1801); *I Virtuosi [I Virtuosi a teatro],* farsa (Venice, Dec. 26, 1801); *Argene,* dramma eroico per musica (Venice, Dec. 28, 1801); *Elisa, ossia Il monte S. Bernardo,* dramma sentimentale per musica (Malta, 1801); *I misteri eleusini,* dramma per musica (Milan, Jan. 6, 1802); *I castelli in*

aria, ossia Gli Amanti per accidente, farsa (Venice, May 1802); *Ercole in Lidia*, dramma per musica (Vienna, Jan. 29, 1803); *Gl'intrighi amorosi*, dramma giocoso (Parma, Carnival 1803); *Le finte rivali*, melodramma giocoso (Aug. 20, 1803); *Alonso e Cora*, dramma per musica (Milan, Dec. 26, 1803; rev. as *Cora* for Naples, 1815); *Amor non ha ritegno* [*La fedeltà delle vedove*], melodramma eroicomico (Milan, May 18, 1804); *I due viaggiatori*, dramma giocoso (Florence, summer 1804); *Zamori, ossia L'Eroe dell'Indie*, dramma per musica (Piacenza, Aug. 10, 1804; inaugural perf. at the Nuovo Teatro Communale); *Eraldo ed Emma*, dramma eroico per musica (Milan, Jan. 8, 1805); *Di locanda in locanda e sempre in sala*, farsa (June 5, 1805); *L'amor coniugale* [*Il custode di buon cuore*], dramma giocoso (Padua, July 26, 1805); *La rocca di Frauenstein*, melodramma eroicomico (Venice, Oct. 26, 1805); *Gli Americani* [*Idalide*], melodramma eroico (Venice, Carnival 1806); *Palmira, o sia Il trionfo della virtù e dell'amore*, dramma per musica (Florence, fall 1806); *Il piccolo compositore di musica*, farsa (Venice, 1806); *Nè l'un, nè l'altro*, dramma giocoso (Milan, Aug. 17, 1807); *Belle ciarle e tristi fatti* [*L'imbroglio contro l'imbroglio*], dramma giocoso (Venice, Nov. 1807); *Adelasia e Aleramo*, melodramma serio (Milan, Dec. 25, 1807); *I cherusci*, dramma per musica (Rome, Carnival 1808); *Il vero originale*, burletta per musica (Rome, Carnival 1808); *La finta sposa, ossia Il Barone burlato*, dramma giocoso (Rome, spring 1808); *Il matrimonio per concorso*, dramma giocoso (Bologna, Carnival 1809); *Il ritorno di Ulisse*, azione eroica per musica (Venice, Carnival 1809); *Amor non soffre opposizione*, dramma giocoso (Venice, Carnival 1810); *Raùl di Créqui*, melodramma serio (Milan, Dec. 26, 1810); *Il sacrifizio d'Ifigenia* [*Ifigenia in Aulide*], azione seria drammatica per musica (Brescia, Carnival 1811); *L'amor figliale* [*Il Disertore*], farsa sentimentale (Venice, Carnival 1811); *La rosa bianca e la rosa rossa* [*Il trionfo dell'amicizia*], melodramma eroica (Genoa, Feb. 21, 1813); *Medea in Corinto*, melodramma tragico (Naples, Nov. 28, 1813); *Tamerlano*, melodramma serio (Milan, Carnival 1813); *Elena* [*Elena e Costantino*], dramma eroicomico per musica (Naples, Carnival 1814); *Atar, o sia Il serraglio d'Ormus*, melodramma serio (Genoa, June 1814); *Le due duchesse, ossia La caccia dei lupi* [*Le due amiche*], dramma semiserio per musica (Milan, Nov. 7, 1814); *La Figlia dell'aria, ossia La vendetta di Giunone*, dramma per musica (Naples, Lent 1817); *Nennone e Zemira*, dramma per musica (Naples, March 22, 1817); *Amor avvocato*, commedia per musica (Naples, spring 1817); *Lanassa*, melodramma eroico (Venice, Carnival 1818); *Alfredo il grande*, melodramma serio (Rome, Feb. 1818); *Le Danaide* [*Danao*], melodramma serio (Rome, Carnival 1819); *Fedra*, melodramma serio (Milan, Dec. 25, 1820); *Demetrio*, dramma per musica (Turin, Carnival 1824).

ORATORIOS: *Iacob a Labano fugiens* (Venice, 1791); *Sisara* (Venice, 1793); *Tobia, o Tobiae matrimonium* (Venice, 1794); *La Passione* (Forli, 1794); *David in spelunca Engaddi* (Venice, 1795); *Il sacrifizio di Iefte* (Forli; year unknown); *Samuele* (Bergamo, 1821); *S. Luigi Gonzaga* (Bergamo, 1822); also the sacred dramas *Ifigenia in Tauride* (Florence, spring 1817) and *Atalia* (Naples, Lent 1822). He also composed about 50 cantatas, 18 masses, over 200 Mass movements, 2 Requiems, 20 Requiem movements, 43 hymns, 14 antiphons, 13 motets, etc. His secular vocal works include over 40 canzonettas, arias, songs, lieder, etc. His instrumental works include 2 syms., 2 piano concertos, chamber music, and keyboard pieces.

WRITINGS: In addition to his *Breve notizie storiche della vita e delle opere di Giuseppe Haydn* (Bergamo, 1809) and *Regolamento delle Lezioni Caritatevoli di musica* (Bergamo, 1822), many other writings remain in MS.

BIBL.: G. Calvi, *Musica sacra di S. M.* (Milan, 1848); G. Finazzi, *Per la solenne inaugurazione del monumento eretto alla memoria del celebre maestro G.S. M. nella basilica di S. Maria Maggiore in Bergamo* (Bergamo, 1853); F. Alborghetti and M. Galli, *Gaetano Donizetti e G.S. M.: Notizie e documenti* (Bergamo, 1875); C. Schmidl, *Cenni biografici su G.S. M.* (Trieste, 1901); C. Scotti, *G.S. M.: Discorso* (Bergamo, 1903); H. Kretzschmar, "Die musik geschichtliche Bedeutung S. M.s," *Jahrbuch der Musikbibliothek Peters 1904;* L. Schiedermair, *Beiträge zur Geschichte der Oper um die Wende des 18. und 19. Jahrhunderts: S. M.* (2 vols., Leipzig, 1907 and 1910); A. Gazzaniga, *Il Fondo musicale M. della biblioteca civica di Bergamo* (Bergamo, 1963); M. Carner, "S. M. and His *L'amor coniugale*," *Music & Letters* (July 1971); J. Freeman, "Johann S. M. and His *Ifigenia in Aulide*," *Musical Quarterly* (April 1971); A. Gazzaniga, "Su *L'amor coniugale* di G.S. M.," *Nuova Rivista Musicale Italiana* (Sept.–Oct. 1971); J. Allitt, *J.S. M.* (Shaftesbury, 1989).

Mayseder, Joseph, distinguished Austrian violinist, pedagogue, and composer; b. Vienna, Oct. 26, 1789; d. there, Nov. 21, 1863. He was a pupil of Suche and Wranitzky (violin) and of E. Förster (piano and composition). He joined the famous Schuppanzigh Quartet as 2nd violin; became concertmaster of the Court Theater orch. in 1810; entered the Court Orch. in 1816; became solo violinist at the Court Opera in 1820 and chamber violinist to the Emperor in 1835; music director of the court chapel in 1836–37. He never went on tours, and rarely gave concerts; yet he was a finished virtuoso, admired even by Paganini. In Vienna he was very successful as a teacher. His works include 3 violin concertos, a Mass (1848), 5 string quintets, 8 string quartets, trios, and solo violin pieces.

BIBL.: E. Hellsberg, *J. M.* (diss., Univ. of Vienna, 1955).

Mayuzumi, Toshirō, eminent Japanese composer; b. Yokohama, Feb. 20, 1929. He studied with T. Ikenouchi and A. Ifukube at the National Univ. of Fine Arts and Music in Tokyo (1945–51); then took courses at the Paris Cons. with Aubin (1951–52). Returning to Japan, he organized the modern group Ars Nova Japonica and also worked at the electronic music studio in Tokyo. His style of composition embodies sonorous elements from traditional Japanese music, serial techniques, and electronic sounds, all amalgamated in a remarkably effective manner; he is also a successful composer of film scores, including that for *The Bible.*

WORKS: Violin Sonata (1946); *Divertimento* for 10 Instruments (1948); *Symphonic Mood* (1950); *Sphenogramme* for Voice and Instruments (ISCM Festival, Frankfurt, June 25, 1951); *Ectoplasme* for Electronic Instruments, Percussion, and Strings (ISCM Festival, Stockholm, June 5, 1956); *Mikrokosmos* for 7 Instruments (Karuizawa, Aug. 12, 1957); *Phonologie symphonique* (Tokyo, May 28, 1957); *Nirvana Symphony* (Tokyo, April 2, 1958); *U-So-Ri*, oratorio (Tokyo, June 12, 1959); *Mandala-Symphonie* (Tokyo, March 27, 1960); *Bunraku* for Cello (1960); *Music with Sculpture* for Winds (Pittsburgh, June 29, 1961); *Prelude* for String Quartet (1961); *Samsara*, symphonic poem (Tokyo, June 12, 1962); *Texture* for Band (Pittsburgh, June 10, 1962); *Essay in Sonorities* (Osaka, Jan. 21, 1963); *Bugaku*, ballet (N.Y., March 20, 1963); *Fireworks* for Band (Pittsburgh, June 13, 1963); *Pratidesana*, Buddhist cantata (Kyoto, Sept. 5, 1963); *The Ritual Overture* for Band (Pittsburgh, July 2, 1964); *The Birth of Music*, symphonic poem (Tokyo, Oct. 10, 1964); *Showa Tempyo Raku* (Old and Present Music), symphonic poem (Tokyo, Oct. 31, 1970); *Kinkakuji* (The Temple of the Golden Pavilion), opera (Berlin, June 23, 1976); *Aria in G* for Violin Solo and Orch. (1978); *The Kabuki*, ballet (1985); *Perpetuum mobile* for Orch. (1989).

Mazas, Jacques-Féréol, French violinist, teacher, and composer; b. Lavaur, Tarn, Sept. 23, 1782; d. Bordeaux, Aug. 25, 1849. He was a pupil of Baillot at the Paris Cons., winning 1st prize as violinist (1805); then played in the orch. of the Italian Opera in Paris; toured Europe (1811–27); then was a teacher in Orléans (from 1831), and director of a music school in Cambrai (1837–41). He spent the last years of his life in Bordeaux. He wrote a method for violin (new ed. by J. Hrímalý) and numerous valuable studies; also a method for viola; concertos, string quartets, trios, violin duets, fantasias, variations, romances, etc.; also 3 operas, one of which, *Le Kiosque*, was performed in Paris in 1842. A set of 6 études was publ. in a new ed. by Hubay.

Mazura, Franz, Austrian bass-baritone; b. Salzburg, April 21, 1924. He studied in Detmold; made his operatic debut in

Kassel (1949); later appeared at the opera houses of Mainz, Braunschweig, and Mannheim. In 1963 he made his 1st appearance at the Berlin Städtische Oper and in 1967 at the Hamburg State Opera; also sang at the Bayreuth Festivals (from 1971). In 1979 he sang Dr. Schön in the premiere of the 3-act version of *Lulu* in Paris, which role he also sang at his Metropolitan Opera debut in N.Y. (Dec. 12, 1980). In addition to the Wagnerian repertoire, he sang Pizzaro in *Fidelio*, Jochanaan in *Salome*, and Moses in Schoenberg's *Moses und Aron*.

Mazzinghi, Joseph, English pianist and composer of Corsican descent; b. London, Dec. 25, 1765; d. Downside, near Bath, Jan. 15, 1844. He was the son of Thomas Mazzinghi, a wine merchant, who played violin at Marylebone Gardens and was active as a composer. He studied with J.C. Bach in London; he was a mere child when his father died, and succeeded him as organist of the Portuguese Chapel at 10. He subsequently took lessons with Bertoni, Sacchini, and Anfossi during their British sojourns. He was music director (1785–94) and harpsichordist (1785–98) at the King's Theatre in London; then taught piano. He wrote prolifically, producing dramatic works, ballets, sonatas, piano pieces, songs, glees, etc., all of little merit.

Mazzocchi, Domenico, Italian composer, brother of **Virgilio Mazzocchi**; b. Veja, near Città Castellana (baptized), Nov. 8, 1592; d. Rome, Jan. 21, 1665. A learned Roman lawyer, he studied music with Nanini; in 1621 he entered the service of Cardinal Ippolito Aldobrandini. He publ. *Madrigali a 5 voci in partitura* (1638), in which appear, for the 1st time, the conventional symbols for *crescendo* ($<$) and *decrescendo* ($>$), *piano* (*p*), *forte* (*f*), and *trillo* (*tr*), which he explains in a preface. He also composed the operas *La catena d'Adone* (Rome, 1626) and *L'innocenza difesa*, several oratorios, and various pieces of church music.
Bibl.: A. Cardinali, *Cenni biografici su D. e Virgilio M.* (Subiaco, 1926); W. Witzenmann, "D. M., 1592–1665: Dokumente und Interpretationen," *Analecta Musicologica*, 8 (1970).

Mazzocchi, Virgilio, Italian composer, brother of **Domenico Mazzocchi**; b. Veja (baptized), July 22, 1597; d. there, Oct. 3, 1646. He studied music with his brother in Rome; served as maestro di cappella at the Chiesa del Gesù; then was at St. John Lateran (1628–29). In 1629 he was engaged at the Cappella Giulia at St. Peter's, and served there until his death. He wrote the opera *Chi soffre, speri* with Marazzoli (Rome, Feb. 27, 1639), which was a revision of *Il facone* (Rome, Feb. 1637); excerpts from it were publ. by H. Goldschmidt; an *Argomento et allegoria* relating to it was publ. at the time of its 1st performance; a copy is in the Library of Congress in Washington, D.C.
Bibl.: A. Salza, "M.," *Rivista Musicale Italiana* (1917); A. Cardinali, *Cenni biografici su Domenico e V. M.* (Subiaco, 1926).

Mazzolani, Antonio, Italian composer; b. Ruina, near Ferrara, Dec. 26, 1819; d. Ferrara, Jan. 25, 1900. He studied with Zagagnoni (composition) and Lodi (piano); wrote the operas *Gismonda* (Ferrara, May 17, 1854) and *Enrico Charlis* (Ferrara, Nov. 25, 1876); his choruses, with extensive soli, were very popular in Italy during his time.

Mazzoleni, Ettore, Canadian conductor, teacher, and composer of Italian-Swiss descent; b. Brusio, Switzerland, June 19, 1905; d. in an automobile accident in Oak Ridges, near Toronto, June 1, 1968. He studied mathematics and music at Oxford Univ. (B.A., 1927; B.Mus., 1927) and piano at the Royal College of Music in London, where he later taught (1927–29). He then settled in Toronto, where he was music master and later an English instructor at Upper Canada College (1929–45); also taught music history at the Toronto Cons. (from 1932) and conducted its sym. orch. (from 1934); was made its principal in 1945, continuing in that capacity when it became the Royal Cons. of Music of Toronto in 1952; retired in 1966. He was associate conductor of the Toronto Sym. Orch. (1942–48); also appeared as a conductor in other Canadian cities.

In 1949 he became a naturalized Canadian citizen. He made several transcriptions of folk songs for various instrumental and vocal groups.

Mazzucato, Alberto, Italian violinist, composer, and writer on music; b. Udine, July 28, 1813; d. Milan, Dec. 31, 1877. He 1st studied mathematics; then turned to music, his teacher being Bresciano in Padua, where his 1st opera, *La Fidanzata di Lammermoor*, was given (Feb. 24, 1834); he wrote 8 more operas: *Don Chisciotte* (Milan, April 26, 1836), *Esmeralda* (Mantua, Feb. 10, 1838; his most successful stage work), *I Corsari* (Milan, Feb. 15, 1840), *I due sergenti* (Milan, Feb. 27, 1841), *Luigi V, re di Francia* (Milan, Feb. 25, 1843), *Hernani* (Genoa, Dec. 26, 1843), *Alberico da Romano* (Padua, 1847), and *Fede* (not perf.). Verdi's ascendance soon put him into the shade. He joined the faculty of the Milan Cons. in 1839, and from 1872 until his death was its director. From 1859 to 1868 he was concertmaster in the orch. of La Scala, Milan. He wrote for the *Gazzetta Musicale di Milano* (1845–56); then was its ed. (1856–58). He publ. *Trattato d'estetica musicale*.

McAllester, David (Park), American ethnomusicologist; b. Everett, Mass., Aug. 6, 1916. He studied anthropology at Harvard Univ. (B.A., 1934) and Columbia Univ. (Ph.D., 1939); taught anthropology at Wesleyan Univ. from 1947; from 1972 he served as prof. of anthropology and music there. He devoted much time to the study of American Indian culture.
Writings: *Peyote Music* (N.Y., 1949); *Enemy Way Music* (Cambridge, Mass., 1954); *The Myth and Prayers of the Great Star Chant* (Santa Fe, N.Mex., 1956); ed. *Readings in Ethnomusicology* (N.Y., 1971); with S. McAllester, *Hogans: Navajo Houses and House Songs* (Middletown, Conn., 1980).

McArthur, Edwin, American conductor, piano accompanist, and song composer; b. Denver, Sept. 24, 1907; d. N.Y., Feb. 24, 1987. He studied at the Juilliard School of Music in N.Y.; worked as an organist and voice coach, and also had success as an accompanist. He was best known for his conducting and coaching of Wagner's works. In 1941 he became the 1st native American to conduct an opera at the Metropolitan Opera in N.Y., and won critical acclaim when he led Kirsten Flagstad and Lauritz Melchior in *Tristan und Isolde*. In 1966 he wrote about his long friendship with the great soprano in *Flagstad: A Personal Memoir*. He was the music director of the St. Louis Municipal Opera (1945–50); then conducted the Harrisburg (Pa.) Sym. Orch. (1950–74). From 1967 to 1972 he served as director of the opera dept. at the Eastman School of Music in Rochester, N.Y. He retired to private coaching of opera.

McBride, Robert (Guyn), American composer; b. Tucson, Ariz., Feb. 20, 1911. He learned to play clarinet, saxophone, organ, and piano; played in dance bands as a youth. He studied music theory at the Univ. of Arizona (1928–35); was a member of the Tucson Sym. Orch. (1928–35). From 1935 to 1946 he taught wind instruments at Bennington (Vt.) College; was then arranger for Triumph Films, N.Y. (1946–57); from 1957 to 1978 he was on the music faculty of the Univ. of Arizona. An exceptionally prolific composer, he wrote over 1,000 pieces in various genres, many of them on American or Mexican themes with an infusion of jazz elements.
Works: orch.: *Mexican Rhapsody* (1934); *Side Show* (1944); Violin Concerto (1954); *Hill Country Symphony* (1964); *Symphonic Melody* (1968); *Folk-Song Fantasy* (1973); *Light Fantastic* (1976–77). **chamber:** *Workout* for Oboe and Piano (1936); *Swing Stuff* for Clarinet and Piano (1938); *Jam Session* for Woodwind Quintet (1941); *Swing Foursome* for String Quartet (1957); *5 Winds Blowing* for Wind Quintet (1957); *Lament for the Parking Problem* for Trumpet, Horn, and Trombone (1968).

McCabe, John, esteemed English pianist, music educator, and composer; b. Huyton, April 21, 1939. He learned to play piano, violin, and cello as a child; studied with Proctor Gregg (composition) at the Univ. of Manchester and with Pitfield (composition) and Green (piano) at the Royal Manchester College of Music; later took courses at the Munich Academy of

Music (1964–65) and also studied privately there with Genzmer. He was pianist-in-residence at Univ. College, Cardiff (1965–67); then settled in London as a pianist, excelling in the music of Haydn and contemporary composers; was director of the London College of Music from 1983. In 1985 he was made a Commander of the Order of the British Empire.

WORKS: THEATER: *The Lion, the Witch, and the Wardrobe,* children's opera (1968; Manchester, April 29, 1969); *This Town's a Corporation Full of Crooked Streets,* entertainment for Speaker, Tenor, Children's Choir, Mixed Choir, and Instrumental Ensemble (1969); *Notturni ed Alba,* ballet (1970); *The Teachings of Don Juan,* ballet (Manchester, May 30, 1973); *The Play of Mother Courage,* chamber opera (Middlesbrough, Oct. 3, 1974); *Mary Queen of Scots,* ballet (1975; Glasgow, March 3, 1976). **ORCH.:** 2 violin concertos: No. 1, *Sinfonia concertante* (1959); No. 2 (Birmingham, March 20, 1980); Concerto for Chamber Orch. (1962; rev. 1968); *Concerto funèbre* for Viola and Chamber Orch. (1962); *Variations on a Theme of Hartmann* (1964; Manchester, Nov. 24, 1965); *Chamber Concerto* for Viola, Cello, and Orch. (1965); *Concertante* for Harpsichord and Chamber Ensemble (1965); 3 syms.: No. 1, *Elegy* (1965; Cheltenham, July 4, 1966); No. 2 (Birmingham, Sept. 26, 1971); No. 3, *Hommages* (London, July 11, 1978); 3 piano concertos: No. 1 (1966); No. 2, *Sinfonia concertante* (1970; Middlesbrough, Nov. 23, 1971); No. 3, *Dialogues* (1976; rev. 1977; Liverpool, Aug. 5, 1977); Concertino for Piano Duet and Orch. (1968); *Concertante Music* (Bath, June 24, 1968); *Metamorphosen* for Harpsichord and Orch. (1968; Liverpool, Feb. 19, 1972); *Concertante Variations on a Theme of Nicholas Maw* for Strings (1970; Bristol, March 3, 1971); Oboe d'Amore Concerto (Portsmouth, April 26, 1972); *The Chagall Windows* (1974; Manchester, Jan. 9, 1975); *Sonata on a Motet* for String Orch. (Manchester, March 20, 1976); *Jubilee Suite* (London, April 17, 1977); Clarinet Concerto (1977; London, July 11, 1978); *The Shadow of Light* (London, Dec. 6, 1979); Concerto (1982; London, Feb. 10, 1983); *Tuning* ('s Hertogenbosch, July 27, 1985); *Fire at Durilgai* (London, Aug. 7, 1989). **CHAMBER:** 5 string quartets (1960, 1972, 1979, 1982, 1989); Partita for String Quartet (1960); Sym. for 10 Wind Instruments (1964); String Trio (1965); *Nocturnal* for Piano Quintet (1966); *Fantasy* for Brass Quartet (1967); *Rounds* for Brass Quintet (1967); Oboe Quartet (1968); Concerto for Piano and Wind Quintet (1969); *Canzona* for Wind and Percussion (1970); *The Goddess Trilogy* for Horn and Piano: 1, *The Castle of Arianrhod* (1973); 2, *Floraison* (1975); 3, *Shape-Shifter* (1975); *Desert I: Lizard* for Flute, Oboe, Clarinet, Bassoon, and Percussion (1981); *Desert II: Horizon* for 10 Brass Instruments (1981); *Desert III: Landscape* for Violin, Cello, and Piano (1982); *Desert IV: Vista* for Recorder (1983); *Rainforest* for 10 Players (N.Y., Nov. 30, 1984); piano pieces; organ works. **VOCAL:** *Voyage,* cantata for Vocal Soloists, Boys' Choir, Mixed Choir, and Organ (Worcester, Aug. 30, 1972); *Stabat Mater* for Soprano, Chorus, and Orch. (Northampton, Oct. 28, 1976); *Reflections of a Summer Night,* cantata for Chorus and Orch. (1977; Fishguard, July 26, 1978); *Scenes from America Deserta* for 6 Voices (1986); works for solo voices, including *Time Remembered* for Soprano and Instrumental Ensemble (Malvern, Oct. 4, 1973).

BIBL.: R. Maycock, "Variations on a Form: J. M.'s String Quartets," *Musical Times* (July 1989).

McCalla, James, American musicologist; b. Lawrence, Kans., Aug. 25, 1946. He received a B.Mus. in piano and a B.A. in French from the Univ. of Kansas in Lawrence (1968), and an M.M. in music literature from the New England Cons. of Music in Boston (1973); then took a Ph.D. in musicology, specializing in 20th-century music, with Kerman at the Univ. of Calif. at Berkeley (1976, with the diss. *"Between Its Human Accessories": The Art of Stéphane Mallarmé and Pierre Boulez*). He taught at the Univ. of Virginia (1976–78), the State Univ. of N.Y. at Stony Brook (1978–85), and Bowdoin College in Maine (from 1985). His textbooks include *Jazz: A Listener's Guide* (Englewood Cliffs, N.J., 1982) and *Chamber Music of*

Our Time (1991). His research employs literary critique to analyze the interface between complex musical and textual works, with subjects including indeterminacy and jazz.

McCartney, (John) Paul, English rock-'n'-roll singer, guitarist, pianist, organist, and composer, member of the famous Liverpudlian quartet The Beatles; b. Liverpool, June 18, 1942. He picked out chords on a family piano (his father was an amateur ragtime player), and at puberty began playing a left-handed guitar. He was the only Beatle who attended college, and studied English literature. Fascinated by Elvis Presley, he tried to emulate the spirit of American rock 'n' roll *à l'anglaise*. With fellow Liverpudlians John Lennon, George Harrison, and Stuart Sutcliffe, he formed the group known as the Silver Beatles, which later took the name The Beatles. They played at Liverpool's Casbah Club (1959), and then at the Cavern Club (1961), where they were joined by the drummer Pete Best. After the death of Sutcliffe (1962) and the departure of Best, Richard Starkey, known as Ringo Starr, joined the group and history was made when they appeared at the London Palladium in 1963. Their fruitful and lucrative association continued until the breakup of the group in 1970, when McCartney went to court to end the partnership and asked for an accounting of assets and income. He subsequently was active with his own group, Wings. In 1990 he made a phenomenally successful tour of the U.S. Endowed with an authentic poetic gift, McCartney infused a literary quality into the lyrics used by The Beatles, fashioning them in archaic English prosody, which in combination with the modal harmony of the arrangements imparted a somewhat distant quality to their products. Like his co-Beatles, McCartney went through a period of transcendental meditation when he sat at the feet of a hirsute Indian guru, but his British common sense soon overrode this metaphysical infatuation.

BIBL.: H. Davies, *The Beatles* (N.Y., 1968); G. Geppert, *Songs der Beatles. Texte und Interpretationen* (2nd ed., Munich, 1968); N. Rorem, "The Beatles," *N.Y. Review of Books* (Jan. 18, 1968); E. Davies, "The Psychological Characteristics of Beatle Mania," *Journal of the History of Ideas* (April–June 1969); P. McCabe and R. Schonfeld, *Apple to the Core: The Unmaking of the Beatles* (N.Y., 1972); F. Seloron, *Les Beatles* (Paris, 1972); W. Mellers, *Twilight of the Gods: The Music of the Beatles* (N.Y., 1973); T. O'Grady, *The Beatles: A Musical Evolution* (Boston, 1983); C. Flippo, *Yesterday: The Unauthorized Biography of P. M.* (N.Y., 1988).

McCauley, William (Alexander), Canadian conductor and composer; b. Tofield, Alberta, Feb. 14, 1917. He studied at the Univ. of Toronto (M.B., 1947), with Margaret Parsons (piano, 1947) and Healy Willan (composition) at the Toronto Cons., and with Howard Hanson and Bernard Rogers at the Eastman School of Music in Rochester, N.Y. (M.M., 1959; D.M.A., 1960); also was a conducting pupil of Monteux in Hancock, Maine (summer 1959). He was 1st trombone for the Ottawa Phil. and the National Film Board (1947–49); then was music director of Crawley Films (1949–60), where he composed and conducted music for over 100 television films and documentaries; then was music director of York Univ. (1960–69), the O'Keefe Centre (1960–87), Christopher Chapman Films (1969–70), Seneca College (1970–78), and the North York Sym. Orch. (1972–88). His music is pleasing, lyrical, and inoffensive, with some officious modernities.

WORKS: ORCH.: *Newfoundland Scene* (1952); *Saskatchewan Suite* (1956); *5 Miniatures* for Flute and Strings (1958); *Contrasts* (1958); Horn Concerto (1959); *5 Miniatures* for Bass Trombone, Harp, and Strings (1959); *Theme and Deviations* (1960); *Wilderness,* music from the film (1963); *Canadian Folk Song Fantasy* for Symphonic Band (1966); *Metropolis,* concert suite for Symphonic Band (1967); *2 Nocturnes* for Strings (1968); *Sunday Morning at Wahanowin* for String Orch. (1968); *Concerto grosso* for Brass Quintet and Orch. (1973); *Christmas Carol Fantasies* (1975). **CHAMBER:** *5 Miniatures* for 6 Percussionists (1962); *5 Miniatures* for 10 Winds (1968); *5 Miniatures* for 4 Saxophones (1972); *Miniature Overture* for Brass Quintet

(1973); *Kaleidoscope québécois* for Flute, Clarinet, Violin, Cello, and 2 Pianos (1974); *5 Miniatures* for Brass Quintet (1974); also *Space Trip* for Piano (1968); choruses; songs, many with instrumental accompaniment.

McClain, Ernest Glenn, American music scholar; b. Canton, Ohio, Aug. 6, 1918. He studied at Oberlin College (B.Mus., 1940), Northwestern Univ. (M.Mus., 1946), and Columbia Univ. (Ed.D., 1959). He was band director at Denison Univ. (1946–47) and the Univ. of Hawaii (1947–50); then taught at Brooklyn College, City Univ. of N.Y., from 1950 until his retirement in 1981. He developed an effective way of teaching tuning systems using the monochord. His articles and books are sophisticated explorations of the interface between acoustics, mathematics, philosophy, and religion in ancient and medieval cultures.

WRITINGS: *The Myth of Invariance: The Origin of the Gods, Mathematics, and Music from the Rig-Veda to Plato* (Boulder, Colo., 1976); *The Pythagorean Plato: Prelude to the Song Itself* (York Beach, Maine, 1978); *Meditations through the Quran: Tonal Images in an Oral Culture* (1981).

McClary, Susan, progressive American musicologist; b. St. Louis, Mo., Oct. 2, 1946. She studied piano at Southern Illinois Univ. (B.Mus., 1968) and musicology at Harvard Univ. (A.M., 1971; Ph.D., 1976, with the diss. *The Transition from Modal to Tonal Organization in the Works of Monteverdi*). She taught at Harvard Univ. (1969–73) and Trinity College in Hartford, Conn. (1977); joined the faculty of the Univ. of Minnesota in 1977, becoming a prof. in 1990; was acting director of its Center for Humanistic Studies (1984–85) and director of its Collegium Musicum. Her early research disputed the view of 17th-century music that treats it as primitive tonality, arguing instead for its theoretical integrity. From 1982 she publ. articles on the political, economic, and feminist critique of music, on subjects including Mozart, Madonna, Bach, and Laurie Anderson; these studies won her attention and infamy and led to her being called "the 1st radical feminist musicologist." Her books include *Feminine Endings: Music, Gender, and Sexuality* (Minneapolis, 1990) and *Power and Desire in Seventeenth-Century Music* (Princeton, 1991); also co-ed., with R. Leppert, *Music and Society: The Politics of Composition, Performance and Reception* (Cambridge, 1987).

McCorkle, Donald M(acomber), American musicologist; b. Cleveland, Feb. 20, 1929; d. Vancouver, Feb. 6, 1978. He studied at Brown Univ., at Bradley Univ. (B.Mus., 1951), and with W. Apel and P. Nettl at Indiana Univ. (M.A., 1953; Ph.D., 1958, with the diss. *Moravian Music in Salem: A German-American Heritage*). He was assistant prof. of musicology at Salem College, Winston-Salem, N.C. (1954–64); was also director of the Moravian Music Foundation (1956–64); then was prof. of musicology at the Univ. of Maryland (1964–72); subsequently was a prof. and head of the music dept. at the Univ. of British Columbia (1972–75).

McCormack, John, famous Irish-born American tenor; b. Athlone, June 14, 1884; d. "Glena," Booterstown, County Dublin, Sept. 16, 1945. In 1902 he became a member of the Palestrina Choir of Dublin's Cathedral, where he received lessons from the choirmaster, Vincent O'Brien. In 1903 he won the gold medal in the tenor section of the Feis Ceoil (National Music Festival) in Dublin, and began making concert appearances there; 1st sang in the U.S. at the St. Louis Exposition in 1904; that same year he commenced making recordings. After vocal studies with Vincenzo Sabatini in Milan (1905), he made his operatic debut under the name Giovanni Foli in the role of Fritz in *L'Amico Fritz* in Savona (Jan. 13, 1906); then went to London, where he began appearing in concerts in 1907; made his Covent Garden debut as Turiddu (Oct. 15, 1907), and subsequently sang there during the 1908–14 summer seasons in such roles as Edgardo, the Duke in *Rigoletto*, Rodolfo, Count Almaviva in *Il Barbiere di Siviglia*, Pinkerton, Gounod's Romeo, Cavaradossi, and Elvino. He made his U.S. operatic debut as Alfredo in *La Traviata* at the Manhattan

Opera House (Nov. 10, 1909); chose that same role for his Metropolitan Opera debut in N.Y. (Nov. 29, 1910), remaining on the company's roster until 1911 and returning from 1912 to 1914 and from 1917 to 1919; also sang with the Chicago Opera (1910–11). After making his formal concert debut at the Manhattan Opera House (Nov. 18, 1909), McCormack devoted much of his time to a concert career, which he furthered through his many recordings. After World War I, he made few appearances in opera, giving his last performance as Gritzko in Mussorgsky's *The Fair at Sorochinsk* in Monte Carlo on March 25, 1923. He applied for American citizenship in 1914; this action, coupled with his strong support of the Irish cause, cost him the support of the British public during World War I. He became a naturalized U.S. citizen in 1919. After an absence of 10 years, he made a triumphant return to England at a Queen's Hall Concert in London in 1924. In subsequent years he pursued a far-flung concert career with enormous success, although his vocal powers began to wane about 1930. He bade his farewell to the U.S. in Buffalo on March 17, 1937. He gave his last concert in London at the Royal Albert Hall on Nov. 27, 1938. At the outbreak of World War II (1939), he came out of retirement to aid the Red Cross; sang on the radio; continued to make recordings until 1942. He received a number of honors, including being made a Papal Count by Pope Pius XI in 1928. McCormack was an incomparable recitalist, his repertoire ranging from the works of the great masters to popular Irish songs and ballads.

BIBL.: P. Key, *J. M.: His Own Life Story* (Boston, 1918); L. Strong, *J. M.* (London, 1941); L. McCormack (his widow), *I Hear You Calling Me* (Milwaukee, 1949); L. MacDermott Roe, *J. M.: The Complete Discography* (London, 1956; 2nd ed., 1972); R. Foxall, *J. M.* (London, 1963); G. Ledbetter, *The Great Irish Tenor* (London, 1977).

McCoy, Seth, black American tenor and teacher; b. Sanford, N.C., Dec. 17, 1928. He studied at the North Carolina Agricultural and Technical College (graduated, 1950), then pursued vocal training with Pauline Thesmacher at the Cleveland Music School Settlement and with Antonia Lavanne in N.Y. He 1st gained notice as a soloist with the Robert Shaw Chorale (1963–65), with which he toured throughout the U.S. and South America; later appeared with the Bach Aria Group (1973–80); also was a soloist with such leading U.S. orchs. as the N.Y. Phil., Boston Sym. Orch., Chicago Sym. Orch., and Los Angeles Phil. In 1978 he made his European debut at the Aldeburgh Festival. On Feb. 17, 1979, he made his Metropolitan Opera debut in N.Y. as Tamino. His London debut was as soloist in Bach's *Christmas Oratorio* in 1986. He taught at the Eastman School of Music in Rochester, N.Y. (from 1982).

McCoy, William J., American composer; b. Crestline, Ohio, March 15, 1848; d. Oakland, Calif., Oct. 15, 1926. His family moved to California when he was a child; he began to compose at the age of 12; then was sent to N.Y. to study with William Mason; he later studied at the Leipzig Cons. with Reinecke and Hauptmann. His Sym. in F was conducted in Leipzig by Reinecke in 1872. He returned to California and wrote some theater music for the Bohemian Club there (*Harmadryads, The Cave Man,* etc.); also wrote an opera, *Egypt* (2 acts presented at the Berkeley Music Festival, Sept. 17, 1921), for which he received the Bispham Medal of the American Opera Soc. of Chicago; *Yosemite,* overture; Violin Concerto; a suite from *A Masque of Apollo* (*Prelude, Dance,* and *The Naiad's Idyl*); numerous songs; and a textbook, *Cumulative Harmony.*

McCracken, James (John Eugene), remarkable American tenor; b. Gary, Ind., Dec. 16, 1926; d. N.Y., April 29, 1988. After working at the Roxy Theatre in N.Y., he sang at Radio City Music Hall and appeared in minor roles on Broadway; following formal vocal studies with Wellington Ezekiel, he made his operatic debut as Rodolfo with the Central City Opera in Colorado (1952). On Nov. 21, 1953, he made his 1st appearance at the Metropolitan Opera in N.Y. as Parpignol; continued to sing minor roles there until he decided to try his fortune in Europe in 1957. After further vocal training with Marcello

Conati in Milan, he joined the Zürich Opera in 1959 and proved himself in major roles there. He soon gained wide recognition for his portrayal of Verdi's Otello, a role he sang to great acclaim at the Metropolitan Opera on March 10, 1963; remained on its roster until quitting the company in a dispute with the management in 1978. In 1983 he returned to the Metropolitan Opera as a participant in its Centennial Gala; he rejoined its roster in 1984, singing there with distinction until his death. He also appeared as a guest artist with major U.S. and European opera houses, and as a soloist with leading orchs. He often made joint appearances with his wife, **Sandra Warfield.** In addition to Otello, he won renown as Canio, Florestan, Don José, Radames, Samson in Saint-Saëns's opera, and Bacchus in Strauss's *Ariadne auf Naxos*. With his wife, he publ. the memoir *A Star in the Family* (ed. by R. Daley; N.Y., 1971).

BIBL.: B. Paolucci, "America's Heroic Tenor: J. M.," *Ovation* (Sept. 1985).

McCutchan, Robert Guy, American choral conductor and hymnologist; b. Mount Ayr, Iowa, Sept. 13, 1877; d. Claremont, Calif., May 15, 1958. He was active as a music educator and choral conductor in the schools and churches of Iowa, Kansas, and Indiana; made a thorough study of American hymnals and publ. a valuable compilation, *Our Hymnody* (Nashville, 1937; 2nd ed., 1942; contains detailed biographical information on American hymn composers); also *Hymn Tune Names: Their Sources and Significance* (Nashville, 1957).

McDaniel, Barry, American baritone; b. Lyndon, Kans., Oct. 18, 1930. He studied at the Juilliard School of Music in N.Y.; then was awarded a Fulbright scholarship in Germany; he took voice lessons in Stuttgart; made his operatic debut with the Württemberg State Theater there in 1959; subsequently sang with the Karlsruhe Opera, the Städtische Oper in Berlin, the Bavarian State Opera in Munich, and the Vienna State Opera; also made guest appearances at the Salzburg and Bayreuth festivals. On Jan. 19, 1972, he sang the role of Pelléas in Debussy's *Pelléas et Mélisande* in his debut with the Metropolitan Opera in N.Y. His operatic repertoire is quite extensive; he is equally adept in Baroque operas and in modern roles.

McDermott, Vincent, American composer; b. Atlantic City, N.J., Sept. 5, 1933. He studied with Rochberg at the Univ. of Pa. (B.F.A. in composition, 1959; Ph.D. in music history and theory, 1966) and took a course in music history at the Univ. of Calif. at Berkeley (M.A., 1961); also received instruction in composition from Milhaud and Stockhausen. He studied the tabla at the Ali Akbar Khan College in Oakland, Calif. (1973), and the Javanese gamelan at the Akademi Seni Karawitan Indonesia in Surakarta (1971, 1978). He taught at the Hampton Inst. in Virginia (1966–67), at the Wisconsin Cons. of Music in Milwaukee (1967–77), and at Lewis and Clark College in Portland, Oreg. (from 1971); in 1980 he held the directorship of the Venerable Showers of Beauty gamelan. His music draws freely upon both Western and Eastern elements.

WORKS: STAGE: *A Perpetual Dream*, chamber opera (1978); *Spirits among the Spires*, chamber opera (1987); *The King of Bali* for Singers, Puppets, and Gamelan (Portland, Oreg., April 20, 1990). **ORCH.:** *Siftings upon Siftings* (1976); *Solonese Concerto* for Piano, Voice, and Orch. (1979); *Prelude, Waltz, and Chorale* for String Quartet and Chamber Orch. (1985). **CHAMBER:** *3 for 5* for Flute, Alto Saxophone, Vibraphone, Piano, Tabla or Bongos, and Cymbal (1970); *Komal Usha-Rudra Nisha* for Sitar, Flute, Guitar, and Double Bass (1972); *Time Let Me Plan and Be Golden in the Mercy of His Means* for Guitar and Harpsichord (1973); *Dreams, Listen* for Viola and Piano (1974); *Kagoklaras* for Prepared Piano and Gamelan (1981); *The Bells of Tajilor* for Gamelan (1984). **VOCAL:** *Mixes,* Cantata No. 1, for Voices, Violin, and Percussion (1971); *Thou Restless Ungathered,* Cantata No. 2, for Soprano or Tenor, Clarinet, and Tape (1973); *Swift Wind,* Cantata No. 3, for High Voice and Double Bass (1974); *Slayer of Time, Ancient of Days,* Cantata No. 4, for Soloists, Chorus, English Horn, Guitar, and Percussion (1977); *Laudamus* (1980); *The Book of the Lover,* the Beloved, and the Alone for Voice and Instruments (1980); *Tagore Songs* for Soprano and Guitar (1981); *Sweet-breathed Minstrel* for 2 Voices, Viola, and Gamelan (1982); *The Dark Laments of Ariadne and of Attis,* 2 songs after Catullus for Soprano, Narrator, Viola, and Tape (1983). **TAPE AND MIXED MEDIA:** *He Who Ascends by Ecstasy into Contemplation of Sublime Things Sleeps and Sees a Dream* for Piano and Tape (1972); *Pictures at an Exhibition,* multimedia piece (1975); *Orpheus* for Tape and Video (1975); *Rain of Hollow Reeds* for Tape (1977); *A Perpetual Dream* for Voice, Tape, and 1 or 2 Dancers (1978); *Execution—what! what? what,* multimedia piece (1980).

McDonald, Harl, American pianist, music administrator, and composer; b. near Boulder, Colo., July 27, 1899; d. Princeton, N.J., March 30, 1955. He studied at the Univ. of Southern Calif. in Los Angeles (Mus.B., 1921); continued his studies in Leipzig at the Cons. and the Univ. (diploma, 1922). He made tours of the U.S. as a pianist from 1923; taught at the Philadelphia Musical Academy (1924–26) and the Univ. of Pa. (1926–46), where he later was a prof. and director of its music dept.; was also general manager of the Philadelphia Orch. (1939–55).

WORKS (all 1st perf. in Philadelphia unless otherwise given): **ORCH.:** 4 syms.: No. 1, *The Santa Fé Trail* (Nov. 16, 1934); No. 2, *The Rhumba Symphony* (Oct. 4, 1935); No. 3, *Lamentations of Fu Hsuan,* for Orch., Chorus, and Soprano Solo (Jan. 3, 1936); No. 4 (April 8, 1938); *Festival of the Workers* (April 26, 1934); *3 Poems on Traditional Aramaic Themes* (Dec. 18, 1936); Concerto for 2 Pianos and Orch. (April 2, 1937); Violin Concerto (March 16, 1945); *Saga of the Mississippi* (April 9, 1948); *From Childhood,* suite for Harp and Orch. (Jan. 17, 1941); 2 nocturnes: *San Juan Capistrano* (Boston, Oct. 30, 1939); *Arkansas Traveler,* humoresque (Detroit, March 3, 1940); *Bataan,* tone poem (Washington, D.C., July 3, 1942). **CHAMBER:** 2 piano trios (1931, 1932); *Fantasy* for String Quartet (1932); *Quartet on Negro Themes* (1933); also many choral works.

McDonald, Susann, noted American harpist and pedagogue; b. Rock Island, Ill., May 26, 1935. She began harp study when she was 6, then took lessons with Marcel Grandjany in N.Y. (1948) and Marie Ludwig in Chicago (1948–52); continued her training in Paris at the École Normale de Musique and privately with Henriette Renié (1952; 1953–55); was also a scholarship student of Lily Laskine at the Paris Cons. (1954–55), graduating with the premier prix in 1955, the 1st American to attain that distinction for harp. She subsequently pursued an outstanding concert career, playing with most of the leading orchs. of the world and appearing as a recitalist in the major music centers. She was artist-in-residence (1963–70) and associate prof. (1970–81) at the Univ. of Arizona; was also a lecturer at the Univ. of Southern Calif. in Los Angeles (1966–81) and head of the harp dept. at the Juilliard School in N.Y. (1975–85); was chairman of the harp dept. at the Indiana Univ. School of Music in Bloomington (from 1981); served as artistic director of the World Harp Congress (from 1981). She ed. a number of works for her instrument. A remarkable virtuoso, she maintains an extensive repertoire, which ranges from early works to contemporary scores.

McDowell, John Herbert, American composer; b. Washington, D.C., Dec. 21, 1926; d. Scarsdale, N.Y., Sept. 3, 1985. He studied at Colgate Univ. (B.A., 1948) and at Columbia Univ. with Otto Luening, Jack Beeson, and Roger Goeb (M.A., 1957); held a Guggenheim fellowship in 1962. He devoted his energies chiefly to music for the theater and dance.

WORKS: Cantata, *Good News from Heaven* (1957); *Four Sixes and a Nine* for Orch. (1959); *Accumulation* for 35 Flutes, Strings, and Percussion (1964); 100-odd pieces for dance, among them *Insects and Heroes* (1961); *From Sea to Shining Sea,* an homage to Ives (1965); *Dark Psalters* (1968).

McEwen, Sir John (Blackwood), Scottish composer and pedagogue; b. Hawick, April 13, 1868; d. London, June 14,

1948. He studied at Glasgow Univ. (M.A., 1888) and at the Royal Academy of Music in London with Corder, Matthay, and Prout; taught piano in Glasgow (1895–98) and composition at the Royal Academy of Music in London (1898–1936); in 1924 he succeeded Alexander Mackenzie as principal, retiring in 1936. He was knighted in 1931. He continued to compose until his last years.

WORKS: 2 syms.: No. 1 (1892–98); No. 2, *Solway* (1911); 4 orch. suites (1893–1941); Viola Concerto (1901); 17 string quartets (1893–1947); 7 violin sonatas (1913–39); 7 Bagatelles "Nugae" for Strings (1912); *Scottish Rhapsody* for Violin and Piano (1915); Viola Sonata (1930); piano pieces; songs.

McFerrin, Bobby (Robert), gifted black American popular vocalist, son of **Robert McFerrin;** b. N.Y., March 11, 1950. He studied music theory from the age of 6 and played piano in high school, forming a quartet that copied the styles of Henry Mancini and Sergio Mendes. In 1970 he heard Miles Davis's fusion album *Bitches Brew* and completely changed his musical direction. He studied music at Sacramento State Univ. and at Cerritos College; then played piano professionally until 1977, when he began to develop his voice; toured in 1980 with jazz vocalist Jon Hendricks, and debuted a solo act in 1982. His recordings include *Bobby McFerrin* (1982), *The Voice* (1984), *Spontaneous Improvisation* (1986), *Simple Pleasures* (1988; includes the song *Don't Worry, Be Happy*, which made him a household name), and *Medicine Music* (1991); also made several music videos and sang with Herbie Hancock, Yo-Yo Ma, Manhattan Transfer, and others. In 1989 he established the 11-voice ensemble Voicestra, with which he created the sound track for *Common Threads*, a 1989 documentary on the AIDS quilt; the group's 1st concert tour, in 1990, received critical acclaim. McFerrin began studying conducting in 1989, making his debut with a performance of Beethoven's Sym. No. 7 with the San Francisco Sym. on March 11, 1990. Technically, McFerrin is a virtuoso, using a remarkable range of voices with sophisticated control and accompanying them with body percussion, breath, and other self-generated sounds. Esthetically, he fuses a number of musical styles, including jazz, rock, and New Age, in a brilliant palette; his solo and ensemble shows are based on various improvisatory structures through which he produces highly polished, expertly burnished works.

McFerrin, Robert, black American baritone, father of **Bobby McFerrin;** b. Marianna, Ariz., March 19, 1921. He studied at Fisk Univ. in Nashville, Chicago Musical College (B.M., 1948), and Kathryn Turney Long School in N.Y. In 1949 he appeared in Kurt Weill's *Lost in the Stars*, in William Grant Still's *Troubled Island* (with the N.Y. City Opera), and as Amonasro in *Aida* (with Mary Cardwell Dawson's National Negro Opera Co.); joined the New England Opera Co. in 1950, creating roles in Marc Connelly's play *The Green Pastures* (N.Y., 1951; music by Hall Johnson) and *My Darlin' Aida* (1952), a version of Verdi's opera set in the Confederacy. He won the Metropolitan Auditions of the Air in 1953; became the 1st black male to join the company, making his debut on Jan. 27, 1955, as Amonasro. After singing in Naples at the Teatro San Carlo, he sang the role of Porgy (played by Sidney Poitier) in the film version of Gershwin's *Porgy and Bess* (1959); also sang on the recording. He toured internationally, giving recitals of arias, art songs, and spirituals.

McGegan, Nicholas, English keyboard player, flutist, and conductor; b. Sawbridgeworth, Hertfordshire, Jan. 14, 1950. He studied piano at London's Trinity College of Music (1968) and also learned to play the flute, specializing in the Baroque flute; pursued his education at Corpus Christi College, Cambridge (B.A., 1972), and at Magdalen College, Oxford (M.A., 1976). He was active as a flutist, harpsichordist, fortepianist, and pianist in London, where he was also a prof. of Baroque flute (1973–79) and music history (1975–79) and director of early music (1976–80) at the Royal College of Music. From 1979 to 1984 he was artist-in-residence at Washington Univ. in St. Louis; then became music director of the Philharmonia

Baroque Orch. in San Francisco (1985), the Ojai (Calif.) Festival (1988), and the Göttingen Handel Festival (1991); also appeared widely in Europe and North America as a guest conductor.

McGhee, Brownie (Walter), black American blues guitarist, singer, and songwriter; b. Knoxville, Tenn., Nov. 30, 1915. He was known for his deft guitar playing and mellifluous singing in partnership with Sonny Terry, the blues harmonica player; Terry wailed vocally and instrumentally and McGhee melded this into a smooth, closely integrated blend. During their 40-year association (1939–79), they appeared in concert and at blues and folk music festivals throughout the U.S., Europe, New Zealand, and Australia. They also recorded some 30 record albums, many of which featured McGhee's songs: *Life Is a Gamble, Tell Me Why, Blues Had a Baby (And They Called It Rock and Roll), Walk On, Hole in the Wall, I Couldn't Believe My Eyes, My Father's Words, Watch Your Close Friend,* and *Rainy Day*.

McGibbon, William, Scottish violinist and composer; b. Edinburgh, c.1690; d. there, Oct. 3, 1756. He studied violin in his youth with William Corbett in London, then became principal violinist of the Edinburgh Musical Soc. His extant works include 18 trio sonatas in 3 vols. (Edinburgh, 1729 and 1734; London, c.1745), 6 sonatas for Violin and Basso Continuo (Edinburgh, 1740), 6 sonatas for 2 Flutes (London, 1748), and variations on popular tunes for Solo Violin.

McGill, Josephine, American composer; b. Louisville, Ky., Oct. 20, 1877; d. there, Feb. 24, 1919. She studied with Alexander Lambert at the N.Y. College of Music; collected material for the publication *Folk Songs of the Kentucky Mountains* (1917, 1922, 1926, and 1937); also wrote songs.

McGlaughlin, William, American conductor; b. Philadelphia, Oct. 3, 1943. He studied at Temple Univ. (B.M., 1967; M.M., 1969); played trombone in the Pittsburgh Sym. Orch. and the Philadelphia Orch., and was founder-conductor of the Pittsburgh Sym. Players and the Pittsburgh Camerata (1973). He became assistant conductor of the Pittsburgh Chamber Orch. in 1975; was also a conductor with the St. Paul (Minn.) Chamber Orch. (1975–78). He was music director of the Eugene (Oreg.) Sym. Orch. (1981–85) and the Tucson Sym. Orch. (1983–87). In 1986 he became music director of the Kansas City (Mo.) Sym. Orch. and of the San Francisco Chamber Orch.

McGurty, Mark, remarkably gifted American composer whose music possesses an aura of new classicism; b. Newark, N.J., April 28, 1955. He studied at the Juilliard School in N.Y., where his major teachers were David Diamond and Elliott Carter. He also took lessons in violin with Frank Scocozza, piano with Frances Goldstein, and conducting with Abraham Kaplan. However, he did not at once pursue the occupation of a professional composer or performer, but had to earn a living elsewhere. He was manager of the Orquesta Filarmónica de Caracas in Venezuela (1979–83); concurrently was active as an instructor at the Simon Bolivar Univ. in Caracas, and occasional director for the Opera Nacional of Caracas. His next engagement was with the Opera of the Dominican Republic. In 1985 he moved to California, where he worked on the production of recordings for the Pacific Sym. During all these years, he was intensely working on a number of compositions for theater, orch., and chamber ensembles. In all cases he favors complex ensembles of variegated instruments marked by a resilient rhythmic beat while the flow of governing melody is never muted.

WORKS: BALLETS: *The Castle*, after Kafka (1974); *Journey to the Land of the Tarahumaras* (1975). **ORCH.:** Symphonic Poem (1975); *Variations on a Gregorian Chant* (1976); Concerto for Viola and 24 Players (1982); Concerto for Violin and Orch. (Caracas, 1982); Sym. for Strings (Santo Domingo, 1983); *Concerto grosso* for Piano and Strings (Caracas, 1983); *Dirige Domine* for String Orch. (1985); Concerto for Piano No. 1 (1985); Concerto (1985); Concerto for Piano (Los Angeles, 1987); *Oisin* and the *Gwragedd Annwn* (1988); *Sinfonie pour un tombeau d'Anatole* (1987–88); *Denizens of the Realm Faerie* (Long Beach, Calif., 1990). CHAMBER: Sonata for Violin and Piano (N.Y., 1974); Quintet (N.Y., 1974); Sonata for Piano No. 1 (1975); *Partita for Violin Alone* (1976); 8 string quartets, including No. 1 (N.Y., 1976); No. 3 (1978); No. 4 (Caracas, 1981); No. 5 (1983); No. 7 (Los Angeles, 1987); No. 8, *Armadillo Quartet* (Los Angeles, 1987); Flute Sonata (1977); *Concert Études* for Piano (1983); Chamber Sym. (Caracas, 1983); Woodwind Quintet (1985); Sonata for Piano (Los Angeles, 1985); *Fantasies and Cadenzas* for Oboe Quartet (London, 1987); *Clarinet Alone* (1987); *Sonata and Its Double* for 2 Pianos (1 pianist with midi equipment) (1987); *Whitening* for Soprano and Ensemble (Philadelphia, 1987); *Songs of the Gwrageth Anoon* for 21 Instruments (Los Angeles, 1987); *Sonata for Violin Alone* (1988); *Scene Concertante* for Flute, Harp, and Strings (Los Angeles, 1988).

McHose, Allen Irvine, American music theorist and educator; b. Lancaster, Pa., May 14, 1902; d. Canandaigua, N.Y., Sept. 14, 1986. He studied at Franklin and Marshall College (B.S., 1923; D.F.A., 1948), at the Eastman School of Music in Rochester, N.Y. (B.M., 1928; M.M., 1929), and at Oklahoma City Univ. (D.Mus., 1945). From 1930 to 1967 he was on the faculty at the Eastman School; from 1931 to 1962, he was chairman of the theory dept. there. He developed a theory of musical analysis based upon a statistical survey of works of J.S. Bach, and propounded it persuasively in his books *Contrapuntal Harmonic Technique of the 18th Century* (1947) and *Basic Principles of the Technique of 18th and 19th Century Composition* (1951). He also publ. *Sight Singing Manual* (1944, with R. Tibbs); *Keyboard and Dictation Manual* (1949, with D. White); *Teachers' Dictation Manual* (1948); and *Musical Style 1850–1920* (1950).

McHugh, Jimmy (James Francis), American composer of popular music; b. Boston, July 10, 1894; d. Beverly Hills, May 22, 1969. He was a rehearsal accompanist for the Boston Opera Co. before embarking on composition. He moved to N.Y. in 1921; with Dorothy Fields, he produced the all-black Broadway revue *The Blackbirds of 1928* (1930), which included his greatest hit song, *I Can't Give You Anything but Love, Baby.* In 1930 he went to Hollywood; wrote for films and also composed many popular songs; later led a dance band.

McIntire, Dennis K(eith), American music historian and lexicographer; b. Indianapolis, June 25, 1944. His innate love of music was manifested at a very early age when he discovered his maternal grandmother's Edison Amberola and a cornucopia of playable cylinders. His rejection of the rudiments of formal music schooling did not preclude his being able to give authentic performances of such works as John Cage's famous silent masterpieces, *4'33"* and *0'00".* By 1985 his mastery of musical reproductive technique reached its summit, so that he could play difficult scores on the compact disc player. As a lexicographer, he was autodidact, being mainly inspired by the example of the great Samuel Johnson. His precocious self-assurance was such that at the age of 13 he undertook a systematic attack on imperfections in reference books, beginning with misinformative vols. such as *The Lincoln Library of Essential Information.* After 10 years of badgering its eds., he was made an assistant and research ed. of the aforesaid encyclopedia in 1967. His fascination for reference books spurred him on to consume virtually the entire contents of several voluminous standard sources, among them *Baker's Biographical Dictionary of Musicians, Grove's Dictionary of Music and Musicians,* and even the monumental *Encyclopaedia Britannica.* Appalled by the surprising percentage of errors in such dignified reference publications, he undertook a systematic correspondence with their eds., suggesting corrections and additions. In the meantime, he undertook a thorough study of 20th-century European history at Indiana Univ., but managed to depart the halls of academe without a devastating critique of any deficiencies in instruction; continued to fulfill editorial duties all the while. His capacity of total recall and indefatigability in corresponding

with far corners of the musical world enabled him to make valuable additions to the 7th and 8th eds. of *Baker's* (1984, 1991); he also contributed material to Slonimsky's *Supplement to Music since 1900* (1986). It is no wonder that he became known to intimates as "Dennisimo," the superlative of his 1st name, in appreciation of his quaquaversal and, indeed, immarcescible super-duper contribution to the art of musical lectionary. He also lent assistance to *The Concise Oxford Dictionary of Opera* (1979), *The Oxford Dictionary of Music* (1985), and *The New Everyman Dictionary of Music* (1988); served as an adviser and contributor to *The New Grove Dictionary of American Music* (1986) and as co-consultant ed. (with D. Cummings) of the 12th and 13th eds. of *The International Who's Who in Music* (1990, 1992). From 1991 he was an adviser to the *Encyclopaedia Britannica.* He also was a contributor to *The New Grove Dictionary of Opera* (1992).

McIntyre, Donald (Conroy), New Zealand bass-baritone; b. Auckland, Oct. 22, 1934. He studied at the Guildhall School of Music in London; made his operatic debut as Zachariah in *Nabucco* with the Welsh National Opera in Cardiff (1959); then was a member of the Sadler's Wells Opera in London (1960–67). In 1967 he made his debut as Pizzaro at Covent Garden in London; that same year he made his 1st appearance at the Bayreuth Festival as Telramund, returning there annually until 1981; sang Wotan there during the centenary *Ring* production in 1976. On Feb. 15, 1975, he made his Metropolitan Opera debut in N.Y. as Wotan. He made guest appearances with many of the leading opera houses of the world. In 1977 he was made an Officer of the Order of the British Empire, and in 1985 a Commander of the Order of the British Empire. His other roles include Kaspar in *Der Freischütz,* Attila, Klingsor, Amfortas, the Dutchman, Golaud, and Escamillo.

McKay, George Frederick, American composer; b. Harrington, Wash., June 11, 1899; d. Stateline, Nev., Oct. 4, 1970. He studied at the Univ. of Washington, Seattle, and subsequently at the Eastman School of Music in Rochester, N.Y., with Palmgren and Sinding; graduated in 1923. In 1941 he was appointed to the faculty of the Univ. of Washington, from which he retired in 1968.

WORKS: ORCH.: 4 sinfoniettas (1925–42); *Fantasy on a Western Folk Song* (Rochester, N.Y., May 3, 1933); *Port Royal, 1861,* suite on Negro folk songs for Strings (1939); *Bravura Prelude* for Brass Ensemble (Rochester, N.Y., April 30, 1939); *To a Liberator,* symphonic poem (Indianapolis, March 15, 1940); *Introspective Poem* for Strings (Philadelphia, April 3, 1941); *A Prairie Portrait* (San Francisco, Sept. 4, 1941); *Pioneer Epic* (Oakland, Calif., Feb. 17, 1942). **CHAMBER:** Wind Quintet (1930); Piano Trio (1931); *American Street Scenes,* quintet for Clarinet, Trumpet, Saxophone, Bassoon, and Piano (1935).

McKellar, Kenneth, Scottish tenor; b. Paisley, June 23, 1927. He took a course in philology at the Univ. of Aberdeen and received a B.S. degree; then studied voice at the Royal College of Music in London. He subsequently sang with the Carl Rosa Opera Co. in London; later toured the U.S. as a concert singer. He was also a fine interpreter of traditional Scottish ballads, which he included in his concert programs.

McKinley, Carl, American composer and organist; b. Yarmouth, Maine, Oct. 9, 1895; d. Boston, July 24, 1966. He studied with E.B. Hill at Harvard Univ.; in 1929, was appointed instructor of organ and composition at the New England Cons. of Music in Boston. Many of his works were inspired by American subjects. He wrote *The Blue Flower,* symphonic poem (N.Y., Jan. 18, 1924); *Masquerade,* American rhapsody for Orch. (his most popular work; Chicago North Shore Festival, May 29, 1926); *Caribbean Holiday* (Boston, Nov. 18, 1948); String Quartet, Cello Sonata, and other pieces of chamber music, as well as organ pieces and songs.

McKinley, William Thomas, imaginative American composer; b. New Kensington, Pa., Dec. 9, 1938. He demonstrated musical talents early, becoming a member of the Pittsburgh musicians' union at the age of 11. He studied with Lopatnikoff and Dorian at the Carnegie Inst. of Technology (B.F.A., 1960); with Powell, Wyner, and Moss at Yale Univ. (M.M., 1968; M.F.A., 1969); and with Schuller at the Berkshire Music Center at Tanglewood. He taught composition and theory at the State Univ. of N.Y. at Albany (1968–69), the Univ. of Chicago (1970–73), and the New England Cons. of Music in Boston (from 1973), where he was also composer-in-residence. Among his many honors are a Fromm Fellowship (1963), 5 NEA grants (1975–78), a Naumberg Foundation Grant (1976), the Minnesota Orch.'s 75th Anniversary Orchestral Prize (1979), a Koussevitzky Foundation Fellowship (1983), a music award from the American Academy and Inst. of Arts and Letters (1983), and a Guggenheim fellowship (1985–86). He also performed as a jazz pianist. Though modern in technique and spirit, his music is infused throughout with romanticism.

WORKS: ORCH.: 5 syms.: No. 1 (1976; Minneapolis, Jan. 3, 1979); No. 2 (1978); No. 3 (N.Y., May 18, 1984); No. 4 (1985; N.Y., March 25, 1986); No. 5 (1988; Pasadena, Calif., March 18, 1989); *Circular Forms* (Chicago, April 25, 1972); Concerto (Boston, Dec. 11, 1975); *October* (1976); 2 clarinet concertos (1977, 1990); Cello Concerto (1977); 2 piano concertos (1977, 1987); *The Mountain* (Pittsburgh, Oct. 17, 1982); Sinfonia Concertante (Boston, May 1, 1986); *Boston Overture* (Boston, May 6, 1986); Flute Concerto (1987); Trumpet Concerto (1987); Concerto for Horn and Orch., *Huntington* (1988); *Adagio* for Strings (1989); *New York Overture* (1990). CHAMBER: 7 string quartets (1959–88); Trio for Violin, Piano, and Cello (1962); Trio for 2 Violins and Cello (1971); *TASHI*, quartet for Piano, Clarinet, Violin, and Cello (1976); Sinfonia for String Quartet (1977); Wind Quintet (1980); *Trio appassionata* for Clarinet, Viola, and Piano (1982); Quintet for Viola and String Quartet (1987); piano pieces, including a Quartet (1988). VOCAL: *Deliverance, Amen*, oratorio for Chorus, Chamber Ensemble, and Organ (Boston, Dec. 12, 1983); choruses; songs.

McKinney, Baylus Benjamin, American composer and editor of gospel hymns; b. Heflink, La., July 22, 1886; d. Bryson City, N.C., Sept. 7, 1952. He was educated at Mt. Lebanon Academy in Louisiana, Louisiana College, and the Southwestern Baptist Theological Seminary; then taught at the seminary (1919–32). He was music ed. for the Robert H. Coleman publishing firm in Dallas (1918–35) and for the Baptist Sunday School Board's widely used *Broadman Hymnal* (1941). He wrote both words and music to some 150 gospel hymns and set more than 100 texts to music.

BIBL.: P. Powell, *A Biographical and Bibliographical Study of B.B. M. (1886–1952)* (thesis, New Orleans Baptist Theological Seminary, 1973); W. Reynolds and A. Faircloth, *The Songs of B.B. M.* (Nashville, Tenn., 1974); T. Terry, *B.B. M.: A Shaping Force in Southern Protestant Music* (diss., North Texas State Univ., 1981); R. Hastings, *Glorious Is Thy Name!: B.B. M., the Man and His Music* (Nashville, Tenn., 1986).

McKuen, Rod (Marvin), American minstrel and lyricist; b. Oakland, Calif., April 29, 1933. He ran away from a previously broken home at the age of 11; bummed as a logger and roadman; roped calves and dogged bulls in and out of rodeo shows; became a disc jockey and scriptwriter in a psychological warfare unit during the Korean War. Returning to the U.S., he appeared as a folksy balladeer in San Francisco nightclubs; obtained a music theory book and learned to write tunes; supported himself by playing supporting roles in otherwise unsupportable bit parts in the movies; eked out a posh living by crashing parties and gorging himself on choice comestibles. He became a roving poet, dispensing a plethora of facile country-style songs with monosyllabic assonances for rhymes and a simple appeal of scenes of non-obscene free love against an artificially flavored pastoral landscape. His 1st anthology of verse, *An Autumn Came*, was a failure, but he stumbled into a poetic bonanza with the commercially issued vols. *Stanyan Street* and *Listen to the Warm*. He never indentured himself to an agent, and so was able to reap a lucrative harvest of success, blandly chanting, "I have no special bed, I give myself to those who offer love." He publ. a memoir, *Finding My Father* (N.Y.,

1976), in which he stated, "I was born a bastard; some people spend their entire lives becoming one." His putative natural father was a lumberjack who died about 1965.

McLaughlin, John, English rock and jazz guitarist and bandleader; b. Yorkshire, Jan. 4, 1942. He played piano and guitar as a child, and formed a band as a schoolboy. In 1969 he issued his 1st solo album, *Extrapolation*, which displayed his virtuosity on the guitar. He subsequently got together with Miles Davis, with whom he made *Bitches Brew* and *In a Silent Way*. In 1970 he sought spiritual expansion through a worshipful association with a Bengal mystic, and recorded *My Goal's Beyond*, an album of transcendental meditation containing group improvisation; a further development was his Mahavishnu Orch. (1971), mixing rock and jazz with Hindu religiosity; later organized an acoustic outfit known as Shakti, which used both Western and Eastern instruments; subsequently performed in various duos and trios.

McLean, Barton (Keith), American composer; b. Poughkeepsie, N.Y., April 8, 1938. He studied music education at the State Univ. of N.Y. at Potsdam (B.S., 1960), with Cowell at the Eastman School of Music in Rochester, N.Y. (M.M., 1965), and composition at Indiana Univ. in Bloomington (Mus.D., 1972). He taught at the State Univ. of N.Y. at Potsdam (1960–66). He then was head of theory and composition and director of the electronic music center at Indiana Univ. in South Bend (1969–76); after teaching and serving as director of the electronic music center at the Univ. of Texas in Austin (1976–83), he taught and was co-director at the I-Ear Studios at the Rensselaer Polytechnic Inst. (1987–89). In 1974 he married **Priscilla McLean;** together they toured in the U.S. and abroad as the McLean Mix electro-acoustic music duo. In 1976 and 1982 he received NEA fellowships; also held MacDowell Colony fellowships (1979, 1981, 1984, 1985). Most of his compositional efforts have been devoted to electronic and computer music.

WORKS: ORCH.: *Metamorphosis* (1972). CHAMBER: *Ritual of the Dawn* for 6 Players (1982); *Pathways* for Symphonic Winds (1983); *From the Good Earth*, "foot-stompin' homage to Bartók" for String Quartet (1985). VOCAL: *3 Songs on Sandburg Poems* for Voice and Piano (1970). TAPE AND ELECTRONICS: *The Sorcerer Revisited* for Tape (1975); *Mysteries from the Ancient Nahuatl* for Soloists, Chorus, Narrator, Instrumentalists, and Tape (1978); *Etunytude* for Computer (1982); *In Wilderness Is the Preservation of the World: Voices of the Wild, Passages of the Night*, electronic piece (1985); *Voices of the Wild: Primal Spirits* for McLean Mix Synthesizer, Soloists, and Orch. (1987; Troy, N.Y., Feb. 26, 1988); *Earth Music*, improvisation installation-performance computer piece (1988); *Visions of a Summer Night* for Computer (1988); *Rainforest*, environmental audience-interactive quasi-installation computer piece (1989).

BIBL.: J. Aikin, "B. and Priscilla M.: Composing for Piano, Synthesizer and Electronic Tape," *Keyboard* (Sept. 1983).

McLean, Priscilla (Anne, née **Taylor),** American composer; b. Fitchburg, Mass., May 27, 1942. She studied at Fitchburg State College (B.E.E., 1963) and the Univ. of Lowell (B.M.E., 1965) in Massachusetts, and with Heiden and Beversdorf at Indiana Univ. (M.M., 1969). She was an associate lecturer at Indiana Univ.'s Kokomo campus (1971–73) and at St. Mary's College in Notre Dame, Ind. (1973–76); in 1975–76 she was composer-in-residence at the electronic music center at Indiana Univ.'s South Bend campus, and in 1985 served as visiting prof. of music at the Univ. of Hawaii in Manoa. In 1974 she married **Barton McLean;** together they toured in Europe and the U.S. as the McLean Mix electro-acoustic music duo. She appeared as a singer, pianist, and percussionist, and also played synthesizer and native wooden flutes. She received numerous NEA grants (1979–87) and MacDowell Colony fellowships (1979, 1981, 1984, 1986). Her compositions make innovative use of man-made or animal sounds with synthesized music.

WORKS: ORCH.: *Holiday for Youth* for Concert Band (1965); *Variations and Mosaics on a Theme of Stravinsky* (Indianapolis, April 24, 1975); *A Magic Dwells* for Orch. and Tape (1984);

Voices of the Wild: 1 (Printemps) Rites (Albany, N.Y., Feb. 26, 1988); *Wilderness* for Chamber Orch. (Cleveland, Jan. 15, 1989). CHAMBER: *Spectra I* for Percussion and Synthesizer (1971) and *II* for Percussion and Prepared Piano (1972); *Ah-Syn!* for Autoharp and Synthesizer (1976); *Fire and Ice* for Trombone and Piano (1977); *Beneath the Horizon I* for Tuba Quartet and Taped Whales (1978) and *III* for Tuba and Taped Whale Ensemble (1979); *The Inner Universe*, 8 tone poems for Piano and Tape (1981); *Elan! A Dance to All Rising Things from the Earth* for Instrumental Ensemble (1984). VOCAL: *3 Songs in Season* for Chorus (1963; rev. 1967); *Rainer Maria Poems*, 3 songs for Voice and Violin (1967; rev. 1974); *Messages* for 4 Soloists, Chorus, and Chamber Ensemble (1974); *Fantasies for Adults and Other Children*, 8 songs for Voice and Amplified Piano (1980); *In Celebration* for Chorus (1987); also tape pieces.

McNair, Barbara, black American singer of popular music and actress; b. Racine, Wis., March 4, 1939. She studied music at the Univ. of Southern Calif. in Los Angeles; then went to N.Y., where she sang in Broadway musicals, including *Body Beautiful* (1958) and *The Merry World of Nat King Cole* (1961); she also appeared as a television actress.

McNair, Sylvia, talented American soprano; b. Mansfield, Ohio, June 23, 1956. She studied with Margarita Evans at Wheaton (Ill.) College (B.M., 1978) and with Virginia MacWatters (1978–80), John Wustman (1978–82), and Virginia Zeani (1980–82) at the Indiana Univ. School of Music in Bloomington (M.M., 1982). She made her formal concert debut as a soloist in *Messiah* with the Indianapolis Sym. Orch. (1980). Her operatic debut followed as Sandrina in Haydn's *L'Infedeltà delusa* at N.Y.'s Mostly Mozart Festival (1982). In 1984 she created the title role in Kelterborn's opera *Ophelia* at her European debut at the Schwetzingen Festival, and immediately thereafter sang the role at Berlin's Deutsche Oper. In 1990 she was honored with the Marian Anderson Award. Her extensive repertoire ranges from Monteverdi to contemporary composers.

McNaught, William Gray, English music journalist and editor; b. London, March 30, 1849; d. there, Oct. 13, 1918. He studied at the Royal Academy of Music in London (1872–76); was active as a choral conductor; was founder-ed. of the *School Music Review* (1892–1918); also was ed. of the *Musical Times* (1910–18). His son, also named **William (Gray) McNaught** (b. London, Sept. 1, 1883; d. there, June 9, 1953), was educated at Univ. College School and Worcester College, Oxford; was assistant ed. to his father at the *Musical Times*, and later ed. (1944–53). He publ. *A Short Account of Modern Music and Musicians* (London, 1937), *Beethoven* (London, 1940), and *Elgar* (London, 1947).

McNeill, Lloyd, black American artist, musician, painter, photographer, and poet; b. Washington, D.C., April 12, 1935. He studied art and zoology at Morehouse College (B.A., 1961), painting and printmaking at Howard Univ. (M.F.A., 1963), lithography at the École des Beaux Arts in Paris (1964–65), and sound recording techniques and animation at N.Y. Univ. (1974); also studied composition with Hale Smith and flute with Frank Albright, Eric Dolphy, Harold Jones, and others. A true Renaissance man, McNeill excels in a variety of art forms; his drawings were praised by Picasso, whom he befriended in the 1960s, and have been exhibited widely with his paintings; he also appears in readings of his own poetry. He appeared as a congo drummer with Nina Simone and in a variety of ensembles as a flutist; in 1968 he formed the Lloyd McNeill Band. He taught at Dartmouth College, Spelman College, and Howard Univ.; in 1969 he joined the visual arts faculty at Rutgers Univ. (Mason Gross School of the Arts); subsequently was a prof. there. He produced 6 record albums: *Asha, Tanner Suite, Washington Suite, Treasures, Tori,* and *Elegia*; among his other compositions is *Sketches* for Solo Flute (1986); certain movements are often performed separately (e.g., *Tori Suite,* 3 pieces), while others have been arranged for different instrumental combinations, including *The Falling*

Snow for Flute and Violin (1987) and *Calypso Facto* for Flute and Violin (1987; also arranged for Harpsichord); he also wrote and performed dance pieces and film scores.

McPartland, Jimmy (James), American jazz trumpeter and bandleader; b. Chicago, March 15, 1907; d. Port Washington, N.Y. March 13, 1991. He studied violin, then took up the cornet; at the age of 16, he organized a band with his brother; subsequently played with Bix Beiderbecke, Ben Pollack, and Jack Teagarden. After military service in World War II, he resumed his career by organizing his own quartet in Chicago; later led his own band on tours. He married **Marian McPartland** in 1945.

McPartland, Marian (Margaret, née **Turner),** English jazz pianist and composer; b. Windsor, March 20, 1918. She 1st played violin; then won a scholarship to the Guildhall School of Music in London, where she studied piano. She began her career as a jazz pianist in joint appearances with the jazz pianist Billy Mayerl; in 1945 she married **Jimmy McPartland;** in 1946 she went to America and played in a combo with her husband; in 1951 she organized her own trio. She wrote a number of songs in the popular vein, including the successful *There'll Be Other Times.* A vol. of her collected articles appeared as *All in Good Time* (N.Y., 1987).

McPhatter, Clyde, black American vocalist; b. Durham, N.C., Nov. 15, 1933; d. N.Y., June 13, 1972. His father was a preacher in a Baptist church, and McPhatter began singing gospel songs under his tutelage. Still in school, he formed the Mt. Lebanon Singers, a gospel group; then sang with The Dominoes, a choral ensemble, making a hit with *Have Mercy, Baby.* In 1953 he organized his own group, The Drifters, which established the mix of gospel and pop that came to be known as "soul." His best renditions were the rhythm-and-blues *Money Honey,* and pop favorites *There Goes My Baby, Dance with Me, A Lover's Question,* and *Lover Please.*

McPhee, Colin (Carhart), outstanding American composer and ethnomusicologist; b. Montreal, Canada, March 15, 1900; d. Los Angeles, Jan. 7, 1964. He studied piano and composition with Harold Randolph and Gustav Strube at the Peabody Cons. in Baltimore (graduated, 1921), then took piano lessons with Arthur Friedheim in Toronto (1921–24); continued his studies with Paul Le Flem (composition) and Isidor Philipp (piano) in Paris (1924–26). Returning to the U.S. (1926), he joined the modern movement in N.Y. and was briefly a student of Varèse; wrote scores for the experimental films H_2O and *Mechanical Principles* in 1931. He became infatuated with the gamelan music of Java and Bali; moved to Indonesia in 1931 and, except for brief interruptions, remained there until 1939. He then returned to the U.S. and was a consultant to the Office of War Information during World War II; later was active with the Inst. of Ethnomusicology at the Univ. of Calif. at Los Angeles (1958–64). His *Tabuh-Tabuhan* for 2 Pianos, Orch., and Exotic Percussion, composed and premiered during an interlude in Mexico City (1936), is the quintessential work in his Bali-influenced style. He wrote the books *A House in Bali* (N.Y., 1946), *A Club of Small Men* (N.Y., 1948), and *Music in Bali* (New Haven, 1966).

WORKS: ORCH.: 2 piano concertos: No. 1, *La Mort d'Arthur* (Baltimore, May 26, 1920; not extant); No. 2 (1923; Toronto, Jan. 15, 1924; not extant); *Sarabande* (1927); 3 syms.: No. 1 in 1 movement (1930; not extant); No. 2, *Pastorale* (1957; Louisville, Jan. 15, 1958); No. 3 (1960–62; incomplete); *Tabuh-Tabuhan* for 2 Pianos, Orch., and Exotic Percussion (Mexico City, Sept. 4, 1936); *4 Iroquois Dances* (1944); *Transitions* (1954; Vancouver, March 20, 1955); *Nocturne* for Chamber Orch. (N.Y., Dec. 3, 1958); Concerto for Wind Orch. (1959; Pittsburgh, July 1960). CHAMBER: *Pastorale and Rondino* for 2 Flutes, Clarinet, Trumpet, and Piano (1925; not extant); Concerto for Piano and Wind Octet (1928; Boston, March 11, 1929). VOCAL: *Sea Shanty Suite* for Baritone, Men's Chorus, 2 Pianos, and Timpani (N.Y., March 13, 1929); *From the Revelation of St. John the Divine* for Men's Chorus, 3 Trumpets, 2

Pianos, and Timpani (1935; N.Y., March 27, 1936; not extant). PIANO: 4 *Piano Sketches* (1916); *Invention* (1926); *Kinesis* (1930); *Balinese Ceremonial Music* for 2 Pianos (1934–38).

BIBL.: W. Riegger, "Adolph Weiss and C. M.," in H. Cowell, ed., *American Composers on American Music* (Stanford, Calif., 1933); C. Sigmon, "C. M.," *American Composers Alliance Bulletin*, XII/1 (1964); R. Mead, *Henry Cowell's New Music 1925–1936* (Ann Arbor, 1981); C. Oja, "C. M.—Composer Who Fell in Love with Bali," *N.Y. Times* (Nov. 1, 1982); R. Mueller, *Imitation and Stylization in the Balinese Music of C. M.* (diss., Univ. of Chicago, 1982); C. Oja, "C. M.—A Composer Turned Explorer," *Tempo*, 148 (1984); idem, *C. M. (1900–1964): A Composer in Two Worlds* (diss., City Univ. of N.Y., 1985).

McRae, Carmen, black American jazz vocalist and pianist; b. N.Y., April 8, 1922. She joined Benny Carter's band in 1944; subsequently sang with the bands of Count Basie, Mercer Ellington, and others; made tours in Europe and Japan. She was married to **Kenny Clarke,** and recorded several songs as Carmen Clarke. In 1980 she was a featured performer at N.Y.'s Carnegie Hall.

McShann, Jay "Hootie," black American jazz pianist, blues singer, and bandleader; b. Muskogee, Okla., Jan. 12, 1909. He took up the piano at an early age; led his own group during the big-band era in Kansas City. Among his hits were *Hootie Blues* (a title from which he got his nickname), *Confessin' the Blues*, and *Swingmatism*. The legendary jazz figure Charlie Parker was a member of McShann's band. After a stint in the U.S. Army (1943–45), he resumed his career, working mainly in California. He continued to be active well into old age; in 1974 he toured Europe with the show *The Musical Life of Charlie Parker*; in 1975 he took part in the Montreux Jazz Festival; in 1979 he played at the Alexandra Palace Jazz Festival in London. He publ. *Boogie Woogie and Blues Piano Solos*. He also appeared in the film *The Last of the Blue Devils*.

Meader, George, American tenor; b. Minneapolis, July 6, 1888; d. Los Angeles, Dec. 19, 1963. He studied law at the Univ. of Minnesota (graduated, 1908) and concurrently took vocal lessos with Anna Schoen-René; then studied with Pauline Viardot-Garcia in Paris. He made his operatic debut as the Steersman in *Der fliegende Holländer* in Leipzig (1911); then was a member of the Stuttgart Opera until 1919. Returning to America in 1919, he gave recitals before making his operatic debut with the Metropolitan Opera in N.Y. as Victorin in Korngold's *Die tote Stadt* (Nov. 19, 1921); he left the Metropolitan in 1931 and sang in operetta; was particularly successful in Jerome Kern's *Cat and the Fiddle*.

Meale, Richard (Graham), Australian composer; b. Sydney, Aug. 24, 1932. He was admitted to the New South Wales State Conservatorium of Music at age 12 to study piano with Winifred Burton; also studied harp and clarinet there (1947–55); took a course in Asian music at the Ethnomusicological Inst. at the Univ. of Calif. at Los Angeles (1960); traveled to France and Spain before returning in 1961 to Australia, where he was program planner for the ABC (1962–69); then taught at the Univ. of Adelaide (from 1969). In 1971 he was made a Member of the Order of the British Empire. In his music, he follows the precepts of ethnomusicology, seeking to create a synthesis of primitive natural melorhythms with modernistic counterpoints. His early works reflect the influence of Bartók and Hindemith, the later ones Messiaen and Boulez.

WORKS: BALLETS: *The Hypnotist* (1956); *At 5 in the Afternoon* (1961). ORCH.: *Flute Concerto* (1959); *Sinfonia* for Piano, 4-hands, and Strings (1959); *Homage to García Lorca* for Double String Orch. (1964); *Images (Nagauta)* (1966); *Nocturnes* for Vibraphone, Harp, Celesta, and Orch. (1966–67); *Very High Kings* (1968); *Clouds Now and Then* (1969); *Soon It Will Die* (1969); *Variations* (1970); *Evocations* for Oboe, Chamber Orch., and Violin obbligato (1972); *Virdian* for Strings (1979). CHAMBER: *Rhapsody* for Violin and Piano (1952); Quintet for Oboe and Strings (1952); *Rhapsody* for Cello and Piano (1953); Horn Sonata (1954); Solo Flute Sonata (1957); Divertimento

for Piano Trio (1959); Flute Sonata (1960); *Las Alboradas* for Flute, Violin, Horn, and Piano (1963); *Intersections* and *Cyphers* for Flute, Viola, Vibraphone, and Piano (both 1965; graphic scores); *Interiors/Exteriors* for 2 Pianos and 3 Percussionists (1970); Wind Quintet (1970); *Incredible Floridas*, homage to Rimbaud, for Flute, Guitar, Violin, Cello, Piano, and Percussion (1971); *Plateau* for Wind Quintet (1971); 2 string quartets (1974, 1980); *Fanfare* for Brass (1978). PIANO: *Stonehenge* (1945); *Orenda* (1959; rev. 1968); *Coruscations* (1971).

Mechem, Kirke (Lewis), American composer, conductor, and lecturer on music; b. Wichita, Kans., Aug. 16, 1925. He was a pupil of Harold Schmidt, Leonard Ratner, and Sandor Salgo at Stanford Univ. (B.A., 1951) and of Walter Piston, Randall Thompson, and A. Tillman Merritt at Harvard Univ. (M.A., 1953). After serving as director of music at Menlo College in California (1953–56) and as a teacher and conductor at Stanford Univ. (1953–56), he was active in Vienna (1956–57; 1961–63). He was composer-in-residence at the Univ. of San Francisco's Lone Mountain College (1964–65; 1966–72) and a teacher and conductor at San Francisco State College (1965–66). In his works he adopts a candidly euphonious method of composition, not shirking resolvable dissonances and circumtonal patterns, but faithfully observing basic tonality. He became well known as a composer of choral works and instrumental pieces. His opera *Tartuffe* proved an immediate success at its premiere and was subsequently performed more than 100 times.

WORKS: OPERAS: *Tartuffe*, after Molière (1977–80; San Francisco, May 27, 1980); *John Brown* (1988–89). ORCH.: 2 syms.: No. 1 (1958–59; San Francisco, Jan. 6, 1965); No. 2 (1966; San Francisco, March 29, 1967; rev. 1968; San Francisco, Jan. 15, 1969); *Haydn's Return*, fugue and variations on Haydn's *Farewell Symphony* (1960; Santa Rosa, Calif., Feb. 12, 1961); *The Jayhawk*, overture to a mythical comedy (1974; Topeka, Kans., March 19, 1975). CHAMBER: Suite for 2 Violins (1952–53); Suite for Piano (1954); Trio for Oboe, Clarinet, and Bassoon (1955); Trio for Piano, Violin, and Cello (1956–57); Divertimento for Flute, Violin, Viola, and Cello (1958); String Quartet No. 1 (1962–63); Piano Sonata (1964–65); *Whims*, 15 easy vignettes for Piano (1967; also as *Brass Buttons* for Brass Quintet, 1969); various choral works and songs.

Meck, Nadezhda von, Russian patroness of music, friend and benefactress of Tchaikovsky; b. Znamenskoye, near Smolensk, Feb. 10, 1831; d. Wiesbaden, Jan. 13, 1894. She became interested in Tchaikovsky's music through Nikolai Rubinstein, director of the Moscow Cons., of which she was a patroness. At 1st offering Tchaikovsky commissions, she later granted him a yearly allowance of 6,000 rubles in order that he might compose undisturbed by financial considerations. He lived for long periods in close proximity to her, at Brailov (near Kiev) and in Florence, Italy, but although they carried on an extensive and intimate correspondence (3 vols., Moscow, 1934–36), they never met face to face. Tchaikovsky's allowance was abruptly cut off in 1890 on the pretext of financial difficulties, leading to a complete break between him and Mme. von Meck in 1891. She employed the youthful Debussy as a pianist in her household.

BIBL.: O. Bennigson, "More Tchaikovsky–v.M. Correspondence," *Musical Quarterly* (April 1938).

Medek, Tilo, German composer; b. Jena, Jan. 22, 1940. He studied composition with Wagner-Régeny at the Deutsche Hochschule für Musik in East Berlin; attended classes in musicology with Vetter and E.H. Meyer at Humboldt Univ. in East Berlin (1959–64), and later with Wagner-Régeny at the Deutsche Akademie der Künste (1964–67). In 1977 he moved to West Germany.

WORKS: OPERAS: *Einzug*, short opera after Isaac Babel (1969); *Katharina Blum* (1986); singspiels: *Iche und die Hexe Yu* (1970–71); *Appetit auf Frühkirschen* (1971). BALLET: *David und Goliath* (1972). ORCH.: *Triade* (1964); *Rezitativ und Arie* (1965); *Porträt eines Tangos* (1968); *Das zögernde Lied* (1970); Flute Concerto (1973); *Grosser Marsch* (1974);

Concerto for Piccolo and Orch. (1975; East Berlin, Feb. 2, 1976); *König Johann*, concert overture (1976); Marimba Concerto (1975–76); Cello Concerto No. 1 (East Berlin, Oct. 8, 1978); Organ Concerto (1977–79; Baden-Baden, March 7, 1981); Violin Concerto (1979–80; Cologne, Nov. 14, 1980); *König Johann oder Der Ausstieg* for Organ and Orch. (1980); *Eisenblätter* for Orch. and Organ (1983); Cello Concerto No. 2 (1984); *Rheinische Sinfonie* (1986). CHAMBER: *Tanzstudie* for Horn, Harpsichord, and Piano (1963); Flute Sonata (1963); 3 wind quintets (1965; 1974–76; 1979); String Trio (1965); *Terzinen*, duo for Flute and Piano (1966); *Divertissement* for Wind Quintet and Harpsichord (1967); *Stadtpfeifer*, "Schwanengesang" for Clarinet, Trombone, Cello, and Piano (1973); *Schattenspiele* for Cello (1973); *Sensible Variationen um ein Schubertthema* for Flute, Violin, and Cello (1973); Nonet (1974); *3 Tagzeiten* for Marimba, Piano, and Percussion (1976); *Tagtraum* for 7 Instruments (1976); *Giebichenstein* for 8 Instruments (1976); *Eine Stele für B.A. Zimmermann* for Cello (1976); *Zur Unzeit Erblühtes*, 5 pieces for Marimba (1977); *Erdrauch* for Guitar (1979); *Reliquienschrein* for Organ and Percussion (1980). VOCAL: *Altägyptische Liebeslieder* for 2 Voices and Orch. (1963); *Johann Wallbergens natürliche Zauberkünste 1768* for Narrator, Soprano, and Salon Orch. (1965; Gelsenkirchen, Jan. 18, 1979); *Sintflutbestanden*, triptych for Tenor, Piano, and Horn (1967); *Gethsemane*, cantata (1980). PIANO: *Miszellen I–III* (1965–75); *Kaminstücke*, 12 pieces (1968–70); *Adventskalender*, 24 pieces (1972–73); *Tag- und Nachtstücke* (Book I, Nos. 1–8, 1976–78). ORGAN: *Verschüttete Bauernflöte* (1969); *Praeludium—Choralspiel—Postludium* (1971–78); *Ranken* (1978); *Rückläufige Passacaglia* (1979); *Schnurrpfeifereien* (1979).

Meder, Johann Valentin, German singer, organist, and composer; b. Wasungen, near Meiningen (baptized), May 3, 1649; d. Riga, July 1719. He studied theology in Leipzig and Jena. After serving as a court singer in Gotha (1671), Bremen (1672–73), Hamburg (1673), Copenhagen (1674), and Lübeck (1674), he was Kantor at the Reval Gymnasium (1674–80). From 1687 to 1698 he was Kapellmeister at St. Marien in Danzig; then was Kantor at Königsberg Cathedral, and subsequently in Riga (from 1700). He composed the opera *Die beständige Argenia* (Reval, 1680), an oratorio Passion (1700), and many masses, cantatas, and motets.

Mediņš, family of prominent Latvian musicians, all brothers:
(1) **Jāzeps Mediņš,** conductor and composer; b. Kaunas, Feb. 13, 1877; d. Riga, June 12, 1947. He studied at the Riga Music Inst. (graduated, 1896), where he later was a teacher and director; was a conductor at the Riga Theater (1906–11), the Baku Opera (1916–22), and the Latvian National Opera in Riga (1922–25); later taught piano at the Riga Cons. (1945–47).
    WORKS: Operas: *Vaidelote* (The Priestess; 1922–24; Riga, 1927); *Zemdegi* (The Zemdegs Family; 1947; completed by M. Zariņš); also Sym. No. 2, *Ziedonī* (In Springtime; 1937); Sym. No. 3 (1941); Violin Concerto (1911); String Quartet (1941); other chamber music; choral works; songs.
    BIBL.: M. Zālīte, *J. M.* (Riga, 1951).
(2) **Jēkabs Mediņš,** conductor, teacher, and composer; b. Riga, March 22, 1885; d. there, Nov. 27, 1971. He studied at the Riga Music Inst. (graduated, 1905) and at the Berlin Hochschule für Musik (1910–14); taught at the Jelgava Teachers' Inst. (1921–44), and was director of the People's Cons. there (1921–41); later taught choral conducting at the Riga Cons. (1944–71), serving as its rector (1949–51). He wrote an autobiography, *Silueti* (Silhouettes; Riga, 1968).
    WORKS: Clarinet Concerto (1948); 2 horn concertos (1949, 1962); Kokle Concerto (1952); Organ Concerto (1954); cantatas; chamber music; songs.
(3) **Jānis Mediņš,** conductor and composer; b. Riga, Oct. 9, 1890; d. Stockholm, March 4, 1966. He studied at the Riga Music Inst. (graduated, 1909); was a violist and conductor at the Latvian Opera in Riga (1913–15), then a military bandmaster in St. Petersburg (1916–20). He conducted at the Latvian

National Opera (1920–28); subsequently was chief conductor of the Latvian Sym. Orch. (1928–44); was also a prof. at the Riga Cons. (1929–44). As the Soviet army approached his homeland (1944), he went to Germany; then settled in Stockholm (1948). He wrote an autobiography, *Toni un pustoni* (Tones and Semitones; Stockholm, 1964). He distinguished himself as a composer of both vocal and instrumental works.
    WORKS: STAGE: OPERAS: *Uguns un nakts* (Fire and Night; 1st written as 2 operas, 1913–19; Riga, May 26, 1921; rev. as a single opera, 1924); *Dievi un cilvēki* (Gods and Men; Riga, May 23, 1922); *Sprīdītis* (Tom Thumb; Riga, 1927); *Luteklīte* (The Little Darling), children's opera (Riga, 1939). BALLET: *Mīlas uzvara* (Love's Victory; 1935; the 1st Latvian ballet). ORCH.: Cello Concerto (1928); Piano Concerto (1934); several suites for Orch., including No. 3, *Dzimtene* (The Fatherland; 1933); other orch. pieces and music for band. CHAMBER: 2 piano trios (1930, 1958); Cello Sonata (1945); String Quartet (1946); 2 sonatas for Violin and Piano (1946, 1954); various piano pieces; also 8 cantatas; some 130 songs.

Medtner, Nicolai (actually, **Nikolai Karlovich**), notable Russian pianist and composer of German descent; b. Moscow, Jan. 5, 1880; d. London, Nov. 13, 1951. He 1st studied piano with his mother, and then with his uncle, Theodore Goedicke; in 1892, entered the Moscow Cons., where he took courses with Sapelnikov and Safonov (piano) and Arensky and Taneyev (composition); graduated in 1900, winning the gold medal; that same year he won the Rubinstein prize in Vienna; for the next 2 years he appeared with much success as a pianist in the European capitals; returning to Russia, he taught at the Moscow Cons. (1902–3; 1909–10; 1914–21); then lived in Berlin and Paris; eventually settled in London (1935). He made tours of the U.S. (1924–25; 1929–30) and the Soviet Union (1927). He publ. a collection of essays as *Muza i moda* (The Muse and Fashion; Paris, 1935; Eng. tr., 1951). In Russian music he was a solitary figure; he never followed the nationalist trend, but endeavored to create a new type of composition, rooted in both the Classical and the Romantic traditions; his sets of fairy tales in sonata form are unique examples of his favorite genre. He wrote his best compositions before he left Russia; although he continued to compose during his residence abroad, his late music lacks the verve and Romantic sincerity that distinguish his earlier works. He wrote almost exclusively for the piano and for the voice. A revival of his music was begun in Russia after his death, and a complete ed. of his works appeared in Moscow (12 vols., 1959–63).
    WORKS: 3 piano concertos: No. 1 (1914–18); No. 2 (1920–27; Moscow, March 13, 1927); No. 3 (1940–43; London, Feb. 19, 1944, composer soloist); 3 sonatas for Violin and Piano (1909–10; 1926; 1938); Piano Quintet (1904–49); numerous piano pieces, including 34 *Fairy Tales* (1905–29), *Sonaten-Triade* (1904–8), 6 sonatas (1896–1915), *Sonata romantica* (1931–32), *Sonata minacciosa* (1931–32), and *Sonata idillica* (1935); also various sets of piano pieces, including 4 *Lyric Fragments* (1910–11), 3 sets of *Forgotten Melodies* (1918–20), and 4 sets of *Romantic Sketches for the Young* (1932); also 107 songs.
    BIBL.: V. Yakovlev, *N. M.* (Moscow, 1927); R. Holt, *M. and His Music* (London, 1948); idem, ed., *N. M. (1879–1951): A Tribute to His Art and Personality* (London, 1955); E. Dolinskaya, *N. M.* (Moscow, 1966); H. Milne, "N. M.: A Centenary Appraisal," *Music and Musicians*, XXVIII/5 (1980).

Meerts, Lambert (-Joseph), Belgian violinist and pedagogue; b. Brussels, Jan. 6, 1800; d. there, May 12, 1863. He studied with Lafont and Habeneck at Paris; from 1835, was prof. at the Brussels Cons. Among his instructive works for violin are *Études pour violon avec accompagnement d'un second violon; Mécanisme du violon* (advanced studies); 12 books of studies on rhythm, on motifs by Beethoven.

Meester, Louis de, Belgian composer; b. Roeselare, Oct. 28, 1904; d. Ghent, Dec. 12, 1987. He traveled widely in his youth as a popular musician, being autodidact; lived in Algeria (1928–30); was director of the Meknes Cons., French Morocco (1933–

37); returned to Belgium in 1938 and studied briefly with Jean Absil; served as acoustical director at the Belgian Radio (1945–61). From 1961 to 1969 he was director of the Inst. for Psychoacoustics and Electronic Music at the Univ. of Ghent.

WORKS: OPERAS: *La Grande Tentation de Saint Antoine*, opera buffa (1957; Antwerp, Nov. 11, 1961); *2 is te weinig, 3 is te veel* (2 Is Too Little, 3 Is Too Much; 1966; Palermo, June 13, 1969); *Paradijsgeuzen* (Beggars in Heaven; 1966; Ghent, March 26, 1967); also *Van een trotse vogel*, musical comedy for Narrator and Small Orch. (1948). **ORCH.:** *Magreb* for Viola and Orch. (1946); *Capriccio* (1948); *Sprookjesmuziek* (1949); 2 works serving as introductions for children to instruments of the orch.: *Betje Trompet* for Narrator and Small Orch. (1949) and *Betje Trompet en de Reus* (Betje Trumpet and the Giant) for 2 Narrators and Orch. (1965); *Sinfonietta buffa* (1950); 2 piano concertos (1952, 1956); *La Voix du silence*, cantata for Baritone, Narrators, Female Chorus, and Chamber Orch. (1951–54); *Musica per archi* (1955); *Amalgames* (1956); *Marine* (1957); Concertino for 2 String Orchs. (1965); *Serenade* for Flute, Oboe, and Strings (1967); *Ballade van de gebarste trommel* for Narrator and Orch. (1973); *Tombeau voor P.-P. Rubens* (1977). **CHAMBER:** Cello Sonatina (1945); *Divertimento* for Wind Quintet (1946); 3 string quartets (1947, 1949, 1954); String Trio (1951); *Tafelmuziek* for Flute, Oboe, Violin, Viola, and Cello (1953); Sonata for Solo Guitar (1954); Violin Sonata (1957); *Serenade* for Harpsichord and 11 Strings (1958–59); *Postludium* for Organ and Brass (1959); *Divertimento* for Piano Quartet (1970); *Drie interludes* for Flute and Organ (1975). **PIANO:** Sonata (1946); *3 Nocturnes* (1947); *Variations* for 2 Pianos (1947); *Petite Suite* (1953); *Petites Variations* for Piano (1954); *Mimes* for Piano (1958); Piano Sonatina (1964); also 9 electronic pieces; choruses; film music.

Meeuwisse, Willy, Dutch pianist and composer; b. Arnhem, Dec. 18, 1914; d. Amsterdam, Aug. 6, 1952. He was a student of Sem Dresden in Amsterdam; his *Suite of Old Dutch Dances* for Piano Solo enjoyed a certain popularity; also was active as a concert pianist.

Méfano, Paul, French composer; b. Basra, Iraq, March 6, 1937. He studied at the Paris Cons. with Dandelot, Messiaen, Martenot, and Milhaud; attended seminars of Boulez, Stockhausen, and Pousseur in Basel. He received a grant from the Harkness Foundation for residence in the U.S. (1966–68) and in Berlin (1968–69). In his music he pursues a constructivist style, with an emphasis on rhythmic percussion and electronic sound; the influences of Stravinsky and Varèse are particularly in evidence.

WORKS: OPERA: *Micromegas* for 4 Singers, Narrator, 3 Actors, 10 Instruments, and Tape, after Voltaire (1979). **ORCH.:** *Incidences* for Orch. and Piano (1960); *Interférences* for Chamber Group (1966); *Aurelia* for 3 Choruses, 3 Orchs., and 3 Conductors (1968). **VOCAL:** *Paraboles* for Soprano and Chamber Ensemble (Paris, Jan. 20, 1965); *Lignes* for Bass, Brass, Percussion, Bassoon, and Amplified Double Bass (1968); *La Cérémonie* for 3 Solo Voices, Instrumental Groups, and 12-voice Speaking Chorus (1970); *La Messe des voleurs* for 4 Solo Voices, Chamber Ensemble, and Electronic Equipment (Royan Festival, March 28, 1972). **CHAMBER:** *Ondes, Espaces mouvants* for 12 Players (Metz Festival, Nov. 20, 1975); *Mouvement calme* for String Quartet (1976); *Traits suspendus* for Double-Bass and Flute (1980); also *Intersection*, electronic piece for 2 Generators and Ring Modulator (1971).

Mehta, Mehli, Indian violinist and conductor, father of **Zubin Mehta;** b. Bombay, Sept. 25, 1908. He studied at the Univ. of Bombay and at Trinity College of Music in London (licentiate, 1929). He founded the Bombay Sym. Orch. in 1935; was its concertmaster (until 1945) and then its conductor (until 1955); subsequently was assistant concertmaster of the Hallé Orch. in Manchester (1955–59). He then settled in the U.S., where he played in the Curtis String Quartet in Philadelphia (1959–64); subsequently went to Los Angeles, where he founded the American Youth Sym. Orch. (1964); also taught at the Univ. of Calif. there (1964–76), serving as conductor of its sym. and chamber orchs.

Mehta, Zubin, exuberant, effulgent, and eloquent Indian conductor, son of **Mehli Mehta;** b. Bombay, April 29, 1936. The family belonged to the historic tribe of Parsi nobles, the fire-worshiping followers of Zarathustra who fled en masse from the turbulence of Persia 13 centuries before Zubin Mehta's birth. He was tutored in music by his father; he learned to play violin and piano; when he was 16 he successfully conducted a rehearsal of the Bombay Sym. Orch. Before deciding on a musical career, he took a course in medicine at St. Xavier College in Bombay; but he turned away from the unesthetic training in dissection, and instead went to Vienna, where he practiced to play the double bass at the Academy of Music and took conducting lessons with Hans Swarowsky. During the summers of 1956 and 1957, he attended conducting classes at the Accademia Chigiana in Siena with Carlo Zecchi and Alceo Galliera. In 1957 he graduated from the Vienna Academy of Music, and made his professional debut conducting the Tonkünstler Orch. in the Musikverein. In 1958 he married the Canadian singer Carmen Lasky; they had 2 children, but were divorced in 1964; she married Zubin Mehta's brother Zarin in 1966, thus making Zubin an uncle by marriage of his own children. On July 20, 1969, he married the actress Nancy Kovack in a dual ceremony, Methodist and Zoroastrian. In the meantime his career progressed by great strides; he won the competition of the Royal Liverpool Phil. in 1958, and conducted it for a season as an assistant; later he obtained guest engagements in Austria and Yugoslavia. In 1959 he competed in a conducting test in Tanglewood, and won 2nd prize. In 1960 he received a bona fide engagement to conduct the Vienna Sym. Orch.; that same year he also made a highly successful appearance as a guest conductor with the Philadelphia Orch.; later in 1960 he conducted 2 concerts of the Montreal Sym. Orch. and produced such a fine impression that he was appointed its music director. In 1962 Mehta took the Montreal Sym. Orch. to Russia, where he gave 8 concerts; then conducted 2 concerts with it in Paris and 1 in Vienna, where he took 14 bows in response to a vociferous ovation. In the meantime he received a contract to conduct the Los Angeles Phil., becoming its associate conductor in 1961 and its music director in 1962; he was thus the holder of 2 major conducting jobs, a feat he was able to accomplish by commuting on newfangled jet airplanes; he was also the youngest conductor to function in this dual capacity. His career was now assuming the allure of a gallop, aided by his ability, rare among conductors, to maintain his self-control under trying circumstances. He has the reputation of a bon vivant; his joy of life is limitless. Professionally, he maintains an almost infallible reliability; he conducts all of his scores, even the most mind-boggling modern scores, and operas as well, from memory. He is also a polyglot; not only is he eloquent in English and Hindi, but he is fluent in German, French, and Spanish; he even speaks understandable Russian. He made his debut at the Metropolitan Opera in N.Y. on Dec. 29, 1965, conducting *Aida.* His performances of *Carmen* and *Turandot* were highly praised. In 1967 he resigned his post in Montreal; in 1968 he was named music adviser of the Israel Phil.; in 1977 he became its music director. In 1978 he left the Los Angeles Phil. after he received an offer he could not refuse, the musical directorship of the N.Y. Phil.; in 1980 he toured with it in Europe. In 1991 he left his post with the N.Y. Phil. His association with the Israel Phil. was particularly affectionate; he conducted it during the Six-Day War and at the 25th anniversary of Israel's independence; in 1974 he was given an honorary Ph.D. by Tel Aviv Univ. No Jew could be more Israeli than the Parsi Mehta. *Time* glorified him with a cover story in its issue of Jan. 19, 1968.

BIBL.: M. Bookspan and R. Yockey, *Z.: The Z. M. Story* (N.Y., 1978); P. Hart, *Conductors: A New Generation* (N.Y., 1979).

Méhul, Etienne-Nicolas, famous French composer; b. Givet, Ardennes, June 22, 1763; d. Paris, Oct. 18, 1817. His father apprenticed him to the old blind organist of the Couvent des Récollets in Givet; he then went to Lavaldieu, where he studied with the German organist Wilhelm Hansen, director of music at the monastery there. In 1778 he went to Paris, where he continued his musical studies with Jean-Frédéric Edelmann. His 1st opera to receive a performance was *Euphrosine, ou Le Tyran corrigé* (Théâtre Favart, Paris, Sept. 4, 1790); another opera, *Alonso et Cora* (later known as *Cora*), was staged at the Paris Opéra on Feb. 15, 1791. His next opera, *Adrien*, was in rehearsal by the end of 1791, but the revolutionary turmoil prevented a performance; it finally received its premiere at the Paris Opéra on June 4, 1799. His opera *Stratonice* was given at the Théâtre Favart in Paris on May 3, 1792, and was highly successful. Then followed his opera *Le Jeune Sage et le vieux fou*, which was performed at the same theater on March 28, 1793. In 1793 Méhul became a member of the Inst. National de Musique, which had been organized by the National Convention under the revolutionary regime. He composed a number of patriotic works during these turbulent years of French history, including the popular *Chant du départ* (1st perf. publicly on July 4, 1794). He also continued to compose for the theater, shrewdly selecting subjects for his operas allegorically suitable to the times. In 1794 he was awarded an annual pension of 1,000 francs by the Comédie-Italienne. In 1795 he became one of the 5 inspectors of the newly established Cons., and was also elected to the Institut. He became a member of the Légion d'Honneur in 1804. Between 1795 and 1807 Méhul composed 18 operas, some of which were written in collaboration with other composers. His greatest opera from this period is the biblical *Joseph* (Opéra-Comique, Feb. 17, 1807); its success in Paris led to performances in Germany, Austria, Hungary, Russia, the Netherlands, Belgium, Switzerland, England, Italy, and America. Also noteworthy is his *Chant national du 14 juillet 1800*, an extensive work calling for 2 choirs with an additional group of high voices and orchestral forces. Apart from operas, he composed several syms. In spite of poor health, he continued to teach classes at the Paris Cons.; among his students was Hérold. His last opera was *La Journée aux aventures*, which was given at the Opéra-Comique on Nov. 16, 1816. Although Méhul's operas practically disappeared from the active repertoire, his contribution to the operatic art remains of considerable historical importance. Beethoven, Weber, and Mendelssohn were cognizant of some of his symphonic works.

WORKS: STAGE (all 1st perf. in Paris): **OPERAS:** *Euphrosine, ou Le Tyran corrigé* (Sept. 4, 1790; rev. as *Euphrosine et Coradin*); *Alonso et Cora* (Feb. 15, 1791; later known as *Cora*); *Stratonice* (May 3, 1792); *Le Jeune Sage et le vieux fou* (March 28, 1793); *Horatius Coclès* (Feb. 18, 1794); *Le Congrès des rois* (Feb. 26, 1794; in collaboration with 11 other composers); *Mélidore et Phrosine* (May 6, 1794); *Doria, ou La Tyrannie détruite* (March 12, 1795); *La Caverne* (Dec. 5, 1795); *La Jeunesse d'Henri IV* (May 1, 1797; later known as *Le Jeune Henri*); *La Prise du pont de Lodi* (Dec. 15, 1797); *Adrien, empéreur de Rome* (June 4, 1799; later known as *Adrien*); *Ariodant* (Oct. 11, 1799); *Epicure* (March 14, 1800; in collaboration with Cherubini); *Bion* (Dec. 27, 1800); *L'Irato, ou L'Emporté* (Feb. 17, 1801); *Une Folie* (April 5, 1802); *Le Trésor supposé, ou Le Danger d'écouter aux portes* (July 29, 1802); *Joanna* (Nov. 23, 1802); *Héléna* (March 1, 1803); *Le Baiser et la quittance, ou Une Aventure de garnison* (June 18, 1803; in collaboration with Boieldieu, R. Kreutzer, and Nicolo); *L'Heureux malgré lui* (Dec. 29, 1803); *Les 2 Aveugles de Tolède* (Jan. 28, 1806); *Uthal* (May 17, 1806); *Gabrielle d'Estrées, ou Les Amours d'Henri IV* (June 25, 1806); *Joseph* (Feb. 17, 1807); *Amphion, ou Les Amazones* (Dec. 17, 1811; later known as *Les Amazones, ou La Fondation de Thèbes*); *Le Prince troubadour* (May 24, 1813); *L'Oriflamme* (Feb. 1, 1814; overture by Méhul; remainder in collaboration with H.-M. Berton, R. Kreutzer, and Paer); *La Journée aux aventures* (Nov. 16, 1816); *Valentine de Milan* (Nov. 28, 1822); the opera *Lausus* and the opera-ballet *L'Amour et Psyché* are considered doubtful works in the Méhul canon. **BALLETS:** *Le Jugement de Paris* (March 5, 1793; with music

by Gluck, Haydn, and others); *La Dansomanie* (June 14, 1800; with music by Mozart and others); *Daphnis et Pandrose* (Jan. 14, 1803; with music by Gluck, Haydn, and others); *Persée et Andromède* (June 8, 1810; with music by Haydn, Paer, and Steibelt). He also composed several pieces of incidental music, many choral works (including the *Chant national du 14 juillet 1800*), numerous songs and patriotic works, etc. **ORCH.:** Several syms., including those numbered by Méhul as No. 1 in G minor (1809), No. 2 in D major (1809), No. 3 in C major (1809), and No. 4 in E major (1810). He also composed 2 books of keyboard sonatas: *3 sonates*, book 1 (1783), and *3 sonates*, book 2 (1788); in addition, a chamber music work entitled *Ouverture burlesque*, for Piano, Violin, 3 Mirlitons, Trumpet, and Percussion.

BIBL.: A. Quatremère de Quincy, *Funérailles de M. M.*, *Institut Royal de France* (Paris, 1817); idem, "Notice historique sur la vie et les œuvres de M. M.," *Institut Royal de France: Séance publique de l'Académie Royale des Beaux-Arts du 2 octobre 1819* (Paris, 1819); F.-J. Fétis, "Biographie: M. (Etienne Henri)," *Revue Musicale*, VII (1830); P. Vieillard, *M., Sa vie et ses œuvres* (Paris, 1859); J.-B. Weckerlin, "Les Quatre Versions de la romance de Joseph, opéra de M.," *Revue et Gazette Musicale de Paris*, XLII (1875); A. Pougin, *M.: Sa vie, son génie, son caractère* (Paris, 1889; 2nd ed., 1893); H. Parent de Curzon, "M., Sa vie et son œuvre," *Musiciens du temps passé* (Paris, 1893); R. Brancour, *M.* (Paris, 1912); H. Strobel, "Die Opern von E.N. M.," *Zeitschrift für Musikwissenschaft*, VI (1923–24); C. Barzel, "Notes et documents de musique: La Jeunesse et le roman de M.," *Mercure de France* (Sept. 15, 1932); P.-M. Masson, "L'Œuvre dramatique de M.," *Annales de l'Université de Paris*, XII (Paris, 1937); A. Ringer, "A French Symphonist at the Time of Beethoven: E.N. M.," *Musical Quarterly* (Oct. 1951); W. Dean, "Opera under the French Revolution," *Proceedings of the Royal Musical Association*, XCIV (1967–68); W. Dudley, *Orchestration in the Musique d'harmonie of the French Revolution* (diss., Univ. of Calif., Berkeley, 1968); D. Charlton, *Orchestration and Orchestral Practice in Paris, 1789–1810* (diss., Cambridge Univ., 1973); idem, "Motive and Motif: M. before 1791," *Music & Letters*, LVII (1976).

Mei, Girolamo, eminent Italian scholar and writer on music; b. Florence, May 27, 1519; d. Rome, July 1594. He studied with the scholar Piero Vettori, serving as his assistant in editing and annotating the works of the great Greek and Latin men of letters. Upon the founding of the Accademia de'Umidi (1540; later the Accademia Fiorentia), he became one of its 1st members. After settling in Rome (1559), he was a secretary to Cardinal Giovanni Ricci da Montepulciano (1561–74); then lived in the palace of the nobleman Giovanni Francesco Ridolfi. He publ. *Discorso sopra la musica antica e moderna* (Venice, 1602; reprint, 1968, ed. by G. Massera), the 1st significant study of the tonoi in Greek music. He also left in MS *De modis musicis antiquorum libri IV; De nomi delle corde del monochordo;* and *Trattato di musica: Come potesse tanto la musica appresso gli antichi.* His letters to the members of Bardi's Camerata in Florence are of great historical significance, for they led to a call for the reform of music and the development of monody, which culminated in the rise of the 1st music dramas and the new recitative style. See C. Palisca, ed., *Girolamo Mei (1519–1594): Letters on Ancient and Modern Music to Vincenzo Galilei and Giovanni Bardi*, Musicological Studies and Documents, III (1960; 2nd ed., 1977).

BIBL.: B. Hanning, *The Influence of Humanistic Thought and Italian Renaissance Poetry on the Formation of Opera* (diss., Yale Univ., 1968); C. Palisca, "The 'Camerata Fiorentina': A Reappraisal," *Studi Musicali*, I (1972).

Meibom (Meiboom, Meybom, Meibomius), Marcus, erudite Danish scholar; b. Tönning, Schleswig, 1620 or 1621; d. Utrecht, Feb. 15, 1710. He studied law at the Univ. of Königsberg (1644) and medicine at the Univ. of Leiden (1645), but subsequently devoted himself to philology and mathematics. He was assistant royal librarian in Stockholm (1652–53) before serving King Frederik III of Denmark in Copenhagen (1653–

64), where he held the title of consilarus regius. After serving as director of customs in Elsinore (1664–68), he lived in England (1674–77); then settled in Holland. His major contribution to music was his *Antiquae musicae auctores septem, graece et latine, Marcus Meibomius restituit ac notis explicavit* (2 vols., Amsterdam, 1652), which includes treatises on music by Aristoxenos, Cleonides, Nicomachus, Alypius, Gaudentius Philosophos, Bacchius, Aristides Quintilianus, and Martianus Capella.

Meier, Johanna, American soprano; b. Chicago, Feb. 13, 1938. She was a scholarship student at the Manhattan School of Music in N.Y. She made her debut with the N.Y. City Opera in 1969 as the Countess in Strauss's *Capriccio;* continued to appear there regularly until 1979; made her Metropolitan Opera debut in N.Y. as Strauss's Ariadne on April 9, 1976, and subsequently appeared there regularly; also sang opera in Chicago, Cincinnati, Pittsburgh, Seattle, and Baltimore. In Europe, she had guest engagements in opera in Zürich, Vienna, Hamburg, Berlin, and Bayreuth; also appeared in concerts.

Meier, Waltraud, German mezzo-soprano; b. Würzburg, Jan. 9, 1956. She was a pupil of Dietger Jacob in Cologne. In 1976 she made her operatic debut as Cherubino at the Würzburg Opera, singing there until joining the Mannheim National Theater in 1978; then was a member of the Dortmund Opera (1980–83). In 1980 she appeared as Fricka at the Teatro Colón in Buenos Aires, and in 1984 sang Brangäne at the Paris Opéra and Eboli at London's Covent Garden. From 1984 to 1987 she appeared at the Bayreuth Festivals. From 1986 she sang at the Württemberg State Theater in Stuttgart. In 1987 she made her Metropolitan Opera debut in N.Y. as Fricka, and then sang Venus at the Vienna State Opera. In addition to her roles in operas by Wagner, Verdi, and Strauss, she is a notable concert artist.

Meiland, Jakob, German composer; b. Senftenberg, Lausitz, 1542; d. Hechingen, Dec. 31, 1577. He was a choirboy in the Dresden Hofkapelle; in 1558 he enrolled at the Univ. of Leipzig; in 1563 joined the Kantorei of the Protestant Margrave Georg Friedrich of Brandenburg-Ansbach; in 1564 became its director; in 1565 founded its Hofkapelle and served as its 1st director. He moved to Frankfurt in 1572 and to Celle in 1576. In 1577 he became Kapellmeister to Count Eitel Friedrich von Hohenzollern of Hechingen, but died that same year.
Works: *Cantiones sacrae cum harmonicis numeris, a 5, 6* (Nuremberg, 1564; 4th ed., 1573); *Selectae cantiones, a 5, 6* (1572); *Cantiones aliquot novae . . . quibus adiuncta sunt officia due, a 5* (Frankfurt, 1575); *Sacrae aliquot cantiones latinae et germanicae . . . sequentes duas cantiones in honorem domini Sigismundi Feyerabend et Hieronymi eius filii, a 4, 5* (Frankfurt, 1575); *Harmoniae sacrae selectae ac compositiones divinae, a 5* (Erfurt, 1588); *Cygneae cantiones latinae et germanicae, a 4, 5* (Wittenberg, 1590); 3 Passions; Mass; secular songs; etc.
Bibl.: R. Oppel, *J. M. (1542–1577)* (Pfungstadt, 1911).

Meinardus, Ludwig (Siegfried), German conductor, composer, and writer on music; b. Hooksiel, Oldenburg, Sept. 17, 1827; d. Bielefeld, July 10, 1896. He was a pupil at the Leipzig Cons.; also studied in Berlin, in Weimar (with Liszt), and with Marx in Berlin. From 1853 to 1865 he was conductor of the Singakademie at Glogau; then was a teacher at the Dresden Cons.; from 1874 to 1887 he lived in Hamburg as a composer and critic, then went to Bielefeld. He wrote a kind of autobiography, *Ein Jugendleben* (2 vols., 1874); other writings include *Rückblick auf die Anfänge der deutschen Oper* (1878), *Mattheson und seine Verdienste um die deutsche Tonkunst* (1879), *Mozart: Ein Künstlerleben* (1882), *Die deutsche Tonkunst im 18.–19. Jahrhundert* (1887), *Klassizität und Romantik in der deutschen Tonkunst* (1893), and *Eigene Wege* (1895). He composed 2 operas; 6 oratorios, including *Luther in Worms* (Leipzig, 1876), his most successful score; 2 syms. (c.1875, 1879); many choral works; much chamber music.
Bibl.: C. Kleinschmidt, *L. M., 1827–1896: Ein Beitrag zur*

Geschichte der ausgehenden musikalischen Romantik (Wilhelmshaven, 1985).

Meitus, Yuli (Sergievich), eminent Ukrainian composer; b. Elizavetgrad, Jan. 28, 1903. He studied piano at a local music school, where he soon began to compose. Later he moved to Kharkov, where he composed music to theatrical productions on contemporary revolutionary subjects. In 1924 he wrote a melodeclamation commemorating the death of Lenin, and in 1930 he composed a symphonic suite, *Dneprostroy,* on the subject of the building of the hydroelectric station on the Dnieper River; in the score he included a number of percussion instruments representing various mechanical aspects of the project. During the Russian Civil War (1918–20), he wrote the opera *Perekop,* on the subject of the protracted struggle between the red and white armies on the Crimean Peninsula (Kiev, Jan. 20, 1939). When Russia was invaded by the Nazi armies (1941), Meitus was forced to move to Turkestan in Central Asia. There he produced the operas *Gaidamaki* (Ashkhabad, Oct. 15, 1943) and *Leili and Medzhiun* (Ashkhabad, Nov. 2, 1946). Returning to the Ukraine, he produced the operas *The Young Guard* (Kiev, Nov. 7, 1947), *Dawn over the River Dvina* (Kiev, July 5, 1955), *Stolen Happiness* (Lvov, Galicia, Sept. 10, 1960), and *The Daughter of the Wind* (Odessa, Oct. 24, 1965). There followed *The Brothers Ulyanov* (Ufa, Nov. 25, 1967), on the subject of the family of Lenin, whose real name was Ulyanov (Lenin's brother was executed by hanging for participation in a conspiracy to kill the Czar). Other operas include *Makhtunkuli,* on Turkmenian themes (Ashkhabad, Dec. 29, 1962); *Yaroslav the Wise,* on the rule of an early Russian chieftain (Donetsk, March 3, 1973); *Richard Sorge,* on the life of a German Soviet agent working in Nazi circles in Tokyo (Lvov, 1976); *Ivan the Terrible* (1980–82); and *Maria Volkonskaya,* on the wife of one of the Decembrist rebels against Czar Nicholas I; she followed her husband to his Siberian exile (1986–89). Apart from operas, which constitute his main contribution to Soviet music, Meitus composed a number of instrumental works, which were invariably connected with themes of socialist structures; in this connection, he joined the Assoc. of Revolutionary Ukrainian Composers. It was only when such proletarian groups were disbanded by the Soviet government in 1932 that Meitus devoted himself mainly to opera. He also composed a considerable number of choruses and solo songs to Russian and Ukrainian words. Stylistically, most of his music follows the tenets of socialist realism, observing clear tonality but freely using dissonant harmonies when necessary for dramatic effect; he also applied considerable variety in asymmetrical meters and rhythms, especially in his works based on Turkmenian themes.
Bibl.: Y. Malishev, *Y. M., Essays on His Work* (Moscow, 1962); L. Arkhimovich and I. Mamchur, *Y. M.* (Moscow, 1983).

Mekeel, Joyce, American harpsichordist and composer; b. New Haven, Conn., July 6, 1931. She studied at the Longy School of Music in Cambridge, Mass. (1952–55); received instruction in keyboard playing from Boulanger at the Paris Cons. (1955–57), from Leonhardt (1957), and from Kirkpatrick (1957–59); took courses in theory and composition at Yale Univ. (B.M., 1959; M.M., 1960) and studied privately with Earl Kim (1960–62); completed her education at Boston Univ. (Ph.D., 1983, with the diss. *Social Influences on Changing Audience Behavior in the Mid-Victorian London Theatre*). She made appearances as a harpsichordist, and was a composer for several dance and theater companies (1961–75); taught at the New England Cons. of Music in Boston (1964–70) and at Boston Univ. (from 1970).
Works: **stage:** *Jaywalk* for Viola and Dancer (1969); *Moveable Feast* (1973–75; in collaboration with P. Earls and L. Davidson); *Kisses and Kazoos* (1977); *Alarums and Excursions* for Violin, Viola, Cello, Piano, Flute, Clarinet, Percussion, and Actress/Mezzo-soprano (1978); *Museum* (1980); *Sigil* for String Quintet, Clarinet, English Horn, 2 Horns, 2 Tubas, Harp, Actor, and Actress/Mezzo-soprano (1981); *Journeys of Remembrance* (1986). **orch.:** *String Figures Disentangled by a Flute* for Flute

and String Orch. (Boston, April 2, 1969); *Vigil* (Boston, Oct. 19, 1978). CHAMBER: *Spindrift* for String Quartet (1970); *Hommages* for Brass Quintet (1973); *Rune* for Flute and Percussion (1976); *Tessera* for String Quintet, Saxophone, English Horn, Contrabassoon, Trumpet, Horn, and Harps (1981); *Fertile Vicissitudes* for Harp and Oboe (1981); *Voices* for Violin, Clarinet, and Piano (1983); *An Insomnia of Owls* for Woodwind Quintet (1985); numerous solo works. VOCAL: *White Silence* for Chorus (1965); *Waterwalk* for Speaking Chorus (1970); *Corridors of Dream* for Mezzo-soprano, Flute, Clarinet, Harp, Viola, and Cello (1972); *Toward the Source* for Chorus and Orch. (1974); *Serena* for Mezzo-soprano, Speaker, and Prepared Piano (1975); songs.

Melachrino, George (Miltiades), English conductor of popular music; b. London, May 1, 1909; d. there, June 18, 1965. He studied at London's Trinity College of Music; then conducted his own band; subsequently launched the Melachrino Strings (1945), which he imbued with a sort of black-velvet coloration that made the "Melachrino sound" a byword among music-lovers. He could play every instrument except harp and piano. His recording albums bore titles of irresistible sentimentality, e.g., *Music for Two People Alone, Music for a Nostalgic Traveler* (known in Europe under the name of *Reverie*), and *Music for Relaxation.*

Melani, family of Italian musicians, of whom the most important were the following 3 brothers:

(1) Jacopo Melani, organist and composer; b. Pistoia, July 6, 1623; d. there, Aug. 19, 1676. He became organist (1645) and maestro di cappella (1657) of Pistoia Cathedral. He excelled as a composer of comic operas, which included *Il potesta di Colognole* (Florence, 1657; also known as *La Tancia*), *Ercole in Tebe* (Florence, July 8, 1661), *Il Girello* (Rome, 1668), and *Enea in Italia* (Pisa, 1670).

(2) Atto Melani, alto and composer; b. Pistoia, March 31, 1626; d. Paris, 1714. He was a pupil of Luigi Rossi and Marc'Antonio Pasqualini in Rome. In 1664 he visited Paris, where he won the esteem of Queen Anne and Mazarin; while singing in opera there, he also secretly served as a diplomatic courier; after Mazarin's death, he entered the service of Cardinal Giulio Rospigliosi and became enmeshed in papal politics; in 1679 he returned to Paris, where he was active in politics. He composed various vocal pieces, including solo cantatas and duets.

(3) Alessandro Melani, composer; b. Pistoia, Feb. 4, 1639; d. Rome, Oct. 1703. He sang at Pistoia Cathedral (1650–60) and then served as maestro di cappella in Orvieto and Ferrara. In 1667 he succeeded his brother Jacopo as maestro di cappella of Pistoia Cathedral, but later that year went to Rome to take up that position at S. Maria Maggiore; in 1672 he obtained the same position at S. Luigi dei Francesi, which he held until his death. He composed the operas *L'empio punito* (Rome, 1669), *Il trionfo della continenza considerato in Scipione Africano* (Fano, 1677), *Le reciproche gelosie* (Siena, 1677), *Roberto ovvero Il Carceriere di se medesimo* (Florence, 1681), and *Ama chi t'ama* (Siena, 1682); he also collaborated with B. Pasquini and A. Scarlatti on the opera *S. Dinna* (Rome, 1687). His other works include oratorios, motets, and cantatas.

Melartin, Erkki (Gustaf), Finnish composer; b. Käkisalmi, Feb. 7, 1875; d. Pukinmäki, Feb. 14, 1937. He was a pupil of Wegelius at the Helsinki Music Inst. and of Robert Fuchs in Vienna; taught theory at the Helsinki Music Inst. (1898; 1901–7); succeeded Wegelius as director in 1911, and remained at this post until 1936. His compositions are marked by a lyrical strain, with thematic materials often drawn from Finnish folk songs. WORKS: STAGE: Opera, *Aino* (1907; Helsinki, Dec. 10, 1909); ballet, *Sininen helmi* (The Blue Pearl, 1930); also incidental music. ORCH.: 8 syms. (1902; 1904; 1906–7; 1912; 1916, *Sinfonia brevis*; 1924–25; 2 unfinished); 3 symphonic poems; 3 lyric suites; Violin Concerto; Serenade for Strings; *Karjalaisia kuvia* (Karelian Pictures). CHAMBER: 4 string quartets; Quartet for 2 Trumpets, Trombone, and Horn; Quartet for 4 Horns; Trio for Flute, Clarinet, and Bassoon; 2 violin

sonatas; Sonata for Flute and Harp; piano pieces; violin works; also choruses and about 300 songs.

Melba, Dame Nellie (stage name of **Mrs. Helen Porter Armstrong,** née **Mitchell**), famous Australian soprano; b. Burnley, near Richmond, May 19, 1861; d. Sydney, Feb. 23, 1931. Her father, who had decided objections to anything connected with the stage, was nevertheless fond of music and proud of his daughter's talent. When she was only 6 years old he allowed her to sing at a concert in the Melbourne Town Hall, but would not consent to her having singing lessons; instead, she was taught piano, violin, and harp, and even had instruction in harmony and composition. As she grew older she frequently played the organ in a local church, and was known among her friends as an excellent pianist, while all the time her chief desire was to study singing. Not until after her marriage in 1882 to Captain Charles Armstrong was she able to gratify her ambition, when she began to study with a local teacher, Cecchi; her 1st public appearance as a singer was on May 17, 1884, in a benefit concert in Melbourne. The next year her father received a government appointment in London, and she accompanied him, determined to begin an operatic career. She studied with Mathilde Marchesi in Paris. Melba gave her 1st concert in London (June 1, 1886). Her debut as Gilda at the Théâtre Royal de la Monnaie in Brussels (Oct. 13, 1887) created a veritable sensation; the famous impresario Augustus Harris immediately engaged her for the spring season at London's Covent Garden, where she appeared on May 24, 1888, as Lucia, to only a half-full house. However, she scored a major success at the Paris Opéra as Ophelia in Thomas's *Hamlet* (May 8, 1889); then sang with great success in St. Petersburg (1891), Milan (La Scala, 1893; immense triumph over a carefully planned opposition), Stockholm and Copenhagen (Oct. 1893), N.Y. (Metropolitan Opera, as Lucia, Dec. 4, 1893), and Melbourne (Sept. 27, 1902). From her 1st appearance at Covent Garden she sang there off and on until 1914; besides being one of the most brilliant stars of several seasons at the Metropolitan Opera in N.Y., she also sang with Damrosch's Opera Co. (1898) and at Hammerstein's Manhattan Opera (1906–7 and 1908–9), and made several transcontinental concert tours of the U.S. Bemberg wrote for her *Elaine* (1892), and Saint-Saëns, *Hélène* (1904), in both of which she created the title roles. In 1915 she began teaching at the Albert Street Conservatorium in Melbourne; returned to Covent Garden for appearances in 1919, 1923, and a farewell performance on June 8, 1926. Then she returned to Australia and retired from the stage. Melba was by nature gifted with a voice of extraordinary beauty and bell-like purity; through her art she made this fine instrument perfectly even throughout its entire compass (B-flat–f‴) and wonderfully flexible, so that she executed the most difficult fioritura without the least effort. As an actress she did not rise above the conventional, and for this reason she was at her best in parts demanding brilliant coloratura (Gilda, Lucia, Violetta, Rosina, Lakmé, etc.). On a single occasion she attempted the dramatic role of Brünnhilde in *Siegfried* (Metropolitan Opera, N.Y., Dec. 30, 1896), and met with disaster. In 1918 she was created a Dame Commander of the Order of the British Empire. She was a typical representative of the golden era of opera; a prima donna *assoluta*, she exercised her powers over the public with perfect self-assurance and a fine command of her singing voice. Among her other distinguished roles were Mimi, Else, Nedda, Aida, Desdemona, and Marguerita. As a measure of Melba's universal popularity, it may be mentioned that her name was attached to a delicious dessert (Peach Melba) and also to Melba toast, patented in 1929 by Bert Weil. A motion picture based on her life was produced in 1953 with Patrice Munsel as Melba. She wrote an autobiography, *Melodies and Memories* (London, 1925).

BIBL.: A. Murphy, *M., A Biography* (London, 1909; contains a chapter on singing written by Melba); P. Colson, *M., An Unconventional Biography* (London, 1931); J. Wechsberg, *Red Plush and Black Velvet: The Story of M. and Her Times* (Boston,

1961); G. Hutton, *M.* (Melbourne, 1962); J. Hetherington, *M.* (London, 1967); W. Moran, *N. M.: A Contemporary Review* (Westport, Conn., 1985); T. Radic, *M.: The Voice of Australia* (Melbourne and London, 1986).

Melcer (-Szczawiński), Henryk, esteemed Polish pianist, conductor, teacher, and composer; b. Kalisch, Sept. 21, 1869; d. Warsaw, April 18, 1928. He was a pupil of Noszkowski (composition) and Strobl (piano) at the Warsaw Music Inst. (graduated, 1890); after touring Russia as an accompanist, he received further piano training from Leschetizky in Vienna. After successful concert tours of Russia, Germany, and France, he taught at the Helsinki Cons. (1895–96) and was a prof. at the Lemberg Cons. (1896–99); was director of the Lodz music society (1899–1902) and director-conductor of the Lodz Phil. (from 1902); was conductor of the Warsaw Phil. (1910–12) and Opera (1915–16). He subsequently taught at the Warsaw Cons. (from 1919), serving as head of piano studies (until 1928), orchestration (1925–26), and composition (1925–28).
    Works: 2 operas: *Protasilas i Laodamia* (1902; Paris, 1925) and *Marja* (Warsaw, Nov. 16, 1904); 2 piano concertos: No. 1 (won the Rubinstein prize, 1895); No. 2 (won the Paderewski prize, 1898); *Pani Twardowska,* ballad for Tenor, Chorus, and Orch. (1898); Piano Trio (1895); Violin Sonata (c.1896); songs; piano pieces.

Melchers, Henrik Melcher, Swedish violinist and composer; b. Stockholm, May 30, 1882; d. there, April 9, 1961. He studied at the Stockholm Cons. and with J. Lindegren; later at the Paris Cons. He lived in Paris (1905–19), then in Brussels and Sondershausen. In 1925 he became a prof. at the Stockholm Cons. Among his works are *Swedish Rhapsody* for Orch. (Stockholm, 1914), the symphonic poems *Näcken* (1916) and *La Kermesse* (1919), *Poem* for Violin and Orch. (1922), and songs.

Melchior, Lauritz (real name, **Lebrecht Hommel**), celebrated Danish-born American tenor; b. Copenhagen, March 20, 1890; d. Santa Monica, Calif., March 18, 1973. He studied with Paul Bang at the Royal Opera School in Copenhagen, making his operatic debut in the baritone role of Silvio in *Pagliacci* at the Royal Theater there (April 2, 1913); continued on its roster while studying further with Vilhelm Herold, and then made his tenor debut as Tannhäuser (Oct. 8, 1918). In 1921 he went to London to continue his training with Beigel, and then studied with Grenzebach in Berlin and Bahr-Mildenburg in Munich. On May 24, 1924, he made his Covent Garden debut in London as Siegmund, returning there regularly from 1926 to 1939. He was in Bayreuth in 1924 to study with Kittel; made his 1st appearance at the Festspielhaus there as Siegfried on July 23, 1924, and continued to make appearances there until 1931. On Feb. 17, 1926, he made his Metropolitan Opera debut in N.Y. as Tannhäuser, and quickly established himself as one of its principal artists; with the exception of the 1927–28 season, he sang there regularly until his farewell performance as Lohengrin on Feb. 2, 1950. In 1947 he became a naturalized U.S. citizen. After the close of his operatic career, Melchior appeared on Broadway and in films; also continued to give concerts. He was accorded a preeminent place among the Wagnerian Heldentenors of his era.
    Bibl.: H. Hanse, *L. M.: A Discography* (Copenhagen, 1965; 2nd ed., 1972); S. Emmons, *Tristanissimo: The Authorized Biography of Heroic Tenor L. M.* (N.Y., 1990).

Melichar, Alois, Austrian music critic and composer; b. Vienna, April 18, 1896; d. Munich, April 9, 1976. He studied theory at the Vienna Academy of Music with Joseph Marx (1917–20) and at the Hochschule für Musik in Berlin with Schreker (1920–23). From 1923 to 1926 he was in the Caucasus, where he collected materials on Caucasian folk songs; then lived in Berlin and Vienna. As a composer, he followed the safe footpath of Reger, Pfitzner, and Graener; he wrote a symphonic poem, *Der Dom* (1934); *Rhapsodie über ein schwedisches Volkslied* (1939); *Lustspiel-Ouvertüre* (1942); lieder; film music. As a music critic, he acquired notoriety by his intemperate attacks on better composers than himself. His publications, written in his virulent, polemical manner, include *Die unteilbare Musik* (Vienna, 1952), *Musik in der Zwangsjacke* (Vienna, 1958), and (particularly vicious) *Schönberg und die Folgen* (Vienna, 1960).

Melik-Pashayev, Alexander (Shamilievich), noted Russian conductor; b. Tiflis, Oct. 23, 1905; d. Moscow, June 18, 1964. He studied with N. Tcherepnin at the Tiflis Cons.; was pianist and concertmaster of the Tiflis Opera orch. (1921–24), and then its conductor; after conducting studies with Gauk at the Leningrad Cons. (graduated, 1930), he returned to the Tiflis Opera as chief conductor (1930–31); then conducted at Moscow's Bolshoi Theater, later serving as its chief conductor (1953–62). He was highly esteemed for his interpretations of Russian operas; was awarded 2 Stalin prizes (1942, 1943) and was made a People's Artist of the U.S.S.R. (1951).

Melikov, Arif (Djangirovich), Russian composer; b. Baku, Sept. 13, 1933. He studied the tar (an oriental lute) at the Baku Zeinalla Music College (1948–53) and composition with Kara Karayev at the Gadjibekov Azerbaijan State Cons. (1953–58); in 1965 he joined its faculty. His early music hewed to the tenets of socialist realism, representational and stylistically inoffensive to untutored ears. In his later works he made use of various modern techniques.
    Works: **stage:** Ballets, *The Legend of Love* (Leningrad, March 23, 1961); *The 2* (1969); *Poem of 2 Hearts* (1983); musical, *Waves* (1967); also incidental music to plays; film scores. **orch.:** *symphonic poems:* *Fairy Tale* (1957); *In Memory of Fizuli* (1959); *Metamorphoses* (1963); *Motherland,* with Voice (1964); *The Last Pass* (1976); *Remember* (1978). **other orch.:** Concertino for Flute and Orch. (1956); 6 syms. (1958, 1969, 1975, 1977, 1979–82, 1985); 2 *Suites* (1965); *Suite* for Folk Orch. (1967); *Pictures* for Folk Orch. (1967); 8 *Pieces* (1968); 2 *Suites* (1970); 12 *Pieces* (1971); *Symphonic Dances* (1976). **chamber:** *Suite* for Violin and Piano (1954); *Scherzo* for Violin and Piano (1954); Sonata for Solo Violin (1980); *Scherzo* for 2 Pianos (1983); also vocal works, including *Voice of the Earth,* cantata (1972); choruses; and songs.

Melikyan, Romanos Hovakimi, Armenian composer; b. Kiziyar, northern Caucasus, Dec. 1, 1883; d. Erevan, March 30, 1935. He studied at the Rostov College of Music (graduated, 1905), then with Ippolitov-Ivanov, Taneyev, and Yavorsky in Moscow (1905–7); subsequently with Kalafati and Steinberg at the St. Petersburg Cons. (1910–14). He founded the Tiflis Music League (1908); became director of music at the Armenian House of Culture in Moscow (1918), then founded the Erevan Cons. (1923); was also founder-director of the Erevan Theater of Opera and Ballet (1933). He was a major figure in Armenian music circles; as a composer, he was highly regarded for his songs and folk-song arrangements.
    Bibl.: G. Geodakyan, *R. M.* (Erevan, 1960); K. Tordjyan, *R. M.* (Erevan, 1960).

Melis, Carmen, Italian soprano; b. Cagliari, Sardinia, Aug. 14, 1885; d. Longone al Segrino, Dec. 19, 1967. She studied with Teresina Singer and Carlo Carignani in Milan, Antonio Cotogni in Rome, and Jean de Reszke in Paris; made her operatic debut in Novara in 1905; then sang in Naples (1906) and toured Russia (1907). She was engaged by Hammerstein for the Manhattan Opera, and made her American debut there as Tosca (N.Y., Nov. 26, 1909); subsequently was a member of the Boston Opera Co. (1911–13). Later she became a teacher; her most famous pupil was Renata Tebaldi.

Melkikh, Dmitri, Russian composer; b. Moscow, Feb. 11, 1885; d. there, Feb. 22, 1943. He studied at the People's Cons. in Moscow with Yavorsky, under whose influence he wrote music in archaic Russian modes; his few symphonic works reveal slight traits of French Impressionism. Among his works are 3 syms. (1925, 1933, 1938); 4 string quartets; a symphonic poem, *Alladine et Palomides* (after Maeterlinck); and several song cycles.

Melkus, Eduard, Austrian violinist, conductor, and teacher; b. Baden-bei-Wien, Sept. 1, 1928. He studied violin with Ernst

Moravec at the Vienna Academy of Music (1943–53) and musicology with Schenk at the Univ. of Vienna (1951–53); continued his violin training with Firmin Touche in Paris (1953), Alexander Schaichet in Zürich (1956), and Peter Rybar in Winterthur (1958). After playing in several Swiss orchs., he became prof. of violin and viola at the Vienna Hochschule für Musik (1958); also toured as a soloist in Europe and the U.S.; founded the Capella Academica of Vienna (1965), which he conducted in performances of works ranging from the Renaissance to the early Classical era, utilizing modern instruments as well as original instruments or reproductions.

Mell, Gertrud Maria, Swedish composer, organist, and sea captain; b. Ed, Aug. 15, 1947. She studied at the Lund Cons. (diploma in organ, 1967) and in Stockholm (music teacher's diploma, 1968); later pursued training at the Univ. of Marine Officers in Göteborg (1978–81), passing examinations as a mate (1979), ship mechanic (1979), sea captain (master mariner, 1981), radio telephone operator (1982), and ship engineer (1985). She began her career as a church organist in Ed at age 17 and became adept at improvisation; was organist in Töftedal (1967–76) and also taught music in Ed (1969–71) and Bengtsfors (1972–76). After working as a seaperson on transatlantic ships (1976–78), she pursued both music and navigation; served as organist of the Pater Noster Church in Göteborg (from 1982); also appeared as a recitalist in concert, radio, and television settings, and even made an appearance as a pop singer in her recording *Mermaid* (1977).
    WORKS: ORCH.: 4 syms. (1964, 1965, 1966, 1967); *Melodie aus dem Meer,* symphonic poem (1980; also for Violin and Piano, 1976); *Solvind* (1984; also for Flute and Piano, 1975); *Celeste cordialis* for String Orch. (1985); *Andante,* symphonic poem (1988). **OTHER:** String Quartet No. 1 (1969); piano pieces, including *Fantasie* (1961) and *Impromptu* (1971); organ music; improvisations for both piano and organ; choral works, including *Pater noster* for Soloists, Choir, and Instruments (1983); songs; various pop pieces.

Mellencamp, John "Cougar," popular American rock singer and songwriter; b. Seymour, Ind., Oct. 7, 1951. Born on the wrong side of the tracks, he evinced an early predilection for antisocial, small-town-America behavior; in his teen years, his penchant for beer drinking, pill popping, and girl chasing was relieved only by a love for rock music. After playing guitar in several rock bands, he cheated his way through Vincennes Univ. as a communications major (graduated, 1973), only to resume his quest for rock stardom. He formed his 1st rock band, Trash!, and began to churn out his own unsuccessful songs. Moving to N.Y. in 1975, he signed with the manager Tony DeFries, who groomed him as Johnny Cougar, the centerpiece of the album *Chestnut Street Revisited* (1976). After it bombed, he sojourned in England as a rock reject (1977–78). Back in the U.S., he charted a new course with his rock band Zone and struck a responsive chord with his album *John Cougar* (1979), which included his hit songs *I Need a Lover* and *Taxi Dancer.* His next album, *Nothin' Matters and What if It Did* (1980), featured the popular hits *This Time* and *Ain't Even Done with the Night.* After the moneymaking album *American Fool* (1982), the self-proclaimed "Little Bastard" of heartland rockdom made an impact with his album *Uh-Huh* (1983), the 1st to appear under the cognomen John Cougar Mellencamp. Mellencamp expressed an expanded social conscience in the albums *Scarecrow* (1985), *The Lonesome Jubilee* (1987), and *Big Daddy* (1989).
    BIBL.: M. Torgoff, *American Fool: The Roots and Improbable Rise of J.C. M.* (N.Y., 1986); *Current Biography* (March 1988).

Mellers, Wilfred (Howard), English musicologist and composer; b. Leamington, Warwickshire, April 26, 1914. He studied at Cambridge Univ. (B.A., 1936; M.A., 1939); was a pupil in composition of E. Wellesz and E. Rubbra; received his D.Mus. from the Univ. of Birmingham (1960). He was a lecturer in music at Downing College, Cambridge (1945–48); after serving as a staff tutor in the extramural dept. at the Univ. of Birmingham (1948–59), he served as Andrew W. Mellon Prof. of Music

at the Univ. of Pittsburgh (1960–63); then was prof. of music at the Univ. of York (1964–81). In 1982 he was made an Officer of the Order of the British Empire.
    WRITINGS: *Music and Society: England and the European Tradition* (London, 1946); *Studies in Contemporary Music* (London, 1947); *François Couperin and the French Classical Tradition* (London, 1950; 2nd ed., rev., 1987); *Music in the Making* (London, 1952); *Romanticism and the 20th Century* (London, 1957; 2nd ed., rev., 1988); *The Sonata Principle* (London, 1957; 2nd ed., rev., 1988); *Music in a New Found Land: Themes and Developments in the History of American Music* (London, 1964; 2nd ed., rev., 1987); *Harmonious Meeting: A Study of the Relationship between English Music, Poetry and Theatre, c.1600–1900* (London, 1965); *Caliban Reborn: Renewal in Twentieth-Century Music* (N.Y., 1967); *Twilight of the Gods: The Music of the Beatles* (N.Y., 1973); *Bach and the Dance of God* (N.Y., 1980); *Beethoven and the Voice of God* (London, 1983); *A Darker Shade of Pale: A Backdrop to Bob Dylan* (London, 1984); *Angels of the Night: Popular Female Singers of Our Time* (London, 1986); *The Masks of Orpheus: Seven Stages in the Story of European Music* (Manchester, England, and Wolfeboro, N.H., 1987); *Le Jardin Parfume: Homage to Frederic Mompou* (1989); *Vaughan Williams and the Vision of Albion* (1989).
    WORKS: STAGE: Operas: *The Tragicall History of Christopher Marlowe* (1952); *The Shepherd's Daughter,* chamber opera (1953–54); *Mary Easter,* ballad opera (1957); monodrama, *The Ancient Wound* (Victoria, British Columbia, July 27, 1970). **ORCH.:** *Sinfonia ricercata* (1947); *Alba, in 9 Metamorphoses* for Flute and Orch. (1961); *Noctambule and Sun Dance* for Wind Sym. (1966); *Shaman Songs* for Jazz Paraphernalia (1980); *The Wellspring of Loves,* concerto for Violin and String Orch. (1981); *The Spring of the Year* for Double String Orch. (1985); *Hortus Rosarium* for 11 Solo Strings (1986). **CHAMBER:** String Trio (1945); Sonata for Viola and Piano (1946); *Eclogue* for Treble Recorder, Violin, Cello, and Harpsichord (1961); Trio for Flute, Cello, and Piano (1963); *Ghost Dance* for Flute, Viola, and Harpsichord (1972); *Aubade for Indra* for Clarinet and String Quartet (1981); *The Happy Meadow,* eclogue for Flute and Guitar (1986); piano pieces; also numerous vocal works.

Melles, Carl, Hungarian conductor; b. Budapest, July 15, 1926. He received his musical training in Budapest; in 1951 he was appointed conductor of the Hungarian State Orch. and the Sym. Orch. of Hungarian Radio and Television; was also a prof. at the Budapest Academy of Music (1954–56). After the abortive rebellion in 1956, he led the Radio Orch. of Luxembourg (1958–60); also conducted at Bayreuth and Salzburg. He eventually made his home in Vienna and became a regular conductor of the Vienna Sym. Orch. and on the Austrian Radio.

Mellnäs, Arne, Swedish composer; b. Stockholm, Aug. 30, 1933. In 1953 he entered the Stockholm Musikhögskolan, where he later was a pupil in composition of Erland von Koch, Lars-Erik Larsson, Karl-Birger Blomdahl, and Bo Wallner (1958–61); also studied composition with Blacher at the Berlin Hochschule für Musik (1959), and privately with Max Deutsch in Paris (1961) and Ligeti in Vienna (1962); worked with Gottfried Michael Koenig in Bilthoven (1962–63) and was active at the San Francisco Tape Music Center (1964). After teaching at the Stockholm Citizen's School (1961–63), he taught at the Stockholm Musikhögskolan (from 1963); in 1983 he became chairman of the Swedish section of the ISCM. In 1984 he was elected a member of the Royal Swedish Academy of Music in Stockholm. Mellnäs is one of Sweden's most innovative avant-garde composers; he has done much to advance the cause of contemporary music in his homeland.
    WORKS: Oboe Sonata (1957); Concerto for Clarinet and Strings (1957); *Music* for Orch. (1959); *Chiasmos* for Orch. (1961); *Växlingar* for Flute, or Piccolo, and Clarinet (1961); *Collage* for Orch. (1962); *Per caso* for Saxophone, Trombone, Violin, Double Bass, and 2 Percussionists (1963); *Tombola*

for Horn, Trombone, Electric Guitar, and Piano (1963); electronic pieces: *Cem/63* (1963), *Nite Music* (1964), *Intensity 6.5* (1966; dedicated to the memory of Edgard Varèse, containing electronically modified quotations from Varèse's works, particularly from *Density 21.5*), *Conglomérat* (1968), *Eufoni* (1969), *Monotrem* (1969), *Kaleidovision*, ballet for television (1969), *Appassionato* (1970), *Far Out* (1970), *Splinters* (1970); *Aura* for Orch. (Malmö, June 5, 1964); *Gestes sonores* for Any Ensemble (1964); *Sic transit* for Instruments and Tape (1964); *Succsim* for Chorus (1964); *Siamfoni* for Trumpet, Horn, and Trombone (1964); *Minibuff*, opera for 2 Singers and Tape (1966); *Drones* for Jazz Combo (1967); *Fixations* for Organ (1967); *Quasi niente* for 1 to 4 String Trios (1968); *Spots and Spaces*, after e.e. cummings, for Male Chorus, 11 Strings, and Winds (1968); *Aglepta* for Chorus (1969); *Capricorn Flakes* for Piano, Harpsichord, and Vibraphone (1970); *Cabrillo* for Clarinet, Trombone, Cello, and Percussion (1970); *Schizofoni* for 1, 2, or 3 Pianos (1971); *Noël*, after e.e. cummings, for 2 Sopranos, Children's Chorus, and Instrumental Ensemble (1971); *Transparence* for Orch. (1972); *Vae* for Chorus and Organ (1972); *Ceremus* for Flute, Clarinet, Trumpet, Trombone, Double Bass, and Percussion (1973); *Sub luna* for Soprano, Flute, Violin, and Harp (1973); *Mara Mara Minne* for Chorus and Tape (1973); *Fragile* for Any Kind and Number of Instruments (1973); *Blow* for Wind Orch. (1974); church opera, *Erik the Holy* (Stockholm, May 18, 1976); *Moments musicaux* for Orch. (1977); *Incantations* for Wind Orch. (1978); *Capriccio* for Orch. (1978); *Nocturnes* for Mezzosoprano and Chamber Ensemble (1980); chamber opera, *The Canterville Ghost* (1980); *Pieces fugitives* for Flute, Bassoon, Violin, Guitar, and Harpsichord (1981); chamber opera, *Bed of Roses* (1984); *Stampede* for Saxophone Quartet (1985); Sym. No. 1, *Ikaros* (1986; Stockholm, March 18, 1987); *Gardens* for Flute, Clarinet, Percussion, Violin, Cello, and Piano (1986).

Melnikov, Ivan (Alexandrovich), noted Russian baritone; b. St. Petersburg, March 4, 1832; d. there, July 8, 1906. He was a choirboy in school; was engaged in trade, and for a time served as inspector of Volga boats; he began to study seriously late in life; took lessons with Lomakin (1862); then went to Italy, where he studied with Repetto. He made his operatic debut as Riccardo in *I Puritani* in St. Petersburg (Oct. 6, 1867), where he sang regularly until his farewell performance in *Prince Igor* in 1890; then taught voice. He created the title role in Mussorgsky's *Boris Godunov* (St. Petersburg, Feb. 8, 1874); was particularly esteemed for his portrayals of roles in operas by Glinka, Borodin, and Tchaikovsky.

Melton, James, American tenor; b. Moultrie, Ga., Jan. 2, 1904; d. N.Y., April 21, 1961. He studied with Gaetano de Luca in Nashville and Enrico Rosati in N.Y.; then with Michael Raucheisen in Berlin. He began his career on the radio; made his concert debut in N.Y. on April 22, 1932, and his operatic debut as Pinkerton in *Madama Butterfly* in Cincinnati on June 28, 1938. On Dec. 7, 1942, he appeared for the 1st time with the Metropolitan Opera in N.Y. as Tamino in *Die Zauberflöte;* remained on its roster until 1950; also toured the U.S. as a concert singer and later appeared in films.

Meluzzi, Salvatore, Italian composer; b. Rome, July 22, 1813; d. there, April 17, 1897. He was maestro di cappella at the basilica of St. Peter's in the Vatican, and for 45 years was director of the Cappella Giulia. Thoroughly versed in the art of the early Italian masters, he emulated them in writing masses, Requiems, antiphons, motets, hymns, and Psalms; among his best pieces are a *Stabat Mater* and a *Miserere*.

Membrée, Edmond, French composer; b. Valenciennes, Nov. 14, 1820; d. Château Damont, near Paris, Sept. 10, 1882. He studied at the Paris Cons. with Alkan and Zimmerman (piano) and Carafa (composition).

WORKS: Operas: *François Villon* (Paris, April 20, 1857); *L'Esclave* (Paris, July 17, 1874); *Les Parias* (Paris, Nov. 13, 1876); *La Courte Echelle* (Paris, 1879); also a cantata, *Fingal* (Paris, May 14, 1861); ballads; songs; etc.

BIBL.: L. Mention, *Un Compositeur valenciennois: E. M.* (Paris, 1908).

Menager, Laurent, Luxembourgian composer; b. Luxembourg, Jan. 10, 1835; d. there, Feb. 7, 1902. He was a song composer and a respected pedagogue. A postage stamp was issued in his honor by the government of Luxembourg in 1951.

Menasce, Jacques de, Austrian-born American pianist and composer; b. Bad Ischl (of a French-Egyptian father and a German mother), Aug. 19, 1905; d. Gstaad, Switzerland, Jan. 28, 1960. He studied in Vienna with Sauer (piano) and with J. Marx, Paul Pisk, and Alban Berg (composition). From 1932 to 1940 he gave concerts in Europe as a pianist; in 1941 he went to America, living mostly in N.Y., but continued his concert career in Europe. He became a naturalized American citizen.

WORKS: 2 piano concertos (1935, 1939); *Divertimento* for Piano and String Orch. (1940); 2 ballets: *The Fate of My People* (1945) and *Status Quo* (1947); Violin Sonata (1940); Viola Sonata (1950); choruses; songs; piano pieces.

Menchaca, Angel, Paraguayan music theorist; b. Asunción, March 1, 1855; d. Buenos Aires, May 8, 1924. He was trained as a jurist; also taught history and literature at the National College in Buenos Aires. In 1914 he publ. a provocative book, *Sistema teórico-gráfico de la música,* in which he proposed a new system of notation, employing a basic alphabet of 12 notes and dispensing with the established signatures, staff, etc. He toured Europe for the purpose of lecturing on this device; invented a special keyboard to facilitate its application. He was also a composer; his compositions include songs and school choruses.

Mendel, Arthur, eminent American music scholar; b. Boston, June 6, 1905; d. Newark, N.J., Oct. 14, 1979. He studied at Harvard Univ. (A.B., 1925); also took courses in theory with Nadia Boulanger in Paris (1925–27); returning to America, he was literary ed. of G. Schirmer, Inc. (1930–38); also wrote music criticism in the *Nation* (1930–33); from 1936 to 1953 he conducted in N.Y. a chorus, The Cantata Singers, specializing in Baroque music; taught at the Dalcroze School of Music from 1938; was its president (1947–50); also lectured at Columbia Univ. (1949) and the Univ. of Calif., Berkeley (1951); he was then prof. of music and chairman of the music dept. at Princeton Univ. (1952–67); held the Henry Putnam Univ. Professorship there from 1969 to 1973. He ed. (with H. David) the valuable "documentary biography" *The Bach Reader* (N.Y., 1945; 2nd ed., rev., 1966); ed. Bach's *St. John Passion* (1951), Schütz's *Christmas Story* (1949) and *Musicalische Exequien* (1957), and other works of the Baroque period. He publ. numerous important articles on the history of pitch, reprinted in *Studies in the History of Musical Pitch* (Amsterdam, 1969), and also promoted the possibility of music analysis with the aid of a computer, publ. in *Computers and the Humanities* (1969–70). A Festschrift, *Studies in Renaissance and Baroque Music in Honor of Arthur Mendel,* ed. by R. Marshall, was publ. in Kassel in 1974.

Mendel, Hermann, German music lexicographer; b. Halle, Aug. 6, 1834; d. Berlin, Oct. 26, 1876. He was a pupil of Mendelssohn and Moscheles in Leipzig, and of Wieprecht in Berlin. In 1870 he founded and ed. the *Deutsche Musiker-Zeitung;* also ed. *Mode's Opernbibliothek* (about 90 librettos, with commentaries and biographies of composers) and a *Volksliederbuch.* He publ. 2 small books on Meyerbeer (1868, 1869). His great work was the *Musikalisches Conversations-Lexikon,* which he began to publ. in 1870, but was able to continue only to the letter *M;* the rest was completed by August Reissmann; the entire ed. was in 11 vols.; a supplementary vol. was publ. in 1883.

Mendelsohn, Alfred, Rumanian composer and conductor; b. Bucharest, Feb. 17, 1910; d. there, May 9, 1966. He studied in Vienna with Joseph Marx, Franz Schmidt, Egon Wellesz, and others (1927–31), and at the Bucharest Cons. with Jora (1931–32). From 1946 to 1954 he was conductor of the Rumanian Opera in Bucharest; from 1949, was prof. at the Bucharest Cons., remaining there until his death. An exceptionally prolific composer, he produced a great amount of highly competent, technically accomplished music. Influenced primarily by the programmatic Romanticism of the Vienna School, he also probed the potentialities of motivic structures, suggesting the serial concepts of modern constructivists while remaining faithful to basic tonalitarianism.

WORKS: DRAMATIC: OPERAS: *Meşterul Manole* (1949); *Michelangelo* (Timişoara, Sept. 29, 1964); *Spinoza*, lyrical scene (1966). **OPERETTA:** *Anton Pann* (Bucharest, 1963). **BALLETS:** *Harap alb* (The White Moor; 1948); *Călin* (1956). **ORATORIOS CANTATAS:** *1917* (1956; on the Russian Revolution); *Inimă vitează* (1952); *Canata Bucureştiului* (1953); *Horia* (1955); *1907* (1957; deals with the 1907 peasant uprising in Rumania); *Glasul lui Lenin* (The Voice of Lenin; 1957); *Sub cerul de vară* (1959); *Pentru Marele Octombrie* (1960); *Cei puternici* (1965); also *Imnul iubirii* (The Love Hymn), dramatic sym., with libretto, in 7 tableaus (1946). **ORCH.:** *Suite concertante* for Flute and String Orch. (1957); *Suite* for Chamber Orch. (1940); *Suită comemorativă* for String Orch. (1943); 9 syms.: No. 1 (1944); No. 2, *Veritas* (1947); No. 3, *Reconstrucţia* (1949); No. 4, *Apelul păcii* (1951); No. 5 (1953); No. 6 (1955); No. 7 (1960); No. 8 (1963); No. 9, *Concertante*, for Organ and Orch. (1964); symphonic poems: *Prăbuşirea Doftanei* (Doftana's Assault; 1949); *Eliberarea* (Liberation; 1954); *Va înflori acel Arminden* (The May Tree Will Blossom; 1959); *Schite dobrogene* (Dobrudjan Sketches; 1961); Chamber Sym. (1961); 2 piano concertos (1946, 1949); Cello Concerto (1949); 3 violin concertos (1953, 1957, 1964); Concertino for Harp and Strings (1955); *Divertimento* for Horn and Strings (1957); Concerto Grosso for String Quartet and Strings (1958); Concerto for Organ and Chamber Orch. (1960); Viola Concerto (1965); *Epitaph* (1965); Concerto (1965); Concerto for String Orch. (1965). **CHAMBER:** 10 string quartets (1930–64); Piano Quintet (1953); Harp Quintet (1955); String Sextet (1957); Piano Trio (1959); *Theme and Variations* for 7 Cellos (1963); Octet for 8 Cellos (1963); numerous sonatas for violin, viola, and cello; Piano Sonata (1947) and smaller pieces; song cycles.

Mendelssohn, Arnold (Ludwig), distinguished German organist, pedagogue, and composer, son of a 2nd cousin of **(Jacob Ludwig) Felix Mendelssohn (-Bartholdy);** b. Ratibor, Dec. 26, 1855; d. Darmstadt, Feb. 19, 1933. He studied law at the Univ. of Tübingen (1877), then took courses with Löschhorn (piano), Haupt (organ), and Grell, Kiel, and Taubert (composition) at Berlin's Institut für Kirchenmusik (1877–80). He was organist and music director at the Univ. of Bonn (1880–82), then music director in Bielefeld (1882–85); taught composition at the Cologne Cons. (1885–90); was Hessian master of church music and prof. at the Darmstadt Cons. (1891–1912); thereafter was a prof. at Frankfurt's Hoch Cons.; among his pupils was Hindemith. He championed the music of Schütz and Bach. In his own sacred works, he helped to revitalize Lutheran church music. He wrote a book on esthetics, *Gott, Welt und Kunst* (ed. by W. Ewald; Wiesbaden, 1949).

WORKS: 3 operas: *Elsi, die seltsame Magd* (Cologne, 1896); *Der Bärenhäuter* (Berlin, Feb. 9, 1900); *Der Minneburg* (Mannheim, 1909); incidental music to Goethe's *Paria* (1906) and *Pandora* (1908); 3 syms.; Violin Concerto (1922); sacred choral works, including *Abendkantate* (1881) and 2 other cantatas (both 1912); *Deutsche Messe* (1923); *Geistliche Chormusik* (1926); 3 string quartets; Cello Sonata; 2 piano sonatas; songs.

BIBL.: W. Nagel, *A. M.* (Leipzig, 1906); A. Werner-Jensen, *A. M. als Liederkomponist* (Winterthur, 1976); J. Böhme, *A. M. und seine Klavier- und Kammermusik* (Frankfurt am Main, 1987).

Mendelssohn, Fanny. See **Hensel, Fanny Cäcilia.**

Mendelssohn (-Bartholdy), (Jacob Ludwig) Felix, famous German composer, pianist, and conductor; b. Hamburg, Feb. 3, 1809; d. Leipzig, Nov. 4, 1847. He was a grandson of the philosopher Moses Mendelssohn and the son of the banker Abraham Mendelssohn; his mother was Lea Salomon; the family was Jewish, but upon its settlement in Berlin the father decided to become a Protestant and added Bartholdy to his surname. Mendelssohn received his 1st piano lessons from his mother; subsequently studied piano with Ludwig Berger and violin with Carl Wilhelm Henning and Eduard Rietz; he also had regular lessons in foreign languages and in painting (he showed considerable talent in drawing with pastels); he also had piano lessons with Marie Bigot in Paris, where he went with his father for a brief stay in 1816. His most important teacher in his early youth was Carl Friedrich Zelter, who understood the magnitude of Mendelssohn's talent; in 1821 Zelter took him to Weimar and introduced him to Goethe, who took considerable interest in the boy after hearing him play. Zelter arranged for Mendelssohn to become a member of the Singakademie in Berlin in 1819 as an alto singer; on Sept. 18, 1819, his *19th Psalm* was performed by the Akademie. In 1825 Mendelssohn's father took him again to Paris to consult Cherubini on Mendelssohn's prospects in music; however, he returned to Berlin, where he had better opportunities for development. Mendelssohn was not only a precocious musician, both in performing and in composition; what is perhaps without a parallel in music history is the extraordinary perfection of his works written during adolescence. He played in public for the 1st time at the age of 9, on Oct. 28, 1818, in Berlin, performing the piano part of a trio by Wölffl. He wrote a remarkable octet at the age of 16; at 17 he composed the overture to the incidental music to Shakespeare's *A Midsummer Night's Dream*, an extraordinary manifestation of his artistic maturity, showing a mastery of form equal to that of the remaining numbers of the work, which were composed 15 years later. He proved his great musicianship when he conducted Bach's *St. Matthew Passion* in the Berlin Singakademie on March 11, 1829, an event that gave an impulse to the revival of Bach's vocal music. In the spring of 1829 Mendelssohn made his 1st journey to England, where he conducted his Sym. in C minor (seated, after the fashion of the time, at the keyboard); later he performed in London the solo part in Beethoven's *Emperor* Concerto; he then traveled through Scotland, where he found inspiration for the composition of his overture *Fingal's Cave* (*Hebrides*), which he conducted for the 1st time during his 2nd visit to London, on May 14, 1832; 10 days later he played in London the solo part of his G minor Concerto and his *Capriccio brillante*. He became a favorite of the English public; Queen Victoria was one of his most fervent admirers; altogether he made 10 trips to England as a pianist, conductor, and composer. From 1830 to 1832 he traveled in Germany, Austria, Italy, and Switzerland, and also went to Paris. In May 1833 he led the Lower-Rhine Music Festival in Düsseldorf; then conducted at Cologne in June 1835. He was still a very young man when, in 1835, he was offered the conductorship of the celebrated Gewandhaus Orch. in Leipzig; the Univ. of Leipzig bestowed upon him an honorary degree of Ph.D. Mendelssohn's leadership of the Gewandhaus Orch. was of the greatest significance for the development of German musical culture; he engaged the violin virtuoso Ferdinand David as concertmaster of the orch., which soon became the most prestigious symphonic organization in Germany. On March 28, 1837, he married Cécile Charlotte Sophie Jeanrenaud of Frankfurt, the daughter of a French Protestant clergyman. Five children (Carl, Marie, Paul, Felix, and Elisabeth) were born to them, and their marriage was exceptionally happy. At the invitation of King Friedrich Wilhelm IV, Mendelssohn went in 1841 to Berlin to take charge of the music of the court and in the Cathedral; he received the title of Royal Generalmusikdirektor, but residence in Berlin was not required. Returning to Leipzig in 1842, he organized the famous "Conservatorium." Its splendid faculty comprised, besides Mendelssohn (who taught piano, ensemble playing, and later composition), Schumann, who taught classes in piano and composition; Hauptmann, in music theory; David, in violin; Becker, in organ; and Plaidy and Wenzel, in piano. The Conservatorium was officially opened on April 3, 1843. The financial nucleus of the foundation was a bequest from Blümner of 20,000 thaler, left at the disposal of the King of Saxony for the promotion of the fine arts. Mendelssohn made a special journey to Dresden to petition the King on behalf of the Leipzig Cons. During his frequent absences, the Gewandhaus Concerts were conducted by Hiller (1843–44) and Gade (1844–45). In the summer of 1844 he conducted the Phil. Concerts in London; this was his 8th visit to England; during his 9th visit he conducted the 1st performance of his oratorio *Elijah* in Birmingham, on Aug. 26, 1846. It was in England that the "Wedding March" from Mendelssohn's music to *A Midsummer Night's Dream* began to be used to accompany the bridal procession; the performance of the work was for the marriage of Tom Daniel and Dorothy Carew at St. Peter's Church, Tiverton, on June 2, 1847; the organist was Samuel Reay; it became particularly fashionable, however, when it was played at the wedding of the Princess Royal in 1858. He made his 10th and last visit to England in the spring of 1847; this was a sad period of his life, for his favorite sister, Fanny, died on May 14, 1847. Mendelssohn's own health began to deteriorate, and he died at the age of 38. The exact cause of his early death is not determined; he suffered from severe migraines and chills before he died, but no evidence could be produced by the resident physicians for either a stroke or heart failure. A detailed account of Mendelssohn's illness and death is found in D. Kerner's *Krankheiten grosser Musiker* (Stuttgart, 1969). The news of his death produced a profound shock in the world of music; not only in Germany and England, where he was personally known and beloved, but in distant America and Russia as well, there was genuine sorrow among musicians. Mendelssohn societies were formed all over the world; in America the Mendelssohn Quintette Club was founded in 1849. A Mendelssohn Scholarship was established in England in 1856; its 1st recipient was Arthur Sullivan.

Mendelssohn's influence on German, English, American, and Russian music was great and undiminishing through the years; his syms., concertos, chamber music, piano pieces, and songs became perennial favorites in concerts and at home, the most popular works being the overture *Hebrides*, the ubiquitously played Violin Concerto, the *Songs without Words* for Piano, and the "Wedding March" from incidental music to *A Midsummer Night's Dream*. Professional music historians are apt to place Mendelssohn below the ranks of his great contemporaries Schumann, Chopin, and Liszt; in this exalted company Mendelssohn is often regarded as a phenomenon of Biedermeier culture. A barbaric ruling was made by the Nazi regime to forbid performances of Mendelssohn's music as that of a Jew; his very name was removed from music history books and encyclopedias publ. in Germany during that time. This shameful episode was of but a transitory nature, however; if anything, it served to create a greater appreciation of Mendelssohn's genius following the collapse of the infamous 3rd Reich.

WORKS: STAGE: *Ich, J. Mendelssohn . . .* , Lustspiel (1820); *Die Soldatenliebschaft*, comic opera (1820; Wittenberg, April 28, 1962); *Die beiden Pädagogen*, singspiel (1821; Berlin, May 27, 1962); *Die wandernden Komödianten*, comic opera (1822; dialogue not extant); *Der Onkel aus Boston oder Die beiden Neffen*, comic opera (1823; Berlin, Feb. 3, 1824; dialogue not extant); *Die Hochzeit des Camacho*, op. 10, opera (1825; Berlin, April 29, 1827; dialogue not extant); *Die Heimkehr aus der Fremde*, op. 89, Liederspiel (1829, written for the silver wedding anniversary of Mendelssohn's parents, perf. at their home, Berlin, Dec. 26, 1829); *Der standhafte*, incidental music to Calderón's play (1833); *Trala. A frischer Bua bin i* (1833); *Ruy Blas*, incidental music to Hugo's play (1839); *Antigone*, op. 55, incidental music to Sophocles' play (Potsdam, Oct. 28, 1841); *A Midsummer Night's Dream*, op. 61, incidental music to Shakespeare's play (1842; Potsdam, Oct. 14, 1843); *Oedipus at Colonos*, op. 93, incidental music to Sophocles' play (Potsdam, Nov. 1, 1845); *Athalie*, op. 74, incidental music to Racine's play (Berlin-Charlottenburg, Dec. 1, 1845); *Lorelei*, op. 98, opera (begun in childhood but unfinished; *Ave Maria*, a vintage chorus, and finale to Act I only; Birmingham, Sept. 8, 1852).

ORATORIOS: *St. Paul*, op. 36 (1834–36; Düsseldorf, May 22, 1836, composer conducting); *Elijah*, op. 70 (1846; Birmingham, Aug. 26, 1846, composer conducting); *Christus*, op. 97 (unfinished; Boston, May 7, 1874).

OTHER SACRED: *Die Himmel erzählen* for 5 Voices (1820); *Gott, du bist unsre Zuversicht* for 5 Voices (1820); *Ich will den Herrn nach seiner Gerechtigkeit preisen* for 4 Voices (1820); *Tag für Tag sei Gott gepriesen* for 5 Voices (1820); *Das Gesetz des Herrn ist ohne Wandel* for 5 Voices (1821–22); *Er hat der Sonne eine Hütte gemacht* for 5 Voices (1821–22); *Jube Domine* for Solo Voices and Double Chorus (1822); *Psalm LXVI* for Double Female Chorus and Basso Continuo (1822); *Magnificat in D major* for Chorus and Orch. (1822); *Kyrie in C minor* for Solo Voices and Chorus (1823); *Jesus, meine Zuversicht* for Solo Voices and Chorus (1824); *Salve Regina* in E-flat major for Soprano and Strings (1824); 2 sacred pieces for Chorus: *Wie gross ist der Allmächt'gen Güte* (1824) and *Allein Gott in der Höh' sey Ehr* (1824); *Te Deum in D major* for Double Chorus and Basso Continuo (1826); *Jesu, meine Freude*, chorale cantata for Double Chorus and Strings; *Tu es Petrus* for Chorus and Orch., op. 111 (1827); *Ave Maria Stella* for Soprano and Orch. (1828); *Hora est* for 16 Voices and Organ (1828); 3 sacred pieces for Tenor, Chorus, and Organ, op. 23: *Aus tiefer Not*, *Ave Maria*, and *Mitten*; *Psalm CXV* for Solo Voices, Chorus, and Orch., op. 31 (1830); *Zum Feste der Dreieinigkeit* (*O beata et benedicta*) for 3 Sopranos and Organ (1830); 3 motets for Female Chorus and Organ, op. 39 (1830): *Hear my prayer, O Lord* (*Veni, Domine*), *O praise the Lord* (*Laudate pueri*), and *O Lord, thou hast searched me out* (*Surrexit Pastor*); *Verleih uns Frieden* for Chorus and Orch. (1831); *Te Deum in A major* for Solo Voices, Chorus, and Organ (1832); *Lord have mercy upon us* for Chorus (1833); 2 sacred choruses for Male Chorus, op. 115 (1833); *Responsorium et hymnus* for Male Voices, Cello, and Organ, op. 121 (1833); *Psalm XLII* for Solo Voices, Chorus, and Orch., op. 42 (1837); *Psalm XCV* for Tenor, Chorus, and Orch., op. 46 (1838); *Psalm V, Lord hear the voice* for Chorus (1839); *Psalm XXXI, Defend me, Lord* for Chorus (1839); *Hymn in A major* for Solo Voice, Chorus, and Orch., op. 96 (1840); *Psalm CXIV* for Double Chorus and Orch., op. 51 (1839); *Geistliches Lied* in E-flat major for Solo Voice, Chorus, and Organ (1840); *Psalm C, Jauchzet den Herrn* for Chorus (1842); *Herr Gott, dich loben wir* for Solo Voices, Chorus, Organ, and Orch. (1843); *Psalm XCVIII* for Double Chorus and Orch., op. 91 (1843); *Ehre sei dem Vater* for 8 Voices (1844); *Hear my prayer*, hymn for Soprano, Chorus, and Organ (1844); *Ehre sei dem Vater* in C major for 4 Voices (1845); *Er kommt aus dem kindlichen Alter der Welt* for 6 Voices (1846); *Lauda Sion* for Chorus and Orch., op. 73 (Liège, June 11, 1846); *Die deutsche Liturgie* for 8 Voices (1846); 3 *English Church Pieces* for Solo Voices and Chorus, op. 69 (1847): *Nunc dimittis*, *Jubilate*, and *Magnificat*; 3 Psalms for Solo Voices and Double Chorus, op. 78: *Psalm II* (1843), *Psalm XLIII* (1844), and *Psalm XXII* (1844); 6 *Anthems* for Double Chorus, op. 79: *Rejoice, O ye people*; *Thou, Lord, our refuge hast been* (1843); *Above all praises* (1846); *Lord, on our offences* (1844); *Let our hearts be joyful* (1846); *For our offences* (1844). Other works include: *Ach Gott vom Himmel sieh darein*, chorale cantata for Solo Voices, Chorus, and Orch.; *Cantique pour l'Eglise wallonne de Francfort* (*Venez chantez*) for 4 Voices; *Christe, du Lamm Gottes*, chorale cantata for Chorus and Orch.; *Gloria patri* (*Ehre sei dem Vater*) for 4 Voices; *Glory be to the Father* for 4 Voices; *Gloria* in E-flat major for Solo Voices, Chorus, and Orch. (unfinished); *Kyrie* for Chorus and Orch.; *Kyrie* in A major for 8 Voices; *Vom Himmel hoch*, chorale cantata for Solo Voices, Chorus, and Orch.; etc.

SECULAR CANTATAS: *In feierlichen Tönen*, wedding cantata for Soprano, Alto, Tenor, Chorus, and Piano (1820); *Grosse Festmusik zum Dürerfest* for Solo Voices, Chorus, and Orch. (Berlin, April 18, 1828); *Begrüssung* (*Humboldt Cantata*), festival music for Solo Male Voices, Male Chorus, and Wind (Berlin, Sept. 18, 1828); *Die erste Walpurgisnacht* for Chorus and Orch., op. 60 (1832; Berlin, Jan. 1833; rev. 1843; Leipzig, Feb. 2, 1843); *Gott segne Sachsenland* for Male Voices and Wind (Dresden, June 7, 1843); *An die Künstler,* festival song for Male Voices and Brass, op. 68 (Cologne, June 1846).

CHORAL SONGS: *Einst ins Schlaraffenland zogen* for 4 Male Voices (1820); *Lieb und Hoffnung* for Male Voices (1820); *Jägerlied (Kein bess're Lust in dieser Zeit)* for 4 Male Voices (1822); *Lob des Weines (Seht, Freunde, die Gläser)* for Solo Male Voices and Male Chorus (1822); *Lass es heut am edlen Ort* for 4 Male Voices (1828); *Worauf kommt es überall an* for 4 Male Voices (1837); *Im Freien zu singen* for Mixed Voices, op. 41: 1, *Im Walde* (1838); 2, *Entflieh mit mir* (1838); 3, *Es fiel ein Reif* (1838); 4, *Auf ihrem Grab* (1834); 5, *Mailied* (1838); 6, *Auf dem See* (1838); *Der erste Frühlingstag* for Mixed Voices, op. 48 (1839): 1, *Frühlingsahnung;* 2, *Die Primel;* 3, *Frühlingsfeier;* 4, *Lerchengesang;* 5, *Morgengebet;* 6, *Herbstlied; Ersatz für Unbestand* for 4 Male Voices (1839); *Festgesang* for Male Voices (Leipzig, June 25, 1840; No. 2 adapted by W.H. Cummings for *Hark! the Herald Angels Sing*); 6 male choruses, op. 50: 1, *Türkisches Schenkenlied* (1839–40); 2, *Der Jäger Abschied* (1840); 3, *Sommerlied* (1839–40); 4, *Wasserfahrt* (1839–40); 5, *Liebe und Wein* (1839); 6, *Wanderlied* (1842); *Nachtgesang* for 4 Male Voices (1842); *Die Stiftungsfeier* for 4 Male Voices (1842); *Im Grünen* for Mixed Voices, op. 59: 1, *Im Grünen* (1837); 2, *Frühzeitiger Frühling* (1843); 3, *Abschied vom Wald* (1843); 4, *Die Nachtigall* (1843); 5, *Ruhetal* (1843); 6, *Jagdlied* (1843); *Sahst du ihn herniederschweben,* funeral song for Mixed Voices, op. 116 (1845); *Der Sänger* (1845; Leipzig, Nov. 10, 1846); *Wandersmann* for Male Voices, op. 75: 1, *Der frohe Wandersmann* (1844); 2, *Abendständchen* (1839); 3, *Trinklied;* 4, *Abschiedstafel* (1844); 4 male choruses, op. 76: 1, *Das Lied vom braven Mann;* 2, *Rheinweinlied* (1844); 3, *Lied für die Deutschen in Lyon* (1846); 4, *Comitat;* 6 choruses for Mixed Voices, op. 88: 1, *Neujahrslied* (1844); 2, *Der Glückliche* (1843); 3, *Hirtenlied* (1839); 4, *Die Waldvögelein* (1843); 5, *Deutschland* (1839–43); 6, *Der wandernde Musikant* (1840); 4 choruses for Mixed Voices, op. 100: 1, *Andenken* (1844); 2, *Lob des Frühlings* (1843); 3, *Frühlingslied* (1843–44); 4, *Im Wald* (1839); 4 male choruses, op. 120: 1, *Jagdlied* (1837); 2, *Morgengruss des Thüringischen Sängerbundes* (1847); 3, *Im Süden;* 4, *Zigeunerlied; Lob der Trunkenheit (Trunken müssen wir alle sein)* for 4 Male Voices; *Musikantenprügelei (Seht doch diese Fiedlerbanden)* for 2 Male Voices. Also concert arias: *Che vuoi mio cor?* for Mezzo-soprano and Strings, and *Infelice* for Soprano and Orch., op. 94 (1834; rev. 1843).

SONGS: *Ave Maria* (1820); *Raste Krieger, Krieg ist aus* (1820); *Die Nachtigall (Da ging ich hin)* (1821–22); *Der Verlassene (Nacht ist um mich her)* (1821–22); *Von allen deinen zarten Gaben* (1822); *Wiegenlied (Schlummre sanft)* (1822); *Sanft weh'n im Hauch der Abendluft* (1822); *Der Wasserfall (Rieselt hernieder)* (1823); 12 songs, op. 8 (1828): 1, *Minnelied;* 2, *Das Heimweh* (by Fanny Mendelssohn); 3, *Italien* (by Fanny Mendelssohn); 4, *Erntelied;* 5, *Pilgerspruch;* 6, *Frühlingslied;* 7, *Maienlied;* 8, *Andres Maienlied (Hexenlied);* 9, *Abendlied;* 10, *Romanze;* 11, *Im Grünen;* 12, *Suleika und Hatem* (by Fanny Mendelssohn); *The Garland (Der Blumenkranz)* (1829); 12 songs, op. 9 (1829–30): 1, *Frage;* 2, *Geständnis;* 3, *Wartend;* 4, *Im Frühling;* 5, *Im Herbst;* 6, *Scheidend;* 7, *Sehnsucht* (by Fanny Mendelssohn); 8, *Frühlingsglaube;* 9, *Ferne;* 10, *Verlust* (by Fanny Mendelssohn); 11, *Entsagung;* 12, *Die Nonne* (by Fanny Mendelssohn); 4 songs (1830): 1, *Der Tag (Sanft entschwanden mir);* 2, *Reiterlied (Immer fort);* 3, *Abschied (Leb wohl mein Lieb);* 4, *Der Bettler (Ich danke Gott dir); Seemanns Scheidelied* (1831); *Weihnachtslied (Auf schicke dich recht feierlich)* (1832); 6 songs, op. 19a (1830–34): 1, *Frühlingslied;* 2, *Das erste Veilchen;* 3, *Winterlied;* 4, *Neue Liebe;* 5, *Gruss;* 6, *Reiselied; Mailied (Ich weiss mir'n Mädchen)* (1834); 2 romances: *There be none of beauty's daughters* (1833) and *Sun of the Sleepless* (1834); 2 songs: *Das Waldschloss* (1835) and *Pagenlied* (1835); 6 songs, op. 34 (1834–36): 1, *Minnelied;* 2, *Auf Flügeln des Gesanges;* 3, *Frühlingslied;* 4, *Suleika;* 5, *Sonntagslied;* 6, *Reiselied; Lied einer Freundin (Zarter Blumen leicht Gewinde)* (1837); *Im Kahn* (1837); *O könnt ich zu dir fliegen* (1838); 6 songs, op. 47 (1832–39): 1, *Minnelied;* 2, *Morgengruss;* 3, *Frühlingslied;* 4, *Volkslied;* 5, *Der Blumenstrauss;* 6,

Bei der Wiege; 2 songs: *Todeslied der Bojaren* (1840) and *Ich hör ein Vöglein* (1841); 6 songs, op. 57 (1839–43): 1, *Altdeutsches Lied;* 2, *Hirtenlied;* 3, *Suleika;* 4, *O Jugend;* 5, *Venetianisches Gondellied;* 6, *Wanderlied;* 6 songs, op. 71 (1842–47): 1, *Tröstung;* 2, *Frühlingslied;* 3, *An die Entfernte;* 4, *Schilflied;* 5, *Auf der Wanderschaft;* 6, *Nachtlied;* 3 songs, op. 84 (1831–39): 1, *Da lieg' ich unter den Bäumen;* 2, *Herbstlied;* 3, *Jagdlied;* 6 songs, op. 86 (1831–51): 1, *Es lauschte des Laub;* 2, *Morgenlied;* 3, *Die Liebende schreibt;* 4, *Allnächtlich im Traume;* 5, *Der Mond;* 6, *Altdeutsches Frühlingslied;* 6 songs, op. 99: 1, *Erster Verlust;* 2, *Die Sterne schau'n;* 3, *Lieblingsplätzchen;* 4, *Das Schifflein;* 5, *Wenn sich zwei Herzen scheiden;* 6, *Es weiss und rät es doch keiner;* 2 sacred songs, op. 112: *Doch der Herr, er leitet die Irrenden recht* and *Der du die Menschen lässest sterben;* also *Des Mädchens Klage; Warnung vor dem Rhein; Der Abendsegen (The Evening Service); Gretschen (Meine Ruh ist hin); Lieben und Schweigen (Ich flocht ein Kränzlein schöner Lieder); Es rauscht der Wald; Vier trübe Monden sind entfloh'n; Weinend seh' ich in die Nacht; Weiter, rastlos atemlos vorüber.* Vocal duets: *Ein Tag sagt es dem andern* for Soprano and Alto (1821); 6 duets, op. 63 (1836–45): 1, *Ich wollt' meine Lieb';* 2, *Abschiedslied der Zugvögel;* 3, *Gruss;* 4, *Herbstlied;* 5, *Volkslied;* 6, *Maiglöckchen und die Blümelein;* 3 duets, op. 77 (1836–47): 1, *Sonntagsmorgen;* 2, *Das Aehrenfeld;* 3, *Lied aus "Ruy Blas";* 3 folk songs: 1, *Wie kann ich froh und lustig sein;* 2, *Abendlied;* 3, *Wasserfahrt;* also various canons.

ORCH.: 13 youthful sinfonias for Strings: No. 1, in C major (1821); No. 2, in D major (1821); No. 3, in E minor (1821); No. 4, in C minor (1821); No. 5, in B-flat major (1821); No. 6, in E-flat major (1821); No. 7, in D minor (1821–22); No. 8, in D major (1822); No. 9, in C major (1823); No. 10, in B minor (1823); No. 11, in F major (1823); No. 12, in G minor (1823); No. 13, in C minor (1823; one movement only); syms.: No. 1, in C minor, op. 11 (1824); No. 2, in B-flat major, a sym.-cantata for Solo Voices, Chorus, and Orch., *Lobgesang* or *Hymn of Praise,* op. 52 (Leipzig, June 25, 1840, composer conducting); No. 3, in A minor, *Scottish,* op. 56 (1830–42; Leipzig, March 3, 1842, composer conducting); No. 4, in A major, *Italian,* op. 90 (London, May 13, 1833, composer conducting); No. 5, in D major, *Reformation,* op.107 (1830–32; Berlin, Nov. 15, 1832, composer conducting); Violin Concerto in D minor for Strings (1822; Yehudi Menuhin gave its 1st perf. from the MS, N.Y., Feb. 4, 1952); Piano Concerto in A minor for Strings (1822); Concerto in D minor for Violin, Piano, and Strings (1823); Concerto in E major for 2 Pianos and Orch. (1823; Berlin, Nov. 14, 1824); Concerto in A-flat major for 2 Pianos and Orch. (1824; Stettin, Feb. 20, 1827); Overture in C major for Wind Instruments, op. 24 (1824); *Capriccio brillant* in B minor for Piano and Orch., op. 22 (1825–26; London, May 25, 1832); Overture (*Trumpet* Overture) in C major, op. 101 (1826; rev. 1833); *Ein Sommernachtstraum,* overture for Shakespeare's *A Midsummer Night's Dream,* op. 21 (1826; Stettin, April 29, 1827); *Meeresstille und glückliche Fahrt* (Calm Sea and Prosperous Voyage), overture after Goethe, op. 27 (Berlin, April 18, 1828); *Die Hebriden* or *Fingals Höhle* (The Hebrides or Fingal's Cave), overture, op. 26 (1830; London, May 14, 1832); Piano Concerto No. 1, in G minor, op. 25 (Munich, Oct. 17, 1831, composer soloist); *Die schöne Melusine* (The Fair Melusina), overture after Grillparzer, op. 32 (1833; London, April 7, 1834); *Rondo brillant* in E-flat major for Piano and Orch., op. 29 (1834); *Trauermarsch* in A minor for Wind, op. 103 (1836); Piano Concerto No. 2, in D minor, op. 40 (Birmingham, Sept. 1837, composer soloist); *Serenade and Allegro giocoso,* in B minor, for Piano and Orch., op. 43 (1838); *Ruy Blas,* overture after Hugo, op. 95 (Leipzig, March 1839); March in D major, op. 108 (1841); Violin Concerto in E minor, op. 64 (1844; Leipzig, March 13, 1845; Ferdinand David, soloist; composer conducting).

CHAMBER: Trio in C minor for Violin, Viola, and Piano (1820); Presto in F major for Violin and Piano (1820); Violin Sonata in F major (1820); 15 fugues for String Quartet (1821); Piano Quartet in D minor (1822); Piano Quartet No. 1, in C minor, op. 1 (1822); String Quartet in E-flat major (1823); Piano Quartet No. 2, in F minor, op. 2 (1823); Viola Sonata in C minor (1824); Sextet in D major for Violin, 2 Violas, Cello, Double Bass, and Piano, op. 110 (1824); Clarinet Sonata in E-flat major (1824); Piano Quartet No. 3, in B minor, op. 3 (1825); Violin Sonata in F minor, op. 4 (1825); Octet in E-flat major for 4 Violins, 2 Violas, and 2 Cellos, op. 20 (1825); Quintet No. 1, in A major, for 2 Violins, 2 Violas, and Cello, op. 18 (1826; rev. 1832); String Quartet No. 2, in A major, op. 13 (1827); Fugue in E-flat major for String Quartet (1827); Fugue in E-flat major for String Quartet, op. 81/4 (1827); *Variations concertantes* for Cello and Piano, op. 17 (1829); String Quartet No. 1, in E-flat major, op. 12 (1829); *The Evening Bell* for Harp and Piano (1829); Concert Piece in F major for Clarinet, Basset Horn, and Piano or Orch., op. 113 (1833); Concert Piece in D minor for Clarinet and Basset Horn, op. 114 (1833); string quartets, Nos. 3–5, op. 44 (1837–38); Violin Sonata in F major (1838); Cello Sonata No. 1, in B-flat major, op. 45 (1838); Piano Trio No. 1, in D minor, op. 49 (1839); *Capriccio* in E minor for String Quartet, op. 81/3 (1843); Cello Sonata No. 2, in D major, op. 58 (1843); Quintet No. 2, in B-flat major, op. 87 (1845); Piano Trio No. 2, in C minor, op. 66 (1845); *Lied ohne Worte* in D major for Cello and Piano, op. 109 (1845); String Quartet No. 6, in F minor, op. 80 (1847); *Andante* in E major for String Quartet, op. 81/1 (1847); *Scherzo* in A minor for String Quartet, op. 81/2 (1847).

PIANO: *Andante* in F major (1820); piano piece in E minor (1820); 2 little pieces (1820); 2 little pieces (1820); 5 little pieces (1820); *Largo-Allegro* in C minor (1820); *Recitativo (Largo)* in D minor (1820); Sonata in F minor (1820); Sonata in A minor (1820); *Presto* in C minor (1820); Sonata in E minor (1820); 2 studies (1820); *Allegro* in A minor (1821); Study in C major (1821); Sonata in G minor, op. 105 (1821); *Largo-Allegro molto* in C minor/major (1821–22); 3 fugues: D minor, D minor, and B minor (1822); *Allegro* in D minor (1823); *Fantasia (Adagio)* in C minor (1823); *Rondo capriccioso* in E major, op. 14 (1824); *Capriccio* in F-sharp minor, op. 5 (1825); Fugue in C-sharp minor (1826); Sonata in E major, op. 6 (1826); *7 charakteristische Stücke*, op. 7 (1827); *Fantasia* in E major, on "The Last Rose of Summer," op. 15 (1827); Sonata in B-flat major, op. 106 (1827); Fugue in E minor (1827); *Scherzo* in B minor (1829); *3 fantaisies ou caprices*, op. 16 (1829); *Andante* in A major (1830); *Lieder ohne Worte (Songs without Words)*: 8 books, op. 19 (1829–30), 30 (1833–34), 38 (1836–37), 53 (1839–41), 62 (1842–44), 67 (1843–45), 85 (1834–45), 102 (1842–45); *Fantasia (Sonate écossaise)* in F-sharp minor, op. 28 (1833); *3 Caprices*, op. 33 (1833–35); *Scherzo a capriccio* in F-sharp minor (1835–36); Study in F minor (1836); *Andante* in A-flat major (1836); *Lied* in F-sharp minor (1836); *Prelude* in F minor (1836); *3 Preludes*, op. 104a (1836); *6 Preludes* and *Fugues*, op. 35 (1832–37); *Gondellied (Barcarole)* in A major (1837); *Capriccio* in E major, op. 118 (1837); *Albumblatt (Lied ohne Worte)* in E minor, op. 117 (1837); *Andante cantabile* and *Presto agitato*, in B major (1838); *3 Studies*, op. 104b (1834–38); *Prelude* and *Fugue* in E minor (1827–41); *Variations sérieuses* in D minor, op. 54 (1841); *Variations* in E-flat major, op. 82 (1841); *Variations* in B-flat major, op. 83 (1841); *Kinderstücke (Christmas Pieces)*, op. 72 (1842–47); *Perpetuum mobile* in C major, op. 119; etc.
PIANO DUETS: *Lento-Vivace* in G minor (1820); *Fantasia* in D minor (1824); *Allegro brillant* in A major, op. 92 (1841); *Variations* in B-flat major, op. 83a (1841). For 2 Pianos: *Duo concertant*: Variations on the march from Weber's *Preciosa* (1833; with Moscheles). Also several works for organ, including *3 Preludes* and *Fugues*, op. 37 (1837), and *6 sonatas*, op. 65 (1844–45).

BIBL.: COLLECTED EDITIONS, SOURCE MATERIAL: The 1st collected ed. of his works, *F. M.-B.: Werke: Kritisch durchgesehene Ausgabe*, was ed. by Julius Rietz and publ. by Breitkopf & Härtel (Leipzig, 1874–77); this ed. omits a number of works, however. A new ed. of the complete works, the *Leipziger Ausgabe der Werke F. M.-B.s*, began publication in Leipzig in 1960 by the Internationale Felix-Mendelssohn-Gesellschaft. Breit-

kopf & Härtel publ. a *Thematisches Verzeichnis im Druck erschienener Compositionen von F. M.-B.* (Leipzig, 1846; 2nd ed., 1853; 3rd ed., 1882). Other sources include the following: Y. Rokseth, "Manuscrits de M. à la Bibliothèque du Conservatoire," *Revue de Musicologie*, XV (1934); E. Walker, "An Oxford Collection of M.iana," *Music & Letters*, XIX (1938); M. Schneider, "Eine M.-Sammlung in Basel," *Der Amerbach Bote: Almanach* (Basel, 1947); E. Werner, "M. Sources," *Notes*, II (1954–55); *M.-Festwoche aus Anlass der 150. Wiederkehr des Geburtstages am 3. Februar 1959* (Leipzig, 1959); M. Schneider, *M.-Archiv der Staatsbibliothek Stiftung Preussischer Kulturbesitz* (Berlin, 1965); R. Elvers, *F. M.-B.: Dokumente seines Lebens: Ausstellung zum 125. Todestag* (Berlin, 1972); P. Krause, *Autographen, Erstausgaben und Frühdrucke der Werke von F. M.-B. in Leipziger Bibliotheken und Archiven* (Leipzig, 1972); K. Schultz, ed., *F. M.B.: "Der schöne Zwischenfall in der deutschen Musik"* (Vienna, 1981).
BIOGRAPHICAL: W. Lampadius, *F. M.-B.: Ein Denkmal für seine Freunde* (Leipzig, 1848; Eng. tr., with additional articles by others, N.Y., 1865; 2nd greatly augmented German ed., as *F. M.-B.: Ein Gesammtbild seines Lebens und Wirkens*, Leipzig, 1886); L. Stierlin, *Biographie von F. M.-B.* (Zürich, 1849); J. Benedict, *A Sketch of the Life and Works of the Late F. M.-B.* (London, 1850; 2nd ed., 1853); W. Neumann, *F. M.-B.: Eine Biographie* (Kassel, 1854); A. Reissmann, *F. M.-B.: Sein Leben und seine Werke* (Berlin, 1867; 3rd ed., rev., 1893); H. Barbedette, *F. M.-B.: Sa vie et ses œuvres* (Paris, 1868); C. Mendelssohn-Bartholdy, *Goethe und F. M.-B.* (Leipzig, 1871; Eng. tr., London, 1872; 2nd ed., 1874); S. Hensel, *Die Familie M. 1729–1847, nach Briefen und Tagebüchern* (3 vols., Berlin, 1879; 18th ed., 1924; Eng. tr., 2 vols., London, 1881); J. Sittard, *F. M.-B.* (Leipzig, 1881); W. Rockstro, *M.* (London, 1884; rev. ed., 1911); E. David, *Les M.-B. et Robert Schumann* (Paris, 1886); J. Eckardt, *Ferdinand David und die Familie M.-B.* (Leipzig, 1888); J. Hadden, *M.* (London, 1888; 2nd ed., 1904); S. Stratton, *M.* (London, 1901; 6th ed., 1934); V. Blackburn, *M.* (London, 1904); E. Wolff, *F. M.-B.* (Berlin, 1906; 2nd ed., rev., 1909); C. Bellaigue, *M.* (Paris, 1907; 4th ed., 1920); J. Hartog, *F. M.-B. en zijne werken* (Leyden, 1908); P. de Stoecklin, *M.* (Paris, 1908; 2nd ed., 1927); M. Jacobi, *F. M.-B.* (Bielefeld, 1915); W. Dahms, *M.* (Berlin, 1919; 9th ed., 1922); J. Esser, *F. M.-B. und die Rheinlande* (diss., Univ. of Bonn, 1923); C. Winn, *M.* (London, 1927); J. Cooke, *F. M.-B.* (Philadelphia, 1929); E. Vuillermoz, *Une Heure de musique avec M.* (Paris, 1930); S. Kaufmann, *M.: A Second Elijah* (N.Y., 1934; 2nd ed., 1936); J. Petitpierre, *Le Mariage de M. 1837–1847* (Lausanne, 1937; Eng. tr. as *The Romance of the M.s*, London, 1947); B. Bartels, *M.-B.: Mensch und Werk* (Bremen, 1947); K. Wörner, *F. M.-B.: Leben und Werk* (Leipzig, 1947); M. Schneider, *M. im Bildnis* (Basel, 1953); P. Radcliffe, *M.* (London, 1954; 2nd ed., rev., 1967); R. Sterndale Bennett, "The Death of M.," *Music & Letters*, XXXVI (1955); E. Werner, "New Light on the Family of F. M.," *Hebrew Union College Annual*, XXVI (1955); H. Worbs, *F. M.-B.* (Leipzig, 1956; 2nd ed., 1957); idem, *F. M.-B.: Wesen und Wirken im Spiegel von Selbstzeugnissen und Berichten der Zeitgenossen* (Leipzig, 1958); H. Jacob, *F. M. und seine Zeit: Bildnis und Schicksal eines Meisters* (Frankfurt, 1959–60; Eng. tr., 1963); E. Werner, *M.: A New Image of the Composer and His Age* (N.Y., 1963; 2nd ed., rev. and augmented, Zürich, 1980); E. Rudolph, *Der junge F. M.: Ein Beitrag zur Musikgeschichte des Stadt Berlin* (diss., Humboldt Univ., Berlin, 1964); K.-H. Köhler, *F. M.-B.* (Leipzig, 1966; 2nd ed., rev., 1972); H. Schonberg, *The Great Conductors* (N.Y., 1967); S. Grossmann-Vendrey, *F. M.-B. und die Musik der Vergangenheit* (Regensburg, 1969); M. Hurd, *M.* (London, 1970); W. Reich, *F. M. im Spiegel eigener Aussagen und zeitgenössischer Dokumente* (Zürich, 1970); H. Kupferberg, *The M.s: Three Generations of Genius* (N.Y., 1972); G. Marek, *Gentle Genius: The Story of F. M.* (N.Y., 1972); P. Ranft, *F. M.B.: Eine Lebenschronik* (Leipzig, 1972); Y. Tiénot, *M.: Musicien complet* (Paris, 1972); W. Blunt, *On Wings of Song: A Biography of F. M.* (N.Y., 1974); H. Worbs, *M.-B.* (Hamburg, 1974); D. Jenkins and M. Visocchi, *M. in Scotland* (Lon-

don, 1978); M. Moshansky, *M.* (Tunbridge Wells, 1982); G. Schuhmacher, ed., *F. M.-B.* (Darmstadt, 1982); W. Konold, *F. M.B. und seine Zeit* (Laaber, 1984); R. Elvers, ed., *F. M.: A Life in Letters* (London, 1989).

CRITICAL, ANALYTICAL: F. Zander, *Über M.s Walpurgisnacht* (Königsberg, 1862); C. Seldon, *La Musique en Allemagne: M.* (Paris, 1867); F. Edwards, *The History of M.'s Oratorio "Elijah"* (London, 1896; 2nd ed., 1900); J. Hathaway, *An Analysis of M.'s Organ Works: A Study of Their Structural Features* (London, 1898); O. Mansfield, *Organ Parts of M.'s Oratorios and Other Choral Works Analytically Considered* (London, 1907); idem, "Some Characteristics and Peculiarities of M.'s Organ Sonatas," *Musical Quarterly* (July 1917); H. Waltershausen, *M.s Lieder ohne Worte* (Munich, 1920); J. Koffler, *Die orchestrale Koloristik in den symphonischen Werken von M.* (diss., Univ. of Vienna, 1923); H. Mandt, *Die Entwicklung des Romantischen in der Instrumentalmusik F. M.-B.s* (diss., Univ. of Cologne, 1927); G. Schünemann, "Die Bachpflege der Berliner Singakademie," *Bach-Jahrbuch 1928*; R. Werner, *F. M.-B. als Kirchenmusiker* (Frankfurt, 1930); C. Wilkinson, *How to Interpret M.'s "Songs without Words"* (London, 1930); T. Armstrong, *M.'s "Elijah"* (London, 1931); G. Kinsky, "Was M. Indebted to Weber?," *Musical Quarterly* (April 1933); G. Wilcke, *Tonalität und Modulation im Streichquartett M.s und Schumanns* (Leipzig, 1933); L. Hochdorf, *M.s "Lieder ohne Worte" und der "Lieder ohne Worte"-Stil in seinen übrigen Instrumentalwerken* (diss., Univ. of Vienna, 1938); J. Horton, *The Chamber Music of M.* (London, 1946); L. and H. Tischler, "M.'s Songs without Words," *Musical Quarterly* (Jan. 1948); P. Young, *Introduction to the Music of M.* (London, 1949); D. Mintz, "Melusine: A M. Draft," *Musical Quarterly* (Oct. 1957); idem, *The Sketches and Drafts of Three of M.'s Major Works (Elijah,* Sym. No. 4, and D-minor Trio; diss., Cornell Univ., 1960); S. Vendrey, *Die Orgelwerke von F. M.-B.* (diss., Univ. of Vienna, 1964); J. Werner, *M.'s "Elijah": A Historical and Analytical Guide to the Oratorio* (London, 1965); G. Friedrich, *Die Fugenkomposition in M.s Instrumentalwerk* (Bonn, 1969); F. Krummacher, *M. der Komponist; Studien zur Kompositionsweise am Beispiel der Kammermusik für Streicher* (Habilitationsschrift, Univ. of Erlangen, 1972); M. Thomas, *Das Instrumentalwerk F. M.-B.s: Eine systematisch-theoretische Untersuchung unter besonderer Berücksichtigung der zeitgenössischen Musiktheorie* (Kassel, 1972); C. Dahlhaus, ed., *Das Problem M.* (Regensburg, 1974); B. Pritchard, "M.'s Chorale Cantatas: An Appraisal," *Musical Quarterly* (Jan. 1976); D. Seaton, *A Study of a Collection of M.'s Sketches and Other Autograph Material, Deutsche Staatsbibliothek Berlin "Mus. Ms. Autogr. M. 19"* (diss., Columbia Univ., 1977); F. Krummacher, *M.—der Komponist: Studien zur Kammermusik für Streicher* (Munich, 1978); A. Kurzhals-Reuter, *Die Oratorien F. M.B.s: Untersuchungen zur Quellenlage, Entstehung, Gestaltung und Überlieferung* (Tutzing, 1978); R. Todd, *The Instrumental Music of F. M.B.: Selected Studies Based on Primary Studies* (diss., Yale Univ., 1979); T. Ehrle, *Die Instrumentation in den Symphonien und Ouvertüren von F. M.B.* (Wiesbaden, 1983); R. Todd, *M.'s Musical Education: A Study and Edition of His Exercises in Composition* (Cambridge, 1982); J. Finson and R. Todd, eds., *M. and Schumann: Essays on Their Music and Its Context* (Durham, 1984); G. Vitercik, *The Early Works of F. M.: A Study in Romantic Sonata Style* (diss., State Univ. of N.Y., Stony Brook, 1985); C. Jost, *M.s Lieder ohne Worte* (Tutzing, 1988); M. Pape, *M.s Leipziger Orgelkonzert 1840: Ein Beitrag zur Bach-Pflege im 19. Jahrhundert* (Wiesbaden, 1988).

CORRESPONDENCE: P. Mendelssohn-Bartholdy, *Reisebriefe . . . aus den Jahren 1830–32* (Leipzig, 1861; 5th ed., 1882; Eng. tr. by Lady Wallace as *Letters from Italy and Switzerland*, London, 1862); idem, *Briefe aus den Jahren 1833–47* (Leipzig, 1863; 8th ed., 1915; Eng. tr. by Lady Wallace, London, 1863); L. Nohl, *Musiker-briefe* (Leipzig, 1867); E. Polko, *Erinnerungen an F. M.-B.* (Leipzig, 1868; Eng. tr. by Lady Wallace, London, 1869); E. Devrient, *Meine Erinnerungen an F. M.-B. und seine Briefe an mich* (Leipzig, 1869; Eng. tr. by Lady Macfarren, London, 1869); *Acht Briefe und ein Faksimile* (Leipzig, 1871;

Eng. tr. in *Macmillan's Magazine*, June 1871); F. Hiller, *F. M., Briefe und Erinnerungen* (Cologne, 1874; Eng. tr. by M.E. von Glehn, London, 1874); S. Hensel, *The M. Family, 1729–1847, from Letters and Journals* (2 vols., 1882; reprint, N.Y., 1969); F. Moscheles, *Brief von F. M. an Ignaz und Charlotte Moscheles* (Leipzig, 1888; Eng. tr. as *Letters of F. M.*, London, 1888); M. Friedlaender, "Briefe an Goethe," *Goethe-Jahrbuch* (1891); E. Wolff, *F. M.-B., Meisterbriefe* (Berlin, 1907; 2nd augmented ed., 1909); K. Klingemann, *F. M.-B.s Briefwechsel mit Legationsrat Karl Klingemann* (Essen, 1909); G. Selden-Goth, *M.'s Letters* (selections from the letters, tr. by Lady Wallace, with additional correspondence; N.Y., 1945); R. Sietz, ed., *F. M.-B.: Sein Leben in Briefen* (Cologne, 1948). A new collection of letters is being publ. by the Veröffentlichungen der Historischen Kommission zu Berlin: vol. 1, *Briefe an deutsche Verleger*, ed. by R. Elvers (Berlin, 1968); H.-J. Rothe and R. Szeskus, eds., *Briefe aus Leipziger Archiven* (Leipzig, 1972); R. Elvers, ed., *M.B.: Briefe* (Frankfurt am Main, 1984); M. Citron, ed., *The Letters of Fanny Hensel to F. M.* (Stuyvesant, N.Y., 1987).

Meneely-Kyder, Sarah, American composer, pianist, and sitar player; b. Albany, N.Y., Feb. 18, 1945. She studied music theory and piano at Goucher College (B.A., 1967); also had composition studies with Robert Hall Lewis (from 1966), Earle Brown at the Peabody Cons. in Baltimore (M.M., 1969), and Robert Morris at the Yale School of Music (M.M.A., 1973); also studied the sitar and vina for 10 years. Her early works were serial or atonal in design; later she experimented with controlled improvisation, and spatial and proportional systems; still later she concentrated upon fusing disparate musical styles, making use of North Indian notational systems and instrumentations. She hails from a family of bell manufacturers who established the Meneely Foundry in Troy, N.Y.

WORKS: Concerto for Piano and Orch. (1967); *Homegrown* for Piano (1973); *Lament* for Sitar and Renaissance Instruments (1978); *Filarmonico* for Chorus, Piano, Vibraphone, and Gamelan Chimes (1980; rev. 1986, 1988); *Now I Sing Only 1 Song* for 2 Pianos (1980); *Weep, the Mighty Typhoons* for Mezzo-soprano and Piano (1982); *Narcissus* for Clarinet (1983); *Season Phases* for Piano (1987–88); *The 3 Gunas* for Piano, 4-hands, Violin, Cello, Flute, Clarinet, and Bassoon (1989).

Meneses, António, talented Brazilian cellist; b. Recife, Aug. 23, 1957. His father was 1st hornist in the opera orch. in Rio de Janeiro. António began his musical training when he was 8, then became a pupil of Janigro in Düsseldorf and Stuttgart at 16. He won 2nd prize in the Barcelona International Maria Casals Competition (1976) and in the Rio de Janeiro International Competition (1976); after winning 1st prize in the International ARD Competition in Munich (1977), he captured the prestigious gold medal at the Tchaikovsky Competition in Moscow (1982). He subsequently appeared as soloist with many major European orchs. He made his 1st tour of North America in 1985. His wife is **Cecile Licad.**

Mengal, Jean-Baptiste, Belgian horn player, brother of **Martin-Joseph Mengal;** b. Ghent, Feb. 21, 1792; d. Paris, Dec. 19, 1878. He learned the rudiments of music from his father, who was an experienced horn player, and from his brother, whom he succeeded as 1st horn player at the Ghent municipal theater. In 1812 he entered the Paris Cons., graduating with 1st prize; then played in the orch. of the Grand Opéra. He wrote a number of works for his instrument: fantasies, duets, solos; also publ. a method of horn playing.

Mengal, Martin-Joseph, Belgian horn player and conductor, brother of **Jean-Baptiste Mengal;** b. Ghent, Jan. 27, 1784; d. there, July 4, 1851. He studied with his father; played in Paris orchs.; in 1825 he was appointed director of the Ghent municipal theater; then was conductor in Antwerp; in 1835 he became director of the Ghent Cons. He wrote a number of sacred works; his MSS are preserved at the Ghent Cons.

Mengelberg, Karel (Willem Joseph), Dutch composer and conductor, father of **Misha** and nephew of **(Josef) Willem**

Mengelberg; b. Utrecht, July 18, 1902; d. Amsterdam, July 11, 1984. He studied with Pijper and later took a course at the Hochschule für Musik in Berlin. He conducted theater orchs. in provincial German towns and was a musician with Berlin Radio (1930–33); subsequently was conductor of the municipal band in Barcelona (1933); then went to Kiev, where he was in charge of the music dept. in the Ukrainian film studio. He returned to Amsterdam in 1938.

Works: 2 ballets: *Bataille* (1922) and *Parfait amour* (1945); *3 songs from Tagore's "The Gardener"* for Soprano and Orch. (1925); String Quartet (1938); Sonata for Solo Oboe (1939); Trio for Flute, Oboe, and Bassoon (1940); a short *Requiem* for Orch. (1946); *Divertimento* for Small Orch. (1948); Horn Concerto (1950); *Toccata* for Piano (1950); *Jan Hinnerik* for a cappella Chorus (1950); *Anion*, symphonic sketch (1950); *Soliloquio* for Flute (1951); *Ballade* for Flute, Clarinet, Harp, and String Quartet (1952); *Serenade* for String Orch. (1952); *Recitatief* for Baritone, Viola da Gamba, and Harpsichord (1953); *Suite* for Small Orch. (1954); *Roland Holst*, cantata for Chorus and Small Orch. (1955); *Soneria, Romanza e Mazurca* for Harp (1958); *De bergen* for Orch. (1982). In 1961 he completed the revision, with a simplified orchestration, of Willem Pijper's 2nd Sym. (Pijper's own rev. score was destroyed during a Nazi air raid on Rotterdam in May 1940).

Mengelberg, Kurt Rudolf, German-born musicologist and composer of Dutch descent, nephew of **(Josef) Willem Mengelberg;** b. Krefeld, Feb. 1, 1892; d. Beausoleil, near Monte Carlo, Oct. 13, 1959. He studied piano with Neitzel in Cologne and musicology with Hugo Riemann at the Univ. of Leipzig, receiving his doctorate in 1915. He then went to Amsterdam, where he studied music theory with his uncle; in 1917, through his uncle's intervention, he became artistic assistant of the Concertgebouw Orch. in Amsterdam; then was artistic manager there (1925–35), and finally director (1935–54). Among his publications were the valuable program book *Das Mahler-Fest, Amsterdam Mai 1920* (Vienna, 1920); a biography of Mahler (Leipzig, 1923); *Nederland, spiegeleener beschaving* (The Netherlands, Mirror of a Culture; Amsterdam, 1929); a commemorative publication on the semicentennial of the Concertgebouw (Amsterdam, 1938); *Muziek, spiegel des tijds* (Music, Mirror of Time; Amsterdam, 1948); and a biography of Willem Mengelberg. His compositions are mainly liturgical; among them are *Missa pro pace* (1932), *Stabat Mater* (1940), and *Victimae Paschali laudes* (1946); he also wrote *Symphonic Variations* for Cello and Orch. (1927); Violin Concerto (1930); *Capriccio* for Piano and Orch. (1936); Concertino for Flute and Chamber Orch. (1943); solo songs and piano pieces.

Mengelberg, Misha, Dutch composer, son of **Karel (Willem Joseph) Mengelberg;** b. Kiev, June 5, 1935. He was born in Kiev while his father was working in the U.S.S.R.; went in 1938 to the Netherlands, where he studied with Kees van Baaren at the Royal Cons. in The Hague, graduating in 1964.

Works: He participated in creating an anti-imperialistic collective opera, *Reconstructie* (1968–69; Holland Festival, June 29, 1969; in collaboration with Louis Andriessen, Reinbert de Leeuw, Peter Schat, and Jan van Vlijmen); *Musica* for 17 Instruments (1959); *Medusa* for String Quartet (1962); *Commentary* for Orch. (1965); *Exercise* for Flute (1966); *Omtrent een componistenactie* (Concerning a Composer's Action) for Wind Quintet (1966); *3 Piano Pieces + Piano Piece 4* (1966); *Amaga* for 3 Different Guitars and Electronic Equipment (1968); *Anatoloose* for Orch. and Tape (1968; Holland Festival, July 8, 1971); *Hello Windy Boys* for Double Wind Quintet (1968); *Met welbeleefde groet van de kameel* (With the Very Polite Greetings of the Camel) for Orch. with Electronic Sawing and Excavating Drills (1971–73); *Onderweg* (On the Way) for Orch. (1973; Bergen, Norway, Jan. 13, 1974); *Dressoir* for Wind Instruments and Piano (1977).

Mengelberg, (Josef) Willem, celebrated Dutch conductor, uncle of **Karel (Willem Joseph)** and **Kurt Rudolf Mengelberg;** b. Utrecht, March 28, 1871; d. Chur, Switzerland, March 21, 1951. He studied at the Utrecht Cons., and later at the

Cologne Cons. with Seiss, Jensen, and Wüllner. He was appointed municipal music director in Lucerne in 1891, and his work there attracted so much attention that in 1895 he was placed at the head of the Concertgebouw Orch. in Amsterdam, holding this post for 50 years (resigning in 1945), a record tenure for any conductor; during his directorship, he elevated that orch. to a lofty position in the world of music; was also director of the Museumgesellschaft concerts in Frankfurt from 1908 to 1921. In addition, he became conductor of the Toonkunst choral society in Amsterdam (1898); appeared frequently as guest conductor in all the European countries; in England he was an annual visitor from 1913 until World War II. He 1st appeared with the N.Y. Phil. in 1905; then conducted it regularly from 1922 to 1930, with Toscanini serving as associate conductor in 1929–30. In 1928 he received the degree of Mus.Doc. at Columbia Univ. (*honoris causa*); in 1933 he was appointed prof. of music at Utrecht Univ. During the occupation of the Netherlands by the Germans, Mengelberg openly expressed his sympathies with the Nazi cause, and lost the high respect and admiration that his compatriots had felt for him; after the country's liberation (1945), he was barred from professional activities there, the ban to be continued until 1951, but he died in that year in exile in Switzerland. Mengelberg was an outstanding representative of the Romantic tradition in symphonic conducting. His performances of the Beethoven syms. were notable for their dramatic sweep and power, if not for their adherence to stylistic proprieties. He was a great champion of many of the major composers of his era, including Mahler and Strauss; both men appeared as guest conductors of the Concertgebouw Orch., and became Mengelberg's friends. Mahler dedicated his 5th and 8th syms. to Mengelberg and the Concertgebouw Orch., and Strauss dedicated his *Ein Heldenleben* to the same forces. Mengelberg was the 1st to lead a major cycle of Mahler's works, in Amsterdam in 1920.

Bibl.: H. Nolthenius, *W. M.* (Amsterdam, 1920); A. Van den Boer, *De psychologische beteekenis van W. M. als dirigent* (Amsterdam, 1925); E. Sollitt, *M. and the Symphonic Epoch* (N.Y., 1930); idem, *M. spreckt* (speeches by M.; The Hague, 1935); W. Paap, *W. M.* (Amsterdam, 1960); A. Kozinn, "W. M.: His Art and Tragedy," *Keynote* (Dec. 1986).

Menges, (Siegfried Frederick) Herbert, English conductor, brother of **Isolde (Marie) Menges;** b. Hove (of German parents), Aug. 27, 1902; d. London, Feb. 20, 1972. He played violin as a child; then took piano lessons with Mathilda Verne and Arthur de Greef; later attended courses in composition with Vaughan Williams and Holst at the Royal College of Music in London. He began his conducting career in Brighton, and conducted the Brighton Phil. Soc. (which was founded by his mother) from 1925 until his death. He was also a music director of the Old Vic Theatre (1931–50) in London; in 1945 he became conductor of the Southern Phil. Orch. at Southsea. In 1963 he was made an Officer of the Order of the British Empire.

Menges, Isolde (Marie), English violinist, sister of **(Siegfried Frederick) Herbert Menges;** b. Hove (of German parents), May 16, 1893; d. Richmond, Surrey, Jan. 13, 1976. Both her parents were violinists, and she studied at home; then went to St. Petersburg for lessons with Leopold Auer. She made her London debut on Feb. 4, 1913, and her N.Y. debut on Oct. 21, 1916. In 1931 she was appointed to the faculty of the Royal College of Music in London; also organized the Menges Quartet.

Mengewein, Karl, German composer and teacher; b. Zaunroda, Thuringia, Sept. 9, 1852; d. Berlin, April 7, 1908. From 1876 until 1886 he was a teacher at Freudenberg's Cons., Wiesbaden, and with the latter founded a Cons. in Berlin in 1886, of which he was co-director until 1896. He founded the Oratorienverein (1895) and the next year the "Madrigal" for the production of a cappella music. He wrote an oratorio, *Johannes der Täufer* (1892); festival cantata, *Martin Luther;* operetta, *Schulmeisters Brautfahrt* (Wiesbaden, 1884); overture, *Dornröschen;* several singspiels; a Requiem; female choruses; etc. He also publ. *Die Ausbildung des musikalischen Gehörs* (1908).

Ménil, Félicien de, French musicologist; b. Boulogne-sur-Mer, July 16, 1860; d. Neuilly, near Paris, March 28, 1930. He studied with Henri Maréchal and Lenepveu at the Paris Cons.; undertook extensive travels in America, India, and Africa; returning to Paris, he was appointed prof. of history of music at the École Niedermeyer (1899). His publications include: *Monsigny* (1893); *Josquin des Près* (1897); *L'École flamande du XVᵉ siècle* (Paris, 1895; considerably augmented and publ. as *L'École contrapuntique flamande au XVᵉ et au XVIᵉ siècle*, 1905); *Histoire de la danse à travers les âges* (1904). He was an ardent adherent of Esperanto, and wrote the hymn of the Esperantists (1928).

Mennin (real name, **Mennini**), **Peter,** eminent American composer and music educator, brother of **Louis (Alfred) Mennini**; b. Erie, Pa., May 17, 1923; d. N.Y., June 17, 1983. His family stemmed from Italy; his brother did not cut off the last letter of his name as Peter did. His early environment was infused with music, mostly from phonograph recordings; he studied piano with Tito Spampani. In 1940 he enrolled in the Oberlin Cons. in Ohio, where he took courses in harmony with Normand Lockwood. He quickly learned the basics of composition, and at the age of 18 wrote a sym. and a string quartet. In 1942 he enlisted in the U.S. Army Air Force; was discharged in 1943, and resumed his musical studies at the Eastman School of Music in Rochester, N.Y., where his teachers were Howard Hanson and Bernard Rogers. He worked productively; wrote another sym. in 1944; a movement from it, entitled *Symphonic Allegro*, was performed by the N.Y. Phil., Leonard Bernstein conducting, on March 27, 1945. His 3rd Sym. was performed by Walter Hendl with the N.Y. Phil. on Feb. 27, 1947. Mennin progressed academically as well; he obtained his Ph.D. from the Eastman School of Music in 1947. He received a Guggenheim fellowship grant in 1948; a 2nd Guggenheim grant followed in 1956. From 1947 to 1958 he taught composition at the Juilliard School of Music in N.Y.; in 1958 he assumed the post of director of the Peabody Cons. in Baltimore. In 1962 he received his most prestigious appointment, that of president of the Juilliard School of Music, serving in that capacity until his death. Despite his academic preoccupations, he never slackened the tempo of his activities as a composer; he diversified his syms. by adding descriptive titles; thus his 4th Sym. was subtitled *The Cycle* and was scored for chorus and orch.; his 7th Sym. was called *Variation Symphony*; the 4 movements of his 8th Sym. bore biblical titles. Increasingly also, he began attaching descriptive titles to his other works; his Concertato for Orch. was named *Moby Dick*; there followed a *Canto for Orchestra*, a *Cantata de Virtute*, *Voices*, and *Reflections of Emily*, to texts by Emily Dickinson. Mennin's musical mind was directed toward pure structural forms; his music is characterized by an integrity of purpose and teleological development of thematic materials, all this despite the bold infusion of dissonant sonorities in contrapuntal passages. He held honorary doctorates from the Univ. of Chicago, the Univ. of Wisconsin, Temple Univ., and the Univ. of Heidelberg in Germany.

WORKS: ORCH.: 9 syms.: No. 1 (1942); No. 2 (Rochester, N.Y., March 27, 1945); No. 3 (N.Y., Feb. 27, 1947); No. 4, *The Cycle*, for Chorus and Orch. (N.Y., March 18, 1949); No. 5 (Dallas, April 2, 1950); No. 6 (Louisville, Nov. 18, 1953); No. 7, *Variation Symphony* (Cleveland, Jan. 23, 1964); No. 8, in 4 movements, titled *In Principio, Dies Irae, De Profundis, Laudate Dominum* (N.Y., Nov. 21, 1974); No. 9, *Sinfonia capricciosa* (Washington, D.C., March 10, 1981); *Sinfonia* for Chamber Orch. (Rochester, N.Y., May 24, 1947); *Fantasia* for String Orch. (N.Y., Jan. 11, 1948); *Folk Overture* (Washington, D.C., Dec. 19, 1945); Violin Concerto (1950); Concertato, *Moby Dick* (Erie, Pa., Oct. 20, 1952); Cello Concerto (N.Y., Feb. 19, 1956); Piano Concerto (Cleveland, Feb. 27, 1958); Concertino for Flute, Strings, and Percussion (1945); *Canto for Orchestra* (San Antonio, March 4, 1963); *Cantata de Virtute*

for Tenor, Baritone, Narrator, Chorus, Children's Chorus, and Orch., originally planned as a setting of Robert Browning's poem *The Pied Piper of Hamelin* (Cincinnati, May 2, 1969); *Symphonic Movements* (Minneapolis, Jan. 21, 1971; later perf. under the title *Sinfonia*); *Voices* for Mezzo-soprano, Percussion, Piano, Harp, and Harpsichord, to texts from Thoreau, Melville, Whitman, and Emily Dickinson (N.Y., March 28, 1976); *Reflections of Emily* for Treble Voices, Piano, Harp, and Percussion, to texts from poems by Emily Dickinson (N.Y., Jan. 18, 1979); Flute Concerto (N.Y., May 25, 1988). **CHAMBER:** 2 string quartets (1941, 1951); *Sonata concertante* for Violin and Piano (Washington, D.C., Oct. 19, 1956); Piano Sonata (1963).

Mennini, Louis (Alfred), American composer and music educator, brother of **Peter Mennin**; b. Erie, Pa., Nov. 18, 1920. He studied at the Oberlin Cons. (1939–42); then served in the U.S. Army Air Force (1942–45); subsequently studied composition with Bernard Rogers and Howard Hanson at the Eastman School of Music, Rochester, N.Y. (B.M., 1947; M.M., 1948); was a prof. at the Univ. of Texas (1948–49); then was a prof. of composition at the Eastman School of Music, receiving his doctorate in composition from the Univ. of Rochester in 1961. After serving as dean of the School of Music at the North Carolina School of the Arts in Winston-Salem (1965–71), he became chairman of the music dept. at Mercyhurst College in Erie, Pa., in 1973, where he founded the D'Angelo School of Music and D'Angelo Young Artist Competition. In 1983 he founded the Virginia School of the Arts in Lynchburg, serving as its head until his retirement in 1988. His music is pragmatic and functional, with occasional modernistic touches.

WORKS: CHAMBER OPERAS: *The Well* (Rochester, N.Y., May 8, 1951); *The Rope*, after Eugene O'Neill (Berkshire Music Festival, Aug. 8, 1955). **ORCH.:** *Overtura breve* (1949); 2 syms.: No. 1, *Da chiesa* (1960); No. 2, *Da festa* (1963); *Tenebrae* (1963); Concerto Grosso (1975); also a String Quartet (1961); numerous pieces for violin; piano works.

Menotti, Gian Carlo, remarkable Italian composer; b. Cadegliano, July 7, 1911. He was the 6th of 10 children. He learned the rudiments of music from his mother, and began to compose as a child, making his 1st attempt at an opera, entitled *The Death of Pierrot*, at the age of 10. He studied at the Milan Cons. (1924–27); then went to the U.S., and entered the Curtis Inst. of Music in Philadelphia (1927–33), where he studied with Rosario Scalero; subsequently taught composition there; traveled often to Europe; made his home in Mt. Kisco, N.Y. Although Menotti associated himself with the cause of American music, and spent much of his time in the U.S., he retained his Italian citizenship. As a composer, he is unique on the American scene, being the 1st to create American opera possessing such an appeal to audiences as to become established in the permanent repertoire. Inheriting the natural Italian gift for operatic drama and an expressive singing line, he adapted these qualities to the peculiar requirements of the American stage and to the changing fashions of the period; his serious operas have a strong dramatic content in the realistic style stemming from the Italian *verismo*. He wrote his own librettos, marked by an extraordinary flair for drama and for the communicative power of the English language; with this is combined a fine, though subdued, sense of musical humor. Menotti made no pretensions at extreme modernism, and did not fear to approximate the successful formulas developed by Verdi and Puccini; the influence of Mussorgsky's realistic prosody is also in evidence, particularly in recitative. When dramatic tension required a greater impact, Menotti resorted to atonal and polytonal writing, leading to climaxes accompanied by massive dissonances. His 1st successful stage work was *Amelia Goes to the Ball*, an opera buffa in 1 act (originally to an Italian libretto by the composer, as *Amelia al ballo*), staged at the Academy of Music, Philadelphia, on April 1, 1937. This was followed by another comic opera, *The Old Maid and the Thief*, commissioned by NBC, 1st performed on the radio, April 22, 1939, and on the stage, by the Philadelphia Opera Co., on

Feb. 11, 1941. Menotti's next operatic work was *The Island God*, produced by the Metropolitan Opera, N.Y., on Feb. 20, 1942, with indifferent success; but with the production of *The Medium* (N.Y., May 8, 1946), Menotti established himself as the foremost composer-librettist of modern opera. The imaginative libretto, dealing with a fraudulent spiritualist who falls victim to her own practices when she imagines that ghostly voices are real, suited Menotti's musical talent to perfection; the opera had a long and successful run in N.Y., an unprecedented occurrence in the history of the American lyric theater. A short humorous opera, *The Telephone*, was 1st produced by the N.Y. Ballet Soc., Feb. 18, 1947, on the same bill with *The Medium;* these 2 contrasting works were subsequently staged all over the U.S. and in Europe, often on the same evening. Menotti then produced *The Consul* (Philadelphia, March 1, 1950), his best tragic work, describing the plight of political fugitives vainly trying to escape from an unnamed country but failing to obtain the necessary visa from the consul of an anonymous power; very ingeniously, the author does not include the title character in the cast, since the consul never appears on the stage but remains a shadowy presence. *The Consul* exceeded Menotti's previous operas in popular success; it had a long run in N.Y., and received the Pulitzer Prize. On Christmas Eve, 1951, NBC presented Menotti's television opera *Amahl and the Night Visitors*, a Christmas story of undeniable poetry and appeal; it became an annual television production every Christmas in subsequent years. His next opera was *The Saint of Bleecker Street*, set in a N.Y. locale (N.Y., Dec. 27, 1954); it won the Drama Critics' Circle Award for the best musical play of 1954, and the Pulitzer Prize for 1955. A madrigal ballet, *The Unicorn, the Gorgon and the Manticore*, commissioned by the Elizabeth Sprague Coolidge Foundation, was 1st presented at the Library of Congress, Washington, D.C., Oct. 21, 1956. His opera *Maria Golovin*, written expressly for the International Exposition in Brussels, was staged there on Aug. 20, 1958. In 1958 he organized the Festival of 2 Worlds in Spoleto, Italy, staging old and new works; in 1977 he inaugurated an American counterpart of the festival in Charleston, S.C. In many of the festival productions Menotti acted also as stage director. In the meantime he continued to compose; he produced in quick succession *Labyrinth*, a television opera to his own libretto (N.Y., March 3, 1963); *Death of the Bishop of Brindisi*, dramatic cantata with the text by the composer (Cincinnati, May 18, 1963); *Le Dernier Sauvage*, opera buffa, originally with an Italian libretto by Menotti, produced at the Opéra-Comique in Paris in a French tr. (Oct. 21, 1963; produced in Eng. at the Metropolitan Opera, N.Y., Jan. 23, 1964); *Martin's Lie*, chamber opera to Menotti's text (Bath, England, June 3, 1964); *Help, Help, the Globolinks!*, "an opera in 1 act for children and those who like children" to words by Menotti, with electronic effects (Hamburg, Dec. 19, 1968); *The Most Important Man*, opera to his own libretto (N.Y., March 12, 1971); *The Hero*, comic opera (Philadelphia, June 1, 1976); *The Egg*, a church opera to Menotti's own libretto (Washington Cathedral, June 17, 1976); *The Trial of the Gypsy* for Treble Voices and Piano (N.Y., May 24, 1978); *Miracles* for Boys' Choir (Fort Worth, April 22, 1979); *La loca*, opera to Menotti's own libretto dealing with a mad daughter of Ferdinand and Isabella (San Diego, June 3, 1979); *A Bride from Pluto*, opera (Washington, D.C., April 14, 1982). Among Menotti's non-operatic works are the ballets *Sebastian* (1944) and *Errand into the Maze* (N.Y., Feb. 2, 1947); Piano Concerto No. 1 (Boston, Nov. 2, 1945); *Apocalypse*, symphonic poem (Pittsburgh, Oct. 19, 1951); Violin Concerto (Philadelphia, Dec. 5, 1952, Zimbalist soloist); *Triplo Concerto a Tre*, triple concerto in 3 movements (N.Y., Oct. 6, 1970); *Landscapes and Remembrances*, cantata to his own autobiographical words (Milwaukee, May 14, 1976); *First Symphony*, subtitled *The Halcyon* (Philadelphia, Aug. 4, 1976); Piano Concerto No. 2 (Miami, June 23, 1982); *Nocturne* for Soprano, String Quartet, and Harp (N.Y., Oct. 24, 1982); Double-bass Concerto (N.Y. Phil., Oct. 20, 1983, James VanDemark, soloist; Zubin Mehta conducting); *For the Death of Orpheus* for Tenor, Chorus, and

Orch. (Atlanta, Nov. 8, 1990). He also wrote a number of *pièces d'occasion* such as *Trio for a House-Warming Party* for Piano, Cello, and Flute (1936); *Variations on a Theme by Schumann*; *Pastorale* for Piano and String Orch.; *Poemetti per Maria Rosa* (piano pieces for children); etc. Menotti is the author of the librettos for Samuel Barber's operas *Vanessa* (Metropolitan Opera, N.Y., Jan. 15, 1958) and *A Hand of Bridge* (1959), and wrote a play without music, *The Leper* (Tallahassee, April 22, 1970).

After many years in America, he bought an estate, Yester House, in Scotland, and made it his permanent abode in 1974 with his legally adopted son, Francis Phelan, who thenceforth bore his name.

BIBL.: J. Gruen, *M.: A Biography* (N.Y., 1978); J. Ardoin, *The Stages of M.* (Garden City, N.Y., 1985).

Menter, Joseph, German cellist, father of **Sophie Menter;** b. Teisbach, Bavaria, Jan. 23, 1808; d. Munich, April 18, 1856. He began his career as a violinist; then studied cello with Moralt in Munich, and became a member of the orch. of the Bavarian Royal Opera (1833).

Menter, Sophie, esteemed German pianist and teacher, daughter of **Joseph Menter;** b. Munich, July 29, 1846; d. there, Feb. 23, 1918. She studied piano with Niest in Munich and with Lebert in Stuttgart; made her professional debut in 1867 at the Gewandhaus Concerts in Leipzig, and later took lessons with Tausig and Liszt. In 1872 she married the cellist **David Popper** (divorced, 1886). From 1883 to 1887 she taught piano at the St. Petersburg Cons.; then lived mostly in the Tirol. She composed a number of attractive pieces. Tchaikovsky orchestrated her work *Ungarische Zigeunerweisen* for Piano and Orch., and she played it under his direction in Odessa, on Feb. 4, 1893.

Menuhin, Hephzibah, American pianist, sister of **Yehudi Menuhin;** b. San Francisco, May 20, 1920; d. London, Jan. 1, 1981. Like her brother, she appeared in public at a very early age in San Francisco (1928); studied there and later with Ciampi in Paris; toured widely as a recitalist with her brother in the U.S. and Europe.

Menuhin, Sir Yehudi, celebrated American violinist, brother of **Hephzibah Menuhin;** b. N.Y., April 22, 1916. He was born of Russian-Jewish parents (the family surname was originally Mnuhin). As a child, he was taken to San Francisco, where he began to study violin with Sigmund Anker; in 1923 he began taking lessons with Louis Persinger, who was then concertmaster of the San Francisco Sym. Orch. On Feb. 29, 1924, he made his public debut in Oakland playing Bériot's *Scène de ballet* with Persinger as accompanist; Menuhin was only 7 at the time. On Jan. 17, 1926, when he was 9 years old, he played a recital in N.Y. He made his European debut in Paris on Feb. 6, 1927, with Paul Paray and the Lamoureux Orch. In Paris he began to study with Georges Enesco, who became his most influential teacher, and who guided his future career. Returning to America, Menuhin played the Beethoven Concerto with Fritz Busch and the N.Y. Sym. Orch. on Nov. 25, 1927, winning unanimous acclaim from the public and the press. He subsequently made tours throughout America and Europe; on April 12, 1929, he appeared with Bruno Walter and the Berlin Phil., playing concertos by Bach, Beethoven, and Brahms on the same program; on Nov. 10, 1929, he made his London debut. He continued to pursue his studies with Enesco, and also received additional instruction from Adolf Busch. On the sesquicentennial of the 1st concert given at the Gewandhaus in Leipzig, he appeared as soloist with the Gewandhaus Orch. in the Mendelssohn Concerto (Nov. 12, 1931). In 1935 he completed his 1st world tour, giving concerts in 73 cities in 13 countries, including Australia. He also became active in organizing music festivals; in 1956 he established the Gstaad Festival in Switzerland. In 1959 he made his home in London, and founded the Bath Festival, which he directed until 1968; he also founded the Windsor Festival and directed it from 1969 to 1972. He toured as soloist with his own chamber orch.; later he devoted much time to conducting and musical education. He toured Japan in 1951 and Russia in 1956. In 1963 he founded his own boarding school for musically gifted children at Stoke d'Abernon, Surrey. In 1965 he received an honorary knighthood from Queen Elizabeth II. In 1970 he received honorary citizenship from the community of Saanen, Switzerland, and assumed Swiss national allegiance while preserving his American citizenship. In 1971 he succeeded Barbirolli as president of Trinity College of Music in London. In 1976 he was awarded an honorary doctorate by the Sorbonne of Paris, the 1st musician to be so honored during its entire history. On Sept. 10, 1981, he celebrated the 50th anniversary of his 1st appearance in Leipzig by performing the Brahms Concerto with Kurt Masur and the Gewandhaus Orch. In 1985 he was granted honorary British citizenship, and thereby formally became Sir Yehudi. In 1986 President Mitterand made him a Grand Officer of the Légion d'honneur of France. In 1987 he was made a member of the Order of Merit.

Apart from his musical activities, he became deeply interested in art, politics, and above all, psychology and philosophy. He embraced the cause of oriental religions, practiced yoga exercises, and even lectured on these abstruse subjects. In 1963 he appeared on the BBC in London in a discussion entitled "Yehudi Menuhin and His Guru." He also adopted a health diet, eschewing carbohydrates and some other foods. In his political utterances he antagonized many factions in many lands. He was enthusiastically received in Israel during his tours in 1950, 1951, 1952, and 1953, but aroused Israeli animosity when he gave benefit concerts for Palestinian refugees. He embarrassed the Russians at a music congress in Moscow in 1971 when in his speech, which he read in understandable Russian, he appealed to them on behalf of human rights; he was never invited to Russia again. In the meantime, his artistry suffered somewhat; critics began to notice a certain unsteadiness in his intonation and technique; as a conductor he performed not more than satisfactorily. Still, he never slackened his energetic activities, musical or non-musical. He publ. a collection of essays under the title *Theme and Variations* (London, 1972); an autobiography, *Unfinished Journey* (N.Y., 1977); with Curtis W. Davis, *The Music of Man* (London, 1980), based on the television series of the same title, and *Life Class* (London, 1986).

BIBL.: B. Gavoty, *Y. M. et Georges Enesco* (Geneva, 1955); R. Magidoff, *Y. M.: The Story of the Man and the Musician* (Garden City, N.Y., 1955; 2nd ed., 1973); N. Wymer, *Y. M.* (London, 1961); E. Fenby, *M.'s House of Music* (London, 1969); R. Daniels, *Conversations with M.* (London, 1979); M. Menuhin, *The M. Saga* (London, 1984); D. Menuhin, *Fiddler's Moll* (London, 1985); B. Land, "The Indefatigable Y. M. at Seventy," *Ovation* (June 1986); K. Pohl and A. Zipf-Pohl, eds., *Hommage à Y. M.: Festschrift zum 70. Geburtstag am 22. April 1986* (Baden-Baden, 1986).

Mercadante, (Giuseppe) Saverio (Raffaele), important Italian opera composer and teacher; b. Altamura, near Bari (baptized), Sept. 17, 1795; d. Naples, Dec. 17, 1870. He was born out of wedlock; was taken to Naples when he was about 11. In 1808 he was enrolled in the Collegio di San Sebastiano; he had no means to pay for his tuition; besides, he was over the age limit for entrance, and was not a Neapolitan; to gain admission he had to change his 1st Christian name and adjust his place and date of birth. He studied solfeggio, violin, and flute; also took classes in figured bass and harmony with Furno and counterpoint with Tritto; subsequently studied composition with the Collegio's director, Zingarelli (1816–20). He began to compose while still a student, writing marches, concertos, sinfonias, trios, quartets, and other works. In 1818 he composed 3 ballets; the success of the 3rd, *Il flauto incantato*, encouraged him to try his hand at an opera. His 1st opera, *L'apoteosi d'Ercole*, had a successful premiere in Naples on Jan. 4, 1819. He wrote 5 more operas before *Elisa e Claudio*, produced at La Scala in Milan on Oct. 30, 1821, which established his reputation. Other important operas were *Caritea,*

regina di Spagna (Venice, Feb. 21, 1826); *Gabriella di Vergy* (Lisbon, Aug. 8, 1828); *I Normanni a Parigi* (Turin, Feb. 7, 1832); *I Briganti* (Paris, March 22, 1836); *Il giuramento* (Milan, March 10, 1837; considered his masterpiece); *Le due illustri rivali* (Venice, March 10, 1838); *Elena da Feltre* (Naples, Dec. 26, 1838); *Il Bravo* (Milan, March 9, 1839); *La Vestale* (Naples, March 10, 1840; one of his finest operas); *Il Reggente* (Turin, Feb. 2, 1843); *Leonora* (Naples, Dec. 5, 1844); *Orazi e Curiazi* (Naples, Nov. 10, 1846; a major success in Italy); and *Virginia* (Naples, April 7, 1866; his last opera to be perf., although composed as early as 1845; its premiere was delayed for political reasons). Mercadante wrote about 60 operas in all, for different opera houses, often residing in the city where they were produced; thus he lived in Rome, Bologna, and Milan; he also spent some time in Vienna (where he composed 3 operas in 1824) and in Spain and Portugal (1826–31). From 1833 to 1840 he was maestro di cappella at the Cathedral of Novara; about that time he suffered the loss of sight in one eye, and in 1862 he became totally blind. In 1839 Rossini offered him the directorate of the Liceo Musicale in Bologna, but he served in that post only a short time; in 1840 he was named director of the Naples Cons. in succession to his teacher Zingarelli. Mercadante's operas are no longer in the active repertoire, but they are historically important, and objectively can stand comparison with those of his great compatriots Rossini, Bellini, and Donizetti.

WORKS: OPERAS: *L'apoteosi d'Ercole,* dramma per musica (Teatro San Carlo, Naples, Jan. 4, 1819); *Violenza e costanza, ossia I falsi monetari,* dramma giocoso (Teatro Nuovo, Naples, Jan. 19, 1820; also known as *Il castello dei spiriti*); *Anacreonte in Samo,* dramma per musica (Teatro San Carlo, Naples, Aug. 1, 1820); *Il geloso ravveduto,* melodramma buffo (Teatro Valle, Rome, Oct. 1820); *Scipione in Cartagine,* melodramma serio (Teatro Argentina, Rome, Dec. 26, 1820); *Maria Stuarda regina di Scozia [Maria Stuart],* dramma serio (Teatro Comunale, Bologna, May 29, 1821); *Elisa e Claudio, ossia L'amore protetto dall'amicizia,* melodramma semiserio (Teatro alla Scala, Milan, Oct. 30, 1821); *Andronico,* melodramma tragico (Teatro La Fenice, Venice, Dec. 26, 1821); *Il posto abbandonato, ossia Adele ed Emerico,* melodramma semiserio (Teatro alla Scala, Milan, Sept. 21, 1822); *Amleto,* melodramma tragico (Teatro alla Scala, Milan, Dec. 26, 1822); *Alfonso ed Elisa,* melodramma serio (Teatro Nuovo, Mantua, Dec. 26, 1822); *Didone abbandonata,* dramma per musica (Teatro Regio, Turin, Jan. 18, 1823); *Gli sciti,* dramma per musica (Teatro San Carlo, Naples, March 18, 1823); *Costanzo ed Almeriska,* dramma per musica (Teatro San Carlo, Naples, Nov. 22, 1823); *Gli Amici di Siracusa,* melodramma eroico (Teatro Argentina, Rome, Feb. 7, 1824); *Doralice,* dramma semiserio (Kärnthnertortheater, Vienna, Sept. 18, 1824); *Le nozze di Telemaco ed Antiope,* azione lirica (Kärnthnertortheater, Vienna, Nov. 5, 1824; in collaboration with others); *Il Podestà di Burgos, ossia Il Signore del villaggio,* melodramma semiserio (Kärnthnertortheater, Vienna, Nov. 20, 1824; 2nd version as *Il Signore del villaggio,* in Neapolitan dialect, Teatro Fondo, Naples, May 28, 1825); *Nitocri,* melodramma serio (Teatro Regio, Turin, Dec. 26, 1824); *Ipermestra,* dramma tragico (Teatro San Carlo, Naples, c.1824); *Erode, ossia Marianna,* dramma tragico (Teatro La Fenice, Venice, Dec. 27, 1825); *Caritea, regina di Spagna [Donna Caritea], ossia La morte di Don Alfonso re di Portogallo,* melodramma serio (Teatro La Fenice, Venice, Feb. 21, 1826); *Ezio,* dramma per musica (Teatro Regio, Turin, Feb. 2, 1827); *Il montanaro,* melodramma comico (Teatro alla Scala, Milan, April 16, 1827); *La testa di bronzo, ossia La capanna solitaria,* melodramma eroico comico (private theater of Barone di Quintella, Lisbon, Dec. 3, 1827); *Adriano in Siria,* dramma serio (Sao Carlos, Lisbon, Feb. 24, 1828); *Gabriella di Vergy,* melodramma serio (Sao Carlos, Lisbon, Aug. 8, 1828); *La rappresaglia,* opera buffa (Cadiz, Nov. 20?, 1829); *Don Chisciotte [alle nozze di Gamaccio],* opera buffa (Cadiz, c.1829); *Francesca da Rimini,* melodramma (Madrid, c.1830); *Zaira,* melodramma tragico (Teatro San Carlo, Naples, Aug. 31, 1831); *I Normanni a Parigi,* tragedia lirica (Teatro Regio, Turin, Feb. 7, 1832); *Ismalia, ossia*

Amore e morte, melodramma serio fantastico (Teatro alla Scala, Milan, Oct. 27, 1832); *Il Conte di Essex*, melodramma (Teatro alla Scala, Milan, March 10, 1833); *Emma d'Antiochia*, tragedia lirica (Teatro La Fenice, Venice, March 8, 1834); *Uggero il danese*, melodramma (Teatro Riccardi, Bergamo, Aug. 11, 1834); *La gioventù di Enrico V*, melodramma (Teatro alla Scala, Milan, Nov. 25, 1834); *I due Figaro*, melodramma buffo (1st confirmed perf., Madrid, Jan. 26, 1835); *Francesca Donato, ossia Corinto distrutta*, melodramma semiserio (Teatro Regio, Turin, Feb. 14, 1835); *I Briganti*, melodramma (Théâtre-Italien, Paris, March 22, 1836); *Il giuramento*, melodramma (Teatro alla Scala, Milan, March 10, 1837; also known as *Amore e dovere*); *Le due illustri rivali*, melodramma (Teatro La Fenice, Venice, March 10, 1838); *Elena da Feltre*, dramma tragico (Teatro San Carlo, Naples, Dec. 26, 1838); *Il Bravo [La Veneziana]*, melodramma (Teatro alla Scala, Milan, March 9, 1839); *La Vestale*, tragedia lirica (Teatro San Carlo, Naples, March 10, 1840); *La Solitaria delle Asturie, ossia La Spagna ricuperata*, melodramma (Teatro La Fenice, Venice, March 12, 1840); *Il proscritto*, melodramma (Teatro San Carlo, Naples, Jan. 4, 1842); *Il Reggente*, dramma lirico (Teatro Regio, Turin, Feb. 2, 1843); *Leonora*, melodramma semiserio (Teatro Nuovo, Naples, Dec. 5, 1844); *Il Vascello de Gama*, melodramma romantico (Teatro San Carlo, Naples, March 6, 1845); *Orazi e Curiazi*, tragedia lirica (Teatro San Carlo, Naples, Nov. 10, 1846); *La Schiava saracena, ovvero Il campo di Gerosolima*, melodramma tragico (Teatro alla Scala, Milan, Dec. 26, 1848); *Medea*, tragedia lirica (Teatro San Carlo, Naples, March 1, 1851); *Statira*, tragedia (Teatro San Carlo, Naples, Jan. 8, 1853); *Violetta*, melodramma (Teatro Nuovo, Naples, Jan. 10, 1853); *Pelagio*, tragedia lirica (Teatro San Carlo, Naples, Feb. 12, 1857); *Virginia*, tragedia lirica (Teatro San Carlo, Naples, April 7, 1866).

BALLETS: *Il Servo balordo o La disperazione di Gilotto* (Teatro San Carlo, Naples, Feb. 1, 1818); *Il Califfo generoso* (Teatro Fondo, Naples, 1818); *Il flauto incantato o Le convulsioni musicali* (Teatro San Carlo, Naples, Nov. 19, 1818; rev. version for Teatro alla Scala, Milan, Jan. 12, 1828); *I Portoghesi nelle Indie o La conquista di Malacca* (Teatro San Carlo, Naples, May 30, 1819; in collaboration with Gallenberg).

In addition to his music for the theater, he composed much sacred music, including masses, motets, 8 Magnificats, several Salve Reginas, 2 settings of the *Tantum ergo*, etc.; of particular interest is his *Le sette [ultime] parole di Nostro Signore* for 2 Sopranos, Tenor, Baritone, Mixed Voices, 2 Violas, Cello, and Double Bass (1838); also his *Christus e Miserere* for Alto, Tenor, Bass, Chorus a cappella, English Horn, Horn, Bassoon, and Harp (Cons., Naples, March 19, 1856). He furthermore composed a number of cantatas and hymns with orch., including a hymn for Garibaldi (Naples, 1861) and another designed for the inauguration of a statue to Rossini (Pesaro, Aug. 21, 1864). His orch. music includes sinfonias (actually free variations in the form of an overture), fantasias on themes by other composers, marches, etc. He also wrote a number of chamber music pieces and songs. **BIBL.:** W. Neumann, *S. M.* (Kassel, 1855); R. Colucci, *Biografia di S. M.* (Venice, 1867); F. Florimo, "*S. M.*," in *Cenno storico sulla scuola musicale di Napoli* (2 vols., Naples, 1869–71; 2nd ed., rev. and enl. in 4 vols., 1880–83, as *La scuola musicale di Napoli e i suoi conservatorii*); O. Serena, *I musicisti altamurani . . . in occasione del centenario di S. M.* (Altamura, 1895); G. Bustico, "*S. M. a Novara*," *Rivista Musicale Italiana*, XXVIII (1921); A. Pomè, *Saggio critico sull'opera musicale di S. M.* (Turin, 1925); G. Pannain, "Saggio su la musica a Napoli nel secolo XIX, da M. a Martucci," *Rivista Musicale Italiana*, XXXV (1928); G. de Napoli, *La triade melodrammatica altamurana: Giacomo Tritto, Vincenzo Lavigna, S. M.* (Milan, 1931); G. Solimene, *La patria e i genitori di M.* (Naples, 1940); B. Notarnicola, *S. M.: Biografia critica* (Rome, 1945; 3rd ed., rev., 1951, as *S. M. nella gloria e nella luce; Verdi non ha vinto M.*); F. Schlitzer, *M. e Cammarano* (Bari, 1945); a sesquicentennial publication prepared by the committee "Pro Mercadante," *S. M.: Note e documenti* (Bari, 1945); F. Walker, "M. and Verdi," *Music & Letters* (Oct. 1952 and Jan. 1953); A. Sardone, *M.,*

le due patrie e "La gran madre Italia" (Naples, 1954); E. Brizio, "S. M.: Cause e rimedi di una ingiustizia," *Altamura: Bolletino dell'Archivio* (Jan. 1967); G. Carli Ballola, "Incontro con M.," *Chigiana*, XXVI–XXVII (Florence, 1969–70); M. Rinaldi, "Significato di M.," *Ritratti e fantasie musicale* (Rome, 1970); G. Carli Ballola, "M. e Il Bravo," *Il melodramma italiano dell'ottocento: Studi e ricerche per Massimo Mila* (Turin, 1977); S. Palermo, *S. M.: Biografia, epistolario* (Fasano, 1985).

Mercadier, Jean Baptiste, French music theorist; b. Belesta, Ariège, April 18, 1750; d. Foix, Jan. 14, 1815. He wrote *Nouveau système de musique théorique et pratique* (1776), a critique of Tartini's and Rameau's systems, favoring Rameau.

Mercer, Johnny (John Herndon), American lyricist and composer of popular music; b. Savannah, Ga., Nov. 18, 1909; d. Los Angeles, June 25, 1976. He went to N.Y. as a youth, and attracted the attention of Paul Whiteman; subsequently wrote songs for him, Benny Goodman, and Bob Crosby. In 1940 he went to Hollywood, where he founded Capitol Records. His 1st success as a lyric writer was *Lazybones*, with music by Hoagy Carmichael; another great success was *Accentuate the Positive*, which he wrote for his psychoanalyst. He wrote both words and music for *Something's Gotta Give* and other hits. He received 4 Academy awards for his lyrics. **BIBL.:** R. Bach and G. Mercer, *Our Huckleberry Friend: The Life, Times and Lyrics of J. M.* (Secaucus, N.J., 1982).

Mercer, Mabel, English-born American songstress; b. Burton upon Trent, Staffordshire, Feb. 3, 1900; d. Pittsfield, Mass., April 20, 1984. Her father, a black American, died before she was born; her mother was a white British vaudeville singer. She became a stage performer in her early adolescence; was a dancer in a music hall in London; after World War I she went to Paris, where she made a success as a nightclub singer; became a vedette at Bricktop's. In 1938 she went to America and settled in N.Y. She continued her career as a nightclub singer, but also gave regular recitals of popular songs. In 1983 she received the Medal of Freedom from President Reagan. She was briefly married to jazz musician Kelsey Pharr. **BIBL.:** J. Haskins, *M. M.: A Life* (N.Y., 1987).

Mercure, Pierre, Canadian composer; b. Montreal, Feb. 21, 1927; d. in an ambulance between Avallon and Auxerres, France, Jan. 29, 1966, after an automobile crash while driving from Paris to Lyons. He studied harmony and counterpoint with Marvin Duchow and Claude Champagne and bassoon with Roland Gagnier and Louis Letellier at the Montreal Cons. (1944–49); then studied composition with Boulanger and conducting with Barzin in Paris (1949–50); later studied orchestration with Hoérée and Milhaud and conducting with Fournet there (1962); also took courses with Dallapiccola at the Berkshire Music Center in Tanglewood (1951), and at Darmstadt and Dartington with Pousseur, Nono, and Berio (1962). He played bassoon with the Montreal Sym. Orch. (1947–52); then joined the CBC (1952), where he served as its 1st producer of television music programming (1954–59). In his music, he explored electronic sonorities in combinations with traditional instrumentation. **WORKS:** *Kaléidoscope* for Orch. (1947–48); *Pantomime* for Winds and Percussion (1948); 3 short choreographed pieces: *Dualité*, with Trumpet and Piano; *La Femme archaïque*, with Viola, Piano, and Timpani; and *Lucrèce Borgia*, with Trumpet, Piano, and Percussion (all composed in 1949); *Emprise* for Clarinet, Bassoon, Cello, and Piano (1950); *Cantate pour une joie* for Soprano, Chorus, and Orch. (1955); *Divertissement* for Solo String Quartet and String Orch. (1957); *Triptyque* for Orch. (1959); 6 tape pieces with optional choreography: *Improvisation, Incandesence, Structures métalliques I and II* (all 1961), *Manipulations* (1963), and *Surimpressions* (1964); *Répercussions*, for Japanese Wind Chimes on Tape (1961); *Jeu de Hockey* on Tape (1961); *Structures métalliques III* for Tape (1962); *Tétrachromie*, ballet for 3 Winds, 4 Percussionists, and Tape (1963); *Psaume pour abri*, radiophonic cantata for Narrator, 2 Choirs, Chamber Ensemble, and Tape (Montreal,

May 15, 1963); *Lignes et points* for Orch. (1964; Montreal, Feb. 16, 1965); *H₂O per Severino* for 4–10 Flutes and/or Clarinets (1965); film scores.

Merian, Wilhelm, Swiss musicologist; b. Basel, Sept. 18, 1889; d. there, Nov. 15, 1952. He studied with Nef at the Univ. of Basel (Ph.D., 1915, with the diss. *Die Tabulaturen des Organisten Hans Kotter: Ein Beitrag zur Musikgeschichte des beginnenden 16. Jahrhunderts;* publ. in Leipzig, 1916); subsequently completed his Habilitation there in 1921 with his *Die Klaviermusik der deutschen Koloristen,* and joined its faculty that same year. From 1920 to 1951 he was music critic and music ed. of the *Basler Nachrichten.* With Paul Sacher, he helped to found the Schola Cantorum Basiliensis (1933). **WRITINGS:** ed. *Gedenkschrift zum 50 jährigen Bestehen der Allgemeinen Musikschule in Basel* (1917); *Basels Musikleben im XIX. Jahrhundert* (1920); *Der Tanz in den deutschen Tabulaturbüchern . . .* (1927); *Hermann Suter: Ein Lebensbild als Beitrag zur schweizerischen Musikgeschichte* (1936).

Méric-Lalande, Henriette (Clémentine), French soprano; b. Dunkirk, 1798; d. Chantilly, Sept. 7, 1867. She studied with her father, who was the director of a provincial opera company; made her debut in Nantes in 1814; after vocal studies with García in Paris, she made her 1st appearance there on April 3, 1823, in Castil-Blaze's pasticcio *Les Folies amoureuses;* then continued her training with Bonfichi and Banderali in Milan and took part in the Venice premiere of Meyerbeer's *Il Crociatto in Egitto* (March 7, 1824). She created Bianca in Bellini's *Bianca e Gernando* (Naples, May 30, 1826), Imogene in *Il Pirata* (Milan, Oct. 27, 1827), and Alaide in *La Straniera* (Milan, Feb. 14, 1829), even though Bellini himself declared that she was "incapable of delicate sentiment." She made her London debut in *Il Pirata* at the King's Theatre (April 17, 1830) and appeared in Rossini's *Semiramis* (1831); she retired shortly after creating the title role in Donizetti's *Lucrezia Borgia* (Milan, Dec. 26, 1833).

Mériel, Paul, French composer; b. Mondonbleau, Loire-et-Cher, Jan. 4, 1818; d. Toulouse, Feb. 24, 1897. As a boy, he earned his living playing the violin in theater orchs.; later studied with Napoleão in Lisbon; produced a comic opera, *Cornelius l'argentier,* in Amiens; then settled in Toulouse, where he brought out a symphonic poem, *Le Tasse (Tasso);* a grand opera, *L'Armorique* (1854); and the comic opera *Les Précieuses ridicules* (1877).

Merikanto, Aarre, Finnish composer, son of **(Frans) Oskar Merikanto;** b. Helsinki, June 29, 1893; d. there, Sept. 29, 1958. He studied composition with Melartin at the Helsinki Music Inst.; then in Leipzig with Reger (1912–14) and with Vasilenko in Moscow (1915–16). In 1936 he joined the faculty at the Sibelius Academy in Helsinki, and in 1951 succeeded Palmgren as head of the dept. of composition there; held this post until his death. Like his father, he wrote on themes of Finnish folklore, but some of his early works reveal Russian and French traits. **WORKS: OPERA:** *Juha* (1920–22; Finnish Radio, Helsinki, Dec. 3, 1958; 1st stage perf., Lahti, Oct. 28, 1963). **ORCH.:** 3 piano concertos (1913, 1937, 1955); 3 syms. (1916, 1918, 1953); 4 violin concertos (1916, 1925, 1931, 1954); *Lemminkainen,* symphonic suite (1916); 2 cello concertos (1919; 1941–44); *Pan,* symphonic poem (1924); Concerto for Violin, Clarinet, Horn, and String Sextet (1925); *Concert Piece* for Cello and Chamber Orch. (1926); *Symphonic Study* (1928; mutilated; reconstructed by P. Heininen, 1981; Helsinki, Aug. 26, 1982); *Notturno,* symphonic poem (1929); *Kyllikin ryöstö* (The Abduction of Kyllikki), symphonic poem (1935); *Scherzo* (1937); *3 Impressions* (1940); *Soitelma kesäyölle* (Music to the Summer Night; 1942); *Genesis* for Soprano, Chorus, and Orch. (1956); *Tuhma* (Simpleton) for Male Chorus and Orch. (1956). **CHAMBER:** 2 string quartets (1913, 1939); String Trio (1912); Piano Trio (1917); Nonet (1926); String Sextet (1932); *Partita* for Harp and Woodwinds (1936); also songs.

Merikanto, (Frans) Oskar, Finnish composer, conductor, and organist, father of **Aarre Merikanto;** b. Helsinki, Aug.

5, 1868; d. Hausjärvi-Oiti, Feb. 17, 1924. After preliminary study in his native city, he studied at the Leipzig Cons. (1887–88) and in Berlin (1890–91). Returning to Finland, he became organist of St. John's Church, and from 1911 to 1922 was conductor of the National Opera in Helsinki. He wrote manuals for organ playing. He wrote the 1st opera in Finnish, *Pohjan Neiti* (The Maid of the North; 1899; Vyborg, June 18, 1908); also the operas *Elinan surma* (Elina's Death; Helsinki, Nov. 17, 1910) and *Regina von Emmeritz* (Helsinki, Jan. 30, 1920); various instrumental pieces; organ works; numerous songs, many of which became popular in his homeland. **BIBL.:** Y. Suomalainen, *O. M.* (Helsinki, 1950).

Meriläinen, Usko, Finnish composer; b. Tampere, Jan. 27, 1930. He studied with Aarre Merikanto and Leo Funtek at the Sibelius Academy in Helsinki (1951–55); then took private lessons with Ernst Krenek in Darmstadt and with Wladimir Vogel in Switzerland. In 1956–57 he was a conductor and teacher in Kuopio; subsequently was theater conductor in Tampere (1957–60); then taught at the music inst. there (1961–66) and from 1965 at the Univ. He also served as chairman of the Finnish Composers Assoc. (from 1981). In his music he adopted a pragmatic modern idiom, with structural foundations of tonal and/or dodecaphonic procedures, depending on the basic concept. **WORKS: BALLETS:** *Arius* (1958–60; also 2 suites, 1960, 1962); *Psyche* (1973); also *Alasin* (The Anvil), dance pantomime (1975; also listed as his 4th Sym.). **ORCH.:** 5 syms.: No. 1 (1953–55); No. 2 (1964); No. 3 (1971); No. 4, *Alasin* (The Anvil; 1975; also listed as the dance pantomime under the same name); No. 5 (1976); 2 piano concertos (1955, 1969); Concerto (1956); Chamber Concerto for Violin, 2 Percussionists, and Double String Orch. (1962); *Epyllion* (1963); *Musique du printemps* (1969); Cello Concerto (1975); *Dialogues* for Piano and Orch. (1977); *Mobile—ein Spiel für Orchester* (1977); *A Kinetic Poem* for Piano and Orch. (1981); *Kivenmurskaajat* (The Stone Crushers; 1982); *Visions and Whispers* (1985); *". . . but this is a landscape, monsieur Dali!"* (1986); Flute Concerto (1986). **CHAMBER:** *Partita* for Brass (1954); *4 Bagatelles* for String Quartet (1962); String Quartet (1965); *Divertimento* for Wind Quintet, Harp, Viola, and Cello (1968); *Metamorfora for 7* for Clarinet, Bassoon, Trumpet, Trombone, Percussion, Violin, and Double Bass (1969); *Concerto for 13* for 7 Violins, 3 Violas, 2 Cellos, and Double Bass (1971); *Concerto* for Double Bass and Percussion (1973); *Aspects of the Ballet "Psyche"* for Tape and Instrumental Ensemble (1973); *Simultus for 4* for Flute, Alto Saxophone, Guitar, and Percussion (1979); *Kyma* for String Quartet (1979); *Suvisoitto: Summer Sounds for Flute and Grasshoppers* for Flute and Tape (1979); *Paripeli* (For 2) for Cello and Piano (1980); Sonata for Alto Saxophone and Piano (1982); *Mouvements circulaires en douceur* for 4 Flutes (1985). **PIANO:** Suite (1955); Sonatina (1958); 4 sonatas (1960, 1966, 1972, 1974); *Tre Notturni* (1967); *Papillons* for 2 Pianos (1969); also *Yö, vene ja punaiset purjeet* (Night, a Boat and Red Sails) for Chorus (1987); 2 electro-acoustic works: *The Concert Where I Dozed Off—Consciousness Streaming Free,* radiophonic poem (1982), and *Oratorio Picassolle* (1984).

Merk, Joseph, Austrian cellist and composer; b. Vienna, March 18, 1795; d. Ober-Döbling, June 16, 1852. He was trained in Vienna; in 1818 became 1st cellist at the Vienna Court Opera; in 1823, a teacher at the Cons. He wrote 2 cello concertos, fantasias, polonaises, etc.; his cello études are of value to students.

Merklin, Joseph, German organ builder; b. Oberhausen, Baden, Jan. 17, 1819; d. Nancy, France, June 10, 1905. He worked in his father's workshop in Freiburg; in 1843 went to Brussels; in 1853 took his brother-in-law, F. Schütze, into partnership, changing the name of his firm to Merklin, Schütze & Cie. In 1855 he bought out the Ducroquet firm in Paris; in 1858 he reorganized his partnership as the Société Anonyme pour la Fabrication des Orgues, Établissement Merklin-Schütze. The firm supplied organs to several cathedrals in Europe. Merklin publ. an interesting technical paper, *Notice sur l'électricité appliquée aux grandes orgues* (Paris, 1887), containing some surprising insights on the possible manufacture of electric organs. His nephew Albert Merklin (1892–1925) went to Madrid at the outbreak of World War I in 1914 and established a Spanish branch of the firm. Merklin's Paris factory was acquired by Guttschenritter in 1899, and his branch in Lyons was bought in 1906 by the Swiss organ builder Theodor Kuhn; it was incorporated in 1926 as Société Anonyme des Anciens Établissements Michel, Merklin & Kuhn. After several further changes of ownership, the firm was taken over in 1967 by Fredrich Jakob in Zürich.

Merli, Francesco, Italian tenor; b. Milan, Jan. 27, 1887; d. there, Dec. 12, 1976. He studied with Borghi and Negrini in Milan; made his 1st appearance at Milan's La Scala as Alvaro in Spontini's *Fernando Cortez* (1916), and subsequently sang there regularly until 1942; also appeared at the Teatro Colón in Buenos Aires; between 1926 and 1930 he sang at Covent Garden in London. He made his debut at the Metropolitan Opera in N.Y. as Radames in *Aida* on March 2, 1932; then returned to Italy. He retired from the stage in 1948 and was active mainly as a voice teacher. His other roles included Don José, Otello, Canio, Samson, Calaf, and Dick Johnson.

Merman, Ethel (real name, **Ethel Agnes Zimmerman**), famous American singer of popular music; b. N.Y., Jan. 16, 1908; d. there, Feb. 14, 1984. She was of German-Scottish extraction. She took a commercial course in high school and held several jobs as a secretary while trying to satisfy her desire to be a singing actress. She never took vocal lessons but developed her booming powerful voice naturally. She obtained some bookings at Long Island night spots, and soon attracted the attention of Broadway managers. She auditioned for George Gershwin, who hired her to sing in his musical *Girl Crazy* in 1930; she brought the house down with the hit song *I Got Rhythm*, holding a high C for 16 bars in the coda against the orch. playing the melodic line. Among the musicals in which she starred were Cole Porter's *Anything Goes* (1934), Irving Berlin's *Annie Get Your Gun* (1946) and *Call Me Madam* (1950), and Jule Styne's *Gypsy* (1959). She also sang in 14 movie musicals, among them *There's No Business Like Show Business* and *It's a Mad, Mad, Mad, Mad World*. In 1970 she made her last apperance on Broadway; her last public appearance was in 1982, when she took part in a Carnegie Hall benefit concert. Merman had unbounded confidence in her stardom; she could also act in an uninhibited manner, which suited most of the roles she sang on Broadway. She was arrogant and foul-mouthed in her dealings with agents, managers, directors, and even composers, but she knew how to put the music across; her ability to make the most of each song, and her sense of perfect intonation, made her the darling of Broadway. Indeed, she was dubbed the "queen of Broadway." "Broadway has been very good for me," she once said, "but I've been very good for Broadway." Her private life was tempestuous; she married and divorced 4 times; her daughter from the 2nd marriage committed suicide. In 1983 she underwent surgery to remove a brain tumor. When the news of her death was announced, Broadway theaters observed a minute of silence to honor her memory.
BIBL.: R. Thomas, *I Got Rhythm! The E. M. Story* (N.Y., 1985).

Merola, Gaetano, Italian-American conductor and opera manager; b. Naples, Jan. 4, 1881; d. while conducting a performance of the San Francisco Sym. Orch. at Sigmund Stern Grove in San Francisco, Aug. 30, 1953. He studied at the Naples Cons.; then went to the U.S. in 1899, and was appointed assistant conductor at the Metropolitan Opera in N.Y.; also conducted the Henry Savage English Opera in N.Y. (1903) and at the Manhattan Opera; subsequently became music director and manager of the San Francisco Opera in 1923, where he remained until his death; also conducted opera in Los Angeles (1924–32).

Merriam, Alan P(arkhurst), American anthropologist and ethnomusicologist; b. Missoula, Mont., Nov. 1, 1923; d. in an airplane crash near Warsaw, March 14, 1980. He studied at the Univ. of Montana (B.A., 1947); took courses in anthropology from Melville Herskovits and Richard Waterman at Northwestern Univ. (M.M., 1948; Ph.D., 1951); taught anthropology there in 1953–54 and again from 1956 to 1962, and at the Univ. of Wisconsin (1954–56); in 1962 he became a prof. of anthropology at Indiana Univ. in Bloomington; was chairman of the dept. there from 1966 to 1969. In 1976 he was engaged as a senior scholar in anthropology at the Univ. of Sydney. He was involved in field research among the Flathead Indians and the tribes in Zaire.
WRITINGS: *The Anthropology of Music* (Evanston, Ill., 1964); with F. Gillis, *Ethnomusicology and Folk Music: An International Bibliography of Dissertations and Theses* (Middletown, Conn., 1966); *Ethnomusicology of the Flathead Indians* (Chicago, 1967); *African Music on LP: An Annotated Discography* (Evanston, 1970); *The Arts and Humanities in African Studies* (Bloomington, Ind., 1972).

Merrick, Frank, English pianist and composer; b. Clifton, Bristol, April 30, 1886; d. London, Feb. 19, 1981. He studied piano and composition with his father; made his debut in 1895, then studied piano with Leschetizky in Vienna (1898–1901; 1905). Returning to England, he taught at the Royal Manchester College of Music (1911–29); then became a prof. at the Royal College of Music in London; in 1956 he joined the piano faculty of Trinity College of Music in London. In 1928 he entered a rather ill-conceived contest launched by the Columbia Phonograph Co. to nail down the centenary of Schubert's death by finishing his "Unfinished" Sym. Merrick did finish it, and won a prize. He was married to the pianist Hope Squire and gave duo-piano concerts with her. He championed the music of British composers in his concerts. In 1978 he was made a Commander of the Order of the British Empire. Somewhat off-center in his propensities, proclivities, and predilections, he learned Esperanto and wrote songs to his own texts in that artificial language. He also composed 2 playable piano concertos and some pleasurable instrumental pieces, such as *Celtic Suite* and *Dream Pageant*. He publ. a didactic vol., *Practising the Piano* (London, 1958), and ed. John Field's piano concertos.

Merrill, Robert, noted American baritone; b. N.Y., June 4, 1917. He 1st studied voice with his mother, Lillian Miller Merrill, a concert singer; subsequently took lessons with Samuel Margolis. He began his career as a popular singer on the radio; then made his operatic debut as Amonasro in *Aida* in Trenton, N.J., in 1944. After winning the Metropolitan Opera Auditions of the Air in N.Y., he made his debut there with the Metropolitan Opera on Dec. 15, 1945, as Germont in *La Traviata*. He remained on the roster of the Metropolitan Opera for 30 years; also gave solo recitals. In 1961 he made his European operatic debut as Germont in Venice; sang that same role at his Covent Garden debut in London in 1967. He became a highly successful artist through many radio, television, and film appearances; gave recitals and sang with the major American orchs.; also starred in *Fiddler on the Roof* and other popular musicals. Among his numerous roles were Don José, Iago, Figaro, Rigoletto, Ford, and Scarpia. He was briefly married to the American soprano **Roberta Peters.** He publ. 2 autobiographical books, *Once More from the Beginning* (N.Y., 1965) and *Between Acts* (N.Y., 1977).

Merriman, Nan (actually, **Katherine-Ann**), American mezzo-soprano; b. Pittsburgh, April 28, 1920. She studied with Alexia Bassian in Los Angeles; made her operatic debut as La Cieca in *La Gioconda* with the Cincinnati Summer Opera in 1942; from 1943 she sang with Toscanini and the NBC Sym. Orch.; also appeared in opera at Aix-en-Provence, Edinburgh, and Glyndebourne. She retired in 1965. Her best operatic roles were Gluck's Orfeo, Maddalena in *Rigoletto*, Dorabella in *Così fan tutte*, Emilia in *Otello*, Baba the Turk in *The Rake's Progress*, and Meg in *Falstaff*.

Merritt, A(rthur) Tillman, American musicologist and pedagogue; b. Calhoun, Mo., Feb. 15, 1902. He studied at the Univ. of Missouri (B.A., 1924; B.F.A., 1926) and Harvard Univ. (M.A., 1927); then went to Europe on a J.K. Paine traveling scholarship from Harvard, and studied in Paris with Nadia Boulanger and Paul Dukas; upon his return to America, he taught at Trinity College in Hartford, Conn. (1930–32). In 1932 he joined the faculty of the music dept. of Harvard Univ.; was its chairman from 1942 to 1952 and from 1968 to 1972, when he retired. He publ. the valuable treatise *Sixteenth-century Polyphony: A Basis for the Study of Counterpoint* (Cambridge, Mass., 1939); also ed. works by Janequin. On his retirement, he was honored with a Festschrift, *Words and Music: The Scholar's View* (Cambridge, Mass., 1972).

Merseburger, Carl Wilhelm, German music publisher; b. 1816; d. 1885. In 1849 he purchased the publishing business of Carl Fredrich Meusel in Weissensfels; specializing in school music, he brought out a great number of useful manuals and songbooks; also was the publisher of *Euterpe,* a periodical on education. His successor was his brother Otto Merseburger (1822–1898); the latter was succeeded by his son, Max Merseburger (1852–1935), who headed the firm until 1918, being assisted by Georg Merseburger (1871–1958). The firm's entire stock was destroyed during the air raids on Leipzig in 1944; after the war, Georg's son, Karl Merseburger (1905–78), reconstituted the business in Berlin; it was acquired by Adolf Strube in 1956, and then became a limited company in 1964.
BIBL.: *100 Jahre im Dienste der Musik: Aus der Arbeit des Verlages C. M.* (Leipzig, 1949).

Mersenne, Marin, eminent French mathematician, philosopher, and music theorist; b. La Soultière, near Oizéí, Sept. 8, 1588; d. Paris, Sept. 1, 1648. He studied at the college of Le Mans; then at the Jesuit School at La Flèche (from 1604); then at the Collège Royal and the Sorbonne in Paris from 1609. He began his novitiate at the Nigeon monastery, near Paris (1611), completing it at St. Pierre de Fublaines, near Meaux, where he took holy orders (1612); then served the Minim monastery at the Paris Place Royale, becoming a deacon and a priest. He taught philosophy (1615–17) and theology (1618) at the Nevers monastery, and then was made correcter there. In 1619 he returned to Paris as conventual of the order. He made 3 trips to Italy between 1640 and 1645. He maintained a correspondence with the leading philosophers and scientists of his time. His writings provide source material of fundamental importance for the history of 17th-century music. His correspondence, ed. by C. de Waard and B. Rochot, began publication in Paris in 1932.
WRITINGS (all publ. in Paris): *Quaestiones celeberrimae in Genesim* (1623); *Traité de l'harmonie universelle* (1627); *Questions harmoniques* (1634); *Les préludes de l'harmonie universelle* (1634); *Harmonicorum libri, in quibus agitur de sonorum natura* (1635–36); *Harmonicorum instrumentorum libri IV* (1636; publ. with the preceding as *Harmonicorum libri XII,* 1648; 2nd ed., 1652); etc.
BIBL.: H. Ludwig, *M. M. und seine Musiklehre* (Halle and Berlin, 1935); F. Hyde, *The Position of M. M. in the History of Music* (diss., Yale Univ., 1954); A. Gruber, "M. and Evolving Tonal Theory," *Journal of Music Theory,* XIV (1970).

Mersmann, Hans, distinguished German musicologist; b. Potsdam, Oct. 6, 1891; d. Cologne, June 24, 1971. He studied in Munich with Sandberger and Kroyer, in Leipzig with Riemann and Schering, and with Wolf and Kretzschmar at the Univ. of Berlin, where he received his Ph.D. in 1914 with the dissertation *Christian Ludwig Boxberg und seine Oper "Sardanapalus"* (Ansbach 1698), *mit Beiträgen zur Ansbacher Musikgeschichte;* completed his Habilitation at the Berlin Technische Hochschule in 1921 with his *Grundlagen einer musikalischen Volksliedforschung* (publ. in Leipzig, 1930); was a reader there from 1927. He subsequently occupied various teaching positions at the Stern Cons. in Berlin, and at the Technische Hochschule there, until 1933; was in

charge of the folk-song archives of the Prussian Volksliederkommission (1917–33); also organized numerous seminars on musicology and modern music; from 1924, ed. the periodical *Melos;* wrote music criticism. He was removed from all of his positions by the Nazi regime in 1933; then devoted himself to private musicological research. After the collapse of the 3rd Reich, he taught at the Staatliche Hochschule für Musik in Munich (1946–47); from 1947 to 1958 he was director of the Hochschule für Musik in Cologne. As a historian and analyst of modern music, Mersmann occupied an important position in 20th-century research.
WRITINGS: *Kulturgeschichte der Musik in Einzeldarstellungen* (4 vols., Berlin, 1921–25); *Angewandte Musikästhetik* (Berlin, 1926); *Das Musikseminar* (Leipzig, 1931); *Kammermusik* (vols. 2–4, Leipzig, 1930; vol. 1, Leipzig, 1933); *Eine deutsche Musikgeschichte* (Potsdam, 1934; 2nd ed., rev. and augmented, 1955, as *Musikgeschichte in der abendländischen Kultur;* 3rd ed., 1973); *Volkslied und Gegenwart* (Potsdam, 1936); *Musikhören* (Berlin, 1938; augmented ed., 1952); *Neue Musik in den Strömungen unserer Zeit* (Bayreuth, 1949); *Die Kirchenmusik im XX. Jahrhundert* (Nuremberg, 1958); *Stilprobleme der Werkanalyse* (Mainz, 1963).
BIBL.: W. Wiora, ed., *Musikerkenntnis und Musikziehung. Dankesgaben für H. M. zu seinem 65. Geburtstag* (Kassel, 1957).

Mertens, Joseph, Belgian conductor and composer; b. Antwerp, Feb. 17, 1834; d. Brussels, June 30, 1901. He was 1st violinist at the Opéra in Brussels; was a violin teacher at the Cons.; was conductor of the Flemish Opera there (1878–89); then inspector of the Belgian music schools, and finally director of the Royal Theater at The Hague. He composed a number of Flemish and French operettas and operas which had local success: *De zwaarte Kapitein* (The Hague, 1877); *De Vrijer in de strop* (1866); *La Méprise* (1869); *L'Egoïsa* (1873); *Thécla* (1874); *Liederik l'intendent* (1875).

Mertke, Eduard, pianist and composer; b. Riga, June 17, 1833; d. Cologne, Sept. 25, 1895. He studied with S. von Lützau (piano) and Agthe (theory); appeared in public as a child pianist; toured Russia and Germany; in 1869 he was appointed to the faculty of the Cologne Cons., where he continued to teach until his death. He wrote the operas *Lisa, oder Die Sprache des Herzens* (Mannheim, Feb. 24, 1872), *Resi vom Hemsensteig,* and *Kyrill von Thessalonica;* many piano pieces; technical exercises for piano; also publ. a collection, *Melodies of the Ukraine.*

Mertz, Joseph Kasper, Austrian guitarist and composer; b. Pressburg, Aug. 17, 1806; d. Vienna, Oct. 14, 1856. He moved to Vienna in 1840; gave concerts there and in Germany, using a 10-string guitar. His works for the guitar enjoyed a modicum of popularity; his *Concertino* received 1st prize at the International Competition in Brussels in 1856. He was married to the pianist Josephine Plantin.
BIBL.: F. Buck, *Die Gitarre und ihre Meister* (Vienna, 1926; 2nd ed., Berlin, 1952).

Merula, Tarquinio, significant Italian organist and composer; b. Cremona, 1594 or 1595; d. there, Dec. 10, 1665. In 1616 he received an appointment as organist of S. Maria Incoronata in Lodi. In 1621 he went to Poland, where he served as court organist. Returning to Italy, he became provisional maestro di cappella for the Laudi della Madonna at Cremona Cathedral in 1626; then held a regular appointment from 1627; also became organist of the collegiate church of S. Agata in 1628. He was appointed maestro di cappella of S. Maria Maggiore in Bergamo in 1631, but was dismissed in 1632 for "indecency" shown toward several of his pupils. He then returned to Cremona, where he became maestro di cappella for the Laudi della Madonna at the Cathedral in 1633; however, a dispute with his superiors over salary and other matters led to his resignation in 1635. By 1638 he had found a position as maestro di cappella and organist to the Cathedral in Bergamo next to S. Maria Maggiore. Disagreements with his former employers at S. Maria Maggiore soon developed, and he finally returned to Cremona in 1646 as Cathedral organist and as organist and maestro di cappella for the Laudi della Madonna, holding these positions until his death. He was a versatile composer and wrote both secular and sacred music; remarkably enough for a church organist, he also wrote instrumental music in a concertante style; his ensemble canzonas are especially fine.

WORKS: SACRED VOCAL: *Il primo libro de motetti e sonate concertati*, op. 6, for 2 to 5 Voices (Venice, 1624); *Libro secondo de concerti spirituali con alcune sonate*, op. 8, for 2 to 5 Voices (Venice, 1628); *Pegaso . . . salmi, motetti, suonate . . .* for 2 to 5 Voices, *libro terzo*, op. 11 (c.1633–37); *Concerto . . . messi, salmi . . . concertati*, op. 15, for 2 to 8 and 12 Voices, with Instruments (Venice, 1639); *Arpa Davidica . . . salmi, et messe*, op. 16, *a 4* (Venice, 1640); *Il terzo libro delle salmi et messa concertati*, op. 18, *a 3–4* (Venice, 1652). **SECULAR VOCAL:** *La finta savia*, opera in collaboration with others (Venice, 1643); *Il primo libro de madrigaletti*, op. 4, for 3 Voices and Basso Continuo (Venice, 1624); *Il primo libro de madrigali concertate*, op. 5, for 4 to 8 Voices and Basso Continuo (Venice, 1624); *Satiro e Corisca dialogo musicale*, op. 7, for 2 Voices and Basso Continuo (Venice, 1626); *Madrigali et altre musiche concertate a 1–5, libro secondo*, op. 10 (Venice, 1633); *Curtio precipitato et altri capricii, libro secondo*, op. 13, for 1 Voice (Venice, 1638); *Canzonetta a 3 et 4*, op. 14? (date unknown; not extant). **INSTRUMENTAL:** *Il primo libro delle canzoni*, *a 4*, op. 1 (Venice, 1615); *Il secondo libro delle canzoni da suonare*, op. 9, for 3 Instruments and Basso Continuo (c.1631–33); *Canzoni overo sonate concertate per chiesa e camera, a 2–3, libro terzo*, op. 12 (Venice, 1637); *Il quarto libro delle canzoni da suonare, a 2–3*, op. 17 (Venice, 1651). See A. Sutkowski, ed., *Tarquinio Merula: Opere complete*, I/i (Brooklyn, 1974). **BIBL.:** J. von Wasielewski, *Die Violine im 17. Jahrhundert* (Bonn, 1874); E. Schmitz, *Geschichte der weltlichen Solokantate* (Leipzig, 1914; 2nd ed., rev., 1955); E. van der Straeten, *The History of the Violin* (London, 1933); E. Crocker, *An Introductory Study of the Italian Canzona for Instrumental Ensembles* (diss., Radcliffe College, 1943); N. Fortune, *Italian Secular Song from 1600 to 1635: The Origins and Development of Accompanied Monody* (diss., Cambridge Univ., 1954); W. Newman, *The Sonata in the Baroque Era* (Chapel Hill, 1959; 4th ed., rev., 1983); A. Curtis, "L'opera cembalo-organistica di T. M.," *L'Organo*, I (1960); J. Roche, "Music at S. Maria Maggiore, Bergamo, 1614–1643," *Music & Letters*, XLVII (1966); C. Palisca, *Baroque Music* (Englewood Cliffs, N.J., 1968); J. Roche, *North Italian Liturgical Music in the Early 17th Century* (diss., Cambridge Univ., 1968); A. Colzani, "La cappella della Laudi a Cremona fino al servizio di T. M.," *Contributi e studi di liturgia e musica nella regione padana* (Bologna, 1972); M. Padoan, "T. M. nelle fonte documentarie," ibid.; E. Ferrari Barassi, "T. M. i jego dialog 'Satiro e Corisca,' " *Pagine* (1974).

Merulo (real name, **Merlotti**), **Claudio,** important Italian composer, organist, and music publisher, called da Correggio; b. Correggio, April 8, 1533; d. Parma, May 4, 1604. He studied with Tuttovale Menon and Girolamo Donato. On Oct. 21, 1556, he became organist at the Cathedral in Brescia, succeeding Vincenzo Parabosco; on July 2, 1557, was chosen as 2nd organist at San Marco in Venice; in 1566 he succeeded Padovano as 1st organist, a position he held until 1584. He composed a number of works for state occasions, including intermedi to Frangipane's *Tragedia* for the visit of Henry III of France in 1574. Active as a music publisher between 1566 and 1570, he brought out several 1st eds. of his own works, as well as of works by Primavera, Porta, and Wert. In 1586 he was appointed organist at the court of the Duke of Parma; in 1591 became organist to the company of the Steccata, a position he retained until his death. Merulo was one of the most famous organists of his time. As a composer, he was an important representative of the Venetian school. His organ music is of especial merit; he also composed church music and madrigals.

WORKS: INSTRUMENTAL: *Ricercari d'intabolatura d'organo . . . libro primo* (Venice, 1567); *Messe d'intavolatura d'organo* (Venice, 1568); *Il primo libro de ricercari da cantare a 4* (Venice,

1574); *Canzoni d'intavolatura d'organo a 4 fatte alla francese* (Venice, 1592); *Toccate d'intavolatura d'organo, libro primo* (Rome, 1598); *Toccate d'intavolatura d'organo, libro secondo* (Rome, 1604); *Libro secondo di canzoni d'intavolatura d'organo a fatte alla francese* (Venice, 1606); *Ricercari da cantare a 4 . . . libro secondo* (Venice, 1607); *Ricercari da cantare a 4 . . . libro terzo* (Venice, 1608); *Terzo libro de canzoni d'intavolatura d'organo a 5 fatte alla francese* (Venice, 1611); see S. Dalla Libera, *Claudio Merulo: Toccate per organo,* I–III (Milan, 1959). **SACRED VOCAL:** *Missarum liber primus* for 5 Voices (Venice, 1573); *Liber primus sacrarum cantionum* for 5 Voices (Venice, 1578); *Liber secundus sacrarum cantionum* for 5 Voices (Venice, 1578); *Il primo libro de mottetti* for 6 Voices (Venice, 1583); *Il primo libro de mottetti* for 4 Voices (Venice, 1584); *Il secondo libro de mottetti* for 6 Voices (Venice, 1593); *Sacrorum concentuum* for 5, 8, 10, 12, and 16 Voices (Venice, 1594); *Il terzo libro de mottetti* for 6 Voices (Venice, 1605); *Misse due* for 8 and 12 Voices, with Organ (Venice, 1609). An edition of his sacred music, ed. by J. Bastian in Corpus Mensurabilis Musicae, began publication in 1970. **SECULAR VOCAL:** *Il primo libro de madrigali* for 5 Voices (Venice, 1566); *Il primo libro de madrigali* for 4 Voices (Venice, 1579); *Il primo libro de madrigali* for 3 Voices (Venice, 1580); *Il secondo libro de madrigali* for 5 Voices (Venice, 1580); also intermedi to L. Dolce's drama *Le Troiane* (1566) and Frangipane's *Tragedia* (Venice, July 21, 1574).

BIBL.: A. Catelani, "Memorie della vita e delle opere di C. M.," *Gazzetta Musicale di Milano,* XVIII (1860); Q. Bigi, *Di C. M. da Correggio* (Parma, 1861); *C. M. da Correggio* (Parma, 1905; essays by 8 Italian scholars); A. Einstein, "C. M.'s Ausgabe der Madrigale," *Sammelbände der Internationalen Musik-Gesellschaft,* VIII/2 (1906–7); O. Kinkeldey, *Orgel und Klavier in der Musik des 16. Jahrhunderts* (Leipzig, 1910); A. Einstein, *The Italian Madrigal* (Princeton, 1949); L. Debes, *Die musikalischen Werke von C. M. (1533–1604)* (diss., Julius-Maximilians Univ., Würzburg, 1964); J. Bastian, *The Sacred Music of C. M.* (diss., Univ. of Michigan, 1967).

Messager, André (Charles Prosper), celebrated French composer and conductor; b. Montluçon, Allier, Dec. 30, 1853; d. Paris, Feb. 24, 1929. He studied at the École Niedermeyer in Paris with Gigout, Fauré, and Saint-Saëns (composition), A. Laussel (piano), and C. Loret (organ). In 1874 he became organist at St.-Sulpice. He was active as a conductor at the Folies-Bergère, where he produced several ballets. After conducting Brussels's Eden-Théâtre (1880), he returned to Paris as organist of St. Paul–St. Louis (1881) and as maître de chapelle at Ste. Marie-des-Batignolles (1882–84). He subsequently was music director at the Opéra-Comique (1898–1903); also managed the Grand Opera Syndicate at London's Covent Garden (1901–7). He was conductor of the Concerts Lamoureux (1905) and music director of the Paris Opéra (1907–14); was also conductor of the Société des Concerts du Conservatoire from 1908 until 1919; under the auspices of the French government, he visited the U.S. with that orch., giving concerts in 50 American cities (1918); also toured Argentina (1916). Returning to Paris, he again conducted at the Opéra-Comique; led a season of Diaghilev's Ballets Russes in 1924. As a conductor, he played an important role in Paris musical life; he conducted the premiere of *Pelléas et Mélisande* (1902), the score of which Debussy dedicated to him. His initial steps as a composer were auspicious; his Sym. (1875) was awarded the gold medal of the Société des Compositeurs and performed at the Concerts Colonne (Jan. 20, 1878); his dramatic scene *Don Juan et Haydée* (1876) was awarded a gold medal by the Academy of St. Quentin. He wrote several other works for orch. (*Impressions orientals, Suite funambulesque,* etc.) and some chamber music, but he was primarily a man of the theater. His style may be described as enlightened eclecticism; his music is essentially French, and more specifically Parisian, in its elegance and gaiety. He was honored in France; in 1926 he was elected to the Académie des Beaux Arts. He was married to Hope Temple (real name, Dotie Davis; 1858–

1938), who was the author of numerous songs. His stage works (1st perf. in Paris unless otherwise given) include *François les-Bas-Bleus* (Nov. 8, 1883; score begun by F. Bernicat and completed after his death by Messager); *La Fauvette du temple* (Nov. 17, 1885); *La Béarnaise* (Dec. 12, 1885); *Le Bourgeois de Calais* (April 6, 1887); *Isoline* (Dec. 26, 1888); *La Basoche* (May 30, 1890; greatly acclaimed); *Madame Chrysanthème* (Jan. 26, 1893; to a story similar to Puccini's *Madama Butterfly*, produced 11 years later; but Puccini's dramatic treatment eclipsed Messager's lyric setting); *Le Chevalier d'Harmental* (May 5, 1896); *Véronique* (Dec. 10, 1898); *Les Dragons de l'impératrice* (Feb. 13, 1905); *Fortunio* (June 5, 1907); *Béatrice* (Monte Carlo, March 21, 1914); *Monsieur Beaucaire* (Birmingham, April 7, 1919). Other stage works were *Le Mari de la Reine* (Dec. 18, 1889); *Miss Dollar* (Jan. 22, 1893); *La Fiancée en loterie* (Feb. 15, 1896); *Les P'tites Michu* (Nov. 16, 1897); *La Petite Fonctionnaire* (May 14, 1921); *Passionnément* (Jan. 15, 1926). His ballets include *Fleur d'oranger* (1878); *Les Vins de France* (1879); *Mignons et vilains* (1879); *Les Deux Pigeons* (1886); *Scaramouche* (1891); *Amants éternels* (1893); *Le Chevalier aux fleurs* (1897); *Le Procès des roses* (1897); *Une Aventure de la guimard* (1900). He also wrote incidental music.

BIBL.: Special issue of *Musica*, LXXII (1908); O. Séré, *Musiciens français d'aujourd'hui* (Paris, 1911; 2nd ed., 1921); H. Février, *A. M.; Mon maître, mon ami* (Paris, 1948); M. Augé-Laribé, *A. M., Musicien de théâtre* (Paris, 1951).

Messchaert, Johannes (Martinus), Dutch baritone; b. Hoorn, Aug. 22, 1857; d. Zürich, Sept. 9, 1922. He studied violin, then changed to singing; was a pupil of Stockhausen in Frankfurt and Wüllner in Munich; began his career as a choral conductor in Amsterdam; then appeared as a singer of the German repertoire; was prof. of voice at the Berlin Königliche Hochschule für Musik (1911–20) and at the Zürich Cons. (1920–22).

BIBL.: F. Martienssen, *J. M.: Ein Beitrag zum Verständnis echter Gesangskunst* (Berlin, 1914; 2nd ed., 1920).

Messiaen, Olivier (Eugène Prosper Charles), outstanding French composer and pedagogue; b. Avignon, Dec. 10, 1908. A scion of an intellectual family (his father was a translator of English literature; his mother, Cécile Sauvage, a poet), he absorbed the atmosphere of culture and art as a child. A mystical quality was imparted by his mother's book of verses *L'Âme en bourgeon*, dedicated to her as yet unborn child. He learned to play piano; at the age of 8 composed a song, *La Dame de Shalott*, to a poem by Tennyson. At the age of 11 he entered the Paris Cons., where he attended the classes of Jean and Noël Gallon, Marcel Dupré, Maurice Emmanuel, and Paul Dukas, specializing in organ, improvisation, and composition; he carried 1st prizes in all these depts. After graduation in 1930, he became organist at the Trinity Church in Paris. He taught at the École Normale de Musique and at the Schola Cantorum (1936–39). He also organized, with André Jolivet, Ives Baudrier, and Daniel-Lesur, the group La Jeune France, with the aim of promoting modern French music. He was in the French army at the outbreak of World War II in 1939; was taken prisoner; spent 2 years in a German prison camp in Görlitz, Silesia; he composed there his *Quatuor pour la fin du temps*; was repatriated in 1941 and resumed his post as organist at the Trinity Church in Paris. He was prof. of harmony and analysis at the Paris Cons. (from 1948). He also taught at the Berkshire Music Center in Tanglewood (1948) and in Darmstadt (1950–53). Young composers seeking instruction in new music became his eager pupils; among them were Boulez, Stockhausen, Xenakis, and others who were to become important composers in their own right. He received numerous honors; was made a Grand Officier de la Légion d'Honneur; was elected a member of the Institut de France, the Bavarian Academy of the Fine Arts, the Accademia di Santa Cecilia in Rome, the American Academy of Arts and Letters, and other organizations. He married the pianist **Yvonne Loriod** in 1961. Messiaen is one of the most original of modern composers; in his music he makes use of a wide range of resources, from Gregorian chant to oriental rhythms. A mystic by nature and Catholic by religion, he strives to find a relationship between progressions of musical sounds and religious concepts; in his theoretical writing he strives to postulate an interdependence of modes, rhythms, and harmonic structures. Ever in quest of new musical resources, he employs in his scores the Ondes Martenot and exotic percussion instruments; a synthesis of these disparate tonal elements finds its culmination in his grandiose orch. work *Turangalîla-Symphonie*. One of the most fascinating aspects of Messiaen's innovative musical vocabulary is the phonetic emulation of bird song in several of his works; in order to attain ornithological fidelity, he made a detailed study notating the rhythms and pitches of singing birds in many regions of several countries. The municipal council of Parowan, Utah, where Messiaen wrote his work *Des canyons aux étoiles*, glorifying the natural beauties of the state of Utah, resolved to name a local mountain Mt. Messiaen on Aug. 5, 1978. On Nov. 28, 1983, his 1st opera, *St. François d'Assise*, was premiered, to international acclaim, at the Paris Opéra.

WORKS: OPERA: *St. François d'Assise* (Paris Opéra, Nov. 28, 1983). **ORCH.:** Fugue in D minor (1928); *Le Banquet eucharistique* (1928); *Simple chant d'une âme* (1930); *Les Offrandes oubliées* (1930; Paris, Feb. 19, 1931); *Le Tombeau resplendissant* (1931; Paris, Feb. 12, 1933); *Hymne au Saint Sacrement* (1932; Paris, March 23, 1933); *L'Ascension* (1933; Paris, Feb. 1935); *3 Talas* for Piano and Orch. (Paris, Feb. 14, 1948); *Turangalîla-Symphonie* (1946–48; Boston, Dec. 2, 1949); *Réveil des oiseaux* for Piano and Orch. (Donaueschingen, Oct. 11, 1953); *Oiseaux exotiques* for Piano, 2 Wind Instruments, Xylophone, Glockenspiel, and Percussion (Paris, March 10, 1956); *Chronochromie* (Donaueschingen, Oct. 16, 1960); *7 Haï-kaï* for Piano, 13 Wind Instruments, Xylophone, Marimba, 4 Percussion Instruments, and 8 Violins (1962; Paris, Oct. 30, 1963); *Couleurs de la cité céleste* for Large Orch., with imitations of 2 New Zealand birds and 1 from Brazil (Donaueschingen, Oct. 17, 1964); *Et expecto resurrectionem mortuorum* for 18 Woodwinds, 16 Brass Instruments, and 3 Percussion Instruments (1964; Paris, May 7, 1965); *Des canyons aux étoiles* (1970–74; N.Y., Nov. 20, 1974). **CHAMBER:** *Thème et variations* for Violin and Piano (1932); *Quatuor pour la fin du temps* for Violin, Clarinet, Cello, and Piano (perf. in Stalag 8A, Görlitz, Silesia, with the composer at the piano, Jan. 15, 1941); *Le Merle noir* for Flute and Piano (1951); *Le Tombeau de Jean-Pierre Guézec* for Horn (1971). **VOCAL:** *2 ballades de Villon* (1921); *3 mélodies* (1930); *La Mort du nombre* for Soprano, Tenor, Violin, and Piano (1930; Paris, March 25, 1931); Mass for 8 Sopranos and 4 Violins (1933); *Poèmes pour Mi* for Soprano and Piano (1936; Paris, April 28, 1937; orch. version, 1937; Paris, 1946); *O sacrum convivium!* for Chorus and Organ (1937); *Chants de terre et de ciel*, song cycle for Soprano and Piano to texts by the composer (1938); *Chœurs pour une Jeanne d'Arc* for Chorus a cappella (1941); *3 petites liturgies de la Présence Divine* for 18 Sopranos, Piano, Ondes Martenot, and Orch. (1944; Paris, April 21, 1945); *Harawi*, "chant d'amour et de mort," for Dramatic Soprano and Piano (1945); *5 rechants* for 12-voice Chorus (1949); *La Transfiguration de Notre Seigneur Jésus-Christ*, in 14 sections, for Chorus and Orch. (Lisbon, June 7, 1969). **PIANO:** *8 Preludes* (1929); *Pièce pour le tombeau de Paul Dukas* (1935); *Visions de l'Amen* for 2 Pianos (1942); *20 regards sur l'enfant Jésus* (1944); *Cantéyodjayâ* (1948); *4 études de rythme* (1949); *Catalogue d'oiseaux* (1956–58). **ORGAN:** *Variations écossaises* (1928); *Le Banquet céleste* (1928); *Diptyque* (1929); *Apparition de l'église éternelle* (1932); *L'Ascension*, version of orch. work of 1933 with new 3rd movement (1934); *La Nativité du Seigneur* (1935); *Les Corps glorieux* (1939); *Messe de la Pentecôte* (1950); *Livre d'orgue* (1951); *Verset pour la fête de la dédicace* (1960); *Méditations sur le mystère de la Sainte Trinité* (1969).

WRITINGS: *20 leçons de solfèges modernes* (Paris, 1933); *20 leçons d'harmonie* (Paris, 1939); *Technique de mon langage musical* (2 vols., Paris, 1944; Eng. tr. as *The Technique of My Musical Language*, 2 vols., 1957); individual articles on musical ornithology and other subjects.

BIBL.: B. Gavoty, *Musique et mystique: Le "Cas" M.* (Paris, 1945); V. Zinke-Bianchini, *O. M. Notice biographique; catalogue détaillé des œuvres éditées* (Paris, 1946); C. Rostand, *O. M.* (Paris, 1958); A. Goléa, *Rencontres avec O. M.* (Paris, 1961); C. Samuel, *Entretiens avec O. M.* (Paris, 1967); S. Waumsley, *The Organ Music of O. M.* (Paris, 1969; rev. 1975); R. Johnson, *M.* (Berkeley, Calif., 1975); R. Nichols, *M.* (London, 1975; 2nd ed., 1985); C. Bell, *O. M.* (Boston, 1984); P. Griffiths, *O. M. and the Music of Time* (London, 1985); J. Gallatin, *An Overview of the Compositional Methods in Representative Works of O. M.* (diss., Univ. of Cincinnati, 1986); A. Michaely, *Die Musik O. M.s: Untersuchungen zum Gesamtschaffen* (Hamburg, 1987); T. Hirsbrunner, *O. M., Leben und Werk* (Laaber, 1988); R. Nichols, "M.'s 'Le Merle noir': The Case of a Blackbird in a Historical Pie," *Musical Times* (Dec. 1988).

Messner, Joseph, Austrian organist, conductor, and composer; b. Schwaz, Tirol, Feb. 27, 1893; d. St. Jakob Thurn, near Salzburg, Feb. 23, 1969. He studied at the Univ. of Innsbruck; after his ordination (1918), he took courses in organ and composition with Friedrich Klose; in 1922 he was appointed Cathedral organist in Salzburg; from 1926 to 1967 he led the concerts at the Salzburg Cathedral. At the same time, he gave a seminar in church music at the Mozarteum there. He wrote 4 operas: *Hadassa* (Aachen, March 27, 1925); *Das letzte Recht* (1932); *Ines* (1933); *Agnes Bernauer* (1935); 3 syms.; Violin Concerto; Cello Concerto; String Quartet; several sacred works, including 11 masses.

Mester, Jorge, talented Mexican-born American conductor; b. Mexico City (of Hungarian parents), April 10, 1935. He settled in the U.S. and became a naturalized citizen in 1968. He studied with Morel at the Juilliard School of Music in N.Y.; also with Bernstein at the Berkshire Music Center in Tanglewood (1955) and with A. Wolff in the Netherlands. From 1956 to 1967 he taught conducting at the Juilliard School of Music. In 1964 he led a few exhibitionistic concerts of the parodistic P.D.Q. Bach series in N.Y., inaugurated with a great thud by Peter Schickele. In 1967 he was appointed music director of the Louisville Orch., holding this post until 1979. Following the Louisville Orch.'s unique policy of commissioning new works and then giving their premieres, Mester conducted, during his tenure, something like 200 1st performances, and made about 70 recordings of some of them. Concurrently, he served as musical adviser and principal conductor of the Kansas City Phil. (1971–74). In 1970 he assumed the post of music director of the Aspen Music Festival; in 1980 he was charged with the task of reorganizing the Casals Festival in Puerto Rico; in 1984 he became music director of the Pasadena (Calif.) Sym. Orch.; also rejoined the Juilliard faculty (1980), serving as chairman of the conducting dept. (1984–87). Equally at home in the classical and modern repertoires, in symphonic music and in opera, Mester knows how to impart a sense of color with a precision of technical detail.

Mestres-Quadreny, Josep (Maria), Spanish composer; b. Manresa, March 4, 1929. He studied composition with Cristòfor Taltabull at the Univ. of Barcelona (1950–56); in 1960 he collaborated in the founding of Música Abierta, an organization of avant-garde musical activity; later he joined composers Xavier Benguerel, Joaquim Homs, and Josep Soler in founding the Conjunt Català de Música Contemporània, for the propagation of Catalan music. In 1968 he went to work in an electronic music studio. In his music he consciously attempts to find a counterpart to Abstract Expressionism in art, as exemplified by the paintings of Miró; for this purpose he applies serial techniques and aleatory procedures.

WORKS: Piano Sonata (1957); *Epitafios,* cantata for Soprano, Strings, Harp, and Celesta (1958); opera, *El Ganxo* (1959); *Triade per a Joan Miró,* composed of *Música da cámara I* for Flute, Piano, Percussion, Violin, and Double Bass; *Música da cámara II* for 3 Clarinets, English Horn, Trumpet, Trombone, Percussion, and String Trio; and *3 Moviments per a orquesta de cámara* for 15 Instruments, formed by superimposing the previous 2 works (all 1961); *3 invenció mòvils: I* for Flute, Clarinet, and Piano; *II* for Voice, Trumpet, and Electric Guitar; and *III* for String Quartet (all 1961); *Tramesa a Tàpies* for Violin, Viola, and Percussion (1961); 3 ballets: *Roba i ossos* (Things and Bones; 1961); *Petit diumenge* (Little Sunday; 1962); *Vegetació submergida* (Submerged Vegetation; 1962); *Quartet de Catroc* for String Quartet (1962); *Digodal* for String Orch. (1963); *Concert per a representar,* musical theater for 6 Voices, 6 Instrumentalists, and Tape (1964); *3 cànons en homenatge a Galile,* in 3 versions: for Piano, for Percussion, and for Ondes Martenot, each with Tape (1965, 1968, 1969); *Conversa* for Chamber Orch. (1965); *Suite bufa,* musical theater for Ballerina, Mezzo-soprano, Piano, and Electronic Sound (1966); *Tríptic carnavalesc,* cantata for Soprano, Flute, Clarinet, Trumpet, Trombone, 2 Percussionists, and Piano (1966); *Música per a Anna* for Soprano and String Quartet (1967); String Trio (1968); *Ibemia* for 13 Instrumentalists (1969); *Quadre* for Chamber Orch. (1969); *Micos i Papellones* for Guitar and Metal Percussion (1970); *Double Concerto* for Ondes Martenot, Percussion, and Orch. (1970); *Variacions essencials* for String Trio and Percussion (1970); *Homenatge a Joan Prats* for 6 Actors, Electro-acoustical Installation, String Quartet, 4 Percussionists, Flute, Clarinet, Trumpet, 2 Trombones, and Tuba (1972); *Frigoli-Frigola* and *Aronada* for any number or type of Instruments (1969, 1972).

Metalov, Vasili (Mikhailovich), Russian musicologist and composer; b. Saratov, March 13, 1862; d. Moscow, June 1, 1926. He studied theology and Russian church music in Moscow; became a teacher at the Moscow Synodal School (1894); was made a prof. of the history of Russian church music at the Moscow Cons. (1901). He composed some sacred works.

WRITINGS (all publ. in Moscow unless otherwise given): *Study of the History of Orthodox Church Singing in Russia* (Saratov, 1893; 3rd ed., 1900); *The Strict Style of Harmony: An Attempt to Describe the Principles of Strict Church Harmony* (1897); *The Synodal, Formerly the Patriarchal, Choristers* (1898); *The Alphabet of Church Singing: An Attempt at a Systematic Guide to the Reading of Kryuki in the Singing of Znamenniy Chant in the Period of the Kinovarniy Pometi* (1899); *The Osmoglasiye of Znamenniy Chant: An Attempt at a Guide to the Study of the Osmoglasiye of Znamenniy Chant in Vocal Popevki* (1900); *Divine Singing in the Russian Church: Pre-Mongol Period* (1906); *The Synodal Academy of Church Singing Past and Present* (1911).

Metastasio, Pietro (real name, **Antonio Domenico Bonaventura Trapassi**), famous Italian poet and opera librettist; b. Rome, Jan. 3, 1698; d. Vienna, April 12, 1782. He was the son of a papal soldier named Trapassi, but in his professional career assumed the Greek tr. of the name, both Trapassi (or Trapassamento) and Metastasio meaning transition. He was a learned classicist; began to write plays as a young boy; studied music with Porpora; he achieved great fame in Italy as a playwright; in 1729, was appointed court poet in Vienna by Emperor Charles VI. He wrote 27 opera texts, which were set to music by Handel, Gluck, Mozart, Hasse, Porpora, Jommelli, and many other celebrated composers; some of them were set to music 60 or more times. His librettos were remarkable for their melodious verse, which naturally suggested musical associations; the libretto to the opera by Niccolo Conforto, *La Nitteti* (1754; Madrid, Sept. 23, 1756), was on the same subject as *Aida,* anticipating the latter by more than a century. Metastasio's complete works were publ. in Paris (12 vols., 1780–82) and Mantua (20 vols., 1816–20); they were ed. by F. Gazzani (Turin, 1968) and by M. Fubino (Milan, 1968); see also A. Wotquenne, *Alphabetisches Verzeichnis der Stücke in Versen . . . von Zeno, Metastasio und Goldoni* (Leipzig, 1905).

BIBL.: S. Mattei, *Memorie per servire alla vita del M.* (Colle, 1785); C. Burney, *Memoirs of the Life and Letters of the Abate M.* (London, 1796); M. Zito, *Studio su P. M.* (Naples, 1904); E. Leonardi, *Il melodramma di M.* (Naples, 1909); L. Russo, *P. M.* (Pisa, 1915; 2nd ed., rev., 1921–45, as *M.*); A. della Corte, *L'estetica musicale di P. M.* (Turin, 1922); A. Bonaventura, "*P. M.* musicista," *Musica d'Oggi* (1932); A. Vullo, *Con-*

fronto fra i melodrammi di Zeno e M. (Agrigento, 1935); B. Brunelli, ed., *Tutte le opere di P. M.* (Milan, 1943–54); H. Wolff, "Das Märchen von der Neapolitanischen Oper und M.," *Analecta Musicologica,* IX (1970); R. Monelle, "The Rehabilitation of M.," *Music & Letters,* LVII (1976); M. Muraro, *M. e il mondo musicale* (Florence, 1986).

Metcalf, Frank J(ohnson), American hymnologist; b. Ashland, Mass., April 4, 1865; d. Washington, D.C., Feb. 25, 1945. He studied at Boston Univ. (B.A., 1886); was a clerk in the War Dept. (1893–1935). He owned a private collection of more than 2,000 hymn books; also a MS bibliography containing about 10,000 entries. He publ. *American Psalmondy, or Titles of Books Containing Tunes Printed in America from 1721 to 1820* (N.Y., 1917); *American Writers and Compilers of Sacred Music* (N.Y., 1925); *Stories of Hymn Tunes* (N.Y., 1928); also numerous articles.

Metheny, Pat(rick Bruce), American jazz and rock guitarist and composer; b. Lee's Summit, Mo., Aug. 12, 1954. He played horn in school, took up guitar at age 13, and taught at the Univ. of Miami and at the Berklee College of Music in Boston while still in his teens; played with vibraphonist Gary Burton's quartet (1974–77). From the mid-1970s, he played and toured widely with his own groups, especially with keyboardist Lyle Mays (b. Wausaukee, Wis., Nov. 27, 1953). His recordings include *Bright Size Life* (1975), *Watercolors* (1977), *Pat Metheny Group* (1978; an important success), *Chautauqua* (1979), *American Garage* (1980), *As Falls Wichita, So Falls Wichita Falls* (1981), *Offramp* (1982), *Travels* (1983), *Rejoicing* (1983), *First Circle* (1984), *Song X* (1986; with Ornette Coleman), and *Still Life (Talking)* (1987). His sound tracks include *Twice in a Lifetime* (1985) and *The Falcon and the Snowman* (1985). Metheny is a brilliant performer on both standard and 12-string electric guitars; his music is lyrical and unusual, related to both fusion and New Age.

Methfessel, Albert Gottlieb, German composer; b. Stadtilm, Thuringia, Oct. 6, 1785; d. Heckenbeck, near Gandersheim, March 23, 1869. From 1832 until 1842 he was court composer at Braunschweig, then retired on a pension. His brother, **Friedrich Methfessel** (b. Stadtilm, Aug. 27, 1771; d. there, May 14, 1807), publ. songs with guitar accompaniment.

WORKS: Opera, *Der Prinz von Basra;* oratorio, *Das befreite Jerusalem;* sonatas and sonatinas for Piano; part-songs, publ. in his *Liederbuch, Liederkranz,* and other collections.

Metianu, Lucian, Rumanian composer; b. Cluj, June 3, 1937. He studied with Olah, Vancea, Paul Constantinescu, and Chirescu at the Bucharest Cons. (1957–63).

WORKS: ORCH.: *Cantata de camera* for Chorus and Chamber Orch. (1953); Concerto for String Orch. (1959); 2 *Choreographic Tableaux* (1964); *Echo* (1966); *Ergodica* (1967); *Conexe* for Speaking Chorus and Orch. (1969); *Elogiu* (1969); *Evocare* (1972); *Evolutio II* (1976). **CHAMBER:** Piano Quintet (1960); 2 string quartets (1961, 1968); Piano Sonata (1962); *Pithagoreis* for Tape (1970–71); *Evolutio '73,* sonata for Solo Double Bass (1973); Duo for Double Bass and Cello (1974); *Evolutio '74* for Cello (1974).

Metner, Nikolai. See **Medtner, Nicolai.**

Métra, (Jules-Louis-) Olivier, French composer; b. Le Mans, June 2, 1830; d. Paris, Oct. 22, 1889. An actor's son, he became an actor himself as a boy; was 1st taught music by E. Roche; then was a pupil of Elwart at the Paris Cons. (1849–54). He played violin, cello, and double bass at Paris theaters; then conducted at various dance halls; the masked balls at the Opéra-Comique (1871); the orch. at the Folies-Bergère (1872–77); the balls at the Théâtre Royal de la Monnaie, Brussels (1874–76); finally, the balls at the Paris Opéra. His waltzes, mazurkas, polkas, quadrilles, etc., were extremely popular; at the Folies-Bergère, he produced 19 operettas and ballet divertissements; and at the Opéra, the ballet *Yedda* (Paris, Jan. 17, 1879).

Mettenleiter, Dominicus, German music historian, brother of **Johann Georg Mettenleiter;** b. Tannhausen, near Ellwan-

gen, May 20, 1822; d. Regensburg, May 2, 1868. He collaborated with his brother in the publication of his *Enchiridion chorale* and publ. on his own several valuable works dealing with music in Bavaria: *Aus der musikalischen Vergangenheit bayrischer Städte: Musikgeschichte der Stadt Regensburg* (Regensburg, 1866); *Musikgeschichte der Oberpfalz* (Amberg, 1867); etc. He also wrote a biography of his brother (Brixen, 1866) and of Karl Proske (Regensburg, 1868; 2nd ed., 1895). His valuable music collection was incorporated with Proske's library in Regensburg.

Mettenleiter, Johann Georg, German composer, brother of **Dominicus Mettenleiter;** b. St. Ulrich, near Ulm, April 6, 1812; d. Regensburg, Oct. 6, 1858. He was active as choirmaster and organist at the Regensburg Cathedral. An erudite church composer, he publ. *Manuale breve cantionum ac precum* (1852) and *Enchiridion chorale . . .* (1855), both with added organ accompaniments; also Psalm 95 for 6 Male Voices (1854); other works in MS (masses; a *Stabat Mater; 2 Miserere; Ave Maria* for Double Chorus; etc.).

BIBL.: D. Mettenleiter, *J.G. M.: Ein Künstlerbild* (Brixen, 1866).

Metzger, Heinz-Klaus, German writer on music; b. Konstanz, Feb. 6, 1932. He studied at the Staatliche Musikhochschule in Freiburg (1949–52), then studied composition with Max Deutsch in Paris and musicology in Tübingen (1952–54). He qualified in 1956 at the Akademie für Tonkunst in Darmstadt, where he later was active in the Darmstadt summer courses. His theoretical, philosophical, and cultural writings on modern and avant-garde music were influenced by Theodor Adorno, who recognized his talent. Metzger co-founded the journal *Musik-Konzepte* with Rainer Riehn in 1977. His relationship with Sylvano Bussotti led to his remarkable studies of music considered unanalyzable by other writers, by composers including Bussotti, Schnebel, and Kagel.

Metzler, Valentin, German-born English music publisher and instrument dealer; b. Bingen, date unknown; d. London, 1833. He settled in London about 1788 and opened a shop for the sale of musical instruments; after his death, his son George Richard Metzler (1797–1867) became the owner, and the name of the firm was changed to G. Metzler & Co. In 1816 the firm began to publ. music; in 1867 G. Metzler entered into partnership with Frank Chappell; the firm continued to carry on its business in London until 1930.

Meulemans, Arthur, eminent Belgian composer; b. Aarschot, May 19, 1884; d. Brussels, June 29, 1966. He studied with Edgar Tinel in Mechelen; in 1916 he founded the Limburg School for organ at Hasselt; he then moved to Brussels; conducted the radio orch. there (1930–42); in 1954 he was elected president of the Royal Flemish Academy of Fine Arts. He produced a prodigious amount of highly competent works in all genres.

WORKS: OPERAS: *Vikings* (1919); *Adriaen Brouwer* (1926); *Egmont* (1944; Antwerp, 1960). **ORCH.:** 15 syms.: No. 1 (1931); No. 2 (1933); No. 3, *Dennensymphonie* (1933); No. 4, for Winds and Percussion (1934); No. 5, *Danssymphonie,* with Female Chorus (1939); No. 6, *Zeesymphonie,* with Contralto and Mixed Chorus (1940); No. 7, *Zwaneven* (1942); No. 8, *Herfstsymphonie,* with Soli and Chorus (1942); No. 9 (1943); No. 10, *Psalmen-Symphonie,* with 2 Narrators, Soli, and Chorus (1943); No. 11 (1946); No. 12 (1948); No. 13, *Rembrandt-Symphonie* (1950); No. 14 (1954); No. 15 (1960); 3 sinfoniettas (1952; 1959–60; 1960); 2 ballet suites: *Josaphatpark* (1933) and *De Vogels* (1947); 3 oratorios: *Sacrum mysterium* (1917), *De zeven weeën* (1920), and *De dochter van Jaïrus* (1922); various symphonic poems, suites, and pieces that include: *Meinacht* (1912); *Plinius Fontein* (1913); *Karnaval-Suite* (1926); *Stadspark,* prelude and scherzo (1928); *Vlaamse rapsodie* (1932); *Verworvenheden* (1939); *Adagio* for Strings (1939); 4 *Symphonic Sketches* (1940); *Fusillé à l'aube* (1948); *De Witte,* with Chorus (1949); *Symphonic Triptych* (1951); *Meterologisch Instituut* (1951); *Tableaux* (1952); *Peter Breugel* (1952); *Hertog Jan van Brabant,* with Baritone (1953); *Social Security*, masquerade (1954); *Ionisatie*, choreographic movements (1956); *Relais* (1957), *Symphonic Dances* (1957); *Esquisses symphoniques* (1958); *Divertimento*, with Chorus (1958); *Aforismen* (1961); *Middelheim* (1961); *Partita* (1961); *Cirkus* (1961); *Torenhof* (1963); 2 Concertos for Orchestra (1953, 1956); many works for soloist and orch.: 3 piano concertos (1941, 1956, 1960); 2-Piano Concerto (1959); 3 violin concertos (1942, 1946, 1950); Viola Concerto (1942); 2 cello concertos (1920, 1944); Flute Concerto (1942); Oboe Concerto (1942); *Sonata concertante* for Clarinet and String Orch. (1948); 4-Clarinet Concertino (1963); 4-Clarinet Suite (1964); 4-Saxophone Concerto Grosso (1958); 4-Saxophone Concertino (1962); 2 horn concertos (1940, 1961); Trumpet Concerto (1943); Trombone Concertino (1953); Timpani Concerto (1954); Harp Concerto (1953); Harpsichord Concerto (1958); 2 organ concertos (1942, 1958); Concerto Grosso for 6 Winds, Strings, Harp, and Percussion (1962). CHAMBER: 5 string quartets (1915, 1932, 1933, 1944, 1952); 2 violin sonatas (1915, 1953); Viola Sonata (1953); Cello Sonata (1953); Trumpet Sonata (1959); Piano Trio (1941); String Trio (1941); 2 woodwind trios (1933, 1960); 2 brass trios (1933, 1960); Piano Quartet (1915); Woodwind Quartet (1962); Saxophone Quartet (1953); *Suite* for 4 Trombones (1942); 3 wind quintets (1931, 1932, 1958); Concerto for Organ, Trumpet, Horn, and Trombone (1962); many other works and solo pieces. PIANO: 3 sonatas (1916, 1917, 1951); 3 sonatinas (1927, 1928, 1941); *Refleksen* (1923); *Préludes* (1951); *Atmosferiliën* (1962). ORGAN: Sonata (1915); 2 syms. (1949); 7 *Pieces* (1959); *Pièce héroïque* (1959). He also wrote many pieces for carillon, a cappella choruses, and songs.

BIBL.: M. Boereboom, *A. M.* (Kortrijk, 1951); *Aan Meester A. M. bij zijn tachtigste verjaardag* (Antwerp, 1964).

Mewton-Wood, Noel, brilliant and forward-looking Australian pianist; b. Melbourne, Nov. 20, 1922; d. (by irrationally imbibing a mortal dose of prussic acid at the pitiful age of 31) London, Dec. 5, 1953. He had beneficial study in his hometown; was accepted at the Royal Academy of Music in London at 14; at 17, made an impressive debut at Queen's Hall, London; critics were unanimous in proclaiming him a great pianist. Having played most of the classical repertoire, he turned to musical moderns, assailing and conquering such formidable technical redoubts as Busoni's *Fantasia contrappuntistica* as well as the diatonically challenging Stravinsky Piano Concerto. He himself composed some piano music.

Meybom, Marcus. See **Meibom, Marcus.**

Meyer, Ernst Hermann, German musicologist and composer; b. Berlin, Dec. 8, 1905; d. there, Oct. 8, 1988. His father was a medical doctor of artistic interests who encouraged him to study music; he took piano lessons with Walter Hirschberg and played in chamber music groups. During the economic disarray in Germany in the 1920s, Meyer was obliged to do manual labor in order to earn a living. In 1926 he was able to enroll in the Univ. of Berlin, where he studied musicology with Johannes Wolf, Arnold Schering, Friedrich Blume, Erich Hornbostel, and Curt Sachs; in 1928 he had additional studies with Heinrich Besseler at the Univ. of Heidelberg, obtaining his Ph.D. in 1930 with the dissertation *Die mehrstimmige Spielmusik des 17. Jahrhunderts in Nord- und Mitteleuropa* (publ. in Kassel, 1934). In 1929 he met Eisler, who influenced him in the political aspect of music. In 1930 he joined the German Communist party. He conducted workers' choruses in Berlin and composed music for the proletarian revue *Der rote Stern* (The Red Star). He also attended classes on film music given by Hindemith. In 1931 he took a course in Marxism-Leninism with Hermann Duncker at the Marxist Workers' School in Berlin. He also began a detailed study of works by modern composers; in his own works, mostly for voices, he developed a style characteristic of the proletarian music of the time, full of affirmative action in march time adorned by corrosive discords, and yet eminently singable. When the Nazis bore down on his world with a different march, he fled to London, where, with the help of Alan Bush, he conducted the Labour Choral Union. During World War II, he participated in the Chorus of the Free German Cultural Union in London and wrote propaganda songs; of these, *Radio Moskau ruft Frau Krämer* was widely broadcast to Germany. In 1948 he went to East Berlin, where he was a prof. and director of the musicological inst. of the Humboldt Univ. until 1970. He was acknowledged as one of the most persuasive theoreticians of socialist realism in music; he founded the periodical *Musik und Gesellschaft*, which pursued the orthodox Marxist line. He publ. *English Chamber Music: The History of a Great Art from the Middle Ages to Purcell* (London, 1946; in German as *Die Kammermusik Alt-Englands*, East Berlin, 1958; new ed., rev., 1982, with D. Poulton as *Early English Chamber Music*); *Das Werk Beethovens und seine Bedeutung für das sozialistisch-realistische Gegenwartsschaffen* (East Berlin, 1970); and the autobiographical *Kontraste-Konflikte* (East Berlin, 1979). A Festschrift was publ. in his honor in Leipzig in 1973.

WORKS: OPERA: *Reiter der Nacht* (1969–72; Berlin, Nov. 17, 1973). **ORCH.:** Sym. for Strings (1946–47; rev. 1958); *Symphonischer Prolog*, dedicated to the memory of freedom fighters (1949); Sym. for Piano and Orch. (1961); *Poem* for Viola and Orch. (1962); Violin Concerto (1964); *Serenata pensierosa* (1965); Concerto Grosso (1966); Sym. in B-flat (1967); Harp Concerto (1969); Toccata (1971); *Divertimento* (1973); Concerto for Orch. with Piano obbligato (1975); *Kontraste, Konflikte* (1977); Viola Concerto (1978); *Sinfonietta* (1980); *Berliner Divertimento* (1981); *Kammersinfonie* (1983; transcription of the 5th String Quartet); *Sinfonische widmung* for Orch. and Concertante Organ (1983). **CHAMBER:** Trio for Flute, Oboe, and Harp (1935); Clarinet Quintet (1944); Piano Trio, *Reflections and Resolution* (1948); 6 string quartets (1956, 1959, 1967, 1974, 1978, 1982); *Sonatina Fantasia* for Violin Solo (1966); Viola Sonata (1979); Piano Trio (1980); Violin Sonata (1984). **CHORAL:** *Mansfelder Oratorium* (1950); cantata, *Nun, Steuermann*, after Walt Whitman's *Now Voyager* (1946; rev. 1955); *Gesang von der Jugend* for Soloists, Mixed Chorus, Children's Chorus, and Orch. (1957); *Das Tor von Buchenwald* (1959); *Der Staat* for Chorus and Orch. (1967); *Lenin hat gesprochen* (1970); also more than 200 mass songs; piano pieces; film music.

BIBL.: K. Niemann, *E.H. M.: Für Sie porträtiert* (Leipzig, 1975); M. Hansen, ed., *E.H. M.: Das kompositiorische und theoretische Werk* (Leipzig, 1976); A. Cross, "The Music of E.H. M.," *Musical Times* (Dec. 1980).

Meyer, Kerstin (Margareta), Swedish mezzo-soprano; b. Stockholm, April 3, 1928. She studied at the Royal Academy of Music (1948–50) and at the Opera School (1950–52) in Stockholm; also at the Accademia Chigiana in Siena and at the Salzburg Mozarteum. In 1952 she made her operatic debut as Azucena at the Royal Theater in Stockholm, where she subsequently sang regularly; also made guest appearances in numerous European opera centers and toured widely as a concert artist. In 1960 she made her 1st appearance at London's Covent Garden as Dido in the English-language production of *Les Troyens*. On Oct. 29, 1960, she made her Metropolitan Opera debut in N.Y. as Carmen, remaining on its roster until 1963; also appeared at the Bayreuth Festivals (1962–65). In 1963 she was made a Royal Swedish Court Singer. Following her retirement, she served as director of the Opera School in Stockholm (from 1984). In 1985 she was made an honorary Commander of the Order of the British Empire. She excelled particularly in contemporary operas, most notably in the works of Schuller, Searle, Henze, Maw, and Ligeti; among her standard portrayals were Orfeo, Dorabella, Fricka, Octavian, and Clytemnestra.

Meyer, Krzysztof, remarkable Polish composer; b. Krakow, Aug. 11, 1943. He played piano as a child; then took lessons in composition with Stanislaw Wiechowicz; subsequently undertook formal studies at the State College of Music in Krakow, where he obtained 2 diplomas: in 1965 in composition with Penderecki, and in 1966 in general music theory with Aleksander Frączkiewicz. In 1964, 1966, and 1968 he went to Paris, where he took courses with Boulanger; won several prizes at various competitions in France and in Poland. From 1965 to 1967 he appeared as a pianist with the contemporary music group MW-2; then was a prof. at the Krakow Cons. (1966–87) and at the Cologne Hochschule für Musik (from 1987). Among his honors were the Award of the Minister of Culture and Arts in Poland (1975) and the Medal of the Government of Brazil (1975). In 1984 he received the Gottfried von Herder Prize of Austria. Apart from his activities as a pianist and a composer, he also contributed to Polish music journals, and publ. the 1st Polish-language monograph on Shostakovich, which was also tr. into German. His musical intelligence and acoustical acuity are of the rarest quality. As a composer, he adopts an advanced idiom without ever transcending the practical limits of instrumental and vocal techniques or of aural perception. As a demonstration of his talent for sophisticated mimicry, he composed a Mozartean sym. that is apt to confuse and seduce the most solemn Mozartologist. (It was, perhaps coincidentally, 1st performed on April Fools' Day in 1977.) Nadia Boulanger wrote of Meyer: "Il est un musicien tout à fait exceptionnel" (*Le Figaro*, Paris, May 7, 1970). He completed Dmitri Shostakovich's discarded opera *The Gamblers* (begun in 1942 with only 40 minutes of music completed) in 1980–81; three-fourths of the work is Meyer's "impersonation" of Shostakovich's style; the "completed" opera was premiered in Wuppertal (June 12, 1983).

WORKS: STAGE: Fantastic comic opera, *Cyberiada*, libretto by composer after the novel by Stanislaw Lem (1967–70; Polish TV, 1971); ballet, *The Countess*, based on an opera by S. Moniuszko (1980). **ORCH.:** 6 syms.: No. 1, *4 Fragments for Orchestra* (1964); No. 2, *Epitaphium Stanislaw Wiechowicz in memoriam* for Chorus and Orch. (1967); No. 3, *Symphonie d'Orphée* for Chorus and Orch., after Valéry (1968); No. 4 (1973); No. 5 (1979); No. 6 (1982); *Concerto da camera* for Flute, Percussion, and Strings (1964); Violin Concerto (1965); Cello Concerto (1971–72); Concerto da Camera for Oboe, Percussion, and Strings (1972); Trumpet Concerto (1975); *Fireballs* (1976); *Interludio dramatico* for Oboe and Chamber Orch. (1980); also a Sym. in D in the style of Mozart (1976). **VOCAL:** *Songs of Resignation and Denial* for Soprano, Violin, and Piano (1963); Quartettino for Soprano, Flute, Cello, and Piano (1966); *5 Chamber Pieces* for Soprano, Clarinet, Violin, and Viola (1967); *Polish Chants* for Soprano and Chamber Orch. (1974); *Lyric Triptych* for Tenor and Chamber Orch., after Auden (1976). **CHAMBER:** 7 string quartets (1963, 1969, 1971, 1974, 1977, 1981, 1985); *Quattro colori* for Clarinet, Trombone, Cello, and Piano (1971); Solo Violin Sonata (1975); *3 Pieces* for Percussion and Tape (1976); *Concerto retro* for Flute, Violin, Cello, and Harpsichord (1976); Piano Trio (1980); Flute Sonata (1980); Cello Sonata (1983). **PIANO:** *Aphorism* (1961); 5 sonatas (1962, 1963, 1966, 1968, 1975); *Magic Pictures* (1975); *Children's Suite* (1978); *24 Preludes* (1978); also a Harpsichord Sonata (1973).

Meyer, Leonard B(unce), noted American musicologist and esthetician; b. N.Y., Jan. 12, 1918. He studied at Bard College (1936–38); took courses in philosophy at Columbia Univ. (B.A., 1940) and also received private instruction in composition from Weigl (1938–39) and Wolpe (1939–41); then with Copland at the Berkshire Music Center at Tanglewood (1946) and Luening at Columbia Univ. (M.A., 1948); subsequently took courses in the history of culture at the Univ. of Chicago (Ph.D., 1954). He taught in the music dept. of the Univ. of Chicago (1946–60); was at the Center for Advanced Studies at Wesleyan Univ. (1960–61); then returned to the Univ. of Chicago as a prof. and chairman of its music dept. (1961–70); after serving as the Ernest Bloch Prof. at the Univ. of Calif. at Berkeley (1970–71), he returned to the Univ. of Chicago as a prof. in the humanities (1972–75); then was a prof. of music and humanities at the Univ. of Pa. (from 1975). He publ. an important book dealing with the problems of communication and cultural contexts in the human response to music, *Emotion and Mean-*

ing in Music (Chicago, 1956); also *The Rhythmic Structure of Music* (with G. Cooper; Chicago, 1960); *Music, the Arts, and Ideas: Patterns and Predictions in Twentieth Century Culture* (Chicago, 1967); *Explaining Music: Essays and Explorations* (Berkeley and Los Angeles, 1973); *Style and Music: Theory, History, and Ideology* (Philadelphia, 1989).

BIBL.: E. Narmour and R. Solie, eds., *Explorations in Music, the Arts, and Ideas: Essays in Honor of L.B. M.* (Stuyvesant, N.Y., 1989).

Meyer, Leopold von (called **Leopold de Meyer**), celebrated Austrian pianist; b. Baden, near Vienna, Dec. 20, 1816; d. Dresden, March 5, 1883. He studied with Czerny and Fischhof; at the age of 19, embarked on a series of pianistic tours in Europe; also toured in America (1845–47). At his concerts he invariably included his own compositions, written in a characteristic salon style; his agents spread sensational publicity about him in order to arouse interest. A *Biography of Leopold de Meyer* was publ. in London in 1845.

BIBL.: R. Lott, *The American Concert Tours of L. d.M., Henri Herz, and Sigismond Thalberg* (diss., City Univ. of N.Y., 1986).

Meyer-Helmund, Erik, German composer; b. St. Petersburg, April 25, 1861; d. Berlin, April 4, 1932. He studied music with his father; then in Berlin with Kiel; was 1st a singer, and traveled extensively in Europe, introducing his own songs; from 1911 he lived in Berlin. He is best known as a song composer; more than 200 of his light vocal numbers were publ.; he also composed 5 operas: *Margitta* (Magdeburg, 1889), *Der Liebeskampf* (Dresden, 1892), *Taglioni* (Berlin, 1912), *Traumbilder* (Berlin, 1912), and *Die schöne Frau Marlies* (Altenburg, 1916); also the operettas *Trischka* (Riga, 1894) and *Lucullus* (Riga, 1905); the ballet *Rübezahl* (Leipzig, 1893); male choruses; piano pieces in a Romantic vein (*Wonnetraum*, *Sérénade rococo*, etc.); *Fantasie* for Violin and Orch.; etc.

Meyer-Olbersleben, Max, German pianist, conductor, teacher, and composer; b. Olbersleben, near Weimar, April 5, 1850; d. Würzburg, Dec. 31, 1927. He 1st studied with his father; then with Liszt at Weimar. On Liszt's recommendation, he received a liberal allowance from the government for further study; took lessons in Munich with Cornelius and Rheinberger. In 1876 he became a teacher of piano and theory at Wüllner-Hartung's orch. school in Weimar; in 1877, was appointed to the staff of the Würzburg Cons., of which he became director in 1907; also conducted the famous Liedertafel from 1879. He was a composer of talent and ability; his chamber music is effectively and competently written; he also publ. songs and piano pieces; also wrote a "romantic opera," *Clare Dettin* (Würzburg, 1896), and a comic opera, *Der Haubenkrieg* (Munich, 1902).

Meyer-Siat, Pie, French musicologist; b. Ribeauvillé, Haut-Rhin, Oct. 15, 1913; d. Strasbourg, April 4, 1989. He was educated at the Univ. of Strasbourg; received a degree in philosophy in 1937; took the agrégation in German in 1948; was awarded his Ph.D. in musicology in 1962 with the dissertation *Les Callinet, facteurs d'orgues à Rouffach, et leur œuvre en Alsace*, publ. in Strasbourg, 1965. He was an authority on organs in Alsace; contributed important articles for *Les Cahiers de la Société d'Histoire de Saverne*.

WRITINGS: *L'Orgue Callinet de Masevaux* (Mulhouse, 1962); *L'Orgue Joseph Callinet de Mollau* (Haut-Rhin) (Strasbourg, 1963); *Les Orgues de Niedernai et d'Obernai* (Colmar, 1972); *Stiehr-Mockers, facteurs d'orgues* (Hagenau, 1972); *Historische Orgeln im Elsass, 1489–1869* (Munich, 1983).

Meyerbeer, Giacomo (real name, **Jakob Liebmann Beer**), famous German composer; b. Vogelsdorf, near Berlin, Sept. 5, 1791; d. Paris, May 2, 1864. He was a scion of a prosperous Jewish family of merchants. He added the name Meyer to his surname, and later changed his 1st name for professional purposes. He began piano studies with Franz Lauska, and also received some instruction from Clementi; made his public debut in Berlin when he was 11. He then studied composition with Zelter (1805–7), and subsequently with B.A. Weber. It was as Weber's pupil that he composed his 1st stage work, the ballet-pantomime *Der Fischer und das Milchmädchen*, which was produced at the Berlin Royal Theater (March 26, 1810). He then went to Darmstadt to continue his studies with Abbé Vogler until late 1811; one of his fellow pupils was Carl Maria von Weber. While under Vogler's tutelage, he composed the oratorio *Gott und die Natur* (Berlin, May 8, 1811) and also the operas *Der Admiral* (1811; not perf.) and *Jephthas Gelübde* (Munich, Dec. 23, 1812). His next opera, *Wirth und Gast, oder Aus Scherz Ernst* (Stuttgart, Jan. 6, 1813), was not a success; revised as *Die beyden Kalifen* for Vienna, it likewise failed there (Oct. 20, 1814). However, he did find success in Vienna as a pianist in private musical settings. In Nov. 1814 he proceeded to Paris, and in Dec. 1815 to London. He went to Italy early in 1816, and there turned his attention fully to dramatic composition. His Italian operas—*Romilda e Costanza* (Padua, July 19, 1817), *Semiramide riconosciuta* (Turin, March 1819), *Emma di Resburgo* (Venice, June 26, 1819), *Margherita d'Angiù* (Milan, Nov. 14, 1820), *L'Esule di Granata* (Milan, March 12, 1821), and *Il Crociato in Egitto* (Venice, March 7, 1824)—brought him fame there, placing him on a par with the celebrated Rossini in public esteem. The immense success of *Il Crociato in Egitto* in particular led to a successful staging at London's King's Theatre (July 23, 1825), followed by a triumphant Paris production (Sept. 25, 1825), which made Meyerbeer famous throughout Europe. To secure his Paris position, he revamped *Margherita d'Angiù* for the French stage as *Margherita d'Anjou* (March 11, 1826). He began a long and distinguished association with the dramatist and librettist Eugène Scribe in 1827 as work commenced on the opera *Robert le diable*. It was produced at the Paris Opéra on Nov. 21, 1831, with extraordinary success.

Numerous honors were subsequently bestowed upon Meyerbeer; he was made a Chevalier of the Légion d'Honneur and a Prussian Hofkapellmeister in 1832, a member of the senate of the Prussian Academy of Arts in 1833, and a member of the Institut de France in 1834. He began work on what was to become the opera *Les Huguenots* in 1832; set to a libretto mainly by Scribe, it was accorded a spectacular premiere at the Opéra on Feb. 29, 1836. Late in 1836 he and Scribe began work on a new opera, *Le Prophète*. He also commenced work on the opera *L'Africaine* in Aug. 1837, again utilizing a libretto by Scribe; it was initially written for the famous soprano Marie-Cornélie Falcon; however, after the loss of her voice, Meyerbeer set the score aside; it was destined to occupy him on and off for the rest of his life. In 1839 Wagner sought out Meyerbeer in Boulogne. Impressed with Wagner, Meyerbeer extended him financial assistance and gave him professional recommendations. However, Wagner soon became disenchanted with his prospects and berated Meyerbeer in private, so much so that Meyerbeer was compelled to disassociate himself from Wagner. The ungrateful Wagner retaliated by giving vent to his anti-Semitic rhetoric.

Meyerbeer began work on *Le Prophète* in earnest in 1838, completing it by 1840. However, its premiere was indefinitely delayed as the composer attempted to find capable singers. On May 20, 1842, *Les Huguenots* was performed in Berlin. On June 11, 1842, Meyerbeer was formally installed as Prussian Generalmusikdirektor. From the onset of his tenure, disagreement with the Intendant of the Royal Opera, Karl Theodor von Küstner, made his position difficult. Finally, on Nov. 26, 1848, Meyerbeer was dismissed from his post, although he retained his position as director of music for the royal court; in this capacity he composed a number of works for state occasions, including the opera *Ein Feldlager in Schlesien*, which reopened the opera house on Dec. 7, 1844, following its destruction by fire. The leading role was sung by Jenny Lind, one of Meyerbeer's discoveries. It had a modicum of success after its 1st performance in Vienna under the title *Vielka* in 1847, although it never equaled the success of his Paris operas. In 1849 he again took up the score of *Le Prophète*. As he could find no tenor to meet its demands, he completely revised the score for the celebrated soprano Pauline Viardot-

García. With Viardot-García as Fidès and the tenor Gustave Roger as John of Leyden, it received a brilliant premiere at the Opéra on April 16, 1849, a success that led to Meyerbeer's being made the 1st German Commandeur of the Légion d'Honneur. His next opera was *L'Étoile du nord*, which utilized music from *Ein Feldlager in Schlesien*; its 1st performance at the Opéra-Comique on Feb. 16, 1854, proved an outstanding success. Equally successful was his opera *Le Pardon de Ploërmel* (Opéra-Comique, April 4, 1859). In 1862 he composed a special work for the London World Exhibition, the *Fest-Ouverture im Marschstyl*, and made a visit to England during the festivities. In the meantime, work on *L'Africaine* had occupied him fitfully for years; given Scribe's death in 1861 and Meyerbeer's own failing health, he was compelled to finally complete it. In April 1864 he put the finishing touches on the score and rehearsals began under his supervision. However, he died on the night of May 2, 1864, before the work was premiered. His body was taken to Berlin, where it was laid to rest in official ceremonies attended by the Prussian court, prominent figures in the arts, and the public at large. Fétis was subsequently charged with making the final preparations for the premiere of *L'Africaine*, which was given at the Paris Opéra to notable acclaim on April 28, 1865.

Meyerbeer established himself as the leading composer of French grand opera in 1831 with *Robert le diable*, a position he retained with distinction throughout his career. Indeed, he became one of the most celebrated musicians of his era. Although the grandiose conceptions and stagings of his operas proved immediately appealing to audiences, his dramatic works were more than mere theatrical spectacles. His vocal writing was truly effective, for he often composed and tailored his operas with specific singers in mind. Likewise, his gift for original orchestration and his penchant for instrumental experimentation placed his works on a high level. Nevertheless, his stature as a composer was eclipsed after his death by Richard Wagner. As a consequence, his operas disappeared from the active repertoire, although revivals and several recordings saved them from total oblivion in the modern era.

WORKS: OPERAS: *Jephthas Gelübde* (Munich, Dec. 23, 1812); *Wirth und Gast, oder Aus Scherz Ernst*, Lustspiel (Stuttgart, Jan. 6, 1813; rev. as *Die beyden Kalifen*, Vienna, Oct. 20, 1814; later known as *Alimelek*); *Das Brandenburger Tor*, singspiel (1814; not perf.); *Romilda e Costanza*, melodramma semiserio (Padua, July 19, 1817); *Semiramide riconosciuta*, dramma per musica (Turin, March 1819); *Emma di Resburgo*, melodramma eroico (Venice, June 26, 1819); *Margherita d'Angiù*, melodramma semiserio (Milan, Nov. 14, 1820; rev. as *Margherita d'Anjou*, Paris, March 11, 1826); *L'Almanzore* (1821; not perf.); *L'Esule di Granata*, melodramma serio (Milan, March 12, 1821); *Il Crociato in Egitto*, melodramma eroico (Venice, March 7, 1824); *Robert le diable*, grand opéra (Paris, Nov. 21, 1831); *Les Huguenots*, grand opéra (Paris, Feb. 29, 1836); *Ein Feldlager in Schlesien*, singspiel (Berlin, Dec. 7, 1844; later known as *Vielka*); *Le Prophète*, grand opéra (Paris, April 16, 1849); *L'Étoile du nord*, opéra-comique (Paris, Feb. 16, 1854; much of the music based on *Ein Feldlager in Schlesien*); *Le Pardon de Ploërmel*, opéra-comique (Paris, April 4, 1859; also known as *Le Chercheur du trésor* and as *Dinorah, oder Die Wallfahrt nach Ploërmel*); *L'Africaine*, grand opéra (Paris, April 28, 1865; originally known as *Vasco da Gama*). He also left a number of unfinished operas in various stages of development. Other stage works include *Der Fischer und das Milchmädchen, oder Viel Lärm um einen Kuss* (*Le Passage de la rivière, ou La Femme jalouse; Le Pêcheur et la laitière*), ballet-pantomime (Berlin, March 26, 1810); *Gli amori di Teolinda* (*Thecelindens Liebschaften*), monodrama (Genoa, 1816); *Das Hoffest von Ferrara*, masque (Berlin, Feb. 28, 1843); *Struensee*, incidental music for a drama by Michael Beer, Meyerbeer's brother (Berlin, Sept. 19, 1846); etc.

SACRED: *Gott und die Natur*, oratorio (Berlin, May 8, 1811); *Geistliche Gesänge*, 7 odes after Klopstock, for Soprano, Alto, Tenor, and Bass (Leipzig, 1817 or 1818); *An Gott*, hymn for Soprano, Alto, Tenor, Bass, and Piano (Leipzig, 1817); Psalm

XCI for Soprano, Alto, Tenor, Bass, and Double Mixed Chorus a cappella (Berlin, 1853); *Prière du matin* for 2 Choirs and Piano ad libitum (Paris, 1864); etc.

OCCASIONAL AND SECULAR CHORAL: *Festgesang zur Errichtung des Gutenbergischen Denkmals in Mainz* for 2 Tenors, 2 Basses, Men's Voices, and Piano ad libitum (Mainz, 1835); *Dem Vaterland* for Men's Voices (Berlin, 1842); *Le Voyageur au tombeau de Beethoven* for Bass Solo and Women's Voices a cappella (1845); *Festhymne* for Solo Voices, Chorus, and Piano ad libitum (for the silver wedding anniversary of the King and Queen of Prussia, 1848); *Ode an Rauch* for Solo Voices, Chorus, and Orch. (in honor of the sculptor Christian Rauch; Berlin, 1851); *Maria und ihr Genius*, cantata for Soprano, Tenor, Chorus, and Piano (for the silver wedding anniversary of Prince and Princess Carl, 1852); *Brautgeleite aus der Heimat*, serenade for Chorus a cappella (for the wedding of Princess Luise, 1856); *Festgesang zur Feier des 100-jährigen Geburtsfestes von Friedrich Schiller* for Soprano, Alto, Tenor, Bass, Chorus, and Orch. (1859); *Festhymnus* for Solo Voices, Chorus, and Piano ad libitum (for the coronation of Wilhelm I, 1861); etc.

ORCH.: Sym. in E-flat major (1811); Piano Concerto (1811); Concerto for Piano and Violin (1812); 4 *Fackeltänze* for Military Band or Orch. (1844, 1850, 1856, 1858); *Festmarsch* for the centenary of Schiller's birth (1859); *Krönungsmarsch* for 2 Orchs. (for the coronation of Wilhelm I, 1861); *Fest-Ouverture im Marschstyl* (for the opening of the World Exhibition in London, 1862); etc. He also composed many fine songs, as well as pieces for piano.

BIBL.: A. Morel, *Le Prophète: Analyse critique de la nouvelle partition de G. M.* (Paris, 1849); E. Lindner, *M.s "Prophet" als Kunstwerk beurtheilt* (Berlin, 1850); E. de Mirecourt, *M.* (Paris, 1854); A. de Lasalle, *M., Sa vie et le catalogue de ses œuvres* (Paris, 1864); A. Pougin, *M.: Notes biographiques* (Paris, 1864); H. Blaze de Bury, *M. et son temps* (Paris, 1865); H. Mendel, *G. M.* (Berlin, 1868); J. Schucht, *M.s Leben und Bildungsgang* (Leipzig, 1869); A. Body, *M. aux eaux de Spa* (Brussels, 1885); A. Kohut, *M.* (Leipzig, 1890); E. Destranges, *L'Œuvre théâtral de M.* (Paris, 1893); J. Weber, *M.: Notes et souvenirs d'un de ses secrétaires* (Paris, 1898); J.-G. Prod'homme, "Die Hugenotten-Premiere," *Die Musik*, III/1 (1903–4); H. de Curzon, *M.: Biographie critique* (Paris, 1910); H. Eymieu, *L'Œuvre de M.* (Paris, 1910); L. Dauriac, *M.* (Paris, 1913; 2nd ed., 1930); L. Hirschberg, "M.s religiöse Tonwerke," *Die Musik*, XIII/3 (1914); G. Kruse, "M.s Jugendopern," *Zeitschrift für Musikwissenschaft*, I (1918–19); J. Kapp, *G. M.* (Berlin, 1920; 8th ed., rev., 1932); H. Strelitzer, *M.s deutsche Jugendopern* (diss., Univ. of Münster, 1920); A. Brent Smith, "The Tragedy of M.," *Music & Letters*, VI (1925); E. Istel, "M.'s Way to Mastership," *Musical Quarterly* (Jan. 1926); G. Servières, "Les Transformations et tribulations de *L'Africaine*," *Rivista Musicale Italiana*, XXXIV (1927); R. Haudek, *Scribes Operntexte für M.: Eine Quellenuntersuchung* (diss., Univ. of Vienna, 1928); H. Abert, "G. M.," *Gesammelte Schriften und Vorträge* (Halle, 1929); J. Cooke, *M.* (Philadelphia, 1929); J.-G. Prod'homme, "M. à Paris avant 'Robert le diable,' d'après son journal inédit," *Mercure de France* (April 14, 1936); H. Becker, "M.s Ergänzungsarbeit an Webers nachgelassener Oper 'Die drei Pintos,'" *Die Musikforschung*, VII (1954); idem, *Der Fall Heine-M.: Neue Dokumente revidieren ein Geschichtsurteil* (Berlin, 1958); idem, ed., *G. M.: Briefwechsel und Tagebücher* (4 vols., Berlin, 1960–85); idem, "G. M.," *Leo Baeck Institute: Yearbook*, IX (London, 1964); M. Brod, "Some Comments on the Relationship between Wagner and M.," ibid.; H. Kirchmeyer, "Psychologie des M.-Erfolges," *Neue Zeitschrift für Musik*, 125 (Jg. 1964); J. Klein, "G. M. (1791–1864)," *Music Review*, XXV (1964); J. Meyerowitz, "G. M.," *Musica*, XIX (1965); C. Frese, *Dramaturgie der grossen Opern G. M.s* (Berlin, 1970); S. Döhring, "Les Œuvres tardives de M.," *Schweizerische Musikzeitung/Revue Musicale Suisse*, XCV (1975); M. Loppert, "An Introduction to 'L'Étoile du nord,'" *Musical Times*, CXVI (1975); J. Thomson, "G. M.: The Jew and His Relationship with Richard Wagner," *Musica Judaica*, I (1975–76); H. Becker, *G. M. in Selbstzeugnissen und Bilddokumenten* (Rein-

bek, 1980); J. Fulcher, "M. and the Music of Society," *Musical Quarterly* (April 1981); H. and G. Becker, *G. M.: Ein Leben in Briefen* (Wilhelmshaven, 1983; Eng. tr., 1989); S. Segalini, *M.: Diable ou prophète?* (Paris, 1985).

Meyerowitz, Jan (actually, **Hans-Hermann**), German-born American composer; b. Breslau, April 23, 1913. In 1927 he went to Berlin, where he studied with Gmeindl and Zemlinsky at the Hochschule für Musik. Compelled to leave Germany in 1933, he went to Rome, where he took lessons in advanced composition with Respighi and Casella, and in conducting with Molinari. In 1938 he moved to Belgium and later to southern France, where he remained until 1946; he then emigrated to the U.S., becoming a naturalized citizen in 1951. He married the French singer Marguerite Fricker in 1946. He held a Guggenheim fellowship twice (1956, 1958). In the U.S. he taught at the Berkshire Music Center in Tanglewood (1948–51) and at Brooklyn (1954–61) and City (1962–80) Colleges of the City Univ. of N.Y. He publ. a monograph on Schoenberg (Berlin, 1967) and *Der echte jüdische Witz* (Berlin, 1971). His music is imbued with expansive emotionalism akin to that of Mahler; in his works for the theater there is a marked influence of the tradition of 19th-century grand opera. His technical idiom is modern, enlivened by a liberal infusion of euphonious dissonance, and he often applies the rigorous and vigorous devices of linear counterpoint.

WORKS: OPERAS: *The Barrier*, to a libretto by Langston Hughes (N.Y., Jan. 18, 1950); *Eastward in Eden* (title changed later to *Emily Dickinson*; Detroit, Nov. 16, 1951); *Simoon* (Tanglewood, Aug. 2, 1950); *Bad Boys in School* (Tanglewood, Aug. 17, 1953); *Esther*, libretto by Langston Hughes (Univ. of Illinois, Urbana, May 17, 1957); *Port Town*, libretto by Langston Hughes (Tanglewood, Aug. 4, 1960); *Godfather Death* (N.Y., June 2, 1961); *Die Doppelgängerin*, after Gerhart Hauptmann (title changed later to conform with the original title of Hauptmann's play, *Winterballade*; Hannover, Jan. 29, 1967). ORCH.: *Silesian Symphony* (1957); *Symphony Midrash Esther* (N.Y., Jan. 31, 1957); *Flemish Overture* (Cleveland, 1959); Flute Concerto (1962); Oboe Concerto (1963); *Sinfonia brevissima* (Corpus Christi, Texas, 1965); *6 Pieces for Orchestra* (Pittsburgh, May 27, 1967); *7 Pieces for Orchestra* (Turin, 1972); 6 Songs for Soprano and Orch., after A. von Platen (1976; Cologne, Feb. 12, 1979). CANTATAS: *Music for Christmas* (N.Y., 1954); *The Glory around His Head* (N.Y., April 14, 1955); *Missa Rachel Plorans* (N.Y., Nov. 5, 1955); *The Rabbis* (text from the Talmud; Turin, 1965); several solo cantatas, among them *Emily Dickinson Cantata*; *6 Songs* to poems by August von Platen for Soprano and Orch. (Cologne, Feb. 12, 1977). CHAMBER: Woodwind Quintet (1954); String Quartet (1955); Cello Sonata (1946); Trio for Flute, Cello, and Piano (1946); Violin Sonata (1960); Flute Sonata (1961); Piano Sonata (1958); *Homage to Hieronymus Bosch* for 2 Pianos, 4-hands (1945); songs.

Meyerowitz, Selmar, German conductor; b. Bartenstein, East Prussia, April 18, 1875; d. Toulouse, March 24, 1941. He studied at the Leipzig Cons., and later with Max Bruch in Berlin; in 1897, became assistant conductor at the Karlsruhe Opera under Mottl, with whom he went to America as conductor at the Metropolitan Opera in N.Y. (1903); subsequently conducted at the Prague National Theater (1905–6), the Berlin Komische Oper (1907–10), the Munich Opera (1912–13), and the Hamburg Opera (1913–17); after appearing as a guest conductor with the Berlin Phil., he conducted at the Berlin Radio and the State Opera (1924–33); also toured with the German Grand Opera Co. in the U.S. (1929–31); settled in France (1933).

Mézeray, Louis (-Charles-Lazare-Costard) de, French baritone, conductor, and composer; b. Braunschweig, Nov. 25, 1810; d. Asnières, near Paris, April 1887. As a young man, he conducted theater orchs. in Strasbourg and elsewhere; at 17, he obtained the post of conductor at the Liège Theater; at 20, he became conductor at the Court Theater in The Hague, where he brought out his heroic opera *Guillaume de Nassau*; subsequently he studied with Reicha in Paris; again traveled as a theater conductor in France, and also appeared as a baritone; finally, in 1843, he became chief conductor at the Grand Théâtre in Bordeaux, and brought the standard of performance there to a very high level.

Miaskovsky, Nikolai (Yakovlevich), eminent Russian composer and teacher; b. Novogeorgievsk, near Warsaw, April 20, 1881; d. Moscow, Aug. 8, 1950. His father was an officer of the dept. of military fortification; the family lived in Orenburg (1888–89) and in Kazan (1889–93). In 1893 he was sent to a military school in Nizhny-Novgorod; in 1895 he went to a military school in St. Petersburg, graduating in 1899. At that time he developed an interest in music, and tried to compose; took lessons with Kazanli; his 1st influences were Chopin and Tchaikovsky. In 1902–3 he was in Moscow, where he studied harmony with Glière. Returning to St. Petersburg in 1903, he took lessons with Kryzhanovsky, from whom he acquired a taste for modernistic composition in the impressionist style. In 1906, at the age of 25, he entered the St. Petersburg Cons. as a pupil of Liadov and Rimsky-Korsakov, graduating in 1911. At the outbreak of World War I in 1914, Miaskovsky was called into active service in the Russian army; in 1916 he was removed to Reval to work on military fortifications; he remained in the army after the Bolshevik Revolution of 1917; in 1918 he became a functionary in the Maritime Headquarters in Moscow; was finally demobilized in 1921. In that year he became prof. of composition at the Moscow Cons., remaining at that post to the end of his life. A composer of extraordinary ability, a master of his craft, Miaskovsky wrote 27 syms., much chamber music, piano pieces, and songs; his music is marked by structural strength and emotional élan; he never embraced extreme forms of modernism, but adopted workable devices of tonal expansion short of polytonality, and freely modulating melody short of atonality. His style was cosmopolitan; only in a few works did he inject folkloric elements. His autobiographical notes were publ. in *Sovetskaya Muzyka* (June 1936); S. Shlifstein ed. a vol. of articles, letters, and reminiscences (Moscow, 1959) and a vol. of articles, notes, and reviews (Moscow, 1960).

WORKS: ORCH. (all 1st perf. in Moscow unless otherwise given): SYMS.: No. 1 in C minor, op. 3 (1908; Pavlovsk, June 2, 1914); No. 2 in C-sharp minor, op. 11 (1910–11; July 24, 1912); No. 3 in A minor, op. 15 (1913–14; Feb. 27, 1915); No. 4 in E minor, op. 17 (1917–18; Feb. 8, 1925); No. 5 in D major, op. 18 (1918; July 18, 1920); No. 6 in E-flat minor, op. 23 (1922–23; May 4, 1924); No. 7 in B minor, op. 24 (1922; Feb. 8, 1925); No. 8 in A major, op. 26 (1924–25; May 23, 1926); No. 9 in E minor, op. 28 (1926–27; April 29, 1928); No. 10 in F minor, op. 30 (1927; April 7, 1928); No. 11 in B-flat minor, op. 34 (1931–32; Jan. 16, 1933); No. 12 in G minor, op. 35 (June 1, 1932); No. 13 in B-flat minor, op. 36 (1933; Winterthur, Oct. 16, 1934); No. 14 in C major, op. 37 (1933; Feb. 24, 1935); No. 15 in D minor, op. 38 (1933–34; Oct. 28, 1935); No. 16 in F major, op. 39 (Oct. 24, 1936); No. 17 in G-sharp minor, op. 41 (Dec. 17, 1937); No. 18 in C major, op. 42 (Oct. 1, 1937); No. 19 in E-flat major for Band (Feb. 15, 1939); No. 20 in E major, op. 50 (Nov. 28, 1940); No. 21 in F-sharp minor, op. 51 (Nov. 16, 1940; perf. as a commissioned work as *Symphonie fantaisie* by the Chicago Sym. Orch., Dec. 26, 1940); No. 22 in B minor, op. 54, *Symphonie ballade* (1941; Tbilisi, Jan. 12, 1942); No. 23 in A minor, op. 56, *Symphony-Suite* (1941; July 20, 1942); No. 24 in F minor, op. 63 (Dec. 8, 1943); No. 25 in D-flat major, op. 69 (1946; March 6, 1947); No. 26 in C major, op. 79 (Dec. 28, 1948); No. 27 in C minor, op. 85 (Dec. 9, 1950). OTHER ORCH.: Overture in G major for Small Orch. (1909; rev. 1949); *Molchaniye* (Silence), op. 9, symphonic poem after Poe (1909; June 13, 1914); Sinfonietta in A major, op. 10, for Small Orch. (1910; rev. 1943); *Alastor*, op. 14, symphonic poem after Shelley (1912–13; Nov. 18, 1914); Serenade in E-flat major, op. 32/1, for Small Orch. (Oct. 7, 1929); Sinfonietta in C minor, op. 32/2, for Strings (May 1930); *Lyric Concertino* in G major, op. 32/2, for Small Orch. (Oct. 7, 1929); Violin Concerto in

D minor, op. 44 (Leningrad, Nov. 14, 1938); 2 Pieces, op. 46/1, for Strings (1945); 2 Pieces, op. 46/2, for Violin, Cello, and Strings (1947); *Privetstvennaya uvertyura* (Salutatory Overture) in D major, op. 48, for Stalin's birthday (Dec. 21, 1939); *Zvenya*, op. 65, suite (1908; rev. 1945); Cello Concerto in C minor, op. 66 (March 17, 1945); *Slavonic Rhapsody*, op. 71 (1946); *Divertissement*, op. 80 (1948). Also a cantata, *Kirov s nami* (Kirov Is with Us), op. 61 (1942); marches for military band; choruses; 13 string quartets (1929–49); 2 cello sonatas (1911, rev. 1945; 1948–49); Violin Sonata (1946–47); 9 piano sonatas (1907–49); several sets of piano pieces; song cycles; etc.

BIBL.: L. Sabaneyev, *Modern Russian Composers* (N.Y., 1927); A. Ikonnikov, *M.: His Life and Work* (N.Y., 1946); T. Livanova, *N.Y. M.* (Moscow, 1953); V. Vinogradov, *Spravochnik-putevoditel* (a guide to the syms.; Moscow, 1954); S. Shlifstein, ed., *Notograficheskii spravochnik* (list of works; Moscow, 1962).

Míča, František Adam, Moravian composer; b. Jaroměřice nad Rokytnou, Jan. 11, 1746; d. Lemberg, March 19, 1811. He studied law in Vienna, where he was active in government service. As a composer, he won the esteem of Emperor Joseph II and Mozart. His works include the singspiel *Adrast und Isidore, oder Die Nachtmusik* (Vienna, April 26, 1781), over 25 syms., 4 violin concertos, a Harpsichord Concerto, and many string quartets and other chamber music pieces.

Michael, family of important German musicians:
(1) Rogier Michael, tenor and composer of Netherlandish birth; b. Mons or Bergen op Zoom, c.1552; d. Dresden, after Jan. 25, 1619. As a child, he sang in the Vienna Hofkapelle; in 1564 he entered the Graz Hofkapelle, where he came under the tutelage of the Kapellmeisters Johannes de Cleve and Annibale Padovano; he then studied under Jacob de Brouck there (1567–69). After singing in the Hofkapelle of the Margrave in Ansbach (1572–74), he went to Dresden as a singer and musician in the Hofkapelle; in 1587 he became Hofkapellmeister; his later assistants there were Michael Praetorius and Heinrich Schütz. Among his pupils was Johann Hermann Schein. Michael's output, which includes sacred histories, chorale settings, and motets, represents the Netherlands school at its best. He had 3 sons, all of whom were his pupils.
(2) Tobias Michael, composer; b. Dresden, June 13, 1592; d. Leipzig, June 26, 1657. He was a treble in the Dresden Hofkapelle, where he studied with Andreas Petermann, Präzeptor to the choirboys; after studying at the Schulpforta electoral school and at the Univ. of Leipzig, he pursued training in theology and philosophy at the Univ. of Wittenberg (1613–18). In 1619 he was made Kapellmeister of the Neue Kirche in Sondershausen, Thuringia; after holding a government post, he became Kantor of the Leipzig Thomaskirche in 1631. Among his finest works are the 2 vols. of *Musicalische Seelenlust* (Leipzig, 1634–35; 1637); vol. I includes 30 German motets for 5 Voices and Continuo and vol. II contains 50 sacred concertos. He also wrote sacred songs and occasional pieces.
(3) Christian Michael, organist and composer; b. Dresden, c.1593; d. Leipzig, Aug. 29, 1637. He studied at the Univ. of Leipzig; in 1633 he succeeded his brother Samuel as organist of the Leipzig Nicolaikirche. He prepared the vol. *Tabulatura, darinnen etzliche Praeludia, Toccaten und Couranten uff das Clavier Instrument gesetzt* (Braunschweig, 1639; 2nd ed., 1645).
(4) Samuel Michael, organist and composer; b. Dresden, c.1597; d. Leipzig, between Aug. 14 and 17, 1632. He studied at the Univ. of Leipzig; in 1628 he became organist at the Leipzig Nicolaikirche, where he remained until he died from the plague. He composed collections of vocal and instrumental pieces.

Michael, David Moritz, German violinist, clarinetist, horn player, and composer; b. Keinhausen, near Erfurt, Oct. 21, 1751; d. Neuwied, Feb. 26, 1827. He spent some years as a Hessian army musician; in 1781 he joined the Moravian church; from 1795 to 1815 he lived in the Moravian settlements

at Nazareth and Bethlehem, Pa., and was the leading spirit in the musical performances in both towns; he played violin and most winds, and as a novelty, would amuse his audience by performing simultaneously on 2 horns. A list of programs of the Collegium Musicum at Nazareth, beginning with 1796, is preserved in the Moravian Historical Soc. in Nazareth. He composed 14 woodwind *Parthien*, 2 "Water-music" suites, 18 anthems for Solo Voice or Chorus and Instruments, and *Psalm CIII* for Soloists, Chorus, and Orch.; the greater portion of his MSS are housed in the Moravian Church archives in Bethlehem, and others are in the Moravian Foundation in Winston-Salem, N.C.; see A. Rau and H. David, *A Catalogue of Music by American Moravians, 1742–1842* (Bethlehem, Pa., 1938).
BIBL.: K. Kroeger, "D.M. M.'s Psalm 103: An Early American Sacred Cantata," *Moravian Music Foundation Bulletin*, XXI/2 (1976); D. Roberts, *The Sacred Vocal Music of D.M. M.: An American Moravian Composer* (diss., Univ. of Kentucky, 1978); K. Hahn, *The Wind Ensemble Music of D.M. M.* (thesis, Univ. of Missouri, 1979).

Michaelides, Solon, Greek musicologist, conductor, composer, and teacher; b. Nicosia, Nov. 25, 1905; d. Athens, Sept. 9, 1979. He studied 1st at Trinity College of Music in London; then took courses in composition at the École Normale de Musique in Paris with Nadia Boulanger, and later in conducting with Marcel Labey at the Schola Cantorum. Upon his return to Cyprus, he founded the Limassol Cons. in 1934 and was its director until 1956; subsequently was director of the Salonika State Cons. (1957–70) and permanent conductor of the Sym. Orch. of Northern Greece (1959–70). In 1970 he was pensioned and he moved to Athens. He publ. *The Neo-Hellenic Folk-music* (Limassol, 1948) and *The Music of Ancient Greece: An Encyclopaedia* (London, 1977). Among his compositions are an opera, *Ulysses* (1951; rev. 1972–73); a ballet, *Nausicaa* (1950); *2 Byzantine Sketches* for Strings (1934); *Cypriot Wedding* for Flute and Strings (1935); *2 Greek Symphonic Pictures* (1936); *Byzantine Offering* for Strings (1944); *Archaic Suite* for Flute, Oboe, Harp, and Strings (1954); Piano Concerto (1966); also 2 cantatas: *The Tomb* (1936) and *The Free Besieged* (1955); *Hymn to Freedom*, the Cypriot national anthem (1962); String Quartet (1934); Piano Trio (1946); *Suite* for Cello and Piano (1966); *Suite* for Piano (1966); various piano pieces; songs.

Michalak, Thomas, Polish-American conductor; b. Krakow, Dec. 21, 1940; d. Newark, July 10, 1986. He studied violin in Warsaw; made his debut as a soloist with the Warsaw Phil. at the age of 16. His conducting debut was with the Ballets Russes de Monte Carlo during its tour of the U.S. in 1964. In 1967 he became a member of the faculty at Ithaca College. In 1972 he won 1st prize in the Koussevitzky awards at the Berkshire Music Center. He served on the conducting staff of the Pittsburgh Sym. Orch. (1974); later was music director of the Canton (Ohio) Sym. Orch. (1976–77) and the New Jersey Sym. Orch. in Newark (1977–83); also served as music adviser of the Kansas City Phil. (1981–82).

Michalsky, Donal, American composer; b. Pasadena, Calif., July 13, 1928; d. (asphyxiated in a fire and burned to death with his wife, 2 small children, a house guest, and her daughter) Newport Beach, Calif., Jan. 1, 1976. He studied clarinet as a youth; then attended the Univ. of Southern Calif. in Los Angeles as a student in theory with Halsey Stevens and in orchestration with Ingolf Dahl, obtaining his doctorate in 1965. In 1958 he went to Germany, where he took a course with Wolfgang Fortner in Freiburg im Breisgau. In 1960 he was appointed prof. of composition at the Calif. State College at Fullerton, holding this position until his tragic death. In his music, he adopted a powerful modern idiom in robust dissonant counterpoint, often written in dodecaphonic technique, and yet permeated with a lyric and almost Romantic sentiment.
WORKS: 3 syms.: No. 1, choral sym., *Wheel of Time* (1967); No. 2, *Sinfonia concertante* (1969); No. 3 (1975); Concertino for 19 Wind Instruments and Percussion (1964); Quintet for 2 Trumpets, 2 Trombones, and Piano (1951); *Divertimento*

for 2 Clarinets and Bass Clarinet (1952); *Partita* for Oboe d'Amore, String Trio, and String Orch. (1956); Cello Sonata (1958); *Sonata concertante* for Piano Solo (1961); *Trio Concertino* for Flute, Oboe, and Horn (1961); *Cantata da Requiem* (1962); *Variations* for Clarinet and Piano (1962); *Partita piccola* for Flute and Piano (1964); *3 × 4* for Saxophone Quartet (1972); a number of pieces for band; songs. The MS of his projected opera *Der arme Heinrich* was burned in the fire that took his life.

Micheelsen, Hans Friedrich, German organist and composer; b. Hennstedt, Dithmarschen, June 9, 1902; d. Glüsing, Holstein, Nov. 23, 1973. He studied in Hamburg and Berlin; was active as a church organist until 1938, when he was drafted into the German army; after demobilization, he settled in Hamburg, where he taught at the Hochschule für Musik. He retired in 1962. He wrote primarily choral music and pieces for organ; among his works are a *Luther Mass* (1933); a German Requiem, *Tod und Leben* (1938); an oratorio, *Wachstum und Reife* (1953); *Passion according to St. Mark* (1954); cantata, *Land der Väter* (1955); evangelical mass, *Unser Wandel ist im Himmel* (1957); *St. John's Passion* for chorus a cappella (1961); also a singspiel, *Münchhausen*; Organ Concerto (1952); Suite for Flute and Piano (1970); some songs in the Hamburg dialect.

Michel, Paul-Baudouin, Belgian composer; b. Haine-St.-Pierre, Sept. 7, 1930. He studied humanities at the Mons Cons.; then took composition with Absil at the Queen Elisabeth Music Chapel in Brussels (1959–62) and conducting at the Royal Cons. in Brussels; attended summer courses in Darmstadt with Ligeti, Boulez, Maderna, and Messiaen. He was later appointed director of the Academy of Music in Woluwé-St.-Lambert. His music adheres to the doctrine of precisely planned structural formations in a highly modern idiom.
WORKS: STAGE: *Jeanne la Folle*, opera (1983–87); *Pandora*, ballet (1961). **ORCH.:** *Variations symphoniques* (1960); *5 infra-morphoses* for String Orch. (1963); *Symphonium* (1966); *Concaténation* for Chamber Orch. (1967); *Hors-Temps* (1970); *Confluences* for 2 Chamber Groups (1974); *Lamobylrinthe ou Dovetailed Forms*, concerto for Piano and 21 Instruments (1979); *Humoresque-Nocturne-Rondo* for Chamber Orch. (1979–80); *Trois nocturnes* (1981); Piano Concerto (1986); Harpsichord Concerto (1986); Concertinetto for Piano and Orch. (1987); *Symphonium "Jeanne la Folle"* (1988). **VOCAL:** *Equateur*, cantata (1962); *Rex pacificus*, radiophonic motet for Bass, Chorus, Orch., and Tape (1968); *Le Feu et le monde* for Narrator, Soli, Chorus, Organ, 12 Trumpets, and Percussion (1970); *Systoles—Diastoles* for Soprano and Instruments (1973); *Le Graal gras, ode au pétrole* for Speaker, Soprano, 10 Instruments, and Tape (1980); *Ecce Homo* for Bass and Chorus (1983); *Itinerrance* for Soprano, Clarinet, and Piano (1988). **CHAMBER:** String Trio (1956); Violin Sonata (1960); *Hommage à François Rabelais*, wind quintet (1960); Clarinet Sonatina (1960); String Quartet (1961); *Sérénade concertante* for Violin and Piano (1962); *Motet aléatoire sur le "Veni creator"* for Chorus, 19 Instruments, and Percussion (1962); *Quadrance* for String Quartet (1965); *Conduit et Danse hiératique* for Harp (1964); *Monologue double* for Flute and Tape (1965); *Ultra-morphoses* for Flute, Clarinet, Saxophone, Percussion, Piano, Violin, Viola, and Cello (1965); *Clarbassonance* for Bass Clarinet and Tape (1966); *Bassonance* for Bassoon and Tape (1966); *Oscillonance* for 2 Violins and Piano (1967); *Colloque* for Piano, Trumpet, and Percussion (1967); *Gravures* for 2 Trumpets and Horn (1972); *Intonations* for Brass (1972); *Parelléloide* for Clavichord and Tape (1974); *Trois sur quatre* for Flute, Cello, and Piano (1979); *Décentrement* for Wind Quintet (1980); *Expansion I* for String Quartet (1981); *Versets* for 2 Ondes Martenot (1982); *Ellipse* for 4 Saxophones and 2 Harps (1983); *Poème* for Cello and Piano (1985); *Hommage à Paul Delvaux* for Saxophone and Harpsichord (1986); *Polyèdre* for 2 Percussionists (1988). **PIANO:** *Partita* No. 1 (1955); *Trans-sonance* (1965); *Libration I* (1971; rev. 1973); *Lithophanie* for Prepared Piano (1971); *Variations concentriques* (1971); *Musicoïde* for 2 Prepared Pianos (1971); *Orbe* (1972); also

the organ pieces *Transphonies pour plusieurs nefs* (1969) and *Puzzlephonie* (1972).

Michelangeli, Arturo Benedetti, celebrated Italian pianist and pedagogue; b. Brescia, Jan. 5, 1920. He received his formal music training at the Venturi Inst. in Brescia, where he took violin lessons with Paolo Chiuieri; at the age of 10, he entered the Milan Cons. as a piano pupil of Giuseppe Anfossi, obtaining his diploma at the age of 13. In 1939 he won the Concours International de Piano in Geneva; later joined the piano faculty at the Martini Cons. in Bologna. He was a lieutenant in the Italian air force; after the formal surrender of Italy to the Allies and the German occupation, he was active in the country's anti-Fascist underground; he was taken prisoner by the Germans, but escaped after a few months. Despite these peripeteias, he somehow managed to practice, acquiring a formidable virtuoso technique. However, he also developed idiosyncrasies, often canceling scheduled performances, and engaged in such distracting (and dangerous) activities as automobile racing, skiing, and mountain climbing. Both his virtuosity and his eccentricities contributed to his legend, and his rare concerts were invariably public successes. He toured the U.S. in 1950 and in 1966; played in the Soviet Union in 1964; also gave concerts in South America. Eventually he returned to Italy and dedicated himself mainly to teaching; organized an International Academy for pianists in a rented palazzo in Brescia with a multitude of pianos in soundproof studios; among his pupils were Jörg Demus, Walter Klien, Maurizio Pollini, and Martha Argerich.

Michelet (real name, **Levin**), **Michel,** Russian-American composer; b. Kiev, June 26, 1894. He studied cello in Kiev and at the Vienna Cons. with Julius Klengel; then went to Leipzig, where he took lessons with Max Reger. Returning to Kiev in 1914, he studied composition with Reinhold Glière. He left Russia in 1921; went to Vienna and subsequently to Paris, where he became a composer of film music. In 1941 he made his way from France to the U.S. under difficult wartime conditions, and settled in Hollywood. His music has a certain lyric quality, in a Russian vein, with an infusion of characteristic devices of early French Impressionism. **WORKS:** Opera, *Hannele,* after Hauptmann (1972); Violin Concerto (1943); *Lisztiana,* "romantic trio" for Violin, Cello, and Piano (1943); 2 cello sonatas (1937, 1977); 3 violin sonatas; Sonata for Balalaika and Piano (1972); piano pieces; songs; nearly 200 film scores.

Micheli, Romano, Italian composer and writer on music; b. Rome, c.1575; d. there, after 1659. He studied with Soriano and G.M. Nanino. He was in the service of the Duke of S. Giovanni in Rome (c.1593) and of Gesualdo in Venice (c.1596–98); then was maestro di cappella of Tivoli Cathedral (1609–10), Concordia Cathedral, near Udine (1616), the Metropolitan Church in Aquileia, near Venice (1618–21), and S. Luigi dei Francesi in Rome (1625–36); after serving as a canon in Naples, he returned to Rome about 1644. Micheli excelled as a composer of canons, and claimed to have invented the canoni sopra le vocali di più parole ("canons on the vowels of several words"). He was a highly disputatious individual and engaged in various controversies with his contemporaries via his polemical writings.

Michi, Orazio, eminent Italian harpist and composer, known as **della Arpa** because of his virtuosity; b. Alifa Caserta, c.1595; d. Rome, Oct. 26, 1641. From 1614 to 1623 he was in Rome; after that, with Cardinal Maurizio of Savoy. Until 1914 his works were unknown except for 5 arias publ. in Bianchi's *Raccolta d'arie* (Rome, 1640) and a 6th one publ. by Torchi in vol. 5 of *L'arte musicale in Italia.* Then, A. Cametti publ., in the *Rivista Musicale Italiana* (April 1914), a full description and complete thematic catalog of about 60 cantatas by Michi, which he had discovered in various Italian libraries and which prove that Michi was one of the earliest and most important Roman masters of the monodic style.

Middelschulte, Wilhelm, eminent German organist and teacher; b. Werne, near Dortmund, April 3, 1863; d. there,

May 4, 1943. He studied at the Inst. für Kirchenmusik in Berlin with Löschhorn (piano), Haupt (organ), and Commer and Schröder (composition). After serving as organist at the Church of St. Luke in Berlin (1888–91), he settled in Chicago; was organist at the Cathedral of the Holy Name (1891–95); subsequently was organist at Milwaukee's St. James's Church (1899–1919) and also a prof. of organ at the Wisconsin Cons. of Music there. He was greatly distinguished for his interpretations of Bach. In 1935 he became instructor of theory and organ at the Detroit Foundation Music School; in 1939 he returned to Germany.

BIBL.: J. Becker, "W. M.," *Musical Quarterly* (April 1928).

Middleton, Hubert Stanley, English organist, teacher, and composer; b. Windsor, May 11, 1890; d. London, Aug. 13, 1959. He studied at the Royal Academy of Music in London and at Cambridge Univ. (M.A., 1920). He was appointed organist and director of music at Trinity College, Cambridge, in 1931; also taught at the Royal Academy of Music in London. His specialty was cathedral music. He composed a number of anthems and organ pieces. He was greatly esteemed as an educator, and his teaching methods exercised profound influence on his students, many of whom became educators in their own right.

Midler, Bette, lovable American singer, actress, and comedienne; b. Paterson, N.J., Dec. 1, 1945. She studied drama in Honolulu, then settled in N.Y., where she sang in a variety of gay venues, including bathhouses and clubs, and on Broadway (*Fiddler on the Roof* and *Tommy*); subsequently engaged Barry Manilow as her music director and a backup trio known as The Harlettes and developed a raucous cabaret routine through which she generated a loyal following, becoming known as "The Divine Miss M"; her 1972 album of that name won a gold record; subsequent albums of note include *Bette Midler* (1973), *Songs for the New Depression* (1976), *Live at Last* (1977), and *Broken Blossom* (1977). She starred in the film *The Rose* (1979), based on the life of Janis Joplin, for which she received an Academy Award nomination; her soundtrack LP sold into the millions; other successful films were *Down and Out in Beverly Hills* (1986), *Ruthless People* (1986), *Outrageous Fortune* (1987), and *Beaches* (1989), for which she sang the Grammy Award–winning title song, *Wind beneath My Wings.* Her covers of songs by artists as varied as Bruce Springsteen, Kurt Weill, Hoagy Carmichael, and Tom Waits evidence her great stylistic diversity. Her comedic gifts, an integral aspect of her live performances, are captured on the recording *Mud Will Be Flung Tonight* (1985), in which she revitalizes the spicy, sometimes lewd anecdotes of the late Sophie Tucker. She authored the comic memoirs *A View from a Broad* (N.Y., 1980) and a children's book, *The Saga of Baby Divine* (N.Y., 1983).

BIBL.: J. Spada, *The Divine B. M.* (N.Y., 1984); M. Bego, *B. M., Outrageously Divine: An Unauthorized Biography* (N.Y., 1987); A. Collins, *B. M.* (N.Y., 1989).

Midori (real name, **Goto Mi Dori**), prodigiously gifted Japanese *wunderkind* of the violin; b. Osaka, Oct. 25, 1971. She studied with her mother, Setsu Goto; in 1981, went to the U.S., where she took violin lessons with Dorothy DeLay at the Aspen Music School and continued her training with that mentor at N.Y.'s Juilliard School. She attracted the attention of Zubin Mehta when she was 10 years old; he subsequently engaged her as a soloist with the N.Y. Phil., with which she traveled on an extensive Asian tour that included Hong Kong, Singapore, Korea, Thailand, and her native Japan. There followed concerts with the Berlin Phil., the Boston Sym. Orch., the Chicago Sym. Orch., the Cleveland and Philadelphia Orchs., the Los Angeles Phil., the London Sym. Orch., and other European and American orchs., in programs that included not only classical concertos but also modern works, under the direction of such renowned conductors, besides Mehta, as Bernstein, Previn, Maazel, Dohnányi, Leppard, and Barenboim. She also attracted the attention of popular television programs, and appeared as a guest of President and Mrs.

Reagan at the White House during the NBC television special *Christmas in Washington* (1983). Most importantly, she won the admiration of orch. members for her remarkable artistic dependability. On one occasion, when a string broke on the concertmaster's violin during an orch. introduction, she demonstrated her sangfroid; since she had a few minutes to spare before her entrance as a soloist, she handed her own violin to the player and coolly changed the broken string in time to continue the performance without pause. On Oct. 21, 1990, she made her N.Y. recital debut at Carnegie Hall.

Miedél, Rainer, German-American conductor; b. Regensburg, June 1, 1937; d. Seattle, March 25, 1983. He studied cello with André Navarra in Paris, and conducting with Franco Ferrara in Siena and István Kertész in Salzburg. In 1965 he was engaged as a cellist with the Stockholm Phil.; made his conducting debut with it in 1967. From 1969 to 1976 he was music director of the Gävleborgs Sym. Orch. in Sweden; concurrently served as assistant conductor of the Baltimore Sym. Orch. (1969–72) and then associate conductor (1972–73). In 1976 he was appointed music director of the Seattle Sym. Orch.; in 1980 he traveled with it on its 1st European tour. From 1980 to 1982 he served as interim music adviser of the Florida Phil.; he also had numerous guest conducting engagements throughout Europe and the U.S. His career was ended when he was stricken with a peculiarly deadly form of cancer. He conducted his last concert in Seattle on Jan. 13, 1983.

Mieg, Peter, Swiss composer, critic, and painter; b. Lenzburg, Sept. 5, 1906. He studied composition, piano, and theory with C. Richter in Lenzburg (1921) and piano with H. Münch in Basel and E. Frey in Zürich (1927); pursued academic studies at the Univs. of Zürich and Basel (Ph.D., 1933); later received training in composition from F. Martin (1942–45). In 1933 he commenced writing art, literary, and music criticism for various Swiss publications; in later years, also took up painting while devoting time to composition.

WORKS: BALLETS: *La Fête de la ligne* (1935); *Daphne* (1943–45). ORCH.: Concerto for 2 Pianos and Orch. (1939–42); 2 piano concertos (1947, 1961); Violin Concerto (1948–49); *Concerto da camera* for Strings, Piano, and Timpani (1952); Concerto for Harpsichord and Chamber Orch. (1953); *Concerto veneziano* for String Orch. (1955); Oboe Concerto (1957); Sym. (1958); *Toccata-Arioso-Gigue* for String Orch. (1959); Concerto for Flute and String Orch. (1962); *Rondeau symphonique* (1964); Cello Concerto (1966–67); Concerto for Harp and String Orch. (1970); Concerto for 2 Flutes and String Orch. (1973–74); *Combray* for String Orch. (1977); *Triple concerto le goût italien* for Violin, Viola, Cello, and String Orch. (1978); *Schlossbildermusik* (1980); Concerto for Piano, 4-hands, and String Orch. (1980); *Lenzburger Cäciliensuite* (1981); Double Concerto for Piano, Cello, and Orch. (1983–84); *Ouverture pour Monsieur Lully* for String Orch. (1986). CHAMBER: Violin Sonata (1936); 2 string trios (1936–37; 1984); 3 string quartets (1938; 1944–45; 1987); Divertimento for Oboe and String Trio (1950); Flute Sonata (1963); Wind Quintet (1977); Piano Trio (1984–85); various piano pieces, including 5 sonatas (1944–88); also choral works and songs.

BIBL.: U. Däster, W. Kläy, and W. Labhart, *P. M.: Eine Monographie* (Aarau and Frankfurt am Main, 1976).

Mielck, Ernst, Finnish composer; b. Vyborg, Oct. 24, 1877; d. Locarno, Italy, Oct. 22, 1899 (2 days before his 22nd birthday). He studied piano in St. Petersburg and composition with Max Bruch in Berlin. His early death deprived Finland of a major musical talent. He left several works showing considerable technical skill and inventive power; among these are a String Quartet (1895); *Macbeth Overture* (1895); String Quintet (1896–97); *Finnish Symphony* (1897); *Dramatic Overture* (1898); 2 piano concertos (1895, 1898); *Finnish Suite* for Orch. (1899). A monograph on Mielck was publ. by W. Mauke (Leipzig, 1901).

Mielke, Antonia, German soprano; b. Berlin, c.1852; d. there, Nov. 15, 1907. At 1st she sang chiefly coloratura roles, but

gradually assumed the great dramatic parts, for which she was particularly gifted. She sang the Wagner heroines at the Metropolitan Opera in N.Y. during the season of 1890–91 (succeeding Lilli Lehmann); also toured the U.S. in concert recitals; returning to Germany, she continued her operatic career until 1902, when she settled in Berlin as a teacher.

Miereanu, Costin, Rumanian-born French composer; b. Bucharest, Feb. 27, 1943. He studied with Alfred Mendelsohn, Varga, and Dan Constantinescu at the Bucharest Cons. (1960–66); attended seminars with Günther Becker and Ligeti at the summer courses in new music held in Darmstadt (1967, 1968) and also had sessions with Pierre Schaeffer at the Paris Cons. (1968–69) and with the Groupe de Recherches Musicales there; in 1968 he settled in France, acquiring French citizenship in 1977. His music presents a totality of the cosmopolitan avant-garde: serialism, electronic sound, aleatory production, and musical-verbal theater. Some of his compositions have optional parts for magnetic tape and film.

WORKS: *Donum sacrum Brancusi* for Voice and Orch. (1963); *Espace dernier*, aleatory music for Chorus, 6 Instrumental Groups, and Tape (1965; Royan, April 14, 1973); *Variante* for Clarinet (1966); *Finis coronat opus* for Pianist and 6 Instrumental Groups (1966); *Cadenza* for 1 or More Pianists (1966); *Monostructures I* for 2 Orchs. of Strings and Brass (1967) and *II* for Strings, Brass, and Tape (1967); *Sur-sum corda* for Piano, Violin, Viola, Cello, and Clarinet (1967–68); *Nuit* for Soprano and a cappella Chorus (1968); *Dans la nuit des temps*, aleatory music for Variable Ensemble and Tape (1968–69); *Couleurs du temps* in 3 versions: for String Orch. (1968), for String Quartet and Tape (1968), and for Double String Quartet and Double Bass (1969); *Espaces au-delà du dernier*, aleatory music for Chamber Ensemble (1969); *Espaces II* for 20 Strings, Piano, and Tape (1967–69); *Polymorphies 5 × 7*, in concert version, for ad libitum Chorus, Variable Ensemble, and Tape, or in stage version, for Actors, Chorus, Variable Ensemble, and Tape (1968–69); *Night Music* for Tape (1968–70); *Alba* for 12 Voices and 4 Percussionists (1972; version for 2 Voices and Objects, 1973); *Source de juin* for Flute, Clarinet, Trombone, Trumpet, Electric Guitar, and Percussion (1972); *Altar* in 3 versions that mix Voices, Instruments, Film, and Tape in various combinations (1973); 5 separate works (*Amnar, Rod, Amurg, Zbor,* and *Apo*) all subtitled "réécriture spatio-temporelle," for varying combinations of Instrumental and Vocal Soloists, Chamber Ensembles, Film, and Tape (1973; all 5 works, Paris, Feb. 5, 1974); *Silence Tisse* for Variable Vocal and Instrumental Ensembles (1973–74); *Domingo* for Variable Quintet of Voices and Instruments (1974); *Quintafeira* for 2 Trumpets, Horn, Trombone, and Tuba (1974); *Segundafeira* for 5 Different Flutes (1974); *Luna cinese* for Narrator, 1 Performer, and 1 or More Electrophones (1975); *Planetarium I* for Piano, 2 Flutes, Trombone, and Vibraphone (1975); *Rêve sans (T)rêve*, "kinéaquarium vidéophonique" (1975); *Sempre azzuro* for Variable Ensemble (1975); *Rosario* for Orch. and Optional Tenor (1973–76); *Musiques élementaires pour la Messe*, cycle of 6 pieces for Variable Instruments (1976); *Rosenzeit* for Orch. (1980); *Voyage d'hiver: I, Dies irae* for Soprano, 8 Instruments, and Tape (1982), and *II, Dies irae* for Orch. (1985); *Miroirs célestes* for Orch. (1983); Double Chamber Concerto for Saxophone, Percussion, and Chamber Orch. (1985); *Clair de biche* for Flute, Clarinet, Saxophone, Wind Quintet, and 5 Percussion (1986); *Le Mur d'Airain* for 9 Instrumentalists (1987).

Mies, Paul, noted German musicologist and pedagogue; b. Cologne, Oct. 22, 1889; d. there, May 15, 1976. He studied musicology, mathematics, and physics at the Univ. of Bonn, receiving his Ph.D. there in 1912 with the dissertation *Über die Tonmalerei*; then was active as a teacher of mathematics in Cologne (1919–39) while continuing his musicological work; in 1946 he became director of the Institut für Schulmusik at the Cologne Staatliche Hochschule für Musik, retaining this post until 1954.

WRITINGS: *Stilmomente und Ausdrucksstilformen im*

Brahmsschen Lied (Leipzig, 1923); *Die Bedeutung der Skizzen Beethovens zur Erkenntnis seines Stiles* (Leipzig, 1925; Eng. tr., London, 1929); *Musik im Unterricht der höheren Lehranstalten* (2 vols., Cologne, 1925–26); *Skizzen aus Geschichte und Ästhetik der Musik* (Cologne, 1926); *Das romantische Lied und Gesänge aus Wilhelm Meister; Musik und Musiker in Poesie und Prosa* (2 vols., Berlin, 1926); *Schubert, der Meister des Liedes: Die Entwicklung von Form und Inhalt im Schubertschen Lied* (Berlin, 1928); *Johannes Brahms: Werke, Zeit, Mensch* (Leipzig, 1930); *Der Charakter der Tonarten: Eine Untersuchung* (Cologne, 1948); *Von Sinn und Praxis der musikalischen Kritik* (Krefeld, 1950); with N. Schneider, *Musik im Umkreis der Kulturgeschichte: Ein Taballenwerk aus der Geschichte der Musik, Literatur, bildenden Kunst, Philosophie und Politik Europas* (Rodenkirchen, 1953); *Franz Schubert* (Leipzig, 1954); *Textkritische Untersuchungen bei Beethoven* (Munich and Duisburg, 1957); *Die geistlichen Kantaten Johann Sebastian Bachs und der Hörer von heute* (3 vols., Wiesbaden, 1959–60; 2nd ed., 1964); *Bilder und Buchstaben werden Musik* (Rodenkirchen, 1964); with H. Grundmann, *Studien zum Klavierspiel Beethovens und seiner Zeitgenossen* (Bonn, 1966; 2nd ed., 1970); *Die weltlichen Kantaten Johann Sebastian Bachs und der Hörer von heute* (Wiesbaden, 1967); *Das instrumentale Rezitativ: Von seiner Geschichte und seinen Formen* (Bonn, 1968); *Die Krise der Konzertkadenz bei Beethoven* (Bonn, 1970); *Das Konzert im 19. Jahrhundert: Studien zu Kadenzen und Formen* (Bonn, 1972); ed. *Reihenfolge*, a collection for school orchs.

Migenes-Johnson, Julia, American soprano; b. N.Y., March 13, 1945. She studied at the High School of Music and Art in N.Y., and while still a student sang in a televised concert performance of Copland's *The 2nd Hurricane* under Bernstein's direction; then appeared in *West Side Story* and *Fiddler on the Roof* on Broadway. On Sept. 29, 1965, she made her debut at the N.Y. City Opera as Annina in *The Saint of Bleecker Street*; then pursued training in Vienna, where she sang at the Volksoper; also studied with Gisela Ultmann in Cologne. In 1978 she made her 1st appearance at the San Francisco Opera as Musetta. Her Metropolitan Opera debut in N.Y. took place on Dec. 10, 1979, as Jenny in *The Rise and Fall of the City of Mahagonny*. In 1983 she sang with the Vienna State Opera. She gained international acclaim for her sultry portrayal of Carmen in Francesco Rosi's film version of Bizet's opera in 1984. In 1985 she returned to the Metropolitan Opera as Berg's Lulu. She won accolades for her compelling performances as Strauss's Salome.

Mignan, Edouard-Charles-Octave, French organist and composer; b. Paris, March 17, 1884; d. there, Sept. 17, 1969. He studied at the Paris Cons. with Widor (organ) and Vidal (compostion); was church organist at Orléans and later at the Madeleine in Paris. He wrote a number of melodious orch. suites, a Sym., sacred choruses, numerous motets, and organ pieces.

Mignone, Francisco (Paulo), eminent Brazilian composer; b. São Paulo, Sept. 3, 1897; d. Rio de Janeiro, Feb. 20, 1986. He studied with his father; then took courses in piano, flute, and composition at the São Paulo Cons.; then studied with Ferroni at the Milan Cons. (1920); returning to Brazil, he was appointed to the faculty of the Escola Nacional de Música in Rio de Janeiro (1933), and taught there until 1967. His music shows the influence of the modern Italian school of composition; his piano pieces are of virtuoso character; his orchestration shows consummate skill. In many of his works he employs indigenous Brazilian motifs, investing them in sonorous modernistic harmonies not without a liberal application of euphonious dissonances.

WORKS: OPERAS: *O Contractador dos diamantes* (Rio de Janeiro, Sept. 20, 1924); *O inocente* (Rio de Janeiro, Sept. 5, 1928); *O Chalaça* (1972); operetta, *Mizú* (1937). BALLETS: *Maracatú de Chico-Rei* (Rio de Janeiro, Oct. 29, 1934); *Quadros amazónicos* (Rio de Janeiro, July 15, 1949); *O guarda chuva* (São Paulo, 1954). ORCH.: *Suite campestre* (Rio de Janeiro,

Dec. 16, 1918); *Congada*, from the opera *O Contractador dos diamantes* (São Paulo, Sept. 10, 1922; his most popular piece); *Scenas da Roda*, symphonic dance (São Paulo, Aug. 15, 1923); *Festa dionisiaca* (Rome, Oct. 24, 1923); *Intermezzo lirico* (São Paulo, May 13, 1925); *Momus*, symphonic poem (Rio de Janeiro, April 24, 1933); *Suite brasileira* (Rio de Janeiro, Dec. 9, 1933); *Sonho de um Menino Travesso* (São Paulo, Oct. 30, 1937); *4 fantasias brasileiras* for Piano and Orch. (1931–37); *Seresta* for Cello and Orch. (Rio de Janeiro, March 31, 1939); *Miudinho*, symphonic dance (São Paulo, June 28, 1941); *Festa das Igrejas* (N.Y., April 22, 1942); *Sinfonia tropical* (1958); Piano Concerto (1958); Violin Concerto (1961); Concerto for Violin, Piano, and Orch. (1966); Concertino for Clarinet and Small Orch. (1957); Bassoon Concertino (1957); Concerto for Violin and Chamber Orch. (1975). CHAMBER: 2 sextets (1935, 1968); String Octet (1956); 2 wind quintets (1960, 1962); 2 string quartets (1956, 1957); Sonata for 4 Bassoons (1966); 2 wind trios (1967, 1968); 3 violin sonatas (1964, 1965, 1966); Cello Sonata (1967); 2 sonatas for 2 Bassoons (1960, 1965); 2 sonatas for Flute and Oboe (1969, 1970); *Trifonia* for Oboe, Flute, and Bassoon (1963); *Tetrafonia* for Flute, Oboe, Clarinet, and Trumpet (1963); *Sonata a tre* for Flute, Oboe, and Clarinet (1970); Sonata for Trumpet Solo (1970); Clarinet Sonata (1971). PIANO: 4 sonatas (1941, 1962, 1964, 1967); *Rondo* (1969); several waltzes in Brazilian popular style; *Samba rítmico* for 2 Pianos (1953); *Sonata humorística* for 2 Pianos (1968). VOCAL: oratorio, *Alegrias de Nossa Senhora* (Rio de Janeiro, July 15, 1949); oratorio, *Santa Clara* (1962); many songs.

BIBL.: N. Slonimsky, *Music of Latin America* (N.Y., 1945); autobiographical brochure, *A parte do anjo* (São Paulo, 1947); L. Correa de Azevedo, "F. M.," *Música Brasileña Contemporánea* (Rosario, Argentina, 1952); special issue of *Inter-American Music Bulletin* (1970–71).

Migot, Georges, significant French composer; b. Paris, Feb. 27, 1891; d. Levallois, near Paris, Jan. 5, 1976. He began taking piano lessons at the age of 6; entered the Paris Cons. in 1909; after preliminary courses in harmony, he studied composition with Widor, counterpoint with Gedalge, and music history with Emmanuel; then orchestration with d'Indy and organ with Gigout and Guilmant. Before completing his studies at the Paris Cons., he was mobilized into the French army, was wounded at Longuyon in 1914, and was released from military service. In 1917 he presented in Paris a concert of his own works; received the Lily Boulanger Prize in 1918. He competed twice for the Prix de Rome in 1919 and 1920, but failed to win and abandoned further attempts to capture it. In the meantime, he engaged in a serious study of painting; in fact, he was more successful as a painter than as a composer in the early years of his career; he exhibited his paintings in Paris art galleries in 1917, 1919, 1923, and subsequent years. He also wrote poetry; virtually all of his vocal works are written to his own words. In his musical compositions, he endeavored to recapture the spirit of early French polyphony, thus emphasizing the continuity of national art in history. His melodic writing is modal, often with archaic inflections, while his harmonic idiom is diatonically translucid; he obtains subtle coloristic effects through unusual instrumental registration. Profoundly interested in the preservation and classification of early musical instruments, he served as curator of the Instrumental Museum of the Paris Cons. (1949–61). He wrote *Essais pour une esthétique générale* (Paris, 1920; 2nd ed., 1937); *Appoggiatures résolues et non résolues* (Paris, 1922–31); *Jean-Philippe Rameau et le génie de la musique française* (Paris, 1930); *Lexique de quelques termes utilisés en musique* (Paris, 1947); 2 vols. of poems (Paris, 1950, 1951); *Matériaux et inscriptions* (Toulouse, 1970); *Kaléidoscope et miroirs ou les images multipliées et contraires* (autobiography; Toulouse, 1970).

WORKS: DRAMATIC: *Hagoromo*, "symphonie lyrique et chorégraphique" for Baritone, Chorus, and Orch., to a libretto by Migot and Laloy (Monte Carlo, May 9, 1922); *Le Rossignol en amour*, chamber opera to a libretto by Migot (1926–28; Geneva, March 2, 1937); *Cantate d'amour*, concert opera to a libretto by Migot (1949–50); *La Sulamite*, concert opera to a libretto by Migot (1969–70); *L'Arche*, "polyphonie spatiale" for Soprano, Female Chorus, and Orch., to a poem by Migot (1971; Marseilles, May 3, 1974). ORCH.: SYMS. (some of their material was derived from earlier pieces of chamber music, and their numeration does not follow chronological order): No. 1, *Les Agrestides* (1919–20; Paris, April 29, 1922); No. 2 (1927; Besançon, Sept. 7, 1961); No. 3 (1943–49); No. 4 (1946–47); No. 5, *Sinfonia da chiesa*, for Wind Instruments (Roubaix, Dec. 4, 1955); No. 6 for Strings (1944–51; Strasbourg, June 22, 1960); No. 7 for Chamber Orch. (1948–52); No. 8 for 15 Wind Instruments and 2 Double Basses (1953); No. 9 for Strings (incomplete); No. 10 (1962); No. 11 for Wind Instruments (1963); No. 12 (1954–64; Lille, May 29, 1972); No. 13 (1967); also *Petite symphonie en trois mouvements enchaînés* for String Orch. (1970; Béziers, July 23, 1971). OTHER ORCH.: *Le Paravent de laque aux cinq images* (1920; Paris, Jan. 21, 1923); *Trois ciné-ambiances* (1922); *La Fête de la bergère* (1921; Paris, Nov. 21, 1925); *Prélude pour un poète* (Paris, June 7, 1929); *Le Livre des danceries*, suite (Paris, Dec. 12, 1931); *Le Zodiaque* (1931–39); *Phonie sous-marine* (1962); *Dialogue* for Piano and Orch. (1922–25; Paris, March 25, 1926); *Dialogue* for Cello and Orch. (1922–26; Paris, Feb. 7, 1927); *Suite* for Violin and Orch. (1924; Paris, Nov. 14, 1925); *Suite* for Piano and Orch. (Paris, March 12, 1927); *Suite en concert* for Harp and Orch. (Paris, Jan. 15, 1928); *La Jungle*, "polyphonie" for Organ and Orch. (1928; Paris, Jan. 9, 1932); Piano Concerto (1962; Paris, June 26, 1964); Concerto for Harpsichord and Chamber Orch. (Paris, Dec. 12, 1967). CHAMBER: *Les Parques* for 2 Violins, Viola, and Piano (1909); 3 string quartets (1921, 1957, 1966); Quartet for Flute, Violin, Cello, and Piano (1960); Quartet for Violin, Viola, Cello, and Piano (1961); Quartet for 2 Clarinets, Corno di Bassetto, and Bass Clarinet (1925); Quartet for Saxophones (1955); Quartet for 2 Violins and 2 Cellos (1955); Quintet for Flute, Oboe, Clarinet, Horn, and Bassoon (1954); *Introduction pour un concert de chambre* for 5 Strings and 5 Wind Instruments (1964); Trio for Oboe, Violin, and Piano (1906); Trio for Violin, Viola, and Piano (1918); Piano Trio (1935); Trio for Oboe, Clarinet, and Bassoon (1944); String Trio (1944–45); Trio for Flute, Cello, and Harp (1965); Guitar Sonata (1960); *Sonate luthée* for Harp Solo (1949); 2 sonatas for Violin Solo (1951, 1959); Violin Sonata (1911); *Dialogue No. 1* for Violin and Piano (1923); *Dialogue No. 2* for Violin and Piano (1925); Sonata for Viola Solo (1958); Sonata for Cello Solo (1954); *Dialogue No. 1* for Cello and Piano (1922); *Dialogue No. 2* for Cello and Piano (1929); Sonata for Cello and Piano (1958); *Suite* for 2 Cellos (1962); *Suite* for Flute Solo (1931); Flute Sonata (1945); *Pastorale* for 2 Flutes (1950); *Suite* for English Horn and Piano (1963); Sonata for Clarinet Solo (1953); Sonata for Bassoon Solo (1953). VOCAL: Oratorios: *La Passion* (1939–46; Paris, July 25, 1957); *L'Annonciation* (1943–46); *La Mise au tombeau* (1948–49); *La Résurrection* (1953; Strasbourg, March 28, 1969); also *Mystère orphique* for Voice and Orch. (1951; Strasbourg, March 18, 1964); *La Nativité de Notre Seigneur*, "lyric mystery" for Soloists, Chorus, and Instruments (1954); *Du ciel et de la terre*, "space sym." for a film (1957); *Le Zodiaque*, "chorégraphie lyrique" (1958–60); sacred choruses a cappella; double and triple choruses a cappella; pieces for Voice and Instrument(s); numerous unaccompanied vocal trios and quartets; also much liturgical music; a group of albums of character pieces for piano; numerous works for organ. BIBL.: L. Vallas, *G. M.* (Paris, 1923); P. Wolff, *La Route d'un musicien: G. M.* (Paris, 1933); M. Henrion, "La Musique vocale de G. M.," *Revue Musicale* (Nov. 1946); M. Honegger, "G. M.," *Revue Musicale Suisse* (1954); M. Pinchard, *Connaissance de G. M., musicien français* (Paris, 1959); M. Honegger, ed., *Catalogue des œuvres musicales de G. M.* (Strasbourg, 1977); C. Latham, ed. and tr., *G. M.: The Man and His Work* (Strasbourg, 1982).

Miguez, Leopoldo (Américo), Brazilian conductor and composer; b. Rio de Janeiro, Sept. 9, 1850; d. there, July 6, 1902.

He studied with Nicolau Ribas in Oporto, Portugal; then was active with a publishing firm and as a conductor in Rio de Janeiro, where he championed the cause of Wagner; was director of the Instituto Nacional de Música there (1890–1902). He pursued Wagnerian ideas in his theater works.

WORKS: 2 operas: *Pele amor!* (Rio de Janeiro, 1897) and *Os Saldunes* (Rio de Janeiro, Sept. 20, 1901); Sym. (1882); overtures; symphonic poems; marches; songs; piano pieces.

BIBL.: "L. M. e o Instituto Nacional de Música," *Revista Brasileira de Música* (1940).

Mihalovich, Edmund von (actually, **Ödön Péter József de**), Hungarian composer; b. Fericsancze, Sept. 13, 1842; d. Budapest, April 22, 1929. He studied with Mosonyi in Pest and with Hauptmann in Leipzig; also took lessons with Peter Cornelius in Munich. From 1887 to 1919 he taught at the Academy of Music in Budapest. Although he remained wholly committed to the German school of composition throughout his life, he did support the efforts of Bartók, Kodály, and Weiner in their search for a distinct national school.

WORKS: OPERAS: *Hagbart und Signe* (1867–74; Dresden, March 12, 1882); *Wieland der Schmied* (1876–78; *König Fjalar* (1880–84; unfinished); *Eleane* (1885–87; Budapest, Feb. 16, 1908); *Toldi szerelme* (Toldi's Love; 1880–90; Budapest, March 18, 1893; rev. 1893–94; Budapest, Feb. 28, 1895); *A tihanyi visszhang* (The Echo of Tichany; 1903; unfinished). ORCH.: 4 syms. (1879; 1892; 1899–1900; 1901–2); *Hero und Leander*, ballade (1875); *La Ronde du Sabbat*, symphonic poem (1879); *Faust*, fantasy (1880); also choral works; Violin Sonata; piano pieces; songs.

Mihalovici, Marcel, significant Rumanian-born French composer; b. Bucharest, Oct. 22, 1898; d. Paris, Aug. 12, 1985. He studied composition privately with Cuclin in Bucharest; in 1919 he went to Paris, where he settled; became a French citizen in 1955. He studied violin with Nestor Lejeune, Gregorian chant with Amédée Gastoué, and composition with Vincent d'Indy at the Schola Cantorum (1919–25). With Martinů, Conrad Beck, and Tibor Harsányi, he formed a freely associated "École de Paris," consisting of emigrants, which later attracted several other Parisian composers, among them Alexandre Tcherepnin of Russia, Alexandre Tansman of Poland, and Alexander Spitzmueller of Austria. Mihalovici was a founding member of the modern music society "Triton" (1932); was elected a member of the Institut de France in 1964. He married the noted pianist **Monique Haas.** Mihalovici's music presents a felicitous synthesis of French and Eastern European elements, tinted with a roseate impressionistic patina and couched in euphoniously dissonant harmonies.

WORKS: OPERAS: *L'Intransigeant Pluton* (1928; Paris, April 3, 1939); *Phèdre* (1949; Stuttgart, June 9, 1951); *Die Heimkehr* (Frankfurt, June 17, 1954); *Krapp ou La Dernière Bande*, libretto by Samuel Beckett (1959–60; Bielefeld, Feb. 25, 1961); opera-buffa, *Les Jumeaux* (1962; Braunschweig, Jan. 23, 1963). BALLETS: *Une Vie de Polichinelle* (Paris, 1923); *Le Postillon du Roy* (Paris, 1924); *Divertimento* (Paris, 1925); *Karagueuz*, ballet for marionettes (Paris, 1926); *Thésée au labyrinthe* (1956; Braunschweig, April 4, 1957; rev. as *Scènes de Thésée*, Cologne, Oct. 15, 1958); *Alternamenti* (1957; Braunschweig, Feb. 28, 1958); *Variations* (Bielefeld, March 28, 1960). ORCH.: *Notturno* (1923); *Introduction au mouvement symphonique* (1923; Bucharest, Oct. 17, 1926); *Fantaisie* (1927; Liège, Sept. 6, 1930); *Cortège des divinités infernales* (1928; Bucharest, Dec. 7, 1930); *Chindia* for 13 Wind Instruments and Piano (1929); *Concerto quasi una Fantasia* for Violin and Orch. (1930; Barcelona, April 22, 1936); *Divertissement* (1934); *Capriccio roumain* (1936); *Prélude et Invention* for String Orch. (1937; Warsaw, April 21, 1939); *Toccata* for Piano and Orch. (1938; rev. 1940); *Symphonies pour le temps présent* (1944); *Variations* for Brass and Strings (1946); *Séquences* (1947); *Ritournelles* (1951); 5 syms.: *Sinfonia giocosa* (Basel, Dec. 14, 1951); *Sinfonia partita* for Strings (1952); *Sinfonia variata* (1960); *Sinfonia cantata* for Baritone, Chorus, and Orch. (1953–63); No. 5 for Soprano and Orch. (in memory of Hans Rosbaud, 1966–69;

Paris, Dec. 14, 1971); *Étude en 2 parties* for Piano Concertante, 7 Wind Instruments, Celesta, and Percussion (Donaueschingen, Oct. 6, 1951); *Elegie* (1955); *Ouverture tragique* (1957); *Esercizio* for Strings (1959); *Musique nocturne* for Clarinet, String Orch., Harpsichord, and Celesta (1963); *Aubade* for Strings (1964); *Périples* for Orch. with Piano Concertante (1967; Paris, March 22, 1970); *Prétextes* for Oboe, Bass Clarinet, and Chamber Orch. (1968); *Variantes* for Horn, and Orch. or Piano (1969); *Borne* (1970); *Rondo* (1970); *Chant premier* for Saxophone and Orch. (1973–74); *Follia*, paraphrases (1976–77). VOCAL: Cantata, *La Genèse* (1935–40); *Cantilène* for Mezzo-soprano and Chamber Orch. (1972); *Cascando*, invention for Music and Voice (1962); *Mémorial*, 5 a cappella motets, each dedicated to a different deceased composer (1952); songs, *Abendgesang* (1957), *Stances* (1967), and *Textes* (1974). CHAMBER: 2 violin sonatas (1920, 1941); Piano Quartet (1922); 3 string quartets (1923; 1931; 1943–46); Oboe Sonatina (1924); *Serenade* for String Trio (1929); Sonata for 3 Clarinets (1933); Viola Sonata (1942); Sonata for Violin and Cello (1944); *Egloge* for Flute, Oboe, Clarinet, Bassoon, and Piano (1945); Sonata for Violin Solo (1949); Sonata for Cello Solo (1949); Wind Trio (1955); *Pastorale triste* for Flute and Piano (1958); Bassoon Sonata (1958); Clarinet Sonata (1958); *Improvisation* for Percussion (1961); *Dialogues* for Clarinet and Piano (1965); *Serioso* for Bass Saxophone and Piano (1971); *Récit* for Clarinet (1973); *Melopeia* for Oboe (1973). PIANO: *3 Nocturnes* (1928); *4 Caprices* (1929); *Ricercari* (1941); *3 pièces nocturnes* (1948); Sonata (1964); *Cantus Firmus* for 2 Pianos (1970); *Passacaglia* for the Left Hand (1975); incidental music for productions of *Sappho* (1946), *Le Paradis perdu* (1951), *Meurtre dans la cathédrale* (1952), *Orphée* (1954), *Mélusine* (1957), and *Herakles* (1975).
BIBL.: G. Beck, *M. M.: Esquisse biographique* (Paris, 1954).

Mihály, András, Hungarian composer and conductor; b. Budapest, Nov. 6, 1917. He studied cello with Adolf Schiffer and chamber music with Leo Weiner and Imre Waldbauer at the Budapest Academy of Music (1934–38); took private composition lessons from Paul Kadosa and István Strasser. He played cello in the orch. of the Budapest Opera (1946–47); was a prof. of chamber music (from 1950) and director of the student orch. (from 1987) at the Budapest Academy of Music; also served as director of the New Hungarian Chamber Ensemble; from 1978 to 1987 he was director of the Hungarian State Opera in Budapest. He won the Kossuth Prize (1955) and 3 Erkel Prizes (1952, 1954, 1964); in 1977 he was made an Eminent Artist by the Hungarian government. As a composer, he writes in a compact contrapuntal style oxygenated by a breath of lyricism.
WORKS: Opera: *Együtt és egyedül* (Together and Alone; 1964–65; Budapest, Nov. 5, 1966); 3 syms. (*Sinfonia da Requiem*, 1946; 1950; 1962); cantatas: *My Beloved Hungarian Fatherland* (1952); *The Red Cart* (1957); *Memory and Warning* (1959); *1871* (1960); *Fly, Poem!* (1967); Cello Concerto (1953); Piano Concerto (1954); *Fantasy* for Wind Quintet, String Orch., Harp, Celesta, and Percussion (1955); *Festive Overture* (1959); Violin Concerto, with Piano obbligato (1959); *3 Movements* for Chamber Ensemble (1969); *Monodia* for Orch. (1971); *Musica per 15* (1975); Piano Trio (1940); 3 string quartets (1942, 1960, 1977); *Rhapsody* for Viola and Piano (1947); *Serenade* for Wind Trio (1956); *Suite* for Cello and Piano (1957); Piano Sonata (1958); *3 Apocrypha* for Female Vocal Trio or Chorus, and Clarinet and Percussion (1962); *Movement* for Cello and Piano (1962); song cycles: *Chamber Music*, after Joyce (1958); *Attila József Songs* (1961); and *Psalms of Rapture*, after Radnóti (1969); incidental music to plays and films.
BIBL.: J. Kárpáti, *M. A.* (Budapest, 1965).

Mikhailova, Maria (Alexandrovna), Russian soprano; b. Kharkov, June 3, 1866; d. Moscow, Jan. 18, 1943. She studied in St. Petersburg, and then in Paris and Milan; in 1892 she made her debut at the Imperial Opera in St. Petersburg as Marguerite de Valois in *Les Huguenots;* she remained a member there until 1912. On Oct. 29, 1895, she created the role of

Electra in Taneyev's *Oresteia*. She visited Tokyo in 1907. She made over 300 recordings, achieving a considerable reputation through the gramophone alone.

Mikhashoff, Yvar (Emilian), American pianist and composer; b. Troy, N.Y., March 8, 1941. He studied at the Eastman School of Music in Rochester, N.Y.; then enrolled at the Juilliard School of Music in N.Y. as a student of Beveridge Webster; subsequently studied composition on a Fulbright scholarship with Nadia Boulanger in Paris (1968–69); also studied at the Univ. of Houston (B.M., 1967; M.M., 1968) and the Univ. of Texas in Austin (D.M.A. in composition, 1973). He taught at the State Univ. of N.Y. in Buffalo (from 1973); toured extensively in the U.S. and Europe, being particularly noted for his championship of American music of the 19th and 20th centuries. He also appeared as a multimedia performer. In 1980 he played the principal acting role in the La Scala premiere of Bussotti's opera *La Racine*. In 1982 he organized the Holland Festival's 2-week-long celebration of 200 years of Dutch-American friendship through a series of 9 thematic concerts covering 250 years of American music.
WORKS: Concerto No. 1 for Piano, Winds, and Percussion (1965); Viola Concerto (1969); *Dances for Davia, I and II,* for Flute and Piano (1958, 1979); *Nocturne* for Cello and Piano (1977); *Light from a Distant Garden* for String Quartet (1983); *Grand Bowery Tango* for Flute and Ensemble (1985); *Night Dances* for String Trio (1985); *Twilight Dances* for Violin, Contrabass, Piano, and Percussion (1986); *Evening Dances* for Violin and Piano (1987); piano pieces; several vocal works, including *In Memoriam Igor Stravinsky* for Voice, Flute, Clarinet, and Cello (1971) and *Improvisations on the Last Words of Chief Seattle* for Speaker, Percussion, Mime Dancer, and Syllabist (1976).

Miki, Minoru, Japanese composer; b. Tokushima, March 16, 1930. He studied with Ifukube and Ikenouchi at the National Univ. of Fine Arts and Music in Tokyo (1951–55); was a founder of the Nihon Ongaku Shūdan (Pro Musica Nipponia; 1964), an ensemble dedicated to performing new music for traditional Japanese instruments; later served as its artistic director. He lectured at the Tokyo College of Music; was founder-director of UTAYOMI-ZA (1986), a musical-opera theater.
WORKS: OPERAS: *Mendori Teishu* (A Henpecked Husband), chamber opera (1963); *Shunkin-shō* (Tokyo, 1975); *An Actor's Revenge* (London, 1979); *Toge no muko ni naniga aruka*, choral opera (1983); *Utayomizaru*, musical-opera (1983); *Joruri* (St. Louis, 1985); *At the Flower Garden*, mini-opera (1985). ORCH.: *Trinita sinfonica* (1953); *Sinfonia Gamula* (1957); *Symphony: Joya* (1960); Marimba Concerto (1969); *Jo-no-Kyoku*, prelude for Shakuhachi, Koro, Shamisen, and Strings (1969); *Convexity*, concerto for 3 Groups of Sankyoku and a Japanese Drum (1970); *Ha-no-Kyoku*, koto concerto (1974); *Hote* for Japanese Orch. (1976); *Symphony from Life* (1980); *Concerto Requiem* for Koto and Japanese Instruments (1980); *Kyu-no-Kyoku* (Sym. for 2 Worlds; Leipzig, Nov. 12, 1981); *3 Pieces*: 1, *March 1930*; 2, *August 1945*; 3, *September 1950* (1983). CHAMBER: *Osabai* for 12 Wind Instruments and Percussion (1955); Sextet for Wind Instruments and Piano (1965); *Paraphrase after Ancient Japanese Music* for Soprano and Ensemble of 10 Japanese Instruments (1966); *Figures for 4 Groups* for Various Instruments (1967–69); *Ballades* for Koto (3 vols., 1969, 1976, 1983); *Tennyo* for Koto (1969); *Hakuyo* for Violin and Koto (1973); *Danses concertantes No. 1, 4 Seasons,* for Ensemble of Japanese Instruments (1973–74), *No. 2, Naruto-Hicho,* for Ensemble of Japanese Instruments (1977), *No. 3, A Tale of Hachirō,* for Ensemble of Japanese Instruments (1981), and *No. 4, Kitano-Uta* (1984); *Yui I* for Shō and Piano (1982), *II* for Cello and Koto (1980–83), and *III, Flowers and Water,* for Shakuhachi, Koto, Shamisen, Harp, and String Quartet (1985); *Marimba Spiritual* for Marimba and 3 Percussionists (1984); Trio for Violin, Cello, and Piano (1986); also many choral works, including *Matsu-no-Kyoko* for Women's Chorus and Ensemble of Japanese Instruments (1974), *Sinfonia concertante per Wasan* for Bass, Women's Chorus, Nohkan, Koto, and Orch. (1976),

Taro, cantata for 5 Soloists, Children's Chorus, and 17 Japanese Instruments (1977), and *Awa Kitobun, I, II, III* (1981).

Mikorey, Franz, German composer and conductor; b. Munich, June 3, 1873; d. there, May 11, 1947. He studied in Munich with Thuille and H. Levi; later in Berlin with H. von Herzogenberg; conducted in Bayreuth (1894); then in Prague, Regensburg, Elberfeld, and Vienna; in 1902 he was engaged as court conductor in Dessau; was appointed music director there in 1912. He conducted opera in Helsinki from 1919 to 1924; then returned to Germany. He publ. *Grundlagen des Dirigierens* (1929).
    WORKS: Opera, *Der König von Samarkand* (Dessau, 1910); 2 syms. *(Tragische; An der Adria)*; *Sinfonia engadiana* for Soli, Chorus, and Orch.; Piano Concerto; Piano Quintet; Piano Trio; male choruses; songs.
    BIBL.: E. Hamann, *F. M.* (Leipzig, 1907).

Miksch, Johann Aloys, esteemed Bohemian baritone and teacher; b. Georgental, July 19, 1765; d. Dresden, Sept. 24, 1845. He was a choirboy in Dresden; then a singer at the Court Church (from 1786); was a baritone in the Italian Opera of Dresden (from 1797); was chorus master of the German Opera (from 1820); was pensioned in 1831. He was greatly renowned as a teacher; among his pupils was Schröder-Devrient.
    BIBL.: A. Kohut, *J. M.* (Leipzig, 1890).

Mikuli, Karl (Karol), Polish pianist, conductor, teacher, and composer of Moldavian descent; b. Czernowitz, Oct. 20, 1819; d. Lemberg, May 21, 1897. He 1st studied medicine in Vienna, but his pronounced talent for music made him decide to go to Paris for serious study; there he became a pupil of Chopin (1844); he also studied composition with Reicha. After the outbreak of the Revolution of 1848, he left Paris and made several tours in Russia and Austria; was appointed director of the Lemberg Cons. (1858); 30 years later he established a music school of his own there. His ed. of Chopin's works contains numerous emendations made by Chopin himself as marginal remarks in Mikuli's student copies. He wrote choral works, chamber music, songs, and piano pieces, the latter greatly influenced by Chopin's style.

Mila, Massimo, Italian writer on music; b. Turin, Aug. 14, 1910; d. there, Dec. 26, 1988. He studied literature at the Univ. of Turin; after graduation, he became a regular contributor to many Italian musical publications; was music critic of *L'Espresso* (1955–68) and of *La Stampa* (1968–74). He taught music history at the Turin Cons. (1953–73) and at the Univ. of Turin (from 1960).
    WRITINGS: *Il melodramma di Verdi* (Bari, 1933); *Cent' anni di musica moderna* (Milan, 1944); *W.A. Mozart* (Turin, 1945); *Breve storia della musica* (Milan, 1946; 2nd ed., 1963); *L'esperienza musicale e l'estetica* (Turin, 1950; 3rd ed., 1965); *"La carriera d'un libertino" di Strawinsky* (Milan, 1952); *Cronache musicale, 1955–1959* (Turin, 1959); *La musica pianistica di Mozart* (Turin, 1963); *Le sinfonie di Mozart* (Turin, 1967); *"I vespri siciliani" di Verdi* (Turin, 1973); *Lettura del Don Giovanni di Mozart* (Turin, 1988).
    BIBL.: G. Pestelli, ed., *Il melodramma italiano dell'ottocento: Studi e ricerche per M. M.* (Turin, 1977).

Milán, Luis de, Spanish musician, courtier, and poet; b. Valencia, c.1500; d. after 1561. He was a favorite at the viceregal court of Valencia under Germaine de Foix and her 3rd husband, Don Fernando of Aragón. In 1536 he brought out his most important work, *Libro de música de vihuela de mano intitulado El Maestro* (Valencia), intended as an instruction book for learning to play the vihuela. This was the 1st book of its kind to be publ. in Spain, and is valuable for its many musical examples (*tientos*, fantasias, pavanes, and solo songs with guitar accompaniment: *villancicos*, romances, and *sonetos*), which reveal Milán's high qualities as a composer. He also publ. *El cortesano* (1561), giving a description of courtly life at Valencia in his day.
    BIBL.: J. Trend, *L. d.M. and the Vihuelistas* (Oxford, 1925);

J. Ward, *The Vihuela de Mano and Its Music* (1536–1576) (diss., N.Y. Univ., 1953).

Milanov, Zinka (née **Kunc**), famous Croatian-American soprano; b. Zagreb, May 17, 1906; d. N.Y., May 30, 1989. She studied at the Zagreb Academy of Music, then with Milka Ternina, Maria Kostrenčić, and Fernando Carpi; made her debut as Leonora in *Il Trovatore* in Ljubljana (1927); subsequently was principal soprano of the Zagreb Opera (1928–35), where she sang in over 300 performances in Croatian. After appearing at Prague's German Theater (1936), she was invited by Toscanini to sing in his performance of the Verdi *Requiem* at the Salzburg Festival (1937). She then made her Metropolitan Opera debut in N.Y. as Verdi's Leonora on Dec. 17, 1937; was one of the outstanding members on its roster (1937–41; 1942–47; 1950–66); gave her farewell performance there as Maddalena in *Andrea Chénier* on April 13, 1966. In addition to appearing in San Francisco and Chicago, she also sang at Buenos Aires's Teatro Colón (1940–42), Milan's La Scala (1950), and London's Covent Garden (1966–67). Her brother was the pianist and composer **Božidar Kunc.** She married Predrag Milanov in 1937, but they were divorced in 1946; she then married Ljubomir Ilic in 1947. Blessed with a voice of translucent beauty, she became celebrated for her outstanding performances of roles in operas by Verdi and Puccini.

Milburn, Ellsworth, American composer; b. Greensburg, Pa., Feb. 6, 1938. He studied with Scott Huston at the Univ. of Cincinnati College-Cons. of Music (1956–58); later with Roy Travis and Henri Lazarof at the Univ. of Calif. at Los Angeles (1959–62) and at Mills College in Oakland, Calif., with Milhaud (1966–68). He was a teacher at the Univ. of Cincinnati College-Cons. of Music (1970–75) and at Rice Univ. in Houston (from 1975).
    WORKS: Opera, *Gesualdo* (1973); *5 Inventions* for 2 Flutes (1965); *Massacre of the Innocents* for Chorus (1965); Concerto for Piano and Chamber Orch. (1967); String Trio (1968); *Soli for 5 Players on 10 Instruments* (1968); String Quintet (1969); *Soli II* for 2 Players on Flutes and Double Bass (1970); *Voussoirs* for Orch. (1970); *Soli III* for Clarinet, Cello, and Piano (1971); *Soli IV* for Flute, Oboe, Double Bass, and Harpsichord (1972); Violin Sonata (1972); *Lament* for Harp (1972).

Milde, Hans Feodor von, Austrian baritone; b. Petronell, April 13, 1821; d. Weimar, Dec. 10, 1899. He studied with F. Hauser and M. García; was a life member of the Weimar Court Opera, and created the role of Telramund in *Lohengrin* (1850). His wife, **Rosa Agthé Milde** (b. Weimar, June 25, 1827; d. there, Jan. 26, 1906), also sang in Weimar (1845–67), where she created the role of Elsa in *Lohengrin*.
    BIBL.: N. von Milde, *P. Cornelius. Briefe . . . an F. und R. v.M.* (Weimar, 1901).

Mildenberg, Albert, American composer; b. Brooklyn, Jan. 13, 1878; d. there (N.Y.), July 3, 1918. He was a member of a musical family; studied piano with his mother; then took lessons with Rafael Joseffy (piano) and Bruno Oscar Klein (composition). In 1905 he went to Rome, where he studied with Sgambati; later studied in Paris with Massenet. Returning to America, he became dean of the music dept. of Meredith College in Raleigh, N.C. He wrote a number of songs, many of them to his own texts; also wrote his own opera librettos. His style was in the Italian tradition; Massenet commended his gift of melody. His light opera *The Wood Witch* was produced in N.Y. on May 25, 1903; another comic opera, *Love's Locksmith*, was given in N.Y. in 1912.

Mildenburg, Anna (actually, **Anna von Bellschau-Mildenburg**), famous Austrian soprano, known as **Anna Bahr-Mildenburg;** b. Vienna, Nov. 29, 1872; d. there, Jan. 27, 1947. She studied with Rosa Papier in Vienna and Bernhard Pollini, the director of the Hamburg Opera, who engaged her to make her debut there as Brünnhilde in *Die Walküre* (Sept. 12, 1895) under Mahler's baton. She appeared as Kundry at the Bayreuth Festival (1897), and subsequently sang there with distinction until 1914; likewise was a leading member of the Vienna Court Opera (1898–1917), where she continued to make appearances until 1921; also sang at London's Covent Garden (1906, 1910, 1913). She was a prof. at the Munich Academy of Music (from 1921) and stage director of the Bavarian State Opera there (1921–26); made her farewell appearance as a singer as Clytemnestra in Augsburg (1930). In 1909 she married the playwright Hermann Bahr, with whom she wrote *Bayreuth und das Wagner Theater* (Leipzig, 1910; Eng. tr., London, 1912); also publ. her memoirs (Vienna and Berlin, 1921) and *Darstellung der Werke Richard Wagner aus dem Geiste der Dichtung und Musik* (Leipzig, 1936). She was generally recognized as one of the foremost Wagnerians of her day.

Bibl.: P. Stefan, *A. B.-M.* (Vienna, 1922).

Milder-Hauptmann, (Pauline) Anna, prominent German soprano; b. Constantinople, Dec. 13, 1785; d. Berlin, May 29, 1838. She was the daughter of an Austrian diplomatic official; in Vienna she attracted the notice of Schikaneder. He recommended her to Tomaselli and Salieri, who taught her opera singing. She made her debut as Juno in Süssmayr's *Der Spiegel von Arkadien* in Vienna on April 9, 1803, and soon became so well regarded as an artist and singer that Beethoven wrote the role of Fidelio for her (Vienna, Nov. 20, 1805). After a tour in 1808, she was made prima donna assoluta at the Berlin court. In 1810 she married a Vienna merchant, Hauptmann. In 1812 she went to Berlin, where she created a sensation, particularly as Gluck's heroines (in *Iphigénie en Tauride, Alcestis,* and *Armida*); she left Berlin in 1829; then sang in Russia, Sweden, and Austria. Mendelssohn chose her as a soloist in his revival of Bach's *St. Matthew Passion* in Berlin (1829); she made her farewell appearance in Vienna in 1836. Her voice was so powerful that Haydn reportedly said to her: "Dear child, you have a voice like a house."

Miles, Maurice, English conductor; b. Epsom, Feb. 25, 1908; d. Hereford, June 26, 1985. He studied with Curzon (piano) and with Wood and Reed (conducting) at the Royal Academy of Music in London; later with Krauss at the Salzburg Mozarteum. He was on the staff of the BBC (1930–36); then conducted in Buxton and Bath (1936–39); after service in the British army, he rejoined the BBC (1943). He then was conductor of the Yorkshire Sym. Orch. (1947–54); later conducted the City of Belfast Orch. (1955–66) and the Ulster Orch. (1966–67); also taught at the Royal Academy of Music (from 1953).

Miles, Philip Napier, English composer and conductor; b. Shirehampton, Jan. 21, 1865; d. King's Weston, near Bristol, July 19, 1935. He studied in London with Parry and Dannreuther; organized the Shirehampton Choral Soc. on his own estate and conducted festivals in various localities in England. He wrote several operas: *Westward Ho!* (London, Dec. 4, 1914), *Fire Flies* (Clifton, Oct. 13, 1924; on the same program with his opera *Markheim*), *Good Friday, Demeter,* and *Queen Rosamond;* also some chamber music and many songs.

Bibl.: H. Colles, "P.N. M.," *Music & Letters* (1936).

Miletić, Miroslav, Croatian violinist and composer; b. Sisak, Aug. 22, 1925. He studied in Zagreb; organized there the renowned Pro Arte String Quartet, specializing in performances of modern music.

Works: Operas: *Hasanaginica* and *Der Fall Ru-ženka;* radio opera, *Auvergnanski Senatori* (1957); *Vision,* television ballet (1958); Suite for String Orch. (1955); Violin Concerto (1958); Viola Concerto (1959); Sym. (1959); *Rhapsodic Variations* for Violin and Piano (1962); 4 string quartets; Violin Sonata; *Proportions* for 6 Instruments; *Lamentation* for Viola and Magnetic Tape; piano pieces; Croatian songs arranged for recorder.

Milford, Robin (Humphrey), English composer; b. Oxford, Jan. 22, 1903; d. Lyme Regis, Dec. 29, 1959. He studied with Holst, Vaughan Williams, and R.O. Morris at the Royal College of Music in London. While still a student, he composed a number of works, mostly in small forms, in a clear rhythmic manner, with thematic materials suggesting English folk music.

Works: stage: Opera, *The Scarlet Letter* (1959); Ballet, *The Snow Queen,* after Hans Christian Andersen (1946); oratorio, *The Pilgrim's Progress,* after John Bunyan (1932); *The Forsaken Merman,* after Matthew Arnold, for Tenor, Women's Chorus, Strings, and Piano (1938–50); *A Litany to the Holy Spirit,* after Robert Herrick (1947). **orch.:** Suite for Chamber Orch. (1924); *Miniature Concerto* for Harpsichord and Chamber Orch. (1927); *Miniature Concerto* for Strings (1933); Violin Concerto (1937); *Ariel* for Small Orch. (1940); *Elegiac Meditation* for Viola and Strings (1947); *A Festival* for Strings (1951); *Fishing by Moonlight* for Piano and Strings (1952). **chamber:** Flute Sonata (1944); *Fantasia* for String Quartet (1945); Violin Sonata (1945); Trio for Clarinet, Cello, and Piano (1948); Trio for 2 Violins and Piano (1949); Violin Sonata (1945); piano pieces; songs.

Bibl.: I. Copley, *R. M.* (London, 1985).

Milhaud, Darius, eminent French composer; b. Aix-en-Provence, Sept. 4, 1892; d. Geneva, June 22, 1974. He was the descendant of an old Jewish family, settled in Provence for many centuries. His father was a merchant of almonds; there was a piano in the house, and Milhaud improvised melodies as a child; then began to take violin lessons. He entered the Paris Cons. in 1909, almost at the age limit for enrollment; studied with Berthelier (violin), Lefèvre (ensemble), Leroux (harmony), Gédalge (counterpoint), Widor (composition and fugue), and d'Indy (conducting); played violin in the student orch. under Dukas. He received 1st "accessit" in violin and counterpoint, and 2nd in fugue; won the Prix Lepaulle for composition. While still a student, he wrote music in a bold modernistic manner; became associated with Satie, Cocteau, and Claudel. When Claudel was appointed French minister to Brazil, he engaged Milhaud as his secretary; they sailed for Rio de Janeiro early in 1917; returned to Paris (via the West Indies and N.Y.) shortly after the armistice of Nov. 1918. Milhaud's name became known to a larger public as a result of a newspaper article by Henri Collet in *Comœdia* (Jan. 16, 1920), grouping him with 5 other French composers of modern tendencies (Auric, Durey, Honegger, Poulenc, and Tailleferre) under the sobriquet Les Six, even though the association was stylistically fortuitous. In 1922 he visited the U.S.; lectured at Harvard Univ., Princeton Univ., and Columbia Univ.; appeared as pianist and composer in his own works; in 1925, he traveled in Italy, Germany, Austria, and Russia; returning to France, he devoted himself mainly to composition and teaching. At the outbreak of World War II, he was in Aix-en-Provence; in July 1940 he went to the U.S.; taught at Mills College in Oakland, Calif. In 1947 he returned to France; was appointed prof. at the Paris Cons., but continued to visit the U.S. as conductor and teacher almost annually, despite arthritis, which compelled him to conduct while seated; he retained his post at Mills College until 1971; then settled in Geneva. Exceptionally prolific from his student days, he wrote a great number of works in every genre; introduced a modernistic type of music drama, "opéra à la minute," and also the "miniature symphony." He experimented with new stage techniques, incorporating cinematic interludes; also successfully revived the Greek type of tragedy with vocal accompaniment. He composed works for electronic instruments, and demonstrated his contrapuntal skill in such compositions as his 2 string quartets (No. 14 and No. 15), which can be played together as a string octet. He was the 1st to exploit polytonality in a consistent and deliberate manner; applied the exotic rhythms of Latin America and the West Indies in many of his lighter works; of these, his *Saudades do Brasil* are particularly popular; Brazilian movements are also found in his *Scaramouche* and *Le Bœuf sur le toit;* in some of his works he drew upon the resources of jazz. His ballet *La Création du monde* (1923), portraying the Creation in terms of Negro cosmology, constitutes the earliest example of the use of the blues and jazz in a symphonic score, anticipating Gershwin in this respect. Despite this variety of means and versatility of forms, Milhaud succeeded in establishing a style that was distinctly and identifiably his own; his melodies are nostalgically lyrical or vivaciously rhythmical, according to mood; his instrumental writing is of great complexity and difficulty, and yet entirely within the capacities of modern virtuoso technique; he arranged many of his works in several versions.

WORKS: OPERAS: *La Brebis égarée*, "roman musical" (1910–15; Paris, Dec. 10, 1923); *Le Pauvre Matelot*, "complainte en trois actes" (1926; Paris, Dec. 12, 1927); *Les Malheurs d'Orphée* (Brussels, May 7, 1926); *Esther de Carpentras*, opéra-bouffe (1925; Paris, Feb. 1, 1938); 3 "minute operas": *L'Enlèvement d'Europe* (Baden-Baden, July 17, 1927), *L'Abandon d'Ariane*, and *La Délivrance de Thésée* (Wiesbaden, April 20, 1928); *Christophe Colomb* (Berlin, May 5, 1930); *Maximilien* (Paris, Jan. 4, 1932); *Médée* (Antwerp, Oct. 7, 1939); *Bolivar* (1943; Paris, May 12, 1950); *Le Jeu de Robin et Marion*, mystery play after Adam de la Halle (Wiesbaden, Oct. 28, 1951); *David* (Jerusalem, June 1, 1954); *La Mère coupable*, to a libretto by Madeleine Milhaud, after Beaumarchais (Geneva, June 13, 1966); *Saint Louis, Roi de France*, opera-oratorio (1970–71; Rio de Janeiro, April 14, 1972). **INCIDENTAL MUSIC:** *Agamemnon* (1913; Paris, April 16, 1927); *Les Choéphores* (concert version, Paris, June 15, 1919; stage version, Brussels, March 27, 1935); *Les Euménides* (1922; Antwerp, Nov. 27, 1927); *Jeux d'enfants* (short plays for children for Voice and Instruments): *À propos de bottes* (1932), *Un Petit Peu de musique* (1933), *Un Petit Peu d'exercice* (1937).

BALLETS: *L'Homme et son désir* (Paris, June 6, 1921); *Le Bœuf sur le toit* (Paris, Feb. 21, 1920); *Les Mariés de la Tour Eiffel* (Paris, June 19, 1921; with Honegger, Auric, Poulenc, and Tailleferre); *La Création du monde* (Paris, Oct. 25, 1923); *Salade*, "ballet chanté" (Paris, May 17, 1924); *Le Train bleu*, "danced operetta" (Paris, June 20, 1924); *Polka* for a ballet, *L'Éventail de Jeanne*, homage to Jeanne Dubost, patroness of music (other numbers contributed by Ravel, Ibert, Roussel, and others; Paris, June 16, 1927); *Jeux de printemps* (Washington, D.C., Oct. 30, 1944); *The Bells*, after Poe (Chicago, April 26, 1946); *'adame Miroir* (Paris, May 31, 1948); *Vendange* (1952; Nice, April 17, 1972); *La Rose des vents* (Paris, 1958); *La Branche des oiseaux* (Nice, 1965).

ORCH.: *Suite symphonique* No. 1 (Paris, May 26, 1914); *Suite symphonique* No. 2 (from incidental music to Claudel's *Protée*; Paris, Oct. 24, 1920); 5 syms. for Small Orch.: No. 1, *Le Printemps* (1917), No. 2, *Pastorale* (1918), No. 3, *Sérénade* (1921), No. 4, *Dixtuor à cordes* (1921), No. 5, *Dixtuor d'instruments à vent* (1922); 12 syms. for Large Orch.: No. 1 (Chicago, Oct. 17, 1940, composer conducting); No. 2 (Boston, Dec. 20, 1946, composer conducting); No. 3, *Hymnus ambrosianus*, with Chorus (Paris, Oct. 30, 1947); No. 4 (Paris, May 20, 1948, composer conducting); No. 5 (Turin, Oct. 16, 1953); No. 6 (Boston, Oct. 7, 1955, composer conducting); No. 7 (Chicago, March 3, 1956); No. 8, *Rhodanienne* (Berkeley, Calif., April 22, 1958); No. 9 (Fort Lauderdale, Fla., March 29, 1960); No. 10 (Portland, Oreg., April 4, 1961); No. 11, *Romantique* (Dallas, Dec. 12, 1960); No. 12, *Rural* (Davis, Calif., Feb. 16, 1962); *Cinéma-Fantaisie sur Le Bœuf sur le toit* for Violin and Orch. (Paris, Dec. 4, 1920); *Caramel mou*, a shimmy, for Jazz Band (1920); *5 études* for Piano and Orch. (Paris, Jan. 20, 1921); *Saudades do Brasil*, suite of dances (also for Piano; 1920–21); *Ballade* for Piano and Orch. (1921); *3 Rag Caprices* (Paris, Nov. 23, 1923); *Le Carnaval d'Aix*, for Piano and Orch. (N.Y., Dec. 9, 1926, composer soloist); *2 hymnes* (1927); Violin Concerto No. 1 (1927); Viola Concerto (Amsterdam, Dec. 15, 1929); Concerto for Percussion and Small Orch. (Paris, Dec. 5, 1930); Piano Concerto No. 1 (Paris, Nov. 23, 1934); *Concertino de printemps*, for Violin and Orch. (Paris, March 21, 1935); Cello Concerto No. 1 (Paris, June 28, 1935); *Suite provençale* (Venice, Sept. 12, 1937); *L'Oiseau* (Paris, Jan. 30, 1938); *Cortège funèbre* (N.Y., Aug. 4, 1940); Clarinet Concerto (1941; Washington, D.C., Jan. 30, 1946); Piano Concerto No. 2 (Chicago, Dec. 18, 1941, composer soloist); Concerto for 2 Pianos and Orch. (Pittsburgh, Nov. 13, 1942); *Opus americanum* (San Francisco, Dec. 6, 1943); *Suite française* (for Band, N.Y., June 13, 1945; for Orch., N.Y., July 29, 1945); *Cain and Abel* for Narrator

and Orch. (Hollywood, Oct. 21, 1945); *Le Bal martiniquais* (N.Y., Dec. 6, 1945, composer conducting); *2 Marches* (CBS, N.Y., Dec. 12, 1945); *Fête de la Victoire* (1945); Cello Concerto No. 2 (N.Y., Nov. 28, 1946); *Suite* for Harmonica and Orch. (1942; Paris, May 28, 1947, Larry Adler soloist; also for Violin and Orch., Philadelphia, Nov. 16, 1945, Zino Francescatti soloist); Piano Concerto No. 3 (Prague, May 26, 1946); Violin Concerto No. 2 (Paris, Nov. 7, 1948); *L'Apothéose de Molière* for Harpsichord and Strings (Capri, Sept. 15, 1948); *Kentuckiana* (Louisville, Jan. 4, 1949); Concerto for Marimba, Vibraphone, and Orch. (St. Louis, Feb. 12, 1949); Piano Concerto No. 4 (Boston, March 3, 1950); *West Point Suite* for Band (West Point, May 30, 1952); *Concertino d'hiver* for Trombone and String Orch. (1953); *Ouverture méditerranéenne* (Louisville, May 22, 1954); Harp Concerto (Venice, Sept. 17, 1954); Piano Concerto No. 5 (1955; N.Y., June 25, 1956); Oboe Concerto (1957); Concerto No. 3 for Violin and Orch., *Concerto royal* (1958); *Aubade* (Oakland, Calif., March 14, 1961); *Ouverture philharmonique* (N.Y., Nov. 30, 1962); *A Frenchman in New York* (Boston, June 25, 1963); *Odes pour les morts des guerres* (1963); *Murder of a Great Chief of State*, in memory of John F. Kennedy (Oakland, Calif., Dec. 3, 1963); *Pacem in terris*, choral sym. (Paris, Dec. 20, 1963); *Music for Boston* for Violin and Orch. (1965); *Musique pour Prague* (Prague, May 20, 1966); *Musique pour l'Indiana* (Indianapolis, Oct. 29, 1966); *Musique pour Lisbonne* (1966); *Musique pour Nouvelle Orléans* (commissioned by the New Orleans Sym. Orch., but unaccountably canceled, and perf. for the 1st time in Aspen, Colo., Aug. 11, 1968, composer conducting); *Musique pour l'Univers Claudelien* (Aix-en-Provence, July 30, 1968); *Musique pour Graz* (Graz, Nov. 24, 1970); *Musique pour San Francisco*, "with the participation of the audience" (1971); *Suite in G* (San Rafael, Calif., Sept. 25, 1971); *Ode pour Jerusalem* (1972). **CHAMBER:** 18 string quartets (1912–51), of which No. 14 and No. 15 are playable together, forming an octet (1st perf. in this form in Oakland, Calif., Aug. 10, 1949); 2 violin sonatas (1911, 1917); Sonata for Piano and 2 Violins (1914); *Le Printemps* for Piano and Violin (1914); Sonata for Piano, Flute, Clarinet, and Oboe (1918); Sonatina for Flute and Piano (1922); *Impromptu* for Violin and Piano (1926); *3 caprices de Paganini* for Violin and Piano (1927); Sonatina for Clarinet and Piano (1927); *Pastorale* for Oboe, Clarinet, and Bassoon (1935); *Suite* for Oboe, Clarinet, and Bassoon (1937); *La Cheminée du Roi René*, suite for Flute, Oboe, Clarinet, Horn, and Bassoon (1939); Sonatina for 2 Violins (1940); *Sonatine à trois* for Violin, Viola, and Cello (1940); Sonatina for Violin and Viola (1941); *Quatre visages* for Viola and Piano (1943); 2 viola sonatas (1944); *Elegie* for Cello and Piano (1945); *Danses de Jacarémirim* for Violin and Piano (1945); Sonata for Violin and Harpsichord (1945); Duo for 2 Violins (1945); String Trio (1947); *Aspen Serenade* for 9 Instruments (1957); String Sextet (1958); Chamber Concerto for Piano, Wind Instruments, and String Quintet (1961); String Septet (1964); Piano Quartet (1966); Piano Trio (1968); *Stanford Serenade* for Oboe and 11 Instruments (1969; Stanford, Calif., May 24, 1970); *Musique pour Ars nova* for 13 Instruments, with aleatory episodes (1969); Wind Quintet (1973).

VOCAL: 3 albums of songs to words by Francis Jammes (1910–12); *7 poèmes de la Connaissance de l'Est*, to words by Claudel (1913); *3 poèmes romantiques* for Voice and Piano (1914); *Le Château*, song cycle (1914); *4 poèmes* for Baritone, to words by Claudel (1915–17); *8 poèmes juifs* (1916); *Child poems* (1916); *3 poèmes*, to words by Christina Rossetti (1916); *Le Retour de l'enfant prodigue*, cantata for 5 Voices and Orch. (1917; Paris, Nov. 23, 1922, composer conducting); *Chansons bas*, to words by Mallarmé, for Voice and Piano (1917); *2 poèmes de Rimbaud* for Voice and Piano (1917); Psalm 136 for Baritone, Chorus, and Orch. (1918); Psalm 129 for Baritone and Orch. (1919); *Les Soirées de Pétrograd*, in 2 albums: *L'Ancien Régime* and *La Révolution* (1919); *Machines agricoles* for Voice and 7 Instruments, to words from a commercial catalog (1919); *3 poèmes de Jean Cocteau* for Voice and Piano (1920); *Catalogue de fleurs* for Voice with Piano or 7 Instruments (1920); *Feuilles* *de température* for Voice and Piano (1920); *Cocktail* for Voice and 3 Clarinets (1921); *Psalm 126* for Chorus a cappella (1921); *4 poèmes de Catulle* for Voice and Violin (1923); *6 chants populaires hébraïques* for Voice and Piano (1925); *Hymne de Sion* for Voice and Piano (1925); *Pièce de circonstance*, to words by Cocteau, for Voice and Piano (1926); *Cantate pour louer le Seigneur* for Soli, Choruses, and Orch. (1928); *Pan et Syrinx*, cantata (1934); *Les Amours de Ronsard* for Chorus and Small Orch. (1934); *Le Cygne* for Voice and Piano, to words by Claudel (1935); *La Sagesse*, for Voices and Small Orch., to words by Claudel (1935; Paris Radio, Nov. 8, 1945); *Cantate de la paix*, to words by Claudel (1937); *Cantate nuptiale*, after *Song of Songs* (Marseilles, Aug. 31, 1937); *Les Deux Cités*, cantata a cappella (1937); *Chanson du capitaine* for Voice and Piano (1937); *Les Quatre Éléments* for Soprano, Tenor, and Orch. (1938); *Récréation*, children's songs (1938); *3 élégies* for Soprano, Tenor, and Strings (1939); *Incantations* for Male Chorus (1939); *Quatrains valaisans* for Chorus a cappella, to words by Rilke (1939); *Cantate de la guerre* for Chorus a cappella, to words by Claudel (1940); *Le Voyage d'été*, suite for Voice and Piano (1940); *4 chansons de Ronsard* for Voice and Orch. (1941); *Rêves*, song cycle (1942); *La Libération des Antilles* for Voice and Piano (1944); *Kaddisch* for Voice, Chorus, and Organ (1945); *Sabbath Morning Service* for Baritone, Chorus, and Organ (1947); *Naissance de Vénus*, cantata for Mixed Chorus a cappella (Paris Radio, Nov. 30, 1949); *Ballade-Nocturne* for Voice and Piano (1949); *Barba Garibo*, 10 French folk songs, with Orch. (for the celebration of the wine harvest in Menton, 1953); *Cantate de l'initiation* for Chorus and Orch. (1960); *Cantate de la croix de charité* (1960); *Invocation à l'ange Raphael* for 2 Women's Choruses and Orch. (1962); *Adam* for Vocal Quintet (1964); *Cantate de Psaumes* (Paris, May 2, 1968); choral comedy, *Les Momies d'Égypte* (1972).

PIANO: *Le Printemps*, suite (1915–19); 2 sonatas (1916 and 1949); *Saudades do Brasil*, 12 numbers in 2 books (1921); *3 Rag Caprices* (1922; also for Small Orch.); *L'Automne*, suite of 3 pieces (1932); *4 romances sans paroles* (1933); 2 sets of children's pieces: *Touches noires; Touches blanches* (1941); *La Muse ménagère*, suite of 15 pieces (1944; also for Orch.); *Une Journée*, suite of 5 pieces (1946); *L'Enfant aimé*, suite of 5 pieces (also for Orch.; 1948); *Le Candélabre à sept branches*, piano suite (Ein Gev Festival, Israel, April 10, 1952); *Scaramouche*, version for 2 Pianos (1939); *Le Bal martiniquais*, version for 2 Pianos (1944); *Paris*, suite of 6 pieces for 4 Pianos (1948); *6 danses en 3 mouvements* for 2 Pianos (Paris, Dec. 17, 1970).

WRITINGS: *Études* (essays; Paris, 1926); *Notes sans musique* (autobiography; Paris, 1949; Eng. tr., London, 1952, as *Notes without Music*); *Entretiens avec Claude Rostand* (Paris, 1952); *Ma vie heureuse* (Paris, 1973).

BIBL.: P. Landormy, "D. M.," *Le Ménestrel* (Aug. 14, 21, 28, 1925); G. Augsbourg, *La Vie de D. M. en images* (Paris, 1935); M. Bauer, "D. M.," *Musical Quarterly* (April 1942); G. Beck, *D. M.: Étude suivie du catalogue chronologique complet* (Paris, 1949; supplement, 1957); C. Mason, "The Chamber Music of M.," *Musical Quarterly* (July 1957); J. Roy, *D. M.* (Paris, 1968); A. Braga, *D. M.* (Naples, 1969); C. Palmer, *M.* (London, 1976); P. Collaer, *D. M.* (Geneva and Paris, 1982; with complete catalog of works, eds., writings, trs., and recordings; Eng. tr., 1988).

Millard, Harrison, American composer; b. Boston, Nov. 27, 1829; d. there, Sept. 10, 1895. He sang in the chorus of the Handel and Haydn Soc. as a child; then went to Italy to study voice; was a concert tenor for several years, and made tours in England with the Irish soprano Catherine Hayes. Returning to America in 1854, he became a vocal instructor, 1st in Boston, then (from 1856) in N.Y. He publ. about 350 songs; wrote also many church works, and an opera, *Deborah*, to an Italian libretto (not perf.). He also set to music *Uncle Tom's Cabin* by Harriet Beecher Stowe.

Miller, Dayton C(larence), American physicist and flutist; b. Strongsville, Ohio, March 13, 1866; d. Cleveland, Feb. 22, 1941. After graduation from Baldwin College and Princeton Univ. (D.Sc., 1890), he was prof. of physics at the Case School of Applied Science in Cleveland (from 1893). An early interest in the flute led to his experimentation with various versions of the instrument (including a double-bass flute); he accumulated an extensive collection of flutes and various materials relating to the flute, which he left to the Library of Congress in Washington, D.C. A leading authority in the field of acoustics and light, he was president of the American Physical Soc. (1925–26) and of the Acoustical Soc. of America (1931–32), and vice-president of the American Musicological Soc. (1939). He publ. *The Science of Musical Sounds* (1916; 2nd ed., rev., 1926); *Catalogue of Books and Literary Material Relating to the Flute and Other Musical Instruments* (1935); *Anecdotal History of the Science of Sound to the Beginning of the 20th Century* (1935); *Sound Waves, Their Shape and Speed* (1937); etc.

BIBL.: H. Fletcher, *Biographical Memoir of D.C. M.* (Washington, D.C., 1944); L. Gilliam and W. Lichtenwanger, *The D.C. M. Flute Collection: A Checklist of the Instruments* (Washington, D.C., 1961).

Miller, (Alton) Glenn, famous American trombonist and bandleader; b. Clarinda, Iowa, March 1, 1904; d. during an airplane flight from London to Paris, Dec. 15, 1944. He spent his formative years in Fort Morgan, Colo., where he began his musical training; played with the local Boyd Senter Orch. (1921) and took courses at the Univ. of Colorado; after performing with Ben Pollack's band on the West Coast (1924–28), he followed Pollack to N.Y. and then became active as a freelance musician; helped to found an orch. for Ray Noble (1934), and subsequently studied orchestration with Joseph Schillinger; began experimenting with special effects, combining clarinets with saxophone in the same register. He organized his 1st band in 1937, but it failed to find an audience and dissolved in 1938; that same year he organized another band, which caught on only in 1939 through its radio broadcasts and recordings. It subsequently became one of the most successful aggregations of the day, producing such popular recordings as *Moonlight Serenade* (1939), *In the Mood* (1939), *Tuxedo Junction* (1940), *Chattanooga Choo Choo* (1941), and *A String of Pearls* (1941); it also appeared in the films *Sun Valley Serenade* (1941) and *Orchestra Wives* (1942). Miller joined the U.S. Army Air Force as a captain in 1942 and put together a band for entertaining the troops; it was based in England from 1944. A film, *The Glenn Miller Story*, was produced in 1953.

BIBL.: S. Bedwell, *A G. M. Discography and Biography* (London, 1955; 2nd ed., 1956); J. Flower, *Moonlight Serenade: A Bio-Discography of the G. M. Civilian Band* (New Rochelle, N.Y., 1972); G. Simon, *G. M. and His Orchestra* (N.Y., 1974); J. Green, *G. M. and the Age of Swing* (London, 1976); G. Butcher, *Next to a Letter from Home: Major G. M.'s Wartime Band* (Edinburgh, 1986).

Miller, Mildred, American soprano; b. Cleveland, Dec. 16, 1924. Her parents came from Germany; the original family name was Müller. She studied at the Cleveland Inst. of Music (B.M., 1946), then with Sundelius at the New England Cons. of Music in Boston (diploma, 1948). In 1949 she went to Germany; sang with the Stuttgart Opera and with the Bavarian State Opera in Munich. In 1950 she married the American pilot Wesley W. Posvar. Returning to the U.S., she made her debut with the Metropolitan Opera in N.Y. as Cherubino in *Le nozze di Figaro* (Nov. 17, 1951); remained there until 1975; also appeared widely as a concert singer. She was founder–artistic director of the Pittsburgh Opera Theater (from 1978).

Miller, Mitch(ell William), American oboist, recording executive, and conductor; b. Rochester, N.Y., July 4, 1911. He studied at the Eastman School of Music (B.Mus., 1932); played oboe in the Rochester Phil. (1930–33) and the CBS Sym. Orch. (1935–47); was director of artists and repertoire for the classical division of Mercury Records (1947–50); was in charge of the popular division of Columbia Records (1950–61); starred in his own television program, "Sing-Along with Mitch" (1960–65), which became extremely popular.

Miller, Philip Lieson, American music librarian; b. Woodland, N.Y., April 23, 1906. He studied at the Manhattan Music School and the Inst. of Musical Art; from 1927, he worked in the Music Division of the N.Y. Public Library; was assistant chief (1946–59); chief (1959–66). He was one of the principal founders and 1st president (1966–68) of the Assoc. for Recorded Sound Collections; in 1963–64, was president of the Music Library Assoc. He wrote many articles and reviews, dealing especially with singers and singing, and the books *Vocal Music* (N.Y., 1955) and *The Ring of Words. An Anthology of Song Texts* (N.Y., 1963).

Miller, Robert, American pianist and lawyer; b. N.Y., Dec. 5, 1930; d. Bronxville, N.Y., Nov. 30, 1981. He studied piano with Mathilde McKinney and Abbey Simon; then enrolled at Princeton Univ., where he took classes in composition with Milton Babbitt and Edward T. Cone, graduating in 1952; also studied jurisprudence at Columbia Univ. Law School, graduating in 1957. He was admitted to the bar in 1958 and became a practicing Wall Street lawyer; among his clients were several composers. As a pianist, he made his debut in Carnegie Hall in N.Y. in 1957; had a fairly active, though unhappily brief, career as a recitalist, excelling particularly in ultramodern music. He gave the 1st performance in N.Y. in 1980 of a piano concerto by John Harbison; George Crumb wrote his *Makrokosmos* (vol. II) for him.

Miller, Roger (Dean), American country-music singer and songwriter; b. Fort Worth, Texas, Jan. 2, 1936. He abandoned his formal education before completing the 8th grade; he then set out on his own, took up the guitar and other instruments, and served a stint in the U.S. Army in Korea. After his discharge, he made his way to Nashville; although he never learned to read music, he became a successful composer of songs. He made his 1st song hit with the autobiographical *King of the Road* in 1965; among his later successful recordings were *Rings for Sale* (1972), *I Believe in Sunshine* (1973), and *Everybody Gets Crazy Now and Then* (1981). Trying his hand at a more ambitious project, he wrote the successful score for the musical *Big River: The Adventures of Huckleberry Finn* (1984). It won him a Tony Award for best Broadway musical of 1985.

BIBL.: *Current Biography* (Sept. 1986).

Millet, Luis, Catalan composer and conductor; b. Masnou, near Barcelona, April 18, 1867; d. Barcelona, Dec. 7, 1941. He studied with Vidiella and Pedrell; then became a choral conductor. In 1891 he founded the famous choral society Orfeó Català, which he continued to lead until the last years of his life; was also director of the municipal music school in Barcelona; composed several orch. fantasies on Catalan folk songs and many choral works; publ. 2 books on folk music: *De la canción popular catalana* and *Pel nostre ideal* (1917).

BIBL.: B. Sampler, *L. M.* (Barcelona, 1926).

Milligan, Harold Vincent, American organist, writer on music, and composer; b. Astoria, Oreg., Oct. 31, 1888; d. N.Y., April 12, 1951. He studied with Carl and Noble; was a church organist in Portland, Oreg., before going to N.Y. in 1907; then taught organ at various schools and colleges; was church organist in New Jersey and N.Y.; also lectured on American music. He ed. 4 vols. of 18th-century American songs and, with G. Souvaine, *The Opera Quiz Book* (N.Y., 1948); also wrote a biography of Stephen Foster (N.Y., 1920) and *Stories of Famous Operas* (N.Y., 1950; 2nd ed., rev., 1955). He composed 2 children's operettas, *The Outlaws of Etiquette* (1914) and *The Laughabet* (1918); incidental music; choral works; many songs; organ works.

Millo, Aprile (Elizabeth), talented American soprano; b. N.Y., April 14, 1958. Her father was a tenor and her mother a soprano; after living in Europe, Millo's family moved to Los Angeles when she was 11; during her high school years, she studied voice with her parents and augmented her training by listening to recordings of the great divas. In 1977 she won 1st place in the San Diego Opera competition, received the

Geraldine Farrar Award, and sang in the opening concert of the new opera center there. In 1978 she won 1st prize in the Concorso Internazionale di Voci Verdiane in Busseto and received the Montserrat Caballé Award at the Francisco Viñas competition in Barcelona. In 1981 she sang with the N.Y. City Opera and also joined the Metropolitan Opera's Young Artists Development Program; later studied with Rita Patanè. On Jan. 4, 1983, she made her 1st appearance at La Scala in Milan as Elvira in *Ernani*, a role she repeated with the Welsh National Opera in 1984. She made her Metropolitan Opera debut in N.Y. as Amelia in *Simon Boccanegra* on Dec. 3, 1984, substituting for the ailing Anna Tomowa-Sintow. In 1985 she received the Richard Tucker Award. Subsequently she appeared at the Metropolitan Opera in such roles as Elisabetta in *Don Carlos*, Liù in *Turandot*, Luisa Miller, Leonora in *Il Trovatore*, Desdemona in *Otello*, and Aida. She also sang in concert performances with the Opera Orch. of N.Y., appearing as Giselda in *I Lombardi alla prima crociata* (1986) and as Lida in *La battaglia di Legnano* (1987).

BIBL.: C. Battaglia, "The Remarkable Rise of A. M.," *Ovation* (Nov. 1986); *Current Biography* (April 1988).

Millöcker, Carl, Austrian conductor and composer; b. Vienna, April 29, 1842; d. Baden, near Vienna, Dec. 31, 1899. His father was a jeweler, and Millöcker was destined for that trade, but showed irrepressible musical inclinations and learned music as a child; played the flute in a theater orch. at 16; later took courses at the Cons. of the Gesellschaft der Musikfreunde in Vienna. Upon the recommendation of Franz von Suppé, he received a post as theater conductor in Graz (1864). In 1866 he returned to Vienna; from 1869 to 1883, was 2nd conductor of the Theater an der Wien. He suffered a stroke in 1894, which left him partially paralyzed. As a composer, Millöcker possessed a natural gift for melodious music; although his popularity was never as great as that of Johann Strauss or Lehár, his operettas captured the spirit of Viennese life.

WORKS: Operettas (all 1st perf. in Vienna unless otherwise given): *Der tote Gast* (Graz, Dec. 21, 1865); *Die lustigen Binder* (Graz, Dec. 21, 1865); *Diana* (Jan. 2, 1867); *Die Fraueninsel* (Budapest, 1868); *Drei Paar Schuhe* (Jan. 5, 1871); *Wechselbrief und Briefwechsel*, or *Ein nagender Wurm* (Aug. 10, 1872); *Ein Abenteuer in Wien* (Jan. 20, 1873); *Das verwunschene Schloss* (March 30, 1878); *Gräfin Dubarry* (Oct. 31, 1879); *Apajune der Wassermann* (Dec. 18, 1880); *Die Jungfrau von Belleville* (Oct. 29, 1881); *Der Bettelstudent* (Dec. 6, 1882); his most successful work; popular also in England and America as *Student Beggar*; N.Y., Oct. 29, 1883); *Gasparone* (Jan. 26, 1884); *Der Feldprediger* (Oct. 31, 1884); *Der Vice-Admiral* (Oct. 9, 1886); *Die sieben Schwaben* (Oct. 29, 1887); *Der arme Jonathan* (Jan. 4, 1890; new version by Hentschke and Rixner, 1939; quite successful); *Das Sonntagskind* (Jan. 16, 1892); *Der Probekuss* (Dec. 22, 1894); *Nordlicht, oder Der rote Graf* (Dec. 22, 1896).

BIBL.: C. Preiss, "Versuch einer Biographie C. M.s," *Wochenschrift für Kunst und Musik*, III (1905); F. Racek, "Das Tagebuch C. M.s," *Wiener Schriften*, III (1969).

Mills, Charles (Borromeo), American composer; b. Asheville, N.C., Jan. 8, 1914; d. N.Y., March 7, 1982. A scion of a long line of English settlers in the Carolinas, Mills spent his formative period of life in a rural environment; was active in sports, but at the same time played in dance bands. In 1933 he went to N.Y. and engaged in serious study of composition, 1st with Max Garfield and then with Aaron Copland (1935–37), Roger Sessions (1937–39), and Roy Harris (1939–41). He enjoyed composing; wrote mostly in a severe but eloquent contrapuntal style; in virtually his entire career as a composer, he pursued the ideal of formal cohesion; his style of composition may be described as *Baroque à l'américaine*. His quest for artistic self-discipline led him to the decision to become a Roman Catholic, a faith in which no uncertainty exists. He was baptized according to the Roman Catholic rite on May 14, 1944. In 1952 he was awarded a Guggenheim fellowship;

he also engaged in teaching. In his last works, Mills gradually adopted the serial method of composition, which seemed to respond to his need of strong discipline.

WORKS: ORCH.: 6 syms.: No. 1 (1940); No. 2 (1942); No. 3 (1946); No. 4, *Crazy Horse* (Cincinnati, Nov. 28, 1958); No. 5 for Strings (1980); No. 6 (1981); Piano Concerto (1948); *Theme and Variations* (N.Y., Nov. 8, 1951); Concertino for Oboe and Strings (1957); Serenade for Winds and Strings (1960); *In a Mule-Drawn Wagon* for String Orch. (1968); *Symphonic Ode* for String Orch. (1976). **CHAMBER:** 5 string quartets (1939–58); 6 violin sonatas (1940–77); 2 suites for Solo Violin (1942, 1944); 2 cello sonatas (1940, 1942); Piano Trio (1941); Chamber Concerto for 10 Instruments (1942); Sonata for English Horn and Piano (1946); *Concerto sereno* for Woodwind Octet (1948); *Prologue and Dithyramb* for String Quartet (1951); Brass Quintet (1962); Brass Sextet (1964); *Sonata da chiesa* for Recorder and Harpsichord (1972); *The 5 Moons of Uranus* for Recorder and Piano (1972); *Duo eclogue* for Recorder and Organ (1974). **VOCAL:** *Canticles of the Sun* for Voice and Piano (1945); *The Ascension Cantata* for Tenor and Chorus (1954); *The 1st Thanksgiving*, cantata for Chorus and Organ (1956). **PIANO:** 11 sonatinas (1942–45); 2 sonatas (1941–42); *30 Penitential Preludes* (1945). **JAZZ ENSEMBLE:** *The Centaur and the Phoenix* (1960); *Summer Song* (1960); *Paul Bunyan Jump* (1964).

Mills-Cockell, John, Canadian composer; b. Toronto, May 19, 1943. He studied composition and electronic music at the Univ. of Toronto and at the Royal Cons. of Music there. In 1966 he developed, in collaboration with the writer Blake Parker, artist Michael Hayden, and designer Dick Zander, a method of composition and performance called Intersystems; he joined the rock bands Kensington Market in Toronto (1969), Hydro-Electric Streetcar in Vancouver (1969–70), and Syrinx in Toronto (1970–72), which he founded; then devoted himself to composing and recording. He wrote numerous pieces for mixed media, works utilizing tape, electronic music for films, etc.

Mills, Erie, American soprano; b. Granite City, Ill., June 22, 1953. She attended the National Music Camp in Interlochen, Mich., then studied voice with Karl Trump at the College of Wooster, Ohio, with Grace Wilson at the Univ. of Illinois, and with Elena Nikolaidi. In 1979 she made her professional operatic debut as Ninette in *The Love for 3 Oranges* at the Chicago Lyric Opera; on Oct. 13, 1982, she made her 1st appearance with the N.Y. City Opera as Cunegonde in *Candide*, and subsequently sang there regularly; she made her Metropolitan Opera debut in N.Y. as Blondchen in *Die Entführung aus dem Serail* on Nov. 26, 1987. She also made guest appearances with the Cincinnati Opera, Cleveland Opera, San Francisco Opera, Minnesota Opera, Opera Soc. of Washington, D.C., Santa Fe Opera, Houston Grand Opera, Hamburg State Opera, La Scala in Milan, and Vienna State Opera. On March 17, 1989, she made her N.Y. recital debut. Among her other prominent roles are Rossini's Rosina, Donizetti's Lucia, Offenbach's Olympia, Johann Strauss's Adele, and Richard Strauss's Zerbinetta.

Mills, Kerry (real name, **Frederick Allen**), American composer and music publisher; b. Philadelphia, Feb. 1, 1869; d. Hawthorne, Calif., Dec. 5, 1948. He was active as a violinist; taught violin at a private cons. in Ann Arbor, Mich., known as the Univ. School of Music (1892–93); adopting the name Kerry Mills, he publ. his own cakewalk march *Rufus on Parade* (1895); encouraged by its favorable sales, he moved to N.Y., where he became one of the most important publishers of minstrel songs, cakewalks, early ragtime, and other popular music. His own compositions were particularly successful; *At a Georgia Campmeeting* (1897) became the standard against which all other cakewalks were measured; performed in Europe by John Philip Sousa, it became popular there as well; it was roundly denounced in the Leipzig *Illustrierte Zeitung* (Feb. 5, 1903), and could well have been the inspiration for Debussy's *Golliwog's Cakewalk*. Some of his other hits also reached Eu-

rope; his *Whistling Rufus* (1899) was publ. in Berlin as *Rufus das Pfeifergigerl*. He also wrote the popular song *Meet Me in St. Louis, Louis* (1904) for the Louisiana Purchase Exposition held in St. Louis that year; it was revived for the film of that title starring Judy Garland (1944). He also wrote sacred songs as Frederick Allen Mills.

Mills, S(ebastian) B(ach), outstanding English pianist; b. Cirencester, March 13, 1838; d. Wiesbaden, Dec. 21, 1898. He played before Queen Victoria at the age of 7; studied with Cipriani Potter and Sterndale Bennett; later was a student of Moscheles, Plaidy, Hauptmann, and Rietz at the Leipzig Cons., and finally of Liszt. He played at a Leipzig Gewandhaus concert (Dec. 2, 1858), then went to N.Y., where he obtained a decisive success with the Schumann Piano Concerto, which he performed with the Phil. Soc. on March 26, 1859. He remained in N.Y. until making his last appearance on Nov. 24, 1877. He had a significant and lasting impact upon American pianism through his presentation of 1st American performances of works by Hiller, Liszt, Moscheles, Reinecke et al.

Milner, Anthony (Francis Dominic), English composer and teacher; b. Bristol, May 13, 1925. He studied composition privately with Mátyás Seiber (1944–48); also took courses with R.O. Morris (composition) and Herbert Fryer (piano) at the Royal College of Music in London (1945–47). From 1948 to 1964 he taught at Morley College in London; served as director and harpsichordist of the London Cantata Ensemble (1954–65); was a part-time teacher (1961–80) and principal lecturer (from 1980) at the Royal College of Music; was also a lecturer at King's College, London (1965–71), and senior lecturer (1971–74) and principal lecturer (from 1974) at Goldsmiths' College, London.

WORKS: ORCH.: *Variations* (1958; Cheltenham, July 6, 1959); *Divertimento* for String Orch. (London, Aug. 17, 1961); *Overture: April Prologue* (London, Dec. 5, 1961); *Sinfonia pasquale* for String Orch. (1963; Dorchester, May 5, 1964); Chamber Sym. (1967; London, March 31, 1968); 3 syms.: No. 1 (1972; London, Jan. 17, 1973); No. 2 for Soprano, Tenor, Boys' Choir, Chorus, and Orch. (Liverpool, July 13, 1978); No. 3 (1986; London, Nov. 26, 1987); Concerto for Symphonic Wind Band (Ithaca, N.Y., Oct. 10, 1979); Concerto for String Orch. (1982; Wells, June 19, 1984). **VOCAL:** Cantatas: *Salutatio Angelica* for Contralto or Mezzo-soprano, Chorus, and Chamber Orch. (1948; London, Nov. 11, 1951); *The City of Desolation: A Cantata of Hope* for Soprano, Chorus, and Orch. (Totnes, Devon, Aug. 12, 1955); *The Harrowing of Hell* for Tenor, Bass, and Chorus (BBC, Nov. 14, 1956); *Roman Spring* for Soprano, Tenor, Chorus, and Orch. (London, Oct. 13, 1969); *Midway* for Mezzo-soprano and Chamber Orch. (London, July 10, 1974); *Emmanuel*, Christmas cantata for Countertenor, Soprano, Contralto, Tenor, Bass, Chorus, Audience, and Orch. (1974; Kingston upon Thames, Dec. 13, 1975); other vocal works, including *The Gates of Spring*, ode for Soprano, Tenor, Chorus, and String Orch. (1988), many sacred works, and songs. **CHAMBER:** Quartet for Oboe and Strings (1953); Quintet for Wind Instruments (1964); String Quartet No. 1 (1975); piano music; organ pieces.

BIBL.: S. Dodgson, "Retrospect and Prospect: M. at 60," *Musical Times* (May 1985); J. Siddons, *A. M.: A Bio-Bibliography* (Westport, Conn., 1989).

Milnes, Sherrill (Eustace), distinguished American baritone; b. Downers Grove, Ill., Jan. 10, 1935. He learned to play piano and violin at home, then played tuba in a school band; after a period as a medical student at North Central College in Naperville, Ill., he turned to music; subsequently studied voice with Andrew White at Drake Univ. in Des Moines and with Hermanus Baer at Northwestern Univ. He sang in choral performances under Margaret Hillis in Chicago; then was a member of the chorus at the Santa Fe Opera, where he received his 1st opportunity to sing minor operatic roles. In 1960 he joined Boris Goldovsky's Boston opera company and toured widely with it. He met Rosa Ponselle in Baltimore in 1961, and she coached him in several roles; he 1st appeared with the Baltimore Civic Opera as Gérard in *Andrea Chénier* in 1961. He made his European debut as Figaro in *Il Barbiere di Siviglia* at the Teatro Nuovo in Milan on Sept. 23, 1964; then made his 1st appearance at the N.Y. City Opera on Oct. 18, 1964, singing the role of Valentin in *Faust*. His Metropolitan Opera debut in N.Y. followed in the same role on Dec. 22, 1965. He rose to a stellar position at the Metropolitan, being acclaimed for both vocal and dramatic abilities; also sang with other opera houses in the U.S. and Europe. His notable roles include Don Giovanni, Escamillo, the Count di Luna, Tonio, Iago, Barnaba, Rigoletto, and Scarpia.

Milojević, Miloje, Serbian conductor, musicologist, and composer; b. Belgrade, Oct. 27, 1884; d. there, June 16, 1946. He was taught piano by his mother; then entered the Serbian School of Music at Novi Sad; then studied with Mayer G'schray (piano), Mottl (conducting), and Klose (composition) at the Munich Academy of Music and took courses in musicology with Sandberger and Kroyer at the Univ. of Munich; subsequently studied musicology with Nejedlý at the Univ. of Prague (D.Mus., 1925). He was active as a choirmaster in Belgrade; was conductor of the Collegium Musicum at the Univ. there (1925–41); also wrote music criticism and taught composition at the Academy of Music there (1939–46). He publ. *Elements of Music* (Belgrade, 1922), *Smetana* (Belgrade, 1924), and *Music Studies and Articles* (Belgrade, 1926, 1933, 1953). As a composer, he wrote mostly in small forms; was influenced successively by Grieg, Strauss, Debussy, and Russian modernists; his music contains an original treatment of Balkan folk songs. His piano suite, *Grimaces rythmiques* (in a modern vein), was performed at the Paris Festival on June 26, 1937. His list of works contains choral pieces, chamber music, songs, and piano pieces.

BIBL.: P. Konjović, *M. M.: Kompozitor i muzički pisac* (Belgrade, 1954).

Milsap, Ronnie, blind American country-music singer; b. Robbinsville, N.C., Jan. 16, 1944. He entered the North Carolina State School for the Blind as a child and learned to play the violin, piano, and guitar; while in high school he formed his own rock band, but then turned to country music and went to Nashville, Tenn. Very soon he reached the heights of country music, garnering numerous awards and honors. In 1976 he became a regular member of the Grand Ole Opry.

Milstein, Nathan (Mironovich), celebrated Russian-born American violinist; b. Odessa, Dec. 31, 1904. His father was a well-to-do merchant in woolen goods; his mother was an amateur violinist who gave him his 1st lessons. He then began to study with Piotr Stoliarsky in Odessa, remaining under his tutelage until 1914; then went to St. Petersburg, where he entered the class of Leopold Auer at the St. Petersburg Cons. (1915–17). He began his concert career in 1919, with his sister as piano accompanist. In Kiev he met Vladimir Horowitz, and they began giving duo recitals in 1921; later they were joined by Gregor Piatigorsky, and organized a trio. Russia was just emerging from a devastating civil war, and communications with western Europe were not established until much later. In 1925 Milstein was able to leave Russia; he went to Berlin and then to Brussels, where he met Eugène Ysaÿe, who encouraged him in his career. He gave several recitals in Paris, then proceeded to South America. On Oct. 28, 1929, he made his American debut with the Philadelphia Orch. conducted by Stokowski. In 1942 he became an American citizen. He celebrated the 50th anniversary of his American debut in 1979 by giving a number of solo recitals and appearing as soloist with American orchs. As an avocation, he began painting and drawing, arts in which he achieved a certain degree of self-satisfaction. He also engaged in teaching; held master classes at the Juilliard School of Music in N.Y., and also in Zürich. Milstein was renowned for his technical virtuosity and musical integrity. He composed a number of violin pieces, including *Paganiniana* (1954); also prepared cadenzas for the violin concertos of Beethoven and Brahms. His autobiography was publ. as *From Russia to the West* (N.Y., 1990).

BIBL.: B. Gavoty, *N. M.* (Geneva, 1956); B. Schwarz, *Great Masters of the Violin* (N.Y., 1983).

Milstein, Yakov (Isaakovich), Russian pianist, pedagogue, and writer on music; b. Voronezh, Feb. 4, 1911; d. Moscow, Dec. 4, 1981. He studied piano with Igumnov at the Moscow Cons. (Ph.D., 1942); was a member of its faculty (from 1935). His main interest was an analysis of works of masters of Romantic music; particularly important is his biography of Liszt (Moscow, 1956; Hungarian ed., Budapest, 1965). He contributed an essay on the piano technique of Chopin and Liszt to *The Book of the First International Musicological Congress Devoted to the Works of Chopin* (Warsaw, 1963). He also publ. a monograph on Igumnov (Moscow, 1975).

Milton, John, amateur English composer and father of the great poet John Milton; b. Stanton St. John, near Oxford, c.1563; d. London (buried), March 15, 1647. He was a chorister at Christ Church, Oxford (1572–77); apparently remained at Oxford for several years, and in 1585 went to London, where he was admitted to the Scriveners' Co. in 1600; in that year he married Sarah Jeffrey. He composed 8 anthems for 4 to 6 Voices; 7 Psalm settings; 2 madrigals for 5 Voices; Motet for 6 Voices; *In Nomine* a 6; 4 fantasias a 5 and a 6 (1 ed. in Musica Britannica, IX, 1955; 2nd ed., 1962). See G. Arkwright, ed., *John Milton: Six Anthems*, Old English Edition, XXII (1900), and C. Hill, ed., *Sir William Leighton: The Teares or Lamentations of a Sorrowful Soul*, Early English Church Music, XI (1970).

BIBL.: E. Brennecke, Jr., *J. M. the Elder and His Music* (N.Y., 1938).

Milveden, (Jan) Ingmar (Georg), Swedish composer, organist, and musicologist; b. Göteborg, Feb. 15, 1920. He studied cello and organ; then took a course in composition with Sven Svensson and in musicology with C.A. Moberg at the Univ. of Uppsala (graduated, 1945; Fil.lic., 1951; Ph.D., 1972, with the diss. *Zu den liturgischen "Hystorie" in Schweden. Liturgie-und choralgeschichtliche Untersuchungen*). He was organist at Uppsala's St. Per's Church (1967–78); lectured at the Univ. of Stockholm (1970–73) and at the Univ. of Uppsala (1972–86). He distinguished himself as a composer of church music.

WORKS: *Serenade* for String Orch. (1942); Piano Sonatina (1943); Duo for Flute and Piano (1953; rev. 1975); Trio for Flute, Clarinet, and Viola (1955; rev. 1973); *Canticula linnaeana* for Chorus a cappella (1965); *Mässa i skördetid* (Mass of the Harvest Time) for Congregation, Liturgist, 2 Choruses, 2 Organs, 2 Orch. Groups, and Tape (1969); *Pezzo concertante* for Orch. (1969; Uppsala, Feb. 5, 1970); *Concerto al fresco* for Clarinet and Orch. (1970; Uppsala, Nov. 25, 1971); *Threnodia* for 3 Cellos (1970); church opera, *Vid en Korsväg* (1971; Lund, Nov. 30, 1974); *Nu . . .* , 4 Linne quotations for Solo Voices, Chorus, and Instrumental Groups (1972; Ingesund, March 17, 1974); *Magnificat* for 2 Choral Groups, Organ, Winds, and Percussion (1973); *Toccata* for Organ (1973); *3 assaggi* for Cello (1975); *Musica in honorem Sanctae Eugeniae* for Voices (1982); *Alleluia "Terribilis est"* for Voices (1987); choruses; songs.

Mimaroglu, Ilhan Kemaleddin, Turkish composer and writer on music; b. Constantinople, March 11, 1926. He studied law at the Univ. of Ankara; in 1955 traveled to the U.S. on a Rockefeller fellowship, and settled in N.Y., where he studied theory with Jack Beeson and Chou Wen-Chung, musicology with Paul Henry Lang, and electronic music with Vladimir Ussachevsky at Columbia Univ.; he took lessons in modern composition with Stefan Wolpe, and also received inspiring advice from Edgard Varèse. He was subsequently a recipient of a Guggenheim fellowship (1971–72). He publ. several books in Turkish (*Sounds of America, Jazz as an Art, 11 Contemporary Composers, A History of Music, Little Encyclopedia of Western Music, Diary without Datelines,* etc.). In 1963 he began his association with the Columbia-Princeton Electronic Music Center, where he composed most of his electronic works, among them *Le Tombeau d'Edgar Poe* (1964), *Anacolutha*

(1965), *Preludes* for Magnetic Tape (1966–76), *Wings of the Delirious Demon* (1969), and music for Jean Dubuffet's *Coucou Bazar* (1973). He developed compositional methods viewing electronic music in a parallel to cinema, resulting in works for tape in which recorded performance dominates individual rendition. Concurrently, he displayed a growing political awareness in his choice of texts, conveying messages of New Left persuasion in such works as *Sing Me a Song of Songmy*, a protest chant against the war in Vietnam (1971), *Tract* (1972–74), *To Kill a Sunrise* (1974), and String Quartet No. 4 with Voice obbligato on poems by Nâzim Hikmet (1978). Other works include *Pieces sentimentales* for Piano (1957); *Music Plus 1* for Violin and Tape (1970); *Still Life 1980* for Cello and Tape (1983); *Immolation Scene* for Voice and Tape (1983); *Valses ignobles et sentencieuses* for Piano (1984). He destroyed all of his non-performed compositions, as well as those not recorded for posterity within a year of completion. Since the late 1980s, he has been working on a documentary film in which various composers respond to his question dealing with the condition of the contemporary composer in a cultural environment dominated by commercial determinants.

Minami, Satoshi, Japanese composer; b. Tokyo, July 17, 1955. He studied with Teruyuki Noda and Toshiro Mayuzumi at the Graduate School of the Tokyo Univ. of the Arts (degree, 1983). In 1983 he won 2nd prize in the 52nd Japan Music Competition, and in 1986, 2nd prize in the 2nd World Buddhist Music Festival. His concept of "music on the pluralistic structure" is exemplified in his *UTA no KAGE yori*, op. 13; it utilizes songs taken from an early Japanese song collection called *Manyō*, although without reference to their meanings.
Works: *Reliquiae* for Cello and Piano, op. 1 (1976–79); *Plants II* for 2 Violins and 3 Harps, op. 3, no. 2 (1977–79); *Fresco* for Orch., op. 5 (1980; rev. 1985); *Francesco Parmigianino's Hand,* piano suite with Glockenspiel, Tubular Bells, and Tape, op. 11 (1984); *Tatoereba . . .* for Viola and Piano, op. 14, no. 1 (1986); *The Garden of Joyful Intellection II,* op. 15, no. 3 (1988); *Coloration Project I,* op. 17, no. 1 (1989); *UTA no KAGE yori* for Voice, Harp, Violin, Cello, and Piano, op. 13 (1990).

Minchev, Georgi, Bulgarian composer; b. Sofia, Jan. 29, 1939. He studied composition with Goleminov at the Bulgarian State Cons. in Sofia, graduating in 1963; went to Moscow and studied with Shchedrin (1968–70); in 1972 he traveled to France, Great Britain, and the U.S. on a UNESCO scholarship. Returning to Bulgaria, he became chief of productions at the Committee for Television and Radio in Sofia.
Works: Oratorio, *Starobulgarski hroniky* (Old Bulgarian Chronicles) for Narrator, Soloists, Mixed Chorus, Folk Music Chorus, and Orch. (Sofia, Dec. 22, 1971); Sym. (1967); *Music for 3 Orch.* Groups (1968); *Intermezzo and Aquarelle* for Strings, 2 Flutes, and Harpsichord (1972); *3 Poems* for Mezzo-soprano and Orch. (1973); *Concert Music* for Orch. (1975); Piano Concerto (1976); *Symphonic Prologue* (1980); choruses; solo songs; folk-song arrangements.

Mingus, Charles, remarkable black American jazz double-bass player, pianist, bandleader, and composer; b. Nogales, Ariz., April 22, 1922; d. Cuernavaca, Mexico, Jan. 5, 1979. He was reared in Los Angeles; during his high school years, he studied double bass with Red Callender and Herman Rheinschagen and composition with Lloyd Reese; after working with Barney Bigard (1942), Louis Armstrong (1943), and Lionel Hampton (1947–48), he led his own groups as "Baron Mingus" before attracting notice as a member of Red Norvo's trio (1950–51); then settled in N.Y., where he worked with Billy Taylor, Duke Ellington, Stan Getz, Art Tatum, and Bud Powell. He was head of his own recording company, Debut Records (1952–55); also became active as a composer; worked with various musicians in small combos, and eventually developed a close association with Eric Dolphy. A highly explosive individual, Mingus became known as the "angry man of jazz" for his opposition to the white commercial taint of his art form. After his 2nd recording company (Charles Mingus label, 1964–65)

failed, and his financial situation became desperate, he retired from the public scene (1966–69). After resuming his career, he was awarded a Guggenheim fellowship (1971) and subsequently devoted much time to composing; also led his own groups until being stricken with amyotrophic lateral sclerosis, which sidelined him in 1978. His autobiography, *Beneath the Underdog: His World as Composed by Mingus,* was ed. by N. King (N.Y., 1971). Mingus was a master instrumentalist and a versatile composer, producing both conventionally notated works and dictated pieces. In his unique series of works *Fables* and *Meditations,* he achieved a style that effectively erased the lines between jazz improvisation and notated composition. His influence is likely incalculable. His most important work, the 2-hour *Epitaph* for 30 Instruments, which was discovered by his wife several years after his death, received its premiere performance posthumously in N.Y. on June 3, 1989.
Bibl.: B. Coss, *C. M.: A List of Compositions Licensed by B.M.I.* (N.Y., 1961); D. Morgenstern, "C. M. 1922–1979," *Radio Free Jazz* (Feb. 1979); B. Priestley, *M.: A Critical Biography* (London, 1982); H. Lindemaier and H. Salewski, *The Man Who Never Sleeps: The C. M. Discography 1945–1978* (Freiburg, 1983); J. Coleman and A. Young, *M./M.: Two Memoirs* (Berkeley, 1989).

Minkus, Léon (actually, **Aloisius Ludwig**), Austrian violinist and composer; b. Vienna, March 23, 1826; d. there, Dec. 7, 1917. He went to Russia in his youth, and was engaged by Prince Yusupov as concertmaster of his serf orch. in St. Petersburg (1853–56). From 1862 to 1872 he was concertmaster of the Bolshoi Theater in Moscow. In 1869 the Bolshoi Theater produced its ballet *Don Quixote* to the choreography of the famous Russian ballet master Petipa; its success was extraordinary, and its appeal to the Russian audiences so durable that the work retained its place in the repertoire of Russian ballet companies for more than a century, showing no signs of diminishing popularity. Equally popular was his ballet *La Bayadère,* produced by Petipa in St. Petersburg in 1877; another successful ballet was his *La Fiametta or The Triumph of Love,* originally produced in Paris in 1864. From 1872 to 1885 Minkus held the post of court composer of ballet music for the Imperial theaters in St. Petersburg; he remained in Russia until 1891; then returned to Vienna, where he lived in semi-retirement until his death at the age of 91. The ballets of Minkus never took root outside Russia, but their cursive melodies and bland rhythmic formulas suit old-fashioned Russian choreography to the airiest *entrechat.*

Minnelli, Liza (May), successful American singer of popular music and actress; b. Los Angeles, March 12, 1946. She was the daughter of the legendary songstress **Judy Garland** by her 2nd husband, the film director Vincente Minnelli. She dropped out of high school to devote herself exclusively to singing; made her professional debut as a singer in the 1963 off-Broadway revival of *Best Foot Forward* (1941). In 1965 she appeared in the Broadway musical *Flora, the Red Menace,* for which she won a Tony Award. She established herself as a film actress in *The Sterile Cuckoo* (1969); also starred in the highly acclaimed film *Cabaret* (1972), for which she won an Academy Award. She further won Tony awards for her 1-woman show *Liza* (1974) and for her appearance in the Broadway musical *The Act* (1977); she appeared opposite Dudley Moore in the romantic film comedy *Arthur* (1981) and its sequel, *Arthur on the Rocks* (1988). After starring in the musical *The Rink* (1983–84), she underwent treatment for drug and alcohol dependency in 1984. Following rehabilitation, she made extensive tours in the U.S. and abroad.
Bibl.: J. Parish, *L.!: An Unauthorized Biography* (1975); A. Petrucelli, *L.! L.!: An Unauthorized Biography of L. M.* (1983); J. Spada, *Judy and L.* (1983); *Current Biography* (July 1988).

Minnie Memphis. See **Douglas, Minnie.**

Minoja, Ambrogio, Italian composer and singing teacher; b. Ospitaletto Lodigiano, near Piacenza, Oct. 22, 1752; d. Milan,

Aug. 3, 1825. He studied music in Lodi and Naples; served as maestro al cembalo at La Scala in Milan and at the Teatro Canobbiano there from 1780 to 1802. In 1814 he became censor of the Milan Cons., and held that position until his death. As an instructor of high repute, he publ. books of solfeggi and *Lettere sopra il canto* (Milan, 1812). He composed the operas *Tito nelle Gallie* (La Scala, Milan, Dec. 26, 1786) and *Olimpiade* (Rome, Dec. 26, 1787), several syms., sacred music, and chamber music.

Minton, Yvonne (Fay), noted Australian mezzo-soprano; b. Sydney, Dec. 4, 1938. She studied with Marjorie Walker in Sydney and with Henry Cummings and Joan Cross in London; won the Kathleen Ferrier Prize and the 's Hertogenbosch Competition (both 1961). She sang the role of Maggie Dempster in the premiere of Maw's *1 Man Show* (London, 1964); made her Covent Garden debut in London as Lola in *Cavalleria rusticana* (1965), and subsequently sang there regularly; also sang at the Cologne Opera (from 1969) and at the Bayreuth Festivals (from 1974). She made her 1st appearance in the U.S. in Chicago (1970); made her Metropolitan Opera debut in N.Y. as Octavian in *Der Rosenkavalier* on March 16, 1973; also appeared in concerts with the Chicago Sym. Orch. In 1983 she retired from the operatic stage, but continued her concert career. In 1980 she was made a Commander of the Order of the British Empire. Among her finest roles were Gluck's Orfeo, Cherubino, Sextus in *La clemenza di Tito*, Dorabella, Waltraube, Fricka, Dido, and Brangäne; she also created the role of Thea in Tippett's *The Knot Garden* (1970) and sang the role of the Countess in the 1st perf. of the complete version of Berg's *Lulu* (1979).

Mintz, Shlomo, Russian-born Israeli violinist and conductor; b. Moscow, Oct. 30, 1957. His family emigrated to Israel when he was 2; he became a pupil of Ilona Feher there at age 6; gave his 1st recital (1966) and appeared as soloist in the Mendelssohn Concerto with Mehta and the Israel Phil. (1968); completed his training with Dorothy DeLay at N.Y.'s Juilliard School (1973), the same year in which he made his U.S. debut in the Bruch Concerto No. 1 with Steinberg and the Pittsburgh Sym. Orch. at Carnegie Hall. After making his European debut at the Brighton Festival in England (1976), he made a major tour of Europe (1977). In subsequent years he appeared in all the leading music centers of the world, performing as a soloist with orchs., as a recitalist, and as a chamber music artist. In 1989 he was appointed music adviser of the Israel Chamber Orch.

Miolan, Marie. See **Carvalho, Caroline** (née **Caroline-Marie Felix-Miolan**).

Miranda, Carmen (real name, **Maria do Carmo Miranda da Cunha**), charismatic Portuguese-American singer of popular music and actress; b. Marco de Canaveses, near Lisbon, Feb. 9, 1909; d. Beverly Hills, Calif., Aug. 5, 1955. She spent her formative years in Rio de Janeiro and, after performing throughout South America, made her 1st appearance on Broadway in 1939 in the revue *The Streets of Paris;* she was dubbed the "Brazilian Bombshell." She went on to gain an extensive following via many film appearances, recordings, nightclub engagements, and television appearances. She is particularly remembered for her spiky high-heeled shoes and fantastic headdresses made of fruit; in the movie musical *The Gang's All Here* (1943), with lavish choreography by Busby Berkeley, she comically careened her way through the number *The Lady with the Tutti Frutti Hat.*
    BIBL.: M. Gil-Montero, *Brazilian Bombshell: The Biography of C. M.* (N.Y., 1989).

Mirecki, Franz (actually, **Franciszek Wincenty**), Polish composer, pianist, and singing teacher; b. Krakow (baptized), March 31, 1791; d. there, May 29, 1862. He 1st studied with his father; made his debut as a pianist at the age of 9; later was a student of Hummel in Vienna (1814) and of Cherubini in Paris (1817). He was active as a singing teacher, conductor, and composer in Milan (1822–38) and Genoa (1826–38); also

conducted an Italian opera company on a tour of Portugal, England, and France (1825–26). He returned to Krakow in 1838, running his own school until 1841; also served as director of the local Opera (1844–47).
    WORKS: Operas: *Cyganie* (The Gypsies; Warsaw, May 23, 1822); *Evandro in Pergamo* (Genoa, Dec. 26, 1824); *I due forzati* (Lisbon, March 7, 1826); *Cornelio Bentivoglio* (Milan, March 18, 1844); *Nocleg w Apeninach* (A Night in the Apennines; Krakow, April 11, 1845); numerous piano pieces.

Mirouze, Marcel, French composer and conductor; b. Toulouse, Sept. 24, 1906; d. in an automobile accident in Aude, Aug. 1, 1957. He studied with Busser at the Paris Cons.; conducted the Paris Radio Orch. (1935–40) and in Monte Carlo (1940–43). He wrote an opera, *Geneviève de Paris,* for the 2,000th anniversary of the founding of the city of Paris; it was produced 1st as a radio play with music in 1952, and then on stage in Toulouse in the same year; he also composed 2 ballets, *Paul et Virginie* (1942) and *Les Bains de mer* (1946); 2 symphonic tableaux, *Afrique* (1936) and *Asie* (1938); Piano Concerto (1948); film music; piano pieces; songs.

Mirovitch, Alfred, Russian-American pianist; b. St. Petersburg, May 4, 1884; d. Whitefield, N.Mex., Aug. 3, 1959. He graduated from the St. Petersburg Cons. with the 1st prize in piano as a student of Anna Essipova in 1909; began his concert career in 1911; made 9 world tours; made his American debut in 1921. He conducted master classes in piano at the Juilliard School of Music in N.Y. (1944–52); then joined the faculty of Boston Univ.; was also an ed. of piano music for G. Schirmer, Inc.; likewise wrote some piano pieces.

Miry, Karel, Belgian composer; b. Ghent, Aug. 14, 1823; d. there, Oct. 3, 1889. He studied violin with Jean Andries and composition with Martin Joseph Mergal at the Ghent Cons.; in 1857 he was engaged as a prof. of harmony and counterpoint there; in 1871 he was appointed assistant director; from 1875 he was inspector of music in the municipal schools of Ghent, and from 1881, inspector of state-supported music schools. As a composer, he cultivated the national Flemish style; wrote several syms. and 18 operas and operettas to French and Flemish librettos. His opera *Boucherd d'Avesnes* was 1st staged in Ghent on Feb. 5, 1864, obtaining considerable success. But he owes his fame to the patriotic song *De Vlaamse Leeuw,* which he wrote at the age of 22, and which became the Flemish anthem of Belgium.
    BIBL.: J. Maertens, *De structuurontleding van de symfonieen van K. M.* (1823–1889) (diss., Univ. of Ghent, 1968).

Mirzoyan, Edvard (Mikaeli), Armenian composer; b. Gori, Georgia, May 12, 1921. He studied at the Erevan Cons., graduating in 1941; then went to Moscow and entered the composition class of Litinsky and Peyko at the House of Armenian Culture. In 1948 he was appointed instructor at the Erevan Cons.; in 1965 he became a prof. there; served as president of the Union of Composers of the Armenian S.S.R. (from 1957) and secretary of the Union of Soviet Composers (from 1962). In 1981 he was made a People's Artist of the U.S.S.R. In his music he follows a lucid neo-Classical style, while his thematic materials are of native Armenian provenance. He wrote a String Quartet (1947); the cantatas *Soviet Armenia* (1948) and *Lenin* (in collaboration with Arutyunian, 1950); Sym. for Strings (1962); Cello Sonata (1967); film scores.
    BIBL.: M. Ter-Simonyan, *E. M.* (Moscow, 1969).

Misch, Ludwig, German-American organist, conductor, music critic, and musicologist; b. Berlin, June 13, 1887; d. N.Y., April 22, 1967. He studied music theory with Max Friedlaender at the Univ. of Berlin; simultaneously took courses in law, obtaining his D.Jur. degree at the Univ. of Heidelberg in 1911. He was music critic for the *Allgemeine Musikzeitung* (1909–13); conducted theater orchs. in Berlin, Essen, and Bremen. From 1921 to 1933 he was music critic of the *Berliner Lokalanzeiger.* Under the Nazi regime, he conducted a Jewish madrigal choir in Berlin until he was sent to a concentration camp. In 1947 he emigrated to N.Y., where he became active as an organist and musicologist. He publ. the valuable books *Johannes Brahms* (Bielefeld, 1913; 2nd ed., Berlin, 1922); *Beethoven-Studien* (Berlin, 1950; Eng. tr., Norman, Okla., 1953); tr. and annotated (with D. MacArdle) *New Beethoven Letters* (Norman, 1957); *Die Faktoren der Einheit in der Mehrsätzigkeit der Werke Beethovens: Versuch einer Theorie der Einheit des Werkstils* (Bonn, 1958); *Neue Beethoven-Studien und andere Themen* (Bonn, 1967).

Mischakoff (real name, **Fischberg**), **Mischa,** Russian-born American violinist; b. Proskurov, April 3, 1895; d. Petoskey, Mich., Feb. 1, 1981. Owing to a plethora of Russian-Jewish violinists named Fischberg, he decided to change his name to Mischakoff, formed by adding the Russian ending *-koff* to his 1st name, the Russian diminutive for Michael. He studied with Korguyev at the St. Petersburg Cons., graduating in 1912; made his debut that year in Berlin and then was active as an orch. player and teacher. He emigrated to the U.S. in 1921 and became a naturalized citizen in 1927. He was concertmaster of the N.Y. Sym. Orch. (1924–27), the Philadelphia Orch. (1927–29), the Chicago Sym. Orch. (1930–36), the NBC Sym. Orch. in N.Y. (1937–52), and the Detroit Sym. Orch. (1952–68); then guest concertmaster of the Baltimore Sym. Orch. (1968–69); was also concertmaster and soloist with the Chautauqua Sym. Orch. (summers 1925–65); likewise led his own Mischakoff String Quartet. He taught at the Juilliard School of Music in N.Y. (1940–52), at Wayne State Univ. in Detroit (from 1952), and at various other schools.

Misón, Luis, Spanish flutist, oboist, conductor, and composer; b. probably in Barcelona, date unknown; d. Madrid, Feb. 13, 1776. He was a flutist in the Royal Chapel and the Royal Opera, Madrid (from 1748); became conductor there in 1756; composed stage music; was one of the 1st to introduce the "tonadilla escénica," a sort of miniature comic opera that developed from the musical interludes in early Spanish plays; also wrote "sainetes" (dramatic dialogues), zarzuelas, and 12 sonatas for Flute, Viola, and Bass.

Misra, Mahapurush, Indian virtuoso on the tabla; b. Calcutta, Jan. 1, 1933. He studied with eminent swamis and gurus; toured in Europe in 1959 and in the U.S. in 1961.

Missa, Edmond (Jean Louis), French organist and composer; b. Rheims, June 12, 1861; d. Paris, Jan. 29, 1910. He studied with Massenet at the Paris Cons.; received an honorable mention for the Prix de Rome in 1881; then served as organist at St. Thomas d'Aquin. He wrote a number of operas, including *Babette* (London, Oct. 22, 1900) and *Muguette,* based on Ouida's *2 Little Wooden Shoes* (Paris, March 18, 1903); also orch. works, choruses, songs, and piano pieces.

Mitchell, Donald (Charles Peter), eminent English writer on music and publishing executive; b. London, Feb. 6, 1925. He studied at Dulwich College in London (1939–42) and with A. Hutchings and A.E.F. Dickinson at the Univ. of Durham (1949–50); after noncombatant wartime service (1942–45), he founded (1947) and then became co-ed. (with Hans Keller) of *Music Survey* (1949–52); from 1953 to 1957 he was London music critic of the *Musical Times.* In 1958 he was appointed music ed. and adviser of Faber & Faber Ltd.; in 1965 he became managing director, and in 1976 vice chairman; became chairman in 1977 of its subsidiary, Faber Music. He also ed. *Tempo* (1958–62); was on the music staff of the *Daily Telegraph* (1959–64); in 1963–64 he served as music adviser to Boosey & Hawkes Ltd.; from 1971 to 1976 was prof. of music, and from 1976 visiting prof. of music, at the Univ. of Sussex; in 1973 was awarded by it an honorary M.A. degree; received his doctorate in 1977 from Southampton Univ. with a dissertation on Mahler. He lectured widely in the United Kingdom, U.S., and Australia; contributed articles to the *Encyclopædia Britannica* and other reference publications. As a music scholar, Mitchell made a profound study, in Vienna and elsewhere, of the life and works of Gustav Mahler; was awarded in 1961 the Mahler Medal of Honor by the Bruckner Soc. of America and in 1987 the Mahler Medal of the International Gustav Mahler Soc. His major work

is a Mahler biography: vol. 1, *Gustav Mahler: The Early Years* (London, 1958; rev. ed., 1980); vol. 2, *The Wunderhorn Years* (London, 1976); vol. 3, *Songs and Symphonies of Life and Death* (London, 1985). His other publications include: ed. with H. Keller, *Benjamin Britten: A Commentary on All His Works from a Group of Specialists* (London, 1952); *W.A. Mozart: A Short Biography* (London, 1956); with H.C. Robbins Landon, *The Mozart Companion* (N.Y., 1956; 2nd ed., 1965); *The Language of Modern Music* (London, 1963; 3rd ed., 1970); ed. and annotated Alma Mahler's *Gustav Mahler: Memories and Letters* (London, 1968; 3rd ed., rev., 1973); ed. with J. Evans, *Benjamin Britten, 1913–1976: Pictures from a Life* (London, 1978); *Britten and Auden in the Thirties* (London, 1981); *Benjamin Britten: Death in Venice* (Cambridge, 1987).

Mitchell, Dwike, American jazz pianist; b. Jacksonville, Fla., Feb. 14, 1930. He studied at the Philadelphia Musical Academy; formed a duo with the horn player and bassist Willie Ruff, and played in nightclubs with complete popular acceptance despite their academic education and ability to read music. In 1959 they gave impromptu sessions of jazz in Russia, arousing unrestrained enthusiasm among young Soviet audiences.

Mitchell, Howard, American cellist and conductor; b. Lyons, Nebr., March 11, 1911; d. Ormond Beach, Fla., June 22, 1988. He studied piano and trumpet in Sioux City, Iowa; after studying cello at the Peabody Cons. of Music in Baltimore, he completed his training with Felix Salmond at the Curtis Inst. of Music in Philadelphia (1930–35). He was 1st cellist of the National Sym. Orch. in Washington, D.C. (1933–44); then was its assistant (1944–48), associate (1948–49), and principal (1949–69) conductor. He then became conductor of the SODRE Sym. Orch. in Montevideo.

Mitchell, Joni (born **Roberta Joan Anderson**), Canadian singer and songwriter of popular music; b. McLeod, near Lethbridge, Alberta, Nov. 7, 1943. She was reared in Saskatoon and took piano lessons in childhood; later learned to play guitar; attended the Alberta College of Art in Calgary for a year and sang in a local coffeehouse; then performed in Toronto, where she met and married the folksinger Chuck Mitchell; she kept his last name after their divorce. She wrote the hit song *Both Sides Now* (1968), made famous in Judy Collins's recording; Mitchell included it in her album *Clouds* (1969), which captured a Grammy Award for best folk recording in 1970. Her album *Ladies of the Canyon* (1970) attained gold status; the album *Court and Spark* (1974) also proved highly popular. In her interpretations, she closely followed the folk-song style, with an admixture of jazzy syncopation. For a while she worked as a lyricist for Charles Mingus; after his death in 1979, she wrote a moving song in his memory, somewhat sacrilegiously entitled *God Must Be a Boogie Man.* Other interesting albums include *Hejira* (1976), *Don Juan's Reckless Daughter* (1978), and *Chalk Mark in a Rain Storm* (1988).
    BIBL.: L. Fleischer, *J. M.* (N.Y., 1976).

Mitchell, Leona, talented black American soprano; b. Enid, Okla., Oct. 13, 1948. She was one of 15 children; her father, a Pentecostal minister, played several instruments by ear; her mother was a good amateur pianist. She sang in local church choirs; then received a scholarship to Oklahoma City Univ., where she obtained her B.Mus. degree in 1971. She made her operatic debut in 1972 as Micaëla in *Carmen* with the San Francisco Spring Opera Theater. She then received the $10,000 Opera America grant (1973), which enabled her to study with Ernest St. John Metz in Los Angeles. On Dec. 15, 1975, she made her Metropolitan Opera debut in N.Y. as Micaëla; subsequently sang there as Pamina in *Die Zauberflöte* and Musetta in *La Bohème;* she won critical acclaim for her portrayal of Leonora in *La forza del destino* in 1982.

Mitchell, William J(ohn), American musicologist; b. N.Y., Nov. 21, 1906; d. Binghamton, N.Y., Aug. 17, 1971. He studied at the Inst. of Musical Art in N.Y. (1925–29); then at Columbia Univ. (B.A., 1930); went to Vienna for further studies (1930–

32). Upon his return to N.Y. he was on the staff at Columbia Univ.; received his M.A. there in 1938; became a full prof. in 1952, then served as chairman of the music dept. from 1962 to 1967; concurrently he taught at the Mannes College of Music in N.Y. (1957–68); he subsequently joined the faculty of the State Univ. of N.Y. in Binghamton; was president of the American Musicological Soc. (1965–66). He publ. *Elementary Harmony* (N.Y., 1939; 3rd ed., rev., 1965); ed. and tr. Herriot's *La Vie de Beethoven* (1935) and C.P.E. Bach's *Versuch über die wahre Art das Clavier zu spielen* (1949); was co-ed. of the 1st 3 vols. of *Music Forum* (1967–73).

Mitjana y Gordón, Rafael, eminent Spanish music historian; b. Málaga, Dec. 6, 1869; d. Stockholm, Aug. 15, 1921. He studied music with Eduardo Ocón in Málaga, Felipe Pedrell in Madrid, and Saint-Saëns in Paris; was employed in the Spanish diplomatic service in Russia, Turkey, Morocco, and Sweden. His most important work was the extensive contribution on the history of Spanish music in Lavignac's *Encyclopédie de la musique* (Paris, 1920; Part I, vol. IV). He also wrote numerous valuable works of a critical or historical nature, including: *L'Orientalisme musical et la musique arabe* (Uppsala, 1907); *Catalogue critique et descriptif des imprimés de musique des 16ᵉ et 17ᵉ siècles, conservés à la Bibliothèque de l'Université d'Uppsala* (Uppsala, 1911); *Don Fernando de las Infantas, teólogo y músico* (Madrid, 1911); *Cristóbal de Morales: Estudio crítico biográfico* (Madrid, 1920).

Mitrea-Celarianu, Mihai, Rumanian composer; b. Bucharest, Jan. 20, 1935. He studied with Rogalski, A. Mendelsohn, Vancea, and Negrea at the Bucharest Cons. (1948–53); also took private lessons with Jora (1949–51); was a prof. of harmony and music history in Bucharest (1954–60; 1962–68); then attended summer courses in new music given by Aloys Kontarsky, Caskel, and Karkoschka in Darmstadt (1968), and further studied with the Groupe de Recherches Musicales in Paris (1968–69) and with P. Schaeffer and Pousseur at the Paris Cons. (1968–69). His trademarks in composition are aleatory, electronic, and variable scoring.
WORKS: Violin Sonata (1957); Piano Sonata (1958); *Variations* for Orch. (1958); Piano Sonatina (1960); *Le Chant des étoiles*, cantata for Mezzo-soprano and 33 Instruments (1964); *Glosă (Comment)* for Viola (1965); *Petite histoire d'avant-monde* for Small Chamber Ensemble (1967); *Convergences II (Colinda)* for Electronic Instruments and Percussion (1967), *III (Idéophonie M)*, aleatory music for Narrator, Children's Choir, and 19 Instruments (1968), *IV* for 1 Performer on Optional Instrument or Variable Ensemble (1968), and *V (Jeux dans le blanc)* for Chorus, Percussion, and Tape (1969); *Trei pentru cinci* for Aleatorily Structured Orch. (in collaboration with Miereanu and Bosseur, 1969); *Seth* for 7 Instruments (1969); *ZN*, "idéogramme photographique" for 3, 4, or 5 Performers (1971); *Signaux (Sur l'Océan U)* for 13 Players (1971); *Inaugural 71*, "action" for a Flutist, with Electro-acoustical Devices and a Projector (1971); *Piano de matin (Écoute pour Anne Frank)*, "action" for 5 Instruments, 5 Persons manipulating Divergent Sound Sources, Electro-acoustical Devices, and Projectors (1972); *Prérêve* for Voice, Harpsichord, Flute, and Percussion (1975); *Milchstrassenmusik* for Orch. (1983); *Natalienlied* for 10 Instrumentalists (1986); *Evian, Evian* for Instrumental Ensemble (1987); *Weil Paul Celan* for Vocal Ensemble, Chorus, and Orch. (1988).

Mitropoulos, Dimitri, celebrated Greek-born American conductor and composer; b. Athens, March 1, 1896; d. after suffering a heart attack while rehearsing Mahler's 3rd Sym. with the orch. of the Teatro alla Scala, Milan, Nov. 2, 1960. He studied piano with Wassenhoven and harmony with A. Marsick at the Odeon Cons. in Athens; wrote an opera after Maeterlinck, *Sœur Béatrice* (1918), performed at the Odeon Cons. (May 20, 1919); in 1920, after graduation from the Cons., he went to Brussels, where he studied composition with Paul Gilson; in 1921 he went to Berlin, where he took piano lessons with Busoni at the Hochschule für Musik (until 1924); concurrently was répétiteur at the Berlin State Opera. He became a conduc-

tor of the Odeon Cons. orch. in Athens (1924); was its co-conductor (1927–29) and principal conductor (from 1929); was also prof. of composition there (from 1930). In 1930 he was invited to conduct a concert of the Berlin Phil.; when the soloist Egon Petri became suddenly indisposed, Mitropoulos substituted for him as soloist in Prokofiev's Piano Concerto No. 3, conducting from the keyboard (Feb. 27, 1930). He played the same concerto in Paris in 1932 as a pianist-conductor, and later in the U.S. His Paris debut as a conductor (1932) obtained a spontaneous success; he conducted the most difficult works from memory, which was a novelty at the time; also led rehearsals without a score. He made his American debut with the Boston Sym. Orch. on Jan. 24, 1936, with immediate acclaim; that same year he was engaged as music director of the Minneapolis Sym. Orch.; there he frequently performed modern music, including works by Schoenberg, Berg, and other representatives of the atonal school; the opposition that naturally arose was not sufficient to offset his hold on the public as a conductor of great emotional power. He resigned from the Minneapolis Sym. Orch. in 1949 to accept the post of conductor of the N.Y. Phil.; shared the podium with Stokowski for a few weeks, and in 1950 became music director. In 1956 Leonard Bernstein was engaged as associate conductor with Mitropoulos, and in 1958 succeeded him as music director. With the N.Y. Phil., Mitropoulos continued his policy of bringing out important works by European and American modernists; he also programmed modern operas (*Elektra, Wozzeck*) in concert form. A musician of astounding technical ability, Mitropoulos became very successful with the general public as well as with the musical vanguard whose cause he so boldly espoused. While his time was engaged mainly in the U.S., Mitropoulos continued to appear as guest conductor in Europe; he also appeared on numerous occasions as conductor at the Metropolitan Opera in N.Y. (debut conducting *Salome*, Dec. 15, 1954) and at various European opera theaters. He became an American citizen in 1946. As a composer, Mitropoulos was one of the earliest among Greek composers to write in a distinctly modern idiom.
WORKS: Opera: *Sœur Béatrice* (1918; Odeon Cons., Athens, May 20, 1919); *Burial* for Orch. (1925); Concerto Grosso for Orch. (1928); incidental music for *Electra* (1936) and *Hippolytus* (1937); *Concert Piece* for Violin and Piano (1913); Piano Sonata (1915); *Fauns* for String Quartet (1915); *Piano Piece* (1925); *Passacaglia, Preludio e Fuga* for Piano (c.1925); Violin Sonata, *Ostinata* (in a nearly precise Schoenbergian idiom; 1925–26); *10 Inventions* for Soprano and Piano (1926); *4 Dances from Cythera* for Piano (1926).

Mitsukuri, Shukichi, Japanese composer; b. Tokyo, Oct. 21, 1895; d. Chigasaki, Kanagawa Prefecture, May 10, 1971. He graduated in applied chemistry from the engineering dept. of the Imperial Univ. in Tokyo in 1921; then went to Berlin and studied composition with Georg Schumann; returned to Japan in 1925 and became an Imperial Navy engineering officer. In 1930 he founded a contemporary Japanese composers' society, Shinko Sakkyokuka; in 1954, was appointed a prof. at the Music Academy in Tokyo.
WORKS: ORCH.: *Sinfonietta classica* (Paris, March 6, 1936); *10 Haikai de Basho* (Paris, Dec. 10, 1937); *Elegy* for Chorus and Orch. (1949); 2 syms.: No. 1 (Tokyo, Aug. 22, 1951); No. 2 (1963); Piano Concertino (Tokyo, Aug. 22, 1953); Piano Concerto (Tokyo, April 23, 1955). CHAMBER: Violin Sonata (1935); Piano Quintet (1955); *Night Rhapsody* for Piano (1935); other piano pieces; 3 albums of Japanese folk songs (1950, 1954, 1955).

Mitterer, Ignaz Martin, Austrian composer; b. St. Justina, Feb. 2, 1850; d. Brixen, Aug. 18, 1924. He studied singing with his uncle, Anton Mitterer; piano and organ with B. Huber; was ordained a priest in 1874; studied again (1876–77) at the Kirchenmusikschule in Regensburg with F.X. Haberl; was Kapellmeister at the Cathedral there (1882–84); then at the Cathedral in Brixen; wrote over 200 sacred works.

Mitterwurzer, Anton, famous Austrian baritone; b. Sterzing, April 12, 1818; d. Döbling, near Vienna, April 2, 1876. He studied with his uncle, Johann Gänsbacher; after serving as chorister at St. Stephen's, Vienna, he sang in Austrian provincial theaters. In 1839 he was engaged by the Dresden Court Opera, and remained there until he was pensioned in 1870. He was particularly notable in Wagnerian roles.

Mittler, Franz, Austrian composer and pianist; b. Vienna, April 14, 1893; d. Munich, Dec. 28, 1970. He studied in Vienna with Heuberger and Prohaska; later in Cologne with Fritz Steinbach and Carl Friedberg. From 1921 to 1938 he lived in Vienna as a pianist and accompanist; in 1939 he settled in N.Y. He wrote an opera, *Rafaella* (Duisburg, 1930); Piano Trio; a number of piano pieces. In America he wrote numerous popular songs (*In Flaming Beauty, From Dreams of Thee, Soft through My Heart, Over the Mountains*); also light piano suites: *Manhattan Suite, Suite in 3/4 Time, Newsreel Suite, Boogie-Woogie, Waltz in Blue, 1-Finger Polka.*
BIBL.: D. Mittler Battipaglia, *F. M.: Composer, Pedagogue and Practical Musician* (diss., Univ. of Rochester, 1974).

Miyagi (real name, **Wakabe**), **Michio,** Japanese koto player, teacher, and composer; b. Kobe, April 7, 1894; d. (in a railroad accident) Kariya, near Tokyo, June 25, 1956. He was given the surname of Suga in infancy; became blind at age 7; studied the koto with Nakajima Kengyō II and made his debut when he was 9. He went to Inchon (1908) to teach the koto and shakuhachi; then taught in Seoul. After receiving his certificate as a koto player with highest honors, he was given the professional name of Nakasuga; was known as Michio Miyagi from 1913. He settled in Tokyo (1917); with Seiju Yoshida, he founded the New Japanese Music Movement (1920); became a lecturer (1930) and a prof. (1937) at the Tokyo Music School; taught at the National Univ. of Fine Arts and Music (from 1950). He wrote more than 1,000 works for koto and other Japanese instruments; also an opera, *Kariteibo* (1924); choral works and solo vocal music.
BIBL.: E. Kikkawa, *Miyagi Michio den* (The Life of M. M.; Tokyo, 1962).

Miyoshi, Akira, Japanese composer; b. Tokyo, Jan. 10, 1933. He joined the Jiyû-Gakuen children's piano group at the age of 3, graduating at the age of 6. He studied French literature; in 1951 he began to study music with Hirai, Ikenouchi, and Raymond Gallois-Montbrun, who was in Tokyo at the time. He obtained a stipend to travel to France and took lessons in composition with Henri Challan and again with Gallois-Montbrun (1955–57); upon his return to Japan, he resumed his studies in French literature at the Univ. of Tokyo, obtaining a degree in 1961. In 1965 he was appointed instructor at the Toho Gakuen School of Music in Tokyo.
WORKS: POETICAL DRAMAS: *Happy Prince* (1959) and *Ondine* (1959). **ORCH.:** *Symphonie concertante* for Piano and Orch. (1954); *Mutation symphonique* (1958); *3 mouvements symphoniques* (1960); Piano Concerto (1962); *Duel* for Soprano and Orch. (1964); Concerto (Tokyo, Oct. 22, 1964); Violin Concerto (1965); *Odes metamorphosées* (1968); Concerto for Marimba and String Ensemble (1969); 2 works of musical poesy: *The Red Mask of Death I* for Narrator, Orch., and Electronic Sound (1969) and *II* for Voice, Chorus, Orch., and Electronic Sound (1970); *Ouverture de fête* (1973); *Leos* (1976); *Noesis* (1978). **CHAMBER:** Sonata for Clarinet, Bassoon, and Piano (1953); Violin Sonata (1954–55); Sonata for Flute, Cello, and Piano (1955); *Torse I* for Chamber Orch. (1959), *II* for Chorus, Piano, Electone, and Percussion (1962), *III* for Marimba (1968), *IV* for String Quartet and 4 Japanese Instruments (1972), and *V* for 3 Marimbas (1973); 2 string quartets (1962, 1967); *Conversation,* suite for Marimba (1962); *8 poèmes* for Flute Ensemble (1969); *Transit* for Electronic and Concrete Sounds, Percussion, and Keyboard Instruments (1969); *Hommage à musique de chambre, I, II, III,* and *IV* for Flute, Violin and Piano (1970, 1971, 1972, 1974); *Nocturne* for Marimba, Percussion, Flute, Clarinet, and Double Bass (1973); *Protase de loin à rien* for 2 Guitars (1974); *Concert Étude* for 2 Marimbas

(1977). **PIANO:** Sonata (1958); *In Such Time,* suite (1960); *Études en forme de Sonate* (1967); also choruses; songs.

Mizelle, (Dary) John, American composer; b. Stillwater, Okla., June 14, 1940. He studied trombone at Calif. State Univ. in Sacramento (B.A., 1965) and composition at the Univ. of Calif. at Davis (M.A., 1967) and at the Univ. of Calif. at San Diego (Ph.D., 1977); also studied computer music at Columbia Univ. (1979–83). He taught at the Univ. of South Florida in Tampa (1973–75) and at the Oberlin College Cons. of Music (1975–79); in 1990, joined the faculty of the State Univ. of N.Y. at Purchase. He served as associate ed. of *Source* magazine (1966–69). Interest in Mizelle's music increased greatly when a 25-year retrospective concert was given in N.Y. in 1988; his compositions, which number over 200, have been lauded for their stylistic assimilation of such disparate Western composers as Bartók, Messiaen, and Xenakis, their admixtures of ancient, traditional acoustic, and electronic instruments, the mathematical exactitude of their construction, their generous reliance upon the improvisational skills of performers, and their varied use of extended vocal techniques.
WORKS: 3 string quartets (1964, 1975, 1983); *Green and Red,* quartet for 9 Instruments (1965); *Straight Ahead* for Violin, Flute, Trumpet, Trombone, Percussion, and Tape (1965); *Radial Energy I* for Unspecified Instruments (1967) and *II* for Orch. (1968); *Mass* for Chorus and Live Electronics (1968); *Polyphonies I* for Quadraphonic Tape, Shakuhachi, and Electronics (1975), *II* for Tape and Dance (1976), and *III* for Quadraphonic Tape and Theater (1978); *Soundscape* for Percussion Ensemble (1976); *Quanta I & Hymn to Matter* for 8 Multiphonic Vocalists, Chorus, and Orch. (1972–76); *Polytempus I* for Trumpet and Tape (1976); *Primavera-Heterophony* for 24 Cellos (1977); *Samadhi* for Quadraphonic Tape (1978); *Quanta II & Hymn of the Word* for Wind Ensemble, Percussion, Organ, and 2 Choruses (1979); *Polytempus II* for Marimba and Tape (1979); *Lake Mountain Thunder* for English Horn and Percussion Ensemble (1981); *The Thunderclap of Time I* (1981) and *II* (1982), music for a planetarium; Requiem Mass for Chorus and Orch. (1982); *Sonic Adventures,* 15 process pieces for Various Multiple Instrumental Ensembles (1982); Quintet for Woodwinds (1983); Contrabass Quartet (1983); *Indian Summer* for String Quartet and Oboe (1983); *Sounds* for Orch. (1984); Concerto for Contrabass and Orch. (1974–85); *Genesis* for Orch. (1985); *Blue* for Orch. (1985–86); Percussion Concerto (1985–87); *Parameters* for Percussion Solo and Chamber Orch. (1974–87); *Earth Mountain Fire,* 80 minutes of music for Compact Disk (1987–); *Fossy: A Passion Play,* music theater (1987); *Chance Gives Me What I Want,* dance piece (1988).

Mizler, Lorenz Christoph, learned German music scholar; b. Heidenheim, Franconia, July 25, 1711; d. Warsaw, March 1778. He entered the Ansbach Gymnasium when he was 13; also took music lessons from Ehrmann in Ansbach, and learned to play the violin and flute. In 1731 he enrolled as a theology student at the Univ. of Leipzig; he received his bachelor's degree in 1733, and his master's degree in 1734 with his *Dissertatio, Quod musica ars sit pars eruditionis philosophicae* (2nd ed., 1736; 3rd ed., 1740). He was a friend of J.S. Bach. In 1735 he went to Wittenberg, where he studied law and medicine. Returning to Leipzig in 1736, he gave his disputation *De usu atque praestantia philosophiae in theologia, jurisprudentia, medicina* (Leipzig, 1736; 2nd ed., 1740). In 1737 he joined the faculty of the Univ. of Leipzig, where he lectured on Mattheson's *Neu-eröffnete Orchestre* and music history. In 1738 he also established the Korrespondierende Sozietät der Musicalischen Wissenschaften. He likewise publ. the valuable music periodical *Neu eröffnete musikalische Bibliothek* (1739–54). In 1743 he entered the service of the Polish count Malachowski of Konshie, working as a secretary, teacher, librarian, and mathematician; he learned the Polish language and devoted much time to the study of Polish culture. In 1747 he took his doctorate in medicine at the Univ. of Erfurt; that same year he went to Warsaw, where he was made physician to the court in 1752.

He was ennobled by the Polish court as Mizler von Kolof in 1768. His vast erudition in many branches of knowledge impelled him to publ. polemical works in which he, much in the prevalent manner of 18th-century philosophers, professed omniscience. Thus he publ. the pamphlet *Lusus ingenii de praesenti bello* (Wittenberg, 1735), in which he proposed, by means of a musical game, to advise the German emperor Karl VII on the proper conduct of the war waged at the time. Pugnacious by nature, he derided "the stupidities of conceited self-grown so-called composers making themselves ridiculous" in a lampoon entitled "Musical Stabber" (*Musikalischer Starstecher, in welchem rechtschaffener musikverständigen Fehler bescheiden angemerket, eingebildeter und selbst gewachsener sogenannter Componisten Thorheiten aber lächerlich gemachet werden*, Leipzig, 1739–40). His theoretical writings include *Anfangs-Gründe des General-Basses nach mathematischer Lehr-Art abgehandelt* (an attempt to instruct figured bass by mathematical rules; Leipzig, 1739). He also translated into German Fux's *Gradus ad Parnassum*, with annotations (Leipzig, 1742). He prepared an autobiography for Mattheson's basic biographical music dictionary, *Grundlage einer Ehren-Pforte* (Hamburg, 1740; new ed. by M. Schneider, Berlin, 1910; reprint, 1969).

BIBL.: F. Wöhlke, *L.C. M.: Ein Beitrag zur musikalischen Gelehrtengeschichte des 18. Jahrhunderts* (Würzburg, 1940); J. Birke, *Christian Wolffs Metaphysik und die zeitgenössische Literatur- und Musiktheorie: Gottsched, Scheibe, M.* (Berlin, 1966); H. Federhofer, "Johann Joseph Fux und Johann Mattheson im Urteil L.C. M.s," *Speculum musicae artis: Festgabe für Heinrich Husmann* (Munich, 1970).

Mlynarski, Emil (Simon), Polish violinist, conductor, and composer; b. Kibarty, July 18, 1870; d. Warsaw, April 5, 1935. He studied at the St. Petersburg Cons. (1880–89), taking up both the violin, with Leopold Auer, and piano, with Anton Rubinstein; also took a course in composition with Liadov. He embarked on a career as a conductor; in 1897 he was appointed principal conductor of the Warsaw Opera, and concurrently conducted the concerts of the Warsaw Phil. (1901–5); from 1904 to 1907 he was director of the Warsaw Cons. He achieved considerable success as a conductor in Scotland, where he was principal conductor of the Scottish Orch. in Glasgow (1910–16). He was director of the Warsaw Cons. (1919–22), and of the Warsaw Opera (1918–29). From 1929 to 1931 he taught conducting at the Curtis Inst. of Music in Philadelphia; in 1931 he returned to Warsaw. He composed an opera, *Noc letnia* (Summer Night; 1914; Warsaw, March 29, 1924); Sym., *Polonia* (1910); 2 violin concertos (1897, Paderewski prize; 1914–17); violin pieces.

BIBL.: A. Wach, *Zycie i twórczość Emila M.ego* (Life and Works of E. M.; diss., Univ. of Krakow, 1953); J. Mechanisz, *E. M.: W setną rocznicę urodzin (1870–1970)* (Warsaw, 1970).

Moberg, Carl Allan, eminent Swedish musicologist; b. Östersund, June 5, 1896; d. Uppsala, June 19, 1978. He studied with Norlind at the Univ. of Uppsala (1917–24); then took some lessons with Alban Berg in Vienna, and took a course in musicology with Peter Wagner in Fribourg (1924–27); received his Ph.D. in 1927 from the Univ. of Uppsala; later studied with Handschin in Basel (1934–35). He was a reader (1928–47) and a prof. (1947–61) at the Univ. of Uppsala; was ed. of *Svensk tidskrift för musikforskning* (1945–61) and of *Studia musicologica upsaliensia* (1952–61). Among his achievements was a journey to Lapland in the north to collect native songs. He was honored with a Festschrift on his 65th birthday in 1961. Moberg distinguished himself particularly in the study of music history and ethnomusicology.

WRITINGS: *Kyrkomusikens historia* (Stockholm, 1932); *Tonkonstens historia i Västerlandet* (2 vols., Stockholm, 1935); *Dietrich Buxtehude* (Hälsingborg, 1946); *Die liturgischen Hymnen in Schweden* (Uppsala, 1947); *Musikens historia i Västerlandet intill 1600* (Oslo, 1973).

Mocquereau, Dom André, distinguished French music scholar; b. La Tessoualle, near Cholet, Maine-et-Loire, June 6, 1849; d. Solesmes, Jan. 18, 1930. In 1875 he joined the Order of Benedictines at the Abbey of Solesmes and devoted himself to the study of Gregorian chant under the direction of Dom Pothier; took his vows (1877) and was ordained a priest (1879); was made choirmaster (1889); was its prior (1902–8), during which period the order was expelled from France and found refuge on the Isle of Wight (1903); later returned to Solesmes. He was the founder and ed. of the 1st 13 vols. of Paléographie Musicale. He publ. *Paroissien romain: Liber usualis* (Tournai, 1903; 5th ed., 1905) and *Le Nombre musical grégorien* (2 vols., Tournai, 1908, 1927; Eng. tr., 1932–51).

BIBL.: J. Ward, *De greg. Zangen naar D. M.* (Doornik, 1929); J. de Donostia, *À propos du nombre musical grégorien de D. M.* (Paris, 1930); special issues of *Gregorian Review* (Jan.–Feb. 1955) and *Revue Grégorienne* (Jan.–April 1955).

Mödl, Martha, esteemed German mezzo-soprano, later soprano; b. Nuremberg, March 22, 1912. She studied at the Nuremberg Cons. and in Milan; made her operatic debut as Hänsel in Nuremberg (1942), then sang in Düsseldorf (1945–49) and at the Hamburg State Opera (1947–55), appearing in soprano roles from 1950 with notable success. She sang at London's Covent Garden (1949–50; 1953; 1959; 1966); appeared as Kundry at the resumption of the Bayreuth Festival productions in 1951, and continued to sing there regularly until 1967; sang Leonore in the 1st performance at the rebuilt Vienna State Opera in 1955. On March 2, 1957, she made her Metropolitan Opera debut in N.Y. as Brünnhilde in *Götterdämmerung*, remaining on the roster there until 1960; was again a member of the Hamburg State Opera (1956–75). In 1981 she sang in the premiere of Cerha's *Baal* in Salzburg. She was made both a German and an Austrian Kammersängerin. Among her finest mezzo-soprano roles were Dorabella, Carmen, Eboli, Octavian, the Composer, and Marie in *Wozzeck*; as a soprano, she excelled as Brünnhilde, Isolde, Gutrune, Venus, and Sieglinde.

BIBL.: W. Schäfer, *M. M.* (Hannover, 1967).

Moeck, Hermann, German music publisher and instrument maker; b. Elbing, July 9, 1896; d. Celle, Oct. 9, 1982. He established his publ. business in Celle in 1930; in 1960 he handed it over to his son **Hermann Moeck, Jr.** (b. Lüneburg, Sept. 16, 1922). The firm was influential in the revival of the manufacture of the vertical flute (recorder) and other Renaissance and early Baroque instruments; Moeck also publ. arrangements and authentic pieces for recorders and the theretofore obsolete fidels. Hermann Moeck, Jr., wrote a valuable monograph, *Ursprung und Tradition der Kernspaltflöten* (2 vols., 1951), also publ. in an abridged form as *Typen europäischer Blockflöten* (Celle, 1967).

Moeller, M(athias) P(eter). See **Möller, M(athias) P(eter).**

Moeran, E(rnest) J(ohn), English composer of Anglo-Irish descent; b. Heston, Middlesex, Dec. 31, 1894; d. Kenmare, County Kerry, Ireland, Dec. 1, 1950. His father was a clergyman, and he learned music from hymnbooks; then studied at the Royal College of Music in London; was an officer in the British army in World War I, and was wounded. Returning to London, he took lessons in composition with John Ireland (1920–23); also became interested in folk music; he collected numerous folk songs in Norfolk, some of which were publ. by the Folksong Soc. (1922). In his early music, he was influenced by Ireland and Delius, but later found inspiration in the works of Vaughan Williams, Holst, and Warlock.

WORKS: ORCH.: *In the Mountain Country*, symphonic impression (1921); 2 rhapsodies (1922; 1924, rev. 1941); Sym. (1934–37; London, Jan. 13, 1938); Violin Concerto (London, July 8, 1942); *Rhapsody* for Piano and Orch. (London, Aug. 19, 1943); *Overture to a Masque* (1944); Sinfonietta (1944); Cello Concerto (Dublin, Nov. 25, 1945, with Moeran's wife, Peers Coetmore, as soloist); *Serenade* (London, Sept. 2, 1948). CHAMBER: Piano Trio (1920); String Quartet (1921); Violin

Sonata (1930); String Trio (1931); *Fantasy Quartet* for Oboe, Violin, Viola, and Cello (1946); Cello Sonata (1947); also choral works; piano and organ pieces; many songs.

BIBL.: H. Foss, *Compositions of E.J. M.* (London, 1948); S. Wild, *E.J. M.* (London, 1973); G. Self, *The Music of E.J. M.* (London, 1986).

Moeschinger, Albert, Swiss composer; b. Basel, Jan. 10, 1897; d. Thun, Sept. 25, 1985. He studied in Bern and Leipzig, and with Courvoisier in Munich (1917–23); then taught theory and piano at the Bern Cons. (1937–43). His large output reflects the influences of German neo-Romanticism and French Impressionism.

WORKS: *Die kleine Seejungfrau*, radio opera (1947); *Amor und Psyche*, ballet (1955); 5 syms.; 5 piano concertos; *Ballade symphonique* for Orch. (1957); *Fantaisie concertante* for Flute, Clarinet, Bassoon, and Orch. (1963); *Ignis divinus* for Orch. (1966); *Erratique* for Orch. (1969); *Variations mystérieuses* for Chamber Orch. (1977); *Blocs sonores* for Orch. (1977); 6 string quartets; 2 piano trios; 3 piano quintets; Piano Sextet; 6 wind trios; choral works; organ music; piano pieces.

Moevs, Robert W(alter), American composer and teacher; b. La Crosse, Wis., Dec. 2, 1920. He studied with Piston at Harvard College (A.B., 1942), with Boulanger at the Paris Cons. (1947–51), and at Harvard Univ. (A.M., 1952). From 1952 to 1955 he was a Rome Prize Fellow in music at the American Academy in Rome; he held a Guggenheim fellowship (1963–64). He taught at Harvard Univ. (1955–63); was composer-in-residence at the American Academy in Rome (1960–61); in 1964 joined the faculty of Rutgers Univ. in New Jersey, where he was a prof. (from 1968) and chairman of the music dept. at its New Brunswick campus (1974–81). In addition to his activities as a composer and teacher, he made appearances as a pianist, often in performances of his own works. In 1978 he was awarded the Stockhausen International Prize for his Concerto Grosso for Piano, Percussion, and Orch. As a composer, he developed a compositional method based on intervallic control as opposed to specific pitch sequence that he described as systematic chromaticism.

WORKS: ORCH.: *Passacaglia* (1941); *Introduction and Fugue* (1949); *Overture* (1950); *14 Variations* (1952); *3 Symphonic Pieces* (1954–55; Cleveland, April 10, 1958); Concerto Grosso for Piano, Percussion, and Orch. (1960; 2nd version with Amplified Instruments, 1968); *In Festivitate* for Wind Instruments and Percussion (Dartmouth, N.H., Nov. 8, 1962); *Main-Travelled Roads, Symphonic Piece No. 4* (1973); *Prometheus: Music for Small Orchestra, I* (1980); *Pandora: Music for Small Orchestra, II* (1986). **CHAMBER:** *Spring* for 4 Violins and Trumpets (1950); 2 string quartets: No. 1 (1957; Cambridge, Mass., Feb. 17, 1960); No. 2 (1989); *Variazioni sopra una Melodia* for Viola and Cello (1961); *Musica da camera* for Chamber Ensemble (1965); *Fanfare canonica* for 6 Trumpets (1966); *Paths and Ways* for Saxophone and Dancer (1970); *Musica da camera II* for Chamber Ensemble (1972); Trio for Violin, Cello, and Piano (1980); *Dark Litany* for Wind Ensemble (1987); Woodwind Quintet (1988); solo pieces; various keyboard works. **VOCAL:** *Cantata sacra* for Baritone, Men's Chorus, Flute, 4 Trombones, and Timpani (1952); *Attis* for Tenor, Chorus, Percussion, and Orch. (1958–59; 1963); *Et Nunc, reges* for Women's Chorus, Flute, Clarinet, and Bass Clarinet (1963); *Ode to an Olympic Hero* for Voice and Orch. (1963); *Et Occidentem Illustra* for Chorus and Orch. (1964); *A Brief Mass* for Chorus, Organ, Vibraphone, Guitar, and Double Bass (1968); *The Aulos Player* for Soprano, 2 Choruses, and 2 Organs (1975); songs; choruses.

Moffo, Anna, noted American soprano; b. Wayne, Pa., June 27, 1932. She was of Italian descent. She studied voice at the Curtis Inst. of Music in Philadelphia; later went to Italy on a Fulbright fellowship and studied at the Accademia di Santa Cecilia in Rome. She made her debut as Norina in Spoleto in 1955 and, progressing rapidly in her career, was engaged at La Scala in Milan, at the Vienna State Opera, and in Paris. She made her U.S. debut as Mimi with the Chicago Lyric Opera in 1957; on Nov. 14, 1959, she made her debut at the Metropolitan Opera in N.Y. as Violetta, obtaining a gratifying success; sang regularly at the Metropolitan and other major opera houses in the U.S. and Europe until she suffered a vocal breakdown in 1974; then resumed her career in 1976. In her prime, she became known for her fine portrayals of such roles as Pamina, the 4 heroines in *Les Contes d'Hoffmann*, Gilda, Massenet's Manon, Mélisande, Juliet, Luisa Miller, and Gounod's Marguerite.

Mohaupt, Richard, German composer; b. Breslau, Sept. 14, 1904; d. Reichenau, Austria, July 3, 1957. He studied with J. Prüwer and R. Bilke; began his musical career as an opera conductor; also gave concerts as a pianist. After the advent of the Nazi regime in 1933, he was compelled to leave Germany because his wife was Jewish; he settled in N.Y. in 1939, and continued to compose; was also active as a teacher. In 1955 he returned to Europe.

WORKS: OPERAS: *Die Wirtin von Pinsk* (Dresden, Feb. 10, 1938); *Die Bremer Stadtmusikanten* (Bremen, June 15, 1949); *Double Trouble* (Louisville, Dec. 4, 1954); *Der grüne Kakadu* (Hamburg, Sept. 16, 1958). **BALLETS:** *Die Gaunerstreiche der Courasche* (Berlin, Aug. 5, 1936); *Lysistrata* (1946; rev. for Orch. as *Der Weiberstreik von Athen*, 1955); *Max und Moritz*, dance-burlesque (1945; Karlsruhe, Dec. 18, 1950); *The Legend of the Charlatan*, mimodrama (1949). **ORCH.:** *Stadtpfeifermusik* (1939; ISCM Festival, London, July 7, 1946; rev. for Winds, 1953); Sym., *Rhythmus und Variationen* (1940; N.Y., March 5, 1942); Concerto (1942); Violin Concerto (1945; N.Y., April 29, 1954); *Banchetto musicale* for 12 Instruments and Orch. (1955); *Offenbachiana* (1955). **VOCAL:** *Trilogy* for Alto and Orch. (1951); *Bucolica* for 4 Soloists, Chorus, and Orch. (1955); lieder; children's songs; also chamber music; piano pieces; scores for films and radio; arrangements.

Moiseiwitsch, Benno, outstanding Russian-born English pianist; b. Odessa, Feb. 22, 1890; d. London, April 9, 1963. He studied in Odessa, and won the Anton Rubinstein prize at the age of 9; then went to Vienna at 14 and studied with Leschetizky. He made his British debut in Reading on Oct. 1, 1908, and subsequently made London his home; made his American debut in N.Y. on Nov. 29, 1919, and toured many times in Australia, India, Japan, etc. He became a naturalized British subject in 1937. He represented the traditional school of piano playing, excelling mostly in Romantic music.

BIBL.: M. Moiseiwitsch, *B. M.* (London, 1965).

Mojsisovics (-Mojsvár), Roderich, Edler von, Austrian composer; b. Graz, May 10, 1877; d. there, March 30, 1953. He studied with Degner in Graz, with Wüllner and Klauwell at the Cologne Cons., and with Thuille in Munich. He conducted a choral group in Brünn (1903–7); then taught in various Austrian towns. He became director of the Graz Steiermärkische Musikverein (1912); it became the Graz Cons. in 1920, and he remained as director until 1931; from 1932 to 1935 he taught music history at the Univ. of Graz; then lectured in Munich and Mannheim; he returned to teach at the Graz Cons. from 1945 to 1948. He publ. *Bach-Probleme* (Würzburg, 1931). As a composer, he followed Regerian precepts. Among his stage works were 5 operas, a melodrama, a musical comedy, etc.; also wrote 5 syms.; a symphonic poem, *Stella*; 2 overtures; Violin Concerto; 3 string quartets and other chamber music; choral works; songs; piano pieces; organ works.

BIBL.: K. Haidmayer, *R. v.M.: Leben und Werk* (diss., Univ. of Graz, 1951).

Mokranjac, Stevan (Stojanović), Serbian conductor, musicologist, teacher, and composer; b. Negotin, Jan. 9, 1856; d. Skoplje, Sept. 28, 1914. He studied in Munich with Rheinberger, and in Leipzig with Jadassohn and Reinecke; in 1887 he became director of the Serbian Choral Soc. in Belgrade, with which he also toured. In 1899 he founded the Serbian Music School in Belgrade, and remained its director until his death. He wrote 15 choral rhapsodies on Serbian and Macedonian melodies; a Liturgy of St. John Chrysostomos (publ. in

Leipzig, 1901; also with an Eng. tr. as *Serbian Liturgy*, London, 1919); a Funeral Service ("Opelo"); he compiled a large collection of church anthems according to the Serbian usage and derived from early Byzantine modes; wrote a collection of songs for Mixed Chorus, *Rukoveti* (Bouquets).

BIBL.: P. Konjović, *S.S. M.* (Belgrade, 1956).

Mokranjac, Vasilije, Serbian composer; b. Belgrade, Sept. 11, 1923; d. there, May 27, 1984. He was brought up in a musical enviroment (his father was a cellist, a nephew of **Stevan Mokranjac**). He studied piano and composition at the Belgrade Academy of Music. His early works are Romantic in style, but he gradually began experimenting with serial techniques, while safeguarding the basic tonal connotations.

WORKS: 3 syms.: No. 1 (Belgrade, Feb. 2, 1962); No. 2 (Belgrade, April 1, 1966); No. 3 (Belgrade, Oct. 25, 1968); *Dramatic Overture* (1950); *Concertino* for Piano, String Orch., and 2 Harps (Belgrade, March 15, 1960); chamber music; piano pieces; incidental music for dramatic plays.

Molchanov, Kirill (Vladimirovich), Russian composer; b. Moscow, Sept. 7, 1922; d. there, March 14, 1982. He was attached to the Red Army Ensemble of Song and Dance during World War II; after demobilization, he studied composition with Anatoly Alexandrov at the Moscow Cons., graduating in 1949. From 1973 to 1975 he served as director of the Bolshoi Theater in Moscow and accompanied it on its American tour in 1975. He was primarily an opera composer; his musical style faithfully follows the precepts of socialist realism. His most successful work, the opera *The Dawns Are Quiet Here*, to his own libretto depicting the Russian struggle against the Nazis, was 1st performed at the Bolshoi Theater on April 11, 1975. It became the melodramatic event of the year, accompanied by an unabashed display of tearful emotion; however, its American performance during the visit of the Bolshoi Theater to N.Y. in June 1975 met with a disdainful dismissal on the part of the critics.

WORKS: Operas: *The Stone Flower* (Moscow, Dec. 2, 1950); *Dawn* (1956); *Romeo, Juliet, and Darkness* (1963); *The Unknown Soldier* (1967); *A Woman of Russia* (1969); *The Dawns Are Quiet Here* (Moscow, April 11, 1975); 3 piano concertos (1945, 1947, 1953); cantata, *Song of Friendship* (1955); *Black Box*, suite for Voice, Recitation, and Piano (1968).

BIBL.: Y. Korev, *K. M.* (Moscow, 1971).

Moldenhauer, Hans, German-American musicologist; b. Mainz, Dec. 13, 1906; d. Spokane, Wash., Oct. 19, 1987. He studied music with Dressel, Zuckmayer, and Rosbaud in Mainz; was active as a pianist and choral conductor there. In 1938 he went to the U.S., and settled in Spokane, Wash.; as an expert alpinist, he served in the U.S. Mountain Troops during World War II. He founded the Spokane Cons. (1942), incorporating it as an educational institution in 1946; also continued his own studies at Whitworth College there (B.A., 1945) and at the Chicago Musical College of Roosevelt Univ. (D.F.A., 1951). With his wife, the pianist Rosaleen Moldenhauer (1926–82), he inaugurated a series of radio broadcasts of 2-piano music; the outgrowth of this was the publication of his valuable book *Duo-Pianism* (Chicago, 1950). As a music reseacher, he became profoundly interested in the life and works of Webern; he organized 6 international Webern festivals, in Seattle (1962), Salzburg (1965), Buffalo (1966), at Dartmouth College, Hanover, N.H. (1968), in Vienna (1972), and at Louisiana State Univ., Baton Rouge (1976). His major achievement in research was the formation of the Moldenhauer Archives ("Music History from Primary Sources"), embodying a collection of some 10,000 musical autographs, original MSS, correspondence, etc., of unique importance to musical biography. Particularly rich is the MS collection of works of Webern, including some newly discovered works; for this accomplishment, Moldenhauer was awarded in 1970 the Austrian Cross of Honor for Science and Art. In 1988 the archives became a part of the Library of Congress in Washington, D.C. Moldenhauer's publications concerning Webern include *The Death of Anton Webern: A Drama in Documents* (N.Y., 1961); ed.

with D. Irvine, *Anton von Webern: Perspectives: 1st Webern Festival, Seattle 1962* (Seattle, 1966; catalog of the Webern Archive); *Anton von Webern: Sketches 1926–1945* (N.Y., 1968); with R. Moldenhauer, *Anton von Webern: Chronicle of His Life and Work* (N.Y., 1978). Moldenhauer suffered from Retinitis pigmentosa, and became totally blind in 1980. He remarried in 1982, a few months after his 1st wife's death.

Moldovan, Mihai, Rumanian composer; b. Dej, Nov. 5, 1937; d. Medgidia, Sept. 11, 1981. He studied with Toduţa and Comes at the Cluj Cons. (1956–59); then with Vancea, Vieru, and Jora at the Bucharest Cons. (1959–62); was active in various branches of Rumanian radio and television. His music fuses a Rumanian ethos with modern harmonic textures.

WORKS: OPERAS: *Trepte ale istoriei* (1972); *Micul prinţ* (1977–78). **CANTATAS:** *Soare al păcii* (Sun of Peace; 1962); *Prefigurarea primăverii*, chamber cantata (1962); *Bocet* (1963); *6 stări de nuanţă* (1966); *Cintare omului* (1967); *Luceafăru de ziuă* (1977). **ORCH.:** *Rituale*, suite for Soprano and Orch. (1963); Oboe Concerto (1964); *Texturi* (1967); *Poem* for Chamber Orch., with Ondes Martenot (1967); *Vitralii* (Stained Glass Windows; 1968); *Scoarţe* (Tapestry; 1969); *Tulnice* for 4 Flutes, 8 Horns, Harp, 4 Cellos, 4 Double Basses, and Percussion (1971); *Sinfonia* for Strings (1972); Concerto for Double Bass and Orch. (1973); *Cantemirian* (1976); *Omagiu lui Anton Pann* (1976); *Rezonante* (1976); *Memoria Putnei* for String Orch. (1978). **CHAMBER:** Violin Sonatina (1967); 2 string quartets (1968, 1978); *Incantations* for Clarinet and Piano (1968); *Cadenza I* for Trombone and Percussion, *II* for Double Bass, and *III* for Flute and Percussion (all 1971); *Cîntece străbune* (Ancient Songs) for Soprano, Flute, Clarinet, Horn, Trumpet, Trombone, Piano, Vibraphone, Xylophone, and String Quintet (1972); *Imaginati-vă un spectacol Kabuki* for Chamber Ensemble (1978); *Cadenza V* for Cello and Trumpet (1980).

Molina, Antonio (Jesus), Filipino conductor, music administrator, and composer; b. Manila, Dec. 26, 1894; d. there, Jan. 29, 1980. He studied at the S. Juan de Letran College and at the Univ. of the Philippines Cons.; became a teacher at the latter (1925); was also active as a conductor; was director of the Centro Escolar Univ. Cons. (1948–71). He founded and directed a string group, Rondalla Ideal.

WORKS: *Ritorna Vincitor*, lyric drama (Manila, March 10, 1918); 2 zarzuelas: *Panibuglo* (Manila, April 16, 1918) and *Ang Ilaw* (Manila, Nov. 23, 1918); *The Living Word*, Christmas cantata for Mixed Chorus and Orch. (Manila, Dec. 18, 1936); *Ang batingaw* (The Bells), choral sym. (1972); Piano Quintet, based on native folk songs (1929; Manila, Jan. 21, 1950); Trio (1931); many songs; numerous piano pieces.

Molinari, Bernardino, eminent Italian conductor; b. Rome, April 11, 1880; d. there, Dec. 25, 1952. He studied with Falchi and Renzi at Rome's Liceo di Santa Cecilia (graduated, 1902). He was artistic director of Rome's Augusteo Orch. (1912–43); also conducted throughout Europe and South America. In 1928 he made his American debut with the N.Y. Phil., which he conducted again during the 1929–30 and 1930–31 seasons; he also appeared with other American orchs. He was head of the advanced conducting class at Rome's Accademia di Santa Cecilia (from 1936), serving as a prof. there (from 1939). Molinari championed the modern Italian school, and brought out many works by Respighi, Malipiero, and other outstanding Italian composers; publ. a new ed. of Monteverdi's *Sonata sopra Sonata Maria* (1919) and concert transcriptions of Carissimi's oratorio *Giona*, Vivaldi's *Le quattro stagioni*, etc.; also orchestrated Debussy's *L'Isle joyeuse*.

BIBL.: E. Mucci, *B. M.* (Lanciano, 1941).

Molinari-Pradelli, Francesco, Italian conductor; b. Bologna, July 4, 1911. He studied with d'Ivaldi and Nordio in Bologna, and with Molinari at the Accademia di Santa Cecilia in Rome. In 1938 he launched his career as a conductor; in 1939 he appeared for the 1st time as an opera conductor, leading *L'elisir d'amore* in Bologna. He conducted at Milan's La Scala from 1946; made his 1st appearance at London's Covent Garden in 1955, at the San Francisco Opera in 1957, and at the Vienna State Opera in 1959. On Feb. 7, 1966, he made his Metropolitan Opera debut in N.Y. conducting *Un ballo in maschera*, and remained on the company's roster until 1973. He was also active as a pianist. He was best known as an interpreter of the Italian operatic repertoire.

Molique, (Wilhelm) Bernhard, noted German violinist, teacher, and composer; b. Nuremburg, Oct. 7, 1802; d. Cannstadt, near Stuttgart, May 10, 1869. He 1st studied with his father, making his 1st public appearance when he was 6; after some lessons with Spohr (1815), he studied with Rovelli in Munich (1816–17). He made his formal debut in Vienna on Dec. 28, 1817, and then became a member of the orch. of the Theater an der Wien; was made concertmaster of the Munich Court Orch. (1820) and then of the Stuttgart orch., being granted the title of Musikdirektor. He won fame abroad with extended tours in the Netherlands, Russia, England, and France. The political crisis of 1848 caused him to settle in London, where he was prof. of composition at the Royal College of Music (1861–66); after giving his farewell concert at St. James's Hall (May 3, 1866), he retired to Cannstadt. His works include 6 violin concertos (1827–46); 8 string quartets (1841–53); pieces for violin and piano, and for violin and flute; fantasias, rondos, and other works for solo violin; many songs.

BIBL.: F. Schröder, *B. M. und seine Instrumentalkompositionen* (Stuttgart, 1923).

Molitor, Raphael, German musicologist; b. Sigmaringen, Feb. 2, 1873; d. Beuron, Oct. 14, 1948. He was the son of Johann Baptist Molitor, a cathedral organist; he studied philosophy and theology in the Benedictine Monastery of Beuron; was ordained a priest in 1897; lectured there on canon law (1898–1904); in 1904, was appointed a member of the advisory board of the Editio Vaticana. He was one of the foremost authorities on Gregorian chant.

Moll, Kurt, outstanding German bass; b. Buir, near Cologne, April 11, 1938. He learned to play the guitar and cello and sang in a school choir in his youth; then studied voice at the Cologne Hochschule für Musik and with Emmy Müller. After singing minor roles at the Cologne Opera (1958–61), he sang in Aachen (1961–63), Mainz (1963–66), and Wuppertal (1966–69); subsequently pursued a career of great distinction, appearing regularly in Hamburg, Bayreuth, Salzburg, Vienna, Paris, Milan, and London. He made his U.S. debut as Gurnemanz at the San Francisco Opera in 1974; on Sept. 18, 1978, came his Metropolitan Opera debut in N.Y., in which he essayed the role of the Landgrave; he subsequently appeared there regularly. He made his 1st appearance at the Chicago Lyric Opera as Daland in 1983. He also sang widely as a concert artist and recitalist; made his North American recital debut at N.Y.'s Carnegie Hall in 1984. Among his other notable roles are the Commendatore, Sarastro, King Mark, Pogner, Nicolai's Falstaff, and Baron Ochs.

Möllendorff, Willi von, German pianist and composer; b. Berlin, Feb. 28, 1872; d. Stettin, April 27, 1934. He studied with Bargiel at the Berlin Hochschule für Musik (1891–93); was subsequently active as a pianist and theater conductor in Giessen, Berlin, and Stettin. He was known especially for his experimentation with quarter-tones, for the exposition of which he invented a bichromatic harmonium with a new keyboard. For this instrument he composed an *Adagio religioso* (with Cello Solo); also *5 kleine Stücke*. In addition, he wrote operas, a ballet, 2 syms., choral works, etc.

Mollenhauer, Eduard, German-American violinist and composer; b. Erfurt, April 12, 1827; d. Owatonna, Minn., May 7, 1914. He was a violin pupil of Ernst (1841) and Spohr (1843); after a brief concert career in Germany, he went to London, where he joined Jullien's Orch., of which an older brother, Friedrich Mollenhauer (1818–85), also a violinist, was a member; after a tour with Jullien's Orch. in the U.S. (1853), the brothers settled in N.Y. as teachers; Eduard also appeared as a soloist with the N.Y. Phil. He wrote the operas *The Corsican*

Bride (N.Y., 1861) and *Manhattan Beach, or Love among the Breakers* (1878); 3 syms.; a Violin Concerto; solo pieces for violin; songs. Another brother, **Henry Mollenhauer** (b. Erfurt, Sept. 10, 1825; d. Brooklyn, N.Y., Dec. 28, 1889), was a cellist and teacher; was a member of the Stockholm Royal Orch. (1853); toured the U.S. with Thalberg, Gottschalk, and Carlotta Patti (1856–58); then settled in Brooklyn as a teacher; later founded his own cons.

Mollenhauer, Emil, American violinist and conductor, nephew of **Eduard Mollenhauer;** b. Brooklyn, Aug. 4, 1855; d. Boston, Dec. 10, 1927. He studied violin with his father, Friedrich Mollenhauer; in 1872 he entered Theodore Thomas's orch.; also played with the N.Y. Sym. Soc. He then went to Boston, where he played in the orch. of the Bijou Theatre (1883–84) and the Boston Sym. Orch. (1884–89); then helped to found the Boston Festival Orch., serving as its concertmaster (1889–92) and its conductor (1892–1914); also conducted the German Band (from 1889; renamed as the Boston Band, 1904), the Boston Municipal Band, and the People's Sym. Orch.; likewise was conductor of the Handel and Haydn Soc. (1899–1927).

BIBL.: H. Woelber, "Famous Bandmasters: E. M.," *International Musician*, XXX/6 (1932).

Moller or **Möller, Joachim.** See **Burck, Joachim.**

Moller, John Christopher (real name, **Johann Christoph Möller**), German-American organist, music publisher, concert manager, and composer; b. in Germany, 1755; d. N.Y., Sept. 21, 1803. He was active in London (c.1775–85); then emigrated to the U.S. In 1790 he appeared in N.Y. as a harpsichordist, but left immediately after his concerts for Philadelphia, where he became organist and composer for the Zion German Lutheran Church. From 1790 to 1793 he took part in the City Concerts (with Reinagle, and later Henri Capron) as both manager and performer. Apparently he was also proficient as a pianist, violinist, and performer on the glass harmonica. In 1793 he was joint proprietor, with Capron, of a music store, which he also used as a music school. Because of the destruction of the Zion Church by fire on Dec. 26, 1794, Moller's income was severely reduced, and in 1795 he returned to N.Y.; was organist of the Trinity Episcopal Church; was also active as a concert manager. In 1796 he succeeded Hewitt in the management of the N.Y. City Concerts with the Van Hagens. His attempt to continue this subscription series by himself, when Van Hagen later left for Boston, was unsuccessful.

WORKS: 6 quartettos for Strings (London, c.1775); 6 sonatas for Fortepiano or Harpsichord, Violin, and Cello (London, c.1775); 6 sonatas for Harpsichord or Pianoforte, Violin, and Cello ad libitum (London, c.1782); 2 keyboard concertos; *Dank und Gebet*, cantata (1794); various didactic works; etc.

BIBL.: E. Wolf, *Lutheran Church Music in America during the Eighteenth and Early Nineteenth Centuries* (diss., Univ. of Illinois, 1960; includes text and music of *Dank und Gebet*); R. Stetzel, *J.C. M. (1755–1803) and His Role in Early American Music* (diss., Univ. of Iowa, 1965; includes complete list of works); E. Wolf, "Music in Old Zion, Philadelphia, 1750–1850," *Musical Quarterly* (Oct. 1972).

Möller, M(athias) P(eter), Danish-American organ builder; b. Bornholm, Sept. 29, 1855; d. Hagerstown, Md., April 13, 1937. He was trained as a mechanic before emigrating to the U.S. (1872); after working for the organ-building firm of Derrick & Felgemaker in Erie, Pa., he settled in Hagerstown and founded his own company (1880), which became the largest manufacturer of pipe organs in the U.S. He installed organs throughout the U.S. and made a number of improvements in their construction; later pioneered the development of small, self-contained organs. After his death, his son, M.P. Möller, Jr. (1902–61), served as president of the company; after his death, it was run by other descendants of the founder. Among its notable modern organs are those in the National Shrine of the Immaculate Conception in Washington, D.C. (1965), in Heinz Chapel at the Univ. of Pittsburgh (1970), and at Orchestra Hall in Chicago (1981).

Molloy, James Lyman, Irish composer of light music; b. Cornalaur, King's County, Aug. 19, 1837; d. Wooleys, Buckinghamshire, Feb. 4, 1909. His operettas (*Students' Frolic, My Aunt's Secret, Very Catching*), numerous songs (*Love's Old Sweet Song, London Bridge, The Kerry-dance, The Postilion, Punchinello,* etc.), and Irish melodies with new accompaniments enjoyed great popularity.

Molnár, Antal, distinguished Hungarian musicologist and composer; b. Budapest, Jan. 7, 1890; d. there, Dec. 7, 1983. He studied composition with Herzfeld at the Budapest Academy of Music (1907–10); was a violist in the Waldbauer String Quartet (1910–13) and the Dohnányi-Hubay Piano Quartet (1915–17); taught at the Budapest Academy of Music (1919–59). He received the Franz Joseph Prize (1914) and the Kossuth Prize (1957); in 1970 was made an Eminent Artist of the Hungarian People's Republic.
WRITINGS (all publ. in Budapest, in Hungarian): *The Spirit of the History of Music* (1914); *History of European Music until 1750* (1920); *Spiritual Basis of Bach's and Handel's Music* (1920); *The Sociology of Music History* (1923); *New Music* (1925); *The New Hungarian Music* (1926); *Introduction to Musical Culture* (1928); *Physics and Music* (1930); *Light on Musical History* (1933); *Musical Esthetics and "Geisteswissenschaft"* (1935); *Zoltán Kodály* (1936); *Musical Esthetics* (1938); *Popular Musical Esthetics* (1940); *The Spirit of the New Music* (1948); *The Art of Bartók with Reminiscences of His Life* (1948); *Repertory of the History of Baroque Music* (1959); *Writings on Music* (1961); *The World of the Composer* (1969); *Practical Musical Esthetics* (1971); *On Myself—On Others* (autobiography; 1974).
WORKS: ORCH.: *Grotesque March* (1914); Cello Concerto (1916); *Hungarian Dances* (1917); *Operetta Music* (1920); *Budapest,* overture (1921); *Past and Present* for Violin and Orch. (1923); *Suite* (1925); *Variations on a Hungarian Theme* (1928); *Hungarian Comedy Overture* (1928); *Kuruc-Music* for 4 Tárogatós and Chamber Orch. (1936); *Overture to a Comedy* (1948); Harp Concerto (1952); also *Savitri,* stage music (1912); chamber music; sacred and secular vocal music; piano pieces; organ music; didactic pieces; folk-song arrangements; etc.
BIBL.: *Muzsika,* XIII/1 (1970).

Molter, Johann Melchior, German composer; b. Tiefenort, near Eisenach, Feb. 10, 1696; d. Karlsruhe, Jan. 12, 1765. As a composer, he was typical of his Saxon contemporaries; he attended the Gymnasium in Eisenach, the same institution where Bach had studied earlier. His instrument was the violin, and it was as a violinist that he found employment with a succession of margraves. Like Bach, he was fertile and fathered 8 children. He was even more prolific as a composer than the 2 other great Saxons, Bach and Handel. He wrote something like 170 chamber syms. and is credited with 66 instrumental concertos, not to mention religious works. He traveled to Italy, where he perfected his art of virtuoso instrumental writing. He lived sufficiently long to be impressed by the elegant style of French Rococo music, and some of his works may be described as Gallic.

Momigny, Jérôme-Joseph de, Belgian-French music theorist, publisher, and composer; b. Philippeville, Namur, Jan. 20, 1762; d. Charenton, near Paris, Aug. 25, 1842. He studied music early in life, and at the age of 12 was already engaged as a church organist in St. Omer; in 1785 he went to Lyons. He became involved in the political struggle against the Jacobins in 1793; after their ouster, he was appointed provisional municipal officer, and took part in the resistance against the troops of the National Convention; when that enterprise failed, he fled to Switzerland. After the fall of Robespierre, he returned to Lyons; then went to Paris, where he remained under Napoleon and the restoration of the monarchy. He opened there a successful music publishing business which flourished (1800–1828) and which publ. about 750 works by 153 composers,

including a number of his own compositions and treatises on music, in which he claimed to have invented a new and unfailing system of theory and harmony; the titles alone of some of his tracts, containing such immoderate asseverations as "théorie neuve et générale," "seul système musical qui soit vraiment fondé et complet," "la seule vraie théorie de la musique," etc., reveal his uncommon faith in himself. He bolstered his self-assurance by such declarations as: there can exist only 1 true art of music; there is 1 and only 1 code of morals; there must be a sharp distinction between good and bad combinations of sounds, as there is between right and wrong in morality. By false analogy with order in music, he extolled monarchical rule and publ. numerous pamphlets in support of his reactionary convictions. Not finding a ready response from the authorities, he gradually sank into pathetic solitude and ended his days in an asylum. His tracts, both on music and on politics, are of interest only to investigators of material on depraved mental states, and his own compositions fell into utter desuetude during his lifetime. Riemann publ. a devastating review of Momigny's theories which drove a mortuary nail into his hopes for recognition.
WRITINGS (all publ. in Paris): *Méthode de piano* (1802); *La Première Année de leçons de pianoforte* (1802–3); *Cours complet d'harmonique et de composition* (1803–6; 2nd ed., 1808); *Exposé succint du seul système musical qui soit partout d'accord avec la nature, avec la raison et avec la pratique* (1808); *Le Nouveau Solfège* (1808); *La Seule Vraie Théorie de la musique* (1821); *À l'Académie des Beaux-Arts* (1831); *Cours général de musique* (1834).
WORKS: 3 operas: *Le Baron de Felsheim* (Lyons, before 1800); *La Nouvelle Laitière* (before 1811); *Arlequin Cedrillon* (Paris, 1800); cantatas; songs; chamber music; piano pieces; arrangements and transcriptions.
BIBL.: A. Palm, *J.-J. d.M.* (diss., Univ. of Tübingen, 1957); idem, *J.-J. d.M.: Leben und Werk: Ein Beitrag zur Geschichte der Musiktheorie im 19. Jahrhundert* (Cologne, 1969).

Mompou, Federico, significant Spanish composer; b. Barcelona, April 16, 1893; d. there, June 30, 1987. After preliminary studies at the Barcelona Cons., he went to Paris, where he studied piano with Philipp and composition with Rousseau. He returned to Barcelona during World War I; then was again in Paris from 1921 to 1941, when he once more went back to Spain. His music is inspired by Spanish and Catalan melos, but its harmonic and instrumental treatment is entirely modern. He wrote mostly for piano: *6 impressions intimes* (1911–14); *Scènes d'enfants* (1915); *Suburbis* (1916–17); *3 pessebres* (1918); *Cants magics* (1919); *Festes Llunyanes* (1920); *6 charmes* (1921); *3 variations* (1921); *Dialogues* (1923); a series, *Canción y Danza* (1918–53); *10 preludes* (1927–51); *3 paisajes* (1942, 1947, 1960); *Música callada* (4 albums, 1959–67); *Suite compostelana* for Guitar (1963); choral works and songs.
BIBL.: S. Kastner, *F. M.* (Madrid, 1946); A. Iglesias, *F. M.* (Madrid, 1977); C. Janés, *F. M.: Vida, textos, documentos* (Madrid, 1987); W. Mellers, *Le Jardin Parfume: Homage to F. M.* (1989).

Monaco, Mario del. See **Del Monaco, Mario.**

Monasterio, Jesús de, famous Spanish violinist and pedagogue; b. Potes, near Santander, March 21, 1836; d. Casar del Periedo, Sept. 28, 1903. A child prodigy, he began his training with his father; then studied in Valladolid; played for the Queen in 1843, and she became his patroness; he made his debut in 1845 in Madrid at age 9; studied at the Brussels Cons. with Bériot (violin) and Fétis (theory), graduating with the prix extraordinaire. He subsequently toured throughout Europe; was made honorary violinist at Madrid's royal chapel (1854); was prof. of violin (from 1857) and director (1894–97) at the Madrid Cons.; conducted the Sociedad de Conciertos (1869–76), and was influential in forming a taste for classical music in Spain. He publ. a number of violin pieces, including the popular *Adíos a la Alhambra.*
BIBL.: J. Alonso, *J. d.M.* (Santander, 1954).

Moncada, Eduardo Hernández. See **Hernández Moncada, Eduardo.**

Moncayo García, José Pablo, Mexican composer; b. Guadalajara, June 29, 1912; d. Mexico City, June 16, 1958. He studied with Chávez; from 1932 he was a member of the Mexico Sym. Orch.; was conductor of the National Sym. Orch. (1949–52); in company with Ayala, Contreras, and Galindo (also pupils of Chávez), he formed the so-called Grupo de Los Cuatro for the purpose of furthering the cause of Mexican music.
WORKS: OPERA: *La mulata de Córdoba* (Mexico City, Oct. 23, 1948). **ORCH.:** *Huapango* (1941); Sym. (1944); Sinfonietta (1945); *Homenaje a Cervantes* for 2 Oboes and Strings (Mexico City, Oct. 27, 1947); *Cumbres* (Louisville, June 12, 1954); also piano pieces; choruses.

Mondonville, Jean-Joseph Cassanéa de (de Mondonville was his wife's maiden name), distinguished French violinist, conductor, and composer; b. Narbonne (baptized), Dec. 25, 1711; d. Belleville, near Paris, Oct. 8, 1772. He played in the Holy Week program at the Concert Spirituel in Paris (1734); after appearing at the Concert de Lille, he returned to Paris, where he was made violinist at the royal chapel and chamber (1739); he wrote motets for the Concert Spirituel; was made sous-maître of the royal chapel (1740); became intendant of the "musique de la chapelle" in Versailles (1744); was music director of the Concert Spirituel (1755–62). He composed numerous stage works, oratorios, grand motets, and instrumental pieces.
BIBL.: J.-J. Galibert, *J.-J.C. d.M.* (Narbonne, 1856); F. Hellouin, *M.: Sa vie et son œuvre* (Paris, 1903); A. Tessier, "Madame d.M.," *Revue Musicale* (July 1926); E. Borroff, *The Instrumental Works of J.-J.C. d.M.* (diss., Univ. of Michigan, 1958); idem, "The Instrumental Style of J.-J.C. d.M.," *Recherches sur la Musique Française Classique,* VII (1967).

Monestel, Alejandro, Costa Rican organist and composer; b. San José, April 26, 1865; d. there, Nov. 3, 1950. He studied at the Brussels Cons.; returning to Costa Rica in 1884, he was organist at the San José Cathedral (until 1902); then lived in N.Y. (1902–37), where he was active as a church organist and composer. He wrote 14 masses; 4 Requiems; 5 cantatas; *Rapsodia costarricense* for Orch. (San José, Aug. 28, 1935); arrangements of Costa Rican songs.

Monfred, Avenir de, Russian composer of French descent; b. St. Petersburg, Sept. 17, 1903; d. Paris, April 11, 1974. He studied piano, organ, and composition at the Petrograd Cons., graduating in 1922. In 1924 he went to Paris and studied with Vincent d'Indy at the Schola Cantorum (1925–27). He promulgated an interesting theory of composition, "diatonic polymodality," expounded in detail in his book *The New Diatonic Modal Principle of Relative Music* (N.Y., 1970).
WORKS: 2 syms. (1955, 1957); *Rapsodie juive* for Orch. (1926); symphonic poem, *Vienna, 1850* (1941); symphonic suite, *Manhattan Sketches* (1958); ballet, *Suite New-yorkaise* (Monte Carlo, Nov. 19, 1956); String Quartet (1939); 3 violin sonatas (1922, 1926, 1947); Cello Sonata (1938); many pieces for piano and for organ; choruses; film scores.

Moniuszko, Stanislaw, famous Polish composer; b. Ubiel, Minsk province, Russia, May 5, 1819; d. Warsaw, June 4, 1872. In 1827 his family went to Warsaw, where he studied piano and music with August Freyer; continued his training with Dominick Stefanowica in Minsk and with Rungenhagen in Berlin (1837). He went to Vilnius in 1840; there he served as organist at St. John's; gained attention as a composer when he publ. vol. I of his *Śpiewnik domowy* (Songbook for Home Use; 1843); gained the support of various Polish figures in the arts, and also won the admiration of Glinka, Dargomïzhsky, and Cui in Russia. On Jan. 1, 1848, a concert performance of the 2-act version of his opera *Halka* was given for the 1st time in Vilnius; after he expanded it to 4 acts, it was staged in Warsaw on Jan. 1, 1858, scoring a great success. He then settled in Warsaw (1859), becoming conductor of opera at the Grand Theater; he continued to compose for the stage,

and also taught at the Music Inst. (from 1864); publ. *Pamiętnik do nauki harmonii* (Textbook on Harmony; 1871). Moniuszko holds a revered place in Polish music history as the outstanding composer of opera in his era; he also excelled as a composer of songs.
WORKS: STAGE: OPERAS: *Halka* (1846–47; 2-act version, concert perf., Vilnius, Jan. 1, 1848; 4-act version, 1857; Warsaw, Jan. 1, 1858); *Sielanka* (Idyll; c.1848); *Bettly* (Vilnius, May 20, 1852); *Flis* (The Raftsman; Warsaw, Sept. 24, 1858); *Rokiczana* (1858–59); *Hrabina* (The Countess; 1859; Warsaw, Feb. 7, 1860); *Verbum nobile* (Warsaw, Jan. 1, 1860); *Straszny dwór* (The Haunted Manor; 1861–64; Warsaw, Sept. 18, 1865); *Paria* (1859–69; Warsaw, Dec. 11, 1869); *Trea* (1872; unfinished). **OPERETTAS:** *Nocleg w Apeninach* (A Night's Lodging in the Apennines; Vilnius, 1839); *Ideal czyli Nowa Precioza* (Ideal or The New Preciosa; Vilnius, 1840); *Karmaniol czyli Francuzi lubią zartować* (Carmagnole or The French Like Joking; 1841); *Zólta szlafmyca* (The Yellow Nightcap; 1841); *Nowy Don Quichot czyli Sto szanlestw* (The New Don Quixote or 100 Follies; 1841; Lemberg, 1849); *Loteria* (The Lottery; Minsk, Nov. 1843); *Cyganie* (The Gypsies; 1850; Vilnius, May 20, 1852; rev. as *Jawnuta,* Warsaw, June 5, 1860); *Beata* (1871; Warsaw, Feb. 2, 1872); incidental music to 14 plays; ballets. **ORCH.:** *Bajka* (The Fairy Tale), overture (Vilnius, May 1, 1848); *Kain,* overture (St. Petersburg, March 1856); *Polonaise de concert* (1866); *Uwertura wojenna* (Military Overture; Vilnius, March 19, 1857); also chamber music; vocal works. A complete ed. of his works commenced publication in Krakow in 1965.
BIBL.: A. Walicki, *S. M.* (Warsaw, 1873); A. Poliński, *M.* (Kiev, 1914); H. Opieński, *S. M.: Życie i dziela* (S. M.: Life and Works; Lwow, 1924); S. Niewiadomski, *S. M.* (Warsaw, 1928); F. Kęcki, *A Catalogue of Musical Works of M. Karlowicz and S. M.* (Warsaw, 1936); Z. Jachimecki, *Muzyka kościelna Moniuszki* (M.'s Church Music; Warsaw, 1947); W. Rudziński, *S. M.* (Krakow, 1954; 4th ed., 1972); J. Prosnack, *S. M.* (Krakow, 1964; 2nd ed., 1969); W. Rudziński and M. Stokowska, eds., *S. M.: Listy zebrane* (S. M.: Collected Letters; Krakow, 1969); K. Mazur, *Pierwodruki S.a M.* (The Editions of M.'s Works; Warsaw, 1970).

Monk, Edwin George, English organist, music editor, and composer; b. Frome, Somerset, Dec. 13, 1819; d. Radley, near Oxford, Jan. 3, 1900. He studied with G.A. Macfarren; received a B.Mus. (1848) and D.Mus. (1856) from Oxford. From 1859 to 1883 he was organist of York Minster. He ed. *The Anglican Chant Book* (1850), *The Anglican Choral Service Book* (1858), and *The Anglican Hymn Book* (with R. Corbet Singleton; 1868).

Monk, Meredith (Jane), American composer, singer, and filmmaker; b. Lima, Peru (of American parents), Nov. 20, 1942. She studied eurythmics, the educational method that relates music to movement, from an early age; was educated at Sarah Lawrence College (B.A., 1964), then was a pupil in voice of Vicki Starr, John Devers, and Jeanette Lovetri, in composition of Ruth Lloyd, Richard Averee, and Glenn Mack, and in piano of Gershon Konikow. She pursued an active career as a singer, filmmaker, director, choreographer, recording artist, and composer. In 1968 she organized The House in N.Y., a company devoted to interdisciplinary approaches to the arts; in 1978 she founded there her own vocal chamber ensemble, with which she toured widely in the U.S. and abroad. In 1972 and 1982 she held Guggenheim fellowships; received various ASCAP awards and many commissions. Her powerful soprano vocalizations employ a wide range of ethnic and avant-garde influences. As one of the 1st and most natural of performance artists, she developed a flexible, imaginative theatrical style influenced by dream narrative and physical movement.
WORKS: *16 Millimeter Earrings* for Voice and Guitar (1966); *Candy Bullets and Moon* for Voice, Electric Organ, Electric Bass, and Drums (1967; in collaboration with D. Preston); *Blueprint: Overload/Blueprint 2* for Voice, Echoplex, and Tape (1967); *Juice,* theater cantata for 85 Voices, Jew's Harp, and 2 Violins (1969); *A Raw Recital* for Voice and Electric Organ

(1970); *Needle-Brain Lloyd and the Systems Kid* for 150 Voices, Electric Organ, Guitar, and Flute (1970); *Key,* album of invisible theater for Voice, Electric Organ, Vocal Quartet, Percussion, and Jew's Harp (1970–71); *Plainsong for Bill's Bojo* for Electric Organ (1971); *Vessel,* opera epic for 75 Voices, Electric Organ, Dulcimer, and Accordion (1971); *Paris* for Piano and Vocal Duet (1972); *Education of the Girlchild,* opera for 6 Voices, Electric Organ, and Piano (1972–73); *Our Lady of Late* for Voice and Wine Glass (1972–73); *Chacon* for 25 Voices, Piano, and Percussion (1974); *Anthology and Small Scroll* for Voice and Tape (1975); *Quarry,* opera for 38 Voices, 2 Pump Organs, 2 Soprano Recorders, and Tape (1976); *Venice/Milan* for 15 Voices and Piano, 4-hands (1976); *Songs from the Hill* for Voice (1976–77); *Tablet* for 4 Voices, Piano, 4-hands, and 2 Soprano Recorders (1977); *The Plateau Series* for 5 Voices and Tape (1977); *Dolmen Music* for 6 Voices, Cello, and Percussion (1979); *Recent Ruins* for 14 Voices, Tape, and Cello (1979); *Turtle Dreams (Waltz)* for 4 Voices and 2 Electric Organs (1980–81); *Specimen Days* for 14 Voices, Piano, and 2 Electric Organs (1981); *View No. 1* for Piano, Synthesizer, and Voice (1981); *View No. 2* for Voice and Synthesizer (1982); *Ellis Island* for 2 Pianos (1982); *Tokyo Cha-Cha* for 6 Voices and 2 Electric Organs (1983); *Engine Steps* for Tape Collage (1983); *2 Men Walking* for 3 Voices and Electric Organs (1983); *The Games* for 16 Voices, Synthesizer, Keyboards, Flemish Bagpipes, Bagpipes, Chinese Horn, and Rauschpfeife (1983); *Panda Chant I* for 4 Voices and *II* for 8 Voices (1984); *Graduation Song* for 16 Voices (1984); *Book of Days* for 25 Voices, Synthesizer, and Piano (1985); *Scared Song* for Voice, Synthesizer, and Piano (1986); *I Don't Know* for Voice and Piano (1986); *Double Fiesta* for Voice and 2 Pianos (1986); *String* for Voice (1986); *Window in 7's (for Nurit)* for Piano (1986); *Duet Behavior* for 2 Voices (1987); *The Ringing Place* for 9 Voices (1987); *Do You Be* for 10 Voices, 2 Pianos, Synthesizer, Violin, and Bagpipes (1987); *Book of Days,* film score for 10 Voices, Cello, Shawm, Synthesizer, Hammered Dulcimer, Bagpipe, and Hurdy Gurdy (1988); *Fayum Music* for Voice, Hammered Dulcimer, and Double Ocarina (1988); *Light Songs* for Voice (1988); *Raven* for Piano (1988); *Cat Song* for Voice (1988); *Parlour Games* for 2 Pianos (1988); *Waltz* for 2 Pianos (1988); *Processional* for Piano and Voice (1988); *Atlas,* opera (Houston, Feb. 22, 1991).

Monk, Thelonious "Sphere," noted black American jazz pianist and composer; b. Rocky Mount, N.C., Oct. 10, 1917; d. Englewood, N.J., Feb. 17, 1982. He spent most of his life in Harlem, where he played in nightclubs; gradually surfaced as a practitioner of bebop, set in angular rhythms within asymmetrical bar sequences. His eccentric behavior was signalized by his external appearance; he wore skullcaps and dark sunglasses; time and again he would rise from the keyboard and perform a tap dance. Although not educated in the formal sense, he experimented with discordant harmonies, searching for new combinations of sounds. Paradoxically, he elevated his ostentatious ineptitude to a weirdly cogent modern idiom, so that even deep-thinking jazz critics could not decide whether he was simply inept or prophetically innovative. Monk's own tunes, on the other hand, seemed surprisingly sophisticated, and he gave them impressionistic titles, such as *Crepuscule with Nellie* (Nellie was the name of his wife) and *Epistrophy,* or else ethnically suggestive ones, as in *Rhythm-a-ning.* A profoundly introspective neurotic, he would drop out of the music scene for years, withdrawing into his inner self. During the period between 1973 and 1976, he stayed with an admirer, the Baroness Pannonica de Koenigswarter, in her mansion in Weehawken, N.J., but was visited daily by his wife, Nellie. He made his last public appearance at the Newport Jazz Festival in 1976, but seemed a faint shadow, a weak echo of his former exuberant personality. His song *Criss-Cross* (1951) was used by Gunther Schuller for his *Variations on a Theme of Thelonious Monk.* **BIBL.:** N. Hentoff, *T. M.* (N.Y., 1961); L. Bijl and F. Conté, *M. on Record: A Discography of T. M.* (Amsterdam, 1982); T.

Fitterling, *T. M.: Sein Leben, seine Musik, seine Schallplatten* (Waakirchen, 1987).

Monk, William Henry, English organist, choirmaster, music editor, and composer; b. London, March 16, 1823; d. there, March 1, 1889. He was a pupil of T. Adams, J.A. Hamilton, and G.A. Griesbach; served as organist in various London churches; taught music at King's College in London, the School for the Indigent Blind, the National Training School, etc. He ed. for the Church of Scotland *The Book of Psalms in Metre, Scottish Hymnal, The Psalter,* and *Book of Anthems;* was the music ed. of *Hymns, Ancient and Modern* (1861), for which he composed the tune for the beloved hymn *Abide with me;* also composed many other popular hymn tunes, as well as anthems and service music; likewise ed. collections of hymns and Psalms.

Monleone, Domenico, Italian opera composer; b. Genoa, Jan. 4, 1875; d. there, Jan. 15, 1942. He studied at the Milan Cons.; from 1895 to 1901, was active as a theater conductor in Amsterdam and in Vienna. He attracted attention by producing in Amsterdam (Feb. 5, 1907) an opera, *Cavalleria rusticana,* to a libretto by his brother Giovanni, on the same subject as Mascagni's celebrated work; after its 1st Italian performance (Turin, July 10, 1907), Mascagni's publisher, Sonzogno, brought a lawsuit against Monleone for infringement of copyright. Monleone was forced to change the title; his brother rewrote the libretto, and the opera was produced as *La Giostra dei falchi* (Florence, Feb. 18, 1914). Other operas were: *Una novella di Boccaccio* (Genoa, May 26, 1909); *Alba eroica* (Genoa, May 5, 1910); *Arabesca* (Rome, March 11, 1913; won 1st prize at the competition of the City of Rome); *Suona la ritrata* (Milan, May 23, 1916); *Il mistero* (Venice, May 7, 1921); *Fauvette* (Genoa, March 2, 1926); *La ronda di notte* (Genoa, March 6, 1933); also an opera in Genovese dialect, *Scheüggio Campann-a* (Genoa, March 12, 1928). For some of his works he used the pseudonym W. di Stolzing.

Monn (originally, **Mann**), **Johann Christoph,** Austrian pianist, teacher, and composer, brother of **Matthias Georg Monn;** b. 1726; d. Vienna, June 24, 1782. He served Count Kinsky as a music teacher in Prague (1750); later settled in Vienna as a keyboard teacher. He wrote 6 syms., 3 piano concertos (also attributed to his brother), 10 divertimentos à 3 and a divertimento for Violin and Bass, and various keyboard works, including 8 sonatas, 20 minuets and trios, and a ballo.

Monn, Matthias Georg or **Georg Matthias** (born **Johann Georg Mann**), Austrian organist and composer, brother of **Johann Christoph Monn;** b. Vienna, April 9, 1717; d. there, Oct. 3, 1750. He became organist of Vienna's Karlskirche about 1738. His instrumental music marks a transition from the Baroque to the new style perfected by the composers of the Mannheim school. **WORKS:** 21 syms. (several not extant; a Sym. in E-flat major, formerly attributed to him, is now known to be by F. Pokorny); 7 harpsichord concertos; Cello Concerto (also arranged for Harpsichord); *Concertino fugato* for Violin and Strings; Divertimento for Harpsichord and Strings; 6 string quartets (2 arranged from his syms.); Divertimento for 3 Strings; 8 partitas for 2 Violins and Bass; 2 trios; 2 sonatas and 2 allegros for Violin and Bass; much keyboard music, including 14 sonatas; 8 sets of preludes and versetti for Organ; sacred music, including several masses and a Magnificat. See K. Horwitz and K. Riedel, eds., *Wiener Instrumentalmusik vor und um 1750,* I, Denkmäler der Tonkunst in Österreich, XXXI, Jg. XIX/2 (1908), and W. Fischer, ed., II, ibid., XXXIX, Jg. IXI/2 (1912). **BIBL.:** H. Riemann, "Stamitz oder M.?," *Blätter für Haus- und Kirchenmusik,* XII/7–8 (1907–8); R. Philipp, *Die Messenkomposition der Wiener Vorklassiker G.M. M. und C.Chr. Wagenseil* (diss., Univ. of Vienna, 1938).

Monnikendam, Marius, Dutch music critic, teacher, and composer; b. Haarlem, May 28, 1896; d. Heerlen, May 22, 1977. He studied composition with Sem Dresden, and organ and piano with de Pauw at the Amsterdam Cons.; in 1925 he went to Paris, where he took courses with Aubert and d'Indy at the Schola Cantorum. Returning to the Netherlands, he taught composition at the Rotterdam Cons. and in Amsterdam; also served as music critic of the newspaper combine *De Tijd* and *De Maasbode*. He wrote a number of church works, in which he revived the most ancient form of plainchant, but injected asymmetric rhythms in a modern style; in his larger works, he employed the resources of advanced harmony, including polytonality. He publ. monographs on Franck (Amsterdam, 1949) and Stravinsky (Haarlem, 1951); also *50 Masterpieces of Music* (The Hague, 1953) and *Nederlandse Componisten van heden en verleden* (Amsterdam, 1968).

WORKS: ORCH.: *Arbeid* (Labor), symphonic movement (1931); *Sinfonia super "Merck toch hoe sterck"* for Chamber Orch. (1944); *Mouvement symphonique* (1950); Concerto for Trumpet, Horn, and Orch. (1952); *Variations symphoniques super "Merck toch hoe sterck"* (1954); Concerto for Organ and Strings (1958); *Ouverture* for Organ and Orch. (1960); *Vision* for Chamber Orch. (1963); Concerto for Organ, Wind Instruments, Harp, Double Bass, and Percussion (1968); Piano Concertino (1974). **VOCAL:** 2 Te Deums for Chorus and Orch. (1919, 1946); *Missa Nova* for 3 Voices and Organ (1928); 7 *Boetpsalmen* (7 Penitential Psalms) for Chorus and Orch. (1934); *Noah*, oratorio (1937); *Samson*, oratorio (1938); *Solomon*, oratorio (1939); *Missa antiphonale* (1939); *Sinfonia sacra I* for Male Chorus and Orch. (1947); *Sinfonia sacra II* (*Domine salvum fac*) for Chorus and Orch. (1952); *Passion* for Speaker, Chorus, and Orch. (1948); *Van Riebeeck-Taferelen* for 2 Speakers, Chorus, and Orch. (1952); *Noé ou La Destruction du Premier Monde*, oratorio (1955); *Magnificat* for Soprano, Male Chorus, and Orch. without Strings (1956; transcribed for Mixed Chorus and Full Orch., 1965); *Missa festiva* for Chorus and Orch. (1956); *Lamentations of Jeremiah* for Chorus and Orch. (1956); *Hymne* for Alto, Male Chorus, and Orch. (1957); *Missa solenissima* for Chorus, Organ, and 7 Wind Instruments (1959); *Missa pro defunctis* for 3 Soloists, Organ, and Percussion (1961); *Apocalypse* for Chorus and Organ (1966); *Madrigalesca* for Chorus, 9 Winds, and Percussion (1966); *De Kinderkruistocht* (The Children's Crusade) for Mixed or Female Chorus, 7 Woodwinds, and Percussion (1967); *Via sacra* (Way of the Cross) for Speaker, Chorus, Organ, Percussion, and Projection Slides (1969); *3 psaumes pour le temps présent* for Soloists, Chorus, and Chamber Orch. (1971); *Missa concertanta* for Soloists, Chorus, and Orch. (1971); *Elckerlyc* (Everyman), mystery play for Chorus, Organ, and Orch. (1975; The Hague, May 28, 1976); *Heart Rhythm* for Speaker, Male Chorus, Organ, Double Bass, and Percussion (1975); *Gloria* for Chorus, Organ, and Orch. (1976). **CHAMBER:** Cello Sonata (1925); 2 *toccatas* for Organ (1931, 1970); Concerto for Organ, 2 Trumpets, and 2 Trombones (1956); *10 Inventions* for Organ (1959); *Suite* for Flute, Oboe, Clarinet, Bassoon, and Harp (1960); Piano Sonatina (1967); *Suite biblique* for Piano, 4-hands (1967); *The Bells*, prelude for Organ (1971); *Toccata batalla* for Organ, 2 Trumpets, and 2 Trombones (1972); numerous small organ pieces.

Monod, Jacques-Louis, French pianist, conductor, music editor, and composer; b. Asnières, near Paris, Feb. 25, 1927. He was admitted to the Paris Cons. before he had reached the official entrance age of 9, later studying with Messiaen (1944) and receiving instruction in theory, composition, and analysis from Leibowitz (1944–50); subsequently studied composition with Wagenaar at N.Y.'s Juilliard School of Music and conducting with Rudolf Thomas at Columbia Univ., and then took courses with Blacher and Rufer in Berlin. As a pianist and conductor, he became a proponent of modern music; was married for a time to the American soprano **Bethany Beardslee,** with whom he gave many song recitals; was chief music ed. of the Boelke-Bomart firm (1952–82); was also active as a teacher at various U.S. academic institutions. He wrote orch. works, chamber music, and songs.

Mononen, Sakari (Tuomo), Finnish composer; b. Korpiselkä, July 27, 1928. He studied composition with Nils-Eric Fougstedt and Einar Englund at the Sibelius Academy in Helsinki, graduating in 1962; then was an organist and theory teacher at the Kuopio Music Inst., where he was made head of the church music dept. (1970) and prorector (1976).

WORKS: Orch.: Sym. (1961); Concerto Grosso for Winds and Strings (1968); *Divertimento* (1971); *Legenda con espressione* (1971); *Perspectives* (1972); also 2 suites for Piano (1959, 1970); String Trio (1960); String Quartet (1961); 3 organ sonatas (1963, 1964, 1965); *Vuorela Suite* for a cappella Chorus (1972); Clarinet Sonata (1973).

Monpou, (François Louis) Hyppolite, French organist and composer; b. Paris, Jan. 12, 1804; d. Orléans, Aug. 10, 1841. He became a choirboy at Paris's St.-Germain-l'Auxerrois at age 5; then went to Notre Dame when he was 9; entered Choron's École Royale et Speciale de Chant at age 13; Choron sent him to the Tours Cathedral to study organ; he became its organist (1819). He soon returned to Paris, where he became master accompanist at the Académie Royale; studied harmony with Fétis at Choron's Academy (1822), then became a teacher of singing and maître de chapelle at the College of St. Louis (1825); subsequently was made organist at St. Thomas d'Aquin, St. Nicolas des Champs, and the Sorbonne (1827). He was notably successful as a composer of songs; his opera *Le Planteur* (Paris, March 1, 1839) also proved a popular success.

WORKS: OPERAS (all 1st perf. in Paris): *Les Deux Reines* (Aug. 6, 1835); *Le Luthier de Vienne* (June 30, 1836); *Le Piquillo* (Oct. 31, 1837); *Un Conte d'autrefois* (Feb. 28, 1838); *Perugina* (Dec. 20, 1838); *La Chaste Suzanne* (Dec. 27, 1839); *Le Planteur* (March 1, 1839); *La Reine Jeanne* (Oct. 13, 1840); *Lambert Simnel* (Sept. 1, 1843; completed by A. Adam); *L'Orfèvre* (unfinished); more than 75 songs.

BIBL.: G. Grand, "H. M.," *Revue de Paris*, IX (1868); H. Bachelin, "H. M.," *Le Ménestrel*, XC (1928).

Monrad Johansen, David. See **Johansen, David Monrad.**

Monroe, Bill (William Smith), American country-music singer, mandolin player, and songwriter; b. near Rosine, Ky., Sept. 13, 1911. He studied with his uncle, a fiddler; then played fiddle in a band formed by his brothers Birch and Charlie. In 1938 he organized his own band, the Blue Grass Boys, which gained fame through appearances on the "Grand Ole Opry" radio program in Nashville. His innovations in string-band music led to the development of the bluegrass style, notable for its syncopated rhythm and complex but invariably tonal harmonies. In 1970 he was elected a member of the Country Music Hall of Fame.

BIBL.: J. Rooney, *Bossmen: B. M. & Muddy Waters* (N.Y., 1971); N. Rosenberg, *B. M. and His Blue Grass Boys: An Illustrated Discography* (Nashville, Tenn., 1974); P. Guralnick, "B. M.: Hard-workingman Blues," *Country Music*, IX/9 (1981).

Monsigny, Pierre-Alexandre, noted French composer; b. Fauquembergues, near St.-Omer, Oct. 17, 1729; d. Paris, Jan. 14, 1817. He was educated at the Jesuit college in St.-Omer, where he also received instruction in violin; upon his father's death, he abandoned his studies in order to support his family; took a job in the Paris offices of the receiver-general of the Clergé de France (1749). Several years later he was befriended by the Duke of Orléans, who encouraged him to pursue his musical career; after studying for 5 months with the double-bass player Gianotti, he successfully brought out his 1st opera, *Les Aveux indiscrets* (Théâtre de la Foire St.-Germain, Feb. 7, 1759). In quick succession, and with increasing success, the same theater brought out 3 more of Monsigny's operas: *Le Maître en droit* (Feb. 23, 1760), *Le Cadi dupé* (Feb. 4, 1761), and *On ne s'avise jamais de tout* (Sept. 14, 1761). The members of the Comédie-Italienne, alarmed at the rising prestige of the rival enterprise, succeeded in closing it, by exercise of vested privilege, and took over its best actors. Thereafter Monsigny wrote most of his works for the Théâtre-Italien and the private theaters of the Duke of Orléans, having become the latter's maître d'hôtel in 1768. After scoring a triumph with his *Félix, ou L'Enfant trouvé* (Fontainebleau, Nov. 10, 1777), he abruptly abandoned his career as a composer for the theater. His patron died in 1785 and the new duke abolished Monsigny's job, but retained him as inspector of the canals of Orléans. With the coming of the Revolution, he lost his post; obtained a pension from the Opéra-Comique (1798) and served as Inspector of Musical Education from 1800 until the post was abolished in 1802. His last years were relieved by several pensions; he was made a Chevalier of the Légion d'Honneur (1804) and was elected to Grétry's chair in the Institut de France (1813). Monsigny possessed an uncommon and natural melodic invention, and sensibility in dramatic expression, but his theoretical training was deficient; still, his works attained the foremost rank among the precursors of the French comic operas.

WORKS: (all 1st perf. in Paris unless otherwise given): *Les Aveux indiscrets*, opéra-comique (Feb. 7, 1759); *Le Maître en droit*, opéra-comique (Feb. 23, 1760); *Le Cadi dupé*, opéra-comique (Feb. 4, 1761); *On ne s'avise jamais de tout*, opéra-comique (Sept. 14, 1761); *Le Roy et le fermier*, comédie (Nov. 22, 1762); *Le Nouveau Monde*, divertissement (1763; not perf.); *Rose et Colas*, comédie (March 8, 1764); *Le Bouquet de Thalie*, prologue (Bagnolet, Dec. 25, 1764); *Aline, reine de Golconde*, ballet héroïque (April 15, 1766); *Philémon et Baucis*, comédie (Bagnolet, 1766); *L'Isle sonnante*, opéra-comique (Bagnolet, June 5, 1767); *Le Déserteur*, drame (March 6, 1769); *La Rosière de Salency*, comédie (Fontainebleau, Oct. 25, 1769; in collaboration with Philidor, Blaise, and Swieten); *Pagamin de Monègue*, opéra-comique (c.1770; not perf.); *Le Faucon*, opéra-comique (Fontainebleau, Nov. 2, 1771); *La Belle Arsène*, comédie féerie (Fontainebleau, Nov. 6, 1773; rev. for Paris, Aug. 14, 1775); *Félix, ou L'Enfant trouvé*, comédie (Fontainebleau, Nov. 10, 1777); *Robin et Marion* (n.d.; not perf.).

BIBL.: A. Quatremère de Quincy, *Notice historique sur la vie et les ouvrages de M. de M.* (Paris, 1818); A. Alexandre, "Éloge historique de P.-A. M.," *Mémoires de la Société Royale d'Arras*, II (1819); P. Hédouin, *Notice historique sur P.-A. de M.* (Paris, 1821); F. de Ménil, *Les Grands Musiciens du Nord: M.* (Paris, 1893); A. Pougin, *M. et son temps* (Paris, 1908); P. Druilhe, *M.: Sa vie et son œuvre* (Paris, 1955); L. Fox, " 'La Belle Arsène' by P.-A. M.," *Recherches sur la Musique Française Classique*, IX (1969).

Montagu-Nathan, M(ontagu) (real name, **Montagu Nathan**), English writer on music; b. Banbury, Sept. 17, 1877; d. London, Nov. 15, 1958. He legally changed his name to Montagu Montagu-Nathan on March 17, 1909. He studied in Birmingham; then took violin lessons with Ysaÿe in Brussels, with Heermann in Frankfurt, and with Wilhelmj in London. He appeared as a violinist in Belfast and Leeds, but soon abandoned concerts in favor of music journalism. He learned the Russian language and wrote several books on Russian music: *A History of Russian Music* (London and N.Y., 1914; 2nd ed., 1918); *An Introduction to Russian Music* (London and Boston, 1916); *Contemporary Russian Composers* (London, 1917); *Handbook to the Piano Works of A. Scriabin* (London, 1917); also monographs on Glinka (London, 1916; 2nd ed., 1921), Mussorgsky (London, 1916), and Rimsky-Korsakov (London, 1916).

Montague, Stephen (Rowley), American composer, pianist, and writer on music; b. Syracuse, N.Y., March 10, 1943. He studied with his father, Richard Montague, at St. Petersburg Junior College in Florida (A.A., 1963), with Carlisle Floyd and John Boda at Florida State Univ. (B.M., 1965; M.M., 1967), and with Marshall Barnes, Herbert Brün, Wolf Rosenberg, and David Behrman at Ohio State Univ. (D.M.A., 1972). From 1967 to 1969 he taught at Butler Univ. in Indianapolis; then held a Fulbright scholarship and worked at the Studio for Experimental Music at the Polish Radio in Warsaw (1972–74). He settled in London, where he served as a composer and performer with the Strider Dance Co.; from 1975, he toured throughout the world as a pianist, championing 20th-century music. In 1980 he helped organize the Electro-Acoustic Music Assoc. of Great Britain, serving as its 1st concert director (1983–87) and chairman (from 1988). He contributed articles to The

New Grove Dictionary of American Music (1986). His compositions range from the traditional to electro-acoustic and mixed-media forms.

WORKS: DRAMATIC: *Largo con moto* for Dancer and Tape (1975); *Criseyde* for Soprano, Ocarina, Slides, and Electronics (1976); *Into the Sun*, ballet (Manchester, Oct. 31, 1977); *Footfalls* for Dancer and Electronic Tape (London, Oct. 12, 1979); *I, Giselle*, multimedia dance/theater piece (London, March 15, 1980); *Splitter* for Dancer, Moving Sculpture, and Electronic Tape (Edinburgh, Aug. 21, 1981); *Gravity Is Proving Most Difficult* for Dancer, Clarinet, Electronics, and Slides (London, Aug. 4, 1984); *The Montague Stomp* for 2 Dancers and 6 Instrumentalists (1984); *Median*, ballet (1984; London, Jan. 3, 1985); *Ceremony* for 18 Dancers and Electronic Tape (Eastbourne, Feb. 26, 1986). **ORCH.:** *Argulus* (1968); *Voussoirs* for Orch. and Tape (1972); *Sound Round* for Orch. and Electronics (1973; Manchester, July 11, 1988); *Varshavian Spring* for Chorus and Chamber Orch. (1973; rev. 1980); *At the White Edge of Phrygia* for Chamber Orch. (London, June 20, 1983; also for Orch., 1984; London, Jan. 26, 1989); *Prologue* (London, Jan. 3, 1985); Concerto for Piano and Chamber Orch. (London, June 11, 1988). **CHAMBER:** *Quiet Washes* for 3 Trombones and 3 Pianos (1974); *E pluribus unum*, graphic text score for Any Chamber Group (1976); *Paramell I* for Trombone and Piano (1977), *II: Entity* for 6 Percussionists (1977), *III* for Piano and Audience (1981), *IV* for Tuba and Electronic Tape (1977; also for Bass Trombone and Electronic Tape), *V* for 2 Pianos (1981; also for Solo Piano), and *VI* for Piano, Flute, Clarinet, and Cello (1981); String Quartet: *In Memoriam*, with Electronics (London, June 2, 1989). **ELECTRONIC:** *The Eyes of Ambush* for 1 to 5 Instruments or Voices, and Tape Delay (1973); *Caccia* for Amplified Trombone, Piano, and Tape (1974); *Inundations I*, trio for 3 Amplified Pianos, 12 Pianists, and Electronic Tape (1975); *Frozen Mirrors* for Piano, Viola, Percussion, Electronics, and Tape (1976); *Passim* for Piano, Percussion, and Electronic Tape (1977); Quintet for Piano and 4-Channel Tape (1978); *Gravity's Rainbow* for Flute and Electronics (1980); *Mouth of Anger* for Bass Clarinet, Piano, Percussion, Electronics, and Tape (1981; rev. 1983); Quartet for Electronic Tape (1982); *Tigida Pipa* for 4 Amplified Voices, Percussion, and Tape (1983); *Haiku* for Piano, Electronics, and Tape (1987).

Monte, Philippe de (Filippo di Monte or **Philippus de Monte),** great Belgian composer; b. Mechlin, 1521; d. Prague, July 4, 1603. He went to Italy in his youth and was active there as a singer and teacher. From 1542 to 1551 he was in Naples in the service of the Pinelli family; then went to Rome, where he publ. his 1st book of madrigals (1554); from Rome he proceeded to Antwerp in 1554, and then to England, where he served as chorus praefectus in the private chapel of Philip II of Spain, the husband of the Queen, Mary Tudor. In Sept. 1555 he left England and went to Italy again; in 1567 he was in Rome. On May 1, 1568, he became Imperial Court Kapellmeister to the Emperor Maximilian II in Vienna; he held this position until his death, which occurred while the court was at Prague during the summer of 1603. In 1572 he was appointed treasurer of Cambrai Cathedral, and in 1577, also a canon (residence was not required for either position there). He was greatly esteemed as a composer; he wrote some 1,000 madrigals, about 40 masses, and many other works of sacred music.

WORKS: MASSES: *Missa ad modulum "Benedicta es"* for 6 Voices (Antwerp, 1579); *Liber primus* [7] *missarum* for 5, 6, and 8 Voices (Antwerp, 1587); Mass for 5 Voices (Venice, 1590); none of his other masses were publ. in his lifetime, and most of these remain in MS. **MOTETS:** *Sacrarum cantionum . . . liber primus* for 5 Voices (Venice, 1572); *Sacrarum cantionum . . . liber secundus* for 5 Voices (Venice, 1573); *Sacrarum cantionum . . . liber tertius* for 5 Voices (Venice, 1574); *Libro quarto de motetti* for 5 Voices (Venice, 1575); *Sacrarum cantionum . . . liber quintus* for 5 Voices (Venice, 1579); *Sacrarum cantionum . . . liber sextus* for 5 Voices (Venice, 1584; not extant); *Sacrarum cantionum*

. . . *liber primus* for 6 and 12 Voices (Venice, 1585); *Sacrarum cantionum . . . liber secundus* for 6 Voices (Venice, 1587); *Sacrarum cantionum . . . liber primus* for 4 Voices (Venice, 1596); *Sacrarum cantionum . . . liber septimus* for 5 Voices (Venice, 1600); etc.

MADRIGALI SPIRITUALI: *Il primo libro de madrigali spirituali* for 5 Voices (Venice, 1581); *Il primo libro de madrigali spirituali* for 6 Voices (Venice, 1583); *Il secondo libro de madrigali spirituali* for 6 and 7 Voices (Venice, 1589); *Il terzo libro de madrigali spirituali* for 6 Voices (Venice, 1590); *Eccellenze di Maria vergine* for 5 Voices (Venice, 1593).

MADRIGALS: *Madrigali . . . libro primo* for 5 Voices (Rome, 1554); *Il primo libro de madrigali* for 4 Voices (Venice, 1562); *Il secondo libro de madrigali* for 5 Voices (Venice, 1567); *Il primo libro de' madrigali* for 6 Voices (c.1568; not extant; 2nd ed., Venice, 1569); *Il secondo libro delli madrigali* for 6 Voices (Venice, 1569); *Il secondo libro delli madrigali* for 4 Voices (Venice, 1569); *Il terzo libro delli madrigali* for 5 Voices (Venice, 1570); *Il quarto libro delli madrigali* for 5 Voices (Venice, 1571); *Madrigali . . . libro quinto* for 5 Voices (Venice, 1574); *Il sesto libro delli madrigali* for 5 Voices (Venice, 1575); *Il terzo libro de madrigali* for 6 Voices (Venice, 1576); *Il settimo libro delli madrigali* for 5 Voices (Venice, 1578); *Il quarto libro de madrigali* for 6 Voices (Venice, 1580); *L'ottavo libro delli madrigali* for 5 Voices (Venice, 1580); *Il nono libro de madrigali* for 5 Voices (Venice, 1580); *Il terzo libro de madrigali* for 4 Voices (c.1580; not extant; 2nd ed., Venice, 1585); *Il decimo libro delli madrigali* for 5 Voices (Venice, 1581); *Il quarto libro de madrigali* for 4 Voices (Venice, 1581); *Il primo libro de madrigali* for 3 Voices (Venice, 1582); *Il quinto libro de madrigali* for 6 Voices (Venice, 1584); *L'undecimo libro delli madrigali* for 5 Voices (Venice, 1586); *Il duodecimo libro delli madrigali* for 5 Voices (Venice, 1587); *Il terzodecimo libro delli madrigali* for 5 Voices (Venice, 1588); *Il quartodecimo libro delli madrigali* for 5 Voices (Venice, 1590); *Il sesto libro de madrigali* for 6 Voices (Venice, 1591); *Il settimo libro de madrigali* for 6 Voices (Venice, 1591); *Il quintodecimo libro de madrigali* for 5 Voices (Venice, 1592); *Il sestodecimo libro de madrigali* for 5 Voices (Venice, 1593); *L'ottavo libro de madrigali* for 6 Voices (Venice, 1594); *Il decimosettimo libro delli madrigali* for 5 Voices (Venice, 1595); *Il decimottavo libro delli madrigali* for 5 Voices (Venice, 1597); *Il decimonono libro delli madrigali* for 5 Voices (Venice, 1598); *La fiammetta . . . libro primo* for 7 Voices (Venice, 1599); *Musica sopra Il pastor fido . . . libro secondo* for 7 Voices (Venice, 1600); etc. A complete ed. of his works was edited by C. van den Borren and G. van Doorslaer as *Philippe de Monte: Opera* (31 vols., Bruges, 1927–39; reprint, 1965). R. Lenaerts and others ed. *Philippe de Monte: New Complete Edition* (Louvain, 1975–81).

BIBL.: G. van Doorslaer, *P. d. M.* (Mechelen, 1895); V. Eberstein, *Die Messen P. d. M., mit besonderer Berücksichtigung seiner Parodietechnik* (diss., Univ. of Vienna, 1912); P. Bergmans, *Quatorze lettres inédites du compositeur P. d. M.* (Brussels, 1921); G. van Doorslaer, *La Vie et les œuvres de P. d. M.* (Brussels, 1921); idem, *Deux lettres nouvelles de P. d. M.* (Mechelen, 1927); A. Einstein, "Filippo di M. als Madrigalkomponist," *International Musicological Society Congress Report*, I (Liège, 1930); J. van Nuffel, "P. d. M.," *Proceedings of the Music Association*, 57 (1931); P. Oberg, *The Sacred Music of P. d. M.* (diss., Univ. of Rochester, 1944); A. Einstein, *The Italian Madrigal* (Princeton, 1949); P. Nuten, *De madrigali spirituali van Filip de M.* (Brussels, 1958); G. Michael, *The Parody Mass Technique of P. d. M.* (diss., N.Y. Univ., 1959); R. Lindell, *Die sechs- und siebenstimmige Madrigale von Filippo di M.* (diss., Univ. of Vienna, 1977); I. Bossuyt, "Newly-discovered Part Books of Early Madrigal Collections of Philippus de M. (1521–1603)," *Fontes Artis Musicae*, XXVI (1979); B. Mann, *The Secular Madrigals of Filippo di M., 1521–1603* (Ann Arbor, 1983).

Monte, Toti dal. See **Dal Monte, Toti.**

Montéclair, Michel Pignolet de (real name, **Michel Pignolet**), distinguished French composer, teacher, and music theo-

rist; b. Andelot, Haute-Marne (baptized), Dec. 4, 1667; d. Aumont, Sept. 22, 1737. He became a pupil at the Langres Cathedral choir school (1676), where he was taught by the choirmaster, Jean-Baptiste Moreau; was maître de la musique to the Prince of Vaudémont, whom he followed to Italy; went to Paris (1687), and later added the name of the fortress in his birthplace, "Montéclair," to his own; with Fedeli, he introduced the double bass to the Paris Opéra orch., where he played from 1699 until 3 months before his death; was also active as a teacher, his students including François Couperin's daughters.

WORKS: *Les Festes de l'été*, opera ballet (Opéra, Paris, June 12, 1716); *Jephté*, tragédie lyrique (Opéra, Paris, Feb. 28, 1732); also *Messe de Requiem*, motets, and other sacred works, all of which are lost; various cantatas, several of which were ed. by J. Anthony and D. Akmajian in Recent Researches in the Music of the Baroque Era, XXIX–XXX (1978); airs; *Sérénade ou concert divisez en 3 suites* for Violins, Recorders, and Oboes (Paris, 1697); (6) *Concerts* for 2 Flutes (n.d.; ed. by R. Viollier, N.Y. and Locarno, 1962–64); (6) *Concerts* for Flute and Basso Continuo (n.d.); *Brunètes anciènes et modernes* for Flute or Violin (n.d.); other instrumental music (not extant).

WRITINGS: (all publ. in Paris): *Nouvelle méthode pour apprendre la musique* (1709); *Leçons de musique divisées en quatre classes* (c.1709); *Méthode facile pour apprendre à jouer du violon* (1711–12); *Petite méthode pour apprendre la musique aux enfans et même aux personnes plus avencées en âge* (c.1735); *Principes de musique* (1736).

BIBL.: J. de La Fage, "M. M.," *Revue et Gazette Musicale de Paris*, XXIV (1857); E. Voillard, *Essai sur M.* (Paris, 1879); M. Pincherle, "Elementary Musical Instruction in the 18th Century: An Unknown Treatise by M.," *Musical Quarterly* (Jan. 1948); E. Borrel, "Notes sur l'orchestration de l'opéra *Jephté* de M. (1733) et de la symphonie des *Elémens* de J.F. Rebel (1737)," *La Revue Musicale*, 226 (1955); R. Viollier, "Trois Jephté, trois styles," *Revue de Musicologie*, XLIII (1959); J. Anthony, "French Binary Air within Italian Aria da Capo in M.'s Third Book of Cantatas," *Proceedings of the Royal Musical Association*, CIV (1977–78); J. Sadie, "M., the Viol Player's Composer," *Journal of the Viola da Gamba Society of America*, XV (1978).

Montella, Giovanni Domenico, Italian lutenist, organist, and composer; b. Naples, c.1570; d. there, before July 2, 1607. He studied with Giovanni de Macque; was a lutenist in the academy of Don Fabrizio Gesualdo; in 1591 he was engaged as lutenist in the Spanish viceroy's chapel, where he also was an organist (from 1599). He wrote Psalms and other church music; publ. 4 vols. of *villanelles*, 2 vols. of motets, and 10 vols. of madrigals. Some of his sacred music is included in *Istituzioni e monumenti dell'arte musicale italiano* (vol. V, 1934).

Montemezzi, Italo, eminent Italian opera composer; b. Vigasio, near Verona, Aug. 4, 1875; d. there, May 15, 1952. He was a pupil of Saladino and Ferroni at the Milan Cons., and graduated in 1900; his graduation piece, conducted by Toscanini, was *Cantico dei Cantici*, for Chorus and Orch. He then devoted himself almost exclusively to opera. In 1939 he went to the U.S.; lived mostly in California; in 1949 he returned to Italy. Montemezzi's chief accomplishment was the maintenance of the best traditions of Italian dramatic music, without striving for realism or overelaboration of technical means. His masterpiece in this genre was the opera *L'amore dei tre re* (Milan, April 10, 1913), which became a standard work in the repertoire of opera houses all over the world. Other operas are *Giovanni Gallurese* (Turin, Jan. 28, 1905); *Hellera* (Turin, March 17, 1909); *La nave* (libretto by Gabriele d'Annunzio; Milan, Nov. 1, 1918); *La notte di Zoraima* (Milan, Jan. 31, 1931); *L'incantesimo* (NBC, Oct. 9, 1943, composer conducting); he also wrote *Paolo e Virginia* for Orch. (1929); *Italia mia, nulla fermerà il tuo canto* for Orch. (1944).

BIBL.: L. Tretti and L. Fiumi, eds., *Omaggio a I. M.* (Verona, 1952).

Monteux, Pierre, celebrated French-born American conductor; b. Paris, April 4, 1875; d. Hancock, Maine, July 1, 1964. He studied at the Paris Cons. with Berthelier (violin), Lavignac (harmony), and Lenepveu (composition); received 1st prize for violin (1896); then was a viola player in the Colonne Orch., and later chorus master there; also played viola in the orch. of the Opéra-Comique. He then organized his own series, the Concerts Berlioz, at the Casino de Paris (1911); that same year, he also became conductor for Diaghilev's Ballets Russes; his performances of modern ballet scores established him as one of the finest technicians of the baton. He led the world premieres of Stravinsky's *Petrouchka, Le Sacre du printemps,* and *Le Rossignol;* Ravel's *Daphnis et Chloé;* and Debussy's *Jeux;* conducted at the Paris Opéra (1913–14); founded the Société des Concerts Populaires in Paris (1914); appeared as guest conductor in London, Berlin, Vienna, Budapest, etc. In 1916–17 he toured the U.S. with the Ballets Russes; in 1917, conducted the Civic Orch. Soc., N.Y.; from 1917 to 1919, at the Metropolitan Opera there. In 1919 he was engaged as conductor of the Boston Sym. Orch., and held this post until 1924; from 1924 to 1934 he was associate conductor of the Concertgebouw Orch. in Amsterdam; from 1929 to 1938 he was principal conductor of the newly founded Orch. Symphonique de Paris. From 1936 until 1952 he was conductor of the reorganized San Francisco Sym. Orch. He became a naturalized U.S. citizen in 1942. He appeared as a guest conductor with the Boston Sym. Orch. from 1951, and also accompanied it on its 1st European tour in 1952, and then again in 1956; likewise was again on the roster of the Metropolitan Opera (1953–56). In 1961 (at the age of 86) he became principal conductor of the London Sym. Orch., retaining this post until his death. He was married in 1927 to **Doris Hodgkins** (b. Salisbury, Maine, 1895; d. Hancock, Maine, March 13, 1984), an American singer who co-founded in 1941 the Domaine School for Conductors and Orchestral Players in Hancock, Maine, of which Monteux was director. She publ. 2 books of memoirs, *Everyone Is Someone* and *It's All in the Music* (N.Y., 1965). After Monteux's death, she established the Pierre Monteux Memorial Foundation. As an interpreter, Monteux endeavored to bring out the inherent essence of the music, without imposing his own artistic personality; unemotional and restrained in his podium manner, he nonetheless succeeded in producing brilliant performances in an extensive repertoire ranging from the classics to the 20th century.

Bibl.: H. Schonberg, *The Great Conductors* (N.Y., 1967); D. Schneider, *The San Francisco Symphony Orchestra: Music, Maestros, and Musicians* (Novato, Calif., 1983); J. Canarina, "P. M.: A Conductor for All Repertoire," *Opus* (April 1986).

Monteverdi, Claudio (Giovanni Antonio), great Italian composer, brother of **Giulio Cesare Monteverdi;** b. Cremona (baptized), May 15, 1567; d. Venice, Nov. 29, 1643. His surname is also rendered as Monteverde. He was the son of a chemist who practiced medicine as a barber-surgeon; studied singing and theory with Marc' Antonio Ingegneri, maestro di cappella at the Cathedral of Cremona; he also learned to play the organ. He acquired the mastery of composition at a very early age; he was only 15 when a collection of his 3-part motets was publ. in Venice; there followed several sacred madrigals (1583) and canzonettas (1584). In 1589 he visited Milan, and made an appearance at the court of the Duke of Mantua; by 1592 he had obtained a position at the court in the service of Vincenzo I as "suonatore" on the viol (viola da gamba) and violin (viola da braccio). He came into contact with the Flemish composer Giaches de Wert, maestro di cappella at the Mantuan court, whose contrapuntal art greatly influenced Monteverdi. In 1592 Monteverdi publ. his 3rd book of madrigals, a collection marked by a considerable extension of harmonic dissonance. In 1595 he accompanied the retinue of the Duke of Mantua on forays against the Turks in Austria and Hungary, and also went with him to Flanders in 1599. He married Claudia de Cattaneis, one of the Mantuan court singers, on May 20, 1599; they had 2 sons; a daughter died in infancy. In 1601 he was appointed maestro di cappella in Mantua following the death of Pallavicino. The publication of 2 books of madrigals in 1603 and 1605 further confirmed his mastery of the genre. Having already composed some music for the stage, he now turned to the new form of the opera. *L'Orfeo,* his 1st opera, was given before the Accademia degli Invaghiti in Mantua in Feb. 1607. In this pastoral, he effectively moved beyond the Florentine model of recitative-dominated drama by creating a more flexible means of expression; the score is an amalgam of monody, madrigal, and instrumental music of diverse kinds. In 1607 Monteverdi was made a member of the Accademia degli Animori of Cremona. He suffered a grievous loss in the death of his wife in Cremona on Sept. 10, 1607. Although greatly depressed, he accepted a commission to compose an opera to celebrate the marriage of the heir-apparent to the court of Mantua, Francesco Gonzaga, to Margaret of Savoy. The result was *L'Arianna,* to a text by Rinuccini, presented in Mantua on May 28, 1608. Although the complete MS has been lost, the extant versions of the Lamento d'Arianna from the score testify to Monteverdi's genius in expressing human emotion in moving melodies. In 1614 he prepared a 5-part arrangement of his 6th book of madrigals, also publ. separately (Venice, 1623). He further wrote 2 more works for wedding celebrations, the prologue to the pastoral play *L'Idropica* (not extant) and the French-style ballet *Il ballo delle ingrate.* His patron, Duke Vincenzo of Mantua, died in 1612; and his successor, Francesco, did not retain Monteverdi's services. However, Monteverdi had the good fortune of being called to Venice in 1613 to occupy the vacant post of maestro di cappella at San Marco, at a salary of 300 ducats, which was raised to 400 ducats in 1616. His post at San Marco proved to be the most auspicious of his career, and he retained it for the rest of his life. He composed mostly church music, but did not neglect the secular madrigal forms. He accepted important commissions from Duke Ferdinando of Mantua. His ballet *Tirsi e Clori* was given in Mantua in 1616. In 1619 he publ. his 7th book of madrigals, significant in its bold harmonic innovations. In 1624 his dramatic cantata, *Il combattimento di Tancredi e Clorinda,* after Tasso's *Gerusalemme liberata,* was performed at the home of Girolamo Mocenigo, a Venetian nobleman. The score is noteworthy for the effective role played by the string orch. Other works comprised intermedi for the Farnese court in Parma. A great inconvenience was caused to Monteverdi in 1627 when his son Massimiliano, a medical student, was arrested by the Inquisition for consulting books on the Index Librorum Prohibitorum; he was acquitted. In 1630 Monteverdi composed the opera *Proserpina rapita* for Venice; of it only 1 trio has survived. Following the plague of 1630–31, he wrote a mass of thanksgiving for performance at San Marco (the *Gloria* is extant); in 1632 he took Holy Orders. His *Scherzi musicali* for 1 and 2 Voices was publ. in 1632. Then followed his *Madrigali guerrieri et amorosi,* an extensive retrospective collection covering some 30 years, which was publ. in 1638. In 1637 the 1st public opera houses were opened in Venice, and Monteverdi found a new outlet there for his productions. His operas *Il ritorno d'Ulisse in patria* (1640), *Le nozze d'Enea con Lavinia* (1641; not extant), and *L'incoronazione di Poppea* (1642) were all given in Venice. (Research by Alan Curtis suggests that the latter opera owes its final form to Francesco Sacrati.) The extant operas may be considered the 1st truly modern operas in terms of dramatic viability. Monteverdi died at the age of 76 and was accorded burial in the church of the Frari in Venice. A commemorative plaque was erected in his honor, and a copy remains in the church to this day.

Monteverdi's place in the history of music is of great magnitude. He established the foundations of modern opera conceived as a drama in music. For greater dynamic expression, he enlarged the orch., in which he selected and skillfully combined the instruments accompanying the voices. He was one of the earliest, if not the 1st, to employ such coloristic effects as string tremolo and pizzicato; his recitative assumes dramatic power, at times approaching the dimensions of an arioso. In harmonic usage he introduced audacious innovations, such as the use of the dominant seventh-chord and other dissonant chords without preparation. He is widely regarded as having popularized the terms "prima prattica" and "secunda prattica" to demarcate the polyphonic style of the 16th century from the largely monodic style of the 17th century, corresponding also to the distinction between "stile antico" and "stile moderno." For this he was severely criticized by the Bologna theorist Giovanni Maria Artusi, who publ. in 1600 a vitriolic pamphlet against Monteverdi, attacking the "musica moderna" which allowed chromatic usages in order to achieve a more adequate expression.

WORKS: In addition to various eds. of his works in separate format, G.F. Malipiero edited a complete ed. as *Claudio Monteverdi: Tutte le opere* (16 vols., Asolo, 1926–42; 2nd ed., rev., 1954; vol. 17, supplement, 1966). All of these are now being superseded by 2 new complete eds.: one, by the Fondazione Claudio Monteverdi, began publishing in 1970; the other, ed. by B.B. de Surcy, began issuing simultaneously critical and facsimile eds. in 1972. A list of his works follows:

DRAMATIC: *L'Orfeo*, opera, designated "favola in musica" (Mantua, Feb. 1607; publ. in Venice, 1609); *L'Arianna*, opera (Mantua, May 28, 1608; not extant except for various versions of the Lament); *In ballo delle ingrate*, ballet (Mantua, 1608; publ. in *Madrigali guerrieri et amorosi*, Venice, 1638); Prologue to *L'Idropica*, comedy with music (Mantua, June 2, 1608; not extant); *Tirsi e Clori*, ballet (Mantua, 1616; publ. in *Concerto: Settimo libro*, Venice, 1619); *Le nozze di Tetide*, favola marittima (begun 1616 but unfinished; not extant); *Andromeda*, opera (begun c.1618 but unfinished; libretto extant); *Apollo*, dramatic cantata (unfinished; not extant); *Il combattimento di Tancredi e Clorinda* (Venice, 1624; publ. in *Madrigali guerrieri et amorosi*, Venice, 1638); *La finta pazza Licori* (composed for Mantua, 1627; never perf.; not extant); *Gli amori di Diana e di Endimione* (Parma, 1628; not extant); *Mercurio e Marte*, torneo (Parma, 1628; not extant); *Proserpina rapita*, opera (Venice, 1630; only 1 trio extant); *Volgendo il ciel*, ballet (Vienna, c.1636; publ. in *Madrigali guerrieri et amorosi*, Venice, 1638); *Il ritorno d'Ulisse in patria*, opera (Venice, 1640); *Le nozze d'Enea con Lavinia*, opera (Venice, 1641; not extant); *La vittoria d'Amore*, ballet (Piacenza, 1641; not extant); *L'incoronazione di Poppea*, opera (Venice, 1642).

SECULAR VOCAL: *Canzonette* for 3 Voices (Venice, 1584); *Il primo libro de madrigali* for 5 Voices (Venice, 1587); *Il secondo libro de madrigali* for 5 Voices (Venice, 1590); *Il terzo libro de madrigali* for 5 Voices (Venice, 1592); *Il quarto libro de madrigali* for 5 Voices (Venice, 1603); *Il quinto libro de madrigali* for 5 Voices (Venice, 1605); *Musica tolta da i madrigali di Claudio Monteverde e d'altri autori, e fatta spirituale da Aquilino Coppini* for 5 and 6 Voices (Milan, 1607); *Scherzi musicali di Claudio Monteverde, raccolti da Giulio Cesare Monteverde suo fratello* for 3 Voices (Venice, 1607); *Il secondo libro della musica di Claudio Monteverde e d'altri autori, fatta spirituale da Aquilino Coppini* for 5 Voices (Milan, 1608); *Il terzo libro della musica di Claudio Monteverde e d'altri autori, fatta spirituale da Aquilino Coppini* for 5 Voices (Milan, 1609); *Il sesto libro de madrigali* for 5 Voices, "con uno dialogo," and 7 Voices, with Basso Continuo (Venice, 1614); *Concerto: Settimo libro de madrigali, con altri generi de canti* for 1 to 4 and 6 Voices, with Basso Continuo (Venice, 1619); *Scherzi musicali cioè arie, et madrigali in stil recitativo, con una ciaccona . . . raccolti da Bartholomeo Magni* for 1 and 2 Voices, with Basso Continuo (Venice, 1632); *Madrigali guerrieri et amorosi con alcuni opuscoli in genere rappresentativo, che saranno per brevi episodii frà i canti senza gesto: Libro ottavo* for 1 to 8 Voices and Instruments, with Basso Continuo (Venice, 1638); *Madrigali e canzonette . . . libro nono* for 2 and 3 Voices, with Basso Continuo (Venice, 1651).

SACRED VOCAL: *Sacrae cantiunculae . . . liber primus* for 3 Voices (Venice, 1582); *Madrigali spirituali* for 4 Voices (Brescia, 1583); *Musica tolta da i madrigali di Claudio Monteverde e d'altri autori, e fatta spirituale da Aquilino Coppini* for 5 and 6 Voices (Milan, 1607); *Il secondo libro della musica di Claudio Monteverde e d'altri autori, fatta spirituale da Aquilino*

Coppini for 5 Voices (Milan, 1608); *Il terzo libro della musica di Claudio Monteverdi e d'altri autori, fatta spirituale da Aquilino Coppini* for 5 Voices (Milan, 1609); *Sanctissimae virgini missa senis vocibus ad ecclesiarum choros ac Vespere pluribus decantandaecum nonnullis sacris concentibus ad sacella sive principum cubicula accommodata* for 1 to 3, 6 to 8, and 10 Voices and Instruments, with Basso Continuo (Venice, 1610); *Selva morale e spirituale* for 1 to 8 Voices and Instruments (Venice, 1641); *Messa* for 4 Voices, *et salmi* for 1 to 8 Voices, and *concertati, e parte da cappella, et con le letanie della beata vergine* for 6 Voices (Venice, 1650).

BIBL.: S. Davari, *Notizie biografiche del distinto maestro di musica C. M.* (Mantua, 1884); E. Vogel, "C. M.," *Vierteljahrsschrift für Musikwissenschaft*, III (1887); G. Sommi Picenardi, *C. M. a Cremona* (Milan, 1896); H. Goldschmidt, "M.s Ritorno d'Ulisse," *Sammelbände der Internationalen Musik-Gesellschaft*, IV (1902–3); idem, "C. M.s Oper: Il ritorno d'Ulisse in patria," ibid., IX (1907–8); G. Cesari, "Die Entwicklung der M.schen Kammermusik," *International Musical Society Congress Report*, III (Vienna, 1909); H. Leichtentritt, "C. M. als Madrigalkomponist," *Sammelbände der Internationalen Musik-Gesellschaft*, XI (1909–10); L. Schneider, *Un Précurseur de la musique italienne aux XVIe et XVIIe siècles: C. M.: L'Homme et son temps* (Paris, 1921); A. Tessier, "Les Deux Styles de Monteverde," *Revue Musicale*, III/8 (1922); H. Prunières, *La Vie et l'œuvre de C. M.* (Paris, 1924; Eng. tr., 1926; 2nd French ed., 1931); C. van den Borren, " 'Il ritorno d'Ulisse in patria' de C. M.," *Revue de l'Université de Bruxelles*, III (1925); J. Westrup, "Monteverde's 'Il ritorno d'Ulisse in patria,' " *Monthly Musical Record*, LVIII (1928); G. Malipiero, *C. M.* (Milan, 1929); issue of the *Rassegna Musicale* devoted to M. (Oct. 1929); K. Müller, *Die Technik der Ausdrucksdarstellung in M.s monodischen Frühwerken* (Berlin, 1931); H. Redlich, *C. M.: Ein formgeschichtlicher Versuch* (Berlin, 1932); J. Westrup, "The Originality of Monteverde," *Proceedings of the Musical Association*, LX (1933–34); W. Kreidler, *Heinrich Schütz und der Stile Concitato von C. M.* (Stuttgart, 1934); H. Redlich, "Notationsprobleme in C. M.s 'Incoronazione di Poppea,' " *Acta Musicologica*, X (1938); J. Westrup, "M. and the Orchestra," *Music & Letters*, XXI (1940); idem, "M.'s 'Lamento d'Arianna,' " *Music Review*, I (1940); O. Tiby, *C. M.* (Turin, 1944); D. de' Paoli, *C. M.* (Milan, 1945); H. Redlich, "M.'s Religious Music," *Music & Letters*, XXVII (1946); M. Bukofzer, *Music in the Baroque Era from M. to Bach* (London, 1948); A. Einstein, *The Italian Madrigal* (Princeton, 1949); H. Redlich, *C. M.: Leben und Werk* (Olten, 1949; Eng. tr. and rev., London, 1952); J. Westrup, "M. and the Madrigal," *Score*, I (1949); L. Schrade, *M., Creator of Modern Music* (London, 1950); M. le Roux, *C. M.* (Paris, 1951); C. Sartori, "M.ana," *Musical Quarterly* (July 1952); idem, *M.* (Brescia, 1953); A. Abert, *C. M. und das musikalische Drama* (Lippstadt, 1954); H. Redlich, "C. M.: Some Problems of Textual Interpretation," *Musical Quarterly* (Jan. 1955); W. Osthoff, "Zu den Quellen von M.s Ritorno d'Ulisse in Patria," *Studien zur Musikwissenschaft*, XXIII (1956); D. Arnold, " 'Seconda pratica': A Background to M.'s Madrigals," *Music & Letters*, XXXVIII (1957); W. Osthoff, "M.-Funde," *Archiv für Musikwissenschaft* (1957); idem, "Neue Beobachtungen zu Quellen und Geschichte von M.s 'Incoronazione di Poppea,' " *Die Musikforschung*, XI (1958); G. Pannain, "Studi m.ana," *La Rassegna Musicale*, XXVIII (1958), XIX (1959), XXX (1960), XXXI (1961), and *Quaderni della Rassegna Musicale*, III (1965); R. Roche, *M.* (Paris, 1959); W. Osthoff, *Das dramatische Spätwerk C. M.s* (Tutzing, 1960); C. Gallico, "Newly Discovered Documents Concerning M.," *Musical Quarterly* (Jan. 1962); F. Ghisi, "L'orchestra in M.," in *Karl Gustav Fellerer zum 60. Geburtstag* (Cologne, 1962); D. Arnold, *M.* (London, 1963); R. Tellart, *C. M.: L'Homme et son œuvre* (Paris, 1964); D. Arnold, *M. Madrigals* (London, 1967); G. Barblan et al., *C. M. nel quarto centenario della nascita* (Turin, 1967); H. Redlich, "C. M.: Some Editorial Problems of 1967," *Consort*, 24 (1967); E. Santoro, *La famiglia e la formazione di C. M.: Note biografiche con documenti inediti* (Cremona, 1967); D. Arnold and N. Fortune, eds., *The M.*

Companion (London, 1968; 2nd ed., rev., 1985, as *The New M. Companion*); *Congresso internazionale sul tema C. M. e il suo tempo: Venezia, Mantova e Cremona 1968* (Verona, 1969); N. Anfuso and A. Gianuario, *Preparazione alla interpretazione della Poiēsis M.ana* (Florence, 1971); W. Frobenius, "Zur Notation eines Ritornells in M.s 'L'Orfeo,'" *Archiv für Musikwissenschaft*, XXVIII (1971); K. Mays, *Harmonic Style in the Madrigals of C. M.* (diss., Indiana Univ., 1971); D. Stevens, "M.'s Necklace," *Musical Quarterly* (July 1973); idem, *M.: Sacred, Secular and Occasional Music* (Rutherford, N.J., 1978); D. de' Paoli, *M.* (Milan, 1979); J. Kurtzman, *Essays on the M. Mass and Vespers of 1610* (Houston, 1979); D. Stevens, ed. and tr., *The Letters of C. M.* (London, 1980); D. Arnold, *M. Church Music* (London, 1982); S. Leopold, *C. M. und seine Zeit* (Laaber, 1982); J. Whenham, *Duet and Dialogue in the Age of M.* (Ann Arbor, 1982); J. Roche, *North Italian Church Music in the Age of M.* (Oxford, 1984); P. Fabbri, *M.* (Turin, 1985); F. Noske, "An Unknown Work by M.: The Vespers of St. John the Baptist," *Music & Letters* (April 1985); A. Rosenthal, "M.'s 'Andromeda': A Lost Libretto Found," ibid. (Jan. 1985); D. Stevens, "M.'s Earliest Extant Ballet," *Early Music* (Aug. 1986); G. Tomlinson, *M. and the End of the Renaissance* (Oxford, 1986); D. Blazey, "A Liturgical Role for M.'s *Sonate sopra Sancta Maria*," *Early Music* (May 1989); A. Curtis, "*La Poppea Impasticciata* or, Who Wrote the Music to *L'Incoronazione* (1643)?," *Journal of the American Musicological Society* (Spring 1989); D. Kiel and K. Adams, *C. M.: A Guide to Research* (N.Y., 1989); S. Leopold, *M.: Music in Transition* (Oxford, 1991).

Monteverdi, Giulio Cesare, Italian organist, composer, and writer on music, brother of **Claudio (Giovanni Antonio) Monteverdi**; b. Cremona (baptized), Jan. 31, 1573; d. Salò, Lake Garda, during the plague of 1630–31. In 1602 he entered the service of the Duke of Mantua, where his famous brother was maestro di cappella. He composed the music for the 4th intermedio in Guarini's play *L'Idropica*, which was performed for the wedding celebration of the Mantuan heir-apparent, Francesco Gonzaga, and Margaret of Savoy in 1608. His opera *Il rapimento di Proserpina* was given in Casale Monferrato in 1611. In 1620 he was named maestro di cappella of the Cathedral in Salò. He publ. a collection of 25 motets under the title *Affetti musici, ne quali si contengono motetti a 1–4 et 6 voci, per concertarli nel basso per l'organo* (Venice, 1620). A madrigal for 3 Voices and Continuo (1605) and 2 pieces in his brother's *Scherzi musicali* (Venice, 1607) are extant. He contributed to the collection *Scherzi musicali* an important *Dichiaratione*, in which he expounded at length the musical ideas of his brother and gave a vigorous reply to the attacks on Monteverdi by Artusi; an Eng. tr. is found in O. Strunk, *Source Readings in Music History* (N.Y., 1950).

BIBL.: C. Sartori, "G.C. M. a Salò: Nuovi documenti inediti," *Nuova Rivista Italiana* (Nov.–Dec. 1967).

Montgomery, Kenneth (Mervyn), Irish conductor; b. Belfast, Oct. 28, 1943. He received his formal musical education at the Royal College of Music in London; studied conducting in Siena with Sergiu Celibidache, and in London with Sir Adrian Boult; also had instruction with John Pritchard and Hans Schmidt-Isserstedt. In 1964 he joined the conducting staff of the Glyndebourne Festival; in 1966 he conducted at the Sadler's Wells Opera in London. In 1970 he became assistant conductor of the Western Orch. Soc. at Bournemouth; in 1972, its associate conductor; in 1973 was appointed music director of the Bournemouth Sinfonietta. He was music director of the Glyndebourne Touring Opera (1975–76). From 1976 to 1980 he was principal conductor of the Netherlands Radio; in 1981 he became chief conductor of its Groot Omroep Koor. He was music director of Opera Northern Ireland in Belfast from 1985.

Montgomery, Merle, American music educator, editor, and composer; b. Davidson, Okla., May 15, 1904; d. Arlington, Va., Aug. 25, 1986. She studied at the Univ. of Oklahoma (B.F.A., 1924), with Philipp (piano) and Boulanger (composition) at the American Cons. in Fontainebleau (diploma, 1933),

and at the Eastman School of Music in Rochester, N.Y. (M.M., 1938; Ph.D. in music theory, 1948). She was head of the music dept. at Southwestern Inst. in Weatherford, Okla. (1938–41); after teaching at the Eastman School of Music (1943–45), she went to N.Y. as national educational representative and later vice-president of the Carl Fischer firm; ed. music and books on music; taught at the Westchester Cons.; was president of the National Music Council (1975–79). She composed mainly songs and piano pieces, often using the name Aline Campbell.

Montgomery, Wes (actually, **John Leslie**), outstanding black American jazz guitarist; b. Indianapolis, March 6, 1923; d. there, June 15, 1968. He began his career performing in local clubs; after touring and recording with Lionel Hampton's band (1948–50), he returned to Indianapolis; formed a group with his brothers Buddy, a pianist and vibraphonist, and Monk, a double-bass player; then formed his own trio (1959), which recorded the successful album *The Wes Montgomery Trio* that same year; toured widely from 1963. He won a Grammy Award for his recording of *Goin' Out of My Head* (1965); his album *A Day in the Life* (1967) was the best-selling jazz LP of the year. Montgomery was the leading jazz guitarist of his generation; he was a master electric guitarist, using his thumb in place of a plectrum.

BIBL.: L. Garson and J. Stewart, *W. M. Jazz Guitar Method* (N.Y., 1968); S. Khan, *The W. M. Guitar Folio* (N.Y., 1978); A. Ingram, *W. M.* (1985).

Montoya, Carlos, popular Spanish flamenco guitarist; b. Madrid, Dec. 13, 1903. He began to play the guitar when he was 8; within a few years he performed professionally with various dance groups, and later gave solo recitals which attracted faithful aficionados; he traveled in the U.S., South America, and Japan. He also improvised a number of attractive pieces, among them a *Suite flamenca* for Guitar and Orch. (1966); they were notated by helpers, since Montoya himself never learned to read music.

Montsalvatge, Bassols Xavier, Catalan music critic and composer; b. Gerona, March 11, 1911. He studied with Morera and Pahissa; in 1936 he received the Pedrell prize for his *Pequeña suite burlesca* for Violin and Woodwinds. He wrote the musical fables *El gato con botas* (Barcelona, 1947) and *Viaje a la luna* (in Catalan; Barcelona, 1966); *Sinfonia mediterránea* (1949); a string quartet, *Cuarteto indiano* (1952); *Concierto breve* for Piano and Orch. (1953); 3 *danzas inciertas* for 2 Violins (1956); *Cant espiritual* for Chorus and Orch. (1958); song cycle, 5 *Invocaciones al crucificado* for Soprano and 12 Instruments (1969); also incidental music; film scores; choruses; songs; piano music; organ pieces; guitar works.

BIBL.: M. Valls, *X. M.* (Barcelona, 1969); E. Franco, *X. M.* (Madrid, 1975).

Monza, Carlo, Italian composer; b. Milan, c.1735; d. there, Dec. 19, 1801. He studied with G.A. Fioroni and most likely received instruction from G.B. Sammartini, whom he succeeded as organist (1768) and then as maestro di cappella (1775) at Milan's ducal court. He also held the position of maestro di cappella at the churches of S. Maria Segreta, S. Giovanni in Conca, and the Chiesa della Rosa there. He later became maestro di cappella at Milan Cathedral (1787), but retained his position at the ducal court. Illness ended his tenure at the former (1793), and the French occupation (1796) at the latter. He was a skillful composer of both operas and sacred music.

WORKS: Operas: *Olimpiade* (Milan, May 1753); *Sesostri re d'Egitto* (Milan, Dec. 26, 1759); *Achille in Sciro* (Milan, Feb. 4, 1764); *Temistocle* (Milan, Jan. 1, 1766); *Oreste* (Turin, Carnival 1766); *Demetrio* (Rome, Jan. 3, 1769); *Adriano in Siria* (Naples, Nov. 4, 1769); *Germanico in Germania* (Rome, Jan. 7, 1770); *La Lavandara astuta*, pasticcio (Milan, July 2, 1770); *Nitteti* (Milan, Jan. 22, 1771); *Aristo e Temira* (Bologna, May 1771); *Berenice* (Turin, 1771?); *Antigono* (Rome, Carnival 1772); *Il (finto) cavalier parigino* (Milan, Sept. 3, 1774); *Ales-*

sandro nelle Indie (Bologna, Jan. 1775); *Cleopatra* (Turin, Dec. 26, 1775); *Caio Mario* (Venice, Ascension Fair 1777); *Attilio Regolo* (1777; not perf.); *Ifigenia in Tauride* (Milan, Jan. 1784); *Enea in Cartagine* (Alessandria, Oct. Fair 1784); *Erifile* (Turin, Dec. 26, 1785); also secular cantatas. He wrote much sacred music, including 13 masses, 20 Glorias, 18 offertories, many motets, 11 Magnificats, and 37 hymns. His instrumental music includes several syms., overtures, chamber music, and keyboard pieces.

Moodie, Alma, Australian violinist; b. Brisbane, Sept. 12, 1900; d. Frankfurt am Main, March 7, 1943. She studied with César Thomson in Brussels (1907–10); played at a concert as a child prodigy (with Max Reger); gave concerts in Germany, where she lived most of her life; taught at the Frankfurt Academy of Music. Her prestige as a musician was high in Germany; she performed many new works; Pfitzner wrote his Violin Concerto for her.

Moody, Fanny, English soprano; b. Redruth, Cornwall, Nov. 23, 1866; d. Dundrum, County Dublin, July 21, 1945. She studied with Charlotte Sainton-Dolby, making her debut in a memorial concert for her teacher at Prince's Hall in London (1885); made her operatic debut as Arline in *The Bohemian Girl* with the Carl Rosa Opera Co. in Liverpool (1887), and subsequently was the company's principal soprano until 1898; she married the Irish bass and impresario **Charles Manners** (1890), with whom she founded the Moody-Manners Opera Co. (1898), and thereafter toured widely with it until it was disbanded (1916). Among her best roles were Gounod's Marguerite and Juliet, Verdi's Leonora, and Santuzza.
BIBL.: P. Graves, "The M.-Manners Partnership," *Opera*, IX (1958).

Moog, Robert (Arthur), American designer of electronic instruments; b. Flushing, N.Y., May 23, 1934. He studied at Queens College (B.S. in physics, 1957), Columbia Univ. (B.S. in electrical engineering, 1957), and Cornell Univ. (Ph.D. in engineering physics, 1965). He founded the R.A. Moog Co. in 1954 for the purpose of designing electronic musical instruments; in 1964 he introduced the 1st synthesizer modules; his company was incorporated in 1968, with its headquarters at Trumansburg, N.Y. In 1970 he brought out the Minimoog, a portable monophonic instrument; in 1971 the company became Moog Music and went to Buffalo, N.Y.; in 1973 it became a division of Norlin Industries, with which Moog was associated until 1977. He founded another firm, Big Briar, in Leicester, N.C., which manufactured devices for precision control of analog and digital synthesizers. He was associated with Kurzweil Music Systems of Boston (1984–89). His synthesizers and other electronic devices were used by both classical and rock musicians.
BIBL.: D. Crombie, "The M. Story," *Sound International*, 6 (1978); T. Rhea, "The M. Synthesizer," *Contemporary Keyboard*, VII/3 (1981).

Moór, Emanuel, Hungarian pianist, inventor, and composer; b. Kecskemét, Feb. 19, 1863; d. Mont Pèlerin, near Montreux, Switzerland, Oct. 20, 1931. He studied in Budapest and Vienna; toured the U.S. from 1885 to 1887 as director of the Concerts Artistiques, for which he engaged Lilli Lehmann, Ovide Musin, and other celebrated artists, and also acted as their accompanist. He then lived in London, Lausanne, and Munich. He invented the Moór-Duplex piano, consisting of a double keyboard with a coupler between the two manuals (an octave apart). With the introduction of this piano, a new technique was made possible, facilitating the playing of octaves, tenths, and even chromatic glissandos. Some piano manufacturers (Steinway, Bechstein, Bösendorfer) put the Moór mechanism into their instruments. His 2nd wife, **Winifred Christie** (b. Stirling, Feb. 26, 1882; d. London, Feb. 8, 1965), an English pianist, aided him in promoting the Moór keyboard, and gave many performances on it in Europe and the U.S. She publ. (in collaboration with her husband) a manual of technical exercises for the instrument. Perhaps needless to say, Moór's

invention sank into innocuous desuetude along with phonetic alphabets, Volapük, and similar elucubrations of earnest but impractical innovators.
WORKS: OPERAS: *La Pompadour* (Cologne, Feb. 22, 1902); *Andreas Hofer* (Cologne, Nov. 9, 1902); *Hochzeitsglocken* (Kassel, Aug. 2, 1908; in London as *Wedding Bells*, Jan. 26, 1911); *Der Goldschmied von Paris* (n.d.); *Hertha* (unfinished). **ORCH.:** 8 syms. (1893–1910); 3 piano concertos (1886, 1888, 1906); 4 violin concertos (1905–7); 2 cello concertos (1905–6); Triple Concerto for Violin, Cello, Piano, and Orch. (1907); Harp Concerto (1913); also Requiem (1916); much chamber music; numerous songs.
BIBL.: L. Deutsch, *Die Technik der Doppelklaviatur M.* (Leipzig, 1932); M. Pirani, *E. M.* (London, 1959); H. Shead, *The History of the E. M. Double Keyboard Piano* (1978).

Moor (real name, **Mohr**), **Karel,** Czech conductor, composer, and writer; b. Bělohrad, Dec. 26, 1873; d. Prague, March 30, 1945. He studied at the Prague Cons.; then went for further study to Vienna. From 1900 to 1923 he was active as a theatrical director and conductor in Bohemia and Serbia; then lived mainly in Prague. He achieved his 1st success as a composer with the operetta *Pan profesor v pekle* (Mr. Professor in Hell), produced in Brünn in 1908; his other operas, *Viy*, after Gogol's fantastic tale (1901; Prague, July 14, 1903), and *Hjördis* (1899; rev. 1901; Prague, Oct. 22, 1905), were also successful. A facile writer, he publ. an autobiography in the form of a novel as *Karl Martens* (Prague, 1906); a vol. of reminiscences, *Vzpomínsky* (Pilsen, 1917); and a semi-fictional book, *V dlani osudu* (In the Hands of Fate; Nový Bydžov, 1947).

Moore, Carman (Leroy), versatile black American composer, conductor, teacher, and writer on music; b. Lorain, Ohio, Oct. 8, 1936. He studied with Martin Morris (horn), Peter Brown (cello), and Cecil Isaacs (conducting) at the Oberlin College Cons. of Music; after further studies at Ohio State Univ. (B.M., 1958), he went to N.Y., where he studied at the Juilliard School of Music with Persichetti and Berio (B.M., 1966); completed his studies with Stefan Wolpe (1967). He helped to launch the Soc. of Black Composers in 1968; taught at Manhattanville College (1969–71), Yale Univ. (1969–71), and Queens (1970–71) and Brooklyn (1972–74) Colleges of the City Univ. of N.Y. He presented concerts with his own group, Carman Moore and Ensemble, which he transformed into the Skymusic Ensemble in 1985. In addition to writing music criticism, he publ. a biography of Bessie Smith as *Somebody's Angel Child* (1970) and a textbook on teaching popular music (1980). In his compositions, he makes imaginative use of various genres, ranging from jazz to the avant-garde.
WORKS: THEATRICAL: OPERA: *The Masque of Saxophone's Voice* (1981). **MUSIC THEATER:** *Wild Gardens of the Loup Garou* (1983); *Distraughter, or The Great Panda Scanda* (1983); *Paradise Re-Lost* (1987). **MUSICAL:** *Franklin and Eleanor* (1989). **BALLETS:** *A Musical Offering* (1962); *Catwalk* (1966); *Tryst* (1966); *They Tried to Touch* (1986); *La Dea delle Acque* (Milan, March 29, 1988). **DANCE PIECE:** *Shipwreck* (1989). **INTERMEDIA:** *Broken Suite* for Instrumental Ensemble (1969); *The Illuminated Workingman* for 11 Instruments and Tape (1971); *American Themes and Variations* for Narrator and Instrumental Ensemble (1980); *Sky Dance/Sky Time* for Instrumental Ensemble, Dance Ensemble, and Sculpture (1984); *The Persistence of Green* for Dance, Dance Projections, and Instrumental Ensemble (N.Y., April 16, 1988); *The Magical Turn About Town* for Instrumental Ensemble (N.Y., July 18, 1989); *Tales of Exile* for Dancers and Instrumental Ensemble (N.Y., July 15, 1989); *Magic Circle* for Dancer, Projections, and Instrumental Ensemble (N.Y., Dec. 28, 1989). **ORCH.:** *Sinfonia* (1964); *Saratoga Festival Overture* (1966); *Gospel Fuse* for 4 Women's Voices and Orch. (San Francisco, Jan. 22, 1975); *Wildfires and Field Songs* (N.Y., Jan. 23, 1975); *Hit*, percussion concerto (1978); Concerto for Blues Piano and Orch. (1982); *Concertos (The Theme Is Freedom)* (N.Y., Nov. 11, 1985); Concerto for Jazz Violin and Orch. (1987). **CHAMBER:** Piano Sonata (1963); Mandolin Sonata (1966); Cello Sonata (1966); *Drum*

Major for Chamber Ensemble and Tape (1969); Quartet for Saxophones and Echo Device (1978); *Dawn of the Solar Age* for Brass, Percussion, and Synthesizer (1978); *Music for the Flute Alone* for Flute, Piano, Double Bass, and Tape (1981); *Deep Night with Tree* for Flute and Taped Flute (1986); *Journey to: Journey through* for 9 Instruments (1987); Concerto for Tap and Chamber Ensemble (1989). VOCAL: *Wedding Cantata* for Voices and Instruments (1963); *Variations on a Theme of Abraham Lincoln* for Soprano and Instrumental Ensemble (1973); *The Great American Nebula*, cantata for Narrator, Chorus, Orch., and Synthesizer (1976); *Follow Light* for Chorus, Percussion, and Double Bass (1981); *Celestial Intervals* or *Triptych* for Soprano, Tenor, and Instrumental Ensemble (N.Y., April 14, 1989).

Moore, Dorothy Rudd, black American composer; b. New Castle, Del., June 4, 1940. She studied with Mark Fax at Howard Univ. (B.Mus., 1963), with Nadia Boulanger at the American Cons. at Fontainebleau (1963), and with Chou Wen Chung in N.Y. (1965); then taught at the Harlem School of the Arts (1965–66), N.Y. Univ. (1969), and Bronx Community College (1971); also appeared as a singer in N.Y. and wrote poetry. In 1968 she helped to found the Soc. of Black Composers. She is married to the cellist Kermit Moore, who has given premiere performances of her works.

WORKS: OPERA: *Frederick Douglass* (1979–85). **ORCH.:** *Reflections* for Symphonic Winds (1962); Sym. (1963). **CHAMBER:** *Baroque Suite* for Cello (1965); *Adagio* for Viola and Cello (1965); 3 Pieces for Violin and Piano (1967); *Modes* for String Quartet (1968); *Moods* for Viola and Cello (1969); Piano Trio (1970); *Dirge and Deliverance* for Cello and Piano (1971); *Night Fantasy* for Clarinet and Piano (1978); also piano pieces, including *Dream and Variations* (1974) and *A Little Whimsy* (1982); numerous vocal works, including song cycles (*12 Quatrains from the Rubaiyat* for Soprano and Oboe [1962]; etc.) and songs.

Moore, Douglas (Stuart), distinguished American composer and music educator; b. Cutchogue, N.Y., Aug. 10, 1893; d. Greenport, N.Y., July 25, 1969. He studied at Yale Univ. with D.S. Smith and Horatio Parker; wrote several univ. songs, among them the football song *Good Night, Harvard,* which became popular among Yale students; after obtaining his B.A. (1915) and Mus.Bac. (1917), he joined the U.S. Navy; following the Armistice of 1918, he attended classes of d'Indy at the Schola Cantorum in Paris and also took lessons in organ with Tournemire and in composition with Boulanger, and with Bloch in Cleveland. Returning to the U.S., he served as organist at the Cleveland Museum of Art (1921–23) and at Adelbert College, Western Reserve Univ. (1923–25); in 1925 he received a Pulitzer traveling scholarship in music and spent a year in Europe. In 1926 he was appointed to the faculty of Columbia Univ.; in 1940 he became head of the music dept. there; many American composers were his students. He retired in 1962. A fine craftsman, Moore applied his technical mastery to American subjects in his operas and symphonic works. He achieved popular success with his "folk opera" *The Ballad of Baby Doe,* dealing with the true story of a historical figure during the era of intensive silver mining; the opera was staged on July 7, 1956, at Central City, Colo., where its action took place; the opera had numerous revivals in America, and also in Europe. He publ. the books *Listening to Music* (1932; 2nd ed., augmented, 1937) and *From Madrigal to Modern Music: A Guide to Musical Styles* (1942).

WORKS: OPERAS: *White Wings,* chamber opera (1935; Hartford, Feb. 2, 1949); *The Headless Horseman* (1936; Bronxville, N.Y., March 4, 1937); *The Devil and Daniel Webster* (1938; N.Y., May 18, 1939); *The Emperor's New Clothes,* children's opera (1948; N.Y., Feb. 19, 1949; rev. 1956); *Giants in the Earth* (1949; N.Y., March 28, 1951; rev. 1963; awarded the Pulitzer Prize in Music); *The Ballad of Baby Doe,* folk opera (Central City, Colo., July 7, 1956); *Gallantry,* "soap opera" (1957; N.Y., March 15, 1958); *The Wings of the Dove* (N.Y., Oct. 12, 1961); *The Greenfield Christmas Tree,* Christmas en-

tertainment (Baltimore, Dec. 8, 1962); *Carrie Nation,* to the story of the notorious temperance fighter (Lawrence, Kans., April 28, 1966); also a ballet, *Greek Games* (1930); incidental music; film scores for *Power in the Land* (1940), *Youth Gets a Break* (1940), and *Bip Goes to Town* (1941). **ORCH.:** *The Pageant of P.T. Barnum,* suite (1924; Cleveland, April 15, 1926); *Moby Dick,* symphonic poem (1927); *A Symphony of Autumn* (1930); *Overture on an American Tune* (N.Y., Dec. 11, 1932); *Village Music,* suite (N.Y., Dec. 18, 1941); *In Memoriam,* symphonic poem (1943; Rochester, N.Y., April 27, 1944); Sym. No. 2 in A major (1945; Paris, May 5, 1946); *Farm Journal,* suite for Chamber Orch. (1947; N.Y., Jan. 19, 1948); *Cotillion,* suite for Strings (1952). **CHAMBER:** Violin Sonata (1929); String Quartet (1933); Wind Quintet (1942; rev. 1948); Clarinet Quintet (1946); Piano Trio (1953); also piano pieces, organ music, choral works, and songs.

BIBL.: W. Rhodes, "D. M.'s Music," *Columbia University Quarterly* (Oct. 1940); O. Luening, "D. M.," *Modern Music,* XX/4 (1942); J. Beeson, "In Memoriam D. M. (1893–1969); An Appreciation," *Perspectives of New Music,* VIII/1 (1969); H. Weitzel, *A Melodic Analysis of Selected Vocal Solos in the Operas of D. M.* (diss., N.Y. Univ., 1971); D. Reagan, *D. M. and His Orchestral Works* (diss., Catholic Univ. of America, 1972); H. Gleason and W. Becker, "D. M.," in *20th-Century American Composers* (Bloomington, Ind., 2nd ed., rev., 1981).

Moore, Earl Vincent, American music educator and composer; b. Lansing, Mich., Sept. 27, 1890; d. La Jolla, Calif., Dec. 29, 1987. He studied at the Univ. of Michigan (B.A., 1912; M.A., 1915) and later in Europe with Widor, Holst, Boult, Heger, and others. He was an organist and teacher of theory at the Univ. of Michigan (1914–23); then was director of its School of Music, while continuing to teach (was a prof. there, 1923–46); from 1946 to 1960 he was dean of the School of Music. In 1939–40 he was national director of the WPA Music Project; from 1960 to 1970 he was chairman of the music dept. at the Univ. of Houston. He was a founder-member of the National Assoc. of Schools of Music and its president from 1936 to 1938. He composed parts of the Michigan Union Operas and other pieces, but is famous at the Univ. of Michigan as composer of the football song *Varsity.*

Moore, Gerald, renowned English piano accompanist; b. Watford, July 30, 1899; d. Penn, Buckinghamshire, March 13, 1987. He 1st studied with Wallis Bandey at the local music school; after the family went to Canada in 1913, he continued his studies with Michael Hambourg; then made appearances as a solo recitalist and accompanist; following his return to England (1919), he completed his training with Mark Hambourg. He began recording in 1921 and 1st gained distinction as accompanist to John Coates in 1925; he subsequently achieved well-nigh legendary fame as the preeminent accompanist of the day, appearing with such celebrated singers as Kathleen Ferrier, Dietrich Fischer-Dieskau, Elisabeth Schwarzkopf, Janet Baker, and others. He retired from the concert platform in 1967 but continued to make recordings. He was made a Commander of the Order of the British Empire (1954); was made an honorary D.Litt. by the Univ. of Sussex (1968) and Mus.D. by Cambridge Univ. (1973). As a witty account of his experiences at the piano, he publ. a sort of autobiography, *The Unashamed Accompanist* (London, 1943; rev. 1957), followed by an even more unzipped opus, *Am I Too Loud? Memoirs of an Accompanist* (London, 1962), and concluding with a somewhat nostalgic vol., *Farewell Recital: Further Memoirs* (London, 1978), and a rip-roaring sequel, *Furthermoore* [sic]: *Interludes in an Accompanist's Life* (London, 1983). Of a purely didactic nature are his books *Singer and Accompanist: The Performance of 50 Songs* (London, 1953), *The Schubert Song Cycles* (London, 1975), and *"Poet's Lore" and Other Schumann Cycles and Songs* (London, 1984).

Moore, Grace, popular American soprano; b. Nough, near Del Rio, Tenn., Dec. 5, 1898; d. in an airplane crash near Copenhagen, Jan. 26, 1947. She studied at the Wilson Greene School of Music in Chevy Chase, Md., and with Marafioti in

N.Y.; 1st appeared in musical comedy in N.Y. (1921–26); then continued her studies in Antibes with Richard Berthélemy. Upon returning to America, she made her operatic debut as Mimi at the Metropolitan Opera in N.Y. (Feb. 7, 1928), and sang there off and on until 1946; made successful appearances also at the Paris Opéra-Comique (1928), Covent Garden, London (1935), and other European centers; also sang with the Chicago City Opera (1937); appeared in several motion pictures, including *One Night of Love* (1934). She publ. an autobiography, *You're Only Human Once* (1944). Her finest roles were Mimi, Tosca, Louise, Fiora, and Manon.

Moore, Jerrold Northrop, American editor and writer on music; b. Paterson, N.J., March 1, 1934. He studied at Swarthmore College (B.A., 1955) and Yale Univ. (M.A., 1956; Ph.D., 1959); taught English at the Univ. of Rochester (1958–61), then was curator of historical sound recordings at Yale Univ. (1961–70). He wrote the authoritative biography *Edward Elgar: A Creative Life* (1984); was also an editor of the complete critical ed. of Elgar's works (from 1981). His other publications include *Elgar: A Life in Photographs* (1972), *Elgar on Record: The Composer and the Gramophone* (1974), *A Voice in Time: The Gramophone of Fred Gaisberg* (1976; U.S. ed. as *A Matter of Records*), *Music and Friends: Letters to Adrian Boult* (1979), *Spirit of England: Edward Elgar in His World* (1984), and *Elgar and His Publishers: Letters of a Creative Life* (2 vols., 1987).

Moore, John W(eeks), pioneer American musicologist and lexicographer; b. Andover, N.H., April 11, 1807; d. Manchester, N.H., March 23, 1889. He learned the printer's trade and then went to Brunswick, Maine (1828), where he publ. the 1st weekly newspaper in that state; after living in New Hampshire again (1831–38), he settled in Bellows Falls, Vt., as ed. of the *Bellows Falls Gazette* (1838–55); also ed. the *World of Music* (1843–49), a music journal. His magnum opus was the *Complete Encyclopedia of Music, Elementary, Technical, Historical, Biographical, Vocal, and Instrumental* (1852; reprint, 1972), the 1st comprehensive work of its kind in English. He went to Manchester (1863), where he revived the *World of Music* (1867–70); also brought out a supplement to his encyclopedia (1875; reprint, 1972) and ed. *A Dictionary of Musical Instruments* (1876), an abridged version of his encyclopedia.

Moore, Mary (Louise) Carr, American composer and teacher; b. Memphis, Tenn., Aug. 6, 1873; d. Inglewood, Calif., Jan. 9, 1957. Her father was a cavalry officer in the U.S. Army who sang; her mother authored several theater dramas; her uncle, John Harraden Pratt, was an organist; after the family went to California (1885), she studied composition with her uncle and singing with H.B. Pasmore in San Francisco. She began her career as a teacher, composer, and singer; sang the lead role in her 1st operetta, *The Oracle* (San Francisco, March 19, 1894), but soon devoted herself fully to teaching and composition. She taught in Lemoore, Calif. (1895–1901), and in Seattle (1901–15), where she founded the American Music Center (1909); after teaching in San Francisco (1915–26), she went to Los Angeles as an instructor at the Olga Steeb Piano School (1926–43) and was prof. of theory and composition at Chapman College (1928–47); was a founder of the Calif. Soc. of Composers (1936–38) and the Soc. of Native Composers (1938–44). As a composer, she devoted herself mainly to writing vocal works, particularly operas on American themes; her most important score was *Narcissa, or The Cost of Empire* (Seattle, April 22, 1912), which was awarded the David Bispham Memorial Medal.

WORKS: Operas: *The Oracle* (San Francisco, March 19, 1894); *Narcissa, or The Cost of Empire* (1909–11; Seattle, April 22, 1912); *The Leper* (1912); *Memories* (Seattle, Oct. 31, 1914); *Harmony* (San Francisco, May 25, 1917); *The Flaming Arrow, or The Shaft of Ku'pish-ta-ya* (1919–20; San Francisco, March 27, 1922); *David Rizzio* (1927–28; Los Angeles, May 26, 1932); *Los rubios* (Los Angeles, Sept. 10, 1931); *Flutes of Jade Happiness* (1932–33; Los Angeles, March 2, 1934); *Legende provençale* (1929–35); also *Ka-mi-a-kin* for Orch. (1930); Piano Con-

certo (1933–34); *Kidnap* for Orch. (1937–38); 3 piano trios (1895, 1906, 1941); Violin Sonata (1918–19); 2 string quartets (1926, 1930); String Trio (1936); *Brief Furlough* for Quintet (1942); some 20 pieces for Various Instruments and Piano; 57 piano pieces; 57 choral works; some 250 songs (1889–1952).

BIBL.: "M.C. M.—American Composer," *Christian Science Monitor* (April 16, 1929); M. Couche, "M.C. M.: American Composer," *Music of the West*, IX/6 (1954); C. Smith and C. Richardson, *M.C. M., American Composer* (Ann Arbor, 1989).

Moore, Melba, black American singer of popular music and actress; b. N.Y., Oct. 29, 1945. She studied at Newark's Arts High School and at the Montclair, N.J., State Teachers College; subsequently taught school for several years before setting out on a professional singing career. She served as a vocalist with the orch. of Babs Gonzales (1964); then sang in Broadway musicals, including the highly successful *Hair* (1968–70). She also appeared on the stage as a dramatic actress. Among her recording albums, the eponymous *Peach Melba* attracted attention.

Moore, Thomas, famous Irish poet, ballad singer, and song composer; b. Dublin, May 28, 1779; d. Sloperton Cottage, near Devizes, Wiltshire, Feb. 25, 1852. He had no regular musical training, but learned to play the piano with the aid of the organist William Warren. He was in London from 1799 to 1803; then received a position as a government functionary in Bermuda; however, he stayed there only a few months; then returned to London by way of the U.S. and Canada. In London he became extremely popular as a ballad singer in the houses of the aristocracy; between 1808 and 1834 he publ. *A Selection of Irish Melodies*, with music by John Stevenson. In 1817 he issued his celebrated poem *Lalla Rookh*. An ardent Irish nationalist, he played an important role in the creation and revival of Irish poetry and music. Among his own melodies are *Love thee, dearest; When midst the gay; One dear smile;* and *The Canadian Boat-Song.* He freely borrowed his musical materials from popular Irish tunes and in some cases modified them sufficiently to produce apparently new songs. He also composed short concerted vocal pieces; the terzetto *O lady fair* and the 3-part glee *The Watchman* won wide popularity. In 1895 Stanford publ. *The Irish Melodies of Thomas Moore: The Original Airs Restored.*

BIBL.: S. Gwynn, *T. M.* (London, 1905); W. Trench, *T. M.* (Dublin, 1934).

Moorhead, John, Irish violinist and composer; b. in Ireland, c.1760; d. (suicide) near Deal, March 1804. After studying music in Ireland, he became a theater musician in England. In 1798 he joined the orch. at London's Covent Garden, but became insane and had to be committed in 1802. After his release, he became a navy bandmaster. Then, following a relapse in 1804, he took his own life. He wrote 14 stage works, including the comic operas *Il Bondocani, or The Caliph Robber* (Covent Garden, Nov. 15, 1800; in collaboration with Attwood), *The Cabinet* (Covent Garden, Feb. 9, 1802; in collaboration with Braham, Corri, Davy, and Reeve), and *Family Quarrels* (Covent Garden, Dec. 18, 1802; in collaboration with Braham and Reeve).

Moos, Paul, German writer on music and esthetics; b. Bad Buchau, near Ulm, March 22, 1863; d. Raeren, Belgium, Feb. 27, 1952. He studied with Thuille, Rheinberger, and others at Munich's Akademie der Tonkunst.

WRITINGS: *Moderne Musikästhetik in Deutschland: Historisch-kritische Übersicht* (Berlin and Leipzig, 1902; rev. and augmented 1922, as *Die Philosophie der Musik von Kant bis Eduard von Hartmann*); *Richard Wagner als Ästhetiker* (Berlin and Leipzig, 1906); *Die deutsche Ästhetik der Gegenwart: Mit besonderer Berücksichtigung der Musikästhetik,* I: *Die psychologische Ästhetik* (Berlin and Leipzig, 1920) and II: *Die deutsche Ästhetik der Gegenwart: Versuch einer kritischen Darstellung* (Berlin, 1931).

Mooser, (Jean Pierre Joseph) Aloys, noted Swiss organist and organ builder, great-grandfather of **R(obert) Aloys**

Mooser; b. Niederhelfenschwyl, June 27, 1770; d. Fribourg, Dec. 19, 1839. He studied with his father, the Alsatian organ builder Joseph Anton Mooser (1731–92), who settled in Fribourg in the 1760s; Aloys built the outstanding organ at St. Nicolas's Cathedral there (1824–34).

BIBL.: R.A. Mooser, "A. M., facteur d'orgues à Fribourg," *Nouvelles Étrennes Fribourgeoises*, LXVIII (1935).

Mooser, R(obert) Aloys, Swiss writer on music, great-grandson of **(Jean Pierre Joseph) Aloys Mooser;** b. Geneva, Sept. 20, 1876; d. there, Aug. 24, 1969. His mother was a Russian, and he acquired the knowledge of the Russian language in childhood. He studied with his father and Otto Barblan in Geneva. In 1896 he went to St. Petersburg, where he served as organist at the French church, wrote music criticism for the *Journal de St. Petersbourg*, and made an extensive study of Russian music in the archives. He took courses with Balakirev and Rimsky-Korsakov. In 1909 he returned to Geneva and wrote music criticism for the periodical *La Suisse* (1909–62); was also founder, ed., and publisher of the periodical *Dissonances* (1923–46). His reviews were collected in the vols. *Regards sur la musique contemporaine: 1921–1946* (Lausanne, 1946); *Panorama de la musique contemporaine: 1947–1953* (Geneva, 1953); *Aspects de la musique contemporaine: 1953–1957* (Geneva, 1957); and *Visage de la musique contemporaine, 1957–1961* (Paris, 1962). He wrote the following books on Russian music: *Contribution à l'histoire de la musique russe: L'Opéra comique française en Russie au XVIIIe siècle* (Geneva, 1932; 2nd ed., 1954); *Violonistes-compositeurs italiens en Russie au XVIIIe siècle* (Milan, 1938–50); *Opéras, intermezzos, ballets, cantates, oratorios joués en Russie durant le XVIIIe siècle* (Geneva, 1945; 3rd ed., 1964); *Annales de la musique et des musiciens en Russie au XVIIIe siècle* (of prime importance for new, detailed, and accurate documentation; 3 vols., Geneva, 1948–51); also wrote *Deux violonistes genevois: Gaspard Fritz (1716–1783), Christian Haensel (1766–1850)* (Geneva, 1968).

Morales, Carlos O., Puerto Rican composer; b. San Juan, June 17, 1953. He studied at the Cons. of Music in Puerto Rico, graduating with degrees in guitar performance (1976) and music education (1977); subsequently taught there; also studied at the Accademia Musicale Chigiana in Siena. In 1979 he went to California, where he continued his composition studies. He is known primarily for his transcriptions to guitar of music originally written for the Renaissance laud. He currently is a prof. of music history at the Interamerican Univ. of Puerto Rico in Germán. Among his original compositions are *Thanks after Communion* for Male Chorus (1980); *Etapas* for Flute (1981); 2 symphonic poems, *Guanina* (1981) and *La Campana del Ingenio* (1984); and numerous works for solo guitar, including *Nocturno* (1984) and *Canción de Cuna* (1985).

Morales, Cristóbal de, eminent Spanish composer; b. Seville, c.1500; d. probably in Marchéna, between Sept. 4 and Oct. 7, 1553. He was probably a pupil of Fernández de Castilleja, the maestro de capilla at the Seville Cathedral. Morales was maestro de capilla at Avila Cathedral (1526–28); served in the same capacity in Plasencia (1528–31). In 1535 he entered the papal choir in Rome (until 1540, and again 1541–45); he composed much sacred music during this period. After a brief journey to Spain, he returned to Rome and increased his productivity as a composer; he also traveled in the retinue of the Pope to various towns in Italy. He was maestro de capilla at Toledo Cathedral (1545–47), to the Duke of Arcos in Marchéna (1548–51), and at Málaga Cathedral (1551–53). Morales was one of the outstanding masters of the polyphonic style; he was greatly esteemed by contemporary musicians; Bermudo described him as "the light of Spain in music." His works include more than 25 masses, 18 Magnificats, 2 Lamentations, and numerous motets. A modern ed. is appearing in Monumentos de la Música Española (Madrid, 1952–64).

BIBL.: H. Collet, *Le Mysticisme musical espagnol au XVIe siècle* (Paris, 1913); R. Mitjana y Gordon, *C. d.M., Estudio crítico-biográfico* (Madrid, 1920); F. Piqueras, *Música y músicos toledanos* (Toledo, 1922); J. Trend, "C. M.," *Music & Letters* (Jan. 1925); E. and C. Hernández, *Antología musical* (Barcelona, 1933); R. Stevenson, "C. M., A Fourth-Centenary Biography," *Journal of the American Musicological Society* (Spring 1953); idem, "The Earliest Polyphonic Imprint in South America," *Notes* (March 1967); H. Anglès, "Problemas que presenta la nueva edición de las obras de M. y de Victoria," in J. Robijns et al., eds., *Renaissance-Muziek 1400–1600: Donum natalicium René Bernard Lenaerts* (Louvain, 1969); S. Rubio, *C. d.M.: Estudio crítico de su polifonía* (El Escorial, 1969).

Morales, Melesio, Mexican composer; b. Mexico City, Dec. 4, 1838; d. San Petro de los Pinos, May 12, 1908. He began to compose salon music for piano and soon acquired sufficient technique to write for the stage; produced 2 operas, *Romeo y Julieta* (Mexico City, Jan. 27, 1863) and *Ildegonda* (Mexico City, Dec. 27, 1865); then went to France and Italy for additional study. Returning to Mexico, he taught and composed. His orch. fantasy, *La locomotiva*, was performed at the opening of the Mexico-Puebla railway (Nov. 16, 1869); it anticipated Honegger's *Pacific 231* by more than 50 years. He later produced 2 more operas: *Gino Corsini* (Mexico City, July 14, 1877) and *Cleopatra* (Mexico City, Nov. 14, 1891). Despite his passionate advocacy of national music, he followed conventional Italian models in his own works.

Morales, Olallo (Juan Magnus), Spanish-born Swedish conductor, music critic, and composer; b. Almería (of a Spanish father and Swedish mother), Oct. 15, 1874; d. Tällberg, April 29, 1957. Taken to Sweden as a child, he received his education there, 1st at Göteborg, then at the Stockholm Cons., with W. Stenhammar and others (1891–99), and in Berlin with H. Urban (composition) and Teresa Carreño (piano). In 1901 he returned to Sweden; was conductor of the Göteborg Orch. (1905–9); was a teacher (1917–21) and a prof. (1921–39) at the Stockholm Cons.; was also secretary of the Royal Academy of Music (1918–40). With T. Norlind, he publ. *Kungliga musikaliska akademien* (Royal Academy of Music; Stockholm; vol. I, 1771–1921 [1921]; vol. II, 1921–31 [1932]; vol. III, 1931–41 [1942]); also publ. a handbook on conducting (Stockholm, 1946). His works include a Sym. (1901); several overtures; Violin Concerto (1943); String Quartet; Piano Sonata; *Balada andaluza* for Piano (1946); *Nostalgia* (1920) and other character pieces for piano; choral works; songs.

Moralt, family of German musicians, all brothers and members of the famous Moralt string quartet:

(1) Joseph Moralt, violinist and conductor; b. Schwetzingen, Aug. 5, 1775; d. Munich, Nov. 13, 1855. He was made a supernumerary musician (1787) and concertmaster (1800) in the Munich Hofkapelle; was also concertmaster in the family string quartet; likewise was conductor at the Italian and German Operas in Munich.

(2) Johann Baptist Moralt, violinist and composer; b. Mannheim, March 10, 1777; d. Munich, Oct. 7, 1825. He studied violin with Johann Baptist Geiger and C. Cannabich and composition with Joseph Grätz; wrote 2 syms., much chamber music, and sacred vocal works.

(3) Philipp Moralt, cellist; b. Munich, Dec. 29, 1780; d. there, Jan. 10, 1830. He also played in the Munich municipal band.

(4) Georg Moralt, violist; b. Munich, 1781; d. there, 1818.

Moralt, Rudolf, esteemed German composer, nephew of **Richard Strauss;** b. Munich, Feb. 26, 1902; d. Vienna, Dec. 16, 1958. He studied in Munich at the Univ. and the Academy of Music, his principal teachers being Courvoisier and Schmid-Lindner. After serving as répétiteur at the Bavarian State Opera in Munich (1919–23), he was conductor at the Kaiserslautern Städtische Oper (1923–28; 1932–34) and music director of the German Theater in Brno (1932–34); then conducted opera in Braunschweig (1934–36) and Graz (1937–40); subsequently was a principal conductor at the Vienna State Opera (1940–58); also appeared as a guest conductor in Europe. In addition to his natural affinity for the music of his uncle, he also conducted fine performances of Mozart, Wagner, Johann Strauss, and Pfitzner.

Moran-Olden (real name, **Tappenhorn**), Fanny, German soprano; b. Oldenburg, Sept. 28, 1855; d. Berlin, Feb. 13, 1905. She studied with Haas in Hannover and Götze in Dresden; made her concert debut at the Leipzig Gewandhaus (1877); made her operatic debut under the name Fanny Olden as Norma in Dresden (1878); she then sang at the Frankfurt Opera (1878–84), the Leipzig City Theater (1884–91), and the Munich Court Opera (1891–95). She made her Metropolitan Opera debut in N.Y. on Nov. 28, 1888, as Valentine in *Les Huguenots;* was on its roster until 1889 and again in 1900–1901. In 1896 she toured Europe. After retiring from the stage (1902), she taught voice at Berlin's Klindworth-Scharwenka Cons. She married the tenor Karl Moran (1879) and the baritone Theodor Bertram (1897).

Moran, Robert (Leonard), American composer of the avant-garde; b. Denver, Jan. 8, 1937. He studied piano; went to Vienna in 1957 and took lessons in 12-tone composition with Hans Erich Apostel. Returning to America, he enrolled at Mills College in Oakland Calif., where he attended seminars of Luciano Berio and Darius Milhaud (M.A., 1963); completed his training with Roman Haubenstock-Ramati in Vienna (1963); also painted in the manner of Abstract Expressionism. He was active in avant-garde music circles; with Howard Hersh, he was founder and co-director of the San Francisco Cons.'s New Music Ensemble; was composer-in-residence at Portland (Oreg.) State Univ. (1972–74) and at Northwestern Univ. (1977–78), where he led its New Music Ensemble; also appeared extensively as a pianist in the U.S. and Europe in programs of contemporary music. In his compositions, he combines the "found art" style with aleatory techniques; some of his works are in graphic notation animated by a surrealistic imagination.

Works: operas: *Let's Build a Nut House,* chamber opera in memory of Paul Hindemith (San Jose, April 19, 1969); *Divertissement No. 3: A Lunchbag Opera* for Paper Bags and Instruments (BBC Television, 1971); *Metamenagerie,* department store window opera (1974); *Hitler: Geschichten aus der Zukunft* (1981); *Erlösung dem Erlöser,* music drama for Tape Loops and Performers (1982); *The Juniper Tree,* children's opera (1985; in collaboration with P. Glass). **ballets:** *Spin Again* for Amplified Harpsichord(s) and Electric Keyboards (1980); *Chorale Variations: 10 Miles High over Albania* for 8 Harps (1983). **other stage:** *Durch Wüsten und Wolken* for Shadow Puppets and Instruments (1975); *Marketmenagerie* for Children and Musique Concrète (1975); *Es war einmal,* children's show for Film, Slides, and Musique Concrète (1976); *Music for Gamelan,* incidental music (1978); *Am 29. 11. 1780* for Tape and Dancers (1979). **orch.:** *Interiors* for Orch., Chamber Orch., or Percussion Ensemble (1964; San Francisco, April 12, 1965); *Bombardments* No. 2 for 1 to 5 Percussion (1964); *L'Après-midi du Dracoula* for Any Group of Instruments capable of producing Any Kind of Sound (1966); *Elegant Journey with Stopping Points of Interest* for Any Ensemble (1967); *Jewelencrusted Butterfly Wing Explosions* (1968); *Silver and the Circle of Messages* for Chamber Orch. (San Francisco, April 24, 1970); *Emblems of Passage* for 2 Orchs. (1974); *Angels of Silence* for Viola and Chamber Orch. (1975); *Enantiodromia* for 8 Orchs. and Dancers (1977). **chamber:** *4 Visions* for Flute, Harp, and String Quartet (1964); *Eclectic Boogies* for 13 Percussionists (N.Y., Jan. 14, 1965); *Within the Momentary Illumination* for 2 Harps, Electric Guitar, Timpani, and Brass (Tokyo, Dec. 1, 1965); *Scream Kiss No. 1* for Harpsichord and Stereophonic Tape (1968); *Evening Psalm of Dr. Dracula* for Prepared Piano and Tape (1973); *The Last Station of the Albatross* for 1 to 8 Instruments (1978); *BASHA* for 4 Amplified Clavichords (1983); *Survivor from Darmstadt* for Bass Oboes (1984). **other:** *Smell Piece for Mills College* for Frying Pans and Foods (Mills College, Nov. 20, 1967; originally intended to produce a conflagration sufficiently thermal to burn down the college); *39 Minutes for 39 Autos* for 30 Skyscrapers, 39 Auto Horns,

Moog Synthesizer, and Players, employing 100,000 Persons, directed from atop Twin Peaks in San Francisco, and making use of Autos, Airplanes, Searchlights, and local Radio and Television Stations (San Francisco, Aug. 20, 1969); *Titus* for Amplified Automobile and Players (1969); *Hallelujah,* "a joyous phenomenon with fanfares" for Marching Bands, Drum and Bugle Corps, Church Choirs, Organs, Carillons, Rock-'n'-Roll Bands, Television Stations, Automobile Horns, and Any Other Sounding Implements, commissioned by Lehigh Univ. for the city of Bethlehem, Pa., with the participation of its entire population of 72,320 inhabitants (Bethlehem, April 23, 1971); *Pachelbel Promenade* for Guitar Ensemble, Folk Instruments, String Ensemble, and Jazz Ensemble (1975); *From the Market to Asylum* for Performers (1982); *Music for a Fair* (1984).

Moravec, Ivan, distinguished Czech pianist and pedagogue; b. Prague, Nov. 9, 1930. He studied with Grünfeld at the Prague Cons. (graduated, 1948); after further training with Štěpánova-Kurzova in Prague (1952–53), he attended Michelangeli's master classes in Arezzo (1957, 1958). He made his debut with the Prague Radio (1946); later toured in Europe, making his London debut in 1959; 1st appeared in the U.S. as soloist with the Cleveland Orch. in N.Y. (Jan. 30, 1964). He taught at the Prague Academy of Music (from 1967), where he headed its master class in piano (from 1969). Moravec is particularly noted for his performances of the standard 19th- and 20th-century repertoires.

Morawetz, Oskar, significant Czech-born Canadian composer; b. Světlá nad Sázavou, Jan. 17, 1917. He studied with Jaroslav Křička at the Univ. of Prague (1933–36); after the invasion of Czechoslovakia by the Nazis in 1938, he went to Vienna, where he studied with Julius Isserlis, and then to Paris, where he had lessons with Lévy; emigrated to Canada in 1940, becoming a naturalized citizen in 1946; completed his training at the Univ. of Toronto (B.M., 1944; D.Mus., 1953). He taught at the Royal Cons. of Music of Toronto (1946–51) and at the Univ. of Toronto (1951–82). In 1989 he received the Order of Canada. His music is Classical in format, Romantic in spirit, impressionistic in coloring, and modernistic in harmonic usage.

Works: orch.: *Carnival Overture* (1945; Montreal, July 1, 1947); *Divertimento* for Strings (1948; rev. 1954); 2 syms.: No. 1 (1950–53; 1st complete perf., Toronto, March 5, 1956; each movement is titled for separate perf.: *Fantasy, Dirge,* and *Scherzo*) and No. 2 (1959; Toronto, Feb. 2, 1960); *Overture to a Fairy Tale* (Halifax, Feb. 8, 1957); *Capriccio* (1960); Piano Concerto (1962; Montreal, April 23, 1963); Sinfonietta for Strings (1963; rev. 1983, 1989); *Passacaglia on a Bach Chorale* (Toronto, Nov. 24, 1964); Sinfonietta for Winds and Percussion (1965; Montreal, Feb. 22, 1966); Concerto for Brass Quintet and Chamber Orch. (Toronto, March 28, 1968); *Memorial to Martin Luther King,* elegy for Cello and Orch. (1968; the last movement employs the popular spiritual *Free at Last;* rev. 1973); *Reflections after a Tragedy* (1968); Harp Concerto (1976); Concerto for Clarinet and Chamber Orch. (1989). **vocal:** *Keep Us Free* for Chorus and Orch. (1951); *From the Diary of Anne Frank* for Soprano or Mezzo-soprano, and Orch. (CBC, May 20, 1970); *A Child's Garden of Verses,* after R.L. Stevenson, for Mezzo-soprano or Alto or Baritone, and Orch. (Toronto, Feb. 10, 1973); *Psalm 22: God, Why Have You Forsaken Me?* for Baritone or Mezzo-soprano or Contralto, and Piano or Orch. (1980; orch. version, Toronto, Jan. 4, 1984); *5 Biblical Songs* for Chorus (1981; Vancouver, Sept. 12, 1982); solo songs. **chamber:** 5 string quartets (1944; 1952–55; 1959; 1978; 1990); Duo for Violin and Piano (1947; rev. 1959); 3 violin sonatas (1956; 1965, rev. 1976; 1985); Trio for Flute, Oboe, and Harpsichord or Piano (1960); 2 *Fantasies* for Cello and Piano (1962; rev. 1970); 2 *Preludes* for Violin and Piano (1965); Flute Sonata (1980); Horn Sonata (1980); Oboe Sonata (1980–81); Clarinet Sonata (1981); Bassoon Sonata (1981); Sonata for Viola and Harp (1985–86); Trumpet Sonata (1986); also piano works, including *Sonata tragica* (1945), *Ballade* (1946; rev. 1982), *Scherzo* (1947), *Fantasy in D minor* (1948),

Fantasy on a Hebrew Theme (1951), *Scherzino* (1953), *Fantasy, Elegy and Toccata* (1956), *10 Preludes* (1961), *Suite* (1968), *Fantasy* (1973), and *4 Contrasting Moods* (1985–86).

Mordden, Ethan, American writer on music; b. Heavensville, Pa., Jan. 27, 1949. He studied piano at an early age; was educated in Quaker schools, including Friends Academy in Locust Valley, N.Y.; also studied at the Univ. of Pa. (B.A. in history, 1969). He worked as a musical director and coach in N.Y. (1971–74), then was assistant ed. of *Opera News* (1974–76); also was a visiting fellow at Yale Univ. (1980). He is a regular contributor to the *New Yorker;* won a National Magazine Award in 1989; also wrote for the *N.Y. Times* and *Christopher Street,* among other publications. In addition to his numerous books on music, film, and theater, he publ. fiction on gay life, especially the Buddies Trilogy (*I've a Feeling We're Not in Kansas Anymore* [1985], *Buddies* [1986], and *Everybody Loves You* [1988]); also composed *Reminiscences de Mahagonny* for Piano (1986).

WRITINGS: *Better Foot Forward: The Story of America's Musical Theatre* (1976); *Opera in the Twentieth Century* (1978); *That Jazz!: An Idiosyncratic Social History of the American Twenties* (1978); *A Guide to Orchestral Music* (1979); *The Splendid Art of Opera: A Concise History* (1980); *The Hollywood Musical* (1983); *Demented: The World of the Opera Diva* (1985); *Opera Anecdotes* (1986); *A Guide to Opera Recordings* (1987).

Moreau, Jean-Baptiste, French composer; b. Angers, 1656; d. Paris, Aug. 24, 1733. He was a chorister at Angers Cathedral; then was maître de musique at the cathedrals of Langres (1681–82) and Dijon. By Jan. 1687 he was in Paris; was introduced at the French court by the Dauphine, and was commissioned by Louis XIV to write several divertissements, among them *Les Bergers de Marly* (1687). He won great success with his musical interludes (recitatives and choruses) for Racine's *Esther* (1698) and *Athalie* (1691), performed at the school for young noblewomen at St.-Cyr, where he was musicien ordinaire; also wrote music for Racine's *Cantiques spirituels,* for performance at St.-Cyr. His success at court was marred by his dissolute habits; however, he was greatly esteemed as a teacher of singing and composition; among his pupils were Montéclair, J.F. Dandrieu, Clérambault, and the singers Louise Couperin and his own daughter Marie-Claude Moreau. The music to *Esther* and *Athalie,* and the *Cantiques spirituels,* were publ. in the music supplement to P. Mesnard's *Œuvres de J. Racine* (Paris, 1873).

BIBL.: T. Lavallée, *Histoire de la maison royale de St.-Cyr* (Paris, 1856); A. Taphanel, *Le Théâtre de St.-Cyr* (Paris, 1876); J. Tiersot, "Les Chœurs d'Esther et d'Athalie de M.," *Revue Musicale* (Jan. 1903); K. Meyer, *Der chorische Gesang der Frauen* (Leipzig, 1917); N. Demuth, "A Musical Backwater," *Musical Quarterly* (Oct. 1954).

Moreau, Léon, French composer; b. Brest, July 13, 1870; d. Paris, April 11, 1946. He studied at the Paris Cons.; won the Grand Prix de Rome in 1899. Among his works are the operas *Myriade* and *Pierrot décoré;* the symphonic poems *Sur la mer lointaine* and *Dionysos;* a Piano Concerto; many songs.

Moreira, António Leal, Portuguese composer; b. Abrantes, 1758; d. Lisbon, Nov. 21, 1819. He studied with João de Sousa Carvalho at the Lisbon Seminario Patriarcal; became his assistant in 1775; in 1787 he was appointed mestre de capela of the royal chapel; then served as music director of the Italian Opera Theater (1790–93) and the Teatro San Carlo (1793–1800) in Lisbon. He composed numerous stage works; his opera buffa *Il disertore francese* was given at the Turin Carnival in 1800; also composed 4 masses, 2 Magnificats, and 5 villancicos.

Morel, Auguste-François, French composer; b. Marseilles, Nov. 26, 1809; d. Paris, April 22, 1881. He lived in Paris from 1836 to 1850; then returned to Marseilles, and became director of the Cons. He wrote the opera *Le Jugement de Dieu* (1860); 2 syms.; overtures; much chamber music.

Morel, (Joseph Raoul) François (d'Assise), Canadian pianist and composer; b. Montreal, March 14, 1926. He studied

piano with Trudel, Letondal, and Malépart, composition with Champagne, acoustics with Papineau-Couture, and harmony, counterpoint, and fugue with Isabelle Delorme at the Cons. de Musique de Québec à Montréal (1944–53); was a founding member of the new music group Musique de Notre Temps (1956); taught at Montreal's Inst. Nazareth (1959–61); was director of the Montreal Academy of Music (1972–78); then taught at the Univ. of Montreal and Laval Univ. (from 1979). His music parallels the esthetic fashions of modern times, from Debussyan coloristic imagism to motoric neo-Classicism to the organized sound of Varèse to the stern serialism of the cosmopolitan avant-garde.

WORKS: ORCH.: *Esquisse* (Montreal, Oct. 7, 1947); *Diptyque* for 23 Instruments (1948; rev. 1956; originally *Suite pour petit orchestre*); *Antiphonie* (N.Y., Oct. 16, 1953); *Litanies* for Winds, Brass, Harp, Piano, Celesta, and Percussion (1956; rev. 1970); *Spirale* for Winds, Brass, Harp, Celesta, and Percussion (1956); *Intrada* for Chorus and Orch. (1957); *Rituel de l'espace,* symphonic poem (1956–58; Montreal, April 6, 1960); *Boréal* (1959; Montreal, April 26, 1960); *L'Étoile noire* (Montreal, March 13, 1962); *Trajectoire* (Montreal, April 20, 1967); *Neumes d'espace et Reliefs* (Edmonton, Oct. 29, 1967); *Prismes-Anamorphoses* for Winds, Percussion, Harp, Piano, and Celesta (1967); *Départs* for 14 Solo Strings, Harp, Guitar, and 2 Percussionists (Montreal, March 17, 1969); *Iikkii (Froidure)* for 18 Solo Instruments (Montreal, Feb. 3, 1972); *Radiance* for Small Orch. (1970–72); also works for jazz band, including *Beatnik* (1959) and *Sinfonia* (1963). **CHAMBER:** 2 string quartets (1952; 1962–63); *Cassation* for Woodwind Septet (1954); *Symphonie* for Brass and Percussion (1956); *Rythomologue* for 8 Percussionists (1957; rev. 1970); *Le Mythe de la roche percée* for Double Woodwinds and Percussion (Pittsburgh, June 10, 1961); Brass Quintet (1962); *Requiem* for Winds (1963); *Me duele España,* variations for Guitar (1975); also piano pieces, including *Rondo enfantin* (1949) and *2 études de sonorité* (1952–54); songs.

Morel, Jean, French-American conductor and pedagogue; b. Abbeville, Jan. 10, 1903; d. N.Y., April 14, 1975. He studied piano with Isidor Philipp, music theory with Noël Gallon, music history with Maurice Emmanuel, lyric repertoire with Reynaldo Hahn, and composition with Pierné in Paris; subsequently taught at the American Cons. in Fountainebleau (1921–36). At the outbreak of World War II in 1939, he emigrated to the U.S.; taught at Brooklyn College (1940–43); then conducted opera in Brazil and Mexico. In 1949 he was appointed to the faculty of the Juilliard School of Music in N.Y., and became conductor of the Juilliard Orch. He also conducted at the Metropolitan Opera in N.Y. (1956–62; 1967–68; 1969–71). He gained wide recognition as a teacher of conducting; retired from Juilliard in 1971.

Morell, Barry, American tenor; b. N.Y., March 30, 1927. He studied in N.Y.; made his operatic debut as Pinkerton in *Madama Butterfly* at the N.Y. City Opera (March 26, 1955), a role he also chose for his 1st appearance at N.Y.'s Metropolitan Opera (Nov. 1, 1958); subsequently made guest appearances in Europe and South America.

Morelli (real name, **Zanelli**), **Carlo,** Chilean baritone; b. Valparaiso (of an Italian father and a Chilean mother), Dec. 25, 1897; d. Mexico City, May 12, 1970. He studied voice in Bologna with Angelo Queize, and in Florence with Leopoldo Mugnone. He sang at La Scala, Milan (1922); toured South America (1925–31); made his 1st U.S. appearence with the Chicago Opera in 1932; made his debut at the Metropolitan Opera in N.Y. on Dec. 21, 1935, as Marcello in *La Bohème;* remained there until 1940; then sang with the San Carlo Opera at the City Center, N.Y. (1940–49). In 1949 he settled in Mexico.

Morelot, Stéphen, French scholar; b. Dijon, Jan. 12, 1820; d. Beaumont, Oct. 7, 1899. He was dean of the faculty of jurisprudence at Dijon Univ.; was co-ed. (from 1845) of the *Revue de la Musique Religieuse, Populaire et Classique;* he went to Italy in 1847 to study church music. He publ. numerous essays; his *Manuel de Psalmodie en fauxbourdons à 4 voix . . .* (1855) is an ingenious attempt to revive the ancient style of harmonization.

Morena (real name, **Meyer**), **Berta**, noted German soprano; b. Mannheim, Jan. 27, 1878; d. Rottach-Egern, Oct. 7, 1952. Her buxom beauty attracted the attention of the famous painter von Lenbach, who persuaded her to study voice with Sophie Röhr-Brajnin and Aglaja von Orgeni in Munich; after additional training with Regina de Sales, she made her debut as Agathe in *Der Freischütz* at the Munich Court Opera (1898); remained on its roster until 1927; made her American debut with the Metropolitan Opera in N.Y. as Sieglinde (March 4, 1908), remaining on its roster until 1909; then returned from 1910 to 1912 and in 1924–25. She was regarded in Germany as an intelligent and musicianly singer, excelling particularly in Wagnerian roles, including Elisabeth, Elsa, Eva, Isolde, and the 3 Brünnhildes.
BIBL.: A. Vogl, *B. M. und ihre Kunst* (Munich,1919).

Moreno (Andrade), Segundo Luis, Ecuadorian musicologist and composer; b. Cotacachi, Aug. 3, 1882; d. Quito, Nov. 18, 1972. He played the clarinet in a civil band in Quito. He studied at the Quito Cons.; then was active as a military band leader in various localities in Ecuador; in 1937, took over the newly established Cons. Nacional de Música in Cuenca; later was director of the Guayaquil Cons. (1940–45). He composed mostly for military band; many of his pieces celebrate various patriotic events in Ecuador, as the cantata *La emancipación* (1920), the overture *9 de Julio* (1925), and various pieces on native motifs, among them *3 suites ecuatorianas* for Orch. (1921, 1944, 1945). He publ. *Música y danzas autoctonas del Ecuador* (Quito, 1949) and *La música de los Incas* (Quito, 1957).

Morera, Enrique (Enric), Spanish composer; b. Barcelona, May 22, 1865; d. there, March 11, 1942. As a child, he was taken to Argentina, and studied in Buenos Aires; then took courses at the Brussels Cons. Returning to Barcelona, he studied piano with Albéniz and harmony with Felipe Pedrell. In 1895 he founded the choral society Catalunya Nova, which he conducted until 1909; then taught at the Escuela Municipal de Música in Barcelona (1910–28). He was an ardent propagandist of Catalan music, and wrote a number of songs to Catalan words; also collected 193 melodies of popular origin. His opera *Emporium*, originally to a Catalan text, was performed 1st in Italian (Barcelona, Jan. 20, 1906); he wrote more than 50 other stage works (lyric comedies, zarzuelas, operettas, intermezzos, etc.); several symphonic poems, including *Introducció a l'Atlántida* (1893); Cello Concerto (1917); *Poema de la nit i del dia* for Orch. (1919); chamber music; much choral music; many sardanas.
BIBL.: I. Iglesias, *Enric M.* (Barcelona, 1921); J. Pena, *Enric M.* (Barcelona, 1937).

Morère (real name, **Couladère**), **Jean,** French tenor; b. Toulouse, Oct. 6, 1836; d. Paris, Feb. 1887. He studied with Paul Laget in Toulouse; made his debut as Manrico at the Paris Opéra in 1861, where he sang until 1869; created the title role in Verdi's *Don Carlos* there in 1867; also appeared in Brussels at the Théâtre Royal de la Monnaie (1865–66; 1869–70). He suffered a mental derangement in the wake of the Franco-Prussian War in 1871.

Moreschi, Alessandro, Italian castrato soprano; b. Montecompatri, near Rome, Nov. 11, 1858; d. Rome, April 21, 1922. He studied with Capocci in Rome; from 1883 to 1913 he sang at the Vatican's Sistine Chapel. The last of the castrati, he had a voice of such purity and beauty that he was nicknamed "l'angelo di Roma."
BIBL.: A. Heriot, *The Castrati in Opera* (London, 1956).

Morganfield, Mckinley. See Waters, Muddy.

Mori, Frank (Francis), English conductor and composer, son of **Nicolas Mori**; b. London, March 21, 1820; d. Chaumont, France, Aug. 2, 1873. He was educated by his father; wrote light music; his operetta *The River-Sprite* (London, Feb. 9, 1865) was fairly successful.

Mori, Nicolas, English violinist and music publisher, father of **Frank (Francis) Mori;** b. London (of Italian descent), Jan. 24, 1796; d. there, June 14, 1839. He studied with Barthélemon and appeared as a soloist in one of the latter's concertos when he was 8; then continued his studies with Viotti (1808–14); was a soloist at a Phil. Soc. concert in London (1814), and then became one of its concertmasters (1816); was also concertmaster at the King's Theatre until his death. He married Elizabeth Lavenu, widow of the publisher Lewis Lavenu, in 1819; the firm was known as Mori & Lavenu from about 1818 to 1839. He brought out the English eds. of works by Mendelssohn, and other music; wrote music for violin. An eccentric, he wrote flamboyant advertisements about his career, and shortly before his death announced his own memorial concert, punning on his name ("Memento Mori").
BIBL.: E. Duffin, *Particulars of the Illness and Death of the Late Mr. M. the Violinist* (London, 1839).

Moriani, Napoleone, outstanding Italian tenor; b. Florence, March 10, 1806; d. there, March 4, 1878. He studied with C. Ruga; made his operatic debut in Pacini's *Gli Arabi nelle Gallie* in Pavia in 1833; then sang throughout Italy, garnering great praise for his interpretations of Bellini, Donizetti, and Verdi; he created the role of Enrico in Donizetti's *Maria di Rudenz* in Venice in 1838, and that of Carlo in *Linda di Chamounix* in Vienna in 1842. He sang in Madrid (1844–46) and London (1844–45); made his Paris debut at the Théâtre-Italien (1845), where he returned in 1849–50 before appearing again in Madrid; retired from the stage in 1851. Having sung so many death-laden tenor roles, he became known as "il tenore della bella morte."

Morillo, Roberto García, Argentine composer and music critic; b. Buenos Aires, Jan. 22, 1911. He studied composition with Aguirre and Juan José Castro; later took courses with Gaito and Ugarte. From 1926 to 1930 he was in Paris. Returning to Argentina, he taught at the National Cons. in Buenos Aires and wrote music criticism for *La Nación*. He publ. monographs on Mussorgsky (1943), Rimsky-Korsakov (1945), and Carlos Chávez (1960); also *Julian Bautista en la música española contemporánea* (1949). His music is marked by propulsive rhythms and a strong sense of dissonant counterpoint. Among his works are a symphonic poem, *Berseker* (Buenos Aires, Dec. 29, 1932); Piano Concerto (Buenos Aires, Nov. 7, 1940); *Las pinturas negras de Goya* for Piano, Violin, Cello, Flute, Clarinet, and Bassoon (Montevideo, May 27, 1940); *The Fall of the House of Usher*, after Poe (Buenos Aires, May 12, 1943); 3 syms. (1948, 1955, 1961); *Variaciones olímpicas* for Orch. (1958); *3 pinturas de Piet Mondrian* for Orch. (1960); *Ciclo de Dante Alighieri* for Chamber Orch. (1970); *Dionysos* for Orch. (1971); Quartet for Violin, Cello, Clarinet, and Piano (1937); *Concerto a 9* for 3 Clarinets and Strings (1943); String Quartet (1951); 5 piano sonatas (1935–62); *Cantata de los caballeros* for Soprano and Orch., to words by García Lorca (1965); *Divertimento sobre temas de Paul Klee* for Wind Quintet (1967; orchestrated 1971); *Cantata féstiva* a cappella (1971); also film music.

Morini (real name **Siracusano**), **Erica (Erika),** Austrian-born American violinist; b. Vienna, Jan. 5, 1904. Her father was Italian and her mother Austrian; she studied at her father's school of music in Vienna; then with Ševčík at the Vienna Cons.; made her professional debut at the age of 12; played with the Gewandhaus Orch. in Leipzig under the direction of Nikisch (1918). She made her U.S. debut in N.Y. on Jan. 26, 1921; in subsequent years she played with virtually all the major American orchs.; also toured South America, Australia, and the Orient; eventually settled in N.Y.; became a naturalized citizen in 1943.

Morison, Elsie (Jean), Australian soprano; b. Ballarat, Aug. 15, 1924. She studied with Clive Carey at the Melbourne Cons.; made her London debut at the Royal Albert Hall in London in 1948; then sang with the Sadler's Wells Opera (1948–54) and at Covent Garden (1953–62). She married **Rafael Kubelik**

in 1963. Her roles included Pamina, Susanna, Marzelline, Micaela, and Anne Trulove.

Moritz, Landgrave of Hessen-Kassel, German patron of the arts and composer, called Moritz "der Gelehrte" (the learned); b. Kassel, May 25, 1572; d. Eschwege, March 15, 1632. He succeeded his father in 1592, remaining as landgrave until abdicating in favor of his son during the 30 Years' War in 1627. Having studied music with the court Kapellmeister Georg Otto, he took a deep interest in all the arts and gained a reputation as a great patron of enlightened views and noble generosity. He built the 1st court theater in Germany, the Ottoneum (1605), which he named for his Kapellmeister. He was the patron of Heinrich Schütz. In 1955 the musicological inst. in Kassel was named in his honor as the Landgraf-Moritz-Stiftung. He wrote much sacred music and some instrumental pieces, most of which have not survived.

BIBL.: E. Zulauf, *Beiträge zur Geschichte der landgräflich-hessischen Hofkapelle zu Cassel bis auf die Zeit M. des Gelehrten* (Kassel, 1902); W. Blandenburg, "Landgraf M. von Hessen-Kassel," *Musik und Kirche*, XLII (1972).

Morlacchi, Francesco (Giuseppe Baldassare), prominent Italian conductor and composer; b. Perugia, June 14, 1784; d. Innsbruck, Oct. 28, 1841. He studied with his uncle, the Cathedral organist L. Mazzetti, and with Luigi Caruso in Perugia; then with Zingarelli in Loreto (1803–4) and Padre Mattei at Bologna's Liceo Filarmonica (1805), where he received his diploma of "maestro compositore" for the cantata *Il tempio della gloria*, written in honor of Napoleon's coronation as King of Italy. He demonstrated his contrapuntal skill by composing a *Miserere a 16* (1807); he 1st gained success as a composer for the stage with his operas *La Principessa per ripiego* (Rome, autumn 1809) and *Le Danaidi* (Rome, Feb. 11, 1810). He then was called to Dresden as deputy Kapellmeister of the Italian Opera in 1810, being made Kapellmeister for life in 1811; he retained the latter title until the Italian Opera was closed in 1832. During these years, he wrote some of his most successful stage works, among them *Il nuovo barbiere di Siviglia* (Dresden, May 1816), *La simplicetta di Pirna* (Dresden, Aug. 1817), *La gioventù di Enrico* (Dresden, Oct. 4, 1823), *Il Colombo* (Genoa, June 28, 1828), and *Il Rinnegato* (Dresden, March 1832); also wrote a *Requiem* upon the death of King Friedrich August I of Saxony (1827). In later years he divided his time between Dresden and Italy; stricken with tuberculosis in 1839, he died on his way to his homeland.

BIBL.: "Verzeichnis sämtlicher Compositionen des Kapellmeisters Ritter M. bis 1822," *Allgemeine Musikalische Zeitung*, V (1823); G. Ricci des Ferres-Cancani, *F. M., un maestro italiano alla corte di Sassonia (1785–1841)* (Florence, 1956); B. Brumana and G. Ciliberti, eds., *F. M. e la musica del suo tempo (1785–1841)* (Florence, 1986).

Morley, Thomas, famous English composer; b. Norwich, 1557 or 1558; d. London, Oct. 1602. He studied with William Byrd. From 1583 to 1587 he was organist and master of the choristers at Norwich Cathedral. In 1588 he received his B.Mus. from Oxford. About this time he became organist at St. Paul's Cathedral. By 1591 he had turned spy for the government of Queen Elizabeth I. In 1592 he was sworn in as a Gentleman of the Chapel Royal and was made Epistler and then Gospeller. He was also active as a printer, holding a monopoly on all music publ. under a patent granted to him by the government in 1598. In addition to publishing his own works, he acted as ed., arranger, translator, and publisher of music by other composers. Notable among his eds. was *The Triumphes of Oriana* (1601), a collection of madrigals by 23 composers. He gained distinction as a music theorist; his *A Plaine and Easie Introduction to Practicall Musicke* (1597) became famous as an exposition of British musical schooling of his time.

WORKS: MADRIGALS: *Canzonets, or Little Short Songs to Three Voyces* (London, 1593; 3rd ed., enl., 1602, as *Canzonets . . . with Some Songs added by the Author*); *Madrigalls to Foure Voyces: The First Booke* (London, 1594; 2nd ed., enl., 1600,

as *Madrigalls . . . with Some Songs added by the Author*); *The First Booke of Balletts to Fiue Voyces* (London, 1595; 3rd ed., 1600); *The First Booke of Canzonets to Two Voyces* (London, 1595); *Canzonets or Little Short Aires to Fiue and Sixe Voyces* (London, 1597); he ed. the last 3 in Italian editions as well; he also ed. *Madrigales: The Triumphes of Oriana, to Fiue and Six Voyces Composed by Divers Seurall Aucthors* (London, 1601). **SOLO SONGS:** *The First Booke of Aires or Little Short Songs to Sing and Play to the Lute with the Base-Viol* (London, 1600; it contains the song *It was a lover and his lasse* from Shakespeare's *As You Like It*). Many of the preceding works were ed. by E.H. Fellowes in *The English Madrigal School* (4 vols., 1913 et seq.: I, *Canzonets to 2 Voices* [1595] and *Canzonets to 3 Voices* [1593], rev. by T. Dart, 1956; II, *Madrigals to 4 Voices* [1594], rev. by T. Dart, 1963; III, *Canzonets to 5 and 6 Voices* [1597], rev. by T. Dart, 1966; IV, *Ballets to 5 Voices* [1600], rev. by T. Dart, 1966). *The Triumphes of Oriana* was ed. by E.H. Fellowes in *The English Madrigal School, A Guide to Its Practical Use* (London, 1926; rev. by T. Dart, 1962, in *The English Madrigalists*). *The First Booke of Aires* was ed. by E.H. Fellowes in *The English School of Lutenist Song Writers* (London, 1920–32; rev. by T. Dart, 1966, in *The English Lute-Songs*). Modern eds. of additional works by Morley include H. Andrews and T. Dart, *Collected Motets* (London, 1959), and T. Dart, ed., *Keyboard Works*, in *English Keyboard Music* (London, 1959). Morley ed. *The First Booke of Consort Lessons, made by divers exquisite Authors for sixe Instruments to play together, viz. the Treble Lute, the Pandora, the Citterne, the Base Violl, the Flute, and the Treble Violl* (London, 1599; 2nd ed., corrected and enl., 1611; modern ed. by S. Beck, N.Y., 1959). His treatise *A Plaine and Easie Introduction to Practicall Musicke* (London, 1597) was publ. in a facsimile ed. by E.H. Fellowes (London, 1937); a modernized ed. was publ. by R. Alec Harman (London, 1952; 2nd ed., 1963).

BIBL.: O. Bekker, *Die englischen Madrigalisten William Byrd, T. M. und John Dowland* (Leipzig, 1901); E.H. Fellowes, *English Madrigal Verse* (Oxford, 1920; 3rd ed., rev., 1967, by F. Sternfeld and D. Greer; idem, *The English Madrigal Composers* (Oxford, 1921; 2nd ed., 1948); idem, *The English Madrigal* (Oxford, 1925); J. Pulver, "The English Theorists: XIII—T. M.," *Musical Times*, LXXVI (1935); T. Dart, "M.'s Consort Lessons of 1599," *Proceedings of the Royal Musical Association*, LXXIV (1947–48); J. King, *An Aesthetic and Musical Analysis of the Madrigals of T. M., with Special Reference between Text and Music and Some Comparison with the Madrigals of John Wilby, John Bennet, and the "Triumphs of Oriana"* (diss., Univ. of Toronto, 1950); R. Stevenson, "T. M.'s 'Plaine and Easie' Introduction to the Modes," *Musica Disciplina*, VI (1952); J. Kerman, "M. and the 'Triumphs of Oriana,'" *Music & Letters*, XXXIV (1953); J. Uhler, *M.'s Canzonets for Two Voices* (diss., Univ. of Louisiana, 1954); idem, "T. M.'s Madrigals for Four Voices," *Music & Letters*, XXXVI (1955); idem, *M.'s Canzonets for Three Voices* (Baton Rouge, 1957); D. Brown, "T. M. and the Catholics: Some Speculations," *Monthly Musical Record*, LXXXIX (1959); T. Dart, "M. and the Catholics: Some Further Speculations," ibid.; F. Zimmerman, "Italian and English Traits in the Music of T. M.," *Anuario Musical*, XIV (1959); D. Brown, "The Style and Chronology of T. M.'s Motets," *Music & Letters*, XLI (1960); C. Murphy, *T. M. Editions of Italian Canzonets and Madrigals* (Tallahassee, 1964); W. Shaw, "T. M. of Norwich," *Musical Times*, CVI (1965); D. Greer, "The Lute Songs of T. M.," *Lute Society Journal*, VIII (1966); R. McGrady, "T. M.'s First Booke of Ayres," *Music Review*, XXXIII (1972); M. Chibbett, "Dedications in M.'s Printed Music," *Royal Musical Association Research Chronicle*, XIII (1977); G. Beechey, "M.'s Church Music," *Musical Times* (Sept. 1981).

Mornington, Garret Wesley, 1st Earl of, Irish composer and father of the Duke of Wellington; b. Dublin, July 19, 1735; d. Kensington, May 22, 1781. He studied violin, harpsichord, organ, and composition in his youth; then studied at Trinity College, Dublin (B.A., 1754; M.A., 1757); was made Mus.D. (1764) and served as the 1st prof. of music at the Univ. of

Dublin (1764–74). He was admired as a glee composer; won prizes awarded by the Catch Club (1776, 1777, and 1779), the last for his *Here in cool grot*. Sir Henry Bishop ed. a complete collection of his glees and madrigals (1846).

Moroi, Makoto, Japanese composer, son of **Saburo Moroi**; b. Tokyo, March 12, 1930. He studied with his father and Ikenouchi at the Tokyo National Univ. of Fine Arts and Music (1948–52); also studied Gregorian chant with Paul Anouilh and Renaissance and Baroque music with Eta Harich-Schneider; taught at the Osaka National Univ. of Fine Arts and Music (from 1968). His music partakes of 3 different sources which sometimes fuse into a unified modality: ancient Japanese elements, serialism, and sonorism, i.e., organized sound with electronic instruments.
WORKS: *Composition No. 1* for Orch. (1951–53), *No. 2* for Orch. (1958), *No. 3* for Narrator, Male Chorus, and Orch. (1958), *No. 4* for Narrator, 3 Speaking Sopranos, Chorus, and Orch. (1960), and *No. 5, Ode to Arnold Schoenberg*, for Chamber Orch. (Osaka, Aug. 26, 1961); *Suite classique* for Orch. (1953); *Suite concertante* for Violin and Orch. (Kyoto, Sept. 7, 1963); Piano Concerto (1966); Sym. (Tokyo, Nov. 7, 1968); Concerto for Shakuhachi, String Orch., and Percussion (1970–71); *Pitagorasu no hoshi* (Stars of Pythagoras) for Narrator, Chorus, Tape, and Chamber Orch. (1959); *Cantata da camera No. 1* for Ondes Martenot, Harpsichord, 3 Percussionists, Male Chorus, and Narrator (1959); *Cantata da camera No. 2, Blue Cylinder*, for Narrator, Soprano, Chorus, and Chamber Orch. (1959); *The Red Cocoon* for Narrator, Pantomime, 2 Choruses, Tape, and Orch. (1960); *Phaeton, the Coachman* for Narrator, Solo Voice, Chorus, and Tape (1965); *Vision of Cain*, symphonic sketch for ballet (1966); *Izumo, My Home!* for Baritone, Soprano, Chorus, Orch., and Tape (1970); Sym. for Voice, Percussion, Japanese Instruments, and Tape (1972); *Musica da camera No. 3* for Viola and Wind Quintet (1951); *Musica da camera No. 4* for String Quartet (1954); *Partita* for Flute (1953); *Albumblätter* for Oboe (1953); *Développements rarefiants* for Soprano and Chamber Group (Karuizawa, July 12, 1957); *Ordre* for Cello and Piano (1958); *5 epigrammes* for Flute, Clarinet, Vibraphone, Celesta, Harp, Violin, and Cello (Tokyo, Feb. 29, 1964); *Kusabira* (Mushrooms) for 2 Voices and Electronic Sound (1964); *Toccata, Sarabande and Tarantella* for Strings and Piano (1964); *5 Dialogues* for 2 Shakuhachi (1965); *Les Farces* for Violin (1970); piano pieces: *Alpha and Beta* (1953–54), Sonatina (1966), and *8 Parables* (1967); *Contradiction I and II* (1972) and several other works for Japanese instruments alone.

Moroi, Saburo, Japanese composer, teacher, and writer on music, father of **Makoto Moroi**; b. Tokyo, Aug. 7, 1903; d. there, March 24, 1977. He studied literature at Tokyo Univ. (1926–28), and later took lessons in composition with Max Trapp, orchestration with Gmeindl, and piano with Robert Schmidt at the Hochschule für Musik in Berlin (1932–34). Upon returning to Japan, he was active as a music teacher; was inspector of music and adult education for the Ministry of Culture (1946–64) and director of Tokyo's Gakuen Academy of Music (1967–77); among his students, in addition to his son, were Dan and Irino. Among his numerous publications are *Junsui tai i ho* (Strict Counterpoint; Tokyo, 1949) and *Gakushiki no kenkyū* (Historical Research on Musical Forms; 5 vols., Tokyo, 1957–67).
WORKS: 2 piano concertos (1933, 1977); 5 syms.: No. 1 (Berlin, Oct. 2, 1934), No. 2 (Tokyo, Oct. 12, 1938), No. 3, with Organ (Tokyo, May 26, 1950), No. 4 (Tokyo, March 26, 1951), and No. 5 (Tokyo, 1971); Cello Concerto (1936); Bassoon Concerto (1937); Violin Concerto (1939); *2 Symphonic Movements* (1942); Sinfonietta (1943); *Allegro* for Piano and Orch. (1947); *2 Songs* for Soprano and Orch. (1935); fantasy-oratorio, *A Visit of the Sun* (Tokyo, June 30, 1969); Violin Sonata (1934); String Quartet (1933); Piano Quartet (1935); Viola Sonata (1935); Flute Sonata (1937); String Sextet (1939); String Trio (1940); 2 piano sonatas (1933, 1940); *Preludio ed Allegro giocoso* for Piano (1971).

Moross, Jerome, American composer; b. N.Y., Aug. 1, 1913; d. Miami, July 25, 1983. He studied at the Juilliard School of Music in N.Y. (1931–32) and at N.Y. Univ. (graduated, 1932); became associated with various ballet groups and wrote a number of scores for the dance, most of them on American subjects, all of them in a vivid folklike manner. In 1940 he went to Hollywood as an arranger; collaborated with Aaron Copland on the score for *Our Town*. He held 2 Guggenheim fellowships (1947, 1948). His 1st film score was *Close Up* (1948); his other film scores included *The Cardinal*, *The Proud Rebel*, and *The Big Country*. For Broadway he wrote music for *Parade* (1935). His works for the dance included *Paul Bunyan* (1934); *American Patterns* (1937); *Frankie and Johnny* (1938); *Guns and Castanets* (1939); *The Eccentricities of Davy Crockett* (1946); *Robin Hood* (1946). He also wrote operas: *Susanna and the Elders* (1940); *Willie the Weeper* (1945); *The Golden Apple* (1948–50); *Gentlemen, Be Seated!* (N.Y., Oct. 10, 1963); *Sorry, Wrong Number* (1977); a ballet suite, *The Last Judgment* (1953); several orch. works, including a Sym. (Seattle, Oct. 18, 1943); *Beguine* (N.Y., Nov. 21, 1934); and *A Tall Story* (N.Y., Sept. 25, 1938); chamber music, including Sonatina for Clarinet Choir (1966); Sonatina for Strings, Double Bass, and Piano (1967); Sonatina for Brass Quintet (1968); Sonatina for Woodwind Quintet (1970); Sonatina for Divers Instruments (1972); Sonata for Piano Duet and String Quartet (1975); and Concerto for Flute and String Quartet (1978).

Morphy, Guillermo, Conde de, Spanish courtier and musician; b. Madrid, Feb. 29, 1836; d. Baden, Switzerland, Aug. 28, 1899. He was taken to Germany as a child; there he studied music; took courses with Fétis in Brussels, where he wrote an orch. *Serenata española*, which had several performances. In 1864 he was named "chamber gentleman" to the Prince of Asturias, the future Alfonso XII, and then became his secretary; received his nobiliary title in 1885. He spent much time in Vienna and Paris, and took up the study of Spanish tablature music of the 16th century. His transcriptions (marred by inaccuracies) were publ. posthumously, with an introduction by Gevaert, as *Les Luthistes espagnols du XVIe siècle* (2 vols., Leipzig, 1902; German text by Riemann). In his influential position at the Spanish court, Morphy helped many talented musicians; he was instrumental in procuring a stipend for Albéniz to enable him to study in Brussels.

Morris, Harold, American composer and pianist; b. San Antonio, March 17, 1890; d. N.Y., May 6, 1964. He studied at the Univ. of Texas (B.A.) and the Cincinnati Cons. (M.M., 1922); lectured at the Rice Inst. of Houston (1933), Duke Univ. (1939–40), etc.; was on the faculty of the Juilliard School of Music (1922–39) and Teachers College, Columbia Univ. (1935–46); received many awards; was one of the principal founders of the American Music Guild in N.Y. (1921). In his music, he reveals himself as a Romanticist; in the main direction of his creative development, he was influenced by Scriabin. Many of his works are of programmatic content; some of them include American thematic material.
WORKS: ORCH.: *Poem*, after Tagore's *Gitanjali* (1915; Cincinnati, Nov. 29, 1918); *Dum-A-lum*, variations on a Negro spiritual for Chamber Orch. (1925); 3 syms.: No. 1, after Browning's *Prospice* (1925); No. 2, *Victory* (1943; Chicago, Dec. 23, 1952); No. 3, *Amaranth*, after E.A. Robinson's poem (1946; Houston, March 13, 1948); *Piano Concerto on 2 Negro Themes* (1927; Boston, Oct. 23, 1931); *Suite* for Chamber Orch. (1927; N.Y., Nov. 1, 1941); Violin Concerto (1938; N.Y., May 25, 1939); *Passacaglia and Fugue* (1939); *American Epic* (1942); *Heroic Overture* (1943). CHAMBER: 2 piano trios (1917, 1933); Violin Sonata (1919); 2 string quartets (1928, 1937); 2 piano quintets (1929, 1937); Suite for Piano and Strings (1943); also many works for solo piano, including 4 sonatas (1915, 1915, 1920, 1939) and *Ballade* (1938).

Morris, James (Peppler), outstanding American bass-baritone; b. Baltimore, Jan. 10, 1947. After studies with a local teacher, he won a scholarship to the Univ. of Maryland; concur rently received invaluable instruction from Rosa Ponselle; then continued his studies with Frank Valentino at the Peabody Cons. of Music in Baltimore (1966–68); made his debut as Crespel in *Les Contes d'Hoffmann* with the Baltimore Civic Opera (1967). After further training with Nicola Moscona at the Philadelphia Academy of Vocal Arts (1968–70), he made his Metropolitan Opera debut in N.Y. as the King in *Aida* on Jan. 7, 1971; appeared with the Opera Orch. of N.Y. and sang widely in Europe. In 1975 he scored a notable success as Don Giovanni at the Metropolitan. Although closely associated with the Italian and French repertoires, he appeared as Wotan in *Die Walküre* at the Baltimore Civic Opera in 1984; subsequently sang that role in the San Francisco Opera's *Ring* cycle in 1985, eliciting extraordinary critical acclaim. His other esteemed roles include Count Almaviva, Philip II, the Dutchman, the 4 villains in *Les Contes d'Hoffmann*, Timur in *Le Roi de Lahore*, Scarpia, and Claggart in *Billy Budd*.

BIBL.: *Current Biography* (July 1986).

Morris, R(eginald) O(wen), English composer and pedagogue; b. York, March 3, 1886; d. London, Dec. 14, 1948. He studied at the Royal College of Music in London with Charles Wood; from 1920 to 1926, taught there; after teaching at the Curtis Inst. of Music in Philadelphia (1926–28), he again taught at the Royal College of Music (1928–48). He became best known as a teacher, serving as a discerning mentor to many notable students. He was the brother-in-law of **Vaughan Williams.**

WORKS: Sym. (1935); Violin Concerto (1930); *Concerto piccolo* for 2 Violins and String Orch. (1930); *Fantasy* for String Quartet (1922); other chamber works; songs; folk-song arrangements.

WRITINGS (all publ. in London unless otherwise given): *Contrapuntal Technique in the 16th Century* (Oxford, 1922); *Foundations of Practical Harmony and Counterpoint* (1925); with H. Ferguson, *Preparatory Exercises in Score Reading* (1931); *Figured Harmony at the Keyboard* (1931); *The Structure of Music* (1935); *Introduction to Counterpoint* (1944); *Oxford Harmony* (1946).

BIBL.: W. Mellers, "The Music of R.O. M.," *Musical Opinion*, LXIV (1940–41); E. Rubbra, "R.O. M.: An Appreciation," *Music & Letters* (Jan. 1949).

Morris, Robert (Daniel), English-born American composer, teacher, and music theorist; b. Cheltenham, Oct. 19, 1943. He studied composition at the Eastman School of Music in Rochester, N.Y. (B.Mus., 1965), and at the Univ. of Michigan (M.Mus., 1966; D.M.A., 1969). He taught at the Univ. of Hawaii (1968–69); then was on the faculty of Yale Univ. (1969–77), where he was director of the electronic music studio (1972–77) and chairman of the composition dept. (1973–77). From 1976 to 1980 he served on the staff of the music dept. of the Univ. of Pittsburgh. In 1980 he joined the faculty at the Eastman School of Music. He publ. *Composition with Pitch-Classes: A Theory of Compositional Design* (New Haven, 1987).

WORKS: DRAMATIC: *Hagoromo* for Soprano, Bass, Men's Chorus, 2 Flutes, 3 Violins, String Bass, and Bells (1977); also incidental music. **ORCH.:** *Syzygy* (Ann Arbor, April 13, 1966); *Continua* (New Haven, Dec. 14, 1972); *Streams and Willows*, flute concerto (Pittsburgh, Nov. 12, 1974); *In Different Voices* for Symphonic Band (New Haven, Feb. 28, 1976); *Tapestries* for Chamber Orch. (1976); *Interiors* (Pittsburgh, March 7, 1978); *Cuts* for Large Wind Ensemble (1984; Rochester, N.Y., April 1, 1986); *Just Now and Again* (1987); *Clash* (Rochester, N.Y., May 25, 1988); *Piano in the Winds*, concerto for Piano and Wind Ensemble (1988). **CHAMBER:** *Sangita 67* for Flutes, Strings, and Percussion (1967); *Varnam* for 5 Melody Instruments and Percussion (1972); *Motet on Doo-Dah* for Alto Flute, Double Bass, and Piano (1973); *Not Lilacs* for Alto Saxophone, Trumpet, Piano, and Drums (1974); *Throughout (Anyway)* for 4 Flutes (1975); *The Dreamer Once Removed* for Carillon and 4 Trumpets (1976); String Quartet (1976); *3/4/5* for 3, 4, or 5 Players (1977); *Plexus* for Woodwind Quartet (1978); *Tigers and Lilies* for 12 Saxophones (1979); *Vira* for Tuba,

Flute, Crotales, and Gongs (1980); *Tournament* for 12 or 24 Trombones (1981); *2's Company* for 8 Instruments (1982); *Saraswati's Children* for Melody Instruments, Percussion, and Drone (1985); *Arci* for String Quartet (1988). **PIANO:** *Trip, Tusk, Night Vapors* (1967); *Cairn* (1969); *Phrases* (1970); *Bhayanaka* for Piano, 4-hands (1977); *Either Ether* (1978); *Allies* for Piano, 4-hands (1979); *Variations on a Theme of Steve Reich* (1980); *Diamond* (1982); *4 Voices in 3 Voices* (1983); *Alter Egos* (1985); *Twice* (1987). **VOCAL:** *Forgotten Vibrations* for Soprano and Chamber Ensemble (1967); . . . *Versus* . . . for 5 Altos, Chamber Ensemble, Jazz Ensemble, and Double Bass obbligato (1968); *Lorelei* for Soprano, Bass, Flutes, Cellos, and Piano, 4-hands (1970–71); *Q* for Chorus and Orch. (1976); *Haiku Cycle* for Soprano and Piano (1978); *Hamiltonian Cycle: Chorus* (1979); *4-fold Heart Sutra* for Baritone, Men's Chorus, Piano, and Vibraphone (1984); *Wang River Cycle* for Mezzosoprano and 8 Instruments (1985); *A Time* for Soprano and 8 Instruments (1987–88). **ELECTRONIC:** *Entelechy* for Voice, Cello, Piano, and Electronics (1969); *Phases* for 2 Pianos and Electronics (1970); . . . *Delay* . . . for String Trio and Tape (1971; rev. 1972); *Thunders of Spring over Distant Mountains* (1973); *Bob's Plain Bobs* for 4 Percussionists and Tape (1975); *Curtains* for Pipe Organ and Tape (1976); *Entelechy '77* for Piano and Electronics (1977); *Flux Mandala* for Tape (1977–78); *Shanti* for Clarinet and Tape (1979); *Ghost Dances* for Flutes and Tape (1980); *Aubade* for Tape (1981); *Exchanges* for Piano and Tape (1982); *Night Sky Scroll* for Tape (1984–85); *Amid Flock and Flume* for Flute and Tape (1986).

Morris, Wyn, Welsh conductor; b. Trlech, Feb. 14, 1929. He studied at the Royal Academy of Music in London and the Salzburg Mozarteum; then was apprentice conductor with the Yorkshire Sym. Orch. (1950–51) and conductor of an army band (1951–53). In 1954 he founded the Welsh Sym. Orch.; in 1957 he went to the U.S., where he led the Cleveland Chamber Orch. and other groups. In 1960 he returned to Great Britain; served as conductor of the choir of the Royal National Eisteddfod of Wales (1960–62), of the Royal Choral Soc. of London (1968–70), and of the Huddersfield Choral Soc. (1969–74); then organized the Symphonica of London, with which he gave regular concerts in ambitious programs, particularly of Mahler's music.

Morrison, Jim (James), psychedelic American rock musician; b. Melbourne, Fla., Dec. 8, 1943; d. Paris, July 3, 1971. He studied cinema at the Univ. of Calif., Los Angeles, where he met Ray Manzarek, who was pinch-hitting with a rhythm-and-blues band, Rick and the Ravens, and a jazz drummer, John Densmore. They organized a group called The Doors, in allusion to the doors of perception opening into the surreal worlds as revealed by Aldous Huxley's search for hallucinogenic substances. The Doors had morbid propensities and mixed sex with death in their songs; because of that chimera of intellectuality, The Doors were solemnly discussed on the pages of highbrow magazines. For some years they served as a house band at The Whiskey A Go-Go, a sleazy watering hole for psychedelic hippies on Los Angeles's Sunset Strip. Morrison acted out his exhibitionistic expressionism on the stage for the benefit of the receptive throng. The products of this period were such songs of altered states as *Light My Fire, Break On Through, Love Me 2 Times, People Are Strange, When the Music's Over, My Eyes Have Seen You,* and *The End.* Morrison's erotomania, stooping to such indecencies as dry-humping the microphone and explicit masturbatory gestures, finally led to a bust in Miami in 1969. He went into a decline, and his attempt to return to straight rock with sporadic releases such as *Touch Me, Love Her Madly, Roadhouse Blues, You Make Me Real,* and *L.A. Woman* were but partially successful. In trouble with authorities and besotted with alcohol, he went to Paris and died at age 27 of an apparent heart attack.

Morrison, Van (real name, **George Ivan**), Irish-American rock singer, guitarist, saxophonist, and songwriter; b. Belfast, Aug. 13, 1945. He taught himself to sing and play the guitar, harmonica, and saxophone; after dropping out of high school when he was 16, he set off with his rhythm-and-blues outfit, the Monarchs, for Germany; returning to Belfast, he put together the group called Them (1963), with which he began his recording career. After Them folded (1966), he went to the U.S.; produced the hit song *Brown-Eyed Girl* (1967), and that same year brought out his 1st solo album, *Blowin' Your Mind.* The album *Astral Weeks* (1968) established his expanded consciousness and galactic dreams; went on to record such successful albums as *Moondance* (1970), *Wavelength* (1978), *Into the Music* (1979), and *The Inarticulate Speech of the Heart* (1983).

Morse, Theodore, American music publisher and composer; b. Washington, D.C., April 13, 1873; d. N.Y., May 25, 1924. He settled in N.Y. when he was 14 and worked as a clerk in various publishing firms; after operating his own publishing concern (1898–1900), he worked for the firm of Howley, Haviland, & Dresser; after the firm dissolved (1905), he and Haviland ran their own company until 1910; Morse then operated independently until selling out to Leo Feist in 1915. He became best known as a composer of sentimental ballads, love songs, and novelty pieces; his most successful song was *M-O-T-H-E-R* (1915). His wife, **Alfreda Theodora Strandberg Morse** (b. Brooklyn, July 11, 1890; d. White Plains, N.Y., Nov. 10, 1953), wrote the texts to several of his songs.

Mortari, Virgilio, Italian composer and pianist; b. Passirana di Lainate, near Milan, Dec. 6, 1902. He studied at the Milan Cons. with Bossi and Pizzetti; completed his composition studies at the Parma Cons. (diploma, 1928); after appearances as a concert pianist, he became an instructor at the Cons. Benedetto Marcello in Venice (1933–40); in 1940 he was appointed prof. of music at the Accademia di Santa Cecilia in Rome, remaining at this post until 1973; in 1963 he became vice-president there. With Casella, he publ. *La tecnica dell'orchestra contemporanea* (Milan, 1947; 2nd ed., 1950). He completed Mozart's unfinished score *L'Oca del Cairo* (Salzburg, Aug. 22, 1936). His music combines the traits of the Italian Baroque and the modern French school of composition.

WORKS: OPERAS: *Secchi e Sberlecchi* (Udine, 1927); *La scuola delle moglie* (1930; rev. version, Milan, 1959); *La Figlia del diavolo* (Milan, March 24, 1954); *Il contratto* (Rome, 1964).
BALLETS: *L'allegra piazzetta* (Rome, 1945); *Specchio a tre luci* (Rome, 1973). ORCH.: *Fantasia* for Piano and Orch. (1933); *Notturno incantato* (1940); *Eleonora d'Arborea*, overture (1968); *Tripartita* (1972); also the following concertos: 2 piano concertos (1952, 1960); Viola Concerto (1966); Double-bass Concerto (1966); Violin Concerto (1967); Double Concerto for Violin and Piano (1968); Cello Concerto (1969); Harp Concerto (1972); also Concerto for String Quartet and Orch. (1937), Sonatina for Harp (1938), *Piccola serenata* for Cello (1946), *Piccola serenata* for Violin (1947), *Duettini concertati* for Violin and Double Bass (1966), *Capriccio* for Violin (1967); vocal works: 2 *Funeral Psalms* in memory of Casella for Voice and Instruments (1947); *Stabat Mater* (1947); *Requiem* (1959); *Alfabeto a sorpresa* for 3 Voices and 2 Pianos (1959); songs.

Mortelmans, Ivo (Oscar), Belgian conductor, teacher, and composer, son of **Lodewijk Mortelmans;** b. Antwerp, May 19, 1901; d. Ostend, Aug. 20, 1984. He studied at the Antwerp Cons.; upon graduation, taught academic subjects and music theory in Berchem (1925–66), Deurne (1939–70), and Mortsel (1946–67). He was active as an opera conductor. He wrote an oratorio, *Eeuwig vlecht de bruid haar kroon* (1964), and numerous other choral works, both sacred and secular.

Mortelmans, Lodewijk, Belgian conductor, teacher, and composer, father of **Ivo (Oscar) Mortelmans;** b. Antwerp, Feb. 5, 1868; d. there, June 24, 1952. He was a chorister in the Dominican Church; then studied with Benoit in Antwerp. In 1889 he won the 2nd Belgian Prix de Rome; gained 1st prize with his cantata *Lady Macbeth* in 1893; then taught at the Antwerp Cons. In 1921 he made a tour in the U.S.; was director of the Antwerp Cons. from 1924 to 1933. His finest

creations were his songs to Flemish texts, which prompted Gilson to call him the "Prince of the Flemish song."

WORKS: Opera, *De kinderen der Zee* (Antwerp, 1920); symphonic poems: *Helios* (1894); *Mythe du printemps* (1895); *Avonlied* (1928); *Weemoedig aandenken* (1942); *Eenvoud* (1950); also *Symphonie homérique* (1898); 4 elegies: *In memoriam* (1917), *Elevation du cœur* (1917), *Solitude* (1919), and *Treurdicht* (1925); also a church cantata, *Jong Vlaanderen* (1907); 3 sets of *Miniatures* for Piano; 27 *Old Flemish Folksongs* for Piano; a number of songs to Flemish texts.
BIBL.: J. Broeckx, *L. M.* (Antwerp, 1945).

Mortensen, Finn (Einar), Norwegian teacher and composer; b. Christiania, Jan. 6, 1922; d. there (Oslo), May 21, 1983. He studied harmony with Thorlief Eken (1942) and counterpoint with Klaus Egge (1943) in Oslo; received instruction in composition with Niels Viggo Bentzon in Copenhagen (1956). He taught theory at the Norwegian Correspondence School (1948–66); then composition at the Oslo Cons. (1970–73); subsequently was prof. of composition at the Oslo Musikkhøgskolan (from 1973); also served as chairman of the Norwegian Soc. of Composers (1972–74). In some compositions he adopted a modified 12-tone idiom, supplemented by the devices of permutation and thematic rotation.

WORKS: ORCH.: Sym. (1953; Bergen, Jan. 21, 1963); *Pezzo orchestrale* (1957); *Evolution* (1961); *Tone Colors* (1961); Piano Concerto (Oslo, Sept. 11, 1963); *Fantasia* for Piano and Orch. (Oslo, May 6, 1966); *Per orchestra* (Oslo, Nov. 27, 1967); *Hedda* (1974–75); *Fantasia* for Violin and Orch. (1977). CHAMBER: String Trio (1950); Wind Quintet (1951); Solo Flute Sonata (1953); Duo for Soprano and Violin (1956); Sonatina for Clarinet Solo (1957); Sonatina for Balalaika and Piano (1957); 5 *Studies* for Flute (1957); Sonatina for Solo Viola (1959); Oboe Sonatina (1959); *Fantasia* for Bassoon (1959); Violin Sonata (1959); Viola Sonatina (1959); Piano Quartet (1960); 3 *Pieces* for Violin and Piano (1961–63); *Constellations* for Accordion, Guitar, and Percussion (1971); *Neoserialism I* for Flute and Clarinet (1971), *II* for Flute, Clarinet, and Bassoon (1972), and *III* for Violin, Viola, and Cello (1973); *Suite* for Wind Quintet (1972); *Serenade* for Cello and Piano (1972); 3 *Pieces* for Accordion (1973); *Construction* for Horn (1974–75); *Adagio and Fugue* for 16 Horns (1976); Sonata for Oboe and Harpsichord (1976); *Fantasia* for Trombone (1977); *Suite* for 5 Recorders and String Quintet (1978–79); String Quartet (1981). PIANO: 2 sonatinas (1943, 1949); 2 sonatas (1956, 1977); *Fantasia and Fugue* (1957–58); 2-Piano Sonata (1964); *Drawing* (1966); *Impressions* for 2 Pianos (1971).

Mortensen, Otto (Jacob Hübertz), Danish pianist, teacher, and composer; b. Copenhagen, Aug. 18, 1907; d. Århus, Aug. 30, 1986. He studied with Christiansen (piano), Rung-Keller (organ), and Jeppeson (theory) at the Copenhagen Cons. (1925–29); made his debut as a pianist in Copenhagen (1930); continued his studies in Berlin (1930), with Milhaud and Desormière in Paris (1939), and at the Univ. of Copenhagen (M.A., 1956); taught at the Copenhagen Cons. (1942–66) and at the Univ. of Århus (1966–74). He wrote mostly vocal music, including many songs; also a Sym. (1956); Piano Concerto (1945); 2 string quartets (1937, 1955); Quartet for Flute, Violin, Cello, and Piano (1938); Wind Quintet (1944); Oboe Sonata (1947); piano pieces.

Morthenson, Jan W(ilhelm), Swedish composer; b. Örnsköldsvik, April 7, 1940. He studied composition with Mangs, Lidholm, and Metzger in Stockholm and esthetics at the Univ. of Uppsala; received instruction in electronic techniques from Koenig in Cologne and attended the new music courses in Darmstadt. He devised a "non-figurative" method in which "individual changes in sound are imperceptible"; publ. a treatise on the subject (Copenhagen, 1966).

WORKS: 4 pieces entitled *Coloratura: I* for Strings and Tape (1960), *II* for Orch. (1962), *III* for Chamber Orch. (1962–63), and *IV* for Orch. (1963); 3 *Wechselspiel: I* for Cello (1960), *II* for Flute and 3 Loudspeakers (1961), and *III* for Piano and Percussion (1961); *Canzona* for 6 Choral Groups, Percussion, and Loudspeakers (1961); *Chains-Mirrors*, electro-acoustical work for Soprano (1961); *Some of these . . .* , graphic music for Organ (1961); *Courante I, II, and III*, graphic music for Piano (1962); *Pour Madame Bovary* for Organ (1962); *3 Antiphonia: I* for Orch. (1963), *II* for Chamber Orch. (1963), and *III* for Chamber Orch. (1970); *Eternes* for Organ (1964); computer pieces: *Neutron Star* (1967), *Spoon River* (1967), *Ultra* (1971), and *Sensory Project I* and *II* (1971); electronic pieces: *Interferences* (1967), *Epsilon Eridani* (1967), *Iono-sphères* (1969), and *Zero* (1969); *Decadenza I* for Organ and Tape (1968); *Decadenza II* for Orch. with Tape and Film (1970; Uppsala, Jan. 18, 1972); *Colossus* for Orch. (1970; Berlin, Nov. 26, 1972); *Farewell* for Organ (1970); *Senza* for Strings (1970); *Labor* for Chamber Orch. (1971); *Life* for Tenor, Orch., and Instrumental Group (1972); *Video I* for 8 Solo Strings (1972); *Alla marcia* for Female Chorus, Orch., Tape, and 8 Strobo-scopes (1972–73; Stockholm, March 31, 1974); *5 Pieces* for Orch. (1973); *Soli* for Wind Quintet (1974); *Morendo* for Cho-rus, Orch., and Tape (Swedish Radio, Oct. 21, 1977); *Musica nera* for 9 Instruments, Tape, and Projection (1979); Organ Concerto (1981; Stockholm, Feb. 9, 1982); *Trauma*, radio opera (Swedish Radio, Aug. 30, 1981); *Energia I* for Symphonic Band (1984); *1984* for Orch. and Electronics (Swedish Radio, Sept. 21, 1984); *Materia* for Soprano, Chorus, Synthesizer, and Organ (1985); *Paraphonia* for Orch. (Stockholm, March 29, 1987); *Once* for Clarinet, Cello, and Piano (1988); *Silence XX* for Laser and Tape (1988).

Morton, "Jelly Roll" (Ferdinand Joseph Lemott, La-Mothe, or La Menthe), famous black American (actually, a "Creole-of-color," having mixed African and French-American ancestry) ragtime, blues, and jazz pianist and composer; b. New Orleans, Oct. 20, 1890; d. Los Angeles, July 10, 1941. Born into a French-speaking family that proudly recalled its former days of wealth and position, Morton grew up surrounded by musical instruments and frequently attended performances at the New Orleans French Opera House. He took up piano when he was 10 and began working in the bordellos of Storyville when he was 12; by the time he was 14, he was traveling throughout Louisiana, Mississippi, Alabama, and Florida while making New Orleans his main haunt; he was a colorful and flamboyant figure, given to extravagant boasting and flashy living; in addition to his being a musician, he was a professional gambler (cards and billiards), nightclub owner, and producer; he made and lost several fortunes. As a result of his travels, he assimiliated various black, white, and Hispanic musical idioms to produce a form of music akin to jazz. After performing in Los Angeles (1917–22), he went to Chicago, where he made his 1st solo recordings in 1923 of his own *New Orleans Blues* (1902), *Jelly Roll Blues* (1905), and *King Porter Stomp* (1906) and, with a sextet of his own, *Big Foot Ham* (1923); with his own New Orleans–style band, the Red Hot Peppers, he recorded *Grandpa's Spells* (1911), *The Pearls* (1919), and *Black Bottom Stomp* (1925). He went to N.Y. in 1928, but found himself outside the mainstream of jazz developments; later ran a jazz club in Washington, D.C., where he made infrequent appear-ances as a pianist; in 1938 Alan Lomax, the folklorist, recorded him for the Library of Congress, capturing him on disc playing piano, singing, relating anecdotes, and preserving his view of the history of jazz; the disc was issued in 1948. J. Dapogny ed. *The Collected Piano Music of Ferdinand "Jelly Roll" Morton* (Washington, D.C., 1982).

BIBL.: A. Lomax, *Mister Jelly Roll. The Fortunes of J.R. M., New Orleans Creole and "Inventor of Jazz"* (N.Y., 1950; 2nd ed., 1973); M. Williams, *J.R. M.* (London, 1962); J. Davis and I. Wright, *M.'s Music* (London, 1968); M. Hood and H. Flint, eds., *"J.R." M.: The Original Mr. Jazz* (N.Y., 1975); L. Wright, *Mr. Jelly Lord* (Chigwell, England, 1980); W. Balliett, *J.R., Jabbo and Fats* (N.Y., 1983); L. Gushee, "A Preliminary Chronology of the Early Career of Ferd 'J.R.' M.," *American Music*, III (1985).

Morton, Lawrence, American music critic, impresario, and musicologist, pioneer of modern music and friend to many famous contemporaries; b. Duluth, Minn., July 13, 1904; d. Santa Monica, Calif., May 8, 1987. He earned a living as a film theater organist in Chicago and N.Y. In 1937 he moved to Los Angeles, where he devoted himself mainly to music criticism. In 1954 he joined Peter Yates to organize the famous West Coast concert series Evenings on the Roof (later Monday Evening Concerts), which was devoted to the performance of modern music and lesser-known works from earlier repertoires. He championed Pierre Boulez, and, among lesser lights, Ingolf Dahl, in his programs, as well as Stravinsky, Copland, Schoen-berg, and other celebrated masters. The Lawrence Morton Fund was established in 1987 to facilitate the completion of his historical documentation of the above-named concert se-ries; his rich and extensive archives were donated to the Special Collections aspect of the Research Library at the Univ. of Calif. at Los Angeles.

Morton, Robert, English composer; b. c.1430; d. c.1476. He was a priest; served as clerc (1457–71 or –72) and chappellaine (1457–76) at the Burgundian court chapel choir. Only 8 of his secular works are extant; his songs *N'aray je jamais mieulx que j'ay* and *Le Souvenir de vous me tue* were widely dissemi-nated in his day. A modern ed. of his works was undertaken by A. Atlas (1982).

BIBL.: D. Fallows, *R. M.'s Songs: A Study of Styles in the Mid-Fifteenth Century* (diss., Univ. of Calif., Berkeley, 1978).

Mosca, Giuseppe, Italian composer, brother of **Luigi Mosca;** b. Naples, 1772; d. Messina, Sept. 14, 1839. He studied with Fenaroli at the Cons. of S. Maria di Loreto in Naples; was engaged as répétiteur at the Théâtre-Italien, Paris (1803–10); then was music director at the Teatro Carolino in Palermo (1817–20); later was director of music at a Messina theater (1827). He wrote 42 operas, ballets, and other stage pieces.

Mosca, Luigi, Italian composer, brother of **Giuseppe Mosca;** b. Naples, 1775; d. there, Nov. 30, 1824. He was a pupil of Fenaroli; served as maestro al cembalo at Naples's Teatro San Carlo and also primo maestro di canto at the Cons. (from 1813). He wrote 16 operas, of which *I Pretendenti delusi* (Milan, Sept. 7, 1811) was the most successful.

Moscheles, Ignaz, eminent Czech-born pianist, conductor, pedagogue, and composer; b. Prague, May 23, 1794; d. Leipzig, March 10, 1870. Of a well-to-do family (his father was a Jewish merchant), he was trained in music as soon as his ability was discovered; his 1st piano teacher was Dionys Weber at the Prague Cons. (1804–8); at the age of 14, he performed one of his own concertos at a public concert; then went to Vienna (1808), where he continued his studies with Albrechts-berger and Salieri and earned his living by teaching; his con-spicuous talents won him access to the best circles; a friend of Beethoven, he prepared the piano score of *Fidelio*. He then traveled throughout Europe as a virtuoso (from 1815), winning great applause in the leading music centers; he was a pioneer in developing various modifications of tone by touch, afterward exploited by Liszt. He made his London debut at a Phil. Soc. concert on June 11, 1821; settled in London in 1825 and be-came a teacher at the Royal Academy of Music; was also active as a conductor, serving as co-director of the Phil. Soc. (1832–41); likewise continued to appear as a pianist, and also founded an important series of historical concerts in which he played the works of Bach, Handel, and Scarlatti on the harpsichord. He gave Mendelssohn piano lessons in Berlin (1824); the teacher-pupil relationship between Moscheles and Mendels-sohn developed into a close friendship; the 2 gave the premiere of Mendelssohn's Concerto for 2 Pianos and Orch. in London (July 13, 1829); after founding the Leipzig Cons. (1842), Men-delssohn invited Moscheles to join its faculty (from 1846), where a host of pupils were trained by him with sympathetic consideration, and yet with unflinching discipline in musical matters. He was noted for his energetic, brilliant, and strongly rhythmic playing; his virtuosity equaled his emotional absorp-tion in the music; his romantic pieces for piano expressed clearly his ideas of the extent and the limitations of the instrument. Moscheles tr. Schindler's biography of Beethoven into English (with numerous additions), publ. as *The Life of Beethoven* (2 vols., London, 1841). His wife, **Charlotte** (née **Embden**) **Moscheles** (b. 1805; d. Detmold, Dec. 13, 1889), wrote *Aus Moscheles' Leben* (2 vols., Leipzig, 1872; Eng. tr., London, 1873). His correspondence with Mendelssohn was publ. by his son, F. Moscheles, in 1888, who also publ. his father's memoirs as *Fragments of an Autobiography* (London, 1899). His works include a Sym. (1829); 8 piano concertos (1819–38); other works for Piano and Orch.; several fine sonatas for Piano, including *Sonate mélancolique* (1814), Sonata in D major (1815?), *Grosse sonate* (1816), and *2 grandes sonates* for 4-hands (1816, 1845); many salon and didactic piano pieces; chamber music; songs. A thematic index was publ. in 1885 (reprint, London, 1967).

BIBL.: A. Coleridge, *Recent Music and Musicians as Described in the Diaries and Correspondence of I. M.* (1873; reprint, N.Y., 1970); G. Servières, "M.," *Revue Pleyel* (Dec. 1926); H. Engel, *Die Entwicklung des deutschen Klavierkonzertes von Mozart bis Liszt* (Leipzig, 1927); I. Heussner, *I. M. in seinen Klavier-Sonaten, -Kammermusikwerken, und -Konzerten* (diss., Univ. of Marburg, 1963); J. Roche, "I. M.," *Musical Times* (March 1970); E. Smidak, *Isaak-Ignaz M.: The Life of the Composer and His Encounters with Beethoven, Liszt, Chopin and Mendelssohn* (Aldershot, 1989).

Moscona, Nicola, Greek bass; b. Athens, Sept. 23, 1907; d. Philadelphia, Sept. 17, 1975. He studied at the Athens Cons. with Elena Teodorini. He sang opera in Greece and Eygpt; then was engaged to sing at the Metropolitan Opera in N.Y., and made a successful American debut there as Ramfis in *Aida* (Dec. 13, 1937); remained on its staff until 1962; then went to Philadelphia, where he taught at the Academy of Vocal Arts.

Mosel, Ignaz Franz von, Austrian composer, conductor, and writer on music; b. Vienna, April 1, 1772; d. there, April 8, 1844. He was the 1st conductor of the musical festivals given by Vienna's Gesellschaft der Musikfreunde at the imperial riding school (1812–16); he pioneered the use of the baton in Vienna; was vice-director of the 2 Court Theaters (1820–29); then was principal custos of the Imperial Library (1829–44); was ennobled and made a Hofrat.

WORKS: Operas (all 1st perf. at the Vienna Court Opera): *Die Feuerprobe,* singspiel (April 28, 1811); *Salem,* lyric tragedy (March 5, 1813); *Cyrus and Astyages,* heroic opera (June 13, 1818); much incidental music; instrumental pieces; masses; Psalms; cantatas; songs; arrangements.

WRITING (all publ. in Vienna): *Versuch einer Ästhetik des musikalischen Tonsatzes* (1813); *Über das Leben und die Werke des Anton Salieri* (1827); *Geschichte der k.k. Hofbibliothek in Wien* (1835); *Über die Original-Partitur des Requiems von W.A. Mozart* (1839).

BIBL.: R. Batka, "M.iana," *Musikbuch aus Österreich,* VII–IX (Vienna, 1911–12).

Moser, Andreas, noted German violin pedagogue and music scholar, father of **Hans Joachim Moser;** b. Semlin an der Donau, Nov. 29, 1859; d. Berlin, Oct. 7, 1925. He studied 1st in Zürich with Hegar; also took courses in engineering and architecture in Stuttgart; in 1878 he became a violin pupil of Joachim in Berlin; in 1883–84 he was concertmaster in Mannheim; in 1884 he settled in Berlin. In 1888 he was appointed a teacher at the Hochschule für Musik, a post he held until his death. He publ. valuable studies on the history of the violin.

WRITINGS: *Joseph Joachim, Ein Lebensbild* (Berlin, 1898; 5th ed., rev., 1910; Eng. tr. from 2nd Ger. ed., 1900); with Joachim, *Violinschule* (3 vols., Berlin, 1902–5; 2nd ed., rev., 1959, by M. Jacobsen); ed. *Johannes Brahms im Briefwechsel mit Joseph Joachim* (vols. V and VI of the complete Brahms correspondence, Berlin, 1908); ed. with Joachim, *Briefe von und an Joseph Joachim* (3 vols., Berlin, 1911–13); *Methodik des Violinspiels* (2 vols., Leipzig, 1920); *Geschichte des Violin-*

spiels (Berlin, 1923; 2nd ed., rev. and enl., 1966–67); *Technik des Violinspiels* (2 vols., Leipzig, 1925).

BIBL.: H.J. Moser, "A. M.," in A. Ebel, ed., *Berliner Musikjahrbuch* (Berlin and Leipzig, 1926).

Moser, Edda (Elisabeth), prominent German soprano, daughter of **Hans Joachim Moser;** b. Berlin, Oct. 27, 1938. She studied with Hermann Weissenborn and Gerty König at the Berlin Cons.; made her debut as Kate Pinkerton at the Berlin Städtische Oper (1962); after singing in the Würzburg Opera chorus (1962–63), she sang opera in Hagen and Bielefeld; subsequently appeared with the Frankfurt Opera (1968–71) before joining the Vienna State Opera; also sang in Berlin, Salzburg, Hamburg, etc. She made her U.S. debut as Wellgunde in *Das Rheingold* at the Metropolitan Opera in N.Y. on Nov. 22, 1968, and later appeared there as Donna Anna, the Queen of the Night, and Liù. She maintains an extensive repertoire, singing both coloratura and lyrico-dramatic roles, being equally successful in standard and contemporary works; has also sung widely as a concert artist.

Moser, Hans Joachim, eminent German musicologist, son of **Andreas** and father of **Edda (Elisabeth) Moser;** b. Berlin, May 25, 1889; d. there, Aug. 14, 1967. He studied violin with his father; then took courses in musicology with Kretzschmar and Wolf at the Univ. of Berlin, with Schiedermair at the Univ. of Marburg, and with Riemann and Schering at the Univ. of Leipzig; also studied voice with Oskar Noë and Felix Schmidt, and took courses in composition with H. van Eyken, Robert Kahn, and G. Jenner; he received his Ph.D. from the Univ. of Rostock in 1910 with the dissertation *Die Musikergenossenschaften im deutschen Mittelalter.* Returning to Berlin, he was active as a concert singer (bass-baritone); then served in the German army during World War I. He subsequently completed his Habilitation at the Univ. of Halle in 1919 with his *Das Streichinstrumentenspiel im Mittelalter* (publ. in A. Moser's *Geschichte des Violinspiels,* Berlin, 1923; 2nd ed., rev. and enl., 1966–67). In 1919 he joined the faculty of the Univ. of Halle as a Privatdozent of musicology, and then became a reader there in 1922; he then was a reader at the Univ. of Heidelberg from 1925 to 1927; he was honorary prof. at the Univ. of Berlin from 1927 to 1934, and also served as director of the State Academy for Church and School Music in Berlin from 1927 to 1933; he received the degree of doctor of theology at Königsberg in 1931. He retired from his public positions in 1934 but continued his musicological pursuits in Berlin; he later served as head of the Reichsstelle für Musik-Bearbeitungen from 1940 to 1945. After World War II, he resumed teaching by accepting appointments as a prof. at the Univ. of Jena and the Hochschule für Musik in Weimar in 1947; he then served as director of the Berlin Cons. from 1950 until 1960. Moser was an outstanding music historian and lexicographer; his numerous writings are notable for their erudition. However, his unquestionable scholarship was marred by his ardent espousal of the Nazi racial philosophy; so ferocious was his anti-Semitism that he excluded Mendelssohn from his books publ. during the 3rd Reich. He served as ed. of a projected complete edition of Weber's works (Augsburg and Leipzig, 1926–33), but it remains unfinished. Other works he ed. include *Luthers Lieder, Werke,* XXXV (Weimar, 1923; with O. Albrecht and H. Lucke); *Minnesang und Volkslied* (Leipzig, 1925; 2nd ed., enl., 1933); *Das Liederbuch des Arnt von Aich* (Kassel, 1930; with E. Bernoulli); *Das deutsche Sololied und die Ballade, Das Musikwerk,* XIV (1957; Eng. tr., 1958); *Heinrich Schütz: Italienische Madrigale, Neue Ausgabe sämtlicher Werke,* XXII (Kassel, 1962). He also contributed countless articles to various German music journals; likewise wrote novels, short stories, and a comedy. He also tried his hand at composing, producing the school opera *Der Reisekamerad,* choruses, and songs. He arranged operas by Handel and Weber; wrote an entirely new libretto for Weber's *Euryanthe* and produced it under the title *Die sieben Raben* (Berlin, March 5, 1915).

WRITINGS: *Technik der deutschen Gesangskunst* (Berlin,

1911; 3rd ed., 1955; with Oskar Noë); *Geschichte der deutschen Musik* (3 vols., Stuttgart and Berlin, 1920, 1922, and 1924; 2nd ed., enl., 1968); *Musikalisches Wörterbuch* (Leipzig and Berlin, 1923); *Paul Hofhaimer: Ein Lied- und Orgelmeister des deutschen Humanismus* (Stuttgart and Berlin, 1929; 2nd ed., enl., 1966); *Die Ballade* (Berlin, 1930); *Die Epochen der Musikgeschichte im Überblick* (Stuttgart and Berlin, 1930; 2nd ed., 1956); *Die mehrstimmige Vertonung des Evangeliums* (2 vols., Leipzig, 1931 and 1934); *Musiklexikon* (Berlin, 1932–35; 2nd ed., 1943, withdrawn; 3rd ed., 1951; 4th ed., 1955; supplement, 1963); *Corydon: das ist: Geschichte des mehrstimmigen Generalbass-Liedes und des Quodlibets im deutschen Barock* (2 vols., Braunschweig, 1933); *Die Melodien der Luther-Lieder* (Leipzig and Hamburg, 1935); *Johann Sebastian Bach* (Berlin, 1935; 2nd ed., 1943); *Tönende Volksaltertümer* (Berlin, 1935); *Heinrich Schütz: Sein Leben und Werk* (Kassel, 1936; 2nd ed., rev., 1954; Eng. tr., 1959); *Lehrbuch der Musikgeschichte* (Berlin, 1936; 13th ed., 1959); *Das deutsche Lied seit Mozart* (Berlin and Zürich, 1937; 2nd ed., rev., 1968); *Die Musikfibel* (Leipzig, 1937); *Kleine deutsche Musikgeschichte* (Stuttgart, 1938; 4th ed., 1955); *Allgemeine Musiklehr* (Berlin, 1940); *Christoph Willibald Gluck* (Stuttgart, 1940); *Kleines Heinrich-Schütz-Buch* (Kassel, 1940; Eng. tr., 1967); *Carl Maria von Weber* (Leipzig, 1941; 2nd ed., 1955); *George Friedrich Händel* (Kassel, 1941; 2nd ed., 1952); *Goethe und die Musik* (Leipzig, 1949); *Lebensvolle Musikerziehung* (Vienna, 1952); *Musikgeschichte in hundert Lebensbildern* (Stuttgart, 1952); *Die evangelische Kirchenmusik in Deutschland* (Berlin, 1953); *Musikästhetik* (Berlin, 1953); *Die Musikleistung der deutschen Stämme* (Vienna, 1954); *Die Tonsprachen des Abendlandes* (Berlin and Darmstadt, 1954); *Dietrich Buxtehude* (Berlin, 1957); *Musik in Zeit und Raum* (Berlin, 1960; collected essays); *Bachs Werke: Ein Führer für Musikfreunde* (Kassel, 1964); etc. **BIBL.:** *Festgabe für H.J. M.* (Kassel, 1954; with complete list of writings).

Moser, Rudolf, Swiss composer; b. Niederuzwyl, Jan. 7, 1892; d. in a fall while mountain climbing in Silvaplana, Aug. 20, 1960. He studied theology at Basel Univ. and musicology with Nef there; then studied at the Leipzig Cons. (1912–14) with Reger, Sitt, and Klengel; further with Huber in Basel and Lauber in Geneva. He became conductor of the Cathedral choir in Basel; was also active as a pedagogue. **WORKS:** *Die Fischerin,* singspiel after Goethe (1935); *Der Rattenfänger,* dance play (1950); Concerto Grosso for String Orch. (Basel, June 26, 1927); several suites for orch.; 3 violin concertos; Organ Concerto; Concerto for Violin, Viola, and Cello; Piano Concerto; Viola Concerto; 4 string quartets; Piano Trio; String Sextet; *Das Lied von der Sonne* for Soli, Chorus, Orch., and Organ; *Odes of Horace* for Baritone, Chorus, and Orch.; other vocal music; organ pieces. **BIBL.:** H. Buchli, *R. M.* (Zürich, 1964).

Mosewius, Johann Theodor, German conductor and musicologist; b. Königsberg, Sept. 25, 1788; d. Schaffhausen, Sept. 15, 1858. He began his career as an opera singer in Königsberg, and later in Breslau; was music director of the Königsberg Theater (1814–16); in 1827 he joined the faculty at the Univ. of Breslau; in 1832 he became music director there; in 1831, became director of the Academic Inst. for Church Music in Breslau. By establishing the Singakademie (1825) and giving competent performances of works by composers from Bach to Beethoven, he exercised a cultural influence on the musical life of Breslau. He also publ. articles on composers; of these, 2 were reprinted separately: *J.S. Bach in seinen Kirchencantaten und Choralgesängen* (1845) and *J.S. Bachs Matthäus-Passion* (1852). **BIBL.:** *Verzeichnis von Musikalien aus dem Nachlass des verstorbenen Herrn Dr. J.T. M.* (Breslau, n.d.).

Mosko, "Lucky" (Stephen L.), American composer and conductor; b. Denver, Dec. 7, 1947. He studied conducting and piano with Antonia Brico (1959–65), then entered Yale Univ. as a composition student of Donald Martino and a conducting student of Gustav Meier (B.A., 1969); also studied composition at the Calif. Inst. of the Arts with Mel Powell, Morton Subotnick, and Leonard Stein (M.F.A., 1972). He traveled on a Fulbright grant to Iceland to research folk and contemporary music (1974, 1978). He taught at the Calif. Inst. of the Arts (1970–90); was director of its conducting program (1976–82), conductor of its orch. (1980–82), and founder-director of its Twentieth Century Players (1974–87). He was composer-in-residence at the Aspen Music Festival (1986, 1987); joined the faculty at Harvard Univ. in 1990. Mosko was principal conductor of the San Francisco Contemporary Music Players (from 1987) and the Griffen Ensemble of Boston (from 1990); also was a guest conductor with the San Francisco Sym. (from 1983) and the Los Angeles Phil. (from 1985); was director of the Ojai Music Festival in 1990. Mosko is an important conductor of new music, giving 1st performances of works by Cage, Scelsi, Stockhausen, Xenakis, and others. His own compositions are peculiar, somewhat abstruse, and characterized by wide-ranging fragments of sound in delicately controlled timbral contexts. He is married to the flutist Dorothy Stone. **WORKS:** *Lovely Mansions* for Chamber Ensemble (1971); *Night of the Long Knives* for Soprano and Chamber Ensemble (1974); *3 Clerks in Niches* for Chamber Ensemble (1975); *Darling* for Contrabass (1976); *Rais Murad* for Cello and Piano (1978); *Cosmology of Easy Listening* for Percussion Trio (1979); *Indigenous Music I* for Chorus (1981) and *II* for Solo Instruments and Chamber Ensemble (1984); *Superluminal Connections I* for Chamber Orch. (1985) and *II: The Atu of Tahiti* for Voices and Orch. (1986); *The Road to Tiphareth* for Chamber Ensemble (1986); *for Morton Feldman* for Flute, Cello, and Piano (1987); *Schweres Loos* for Alto, Piccolo, Bass Clarinet, and Violin (1988); *A Garden of Time* for Orch. (1989).

Moskowa, Joseph Napoléon Ney, Prince de la, French statesman and composer; b. Paris, May 8, 1803; d. St.-Germain-en-Laye, July 25, 1857. He was the eldest son of Michel Ney, Duc d'Elchingen and Prince de la Moskowa; he revealed a talent for music as child; was made a member of the Chambre de Paris (1831), and later served as brigadier general under Napoleon III. With A. Adam, he organized the Société de Concerts de Musique Vocale, Religieuse et Classique (1843), which presented works of the Renaissance, Baroque, and Classical periods at his palace; the society publ. 11 vols. of these works as *Recueil des morceaux de musique ancienne.* He composed 2 comic operas, *Le Cent-Suisse* (Paris, June 7, 1840) and *Yvonne* (Paris, March 16, 1855); also some sacred music, including a Mass with Orch. (1831).

Mosolov, Alexander (Vasilievich), Russian composer; b. Kiev, Aug. 11, 1900; d. Moscow, July 12. 1973. He fought in the Civil War in Russia (1918–20); was wounded and decorated twice with the Order of the Red Banner for heroism. After the war, he studied composition with Glière in Kiev; then studied harmony and counterpoint with Glière, composition with Miaskovsky, and piano with Prokofiev and Igumnov at the Moscow Cons. (1922–25). He played his 1st Piano Concerto in Leningrad on Feb. 12, 1928. In his earliest works he adopted modernistic devices; wrote songs to texts of newspaper advertisements. His ballet *Zavod* (Iron Foundry; Moscow, Dec. 4, 1927) attracted attention because of the attempt to imitate the sound of a factory at work by shaking a large sheet of metal. However, Mosolov's attempt to produce "proletarian" music by such means elicited a sharp rebuke from the official arbiters of Soviet music. On Feb. 4, 1936, he was expelled from the Union of Soviet Composers for staging drunken brawls and behaving rudely to waiters in restaurants. He was sent to Turkestan to collect folk songs as a move toward his rehabilitation. After settling in Moscow in 1939, he continued to make excursions to collect folk songs in various regions of Russia. **WORKS: OPERAS:** *Geroy* (The Hero; 1927; Baden-Baden, July 15, 1928); *Plotina* (The Dam; Leningrad, 1929); *The Signal* (1941); *Maskarad* (Masquerade; 1940); also an anti-fascist musical comedy, *Friedrich Barbarossa.* **ORCH.:** 6 syms. (1928, 1932, 1937, 1942, 1947, 1950); 2 piano concertos (1927, 1932); 5 suites: No. 1, *Turkmenian* (1933); No. 2, *Uzbekian Dance*

(1935); No. 3, *Native Lands*, with Folk Instruments (1951); No. 4 (1955); No. 5, *Festive* (1955); Harp Concerto (Moscow, Nov. 18, 1939); Concerto (1943); Cello Concerto (1946); *Elegiac Poem* (1961). VOCAL: 4 oratorios, among them *M.I. Kalinin* (1940) and *Moscow* (1948); patriotic cantata, *Minin and Pozharsky; Kirghiz Rhapsody* for Mezzo-soprano, Chorus, and Orch. (1933); *Ukraine* for Soloist, Chorus, and Orch. (1942). CHAMBER: 2 string quartets (1926, 1942); Trio for Clarinet, Cello, and Piano (1926); Piano Trio (1927); Cello Sonata (1927); Viola Sonata (1928); *Dance Suite* for Piano Trio (1928); also 4 piano sonatas (1923, 1924, 1925, 1926); choruses; songs.

Mosonyi, Mihály (real name, **Michael Brand**), noted Hungarian composer; b. Boldogasszonyfalva, Sept. 4, 1814; d. Pest, Oct. 31, 1870. He learned to play wind instruments and the organ in childhood; went to Magyaróvár as a church officer when he was 15, and taught himself music by copying Hummel's piano exercises; proceeded to Pressburg (c.1832), where he studied piano and theory with Károly Turányi; after serving as a piano teacher in the household of Count Péter Pejachevich in Rétfalu (1835–42), during which time he honed his compositional skills through diligent study of Reicha's theoretical works, he settled in Pest as a teacher of piano and composition. He 1st attracted notice as a composer when his overture was premiered in April 1843. It was followed by his 1st Sym. and a Piano Concerto, the latter anticipating Liszt in the formulation of cyclic development. His 1st work to adopt Hungarian idioms was his 2nd Sym. (Pest, March 30, 1856). Liszt became his friend in 1856 and encouraged him in his work, proposing to produce his German Romantic opera *Kaiser Max auf der Martinswand* (1856–57); the score was never performed. Mosonyi's espousal of Hungarian nationalism led him to abandon his real name in 1859, adopting one that honored his birthplace, the county of Mosen. In his compositions, he gave increasing attention to Hungarian elements, producing his *Hódolat Kazinczy Ferenc szellemenek* (Homage to Kazinczy; 1860) for Piano (later orch.), a Hungarian rhapsody, and *Gyász hangok Széchenyi István halálára* (Funeral Music for Széchenyi; 1860) for Piano (later orch.), which employs the so-called Hungarian ostinato. His 2nd opera, *Szép Ilonka* (Pretty Helen), was premiered at the National Theater in Pest on Dec. 19, 1861, but made little impact. His last opera, *Álmos* (1862), was not performed in his lifetime; its 1st performance took place at Budapest's Royal Hungarian Opera on Dec. 6, 1934.

BIBL.: K. Ábrányi, *Mosonyi Mihály élet és jellemrajza* (M. M., His Biography and Character; Pest, 1872); J. Káldor, *Michael M.* (Dresden, 1936); F. Bónis, *Mosonyi Mihály* (Budapest, 1960); idem, ed., *Magyar zenetörténeti tanulmányok Mosonyi Mihály es Bartók Béla emlékér* (Studies on the History of Hungarian Music, in Memory of M. M. and Béla Bartók; Budapest, 1973).

Moss, David (Michael), American avant-garde percussionist and vocalist; b. N.Y., Jan. 21, 1949. He studied South Indian drumming with Tanjore Ranganathan (1970) and composition with Bill Dixon (1971–73); from 1972, toured Europe, Japan, Australia, and the U.S. as a soloist and leader of his own ensembles in more than 950 concerts; worked with David Van Tieghem, John King, John Zorn, and others. Moss has collaborated with numerous dance, visual, theater, and video artists; his recordings include *Terrain: Solo Percussion and Voice* (1980), *David Moss Dense Band 'Live' in Europe* (1988), and *The Day We Forgot* (1990); he also created and produced new music programs for radio (from 1981). Moss's solo performances combine a wide range of pitched and unpitched percussion, "found" objects, sound sculpture, and electronics with extended vocalizations.

WORKS: *Light no. 18* (1983); *Full House*, duets (1983); *King Lear*, incidental music (1983); *N.Y. Objects & Noise nos. 1 and 2* (1984); *Vox Box* (1984); *Mossmen* (1984); *Intimate Solos* (1985); *Light no. 20* (1985); *Operadio* (1986); *Slow Talking* (1987); *Slant Lines* (1987); *Operadio no. 2* (1987); *Conjuring Calvino* (1988); *Language Linkage nos. 1–3* (1988); *That Tempest* (1989); *After That Tempest* (1989); *Stolen Voice* (1990).

Moss, Lawrence (Kenneth), American composer and teacher; b. Los Angeles, Nov. 18, 1927. He studied at the Univ. of Calif. at Los Angeles (B.A., 1949), at the Eastman School of Music in Rochester, N.Y. (M.A., 1950), and with Leon Kirchner at the Univ. of Southern Calif. in Los Angeles (Ph.D., 1957); held a Fulbright scholarship (1953–54), 2 Guggenheim fellowships (1959–60; 1968–69), and 3 NEA grants (1975, 1977, 1980). He taught at Mills College (1956–59) and Yale Univ. (1960–68); then was a prof. and director of the composition dept. at the Univ. of Maryland at College Park (from 1969); in 1986 he was composer-in-residence at the Rockefeller Center in Bellagio, Italy. His style of composition tends toward polycentric tonality, with sporadic application of serial techniques and electronic sounds.

WORKS: DRAMATIC: OPERAS: *The Brute*, comic opera (1960; Norfolk, Conn., July 15, 1961); *The Queen and the Rebels* (1989). THEATER: *Unseen Leaves* for Soprano, Oboe, Tapes, Slides, and Lights (Washington, D.C., Oct. 20, 1975); *Nightscape* for Soprano, Flute, Clarinet, Violin, Percussion, Dancer, Tape, and Slides (1978); *Dreamscape* for Dancer, Tape, and Lights (1980); *Images* for Clarinet, Tape, and Dancer (1981); *Rites* for Tape, Slides, Lights, and Dancers (1983); *Song to the Floor* for Dancer and Tape (1984); *That Gong-Tormented Sea* for Tape and Dance (1985); *Lesbia's Sparrow* for Singer, Tape, and Dancer (1985); *Incidental Music* for Percussion and Mime/Dancer (1986); *Blackbird* for Clarinet, Mime/Dancer, and Tape (1987). ORCH.: *Suite* (1950); *Scenes* for Small Orch. (1961); *Paths* (1970); *Symphonies* for Brass Quintets and Chamber Orch. (1977); *Clouds* for Chamber Ensemble (1989). CHAMBER: 3 string quartets (1958, 1975, 1980); Violin Sonata (1959); *Music for 5* for Brass Quintet (1963); *Patterns* for Flute, Clarinet, Viola, and Piano (1967); *Auditions* for Woodwind Quintet and Tape (1971); *B.P.: A Melodrama* for Trombone, Piano, and Tape (1976); *Chanson* for Flute Choir (1979); *Aprèsludes* for Flute and Percussion (1983); *Music of Changes* for 7 Performers and Conductor (1986); *Various Birds* for Woodwind Quintet (1987); *Violaria, una dramma per musica* for Viola and Tape (1988); piano pieces. VOCAL: *A Song of Solomon* for Chorus and Piano (1956); *Song of Myself* for Baritone and Chamber Ensemble (1957); *Ariel* for Soprano and Orch. (1969); *Greetings in Close Harmony* for Vocal Quartet and 6 Instruments (1986); solo songs with various accompaniments.

Moss, Piotr, Polish composer; b. Bydgoszcz, May 13, 1949. He graduated from the State Academy of Music in Warsaw; became engaged mainly in composing music for radio, television, and films, in a mandatory semi-classical manner. However, he writes concert pieces in an adult and civilized style.

WORKS: Violin Concerto (1971); Wind Quintet (1971); *Per esempio*, music for 13 Performers (1972); String Quartet (1973); *Charon*, sym. (1973); Piano Concertino (1973); *Vowels* for 12 Voices and Instrumental Ensemble (1974); Piano Trio (1974); *Giorno* for 10 Performers (1975); Cello Concerto (1975); *Poem* for Cello and Orch. (1978); Concerto for Harpsichord and 2 String Orchs. (1980); Sonata for String Quartet (1982); *Incontri* for Orch. (1982; Paris, May 7, 1984); *Musique en trois mouvements* for Cello and Chamber Ensemble (Versailles, Nov. 17, 1983); *Abendmusik*, quartet for Oboe, Violin, Viola, and Cello (1985); *Mesto* for Wind Quartet, Organ, and Percussion (1986; Salzburg, May 27, 1987); *Elegy: Alexander Tansman in memoriam* for 2 Cellos (1986; also for Cello and String Orch., 1987).

Moszkowski, Moritz, famous German pianist, teacher, and composer of Polish descent; b. Breslau, Aug. 23, 1854; d. Paris, March 4, 1925. He studied at the Dresden Cons.; later at the Stern Cons. and at the Kullak Academy in Berlin; then became a teacher at the latter institution. He gave his 1st public concert in Berlin in 1873; then played elsewhere in Germany, and in Paris, where he established his reputation as a pianist; in 1897 he made Paris his headquarters. Among his notable pupils were Josef Hofmann, Wanda Landowska, Joaquín Nin, and Joaquín Turina. As a composer, he is most widely known by his pieces in the Spanish vein, particularly the 2 books of

Spanische Tänze for Piano Solo or Piano Duo; also popular were his études, concert waltzes, gavottes, *Skizzen*, a tarantella, a humoresque, etc. In larger forms he essayed an opera, *Boabdil, der letze Maurenkönig* (Berlin, April 21, 1892), which contains a ballet number that became popular; he also wrote a ballet, *Laurin* (1896); a symphonic poem, *Jeanne d'Arc; Phantastischer Zug* for Orch.; *Aus aller Herren Länder* for Orch.; Violin Concerto; Piano Concerto.

Moszumańska-Nazar, Krystyna, Polish composer; b. Lwow, Sept. 5, 1924. She studied composition with Wiechowicz and piano with Jan Hoffman at the State College of Music in Krakow (1948–55); in 1964 she was appointed to its faculty, serving as its rector (from 1987). In 1988 she received the award of the Polish Composers Union for her life's works and in 1989 received the Award of Merit of the Polish government. Her music is classical in its formal organization, but densely dissonant in harmony.

WORKS: ORCH.: Piano Concertino (1954); 2 overtures (1954, 1956); *Allegro symphonique* (1957); *4 Symphonic Essays* (1957); *Hexaèdre* (1960); *Music for Strings* (1961); *Exodus* for Orch. and Tape (1964); *Variazioni concertanti* for Flute and Chamber Orch. (1965–66); *Intonations* for 2 Choruses and Orch. (1968); *Pour orchestre* (1969; Poznan, March 29, 1973); *Polish Madonnas,* poem for Chorus and Orch. (1974; Krakow, April 23, 1976); *Challenge* for Baritone and Chamber Orch. (Poznan, April 28, 1977); *Rhapsody No. 2* (Krakow, Sept. 12, 1980); Sinfonietta for Chamber String Orch. (1983; Baranow, Sept. 10, 1986); *The Song of Songs* for Soprano, Reciting Voice, Reciting Chorus, and Chamber Ensemble (1984); Concerto (1985–86); *Fresco* (Krakow, Nov. 25, 1988). **CHAMBER:** 5 *Duets* for Flute and Clarinet (1959); *Interpretations* for Flute, Percussion, and Tape (1967); *Implications* for 2 Pianos and Percussion (1968); *Bel canto* for Soprano, Celesta, and Percussion (1972); String Quartet (1973–74); *From End to End Percussion* for Percussionist (1976; Berkeley, Calif., May 24, 1978); *Variants* for Piano and Percussion (1979; London, Feb. 5, 1980); String Quartet No. 2 (1980); *Canzona* for Violin (1988); Fantasy for Marimbaphone (1988); *Music for 5* for Percussion (Munich, Feb. 23, 1989).

Moten, Bennie (Benjamin), prominent black American jazz pianist and bandleader; b. Kansas City, Mo., Nov. 13, 1894; d. there, April 2, 1935. He studied baritone horn and piano; worked in local bands; then organized his own 5-piece group, which evolved into one of the major big bands of the late 1920s and early 1930s; he made many recordings and toured extensively.

Motta, José Vianna da. See **Vianna da Motta, José.**

Mottl, Felix (Josef), celebrated Austrian conductor; b. Unter-Sankt Veit, near Vienna, Aug. 24, 1856; d. Munich, July 2, 1911. After preliminary studies at a seminary, he entered the Vienna Cons. and studied with Door (piano), Bruckner (theory), Dessoff (composition), and Hellmesberger (conducting), graduating with high honors. In 1876 he acted as one of the assistants at the 1st Wagner festival at Bayreuth. In 1881 he succeeded Dessoff as court conductor at Karlsruhe; in 1893 he was appointed Generalmusikdirektor there. He conducted *Tristan und Isolde* at the Bayreuth Festival in 1886; led a Wagner concert in London in 1894; conducted the premiere of part I of Berlioz's *Les Troyens à Carthage, La Prise de Troie* (in German; Karlsruhe, 6, 1890). After conducting at London's Covent Garden (1898–1900), he made his Metropolitan Opera debut in N.Y. conducting *Die Walküre* on Nov. 25, 1903; engaged to conduct *Parsifal* there, he withdrew after protests from the Wagner family over copyright violations. In 1903 he became Generalmusikdirektor of the Munich Court Opera; was conductor of the Vienna Phil. (1904–7). His long intimate relationship with the soprano **Zdenka Fassbender** was legalized in marriage on his deathbed. He ed. vocal scores of the works of Wagner; wrote 4 operas: *Agnes Bernauer* (Weimar, 1880), *Graf Eberstein* (Karlsruhe, 1881), *Fürst und Sänger* (1893), and *Rama;* also a String Quartet; numerous songs. Among his arrangements,

that of Chabrier's *Bourrée fantasque* enjoys continued popularity in the concert hall.

Mottu, Alexandre, Swiss pianist, organist, teacher, and composer; b. Geneva, June 11, 1883; d. there, Nov. 24, 1943. He studied organ with Otto Barblan in Geneva and piano with Teresa Carreño in Berlin. He was appointed prof. of piano and organ at the Geneva Cons. in 1907. His works include various pieces for piano, violin, and organ, and much choral music.

Moulaert, Pierre, Belgian composer and teacher, son of **Raymond (Auguste Marie) Moulaert;** b. Brussels, Sept. 24, 1907; d. there, Nov. 13, 1967. He studied at the Royal Cons. in Brussels with his father and Joseph Jongen, and taught there from 1937 until his death. He was not a prolific composer, and wrote mostly in small forms, but his music has a distinctive quality of fine craftsmanship.

WORKS: *Passepied en Rondo* for Wind Quintet (1940); Concertino for Flute, Oboe, and Strings (1954); String Quartet (1956); *Sérénade* for Orch. (1956); *Petite musique concertante* for Orch. (1961); *Introduction et Fugue* for Flute, Oboe, Clarinet, Bassoon, and Strings (Uccle, March 7, 1963); *Séquences* for Orch. (1964).

Moulaert, Raymond (Auguste Marie), Belgian pianist, teacher, and composer, father of **Pierre Moulaert;** b. Brussels, Feb. 4, 1875; d. there, Jan. 18, 1962. He studied at the Brussels Cons. with Arthur de Greef (piano) and Edgar Tinel (theory); then was appointed to its staff and taught composition (from 1927); concurrently was director of his own music school in St.-Gilles (1913–38); also lectured at the Queen Elizabeth Chapel of Music in Brussels.

WORKS: *Theme and Variations* for Trumpet and Orch. (1910); *Appels pour un tournoi de chevalerie* for Wind Orch. (1923); *Passacaglia* for Orch. (1931); *Symphonie de valses* (1936); Trumpet Concertino (1937); Piano Concerto (1938); *Rhapsodie écossaise* for Clarinet and Orch. (1940); *Tango-caprice* for Saxophone and Orch. (1942); *Études symphoniques* (1943); *Symphonie de fugues* (1942–44); *Eroica* for Horn and Chamber Orch. (1946); *Légende* for Flute and Orch. (1951); *Variations symphoniques* (1952); Sinfonietta for Strings (1955; lost); *Andante* for 4 Horns (1903); *Andante, Fugue et Final* for 4 Saxophones (1907); Sextet for Wind Quintet and Piano (1925); *Passacaglia* for Double Bass (1928); *Études rythmiques* for Percussion (1929); *Divertimento* for String Trio (1936); *Choral varié* for 4 Cellos (1937); *Suite* for 3 Trombones (1939); *Sonata en forme de passacaille* for Cello and Piano (1942); *Concert* for Wind Quintet and Harp (1950); *Bagatelles* for 2 Violins (1960); organ works, including Sonata (1907), 2 *Pieces* (1910), 3 *poèmes bibliques* (1916–20), 2 *Fugues* (1929), and *Prelude et Choral* (1948); piano works, including Sonata (1917), *Toccata* (1938), *Ciels* (1938), and *Études-paraphrases,* after Paganini (1948); 5 sets of *Poèmes de la Vieille France* for variable vocal groups (1917–43); *L'Eau passe,* song cycle for Solo Voice.

Mount-Edgcumbe, Richard, 2nd Earl of, English nobleman and amateur musician; b. Plymouth, Sept. 13, 1764; d. Richmond, Surrey, Sept. 26, 1839. He was the (anonymous) author of the book *Musical Reminiscences, containing an Account of the Italian Opera in England from 1773* (1824; 4th ed., 1834). He also wrote an opera, *Zenobia* (in Italian), which was produced in London on May 22, 1800.

Mouquet, Jules, French composer; b. Paris, July 10, 1867; d. there, Oct. 25, 1946. He studied at the Paris Cons. with Leroux (harmony) and Dubois (composition); won the 1st Prix de Rome in 1896 with his cantata *Mélusine,* the Prix Trémont in 1905, and the Prix Chartier (for chamber music) in 1907; in 1913 he became prof. of harmony at the Paris Cons.

WORKS: 2 oratorios: *Le Sacrifice d'Isaac* and *Le Jugement dernier;* 2 symphonic poems: *Diane et Endymion* and *Persée et Andromède; Danse grecque* for Orch.; *Divertissement grec* for Flute and Harp; Sonata for Flute and Piano; pieces for oboe and piano, bassoon and piano, saxophone and piano, etc.; Septet for Wind Instruments; *Études antiques* for Piano.

Mouret, Jean-Joseph, noted French composer; b. Avignon, April 11, 1682; d. Charenton, Dec. 20, 1738. He is believed to have received his musical training at the Notre Dame des Doms choir school in Avignon. After settling in Paris (1707), he became maître de musique to the Marshal of Noailles; within a year or so, he was made surintendant de la musique at the Sceaux court. He was director of the Paris Opéra orch. (1714–18); became composer-director at the New Italian Theater (1717), remaining there for 2 decades; was also made an ordinaire du Roy as a singer in the king's chamber (1720), and served as artistic director of the Concert Spirituel (1728–34), where he brought out many of his cantatas, motets, and cantatilles. In 1718 he was granted a royal privilege to publ. his own music. Stricken with a mental disorder in 1737, he was placed in the care of the Fathers of Charity in Charenton in 1738. Among his most successful works were the opéra-ballet *Les Fêtes ou Le Triomphe de Thalie* (Paris, Aug. 14, 1714), the comédie lyrique *Le Mariage de Ragonde et de Colin ou La Veillée de village* (Sceaux, Dec. 1714), various divertissements for the Italian Theater, and the *Suites de simphonies* (c.1729; ed. by M. Sanvoisin, Paris, 1970).

BIBL.: A. Pougin, "M.," *Revue et Gazette Musicale de Paris,* XXVI (1859) and XXVII (1860); R. Viollier, "Les Symphonies de J.-J. M.," *Revue de Musicologie,* XVII (1936); idem, "Les Divertissements de J.-J. M. pour la 'Comédie Italienne' à Paris," ibid., XX (1939); C. le Gras, "J.-J. M., 'le musicien des grâces,'" *Mémoires de l'Académie de Vaucluse,* 3rd series, III (Avignon, 1939); R. Viollier, *J.-J. M., le musicien des grâces* (Paris, 1950); M. Barthélemy, "Les Divertissements de J.-J. M. pour les comédies de Dancourt," *Revue Belge de Musicologie,* VII (1953).

Moussorgsky, Modest (Petrovich). See **Mussorgsky, Modest (Petrovich).**

Mouton, Jean, important French composer; b. Holluigue, near Samer, c.1459; d. St. Quentin, Oct. 30, 1522. In 1477 he became a singer and teacher of religion (écolâtre-chantre) at the collegiate church of Notre Dame in Nesle. He became maître de chapelle in Nesle in 1483, and also entered the priesthood. In 1500 he was in charge of the choirboys at the Cathedral of Amiens. In 1501 he was director of music at the collegiate church of St. André in Grenoble, but left his position without permission in 1502. He subsequently entered the service of Queen Anne; later served Louis XII and François I. He was made canon in absentia at St. André in Grenoble, which conferred a benefice on him in 1510, and later was elected a canon at St. Quentin. Pope Leo X made him an apostolic notary. He was the teacher of Adrian Willaert. In his music he followed the precepts of Josquin Des Prez; he particularly excelled in the art of the canon. He composed more than 100 motets, some 15 masses, and over 20 chansons. About 50 of his works were publ. in his lifetime; several collections were publ. posthumously. His *Opera omnia,* ed. by A. Minor, began publication in 1967 in the Corpus Mensurabilis Musicae series of the American Inst. of Musicology.

BIBL.: J. Delporte, "L'École polyphonique franco-flamande: J. M.," *Revue Liturgique et Musicale,* XVI/3 (1932), XVII/4 (1933), XVIII/6 (1934), and XIX/2 (1935); idem, "Nouveaux documents sur J. M.," *Musique et Liturgie,* XXI (1937); F. Lesure, "Un Document sur la jeunesse de J. M.," *Revue Belge de Musicologie,* V (1951); A. Minor, *The Masses of J. M.* (diss., Univ. of Michigan, 1951); R. Dammann, *Studien zu den Motetten von J. M.* (diss., Univ. of Freiburg, 1952); J. Shine, *The Motets of J. M.* (diss., N.Y. Univ., 1953); P. Kast, *Studien zu den Messen des J. M.* (diss., Univ. of Frankfurt, 1955); idem, "Zu Biographie und Werk J. M.s," *Kongressbericht: Wien Mozartjahr 1956;* L. Lockwood, "J. M. and Jean Michel: New Evidence on French Music and Musicians in Italy, 1505–1520," *Journal of the American Musicological Society,* XXXII (1979).

Moyse, Louis, French-American flutist, pianist, and composer, son of **Marcel (Joseph) Moyse;** b. Scheveningen, the Netherlands, July 14, 1912. He was taken to Paris as an infant; learned to play the piano and flute at home; later took private piano lessons with Isidore Philipp (1925–27); in 1930 he entered the Paris Cons., where he studied flute with Philippe Gaubert and composition with Eugène Bigot; he graduated in 1932 with the premier prix in flute; then was his father's teaching assistant at the Paris Cons., and filled in with various jobs playing at movie theaters and restaurants. He served in the French army during World War II; after the war, he organized the Moyse Trio, with his father as flutist, his wife, Blanche Honegger-Moyse, as violinist, and himself as pianist. In 1948 he went with his wife to the U.S.; became an American citizen in 1959; was active at the Marlboro (Vt.) Music Festival (from 1950); was prof. of flute and chamber music at the Univ. of Toronto (from 1975).

WORKS: *Suite* for 2 Flutes and Viola (1957); *4 Dances* for Flute and Violin (1958); Woodwind Quintet (1961); *Divertimento* for Double Woodwind Quintet, 2 Cellos, Double Bass, and Timpani (1961); *4 Pieces* for 3 Flutes and Piano (1965); *3 Pieces* for Flute and Guitar (1968); *Marlborian Concerto* for Flute, English Horn, and Orch. (1969); *A Ballad for Vermont* for Narrator, Soloists, Chorus, and Orch. (1971–72); Flute Sonata (1975); *Serenade* for Piccolo, 4 Flutes, Alto Flute, Bass Flute, and Piano (1977); several collections of didactic flute pieces; various arrangements for flute and instrumental groups of works by Bach, Handel, Telemann, Mozart, Beethoven, and Weber.

Moyse, Marcel (Joseph), celebrated French flutist and pedagogue, father of **Louis Moyse;** b. Saint-Amour, Jura, May 17, 1889; d. Brattleboro, Vt., Nov. 1, 1984. He studied flute with Taffanel at the Paris Cons. (premier prix, 1906); then was solo flutist in several Paris orchs. (Lamoureux, Cologne, Pasdeloup, etc.). In 1932 he succeeded Philippe Gaubert as prof. of flute at the Paris Cons. In 1949 he went to the U.S.; in 1950 he organized, with his son, Rudolf Serkin, Adolf Busch, and Hermann Busch, the Marlboro School and Festival of Music in Brattleboro, Vt.; also conducted master classes in flute and chamber music in Switzerland; gave similar courses in Japan in 1973. At the age of 92 he conducted an instrumental ensemble in the music of Mozart and Dvořák, on Aug. 11, 1981, in N.Y. He publ. a series of excellent flute studies; also wrote 50 variations on the Allemande from Bach's Flute Sonata in A minor and compiled a manual for flute, *Tone Developement through Interpretation.*

Moyzes, Alexander, Slovak composer and teacher, son of **Mikuláš Moyzes;** b. Kláštor pod Znievom, Sept. 4, 1906; d. Bratislava, Nov. 20, 1984. He studied conducting with Ostrčil, composition with Karel and Šín, and organ with Wiedermann at the Prague Cons. (1925–28); then studied in Novák's master class there (1929–30). Upon graduation from the Cons. in 1928, he taught at the Bratislava Academy of Music and Drama (from 1929); was chief music adviser to the Bratislava Radio and a prof. at the Bratislava Cons. (from 1941); became a prof. of composition at the Bratislava College of Musical Arts (1949), serving as its rector (1965–71). He won the State Prize (1956) and was made an Artist of Merit (1961) and a National Artist (1966). His music uses the melodic resources of Slovak folk songs; his Sym. No. 1 is the 1st national Slovak sym.

WORKS: OPERA: *Udatný kráľ* (The Brave King; 1966; Bratislava, 1967). **ORCH.:** 12 syms.: No. 1 (Bratislava, Feb. 11, 1929); No. 2 (1932; rev. 1941); No. 3 (1942; orch. version of the Wind Quintet); No. 4 (1939–47); No. 5 (1948); No. 6 (1951); No. 7 (Bratislava, Oct. 23, 1955); No. 8 (1968); No. 9 (1971); No. 10 (1978); No. 11 (1978); No. 12 (1983); *Symphonic Overture* (1929); Concertino (1933); *Jánošík's Rebels* (1933); *Nikola Šuhaj,* overture (1933); *Down the River Váh,* symphonic suite (1936; rev. 1945); *Dances from the Hron Region* (1950); *February Overture* (1952); *Dances from Gemer,* suite (1955); Violin Concerto (1958); *Sonatina giocosa* for Violin, Chamber String Orch., and Harpsichord (1962); Flute Concerto (1966); *Keeper of the House,* overture (1972); *Bonfires on the Mountains,* symphonic suite (1973); *Musica istropoli-*

tana for Chamber String Orch. (1974); *Music to Woman*, symphonic study (1975; Bratislava, May 13, 1976); *The Tale about Jánošik*, rhapsodic suite (1976). VOCAL: Cantatas: *Svätopluk* (1935); *Znejú piesne na chotari* (Songs Resound in the Meadows; 1948); 2 song cycles: *Jeseň* (In Autumn) for Mezzo-soprano and Orch. or Piano (1960) and *Morning Dew* for Mezzo-soprano and Orch. or Piano (1963). CHAMBER: 4 string quartets (1928, 1969, 1981, 1983); Wind Quintet (1933); *Poetic Suite* for Violin and Piano (1948); *Duetta* for Violin and Piano (1960); *Small Suite* for Violin and Piano (1968); Sonatina for Flute and Guitar (1975); *Divertimento* for Piano (1929); *Jazz Sonata* for 2 Pianos (1932); Piano Sonata (1942).

BIBL.: L. Burlas, *A. M.* (Bratislava, 1956).

Moyzes, Mikuláš, Slovak composer and teacher, father of **Alexander Moyzes;** b. Zvolenská, Slatina, Dec. 6, 1872; d. Prešov, April 2, 1944. He was a non-resident student at the Budapest Academy of Music; then was a music teacher and organist in various Slovak towns; settled in Prešov as a teacher (1908). He was a leading figure in the development of Slovak national music.

WORKS: MELODRAMAS: *Siroty* (Orphans; 1921); *Lesná panna* (Maid of the Woods; 1922); *Čertova rieka* (The Devil's River; 1940). ORCH.: 2 suites (1931, 1935); *Malá vrchovská symfónia* (Little Highland Sym.; 1937); *Naše Slovensko* (Our Slovakia), festival overture (1938); choral works, including *Missa solemnis* (1906) and a *Mass* (1929); 4 string quartets (1926, 1929, 1932, 1943); Wind Sextet (1934); organ pieces; songs; didactic works; folk-song arrangements.

BIBL.: Z. Bokesová, *Sedemdesiatročný M. M.* (M. M. at 70; Bratislava, 1942).

Mozart, Franz Xaver Wolfgang, Austrian pianist and composer, son of **Wolfgang Amadeus Mozart** and often called by his father's name; b. Vienna, July 26, 1791; d. Carlsbad, July 29, 1844. He studied piano with F. Niemetschek in Prague while living with the Dušek family; continued his training with S. Neukomm, Andreas Steicher, Hummel, Salieri, G. Vogler, and Albrechtsberger in Vienna. After a period as a teacher in Lemberg and environs (1807–19), he embarked upon a major tour of Europe as a pianist (1819–21); then returned to Lemberg as a teacher (1822), receiving additional instruction in counterpoint from Johann Mederitsch or Gallus (1826); that same year he organized the Lemberg Cäcilien-Chor. He settled in Vienna (1838); was named honorary Kapellmeister of the Dom-Musik-Verein and the Mozarteum in Salzburg (1841); was made maestro compositore onorario of Rome's Congregazione ed Accademica Santa Cecilia (1842). As a composer, he revealed a gift for pianistic writing.

WORKS: ORCH.: 2 piano concertos: C major, op. 14 (publ. in Leipzig, 1809; ed. by R. Angermüller, Salzburg, 1972), and E-flat major, op. 25 (publ. in Leipzig, 1818); *Konzertvariationen* for Piano and Orch. (1820); Sinfonia in D major; 12 Minuets and Trios (1808). CHAMBER: Piano Quintet, op. 1 (1802; ed. in *Diletto musicale*, no. 180, Vienna, 1966); *Sei piccoli pezzi* for Flute and 2 Horns, op. 11 (1808); 2 violin sonatas: B-flat major, op. 7 (1808), and F major, op. 15 (1813); *Grande Sonate* in E major for Violin or Cello, and Piano, op. 19 (1820; ed. by W. Boettcher for Cello, Mainz, 1969); *Rondo (Sonate)* for Flute and Piano (ed. by R. Ermeler, Wilhelmshaven, 1962). PIANO: Sonata, op. 10 (1808); 12 Polonaises, op. 17 (c.1815), op. 22 (1820), and op. 26 (c.1821); 11 sets of variations; also 4 cantatas, including 1 for Haydn's birthday (1805; not extant); several unaccompanied choral pieces; songs.

BIBL.: A Fuchs, "Biographische Skizze von W.A. M. (dem Sohne)," *Allgemeine Wiener Musik-Zeitung*, IV/11 (1844); idem, "Gedächtnisfeier am Sterbetag W.A. M.s des Sohnes," ibid., V/107 (1845); idem, "W.A. M.'s (des Sohnes) Vermächtnis an das Mozarteum in Salzburg," ibid., V/6 (1845); A. Schmid, "W.A. M. (Sohn)," *Denksteine* (Vienna, 1848); J. Fischer, *W.A. M. (Sohn): Eine biographische Skizze, sowie zwei bisher unbekannte Briefe Mozart's (Vater)* (Carlsbad, c.1888); O. Deutsch, "Der Sohn: Eine Studie über W.A. M. den Jüngeren mit neuen Mitteilungen," *Musica Divina*, II (1914); K. Geiringer, "W.A.

M. the Younger," *Musical Quarterly* (Oct. 1941); A. van der Linden, "Lettres de W.A. M. junior," *Revue Belge de Musicologie*, V (1951); W. Hummel, "W.A. M.s Söhne: Quellen und Schrifttum zur Darstellung ihrer Lebensbilder," *Mozart-Jahrbuch 1954*; idem, *W.A. M.s Söhne* (Kassel and Basel, 1956); A. van der Linden, "Le Dernier Fils de W.A. M.," *Bulletin de la Classe des Beaux-arts de l'Académie Royale de Belgique*, I (1968).

Mozart, (Johann Georg) Leopold, German-born Austrian composer, violinist, and music theorist, father of **Wolfgang Amadeus** and **Maria Anna Mozart;** b. Augsburg, Nov. 14, 1719; d. Salzburg, May 28, 1787. A bookbinder's son, he studied at the Augsburg Gymnasium (1727–35); continued his studies at the Lyceum attached to the Jesuit school of St. Salvator (1735–36). In 1737 he went to Salzburg, where he studied philosophy and law at the Benedictine Univ.; he received his bachelor of philosophy degree in 1738. Subsequently he entered the service of Johann Baptist, Count of Thurn-Valsassina and Taxis, the Salzburg canon and president of the consistory, as both valet and musician. In 1743 he became 4th violinist in the Prince-Archbishop's Court Orch.; also taught violin and keyboard to the choirboys of the Cathedral oratory. In 1757 he became composer to the court and chamber; in 1758 he was promoted to 2nd violinist in the Court Orch.; in 1762 he was appointed Vice-Kapellmeister. He married Anna Maria Pertl of Salzburg on Nov. 21, 1747; of their 7 children, only Maria Anna and Wolfgang survived infancy. He dedicated himself to the musical education of his children, but his methods of presentation of their concerts at times approached frank exploitation, and his advertisements of their appearances were in poor taste. However, there is no denying his great role in fostering his son's career. Leopold was a thoroughly competent composer; the mutual influence between father and son was such that works long attributed to his son proved to be his. He was also important as a music theorist. He produced an influential violin method in his *Versuch einer gründlichen Violinschule* (Augsburg, 1756; 2nd ed., rev., 1769–70; 3rd ed., enl., 1787; facsimile of 1756 ed., Vienna, 1922; also various trs., including one in Eng., London, 1939; 2nd ed., 1951). His *Nannerl-Notenbuch* is a model of a child's music album; it was publ. in 1759; ed. in part by E. Valentin (Munich, 1956; 2nd ed., 1969). M. Seiffert ed. *Leopold Mozart: Ausgewählte Werke* in Denkmäler der Tonkunst in Bayern, XVII, Jg. IX/2 (Leipzig, 1908). His vocal works include sacred cantatas, masses, litanies, school dramas, and secular lieder. He also composed syms.; the famous *Kindersinfonie*, long attributed to Haydn, was in all probability a work by Leopold. On this, see E.F. Schmid, "Leopold Mozart und die Kindersinfonie," *Mozart Jahrbuch 1951*, and R. Münster, "Wer ist der Komponist der 'Kindersinfonie'?," *Acta Mozartiana*, XVI (1969). Other orch. works include several concertos, among them *Die musikalische Schlittenfahrt* (1755); dances; etc. He also composed chamber music and works for the keyboard.

BIBL.: CORRESPONDENCE AND NOTEBOOKS: H. Abert, "L. M.s Notenbuch von 1762," *Gluck-Jahrbuch*, III (1917); A. Schurig, *L. M.s Reiseaufzeichnungen, 1763–1771* (facsimile ed.; Dresden, 1920); O.E. Deutsch and B. Paumgartner, *L. M.s Briefe an seine Tochter* (Salzburg and Leipzig, 1936); E. Anderson, ed. and tr., *Letters of M. and His Family* (3 vols., London and N.Y., 1938; 2nd ed., rev. by A. Hyatt King and M. Carolan, 1966; 3rd ed., rev. by S. Sadie and F. Smart, 1985); E. Müller von Asow, "L. M.s Münchener Reise 1786," *Musikerziehung*, VIII (1954–55); A. Kozár, *Wolfgang Amadeus M. (1756–1791) im Spiegel der Briefe seines Vaters L. M.: Ein Beitrag zur Kulturgeschichte des 18. Jahrhunderts* (diss., Univ. of Graz, 1955); E. Müller von Asow, "Zu L. M.s Wiener Reise 1785," *Musikerziehung*, IX (1955–56); H. Klein, "Unbekannte M.iana von 1766/67," *Mozart Jahrbuch 1957*; D.-R. de Lerma, "The Nannerl Notebook," *Music Review*, XIX (1958); W. Bauer, O.E. Deutsch, and J. Eibl, eds., *M.: Briefe und Aufzeichnungen* (contains letters, notebooks, etc., relating to Leopold; 7 vols., Kassel, 1962–75); W. Plath, "L. M.s Notenbuch für Wolfgang (1762):

Eine Fälschung?," *Mozart Jahrbuch 1971–72* (concerning a spurious notebook).

BIOGRAPHICAL, CRITICAL, ANALYTICAL, ETC.: M. Friedlaender, "L. M.s Klaviersonaten," *Die Musik*, IV/1 (1904); W. Renz, "L. M. als Komponist," ibid., IV/4 (1905); G. Schünemann, "L. M. als Komponist," *Allgemeine Musik-Zeitung*, XXVI (1909); A. Moser, *Geschichte des Violinspiels* (Berlin, 1923; 2nd ed., rev. and enl., 1966–67); K. Gerhartz, "Die Violinschule von L. M. (1756)," *Mozart-Jahrbuch*, III (1929); O.E. Deutsch, "Vater M.s Ende," *National-Zeitung Basel: Sonderausgabe* (May 30, 1937); F. Posch, "L. M. als Mensch, Vater und Erzieher der Aufklärung," *Neues Mozart-Jahrbuch*, I (1941); E. Theiss, *Die Instrumentalwerke L. M.s nebst einer Biographie* (diss., Univ. of Giessen, 1942); E. Schmid, "L. M.," *Lebensbilder aus dem Bayerischen Schwaben*, III (Munich, 1954); idem, "L. M.: Vater und Mentor," *Österreichische Musikzeitschrift*, XI (1956); idem, "Neues zu L. M.s Bildungsgang," *Acta Mozartiana*, III/1 (1956); W. Egk, "Anmerkungen zur Violinschule von L. M.," *Gestalt und Gedanke*, IV (1957); W. Plath, "Beiträge zu M.-Autographie, I: Die Handschrift L. M.s," *Mozart Jahrbuch 1960–61*; J. Kay, *Mein Sohn Wolfgang Amadeus: Glück und Tragik des Vaters L. M.* (Vienna, 1965); W. Lievense, *De familie M. in Nederland: Een reisverslag* (Hilversum, 1965); R. Münster, "Neues zu L. M.s Augsburger Gymnasialjahren," *Acta Mozartiana*, XII (1965); L. Staehelin, *Die Reise der Familie M. durch die Schweiz* (Bern, 1968); L. Wegele, ed., *L. M., 1719–1787: Bild einer Persönlichkeit* (Augsburg, 1969); W. Plath, "Zur Echtheitsfrage bei M.: 2. L. M.," *Mozart Jahrbuch 1971–72*; D. Carlson, *The Sacred Vocal Works of L. M.* (diss., Univ. of Michigan, 1976); A. Layer, *Eine Jugend in Augsburg—L. M. 1719–1787* (Augsburg, 1976); N. Zaslow, "The 'Lambach' Symphonies of Wolfgang and L. M.," *Music and Civilization: Essays Presented to Paul Henry Lang* (N.Y., 1983); C. Eisen, *The Symphonies of L. M. and Their Relationship to the Early Symphonies of Wolfgang Amadeus M.: A Bibliographical and Stylistic Study* (diss., Cornell Univ., 1986); E. Schwerin, *L. M.: Profile of a Personality* (N.Y., 1987).

Mozart, Maria Anna (Walburga Ignatia), Austrian pianist and teacher, daughter of **(Johann Georg) Leopold** and sister of **Wolfgang Amadeus Mozart,** nicknamed "Nannerl"; b. Salzburg, July 30, 1751; d. there, Oct. 29, 1829. She was taught music by her father from her earliest childhood, and appeared in public as a pianist with her brother; after their travels together in Europe, she returned to Salzburg and eventually devoted herself mainly to teaching. In 1784 she married Baron von Berchthold zu Sonnenburg, who died in 1801. She went blind in 1825. Although nearly 5 years older than Wolfgang, she survived him by 38 years.

BIBL.: W. Hummel, ed., *Nannerl M.s Tagebuchblätter mit Eintragungen ihres Bruders Wolfgang Amadeus* (Stuttgart, 1958).

Mozart, Wolfgang Amadeus (baptismal names, **Johannes Chrysostomus Wolfgangus Theophilus**), supreme Austrian genius of music whose works in every genre are unsurpassed in lyric beauty, rhythmic variety, and effortless melodic invention, son of **(Johann Georg) Leopold,** brother of **Maria Anna,** and father of **Franz Xaver Wolfgang Mozart;** b. Salzburg, Jan. 27, 1756; d. Vienna, Dec. 5, 1791. He and his sister, tenderly nicknamed "Nannerl," were the only 2 among the 7 children of Anna Maria and Leopold Mozart to survive infancy. Mozart's sister was 4½ years older; she took harpsichord lessons from her father, and Mozart as a very young child eagerly absorbed the sounds of music. He soon began playing the harpsichord himself, and later studied the violin. Leopold was an excellent musician, but he also appreciated the theatrical validity of the performances that Wolfgang and Nannerl began giving in Salzburg. On Jan. 17, 1762, he took them to Munich, where they performed before the Elector of Bavaria. In Sept. 1762 they played for Emperor Francis I at his palace in Vienna. The family returned to Salzburg in Jan. 1763, and in June 1763 the children were taken to Frankfurt, where Wolfgang showed his skill in improvising at the key-

board. In Nov. 1763 they arrived in Paris, where they played before Louis XV; it was in Paris that Wolfgang's 1st compositions were printed (4 sonatas for Harpsichord, with Violin ad libitum). In April 1764 they proceeded to London; there Wolfgang played for King George III. In London he was befriended by Bach's son Johann Christian Bach, who gave exhibitions improvising 4-hands at the piano with the child Mozart. By that time Mozart had tried his ability in composing serious works; he wrote 2 syms. for a London performance, and the MS of another very early sym., purportedly written by him in London, was discovered in 1980. Leopold wrote home with undisguised pride: "Our great and mighty Wolfgang seems to know everything at the age of 7 that a man acquires at the age of 40." Knowing the power of publicity, he diminished Wolfgang's age, for at the time the child was fully 9 years old. In July 1765 they journeyed to the Netherlands, then set out for Salzburg, visiting Dijon, Lyons, Geneva, Bern, Zürich, Donaueschingen, and Munich on the way. Arriving in Salzburg in Nov. 1766, Wolfgang applied himself to serious study of counterpoint under the tutelage of his father. In Sept. 1767 the family proceeded to Vienna, where Wolfgang began work on an opera, *La finta semplice;* his 2nd theater work was a singspiel, *Bastien und Bastienne,* which was produced in Vienna at the home of Dr. Franz Mesmer, the protagonist of the famous method of therapy by "animal magnetism," which became known as Mesmerism. On Dec. 7, 1768, Mozart led a performance of his *Missa solemnis* in C minor before the royal family and court at the consecration of the Waisenhauskirche. Upon Mozart's return to Salzburg in Jan. 1769, Archbishop Sigismund von Schrattenbach named him his Konzertmeister; however, the position was without remuneration. Still determined to broaden Mozart's artistic contacts, his father took him on an Italian tour. The announcement for a concert in Mantua on Jan. 16, 1770, just a few days before Mozart's 14th birthday, was typical of the artistic mores of the time: "A Symphony of his own composition; a harpsichord concerto, which will be handed to him, and which he will immediately play *prima vista;* a Sonata handed him in like manner, which he will provide with variations, and afterwards repeat in another key; an Aria, the words for which will be handed to him and which he will immediately set to music and sing himself, accompanying himself on the harpsichord; a Sonata for harpsichord on a subject given him by the leader of the violins; a Strict Fugue on a theme to be selected, which he will improvise on the harpsichord; a Trio in which he will execute a violin part *all' improvviso;* and, finally, the latest Symphony by himself." Legends of Mozart's extraordinary musical ability grew; it was reported, for instance, that he wrote out the entire score of *Miserere* by Allegri, which he had heard in the Sistine Chapel at the Vatican only twice. Young Mozart was subjected to numerous tests by famous Italian musicians, among them Giovanni Sammartini, Piccini, and Padre Martini; he was given a diploma as an elected member of the Accademia Filarmonica in Bologna after he had passed examinations in harmony and counterpoint. On Oct. 10, 1770, the Pope made him a Knight of the Golden Spur. He was commissioned to compose an opera; the result was *Mitridate, rè di Ponto,* which was performed in Milan on Dec. 26, 1770; Mozart himself conducted 3 performances of this opera from the harpsichord; after a short stay in Salzburg, they returned to Milan in 1771, where he composed the serenata *Ascanio in Alba* for the wedding festivities of Archduke Ferdinand (Oct. 17, 1771). He returned to Salzburg late in 1771; his patron, Archbishop Schrattenbach, died about that time, and his successor, Archbishop Hieronymus Colloredo, seemed to be indifferent to Mozart as a musician. Once more Mozart went to Italy, where his newest opera, *Lucio Silla,* was performed in Milan on Dec. 26, 1772. He returned to Salzburg in March 1773, but in July of that year he went to Vienna, where he became acquainted with the music of Haydn, who greatly influenced his instrumental style. Returning to Salzburg once more, he supervised the production of his opera *Il Rè pastore,* which was performed on April 23, 1775.

In March 1778 Mozart visited Paris again for a performance of his "Paris" Sym. at a Concert Spirituel. His mother died in Paris on July 3, 1778. Returning to Salzburg in Jan. 1779, he resumed his duties as Konzertmeister and also obtained the position of court organist at a salary of 450 gulden. In 1780 the Elector of Bavaria commissioned from him an opera seria, *Idomeneo*, which was successfully produced in Munich on Jan. 29, 1781. In May 1781 Mozart lost his position with the Archbishop in Salzburg and decided to move to Vienna, which became his permanent home. There he produced the operatic masterpiece *Die Entführung aus dem Serail*, staged at the Burgtheater on July 16, 1782, with excellent success. On August 4, 1782, he married Constanze Weber, the sister of Aloysia Weber, with whom he had previously been infatuated. Two of his finest syms.—No. 35 in D major, "Haffner," written for the Haffner family of Salzburg, and No. 36 in C major, the "Linz"—date from 1782 and 1783, respectively. From this point forward Mozart's productivity reached extraordinary dimensions, but despite the abundance of commissions and concert appearances, he was unable to earn enough to sustain his growing family. Still, melodramatic stories of Mozart's abject poverty are gross exaggerations. He apparently felt no scruples in asking prosperous friends for financial assistance. Periodically he wrote to Michael Puchberg, a banker and a brother Freemason (Mozart joined the Masonic Order in 1784), with requests for loans (which he never repaid); invariably Puchberg obliged, but usually granting smaller amounts than Mozart requested. (The market price of Mozart autographs has grown exponentially; a begging letter to Puchberg would fetch, some 2 centuries after it was written, a hundred times the sum requested.) In 1785 Mozart completed a set of 6 string quartets which he dedicated to Haydn; unquestionably the structure of these quartets owed much to Haydn's contrapuntal art. Haydn himself paid a tribute to Mozart's genius; Mozart's father quoted him as saying, "Before God and as an honest man I tell you that your son is the greatest composer known to me either in person or by name." On May 1, 1786, Mozart's great opera buffa, *Le nozze di Figaro*, was produced in Vienna, obtaining a triumph with the audience; it was performed in Prague early in 1787 with Mozart in attendance. It was during that visit that Mozart wrote his 38th Sym., in D major, known as the "Prague" Sym.; it was in Prague, also, that his operatic masterpiece *Don Giovanni* was produced, on Oct. 29, 1787. It is interesting to note that at its Vienna performance the opera was staged under the title *Die sprechende Statue*, unquestionably with the intention of sensationalizing the story; the dramatic appearance of the statue of the Commendatore, introduced by the ominous sound of trombones, was a shuddering climax to the work. In Nov. 1787 Mozart was appointed Kammermusicus in Vienna as a successor to Gluck, albeit at a smaller salary: he received 800 gulden per annum as against Gluck's salary of 2,000 gulden. The year 1788 was a glorious one for Mozart and for music history; it was the year when he composed his last 3 syms.: No. 39 in E-flat major; No. 40 in G minor; and No. 41 in C major, known under the name "Jupiter" (the Jovian designation was apparently attached to the work for the 1st time in British concert programs; its earliest use was in the program of the Edinburgh Festival in Oct. 1819). In the spring of 1789 Mozart went to Berlin; on the way he appeared as soloist in one of his piano concertos before the Elector of Saxony in Dresden, and also played the organ at the Thomaskirche in Leipzig. His visits in Potsdam and Berlin were marked by his private concerts at the court of Friedrich Wilhelm II; the King commissioned from him a set of 6 string quartets and a set of 6 piano sonatas, but Mozart died before completing these commissions. Returning to Vienna, he began work on his opera buffa *Così fan tutte* (an untranslatable sentence because *tutte* is the feminine plural, so that the full title would be "Thus do all women"). The opera was 1st performed in Vienna on Jan. 26, 1790. In Oct. 1790 Mozart went to Frankfurt for the coronation of Emperor Leopold II. Returning to Vienna, he saw Haydn, who was about to depart for London. In 1791, during his last year

of life, he completed the score of *Die Zauberflöte*, with a German libretto by Emanuel Schikaneder. It was performed for the 1st time on Sept. 30, 1791, in Vienna. There followed a mysterious episode in Mozart's life; a stranger called on him with a request to compose a Requiem; the caller was an employee of Count Franz von Walsegg, who intended to have the work performed as his own in memory of his wife. Mozart was unable to finish the score, which was completed by his pupil Süssmayr, and by Eybler.

The immediate cause of Mozart's death at the age of 35 has been the subject of much speculation. A detailed examination of his medical history is found in P. Davies, "Mozart's Illnesses and Death—1: The Illnesses, 1756–90" and "2: The Last Year and the Fatal Illness," *Musical Times* (Aug. and Oct. 1984). Almost immediately after the sad event, myths and fantasies appeared in the press; the most persistent of them all was that Mozart had been poisoned by Salieri out of professional jealousy; this particularly morbid piece of invention gained circulation in European journals; the story was further elaborated upon by a report that Salieri confessed his unspeakable crime on his deathbed in 1825. Pushkin used the tale in his drama *Mozart and Salieri*, which Rimsky-Korsakov set to music in his opera of the same title; a fanciful dramatization of the Mozart-Salieri rivalry was made into a successful play, *Amadeus*, by Peter Shaffer, which was produced in London in 1979 and in N.Y. in 1980; it subsequently gained wider currency through its award-winning film version of 1984. The notion of Mozart's murder also appealed to the Nazis; in the ingenious version propagated by some German writers of the Hitlerian persuasion, Mozart was a victim of a double conspiracy of Masons and Jews who were determined to suppress the flowering of racial Germanic greatness; the Masons, in this interpretation, were outraged by his revealing of their secret rites in *Die Zauberflöte*, and allied themselves with plutocratic Jews to prevent further spread of his dangerous revelations. Another myth related to Mozart's death that found its way into the majority of Mozart biographies and even into respectable reference works was that a blizzard raged during his funeral and that none of his friends could follow his body to the cemetery; this story is easily refuted by the records of the Vienna weather bureau for the day (see N. Slonimsky, "The Weather at Mozart's Funeral," *Musical Quarterly*, Jan. 1960). It is also untrue that Mozart was buried in a pauper's grave; his body was removed from its original individual location because the family neglected to pay the mandatory dues.

The universal recognition of Mozart's genius during the 2 centuries since his death has never wavered among professional musicians, amateurs, and the general public. In his music, smiling simplicity was combined with somber drama; lofty inspiration was contrasted with playful diversion; profound meditation alternated with capricious moodiness; religious concentration was permeated with human tenderness. Devoted as Mozart was to his art and respectful as he was of the rules of composition, he was also capable of mocking the professional establishment. A delightful example of this persiflage is his little piece *Ein musikalischer Spass*, subtitled "Dorf Musikanten," a "musical joke" at the expense of "village musicians," in which Mozart all but anticipated developments of modern music, 2 centuries in the future; he deliberately used the forbidden consecutive fifths, allowed the violin to escape upward in a whole-tone scale, and finished the entire work in a welter of polytonal triads. Mozart is also the only great composer to have a town named after him—the town of Mozart, in the province of Saskatchewan, Canada, lying between Synyard and Elfros on a CPR main line that skirts the south end of Big Quill Lake. It consists of 2 elevators, a covered curling rink, a Centennial hall, a co-op store, and a handful of well-kept homes. A local recounts that the town was named in the early 1900s by one Mrs. Lunch, the wife of the stationmaster, who was reportedly a talented musician and very well thought of in the community. She not only named the town Mozart but also brought about the naming of the streets after other, equally famous musicians: Chopin, Wagner, and Liszt.

The variety of technical development in Mozart's works is all the more remarkable considering the limitations of instrumental means in his time; the topmost note on his keyboard was F above the 3rd ledger line, so that in the recapitulation in the 1st movement of his famous C major Piano Sonata, the subject had to be dropped an octave lower to accommodate the modulation. The vocal technique displayed in his operas is amazing in its perfection; to be sure, the human voice has not changed since Mozart's time, but he knew how to exploit vocal resources to the utmost. This adaptability of his genius to all available means of sound production is the secret of the eternal validity of his music, and the explanation of the present popularity of mini-festivals, such as the N.Y. concert series advertised as "Mostly Mozart."

In the list of Mozart's works given below, the K. numbers represent the system of identification established by L. von Köchel in his *Chronologisch-thematisches Verzeichnis sämtlicher Tonwerke Wolfgang Amade Mozarts* (Leipzig, 1862; 6th ed., rev. by F. Giegling, A. Weinmann, and G. Sievers, Wiesbaden, 1964); the rev. K. numbers of the 6th ed. are also included.

WORKS: OPERAS AND OTHER COMPOSITIONS FOR THE STAGE: *Apollo et Hyacinthus*, K.38, Latin intermezzo (Salzburg Univ., May 13, 1767); *La finta semplice*, K.51; 46a, opera buffa (Archbishop's palace, Salzburg, May 1?, 1769); *Bastien und Bastienne*, K.50; 46b, singspiel (Franz Mesmer's residence, Vienna, Sept.?–Oct.? 1768); *Mitridate, rè di Ponto*, K.87; 74a, opera seria (Regio Ducal Teatro, Milan, Dec. 26, 1770); *Ascanio in Alba*, K.111, festa teatrale (Regio Ducal Teatro, Milan, Oct. 17, 1771); *Il sogno di Scipione*, K.126, serenata (Archbishop's palace, Salzburg, May? 1772); *Lucio Silla*, K.135, opera seria (Regio Ducal Teatro, Milan, Dec. 26, 1772); *La finta giardiniera*, K.196, opera buffa (Munich, Jan. 13, 1775; also produced as a singspiel, *Die verstellte Gärtnerin*, Augsburg, May 1, 1780); *Il Rè pastore*, K.208, dramma per musica (Archbishop's palace, Salzburg, April 23, 1775); *Semiramis*, K.Anh. 11; 315e, duodrama (not extant); *Thamos, König in Ägypten*, K.345; 336a, music for Gebler's play; *Zaide*, K.344; 336b, singspiel (unfinished; dialogue rewritten and finished by Gollmick, with overture and finale added by Anton André, Frankfurt, Jan. 27, 1866); *Idomeneo, rè di Creta*, K.366, opera seria (Hoftheater, Munich, Jan. 29, 1781); *Die Entführung aus dem Serail*, K.384, singspiel (Burgtheater, Vienna, July 16, 1782); *L'oca del Cairo*, K.422, opera buffa (unfinished); *Lo Sposo deluso*, K.430; 424a, opera buffa (unfinished); *Der Schauspieldirektor*, K.486, singspiel (Schönbrunn Palace, Heitzing [suburb of Vienna], Feb. 7, 1786); *Le nozze di Figaro*, K.492, opera buffa (Burgtheater, Vienna, May 1, 1786); *Il dissoluto punito, ossia Il Don Giovanni*, K.527, opera buffa (National Theater, Prague, Oct. 29, 1787); *Così fan tutte, ossia La scuola degli amanti*, K.588, opera buffa (Burgtheater, Vienna, Jan. 26, 1790); *Die Zauberflöte*, K.620, singspiel (Theater auf der Wieden, Vienna, Sept. 30, 1791); *La clemenza di Tito*, K.621, opera seria (National Theater, Prague, Sept. 6, 1791). Arias and scenes for Voice and Orch.: 39 for Soprano (4 not extant); 1 for Alto; 11 for Tenor (1 with only 48 bars extant); 8 for Bass. Duets for Solo Voices and Orch.: 1 for 2 Tenors; 1 for Soprano and Tenor; 2 for Soprano and Bass. Ensembles for Solo Voices and Orch.: 1 for Soprano, Tenor, and Bass; 1 for Tenor and 2 Basses; 1 for Soprano, Tenor, and 2 Basses; 1 for Soprano, Alto, Tenor, and Bass (not extant). Ensembles for Solo Voices, and Piano or other Instruments: 1 for 2 Sopranos; 5 for 2 Sopranos and Bass; 2 for Soprano, Tenor, and Bass; 1 for 2 Sopranos and Bass; 1 for Soprano, 2 Tenors, and Bass. 34 songs for Solo Voices, with Piano (2 with Mandolin; 2 Masonic songs, with Male Chorus). Numerous canons.

MASSES, ORATORIOS, CANTATAS, ETC.: Kyrie in F major, K.33 (1766); *Die Schuldigkeit des ersten Gebots*, K.35, sacred drama (1767; part 1 by Mozart, part 2 by Michael Haydn, part 3 by Adlgasser; Salzburg, March 12, 1767); *Grabmusik*, K.42; 35a, cantata (1767; Salzburg Cathedral, April 7, 1767); *Missa solemnis* in C minor, K.139; 47a, "Waisenhausmesse" (1768; Vienna, Dec. 7, 1768); *Missa brevis* in C major, K.49; 47d (1768; only fragments extant); *Missa brevis* in D minor, K.65; 61a (1769;

Collegiate Church, Salzburg, Feb. 5, 1769); *Missa* in C major, K.66, "Dominicus" (1769; St. Peter, Salzburg, Oct. 15, 1769); *La Betulia liberata*, K.118; 74c, oratorio (1771); *Missa brevis* in G major, K.140; C 1.12 (1773; may not be by Mozart); *Missa* in C major, K.167, "In honorem Ssmae Trinitatis" (1773); *Missa brevis* in F major, K.192; 186f (1774); *Missa brevis* in D major, K.194; 186h (1774); *Missa brevis* in C major, K.220; 196b, "Spatzenmesse" (1775–76); *Missa* in C major, K.262; 246a (1775); *Missa* in C major, K.257, "Credo" (1776); *Missa brevis* in C major, K.258, "Spaur" (1776); *Missa brevis* in C major, K.259, "Organ Solo" (1776); *Missa brevis* in B-flat major, K.275; 272b (1777; St. Peter, Salzburg, Dec. 21, 1777); *Missa* in C major, K.317, "Coronation" (1779); *Missa solemnis* in C major, K.337 (1780); Kyrie in D minor, K.341; 368a (1780–81); *Missa* in C minor, K.427; 417a (1782–83; unfinished; Kyrie and Gloria, St. Peter, Salzburg, Oct. 25, 1783); *Dir, Seele des Weltalls*, K.429; 468a, cantata (1785; unfinished); *Davidde penitente*, K.469, oratorio (1785; music from the *Missa* in C minor, K.427; 417a, 2 arias excepted); *Die Maurerfreude*, K.471, cantata (1785; "Zur gekronten Hoffnung" Lodge, Vienna, April 24, 1785); *Die ihr des unermesslichen Weltalls Schöpfer ehrt*, K.619, cantata (1791); *Eine kleine Freimaurer-Kantate*, K.623 (1791; "Zur neugekronten Hoffnung" Lodge, Vienna, Nov. 18, 1791); Requiem in D minor, K.626 (1791; unfinished; completed by Franz Xaver Süssmayr). Also the following: *God Is Our Refuge* in G minor, K.20, motet (1765); *Stabat Mater*, K.33c (1766; not extant); *Scande coeli limina* in C major, K.34, offertory (1767); *Veni Sancte Spiritus* in C major, K.47 (1768); *Benedictus sit Deus* in C major, K.117; 66a, offertory (1768); *Te Deum* in C major, K.141; 66b (1769); *Ergo interest* in G major, K.143; 73a, motet (1773); Miserere in A minor, K.85; 73s (1770); *Cibavit eos* in A minor, K.44; 73u, antiphon (1770; may not be by Mozart); *Quaerite primum* in D minor, K.86; 73v, antiphon (1770); *Regina coeli* in C major, K.108; 74d (1771); *Inter natos mulierum* in G major, K.72; 74f, offertory (1771); *Regina coeli* in B-flat major, K.127 (1772); *Exsultate, jubilate* in F major, K.165; 158a, motet (1773; Milan, Jan. 17, 1773); *Tantum ergo* in D major, K.197; C 3.05 (1774; may not be by Mozart); *Sub tuum praesidium* in F major, K.198; C 3.08, offertory (1774; may not be by Mozart); *Misericordias Domini* in D minor, K.222; 205a, offertory (1775); *Venite populi* in D major, K.260; 248a (1776); *Alma Dei creatoris* in F major, K.277; 272a, offertory (1777); *Sancta Maria, mater Dei* in F major, K.273, gradual (1777); Miserere, K.Anh. 1; 297a (1778; not extant); *Kommet her, ihr frechen Sünder* in B-flat major, K.146; 317b, aria (1779); *Regina coeli* in C major, K.276; 321b (1779?); *O Gottes Lamm; Als aus Aegypten*, K.343; 336c, 2 German sacred songs (1787?); *Ave verum corpus* in D major, K.618, motet (1791). Additional works: *Litaniae Lauretanae* in B-flat major, K.109; 74e (1771); *Litaniae de venerabili altaris sacramento* in B-flat major, K.125 (1772); *Litaniae Lauretanae* in D major, K.195; 186d (1774); *Dixit Dominus, Magnificat* in C major, K.193; 186g (1774); *Litaniae de venerabili altaris sacramento* in E-flat major, K.243 (1776); *Vesperae de Dominica* in C major, K.321 (1779); *Vesperae solennes de confessore* in C major, K.339 (1780).

ORCH.: SYMS.: No. 1 in E-flat major, K.16 (1764–65); A minor, K.Anh. 220; 16a "Odense" (1768?; considered lost until discovered in Odense in 1982; may not be by Mozart); No. 4 in D major, K.19 (1765); F major, K.Anh. 223; 19a (1765; considered lost until discovered in 1980); C major, K.Anh. 222; 19b (1765; not extant); No. 5 in B-flat major, K.22 (1765); No. 43 in F major, K.76; 42a (1767; may not be by Mozart); No. 6 in F major, K.43 (1767); No. 7 in D major, K.45 (1767); G major, K.Anh. 221; 45a, "Old Lambach" (1768); No. 55 in B-flat major, K.Anh. 214; 45b (1768); No. 8 in D major, K.48 (1768); D major, K.Anh. 215; 66c (1769; not extant); B-flat major, K.Anh. 217; 66d (1769; not extant); B-flat major, K.Anh. 218; 66e (1769; not extant); No. 9 in C major, K.73 (1772); No. 44 in D major, K.81; 731 (1770; may be by Leopold Mozart); No. 47 in D major, K.97; 73m (1770); No. 45 in D major, K.95; 73n (1770); No. 11 in D major, K.84; 73q (1770; may not be by Mozart); No. 10 in G major, K.74 (1770); No. 42

in F major, K.75 (1771); No. 12 in G major, K.110; 75b (1771); D major, K.120; 111a (1771; finale only; perf. with the overture to *Ascanio in Alba*, K.111, forming a sym.); No. 46 in C major, K.96; 111b (1771); No. 13 in F major, K.112 (1771); No. 14 in A major, K.114 (1771); No. 15 in G major, K.124 (1772); No. 16 in C major, K.128 (1772); No. 17 in G major, K.129 (1772); No. 18 in F major, K.130 (1772); No. 19 in E-flat major, K.132 (1772; with alternative slow movements); No. 20 in D major, K.133 (1772); No. 21 in A major, K.134 (1772); No. 50 in D major, K.161, 163; 141a (1772); No. 26 in E-flat major, K.184; 161a (1773); No. 27 in G major, K.199; 161b (1773); No. 22 in C major, K.162 (1773); No. 23 in D major, K.181; 162b (1773); No. 24 in B-flat major, K.182; 173dA (1773); No. 25 in G minor, K.183; 173dB (1773); No. 29 in A major, K.201; 186a (1774); No. 30 in D major, K.202; 186b (1774); No. 28 in C major, K.200; 189k (1774); D major K.121; 207a (1774–75; finale only; perf. with the overture to *La finta giardiniera*, K.196, forming a sym.); D major (4 movements from the Serenade in D major, K.204; 213a); C major, K.102; 213c (1775; finale only; perf. with versions of the overture and 1st aria from *Il Rè pastore*, K.208); D major (4 movements from the Serenade in D major, K.250; 248b); No. 31 in D major, K.297; 300a, "Paris" (1778: with 2 slow movements); No. 32 in G major, K.318 (1779; in 1 movement); No. 33 in B-flat major, K.319 (1779); D major (3 movements from the Serenade in D major, K.320, "Posthorn"); No. 34 in C major, K.338 (1780); C major, K.409; 383f (1782; minuet only; may have been intended for the Sym. No. 34 in C major, K.338); No. 35 in D major, K.385, "Haffner" (1782); No. 36 in C major, K.425, "Linz" (1783); No. 37 in G major, K.444; 425a (1783?; only the introduction is by Mozart; remainder by Michael Haydn); No. 38 in D major, K.504, "Prague" (1786); No. 39 in E-flat major, K.543 (1788); No. 40 in G minor, K.550 (1788); No. 41 in C major, K.551, "Jupiter" (1788). A sym. listed as K.Anh. 8; 311A was never composed.

PIANO CONCERTOS: No. 5 in D major, K.175 (1773); No. 6 in B-flat major, K.238 (1776); No. 8 in C major, K.246 (1776); No. 9 in E-flat major, K.271 (1777); No. 12 in A major, K.414; 385p (1782); No. 11 in F major, K.413; 387a (1782–83); No. 13 in C major, K.415; 387b (1782–83); No. 14 in E-flat major, K.449 (1784); No. 15 in B-flat major, K.450 (1784); No. 16 in D major, K.451 (1784); No. 17 in G major, K.453 (1784); No. 18 in B-flat major, K.456 (1784); No. 19 in F major, K.459 (1784); No. 20 in D minor, K.466 (1785); No. 21 in C major, K.467 (1785); No. 22 in E-flat major, K.482 (1785); No. 23 in A major, K.488 (1786); No. 24 in C minor, K.491 (1786); No. 25 in C major, K.503 (1786); No. 26 in D major, K.537, "Coronation" (1788); No. 27 in B-flat major, K.595 (1788?–91). Also No. 10 in E-flat major, for 2 Pianos, K.365; 316a (1779); No. 7 in F major, for 3 Pianos, K.242 (1776); Rondo in D major, K.382 (1782; new finale for No. 5 in D major, K.175); Rondo in A major, K.386 (1782).

VIOLIN CONCERTOS: No. 1 in B-flat major, K.207 (1773?); No. 2 in D major, K.211 (1775); No. 3 in G major, K.216 (1775); No. 4 in D major, K.218 (1775); No. 5 in A major, K.219 (1775). Also the following: Concertone in C major for 2 Violins, K.90; 186e (1774); Adagio in E major for Violin, K.261 (1776; for Violin Concerto No. 5); Rondo in B-flat major for Violin, K.269; 261a (1776); Sinfonia concertante in E-flat major for Violin and Viola, K.364; 320d (1779); Rondo in C major for Violin, K.373 (1781); Andante in A major for Violin, K.470 (1785; not extant).

WIND INSTRUMENTS: Concerto for Trumpet, K.47c (1768; not extant); Concerto for Bassoon in B-flat major, K.191; 186e (1774); Concerto for Oboe, K.271k (1777; not extant; perhaps a version of K.314; 285d below); Concerto for Flute in G major, K.313; 285c (1778); Concerto for Oboe or Flute in C/D major, K.314; 285d (1778; oboe version may be for K.271k above); Andante for Flute in C major, K.315; 285e (1779–80); Sinfonia concertante for Flute, Oboe, Bassoon, and Horn, K.Anh. 9; 297B (1778?; not extant; may not have been composed); Sinfonia concertante in E-flat major for Oboe, Clarinet, Bassoon, and Horn, K.Anh. 9; C 14.01 (doubtful); Concerto for Flute

and Harp in C major, K.299; 297c (1778); Sinfonia concertante in G major for 2 Flutes, 2 Oboes, and 2 Bassoons, K.320 (movements 3 and 4 of the Serenade in D major, K.320, "Posthorn"); Rondo for Horn in E-flat major, K.371 (1781; unfinished); concertos for Horn: No. 1 (old No. 2) in E-flat major, K.417 (1783); No. 2 (old No. 4) in E-flat major, K.495 (1786); No. 3 in E-flat major, K.447 (1783?); No. 4 (old No.1) in D major, K.412; 386b (1791; unfinished finale completed by Süssmayr, 1792); Concerto for Clarinet in A major, K.622 (1791).

SERENADES, DIVERTIMENTOS, CASSATIONS, ETC.: *Gallimathias musicum,* K.32 (1766); 6 divertimentos, K.41a (1767; not extant); Cassation in D major, K.100; 62a (1769); Cassation in G major, K.63 (1769); Cassation in C major (1769; not extant); Cassation in B-flat major, K.99; 63a (1769); Divertimento in E-flat major, K.113 (1771); Divertimento in D major, K.131 (1772); Divertimento in D major, K.136; 125a (1772); Divertimento in B-flat major, K.137; 125b (1772); Divertimento in F Major, K.138; 125c (1772); Divertimento in D major, K.205; 167a (1773?); Serenade in D major, K.185; 167a (1773); Serenade in D major, K.203; 189b (1774); Serenade in D major, K.204; 213a (1775); *Serenata notturna* in D major, K.239 (1776); Divertimento in F major, K.247 (1776); Serenade in D major, K.250; 248b, "Haffner" (1776); Divertimento in D major, K.251 (1776); *Notturno* in D major, K.286; 269a (1776–77); Divertimento in B-flat major, K.287; 271h (1777); Serenade in D major, K.320, "Posthorn" (1779); Divertimento in D major, K.334; 320b (1779–80); *Maurerische Trauermusik* in C minor, K.477; 479a (1785); *Ein musikalischer Spass* in F major, K.522 (1787; satirical; employs deliberate discords, consecutive fifths, etc.); *Eine kleine Nachtmusik* in G major, K.525 (1787). Also 14 divertimentos for Wind Ensemble; 15 marches (2 not extant); 56 German dances, ländler, and 58 Contredanses (10 not extant, 9 doubtful); ballet, *Les Petits Riens,* K.Anh. 10; 299b (1778; Opéra, Paris, June 11, 1778); etc.

CHAMBER: STRING QUARTETS: G major, K.80; 73f (1770); D major, K.155; 134a (1772); G major, K.156; 134b (1772); C major, K.157 (1772–73); F major, K.158 (1772–73); B-flat major, K.159 (1773); E-flat major, K.160; 159a (1773); F major, K.168 (1773); A major, K.169 (1773); C major, K.170 (1773); E-flat major, K.171 (1773); B-flat major, K.172 (1773); D minor, K.173 (1773); G major, K.387 (1782); D minor, K.421; 417b (1783); E-flat major, K.428; 421b (1783); B-flat major, K.458, "Hunt" (1784); A major, K.464 (1785); C major, K.465, "Dissonance" (1785); D major, K.499, "Hoffmeister" (1786); D major, K.575, "Prussian" (1789); B-flat major, K.589, "Prussian" (1790); F major, K.590, "Prussian" (1790); Adagio and Fugue in C minor, K.46 (1788).

STRING QUINTETS (2 Violins, 2 Violas, and Cello): B-flat major, K.174 (1773); C major, K.515 (1787); G minor, K.516 (1787); C minor, K.406; 516b (1788; an arrangement of K.88); D major, K.593 (1790); E-flat major, K.614 (1791).

STRINGS AND WIND INSTRUMENTS: Duo in B-flat major for Bassoon and Cello, K.292; 196c (1775); Quartet in D major for Flute, Violin, Viola, and Cello, K.285 (1777); Quartet in G major for Flute, Violin, Viola, and Cello, K.285a (1778); Quartet in C major for Flute, Violin, Viola, and Cello, K.Anh. 171; 285b (1781–82); Quartet in A major for Flute, Violin, Viola, and Cello, K.298 (1786–87); Quartet in F major for Oboe, Violin, Viola, and Cello, K.370; 368b (1781); Quintet in E-flat major for Horn, Violin, 2 Violas, and Cello, K.407; 386c (1782); Quintet in A major for Clarinet, 2 Violins, Viola, and Cello, K.581 (1789).

STRING SONATAS, DUOS, AND TRIOS: Solos for Cello and Bassoon, K.33b (1766; not extant); *Nachtmusik* for 2 Violins and Bassoon, K.41g (1767; not extant); Sonata in C major for Violin and Bassoon, K.46d (1768); Sonata in F major for Violin and Bassoon, K.46e (1768); Trio in B-flat major for 2 Violins and Bassoon, K.266; 271f (1777); 4 preludes for Violin, Viola, and Cello, K.404a (1782; may not be by Mozart); Duo in G major for Violin and Viola, K.423 (1783); Duo in B-flat major for Violin and Viola, K.424 (1783); Trio in E-flat major for Violin, Viola, and Cello, K.563 (1788).

KEYBOARD AND OTHER INSTRUMENTS: Divertimento in B-flat major for Piano, Violin, and Cello, K.254 (1776); Trio in D minor for Piano, Violin, and Cello, K.442 (1783?–90; unfinished; completed by M. Stadler); Quintet in E-flat major for Piano, Oboe, Clarinet, Bassoon, and Horn, K.452 (1784); Quartet in G minor for Piano, Violin, Viola, and Cello, K.478 (1785); Quartet in E-flat major for Piano, Violin, Viola, and Cello, K.493 (1786); Trio in G major for Piano, Violin, and Cello, K.496 (1786); Trio in E-flat major for Piano, Clarinet, and Viola, K.498 (1786); Trio in B-flat major for Piano, Violin, and Cello, K.502 (1786); Trio in E major for Piano, Violin, and Cello, K.542 (1788); Trio in C major for Piano, Violin, and Cello, K.548 (1788); Trio in G major for Piano, Violin, and Cello, K.564 (1788); Adagio and Rondo in C minor for Glass Harmonica, Flute, Oboe, Viola, and Cello, K.617 (1791).

KEYBOARD AND VIOLIN SONATAS: C major, K.6 (1762–64); D major, K.7 (1762–64); B-flat major, K.8 (1763–64); G major, K.9 (1763–64); B-flat major, K.10 (1764); G major, K.11 (1764); A major, K.12 (1764); F major, K.13 (1764); C major, K.14 (1764); B-flat major, K.15 (1764); E-flat major, K.26 (1766); G major, K.27 (1766); C major, K.28 (1766); D major, K.29 (1766); F major, K.30 (1766); B-flat major, K.31 (1766); G major, K.301; 293a (1778); E-flat major, K.302; 293b (1778); C major, K.303; 293c (1778); A major, K.305; 293d (1778); C major, K.296 (1778); E minor, K.304; 300c (1778); D major, K.306; 300l (1778); B-flat major, K.378; 317d (1779?); B-flat major, K.372 (1781; unfinished; completed by M. Stadler); G major, K.379; 373a (1781); F major, K.376; 374d (1781); F major, K.377; 374e (1781); E-flat major, K.380; 374f (1781); C major, K.403; 385c (1782; unfinished; completed by M. Stadler); C major, K.404; 385d (1782?; unfinished); A major, K.402; 385e (1782; unfinished; completed by M. Stadler); C minor, K.396; 385f (1782; 1 movement only; completed by M. Stadler); B-flat major, K.454 (1784); E-flat major, K.481 (1785); A major, K.526 (1787); F major, K.547, "für Anfänger" (1788); Variations in G major, K.359; 374a (1781); Variations in G minor, K.360; 374b (1781).

SONATAS FOR KEYBOARD SOLO: G major, K.Anh. 199; 33d (1766; not extant); B-flat major, K.Anh. 200; 33e (1766; not extant); C major, K.201; 33f (1766; not extant); F major, K.202; 33g (1766; not extant); C major, K.279; 189d (1775); F major, K.280; 189e (1775); B-flat major, K.281; 189f (1775); E-flat major, K.282; 189g (1775); G major, K.283; 189h (1775); D major, K.284; 205b (1775); C major, K.309; 284b (1777); D major, K.311; 284c (1777); A minor, K.310; 300d (1778); C major, K.330; 300h (1781–83); A major, K.331; 300i (1781–83); F major, K.332; 300k (1781–83); B-flat major, K.333; 315c (1783–84); C minor, K.457 (1784); F major, K.533 (1788); C major, K.545, "für Anfänger" (1788); F major, K.Anh. 135; 547a (1788; may not be by Mozart); B-flat major, K.570 (1789); D major, K.576 (1789).

KEYBOARD DUET: Sonata in C major, K.19d (1765); Sonata in D major, K.381; 123a (1772); Sonata in B-flat major, K.358; 186c (1773–74); Sonata in F major, K.497 (1786); Sonata in C major, K.521 (1787). Also: Sonata in D major for 2 Keyboards, K.448; 375a (1781); 17 variations for Keyboard Solo (1 not extant) and 1 for Piano Duet; many miscellaneous pieces; 17 sonatas for Organ, most with 2 Violins and Bassoon; etc.

Since the publication of the Breitkopf & Härtel ed. of Mozart's works, the list of doubtful and spurious compositions has grown extensively. The pioneering research of Wyzewa and Saint-Foix has been followed by the important studies of Plath, Tyson, and other scholars. For detailed information, see the bibliography below. A selected compilation of doubtful and spurious works follows (those noted in the list of works above are excluded):

MASSES: F major, K.116; 90a, by Leopold Mozart; E-flat major, K.Anh. 235f; C 1.02, by B. Schack; G major, K.Anh. 232; C 1.04, "12th Mass"; G major, K.deest; C 1.18, "Missa solemnis pastorita"; D minor, K.Anh. 237; C 1.90, "Requiem brevis"; Kyrie in C major, K.340; C 3.06; Kyrie in C major, K.221; A1, by Eberlin. Also: *Lacrimosa* in C minor, K.Anh. 21; A2, by Eberlin; *Justum deduxit Dominus*, hymn, K.326; A4, by

Eberlin; *Adoramus te*, hymn, K.327; A10, by Q. Gasparini; *De profundis clamavi*, Psalm, K.93; A22, by Reutter; *Salve Regina*, K.92; C 3.01; *Tantum ergo* in B-flat major, K.142; C 3.04; *Offertorium sub exposito venerabili*, K.177 and 342; C 3.09, by Leopold Mozart.

SYMS.: No. 2, in B-flat major, K.17; C 11.02; B-flat major, K.Anh. 216; C 11.03; No. 3, in E-flat major, K.18; A51, by C.F. Abel; G major, "New Lambach" (1768; by L. Mozart); F major, K.98; C 11.04; B-flat major, K.311a; C 11.05, the "2nd Paris" Sym. Also: Fugue in D major, K.291; A52, by M. Haydn, finished by S. Sechter.

PIANO CONCERTOS: The 1st 4 piano concertos, K.37, 39, 40, and 41, are arrangements of sonata movements by Raupach, Honauer, Schobert, Eckard, and C.P.E. Bach; the 5th Piano Concerto, K.107, consists of arrangements of 3 sonatas by Johann Christian Bach.

VIOLIN CONCERTOS: Two violin concertos, 1 in D major, K.271a; 271i, the other in E-flat major, K.268; C 14.04, may contain some music composed by Mozart. The Violin Concerto in D major, K.Anh. 294a; C 14.05, the "Adelaide" Concerto, which was widely performed after its alleged discovery in 1931, was actually composed by the French violinist Marius Casadesus; it was supposedly dedicated to Princess Adelaide, the daughter of Louis XV, by the boy Mozart during his visit to Paris at the age of 10. Also: *Sinfonia concertante* in A major for Violin, Viola, and Cello, K.Anh. 104; 320e.

SONATAS FOR KEYBOARD AND VIOLIN: K.55–60; C23.01–6 and K.61, by Raupach.

BIBL.: COLLECTED EDITIONS, SOURCE MATERIAL: The 1st collected edition of Mozart's works was ed. by L. von Köchel et al. as *W.A. M.s Werke*; it was publ. by Breitkopf & Härtel (74 vols. in 24 series, Leipzig, 1877–83; 11 supplementary vols., Leipzig, 1877–1910). A new critical edition, *W.A. M.: Neue Ausgabe Sämtlicher Werke*, ed. by E. Schmid et al., began publishing in Kassel in 1955; it is sponsored by the Internationale Stiftung Mozarteum Salzburg.

The standard thematic catalog is L. von Köchel, ed., *Chronologisch-thematisches Verzeichnis sämtlicher Tonwerke W. Amade M.s* (Leipzig, 1862; 3rd ed., extensively rev. by A. Einstein, Leipzig, 1937; reprint, with supplement, Ann Arbor, 1947; 6th ed., a major revision, by F. Giegling, A. Weinmann, and G. Sievers, Wiesbaden, 1964; the 6th ed. contains a rev. K. numbering system; further supplementary material is found in the *M.-Jahrbuch 1971–2*, as prepared by P. van Reijen).

See also the following: Mozart's own *Verzeichnuss aller meiner Werke* (facsimile ed. by O. Deutsch as *W.A. M.: Verzeichnis aller meiner Werke: Faksimile der Handschrift mit dem Beiheft "M.s Werkverzeichnis 1784–1791,"* Vienna, 1938; Eng. ed., 1956; also another ed. by E. Müller von Asow as *W.A. M.: Verzeichnis aller meiner Werke und Leopold M.: Verzeichnis der Jugendwerke W.A. M.s*, Vienna, 1943; 2nd ed., 1956); A. André, *Thematischer Katalog wie M. solchen von 1784–91 eigenhändig geschrieben hat* (Offenbach, 1805; 2nd ed., augmented, 1828); K. Moyses, *Systematischer Katalog der im M.eum befindlichen Autographe M.s* (Salzburg, 1862); C. von Wurzbach, *M.-Buch* (Vienna, 1869); J. Horner, *Katalog des M.s-Museums zu Salzburg* (Salzburg, 1882; 2nd ed. by J. Engl, 1898); H. de Curzon, *Essai de bibliographie mozartienne: Revue critique des ouvrages relatifs à W.A. M. et ses œuvres* (Paris, 1906); L. Schiedermair, *W.A. M.s Handschrift in zeitlich geordneten Nachbildungen* (Bückeburg and Leipzig, 1919); M. Blaschitz, *Die Salzburger M.-Fragmente* (diss., Univ. of Bonn, 1924); O. Keller, *W.A. M.: Bibliographie und Ikonographie* (Berlin, 1927); O. Deutsch and C. Oldman, "M.-Drucke: Eine bibliographisches Ergänzung zu Köchels Werkverzeichnis," *Zeitschrift für Musikwissenschaft*, XIV (1931–32); C. Oldman, "M. and Modern Research," *Proceedings of the Royal Musical Association*, LVIII (1931–32); H. Farmer and H. Smith, *New M.iana: The M. Relics in the Zavertal Collection at the University of Glasgow* (Glasgow, 1935); O. Deutsch, "M.s Nachlass: Aus den Briefen Constanzes an den Verlag André," *M.-Jahrbuch 1953*; idem, "M.s Verleger," *M.-Jahrbuch 1955*; A. Hyatt King, *M. in the British Museum* (London, 1956); H. Moldenhauer,

"Übersicht der Musikmanuskripte W.A. M.s in den Vereinigten Staaten von Amerika (1956)," *M.-Jahrbuch 1956;* L. Nowak, "Die Wiener M.-Autographen," *Österreichische Musikzeitschrift,* XI (1956); M. and C. Raeburn, "M.'s Manuscripts in Florence," *Music & Letters* (Oct. 1959); W. Plath, "Beiträge zur M.-Autographie I: Die Handschrift Leopold M.," *M.-Jahrbuch 1960–61;* O. Schneider and A. Algatzy, *M.-Handbuch: Chronik, Werk, Bibliographie* (Vienna, 1962); A. Abert, "Methoden der M.forschung," *M.-Jahrbuch 1964;* H. Engel, "Probleme der M.forschung," *M.-Jahrbuch 1964;* G. Rech, "M.: Results of Present-Day Research on His Works," *Universitas,* VII (1965); G. Croll, "Zu den Verzeichnissen von M.s nachgelassenen Fragmenten und Entwurfen," *Österreichische Musikzeitschrift,* XXI (1966); K. Pfannhauser, "Epilegomena M.iana," *M.-Jahrbuch 1971–2;* W. Plath, "Leopold Mozarts Notenbuch für Wolfgang (1762): Eine Fälschung?," *M.-Jahrbuch 1971–2;* W. Plath et al., "Zur Echtheitsfrage bei M.," *M.-Jahrbuch 1971–2;* N. Zaslaw, "A Rediscovered M. Autograph at Cornell University," *M.-Jahrbuch 1971–2;* D. Leeson and D. Whitwell, "M.'s Thematic Catalogue," *Musical Times* (Aug. 1973); A. Hyatt King, "Some Aspects of Recent M. Research," *Proceedings of the Royal Musical Association,* C (1973–74); R. Angermüller and O. Schneider, "M.-Bibliographie (bis 1970)," *M.-Jahrbuch 1975;* W. Senn, "Beiträge zur M.forschung," *Acta Musicologica,* XLVIII (1976); W. Plath, "Beiträge zur M.-Autographie II: Schriftchronologie 1770–1780," *M.-Jahrbuch 1976–7;* R. Angermüller and O. Schneider, *M.-Bibliographie 1971–1975 mit Nachträgen bis 1970* (Kassel, 1978); O. Wessely, "Ergänzerungen zur M.-Bibliographie," *Studien zur Musikwissenschaft,* XXIX (1978); A. Hyatt King, *A M. Legacy: Aspects of the British Library Collections* (London, 1984); G. Haberkamp, *Die Erstdrucke der Werke von W.A. M.: Bibliographie* (Tutzing, 1986); R. Angermüller and O. Schneider, *M.-Bibliographie, 1981–1985: Mit Nachträgen zur M.-Bibliographie bis 1980* (Kassel and N.Y., 1987); B. Hastings, *W.A. M.: A Guide to Research* (N.Y., 1989).

YEARBOOKS AND OTHER PUBLICATIONS.: *Jahresbericht des M.eums* (Salzburg, 1880–1917); *Mitteilungen für die M.gemeinde in Berlin* (Berlin, 1895–1925); *M.eums-Mitteilungen* (Salzburg, 1918–21); *M.-Jahrbuch* (3 vols., Munich, 1923, 1924, and 1929); *Wiener Figaro* (issued by the M.gemeinde of Vienna, 1931); *Neues M.-Jahrbuch* (3 vols., Regensburg, 1941–43); *M.-Jahrbuch* (Salzburg, 1950); *Mitteilungen der Internationalen Stiftung M.eum* (Salzburg, 1952); *Acta M.iana* (issued by the Deutschen M.-Gesellschaft of Augsburg, 1954).

CORRESPONDENCE: L. Nohl, *M.s Briefe nach den Originalen herausgegeben* (Salzburg, 1865; Eng. tr. by Lady Wallace, London, 1866; 2nd German ed., augmented, Leipzig, 1877); H. de Curzon, *Nouvelles lettres des dernières années de la vie de M.* (Paris, 1898); K. Storck, *M.s Briefe in Auswahl* (Stuttgart, 1906); A. Leitzmann, *M.s Briefe ausgewählt* (Leipzig, 1910); M. Weigel, *M.s Briefe* (Berlin, 1910); H. Leichtentritt, *M.s Briefe* (Berlin, 1912); L. Schiedermair, *Die Briefe W.A. M.s und seiner Familie: Erste kritische Gesamtausgabe* (5 vols., of which the last is an iconography, Munich and Leipzig, 1914); E. Anderson, ed. and tr., *Letters of M. and His Family* (the most extensive collection in Eng.; 3 vols., London and N.Y., 1938; 2nd ed., rev. by A. Hyatt King and M. Carolan, 1966; 3rd ed., rev. by S. Sadie and F. Smart, 1985); E. Müller von Asow, ed., *Gesamtausgabe der Briefe und Aufzeichnungen der Familie M.* (5 vols., Berlin, 1942); W. Bauer, O. Deutsch, and J. Eibl, eds., *M.: Briefe und Aufzeichnungen* (the standard ed., with commentaries; 7 vols., Kassel, 1962–75).

BIOGRAPHICAL: F. von Schlichtegroll, "Johannes Chrysostomus W. Gottlieb M.," *Nekrolog auf das Jahr 1791* (Gotha, 1793; new ed. by L. Landshoff, Munich, 1924); F. Niemtschek, *Leben des k. k. Kapellmeisters W. Gottlieb M. nach Originalquellen beschrieben* (Prague, 1798; 2nd ed., augmented, 1808; facsimile reprint of the latter, 1905; Eng. tr., London, 1956); I. Arnold, *M.s Geist: Seine kurze Biographie und ästhetische Darstellung* (Erfurt, 1803); idem, *Galerie der berühmtesten Tonkünstler des 18. und 19. Jahrhunderts . . . W.A. M. und Joseph Haydn: Versuch einer Parallele* (Erfurt, 1810; 2nd ed., 1816); Stendhal, *Lettres . . . sur le célèbre compositeur Haydn: Suivies d'une vie de M. et considérations sur Métastase* (Paris, 1814; 2nd ed., rev., as *Vies de Haydn, de M. et de Métastase;* Eng. tr., 1972); P. Lichtenthal, *Cenni biografici intorno al celebre maestro W.A. M.* (Milan, 1816); G. von Nissen, *Biographie W.A. M.s nach Originalbriefen* (Leipzig, 1828); A. Oulibicheff, *Nouvelle biographie de M., suivie d'un aperçu sur l'histoire générale de la musique* (3 vols., Moscow, 1843; German tr. by L. Gantter, Stuttgart, 1859; Russian tr. by M. Tchaikovsky, Moscow, 1890); E. Holmes, *The Life of M.* (London, 1845; 2nd ed., 1878); O. Jahn, *W.A. M.* (4 vols., Leipzig, 1856–59; 2nd ed., 1867; Eng. tr. by P. Townsend, London, 1882; German revisions by H. Deiters, 3rd ed., 1891–93, and 4th ed., 1905–7; exhaustively rewritten and rev. by H. Abert as *W.A. M.: Neu bearbeitete und erweiterte Ausgabe von Otto Jahns "M.,"* 2 vols., Leipzig, 1919–21, rendering it the standard biography; further revision by A.A. Abert, 2 vols., Leipzig, 1955–56); L. Nohl, *M.* (Leipzig, 1863; 2nd ed., augmented, as *M.s Leben,* 1877; Eng. tr. by Lady Wallace, London, 1877; 3rd German ed., rev. by P. Sakolowski, Berlin, 1906); C. Pohl, *M. und Haydn in London* (Vienna, 1867); L. Nohl, *M. nach den Schilderungen seiner Zeitgenossen* (Leipzig, 1880); G. Nottebohm, *M.iana* (Leipzig, 1880); V. Wilder, *M., L'Homme et l'artiste* (Paris, 1880; 4th ed., 1889; Eng. tr., London, 1908); L. Meinardus, *M.: Ein Künstlerleben* (Leipzig, 1882); F. Gehring, *M.* (London, 1883; 2nd ed., 1911); L. Klasen, *W.A. M.: Sein Leben und seine Werke* (Vienna, 1897); O. Fleischer, *M.* (Berlin, 1899); R. Procházka, *M. in Prag* (Prague, 1899; rev. and augmented ed. by P. Nettl as *M. in Böhmen,* Prague, 1938); E. Breakspeare, *M.* (London, 1902); E. Prout, *M.* (London, 1903); L. Mirow, *M.s letzte Lebensjahre: Eine Künstlertragödie* (Leipzig, 1904); C. Belmonte, *Die Frauen im Leben M.s* (Augsburg, 1905); C. Bellaigue, *M.* (Paris, 1906); F. Lentner, *M.s Leben und Schaffen* (Innsbruck, 1906); H. von der Pfordten, *M.* (Leipzig, 1908); K. Storck, *M.: Sein Leben und Schaffen* (Stuttgart, 1908); W. Flower, *Stray Notes on M. and His Music* (Edinburgh, 1910); L. Schmidt, *W.A. M.* (Berlin, 1912); T. de Wyzewa and G. de Saint-Foix, *W.A. M.: Sa vie musicale et son œuvre de l'enfance à la pleine maturité* (a useful study, especially on the origin and development of M.'s style; 5 vols., Paris, 1912–46; vols. 3–5 by Saint-Foix alone); A. Schurig, *W.A. M.: Sein Leben und sein Werk* (2 vols., Leipzig, 1913; 2nd ed., 1923; French tr., 1925); H. de Curzon, *M.* (Paris, 1914; 2nd ed., 1927); E. Engel, *W.A. M.* (Vienna, 1914); J. Kreitmeier, *W.A. M.: Eine Charakterzeichnung des grossen Meisters nach literarischen Quellen* (Düsseldorf, 1919); L. Schiedermair, *M.: Sein Leben und seine Werke* (Munich, 1922; 2nd ed., rev., 1948); E. Blümml, *Aus M.s Freundes und Familien Kreis* (Vienna, 1923); O. Keller, *W.A. M.* (Berlin, 1926); B. Paumgartner, *M.* (Berlin, 1927; 6th ed., 1967); D. Hussey, *W.A. M.* (London, 1928; 2nd ed., 1933); M. Morold, *M.* (Vienna, 1931); R. Tenschert, *M.* (Leipzig, 1931); M. Davenport, *M.* (N.Y., 1932); H. Ghéon, *Promenades avec M.* (Paris, 1932; 7th ed., 1948; Eng. tr. as *In Search of M.,* London, 1934); S. Sitwell, *M.* (N.Y., 1932); R. Haas, *W.A. M.* (Potsdam, 1933; 2nd ed., 1950); E. Schmid, *W.A. M.* (Lübeck, 1934; 3rd ed., 1955); J. Talbot, *M.* (London, 1934); E. Blom, *M.* (London, 1935; 3rd ed., rev. by J. Westrup, 1975); A. Boschot, *M.* (Paris, 1935; 2nd ed., 1949); C. Perriolat, *M., Révélateur de la beauté artistique* (Paris, 1935); A. Kolb, *M.* (Vienna, 1937); W. Turner, *M.: The Man and His Works* (London and N.Y., 1938; 3rd ed., 1966); I. Gyomai, *Le Cœur de M.* (Paris, 1939); W. Goetz, *M.: Sein Leben in Selbstzeugnissen, Briefen und Berichten* (Berlin, 1941); E. Komorzynski, *M.* (Berlin, 1941; Vienna, 1955); G. Schaeffner, *W.A. M.* (Bern, 1941); A. Albertini, *M.: La vita, le opere* (Milan, 1942); E. Valentin, *Wege zu M.* (Regensburg, 1942); A. Einstein, *M.: His Character, His Work* (N.Y., 1945; German ed., 1947; 4th ed., 1960); P. Espil, *Les Voyages de Chérubin, ou L'Enfance de M.* (Bayonne, 1946); M. Mila, *W.A. M.* (Turin, 1946); E. Valentin, *M.* (Hameln, 1947); R. Tenschert, *W.A. M.* (Salzburg, 1951; Eng. tr., London, 1952); M. Kenyon, *M. in Salzburg* (London, 1952); K. Röttger, *W.A. M.* (Stuttgart, 1952); M. Brion, *M.* (Paris, 1955); J. Dalchow, *W.A. M.s Krankheiten, 1756–1763* (Bergisch Gladbach, 1955); N.

Medici di Marignano and R. Hughes, *A M. Pilgrimage: Being the Travel Diaries of Vincent and Mary Novello in the Year 1829* (London, 1955); A. Ostoja, *M. e l'Italia* (Bologna, 1955); E. Schenk, *W.A. M.: Eine Biographie* (Vienna and Zürich, 1955; 2nd ed., rev., 1975; Eng. tr. in an abridged ed. as *M. and His Times*, N.Y., 1959); G. Barblan and A. Della Corte, *M. in Italia* (Milan, 1956); C. Fusero, *M.* (Turin, 1956); F. Hadamowsky and L. Nowak, *M.: Werk und Zeit* (Vienna, 1956); D. Kerner, "W.A. M.s Krankheiten und sein Tod," *Neue Zeitschrift für Musik* (Dec. 1956); E. Blom, "M.'s Death," *Music & Letters* (Oct. 1957); J. Burk, *M. and His Music* (N.Y., 1959); J. and B. Massin, *W.A. M.: Biographie, histoire de l'œuvre* (Paris, 1959; 2nd ed., 1970); C. Haldane, *M.* (London, 1960); O. Deutsch, *M.: Die Dokumente seines Lebens, gesammelt und erläutert* (an invaluable study; Kassel, 1961; Eng. tr. as *M.: A Documented Biography*, Palo Alto, Calif., 1965; 2nd ed., 1966; supplement, 1978); idem, "Die Legende von M.s Vergiftung," *M.-Jahrbuch 1964*; S. Sadie, *M.* (London, 1965); C. Bär, *M.: Krankheit, Tod, Begräbnis* (Kassel, 1966; rev. ed., 1972); A. Hyatt King, *M.: A Biography with a Survey of Books, Editions and Recordings* (a useful study; London, 1970); M. Levey, *The Life and Death of M.* (London, 1971); H. Schuler, *Die Vorfahren W. M.s* (Essen, 1972); J. Eibl, "Die M.s und der Erzbischof," *Österreichische Musikzeitschrift*, XXX (1975); A. Hutchings, *M.: The Man, the Musician* (London and N.Y., 1976); W. Hildesheimer, *M.* (Frankfurt, 1977; Eng. tr., 1979); C. Bär, "Er war . . . kein guter Wirth: Eine Studie über M.s Verhältnis zum Geld," *Acta M.iana*, XXV (1978); I. Keys, *M.: His Life in His Music* (St. Albans, 1980); R. Angermüller, *"Auf Ehre und Credit": Die Finanzen des W.A. M.* (Munich, 1983); J. Féron, *M.: L'Avenir d'un enfant prodige* (Paris, 1983); A. Steptoe, "M. and Poverty: A Re-examination of the Evidence," *Musical Times* (April 1984); M. Morrow, "M. and Viennese Concert Life," ibid. (Aug. 1985); K. Pahlen, *Das M.-Buch: Chronik von Leben und Werk* (Zürich, 1985); P. Autexier, *M.* (Paris, 1987); P. Davies, "M.'s Manic-Depressive Tendencies," *Musical Times* (March–April 1987); J. Hocquard, *M.: L'Amour, la mort* (Paris, 1987); P. Young, *M.* (N.Y., 1987); H.C. Robbins Landon, *1791: M.'s Last Year* (London, 1988); P. Davies, *M. in Person: His Character and Health* (Westport, Conn., 1989); H.C. Robbins Landon, *M.: The Golden Years* (N.Y., 1989); idem, ed., *The M. Compendium* (N.Y., 1990); idem, *M. and Vienna* (N.Y., 1991).

ICONOGRAPHY: R. Tenschert, *W.A. M. 1756–1791: Sein Leben in Bildern* (Leipzig, 1935); R. Bory, *La Vie et l'œuvre de W.-A. M. par l'image* (Geneva, 1948; in Eng. as *The Life and Works of W.A. M. in Pictures*, Geneva, 1948); G. Rech, *W.A. M.: Ein Lebensweg in Bildern* (Munich and Berlin, 1955); R. Petzoldt, *W.A. M.: Sein Leben in Bildern* (Leipzig, 1956); E. Valentin, *M.: Eine Bildbiographie* (Munich, 1959; Eng. tr., 1959); O. Deutsch, *M. und seine Welt in zeitgenössischen Bildern* (Kassel, 1961; in German and Eng.).

MOZART AND FREEMASONRY: O. Deutsch, *M. und die Wiener Logen: Zur Geschichte seiner Freimaurer-Kompositionen* (Vienna, 1932); P. Nettl, *M. und die königliche Kunst: Die freimaurerische Grundlage der Zauberflöte* (Berlin, 1932; 2nd ed., 1956); P. Nettl, *M. and Masonry* (N.Y., 1957); J. Chailley, *"La Flûte enchantée," opéra maconnique: Essai d'explication du livret et de la musique* (Paris, 1968; Eng. tr. as *The Magic Flute, Masonic Opera*, N.Y., 1971; London, 1972); F. Smyth, "Brother M. of Vienna," *Ars Quatuor Coronatorum*, 87, Transactions of Quatuor Coronati Lodge No. 2076, London (Lodge of research; 1974); K. Thomson, "M. and Freemasonry," *Music & Letters* (Jan. 1976); idem, *The Masonic Thread in M.* (London, 1977); D. Heartz, "La clemenza di Sarastro: Masonic Benevolence in M.'s Last Operas," *Musical Times* (March 1983); H.C. Robbins Landon, *M. and the Masons* (London, 1983); J. Elenor, "Masonic Mediants: Notes on a Three-Keyed Opera," *Musical Times* (June 1987).

CRITICAL AND ANALYTICAL: GENERAL: A. Hammerle, *M. und einige Zeitgenossen: Neue Beiträge für Salzburgische Geschichte, Literatur und Musik* (Salzburg, 1877); K. Prieger, *Urtheile bedeutender Dichter, Philosophen und Musiker über M.*

(Wiesbaden, 1885–86); E. Komorzynski, *M.s Kunst der Instrumentation* (Stuttgart, 1906); A. Cametti, *M. a Roma* (Rome, 1907); G. Schünemann, ed., *M. als achtjahriger Komponist: Ein Notenbuch Wolfgangs* (Leipzig, 1909; Eng. tr., 1909); W. Nagel, *M. und die Gegenwart* (Langensalza, 1912); A. Leitzmann, *M.s Persönlichkeit* (Leipzig, 1914); R. Lach, *W.A. M. als Theoretiker* (Vienna, 1918); E. Lert, *M. auf dem Theater* (Berlin, 1918; 4th ed., 1922); H. Mersmann, *M.* (vol. 4 of *Kulturgeschichte der Musik in Einzeldarstellungen*, Berlin, 1925); V. Heinrich, *Komik und Humor bei M.* (Vienna, 1931); W. Lüthy, *M. und die Tonartencharakteristik* (Strasbourg, 1931); D. Tovey, *Essays in Musical Analysis* (7 vols., London, 1935–44); C. Thieme, *Der Klangstil des M.orchesters* (Leipzig, 1936); P. Hirsch, "Some Early M. Editions," *Music Review*, I (1940); H. Deininger, ed., *Augsburger M.buch: Zeitschrift des historischen Vereins für Schwaben*, LV–LVI (Augsburg, 1942–43); H. Socnik, *Das Pedal bei M.* (Danzig, 1943); M. Mila, *Saggi M.iani* (Milan, 1945); J. Chantavoine, *M. dans M.* (Paris, 1948); E. Schmid, *Ein schwäbisches M.buch* (Stuttgart, 1948); R. Elvers, *Untersuchungen zu den Tempi in M.s Instrumentalmusik* (diss., Univ. of Berlin, 1952); A. Hyatt King, *M. in Retrospect: Studies in Criticism and Bibliography* (London, 1955; 3rd ed., 1970); I. Bruce, "A Note on M.'s Bar-rhythms," *Music Review*, XVII (1956); A. Einstein, *Essays on Music* (N.Y., 1956); H. Engel, "M.s Instrumentation," *M.-Jahrbuch 1956*; R. Giazotto, *Annali M.iani* (Milan, 1956); H.C. Robbins Landon and D. Mitchell, eds., *The M. Companion* (N.Y. and London, 1956; 2nd ed., 1965); P. Schaller and H. Kühner, eds., *M.-Aspekte* (Olten and Freiburg, 1956); E. Schmid, "M. and Haydn," *Musical Quarterly* (April 1956); H. Albrecht, ed., *Die Bedeutung der Zeichen Keil, Strich, und Punkt bei M.* (Kassel, 1957); A. Della Corte, *Tutto il teatro di M.* (Turin, 1957); W. Siegmund-Schultze, *M.s Melodik und Stil* (Leipzig, 1957); H. Engel, "Haydn, M. und die Klassik," *M.-Jahrbuch 1959*; G. Massenkeil, *Untersuchungen zum Problem der Symmetrie in der Instrumentalmusik W.A. M.s* (Wiesbaden, 1962); *Neues Augsburger M.buch: Zeitschrift des historischen Vereins für Schwaben*, LXII–LXIII (Augsburg, 1962); I. Eisley, "M. and Counterpoint: Development and Synthesis," *Music Review*, XXIV (1963); P. Lang, ed., *The Creative World of M.* (N.Y., 1963); *M.gemeinde Wien 1913 bis 1963: Forschung und Interpretation* (Vienna, 1964); S. Davis, "Harmonic Rhythm in M.'s Sonata Form," *Music Review*, XXVII (1966); M. Flothuis, *M.s Bearbeitungen eigener und fremder Werke* (Salzburg, 1969); K. Marx, *Zur Einheit der zyklischen Form bei M.* (Stuttgart, 1971); M. Schmid, *M. und die Salzburger Tradition* (Tutzing, 1976); F. Holbock, *W.A. M.: Der Salzburger Domorganist und seine Beziehungen zur katholischen Kirche* (Stein am Rhein, 1978); C. Floros, *M. Studien I: Zu M.s Sinfonie, Opern- und Kirchenmusik* (Wiesbaden, 1979); R. Leavis, "M.'s Divertimentos for Mixed Consort," *Musical Times* (June 1980); B. Brophy, "Da Ponte and M.," *Musical Times* (July 1981); A. Tyson, "The M. Fragments," *Journal of the American Musicological Society*, XXXIV (1981); G. Pestelli, *The Age of M. and Beethoven* (Cambridge, 1984); G. Born, *M.s Musiksprache: Schlüssel zu Leben und Werk* (Munich, 1985); G. Gruber, *M. und die Nachwelt* (Salzburg, 1985); A. Tyson, *M.: Studies of the Autograph Scores* (Cambridge, Mass., 1987); J. Webster, "To Understand Verdi and Wagner We Must Understand M.," *19th Century Music* (Fall 1987); J.-P. Marty, *The Tempo Indications of M.* (New Haven, 1988); W. Crutchfield, "The Prosodic Appoggiatura in the Music of M. and His Contemporaries," *Journal of the American Musicological Society* (Summer 1989).

OPERA AND VOCAL MUSIC: A. Oulibicheff, *M.s Opern: Kritische Erläuterungen* (Leipzig, 1848); W. Pole, *The Story of M.'s Requiem* (London, 1879); C. Gounod, *Le Don Juan de M.* (Paris, 1890; Eng. tr., 1895); A. Farinelli, *Don Giovanni: Note critiche* (Turin, 1896); A. Weltner, *M.s Werke und die Wiener Hoftheater: Statistisches und Historisches* (Vienna, 1896); K. Söhle, *M. Dramatisches Zeitbild* (Leipzig, 1907); E. Dent, *M.'s Operas: A Critical Study* (London, 1913; 2nd ed., 1947); H. Cohen, *Die dramatische Idee in M.s Operntexten* (Berlin, 1916); H. von Waltershausen, *Die Zauberflöte* (Munich, 1920); A. Lorenz,

"Das Finale in M.s Meisteropern," *Die Musik*, XIX (1926–27); E. Blom, "The Literary Ancestry of Figaro," *Musical Quarterly* (Oct. 1927); R. Dumesnil, *Le "Don Juan" de M.* (Paris, 1927; 2nd ed., 1955); O. Beer, *M. und das Wiener Singspiel* (Vienna, 1932); K. Rosenthal, "The Salzburg Church Music of M. and His Predecessors," *Musical Quarterly* (Oct. 1932); S. Anheisser, "Die Urfassung des Figaro," *Zeitschrift für Musikwissenschaft*, XV (1932–33); F. Brukner, *Die Zauberflöte: Unbekannte Handschriften und seltene Drucke aus der Frühzeit der Oper* (Vienna, 1934); P. Stefan, *Die Zauberflöte: Herkunft, Bedeutung, Geheimnis* (Vienna, 1937); E. Komorzynski, "Die Zauberflöte: Entstehung und Bedeutung des Kunstwerks," *Neues M.-Jahrbuch* (vol. I, Regensburg, 1941); K. Rosenthal, "M.'s Sacramental Litanies and Their Forerunners," *Musical Quarterly* (Oct. 1941); P. Jouve, *Le Don Juan de M.* (Freiburg, 1942; 3rd ed., Paris, 1948; Eng. tr., London, 1957); L. Conrad, *M.s Dramaturgie der Oper* (Würzburg, 1943); E. Wellesz, "Don Giovanni and the Dramma Giocoso," *Music Review*, IV (1943); C. Benn, *M. on the Stage* (London, 1946; 2nd ed., 1947); S. Levarie, *M.'s "Le nozze di Figaro": A Critical Analysis* (Chicago, 1952); D. Lauener, *Die Frauengestalten in M.s Opern* (Zürich, 1954); K. Fellerer, *M.s Kirchenmusik* (Salzburg, 1955); M. Brown, "M.'s Songs for Voice and Piano," *Music Review*, XVII (1956); A. Greither, *Die sieben grossen Opern M.s: Versuche über das Verhältnis der Texte zur Musik* (Heidelberg, 1956; 2nd ed., enl., 1977); C. Raeburn, "Die textlichen Quellen des 'Schauspieldirektor,'" *Österreichische Musikzeitschrift*, XIII (1958); E. Hess, "Zur Ergänzung des Requiems von M. durch F.X. Süssmayr." *M.-Jahrbuch 1959*; T. Volek, "Über den Ursprung von M.s Oper 'La clemenza di Tito,'" *M.-Jahrbuch 1959*; I. Kecskeméti, "Beiträge zur Geschichte von M.s Requiem," *Studia Musicologica Academiae Scientiarum Hungaricae*, I (1961); S. Kunze, "M.s Schauspieldirektor," *M.-Jahrbuch 1962–3*; K. Marguerre, "M. und Süssmayr," *M.-Jahrbuch 1962–3*; A. Livermore, "The Origins of Don Juan," *Music & Letters* (July 1963); B. Brophy, *M. the Dramatist: A New View of M., His Operas and His Age* (London and N.Y., 1964; new ed., 1988); O. Deutsch, "Zur Geschichte von M.s Requiem," *Österreichische Musikzeitschrift*, XIX (1964); C. Floros, "Das 'Programm' in M.s Meisterouverturnen," *Studien zur Musikwissenschaft*, XXVI (1964); C. Raeburn, "Die Entführungsszene aus 'Die Entführung aus dem Serail,'" *M.-Jahrbuch 1964*; A. Rosenberg, *Die Zauberflöte: Geschichte und Deutung* (Munich, 1964); A. Livermore, "Così fan tutti: A Well-kept Secret," *Music & Letters* (Oct. 1965); R. Moberly and C. Raeburn, "M.'s 'Figaro'; The Plan of Act III," *Music & Letters* (April 1965); L. Nowak, "Das Requiem von W.A. M.," *Österreichische Musikzeitschrift*, XX (1965); P. Branscombe, "'Die Zauberflöte': Some Textual and Interpretative Problems," *Proceedings of the Royal Musical Association*, XCII (1965–66); M. Chusid, "The Significance of D minor in M.'s Dramatic Music," *M.-Jahrbuch 1965–6*; G. Gruber, "Das Autograph der 'Zauberflöte,'" *M.-Jahrbuch 1967* and *1968–70*; D. Heartz, "The Genesis of M.'s Idomeneo," *M.-Jahrbuch 1967*; K.-H. Köhler, "M.s Kompositionsweise: Beobachtungen am Figaro-Autograph," *M.-Jahrbuch 1967*; R. Moberly, *Three M. Operas: Figaro, Don Giovanni, The Magic Flute* (London, 1967; N.Y., 1968); S. Döhring, "Die Arienformen in M.s Opern," *M.-Jahrbuch 1968–70*; H. Federhofer, "Die Harmonik als dramatischer Ausdrucksfaktor in M.s Meisteropern," *M.-Jahrbuch 1968–70*; E. Batley, *A Preface to The Magic Flute* (London, 1969); C. Henning, "Thematic Metamorphoses in Don Giovanni," *Music Review*, XXX (1969); A. Abert, *Die Opern M.s* (Wolfenbüttel, 1970; in Eng. in *The New Oxford History of Music*, vol. VII, London, 1973); B. Brophy, "'Figaro' and the Limitations of Music," *Music & Letters* (Jan. 1970); F. Beyer, "M.s Komposition zum Requiem: Zur Frage der Ergänzung," *Acta M.iana*, XVIII (1971); A. Dunning, "M.s Kanons," *M.-Jahrbuch 1971–2*; C. Rosenthal, "Der Einfluss der Salzburger Kirchenmusik auf M.s kirchenmusikalische Kompositionen," *M.-Jahrbuch 1971–2*; H. Eggebrecht, *Versuch über die Wiener Klassik: Die Tanzszene in M.s "Don Giovanni"* (Wiesbaden, 1972); S. Kunze, *Don Giovanni vor M.: Die Tradition der Don Giovanni-Opern im italienischen Buffo-Theater des 18. Jahrhunderts* (Munich, 1972); R. Moberly, "M. and His Librettists," *Music & Letters* (April 1973); D. Heartz, "Tonality and Motif in Idomeneo," *Musical Times* (May 1974); R. Moberly, "The Influence of French Classical Drama on M.'s 'La clemenza di Tito,'" *Music & Letters* (July 1974); K. Fellerer, "Liturgische Grundlagen der Kirchenmusik M.s," in *Festschrift Walter Senn* (Munich and Salzburg, 1975); G. Gruber, "Bedeutung und Spontaneität in M.s 'Zauberflöte,'" ibid.; H. Scheel, "'Le Mariage de Figaro' von Beaumarchais und das Libretto der 'Nozze di Figaro' von Lorenzo da Ponte," *Die Musikforschung*, XXVIII (1975); A. Tyson, "'La clemenza di Tito' and Its Chronology," *Musical Times* (March 1975); W. Mann, *The Operas of M.* (London, 1977); F. Noske, *The Signifier and the Signified: Studies in the Operas of M. and Verdi* (The Hague, 1977); D. Heartz, "M., His Father and 'Idomeneo,'" *Musical Times* (March 1978); C. Osborne, *The Complete Operas of M.* (London, 1978); C. Ballantine, "Social and Philosophical Outlook of M.'s Operas," *Musical Quarterly* (Oct. 1981); P. Branscombe, "Cosi in Context," *Musical Times* (July 1981); R. Donington, "Don Giovanni Goes to Hell," *Musical Times* (July 1981); D. Heartz, "'Che mi sembra di morir'; Donna Elvira and the Sextet," *Musical Times* (July 1981); A. Tyson, "Le nozze di Figaro: Lessons from the Autograph Score," *Musical Times* (July 1981); B. Williams, "M.'s Comedies and the Sense of an Ending," *Musical Times* (July 1981); C. Gianturco, *M.'s Early Operas* (London, 1982); W. Allanbrook, *Rhythmic Gesture in M.: Le nozze di Figaro and Don Giovanni* (Chicago and London, 1984); S. Kunze, *M.s Opern* (Stuttgart, 1984); K. Fellerer, *Die Kirchenmusik W.A. M.s* (Laaber, 1985); S. Henze-Döhring, *Opera seria, Opera buffa and M.s Don Giovanni: Zur Gattungskonvergenz in der italienischen Oper des 18. Jahrhunderts* (Laaber, 1986); J. Hocquard, *La Clemenza di Tito K. 621* (n.p., 1986); J. Kaiser, *Who's Who in M.'s Operas: From Alfonso to Zerlina* (London, 1986); B. Blomhert, *The Harmoniemusik of "Die Entführung aus dem Serail" by W.A. M.: Study about its Authenticity and Critical Edition* (The Hague, 1987); S. Corse, *Opera and the Uses of Language: M., Verdi, and Britten* (London and Toronto, 1987); J. Kristek, ed., *M.'s Don Giovanni in Prague* (Prague, 1987); T. Bauman, *W.A. M.: Die Entführung aus dem Serail* (Cambridge, 1988); T. Carter, *W.A. M.: Le Nozze di Figaro* (Cambridge, 1988); R. Maunder, *M.'s Requiem: On Preparing a New Edition* (Oxford, 1988); A. Steptoe, *The M.-Da Ponte Operas: The Cultural and Musical Background to Le nozze di Figaro, Don Giovanni, and Così fan tutte* (Oxford, 1988); D. Heartz, *M.'s Operas* (Berkeley, 1990).

ORCHESTRAL: D. Schultz, *M.s Jugendsinfonien* (Leipzig, 1900); H. Schenker, "M.: Sinfonie g-Moll," *Das Meisterwerk in der Musik*, II (1926); A. Dickinson, *A Study of M.'s Last Three Symphonies* (London, 1927; 2nd ed., 1940); G. de Saint-Foix, *Les Sinfonies de M.* (Paris, 1932; Eng. tr., 1947); N. Broder, "The Wind Instruments in M.'s Symphonies," *Musical Quarterly* (July 1933); C. Girdlestone, *W.A. M. et ses concertos pour piano* (2 vols., Paris, 1939; 3rd ed., 1978; in Eng., 1 vol., London and Norman, Okla., 1948); A. Hutchings, *A Companion to M.'s Piano Concertos* (London, 1948; 2nd ed., 1950); H. Engel, "Über M.s Jugendsinfonien," *M.-Jahrbuch 1951*; G. Hausswald, *M.s Serenaden: Ein Beitrag zur Stilkritik des 18. Jahrhunderts* (Leipzig, 1951; 2nd ed., rev., 1975); H. Engel, "Der Tanz in M.s Kompositionen," *M.-Jahrbuch 1952*; J. David, *Die Jupiter-Sinfonie: Eine Studie über die thematisch-melodischen Zusammenhänge* (Göttingen, 1953); E. Simon, "Sonata into Concerto: A Study of M.'s First Seven Concertos," *Acta Musicologica*, XXXI (1959); A. Abert, "Stilistischer Befund und Quellenlage: Zu M.s Lambacher Sinfonie KV Anh. 221–45a," *Festschrift Hans Engel* (Kassel, 1964); H. Tischler, *A Structural Analysis of M.'s Piano Concertos* (N.Y., 1966); D. Forman, *M.'s Concerto Form: The First Movements of the Piano Concertos* (London, 1971); P. Benary, "Metrum bei M.: Zur metrischen Analyse seiner letzten drei Sinfonien," *Studien zur Musikwissenschaft*, CXIV (1974); S. Wollenberg, "The Jupiter Theme: New Light on Its Creation," *Musical Times* (Sept. 1975); A. Hyatt King, *M. Wind and String Concertos* (London, 1978);

N. Zaslaw, "M.'s Paris Symphonies," *Musical Times* (Sept. 1978); C. Wolff, "Zur Chronologie der Klavierkonzert-Kadenzen M.s," *M.-Jahrbuch 1978–9;* A. Tyson, "The Two Slow Movements of M.'s Paris Symphony K297," *Musical Times* (Jan. 1981); R. Dearling, *The Music of W.A. M.: The Symphonies* (Rutherford, N.J., 1982); E. Smith, *M. Serenades, Divertimenti and Dances* (London, 1982); L. Ferguson, *"Col Basso" and "Generalbass" in M.'s Keyboard Concertos: Notation, Performance, Theory, and Practice* (diss., Princeton Univ., 1983); N. Zaslaw, "The 'Lambach' Symphonies of W. and Leopold M.," *Music and Civilization: Essays Presented to Paul Henry Lang* (N.Y., 1983); J. Larsen, "M.'s 'Odense' Symphony," *Music & Musicians* (Feb. 1985); C. Eisen, *The Symphonies of Leopold M. and Their Relationship to the Early Symphonies of W.A. M.: A Bibliographical and Stylistic Study* (diss., Cornell Univ., 1986); S. Sadie, *M. Symphonies* (London, 1986); J. Larsen and K. Wedin, eds., *Die Sinfonie KV 16a "del Sigr. M.": Bericht über das Symposium in Odense anlässlich der Erstaufführung des wiedergefundenen Werkes Dezember 1984* (Odense, 1987); C. Eisen, "New Light on M.'s 'Linz' Symphony, K.425," *Journal of the Royal Musical Association,* 113/1 (1988); W. Malloch, "Carl Czerny's Metronome Marks for Haydn and M. Symphonies," *Early Music* (Feb. 1988); C. Eisen, "Problems of Authenticity among M.'s Early Symphonies: The Examples of K.Anh. 220 (16a) and 76 (42a)," *Music & Letters* (Nov. 1989); R. Levin, *Who Wrote the M. Four-Wind Concertante?* (Stuyvesant, N.Y., 1989); N. Zaslaw, *M.'s Symphonies: Context, Performance Practice, Reception* (Oxford, 1990). **CHAMBER MUSIC:** T. Dunhill, *M.'s String Quartets* (London, 1927; 2nd ed., 1948); A. Einstein, "M.'s Ten Celebrated String Quartets," *Music Review,* III (1942); W. Fischer, "M.s Weg von der begleiteten Klaviersonata zur Kammermusik mit Klavier," *M.-Jahrbuch 1956;* K. Marguerre, "M.s Klaviertrios," *M.-Jahrbuch 1960–61;* A. Hyatt King, *M. Chamber Music* (London, 1968); W. Hummeke, *Versuch einer strukturwissenschaftlichen Darstellung der ersten und vierten Sätze der zehn letzten Streichquartette von W.A. M.* (Münster, 1970); I. Hunkemöller, *W.A. M.s frühe Sonaten für Violine und Klavier* (Bern and Munich, 1970); D. Leeson and D. Whitwell, "M.'s 'Spurious' Wind Octets," *Music & Letters* (Oct. 1972); R. Hellyer, "M.'s Harmoniemusik," *Music Review,* XXXIV (1973); A. Tyson, "New Light on M.'s 'Prussian' Quartets," *Musical Times* (Feb. 1975); C. Wolff, ed., *The String Quartets of Haydn, M., and Beethoven: Studies of the Autograph Manuscripts* (a valuable investigation; Cambridge, Mass., 1980); R. Hellyer, "M.'s Harmoniemusik and Its Publishers," *Musical Times* (July 1981); M. Flothuis, *W.A. M.: Streichquintett G-moll, KV 516* (Munich, 1987); E. Cavett-Dunsby, "M.'s 'Haydn' Quartets: Composing Up and Down without Rules," *Journal of the Royal Musical Association,* 113/1 (1988). **KEYBOARD:** F. Lorenz, *W.A. M. als Clavier-Componist* (Breslau, 1866); F. Marks, *Questions on M.'s Pianoforte-sonatas* (London, 1929); N. Broder, "M. and the 'Clavier,'" *Musical Quarterly* (Oct. 1941); H. Dennerlein, *Der unbekannte M.: Die Welt seiner Klavierwerke* (Leipzig, 1951); P. and E. Badura-Skoda, *M.-Interpretation, Anregungen zur Interpretation der Klavierwerke* (Vienna and Stuttgart, 1957; rev. ed. in Eng. as *Interpreting M. on the Keyboard,* N.Y., 1962); R. Rosenberg, *Die Klaviersonaten M.s: Gestalt- und Stilanalyse* (Hofheim, Hesse, 1972); E. McKay, *The Impact of the New Pianofortes on Classical Keyboard Style: M., Beethoven and Schubert* (West Hagley, West Midlands, 1987). **MISCELLANEOUS:** C. Roleff, ed., *M.iana* (Tutzing, 1988); G. Snell, ed., *Viva M.: An Anthology of Appreciation* (San Jose, Calif., 1989).

Mraczek (actually, **Mraček**), **Joseph Gustav,** Czech composer; b. Brünn, March 12, 1878; d. Dresden, Dec. 24, 1944. He received his 1st instruction from his father, the cellist Franz (František) Mraček (1842–98); was a chorister in various churches in Brünn before going to Vienna, where he studied with Hellmesberger, Stocker, and Löwe at the Cons.; from 1897 to 1902, was concertmaster at the Stadttheater in Brünn;

then taught violin at the Cons. there (1898–1919). He settled in Dresden and conducted the Phil. (1919–24) and taught composition at the Cons. (from 1919). **WORKS: OPERAS:** *Der glaserne Pantoffel* (Brünn, 1902); *Der Traum* (Brünn, Feb. 26, 1909); *Aebelö* (Breslau, 1915); *Ikdar* (Dresden, 1921); *Herrn Dürers Bild oder Madonna am Wiesenzaun* (Hannover, Jan. 29, 1927); *Der Liebesrat* (not perf.); *Der arme Tobias* (1936). **ORCH.:** *Rustans Traum,* symphonic poem (1911); *Max und Moritz,* symphonic burlesque (1911); *Orientalische Skizzen* for Chamber Orch. (1918); *Eva,* symphonic poem (1922); *Variété,* scenes (1928); also Piano Quintet; String Quartet; choral works; piano pieces; songs. **BIBL.:** E. Müller, *J.G. M.* (Dresden, 1917).

Mravina (original name, **Mravinskaya**), **Evgeniya (Konstantinovna),** noted Russian soprano; b. St. Petersburg, Feb. 16, 1864; d. Yalta, Oct. 25, 1914. She studied in St. Petersburg with Pryanishnikov, and later with Désirée d'Artôt in Berlin; then sang in Italy. After returning to Russia, she joined the Maryinsky Theater in St. Petersburg in 1886, remaining on its roster until 1900. In 1891–92 she toured in England, France, Belgium, and Germany. She had the privilege of going over the part of Marguerite in *Faust* with Gounod, and the part of Mignon in the opera of that name by Thomas with the composer himself. She gave brilliant renditions of Italian soprano roles; was greatly praised in Russia for her performances of the Russian operatic parts. She retired from the operatic stage in 1900 but continued to appear in recital. **BIBL.:** A. Grigorieva, *E.K. M.* (Moscow, 1970).

Mravinsky, Evgeni (Alexandrovich), eminent Russian conductor; b. St. Petersburg, June 4, 1903; d. there (Leningrad), Jan. 19, 1988. He studied biology at St. Petersburg Univ.; then joined the Imperial Ballet as a pantomimist and rehearsal pianist; in 1924 he enrolled in the Leningrad Cons., where he studied conducting with Gauk, graduating in 1931; also took additional training with Malko; had courses in composition with Vladimir Shcherbachev; then was conductor of the Leningrad Theater of Opera and Ballet (1932–38). In 1938 he was appointed principal conductor of the Leningrad Phil. Mravinsky represented the best of the Soviet school of conducting, in which technical precision and fidelity to the music were combined with individual and even Romantic interpretations. He was especially noted for his fine performances of Tchaikovsky's operas, ballets, and syms.; he gave 1st performances of several syms. of Prokofiev and Shostakovich; also conducted works by Bartók and Stravinsky. In 1973 he was awarded the order of Hero of Socialist Labor. **BIBL.:** V. Bogdanov-Berezovsky, *The Soviet Conductor M.* (Leningrad, 1956); V. Fomin, *M. Conducts* (Leningrad, 1976).

Mshvelidze, Shalva (Mikhailovich), Russian ethnomusicologist, teacher, and composer; b. Tiflis, May 28, 1904; d. there (Tbilisi), March 4, 1984. He studied with Bagrinovsky at the Tiflis Cons., graduating in 1930, and with Shcherbachev, Tyulin, Steinberg, and Ryazanov at the Leningrad Cons. He was made a teacher (1929) and a prof. (1942) at the Tbilisi Cons. He was a leading figure in Georgian music. **WORKS: OPERAS:** *Legend of Tariel* (Tbilisi, Feb. 25, 1946; rev. 1966); *The Grandmaster's Right Hand* (Tbilisi, June 3, 1961); *Widow of a Soldier* (1967); *Aluda Ketelauri* (1972). **ORATORIOS:** *Caucasiana* (1949); *The Legacy of Posterity,* for the centennial of Lenin's birth (1970). **ORCH.:** 5 syms. (1943, 1944, 1952, 1968, 1974); 4 symphonic poems: *Azar* (1933); *Zviadauri* (1940); *Mindia* (1949); *Youngling and Tiger* (1962); also chamber music; songs; incidental music to about 25 plays; film scores. **BIBL.:** V. Donadze, *S. M.* (Tbilisi, 1946); A. Shaverzashvili, *Fugi S. M.* (Tbilisi, 1964); A. Tsulukidze, *S. M.* (Tbilisi, 1964).

Muck, Karl, great German conductor; b. Darmstadt, Oct. 22, 1859; d. Stuttgart, March 3, 1940. He received his 1st musical instruction from his father; also studied piano with Kissner in Würzburg; later pursued academic studies (classical philology) at the Univs. of Heidelberg and Leipzig (Ph.D., 1880).

He also attended the Leipzig Cons., and shortly before graduation made a successful debut as pianist with the Gewandhaus Orch. However, he did not choose to continue a pianistic career; he obtained a position as chorus master at the municipal opera in Zürich; his ability soon secured him the post of conductor there; in subsequent years he was theater conductor in Salzburg, Brünn, and Graz; there Angelo Neumann, impresario of a traveling opera company, heard him, and engaged him as conductor for the Landestheater in Prague (1886), and then as Seidl's successor for his traveling Wagner Co. It was during those years that Muck developed his extraordinary qualities as a masterful disciplinarian and faithful interpreter possessing impeccable taste. In 1889 he conducted the Wagner tetralogy in St. Petersburg, and in 1891, in Moscow. In 1892 he was engaged as 1st conductor at the Berlin Royal Opera, and also frequently conducted sym. concerts of the Royal Chapel there. From 1894 to 1911 he led the Silesian Music Festivals; in 1899 he conducted the Wagner repertoire at London's Covent Garden. He also appeared, with outstanding success, in Paris, Rome, Brussels, Madrid, Copenhagen, and other European centers. In 1901 he was selected to conduct the performances of *Parsifal* at Bayreuth; appeared there regularly until 1930. Muck was one of the conductors of the Vienna Phil. (1904–6); then was conductor of the Boston Sym. Orch. (1906–8) before returning to Berlin as Generalmusikdirektor. He returned to America in 1912 and again assumed the post of conductor of the Boston Sym. Orch.; held that post with the greatest distinction until the U.S. entered World War I in 1917. Muck's position then became controversial; a friend of Kaiser Wilhelm II, he saw no reason to temper his ardent German nationalism, nor was he inclined to alter certain aspects of his private life. Protests were made against his retention as conductor, but despite the efforts to defend him by Major Higginson, the founder of the Boston Sym. Orch., Muck's case proved hopeless. In order to avoid prosecution under the Mann Act, he subsequently submitted to being arrested at his home on March 25, 1918, as an enemy alien and was interned until the end of the war. In 1919 he returned to Germany; conducted the Hamburg Phil. from 1922 until his retirement in 1933. Muck was one of the foremost conductors of his era. A consummate musician, endowed with a masterful technique, he was renowned for his authoritative performances of the revered Austro-German repertoire. His sympathies were wide, however, and he programmed such contemporary musicians as Mahler, Debussy, Sibelius, and even Schoenberg and Webern at his concerts. His penchant for stern disciplinarianism and biting sarcasm made him a feared podium figure for the musicians who played under him, but the results he obtained were exemplary.

BIBL.: W. Zinne, "C. M.," *Die Musik*, XVII (1924–25); N. Stücker, *K. M.* (Graz, 1939); I. Lowens, "L'Affaire-M.," *Musicology* I/3 (1947); H. Schonberg, *The Great Conductors* (N.Y., 1967); J. Baker-Carr, *Evening at Symphony: A Portrait of the Boston Symphony Orchestra* (Boston, 1977).

Muczynski, Robert, American composer, pianist, and teacher; b. Chicago, March 19, 1929. He received training from Walter Knupfer (piano) and A. Tcherepnin (composition) at De Paul Univ. (B.M., 1950; M.M., 1952), playing his own *Divertimento* for Piano and Orch. at his graduation; pursued further training with Tcherepnin in Nice (summer 1961). In 1958 he made his N.Y. recital debut, and in subsequent years continued to be active as a pianist; taught at De Paul Univ. (1955–58) and served as chairman of the piano dept. at Loras College in Dubuque, Iowa (1956–59); in 1964–65 he was a visiting lecturer at Roosevelt Univ. in Chicago; then was a prof. and head of the composition dept. at the Univ. of Arizona in Tucson from 1965 until 1988, when he became prof. emeritus. He is a particularly fine composer of chamber music and piano pieces, whose output reflects the influence of Bartók and Piston, among others.

WORKS: ORCH.: *Divertimento* for Piano and Orch. (1951–52); Sym. No. 1 (1953); Piano Concerto (1954; Louisville, Jan. 12, 1955); *Galena: A Town*, suite (1957–58); *Dovetail Overture* (Oakland, Calif., March 13, 1960); *Dance Movements* for Chamber Orch. (1962–63); *Symphonic Dialogues* (Washington, D.C., Oct. 31, 1965); *Charade* (1970–74); *A Serenade for Summer* for Chamber Orch. (1976; Tucson, Sept. 15, 1978); *Symphonic Memoir* (1978; Tucson, Jan. 11, 1979); Concerto for Alto Saxophone and Chamber Orch. (Kalamazoo, Mich., Oct. 31, 1981). **CHAMBER:** *Allegro deciso* for Brass Sextet and Timpani (1952); *Fragments* for Woodwind Trio (1958); Trumpet Trio (1959); *3 Designs* for 3 Timpani (1960); Sonata for Flute and Piano (1960–61); *Movements* for Wind Quintet (1962); 3 piano trios (1966–67; 1975; 1986–87); *Gallery*, suite for Cello (1966); Sonata for Cello and Piano (1968); *Fantasy Trio* for Clarinet, Cello, and Piano (1969); *Voyage*, 7 pieces for Trumpet, Horn, and Trombone (1969); Sonata for Alto Saxophone and Piano (1970); Trio for Violin, Viola, and Cello (1971–72); *Time Pieces* for Clarinet and Piano (1983); Wind Quintet (1985); also numerous piano pieces. **VOCAL:** *Alleluia* for Chorus (1961); *I Never Saw a Moor* for Chorus (1967); *Synonyms for Life* for Chorus and Piano (1973).

Mudarra, Alonso de, Spanish vihuelist and composer; b. Palencia diocese, c.1508; d. Seville, April 1, 1580. He became a canon (1546) and was elected major domo (1568) at Seville Cathedral. He publ. the important vol. *Tres libro de música en cifras para vihuela* (Seville, 1546; ed. in Monumentos de la Música Española, VII, 1949).

BIBL.: M. Schneider, "Un villancico de A. d.M. procedente de la música popular granadina," *Anuario Musical*, X (1955).

Muddy Waters. See **Waters, Muddy.**

Mudge, Richard, English clergyman and composer; b. Bideford, 1718; d. Bedworth, Warwickshire, April 3, 1763. He studied at Pembroke College, Oxford (B.A., 1738; M.A., 1741); after ordination, he was made vicar in Great Packington (1735) and rector of Bedworth (1756). He publ. a set of *Six Concertos in seven parts . . . to which is added a "Non nobis Domine" in eight parts* (London, 1749); also wrote a *Medley Concerto, with French Horns.*

BIBL.: S. Flint, *M. Memoirs* (1883).

Mudie, Thomas Molleson, English composer and organist of Scottish descent; b. London, Nov. 30, 1809; d. there, July 24, 1876. He studied at the Royal Academy of Music in London with Crotch and Potter; then taught piano there (1832–44); was organist at Galton, Surrey (1834–44); then taught at Edinburgh (1844–63), eventually returning to London. He wrote 5 syms. (1827–37); Piano Quintet (1843); Piano Trio (1843); sacred vocal works; piano pieces; songs.

Mueller, Otto-Werner, German-American conductor and pedagogue; b. Bensheim, June 23, 1926. He studied at the Frankfurt Musisches Gymnasium; was made music director of the Stuttgart Radio's chamber music dept. (1945), where he founded and conducted its chamber choir; then became conductor at the Heidelberg Theater (1947). After moving to Canada in 1951, he conducted with the CBC and joined the faculty of the Montreal Cons. (1958). He was founder-director of the Victoria School of Music in British Columbia (1963–65) and music director of the Victoria Sym. Orch. (1963–67); then went to the U.S., where he was prof. of music at the Univ. of Wisconsin (1967–77) and of conducting at the Yale Univ. School of Music (1977–87); subsequently directed orch. studies at N.Y.'s Juilliard School (from 1987).

Mueller (Müller) von Asow, Erich H(ermann), noted German musicologist; b. Dresden, Aug. 31, 1892; d. Berlin, June 4, 1964. He studied with Riemann and Schering at the Univ. of Leipzig (Ph.D., 1915, with the diss. *Die Mingottischen Opernunternehmungen, 1732–1756*; publ. in Dresden, 1917, as *Angelo und Pietro Mingotti: Ein Beitrag zur Geschichte der Oper im XVIII. Jahrhundert*). During World War I, he was active as a military bandmaster; after serving as assistant director of Leipzig's Neue Theater, he was artistic director of Dresden's international festival for modern music (1917–18); was director of the Wernow Theater (1918–19) and then was active as a music critic in Berlin and Dresden; joined the staff of Dresden's Pädagogium der Tonkunst (1926), serving as its director (1927–33). He went to Austria (1936); was briefly under arrest by the Gestapo (1943); returned to Germany in 1945, where he founded the Internationales Musiker-Brief-Archiv in Berlin.

WRITINGS: *Joseph Gustav Mraczek* (Dresden, 1917); *Die Musiksammlung der Bibliothek zu Kronstadt* (Kronstadt, 1930); *Dresdner Musikstätten* (Dresden, 1931); *Egon Kornauth: Ein Bild von Leben und Schaffen des mährischen Komponisten* (Vienna, 1941); *Max Reger und seine Welt* (Berlin, 1944); *Richard Strauss: Thematisches Verzeichnis* (3 vols., Vienna and Wiesbaden, 1959–74; completed by A. Ott and F. Trenner); also ed. numerous vols.

Muench, Gerhart, German-born Mexican pianist and composer; b. Dresden, March 23, 1907; d. Tacámbaro, Nov. 9, 1988. He studied piano with his father, a prof. at the Dresden Cons.; gave a public piano recital in Dresden at the age of 9. His auspicious career was halted by the Nazi takeover in Germany; Muench was drafted into the German army, but was discharged in 1944 as physically unfit; he emigrated to America in 1947; settled in Mexico in 1953; taught at the Univ. Nacional in Mexico City. In his piano recitals he introduced the new music of Stockhausen, Boulez, Pousseur, and others to Mexican audiences.

WORKS: CHAMBER OPERA: *Tumulus Veneris* (1950). ORCH.: *Concerto da camera* for Piano and Chamber Orch. (1926); *Capriccio variato* for Piano and Orch. (1941); *Vocationes* for Piano and Chamber Orch. (1951); Bassoon Concerto (1956); *Muerte sin fin* (1957); Concerto for Piano and Strings (1957); Violin Concerto (1959); *Labyrinthus Orphei* (1965); *Itinera duo* for Piano and Orch. (1965); *Oxymora* (1967); *Auditur* (1968); *Epitomae tacambarensiae* (1974). CHAMBER: Cello Sonata (1938); *Tesauras Orphei* for Oboe, Clarinet, Viola, Double Bass, and Harp (1957); *Evoluta* for 2 Pianos (1961); *Pièce de résistance* for Piano (1962); *Tessellata tacambarensia,* cycle of 9 chamber pieces for various instrumental groups or soloists (1964–76); *Asociaciones* for Soprano and Instruments (1969); *Out of Chaos* for Cello and Piano (1975); *Signa Flexanima* for Piano Trio (1975); *Tetrálogo* for String Quartet (1977); *Mini-Dialogos* for Violin and Cello (1977); *Proenza* for Piano Trio (1977); *Yuriko* for Violin and Piano (1977); also 5 masses; choruses; songs.

Muffat, Georg, eminent French-born German organist and composer of Scottish descent, father of **Gottlieb (Theophil) Muffat;** b. Mégève, Savoy (baptized), June 1, 1653; d. Passua, Feb. 23, 1704. He went to Alsace in childhood; after studies with Lully and others in Paris (1663–69), he returned to Alsace as a student at the Jesuit college in Sélestat and continued his studies in Molsheim (from 1671), where he was made organist of the exiled Strasbourg Cathedral chapter; by 1674 he was in Ingolstadt as a law student; with war imminent, he went to Vienna and found a patron in Emperor Leopold I. After a sojourn in Prague (1677–78), he became organist and chamber musician to Archbishop Max Gandolf, Count of Kuenberg, in Salzburg; during his tenure, he was allowed a leave of absence to pursue his training with Pasquini in Rome, where he was befriended by Corelli. In 1690 he was appointed Kapellmeister at the court of Johann Philipp of Lamberg, Bishop of Passau. Muffat was a significant composer who helped introduce the French and Italian styles of his era to the German-speaking lands. He wrote the valuable treatise *Regulae concentuum partiturae* (c.1699; ed. by H. Federhofer, Musicological Studies and Documents, IV, 1961).

WORKS: *Armonico tributo,* 5 sonatas for Strings and Basso Continuo (Salzburg, 1682); *Apparatus musico-organisticus,* 12 toccatas, a ciaccona, a passacaglia, and an aria with variations for Organ (Salzburg, 1690); *Suavioris harmoniae instrumentalis hyporchematicae florilegium primum,* 7 suites for Orch., *a 4* or 5, and Basso Continuo (Augsburg, 1695); *Florilegium secundum,* 8 suites for Orch., *a 4,* and Basso Continuo (Passau, 1698); *Ausserlesene Instrumental-Music,* 12 concerti grossi (Passau, 1701); other extant works include a Sonata for Violin

and Basso Continuo (1677) and various preludes and dances for Keyboard.

BIBL.: L. von Stollbrock, *Die Komponisten G. und Gottlieb M.* (Rostock, 1888); idem, "G. M. und sein 'Florilegium,'" *Monatshefte für Musikgeschichte,* XXII (1890); idem, "G. M.s musiktheoretische Abhandlung," ibid., XXIII (1891); A. Schering, "G. M.: 'Ausserlesene mit Ernst und Lust gemengte Instrumental-Musik,' 1701," *Zeitschrift der Internationalen Musik-Gesellschaft,* V (1903–4); A. Goehlinger, "Georges M.," *Caecilia,* LXII (1954); R. Walter, "G. M. und sein 'Apparatus musico-organisticus,'" *Musik und Altar,* XI (1959); K. Cooper and J. Zsako, "G. M.'s Observations on the Lully Style of Performance," *Musical Quarterly,* LIII (1967); W. Kolneder, *G. M. zur Aufführungspraxis* (Strasbourg, 1970); S. Harris, "Lully, Corelli, M. and the Eighteenth-century String Body," *Music & Letters,* LIV (1973); I. Stampfl, *G. M.: Orchesterkompositionen: Ein musikhistorischer Vergleich der Orchestermusik, 1670–1710* (Passau, 1984).

Muffat, Gottlieb (Theophil), distinguished German organist and composer, son of **Georg Muffat;** b. Passau (baptized), April 25, 1690; d. Vienna, Dec. 9, 1770. He most likely received his initial training from his father; by 1711 was in Vienna, where he continued his education as a Hofscholar under Fux; later studied abroad. He was officially named court organist in 1717, his duties including performing for the Hofkapelle and serving as continuo accompanist for the opera; later became a teacher to the children of the royal family; was made 2nd organist (1729) and 1st organist (1741), retaining the latter position until he was pensioned (1763). Muffat was a notable representative of the late Baroque era, producing a large body of fine keyboard music. He publ. 72 *Verseltsammt 12 Toccaten (besonders zum Kirchen-Dienst bey Choral-Aemtern und Vesperen dienlich)* (Vienna, 1726) and *Componimenti musicali per il cembalo,* 6 suites and a ciaccona (Augsburg, c.1739); other works include 32 ricercari, 24 toccatas with 24 capriccios, various other capriccios, 19 canzonas, preludes, fugues, partitas, 2 organ masses, etc.

BIBL.: L. von Stollbrock, *Die Komponisten Georg und G. M.* (Rostock, 1888); E. von Werra, "Georg Muffat . . . und G. M. . . . : Bio-bibliographische Studien," *Kirchenmusikalisches Jahrbuch,* VIII (1893); P. Robinson, "M.'s 'Componimenti,'" *Zeitschrift der Internationalen Musik-Gesellschaft,* IX (1907–8); J. Knöll, *Die Klavier- und Orgelwerke Theophile* (diss., Univ. of Vienna, 1916); S. Morris, *G. M.'s Clavier Suites* (diss., Boston Univ., 1959); S. Dahms, "Neues zur Chronologie der Opern von Biber und M.," *Österreichische Musikzeitschrift,* XXIX (1974); S. Wollenberg, "The Keyboard Suites of G. M. (1690–1770)," *Proceedings of the Royal Musical Association,* CII (1975–76); B. Baselt, "M. and Handel: A Two-Way Exchange," *Musical Times,* CXX (1979).

Mugellini, Bruno, Italian composer; b. Potenza, Dec. 24, 1871; d. Bologna, Jan. 15, 1912. He studied with Busi and Martucci in Bologna; appeared as a concert pianist in Italy; then was appointed prof. of piano at the Liceo Musicale in Bologna (1898), and succeeded Martucci as its director in 1911. He wrote an opera, *Catullo;* a symphonic poem, *Alla Fonte del Clitumno;* Piano Quartet; Cello Sonata; several sonatas and other pieces for piano; church music.

Mugnone, Leopoldo, noted Italian conductor; b. Naples, Sept. 29, 1858; d. there, Dec. 22, 1941. He studied with Cesi and Serrao at the Naples Cons.; began to compose as a young student; when he was 16, he produced a comic opera, *Don Bizarro e le sue figlie* (Naples, April 20, 1875); other operas were *Il Biricchino* (Venice, Aug. 11, 1892; fairly successful) and *Vita Brettone* (Naples, March 14, 1905). He also composed an attractive Neapolitan song, *La Rosella,* and other light music. But it was as a fine opera conductor that Mugnone achieved fame; his performances of Italian stage works possessed the highest degree of authority and an intense musicianly ardor. He also brought out Wagner's music dramas in Italy; conducted the 1st performances of Mascagni's *Cavalleria rusticana*

(Rome, May 17, 1890) and Puccini's *Tosca* (Rome, Jan. 14, 1900).

Mühlfeld, Richard (Bernhard Herrmann), famous German clarinetist; b. Salzungen, Feb. 28, 1856; d. Meiningen, June 1, 1907. He 1st studied the violin and played in the Meiningen Court Orch.; then practiced on the clarinet without a teacher, and in 1876 became 1st clarinetist at the Saxe-Meiningen court. From 1884 to 1896 he was 1st clarinetist at the Bayreuth Festivals; became music director of the Meiningen Court Theater (1890). Brahms wrote for him the Trio, op. 114 (for Clarinet, Cello, and Piano), the Quintet, op. 115 (for Clarinet, 2 Violins, Viola, and Cello), and the 2 clarinet sonatas, op. 120.

BIBL.: P. Weston, *Clarinet Virtuosi of the Past* (London, 1971).

Mühling, August, German organist and composer; b. Raguhne, Sept. 26, 1786; d. Magdeburg, Feb. 3, 1847. He was for many years organist at the Magdeburg Cathedral; wrote the oratorios *Abbadona, Bonifazius, David, and Die Leidensfeier Jesu;* 2 syms.; Concerto for Bassoon and Orch.; 3 string quartets; Quintet for Flute, 2 Violins, Viola, and Cello; sacred duets and songs.

Mul, Jan, Dutch composer; b. Haarlem, Sept. 20, 1911; d. Overveen, Dec. 30, 1971. He studied with H. Andriessen and with Sem Dresden at the Amsterdam Cons.; was an organist and choral conductor in Overveen (1931–60); served as music ed. of the Amsterdam daily *De Volkskrant* and chairman of the Guild of Dutch Composers. He orchestrated Dresden's opera *François Villon* from the vocal score for the production at the Holland Festival (Amsterdam, June 12, 1958) and Sweelinck's *Keyboard Variations on an Old Song* (Amsterdam, June 12, 1963). He wrote some fine sacred choral music; his secular works show the influence of the French modern school.

WORKS: OPERAS: *De Varkenshoeder* (The Swineherd), after H.C. Andersen (Amsterdam, June 25, 1953); *Bill Clifford* (Hengelo, Oct. 5, 1964). **VOCAL:** Several masses; *Stabat Mater* for Chorus and Small Orch. (1934); *4 Coplas* for Voice and Orch. (1936); *Egmont onthalsd* (Egmont Beheaded) for Chorus and Orch. (1938); Sonata for Mezzo-soprano, Baritone, and Small Orch. (1940–53); *Galant Quartet* for Soprano and Small Orch. or Flute, Cello, and Piano (1952); *Lettre de M. l'Abbé d'Olivet à M. le President Bouhier* for Baritone and Orch. (1962); *The Old Familiar Faces* for Bass and Chamber Orch. (1969); *L'Homme désarmé,* cantata (1970–71; Leiden, Sept. 25, 1973). **ORCH.:** Piano Concerto (1938); *Felicitatie* (1952); Concerto (1956); Sinfonietta (1957; orchestration of his Piano Sonata); *Mein junges Leben* (1961); Concerto for Piano, 4-hands, and Small Orch. (1962); *Confetti musicali* (1965); *Ik, Jan Mul* (I, Jan Mul; 1965); *Divertimento* for Piano and Orch. (1967); *Balladino* for Cello and Orch. or Piano (1968); *Variazioni "I due orsini"* (1968). **PIANO:** 2 sonatinas (1928, 1942); Sonata (1940); *Intervallen,* 6 inventions (1942; orchestrated in 1954); 2-piano Sonata (1953); *Les Donemoiselles,* punning tribute to the Dutch Soc. Donemus, 6 small pieces (1968); also an Organ Sonata (1942). **CHAMBER:** Quintet for Clarinet, Bassoon, Violin, Viola, and Cello (1957); Trio for 2 Violins and Double Bass (1969).

Mulder, Ernest Willem, Dutch composer; b. Amsterdam, July 21, 1898; d. there, April 12, 1959. He studied at the Toonkunst Cons. in Amsterdam, and later taught there; was a lecturer at the Univ. of Utrecht (1938–47), director of the Bussum Music School, and conductor of the Toonkunst Musical Soc. He specialized in sacred music.

WORKS: Opera, *Dafne* (1932–34); *3 chansons* for Soprano and Orch. (1921–28); *Sinfonia sacra I* for 6 Soloists, Chorus, and Orch. (1922–32), *II, Dialogue mystique,* for Baritone, Chorus, and Orch. (1936–40), *III, super psalmos,* for Orch. (1948), and *IV, super passionem,* for Orch. (1949–50); *Requiem (Missa pro defunctis)* for Soloists, Chorus, and Orch. (1927–32); Piano Concerto (1935); *Holland* for Chorus and Orch. (1942); *Maria-motetten,* 5 pieces for Soprano and Various Instrumental Ensembles (1945); *Stabat Mater dolorosa* for Soloists, Chorus,

and Orch. (1948); *Te Deum laudamus* for Chorus and Orch. (1951); *Symphonietta* for Medium Voice and Orch. (1958); 2 violin sonatas (1920); *Ars contrapunctica,* collection of 7 small works for various instrumental combinations (1938–40); *Sonata (in modo classico)* for Solo Violin (1941); Trio for 3 Bassoons (1942); String Quartet (1942); Sextet for Wind Quintet and Piano (1946); Quartet for Oboe, Bassoon, Cello, and Harp (1946); songs.

Mulder, Herman, Dutch composer; b. Amsterdam, Dec. 12, 1894; d. there, April 28, 1989. He studied harmony and voice, and had a brief career as a concert singer.

WORKS: ORCH.: 14 syms.: No. 1 (1940); No. 2 (1952); No. 3 (1954); No. 4 (1959–60); No. 5 (1961); No. 6 (1962); No. 7 (1964); No. 8 (1967); No. 9 (1968); No. 10 (1971); No. 11 (1972–73); No. 12 (1974–75); No. 13, *Sinfonia concertante* (1976); No. 14, *De laatste roep* for Choir and Orch. (1981); *Suite* (1941); Piano Concerto (1943); Concerto (1956); Concertino for Piano, 9 Wind Instruments, and Percussion (1964); Violin Concerto (1964); Concertino for Violin and String Orch. (1964); Concertino for Oboe and Orch. (1966); *Music* for Violin and Chamber Orch. (1967); 2-piano Concerto (1968); *Ouverture* (1967–70); *Capriccio* (1970); *Funerailles* (1971); *De snaren hebben getrild,* cantata for Soprano and Orch. (1977); *Introduction, Chaconne, and Finale* (1978). **CHAMBER:** 13 string quartets (Nos. 7–13, 1951–70); 5 sonatas, 1 each for Oboe, Flute, Clarinet, Horn, and Bassoon, all with Piano (1943–45); Piano Quintet (1947); English Horn Sonata (1950); 3 cello sonatinas (1956, 1956, 1967); 2 string quintets, with 2 Violas (1956, 1972); 2 string sextets (1957, 1973); 6 violin sonatas (1958–82); Viola Sonata (1960); Trio for Flute, Oboe, and Bassoon (1960); String Quintet, with 2 Cellos (1961); 2 wind quintets (1961, 1966); 2 piano trios (1965, 1978); Piano Quartet (1965); Violin Sonatina (1972); 2 string trios (1972); 2 Divertimenti for Violin (1978); also *Droomland* (Dreamland) for Baritone or Contralto and Piano (1949; orchestrated 1971); various works for solo piano, including 6 sonatas; songs.

Muldowney, Dominic (John), English composer; b. Southampton, July 19, 1952. He studied with Jonathan Harvey at Southampton Univ. and later with Birtwistle in London and with Bernard Rands and David Blake at York Univ.; in 1976 he was appointed composer-in-residence at the National Theatre in London. He belongs to a group of English composers who reject esoteric musical abstractions and doctrinaire methodology in favor of an art which is readily accessible to a wide range of listeners.

WORKS: *An Heavyweight Dirge* for Tenor and Baritone Soli, with Mezzo-soprano and 6 Players (1971; York, Feb. 1972); *Driftwood to the Flow* for 18 Strings (1972); *Klavier-Hammer* for 1 or more Pianos (1973); *Music at Chartres* for 16 Instruments (1974); 2 string quartets (1973, 1980); Cantata for Soloists, 2 Speakers, 2 Cellos, Percussion, and Chorus (1974); *Solo/Ensemble* for Chamber Group (1974); *The Earl of Essex's Galliard* for 3 Actors, Dancer, and 7 Instruments (1976; Oxford, July 8, 1980); *Double Helix* for 8 Players (1977); *A Garland of Chansons* for 6 Oboes and 3 Bassoons (1978); *3 Hymns to Agape* for 4 Players (1978); *Macbeth,* ballet (1979); 5 Psalms for Choir, Soprano, Tenor, Instruments, and Tape (1979; Horsham, Dec. 6, 1980); Concerto for 4 Violins and Strings (1980); *5 Theatre Poems* for Mezzo-soprano and Instruments, after Brecht (1980–81; London, April 26, 1982); Piano Trio (1980; Bath, May 25, 1982); *In Dark Times* for 4 Soloists and Chamber Group, after Brecht (1981; London, Feb. 23, 1982); *The Duration of Exile* and *A Second Show* for Mezzo-soprano and Chamber Group (London, June 2, 1983); Piano Concerto (London, July 27, 1983); Saxophone Concerto (1984); Sinfonietta (1986).

Mulè, Giuseppe, Italian composer; b. Termini, Imerese, Sicily, June 28, 1885; d. Rome, Sept. 10, 1951. He studied at the Palermo Cons.; graduated as a cellist as well as in composition. In 1922 he was engaged as director of the Palermo Cons. (until 1925); in 1925 he succeeded Respighi as director of the Accademia di Santa Cecilia in Rome; remained there until 1943. He wrote mostly for the stage, and was particularly successful in providing suitable music for revivals of Greek plays. He composed numerous operas in the tradition of the Italian *verismo*: *La Baronessa di Carini* (Palermo, April 16, 1912); *La Monacella della fontana* (Trieste, Feb. 17, 1923); *Dafni* (Rome, March 14, 1928); *Liolà* (Naples, Feb. 2, 1935); *Taormina* (San Remo, 1938); *La zolfara* (Rome, 1939); also the oratorio *Il Cieco di Gerico* (1910); 2 symphonic poems, *Sicilia canora* (1924) and *La Vendemmia* (1936); also *3 canti siciliani* for Voice and Orch. (1930); a String Quartet and other chamber music; songs.

Müller, Adolf, Jr., Austrian composer and conductor, son of **Adolf Müller, Sr.;** b. Vienna, Oct. 15, 1839; d. there, Dec. 14, 1901. After completing his education in Vienna, he was engaged as a theater conductor in the provinces; was conductor of the German Opera at Rotterdam (1875–83); after that at the Theater an der Wien, where his father had directed before him. He produced a number of operas: *Heinrich der Goldschmidt* (Magdeburg, 1867), *Waldmeisters Brautfahrt* (Hamburg, Feb. 15, 1873), *Van Dyke* (Rotterdam, 1877), etc.; and the Viennese operettas *Der Hofnarr* (Nov. 20, 1886; his greatest success), *Der Teufels Weib* (Nov. 22, 1890), *Der Millionen-Onkel* (Nov. 5, 1892), *General Gogo* (Feb. 1, 1896), and *Der Blondin von Namur* (Oct. 15, 1898).

Müller, Adolf, Sr. (real name, **Matthias Schmid**), Austrian conductor and composer, father of **Adolf Müller, Jr.;** b. Tolna, Oct. 7, 1801; d. Vienna, July 29, 1886. He was orphaned at an early age and reared by an aunt; studied with Joseph Rieger, the Brünn Cathedral organist, and with Joseph von Blumenthal in Vienna; after appearances as a singer and actor, he became a prolific composer for the Viennese theater; was conductor of the Theater an der Wien (1828–78) and also conducted at the Leopoldstadt Theater. He wrote almost 600 scores for the stage, some sacred music, chamber pieces, and about 400 songs.

BIBL.: A. Bauer, *Die Musik Adolph M.s in den Theaterstücken Johann Nestroys* (diss., Univ. of Vienna, 1935).

Müller, August Eberhard, German organist and composer; b. Nordheim, Hannover, Dec. 13, 1767; d. Weimar, Dec. 3, 1817. He studied keyboard playing with his father, Matthäus Müller, an organist; after receiving instruction in harmony and composition from J.C.F. Bach in Bückeburg, he studied law in Göttingen (1786). He was an organist at various churches at Magdeburg and Leipzig; in 1800 he became assistant to Johann Adam Hiller at the Thomasschule in Leipzig, and succeeded him as Kantor there in 1804; also was music director of the Thomaskirche and Nikolaikirche. In 1810 he became court conductor in Weimar. He wrote a singspiel, *Der Polterabend* (Weimar, 1813 or 1814); 11 flute concertos; 2 keyboard concertos; cantatas; 17 keyboard sonatas and other works for keyboard; chamber music. He publ. a practical piano method (1805; actually the 6th ed. of G. Löhlein's *Clavier-Schule*, rev. by Müller; Kalkbrenner's method is based on it; Czerny publ. the 8th ed. in 1825) and a method for the flute. He also publ. cadenzas for, and a guide to the interpretation of, Mozart's concertos; arranged piano scores of Mozart's operas (very popular in his time).

BIBL.: G. Haupt, *A.E. M.'s Leben und Klavierwerke* (Leipzig, 1926).

Müller, Friedrich, German clarinetist, conductor, and composer; b. Orlamünde, Dec. 10, 1786; d. Rudolstadt, Dec. 12, 1871. In 1803 he entered the royal orch. at Rudolstadt as a clarinet player; in 1831 he became its conductor; was pensioned in 1854. He wrote 2 syms.; 2 clarinet concertos and other music for clarinet; also clarinet studies; a Quartet for Clarinet and Strings; etc.

Müller, George Godfrey (actually, **Georg Gottfried**), German-American minister, violinist, and composer; b. Gross Hennersdorf, Saxony, May 22, 1762; d. Lititz, Pa., March 19, 1821. He went to America in 1784, and spent the major part of his life at Lititz, as a member of the culturally important group of Moravians in America. His works are listed by A.G. Rau

and H.T. David in *A Catalogue of Music by American Moravians* (Bethlehem, Pa., 1938), and his music is represented in vol. I of the series Music by the Moravians in America (1938).

Müller, Gottfried, German composer; b. Dresden, June 8, 1914. He studied with Tovey in Edinburgh and with Straube in Leipzig; was an instructor at the Hochschule für Musik in Leipzig and, from 1952 to 1961, an organist in Berlin. In 1961 he was appointed prof. of composition at the Nuremberg Cons. Among his works are a set of orch. variations on a German folk song, which became popular; *Deutsches Heldenrequiem* (1934); *Capriccio* (1959); *Dürersymphonie* (1962); Concertino for 3 Pianos (1963); String Quartet (1966); Concerto for 2 Pianos and Orch. (1967); Piano Concerto (1969).

Müller, Heinrich Fidelis, German composer and choirmaster; b. Fulda, April 23, 1827; d. there, Aug. 30, 1905. He was for many years choirmaster at the Cologne Cathedral; composed the oratorios *Weihnachtsoratorium, Die heilige Elisabeth,* and *Die Passion unseres Herrn*; several masses, motets, choruses, etc.

Müller, Iwan, German clarinetist, basset-horn player, instrument maker, and composer; b. Reval, Estonia, Dec. 14, 1786; d. Bückeburg, Feb. 4, 1854. He toured throughout Europe; served as a chamber musician at the St. Petersburg imperial court (1800–1807); developed an 18-key basset horn (1808) and a 13-key clarinet (1809), and also claimed for himself the invention of the alto clarinet; made Paris his headquarters (1809). Although he faced the opposition of conservative instrument makers, his improved clarinet eventually won general popularity. He spent the last years of his life at Bückeburg as a court musician; publ. a method for his new instruments; composed 6 clarinet concertos and 2 clarinet quartets.

BIBL.: W. Tenney, "I. M. and His New Clarinet," *Woodwind Magazine,* III (1951); F. Rendall, *The Clarinet* (London, 1954; 3rd. ed., 1971); P. Weston, *Clarinet Virtuosi of the Past* (London, 1971).

Müller, Maria, Austrian soprano; b. Leitmeritz, Jan. 29, 1898; d. Bayreuth, March 13, 1958. She studied with Erik Schmedes in Vienna and Max Altglass in N.Y.; made her debut as Elsa in Linz in 1919; then sang at the German Theater in Prague (1921–23) and at the Bavarian State Opera in Munich (1923–24). On Jan. 21, 1925, she made her Metropolitan Opera debut in N.Y. as Sieglinde, remaining on its roster until 1935. In 1926 she joined the Berlin Städtische Oper and later the Berlin State Opera; also sang at the Wagner festivals in Bayreuth (1930–44) and in Salzburg.

Müller, Peter, German composer; b. Kesselstadt, near Hanau, June 9, 1791; d. Langen, Aug. 29, 1877. He taught music at various schools in Germany; wrote the popular *Jugendlieder*; also male choruses; organ pieces; etc. In 1839 he became pastor at Staden. His opera (after Bulwer-Lytton), *Die letzten Tage von Pompeii,* was produced at Darmstadt on Dec. 25, 1853; he also wrote 7 string quintets and other chamber music.

Müller, Sigfrid Walther, German composer; b. Plauen, Jan. 11, 1905; d. in a Russian prison camp in Baku, Nov. 2, 1946. He studied at the Leipzig Cons. with Karg-Elert and Martienssen; also church music and organ with Straube; taught at the Leipzig Cons. (1929–32) and at the Hochschule für Musik in Weimar (1940–41); then was in the German army on the eastern front. His output comprised 62 opus numbers, mostly chamber music and organ works; also an opera, *Schlaraffenhochzeit* (Leipzig, 1937); *Böhmische Musik* for Orch.; *Gohliser Schlossmusik* for Small Orch.; Concerto for Flute and Chamber Orch. (1941).

Müller, Wenzel, prominent Austrian conductor and composer; b. Tyrnau, Moravia, Sept. 26, 1767; d. Baden, near Vienna, Aug. 3, 1835. He studied with the Kornitz schoolmaster, learning to play all the instruments of the orch. and beginning to compose as a child; continued his studies at the Raigern Benedictine foundation, where he received further instruction from its choirmaster, Maurus Haberbauer; subsequently completed his studies with Dittersdorf in Johannisberg. In 1782 he became 3rd violinist in Waizhofer's theater company in Brünn, attracting notice with his successful singspiel *Das verfehlte Rendezvouz, oder Die weiblichen Jäger*; after a concert tour with the Willmann family (1786), he settled in Vienna as Kapellmeister at the Leopoldstädter-Theater. His 1st success as a composer there came with his singspiel *Das Sonnenfest der Braminen* (Sept. 9, 1790); it was followed by such popular stage works as (*Kaspar*) *Der Fagottist, oder Die Zauberzither* (June 8, 1791), *Die Schwestern von Prag* (March 11, 1794), *Das lustige Beilager* (Feb. 14, 1797), *Die zwölf schlafenden Jungfrauen* (Oct. 12, 1797), and *Die Teufelsmühle am Wienerberg* (Nov. 12, 1799). After serving as Kapellmeister at Prague's German Opera (1807–13), he returned to the Leopoldstädter-Theater as Kapellmeister in 1815; among the subsequent popular scores he wrote for it were *Tankredi* (April 25, 1817), *Der verwunschene Prinz* (March 3, 1818), *Aline, oder Wien in einem andern Weltteil* (Oct. 9, 1822), *Der Barometermacher auf der Zauberinsel* (Dec. 18, 1823), *Die gefesselte Phantasie* (Jan. 8, 1828), and *Der Alpenkönigund der Menschenfeind* (Oct. 17, 1828). His daughter was the soprano **Therese Grünbaum**. Müller was the most successful composer of light stage works for the Vienna theater of his day, and several of his works remain a part of the Austrian repertoire. A prolific composer, he produced some 250 theatrical pieces alone. He also wrote syms., sacred music, chamber music, piano pieces, and several enduring songs.

BIBL.: W. Blum, "W. M., der eigentliche Schöpfer echter Volks-Musik," *Allgemeine Theater-Zeitung*, XXVIII/161–2 (Vienna, 1835); W. Krone, *W. M.: Ein Beitrag zur Geschichte der komischen Oper* (Berlin, 1906); L. Raab, *W. M.: Ein Tonkünstler Altwiens* (Baden, 1928).

Müller-Blattau, Joseph (Maria), noted German musicologist; b. Colmar, Alsace, May 21, 1895; d. Saarbrücken, Oct. 21, 1976. He studied musicology with Friedrich Ludwig at the Univ. of Strasbourg, and composition and conducting with Pfitzner and organ with Ernst Münch at the Strasbourg Cons. He served in the German army during World War I; after the Armistice of 1918, he resumed his studies in musicology with Wilibald Gurlitt at the Univ. of Freiburg im Breisgau (Ph.D., 1920, with the diss. *Grundzüge einer Geschichte der Fuge*; publ. in Königsberg, 1923; 3rd ed., rev., 1963). He then completed his Habilitation at the Univ. of Königsberg in 1922 with his *Die Kompositionslehre Heinrich Schützens in der Fassung seines Schülers Christoph Bernhard* (publ. in Leipzig, 1926; 2nd ed., 1963). He taught at the Univ. of Königsberg; was promoted to reader there in 1928; then taught at the Univs. of Frankfurt (1935–37) and Freiburg im Breisgau (1937–39); subsequently served in military administration (1939–42); then lectured at the Univ. of Strasbourg during the last years of World War II. From 1952 to 1958 he was director of the Staatliche Hochschule für Musik in Saarbrücken; he also taught at the Univ. of Strasbourg from 1952 to 1964. He was the editor of the abortive 12th ed. of Riemann's *Musiklexikon* (1937–39), of which only a few issues appeared before the outbreak of World War II made further publication impossible.

WRITINGS: *Das Elsass, ein Grenzland deutscher Musik* (Freiburg, 1922); *Geschichte der Musik in Ost- und Westpreussen von der Ordenszeit bis zur Gegenwart* (Königsberg, 1931; 2nd ed., enl., 1968); *Hamann und Herder in ihren Beziehungen zur Musik* (Königsberg, 1931); *Das deutsche Volkslied* (Berlin, 1932; 2nd ed., 1958); *Einführung in die Musikgeschichte* (Berlin, 1932; 2nd ed., 1941); *Johannes Brahms* (Potsdam, 1933); *Georg Friedrich Händel* (Potsdam, 1933; 2nd ed., 1959); *Zur Erforschung des ostpreussischen Volksliedes* (Halle, 1934); *Johann Sebastian Bach* (Leipzig, 1935; 2nd ed., Stuttgart, 1950); *Geschichte der deutschen Musik* (Berlin, 1938; 3rd ed., 1942); *Hans Pfitzner* (Potsdam, 1940; 2nd ed., rev., 1969); *Gestaltung—Umgestaltung: Studien zur Geschichte der musikalischen Variation* (Stuttgart, 1950); *Das Verhältnis von Wort und Ton in der Geschichte der Musik: Grundzüge und Probleme* (Stutt-

gart, 1952); *Die Volksliedsammlung des jungen Goethe* (Kassel, 1955); *Von der Vielfalt der Musik: Musikgeschichte—Musikerziehung—Musikpflege* (Freiburg, 1966); *Goethe und die Meister der Musik* (Stuttgart, 1969).

BIBL.: W. Salmen, ed., *Festgabe für J. M.-B. zum 65. Geburtstag* (Saarbrücken, 1960; 2nd ed., 1962); C.-H. Mahling, ed., *Zum 70. Geburtstag von J. M.-B.* (Kassel, 1966).

Müller-Hartmann, Robert, German composer; b. Hamburg, Oct. 11, 1884; d. Dorking, Surrey, Dec. 15, 1950. He studied at the Stern Cons. in Berlin; was a lecturer on music at Hamburg Univ. (1923–33); in 1937 he settled in England, where he worked mainly as an arranger and translator. He wrote a number of symphonic works, some of which were 1st performed by Richard Strauss and Karl Muck: a Sym., a Symphonic Ballad, several sets of variations, etc.; a Trio for Flute, Violin, and Viola; 2 violin sonatas; many organ works; piano pieces.

Müller-Hermann, Johanna, Austrian composer and pedagogue; b. Vienna, Jan. 15, 1878; d. there, April 19, 1941. She studied with Karl Nawratil, Josef Labor, Guido Adler, Zemlinsky, and J.B. Foerster; began to compose at an early age, in a Romantic vein, influenced chiefly by Mahler and Max Reger; was regarded as one of the foremost European women composers of orch. and chamber music of her time. She wrote an oratorio, *In Memoriam*, to Walt Whitman's words; a Sym. for Voices with Orch.; a Symphonic Fantasy on Ibsen's play *Brand*; String Quartet; String Quintet; Piano Quintet; Violin Sonata; Cello Sonata; Piano Sonata; several song cycles.

Müller-Kray, Hans, German conductor; b. Essen, Oct. 13, 1908; d. Stuttgart, May 30, 1969. He studied piano, cello, and theory in Essen; then was a conductor at the Essen Theater. He conducted in Münster (1934–41), Frankfurt (1942–45), and Wiesbaden (1945–48). In 1948 he became chief conductor of the Stuttgart Radio Sym. Orch., a post he held until his death. He was also a composer; wrote several ballet scores and other works.

Müller Quartets. Two famous German string quartets, the 1st to undertake regular concert tours, their members being: **(1) The brothers Karl** (1797–1873), **Gustav** (1799–1855), **Theodor** (1802–75), and **Georg** (1808–55); they were all born in Braunschweig and belonged to the orch. there, Karl as concertmaster, Theodor as cellist, Gustav as violinist, and Georg as conductor. Their artistic tours included not only all the large German cities, but also Vienna and Paris (1833), Copenhagen (1838), St. Petersburg (1845), and the Netherlands (1852).

BIBL.: L. Köhler, *Die Gebrüder M. und das Streichquartett* (Leipzig, 1858); E. Stier, "Das Streichquartett der Gebrüder M.," *Braunschweigisches Archiv* (July 1913).

(2) The four sons of Karl, all born in Braunschweig (this quartet was organized in 1855, after the death of 2 members of the 1st one); **Karl,** 1st violin (b. April 14, 1829; d. Stuttgart, Nov. 11, 1907); **Hugo,** 2nd violin (b. Sept. 21, 1832; d. Braunschweig, June 26, 1886; **Bernhard,** viola (b. Feb. 24, 1825; d. Rostock, Sept. 4, 1895); and **Wilhelm,** cello (b. June 1, 1834; d. N.Y., Sept. 7, 1897). For 10 years they constituted the court quartet at Meiningen; then, after extended and successful travels, they settled in Rostock as members of the city orch., Karl being appointed music director. The quartet was broken up by the appointment of Wilhelm (1873) to succeed Sweerts as 1st cello in the Royal Orch. at Berlin, and prof. in the Hochschule für Musik. Karl lived from then on in Stuttgart and Hamburg; was also a composer.

Müller-Reuter, Theodor, German conductor and composer; b. Dresden, Sept. 1, 1858; d. there, Aug. 11, 1919. He studied piano with Alwin Wieck in Dresden and Clara Schumann in Frankfurt; also took lessons in composition with E.J. Otto and Meinardus in Dresden. He taught piano at the Strasbourg Cons. (1879–87), and at Dresden; subsequently conducted the Concert Soc. in Krefeld (1893–1918), returning to Dresden shortly before his death. He wrote the operas *Ondolina* (Strasbourg, 1883) and *Der tolle Graf* (Nuremberg, 1887), and many choral works; publ. *Lexikon der deutschen Konzert-Literatur* (Leipzig, 1909; supplement, 1921); also a vol. of reminiscences and essays, *Bilder und Klänge des Friedens; Musikalische Erinnerungen und Aufsätze* (Leipzig, 1919).

Müller von Kulm, Walter, Swiss composer; b. Kulm, Aug. 31, 1899; d. Arlesheim, near Basel, Oct. 3, 1967. He studied in Aarau and at the conservatories and in Basel and Zürich, and took courses in musicology, philosophy, and psychology at the Univ. of Basel; was director of the Basel Cons. (1947–64). He publ. the manual *Grundriss der Harmonielehre* (Basel, 1948). Among his works were the opera *Der Erfinder* (1944); a ballet, *Die blaue Blume* (1936); the oratorios *Vater unser* (1945) and *Petrus* (1960); Sym. (1928); chamber music; keyboard pieces; etc.

Müller-Zürich (real name, **Müller**), **Paul,** esteemed Swiss conductor and composer; b. Zürich, June 19, 1898. He studied with Andreae and Jarnach at the Zürich Cons. (1917–19) and in Paris and Berlin; then taught in Zürich at the Cons. (1927–69) and at the Univ. (1959–70); was active as a choral and sym. conductor, serving as director of the Elisabeth Schmid Choir (1931–39), the Lucerne Chamber Orch. (1948–55), and other ensembles. His music evolved from early Romantic influences to reflect neo-Baroque practices in a contemporary, tonal style.

Works: orch.: *Little Symphony* (1920); *Little Serenade* for Chamber Orch. (1921); *Hymnus* (1927); Concerto for Viola and Small Orch. (1934); Concerto for Violin and Small Orch. (1935); Concerto for Organ and Strings (1938); Sym. for Strings (1944); Sym. (1947); Sym. for Flute and Strings (1952); Cello Concerto (1954); *Sinfonischer Prolog* (1955); *Sinfonische Suite* (1956–57); Violin Concerto No. 2 (1957); Concerto for 2 Violins, Harpsichord, and Strings (1958); Sinfonietta (1964); *Sonata* for Strings (1967–68); *Consenso,* suite (1974). **chamber:** Erinne Quintet (1919); 2 string quartets (1921, 1960); 3 violin sonatas (1922, 1941, 1952); *Marienleben* for 10 Instruments (1928); *Präludium, Arie und Fuge* for Oboe, Bassoon, Horn, Trumpet, and String Quintet (1933); *Petite sonate* for Clarinet and Piano (1942); *Fantasie und Fugue* for Violin and Organ (1949); String Trio (1950); *Canzone* for String Quartet (1961); Trio for Flute, Clarinet, and Piano (1965–66); Sonata for Solo Viola (1979); *Fantasie* for Oboe and Organ (1980); *Serenata turicensis* for Basset Horn, Viola, and Cello (1981); also dramatic pieces, choral music, organ works, and songs.

Bibl.: F. Jakob, *P. M.: Biographie und Werkverzeichnis* (Zürich, 1963).

Mulligan, Gerry (Gerald Joseph), outstanding American jazz baritone saxophonist and arranger; b. N.Y., June 4, 1927. His formative years were spent in Philadelphia, where he learned to play piano; played reed instruments and worked professionally as an arranger while still in his teens; then went to N.Y. (1946), where he played reed instruments and wrote arrangements for Gene Krupa's big band; after performing with Miles Davis (1948–50), he acquired a reputation as one of the finest baritone saxophonists of his era. In 1952 he formed the 1st of several "piano-less" quartets, with which he toured extensively and made recordings; led his own big band on a tour of Europe in 1960 and of Japan in 1964; also made appearances with various jazz notables, and began playing the soprano saxophone. He was an important figure in the development of "cool" jazz, remaining a protean figure in jazz circles for decades.

Bibl.: A. Morgan and R. Horricks, *G. M.: A Biography, Appreciation, Record Survey and Discography* (London, 1958); A. Tercinet, "Discographie de G. M.," *Jazz Hot,* 335 and 336 (1977); J. Klinkowitz, *Listen: G. M.: An Aural Narrative in Jazz* (N.Y., 1991).

Mullings, Frank (Coningsby), distinguished English tenor; b. Walsall, March 10, 1881; d. Manchester, May 19, 1953. He studied voice in Birmingham; made his debut in Coventry in 1907 as Faust; then sang Tristan in London in 1913, and performed the role of Otello in Manchester in 1916. In 1919

he was the 1st to sing Parsifal in English, at Covent Garden in London. From 1922 to 1926 he was the principal dramatic tenor of the British National Opera Co., and appeared with it as Apollo in the 1st performance, in 1924, of Rutland Boughton's *Alkestis.* He taught at the Birmingham School of Music (1927–46) and at the Royal Manchester College of Music (1944–49). His other roles included Siegfried, Tannhäuser, Canio, and Radames.

Mullova, Viktoria, Russian violinist; b. Moscow, Nov. 27, 1959. She began violin lessons in childhood and made her public debut as soloist in Vieuxtemps's 5th Concerto when she was 12; studied in Moscow with Bronin at the Central Music School (1969–78) and with Kogan at the Moscow Cons. She won 1st prize in the Sibelius Competition in Helsinki in 1981 and took the Gold Medal in the Tchaikovsky Competition in Moscow in 1982. She then left Russia to pursue an international career, touring as a concert recitalist and appearing as soloist with major orchs.

Mumma, Gordon, innovative American composer, performer, electronic-music engineer, teacher, and writer on music; b. Framingham, Mass., March 30, 1935. He received private instruction in piano, horn, and composition; attended the Univ. of Michigan in Ann Arbor (1952–53). In 1958 he became cofounder of Ann Arbor's Cooperative Studio for Electronic Music, remaining active with it until 1966; also was co-director of the ONCE Festival and ONCE Group there (1960–66). He helped to develop a revolutionary theatrical art based on projected images, resulting in an esthetic medium called "Manifestations: Light and Sound" and, later, "Space Theatre"; in 1964 he participated in a memorable presentation of "Space Theatre" at Venice's Biennial Exhibition, a pioneering demonstration of the electronic light show. Having attended the Inst. of Science and Technology at the Univ. of Michigan (1959–62), he returned there as a research associate in acoustics and seismics (1962–63). From 1966 to 1974 he was active as a composer and performer with the Merce Cunningham Dance Co. in N.Y.; also was active with the Sonic Arts Union in N.Y. (from 1966). He taught at the Univ. of Illinois at Urbana (1969–70) and at the Univ. of Calif. at Santa Cruz (1973–75), where he subsequently was a prof. of music (from 1975). He also was a visiting lecturer at Brandeis Univ. (1966–67), the State Univ. of N.Y. at Buffalo (1968), and the Ferienkurse für Neue Musik in Darmstadt (1974); in 1981 he held the Darius Milhaud Professorship at Mills College in Oakland, Calif.; after serving as a visiting prof. at the Univ. of Calif. at San Diego (1985, 1987), he returned to Mills College as Distinguished Visiting Composer in 1989. Mumma has contributed various articles on contemporary music to journals and other publications. He pioneered the process of "cybersonic music," the control of acoustical and electronic media by means of feedback; also applied computer techniques to composition.

Works: *Sinfonia* for 12 Instruments and Tape (1958–60; Ann Arbor, March 4, 1961); *Megaton for William Burroughs,* live electronic piece for 10 Electronic, Acoustic, and Communication Channels (1963; Ann Arbor, Feb. 28, 1964); *Mographs,* pieces for Various Combinations of Pianos and Pianists (1962–64); *Music for the Venezia Space Theatre* for 4-channel Magnetic Tape with Live Electronic Music (Venice, Sept. 1, 1964); *The Dresden Interleaf 13 February 1945,* quadraphonic electronic music on magnetic tape (Ann Arbor, Feb. 13, 1965); *Horn* for Cybersonic Horn and Voices (1965); *Mesa,* live electronic music for Cybersonic Bandoneon (St. Paul de Vence, France, Aug. 6, 1966); *Hornpipe* for Cybernetic Horn and Waldhorn (1967); *Schoolwork* for Bowed Psaltery, Piano Melodica, and Bowed Crosscut Saw (1970); *Telepos* for Dancers, Telemetry Belts, and Accelerometers (1971; N.Y., Feb. 2, 1972); *Cybersonic Cantilevers,* cybersonic electronic system with public participation (Syracuse, N.Y., May 19, 1973); *Some Voltage Drop,* variable-duration theater piece with electro-acoustical implementation (Paris, Oct. 13, 1974); *Earheart: Flights, Formations, and Starry Nights* for Dancers and Electronics (Portland, Oreg., Sept. 9, 1977); *Echo-BCD* for Dancers and Electronics (Port land, Oreg., Oct. 15, 1978); *11 Note Pieces and Decimal Passacaglia* for Harpsichord (1979); *Pontpoint* for Dancers and Electronics (1979; Portland, Oreg., March 14, 1980); *Retrospect*, stereophonic electro-acoustic music (1962–82; Santa Cruz, Calif., Oct. 6, 1982); *Faisandage et galimafrée*, divertimento for Trios of Diverse Instruments (Santa Cruz, Calif., June 10, 1984); *Epifont (Spectral Portrait in memoriam George Cacioppo)*, stereophonic electro-acoustic music on magnetic tape (1984; Ann Arbor, Mich., April 14, 1985); *Than Particle* for Solo Percussion and Digital Computer (Los Angeles, Nov. 7, 1985); *Aleutian Displacement* for Chamber Orch. (1987); *Orait* for Dancers and Vocal Ensemble (Santa Cruz, Calif., June 17, 1988); *Ménages à deux* for Violin, Piano, Vibraphone, and Marimba (1989; Berkeley, Calif., Feb. 10, 1990).

Munch (originally, **Münch**), **Charles**, eminent Alsatian conductor, son of **Ernst Münch**; b. Strasbourg, Sept. 26, 1891; d. Richmond, Va., Nov. 6, 1968. He studied violin at the Strasbourg Cons. and with Lucien Capet in Paris; at the outbreak of World War I (1914), he enlisted in the German army; made a sergeant of artillery, he was gassed at Peronne and wounded at Verdun; after the end of the war (1918) and his return to Alsace-Lorraine (1919), he became a French citizen. Having received further violin training from Carl Flesch in Berlin, he pursued a career as a soloist; was also prof. of violin at the Leipzig Cons. and concertmaster of the Gewandhaus Orch. there. On Nov. 1, 1932, he made his professional conducting debut in Paris with the Straram Orch.; studied conducting with Alfred Szendrei there (1933–40). He quickly rose to prominence; was conductor of Paris's Orch. de la Société Philharmonique (1935–38) and became a prof. at the École Normale de Musique (1936). In 1938 he became music director of the Société des Concerts du Conservatoire de Paris, remaining in that post during the years of the German occupation during World War II; refusing to collaborate with the Nazis, he gave his support to the Résistance, being awarded the Légion d'honneur in 1945. He made his U.S. debut as a guest conductor of the Boston Sym. Orch. on Dec. 27, 1946; a transcontinental tour of the U.S. with the French National Radio Orch. followed in 1948. In 1949 he was appointed music director of the Boston Sym. Orch., which he and Monteux took on its 1st European tour in 1952; they took it again to Europe in 1956, also touring in the Soviet Union, making it the 1st U.S. orch. to do so. After retiring from his Boston post in 1962, Munch made appearances as a guest conductor; also helped to launch the Orch. de Paris in 1967. Munch acquired an outstanding reputation as an interpreter of the French repertoire, his performances being marked by spontaneity, color, and elegance. French music of the 20th century also occupied a prominent place on his programs; he brought out new works by Roussel, Milhaud, Honegger, and others. He wrote *Je suis chef d'orchestre* (Paris, 1954; Eng. tr., N.Y., 1955).

BIBL.: P. Olivier, *C. M.: Une Biographie par le disque* (Paris, 1987).

Münch, Ernst, Alsatian organist and choral conductor, father of **Charles Munch**; b. Niederbronn, Dec. 31, 1859; d. Strasbourg, April 1, 1928. He was appointed organist at St. Wilhelm (St. Guillaume) Church in Strasbourg in 1882, where he founded a choir which attained a great renown for its performance of Bach's cantatas and passions; Albert Schweitzer served as organist at these performances.

Münch, Hans, Alsatian-born Swiss conductor and composer, nephew of **Ernst Münch**; b. Mulhouse, March 9, 1893; d. Basel, Sept. 7, 1983. His father, Eugen Münch, was a conductor. After studying with Albert Schweitzer, he settled in Basel (1912) and became a naturalized Swiss citizen; took courses with Hans Huber (composition), Adolf Hamm (organ), and Emil Braun (cello) at the Cons.; played cello in the city orch. (1914–16); then taught piano at the Cons. (1918–32) and conducted the Bach Choir (1921–26); subsequently led the Gesangverein and the Liedertafel, was conductor of the Allgemeine Musikgesellschaft (1935–66), and served as director of the Music School and Cons. (1935–47). He composed a

Sym. (1951), *Symphonische Improvisationen* (1971), and several cantatas.

Münchinger, Karl, German conductor; b. Stuttgart, May 29, 1915; d. there, March 13, 1990. He studied at the Hochschule für Musik in Stuttgart; then with Abendroth at the Leipzig Cons.; from 1941 to 1943 he was 1st conductor of the orch. in Hannover, and in 1945 founded the Stuttgart Chamber Orch. He toured America, Japan, and Russia; made his U.S. debut in San Francisco in 1953, and during the following season made a U.S. tour with his Stuttgart Chamber Orch.; he visited the U.S. again in 1977. In 1966 he organized the "Klassische Philharmonie" in Stuttgart, with which he gave regular performances. He retired in 1988.

Munclinger, Milan, Czech flutist and conductor; b. Košice, July 3, 1923; d. Prague, March 30, 1986. He began to study the flute in his youth; then enrolled at the Prague Cons.; also studied at the Prague Academy of Musical Arts and the Univ. of Prague. He gained distinction as founder-conductor of the Ars Ridiviva ensemble (1951), with which he gave performances of the Baroque and Classical repertoires with much success; also toured widely with his ensemble.

Münnich, Richard, German music educator and theorist; b. Berlin, June 7, 1877; d. Weimar, July 4, 1970. He studied piano with his father, and cello with Otto Hutscenreuter; then took courses at the Univ. of Berlin with Max Friedlaender and Carl Stumpf (Ph.D., 1902). He subsequently devoted himself to music education; held various teaching posts in Berlin and Stettin; taught music theory at the Klindworth-Scharwenka Cons. in Berlin (1910–35); in 1935 he was appointed prof. and director at the Hochschule für Musik in Weimar; he retired in 1964. He publ. a number of practice books for school, among them *Widerholungsbüchlein für den Musikunterricht an höheren Schulen* (4th ed., 1928) and *Jale, Ein Beitrag zur Tonsilbenfrage und zur Schulmusik-Propädeutik* (Lahr, 1930; new ed., Wolfenbüttel, 1959). In his numerous writings on harmony he followed Riemann's analytical theories. A Festschrift was presented to him on his 70th birthday (1947).

Munrow, David (John), gifted English recorder player; b. Birmingham, Aug. 12, 1942; d. (suicide) Chesham Bois, Buckinghamshire, May 15, 1976. He studied English at Pembroke College, Cambridge; during this period (1961–64), he founded an ensemble for the furtherance of early English music and organized a recorder consort. In 1967 he formed the Early Music Consort of London, with which he gave many successful concerts of medieval and Renaissance music; also was active with his own BBC radio program. He lectured on the history of early music at the Univ. of Leicester (from 1967) and was prof. of recorder at London's Royal Academy of Music (from 1969); publ. the vol. *Instruments of the Middle Ages and Renaissance* (London, 1976). He killed himself for obscure reasons in his early maturity.

Munsel, Patrice (Beverly), American soprano; b. Spokane, Wash., May 14, 1925. She studied in N.Y. with William Herman and Renato Bellini; won an audition at the Metropolitan Opera and made a successful debut there on Dec. 4, 1943, in the role of Philine in Thomas's *Mignon*, being the youngest singer to appear there to that time; she remained on the staff until 1958, excepting the 1945–46 season. She subsequently made several European tours. Her best roles were Gilda, Lucia, Rosina, Violetta, and Lakmé. She portrayed Melba in a motion picture on Melba's life (1953); also made successful appearances in operetta and in Broadway musicals.

Munz, Mieczyslaw, esteemed Polish-American pianist and pedagogue; b. Krakow, Oct. 31, 1900; d. N.Y., Aug. 25, 1976. He studied piano and composition at the Vienna Academy of Music, and later at the Hochschule für Musik in Berlin; his principal teacher there was Ferruccio Busoni. He made a brilliant debut in Berlin in 1920 as soloist in 3 works on the same program: the Brahms Piano Concerto in D minor, Liszt's Piano Concerto in A, and *Variations symphoniques* by Franck. His American debut took place in a solo recital in N.Y. on

Oct. 20, 1922; he subsequently was soloist with a number of orchs. in the U.S.; also toured Europe, South America, Australia, and Japan. He taught at the Cincinnati College-Cons. of Music (1925–30); then was on the faculty of the Curtis Inst. of Music in Philadelphia (1930–32; 1941–63); from 1946 to 1965 he taught at the Peabody Inst.; also was a prof. of piano at the Juilliard School of Music in N.Y. (1963–75). In 1975 he was given a tenured appointment at the Toho Gakuen School of Music in Tokyo, but he was forced to return to the U.S. due to illness. He was highly esteemed as a teacher; his students included Emanuel Ax and Ilana Vered. His piano playing was distinguished by a fine Romantic flair supported by an unobtrusive virtuoso technique.

Muradeli, Vano (Ilyich), Russian composer; b. Gori, Georgia, April 6, 1908; d. Tomsk, Siberia, Aug. 14, 1970. As a child he improvised songs, accompanying himself on the mandolin; he studied with Barchudarian and Bagrinsky at the Tiflis Cons. (graduated, 1931) and with Shekhter and Miaskovsky at the Moscow Cons. (graduated, 1934). His early compositions were influenced by his native folk music; he wrote a *Georgian Suite* for Piano (1935) and incidental music to plays on Caucasian subjects. His 1st important work was a sym. in memory of the assassinated Soviet dignitary Kirov (Moscow, Nov. 28, 1938); his 2nd Sym. (1946) received a Stalin prize. The performance of his opera *Great Friendship* (Moscow, Nov. 7, 1947) gave rise to an official condemnation of modernistic trends in Soviet music, culminating in the resolution of the Central Committee of the Communist Party of Feb. 10, 1948, which described the opera as "chaotic, inharmonious, and alien to the normal human ear." His reputation was rehabilitated by his subsequent works: *The Path of Victory*, symphonic poem for Chorus and Orch. (1950); a series of choruses (*Stalin's Will Has Led Us; Song of the Fighters for Peace; Hymn to Moscow*, which received a Stalin prize in 1951); and an opera, *October* (Moscow, April 22, 1964).

Murakumo, Ayako, Japanese composer; b. Gifu Prefecture, Feb. 25, 1949. She graduated from the Graduate School of Aichi Prefecture Univ. of the Arts (degree, 1982); received the Nagoya City Cultural Promotion Prize (1985), the Incentive Prize for Original Theatrical Art from the Agency of Cultural Affairs (1986), and an award from the Kyūshū competition (1988).

Works: *Hishō* for Orch. (1980); *Chronos* for Orch. (1982); *Wave* for Orch. (1982); *Reflection* for Flute, Clarinet, Cello, and Percussion (1982); *Projection* for Mezzo-soprano, Cello, and Piano (1984); *Fūha* for Flute, Cello, and Piano (1984); *Chiku-in Sō-Sho* for Shakuhachi and Koto (1985); *Ondine* for Mixed Chorus (1985); *Interspersion* for Viola, Cello, and Contrabass (1988); *Polymorph II* for Recorder and Guitar (1989).

Muratore, Lucien, prominent French tenor and teacher; b. Marseilles, Aug. 29, 1876; d. Paris, July 16, 1954. He studied at the Marseilles Cons., graduating with honors in 1897, but began his career as an actor. Later he studied opera at the Paris Cons.; made his opera debut at the Paris Opéra-Comique on Dec. 16, 1902, in Hahn's *La Carmélite*, with extraordinary success. Muratore also sang in the premieres of several operas by Massenet: *Ariane* (1906), *Bacchus* (1909), and *Roma* (1912); Février's *Monna Vanna* (1909) and Giordano's *Siberia* (1911); etc. In 1913 he made his American debut with the Boston Opera Co.; on Dec. 15, 1913, he sang Faust with the Chicago Opera Co. In 1914 he joined the French army; then returned to the Chicago Grand Opera (1915–19; 1920–22). In 1922 he went back to France; for 7 years he served as mayor of the town of Biot. He was married 3 times; his 1st 2 marriages (to Marguerite Bériza, a soprano, and to the famous prima donna **Lina Cavalieri**) ended in divorce; his 3rd wife was Marie Louise Brivaud.

Muris, Johannes de (original French rendering may have been **Jehan des Murs, de Murs, de Meurs,** etc.), important French music theorist, astronomer, and mathematician; b. in the diocese of Lisieux, Normandy, c.1300; d. c.1351. He was long confused with Julian des Murs, a Master of the Children

of the Sainte-Chapelle of Paris (c.1350), who later served as secretary to Charles V of France; it seems most likely, however, that the 2 were close relatives. Johannes de Muris is listed as a baccalaureate student in the Faculty of Arts in Paris in 1318. During the next few years he was active in Evreux and Paris; was associated with the Collège de Sorbonne in Paris, where he achieved the academic degree of Magister. In 1326–27 he was at the monastery of Fontevrault (Maine-et-Loire); it is known that Julian des Murs was his clerk at this time. In 1332–33 he was in Evreux; then returned to Paris, where he was again associated with the Sorbonne (1336–37). From 1338 to 1342 he was in service at the court of the King of Navarra, Philippe d'Evreux. In 1342 he was one of the 6 canons of the collegiate church in Mezières-en-Brenne (Indre); in 1344 he went, at the invitation of Pope Clement VI, to Avignon, where he participated in the conference on the reform of the calendar. There is extant a letter in verse which he wrote to Philippe de Vitry.

The writings by Muris pose problems; titles and versions of the various works attributed to him are questionable. Those that appear authentic are as follows: *Ars novae musicae* or *Notitia artis musicae* (1321; although he gave it the title *Summa musicae*, the work is always known by the 2 preceding titles in order to avoid confusion with a spurious work of the same name); *Questiones super partes musicae* or *Compendium musicae practicae* (c.1322; apparently a condensed version of the 2nd book of the *Ars novae musicae*); *Musica speculativa secundum Boetium* (June 1323). Some scholars also attribute to him *Libellus cantus mensurabilis* (*secundum Johannes de Muris*) (c.1340) and *Ars contrapuncti secundum Johannes de Muris* (after 1340). The *Speculum musicae* (c.1325), long attributed to Muris, has been proved to be a work by Jacques de Liège.

Bibl.: R. Hirschfeld, *J. d.M.: Seine Werke und seine Bedeutung als Verfechter des Classischen in der Tonkunst: Eine Studie* (Leipzig, 1884); H. Riemann, *Geschichte der Musiktheorie im IX.–XIX. Jahrhundert* (Leipzig, 1898; 2nd ed., rev., 1921; Eng. tr., 1967); W. Grossmann, *Die einleitenden Kapitel des Speculum Musicae von J. d.M.: Ein Beitrag zu Musikanschauung des Mittelalters* (Leipzig, 1924; erroneous in ascribing the authorship of *Speculum musicae* to Muris); L. Gushee, "New Sources for the Biography of J. d.M.," *Journal of the American Musicological Society,* XXII (1969); U. Michels, *Die Musiktraktate des J. d.M.* (Wiesbaden, 1970); M. Haas, "Musik zwischen Mathematik und Physik: Zur Bedeutung der Notation in den 'Notitia artis musicae' des J. d.M. (1321)," in *Festschrift für Arno Volk* (Cologne, 1974).

Muro, Bernardo de, Italian tenor; b. Tempio Pausanio, Sardinia, Nov. 3, 1881; d. Rome, Oct. 27, 1955. He studied at the Accademia di Santa Cecilia in Rome and with Alfredo Martinio; made his debut as Turiddu in *Cavalleria rusticana* at Rome's Teatro Costanzi in 1910; in 1911 he appeared at Milan's La Scala as Folco in Mascagni's *Isabeau* and returned there in the title role of *Don Carlos* in 1912; then sang in various Italian music centers, winning admiration for his portrayal of Otello; also appeared in Europe and South America. After marrying the American soprano Barbara Wait, he toured with U.S. with minor opera companies; following his retirement from the stage (1943), he devoted himself to teaching. He never became a star in the operatic firmament, yet knowledgeable critics regarded him as worthy of comparison with Caruso, both in the carrying force of his natural voice and in emotional appeal. He wrote an autobiographical vol., *Quandro ero Folco* (Milan, 1956).

Murphy, "Turk" (Melvin E.), American jazz trombonist and bandleader; b. Palermo, Calif., Dec. 16, 1915; d. San Francisco, May 30, 1987. After studying music theory, he took up the cornet and trombone; subsequently led his own band. He achieved distinction by reviving ragtime and jazz numbers from the early period of popular music.

Bibl.: J. Goggin, *T. M.: Just for the Record* (San Francisco, 1982).

Murray, Ann, Irish mezzo-soprano; b. Dublin, Aug. 27, 1949. She studied at the Royal Manchester College of Music and in London. In 1974 she made her operatic debut as Alceste at Glasgow's Scottish Opera, and then appeared regularly at London's English National Opera; in 1976 she made her Covent Garden debut in London as Cherubino, and subsequently sang there frequently. On Oct. 18, 1985, she made her Metropolitan Opera debut in N.Y. as Sextus in *La clemenza di Tito.* She also sang as a guest artist with various opera houses and festivals at home and abroad, and likewise pursued a notably successful career as a concert artist. Among her finest roles are Handel's Xerxes, Mozart's Dorabella and Zerlina, and Strauss's Composer. Her husband is **Philip Langridge.**

Murray, (Morna) Anne, Canadian singer of popular and country-western music; b. Springhill, Nova Scotia, June 20, 1945. She attended Mount St. Vincent Univ. in Halifax; graduated from the Univ. of New Brunswick in Fredericton with a bachelor's degree in physical education in 1966. She made appearances on Canadian television and several recordings; in 1970 she gained international recognition with her album *Snowbird.* After several more successful albums, she received the 1974 Grammy award as best female country vocalist for her recording of *Love Song.* Other successful albums followed, including *New Kind of Feeling* (1979), which won her a platinum award. In 1981 she again won the Grammy award as best female country vocalist for her recording of *Could I Have This Dance?* from the movie *Urban Cowboy.*

Murray, Bain, American composer; b. Evanston, Ill., Dec. 26, 1926. He studied with H. Elwell at Oberlin College (A.B., 1951) and Thompson and Piston at Harvard Univ. (A.M., 1952); also received instruction from Boulanger in Paris. He taught at Harvard Univ. (1954–55), Oberlin College (1955–60), and Cleveland State Univ. (from 1960), where he was head of its theory and composition dept. (from 1966).
 Works: Opera-oratorio, *The Legend* (1986; Cleveland, May 8, 1987); ballet, *Peter Pan; Epitaph* for Strings; many choral works; song cycles with orch. or chamber orch.; solo songs; 2 string quartets; Trio for Flute, Cello, and Piano; Woodwind Quintet; piano pieces.

Murray, Michael, American organist; b. Kokomo, Ind., March 19, 1943. He studied with Dorothy Cleveland Hopkins in Kokomo (1958–59), Mallory Bransford in Indianapolis (1959–61), Haskell Thomson at Oberlin College (1961; 1965), and Marcel Dupré in Paris (1961–64). He served as organist (1967–80) and music director (1970–80) at Cleveland Heights Christian Church. He formally launched his career as a concert artist with a series of the complete organ works of J.S. Bach in Cleveland (1968–69). He made his European debut in Leiden, the Netherlands, in 1972; thereafter he regularly toured the U.S. and Europe, making his N.Y. debut at St. James Episcopal Church in 1986. He was a contributor of articles to the journals *Diapason* and *American Organist;* publ. *Marcel Dupré: The Work of a Master* (Boston, 1985).

Murray, Thomas (Mantle), American organist and choral conductor; b. Los Angeles, Oct. 6, 1943. He studied with Clarence Mader (organ) and Howard Swan (choral conducting) at Occidental College (B.A., 1965), then was organist at Los Angeles's Immanuel Presbyterian Church (1965–73) and organist and choirmaster at Boston's St. Paul's Episcopal Church (1973–80). He taught at the Yale Univ. School of Music from 1981 and toured widely as a recitalist, acquiring a fine reputation as an interpreter of the Romantic organ repertoire.

Murrill, Herbert (Henry John), English organist, choral conductor, broadcasting executive, and composer; b. London, May 11, 1909; d. there, July 24, 1952. He studied at the Royal Academy of Music in London with York Bowen, Stanley Marchant, and Alan Bush (1925–28); then was an organ scholar at Worcester College, Oxford (1928–31), where he took courses with Ernest Walker and Sir Hugh Allen. He occupied various posts as organist and choral director; was prof. of composition at the Royal Academy of Music (1933–52); joined the staff of the BBC (1936), where he was program organizer (1942); after working in the British intelligence service (1942–46), he returned to the BBC as assistant head (1948) and head (1950) of music. His relatively small output was in a modern vein, exemplified by a "jazz opera," *Man in Cage* (London, 1930). He also wrote 2 cello concertos (1935; 1950, *El cant dels ocells*), choral works, chamber music, piano pieces, and songs.

Murschhauser, Franz Xaver Anton, German music theorist and composer; b. Zabern, near Strasbourg (baptized), July 1, 1663; d. Munich, Jan. 6, 1738. He studied with J.K. Kerll in Munich; from 1691 he was music director of the Frauenkirche there. He wrote the theoretical treatise *Academia musicopoetica bipartita, oder Hohe Schule der musikalischen Compositions,* the 1st part of which appeared in 1721, provocatively described as being intended "to give a little more light to the excellent Herr Mattheson." The latter retaliated with such devastating effect in his *Die melopoetische Licht-Scheere* (vol. I, *Critica musica,* 1722) that Murschhauser refrained from publishing the 2nd part of his work. His compositions for organ are reprinted in Denkmäler der Tonkunst in Bayern, XXX, Jg. XVIII (1917), ed. by M. Seiffert, with a biographical sketch.
 Bibl.: M. Vogeleis, "F.X.A. M.," *Kirchenmusikalisches Jahrbuch* (1901).

Murska, Ilma di, Croatian soprano; b. Zagreb, Jan. 4, 1836; d. Munich, Jan. 14, 1889. She studied with Mathilde Marchesi in Vienna and Paris; made her debut in Florence (1862). After a European tour, she was engaged at the Vienna Court Opera. She made her London debut as Lucia (May 11, 1865) and was favorably received there until 1873; toured America (debut as Amina in N.Y., Oct. 7, 1873) and Australia (1873–76); was again in London in 1879. She was greatly admired for the quality of her voice and stage presence, but her voice and health deteriorated so rapidly that reviewers were embarrassed by her pathetic vocal display at her last N.Y. appearance (Dec. 29, 1887). She taught unsuccessfully at the National Cons. there (1888) and then returned to Germany, where she died in poverty. She also composed a few works, including *Farewell,* a polka for Piano, and *Ritrono,* a waltz for Piano. Her life was filled with turbulence and a fabricated background: 2 marriages, an illegitimate daughter whose legitimacy was established by fabricating a 3rd marriage, lawsuits with opera companies, and injudicious advice from friends. Learning of her death, her daughter, with whom she was living, distraughtly committed suicide.

Musard, Philippe, famous French conductor and composer; b. Tours, Nov. 8, 1792; d. Auteuil, Paris, March 30, 1859. He studied music privately with Reicha. He organized his own Concerts-Musard in Paris, at which he presented popular works and dance music; the remarkable cornetist Dufresne became an added attraction, and Musard wrote special solo pieces for him; he also conducted balls at the Paris Opéra (1835–36), at which his orch. of 70 musicians won great acclaim; led popular concerts at London's Drury Lane and Lyceum Theatre (1840–41); remained a successful figure in France until his retirement in 1852. His quadrilles and galops enjoyed immense popularity, and he earned the sobriquet "le roi des quadrilles." His son Alfred Musard (1828–81) was also a composer of quadrilles, and a bandleader.

Musgrave, Thea, remarkable Scottish composer; b. Barnton, Midlothian, May 27, 1928. She pursued preliminary medical studies at the Univ. of Edinburgh, and concurrently studied with Mary Grierson (musical analysis) and Hans Gál (composition and counterpoint), receiving her B.Mus. (1950) and winning the Donald Tovey Prize; then studied privately and at the Paris Cons. with Boulanger (1952–54); later was a scholarship student of Copland at the Berkshire Music Center in Tanglewood (1959). She taught at the Univ. of London (1958–65), then was a visiting prof. of composition at the Univ. of Calif. at Santa Barbara (1970); also lectured at various other U.S. and English univs.; likewise made appearances as a conductor on both sides of the Atlantic. She held 2 Guggenheim fellowships (1974–75; 1982). In 1971 she married the American violinist Peter Mark, who later served as conductor of the Virginia Opera Assoc. in Norfolk. She was named Distinguished Prof. of Music at Queens College in N.Y. in 1987. At the outset of her career, she followed the acceptable modern style of composition, but soon the diatonic lyricism of the initial period of her creative evolution gave way to increasingly chromatic constructions, eventually systematized into serial organization. She described her theatrical works as "dramatic abstracts" in form, because even in the absence of a programmatic design, they revealed some individual dramatic traits. Appreciated by critics and audiences alike, her compositions, in a variety of styles but invariably effective and technically accomplished, enjoyed numerous performances in Europe and America.

WORKS: OPERAS: *The Abbott of Drimock*, chamber opera (London, 1955); *The Decision* (1964–65; London, Nov. 30, 1967); *The Voice of Ariadne* (1972–73; Aldeburgh, June 11, 1974); *Mary, Queen of Scots* (1976; Edinburgh, Sept. 6, 1977); *A Christmas Carol* (Norfolk, Va., Dec. 7, 1979); *An Occurrence at Owl Creek Bridge*, radio opera (1981; London, Sept. 14, 1982); *Harriet, the Woman Called Moses* (Norfolk, Va., March 1, 1985). **BALLETS:** *A Tale for Thieves* (1953); *Beauty and the Beast* (London, Nov. 19, 1969); *Orfeo* (1975; BBC-TV, March 17, 1977; as *Orfeo II* for Flute and Strings, Los Angeles, March 28, 1976; as *Orfeo I* for Flute and Tape, Chichester, July 5, 1976). **ORCH.:** *Divertimento* for String Orch. (1957); *Obliques* (1958); *Scottish Dance Suite* (1959); *Perspectives* (1961); *Theme and Interludes* (1962); *Sinfonia* (1963); *Festival Overture* (1965); *Nocturnes and Arias* (1966); *Variations* for Brass Band (1966); *Concerto for Orchestra* (1967); Clarinet Concerto (London, Feb. 5, 1969; a deft, chic virtuoso piece, requiring the soloist to promenade among members of the orch.); *Night Music* for Chamber Orch. (1969); *Memento vitae* (1969–70); Horn Concerto (1971); Viola Concerto (London, Aug. 13, 1973); *Peripeteia* (1981); *Moving into Aquarius* (1984; London, Jan. 23, 1985; in collaboration with R.R. Bennett); *The Seasons* (London, Dec. 4, 1988); *Rainbow* (Glasgow, Oct. 8, 1990). **CHAMBER:** String Quartet (1958); *Colloquy* for Violin and Piano (1960); Trio for Flute, Oboe, and Piano (1960); *Serenade* for Flute, Clarinet, Harp, Viola, and Cello (1961); Chamber Concerto No. 1 for 9 Instruments (1962); Chamber Concerto No. 2 for 5 Instruments (1966); Chamber Concerto No. 3 for 8 Instruments (1966); *Sonata for 3* for Flute, Violin, and Guitar (1966); *Impromptu No. 1* for Flute and Oboe (1967); *Music* for Horn and Piano (1967); *Soliloquy No. 1* for Guitar and Tape (1969); *Elegy* for Viola and Cello (1970); *Impromptu No. 2* for Flute, Oboe, and Clarinet (1970); *From 1 to Another I* for Viola and Tape (1970; arranged as *From 1 to Another I* for Viola and 15 Strings, 1980); *Space Play*, concerto for 9 Instruments (London, Oct. 11, 1974); *Fanfare* for Brass Quintet (1982); *Pierrot* for Clarinet, Violin, and Piano (1985); *The Golden Echo I* for Horn and Tape (1986; as *The Golden Echo II* for Solo Horn and 16 Accompanying Horns, 1986); *Narcissus* for Flute with Digital Delay (1987). **VOCAL:** *4 Madrigals* for Chorus (1953); *A Suite o' Bairnsangs* for Voice and Piano (1953); *Cantata for a Summer's Day* for Vocal Quartet, Speaker, Flute, Clarinet, String Quartet, and Double Bass (1954); *Song of the Burn* for Chorus (1954); *5 Love Songs* for Tenor and Guitar (1955); *A Song for Christmas* for Voice and Piano (1958); *Triptych* for Tenor and Orch. (1959); *The Phoenix and the Turtle* for Chorus and Orch. (1962); *The 5 Ages of Man* for Chorus and Orch. (1964); *Memento creatoris* for Chorus (1967); *Rorate coeli* for Chorus (1974); *The Last Twilight* for Chorus, Brass, and Percussion (Santa Fe, July 20, 1980); *The Lord's Prayer* for Chorus and Organ (1983); *Black Tambourine* for Women's Voices, Piano, and Percussion (1985); *For the Time Being: Advent* for Narrator and Chorus (1986; London, April 27, 1987).

BIBL.: D. Hixon, *T. M.: A Bio-Bibliography* (Westport, Conn., 1984).

Mushel, Georgi, Russian pianist and composer; b. Tambov, July 29, 1909. He studied piano with Oborin and composition with Miaskovsky at the Moscow Cons.; during World War II, he moved to Tashkent in Uzbekistan, where he composed the 1st opera on Uzbek themes, *Farkhad i Shirin,* as well as other works inspired by Uzbek folklore.

Musicescu, Gavriil, Rumanian choral conductor, teacher, and composer; b. Ismail, March 20, 1847; d. Iaşi, Dec. 21, 1903. He studied at the Iaşi Cons. and later at the St. Petersburg Cons. In 1872 he was appointed a prof. at the Iaşi Cons.; became its director in 1901. He composed liturgical hymns and Psalms as well as secular choral works and songs for solo voice; in his secular works, he utilized folk songs; also made arrangements of folk songs. A selected vol. of his music was ed. by G. Breazul (Bucharest, 1958).

BIBL.: G. Breazul, *G. M.* (Bucharest, 1962).

Musin, Ovide, Belgian violinist, teacher, and composer; b. Nandrin, near Liège, Sept. 22, 1854; d. N.Y., Nov. 24, 1929. He studied with Heynberg and Léonard at the Liège Cons., taking 1st violin prize at the age of 13; he won the gold medal at 15; toured Europe from 1874 to 1882 with remarkable success. In 1883 he went to America; between 1892 and 1897 he made 2 world tours. From 1897 to 1908 he taught at the Liège Cons.; in 1908 he established himself in N.Y., and opened his own school of music. He publ. a number of brilliant violin pieces; also the instructive works *System of Daily Practice* (1899) and *The Belgian School of the Violin* (4 vols.; 1916; a combination of his own methods with those of his teacher Léonard); also publ. a book, *My Memories* (1920). His wife, **Annie Louise Tanner-Musin** (b. Boston, Oct. 3, 1856; d. there, Feb. 28, 1921), was a well-known coloratura soprano.

Mussolini, Cesare, Italian composer and music theorist; b. Romagna, 1735; d. probably in London, date unknown. He went to London (1780), where he publ. *A New and Complete Treatise on the Theory and Practice of Music, with Solfeggios* (1795); also wrote canzonets. He was an ancestor of Benito Mussolini.

Mussorgsky, Modest (Petrovich), great Russian composer; b. Karevo, Pskov district, March 21, 1839; d. St. Petersburg, March 28, 1881. He received his 1st instruction on the piano from his mother; at the age of 10, he was taken to St. Petersburg, where he had piano lessons with Anton Herke, remaining his pupil until 1854. In 1852 he entered the cadet school of the Imperial Guard; composed a piano piece entitled *Porte enseigne Polka,* which was publ. (1852); after graduation (1856), he joined the regiment of the Guard. In 1857, he met Dargomyzhsky, who introduced him to Cui and Balakirev; he also became friendly with the critic and chief champion of Russian national music, Vladimir Stasov. These associations prompted his decision to become a professional composer. He played and analyzed piano arrangements of works by Beethoven and Schumann; Balakirev helped him to acquire a knowledge of form; he tried to write music in classical style, but without success; his inner drive was directed toward "new shores," as Mussorgsky expressed it. The liquidation of the family estate made it imperative for him to take a paying job; he became a clerk in the Ministry of Communications (1863), being dismissed 4 years later. During this time, he continued to compose, but his lack of technique compelled him time and again to leave his various pieces unfinished. He eagerly sought professional advice from his friends Stasov (for general esthetics) and Rimsky-Korsakov (for problems of harmony); to the very end of his life, he regarded himself as being only half-educated in music, and constantly acknowledged his inferiority as a craftsman. But he yielded to no one in his firm faith in the future of national Russian music. When a group of composers from Bohemia visited St. Petersburg in 1867, Stasov publ. an article in which he for the 1st time referred to the "mighty handful of Russian musicians" pursuing the ideal of national art. The expression was picked up derisively by some journalists, but it was accepted as a challenge by Mussorgsky and his comrades-in-arms, Balakirev, Borodin, Cui, and Rimsky-

Korsakov, the "mighty 5" of Russian music. In 1869 he once more entered government service, this time in the forestry dept. He became addicted to drink, and had epileptic fits; he died a week after his 42nd birthday. The significance of Mussorgsky's genius did not become apparent until some years after his death. Most of his works were prepared for publication by Rimsky-Korsakov, who corrected some of his harmonic crudities, and reorchestrated the symphonic works. Original versions of his music were preserved in MS, and eventually publ. But despite the availability of the authentic scores, his works continue to be performed in Rimsky-Korsakov's eds., made familiar to the whole musical world. In his dramatic works, and in his songs, Mussorgsky draws a boldly realistic vocal line, in which inflections of speech are translated into a natural melody. His 1st attempt in this genre was an unfinished opera, *The Marriage*, to Gogol's comedy; here he also demonstrated his penetrating sense of musical humor. His ability to depict tragic moods is revealed in his cycle *Songs and Dances of Death*; his understanding of intimate poetry is shown in the children's songs. His greatest work is the opera *Boris Godunov* (to Pushkin's tragedy), which has no equal in its stirring portrayal of personal destiny against a background of social upheaval. In it, Mussorgsky created a true national music drama, without a trace of the Italian conventions that had theretofore dominated the operatic works by Russian composers. He wrote no chamber music, perhaps because he lacked the requisite training in contrapuntal technique. Of his piano music, the set of pieces *Pictures at an Exhibition* (somewhat after the manner of Schumann's *Carnaval*) is remarkable for its vivid representation of varied scenes (it was written to commemorate his friend, the painter Victor Hartmann, whose pictures were the subjects of the music); the work became famous in the brilliant orchestration of Ravel. Although Mussorgsky was a Russian national composer, his music influenced many composers outside Russia, and he came to be regarded as the most potent talent of the Russian national school. The paintings of Victor Hartmann that inspired *Pictures at an Exhibition* were reproduced by Alfred Frankenstein in his article on the subject in the *Musical Quarterly* (July 1939); he also brought out an illustrated ed. of the work (1951).

WORKS: OPERAS: *Salammbô* (1863–66; unfinished); *Zhenitba* (The Marriage), comic opera (1868; only Act 1 completed; St. Petersburg, April 1, 1909; completed and orchestrated by A. Tcherepnin; Essen, Sept. 14, 1937); *Boris Godunov* (1st version, with 7 scenes, 1868–69; Leningrad, Feb. 16, 1928; 2nd version, with prologue and 4 acts, 1871–72, rev. 1873; St. Petersburg, Feb. 8, 1874; rev. and reorchestrated by Rimsky-Korsakov, 1896; St. Petersburg, Dec. 10, 1896); *Khovanshchina* (1872–80; completed and orchestrated by Rimsky-Korsakov; St. Petersburg, Feb. 21, 1886); *Sorochinskaya yarmarka* (The Fair at Sorochinsk), comic opera (1874–80; completed by Cui, Liadov, Karatigin, and others; Moscow, Oct. 21, 1913; also arranged and orchestrated by N. Tcherepnin; Monte Carlo, March 17, 1923). **ORCH.:** *Scherzo* (1858; St. Petersburg, Jan. 23, 1860; originally for Piano); *Alla marcia notturna* (1861); *Ivanova noch' na Lisoy gore* (A Night on Bald Mountain; 1860–67; reorchestrated by Rimsky-Korsakov; St. Petersburg, Oct. 27, 1886; originally for Piano); *Intermezzo symphonique in modo classico* (1867; originally for Piano); *Vyzatiye Karsa* (The Capture of Kars), march (1880). **CHORAL:** *Marsh Shamilya* (Shamil's March) for Tenor, Bass, Chorus, and Orch. (1859); *Porazheniye Sennakheriba* (The Destruction of Sennacherib) for Chorus and Orch. (St. Petersburg, March 18, 1867; rev. 1874); *Iisus Navin* (Jesus Navin) for Alto, Bass, Chorus, and Piano (1874–77); 3 vocalises for 3 Women's Voices (1880); 5 Russian folksongs arranged for 4 Male Voices (1880; No. 5 unfinished). **PIANO:** *Porte-enseigne polka* (1852); *Souvenir d'enfance* (1857); 2 sonatas (1858; not extant); 2 *Scherzos* (both 1858); *Impromptu passion: Jeux d'enfants—Les Quatre Coins: Ein Kinderscherz* (1859; rev. 1860); Allegro and Scherzo for a Sonata for Piano, 4-hands (1860); *Preludio in modo classico* (1860; not extant); *Intermezzo in modo classico* (1860–61; orchestrated 1867; rearranged for Piano, 1867); *Menuet monstre* (1861; not extant); *Iz vospomina-*

niy detstva (From Memories of Childhood; 1865); *La Capricieuse* (1865); *Shveyg* (The Seamstress; 1871); *Kartinki s vistavki* (Pictures at an Exhibition), suite (1874; *Promenade; Gnomus; Il vecchio castello; Tuileries; Bydlo; Ballet des poussins dans leurs coques; Deux juifs, l'un riche et l'autre pauvre; Limoges—Le Marché; Catacombae; Cum mortuis in lingua mortua; La Cabane sur des pattes de poule; La Grande Porte de Kiev;* French titles by Mussorgsky; orchestrated by Ravel, 1922); *Burya no Chernom more* (Storm on the Black Sea; 1879; not extant); *Na yuzhnom bere Krima* (On the Southern Shore of the Crimea; 1880); *Méditation* (1880); *Une Larme* (1880); *Au villa* (c.1880); transcriptions of dances from the opera *The Fair at Sorochinsk;* many fragments from youthful works, etc. **SONGS:** *King Saul* (1863); *Cradle Song* (1865); *Darling Savishna* (1866); *The Seminarist* (1866); *Hopak* (1866); *On the Dnieper* (1879); *The Classicist* (satirical; 1867); *The Garden by the Don* (1867); *The Nursery*, children's song cycle (1868–72); *Rayok* (The Peep Show), musical lampoon at assorted contemporaries (1870); *Sunless*, song cycle (1874); *Forgotten* (1874); *Songs and Dances of Death*, cycle of 4 songs (1875–77); *Mephistopheles' Song of the Flea* (1879); etc. A collected ed. of his works was compiled by P. Lamm (8 vols., Moscow, 1928–34; 1939).

BIBL.: The Russian literature on Mussorgsky is extensive. A collection of letters and documents was publ. by A. Rimsky-Korsakov (Moscow, 1932); materials, largely taken from this vol., were tr. and ed. by J. Leyda and S. Bertensson as *The M. Reader* (N.Y., 1947). See also V. Stasov, *M.* (St. Petersburg, 1881); V. Baskin, *M.* (Moscow, 1887); P. d'Alheim, *M.* (Paris, 3rd ed., 1896); M. Olénine-d'Alheim, *Le Legs de M.* (Paris, 1908); M.D. Calvocoressi, *M.* (Paris, 1907; 2nd French ed., 1911; Eng. tr., London, 1919); R. Newmarch, "M.'s Operas," *Musical Times* (July 1913); M. Montagu-Nathan, *M.* (London, 1916); O. von Riesemann, *M.* (Munich, 1925; in Eng., N.Y., 1935); A. Swan, "M. and Modern Music," *Musical Quarterly* (April 1925); R. Godet, *En marge de Boris Godunov* (Paris, 1927); K. von Wolfurt, *M.* (Stuttgart, 1927); I. Glebov, *M.* (Leningrad, 1928); H. van Dalen, *M.* (The Hague, 1930); M.D. Calvocoressi, "M.'s Musical Style," *Musical Quarterly* (Oct. 1932); Y. Keldish, *Lyricism in M.'s Songs* (Moscow, 1933); M.D. Calvocoressi, "M.'s Youth," *Musical Quarterly* (Jan. 1934); V. Fedorov, *M.* (Paris, 1935); M. Tibaldi Chiesa, *M.* (Milan, 1935); G. Abraham and M.D. Calvocoressi, "M.," in *Masters of Russian Music* (London, 1936); C. Barzel, *M.* (Paris, 1939); G. Orlov, *Chronicle of the Life and Works of M.* (Moscow, 1940); G. Gavazzeni, *M. e la musica russa dell' 800* (Florence, 1943); M.D. Calvocoressi, *M.* (completed by G. Abraham, London, 1946; 2nd ed., rev., 1974); R. Hofmann, *M.* (Paris, 1952); M.D. Calvocoressi, *M. M., His Life and Works* (London, 1956; ed. by G. Abraham; a completely different book from the earlier ones by Calvocoressi); V. Serov, *M. M.* (N.Y., 1968); L. Hübsch, *M. M.: Bilder einer Ausstellung* (Munich, 1978); R. Oldani, *New Pespectives on M.'s Boris Godunov* (diss., Univ. of Michigan, 1978); M. Schandert, *Das Problem der originalen Instrumentation des Boris Godunov von M.P. M.* (Hamburg, 1979); E. Reilly, *A Guide to M.: A Scorography* (N.Y., 1980); M. Brown, ed., *M.: In Memoriam 1881–1981* (Ann Arbor, 1982); P. Weber-Bockholdt, *Die Lieder M.s: Herkunft und Erscheinungsform* (Munich, 1982); A. Orlova, *M.'s Days and Works: A Biography in Documents* (Ann Arbor, 1983); R. Taruskin, "M. vs. M.: The Versions of *Boris Godunov*," *19th Century Music* (Fall 1984 and Spring 1985); C. Emerson, *Boris Godunov: Transpositions of a Russian Theme* (Bloomington and Indianapolis, 1986); R. Taruskin, "Handel, Shakespeare, and M.: The Sources and Limits of Russian Musical Realism," *Studies in the History of Music* (vol. 1, N.Y., 1987); E. Garden, "Three Nights on Bare Mountain," *Musical Times* (July 1988).

Mustel, Victor, celebrated French builder of harmoniums; b. Le Havre, June 13, 1815; d. Paris, Jan. 26, 1890. He began as a carpenter; in 1844 he went to Paris, where he worked in several shops, becoming foreman in Alexandre's harmonium factory; established himself in 1853; the following year he invented the harmonium with "double expression," which won 1st prize at the Paris Exposition of 1855; from 1866 the firm was famous as V. Mustel & ses Fils. He also constructed an instrument consisting of graduated tuning forks in a resonance box, operated by a keyboard; this was patented in 1886 by his son Auguste Mustel (1842–1919) as the "Celesta." Tchaikovsky heard the celesta in Paris and became so enchanted with it that he used it for the 1st time in any score in his ballet *The Nutcracker*.

Müthel, Johann Gottfried, German organist and composer; b. Mölln, Jan. 17, 1728; d. Bienenhof, near Riga, July 14, 1788. He studied at Lübeck and became court organist at Schwerin in 1747. In 1750 he traveled to Leipzig to see Bach, and remained with him for a few days before Bach's death. He then journeyed to Potsdam, where he met Carl Philipp Emanuel Bach. In 1753 he went to Riga, where he became an organist at the Lutheran church in 1755. Among his extant works are 10 harpsichord concertos (6 ed. in Denkmäler Norddeutscher Musik, III–IV, Munich, 1975), a Concerto for 2 Bassoons and Strings, sonatas for Harpsichord, and organ music.

BIBL.: R. Campbell, *J.G. M.* (diss., Indiana Univ., 1966).

Muti, Riccardo, greatly talented Italian conductor; b. Naples, July 28, 1941. His father was a physician who possessed a natural Neapolitan tenor voice; after receiving instruction in violin and piano from his father, Riccardo studied composition with Jacopo Napoli and Nino Rota at the Conservatorio di Musica San Pietro a Majella in Naples, taking a diploma in piano; then studied conducting with Antonino Votto and composition with Bruno Bettinelli at the Verdi Cons. in Milan; also attended a seminar in conducting with Franco Ferrara in Venice (1965). After winning the Guido Cantelli Competition in 1967, he made his formal debut with the RAI in 1968; then conducted in several of the major Italian music centers. His success led to his appointment as principal conductor of the Teatro Comunale in Florence in 1970; also conducted at the Maggio Musicale Fiorentino, becoming its artistic director in 1977. In the meantime, he began his advancement to international fame with guest conducting appearances at the Salzburg Festival in 1971 and with the Berlin Phil. in 1972. He made his U.S. debut with the Philadelphia Orch. on Oct. 27, 1972. In 1973 he conducted at the Vienna State Opera, and that same year became principal conductor of the New Philharmonia Orch. in London (it resumed its original name of Philharmonia Orch. in 1977). In 1974 he conducted the Vienna Phil. and in 1977 appeared at London's Covent Garden. His successful appearances with the Philadelphia Orch. led to his appointment as its principal guest conductor in 1977. In 1979 he was also named music director of the Philharmonia Orch. In 1980 he succeeded Eugene Ormandy as music director of the Philadelphia Orch., and subsequently relinquished his posts in London and Florence in 1982. In 1986 he became music director of Milan's La Scala, but retained his Philadelphia position. Muti announced his resignation as music director of the Philadelphia Orch. in 1990, but agreed to serve as its laureate conductor from 1992. His brilliance as a symphonic conductor enabled him to maintain, and even enhance, the illustrious reputation of the Philadelphia Orch. established by Stokowski and carried forward by Ormandy. Unlike his famous predecessors, he excels in both the concert hall and the opera pit.

BIBL.: D. Webster, "R. M.," *Ovation* (Feb. 1983); H. Waleson, "R. M.: A Tale of Two Cities," ibid. (Dec. 1988).

Mutter, Anne-Sophie, talented German violinist; b. Rheinfelden, June 29, 1963. At the age of 6 she won "1st Prize with Special Distinction" at the "Jungen Musiziert" National Competition, the youngest winner in its annals. In 1976 she came to the notice of Herbert von Karajan during her appearance at the Lucerne Festival; in 1977 he invited her to be a soloist with him and the Berlin Phil. at the Salzburg Easter Festival; this was the beginning of an auspicious career. She subsequently appeared regularly with Karajan and the Berlin Phil., and also recorded standard violin concertos with him; likewise

appeared as soloist with many other leading conductors and orchs. on both sides of the Atlantic. She held the 1st International Chair of Violin Studies at London's Royal Academy of Music (from 1986). On Dec. 14, 1988, she made her N.Y. recital debut.

BIBL.: D. Stearns, "Beauty and the Bow," *Ovation* (April 1988).

Muzio, Claudia (real name, **Claudina Muzzio**), oustanding Italian soprano; b. Pavia, Feb. 7, 1889; d. Rome, May 24, 1936. She studied with Casaloni in Turin and Viviani in Milan; made her debut as Manon in Arezzo (Jan. 15, 1910); then sang in Italy, South America, France, and England; made her Metropolitan Opera debut in N.Y. as Tosca (Dec. 4, 1916), remaining on its roster until 1922; created the role of Giorgetta in Puccini's *Il tabarro* there (Dec. 14, 1918). In 1922 she made her 1st appearance with the Chicago Opera as Aida, and continued to sing there regularly until 1932; also sang in South America and again at La Scala (1926–27); after returning to the Metropolitan (1933–34), she pursued her career mainly in Rome. She was one of the most gifted dramatic sopranos of her time, excelling in such roles as Desdemona, Mimi, Santuzza, Margherita in *Mefistofele*, Violetta, and Madeleine de Coigny.

BIBL.: H. Barnes, *C. M.: A Biographical Sketch and Discography* (Austin, Texas, 1947); J. Richards, "C. M.," *Record Collector*, XVII (1968); J. Steane, "C. M.: A Centenary Tribute," *Musical Times* (Feb. 1989).

Muzio, (Donnino) Emanuele, Italian conductor and composer; b. Zibello, Aug. 24, 1821; d. Paris, Nov. 27, 1890. He began his studies with Ferdinando Provesi; then studied piano with Margherita Barezzi (Verdi's 1st wife), and composition with Verdi himself; was one of the very few pupils Verdi ever had. In 1850 he was engaged as conductor of the Théâtre du Cirque in Brussels; he later traveled to England and America; settled in Paris in 1875 as a singing teacher. Carlotta Patti and Clara Louise Kellogg were his pupils. He wrote several operas: *Giovanna la pazza* (Brussels, April 8, 1851); *Claudia* (Milan, Feb. 7, 1853); *Le due regine* (Milan, May 17, 1856); *La Sorrentina* (Bologna, Nov. 14, 1857); also many songs and piano pieces.

BIBL.: A. Belforti, *E. M., l'unico alievo di Giuseppe Verdi* (Fabriano, 1895); L. Garibaldi, ed., *Giuseppe Verdi nelle lettere di E. M. ed Antonio Barezzi* (Milan, 1931).

Myagi, Ester, Estonian composer; b. Tallinn, Jan. 10, 1922. She studied at the Tallinn Cons. and with Shebalin at the Moscow Cons. In 1954 she was appointed instructor in music theory at the Tallinn Cons. In her music she cultivates Romantic motifs. Her principal work is a cantata, *Kalevipoja teckond Soome*, written under the influence of Sibelius (1954). She also wrote a Sym. (1969), several pieces of chamber music, and choruses.

Mycielski, Zygmunt, Polish music critic and composer; b. Przeworsk, Aug. 17, 1907; d. Warsaw, Aug. 5, 1987. He studied with Rizzi in Krakow and with Dukas and Boulanger at the Paris École Normale de Musique, where he was a member of the Soc. of Young Polish Musicians (1928–36). After World War II, he became active as a journalist; ed. the principal Polish music magazine, *Ruch Muzyczny* (1945–48; 1960–68); publ. 2 collections of essays: *Uzieczki z pieciolinii* (Flight of the Staff Lines; Warsaw, 1956) and *Notatki o muzyce i muzykach* (Notes on Music and Musicians; Krakow, 1961). His music, couched in a modern idiom, contains elements of Polish folk inflections, but dodecaphonic usages are also encountered.

WORKS: Piano Trio (1934); *Lamento di Tristano* for Small Orch., in memory of Szymanowski (1937); 5 *Symphonic Essays* (1945); *Portrait of a Muse* for Narrator, Chorus, and 15 Instruments (1947); 6 syms.: No. 1 (1947); *Polish Sym.* (1951); No. 2 (1960); No. 3, *Sinfonia breve* (1967; Warsaw, Sept. 23, 1972); No. 4 (1972–73; Poznan, April 2, 1976); No. 5 (1977); *Silesian Overture* (1948); *Zabawa w Lipinach* (Merrymaking at Lipiny), ballet (1953); Piano Concerto (1954); *Variations* for String Orch. (1980); *Portrait of a Muse* for Narrator, Chorus, and

15 Instruments (1947); *Nowy lirnik mazowiecki* (New Mazovian Bard), 9 songs and finale for Soprano, Baritone, Chorus, and Orch. (1955); *5 Preludes* for Piano Quintet (1967); Psalms for Baritone, Chorus, and Orch. (1982); *Liturgia sacra* for Chorus and Orch. (1983–84); songs.

Myers, Rollo (Hugh), English music critic and writer on music; b. Chislehurst, Kent, Jan. 23, 1892; d. Chichester, Jan. 1, 1985. He studied briefly at the Royal College of Music in London; then was music correspondent for English newspapers in Paris (1919–34); was a member of the staff of the BBC in London (1935–44); was active as music journalist and ed.; publ. the books *Modern Music: Its Aims and Tendencies* (London, 1923); *Music in the Modern World* (London, 1939; 2nd ed., rev., 1948); *Debussy* (London, 1948); *Erik Satie* (London, 1948); *Introduction to the Music of Stravinsky* (London, 1950); *Ravel: Life and Works* (London, 1960); *Emmanuel Chabrier and His Circle* (London, 1969); *Modern French Music* (Oxford, 1971); also ed. an anthology, *Twentieth Century Music* (London, 1960; 2nd ed., enl., 1968).

Mysliveček (Mysliweczek; Mislivecček), Josef, famous Bohemian composer, called "Il divino Boemo" and "Il Venatorini" in Italy; b. Ober-Sárka, near Prague, March 9, 1737; d. Rome, Feb. 4, 1781. His father was a miller. He was a pupil at the Normalschule of the Dominicans of St. Jilgi (1744–47) and the Jesuit Gymnasium (1748–53), where he received his 1st instruction in music; he also sang in the choir of St. Michal under Felix Benda. He then was apprenticed as a miller, being made a master miller in 1761. He also pursued his musical studies, taking courses in counterpoint with František Habermann and organ with Josef Seger. In 1760 he publ. anonymously a set of 6 sinfonias, named after the 1st 6 months of the year. Determined upon a career as a composer, he went to Venice in 1763 to study the art of operatic writing with Giovanni Pescetti. His 1st opera, *Medea*, was produced in Parma in 1764. While in Parma, he met the singer Lucrezia Aguiari, who became his mistress in the 1st of his many romantic liaisons. He was commissioned to write another opera, *Il Bellerofonte*, for the Teatro San Carlo in Naples, where it was performed with considerable success on Jan. 20, 1767. This led to other commissions from Italian theaters. His opera *Ezio* (Naples, June 5, 1775) and his oratorio *Isacco figura del Redentore* (Florence, March 10, 1776) were successfully performed in Munich in 1777; his career was blunted, however, by syphilis and disfiguring facial surgery. He returned to Italy but never regained his social standing. He succumbed at the age of 43. Mysliveček was one of the most significant Bohemian composers; his operas and oratorios were frequently performed and publ. in his lifetime. Mozart expressed admiration of his talent.

Works: operas: *Medea* (Parma, 1764); *Il Bellerofonte* (Naples, Jan. 20, 1767); *Farnace* (Naples, Nov. 4, 1767); *Il trionfo di Clelia* (Turin, Dec. 26, 1767); *Il Demofoonte* (Venice, Jan. 1769); *L'Ipermestra* (Florence, March 28, 1769); *La Nitteti* (Bologna, spring 1770); *Montezuma* (Florence, Jan. 23, 1771); *Il gran Tamerlano* (Milan, Dec. 26, 1771); *Il Demetrio* (Pavia, Jan. 25, 1773); *Erifile* (Munich, 1773); *Romolo ed Ersilia* (Naples, Aug. 13, 1773); *La clemenza di Tito* (Venice, Dec. 26, 1773); *Antigona* (Turin, Carnival 1774); *Atide* (Padua, June 1774); *Artaserse* (Naples, Aug. 13, 1774); *Il Demofoonte* (Naples, Jan. 20, 1775); *Ezio* (Naples, June 5, 1775); *Merope* (Naples, 1775); *Adriano in Siria* (Florence, fall 1776); *Las Calliroe* (Naples, May 30, 1778); *L'Olimpiade* (Naples, Nov. 4, 1778); *La Circe* (Venice, May 1779); *Il Demetrio* (Naples, Aug. 13, 1779); *Armida* (Milan, Dec. 26, 1779); *Medonte* (Rome, Jan. 1780); *Antigono* (Rome, April 1780). **oratorios:** *La famiglia di Tobia* (Florence, May 24, 1771); *Giuseppe riconosciuto* (Padua, 1771); *La Passione di Gesù Cristo* (Prague, 1773); *La liberazione d'Israele* (1775); *Isacco figura del Redentore* (Florence, March 10, 1776); also sinfonias, overtures, keyboard concertos, sonatas for keyboard, string quartets, trios.

Bibl.: H. Wilkemann, *Joseph Mysliweczek als Opernkomponist* (diss., Univ. of Vienna, 1915); M. Pincherle, "Un Oublié: Il divino Boemo," *Feuillets d'histoire de violon* (Paris, 1927); G. de Saint-Foix, "Un Ami de Mozart: Joseph Mysliweczek," *La Revue Musicale*, IX/4–6 (1928); P. Nettl, "Mozart und M.," *Prager Rundschau*, VII (1937); idem, *Mozart in Böhmen* (Prague, 1938); J. Čeleda, *J. M., tvůrce pražského nářeči hudebniho rokoka tereziánského* (J. M.: Creator of the Prague Dialect of Theresian Musical Rococo; Prague, 1946); U. Prota-Giurleo, "L'Abate Galiani messo in imbarazzo da un musicista boemo," *Nostro Tempo* (1957); S. Špatová-Ramešová, *Il divino Boemo* (Prague, 1957); R. Pečman, *J. M. und sein Opernepilog* (Brno, 1970; includes bibliography and list of sources).

Mysz-Gmeiner, Lula (née **Gmeiner**), noted Hungarian contralto; b. Kronstadt, Transylvania, Aug. 16, 1876; d. Schwerin, Aug. 7, 1948. She studied violin in her native town, and singing in Berlin with Etelka Gerster and Lilli Lehmann; made her concert debut in Berlin in 1899; then traveled in Europe as a concert singer; was greatly praised for her interpretations of German lieder. She was a prof. at the Berlin Hochschule für Musik (1920–45), numbering among her students Peter Anders and Elisabeth Schwarzkopf.

Myszuga, Alexander, Polish tenor of Ukrainian descent; b. Nowy Witków, near Lemberg, June 7, 1853; d. Schwarzwald, near Freiburg im Breisgau, March 9, 1922. He studied voice in Lemberg, Milan, and Paris, adopting the name Filippi for his stage appearances in Italy. He sang in Italy, Vienna, and Prague in both lyrical and dramatic roles in French and Italian operas; he was also noted for singing tenor parts in Polish operas. In later years he taught voice in Kiev and Stockholm.

Bibl.: O. Lada, "A. M.," *Ruch Muzyczny*, X/9 (1966).

N

Nabokov, Nicolas (actually, Nikolai), distinguished Russian-born American composer; b. near Lubcha, Novogrudok district, Minsk region, April 17, 1903; d. N.Y., April 6, 1978. He was a scion of a distinguished Russian family; his uncle was a liberal member of the short-lived Duma (Russian parliament); the famous writer Vladimir Nabokov was his 1st cousin. (The name is pronounced with stress on the 2nd syllable, Nabókov.) Nabokov received his early education with Rebikov in St. Petersburg and in Yalta; after taking courses at the Stuttgart Cons. (1920–22), he continued his studies with Juon and Busoni at the Berlin Hochschule für Musik (1922–23); finally moved to Paris, where he was introduced to Diaghilev, who commissioned him to write his 1st major score, the ballet-oratorio *Ode: Méditation sur la majesté de Dieu* (1927), for the Ballets Russes. In 1933 he went to the U.S., and in 1939 became a naturalized citizen; taught at Wells College in Aurora, N.Y. (1936–41) and at St. John's College in Annapolis (1941–44); after working for the U.S. government in Berlin (1944–47), he taught at the Peabody Cons. of Music in Baltimore (1947–52). From 1951 to 1963 he was secretary-general of the Congress for Cultural Freedom; then served as artistic director of the Berlin Music Festivals (1963–68); lectured on esthetics at the State Univ. of N.Y. at Buffalo (1970–71) and at N.Y. Univ. (1972–73). He was elected to membership in the National Inst. of Arts and Letters in 1970. In addition to writing articles for various periodicals, he wrote a book of essays, *Old Friends and New Music* (Boston, 1951), and the vols. *Igor Stravinsky* (Berlin, 1964) and *Bagazh: Memoirs of a Russian Cosmopolitan* (N.Y., 1975). In his music he adopted a cosmopolitan style, with an astute infusion of fashionable bitonality; in works of Russian inspiration, he reverted to melorhythms of Russian folk songs.

WORKS: STAGE: OPERAS: *The Holy Devil,* on the subject of Rasputin (Louisville, Ky., April 16, 1958; rev. as *Der Tod des Grigorij Rasputin,* Cologne, Nov. 27, 1959); *Love's Labour's Lost,* to a libretto of W.H. Auden after Shakespeare (1970–73; Brussels, Feb. 7, 1973). **BALLETS:** *Ode: Méditation sur la majesté de Dieu,* ballet-oratorio (1927; Paris, June 6, 1928); *La vie de Polichinelle* (Paris, 1934); *Union Pacific* (Philadelphia, April 6, 1934); *The Last Flower* (1941); *Don Quixote* (1966); *The Wanderer* (1966). **ORCH.:** 3 syms.: No. 1, *Symphonie lyrique* (Paris, Feb. 16, 1930); No. 2, *Sinfonia biblica* (N.Y., Jan. 2, 1941); No. 3, *A Prayer* (N.Y., Jan. 4, 1968); Piano Concerto (1932); *Le Fiancé,* overture (1934); Flute Concerto (1948); *Les Hommages* (Philadelphia, Nov. 6, 1953); *Symphonic Variations* (1967). **VOCAL:** *Job,* oratorio for Men's Voices and Orch. (1933); *Collectionneur d'échos* for Soprano, Bass, and 9 Percussion Instruments (1933); *The Return of Pushkin,* elegy for Soprano or Tenor and Orch. (Boston, Jan. 2, 1948); *America Was Promises,* cantata for Alto, Baritone, and Men's Voices (N.Y., April 25, 1950); *Vita nuova* for Soprano, Tenor, and Orch. (Boston, March 2, 1951); *Symboli chrestiani* for Baritone and Orch. (1953); *Quatre poèmes de Boris Pasternak* for Voice and Piano (1961; arr. for Voice and Strings, 1969); *5 Poems by Anna Akhmatova* for Voice and Orch. (1964). **CHAMBER:** *Serenata estiva* for String Quartet (1937); Bassoon Sonata (1941); *Canzone, Introduzione, e Allegro* for Violin and Piano (1950); 2 piano sonatas (1926, 1940); piano pieces.

Nachbaur, Franz (Ignaz), German tenor; b. Giessen, near Friedrichshafen, March 25, 1830; d. Munich, March 21, 1902. He studied with Pischek in Stuttgart and Lamperti in Milan; made his debut in Passau (1857); then sang in Basel (1857), Hannover (1859–60), Prague (1860–63), and Darmstadt (1863–68). He made his 1st appearance at the Munich Court Opera on June 24, 1867, in Flotow's *Alessandro Stradella*; subsequently was one of its principal members, and was chosen to create the roles of Walther von Stolzing in *Die Meistersinger von Nürnberg* (June 21, 1868) and Froh in *Das Rheingold* (Sept. 22, 1869); he made his London debut in Euryanthe at Drury Lane (1882); gave his farewell performance at the Munich Court Opera as Chapelou in Adam's *Le Postillon de Longjumeau* on Oct. 13, 1890, his 1,001st appearance there.

Nadel, Arno, German composer; b. Vilnius, Oct. 3, 1878; d. in the Auschwitz concentration camp, March 1943. He studied in Königsberg with Birnbaum and Schwalm; then at the Jewish Seminary in Berlin with Loewengard and L. Mendelssohn; in 1916 he became conductor of the Jewish Community Choir in Berlin. He compiled several anthologies of Jewish songs, among them *Jontefflieder*, in 10 vols. (1919); *Jüdische Volkslieder*, in 2 vols. (Leipzig, 1921; new ed., 1926).

Nadermann, François Joseph, French harp virtuoso and composer; b. Paris, 1781; d. there, April 2, 1835. He was a pupil of Krumpholtz; from 1816, served at the Royal Chapel; in 1825, he was appointed a prof. at the Paris Cons. He joined his brother Henri in the management of the harp-making business founded by their father. He composed 2 harp concertos and various other pieces for the instrument.

Nagano, Kent (George), American conductor; b. Morro Bay, Calif. (of Japanese-American parents), Nov. 22, 1951. He studied at Oxford Univ. (1969) with Grosvenor Cooper at the Univ. of Calif. in Santa Cruz (B.A., 1974), at San Francisco State Univ. (M.M., 1976), and at the Univ. of Toronto; also had instruction in conducting from Laszlo Varga in San Francisco. He was associated with Sarah Caldwell's Opera Co. of Boston (1977–79); was made music director of the Berkeley (Calif.) Sym. Orch. (1978) and of the Ojai (Calif.) Music Festival (1984). While working as an assistant conductor with the Boston Sym. Orch., he was called upon to substitute for Ozawa at the last moment and led a notably successful performance of Mahler's 9th Sym. without benefit of rehearsal (Nov. 30, 1984). In 1985 he was the 1st co-recipient (with Hugh Wolff) of the Affiliate Artist's Seaver Conducting Award. He subsequently appeared as a guest conductor with various orchs. on both sides of the Atlantic. In 1989 he became chief conductor of the Opéra de Lyon.

    BIBL.: P. Moor, "K. N.," *Musical America* (Nov. 1987).

Nagel, Wilibald, German pianist and musicologist; b. Mülheim-an-der-Ruhr, Jan. 12, 1863; d. Stuttgart, Oct. 17, 1929. He studied in Berlin with Ehrlich, Spitta, Bellermann, and others. In 1888 he was appointed a lecturer in music history at the Univ. of Zürich; then lived in London (1893–96), where he studied early English music. Returning to Germany, he completed his Habilitation at Darmstadt's Grossherzogliche Technische Hochschule with his *Die Entwicklung der Musik in Frankreich und England* (1898; publ. in Berlin, 1898); then served on its faculty as a prof. from 1905 to 1913. He then settled in Stuttgart, where he ed. the *Neue Musikzeitung* (1917–21); from 1921, was a prof. at the Hochschule für Musik; also made frequent appearances as a concert pianist. He wrote the valuable article "Annalen der englischen Hofmusik von der zeit Heinrichs VIII. bis zum Tode Karls I., 1509–1649," *Monatshefte für Musikgeschichte,* XXVI–XXVII (1894–95).

    WRITINGS: *Die dramatisch-musikalischen Bearbeitungen der Genovefa-Legende. Ein Beitrag zur Geschichte der Oper* (Leipzig, 1889); *Johannes Brahms als Nachfolger Beethoven's* (Leipzig and Zürich, 1892); *Geschichte der Musik in England* (2 vols., Strasbourg, 1894, 1897); *Annalen der englischen Hofmusik, 1509–1649* (1894); *Beethoven und seine Klaviersonaten* (2 vols., Langensalza, 1903, 1905; 3rd ed., 1933); *Der Musik im täglichen Leben: Ein Beitrag zur Geschichte der musikali-*

schen Kultur unserer Tage (Langensalza, 1907); *Über die Strömungen im unserer Musik: Kritische Randbemerkungen zur modernen Kunst* (Langensalza, 1913); *Die Klaviersonaten von Johannes Brahms: Technisch-ästhetische Analysen* (Stuttgart, 1915); *Wilhelm Mauke* (Vienna and Leipzig, 1919); *Johannes Brahms* (Stuttgart, 1923).

Nägeli, Hans Georg, Swiss music publisher, writer on music, and composer; b. Wetzikon, near Zürich, May 26, 1773; d. there, Dec. 26, 1836. He founded a music shop and lending library, and then his own publ. firm (1792); management of the latter passed to J.C. and Kaspar Hug in 1807, and Nägeli left it to form his own firm in 1818. He founded in Zürich the Singinstitut (1805), the Sängerverein (1826), and the Musikalischer Frauenverein (1828); taught in a primary school and championed the Pestalozzian system; wrote a singing manual and many pamphlets, his most significant essays appearing in *Vorlesungen über Musik mit Berücksichtigung der Dilettanten* (1826); W. Reich ed. a collection of his articles as *Von Bach zu Beethoven* (Basel, 1945). In spite of disagreements, he was a close friend of Beethoven; publ. the periodical *Répertoire des Clavecinistes* (from 1803), in which he brought out piano pieces by contemporary composers, including the 1st ed. of Beethoven's op. 31 sonatas. As a composer, he wrote some estimable choral works and solo songs, the latter presaging Schubert.

    BIBL.: Biographical sketches by Ott (1838), Bierer (1844), Keller (1848), and Schneebeli (1873); H. Kling, *Beethoven et ses relations avec N.* (1912); R. Hunziker, *H.G. N.: Gedächtnisrede* (Winterthur, 1924); idem, *H.G. N.* (Zürich, 1938); A. Cherbuliez, *Der unbekannte N.* (Chur, 1938); J. Hassan, *Die Welt- und Kunstanschauung H.G. N.s mit besonderer Berücksichtingung der Musik* (diss., Univ. of Zürich, 1947); H. Schattner, *Volksbildung durch Musikerziehung: Leben und Wirken H.G. N.s* (diss., Univ. of Saarbrücken, 1960).

Naginski, Charles, American composer; b. Cairo, Egypt, May 29, 1909; d. (drowned) Lenox, Mass., Aug. 4, 1940. He was taken to America at an early age; studied piano with his father and other teachers; from 1928 to 1933, held a fellowship at the Juilliard Graduate School as a pupil in composition of Rubin Goldmark.

    WORKS: *Suite* for Orch. (1931); 2 syms. (1935, 1937); *1936,* orch. poem (1936); Sinfonietta for Orch. (1937); *3 Movements for Chamber Orch.* (1937); *The Minotaur,* ballet for Orch. (1938); *Nocturne and Pantomime* for Orch. (1938); *5 Pieces from a Children's Suite* for Orch. (Boston, 1940); *Movement for Strings;* 2 string quartets (1933); songs.

Nancarrow, Conlon, remarkable American-born Mexican composer, innovator in the technique of recording notes on a player-piano roll; b. Texarkana, Ark., Oct. 27, 1912. He played the trumpet in jazz orchs.; then took courses at the Cincinnati College-Cons. of Music (1929–32); subsequently traveled to Boston, where he became a private student of Nicolas Slonimsky, Walter Piston, and Roger Sessions. In 1937 he joined the Abraham Lincoln Brigade and went to Spain to fight in the ranks of the Republican Loyalists against the brutal assault of General Franco's armies. Classified as a premature anti-Fascist after the Republican defeat in Spain, he was refused a U.S. passport and moved to Mexico City, where he remained for 40 years, eventually obtaining Mexican citizenship (1956). In 1981, with political pressures defused in the U.S., Nancarrow was able to revisit his native land and to participate in the New American Music Festival in San Francisco. In 1982 he was a composer-in-residence at the Cabrillo Music Festival in Aptos, Calif.; also traveled to Europe, where he participated at festivals in Austria, Germany, and France. An extraordinary event occurred in his life in 1982, when he was awarded the "genius grant" of $300,000 by the MacArthur Foundation of Chicago, enabling him to continue his work without any concerns about finances. The unique quality of Nancarrow's compositions is that they can be notated only by perforating player-piano rolls to mark the notes and rhythms, and can be performed only by activating such piano rolls. This method of composition gives him total freedom in conjuring up the most complex contrapuntal, harmonic, and rhythmic combinations that no human pianist or number of human pianists could possibly perform. The method itself is extremely laborious; a bar containing a few dozen notes might require an hour to stamp out on the piano roll. Some of his studies were publ. in normal notation in Cowell's *New Music Quarterly*. Copland, Ligeti, and other contemporary composers expressed their appreciation of Nancarrow's originality in high terms of praise. On Jan. 30, 1984, Nancarrow gave a concert of his works in Los Angeles, in a program including his *Prelude and Blues for Acoustic Piano* and several of his studies. An audiovisual documentary on Nancarrow was presented on slides by Eva Soltes. A number of Nancarrow's *Studies for Player Piano* that could be adequately notated were publ. in *Soundings 4* (1977), accompanied with critical commentaries by Gordon Mumma, Charles Amirkhanian, John Cage, Roger Reynolds, and James Tenney. On Oct. 15, 1988, his 3rd String Quartet was given its premiere performance in Cologne by the London-based Arditti Quartet, perhaps the only ensemble in the world capable of realizing Nancarrow's exceedingly complex score.

BIBL.: P. Carlsen, *The Player-Piano Music of C. N.: An Analysis of Selected Studies* (Brooklyn, 1988).

Nanino (Nanini), Giovanni Bernardino, Italian composer and teacher, brother of **Giovanni Maria Nanino;** b. c.1560; d. Rome, 1623. He was a boy soprano at Vallerano Cathedral; studied music with his brother. From 1591 to 1608 he was maestro di cappella at S. Luigi dei Francesi in Rome. His brother lived with him in a home maintained by the church, and they boarded and taught the boy sopranos. He subsequently was maestro di cappella at S. Lorenzo in Damaso, the small church in the home of Cardinal Montalto. He was a significant composer and teacher in his day.

WORKS: SACRED: *Motecta* for 2 to 4 Voices (Rome, 1610); *Motecta, liber secundus* for One to 5 Voices, with Basso Continuo (Rome, 1611); *Motecta, liber tertius* for One to 5 Voices, with Basso Continuo (Rome, 1612); *Motecta, liber quartus* for 1 to 5 Voices, with Basso Continuo (Rome, 1618); *Salmi vespertini* for 4 to 8 Voices (Rome, 1620; ed. by K. Proske, *Musica divina*, I/3 and II/2, Regensburg, 1860–74); *Venite exultemus* for 3 Voices, with Basso Continuo (Assisi, 1620); etc. **SECULAR:** *Il primo libro de madrigali* for 5 Voices (Venice, 1588); *Il secondo libro de madrigali* for 5 Voices (Venice, 1599); *Il terzo libro de madrigali* for 5 Voices (Rome, 1612); etc.

BIBL.: H.-W. Frey, "Die Kapellmeister an der französischen Nationalkirche San Luigi dei Francesi in Rom im 16. Jahrhundert," *Archiv für Musikwissenschaft*, XXIII (1966).

Nanino (Nanini), Giovanni Maria, important Italian composer and teacher, brother of **Giovanni Bernardino Nanino;** b. Tivoli, 1543 or 1544; d. Rome, March 11, 1607. He was a boy soprano at Vallerano Cathedral, and was a pupil of Palestrina in Rome. Following Palestrina's resignation as maestro di cappella at S. Maria Maggiore in 1567, Nanino was named his successor. From 1575 to 1577 he was maestro di cappella at S. Luigi dei Francesi. In 1577 he became a tenor in the papal choir, remaining a member until his death; he also was elected to the position of maestro di cappella several times after 1586. He continued an association with S. Luigi dei Francesi; after his brother was made maestro di cappella there in 1591, he lived with his brother in a home maintained by the church, where they boarded and taught the boy sopranos. His pupils included Paolo Agostino, Felice Anerio, Antonio Brunelli, and other outstanding musicians. Nanino was one of the most significant composers and teachers of the Roman school. His sacred and secular works are of great merit.

WORKS: SACRED: *Motecta . . . nova inventione elaborata* for 3 to 5 Voices (Venice, 1586; 4 are found in K. Proske, ed., *Musica divina*, I/2, 4, Regensburg, 1854–62; 14 are in R. Schuler, *The Life and Liturgical Works of Giovanni Maria Nanino*, diss., Univ. of Minnesota, 1963); 5 Lamentations in F. Haberl, "G.M. Nanino," *Kirchenmusikalisches Jahrbuch*, VI (1891); 2 canons ed. by A. Cametti in *Rivista Musicale Italiana*, XXXV

(1928); 14 motets are in R. Schuler, *G.M. Nanino: Fourteen Liturgical Works* (Madison, Wis., 1969). **SECULAR:** *Il primo libro de' madrigali* for 5 Voices (Venice, c.1571; not extant; 2nd ed., 1579); *Madrigali* for 5 Voices (Venice, 1581; with 13 pieces by A. Stabile); *Il terzo libro de madrigali* for 5 Voices (Venice, 1586; with one piece by G.B. Nanino); *Il primo libro delle canzonette* for 3 Voices (Venice, 1593); also *157 Contrappunti e canoni a 2–11 voci* (in MS).

BIBL.: F. Haberl, "G.M. N.," *Kirchenmusikalisches Jahrbuch*, VI (1891); G. Radiciotti, *G.M. N., musicista tiburtino . . . Vita ed opere* (Pesaro, 1909); R. Schuler, *The Life and Liturgical Works of G.M. N.* (diss., Univ. of Minnesota, 1963); H.-W. Frey, "Die Gesänge der Sixtinischen Kapelle an den Sonntagen und hohen Kirchenfesten des Jahres 1616," *Mélanges Eugène Tisserant* (Vatican City, 1964); idem, "Die Kapellmeister an der französischen Nationalkirche San Luigi dei Francesi in Rom im 16. Jahrhundert," *Archiv für Musikwissenschaft*, XXII (1965) and XXIII (1966).

Napoli, Gennaro, Italian composer, father of **Jacopo Napoli;** b. Naples, May 19, 1881; d. there, June 28, 1943. He was a pupil of d'Arienzo and de Nardis at the Royal Cons. in Naples; in 1906, won the Pensionato Nazionale per la Musica; in 1912, became a teacher of composition at the Liceo Musicale in Naples; in 1915, joined the staff of the Royal Cons.; in 1926, became its assistant director; was ed. of *L'Arte pianistica*. He wrote *Bassi imitati e fugati* (1915).

WORKS: Opera, *Jacopo Ortis;* dramatic scene, *Armida abbandonata* (1906); *In montagna,* orch. suite (1906); Sym. in D minor; *Il sole risorto* for Soli, Chorus, and Orch. (1909); piano pieces; songs; etc.

Napoli, Jacopo, Italian composer, son of **Gennaro Napoli;** b. Naples, Aug. 26, 1911. He studied at the Cons. San Pietro a Majella in Naples, with his father and S. Cesi; was subsequently appointed to the faculty, and eventually became director (1954–62); subsequently was director of the Milan Cons. (1962–72) and then of the Rome Cons. (1972–76). He specialized in opera, often with a Neapolitan background, which gave him the opportunity to use Neapolitan songs in his scores. His operas include *Il Malato immaginario* (Naples, 1939); *Miseria e nobiltà* (Naples, 1945); *Un curioso accidente* (Bergamo, 1950); *Masaniello* (1951; won a prize at La Scala, Milan); *I Peccatori* (1954); *Il tesoro* (Rome, 1958); *Il rosario* (Brescia, 1962); *Il povero diavolo* (Trieste, 1963); *Il Barone avaro* (Naples, 1970).

Nápravník, Eduard (Francevič), celebrated Czech-born Russian conductor; b. Býšt, near Hradec Králové, Aug. 24, 1839; d. Petrograd, Nov. 23, 1916. He began his musical training with Půhonný, the village school master, and then with his uncle, Augustin Svoboda, in Dašice; subsequently went to Prague, where he took courses with Blažek and Pitsch at the Organ School; after further studies at the Maydl Inst. (1856–61), he joined its faculty; also received instruction in orchestration from Kittl. He then was engaged to conduct the private orch. of the Russian nobleman Yussupov in St. Petersburg (1861–63); after serving as répétiteur and organist at the Imperial Opera, he was named its 2nd conductor in 1867; he subsequently was its chief conductor from 1869 until his death; also was the conductor of the concerts of the St. Petersburg branch of the Russian Musical Society (1869–81), the Red Cross Concerts (1869–87), and the Patriotic Concerts (1871–87). He became greatly renowned as a thorough musician, possessing a fabulous sense of pitch and rhythm and exceptional ability as a disciplinarian. His reputation and influence were very great in Russian operatic affairs; Dostoyevsky, in one of his novels, uses Nápravník's name as a synonym for a guiding spirit. Nápravník conducted the premieres of operas by Tchaikovsky, Mussorgsky, Dargomyzhsky, N. Rubinstein, and Rimsky-Korsakov, and also introduced many non-Russian works to his adopted homeland. His interpretations of the Russian repertoire established a standard emulated by other Russian conductors; yet he was deficient in emotional inspiration; his performances of symphonic works were regarded as competent but not profound. He was himself a composer of several operas in the Russian style, imitative of Tchaikovsky; one of them, *Dubrovsky* (St. Petersburg, Jan. 15, 1895), has become part of the active repertoire in Russia. His other operas, all premiered in St. Petersburg, were *Nizhegorotzy* (Jan. 8, 1869), *Harold* (Nov. 23, 1886), and *Francesca da Rimini* (Dec. 9, 1902). He also wrote 4 syms. (c.1860; 1873; 1874, *The Demon;* 1879); overtures; Piano Concerto (1877); some chamber music; piano pieces.

    BIBL.: P. Weymarn, *E.F. N.* (St. Petersburg, 1881); N. Findeisen, *E.F. N.* (St. Petersburg, 1898); V. Walter, *E.F. N.: Ksoletiyu yevo artisticheskoy deyatelnosti 1863–1913* (St. Petersburg, 1914).

Nardini, Pietro, Italian violinist and composer; b. Livorno, April 12, 1722; d. Florence, May 7, 1793. He was a pupil of Tartini at Padua; from 1762 to 1765, was solo violinist in the Stuttgart Court Orch.; lived with Tartini until the latter's death in 1770; then was maestro of the court music at Florence. Both Leopold Mozart and Schubart praised his playing. Among his works are 16 violin concertos; 6 sonatas for Violin and Bass; 6 violin solos; 6 viola duets; 6 string quartets.

    BIBL.: A. Moser, *Geschichte des Violinspiels* (Berlin, 1923; 2nd ed., rev. and enl., 1966–67); C. Pfäfflin, *P. N.: Seine Werke und sein Leben* (Stuttgart, 1930; 2nd ed., 1936); C. Sartori, "*P. N.,* violinista dell'amore," *Musicisti toscani,* II, *Chigiana,* XII (1956).

Nares, James, English organist, teacher, and composer; b. Stanwell, Middlesex (baptized), April 19, 1715; d. London, Feb. 10, 1783. He was a chorister in the Chapel Royal under Gates; also studied with Pepusch. After briefly serving as assistant to John Pigott, the organist of St. George's Chapel, Windsor Castle, he became organist of York Minster in 1735; in 1756 he succeeded Greene as one of the organists to the Chapel Royal; he received a Mus.D. from Cambridge Univ. in 1757; was Master of the Children at the Chapel Royal, 1757–80. He publ. a dramatic ode, *The Royal Pastoral* for Soloists, Chorus, and Orch. (c.1769) and *A Collection of Catches, Canons and Glees* (c.1775).

Narmour, Eugene, American musicologist; b. Deming, N.J., Oct. 27, 1939. He studied at the Eastman School of Music in Rochester, N.Y. (B.M., 1961; M.A., 1962), and with Leonard Meyer, Grosvenor Cooper, and Howard M. Brown at the Univ. of Chicago (Ph.D., 1974); taught at East Carolina Univ. (1963–67), the Univ. of Chicago (1968–71), and the Univ. of Pa. (from 1971), where he became a prof. (1987) and also served as dept. chairman and conductor of the univ. orch.; was a Fellow at Oxford (1984, 1989–90); lectured widely in North America, Europe, and Asia. His 1st book, *Beyond Schenkerism: The Need for Alternatives in Music Analysis* (Chicago, 1977), was an important turning point in contemporary analysis, focusing on the interface between music theory and cognition and addressing problems of composition and perception. His other publications include *The Analysis and Cognition of Basic Melodic Structures* (Chicago, 1990) and *The Analysis and Cognition of Melodic Complexity* (Chicago, 1991).

Narváez, Luis de, Spanish vihuelist and composer who flourished from 1530 to 1550. He was a native of Granada; served as music teacher to the children in the chapel of Prince Philip (later Philip II), and had the opportunity to travel throughout northern Europe. He publ. *Los seys libros del Delphin de música de cifra para tañer vihuela* (Valladolid, 1538; in tablature), containing the earliest examples of variation form and the use of symbols for tempo indications in Spain; it was reprinted in modern notation by E. Pujol in Monumentos de la Música Española (Vol. 3, Barcelona, 1945) and G. Tarragó (Madrid, 1971).

Nash, Heddle, English tenor; b. London, June 14, 1896; d. there, Aug. 14, 1961. He was a chorister at Westminster Abbey; then studied in London and with Giuseppe Borgatti in Milan; made his operatic debut in Milan in 1924 as Count Almaviva; then returned to London, where he sang at the Old Vic Theatre and at the Sadler's Wells Opera Co. (1925) and with the British

National Opera Co. (1926–29). He was a leading tenor at Covent Garden (1929–39 and 1947–48); also had engagements at the Glyndebourne Festivals (1934–38); was particularly noted for his fine performances in operas by Mozart and Rossini. His son, **John Heddle Nash** (b. London, March 30, 1928), was a baritone.

Nasidze, Sulkhan, Russian composer; b. Tiflis, March 17, 1927. He studied piano and composition at the Tbilisi Cons.; in 1963 joined its staff; in 1974 became artistic director of the State Phil. of Georgia in Tbilisi. His music is imbued with Georgian melorhythms, and is set in a fairly advanced idiom. He wrote the oratorio *Fatherland Mine* (1967); cantata, *Spring, Spring!* (1975); 5 syms. (1958, 1964, 1970, 1972, 1975); *Rhapsody* on themes of old Tiflis for Orch. (1964); 2 piano concertos (1954, 1961); Cello Concerto (1974); Piano Trio (1958); 2 string quartets (1968, 1971); *Polyphonic Sonata* for Piano; vocal cycles; choruses.

Nasolini, Sebastiano, Italian composer; b. Piacenza, c.1768; d. probably in Naples, c.1816. He most likely studied at the ducal chapel in Venice; was maestro al cembalo at the S. Pietro theater in Trieste (1787–90); was also maestro di cappella at the Cathedral of S. Giusto there (1788–90); then was mainly active in Venice as a composer for the theater. He was a highly successful composer of popular stage works; among his extant operas are *La morte di Semiramide* (Padua, Oct. 1790), *La morte di Cleopatra* (Vicenza, June 22, 1791), *Merope* (Venice, Jan. 21, 1796), *Il Medico di Lucca* (Venice, 1797), *Gli umori contrarii* (Venice, June 1798), *Il trionfo di Clelia* (Milan, Dec. 26, 1798), and *Achille* (Modena, June 23, 1806). He also composed pasticcios, oratorios, and cantatas.

    BIBL.: E. de Giovanni, *Giuseppe Nicolini e S. N.* (Piacenza, 1927); C. Anguissola, *Geminiano Giacomelli e S. N.: Musicisti placentini* (Piacenza, 1935).

Nastasijević, Svetomir, Serbian composer; b. Gornje Milanovec, April 1, 1902; d. Belgrade, Aug. 17, 1979. He studied engineering and architecture; at the same time he learned to play the violin; wrote music criticism and publ. 2 manuals on music theory. His works include the music drama *Medjuluško blago* (The Treasure of the Medjuluzje; Belgrade, March 4, 1937); *Durad Branković,* national opera from medieval Serbian history (Belgrade, June 12, 1940); several symphonic poems and choruses. In his operas, he adopts the Wagnerian system of leitmotifs.

Nat, Yves, French pianist; b. Béziers, Dec. 28, 1890; d. Paris, Aug. 31, 1956. He studied at the Paris Cons. with Diémer; was appointed a prof. of piano there in 1934. He gave numerous recitals in France, where his reputation was very high; made an American tour as accompanist in 1911 and in 1914 (with Luisa Tetrazzini).

Nataletti, Giorgio, Italian ethnomusicologist; b. Rome, June 12, 1907; d. there, July 16, 1972. He studied at the Pesaro Cons., then pursued ethnomusicological research in Italy, the Maritime Alps, and Tunisia (from 1926). He was technical director of Le Arti di le Tradizioni Popolari dell'OND (ENAL) (1926–36; 1946–61) and secretary of the Comitato Nazionale delle Arti Popolari (1947–52). In 1948, with I. Pizzetti and others, he founded the Centro Nazionale Studi di Musica Popolare. In addition, he was active as broadcaster and music director of the RAI; also was artistic director of RCA Italiana and taught folk music (from 1940) and music history (from 1961) at the Rome Cons. With A. Lomax and D. Carpitella, he prepared the Italian section of *The Columbia World Library of Folk and Primitive Music* (vols. XV and XVI).

    WRITINGS (all publ. in Rome unless otherwise given): With G. Petrassi, *Canti della campagna romana* (Milan, 1930); *Musica e canti della patria* (Tunis, 1933); *Trenta ninna nanne popolari italiene* (1934); *Catalogo del Museo strumentale di Tunisi* (1935); *I poeti a braccio della campagna romana* (1936); *La raccolta dei canti popolari della CIATP* (1936); *Verdi e le sue medaglie* (1941); *Il folklore musicale Italia* (1948); *La musica folklorica italiana nel cinema* (1959).

BIBL.: *1922–1962: Quaranti anni di attività di G. N.* (Rome, 1962).

Natanson, Tadeusz, Polish composer and pedagogue; b. Warsaw, Jan. 26, 1927; d. Wroclaw, Nov. 10, 1990. He studied composition with K. Wilkomirski, P. Perkowski, and S. Poradowski at the Wroclaw Academy of Music (1952–56); was on its faculty (from 1957), and also taught at the Warsaw Academy of Music (from 1977), where he received his Ph.D. (1977; with a diss. on music therapy as a function of music). He also taught at the Univ. of Silesia in Cieszyn (from 1983), where he served as head of the Inst. for Music Therapy (from 1984).

WORKS: STAGE: *Tamango*, opera (1972); *Quo Vadis,* ballet-pantomime (1970). **ORCH.:** *Toccata* (1956); 2 piano concertos (1956, 1980); *Polifonie* for 2 String Orchs. (1958); *Rondo concertante* for Violin and Orch. (1958); Double Concerto for 2 Saxophones and Orch. (1959); 7 syms.: No. 1 for Piano and Orch., *Wroclaw* (1961); No. 2 (1964); No. 3, "John Kennedy in Memoriam" (1965); No. 4 (1969); No. 5 for Baritone, Chorus, and Orch. (1974); No. 6 (1980); No. 7 (1982); *Concerto breve* for Trombone and Orch. (1963); Viola Concerto (1971); *Triptyque* (1976); *Symphoniette classique* (1979). **VOCAL:** *Satires* for Chorus and Instrumental Ensemble (1960); *I Prayed to Jehovah* for Reciter and Orch. (1964); *Cain's Question* for Reciter and Orch. (1967; also for Reciter and Men's Voices); *A Salt Shaker Full of Pepper* for Men's Chorus (1968); *Familiale* for Reciter and Chamber Ensemble (1979). **CHAMBER:** 2 wind quartets (1960, 1987); Toccata for 2 Clarinets, 2 Horns, and Piano (1964); 2 trios for Violin, Cello, and Piano (1965, 1966); Oboe Sonata (1977); *Sonata antiqua* for Wind Quintet (1978); Sextet for 3 Trumpets and 3 Trombones (1981).

Nathan, Hans, German-born American musicologist; b. Berlin, Aug. 5, 1910; d. Boston, Aug. 4, 1989. He took courses in musicology at the Univ. of Berlin (Ph.D., 1934); studied piano with Rudolph Schmidt and Claudio Arrau, theory with Grete von Zieritz, and conducting with Michael Taube; was active as a music critic in Berlin (1932–36). In 1936 he went to the U.S.; became an American citizen in 1944; from 1936 to 1938 he did postgraduate study at Harvard Univ. After a year of teaching at Tufts Univ., he joined the faculty of Michigan State Univ. in East Lansing in 1946; held a Guggenheim fellowship in 1957; was a visiting prof. at the Inst. for Advanced Study in Princeton, N.J., in 1957–58 and again in the summer of 1979; he retired in 1981. He wrote *Das Rezitativ der Frühopern Richard Wagners* for his diss. at the Univ. of Berlin (1934); in the U.S. he devoted himself chiefly to subjects of American music; publ. the valuable books *Dan Emmett and the Rise of Early Negro Minstrelsy* (Norman, Okla., 1962) and *William Billings: Data and Documents* (Detroit, 1976). He was the ed. of vol. 2 (1977) of the complete, critical ed. of works by William Billings, in 4 vols.; contributed articles on folk music, history, and modern biography to various publications.

Nathan, Isaac, English-born Australian composer of Polish-Jewish descent; b. Canterbury, 1790; d. Sydney, Jan. 15, 1864. He studied singing and composition with D. Corri in London; collaborated with Byron on the *Hebrew Melodies* (1815–19), his most successful effort; served as music librarian to George IV; also maintained a music publishing business. In 1841 he moved to Australia, where he continued his enterprises; also continued to compose, being the 1st to write operas in Australia.

WRITINGS: *An Essay on the History and Theory of Music, and on the Qualities, Capabilities and Management of the Human Voice* (1823; 2nd ed., 1836, as *Musurgia Vocalis*) and *Memoirs of Madame Malibran de Bériot* (1836).

WORKS: STAGE: Comic operas: *Sweethearts and Wives* (London, July 7, 1823) and *The Alcaid, or The Secrets of the Office* (London, July 14, 1824); operatic farce, *The Illustrious Stranger, or Married and Buried* (London, Oct. 1, 1827); opera, *Don John of Austria* (Sydney, May 3, 1847); songs; piano pieces.

BIBL.: C. Berti, *I. N.: Australia's First Composer* (Sydney, 1922); O. Phillips, *I. N.: Friend of Byron* (London, 1940); E. Dibdin, "I. N.," *Music & Letters,* XXII (1941); C. Mackerras, *The Hebrew Melodist: A Life of I. N.* (Sydney, 1963).

Nathan, Montagu. See **Montague-Nathan, M(ontagu).**

Natorp, Bernhard Christoph Ludwig, German vocal pedagogue; b. Werden-am-Ruhr, Nov. 12, 1774; d. Münster, Feb. 8, 1846. He studied theology and pedagogics at Halle Univ.; became a pastor at Essen in 1798; counselor of the Consistory at Potsdam in 1808; general superintendent at Münster in 1819.

WRITINGS: *Anleitung zur Unterweisung im Singen für Lehrer in Volksschulen* (2 courses, 1813, 1820); *Lehrbüchlein der Singekunst* (2 courses, 1816, 1820); *Über den Gesang in den Kirchen der Protestanten* (1817); *Über den Zweck, die Einrichtung und den Gebrauch des Melodienbuchs für den Gemeindegesang in den evangelischen Kirchen* (1822); *Melodienbuch* (1822); *Choralbuch für evangelische Kirchen* (1829; harmonized in 4 parts with preludes and interludes by Rinck; 4th ed., 1885); and *Über Rincks Präludien* (1834).

BIBL.: H. Knab, *B.C.L. N.* (Kassel, 1933).

Natra, Sergiu, Rumanian-born Israeli composer; b. Bucharest, April 12, 1924. He studied composition with Leon Klepper at the Bucharest Cons. (1945–52); emigrated to Israel in 1961, where he became active mainly as a teacher; became a teacher at the Rubin Academy of Music in Tel Aviv (1975); was prof. at the Univ. of Tel Aviv (from 1976).

WORKS: *Divertimento in a Classical Style* for String Orch. (1943); *March and Chorale* for Orch. (1944); String Quartet (1947); *Suite* for Orch. (1948); Sym. No. 1 (1952); *4 Poems* for Baritone and Orch. (1958); *Music for Violin and Harp* (1959); Sinfonia for Strings (1960); *Toccata* for Orch. (1963); *Music for Harpsichord and 6 Instruments* (1964); Sonatina for Solo Harp (1965; rev. 1978); *Music for Oboe and Strings* (1965); *Variations* for Piano and Orch. (1966); *Song of Deborah* for Mezzo-soprano and Chamber Orch. (1967); *Commentary on Nehemia* for Baritone, Chorus, and Orch. (1967); 3 solo sonatinas: for Trombone, for Trumpet, and for Oboe (all 1969); *Environment for an Exhibition,* sound collage on tape (1970); Piano Trio (1971); *Pages from a Composer's Diary* for Chamber Orch. (1978); *Diary of a Choreographer,* ballet (1982); *Miracle of the Peoples,* cantata (1984); *Music for Nicanor* (Zabaleta) for Harp, Flute, Clarinet, and String Quartet (1988).

Nattiez, Jean-Jacques, French music theorist; b. Amiens, Dec. 30, 1945. He served on the music faculty of the Univ. of Montreal (from 1972), where he also was director of the Groupe de Recherches en Sémiologie Musicale (1974–80); initiated numerous publications in musical semiotics and authored the 1st major study in the discipline, *Fondements d'une sémiologie de la musique* (Paris, 1975). He also ed. and contributed articles to several vols. of the journal of musical semiotics, *Musique en Jeu* (1971–78). He is co-director, with Pierre Boulez, of the series Musique/Passé/Présent. Nattiez is the leading proponent of musical semiotics, delineating syntactic structures that recall the earlier studies of Ruwet.

WRITINGS: *"Densité 21.5" de Varèse: Essai d'analyse sémiologique* (Montreal, 1975); *Fondements d'une sémiologie de la musique* (Paris, 1975); *Tétralogies (Wagner, Boulez, Chéreau), essai sur l'infidélité* (Paris, 1983); *De la sémiologie à la musique* (Montreal, 1987); *Musicologie générale et sémiologie* (Paris, 1987; vol. I of a radically rev. ed. of his *Fondements*); *Proust musicien* (Paris, 1989); ed. *Pierre Boulez, John Cage: Correspondance et documents* (vol. I, Basel, 1990).

Naudin, Emilio, Italian-born French tenor; b. Parma (of French parents), Oct. 23, 1823; d. Boulogne-sur-Mer, May 5, 1890. He was a pupil of Panizza in Milan; made his debut in Pacini's *Saffo* in Cremona (1843); appeared in Vienna, St. Petersburg, London, Madrid, and Paris (from 1862, at the Théâtre-Italien). He created the role of Vasco da Gama in *L'Africaine* (in accordance with a stipulation in Meyerbeer's will); retired in 1879.

Naujalis, Juozas, Lithuanian organist, teacher, and composer; b. Raudondvaris, near Kaunas, April 9, 1869; d. Kaunas, Sept. 9, 1934. He studied at the Warsaw Musical Inst.; served as an organist in various Lithuanian towns; in 1919, became director of the Music School in Kaunas, later of the State Music Inst. His compositions include masses, a Lithuanian church hymn, piano and organ works, etc.

Naumann, Emil, German music scholar and composer, grandson of **Johann Gottlieb Naumann;** b. Berlin, Sept. 8, 1827; d. Dresden, June 23, 1888. He was a pupil of Schnyder von Wartensee in Frankfurt, and then of Mendelssohn in Leipzig (1842); he studied at the Leipzig Cons. (1843–44); later took courses at the Univ. of Bonn; received his Ph.D. at the Univ. of Berlin in 1867 with the dissertation *Das Alter der Psalmengesänge*. In 1850 he became Hofkirchen-Musikdirektor in Berlin. In 1873 he was made a lecturer in music history at the Dresden Cons. In his works he faithfully followed the methods of his revered teacher Mendelssohn, without ever attaining the melodic grace and harmonic lucidity that made Mendelssohn's music a perennial art. Naturally, he opposed Wagner's innovations and wrote critically about "the music of the future."

WORKS: STAGE: *Judith*, opera (Dresden, 1858); *Die Mühlenhexe*, singspiel (Berlin, 1861); *Loreley*, grand opera (Berlin, 1889). **VOCAL:** *Christus der Friedensbote*, oratorio (Dresden, 1848); *Missa solennis* (1851); *Die Zerstörung Jerusalem's durch Titus*, cantata (1855); *12 Psalms in Psalmen auf alle Sonn- und Fest-Tage des evangelischen Kirchenjahres* for *Musica sacra*, vols. VIII–X (Berlin and Posen, 1855); *Dank- und Jubel-Cantate zur Feier der Siege Preussens im Jahre 1866*. Also, Sonata for Piano and Violin, and several overtures.

WRITINGS: *Ueber Einführung des Psalmengesanges in die evangelische Kirche* (Berlin, 1856); *Die Tonkunst in ihren Beziehungen zu den Formen und Entwickelungsgesetzen alles Geisteslebens* (2 vols., Berlin, 1869–70); *Ludwig van Beethoven: Zur hundertjährigen Geburtstagsfeier* (Berlin, 1871); *Deutsche Tondichter von Sebastian Bach bis auf die Gegenwart* (Berlin, 1871; 6th ed., 1895); *Nachklänge: Eine Sammlung von Vorträgen und Gedenkblättern* (Berlin, 1872); *Deutschlands musikalische Heroen in ihrer Rückwirkung auf die Nation* (Berlin, 1873); *Italienische Tondichter von Palestrina bis auf die Gegenwart* (Berlin, 1874–75; 2nd ed., 1883); *Das goldene Zeitalter der Tonkunst in Venedig* (Berlin, 1876); *Musikdrama oder Oper? Eine Beleuchtung der Bayreuther Bühnenfestspiele* (Berlin, 1876); *Zukunftsmusik und die Musik der Zukunft* (Berlin, 1877); *Darstellung eines bisher unbekannt gebliebenen Stylgesetzes im Aufbau des classischen Fugenthemas* (Berlin, 1878); *Illustrierte Musikgeschichte* (2 vols., Berlin and Stuttgart, 1880–85; Eng. tr. by F. Ouseley, 1882–86; 10th German ed., 1934, by E. Schmitz); *Der moderne musikalische Zopf* (Berlin, 1880).

Naumann, (Karl) Ernst, German organist, conductor, and composer, grandson of **Johann Gottlieb Naumann;** b. Freiberg, Saxony, Aug. 15, 1832; d. Jena, Dec. 15, 1910. He studied in Leipzig with Hauptmann, Richter, Wenzel, and Langer; received his Ph.D. in 1858 from the Univ. of Leipzig with the dissertation *Über die verschiedenen Bestimmungen der Tonverhältnisse und die Bedeutung des pythagoreischen oder reinen Quintensystems für unsere heutige Musik* (pub. in Leipzig, 1858); also took organ lessons in Dresden with Johann Schneider. In 1860 he was appointed music director and director of academic concerts at the Univ. of Jena; also served as city organist; was made a prof. in 1877; retired in 1906. He ed. 6 vols. of Bach's cantatas and works for keyboard for the collected edition of the Bach Gesellschaft, and later ed. several organ works for the Neue Bach Gesellschaft. He also ed. a practical edition of Bach's organ music in 9 vols. (1899–1904). His own compositions include chamber music, sacred works, and lieder.

Naumann, Johann Gottlieb, distinguished German composer and conductor, grandfather of **Emil** and **(Karl) Ernst Naumann;** b. Blasewitz, near Dresden, April 17, 1741; d. Dresden, Oct. 23, 1801. He received his 1st instruction in music at the Dresden Kreuzschule. In 1757 the Swedish violinist Anders Wesström took him to Italy, where he received

valuable instruction from Tartini in Padua, Padre Martini in Bologna, and Hasse in Venice. His intermezzo *Il tesoro insidiato* was premiered in Venice on Dec. 28, 1762. In 1764 he returned to Dresden, where he was appointed 2nd church composer to the court; in 1765 he was named chamber composer. He made return trips to Italy (1765–68; 1772–74), where he brought out several operas. In 1776 he was appointed Kapellmeister in Dresden. In 1777 he visited Stockholm at the invitation of Gustavus III, and was charged with reorganizing the Hofkapelle. His most popular opera, *Cora och Alonzo*, received its 1st complete performance in Stockholm during the consecration of the New Opera House on Sept. 30, 1782. Another important opera, *Gustaf Wasa*, was premiered there on Jan. 19, 1786, and was considered the Swedish national opera for many years. In 1785–86 he visited Copenhagen, where he carried out some reforms at the Hofkapelle and court opera. He composed the opera *Orpheus og Eurydike* for the Danish king's birthday, and it was premiered in Copenhagen on Jan. 31, 1786. He was named Oberkapellmeister for life in Dresden in 1786. At the request of Friedrich Wilhelm II, he made several visits to Berlin, where his operas *Medea in Colchide* (Oct. 16, 1788) and *Protesilao* (Jan. 26, 1789) were premiered at the Royal Opera. He also wrote masses, cantatas, oratorios, and lieder.

WORKS: STAGE (all 1st perf. at the Kleines Kurfürstliches Theater in Dresden unless otherwise given): *Il tesoro insidiato*, intermezzo (Teatro San Samuele, Venice, Dec. 28, 1762); *Li creduti spiriti*, opera buffa (Teatro San Cassiano, Venice, Carnival 1764; in collaboration with 2 other composers); *L'Achille in Sciro*, opera seria (Teatro San Cecilia, Palermo, Sept. 5, 1767); *Alessandro nelle Indie*, opera seria (1768; unfinished); *La clemenza di Tito*, opera seria (Feb. 1, 1769); *Il villano geloso*, opera buffa (1770); *Solimano*, opera seria (Teatro San Benedetto, Venice, Carnival 1773); *L'isola disabitata*, azione per musica (Venice, Feb. 1773); *Armida*, opera seria (Teatro Nuovo, Padua, June 13, 1773); *Ipermestra*, opera seria (Teatro San Benedetto, Venice, Feb. 1, 1774); *La villanella incostante*, opera buffa (Teatro San Benedetto, Venice, Fall 1773); *L'Ipocondriaco*, opera buffa (March 16, 1776); *Amphion*, prologue and opera-ballet (Royal Theater, Stockholm, Jan. 1, 1778); *Elisa*, opera seria (April 21, 1781); *Cora och Alonzo*, opera seria (New Opera House, Stockholm, Sept. 30, 1782); *Osiride*, opera seria (Oct. 27, 1781); *Tutto per amore*, opera buffa (March 5, 1785); *Gustaf Wasa*, lyric tragedy (New Opera House, Stockholm, Jan. 19, 1786); *Orpheus og Eurydike*, opera seria (Royal Theater, Copenhagen, Jan. 31, 1786); *La reggia d'Imeneo*, festa teatrale (Oct. 21, 1787); *Medea in Colchide*, opera seria with ballet (Royal Opera, Berlin, Oct. 16, 1788); *Protesilao*, opera seria with ballet and choruses (Royal Opera, Berlin, Jan. 26, 1789; in collaboration with J.F. Reichardt); *La dama soldato*, opera buffa (March 30, 1791); *Amore giustificato*, festa teatrale (May 12, 1792); *Aci e Galatea ossia I ciclopi amanti*, opera buffa (April 25, 1801). **ORATORIOS** (all performed in Dresden unless otherwise given): *La passione di Gesù Cristo* (Padua, 1767); *Isacco, figura del Redentore* (1772); *S. Elena al calvario* (1775); *Giuseppe riconosciuto* (1777); *Il ritorno del figliolo prodigo* (1785); *La morte d'Abel* (1790); *Davide in Terebinto, figura del Salvatore* (1794); *I Pellegrini al sepolcro* (1798); *Il ritorno del figliolo prodigo* (1800); *Betulia liberata* (1805); also masses, including a *Missa solenne* in A-flat major (Vienna, 1804), and sacred cantatas. **LIEDER:** *Freimaurerlieder . . . zum Besten der neuen Armenschule* (publ. in Leipzig, 1775); *40 Freymäurerlieder zum Gebrauch der teutschen auch französischen Tafellogen* (publ. in Berlin, 1782; 2nd ed., 1784); *Sammlung von Liedern* (publ. in Pförten, 1784); *Sechs neue Lieder* (publ. in Berlin, 1795); *25 neue Lieder verschieden Inhalts* (publ. in Dresden, 1799); etc. His instrumental works include sinfonias, a Keyboard Concerto, quartets, sonatas for Keyboard and Violin, sonatas for Glass Harmonica, etc.

BIBL.: A. Meissner, *Bruckstücke zur Biographie J.G. N.'s* (2 vols., Prague, 1803–4; 2nd ed., Vienna, 1814); F. Rochlitz, "J.G. N. und sein Vater-Unser, nach Klopstock," *Für Freunde der Tonkunst*, III (Leipzig, 1830); F. Mannstein, *Vollständiges*

Verzeichnis aller Kompositionen des Kurfürstlich Sächsischen Kapellmeisters N. (Dresden, 1841); G. Schweizer, Biographie von J.G. N. (3 vols., Zürich, 1843–45); M. Nestler, Der kursächsische Kapellmeister N. aus Blasewitz (Dresden, 1901); R. Engländer, J.G. N. als Opernkomponist (1741–1801) (Leipzig, 1922); R. Engländer, "Die Dresdner Instrumentalmusik in der Zeit der Wiener Klassik," Uppsala Universitets årsskrift 1956, no. 5.

Naumann, Siegfried, Swedish composer and conductor; b. Malmö, Nov. 27, 1919. He received instruction in violin, theory, and composition from his father, then studied with Wolf (violin) and Myrtelius (instrumentation), and also took courses with Melchers, Mann, and Broström at the Stockholm Musikhögskolan (1942–45); after conducting the Örnsköldsvik Music Society (1945–49), he studied composition with Pizzetti at Rome's Accademia di Santa Cecilia (1949–53); also with Malipiero and Orff. He later received instruction in conducting at the Salzburg Mozarteum and with Furtwängler and Scherchen. He was conductor of the Gävle Sym. Orch. (1954–55); in 1962 he founded the Musica Nova ensemble, which he conducted on tours of Scandinavia, Germany, and England; was its conductor until 1977. He taught conducting at the Stockholm Musikhögskolan (1963–83), becoming a prof. there in 1976; then taught at the Malmö Musikhögskolan and Teaterhögskolan (from 1983). He wrote 3 syms. and some other works in a traditionally acceptable infra-modern idiom, but at the age of 40 decided to adopt an austere structural style governed by serial procedures and diversified by aleatory passages. To mark this decisive avatar, he designated his 1st serial work, Ruoli (Roles) for 4 Clarinets, as op. 1 (1959). His subsequent compositions in this modern style are: 7 Sonetti di Petrarca for Tenor, Harp, Vibraphone, and 4 Cellos (1959); Phaedri: 4 Fabulae for Soli, Chorus, and 8 Instruments (1961); Improvviso sopra 28 strutture for Keyboard and Percussion Instruments (1961); Transformations for Orch. (1962; Gävleborg, April 29, 1962); Risposte I for Flute and Percussion (1963); Risposte II for Piano, Hammond Organ, Electric Guitar, Trombone, and Percussion (1963); Il cantico del sole for Soli, Chorus, 10 Solo Instruments, and Orch. (1963; I.S.C.M. Festival, Stockholm, Sept. 14, 1966); Cadenza for 9 Players (1964); Missa in onore della Madonna de Loreto for Chorus, Organ, and Percussion (1964); Spettacolo I for Soprano and Orch. (1967); Spettacolo II for 3 Soli, Chorus, and Orch. (1969); Estate for Chamber Orch. (1968); Ljudposter (Soundposts) for Wind Orch. (1970); Due cori su testi latini for Chorus, Double Bass, Hammond Organ, and Percussion (1970); Teatro strumentale for Chamber Ensemble (1971); Il cielo del ponte a Moriano, dialogue for Tenor, Chorus, and Chamber Orch. (1972); Materialstudier i improvisation for Orch. (1974); Fanfarer for Wind Ensemble (1974–76); Strutture per Giovanni, Version B for Wind Orch. (1980); Ljudspel/Giuoco di suono for 3 Instrumental Groups (1984); Och lärka slår och Skånes somrar ila for Chorus and Orch. (Malmö, Sept. 8, 1985); Strutture for Orch. (1986); Tripla for Flute, Cello, and Piano (1987).

Nauwach, Johann, German composer; b. Brandenburg, c.1595; d. probably in Dresden, c.1630. By 1607 he was a choirboy in Dresden; in 1612 he was sent to Italy for further study by the Elector of Saxony; he studied in Turin and Florence, receiving instruction on the lute from Lorenzo Allegri; in 1618 he returned to Dresden, and was later made a chamber musician. His 1st collection of songs shows the major influence of Caccini and other Italian monodists, while the 2nd collection is historically important as the 1st German vol. of continuo lieder.

WORKS: Libro primo di arie passeggiate a una voce per cantar e sonar nel chitarrone (Dresden, 1623); Erster Theil teutscher Villanellen mit 1, 2 und Stimmen auf der Tiorba Laute, Clavicymbel und andere Instrumenta gerichtet (Dresden, 1627).

BIBL.: A. Einstein, "Ein unbekannter Druck aus der Frühzeit der Monodie," Sammelbände der Internationalen Musik-Gesellschaft, XIII (1911–12); W. Vetter, Das frühdeutsche Lied, II (Münster, 1928); R. Thomas, Poetry and Song in the German Baroque (Oxford, 1963); J. Baron, Foreign Influences on the German Secular Solo Continuo Lied in the Mid-seventeenth Century (diss., Brandeis Univ., 1967).

Nava, Gaetano, Italian vocal pedagogue; b. Milan, May 16, 1802; d. there, March 31, 1875. He was taught by his father, **Antonio Maria Nava** (1775–1826) and Pollini; then at the Milan Cons. from 1817 to 1824 by Orlandi, Ray, Piantanida, and Frederici. From 1837 he was a prof. of solfeggio at the Cons., and of choral singing, from 1848. He wrote a great number of excellent solfeggi and vocalises; also Metodo pratico di vocalizzazione.

Navarra, André (-Nicolas), noted French cellist and pedagogue; b. Biarritz, Oct. 13, 1911; d. Siena, July 31, 1988. He studied at the Paris Cons. with J. Loeb (cello) and Tournemire (chamber music), winning a premier prix at 16. He was a member of the Krettly String Quartet (1929–35); made his debut as a soloist with the Paris Colonne Orch. (1931). He was prof. of cello at the Paris Cons. (from 1949) and at the North West German Music Academy (from 1958); also taught in Siena (1954–88). He gave premiere performances of cello concertos by Jolivet (1962) and Tomasi (1970).

Navarrini, Francesco, distinguished Italian bass; b. Citadella, 1853; d. Milan, Feb. 23, 1923. He studied with Giuseppe Felix and Carlo Boroni in Milan; made his debut as Alfonso in Lucrezia Borgia in Ferrara in 1876. From 1883 to 1900 he was a member of La Scala in Milan; created the role of Lodovico in Verdi's Otello there (Feb. 5, 1887); then toured in England, France, and Russia. He made his 1st American appearance in 1902 as a member of Mascagni's traveling opera co. A giant of a man (he measured 6-and-a-half feet), he imposed his presence in heroic and buffo bass roles, including roles in Wagner's operas.

Navarro, "Fats" (Theodore), American jazz trumpeter; b. Key West, Fla., Sept. 24, 1923; d. N.Y., July 7, 1950. He first took up the tenor saxophone, then mastered the trumpet; subsequently played with several groups, including those of Andy Kirk (1943–44) and Billy Eckstine (1945–46); he later worked in N.Y. as a leading exponent of the bop style.

Navarro, (Luis Antonio) García, Spanish conductor; b. Chiva, April 30, 1941. He was educated at the Valencia Cons., where he studied oboe; also took courses at the Madrid Cons. He then went to Vienna to study conducting with Hans Swarowsky, Karl Oesterreicher, and Reinhold Schmid; also took composition lessons with Alfred Uhl. In 1967 he won 1st prize at the conducting competition in Besançon. He was music director of the Valencia Sym. Orch. (1970–74); then was associate conductor of the Noordhollands Phil. in Haarlem (1974–78), and music director of Lisbon's Portuguese Radio Sym. Orch. (1976–82) and National Opera at the São Carlos Theater (1980–82). In 1979 he made his debut as an opera conductor at London's Covent Garden, and then appeared for the 1st time in the U.S. in 1980. He was Generalmusikdirektor of the Württemberg State Theater in Stuttgart from 1987.

Navarro, Juan, distinguished Spanish composer; b. Seville or Marchena, c.1530; d. Palencia, Sept. 25, 1580. He was a pupil of Fernández de Castilleja in Seville; sang as a tenor in the choir of the Duke of Arcos at Marchena in 1549; then sang at the Cathedral in Jaén; joined the choir at Málaga Cathedral in 1553; in 1554, applied unsuccessfully for the post of maestro de capilla there (F. Guerrero was the successful candidate); was maestro de capilla at the Cathedrals in Ávila (1563–66), Salamanca (1566–74), Ciudad Rodrigo (1574–78), and Palencia (from 1578). Navarro's Psalmi, Hymni ac Magnificat totius anni . . . for 4 voices were publ. at Rome in 1590 (modern ed. by S. Rubio, Madrid, 1978). Other works include motets, psalms, hymns, villanescas, and songs.

BIBL.: G. Chase, "J. N. Hispalensis and J. N. Gaditanus," Musical Quarterly (April 1945); R. Stevenson, Spanish Cathedral Music in the Golden Age (Berkeley, Calif., 1961).

Navas, Juan (Francisco) de, Spanish harpist and composer who flourished in Madrid from 1659 to 1709. He was a musician in the royal chapel by 1659; was a subordinate maestro de capilla there by 1683. He wrote numerous secular works, including some interesting Pasacalles with guitar accompaniment; also contributed Act 2 to the 3-act zarzuela *Apolo y Dafne;* likewise wrote some sacred music.

Navrátil, Karel, Czech composer; b. Prague, April 24, 1867; d. there, Dec. 23, 1936. He was a pupil of Ondříček (violin) and G. Adler (theory); lived in Prague.

Works: Lyric drama, *Hermann;* opera, *Salammbô;* 2 syms.; symphonic poems: *Der weisse Berg, Lipany, Jan Hus, Žižka,* and *Žalco;* Violin Concerto; 2 piano concertos; Sonata for Violin; Sonata for Viola; men's choruses; songs.

Naylor, Bernard (James), English-born Canadian organist, conductor, and composer, son of **Edward (Woodall) Naylor;** b. Cambridge, Nov. 22, 1907; d. Keswick, Cumbria, England, May 20, 1986. He studied composition with Vaughan Williams, Holst, and Ireland at the Royal College of Music in London (1924–27); then served as conductor of the Oxford Univ. Opera Club (1927–31). In 1932 he went to Canada, where he was active in Winnipeg as conductor of its Male Voice Choir, Phil. Choir, and Sym. Orch.; returned to England in 1936 and was organist and director of music at Queen's College, Oxford, until 1939; once more in Canada, he conducted the Little Sym. Orch. in Montreal (1942–47); returned again to England and taught at Oxford (1950–52) and at Reading Univ. (1952–59). He moved permanently to Canada in 1959. As a composer, he specialized in sacred choral music.

Works: *Variations* for Small Orch. (1960); String Trio (1960); *The Living Fountain,* cycle of 4 songs for Tenor and String Orch. (1947); *Missa da camera* for 4 Vocal Soloists, Chorus, and Chamber Orch. (1954–66); *The Resurrection According to Saint Matthew,* Easter cantata (1965); *The Nymph Complaining for the Death of Her Faun* for Mezzo-soprano, Flute, Oboe, Clarinet, Bassoon, and String Quartet (1965); *Festal Te Deum* for Chorus and Orch. (1968); *Scenes and Prophecies* for Soprano, Chorus, Brass, and Percussion (1968–69); several a cappella choruses, including *9 Motets* (1952), *Magnificat & Nunc Dimittis* (1964), and *Missa sine Credo* (1969); songs.

Naylor, Edward (Woodall), English organist and composer, son of **John** and father of **Bernard (James) Naylor;** b. Scarborough, Feb. 9, 1867; d. Cambridge, May 7, 1934. He studied with his father; then at Emmanuel College, Cambridge (B.A., 1887; Mus.B. and M.A., 1891; Mus.D., 1897) and at London's Royal College of Music (1888–92). He was organist at St. Michael, Chester Square (1889–96) and St. Mary, Kilburn (1896–97); then was assistant master at the Leys School and organist at Emmanuel College, Cambridge, where he also was a lecturer (from 1902). He publ. *Shakespeare and Music* (London, 1896; 2nd ed., 1931), *An Elizabethan Virginal Book* (London, 1905), *Shakespeare Music* (London, 1912; 2nd ed., 1928), and *The Poets and Music* (London, 1928). Among his works were an opera, *The Angelus* (London, Jan. 27, 1909; won the Ricordi prize); *Tokugawa,* overture (Tokyo, 1919); sacred music; men's choruses; chamber music; etc.

Naylor, John, English organist and composer, father of **Edward (Woodall) Naylor;** b. Stanningley, near Leeds, June 8, 1838; d. at sea, May 14, 1897. He was a choirboy at Leeds Parish Church; received a Mus.D. from Cambridge Univ. in 1872; was organist at various churches in England; in 1883, became organist and choirmaster of York Minster, and also (from 1892) conductor of the York Musical Society.

Works: 4 cantatas: *Jeremiah, The Brazen Serpent, Meribah,* and *Manna;* church services, anthems, hymns, part-songs, organ pieces, and a well-known book of chants.

Nazareth (Nazaré), Ernesto (Júlio de), Brazilian pianist and composer; b. Rio de Janeiro, March 20, 1863; d. there, Feb. 4, 1934. He was a pioneer in fostering a national Brazilian type of composition, writing pieces in European forms with Brazilian melorhythmic inflections, pointedly entitled *Fado brasileiro, Tango brasileiro, Valsa brasileira, Marcha brasileira,* etc.; he also composed original dances in the rhythms of the samba and chôro. In his declining years, he became totally deaf.

Bibl.: J. Diniz, *N.: Estudos analíticos* (Reclife, 1963).

Near, Holly, American popular vocalist, songwriter, and actress; b. Ukiah, Calif., June 6, 1949. She sang in public from childhood; also worked in film and television and had a leading role on Broadway in the rock musical *Hair.* She took a commercially and artistically independent stance with her music, forming the Redwood label to record *Hang In There* (1973), *Live Album* (1974), *You Can Know All I Am* (1976), and *Imagine My Surprise* (1979), all of which became known largely by word of mouth, launching one of the most successful careers in the "women's music" genre. Her later recordings include *Fire in the Rain* (1981), *Speed of Light* (1982), *Journeys* (1983), *Watch Out!* (1984), *Sing to Me the Dream* (1984), *Harp* (1985, with Arlo Guthrie and Pete Seeger), *Singing with You* (1986), *Don't Hold Back* (1987), *Sky Dances* (1989), and *Singer in the Storm* (1990). While preferring smaller venues for her performances, she appeared at Carnegie Hall in N.Y. and the Royal Albert Hall in London; also made film and television appearances, participated in benefit concerts, and engaged in philanthropic work. With Meg Christiansen and Cris Williamson, she is one of the most important and influential musicians in the feminist/lesbian community; her excellent voice, flexible acting skills, and fiery personality have won her a large and general audience. Her autobiography was publ. as *Fire in the Rain, Singer in the Storm* (N.Y., 1990).

Neary, Martin (Gerard James), English organist and conductor; b. London, March 28, 1940. He was an organ scholar at Gonville and Caius College, Cambridge; then went to the U.S., where he was a conducting scholar at the Berkshire Music Center at Tanglewood (1963). Back in England, he was assistant organist (1963–65) and organist (1965–71) at St. Margaret's, Westminster, and then organist and master of the music at Winchester Cathedral (from 1972); was also founder-conductor of the Martin Neary Singers (from 1972). From 1963 to 1972 he served as prof. of organ at London's Trinity College of Music. He toured extensively throughout Europe as a recitalist, making his 1st tour of North America in 1963. He acquired a fine reputation as a proponent of contemporary music, giving premiere performances of many organ works by British composers.

Neate, Charles, English pianist, cellist, and composer; b. London, March 28, 1784; d. Brighton, March 30, 1877. He studied music with James Windsor and later took piano lessons with John Field; he further studied cello with W. Sharp and composition with Wölff. He started his career as a pianist at London's Covent Garden in the Lenten Oratorio performances (1800); in 1813, became one of the founders of the London Phil. Society, with which he appeared as performer and conductor; in 1815 he went to Vienna, where he succeeded in entering into a friendly relationship with Beethoven. He composed 2 piano sonatas; a Quintet for Piano, Woodwinds, and Double Bass; 2 piano trios; also publ. *An Essay on Fingering* (1855). Literature on Beethoven frequently mentions Neate's relationship with him.

Bibl.: E. Anderson, "C. N.: A Beethoven Friendship," in W. Gerstenburg, J. LaRue, and W. Rehm, eds., *Festschrift Otto Erich Deutsch* (Kassel, 1963).

Neblett, Carol, American soprano; b. Modesto, Calif., Feb. 1, 1946. She studied voice privately with William Vennard, then with Lotte Lehmann and Pierre Bernac at the Univ. of Southern Calif. in Los Angeles; quitting school before graduating (1965), she toured as a soloist with the Roger Wagner Chorale; then made her operatic debut as Musetta with the N.Y. City Opera (March 8, 1969). She garnered wide public exposure when she appeared as Thaïs with the New Orleans Opera (1973), choosing to disrobe at the close of Act 1; subsequently made debuts with the Chicago Lyric Opera (Chrysothemis in *Elektra,* 1975), the Dallas Civic Opera (Antonia in

Les Contes d'Hoffmann, 1975), the Vienna State Opera (1976), and London's Covent Garden (1977); also sang widely as a soloist with U.S. orchs. In 1975 she married **Kenneth Schermerhorn.**

Nebra (Blasco), José (Melchor de), Spanish composer; b. Catalayud, Zaragoza (baptized), Jan. 6, 1702; d. Madrid, July 11, 1768. He studied with his father, **José (Antonio) Nebra** (b. La Hoy [baptized], Nov. 23, 1672; d. Cuenca, Dec. 4, 1748), maestro de capilla of Cuenca Cathedral (1729–48). He became principal organist of the royal chapel and of the Descalzas Reales Convent in Madrid (1724); was made deputy director of the royal chapel and head of the royal choir school (1751). Together with Literes, he was engaged to reconstruct and compose new music when the archives of the Royal Chapel were destroyed in the fire of 1734. He was a prolific composer; wrote about 20 operas and a great deal of sacred music. His Requiem for Queen Barbara (1758) is reproduced in Eslava's *Lira Sacro-Hispana.*

BIBL.: N. Solar-Quintes, "El compositor español J.d. N. (†II–IV-1768): nuevas aportaciones para su biografía," *Analecta Musicologica,* IX (1954); D. Preciado, "J. N. (1709–1782) 52 años largos de organista en La Seo de Zaragoza (1730–1782)," *Tesoro sacro musical,* LX (1977).

Nechayev, Vasily, Russian pianist and composer; b. Moscow, Sept. 28, 1895; d. there, June 5, 1956. He studied at the Moscow Cons. with Goldenweiser (piano), graduating in 1917; then took composition lessons with Vasilenko. In 1925 he joined the staff of the Moscow Cons. He made a systematic study of the folk songs of the Ural region and made arrangements of folk songs of other lands. He composed the operas *7 Princesses,* after Maeterlinck (1923), and *Ivan Bolotnikov* (1930); a Septet, Quartet, Violin Sonata, Cello Sonata, songs, and a number of piano pieces.

Nedbal, Oskar, distinguished Czech violist, conductor, and composer; b. Tábor, Bohemia, March 26, 1874; d. (suicide) Zagreb, Dec. 24, 1930. He was a pupil of Bennewitz (violin), Knittl and Stecker (theory), and Dvořák (composition) at the Prague Cons., where he graduated in 1892. From 1891 to 1906 he played viola in the famous Bohemian String Quartet; from 1896 to 1906 he conducted the Czech Phil.; from 1906 to 1918, was conductor of the Tonkünstler-Orch. in Vienna; later was director of the Slovak National Theater in Bratislava (1923–30) and a conductor with the Radio there (1926–30). He was a notable interpreter of Czech music, and also was admired for his fine performances of the standard repertory.

WORKS: STAGE: OPERA: *Sedlák Jakub* (Peasant Jacob; 1919–20; Brno, Oct. 13, 1922; rev., Bratislava, Dec. 15, 1928). **OPERETTAS:** *Die keusche Barbora* (Vienna, Oct. 7, 1911); *Polenblut* (Vienna, Oct. 25, 1913); *Die Winzerbraut* (Vienna, Feb. 11, 1916); *Die schöne Saskia* (Vienna, Nov. 16, 1917); *Eriwan* (Vienna, Nov. 29, 1918). **BALLETS:** *Pohádka o Honzovi* (Legend of Honza; Prague, Jan. 24, 1902); *Z pohádky do pohádky* (From Fairy Tale to Fairy Tale; Prague, Jan. 25, 1908); *Princezna Hyacinta* (Prague, Sept. 1, 1911); *Des Teufels Grossmutter* (Vienna, April 20, 1912); *Andersen* (Vienna, March 1, 1914); also a *Scherzo caprice* for Orch. (1892) and piano pieces.

BIBL.: J. Květ, *In memoriam O.a N.a* (Bratislava, 1931); idem, *O. N.* (Prague, 1947); M. Šulc, *O. N.* (Prague, 1959); A. Buchner, *O. N.: Život a dílo* (O N.: Life and Works; Prague, 1976).

Neefe, Christian Gottlob, German composer and conductor; b. Chemnitz, Feb. 5, 1748; d. Dessau, Jan. 26, 1798. He studied music in Chemnitz with Wilhelmi, the city organist; also with C.G. Tag, the cantor of Hohenstein. He began to compose when he was 12, and studied the textbooks of Marpurg and C.P.E. Bach. He studied law at the Univ. of Leipzig (1769–71); subsequently continued his studies in music with A. Hiller; then succeeded Hiller as conductor of Seyler's traveling opera troupe (1776). In 1779 he became conductor of the Grossmann-Hellmuth opera enterprise in Bonn. Neefe's name is especially honored in music history because about 1780 Beethoven was his pupil in piano, organ, figured-bass practice, and composition in Bonn; there is evidence that Neefe realized the greatness of Beethoven's gift even as a child. In 1782 he was named court organist. After the Grossmann theater closed in 1784, he devoted himself mainly to teaching as a means of support. The theater was reopened in 1789, and Neefe served as its stage director until 1794, when the French army occupied Bonn and the theater was closed again. He then moved to Dessau, becoming music director of its theater in 1796. His autobiography, *Lebenslauf von ihm selbst geschrieben,* dated 1782, was revised by F. Rochlitz for publ. in the *Allgemeine musikalische Zeitung* (1798–99; Eng. tr. in P. Nettl, *Forgotten Musicians,* N.Y., 1951).

WORKS: *Die Apotheke,* comic opera (Berlin, Dec. 13, 1771); *Amors Guckkasten,* operetta (Leipzig, May 10, 1772); *Die Einsprüche,* operetta (Leipzig, Oct. 16, 1772); *Zemire und Azor* (Leipzig, March 5, 1776; not extant); *Heinrich und Lyda,* singspiel (Berlin, March 26, 1776); *Die Zigeuner* (Frankfurt, Nov. 1777); *Sophonisbe,* monodrama (Mannheim, Nov. 3, 1778); *Adelheit von Veltheim,* opera (Frankfurt, Sept. 23, 1780); lieder; concertos; keyboard music.

BIBL.: M. Stöpgeschoff, *N. als Liederkomponist* (diss., Univ. of Bonn, 1924); I. Leux, *C.G. N., 1748–98: Biographie und Instrumentalkompositionen* (Leipzig, 1925); A. Becker, *C.G. N. und die Bonner Illuminaten* (Bonn, 1969).

Neel, (Louis) Boyd, English-born Canadian conductor; b. Blackheath, Kent, July 19, 1905; d. Toronto, Sept. 30, 1981. He studied at the Royal Naval College in Dartmouth; after taking medical courses at Caius College, Cambridge (B.A., 1926; M.A., 1930), he studied theory and orchestration at the Guildhall School of Music in London (1931). In 1932 he organized the Boyd Neel Orch., which gave its 1st performance in London on June 22, 1933; it quickly gained a fine reputation, excelling in performances of contemporary British music; also played Baroque works. He commissioned Britten's *Variations on a Theme of Frank Bridge* and conducted its premiere at the Salzburg Festival in 1937. He remained active with his ensemble until 1952; also appeared as a conductor with various English orchs. and theaters. He conducted at the Sadler's Wells Theatre (1945–47) and with the D'Oyly Carte Opera (1948–49); was also conductor of the Robert Mayer Children's Concerts (1946–52). After serving as founder-conductor of the Hart House Orch. in Toronto (1954–71), with which he made many tours, he conducted the Mississauga Sym. Orch. (1971–78); was also dean of the Royal Cons. of Music of Toronto (1953–71). He became a naturalized Canadian citizen in 1961; was made a Commander of the Order of the British Empire (1953) and an Officer of the Order of Canada (1973). His book, *The Story of an Orchestra* (London, 1950), recounted his years with the Boyd Neel Orch.

Nef, Albert, Swiss conductor and composer, brother of **Karl Nef;** b. St. Gallen, Oct. 30, 1882; d. Bern, Dec. 6, 1966. He studied at the Leipzig Cons. and with Kretzschmar in Berlin (Ph.D., 1906); from 1907, was an opera conductor in Lübeck, Neustrelitz, and Rostock; from 1912, was in Bern, and was conductor of the Orch. Society there from 1922; from 1920, was president of the Swiss Stage Artists' Alliance. He was the author of *Das Lied in der deutschen Schweiz Ende des 18. und am Anfang des 19. Jahrhunderts* (1909); also of *50 Jahre Berner Theater* (Bern, 1956). He composed a singspiel, *Graf Strapinski* (Bern, 1928); *Appenzeller Tänze* for Orch. (1926); *Wanderschaft,* song cycle for Tenor, Mixed Chorus, and Orch. (Bern, 1924); choruses; piano pieces; songs.

Nef, Karl, Swiss musicologist, brother of **Albert Nef;** b. St. Gallen, Aug. 22, 1873; d. Basel, Feb. 9, 1935. He entered the Leipzig Cons. in 1891, studying with Reckendorf (piano), Julius Klengel (cello), and Jadassohn (theory); attended Kretzschmar's lectures on musicology at the Univ., and in 1896 received a Ph.D. with his dissertation *Die Collegia musica in der deutschen reformierten Schweiz* (publ. in St. Gallen, 1897); subsequently completed his Habilitation in 1900 at the Univ. of Basel. He settled in Basel in 1897; from 1897 to 1925 he was music critic of the *Basler Nachrichten* and from 1898 to 1909, ed. the *Schweizerische Musikzeitung;* in 1900, became Privatdozent for musicology at the Univ.; in 1909, became associate prof.; in 1923, prof.

WRITINGS: *Schriften über Musik und Volksgesang* (Bern, 1908); *Einführung in die Musikgeschichte* (Basel, 1920; 3rd ed., 1945; Eng. tr. as *Outline of the History of Music,* N.Y., 1935); *Geschichte der Sinfonie und Suite* (Leipzig, 1921); *Geschichte unserer Musikinstrumente* (Leipzig, 1926; new ed., 1949); *Die neun Sinfonien Beethovens* (Leipzig, 1928); *Aufsätze* (Basel, 1936).

BIBL.: *Festschrift K. N. zum 60. Geburtstag* (Zürich, 1933).

Negrea, Marţian, Rumanian composer; b. Vorumloc, Transylvania, Feb. 10, 1893; d. Bucharest, July 13, 1973. He studied with Timotei Popovici at the Andréien Seminary in Sibiu (1910–14); then took courses with Franz Schmidt and Mandyczewski at the Vienna Academy of Music (1918–21). Returning to Rumania, he was a prof. of harmony at the Cluj Cons. (1921–41) and at the Bucharest Cons. (1941–63). His music is marked by a Romantic quality; almost all of his compositions are programmatic in intent and folkloric in content. Thematically, he applies elements of Transylvanian melorhythms.

WORKS: Opera: *Marin Pescarul* (Marin the Fisherman; 1933; Cluj, Oct. 3, 1934); *Fantezie simfonică* (1921); 2 *Rapsodia română* for Orch. (1938, 1950); *Poveşti din Grui* (Fairytale from Grui), symphonic poem (1940); *Divertissement* for Orch. (1951); *Prin munţii apuseni* (Through the Western Mountains), suite for Orch. from music to the film (1952); *Recrutul* (The Recruit), symphonic suite (1953); *Simfonia primăverii* (Spring Symphony, 1956); *Sărbătoarea muncii* (Celebration of Work), symphonic poem (1958); Concerto for Orch. (1963); *Requiem* for Soloists, Chorus, and Orch. (1957); *Oratoriul patriei* for Narrator, Soloists, Chorus, and Orch. (1959); *Prelude and Fugue* for String Quartet (1920); 4 *Pieces* for Harp (1945); String Quartet (1949); 4 *Rumanian Sketches* for Clarinet and Piano (1958); *Suite* for Clarinet and Piano (1960); Piano Sonata (1921); Piano Sonatina (1922); choruses; songs.

Negri, Gino, Italian composer; b. Milan, May 25, 1919. He studied at the Milan Cons. with Renzo Bossi, graduating in 1942. In 1959 he was appointed artistic director of the Teatro del Popolo in Milan. He wrote a number of light operas, all to his own librettos, among them *Vieni qui, Carla* (Milan, Feb. 28, 1956); *Massimo* (Milan, April 12, 1958); *Il tè delle tre* (Como, Sept. 12, 1958); *Il Circo Max* (Venice, Sept. 23, 1959); *Publicità, ninfa gentile* (Milan, 1970).

Negri, Vittorio, Italian conductor, record producer, and musicologist; b. Milan, Oct. 16, 1923. He was educated at the Milan Cons., graduating with a degree in composition and conducting in 1946; began his professional career at the Salzburg Mozarteum, working with Bernhard Paumgartner; then served as a guest conductor of the Orch. del Teatro alla Scala in Milan, the Orch. National de France in Paris, the Dresden Staatskapelle, and the Boston Sym. Orch.; also made festival appearances in Salzburg, Montreux, Monte Carlo, and Versailles.

Neidhardt (Neidhart, Nithart) von Reuenthal, German Minnesänger; b. c.1180; d. c.1240. Born into a knightly family, he was in the service of Duke Otto II of Bavaria in Landshut; went to Austria (1232). He was in all probability the earliest German musician whose songs are extant. These are found in MS collections of the late 14th century; a complete list of sources is in Hagen's *Minnesinger* (vol. 4; 1838). An ed. of Neidhardt's songs, with facsimile reproductions and transcriptions in modern notation, was brought out by W. Schmieder in Denkmäler der Tonkunst in Österreich, LXXI, Jg. XXXVII (1930). Another collection, *Neidhardt-Lieder,* ed. by F. Gennrich, was publ. as no. 9 in the series Summa Musica Medii Aevi (Darmstadt, 1962).

BIBL.: L. Erk and F. Böhme, *Deutscher Liederhort* (Leipzig, 1894); H. Rietsch, *Die deutsche Liedweise* (1904); S. Singer, *Neidhartstudien* (Tübingen, 1920); E. Wiessner, *Kommentar zu Neidharts Liedern* (Leipzig, 1954); idem, *Vollständiges Wörterbuch zu Neidharts Liedern* (Leipzig, 1954); A. Hatto and R. Taylor, *The Songs of Neidhart von Reuental* (Manchester, 1958); D. Boueke, *Materialien zur Neidhart-Überlieferung* (Munich, 1967); K. Kohrs, "Zum Verhältnis von Sprache und Musik in den Liedern Neidharts von Reuental," *Deutsche Vierteljahrsschrift für Literaturwissenschaft und Geistesgeschichte,* XLIII/4 (1969); E. Simon, "Neidharte and Neidhartiana: Notes on the History of a Song Corpus," *Beiträge zur Geschichte der deutschen Sprache und Literatur,* XCIV (1972).

Neidlinger, Gustav, German bass-baritone; b. Mainz, March 21, 1910. He received his musical training in Frankfurt; then sang with the operas in Mainz (1931–34), Hamburg (1936–50), and Stuttgart (from 1950). In 1952 he made his 1st appearance at the Bayreuth Festival; in 1953 he sang at La Scala in Milan; in 1956 at the Vienna State Opera. He also sang at Covent Garden in London (1963) and the Teatro Colón in Buenos Aires (1968). He made his Metropolitan Opera debut in N.Y. on Nov. 17, 1972, as Alberich in Wagner's *Siegfried.* It was in Wagnerian roles that he gained his best successes.

Neighbour, O(liver) W(ray), English music bibliographer and musicologist; b. Merstham, Surrey, April 1, 1923. He pursued the study of modern languages at Birbeck College (B.A., 1950); joined the dept. of printed books at the British Museum (1946); then was on the music room staff (1951–76), subsequently serving as its superintendent (1976–85). He publ. *English Music Publishers: Plate Numbers in the First Half of the Nineteenth Century* (with A. Tyson; London, 1965) and *Consort and Keyboard Music,* vol. III of *The Music of William Byrd* (London, 1978); also ed. *Music and Bibliography: Essays in Honour of Alec Hyatt King* (London, 1980).

Neikrug, Marc (Edward), American pianist and composer; b. N.Y., Sept. 24, 1946. He studied at the Detmold North West German Music Academy with Giselher Klebe and at the Berkshire Music Center at Tanglewood with Gunther Schuller; was composer-in-residence at the Marlboro Music Festival (1972); also studied at the State Univ. of N.Y. at Stony Brook (M.M., 1971); received an N.E.A. grant (1974). As a performer, he became well known as a duo recitalist with Pinchas Zukerman.

WORKS: STAGE: *Through Roses* for Actor and 7 Instrumentalists (1980). **ORCH.:** Piano Concerto (1966); Clarinet Concerto (1970); Viola Concerto (1974; Boston, Oct. 14, 1979); *Eternity's Sunrise* (1980); Violin Concerto (1985); Flute Concerto (Pittsburgh, Sept. 8, 1989). **CHAMBER:** 2 string quartets (1970, 1972); Cello Sonata (1971); Suite for Cello and Piano (1974); *Rituals* for Flute and Harp (1976); 3 *Fantasies* for Violin and Piano (1977); Violin Sonata; Sonata for Cello Solo; Quartet for Flute and String Trio; Concertino for 7 Instruments (Boston, April 17, 1977); *Continuum* for Cello and Piano (1978); *Kaleidoscope* for Clarinet and Piano (1979); also a Piano Sonata (1972) and *Cycle for 7* for Piano (1978).

Neitzel, Otto, German pianist, conductor, music critic, and composer; b. Falkenburg, Pomerania, July 6, 1852; d. Cologne, March 10, 1920. He was a pupil at Kullak's Academy in Berlin; studied also at the Univ. (Ph.D., 1875); then made a concert tour, as pianist, with Pauline Lucca and Sarasate; in 1878, became conductor of the Musikverein at Strasbourg, where (1879–81) he also conducted at the City Theater. From 1881 to 1885 he taught at the Moscow Cons.; then at the Cologne Cons.; from 1887, was also critic for the *Kölnische Zeitung;* he visited the U.S. in 1906–7 as a lecturer, pianist, and conductor; in 1919, became a member of the Academy of Arts in Berlin. He wrote *Führer durch die Oper des Theaters der Gegenwart* (3 vols., 1890–93; 4th ed., 1908); *Beethovens Symfonien nach ihrem Stimmungsgehalt erläutert* (1891; 6th ed., 1924); *Saint-Saëns* (1899); *Aus meiner Musikantenmappe* (1914).

WORKS: Operas: *Die Barbarina* (Wiesbaden, Nov. 15, 1905) and *Der Richter von Kaschau* (Darmstadt, March 31, 1916); Piano Concerto (1900); *Capriccio* for Piano and Orch.; etc.

Nejedlý, Vít, Czech composer, son of **Zdeněk Nejedlý;** b. Prague, June 22, 1912; d. Dukla, Slovakia, Jan. 1, 1945. He studied composition with Jeremiáš and conducting with Talich at the Charles Univ. in Prague, obtaining his Ph.D. in 1936; after the occupation of Czechoslovakia by the Nazis in 1939, he went to the Soviet Union, where he was an ed. of Czech programs for Radio Moscow foreign broadcasts; in 1943, joined the Czechoslovak contingent of the Red Army, and moved with it to the borders of Czechoslovakia, when he died of typhoid fever.

Works: Opera, *Tkalci* (The Weavers), after Hauptmann (1938; completed by Jan Hanuš; Pilsen, May 7, 1961); melodrama, *The Dying* (1933); 3 syms.: No. 1 (1931); No. 2, *Bídy a smrti* (Poverty and Death, 1934); No. 3, *Španělská* (Spanish, 1937–38; dedicated to the Spanish Loyalist Army); *Overture to Verhaeren's Dawn* (1932); *Commemoration* for Orch. (1933); *Sinfonietta* (1937); *Dramatic Overture* (1940); *Lidová suita* (*Popular Suite*) for Orch. (1940); 2 cantatas, *Den* (The Day, 1935) and *To You* (1943); 2 *Compositions* for Wind Quintet (1934); 2 *Compositions* for Nonet (1934); *Small Suite* for Violin and Piano (1935); String Quartet (1937); Concertino for Nonet (1940); *Fantasy* for Piano (1937); many songs; military marches and choruses.

Bibl.: J. Plavec, *Vzpominky na Vita Nejedlého* (Memories of N.; Prague, 1948); J. Jiránek, *V. N.* (Prague, 1959).

Bibl.: A. Dette, *Die Barbarina* (Fulda, 1913).

Nejedlý, Zdeněk, Czech musicologist and politician, father of **Vit Nejedlý**; b. Litomyšl, Feb. 10, 1878; d. Prague, March 9, 1962. He studied in Prague with Fibich, and took courses with Jaroslav Goll (history) and Hostinský (esthetics) at the Charles Univ., where he qualified in 1900; was an archivist at the National Museum (1899–1909); joined the staff of the Charles Univ. (1905), serving as a reader (1908–19) and prof. (1919–39) in musicology. He joined the Czech Communist Party in 1929; after the Nazi occupation of his country (1939), he went to the Soviet Union and was a prof. of history at the Univ. of Moscow. After the liberation of Czechoslovakia (1945), he returned to Prague; was minister of education (1948–53) and deputy premier (1953).

Writings (all publ. in Prague): *Zdenko Fibich, zakladatel scénického melodramu* (Zdenko Fibich, Founder of the Scenic Melodrama; 1901); *Katechismus estetiky* (A Manual of Esthetics; 1902); *Dějinv české hudby* (A History of Czech Music; 1903); *Dějiny předhusitského v Čechách* (A History of Pre-Hussite Song in Bohemia; 1904; 2nd ed., 1954, as *Dějiny husitského zpěvu*); *Počátky husitského zpěvu* (The Beginnings of Hussite Song; 1907; 2nd ed., 1954–55, as *Dějiny husitského zpěvu*); *Zpěvohry Smetanovy* (Smetana's Operas; 1908; 3rd ed., 1954); *Josef Bohuslav Foerster* (1910); *Dějiny husitského spěvu za válek husitských* (A History of Hussite Song during the Hussite Wars; 1913; 2nd ed., 1955–56, as *Dějiny husitského zpěvu*); *Gustav Mahler* (1913; 2nd ed., 1958); *Richard Wagner* (1916; 2nd ed., 1961); *Všeobecné dějiny hudby, I: O původy hudby, Antika* (A General History of Music, I: Origin and Antiquity; 1916–30); *Vítězslav Novák* (1921; articles and reviews); *Otakara Hostinského estetika* (Otakar Hostinský's Esthetics; 1921); *Smetana* (1922); *Bedřich Smetana* (4 vols., 1924–33; 2nd ed., 1950–54); *Zdeňka a Fibicha milostný denik* (Zdeněk Fibich's Erotic Diary; 1925; 2nd ed., 1949); *Otakar Ostrčil, Vzrůst a uzráni* (Otakar Ostrčil: Growth and Maturity; 1935; 2nd ed., 1949); *Sovětská hudba* (Soviet Music; 1936–37); *Otakar Hostinský* (1937; 2nd ed., 1955); *Kritiky* (2 vols., 1954, 1965).

Bibl.: J. Teichmann, *Z. N.* (Prague, 1938); V. Pekárek, *Z. N.* (Prague, 1948); J. Jiránek, *Z. N.* (Prague, 1952); A. Sychra, *Estetika Z.a Nejedlého* (Z. N.'s Esthetics; Prague, 1956); F. Cervinka, *Z. N.* (Prague, 1959); V. Pekárek and J. Kubát, eds., *Na pamět' Z.a Nejedlého* (In Memory of Z. N.; Prague, 1966); *Z. N.: Doba—život—dilo* (Z. N.: Times—Life—Work; Prague, 1975); M. Ransdorf, *Z. N.* (Prague, 1988).

Nelhybel, Vaclav, Czech-born American composer and conductor; b. Polanka nad Odrou, Sept. 24, 1919. He studied composition and conducting with Řídký at the Prague Cons. (1938–42) and musicology at the Univ. of Prague (1938–42);

in 1942, went to Switzerland and took courses in medieval and Renaissance music at the Univ. of Fribourg; was affiliated with the Swiss Radio (1946–50); then was music director of Radio Free Europe in Munich (1950–57). In 1957 he settled in the U.S., becoming a citizen in 1962; subsequently evolved energetic activities as a lecturer and guest conductor at American colleges and high schools. As a composer, he is especially notable for his fine pieces for the symphonic band. His harmonic idiom is of a freely dissonant texture, with melorhythmic components gravitating toward tonal centers. In 1976 he accomplished the setting for organ, brass, and timpani of 52 hymns and 6 church pieces, publ. in a collection entitled *Festival Hymns and Processionals*.

Works: stage: operas: *A Legend* (1953–54); *Everyman*, medieval morality play (Memphis, Oct. 30, 1974); *The Station* (1978). **ballets:** *In the Shadow of a Lime Tree* (1946); *The Cock and the Hangman* (Prague, Jan. 17, 1947). **orch.:** Sym. No. 1 (1942); *Ballade* (1946); *Etude symphonique* (1949); Concertino for Piano and Chamber Orch. (1949); *Sinfonietta Concertante* (1960); Viola Concerto (1962); *Houston Concerto* (1967); *Concertino da camera* for Cello, 15 Winds, and Piano (1971); *Polyphonies* (1972); *Toccata* for Harpsichord, 13 Winds, and Percussion (1972); *Cantus and Ludus* for Piano, 17 Winds, and Percussion (1973); *Polyphonic Variations* for Strings and Trumpet (1975); *Slavonic Triptych* (1976). **symphonic band:** *Caucasian Passacaglia* (1963); *Concerto Antiphonale* for 14 Brasses (1964); *Symphonic Requiem*, with Baritone in the last of its 4 movements (1965); *Estampie*, with Antiphonal Brass Sextet (1965); *Yamaha Concerto* (1971); *Introit*, with Solo Chimes (1972); *Dialogues*, with Piano Solo (1976); *Ritual* (1978). **vocal:** *Caroli antiqui varii*, 7 a cappella choruses for 7 Voices (1962); *Epitaph for a Soldier* for Soloists and a cappella Chorus (1964); *Peter Piper* for Chorus, and Clarinet Choir or Piano (1965); *Cantata pacis* for 6 Soloists, Chorus, Winds, Percussion, and Organ (1965); *Dies ultima* for 3 Soloists, Mixed Chorus, Speaking Chorus, Orch., and Jazz Band (1967); *Sine nomine* for 4 Soloists, Chorus, Orch., and Tape (1968); *America Sings* for Baritone, Chorus, and Band (1974); *Estampie natalis* for Double Chorus, Piccolo, Viola, Cello, and Percussion (1976); *6 Fables for All Time* for Narrator, Chorus, and Orch. (Ridgefield, Conn., Oct. 25, 1980; Skitch Henderson, narrator). **chamber:** *3 Organa* for 4 Bassoons (1948); 2 string quartets (1949, 1962); 3 wind quintets (1948, 1958, 1960); Quartet for 4 Horns (1957); Quartet for Piano and 3 Brass Instruments (1959); *4 Miniatures* for String Trio (1959); *Numismata* for Brass Septet (1961); Brass Trio (1961); 2 brass quintets (1961, 1965); *Impromptus* for Wind Sextet (1963); 9 clarinet trios (1963); *Scherzo concertante* for Horn and Piano (1963); *3 Pieces* for Saxophone Quartet (1965); *Quintetto concertante* for Violin, Trombone, Trumpet, Xylophone, and Piano (1965); Concerto for Percussion (1972); *Concerto spirituoso No. 1* for 12 Flutes, Electric Harpsichord, and Voice (1974); *No. 2* for 12 Saxophones, Electric Harpsichord, and Voice (1974); *No. 3* for Electric Violin, English Horn, Horn, Tuba, Vibraphone, Winds, Percussion, and Voice (1975); *No. 4* for Voice, String Quartet, and Chamber Orch. (1977); *Oratio No. 1* for Piccolo, Trumpet, Chimes, and String Quartet or String Orch. (1974) and *No. 2* for Oboe and String Trio (1976); *Music for 6 Trumpets* (1975); *Ludus* for 3 Tubas (1975); Bassoon Quartet (1976); *Variations* for Harp (1977). **piano:** *103 Short Pieces* (1965). **organ:** *Trois danses liturgiques* (1964); *26 Short Preludes* (1972); *Preambulum*, with Timpani (1977).

Nelle, Wilhelm, German writer on music; b. Schwöbber, near Hameln, May 9, 1849; d. Münster, Oct. 15, 1918. He studied theology in Halle and Tübingen, where he also studied music with Robert Franz and Otto Scherzer. From 1872 he was active as a priest in various German cities. In 1895 he founded the Evangelischer Kirchengesang-Verein für Westfalen. He was prominent in the reform and organization of Evangelical church music in Germany.

Writings: *Das evangelische Gesangbuch von 1835* (1883); *Liederbüchlein, 25 geistliche und weltliche Lieder* (1891); *Cho-*

ralbuch zum Rheinisch-Westfälischen evangelischen Gesangbuch (with Hollenberg, 1892; 3rd ed., 1908); *Die Festmelodien des Kirchenjahres charakterisiert* (1895; 2nd ed., 1904, as *Aus dem evangelischen Melodienschatz*, I); *Geschichte des deutschen evangelischen Kirchenliedes* (1904; 3rd ed., 1928); *Chorbuch* (with J. Plath, 1917).

Nelson, John (Wilton), American conductor; b. San José, Costa Rica (of American parents), Dec. 6, 1941. He studied at Wheaton (Ill.) College and with Morel at the Juilliard School of Music in N.Y.; was music director of the Indianapolis Sym. Orch. (1976–87), the Caramoor Festival (1983–90), and the Opera Theatre of St. Louis (from 1985).

Nelson, Judith (Anne) (née **Manes**), American soprano; b. Chicago, Sept. 10, 1939. She studied at St. Olaf College in Northfield, Minn.; then sang with music groups at the Univ. of Chicago and the Univ. of Calif., Berkeley; made her operatic debut as Drusilla in Monteverdi's *L'incoronazione di Poppea* in Brussels in 1979. She appeared widely as a soloist and recitalist. Although she is particularly noted for her performances of Baroque music, she also introduced compositions by American and English composers.

Nelson, Oliver (Edward), black American saxophonist, composer, and arranger; b. St. Louis, June 4, 1932; d. Los Angeles, Oct. 27, 1975. He studied piano, saxophone, taxidermy, dermatology, and embalming. After serving in the Marines, he studied composition with Robert Wykes at Washington Univ. in St. Louis (1954–58); had private lessons with Elliott Carter in N.Y. and George Tremblay in Los Angeles; in the 1950s and early 1960s, he played saxophone in several jazz orchs., among them those led by Wild Bill Davis, Louis Bellison, Duke Ellington, and Count Basie; then moved to Hollywood. He publ. a valuable saxophone improvisation book, *Patterns for Jazz* (Los Angeles, 1966; originally titled *Patterns for Saxophone*).

WORKS: Saxophone Sonata (1957); *Songs* for Contralto and Piano (1957); Divertimento for 10 Woodwinds and Double Bass (1957); *Afro-American Sketches* for Jazz Ensemble (1960); *Blues and the Abstract Truth* for Jazz Ensemble (1960); Woodwind Quintet (1960); *Dirge* for Chamber Orch. (1961); *Soundpiece* for Contralto, String Quartet, and Piano (1963); *Soundpiece* for Jazz Orch. (1964); *Patterns* for Jazz Ensemble (1965); *A Study in 5/4* for Wind Ensemble (1966); Concerto for Xylophone, Marimba, Vibes, and Wind Orch. (1967); *The Kennedy Dream Suite* for Jazz Ensemble (1967); *Jazzhattan Suite* for Jazz Orch. (N.Y., Oct. 7, 1967); Septet for Wind Orch. (1968); *Piece* for Orch. and Jazz Soloists (1969); *A Black Suite* for Narrator, String Quartet, and Jazz Orch. (1970); *Berlin Dialogue* for Jazz Orch. (Berlin, 1970); *Concert Piece* for Alto Saxophone and Studio Orch. (1972); *Fugue and Bossa* for Wind Orch. (1973); also a sterling jazz arrangement of Prokofiev's *Peter and the Wolf* (1966) and music for films and television.

BIBL.: D. Baker et al., eds., *The Black Composer Speaks* (Metuchen, N.J., 1978).

Nelson, Prince Roger. See Prince.

Nelson, Robert U(riel), American musicologist; b. Brush, Colo., Sept. 16, 1902. He studied at the Univ. of Calif., Berkeley (A.B., 1923); later worked with Gaston Déthier and Percy Goetschius at the Inst. of Musical Art, N.Y. (diplomas in piano and organ, 1925), and with Walter Piston and Willi Apel at Harvard Univ. (M.A., 1937; Ph.D., 1944). He also studied composition with Gustav Holst and Eugene Zador. From 1925 to 1937 he was a faculty member at Washington State Univ.; in 1938, became an instructor at the Univ. of Calif., Los Angeles; was a prof. from 1955; retired in 1970. He publ. a valuable study, *The Technique of Variation* (Berkeley, 1948); contributed numerous articles to music magazines.

Nelson, Ron(ald Jack), American composer; b. Joliet, Ill., Dec. 14, 1929. He studied composition with Howard Hanson, Bernard Rogers, Louis Mennini, and Wayne Barlow at the Eastman School of Music in Rochester, N.Y. (B.Mus., 1952; M.Mus., 1953; D.M.A., 1956); in the interim, went to Paris on a Fulbright grant, where he took courses with Tony Aubin at the École Normale de Musique (1955). In 1956 he joined the music staff of Brown Univ. in Providence, R.I.; was chairman of the music dept. there from 1963 to 1973. His orch., band, and choral pieces have been widely performed. He should not be confused with the American church musician and composer Ronald Axel Nelson (b. Rockford, Ill., April 29, 1927).

WORKS: STAGE: OPERAS: *The Birthday of the Infanta* (Rochester, N.Y., May 14, 1956) and *Hamaguchi* (1981). **BALLET:** *Dance in Ruins* (1954). **ORCH.:** *Sarabande: For Katharine in April* (1954); *Savannah River Holiday* (1955; also for Band, 1973); *This Is the Orchestra* for Narrator and Orch. (1960); *Jubilee* (1960); *Overture for Latecomers* (1961); *Toccata* (1961); *Rocky Point Holiday* (1969; also for Band, 1969); *Trilogy: JFK—MLK—RFK* for Orch. and Tape (in memory of President John F. Kennedy, Martin Luther King, and Robert F. Kennedy; 1969); *5 Pieces for Orchestra after Paintings by Andrew Wyeth* (1976); *Meditation and Dance* (1977); *Fanfare for a Celebration* (1983; also for Band, 1982); *Elegy* for Strings (1988). **BAND:** *Mayflower Overture* (1958); *Rocky Point Holiday* (1969; also for Orch., 1969); *Savannah River Holiday* (1973; also for Orch., 1955); *Fanfare for a Celebration* (1982; also for Orch., 1983); *Medieval Suite* (1982); *Aspen Jubilee* (1984). **OTHER INSTRUMENTAL:** *Pebble Beach Sojourn* for Organ, Brass, and Percussion (1983); *Danza Capriccio* for Alto Saxophone and Wind Ensemble (1988); *Morning Alleluias for the Winter Solstice* for Wind Ensemble (1989). **VOCAL:** *The Christmas Story*, cantata (1958); *Triumphal Te Deum* (1963); *What Is Man?*, oratorio (1964); *Meditation of the Syllable OM*, with Narrator (1970); *Mass of St. La Salle* (1981); *Te Deum Laudamus* for Chorus and Wind Ensemble (1985); other choral works; songs; piano pieces.

Nelson, Willie (Hugh), American country-music singer, guitarist, and songwriter; b. Abbott, Texas, April 30, 1933. For a short time he attended Baylor Univ. in Waco, Texas; then made appearances in local honky-tonk bars; also began to write songs, which included *Hello Walls*, *Crazy*, and *Night Life*, made famous by leading singers of the day. He then went to Nashville, Tenn., where he played bass in the band of Ray Price, and gained renown with such songs as *The Party's Over* and *Little Things* in his many appearances with the Grand Ole Opry. He eventually returned to Texas and became instrumental in the development of the "Austin sound," a.k.a. "outlaw country" or "redneck rock." With the album *Red-headed Stranger* (1975), he gained success and went on to produce a number of others, including *Stardust* (1978), *Willie and Family Live* (1978), *Honeysuckle Rose* (1980), *Always on My Mind* (1982), and *Angel Eyes* (1984). He also became a competent actor, making appearances in the films *Electric Horseman* (1979) and *Honeysuckle Rose* (1980). His autobiography was publ. as *Willie* (N.Y., 1988).

Nelsova (real name, **Katznelson**), **Zara,** brilliant Canadian-born American cellist of Russian descent; b. Winnipeg, Dec. 23, 1918. Her father, a flutist, gave her music lessons; she later studied with Dezso Mahalek (1924–28). In 1929 she went to London, where she continued her studies with Herbert Walenn (until 1935). In 1931, at the age of 13, she appeared as soloist with the London Sym. Orch. With her 2 sisters, a pianist and a violinist, she organized a group billed as the Canadian Trio, and toured in England, Australia, and South Africa. Returning to Canada, she served as principal cellist of the Toronto Sym. Orch. (1940–43); she was also a member of another Canadian Trio, this time with Kathleen Parlow and Sir Ernest MacMillan (1941–44). In 1942 she made her U.S. debut at Town Hall in N.Y.; also continued her studies, receiving valuable instruction from Feuermann, Casals, and Piatigorsky. In 1962 she joined the faculty of the Juilliard School of Music in N.Y. In 1953 she became an American citizen. From 1963 to 1973 she was the wife of the American pianist **Grant Johannesen.** She received rather rapturous press reviews for her lyrical interpretations of classical and modern cello music in a purportedly "Russian" (i.e., wonderful) style.

Nelsson, Woldemar, Russian conductor; b. Kiev, April 4, 1938. His father, a conductor, gave him violin lessons in Kiev; after conducting studies at the Novosibirsk Cons., he attended master classes at the Moscow Cons. and the Leningrad Cons. He won 1st prize in the All-Union Conducting Competition in Moscow (1971); then became assistant to Kondrashin and the Moscow Phil.; also appeared as a guest conductor throughout the Soviet Union. In 1977 he emigrated to West Germany, where he served as Generalmusikdirektor of the Kassel State Theater (1980–87). From 1980 he was a regular conductor at the Bayreuth Festivals.

Němeček, Franz Xaver. See **Niemtschek, Franz Xaver.**

Nemescu, Octavian, avant-garde Rumanian composer; b. Pascani, March 29, 1940. He studied with Jora, Alfred Mendelsohn, Vieru, Ciortea, Vancea, and Paul Constantinescu at the Bucharest Cons. (1956–63); attended the summer courses of new music held in Darmstadt (1972); taught asymptotic approximations from infinitude to infinitesimality.

Works: Clarinet Sonata (1961–62); *Poliritmii* for Clarinet, Piano, and Prepared Piano (1962–63); *Triunghi (Triangle)* for Orch. (1964; Bucharest, Dec. 3, 1967); *Patru dimensiuni în timp (4 Dimensions in Time): I* for Orch. (1965), *II* for Chorus and Orch. (1966), *III* for Orch. (1967), and *IV* for Orch. (1968); *Combinaţii în cercuri (Combinations of Circles)* for Cello, Tape, and Multimedia Action (1965); *Plurisens,* cycle for Variable Group and Multimedia Action (1965–68); *Memorial I–V* for various combinations of Instruments, Tape, and Multimedia Action (1968–70); *Concentric* and *Efemeride,* both for Variable Ensemble, Tape, and Multimedia Action (1968–69); *Ego,* multimedia spectacle (1970); *Le Roi va mourir* for an Instrumentalist, Clock, Tape, and Multimedia Action (1971–72); *Ulysse* for Variable Group, Tape, and Multimedia Action (1972–73); *Jeu des sens,* music for a pair of ears, eyes, hands, a nose, and a mouth (1973–74); *Pourras-tu seul?* and *Cromoson,* both "imaginary music" (1973–74); *Natural!,* space music (1973–74); *Kalendrier,* permanent music for the atmosphere of a room (1974); *Sugesti II* for Chamber Ensemble (1974); *Sugestii III: "Cumpăna porţii"* for Viola and Tape (1977–78); *Sugestii IV* for Piano (1979); *Combinaţii în cercuri* for Chamber Ensemble and Tape (1979–80); *Sugestii V* for Clarinet, Piano, and Tape (1981); *Natural-Cultural* for Chamber Ensemble and Tape (1973–83); *Metabizantinirikon* for Clarinet and Tape (1983–84).

Németh, Mária, Hungarian soprano; b. Körmend, March 13, 1897; d. Vienna, Dec. 28, 1967. She studied with Georg Anthes and Géza Laszló in Budapest, Giannina Russ in Milan, Fernando De Lucia in Naples, and Felicie Kaschowska in Vienna; made her debut as Sulamith in *Königin von Saba* in Budapest in 1923. In 1924 she became a member of the Vienna State Opera, where she remained until 1946; also made appearances at Covent Garden in London, La Scala in Milan, Munich, Rome, Paris, and Salzburg. She sang both lyric and coloratura roles during her career, excelling as the Queen of the Night, Aida, Donna Anna, and Tosca, among others.

Nemiroff, Isaac, American composer; b. Cincinnati, Feb. 16, 1912; d. N.Y., March 5, 1977. He studied at the Cincinnati Cons., and with Stefan Wolpe at the N.Y. College of Music; taught at various music schools in N.Y. and Brooklyn.

Works: Duo for Violin and Cello (1939); Concerto for Oboe and String Orch. (1955); Concertino for Flute, Violin, and String Orch. (1958); *Lorca,* solo cantata for Voice, Flute, and Strings (1963); Woodwind Quintet (1968); Quintet for Flute, Clarinet, Cello, Voice, and Piano (1969); *Atomyriades* for Oboe (1972); Duo for Oboe and Bass Clarinet (1973); 2 string quartets; 2 violin sonatas; Saxophone Sonata.

Nemtin, Alexander, Russian composer; b. Perm, July 13, 1936. He studied at the Moscow Cons., graduating in 1960. He writes music in different genres, but his most notable creation is an intimately plausible reification of Scriabin's *Acte préalable,* the "preliminary act" of the planned *Mysterium.* Nemtin put together the score from sketches left by Scriabin,

supplemented by materials from his late opus numbers, endeavoring to recreate Scriabin's symphonic textures. The 1st part of this work was performed in Moscow on March 16, 1973.

Nenna, Pomponio, Italian composer; b. Bari, near Naples, c.1550. d. probably in Rome, before Oct. 22, 1613. He was in the service of Gesualdo in Naples (c.1594–99); was in Rome by 1608. Held in high regard by his contemporaries, he was created a Knight of the Golden Spur in 1603. He publ. 6 books of madrigals for 5 Voices from 1582 to 1618, and a book of madrigals for 4 Voices (1613). Some of his madrigals were ed. by E. Dagnino in Pubblicazioni dell'Istituto Italiano per la Storia della Musica, *Monumenti,* II (1942).

Nenov, Dimiter, Bulgarian composer and pianist; b. Razgrad, Jan. 1, 1902; d. Sofia, Aug. 30, 1953. He went to Dresden to study architecture at the Technische Hochschule and piano with Feling and composition with Blumer and Bitner at the Cons.; after working as an architect, he continued his studies with Petri in Zakopane (1931) and attended the Bologna Cons. (1932). He taught piano in Sofia (1930–33), then at the State Academy of Music there (1933–35), where he later was made a reader (1937) and a prof. (1943).

Works: 2 syms. (1922; 1923, unfinished); *Ballad* for Orch. (1926); Piano Concerto (1932–36); 2 ballads for Piano and Orch. (1942, 1943); *Rhapsodic Fantasy* for Orch. (1942–52); Violin Sonata (1921); Piano Sonata (1922).

Bibl.: L. Nikolov, ed., *D. N.: spomeni i materijali* (Sofia, 1969).

Nepomuceno, Alberto, important Brazilian composer; b. Fortaleza, July 6, 1864; d. Rio de Janeiro, Oct. 16, 1920. He studied in Rome, Berlin, and Paris, returning to Brazil in 1895. In 1902 he was appointed director of the Instituto Nacional de Música in Rio de Janeiro, remaining only for a few months; he returned to this post in 1906, holding it until 1916. In 1910 he conducted Brazilian music at the International Exposition in Brussels. In some of his music he introduced thematic material from Brazilian folk music.

Works: Operas: *Artemis* (Rio de Janeiro, June 14, 1898); *O Garatuja* (Rio de Janeiro, Oct. 26, 1904); *Abul* (1899–1905; Buenos Aires, June 30, 1913); Sym. (1894; publ. 1937); *Série brasileira* for Orch. (1892; contains a popular batuque); chamber music; over 80 songs; piano and organ pieces.

Neri, Giulio, Italian bass; b. Turilla di Siena, May 21, 1909; d. Rome, April 21, 1958. He studied with Ferraresi in Florence; made his debut at the Teatro delle Quattro Fontane in Rome in 1935; then sang at the Teatro Reale dell'Opera in Rome, where he soon established himself as a principal bass; also made guest appearances at La Scala in Milan, Florence, Venice, London, and Munich. An outstanding Verdi interpreter, he was equally distinguished as a Wagnerian.

Neri, Saint Donna Filippo, outstanding Roman Catholic churchman; b. Florence, July 21, 1515; d. Rome, May 26, 1595. He was educated in Florence; by 1534, was in Rome; in 1548 he founded the Confraternità della Ss. Trinità; in 1551, took Holy Orders. He began giving lectures on religious subjects and holding spiritual exercises in his living quarters at S. Girolamo della Carità in 1552; by 1554 he was active in the oratory of the church there. These meetings invariably ended with the singing of hymns, or *laudi spirituali,* for which the poet Ancina wrote many of the texts, while Giovanni Animuccia, maestro di cappella at the Vatican and music director of the Oratory, set them to music. In 1575 the Congregation of the Oratory, as a seminary for secular priests, was officially recognized by Pope Gregory XIII, and in 1578 the Congregation transferred its headquarters to the church of Santa Maria in Vallicella. Neri, however, remained at S. Girolamo until 1583; Victoria lived with him there, serving as chaplain. Neri was also a friend and spiritual adviser of Palestrina. From the musical practice of the Oratory there eventually developed the form that we know as "oratorio." It was not until about 1635–40 that this form actually began to receive the title of oratorio, from the place where the performances were given. Neri was beatified on May 25, 1615, and canonized on March 12, 1622.

BIBL.: P. Bacci, *Vita di S.F. N., fiorentino* (Rome, 1622; Eng. tr., 2 vols., St. Louis, 1903); A. Alaleona, *Studi su la storia dell'oratorio musicale in Italia* (Turin, 1908; 2nd ed., 1945, as *Storia dell'oratorio musicale in Italia*); L. Ponnelle and L. Bourdet, *Saint Philippe Néri et la société romaine de son temps (1515–1595)* (Paris, 1918; Eng. tr., London, 1932); C. Gasbarri, *L'oratorio filippino* (Rome, 1957); G. Incisa della Rocchetta and N. Vian, eds., *Il primo processo per S.F. N. nel codice vaticano latino 3789e in altri esemplari dell'archivo dell'Oratorio di Roma,* Studi e Testi, CXCI, CXCVI, CCV, CCXXIV (Rome, 1957–63); M. Trevor, *Apostle of Rome: A Life of Philip N., 1515–1595* (London, 1966); H. Smither, *A History of the Oratorio,* Vol. 1 (Chapel Hill, 1977).

Nerini, Emile, French composer; b. Colombes, near Paris, Feb. 2, 1882; d. Paris, March 22, 1967. Son of a piano manufacturer, he studied with Decombes, Diémer, Lenepveu, and Caussade at the Paris Cons.

WORKS: Lyric dramas: *Manoël* (Paris, May 11, 1905); *Le Soir de Waterloo* (Paris, April 17, 1910); *L'Épreuve dernière* (Monte Carlo, March 16, 1912); *Mazeppa* (Bordeaux, 1925); operetta, *Mademoiselle Sans-Gêne* (1944; Bordeaux, 1966); *Bacchus* for Chorus and Orch.; programmatic pieces for Orch. (*Parmi les roses, Solitude, Rêve oriental,* etc.); chamber music; instrumental sonatas; songs; etc.

Nero, Peter (Bernard), popular American pianist and conductor; b. N.Y., May 22, 1934. He studied at the Juilliard School of Music in N.Y.; then toured as a pianist with Paul Whiteman; subsequently launched a highly successful career as a pianist in the popular music genres. He also appeared as a conductor in his own arrangements of popular music and in his original compositions; he wrote the score for the film *A Sunday in New York,* in which he also played a cameo part.

Neruda, family of Moravian musicians: **(1) Josef Neruda,** organist and teacher; b. Mohelno, Jan. 16, 1807; d. Brünn, Feb. 18, 1875. He studied at the Benedictine monastery of Rajhrad; taught piano in Olmütz (1825–32); was organist of Brünn Cathedral (1832–44). He also appeared in concerts throughout Europe with his children, who were as follows: **(2) Amálie Nerudová,** pianist and teacher; b. Brünn, March 31, 1834; d. there, Feb. 24, 1890. She studied with her father; in addition to making tours of Europe with her family, she played in a trio with her brother Viktor and her sister Wilma (1848–52); then was active mainly as a performer and teacher in Brünn. **(3) Viktor Neruda,** cellist; b. Brünn, 1836?; d. St. Petersburg, 1852. He studied with his father; played in a trio with his sisters Amálie and Wilma (from 1848); also toured Europe with his family, dying during a visit to Russia. **(4) Wilma Maria Francisca (Vilemína Maria Franziška) Neruda,** esteemed violinist and teacher; b. Brünn, March 21, 1838?; d. Berlin, April 15, 1911. She studied with her father and with Leopold Jansa in Vienna, making her debut there (1846). After touring Germany with her family (1848), she gave concerts in London (1849); was soloist at a Phil. Soc. concert there (June 11, 1849). She played in a trio with her sister Amálie and her brother Viktor (1848–52), and subsequently pursued a distinguished solo career; was made chamber virtuoso by the Swedish king in 1863. In 1864 she married the Swedish conductor and composer **Ludvig Norman**; they separated in 1869. She was prof. of violin at the Stockholm Cons. (1867–70); gave annual concerts in London from 1869 and was greatly admired there; in 1876 the Duke of Edinburgh (later of Saxe-Coburg-Gotha) and the earls of Dudley and Hardwicke presented her with an outstanding Stradivarius dating from 1709. She continued to give concerts throughout Europe while remaining closely associated with the musical life of England; also appeared as a chamber music artist, and gave recitals with **Charles Hallé** from 1877, marrying him in 1888. The Prince of Wales (later Edward VII), with the support of the kings of Sweden and Denmark, launched a public subscrip-

tion in her honor in 1896. She toured the U.S. in 1899, and in 1900 settled in Berlin, where she taught at the Stern Cons.; was made violinist to Queen Alexandra in 1901. **(5) Marie (Arlbergová) Neruda,** violinist; b. Brünn, March 26, 1840; d. Stockholm, 1922. She studied with her father, then appeared in concerts on tours of Europe with her family; later settled in Stockholm. **(6) Franz (František Xaver Viktor) Neruda,** cellist and composer; b. Brünn, Dec. 3, 1843; d. Copenhagen, March 20, 1915. He studied violin with his father, and then took up the cello on his own (1852); appeared on tours of Europe with his family. After further cello training with Brezina in Brünn and with Servais in Warsaw (1859), he made a successful tour of Scandinavia with his sisters Wilma and Marie (1861–64); then settled in Copenhagen as a member of the royal orch. (1864–76). He was a founder of the Soc. for Chamber Music and its string quartet (1868); performed widely with it until pursuing his career in England (1876–79). He then founded his own string quartet in Copenhagen, with which he was active from 1879 to 1889. After serving as a prof. at the St. Petersburg Cons. (1889–91), he returned to Copenhagen as conductor of the concerts of the Music Soc. (1891–1915); concurrently conducted the concerts of the Stockholm Music Soc.; was also active as a piano teacher. He wrote 5 cello concertos; *Fra Bøhmerwald,* a set of orch. works; chamber music; pieces for Cello and Piano; organ works; piano pieces; songs.

Nessler, Victor E(rnst), Alsatian composer; b. Baldenheim, Jan. 28, 1841; d. Strasbourg, May 28, 1890. He studied in Strasbourg, where he produced his 1st opera, *Fleurette* (1864); then continued his studies in Leipzig with M. Hauptmann, being made chorusmaster at the Stadttheater (1870) and later at the Carola-Theater. He established his reputation as a composer for the theater with his opera *Der Rattenfänger von Hameln* (Leipzig, March 19, 1879). An even greater success was achieved by his opera *Der Trompeter von Säkkingen* (Leipzig, May 4, 1884), which entered the repertoire of many European opera houses. In both operas Nessler adroitly appealed to the Romantic tastes of the German audiences, even though from a purely musical standpoint these productions offered little originality. His other operas premiered in Leipzig were *Dornröschens Brautfahrt* (1867), *Irmingard* (1876), *Der wilde Jäger* (1881), and *Otto der Schütz* (1886); his last opera was *Die Rose von Strassburg* (Munich, 1890). He also wrote the operettas *Die Hochzeitsreise* (1867), *Nachtwächter und Student* (1868), and *Am Alexandertag* (1869).

BIBL.: C. Schneider, "V. N., compositeur alsacien du *Trompette de Säkkingen,*" *La Musique en Alsace hier et aujourd'hui* (Strasbourg, 1970).

Nesterenko, Evgeni (Evgenievich), distinguished Russian bass; b. Moscow, Jan. 8, 1938. He 1st studied architectural engineering; graduated from the Leningrad Structural Inst. in 1961; then enrolled in the Leningrad Cons., where he studied voice with Lukanin. He began his opera career at the Maly Theater in Leningrad (1963–67); then was a member of the Kirov Opera and Ballet Theater there (1967–71). In 1970 he won 1st prize at the Tchaikovsky Competition in Moscow; in 1971 he joined the Bolshoi Theater. He then engaged on a European concert tour; also sang in the U.S. In 1975 he was appointed chairman of the voice dept. at the Moscow Cons. He excelled in such roles as Boris Godunov and Méphistophélès. In 1982 he was awarded the Lenin Prize.

Nestyev, Izrail (Vladimirovich), Russian musicologist; b. Kerch, April 17, 1911. He studied at the Moscow Cons., graduating in 1937; during World War II, he served as a military correspondent; subsequently was in charge of the programs of Moscow Radio (1945–48); in 1956 he joined the staff of the Moscow Cons., conducting seminars on European music. He is the author of the standard biography of Prokofiev (Moscow, 1946; Eng. tr., N.Y., 1946; rev. ed., Moscow, 1957; Eng. tr., Stanford, Calif., 1960, with a foreword by N. Slonimsky; new ed. rev. and augmented, Moscow, 1973); other books are *Popular Song as Foundation of Musical Creativity* (Moscow, 1961); *How to Understand Music* (Moscow, 1962); *Hanns Eisler* *and His Songs* (Moscow, 1962); *Puccini* (Moscow, 1963); *Béla Bartók, Life and Works* (Moscow, 1969). He was a co-ed. of the symposium *Sergei Prokofiev; Articles and Materials* (Moscow, 1962) and of *European Music of the 20th Century; Materials and Documents* (Moscow, 1975).

Nettl, Bruno, distinguished Czech-born American ethnomusicologist, son of **Paul Nettl;** b. Prague, March 14, 1930. He was taken to the U.S. in 1939; studied at Indiana Univ. (A.B., 1950; M.A., 1951; Ph.D., 1953, with the diss. *American Indian Music North of Mexico: Its Styles and Areas;* publ. as *North American Indian Musical Styles,* Philadelphia, 1954); he also received an M.A. degree in library science from the Univ. of Michigan in 1960. He taught at Wayne State Univ. (1953–64); in 1964 he joined the faculty of the Univ. of Illinois at Urbana, becoming a prof. of music and anthropology in 1967. He ed. the periodical *Ethnomusicology* (1961–65), serving as president of the Society for Ethnomusicology (1969–71); was also ed. of the yearbook of the International Folk Music Council (1974–77), and contributed articles to scholarly journals.

WRITINGS: *Music in Primitive Culture* (Cambridge, Mass., 1956); *An Introduction to Folk Music in the United States* (Detroit, 1960; 3rd ed., rev. and augmented by H. Myers, 1976, as *Folk Music in the United States, an Introduction*); *Cheremis Musical Styles* (Bloomington, Ind., 1960); *Reference Materials in Ethnomusicology* (Detroit, 1961; 2nd ed., rev., 1968); *Theory and Method in Ethnomusicology* (N.Y., 1964); *Folk and Traditional Music of the Western Continents* (Englewood Cliffs, N.J., 1965; 3rd ed., rev. by V. Goertzen, 1990); with B. Foltin, Jr., *Daramad of Chahargah: A Study in the Performance Practice of Persian Music* (Detroit, 1972); with C. Hamm and R. Byrnside, *Contemporary Music and Music Cultures* (Englewood Cliffs, N.J., 1975); ed. *Eight Urban Musical Cultures, Tradition and Change* (Urbana, Ill., 1978); *The Study of Ethnomusicology: 29 Issues and Concepts* (Urbana, Ill., 1983); *The Western Impact on World Music: Change, Adaptation, and Survival* (N.Y., 1985); *Blackfoot Musical Thought: Comparative Perspectives* (Kent, Ohio, 1989).

Nettl, Paul, eminent Czech-born American musicologist, father of **Bruno Nettl;** b. Hohenelbe, Bohemia, Jan. 10, 1889; d. Bloomington, Ind., Jan. 8, 1972. He studied jurisprudence (Jur.D., 1913) and musicology (Ph.D., 1915) at the German Univ. of Prague; from 1920 to 1937 was on its faculty. In 1939 he emigrated to the U.S.; became a naturalized U.S. citizen (1945). After teaching at Westminster Choir College and in N.Y. and Philadelphia, he was a prof. of musicology at Indiana Univ. in Bloomington (1946–59); remained a part-time teacher there until 1963.

WRITINGS: *Vom Ursprung der Musik* (Prague, 1918); *Alte jüdische Spielleute und Musiker* (Prague, 1923); *Musik und Tanz bei Casanova* (Prague, 1924); *Musik-Barock in Böhmen und Mähren* (Brünn, 1927); *Der Prager Kaufruf* (Prague, 1930); *Das Wiener Lied im Zeitalter des Barock* (Vienna, 1934); *Mozart in Böhmen,* after Prochazka's *Mozart in Prag* (Prague, 1938); *The Story of Dance Music* (N.Y., 1947); *The Book of Musical Documents* (N.Y., 1948); *Luther and Music* (N.Y., 1948); *Casanova und seine Zeit* (Esslingen, 1949); *Goethe und Mozart: Eine Betrachtung* (Esslingen, 1949); *The Other Casanova* (N.Y., 1950); *Forgotten Musicians* (N.Y., 1951); *National Anthems* (N.Y., 1952; 2nd ed., enl., 1967); *Beethoven Encyclopedia* (N.Y., 1956; 2nd ed., rev., 1967, as *Beethoven Handbook*); *Mozart and Masonry* (N.Y., 1957); *Beethoven und seine Zeit* (Frankfurt, 1958); *Georg Friedrich Händel* (Berlin, 1958); *Mozart und der Tanz* (1960); *The Dance in Classical Music* (N.Y., 1963); R. Daniel, ed., *P.N.: Selected Essays* (Bloomington, 1975).

BIBL.: T. Atcherson, *Ein Musikwissenschaftler in zwei Welten: Die musikwissenschaftlen und literarischen Arbeiten von P. N.* (Vienna, 1962).

Neubauer, Franz Christoph, Czech violinist and composer; b. Melník, March 21, 1750; d. Bückeburg, Oct. 11, 1795. He was taught violin by the village schoolmaster; led a wandering life; produced an operetta, *Ferdinand und Yariko,* in Munich (1784); then proceeded to Vienna, where he met Mozart and

Haydn; from 1790 to 1794 he served as Kapellmeister to Prince Weilburg; in 1795, succeeded Johann Christoph Friedrich Bach as court Kapellmeister at Bückeburg. He was a prolific composer; publ. 10 syms. (1791–95); *La bataille* for Orch. (1794; contains sounds imitative of battle); Flute Concerto (1795); Piano Concerto (publ. 1798); Cello Concerto (n.d.); 25 quartets (1785–93); also various other chamber music pieces; choral works; songs; piano pieces.

BIBL.: F. von Schlichtegroll, *Nekrolog auf das Jahr 1795,* II (Gotha, 1798; ed. by R. Schaal, Kassel and Basel, 1954); R. Sjoerdsma, *The Instrumental Works of F.C. N. (1760–95)* (diss., Ohio State Univ., 1970).

Neuendorff, Adolph (Heinrich Anton Magnus), German-American conductor, impresario, and composer; b. Hamburg, June 13, 1843; d. N.Y., Dec. 4, 1897. He went to N.Y. in 1854 and studied violin with Matzka and Weinlich, and piano with Schilling. He appeared both as a concert violinist and pianist; gave violin concerts in Brazil in 1861. In 1864 he went to Milwaukee, then a center of German music, and served as music director of the German theater; subsequently moved to N.Y., where he conducted German opera, including 1st American performances of *Lohengrin* (April 3, 1871) and *Die Walküre* (April 2, 1877); in 1878–79 he conducted the N.Y. Phil.; from 1884 to 1889 he was in Boston and became the 1st conductor of the Music Hall Promenade Concerts (later Boston Pops); then conducted the Emma Juch Grand Opera Co. (1889–91); he then followed his wife, the singer Georgine von Januschowsky, to Vienna, where she was prima donna and he a conductor at the Hofoper (1893–95); returning to N.Y., he served as director of music at Temple Emanu-El (1896) and as conductor at the Metropolitan Opera (1897). He wrote the comic operas *Der Rattenfänger von Hameln* (1880), *Don Quixote* (1882), *Prince Waldmeister* (1887), and *The Minstrel* (1892); 2 syms. (1878, 1880); other orch. works; quartets for Male Voices; songs.

Neuhaus, Heinrich (Gustavovich), eminent Russian pianist and pedagogue; b. Elizavetgrad, April 12, 1888; d. Moscow, Oct. 10, 1964. He studied piano with his father, **Gustav Neuhaus** (1847–1938); other musical members of the family were his uncle, **Felix Blumenfeld,** and his 1st cousin, **Karol Szymanowski.** Neuhaus began giving concerts at the age of 9; he made a concert tour in Germany in 1904, then studied composition with Paul Juon in Berlin; from 1912 to 1914 he took piano lessons with Leopold Godowsky in Vienna. Returning to Russia, he taught piano at the Kiev Cons. (1918–22); then was a prof. from 1922 to his death at the Moscow Cons. Among his outstanding students were Emil Gilels, Sviatoslav Richter, Yakov Zak, and Radu Lupu. He excelled as an interpreter of the Romantic and 20th-century Russian repertory; publ. *Ob iskusstve fortepiannoy igri* (The Art of Piano Playing; Moscow, 1958; 3rd ed., 1967; Eng. tr., London, 1973).

BIBL.: V. Delson, *H. N.* (Moscow, 1966).

Neuhaus, Rudolf, German conductor; b. Cologne, Jan. 3, 1914; d. Dresden, March 7, 1990. He 1st studied violin; then took conducting lessons with Hermann Abendroth, and also studied music theory with Philipp Jarnach at the Cologne Hochschule für Musik (1932–34). He was music director of the Landestheater in Neustrelitz (1934–44); then was conductor of the Landestheater in Schwerin (1945–50), serving as its Generalmusikdirektor from 1950 to 1953. In 1953 he joined the Dresden State Opera, where he was deputy Generalmusikdirektor until 1975; was noted for his performances of operas of Wagner and Richard Strauss. From 1953 he was a member of the faculty of the Dresden Hochschule für Musik; in 1959, was named prof. there.

Neukomm, Sigismund, Ritter von, Austrian pianist, conductor, writer on music, and composer; b. Salzburg, July 10, 1778; d. Paris, April 3, 1858. He began his musical studies when he was 7, with Franz Xaver Weissauer, the Salzburg Cathedral organist; then studied theory with Michael Haydn; took courses in philosophy and mathematics at the Univ. there, being made honorary organist of the Univ. church (c.1792) and chorus master of the court theater (1796). He continued his studies in Vienna with Joseph Haydn (1797–1804); was active as a teacher. After serving as conductor of the German Theater in St. Petersburg (1804–8), he went to Paris; became a friend of Cherubini, Gossec, Grétry, Monsigny, and other prominent musicians; was pianist to Prince Talleyrand, in which capacity he went to the Congress of Vienna (1814), where his Requiem in C minor in memory of Louis XVI was given (Jan. 21, 1815); that same year he was ennobled by Louis XVII and was made Chevalier of the Légion d'honneur. He was taken to Rio de Janeiro by the Duke of Luxembourg (1816), and became active at the court of John VI of Portugal; after the outbreak of the revolution (1821), he accompanied John VI to Lisbon, and then returned to Paris. After again serving Talleyrand, he traveled widely (from 1826); visited England in 1829, and thereafter made frequent trips between London and Paris. Many of his articles appeared in the *Revue et Gazette Musicale de Paris*. His autobiography was publ. as *Esquisses biographiques de Sigismond Neukomm* (Paris, 1859). **Elisabeth Neukomm** (1789–1816), his sister, gained fame in Vienna as a soprano. A prolific composer, he produced over 1,300 works.

WORKS: STAGE: *Die Nachtwächter*, intermezzo (Vienna, 1804); *Die neue Oper oder Der Schauspieldirektor*, intermezzo (Vienna, 1804); *Alexander am Indus*, opera (St. Petersburg, Sept. 27, 1804); *Musikalische Malerei*, farce (Moscow, May 1, 1806); *Arkona*, melodrama (Würzburg, Sept. 21, 1808); *Niobé*, tragédie lyrique (Montbéliard, 1809); also incidental music to plays. **SACRED VOCAL:** Oratorios; cantatas; 48 masses; 27 offertories; 2 Passions; 11 Te Deums; 73 motets and anthems; 236 hymns and chorales; 243 chants and songs; etc. Other vocal works include 36 choruses, over 150 canons, over 160 quartets and trios, and over 275 arias, songs, romances, etc. **INSTRUMENTAL:** 2 syms.; 5 overtures; Piano Concerto; 6 phantasies for Orch.; various marches; chamber music; piano music; pieces for Harmonium; arrangements; etc.

BIBL.: G. Pellegrini-Brandacher, *S.R. v.N. (und seine Oratorien)* (diss., Univ. of Munich, 1936); idem, "S.R. v.N.: Ein vergessener Salzburger Musiker," *Mitteilungen der Salzburger Landeskunde*, LXXVI (1936); L. Corrêa de Azevedo, "S. N., An Austrian Composer in the New World," *Musical Quarterly* (Oct. 1959); A. Seebohm, *Das deutsche Klavierlied S. N.s: Ein Beitrag zur Musikgeschichte des frühen 19. Jahrhunderts* (diss., Univ. of Vienna, 1968); R. Angermüller, "S.R. v.N. (1778–1858) und seine Lehrer Michael und Joseph Haydn: Eine Dokumentation," *Haydn-Studien*, III (1973); idem, *S. N.: Werkverzeichnis, Autobiographie, Beziehung zu seinen Zeitgenossen* (Munich, 1977).

Neumann, Angelo, Austrian tenor and opera administrator; b. Vienna, Aug. 18, 1838; d. Prague, Dec. 20, 1910. He began a mercantile career, but deserted it after taking vocal lessons from Stilke-Sessi; made his debut in Berlin in 1859, then sang in Krakow, Oldenburg, Pressburg, Danzig, and at the Vienna Court Opera (1862–76); from 1876 to 1882 he was manager of the Leipzig Opera; then gathered together a traveling company for producing Wagner operas, journeying as far as Italy; from 1882 to 1885 he was manager of the Bremen Opera; then until his death, of the Prague Deutsches Theater. He publ. *Erinnerungen an Richard Wagner* (1907; Eng. tr. by E. Livermore, 1908).

Neumann, Franz (František), Czech conductor and composer; b. Přerov, Moravia, June 16, 1874; d. Brno, Feb. 24, 1929. He was a pupil at the Leipzig Cons.; was répétiteur in Karlsruhe and Hamburg; then conductor in Regensburg, Linz, and Reichenberg; in 1904, became 2nd conductor in Frankfurt; subsequently was named 1st conductor (1919) and director (1925) of the Brno National Opera. He composed the operas *Die Brautwerbung* (Linz, 1901), *Liebelei* (Frankfurt, Sept. 18, 1910), *Herbststurm* (Berlin, April 9, 1919), *Beatrice Caracci* (Brno, April 29, 1922; in Czech), and *Leyer und Schwert* (publ. 1901; not produced); 2 ballets; men's choruses; etc.

Neumann, Frederick (actually, **Fritz**), distinguished Austrian-born American violinist and musicologist; b. Bielitz, Dec. 15, 1907. He studied violin with Ondříček, Ševčík, and Marteau in Prague, and also took courses at the Univ. of Berlin (Ph.D., 1934, in political science and economics); subsequently studied violin with H. Kaplan in Berlin and A. Busch in Basel. He emigrated to the U.S. in 1939, and served as head of the string dept. of the Cornish School of Music and Arts in Seattle (1939–42); during World War II (1942–45), he was in the intelligence service of the U.S. Army, becoming a naturalized U.S. citizen (1943). After the war, he studied at Teachers College, Columbia Univ. (M.A., 1947), and at Columbia Univ. (Ph.D., 1952). He was prof. of music and concertmaster of the orch. at the Univ. of Miami (1948–51) and prof. of music at the Univ. of Richmond (Va.) (1955–78); also was concertmaster of the Richmond Sym. Orch. (1957–64), and a visiting prof. at Princeton (1970–71), Yale (1975–76), and Indiana (1978–79) univs. He made valuable contributions to the field of 17th- and 18th-century performance practices. He publ. the books *Contemporary Violin Technique* (with F. Galamian; 2 vols., N.Y., 1966, 1977), *Violin Left Hand Technique: A Critical Survey of the Literature* (Urbana, Ill., 1969), *Ornamentation in Baroque and Post-Baroque Music* (Princeton, N.J., 1978), *Essays in Performance Practice* (Ann Arbor, Mich., 1982), *Ornamentation and Improvisation in Mozart* (Princeton, N.J., 1986), and *New Essays on Performance Practice* (Ann Arbor, Mich., 1989).

Neumann, Václav, prominent Czech conductor; b. Prague, Sept. 29, 1920. He studied violin with J. Micka and conducting with Pavel Dědeček and Metod Dolež at the Prague Cons. (1940–45). While still a student, he was active as a chamber-music player; became a founding member of the Smetana Quartet (1945); that same year he was made 1st violist of the Czech Phil., making his conducting debut in 1948. He was chief conductor of the Karlovy Vary Sym. Orch. (1951–54) and of the Brno Sym. Orch. (1954–56); then conducted at East Berlin's Komische Oper (1956–64), and concurrently was conductor of Prague's FOK Sym. Orch. From 1964 to 1968 he held the post of 2nd conductor of the Czech Phil.; during that same period, he was the conductor of the Gewandhaus Orch. and Generalmusikdirektor of the Opera in Leipzig; then held the latter post at the Württemberg State Theater in Stuttgart (1969–72). He was chief conductor of the Czech Phil. (1968–89), touring widely with it in Europe and abroad.

Neumann, Věroslav, Czech composer; b. Citoliby, near Louny, May 27, 1931. He studied theory with Jaroslav Řídký at the Prague Academy of Musical Arts (1950–54). After a few works in a traditional style, he adopted the 12-tone method of composition.

WORKS: *Glorie*, radio opera (1970). **ORCH.:** *Panoráma Prahy* (Panorama of Prague) for Baritone and Orch. (1962); *Peace Symphony* (1964); *Ode* (1966); *Pozvánka na koktejl* (Invitation to Cocktails; 1969); *Dedication* for Chamber Orch. (1977); Concerto for Trumpet, Strings, and Tape (1980); *Symphonic Dances* (1982–83). **CHORAL:** *Intervals*, children's choral cycle (1971); *What Is Lovely in the World* for Children's Choir and Orch. (1983); *In Bohemia*, small cantata for Girl's Chorus and Orch. (1984). **CHAMBER:** *Omaggio a Prokofiev* for 2 Violins (1969); String Quartet (1969); *5 Dramatic Sequences* for Cello and Piano (1978); *Syrinx* for 2 Flutes and Piano (1981); also *3 Pieces* for Organ (1977).

Neumann, Werner, respected German musicologist; b. Königstein, Jan. 21, 1905. He studied piano and theory at the Leipzig Cons., and musicology with Kroyer and Zenck at the Univ. of Leipzig (Ph.D., 1938, with the diss. *J.S. Bachs Chorfuge: Ein Beitrag zur Kompositions-Technik Bachs*; publ. in Leipzig, 1938; 2nd ed., 1950), where he also took courses in psychology and philosophy. He taught at the Leipzig Hochschule für Musik; in 1950 he founded the Leipzig Bach Archive, and in 1953 became co-ed. of the *Bach-Jahrbuch* and the Neue Bach-Ausgabe, retiring in 1973. The vol. *Bach-Studien*, V (Leipzig, 1975), was publ. as a Festschrift in his honor.

WRITINGS: *Handbuch der Kantaten Johann Sebastian Bachs* (Leipzig, 1947; 4th ed., 1971); *Auf den Lebenswegen Johann Sebastian Bachs* (Berlin, 1953; 4th ed., 1962); *Johann Sebastian Bach: Sämtliche Kantatatexte* (Leipzig, 1956; 2nd ed., 1967); *Bach: Eine Bildbiographie* (Munich, 1960; 2nd ed., 1961; Eng. tr., 1961, as *Bach and His World*; 2nd ed., 1969); ed. with H.-J. Schulze, *Schriftstücke von der Hand Johann Sebastian Bachs*, Bach-Dokumente, I (Leipzig, 1963); ed. with H.-J. Schulze, *Fremdschriftliche und gedruckte Dokument zur Lebensgeschichte Johann Sebastian Bachs 1685–1750*, Bach-Dokumente, II (Leipzig, 1969); ed. *Bilddokumente zur Lebensgeschichte Johann Sebastian Bachs*, Bach-Dokumente, IV (Leipzig, 1978).

Neumark, Georg, German poet, novelist, viol player, and composer; b. Langensalza, March 3, 1621; d. Weimar, July 8, 1681. He studied in Schleusingen and Gotha; led a wandering life until settling at the Weimar court as a chancellor and librarian. He wrote both sacred and secular poetry, many texts being set to his own music. His most important collection was publ. as *Georg Neumarks. . .Poetisch- und musikalisches Lustwäldchen* (Hamburg, 1652; augmented ed., Jena, 1657, as *Fortepflanzter musikalisch poetischen Lustwald*); his hymns *Wer nur den lieben Gott lässt walten* and *Ich lass Gott in allem walten* have become standard Lutheran chorales, the former being used by Bach in his cantata BWV 197.
BIBL.: F. Knauth, *G. N., Leben und Dichten* (Langensalza, 1881).

Neupert, Edmund, Norwegian-American pianist and pedagogue; b. Christiania, April 1, 1842; d. N.Y., June 22, 1888. He studied at Kullak's Academy in Berlin; then taught there. In 1868 he went to Denmark, where he taught piano at the Copenhagen Cons.; for 2 years he was a piano instructor at the Moscow Cons. (1881–83); then emigrated to the U.S. and settled in N.Y. as a piano teacher. His collections of piano studies were much in use by American teachers.

Neusidler, Hans, eminent German lutenist, lute maker, intabulator, and composer, father of **Melchior Neusidler;** b. Pressburg, c.1508; d. Nuremberg, Feb. 2, 1563. He settled in Nuremberg in 1530; took the oath of citizenship in 1531. In addition to his important vols. of lute music, he was active as a lute maker. He was twice married, and fathered 17 children. Among his intabulations for lute, all of which were publ. in Nuremberg, are *Ein newgeordent künstlich Lautenbuch in zwen Theyl gethylt: Der erst für die anfahenden Schuler* (1536; 20th ed. by H. Mönkemeyer in Die Tabulatur, I, Hofheim am Taunus, 1965), *Ein newes Lautenbüchlein mit vil schonen Liedern* (1540), *Das erst Buch: Ein newes Lautenbüchlein mit vil feiner lieblichen Liedern für die jungen Schuler* (1544), *Das erst Buch: Ein newes Lautenbüchlein mit vil feiner lieblichen Liedern, für die jungen Schuler* (1547), and *Das ander Buch: Ein new künstlich Lauten Buch erst yetzo von newem gemacht für junge und alte Schuler* (1549).

Neusidler, Melchior, distinguished German lutenist, intabulator, and composer, son of **Hans Neusidler;** b. Nuremberg, 1531; d. Augsburg, 1590. Around 1551 he went to Augsburg, where he became a citizen in 1552; was leader of the "stille musica," a group of musicians who played in the residences of the major members of the city; also performed with municipal musicians at public events; was in Italy (1565–66); was in Innsbruck (1580–81). His younger brother, **Conrad Neusidler** (b. Nuremberg [baptized], Feb. 13, 1541; d. Augsburg, c.1604), was also a lutenist and composer; he went to Augsburg in 1562.
WORKS: INTABULATIONS FOR LUTE: *Il primo libro intabolatura di liuto di . . . Neysidler . . . ove sono madrigali, canzon francesi, pass'emezi, saltarelli & alcuni suoi ricercari* (Venice, 1566); *Il secondo libro intabolatura di liuto di Neysidler* (Venice, 1566); *Teütsch Lautenbuch, darinnenn künstliche Muteten, liebliche italianische, frantzösische, teütsch Stuck* (Strasbourg, 1574).

BIBL.: A. Layer, "M. N.," *Lebensbilder aus dem bayerischen Schwaben*, V (1956).

Nevada (real name, **Wixom**), **Emma,** noted American soprano, mother of **Mignon (Mathilde Marie) Nevada;** b. Alpha, near Nevada City, Calif., Feb. 7, 1859; d. Liverpool, June 20, 1940. She studied from 1877 with Marchesi in Vienna; made her operatic debut as Amina at London's Her Majesty's Theatre (May 17, 1880); sang in the leading Italian music centers, including Milan's La Scala (1881). Her 1st appearance in Paris was at the Opéra-Comique, May 17, 1883, as Zora in F. David's *Perle du Brésil*. During the season of 1884–85, she was a member of Col. Mapleson's company at the Academy of Music in N.Y., singing on alternate nights with Patti. She sang in Chicago at the Opera Festival in 1885, and again in 1889. She then sang mostly in Europe; retired in 1910.
BIBL.: W. Armstrong, ed., "Reminiscences of E. N.," *New York Tribune Sunday Magazine* (Oct. 28, 1906).

Nevada, Mignon (Mathilde Marie), American soprano, daughter of **Emma Nevada;** b. Paris (of American parents), Aug. 14, 1886; d. Long Melford, England, June 25, 1971. She studied with her mother; made her debut at the Teatro Costanzi, Rome, as Rosina in *Il Barbiere di Siviglia* in 1907; then sang a season at the Teatro San Carlos in Lisbon; after a season at the Pergola Theater in Florence, she made her London debut at Covent Garden as Ophelia (Oct. 3, 1910), and sang there in subsequent seasons; also appeared at the Théâtre Royal de la Monnaie in Brussels, and (1923) at La Scala in Milan; during World War II, she engaged in war work at Liverpool, England; from 1954, lived in London.

Neveu, Ginette, brilliant French violinist; b. Paris, Aug. 11, 1919; d. in an airplane disaster in San Miguel, Azores Islands, Oct. 28, 1949. She was a grandniece of **Widor;** studied with her mother, making her debut when she was 7 as soloist with the Colonne Orch. in Paris; after further studies at the Cons. there, she won the premier prix at age 11; then completed her training with Enesco and Flesch. She won the Wieniawski Competition (1935), and then embarked on an acclaimed career as a virtuoso, touring Poland and Germany that same year, the Soviet Union (1936), and the U.S. and Canada (1937). After the close of World War II, she made her London debut (1945); then appeared in South America, Boston, and N.Y. (1947). Her tragic death occurred on a flight to the U.S. for a concert tour; her brother, Jean-Paul, a talented pianist and her accompanist, also lost his life. Her performances were notable for their controlled and yet impassioned intensity, ably supported by a phenomenal technique.
BIBL.: M.-J. Ronze-Neveu, *G. N.: La Fulgurante Carrière d'une grande artiste* (Paris, 1952; Eng. tr., London, 1957).

Nevin, Arthur (Finley), American composer and pedagogue, brother of **Ethelbert (Woodbridge) Nevin;** b. Edgeworth, Pa., April 27, 1871; d. Sewickley, Pa., July 10, 1943. He received musical training at home, mainly from his father; then studied at the New England Cons. of Music in Boston (1889–93); in 1893 he went to Berlin, where he studied piano with Klindworth and composition with Boise and Humperdinck. Returning to the U.S., he devoted himself to teaching, research, composition, and conducting; lived with the Blackfoot Indians in Montana (summers, 1903, 1904), and later wrote and lectured on his experiences. He was a prof. of music at the Univ. of Kansas (1915–20) and director of the municipal music dept. of Memphis, Tenn. (1920–22); he settled in Sewickley as a private teacher (1926).
WORKS: *Poia*, opera (Berlin, April 23, 1910); *A Daughter of the Forest*, opera (Chicago, Jan. 5, 1918); *A Night in Yaddo Land*, masque (N.Y., 1900); 2 cantatas: *The Djinns* (N.Y., 1913) and *Roland*; *Bakawali Dances* for Orch.; 3 orch. suites, including *Lorna Doone* and *Love Dreams*; chamber music; piano pieces; songs.

Nevin, Ethelbert (Woodbridge), popular American composer, brother of **Arthur (Finley) Nevin;** b. Edgeworth, Pa., Nov. 25, 1862; d. New Haven, Conn., Feb. 17, 1901. After preliminary musical studies in America, he went to Germany, where he took lessons in singing and piano with Franz Böhme in Dresden (1877–78); returning to the U.S., he studied piano with Benjamin J. Lang and harmony with Stephen A. Emery in Boston (1881–83). In 1884 he went again to Germany to study piano with Karl Klindworth in Berlin (1884–86); then lived in Europe before finally settling in New Haven in 1897. He had a natural talent for melodious songs and piano pieces in a semi-Classical manner. His *The Rosary* (1898) achieved tremendous popularity, selling over a million copies within a decade; another favorite was his song *Mighty Lak' a Rose* (1901); his "Narcissus" from the piano suite *Water Scenes* (1891) was a perennial favorite in American parlors.

WORKS: *Floriane's Dream*, pantomime (N.Y., March 24, 1898); *The Quest*, cantata (1902); choruses; *Captive Memories*, song cycle for Baritone, 4 Voices, and Piano (1899); many other songs; piano suites: *Water Scenes* (1891), *Maggio in Toscana* (1896), and *A Day in Venice* (1898); other piano pieces; etc.

BIBL.: V. Thompson, *The Life of E. N.* (Boston, 1913); F. Rogers, "Some Memories of E. N.," *Musical Quarterly* (July 1917); J. Howard, *E. N.* (N.Y., 1935).

Neway, Patricia, American soprano; b. N.Y., Sept. 30, 1919. She was educated at Notre Dame College for women; received vocal instruction from Morris Gesell, who later became her husband; made her stage debut as Fiordiligi at the Chautauqua Festival in 1946. After several appearances in minor roles, she achieved her 1st significant success as Magda Sorel in Menotti's opera *The Consul* (Philadelphia, March 1, 1950); created the role of the Mother in another Menotti opera, *Maria Golovin*, at the Brussels World's Fair (Aug. 20, 1958). Her repertoire also included parts in operas by Alban Berg and Benjamin Britten.

Newbould, Brian, English musicologist; b. Kettering, Feb. 26, 1936. He studied at the Univ. of Bristol (B.Mus., 1958; M.A., 1961) and was a lecturer at the Royal Scottish Academy of Music in Glasgow (1960–65) and at the Univ. of Leeds (1965–79). He became prof. of music and head of the music dept. at the Univ. of Hull in 1979. He prepared effective realizations of Schubert's Sym. No. 7, D. 729, and Sym. No. "10," D. 936a; also completed the scherzo and trio of Schubert's Sym. No. 8, D. 759, "Unfinished."

Newcomb, Ethel, American pianist; b. Whitney Point, N.Y., Oct. 30, 1875; d. there, July 3, 1959. She went to Vienna in 1895, and studied with Leschetizky until 1903; served as his assistant from 1904 to 1908; made her debut on Feb. 28, 1903, with the Vienna Sym. Orch.; returning to America, she appeared in recitals; then settled at her home in Whitney Point. She publ. *Leschetizky as I Knew Him* (London, 1921).

Newlin, Dika, American writer on music and composer; b. Portland, Oreg., Nov. 22, 1923. She studied piano and theory at Michigan State Univ. (B.A., 1939) and at the Univ. of Calif., Los Angeles (M.A., 1941); later took courses at Columbia Univ. in N.Y. (Ph.D., 1945, with the diss. *Bruckner-Mahler-Schoenberg*; publ. in N.Y., 1947; 2nd ed., rev., 1978); concurrently received instruction in composition from Farwell, Schoenberg, and Sessions, and in piano from Serkin and A. Schnabel. She taught at Western Maryland College (1945–49), Syracuse Univ. (1949–51), Drew Univ. (1952–65), North Tex. State Univ. (1965–73), and Virginia Commonwealth Univ. (from 1978). She ed. and tr. several books by and about Schoenberg; also publ. *Schoenberg Remembered: Diaries and Recollections, 1938–1976* (N.Y., 1980). Her compositions follow the Schoenbergian idiom and include 3 operas, a Sym. for Chorus and Orch., a Piano Concerto, chamber music, piano pieces, and songs.

BIBL.: T. Albrecht, ed., *D. Caecilia: Essays for D. N., November 22, 1988* (Kansas City, Mo., 1988).

Newman, Alfred, American film composer and conductor, uncle of **Randy Newman;** b. New Haven, Conn., March 17, 1900; d. Los Angeles, Feb. 17, 1970. He studied piano with Sigismund Stojowski and composition with Rubin Goldmark; also had private lessons with Schoenberg in Los Angeles. He began his career in vaudeville shows billed as "The Marvelous Boy Pianist"; later, when he led theater orchs. on Broadway, he was hailed as "The Boy Conductor" and "The Youngest Conductor in the U.S." In 1930 he went to Hollywood and devoted himself entirely to writing film music; he wrote about 230 film scores; 45 of this number were nominated for awards of the Motion Picture Academy, and 9 were winners. Among his most successful scores were *The Prisoner of Zenda* (1937), *The Hunchback of Notre Dame* (1939), *Wuthering Heights* (1939), *Captain from Castille* (1947), *The Robe* (1953), and *The Egyptian* (1954; partly written by the original assignee, Bernard Herrmann). Stylistically he followed an eclectic type of theatrical Romanticism, often mimicking, almost literally, the most popular works of Tchaikovsky, Rachmaninoff, Wagner, and Liszt, and amalgamating these elements in colorful free fantasia; in doing so, he created a category of composition that was to become known, with some disdain, as "movie music."

BIBL.: F. Steiner, *The Making of an American Film Composer: A Study of A. N.'s Music in the First Decade of the Sound Era* (diss., Univ. of Southern Calif., 1981).

Newman, Anthony, American harpsichordist, pianist, organist, conductor, and composer; b. Los Angeles, May 12, 1941. He studied piano and organ; in 1959 he went to Paris, where he took courses at the École Normale de Musique with Pierre Cochereau and Nadia Boulanger; returning to the U.S., he studied organ at the Mannes College of Music in N.Y. (B.S., 1962) and composition with Leon Kirchner and Luciano Berio at Harvard Univ. (M.A., 1963); received his D.M.A. from Boston Univ. in 1966. He made his professional debut at Carnegie Hall in N.Y. in 1967, in a recital featuring the pedal harpsichord; subsequently toured widely as a harpsichordist, organist, pianist, and fortepianist. He served on the faculty of the Juilliard School in N.Y. (1968–73), at the State Univ. of N.Y. at Purchase (1968–75), and at the Indiana Univ. School of Music in Bloomington (1978–81); also gave master classes. His own compositions are in a neo-Baroque style. He publ. *Bach and the Baroque: A Performing Guide with Special Emphasis on the Music of J.S. Bach* (N.Y., 1985).

WORKS: ORCH.: Orch. Cycle I (1975); Violin Concerto, composed for the 50th anniversary of the Indianapolis Sym. Orch. (Indianapolis, Oct. 26, 1979); *Sinfonia for a Great Occasion* (Milwaukee, March 25, 1989). **CHAMBER:** Violin Sonata (1976); Cello Sonata (1977); Sonata for Double Bass and Piano (1981); Piano Trio (1980); Piano Quintet (1981). **PIANO:** Piano Cycle I (1976). **ORGAN:** *Bhajeb* (1970); *Symphony in the French Manner* (1979); *Prelude and Contrapunctus* (1981). **GUITAR:** *Variations and Grand Contrapunctus* (1979); Suite for Guitar (1982).

BIBL.: J. Braider, "A. N.: Renaissance Man of the Classical Keyboard," *Contemporary Keyboard* (Dec. 1980).

Newman, Ernest (real name, **William Roberts),** renowned English music critic and writer on music; b. Everton, Lancashire, Nov. 30, 1868; d. Tadworth, Surrey, July 7, 1959. He was educated at Liverpool College and the Univ. of Liverpool; while employed as a bank clerk (1889–1904), he pursued various studies on his own and began to publ. books on music; assumed his *nom de plume* to symbolize an "earnest new man." In 1904 he accepted an instructorship in Birmingham's Midland Inst., and took up music as a profession; in 1905–6 he was in Manchester as critic of the *Guardian;* from 1906 to 1918, in Birmingham as critic for the *Daily Post;* in 1919–20, in London as critic for the *Observer;* from 1920 to 1958, was on the staff of the *London Sunday Times;* from 1923, was also a contributor to the *Glasgow Herald;* in 1924–25, was guest critic of the *N.Y. Evening Post.* One of the best equipped and most influential of English music critics, he continued to write his regular column in the *Sunday Times* in his 90th year.

WRITINGS: All publ. in London: *Gluck and the Opera* (1895); *A Study of Wagner* (1899); *Wagner* (1904); *Musical Studies*

(1905; 3rd ed., 1914); *Elgar* (1906); *Hugo Wolf* (1907); *Richard Strauss* (1908); *Wagner as Man and Artist* (1914; 2nd ed., 1924); *A Musical Motley* (1919); *The Piano-Player and Its Music* (1920); *Confessions of a Musical Critic* (1923); *Solo Singing* (1923); *A Musical Critic's Holiday* (1925); *The Unconscious Beethoven* (1927); *What to Read on the Evolution of Music* (1928); *Stories of the Great Operas* (3 vols., 1929–31); *Fact and Fiction about Wagner* (1931); *The Man Liszt* (1934); *The Life of Richard Wagner* (4 vols., 1933, 1937, 1941, 1946); *Opera Nights* (1943; U.S. ed. as *More Stories of Famous Operas*); *Wagner Nights* (1949; U.S. ed. as *The Wagner Operas*); *More Opera Nights* (1954; U.S. ed. as *17 Famous Operas*); *From the World of Music: Essays from "The Sunday Times"* (selected by F. Aprahamian; London, 1956); *More Musical Essays* (2nd selection from the *Sunday Times*, London, 1958); *Testament of Music* (selected essays; 1962); *Berlioz, Romantic Classic* (ed. by P. Heyworth; 1972). **Bibl.:** H. van Thal, ed., *Fanfare for E. N.* (London, 1955); V. Newman, *E. N.: A Memoir by His Wife* (London, 1963).

Newman, Randy, American societal singer, pianist, and songwriter, nephew of **Alfred Newman;** b. Los Angeles, Nov. 28, 1943. He spent his childhood in southern Calif., where he took regular music lessons. His songs often veered toward the unacceptable, unthinkable, and inconceivable, as while ostensibly attacking the rednecks he used the word "nigger." In 1977 he produced the album *Little Criminals*, which assailed the bigots, but in which one number, *Short People*, was misconstrued as an attack on people short of stature and picayune in mind. As a result, his songs were dropped at some radio stations. He recouped with the album *Born Again* (1979); then brought out the albums *Ragtime* (1981) and *Trouble in Paradise* (1983). He also wrote several film scores.

Newman, William S(tein), distinguished American music scholar; b. Cleveland, April 6, 1912. He studied piano with Riemenschneider and Arthur Loesser; composition with Elwell and Shepherd in Cleveland; received his Ph.D. at Western Reserve Univ. in 1939 with the dissertation *The Present Trend of the Sonata Idea*; then pursued postdoctoral studies with Lang and Hertzmann at Columbia Univ. in 1940; during World War II, he served in the U.S. Army Air Force Intelligence. From 1945 to 1970 he taught at the Univ. of North Carolina at Chapel Hill; became prof. emeritus in 1976. He focused most of his research on the evolution of the instrumental sonata. His chief project was *A History of the Sonata Idea* (Chapel Hill; Vol. I, *The Sonata in the Baroque Era*, 1959; 4th ed., rev., 1983; Vol. II, *The Sonata in the Classic Era*, 1963; 3rd ed., rev., 1983; Vol. III, *The Sonata since Beethoven*, 1969; 3rd ed., rev., 1983). He also publ. *The Pianist's Problems* (N.Y., 1950; 4th ed., 1984), *Understanding Music* (N.Y., 1953; 3rd ed., rev., 1967), *Performance Practices in Beethoven's Piano Sonatas* (N.Y., 1971), and *Beethoven on Beethoven: Playing His Piano Music His Way* (N.Y. and London, 1989). He contributed articles to various reference works and music journals.

Newmarch, Rosa (Harriet) (née **Jeaffreson**), English writer on music; b. Leamington, Dec. 18, 1857; d. Worthing, April 9, 1940. Growing up in an artistic atmosphere, she entered the Hetherley School of Art to study painting, but after a time abandoned that career for literary pursuits; settled in London in 1880 as a contributor to various journals. There she married Henry Charles Newmarch in 1883. She visited Russia in 1897 and many times afterward; established contact with the foremost musicians there; her enthusiasm for Russian music, particularily that of the Russian national school of composition, was unlimited, and she publ. several books on the subject which were of importance to the appreciation of Russian music in England, though her high-pitched literary manner was sometimes maintained to the detriment of factual material. **Writings:** All publ. in London unless otherwise given: *Tchaikovsky: His Life and Works* (1900; 2nd ed., 1908, ed. by E. Evans); *Henry J. Wood* (1904); *The Russian Opera* (1914); *A Quarter of a Century of Promenade Concerts at Queen's Hall* (1928); *The Concert-goer's Library of Descriptive Notes* (6 vols.,

1928–48); *The Music of Czechoslovakia* (Oxford, 1942); *Jean Sibelius* (1944).

Newmark, John (real name, **Hans Joseph Neumark),** German-born Canadian pianist; b. Bremen, June 12, 1904. He studied piano with Karl Boerner in Bremen (1912–19) and Annie Eisele in Leipzig (1920–21). He began his career as an accompanist to Szymon Goldberg (1925); with August Wenzinger, he founded the Neue Kammermusik society in Bremen for the performance of modern music (1929); was director of music programs for the Bremen Radio (1930–33). After going to London (1939), he was interned as an alien (1940), and sent to Canada; after his release, he studied harmony and conducting with Mazzoleni in Toronto (1942). Following World War II, he pursued a far-flung career as an accompanist, traveling all over the world with the most celebrated artists of the day. He became a naturalized Canadian citizen in 1946, and in 1974 was made an Officer of the Order of Canada.

Newsom, Hugh Raymond, American concert manager and composer; b. Cawnpore, India (of American parents), Dec. 20, 1891; d. Baltimore, May 19, 1978. He was taken to America as an infant; studied at the Oberlin (Ohio) Cons. and with Chadwick at the New England Cons. of Music in Boston. He became a successful concert manager; in 1937, married the harpist Marjorie Brunton. In the meantime, he composed industriously, producing works which were disarmingly euphonious in an attractive lyric vein. He wrote an oratorio-drama, *The Divine Tragedy*; several other oratorios; a Harp Concerto (N.Y., Nov. 6, 1968, Brunton soloist); song cycles; character pieces for Piano.

Newton, Ivor, English pianist; b. London, Dec. 15, 1892; d. there, April 21, 1981. He studied piano with Arthur Barclay; then went to Berlin, where he studied lieder with Zur Mühlen and the art of accompaniment with Conraad van Bos. An earnest student of the history of song and the proper role of accompaniment, he became one of the most appreciated piano accompanists of the time, playing at recitals with celebrated singers and instrumentalists, among them Dame Nellie Melba, John McCormack, Fyodor Chaliapin, Kirsten Flagstad, Pablo Casals, Yehudi Menuhin, and Maria Callas. His career, which spanned more than 60 years, is chronicled in his interesting autobiography, *At the Piano—Ivor Newton* (London, 1966). In 1973 he was made a Commander of the Order of the British Empire.

Newton, Wayne, American singer of popular music; b. Roanoke, Va., April 3, 1942. He began his career on television as a pop singer; was then propelled to commercial greatness at the neon-lighted casinos of Las Vegas and other artistically repugnant but monetarily attractive haunts; he also shrewdly invested his lucre in real-estate ventures; his recordings sold into the millions. An additional plus was his loud proclamation of the American virtues of legitimate motherhood, honest capitalism, and right-wing Republicanism.

Newton-John, Olivia, English rock, country-music, and pop singer; b. Cambridge, Sept. 26, 1948. She was taken to Australia as a child; returning to England at the age of 16, she began making appearances as a folksinger; eventually turned to country music. She made her 1st tour of America in 1974, becoming a part of the "Nashville scene." Among her most popular songs were *Have You Never Been Mellow* and *I Honestly Love You*; she also appeared in the highly successful, if tawdry, film *Grease* (1978). In 1988 she brought out the album *The Rumour*.

Ney, Elly, German pianist; b. Düsseldorf, Sept. 27, 1882; d. Tutzing, March 31, 1968. She was a piano student of Leschetizky and Sauer in Vienna; made her debut in Vienna in 1905; gave successful recitals in Europe and America; then devoted herself mainly to teaching; lived mostly in Munich. She was married to **Willem van Hoogstraten** (1911–27); in 1928 she married P.F. Allais of Chicago. She publ. an autobiography, *Ein Leben für die Musik* (Darmstadt, 1952; 2nd ed., 1957, as *Erinnerungen und Betrachtungen; Mein Leben aus der Musik*). **Bibl.:** C. von Pidoll, *E. N.* (Leipzig, 1942); Z. Maurina, *Be-*

gegnung mit E. N. (Memmingen, 1956); E. Valentin, *E. N.,*
Symbol einer Generation (Munich, 1962).

Nezhdanova, Antonina (Vasilievna), distinguished Russian
soprano; b. Krivaya Balka, near Odessa, June 16, 1873; d.
Moscow, June 26, 1950. She studied at the Moscow Cons.
(graduated, 1902); made her debut as Antonida in *A Life for*
the Tsar in Moscow (1902); shortly thereafter, became a principal member of the Bolshoi Theater there, remaining on its
roster for almost 40 years; also appeared in other Russian
music centers, as both an opera singer and a concert singer;
sang Gilda in Paris (1912). She taught at the Stanislavsky
Opera Studio and the Bolshoi Theater Opera Studio (from
1936); was prof. of voice at the Moscow Cons. (from 1943).
Her husband was **Nikolai Golovanov.** She was made a People's Artist of the U.S.S.R. (1936). She was notably successful
in lyric, coloratura, and dramatic roles, her range extending
to high G; in addition to Antonida, she excelled as Tatiana,
Marguerite, Marfa, Lakme, and Juliette. Her memoirs were
publ. posthumously in Moscow (1967).
 Bibl.: M. Lvov, *A.V. N.* (Moscow, 1952); G. Polyanovsky,
A. N. (Moscow, 1970).

Nibelle, Adolphe-André, French composer of operettas; b.
Gien, Loiret, Oct. 9, 1825; d. Paris, March 11, 1895. He wrote
numerous operettas for Paris, the most successful being *Le*
Loup-Garou (1858), *Les Filles du lac* (1858), *L'Arche-Marion*
(1868), *La Fontaine de Berny* (1869), *Le 15 août* (1869), *Les*
Quatre Cents Femmes d'Ali-Baba (1872), and *L'Alibi* (1873);
also publ. *Heures musicales* (24 songs).

Nicholls, Agnes, English soprano; b. Cheltenham, July 14,
1877; d. London, Sept. 21, 1959. She studied singing with
Visetti at the Royal College of Music in London; made her
operatic debut in Manchester on Nov. 20, 1895, as Dido in a
revival of Purcell's opera. From 1901 to 1924 she sang with
the Denhof, Beecham, and British National Opera companies.
On July 15, 1904, she married the conductor **Hamilton Harty.**
She was quite successful in Wagnerian roles; in 1908 she
sang Sieglinde in *Die Walküre* at Covent Garden under the
direction of Hans Richter.

Nichols, "Red" (Ernest Loring), American jazz cornetist
and bandleader; b. Ogden, Utah, May 8, 1905; d. Las Vegas,
June 28, 1965. His father taught him cornet, and he played
in his father's brass band from the age of 12. He then cut a
swath in the world of popular music with his own band, advertised as "Red Nichols and His Five Pennies" (actually, the
number of "Pennies" was 10); among its members were such
future celebrities as Jimmy Dorsey, Benny Goodman, and
Glenn Miller. A maudlin motion picture, *The Five Pennies,*
was manufactured in 1959, and catapulted Nichols into the
stratosphere of jazzdom. Heuristic exegetes of European her-
meneutics bemoaned the commercialization of his style, giving
preference to his earlier, immaculate, jazzification.
 Bibl.: G. Johnson, *The Five Pennies: The Biography of Jazz*
Band Leader R. N. (N.Y., 1959).

Nicholson, George (Thomas Frederick), English composer
and pianist; b. Great Lumley, Sept. 24, 1949. He was educated
at the Univ. of York (B.A. in English and music, 1971; Ph.D.
in composition, 1979), his mentors in music being Bernard
Rands and David Blake. He then was active as a teacher and
performer; from 1988 he served as lecturer in music and director of composition at the Univ. of Keele.
 Works: ORCH.: *1132* (1976); *The Convergence of the Twain*
for Chamber Orch. (1978); Chamber Concerto for 13 Instruments (1979–80); *Sea-Change* for 14 Strings (1988). **CHAMBER:**
Recycle for 11 Instruments (1975–76); 2 string quartets (1976–
77; 1984–85); Brass Quintet (1977); *Winter Music* for Clarinet,
Harp, and Percussion (1978); *Ancient Lights* for 7 Instruments
(1982); *Sound Progressions Newly Minted* for Brass Quintet
(1983); *Piano Sonata* (1983); *Stilleven* for 5 Instruments
(1985); *Romanza* for Violin and Piano (1987); *All Systems Go*
for Piano (1989). **VOCAL:** *Alla Luna* for Soprano, Clarinet, and
Piano (1981); *Aubade* for Soprano and 5 Instruments (1981);
The Arrival of the Poet in the City for Narrator and 7 Instru-

ments (1982–83); *A World of Imagination* for Chorus (1984);
Blisworth Tunnel Blues for Soprano and Chamber Orch. (1986–
87); songs.

Nicodé, Jean-Louis, German pianist, conductor, and composer; b. Jerczik, near Posen, Aug. 12, 1853; d. Langebrück,
near Dresden, Oct. 5, 1919. He was taught by his father and
by the organist Hartkäs; in 1869, entered Kullak's Academy
in Berlin, where he studied piano with Kullak, harmony with
Wüerst, and counterpoint and composition with Kiel. He made
a concert tour (1878) with Artôt through Galicia and Rumania;
from 1878 to 1885, was a piano teacher at the Dresden Cons.,
and from 1885 to 1888, was conductor of the Dresden Phil.;
established the Nicodé Concerts in 1893, and, in order to enlarge their scope by the production of larger choral works,
formed the Nicodé Chorus in 1896. In 1900 he abandoned
these concerts, retired to Langebrück, and devoted himself
to composition. He wrote 2 expansive symphonic works: *Das*
Meer for Soloists, Men's Voices, Orch., and Organ (1889) and
Gloria! ein Sturm- und Sonnenlied for Boy's Voices, Men's
Voices, Orch., and Organ (1905); several other symphonic
works; some chamber music; songs; piano pieces.
 Bibl.: T. Schäfer, *J.-L. N.: Ein Versuch kritischer Würdigung*
und Erläuterung seines Schaffens (Berlin, 1907); O. Taubmann,
J.-L. N., (Leipzig, 1909).

Nicolai, (Carl) Otto (Ehrenfried), famous German composer and conductor; b. Königsberg, June 9, 1810; d. Berlin,
May 11, 1849. He studied piano at home; in 1827 he went
to Berlin, where he took lessons in theory with Zelter; he
also took courses with Bernhard Klein at the Royal Inst. for
Church Music. On April 13, 1833, he made his concert debut
in Berlin as a pianist, singer, and composer. He then was
engaged as organist to the embassy chapel in Rome by the
Prussian ambassador, Bunsen. While in Italy, he also studied
counterpoint with Giuseppe Baini. In 1837 he proceeded to
Vienna, where he became a singing teacher and Kapellmeister
at the Kärnthnertortheater. In 1838 he returned to Italy; on
Nov. 26, 1839, he presented in Trieste his 1st opera, *Rosmonda*
d'Inghilterra, given under its new title as *Enrico II.* His 2nd
opera, *Il Templario,* was staged in Turin on Feb. 11, 1840.
In 1841 he moved to Vienna, where he was appointed court
Kapellmeister in succession to Kreutzer. Nicolai was instrumental in establishing sym. concerts utilizing the musicians
of the orch. of the Imperial Court Opera Theater; on March
28, 1842, he conducted this ensemble featuring Beethoven's
7th Sym.; this became the inaugural concert of the celebrated
Vienna Phil. In 1848 he was appointed Kapellmeister of the
Royal Opera in Berlin. On March 9, 1849, his famous opera
Die lustigen Weiber von Windsor, after Shakespeare, was given
at the Berlin Royal Opera; it was to become his only enduring
creation. Nicolai died 2 months after its production. In 1887
Hans Richter, then conductor of the Vienna Phil., inaugurated
an annual "Nicolai-Konzert" in his memory, and it became a
standard occasion. It was conducted by Gustav Mahler (1899–
1901); by Felix Weingartner (1909–27); by Wilhelm Furtwängler (1928–31, 1933–44, and 1948–54); by Karl Böhm (1933–
57 and 1964–80); and by Claudio Abbado in 1980 and 1983.
 Works: OPERAS: *Enrico II* (original title, *Rosmonda d'In-*
ghilterra; Trieste, Nov. 26, 1839); *Il Templario* (Turin, Feb. 11,
1840; rev. as *Der Tempelritter,* Vienna, Dec. 20, 1845); *Gildippe*
ed Odoardo (Genoa, Dec. 26, 1840); *Il proscritto* (Milan, March
13, 1841; rev. as *Die Heimkehr des Verbannten,* Vienna, Feb.
3, 1846); *Die lustigen Weiber von Windsor* (Berlin, March 9,
1849). **SACRED:** *Pater noster* for 8 Voices, op. 33; *In assumptione*
Beatae Mariae Virginis, offertory for 5 Voices, op. 38; *Salve re-*
gina for Soprano and Orch., op. 39; *Te Deum* for Solo Voices,
4 Voices, and Orch.; *Mass in D major* for 4 Solo Voices, 4
Voices, and Orch.; Psalms, motets, etc. **SECULAR CHORAL:** *Preus-*
sens Stimme for 4 Voices and Orch., op. 4; *6 lieder* for 4 Voices,
op. 6; *Verschiedene Empfindungen an einem Platz* for Soprano,
2 Tenors, Bass, and Piano, op. 9; *3 Königslieder der älteren*
Berliner Liedertafel for 4 Male Voices, op. 10; *Gesänge* for 4
Male Voices, op. 17; etc. **ORCH.:** *In morte di Vincenzo Bellini,*

a funeral march; syms.: No. 1, in C minor (1831), and No. 2, in D major (1835; rev. 1845); *Kirchliche Festouvertüre über . . . Ein feste Burg* for 4 Voices, Organ, and Orch., op. 32 (1844); *Weihnachtsouvertüre über Vom Himmel hoch* for 4 Voices ad libitum and Orch. Also chamber music; solo songs.

BIBL.: H. Mendel, *O. N.: Eine Biographie* (Berlin, 1866; 2nd ed., 1868); B. Schröder, ed., *O. N.: Tagebücher nebst biographischen Ergänzungen* (Leipzig, 1892); "O. N.s Briefe aus den Jahren 1832–48," *Deutsche Rundschau* (Jan. 1897); G. Kruse, "Falstaff und Die lustigen Weiber," *Die Musik*, VI/4 (1906–7); idem, "O. N. als Sinfoniker," *Allgemeine Musik-Zeitung*, XXXV (1908); idem, "Goethe, Zelter und O. N.," *Goethe-Jahrbuch*, XXXI (1910); idem, "O. N.s italienische Opern," *Sammelbände der Internationalen Musik-Gesellschaft*, XII/2 (1910–11); idem, *O. N.: Ein Künstlerleben* (Berlin, 1911); idem, *O. N.s musikalische Aufsätze* (Regensburg, 1913); W. Altmann, ed., *O. N.: Briefe an seinen Vater* (Regensburg, 1924); G. Kruse, "O. N.s 'Lustigen Weiber' . . . mit unbekannt gebliebenen Nummern," *Die Musik*, XXVIII (1936); W. Altmann, ed., *O. N.s Tagebücher* (Regensburg, 1937); E. Schliepe, "Das wiederentdeckte 'Tedeum' von O. N.," *Die Musik*, XXXI (1939); W. Jerger, ed., *O. N.: Briefe an die Wiener Philharmoniker* (Vienna, 1942); H. Kraus and K. Schreinzer, eds., *Wiener Philharmoniker 1842–1942* (Vienna, 1942); A. Würz, "O. N.: Eine Betrachtung zu seinem Gedenken," *Neue Musikzeitschrift* (April 1949); J. Klein, "Verdi and N.: A Strange Rivalry," *Music Review*, XXXII (1971); U. Konrad, *O. N., 1810–1849: Studien zu Leben und Werk* (Baden-Baden, 1986).

Nicolau, Antonio, Catalan composer and conductor; b. Barcelona, June 8, 1858; d. there, Feb. 26, 1933. He studied in Barcelona with Balart and Pujol; also in Paris, where he lived for 8 years; then became conductor of the Sociedad de Conciertos de Barcelona, with which he gave many important 1st performances in Spain; was director of the Barcelona Municipal Music School from 1896 and teacher of many of the leading Catalan musicians, including Lamote de Grignon.

WORKS: OPERAS: *La tempestad* (Barcelona, 1877); *Constanza* (Barcelona, 1878); *Corazon de fuego* (Madrid, 1878); *Un rapto* (Madrid, 1887); also *Athalia*, sym. (1876); *El triunfo de Venus*, symphonic poem (Paris, 1882); many choral works.

Nicolet, Aurèle, prominent Swiss flutist and pedagogue; b. Neuchâtel, Jan. 22, 1926. He was educated in Zürich and Paris; then played flute in Swiss orchs.; later joined the Berlin Phil. (1950–59). He was a prof. at the Berlin Hochschule für Musik (1953–65); then taught at the Hochschule für Musik in Freiburg; also gave summer classes at the Salzburg Mozarteum. Apart from his activities as a pedagogue, he developed a wide international career giving concerts as a soloist with orchs., recitalist, and chamber-music player.

Nicolini (real name, **Ernest Nicolas**), French tenor; b. Saint-Malo, Feb. 23, 1834; d. Pau, Jan. 19, 1898. He studied at the Paris Cons. In July 1857 he made his operatic debut in Halévy's *Les Mousquetaires de la Reine* at the Paris Opéra-Comique, and then sang there until 1859. He subsequently studied in Italy, where he adopted the name Nicolini and appeared at Milan's La Scala in 1859–60. Returning to Paris, he was a member of the Théâtre-Italien (1862–69); on May 29, 1866, he made his debut at London's Covent Garden as Edgardo opposite Patti's Lucia. He returned to London to sing at Drury Lane (1871) and at Covent Garden (1872–84); toured Europe, the U.S., and South America with Patti, marrying her on Aug. 10, 1886; that same year he bade his farewell to the operatic stage as Almaviva in *Il barbiere di Siviglia* at Drury Lane. Among his finest roles were Roméo and Faust.

Nicolini (real name, **Nicolo Grimaldi**), renowned Italian castrato alto; b. Naples (baptized), April 5, 1673; d. there, Jan. 1, 1732. He studied with Provenzale in Naples, making his debut there as a page in his *La Stellidaura vendicata* (1685); then entered the Cappella del Tesoro di S. Gennaro at Naples Cathedral (1690) and the Naples Royal Chapel (1691); he appeared in opera in Naples (1697–1724); also in Venice

(1700–1731), being made a Knight of the Order of San Marco (1705). He made his London debut at the Queen's Theatre in Haym's arrangement of A. Scarlatti's *Pirroe Demetrio* (Dec. 14, 1708), and subsequently was its leading singer until 1712; he created Handel's Rinaldo (Feb. 24, 1711). He returned to London to create Handel's Amadigi (May 25, 1715), singing there until 1717. He then pursued his career in his homeland, remaining active until his death. At the zenith of his career, he was held in the highest esteem by his contemporaries, being celebrated for his remarkable vocal gifts and dramatic abilities.

BIBL.: E. Faustini-Fasini, "Gli astri maggiori del 'bel canto' napolitano: Il Cav. Nicola Grimaldi detto 'Nicolini'," *Note d'archivio per la storia musicale*, XII (1935).

Niculescu, Ştefan, Rumanian composer and musicologist; b. Moreni, July 31, 1927. He studied at the Bucharest Cons. with Mihail Jora, Ion Dumitrescu, Tudor Ciortea, Theodor Rogalski, and others; attended the summer courses on advanced music in Darmstadt; also worked in an electronic studio in Munich (1966); from 1963, was on the staff of the Bucharest Cons. In his music he follows the median course of serialism, without excluding tonality. He publ. a monograph on Georges Enesco (Bucharest, 1971) and several analytic articles on the music of Webern, Xenakis, Boulez, Ligeti, and Cage.

WORKS: STAGE: *Cartea cu "Apolodor,"* opera (1975); *Le Prince né des larmes*, ballet (1982). **ORCH.:** 3 syms.: No. 1 (1955–56); No. 2, *Opus Dacicum* (1978–80); No. 3, *Cantos* (1984); *Hétéromorphie* (1967); *Formants* for 17 Solo Strings (1968); *Unisonos I* (Mainz, Sept. 26, 1970); *Unisonos II* (Graz, Oct. 17, 1972); *Ison II*, concerto for Winds and Percussion (1975–76); *Synchrony II, Omaggio a Enescu e Bartók* (1981). **CHAMBER:** Clarinet Sonata (1954–55); String Trio (1957; rev. 1976); *Inventions* for Clarinet and Piano (1963); *Inventions* for Viola and Piano (1965); *Triplum I* for Flute, Cello, and Piano (1971); *Ison I*, variations for 14 Instrumental Soloists (1971); *Triplum II* for Clarinet, Cello, and Piano (1972); *Synchrony I* for 2 to 12 Instruments (1979); *Echoes II* for Violin and Synthesizer (1984); *Octuplum* for 8 Instruments (1985); piano pieces; numerous vocal works, including *Fragments I* for Voices and Instruments (1976) and *Fragments II and III* for Voices and Solo Instruments (1977).

Niecks, Frederick (actually, **Friedrich**), German-English writer on music; b. Düsseldorf, Feb. 3, 1845; d. Edinburgh, June 24, 1924. He studied the violin under Langhans, Grünewald, and Auer, and composition with J. Tausch; made his debut (as a violinist) at Düsseldorf in 1857; until 1867 he was a member of the orch. there, the last years as concertmaster; in 1868, became organist at Dumfries, Scotland, and viola player in a quartet with A.C. Mackenzie. After teaching at the Univ. of Leipzig (1877–78) and travels in Italy, he won a position in London as critic for the *Monthly Musical Record* and *Musical Times*; in 1891, was appointed Reid Prof. of Music at Edinburgh Univ. In 1901 Niecks founded the Music Education Society. He was made a Mus.Doc. (*honoris causa*) by Dublin Univ. in 1898; LL.D. by Edinburgh Univ. After his retirement in 1914, he lived in Edinburgh.

WRITINGS: All publ. in London unless otherwise given: *A Concise Dictionary of Musical Terms* (2nd ed., 1884; 5th ed., rev. and enl., 1900); *Frederick Chopin as a Man and Musician* (1888; 3rd ed., 1902); *Musical Education and Culture* (Edinburgh, 1892); *Programme Music in the Last Four Centuries* (1907); *Robert Schumann* (ed. by C. Niecks; 1925).

Niedermeyer, (Abraham) Louis, Swiss composer; b. Nyon, April 27, 1802; d. Paris, March 14, 1861. He was a pupil in Vienna of Moscheles (piano) and Förster (composition); in 1819, of Fioravanti in Rome and Zingarelli in Naples. He lived in Geneva as an admired song composer, and settled in Paris in 1823; there he brought out 4 unsuccessful operas (*La casa nel bosco*, May 28, 1828; *Stradella*, March 3, 1837; *Marie Stuart*, Dec. 6, 1844; *La Fronde*, May 2, 1853). He then bent his energies to sacred composition, and reorganized Choron's Inst. for Church Music as the École Niedermeyer, which eventually became a flourishing inst. with government subvention; he also founded (with d'Ortigue) a journal for church music, *La Maîtrise* (1857–61); they also publ. *Traité théorique et pratique de l'accompagnement du plain-chant* (Paris, 1857; 2nd ed., 1876; Eng. tr., N.Y., 1905). He wrote masses, motets, hymns, romances (*Le Lac; Le Soir; La Mer; L'Automne;* etc.), organ preludes, piano pieces, etc.

BIBL.: A. Niedermeyer, *L. N.: Son œuvre et son école* (Paris, n.d.); *Vie d'un compositeur moderne* (by Niedermeyer's son; Fontainebleau, 1892); M. Galerne, *L'École N.* (Paris, 1928).

Nielsen, Alice, American soprano; b. Nashville, Tenn., June 7, 1868?; d. N.Y., March 8, 1943. She was of partly Danish, partly Irish extraction; sang in a church choir in Kansas City; then joined the Burton Stanley Opera Co., where she sang in operettas; she made her debut as a grand-opera singer in Naples as Marguerite in *Faust* (Dec. 6, 1903); made her 1st American appearance in N.Y. (Nov. 10, 1905). In 1908 she toured with the San Carlo Co. in the U.S.; then achieved the status of a prima donna with the Boston Opera Co. (1909–13) and also sang with the Metropolitan Opera. She eventually settled in N.Y. as a singing teacher.

Nielsen, Carl (August), greatly significant Danish composer; b. Sortelung, near Nørre-Lyndelse, June 9, 1865; d. Copenhagen, Oct. 3, 1931. He received violin lessons in childhood from his father and the local schoolteacher; played 2nd violin in the village band, and later in its amateur orch. After studying cornet with his father, he played in the Odense military orch. (1879–83), serving as its signal horn and alto trombone player; also taught himself to play piano. While in Odense, he began to compose, producing several chamber pieces; then received financial assistance to continue his training at the Royal Cons. in Copenhagen, where he studied violin with V. Tofte, theory with J.P.E. Hartmann and Orla Rosenhoff, and music history with N. Gade and P. Matthison-Hansen (1884–86). He was a violinist in Copenhagen's Royal Chapel Orch. (1889–1905); in the interim, he achieved his 1st success as a composer with his *Little Suite* for Strings (1888); then continued private studies with Rosenhoff for a number of years. In 1901 he was granted an annual pension; he was conductor of the Royal Theater (1908–14) and the Musikföreningen (1915–27) in Copenhagen; also appeared as a guest conductor in Germany, the Netherlands, Sweden, and Finland; taught theory and composition at the Royal Cons. (1916–19), being appointed its director a few months before his death. The early style of Nielsen's music, Romantic in essence, was determined by the combined influences of Gade, Grieg, Brahms, and Liszt, but later on he experienced the powerful impact of modern music, particularly in harmony, which in his works grew more and more chromatic and dissonant; yet he reserved the simple diatonic progressions, often in a folk-song manner, for his major climaxes; in his orchestration he applied opulent sonorities and colorful instrumental counterpoint; there are instances of bold experimentation in some of his works, as, for example, the insertion of a snare-drum solo in his 5th Sym., playing independently of the rest of the orch.; he attached somewhat mysterious titles to his 3rd and 4th syms. (*Expansive* and *Inextinguishable*). Nielsen is sometimes described as the Sibelius of Denmark, despite obvious dissimilarities in idiom and sources of inspiration; while the music of Sibelius is deeply rooted in national folklore, both in subject matter and melodic derivation, Nielsen seldom drew on Danish popular modalities; Sibelius remained true to the traditional style of composition, while Nielsen sought new ways of modern expression. It was only after his death that Nielsen's major works entered the world repertoire; festivals of his music were organized on his centennial in 1965, and his syms. in particular were played and recorded in England and America, bringing him belated recognition as one of the most important composers of his time. In 1988 Queen Margrethe II dedicated the Carl Nielsen Museum in Odense. His writings include *Levende musik* (Copenhagen, 1925; Eng. tr. as *Living Music*, London, 1953) and *Min fynske barndom* (Copenhagen, 1927; Eng. tr. as *My Childhood*, London, 1953).

WORKS: (all 1st perf. in Copenhagen unless otherwise given): **STAGE:** *Saul og David*, opera (1898–1901; Nov. 28, 1902); *Maskarade*, opera (1904–6; Nov. 11, 1906); *Snefrid*, melodrama (1893; April 10, 1894; rev. 1899); incidental music to A. Munch's *En aften paa Giske* (1889; Jan. 15, 1890), G. Wied's *Atalanta* (Dec. 19, 1901), Drachmann's *Hr. Oluf han rider*— (Master Oluf Rides—; Oct. 9, 1906), L. Holstein's *Tove* (1906–8; March 20, 1908), L. Nielsen's *Willemoes* (1907–8; Feb. 7, 1908), O. Benzon's *Foraeldre* (Feb. 9, 1908), J. Aakjaer's *Ulvens søn* (Århus, Nov. 14, 1909), A. Oehlenschlaeger's *Hagbarth og Signe* (June 4, 1910), Oehlenschlaeger's *Sankt Hansaftenspil* (June 3, 1913), Christiansen's *Faedreland* (1915; Feb. 5, 1916), H. Rode's prologue to the Shakespeare Memorial Celebrations (Elsinore, June 24, 1916), J. Sigurjónsson's *Løgneren* (Feb. 15, 1918), Oehlenschlaeger's *Aladdin*, op. 34 (1918–19; Feb. 15 and 22, 1919), Rode's *Moderen*, op. 41 (1920; Jan. 30, 1921), Christiansen's *Cosmus* (1921–22; Feb. 25, 1922), H. Bergstedt's *Ebbe Skammelsen* (June 25, 1925), S. Michaelis's *Amor og Digteren*, op. 54 (Odense, Aug. 12, 1930), and N. Grundtvig's *Paaske-aften* (April 4, 1931).

ORCH.: 6 syms.: No. 1, op. 7 (1890–92; March 14, 1894); No. 2, op. 16, *Die fire temperamenter* (The 4 Temperaments; Dec. 1, 1902); No. 3, op. 27, *Sinfonia espansiva* (1910–11; Feb. 28, 1912); No. 4, op. 29, *Det uudslukkelige* (The Inextinguishable; 1914–16; Feb. 1, 1916); No. 5, op. 50 (Jan. 24, 1922); No. 6, *Sinfonia semplice* (Dec. 11, 1925); *Little Suite* for Strings, op. 1 (Sept. 8, 1888; rev. 1889); *Symphonic Rhapsody* (1888; Feb. 24, 1893; not extant); *Helios*, overture, op. 17 (Oct. 8, 1903); *Saga-drøm* (Dream of Saga), op. 39 (April 6, 1908); Violin Concerto, op. 33 (1911; Feb. 28, 1912); paraphrase on "Naermere Gud til dig" ("Near My God to Thee") for Wind Orch. (1912; Aug. 22, 1915); *Pan og Syrinx*, op. 49, pastorale (Feb. 11, 1918); Flute Concerto (Paris, Oct. 21, 1926); *En fantasirejse til Faerøerne* (A Fantasy-Journey to the Faroe Islands), rhapsodic overture (Nov. 27, 1927); Clarinet Concerto, op. 57 (Humlebaek, Sept. 14, 1928); *Bohmisk-Dansk folketone* (Bohemian and Danish Folk Tunes), paraphrase for Strings (Nov. 1, 1928).

CHORAL: *CANTATAS:* For the Lorens Frølich Festival (1900), the Students' Assoc. (1901), the anniversary of the Univ. of Copenhagen, op. 24 (1908), the commemoration of Feb. 11, 1659 (1909), the national exhibition in Århus (1909; in collaboration with E. Bangert), the commemoration of P. Krøyer (1909), the centenary of the Merchants' Committee (1917), the centenary of the Polytechnic High School (1929), the 50th anniversary of the Danish Cremation Union (1930), the 50th anniversary of the Young Merchants' Education Assoc. (1930), and *Digtning i sang og toner*, for the opening of the swimming baths (1930); *Hymnus amoris* for Soprano, Tenor, Baritone, Chorus, and Orch., op. 12 (April 27, 1897); *Søvnen* (Sleep) for Chorus and Orch., op. 18 (1903–4; March 21, 1905); *Fynsk foraar* (Springtime in Funen), lyrical humoresque for Soprano, Tenor, Bass, Chorus, and Orch., op. 42 (1921; Odense, July 8, 1922); *Hyldest til Holberg* for Solo Voices, Chorus, and Orch. (1922); *Hymne til kunsten* for Soprano, Tenor, Chorus, and Wind Orch. (1929). *UNACCOMPANIED CHORAL:* *Sidskensang* (1906); *Kom Guds engel* (1907); *Aftenstemning* (1908); *Paaskeliljen* (1910); *Der er et yndigt land* (1924); 2 school songs (1929); 3 Motets, op. 55 (1929; April 30, 1930); *Til min fødeø* (1929); 6 Rounds (1930); etc. *SOLO VOCAL:* 2 melodramas: *Franz Neruda in memoriam* for Speaker and Orch. (1915) and *Island* for Speaker and Piano (1929). *SONGS:* 5 Songs, op. 4 (1891); *Viser og vers*, op. 6 (1891); 6 Songs, op. 10 (1894); *Du danske mand* (1906); Strophic Songs, op. 21 (1902–7); *De unges sang* (1909); Hymns and Sacred Songs (1913–14); 20 Danish Songs (vol. I, 1914; in collaboration with T. Laub); 20 Danish Songs (vol. II, 1914–17; in collaboration with Laub); *Studie efter naturen* (1916); *Blomstervise* (1917); 20 Popular Melodies (1917–21); 4 Popular Melodies (1922); *Balladen om bjørnen*, op. 47 (1923); 10 Little Danish Songs (1923–24); 4 Jutish Songs (1924–25); *Vocalise-étude* (1927); etc.

CHAMBER: 5 string quartets: (1882–83); op. 13 (1887–88; rev. 1897–98); op. 5 (1890); op. 14 (1897–98); *Piacevolezza,* op. 19 (1906; rev. as the Quartet in F major, op. 44, 1919); Piano Trio (1883); String Quintet for 2 Violins, 2 Violas, and Cello (1888); *Ved en ung kunstners baare* (At the Bier of a Young Artist) for String Quartet and Double Bass (1910); *Serenata in vano* for Clarinet, Bassoon, Horn, Cello, and Double Bass (1914); Wind Quintet, op. 43 (1922); Sonata No. 1 for Violin and Piano (1881–82); Sonata for Violin and Piano, op. 9 (1895); Sonata No. 2 for Violin and Piano, op. 35 (1912); Duet for 2 Violins (1882–83); *Fantasistykke* for Clarinet and Piano (c.1885); 2 *Fantasistykker* for Oboe and Piano, op. 2 (1889); *Canto serioso* for Horn and Piano (1913); Prelude and Theme with Variations for Violin, op. 48 (1923); *Preludio e presto* for Violin, op. 52 (1927–28); *Allegretto* for 2 Recorders (1931).

KEYBOARD: *PIANO:* 2 character pieces (1882–83); 5 pieces, op. 3 (1890); *Symphonic Suite,* op. 8 (1894); *Humoreske-bagateller,* op. 11 (1894–97); *Fest-praeludium:* "Ved Aarhundredskiften" (1900); *Drømmen om "Glade Jul"* (1905); Chaconne, op. 32 (1916); Theme and Variations, op. 40 (1917); Suite "Den Luciferiske," op. 45 (1919–20); 3 pieces, op. 59 (1928); *Klaviermusik for smaa og store,* op. 53 (2 vols., 1930). **ORGAN:** 29 Little Preludes, op. 51 (1929); 2 Preludes (1930); *Commotio,* op. 58 (1931).

BIBL.: H. Seligmann, *C. N.* (Copenhagen, 1931); K. Jeppesen, "C. N.: A Danish Composer," *Music Review* (1946); T. Meyer and F. Schandorf Petersen, *C. N.: Kunstneren og mennesket* (2 vols., Copenhagen, 1947–48); H. Riis-Vestergaard, *C. N.s symfoniske stil, dens forudsaetninger og saerpraeg* (diss., Univ. of Copenhagen, 1952); I. Møller and T. Meyer, eds., *C. N.s breve i udvalg og med kommentarer* (Copenhagen, 1954); K. Jeppesen, "C. N. paa hundredaarsdagen: Nogle erindringer," *Dansk aarbog for musikforskning,* IV (1964–65); J. Balzer, ed., *C. N. i hundredåret for hans fødsel* (Copenhagen, 1965; Eng. tr., 1965); J. Fabricius, *C. N. 1865–1931: A Pictorial Biography* (Copenhagen, 1965); D. Fog and T. Schousboe, *C. N.: kompositioner: En bibliografi* (Copenhagen, 1965); R. Simpson, "C. N. and Tonality," *Dansk musiktidsskrift,* XL (1965); idem, *Sibelius and N.: A Centenary Essay* (London, 1965); A. Telmányi, *Mit barndomschjem* (Copenhagen, 1965); J. Waterhouse, "N. Reconsidered," *Musical Times,* CVI (1965); T. Schousboe, ed., *C. N.: Dagbøger og brevvesling med Anna Marie Carl Nielsen* (2 vols., Copenhagen, 1983); M. Miller, *C. N.: A Guide to Research* (N.Y., 1987).

Nielsen, (Carl Henrik) Ludolf, Danish violist, conductor, and composer; b. Nørre-Tvede, Jan. 29, 1876; d. Copenhagen, Oct. 16, 1939. He was a pupil of V. Tofte (violin), A. Orth (piano), Bondesen (harmony), and O. Malling and J.P.E. Hartmann (composition) at the Copenhagen Cons. (1896–98); then was a violist at the Tivoli and violist and deputy conductor at the Palekoncerter. He won the Ancker stipend and traveled in Germany, Austria, and Italy (1907); later played in the Bjørvig Quartet; subsequently was conductor of the musical society Euphrosyne (1914–20). His music represents an expansive late Romantic style.

WORKS: OPERAS: *Isbella* (Copenhagen, Oct. 8, 1915); *Uhret* (The Clock; 1911–13); *Lola* (1917–20). **BALLETS:** *Lackschmi* (1921; Copenhagen, March 4, 1922); *Rejsekammeraten* (1928); also incidental music to plays; music for radio. **ORCH.:** 3 syms.: No. 1, op. 3 (1903); No. 2, op. 19 (1909; Copenhagen, April 25, 1910); No. 3, op. 32 (1913; Copenhagen, May 4, 1914); other orch. works. **CHAMBER:** 3 string quartets (1900, 1904, 1920); also choral works; songs; piano pieces; organ music.

Nielsen, Ludwig, Norwegian organist, conductor, and composer; b. Borge in Østfold, Feb. 3, 1906. He studied with Sandvold and Lange at the Oslo Cons., then with Straube, Raphael, and Hochkofler at the Leipzig Cons. (1931–32) and with Steenberg and Walle-Hansen in Oslo. He was organist at the Høvik Church, Baerum, Akershus (1924–32), and organist and choirmaster at Trondheim Cathedral (1935–76); also taught at the Oslo Cons. (1934–35) and the Trondheim Music School (from 1942). He distinguished himself primarily as a composer of sacred music. Among his organ works are a Concerto for Organ and Strings (1965), chorales, fugues, fantasies, and other pieces; his choral works include a *Te Deum* (1944–45), the oratorio *Draumkvedet* (1962), and motets.

BIBL.: B. Moe, *L. N.* (diss., Univ. of Trondheim, 1974).

Nielsen, Riccardo, Italian composer; b. Bologna, March 3, 1908; d. Ferrara, Jan. 30, 1982. He studied with Alfredo Casella and Carlo Gatti; began composing in the Italian Baroque manner but eventually made a decisive turn toward the 12-tone technique of composition. He occupied various administrative and teaching positions; from 1946 to 1950, was director of the Teatro Comunale in Bologna; in 1952, became director of the Liceo Frescobaldi in Ferrara, where he also taught composition. He publ. a theoretical work, *Le forme musicali* (Bologna, 1961).

WORKS: *Sinfonia concertante* for Piano and Orch. (1932); Violin Concerto (1932); *Divertimento* for Clarinet, Bassoon, Trumpet, Violin, Viola, and Cello (1934); Concerto for Orch. (1935); *Musica per archi* (1946); monodrama, *L'Incubo* (Venice, 1948); radio opera, *La via di Colombo* (1953); *Variations* for Orch. (1956); *Requiem nella miniera* (1957); *Invenzioni e sinfonie* for Soprano and Orch. (1959); *Varianti* for Orch. (1965); *6 + 5 fasce sonore* for Strings (1968); Piano Quartet (1961); *7 aforismi* for Clarinet and Piano (1958); Cello Sonata (1958); *Cadenza a due* for Cello and Piano (1967); Chamber Cantata for Voice, Women's Chorus, and Instruments (1969); *Ganymed* for Soprano, Clarinet, Cello, and Piano (1958); *4 poesie di Apollinaire* for Voice and Piano (1961).

Nielsen, Svend, Danish composer; b. Copenhagen, April 20, 1937. He studied music theory with Vagn Holmboe at the Royal Danish Cons. of Music in Copenhagen, graduating in 1967; then continued to take lessons in advanced composition with Per Nørgård; in 1969 he became an instructor at the Royal Danish Cons. of Music in Copenhagen. Among his works are *Duetter* for Soprano, Contralto, Flute, Cello, Vibraphone, and Percussion (1964); *Prisma-suite* for Contralto, Flute, Viola, and Strings (1965); *Metamorfoser* for 23 Solo Strings (1968); chamber opera, *Bulen* (1968); *Nuages* for Orch. (1972); Sym. (1978–79); Violin Concerto (1985).

Nielsen, Tage, Danish composer, pedagogue, and administrator; b. Copenhagen, Jan. 16, 1929. He studied musicology at the Univ. of Copenhagen (M.A., 1955), but was mainly autodidact as a composer. In 1951 he joined the staff of the Danish Radio in Copenhagen, serving as deputy head of its music dept. (1957–63); then was director (1963–83) and a prof. (1964–83) at the Århus Academy of Music; subsequently was director of the Danish Academy in Rome (1983–89). In his 1st mature works, he composed along the lines of the modern Darmstadt school; after writing in the style of the Danish New Simplicity mode, he adopted a neo-Romantic means of expression.

WORKS: ORCH.: *Intermezzo gaio* (1952; rev. 1963); *4 miniaturer* for String Orch. (1963); *Bariolage* (1965; Århus, Feb. 7, 1966); *Il giardino magico* (1967–68; Århus, Feb. 24, 1969); *Lamento* (1978); *Passacaglia* (1981; Copenhagen, Nov. 24, 1983). **CHAMBER:** 2 *Impromptus* for Viola and Organ (1967); *Praeludium og fuga* for Clarinet, Cello, and Piano (1983); *Salon,* trio for Flute, Viola, and Harp (1984); *Paesaggi* for 2 Pianos (Rome, May 25, 1985); *3 Opera Fragments* for 12 Instruments and Percussion (1986; Humlebaek, May 28, 1988); *Tramonto* for Cello and Percussion (1989); many works for Solo Instruments, including *Marker og enge* (Fields and Meadows), divertimento for Organ (1971), and *Opstilling og landskab* (Arrangement and Landscape) for Flute (1981). **VOCAL:** *Attisk sommer* (Attic Summer) for Soprano, Guitar, and Percussion (1974); *3 Shakespeare Fragments* for Soprano, Oboe, Cello, and Piano (1977–78); *3 Black Madrigals* for Chorus (1978); *2 Choral Songs* for Chorus (1984); *In tribulatione mea,* motet for Chorus (1985); songs.

Niemann, Albert, greatly respected German tenor; b. Erxleben, near Magdeburg, Jan. 15, 1831; d. Berlin, Jan. 13, 1917.

He began his career as an actor and dramatist; joined the Dessau Opera (1849), where he sang in the chorus and appeared in minor roles; then had lessons with F. Schneider and Nusch; sang in Halle from 1852 to 1854; then in Hannover; then went to Paris, where he studied with Duprez. In 1866 he was engaged at the Berlin Royal Opera, remaining on its roster until 1888. Wagner thought highly of him, and asked him to create the role of Tannhäuser in Paris (March 13, 1861) and of Siegmund at the Bayreuth Festival (Aug. 14, 1876). From 1886 to 1888 he was a member of the Metropolitan Opera in N.Y.; his debut there was in his star role as Siegmund (Nov. 10, 1886); then he sang Tristan at the American premiere of *Tristan und Isolde* (Dec. 1, 1886) and Siegfried in *Götterdämmerung* (Jan. 25, 1888) there. He publ. *Erinnerungen an Richard Wagner* (Leipzig, 1907; Eng. tr., 1908); his correspondence with Wagner was ed. by W. Altmann (Berlin, 1924).

BIBL.: R. Sternfeld, *A. N.* (Berlin, 1904).

Niemann, Walter, German writer on music and composer; b. Hamburg, Oct. 10, 1876; d. Leipzig, June 17, 1953. He was a pupil of his father, Rudolph (Friedrich) Niemann, and of Humperdinck (1897); from 1898 to 1901, studied at the Leipzig Cons. with Reinecke and von Bose, and at the Univ. with Riemann and Kretzschmar (musicology); received a Ph.D. in 1901 with the dissertation *Über die abweichende Bedeutung der Ligaturen in der Mensuraltheorie der Zeit vor Johannes de Garlandia* (publ. in Leipzig, 1902; reprint, Wiesbaden, 1971); from 1904 to 1906, was ed. of the *Neue Zeitschrift für Musik* in Leipzig; in 1906–7, was a teacher at the Hamburg Cons.; in 1907–17, was again in Leipzig as a writer and critic of the *Neueste Nachrichten*, then gave up this position to devote himself to composition. Besides a Violin Sonata and a few works for orch. and string orch., he wrote numerous piano pieces (over 150 opus numbers).

WRITINGS: All publ. in Leipzig unless otherwise given: *Musik und Musiker des 19. Jahrhunderts* (1905); *Die Musik Skandinaviens* (1906); *Das Klavierbuch* (1907; 5th ed., 1920); with G. Schjelderup, *Edvard Grieg: Biographie und Würdigung seiner Werke* (1908); *Das Norlandbuch* (Weimar, 1909); *Die musikalische Renaissance des 19. Jahrhunderts* (1911); *Taschenlexikon für Klavierspieler* (1912; 4th ed., 1918, as *Klavierlexikon*); *Die Musik seit Richard Wagner* (1913; 5th and later eds. as *Die Musik der Gegenwart seit Wagner*); *Jean Sibelius* (1917); *Die nordische Klaviermusik* (1918); with O. Klauwell, *Die Formen der Instrumentalmusik* (2nd ed., 1918); *Die Virginalmusik* (1919); *Meister des Klaviers* (1919); *Brahms* (1920; 14th ed., 1933; Eng. tr., N.Y., 1929).

Niemtschek (Niemetschek, Němeček), Franz Xaver, Czech writer on music; b. Sadská, near Poděbrady, July 24, 1766; d. Vienna, March 19, 1849. He studied at the Prague Gymnasium (1776–82); then studied philosophy at the Univ. of Prague (Ph.D., 1800), where he was a prof. of philosophy (1802–20). He is known in musical annals for his biography of Mozart, whom he greatly admired and evidently knew personally: *Leben des k. k. Kapellmeisters Wolfgang Gottlieb Mozart* (Prague, 1798; 2nd ed., 1808; in Eng., London, 1956).

Nietzsche, Friedrich (Wilhelm), celebrated German philosopher; b. Röcken, near Lützen, Oct. 15, 1844; d. Weimar, Aug. 25, 1900. He was prof. of classical philology at the Univ. of Basel (1869–79); was at 1st a warm partisan of Wagner, whom he championed in *Die Geburt der Tragödie aus dem Geiste der Musik* (1872; 2nd ed., 1874) and *Richard Wagner in Bayreuth* (1876). In *Der Fall Wagner* and *Nietzsche contra Wagner* (both 1888) and in *Götzendämmerung* (1889), he turned against his former idol and became a partisan of Bizet. Nietzsche tried his hand at composition, producing both sacred and secular choral works, songs, and piano pieces; see C. Jang, ed., *Friedrich Nietzsche: Der musikalische Nachlass* (Kassel, 1977).

BIBL.: E. Förster-Nietzsche, *Das Leben F. N.s* (2 vols., Leipzig, 1895–1904; Eng. tr. [condensed], N.Y., 1912–15); J. Zeitler, *N.s Ästhetik* (Leipzig, 1900); T. Lessing, *Schopenhauer, Wagner, N.* (Munich, 1906); H. Bélart, *F. N. und Richard*

Wagner (Berlin, 1907); P. Lasserre, *Les Idées de N. sur la musique. La Période Wagnérienne (1871–6)* (Paris, 1907; new ed., 1930); H. Bélart, *F. N.s Freundschaftstragödie mit R. Wagner* (Dresden, 1912); E. Förster-Nietzsche, *Wagner und N. zur Zeit ihrer Freundschaft* (Munich, 1915); "Wagner and N.: The Beginning and End of Their Friendship," *Musical Quarterly* (July 1918; selection from E. Förster-Nietzsche's book, tr. by C. Kerr); W. Dahms, *Die Offenbarung der Musik. Eine Apotheose F. N.s* (1922); L. Griesser, *N. und Wagner* (1923); K. Hildebrandt, *Wagner und N., Ihr Kampf gegen das 19. Jahrhundert* (Breslau, 1924); H. Baugh, "N. and His Music," *Musical Quarterly* (April 1926); J. Verweyen, *Wagner und N.* (Stuttgart, 1926); E. Gürster, *N. und die Musik* (1929); J. Huneker, *Essays* (N.Y., 1929); E. Eckertz, *N. als Künstler* (Munich, 1930); G. Foster, *F. N.* (N.Y., 1931); P. Dippel, *N. und Wagner* (1934); E. Ruprecht, *Der Mythos bei Wagner und N.* (Berlin, 1938); J. Klein, "N.'s Attitude to Bizet," *Music Review*, XXI (1960); F. Love, *Young N. and the Wagnerian Experience* (Chapel Hill, 1963); D. Fischer-Dieskau, *Wagner und N.: Der Mystagogue und sein Abtrünniger* (Stuttgart, 1974; Eng. tr. as *Wagner and N.*, N.Y., 1976 and London, 1978); F. Love, "N., Music and Madness," *Music & Letters*, LX (1979); F.-P. Hudek, "*Die Tyrannei der Musik*": *N.s Wertung des wagnerischen Musikdramas* (Würzburg, 1989).

Niewiadomski, Stanislaw, Polish composer and music critic; b. Soposzyn, Galicia, Nov. 4, 1859; d. Lwow, Aug. 15, 1936. He studied in Lemberg (Lwow) (with Mikuli), Vienna (with F. Krenn), and Leipzig (with Jadassohn); in 1886–87 and 1918–19, was manager of the Lwow Opera; from 1885 to 1914, was music critic there; from 1887 to 1914, was a teacher at the Lwow Cons.; from 1918 to 1921, was ed. of the *Gazeta Muzyczna*; from 1919, was a music critic in Warsaw and a teacher at the Cons. there; in 1929, became director of the Warsaw Music Inst. He composed 2 syms., 4 overtures, a String Quartet, numerous songs, and piano pieces (about 500 works); also publ. biographies of Chopin and Moniuszko.

Nigg, Serge, French composer; b. Paris, June 6, 1924. He studied composition with Messiaen and Simone Plé-Caussade at the Paris Cons. (1941–46) and privately with René Liebowitz (1946–48), mainly the Schoenbergian method of composition with 12 tones. Nigg became one of the earliest representatives of dodecaphony in France; however, under the influence of his political convictions, he later abandoned modern techniques and began writing in a manner accessible to a broad public. In 1959 he formed, with Durey and others, the Assoc. of Progressive Musicians, advocating socialist realism in music.

WORKS: STAGE: 2 ballets: *Billard* (1951; Amsterdam, 1951) and *L'Etrange Aventure de Gulliver à Lilliput* (1958; for radio; concert version for 12 Instruments). **ORCH.:** *Timour*, symphonic poem (1944); Concertino for Piano, Wind Instruments, and Percussion (1946); *3 mouvements symphoniques* (1947); *Pour un poète captif*, symphonic poem appealing for the liberation of a radical poet imprisoned for political disturbances (1950); 2 piano concertos: No. 1 (1954; Paris, Jan. 10, 1955) and No. 2 (1970–71; Strasbourg, June 10, 1971); Violin Concerto (1957; Paris, May 27, 1960); *Musique funèbre* for Strings (1958); *Jérôme Bosch Symphonie* (Strasbourg, June 21, 1960); Concerto for Flute and Strings (1961); *Visages d'Axël*, suite in 2 parts (Paris, Sept. 4, 1967); *Fulgar* for Band, Percussion, 2 Harps, Piano, Celesta, and Tubular Chimes (Paris, Oct. 9, 1969); *Scènes concertantes* for Piano and Strings (Paris Radio, March 26, 1976); *Millions d'oiseaux d'or* (1980–81; Toulouse Orch. on U.S. tour, Boston, March 20, 1981). **VOCAL:** *Perséphone*, melodrama (1942); *Le Fusillé inconnu*, oratorio (1949); *Les Vendeurs d'indulgences*, cantata (1953); *Prière pour le premier jour d'été*, cantata for Speaker, Chorus, and Orch. (1955); *La Croisade des Enfants*, oratorio for Narrator, Baritone, Children's Chorus, Mixed Chorus, and Small Orch. (1959); *Histoire d'œuf* for 2 Speakers, 6 Percussionists, and Piano (1961); *Le Chant du dépossédé*, after Mallarmé, for Narrator, Baritone, and Orch. (Strasbourg, June 25, 1964). **CHAMBER:** *Variations* for Piano and 10 Instruments (1946; Paris, Jan. 29, 1947);

Quintet for Flute, String Trio, and Harp (1952); Solo Violin Sonata (1965); *Pièce* for Trumpet and Piano (1972); *Pièce* for Flute and Piano (1976). PIANO: *Fantaisie* (1942); *Le Tombeau de Jérôme Bosch* (1958); 2 sonatas (1943, 1965).

Niggli, Arnold, Swiss writer and editor; b. Aarburg, Dec. 20, 1843; d. Zürich, May 30, 1927. He studied law at Heidelberg, Zürich, and Berlin. From 1875 to 1909, he was secretary to the town council at Aarau; from 1890 to 1898, was ed. of the *Schweizerische Musikzeitung;* later, he lived in Zürich. He publ. *Die Schweizerische Musikgesellschaft; Eine musik- und kulturgeschichtliche Studie* (1886), *Geschichte des eidgenössischen Sängervereins, 1842–92,* and short studies of a number of great composers and performers (some of them in Waldersee's *Sammlung musikalischer Vorträge*).

Nikisch, Arthur, famous Austrian conductor of Moravian and Hungarian descent; b. Lébényi Szent-Miklós, Oct. 12, 1855; d. Leipzig, Jan. 23, 1922. His father was head bookkeeper to Prince Lichtenstein. Nikisch attended the Vienna Cons., studying with Dessoff (composition) and Hellmesberger (violin), graduating in 1874. While still a student, he had the honor of playing among the 1st violins under Wagner's direction at the laying of the cornerstone of the Bayreuth Theater (1872). He was at first engaged as a violinist in the Vienna Court Orch. (1874–77); then was chorusmaster (1877–78), 2nd conductor (1878–79), and 1st conductor (1879–89) of the Leipzig City Theater. In 1889 he was engaged as conductor of the Boston Sym. Orch., with excellent success, remaining at this post until 1893. Returning to Europe, he was music director of the Budapest Opera (1893–95); also conducted the Phil. Concerts; from 1895, was conductor of the Gewandhaus Orch. in Leipzig, and of the Berlin Phil. From 1897 he was in constant demand as a visiting conductor, and made a number of extended tours with the Berlin Phil.; he directed many of the concerts of the London Phil. Society, and works of Wagner and Richard Strauss at Covent Garden; in 1912 he made a tour of the U.S. with the London Sym. Orch. From 1902 to 1907, he was director of studies at the Leipzig Cons.; in 1905–6, general director of the Stadttheater. As a sym. conductor, he possessed an extraordinary Romantic power of musical inspiration; he was the 1st of his profession to open the era of "the conductor as hero," exercising a peculiar magnetism on his audiences equal to that of virtuoso artists; his personal appearance, a poetic-looking beard and flowing hair, contributed to his success. His son **Mitja Nikisch** (b. Leipzig, May 21, 1899; d. Venice, Aug. 5, 1936) was an excellent pianist; he toured South America in 1921; made his U.S. debut in N.Y., Oct. 23, 1923.
BIBL.: F. Pfohl, *A. N. als Mensch und als Künstler* (Leipzig, 1900; 2nd ed., 1925); E. Segnitz, *A. N.* (Leipzig, 1920); H. Chevalley, ed., *A. N., Leben und Wirken* (Berlin, 1922; 2nd ed., 1925); A. Dette, *A. N.* (Leipzig, 1922); H. Schonberg, *The Great Conductors* (N.Y., 1967); W. Stresemann, *The Berlin Philharmonic from Bülow to Karajan* (in German and Eng.; Berlin, 1979).

Nikolais, Alwin (Theodore), American choreographer, stage director, and composer; b. Southington, Conn., Nov. 25, 1912. He studied piano; played in movie houses for the silent films. In 1929 he began to study dance with a pupil of Mary Wigman; became director of the Hartford (Conn.) Parks Marionette Theater and later chairman of the dance dept. of the Hartt School of Music there. From 1942 to 1946 he served in military counterintelligence in Europe; then studied with Hanya Holm in N.Y. He became director of the Henry Street Settlement Playhouse (1948), where he organized the Alwin Nikolais Dance Theatre. He wrote music for many of his dance productions, including works in the electronic medium. His principal choreographic innovation is the technique of body extension by tubular projections and disks attached to the head and upper and nether limbs, so that a biped dancer becomes a stereogeometrical figure; often in his productions clusters of dancers form primitivistic ziggurats.

Nikolayev, Leonid (Vladimirovich), Russian pianist, pedagogue, and composer; b. Kiev, Aug. 13, 1878; d. Tashkent, Oct. 11, 1942. He was a pupil of Sergei Taneyev and Ippolitov-Ivanov at the Moscow Cons.; then settled in St. Petersburg, where he became prof. of piano at the Cons. in 1906, achieving a fine reputation as a teacher; among his piano pupils was Shostakovitch. Nikolayev went to Tashkent in Central Asia after the German invasion of Russia in 1941, and died there shortly afterward. He composed several symphonic works; *Hymn to Beauty* for Soli, Chorus, and Orch.; 3 string quartets; Cello Sonata; Violin Sonata; a number of piano works; etc.
BIBL.: S. Savshinsky, *L.V. N.* (Moscow, 1960).

Nikolayeva, Tatiana (Petrovna), esteemed Russian pianist, pedagogue, and composer; b. Bezhitz, May 4, 1924. She began her piano training with Goldenweiser at Moscow's Central Music School, continuing as his pupil at the Moscow Cons. (graduated, 1947); also studied composition there with Golubev (graduated, 1950). After a highly successful series of concerts in Russia, she won 1st prize at Leipzig's Bach festival for her performance of Bach's clavier works (1950); subsequently toured in Eastern Europe and later made visits to Western Europe; gave several highly acclaimed recitals in London (1986). She was a teacher (1959–65) and a prof. (from 1965) at the Moscow Cons. She was a remarkably gifted virtuoso; Shostakovich wrote his 24 Preludes and Fugues expressly for her. She was made an Honored Artist of the RSFSR in 1955. Among her works are several syms.; 2 piano concertos; Piano Quintet; Piano Sonata; many piano pieces.

Nikolov, Lazar, Bulgarian composer; b. Burgas, Aug. 26, 1922. He studied composition with Vladigerov at the Bulgarian State Cons. in Sofia (1942–47); in 1961, joined its faculty. An experimenter by nature, he was one of the few composers in Bulgaria who adopted modern procedures of composition, melodically verging on atonality and harmonically on polytonality.
WORKS: 2 operas: *Prometheus Bound,* chamber opera (1963–69; Ruse, March 24, 1974), and *Uncles* (1975); 2 piano concertos: No. 1 (1947–48; Ruse, Nov. 21, 1949) and No. 2 (1954–55; Sofia, Feb. 28, 1963); Concerto for String Orch. (1949; Ruse, Nov. 30, 1951); Violin Concerto (1951–52; Varna, March 25, 1955); 2 syms.: No. 1 (1953; Varna, Feb. 16, 1956) and No. 2, with 2 Pianos (1960–61); Piano Concertino (1964); *Symphonies* for 13 Strings (1965); *Divertimento concertante* for Chamber Orch. (1968); Cello Concertino (1973); *Chants for Soloists, Chorus, and Chamber Instrumental Group* (1969); Violin Sonata (1953–54); Viola Sonata (1955); Piano Quintet (1958–59); Flute Sonata (1962); Cello Sonata (1962); Clarinet Sonata (1962); 2 string quartets (1965, 1970); Sonata for 2 Harps (1971); Double-bass Sonata (1972); Bassoon Sonata (1976); Oboe Sonata (1976); 4 piano sonatas (1950, 1952, 1955, 1964); 2-piano Sonata (1952).

Nikolovski, Vlastimir, Macedonian composer; b. Prilep, Dec. 20, 1925. Both his parents were professional musicians; from them he received elementary musical education. In 1944 he obtained a baccalaureate in Prilep; subsequently studied music theory with Evlahov at the Leningrad Cons. In 1955 he returned to Yugoslavia, where he took courses at the Belgrade Academy of Music. Upon graduation, he settled in Skopje and became active as a teacher and as director of musical programming for the state radio. In 1976 he was appointed a corresponding member of the Academy of Arts of Macedonia. In his music he makes use of a number of native instruments, particularly in the percussion section. Among his works are 3 syms., a Piano Concerto, 2 oratorios, a Violin Sonata, a Cello Sonata, a Piano Sonata, a String Quartet, and a number of choruses on Macedonian themes.

Niles, John Jacob, American folksinger, folk-music collector, and composer; b. Louisville, Ky., April 28, 1892; d. at his Boot Hill farm, near Lexington, Ky., March 1, 1980. He began collecting and transcribing Appalachian songs when he was 15, and subsequently traveled throughout the Southern Appalachians; studied at the Cincinnati Cons. (1919), and later took courses at the Univ. of Lyons and at the Paris Schola Cantorum; after making his debut as an opera singer in Massenet's *Manon* with the Cincinnati Opera (1920), he devoted himself to teaching, performing folk music, collecting, and composing. His own works include such favorites as *I Wonder as I Wander*, *Go 'way from my Window*, and *Black Is the Color of My True Love's Hair*. With Douglas Moore, he also brought out *Songs My Mother Never Taught Me* (1929). Many of his works were included in the collection *The Songs of John Jacob Niles* (1975). The greater part of his MSS, field notebooks, instruments, etc., are housed in the John Jacob Niles Collection at the Univ. of Kentucky; other material is at the Library of Congress. Among his publications are *7 Kentucky Mountain Songs* (1929); *7 Negro Exultations* (1929); *Songs of the Hill Folk* (1934); *10 Christmas Carols* (1935); *More Songs of the Hill Folk* (1936); *Ballads and Tragic Legends* (1937); *The Anglo-American Ballad Study Book* (1945); *The Anglo-American Carol Study Book* (1948); *The Shape-Note Study Book* (1950).

Nilsson, (Märta) Birgit, greatly renowned Swedish soprano; b. Västra Karups, May 17, 1918. She studied with Joseph Hislop at the Royal Academy of Music in Stockholm; made her debut as Agathe in *Der Freischütz* at the Royal Theater in Stockholm (1946), gaining her 1st success as Verdi's Lady Macbeth (1947); then sang major roles in operas by Wagner, Puccini, and Strauss with increasing success. She first appeared as Brünnhilde in *Götterdämmerung* in Stockholm during the 1954–55 season, and sang this role in the *Ring* cycle for the 1st time in Munich during the same season; likewise appeared at the Vienna State Opera (1954) and at the Bayreuth Festival (1954), to which she returned regularly from 1959 to 1970. On Aug. 9, 1956, she made her U.S. debut at the Hollywood Bowl; then sang Brünnhilde in *Die Walküre* at the San Francisco Opera (Oct. 5, 1956); subsequently made her 1st appearance at London's Covent Garden (1957). She made her long-awaited Metropolitan Opera debut in N.Y. as Isolde on Dec. 19, 1959. She was universally acclaimed as one of the greatest Wagnerian dramatic sopranos of all time. After an absence of 5 years, she returned to the Metropolitan Opera for a gala concert on Nov. 4, 1979. She then rejoined the co., appearing as Elektra in 1980. She retired from the operatic stage in 1982. In addition to her brilliant Wagnerian roles, she excelled as Beethoven's Leonore, Puccini's Turandot, and Strauss's Salome and Elektra. She publ. *Mina minnesbilder* (Stockholm, 1977; Eng. tr. as *My Memoirs in Pictures*, Garden City, N.Y., 1981).

Nilsson, Bo, Swedish composer of ultramodern tendencies; b. Skellefteå, May 1, 1937. Largely autodidact, he experimented with techniques of serial composition, the phonetic possibilities of vocal music, and electronic sonorities; attended seminars on modern techniques in Cologne and Darmstadt. His works are constructed on precise quasi-mathematical, serial principles, and are often given abstract titles in German. He publ. his memoirs as *Livet i en mössa* (Life in a Cap; 1984).

WORKS: *Frequenzen* for Piccolo, Flute, Percussion, Guitar, Xylophone, Vibraphone, and Double Bass (1955–56); *Bewegungen* for Piano (1956); *Schlagfiguren* for Piano (1956); *Buch der Veränderungen* for Orch. (1957); *Zeiten im Umlauf* for 8 Woodwinds (1957); *Kreuzungen* for Flute, Vibraphone, Guitar, and Xylophone (1957); *Audiogramme* for Tape (1957–58); *Ett blocks timme*, chamber cantata for Soprano and 6 Instrumentalists (1957–58); *20 Gruppen* for Piccolo, Oboe, and Clarinet, or any 3 Instruments (1958); *Quantitäten* for Piano (1958); *Plexus* for Orch. (1959); *Stenogramm* for Percussion or Organ (1959); *Reaktionen* for 1–4 Percussionists (1960); *Szenes I–IV: I* for 2 Flutes, 2 Trumpets, Piano, Harp, and 2 Percussionists (1960); *II* for 6 Trumpets, 6 Violins, 4 Percussionists, Piano, Harp, Celesta, and Vibraphone (1961); *III* for Chamber Orch. (1961); *IV* for Saxophone, Orch., and Chorus (1974–75); *Versuchungen* (Temptations) for 3 Orch. Groups (1961); *La Bran* for Chorus and Orch. (1961); *Entrée* for Tape and Orch. (1963); *Litanei über das verlorene Schlagzeug* for Orch. without Percussion, to conform to the title (1965); *Déjà-vu* for Wind Quartet (1967); *Revue* for Orch. (1967); *Attraktionen* for String Quartet

(1968); *Design* for Violin, Clarinet, and Piano (1968); *Rendezvous* for Piano (1968); *Quartets* for 36 Winds, Percussion, and Tape (1969); *Caprice* for Orch. (1970); *Exit* for Tape and Orch. (1970); *Eurythmical Voyage* for Piano, Tape, and Orch. (1970); *Déjà-connu* for Wind Quintet (1973); *Nazm* for Speakers, Vocal Soloists, Chorus, Orch., and Tape (1972–73); *Déjà connu, déjà entendu* for Wind Quintet (1976); *La Bran* for Saxophone, Chorus, and Orch. (1963–76; Stockholm, March 19, 1976); Piano Quintet (1979); *Wendepunkt* for Brass and Live Electronics (1981); *Carte postale a Sten Frykberg* for Brass Quintet (1985).

Nilsson, Christine (real name **Kristina Törnerhjelm**), admired Swedish soprano; b. Sjöabol, near Växjö, Aug. 20, 1843; d. Stockholm, Nov. 22, 1921. Her teachers were Baroness Leuhausen, and F. Berwald in Stockholm; with him she continued study in Paris, and on Oct. 27, 1864, made her debut, as Violetta in *La Traviata*, at the Théâtre-Lyrique, where she was engaged for 3 years. After successful visits to London, she was engaged from 1868 to 1870 at the Paris Opéra; then made long tours with Strakosch in America (1870–72), and sang in the principal continental cities. In 1872 she married Auguste Rouzaud (d. 1882); her 2nd husband (married 1887) was the Spanish count Angel Vallejo y Miranda. She revisited America in the winters of 1873, 1874, and 1883, making her debut on the opening night of the Metropolitan Opera House in N.Y. on Oct. 22, 1883, as Marguerite in *Faust*. Her voice was not powerful, but it was brilliant. She excelled as Marguerite and Mignon.

BIBL.: B. Carlsson, *K. N.* (Stockholm, 1922); T. Norlind, *K. N.* (Stockholm, 1923); H. Headland, *C. N., the Songbird of the North* (Rock Island, Ill., 1943).

Nilsson, Leo, Swedish composer; b. Malmö, Feb. 20, 1939. He studied organ and music pedagogy at the Stockholm Musikhögskolan (1958–62); after working at the electronic-music studio of the ORTF in Paris, he returned to Sweden and was active in electronic-music circles; collaborated with Ralph Lundsten for a time, and also organized his own electronic-music studio in Skåne; taught at the Stockholm Musikhögskolan (from 1982). He composed various experimental works utilizing electronics.

WORKS: *Vilda livet fortsätter*, electronic score (1974); *Star-75*, multimedia piece (1975); *Zoo*, intermedia piece (1975); *String Play Video*, video piece (1976); *Vad speglar ögat själens spegel*, electronic score (1976); *Identitet* for Trombone, Violin, Double Bass, Synthesizer, and Electronics (1978); *Incostante* for Instrument and Electronics (1978); *Musica mobile*, electronic score (1978); *Signs of Presence*, sonographic piece (1978); *Sonata grafica Y* for Brass Quintet and Live Electronics (1978); *Va-et-vient monsieur Satie* for Piano and Live Electronics (1979); *Lek*, electronic score (1979); *Stenens hjärta*, electronic score (1979); *Animagica* (1980); *Sonata infernale*, electronic score (1981); *Early Ear*, electronic score (1982); *An der Quelle* for Piano (1983); *Musique d'ameublement* for 16 Winds, Cello, and Tape (Stockholm, Oct. 5, 1983); *Niente subito* for Cello and Tape (1983); *Svart vår-vår tiger* for Narrator, Piano, Cello, Live Electronics, and Tape (1983); *Voice of Glass*, electroacoustic piece (1985); *Passage* for Amplified Viola and Percussion (1986).

Nilsson, Torsten, Swedish organist, choirmaster, teacher, and composer; b. Höör, Jan. 21, 1920. He studied church music and pedagogy at the Stockholm Musikhögskolan (1938–42); also had instruction in organ from Alf Lindner and in organ and composition from Anton Heiller in Vienna (1961, 1965). He was organist in Köping (1943–53), Hälsingborg (1953–62), and at the Oscar Church in Stockholm (1962–79); also was conductor of the Oscar Motet Choir. He taught theory at the Stockholm Citizen's School (1962–73) and liturgical singing at the Stockholm Theological Inst. (1964–70) and the Univ. of Uppsala (1966–70). He excels in liturgical works; in his organ music he introduces many innovations, such as static tone-clusters and specified periods of thematic improvisation.

WORKS: CHURCH OPERA-ORATORIOS: *Ur jordens natt* (Out of the Night of the Earth) for Improvising Soli and Vocal

Groups, with Organ (Stockholm, April 12, 1968); *Dantesvit* (Dante Suite) for Soli, Vocal Group, Percussion, Organ, Harpsichord, and Tape (Stockholm, April 23, 1969); *Skapelse* (The Creation) for Narrator, Chorus, Organ, and Instruments (Stockholm, May 11, 1970); *Ur jordens natt. Del 2* (Out of the Night of the Earth, Part 2; Stockholm, April 12, 1974); *Den sista natten* (The Last Night) for 2 Actors, Mixed and Children's Chorus, Flute, Harp, Organ, and Percussion (Stockholm, Nov. 25, 1973). OPERA: *Malin: Pictures of History* for Chorus and Archaeological Instruments (1987; Nashville, Tenn., April 8, 1988). ORCH.: 2 concertos: No. 1 for Piano and String Orch. (1974–77); No. 2, *On the Threshold* for Piano, Wind Instruments, and Percussion (1975); Concerto for Trombone and Strings (1978); *Om ett brev*, lyric suite for String Orch. (1983); *A Lyric Suite* for Strings (1986–87). CHAMBER: Concertino for Trombone and Organ (1978); *Verwerfungen* for Organ and Percussion (1980); Rondo for Trombone (1981); Concertino for Trombone and Organ (1981–85); Concertino for Horn and Brass Quartet or Organ (1983); *Signals with 7 Structures* for Organ and 5 Percussionists (1985); *Rondo Sueziae* for Trombone and Piano (1987); *Revelations*, concerto for Organ and Piano (1988); organ music; piano pieces; various vocal works.

BIBL.: B. Huldt, "A Portrait of T. N.," *Nordic Sounds* (June 1987).

Nimas, Lithuanian composer and conductor; b. Viduklé, April 17, 1907. He studied with his father, an organist, then went to Prague, where he took advanced composition lessons with Jaroslav Křička and Alois Hába; subsequently occupied various conducting posts in Lithuania. After numerous misadventures during World War II, he finally emigrated to the U.S. His music reflects the influences of Scriabin and the French Impressionists. He wrote a Trumpet Concerto, 2 string quartets, and piano pieces.

Nimsgern, Siegmund, German bass-baritone; b. St. Wendel, Jan. 14, 1940. He took vocal lessons with Sibylle Fuchs, Jakob Stämpfli, and Paul Lohmann in Saarbrücken; sang at the Saarbrücken Opera (1967–71) and then at the Deutsche Oper am Rhein in Düsseldorf (1971–74); later engaged on an international career, appearing in Milan, Paris, Montreal, San Francisco, and London. On Oct. 2, 1978, he made his Metropolitan Opera debut in N.Y. as Pizarro.

Nin (y Castellanos), Joaquín, Spanish-born Cuban pianist and composer, father of **Joaquín (María) Nin-Culmell;** b. Havana, Sept. 29, 1879; d. there, Oct. 24, 1949. He studied piano with Carlos Vidiella in Barcelona and M. Moszkowski in Paris; composition with d'Indy at the Schola Cantorum there; taught piano there (1905–8); lived in Berlin, Havana, and Brussels, then settled in Paris; was a member of the French Legion of Honor, the Cuban Academy, etc. He was especially noted as an interpreter of early piano music. He championed the music of Bach and works by early Spanish composers, advocating their performance on the piano as opposed to the harpsichord. He wrote articles on esthetics; ed. 2 valuable collections of keyboard music: *16 sonatas anciennes d'auteurs espagnols* (Paris, 1925) and *17 sonates et pièces anciennes d'auteurs espangols* (Paris, 1929); these 2 collections contained the 1st contemporary eds. of Padre Antonio Soler, and led to the rediscovery of Spain's outstanding 18th-century master; also ed. *Sept chants lyriques espagnols anciens* (1926) and *Sept chansons picaresques espangoles anciennes* (1926), both for Voice and Piano, 10 pieces by Herrando for Violin and Piano (1937), and *Vocalise* (*Chant elégiaque*) for Voice and Piano.

WORKS: *20 cantos populares españoles* for Voice and Piano (1923); *10 noëls espagnols* for Voice and Piano (1932); *Aus jardín de Lindaraja* for Violin and Piano (1927); *5 commentarios* for Violin and Piano (1929); many solo piano pieces, including *Danza ibérica* (1926); *Mensaje a Claude Debussy* (1929); *Cadena de valses* (1929); *"1830" variaciones* (1930); *Canto de cuna para los huérfanos de España* (1939).

Nin-Culmell, Joaquín (María), Cuban-American pianist and composer, son of **Joaquín Nin (y Castellanos);** b. Berlin, Sept. 5, 1908. He studied piano in Paris at the Schola Cantorum; later took lessons in composition at the Paris Cons. with Paul Dukas; from 1930 to 1934 had composition lessons in Granada with Manuel de Falla; then studied piano with Cortot and Viñes. He emigrated to the U.S. in 1938, where he taught at Williams College in Williamstown, Mass. (1940–50) and the Univ. of Calif. in Berkeley (1950–74). His music retains its Spanish influence à la Falla, but he employs modern harmonies and characteristic asymmetrical rhythms of the cosmopolitan contemporary school.

WORKS: STAGE: *La Celestina*, opera (1965–); 3 ballets: *Don Juan* (1958–59); *El burlador de Sevilla* (1965); *Le Rêve de Cyrano* (1978); incidental music to Lorca's *Yerma* (1956; rev. 1988) and Shakespeare's *Cymbeline* (1980). ORCH.: *Homage to Falla* (1933); Piano Concerto (Rochester [N.Y.] Phil. in Williamstown, Mass., Dec. 5, 1946, composer soloist); *3 piezas antiguas españolas* (1959–61); *Diferencias* (1962); Cello Concerto (1962–63). CHAMBER: Piano Trio (1929); Piano Quintet (1934–36); *Celebration for Julia* for String Quartet and Glockenspiel in memory of the music patroness Julia Hanes Hurley (1981; N.Y., March 3, 1982); works for Piano, including *Tres impresiones* (1929), *Sonata breve* (1932), *Tonadas I-VI* (1956–61), *Alexandro y Luis* (1983), and *Doce Danzas Cubanas* (1985); works for Guitar, including 6 *Variations on a Theme by Luis de Milán* (1945). VOCAL: *Missa in honorem Sanctae Rosae* for Chorus and Brass (1963); Cantata for Mezzo-soprano and Strings (1965–66); *Dedication Mass* for Mixed Chorus and Organ (1970); *Ragpicker's Song* for Men's Chorus and Piano (1988).

Nini, Alessandro, Italian composer; b. Fano, near Pesaro, Nov. 1, 1805; d. Bergamo, Dec. 27, 1880. He studied with Luigi Palmerini at the Liceo Musicale in Bologna. In 1830 he accepted the post of director of the singing school in St. Petersburg, returning to Italy in 1837. Eventually he moved to Bergamo, where he was maestro di cappella at S. Maria Maggiore (1847–77) and director of the Istituto Musicale. He wrote 7 operas as well as syms., some chamber music, and cantatas. He was commended as a composer by Rossini and Verdi.

Nisard, Théodore (pen name of **Abbé Théodule-Eléazar-Xavier Normand**), Belgian organist and writer on music; b. Quaregnon, near Mons, Jan. 27, 1812; d. Jacqueville, Seine-et-Marne, Feb. 29, 1888. He was a chorister at Cambrai, and also studied music at Douai; attended the priests' seminary at Tournai and was ordained in 1835; in 1839, was appointed director of the Enghien Gymnasium, occupying his leisure with the study of church music. In 1842 he became 2nd chef de chant and organist at St. Germain des Prés, Paris; but soon devoted himself wholly to literary work; he publ. the 1st transcription of the Antiphonary of Montpellier (neumes and Latin letter notation from A to P), discovered by Danjou in 1847. Of his numerous books on plainchant the most important are a revised ed. of Jumilhac's *La Science et la pratique du plain-chant* (1847; with Le Clercq) and *Dictionnaire liturgique, historique et pratique du plain-chant et de musique d'église au moyen âge et dans les temps modernes* (1854; with d'Ortigue). He also publ. *De la notation proportionelle au moyen âge* (1847); *Etudes sur les anciennes notations musicales de l'Europe* (1847); *Etudes sur la restauration du chant grégorien au XIXe siècle* (1856); *Du rythme dans le plain chant* (1856); *Les Vrais Principes de l'accompagnement du plain-chant sur l'orgue d'après les maîtres des XVe et XVIe siècles* (1860); *Des chansons populaires chez les anciens et chez les Français* (1867); *L'Archéologie musicale et le vrai chant grégorien* (1890; 2nd ed., 1897). All of these works were publ. in Paris.

Nissen, Georg Nikolaus, Danish statesman and music scholar; b. Haderslev, Jan. 22, 1761; d. Salzburg, March 24, 1826. He entered the diplomatic service in 1792, becoming the Danish chargé d'affaires in Vienna in 1793; commenced a friendship with Mozart's widow, Constanze (1797), and later became her husband (1809); after a period in Copenhagen (1810–20), he settled in Salzburg. He collected materials for a biography of Mozart, which was completed and publ. by Johann Feurstein as *Biographie W.A. Mozarts: nach Originalbriefen, Sammlungen alles über ihn Geschriebenen, mit vielen neuen Beylagen, Steindrucken, Musikblättern und einem Facsimile* (Leipzig, 1828; supplement, 1829; 2nd ed., 1849).

BIBL.: R. Münster, "N.s 'Biographie W.A. Mozarts': zu ihrer Entstehungsgeschichte," *Acta Mozartiana,* IX/1 (1962).

Nissen, Hans Hermann, distinguished German bass-baritone; b. Zippnow, near Marienwerder, West Prussia, May 20, 1893; d. Munich, March 28, 1980. He studied with Julius von Raatz-Brickmann in Berlin, where he made his concert debut (1920); then made his operatic debut as the Caliph in *Der Barbier von Bagdad* at the Berlin Volksoper (1924); subsequently joined the Bavarian State Opera in Munich (1925). In 1930 he went to the U.S., where he was a member of the Chicago Civic Opera (until 1932); on Nov. 23, 1938, he made his debut with the Metropolitan Opera in N.Y., as Wotan, and remained with it for a season. He then rejoined the Bavarian State Opera in Munich, retiring in 1967. He remained in Munich as a voice teacher.

Nissman, Barbara, American pianist; b. Philadelphia, Dec. 31, 1944. She was educated at the Univ. of Michigan (B.M., 1966; M.M., 1966; D.M.A., 1969); her principal mentor was György Sandor. In 1971 she made her U.S. orch. debut as soloist with Ormandy and the Philadelphia Orch.; she subsequently appeared as soloist with leading orchs. throughout the U.S. and Europe, and also gave concerts in Latin America and the Far East. She has become particularly known for her performances of contemporary music, most especially the works of Ginastera, who dedicated his 3rd piano sonata to her.

Nivers, Guillaume Gabriel, French organist, music theorist, and composer; b. probably in Paris, c.1632; d. there, Nov. 30, 1714. He most likely received his education at the Univ. of Paris (M.A., 1661); was organist of St. Sulpice from the early 1650s; was also made one of the 4 organists of the royal chapel (1678), master of music to the queen (1681), and head of music at the Maison Royale de St. Louis, the convent school in St. Cyr for young women of the nobility. He was a leading figure in the development of the French organ school.

WRITINGS: *Traité de la composition de musique* (Paris, 1667; 4th ed., 1712; Eng. tr. edited by A. Cohen in Music Theorists in Translation, III, Brooklyn, 1961); *Dissertation sur le chant grégorien* (Paris, 1683); *L'art d'accompagner sur la basse continue* (see *Motets à voix seule . . .* below); *Méthode certaine pour apprendre le plein-chant de l'Église* (Paris, 1699).

EDITIONS: *Graduale romanum juxta missale . . . in usum et gratiam monialum ordinis Augustini* (Paris, 1658); *Antiphonarium romanum juxta breviarum* (Paris, 1658); *Passiones D. N. J. C. cum benedictione cerei paschalis* (Paris, 1670); *Lamentationes Jeremiae prophetae* (Paris, 1689); *Graduale monasticum juxta missale . . . in usum et gratiam monialum ordinis S. Benedicti* (Paris, 1696); *Antiphonarium monasticum juxta breviarum* (Paris, 1696); *Le Processionel avec les saluts suivant l'antiphonaire des religeuses* (Paris, 1706).

WORKS: SACRED VOCAL: *Motets à voix seule . . . et quelques autres motets à deux voix propres pour les religieuses avec L'Art d'accompagner sur la basse continue, pour l'orgue et le clavecin* (Paris, 1689; 4th ed., 1741); *Chants et motets à l'usage de l'église et communauté des Dames de la Royale Maison de St.-Louis à St.-Cyr* (with Clérambault; Paris, 1692); etc. ORGAN: *Livre d'orgue contenant cent pièces de tous les tons de l'Église* (Paris, 1665); 2: *Livre d'orgue contenant la messe et les hymnes de l'Église* (Paris, 1667); 3: *Livre d'orgue des huit tons de l'Église* (Paris, 1675).

BIBL.: W. Pruitt, *The Organ Works of G.G. N.* (diss., Univ. of Pittsburgh, 1969); idem, "The Organ Works of G.G. N. (1632–1714)," *Recherches sur la musique française classique,* XV (1973).

Nixon, Marni (née **Margaret Nixon McEathron**), American soprano; b. Altadena, Calif., Feb. 22, 1930. She studied with Carl Ebert at the Univ. of Southern Calif. in Los Angeles, Jan Popper at Stanford Univ., and Boris Goldovsky and Sarah Caldwell at the Berkshire Music Center at Tanglewood. She pursued a multifaceted career; sang on the soundtrack of the films *The King and I, West Side Story,* and *My Fair Lady,* and also starred in her own children's program on television; appeared in musical comedy and opera; was a soloist with major orchs. in the U.S. and abroad. She taught at the Calif. Inst. of the Arts (1969–71) and the Music Academy of the West in Santa Barbara (from 1980).

Nixon, Roger, American composer; b. Tulare, Calif., Aug. 8, 1921. He studied clarinet with a local teacher; in 1940, attended a seminar in composition with Arthur Bliss at the Univ. of Calif., Berkeley, and in 1941, with Ernest Bloch. From 1942 to 1946 he was in the U.S. Army; he returned in 1947 to Berkeley, where he had fruitful sessions with Sessions (M.A., 1949; Ph.D., 1952); in the summer of 1948 he took private lessons with Schoenberg. In 1960 he joined the staff of San Francisco State College. A prolific composer, he writes in a consistent modern idiom anchored in fluctuating tonality and diversified by atonal protuberances. His music is marked by distinctly American melorhythms; his miniature opera, *The Bride Comes to Yellow Sky,* is an exemplar of adroit modernistic Westernism fashioned in a non-ethnomusicological manner.

WORKS: OPERA: *The Bride Comes to Yellow Sky* (Eastern Illinois Univ., Feb. 20, 1968; rev. version, San Francisco State College, March 22, 1969). ORCH.: *Air for Strings* (1953); Violin Concerto (1956); *Elegiac Rhapsody* for Viola and Orch. (1962); *3 Dances* (1963); Viola Concerto (1969; San Francisco, April 29, 1970); *San Joaquin Sketches* for Orch. or Band (1982); various works for Band, including *Chamarita!* (1980), *California Jubilee* (1982), and *Golden Jubilee* (1985). CHAMBER: String Quartet No. 1 (1949); *Conversations* for Violin and Clarinet (1981); *Music for Clarinet and Piano* (1986). VOCAL: *Christmas Perspectives* for Chorus (1980); *Festival Mass* for Chorus (1980); *Chaunticleer* for Men's Voices (1984); *The Canterbury Tales* for Chorus (1986); *The Daisy* for Chorus (1987); other choral works; song cycles and songs; etc.

Niyazi (real name, **Taghi-zade-Khadzhibekov**), Russian conductor and composer; b. Tiflis, Aug. 20, 1912; d. Baku, Aug. 2, 1984. His father was the well-known composer Zulfugar Khadzhibekov. He studied music in Moscow, Erevan, and Baku. From 1937 to 1965 he served, off and on, as conductor of the Azerbaijani Ballet. In 1961 he was named principal conductor of the Leningrad Theater of Opera and Ballet. He conducted a number of 1st performances of works by Azerbaijani composers.

WORKS: Opera, *Hosrov and Shirin* (1942); ballet, *Chitra,* after Rabindranath Tagore (1961); *In Combat,* symphonic poem (1944); popular concert pieces; songs.

BIBL.: E. Abasova, N. (Baku, 1965).

Nketia, J(oseph) H(ansen) Kwabena, Ghanaian ethnomusicologist; b. Mampong Ashanti, near Kumasi, June 22, 1921. He attended Teacher Training College in Akropong-Akwapim (1937–40); then taught music and languages at Presbyterian Training College there (1942–44; 1949–52), where he made his 1st collection of Akan songs (publ. 1949), and composed original works and arrangements of Ghanaian music. He also studied at the School of Oriental and African Studies, Univ. of London (1944–46; B.A., 1949), where he developed an interdisciplinary approach to ethnomusicology. He taught at the Univ. of Ghana (1951–81) and at the Univ. of Calif., Los Angeles (1969–83); became Andrew Mellon Prof. of Music at the Univ. of Pittsburgh in 1983; also was director of the Inst. of African Studies at the Univ. of Ghana (1965–80). His numerous publications include collections and studies of African music and performance (publ. in Ghana), as well as the important *Music of Africa* (N.Y., 1974; won the ASCAP–Deems Taylor Award).

Nobel, Felix de, Dutch pianist and choral conductor; b. Haarlem, May 27, 1907; d. Amsterdam, March 25, 1981. He studied piano with Martha Autengruber and composition with Sem Dresden at the Amsterdam Cons.; from 1939 to 1973, led the Netherlands Chamber Choir. He was chiefly known as an excellent accompanist for singers; made arrangements of Dutch, Irish, and Jewish folk songs for women's chorus. In 1965 he was awarded the Elizabeth Sprague Coolidge Memorial Medal.

Noble, Ray(mond Stanley), English bandleader, composer, and arranger, nephew of **(Thomas) Tertius Noble;** b. Brighton, Dec. 17, 1903; d. London, April 2, 1978. He received a thorough musical training at Cambridge; formed a band in London, assembled mostly from hotel orch. groups. Most of his arrangements were of English folk tunes; then he began to compose; among his most popular songs was *Goodnight, Sweetheart,* which subsequently became his theme song on American radio shows. In 1934 he went to the U.S.; Glenn Miller helped him to assemble musicians for his band, and he opened at the Rainbow Room in N.Y. on June 1, 1935, seated at a white grand piano on a rotating platform, making tours among the guests at the floorside, and returning to the bandstand at the end of each number. He became extremely successful on network radio shows, appearing not only as a bandleader and composer but also as an actor, usually in the role of a comical Englishman. Besides his theme song—*Goodnight, Sweetheart*—he composed *The Very Thought of You, By the Fireside, The Touch of Your Lips,* and several other hit songs. His *Cherokee,* originally a section of his *American Indian Suite,* became a perennial favorite. Noble demonstrated, in a chorus he wrote for 5 saxophones, his expertise in purely contrapuntal writing with a jazz flavor.

Noble, (Thomas) Tertius, English organist and composer, uncle of **Ray(mond Stanley) Noble;** b. Bath, May 5, 1867; d. Rockport, Mass., May 4, 1953. He studied organ with Parratt at the Royal College of Music in London, where he also took courses in music theory with Bridge and Stanford. He was subsequently employed as a church organist in Colchester and Cambridge. In 1898 he organized the York Sym. Orch., which he conducted until 1912; he then emigrated to America and served as organist at St. Thomas's Episcopal Church in N.Y. until 1947; he gave his final organ recital, playing his own works, in N.Y. on Feb. 26, 1947. He publ. *The Training of the Boy Chorister* (N.Y., 1943).

Nobre, Marlos, Brazilian composer, conductor, and pianist; b. Recife, Feb. 18, 1939. He studied piano and composition at the Pernambuco Cons. (graduated, 1955) and at the Ernani Braga Inst. (graduated, 1959); in 1960, went to Rio de Janeiro, where he took composition lessons with H.J. Koellreutter; later studied with Camargo Guarnieri at the São Paulo Cons. (1961–62) and with Alberto Ginastera in Buenos Aires (1963–64); took a course in electronic music with Ussachevsky at Columbia Univ. (1969); was music director of the National Sym. Orch. of Brazil (1971–76); then was president of the National Music Inst. of the National Foundation of the Arts (1976–79). Despite a somewhat quaquaversal efflux of styles and idioms to which he was exposed during his student days, he succeeded in forming a strongly individual manner of musical self-expression, in which sonorous and structural elements are effectively combined with impressionistic, pointillistic, and serial techniques, supplemented by restrained aleatory procedures. He is one of the few contemporary Latin-American composers who does not disdain to make use of native melorhythmic inflections, resulting in ingratiating harmoniousness.

WORKS: Concertino for Piano and Strings (1959); *Variations* for Oboe (1960); Piano Trio (1960); *Theme and Variations* for Piano (1961); *16 Variations* for Piano (1962); Solo Viola Sonata (1963); *Divertimento* for Piano and Orch. (Rio de Janeiro, Nov. 10, 1965); *Rhythmic Variations* for Piano and Percussion (1963); *Ukrínmakrinkrín* for Soprano, Wind Instruments, and Piano, to a text derived from primitive Brazilian Negro and Indian rituals (Buenos Aires, Nov. 20, 1964); *Modinha* for Voice, Flute, and Viola (1966); *Sonata breve* for Piano (1966); *Canticum instrumentale* for Flute, Harp, Piano, and Timpani (1967); String Quartet No. 1 (1967); *Rhythmetron*

for 32 Percussion Instruments (1968; choreographed 1969); *Convergencias* for Orch. (Rio de Janeiro, June 11, 1968); Wind Quintet (1968); *Tropicale* for Flute, Clarinet, Piano, and Percussion (1968); *Desafio I* for Viola and String Orch. (1968), *II* for Cello and String Orch. (1968), *III* for Violin and String Orch. (1968), *IV* for Double Bass and String Orch. (1977), *V* for 6 Cellos (1977), *VI* for String Orch. (1979), and *VII* for Piano and String Orch. (1980); *Concerto breve* for Piano and Orch. (Rio de Janeiro, May 27, 1969); *Ludus instrumentalis* for Chamber Orch. (1969); *Mosaico* for Orch. (Rio de Janeiro, May 12, 1970); *Biosfera* for String Orch. (1970; Lisbon, Jan. 27, 1971); *Sonancias* for Piano and Percussion (1972); *O canto multiplicado* for Voice and String Orch. (1972); *In memoriam* for Orch. (Rio de Janeiro, Sept. 18, 1976); Concerto for String Orch. (1975–76); Guitar Concerto (1980); Concerto No. 2 for String Orch. (1981).

Nobutoki, Kiyoshi, Japanese composer and pedagogue; b. Kyoto, Dec. 29, 1887; d. Tokyo, Aug. 1, 1965. He studied music in Japan and in Germany; composed a militant cantata, *Kaidō Tōsei* (Along the Coast, Conquer the East; Tokyo, Nov. 26, 1940), and other choral works; was primarily engaged in educational work in Tokyo.

Noda, Ken, Japanese-American pianist and composer; b. N.Y., Oct. 5, 1962. He studied piano with Adele Marcus at the Juilliard School in N.Y.; also had lessons in composition with Sylvia Rabinof and Thomas Pasatieri. He made his professional debut as a soloist with the Minnesota Orch. in Beethoven's 3rd Piano Concerto (Minneapolis, May 14, 1977); then made his London debut with the English Chamber Orch. (1979). After further studies with Daniel Barenboim in Paris (1979–83), he appeared with major orchs. on both sides of the Atlantic.

WORKS: OPERAS: *The Canary* (Brevard, N.C., Music Festival, Aug. 18, 1973); *The Swing* (1974); *The Rivalry* (1976); *The Highwayman* (1979); *The Magic Turtle* (1980); also *A Zoo Suite* for Piano (1973); *Piano Sonatina* (1974); *Prelude and Canon* for Piano (1974); *An Emily Dickinson Song Cycle* (1977); *A Christina Rossetti Song Cycle* (1977); *A Cycle of German Poems* (1977).

Noda, Teruyuki, Japanese pianist and composer; b. Mie Prefecture, June 15, 1940. He studied at the Tokyo Univ. of Arts with Tomojiro Ikenouchi and Akio Yashiro.

WORKS: *Symphony in One Movement* (1963); Trio for Violin, Horn, and Piano (1963); Quartet for Horn, Cello, Timpani, and Piano (1965); *Choral Symphony* (Tokyo, July 10, 1968); *Mattinata* (Morning Song) for Marimba, 3 Flutes, and Contrabass (Tokyo, Oct. 4, 1968); *A Mirror or A Journey,* symphonic radio piece with Monologue (1968); 2 quartets for Japanese Instruments (1969, 1973); *Dislocation* for Orch. (Tokyo, Feb. 10, 1971); *Mutation* for 4 Japanese Instruments and Orch. (1971); *Shi-sha-no-Sho (Livre de mort)* for Mixed Chorus (1971); Piano Concerto (1977); *Poems I* and *II* for 7 Instruments (1980); Sym. No. 2 (1983); *Novelette* for String Quartet (1983); Guitar Concerto (1984).

Nodermann, Preben (Magnus Christian), Danish organist and composer; b. Hjørring, Jan. 11, 1867; d. Lund, Nov. 14, 1930. He was a pupil of O. Malling in Copenhagen (1888–90); From 1899 to 1903, was organist in Malmö; then was director of music at Lund Cathedral. He publ. *Studier i svensk hymnologi* (1911).

WORKS: STAGE: *König Magnus,* opera (Hamburg, Oct. 8, 1898); *Gunnlögs Saga,* opera (not perf.); *Rokoko,* opera (Leipzig, 1923); *Prinz Inkognito,* operetta (Copenhagen, 1909; publ. as *Die Jungfernstadt*); also motets; sacred and secular choruses; pieces for Violin and Piano; organ preludes; etc.

Noehren, Robert, American organist, organ builder, and composer; b. Buffalo, N.Y., Dec. 16, 1910. He studied at the Inst. of Musical Art in N.Y. and at the Curtis Inst. of Music in Philadelphia; served in the U.S. Army in World War II. After demobilization, he studied at the Univ. of Michigan, receiving his B.Mus. degree in 1948. He taught at Davidson College in N.C. (1946–49) and at the Univ. of Michigan (1949–76); also toured extensively as a recitalist in North America and overseas. He built organs for churches in Milwaukee, Buffalo, San Francisco, and other cities. Among his works are a number of solo organ pieces, including 2 sonatas.

Noelte, A. Albert, German-American music pedagogue and composer; b. Starnberg, March 10, 1885; d. Chicago, March 2, 1946. He went to the U.S. in 1901 and studied music and literature in Boston; in 1908 he returned to Germany but frequently visited the U.S.; in 1931, settled there and was appointed a prof. at Northwestern Univ. in Evanston, Ill. He earned a fine reputation as a teacher; many American scholars and composers were his pupils. He composed an orch. piece, *Prologue to a Romantic Drama,* which was performed in Chicago on Jan. 16, 1941, and a number of other pieces of little consequence. His opera *François Villon* was produced in Karlsruhe in 1920.

Nohl, (Karl Friedrich) Ludwig, German writer on music; b. Iserlohn, Westphalia, Dec. 5, 1831; d. Heidelberg, Dec. 15, 1885. He studied jurisprudence at Bonn (1850), Heidelberg, and Berlin; entered the legal profession against his own desire, to please his father. In music he was instructed by Dehn; later (1857–58) by Kiel, in Berlin. Having embraced music as his profession, he took his Ph.D. at Heidelberg in 1860; subsequently went to Munich (1861), where he was an honorary prof. at the Univ. (1865–68); after living in Badenweiler (1868–72), he settled in Heidelberg as a private lecturer, becoming a prof. at the Univ. in 1880. He publ. biographies and eds. of letters of several great composers, but these have been superseded by modern scholarship. Among his writings are *Musikalisches Skizzenbuch* (1866); *Musiker-Briefe* (1867); *Beethovens Leben* (3 vols., 1867–77); *Neues Skizzenbuch* (1869); *Gluck und Wagner* (1870); *Die Beethoven-Feier und die Kunst der Gegenwart* (1871); *Beethoven, Liszt, Wagner* (1874); *Beethoven nach den Schilderungen seiner Zeitgenossen* (1877; in Eng. as *Beethoven as Depicted by His Contemporaries,* 1880); *Mozart nach den Schilderungen seiner Zeitgenossen* (1880); *Richard Wagners Bedeutung für die nationale Kunst* (1883); *Das moderne Musikdrama* (1884); *Die geschichtliche Entwickelung der Kammermusik* (1885).

Nola, Giovanni Domenico del Giovane da, distinguished Italian composer; b. Nola, c.1515; d. Naples, May 1592. He was made maestro di cappella at Naples's Ss. Annunziata (1563). He excelled as a composer of both sacred and secular vocal music.
WORKS: SACRED VOCAL: *Liber primus motectorum* for 5 Voices (Venice, 1549); *Cantiones vulgo motecta appellatae . . . monis generis instrumentis cantatu commodissimae . . . liber primus* for 5 to 6 Voices (Venice, 1575; not extant). SECULAR VOCAL: *Canzoni villanesche . . . liber primo et secondo* for 3 Voices (Venice, 1541; not extant; 2nd ed. publ. separately as 2 books, Venice, 1545); *Madrigali* for 4 Voices (Venice, 1545); *Il secondo libro de madrigali* for 5 Voices (Rome, 1564); *Il primo libro delle villanelle alla napolitana* for 3 to 4 Voices (Venice, 1567); *Il quarto libro di madrigali* for 5 to 6 Voices (not extant).
BIBL.: L. Cammarota, *Gian Domenico del Giovane da Nola: I documenti biografici d l'attività presso la SS. Annunziata con l'opera completa* (Rome, 1973).

Nolte, Ewald V(alentin), American organist, choirmaster, teacher, and composer; b. Utica, Nebr., Sept. 21, 1909. He studied music with Albert Noelte (not a relation) at Northwestern Univ. in Evanston, Ill. (M.Mus., 1945; Ph.D., 1954), and with Paul Hindemith and Leo Schrade (1950–51) at Yale Univ. His professional career was devoted mainly to education and to conducting church choruses. From 1944 to 1964 he was on the music faculty of Northwestern Univ., and from 1964 to 1980, at Salem College; From 1964 to 1972, he was executive director of the Moravian Music Foundation. He publ. a series of anthologies, *Music for Young Americans;* arranged American folk songs; supplied accompaniments to hymns; composed choral sacred music; ed. numerous works from the Moravian Foundation Archives.

Noni, Alda, Italian soprano; b. Trieste, April 30, 1916. She studied in Trieste and in Vienna; made her debut in Ljubljana in 1937 as Rosina in *Il Barbiere di Siviglia;* then sang at the Vienna State Opera (1942–44). In 1946 she appeared in London as Norina in Donizetti's *Don Pasquale;* also sang at the Glyndebourne Festivals (1950; 1952–54). She was entrusted by Richard Strauss with the role of Zerbinetta in the Vienna production of *Ariadne* in 1944. She became best known for her soubrette roles in Italian operas.

Nono, Luigi, remarkable Italian composer who earned a unique place in the history of modern music through his consistent devotion to social problems; b. Venice, Jan. 29, 1924; d. there, May 8, 1990. He became a student at the Venice Cons. (1941), where he received instruction in composition with Malipiero (1943–45); also studied law at the Univ. of Padua (graduated, 1946); later had advanced harmony and counterpoint lessons with Maderna and Scherchen. A man of extraordinary courage, he joined the Italian Communist Party while the country was still under the dictatorship of Mussolini, and was an active participant in the Italian Resistance Movement against the Nazis. In 1975 he was elected to the Central Committee of the Communist Party, and remained a member until his death. Although his works were extremely difficult to perform and practically all of them were devoted to Leftist propaganda, he found support among a number of liberal composers and performers. At the end of his life, he acquired an enormous reputation as a highly original composer in the novel technical idiom as well as a fearless political agitator. In his technique of composition, he followed the precepts of Arnold Schoenberg without adhering to the literal scheme of dodecaphonic composition. As a resolutely "engaged" artist, Nono mitigated the antinomy between the modern idiom of his music and the conservative Soviet ideology of Socialist Realism by his militant political attitude and his emphasis on revolutionary subjects in his works, so that even extreme dissonances may be dialectically justified as representing the horrors of Fascism. He made several visits to the Soviet Union, the last in 1988, but his works are rarely performed there because of the intransigence of his idiom. He made use of a variety of techniques: serialism, "sonorism" (employment of sonorities for their own sake), aleatory and concrete music, and electronics. Perhaps his most militant composition, both politically and musically, is his opera *Intolleranza 1960,* utilizing texts by Brecht, Eluard, Sartre, and Mayakovsky; the work is a powerful protest against imperialist policies and social inequities. At its production in Venice on April 13, 1961, a group of neo-Fascists showered the audience with leaflets denouncing Nono for his alleged contamination of Italian music by alien doctrines, and even making a facetious allusion to his name as representing a double negative. Nono was married to Schoenberg's daughter, Nuria, in 1955; they separated on friendly terms after several years; they had 2 daughters. Nuria settled in her father's last residence in Los Angeles, while Nono traveled widely in Europe. He died of a liver ailment at the age of 66.
WORKS: *Variazioni canoniche* for Orch., based on the 12-tone row of Schoenberg's *Ode to Napoleon Buonaparte* (Darmstadt, Aug. 27, 1950); *Polifonica, monodia, ritmica* for Flute, Clarinet, Bass Clarinet, Saxophone, Horn, Piano, and Percussion (Darmstadt, July 10, 1951); *España en el corazón* for Voices and Instruments, to words by Lorca (Darmstadt, July 21, 1952); ballet, *Der rote Mantel* (Berlin, Sept. 20, 1954); *La Victoire de Guernica* for Voices and Orch. (1954); *Canti* for 13 Instruments (Paris, March 26, 1955); *Incontri* for 24 Instruments (Darmstadt, May 30, 1955); *Varianti* for Violin, Strings, and Woodwinds (Donaueschingen, Oct. 20, 1957); *La terra e la compagna* for Soli, Chorus, and Instruments (Hamburg, Jan. 13, 1958); *Il canto sospeso* for Solo Voices, Chorus, and Orch., to texts from letters by young men and women condemned to death by the Fascists (Cologne, Oct. 24, 1956); *Intolleranza 1960,* opera (1960–61; Venice, April 13, 1961); *Sarà dolce tacere* for 8 Solo Voices, to texts from "La terra e la morte" by Cesare Pavese (Washington, D.C., Feb. 17, 1961); *La fabbrica illumi-*

nata for Voice and Magnetic Tape (1964); music for the documentary play *Die Ermittlung* by Peter Weiss, dealing with the trial of Nazi guards (Frankfurt, Oct. 19, 1965); *Sul ponte di Hiroscima*, commemorating the victims of the atomic attack on Hiroshima, for Soloists and Orch. (1962); *A Floresta é jovem e cheja de vida*, oratorio to texts from declarations by the Vietnam guerrilla fighters (1966); *Per Bastiana* for Electronic Tape and 3 Orch. Groups (1967); *Non consumiano Marx* for Electronic Sound (1968); *Voci destroying Muros* for Women's Voices and Instruments in Mixed Media, featuring a machine gun pointed toward the audience (1970); *Y entonces comprendió* for Voices and Magnetic Tape, dedicated to Ché Guevara (1970); *Ein Gespenst geht um in der Welt* for Voice and Orch., to words from the Communist Manifesto (Cologne, Feb. 11, 1971); *Como una ola de fuerza y luz* for Singer, Piano, Magnetic Tape, and Orch. (1972); 2 piano concertos (1972, 1975); *Al gran sole carico d'amore*, opera (1974); *. . . sofferte onde serene . . .* for Piano and Tape (1976); *Con Luigi Dallapiccola* for 6 Percussionists and Live Electronics (1979); *Fragmente-Stille, an Diotima* for String Quartet (1979–80); *Das atmende Klarsein* for Bass Flute, Choir, and Live Electronics (1980–81); *Quando stanno morendo . . .* for 4 Female Voices, Bass Flute, Cello, and Live Electronics (1982); *Omaggio a György Kurtág* for Trombone and Live Electronics (1983); *A C. Scarpa architetto, ai suo infiniti possibili* for Orch. (1984); *Guai ai gelidi mostri* for 2 Altos, Flute, Clarinet, Tuba, Viola, Cello, Double Bass, and Live Electronics (1984); *Prometeo, Tragedia dell'ascolto* (1984; rev. 1985); *A Pierre: Dell'azzurro silenzio, inquietum* for Chorus, Flute, Clarinet, and Live Electronics (1985); *Risonanze erranti a M. Cacciari* for Alto, Flute, Tuba, Percussion, and Live Electronics (1986); *Découvrir la subversion: Omaggio a E. Jabés* for Mezzo-soprano, Narrator, Tuba, Horn, and Live Electronics (1987); *No hay caminos, hay que caminar. . . A. Tarkovsky* for Orch. (1987).

BIBL.: J. Stenzl, ed., *L. N.: Texte: Studien zu seiner Musik* (Zürich, 1975); F. Spangemacher, *L. N., die elektronische Musik* (Regensburg, 1983).

Noone, Jimmy, black American jazz clarinetist and bandleader; b. Cut-Off, La., April 23, 1895; d. Los Angeles, April 19, 1944. He first took up the guitar; began to play the clarinet at age 15; then studied with Sidney Bechet in New Orleans; subsequently made appearances there with Bechet's orch.; later played in Chicago and N.Y., appearing with various bands and leading his own groups. His limpid style of playing was preserved on many fine recordings.

BIBL.: W. Kenney, III, "J. N.: Chicago Classic Jazz Clarinetist," *American Music* (Summer 1986).

Norby, Erik, Danish composer; b. Copenhagen, Jan. 9, 1936. He studied with Leif Kayser at the Royal Danish Cons. of Music in Copenhagen (graduated with a diploma in composition and theory, 1966) and with Per Nørgård at the Jutland Cons.; subsequently taught at the Alborg Cons. until 1975. His music reveals deft handling of styles ranging from the late Romantic to Darmstadt schools. He withdrew several of his scores after incorporating them into later compositions.

WORKS: ORCH.: *Folkesang-suite* (1962); *Variations* (1963); *Music for 8 Sextets* (1966); *Nocturne* (1969); *Corps celeste*, symphonic poem (1970); *Regnbueslangen* (The Rainbow Snake), symphonic poem (Copenhagen, Nov. 20, 1975); *Illuminations*, capriccio for Flute and Strings (1978); *Edvard Munch Triptych* for Chorus and Orch. (Danish Radio, Oct. 11, 1979); *3 Dances* for Wind Orch. (1983). **CHAMBER:** *Illustrations* for 6 Percussion (1965); *Schubert Variations* for 4 Flutes (1974); *Kuhlau Metamorphoses* for 4 Flutes (1978); *Partita* for Flute and Organ (1981); *Tivoli Collage* for 5 Percussion (1983). Also several choral works, including a cantata for the 150th anniversary of the Copenhagen Cathedral (1979), and *Abendstern* for Soprano, English Horn, Harp, and Cello from *Des Knaben Wunderhorn* (1984); organ pieces.

BIBL.: K. Ketting, "E. N.," *Nordic Sounds* (March 1986).

Nordal, Jón, Icelandic composer; b. Reykjavík, March 6, 1926. He studied with Kristjánsson and Thórarinsson at the Reykjavík College of Music; then in Zürich with Burkhard (1949–51); finally in Paris and Rome (1956–57) and in Darmstadt (1957). He taught at the Reykjavík College of Music before becoming its director in 1959. In 1968 he became a member of the Royal Swedish Academy. His early works are in the neo-Classical mold, but in the course of time he adopted colorism in the French impressionist vein.

WORKS: ORCH.: *Concerto Grosso* (1950); *Concerto* (1954); *Sinfonietta seriosa* (1954); Piano Concerto (1957); *Brotaspil* (A Play of Fragments; 1963); *Adagio* for Flute, Harp, Piano, and String Orch. (1965); *Stiklur* (1969); *Canto elegiaco* for Cello and Orch. (1971); *Leidsla* (Rapture; 1973); *Epitafion* (1974); *Langnaetti* (The Winter Night; 1976); *Tvisöng* (Twinsong), double concerto for Violin, Viola, and Orch. (1979); *Tileinkun* (Dedication; 1981); *Choralis* (Washington, D.C., Nov. 23, 1982); Cello Concerto (1983). **CHAMBER:** Violin Sonata (1952); *Rórill* for Flute, Oboe, Clarinet, and Bass Clarinet; Duo for Violin and Cello (1983).

Nordgren, Pehr Henrik, Finnish composer; b. Saltvik, Jan. 19, 1944. He studied composition with Kokkonen and musicology at the Univ. of Helsinki, and composition and traditional Japanese music at the Tokyo Univ. of Arts and Music (1970–73). In his works he utilizes traditional and advanced harmonies and both Western and traditional Japanese instruments.

WORKS: STAGE: *Den svarte munken* (The Black Monk), chamber opera (1981; Stockholm, March 20, 1984); *Alex*, television opera (1983; Helsinki, Sept. 6, 1986). **ORCH.:** *Epiphrase* (1966); *Euphonie I* (Helsinki, Feb. 25, 1967), *II* (1967; Helsinki, Jan. 30, 1969), *III* (Lahti, April 12, 1975), and *IV* (1981); *Minore* (1968); 3 violin concertos: No. 1 (1969; Helsinki, Feb. 12, 1970); No. 2 for Violin and Strings (Helsinki, Nov. 15, 1977); No. 3 for Violin and Strings (1981; Kaustinen, Jan. 31, 1982); 3 viola concertos: No. 1 (1970); No. 2 (Helsinki, Dec. 7, 1979); No. 3 for Viola and Chamber Orch. (Vaasa, July 2, 1986); Concerto for Clarinet, Folk Instruments, and Small Orch. (1970; Helsinki, April 22, 1971); *The Turning Point* (1972; Helsinki, March 12, 1974); *Autumnal Concerto* for Traditional Japanese Instruments and Orch. (Helsinki, Aug. 28, 1974); Sym. (Turku, Oct. 10, 1974); *Koko maailma valittanee* (The Whole World Will Lament) for Strings (1966–74); Piano Concerto (Helsinki, April 22, 1975); *Pelimannimuotokuvia* (Portraits of Country Fiddlers) for Strings (Seinäjoki, April 5, 1976); *Summer Music* (Kaustinen, July 18, 1977); Sym. for Strings (1978; Kokkola, Jan. 14, 1979); 2 cello concertos: No. 1 for Cello and Strings (Kuhmo, July 28, 1980); No. 2 (Helsinki, March 21, 1984); Concerto for Strings (1982; Kokkola, Nov. 27, 1983); *Elegy to Vilho Lampi* (1984; Oulu, Feb. 21, 1985); Concerto for Kantele and Small Orch. (Joensuu, June 19, 1985); *Tanse-Choral* for 15 Strings (Kokkola, Jan. 6, 1986); *HATE-LOVE* for Cello and Strings (1987); Sym. No. 2 (1989). **CHAMBER:** 5 string quartets (1967, 1968, 1976, 1983, 1986); *Nachtwache*, suite from the music to the radio play by Nelly Sachs, for Chamber Ensemble (1967); *Neljä kuolemankuvaa* (4 Pictures of Death) for Chamber Ensemble (1968); *Kolme maanitusta* (3 Enticements): Wind Quintet No. 1 (1970); Quartet No. 1 for Traditional Japanese Instruments (1974); Wind Quintet No. 2 (1975); *Seita*, Quartet No. 2, for Traditional Japanese Instruments (1978); Piano Quintet (1978); Piano Trio (1980); *Equivocations* for Kantele and String Trio (1981). **VOCAL:** *Agnus Dei* for Soprano, Baritone, Chorus, and Orch. (1970; Helsinki, May 11, 1971); *Kuninkaan kämmenellä* (In the Palm of the King's Hand), cantata for Soprano, Baritone, Chorus, and Orch. (1979; Kokkola, Feb. 24, 1980); *Taivaanvalot* (The Lights of Heaven) for Soprano, Tenor, Chorus, Children's Chorus, and Orch. (Kaustinen, Feb. 3, 1985).

Nordheim, Arne, significant Norwegian composer; b. Larvik, June 20, 1931. He studied organ, piano, and theory at the Oslo Cons. (1948–52); received instruction in composition from Karl Andersen, Conrad Baden, and Bjarne Brustad there and from Vagn Holmboe in Copenhagen (1955); then was a music critic of Oslo's *Dagbladet* (1960–68). As a composer, he joined the avant-garde circles; experimented in pointillistic tone color; adopted a motivic method of melorhythmic structures without formal development.

WORKS: *Epigram* for String Quartet (1954); String Quartet (1956); *Aftonland* (Evening Land), song cycle for Soprano and Chamber Ensemble (1957); *Canzona per orchestra* (Bergen, June 11, 1961); *Katharsis*, ballet based on the legend of St. Anthony, for Orch. and Tape (1962); *Kimaere*, ballet (1963); *Partita* for Viola, Harpsichord, and Percussion (1963); *Epitaffio* for Orch. and Tape (1963); *Favola*, musical play for Soloists, Chorus, Orch., and Tape (1965); electronic pieces: *Evolution* (1966), *Warsawa* (1967–68), *Solitaire* (1968), *Pace* (1970), and *Lux et tenebrae* (1971); *3 Responses* for Percussion Groups and Tape (1967); *Eco* for Soprano, Chorus, and Orch. (1967–68); *Colorazione* for Hammond Organ, 2 Percussionists, and Tape (1967–68); *Signaler* for Accordion, Percussion, and Electric Guitar (1967); incidental tape music for Ibsen's *Peer Gynt* (1969); *Floating* for Orch. (Graz, Oct. 20, 1970); *Dinosaurus* for Accordion and Tape (1971); *Listen* for Piano (1971); *Partita II* for Electric Guitar (1971); *Greening* for Orch. (Los Angeles, April 12, 1973); *Zimbel* for Orch. (1974); *Spur* for Accordion and Orch. (1974); *Doria* for Tenor and Orch. (1974–75); 3 ballets: *Strender* (1974), *Aridadne*, with Tape and 2 Sopranos (1977), and *The Tempest*, with Tape (1979); *Be Not Afeared*, after Shakespeare, for Soprano, Baritone, Ensemble, and Tape (1978); *Tempora noctis* for Soprano, Mezzo-soprano, Orch., and Tape (1979); ballet, *The End of Time* (1981); *Tenebrae*, concerto for Cello and Orch. (1981–82; Washington, D.C., Nov. 23, 1982); *Tenebrae* for Cello and Orch. (1982); *Aurora* for 4 Soli, Chorus, 2 Percussionists, and Tape (1984); *Varder* for Trumpet and Orch. (1986); *Rendez-vous* for String Orch. (1987).

Nordica (real name, **Norton**), **Lillian**, distinguished American soprano; b. Farmington, Maine, Dec. 12, 1857; d. Batavia, Java, May 10, 1914. She studied with John O'Neill at the New England Cons. of Music in Boston (graduated, 1876); continued her training with Marie Maretzek in N.Y. (1876), where she made her formal debut as soloist with Gilmore's Grand Boston Band (Sept. 30, 1876); toured with it in the U.S. and later in Europe (1878). After coaching from François Delsarte and Emilio Belari in Paris, she studied with Antonio Sangiovanni at the Milan Cons., who suggested she adopt the stage name Nordica. It was under that name that she made her operatic debut as Donna Elvira at the Teatro Manzoni there (March 8, 1879). In St. Petersburg, she sang for Czar Alexander II a week before he was assassinated in March 1881. After making appearances in several German cities, she went to Paris to study with Giovanni Sbriglia (1881–82); she made her Paris debut on July 22, 1882, as Marguerite, at the Opéra; on Jan. 22, 1883, she married Frederick A. Gower. With him she returned to America and made her American debut as Marguerite with Mapleson's company at N.Y.'s Academy of Music on Nov. 26, 1883. In 1884 she began proceedings for divorce from her 1st husband, but he mysteriously disappeared while attempting to cross the English Channel in a balloon. She made her debut at Covent Garden in London on March 12, 1887, as Violetta; sang there again in 1898, 1899, and 1902. She first sang at the Metropolitan Opera in N.Y. on Dec. 18, 1891, as Valentine in *Les Huguenots*. She was heard for the 1st time as Isolde at the Metropolitan on Nov. 27, 1895, scoring an overwhelming success. From then on she sang chiefly Wagnerian roles; she continued to appear off and on at the Metropolitan until 1909, when she began to make extended concert tours. Her farewell appearance was at a concert in Melbourne on Nov. 25, 1913. In 1896 she married the Hungarian tenor Zoltan Doeme, from whom she was divorced in 1904; in 1909 she married the banker George W. Young in London. She died while on a trip around the world. **BIBL.:** I. Glackens, *Yankee Diva: L. N. and the Golden Days of Opera* (N.Y., 1963).

Nordoff, Paul, American composer and music therapist; b. Philadelphia, June 4, 1909; d. Herdecke, Germany, Jan. 18, 1977. He studied piano with Olga Samaroff at the Philadelphia Cons. (B.M., 1927; M.M., 1932) and composition with Rubin Goldmark at the Juilliard School of Music in N.Y. (1928–33); later received the degree of Bachelor of Music Therapy at Combs College (1960). He taught composition at the Philadelphia Cons. (1937–42), Michigan State College (1945–49), and Bard College (1949–59); held 2 Guggenheim fellowships (1933, 1935). From 1959 he devoted himself mainly to music therapy for handicapped children. With C. Robbins, he publ. *Music Therapy for Handicapped Children: Investigations and Experience* (N.Y., 1965), *Music Therapy in Special Education* (N.Y., 1971), *Therapy in Music for Handicapped Children* (N.Y., 1971), and *Creative Music Therapy: Individualized Treatment for the Handicapped Child* (N.Y., 1977).

WORKS: STAGE: OPERAS: *Mr. Fortune* (1936–37; rev. 1956–57); *The Sea Change* (1951). **OPERETTA:** *The Masterpiece* (1940; Philadelphia, Jan. 24, 1941). **BALLETS:** *Every Soul Is a Circus* (1937); *Salem Shore* (1943); *Tally Ho* (1943). **ORCH.:** *Prelude and 3 Fugues* for Chamber Orch. (1932–36); Piano Concerto (1935); Suite (1938); Concerto for Violin, Piano, and Orch. (1948); Violin Concerto (1949); *The Frog Prince* for Narrator and Orch. (1954); *Winter Symphony* (1954); *Spring Symphony* (1956); *Gothic Concerto* for Piano and Orch. (1959). **CHAMBER:** Piano Quintet (1936); Quintet for Winds and Piano (1948); Sonata for Violin and Piano (1950); Sonata for Flute and Piano (1953); also choral works, songs, piano pieces, and many works for handicapped children.

Nordqvist, (Johan) Conrad, Swedish conductor, organist, and composer; b. Vänersborg, April 11, 1840; d. Charlottenlund, April 16, 1920. He was a pupil of the Stockholm Cons. (1856); joined the court orch. in 1859 as a viola player; in 1864, became regimental bandmaster; in 1876, became chorus master at the Royal Opera; then was court conductor (1885–92; 1897–1908). From 1870 to 1872, from 1880 to 1900, and from 1910 to 1916 he taught at the Stockholm Cons.; then occupied various posts as organist and conductor. He wrote a funeral march for the obsequies of Charles XV (1872) and a festival march for the golden wedding anniversary of Oscar II (1897), besides ballets, piano pieces, and songs.

Nordraak, Rikard, Norwegian composer; b. Christiania, June 12, 1842; d. Berlin, March 20, 1866. He was a pupil of Kiel and Kullak in Berlin; was a composer with a strong Norwegian nationalist tendency; was a close friend of Grieg, upon whom he exerted a considerable influence, and who wrote a funeral march in his memory. He wrote the Norwegian national anthem, *Ja, vi elsker dette landet* (Yes, We Love This Land), which was first sung on Norway's national day (May 17, 1864). His other works include incidental music to Björnson's *Maria Stuart i Skotland* (1864–65; Christiania, 1867) and *Sigurd Slembe: Kaares sang* (Copenhagen, 1865), several unaccompanied male choruses, songs, and piano pieces. His death at the age of 23 was a grievous loss to Norway's music. **BIBL.:** L. Greni, *R. N.* (Oslo, 1941); A. van E. Sein, *R. N.* (Oslo, 1942).

Noren, Heinrich (real name, **Heinrich Suso Johannes Gottlieb**; in 1916 he added his wife's name, Noren, to his own), Austrian violinist and composer; b. Graz, Jan. 5, 1861; d. Rottach, Bavaria, June 6, 1928. He studied violin with Vieuxtemps in Brussels (1878) and with Massart in Paris (1883); composition with Gernsheim and Bussler in Berlin; in 1895 he settled in Krefeld, where he founded his own music school. He then taught at the Stern Cons. in Berlin (1901–7); in 1915 he moved to Rottach. His name attracted attention with the performance of his orch. variations, *Kaleidoskop* (Dresden, July 1, 1907), in which the last movement, dedicated to "a famous contemporary," was a variation on a theme from *Ein Heldenleben* by Richard Strauss. The publishers of Strauss instituted a lawsuit against Noren, which created a ripple of excitement in musical circles. Noren also composed an opera, *Der Schleier der Beatrice*; Sym.; Violin Concerto; and some chamber music.

Norena, Eidé (real name, **Kaja Andrea Karoline Hansen-Eidé**), Norwegian soprano; b. Horten, April 26, 1884; d. Lausanne, Nov. 19, 1968. She studied voice with Ellen Gulbranson in Christiania; later in Weimar, London, and Paris; was a pupil of Raimund von Zur Mühlen; began her career as a concert singer in Scandinavia. She made her operatic debut as Amor in Gluck's *Orfeo* in Christiania (1907), subsequently singing at the National Theater there (1908–18). After appearances at Stockholm's Royal Theater, she sang at La Scala in Milan, Covent Garden in London, and at the Paris Opéra. She was a member of the Chicago Opera (1926–28); from 1933 to 1938, of the Metropolitan Opera in N.Y. (made her debut as Mimi, on Feb. 9, 1933); toured the U.S. in concert.

Nørgård, Per, prominent Danish composer and pedagogue; b. Gentofte, near Copenhagen, July 13, 1932. He began piano lessons when he was 8; in 1949 he became a private composition pupil of Holmboe; after entering the Royal Danish Cons. of Music in Copenhagen (1952), he continued his training with Holmboe there and also took courses with Høffding (theory), Koppel (piano), and Jersild (solfège), passing his examinations in theory, composition, and pedagogy (1955); following further studies with Nadia Boulanger in Paris (1956–57), he was awarded the Lily Boulanger Prize in 1957. He was a music critic for Copenhagen's *Politiken* (1958–62); also taught at the Odense Cons. (1958–60); after teaching at the Royal Danish Cons. of Music in Copenhagen (1960–65), he joined the faculty of the Århus Cons. in 1965, where he was made prof. of composition in 1987. In 1988 he was awarded the Henrik-Steffens-Preis of Germany. After a period of adolescent emulation of Sibelius, he plunged into the mainstream of cosmopolitan music-making, exploring the quasi-mathematical serial techniques based on short tonal motifs, rhythmic displacement, metrical modulation, pointillism, graphic notation, and a "horizontal" invariant fixing certain notes to specific registers; then shifted to a pointillistically impressionistic colorism evolving in a tonal bradykinesis.

WORKS: STAGE: OPERAS: *The Labyrinth* (1963; Copenhagen, Sept. 2, 1967); *Gilgamesh* (1971–72; Århus, May 4, 1973); *Siddharta* (1977–79; Stockholm, March 18, 1983); *The Divine Tivoli,* chamber opera (1982). **BALLETS:** *Le Jeune Homme à marier* (1964; Danish Television, April 2, 1965; 1st stage perf., Copenhagen, Oct. 15, 1967); *Tango Chicane* (Copenhagen, Oct. 15, 1967); *Trio* for 3 Dancers and Percussion (Paris, Dec., 1972). **ORCH.:** *Metamorphose* for Strings (1952); 5 syms.: No. 1, *Sinfonia austera* (1954; Danish Radio, Aug. 19, 1958); No. 2 (Århus, April 13, 1970); No. 3 (1972–75; Copenhagen, Sept. 2, 1976); No. 4, *Indian Rose Garden and Chinese Witch Lake* (Hamburg, Oct. 30, 1981); No. 5 (1990); *Constellations,* concerto for 12 Solo Strings or 12 String Groups (Copenhagen, Nov. 3, 1958); *Lyse Danse* for Chamber Orch. (1959); *Fragment VI* for 6 Orch. Groups: Winds, Brass, Percussion, Harp, Pianos, Timpani (1959–61; Århus, Feb. 12, 1962); *Iris* (Copenhagen, May 19, 1967); *Luna, 4 Phases* (Danish Radio, Sept. 5, 1968); *Recall* for Accordion and Orch. (1968); *Voyage into the Golden Screen* for Chamber Orch. (Copenhagen, March 24, 1969); *Mosaic* for 16 Winds (1969); *Doing* for Wind Orch. (1969); *Dream Play* for Chamber Orch. (1975); *Twilight* for Orch. and Conga Player Obbligato with Dancer ad libitum (1976–77); *For a Change,* percussion concerto (1982); *Burn* (Glasgow, Sept. 17, 1984); *Between* for Cello and Orch. (Copenhagen, Aug. 30, 1985); *Prelude to Breaking* (Göteborg, Sept. 26, 1986); *Remembering Child* for Viola and Chamber Orch. (St. Paul, Minn., Sept. 12, 1986); *Helle Nacht,* violin concerto (1987); *Pastorale* for String Orch. (1988); *King, Queen, and Ace* for Harp and Chamber Ensemble (1989). **CHAMBER:** Quintet for Flute, Violin, Viola, Cello, and Piano (1951–52); *Suite* for Flute and Piano (1952); *Solo intimo* for Cello (1953); *Diptychon* for Violin and Piano (1953); 2 trios for Clarinet, Cello, and Piano (1955, 1974); *Songs from Aftonland* for Contralto, Flute, Harp, Violin, Viola, and Cello (1956); 3 string quartets: No. 1, *Quartetto brioso* (1958); No. 2, *In 3 Spheres* (1965); No. 3, *Inscape* (1969); *Miniatures* for String Quartet (1959); *Waves*

for Percussion (1969); *Returns* for Guitar (1976); *I Ching* for Percussion (1982); *9 Friends* for Harmonica or Piano (1985); *Tintinnabulary* for String Quartet (1986); *Lin* for Clarinet, Cello, and Piano (1986); *Hut ab* for 2 Clarinets (1988); *Syn* for Brass Quintet (1988); *Swan Descending* for Harp (1989). **PIANO:** 2 sonatas (1952, 1957); *Sketches* (1959); *9 Studies* (1959); *4 Fragments* (1959–60); *Grooving* (1967–68); *Turn* (1973); *Achilles and the Tortoise* (1983). **ORGAN:** *Canon* (1971); *Triapartita* (1988). **VOCAL:** *Triptychon* for Mixed Voices and Wind Instruments or Organ (1957); *Nocturnes,* suite for Soprano and Piano or 19 Instruments (1961–62); *3 Love Songs* for Contralto and Orch. (1963); *Prism* for 3 Vocalists and Instrumental Ensemble (1964); *The Fourth Day* for Chorus and Orch. (1984–85; 4th movement of a collaborative work, *Hexaemeron,* depicting the 7 days of creation); *Entwicklungen* for Alto and Instrumental Ensemble (1986); *L'Enfant et l'aube* for Soprano, Tenor, and Chamber Ensemble (Radio France, Paris, June 7, 1988).

Nørholm, Ib, Danish composer; b. Copenhagen, Jan. 24, 1931. He studied theory with Holmboe, music history with Hjelmborg, and form and analysis with Bentzon and Høffding at the Royal Danish Cons. of Music in Copenhagen (1950–54), passing his examinations in theory and music history (1954), organ and teaching (1955), and sacred music (1956). He was active as a music critic (1956–64); was a church organist in Elsinore (1957–63) and then at Copenhagen's Bethlemskirken (from 1964); also taught part-time at the Royal Danish Cons. of Music in Copenhagen (from 1961) and at the Odense Cons.; subsequently taught theory at the Royal Danish Cons. of Music in Copenhagen (from 1973). His musical idiom is permeated with Scandinavian lyricism, even when he introduces modernistic devices.

WORKS: STAGE: Opera, *Invitation to a Beheading,* after Vladimir Nabokov's novel (1965, Danish Television, Oct. 10, 1967); chamber opera, *Den unge Park* (The Young Park; Århus, Oct. 14, 1970); chorus opera, *The Garden Wall,* for 20 Singers and Chamber Ensemble (1976); chamber opera, *The Revenge of the Truth* (1985). **ORCH.:** 7 syms.: No. 1 (Danish Radio, Aug. 13, 1959); No. 2, *Isola Bella* (Copenhagen, April 27, 1972); No. 3, *Day's Nightmare* (Copenhagen, Oct. 9, 1973); No. 4, *Modskabelse,* for Soloists, Chorus, and Orch. (1979); No. 5 (1981); No. 6 (1982); No. 7, *Ecliptical Instincts* (Copenhagen, May 20, 1983); *Fluctuations* for 34 Solo Strings, 2 Harps, Harpsichord, Mandolin, and Guitar (1962); *Relief I* and *II* for Chamber Ensemble (both 1963) and *III* for Orch. (1964); *Serenade of Cincinnatus* for Chamber Orch. (1964); *Exile* (Copenhagen, Sept. 8, 1966); *Efter Ikaros* (After Icarus), suite (1967); *Jongleurs-69* for Soloists, Chorus, Ensembles, Loudspeaker Voice, and Orch. (Odense, Nov. 25, 1969); *Tys og lovsang* (Light and Hymn of Thanksgiving) for Soloists, Chorus, Organ, and Instrumental Ensemble (Copenhagen Cathedral, Dec. 5, 1972); *Day's Nightmare II* for Soloists, Chorus, and Orch. (Copenhagen, Nov. 29, 1973); *Heretic Hymn,* fresco (1974); *Proprium Missae Dominicae Pentacostis* for 2 Choruses, Winds, and Organ (1977); *Idylles d'Apocalypse* for Organ and 20 Instruments (1980); *Lux Secunda* for Soprano, Baritone, Chorus, and Small Orch. (1984). **CHAMBER:** *Rhapsody* for Viola and Piano (1955); 7 string quartets: No. 1, *In Vere* (1955); No. 2, *5 Impromptus* (1965); No. 3, *From My Green Herbarium* (1966); No. 4, *September—October—November* (1966); No. 5 (1976); No. 6, *Skygerne Frosner* (1978); No. 7, *En passant* (1985); *Tombeau* for Cello and Piano (1956); Violin Sonata (1956–57); Trio for Clarinet, Cello, and Piano (1957); *Mosaic Fragments* for Flute and String Trio (1958); Piano Trio (1959); *Signature from a Province* for Piano (1970); *Dialogue in 3 Courses* for Guitar, Accordion, and Percussion (1972); Guitar Sonata (1976); *Essai prismatique* for Piano Trio (1979); *The Garden with Paths That Part* for 7 Instruments (1982); *6 Short Motets* (1986); songs.

Norlind, (Johan Henrik) Tobias, distinguished Swedish musicologist; b. Vellinge, May 6, 1879; d. Stockholm, Aug. 13, 1947. He studied piano and music in Lund; then went to

Germany, where he took courses in composition with Jadassohn at the Leipzig Cons. (1897–98) and with Thuille in Munich (1898–99); he also studied musicology with Sandberger at the Univ. of Munich, and subsequently with Friedlaender at the Univ. of Berlin. Returning to Sweden in 1900, he attended the univs. of Uppsala and Lund, obtaining the degree of Ph.D. in 1909. He then held several positions as an instructor in colleges and univs.; taught music history at the Stockholm Cons. (1918–45).

WRITINGS: All publ. in Stockholm unless otherwise given: *Svensk musikhistoria* (Hälsingborg, 1901; 2nd ed., 1918; abr. Ger. tr., 1904); *Allmänt musiklexikon* (1912–16; 2nd ed., 1927–28); *Jenny Lind: en minnesbok till hundraårsdagen* (1919); *Allmän musikhistoria* (1922); *Kristina Nilsson, sångerskan och konstärinnan* (1923); *Beethoven och hans tid* (1924–25); with E. Trobäck, *Kunglia hovkapellets historia 1526–1926* (1926); *Systematik der Saiteninstrumente*: Vol. I, *Geschichte der Zither* (1936), and Vol. II, *Geschichte des Klaviers* (1939; 2nd ed., 1941); *Bilder ur svenska musikens historia från äldsta tid till medeltidens slut* (1947).

BIBL.: C. Moberg, "T. N.," *Die Musikforschung*, II (1949).

Norman, Jessye, exceptionally gifted black American soprano; b. Augusta, Ga., Sept. 15, 1945. She received a scholarship to study at Howard Univ. in Washington, D.C. (1961), where she had vocal lessons from Carolyn Grant; continued her training at the Peabody Cons. of Music in Baltimore and at the Univ. of Michigan, where her principal teachers were Pierre Bernac and Elizabeth Mannion. She won the Munich Competition (1968), and then made her operatic debut as Elisabeth in *Tannhäuser* at the Berlin Deutsche Oper (1969); appeared in the title role of *L'Africaine* at Florence's Maggio Musicale (1971), and the following year sang Aida at Milan's La Scala and Cassandra in *Les Troyens* at London's Covent Garden; subsequently made major recital debuts in London and N.Y. (1973). After an extensive concert tour of North America (1976–77), she made her U.S. stage debut as Jocasta in *Oedipus rex* and as Purcell's Dido on a double bill with the Opera Co. of Philadelphia on Nov. 22, 1982. She made her Metropolitan Opera debut in N.Y. as Cassandra on Sept. 26, 1983. In 1986 she appeared as soloist in Strauss's *Vier letzte Lieder* with the Berlin Phil. during its tour of the U.S. On Sept. 20, 1989, she was the featured soloist with Zubin Mehta and the N.Y. Phil. in its opening concert of its 148th season, which was telecast live to the nation by PBS. Her extraordinary repertory ranges from Purcell to Richard Rodgers; she commended herself in Mussorgsky's songs, which she performed in Moscow in the original Russian; in her recitals she gave performances of the classical German repertory as well as contemporary masterpieces, such as Schoenberg's *Gurrelieder* and the French moderns, which she invariably performed in the original tongue. This combination of scholarship and artisty contributed to her consistently successful career as one of the most versatile concert and operatic singers of her time.

Norman, (Fredrick Vilhelm) Ludvig, Swedish conductor and composer; b. Stockholm, Aug. 28, 1831; d. there, March 28, 1885. He studied piano and composition at the Leipzig Cons. with Moscheles, Hauptmann, and Rietz (1848–53); returning to Stockholm, he taught at the Cons. (1858–61); was made conductor of the royal orch. (1861); was founder-conductor of the Nya Harmoniska Sallskapet (1869–78); later was active with the Musikförening and the Konsertförening. He married the violinist **Wilma Neruda** in 1864 (separated, 1869). He publ. *Musikaliska uppsatser och kritiker* (Stockholm, 1888).

WORKS: 3 syms. (1858, 1871, 1881); Konsertstycke for Piano and Orch. (1875); 4 overtures; 2 cantatas; String Sextet (1854); String Octet (1866–67); String Quintet (1870); 6 string quartets; Piano Quintet (1856–57); Piano Trio (1871–72); Sextet for Piano, 2 Violins, Viola, Cello, and Double Bass (1868–69); Cello Sonata (1867); Viola Sonata (1869); piano pieces; songs.

BIBL.: J. Bagge, *Förteckning öfver L. N.s tonvert* (Stockholm, 1886).

Norrington, Roger (Arthur Carver), scholarly English conductor; b. Oxford, March 16, 1934. He was educated at Clare College, Cambridge, and the Royal College of Music in London; was active as a tenor. In 1962 he founded the Schütz Choir in London, with which he first gained notice as a conductor. From 1966 to 1984 he was principal conductor of the Kent Opera, where he produced scores by Monteverdi utilizing his own performing eds.; served as music director of the London Baroque Players (from 1975) and the London Classical Players (from 1978); also was principal conductor of the Bournemouth Sinfonietta (1985–89). On April 2, 1989, he made an auspicious N.Y. debut at Carnegie Hall conducting Beethoven's 8th and 9th syms. In 1990 he became music director of the Orch. of St. Luke's in N.Y. In 1980 he was made an Officer of the Order of the British Empire; in 1990, a Commander of the Order of the British Empire. Norrington entered controversy by insisting that the classical tempo is basic for all interpretation. He also insisted that Beethoven's metronome markings, not usually accepted by performers, are in fact accurate reflections of Beethoven's inner thoughts about his own music. He obtained numerous defenders of his ideas (as one critic put it, "inspired literalism") for the interpretation of classical music, which aroused sharp interest as well as caustic rejection. However that might be, his performances, especially in the U.S., received a great deal of attention, and he was particularly praised for the accuracy and precision of his interpretations. In 1985 he began an annual series of musical "experiences": weekends devoted to in-depth exploration of some major classical work, comprising lectures, open rehearsals, research exhibits, and performances of other works by the same composer (which have included Haydn and Berlioz as well as the inevitable Beethoven) and his contemporaries, selected to explicate the musical centerpiece.

BIBL.: E. Greenfield, "R. N.," *Musical America* (July 1989); N. Kenyon, "R. N.: The Forward March of Early Music," *Ovation* (June 1989).

North, Alex, gloriously gifted American composer and conductor with a predilection for uniquely colored film music; b. Chester, Pa., Dec. 4, 1910. His father, a blacksmith, was an early immigrant from Russia. North studied piano and music theory at the Curtis Inst. of Music in Philadelphia; later received a scholarship to study at the Juilliard School of Music in N.Y., where he took courses in composition (1929–32). A decisive change in his life came with his decision to go to Russia as a technology specialist at a time when Russia was eager to engage American technicians. He became fascinated with new Russian music and received a scholarship to attend the Moscow Cons., where he studied composition with Anton Weprik and Victor Bielyi (1933–35). He also was music director of the propaganda group of German Socialists called "Kolonne Links" (Column to the Left!). He mastered the Russian language and acquired a fine reputation in Russia as a true friend of Soviet music. Returning to the U.S., he took additional courses in composition with Aaron Copland (1936–38) and Ernst Toch (1938–39). In 1939 he conducted 26 concerts in Mexico as music director of the Anna Sokolow Dance Troupe; during his stay in Mexico City, he had some instruction from Silvestre Revueltas. In 1942 North entered the U.S. Army; promoted to captain, he became responsible for entertainment programs in mental hospitals. He worked closely with the psychiatrist Karl Menninger in developing a theatrical genre called "psychodrama," which later became an accepted mode of psychological therapy. During his Army years, North also worked with the Office of War Information, composing scores for over 25 documentary films. During all these peregrinations he developed a distinct flair for theater music, while continuing to produce estimable works in absolute forms. His concerto, *Revue for Clarinet and Orch.*, was performed by Benny Goodman in N.Y. under the baton of Leonard Bernstein on Nov. 18, 1946. He further expanded his creative talents to write a number of modern ballets. The result of these multifarious excursions into musical forms was the formation of a style peculiarly recognizable as the specific art of North. His concentrated efforts, however, became directed mainly toward the art of film music, a field in which he triumphed. John Huston stated in 1986 that "it is the genius of Alex North to convey an emotion to the audience"; other directors praised North's cine-musical abilities in similar terms. Among the writers with whom he worked were Tennessee Williams, John Steinbeck, and Arthur Miller. But no success is without disheartening frustration. North was commissioned to write the score for *2001: A Space Odyssey*, on which he worked enthusiastically. But much to his dismay, the director, Stanley Kubrick, decided to replace it by a pasticcio that included such commonplaces as *The Blue Danube Waltz*. North refused to be downhearted by this discomfiture and used the discarded material for his 3rd Sym. He was nominated 15 times for an Academy Award for best film music, but it was not until 1986 that the Academy of Motion Picture Arts and Sciences finally awarded him an Oscar for lifetime achievement. Among his outstanding scores are *A Streetcar Named Desire* (1951), *Death of a Salesman* (1951), *Viva Zapata!* (1952), *The Rose Tattoo* (1955), *The Bad Seed* (1956), *The Rainmaker* (1956), *The Sound and the Fury* (1959), *Spartacus* (1960), *The Children's Hour* (1961), *The Misfits* (1961), *Cleopatra* (1963), *The Agony and the Ecstasy* (1965), *Who's Afraid of Virginia Woolf?* (1966), *The Shoes of the Fisherman* (1968), *Shanks* (1973), *Bite the Bullet* (1975), *Dragonslayer* (1981), *Under the Volcano* (1984), *Prizzi's Honor* (1985), *The Penitent* (1986), *The Dead* (1987), and *Good Morning, Vietnam* (1988). His song *Unchained Melody* (1955) became a popular hit.

WORKS: STAGE: BALLETS: *Ballad in a Popular Style,* for Anna Sokolow (1933); *Case History* (1933); *War Is Beautiful* (1936); *Slaughter of the Innocents* (N.Y., Nov. 14, 1937); *American Lyric,* for Martha Graham (N.Y., Dec. 26, 1937); *Inquisition* (1938); *Lupe* (1940); *Design for 5* (1941); *Exile* (Mansfield, March 3, 1941); *Golden Fleece,* for Hanya Holm (Mansfield, March 17, 1941); *Clay Ritual* (Hartford, Conn., May 20, 1942); *Intersection* (1947); *A Streetcar Named Desire* (Montreal, Oct. 9, 1952); *Daddy Long Legs Dream Ballet* (1955; for Fred Astaire and Leslie Caron in the film *Daddy Long Legs*); *Mal de siècle* (Brussels, July 3, 1958). **CHILDREN'S OPERA AND THEATER:** *The Hither and Thither of Danny Dither* (1941); *Little Indian Drum* for Narrator and Orch. (N.Y., Oct. 19, 1947). **ORCH.:** *Rhapsody* for Piano and Orch. (N.Y., Nov. 11, 1941); *Revue* for Clarinet and Orch. (N.Y., Nov. 18, 1946); Sym. No. 1 (1947); *Morning Star Cantata* for Chorus and Orch. (N.Y., May 18, 1947); *Negro Mother Cantata* for Chorus and Orch. (N.Y., May 17, 1948); *Holiday Set* (Saratoga, N.Y., July 10, 1948); Sym. No. 2 (1968); Sym. No. 3 (1971; based upon unused original score for *2001: A Space Odyssey*); also a Trio and a Quintet for Wood winds.

North, Roger, English lawyer and writer on music; b. probably in Tostock, Suffolk, c.1651; d. Rougham, March 1, 1734. He was a member of Parliament; served as Queen's Attorney General under James II until the Revolution of 1688. His writings were not publ. during his lifetime and have only recently been recognized as significant contributions to music. See J. Wilson, ed., *Roger North on Music: Being a Selection from His Essays Written during the Years c.1695–1728* (London, 1959); M. Chan and J. Kassler, eds., *Roger North's Cursory Notes of Musicke* (c.1698–c.1703): *A Physical, Psychological and Critical Theory* (Kensington, N.S.W., 1986); idem and J. Hine, *Roger North's Writings on Music to c.1703: A Set of Analytical Indexes* (Kensington, N.S.W., 1986); idem, *Roger North's The Musical Grammarian and Theory of Sounds* (Kensington, N.S.W., 1988).

Norvo, Red (real name, **Kenneth Norville**), American jazz xylophonist, vibraphonist, and bandleader; b. Beardstown, Ill., March 31, 1908. He played piano and xylophone while attending classes in mining engineering at the Univ. of Missouri (1926–27); later joined Paul Whiteman's orch. In 1935 he organized his own band in N.Y.; also worked with Benny Goodman (1944–45) and Woody Herman (1945–46). He was temporarily married to the blues singer **Mildred Bailey.**

Noske, Frits (Rudolf), Dutch musicologist; b. The Hague, Dec. 13, 1920. He studied cello and theory at the Amsterdam Cons. and at the Royal Cons. in The Hague (1940–45), then pursued musicological training with Bernet Kempers and Smits van Waesberghe at the Univ. of Amsterdam (Ph.D., 1954, with the diss. *La Mélodie française de Berlioz à Duparc*; publ. in Amsterdam, 1954; Eng. tr., rev., 1970); also had lessons with Masson at the Sorbonne in Paris (1949–50). He taught music history at the Amsterdam Cons. and at the Bussum Toonkunst Music School; was librarian at the Amsterdam Music Library (1951–54), and subsequently was its director (1954–68); also was a reader in musicology at the Univ. of Leiden (1965–68) and prof. of musicology at the Univ. of Amsterdam (from 1968).

WRITINGS: *Forma formans: Een struutuuranalytische methode, toegepast op de instrumentale muziek van Jan Pieterszoon Sweelinck* (Amsterdam, 1969; Eng. tr., rev., 1976, in the *International Review of the Aesthetics and Sociology of Music*, VII); *The Signifier and the Signified: Studies in the Operas of Mozart and Verdi* (The Hague, 1977); *Sweelinck* (Oxford, 1988).

Noskowski, Zygmunt (Sigismund von), significant Polish conductor and composer; b. Warsaw, May 2, 1846; d. there, July 23, 1909. He studied at the Warsaw Music Inst.; then became an instructor in a school for the blind, and devised a music notation for the blind. He subsequently studied composition with Kiel in Berlin. After a brief period of professional activities in Western Europe, he returned to Warsaw and was director of the Music Society (1881–1902); in 1888 he was appointed a prof. at the Warsaw Cons.; later was director of the Warsaw Phil. (1905–8) and Opera (1907–9). He wrote the operas *Livia Quintilla* (Lemberg, Feb. 1, 1898), *Wyrok* (The Judgement; Warsaw, Nov. 15, 1906), and *Zemsta za mur graniczny* (Revenge for the Boundary Wall), after A. Fredro's *Zemsta* (Warsaw, 1909); 3 syms.: No. 1 (1874–75); No. 2, *Elegiac* (1875–79); No. 3, *Od wiosny do wiosny* (From Spring to Spring; 1903); *Morskie Oko*, symphonic overture (1875); *Step* (The Steppe), symphonic poem (1896–97); *Z zycia narodu* (From the Life of the Nation), symphonic variations (1901); chamber music; songs.

BIBL.: A. Sutkowski, *Z. N.* (Krakow, 1957); W. Wrónski, *Materialy z życia i twórczości Z. N.ego* (Krakow, 1960).

Noté, Jean, Belgian baritone; b. Tournai, May 6, 1859; d. Brussels, April 1, 1922. He studied at the Ghent Cons.; made his debut in a concert in Ghent in 1883; then sang opera in Lille, Brussels, Lyons, Marseilles, etc. He made his N.Y. Metropolitan Opera debut on Dec. 3, 1908, as Escamillo. In 1913 he joined the Paris Opéra, and remained on its roster until his death. Among his finest roles were Hamlet, Beckmesser, Rigoletto, and Wolfram.

Notker "Balbulus" (the latter nickname meaning "stammerer"), music theorist and composer; b. Elgg, near Zürich (or Jonschwyl, near St. Gallen), c.840; d. April 6, 912. He was a monk at the St. Gallen monastery. He was one of the earliest and most important writers of sequences; his *Liber hymnorum* (sequence texts of the year 884) is of particular interest. Several short treatises on music ascribed to him are most likely by others, including Notker Labeo (b. c.950; d. St. Gallen, June 29, 1022), a monk at St. Gallen, known as Notker the German.

BIBL.: A. Henschel, *Zehn Sequenzen des N. B., aus den ältesten Quellen übertragen und mit der Überlieferung verglichen* (diss., Univ. of Erlangen, 1924); R. van Doren, *Etude sur l'influence musicale de l'Abbaye de St. Gall* (1925); H. Husmann, "Die St. Galler Sequenztradition bei N. und Ekkehard," *Acta Musicologica*, 26 (1954); R. Crocker, *The Early Medieval Sequence* (Berkeley, Calif., 1977).

Nottebohm, (Martin) Gustav, distinguished German musicologist; b. Lüdenscheid, Westphalia, Nov. 12, 1817; d. Graz, Oct. 29, 1882. He studied with Berger and Dehn in Berlin (1838–39); then with Mendelssohn and Schumann in Leipzig (1840–45); finally with Sechter in Vienna (1846), where he settled as a music teacher. He revised the Beethoven ed. publ. by Breitkopf & Härtel, prepared thematic catalogues of the works of Beethoven and Schubert, and edited some of the works of Mozart. Of particular importance are his studies of Beethoven's sketchbooks.

WRITINGS: All publ. in Leipzig unless otherwise given: *Ein Skizzenbuch von Beethoven* (1865; 2nd ed., 1924, by P. Mies, as *Zwei Skizzenbücher von Beethoven aus den Jahren 1801 bis 1803*); *Thematisches Verzeichniss der im Druck erschienenen Werke von Ludwig van Beethoven* (2nd ed., 1868, reprint, 1969); *Beethoveniana* (1872; 2nd ed., 1925); *Beethovens Studien* (1873; includes Beethoven's exercise books under Haydn, Albrechtsberger, and Salieri); *Thematisches Verzeichniss der im Druck erschienenen Werke von Franz Schubert* (Vienna, 1874); *Mozartiana* (1880); E. Mandyczewski, ed., *Zweite Beethoveniana* (1887; 2nd ed., 1925).

Nouguès, Jean, French composer; b. Bordeaux, April 25, 1875; d. Auteuil, Aug. 28, 1932. He showed marked precocity as a composer, having completed an opera, *Le Roi du Papagey,* before he was 16. After regular study in Paris, he produced his opera *Yannha* at Bordeaux in 1897. The next 2 operas, *Thamyris* (Bordeaux, 1904) and *La Mort de Tintagiles* (Paris, 1905), were brought out without much success; but after the production of his spectacular *Quo Vadis?* (text by H. Cain, after Sienkiewicz's famous novel; Nice, Feb. 9, 1909), he suddenly found himself famous. The work was given in Paris on Nov. 26, 1909, and in N.Y. on April 4, 1911; had numerous revivals in subsequent years. His later operas failed to measure up to *Quo Vadis?;* they included *L'Auberge rouge* (Nice, Feb. 21, 1910), *La Vendetta* (Marseilles, 1911), *L'Aiglon* (Rouen, Feb. 2, 1912), and *Le Scarabée bleu* (1931).

Nourrit, Adolphe, celebrated French tenor; b. Montpellier, March 3, 1802; d. (suicide) Naples, March 8, 1839. He studied voice with the elder Manuel García; at the age of 19, he made his debut as Pylaides in Gluck's opera *Iphigénie en Tauride* at the Paris Opéra (Sept. 10, 1821), with excellent success. He soon became known in Paris as one of the finest tenors of his generation, and famous opera composers entrusted him with leading roles at the premieres of their works; thus, he appeared in the title role of Meyerbeer's *Robert le Diable* (Paris, Nov. 21, 1831) and as Raoul in *Les Huguenots* (Paris, Feb. 29, 1836); in the title role in Rossini's *Le Comte Ory* (Paris, Aug. 20, 1828) and as Arnold in his *Guillaume Tell* (Paris, Aug. 3, 1829); as Masaniello in Auber's *La Muette de Portici* (Paris, Feb. 29, 1828); as Eléazar in Halévy's *La Juive* (Paris, Feb. 23, 1835); and others. He then traveled in Italy in Dec. 1837, and was particularly successful in Naples. His career seemed to be assured, but despite all these successes, vocal problems and a liver ailment led to depression, and he killed himself by jumping from the roof of his lodging in Naples.

BIBL.: M. Quicherat, *A. N.: Sa vie* (3 vols., Paris, 1867); E. Boutet de Monvel, *Un Artiste d'autrefois, A. N.* (2 vols., Paris, 1903); F. Rogers, "A. N.," *Musical Quarterly* (Jan. 1939).

Nováček, Ottokar (Eugen), Czech-American violinist and composer; b. Weisskirchen, Hungary, May 13, 1866; d. N.Y., Feb. 3, 1900. He studied violin with his father, Martin Joseph Nováček, and with Brodsky at the Leipzig Cons., graduating in 1885. In 1891 he was engaged to join the Boston Sym. Orch.; then played in the Damrosch Orch. in N.Y. (1892–93). In America, Nováček began to compose; his name became known chiefly through his brilliant *Perpetuum mobile* for Violin and Orch.; he also wrote a Piano Concerto; 3 string quartets; *8 Concert-Caprices* for Violin and Piano; *Bulgarian Dances* for Violin and Piano; and songs.

Nováček, Rudolf, Czech violinist and composer; b. Bela Crkva, April 7, 1860; d. Prague, Aug. 12, 1929. He lived mostly in Temesvár; also held occasional positions as violin teacher and conductor in Rumania, Bulgaria, and Russia. His Sinfonietta for Wind Instruments (Prague, Nov. 11, 1888) became popular.

Novães, Guiomar, extraordinary Brazilian pianist; b. São João da Bôa Vista, Feb. 28, 1895; d. São Paulo, March 7, 1979. She was the 17th of 19 offspring in a highly fecund family;

studied piano with Luigi Chiafarelli; soon began performing in public recitals. The Brazilian government sent her to France to take part in a competition for entering the Paris Cons.; she won 1st place among 389 contestants from a jury that included Debussy and Fauré; Debussy praised her for "the power of total inner concentration, rare among artists." She enrolled in the class of Isidor Philipp, who later described her as a true "force of nature." She graduated from the Paris Cons. in 1911, and made a successful concert tour in France, England, and Italy. She made her U.S. debut at a N.Y. recital on Nov. 11, 1915, and subsequently made numerous tours of the U.S. Reviewing one of her concerts, James Huneker described her as "the Paderewska of the Pampas." In 1922 she married the Brazilian composer **Octavio Pinto.** She made her home in São Paulo, with frequent sojourns in N.Y. In 1956 the Brazilian government awarded her the Order of Merit as a goodwill ambassador to the U.S. She made her last U.S. appearance in 1972. She was especially praised for her interpretations of the music of Chopin, Schumann, and other composers of the Romantic era; she also played pieces by South American composers, including some works written for her by her husband. Her playing was notable for its dynamic colors; she exuded a personal charm, while often disregarding the more pedantic aspects of the music.

Novák, Jan, Czech composer; b. Nová Říše na Morave, April 8, 1921; d. Ulm, Germany, Nov. 17, 1984. He studied composition with Petrželka at the Brno Cons. (1940–46; interrupted by the Nazi occupation) and Bořkovec at the Prague Academy of Musical Arts (1946–47), then with Copland at the Berkshire Music Center at Tanglewood (1947) and Martinů in N.Y. (1947–48). He subsequently made his home in Brno; being outside his homeland at the time of the Soviet invasion (1968), he chose not to return, and went to Denmark before settling in Rovereto, Italy (1970), where he taught piano at the municipal music school. Predictably, his works ceased to be performed in his native land until the Communist regime collapsed in 1989. His early music is influenced by Martinů; with the Concertino for Wind Quintet (1957) and the *Capriccio* for Cello and Orch. (1958), he adopted jazz elements; beginning in 1958 he applied dodecaphonic techniques, and after 1960 his interest in all things Latin and vocal almost completely dominates his output.

WORKS: STAGE: *Svatební Košile* (The Specter's Bride), ballet-ballad (1954; Plzeň, 1955); *Komedie o umučenie a slavném vzkříšení Pána a spasitele našeho Ježíše Krista* (Play of the Passion and Glorious Resurrection of the Lord Our Savior Jesus Christ; Brno, 1965); *Dulcitius,* lyric drama (1977); *Aesopia,* fable-cantata with introit and exit (1981; version for 2 Pianos and Orch. as *Aesopia minora*). **ORCH.:** Oboe Concerto (1953); 2–piano Concerto (1954); *Capriccio* for Cello and Orch. (1958); *Variations on a Theme of Martinů* (1959; orchestration of a 1949 piece for 2 Pianos); *Musica Caesariana* for Wind Orch. (1960); *Concentus Eurydicae* for Guitar and String Orch. (1971); *Odarum contentus,* 5 Meditations for String Orch. (1973); *Concentus biiugis* for Piano, 4-hands, and Small Orch. (1976); *Ludi symphoniaci I* (1978); *Choreae vernales* for Flute, Harp, Celeste or Piano, and Small Orch. (1980); *Ludi concentantes* for 18 Instruments (1981); *Symphonia bipartita* (1983). **VOCAL:** *Píseň Závišova* (Songs of Zavis) for Tenor and Orch. (1957); *Passer Catulli* for Bass and 9 Instruments (1961); *Ioci vernales* for Bass, 8 Instruments, and Bird Songs on Tape (1964); *Testamentum* for Chorus and 4 Horns (1966); *Dido,* oratorio after Virgil (1967); *Ignis pro Ioanne Palach,* cantata (1968; Prague, April 15, 1969); *Planctus Troadum,* chamber cantata after Seneca, for Contralto, Female Chorus, 8 Cellos, 2 Double Basses, and 2 Percussionists (1969); *Vernalis temporis symphonia* for Soli, Chorus, and Orch. (1982); songs and choruses. **CHAMBER:** *Ioci pastorales* for Oboe, Clarinet, Horn, and Bassoon (1974); *Rosarium,* 9 divertimenti for 2 Guitars (1975); *Quadricinium fidium I* for String Quartet (1978); *Sonata solis fidibus* for Solo Violin (1980); *Sonata da chiesa I* for Violin and Organ and *II* for Flute and Organ (both 1981); *Sonata rustica* for Accordion and Piano (1982); *Aeolia* for 2 Flutes and Piano (1983); pieces for Piano, including *Variations on a Theme of Martinů* for 2 Pianos (1949; orchestrated 1959); harpsichord and organ works.

Novák, Johann Baptist (actually, **Janez Krstnik**), Slovenian composer; b. Ljubljana, c. 1756; d. there, Jan. 29, 1833. He served as a government clerk and at the same time studied music; in 1799–1800, was conductor, and from 1808 to 1929, music director, of the Phil. Society in Ljubljana; he gave concerts as a singer and violinist. A close contemporary of Mozart, he composed in a Mozartean manner. His historical importance lies in his incidental music to T. Linhart's play *Ta veseli dan, ali Matiček se ženi* (A Happy Day, or Matiček Is Getting Married; 1790), which is based on Beaumarchais's comedy that served for Mozart's great opera *Le nozze di Figaro*. Novák later renamed his work *Figaro*. His music forms a striking parallel to Mozart's procedures and yet contains some original traits.

BIBL.: D. Cvetko, "J.B. N.—ein slowenischer Anhänger Mozarts," *Bericht über den Internationalen Musikwissenschaftlichen Kongress Wien, Mozartjahr, 1956.*

Novák, Milan, Slovak composer; b. Trahovice, Aug. 12, 1927. He studied piano with Kafenda, composition with Alexander Moyzes, and conducting with Talich at the Bratislava Cons. In 1955 he was appointed conductor of the Military Artistic Ensemble in Bratislava.

WORKS: 2 ballets: *Where the Play Ends* (1964) and *Ballad about a Tree* (1967); Concertino for Trumpet, Strings, Piano, 4-hands, and Percussion (1964); *Reminiscences* for Cello and Orch. (1969); Concerto for Harp and Chamber Orch. (1972); *Mountains and the Heart*, song cycle for Bass and Orch. (1973); *30 Happy Years*, cantata for Children's Chorus and Orch. (1975); *So that There Is Life on Earth*, cantata (1976); Clarinet Sonatina (1959); Cello Sonatina (1961); String Quartet (1975); *Music* for Flute and String Quartet (1975); *Divertimento* for Oboe, Clarinet, and Bassoon (1980); *4 Preludes* for Orch. (1981); *Music* for Trumpet and Strings (1984); music for theater and films.

Novák, Vitězslav (Augustín Rudolf), eminent Czech composer and pedagogue; b. Kamenitz, Dec. 5, 1870; d. Skuteč, July 18, 1949. He studied in Jindřichův Hradec with Vilém Pojman; subsequently won a scholarship to study law at the Univ. of Prague, but concentrated his studies on music at the Prague Cons., where he received instruction in piano from Jiránek, harmony from Knittl, and counterpoint from Strecker; later attended Dvořák's master class there. After graduating in 1892, he continued to study piano until 1896 and also remained a student of philosophy at the Univ. until 1895. He then taught privately and was active as a folk-song collector; through such orch. works as *V tatrách* (In the Tatra Mountains; 1902), *Slováckà svita* (Slovak Suite; 1903), and *O věčne touzé* (Eternal Longing; 1903–5), the cantata *Bouře* (The Storm; 1910), and the piano tone poem *Pan* (1910), he acquired a notable reputation as a composer; he devoted himself to teaching, serving as a prof. at the Prague Cons. (1909–39). His importance as a composer was enhanced in later years by such works as the *Podzimní symfonie* (Autumn Sym.; 1931–34) and *Jihočeská svita* (South Bohemian Suite) for Orch. (1936–37). He was honored with the title of National Artist of the Czech Republic in 1945. The 1st vol. of his unfinished autobiography, *O sobě a jiných*, was publ. in Prague in 1946. Novák's earliest works followed the general line of German Romanticism; Brahms was so impressed with them that he recommended Novák to his own publisher, Simrock. Novák's interest in folk music made a substantial impact on his music, although he rarely incorporated original folk material in his compositions. His late works espoused patriotic themes.

WORKS (all 1st perf. in Prague unless otherwise given): **STAGE:** *Zvikovský rarášek* (The Imp of Zvikov), comic opera (1913–14; Oct. 10, 1915); *Karlštejn*, opera (1914–15; Nov. 18, 1916); *Lucerna* (The Lantern), musical fairy tale (1919–22; May 13, 1923); *Dědův odkaz* (Old Man's Bequest; 1922–25;

Brno, Jan. 16, 1926); 2 ballet-pantomimes: *Signorina Gioventu* (1926–28; Feb. 10, 1929) and *Nikotina* (Feb. 10, 1929); incidental music to F. Rachlik's *Žižka* (1948). **ORCH.:** *Korzár* (The Corsair), overture (1892; Nov. 20, 1927; rev. 1943); Serenade in F major for Small Orch. (Sept. 27, 1895); Piano Concerto (1895; Nov. 21, 1915); *Maryša*, dramatic overture (1898; Jan. 28, 1899); *V. Tatrách* (In the Tatra Mountains), symphonic poem (1902; Dec. 7, 1907); *Slováckà svita* (Slovak Suite) for Small Orch. (1903; Feb. 4, 1906); *O věčné touze* (Eternal Longing; 1903–5; Feb. 8, 1905); Serenade for Small Orch. (1905; March 6, 1906); *Toman a lesni panna* (Toman and the Wood Nymph), symphonic poem (1906–7; April 5, 1908); *Lady Godiva*, overture (Nov. 24, 1907); *Podzimni symfonie* (Autumn Sym.) for Men's Chorus, Women's Chorus, and Orch. (1931–34; Dec. 18, 1934); *Jihočeská svita* (South Bohemian Suite; Dec. 22, 1937); *De profundis*, symphonic poem (Brno, Oct. 9, 1941); *Svatováclavský triptych* (St. Wenceslas Triptych) for Organ and Orch. (1941; March 6, 1942); *Májová symfonie* (May Sym.) for Solo Voices, Chorus, and Orch. (1943; Dec. 5, 1945). **CHAMBER:** Sonata for Violin and Piano (1891); Piano Trio (1892); Piano Quartet (1894; rev. 1899); Piano Quintet (1896; rev. 1897); 3 string quartets (1899, 1905, 1938); *Piano Trio quasi una ballata* (1902); Sonata for Cello and Piano (1941); various piano pieces; also choral works, songs, and arrangements of folk songs.

BIBL.: Z. Nejedlý, *V. N.: Studie a kritiky* (Prague, 1921); B. Vomáčka and S. Hanuš, eds., *Sbornik na počest 60. narozenin V.a N.a* (Prague, 1930); A. Srba, ed., *V. N.: Studie a vzpominky* (Prague, 1932; supplements, 1935, 1940); A. Hába, *V. N.: K 70. narozeninám* (Prague, 1940); V. Štěpán, *N. a Suk* (Prague, 1945); K. Hoffmeister, *Tvorba V.a N.a z let 1941–1948* (Prague, 1949); V. Lébl, "Postledmí tvůrci období V.a N.a" (V. N.'s Last Creative Period), *Hudebni Rozhledy*, XI (1958); idem, *V. N.: Zivot a dilo* (Prague, 1964); idem, *V. N.* (Prague, 1968; in Eng.); special issue of *Hudebni Věda*, VIII (1971); K. Padrta and B. Štědroň, ed., *Národni umelec V. N., Studie a vzpominsky k 100. výroci narozeni* (Studies and Reminiscences on the 100th Anniversary of V. N.'s Birth; České Budějovice, 1972).

Novello, (Joseph) Alfred, prominent English music publisher, son of **Vincent** and brother of **Clara (Anastasia) Novello;** b. London, Aug. 12, 1810; d. Genoa, July 16, 1896. He joined his father's music publishing venture when he was 19 and was instrumental in making it a commercial success as Novello & Co.; the firm prospered by bringing out eds. of the classics, most notably of choral music. He was also active as a bass singer, organist, choirmaster, and composer. He retired to Genoa in 1856.

Novello, Clara (Anastasia), outstanding English soprano, daughter of **Vincent** and sister of **(Joseph) Alfred Novello;** b. London, June 10, 1818; d. Rome, March 12, 1908. Having studied piano and singing in London, she entered the Paris Institution de Musique Religieuse in 1829, but returned home the following year because of the revolution. She won the approbation of Rossini, and became his friend for life. After a successful concert debut on Oct. 22, 1832, at Windsor, she was engaged for the Phil. Society, the Antient Concerts, and the principal festivals. In 1837 Mendelssohn engaged her for the Gewandhaus concerts in Leipzig; following additional studies in Milan (1839), she made her operatic debut as Rossini's Semiramide in Bologna (1841); sang with great success in the principal Italian cities. On Nov. 22, 1843, she married Count Gigliucci, withdrawing to private life for several years; she reappeared in 1850, singing in concert and opera (chiefly in England and Italy). After her farewell appearance in London in 1860, she retired to Rome. Schumann greatly admired her, and coined the term Novelette for some of his pieces as an affectionate homage to her.

BIBL.: V. Gigliucci, *C. N.'s Reminiscences, compiled by her daughter* (London, 1910; with memoir by A. Coleridge); A. Mackenzie-Grieve, *C. N., 1818–1908* (London, 1955).

Novello, Vincent, English organist, conductor, editor, music publisher, and composer, father of **Clara (Anastasia)** and

(Joseph) Alfred Novello; b. London, Sept. 6, 1781; d. Nice, Aug. 9, 1861. He was a chorister at the Sardinian Embassy Chapel in London, where he studied organ with Welbe; later was deputy organist to Webbe and Danby, and from 1797 to 1822, organist at the chapel of the Portuguese Embassy. He was pianist to the Italian Opera in 1812; was a founder of the Phil. Society in 1813, sometimes conducting its concerts; from 1840 to 1843, was organist at the Roman Catholic Chapel in Moorfields. In 1811 he founded the great London music publishing firm of **Novello & Co.** Himself a composer of sacred music (masses, motets, anthems, Kyries, etc.), he gathered together and publ. excellent collections: *A Collection of Sacred Music* (1811; 2 vols.); *Purcell's Sacred Music* (1829; 5 vols.); *Croft's Anthems; Greene's Anthems; Boyce's Anthems;* masses by Haydn, Mozart, Beethoven; etc. He retired to Nice in 1848.

BIBL.: M. Cowden-Clarke, *Life and Labours of V. N.* (London, 1864); W. Barclay Squire, "Some N. Correspondence," *Musical Quarterly* (April 1917); N. Medici and R. Hughes, *A Mozart Pilgrimage* (London, 1955; travel diaries of V. N. and his wife); M. Hurd, *V. N.—and Company* (Borough Green, 1981).

Novello & Co., one of the world's leading music publishing firms. **Vincent Novello** began editing and publishing works at his own expense in London in 1811; his son, **(Joseph) Alfred Novello,** became active with his father at age 19, and the 2 developed their activities into the successful commercial enterprise known as Novello & Co. The firm prospered by publishing affordable eds. of the classics, concentrating on the choral literature. **Henry Littleton** (b. London, Jan. 2, 1823; d. there, May 11, 1888) joined the business in 1841; following the retirement of the younger Novello in 1856, he became manager of the firm; subsequently was made a partner (1861) and sole proprietor (1866). He acquired the business of Ewer and Co. in 1867, creating the firm of Novello, Ewer & Co. On his retirement in 1887 he was succeeded by his sons, Alfred H. and Augustus J. Littleton, and his sons-in-law, George T.S. Gill and Henry W. Brooke. In 1898 the firm became Novello & Co., Ltd. It became a part of the Granada group of companies in 1970. In addition to bringing out works by leading English composers of the 20th century, it also publ. the highly respected music journal *Musical Times;* founded in 1844 by Joseph Mainzer, it was acquired by Novello in 1846 and remains the oldest continuously issued music periodical in the world; it was publ. by Orpheus Publications from 1988.

BIBL.: J. Bennett, *A Short History of Cheap Music as Exemplified in the Records of the House of N., Ewer & Co.* (London, 1887); "The N. Centenary, 1811–1911," *Musical Times* (June 1911); M. Hurd, *V. N.—and Company* (Borough Green, 1981).

Novello-Davies (real name, **Davies**), **Clara,** Welsh singer, choral conductor, and composer; b. Cardiff, April 7, 1861; d. London, March 1, 1943. Her father (who was also her 1st teacher) called her "Clara Novello" after the celebrated singer of that name, and she adopted the combined name professionally. She sang at concerts; in 1881 she turned to choral conducting; organized a Royal Welsh Ladies' Choir, with which she traveled with fine success in Great Britain, France, America, and South Africa; at the World's Fair in Chicago (1893) and at the Paris Exposition (1900) the chorus was awarded 1st prize. She was commended by Queen Victoria (1894) and by King George V and Queen Mary (1928). She publ. a number of successful songs (*A Voice from the Spirit Land, The Vigil, Comfort,* etc.); authored *You Can Sing* and an autobiography, *The Life I Have Loved* (London, 1940). Her son, **Ivor Novello** (real name, David Ivor Davies) (b. Cardiff, Jan. 15, 1893; d. London, March 6, 1951), was a composer, playwright, and actor; at his mother's request, he wrote the popular World War I song *Till the Boys Come Home* (*Keep the Home Fires Burning;* 1914); wrote musical comedies and revues, and was also active as an actor; after working as a playwright, he resumed composing for the stage; his most successful musical was *The Dancing Years* (London, March 23, 1939).

BIBL.: S. Wilson, *I.* (London, 1975).

Noverre, Jean-Georges, Swiss-French choreographer; b. Paris, April 29, 1727; d. St.-Germain-en-Laye, Oct. 19, 1810. He studied in Paris; danced in Fontainebleau (1743) and then in Berlin; subsequently was principal dancer in Strasbourg (1750–54) and at the Paris Opéra-Comique (1754–55). He later was active in London (1755–57), Lyons (1757–60), Stuttgart (1760–67), Vienna, and Milan (1774–76), Vienna again (1776), the Paris Opéra (1776–81), and London once more (1781–82; 1787–89); retired in 1794. He is credited with introducing dramatic action into the ballet (ballet-pantomime). He publ. *Lettres sur la danse, et sur les ballets* (Lyons and Stuttgart, 1760; 2nd ed., 1783; Eng. tr., London, 1782).

BIBL.: C. Noverre, *Life and Works of the Chevalier N.* (London, 1882); H. Abert, "J.G. N. und sein Einfluss auf die dramatische Balletkomposition," *Jahrbuch der Musikbibliothek Peters 1908;* H. Niedecken, *J.G. N.: Sein Leben und seine Beziehungen zur Musik* (Halle, 1914); D. Lynham, *The Chevalier N.: Father of Modern Ballet* (London, 1950); P. Tugal, *J.-G. N. der grosse Reformator des Tanzes* (Berlin, 1959).

Novikov, Anatoly (Grigorievich), Russian composer; b. Skopin, Oct. 30, 1896; d. Moscow, Sept. 23, 1984. He studied at the Moscow Cons. with Glière, Vasilenko, and Catoire; devoted himself to organizing choral groups in the Soviet Military Academy; composed a number of patriotic songs which entered the Soviet popular repertoire, among them 5 *Bullets;* he also wrote the political cantata *We Need Peace* (1954) and some lively musical comedies. On his 80th birthday he was awarded the order of Hero of Socialist Labor, the Order of Lenin, and the Sickle and Hammer gold medal.

Novotná, Jarmila, Czech soprano; b. Prague, Sept. 23, 1907. She studied with Destinn in Prague; made her debut as Mařenka in *The Bartered Bride* there (1925), then continued her studies in Milan. She sang in Berlin (from 1928); was a member of the Vienna State Opera (1933–38), where she gained distinction as Octavian; also created the title role in Lehar's *Giuditta* (1934). She made her American debut at San Francisco as Madama Butterfly (Oct. 18, 1939); first sang at the Metropolitan Opera in N.Y. as Mimi in *La Bohème* on Jan. 5, 1940; remained on its staff until 1951; was there again from 1952 to 1956; also appeared in films and on Broadway. Her other fine roles included Pamina, Donna Elvira, Violetta, Mélisande, and various roles in Czech operas.

Nowak, Leopold, eminent Austrian musicologist; b. Vienna, Aug. 17, 1904; d. there, May 27, 1991. He studied piano and organ with Louis Dité and counterpoint with Franz Schmidt at the Vienna Academy of Music; then took courses in musicology with Guido Adler and Robert Lach at the Univ. of Vienna; received his Ph.D. there in 1927 with the dissertation *Das deutsche Gesellschaftslied bei Heinrich Finck, Paul Hofhaymer und Heinrich Isaac;* publ. in an augmented version as "Das deutsche Gesellschaftslied in Österreich von 1480 bis 1550," *Studien zur Musikwissenschaft,* XVII, 1930; completed his Habilitation in 1932 with his *Grundzüge einer Geschichte des Basso ostinato* (publ. in Vienna, 1932). He lectured at the Univ. of Vienna from 1932 until 1973; in 1945 he became ed. of the critical edition of Bruckner's works; from 1946 to 1969 he was director of the music division of the Nationalbibliothek in Vienna, where he compiled valuable catalogues for special exhibitions on Bruckner, Bach, Mozart, Haydn, and others. His exhaustive studies on the life and music of Bruckner are of prime value.

WRITINGS: *Franz Liszt* (Innsbruck, 1936); *Te Deum laudamus: Gedanken zur Musik Anton Bruckners* (Vienna, 1947); *Joseph Haydn* (Vienna, 1951; 3rd ed., 1965); *Gegen den Strom: Leben und Werk von Emil Nikolaus von Reznicek* (with F. von Reznicek, the composer's daughter; Vienna, 1960); *Anton Bruckner: Musik und Leben* (a brief study; Vienna, 1964); *Reden und Ansprachen* (Vienna, 1964); *Anton Bruckner: Musik und Leben* (a voluminous pictorial biography; Linz, 1973); *Das Geburtshaus Anton Bruckners [Ansfelden]: Führer* (Linz, 1975).

BIBL.: F. Grasberger, ed., *Bruckner-Studien: L. N. zum 60. Geburtstag* (Vienna, 1964).

Nowak, Lionel (Henry), American pianist, teacher, and composer; b. Cleveland, Sept. 25, 1911. He studied piano with Beryl Rubinstein and Edwin Fischer, and took courses in composition with Herbert Elwell, Roger Sessions, and Quincy Porter at the Cleveland Inst. of Music (B.Mus., 1933; M.Mus., 1936). In 1924 he made his formal debut as a soloist with the Cleveland Orch.; was director of music at Fenn College in Cleveland (1932–38) and of the Doris Humphrey-Charles Weidman Modern Dance Co. (1938–42). He was prof. of music at Converse College in Spartanburg, S.C. (1942–46); also conducted the Spartanburg Sym. Orch. (1942–45); was prof. of music at Syracuse Univ. (1946–48) and at Bennington (Vt.) College (from 1948). Following a stroke in 1980, he composed works for piano, right-hand, and also commissioned such scores from other composers. He wrote some effective dance pieces.

WORKS: DANCE: *Square Dances* (1938); *Danzas mexicanas* (1939); *On My Mother's Side* (1939); *The Green Land* (1941); *Flickers* (1942); *House Divided* (1944); *Story of Mankind* (1946). **ORCH.:** Piano Concerto (1944); *Concert Piece* for Timpani and Strings (1961). **CHAMBER:** Oboe Sonata (1949); *Orrea Pernel*, sonata for Violin (1950); 3 cello sonatas (1950, 1951, 1960); *Diptych* for String Quartet (1951); Quartet for Oboe and Strings (1952); Piano Trio (1954); *Soundscapes:* for Piano (1964), String Quartet (1970), Bassoon and Piano (1971), Violin, Piano, and Percussion (1971), and Woodwind Trio (1973); Suite for 2 Cellos (1981); Suite for Flute and Harpsichord (1989); vocal pieces.

Nowowiejski, Felix, Polish organist, conductor, and composer; b. Wartenburg, Feb. 7, 1877; d. Poznan, Jan. 18, 1946. He studied with Bussler at the Stern Cons. in Berlin, with Bruch at the Königliche Musikakademie, and with Friedlaender, Ballermann, and Dessoir at the Univ.; also received some instruction from Dvořák in Prague; won the Paderewski Prize in 1903. He was director of the Krakow Music Soc. (1909–14) and a prof. at the Poznan Cons. (1920–27). A competent composer, he followed the line of German Romanticism.

WORKS: 2 operas: *Emigranci* (The Emigrants; 1917) and *Legenda Baltyku* (Baltic Legend; Poznan, 1924); several ballets; 5 syms. (1903–41; 1st not extant); Cello Concerto (1938); Piano Concerto (1941); much choral music, including oratorios, masses, cantatas, patriotic works, etc.; also songs; piano pieces; organ music.

BIBL.: J. Boehm, *F. N.* (Olsztyn, 1968).

Nozzari, Andrea, Italian tenor; b. Vertrova, near Bergamo, 1775; d. Naples, Dec. 12, 1832. He studied with Petrobelli in Bergamo; made his operatic debut in 1794; then made appearances in Rome, Milan, and Paris; was a principal tenor in Naples (1811–25); created tenor roles in several operas of Rossini; then retired and taught singing.

Nucci, Leo, prominent Italian baritone; b. Castiglione dei Pepuli, near Bologna, April 16, 1942. He studied with Giuseppe Marchesi and Ottaviano Bizzarri; made his debut as Rossini's Figaro in Spoleto (1967). After singing in the chorus of Milan's La Scala (1969–75), he attracted attention with his portrayal of Schaunard in *La Bohème* at Venice's Teatro La Fenice (1975); then was engaged as a member of La Scala, where he appeared as Rossini's Figaro, Rodrigo in *Don Carlos*, Miller in *Luisa Miller*, Marcello, and Sharpless. In 1978 he made his 1st appearance at the Vienna State Opera and at London's Covent Garden; he made his Metropolitan Opera debut in N.Y. as Renato in *Un ballo in Maschera* on Feb. 22, 1980. He first sang at the Paris Opéra and the Chicago Lyric Opera in 1981. He also sang in San Francisco, Berlin, Rome, Hamburg, and Geneva.

Nucius (Nucis, Nux), Johannes, German composer and music theorist; b. Görlitz, c.1556; d. Himmelwitz, March 25, 1620. He studied music with Johannes Winckler, the cantor of the Görlitz Gymnasium; c.1586 he took Holy Orders at the monastery of Rauden; in 1591, was made abbot of the monastery of Himmelwitz in Silesia. He publ. 50 *Modulationes sacrae modis musicis* for 5 and 6 Voices (Prague, 1591; 2nd ed., 1609, as *Cantionum sacrarum liber primus*); 52 *Cantionum sacrarum diversarum vocum, liber secundus*, some for 7, others for 8, Voices (Liegnitz, 1609); a theoretical work, *Musices poeticae sive De compositione cantum praeceptiones ultissimae* (Neisse, 1613). A selected ed. of his motets was brought out by J. Kendermann in Das Erbe Deutscher Musik, 2nd series, V (1968).

BIBL.: B. Widmann, *J. N., Abt von Himmelwitz* (Bregenz, 1921); E. Kirsch, *Von der Persönlichkeit und dem Stil des schlesischen Zisterzienser-Komponisten J. N.* (Breslau, 1926).

Nuitter (real name, **Truinet**), **Charles Louis Etienne,** French writer on music; b. Paris, April 24, 1828; d. there, Feb. 23, 1899. He was a lawyer by profession; also became interested in the theater; was custodian of the archives of the Paris Opéra (from 1866). He changed his real name, Truinet, to Nuitter by anagrammatic transposition of letters, and under that name wrote librettos for many operas and operettas, including some by Offenbach; also tr. librettos of operas by Weber, Mozart, Wagner, and Verdi; wrote scenarios for Delibes (*Coppélia*) and others. He publ. *Le Nouvel Opéra* (1875); *Les Origines de l'opéra français* (1886; with Thoinan); many articles in music magazines.

Nummi, Seppo (Antero Yrjönpoika), Finnish composer, music critic, and festival administrator; b. Oulu, May 30, 1932; d. Tampere, Aug. 1, 1981. He studied at the Univ. of Helsinki and at the Sibelius Academy; his private composition teacher was Yrjö Kilpinen. He began writing music criticism for the newspaper *Uusi Suomi* in 1953; in 1967 he founded the Savonlinna Opera Festival; then was executive director of the Helsinki Festival (1969–77). As a composer, he is best known for his many songs in a fine lyrical mode, in the tradition of Hugo Wolf and Kilpinen; he also wrote some chamber music. He publ. *Musica fennica* (with T. Makinen; Helsinki, 1965; tr. into Eng. and several other languages) and *Modern Musik* (Stockholm, 1966; also in Finnish).

Nunes, Emmanuel, Portuguese-born French composer; b. Lisbon, Aug. 31, 1941. He studied at Lisbon's Music Academy and at the Ferienkurse at Darmstadt (1963–65); then settled in Paris, where he became active in French and German avant-garde circles. He attended the Rheinische Musikhochschule in Cologne (1965–67), where he studied with Pousseur and Stockhausen. He was awarded 1st prize in musical esthetics at the Paris Cons. He was resident composer to Berlin's DAAD (1978–79). He holds the Chair of Composition at Freiburg's Hochschule für Musik (Institut für Neue Musik), and lectures regularly at the Paris Cons. His works are technically assured and inventive; in the 1980s they became increasingly compact, tense, and extreme in character. Many of his compositions, which include *Seuils I-II* for Orch. (1966–67), *Esquisses* for String Quartet (1967; rev. 1980), and *Musik der Frühe* for Chamber Orch. (1980–84), were commissioned by the Gulbenkian Foundation, Radio France, and the French Ministry of Culture.

Nunó, Jaime, Spanish organist, conductor, and composer; b. San Juan de las Abadesas, Sept. 8, 1824; d. Auburndale, N.Y., July 18, 1908. He studied with Mercadante in Italy; in 1851, went to Cuba, and in 1854 to Mexico, where he was appointed chief of military bands; won 1st prize in a competition for choosing the Mexican national anthem, which was first sung on Sept. 15, 1854. Subsequently he was active as an impresario for Italian opera companies in Cuba, Mexico, and the U.S.

Nurimov, Chari, Russian composer; b. Buiramali, Turkmenia, Jan. 1, 1941. He studied with Litinsky at the Gnessin Inst. in Moscow (graduated, 1964); returning to Turkmenia, he worked for the Ashkhabad radio and taught at the music inst. He received awards as a national Turkmenian composer; his Trumpet Concerto became popular.

WORKS: BALLETS: *The End of Sukhovei* (1967); *Immortality*

(1972); *A Kughitang Tragedy* (1976). ORCH.: Overture in E minor (1959); Overture in A minor (1961); Sym. No. 1 (1963); Trumpet Concerto (1968); Concerto-Poem for Voice and Orch. (1971); Piano Concerto (1973); Overture (1974); *Ghazels* for Oboe, Percussion, Piano, and Strings (1976); *The Flame of October*, poem (1979); Sinfonietta (1981); *Destan Concerto* for Flute, Oboe, Percussion, Piano, and Strings (1983). CHAMBER: Suite for String Quartet (1960); Partita for String Quartet (1963); *The Tekin Frescoes* for 11 Instruments (1969); Woodwind Quintet (1979); String Quartet (1980). WITH PIANO: Sonata for Violin (1961); Oboe Sonatina (1964); Concert Piece for Trombone (1971); *Pastoral* for Flute (1973). SOLO PIANO: 2 sonatinas (1960, 1965); 3 Fugues (1962); Impromptu-Fantasia (1964); 12 Polyphonic Pieces (1968). Also over 70 songs; film music.

Nurock, Kirk, innovative American composer and originator of "natural sound"; b. Camden, N.J., Feb. 28, 1948. He held scholarships for study at the Juilliard School in N.Y. and at the Eastman School of Music in Rochester, N.Y. His teachers in composition were Persichetti, Sessions, and Berio. He was awarded the Elizabeth Sprague Coolidge Prize in chamber music in 1970. From his earliest essays in composition, he adhered to extraordinary and unusual sound production; became active as a conductor of idiosyncratic theater productions, among them the temporarily objectionable musical *Hair*, which aroused indignant protests on the part of tender-minded listeners. He further developed a natural ability to perform advanced keyboard jazz music. In 1971 he developed an experimental vocal technique which he called "natural sound," founded on the assumption that every person's vocal cords, as well as other parts of their bodies, are capable of producing variegated sound. In several works he annexed animal noises; the most challenging of them being *Sonata for Piano and Dog* (1982) and *Gorilla, Gorilla* for Solo Piano (1988). Audience participation is welcomed as an integral part of "natural sound" productions. Several of Nurock's works are specifically scored for untrained, improvisatory participants. Interestingly enough, many newspaper reviews of his presentations seem to revive the alarmed outcries of shocked innocence that greeted 1st performances of the now-recognized works of Prokofiev, Stravinsky, Schoenberg, and Varèse.

WORKS: DRAMATIC: *Mowgli*, musical theater work after Kipling's *Jungle Book*, with 12 Singing Actors and 6 Musicians (1978–84). ORCH.: *Accumulations* (1968); *Assemblage* (1969). CHAMBER: *Clarinet Chant* for 6 Clarinets and Bass Clarinet (1970); *Creature Memory* (1979); *The Incurable Dorothy Parker*, song cycle for Soprano and Piano (Philadelphia, Nov. 10, 1986). "NATURAL SOUND," INCLUDING ANIMALS: *Elemental Chant* (1972); *Audience Oratorio*, with Audience Participation (1975); *Howl* for 20 Voices and 4 Canines (N.Y., Jan. 15, 1980); *Bronx Zoo Events* (Bronx Zoo, N.Y., Oct. 24, 1980); *Sonata for Piano and Dog* (1982; N.Y., March 16, 1983); *Expedition* for Jazz Trio and Siberian Husky (N.Y., Jan. 14, 1984); *Sendings* for 5 Winds and 4 Creatures (N.Y., March 17, 1984); *Haunted Messages* for Piano and Barking Audience (1984; N.Y., March 20, 1990); *Listening Bach* for Orch., Chorus, Narrator, and Animals (1986–88); *Gorilla, Gorilla* for Piano (N.Y., March 19, 1988); also *3 Screams* for 2 Amplified Pianos (N.Y., March 20, 1990); numerous ensemble numbers for plays.

Nussio, Otmar, Italian composer; b. Grosseto, Oct. 23, 1902. He studied flute, piano, and composition at the Cons. in Milan and with Respighi in Rome. He conducted concerts of light music and wrote a number of overtures and orch. suites, among them *Escapades musicales* (1949); *Rubensiana* (Rubens House, Antwerp, May 21, 1950); *Tzigana* (1954); *Portraits musicaux* (1955); *Episodio* (1958); *Monologhi di vita e di morte* (1958); and *Alborada* (1971); also a Flute Concerto (1936); Piano Concerto (1960); *Cantata ticinese* for Voices and Orch. (1962); *Passatempo donchisciottesco* for Clarinet and Orch. (1971).

Nyiregyházi, Erwin, remarkable but eccentric Hungarian-American pianist; b. Budapest, Jan. 19, 1903; d. Los Angeles,

April 13, 1987. He absorbed music by a kind of domestic osmosis, from his father, a professional tenor, and his mother, an amateur pianist. An exceptionally gifted *wunderkind*, he had perfect pitch and a well-nigh phonographic memory as a very small child; played a Haydn sonata and pieces by Grieg, Chopin, and himself at a concert in Fiume at the age of 6. In 1910 he entered the Budapest Academy of Music, studying theory with Albert Siklós and Leo Weiner, and piano with István Thomán. In 1914 the family moved to Berlin, where he became a piano student of Ernst von Dohnányi. He made his debut in Germany playing Beethoven's 3rd Piano Concerto with the Berlin Phil. (Oct. 14, 1915). In 1916 he began studying with Frederic Lamond, a pupil of Liszt, who was instrumental in encouraging Nyiregyházi to study Liszt's music, which was to become the most important part of his concert repertoire. In 1920 he went to the U.S.; his American debut (Carnegie Hall, N.Y., Oct. 18, 1920) was sensationally successful; the word "genius" was freely applied to him by critics usually restrained in their verbal effusions. Inexplicably, his American career suffered a series of setbacks; he became involved in a lawsuit with his manager; he married his next manager, a Mrs. Mary Kelen, in 1926, but divorced her a year later. He then went to California, where he became gainfully employed as a studio pianist in Hollywood; in 1930 he made a European tour; then lived in N.Y. and in Los Angeles. Beset by personal problems, he fell into a state of abject poverty, but resolutely refused to resume his concert career; he did not even own a piano. He married frequently, and as frequently divorced his successive wives. In 1972 he married his 9th wife, a lady 10 years his senior; she died shortly afterward. Attempts were made in vain by friends and admirers in Calif. to induce him to play in public; a semi-private recital was arranged for him in San Francisco in 1974; a recording of his playing of Liszt was issued in 1977; it was greeted with enthusiastic reviews, all expressing regret for his disappearance from the concert stage. Nyiregyházi composed several hundred works, mostly for piano; they remain in MS. As a child, Nyiregyházi was the object of a "scientific" study by Géza Révész, director of the Psychological Laboratory in Amsterdam, who made tests of his memory, sense of pitch, ability to transpose into different keys at sight, etc.; these findings were publ. in German as *Psychologische Analyse eines musikalisch hervorragenden Kindes* (Leipzig, 1916) and in Eng. as *The Psychology of a Musical Prodigy* (London, 1925), but the examples given and the tests detailed in the book proved to be no more unusual than the capacities of thousands of similarly gifted young musicians.

Nystedt, Knut, esteemed Norwegian choral conductor, organist, pedagogue, and composer; b. Christiania, Sept. 3, 1915. He studied organ with Arild Sandvold, conducting with Øivin Fjeldstad, and composition with Per Steenberg and Bjarne Brustad at the Oslo Cons. (1931–43); then pursued training with Ernest White (organ) and Aaron Copland (composition) in N.Y. (1947). From 1946 to 1982 he was organist at Oslo's Torshov Church; also was a prof. of choral conducting at the Oslo Cons. (1964–85). In 1950 he founded Det Norske Solistokor (the Norwegian Soloist Choir), which he conducted for the 1st time in Oslo on May 23, 1951; in subsequent years he developed it into one of the finest choral groups in the world, conducting it in a comprehensive literature with a special regard for contemporary scores. In 1960 he conducted it for the 1st time in the U.S.; later led it on tours of Japan, Korea, Hong Kong, and Thailand (1978), China (1982), and Israel (1984, 1988). On March 18, 1990, he conducted his farewell concert as its conductor in Oslo. In 1966 he was made a Knight of the Order of St. Olav; in 1978 he was awarded the Spellemannsprisen; in 1980 he received the music prize of the Norwegian Council for Cultural Affairs. He is an outstanding composer of choral music; his orch. works have also won approbation both at home and abroad.

WORKS: STAGE: *Med krone og stjerne* (With Crown and Star), Christmas opera (1971). ORCH.: *Høgfjell* (The Mountains), suite (1940–41); *Concerto grosso* for 3 Trumpets and Strings (1946); *Spenningens land* (Land of Suspense), symphonic fantasy (1947; Oslo, Sept. 29, 1948); *Festival Overture* (1950); Sym. for Strings (1950); Concertino for English Horn, Clarinet, and Strings (1952); *De syv segl* (The 7 Seals), visions (1958–60); *Collocations* (1963); *Mirage* (1974); *Fisken* (Fish; 1976); *Exsultate* (1980; Oslo, Sept. 5, 1985; also for Organ); *Sinfonia del mare* (1983); Horn Concerto (Helsinki, Oct. 13, 1986); also works for Band. **CHAMBER:** 5 string quartets (1938; 1948; 1956; 1966, Norwegian Radio, Feb. 6, 1989; 1988); *The Moment* for Soprano, Celesta, and Percussion (1962); *Pia memoria,* Requiem for 9 Brass Instruments (1971); *Rhapsody in Green* for Brass Quintet (1978); *Music* for 6 Trombones (1980); organ pieces. **CHORAL:** *Nådevegen,* oratorio for Soli, Chorus, and Orch. (1943–46); *Norge mitt land* (Norway, My County) for Baritone, Chorus, and Orch. (1944); *De profundis* (1964); *Spes Mundi* (The Hope of the World), Mass for Chorus, Drama Group, Trumpet, Organ, Percussion, Narrator, and Congregation (1970); *Dies Irae* for 4 Choruses, Wind, and Percussion (1976); *A Hymn of Human Rights* for Chorus, Organ, and Percussion (1982; Des Moines, Iowa, March 6, 1983); *For a Small Planet* for Chorus, String Quartet, Harp, and Narrator (1983; Eugene, Oreg., July 13, 1984); *Missa Brevis* (1984; Bergen, June 17, 1985); *The Lamentations of Jeremiah* (1985); *Stabat Mater* for Chorus and Cello (1986); *Salomo* (Song of Songs) for Soli, Chorus, Dancers, Instruments, and Organ (1990).

Nystroem, Gösta, Swedish composer; b. Silvberg, Oct. 13, 1890; d. Särö, near Göteborg, Aug. 9, 1966. He studied piano, harmony, and composition with his father; then piano and harmony with Lundberg and Bergenson in Stockholm; took courses at the Cons. there (1913–14), and also studied composition with Hallén; after further training in Copenhagen and Germany, he went to Paris (1920) and studied composition and instrumentation with d'Indy and Sabaneyev and conducting with Chevillard; subsequently wrote music criticism in Göteborg (1932–47). After following neo-Baroque practices, he developed an independent mode of composition.

WORKS: DRAMATIC: Radio drama, *De Blinda* (The Blind, 1949); ballet, *Ungersvennen och de sex prinsessorna* (The Young Lad and the 6 Princesses, 1951); radio opera, *Herr Arnes penningar* (Sir Arne's Hoard), based on a novel by Selma Lagerlöf (Swedish Radio, Nov. 26, 1959). **ORCH.:** *Rondo capriccioso* for Violin and Orch. (1917; rev. 1920); symphonic poem, *Is havet* (The Arctic Ocean, 1924); symphonic poem, *Babels torn* (The Tower of Babel, 1928); 2 concertos for String Orch. (1930, 1955); 6 syms.: No. 1, *Sinfonia breve* (1931; Göteborg, Oct. 19, 1932); No. 2, *Sinfonia espressiva* (1932–35; Göteborg, Feb. 18, 1937); No. 3, *Sinfonia del mare,* with Soprano Solo (1947–48; Stockholm, March 24, 1949); No. 4, *Sinfonia Shakespeareana* (Göteborg, Nov. 5, 1952); No. 5, *Sinfonia seria* (Stockholm, Oct. 9, 1963); No. 6, *Sinfonia Tramontana* (1965; Stockholm, Oct. 30, 1966); 4 suites of incidental music: No. 1, *Konungen* (The King, 1933; after Lagerkvist); No. 2, *The Tempest* (1934; after Shakespeare); No. 3, *Bödeln* (The Hangman, 1935); No. 4, *The Merchant of Venice* (1936; after Shakespeare); *Suite* for Small Orch. (1950); *Partita* for Flute, Strings, and Harp (1953); Violin Concerto (1954); *Concerto ricercante* for Piano and Orch. (1959; Stockholm, May 15, 1960); *Summer Music* for Soprano and Orch. (1964); 2 string quartets (1956, 1961); 3 *Havsvisioner* (*Visions of the Sea*) for a cappella Chorus (1956); piano pieces, among them the sentimental *Regrets* (1923; also for Orch.); songs.

BIBL.: P. Christensen, *The Orchestral Works of G. N.: A Critical Study* (diss., Univ. of Washington, 1961; publ. in London, 1965).

Oakeley, Sir Herbert (Stanley), English composer and teacher; b. Ealing, Middlesex, July 22, 1830; d. Eastbourne, Oct. 26, 1903. He was educated at Christ Church, Oxford (B.A., 1853; M.A., 1856), where he studied organ and harmony with S. Elvey; subsequently had lessons with Plaidy, Moscheles, and Papperitz at the Leipzig Cons., J. Schneider in Dresden, and Breidenstein in Bonn. In 1865 he was appointed a prof. of music at Edinburgh Univ., and held this post until 1891; was influential in the musical affairs of Scotland in general; was knighted in 1876. He wrote a cantata, *A Jubilee Lyric* (1887) and *Suite in the Olden Style* for Orch. (1893); also church music, choruses, piano pieces, and arrangements of Scottish melodies.

BIBL.: E. Oakeley, *The Life of Sir H.S. O.* (London, 1904).

Oberhoffer, Emil (Johann), German-born American conductor; b. near Munich, Aug. 10, 1867; d. San Diego, May 22, 1933. He received his initial musical training from his father, an organist; learned to play violin and organ; later studied piano in Paris with Isidor Philipp. He went to N.Y. (1885) and became a naturalized citizen (1893); in 1897, settled in St. Paul, Minn.; became conductor of the Schubert Club chorus and orch. and the Apollo Club; was also prof. of music at the Univ. of Minnesota (1902–5). He became conductor of the Phil. Choral Society in Minneapolis (1901), and having succeeded in securing an endowment for the establishment of a permanent orch., gave his 1st concert with the newly-organized Minneapolis Sym. Orch. on Nov. 5, 1903; he remained its conductor until 1923; then settled in Los Angeles. Upon the death of Walter Henry Rothwell (1927), the conductor of the Los Angeles Phil., he led the remaining concerts of the 1926–27 season with that orch.

Oberlin, Russell (Keys), American countertenor; b. Akron, Ohio, Oct. 11, 1928. He studied at the Juilliard School of Music in N.Y., graduating in 1951; in 1952 he joined the N.Y. Pro Musica Antiqua, appearing as a soloist in works from the medieval and Renaissance periods; in 1960 he sang the role of Oberon in Britten's *A Midsummer Night's Dream* at Covent Garden, London. In 1966 he joined the faculty at Hunter College in N.Y.

Oberthür, Charles (actually, **Karl**), German-English harpist and composer; b. Munich, March 4, 1819; d. London, Nov. 8, 1895. He studied with Elise Brauchle and G.V. Röder in Munich; after playing at various theaters in Switzerland and Germany, he went to London in 1844; established himself as a teacher there. He wrote 2 operas; several cantatas; a symphonic legend, *Lorelei*, for Harp and Orch.; a Nocturne for 3 Harps; many elegant soli for Harp (*Elégie, Pensées musicales, Réveil des elfes, Miranda, Le Sylphe,* etc.).

Oborin, Lev (Nikolaievich), Russian pianist and pedagogue; b. Moscow, Sept. 11, 1907; d. there, Jan. 5, 1974. He studied with Elena Gnessina at the Gnessin Music School in Moscow and with Igumnov at the Moscow Cons. (graduated, 1926). He made his debut in 1924; won the Chopin Competition in Warsaw (1927), then toured widely; was also on the faculty of the Moscow Cons. (1928–74). He was made a People's Artist of the U.S.S.R. in 1964. He was known for his wide sympathies as an interpreter, ranging from the classics to the Soviet school; was soloist in the premiere of Khachaturian's Piano Concerto.

He also composed; wrote piano sonatas and other works for piano, as well as several orch. pieces.

Bibl.: S. Khentova, *L. O.* (Moscow, 1964).

Obouhov, Nicolas (actually, **Nikolai**), remarkable Russian composer; b. Kursk, April 22, 1892; d. Paris, June 13, 1954. He studied at the St. Petersburg Cons. with Nikolai Tcherepnin and Maximilian Steinberg; after the Revolution he emigrated to Paris, where he received instruction from Ravel. As early as 1914 he began experimenting with harmonic combinations containing 12 different notes without duplication (he called his system "absolute harmony"). In 1915 he devised a special notation for this type of harmony, entirely enharmonic, with crosses indicating sharps or flats; several composers, among them Honegger, wrote pieces in Obouhov's notation. He gave a demonstration of his works written and notated in this system in Petrograd at a concert organized by the eds. of the review *Muzykalnyi Sovremennik* on Feb. 3, 1916. He devoted his entire life to the composition of his magnum opus, *Le Livre de vie*, for Solo Voices, Chorus, 2 Pianos, and Orch. The MS score, some 2,000 pages long, was deposited after his death at the Bibliothèque Nationale in Paris. A mystic, Obouhov signed his name "Nicolas l'illuminé" and used his own blood to mark sections in the score; the finale represented the spiritual and religious apotheosis in which both the old and the new Russian societies and political factions become reunited. In this and some other scores Obouhov introduced shouting, screaming, sighing, and groaning sounds for the voice parts. A section of *Le Livre de vie* was performed by Koussevitzky in Paris on June 3, 1926. In quest of new sonorities, Obouhov devised an electronic instrument, the "croix sonore," in the form of a cross, and composed works for it, which were performed by Mme. Aussenac de Broglie. He publ. *Traité d'harmonie tonale, atonale et totale* (Paris, 1946), which presents an exposition of his system.

Bibl.: B. de Schloezer, "N. O.," *Revue Musicale* (1921); C. Laronde, *Le Livre de vie de N. O.* (Paris, 1932).

Oboussier, Robert, Swiss composer; b. Antwerp (of Swiss parents), July 9, 1900; d. (stabbed to death by his roommate), Zürich, June 9, 1957. He studied at the Zürich Cons. with Volkmar Andreae and Philipp Jarnach (composition); then with Siegfried Ochs in Berlin (conducting). He then lived in Florence (1922–28); was music ed. of the *Deutsche Allgemeine Zeitung;* but in 1939 political conditions in Germany impelled him to leave for Switzerland; in 1942 he became director of the Central Archive of Swiss Music, and in 1948 of Suisa (the Swiss association of writers, composers, and publishers). Of cosmopolitan background, he combined in his music the elements of both Germanic and Latin cultures. He publ. *Der Sänger* (with others; Berlin, 1934; 2nd ed., rev., 1959) and *Die Sinfonien Beethovens* (Berlin, 1937); also a collection of critical reviews, *Berliner Musik-Chronik 1930–38* (1969).

Works: Opera, *Amphitryon* (1948-50; Berlin, March 13, 1951); *Trilogia sacra* for Solo Voices, Chorus, and Orch. (1925–29); Piano Concerto (1932–33; rev. 1944); Sym. (1935–36); *Antigone* for Voice and Orch. (1938–39); *Chant de deuil* for Orch. (1942–43); *Introitus* for Strings (1946); *3 Psaumes* for Soli, Chorus, and Orch. (1946–47); Violin Concerto (1952–53); chamber music; songs; piano pieces.

Bibl.: K. Wörner, "R. O.," *Musica* (Oct. 1954); F. Wohlfahrt, "Das Werk R. O.s," *Schweizerische Musikzeitung/Revue musicale suisse,* XCIX (1959).

Obradović, Aleksandar, Yugoslav composer; b. Bled, Aug. 22, 1927. After preliminary study at the Belgrade Academy of Music (graduated, 1952), he went to London, where he took courses with Lennox Berkeley (1959–60). In 1966–67 he studied at the Columbia-Princeton electronic music center in N.Y. He was a prof. at Belgrade's Stanković Music School (1953–54); then served on the faculty at the Belgrade Academy of Music (from 1954), where he was rector from 1979 to 1983. Formally, his music adheres to the architectonic Classical design with strongly discernible tonal centers, but he experiments

with atonal thematics and polytonal harmonies; in some of his works he applies explicit dodecaphonic formulas.

Works: STAGE: *Prolećni uranak* (Spring's Awakening), ballet (1949). **ORCH.:** 6 syms.: No. 1 (1952; Belgrade, March 11, 1953); No. 2 (1959–61; Belgrade, Jan. 22, 1965); No. 3, *Mikrosimfonija* for Tape and Orch. (1967; Opatija, Oct. 27, 1968); No. 4 (Belgrade, May 24, 1972); No. 5, *Intima* (1973; Opatija, Nov. 17, 1974); No. 6 (Belgrade, May 12, 1978); *Symphonic Kolo* (1949); *Symphonic Scherzo* (1955); *Plameni vjetar* (Flaming Wind), song cycle for Baritone and Orch. (1955; Belgrade, Jan. 13, 1959); Concertino for Piano and String Orch. (1956); Concerto for Clarinet and String Orch. (1958; Belgrade, May 26, 1959); *Symphonic Epitaph* for Narrator, Chorus, and Orch. (Belgrade, May 21, 1959); *Scherzo-Overture* (1959); *Kroz svemir* (Through the Universe), suite (1961); *Scherzo in modo dodecaphonico* (Belgrade, May 24, 1962); *Prelude and Fugue* for Voice and String Orch. (1963); *Epitaph H* for Orch. and Tape (Berlin, Oct. 6, 1965); *Sutjeska* for Narrator, Chorus, and Orch. (1968); *Dramatična fuga* for Wind Orch. (Belgrade, Nov. 17, 1972); Cello Concerto (1979; Belgrade, April 23, 1980). **CHAMBER:** Quintet for Flute, Clarinet, and String Trio (1950); *Platani* for Chamber Ensemble (1964); *Microsonata I* for Clarinet (1969); *Microsonata II* for Bassoon (1971); choruses. Also songs; electronic pieces.

Obraztsova, Elena (Vasilievna), outstanding Russian mezzo-soprano; b. Leningrad, July 7, 1937. Her father was an engineer who played the violin. She studied at the Leningrad Cons., graduating in 1964; made her operatic debut as Marina in *Boris Godunov* at Moscow's Bolshoi Theater (1963); won 1st prize at the Tchaikovsky Competition in Moscow in 1970. She made her 1st tour of the U.S. with the Bolshoi troupe in June–July 1975; on Oct. 12, 1976, she made her Metropolitan Opera debut in N.Y. as Amneris in Verdi's *Aïda*. She appeared in recital in N.Y. in 1987, and was also invited to sing again at the Metropolitan Opera after an absence of some 10 years. In 1973 she was named a National Artist of the RSFSR and in 1976 she was awarded the Lenin prize. She possesses a remarkably even tessitura, brilliant in all registers; her roles include virtually the entire Russian operatic repertoire, and such standard roles as Norma, Carmen, Eboli, and Dalila.

Obrecht (Obreht, Hobrecht, Obertus, Hobertus), Jacob, famous Netherlandish composer; b. probably in Bergen-op-Zoom, Nov. 22, 1450 or 1451; d. Ferrara, 1505. He is 1st mentioned as zangmeester in Utrecht (c.1476–78); then became choirmaster for the Corp. of Notre Dame at St. Gertrude in Bergen-op-Zoom (1479); took Holy Orders, and said his 1st Mass as an ordained priest on April 23, 1480. He was made maître des enfants at Cambrai (July 28, 1484), but was dismissed for his neglect of the choirboys as well as financial irregularities (1485); then was made succentor at St. Donatian in Bruges (Oct. 13, 1486). At the invitation of the Duke of Ferrara, he obtained a leave of absence to travel to Italy; arrived in Ferrara in Dec. 1487, returning to Bruges Aug. 15, 1488; was made maître de chapelle there in 1490; obtained remission from his position on Jan. 24, 1491. By 1494 he was at Notre Dame in Antwerp, serving as Capellanie magister in 1495; he returned to St. Gertrude in Bergen-op-Zoom in 1496–97, and then received a benefice connected to the altar of St. Josse in Notre Dame at Antwerp in 1498. He was again at St. Donatian in Bruges from 1499 until his retirement in 1500; then lived in Bergen-op-Zoom and made visits to Antwerp; in 1504 returned to the ducal court in Ferrara, where he died of the plague. Obrecht was one of the leading composers of his era, his masses and motets being of particular importance. He also wrote chansons, many to Dutch texts. Petrucci publ. *Misse Obreht* (Venice, 1503), which contained several of his finest masses. An extensive ed. of his works was prepared by J. Wolf and publ. as *Werken van Jacob Obrecht* by the Vereeniging voor Noord-Nederlands Musiekgeschiedenis (7 vols., Amsterdam and Leipzig, 1908–21). Since its appearance, additional works by Obrecht have been discovered while others formerly attributed to him have been determined to be spurious;

the *Passio Domini nostri Jesu Christi* is now considered a doubtful work, since early sources attribute it to Antoine Longueval and J. a la Venture. A. Smijers ed. *Jacob Obrecht: Opera omnia, editio altera* (9 vols., 1953–64). The *New Obrecht Edition*, under general ed. C. Maas, commenced publication in 1983.

BIBL.: O. Gombosi, *J. O.: Eine stilkritische Studie* (Leipzig, 1925); A. Smijers, "J. O.," *Tijdschrift van de Vereeniging voor Nederlandse muziekgeschiedenis*, XII/1 (1926); A. Pirro, "O. à Cambrai," ibid., XII/2 (1927); A. Smijers, "De Matteus-passie van J. O.," ibid., XIV/3 (1935); O. Strunk, "Origins of the L'homme armé Mass," *Bulletin of the American Musicological Society*, II (1937); A. Piscaer, "J. O.," *Sinte Geertruydsbronnen* (Bergen-op-Zoom, 1938); M. Kyriazis, *Die Cantus firmus-Technik in den Messen O.s* (Bern, 1952); M. Antonowytsch, "Renaissance-Tendenzen in der Fortuna-desperata-Messen von Josquin und O.," *Die Musikforschung*, IX (1956); B. Murray, "New Light on J. O.'s Development: A Biographical Study," *Musical Quarterly*, XLIII (1957); A. Salop, *The Masses of J. O. (1450–1505), Structure and Style* (diss., Indiana Univ., 1959); R. Lenaerts, "J. O.," *Musica*, XV (1961); A. Salop, "J. O. and the Early Development of Harmonic Polyphony," *Journal of the American Musicological Society*, XVII (1964); L. van Hoorn, *J. O.* (The Hague, 1968); R. Todd, "Retrograde, Inversion, Retrograde-Inversion, and Related Techniques in the Masses of O.," *Musical Quarterly*, LXIV (1978); M. Picker, *Johannes Ockeghem and J. O.: A Guide to Research* (N.Y., 1988).

Obretenov, Svetoslav, Bulgarian choral conductor and composer; b. Provadia, Nov. 25, 1909; d. Sofia, May 16, 1955. He studied at the Sofia Cons.; was active as a choral conductor. He wrote mostly for chorus; his oratorio *The Partisans* was performed for the 1st time in Sofia on June 25, 1949.

BIBL.: V. Krstev, *S. O.* (Sofia, 1959).

O'Brien, Eugene, American composer and teacher; b. Paterson, N.J., April 24, 1945. He studied with Robert Beadell at the Univ. of Nebraska (B.M., 1967; M.M., 1969) and on a Fulbright fellowship with Bernd Alois Zimmermann at the Cologne Staatliche Hochschule für Musik (1969–70); after further training with John Eaton and Iannis Xenakis at Indiana Univ. (1970–71), he completed his studies with Donald Erb at the Cleveland Inst. of Music (D.M.A., 1983). In the meantime, he taught composition at the Cleveland Inst. of Music (1973–81), subsequently serving as its composer-in-residence and as chairman of its composition and theory dept. (1981–85); he was associate prof. of music and chairman of the composition dept. at the school of music at the Catholic Univ. of America in Washington, D.C. (1985–87); then associate prof. of music at the Indiana Univ. School of Music (from 1987). He held the Rome Prize Fellowship at the American Academy in Rome (1971–73); also received N.E.A. fellowships (1977, 1979) and a Guggenheim fellowship (1984–85).

WORKS: BALLET: *Taking Measures* (Cleveland, Oct. 10, 1984). **ORCH.:** Sym. (Lincoln, Nebr., May 16, 1969); Cello Concerto (1971; Rome, Dec. 5, 1972); *Dédales* for Soprano and Orch. (1973; Rome, Dec. 18, 1976); *Rites of Passage* (1978); *Dreams and Secrets of Origin* for Soprano and Orch. (Cleveland, Oct. 19, 1987); Alto Saxophone Concerto (1989). **CHAMBER:** *Ambages* for Piano, 4–hands (1972); *Intessitura* for Cello and Piano (1975); *Embarking for Cythera* for 8 Instruments (1978); *Tristan's Lament* for Cello (1979); *Allures* for Percussion Trio (1979); *Fancies and Goodnights* for Flute, Viola, and Harp (1981); *Black Fugatos* for 5 Instruments (1983); *Psalms and Nocturnes* for Flute, Viola da Gamba, and Harpsichord (1985); *Close Harmony* for 2 Pianos (1986); *Mysteries of the Horizon* for 11 Instruments (1987). **VOCAL:** *Ceremony after a Fire Raid* for Baritone and String Quartet (1965); *Requiem Mass* for Soprano, Chorus, and Wind Ensemble (1966); *Nocturne* for Soprano and 10 Instruments (1968); *Elegy for Bernd Alois Zimmermann* for Soprano, Trumpet, 2 Percussion, and Cello (1970); *Lingual* for Soprano, Flute, and Cello (1972).

Obukhova, Nadezhda (Andreievna), Russian mezzo-soprano; b. Moscow, March 6, 1886; d. Feodosiya, Aug. 14, 1961. She studied with Masetti at the Moscow Cons., graduating

in 1912. She made her debut at the Bolshoi Theater there in 1916 as Pauline in *The Queen of Spades*; remained on its roster until 1948. In addition to the Russian repertoire, she was noted for her portrayals of Carmen, Dalila, Amneris, and others. She was greatly esteemed in Russia; in 1943 she was awarded the State Prize of the U.S.S.R.

BIBL.: E. Grosheva, *N. O.* (Moscow, 1953); G. Polyanovsky, *My Meetings with N. O.* (Moscow, 1971).

Očenáš, Andrej, Slovak composer; b. Selce, near Banská Bystrica, Jan. 8, 1911. He studied composition with Alexander Moyzes at the Bratislava Academy of Music, graduating in 1937; then took a course with Vitězslav Novák at the Prague Cons., graduating in 1939. He worked at the Czech Radio in Bratislava (1939–50) and was music deputy to the regional director of broadcasting there (1956–62); taught at the Bratislava Cons. (1943–73); was director there from 1950 to 1954. His music is imbued with a Slovak ethos.

WORKS: STAGE: Musical play, *Rok na dedine* (Year in a Village; Bratislava, Dec. 11, 1948); other stage works: *At the Brigand's Ball* (1941); *Highlander's Songs*, ballet (1954–56); *The Romance of the Rose*, "stage symphony" for Narrator, Solo Singers, Chorus, and Orch. (1969–71). **ORCH.:** *Tales of My Native Land* (1943); *Resurrection*, symphonic cycle (1945–53); *To My Nation*, symphonic cycle (1947); Cello Concerto (1952); *Ruralia Slovaca* for String Orch., 2 Flutes, 2 Clarinets, 2 Trumpets, Horns, and Piano (1957); Piano Concerto (1959); *Concertino rustico* for Cimbalom, Strings, and Piano (1963); Sinfonietta (1966); *About Earth and Man*, sym. for Chorus and Small Orch. (1970); *The Flames of May*, prelude (1972); Violin Concerto (1974); *The Depiction of Life*, symphonic cycle (1980); *Gilding of Traditions* (1984); various choral works, including *Prophecies*, a cantata tetralogy (1949–52). **CHAMBER:** 2 string quartets (*Pictures of the Soul*, 1942; *Étude*, 1970); Concertino for Flute and Piano (1961–62); Piano Trio (1967); *Frescoes* for Violin and Piano (1967); *Poem of the Heart* for Violin (1968); *Don Quixote*, duo for Violin and Cello (1969); *Zvony* (The Bells), piano sonata (1972); piano pieces; songs.

Ochman, Wieslaw, Polish tenor; b. Warsaw, Feb. 6, 1937. He studied in Krakow, Bytom, and Warsaw; made his debut as Edgardo in *Lucia di Lammermoor* in Bytom (1959), appearing there regularly until 1963; then sang in Krakow and Warsaw. He subsequently made debuts at Berlin's Deutsche Oper (1966), the Hamburg State Opera (1967), the Chicago Lyric Opera (1972), the San Francisco Opera (1972), the Paris Opéra (1974), and the Vienna State Opera (1975); made his Metropolitan Opera debut in N.Y. as Arrigo in *Les Vêpres siciliennes* (March 12, 1975). Among his best known roles were those in Mozart's operas as well as Count Almaviva in *Le barbiere di Siviglia*, Ernesto in *Don Pasquale*, the Duke of Mantua, and Cavaradossi.

Ochs, Siegfried, German choral conductor and composer; b. Frankfurt am Main, April 19, 1858; d. Berlin, Feb. 5, 1929. He entered the Berlin Hochschule für Musik (1877), where his mentors were F. Kiel (theory), Joachim (ensemble playing), and Adolf Schulze (choral singing); later continued private studies with Kiel and Barth, and also attended the Univ. In 1882 he organized in Berlin a choral union under his own name, working in close collaboration with the Berlin Phil.; was known as the Phil. Choir from the 1887–88 season until being merged with the chorus of the Berlin Hochschule für Musik (1920), where he served as director of the oratorio dept. He publ. *Der deutsche Gesangverein* (4 vols., Berlin, 1923–28) and *Über die Art, Musik zu Hören* (Berlin, 1926), as well as an autobiography, *Geschehenes, Gesehenes* (Leipzig, 1922). Among his works were a comic opera, *Im Namen des Gesetzes* (Hamburg, Nov. 3, 1888), 2 operettas, song cycles, and choral arrangements of German folk songs.

BIBL.: M. Stappenbeck, *Chronik des Philharmonischen Chors in Berlin 1882-1932* (Berlin, 1932); K. Singer, *S. O., Der Bergründer des Philharmonischen Chors* (Berlin, 1933).

Ockeghem (Okeghem, Okengheim, Ockenheim, etc.**), Johannes (Jean, Jehan de),** great Flemish composer; b. c.1410;

d. probably in Tours, Feb. 6, 1497. He may have been a pupil of Binchois. He is 1st listed among the vicaires-chanteurs at Notre Dame in Antwerp on June 24, 1443, and served there until 1444; by 1446 he was in the service of Charles I, Duke of Bourbon, in Moulins, remaining there until at least 1448. By 1452 he was in the service of Charles VII of France as 1st among the singer-chaplains who were non-priests; by 1454 he was premier chapelain. He subsequently served Louis XI and Charles VIII; in 1459 the latter made him treasurer of the church of St. Martin-de-Tours. Under Louis XI, he also was a canon at Notre Dame in Paris from 1463 to 1470. He likewise was a chaplain at St. Benoît. In Jan. 1470 he traveled to Spain at the King's expense. In 1484 he journeyed to Bruges and Dammes. Upon his death, Guillaume Crétin wrote a poetic "Déploration," and Josquin Des Prez and Lupi composed musical epitaphs. With his contemporaries Dufay and Josquin, Ockeghem ranks among the foremost masters of the Franco-Flemish style of composition in the 2nd half of the 15th century. Among his settings of the Mass is the earliest extant polyphonic Requiem. The inventiveness displayed in his masses is only excelled in his superb motets. His achievements in the art of imitative counterpoint unquestionably make his music a milestone on the way to the a cappella style of the coming generations. A major ed. of his works is found in D. Plamenac, editor, *J. Ockeghem: Sämtliche Werke*, in the Publikationen Älterer Musik, Jg. 1/2 (Leipzig, 1927), which contains 8 masses; a 2nd ed., rev., 1959, was publ. as *Masses I–VIII* in *J. Ockeghem: Collected Works*, I (N.Y.); *Masses and Mass Sections IX–XVI* appeared in the same ed. as vol. II (N.Y., 1947; 2nd ed., 1966). **BIBL.:** E. Thoinan, *Déploration de Guillaume Crétin sur le trépas de J. O., musicien, premier chaplain du roi de France et trésorier de Saint-Martin de Tours* (Paris, 1864); A. Schering, "Ein Rätseltenor Okeghems," in the Kretzschmar Festschrift (Leipzig, 1918); D. Plamenac, *J. O. als Motetten- und Chanson-komponist* (diss., Univ. of Vienna, 1925); idem, "Autour d'Ockeghem," *Revue de Musicologie*, IX (1927–28); W. Stephan, *Die burgundisch-niederländische Motette zur Zeit Ockeghems* (Kassel, 1937); A. Smijers, "Van Ockeghem tot Sweelinck," *Algemeene musiekgeschiedenis* (Utrecht, 1938); E. Krenek, "A Discussion of the Treatment of Dissonances in Okeghem's Masses as Compared with the Contrapuntal Theory of Joh. Tinctoris," *Hamline Studies in Musicology*, II (1947); idem, *J. O.* (N.Y., 1953); B. Meier, "Caput: Bemerkungen zur Messe Dufays und Ockeghems," *Die Musikforschung*, VII (1954); C. Dahlhaus, "Ockeghems 'Fuga trium vocum,'" ibid., XIII (1960); R. Zimmermann, "Stilkritische Anmerkungen zum Werk Ockeghems," *Archiv für Musikwissenschaft*, XXII (1965); M. Henze, *Studien zu den Messenkompositionen J. O.* (Berlin, 1968); F. Lesure, "Ockeghem à Notre-Dame de Paris (1463–1470)," *Essays in Musicology in Honor of Dragan Plamenac* (Pittsburgh, 1969); E. Lowinsky, "Ockeghem's Canon for Thirty-Six Voices: An Essay in Musical Iconography," ibid.; *J. O. en zijn tijd* (Dendermonde, 1970); E. Houghton, *Rhythmic Structure in the Masses and Motets of J. O.* (diss., Univ. of Calif., Berkeley, 1971); M. Picker, *J. O. and Jacob Obrecht: A Guide to Research* (N.Y., 1988).

O'Connell, Charles, American conductor and recording executive; b. Chicopee, Mass., April 22, 1900; d. N.Y., Sept. 1, 1962. He studied at the Catholic School and College of the Holy Cross (B.A., 1922); also studied organ in Paris with Widor. From 1930 to 1944 he was head of the artist and repertoire dept. of the RCA Victor Red Seal label, then music director of Columbia Masterworks (1944–47). He publ. *The Victor Book of the Symphony* (1934; new ed., 1948); *The Victor Book of the Opera* (1937); *The Other Side of the Record* (relating personal experiences in dealing with musical celebrities; N.Y., 1947); *The Victor Book of Overtures, Tone Poems and Other Orchestral Works* (1950).

O'Connor, Sinead, Irish popular vocalist and songwriter; b. Dublin, Dec. 8, 1967. In 1985 she moved to London, where she wrote and produced her successful 1st album, *The Lion and the Cobra* (1987); then toured North America and Europe (1988), becoming an instant hit due to her intensely personal, emotionally fragile songs and her unusual appearance—a delicate face with high cheekbones framed by a shaved head. The success of her 2nd album, *I Do Not Want What I Haven't Got* (1989), paralleled her 1st. She made her acting debut in *Hush-A-Bye Baby* (1989), an Irish television movie, for which she also wrote and performed the score.

Odak, Krsto, Croatian composer; b. Siverić, Dalmatia, March 20, 1888; d. Zagreb, Nov. 4, 1965. He studied composition with P. Hartmann in Munich (1912–13) and with Novák in Prague (1919–22). Upon his return to Yugoslavia, he was prof. of composition at the Zagreb Academy of Music, retiring in 1961. **WORKS: OPERAS:** *Dorica pleše* (Dorica Dances; Zagreb, April 16, 1934); *Majka Margarita* (Mother Margaret), radio opera (Zagreb, March 25, 1955). **ORCH.:** 4 syms. (1940, 1951, 1961, 1965); 2 passacaglias (1938, 1955); Concertino for Bassoon and Strings (1958). **CHAMBER:** 4 string quartets (1923, 1927, 1934, 1956); Violin Sonata (1922); Flute Sonata (1946); also *Radost* (Gaiety), cantata (1959); 2 *Old Slavonic Masses*; motets; songs; incidental music; film scores.

Odaka, Hisatada. See **Otaka, Hisatada.**

O'Day, Anita (real name, **Anita Belle Colton**), American jazz singer; b. Kansas City, Mo., Oct. 18, 1919. She began her career in Chicago as a vocalist with the Max Miller Combo in 1939, and became one of the leading jazz singers of the era; she sang with the big bands of Gene Krupa, Roy Eldridge, and Stan Kenton, and she also gave solo recitals. In spite of her heroine addiction, she remained one of the leading jazz singers of her time; celebrated her 50th year as a jazz singer at N.Y.'s Carnegie Hall (1985). She publ. an autobiography, *High Times, Hard Times* (with G. Eells; N.Y., 1981; new ed., 1989).

Oddone Sulli-Rao, Elisabetta, Italian composer; b. Milan, Aug. 13, 1878; d. there, March 3, 1972. She studied at the Milan Cons.; composed a one-act opera, *A gara colle rondini* (Milan, 1920), and a children's opera, *Petruccio e il cavallo cappuccio* (Milan, 1916); also several oratorios; chamber music; and a number of songs. She did some valuable work on dissemination of Italian folk songs; publ. *Canzoniere popolare italiano*, *Canzoncine per bimbi*, *Cantilene popolari dei bimbi d'Italia*, etc.

Odetta (a.k.a. **Odetta Holmes Felious Gordon**), black American folk singer and guitarist; b. Birmingham, Ala., Dec. 31, 1930. Her family moved to Los Angeles when she was a child; she studied voice at Los Angeles City College, and also learned to play the guitar. She sang in nightclubs in California; made her concert debut in N.Y. in 1959; then appeared on the radio, and took singing parts in several films, including *Sanctuary* (1960). In 1974 she made a tour in the Soviet Union which attracted much attention; the Russians were stunned by the spectacle of a black woman singing Negro spirituals and accompanying herself on the guitar.

Odington, Walter, English music theorist and scientist who fluorished from 1298 to 1316, known as Walter of Evesham. He was a monk at Evesham, a Benedictine abbey near Worcester; was at Oxford (c.1316). He was one of the chief medieval writers on mensural notation; his *De speculatione musices* (MS in Corpus Christi College, Cambridge) was printed by Coussemaker in 1864 (*Scriptores*, I; modern ed. by F. Hammond, *Walteri Odington Summa de speculatione musicae*, in Corpus Scriptorum de Musica, XIV, 1970). This work is particularly valuable for the light it throws on musical rhythm as practiced in the late 13th century; it also discusses intervals, notation, musical instruments, and musical forms (rondellus, motet, etc.). His views on consonance and dissonance are interesting for their acceptance of thirds and sixths as legitimate consonances. He was also noted as an astronomer. **BIBL.:** J. Wolf, "Early English Musical Theorists," *Musical Quarterly* (Oct. 1939).

Odnoposoff, Adolfo, Argentine cellist, brother of **Ricardo Odnoposoff;** b. Buenos Aires, Feb. 22, 1917. He studied with

Alberto Schiuma; then went to Berlin, where he took lessons with Feuermann, and to Paris, where he became a student of Diran Alexanian. He was subsequently active as a concert cellist in Palestine (1936–38), Peru (1938–40), Chile (1940–44), Havana (1944–58), and Mexico City, where he also taught at the Cons. Nacional de Música (1958–64); then was a prof. of cello and chamber music at the Cons. of Music in San Juan, Puerto Rico. In 1975 he became a prof. of cello at North Texas State Univ. in Denton. Several Latin American composers (Roque Cordero, Rodolfo Halffter, Eduardo Mata, Floro Ugarte, Antonio Tauriello, and others) wrote special works for him.

Odnoposoff, Ricardo, Argentine violinist, brother of **Adolfo Odnoposoff;** b. Buenos Aires, Feb. 24, 1914. He studied with Aaron Klasse in Buenos Aires (1919–26), Rudolph Deman in Berlin (1927–28), and Carl Flesch at the Berlin Hochschule für Musik (1928–32). A precocious musician, he played in public as an infant; was a soloist with the Berlin Phil. at 17; won 1st prize at the Vienna (1932) and Ysaÿe (1937) competitions; evolved a brilliant career as a concert violinist, appearing in all parts of the world. He taught at the Vienna (1956), Stuttgart (from 1964), and Zürich (1975–84) Hochschules für Musik.

Odo de Cluny, composer; b. in the Maine, 878 or 879; d. Tours, Nov. 18, 942. A pupil of Rémy d'Auxerre in Paris, he took Holy Orders at 19, and in 899 was canon and choir singer at Tours; in 909 he entered the Benedictine monastery at Baume, near Besançon, and then was successively abbot at Aurillac, Fleuri, and (from 927) Cluny. The famous treatise *Dialogus de musica* (also known as *Enchiridion musices*) is attributed to him without foundation (it is printed in Gerbert's *Scriptores* and, in Eng. tr., in O. Strunk's *Source Readings in Music History,* N.Y., 1950). It is most likely of north Italian origin. In the development of pitch notation through letter-names, the treatise was the 1st to give a complete series (2 octaves and a fifth) of letter-names (G, A, B, C, D, E, F, G, etc.) corresponding to our modern series; but whereas we change from capital to lower-case letters at *c* to designate the pitches of the 2nd octave, in its system the change was made at *a.* The treatise was also the 1st to add the sign *gamma* (Greek "G") to designate the note corresponding to G on the 1st line of our bass clef. It distinguished between b flat and b natural (b *rotundum* and b *quadratum*), but only at one point in the gamut, namely, the note lying one degree below middle C in our system. Odo's only extant compositions are 3 hymns and 12 antiphons.

BIBL.: T. Nisard, *St.-O. d.C.* (Paris, 1866); M. Huglo, "L'Auteur du *Dialogue sur la musique* attribué à O.," *Revue de Musicologie* (1969).

O'Dowd, George Alan. See Boy George.

O'Dwyer, Robert, English-Irish composer and conductor; b. Bristol, Jan. 27, 1862; d. Dublin, Jan. 6, 1949. He was a conductor of the Carl Rosa Opera Co. in London and on tour (1891); then with the Arthur Rousbey Opera Co. in England and Ireland (1892–99); in 1899, became music director at the Univ. of Ireland in Dublin; from 1914 to 1939, was prof. of music there; was music director (from 1901) of the Gaelic League choir, for which he arranged many Irish songs. He wrote one of the earliest operas with a Gaelic text, *Eithne* (Dublin, May 16, 1910); also composed songs with Gaelic words; organ pieces. He left a book in MS, *Irish Music and Its Traditions.*

Oehl, Kurt (Helmut), eminent German musicologist; b. Mainz, Feb. 24, 1923. He was educated at the Mainz Cons. and at the Johannes Gutenberg Univ. in Mainz; obtained his Ph.D. (1952) with the dissertation *Beitrage zur Geschichte der deutschen Mozart-Übersetzungen.* After working as a dramaturg (1952–60), he became a member of the editorial staff of the *Riemann Musiklexikon* in 1960. In this capacity, he helped to prepare the vol. on musical terms and historical subjects (*Sachteil*) for the 12th ed. (Mainz, 1967); also served as a biographical ed. for the *Supplement* (2 vols.; Mainz, 1972,

1975). He then became an ed. for the *Brockhaus-Riemann Musiklexikon* (2 vols.; Mainz, 1978–79; supplement, 1989). With K. Pfarr, he publ. *Musikliteratur im Überblick: Eine Anleitung zum Nachschlagen* (Mainz, 1988); taught at the Johannes Gutenberg Univ. (1973–87).

Oestvig, Karl (Aagaard), Norwegian tenor; b. Christiania, May 17, 1889; d. there (Oslo), July 21, 1968. He studied in Cologne; made his debut at the Stuttgart Opera in 1914; remained on its roster until 1919; was then a member of the Vienna State Opera (1919–27), where he created the role of the Emperor in Strauss's *Die Frau ohne Schatten* in 1919; also sang at the Berlin State Opera and the Städtische Oper; made concert tours of Europe and North America. He retired from the stage in 1932 and devoted himself to teaching; accepted the post of director of the Oslo Opera (1941) during the Nazi occupation of Norway, an action which brought him disgrace after the liberation. He was married to the soprano Maria Rajdl. Among his finest roles were Walther von Stolzing, Lohengrin, and Parsifal.

Offenbach, Jacques (actually, **Jacob**), famous French composer of German descent; b. Cologne, June 20, 1819; d. Paris, Oct. 5, 1880. He was the son of a Jewish cantor, whose original surname was Eberst; Offenbach was the town where his father lived. He studied violin before taking up the cello when he was 9; after training with Joseph Alexander and Bernhard Breuer in Cologne, he settled in Paris (1833); following cello studies with Vaslin at the Cons. (1833–34), he played in the orch. of the Opéra-Comique; also received further instruction from Louis Norblin and Halévy; then pursued a career as a soloist and chamber music artist (from 1838); subsequently was a conductor at the Théâtre-Français (1850–55). His *Chanson de Fortunio* for Musset's *Chandelier* (1850) proved tremendously popular. In 1855 he ventured to open his own theater, the Bouffes-Parisiens, at the Salle Marigny; late that year it moved to the Salle Choiseul, where he scored his 1st great success with the operetta *Orphée aux enfers* (Oct. 21, 1858). His *La Belle Hélène* (Variétés, Dec. 17, 1864) proved to be one of his most celebrated works, soon taken up by theatrical enterprises all over the world. Having abandoned the management of the Bouffes-Parisiens in 1866, he nevertheless continued to write for the stage. His *La Vie parisienne* (Palais Royal, Oct. 31, 1866), *La Grande-Duchesse de Gérolstein* (Variétés, April 12, 1867), and *La Périchole* (Variétés, Oct. 6, 1868) were notably successful. In 1873 he took over the management of the Théâtre de la Gaîté, where he brought out his rev. version of *Orphée aux enfers* as an opéra-féerique (Feb. 7, 1874). In 1876 he undertook a tour of the U.S., describing his impressions in *Notes d'un musicien en voyage* (Paris, 1877) and *Offenbach en Amérique* (Paris, 1877; Eng. tr., 1877, as *Offenbach in America*; republ. as *Orpheus in America*, Bloomington, Ind., 1957). His only grand opera, the masterpiece *Les Contes d'Hoffmann*, remained unfinished at his death; recitatives were added by E. Guiraud with the famous barcarolle from Offenbach's *Die Rheinnixen* (1864), in which the tune was used for a ghost song; the completed score was premiered at the Opéra-Comique in Paris (Feb. 10, 1881) with instantaneous success, and subsequently was performed on both sides of the Atlantic. Offenbach is a master of the operetta; his music is characterized by an abundance of flowing, rollicking melodies, seasoned with ironic humor, suitable to the extravagant burlesque of the situations. His irreverent treatment of mythological characters gave Paris society a salutary shock; his art mirrored the atmosphere of precarious gaiety during the 2nd Empire.

WORKS: STAGE (all 1st perf. in Paris unless otherwise given): *L'Alcôve* (April 24, 1847); *Le Trésor à Mathurin* (May 1853; rev. as *Le Mariage aux lanternes,* Oct. 10, 1857); *Pépito* (Oct. 28, 1853); *Luc et Lucette* (May 2, 1854); *Oyayaie, ou La Reine des îles* (June 26, 1855); *Entrez, messieurs, mesdames* (July 5, 1855); *Les Deux Aveugles* (July 5, 1855); *Une Nuit blanche* (July 5, 1855); *Le Rêve d'une nuit d'été* (July 30, 1855); *Le Violoneux* (Aug. 31, 1855); *Madame Papillon* (Oct. 3, 1855); *Paimpol et Périnette* (Oct. 29, 1855); *Ba-ta-clan* (Dec. 29, 1855);

Élodie, ou Le Forfait nocturne (Jan. 19, 1856); *Le Postillon en gage* (Feb. 9, 1856); *Trombalcazar, ou Les Criminels dramatiques* (April 3, 1856); *La Rose de Saint-Flour* (June 12, 1856); *Les Dragées du baptême* (June 18, 1856); *Le "66"* (July 31, 1856); *Le Savetier et le financier* (Sept. 23, 1856); *La Bonne d'enfants* (Oct. 14, 1856); *Les Trois Baisers du diable* (Jan. 15, 1857); *Croquefer, ou Le Dernier des paladins* (Feb. 12, 1857); *Dragonette* (April 30, 1857); *Vent du soir, ou L'Horrible Festin* (May 16, 1857); *Une Demoiselle en lôterie* (July 27, 1857); *Les Deux Pêcheurs* (Nov. 13, 1857); *Mesdames de la Halle* (March 3, 1858); *La Chatte métamorphosée en femme* (April 19, 1858); *Orphée aux enfers* (Oct. 21, 1858; rev. version, Feb. 7, 1874); *Un Mari à la porte* (June 22, 1859); *Les Vivandières de la grande armée* (July 6, 1859); *Geneviève de Brabant* (Nov. 19, 1859; rev. version, Dec. 26, 1867; 2nd rev. version, Feb. 25, 1875); *Le Carnaval des revues* (Feb. 10, 1860); *Daphnis et Chloé* (March 27, 1860); *Barkouf* (Dec. 24, 1860); *La Chanson de Fortunio* (Jan. 5, 1861); *Le Pont des soupirs* (March 23, 1861; rev. version, May 8, 1868); *M. Choufleuri restera chez lui le . . .* (May 31, 1861); *Apothicaire et perruquier* (Oct. 17, 1861); *Le Roman comique* (Dec. 10, 1861); *Monsieur et Madame Denis* (Jan. 11, 1862); *Le Voyage de MM. Dunanan père et fils* (March 23, 1862); *Les Bavards* or *Bavard et bavarde* (Bad Ems, June 11, 1862); *Jacqueline* (Oct. 14, 1862); *Il Signor Fagotto* (Bad Ems, July 11, 1863); *Lischen et Fritzchen* (Bad Ems, July 21, 1863); *L'Amour chanteur* (Jan. 5, 1864); *Die Rheinnixen* (Vienna, Feb. 4, 1864); *Les Géorgiennes* (March 16, 1864); *Jeanne qui pleure et Jean qui rit* (Bad Ems, July 1864); *Le Fifre enchanté, ou Le Soldat magicien* (Bad Ems, July 9, 1864); *La Belle Hélène* (Dec. 17, 1864); *Coscoletto, ou Le Lazzarone* (Bad Ems, July 24, 1865); *Les Refrains des bouffes* (Sept. 21, 1865); *Les Bergers* (Dec. 11, 1865); *Barbe-bleue* (Feb. 5, 1866); *La Vie parisienne* (Oct. 31, 1866); *La Grande-Duchesse de Gérolstein* (April 12, 1867); *La Permission de dix heures* (Bad Ems, July 9, 1867); *La Leçon de chant* (Bad Ems, Aug. 1867); *Robinson Crusoé* (Nov. 23, 1867); *Le Château à Toto* (May 6, 1868); *L'Île de Tulipatan* (Sept. 30, 1868); *La Périchole* (Oct. 6, 1868; rev. version, April 25, 1874); *Vert-vert* (March 10, 1869); *La Diva* (March 22, 1869); *La Princesse de Trébizonde* (Baden-Baden, July 31, 1869; rev. version, Paris, Dec. 7, 1869); *Les Brigands* (Dec. 10, 1869); *La Romance de la rose* (Dec. 11, 1869); *Mam'zelle Moucheron* (c.1870; rev. version by Delibes, May 10, 1881); *Boule de neige* (Dec. 14, 1871; rev. version of *Barkouf*); *Le Roi Carotte* (Jan. 15, 1872); *Fantasio* (Jan. 18, 1872); *Fleurette, oder Näherin und Trompeter* (Vienna, March 8, 1872); *Der schwarze Korsar* (Vienna, Sept. 21, 1872); *Les Braconniers* (Jan. 29, 1873); *Pomme d'api* (Sept. 4, 1873); *La Jolie Parfumeuse* (Nov. 29, 1873); *Bagatelle* (May 21, 1874); *Madame l'archiduc* (Oct. 31, 1874); *Whittington* (London, Dec. 26, 1874); *Les Hannetons* (April 22, 1875); *La Boulangère a des écus* (Oct. 19, 1875); *Le Créole* (Nov. 3, 1875); *Le Voyage dans la lune* (Nov. 26, 1875); *Tarte à la crème* (Dec. 14, 1875); *Pierrette et Jacquot* (Oct. 13, 1876); *La Boîte au lait* (Nov. 3, 1876); *Le Docteur Ox* (Jan. 26, 1877); *La Foire Saint-Laurent* (Feb. 10, 1877); *Maître Péronilla* (March 13, 1878); *Madame Favart* (Dec. 28, 1878); *La Marocaine* (Jan. 13, 1879); *La Fille du tambour-major* (Dec. 13, 1879); *Belle Lurette* (Oct. 30, 1880; completed by Delibes); *Les Contes d'Hoffmann* (Feb. 10, 1881; completed by Guiraud). **VAUDEVILLES AND INCIDENTAL MUSIC:** *Pascal et Chambord* (March 2, 1839); *Le Brésilien* (May 9, 1863); *Le Gascon* (Sept. 2, 1873); *La Haine* (Dec. 3, 1874). **BALLETS:** *Arlequin barbier* (July 5, 1855); *Pierrot clown* (July 30, 1855); *Polichinelle dans le monde* (Sept. 19, 1855); *Les Bergers de Watteau* (June 24, 1856); *Le Papillon* (Nov. 26, 1860); much other dance music. Also various works for Cello, including *Prière et Boléro* for Cello and Orch. (1840); *Musette, Air de ballet du 17ᵐᵉ siècle* for Cello and Orch. (1843); *Hommage à Rossini* for Cello and Orch. (1843); *Concerto militaire* (1848); Concerto Rondo (c.1850; discovered by A. de Almeida in 1983); *Concertino* (1851); many pieces for Cello and Piano; several works for Solo Cello; pedagogical pieces; songs; etc.

BIBL.: E. de Mirecourt, *Les Contemporains: Auber, O.* (Paris, 1869); Argus, *Célébrités dramatiques: J. O.* (Paris, 1872); A.

Jullien, "M. O., critique: Sa profession de foi," *Airs variés* (Paris, 1877); A. Wolff, "J. O.," *La Gloire à Paris* (Paris, 1886); A. Martinet, *O.: Sa vie et son œuvre* (Paris, 1887); P. Bekker, *J. O.* (Berlin, 1909); R. Grau, "When O. Came to Town," *Musical America* (1913); R. Northcott, *J. O.: A Sketch of His Life and a Record of His Operas* (London, 1917); E. Rieger, *O. und seine Wiener Schule* (Vienna, 1920); L. Schneider, *O.* (Paris, 1923); R. Brancour, *O.* (Paris, 1929); A. Henseler, *Jakob O.* (Berlin, 1930); H. Kristeller, *Der Aufstieg des Kölners J. O.: Ein Musikerleben in Bildern* (Berlin, 1931); S. Kracauer, *J. O. und das Paris seiner Zeit* (Amsterdam, 1937; 2nd ed., 1962; Eng. tr., 1937); S. Sitwell, *La Vie Parisienne: A Tribute to O.* (London, 1937); J. Brindejont-Offenbach, *O., mon grand-père* (Paris, 1940); A. Decaux, *O., roi du Second Empire* (Paris, 1958; 3rd ed., 1975); A. Silbermann, *Das imaginäre Tagebuch des Herrn J. O.* (Berlin, 1960); O. Schneidereit, *J. O.* (Leipzig, 1966); P. Jacob, *J. O. in selbstzeugnissen und Bilddokumenten* (Hamburg, 1969); A. Lamb, "How O. Conquered London," *Opera*, XX (1969); F. Mailer, "J. O.—ein Pariser in Wien," *Österreichische Musikzeitschrift*, XXVII (1972); R. Pourvoyeur, *J. O.: Essay in Toengepaste Muziek- en Toneelsociologie* (Brussels, 1977); A. Faris, *J. O.* (London, 1980); P. Gammond, *O.: His Life and Times* (Tunbridge Wells, 1980; 2nd ed., rev., 1986); J. Harding et al., *O., 1819–1880: A Tribute* (London, 1980); R. Pourvoyeur, *O.: Idillio e Parodia* (Turin, 1980); *Musical Times* (Oct. 1980).

Ogden, Will (actually, **Wilbur Lee**), American composer; b. Redlands, Calif., April 19, 1921. He studied at the Univ. of Wisconsin in Madison (B.M., 1942) and at Hamline Univ. in St. Paul, Minn. (M.A., 1947); after graduate studies at the Univ. of Calif. in Berkeley (1949–50) and at Indiana Univ. in Bloomington (1950–52), he went to Paris on a Fulbright grant and attended the École Normale de Musique (1952–53); returning to the U.S., he obtained his Ph.D. in 1955 from Indiana Univ. with the dissertation *Series and Structure: An Investigation into the Purpose of the Twelve-Note Row in Selected Works of Schoenberg, Webern, Krenek, and Leibowitz*; his teachers in the U.S. included Krenek, Sessions, Bukofzer, Apel, and P. Nettl, and in Paris, Leibowitz. He taught at the Univ. of Texas in Austin (1947–50), at St. Catherine College in St. Paul, Minn. (1954–55), and at Illinois Wesleyan Univ. in Bloomington (1956–65); then became a prof. at the Univ. of Calif. in San Diego (1966), where he served as founder-chairman of its music dept. (1966–71). His compositions display an effective utilization of serial procedures.

WORKS: STAGE: *The Awakening of Sappho*, chamber opera (1976–80). **ORCH.:** *Movements for Dance* for Chamber Orch. (1948); *Diversions* for Wind Band (1964); *5 Comments and Capriccio* (1979); *5 Preludes* for Violin and Chamber Orch. (1985). **CHAMBER:** String Quartet (1947); *Palindrome and Variations* for String Quartet (1961–62); *Suite* for Flute and Double Bass (1978); *6 Small Trios* for Marimba, Trumpet, and Piano (1982); *Serenade* for Wind Quintet (1986–87); piano pieces. **VOCAL:** *3 Statements* for Chorus (1955); *Intrada* for Women's Voices and Instruments (1957); *3 Sea Choruses* (1959; 1960–76); *Orpheus Song* for Chorus (1963); *Un Tombeau de Jean Cocteau II* for Soprano, Clarinet or Mime, Pianist or Conductor, and 13 Instruments (1972); *Un Tombeau de Jean Cocteau III* for Narrator, Soprano, Oboe or Mime, Piano, Slides, and Tape (1976–77); *Summer Images and Reflections*, song cycle for Soprano, Flute, Clarinet, Trumpet, and Piano (1984–85); *Hurricane* for Soprano, Baritone, and Percussion (1985; rev. 1986); songs.

Ogdon, John (Andrew Howard), remarkable English pianist; b. Manchester, Jan. 27, 1937; d. London, Aug. 1, 1989. He studied with Iso Elinson at the Royal Manchester College of Music (1945); began his career while still a student, premiering works by Goehr and Maxwell Davies; made his London debut as soloist in the Busoni Piano Concerto (1958). After winning joint 1st prize (with Ashkenazy) at the Tchaikovsky Competition in Moscow (1962), he pursued a far-flung international career; taught at the Indiana Univ. School of Music in

Bloomington (1976–80). His extraordinary talent and success were marred by the tragedy of his life, acute schizophrenia. His father, Howard Ogdon, who also had the disease, described his misfortunes in *Kingdom of the Lost*. His wife also wrote a book, *Virtuoso: The Story of John Ogdon* (London, 1981), in which she described in detail Ogdon's suffering. Physically he presented a picture of astute well-being, being large of body, powerful of manual dexterity, and sporting a spectacular triangular beard. Despite numerous stays in sanatoriums, electric shock and drug treatment, and suicide attempts, he continued to appear as a concert artist. He maintained a vast repertory. His death at the age of 52 was mourned by a multitude of friends and admirers.

Ogihara, Toshitsugu, Japanese composer; b. Osaka, June 6, 1910. He studied composition with Matsudaira at Nihon Univ.; took private lessons with A. Tcherepnin during the latter's stay in Japan. His music follows the classical models.

Works: Ballet, *Springtime* (1973). **orch.:** 2 *Movements* for Percussion and Orch. (1942); *Sôshun no Hiroba*, symphonic poem (1955); Sym. No. 1 (1958); *Rhapsody* (1960); 2 violin concertos (1962, 1963); Violin Concertino (1962); *Capriccio* for String Orch. (1964); 4 *Pieces* for Horn and String Orch. (1972); *Fancy Parade* (1983). **chamber:** 4 string quartets (1940, 1949, 1953, 1969); 2 string trios (1947, 1961); Violin Sonata (1959); Concerto for Clarinet and String Quartet (1955); *Capriccio* for Woodwinds and Strings (1958); Trio for Clarinet, Cello, and Piano (1962); English Horn Sonata (1962); Quartet for 4 Flutes (1963); Trio for Flute, Violin, and Piano (1965); Piano Quintet (1970); 7 *Poems* for Soprano, Violin, Cello, and Piano (1971); *Serenade* for Cello, Violin, and Clarinet (1972); 4 *Pieces* for Tuba, 3 Tenor Trombones, and Bass Trombone (1972); 2 *Suites* for Flute and Piano (1974); *Duet* No. 1 for Violin and Piano (1983); Suite for Flute and Piano (1984); piano pieces, including a *Fantasia* (1984); songs.

Oginski, Prince Michal Kleofas, Polish composer; b. Guzow, near Warsaw, Sept. 25, 1765; d. Florence, Oct. 15, 1833. He was a Polish nobleman of a musical family; his uncle, **Michal Kazimierz Oginski** (b. Warsaw, 1728; d. there, May 31, 1800), was an amateur composer of some talent. He studied violin and piano with Jozef Kozlowski in Guzow (1773–78); later with Viotti (1798) and Baillot (1810). He was active as a diplomat; he left Poland after its partition, and agitated in Turkey and France for the Polish cause. In 1799 he wrote an opera, *Zélis et Valcour ou Bonaparte au Caire*, to ingratiate himself with Napoleon. Of historical interest are his polonaises, many of which were publ.; the one in A minor, known as *Death Polonaise*, became extremely popular; he also wrote mazurkas and waltzes for Piano, and a patriotic Polish march (1825). His son, **Franciszek Krawery Oginski** (1801–37), was also a composer; wrote piano pieces and songs.

Ogura, Roh, Japanese composer; b. Kitakyūshu, Jan. 19, 1916. He studied with Fukai, Sugawara, and Ikenouchi; then was engaged in teaching.

Works: **Opera:** *Neta* (1957). **orch.:** *Orly—A Bugbear at Sea* for Narrator and Orch. (1963); Sym. in A (1941); Piano Concerto (Tokyo, March 24, 1946); Sym. in F (Tokyo, April 25, 1951); 5 *Movements on Japanese Folk Songs* for Orch. (1957); Sym. in G (1968); Violin Concerto (1971); Cello Concerto (1980). **chamber:** 3 string quartets (1941, 1946, 1954); Violin Sonata (1950); Violin Sonatina (1960); *Divertimento* for 7 Winds (1964); *Divertimento* for 8 Winds (1972); *Dance Suite* for 2 Pianos (1953); also choruses; songs.

Ohana, Maurice, French composer and pianist; b. Casablanca (of Spanish parents), June 12, 1914. He studied piano with Frank Marshall in Barcelona and with Lazare Lévy at the Paris Cons.; also had lessons in counterpoint with Daniel Lesur at the Schola Cantorum (1937–40). Following service in the British Army during World War II, he completed his training with Alfredo Casella at Rome's Accademia di Santa Cecilia (1944–46), then settled in Paris. In 1981 he was made a Com-

mandeur des Arts et Lettres. He won the Prix National de Musique (1975) and the Honegger (1982) and Ravel (1985) prizes.

Works: **operas:** *Syllabaire pour Phèdre* (1967; Paris, Feb. 5, 1968); *Autodafé* (Lyons, May 23, 1972); *Trois contes de l'Honorable Fleur* (Avignon, July 16, 1978); *La Célestine* (1982–86; Paris, June 13, 1988). **radiophonic scores:** *Les Hommes et les autres* (1955); *Histoire véridique de Jacotin* (1961); *Hélène* (1963); *Les Héraclides* (1964); *Iphigénie en Tauride* (1965); *Hippolyte* (1965–66); film music. **orch.:** *Trois graphiques*, concerto for Guitar and Orch. (1950–57; BBC, London, Feb. 1961); *Synaxis* for 2 Pianos, 4 Percussionists, and Orch. (1965–66); *Chiffres de clavecin* for Harpsichord and Chamber Orch. (1967–68); *Silenciaire* for 6 Percussion and String Orch. (1969); *T'harân-Ngô* (Paris, Oct. 1974); *Anneau du Tamarit* for Cello and Orch. (1976); *Livre des Prodiges* (Lyons, Oct. 4, 1979); *Crypt* for String Orch. (1980); Piano Concerto (1980–81); Cello Concerto No. 2 (1988–89). **chamber:** *Tiento* for Guitar (1955); *Quatre improvisations* for Flute (1961); *Cinq séquences* for String Quartet (1963); *Signes* for Flute, 2 Guitars, Piano, and 4 Percussion (1965); *Syrtes* for Cello and Piano (1970); *Sacral d'Ilx* for Harpsichord, Oboe, and Horn (1975); *Satyre* for 2 Flutes (1976); String Quartet No. 2 (1980); *Kypris* for 4 Instruments (1985); piano pieces; harpsichord music. **vocal:** *Llanto por Ignacio Sanchez Mejias* for Baritone, Reciter, Women's Voices, and Instrumental Ensemble (Paris, May 22, 1950); *Cantigas* for Soprano, Mezzo-soprano, Chorus, and Instrumental Ensemble (1953); *Récit de l'ano zéro*, scenic oratorio (1958–59); *Tombeau de Claude Debussy* for Soprano, Guitar, and Chamber Orch. (1962; Paris, Jan. 8, 1964); *Cris* for 12 Voices (1968); *Stream* for Bass and String Trio (1970); *Office des oracles* for 3 Vocal Groups and Instruments (Ste. Baume, Aug. 9, 1974); *Lys de Madrigaux* for Women's Chorus and Instrumental Ensemble (Paris, June 1, 1976); *Messe* for Soprano, Mezzo-soprano, Chorus, and Instrumental Ensemble (Avignon, July 30, 1977); *Lux Noctis—Die Solis* for 4 Choral Groups and 2 Organs (1981–88; Paris, Dec. 9, 1988); *Swan Songs* for 12 Voices (1988).

Bibl.: N. Quist, *M. O.* (diss., Univ. of Heidelberg, 1973).

O'Hara, Geoffrey, Canadian-born American composer; b. Chatham, Ontario, Feb. 2, 1882; d. St. Petersburg, Fla., Jan. 31, 1967. He settled in the U.S. in 1904; became an American citizen in 1919. He studied with Homer Norris and J. Vogler; then acted in vaudeville as a pianist, singer, and composer; wrote the song *Your eyes have told me* for Caruso. In 1913 he was appointed an instructor in American Indian music as part of a program of the Dept. of the Interior; in 1917, became an army song leader; was instructor in community singing at Teachers College, Columbia Univ. (1936–37); charter member of ASCAP (1914). He wrote the operettas *Peggy and the Pirate* (1927), *Riding Down the Sky* (1928), *The Count and the Coed* (1929), and *The Smiling Six-pence* (1930); also wrote about 300 songs, of which the following were extremely popular: *K-K-K-Katy, I Love a Little Cottage, The Living God, I Walked Today Where Jesus Walked,* and *Give a Man a Horse He Can Ride.*

Ohlsson, Garrick (Olof), talented American pianist; b. Bronxville, N.Y., April 3, 1948. He entered the preparatory division of the Juilliard School of Music in 1961 as a student of Sascha Gorodnitzki and later of Rosina Lhévinne (B.Mus., 1971); also studied privately with Olga Barabini and Irma Wolpe. He won the Busoni (1966) and Montreal (1968) competitions; then made his N.Y. recital debut on Jan. 5, 1970; later that year he gained international recognition when he became the 1st American pianist to win the prestigious quinquennial Chopin Competition in Warsaw. A Polish writer described Ohlsson as a "bear-butterfly" for his ability to traverse the entire spectrum of 18 dynamic degrees discernible on the modern piano, from the thundering fortissimo to the finest pianissimo, with reference also to his height (6 foot, 4 inches), weight (225 lbs.), and stretch of hands (an octave and a fifth in the left hand and an octave and a fourth in the right hand).

His interpretations are marked by a distinctive Americanism, technically flawless and free of Romantic mannerisms.

Ohms, Elisabeth, Dutch soprano; b. Arnhem, May 17, 1888; d. Marquardstein, Oct. 16, 1974. She studied in Amsterdam, Frankfurt, and Berlin; made her debut in Mainz in 1921; in 1922 she joined the Bavarian State Opera in Munich, of which she was a principal member until 1936; also sang at La Scala in Milan (1927–29), at Covent Garden in London (1928–29, 1935), and at the Bayreuth Festival (1931). On Jan. 17, 1930, she made her debut with the Metropolitan Opera in N.Y. as Brünnhilde; remained on its roster until 1932. She excelled in Wagner's operas; among her finest roles were Brünnhilde, Kundry, Venus, and Isolde.

Oistrakh, David (Fyodorovich), great Russian violinist; b. Odessa, Sept. 30, 1908; d. Amsterdam, Oct. 24, 1974. He studied violin as a child with Stoliarsky in Odessa; made his debut there at the age of 6; then continued his studies with Stoliarsky at the Odessa Cons. (1923–26); then appeared as soloist in Glazunov's Violin Concerto under the composer's direction in Kiev in 1927. In 1928 he went to Moscow; in 1934, was appointed to the faculty of the Moscow Cons. His name attracted universal attention in 1937 when he won 1st prize at the Ysaÿe Competition in Brussels, in which 68 violinists from 21 countries took part. He played in Paris and London in 1953 with extraordinary success; made his 1st American appearances in 1955, as soloist with major American orchs. and in recitals, winning enthusiastic acclaim; also made appearances as a conductor from 1962. He died while on a visit to Amsterdam as a guest conductor with the Concertgebouw Orch. Oistrakh's playing was marked, apart from a phenomenal technique, by stylistic fidelity to works by different composers of different historical periods. Soviet composers profited by his advice as to technical problems of violin playing; he collaborated with Prokofiev in making an arrangement for violin and piano of his Flute Sonata. (He also played a chess match with Prokofiev.) A whole generation of Soviet violinists numbered among his pupils, 1st and foremost his son **Igor Oistrakh** (b. Odessa, April 27, 1931), who has had a spectacular career in his own right; he won 1st prize at the International Festival of Democratic Youth in Budapest (1949) and the Wieniawski Competition in Poznan (1952); some critics regarded him as equal to his father in virtuosity.

BIBL.: V. Bronin, *D. O.* (Moscow, 1954); I. Yampolsky, *D. O.* (Moscow, 1964); D. Naberin, *D. und Igor O.* (Berlin, 1968); V. Josefowitsch, *D. O.* (Stuttgart, 1977); Y. Soroker, *D. O.* (Jerusalem, 1982); B. Schwarz, *Great Masters of the Violin* (N.Y., 1983); H. Temianka, "D. O.: Memories of a Friendship," *Ovation* (Aug. 1985).

Okeghem, Johannes. See **Ockeghem, Johannes.**

Oki, Masao, Japanese composer; b. Iwata, Shizuoka, Oct. 3, 1901; d. Kamakura, April 18, 1971. He studied engineering and music; then devoted himself mainly to teaching and composition. He wrote 6 syms., of which the 5th was subtitled *Atomic Bomb*; it was performed in Tokyo on Nov. 6, 1953; the 6th Sym. (1970) was entitled *Vietnam*. His other works included a cantata, *Take Back the Human* (1961–63); a String Quartet; and some choral works.

Olah, Tiberiu, Rumanian composer; b. Arpăşel, Jan. 2, 1928. He studied at the Cluj Cons. (1946–49) and the Moscow Cons. (1949–54); in each of the years from 1966 to 1971, he attended the summer courses in new music at Darmstadt. In 1954 he joined the faculty of the Bucharest Cons. In his music he adopts a strong contrapuntal style, with some excursions into the atonal domain and dodecaphonic organization.

WORKS: Piano Sonatina (1950); String Quartet (1952); Trio for Violin, Clarinet, and Piano (1954); *Little Suite* for Orch. (1954); 2 syms. (1952–55; 1985–87); Violin Sonatina (1955); 4 cantatas: *Cantata* for Female Chorus, 2 Flutes, Strings, and Percussion (1956); *Prind visele aripi* (Dreams Become Reality, 1959); *Lumina lui Lenin* (The Light of Lenin, 1959); *Constelaţia omului* (The Galaxy of Man, 1960); a cycle of 5 works inspired by the works of the Rumanian sculptor Constantin

Brâncuşi: *Coloana fără sfîrşit* (Endless Column), symphonic poem (1962); 2 sonatas for Solo Clarinet (1963, 1982); *Spaţiu şi ritm* (Space and Rhythm), étude for 3 Percussion Groups (1964); *Poarta sărutului* (Archway of the Kiss), symphonic poem (1966); *Masa tăcerii* (The Table of Silence), symphonic poem (1967–68); 5 *Pieces* for Orch. (1966); *Echinocţii* (Equinoxes) for Voice, Clarinet, and Piano (1967); *Translations* for 16 Strings (1968); *Perspectives* for 13 Instruments (1969); Sonata for Solo Cello (1971); *Invocations* for Various Instruments (1971); *Crescendo* for Orch. (1972); *Evenimente 1907* for Orch. (1972); *Time of Memory* for Chamber Ensemble (1973; N.Y., Dec. 6, 1974); *Harmonies*: No. 1 for Orch. (1975), No. 2 for Winds and Percussion (1976), No. 3 for Orch. (1977–78), and No. 4, a concerto for 23 Instruments (1981); Sonata for Solo Flute (1978); Sonata for Violin and Percussionist (1985); Sonata for Saxophone and Tape (1986).

Olczewska, Maria (real name, **Marie Berchtenbreitner**), prominent German mezzo-soprano; b. Ludwigsschwaige bei Donauwörth, near Augsburg, Aug. 12, 1892; d. Klagenfurt, Austria, May 17, 1969. She studied with Karl Erler in Munich; began her career singing in operetta; made her operatic debut in Krefeld (1915), then appeared in Leipzig (1916–20) and Hamburg (1920–23); also in Vienna (1921–23). She was a favorite at London's Covent Garden in Wagnerian roles (1924–32); also sang in Munich (1923–25) and again in Vienna (1925–30); likewise appeared in Chicago (1928–32). She made her Metropolitan Opera debut in N.Y. as Brangäne on Jan. 16, 1933, remaining on its roster until 1935. From 1947 to 1949 she taught at the Academy of Music. She had a powerful voice, which made it possible for her to master the Wagner roles; but she was also excellent in dramatic parts, such as Carmen. Furthermore, she had a genuine talent as a stage actress. She was married for a time to the bass-baritone **Emil Schipper.**

Oldberg, Arne, American composer; b. Youngstown, Ohio, July 12, 1874; d. Evanston, Ill., Feb. 17, 1962. He studied composition with Middelschulte; then went to Vienna, where he was a piano pupil of Leschetizky (1893–95); also took courses with Rheinberger in Munich. Returning to America in 1899, he became head of the piano dept. at Northwestern Univ.; retired in 1941. Most of his orch. works were performed by the Chicago Sym. Orch., among them *Paolo and Francesca* (Jan. 17, 1908), *At Night* (April 13, 1917), Sym. No. 4 (Dec. 31, 1942), Sym. No. 5 (Jan. 19, 1950), and *St. Francis of Assisi* for Baritone and Orch. (Ravinia Festival, July 16, 1954). Other works are: *Academic Overture* (1909); *The Sea*, symphonic poem (1934); 2 piano concertos, of which the 2nd won the Hollywood Bowl prize and was performed there (Aug. 16, 1932); Violin Concerto (1933; Chicago, Nov. 7, 1946); 2 rhapsodies for Orch.; chamber music; piano pieces.

Oldham, Arthur (William), English pianist, chorus master, and composer; b. London, Sept. 6, 1926. He studied at the Royal College of Music with Herbert Howells, and privately with Benjamin Britten. He was music director of the Ballet Rambert; served as chorus master of Scottish Opera in Glasgow (1966–74) and was director of the London Sym. Orch. Chorus (1969–76). He wrote the ballets *Mr. Punch* (1946), *The Sailor's Return* (1947), *Circus Canteen* (1951), and *Bonne-Bouche* (1952); a symphonic poem, *The Apotheosis of Lucius* (1952); a musical for children, *The Land of Green Ginger* (1964); *Hymns for the Amusement of Children* for Voices and Organ (1962); various sacred and secular choral works.

Oldman, C(ecil) B(ernard), English librarian and bibliographer; b. London, April 2, 1894; d. there, Oct. 7, 1969. He studied at Exeter College, Oxford; in 1920, received an appointment in the Dept. of Printed Books in the British Museum; from 1948 to 1959, was Principal Keeper. He was an authority on Haydn, Mozart, and Beethoven bibliographical matters; annotated the letters of Constanze Mozart to J.A. André in E. Anderson's *The Letters of Mozart and His Family* (3 vols., London, 1938; 2nd ed., rev., 1966 by A. Hyatt King and M.

Carolan; 3rd ed., rev., 1985 by S. Sadie and F. Smart); his essay "Musical First Editions" in J. Carter, ed., *New Paths in Book-collecting* (London 1934) was publ. separately (1938).

Oldroyd, George, English organist and composer; b. Healey, Yorkshire, Dec. 1, 1886; d. London, Feb. 26, 1951. He studied organ and music theory with Eaglefield Hull; violin with Frank Arnold. After a year in Paris as organist of the English Church there (1915), he played at various London churches; taught at Trinity College of Music; from 1949 he was prof. at the Univ. of London. He wrote a number of sacred works, of which a *Stabat Mater* is notable; publ. *The Technique and Spirit of Fugue: An Historical Study* (London, 1948); *Polyphonic Writing for Voices, in 6 and 8 Parts* (London, 1953); and some essays on Gregorian chant.

Olenin, Alexander, Russian composer, brother of **Marie (Alexeievna) Olénine d'Alheim;** b. Istomino, Riazan district, June 13, 1865; d. Moscow, Feb. 15, 1944. He studied with P. Pabst and with Erdmannsdörfer; lived most of his life in Moscow. He wrote an opera in a folk style, *Kudeyar* (Moscow, Nov. 26, 1915); a symphonic poem, *After the Battle; Préludes prairiales* for 2 Oboes, Violin, and Piano (1927); Piano Sonata; Violin Sonata; several song cycles (*The Street, The Peasant's Son, The Autumn, Home,* etc.); 52 songs to texts by Heine.

Olénine d'Alheim, Marie (Alexeievna), Russian soprano, sister of **Alexander Olenin;** b. Istomino, Riazan district, Oct. 2, 1869; d. Moscow, Aug. 27, 1970, at the age of 100. She studied in Russia and later in Paris; made her debut in Paris in 1896. Through her brother she met Stasov, Balakirev, and Cui, and became interested in Russian vocal music. In 1893 she married the French writer Pierre d'Alheim (1862–1922), tr. of the text of *Boris Godunov;* together they organized, in Moscow and in Paris, numerous concerts and lectures on Russian music, particularly on Mussorgsky; she was an outstanding interpreter of Russian songs; publ. a book, *Le Legs de Mussorgsky* (Paris, 1908). In 1935 she settled in Paris as a voice teacher; in 1949, joined the French Communist Party; in 1959 she returned to Russia.

Olevsky, Julian, German-born American violinist; b. Berlin, May 7, 1926; d. Amherst, Mass., May 25, 1985. After studies in Germany, he went with his family to Buenos Aires (1935), where he made his debut at age 10; then settled in the U.S. (1947), becoming a naturalized citizen (1951). He made his N.Y. debut at Town Hall (1949); taught at the Univ. of Massachusetts in Boston (1967–74).

Oliphant, Thomas, Scottish music editor, cataloguer, writer, and composer; b. Condie, Perthshire, Dec. 25, 1799; d. London, March 9, 1873. He studied in Winchester and was temporary assistant at the British Museum in London (1841–50), where he prepared over 24,000 catalogue entires. He publ. in London *A Brief Account of the Madrigal Society* (1835), *A Short Account of Madrigals* (1836), *La Musa Madrigalesca: or a collection of madrigals, ballets, roundelays &c. chiefly of the Elizabethan age. With remarks and annotations* (1837), and *Catalogue of Manuscript Music in the British Museum* (1842); also publ. collections of glees, catches, and rounds.

Olitzka, Rosa, German-American contralto and teacher, aunt of **Walter Olitzki;** b. Berlin, Sept. 6, 1873; d. Chicago, Sept. 29, 1949. She studied with Désirée Artôt and Julius Hey; sang at Berlin (1891); then was engaged at the Hannover Opera (1892–93), at Covent Garden in London (1894), and in N.Y. with the German Opera Co. (1895–97); was also with the Metropolitan Opera (1895–97, 1899–1901). After a season with the Chicago Grand Opera (1910–11), she made guest appearances in opera and concert in Europe and North America; later taught voice in Chicago.

Olitzki, Walter, German-American baritone, nephew of **Rosa Olitzka;** b. Hamburg, March 17, 1903; d. Los Angeles, Aug. 2, 1949. After a career in Germany, he appeared as Beckmesser at the Metropolitan Opera in N.Y. (Dec. 2, 1939); he specialized in Wagnerian roles; was with the Metropolitan Opera until 1947.

Oliveira, Elmar, talented American violinist; b. Waterbury, Conn., June 28, 1950. He studied violin with Raphael Bronstein on a scholarship at the Hartt College of Music in Hartford, Conn. and later at the Manhattan School of Music in N.Y. He made his formal debut as a soloist with the Hartford (Conn.) Sym. Orch. (1964); appeared with Bernstein at a N.Y. Phil. Young People's Concert (1966), which was telecast to the nation; made his N.Y. recital debut at Town Hall (1973). After winning the Naumburg Award in 1975, he became the 1st American violinist to capture the Gold Medal at the Tchaikovsky Competition in Moscow (1978); thereafter he pursued a rewarding international career. In 1990 he joined the faculty of the Manhattan School of Music in N.Y. His enormous repertoire ranges from the standard literature to contemporary works.

BIBL.: B. Martin, "E. O.," *Ovation* (Oct. 1984).

Oliveira, Jocy de, Brazilian pianist and avant-garde composer; b. Curitiba-Parana (of French and Portuguese descent), April 11, 1936. She studied piano in São Paulo with J. Kliass and in Paris with Marguerite Long; then traveled to the U.S.; obtained her M.A. at Washington Univ. in St. Louis in 1968. She appeared as a piano soloist with major orchs. in Europe and America, specializing in the modern repertoire; in 1966 she played the piano part in Stravinsky's *Capriccio* in St. Louis, under Stravinsky's direction. As a composer, she occupies the aphelion of ultra-modernism, experimenting in electronic, environmental, theatrical, cinematic, and television media, as exemplified by *Probabilistic Theater* I, II, and III for Musicians, Actors, Dancers, Television and Traffic Conductor, and other environmental manifestations. Her *Polinteracões I, II, III* present the culmination of "total music" involving the visual, aural, tactile, gustatory, and olfactory senses, with an anatomic chart serving as a score for guidance of the participants, supplemented by a phonemic table indicating the proper verbalization of vocal parts. (Complete score and illustrations were reproduced in *Source,* no. 7, Sacramento, Calif., 1970.) A performance of *Polinteracões* was attempted on the occasion of the Catalytic Celebration of the 10th Anniversary Festival of the New Music Circle in St. Louis on April 7, 1970, but was stopped by the management as a noisy, noisome nuisance. She also composed a number of advanced sambas, precipitating the vogue of the Brazilian bossa nova. Active in belles-lettres, she penned a sociological fantasy, *O 3° Mundo* (The Third World), a controversial play, *Apague meu* (Spotlight), poetical works, etc. She married the Brazilian conductor and composer **Eleazar de Carvalho.**

Oliver, Henry Kemble, American composer; b. Beverly, Mass., Nov. 24, 1800; d. Salem, Aug. 12, 1885. He was a chorister at Park Street Church in Boston; graduated from Dartmouth College in 1818; played the organ in various churches in Salem and Boston; in 1826, founded and managed the Salem Mozart Assoc.; subsequently went to Lawrence, Mass., where he was mayor in 1859; later was also mayor of Salem; from 1861 to 1865, was treasurer of the State of Massachusetts. He was given B.A. and M.A. degrees by Harvard Univ. (1862) and was made a Mus.Doc. by Dartmouth College (1883). He wrote many well-known hymn tunes (*Federal Street, Morning, Harmony Grove, Beacon Street, Hudson*), motets, chants, and a *Te Deum;* publ. *The National Lyre* (1848; with Tuckerman and Bancroft; contains many of his own compositions), *Oliver's Collection of Hymn and Psalm Tunes* (1860), and *Original Hymn Tunes* (1875).

BIBL.: F. Metcalf, *American Writers and Compilers of Sacred Music* (N.Y., 1925).

Oliver, John, American conductor; b. Teaneck, N.J., June 4, 1939. He studied at the Univ. of Notre Dame (B.M., 1961) and the New England Cons. of Music (M.M. in choral conducting, 1967). After serving as an assistant to Erich Leinsdorf at the Berkshire Music Center at Tanglewood (1968–70), he was named head of vocal and choral activities there; founded his own John Oliver Chorale in 1977. He joined the staff of the Mass. Inst. of Technology in 1964; was a technical instructor there in the humanities dept. (1970–77), then lecturer (1977–81) and, from 1981, senior lecturer.

Oliver, "King" (Joseph), outstanding black American jazz cornetist and bandleader, uncle of **Ulysses (Simpson) Kay;** b. on a plantation near Abend, La., May 11, 1885; d. Savannah, Ga., April 8, 1938. In 1907 he was working in Storyville, the brothel district of New Orleans) with the Melrose Brass Band; in subsequent years he was with a number of other brass bands there, and in 1915 he formed his own group, eventually known as the Creole Jazz Band; in 1917 he acquired the nickname "King," traditionally reserved for the leading jazz musicians. Also in 1917, the government closed the bordellos in Storyville, putting most of the musicians (among others) out of work; the following year Oliver moved his band to Chicago, leading a migration of jazz musicians to the city that was largely responsible for the dispersion of the black New Orleans jazz style throughout the country. In 1922 Louis Armstrong, whom he had known in New Orleans, joined the band, helping to make it the most polished exponent of New Orleans collectively improvised jazz; the group's 1923 recordings were the most influential early jazz recordings ever made; they have been reissued by the Smithsonian Inst. Subsequent bands formed by Oliver remained a potent force in jazz until around 1928.

BIBL.: W. Allen and B. Rust, *K. Joe O.* (London, 1957); E. Souchon, "K. O.: A Very Personal Memoir," *Jazz Review,* III/4 (1960); M. Williams, *K. O.* (London, 1960).

Oliver, Stephen (Michael Harding), English composer; b. Chester, March 10, 1950. He studied at Worcester College, Oxford (1968–72), where he received instruction in composition from Leighton and in electronic music from Sherlaw Johnson; then devoted himself mainly to composition, with emphasis on the theater.

WORKS: STAGE: OPERAS: *The Duchess of Malfi* (1971; rev. version, Santa Fe, N.Mex., Aug. 5, 1978); *Tom Jones* (1975; Snape, April 6, 1976); *The Girl and the Unicorn* (London, Dec. 9, 1978); *A Man of Feeling* (London, Nov. 17, 1980); *Sasha* (1982; Banff, Canada, April 7, 1983); *Beauty and the Beast* (Italian version, *Bella e la Bestia,* Batignano, July 26, 1984; Eng. version, London, June 21, 1985). *OTHER THEATER:* *Slippery Souls,* Christmas drama (1969; rev. 1976); *3 Instant Operas* for Child Performers (1973); *Bad Times,* dramatic sketch for Baritone and String Quartet (1975); *The Waiter's Revenge,* "an absurd fable" (1976); *A Stable Home,* dramatic Christmas cantata (1977); *Jacko's Play,* children's operetta (1979); *Nicholas Nickelby,* incidental music (1980); *Euridice,* arrangement of Peri's opera (1981); *Peter Pan,* incidental music (1982); *Blondel,* musical (1983); *Britannia Preserv'd,* masque (1984); *The Ring* for 4 Singers and Orch. (1984). **ORCH.:** *The Boy and the Dolphin* (1974); Sym. (Liverpool, May 23, 1976; rev. version, Kuopio, Finland, Oct. 13, 1983); *Ricercare No. 2* for Winds (1981). **CHAMBER:** *Music for the Wreck of the Deutschland* for Piano Quintet (1972); *Ricercare No. 1* for Clarinet, Violin, Cello, and Piano (1973); *The Dong with a Luminous Nose* for Narrator and 5 String Quartets (1976); Guitar Sonata (1978); *The Key to the Zoo* for Narrator, 2 Oboes, Bassoon, and Harpsichord (1980); *Ricercare No. 3* for Guitar, Viola, and Cello (1983). **CHORAL:** *The Elixir,* Lenten anthem (1976); *The Child from the Sea* for Treble Solo, Chorus, and Orch. (1980); *A String of Beads* for Chorus and Orch. (1980); *Namings* for Chorus and Brass Quintet (1981); *Trinity Mass* (1981).

Olivero, Magda (actually, **Maria Maddalena**), remarkable Italian soprano; b. Saluzzo, near Turin, March 25, 1912. She studied at the Turin Cons.; made her debut as Lauretta in *Gianni Schicchi* in Turin in 1933; then sang in the Italian provinces. She temporarily retired from the stage when she married in 1941, but resumed her career in 1951; made successful appearances at La Scala in Milan, and in Paris and London. On Nov. 4, 1967, she made her U.S. debut in Dallas in the title role of Cherubini's *Medea;* she was 63 years old when she made her 1st appearance with the Metropolitan

Opera in N.Y., on April 3, 1975, as Tosca; on Dec. 5, 1977, she gave a highly successful recital in a program of Italian art songs at Carnegie Hall, N.Y. Among her operatic roles were Violetta, Fedora, Liù, Suor Angelica, and Minnie; she was praised mainly for her dramatic penetration of each character and her fine command of dynamic nuances.

Oliveros, Pauline, American composer; b. Houston, May 30, 1932. Her mother and grandmother, both piano teachers, taught her the rudiments of music; received instruction in violin from William Sydler, accordion from Marjorie Harrigan, and horn from J.M. Brandsetter; studied composition with Paul Koepke and accordion with William Palmer at the Univ. of Houston (1949–52); continued her studies at San Francisco State College (B.A., 1957) and privately with Robert Erickson (1954–60). She was co-director of the San Francisco Tape Music Center (1961–65); after it became the Mills Tape Music Center, she was its director (1966–67); then taught at the Univ. of Calif. at San Diego (1967–81); held a Guggenheim fellowship (1973–74). She publ. *Pauline's Proverbs* (1976) and *Software for People: Collected Writings 1963–80* (1984). Initiated into modern harmony, the art of asymmetrical rhythms, group improvisation, and acoustical sonorism by Robert Erickson, she gradually expanded her receptivity into the range of subliminal sounds derived from the overtone series, differential tones, and sonic abstractions. In 1960 she composed a Piano Sextet which explored a variety of such elusive tonal elements; it received the Pacifica Foundation National Prize. Advancing further into the domain of new sonorities, she wrote a choral work, *Sound Patterns,* to wordless voices (1962), which received a prize in the Netherlands. While in San Diego, she was able to develop her ideas still further. Taking advantage of her skill as a gardener, she arrayed garden hoses and lawn sprinklers as part of a musical ensemble accompanied by the sounds of alarm clocks and various domestic utensils. Occasionally, a musician was instructed to bark. To this enriched artistic vocabulary was soon added a physical and psychosomatic element; performers acted the parts of a magician, a juggler, and a fortune-teller. Page turners, piano movers, and floor sweepers were listed as performing artists. In her later works she reduced such kinetic activities and gradually began to compose ceremonial works of sonic meditation, sotto voce murmuration, lingual lallation, and joyful ululation, with the purpose of inducing an altered state of consciousness; sometimes an exotic but usually digestible meal was served at leisurely intervals. She often presided over such sessions, singing and playing her faithful accordion; sometimes this music was left to be unheard by ordinary ears, but it could be perceived mystically. In 1977 she obtained 1st prize from the city of Bonn for a work commemorating the sesquicentennial of Beethoven's death; the piece was verbally notated with the intention to subvert perception of the entire city so that it would become a perceptual theater. As she moved higher into the realm of cosmic consciousness, she introduced the psychic element into her works; in 1970 she drew an equation for an indefinite integral of the differential *psi* (for psychic unit), to create the state of Oneness.

WORKS: *Variations for Sextet* for Flute, Clarinet, Trumpet, Horn, Cello, and Piano (1960); *Sound Patterns* for Chorus (1961); Trio for Trumpet, Piano, and Page Turner (1961); Trio for Trumpet, Accordion, and Double Bass (1961); *7 Passages* for 2-channel Tape, Mobile, and Dancer (1963); *Five for Trumpet and Dancer* (1964); *Duo* for Accordion and Bandoneon, with possible Mynah Bird Obbligato (1964); *Apple Box Orchestra* for 10 Performers, Amplified Apple Boxes, etc. (1964); *Pieces of Eight* for Wind Octet and a number of Props, including a Cash Register (1965); *7 Sets of Mnemonics,* multimedia piece (1965); *George Washington Slept Here* for Amplified Violin, Film Projections, and Tape (1965); *Bye Bye Butterfly* for Oscillators, Amplifiers, and Tapes (1965); *Winter Light* for Tape, Mobile, and Figure (1965); *Participle Dangling in Honor of Gertrude Stein* for Tape, Mobile, and Work Crew (1966); *Theater Piece for Trombone Player* for Garden Hose,

Instruments, and Tape (1966); *Night Jar* for Viola d'Amore (1968); *Festival House* for Orch., Mimes, Light, and Film Projections (1968); *Double Basses at Twenty Paces* for 2 Double Basses, Tape, and Projections (1968); *The Dying Alchemist Preview* for Narrator, Violinist, Trumpet, Piccolo, Percussion, and Slides (1969); *The Wheel of Fortune*, suggested by the trump cards in the tarot deck, for Clarinet (1969); *Aeolian Partitions* for Flute, Clarinet, Violin, Cello, and Piano (1969); *To Valerie Solanis and Marilyn Monroe, in Recognition of Their Desperation*, verbally notated score (1970; Solanis, the founder of SCUM, i.e. the Society to Cut Up Men, tried unsuccessfully to shoot the pop artist Andy Warhol; Monroe committed suicide); *Meditation on the Points of the Compass* for Chorus and Percussion (1970); *Bonn Feier*, intended to convert the city of Bonn into an imagined total theater (1971); *Post Card Theater*, multimedia event (1972); *Phantom Fathom*, mixed-media event with an Exotic Potluck Dinner (1972); *1000 Acres* for String Quartet (1972); *Sonic Images*, subliminal auditory fantasy (1972); *Crow Two*, ceremonial opera (1974); *Rose Mountain Slow Runner* for Voice and Accordion (1975; renamed *Horse Sings from Cloud*, inspired by a dream image of a horse lifted to a cloud by birds); *Willow Brook Generations and Reflections* for Wind Instruments and Vocalists (1976); *The Yellow River Map*, ceremonial meditation for a lot of people (1977); *King Kong Sings Along* for Chorus (1977); *Rose Moon*, ceremonial for Chorus and Percussion (1977); *The Witness* for Virtuoso Instrumentalists (1978); *El relicario de los animales* for Soprano and 20 Instruments (1979); *Carol Plantamura* for Voice and 20 Instruments (1979); *Gone with The Wind, 1980* for Assorted Ensembles (1980); *Wheel of Times*, for String Quartet and Electonics (1982); *The Mandala* for 4 Clarinets, 8 Crystal Glasses, Bass Drum, and Finger Cymbals (timeless date of composition).

BIBL.: H. von Gunden, *The Music of P. O.* (Metuchen, N.J., 1983).

d'Ollone, Max(imilien-Paul-Marie-Félix), French conductor, writer on music, and composer; b. Besançon, June 13, 1875; d. Paris, May 15, 1959. He studied with Lavignac, Massenet, and Lenepveu at the Paris Cons.; received the Grand Prix de Rome in 1897 with his cantata *Frédégonde*; was active as an opera conductor in Paris and the French provinces. He wrote the books *Le langage musical* (Paris and Geneva, 1952) and *Le Théâtre lyrique et le public* (Paris, 1955). A prolific composer, he wrote 5 operas: *Le Retour* (Angers, Feb. 13, 1913), *Les Uns et les autres* (Paris, Nov. 6, 1922), *L'Arlequin* (Paris, Dec. 24, 1924), *George Dandin* (Paris, March 19, 1930), and *La Samaritaine* (Paris, June 25, 1937); also *Dans la cathédrale* for Orch. (1906); *Fantaisie* for Piano and Orch. (1899); chamber music; many songs.

Olman, Abe, American songwriter; b. Cincinnati, Dec. 20, 1888; d. Rancho Mirage, Calif., Jan. 4, 1984. He worked as a song demonstrator in Cleveland in 1910; then moved to Chicago, where he established a music publishing firm, La Salle Music. From 1946 to 1956 he was a director of ASCAP. Among his hits were *Oh, Johnny Oh* and *Down among the Sheltering Palms*, which was sung by Al Jolson. He supplied many songs to movie musicals in the early years of the talkies.

Olmeda de San José, Federico, Spanish organist, musicologist, and composer; b. Burgos de Osma, 1865; d. Madrid, Feb. 11, 1909. He studied violin, organ, and music theory at Burgos Cathedral; was appointed organist at Tudela Cathedral in 1887; in 1907, went to Madrid as choirmaster of the Convent of Las Descalzas Reales; founded and ed. the review *La Voz de la Música* (1907). His most significant writings were *Memoria de un viaje a Santiago de Galicia* (1895) and *Discurso sobre la orquesta religiosa* (Burgos, 1896); also ed. *Folklore de Castilla* (Burgos, 1902). He composed 4 syms.; a symphonic poem, *Paraíso perdido*; an *Oda* for String Orch.; several church works; *32 rimas* for Piano (1890–91); organ pieces.

Olsen, Ole, Norwegian composer; b. Hammerfest, July 4, 1850; d. Oslo, Nov. 9, 1927. He studied with Fredrik and

Just Lindeman in Trondheim (1865–69) and with David, Paul, and Reinecke in Leipzig (1870–74); then was active as a music teacher in Christiania; was conductor of the Music Society there (1877–80), instructor of music at the Military Academy (1887–1903), and inspector of military music (1899–1919). He wrote the operas *Stig Hvide* (1876), *Stallo* (1902), and *Klippeøerne* (1905), which were not produced, and *Lajla* (1893, Christiania, Oct. 8, 1908); also some incidental music; a Sym. (1878); the symphonic poems *Aasgaardsreien* (1878) and *Alfedans* (1880); Horn Concerto (Christiania, April 1, 1905); many military marches; numerous choruses; songs; piano music.

BIBL.: A. Dahl, *O. O.* (Christiania, 1910).

Olsen, Poul Rovsing, Danish composer and ethnomusicologist; b. Copenhagen, Nov. 4, 1922; d. there, July 2, 1982. He studied law at the Univ. of Århus (1940–42) and at the Univ. of Copenhagen (1942–48); concurrently, studied harmony and counterpoint with Jeppesen and piano with Christiansen at the Copenhagen Cons. (1943–46); later studied composition with Boulanger and analysis with Messiaen in Paris (1948–49). Between 1958 and 1963 he took part in ethnomusicological expeditions to Arabia, India, Greece, and eastern Greenland and wrote numerous valuable papers on the folklore and musical cultures of the areas he visited. He worked until 1960 for the Danish Ministry of Education as a legal expert on music copyright; served as chairman of the Danish Society of Composers (1962–67); taught ethnomusicology at the Univ. of Lund, Sweden (1967–69), and subsequently at the Univ. of Copenhagen. He was president of the International Council of Traditional Music (formerly the International Folk Music Council) from 1977 until his death. He was a music critic for the newspapers *Morgenbladet* (1945–46), *Information* (1949–54), and *Berlingske Tidende* (1954–74). Much of his music embodies materials of non-European cultures, reflecting the influence of his travels. His *Elegy* for Organ (1953) is the 1st serial work written by a Danish composer.

WRITINGS: *Musiketnologi* (Copenhagen, 1974); with J. Jenkins, *Music and Musical Instruments in the World of Islam* (London, 1976).

WORKS: STAGE: 2 operas: *Belisa*, after García Lorca (1964; Copenhagen, Sept. 3, 1966) and *Usher*, after Poe (1980); 4 ballets: *Ragnarök* (Twilight of the Gods; 1948; Copenhagen, Sept. 12, 1960); *La Création* (1952; Copenhagen, March 10, 1961); *Brylluppet* (The Wedding; 1966; Copenhagen, Sept. 15, 1969); *Den Fremmede* (The Stranger; 1969; Copenhagen, July 17, 1972). **ORCH.:** *Symphonic Variations* (1953); Piano Concerto (1953–54); *Sinfonia I* (1957–58; Copenhagen, April 13, 1959); *Sinfonia II, Susudil*, based on Arab and Turkish modes (Copenhagen, Oct. 31, 1966); *Capriccio* (1961–62); *Et russisk bal* (The Russian Ball), 3 dances (1965); *Au Fond de la nuit* for Chamber Orch. (1968); *Randrussermarchen* (1977); *Lux Coelestis* (1978). **VOCAL:** *Schicksalslieder*, after 4 Hölderlin poems, for Soprano or Tenor, and 7 Instruments (1953); *Evening Songs* for Mezzo-soprano and Flute (1954); *Alapa-Tarana*, vocalise for Mezzo-soprano and Percussion (1959); *A l'inconnu* for Soprano or Tenor, and 13 Instruments (1962); *Kejseren* (The Emperor) for Tenor, Male Chorus, and Orch. (1963; Copenhagen, Sept. 5, 1964); *A Song of Mira Bai* for Chorus, 3 Trumpets, and Percussion (1971); *Air* for Mezzo-soprano, Saxophone, and Piano (1976); *The Planets* for Mezzo-soprano, Flute, Viola, and Guitar (1978). **CHAMBER:** *2 Pieces* for Clarinet and Piano (1943); *Romance* for Cello and Piano (1943); Violin Sonata (1946); 2 string quartets (1948, 1969); Serenade for Violin and Piano (1949); 2 piano trios (1950, 1976); *Prolana* for Clarinet, Violin, and Piano (1955); Cello Sonata (1956); *The Dream of Pan* for Flute (1959); *Nouba*, 6 movements for Harp (1960); *Passacaglia* for Flute, Violin, Cello, and Piano (1960); *Patet* for 9 Musicians (1966); *How to Play in D major without Caring about It*, fantasy for 2 Accordions (1967); *Arabesk* for 7 Musicians (1968); *Shangri-La* for Flute, Viola d'Amore, and Piano (1969); *Pour une Viola d'Amour* (1969); *Rencontres* for Cello and Percussion (1970); *Poème* for Accordian, Guitar, and Percussion (1973); Concertino for Clarinet, Violin, Cello, and Piano

(1973); *Partita* for Cello (1974); *Nostalgie* for Guitar (1976); *Danse élégiaque* for Flute and Guitar (1978); *A Dream of Violet* for String Trio (1982). PIANO: 3 sonatinas (1941, 1951, 1967); *Theme with Variations* (1947); 2 sonatas for Piano, 4-hands (1948, 1967); *12 Preludes* (1948); 2 sonatas (1950, 1952); 3 *Nocturnes* (1951); *Medardus*, suite (1956); 5 *Inventions* (1957); *Bagatelles* (1962); *Images* (1965); *4 Innocent Sonatas* (1969); *Many Happy Returns* (1971).

Olsen, (Carl Gustav) Sparre, Norwegian composer; b. Stavanger, April 25, 1903; d. Oslo, Nov. 8, 1984. He studied composition with Valen and Brustad in Christiania (1925–30), Butting in Berlin, in Vienna, and with Grainger in London; was violinist in the Christiania Phil. (1923–33); was active as a music teacher, music critic, and choral conductor in Bergen (1934–40). In 1936 he received a government life pension; in 1968, was awarded the Order of St. Olav. He publ. the books *Percy Grainger* (Oslo, 1963), *Tor Jonsson-Minne* (Oslo, 1968), and *Sparretonar* (Oslo, 1973). His music followed the national tradition.

WORKS: 2 *Edda Songs* for Voice and Orch. or Piano (1931); *Draumkvedet* (The Dream Ballad) for Narrator, Soloists, Chorus, and Orch. (Bergen, April 19, 1937); 3 *Symphonic Fantasias*: No. 1 (Oslo, Sept. 21, 1939); No. 2 (Oslo, Oct. 6, 1957); No. 3 (Bergen, Nov. 28, 1974); *Serenade* for Flute and String Orch. (1954); *Intrada* for Orch. (1956); *Canticum* for Orch. (1972); Wind Quintet (1946); String Quartet (1972); *Metamorfose* for Cello (1982); songs; sacred choruses.

Olson, Lynn (Freeman) American composer and piano pedagogue; b. Minneapolis, June 5, 1938; d. N.Y., Nov. 18, 1987. He studied at the Univ. of Minnesota; after graduation, he devoted himself mainly to musical education; ran a successful radio series under the inviting title "It's Time for Music." He publ. hundreds of semi-classical piano pieces suitable for teaching, songs, and choruses.

Olsson, Otto (Emanuel), eminent Swedish organist, pedagogue, and composer; b. Stockholm, Dec. 19, 1879; d. there, Sept. 1, 1964. He studied with Lagergren and Dente at the Stockholm Cons. (1897–1901); from 1908 until 1945, taught there; was organist of the Gustav Vasa Church in Stockholm (1908–56); became a member of the Royal Academy of Music in 1915.

WORKS: *Requiem* for Soli, Chorus, and Orch. (1903; Stockholm, Nov. 14, 1976); *Te Deum* for Chorus, Strings, Harp, and Organ (1906); many other choral works; 3 string quartets (1903, 1906, 1947); 2 organ syms. (1903, 1918); 3 sets of *Preludes and Fugues* for Organ (1910–11, 1918, 1935); piano pieces; songs.

Oncina, Juan, Spanish tenor; b. Barcelona, April 15, 1925. He studied in Barcelona; made his debut there as Massenet's Des Grieux in 1946. He then went to Italy and became a leading interpreter of Italian opera. From 1952 to 1961 he was a regular member of the Glyndebourne Festival Opera.

Ondříček, family of Czech musicians:
(1) Ignac Ondříček, violinist and conductor; b. Krusovice, May 7, 1807; d. Prague, Feb. 8, 1871. He studied with Simon Pergler, the local schoolmaster; after playing in his teacher's band, he settled in Prague (1839), where he conducted his own band (1855–70).
(2) Jan Ondříček, violinist and conductor, son of the preceding; b. Bělec, near Bratronice, May 6, 1832; d. Prague, March 13, 1900. He studied with his father and with Mořic Mildner (violin) and Dvořák (theory); then conducted his own band. He had 15 children, including the following:
(3) František Ondříček, eminent violinist and pedagogue; b. Prague, April 29, 1857; d. Milan, April 12, 1922. He studied with his father, and then with Bennewitz at the Prague Cons. (1873–76), where he won a 1st prize; then with Massart at the Paris Cons. (1879–81), where he won a premier prix. He gave the premiere of Dvořák's Violin Concerto in Prague (1883); after extensive tours of Europe, the U.S., and the Far East, he was made Kammervirtuos in Vienna (1888); founded his

own quartet (1907); also taught at the New Vienna Cons. (1909–12) and gave master classes at the Prague Cons. (1919–22). He acquired a notable reputation as a virtuoso; also composed many violin pieces, as well as cadenzas and paraphrases, fantasias, and arrangements of themes by other composers. With S. Mittelmann, he publ. *Neue Methode zur Erlangung der Meistertechnik des Violinspiels auf anatomisch-physiologischer Grundlage* (2 vols., Vienna, 1909).

BIBL.: B. Sich, *F. O.* (Prague, 1947).
(4) Emanuel Ondříček, violinist and pedagogue; b. Pilsen, Dec. 6, 1882; d. Boston, Dec. 30, 1958. He studied with his father, then with Ševčik at the Prague Cons. (1894–99); after touring Europe, he emigrated to the U.S. (1912); then taught in Boston and N.Y. He publ. *The Mastery of Tone Production and Expression on the Violin* (1931).

Onégin, (Elisabeth Elfriede Emilie) Sigrid (née **Hoffmann**), noted German contralto; b. Stockholm (of a German father and a French mother), June 1, 1889; d. Magliaso, Switzerland, June 16, 1943. She studied in Frankfurt with Resz, in Munich with E.R. Weiss, and with di Ranieri in Milan. She made her 1st public appearance, using the name **Lilly Hoffmann,** in Wiesbaden, Sept. 16, 1911, in a recital, accompanied by the Russian pianist and composer **Eugene Onégin** (b. St. Petersburg, Oct. 10, 1883; d. Stuttgart, Nov. 12, 1919; real name, Lvov; he was a grandnephew of **Alexis Lvov,** composer of the Russian Czarist hymn). She married him on May 25, 1913; after his death, she married a German doctor, Fritz Penzoldt (Nov. 20, 1920). She made her 1st appearance in opera as Carmen, in Stuttgart, on Oct. 10, 1912; made her 1st appearance in London in 1913; was a member of the Bavarian State Opera in Munich (1919–22). On Nov. 22, 1922, she made her Metropolitan Opera debut in N.Y. as Amneris, continuing on its roster until 1924. She subsequently sang in Berlin, at London's Covent Garden, the Salzburg Festival, in Zürich, and at the Bayreuth Festivals. She made her last appearances in the U.S. as a recitalist in 1938. Among her most distinguished roles were Gluck's Orfeo, Eboli, Fidès in *Le Prophéte*, Erda, Lady Macbeth, Fricka, Waltraute, and Brangäne.

BIBL.: F. Penzoldt, *Alt-Rhapsodie*; S. O., *Leben und Werk* (Magdeburg, 1939; 3rd ed., 1953).

O'Neill, Norman (Houstoun), English conductor and composer; b. London, March 14, 1875; d. there, March 3, 1934. He was a direct descendant of **John Wall Callcott;** his father was a painter. He studied in London with Arthur Somervell, and later with Knorr in Frankfurt. Returning to London in 1899, he married the pianist **Adine Rückert** (1875–1947). He wrote incidental music for the Haymarket Theatre, of which he was music director from 1908 to 1919 and again 1920 to 1934; also composed 3 ballets, orch. works, chamber music, choral works, piano pieces, and songs.

BIBL.: D. Hudson, *N. O.: A Life of Music* (London, 1945).

Ono, Yoko, Japanese-born American vocalist, songwriter, and performance artist; b. Tokyo, Feb. 18, 1933. She was born to a wealthy banking family; in 1947 moved to N.Y., where she entered Sarah Lawrence College (1953). She became active in Manhattan conceptual-art circles, and in 1966 met **John Lennon** of the Beatles; they became companions and collaborators, marrying in 1969. Under her influence, Lennon became interested in avant-garde ideas that drew him away from rock, contributing to the breakup of the Beatles in 1970. After Lennon's death in 1980, Ono produced several posthumous collaborations. Her solo recordings include *Yoko Ono/Plastic Ono Band* (1970), *Fly* (1971), *Approximately Infinite Universe* (1973), *Feeling the Space* (1973), *Seasons of Glass* (1981), *It's Alright* (1982), and *Every Man Has a Woman* (1984). Her recordings with Lennon include *Unfinished Music no. 1: 2 Virgins* (1968), *Unfinished Music no. 2: Life with the Lions* (1969), *Wedding Album* (1969), *Live Peace in Toronto 1969* (1970), *Double Fantasy* (1980), *Milk and Honey* (1982), and *Heart Play: Unfinished Dialogue* (1983). Ono's work is often bizarre, her shrill tremolo voice moving over a fluid, arrhythmic background reflecting Asian influences; some of her recordings, notably those between 1980 and 1984, are popular in style.

BIBL.: J. Cott and C. Doudna, eds., *The Ballad of John and Yoko* (N.Y., 1982).

Onofri, Alessandro, Italian organist and composer; b. Spoleto, May 29, 1874; d. Varese, Aug. 27, 1932. He studied in Rome with Mascagni, Rossi, and others; in 1904, settled in Boston, where he was a church organist. He wrote the operas *Biancospino* (Venice, March 31, 1910) and *Assiuolo* (Rome, Sept. 25, 1912); the light operas *La famiglia modello* (Livorno, 1913) and *Il bocciuolo di rosa* (Rome, 1916); a set of American dances for Piano.

Onslow, (André) Georges (Louis), noted French composer of English descent; b. Clermont-Ferrand, July 27, 1784; d. there, Oct. 3, 1853. He was the grandson of the 1st Lord Onslow; studied in London with Hüllmandel, Dussek, and Cramer (piano) and in Paris with Reicha (composition). He wrote 3 comic operas, produced in Paris: *L'Alcalde de la Vega* (Aug. 10, 1824), *Le colporteur, ou L'enfant du bûcheron* (Nov. 22, 1827), and *Guise, ou Les états de Blois* (Sept. 8, 1837); 4 syms.; other orch. music. However, these works failed to maintain interest; Onslow's real achievement was the composition of a great number of chamber works, in which he demonstrated an uncommon mastery of counterpoint; he wrote 34 string quintets; 35 string quartets; 6 piano trios; Sextet for Flute, Clarinet, Horn, Bassoon, Double Bass, and Piano; Nonet for Violin, Viola, Cello, Double Bass, Flute, Oboe, Clarinet, Bassoon, and Horn; Septet for Flute, Oboe, Clarinet, Horn, Bassoon, Double Bass, and Piano; violin sonatas; cello sonatas; piano sonatas, 4-hands; piano pieces. He was struck by a stray bullet during a hunting expedition in 1829 and became deaf in one ear; his Quintet No. 15, subtitled *Le Quintette de la balle* (Quintet of the Bullet), was the musical rendering of this episode.

BIBL.: L. Halévy, *Notice sur O.* (Paris, 1855); C. Vulliamy, *The O. Family, 1528–1874* (London, 1953); C. Nobach, *Untersuchungen zu G. O.s Kammermusik* (Basel, 1985).

Oosterzee, Cornelie van, Dutch-German composer; b. Batavia, Java, Aug. 16, 1863; d. Berlin, Aug. 8, 1943. She studied in Berlin, and settled there in 1890; her opera *Das Gelöbnis* was produced in Weimar on May 1, 1910.

Opieński, Henryk, Polish conductor, music scholar, teacher, and composer; b. Krakow, Jan. 13, 1870; d. Morges, Switzerland, Jan. 21, 1942. He studied with Zeleński in Krakow, with Vincent d'Indy in Paris, and with H. Urban in Berlin; then went to Leipzig, where he studied musicology with Riemann and conducting with Nikisch. In 1907 he was appointed an instructor at the Warsaw Musical Society; from 1908 to 1912 he conducted the Warsaw Opera; in 1912 he went again to Germany, where he took his degree of Ph.D. (Univ. of Leipzig, 1914). He spent the years of World War I at Morges, Switzerland; returning to Poland, he was director of the Poznan Cons. (1919–26); then settled again in Morges. He publ. several books and essays on Chopin (Lemberg, 1910; 2nd ed., 1922; Warsaw, 1911; Warsaw, 1912, etc.); also the collected letters of Chopin, in Polish, German, French, and Eng. (1931); other writings include a history of Polish music (Warsaw, 1912; 2nd ed., 1922); *La Musique polonaise* (Paris, 1918; 2nd ed., 1929); a valuable monograph on Moniuszko (Warsaw, 1924); a monograph on Paderewski (Lemberg, 1910; 2nd ed., Warsaw, 1928; in French, Lausanne, 1928; 2nd ed., 1948).

WORKS: Operas: *Maria* (1904; Poznan, April 27, 1923) and *Jakub lutnista* (Jacob the Lutenist; 1916–18; Poznan, Dec. 21, 1927); oratorio, *The Prodigal Son* (1930); symphonic poems: *Lilla Weneda* (1908) and *Love and Destiny* (1912); *Scènes lyriques en forme de quatuor* for String Quartet; violin pieces; songs; an album of 15 Polish songs (with French words; 1928); another album of 15 Polish songs (with Eng. words; 1936).

BIBL.: A. Forenerod, *H. O.* (Lausanne, 1942).

Oppens, Ursula, talented American pianist; b. N.Y., Feb. 2, 1944. She studied economics and English literature at Radcliffe College (B.A., 1965); then studied with Rosina Lhévinne and Leonard Shure at the Juilliard School of Music in N.Y. She won 1st prize at the Busoni Competition in Italy in 1969; co-founded Speculum Musicae in N.Y., a chamber music ensemble devoted to performing contemporary music; also appeared with other chamber music groups, as a recitalist, and as a soloist with major U.S. orchs. In 1976 she was awarded the Avery Fisher Prize. Her expansive repertory ranges from the classics to the cosmopolitan avant-garde.

Orbán, György, Rumanian-born Hungarian composer; b. Tîrgu-Mureș, July 12, 1947. He studied with Sigismund Toduța and János Jagamas at the Cluj Cons. (1968–73), where he then taught theory until 1979; subsequently settled in Hungary and worked as a music ed. for Editio Musica Budapest.

WORKS: ORCH.: *Öt kánon József Attila verseire* (5 Canons to Poems by Attila József) for Soprano and Chamber Ensemble (1977); Triple Sextet for Chamber Ensemble (1980); 2 serenades (1984, 1985). **CHAMBER:** 2 duos: No. 1 for Soprano and Clarinet (1979) and No. 2 for Soprano and Double Bass (1987); Wind Quintet (1985); *Sonata concertante per clarinetto e pianoforte* (1987); Brass Quintet No. 1 (1987); Sonata for Bassoon and Piano (1987). **SOLO INSTRUMENTAL:** Sonata for Violin (1970); *Hymn* for Cimbalom (1980); *Hymn* for Piano (1980); Suite for Piano (1986); 2 piano sonatas (1987, 1987). **CHORAL:** *Virágénekek nöi karra* (Flower Songs for Female Choir), cycle of 9 choruses (1978); *Motetta* (1978); *Kóruskönyv S.A. emlékére* (Chorus Book in Memory of S.A. No. 1), cycle of 5 choruses (1984); *Medálík könyve 1* (Book of Medallions No. 1), cycle of 10 choruses (1987); *Stabat Mater* (1987).

Orbison, Roy (Kelton), American rock singer, guitarist, and songwriter; b. Wink, Tex., April 23, 1936; d. Hendersonville, Tenn., Dec. 6, 1988. He studied geology at North Tex. State College; after performing with local rockabilly bands, he began a recording career in 1956; also was active as a songwriter in Nashville, Tenn. He possessed an excellent lyric tenor voice, so unusual among the common breed of rockers that he won a distinctive niche uncontested by others in the field of popular music. Among his hit songs were *Crying, Many Moods,* and *Regeneration.* His song *Oh, Pretty Woman* became his identification number. Among his anthologies were such albums as *Orbisongs* and *There Is Only One Roy Orbison.* Shortly before his death in 1988, he joined George Harrison, Bob Dylan, and others to produce the album, *The Traveling Wilburys,* on which he added prominent vocals to the songs *Not Alone Anymore, End of the Line,* and *Handle With Care.*

BIBL.: A. Clayson, *Only the Lonely: R. O.'s Life and Legacy* (N.Y., 1989).

Orbón (de Soto), Julián, Spanish-American composer; b. Avilés, Aug. 7, 1925; d. Miami Beach, May 20, 1991. He received the rudiments of a musical education from his father, a professional pianist; after studies at the Oviedo Cons. (1935), he went with his family to Havana, where he studied theory with Ardévol; completed his training with Copland at the Berkshire Music Center in Tanglewood (1946). He was director of his father's Orbón Cons. in Havana (1946–60); taught at the National Cons. in Mexico City (1960–63). In 1964 he settled in N.Y. He held 2 Guggenheim fellowships (1959, 1969). His works reveal Spanish and Cuban stylistic traits; his early neo-Classical bent gave way to a more expressive Romantic style in later scores.

WORKS: Sym. in C major (1945); *Tres versiones sinfónicas* (1953); *Danzas sinfónicas* (1955); Concerto Grosso (1958); *Partita* No. 3 for Orch. (1965–66); *Oficios de 3 días* for Chorus and Orch. (1970); *Partita* No. 4 for Piano and Orch. (1983; Dallas, April 11, 1985); sacred and secular choral works; String Quartet (1951); *Partita* No. 1 for Harpsichord (1963); *Partita* No. 2 for Keyboard Instruments and String Quartet (1964); numerous piano pieces.

Orchard, William (Arundel), English-born Australian pianist, conductor, and composer; b. London, April 13, 1867; d. during a voyage in the South Atlantic off the coast of South Africa (23°49′S; 9°33′E), April 17, 1961. He studied in London and Durham; in 1903, went to Australia and lived in Sydney, where he was active as a conductor and music educator; served as director of the New South Wales State Cons. (1923–34); later taught at the Univ. of Tasmania. He wrote an opera, *The Picture of Dorian Gray*, after Oscar Wilde; a Violin Concerto; String Quartet; String Quintet; choruses; songs. He publ. 2 books dealing with Australian music: *The Distant View* (Sydney, 1943) and *Music in Australia* (Melbourne, 1952).

Ordonez or **Ordoñez, Carlos d'**, Austrian composer of Spanish extraction; b. Vienna, April 19, 1734; d. there, Sept. 6, 1786. He was employed as a clerk, but studied violin and performed successfully at chamber music concerts. He wrote numerous singspiels and much instrumental music, some of which was publ. during his lifetime. His singspiel *Diesmal hat der Mann den Willen* was performed in Vienna on April 22, 1778; his marionette opera *Alceste* was introduced by Haydn in Esterház on Aug. 30, 1775. Ordonez developed an excellent métier, and several of his syms. possessed enough merit to be misattributed to Haydn.
BIBL.: A. Brown, *Carlo d'Ordoñez (1734–1786): A Thematic Catalogue* (Detroit, 1978); idem, "The Symphonies of C. d'Ordoñez," *Haydn Yearbook*, XII (Cardiff, 1981).

Orefice, Giacomo, Italian pianist, music critic, teacher, and composer; b. Vicenza, Aug. 27, 1865; d. Milan, Dec. 22, 1922. He studied piano with Busi and composition with Mancinelli at the Bologna Liceo Musicale (diploma, 1885). He taught at the Milan Cons. (1909–22); was also active as a music critic. He publ. the study *Luigi Mancinelli* (Rome, 1921); ed. Monteverdi's *Orfeo* (Milan, 1909) and Rameau's *Platée*. As a composer of operas, he followed in the verismo school.
WORKS: OPERAS: *L'oasi* (Bologna, 1885); *Mariska* (Turin, Nov. 19, 1889); *Consuelo* (Bologna, Nov. 27, 1895); *Il Gladiatore* (Madrid, March 20, 1898); *Chopin* (Milan, Nov. 25, 1901); *Cecilia* (Vicenza, Aug. 16, 1902); *Il Mosè* (Genoa, Feb. 18, 1905); *Il pane d'altrui* (Venice, Jan. 19, 1907); *Radda* (Milan, Oct. 25, 1912); *I Castello dei sogni* (not perf.). 2 syms. (1892, 1911); *Sinfonia del bosco* (1898); *Anacreontiche*, suite for Orch. (1917); *Laudi francescane*, suite for Orch. (1920); *La soubrette*, ballet (Milan, 1907); chamber music; piano pieces; songs.
BIBL.: A. Bassi, *G. O.: tradizione e avanguardia nel melodramma del primo '900* (Padua, 1987).

Orel, Alfred, distinguished Austrian musicologist; b. Vienna, July 3, 1889; d. there, April 11, 1967. He studied law at the Univ. of Vienna, graduating in 1912; then was employed in the Ministry of Finance until 1918; subsequently studied musicology with Guido Adler at the Univ. of Vienna, where he received his Ph.D. in 1919 with the dissertation *Die Hauptstimme in den "Salve regina" der Trienter Codices*; he completed his Habilitation there in 1922 with his *Über rhythmische Qualität in mehrstimmigen Tonsätzen des 15. Jahrhunderts*. He was director of the music division of the Vienna Stadtbibliothek (1918–40); was also librarian of the Inst. of Musicology (1918–22) and a reader in music history (1929–45) at the Univ. of Vienna. He was particularly noted for his work on the life and music of Anton Bruckner.
WRITINGS: *Unbekannte Frühwerke Anton Bruckners* (Vienna, 1921; with an ed. of the Overture in G minor); *Ein Wiener Beethoven-Buch* (Vienna, 1921); *Anton Bruckner: Das Werk—Der Künstler—Die Zeit* (Vienna and Leipzig, 1925); *Wiener Musikerbriefe aus zwei Jahrhunderten* (Vienna, 1925); *Beethoven* (Vienna, 1927); with R. Stöhr and H. Gál, *Formenlehre der Musik* (Leipzig, 1933; 2nd ed., 1954); *Anton Bruckner, 1824–1896: Sein Leben in Bildern* (Leipzig, 1936); *Kirchenmusikalische Liturgik* (Augsburg, 1936); *Franz Schubert, 1797–1828: Sein Leben in Bildern* (Leipzig, 1939); *Aufsätze und Vorträge* (Vienna and Berlin, 1939); *Ein Harmonielehrekolleg bei Anton Bruckner* (Vienna and Berlin, 1940); *Der junge Schubert* (Vienna, 1940); *Mozarts deutscher Weg: Eine Deutung aus Briefen* (Vienna, 1940; 2nd ed., 1943); *Grillparzer und Beethoven* (Vienna, 1941); *Mozart in Wien* (Vienna, 1944); *Hugo Wolf: Ein Künstlerbildnis* (Vienna, 1947); *Johannes Brahms: Ein Meister und sein Weg* (Olten, 1948); *Goethe als Operndirek-*

tor (Bregenz, 1949); *Bruckner-Brevier: Briefe, Dokumente, Berichte* (Vienna, 1953); *Musikstadt Wien* (Vienna, 1953); *Mozart, Gloria Mundi* (Salzburg, 1956); ed. *Johannes Brahms und Julius Allgeyer: Eine Künstlerfreundschaft in Briefen* (Tutzing, 1964).
BIBL.: H. Federhofer, ed., *Festschrift A. O. zum 70. Geburtstag überreicht von Kollegen, Freunden und Schülern* (Vienna and Wiesbaden, 1960).

Orel, Dobroslav, Czech ecclesiastical music scholar; b. Ronov, near Prague, Dec. 15, 1870; d. Prague, Feb. 18, 1942. He studied music with Novák and Hostinský in Prague; later musicology with Guido Adler at the Univ. of Vienna. In 1914 he received a Ph.D. there with the dissertation *Der Mensuralkodex Speciálník, Ein Beitrag zur Geschichte der Mensuralmusik und der Notenschrift in Böhmen bis 1540*. He was ordained a priest; was a prof. at the Prague Cons. (1907–19); from 1909 to 1918 he was ed. of the Prague church music periodical *Cyrill;* from 1921 to 1938, he was a prof. of musicology at the Komensky Univ., Bratislava; was active as a conductor of various choral societies. He greatly distinguished himself as an authority on Czech liturgical music.
WRITINGS (all in Czech, and publ. in Bratislava unless otherwise given): *A Theoretical and Practical Manual of Roman Plainsong* (Hradec Králové, 1899); *A Czech Hymnbook* (Prague, 1921; 5th ed., 1936); *The Franus Hymnbook* (Prague, 1922); *The Beginnings of Polyphony in Bohemia* (1925); *Ján Levoslav Bella* (1924); *František Liszt a Bratislava* (1925); *Musical Sources in the Franciscan Library in Bratislava* (1930); *St. Wenceslas Elements in Music* (Prague, 1937); J. Potúček, ed., *Contributions to the History of Slovak Music* (1968).

Orff, Carl, outstanding German composer; b. Munich, July 10, 1895; d. there, March 29, 1982. He took courses with Beer-Walbrunn and Zilcher at the Munich Academy of Music (graduated, 1914); later had additional instruction from Heinrich Kaminski in Munich. He was a conductor at the Munich Kammerspiele (1915–17); after military service during World War I (1917–18), he conducted at the Mannheim National Theater and the Darmstadt Landestheater (1918–19); later was conductor of Munich's Bach Society (1930–33). Orff initiated a highly important method of musical education, which was adopted not only in Germany but in England, America, and Russia; it stemmed from the Günther School for gymnastics, dance, and music which Orff founded in 1924 with Dorothee Günther in Munich, with the aim of promoting instrumental playing and understanding of rhythm among children; he commissioned the piano manufacturer Karl Maendler to construct special percussion instruments that would be extremely easy to play; the "Orff instruments" became widely adopted in American schools. Orff's ideas of rhythmic training owe much to the eurhythmics of Jaques-Dalcroze, but he simplified them to reach the elementary level; as a manual, he compiled a set of musical exercises, *Schulwerk* (1930–35, rev. 1950–54). He also taught composition at the Munich Staatliche Hochschule für Musik (1950–55). As a composer, Orff sought to revive the early monodic forms and to adapt them to modern tastes by means of dissonant counterpoint, with lively rhythm in asymmetrical patterns, producing a form of "total theater." His most famous score is the scenic oratorio *Carmina Burana* (Frankfurt, June 8, 1937); the words (in Latin and German) are from 13th-century student poems found in the Benediktbeuren monastery in Bavaria ("Burana" is the Latin adjective of the locality). His other works include: *Der Mond*, opera, after a fairy tale by Grimm (1937–38; Munich, Feb. 5, 1939; rev. version, Munich, Nov. 26, 1950); *Die Kluge*, opera, also after a fairy tale by Grimm (1941–42; Frankfurt, Feb. 20, 1943); *Catulli Carmina*, scenic cantata after Catullus (Leipzig, Nov. 6, 1943); *Die Bernauerin*, musical play (1944–45; Stuttgart, June 15, 1947); *Antigonae*, musical play after Sophocles (1947–48; Salzburg, Aug. 9, 1949); *Trionfo di Afrodite* (1950–51; 3rd part of a triology under the general title *Trionfi*, the 1st and 2nd parts being *Carmina Burana* and *Catulli Carmina*; Milan, Feb. 13, 1953); *Astutuli*, opera-ballet (1945–46; Munich, Oct. 20, 1953); *Comoedia de Christi Resurrectione*, Easter cantata (1955; Munich, March 31, 1956); *Oedipus der Tyrann*, musical play after Sophocles (1957–58; Stuttgart, Dec. 11, 1959); *Ludus de nato infante mirificus*, Nativity play (Stuttgart, Dec. 11, 1960); *Prometheus*, opera (1963–67; Stuttgart, March 24, 1968); *Rota* for Voices and Instruments, after the canon *Sumer is icumen in*, composed as a "salute to youth" for the opening ceremony of the Munich Olympics (1972); stage play *De temporum fine comoedia* (Salzburg, 1973). He further wrote a dance play, *Der Feuerfarbene* (1925); *Präludium* for Orch. (1925); Concertino for Wind Instruments and Harpsichord (1927); *Entrata* for Orch., based on melodies of William Byrd (1928; rev. 1940); Festival Music for Chamber Orch. (1928); *Bayerische Musik* for Small Ensemble (1934); *Olympischer Reigen* for Various Instruments (1936); 3 stage works after Monteverdi: *Klage der Ariadne* (Karlsruhe, 1925; rev. version, Gera, 1940); *Orpheus* (Mannheim, April 17, 1925; 2nd version, Munich, Oct. 13, 1929; 3rd version, Dresden, Oct. 4, 1940); *Tanz der Spröden* (Karlsruhe, 1925; rev. version, Gera, 1940).

BIBL.: W. Trittenhoff, *O.-Schulwerk: Einführung* (Mainz, 1930); A. Liess, *C. O.: Idee und Werk* (Zürich, 1955; 2nd ed., rev., 1977; Eng. tr., 1966); K. Ruppel, G. Sellner, and W. Thomas, *C. O., ein Bericht in Wort und Bild* (Mainz, 1955; 2nd ed., rev., 1960; Eng. tr., 1960); I. Kiekert, *Die musikalische Form in den Werken C. O.s* (Regensburg, 1957); M. Devreese-Papgnies, *Sur les traces du Schulwerk de C. O., Méthodologie pour l'usage des instruments d'orchestre scolaire* (Brussels, 1968); F. Willnauer, ed., *Prometheus: Mythos, Drama, Musik: Beiträge zu C. O.s Musikdrama nach Aischylos* (Tübingen, 1968); U. Klement, *Das Musiktheater C. O.s: Untersuchungen zu einem bürgerlichen Kunstwerk* (diss., Univ. of Leipzig, 1969); G. Keetman, *Elementaria: Erster Umgang mit dem O. Schulwerk* (Stuttgart, 1970; Eng. tr., 1974); R. Münster, ed., *C. O.: das Bühnenwerk* (Munich, 1970); H. Wolfgart, ed., *Das O.- Schulwerk im Dienste der Erziehung und Therapie behinderter Kinder* (Berlin, 1971); W. Thomas, *C. O.: De temporum fine comoedia. . .eine Interpretation* (Tutzing, 1973); G. Orff, *The O. Music Therapy* (London, 1980); U. Klement, *Das Musiktheater C. O.s* (Leipzig, 1982); H. Leuchtmann, *C. O.: ein Gedenkbuch* (Tutzing, 1985).

Orgad, Ben-Zion, German-born Israeli composer; b. Gelsenkirchen, Aug. 21, 1926. He went to Palestine in 1933, where he studied composition with P. Ben-Haim (1942–47); also took courses at the Rubin Academy of Music (graduated, 1947); later studied composition with Copland at the Berkshire Music Center in Tanglewood (1949, 1952, 1961) and with Irving Fine and Harold Shapero at Brandeis Univ. (M.F.A. in musicology, 1962). He subsequently worked for the Israeli Ministry of Education and Culture.

WORKS: *Toccata* for Piano (1946); *Ballade* for Flute (1947); *Hatsvi Israel* (The Beauty of Israel), sym. for Baritone and Orch. (1949); biblical cantata, *Isaiah's Vision* (1952); *Min He'afar* (Out of the Desert), quintet for Mezzo-soprano or Contralto, Flute, Bassoon, Viola, and Cello (1956); *Building the King's Stage* for Orch. (1957); *Monolog* for Viola (1957); Septet for Clarinet, Bassoon, Horn, Violin, Viola, Cello, and Double Bass (1959); *Music for Orch.*, with Solo Horn (1960); String Trio (1961); *7 Variations on C* for Piano (1961); *Tak'sim* for Harp (1962); *Movement on A* for Orch. (1965); *Kaleidoscope* for Orch. (1965); *Mizmorim*, cantata on Psalms (1966–67); *Songs of an Early Morning* for Mezzo-soprano, Baritone, and Chamber Orch. (1968); *Landscapes* for Wind Quintet (1969); *First Watch* for String Orch. (1969); *Melodic Dialogues on 3 Scrolls* for Violin, Oboe, Percussion, String Quartet, and String Orch. (1969); *Songs without Words*, sextet for Violin, Cello, Flute, Clarinet, Percussion, and Piano (1970); *Ballade* for Orch. (1971); *A Tale of a Pipe* for Soloists, Women's Chorus, and 19 Instruments (1971); *The Second Watch* for Chamber Orch. (1973; rev. version, 1982); *Sufferings for Redemption*, cantata for Mezzo-soprano, Women's Chorus, and Chamber Orch. (1974); *Dialogues on the First Scroll* for Chamber Orch. (1975); *Hallel* for Orch. (1979); *She'arim* for Brass Orch. (1986); *Sh'ar Larashut* for Chorus (1988).

Orgeni, Aglaja (real name, **Anna Maria von Görger St. Jorgen**), respected Hungarian soprano and teacher; b. Roma Szombat, Dec. 17, 1841; d. Vienna, March 15, 1926. She was a pupil of Pauline Viardot-García at Baden-Baden; made her debut on Sept. 28, 1865, as Amina, at the Berlin Royal Opera; made her 1st appearance in London on April 7, 1866, as Violetta, at Covent Garden; she sang later in Vienna, Dresden, Berlin, Copenhagen, etc.; from 1886, taught singing at the Dresden Cons.; was made a Royal Professor in 1908 (the 1st case of the title being conferred on a woman). In 1914 she settled in Vienna. Among her distinguished pupils were Erika Wedekind and Edyth Walker. She was held in high esteem for such roles as Agathe in *Der Freischütz*, Marguerite in *Faust*, Leonora in *Il Trovatore*, and Valentine in *Les Huguenots*.

BIBL.: E. Brand, *A. O.* (Munich, 1931).

O'Riley, Christopher, talented American pianist; b. Chicago, April 17, 1956. He began piano lessons with Lilli Simon when he was only 4; later studied with Russell Sherman at the New England Cons. of Music in Boston. After winning 2nd prize in the Montreal Competition (1980), 5th prize in both the Van Cliburn and Leeds competitions (1981), and 6th prize in the Busoni Competition (1981), he made his formal recital debut in N.Y. in 1981; that same year he made his European debut in a recital in Amsterdam. He subsequently appeared as soloist with leading orchs. of the U.S. and Europe, gave recitals, and played in chamber music concerts. His programs often include rarely heard works both in the standard and the contemporary piano literature.

Orlandini, Giuseppe Maria, prominent Italian composer; b. Florence, March 19, 1675; d. there, Oct. 24, 1760. He most likely received his musical training in Florence; served as maestro di cappella at the court of Tuscany during most of his career; also held that position in Florence at the Cathedral (1732–60) and at S. Michele (1734–57). His *Serpilla e Bacocco* was one of the most celebrated stage works of the 18th century.

WORKS: OPERAS: *Artaserse* (Naples, 1708; additional music by F. Mancini); *L'amor generoso* (Pratolino, 1708; additional music by R. Cerruti); *L'odio e l'amore* (Genoa, 1709); *La fede tradita e vendicata* (Genoa, 1709); *Ataulfo re de'Goti, ovvero La forza della virtù* (Rome, Carnival 1712); *L'innocenza difesa* (Ferrara, 1712); *Teuzzone* (Ferrara, 1712); *Carlo, re d'Alemagna* (Bologna, Oct. 28, 1713); *Nerone fatto Cesare* (Venice, Carnival 1715; in collaboration with others); *Amore e maestà* (Florence, 1715; rev. as *Arsace*, London, Jan. 1, 1721); *I veri amici* (Naples, Nov. 26, 1715); *Griselda, ovvero La virtù al cimento* (Brescia, Carnival 1716); *La Merope* (Bologna, Oct. 24, 1717); *Lucio Papirio* (Naples, Dec. 11, 1717; additional music by F. Feo); *Antigona* (Venice, Carnival 1718; rev. as *La fedeltà coronata*, Bologna, 1727); *Le amazoni vinte da Ercole* (Reggio Emilia, April 1718); *Ifigenia in Tauride* (Venice, Carnival 1719); *Il carciere di se stesso* (Turin, Dec. 26, 1719); *Paride* (Venice, Carnival 1720); *Il Farasmene* (Bologna, Nov. 1720; rev. as *L'amor tirannico*, Pesaro, Carnival 1722); *Nerone* (Hamburg, 1720); *Nino* (Rome, Jan. 7, 1722; with additional music by A. Tinazzoli, Pesaro, Carnival 1723); *Semiramide* (Turin, Carnival 1722); *Ormisda* (Bologna, 1722); *Alessandro Severo* (Milan, Jan. 1723); *L'Oronta* (Milan, Jan. 1723); *Berenice* (Venice, Carnival 1725); *Adelaide* (Genoa, Carnival 1726; with additional music by others, Mantua, Carnival 1731); *La fida ninfa* (Venice, 1730); *Massimiano* (Venice, Carnival 1731); *Ifigenia in Aulide* (Florence, Carnival 1732); *Temistocle* (Florence, Carnival 1737); *Le nozze di Perseo e Andromeda* (Florence, 1738); *Arianna* (Florence, Jan. 1739); *Venceslao* (Florence, Dec. 26, 1741); *Vologeso re de'Parti* (Florence, Jan. 1742); *Lo scialacquatore* (Florence, 1744). **INTERMEZZOS:** *Madama Dulcinea e il cuoco del Marchese del Bosco, ovvero La preziosa ridicola* (Rome, 1712); *Lisetta e Delfo* (Rome, Carnival 1713); *Il Marito giocatore e la moglie becchatona* (Venice, Jan. 1719; best known as *Serpilla e Bacocco*; *Melinda e Tiburzio* (Venice, Carnival 1721; rev. as *La Donna nobile*, Venice, Carnival 1730); *Il bottegaro gentiluomo, ovvero Larinda e Vanesio* (Florence, Carnival 1721); *L'Ammalato immaginario* (Florence, Carnival 1725);

Un vecchio innamorato (Florence, Carnival 1732); *Porsugnacco e Grilletta* (Milan, 1727); *Grullo e Moschetta* (Venice, Carnival 1725); *Il Marito geloso* (St. Petersburg, 1734); *Balbo e Dalisa* (Rome, Carnival 1740); also 8 oratorios (only librettos extant).

Orlov, Nikolai (Andreievich), talented Russian pianist; b. Elets, Orlov district, Feb. 26, 1892; d. Grantown-on-Spey, Scotland, May 31, 1964. He studied in Moscow at the Gnessin Music School and then with Igumnov at the Cons. (graduated, 1910); also studied privately with Taneyev. He launched his career in 1912; was also a teacher at the Phil. School (1913–15) and a prof. at the Cons. (1916–21) in Moscow; then toured extensively in Europe, the U.S., and Latin America, settling in England in 1948. He was one of the finest Russian pianists of his day.

Ormandy, Eugene (real name, **Jenö Blau**), outstanding Hungarian-born American conductor; b. Budapest, Nov. 18, 1899; d. Philadelphia, March 12, 1985. He studied violin with his father; entered the Royal Academy of Music in Budapest at the age of 5; began studying with Hubay at 9, and received an artist's diploma at 13; received a teacher's certificate in 1917; then was concertmaster of the Blüthner Orch. in Germany; also gave recitals and played with orchs. as a soloist. In 1921 he went to the U.S.; became an American citizen in 1927; obtained the position of concertmaster of the Capitol Theater Orch., N.Y., and remained there for 2½ years; made his debut as conductor with that orch. in Sept. 1924; in 1926, became its associate music director; in 1929, conducted the N.Y. Phil. at Lewisohn Stadium; in 1930, became guest conductor with the Robin Hood Dell Orch., Philadelphia; on Oct. 30, 1931, conducted the Philadelphia Orch. In 1931 he was appointed music director of the Minneapolis Sym. Orch.; in 1936, was engaged as associate conductor of the Philadelphia Orch. (with Stokowski); on Sept. 28, 1938, became music director, and traveled with it on transcontinental tours in 1937, 1946, 1948, 1957, 1962, 1964, 1971, 1974, and 1977; in 1949, made an extended tour in England; in the spring of 1955, presented concerts with it in 10 European countries; in the summer of 1958 he led it on another European tour (including Russia). He appeared on numerous occasions as guest conductor with European orchs.; in Australia (summer of 1944); South America (summer of 1946); Latin America (1966); the Far East (1967, 1978); and Japan (1972). In 1970 he received the Presidential Medal of Freedom. In 1973 he took the Philadelphia Orch. to China and led it in several cities there; this was the 1st appearance of an American sym. orch. in the People's Republic of China. Ormandy was made an officer of the French Legion of Honor (1952; was promoted to Commander in 1958); was made a Knight of the Order of the White Rose of Finland (1955); became a holder of the medal of the Bruckner Society (1936); received an honorary Mus.D. from the Univ. of Pa. In 1976 he was named an honorary Knight Commander of the Order of the British Empire by Queen Elizabeth II in honor of the American Bicentennial; altogether, he received 26 awards and 23 honorary doctorates. In his interpretations, Ormandy revealed himself as a Romanticist; he excelled in the works of Beethoven, Schumann, and Richard Strauss, conducting all scores from memory. After 42 seasons as music director of the Philadelphia Orch., he retired at the close of the 1979–80 season, and was named Conductor Laureate.
BIBL.: H. Schonberg, *The Great Conductors* (N.Y., 1967); H. Kupferberg, *Those Fabulous Philadelphians* (N.Y., 1969); idem, "E. O.," *Ovation* (Feb. 1984).

Ornithoparchus (Greek form of his real name, **Vogelsang**), **Andreas,** German music scholar; b. Meiningen, c.1485; d. Münster, c.1535. He matriculated at the Univ. of Rostock (M.A., 1512) and at the Univ. of Tübingen (M.A., 1515); was rector of the parochial school in Münster in 1515; also matriculated at Wittenberg (1516), Leipzig (1516), and Greifswald (1518). He publ. a valuable theoretical treatise, *Musice activae micrologus* (Leipzig, 1517; 6th ed., 1540; Eng. tr. by J. Dowland, London, 1609; reprint 1977).

BIBL.: J. Lyra, *A. O. aus Meiningen . . . und dessen Lehre von den Kirchenaccenten* (Gütersloh, 1877).

Ornstein, Leo, remarkable Russian-born American pianist and composer; b. Kremenchug, Dec. 11, 1892. The son of a synagogal cantor, he studied music at home; then with Vladimir Puchalski in Kiev and, at the age of 10, with Essipova at the St. Petersburg Cons. As a consequence of anti-Semitic disturbances in Russia, the family emigrated to the U.S. in 1907. Ornstein studied piano with Bertha Feiring Tapper and Percy Goetschius at the Inst. of Musical Art in N.Y. He gave his 1st concert in N.Y., as a pianist, on March 5, 1911; then played in Philadelphia and other cities. About 1910 he began to compose; he experimented with percussive sonorities, in dissonant harmonies; made a European tour in 1913–14; played in Norway, Denmark, and in Paris; appeared in London on March 27, 1914, in a piano recital announced as "futuristic music" and featuring his Sonata and other works. Returning to the U.S. early in 1915, he gave a series of recitals at the Bandbox Theater in N.Y., comprising works by Debussy, Ravel, Schoenberg, Scriabin, and other modern composers as well as his own; his *Danse sauvage* excited his audiences by its declared wildness and placed him in the center of controversy; he was hailed as the prophet of a new musical era. After several years as an active virtuoso, he turned mainly to teaching; was made head of the piano dept. of the Philadelphia Musical Academy (1920); also founded the Ornstein School of Music in Philadelphia (1940), and continued to teach until 1955. His 90th birthday was celebrated by a special concert of his works in N.Y. in 1982.
WORKS: ORCH.: *3 Moods: Anger, Peace, Joy* (1914); *The Fog,* symphonic poem (1915); *Evening Song of the Cossack* for Chamber Orch. (1923); Piano Concerto (1923; Philadelphia, Feb. 13, 1925); *Lysistrata Suite* (1930); *Nocturne and Dance of the Fates* (St. Louis, Feb. 12, 1937); 2 violin sonatas (c.1915, c.1918); *3 Russian Impressions* for Violin and Piano (1916); 2 cello sonatas (c.1918, c.1920); Piano Quintet (1927); 3 string quartets (?, c.1929, 1976); *Hebraic Fantasy* for Violin and Piano (1975); numerous piano works, including 6 sonatas and many solo pieces; pieces for children; *3 Russian Choruses* (1918); songs.
BIBL.: C. Van Vechten, *Music and Bad Manners* (N.Y., 1916); C. Buchanan, "O. and Modern Music," *Musical Quarterly* (April 1918); F. Martens, *L. O.: The Man, His Ideas, His Work* (N.Y., 1918); P. Rosenfeld, *Musical Chronicle, 1917–1923* (N.Y., 1923); idem, *An Hour with American Music* (N.Y., 1929); V. Perlis, "The Futurist Music of L. O.," *Notes* (June 1975); T. Darter, Jr., *The Futurist Piano Music of L. O.* (diss., Cornell Univ., 1979).

Orozco, Rafael, Spanish pianist; b. Córdoba, Jan. 24, 1946. He studied at the Córdoba Cons., then at the Madrid Cons., where he graduated in 1964; also took piano lessons with Alexis Weissenberg at the Accademia Chigiana in Siena; in 1966 he won the Leeds Competition; subsequently toured extensively, receiving praise as a fine interpreter of the Romantic repertoire.

Orr, C(harles) W(ilfred), English composer; b. Cheltenham, July 31, 1893; d. Painswick, Gloucestershire, Feb. 24, 1976. He studied at the Guildhall School of Music in London; wrote songs in the manner of German lieder, to words by English poets; his set of 7 songs to texts from Housman's *A Shropshire Lad* is notable.
BIBL.: S. Northcote, "The Songs of C.W. O.," *Music & Letters,* XVIII (1937).

Orr, Robin (actually, **Robert Kemsley**), Scottish organist, teacher, and composer; b. Brechin, June 2, 1909. He studied organ with Alcock, piano with Benjamin, and composition with Moule at the Royal College of Music in London (1926–29); then took courses with Rootham and Dent at Pembroke College, Cambridge (Mus.B., 1932; M.A., 1938); later received instruction in composition from Casella at the Accademia Chigiana in Siena and from Boulanger in Paris. He was director of music at Sidcot School, Somerset (1933), and assistant lecturer in music at the Univ. of Leeds (1936–38); served as organist at St. John's College, Cambridge (1938–41; 1945–47); then was a lecturer in music at the Univ. there (1947–56), receiving his Mus.D. (1951); also was prof. of composition at the Royal College of Music (1950–56). He was prof. of music at the univs. of Glasgow (1956–65) and Cambridge (1965–76); was also chairman of the Scottish Opera in Glasgow (1962–76). He was made a Commander of the Order of the British Empire in 1972.

WORKS: OPERAS: *Full Circle* (1967; Perth, April 10, 1968); *Hermiston* (1975); *On the Razzle* (Glasgow, June 27, 1988). **ORCH.:** 3 syms.: No. 1, *Symphony in 1 Movement* (London, Dec. 12, 1963); No. 2 (1971); No. 3 (1978); *Verses from Ogden Nash* for Medium Voice and Strings (1978); *Journeys and Places* for Mezzo-soprano and String Quintet (1971). Also String Quartet; choral pieces; songs.

Orrego-Salas, Juan (Antonio), Chilean composer and music educator; b. Santiago, Jan. 18, 1919. He studied at the School of Architecture of the Catholic Univ. of Santiago (graduated, 1943); studied composition with Humberto Allende and Domingo Santa Cruz at the National Cons. of Music of the Univ. of Chile (1936–43); went to the U.S. and attended classes in musicology with Paul Henry Lang and George Herzog at Columbia Univ. in N.Y. (1944–45); subsequently studied composition with Randall Thompson at Princeton Univ. (1945–46) and with Aaron Copland at Tanglewood, Mass. (summer 1946); in 1953, received a diploma as Profesor Extraordinario de Composición (Ph.D.) from the Univ. of Chile; was awarded the honorary degree of Doctor Scientiae by the Catholic Univ. of Santiago (1971). From 1942 to 1961 he taught at the Univ. of Chile; in 1961, was engaged as director of the Latin American Music Center and a prof. at Indiana Univ. in Bloomington (until 1987); was also chairman of its composition dept. (1975–80). In his extensive output as a composer, Orrego-Salas has revealed himself as an assured master of neo-Classical techniques.

WORKS: STAGE: *El retablo del rey pobre,* opera-oratorio for 3 Sopranos, Mezzo-soprano, Contralto, 2 Tenors, Baritone, Chorus, and Small Orch. (1950–52); 3 ballets: *Juventud* (after Handel's *Solomon*; Santiago, Nov. 19, 1948); *Umbral del sueño* (Santiago, Aug. 8, 1951); *The Tumbler's Prayer* (concert perf., Santiago, Nov. 1960; stage perf., Santiago, Oct. 1961). **ORCH.:** *Escenas de cortes y pastores,* 7 symphonic scenes (1946; Santiago, May 16, 1947); *Obertura festiva* (Santiago, April 1948); 4 syms.: No. 1 (1949; Santiago, July 14, 1950); No. 2, *a la memoria de un vagabundo* (1954; Minneapolis, Feb. 17, 1956); No. 3 (Washington, D.C., April 22, 1961); No. 4, "of the distant answer" (1966; Bloomington, Ind., 1967); 2 piano concertos: No. 1 (Santiago, Nov. 24, 1950); No. 2 (1985); *Concierto de cámera* for Flute, Oboe, Clarinet, Bassoon, 2 Horns, Harp, and String Orch. (Santiago, Nov. 28, 1952); *Serenata concertante* (1954; Louisville, May 14, 1955); *Jubileaus musicus,* "ad honorem Universitatis Sanctae Mariae" (Valparaíso, Chile, Dec. 15, 1956); *Psalms* for Wind Orch. (Pittsburgh, July 1962); *Concerto a tre* for Violin, Cello, Piano, and Orch. (1962; Washington, D.C., May 7, 1965); Concerto for Wind Orch. (Pittsburgh, June 1964); *Volte* for Chamber Ensemble (Rochester, N.Y., Dec. 11, 1971); *Variaciones serenas* for String Orch. (Santiago, Nov. 23, 1971); Concerto for Oboe and String Orch. (1980; Santiago, June 16, 1981); Violin Concerto (1983; Bloomington, Ind., Oct. 3, 1984); *Riley's Merriment,* scherzo (Indianapolis, Oct. 7, 1986); Fantasia for Piano and Wind Orch. (1986; San Antonio, April 29, 1987). **CHAMBER:** Violin Sonata (N.Y., April 1945); *Suite* for Bandoneon (1952; Paris, June 2, 1953); Sextet for Clarinet, String Quartet, and Piano (1953; Tanglewood, Mass., Aug. 15, 1954); 2 divertimentos for Flute, Oboe, and Bassoon (Santiago, Aug. 23, 1956); String Quartet No. 1 (1957; Washington, D.C., April 19, 1958); *Sonata a quattro* for Flute, Oboe, Harpsichord, and Double Bass (Washington, D.C., Oct. 31, 1964); 2 trios for Violin, Cello, and Piano: No. 1 (Caracas, May 12, 1966); No. 2 (1977; N.Y., May 13, 1981); *Esquinas* for Guitar (1971); *Serenata* for Flute and Cello

(Columbus, Ohio, Feb. 22, 1972); *Sonata de Estío* for Flute and Piano (1972; Bloomington, Ind., Oct. 27, 1974); *Presencias* for 7 Instruments (1972; Washington, D.C., May 5, 1977); *Variations for a Quiet Man* for Clarinet and Piano (1980; Miami, Oct. 3, 1982; dedicated to Aaron Copland); *Tangos* for 11 Players (Miami, Oct. 2, 1982); *Balada* for Cello and Piano (Bloomington, Ind., Sept. 26, 1983); *Glosas* for Violin and Guitar (1984). **PIANO:** 2 suites (1946, 1951); *Variaciones y fuga sobre el tema de un pregón* (1946); *Diez piezas simples* (1951); *Canción y danza* (1951); *Rústica* (1952); Sonata (1967); *Dialogues in Waltz* for Piano, 4-hands (1984); *Rondo-Fantasia* (1984). **VOCAL:** *Canciones en tres movimientos* for Soprano and String Quartet (1945); *Cantata de Navidad* for Soprano and Orch. (Rochester, N.Y., Oct. 23, 1946); *Canciones castellanas* for Soprano and 8 Instruments (Santiago, Dec. 12, 1948); *Cantos de Advenimiento* for Female Voice, Cello, and Piano (Santiago, June 26, 1948); *América, no en vano invocamos tu nombre,* cantata for Soprano, Baritone, Men's Chorus, and Orch. (Ithaca, N.Y., May 10, 1966); *Missa "in tempore discordiae"* for Tenor, Chorus, and Orch. (1968–69; Louisville, April 20, 1979); *Palabras de Don Quijote* for Baritone and Chamber Ensemble (Washington, Oct. 31, 1970) *The Days of God,* oratorio for Soloists, Chorus, and Orch. (1974–76; Washington, D.C., Nov. 2, 1976). *Un Canto a Bolivar,* cantata for Men's Voices and Folk Instruments (1980–81); *Biografía Mínima de Salvador Allende* for Voice, Guitar, Trumpet, and Percussion (San Diego, Aug. 16, 1983); *Ash Wednesday,* 3 songs for Mezzo-soprano and String Orch. (1984).

Orsi, Romeo, Italian clarinetist and manufacturer of wind instruments; b. Como, Oct. 18, 1843; d. Milan, June 11, 1918. He studied at the Royal Cons. of Milan (1856–64); in 1873, became a prof. of clarinet there; was 1st clarinetist of La Scala (1871–1911); gave concerts in Italy and in Paris. In 1881 he constructed a combination clarinet capable of performing both B-flat and A clarinet parts; it had a temporary acceptance among orch. players; he also manufactured a bass clarinet in A for use in Verdi's *Otello;* publ. a method for the saxophone.

Orth, John, American pianist, teacher, and composer; b. Annweiler, Bavaria, Dec. 2, 1850; d. Boston, May 3, 1932. His parents settled in Taunton, Mass., when he was a year old; studied organ with his father; then went to Germany, where he took courses with Kullak and Deppe (piano); also had lessons with Liszt; studied composition with Faiszt, Weitzmann, Kiel, and P. Scharwenka. In 1875 he settled in Boston as a pianist and teacher; in lecture-recitals he became a propagandist for Liszt's music in America. In 1883 he married his pupil Lizette E. Blood, known as **L.E. Orth** (d. Boston, Sept. 14, 1913), who was herself a composer of songs and piano pieces. Orth publ. a number of teaching pieces for piano.

Orthel, Léon, Dutch composer and pianist; b. Roosendaal, North Brabant, Oct. 4, 1905; d. The Hague, Sept. 6, 1985. He studied composition with Johan Wagenaar at the Royal Cons. of The Hague (1921–26) and with Paul Juon at the Hochschule für Musik in Berlin (1928–29). From 1941 to 1971 he taught piano and theory at the Royal Cons. of The Hague; concurrently taught composition at the Amsterdam Cons. (1949–71); was chairman of the Composers' Section of the Royal Dutch Society of Musicians (1947–70) while continuing to appear as a pianist.

WORKS: ORCH.: 6 syms.: No. 1 (1931–33); No. 2, *Piccola sinfonia* (1940; Rotterdam, Oct. 31, 1941); No. 3 (1943); No. 4, *Sinfonia concertante* for Piano and Orch. (1949); No. 5, *Musica iniziale* (1959–60); No. 6 (1960–61); *Concertstuk* for Violin and Orch. (1924); *Scherzo* for Piano and Orch. (1927); 2 cello concertos (1929, 1984); *Concertino alla burla* for Piano and Orch. (1930); 2 *Scherzos* (1954–55, 1956–57); *3 movimenti ostinati* (1971–72; Amsterdam, Sept. 1, 1973); *Album di disegni* (1976–77); *Evocazione* (1977); Suite No. 2 (1980); *Music* for Double Bass and Orch. (1981). **CHAMBER:** 2 violin sonatas (1924, 1933); 2 cello sonatas (1925, 1958); 5 *pezzettini* for Clarinet and Piano (1963); String Quartet (1964); Viola Sonata (1964–65); *Ballade* for Flute and Piano (1970); 8 *abbozzi* for

Flute, Cello, and Piano (1971); 5 *Schizzetti* for Harp (1977). PIANO: Sonata (1923); *4 Pieces* (1923–24); 9 sonatinas (1924; *Minatuure sonatine*, 1942; 1945; 1953; for the left hand, 1959; 1974; *Uit 1920 en 1922*, 1975; *Sonatina capricciosa*, 1975; 1977); pieces for children; also 13 separate song cycles to texts by Rilke (1934–72).

d'Ortigue, Joseph (-Louis), French writer on music; b. Cavaillon, Vaucluse, May 22, 1802; d. Paris, Nov. 20, 1866. He studied music with H. Blaze and Castil-Blaze; after training for the law in Aix-en-Provence, he settled in Paris (1829), where he wrote articles on music for various journals. In 1857 he founded *La Maîtrise* (with L. Niedermeyer) and in 1862 the *Journal des Maîtrises* (with F. Clément), both periodicals for church music; in 1863 he became ed. of *Le Ménestrel*; succeeded Berlioz as critic for the *Journal des Débats* (1864). He exercised considerable influence on musical life in Paris.
WRITINGS (all publ. in Paris): *Le balcon de l'Opéra* (1833); *De l'école musicale italienne et de l'administration de l'Académie royale de musique à l'occasion de l'opéra de M.H. Berlioz* (1839; 2nd ed., 1840, as *Du Théâtre italien et de son influence sur le goût musical français*); *Abécédaire de plain-chant* (1841); *Dictionnaire liturgique, historique et théorique de plain-chant et de musique de l'église, au Moyen-Age et dans les temps modernes* (1853); *Introduction à l'étude comparée des tonalités, et principalement du chant grégorien et de la musique moderne* (1853); *Traité théorique et pratique de l'accompagnement du plain-chant* (with Niedermeyer; 1857; Eng. tr., N.Y., 1905); *La Musique à l'église* (1861).
BIBL.: M. Barber, *J. d'O.* (Paris, 1919).

Ortiz, Cristina, Brazilian-born English pianist; b. Bahia, April 17, 1950. She studied in Rio de Janeiro; after training with Magda Tagliaferro in Paris, she won 1st prize in the Van Cliburn Competition (1969); made her N.Y. recital debut in 1971. Following further studies with R. Serkin at the Curtis Inst. of Music in Philadelphia, she pursued an international career (from 1973).

Ortiz, Diego, Spanish music theorist and composer; b. Toledo, c.1510; d. probably in Naples, c.1570. He was maestro de capilla at the viceregal court in Naples (1558–65). He was one of the earliest masters of variations (divisions). His greatest work is *Trattado de glosas sobre clausulas y otros géneros de puntos en la música de violones* (Rome, 1553; modern ed. by M. Schneider, Berlin, 1913; 3rd ed., Kassel, 1967), containing early examples of instrumental variations and ornamental cadenzas (for Viola da Gamba alone with harpsichord). An Italian version of this work was also publ. at Rome in 1553 (*Il primo libro de Diego Ortiz Toletano*, etc.). In addition, he publ. a vol. of sacred music at Venice in 1565 (hymns, motets, Psalms, etc., for 4 to 7 Voices). Some motets by him (in lute tablature) were included in Valderrábano's *Silva de Sirenas* (1547).
BIBL.: J. Subirá, *La música en la Casa de Alba* (Barcelona, 1927); R. Borrowdale, *The "Musices Liber Primus" of D. O., Spanish Musician* (diss., Univ. of Southern Calif., 1952); P. Strassler, *Hymns for the Church Year, Magnificats, and other Sacred Choral Works of D. O.* (diss., Univ. of North Carolina, 1966).

Ortmann, Otto Rudolph, American music educator; b. Baltimore, Jan. 25, 1889; d. there, Oct. 22, 1979. After studying at the Peabody Cons. of Music in Baltimore, he joined its faculty (1917–41), serving as its director (1928–41); also taught the psychology of music at Johns Hopkins Univ. (1921–24) and was on the music faculty at Goucher College (1942–57), serving as its music dept. chairman (1948–57); subsequently gave private instruction in piano, voice, and corrective speech despite advanced age and almost total blindness. Among his publications are *The Physical Basis of Piano Touch and Tone* (1925) and *The Psychological Mechanics of Piano Technique* (1929; 2nd ed., 1962).

Orto (real name, **Dujardin**), **Marbrianus de,** Franco-Flemish singer and composer; b. probably in the Tournai diocese, c.1460; d. Nivelles, c.Feb. 1529. He was the illegitimate off-

spring of a priest; sang in the papal choir in Rome (1483–99?); was also dean of the collegiate church of St. Gertrude in Nivelles (1489–96); in 1505 he was in the service of Philip the Fair of Burgundy, and was legitimized; went to Spain with him in 1506, and was ennobled. After Philip's death that same year, he entered the service of his son, Archduke Charles, later Emperor Charles V, being active at his chapel until at least 1518. Petrucci publ. a book of 5 masses by him (Venice, 1505), as well as 11 chansons for 4 voices in the *Odhecaton* (1500–1503) and a Lamentation in *Lamentationum Jeremias prophetae liber I* (1506).
BIBL.: G. van Doorslaer, "La Chapelle musicale de Philippe le Beau," *Revue Belge d'Archéologie et d'Histoire de l'Art*, IV (1934).

Ory, "Kid" (Edward), black American jazz trombonist and bandleader; b. La Place, La., Dec. 25, 1886; d. Honolulu, Jan. 23, 1973. He played the banjo as a child; then took up trombone; later joined bands led by Louis Armstrong and King Oliver. After a hiatus from performing (1933–42), he organized his own band and toured with it in Europe (1956–59). He was known for his "tailgate" style of trombone playing. He was the composer of the well-known *Muskrat Ramble*.
BIBL.: R. Dixon, *K. O.: A Biography, Appreciation, Record Survey and Discography* (London, 1958).

Osborne (real name, **Eisbein**), **Adrienne,** American contralto; b. Buffalo, Dec. 2, 1873; d. Zell am Ziller, Austria, June 15, 1951. She studied with August Götze and Max Stägemann in Leipzig; later with **Felix von Kraus,** whom she married in 1899. She sang at the Municipal Opera in Leipzig; in 1908 settled in Munich, where she received the rank of Royal Chamber Singer. After the death of her husband in 1937, she went to Zell am Ziller.

Osborne, Bobby (Robert, Jr.) (b. Hyden, Ky., Dec. 7, 1931) and **Sonny** (b. Hyden, Oct. 29, 1937), American country-music singers and instrumentalists. They learned to play the banjo and mandolin, and in 1953 began to make appearances on the radio, billed as the Osborne Brothers, and to take their bluegrass renditions to college campuses and other country-music haunts; their use of amplified electric guitars contributed to their success. Their hits included *Midnight Flyer, Rocky Top*, and *Georgia Pinewoods*.

Osborne, Nigel, English composer; b. Manchester, June 23, 1948. He studied with Egon Wellesz and Kenneth Leighton at Oxford (B.Mus., 1970), then worked with Witold Rudziński and at the Polish Radio Experimental Studio in Warsaw (1970–71); later was a lecturer in music at the Univ. of Nottingham (from 1978), where he held the title of special prof. in composition (from 1989). He won the Radio Suisse Romande Opera prize for his cantata *7 Words* in 1971; was awarded a Gaudeamus prize in 1973 and a Radcliffe prize in 1977. In his compositions he presents olden modalities enhanced by modern techniques, including electronics.
WORKS: *Beautiful Thing I* and *II* for Chamber Ensemble (1969–70); *7 Words*, cantata (1969–71); *Heaventree* for Chorus a cappella (1973); *Kinderkreuzzug* for Chorus and Chamber Ensemble (1974); *Musica da camera* for Violin, Tape, and Audience (1975); *The Sickle* for Soprano and Small Orch. (1975); *Passers By* for Bass Recorder, Cello, Electronic Synthesizer, and Diapositive (1976); Cello Concerto (1977); *Orlando furioso* for Chorus, Wind Band, and Percussion (1978); *In camera* for Chamber Ensemble (1979); Concerto for Flute and Chamber Orch. (London, May 23, 1980); Piano Sonata (1981); *Sinfonia I* (London, Aug. 2, 1982) and *II* (1983); *Cantata piccolo* for Soprano and String Quartet (1982); *Fantasia* for Ensemble (1983); *Wildlife* for Ensemble (1984); *Alba* for Mezzo-soprano, Ensemble, and Tape (1984); *Zansa* for Ensemble (1985); *Pornography* for Mezzo-soprano and Ensemble (1985); *Hell's Angels*, opera (London, Jan. 4, 1986); *The Electrification of the Soviet Union*, opera (1986; Glyndebourne, Oct. 5, 1987).
BIBL.: N. O'Loughlin, "The Music of N. O.," *Musical Times* (May 1980); *New Sounds, New Personalities: British Composers*

of the Late 1980s: Conversations with Paul Griffiths (Winchester, Mass., 1985); P. Driver, "O.'s 'Electrification of the Soviet Union,' " *Musical Times* (Oct. 1987).

Osborn-Hannah, Jane, American soprano; b. Wilmington, Ohio, July 8, 1873; d. N.Y., Aug. 13, 1943. She received her 1st singing lessons from her mother; then went to Europe, where she studied with Marchesi and Sbriglia in Paris; was engaged at the Leipzig Opera (1904–7); then sang in Dresden, Berlin, and Munich; appeared in London in 1908; made her American debut at the Metropolitan Opera in N.Y. as Elisabeth (Jan. 5, 1910) and sang there until 1911; was a member of the Chicago Grand Opera (1910–14); was particularly notable in Wagnerian roles. She was married to Frank Hannah, American consul at Magdeburg.

Osghian, Petar, Serbian composer; b. Dubrovnik, April 27, 1932. He studied at the Belgrade Academy of Music; was on its faculty (from 1964). He adopted a free neo-Romantic style of composition.

Works: *Poema eroico* for Orch. (Belgrade, Dec. 8, 1959); *Symphoniette* for Strings (Belgrade, Dec. 20, 1960); Concerto for Orch. (Belgrade, Feb. 25, 1964); *Sigogis* for Chamber Orch. (Zagreb, May 12, 1967); *Differencias* for Violin and Orch. (1970); String Quartet (1958); Divertimento for Double String Quartet (1973); numerous piano pieces.

Osten, Eva von der, German soprano; b. Insel, Aug. 19, 1881; d. Dresden, May 5, 1936. She studied with August Iffert and Marie Söhle in Dresden; made her debut as Urbain in *Les Huguenots* in Dresden in 1902; was a principal member of the Dresden Court (later State) Opera until 1927; created the role of Octavian in *Der Rosenkavalier* there in 1911; also appeared at London's Covent Garden (1912–14) and in the U.S. with the German Opera Co. (1923–24). After her retirement from the stage, she became a producer of opera in Dresden. She was married to the Czech bass-baritone **Friedrich Plaschke.** Among her most outstanding roles were Kundry, Ariadne, and Tosca.

Osterc, Slavko, Yugoslav composer; b. Veržej, June 17, 1895; d. Ljubljana, May 23, 1941. He began his training with Beran in Maribor; then studied at the Prague Cons. (1925–27); subsequently taught at Ljubljana's Cons. and Academy of Music. He experimented with various techniques, including quarter-tone writing.

Works: STAGE: OPERAS: *Krst pri Savici* (Baptism at the Savica; 1921); *Iz komične opere* (1928); *Krog s kredo* (The Chalk Circle; 1928–29); *Salome* (1919–30); *Medea* (1930); *Dandin v vicah* (Dandin in Purgatory; 1930). BALLETS: *Iz Satanovega dnevnika* (From Satan's Diary; 1924); *Maska rdeče smrti* (The Masque of the Red Death; 1930); *Illusions* (1938–40); *Illegitimate Mother* (1940). ORCH.: Sym. (1922); Concerto (1932); *Passacaglia and Chorale* (ISCM Festival, Warsaw, April 14, 1934); Concerto for Piano and Wind Instruments (ISCM Festival, Prague, Sept. 1, 1935); *Mouvements symphonique* (1936; ISCM Festival, London, June 24, 1938); *Nocturne* for Strings (1940). CHAMBER: 2 string quartets (1927, 1934); Sonata for 2 Clarinets (1929); Wind Quintet (1932); Saxophone Sonata (1935); piano pieces; organ music.

Osthoff, Helmuth, distinguished German musicologist, father of **Wolfgang Osthoff;** b. Bielefeld, Aug. 13, 1896; d. Würzburg, Feb. 9, 1983. He studied music in Bielefeld and in Münster. He served in the German army during World War I; after the Armistice, he resumed his studies at the Univ. of Münster (1919), and later (1920–22) took courses with Wolf, Kretzschmar, and Schünemann at the Univ. of Berlin, where he received his Ph.D. in 1922 with the dissertation *Der Lautenist Santino Garsi da Parma: Ein Beitrag zur Geschichte der oberitaliensischen Lautenmusik der Spätrenaissance* (publ. in Leipzig, 1926). He subsequently studied conducting with Brecher, composition with Klatte, and piano with Kwast at Berlin's Stern Cons. (1922–23). From 1923 to 1926 he served as répétiteur at the Leipzig Opera; in 1926 he became assistant lecturer to Arnold Schering in the dept. of musicology at the

Univ. of Halle; in 1928 he was appointed chief assistant to Schering in the dept. of music history at the Univ. of Berlin; completed his Habilitation there in 1932 with his treatise *Die Niederländer und das deutsche Lied 1400–1640* (publ. in Berlin, 1938). In 1938 he became a prof. and director of the inst. of musicology at the Univ. of Frankfurt, positions he held until his retirement in 1964. He was especially noted for his astute studies of Renaissance music. His other publications include *Adam Krieger; Neue Beiträge zur Geschichte des deutschen Liedes in 17. Jahrhundert* (Leipzig, 1929; 2nd ed., 1970); *Johannes Brahms und seine Sendung* (Bonn, 1942); *Josquin Desprez* (2 vols., Tutzing, 1962–65). A Festschrift was publ. in Tutzing in 1961 to honor his 65th birthday, a 2nd in 1969 for his 70th birthday (contains a bibliography of his writings), and a 3rd in 1977 for his 80th birthday.

Osthoff, Wolfgang, German musicologist, son of **Helmuth Osthoff;** b. Halle, March 17, 1927. He studied piano and theory at the Frankfurt Staatliche Hochschule für Musik (1939–43); then took lessons in conducting with Kurt Thomas (1946–47). He subsequently studied musicology with his father at the Univ. of Frankfurt (1947–49) and with Georgiades at the Univ. of Heidelberg (1949–54); received his Ph.D. there in 1954 with the dissertation *Das dramatische Spätwerk Claudio Monteverdis* (publ. in Tutzing, 1960). He taught at the Univ. of Munich (1957–64); completed his Habilitation there in 1965 with his *Theatergesang und darstellende Musik in der italienischen Renaissance* (publ. in Tutzing, 1969). He became a lecturer at the Univ. of Munich in 1966. In 1968 he was named a prof. of musicology at the Univ. of Würzburg. In addition to many scholarly articles dealing with music history from the 15th to the 19th century, he also contributed to many music reference works.

Bibl.: M. Just and R. Wiesend, eds., *Liedstudien: W. O. zum 60. Geburtstag* (Tutzing, 1989).

Östman, Arnold, Swedish conductor; b. Malmö, Dec. 24, 1939. He studied art history at the Univ. of Lund and music history at the univs. of Paris and Stockholm; was artistic director of the Vadstena Academy (1969–79), where he conducted many 17th- and 18th-century operas; also commissioned and conducted numerous contemporary operas. He was general administrator and music director of the Drottningholm Court Theater (from 1979), where he attempted performances of operas in "authentic style" utilizing period instruments; was also closely associated with the Cologne Opera, taking its productions of *Il matrimonio segreto* on tour to London (1983) and Washington, D.C. (1986).

Ostrčil, Otakar, eminent Czech conductor and composer; b. Smichov, near Prague, Feb. 25, 1879; d. Prague, Aug. 20, 1935. He studied languages at the Univ. of Prague, and then taught at a school in Prague (until 1919); at the same time he took courses in piano with Adolf Mikeš (1893–95) and studied composition privately with Fibich (1895–1900). From 1908 to 1922 he conducted the amateur orch. association in Prague; also conducted opera there (from 1909); in 1920 he succeeded Karel Kovařovic as principal conductor at the Prague National Theater. In his compositions, Ostrčil continued the Romantic tradition of Czech music, with some modern elaborations revealing the influence of Mahler.

Works: OPERAS: *Vlasty skon* (The Death of Vlasta; Prague, Dec. 14, 1904); *Kunálovy oči* (Kunala's Eyes; Prague, Nov. 25, 1908); *Poupě* (The Bud; 1909–10; Prague, Jan. 25, 1911); *Legenda z Erinu* (The Legend of Erin; 1913–19; Brno, June 16, 1921); *Honzovo království* (Honza's Kingdom; 1928–33; Brno, May 26, 1934). ORCH.: Sym. (1905); Sinfonietta (1921); *Léto* (Summer), symphonic poem (1925–26); *Křížová cesta* (Way of the Cross), symphonic variations (1928). Also several choral works; String Quartet; Trio for Violin, Viola, and Piano; several song cycles.

Bibl.: Z. Nejedlý, *O. O.: vzrůst a uzrání* (O. O.: Development and Maturity; Prague, 1935); J. Bartoš, *O. O.* (Prague, 1936).

Oswald, John, provocative Canadian composer and sound engineer; b. Kitchener-Waterloo, May 30, 1953. In 1989 he produced and distributed, free of charge, *Plunderphonic*, a CD anthology of original pieces made up of "plunderphones" ("electroquotes or macrosamples of familiar sound") derived from revised performances of recordings by well-known artists, including James Brown, Lorin Maazel with the Cleveland Orch., George Harrison, Dolly Parton, Glenn Gould, Bing Crosby, Michael Jackson, and Count Basie. Oswald's "plunderphones" are the substance of each of his 24 tracks, themselves sequenced into typical genre groupings, with the exception of "compilation tracks of a particular performer, juxtapositions of complimentary performances by unrelated performers, unusual rearrangements of existing compositions, and the James Brown tracks, which are vehicles for various types and sources of appropriation." Virtually no extraneous music is added, all of the sounds heard being accurate, unprocessed reproductions of the originals. The overall effect is both less and more complicated than Oswald's explanation—repelling and compelling, with referential musical modules flitting around like bytes of information in the bowels of a computer. Oswald is actively involved in the issue of copyright morality; he lectured widely on the subject and also wrote extensively for a variety of publications (*Keyboard*, *The Whole Earth Review*, *Grammy Pulse*, etc.). *Plunderphonic* itself carries no copyright warning; in its place is a "shareright" insignia, which encourages reproduction but prohibits sale. Since 1980 Oswald has been director of Mystery Laboratory of Toronto, the "aural research, production, and dissemination facility" where *Plunderphonic* was produced; he is also music director of the North American Experience Dance Co. (from 1987) and co-founder of *Musicworks*, an informative Canadian journal which emphasizes the experimental and avant-garde. Among his other compositions are *Burroughs*, vocal concrète (1974); *Warm Wind Pressure and Aura* for Ensemble without Instruments (1979); and *Fossils*, vocal concrète (1985); he also wrote 3 full-length dance scores: *Skindling Shades* for Tape (1987), *Wounded* for Miming Musicians (1988), and *Zorro* for a cappella Duet (1989); numerous tape pieces, including *Jazz Edit* (1982) and *Bell Speeds* (1983).

Otaka, Hisatada, Japanese conductor and composer; b. Tokyo, Sept. 26, 1911; d. there, Feb. 16, 1951. He studied composition with Joseph Marx in Vienna; also took lessons in conducting with Felix Weingartner at the Vienna Academy of Music (1934–38); returned to Japan in 1940; conducted the Nippon Sym. Orch. (1942–51) in Tokyo.
WORKS: 2 *Japanese Suites* for Orch.: No. 1 (Budapest, Nov. 8, 1938) and No. 2 (Vienna, Nov. 3, 1939); Sinfonietta for Strings (1937); *Midare* for Orch. (Berlin, Dec. 10, 1939); Cello Concerto (Tokyo, May 23, 1943); *Rhapsody* for Piano and Orch. (Tokyo, Dec. 10, 1943); *Fatherland* for Orch. (Tokyo, Oct. 22, 1945); Sym. (1948); Flute Concerto (Tokyo, March 5, 1951); Violin Sonata (1932); 2 string quartets (1938, 1943); Piano Trio (1941); many piano pieces and songs.

Otaka, Tadaaki, Japanese conductor; b. Kamakura, Nov. 8, 1947. He received his training at the Toho Gakuen School of Music in Tokyo and at the Hochschule für Musik in Vienna; taught at the Toho Gakuen School of Music (from 1970) and appeared as a conductor in Japan. He served as principal conductor of the Tokyo Phil. (from 1974), the Sapporo Sym. Orch. (from 1981), and the BBC Welsh Sym. Orch. in Cardiff (from 1987).

Otaño (y Eugenio), (José María) Nemesio, Spanish composer and musicologist; b. Azcoitia, Dec. 19, 1880; d. San Sebastián, April 29, 1956. He studied with V. Arregui and V. Goicoechea; became a Jesuit priest; founded the Schola Cantorum at Comillas in 1911 and, in 1907, the journal *Música Sacro-Hispana*, of which he was ed. until 1922. He energetically supported the study of Spanish folk music; made a study of the Spanish *villancico*; from 1940 to 1951, was director of the Madrid Cons. He publ. an important collection of old and new Spanish organ music, *Antología de organistas españoles*; an essay on folklore, *El canto popular montañés*; a collection of Spanish military music of the 18th century (Burgos, 1939); also composed a number of sacred works; wrote *La música*

religiosa y la legislación eclesiástica (Barcelona, 1912) and *Antonio Eximeno* (Madrid, 1943).

Otescu, Ion (Nonna), Rumanian composer and conductor; b. Bucharest, Dec. 15, 1888; d. there, March 25, 1940. He studied at the Bucharest Cons. with Kiriac and Castaldi (1903–7); then with Widor at the Paris Cons. and with d'Indy at the Schola Cantorum (1908–11). He was a prof. of composition at the Bucharest Cons. (1913–40) and its director (1918–40). He also conducted opera at the National Theater (1921–39); from 1927, led the concerts of the Bucharest Phil.; was a founding member (1920) of the Society of Rumanian Composers.
WORKS: Musical comedy, *Bubi* (1903); 2 operas: *Ilderim* (libretto by Queen Marie of Rumania; Bucharest, 1920) and *De la Matei cetire* (1938; rev. and completed by A. Stroe; Cluj, Dec. 27, 1966); 2 ballets: *Ileana Cosînzeana* (1918) and *Rubinul miraculos* (1919); *Idilă* for String Orch. (1908); symphonic poems: *Templul din Gnid* (1908), *Legenda trandafirului roşu* (1910), *Narcis* (1911), and *Vrăjile Armidei* (1915); *Din bătrîni*, symphonic sketch (1912); *Peisaj de iarnă*, symphonic tableau (1913); *Scherzo* for Orch. (1923); songs.

Othegraven, August von, German composer; b. Cologne, June 2, 1864; d. Wermelskirchen, March 11, 1946. He studied at the Cologne Cons.; from 1889, taught there; became a prof. in 1914. He composed chiefly for chorus; his oratorio *Marienleben* (Cologne, 1919) was fairly successful; he also wrote a musical fairy tale, *Die schlafende Prinzessin* (Cologne, 1907), and an operetta, *Poldis Hochzeit* (Cologne, 1912).
BIBL.: B. Voss, *A. v.O., Leben und Werk* (Cologne, 1961).

Othmayr, Caspar, celebrated German composer; b. Amberg, March 12, 1515; d. Nuremberg, Feb. 4, 1553. He was a choirboy at the courts in Neumarkt and Amberg; matriculated at the Univ. of Heidelberg (1533), subsequently receiving the degrees of Bachelor, Licentiate, and Master of Arts there. He became Rektor of the Lateinschule at Heilbronn's Cistercian monastery (1545) and then provost of the St. Gumbertus monastery in Ansbach (1547). He was greatly esteemed not only for his sacred works but also for his ingenious polyphonic settings of secular songs.
WORKS (all publ. in Nuremberg): (10) *Cantilena aliquot elegantes ac piae* for 4 to 5 Voices (1546); (2) *Epitaphium D. Martini Lutheri* for 5 Voices (1546); (34) *Symbola illustrissimorum principum, nobilium, aliorumque . . . virorum* for 5 Voices (1547); (41) *Bicinia sacra* (1547); (30) *Tricinia* (1549); (50) *Reutterische und jegerische Liedlein* for 4 to 5 Voices (1549); other songs and motets in various contemporary collections. See H. Albrecht, ed., *Caspar Othmayr: Ausgewählte Werke*, Das Erbe Deutscher Musik, 1st series, XVI (1941) and XXVI (1956).
BIBL.: H. Albrecht, *C. O.: Leben und Werk* (Kassel, 1950).

Ott, David, American composer; b. Crystal Falls, Mich., July 5, 1947. He studied at the Univ. of Wisconsin, Platteville (B.S. in music education, 1969); after training in piano with Alfonso Montecino at the Indiana Univ. School of Music (M.M., 1971), he took courses in theory and composition at the Univ. of Kentucky (D.M.A., 1982). He taught at Houghton (N.Y.) College (1972–75), the Univ. of Kentucky, Lexington (1976–77), Catawba College, Salisbury, N.C. (1977–78), Pfeiffer College, Misenheimer, N.C. (1978–82), and DePauw Univ., Greencastle, Ind. (from 1982); also was active as an organist and conductor.
WORKS: STAGE: *Lucinda Hero*, opera (1985); *Visions: The Isle of Patmos*, ballet (1988). **ORCH.:** *Genesis II* (1980); Piano Concerto (1983); *Short Symphony* for Chamber Orch. (1984); Percussion Concerto (1984); Cello Concerto (1985); *Water Garden* (1986); *Celebration at Vanderburgh* (1987); Saxophone Concerto (1987); Viola Concerto (1988); Concerto for 2 Cellos and Orch. (1988); *DodecaCelli* (1988); *Vertical Shrines* (1989); *Music of the Canvas* (Indianapolis, Oct. 11, 1990); Triple Brass Concerto for Trumpet, Trombone, Horn, and Orch. (1990). **CHAMBER:** Viola Sonata (1982); *Sabado* for Woodwind Quintet (1985); Trombone Sonata (1986); String Quartet No. 1 (1989);

5 *Interludes* for Cello and Piano (1990). Also organ pieces; choral works; songs.

Otte, Hans, German composer and pianist; b. Plauen, Dec. 3, 1926. He studied composition with Hindemith and Johann Nepomuk David, piano with von Pozniak and Gieseking, organ with Germani, and conducting with Abendroth; in 1959 won the Prix de Rome; that same year became head of the music section of Radio Bremen, where he founded the Pro Musica Nova and Pro Musica Antiqua festivals (1961), his unorthodox programming bringing him international attention. He served as president of the German Music Council (1969–72); also publ. articles on contemporary esthetics. His early compositions followed Hindemith; later he adopted serial and aleatoric techniques, and still later he evolved a sort of gentle minimalism. Among his compositions are *Momente* for Orch. (1958); *Nolimentangere* for Actress, Piano, Film, and Sound Track (1966–67); and *Das Buch der Klänge* for Piano (1979–82; Metz, 1982).

Otter, Anne Sofie von, Swedish mezzo-soprano; b. Stockholm, May 9, 1955. She began her training at the Stockholm Musikhögskolan; then studied with Erik Werba in Vienna and Geoffrey Parsons in London, and later with Vera Rozsa. In 1982 she joined the Basel Opera; in 1984 she sang at the Aix-en-Provence Festival. She made her 1st appearance at London's Covent Garden in 1985 as Cherubino; that same year she made her U.S. debut as soloist in Mozart's C-minor Mass with the Chicago Sym. Orch. In 1987 she sang at La Scala in Milan and at the Bavarian State Opera in Munich. In 1988 she appeared as Cherubino at the Metropolitan Opera in N.Y. She sang widely as a soloist with major orchs. and as a recitalist. Her other operatic roles include Gluck's Orfeo, Mozart's Idamantes and Dorabella, Tchaikovsky's Olga, and R. Strauss's Octavian.

Otterloo, (Jan) Willem van, prominent Dutch conductor; b. Winterswijk, Dec. 27, 1907; d. in a automobile accident in Melbourne, Australia, July 27, 1978. He studied with Orobio de Castro (cello) and Sem Dresden (composition) at the Amsterdam Cons.; after graduation, he was engaged as cellist in the Utrecht Sym. Orch. (1932); from 1933 to 1937, served as its assistant conductor, and from 1937 to 1949, as its chief conductor. He was chief conductor of the Residente Orch. in The Hague (1949–73); took it on a tour of the U.S. in 1963. He was also chief conductor (1967–68) and principal guest conductor (1969–71) of the Melbourne Sym. Orch.; then was chief conductor of the Sydney Sym. Orch. from 1973 until his tragic death; was also Generalmusikdirektor of the Düsseldorf Sym. Orch. (1974–77). His unmannered readings of the classics were esteemed. He also composed, producing a Sym., suites for Orch., chamber music, etc.

Ottman, Robert W(illiam), American music theorist and pedagogue; b. Fulton, N.Y., May 3, 1914. He studied music theory with Bernard Rogers at the Eastman School of Music in Rochester, N.Y. (M.Mus., 1943). He served in U.S. Army infantry (1943–46); then took lessons in composition with Alec Rowley at Trinity College of Music in London; in 1946, was engaged as a lecturer in music at North Texas State Univ., from which he also received his Ph.D. (1956); became prof. emeritus in 1980.

WRITINGS (all publ. in Englewood Cliffs, N.J., unless otherwise given): *Music for Sight Singing* (1956; 3rd ed., 1986); with P. Kreuger, *Basic Repertoire for Singers* (San Antonio, 1959); *Elementary Harmony, Theory and Practice* (1961; 3rd ed., 1983); *Advanced Harmony, Theory and Practice* (N.Y., 1961; 3rd ed., 1984); with F. Mainous, *The 371 Chorales of J.S. Bach* (N.Y., 1966; with Eng. texts); with F. Mainous, *Rudiments of Music* (1970; 2nd ed., 1987); *Workbook for Elementary Harmony* (1974; 2nd ed., 1983); with F. Mainous, *Programmed Rudiments of Music* (N.Y., 1979); *More Music for Sight Singing* (1981).

Otto, (Ernst) Julius, German choral conductor and composer; b. Königstein, Sept. 1, 1804; d. Dresden, March 5, 1877. He studied with Weinlig in Dresden; then was a teacher there. In 1830 he was appointed cantor at the Kreuzkirche, and held this position for 45 years; his choir became one of the most celebrated in Germany; he also conducted several choral societies. His best works are the excellent male choruses in his collection *Ernst und Scherz*, which became extremely popular (*Burschenfahrten, Gesellenfahrten, Soldatenleben, Der Spinnabend, Der Sängersaal,* etc.); also 2 grand operas and 4 comic operas for amateur performance (*Die Mordgrundbruck bei Dresden* is the best); 3 oratorios; many songs for Solo Voice (*In die Ferne, Des deutschen Rheines Braut,* etc.); piano sonatas, rondos, etc.

BIBL.: A. Scheumann, *J. O.* (Dresden, 1904).

Otto, Lisa, German soprano; b. Dresden, Nov. 14, 1919. She was educated at the Hochschule für Musik in Dresden; made her debut as Sophie in 1941 at the Landestheater in Beuthen. She was a member of the Dresden State Opera (1946–51); then joined the Berlin Städtische Oper (1952); also sang in Salzburg (from 1953), and made tours of the U.S., South America, and Japan. She was made a Kammersängerin in 1963. She became best known for her roles in Mozart's operas.

Ötvos, Gabor, Hungarian conductor; b. Budapest, Sept. 21, 1935. He was educated at the Franz Liszt Academy of Music in Budapest; left Hungary in 1956 and settled in Italy. He conducted in Venice and Trieste; then went to Germany. From 1967 to 1972 he was 1st conductor and deputy Generalmusikdirektor of the Frankfurt Opera. He also conducted in America; made his Metropolitan Opera debut in N.Y. on Oct. 27, 1971. In 1972 he became Generalmusikdirektor of Augsburg, a post he held until 1981, when he was appointed chief conductor of the Royal Danish Theater in Copenhagen.

Oudin, Eugène (Espérance), American baritone of French descent; b. N.Y., Feb. 24, 1858; d. London, Nov. 4, 1894. He studied law at Yale Univ.; made his debut in N.Y., on Aug. 30, 1886, in an operetta. On Jan. 31, 1891, he created the role of Ivanhoe in London in Arthur Sullivan's opera of that name, and won immediate acclaim. He remained in England most of his life, but also made several appearances in Europe, including Russia; scored notable successes in Wagnerian roles, especially Wolfram and Telramund.

Oudrid (y Segura), Cristóbal, Spanish conductor and composer; b. Badajoz, Feb. 7, 1825; d. while conducting a rehearsal at the Teatro Real in Madrid, March 12, 1877. He studied music with his father; acquired his craft by arranging works of Haydn and Mozart for wind instruments; in 1844 he went to Madrid, where he conducted Italian opera (from 1867) and was director of the Teatro Real (from 1870). He showed a decided talent for writing melodious zarzuelas, among them *Buenas noches, Señor Don Simon* (Madrid, April 16, 1852), *El postillon de la Rioja* (Madrid, June 7, 1856), and *El último mono* (Madrid, May 30, 1859).

BIBL.: A. Pena y Goni, *La opera española en el siglo XIX* (Madrid, 1881).

Oulibicheff, Alexander Dmitrievich, Russian government official and writer on music; b. Dresden, April 13, 1794; d. Lukino, near Nizhny-Novgorod, Feb. 5, 1858. He studied violin at home in Dresden, where his father was Russian ambassador; was educated in Germany. When the family returned to Russia in 1810, he was employed in the Ministry of Finance (1812), and later in the Ministry of Foreign Affairs (1816–30). He was the ed. of the periodical *Journal de St. Petersbourg* (1812–30); retired to his estate at Lukino in 1841. His greatest admiration was for Mozart, which resulted in his magnum opus, *Nouvelle biographie de Mozart, suivie d'un aperçu sur l'histoire générale de la musique et de l'analyse des principales oeuvres de Mozart* (3 vols., Moscow, 1843; 2nd Ger. tr., Stuttgart, 1859; Russian tr., Moscow, 1890). By way of praising Mozart, he inserted deprecating remarks on Beethoven's later style; when he was taken to task for this lack of appreciation (by Lenz and others), he publ. *Beethoven, ses critiques et ses glossateurs* (Leipzig and Paris, 1857), in which he emphatically reiterated his sharp criticism of Beethoven's harmonic and formal procedures.

Oury, Anna Caroline (née **de Belleville**), German pianist and composer; b. Landshut, June 24, 1808; d. Munich, July 22, 1880. Her father, a French nobleman, was director of the Bavarian Court Opera in Munich. She studied with Czerny in Vienna; made her debut there; then gave concerts in Munich and in Paris; settled for many years in London, where she married the violinist **Antonio James Oury** in 1831; toured with him in Russia, Germany, Austria, and France. She wrote a number of piano pieces in the salon style, of which nearly 200 were publ.

Oury, Antonio James, English violinist of Italian descent; b. London, 1800; d. Norwich, July 25, 1883. After studying violin at an early age with his father, he took lessons with Mori, Spagnoletti, and Kiesewetter; later studied violin with Baillot, Kreutzer, and Lafont and conducting with Fétis in Paris. He made his London debut at a benefit concert for Kiesewetter's widow and children (Feb. 20, 1828), and later that year played at a Phil. Soc. concert; also was active as a theater musician. After marrying the pianist and composer **Anna Caroline** (née **de Belleville**) **Oury** (1831), he toured widely with her in Europe until 1847; also was a prof. at London's Royal Academy of Music.

Ouseley, Sir Frederick (Arthur) Gore, English organist, pianist, music theorist, and composer; b. London, Aug. 12, 1825; d. Hereford, April 6, 1889. He was the son of Sir Gore Ouseley, ambassador to Persia and Russia. He studied classics and theology with James Joyce, vicar of Dorking (1840–43); inherited his father's title of baronet (1844) and his considerable wealth; completed his education at Christ Church, Oxford (B.A., 1846; M.A., 1849; D.Mus., 1854). He was ordained a priest in 1849; was curate at St. Barnabas, Pimlico (1849–51); founded the College of St. Michael and All Angels, Tenbury (1854), serving as warden and vicar of the new parish; was also made precentor of Hereford Cathedral (1855), and later canon residentiary there (1886); likewise was prof. of music at the Univ. of Oxford (1855–89). He was a fine organist, and excelled in fugal improvisation. Among his compositions are an opera, *L'isola disabitata* (1834), and other secular vocal works, 3 overtures, 2 oratorios, numerous anthems, church services, chamber music, organ works, and piano pieces. He publ. *A Treatise on Harmony* (1868); *A Treatise on Counterpoint, Canon, and Fugue, based on Cherubini* (1869); *A Treatise on Musical Form and General Composition* (1875). He left his fine music library to St. Michael's College, Tenbury. **BIBL.:** F. Havergal, *Memorials of F.A.G. O., Bart.* (London, 1889); F. Joyce, *Life of Rev. Sir F.A.G. O., Bart., etc.* (London, 1896); H. Colles, "Sir F. O. and his Foundation," in M. Alderson and H. Colles, *History of St. Michael's College, Tenbury* (London, 1943); W. Shaw, ed., *Sir F. O. and St Michael's, Tenbury: A Chapter in the History of English Church Music and Ecclesiology* (Birmingham, 1988).

Ousset, Cécile, French pianist; b. Tarbes, March 3, 1936. A child prodigy, she made her public debut when she was only 5; studied with Marcel Ciampi at the Paris Cons., where she graduated with the premier prix at age 14; subsequently toured throughout the world with notable success, excelling in the Romantic and impressionist repertoire.

Ovchinnikov, Viacheslav, Russian conductor and composer; b. Voronezh, May 29, 1936. He studied composition with Khrennikov at the Moscow Cons., graduating in 1962; also studied conducting with Lev Ginzburg; upon graduation he conducted various orchs. in Moscow and on Soviet radio, television, etc. He composed an opera, *On the Dawn of Misty Youth* (1974–78); ballet, *Sulamith* (1962); oratorio, *Hymn to the Fatherland* (1974); for Orch.: heroic poem, *Yuri Gagarin* (1974); 3 syms. (1956, 1973, 1978); 6 symphonic suites (1955–72); *Elegy in Memory of Rachmaninoff* (1973); also made orch. arrangements of Rachmaninoff's piano works; wrote the background score for the film *War and Peace* (1961–67) and other film music; also choruses, songs, piano pieces.

Overton, Hall (Franklin), American composer; b. Bangor, Mich., Feb. 23, 1920; d. N.Y., Nov. 24, 1972. He studied piano at the Chicago Musical College; served in the U.S. Army overseas (1942–45). After World War II, he studied composition with Persichetti at the Juilliard School of Music, N.Y., graduating in 1951; also took private lessons with Wallingford Riegger and Darius Milhaud. At the same time, he filled professional engagements as a jazz pianist and contributed to the magazine *Jazz Today*. He was awarded 2 Guggenheim fellowships (1955, 1957); also taught at Juilliard (1960–71), the New School for Social Research in N.Y. (1962–66), and at the Yale Univ. School of Music (1970–71). **WORKS: OPERAS:** *The Enchanted Pear Tree*, after Boccaccio's *Decameron* (N.Y., Feb. 7, 1950); *Pietro's Petard* (N.Y., June 1963); *Huckleberry Finn*, after Mark Twain (N.Y., May 20, 1971). **ORCH.:** 2 syms.: No. 1 for Strings (1955); No. 2 (1962); *Interplay* (1964); *Sonorities* (1964); *Rhythms* for Violin and Orch. (1965); *Pulsations* for Chamber Orch. (1972). **CHAMBER:** 3 string quartets (1950, 1954, 1967); String Trio (1957); Viola Sonata (1960); Cello Sonata (1960); various piano works, including *Polarities* Nos. 1 (1959) and 2 (1971), and a Sonata (1963); songs.

Owen, Morfydd Llwyn, Welsh composer, pianist, and singer; b. Treforest, Oct. 1, 1891; d. Gowerton, near Swansea, Sept. 7, 1918. She studied with David Evans at the Univ. of South Wales in Cardiff (B.M., 1912), then with F. Corder at the Royal Academy of Music in London (1912–17), where she later taught. On Feb. 4, 1917, she married Ernest Jones, the Welsh disciple and biographer of Sigmund Freud. Her early death from complications following an operation for appendicitis was greatly lamented, for she had already established herself as a promising composer of vocal works. Her Nocturne for Orch. received the Lucas Prize in Composition from the Royal Academy of Music. She appeared frequently at the semi-annual Eisteddfods, both as a vocalist and as a composer. A 4-vol. ed. of her works, containing a biographical memoir by Jones, was publ. in London (1924). **WORKS: ORCH.:** *Ave Maria* for Soprano, Chorus, and Orch. (1912); Nocturne (1913; Dallas, Tex., June 23, 1987); *Choric Songs* for Chorus and Orch. (1913); *Morfa Rhuddlan*, tone poem (1914); *Towards the Unknown Region*, vocal scena after Walt Whitman for Tenor and Orch. (1915); *The Passing of Branwen* (1917). **CHAMBER:** Romance for Violin and Piano (1911); Piano Trio (1912). **PIANO:** Sonata (1910); Étude (1911); Rhapsody in C-sharp minor (1911); *Prelude after the Style of Bach* (1912); *Fantasie appassionata* (1912); Rhapsodie (1913); Prelude (1913); 3 preludes: *Waiting for Eirlys, Beti Bwt*, and *Nant-y-ffrith* (1914–15); *Preludio e Fuga grotesca* (1914); humoresque, *Little Eric* (1915); *Talyllyn* (1916); 3 Welsh Impressions: *Llanbynmair, Glantaf*, and *Beti Bwt* (1917). **CHORAL:** *The Refugee*, after Schiller (1910); *Fierce Raged the Tempest*, after Thring (1911); *Sweet and Low*, after Tennyson (1911); *Jubilate* (1913); also *Pro Patria*, cantata (1915); songs; hymns. **BIBL.:** L. Haydn, "M.L. O. (1891–1918)," *Welsh Music* (Spring 1918); K. Jones, "The Enigma of M. O.," ibid. (Winter 1975–76); V. Brome, *Ernest Jones: Freud's Alter Ego* (N.Y., 1983); R. Davies, "To Our Lady of Sorrows: A Visit to M.," *Welsh Music* (Winter 1988–89).

Owen, Richard, American lawyer, judge, and composer; b. N.Y., Dec. 11, 1922. He graduated from Dartmouth College in 1947 and from Harvard Law School in 1950; subsequently he served as a senior trial attorney, and then was appointed to the bench by President Nixon to the U.S. District Court in N.Y. (1974). In between he attended night school at the Mannes School of Music, took courses in harmony and counterpoint with Vittorio Giannini and Robert Starer, and attended the Berkshire Music Center at Tanglewood; in 1986 he ran in (and finished) the N.Y. Marathon. He wrote several operas deeply influenced by Puccini and Menotti, including *Dismissed with Prejudice* (1956), *A Moment of War* (1958), *A Fisherman Called Peter* (1965), *Mary Dyer* (dealing with a woman Quaker who was hanged in Boston on June 1, 1660; N.Y., June 12,

1976, with Owen's wife singing the title role), *The Death of the Virgin* (N.Y., March 31, 1983), *Abigail Adams* (N.Y., March 18, 1987), and the children's opera *Tom Sawyer* (N.Y., April 2, 1989).

BIBL.: C. Mann, "With Libretto and Justice for All," *Pursuits* (Spring 1988).

Owens, "Buck" (Alvis Edgar, Jr.), American country-music singer, guitarist, and songwriter; b. Sherman, Tex., Aug. 12, 1929. He took up the piano in his youth, and then the electric guitar; he began playing in honky-tonks when he was 16, and later established himself as one of the most successful country-music entertainers; made many appearances on radio, television, and on tours. He was co-host (with Roy Clark) of the inane but highly successful "Hee Haw" television program (1969–86).

Ozawa, Seiji, brilliant Japanese conductor; b. Fenytien, China (of Japanese parents), Sept. 1, 1935. His father was a Buddhist, his mother a Christian. The family went back to Japan in 1944, at the end of the Japanese occupation of Manchuria. Ozawa began to study piano; at 16 he enrolled at the Toho School of Music in Tokyo, where he studied composition and conducting; one of his teachers, Hideo Saito, profoundly influenced his development as a musician; he graduated in 1959 with 1st prizes in composition and conducting. By that time he had already conducted concerts with the NHK (Japan Broadcasting Corp.) Sym. Orch. and the Japan Phil.; upon Saito's advice, he went to Europe; to defray his expenses he became a motor-scooter salesman for a Japanese firm, and promoted the product in Italy and France. In 1959 he won 1st prize at the international competition for conductors in Besançon, and was befriended by Charles Munch and Eugène Bigot; he then studied conducting with Bigot in Paris. Munch arranged for Ozawa to go to the U.S. and to study conducting at the Berkshire Music Center in Tanglewood; in 1960 he won its Koussevitzky Prize, and was awarded a scholarship to work with Herbert von Karajan and the Berlin Phil. Leonard Bernstein heard him in Berlin and engaged him as an assistant conductor of the N.Y. Phil. On April 14, 1961, he made his 1st appearance with the orch. at Carnegie Hall; later that year, he accompanied Bernstein and the orch. on its tour of Japan. In 1962 he was invited to return as a guest conductor of the NHK Sym. Orch., but difficulties arose between him and the players, who objected to being commanded in an imperious manner by one of their own countrymen; still, he succeeded in obtaining engagements with other Japanese orchs., which he conducted on his periodic visits to his homeland.

After serving as sole assistant conductor of the N.Y. Phil. (1964–65), Ozawa's career advanced significantly; from 1964 to 1968 he was music director of the Ravinia Festival, the summer home of the Chicago Sym. Orch.; in 1969 he served as its principal guest conductor; from 1965 to 1969 he also was music director of the Toronto Sym. Orch., which he took

to England in 1965. From 1970 to 1976 he was music director of the San Francisco Sym. Orch., and then its music adviser (1976–77); took it on an extensive tour of Europe, garnering exceptional critical acclaim. Even before completing his tenure in San Francisco, he had begun a close association with the Boston Sym. Orch.; with Gunther Schuller, he became co-artistic director of its Berkshire Music Center in 1970; in 1972 he assumed the post of music adviser of the Boston Sym. Orch., and in 1973 he became its music director, and sole artistic director of the Berkshire Music Center, an astonishing event in American music annals, marking the 1st time an oriental musician was chosen solely by his merit to head the Boston Sym. Orch., which was for years since its foundation the exclusive preserve of German, and later French and Russian, conductors. In 1976 Ozawa took the Boston Sym. Orch. on a tour of Europe; in 1978 he escorted it to Japan, where those among Japanese musicians who had been skeptical about his abilities greeted his spectacular ascendance with national pride. Another unprecedented event took place in the spring of 1979, when Ozawa traveled with the Boston Sym. Orch. to the People's Republic of China on an official cultural visit; in Aug. 1979 Ozawa and the orch. went on a tour of European music festivals. The centennial of the Boston Sym. Orch. in 1981 was marked by a series of concerts, under Ozawa's direction, which included appearances in 14 American cities and a tour of Japan, France, Germany, Austria, and England.

With dormant racial prejudices finally abandoned in American society, Ozawa's reputation rose to universal recognition of his remarkable talent. He proved himself a consummate master of orchestral playing, equally penetrating in the classical repertoire as in the works of modern times; his performances of such demanding scores as Mahler's 8th Sym. and Schoenberg's *Gurrelieder* constituted proofs of his commanding technical skill, affirmed *a fortiori* by his assured presentation of the rhythmically and contrapuntally intricate 4th Sym. of Charles Ives. All these challenging scores Ozawa consuetudinarily conducted from memory, an astonishing feat in itself. He was married twice: 1st to the Japanese pianist Kyoko Edo, and 2nd, to a Eurasian, Vera Ilyan. He received an honorary doctorate in music from the Univ. of San Francisco in 1971, and one from the New England Cons. of Music in 1982. His remarkable career was the subject of the documentary film "Ozawa," which was telecast by PBS in 1987.

Ozim, Igor, Slovenian violinist and teacher; b. Ljubljana, May 9, 1931. He studied with Leon Pfeifer at the Ljubljana Academy of Music and with Rostal in London (1949–51), then won the Flesch (1951) and Munich (1953) competitions. He toured widely in Europe and the U.S.; also taught at the Ljubljana Academy of Music (1960–63) and then at the Cologne Hochschule für Musik. In 1990 he served on the jury of the International Violin Competition of Indianapolis. He was a notable advocate of contemporary music.

P

Paap, Wouter, eminent Dutch musicologist and composer; b. Utrecht, May 7, 1908; d. Lage Vuursche (Baarn), Oct. 7, 1981. He studied piano and music theory at the Utrecht School of Music (1928–32); taught at the Netherland's Inst. for Catholic Church Music (1934–47); was founder-ed. of the journal *Mens en Melodie* (1946–75).

WRITINGS: *Anton Bruckner* (Bilthoven, 1936); *Toscanini* (Amsterdam, 1938); *Mens en melodie: Inleiding tot de muziek* (Utrecht, 1940); *Ludwig van Beethoven* (Amsterdam, 1941); *Moderne kerkmuziek in Nederland* (with E. Reeser; Bilthoven, 1942); *De symfonieën van Beethoven* (Utrecht, 1946); *Die kunst van het moduleren* (Utrecht, 1948); *Eduard van Beinum* (Baarn, 1956); *De symfonie* (Bilthoven, 1957); ed. *Algemene muziekencyclopedie* (with A. Corbet; 6 vols., Amsterdam, 1957–63; suppl. ed. by J. Robijns, Ghent, 1972); *Willem Mengelberg* (Amsterdam and Brussels, 1960); *Muziek, moderne en klassiek* (Utrecht, 1961); *Mozart: Portret van een muziekgenie* (Utrecht, 1962); *Honderd jaar muziekonderwijs te Utrecht* (Utrecht, 1974); *Een eeuw koninklijke Nederlandse toonkunstenaars vereniging* (Amsterdam, 1975).

WORKS: *Sterre der zee* for Soprano, Chorus, and Orch. (1937); Sinfonietta for Chamber Orch. (1938); *Wals* for Chamber Orch. (1940); *Declamatorium* for Recitation with Orch. (1940); *Passacaglia* for Orch. (1943); *Muziek ter Bruiloft,* solo cantata for Tenor and Orch. (1945); *Studentenmuziek* for String Orch. (1948); *Guirlanden van Muziek* for String Orch. (1951); *Ballet Suite* for Chamber Orch. (1953); *Luchtige suite* for Carillon (1955); *Overture Electora* for Orch. (1956); *5 Liederen* for Voice and Orch. (1956); *Trompetten en klaretten,* 3 pieces for Wind Orch. (1960); Sonatina for Carillon (1963); various pieces for Wind Instruments.

Pablo (Costales), Luis (Alfonso) de, Spanish composer; b. Bilbao, Jan. 28, 1930. He studied jurisprudence at Madrid Univ., receiving a law degree in 1952. He attended the Cons. of Madrid; traveled to Paris, where he received musical advice from Messiaen and Boulez; also took courses at the summer seminars for new music at Darmstadt. Returning to Spain, he organized the modern performance groups Tiempo y Música (1958–65) and Alea; also founded an electronic music studio. He was a visiting Slee Prof. at the State Univ. of N.Y. in Buffalo (1973–74); then became prof. of contemporary musical analysis at the Univs. of Ottawa and Montreal (1974); was made president of the Spanish section of the ISCM in 1981. In his youth he followed the precepts of the national school, with the music of Manuel de Falla as principal influence, but soon he adopted hyperserial techniques, in which whole tonal complexes, chords, or groups of chords become thematic units; similarly, dynamic processes assume the role of compositional determinants, eventually attaining the ultimate libertarianism in promiscuous cross-fertilization of all media, all styles, and all techniques of musical composition.

WORKS: *Coral* for Woodwinds (1953); *Comentarios* for Soprano, Piccolo, Vibraphone, and Double Bass (1956); Clarinet Quintet (1954); 2 string quartets (1955, 1957); *Elegía* for String Orch. (1956); Harpsichord Concerto (1956); *Radial* for 24 Instruments (1960); *Polar* for Voice, Saxophone, Bass Clarinet, and Percussion (1961); *4 Inventions* for Orch. (1955–62); *Tom-*

beau for Orch. (1963); 6 *Modulos:* No. 1, for Chamber Ensemble (1965); No. 2, for Double Orch. (1966); No. 3, for 17 Instruments (1967); No. 4, *Ejercicio,* for String Quartet (1965); No. 5, for Organ (1967); No. 6, *Parafrasis,* for 24 Instruments (1968); *Sinfonías* for 17 Wind Instruments (1955–66); *Cesuras* for Double Trio of Woodwinds and Strings (1964); *Imaginario I* for Harpsichord and 3 Percussionists (1967); *Imaginario II* for Orch. (1967); *Heterogéneo* for 2 Narrators, Hammond Organ, and Orch. (1968; Donaueschingen, Oct. 18, 1970); *Protocolo,* opera (1968; Paris, Oct. 23, 1970); *Quasi una fantasia* for String Sextet and Orch. (1968; Paris, April 17, 1972); *Por diversos motivos* for Voice, Projected Images, and Chamber Orch. (1969); *Oroïtaldi* for Orch. (1971); *Eléphants ivres* (Drunken Elephants), in 4 parts, for differing orch. formations (1972–73); *Je mange, tu manges* for Small Orch. and Tape (1972; Royan, April 14, 1973); *Masque* for Flute, Clarinet, Piano, and Percussion (1973); *Vielleicht* for 6 Percussionists (1973); *Dejame hablar* for 11 Strings (1974); *Homogeneo* for 32 Instruments (1974); *Al Son que Tocan* for 8 Instruments, Voice, and Tape (1974); *Portrait imaginé* for 12 Voices, 18 Instruments, and Tape (1975); *Zurezko Olerkia* for 8 Voices, 4 Percussionists, and Txalaparta (1975); *Credo* for Double Wind Quintet (1976); *Tinieblas del agua* for Orch. (Metz, Nov. 18, 1978); String Trio (1978); 2 piano concertos: No. 1 (1978–79; Madrid, March 1, 1980) and No. 2, with Strings and 2 Marimbas (1979); *Sonido de la guerra* for Soprano, Tenor, Small Female Chorus, and 6 Instruments (1980); *Kiu,* opera (1979–82; Madrid, April 1983); *Cinco meditaciones* for 15 Instruments (1983–84); *Seremata* for Winds and Chorus (1984–85); *Fragmento* for String Quartet (1985).

Pabst, Louis, German pianist, teacher, and composer, brother of **Paul Pabst;** b. Königsberg, July 18, 1846; d. Moscow, 1903. He made his 1st appearance as a pianist in his native city in 1862; was in England from 1867 to 1869; then established a music school in Riga (1869–75); subsequently toured Australia; there he founded the Academy of Music of Melbourne (1887); revisited London in 1894; in 1897, went again to Russia; became an instructor at the music school of the Phil. Society in Moscow in 1899; in 1903, became court councillor of the Ministry of the Interior. He publ. a number of piano pieces.

Pabst, Paul, German pianist and teacher, brother of **Louis Pabst;** b. Königsberg, May 27, 1854; d. Moscow, June 9, 1897. He studied with Liszt; went to Russia, and taught at the Moscow Cons. He made a number of effective paraphrases for piano of operatic works; particularly well known was the one of *Eugene Onegin.*

Pacchiarotti, Gasparo, famous Italian castrato soprano; b. Fabriano, near Ancona (baptized), May 21, 1740; d. Padua, Oct. 28, 1821. He studied with Bertoni at San Marco in Venice, where he was principal soloist (1765–68); was primo uomo in Palermo (1770–71) before singing in Naples (1771–76). After appearing throughout Italy, he was engaged for the inaugural operation productions at Milan's La Scala (Aug.–Sept. 1778). He sang at the King's Theatre in London (1778–80), returning there 1781–84; also appeared at the Tuileries before the French court (1782). Having served as primo uomo at Venice's Teatro S. Benedetto (1784–91), he once more sang in London (1791), appearing in concert as well as opera. He sang in the inaugural season at Venice's Teatro La Fenice (1792–93) before retiring to his estate in Padua. He later sang for Napoleon in Padua (1796) and at Bertoni's funeral at San Marco (June 28, 1814). Pacchiarotti was acclaimed as the greatest castrato of his day, his voice ranging from *c″* to B flat. A. Calegari publ. *Modi generali del canto premessi alle maniere parziali onde adornace o rifiorice le nude o semplici melodie o cantilene giusta il metodo di Gasparo Pacchiarotti* (Milan, 1836).
BIBL.: G. Pacchiarotti (his adopted son), *Cenni biografici intorno a G. P.* (Padua, 1844); R. Sassi, *Un celebre musico fabrianese, G. P.* (*col testamento*) (Fabriano, 1935); A. Heriot, *The Castrati in Opera* (London, 1956).

Pacchierotti, Ubaldo, Italian composer and conductor; b. Cervarese-Croce (Padua), Oct. 30, 1875; d. Milan, April 18, 1916. He studied at the Cons. S. Pietro a Majella in Naples; conducted in Livorno and Buenos Aires.
WORKS: Operas: *La lampada* (Buenos Aires, 1899); *L'albatro* (Milan, 1905); *Eidelberga mia!* (Genoa, Feb. 27, 1908); *Il Santo* (Turin, 1913); and other works.
BIBL.: C. Rietmann, "U. P.," *Pensiero Musicale* (Nov.–Dec. 1926).

Pachelbel, Charles Theodore (actually, **Carl Theodor**), German-American organist, harpsichordist, teacher, and composer, son of **Johann** and brother of **Wilhelm Hieronymus Pachelbel;** b. Stuttgart (baptized), Nov. 24, 1690; d. Charleston, S.C. (buried), Sept. 15, 1750. He emigrated to Boston c.1732; served as organist at Trinity Church in Newport, R.I.; then went to N.Y. and appeared in concerts as a harpsichordist (Jan. 21 and March 8, 1736); then was organist at St. Philip's Church in Charleston (1737–50); gave his 1st public concert in his home there (Nov. 22, 1737); founded his own singing school (1749). His only extant work, a *Magnificat* for 8 Voices (modern ed., N.Y., 1937), was written before his emigration to the U.S.
BIBL.: O. Sonneck, *Early Concert-Life in America* (1731–1800) (Leipzig, 1907); J. Howard, *Our American Music* (N.Y., 1931; 4th ed., rev., 1965); V. Redway, "A New York Concert in 1736," *Musical Quarterly* (April 1936); idem, "C.T. P.," *Musical Emigrant," Journal of the American Musicological Society* (Spring 1952); R. Stevenson, "Caribbean Music History," *Inter-American Music Review,* IV/1 (1981).

Pachelbel, Johann, celebrated German organist, pedagogue, and composer, father of **Charles Theodore (Carl Theodor)** and **Wilhelm Hieronymus Pachelbel;** b. Nuremberg (baptized), Sept. 1, 1653; d. there (buried), March 9, 1706. He studied music in Nuremberg with Heinrich Schwemmer; received instruction in composition and instrumental performance from G.C. Wecker; pursued his academic studies at the local St. Lorenz school; also attended the lectures at the Auditorium Aegidianum. He then took courses briefly at the Univ. of Altdorf (1669–70), and served as organist at the Lorenzkirche there. He subsequently was accepted as a scholarship student at the Gymnasium Poeticum in Regensburg, and took private music lessons with Kaspar Prentz. In 1673 he went to Vienna as deputy organist at St. Stephen's Cathedral. In 1677 he assumed the position of court organist in Eisenach. In 1678 he became organist at the Protestant Predigerkirche in Erfurt. It was in Erfurt that he established his reputation as a master organist, composer, and teacher. He was a friend of the Bach family, and was the teacher of Johann Christoph Bach, who in turn taught Johann Sebastian Bach. On Oct. 25, 1681, Pachelbel married Barbara Gabler; she and their infant son died during the plague of 1683. He then married Judith Drommer on Aug. 24, 1684; they had 5 sons and 2 daughters. In addition to Carl and Wilhelm, their son Johann Michael became an instrument maker and their daughter Amalie became a painter. In 1690 he accepted an appointment as Württemberg court musician and organist in Stuttgart. However, with the French invasion in the fall of 1692, he fled to Nuremberg, and in Nov. of that year he became town organist in Gotha. In 1695 he succeeded Wecker as organist at St. Sebald in Nuremberg, a position he held until his death. Pachelbel was one of the most significant predecessors of Johann Sebastian Bach. His liturgical organ music was of the highest order, particularly his splendid organ chorales. His non-liturgical keyboard music was likewise noteworthy, especially his fugues and variations (of the latter, his *Hexachordum Apollinis* of 1699 is extraordinary). He was equally gifted as a composer of vocal music. His motets, sacred concertos, and concertato settings of the Magnificat are fine examples of German church music. He was a pioneer in notational symbolism of intervals, scales, and pitch levels arranged to correspond to the meaning of the words. Thus, his setting of the motet *Durch Adams Fall* is accomplished by a falling figure in the bass; exaltation is expressed by a rising series of arpeggios in a major key; steadfast faith is conveyed by a repeated note; satanic evil is translated into an ominous figuration of a broken diminished-seventh-chord. Generally speaking, joyful moods are portrayed by major keys, mournful states of soul by minor keys, a practice which became a standard mode of expression through the centuries.

WORKS: In addition to various separate editions of his works, major publications include M. Seiffert and A. Sandberger, eds., *Johann Pachelbel: Klavierwerke*, in Denkmäler der Tonkunst in Bayern, II, Jg. II/1 (1901); M. Seiffert, ed., *Johann Pachelbel: Orgelkompositionen*, in Denkmäler der Tonkunst in Bayern, VI, Jg. IV/1 (1903); K. Matthaei and W. Stockmeier, eds., *Johann Pachelbel: Ausgewählte Orgelwerke* (vols. 1–4 by Matthaei, Kassel, 1928–36; vols. 5–6 by Stockmeier, Kassel, 1972–74).

CHORALES FOR ORGAN: 8 *Choräle zum Praeambulieren* (Nuremberg, 1693). Fugues: *Ach Gott, vom Himmel sieh darein; Ach Herr, mich armen Sünder; Christe, der du bist Tag und Licht; Da Jesus an dem Kreuze stund* (may not be by Pachelbel); *Der Herr ist mein getreuer Hirt* (2 versions); *Dies sind die heil'gen zehn Gebot; Es woll uns Gott genädig sein* (2 versions); *In dich hab' ich gehoffet, Herr; Wo Gott zum Haus nicht gibt sein Gunst.* Three-part Cantus firmus: *Allein Gott in der Höh sei Ehr* (may not be by Pachelbel); *Christ unser Herr zum Jordan kam; Durch Adams Fall; Erbarm dich mein, o Herre Gott; Erhalt uns Herr, bei deinem Wort* (may not be by Pachelbel); *Gelobet seist du, Jesu Christ; Gott Vater, der du deine Sonn; Herr Gott, dich loben alle wir; Ich hab' mein' Sach' Gott heimgestellt; Ich ruf zu dir; Jesus Christus, unser Heiland, der den Tod* (2 versions); *Kommt her zu mir, spricht Gottes Sohn; Lob sei Gott in des Himmels Thron; Meine Seele erhebt den Herren* [tonus peregrinus] (2 versions); *Nun freut euch, lieben Christen g'mein'; O Mensch bewein dein Sünde gross; Vom Himmel hoch da komm ich her; Warum betrübst du dich, mein Herz; Was mein Gott will, das g'scheh allzeit; Wenn wir in höchsten Nöten sein; Wie schön leuchtet der Morgenstern; Wo Got der Herr nicht bei uns hält* (2 versions); *Wo Gott zum Haus nicht gibt sein Gunst.* Four-part Cantus firmus: *Gott hat das Evangelium; Gott Vater, der du deine Sonn'; Komm, Gott Schöpfer, heiliger Geist; Mag ich Unglück nicht widerstahn; Nun lasst uns Gott dem Herren; Vater unser im Himmelreich.* Combination-form: *Ach Gott, vom Himmel sieh darein; Ach Herr, mich armen Sünder; Ach wie elend ist unsre Zeit; Allein Gott in der Höh sei Ehr* (may not be by Pachelbel); *An Wasserflüssen Babylon* (2 versions); *Auf meinen lieben Gott; Christ lag in Todesbanden; Der Tag der ist so freudenreich; Durch Adams Fall; Ein feste Burg; Es spricht der Unweisen Mund wohl; Herr Christ, der einig Gott's Sohn; Herr Jesu Christ, ich weiss gar wohl; Ich ruf zu dir; Nun komm der Heiden Heiland; O Lamm Gottes unschuldig; Vater unser im Himmelreich; Vom Himmel hoch da komm ich her; Warum betrübst du dich, mein Herz; Wenn mein Stündlein vorhanden ist; Wenn wir in höchsten Nöten sein; Wo Gott der Herr nicht bei uns hält.* Bicinia: *Durch Adams Fall; Es spricht der unweisen Mund wohl* (may not be by Pachelbel); *Jesus Christus, unser Heiland, der von uns; Was mein Gott will, das g'scheh allzeit.* Other kinds: *Allein zu dir, Herr Jesu Christ* (2 versions); *Nun lob, mein' Seel', den Herren; Wir glauben all' an einen Gott.* He also composed 95 Magnificat fugues. His non-liturgical music for organ includes 26 fugues, 16 toccatas, 7 preludes, 6 fantasias, 6 ciacconas, 3 ricercari, etc. Additional keyboard music includes his arias with variations known as *Hexachordum Apollinis, sex arias exhibens . . . quam singulis suae sunt subjectae variationes* (Nuremberg, 1699), about 17 suites, and the following chorale variations: *Ach was soll ich Sünder machen; Alle Menschen müssen sterben; Christus, der ist mein Leben; Freu dich sehr, o meine Seele* [*Treuer Gott, ich muss dir klagen*]; *Herzlich tut mich verlangen; Was Gott tut, das ist wohlgetan; Werde munter, mein Gemüte.*

CHAMBER: *Canon and Gigue* in D major for 3 Violins and Basso Continuo (the *Canon* is one of his most famous works, being extremely popular with modern audiences; it has been publ. and republ. in numerous arrangements for various instru-

ments); *Musicalische Ergötzung bestehend in 6 verstimmten Partien* for 2 Violins and Basso Continuo (Nuremberg, 1695); *Partie* in G major for 2 Violins, 2 Violas, Cello, and Basso Continuo.

VOCAL: Motets for 2 4-part choruses: *Der Herr ist König, darum toben die Völker; Der Herr ist König und herrlich geschmückt; Gott ist unser Zuversicht; Jauchzet dem Herrn; Jauchzet Gott, alle Lande; Nun danket alle Gott; Singet dem Herrn; Tröste uns Gott;* also the unfinished *Der Herr ist König und herrlich geschmückt* for 5 Voices and Basso Continuo; in addition, 2 Latin motets: *Exsurgat Deus* and *Paratum cor meum.* Sacred concertos: *Christ lag in Todesbanden* for 4 Voices, 2 Violins, 3 Violas, and Basso Continuo; *Der Name des Herren sei gelobet* for 3 Voices, 2 Violins, and Basso Continuo; *Gott ist unser Zuversicht* for 4 Voices, 2 Violins, 2 Violas, Bassoon, and Basso Continuo; *Gott sei uns gnädig* for 5 Voices, 5 Trumpets, Timpani, 2 Violins, 4 Violas, Bassoon, Basso Continuo, and Organ; *Jauchzet dem Herrn, alle Welt* for 5 Voices, 2 Oboes, 2 Violins, 3 Violas, Viole, and Basso Continuo; *Jauchzet dem Herrn, alle Welt* for 5 Voices, 4 Trumpets, Timpani, 2 Violins, 3 Violas, Bassoon, and Basso Continuo; *Kommt her zu mir* for 4 Voices, 2 Violins, 2 Cornets, and Basso Continuo; *Lobet den Herrn in seinem Heiligtum* for 5 Voices, 2 Flutes, Bassoon, 5 Trumpets, Trombone, Timpani, Cymbal, Harp, 2 Violins, 3 Violas, Basso Continuo, and Organ; *Meine Sünde betrüben mich* for Voice, Chorus of 4 Voices, 4 Viole da Gamba, Bassoon/Viole, and Basso Continuo (fragment only extant); etc. Arias: *Auf, werte Gäst* for Voice, 2 Violins, and Basso Continuo; *Augen, streuet Perlen-Tränen* for 2 Voices, 4 Violas, Viola pro Basso, and Organ; *Das angenehmste Wetter* for Voice, 2 Violins, and Basso Continuo (unfinished); *Das Gewitter* for Voice, 2 Violins, and Basso Continuo; *Das Jahr fängt an* for Voice, 2 Violins, 2 Violas, and Basso Continuo; *Der Widder Abrahams* for 2 Voices, 2 Violins, and Basso Continuo; *Die freuderfüllten Abendstunden* for Voice, 2 Violins, 2 Violas, and Basso Continuo; *Es muss die Sinne ja erfreuen* for Voice, 2 Violins, and Basso Continuo; *Geliebtes Vaterherz* for Voice, 2 Violins, 2 Violas, and Basso Continuo/Viole; *Guter Walter unsers Rats* for Voice, 2 Violins, 2 Violas, and Basso Continuo; *Hör, grosser Mäcenat* for Voice, 2 Violins, 2 Violas, and Basso Continuo; *Mäcenas lebet noch* for Voice, 2 Violins, 2 Violas, Trumpet, and Basso Continuo; *Mein Leben, dessen Kreuz* for Voice, 4 Violas, Viola pro Basso, and Organ; *O grosses Musenlicht* for Voice, 2 Viole da Gamba, and Basso Continuo; *So ist denn dies der Tag* for Voice, Chorus of 4 Voices, 2 Violins, 3 Violas, 4 Trumpets, Timpani, and Basso Continuo; *So ist denn nur die Treu* for 2 Voices, Chorus of 5 Voices, 2 Flutes, 2 Violins, 3 Violas, and Basso Continuo; *Voller Wonder, voller Kunst* for 4 Voices and Basso Continuo (unfinished); *Wie nichtig, ach* for Voice, 3 Violas, and Basso Continuo; *Wohl euch, die ihr in Gott verliebt* for 4 Voices (unfinished). Music for Vespers: *Ingressus* in C major for 4 Voices, 2 Violins, Viola, and Basso Continuo; *Ingressus* in C major for 4 Voices, 3 Violas, Bassoon, and Basso Continuo; *Ingressus* in C major for 5 Voices, 4 Trumpets, Timpani, 2 Violins, 3 Violas, Bassoon, Basso Continuo, and Organ; *Ingressus* in D major for 4 Voices, 2 Violins, Viola, and Basso Continuo; *Ingressus* in D major for 4 Voices, 2 Violins, 3 Violas, Bassoon, and Basso Continuo; *Ingressus* in D minor for 5 Voices, 2 Violins, 3 Violas, Bassoon, and Basso Continuo; *Ingressus* in F major for 5 Voices, 2 Violins, 4 Violas, Bassoon, and Basso Continuo; *Ingressus* in G major for 4 Voices, 2 Violins, 3 Violas ad libitum, Bassoon ad libitum, and Basso Continuo; *Ingressus* in G minor for 4 Voices, 2 Violins, Bassoon, and Basso Continuo; *Ingressus* in G minor for 5 Voices, 2 Violins, Viola, 2 Viole da Gamba, Bassoon, and Basso Continuo; *Ingressus* in A major for 5 Voices, 2 Violins, 3 Violas, Bassoon, and Basso Continuo; *Ingressus* in A minor for 5 Voices, 2 Violins, 3 Violas, Bassoon, and Basso Continuo; *Magnificat* in C major for 5 Voices, 2 Oboes, 2 Violins, 3 Violas, Bassoon, and Basso Continuo; *Magnificat* in C major for 5 Voices, 4 Trumpets, Timpani, 2 Violins, Viola, 2 Viole da Gamba, Bassoon, Basso Continuo, and Organ; *Magnificat* in C major for 4 Voices, 2 Trumpets, 2 Violins, 2 Violas, and Basso Continuo; *Magnificat* in C major for 5 Voices, 4 Trumpets, Timpani, 2 Violins, Viola, 2 Viole da Gamba, Bassoon, and Basso Continuo; *Magnificat* in D major for 5 Voices, 2 Violins, 2 Cornets/Oboes, 3 Violas, Bassoon, and Basso Continuo; *Magnificat* in D major for Double Chorus of 5 Voices and Double Orch., each with 2 Violins, 3 Violas, Bassoon, and Basso Continuo; *Magnificat* in D major for 4 Voices and 4 Violas ad libitum; *Magnificat* in E-flat major for 4 Voices, 2 Violins, 3 Violas, Bassoon, Basso Continuo, and Organ; *Magnificat* in F major for 4 Voices, 2 Violins, Bassoon, and Basso Continuo; *Magnificat* in F major for 5 Voices, 2 Violins, and Basso Continuo; *Magnificat* in G major for 4 Voices, 2 Violins, and Basso Continuo; *Magnificat* in G minor for 4 Voices; *Magnificat* in B-flat major for 5 Voices, 2 Oboes, 2 Violins, 3 Violas, Bassoon, Basso Continuo, and Organ. He also composed a *Missa* in C major for 4 Voices, 2 Violins, Clarino, and Basso Continuo, and a *Missa brevis* in D major for 4 Voices.

BIBL.: J. Mattheson, *Grundlage einer Ehren-Pforte* (Hamburg, 1740; new ed. by M. Schneider, Berlin, 1910; reprint, 1969); P. Spitta, *Johann Sebastian Bach* (2 vols., Leipzig, 1873–80; Eng. tr. by C. Bell and J. Fuller Maitland, 3 vols., London, 1884–85; 2nd ed., 1899; reprint, 2 vols., N.Y., 1951); A. Ritter, "Tabulatur Buch . . . von J. P. n . . . 1704," *Monatshefte für Musikgeschichte*, VI (1874); idem, *Zur Geschichte des Orgelspiels im 14. bis zum Anfange des 18. Jahrhunderts* (Leipzig, 1884); M. Seiffert, *Geschichte der Klaviermusik* (Leipzig, 1899); M. Seiffert, "J. P.s musikalische Sterbensgedanken," *Sammelbände der Internationalen Musik-Gesellschaft*, V (1903–4); G. Beckmann, "J. P. als Kammerkomponist," *Archiv für Musikwissenschaft*, I (1918–19); F. Blume, *Die evangelische Kirchenmusik*, in Bücken's *Handbuch der Musikwissenschaft*, X (1931; 2nd ed., rev., as *Geschichte der evangelischen Kirchenmusik*, 1965; Eng. tr. as *Protestant Church Music: A History*, 1974); O. Kaul, "Zwei unbekannte Kompositionen von J. P.," *Zeitschrift für Musikwissenschaft*, XVI (1933–34); G. Frotscher, *Geschichte des Orgelspiels und der Orgelkomposition*, I (Berlin, 1935; 3rd ed., enl., 1966); E. Doflein, "P.s Kammermusik," *Zeitschrift für Hausmusik*, VII (1938); E. von Rumohr, *Der Nürnbergische Tasteninstrumentalstil im 17. Jahrhundert, dargestellt an Arie, Variation und Suite* (diss., Univ. of Münster, 1938); E. Born, *Die Variation als Grundlage handwerklicher Gestaltung im musikalischen Schaffen J. P.s* (Berlin and Frankfurt, 1941); H. Woodward, *A Study of the Tenbury Manuscripts of J. P.* (diss., Harvard Univ., 1952); K. Matthaei, "J. P.: Zu seinem 300. Geburtstag," *Musik und Gottesdienst*, VII (1953); H. Moser, "J. P.: Zur 300. Wiederkehr seines Geburtstages," *Musik und Kirche*, XXIII (1953); H. Eggebrecht, "J. P. als Vokalkomponist," *Archiv für Musikwissenschaft*, XI (1954); E. Nolte, *The Instrumental Works of J. P.* (diss., Northwestern Univ., 1954); H. Eggebrecht, "J. P.: Zu seinem 250. Todestag," *Musica*, X (1956); E. Nolte, "The Magnificat Fugues of J. P.: Alternation or Intonation?," *Journal of the American Musicological Society*, IX (1956); idem, "Classic Contract between P. and Erfurt Church," *Diapason*, XLVIII (1957); S. Orth, "J. P.: Sein Leben und Wirken in Erfurt," *Aus der Vergangenheit der Stadt Erfurt*, II/4 (1957); F. Riedel, *Quellenkündliche Beiträge zur Geschichte der Musik in der 2. Hälfte des 17. Jahrhunderts* (Kassel, 1960); H. Samuel, *The Cantata in Nuremberg during the Seventeenth Century* (diss., Cornell Univ., 1963); H. Eggebrecht, "Das Weimarer Tabulaturbuch von 1704," *Archiv für Musikwissenschaft*, XXII (1965); F. Krummacher, "Kantate und Konzert im Werk Johann P.s," *Die Musikforschung*, XX (1967).

Pachelbel, Wilhelm Hieronymus, German organist, harpsichordist, and composer, son of **Johann** and brother of **Charles Theodore (Carl Theodor) Pachelbel**; b. Erfurt (baptized), Aug. 29, 1686; d. Nuremberg, 1764. His only known teacher was his father, who gave him instruction in both keyboard instruments and composition. He is believed to have begun his career as an organist in Fürth; then was organist of the Predigerkirche in Erfurt. In 1706 he became organist of the Jakobikirche in Nuremberg; that same year was named organist

at St. Egidien there. In 1719 he became organist at St. Sebald, a post he held until his death. Little of his music is extant, all of it being for keyboard instruments. He publ. *Musicalisches Vergnügen bestehend in einem Praeludio, Fuga und Fantasia, sowohl auf die Orgel als auch auf das Clavier . . . vorgestellt und componiert* in D major (Nuremberg, 1725?) and *Praeludium und Fuga* in C major (Nuremberg, 1725?). He also composed *Fantasia super "Meine Seele, lass es gehen"; Fantasia* in B-flat major; *O Lamm Gottes unschuldig* for Clavier; *Toccata* in G major. See H.J. Moser and T. Fedtke, *Wilhelm Hieronymus Pachelbel: Gesamtausgabe der erhaltenen Werke für Orgel und Clavier* (Kassel, 1957).

BIBL.: J. Mattheson, *Grundlage einer Ehren-Pforte* (Hamburg, 1740; new ed. by M. Schneider, Berlin, 1910; reprint, 1969); A. Ritter, *Zur Geschichte des Orgelspiels im 14. bis zum Anfange des 18. Jahrhunderts* (Leipzig, 1884); M. Seiffert, *Geschichte der Klaviermusik* (Leipzig, 1899); G. Frotscher, *Geschichte des Orgelspiels und der Orgelkomposition*, I (Berlin, 1935; 3rd ed., enl., 1966); F. Riedel, *Quellenkündliche Beiträge zur Geschichte der Musik in der 2. Hälfte des 17. Jahrhunderts* (Kassel, 1960).

Pachler-Koschak, Marie Leopoldine, Austrian pianist; b. Graz, Oct. 2, 1792; d. there, April 10, 1855. She was an enthusiastic admirer of Beethoven, who wrote to her in 1817: "I have found no one, not excepting the great pianists, who interprets my compositions as well as you." In 1816 she married Dr. Karl Pachler, a lawyer in Graz. In their house Franz Schubert spent several weeks in the summer of 1827. Schubert wrote a little 4-hand march for their son, Faust Pachler, who publ. *Beethoven und M. Pachler-Koschak* (Berlin, 1866), which contains valuable details concerning Beethoven's last days.

Pachmann, Vladimir de, eccentric Russian-born Italian pianist; b. Odessa, July 27, 1848; d. Rome, Jan. 6, 1933. He received his primary music education at home from his father, an Austrian lawyer and amateur musician; his mother was Turkish. He then was a pupil of J. Dachs at the Vienna Cons. (1866–68), graduating with the Gold Medal. He began his concert career with a tour of Russia in 1869; he was 40 years old before he made a decisive impact on the international scene; his 1st American tour, in 1891, was sensationally successful, and it was in America that he began exhibiting his curious eccentricities, some of them undoubtedly calculated to produce shock effect: he made grimaces when he did not like his own playing and shouted "Bravo!" when he played a number to his satisfaction; even more bizarre was his crawling under the grand piano after the concert, claiming that he was looking for the wrong notes he had accidentally hit; all this could be explained as idiosyncratic behavior; but he also allowed himself to mutilate the music itself, by inserting arpeggios between phrases and extra chords at the end of a piece. Most American critics were outraged by his shenanigans, but some, notably Philip Hale, found mitigation in the poetic quality of his interpretations. Pachmann was particularly emotional in playing Chopin, when his facial contortions became quite obnoxious; James Huneker dubbed him "Chopinzee." Pachmann did not lack official honors; in 1885, on his tour of Denmark, he was made a Knight of the Order of Danebrog; in 1916 the Royal Phil. Society of London awarded him its Gold Medal. He made his last tour of the U.S. in 1925; spent his last years in Italy, becoming a naturalized Italian citizen in 1928. His personal life was turbulent; he married frequently (the exact number of his wives is in dispute). His 1st wife was his pupil, the Australian Maggie Oakey (1864–1952), who toured as Marguerite de Pachmann from the time of their marriage (1884) until their divorce (1895); she later married a French lawyer, becoming known as Marguerite de Pachmann-Labori. Pachmann and his 1st wife had a son, Adrian de Pachmann (c.1893–1937), who also became a pianist.

BIBL.: K. Sorabji, "P. and Chopin," *Around Music* (London, 1932).

Pacini, Giovanni, Italian composer; b. Catania, Feb. 17, 1796; d. Pescia, Dec. 6, 1867. He was a pupil of Marchesi and Padre

Mattei at Bologna, and of Furlanetto at Venice; his 1st opera was *Don Pomponio* (1813; not perf.); then came *Annetta e Lucinda* (Milan, Oct. 17, 1813); up to 1835 he had produced over 40 operas on various Italian stages, when the failure of *Carlo di Borgogna* (Feb. 21, 1835) at Venice temporarily checked the flow of dramatic composition; he went to Viareggio, near Lucca, and established a very successful school of music, for which he wrote several short treatises, *Corso teoretico-pratico di lezioni di armonia* (Milan, c.1844), and *Cenni storici sulla musica e trattato di contrappunto* (Lucca, 1864), and built a private theater. Later he removed the school to Lucca. In 1840 Pacini, who prided himself on rapid work, wrote his dramatic masterpiece, *Saffo*, in 28 days (Naples, Nov. 29, 1840). Forty more operas followed up to 1867; the best were *Medea* (Palermo, Nov. 28, 1843), *La Regina di Cipro* (Turin, Feb. 7, 1846), and *Niccolò de Lapi* (1857; Florence, Oct. 29, 1873). Pacini also wrote numerous oratorios, cantatas, masses, etc.; a *Dante* sym.; an Octet; 6 string quartets; other chamber music, vocal duets, and arias. He excelled in melodic invention, although his early style prompted Rossini to exclaim "God help us if he knew music: no one could resist him." He was also an active contributor to several musical papers; publ. memoirs, *Le mie memorie artistiche* (Florence, 1865; enlarged by Cicconetti, 1872; rev. by F. Magnani, 1875). His brother, **Emilio Pacini** (b. 1810; d. Neuilly, near Paris, Dec. 2, 1898), was a distinguished librettist.

BIBL.: G. P. (Pescia, 1896); M. Davini, *Il maestro G. P.* (Palermo, 1927); A. Cametti, "La musica teatrale a Roma cento anni fa: 'Il corsaro' di P.," *Annuario della R. accademia di Santa Cecilia* (Rome, 1931); F. Lippmann, "G. P.: Bemerkungen zum Stil seiner Opern," *Chigiana*, XXIV (1967).

Pacini, Leonardo, Italian composer; b. near Pistoia, May 26, 1885; d. Viareggio, April 13, 1937. He was a pupil of Pizzetti at Florence; in 1921, graduated from the Liceo Martini of Bologna. He was a Franciscan friar.

WORKS: OPERAS: *Alla Muda* (1924; Viareggio, 1925) and *Mirta*; operetta, *Il Pirata* (Viareggio, 1927); oratorios: *Transitus Divi Dominici* (Bologna, 1921) and *Frate Francesco* (Viareggio, 1929); cantatas: *La Sagra dei Caduti* (1922); *Portiuncola Pia*; *Clara Discipula* (Viareggio, 1924); *Sinfonia del giglio* for Chorus and Orch.; Psalms, motets, and other church music; chamber music; songs; etc.

Paciorkiewicz, Tadeusz, Polish composer and organist; b. Sierpc, Oct. 17, 1916. He studied organ with Rutkowski at the Warsaw Cons. (graduated, 1942) and composition with Sikorski at the Lodz State College of Music (graduated, 1951); taught in music schools in Plock (1945–49) and Lodz (1949–59); also taught at the Warsaw State College of Music (from 1954), becoming a permanent faculty member (1959); was dean of its composition, theory, and conducting dept. (1963–69), and then its rector (1969–71).

WORKS: STAGE: OPERAS: *Ushico*, radio opera (1962); *The Maiden from the Dormer Window* (1964); *Ligea*, radio opera (1967). **BALLET:** *Warsaw Legend* (1959). **ORCH.:** 2 piano concertos (1952, 1954); 2 syms. (1953, 1957); Violin Concerto (1955); *Duet koncertujacy* for Organ and Orch. (1962); Organ Concerto (1967); *Divertimento* for Clarinet and String Orch. (1968); Trombone Concerto (1971); Viola Concerto (1975–76); *Concerto alla Barocco* (1979); Concerto for Harp, Flute, and String Orch. (1980); Oboe Concerto (1982); Concerto for 2 Violins and Orch. (1983); Horn Concerto (1986). **VOCAL:** *De Revolutionibus*, oratorio for 4 Solo Voices, Reciter, Boys' Chorus, Chorus, Organ, and Orch. (1972); 2 *Psalms* for Soprano and Organ (1985). **CHAMBER:** Wind Quintet (1951); Violin Sonata (1954); 2 string quartets (1960, 1982); 4 caprices: *Quasi una sonata* for Clarinet and Piano (1960); Trio for Flute, Viola, and Harp (1966); 6 *Miniatures* for 4 Trombones (1972); Piano Quintet (1972); *Concertante Duet* for Clarinet and Piano (1973); Cello Sonata (1974–75); 3 *Musical Moments* for 5 Clarinets (1985); also an Organ Sonata (1946–47) and other pieces for Organ; piano works.

Pacius, Fredrik (actually, **Friedrich**), significant German-born Finnish conductor, teacher, and composer; b. Hamburg, March 19, 1809; d. Helsinki, Jan. 8, 1891. He studied violin with Spohr and composition with Hauptmann in Kassel; after playing violin in Stockholm's Royal Chapel (1828–34), he settled in Helsinki (1835) as a lecturer at the Univ., being promoted to prof. (1860); also founded a choral society (1835) and regular sym. concerts (1845). Pacius is acknowledged as the father of Finnish music; his works owe much to the German Romanticists, especially Spohr and Mendelssohn, and to Finnish folk music. His setting of J. Runeberg's Swedish poem *Vårt land* became the Finnish national anthem in 1843; it was set to Finnish words as *Maamme* in 1848. He also wrote the 1st Finnish opera, *Kung Karls jakt* (to a Swedish libretto; Helsinki, March 24, 1852), as well as the opera *Loreley* (Helsinki, April 28, 1887) and incidental music to *Prinsessan af Cypern* (1860), both to Swedish texts, one movement of a sym., a Violin Concerto (1845), other orch. works, part-songs, and songs.

BIBL.: M. Colan-Beaurain, *F. P.* (Helsinki, 1921); O. Andersson, *Den unge P. och musiklivet i Helsingfors på 1830–talet* (Helsinki, 1938); J. Rosas, *F. P. som tonsättare* (Turku, 1949); K. Maasalo, "F. P.," *Suomalaisia sävellyksiä*, II (Borgå, 1969).

Paderewski, Ignacy (Jan), celebrated Polish pianist and composer; b. Kurylowka, Podolia (Russian Poland), Nov. 18, 1860; d. N.Y., June 29, 1941. His father was an administrator of country estates; his mother died soon after his birth. From early childhood, Paderewski was attracted to piano music; he received some musical instruction from Peter Sowinski, who taught him 4-hand arrangements of operas. His 1st public appearance was in a charity concert at the age of 11, when he played piano with his sister. His playing aroused interest among wealthy patrons, who took him to Kiev. He was then sent to Warsaw, where he entered the Cons., learned to play trombone, and joined the school band. He also continued serious studies of piano playing; his teachers at the Warsaw Cons. were Schlözer, Strobl, and Janotha. In 1875 and 1877 he toured in provincial Russian towns with the Polish violinist Cielewicz; in the interim periods he took courses in composition at the Warsaw Cons., and upon graduation in 1878 he was engaged as a member of the piano faculty there. In 1880 he married a young music student named Antonina Korsak, but she died 9 days after giving birth to a child, on Oct. 10, 1880. In 1882 he went to Berlin to study composition with Kiel; there he met Anton Rubinstein, who gave him encouraging advice and urged him to compose piano music. He resigned from his teaching job at the Warsaw Cons. and began to study orchestration in Berlin with Heinrich Urban. While on a vacation in the Tatra Mountains (which inspired his *Tatra Album* for piano) he met the celebrated Polish actress Modjeska, who proposed to finance his further piano studies with Leschetizky in Vienna. Paderewski followed this advice and spent several years as a Leschetizky student. He continued his career as a concert pianist. On March 3, 1888, he gave his 1st Paris recital, and on Nov. 10, 1888, played a concert in Vienna, both with excellent success. He also began receiving recognition as a composer. Anna Essipoff (who was married to Leschetizky) played his piano concerto in Vienna under the direction of Hans Richter. Paderewski made his London debut on May 9, 1890. On Nov. 17, 1891, he played for the 1st time in N.Y., and was acclaimed with an adulation rare for pianists; by some counts he gave 107 concerts in 117 days in N.Y. and other American cities and attended 86 dinner parties; his wit, already fully developed, made him a social lion in wealthy American salons. At one party, it was reported, the hostess confused him with a famous polo player who was also expected to be a guest, and greeted him effusively. "No," Paderewski is supposed to have replied, "he is a rich soul who plays polo, and I am a poor Pole who plays solo." American spinsters beseeched him for a lock of his luxurious mane of hair; he invariably obliged, and when his valet observed that at this rate he would soon be bald, he said, "Not I, my dog." There is even a story related by a gullible biographer that Paderewski could charm beasts by his art and that a spider used to come down from the ceiling in Paderewski's lodgings in Vienna and sit at the piano every time Paderewski played a certain Chopin étude. Paderewski eclipsed even Caruso as an idol of the masses. In 1890 he made a concert tour in Germany; also toured South America, South Africa, and Australia. In 1898 he purchased a beautiful home, the Villa Riond-Bosson on Lake Geneva, Switzerland; in 1899 he married Helena Gorska, Baroness von Rosen. In 1900, by a deed of trust, Paderewski established a fund of $10,000 (the original trustees were William Steinway, Major H.L. Higginson, and Dr. William Mason), the interest from which was to be used for triennial prizes given "to composers of American birth without distinction as to age or religion" for works in the following categories: syms., concertos, and chamber music. In 1910, on the occasion of the centennial of Chopin's birth, Paderewski donated $60,000 for the construction of the Chopin Memorial Hall in Warsaw; in the same year he contributed $100,000 for the erection of the statue of King Jagiello in Warsaw, on the quinquecentennial of his victory over the Teutonic Knights in 1410. In 1913 he purchased a ranch in Paso Robles in Calif.

Although cosmopolitan in his culture, Paderewski remained a great Polish patriot. During the First World War he donated the entire proceeds from his concerts to a fund for the Polish people caught in the war between Russia and Germany. After the establishment of the independent Polish state, Paderewski served as its representative in Washington; in 1919 he was named prime minister of the Polish Republic, the 1st musician to occupy such a post in any country at any period. He took part in the Versailles Treaty conference; it was then that Prime Minister Clemenceau of France welcomed Paderewski with the famous, if possibly apocryphal, remark: "You, a famous pianist, a prime minister! What a comedown!" Paderewski resigned his post on Dec. 10, 1919. He reentered politics in 1920 in the wake of the Russian invasion of Poland that year, when he became a delegate to the League of Nations; he resigned on May 7, 1921, and resumed his musical career. On Nov. 22, 1922, he gave his 1st concert after a hiatus of many years at Carnegie Hall in N.Y. In 1939 he made his last American tour. Once more during his lifetime Poland was invaded, this time by both Germany and Russia. Once more Paderewski was driven to political action. He joined the Polish government-in-exile in France and was named president of its parliament on Jan. 23, 1940. He returned to the U.S. on Nov. 6, 1940, a few months before his death. At the order of President Roosevelt, his body was given state burial in Arlington National Cemetery, pending the return of his remains to Free Poland. Paderewski received many honors. He held the following degrees: Ph.D. from the Univ. of Lemberg (1912); D.Mus. from Yale Univ. (1917); Ph.D. from the Univ. of Krakow (1919); D.C.L. from Oxford Univ. (1920); LL.D. from Columbia Univ. (1922); Ph.D. from the Univ. of Southern Calif. (1923); Ph.D. from the Univ. of Poznan (1924); and Ph.D. from the Univ. of Glasgow (1925). He also held the Grand Cross of the French Legion of Honor (1922). A postage stamp with his picture was issued in Poland in 1919, and 2 postage stamps honoring him in the series "Men of Liberty" were issued in the U.S. in 1960.

As an artist, Paderewski was a faithful follower of the Romantic school, which allowed free, well-nigh improvisatory declensions from the written notes, tempi, and dynamics; judged by 20th-century standards of precise rendering of the text, Paderewski's interpretations appear surprisingly free, but this very personal freedom of performance moved contemporary audiences to ecstasies of admiration. Also, Paderewski's virtuoso technique, which astonished his listeners, has been easily matched by any number of pianists of succeeding generations. Yet his position in the world of the performing arts remains undiminished by the later achievements of younger men and women pianists. As a composer, Paderewski also belongs to the Romantic school. At least one of his piano pieces, the *Menuet in G* (which is a movement of his set of 6 *Humoresques*

for piano), achieved enormous popularity. His other compositions, however, never sustained a power of renewal and were eventually relegated to the archives of unperformed music. His opera *Manru* (1897–1900), dealing with folk life in the Tatra Mountains, was produced in Dresden on May 29, 1901, and was also performed by the Metropolitan Opera in N.Y. on Feb. 14, 1902. Another major work, a Sym. in B minor, was first performed by the Boston Sym. Orch. on Feb. 12, 1909. His other works included a Piano Concerto in A minor (1888); *Fantaisie polonaise* for Piano and Orch. (1893); Violin Sonata (1880); songs; and the following compositions for piano solo: *Prelude and Capriccio; 3 Pieces (Gavotte, Mélodie, Valse mélancholique); Krakowiak; Élégie; 3 Polish Dances; Introduction and Toccata; Chants du voyageur* (5 pieces); *6 Polish Dances; Album de mai* (5 pieces), *Variations and Fugue; Tatra Album* (also arr. for Piano, 4-hands); *6 Humoresques de concert* (which includes the famous *Menuet in G*); *Dans le désert; Miscellanea* (7 pieces); *Légende;* Sonata in E-flat minor (1903). A complete list of Paderewski's works was publ. in the *Bolletino bibliografico musicale* (Milan, 1932).

BIBL.: F. Buffen, *I. P.* (N.Y., 1891); C. Tretbar, *P.: A Biographical Sketch* (N.Y., 1892); H. Finck, *P. and His Art* (N.Y., 1895); A. Nossig, *P.* (Leipzig, 1901); E. Baughan, *I. P.* (London, 1908); A. Chybiński, *P.* (Warsaw, 1910); S. Popielowna, *I. P.* (Tarnow, 1919); F. Martens, *P.* (N.Y., 1923); B. Sidorowicz, *I. P.* (Poznan, 1924); J. Cooke, *P.* (Philadelphia, 1928); H. Opieński, *I.J. P.* (Warsaw, 1928; 3rd ed., rev. and augmented, 1960); C. Philips, *P.* (N.Y., 1933); R. Landau, *I. P.: Musician and Statesman* (N.Y., 1934); *P.'s Diamond Anniversary* (N.Y., 1936); M. Lawton, *The P. Memoirs* (to 1914 only; N.Y., 1938); E. Ligocki, *Homage to P.* (Edinburgh, 1941); A. Gronowicz, *P.: Pianist and Patriot* (Edinburgh, 1943); B. Sarrazin, *Imageries de P.* (Annonay, 1945); A. Baumgartner, *La Vérité sur le prétendu drame P.* (Geneva, 1948); S. Giron, *Le Drame P.* (Geneva, 1948); A. Strakacz, *P. as I Knew Him* (New Brunswick, N.J., 1949); C. Kellogg, *P.* (N.Y., 1956); J. Cieplinski, *I. P.* (N.Y., 1960); R. and P. Hume, *The Lion of Poland: The Story of P.* (N.Y., 1962); R. Halski, *P.* (London, 1964); W. Dulaba, *I. P.* (Krakow, 1966); A. Zamoyski, *P.* (N.Y., 1982); J. Hoskins, *I.J. P., 1860–1941: A Biographical Sketch and a Selective List of Reading Materials* (Washington, D.C., 1984); E. Lipmann, *P., l'idole des années folles* (1984).

Padilla, Lola Artôt de, Spanish soprano; b. Sèvres, near Paris, Oct. 5, 1876; d. Berlin, April 12, 1933. She was the daughter of **Mariano Padilla y Ramos** and **Désirée Artôt.** After vocal training with her mother, she sang in salons and concerts; made her operatic debut at the Paris Opéra-Comique in 1903. Later she toured as a concert singer through Europe; was engaged at the Komische Oper in Berlin from 1905 to 1908 as prima donna; from 1909 to 1927, was a member of the Royal (later State) Opera in Berlin.

Padilla y Ramos, Mariano, Spanish baritone; b. Murcia, 1842; d. Auteuil, near Paris, Nov. 23, 1906. He studied with Mabellini and Ronconi in Florence; made his debut in Messina; sang in opera with great success in Italy, Austria, Germany, and Russia. In 1869 he married the soprano **Désirée Artôt.**

Paër, Ferdinando, significant Italian composer; b. Parma, June 1, 1771; d. Paris, May 3, 1839. He studied with Francesco Fortunati and Gaspare Ghiretti in Parma, producing his 1st stage work, the prose opera *Orphée et Euridice,* there in 1791. On July 14, 1792, he was appointed honorary maestro di cappella to the court of Parma, bringing out his opera *Le astuzie amorose* that same year at the Teatro Ducale there. His finest work of the period was *Griselda, ossia La virtù al cimento* (Parma, Jan. 1798). In 1797 he was appointed music director of the Kärnthnertortheater in Vienna. While there, he made the acquaintance of Beethoven, who expressed admiration for his work. It was in Vienna that he composed one of his finest operas, *Camilla, ossia Il sotteraneo* (Feb. 23, 1799). Another fine opera was his *Achille* (Vienna, June 6, 1801). After a visit to Prague in 1801, he accepted the appointment of court Kapellmeister in Dresden. Three of his most important operas were premiered there: *I Fuorusciti di Firenze* (Nov. 27, 1802), *Sargino, ossia L'Allievo dell'amore* (May 26, 1803), and *Leonora, ossia L'amore conjugale* (Oct. 3, 1804), a work identical in subject with that of Beethoven's *Fidelio* (1805). In 1806 he resigned his Dresden post and accepted an invitation to visit Napoleon in Posen and Warsaw. In 1807 Napoleon appointed him his maître de chapelle in Paris, where he also became director of the Opéra-Comique. Following the dismissal of Spontini in 1812, he was appointed director of the Théâtre-Italien. One of his most successful operas of the period, *Le Maître de chapelle* (Paris, March 29, 1821), remained in the repertoire in its Italian version until the early years of the 20th century. Paër's tenure at the Théâtre-Italien continued through the vicissitudes of Catalani's management (1814–17) and the troubled joint directorship with Rossini (1824–27). After his dismissal in 1827, he was awarded the cross of the Légion d'honneur in 1828; was elected a member of the Inst. of the Académie des Beaux Arts in 1831. He was appointed director of music of Louis Philippe's private chapel in 1832. Paër was one of the most important Italian composers of opera in his era. His vocal writing was highly effective, as was his instrumentation. Nevertheless, his operas have disappeared from the active repertoire. His *Leonora*, however, was revived and recorded in the 1970s by the Swiss conductor Peter Maag.

BIBL.: T. Massé and A. Deschamps, *De MM. P. et Rossini* (Paris, 1820); F. Paër, *M. P., ex-directeur du Théâtre-Italien, à MM les dilettans* (Paris, 1827); C. de Colobrano, *Funérailles de F. P.* (Paris, 1893); R. Engländer, "F. P. als sächsischer Hofkapellmeister," *Neues Archiv für sächsische Geschichte und Alterthumskunde,* I (1929); idem, "P.s *Leonora* und Beethoven's *Fidelio,*" *Neues Beethoven-Jahrbuch,* IV (1930); G. Tabaldini, "F. P.," *Aurea Parma,* II (1939).

Paganelli, Giuseppe Antonio, Italian composer; b. Padua, March 6, 1710; d. probably in Madrid, c.1762. He was employed as a harpsichordist in an Italian opera company; was in Venice (1732), then at Bayreuth (1737–38). In 1755 he went to Madrid. His *Divertisement de le Beau Sexe* (6 sonatas) was ed. by G. Tagliapietra (Milan, 1936). In addition to 11 operas, he composed a number of instrumental works which were popular in his day.

BIBL.: E. Schenk, *G.A. P.* (Salzburg, 1928); W. Newman, *The Sonata in the Classic Era* (Chapel Hill, 1963; 3rd ed., rev., 1983).

Paganini, Niccolò, legendary Italian violinist; b. Genoa, Oct. 27, 1782; d. Nice, May 27, 1840. His father, a poor dockworker, gave him his 1st lessons on the mandolin and violin; he then studied with Giovanni Servetto, a violinist in the theater orch. By this time the young Paganini was already composing; he also began to study harmony with Francesco Gnecco, and subsequently studied violin with Giacomo Costa, who arranged for him to play in local churches. His 1st documented public appearance took place at the church of S. Filippo Neri on May 26, 1794. It was about this time that he was indelibly impressed by the Franco-Polish violin virtuoso Auguste Frédéric Durand (later billed as Duranowski), who was a brilliant showman. Having made phenomenal progress in his studies, he was sent to Parma in 1795 to study with Alessandro Rolla. To defray the costs of the journey, he gave a special concert on July 31, 1795. Upon his arrival in Parma, Rolla is reported to have told him that there was nothing left to teach him and suggested that he study composition with Paër instead. Paër, in turn, sent him to his own teacher, Gasparo Ghiretti. After study with both Ghiretti and Paër, Paganini returned to Genoa (1796), appearing as a violinist in private performances. With Napoleon's invasion of Italy, the family moved to Ramairone; by 1800 he was with his father in Livorno, where he gave concerts; he also appeared in Modena. They returned to Genoa in 1801; that same year, in the company of his older brother Carlo, who was also a violinist, he went to Lucca to play at the Festival of Santa Croce. His appearance there on Sept. 14, 1801, was a brilliant success. He settled there, becoming concertmaster of the National Orch.

As a soloist, Paganini captivated his auditors by his pyrotechnics. During an engagement in Livorno he so impressed a wealthy French merchant that he was rewarded with a valuable violin. With the arrival of Princess Elisa Baciocchi, the sister of Napoleon, as ruler of Lucca (1805), musical life there was reorganized. The 2 major orchs. were dissolved and replaced by a chamber orch. Paganini was retained as 2nd violinist, and then was made solo court violinist (1807). After the chamber orch. itself was dissolved (Jan. 1, 1808), he played in the court string quartet and also served as violin teacher to Prince Felix Baciocchi. Dissastisfied with his position, he broke with the court in Dec. 1809, and pursued a career as a virtuoso. He came to national prominence in 1813 with a series of sensationally successful concerts in Milan. He subsequently toured throughout Italy, his renown growing from year to year and his vast technical resources maturing and augmenting such that he easily displaced the would-be rivals Lafont in Milan (1816) and Lipinski in Piacenza (1818). In 1824 he met the singer **Antonia Bianchi,** who became his mistress; she bore him a son, Achilles, in 1825, whom Paganini had legitimized in 1837. In 1827 he was made a Knight of the Golden Spur by Pope Leo XII. When he left Italy for his 1st tour abroad in 1828, he immediately gained a triumph with his opening concert in Vienna (March 29). He gave 14 concerts during his stay in Vienna, and was accorded the honorary title of chamber virtuoso by the Emperor and presented with the city's medal of St. Salvator. He made his 1st appearance in Berlin on March 4, 1829. He also played in Frankfurt, Darmstadt, Mannheim, and Leipzig. In 1831 he made his Paris (March 9) and London (June 3) debuts. He subsequently gave concerts throughout Great Britain (1831–33).

Paganini's artistic fortunes began to decline in 1834; his long-precarious health was ruined, but he had managed to retain his fame and considerable wealth. He continued to give sporadic concerts in subsequent years, but he spent most of his time at his villa in Parma, making occasional visits to Paris. A critical illness in Oct. 1838 led to the loss of his voice; in Nov. 1839 he went to Nice for his health, and died there the following spring.

Paganini's stupendenous technique, power, and control, as well as his romantic passion and intense energy, made him the marvel of his time. He also was not above employing certain tricks of virtuosity, such as tuning up the A string of his violin by a semitone or playing the *Witches' Dance* on one string after severing the other 3 on stage, in sight of his audience, with a pair of scissors. He was also a highly effective composer for the violin, and gave regular performances of his works at his concerts with great success. Outstanding among his compositions are the 24 *Caprices* for Solo Violin, the *Moto perpetuo* for Violin and Orch., and several of the violin concertos. His collected works are being publ. in an Edizione Nazionale, ed. by L. Ronga et al. (1976–). See also M. Moretti and A. Sorento, *Catalogo tematico delle musiche di Niccolò Paganini* (1983). Paganini prepared a brief autobiography, which was publ. in the *Allgemeine musikalische zeitung,* XXXII (1830). His letters were ed. by E. Neill (Genoa, 1982).

WORKS: VIOLIN AND ORCH.: Violin concertos: E minor (1815?); No. 1, in E-flat major, op. 6 (1817?); No. 2, in B minor, op. 7 (1826); No. 3, in E major (1826); No. 4, in D minor (1830); No. 5, in A minor (1830); various other works for Violin and Orch. **CHAMBER:** 3 string quartets (1800–1805); 21 quartets for various combinations of instruments (1806–20); *Centone di sonate,* 18 sonatas; other sonatas; works for Solo Violin, including 24 *Caprices* (1805).

BIBL.: Valuable information may be found in *Quaderno dell'Istituto di studi P.ani* (1972–); see also K. Guhr, *Über P.s Kunst, die Violine zu spielen* (Mainz, 1830; Eng. tr. by S. Novello, 1831); G. Imbert de Laphalèque, *Notice sur le célèbre violoniste N. P.* (Paris, 1830); J. Schottky, *P.s Leben und Treiben als Künstler und als Mensch* (Prague and Hamburg, 1830; 2nd ed., 1909); F. Schütz, *Leben, Charakter und Kunst des Ritters N. P.* (Ilmenau, 1830); G. Conestabile, *Vita di N. P.* (Perugia, 1851; 2nd ed., rev., 1936, by F. Mompellio); F.-J. Fétis, *Notice* *biographique sur N. P.* (Paris, 1851; Eng. tr., 1852; 2nd ed., 1876); O. Bruni, *N. P., Racconto storico* (Florence, 1873; new ed., 1903); J.-G. Prod'homme, *P.* (Paris, 1907; Eng. tr., 1911; 2nd French ed., 1927); S. Stratton, *N. P.: His Life and Work* (London, 1907); A. Bonaventura, *P.* (Modena, 1911; 4th ed., 1939); J. Kapp, *N. P.* (Berlin, 1913; 15th ed., rev., 1969); E. Istel, *N. P.* (Leipzig, 1919); J. Siber, *P.* (Berlin, 1920); L. Day, *P. of Genoa* (N.Y., 1929); A. Günther, *P. in Lucca* (Munich, 1929); A. Montanelli, *P. a Forlì* (Forlì, 1930); A. Codignola, *P. intimo* (Genoa, 1935); J. Pulver, *P., the Romantic Virtuoso* (London, 1936); R. de Saussine, *P. le magicien* (Paris, 1938; Eng. tr., 1954); I. Pizzetti, *N. P.* (Turin, 1940); M. Tibaldi Chiesa, *P.: La vita e l'opera* (Milan, 1940; 2nd ed., 1944); N. Podenzani, *Il Romanzo di N. P.* (Milan, 1944); H. Spivacke, *P.ana* (Washington, D.C., 1945); T. Valensi, *P.* (Nice, 1950); G. de Courcy, *P.: The Genoese* (2 vols., Norman, Okla., 1957; 2nd ed., rev., 1977); R. de Saussine, *P.* (Milan, 1958); A. Armando, *P.: Eine Biographie* (Hamburg, 1960); A. Codignola, *Arte e magio di N. P.* (Milan, 1960); D. Botti, *P. e Parma* (Parma, 1961); G. de Courcy, *Chronology of N. P.'s Life* (Wiesbaden, 1961); P. Berri, *P.: Documenti e testimonianze* (Genoa, 1962); A. Kendall, *P.* (London, 1982); J. Sugden, *P.* (N.Y., 1982; 2nd ed., rev., 1986); B. Schwarz, *Great Masters of the Violin* (N.Y., 1983).

Page, "Hot Lips" (Oran Thaddeus), black American jazz trumpeter and singer; b. Dallas, Jan. 27, 1908; d. N.Y., Nov. 5, 1954. He took up the trumpet when he was 12 years of age; was a member of the Blue Devils (1927–30); then played in Bennie Moten's band in St. Louis (1931–35) and briefly with Count Basie (1935–36); also with Artie Shaw (1941–42). He was esteemed as both a blues trumpeter and a singer.

Page, Jimmy, English rock guitarist; b. Heston, Middlesex, Jan. 9, 1945. He studied art; then turned to guitar and became one of the most successful "ghost guitarists" on records for which others took credit. In 1966 he joined The Yardbirds as a lead guitarist; the group broke up, and Page went over to another band bearing the inexplicable name Led Zeppelin (some rockologists maintain the Led is a deliberate misspelling of Lead, and that Led Zeppelin is a heteronymous appellation for a "heavy metal" sound, like a dirigible that cannot fly). Led Zeppelin led a successful American tour in 1969, precipitating a "heavy metal" craze, and its albums, including songs such as *Communication Breakdown*, sold prodigiously. Another album, *Led Zeppelin II*, containing the hits *Whole Lotta Love* and *Ramble On*, was even more successful. During their 5th American tour in 1970, the group recorded the album *Led Zeppelin III*, which contained the provocative *Immigrant Song*. In 1976 Led Zeppelin issued its certified platinum award album, *Presence*. In America, the group became the greatest crowd-gathering magnet, but in 1980, one of their charter members was found dead, drowned in his own vomit. This was the signal for Led Zeppelin to disgorge.

Page, John, English tenor and anthologist; b. c.1760; d. London, Aug. 16, 1812. He was a lay clerk at St. George's, Windsor; Gentleman of the Chapel Royal; vicar-choral at St. Paul's. He compiled *Harmonica sacra* (3 vols., 1800; a collection of 74 anthems by eminent English composers of the 16th–18th centuries); *Festive Harmony* (4 vols., 1804; madrigals, glees, and elegies); *Collection of Hymns* (1804); *The Burial Service, Chant, Evening Service, Dirge and Anthems App. to be Perf. at the Funeral of Lord Nelson* (1806); anthems, Psalms, etc.

Page, Patti (real name, **Clara Ann Fowler**), American pop singer; b. Claremore, Okla., Nov. 8, 1927. She sang in a church choir in Tulsa; then appeared on a local radio program, adopting the name Patti Page. She subsequently became a pop recording artist, her 1st hit being *Confess* (1948); gained fame with her recording of *Tennessee Waltz* in 1950, which became the official state song of Tennessee; in later years she made guest appearances in pop concerts with U.S. orchs.

Page, Robert, American conductor; b. Abilene, Tex., April 27, 1927. He studied at Abilene Christian College; then received an M.M. from Indiana Univ.; also did advanced study at N.Y. Univ. He was director of choral activities at Temple Univ. in Philadelphia (1956–75); then was chairman of the dept. of music at Carnegie-Mellon Univ. in Pittsburgh (1975–80; also was director of choruses (1971–89) and assistant conductor (1979–89) of the Cleveland Orch.; was concurrently music director of the Mendelssohn Choir of Pittsburgh; while retaining the latter post, he also served as director of special projects and choral activities of the Pittsburgh Sym. Orch. (from 1989).

Pagliughi, Lina, American-born Italian soprano; b. N.Y., May 27, 1907; d. Rubicone, Oct. 2, 1980. She was encouraged to pursue a career as a singer by Tetrazzini; studied voice in Milan with Manlio Bavagnoli; made her operatic debut at the Teatro Nazionale in Milan as Gilda in 1927; then made appearances throughout Italy; sang at La Scala in Milan in 1930, and continued to make appearances there until 1947; then sang with Italian Radio until her retirement in 1956. She was married to the tenor Primo Montanari. She was best known for her roles in operas by Rossini, Bellini, and Donizetti.

Pahissa, Jaime, Catalan-born Argentine writer on music, teacher, and composer; b. Barcelona, Oct. 7, 1880; d. Buenos Aires, Oct. 27, 1969. He was a practicing architect for 4 years before turning to music as a profession; studied composition with Morera in Barcelona. He associated himself with the Catalan nationalist movement in art, obtaining his 1st important success in 1906 with the Romantic opera *La presó de Lledida* (The Prison of Lérida), which had 100 consecutive performances in Barcelona; it was later revised and produced in Barcelona on Feb. 8, 1928, as *La Princesa Margarita*, again obtaining a notable success. Other operas produced in Barcelona were *Gala Placidía* (Jan. 15, 1913) and *Marianela* (March 31, 1923). Among his orch. works the most remarkable is *Monodía*, written in unisons, octaves, double octaves, etc., without using any other intervals, and depending for its effect only on instrumental variety (Barcelona, Oct. 12, 1925); in a different vein is his *Suite Intertonal* (Barcelona, Oct. 24, 1926), based on his own method of free tonal and polytonal composition. In 1935 Pahissa emigrated to Argentina, settling in Buenos Aires, where he continued to compose; he also established himself as a teacher and writer. He publ. in Buenos Aires several books: *Espíritu y cuerpo de la música* (1945); *Los grandes problemas de la música* (1945; 2nd ed., 1954); *Vida y obra de Manuel de Falla* (1947; Eng. tr., London, 1954); *Sendas y cumbres de la música española* (1955).

Paik, Byung-Dong, Korean composer and pedagogue; b. Seoul, Jan. 26, 1936. He was educated at Seoul National Univ.; in 1969 went to Germany, where he studied music theory with Fritz von Block and Alfred Koerppen and composition with Isang Yun at the Hannover Hochschule für Musik. He returned to Korea in 1971 and subsequently served as a prof. at the Seoul National Univ. Among his awards are the Annual Korean New Composer's Prize (1962, for his *Symphony in 3 Movements*), the 5th Wolgan Musicians Prize (1975), the 1st Korean National Composer's Prize (1977, for his *Zweite Streichquartett*), and the Cultural Prize of Seoul (1983). Several of his works combine Korean musical traditions and instruments with contemporary Western instruments and practices. His style of composition tends toward strict formal procedures utilizing academic musical vocabularies. He publ. *Music Theory* (1977), *Harmony* (1984), and *Music for One's Culture* (1985); also collections of essays, *Seven Fermatas* (1979) and *Sound of Whisper* (1981).

WORKS (all 1st perf. in Seoul unless otherwise given): **ORCH.:** *Symphony in 3 Movements* (1962; July 9, 1963); Cello Concerto (Oct. 30, 1969); *Stimmung* (1971; March 28, 1974); Viola Concerto (Oct. 11, 1972); Piano Concerto (March 26, 1974); *Metamorphosen für 83 Spieler* (Oct. 23, 1974); *Requiescat* for 3 Oboes and Orch. (1974; Feb. 11, 1976); *Youlmok* for Strings (June 23, 1982); *Sansudo* (Sept. 22, 1984); *Pogu* (Pusan, May 2, 1986); *In September* (1987). **CHAMBER:** *Zeite Streichquartett* (Nov. 29, 1977); *Sori* for Flute, Guitar, and Cello (Tokyo, Feb. 26, 1981); Piano Trio (June 30, 1985); *Zweite*

Kammerkonzert (March 11, 1988); *Contra* for Marimbaphone and 2 Percussion (Tokyo, June 21, 1988); 5 Pieces for Cello and Contrabass (March 9, 1989). **TRADITIONAL KOREAN INSTRUMENTS:** *Shin Byul Gock* (April 18, 1972); *Un-Rack* (April 14, 1976); *3 Essays of GAYO* (Dec. 13, 1985); *Hwan Myung* (May 17, 1988); also numerous works for Solo Instruments; dance music; vocal works, including songs.

Paik, Kun-Woo, Korean pianist; b. Seoul, March 10, 1946. He studied music with his father, making his public debut when he was 8. He went to the U.S. in 1960 to continue his studies at the Juilliard School of Music in N.Y. with Rosina Lhévinne; won the Naumburg Award, and also studied with Ilona Kabós in London and Wilhelm Kempff in Italy. He subsequently developed a fine concert career, appearing as soloist with leading orchs. of North America as well as in Europe.

Paik, Nam June, Korean-American avant-garde composer and experimenter in the visual arts; b. Seoul, July 20, 1932. He studied first at the Univ. of Tokyo; then took courses in music theory with Thrasybulos Georgiades in Munich and with Wolfgang Fortner in Freiburg im Breisgau. Turning toward electronics, he did experimental work at the Electronic Music Studio in Cologne (1958–60); attended the summer seminars for new music at Darmstadt (1957–61). In his showings he pursues the objective of total art as the sum of integrated synesthetic experiences, involving all sorts of actions: walking, talking, dressing, undressing, drinking, smoking, moving furniture, engaging in quaquaversal commotion intended to demonstrate that any human or inhuman action becomes an artistic event through the power of volitional concentration of an ontological imperative. Paik attracted attention at his duo recitals with the topless cellist Charlotte Moorman, at which he acted as a surrogate cello, with his denuded spinal column serving as the fingerboard for Moorman's cello bow, while his bare skin provided an area for intermittent pizzicati. About 1963 Paik began experimenting with videotape as a medium for sounds and images; his initial experiment in this field was *Global Groove*, a high-velocity collage of intermingled television bits, which included instantaneous commercials, fragments from news telecasts, and subliminal extracts from regular programs, subjected to topological alterations. His list of works (some of them consisting solely of categorical imperatives) includes *Ommaggio a Cage* for piano demolition, breakage of raw eggs, spray painting of hands in jet black, etc. (Düsseldorf, Nov. 13, 1959); *Symphony for 20 Rooms* (1961); *Variations on a Theme of Saint-Saëns* for Cello and Piano, with the pianist playing *Le Cygne* while the cellist dives into an oil drum filled with water (N.Y., Aug. 25, 1965, composer at the keyboard, cellist Moorman in the oil drum); *Performable Music*, wherein the performer is ordered to make with a razor an incision of no less than 10 centimeters on his left forearm (Los Angeles, Dec. 2, 1965); *Opéra sextronique* (1967); *Opéra électronique* (1968); *Creep into the Vagina of a Whale* (c.1969); *Young Penis Symphony*, a protrusion of 10 erectile phalluses through a paper curtain (c.1970; first perf. at "La Mamelle," San Francisco, Sept. 21, 1975, under the direction of Ken Friedman, who also acted as one of the 10 performers). Of uncertain attribution is a sym. designated as No. 3, which Paik delegated to Friedman, who worked on it in Saugus, Calif., the epicenter of the earthquake of Feb. 9, 1971, and of which the earthquake itself constituted the finale.

BIBL.: C. Tomkins, "Video Visionary," *New Yorker* (May 5, 1975).

Pailliard, Jean-François, noted French conductor; b. Vitry-le-François, April 12, 1928. He received his musical training at the Paris Cons.; later took courses in conducting with Igor Markevitch at the Salzburg Mozarteum. In 1953 he founded the Jean-Marie Leclair Instrumental Ensemble, which became the Jean-François Pailliard Chamber Orch. in 1959, with which he toured widely; also appeared extensively as a guest conductor. He ed. the series Archives de la Musique Instrumentale; publ. the study *La musique française classique* (Paris, 1960).

Paine, John Knowles, prominent American composer and pedagogue; b. Portland, Maine, Jan. 9, 1839; d. Cambridge, Mass., April 25, 1906. His father ran a music store, and conducted the band in Portland. He studied organ, piano, harmony, and counterpoint with Hermann Krotzschmar, then took courses with K. Haupt (organ), W. Wieprecht (orchestration and composition), and others in Berlin (1858–61); concurrently appeared as an organist and pianist in Germany and England. He settled in Boston, becoming organist of the West Church (1861); joined the faculty of Harvard Univ. (1862), where he also was organist at its Appleton Chapel; was prof. of music at Harvard (1875–1906), the 1st to hold such a position at a U.S. univ.; was made a member of the National Inst. of Arts and Letters (1898), and was awarded the honorary degrees of M.A. from Harvard (1869) and Mus.D. from Yale (1890). He greatly distinguished himself as a teacher, serving as mentor to J.A. Carpenter, F.S. Converse, A. Foote, E.B. Hill, D.G. Mason, W. Spalding, and many others. He publ. *The History of Music to the Death of Schubert* (Boston, 1907).

WORKS: STAGE: *Il pescaballo*, comic opera (1862; music not extant); *Azara*, grand opera (1883–98; concert perf., Boston, May 7, 1903); incidental music to Sophocles's *Oedipus tyrannus* (1880–81; Cambridge, Mass., May 17, 1881; rev. 1895) and to Aristophanes's *The Birds* (1900; Cambridge, May 10, 1901). **ORCH.:** 2 syms.: No. 1 (1875; Boston, Jan. 26, 1876); No. 2, *In the Spring* (1879; Cambridge, March 10, 1880); *As You Like It*, overture (c.1876); 2 symphonic poems: *The Tempest* (c.1876) and *An Island Fantasy* (c.1888); Duo Concertante for Violin, Cello, and Orch. (c.1877); *Lincoln: A Tragic Tone Poem* (c.1904–6; unfinished). **CHAMBER:** String Quartet (c.1855); Piano Trio (c.1874); Violin Sonata (1875; rev. c.1905); *Romanza and Scherzo* for Cello and Piano (c.1875); *Larghetto and Scherzo* for Violin, Cello, and Piano (c.1877). **CHORAL:** *Domine salvum fac* for Men's Chorus and Orch. (1863); *Mass* for Soloists, Chorus, Organ, and Orch. (1865; Berlin, Feb. 16, 1867); *St. Peter*, oratorio for Soloists, Chorus, Organ, and Orch. (1870–72; Portland, Maine, June 3, 1873); *Centennial Hymn* for Chorus, Organ, and Orch. (Philadelphia, 1876); *The Realm of Fancy*, cantata for Soloists, Chorus, and Orch. (1882); *Phoebus, Arise!*, cantata for Tenor, Men's Chorus, and Orch. (1882); *The Nativity*, cantata for Soloists, Chorus, and Orch. (1883; rev. 1903); *Song of Promise*, cantata for Soprano, Chorus, Organ, and Orch. (1888); *Columbus March and Hymn* for Chorus, Organ, and Orch. (1892; Chicago, 1893); *Hymn of the West* for Chorus and Orch. (1903; St. Louis, 1904); etc.; also songs; piano music; organ works. His complete organ works were ed. by W. Leupold (Dayton, Ohio, 1975), and his complete piano works were ed. by J. Schmidt (N.Y., 1984).

BIBL.: J. Mathews, "Music in American Universities—in Harvard University—an Interview with J.K. P.," *Music*, IX (1896); L. Elson, "J.K. P.," *Étude*, XXIV (1906); M. DeWolfe Howe, "J.K. P.," *Musical Quarterly* (July 1939); K. Roberts, *J.K. P.* (thesis, Univ. of Michigan, 1962); J. Huxford, *J.K. P.: Life and Works* (diss., Florida State Univ., 1968); R. Smith, "American Organ Composers: J.K. P.," *Music: The AGO and RCCO Magazine*, X/2 (1976); J. Schmidt, *The Life and Works of J.K. P.* (Ann Arbor, Mich., 1980).

Paisible, Louis Henri, French violinist and composer; b. St. Cloud, near Paris, July 21, 1748; d. (suicide) St. Petersburg, March 19, 1782. He studied with Gaviniès; played in the orch. of the Concert Spirituel in Paris; then traveled through Europe; in 1778 he was engaged at the Russian court in St. Petersburg. Although well received at first, he was unable to make headway with a series of concerts for which he solicited subscriptions; deprived of resources, he shot himself. Twelve of his string quartets and 4 violin concertos have been publ. in Paris and London.

BIBL.: R. Mooser, *Annales de la musique et des musiciens en Russie au XVIIIᵉ siècle* (Vol. II, Geneva, 1950); M. Antoine, "De quelques musiciens nommés P.," *Recherches sur la Musique Française Classique*, XV (1975).

Paisiello, Giovanni, famous Italian composer; b. Roccaforzata, near Taranto, May 9, 1740; d. Naples, June 5, 1816. He studied at the Jesuit school in Taranto, and then at the Conservatorio di S. Onofrio in Naples (1754–63). He began his career as an opera composer by writing works for the Marsigli-Rossi Theater in Bologna in 1764. He settled in Naples in 1766, and proceeded to write over 40 operas during the next decade. Outstanding works from this period include *Le finte contesse* (Rome, Feb. 1766), *L'idolo cinese* (Naples, 1767), and *La Frascatana* (Venice, 1774). In 1776 he was invited to Russia, where he was appointed maestro di cappella to the Empress Catherine II in St. Petersburg. He composed one of his most celebrated operas there, *Il Barbiere di Siviglia* (Sept. 26, 1782), which remained popular in Italy until the appearance of Rossini's masterpiece in 1816. In 1783 Ferdinand IV of Naples made him compositore della musica de' drammi. In 1784 he left Russia for Naples, making a stop in Vienna, where he brought out one of his finest scores, *Il Re Teodoro in Venezia* (Aug. 23, 1784). His success in Naples led to his additional appointment in 1787 as maestro della real camera, in which capacity he was responsible for secular music at the court. Between 1784 and 1799 he composed several noteworthy operas, including *Le gare generose* (Naples, 1786), *L'amore contrastato* (Naples, 1788), *Nina, o sia La Pazza per amore* (Caserta, June 25, 1789), and *I Zingari in fiera* (Naples, Nov. 21, 1789). After Republican troops took control of Naples in Jan. 1799, Paisiello was named maestro di cappella nazionale by the new government on May 4, 1799. However, with the return of the Royalists in June 1799, he fell into disfavor with the court; was eventually granted a pardon, and restored to his posts on July 7, 1801. Ferdinand subsequently allowed him to serve as Napoleon's maître de chapelle in Paris from April 1802 until his return to Naples in Aug. 1804. He was made a member of the Légion d'honneur in 1806. He was further honored with membership in the Institut, taking the place of the deceased Haydn in 1809. After Joseph Bonaparte became King of Naples in 1806, Paisiello was appointed director of secular and sacred music at the court; he continued to hold these positions under Joachim Murat, Joseph's successor as King (1808–15); he also served as one of the directors of the new college of music (1807–13). In 1815 Ferdinand returned to the throne, and Paisiello lost all of his posts with the exception of that of maestro della real cappella.

Paisiello's success as a composer of comic operas equaled that of Piccini and Cimarosa. He was extraordinarily prolific; his operas alone number over 90, a few of which have been revived in the 20th century. Although he employed instrumental effects that were rare in Italy, he avoided the over-elaborate numbers in his operas which marked the works of many of his contemporaries, obtaining his results by melodic invention, and by the grace, beauty, and dramatic faithfulness of his conceptions.

BIBL.: I. Arnold, *G. P.: Seine kurze Biographie* (Erfurt, 1810); J. Le Sueur, *Notice sur P.* (Paris, 1816); Quatremère de Quincy, *Notice historique de P.* (Paris, 1817); G. de Dominicis, *Saggio su la vita del Cavalier Don G. P.* (Moscow, 1818); F. Schizzi, *Della vita e degli studi di G. P.* (Milan, 1833); C. Pupino, *P.* (Naples, 1908); S. Panareo, *P. in Russia* (Trani, 1910); U. Prota-Giurleo, *P. ed i suoi primi trionfi a Napoli* (Naples, 1925); A. Cametti, *P. e la corte di Vienna* (Rome, 1929); G. Speziale, *G. P.* (Naples, 1931); E. Faustini-Fasini, *L'ultima opera di P., I pittagorici* (Taranto, 1937); idem, *Opere teatrali, oratori e cantate di G. P.* (Bari, 1940); A. Ghislanzoni, *G. P.: Valutazioni critiche rettificate* (Rome, 1969); J. Hunt, *G. P.: His Life as an Opera Composer* (N.Y., 1975); M. Robinson and U. Hofman, *G. P. (1740–1816): A Thematic Catalogue of His Music* (Stuyvesant, N.Y., 1990).

Paita, Carlos, Argentine conductor; b. Buenos Aires, March 10, 1932. He studied piano with Juan Neuchoff, composition with Jacobo Fischer, and conducting with Artur Rodzinski; greatly impressed by Furtwängler's concerts in Argentina, he became determined to pursue a conducting career. After ap-

pearances in Buenos Aires, he conducted in Europe; made his U.S. debut as a guest conductor with the Houston Sym. Orch. (1979). He was active mainly in South America and Europe; recorded with an orch. in London created especially for him. A conductor of passionate Latin tempermant, he won both fervent admirers and intrepid detractors with his supercharged performances of the Romantic repertory.

Pakhmutova, Alexandra (Nikolaievna), Russian composer; b. Beketovka, near Stalingrad, Nov. 9, 1929. She studied at the Moscow Cons. with Shebalin, graduating in 1953. She was particularly successful in the genre of urban ballads, close to contemporary reality; of these, especially popular were her *Songs of Turbulent Youth* (1961); *Cuba, My Love*, (1962); *Keep Your Heart Young* (1963); *Young Eagles Learn to Fly* (1965); *A Coward Will Not Play Hockey* (1968); *Let Us Embrace the Sky* (1966); *Gagarin's Constellation* (1971); *Sport Heroes* (1972); *Hope* (1974). Her Trumpet Concerto acquired great popularity in Russia.

WORKS: STAGE: Ballet, *Lucid Vision* (1973). **ORCH.:** *Russian Suite* (1952); Trumpet Concerto (Moscow, June 11, 1955); Concerto (1971). **VOCAL:** *Lenin Is in Our Hearts*, suite for Narrator, Children's Chorus, and Orch. (1957); *Young Pioneer Songs*, cantata (1972); choruses; songs. **CHAMBER:** *4 Miniatures on Russian Folk Themes* for String Quartet (1950); *Nocturne* for Horn and Piano (1956).

BIBL.: E. Dobrynina, *A. P.* (Moscow, 1973).

Paladilhe, Emile, French composer; b. Montpellier, June 3, 1844; d. Paris, Jan. 6, 1926. He entered the Paris Cons. in 1853; was a pupil of Marmontel (piano), Benoist (organ), and Halévy (counterpoint); won 1st prize for piano and organ in 1857; won the Grand Prix de Rome in 1860 with the cantata *Le Czar Ivan IV* (Paris Opéra, 1860). He brought out the comic opera *Le Passant* in Paris (April 24, 1872), followed by *L'Amour africain* (May 8, 1875); *Suzanne* (Dec. 30, 1878); *Diana* (Feb. 23, 1885); the opera *Patrie* (Dec. 20, 1886); and *Les Saintes Maries de la mer*, a sacred lyric drama (Montpellier, 1892). He also produced 2 masses; Sym.; numerous songs (*Mandolinata, Premières pensées, Mélodies écossaises*). In 1892 he succeeded Guiraud as member of the Institut de France.

Palange, Louis S(alvador), American conductor, composer, and arranger; b. Oakland, Calif., Dec. 17, 1917; d. Burbank, Calif., June 8, 1979. He played the clarinet and bassoon in school bands; also studied composition with his father and at Mills College with Domenico Brecia before going to Los Angeles (1936), where he continued his studies with Wesley La Violette. He subsequently pursued a varied career as a conductor, composer, and arranger, working mainly in Los Angeles from 1946.

WORKS: ORCH.: 2 syms.: No. 1, *Invasion* (1946); No. 2 (1950; Los Angeles, March 22, 1968); tone poems: *Evangeline* (1943) and *The Plagues of Egypt* (1945); *Pictures* for Flute and Orch. (1948); *Poker Deck Ballet Suite* (1949; Redondo Beach, Calif., Dec. 9, 1960); *A Romantic Concerto* for Piano and Orch. (1949); 2 violin concertos (1950, n.d.). **SYMPHONIC BAND:** *Symphony in Steel* (1940; Los Angeles, March 8, 1941); *Hollywood Panorama*, tone poem (1950; Burbank, Sept. 21, 1952); various other pieces. **CHAMBER:** *Classical Trio* for Flute, Violin, and Viola (1942); *4 Generations* for String Quartet (1950); also film scores and arrangements for Band or Orch.

Palau Boix, Manuel, Spanish conductor, teacher, and composer; b. Alfara de Patriarca, Jan. 4, 1893; d. Valencia, Feb. 18, 1967. He studied first at the Valencia Cons.; later in Paris, where he took lessons from Koechlin and Ravel. Returning to Valencia, he established himself as a teacher, conductor, and composer. Most of his thematic material is inspired by Catalan folk songs; his instrumental music usually bears programmatic content; his technique of composition follows the French impressionistic procedures.

WORKS: ORCH.: 3 syms. (1945, 1946, 1950); *Poemas de juventud* (1926); *Gongoriana* (1927); *Siluetas* (1928); *Homenaje a Debussy* (1929); *Valencia* for Piano and Orch. (1936); *Marcha burlesca* (1936); *Divertimento* (1938); *Poemes de Ilum* (1939); *Concierto dramático* for Piano and Orch. (1948); *Mascarada* *sarcástica* (1949); other works include zarzuelas, choral music, chamber works, songs, and piano pieces.

BIBL.: A. Mingote, *M. P.* (Valencia, 1946); F. León Tello, *La obra pianistica de M. P.* (Valencia, 1956).

Palazzesi, Matilde, Italian soprano; b. Montecarotto, March 1, 1802; d. Barcelona, July 3, 1842. She studied with Giacomo Solarto in Pesaro; made her debut in the title role of Rossini's *Zelmira* in 1824 in Dresden; sang with the Italian Opera there until 1833; then appeared at La Scala in Milan and other Italian opera houses; went to Barcelona, where she sang at the Opera from 1841. She was a leading interpreter of Mozart, Rossini, Bellini, Donizetti, and Spontini.

BIBL.: B. Padovano, *M. P.* (1953).

Páleníček, Josef, Czech composer and pianist; b. Travnik, Yugoslavia, July 19, 1914; d. Prague, March 7, 1991. He studied with Otakar Šín and Vítězslav Novák at the Prague Cons.; then went to Paris and took lessons with Albert Roussel (1936–37). He traveled as pianist in the Czech Trio; in 1963, was appointed to the staff of the Prague Academy of Music. In 1977 he received the State Prize for his interpretations of Janáček's piano works, his specialty.

WORKS: 3 piano concertos: No. 1, with String Orch. and Timpani (1939); No. 2 (1953); No. 3, for young pianists, with Small Orch. (1961); Saxophone Concerto (1944); Concertino for Orch. (1937–45); Flute Concerto (1955); *Concertino da camera* for Clarinet and Orch. (1957); *Symphonic Variations on an Imaginary Portrait of Ilya Ehrenburg* for Orch. (1971); Cello Concerto (1973); Sinfonietta for String Orch. (1977); *Kytice* (Bouquet), ballet (1980–82); oratorio, *Song of Man* (1952–58); Piano Quintet (1933); *Preludium a capriccio* for Violin and Piano (1935); Clarinet Sonatina (1936); *Choral Variations* for Cello and Piano (1942); *Little Suite* for Clarinet and Piano (1943); String Quartet No. 1 (1954); *Masks,* 2 pieces for Saxophone and Piano (1957); *Little Suite* for Violin and Piano (1958); *Trio Sonata* for Mezzo-soprano, Oboe, and Piano (1965); *Variations* for Cello and Piano (1972); *Rondo concertante* for Cello and Piano (1972); *Suita in modo antico* for Cello and Piano (1973); *Concertant Etudes* for Double Bass and Piano (1975); *Tre concertini* for Clarinet and Piano (1977); Piano Sonata (1936); *Piano Sketchbook,* cycle of 5 pieces (1939); instructive works for children.

Palester, Roman, Polish composer; b. Śniatyň, Dec. 28, 1907; d. Paris, Aug. 25, 1989. He studied piano with Soltysowa at the Lwow Cons. and composition with Sikorski at the Warsaw Cons.; subsequently obtained composition and theory diplomas from the Univ. of Warsaw (1931). He divided his time between Poland and France; taught at the Warsaw Cons. from the end of World War II until 1948; then settled in Paris. In his music he adopted the modernistic devices of the French school, but preserved elements of Polish folk songs in the thematic structure of his works; harmonically he did not choose to transcend the limits of enhanced tonality. Several of his works were performed at festivals of the ISCM: *Symphonic Music* (London, July 27, 1931); *Danse polonaise* for Orch. (Barcelona, April 22, 1936); Violin Concerto (London, July 14, 1946). Other works are: 5 syms.: No. 1 (1935); No. 2 (1942); No. 3 for 2 Chamber Orchs. (1945); No. 4 (1951; rev. 1972); No. 5 (1977–81; Warsaw, Sept. 23, 1988); *Requiem* (1948); Sonatina for 3 Clarinets (1936); Concertino for Piano and Orch. (1942); *Serenade* for 2 Flutes and String Orch. (Krakow, Nov. 9, 1947); 2 string trios (1945, 1958); *Passacaglia* for Orch. (1950); *Sonnets for Orpheus* for Voice and Chamber Orch. (1952); *Variations* for Orch. (1955); Concertino for Harpsichord and Instrumental Ensemble (1955); opera, *La Mort de Don Juan* (1959–60; Brussels, 1965); *Varianti* for 2 Pianos (1963); *Metamorphosen* for Orch. (1965–66); 2 piano sonatas (1968, 1975); Trio for Flute, Viola, and Harp (1969); Duo for 2 Violins (1972); *Suite à quatre* for Oboe and String Trio (1973); *Passacaglia and Variations* for Piano (1974); *Songs,* after Milosz, for Soprano and Chamber Orch. (1976); Viola Concerto (1977–78); *Te Deum* for 3 Choirs and Instruments (1978–79).

Palestrina, Giovanni Pierluigi da, great Italian composer; b. probably in Palestrina, near Rome, 1525 or 1526; d. Rome, Feb. 2, 1594. In his letters he customarily signed his name as Giovanni Petraloysio. He is first listed as a choirboy at S. Maria Maggiore in 1537; it is likely that he studied with each of the maestri of the period, Robin Mallapert, one Robert, and Firmin Lebel. In 1544 he was appointed organist of the cathedral of S. Agapit in Palestrina, where his duties also included teaching music to the canons and choirboys. On June 12, 1547, he married Lucrezia Gori; they had 3 sons, Rodolfo (1549–72), Angelo (1551–75), and Iginio (1558–1610). In 1550 the bishop of Palestrina, Cardinal Giovanni Maria Ciocchi del Monte, was elected pope, taking the name of Julius III. On Sept. 1, 1551, he appointed Palestrina maestro of the Cappella Giulia in succession to Mallapert; Palestrina dedicated his 1st book of masses to him in 1554. On Jan. 13, 1555, the pope rewarded him by making him a member of the Cappella Sistina even though he was a married man; he was admitted without taking the entrance examination and without receiving the approval of the other singers. In Sept. 1555 Pope Paul IV dismissed Palestrina and 2 other singers after invoking the celibacy rule of the chapel, although he granted each of them a small pension. On Oct. 1, 1555, Palestrina became maestro di cappella of the great church of St. John Lateran, where his son Rodolfo joined him as a chorister. Palestrina's tenure was made difficult by inadequate funds for the musical establishment, and he resigned his post in July 1560. From 1561 to 1566 he was maestro di cappella of S. Maria Maggiore. In 1562–63 the Council of Trent took up the matter of sacred music. Out of its discussions arose a movement to advance the cause of intelligibility of sacred texts when set to music. Palestrina's role with this Council remains a matter of dispute among historians, but his *Missa Pape Marcelli* is an outstanding example of a number of its reforms. From 1564 he was also in charge of the music at the summer estate of Cardinal Ippolito II d'Este in Tivoli, near Rome. He apparently took up a full-time position in the Cardinal's service from 1567 to 1571. From 1566 to 1571 he likewise taught at the Seminario Romano, where his sons Rodolfo and Angelo were students. In 1568 the court of Emperor Maximilian II offered him the position of imperial choirmaster in Vienna, but Palestrina demanded so high a salary that the offer was tacitly withdrawn. In April 1571, upon the death of Giovanni Animuccia, he resumed his post as maestro of the Cappella Giulia. In 1575 his salary was increased to forestall his move to S. Maria Maggiore. In 1577, at the request of Pope Gregory XIII, Palestrina and Annibale Zoilo began the revision of the plainsongs of the Roman Gradual and Antiphoner. Palestrina never completed his work on this project; the revision was eventually completed by others and publ. as *Editio Medicaea* in 1614. In 1580, having lost his eldest sons and his wife to the plague, he made a decision to enter the priesthood; he soon changed his mind, however, and instead married Virginia Dormoli, the widow of a wealthy furrier, on Feb. 28, 1581. In succeeding years he devoted much time to managing her fortune while continuing his work as a musician. In 1583 he was tendered an offer to become maestro at the court of the Duke of Mantua, but again his terms were rejected as too high. In 1584 he publ. his settings of the *Song of Solomon.* In 1593 he began plans to return to Palestrina as choirmaster of the cathedral, but he was overtaken by death early the next year. He was buried in the Cappella Nuova of old St. Peter's Church.

With his great contemporaries Byrd and Lassus, Palestrina stands as one of the foremost composers of his age. He mastered the polyphonic style of the Franco-Flemish school, creating works of unsurpassing beauty and technical adroitness. His sacred music remains his most glorious achievement. Highly prolific, he composed 104 masses, over 375 motets, 68 offertories, over 65 hymns, 35 Magnificats, over 140 madrigals (both sacred and secular), Lamentations, litanies, and Psalms. The 1st complete edition of his works, *Giovanni Pierluigi da Palestrina: Werke,* was ed. by F.X. Haberl et al. (33 vols., Leipzig, 1862–1903). A new complete edition, *Giovanni Pierluigi da*

Palestrina: Le opere, ed. by R. Casimiri and his successors, began publication in Rome in 1939.

Bibl.: G. Baini, *Memorie storico-critiche della vita e delle opere di G.P.* (Rome, 1828; reprint, 1966); C. von Winterfeld, *J.P. v.P.* (Breslau, 1832); F. Kandler, *Über das Leben und die Werke des G.P. d.P. . . . nach den Memorie storico-critiche des Abbate G. Baini verfasst* (Leipzig, 1834); G. Campori, *Delle relazioni di Orlando di Lasso e G.P. coi principi estensi* (Rome, 1870); P. Wagner, *P. als weltlicher Komponist* (Strasbourgh, 1890); A. Cametti, *Cenni biografici di G.P. d.P.* (Milan, 1894); G. Cascioli, *La vita e le opere di G.P. d.P.* (Rome, 1894); G. Félix, *P. et la musique sacrée (1594–1894)* (Lille, 1896); C. Respighi, *G.P. d.P. e l'emendazione del Graduale romano* (Rome, 1900); M. Brenet, *P.* (Paris, 1905; 3rd ed., 1910); J. Gloger, *Die "Missa Prima." Eine Studie über den P.stil* (Leobschütz, 1910); E. Schmitz, *G.P. P.* (Leipzig, 1914; 2nd ed., 1954); K. Weinmann, *P.s Geburtsjahr* (Regensburg, 1915); R. Casimiri, *Il Codice 59 dell' Archivio musicale lateranense, autografo di G.P. d.P.* (Rome, 1919); Z. Pyne, *P.: His Life and Times* (London, 1922); K. Jeppesen, *P.stil med saerligt henblik paa dissonansbehandlingen* (Copenhagen, 1923; German tr., 1925; Eng. tr., 1927; 2nd ed., 1946, as *The Style of P. and the Dissonance*); A. Cametti, *P.* (Milan, 1925); K. Fellerer, *Der P.stil und seine Bedeutung in der vokalen Kirchenmusik des 18. Jahrhunderts* (Augsburg, 1929); idem, *P.* (Regensburg, 1930; 2nd ed., 1960); O. Ursprung, *Die katholische Kirchenmusik* (Potsdam, 1931); H. Coates, *P.* (London, 1938); J. Samon, *P., ou La Poésie de l'exactitude* (Geneva, 1940); A. Einstein, *The Italian Madrigal* (Princeton, 1949); E. Paccagnella, *P.: Il linguaggio melodico e armonico* (Florence, 1957); H. Andrews, *An Introduction to the Technique of P.* (London, 1958); E. Ferraci, *Il P.* (Rome, 1960); S. Klyce, *P. and His "Missa Pape Marcelli": An Analysis for Performance* (diss., Indiana Univ., 1969); T. Day, *P. in History* (diss., Columbia Univ., 1970); L. Lockwood, Norton Critical Score ed. of the *Pope Marcellus Mass* (N.Y., 1975; includes background and analysis); A. Monterosso Vacchelli, *La messa L'Homme armé di P.: Studio paleografico ed edizione critica,* vol. VII, Istituta et Monumenta (1979).

Paliashvili, Zakhari (Petrovich), significant Georgian composer and pedagogue; b. Kutaisi, Aug. 16, 1871; d. Tiflis, Oct. 6, 1933. His father was a singer and his siblings were active in Georgian music; he studied with his older brother Ivan; later, in 1887, he went to Tiflis, where he joined a Georgian national chorus; also studied horn with Mosko (1891–95) and theory with Klenovsky (1895–99) at the music school there; then took a course with Taneyev at the Moscow Cons. (1900–1903). Returning to Tiflis (1903), he assisted in the founding of the Georgian Phil. Soc. (1905) and directed its music school (1908–17). He publ. 2 collections of folk songs with native harmonies in 5 Georgian dialects under the pseudonym Palia (1910). Following the revolution, he became affiliated with the Tiflis Cons. (1917; prof., 1919; director, 1919; 1923; 1929–32). He was one of the founders of the nationalistic school of Georgian music; with Arakishvili and Balanchivadze, he incorporated native elements into established musical formulas. Their operas were the 1st to use the Georgian language; his own opera *Abesalom and Eteri* (1919) was based upon a Georgian epic. He was awarded many honors during his life, including that of being made a National Artist of Georgia (1925). The Tbilisi opera house was named for him (1937), as was the Georgian State Prize (1971).

Works: 3 operas: *Abesalom and Eteri* (Tiflis, Feb. 21, 1919), *Daisi* (Twilight; Tiflis, Dec. 19, 1923), and *Latavra* (Tiflis, March 16, 1928); *Georgian Suite* for Orch. (1928); choruses; many songs for Voice and Piano.

Bibl.: S. Kashmadze, *Z. P.* (Tbilisi, 1948); K. Tbileli, "About the National Musical Language of the Opera by Z. P., 'Daisi,'" *Sovetskaya Muzyka* (1951); V. Donadze, *Z. P.* (Moscow, 1958; 2nd ed., 1971); L. Danilevich, "The Operas of Z. P. and A. Spendiarov," *About Soviet Music* (Moscow, 1962); S. Aslanishvili, *The Road to "Abesalom"* (Tbilisi, 1971); A. Tsulukidze,

Z. P. (Tbilisi, 1971); I. Zarubishvili, "The Opera of Z. P. 'Abesalom and Eteri,'" *Theatrical Portraits in Opera and Music* (Tbilisi, 1972); P. Khuchua, *Z. P.* (Tbilisi, 1974).

Palisca, Claude V(ictor), American musicologist; b. Fiume, Yugoslavia, Nov. 24, 1921. He was taken to the U.S. as a child; became a naturalized U.S. citizen in 1929. He studied at Queens College (B.A., 1943) with Karol Rathaus (composition), and then at Harvard Univ. with Walter Piston and Randall Thompson (composition) and with Otto Kinkeldey, Gombosi, and Davison (musicology); obtained his M.A. in 1948, and his Ph.D. in 1954 with the diss. *The Beginnings of Baroque Music: Its Roots in Sixteenth-century Theory and Polemics.* He was a member of the faculty at the Univ. of Illinois at Urbana (1953–59); in 1959 he joined the staff of Yale Univ. He held a John Knowles Paine Traveling Fellowship (1949–50), a Fulbright grant for Italy (1950–52), and a Guggenheim fellowship (1960–61). He was president of the American Musicological Society (1970–72); was made a member of the American Academy of Arts and Sciences in 1986.

Writings: *Girolamo Mei: Letters on Ancient and Modern Music to Vincenzo Galilei and Giovanni Bardi* (Rome, 1960; 2nd ed., Stuttgart, 1977); with others, *Seventeenth-Century Science and the Arts* (Princeton, N.J., 1961); with others, *Musicology* (Englewood Cliffs, N.J., 1963); *Baroque Music* (Englewood Cliffs, N.J., 1968; 2nd ed., 1981); ed. and tr. with G. Marco, G. Zarlino's *Le istitutioni harmoniche,* part III, 1558, as *The Art of Counterpoint* (New Haven and London, 1968); ed. *Norton Anthology of Western Music* (2 vols., N.Y., 1980; 2nd ed., 1988); ed. with D. Kern Holoman, *Musicology in the 1980's: Methods, Goals, Opportunities* (N.Y., 1982); *Humanism in Italian Renaissance Musical Thought* (New Haven and London, 1985); *The Florentine Camerata: Documentary Studies and Translations* (New Haven, 1988).

Palkovský, Oldřich, Czech composer, father of **Pavel Palkovský;** b. Brušperk, Feb. 24, 1907; d. Gottwaldov, March 15, 1983. He studied with Petrželka at the Brno Cons. (1925–31) and Suk at the Prague Cons. (1931–33); was director of the State Testing Commission for Music (1939–54), and taught at the Kroměříž branch of the Brno Cons. (1950–67).

Works: orch.: 6 syms. (1933–34; 1939; 1944; 1947; 1956–57; 1962); Concerto for Cimbalom and Small Orch. (1952–53); *Scherzo capriccio* (1953); *Morvarian Dances* (1956); *Variations and Fugue* for Cimbalom, String Orch., and Timpani (1959); Flute Concerto (1959); Oboe Concerto (1961); Accordion Concerto (1961); *3 Symphonic Movements* (1971); Sinfonietta (1978); Small Suite (1981). **chamber:** 10 string quartets (1931–81); 2 piano trios (1940, 1968); Violin Sonata (1942); 2 viola sonatas (1944, 1966); Concertino for Winds (1945); Cello Sonata (1946); Clarinet Sonata (1947); 4 wind quintets (1949–79); Quartet for Flute, Violin, Viola, and Cello (1950); Horn Sonata (1963); *Chamber Music* for 8 Instruments (1964); *Balladic Sonata* for Bassoon and Piano (1969); *Sonnets* for Flute, Bass Clarinet, and Piano (1969); Sonata for Tuba and Piano (1978); Sonata for Trumpet and Piano (1980); Sextet for Wind Instruments (1981); Wind Quartet (1982); piano pieces; songs.

Palkovský, Pavel, Czech composer, son of **Oldřich Palkovský;** b. Zlín, Dec. 18, 1939. He studied composition with Schaefer at the Brno Cons., graduating in 1960, and with Kapr at the Janáček Academy of Music in Brno, graduating in 1964.

Works: Cello Sonata (1963); 2 syms.: No. 1 (1964) and No. 2 for Piano and Orch. (1968–69); *Chamber Music I* for Strings, Piano, and Percussion (1964); *Chamber Music II* for Piano, Organ, Celesta, and Percussion (1968); Horn Sonata (1967); *3 Studies* for Accordion and 9 Winds (1969); Trio for 3 Accordions (1969); Suite for Tuba and Piano (1979); *Musica polyphonica* for Clarinet and Piano (1983).

Pallandios, Menelaos, Greek composer and pedagogue; b. Piraeus, Feb. 11, 1914. He studied with Mitropoulos in Athens and with Alfredo Casella in Rome; in 1936, became an instructor at the Athens Cons., and in 1962 was appointed its director. In 1969 he was elected to the Athens Academy. He wrote music to several ancient Greek tragedies, endeavoring to re-create the classical modes in modern investiture.

WORKS: STAGE: OPERA: *Antigone* (1942). **BALLETS:** *Pombi ston Aheronta* (Procession Towards Acheron; 1942); *Prosefhi se archaeo nao* (Prayer in the Ancient Temple; 1942); *Electra* (1944); *Penthesilea* (1944); *3 Archaic Suites* (1949); *Greek Triptych* (1960); also incidental music to Greek dramas; film scores. **ORCH.:** *Suite in Ancient Style* for Strings (1941); *Prosefhi stin Akropoli* (Prayer on the Akropolis; 1942); *Narcissus* (1942); *Greek Classical Overture* (1944); Sym. (1948); *Divertimento* (1952); Piano Concerto (1958). **CHAMBER:** *5 Character Pieces* for Oboe, Clarinet, and Bassoon (1962); piano music.

BIBL.: M. Pallandios, ed., *M.G. P.*, *moussourgos* (Athens, 1968).

Pallavicino, Benedetto, Italian composer; b. Cremona, 1551; d. Mantua, Nov. 26, 1601. He was a court musician in Mantua from 1583 and maestro di cappella to the Duke from 1596. Monteverdi mentions Pallavicino's death in a letter applying for his post to the Duke of Mantua (Nov. 28, 1601). Pallavicino was a particularly distinguished composer of madrigals.

WORKS: SACRED: *Liber primus missarum* for 4 to 6 Voices (Venice, 1603); *Sacrae Dei laudes* for 8, 12, and 16 Voices (Venice, 1605); motet for 5 Voices, etc. **SECULAR:** *Il primo libro de madrigali* for 4 Voices (Venice, 1579); *Il primo libro de madrigali* for 5 Voices (Venice, 1581); *Il secondo libro de madrigali* for 5 Voices (Venice, 1584); *Il terzo libro de madrigali* for 5 Voices (Venice, 1585); *Il primo libro de madrigali* for 6 Voices (Venice, 1587); *Il quatro libro de madrigali* for 5 Voices (Venice, 1588); *Il quinto libro de madrigali* for 5 Voices (Venice, 1593); *El sesto libro de madrigali* for 5 Voices (Venice, 1600); *Il settimo libro de madrigali* for 5 Voices (Venice, 1604); *L'ottavo libro de madrigali* for 5 Voices (Venice, 1612).

BIBL.: T. Bridges, *The Madrigals of B. P.* (diss., Univ. of Calif., 1952); G. Sartori, "Monteverdiana," *Musical Quarterly* (July 1952); P. Flanders, *The Five-Part Madrigals of B. P.* (diss., N.Y. Univ., 1972); idem, *A Thematic Index to the Works of B. P.* (Hackensack, N.J., 1974).

Pallavicino, Carlo, Italian composer; b. Salò, near Brescia, date unknown; d. Dresden, Jan. 29, 1688. He served as an organista ai concerti at S. Antonio in Padua in 1665–66, and in 1673–74 was maestro dei concerti there. He became a Vice-Kapellmeister at the Dresden court in 1667; was named Kapellmeister in 1672. In 1674 he was named maestro di coro of the Ospedale degli Incurabili in Venice. In succeeding years he became one of the leading opera composers in Venice. In 1685 he accepted an invitation from the Elector Johann Georg III of Saxony to resume his former post as Dresden Kapellmeister. On Jan. 1, 1687, he assumed his duties as director of theater and chamber music. Thirteen of his operas are extant.

BIBL.: J. Smith, "C. P.," *Proceedings of the Royal Musical Association*, XCVI (1969–70).

Pallemaerts, Edmundo, Belgian composer and teacher; b. Mechelen, Dec. 21, 1867; d. Buenos Aires, April 20, 1945. He studied music with De Greef and Kufferath at the Brussels Cons.; settled in Buenos Aires in 1889, and founded there the Cons. Argentino, of which he was the 1st director (1894). He wrote a *Fantasia Argentina* for Orch.; many minor works for Piano; also songs.

Pallo, Imre, Hungarian-American conductor; b. Budapest, May 15, 1941. He studied with Kodály at the Budapest Academy of Music; then took courses in conducting with Hans Swarowsky at the Vienna Academy of Music. He was music assistant to Herbert von Karajan and Karl Böhm at the Vienna and Salzburg festivals (1962–64). He made his American debut with the National Sym. Orch., Washington, D.C., in 1973. He then became a regular conductor at the N.Y. City Opera. In addition, he served as music director of the Hudson Valley Phil. Orch. at Poughkeepsie, N.Y. (from 1976); also held the title of 1st conductor at the Frankfurt Opera (from 1987).

Palm, Siegfried, noted German cellist, pedagogue, and opera administrator; b. Barmen, April 25, 1927. He studied cello with his father, a member of the City Orch. in Wuppertal.

After playing in the City Orch. in Lübeck (1945–47), he joined the North German Radio Sym. Orch. in Hamburg (1947). He served as a member of the Cologne Radio Sym. Orch. (1962–67); in 1962, joined the faculty of the Cologne Hochschule für Musik; was appointed its director in 1972. From 1977 to 1981 he was general administrator of the Deutsche Oper in West Berlin, without abandoning his career as a cellist. He traveled widely in Africa and Asia with the purpose of studying native music. He commissioned several modern composers, among them Blacher, Kagel, Keleman, Ligeti, Penderecki, Xenakis, and Zimmermann, to write special works which he performed in world premieres. He also contributed scholarly treatises on the new techniques of string instruments.

Palma, Athos, Argentine composer; b. Buenos Aires, June 7, 1891; d. Miramar, Jan. 10, 1951. He studied with C. Troiani (piano) and other teachers in Buenos Aires; in 1904, went to Europe, returning to Buenos Aires in 1914. There he was busily engaged as a teacher. He publ. *Teoría razonada de la música* (5 vols., n.d.) and *Tratado completo de armonía* (1941). His music follows the Italian tradition, although the subject matter is derived from South American history and literature.

WORKS: 2 operas: *Nazdah* (Buenos Aires, June 19, 1924) and *Los Hijos del Sol* (Buenos Aires, Nov. 10, 1928); *Cantares de mi tierra* for Strings (1914); symphonic poems: *Jardines* (1926) and *Los Hijos del Sol* (1929); Cello Sonata (1912); Violin Sonata (1924); Piano Sonata; many songs.

BIBL.: N. Lamuraglia, *A. P.: Vida, arte, educación* (Buenos Aires, 1954).

Palmer, Felicity (Joan), English soprano; b. Cheltenham, April 6, 1944. She studied at the Guildhall School of Music in London (1962–67) and with M. Schech at the Munich Hochschule für Musik; was a member of the John Alldis Choir and the Purcell Consort; in 1970 she won the Kathleen Ferrier Memorial Scholarship, the same year she made her formal debut in Purcell's *Dioclesian* at London's Queen Elizabeth Hall; made her operatic debut as Dido with the Kent Opera (1971); her U.S. operatic debut followed as Mozart's Countess with the Houston Grand Opera in 1973. Her concert and operatic repertory ranges from early music to the avant-garde.

Palmer, Horatio R(ichmond), American pedagogue and composer; b. Sherburne, N.Y., April 26, 1834; d. Yonkers, N.Y., Nov. 15, 1907. He was taught by his father and sister, later by various teachers in N.Y., Berlin, and Florence. He settled in Chicago after the Civil War, serving as music director of the Second Baptist Church. Returning to N.Y. (1874), he founded the Church Choral Union (1881), and conducted it in many concerts; was also music director at Chatauqua (1888–1901). He wrote the popular hymn tunes *Yield Not to Temptation* (1868) and *Vincent* (1887); publ. such collections as *The Song Queen* (1867), *The Song Monarch* (1874), and *The Choral Union* (1884); also publ. a number of pedagogical books, including *Palmer's Theory of Music* (1876) and *The Common Sense Music Reader* (1883).

BIBL.: G. Jones, "Dr. P.," *The Musician*, IV (1899).

Palmer, Robert (Moffat), American composer; b. Syracuse, N.Y., June 2, 1915. He studied at the Eastman School of Music in Rochester, N.Y., with Howard Hanson and Bernard Rogers (B.M., 1938; M.M., 1940); also studied with Roy Harris (1939), Aaron Copland (1940), and Quincy Porter; held 2 Guggenheim fellowships (1952–53; 1960–61) and a Fulbright Senior fellowship for study in Italy (1960–61). From 1940 to 1943 he was on the faculty at the Univ. of Kansas; from 1943 to 1980, taught at Cornell Univ. In his music he generally adhered to neo-Classical principles while producing works of a distinctive originality.

WORKS: ORCH.: *Poem* for Violin and Chamber Orch. (1938); Concerto for Small Orch. (1940); *K 19*, symphonic elegy for Thomas Wolfe (1945); Chamber Concerto for Violin, Oboe, and Strings (1949); *Variations, Chorale and Fugue* (1947; rev. 54); 2 syms. (1953, 1966); *Memorial Music* (1960); *Centennial Overture* (1965); *Choric Songs and Toccata* for Band (1968); Piano Concerto (1971); *Overture on a Southern Hymn* for Symphonic Band (1979); Concerto for 2 Pianos, 2 Percussion, Strings, and Brass (1984). VOCAL: *Abraham Lincoln Walks at Midnight* for Chorus and Orch. (1948); *Carmina amoris* for Soprano, Clarinet, Violin, and Piano (1951; also for Soprano and Chamber Orch.); *Of Night and the Sea*, chamber cantata (1956); *Nabuchodonosor*, dramatic oratorio (1964); *Portents of Aquarius* (*Visions and Prophecies*) for Narrator, Chorus, and Organ (1975). CHAMBER: 4 string quartets (1939; 1943, rev. 1947; 1954; 1959); 2 piano quartets (1947, 1973); Piano Quintet (1950); Viola Sonata (1951); Quintet for Clarinet, Strings, and Piano (1952, rev. 1953); Violin Sonata (1956); Piano Trio (1958); *Organon I* for Flute and Clarinet (1962) and *II* for Violin and Viola (1975); Trumpet Sonata (1972); *Sinfonia Concertante* for 9 Instruments (1972); 2 cello sonatas (1978, 1983). PIANO: 3 sonatas (1938, rev. 1946; 1942, rev. 1948; 1979); Sonata for 2 Pianos (1944); Sonata for Piano, 4-hands (1952); *Evening Music* (1956); 7 *Epigrams* (1957–59); *Morning Music* (1973).

BIBL.: W. Austin, "The Music of R. P.," *Musical Quarterly* (Jan. 1956).

Palmgren, Selim, eminent Finnish composer; b. Björneborg, Feb. 16, 1878; d. Helsinki, Dec. 13, 1951. He studied piano and composition at the Helsinki Cons. (1895–99); then went to Berlin, where he continued his piano studies with Ansorge, Berger, and Busoni. Returning to Finland, he became active as a choral conductor in Helsinki (1902–4); from 1909 to 1912 he was director of the Music Society in Turku. In 1921 he made a tour of the U.S. as a pianist; from 1923 to 1926 he taught piano and composition at the Eastman School of Music in Rochester, N.Y.; then returned to Helsinki; became a prof. of harmony and composition at the Sibelius Academy in 1936, remaining there until his death. He was married to the Finnish soprano Maikki Pakarinen in 1910, after her divorce from Armas Järnefelt. He publ. *Minusta tuli muusikko* (Helsinki, 1948). He excelled in piano compositions, often tinged with authentic Finnish colors; some of his pieces are marked by effective impressionistic devices, such as whole-tone scales and consecutive mild dissonances. Among his piano miniatures, *May Night* enjoyed considerable popularity with music students and their teachers.

WORKS: 2 operas: *Daniel Hjort* (Turku, April 15, 1910; rev. version, Helsinki, 1938) and *Peter Schlemihl*; 5 piano concertos: No. 1 (1903); No. 2, *Virta* (The Stream; 1913); No. 3, *Metamorphoses* (1915); No. 4, *Huhtikuu* (April; 1924–26); No. 5 (1939–41); Pastorale for Orch. (1920); *Turun lilja* (The Lily of Turku), cantata (1929); *Ballet Music* for Orch. (1944); *Concert Fantasy* for Violin and Orch. (1945); piano pieces, including 2 sonatas; *Fantasia*; 24 *Preludes*; *Ballade* (in the form of a theme with variations); *Finnische Lyrik* (12 pieces); *Finnische Suite* (*The Seasons*); *Maskenball*, suite; 24 *Études* (1921–22); etc.; songs and men's choruses.

BIBL.: K. Maasalo, "S. P.," *Suomalaisia Sävellyksiä*, II (Borgå, 1969).

Palombo, Paul (Martin), American composer; b. Pittsburgh, Sept. 10, 1937. He was trained in electronics; studied composition at the Peabody Cons. in Baltimore and at the Eastman School of Music in Rochester, N.Y. (Ph.D., 1969), with Wayne Barlow and Bernard Rogers; in 1969 he was appointed to the faculty of the Univ. of Cincinnati College-Cons. of Music; in 1973, assumed the direction of the electronic music studio there; remained until 1978; then was director of the music school of the Univ. of Washington in Seattle (1978–81); in 1981 he became dean of the College of Fine Arts at the Univ. of Wisconsin in Stevens Point.

WORKS: *Serenade* for String Orch. (1964); Piano Sonata (1965); Sinfonietta for Chamber Orch. (1965); Cello Sonata (1966); String Quartet No. 1 (1966–67); *Movement* for Orch. (1967); *Variations* for Orch. (1967–68); *Proteus*, ballet for Tape and Orch. (1969); *Morphosis*, electronic ballet (1970); *Metatheses* for Flute, Oboe, Double Bass, and Harpsichord (1970); *Montage* for Violin and Piano (1971); *Crystals*, electronic multimedia score (1971); *Ritratti anticamente* for Viola and Piano

(1972; rev. 1974); 4 *Sonos: I* for Harpsichord and Tape (1972); *II* for Harp and Tape (1972); *III* for Double Bass and Tape (1973); *IV* for String Trio and Tape (1974); *Etcetera*, electronic ballet (1973); *Stegowagenvolkssaurus*, electronic music for a sculpture (1973–74); *Variants* for Harpsichord (1975); *Laser Music* for Tape (1975); *Music for Triceratops Americus* for Electronics (1977); *The Dance* for Dance Band (1980); *Variatione da camera* for Flute, Clarinet, Viola, Cello, Piano, and 2 Percussion (1980); *Moody Blues* for Voices and Dance Band (1981); *Morning Memories* for Voice and Piano (1981); *It's Over* for Voice and Piano (1981).

Pálsson, Páll (Pampichler), Icelandic composer and conductor; b. Graz (of Icelandic parents), May 9, 1928. He studied with Michl, Mixa, and Brugger in Graz and conducting at the Hamburg Hochschule für Musik (1959–60); settled in Iceland in 1949 and was 1st trumpet player in the Iceland Sym. Orch. He was director of the Reykjavík Male Choir (from 1964) and artistic director of the Reykjavík Chamber Ensemble (from 1974).

WORKS: Divertimento for 18 Winds (1963); *Hringspil I* for Violin, Viola, Clarinet, and Bassoon (1964) and *II* for 2 Trumpets, Horn, and Trombone; *Crystals* for String Quartet and Wind Quintet (1970); *Requiem* for a cappella Chorus (1970); *Dialog* for Orch. (1973); *Mixed Things* for Flute and Piano (1977); *Hugledhing um L* (Meditation über L) for Orch. (1977; the "L" is for Ludwig van Beethoven); Clarinet Concerto (Reykjavík, Jan. 6, 1983).

Pampanini, Rosetta, Italian soprano; b. Milan, Sept. 2, 1896; d. Corbola, Aug. 2, 1973. She studied with Emma Molajoli in Milan; made her debut as Micaela in Rome in 1920; then continued her vocal studies; in 1925 she joined La Scala in Milan, remaining on its roster until 1937, with the exception of the 1931–33 seasons; also sang at Covent Garden in London (1928, 1929, 1933) and in Chicago (1931–32). After retiring in 1942, she taught voice. She was particularly admired for her Puccini roles, most notably Manon, Cio-Cio-San, and Mimi.

Panassié, Hugues, French writer on music; b. Paris, Feb. 27, 1912; d. Montauban, Dec. 8, 1974. He founded the Hot Club de France (1932); lectured on jazz at the Sorbonne (1937) and in the U.S. (1938).

WRITINGS: All publ. in Paris unless otherwise given: *Le Jazz Hot* (1934; Eng. tr. as *Hot Jazz*, N.Y., 1936); *The Real Jazz* (N.Y., 1942; French tr. as *La Véritable Musique de jazz*, Paris, 1946); *La Musique de jazz et le swing* (1945); *Douze années de jazz* (1927–1938) (1946); *Louis Armstrong* (1947); *Jazz panorama* (1950); *Discographie critique* (1951); with M. Gautier, *Dictionnaire du jazz* (1954; Eng. tr. as *Dictionary of Jazz*, London, 1956; U.S. ed. as *Guide to Jazz*, Boston, 1956).

Pandolfini, Angelica, Italian soprano, daughter of **Francesco Pandolfini;** b. Spoleto, Aug. 21, 1871; d. Lenno, July 15, 1959. She studied with Jules Massart in Paris; made her debut as Marguerite in 1894 in Modena; after singing in the Italian provinces, she appeared at La Scala in Milan (1897–99; 1906). She created the title role in *Adriana Lecouvreur* at the Teatro Lirico in Milan in 1902; retired from the stage in 1908. She was best known for her convincing portrayals of *verismo* roles.

Pandolfini, Francesco, Italian baritone, father of **Angelica Pandolfini;** b. Termini Imerese, Palermo, Nov. 22, 1836; d. Milan, Feb. 15, 1916. He studied with Ronconi and Vannuccini in Florence; made his debut in *Gemma di Vergy* in Pisa in 1859; then sang throughout Italy. In 1871 he appeared with notable success at La Scala in Milan; he created the role of Arnoldo in *I Lituani* by Ponchielli there in 1874; also sang at Covent Garden in London (1877, 1882); retired from the stage in 1890.

Panerai, Rolando, Italian baritone; b. Campi Bisenzio, near Florence, Oct. 17, 1924. He studied at the Florence Cons. with Frazzi; also with di Armani and G. Tess in Milan; after winning 1st prize in the voice competition in Spoleto, he made his debut as Faraone in *Mosè* in Naples (1947); in 1951 he joined La Scala in Milan; also sang at Covent Garden in London, the Vienna State Opera, and the Salzburg Festivals. He specialized in the Italian repertoire.

Panizza, Ettore, Argentine conductor and composer of Italian extraction; b. Buenos Aires, Aug. 12, 1875; d. Milan, Nov. 27, 1967. He studied at the Milan Cons., graduating in 1898 with prizes for piano and composition. From 1907 to 1914 and again in 1924 he conducted at London's Covent Garden. He made his 1st appearance at the Teatro Colón (1908), conducting there regularly from 1921. He joined the roster of Milan's La Scala (1916), serving as assistant to Toscanini (1921–29); was a regular conductor there (1930–32; 1946–48); also conducted at the Chicago Civic Opera (1922–24) and N.Y.'s Metropolitan Opera (1934–42). He publ. an autobiography, *Medio siglo de vida musical* (Buenos Aires, 1952).

WORKS: Operas: *Il Fidanzato del mare* (Buenos Aires, Aug. 15, 1897); *Medio evo latino* (Genoa, Nov. 17, 1900); *Aurora* (Buenos Aires, Sept. 5, 1908); *Bisanzio* (Buenos Aires, July 25, 1939); also *Il Re della foresta* for Soli, Chorus, and Orch.; *Tema con variaciones* for Orch.; Violin Sonata; Cello Sonata; String Quartet; piano pieces; songs.

Pankiewicz, Eugeniusz, Polish pianist and composer; b. Siedlce, Dec. 15, 1857; d. Tworki, near Warsaw, Dec. 24, 1898. He studied piano in Lublin; then went to Warsaw to study with J. Wieniawski; later took master classes with Leschetizky in St. Petersburg; he also studied composition with W. Zelenski (1880–81) and Z. Noskowski (1881–83) in Warsaw. He subsequently taught piano at the Warsaw Music Inst.; was confined to a mental hospital (from 1895). He became best known for his attractive songs and piano miniatures, the latter revealing the influence of Chopin.

BIBL.: W. Poźniak, *E. P.* (Krakow, 1958; with thematic catalogue of works).

Pannain, Guido, distinguished Italian musicologist and composer; b. Naples, Nov. 17, 1891; d. there, Sept. 6, 1977. He studied composition with C. de Nardis at the Naples Cons.; after graduating in 1914, he was prof. of music history at the Naples Cons. (1915–61); also wrote music criticism. As a musicologist, he devoted much of his time to the study of Neapolitan music.

WRITINGS: *La teoria musicale di G. Tinctoris* (Naples, 1913); *Le origini della scuola musicale napoletana* (Naples, 1914); *Le origini e lo sviluppo dell'arte pianistica in Italia dal 1500 fino al 1730 circa* (Naples, 1917); *Lineamenti di storia della musica* (Naples, 1922; 9th ed., rev., 1970); *Musica e musicisti in Napoli nel secolo XIX* (Naples, 1922); *Musicisti dei tempi nuovi* (Milan, 1932; Eng. tr. as *Modern Composers,* 1932; 2nd Italian ed., 1954); with A. della Corte, *Storia della musica* (Turin, 1936; 4th ed., 1964); *Il Conservatorio di musica di S. Pietro in Maiella* (Florence, 1942); *La vita del linguaggio musicale* (Milan, 1947; 2nd ed., 1956); *Ottocento musicale italiano: Saggi e note* (Milan, 1952); *L'opera e le opere ed altri scritti di letteratura musicale* (Milan, 1958); *Giuseppe Verdi* (Turin, 1964); *Richard Wagner: Vita di un artista* (Milan, 1964).

WORKS: Operas: *L'Intrusa* (1926; Genoa, 1940); *Beatrice Cenci* (Naples, Feb. 21, 1942); *Madame Bovary* (Naples, April 16, 1955); also a *Requiem* (1912) and a *Stabat Mater* (1969); orch. works, including 2 violin concertos (1930, 1960); Viola Concerto (1955); Harp Concerto (1959); Piano Concerto (1969).

Panofka, Heinrich, Silesian violinist, music critic, singing teacher, and composer; b. Breslau, Oct. 3, 1807; d. Florence, Nov. 18, 1887. He began his career as a violinist; after playing some concerts in Germany, he went to Paris in 1832 and began taking singing lessons with Bordogni. With Bordogni he organized, in 1842, the Académie du Chant des Amateurs, which failed to prosper. In 1847 he went to London, where he became a fashionable singing teacher; eventually he went to Florence, spending his last days there. He publ. a manual, *L'Art de chanter* (Paris, 1854) and *Abécédaire vocal* (Paris, 1858); his *Voix de chanteurs* (Paris, c.1870) reflects his studies in Italy.

Panseron, Auguste-Mathieu, French singing teacher and composer; b. Paris, April 26, 1795; d. there, July 29, 1859. His father, who orchestrated many operas for Grétry, taught him until he entered the Paris Cons. in 1804; he studied under Gossec, Levasseur, and Berton, winning the Prix de Rome in 1813. After study in Bologna, Rome, Naples, Vienna (with Salieri), and Munich, he returned to Paris in 1818, taught singing, was an accompanist at the Opéra-Comique, and wrote 4 1-act operas; became a prof. of solfeggio at the Cons. in 1826, of vocalization in 1831, and of singing in 1836. From 1825 to 1840 he brought out some 200 *romances;* he also composed church music, but attained real eminence as a vocal teacher and as a writer of instructive works on singing.

Pantaleoni, Adriano, Italian baritone, brother of **Romilda Pantaleoni;** b. Udine, Oct. 7, 1837; d. there, Dec. 18, 1908. He studied in Udine and Milan; was a principal member of La Scala in Milan (1871–77; 1896); also sang in London and the U.S. (1879); after his retirement, he taught voice in Udine and Trieste. He was particularly noted for his roles in Verdi's operas.

Pantaleoni, Romilda, Italian soprano, sister of **Adriano Pantaleoni;** b. Udine, 1847; d. Milan, May 20, 1917. She studied with Prati, Rossi, and Lamperti in Milan; made her debut at the Teatro Carcano in Milan in Foroni's *Margherita* in 1868; then sang in Turin and at La Scala in Milan, where she created the role of Desdemona in Verdi's *Otello* in 1887 and Tigrana in Puccini's *Edgar* in 1889.

Panufnik, Andrzej, eminent Polish-born English conductor and composer; b. Warsaw, Sept. 24, 1914. His father was a Polish manufacturer of string instruments, his mother an Englishwoman who studied violin in Warsaw. He began his musical training with his mother; after studying composition with Sikorski at the Warsaw Cons. (diploma, 1936), he took conducting lessons with Weingartner at the Vienna Academy of Music (1937–38); subsequently completed his training with Gaubert in Paris, and also studied in London (1938–39). He returned to Warsaw in 1939, remaining there during the Nazi occupation, playing piano in the underground; after the liberation, he conducted the Krakow Phil. (1945–46) and the Warsaw Phil. (1946–47); he then left his homeland in protest of the Communist regime (1954), settling in England, where he became a naturalized British citizen (1961); after serving as music director of the City of Birmingham Sym. Orch. (1957–59), he devoted himself to composition. His wife, Scarlett Panufnik, publ. *Out of the City of Fear* (London, 1956), recounting his flight from Poland; his autobiography was publ. as *Composing Myself* (London, 1986). In 1988 he appeared as a guest conductor of his own works with the N.Y. Chamber Sym. and in 1990 with the Chicago Sym. Orch. In his early years he belonged to the vanguard group of Polish composers. He made use of advanced techniques, including quarter-tones, and made certain innovations in notation; in several of his orch. works, he left blank spaces in the place of rests to indicate inactive instrumental parts. In his later music he adopted a more circumspect idiom—expressive, direct, and communicative. His compositions to 1944 were destroyed during the Warsaw uprising.

WORKS: ORCH.: *Tragic Overture* (1942; Warsaw, 1943; reconstructed 1945; rev. 1955); *Nocturne* (1947; Paris, 1948; rev. 1955); *Lullaby* for 29 Strings and 2 Harps (1947; Krakow, 1948; rev. 1955); *Divertimento* for Strings, after trios by Felix Janiewicz (1947; Krakow, 1948; rev. 1955); *Sinfonica rustica* (1948; Krakow, 1949; rev. 1955); *Old Polish Suite* for String Orch. (1950; Warsaw, 1951; rev. 1955); *Concerto in modo antico* for Trumpet and Orch. (Krakow, 1951; rev. 1955); *Heroic Overture* (Helsinki, July 27, 1952; rev. 1969); *Rhapsody* (1956; BBC, London, Jan. 11, 1957); *Sinfonica elegiaca* (Houston, Nov. 21, 1957; rev. 1966); *Polonia* (London, Aug. 21, 1959); Piano Concerto (Birmingham, England, Jan. 25, 1962; rev. 1970, 1972, 1982); *Landscape* for String Orch. (1962; rev.

1965; Twickenham, Nov. 13, 1965); *Autumn Music* (1962; rev. 1965; Paris, Jan. 16, 1968); *Sinfonia sacra* (1963; Monte Carlo, Aug. 12, 1964); *Jagiellonian Triptych* for String Orch. (London, Sept. 24, 1966); *Katyń Epitaph* (1967; N.Y., Nov. 17, 1968; rev. 1969); Concerto for Violin and Strings (1971; London, July 18, 1972); *Sinfonia concertante* for Flute, Harp, and Strings (1973; London, May 20, 1974); *Sinfonia di sfere* (1974–75; London, April 13, 1976); *Sinfonia mistica* (1977; Middlesbrough, England, Jan. 17, 1978); *Metasinfonia* for Organ, Timpani, and Strings (Manchester, England, Sept. 9, 1978); *Concerto festivo* (London, June 17, 1979); Concertino for Timpani, Percussion, and Strings (1979–80; London, Jan. 24, 1981); *Sinfonia votiva* (1981; Boston, Jan. 28, 1982; rev. 1984); *A Procession for Peace* (London, July 16, 1983); *Arbor cosmica*, 12 evocations for 12 Strings or String Orch. (1983; N.Y., Nov. 14, 1984); Concerto for Bassoon and Small Orch. (1985; Milwaukee, May 18, 1986); Sym. No. 9, *Sinfonia di speranza* (1986; London, Feb. 25, 1987); *Harmony* (N.Y., Dec. 16, 1989); Sym. No. 10 (1989; Chicago, Feb. 1, 1990). VOCAL: *5 Polish Peasant Songs* for Soprano or Treble Voices, 2 Flutes, 2 Clarinets, and Bass Clarinet (1940; reconstructed 1945; Krakow, 1945; rev. 1959); *Song to the Virgin Mary* for Unaccompanied Chorus or 6 Solo Voices (London, April 26, 1964; rev. 1969); *Universal Prayer* for Soloists, Chorus, 3 Harps, and Organ (1968–69; N.Y., May 24, 1970); *Thames Pageant*, cantata for Young Players and Singers (1969; Twickenham, Feb. 7, 1970); *Winter Solstice* for Soprano, Baritone, Chorus, 3 Trumpets, 3 Trombones, Timpani, and Glockenspiel (Kingston-upon-Thames, Dec. 16, 1972); *Invocation for Peace* for Treble Voices, 2 Trumpets, and 2 Trombones (Southampton, England, Nov. 28, 1972). CHAMBER: Piano Trio (1934; Warsaw, 1935; reconstructed 1945; rev. 1977); *Triangles* for 3 Flutes and 3 Cellos (BBC-TV, April 14, 1972); 2 string quartets: No. 1 (London, Oct. 19, 1976); No. 2, *Messages* (St. Asaph's Cathedral, North Wales, Sept. 25, 1980); piano works, including *Reflections* (1968; London, April 21, 1972) and *Pentasonata* (1984; Aldeburgh, June 23, 1989).

BIBL.: H. Truscott, "The Symphonies of A. P.," *Musical Times* (July 1989).

Panula, Jorma, Finnish conductor and composer; b. Kauhajoki, Aug. 10, 1930. He studied in Helsinki at the School of Church Music and with Leo Funtek at the Sibelius Academy (1948–53); then pursued conducting studies with Dean Dixon in Lund (1953), and with Albert Wolff (1957) and Franco Ferrara (1958) in Hilversum. He conducted theater orchs. in Lahti (1953–55), Tampere (1955–58), and Helsinki (1958–62); after conducting the Finnish National Opera (1962–63), he conducted the Turku Phil. (1963–65), the Helsinki Phil. (1965–72), the Århus Sym. Orch. in Denmark (1972–75), and the Espoo City Orch. (from 1986); also appeared as a guest conductor throughout Europe and in North America. He served as a prof. of conducting at the Sibelius Academy (from 1972), the Stockholm Musikhögskolan (from 1980), and the Copenhagen Royal Danish Cons. of Music (from 1986).

WORKS: STAGE: 2 folk operas: *Jaakko Ilkka* (1978) and *Jokiooppera* (The River Opera; 1982); *Vallan Miehet* (Men of Power), television opera (1987); musicals; scores for films, radio, and television. ORCH.: Violin Concerto (1954); *Adagio and Allegro* (1957); *Orkesteriesittely* (Orchestral Introduction; 1965); *Jazz Capriccio* for Piano and Orch. (1965); Concertino (1972); also choral music; numerous arrangements of folk music.

Panum, Hortense, Danish musicologist; b. Kiel, Germany (of Danish parents), March 14, 1856; d. Copenhagen, April 26, 1933. Her father, a prof. of physiology at Kiel Univ., returned to Copenhagen in 1864. She studied music history with W. Tappert in Berlin (1886–87). After her return to Denmark, she devoted herself to historical studies (especially concerning early instruments).

WRITINGS: *Illustreret musikhistorie* (1895–1905; Part II by W. Behrend); *Musiken og musiklivet i Danmark för anno 1880* (1904); *Musiken og musiklivet i Danmark efter anno 1800* (1906); *Haydn, Mozart, og Beethoven* (1908); *Middelalderens strengeinstrumenter og dares Forlöbere i Oldtiden* (I, 1915; II, 1928; III, 1931; Eng. ed. in one vol., by J. Pulver, as *The Stringed Instruments of the Middle Ages, Their Evolution*, etc., London, 1939; *Af musikhistoriens Billedbog* (1916; 2nd ed., 1930); *Langelegen som dansk folkeinstrument* (1918); *Illustreret musiklexikon* (1924–26; with W. Behrend and O. Sandvik; new ed., 1940).

Panzéra, Charles (Auguste Louis), noted Swiss-born French baritone; b. Geneva, Feb. 16, 1896; d. Paris, June 6, 1976. He studied at the Paris Cons.; made his debut as Albert in *Werther* at the Paris Opéra-Comique in 1919; then gave concerts in Europe and America; also taught at the Juilliard School in N.Y. In 1949 he was appointed a prof. at the Paris Cons. He excelled in the interpretation of French songs. He publ. *L'Art de chanter* (Paris, 1945), *L'Amour de chanter* (Paris, 1957), *L'Art vocal: 30 leçons de chant* (Paris, 1959), and *Votre voix: Directives générales* (Paris, 1967).

Papaioannou, Yannis (Andreou), Greek composer; b. Kavala, Jan. 6, 1911; d. Athens, May 11, 1989. He studied piano and music theory at the Hellenic Cons. in Athens (1922–34); then had some composition lessons with Honegger in Paris (1949). In 1953 he was appointed to the staff of his alma mater. His music traversed from a fairly conservative neo-Classical idiom to dodecaphony and eventually integral serialism.

WORKS: ORCH.: *Idyll* (1938); *Choreographic Prelude* (1939); symphonic poems: *The Corsair* (1940); *Poem of the Forest* (1942); *Vassilis the Albanian* (1945); *Matins of Souls* (1947); *Pygmalion* (1951); *Hellas* (1956); *Symphonic Tableau* (1968); 5 syms. (1946, 1951, 1953, 1963, 1964); *Triptych* for Strings (1947); Piano Concerto (1950); *Concerto for Orchestra* (1954); 3 suites for Orch. (Nos. 1 and 2, *Pictures from Asia*; No. 3, *Egypt*, 1961); Concertino for Piano and String Orch. (1962); *India*, suite (1969); *4 Orphic Hymns* for Narrator and Instrumental Ensemble (1971); Concerto for Violin and Chamber Orch. (1971); Concerto for Violin, Piano, and Orch. (1972–73). VOCAL: *Daphnis and Chloe* for Chorus and Orch. (1934); *Sarpidon's Funeral*, cantata (1965); *3 Byzantine Odes* for Soprano and Chamber Ensemble (1966); *Electra Monologues* for Soprano and Instrumental Ensemble (1968); *Footsteps* for Mezzo-soprano, Narrator, Chorus, and Instrumental Ensemble (1969). CHAMBER: Violin Sonata (1947); *Winter Fantasy*, ballet for Flute, Clarinet, Violin, Cello, and Piano (1950); String Quartet (1959); *Suite* for Guitar (1960); Sonatina for Flute and Guitar (1962); Quartet for Flute, Clarinet, Guitar, and Cello (1962); Trio for Oboe, Clarinet, and Bassoon (1962); *Archaic* for 2 Guitars (1962); String Trio (1963); Trio for Flute, Viola, and Guitar (1968); Quartet for Oboe, Clarinet, Viola, and Piano (1968); *5 Characters*, brass quintet (1970); *Aphigissis* (Narration) for Violin (1970); *The Harlequin's Prattling* for Tuba (1971); *Portrait* for Tuba (1972); *Syneirmoi* (Associations) for 9 Instruments (1973); *Echomorphes* (Sound-figures) for Violin (1975); *Rhythms and Colors* for Cello (1976); *Puck* for Cello (1976); Piano Trio (1977); Piano Sonata (1958); other pieces for Piano; also choruses, songs, theater music.

Papandopulo, Boris, Croatian conductor and composer; b. Bad Honnef am Rhein, Feb. 25, 1906. He studied in Zagreb and Vienna; in 1959 was appointed conductor of the National Theater in Zagreb; from 1964 to 1968 he conducted in Split and Rijeka; later filled engagements as a guest conductor in Yugoslavia. His operas and most of his instrumental works are written in a national Croatian idiom; but he also experimented with the 12-tone techniques, as exemplified by his pointedly titled *Dodekafonski concert* for 2 Pianos (1961).

WORKS: OPERAS: *Amiftrion* (Zagreb, Feb. 17, 1940); *Sunčanica* (The Sun Girl; Zagreb, June 13, 1942); *Rona* (Rijeka, May 25, 1955); *Marulova Pisan* (Marul's Song; Split, Aug. 14, 1970); *Madame Buffault* (1972). BALLETS: *Zlato* (Gold; Zagreb, May 31, 1930); *Žetva* (The Harvest; Sarajevo, March 25, 1950); *Intermezzo* (Sarajevo, May 25, 1953); *Beatrice Cenci* (Gelsenkirchen, 1959); *Gitanella* (1965); *Doktor Atom*, subtitled $Qu + H^3 + H^2 = He^4 + n + 9$ (Rijeka, Oct. 29, 1966); *Ljudi u hotelu* (People in a Hotel; Vienna, May 27, 1967); *Teuta* (1973). ORCH.: 2 syms.: No. 1 (1930) and No. 2 (Zagreb, May 8, 1946); Sinfonietta (1938); 4 piano concertos (1938, 1942, 1947, 1958); Concerto for Harpsichord and String Orch. (1962); Double-bass Concerto (1968); Concerto for 4 Timpani and Orch. (1969); also many cantatas; choruses; songs; 5 string quartets (1927, 1933, 1945, 1950, 1970); Piano Quartet (1938); Clarinet Quintet (1940); Sonata for Viola and Piano (1956); *Mozaik* for Strings and Jazz Quartet (1963); piano pieces.

Papi, Gennaro, Italian-American conductor; b. Naples, Dec. 21, 1886; d. N.Y., Nov. 29, 1941. He studied with de Nardis at the S. Pietro a Majella Cons. in Naples (graduated 1904); was an assistant conductor in Warsaw (1909–10), Turin (1911), London (Covent Garden, 1911–12), Milan, Odessa, and Buenos Aires; from 1913 to 1916, was assistant to Toscanini at N.Y.'s Metropolitan Opera; from 1916 to 1926, a conductor there; from 1925 to 1932, a conductor of the Chicago Civic Opera; then made appearances in Milan, Mexico City, and Buenos Aires until 1935, when he was reengaged at the Metropolitan; he remained with the company until his death.

Papier, Rosa, Austrian mezzo-soprano; b. Baden, near Vienna, Sept. 15, 1858; d. Vienna, Feb. 9, 1932. She sang at the Vienna Court Opera; later taught at the Vienna Cons. In 1881 she married the pianist Hans Paumgartner; their son was the conductor and musicologist **Bernhard Paumgartner.**

Papineau-Couture, Jean, Canadian composer; b. Outremont, Montreal, Nov. 12, 1916. He studied piano with Françoise D'Amour (1926–39) and counterpoint with Gabriel Cusson (1937–40) in Montreal, and also received further piano training there with Léo-Pol Morin (1939–40); then studied composition with Quincy Porter, conducting with Francis Findlay, and piano with Beveridge Webster at the New England Cons. of Music in Boson (B.Mus., 1941); subsequently studied with Nadia Boulanger at the Longy School in Cambridge, Mass. (1941–43), continuing his studies with her in Wis. and Calif. He taught at Brebeuf College (1945–46); then at the Cons. de Musique du Québec à Montréal (1946–63) and the Univ. of Montreal (1951–85), where he was dean of the music faculty (1968–73); was founding president of the Société de Musique Contemporaine du Québec (1966–73). He was made an Officer of the Order of Canada in 1969. His music evolved from a neo-Baroque idiom to Expressionism, with judicious excursions into serial techniques.

WORKS: STAGE: *Papotages* (Tittle-Tattle), ballet (1949; Montreal, Nov. 20, 1950). ORCH.: Concerto grosso for Small Orch. (1943; rev. 1955); Sym. (1947–48; rev. 1956); Concerto for Violin and Chamber Orch. (1951); *Poème* for Orch. (1952); *Prélude* for Orch. (1953); 5 *Pièces concertantes*: No. 1, *Repliement* (Folding Back), for Piano and String Orch. (1956); No. 2, *Eventails,* for Cello and Chamber Orch. (1959); No. 3, *Variations,* for Flute, Clarinet, Violin, Cello, Harp, and String Orch. (1959); No. 4, *Additions,* for Oboe and String Orch. (1959); No. 5, *Miroirs* (1963); 3 *Pieces* (1961); Piano Concerto (1965; Toronto, Feb. 6, 1966); *Oscillations* (1969); *Obsession* for 16 Players (1973); *Clair-obscur* for Double Bassoon, Double Bass, and Orch. (1986); *Nuit polaire* for Contralto and 10 Instruments (1986). VOCAL: *Eglogues* for Alto, Flute, and Piano (1942); *Psaume CL* for Soprano, Tenor, Chorus, Wind Ensemble, and 1 or 2 Organs (1954); *Paysage* for 8 Narrators, 8 Singers, Wind Quintet, String Quintet, Piano, Harp, and Percussion (1968; Zagreb, May 9, 1969); *Contraste* for Voice and Orch. (1970); *Prouesse* for Alto (1985). CHAMBER: Violin Sonata (1944; rev. 1953); *Aria* for Violin (1946); *Suite* for Flute, Clarinet, Bassoon, Horn, and Piano (1947); 2 string quartets (1953, 1967); *Suite* for Violin (1956); *Eclosion,* stage music for a Mime, Violin, Piano, and Tape (1961); *Fantaisie* for Wind Quintet (1963); *Canons* for Brass Quintet (1964); Sextet for Oboe, Clarinet, Bassoon, Violin, Viola, and Cello (1967); *Nocturnes* for Flute, Clarinet, Violin, Cello, Harpsichord, Guitar, and Percussion (1969); *Dyarchie* for Harpsichord (1971); Trio for Clarinet, Viola, and Piano (1974); *Départ* for Alto Flute (1974); *Versegères*

for Bass Flute (1975); *Slano* for String Trio (1975); *J'aime les tierces mineures* for Flute (1976); *Le Débat du cœur et du corps* for Narrator, Cello, and Percussion (1977); *Exploration* for Guitar (1983); *Arcadie* for 4 Flutists (1986); piano pieces.

Pâque, (Marie Joseph Léon) Désiré, remarkable Belgian-born French conductor, teacher, and composer; b. Liège, May 21, 1867; d. Bessancourt, Val d'Oise, Nov. 20, 1939. He began to compose as a child; wrote a Mass at the age of 12; studied at the Liège Cons., where he was a prof. of music theory until 1897. He was a conductor and prof. of composition in Athens (1900–3); then was a prof. of organ at the Lisbon Cons. (1904), and also conducted at the Portuguese court; subsequently traveled throughout Europe (from 1909), settling in Paris in 1914. He wrote 144 opus nos.; his production falls into 3 periods: cosmopolitan and formal (1886–1908); freely episodic, in an *adjonction constante* of recurrent themes (1909–18); atonal and polytonal (1919–39). His last manner was exemplified by *10 pièces atonales pour la jeunesse* for Piano (1925). The bulk of his music remains in MS. Other works include an opera, *Vaima* (1903; Ostend, 1904); 8 syms. (1895, 1905, 1912, 1916, 1919, 1927, 1934, 1936); 2 piano concertos (1888, 1935); Cello Concerto (1893); *Ouverture sur 3 thèmes bulgares* (Ostend, Aug. 17, 1895); *Ouverture libre* (1899; Munich, Dec. 29, 1911); Requiem (1900); 10 string quartets (1892–1939); 3 piano quintets (1896, 1924, 1938); 2 sextets (1909, 1919); 5 suites for Piano, Violin, and Viola (1891–96); 3 piano trios (1903–30); 4 violin sonatas (1890–1934); 4 piano sonatas (1911); Viola Sonata (1915); 13 albums of piano pieces; choral works.

BIBL.: A. Coeuroy, "D. P.," *La Revue Musicale,* III/1 (1921).

Paradies (originally **Paradisi**), (**Pietro**) **Domenico,** Italian composer and harpsichordist; b. Naples, 1707; d. Venice, Aug. 25, 1791. He was a pupil of Porpora; brought out several operas in Italy; in 1746, went to London, where he earned a living mainly as a teacher of harpsichord playing, but also produced several operas, including *Fetonte* (London, Jan. 17, 1747) and *La forza d'amore* (London, Jan. 19, 1751); also composed several symphonic overtures, 2 organ concertos, and cantatas. He publ. *12 sonate di gravicembalo* (London, 1754). Toward the end of his life he returned to Italy. Some of his MSS are preserved in the Fitzwilliam Museum at Cambridge; his sonatas were brought out by G. Benvenuti and D. Cipollini in Milan (1920).

Paradis, Maria Theresia von, noted Austrian pianist, organist, singer, and composer; b. Vienna, May 15, 1759; d. there, Feb. 1, 1824. She was the daughter of Josef von Paradis, the imperial court secretary; she studied piano with L. Koželuh, singing with Richter, singing and dramatic composition with Salieri, dramatic composition with Vogler, and theory with Friberth; appeared in concerts in Vienna (from c.1775). She was blind from her 5th year; Mesmer became interested in her condition and attempted to cure her, without effect (1777–78). She set out on a major concert tour in 1783, visiting Salzburg, Frankfurt, Mainz, and other cities; in 1784 arrived in Paris, where she was highly praised for her appearances as both a keyboard artist and a singer at the Concert Spirituel; Mozart composed a concerto for her. She went to London in late 1784 and appeared at court and in public concerts; returned to Vienna in 1786, and continued to make tours until founding her own music inst. there (1808). Her friend and librettist, Johann Riedinger, invented a notation system for her, and she became a skilled composer. Much of her music is not extant.

WORKS: Stage: *Ariadne und Bacchus,* melodrama (Laxenburg, June 20, 1791); *Der Schulkandidat,* ländliches singspiel (Vienna, Dec. 5, 1792); *Rinaldo und Alcine, Die Insel der Verführung,* comic opera (Prague, June 30, 1797); 2 piano concertos; 3 cantatas; 4 piano sonatas (Amsterdam, 1778); 12 piano sonatas (Paris, 1792); Piano Trio (Vienna, 1800); other piano music; songs; etc.

BIBL.: E. Komorzynski, "Mozart and M.T. P.," *Mozart-Jahrbuch* (Salzburg, 1952); H. Ullrich, "M.T. P. in London," *Music*

& *Letters* (Jan. 1962); idem, "Die erste öffentliche Musikschule der M.T. P. in Wien (1808–24)," *Musikerziehung*, XVI (1962–63); idem, "M.T. P.: Werkverzeichnis," *Beiträge zur Musikwissenschaft*, V (1963).

Paranov, Moshe, American pianist, conductor, and music educator; b. Hartford, Conn., Oct. 28, 1895. He studied piano with Julius Hartt and Harold Bauer and composition with Ernest Bloch and Rubin Goldmark. He married Hartt's daughter, Pauline; was co-founder of the Hartt School of Music in Hartford (1920); was its director (1938–57); after it became part of the Univ. of Hartford, he was its president (1957–71). He was conductor of the Hartford Opera Guild, the Hartt Sym. Orch., and the Hartt Opera Theater (1942–71); was also conductor of the Hartford Sym. Orch. (1947–53).

Paratore, Anthony (b. Boston, June 17, 1944) and his brother **Joseph** (b. Boston, March 19, 1948), outstanding American duo-pianists. They followed separate courses of study as pianists, graduating from the Boston Univ. School of Fine and Applied Arts; both entered the Juilliard School of Music in N.Y., in the class of Rosina Lhévinne, who suggested that they try a career as duo-pianists; they subsequently appeared as duo-pianists with Arthur Fiedler and the Boston Pops Orch., and then made their N.Y. recital debut in 1973. In 1974 they won 1st prize at the Munich International Competition, and scored international successes as duo-pianists. In addition to the standard repertory, they also perf. contemporary works; commissioned and gave the premiere of Michael Schelle's Concerto for 2 Pianos and Orch. (Indianapolis, Jan. 14, 1988).

Paray, Paul, distinguished French conductor and composer; b. Le Tréport, May 24, 1886; d. Monte Carlo, Oct. 10, 1979. He began his musical education with his father, a church organist; in 1904 he entered the Paris Cons. as a composition student; studied there with Leroux, Caussade, Lenepveu, and Vidal; received the Premier Grand Prix de Rome with his cantata *Yanitza* (1911). He was drafted into the French army during World War I and was taken prisoner by the Germans; composed a String Quartet while interned at Darmstadt; after the Armistice (1918), he became conductor of the orch. of the Casino de Cauterets. Substituting for an ailing André Caplet, Paray made his Paris debut on Feb. 20, 1920, and soon became assistant conductor of the Lamoureux Orch., succeeding Chevillard as 1st conductor in 1923; was appointed conductor of sym. concerts in Monte Carlo in 1928, and in 1932 succeeded Pierné as conductor of the Concerts Colonne, remaining until the orch. was disbanded by the Nazi occupiers of Paris in 1940; conducted briefly in Marseilles and, following the liberation of Paris, resumed his duties with the Concerts Colonne (1944–52). Paray made his American debut in N.Y. on July 24, 1939, in a program of French music. In 1952 he became music director of the reorganized Detroit Sym. Orch., and on Oct. 18, 1956, inaugurated the new Ford Auditorium in Detroit in a program that included his own *Mass for the 500th Anniversary of the Death of Joan of Arc,* a work first heard in the Cathedral in Rouen, France, in 1931; he resigned in 1963 and returned to France, though he continued to guest-conduct internationally. In July 1977, at the age of 91, he conducted an orch. concert in honor of Marc Chagall's 90th birthday celebration in Nice, and, at age 92, made his last conducting appearance in the U.S., leading the orch. of the Curtis Inst. of Music in Philadelphia. As a conductor, he concentrated on the Classics and Romantics, and French music. He was the composer of several highly competent works, including, besides *Yanitza* and his *Mass,* a ballet entitled *Artémis troublée* (Paris, April 28, 1922, perf. as a symphonic poem, *Adonis troublé*); *Fantaisie* for Piano and Orch. (Paris, March 25, 1923); 2 full syms., in C (1935) and in A (1940); Sym. for Strings; String Quartet (1918); Violin Sonata (1908); Cello Sonata (1919); piano pieces.
BIBL.: W. Landowski, *P. P.* (Lyons, 1956); N. Shear, "P. P. at 92: A Link with History," *High Fidelity/Musical America* (March 1979).

Parelli (real name, **Paparella**), **Attilio,** Italian conductor and composer; b. Monteleone d'Orvieto, near Perugia, May 31, 1874; d. there, Dec. 26, 1944. He studied at the Accademia di Santa Cecilia in Rome, graduating in 1899; held various posts as a conductor in Italy and France; went to the U.S. as assistant conductor to Campanini at the Manhattan Opera in N.Y. (1906); also conducted for the Chicago Grand Opera Co. In 1925 he returned to Europe. He wrote the operas *Hermes* (Genoa, Nov. 8, 1906); *I dispettosi amanti* (Philadelphia, March 6, 1912); *Fanfulla* (Trieste, Feb. 11, 1921); Sym.; orch. suite, *Rapsodia umbra*; symphonic poem, *La Chimera*; songs.

Parent, Armand, Belgian violinist and composer; b. Liège, Feb. 5, 1863; d. Paris, Jan. 19, 1934. He was a pupil at the Liège Cons. of L. Massart (violin) and S. Dupuis (harmony); then settled in Paris. From 1883 to 1889 he was concertmaster with the Colonne Orch.; from 1900, a prof. of violin at the Schola Cantorum. In 1892 he founded (with Loiseau, Vieux, and Fournier) the Quatuor Parent, which for many years enjoyed an excellent reputation. Parent wrote 2 string quartets, a String Quintet, a Violin Sonata, and a number of minor pieces for violin and piano; also *Gymnastique du violon,* 20 *études de virtuosité, Études pour violon, Exercises pour le violon d'après les 17 quatuors de Beethoven,* and a 5-part *Méthode complète.*

Parepa-Rosa, Euphrosyne (née **Parepa de Boyescu**), prominent Scottish soprano; b. Edinburgh, May 7, 1836; d. London, Jan. 21, 1874. Her father was Baron Georgiades de Boyescu of Bucharest, and her mother the soprano Elizabeth Seguin. After studying with her mother, she made her debut as Amina in *La Sonnambula* in Malta (1855); then sang in Italy, Madrid, and Lisbon. She made her 1st London appearance as Elvira in *I Puritani* with the Royal Italian Opera at the Lyceum Theatre (May 21, 1857); appeared at Covent Garden and Her Majesty's Theatre (1859–65), becoming a great favorite of the English public; also sang in Germany. She then toured the U.S. with Theodore Thomas's orch. and with Carl Rosa (1865); she married Rosa in 1867, and together they formed an opera company in which she starred as the principal soprano; returned to Covent Garden (1872), but illness forced her to give up her career the following year. Her husband founded the Parepa-Rosa Scholarship at the Royal Academy of Music in her memory.

Pareto, Graziella (actually, **Graciela**), Spanish soprano; b. Barcelona, March 6, 1888; d. Rome, Sept. 1, 1973. She studied with Vidal in Milan; made her debut as Micaela in Barcelona in 1906; then sang at the Teatro Colón in Buenos Aires, in Turin, and in St. Petersburg. In 1914 she appeared at La Scala in Milan; subsequently sang at Covent Garden in London (1920), in Chicago (1923–25), and in Salzburg (1931). Among her prominent roles were Rosina, Ophelia, Marguerite de Valois, Violetta, and Norina.

Paribeni, Giulio Cesare, Italian music critic, teacher, and composer; b. Rome, May 27, 1881; d. Milan, June 13, 1960. He studied at the Univ. of Rome and at the Liceo di S. Cecilia of Rome; was first a conductor, then, from 1911 to 1915, head of the publishing firm of Sonzogno; from 1914, was a teacher of composition and harmony at the Royal Cons. in Milan; from 1922, an opera critic of *L'Ambrosiano* in Milan. He was the author of *Storia e teoria della antica musica greca* (Milan, 1912) and *Muzio Clementi,* a biography (Milan, 1921); also, a composer of orch. works, chamber music, and church music.

Parík, Ivan, Slovak composer; b. Bratislava, Aug. 17, 1936. He studied composition with Očenáš at the Bratislava Cons.; then with Cikker and Alexander Moyzes at the Bratislava Academy of Music, graduating in 1962; was then appointed to its faculty. In his music he utilizes a wide range of contemporary resources, from serialism to pointillistic minimalism and expressionistic abstractions.

WORKS: *Music* for 4 String Instruments (1958); 2 *Songs,* to Japanese poetry, for Mezzo-soprano, Violin, Clarinet, Xylophone, and Gong (1960); Sonata for Flute Solo (1962); *Epitaph* for Flute, Viola, and Cello (1962); *Music for 3* for Flute, Oboe, and Clarinet (1964); *Koláže* (Collage) for a variable Chamber Ensemble (1968); *Exercises* for Trumpet (1968); *Vežová hudba* (Tower Music) for 12 Brasses, 2 Tapes, and Bells (1969); *Sonata-Canon* for Flute and Tape (1971); *Meditation* for Viola and Piano (1975); *Epitaph* for Flute and Guitar (1975); electronic pieces.

Parish-Alvars, Elias, remarkable English harpist; b. Teignmouth, Feb. 28, 1808; d. Vienna, Jan. 25, 1849. He studied with F. Dizi and N. Bochsa; after a tour of Germany when he was 15, he completed his studies with T. Labarre. He made tours of Europe from 1834, making his home in Vienna; appeared in the Far East (1838–42), then played in Leipzig and London (1842), in Dresden and Prague (1843), and again in London (1844, 1846); subsequently was made a chamber musician at the Viennese court (1847). He wrote an opera, a Sym., 2 piano concertos, and many works for harp, including 2 concertos, a Concertino for 2 Harps, duos for harp and piano, and some 80 virtuoso pieces for solo harp.

Parkening, Christopher (William), outstanding American guitarist; b. Los Angeles, Dec. 14, 1947. He began guitar lessons when he was 11 with Celedonio and Pepe Romero in Los Angeles, making his public recital debut in 1959; when he was 15 he entered Andrés Segovia's master class at the Univ. of Calif., Berkeley; also received instruction from cellist Gregor Piatigorsky and harpsichordist Malcolm Hamilton. He attended the Univ. of Calif., Los Angeles (1964–65); then entered the Univ. of Southern Calif. as a cello student of Gabor Retjo (there were no guitar teachers on its faculty); by the close of his sophomore year, he was asked by the Univ. to teach guitar, thus initiating its guitar studies; was head of its guitar dept. (1971–75). In the meantime, he launched a brilliant career as a guitar virtuoso; after his 1st major tour of North America (1969), he regularly performed throughout the U.S. and Canada; also made extensive tours throughout the world, garnering acclaim as one of the foremost masters of his instrument. He publ. a valuable guitar method (1973) and made effective transcriptions of works by Bach, Dowland, Debussy, Ravel, and others. **BIBL.:** L. Valdes, "C. P.: Poet of the Guitar," *Ovation* (Jan. 1987); *Current Biography* (April 1987).

Parker, Charlie (Charles Christopher, Jr.), noted black American jazz alto saxophonist, known as Bird or Yardbird; b. Kansas City, Kans., Aug. 29, 1920; d. N.Y., March 12, 1955. He was self-taught, on an alto saxophone given to him at age 13 by his mother; at 15 he left school and became a professional musician. He was a member of Jay McShann's band (1937–44), with which he toured and made his 1st recordings (1941); after performing in Earl Hines's band (1942–44), which included Dizzy Gillespie and other young jazz artists, he played in Billy Eckstine's band (1944–45); after work they would meet in a club called Minton's, and there gradually evolved the new style of bebop. Parker became the acknowledged leader of this style as he developed an improvising technique characterized by virtuosic speed, intense tone, complex harmonies, and florid melodies having irregular rhythmic patterns and asymmetric phrase lengths. After the mid-1940s he usually worked in small combos led either by himself or by one of the other members of the small, close-knit circle of bopsters; occasionally he also worked with larger ensembles (including a string orch. for which he wrote the arrangements). As a composer, he usually worked with the 12-bar blues patterns (but always in an unstereotyped manner; he made 175 blues recordings, all markedly different) or with chord progressions of well-known "standard" tunes: his *Ornithology*, for instance, is based on the progressions of *How High the Moon*. He achieved a prominence that made him a living legend (a leading N.Y. club, Birdland, was named after him); his life, though, in addition to being tragically short, was plagued by the consequences of narcotics addiction (acquired when he was in his mid-teens) and alcoholism. He had a nervous breakdown in 1946, and was confined at Camarillo State Hospital in Calif. for 6 months;

because of suspected narcotics possession, the N.Y. City police rescinded his cabaret license in 1951, thereby denying him the right to work in N.Y. clubs; he attempted suicide twice in 1954, and subsequently entered Bellevue Hospital in N.Y. He died in the N.Y. apartment of a fervent admirer, the Baroness Pannonica de Koenigswarter, the sister of Lord Rothschild. His life was the subject of the 1988 film, *Bird*. **BIBL.:** M. Harrison, *C. P.* (London, 1960); R. Reisner, *Bird: The Legend of C. P.* (N.Y., 1961); J. Jepsen, *A Discography of C. P.* (Copenhagen, 1968); T. Williams, "C. P. Discography," *Discographical Forum* (Sept. 1968–Sept. 1970); D. Morgenstern et al., *Bird and Diz: a Bibliography* (N.Y., 1973); R. Russell, *Bird Lives: The High Life and Hard Times of C. (Yardbird) P.* (N.Y., 1973); T. Owens, *C. P.: Techniques of Improvisation* (diss., Univ. of Calif., Los Angeles, 1974); L. Koch, "Ornithology: A Study of C. P.'s Music," *Journal of Jazz Studies* (Dec. 1974 and June 1975); P. Koster and D. Bakker, *C. P.* (4 vols., Alphen aan den Rijn, the Netherlands, 1974–76); C. Parker and F. Paudras, *To Bird with Love* (Poitiers, France, 1981); B. Priestly, *C. P.* (N.Y., 1984); G. Giddins, *Celebrating Bird: The Triumph of C. P.* (N.Y., 1987); L. Koch, *Yardbird Suite: A Compendium of the Music and Life of C. P.* (Bowling Green, Ohio, 1988).

Parker, Henry Taylor, American critic and writer on music; b. Boston, April 29, 1867; d. there, March 30, 1934. He attended Harvard Univ.; then served as N.Y. correspondent of the *Boston Evening Transcript* and later as its London correspondent; in 1905 he became the newspaper's principal drama and music critic, holding this position until his death. Although not trained as a musician (he could not read notes), Parker possessed an extraordinary sense of esthetic values, and often gave unstinting praise to composers of the modern school who were disdained by the musical establishment; he was equally capable of appreciating fresh talents among performers. He wrote a curiously antiquated prose, employing archaic turns of phrase, but his articles, often very long, were uniquely artistic. He signed his name H.T.P., which was facetiously deciphered by some as an acronym for "Hard To Please," or "Hell To Pay." He publ. a collection of essays on music, *Eighth-Notes* (N.Y., 1922). **BIBL.:** D. McCord, *H.T. P.; Portrait of a Critic* (N.Y., 1935).

Parker, Horatio (William), eminent American composer and pedagogue; b. Auburndale, Mass., Sept. 15, 1863; d. Cedarhurst, N.Y., Dec. 18, 1919. He studied piano with John Orth, theory with Emery, and composition with Chadwick in Boston; subsequently went to Germany, where he took courses in organ and composition with Rheinberger in Munich (1882–85); under his tutelage he wrote a cantata, *King Trojan* (1885). Returning to the U.S., he settled in N.Y. and taught at the cathedral schools of St. Paul and St. Mary (1886–90), at the General Theological Seminary (1892), and at the National Cons. of Music (1892–93); was organist and choirmaster at St. Luke's (1885–87), St. Andrew's (1887–88), and the Church of the Holy Trinity (1888–93); in 1893 he went to Boston as organist and choirmaster at Trinity Church, remaining there until 1902. He attracted attention with the 1st performance of his oratorio *Hora novissima* (N.Y., May 3, 1893), in which he demonstrated his mastery of choral writing, while his harmonic and contrapuntal style remained securely tied to German practices. In 1894 he was engaged as a prof. of theory at Yale Univ.; in 1904 he became dean of its School of Music, and remained there until his death. Many American composers received the benefit of his excellent instruction; among them was Charles Ives, who kept his sincere appreciation of Parker's teaching long after he renounced Parker's conservative traditions. In 1895 he founded the New Haven Sym. Orch., which he conducted until 1918. Parker conducted performances of his works in England in 1900 and 1902; received an honorary degree of Mus.Doc. at Cambridge Univ. in 1902. Returning to the U.S., he served as organist and choirmaster at the collegiate church of St. Nicholas in Boston from 1902 to 1910. He continued to compose industriously, without making any concessions to the emerging modern schools of composition; his choral works are particularly notable. In 1911 his opera *Mona* won the $10,000 prize offered by the Metropolitan Opera in N.Y., and was produced there on March 14, 1912; he also won a prize offered by the National Federation of Women's Clubs for his 2nd opera, *Fairyland*, which was produced in Los Angeles on July 1, 1915. Neither of the operas possessed enough power to survive in the repertoire.

WORKS: STAGE: Operas: *Mona* (1910; Metropolitan Opera, N.Y., March 14, 1912) and *Fairyland* (1914; Los Angeles, July 1, 1915); incidental music to *The Eternal Feminine* for Chorus and Orch. (1903–4; New Haven, Nov. 7, 1904; not extant) and *The Prince of India* for Voice, Chorus, and Orch. (1905; N.Y., Sept. 24, 1906); masque, *Cupid and Psyche* (New Haven, June 16, 1916); *An Allegory of War and Peace* for Chorus and Band (New Haven, Oct. 21, 1916). ORCH.: *Concert Overture* (Munich, July 7, 1884); *Regulus*, overture héroique (1884); *Venetian Overture* (1884); Sym. in C major (Munich, May 11, 1885); *Count Robert of Paris*, overture (N.Y., Dec. 10, 1890); *A Northern Ballad*, symphonic poem (Boston, Dec. 29, 1899); Organ Concerto (Boston, Dec. 26, 1902); *Vathek*, symphonic poem (1903); *Collegiate Overture*, with Men's Chorus (Norfolk Festival, June 7, 1911). CHAMBER: String Quartet (1885; Detroit, Nov. 29, 1887); Suite for Piano, Violin, and Cello (1893); String Quintet (1894; Boston, Jan. 21, 1895); Suite for Piano and Violin (1894; Boston, Jan. 15, 1895). CHORAL: *Psalm* for Soprano, Women's Chorus, Organ, and Harp (Munich, Dec. 23, 1884; publ. as *The Lord Is My Shepherd*, 1904); *Ballade* for Chorus and Orch. (Munich, July 7, 1884; publ. as *The Ballad of a Knight and His Daughter*, 1891); *König Trojan*, ballad for Tenor, Baritone, Chorus, and Orch. (Munich, July 15, 1885; publ. as *King Trojan*, 1886); *Idylle*, cantata for Tenor, Bass, Chorus, and Orch. (1886); *Normannenzug*, cantata for Men's Chorus and Orch. (1888; publ. as *The Norsemen's Raid*, 1911); *Dream-King and His Love*, cantata for Tenor, Chorus, and Orch. (1891; N.Y., March 30, 1893); *The Holy Child*, Christmas cantata for Soprano, Tenor, Bass, Chorus, and Piano or Organ (1893); *The Legend of St. Christopher*, dramatic oratorio for Solo Voices, Chorus, and Orch. (1897; N.Y., April 15, 1898); *Adstant angelorum chori*, motet for 8 Voices (N.Y., March 16, 1899); *A Wanderer's Psalm*, cantata for Solo Voices, Chorus, and Orch. (Hereford, England, Sept. 13, 1900); *Hymnos Andron* for Solo Voices, Men's Chorus, and Orch. (New Haven, Oct. 23, 1901; publ. as *Greek Festival Hymn*, 1901); *A Star Song*, lyric rhapsody for Solo Voices, Chorus, and Orch. (1901; Norwich, England, Oct. 23, 1902); *King Gorm the Grim*, ballad for Chorus and Orch. (1907; Norfolk Festival, June 4, 1908); *A Song of Times*, cantata for Soprano, Chorus, Bugle Corps, Band or Orch., and Organ (Philadelphia, Dec. 1, 1911); *Morven and the Grail*, oratorio for Solo Voices, Chorus, and Orch. (Boston, April 13, 1915); *The Dream of Mary*, morality for Solo Voices, Children's Chorus, Chorus, Congregation, Organ, and Orch. (Norfolk Festival, June 4, 1918); also other cantatas, choruses, part-songs, anthems, and services.

BIBL.: G. Chadwick, *H. P.* (New Haven, 1921); D. Smith, "A Study of H. P.," *Musical Quarterly* (April 1930); I. Parker Semler, with P. Underwood, *H. P.: A Memoir for His Grandchildren* (N.Y., 1942); W. Kearns, *H. P. 1863–1919: A Study of His Life and Music* (diss., Univ. of Illinois, 1965); idem, "H. P. and the English Choral Societies, 1899–1902," *American Music* (Spring 1986).

Parker, J(ames) C(utler) D(unn), American organist, teacher, and composer; b. Boston, June 2, 1828; d. Brookline, Mass., Nov. 27, 1916. He studied law in Boston, and music in Leipzig (1851–54) under Moscheles, Hauptmann, Richter, Plaidy, and Rietz; then lived in Boston; was organist and choir director of Trinity Church (1864–91) and a prof. at the New England Cons. of Music (1871–97). His compositions include *Redemption Hymn* for Alto and Chorus (1877), *The Blind King*, ballad for Baritone, Men's Voices, and Orch. (1883), *St. John*, cantata for Solo Voices, Chorus, and Orch. (1890), and *The Life of Man*, oratorio for Solo Voices, Chorus, and Orch. (1894).

He publ. a *Manual of Harmony* (1855) and *Theoretical and Practical Harmony* (1870).

Parlow, Kathleen, Canadian violinist and teacher; b. Calgary, Alberta, Sept. 20, 1890; d. Oakville, Ontario, Aug. 19, 1963. Her family moved to San Francisco when she was a child, and she had her early instruction in violin there; in 1906 she was sent to St. Petersburg, where she was accepted by Leopold Auer in his violin class at the Cons. She subsequently developed an extensive concert career; played in England, Scandinavia, the U.S., and the Orient. From 1929 to 1936 she was a violin instructor at Mills College in Oakland, Calif.; in 1941, joined the faculty of the Royal Cons. of Music in Toronto; there she organized in 1941 the Parlow String Quartet. She was head of the string dept. at the London (Ontario) College of Music (from 1959). The Kathleen Parlow Scholarship was established at the Univ. of Toronto from proceeds from her estate.

BIBL.: M. French, *K. P.: A Portrait* (Toronto, 1967).

Parnas, Leslie, American cellist and teacher; b. St. Louis, Nov. 11, 1931. He studied with Piatigorsky at the Curtis Inst. of Music in Philadelphia (1948–53); won a number of prizes, including 2nd prize in the Geneva Competition (1957), the Prix Pablo Casals in the International Cello Competition in Paris (1957), and the joint 2nd prize (no 1st prize was given) in the Tchaikovsky Competition in Moscow (1962). He was 1st cellist in the St. Louis Sym. Orch. (1954–62); then appeared worldwide as a soloist with orchs., recitalist, and chamber-music player. He taught at Boston Univ. (from 1962) and the St. Louis Cons. of Music (from 1982).

Parodi, Lorenzo, Italian pedagogue and composer; b. Genoa, Aug. 10, 1856; d. there, March 28, 1926. He studied in Genoa with Guiraud and in Paris with Massenet; taught esthetics and music history and was director of Genoa's Liceo Amilcare Zanella.

WORKS: Oratorios: *Joannes Baptista* and *Calvario*; masses and hymns; cantatas; a *Stabat Mater*; *Suite greca* and *Ouverture triomphale* for Orch.; pieces for Violin, and for Piano; songs.

Parratt, Sir Walter, eminent English organist, teacher, and composer; b. Huddersfield, Feb. 10, 1841; d. Windsor, March 27, 1924. He was a pupil of his father, the organist of the Huddersfield Parish Church; became a pupil of George Cooper (1851), and also began playing the organ in various churches; was made organist of Great Witley Church and private organist to the Earl of Dudley (1864), at the Wigan Parish Church (1868), at Magdalen College, Oxford (1872), and finally at St. George's Chapel, Windsor (1882); was also made private organist to the Queen (1892). He was prof. of organ at the Royal College of Music in London (1883–1923), prof. of music at Oxford Univ. (1908–18), and dean of music at London Univ. (1916–24). Parratt served as Master of the Queen's (later King's) Music (1893–1924). A distinguished recitalist and teacher, he received honorary doctorates in music from the Univs. of Oxford (1894), Cambridge (1910), and Durham (1912); was knighted (1892); became a Member (1901), Commander (1917), and Knight Commander (1921) of the Royal Victorian Order. Among his compositions were the Obitt Service, 4 anthems, and other sacred works, incidental music, songs, organ pieces, and piano music.

BIBL.: F. Edwards, "Sir W. P., Master of the King's Musick," *Musical Times* (July 1902); D. Tovey and G. Parratt, *W. P., Master of Music* (London, 1941).

Parris, Herman, Russian-American physician and composer; b. Ekaterinoslav, Oct. 30, 1903; d. Philadelphia, Jan. 14, 1973. He was taken to America in his infancy; studied at the Jefferson Medical College in Philadelphia, obtaining his M.D. in 1926. Concurrently he studied music at the Univ. of Pa., and graduated in 1921. He was a diligent and competent composer; wrote 4 syms. (1946, 1947, 1949, 1952), 8 piano concertos (1946–53), 4 string quartets (1946, 1948, 1960, 1964), 22 piano sonatas (1946–65), 115 piano preludes (1946–65), *Hebrew Rhapsody* for Orch. (1949), *Lament* for String Orch. (in memory of O. Downes; 1956), and various pieces of chamber music. All these compositions remain largely in limbo, and are seldom if ever visibly, audibly, or plausibly performed, but once in his lifetime he gained a flickering moment of notoriety when he produced an orch. piece entitled *Hospital Suite*, realistically portraying bloody events in the sickroom; it was brought to light in a collegiate spirit by the Doctors' Orch. Society in N.Y. on May 13, 1948. Unfortunately, no further performances were given (all the patients in the suite died).

Parris, Robert, American composer and pianist; b. Philadelphia, May 21, 1924. He studied piano as a youth; enrolled at the Univ. of Pa. (B.S., 1945; M.S., 1946); then studied composition with Peter Mennin at the Juilliard School of Music in N.Y. (B.S., 1948) and with Ibert and Copland at the Berkshire Music Center in Tanglewood (1950–51); in 1952–53 he received a Fulbright fellowship to study with Honegger at the École Normale de Musique in Paris. He taught at several univs. before settling in Washington, D.C., where he joined the faculty of George Washington Univ. in 1963; was also active as a music critic and contributor to various journals. His music is distinguished by strong formal structure and tonal cohesion; when pragmatically justifiable, he applies serialistic techniques with deliberate circumspection.
WORKS: ORCH.: Symphonic Movement No. 1 (1948); *Harlequin's Carnival* (1949); Symphonic Movement No. 2 (1951); Sym. (1952); Piano Concerto (1954); Concerto for 5 Kettledrums and Orch. (1955; Washington, D.C., March 25, 1958); Viola Concerto (1956; Washington, D.C., May 20, 1971); Violin Concerto (1958); Flute Concerto (1964); Concerto for Trombone and Chamber Orch. (Washington, D.C., Sept. 19, 1964); Concerto for Percussion, Violin, Cello, and Piano (1967); *The Phoenix*, concerto for Timpani and Orch. (1969; Detroit, Jan. 2, 1970); *The Messengers* (1974; Albany, N.Y., March 14, 1975; later retitled *Angels*); *Rite of Passage* for Clarinet, Electric Guitar, and Chamber Orch. (1978); *The Unquiet Heart* for Violin and Orch. (1981); *Chamber Music for Orchestra* (1984; Glasgow, Feb. 12, 1985). **CHAMBER:** 2 string trios (1948, 1951); 2 string quartets (1951, 1952); Sonatina for Brass (1948); Sonatina for Winds (1954); Sonata for Viola and Piano (1956); Sonata for Violin and Piano (1956); Quintet for Violin, Cello, Flute, Oboe, and Bassoon (1957); Trio for Clarinet, Piano, and Cello (1959); Sinfonia for Brass (1963); Sonatina for Recorder Quartet (1964); Duo for Flute and Violin (1965); Sonata for Solo Violin (1965); *The Book of Imaginary Beings* for Flute, Violin, Viola, Cello, and Percussion (1972); *The Book of Imaginary Beings, Part II*, for Clarinet, Violin, Viola, Cello, and Percussion (1983); 3 Duets for Electric Guitar and Amplified Harpsichord (1984). **VOCAL:** *Night* for Baritone, String Quartet, and Clarinet (1951); *Alas, for the Day*, cantata (1954); *Mad Scene* for Soloists and Chamber Orch. (1960); *The Raids: 1940* for Soprano, Piano, and Violin (1960); *Hymn for the Nativity* for Chorus and Brass Ensemble (1962); *Dreams* for Soprano and Chamber Orch. (1976); *Cynthia's Revells* for Baritone, Piano, and Optional Guitar (1979).

Parrish, Carl, American musicologist and composer; b. Plymouth, Pa., Oct. 9, 1904; d. (as a result of injuries incurred in an automobile accident) Valhalla, N.Y., Nov. 27, 1965. He studied at the American Cons. in Fontainebleau (1932), the MacPhail School of Music (B.M., 1933), Cornell Univ. (M.A., 1936), and Harvard Univ. (Ph.D, 1939, with the diss. *The Early Piano and Its Influences on Keyboard Technique and Composition in the Eighteenth Century*). He taught at Wells College (1929–43), Fisk Univ. (1943–46), Westminster Choir College (1946–49), and Pomona College (1949–53); from 1953 to 1965 he was a prof. at Vassar College. He publ. *The Notation of Medieval Music* (N.Y., 1957; 2nd ed., 1959) and *A Treasury of Early Music* (N.Y., 1958). With J. Ohl, he publ. *Masterpieces of Music before 1750* (N.Y., 1951). He wrote orch. pieces, choral music, a String Quartet, a song cycle, piano pieces, and folksong arrangements for chorus.

Parrott, Andrew, English conductor; b. Walsall, March 10, 1947. He studied at Oxford Univ., where he pursued research into the performing practices of 16th- and 17th-century music. In 1973 he founded the Taverner Choir, and subsequently the Taverner Consort and Players. He conducted Monteverdi's *Vespers* at London's Promenade Concerts in 1977; gave the 1st performance in London of Bach's *B-minor Mass* with period instruments; also presented in authentic style the *St. Matthew Passion* and the *Brandenburg Concertos*. He appeared as a guest conductor with the English Chamber Orch., the London Bach Orch., and the Concerto Amsterdam. In 1989 he became artistic director of Kent Opera.

Parrott, (Horace) Ian, English composer and writer on music; b. London, March 5, 1916. He studied at London's Royal College of Music (1932–34) and at New College, Oxford (D.Mus., 1940); taught at Malvern College (1937–39). After military service during World War II, he taught at the Univ. of Birmingham (1947–50) and at the Univ. College of Wales in Aberystwyth (1950–83).
WRITINGS: (all publ. in London unless otherwise given): *Pathways to Modern Music* (1947); *A Guide to Musical Thought* (1955); *Method in Orchestration* (1957); *The Music of "An Adventure"* (1966); *The Spiritual Pilgrims* (Llandybie, 1969); *Elgar* (1971; 2nd ed., 1977); *The Music of Rosemary Brown* (1978); *A Musician's Credo* (1986).
WORKS: STAGE: OPERAS: *The Sergeant-Major's Daughter* (Cairo, 1943); *The Black Ram* (1951–53; BBC concert perf., 1957); *Once Upon a Time* (1958–59; Christchurch, 1960); *The Lady of Flowers*, chamber opera (1981; Colchester, Sept. 17, 1982). **BALLET:** *Maiden in Birmingham* (1949; BBC, 1951). **ORCH.:** 5 syms. (1946–79); *El Alamein*, symphonic prelude (1944); *Luxor*, symphonic impression (1948); Piano Concerto (1948); *Pensieri* for Strings (1950); *Romeo and Juliet*, overture (1953); *Variations on a Theme of Dufay* (1955); *Solemn Overture* (1956); English Horn Concerto (1956); 4 *Shakespeare Dances* (1956); *Y Dair* (The 3 Ladies; 1958); *Seithenen Overture* (1959); *Concerto breve* for Cello and Orch. (1961); *The 3 Moorish Princesses* for Narrator and Orch. (1964); Suite for Violin and Orch. (1965); Concerto for Trombone and Wind Instruments (1967); Concertino for 2 Guitars and Small Orch. (1973). **CHAMBER:** 4 string quartets (1946, 1956, 1957, 1963); Oboe Quintet (1946); 2 wind quintets (1948, 1970); *Fantasy Trio* for Violin, Cello, and Piano (1950); *Family Prelude and Fugue* for Strings and Piano (1956); Septet for Flute, Clarinet, String Quartet, and Piano (1962); *Reaching for the Light* for Harpsichord, Piano, and Glockenspiel (1971); *Fanfare and March* for Brass Quartet (1973); *Arfon* for Harp (1978); *My Cousin Alice* for Chorus, Piano, and Tape (1982); *Kaleidoscope* for Piano Trio (1985); *Anthem of Dedication* for Chorus and Organ (1985); piano pieces; organ works, including 2 suites (1977, 1986).

Parry, Sir (Charles) Hubert (Hastings), eminent English composer and pedagogue; b. Bournemouth, Feb. 27, 1848; d. Knight's Croft, Rustington, Oct. 7, 1918. While at Eton, from 1861, he studied composition with G. Elvey; took part in the concerts of the Musical Society as pianist, organist, violinist, and composer. At 19, while still a student at Eton, he took his Mus.B. at Oxford (1867); then had composition lessons with Henry Hugo Pierson, Bennett, and Macfarren at Exeter College, Oxford (B.A., 1870); also took piano lessons from Dannreuther (1872–79). His public career as a composer began with the production of an *Intermezzo religioso* for Strings at the Gloucester Festival of 1868. In 1883 Parry was appointed Choragus at Oxford Univ.; that same year he joined the faculty of London's Royal College of Music, serving as its director (1894–1918); was also prof. of music at Oxford Univ. (1900–8). He was knighted in 1898, and made a baronet in 1903.
WRITINGS: All publ. in London: *Studies of Great Composers* (1886; 8th ed., 1904); *Summary of the History and Development of Mediaeval and Modern European Music* (1893); *The Art of Music* (1893; enlarged as *The Evolution of the Art of Music*, 1896; 2nd ed., rev., 1934 by H. Colles); *The Music of the Seventeenth Century*, Vol. III of *The Oxford History of Music* (1902; 2nd ed., rev. 1938 by E. Dent); *Johann Sebastian Bach:*

The Story of the Development of a Great Personality (1909; 2nd ed., 1934); *Style in Musical Art* (1911).

Works: Opera, *Guinevere* (1885–86); 5 syms. (1878–82; 1883; 1889; 1889; 1912); *Overture to an Unwritten Tragedy* (1893); Piano Concerto in F-sharp (1878–79); *Suite moderne* (1886); *Lady Radnor's Suite* for Strings (1894); *An English Suite* (publ. posthumously, 1921); symphonic poem, *From Death to Life* (1914); other works for orch.; 3 oratorios: *Judith* (Birmingham, 1888); *Job* (Gloucester, 1892); *King Saul* (Birmingham, 1894); *Scenes from Shelley's Prometheus Unbound* (Gloucester, 1880); choral song, *Jerusalem* (1916); many anthems, hymns, motets, odes, part-songs, etc.; 3 string quartets (1867, 1868, 1878–80); 3 piano trios (1878, 1884, 1884–90); String Quintet (1884); Piano Quartet (1879); Nonet for Winds (1877); Fantasie-Sonata for Violin and Piano (1878); Cello Sonata (1883); songs; organ works; piano pieces.

Bibl.: R. Morris, "H. P.," *Music & Letters* (April 1920); C. Graves, *H. P., His Life and Works* (2 vols., London, 1926); G. Greene, *Two Witnesses: A Personal Recollection of H. P. and Friedrich von Hügel* (London, 1930); J. Fuller Maitland, *The Music of P. and Stanford* (Cambridge, 1934); J. Dibble, "P. and Elgar: A New Perspective," *Musical Times* (Nov. 1984).

Parry, John, esteemed blind Welsh harper; b. Bryn Cynan, c.1710; d. Ruabon, Oct. 7, 1782. He studied the Welsh triple harp with Robert Parry of Llanllyfni and Stephan Shon Jones of Penrhyndeudraeth; was harper to Sir Watkins Williams Wynn of Wynnstay, Ruabon (1734–49), continuing in that capacity under his patron's son, Sir Watkins Williams Wynn, II; the Prince of Wales was also his patron. He publ. *Antient British Music, or, A Collection of Tunes, never before published, which are retained by the Cambro-Britons (more particularly in North Wales)* for Harp, Harpsichord, Violin or Flute, and Basso Continuo (with E. Williams; London, 1742); *A Collection of Welsh, English & Scotch Airs with new Variations* (1760–65); *4 New Lessons* for Harp or Harpsichord (London, 1761; also 12 airs for Guitar); *Twelve Airs* for Guitar or 2 Guitars (London, c.1765); *British Harmony, being a Collection of Antient Welsh Airs, the Traditional Remains of those originally sung by the Bards of Wales* (Ruabon and London, 1781; 2nd ed., c.1809, as *Cambrian Harmony*).

Parry, John, Welsh instrumentalist, writer on music, and composer, known as "Bardd Alaw" ("master of song"); b. Denbigh, Feb. 18, 1776; d. London, April 8, 1851. He became a member (1793) and master (1795) of the Denbighshire militia band. In 1807 he settled in London, where he taught the flageolet; was made composer to Vauxhall Gardens (1809). He wrote various works for the stage (from 1814); also appeared as a conductor of the Welsh cymrodorio and eisteddfodau in various locales for many years, being named Bardd Alaw at the Powys Eisteddfod (1820); likewise was music critic for the *Morning Post* (1834–49). His most successful stage work was the musical drama *Ivanhoe or The Knight Templar* (Covent Garden, London, March 2, 1820), which included the popular song *The Lullaby.* He also wrote incidental music, harp sonatas, part-songs, glees, songs, etc. He ed. a collection of Welsh music as *The Welsh Harper* (1839–48). His writings, all publ. in London, include *Il Puntello, or The Supporter* (1832), *An Account of the Rise and Progress of the Harp* (1834), and *An Account of the Royal Musical Festival Held in Westminster Abbey in 1834* (1834). His son, **John Orlando Parry** (b. London, Jan. 3, 1810; d. East Molesey, Surrey, Feb. 20, 1879), was a pianist and comic singer; studied harp with Bochsa; later voice with Lablache in Naples; after a successful career as a singer, he retired from the stage (1853), and was active as organist at St. Jude's, Southsea, and as a teacher; wrote glees and dances for piano.

Bibl.: C. Andrews and J. Orr-Ewing, *Victorian Swandsdown: Extracts from the Early Travel Diaries of J.O. P.* (London, 1935).

Parry, Joseph, Welsh composer; b. Merthyr Tydfil, May 21, 1841; d. Penarth, near Cardiff, Feb. 17, 1903. His parents emigrated to America, but he returned to Britain, won Eisteddfod prizes for songs, and entered the Royal Academy of Music in 1868, studying under Bennett, Garcia, and Steggall; received his Mus.Bac. degree from Cambridge in 1871. He was prof. of music at the Univ. of Wales in Aberystwyth (1873–79); received his Mus.D. from Cambridge (1878), and then ran his own music school in Swansea (1881–88); subsequently lectured at the Univ. College of South Wales and Monmouthshire in Cardiff. He wrote some 400 hymn tunes, the most celebrated being *Aberystwyth* (1877).

Works: operas: *Blodwen* (Aberdare, 1878); *Virginia* (Aberdare, 1883); *Arianwen* (Cardiff, 1890); *Sylvia* (Cardiff, 1895); *King Arthur* (1897); *Ceridwen* (Liverpool, 1900); *The Maid of Cefn Ydfa* (Cardiff, 1902). **oratorios:** *The Prodigal Son* (Chester, 1866); *Emmanuel* (London, 1880); *Saul of Tarus* (Rhyl and Cardiff, 1892). **cantatas:** *The Birds* (Wrexham, 1873); *Jerusalem* (Cambridge, 1878); *Joseph* (Swansea, 1881); *Nebuchadnezzar* (London, 1884); *Cambria* (Llandudno, 1896); also syms.; overtures; String Quartet; anthems; songs; piano pieces; ed. and harmonized *Cambrian Minstrelsie* (6 vols., Edinburgh, 1893).

Bibl.: E. Evans et al., *Cofiant Dr. J. P.* (Cardiff and London, 1921).

Parsch, Arnošt, Czech composer and teacher; b. Bučovice, Moravia, Feb. 12, 1936. He was a pupil of J. Podešva and M. Ištvan; later took courses at the Janáček Academy of Music in Brno; subsequently served on its faculty.

Works: orch.: *Suite* for Strings (1963); Concerto for Winds, Percussion, and Piano (1964); Sonata for Chamber Orch. (1967); 2 syms. (1967, 1973); *Musica concertante con ommagio* (1970); *The Flight* (1973); *The Bird Flew above the Clouds* for Oboe and Orch. (1975); Double Concerto for Flute, Trumpet, and Orch. (1977); *The Message* for 2 String Orchs. (1978); *Divisi. Non divisi!* (1979); Sym.-Concerto for Horn and Orch. (1982); *Rondo* for Orch., with Concertante Violin (1983); 2 *Rondos* for Strings (1984); *Poema,* concerto for Cimbalom and Orch. (1986); Concerto for Bass Clarinet, Piano, and Orch. (1989). **chamber:** *Music* for String Quartet and Percussion (1964); *Trasposizioni I* for Flute, Oboe, Clarinet, Bassoon, and Horn (1967); Organ Sonata (1968); 2 string quartets (1970, 1973); *Esercizii per uno, due, tre e quatro* for 2 Flutes, Guitar, and Cello (1971); *Quatro pezzi per quatro stromenti* for Violin, Clarinet, Double Bass, and Piano (1972); *Early Spring* for Reciter, Flute, Bass Clarinet, and Piano (1972); *Hold Fast!* for 2 Trumpets, Horn, 2 Trombones, and Tuba (1979); *Drawings* for Violin, Clarinet, and Piano (1989). **vocal:** *Simple Truths* for Soprano, 2 Flutes, Guitar, and Cello (1973); *The Sun Rose Once,* cantata for Chorus, Clarinet, Saxophone, and Jazz Orch., after a text by Sitting Bull (1974); *Kings' Ride* for Tenor, Bass, Chorus, and Chamber Ensemble (1984); *Invocation of Love,* 5 songs for Tenor and Piano (1987). **electroacoustic:** *Poetica No. 3* (1967); *Trasposizioni II* (1969) and *III* (1970); *Rotae rotarum* (1971); *Prologos* (1971); *Labyrinthos* (1972); *In High Mountains* (1973); *Daybreak* (1983); *Metamorphoses of Time* (1989).

Parsley, Osbert, English singer and composer; b. 1511; d. Norwich, 1585. He was a "singing-man" at Norwich Cathedral for some 50 years. He wrote both Latin and English sacred music, excelling in the former; several of his instrumental pieces are also extant. See E. Fellowes, Tudor Church Music, X (1929).

Bibl.: J. Morehen, "The Instrumental Consort Music of O. P.," *The Consort*, XXX (1974).

Parsons, Albert Ross, American piano pedagogue; b. Sandusky, Ohio, Sept. 16, 1847; d. Mount Kisco, N.Y., June 14, 1933. He studied with F.L. Ritter in N.Y.; then took piano lessons with Moscheles, Reinecke, Wenzel, and Papperitz at the Leipzig Cons. and music theory with Richter and Paul there; later he received additional instruction with Tausig, Kullak, Weitzmann, and Wüerst in Berlin. In 1871 he settled in N.Y., where he earned the reputation of a piano teacher according to the best German traditions of the art. He publ. the manuals *The Science of Pianoforte Practice* (1886) and

The Virtuoso Handling of the Pianoforte (1917), and wrote some vocal and piano music.

Parsons, Geoffrey (Penwill), prominent Australian pianist; b. Sydney, June 15, 1929. He studied with Winifred Burston at the New South Wales State Conservatorium of Music (1941–48) and with F. Wührer in Munich (1956); settled in London (1950), where he established himself as a fine accompanist, appearing with such leading musicians as Hans Hotter, Elisabeth Schwarzkopf, Nicolai Gedda, and Dame Janet Baker. He was made a Commander of the Order of the British Empire in 1977.

Parsons, Gram (real name, **Cecil Connor**), short-lived American country-rock singer, guitarist, and songwriter; b. Winter Haven, Fla., Sept. 5, 1946; d. Joshua Tree National Monument, Calif., Sept. 19, 1973. He twanged the guitar in Georgia bands, and somehow managed to take time out to study theology at Harvard; it was in those patrician surroundings that he organized a country-rock group, which he called The International Submarine Band. He also contributed to the Byrds in their famous album *Sweetheart of the Rodeo.* On his own he put out *Hickory Wind* and *One Hundred Years from Now.* In 1968 he formed the Flying Burrito Brothers, which recorded his greatest success, *The Gilded Palace of Sin.* There followed *Burrito Deluxe* and *The Last of the Red Hot Burritos.* Just before dying of immoderate drug use, he composed his last song, ironically titled *Grievous Angel.*

Pärt, Arvo, remarkably inventive Estonian composer; b. Paide, Sept. 11, 1935. He studied composition with Heino Eller at the Tallinn Cons., graduating in 1963; from 1958 to 1967 he was attached to the music division of Estonian Radio. In 1980 he emigrated to the West, settling in West Berlin (1982). He began to compose in a traditional manner, writing instrumental pieces in a neo-Baroque idiom, strict to form, freely dissonant in harmony; under the influence of Western musical modernism, he gradually levitated toward the empyreal emporium of empiric sonorism, without renouncing, however, the historic foundation of tonality. The spectrum of his musical vocabulary extends from abecedarian minimalism to quaquaversal polytonality, from impressionistic pointillism to austere serialism. One of his specialities is a technique he calls "tintinnabula," in which he applies shifting phases of a given chord. Pärt was the 1st Estonian composer to use the authentic Schoenbergian method of composition with 12 different tones related only to one another to form melodic and harmonic dodecaphonic structures. He applied it in his arresting *Nekrolog,* dedicated to the victims of the Holocaust. Extending the concept of integral dodecaphony, he makes use of pandiatonic and panpentatonic tone-clusters, culminating in the formation of a Brobdingnagian blob of "white noise." He occasionally resorts to aleatory proceedings; also harks upon occasion back to historic antecedents in applying the austere precepts of *ars antiqua.* In this, Pärt commends himself as a true *Homo ludens,* a musician playing a diversified game.

WORKS: ORCH.: *Nekrolog,* dedicated to the victims of Fascism (1960); 3 syms.: No. 1, *Polyphonic* (1963); No. 2 (1966); No. 3 (1971); *Perpetuum mobile* (1963); *Collage on the Theme B-A-C-H* for Strings, Oboe, and Harpsichord (1964); *Pro et contra* for Cello and Orch. (1964); *Wenn Bach Bienen gezüchtet hätte* (If Bach Had Raised Bees), on the theme B-A-C-H, concertino for Harpsichord, Electric Bass Guitar, Electronic Tape, and Ensemble (1978; Graz, Oct. 7, 1983; version B for Harpsichord and 20 Strings, 1980); *Cantus in Memory of Benjamin Britten* for String Orch. and Glockenspiel (1977); *Tabula Rasa* ("scraped tablet," alluding to the epistemological philosophy of John Locke), concerto for Violin, String Orch., and Prepared Piano (1977); *Fratres I,* version B, for String Orch. and Percussion (1977–82; Göteborg, May 19, 1983); Concerto for Violin, Cello, and Chamber Orch. (1978–79; London, April 23, 1981); *Spiegel im Spiegel* (Mirror in Mirror), version B, for Violin, Piano, and Strings (1980); Cello Concerto (1983); *Festina lente* for String Orch. (1989).

VOCAL: *Meie aed* (Our Garden), cantata for Children's Cho-

rus and Orch. (1959); *Maailma samm* (The World's Stride), oratorio (1961); *Solfeggio* for Mixed Chorus and String Quartet (1964); *Credo* for Piano, Mixed Chorus, and Orch. (1968); *Laul armastatule* (Song for the Beloved), cantata-sym. to poems by Rustaveli (1973); *Calix (Dies irae)* for Chorus, Organ, Trumpet, Trombone, Glockenspiel, Tam-tam, 2 Electric Guitars, and Kettledrum (1976); *Modus (Tintinnabulum 2)* for Soprano and Instrumental Ensemble (1976); *Missa sillabica* for 4 Voices or Chamber Choir, and 6 Instruments (1977); *Cantate Domino canticum novum (Psalm 95)* for 4 Voices and 4 Instruments (1977); *De profundis* for Male Chorus, Organ, and Percussion ad lib. (1970); *Summa* for Tenor, Baritone, and 6 Instruments (1978); *Passio Domini nostri Jesu Christi secundum Joannem* for Chorus and Ensemble (Munich, Nov. 28, 1982); 2 *Slavic Psalms* for Vocal Quintet (1984); *Te Deum* for 3 Choruses and Orch. (1984–86); 7 *Magnificat-Antiphones* for Chorus (1988); *Miserere* for 5 Solo Voices, Chorus, and Orch. (1989).

CHAMBER: String Quartet (1959); Quintettino for 5 Wind Instruments (1964); *Musica syllabica* for 12 Instruments (1964); *Kriips ja punkt* (Dash and Dot) for Ensemble (1967); *Fratres I,* version A, for String Quintet and Wind Quintet (1977), and version C, for Nonet (1977); *Fratres II* for Violin (1980); *Fratres III* for Cello (1980); *Arbos* for 7 Instruments (1977); *Spiegel im Spiegel,* version A, for Violin and Piano (1978); *Pari Intervallo,* version A, for 4 Instruments (1980); *Die Brüder* for Violin and Piano (1980).

KEYBOARD: PIANO: 2 sonatinas (1958, 1959); *Partita* (1959); *Diagrams,* aleatory work (1964); *Für Alina* (1976); *Variationen zur Gesundung von Arinuschka* (Variations for Arinuschka's Recuperation) (1977); *Pari Intervallo,* version C (1980). **ORGAN:** *Trivium* (1976); *Annum per annum* (1980); *Pari intervallo,* version B (1980).

BIBL.: P. Hillier, "A. P.—Magister Ludi," *Musical Times* (March 1989); J. McCarthy, "An Interview with A. P.," ibid.

Partch, Harry, innovative American composer, performer, and instrument maker; b. Oakland, Calif., June 24, 1901; d. San Diego, Sept. 3, 1974. Largely autodidact, he began experimenting with instruments capable of producing fractional intervals, which led him to the formulation of a 43-tone scale; he expounded his findings in his book, *Genesis of a Music* (1949; 2nd ed., rev. and augmented, 1974). Among new instruments constructed by him are elongated violas, a chromelodeon, kitharas with 72 strings, harmonic canons with 44 strings, boos (made of giant Philippine bamboo reeds), cloud-chamber bowls, blow-boys (a pair of bellows with an attached automobile horn), etc. Seeking intimate contact with American life, he wandered across the country, collecting indigenous expressions of folkways, inscriptions on public walls, etc., for texts in his productions.

WORKS: 17 *Lyrics by Li Po* for Voice and Adapted Viola (1930–33; San Francisco, Feb. 9, 1932); 2 *Psalms* for Voice and Adapted Viola (1931; San Francisco, Feb. 9, 1932; rev. 1941); *The Potion Scene from Romeo and Juliet* for Voice and Adapted Viola (1931; San Francisco, Feb. 9, 1932; rev. 1955); *The Wayward Barstow: 8 Hitchhiker Inscriptions from a Highway Railing at Barstow, California* for Voice and Adapted Guitar (1941; N.Y., April 22, 1944; rev. 1954); *U.S. Highball: A Musical Account of a Transcontinental Hobo Trip* for Voices, Guitar I, Kithara, and Chromelodeon (1943; N.Y., April 22, 1944; rev. 1955); *San Francisco: A Setting of the Cries of 2 Newsboys on a Foggy Night in the 20s* for 2 Baritones, Adapted Viola, Kithara, and Chromelodeon (1943; N.Y., April 22, 1944); *The Letter: A Depression Message from a Hobo Friend* for Intoning Voices and Original Instruments (1943; N.Y., April 22, 1944); *Dark Brother* for Voice, Chromelodeon, Adapted Viola, Kithara, and Bass Marimba (1942–43); 2 *Settings from Joyce's Finnegans Wake* for Soprano, Kithara, and 2 Flutes (1944); *Yankee Doodle Fantasy* for Soprano, Tin Flutes, Tin Oboes, Flex-atones, and Chromelodeon (N.Y., April 22, 1944); 11 *Intrusions* for Large Ensemble of Original Instruments (1946–50); *Plectra and Percussion Dances* for Voices and Original Instruments (1949–52; Berkeley, Calif., Nov. 19, 1953); *Oedipus,* dance music for 10 Solo Voices and Original Instruments, after Sophocles (1951; Oakland, Calif., March 14, 1952; rev. 1952–54); *2 Settings from Lewis Carroll* for Voice and Original Instruments (Mill Valley, Calif., Feb. 13, 1954); *Ulysses at the Edge* for Alto Saxophone or Trumpet, Baritone Saxophone, and Original Instruments (1955; adapted to *The Wayward*); *The Bewitched*, dance satire for Soprano and Ensemble of Traditional and Original Instruments (1955; Urbana, Ill., March 26, 1957); *Windsong*, film score (1958; rev. as the ballet *Daphne of the Dunes*, 1967); *Revelation in the Courthouse Park* for 16 Solo Voices, 4 Speakers, Dancers, and Large Instrumental Ensemble (1960; Urbana, Ill., April 11, 1962); *Rotate the Body in All Its Planes*, film score (Urbana, Ill., April 8, 1961); *Bless This Home* for Voice, Oboe, and Original Instruments (1961); *Water! Water!*, farcical "intermission" (1961; Urbana, Ill., March 9, 1962); *And on the 7th Day Petals Fell in Petaluma* for Large Ensemble of Original Instruments (1963–66; Los Angeles, May 8, 1966); *Delusion of the Fury: A Ritual of Dream and Delusion*, dramatic piece for Large Ensemble (1965–66; Los Angeles, Jan. 9, 1969); *The Dreamer That Remains: A Study in Loving*, film score (1972).

BIBL.: O. Daniel, "H. P.," *Music at Home*, I/6 (1955); A. Woodbury, "H. P.: Corporeality and Monophony," *Source*, I/2 (1967); M. Bowen, "H. P.," *Music and Musicians*, XVI/5 (1968); J. Cott, "The Forgotten Visionary," *Rolling Stone*, no. 158 (1974); B. Johnston, "The Corporealism of H. P.," *Perspectives of New Music*, XIII/2 (1975); G. Hackbarth, *An Analysis of H. P.'s "Daphne of the Dunes"* (Ann Arbor, 1979); J. Smith, "The P. Reverberations: Notes on a Musical Rebel," *San Diego Weekly Reader* (Sept. 25, 1980).

Parton, Dolly (Rebecca), successful American singer, guitarist, and songwriter of country and pop-rock music; b. Locust Ridge, near Sevierville, Tenn., Jan. 19, 1946. Born into a poverty-stricken family, she began to sing as a child; after graduating from high school, she went to Nashville, Tenn., to seek her fortune; in 1967 she became a member of Porter Wagoner's band. She quickly assumed a leading place among country-music stars; in 1976 she moved into the pop-rock field, and toured widely with her own group, Gypsy Fever. She composed such popular songs as *Coat of Many Colors, Tennessee Mountain Home, Joshua, Jolene,* and *Love Is Like a Butterfly;* she was particularly successful with the country album *Here You Come Again* and the pop-rock album *Heartbreaker.* To top it all, she made herself famous by appearing as one of the 3 rather odd secretaries in the comedy film *9 to 5* (1980), for which she wrote and recorded the theme song.

BIBL.: L. Scobey, *D.: Daughter of the South* (N.Y., 1977).

Partos, Oedoen (actually, **Ödön**), Hungarian-born Israeli composer and violist; b. Budapest, Oct. 1, 1907; d. Tel Aviv, July 6, 1977. He studied violin with Hubay and composition with Kodály at the Royal Academy of Music in Budapest (1918–24). In 1938 he went to Palestine; was 1st violist in the Palestine Sym. Orch. (later Israel Phil.) from 1938 to 1956. In 1951 he was appointed director of the Tel Aviv Academy of Music (later the Israel Rubin Academy of Tel Aviv Univ.); from 1961, he was a prof. there. He was the soloist for the premieres of his 3 viola concertos. His early works followed the rhythmical and melodic patterns of the oriental tradition, emphasized the chromatic melodic turns, and developed a free accumulation of variations on a theme that is never stated in its entirety. In 1971 he went to the Netherlands and experimented with the possibilities of 31-tone scales proposed by the 17th-century Dutch physicist and mathematician Christiaan Huygens.

WORKS: 2 string quartets: No. 1, *Concertino* (1932; rev. 1939; N.Y., May 24, 1941), and No. 2, *Tehilim* (Psalms; 1960; also for String Orch., without Double Basses, 1960); *4 Folk Songs* for Alto and String Quartet (1939); *Yizkor* (*In memoriam*) for Viola or Violin or Cello, and String Orch. (1947); *Rondo* for Violin and Piano (1947); *4 Israeli Tunes* for Violin or Viola or Cello, and Piano (1948); 3 viola concertos: No. 1, *Songs of Praise* (Tel Aviv, Jan. 22, 1949); No. 2 (1957); No. 3, *Sinfonia concertante* (Jerusalem, 1963); *Ein Gev*, symphonic fantasy (1951–52; Ein Gev, Oct. 1, 1953; UNESCO Prize, 1952; Israel State Prize, 1954); *Oriental Ballad* for Viola and Cello, and Orch. or Piano (1956); Violin Concerto (1958); *Maqamat* for Flute and String Quartet (1959); *Agada* (*A Legend*) for Viola, Piano, and Percussion (1960; ISCM Festival, London, June 6, 1962); *Iltur* (*Improvisation*) for 12 Harps (1960); *Prelude* for Piano (1960); *Dmuyoth* (*Images*) for Orch. (1960); *Daughter of Israel*, cantata (1961); *5 Israeli Songs* for Tenor, Oboe, Piano, and Cello (1962); *Symphonic Movements* (1966); *Arpiliyot* (*Nebulae*) for Wind Quintet (1966); *Netivim* (*Paths*), symphonic elegy (1969); *Shiluvim* (*Fuses*) for Viola and Chamber Orch. (Tel Aviv, June 21, 1970); Concertino for Flute and Piano (1969); *Metamorphoses* for Piano (1971); *Music for Chamber Orch.* (1971); *3 Fantasies* for 2 Violins (1972; composed in the 31-tone system); *Arabesque* for Oboe and Chamber Orch. (1975); *Ballad*, piano quartet (1977); *Fantasy*, piano trio (1977); *Invenzione* a 3 (*Homage à Debussy*) for Flute, Harp, and Viola (1977).

BIBL.: W. Elias, *O. P.* (Tel Aviv, 1978).

Partridge, Ian, English tenor; b. London, June 12, 1938. He received his musical training at New College, Oxford, Clifton College, the Royal College of Music, and the Guildhall School of Music. He first sang in the Westminster Cathedral Choir; then began a solo career. He specialized in German lieder; often appeared in local duos with his sister, the pianist Jennifer Partridge.

Pasatieri, Thomas, talented American opera composer; b. N.Y., Oct. 20, 1945. He began to play the piano by spontaneous generation, and picked up elements of composition, particularly vocal, by a similar subliminal process; between the ages of 14 and 18 he wrote some 400 songs. He persuaded Nadia Boulanger to take him as a student by correspondence between Paris and N.Y. when he was 15; at 16 he entered the Juilliard School of Music, where he became a student of Vittorio Giannini and Vincent Persichetti; he also took a course with Darius Milhaud in Aspen, Colo., where his 1st opera, *The Women*, to his own libretto, was performed when he was only 19. It became clear to him that opera was his natural medium, and that the way to achieve the best results was by following the evolutionary line of Italian operatic productions characterized by the felicity of *bel canto*, facility of harmonic writing, and euphonious fidelity to the lyric and dramatic content of the subject. In striving to attain these objectives, Pasatieri ran the tide of mandatory inharmoniousness; while his productions were applauded by hoi polloi, they shocked music critics and other composers; one of them described Pasatieri's music as "a stream of perfumed urine." This attitude is akin to that taken by some toward Vittorio Giannini and Gian Carlo Menotti (interestingly, all 3 are of Italian genetic stock). From 1967 to 1969 Pasatieri taught at the Juilliard School; then was engaged at the Manhattan School of Music (1969–71); from 1980 to 1983 he was Distinguished Visiting Prof. at the Univ. of Cincinnati College-Cons. of Music.

WORKS: OPERAS: *The Women* (Aspen, Aug. 20, 1965); *La Divina* (N.Y., March 16, 1966); *Padrevia* (N.Y., Nov. 18, 1967); *Calvary* (Seattle, April 7, 1971); *The Trial of Mary Lincoln*, television opera (Boston, Feb. 14, 1972); *Black Widow* (Seattle, March 2, 1972); *The Seagull*, after Chekhov (Houston, March 5, 1974); *Signor Deluso*, after Molière's *Sganarelle* (Vienna, Va., July 27, 1974); *The Penitentes* (Aspen, Aug. 3, 1974); *Inez de Castro* (Baltimore, April 1, 1976); *Washington Square*, after Henry James (Detroit, Oct. 1, 1976); *Three Sisters*, after Chekov (1979; Columbus, Ohio, March 13, 1986); *Before Breakfast* (N.Y., Oct. 9, 1980); *The Goose Girl*, children's opera (Fort Worth, Tex., Feb. 15, 1981); *Maria Elena* (Tucson, April 8, 1983). **OTHER:** *Héloïse and Abelard* for Soprano, Baritone, and Piano (1971); *Rites de passage* for Voice and Chamber Orch. or String Quartet (1974); *3 Poems of James Agee* for Voice and Piano (1974); *Far from Love* for Soprano, Clarinet, and Piano (1976); *Permit Me Voyage*, cantata for Soprano, Chorus, and Orch. (1976); *Mass* for 4 Solo Voices, Chorus, and Orch. (1983); 2 piano sonatas (1976) and other piano works.

Pasdeloup, Jules-Étienne, famous French conductor; b. Paris, Sept. 15, 1819; d. Fontainebleau, Aug. 13, 1887. He studied piano with Laurent and Zimmerman at the Paris Cons., winning premiers prix for solfège (1832) and piano (1834); then was on its faculty (1841–68). He organized the Société des Jeunes Artistes' sym. concerts in Paris, where he conducted for the 1st time on Feb. 20, 1853; these became the Société des Jeunes Artistes du Conservatoire Impérial de Musique concerts, which he conducted from 1856 to 1865. He founded the Concerts Populaires de Musique Classique, conducting its 1st concert on Oct. 27, 1861, and with it championed the works of the great masters as well as those by contemporary French composers; also founded the Société des Oratorios (1868), and was a conductor at the Théâtre-Lyrique (1868–70). His Concerts Populaires gradually lost ground in competition with the concerts of Colonne and Lamoureux, and were abandoned in 1884; they were revived in 1886–87. A grand popular music festival at the Trocadéro (1884), instituted for his benefit, netted him nearly 100,000 francs.

BIBL.: A. Elwart, *Histoire des Concerts populaires de musique classique* (Paris, 1864); J. Jullien, "J. P. et les Concerts Populaires," *Musique: Mélanges d'histoire et de critique* (Paris, 1896); H. Schonberg, *The Great Conductors* (N.Y., 1967); E. Bernard, "J. P. et les Concerts Populaires," *Revue de Musicologie*, LVII (1971).

Pasero, Tancredi, noted Italian bass; b. Turin, Jan. 11, 1893; d. Milan, Feb. 17, 1983. He studied in Turin; made his debut in 1917 as Rodolfo in *La Sonnambula* in Vicenza; from 1924 to 1930 he sang at the Teatro Colón in Buenos Aires; in 1926 he joined La Scala in Milan, remaining on its roster until 1952. He made his Metropolitan Opera debut in N.Y. on Nov. 1, 1929, as Alvise in *La Gioconda*; continued on its roster until 1933. His repertoire was extensive and included Italian, German, French, and Russian operas; he excelled in Verdi's operas, and made a distinctive appearance as Mussorgsky's Boris Godunov.

BIBL.: C. Clerico, *T. P.: Voce verdiana* (Scomegna, 1985).

Pashchenko, Andrei (Filippovich), prolific Russian composer; b. Rostov, Aug. 15, 1883; d. Moscow, Nov. 16, 1972. He studied with Wihtol and Steinberg at the St. Petersburg Cons., graduating in 1917; occupied various clerical positions; was librarian of the St. Petersburg Court Orch. (from 1911), remaining with it when it became the State Orch. (1917) and the Leningrad Phil. (1924); left his post in 1931; in 1961 he went to live in Moscow. An exceptionally fertile composer, he wrote some 14 operas and 15 syms.; the style of his music is a natural continuation of the traditions of the Russian national school; in his later works he allowed a certain influx of impressionistic harmonies and unresolved dissonant combinations.

WORKS: Operas: *Eagles in Revolt* (Leningrad, Nov. 7, 1925); *King Maximilian* (1927); *The Black Cliff* (Leningrad, June 12, 1931); *The Pompadours* (1939); *Jester Balakirev* (1949); *The Capricious Bride* (1956); *Radda and Loyko* (1957); *Nila Snishko* (1961); *The Great Seducer* (1966); *Woman, This Is the Devil* (1966); *African Love* (1966); *The Horse in the Senate* (1967); *Portrait* (1968); *Master and Margarita* (1971); 15 syms. (1915, 1929, 1933, 1938, 1952, 1954, 1956, 1957, 1958, 1963, 1964, 1966, 1969, 1969, 1970); 4 sinfoniettas (1943, 1945, 1953, 1964); *Volga Fantasy* for Orch. (1961); *Ukrainiada,* symphonic poem (1963); *Icarus,* symphonic poem (1964); *Dance Triptych* for Orch. (1965); *The Voice of Peace,* symphonic poem (1971); *Poem of Stars,* symphonic poem (1971); Cello Concerto (1964); 9 string quartets; numerous works for chorus.

BIBL.: Y. Meylikh, *A.F. P.* (Leningrad, 1960).

Pashkevich, Vasily (Alexeievich), Russian violinist and composer; b. c.1740; d. St. Petersburg, March 20, 1797. In 1763 he was admitted as a violinist to the 2nd court orch. in St. Petersburg. His Russian opera *A Carriage Accident* was performed in St. Petersburg on Nov. 7, 1779; in 1782 he presented 2 comic operas in Russian: *The Miser* (Moscow) and *The Pasha of Tunis* (St. Petersburg). In 1783 he became a violinist in the 1st court orch. In 1786 was commissioned by Catherine the Great to write a comic Russian opera, *Fevey,* for which the Empress herself wrote the libretto. It was produced in St. Petersburg on April 19, 1786, and Pashkevich received an award of 1,000 rubles. He was then made chief of ball music at the Imperial Palace and concertmaster of the 1st court orch. (1786); received the honorary rank of colonel. In 1790 he collaborated with Sarti and Canobbio on another Russian opera to a text of Catherine the Great, *The Early Reign of Oleg,* which was first produced at the palace, and publicly performed in St. Petersburg on Nov. 2, 1790. In collaboration with Martín y Soler, he wrote still another comic opera to a text by the Empress, *Fedul and His Children* (perf. at the palace, Jan. 27, 1791; publicly, St. Petersburg, March 2, 1791). His Mass according to the Russian Orthodox liturgy was publ. in Moscow in 1796.

BIBL.: R. Mooser, *Annales de la musique et des musiciens en Russie au XVIIIe siècle* (Vol. II, Geneva, 1951).

Pasini (-Vitale), Lina, Italian soprano; b. Rome, Nov. 8, 1872; d. there, Nov. 23, 1959. She studied in Rome; made her debut in 1893 as Cecilia in Cilea's *Tilda* at the Teatro dal Verme in Milan; then sang at La Scala in Milan, Turin, the Teatro Colón in Buenos Aires, Rome, and Naples; retired from the stage in 1928. She married the conductor Edoardo Vitale in 1897. At the height of her career, she was widely regarded as one of the finest Wagnerian sopranos on the Italian stage. Her sister, Camilla Pasini (b. Rome, Nov. 6, 1875; d. there, Oct. 29, 1935), was also a soprano; she studied in Rome; created the role of Musetta in *La Bohème* (Turin, 1896); retired from the stage in 1905.

Paskalis, Kostas, Greek baritone; b. Levadia, Sept. 1, 1929. He studied at the Athens Cons.; made his debut as Rigoletto in Athens in 1951, singing at the Opera there until 1958. In 1958 he made his 1st appearance with the Vienna State Opera, and subsequently sang there regularly; also sang in Berlin, Moscow, Leningrad, and London. On Feb. 17, 1965, he made his Metropolitan Opera debut in N.Y. as Carlo in *La forza del destino.*

Pasmore, Henry Bickford, American singing teacher and composer; b. Jackson, Wis., June 27, 1857; d. San Francisco, Feb. 23, 1944. He studied in San Francisco; then went to Leipzig and London, where he took courses in singing with various teachers. Returning to America, he taught singing at the Univ. of the Pacific, San Jose, at Stanford Univ., and at Mills College. He wrote an exotic opera, *Lo-ko-rah;* another opera on a libretto based on Californian history, *Amor y oro;* an overture, *Miles Standish;* a symphonic poem, *Gloria California;* a Mass; several cantatas; church music; songs.

Pasquali, Francesco, Italian composer; b. Cosenza, c.1590; d. after 1635. He studied in Rome, and remained there for most of his life. Between 1615 and 1633 he brought out 3 books of madrigals for 1 to 5 Voices, and several vols. of secular and sacred songs for 1, 2, 3, 4, and 5 voices.

Pasquali, Niccolò, Italian violinist and composer; b. c.1718; d. Edinburgh, Oct. 13, 1757. He went to Edinburgh (1740) and then to London (c.1743); was in Dublin (1748–49), again in London (1750–51), again in Dublin (1751–52), and then settled in Edinburgh, where he publ. the valuable treatise *Thorough-bass made easy* (1757); also publ. *The Art of Fingering the Harpsichord* (Edinburgh, 1758). His extant works include 12 overtures (London, 1751), 6 sonatas for Violin and Basso Continuo (1744), 2 sets of 3 sonatas for 2 Violins, Viola, and Basso Continuo (1750), many minuets, and numerous songs.

Pasquini, Bernardo, eminent Italian organist, harpsichordist, pedagogue, and composer; b. Massa di Valdinievole, near Lucca, Dec. 7, 1637; d. Rome, Nov. 21, 1710. He settled in Rome (1650); studied with Vittori and Cesti; was organist at Chiesa Nuova (1661–63), S. Maria Maggiore (1663), S. Maria in Aracoeli (1664–1710), and S. Luigi dei Francesi (1673–75); was also 1st organist at the Oratory of SS. Crocifisso (1664–

85); served as harpsichordist and music director to Prince Giambattista Borghese; was the teacher of Della Ciaja, Durante, and G. Muffat; became a member of the Arcadian Academy (1706). Although greatly esteemed as a keyboard player, little of his music was publ. in his lifetime; many of his vocal works are lost. He excelled as a composer of keyboard suites and variations.

WORKS (all 1st perf. in Rome unless otherwise given): **OPERAS**: *La sincerità con la sincerità, overo Il Tirinto* (Ariccia, 1672); *La forza d'amore* (Rome, 1672; rev. as *Con la forza d'amor si vince amore*, Pratolino, near Florence, 1679); *L'amor per vendetta, overo L'Alcasta* (Jan. 27, 1673); *Tespolo tutore* (1675); *La Donna ancora è fidele* (Carnival 1676); *La caduta del regno dell'Amazzoni* (1678); *Dov'è è pietà* (Carnival 1679); *L'Idalma, overo Chi la duca la vince* (Carnival 1680); *Il Lisimaco* (Carnival 1681); *La Tessalonica* (Jan. 31, 1683); *L'Arianna* (Carnival 1685); *Santa Dinna* (Carnival 1687; in collaboration with A. Melani and A Scarlatti); *L'Eudossia* (Feb. 6, 1692). **ORATORIOS**: *L'Agar* (March 17, 1675); *L'Assuero* (April 15, 1675); *Sant'Alessio* (1676); *Sant'Agnese* (1677); *Sant'Eufrasia* (c.1677); *Salutazione angelica* (Messina, 1681); *Divae clarae triumphus* (March 20, 1682); *L'idolatria di Salomone* (1686); *I fatti di Mosè nel deserto* (Modena, 1687); *Il martirio dei santi* (Modena, 1687); *L'Abramo* (Palermo, 1688); *La sete di Christo* (1689); *La caduta di Salomone* (Florence, 1693); *L'Ismaele* (Florence, 1693); *David trionfante contro Goliath* (Florence, 1694). Other vocal works include some 60 cantatas, of which 50 are for Solo Voice, 2 canzonettas, solo motets and arias, etc. His keyboard music includes sonatas, dances, toccatas, variations, etc. See M. Haynes, ed., *Bernardo Pasquini: Collected Works for a Keyboard*, Corpus of Early Keyboard Music, V/1–7 (1964–68).

BIBL.: V. Virgili, *B. P.* (Pescia, 1908); A. Bonaventura, *B. P.* (Ascoli Piceno, 1923); E. Luin, *B. P. e il suo tricentenario* (Rome, 1939); W. Heimrich, *Die Orgel- und Cembalo-Werke B. P.s* (diss., Free Univ. of Berlin, 1958); M. Haynes, *The Keyboard Works of B. P.* (diss., Indiana Univ., 1960); G. Crain, *The Operas of B. P.* (diss., Yale Univ., 1965).

Pasquini, Ercole, significant Italian organist and composer; b. Ferrara, c.1550; d. Rome, between 1608 and 1619. He studied with Alessandro Milleville; was organist in Ferrara and then at the Cappella Giulia at St. Peter's in Rome (1597–1608); was also organist at S. Spirito in Saxia (1604). He was one of the leading masters of keyboard composition in his era; in addition to some 30 keyboard pieces, several sacred vocal works are extant. See W. Shindle, ed., *Ercole Pasquini: Collected Keyboard Works*, Corpus of Early Keyboard Music, XII (1966).

BIBL.: W. Shindle, *The Keyboard Works of E. P.* (diss., Indiana Univ., 1963).

Pasquotti, Corrado, Italian composer; b. Vittorio Veneto, March 11, 1954. He studied in Padua, Venice, and Milan. In 1977 he received the diploma of merit of the Teatro Angelicum in Milan. He subsequently taught at the Cons. Rossini of Pesaro. In his works he strives to achieve intimate synergy of visual images and auditory projections; his written scores literally follow the parameters of a given painting, with notes corresponding to the lines of the design and rests occupying the spaces of the object; depending on a chart for such correspondences, different musical versions are achieved in actual performances. A typical product of this method is *Forma Magistra Ludi* for Chamber Orch., to images by Yasmin Brandolini d'Adda (1980). He also composed a string quartet, *Quartet "i reflessi"* (1983).

Pass, Joe (real name, **Joseph Anthony Jacobi Passalaqua**), outstanding American jazz guitarist; b. New Brunswick, N.J., Jan. 13, 1929. He took up the guitar as a schoolboy, cutting short his education to pursue a career in music. Unfortunately, he succumbed to drug addiction, was caught, and sentenced to prison; after spending years in halfway houses and hospitals, he was placed at the famous Synanon Foundation clinic in Santa Monica, Calif., where he was finally cured. As a souvenir of this confinement, he recorded a jazz album with his fellow

inmates, *Sounds of Synanon* (1962). He subsequently achieved a premier standing among jazz guitarists, attracting acclaim with his 1st solo album, aptly named *Virtuoso* (1973). Pass worked with many jazz greats, among them Ella Fitzgerald and Oscar Peterson.

Passereau, Pierre, French composer who flourished in the 1st half of the 16th century. He was chapel singer to the Duke of Angoulême, later Francis I; 23 of his chansons were publ. in contemporary anthologies (1533–47); G. Dottin ed. his complete works (1967).

Passy, (Ludvig Anton) Edvard, Swedish pianist, organist, teacher, and composer; b. Stockholm, Sept. 3, 1789; d. Drottningholm, Aug. 16, 1870. He received his 1st music instruction from his brother; then studied with L. Piccinni in Stockholm, with John Field in St. Petersburg, and with Eggert in Stockholm. After several successful tours of Germany, he settled in his native city as a highly esteemed teacher, and pianist in the royal orch. (1818–23) and organist of the royal chapel (1833–66). He wrote 2 operas; 2 piano concertos; Fantasy for Piano and Orch.; 4 string quartets; Piano Trio; choruses; songs; organ works; many virtuoso piano pieces.

Pasta, Giuditta (Maria Costanza) (née **Negri**), famous Italian soprano; b. Saronno, near Milan, Oct. 28, 1797; d. Blevio, Lake Como, April 1, 1865. She studied with Asioli at the Milan Cons. and with Giuseppe Scappa, making her debut in his *Le tre Eleonore* at the Teatro degli Accademici Filodrammatici in Milan (1815); then made her Paris debut in Paër's *Il Principe di Taranto* (1816) and her London debut as Telemachus in Cimarosa's *Penelope* at the King's Theatre (Jan. 11, 1817); after further studies with Scappa, she sang in Venice, Padua, Rome, Brescia, Trieste, and Turin. She then returned to Paris and made a sensational appearance as Desdemona in Rossini's *Otello* at the Théâtre-Italien (June 5, 1821), her voice being acclaimed as a vocal phenomenon and her dramatic abilities without equal; she continued to sing there, appearing in the premiere of Rossini's *Il viaggio a Reims* (June 19, 1825); also sang in London from 1824. She created the title role in Pacini's *Niobe* at Naples's Teatro San Carlo (Nov. 19, 1826); after singing in Vienna (1829), she created the title role in Donizetti's *Anna Bolena* (Milan, Dec. 26, 1830) and Amina in Bellini's *La Sonnambula* (Milan, March 6, 1831); then created the title role in Bellini's *Norma* at Milan's La Scala (Dec. 26, 1831) and *Beatrice di Tenda* in Venice (March 16, 1833). After appearances in London (1837) and St. Petersburg (1840), she virtually abandoned the stage due to the wretched condition of her voice. At the apex of her career, she astounded her auditors by the range of her voice, which encompassed A in the low register to D in the high treble; combined with her rare dramatic gifts, she had few equals on the operatic stage.

BIBL.: M. Ferranti-Giulini, *G. P. e i suoi tempi* (Milan, 1935).

Pasterwitz, Georg (actually **Robert) von,** Austrian composer; b. Bierhütten, near Passau, June 7, 1730; d. Kremsmünster, Jan. 26, 1803. He studied music with Eberlin in Salzburg; after touring Europe, entered the order of the Benedictines in 1755; was choirmaster at the monastery in Kremsmünster (1767–83); lived in Vienna (1785–94); in 1794 he became dean of his monastery's Upper School (until 1801). He publ. 24 *Fughe* for Organ or Harpsichord and 300 *Themata und Versetten* for Organ or Piano. In MS there exists about 20 masses, numerous Psalms, offertories, vespers, motets, etc.; also several operas, intermezzi, and detached arias interpolated in various operas of other composers.

BIBL.: W. Kaas-Cornelius, *G. v.P. als Kirchenkomponist* (diss., Univ. of Vienna, 1925); M. Tremmel, "G. v.P.," *Monatshefte für katholische Kirchenmusik*, XII (1930); A. Kellner, *Musikgeschichte des Stiftes Kremsmünster* (Kassel, 1956).

Patachich, Iván, Hungarian composer; b. Budapest, June 3, 1922. He studied with Albert Siklós, János Viski, and Ferenc Szabó at the Budapest Academy of Music; after working as a theater conductor, he became music director of the Budapest Film Studio in 1952; established the electronic music studio

EXASTUD (Experimentum Auditorii Studii) in Budapest in 1971.
WORKS: STAGE: OPERAS: *Theomachia* (1962); *Fuente ovajuna* (1969); *Brave New World* (1988–89). **BALLETS:** *Fekete-fehér* (Black and White; 1958); *Bakaruhában* (Sunday Romance; 1963); *Mngongo and Mlaba* (1965); *Studio sintetico* (1973). **PANTOMIME:** *Möbius tér* (Mobius Space; 1980). **ORCH.:** 2 harp concertos (1956, 1968); *Poema sinfonico* (1958); Flute Concerto (1958); Viola Concerto (1959); Oboe Concerto (1959); *Serenata* for Strings (1960); Guitar Concerto (1961); *Concerto breve* for Cello and Orch. (1962); 2 divertimentos (1962, 1969); 2 piano concertos (1963, 1968); *Sinfonietta Savariensis* (1964); Violin Concerto (1964); 2 syms. (1965, 1966); *Quadri di Picasso* (1965); Bassoon Concerto (1965); Concerto for 3 Percussionists and Orch. (1966); Concerto for Violin, Piano, and Strings (1969); Organ Concerto (1972); *Presentazioni,* concertino for Cimbalom or Marimba, and Orch. (1975); *Coordinate* (1979); Trumpet Concerto (1985); *Naconxypan szigetén* (On the Island of Naconxypan), 5 symphonic poems (1986); *DX7 Reports No. 2* for Synthesizer and Orch. (1987); Trombone Concerto (1988). **CHAMBER:** 2 sonatas for Violin and Piano (1948, 1964); Sextet for Harp and Winds (1957); Quintet for Harp, Flute, and Strings (1958); Trio for Violin, Viola, and Harp (1958); Wind Quintet (1960); Quartet for 2 Harps, Viola, and Double Bass (1962); 2 piano trios (1962, 1967); Sonata for Viola and Piano (1962); Sonata for Cello and Piano (1963); Sonata for Harp and Horn (1964); Wind Trio (1965); String Trio (1965); *Elementi* for Percussion (1966); *Quattro studii* for 6 Percussionists (1968); *Costruzioni* for 4 Percussionists (1969); Sonata for Oboe and Harp (1971); *Bagatelli* for Organ, Flute, and Horn (1971); *Proporzioni* for 4 Percussionists (1972); *Ja amidohele,* quintet for 5 Cellos (1976); *Quintetto* for Trombone and Tuba (1981); Trio for Bassoons (1982); *Terzettino* for Saxophones (1987); *Quartettino* for Trombones (1988); *Anpro-Sifi* for Percussion Quartet (1988); *Play 88* for Saxophone Quartet (1988); also piano pieces, including Sonata (1965) and Sonatina (1966). **VOCAL: CANTATAS:** *Szirtország* (Country of Cliffs) for Chorus and Orch. (1953); *Music of the Bible* for Tenor, Chorus, and Orch. (1968); *Cantus Profani Silvae* for Chorus and Tape (1978); *Canti stravaganti* for Chorus and Tape (1981); *Az éjszaka csodái* (Miracles of the Night) for Chorus, Orch., and Tape (1985); *Cantus discipulus* for Chorus and Tape (1986); *Miracle of the Hermit Thrush* for Chorus, Orch., and Tape (1987). **OTHER:** *Missa simplex* for Chorus and Organ (1949); *Messe di Santa Marguerita* for Chorus and Orch. (1967); *Canticum Canticorum* for Chorus and Instruments (1985); also live electronic scores and tape pieces.

Patanè, Giuseppe, Italian conductor; b. Naples, Jan. 1, 1932; d. (fatally stricken while conducting *Il Barbiere di Siviglia* at the Bavarian State Opera) Munich, May 30, 1989. He was a son of **Franco Patanè** (1908–68), a conductor; studied at the Cons. S. Pietro a Majella in Naples; made his debut as a conductor at the age of 19, when he led a performance of *La Traviata* at the Teatro Mercadante in Naples; he was subsequently 2nd conductor at the Teatro San Carlo in Naples (1951–56); became principal conductor of the Linz Landestheater in 1961, and in 1962 to 1968 was a conductor of the Deutsche Oper in Berlin; he further filled engagements at La Scala in Milan, at the Vienna State Opera, and in Copenhagen. In 1978 he conducted at the Metropolitan Opera in N.Y.; in 1982 he was appointed co-principal conductor of the American Sym. Orch. in N.Y., remaining at this post until 1984; then was chief conductor of the Mannheim National Theater (from 1987) and of the Munich Radio Orch. (from 1988).

Patey, Janet (Monach) (née **Whytock**), greatly esteemed Scottish contralto; b. London, May 1, 1842; d. Sheffield, Feb. 28, 1894. She studied with Wass, making her debut under the name Ellen Andrews in Birmingham in 1860; then continued her studies with Mrs. Sims Reeves and Ciro Pinsuti. In 1866 she married the baritone **John (George) Patey** (b. Stonehouse, Devon, 1835; d. Falmouth, Dec. 4, 1901); he studied in Paris and Milan, and then made his London debut (1858);

appeared in light roles at Covent Garden and the Italian Opera at the Lyceum Theatre. The 2 then traveled extensively together, both at home and overseas; she became duly recognized as the leading British contralto by 1870; made a tour of the U.S. in 1871.

Patinkin, Mandy, American singer and actor; b. Chicago, Nov. 30, 1952. He grew up on Chicago's South Side, the son of a scrap-metal dealer; began singing in temple when he was 8, later becoming involved in community theater. He spent 2 years at the Univ. of Kansas; then went to the Juilliard School in N.Y., where he studied acting. His 1st important Broadway appearance was as Che Guevara in *Evita* (1978), for which he won a Tony Award. He created the title role in Sondheim's *Sunday in the Park with George* (1984), and delivered a virtuoso performance in the concert version of Sondheim's *Follies* in 1985, performing the trio *Buddy's Blues* as a solo. He has performed extensively with the N.Y. Shakespeare Festival in classical and contemporary roles; his film appearances include *Yentl* (1983), *The Princess Bride* (1987), and *Dick Tracy* (1990). His solo album *Mandy Patinkin* (1989) includes American popular tunes such as *Sonny Boy* among the more expected Sondheim and contemporary songs. He is an expressive actor with an extraordinarily beautiful tenor voice, and one of the most skilled performers in musical theater.

Patiño, Carlos, eminent Spanish composer; b. Santa María del Campo, date unknown; d. Madrid, Sept. 5, 1675. He settled in Madrid, where he became chaplain and maestro de capilla at the Monasterio de la Encarnación (1628); held the latter title at the royal chapel (from 1633); was rector of the college of choirboys (from 1648). He holds an important place in Spanish music history for supplanting the Italian madrigal style for one of Spanish provenance. He produced a large body of sacred music; among his finest works are 6 masses for 4 and 8 Voices and 2 masses for 12 Voices, 17 sacred Latin works, and 24 sacred Spanish compositions (tonos and villancicos); he also wrote theater pieces, most notably cuatros de empezar, which were sung as preludes to dramatic works.

Paton, Mary Ann, distinguished Scottish soprano; b. Edinburgh, Oct. 1802; d. Bulcliffe Hall, Chapelthorpe, July 21, 1864. Of a musical family, she sang in concerts as a child; made her 1st operatic appearance as Susanna in *Le nozze di Figaro* (London, Aug. 3, 1822). She sang the part of Rezia in the premiere of Weber's *Oberon* in London (April 12, 1826) and was praised by Weber himself. She had a very fine voice, and could sing lyric and coloratura parts with equal brilliance. She was married to the tenor Joseph Wood.
BIBL.: "Miss P.," *Quarterly Musical Magazine and Review,* V (London, 1823); J. Wood, *Memoir of Mr. and Mrs. Wood* (Philadelphia, 1840).

Patterson, Annie Wilson, Irish organist, folk song collector, writer on music, and composer; b. Lurgan, Oct. 27, 1868; d. Cork, Jan. 16, 1934. She studied organ with Robert Stewart at the Royal Irish Academy of Music; also studied at the Royal Univ. of Ireland (Mus.B., B.A., 1887; Mus.D., 1889); held several posts as an organist before being made organist at Cork's Shandon Church (1904); was named to the chair of Irish music at the Univ. College, Cork (1924). She organized the Feis Ceoil (Irish Music Festival), held annually from 1897.
WRITINGS: All publ. in London: *The Story of Oratorio* (1902); *Schumann* (1903; 2nd ed., rev., 1934); *The Profession of Music* (1926); *Great Minds in Music* (1926); *The Music of Ireland* (1926).
WORKS: 2 operas: *The High-King's Daughter* and *Oisin;* symphonic poems; cantatas; choruses; songs; arrangements of Irish airs; etc.

Patterson, Franklin Peale, American composer; b. Philadelphia, Jan. 5, 1871; d. New Rochelle, N.Y., July 6, 1966. He studied at the Univ. of Pa., and later in Munich with Thuille and Rheinberger. He wrote several operas, including *The Echo* (Portland, Oreg., June 9, 1925), which won the David Bispham Memorial Medal.

Patterson, Paul (Leslie), English composer; b. Chesterfield, June 15, 1947. He was a pupil of Richard Stoker at the Royal Academy of Music (1964–68) and then studied with Richard Rodney Bennett (1968–70). In 1970 he was made prof. of composition at the Royal Academy of Music, where he also served as head of composition and 20th-century music (from 1985); he likewise was director of contemporary music at Warwick Univ. (1974–80).

WORKS: Wind Quintet (1967); Trumpet Concerto (1969); *Piccola sinfonia* (1971); Horn Concerto (1971); *Fiesta sinfonica* (1972); *Requiem* (1974); Clarinet Concerto (1976); *Cracovian Counterpoints* for 14 Instruments (1977); Concerto for Orch. (1981); *Sinfonia* for Strings (1982); *Mass of the Sea* for Soloists, Chorus, and Orch. (1984); *Stabat Mater* (1986); String Quartet (1986); Harmonica Concerto (1986); *Te Deum* (1988).

Patti, family of prominent Italian singers:

(1) **Salvatore Patti,** tenor; b. Catania, 1800; d. Paris, Aug. 21, 1869. He was 2nd tenor at Palermo's Teatro Carolino (1825–26); after singing throughout Sicily, Italy, and Spain, he settled in N.Y. (1844), where he became active as an opera manager. His wife was the soprano Caterina Chiesa Barilli-Patti (b. Rome, date unknown; d. there, Sept. 6, 1870); she studied with her 1st husband, Barilli; created the role of Eleanora in Donizetti's *L'assedio di Calais* (Naples, Nov. 19, 1836); later sang in N.Y. before retiring to Rome. She had 4 children by her 1st husband, all of whom became singers; she had 3 daughters by her 2nd husband:

(2) **Amalia Patti,** singer; b. Paris, 1831; d. there, Dec. 1915. She appeared in opera and concert in the U.S. until marrying **Maurice Strakosch.**

(3) **Carlotta Patti,** soprano; b. Florence, Oct. 30, 1835; d. Paris, June 27, 1889. She studied with her parents and with Henri Herz in Paris; made her concert debut in N.Y. (1861); sang opera at the Academy of Music there (1862), but due to lameness decided to pursue a concert career; toured in the U.S. and Europe. After marrying the cellist Ernest de Munck (1871), she settled in Paris as a voice teacher.

(4) **Adelina** (actually, **Adela Juana Maria**) **Patti,** greatly celebrated soprano; b. Madrid, Feb. 19, 1843; d. Craig-y-Nos Castle, near Brecon, Wales, Sept. 27, 1919. She was taken to N.Y. (1844), where she began study with her half-brother, Ettore Barilli, and made her 1st public appearance at a charity concert at Tripler's Hall when she was 7; then toured the U.S. as a child prodigy with her brother-in-law **Maurice Strakosch,** and with Ole Bull; later toured with Gottschalk (1857). As the "little Florinda," she made her formal debut as Lucia in N.Y. on Nov. 24, 1859; her European debut followed at London's Covent Garden as Amina in *La Sonnambula* on May 16, 1861; she was hailed as the true successor of Grisi, and subsequently returned to Covent Garden each season for the next 25 years. She sang in Berlin (1861); then in Brussels, Amsterdam, and The Hague (1862); appeared as Amina at the Théâtre-Italien in Paris (Nov. 19, 1862), a role she sang at Vienna's Karlstheater (1863); made her 1st tour of Italy in 1865–66. She married the Marquis de Caux in Paris in 1868; soon after their divorce in 1885, she married the tenor **Nicolini;** after his death in 1898, she married the Swedish nobleman Baron Rolf Cederström in 1899. Patti made her 1st appearance at Milan's La Scala as Violetta on Nov. 3, 1877. She returned to the U.S. for a concert tour in 1881–82, then sang in opera there under the auspices of J.H. Mapleson during the next 3 seasons, earning as much as $5,000 per performance; in 1886–87 again toured the U.S. under the auspices of H.E. Abbey, who presented her at the Metropolitan Opera in N.Y. in the spring of 1887, and then again in 1890 and 1892; her final tour of the U.S. followed in 1903. She made her last appearance at Covent Garden in 1895; her operatic farewell took place in Nice in 1897. Her official farewell concert was given at London's Albert Hall on Dec. 1, 1906. Her last public appearance was at a benefit concert for the Red Cross in that same hall on Oct. 20, 1914. Patti was one of the greatest coloraturas of the 19th century. Although her voice was not one of great power, it possessed a wide range, wonderful flexibility, and perfect evenness. In addition to Amina and Lucia, she was renowned for such roles as Zerlina, Rosina, Norina, Elvira, Martha, Adina, and Gilda; she was also esteemed as Aida and Gounod's Marguerite.

BIBL.: T. de Grave, *Le Biographie d'A. P.* (Paris, 1865); G. de Charnacé, *A. P.* (Paris, 1868); G. Dalmazzo, *A. P.'s Life* (London, 1877); L. Lauw, *Fourteen Years with A. P.* (London, 1884); H. Klein, *The Reign of P.* (N.Y., 1920).

Pattiera, Tino, Yugoslav tenor; b. Čavtat, near Ragusa, June 27, 1890; d. there, April 24, 1966. He studied at the Vienna Academy of Music with Ranieri; in 1915 he joined the Dresden Court (later State) Opera, where he was a principal member of the company until 1941; also sang with the Berlin State Opera (1924–29); was a guest artist in Chicago, Vienna, Budapest, Paris, Prague, and other music centers. He gave his farewell concert in Dresden in 1948; from 1950 he taught voice at the Vienna Academy of Music. He was most renowned for the lyric roles in Verdi's operas.

Pattison, Lee, American pianist; b. Centralia, Wis., July 22, 1890; d. Claremont, Calif., Dec. 22, 1966. He first studied at the New England Cons. of Music in Boston; later in Berlin with Schnabel. In 1916 he formed a duo-piano team with Guy Maier; they gave a number of successful concerts until 1931, when the partnership was dissolved. From 1932 to 1937 he was head of the piano dept. at Sarah Lawrence College; also taught at the Juilliard Summer School; lived mostly in N.Y. His compositions include *Florentine Sketches* for Piano and a piano suite of 7 pieces, *Told in the Hills.*

Patzak, Julius, distinguished Austrian tenor; b. Vienna, April 9, 1898; d. Rottach-Egern, Bavaria, Jan. 26, 1974. He studied musicology and conducting with Adler, Schmidt, and Mandyczewski at the Univ. of Vienna; was autodidact as a singer; made his debut as Radames in Reichenberg (1923). After singing in Brno (1927–28), he was a principal member of the Bavarian State Opera in Munich (1928–45) and the Vienna State Opera (1945–59); first appeared at London's Covent Garden as Tamino (1938), returning there with the visiting Vienna State Opera (1947), and then singing there regularly (1951–54). He was a teacher at the Vienna Academy of Music and the Salzburg Mozarteum; retired from the stage in 1966. He was noted for his roles in Mozart's operas, but he became best known for his compelling portrayals of Beethoven's Florestan and Pfitzner's Palestrina.

Pauer, Ernst, Austrian pianist, teacher, editor, and composer, father of **Max von Pauer;** b. Vienna, Dec. 21, 1826; d. Jugenheim, near Darmstadt, May 9, 1905. He studied piano with Mozart's son, F.X.W. Mozart, and composition with Sechter. In 1851 he went to London; taught at the Royal Academy of Music (1859–64); in 1861 he began a series of historical performances of harpsichord and piano music in chronological order, which attracted considerable attention. After a number of concerts in Germany and Austria, he was appointed pianist to the Austrian court (1866); served as prof. of piano at London's National Training School for Music (from 1876), remaining there when it became the Royal College of Music (1883); retired to Jugenheim (1896). He publ. in London a number of educational works, among them *The Art of Pianoforte Playing* (1877); *Musical Forms* (1878); *The Elements of the Beautiful in Music* (1877); also, *The Birthday Book of Musicians and Composers* (1881) and *A Dictionary of Pianists and Composers for the Pianoforte* (1895); he further brought out collections for piano students: *The New Gradus ad Parnassum; Classical Companion: Celebrated Concert-studies;* and *Cultures of the Left Hand.* He made excellent arrangements of syms. by Beethoven and Schumann, for piano solo, piano, 4-hands, and piano, 8-hands; also arranged Mendelssohn's orch. works for piano, 4-hands and 8-hands; these arrangements were widely used in the 19th century and were extremely useful for young pianists until the advent of the phonograph administered a lethal blow to this type of musical activity.

Pauer, Jiří, Czech composer and arts administrator; b. Libušín, near Kladno, Feb. 22, 1919. He studied composition with Otakar Šín; then with Alois Hába at the Prague Cons. (1943–46) and with Bořkovec at the Prague Academy of Musical Arts (1946–50). He occupied various administrative posts with the Ministry of Education and Culture and with the Czech Radio; was artistic director of the Opera of the National Theater in Prague (1953–55; 1965–67; 1979–89); also taught at the Prague Academy. He was director of the Czech Phil. from 1958 to 1980. His music follows the pragmatic precepts of socialist realism in its modern application, broadly lyrical and tensely dramatic by turns.

WORKS: STAGE: OPERAS: *Žvanivý Slimejš* (Prattling Snail; 1949–50; Prague, April 5, 1958); *Zuzana Vojířová* (1954–57; Prague, May 11, 1958); *Červená Karkulka* (Little Red Riding Hood; 1959; Olomouc, 1960); *Manželské kontrapunkty* (Marital Counterpoints; 1961; 3 operatic satirical sketches, Ostrava, 1962; 2nd version as 5 satires, Liberec, 1967); *Zdravý nemocný* (The Imaginary Invalid), after Molière (1966–69; Prague, May 22, 1970). **MONODRAMA:** *Labutí píseň* (The Swan Song; 1973). **BALLET:** *Ferda Mravenec* (Ferdy the Ant; 1975). **ORCH.:** *Comedy Suite* (1949); Bassoon Concerto (1949); *Youth Suite* (1951); *Scherzo* (1951); *Children's Suite* for Chamber Orch. (1953); *Rhapsody* (1953); Oboe Concerto (1954); Horn Concerto (1958); Sym. (1963); *Commemoration,* symphonic picture (1969); *Canto festivo* (1970–71); Trumpet Concerto (1972); *Initials* (1974); *Aurora,* overture for Large Wind Orch. (1976; also for Orch., 1978); Sym. for Strings (1978); Concerto for Marimba and String Orch. (1984); *Suite* (1987). **CHAMBER:** *Partita* for Harp (1947); *Divertimento* for 3 Clarinets (1949); *Capriccio* for Flute or Oboe or Clarinet or Bassoon and Piano (1952); Violin Sonatina (1953); Cello Sonata (1954); 4 string quartets (1960, 1969, 1970, 1976); *Divertimento* for Nonet (1961); Wind Quintet (1961); Piano Trio (1963); *Concertant Music* for 13 Winds (1971); *Intrada* for 3 Pianos, 3 Trumpets, and 3 Trombones (1975); *Characters* for Brass Quintet (1977–78); *Episodes* for String Quartet (1980); Trio for 3 Horns (1986); Sonata for Violin and Piano (1987); Nonet No. 2 (1988–89); piano pieces; also cantatas; choruses; songs.

Pauer, Max von, eminent Austrian pianist and teacher, son of **Ernst Pauer;** b. London, Oct. 31, 1866; d. Jugenheim, May 12, 1945. He studied with his father and with V. Lachner; embarked on several successful concert tours in Germany; in 1887, was appointed prof. of piano at the Cologne Cons.; in 1897, became a prof. at the Stuttgart Cons.; was its director from 1908 to 1920; in 1920 it became the Hochschule für Musik, which he directed until 1924; then he was director of the Leipzig Cons. (1924–32) and of the Mannheim Hochschule für Musik (1933–34). He made an American tour in 1913–14. Following his father's excellent example in arranging Classical syms. for piano, he made transcriptions of syms. by Mozart and Haydn for piano solo and piano, 4-hands. He publ. an ironic autobiography, *Unser seltsames Ich: Lebensschau eines Künstlers* (Stuttgart, 1942).

Pauk, György, Hungarian-born English violinist; b. Budapest, Oct. 26, 1936. He studied at the Franz Liszt Academy of Music in Budapest. After the unsuccessful Hungarian rebellion of 1956, he went to the Netherlands. He then won several violin competitions, including the prestigious Long–Thibaud Competition in Paris in 1959; eventually made his home in England. With the pianist Peter Frankl and the cellist Ralph Kirshbaum, he formed a successful concert trio.

Paul, Les (real name, **Lester Polfus**), American guitarist and inventor; b. Waukesha, Wis., June 9, 1915. He was mainly autodidact as a guitarist; after performing as a country-music artist, he formed his own jazz group, the Les Paul Trio, which appeared with Fred Waring, Bing Crosby, and the Andrews Sisters. His interest in guitar amplification led to his development of the solid-body electric guitar (1941); later he experimented with recording techniques, being the initiator of so-called "sound-on-sound" or overdubbing technique. He made a number of recordings with his wife, the singer Mary Ford

(née Colleen Summers; b. Pasadena, Calif., July 7, 1924; d. Los Angeles, Sept. 30, 1977).
BIBL.: *Current Biography* (Aug. 1987).

Paul, Oscar, German music scholar; b. Freiwaldau, April 8, 1836; d. Leipzig, April 18, 1898. He studied with Plaidy, Richter, and Hauptmann at the Univ. of Leipzig (Ph.D., 1860); was prof. of music history, piano, and composition at the Leipzig Cons. (from 1869) and prof. extraordinarius at the Univ. of Leipzig (from 1872); was also music critic of the *Leipziger Tagblatt.* He adapted Hauptmann's *Lehre von der Harmonik* for practical usages and publ. the result under the title *Lehrbuch der Harmonik* (Leipzig, 1880; in Eng., N.Y., 1885). He also publ. *Geschichte des Klaviers* (Leipzig, 1869); *Handlexikon der Tonkunst* (Leipzig, 1871–73); *Musikalische Instrumente* (Braunschweig, 1874).

Paul, Thomas (Warburton), distinguished American bass; b. Chicago, Feb. 22, 1934. He studied with Howard Swan and Robert Gross at Occidental College in Los Angeles (B.A., 1956); then took courses in conducting with Jean Morel and Frederic Waldman at the Juilliard School of Music in N.Y.; also studied voice privately in N.Y. He made his vocal debut in Handel's *Belshazzar* at Carnegie Hall on April 10, 1961. He sang with the N.Y. City Opera (1962–71; debut Oct. 4, 1962), and with other U.S. opera companies. He made his European debut in Zürich on April 3, 1976, in a performance of Bach's *St. Matthew Passion.* In 1980 he made his recital debut in N.Y. He made many appearances as a soloist with the major North American orchs. He was a visiting prof. (1971–74) and prof. (from 1974) at the Eastman School of Music in Rochester, N.Y., and also taught at the Aspen Music School. His finest roles include Boris Godunov, Figaro, and Méphistophélès.

Paull, Barberi, American composer of the avant-garde; b. N.Y., July 25, 1946. She began to play piano as an infra-adolescent, in private and in public; with the awakening of consciousness, she opted for jazz and multimedia forms of self-expression, but went through the motions of academic training at the Juilliard School of Music in N.Y., where she studied composition with Hall Overton and Jacob Druckman (1970–71); later she took courses with Charles Wuorinen at the Manhattan School of Music (1972) and attended the Musical Theatre Workshop conducted by Lehman Engel (1973). Then, in a dash of feminist self-assertion, she founded the Barberi Paull Musical Theatre, Inc., and presented with it a series of mixed-media events. In her compositions she elevates eclecticism to an article of democratic faith, embracing jazz, pop tunes, and electronic sound in a context of ostentatious and unapologetic cosmic sentimentality.

WORKS: Electronic ballet, *Time* (1971); *Earth Pulse,* choreographic cantata, making use of musique concrète (1971); *The Mass* for Tape, Percussion, and Visual Projections (1974); *A Land Called The Infinity of Love* for Multimedia (1975); *Sheer Silver Sheen Flower Sky* for Chorus (1971–74); *O Wind* for Mezzo-soprano and String Quartet (1975); *Song for Orchestra* (1977); *A Christmas Carol,* after Dickens, for Chorus and Instrumental Trio (1977; also in a jazz version); many unabashed pop tunes.

Paulli, Holger Simon, Danish violinist, conductor, and composer; b. Copenhagen, Feb. 22, 1810; d. there, Dec. 23, 1891. He studied violin with Schall and Wexschall; at the age of 12, entered the court orch. in Copenhagen; then was its concertmaster (1849–63) and principal conductor (1863–83). In 1866 he was appointed co-director, with Gade and Hauptmann, of the newly founded Copenhagen Cons. He was an admirer of Wagner, and conducted the 1st performances in Denmark of *Lohengrin* (1870) and *Die Meistersinger von Nürnberg* (1872). He composed a singspiel, *Lodsen* (The Pilot), which was produced in Copenhagen on Sept. 25, 1851; also wrote some ballet music, violin pieces, and songs.

Paulson, Gustaf, Swedish composer and organist; b. Hälsingborg, Jan. 22, 1898; d. there, Dec. 17, 1966. He studied composition in Copenhagen with Peder Gram; from 1929 until his death, served as church organist in Hälsingborg. He was an extraordinarily prolific composer. His music reflected the type of Scandinavian Romanticism associated with Sibelius and Nielsen, pervaded by streaks of coherent polyphony.

WORKS: ORCH: 13 syms.: No. 1 (1928); No. 2 (1933); No. 3, *Sinfonia da chiesa* (1945); No. 4, *Uppstandelse* (The Resurrection; 1947); No. 5, *Aron Bergenson in memoriam* (1948); No. 6 (1952); No. 7 (1953); No. 8 (1954); No. 9 (1956); No. 10 (1957); No. 11, *Stabat Mater* (1959; Hälsingborg, March 26, 1961); No. 12 (1963; Hälsingborg, Nov. 28, 1963); No. 13 (1966); 2 sinfonias for String Orch. (1953, 1954); 19 concertos: 2 for Piano (1940, 1961); 2 for Cello (1944, 1957); 2 for Oboe (1950, 1957); 2 for English Horn, with Strings (1958, 1959); 2 for Clarinet (1958, 1959); one each for Bassoon (1959); for Saxophone (1959); for Violin (1960); for Flute, with Female Choir, *Arets tider* (1962); for Horn (1964); for Trombone (1965); for Trumpet (1965); for Viola (1965); for Double Bass (1965–66); *Symphonic Variations* (1934); *Metamorphoses on a Theme by Clementi* (1951); *Passion* for Cello and Orch. (1961). VOCAL: *Stabat Mater* for Soli, Female Chorus, Strings, and Percussion (1956; Hälsingborg, March 17, 1957); *Vid korset*, oratorio (1957); songs. CHAMBER: 5 string quartets; Violin Sonata (1958); Cello Sonata (1960); piano pieces; organ pieces.

Paulus, Olaf, Norwegian organist and composer; b. Christiania, Jan. 25, 1859; d. Stavanger, June 29, 1912. He was a pupil of C. Cappelen and J. Svendsen; also studied at the Leipzig Cons.; from 1889 he was organist at the Cathedral in Stavanger; made a trip to the U.S. in 1902, directing choral concerts in Minneapolis and St. Paul. In his native country he was highly esteemed as a national composer; his men's choruses were in the repertoire of all Norwegian societies; he also wrote songs and piano pieces, and ed. a collection of songs, *De 1,000 hjems sange* (Home Songs; 1888).

Paulus, Stephen (Harrison), American composer; b. Summit, N.J., Aug. 24, 1949. He studied with Paul Fetler and Dominick Argento at the Univ. of Minnesota (B.M., 1971; M.M., 1974; Ph.D., 1978). In 1973 he founded the Minnesota Composers Forum in Minneapolis with Libby Larsen, and was managing composer until 1984; he served as composer-in-residence of the Minnesota Orch. (1983–87) and the Atlanta Sym. Orch. (from 1988). In 1983 he held a Guggenheim fellowship. Paulus has demonstrated fine craftsmanship in both vocal and instrumental writing.

WORKS: OPERAS: *The Village Singer* (1977; St. Louis, June 9, 1979); *The Postman Always Rings Twice* (1981; St. Louis, June 19, 1982; also an orch. suite, Minneapolis, July 26, 1986); *The Woodlanders* (1984; St. Louis, June 13, 1985). ORCH.: *Spectra* for Small Orch. (Houston, April 12, 1980); *Translucent Landscapes* (Peninsula Music Festival, Aug. 6, 1982); *7 Short Pieces* (1983; Minneapolis, Feb. 9, 1984); Divertimento for Harp and Chamber Orch. (1983); *Concerto for Orchestra* (Minneapolis, April 6, 1983); *Ordway Overture* (1984); *Reflections: 4 Movements on a Theme of Wallace Stevens* (1984; St. Paul, Minn., March 22, 1985); *Symphony in 3 Movements (Soliloquy)* (1985; Minneapolis, Jan. 15, 1986); *Ground Breaker*, overture (Minneapolis, Oct. 7, 1987); Violin Concerto (Atlanta, Nov. 5, 1987); *Night Speech* (Spokane, Wash., April 21, 1989); *Concertante* (Atlanta, April 27, 1989); *Symphony for Strings* (Oregon Bach Festival, July 5, 1989); *Street Music* (1990). CHAMBER ENSEMBLE: *Exploration* (1974); *Village Tales: A Tree of Life* (1975); *Graphics* (1977); *Lunar Maria* (1977). OTHER CHAMBER: *Colors* for Brass Quintet (1974); Wind Suite for Woodwind Quartet (1975); 2 string quartets: No. 1, *Music for Contrasts* (1980); No. 2 (1987); *Courtship Songs for a Summer's Eve* for Flute, Oboe, Cello, and Piano (1981); Partita for Violin and Piano (1986); *American Vignettes* for Cello and Piano (1988); *Fantasy in 3 Parts* for Flute and Guitar (1989). VOCAL: *Personals* for Chorus, Flute, and Percussion (1975); *Canticles: Songs and Rituals for Easter and the May* for Soloists, Chorus, and Orch. (1977); *North Shore* for Soloists, Chorus, and Orch. (1977); *Letters for the Times* for Chorus and Chamber Ensemble (1980); *Echoes between the Silent Peaks* for Chorus and

Chamber Ensemble (1984); *Letters from Colette* for Soprano and Chamber Ensemble (1986); *Madrigali di Michelangelo* for Chorus (1987); *Voices* for Chorus and Orch. (1988); *4 Preludes on Playthings of the Wind* for Chorus (1990).

Pauly, Rosa (Rose née **Pollak),** noted Hungarian soprano; b. Eperjes, March 15, 1894; d. Kfar Shmaryahn, near Tel Aviv, Dec. 14, 1975. She studied voice with Rosa Papier in Vienna, and made her operatic debut at the Vienna State Opera as Desdemona in Verdi's *Otello* in 1918. She subsequently sang in Hamburg, Cologne, and Mannheim. From 1927 to 1931 she was a member of the Kroll Opera in Berlin; also of the Vienna State Opera (1929–35); in 1934 she sang the challenging role of Elektra in Strauss's opera in Salzburg, gathering encomiums; in 1935 she appeared at La Scala in Milan. She made her American debut as Elektra in a concert performance with the N.Y. Phil. on March 21, 1937; sang it again at her 1st appearance with the Metropolitan Opera in N.Y. on Jan. 7, 1938; appeared there until 1940; also sang at the Teatro Colón in Buenos Aires in 1939. In 1946 she went to Palestine, and devoted herself to teaching in Tel Aviv. She was esteemed for her roles in the operas of Mozart, Verdi, and Wagner, but most particularly for her compelling portrayals of such Strauss roles as Elektra, the Dyer's Wife, and Helena.

Paumann, Conrad, significant German organist and composer; b. Nuremberg, between 1410 and 1415; d. Munich, Jan. 24, 1473. He was blind from birth; through the patronage of Ulrich Grundherr, and later his son Paul Grundherr, he was able to obtain instruction in music. By 1446 he was appointed organist at St. Sebald in Nuremberg; in 1447 he became town organist. In 1450 he was called to Munich to serve as court organist to Duke Albrecht III of Bavaria. He won great renown as an organist, and traveled to Austria and Italy. He also achieved mastery as a player on the harp, the lute, and the recorder; he was particularly noted for his improvisations. Some of his extant works have been publ. in *Das Erbe deutscher Musik*, 1st series (1958); see also the *Fundamentum organisandi magistri Conradi Paumanns ceci de Nürenberga anno 1452* as ed. by W. Apel in *Keyboard Music of the Fourteenth and Fifteenth Centuries*, Corpus of Early Keyboard Music, I (1963).

BIBL.: F. Arnold and H. Bellerman, "Das Locheimer Liederbuch nebst der Ars organisandi von C. P.," *Jahrbuch für musikalische Wissenschaft*, II (1867); L. Schrade, *Die handschriftliche Überlieferung der ältesten Instrumental-Musik* (Lahr, 1931); B. Wallner, "K. P.," in *Münchner Characterköpfe der Gotik* (Munich, 1938); T. Göllner, *Formen früher Mehrstimmigkeit in deutschen Handschriften des späten Mittelalters* (Tutzing, 1961); F. Krautwurst, "K. P. in Nördlingen," *Festschrift für Heinrich Besseler* (Leipzig, 1961); F. Krautwurst, "Neues zur Biographie K. P.s," *Jahrbuch für fränkische Landesforschung*, XXII (1962); C. Wolff, "C. P.s Fundamentum organisandi und seine verschiedenen Fassungen," *Archiv für Musikwissenschaft*, XXV (1968).

Paumgartner, Bernhard, eminent Austrian musicologist and conductor; b. Vienna, Nov. 14, 1887; d. Salzburg, July 27, 1971. He was a son of the pianist Hans Paumgartner (1843–96) and the mezzo-soprano **Rosa Papier.** He learned to play the horn, violin, and piano in his youth; began to conduct while still in school. After receiving a doctorate in law from the Univ. of Vienna (1911), he studied musicology privately with Adler; was répétiteur at the Vienna Court Opera (1911–12); then was director of the Salzburg Mozarteum (from 1917), which he headed until 1938, and again from 1945 to 1959; was also closely associated with the Salzburg Festival from its founding (1920), serving as its president (1960–71). He also composed; wrote the operas *Die Höhle von Salamanca* (Dresden, 1923) and *Rossini in Neapel* (Zürich, March 27, 1936), various other stage pieces, including several ballets, orch. music, songs, etc.

WRITINGS: *Mozart* (Berlin, 1927; 6th ed., augmented, 1967); *Franz Schubert: Eine Biographie* (Zürich, 1943; 3rd ed., 1960); *Johann Sebastian Bach: Leben und Werk, I: Bis zur Berufung nach Leipzig* (Zürich, 1950); *Erinnerungen* (Salzburg, 1969); G. Croll, ed., *Bernhard Paumgartner: Vorträge und Essays* (Salzburg, 1972).

BIBL.: E. Preussner, ed., *Wissenschaft und Praxis: Eine Festschrift zum 70. Geburtstag von B. P.* (Zürich, 1957); G. Croll, ed., *B. P.* (Salzburg and Munich, 1971).

Paunović, Milenko, Serbian composer; b. Šajkaš, Nov. 28, 1889; d. Belgrade, Oct. 1, 1924. He studied in Leipzig with Reger and Riemann; became a choral conductor in Novi Sad. In his music he followed Wagnerian concepts, and wrote several music dramas to his own texts; also a *Yugoslav Symphony* (Ljubljana, March 17, 1924).

Paur, Emil, Austrian conductor; b. Czernowitz, Bukovina, Aug. 29, 1855; d. Mistek, Bohemia, June 7, 1932. He was trained in the rudiments of music by his father, and played the violin and piano in public at the age of 8; at 11 he entered the Vienna Cons., where he studied violin with J. Hellmesberger, Sr., and composition with Dessoff, graduating in 1870; was 1st court conductor in Mannheim (1880–91), where he also led the sym. concerts; then was conductor of the Leipzig Stadttheater (1891–93). He achieved an excellent reputation as a competent drillmaster, and in 1893 was engaged as conductor of the Boston Sym. Orch. to succeed Nikisch; he held this post for 5 seasons; from 1898 to 1902 he conducted the N.Y. Phil.; during the season of 1899–1900, he led the Wagner repertoire at the Metropolitan Opera in N.Y.; from 1899 to 1902 he served as director of the National Cons. in N.Y., succeeding Dvořák; from 1902 to 1904 he filled engagements in Europe; in 1904 he was again engaged in the U.S., as conductor of the Pittsburgh Sym. Orch. (until 1910). In 1912 he returned to Berlin, but failed to impress the fastidious concert audiences there; after a brief tenure as director of the Berlin Royal Opera (1912), he pursued a career as a guest conductor in Europe. He also composed; wrote a sym., *In der Natur*, a Violin Concerto, and chamber music.

Pavarotti, Luciano, greatly renowned Italian tenor; b. Modena, Oct. 12, 1935. His father, a baker by trade, sang in the local church choir; Luciano learned to read music and began singing with the boy altos; later joined his father in the choir, and also sang in the chorus of the local Teatro Comunale and the amateur Chorale Gioacchino Rossini. To prepare himself for a career as a schoolteacher, he attended the local Scuola Magistrale; then taught in an elementary school, augmenting his income by selling insurance. In the meantime, he began vocal studies with Arrigo Polo in Modena (1955), then went to Mantua, where he continued his training with Ettore Campogalliani (1960). He made his operatic debut as Rodolfo in *La Bohème* at the Teatro Municipale in Reggio Emilia on April 29, 1961. He obtained his 1st major engagement when he appeared as the Duke of Mantua at the Teatro Massimo in Palermo (March 15, 1962). His 1st important appearance outside his homeland was as Edgardo with the Netherlands Opera in Amsterdam (Jan. 18, 1963). On Feb. 24, 1963, he made his Vienna State Opera debut as Rodolfo, a role he also sang for his 1st appearance at London's Covent Garden (Sept. 21, 1963). On Feb. 15, 1965, he made his U.S. debut as Edgardo opposite Joan Sutherland's Lucia with the Greater Miami Opera. After his 1st appearance at Milan's La Scala as Alfredo (April 28, 1965), he made a summer tour of Australia with the Sutherland Williamson International Grand Opera Co., a venture featuring the celebrated diva. He subsequently scored his 1st triumph on the operatic stage when he essayed the role of Tonio in *La Fille du régiment* at Covent Garden (June 1, 1966); with insouciant aplomb, he tossed off the aria *Pour mon âme*, replete with 9 successive high C's, winning an ovation. He was dubbed the "King of the High C's," and a brilliant international career beckoned. He made his debut at the San Francisco Opera as Rodolfo (Nov. 11, 1967), a role he chose for his 1st appearance at the Metropolitan Opera in N.Y. (Nov. 23, 1968). In subsequent seasons he became a mainstay at both houses, and also appeared regularly with other opera houses on both sides of the Atlantic. He also made

frequent appearances in solo recitals and concerts with orchs. In 1977 he starred as Rodolfo in the 1st "Live from the Met" telecast by PBS. In 1978 he made an acclaimed solo recital debut at the Metropolitan Opera, which was also telecast by PBS. In 1980 he founded the Opera Co. of Philadelphia/Luciano Pavarotti International Voice Competition. On Oct. 22, 1983, he was one of the featured artists at the Metropolitan Opera Centennial Gala. In 1984 he gave a concert before 20,000 admirers at N.Y.'s Madison Square Garden, which was also seen by millions on PBS. He celebrated the 25th anniversary of his operatic debut by singing his beloved Rodolfo at the Teatro Comunale in Modena on April 29, 1986. In 1988 he sang Nemorino at the Berlin Deutsche Oper, eliciting thunderous applause and no less than 15 curtain calls. On Jan. 9, 1989, he appeared in concert with the N.Y. City Opera orch. in a special program at Avery Fischer Hall at N.Y.'s Lincoln Center for the Performing Arts, which was televised live by PBS. In 1990 he appeared at the Bolshoi Theater in Moscow.

The most idolized tenor since Caruso, Pavarotti made such roles as Nemorino in *L'elisir d'amore*, Riccardo in *Un ballo in maschera*, Fernando in *La Favorite*, Manrico in *Il Trovatore*, Cavaradossi in *Tosca*, and Radames in *Aida*, as well as the ubiquitous Rodolfo, virtually his own. Indeed, through recordings and television appearances, he won an adoring global following. Always of a jocular rotundity, he announced in 1988 that he had succeeded in dropping 85 pounds from his original body weight. His autobiography was publ. as *Pavarotti: My Own Story* (with W. Wright; Garden City, N.Y., 1981).

BIBL.: M. Mayer, *Grandissimo P.* (Garden City, N.Y., 1986; with career chronology and discography by G. Fitzgerald).

Payne, Anthony (Edward), English composer and music critic; b. London, Aug. 2, 1936. He studied at Dulwich College and the Univ. of Durham (1958–61); was a music critic for the London *Daily Telegraph* (1965–87) and the *Independent* (from 1987). In 1966 he married **Jane Manning**. His style of composition is structurally disciplined, but inwardly Romantic and inspired by northern moods and modes.

WORKS: ORCH.: *Suite from a Forgotten Ballet* (1955; rev. 1986); *Contrapuncti* for String Quartet and Strings (1958; rev. 1979); *Concerto for Orchestra* (1974; London, Jan. 8, 1975); *Songs of the Clouds* (1979–80; Cheltenham, June 29, 1980); *Spring's Shining Wake* (1980–81; BBC, Dec. 21, 1983); *Songs and Seascapes* for String Orch. (London, June 6, 1984); *The Spirit's Harvest* (London, July 31, 1985); *Half-heard in the Stillness* (Derby, Sept. 17, 1987). **CHAMBER:** *Sonatas and Ricercars* for Flute, Oboe, Clarinet, Bassoon, and Horn (1970; BBC, May 28, 1974); *String Quartet* (London, Dec. 4, 1978); *The Stones and Lonely Places Sing* for Flute, Clarinet, Horn, and Piano (London, Sept. 2, 1979); *A Day in the Life of a Mayfly* for Flute, Clarinet, Percussion, Piano, Violin, and Cello (London, Sept. 25, 1981); *The Song Streams in the Firmament* for Clarinet, String Quartet, and Double Bass (N.Y., April 19, 1986); *Fanfares and Processional* for Horn, 4 Trumpets, 4 Trombones, and Tuba (London, Sept. 19, 1986); *Echoes of Courtly Love* for Horn, Trumpet, Flugelhorn, Trombone, and Tuba (1987; London, May 13, 1988); *Consort Music* for 2 Violins, 2 Violas, and Cello (Cambridge, July 27, 1987); *Sea Change* for Flute, Clarinet, Harp, and String Quartet (London, June 12, 1988). **VOCAL:** *Phoenix Mass* for Chorus, 3 Trumpets, and 3 Trombones (1965–72; BBC, Oct. 2, 1973); *2 Songs without Words* for Men's Vocal Quintet (1970; London, Feb. 4, 1971); *1st Sight of Her and After* for 16 Solo Voices (London, Dec. 11, 1975); *The World's Winter* for Soprano, Flute, Oboe, Clarinet, Horn, Harp, and String Trio (Cheltenham, July 4, 1976); *A Little Whitsuntide Cantata* (1977; rev. 1984); *Alleluias and Hockets* for Chorus and 10 Instruments (1987); choruses; songs.

WRITINGS: *Schoenberg* (London, 1968); with L. Foreman, *Frank Bridge* (London, 1976); *Frank Bridge: Radical and Conservative* (London, 1984).

Paz, Juan Carlos, significant Argentine composer; b. Buenos Aires, Aug. 5, 1901; d. there, Aug. 25, 1972. He studied composition with Constantino Gaito in Argentina and later with Vincent d'Indy in Paris; in 1929, with several young composers of radical tendencies, he organized in Buenos Aires the "Grupo Renovación," and in 1937 inaugurated a series of concerts of new music; became a music critic and author of several books. His early works, after 1921, are marked by strong polyphony, in a neo-Classical style; about 1927, he adopted atonal and polytonal procedures; in 1934 he began to compose almost exclusively in the 12-tone idiom; after 1950 he modified his musical language, adopting a less rigid and more personal style of composition.

WORKS: ORCH.: *Canto de Navidad* (1927; instrumented 1930); *Movimiento sinfónico* (1930); Suite for Ibsen's *Juliano Emperador* (1931); *3 Pieces* (1931); *Passacaglia* (1936; ISCM Festival, Paris, June 25, 1937; rev. 1952–53); *Música* (*Preludio y fuga*) (1940); *Passacaglia* for String Orch. (1944; rev. 1949); *Rítmica constante* (1952); *6 superposiciones* (1954); *Transformaciones canónicas* (1955–56); *Música* for Bassoon, Strings, and Percussion (1955–56); *Continuidad 1960* (1960–61; Caracas, May 11, 1966); *Estructuras 1962* for Chamber Orch. (1962); *Música* for Piano and Orch. (1964; Washington, D.C., May 12, 1965). **CHAMBER:** *Tema y transformaciones* for 11 Winds (1929); Wind Octet (1930); 3 sonatinas: No. 1 for Clarinet and Piano (1930); No. 2 for Flute and Clarinet (1932); No. 3 for Oboe and Bassoon (1933; later transcribed for Piano); *Concierto No. 1* for Flute, Oboe, Clarinet, Bassoon, Trumpet, and Piano (1932) and *No. 2* for Oboe, Trumpet, 2 Trombones, Bassoon, and Piano (1935); *4 Composiciónes dodecafónica*: No. 1 for Flute, English Horn, and Cello (1934; lost); No. 2 for Flute and Piano (1935); No. 3 for Clarinet and Piano (1937); No. 4 for Violin (1938); Overture for 12 Instruments (1936); *4 pieces* for Clarinet (1936); *3 Composiciónes en trío*: No. 1 for Flute, Clarinet, and Bassoon (1937); No. 2 for Clarinet, Trumpet, and Alto Saxophone (1938); No. 3 for Flute, Oboe, and Bass Clarinet or Bassoon (1940; rev. 1945); 2 string quartets (1938, 1940–43); *Música* for Flute, Saxophone, and Piano (1943); *Dédalus 1950* for Flute, Clarinet, Violin, Cello, and Piano (1950–51); *Continuidad 1953* for Piano and Percussion (1953–54); *3 contrapuntos* for Clarinet, Electric Guitar, Celesta, Trumpet, Trombone, and Cello (1955); *Invención* for String Quartet (1961); *Concreción* for Flute, Clarinet, Bassoon, Horn, Trumpet, Trombone, and Tuba (1964). **KEYBOARD: PIANO:** 3 sonatas (1923, 1925, 1935); *Tema con transformaciones* (1928); *3 movimientos de jazz* (1932); Sonatina No. 3 (1933; originally for Oboe and Bassoon); *10 piezas sobre una serie dodecafónica* (1936); *Música 1946*; *Núcleos*, 1st series (1962–64). **ORGAN:** *Galaxia 64* (1964). **BIBL.:** J. Beschinsky, *J.C. P.* (Buenos Aires, 1964); J. Romano, "J.C. P.," *Boletín Latino-Americano de Música*, no. 54 (1966); idem, *J.C. P.: Tribulaciones de un músico* (Buenos Aires, 1970).

Peabody, George, American businessman and philanthropist; b. South Danvers, Mass., Feb. 18, 1795; d. London, Nov. 4, 1869. He was the founder of George Peabody & Co., which specialized in American securities and foreign exchange. In 1837 he settled in England, where he conducted a thriving business; in 1857 he disbursed $1,500,000 for the founding of the Peabody Inst. in Baltimore, which later established the Peabody Cons. of Music.

Pearce, S(tephen) Austen, English-American organist and composer; b. Brompton, Kent, Nov. 7, 1836; d. Jersey City, N.J., April 9, 1900. He studied at Oxford Univ. (Mus.B., 1859; Mus.D., 1864). In 1872 he settled in America; taught vocal music at Columbia College in N.Y.: also at the Peabody Inst. in Baltimore. He wrote an opera, *La Belle Américaine*; dramatic oratorio, *Celestial Visions;* church cantata, *The Psalm of Praise;* piano pieces; songs; compiled *A Pocket Dictionary of Musical Terms* in 21 languages (N.Y., 1889).

Pears, Sir Peter (Neville Luard), renowned English tenor; b. Farnham, June 22, 1910; d. Aldeburgh, April 3, 1986. He began his career as temporary organist at Hertford College, Oxford (1928–29), then was director of music at the Grange School, Crowborough (1930–34). He was a scholarship student at the Royal College of Music in London (1933–34); concurrently sang in the BBC Chorus, and then was a member of the BBC Singers (1934–38) and the New English Singers (1936–38). During this period he received vocal instruction from Elena Gerhardt and Dawson Freer. In 1936 he also met Benjamin Britten; they gave their 1st joint recital in 1937, and thereafter remained lifelong personal and professional companions. After singing in the Glyndebourne Chorus (1938), he accompanied Britten to the U.S. (1939); continued his vocal training with Thérèse Behr and Clytie Hine-Mundy. In 1942 he returned to England with Britten, making his stage debut that same year in the title role of *Les Contes d'Hoffmann* at London's Strand Theatre. In 1943 he joined the Sadler's Wells Opera Co., gaining fame when he created the title role in Britten's *Peter Grimes* (June 7, 1945). In 1946 he became a member of the English Opera Group, and thereafter greatly distinguished himself in operas by Britten; among the roles he created were Albert Herring, the Male Chorus in *The Rape of Lucretia*, Captain Vere in *Billy Budd*, Essex in *Gloriana*, Quint in *The Turn of the Screw*, Flute in *A Midsummer Night's Dream* (was co-librettist with the composer), the Madwoman in *Curlew River*, Sir Philip Wingrave in *Owen Wingrave*, and Aschenbach in *Death in Venice*. It was in the latter role that he made his Metropolitan Opera debut in N.Y. on Oct. 18, 1974. He was one of the founders of the Aldeburgh Festival (1948), serving as a director and as a teacher of master classes until his death. Pears also sang in several 1st performances of Britten's non-operatic works, including the *Serenade* for Tenor, Horn, and Strings, the *Michelangelo Sonnets*, and the *War Requiem*. He also excelled in the works of other English composers, among them Elgar, Holst, Vaughan Williams, and Walton, as well as those by Schütz, Bach, Mozart, Schubert, and Schumann. He was made a Commander of the Order of the British Empire in 1957, and was knighted in 1978. **BIBL.:** M. Thorpe, ed., *P. P.: A Tribute on His 75th Birthday* (London, 1985).

Pearsall, Robert Lucas, English antiquarian and composer; b. Clifton, March 14, 1795; d. Wartensee, Lake Constance, Aug. 5, 1856. He studied law and music; as a boy of 13 he wrote a cantata, *Saul and the Witch of Endor.* He lived many years in Germany, where he publ. many of his compositions; was in London on several extended visits; in 1842, purchased a castle on Lake Constance, and remained there for the rest of his life. As a composer, he was at his best in many ingenious madrigals; particularly popular were his part-songs, *Sir Patrick Spens, The Hardy Norseman*, and *O who will o'er the downs so free;* he ed. early church music in Germany; publ. an *Essay on Consecutive Fifths and Octaves in Counterpoint* (London, 1876). **BIBL.:** W. Barclay Squire, "Letters of R.L. P.," *Musical Quarterly*, V (1919) and VI (1920), *Musical Times*, LXI (1920), LXIII (1922), LXIV (1923), and XV (1924); E. Hunt, "R.L. P.," *Proceedings of the Royal Musical Association*, LXXXII (1955–56); idem, *R.L. P., the "Compleat Gentleman" and his Music* (Chesham Bois, 1971).

Pechner, Gerhard, German-American baritone; b. Berlin, April 15, 1903; d. N.Y., Oct. 21, 1969. He trained in Berlin; made his 1st appearance as an opera singer in Berlin in 1927; was compelled to leave Germany in 1933; from 1933 to 1939 he was on the staff of the German Theater in Prague. In 1940 he was engaged by the San Francisco Opera, and on Nov. 27, 1941, made his debut at the Metropolitan Opera in N.Y.; remained there until 1965, and sang there again in 1966–67.

Pedersøn, Mogens, significant Danish composer; b. c.1583; d. probably in Copenhagen, Jan. or Feb. 1623. As a result of the patronage of King Christian IV, he was sent to Venice to study with Giovanni Gabrieli (1599–1600); upon his return to Copenhagen, he worked under Borchgrevinck (1600–1603);

then became an instrumentalist in the royal chapel. After further studies in Italy (1605–9), he returned to Copenhagen to enter the royal chapel once again; was sent by the King to England to serve his sister, Anne, queen to James I (1611). Following his return to Copenhagen (1614), he again was active in the royal chapel, becoming its assistant director (1618). Pedersøn greatly distinguished himself as a composer of both sacred and secular music.

Works: *Madrigali, libro primo* for 5 Voices (Venice, 1608; ed. in Dania Sonans, I, Copenhagen, 1933); *Madrigali, libro secondo* for 5 Voices (1611?; greater portion not extant except for 10 madrigals; ed. in Dania Sonans, III, Egtved, 1967); *Pratum spirituale* for 5 Voices (Copenhagen, 1620; ed. in Dania Sonans, I, Copenhagen, 1933); 2 madrigaletti for 3 Voices (1619; ed. in Dania Sonans, II, Egtved, 1966); 2 pavanes for 5 Viols (MS).

Pederzini, Gianna, noted Italian mezzo-soprano; b. Vò di Avio, Feb. 10, 1903; d. Rome, March 12, 1988. She studied with De Lucia in Naples; made her debut as Preziosilla in 1923 in Messina; in 1930 she joined La Scala in Milan, where she sang until 1943; also appeared in Rome (1939–52), at Covent Garden, London (1931), and at the Teatro Colón in Buenos Aires (1937–39; 1946–47). She returned to La Scala in 1956–57, creating the role of the Prioress in Poulenc's *Dialogues des Carmélites.* She was an outstanding interpreter of roles in Rossini's operas; was also greatly admired for her interpretation of Carmen.

Pedrell, Carlos, Uruguayan composer, nephew of **Felipe Pedrell;** b. Minas, Oct. 16, 1878; d. Montrouge, near Paris, March 3, 1941. He studied in Madrid with his uncle; later went to Paris, where he took lessons with d'Indy and Bréville at the Schola Cantorum. Returning to South America, he was inspector of music in the Buenos Aires schools; lectured at the Univ. of Tucumán; in 1921 he went to Paris, where he remained for the rest of his life. His works are cast in the French style, but the rhythmic elements are related to Spanish and South American sources; his songs, with richly developed accompaniments, are the best among his works.

Works: STAGE: OPERAS: *Ardid de Amor* (Buenos Aires, June 7, 1917); *Cuento de Abril; La Guitare* (Madrid, 1924). **BALLETS:** *La Rose et le gitan* (Antwerp, 1930); *Alleluia* (Buenos Aires, 1936). **ORCH.:** *Une Nuit de Schéhérazade* (1908); *Danza y canción de Aixa* (1910); *En el estrado de Beatriz* (1910); *Fantasia Argentina* (1910); *Ouverture catalane* (1912); *Pastorales* for Voice and Orch. (Paris, 1928); choruses; songs. **BIBL.:** A. Suarès, "C. P.," *Revue Musicale* (June 1931).

Pedrell, Felipe, eminent Spanish musicologist and composer, uncle of **Carlos Pedrell;** b. Tortosa, Feb. 19, 1841; d. Barcelona, Aug. 19, 1922. He became a chorister at Tortosa Cathedral when he was about 7, receiving instruction from Juan Antonio Nin y Serra. In 1873 he went to Barcelona as deputy director of the Light Opera Co., where he produced his 1st opera, *L'ultimo Abenzeraggio* (April 14, 1874). After a visit to Italy (1876–77) and a sojourn in Paris, he settled in Barcelona (1881), where he devoted himself mainly to musicological pursuits. In 1882 he founded the journals *Salterio Sacro-Hispano* and *Notas Musicales y Literarias,* both of which ceased publication in 1883. He then was founder-ed. of the important journal *La Illustración Musical Hispano-Americana* (1888–96). During this period, he worked on his operatic masterpiece, the trilogy *Los Pirineos/Els Pirineus* (1890–91), and also publ. the book *Por nuestra música* (1891), which served as its introduction and as a plea for the creation of a national lyric drama based on Spanish folk song. In 1894 he went to Madrid, where he was named prof. of choral singing at the Cons. and prof. of advanced studies at the Ateneo; was also elected a member of the Royal Academy of Fine Arts. Upon his return to Barcelona (1904), he devoted himself to writing, teaching, and composing. Among his outstanding pupils were Albéniz, Falla, Granados, and Gerhard. Although Pedrell was admired as a composer by his contemporaries, his music has not obtained recognition outside his homeland. His lasting achievement rests upon his distinguished work as a musicologist, in which he did much to restore interest in both historical and contemporary Spanish sacred music.

WRITINGS: *Gramática musical o manual expositivo de la teoria del solfeo, en forma de diálogo* (Barcelona, 1872; 3rd ed., 1883); *Las sonatas de Beethoven* (Barcelona, 1873); *Los músicos españoles en sus libros* (Barcelona, 1888); *Por nuestra música* (Barcelona, 1891); *Diccionario técnico de la música* (Barcelona, 1894; 2nd ed., 1899); *Diccionario biográfico y bibliográfico de músicos y escritores de música españoles, portugueses y hispano-americanos antiguos y modernos* (Barcelona, 1895–97); *Emporio científico e histórico de organografía musical española antigua* (Barcelona, 1901); *Prácticas preparatorias de instrumentación* (Barcelona, 1902); *La cançó popular catalana* (Barcelona, 1906); *Documents pour servir à l'histoire de théâtre musical: La Festa d'Elche ou le drame lyrique liturgique espagnol* (Paris, 1906); *Musicalerias* (Valencia, 1906); *Catàlech de la Biblioteca musical de la Diputació de Barcelona* (Barcelona, 1909); *Músicos contemporáneos y de otros tiempos* (Paris, 1910); *Jornadas de arte* (Paris, 1911; memoirs and articles, 1841–91); *Orientaciones* (Paris, 1910; memoirs and articles, 1892–1902); *La lírica nacionalizada* (Paris, 1913); *Tomás Luis de Victoria Abulense* (Valencia, 1918); *P. Antonio Eximeno* (Madrid, 1920); *Jornadas postreras* (Valls, 1922; autobiography); *Musiquerias* (Paris, n.d.; autobiography).

EDITIONS: *Hispaniae schola musical sacra* (Barcelona, 1894–98); *Teatro lirico español anterior al siglo XIX* (La Coruña, 1897–98); *T.L. de Victoria: Opera omnia* (Leipzig, 1902–13); *El organista litúrgico español* (Barcelona, 1905); *Antología de organistas clásicos españoles* (Madrid, 1908); *Cancionero musical popular español* (Valls, 1918–22; 2nd ed., 1936); with H. Anglès, *Els madrigals i la missa de difunts d'en Brudieu* (Barcelona, 1921).

BIBL.: G. Tebaldini, *F. P. ed il dramma lirico spagnuolo* (Turin, 1897); R. Mitjana, *La música contemporanea en España y F. P.* (Málaga, 1901); H. de Curzon, *F. P. et "Les Pyrénées"* (Paris, 1902); "F. P.," *La Nouvelle Revue* (Jan. 1912); A. Reiff, "F. P.," *Zeitschrift für Musikwissenschaft* (Feb. 1921); L. Villalba Muñoz, *F. P.: Semblanza y biografia* (Madrid, 1922); M. Falla, "F. P.," *Revue Musicale* (Feb. 1923); E. Istel, "F. P.," *Musical Quarterly* (April 1925); F. Bonastre, *F. P.: Acotaciones a una idea* (Tarragona, 1977).

Pedrollo, Arrigo, Italian composer; b. Montebello Vicentino, Dec. 5, 1878; d. Vicenza, Dec. 23, 1964. He studied at the Milan Cons. (1891–1900); at his graduation, wrote a Sym., which was performed by Toscanini. He was the director of the Istituto Musicale in Vicenza (1920–30); then a prof. of composition at the Milan Cons. (1930–41); from 1942 to 1959, was director of the Vicenza Cons. In 1914 he won the Sonzogno competition with his opera *Juana.* His other operas include *Terra promessa* (Cremona, 1908); *La Veglia* (Milan, Jan. 2, 1920); *L'Uomo che ride* (Rome, March 6, 1920); *Maria di Magdala* (Milan, 1924); *Delitto e castigo,* after Dostoyevsky's *Crime and Punishment* (Milan, Nov. 16, 1926); *L'Amante in trappola* (Verona, Sept. 22, 1936); *Il Giglio di Ali* (1948). He also wrote orch. pieces, chamber music, choral works, and songs.

Pedrotti, Carlo, eminent Italian conductor and composer; b. Verona, Nov. 12, 1817; d. there (suicide), Oct. 16, 1893. He studied with Domenico Foroni in Verona, where he first gained success as a composer with his opera *Lina* (May 2, 1840). After serving as conductor of the Italian Opera in Amsterdam (1841–45), he returned to Verona; there he was active as a teacher, opera coach, and conductor at the Teatro Filarmonico and at the Teatro Nuovo, where he brought out his finest opera, *Tutti in maschera* (Nov. 4, 1856). In 1868 he was called to Turin as director of the Liceo Musicale and as director and conductor of the Teatro Regio, where he reorganized the musical life of the city; he also founded and conducted the weekly series of Concerti Popolari, in which he presented the Italian premieres of many historical and contemporary works. In 1882 he went to Pesaro as the 1st director of the newly founded Liceo Musicale, a position he held until ill

health compelled him to resign in 1893; that same year he took his own life by drowning himself in the Adige River. Pedrotti excelled as a composer of opera buffa; however, his importance today rests upon his work as a conductor.
BIBL.: T. Mantovani, *C. P.* (Pesaro, 1894); L. Torchi, "C. P.," *Rivista Musicale Italiana,* I (1894); C. Bianchi, "C. P. a Torino," *Musicalbrandé* (Turin, Dec. 1962).

Peellaert, Augustin-Philippe (-Marie-Ghislain), South Netherlands composer; b. Bruges, March 12, 1793; d. Brussels, April 16, 1876. He studied in Paris with Momigny; in 1832, became a member of the executive board of the Brussels Cons. He wrote masses and other sacred works; chamber music; songs; several operas, of which the following were produced in Brussels: *L'Heure du rendez-vous* (1821); *Agnès Sorel* (Aug. 30, 1823); *Le Barmècide* (1824); *Teniers ou La Noce flamande* (Feb. 21, 1825); *L'Exilé* (1827); *Faust* (1834); *Le Coup de pistolet* (1836); *Louis de Male* (1838); publ. an autobiography, *Cinquante ans de souvenirs* (Brussels, 1867).

Peerce, Jan (real name, **Jacob Pincus Perelmuth**), noted American tenor; b. N.Y., June 3, 1904; d. there, Dec. 15, 1984. He played the violin in dance bands, and sang at various entertainment places in N.Y. In 1932 he was engaged as a singer at Radio City Music Hall in N.Y.; made his operatic debut in Philadelphia as the Duke of Mantua in *Rigoletto* (May 14, 1938), and gave his 1st solo recital in N.Y. on Nov. 7, 1939. His lyrical voice attracted attention, and he was engaged by the Metropolitan Opera in N.Y.; made his debut there as Alfredo in *La Traviata* on Nov. 29, 1941; sang also the parts of Cavaradossi in *Tosca,* Rodolfo in *La Bohème,* and Faust in Gounod's opera; remained on the staff of the Metropolitan until 1966, appearing again in 1967–68; retired in 1982. He was the brother-in-law of **Richard Tucker.**
BIBL.: A. Levy, *The Bluebird of Happiness: The Memoirs of J. P.* (N.Y., 1976).

Peeters, Flor, outstanding Belgian organist, pedagogue, and composer; b. Tielen, July 4, 1903; d. Antwerp, July 4, 1986. He studied organ with Depuydt and Gregorian chant with van Nuffel at the Lemmens Inst. in Mechelen; he succeeded Depuydt as prof. of organ there in 1925, holding this position until 1952. He became a prof. of organ at the Antwerp Cons. in 1948, and was its director from 1952 to 1968. He was elevated to the peerage as Baron Peeters by King Baudoin in 1971. He composed nearly 500 works for organ alone, and also wrote much sacred choral music. His works for organ include *Passacaglia and Fugue* (1938); *Sinfonia* (1940); *Organ Concerto* (1944); *Lied Symphony* (1948); *30 Short Chorale Preludes* (1959); *213 Hymn Preludes for the Liturgical Year* (24 installments, 1959–67); *6 Lyrical Pieces* (1966). He also publ. *Anthologia pro organo* (4 vols., Brussels, 1949–59); *Ars organi* (3 vols., Brussels, 1952–54); *Little Organ Book* (Boston, 1957); etc.
BIBL.: P. Visser, *F. P., Organist* (Turnhout, 1950); J. Lade, "The Organ Music of F. P.," *Musical Times,* CIX (1968); J. Hofmann, *F. P.: His Life and His Organ Works* (Fredonia, 1978).

Peiko, Nikolai, Russian composer; b. Moscow, March 25, 1916. He studied with Litinsky, Rakov, and Miaskovsky at the Moscow Cons. (1933–40). After graduation he was commissioned to collect folk-song materials in the remote Yakutsk district of Siberia, and produced *Suite on a Yakutsk Theme* for Orch. (1941); then investigated Bashkir folk music and composed a Bashkir opera, *Aikhylu* (1943). Returning to Moscow, he was appointed to the faculty of the Moscow Cons. (1942–59); also taught at the Gnessin Musical Inst. in Moscow. His music faithfully follows the precepts of socialist realism, national in thematic derivation and realistic in social content. His 1st and 5th syms. are inspired by the heroism and suffering of the war of 1941–45; his 4th Sym. depicts the glory of the 1917 Soviet Revolution.
WORKS: STAGE: *Aikhylu,* opera on a Bashkir subject (1943; rev. 1953); 2 ballets: *Spring Winds,* on a Tatar subject (1950)

and *Jeanne d'Arc* (1957). **ORCH.:** *Suite on Yakutsk Themes* (1941); Piano Concerto (1943; rev. 1954); 7 syms.: No. 1 (1945); No. 2 (1946); No. 3 (1957); No. 4 (1965); No. 5 (1968); No. 6 (1972); No. 7, for Russian Folk Instruments (1977); *From Russia's Remote Past,* suite (1949); *Moldavian Suite* (1950; Moscow, Dec. 14, 1950); *Festive Overture* on Kabardin themes (1951); *2 Concert Fantasies* for Violin and Orch., on Finnish themes (1953, 1965); *Symphonic Ballad* (1959); *Concerto-Symphony* (1974); *In the Throes of War,* 5 symphonic tableaux (1975); *Concerto-Poem* for Clarinet, Balalaika, and Orch. (1979). **CHAMBER:** Piano Quintet (1961); 3 string quartets (1964, 1965, 1966); *Decimet* for 10 Instruments (1971); Violin Sonata (1976). **PIANO:** 2 sonatinas (1942, 1957); *Sonatina Fairy Tale* (1943); 2 sonatas (1951, 1975).
BIBL.: G. Grigorieva, *N. P.* (Moscow, 1965).

Peinemann, Edith, German violinist; b. Mainz, March 3, 1937. She learned the rudiments of music from her father, concertmaster of the Mainz orch.; continued her studies with Heinz Stanske in Heidelberg (1951–53) and Max Rostal in London (1953–56), where she also took courses at the Guildhall School of Music. At the age of 19 she won the Munich International Competition, and then played with many major German orchs.; also gave duo recitals with the Austrian pianist Jörg Demus. In 1962 she made her 1st tour of America. She was a prof. at the Frankfurt Hochschule für Musik (from 1976).

Peixinho, Jorge (Manuel Rosada Marques), Portuguese pianist and composer; b. Montijo, Jan. 20, 1940. He studied piano at the Lisbon Cons. (1951–58); then took lessons with Goffredo Petrassi at Rome's Accademia di Santa Cecilia (1959–61) and with Luigi Nono in Venice; attended the seminars of Boulez and Stockhausen at the Basel Cons. (1962–63); in addition, worked at the electronic studio in Ghent (1972–73). In 1974 he was appointed to the music faculty at the New Univ. of Lisbon.
WORKS: *Alba* for Soprano, Contralto, Female Chorus, and 11 Instruments (1959); *Fascinação* for Soprano, Flute, and Piano (1959); *Políptico* for Chamber Orch. (1960); *Sobreposições* for Orch. (1960); *Episodes* for String Quartet (1960); Saxophone Concerto (1961); *Sucessões simétricas* for Piano (1961); *Collage I* for 2 Pianos (1962); *Diafonia* for Harp, Celesta, Piano, Harpsichord, Metal Percussion, and 12 Strings (1963); *Morfocromia* for 2 Instrumental Groups (1963); *Dominó* for Flute and Percussion Groups (1964); *Sequência* for Flute in G, Celesta, Vibraphone, and Percussion (1964); *Kinetofonias* for 25 Strings (1965); *Situação 66* for Flute, Clarinet, Trumpet, Harp, and Viola (1966); *Harmónicos* for Piano and 2 Tapes (1967); *Nomos* for Orch. (1967); *Eurídice Reamada* for 5 Soloists, Chorus, and Orch. (1968); *As Quatro Estações* for Trumpet, Cello, Harp, Piano, and Tape (1968); *CDE* for Clarinet, Violin, Cello, and Piano (1970); *A Idade do Ouro* for Clarinet, Violin, Harp, Piano, Organ, and Tape (1970); *A Lira Destemperada* for Soprano, Trombone, and Percussion (1972); *Voix* for Soprano and Chamber Orch. (1972); *Morrer em Santiago* for 6 Percussionists (1973); *Elegia a Amilcar Cabral* for 4-track Tape (1973); incidental and film music.

Pelemans, Willem, Belgian composer; b. Antwerp, April 8, 1901. He studied music history at the Cons. of Malines; then engaged in music journalism. A highly prolific composer, he adopted an attractive idiom of writing music in a Romantic manner.
WORKS: STAGE: *De mannen van Smeerop,* comic opera (1952; Brussels, 1963); 3 chamber operas: *La Rose de Bakawali* (1938); *Le Combat de la vierge et du diable* (1949); *De nozem en de nimf* (1960); musical tale, *Het tinnen soldaatje (Le Petit Soldat de plomb),* after Andersen (1945); lyrical drama, *Floris en Blancefloer* (1947); 3 ballets: *Miles gloriosus* (1945); *Herfstgoud* (Autumnal; 1959); *Pas de quatre* (1969); oratorio, *De wandelende jood* (1929); cantatas: *Diederik en Katrina* (1957); *De vogel van sneeuw* (1964); *Piet en de pijp (Pierre et la pipe)* for children (1963); *'t Pelske* (1976). **ORCH.:** 6 syms. (1936, 1937, 1937, 1938, 1938, 1939); 8 ballades (1933–35); 5 concertinos for Chamber Orch. (1948; 1949; 1950; for Strings, 1958;

1966); *Schetsen voor een buffa-opera* for Chamber Orch. (1952); *Ouvertura buffa* (1959); *Petite suite* (1962); concertos: 7 for Orch. (1948–83); 3 for Piano (1945, 1950, 1967); one each for Harpsichord (1931); for Violin (1954); for Viola (1963); for 2 Trumpets, with Strings (1963); for Organ (1965); for 2 Pianos (1973); for Saxophone (1976); for Clarinet Quartet (1983). **CHAMBER:** Sextet for Brasses (1968); *Petite suite* for String Sextet (1967); 2 wind quintets (1948, 1968); Quintet for Flute, Clarinet, Violin, Viola, and Cello (1950); Quintet for Harp, Flute, Violin, Viola, and Cello (1962); 8 string quartets (1942–70); 2 quartets for Clarinets (1961, 1976); Saxophone Quartet (1965); Wind Quartet (1965); Piano Quartet (1967); 3 piano trios (1932, 1942, 1972); *Pas de trois* for Piano Trio; 3 trios for Oboe, Clarinet, and Bassoon (1940, 1941, 1960); 2 sonatas for Flute, Oboe, and Piano (1955, 1956); String Trio (1945); Trio for 2 Violins and Piano (1957); Brass Sonata for Trumpet, Horn, and Trombone (1955); Trio for 2 Oboes and English Horn (1971); 3 violin sonatas (1942); Solo Violin Sonata (1955); Viola Sonata (1945); Cello Sonata (1959); Solo Cello Sonata (1947); Sonata for Cello and Bassoon (1946); Sonata for Flute, and Harpsichord or Piano (1959); Sonata for Flute and Harp (1967); Clarinet Sonata (1961); *Concertstuk* for Clarinet and Piano (1967); Sonata for 2 Guitars (1967); *Suite* for 2 Guitars (1968); *6 Etudes* for 2 Guitars (1974). **KEYBOARD:** *HARPSICHORD:* 6 *Nocturnes* (1930); 7 *personages van James Ensor* (1933); *Studie* (1966). *PIANO:* 19 sonatas (1935–69); Sonata for 4 hands (1961); 3 toccatas (1948, 1951, 1951); 4 suites (1932–33); *10 Banalities* (1944); 2 sonatas for 2 Pianos (1947, 1954). **VOCAL:** *3 Liederen* for Vocal Quartet and Wind Quintet (1944); *Japanese verzen* for Soprano, Alto, Baritone, and Piano (1958); *Haikai* for Middle Voice, Flute ad lib., and Harp (1967); *Van Ostaijen*, suite for Soprano, Tenor, Women's Chorus, Men's Chorus, and Orch. (1980–81).

Pelissier, Victor, French-American horn player, arranger, and composer; b. probably in Paris, c.1745; d. c.1820. His name appears first in 1792 on Philadelphia concert programs as "first horn of the Theatre in Cape François." In 1793 he went to N.Y., where he lived for many years, and became the principal horn player, also composer and arranger, of the Old American Co. He composed one of the earliest and most influential melodramas in the U.S., *Ariadne Abandoned by Theseus in the Isle of Naxos* (N.Y., 1797); also publ. the collection *Pelissier's Columbia Melodies* (12 vols., Philadelphia, 1811–12; ed. by K. Kroeger in Recent Researches in American Music, XIII-XIV, 1984), consisting of piano arrangements of instrumental works, dances, and songs. His other works include the operas *Edwin and Angelina, or The Banditti* (N.Y., Dec. 19, 1796) and *Sterne's Maria, or The Vintage* (N.Y., Jan. 14, 1799), various pantomimes, most of them lost, incidental music, most notably to W. Dunlap's *The Voice of Nature* (N.Y., 1803), a number of instrumental pieces, etc.

BIBL.: J. Parker, "Musical Reminiscences of P.," *The Euterpeiad,* III/3 (1822); O. Sonneck, *Early Opera in America* (N.Y., 1915); J. Howard, *Our American Music* (N.Y., 1931; 4th ed., rev., 1965); J. Mates, *The American Musical Stage before 1800* (New Brunswick, N.J., 1962).

Pellegrini, Vincenzo, Italian composer and organist; b. Pesaro, date unknown; d. Milan, c.1631. He became a priest, serving at Pesaro Cathedral (1594–1612); then was maestro di cappella at Milan Cathedral (1612–31). His extant works include *Canzoni de intavolatura d'organo fatte alla francese, libro primo* (Venice, 1599; ed. in Corpus of Early Keyboard Music, XXXV, 1972); *Missae* for 4 to 5 Voices (Venice, 1603); sacred vocal pieces with organ accompaniment, publ. under the title *Concerti ecclesiastici da 1, 2, 3, 5 e 6 voci* (Venice, 1619); other compositions are in the collections *Parnassus musicus Ferdinandoeus* (Venice, 1615).

Pelletier, (Louis) Wilfred, noted Canadian conductor and music educator; b. Montreal, June 20, 1896; d. N.Y., April 9, 1982. His father, a baker by trade, was an amateur musician who gave Pelletier his primary instruction; at the age of 14 he played piano in the orch. of the National Theatre in Mon-

treal; in 1915 he won the Prix d'Europe and went to Paris, where he studied piano with Isidor Philipp, composition with Charles-Marie Widor, and opera repertoire with Camille Bellaigue. In 1917 he returned to America and was engaged as rehearsal pianist at the Metropolitan Opera in N.Y.; in 1921 he was appointed an assistant conductor there; from 1928 to 1950 he was a principal conductor there, specializing in the French repertoire; in 1936 he founded the popular Metropolitan Opera Auditions of the Air. He also was active as a conductor in Canada; from 1935 to 1951 he was conductor of the Société des Concerts Symphoniques de Montréal, and from 1951 to 1966, of the Orchestre Symphonique de Québec. From 1943 to 1961 he served as director of the Cons. de Musique in Montreal. In 1968 he was made a Companion of the Order of Canada. He was married consecutively to 2 sopranos: **Queena Mario** (1925–36) and (from 1937) **Rose Bampton.** He publ. an autobiographical sketch, *Une Symphonie inachevée* (Quebec, 1972).

Pembaur, Joseph, Jr., Austrian pianist, son of **Joseph Pembaur, Sr.;** b. Innsbruck, April 20, 1875; d. Munich, Oct. 12, 1950. He was a pupil of his father; then studied with Rheinberger and Thuille at the Munich Academy of Music; was a prof. of piano at the Munich Musikschule (1897–1900); subsequently was on the faculty of the Leipzig Cons. (1902–21); in 1921, was appointed a prof. at the Munich Academy of Music. He wrote a Violin Sonata and a number of songs; publ. *Von der Poesie des Klavierspiels* (1910; 2nd ed., 1911).

BIBL.: C. Werner, *J. P. zum 60. Geburtstag* (Berlin, 1935).

Pembaur, Joseph, Sr., Austrian composer and teacher; b. Innsbruck, May 23, 1848; d. there, Feb. 19, 1923. He studied at the Vienna Cons. with Bruckner and in Munich with Rheinberger and others. In 1874 he was appointed director of the Innsbruck Music School; retired in 1918.

WORKS: Opera: *Der Bauer von Langwall* (Innsbruck, May 2, 1898); symphonic tableau, *In Tirol*; Requiem (in memory of the Tyrolese fallen in World War I; 1916); Organ Sonata; numerous male choruses a cappella.

Pembaur, Karl Maria, Austrian organist and conductor, son of **Joseph Pembaur, Sr.;** b. Innsbruck, Aug. 24, 1876; d. Dresden, March 6, 1939. He studied with his father; then with Rheinberger at the Munich Academy of Music. In 1901 he went to Dresden, where he became court organist and choral conductor; also conducted at the Dresden Opera. He wrote the singspiel *Seien Sie vorsichtig*; *Geistliche Sonette* for 5 Solo Voices and Piano; *Bergbilder* for Woodwind Quintet and Piano; marches; songs; publ. *Drei Jahrhunderte Kirchenmusik am sächsischen Hofe* (Dresden, 1920).

Peñalosa, Francisco de, important Spanish composer; b. Talavera de la Reina, c.1470; d. Seville, April 1, 1528. In 1498 he became a singer in the chapel choir of Ferdinand V; the King obtained a canonry (in absentia) for him in 1505 at the Seville Cathedral; in 1506 the Cathedral authorities revoked the appointment, but by 1510 he was able to fulfill the residence requirement. In 1511 the King made him maestro de capilla to his grandson. In 1512 he went to the royal monastery of S. Pedro de Cardeña, near Burgos. In 1516 he returned to Seville, where he assumed administrative duties at the Cathedral. In 1517 he became chamberlain and singer at the papal chapel; in 1518 he resigned his canonry at Seville Cathedral to become archdeacon of Carmona. In 1521 he resumed his canonry at Seville Cathedral, where he remained until his death. Peñalosa was one of the most important composers of his era, a master of polyphonic sacred and secular music. His sacred works include masses, Magnificats, motets, and hymns. Some of them are found in H. Eslava y Elizondo, ed., Lira Sacro-Hispaña (1st series, vol. I, Madrid, 1869).

BIBL.: R. Stevenson, *La musica en la Catedral de Sevilla, 1478–1606: Documentos para su estudio* (Los Angeles, 1954); idem, *Spanish Music in the Age of Columbus* (The Hague, 1960); idem, "The Toledo Manuscript Polyphonic Choirbooks," *Fonte Artis Musicae,* XX (1973).

Peña y Goñi, Antonio, Spanish writer on music and composer; b. San Sebastían, Nov. 2, 1846; d. Madrid, Nov. 13, 1896. He studied at the Madrid Cons; for 30 years he was music critic of the periodical *El Imparcial*, in which he carried on earnest propaganda for Wagner, whom he knew personally. He composed *¡Viva Hernani!*, a "patriotic Basque song" for Soloist, Chorus, and Orch. (Madrid, Dec. 21, 1875), and some orch., choral, and piano works; publ. the important historical book *La opera española y la música dramática en España en el siglo XIX* (Madrid, 1881).

Penderecki, Krzysztof, celebrated Polish composer; b. Debica, Nov. 23, 1933. (His name is pronounced Kzhýshtov Penderétskee, not Penderekee.) He was educated in Krakow, where he took courses at the Jagellonian Univ.; after private composition studies with F. Skolyszewski, he received instruction in theory from A. Malawski and S. Wiechowicz at the State Higher School of Music (1955–58); was a lecturer in composition there (1958–66), remaining with it when it became the Academy of Music as rector (1972–87) and as prof. (from 1972); also was prof. of composition at the Essen Folkwang Hochschule für Musik (1966–68) and at Yale Univ. (from 1973). He rapidly acquired a reputation as one of the most original composers of his time, receiving numerous honors: received honorary memberships in the Royal Academy of Music in London (1975), the Akademie der Künste of the German Democratic Republic (1975), the Royal Academy of Music in Stockholm (1975), etc.; was awarded the Herder Prize of the Federal Republic of Germany (1977), the Grand Medal of Paris (1982), the Sibelius Prize of Finland (1983), the Premio Lorenzo il Magnifico of Italy (1985), etc.; received honorary doctorates from several univs. After a few works of an academic nature, he developed a hyper-modern technique of composition in a highly individual style, in which no demarcation line is drawn between consonances and dissonances, tonal or atonal melody, traditional or innovative instrumentation; an egalitarian attitude prevails toward all available resources of sound. While his idiom is naturally complex, he does not disdain tonality, even in its overt triadic forms. In his creative evolution, he has bypassed orthodox serial procedures; his music follows an athematic course, in constantly varying metrical and rhythmic patterns. He utilizes an entire spectrum of modern sonorities, expanding the domain of tone to unpitched elements, making use of such effects as shouting, hissing, and verbal ejaculations in vocal parts, at times reaching a climax of aleatory glossalalia; tapping, rubbing, or snapping the fingers against the body of an instrument; striking the piano strings by mallets, etc. For this he designed an optical notation, with symbolic ideograms indicating the desired sound; thus a black isosceles triangle denotes the highest possible pitch; an inverted isosceles triangle, the lowest possible pitch; a black rectangle for a sonic complex of white noise within a given interval; vertical lines tied over by an arc for arpeggios below the bridge of a string instrument; wavy lines of varying amplitudes for extensive vibrato; curvilinear figures for aleatory passages; dots and dashes for repetitions of a pattern; sinusoidal oscillations for quaquaversal glissandos; etc. He applies these modern devices to religious music, including masses in the orthodox Roman Catholic ritual. Penderecki's most impressive and most frequently perf. work is his *Tren pamieci ofiarom Hiroszimy* (Threnody in Memory of Victims of Hiroshima) for 52 String Instruments (1959–60), rich in dynamic contrasts and ending on a tone cluster of 2 octavefuls of icositetraphonic harmony.

Works: *Psalmy Dawida* (Psalms of David) for Chorus, 2 Pianos, Celesta, Harp, 4 Double Basses, and Percussion (1958; Krakow, June 26, 1962); *Emanacje* (Emanations) for 2 Orchs. of String Instruments (1958–59); *Strofy* (Strophes) for Soprano, Narrator, and 10 Instruments (Warsaw, Sept. 17, 1959); *3 Miniatures* for Violin and Piano (1959); *Anaklasis* for 42 Strings and Percussion (1959–60; Baden-Baden, Oct. 16, 1960); *Wymiary czasu i ciszy* (Dimensions of Time and Silence) for Wordless Chorus, Strings, and Percussion (Warsaw, Sept. 18, 1960); *Tren pamieci ofiarom Hiroszimy* (Threnody in Memory

of Victims of Hiroshima) for 52 String Instruments (1959–60; Warsaw Radio, May 31, 1961); String Quartet No. 1 (1960); *Fonogrammi* for 3 Flutes, Strings, and Percussion (1961); *Psalmus*, electronic music (1961); *Polymorphia* for 48 String Instruments (1961; Hamburg, April 16, 1962; perf. as a ballet under the title *Noctiphobie*, Amsterdam, 1970); *Stabat Mater* for 3 Choruses a cappella (1962; an independent section of the *St. Luke Passion*); *Kanon* for 52 String Instruments and Tape (Warsaw, Sept. 20, 1962); *Fluorescences* for Orch. (Baden-Baden, Oct. 21, 1962); *Cantata in honorem almae matris Universitatis Jagellonicae* for Chorus and Orch. (1964); *Mensura Sortis* for 2 Pianos (1964); *Sonata* for Cello and Orch. (1964); *Capriccio* (No. 1) for Oboe and 11 Strings (1965); *Passio et mors Domini Nostri Jesu Christi secundum Lucam* for Narrator, Soprano, Baritone, Bass, Boys' Chorus, 3 Mixed Choruses, and Orch. (1962–65; Münster, March 30, 1966); *De natura sonoris* (No. 1) for Orch. (Royan, April 7, 1966); *Dies irae*, oratorio for Soprano, Tenor, Bass, Chorus, and Orch. (1966–67; Krakow, April 14, 1967; also perf. 2 days later as a commemorative service at the site of the Nazi concentration camp at Oświecim-Brzezinka); Concerto for Violino Grande and Orch. (Östersund, Sweden, July 1, 1967; rev. version, Hanover, N.H., Aug. 4, 1968; the solo instrument is specially constructed with 5 strings); *Capriccio* (No. 2) for Violin and Orch. (Donaueschingen, Oct. 22, 1967); *Pittsburgh Overture* for Wind Ensemble (1967); *Capriccio per Siegfried Palm* for Cello (1968); String Quartet No. 2 (1968); *De natura sonoris No. 2* for Winds, Percussion, and Strings (1968; N.Y., Dec. 3, 1971); opera, *Die Teufel von Loudun*, dealing with a *furor uterinus* among nuns of Loudun struck by a multifutuent incubus personified by a neighboring monastic youth (Hamburg, June 20, 1969); *Utrenja* (Morning Prayer) in 2 parts (1969–71): *Grablegung Christi* for Soprano, Contralto, Tenor, Bass, Basso Profundo, 2 Choruses, and Orch., to a text in old Slavonic (Altenberg Cathedral, April 8, 1970), and *Auferstehung Christi* for the same Soloists, Boys' Chorus, 2 Mixed Choruses, and Orch. (Münster Cathedral, May 28, 1971); *Kosmogonia* for Soprano, Tenor, Bass, Chorus, and Orch. (United Nations, N.Y., Oct. 24, 1970); *Actions* for Jazz Ensemble (Donaueschingen, Oct. 17, 1971); *Prélude* for Winds, Percussion, and Double Basses (Amsterdam, July 4, 1971); *Partita*, concerto for Harpsichord, 4 other Electronically Amplified Solo Instruments, and Chamber Orch. (1971; Rochester, N.Y., Feb. 11, 1972); Cello Concerto (Baltimore, March 8, 1972); *Ecloga VIII* for 6 Male Voices a cappella (Edinburgh Festival, Aug. 21, 1972); *Ekecheireia* for Tape (1972); *Canticum canticorum Salomonis* for 16-voice Chorus, Chamber Orch., and ad libitum Dance Pair (1970–73; Lisbon, June 5, 1973); Sym. No. 1 (London, July 19, 1973); *Intermezzo* for 24 Strings (1973); *Magnificat* for Bass Solo, Vocal Group, 2 Choruses, Boys' Chorus, and Orch. (Salzburg, Aug. 17, 1974); *Als Jakob erwachte* for Voices, Orch., and 12 Ocarinas (Monte Carlo, Aug. 14, 1974); Violin Concerto (1976; Basel, April 27, 1977); opera, *Raj utracony* (Paradise Lost), after Milton (1976–78; Chicago, Nov. 29, 1978); *De profundis* for Chorus and Orch. (Graz, Oct. 16, 1977); *Te Deum* for Soloists, Chorus, and Orch. (Assisi, Sept. 27, 1980); Sym. No. 2, *Christmas Symphony* (N.Y., May 1, 1980); *Lacrimosa* for Soprano, Chorus, and Orch. (1980); *Capriccio* for Tuba (1980); *Polish Requiem* for 4 Soloists, Chorus, and Orch. (1980–84; Stuttgart, Sept. 28, 1984); *Agnus Dei* for Chorus (1981); Cello Concerto No. 2 (1981–82; West Berlin, Jan. 11, 1983); Concerto for Viola, Strings, Percussion, and Celesta (Caracas, July 24, 1983); *Cadenza* for Viola (1984; also for Violin, 1987); opera, *Die schwarze Maske* (1984–86; Salzburg, Aug. 15, 1986); *Per Slava* for Cello (1986); *Song of Cherubim* for Chorus (1987); *Veni creator* for Chorus (1987); *Prelude for Clarinet in B flat* (1987); *Der unterbrochene Gedanke* for String Quartet (1988); *Ubu Rex*, opera (Munich, July 6, 1991).

Bibl.: K. Lisicki, *Szkice o K. Pendereckim* (Warsaw, 1973); W. Schwinger, *P.: Begegnungen, Lebensdaten, Werkkommentare* (Stuttgart, 1979); R. Robinson, *K. P.* (1983); idem, "K. P.," *Ovation* (Nov. 1983; an interview); R. Robinson and A. Winold, *A Study of the P. St. Luke Passion* (Celle, 1983);

P. Moor, "K. P.," *Musical America* (July 1988); W. Schwinger, *K. P.: His Life and Work* (London, 1989).

Penherski, Zbigniew, Polish composer; b. Warsaw, Jan. 26, 1935. He studied composition with Stefan Poradowski at the Poznan Cons. (1955–56) and with Tadeusz Szeligowski at the Warsaw Cons. (1956–59).

WORKS: OPERAS: *Girls Through Will* (1961); *The Little Prince* (1962); *Samson Put on Trial* (1967; Warsaw, Sept. 23, 1969); *Mice* (1971–72); *The Fall of Peryn* (1972; Poznan, Oct. 6, 1974); *Edgar, Son of Walpor* (1982); *The Island of the Roses* (1989). **ORCH.:** *Mazurian Chronicles II* for Orch. and Tape (1973; new version, Glasgow, Sept. 27, 1985); *Anamnesis* (1975; Krakow, May 19, 1978); *String Play* for String Orch. (Ludzmierz, March 2, 1980); *Scottish Chronicles* (Glasgow, March 29, 1987). **CHAMBER:** *Street Music* for Chamber Ensemble (1966); String Quartet (1966); Quartet for Keyboard and 3 Optional Instruments (1970); *Incantation I* for 6 Percussionists (1972); *Incantation II* for 7 Performers (1976); *Jeux partis* for Saxophone and Percussion (1984); piano pieces, including *4 Preludes* (1956) and *Studies in Color* (1961). **VOCAL:** *Ostinata* for Chorus and Orch. (1960); *Choral Pictures* (1960); *3 Gipsy Songs* for Women's Chorus (1961); *Contrasts* for Vocal Ensemble, Selected Instruments, and String Orch. (1962; Lublin, March 5, 1965); *Musica humana* for Baritone, Chorus, and Orch. (1963; Warsaw, Jan. 20, 1967); *Missa abstracta* for Tenor, Narrator, Chorus, and Orch. (Kragujevac, Yugoslavia, Oct. 21, 1966); *Hymnus laudans* for Chorus and Chamber Orch. (1970; Wroclaw, Feb. 24, 1972); *3 Impressions* for Soprano, Piano, and 4 Percussionists (1985); also tape pieces and didactic works.

Penna, Lorenzo, Italian composer; b. Bologna, 1613; d. there, Oct. 31, 1693. He studied at the Univ. of Ferrara. In 1630 he entered the Carmelite monastery of S. Martino in Bologna; became maestro di cappella at S. Illario in Casale Monferrato (1656); in 1665 he received his doctorate in theology from the Univ. of Ferrara; was then maestro di cappella at S. Cassiano in Imola (1667–69); in 1669 he entered the Carmelite Order in Mantua, remaining until 1672; subsequently was maestro di cappella at the church of the Carmine in Parma (1672–73). In 1676 he became a member of the Accademia dei Filarmonici in Bologna, where he remained until his death.

WORKS: *Messe e salmi concertati* for 5 Voices, 2 Violins ad libitum, and Basso Continuo (1656); *Psalmorum totius anni modulatio . . .* for 4 to 5 Voices (1669); *Correnti francesi a quattro,* with String Instruments (1673; designated as "Sonate" in the dedication); *Il sacro Parnaso delli salmi festivi* for 4 to 8 Voices (1677); *Reggia del sacro Parnaso . . .* for 4 to 8 Voices (1677); *Galeria del sacro Parnaso . . .* for 4 to 8 Voices, with Instrumental Accompaniment ad libitum (1678). **WRITINGS:** *Li primi albori musicali per li principianti della musica figurata* (Bologna, 1672; 5th ed., 1696); *Direttorio del canto fermo* (1689). **BIBL.:** J.-H. Lederer, *L. P. und seine Kontrapunkttheorie* (diss., Univ. of Graz, 1970); idem, "Zur Lebensgeschichte L. P.s: Eine biographisch-bibliographische Studie," *Kirchenmusikalisches Jahrbuch,* LV (1971); idem, "Zur Kontrapunkttheorie L. P.s," *Studien zur Musikwissenschaft,* XXVIII (1977).

Pennario, Leonard, brilliant American pianist; b. Buffalo, July 9, 1924. He received instruction from Guy Maier, Isabelle Vengerova, and Olga Steeb (piano) and Ernst Toch (composition); played in public at 7; made his formal debut as soloist in the Grieg Concerto with the Dallas Sym. Orch. when he was 12; made his Carnegie Hall debut as soloist in Liszt's 1st Concerto with the N.Y. Phil (Nov. 17, 1943); toured Europe for the 1st time (1952); subsequently appeared throughout the world. He played chamber music with Heifetz and Piatigorsky; was active as a teacher.

Penniman, Richard Wayne, pioneering black American rock 'n' roll singer and songwriter, known as "Little Richard" and extolled by his followers as the "King of Rock 'n' Roll"; b. Macon, Ga., Dec. 5, 1932. Possessed by religious fervor, he sang in local church choirs, then switched to a traveling medicine show. He won a talent contest in Atlanta at the age of 19, recorded "demo" (demonstration) records, and hit the proverbial jackpot with *Tutti Frutti* (1954). Some of his hits were focused on girls, some with first-name titles: *Lucille, Jenny, Jenny,* and *The Girl Can't Help It* (which was the title song of a film he appeared in). Other smash hits were *Keep a-Knockin', Good Golly, Miss Molly, Long Tall Sally,* and *Slippin' and Slidin'.* He was the harbinger of the unrestrained but puissant manner of American music that produced such individuals as Mick Jagger, Jerry Lee Lewis, James Brown, and Jimi Hendrix. Then, in the midst of his popular and commercial successes, he suddenly hit the religion trail, went to college in Alabama to study theology, embraced the ministry, toured the gospel circuit, and denounced rock 'n' roll as the tool of the devil. Still, he put out an autobiographical album entitled *The King of Rock and Roll* before abandoning the sinful world for God. His personal hosannas survived in his early albums, *Here's Little Richard, Fabulous Little Richard,* and (more to the point) *Wild and Frantic Little Richard.*

BIBL.: C. White, *The Life and Times of Little Richard: The Quasar of Rock* (1984); *Current Biography* (Sept. 1986).

Pentenrieder, Franz Xaver, German composer; b. Kaufbeuren, Bavaria, Feb. 6, 1813; d. Munich, July 17, 1867. He studied with Kalcher and Stunz; became conductor at the Munich Court Opera; wrote a successful opera, *Die Nacht zu Paluzzi* (Munich, Oct. 2, 1840); perf. widely in Germany); a comic opera, *Das Haus ist zu verkaufen* (Leipzig, 1846); a number of church works; songs. As a result of an accident, he became insane, and spent the last few years of his life in an asylum.

Pentland, Barbara (Lally), Canadian composer; b. Winnipeg, Jan. 2, 1912. After taking piano lessons at a Montreal boarding school, she went to N.Y. and studied with Frederick Jacobi and Bernard Wagenaar at the Juilliard School of Music (1936–39); also took summer courses with Aaron Copland at the Berkshire Music Center in Tanglewood (1941 and 1942). She was an instructor at the Toronto Cons. (1943–49) and with the music dept. of the Univ. of British Columbia in Vancouver (1949–63). In her compositions she adopts a pragmatic method of cosmopolitan modernism, employing dissonant linear counterpoint and dodecaphonic melodic structures within the framework of Classical forms.

WORKS: STAGE: *The Lake,* chamber opera (1952; Vancouver, March 3, 1954); *Beauty and the Beast,* ballet-pantomine for 2 Pianos (1940). **ORCH.:** *Concert Overture* (1935); *2 Pieces* for Strings (1938); *Lament* (1939); *Holiday Suite* for Chamber Orch. (1941); *Arioso and Rondo* (1941); Concerto for Violin and Small Orch. (1942); 4 syms.: No. 1 (1945–48); No. 2 (1950; Toronto, Feb. 9, 1953); No. 3, *Symphony in 10 Parts* for Chamber Ensemble (1957; Vancouver, Sept. 18, 1959); No. 4 (1959); *Colony Music* for Piano and Strings (1947); *Variations on a Boccherini Theme* (1948); Concerto for Organ and Strings (1949); *Ave atque vale* (1951); *Ricercar* for Strings (1955); Concerto for Piano and String Orch. (1956); *Strata* for String Orch. (1964); *Ciné scene* for Chamber Orch. (1968); *News,* to a text from the news media, for Virtuoso Voice and Orch. (1970); *Variations concertante* for Piano and Small Orch. (1970); *Res musica* for String Orch. (1975). **CHAMBER:** Piano Quartet (1939); Cello Sonata (1943); 5 string quartets (1945, 1953, 1969, 1980, 1985); *Vista* for Violin and Piano (1945); Violin Sonata (1946); Wind Octet (1948); *Weekend Overture* for Resort Combo of Clarinet, Trumpet, Piano, and Percussion (1949); Solo Violin Sonata (1950); Solo Flute Sonatina (1954); Piano Trio (1962); *Variations* for Viola (1965); *Trio con Alea* for String Trio (1966); Septet for Horn, Trumpet, Trombone, Violin, Viola, Cello, and Organ (1967); *Reflections* for Freebass Accordion (1971); *Interplay* for Accordion and String Quartet (1972); *Occasions* for Brass Quintet (1974); *Disasters of the Sun* for Mezzo-soprano, 9 Instruments, and Tape (1976); *Trance* for Flute, Piano, and Harp (1978); *Eventa* for Flute, Clarinet, Trombone, 2 Percussion, Harp, Violin, and Cello (1978); *Elegy* for Horn and Piano (1980); *Tellus* for Flute,

Cello, Piano, Percussion, and Celesta (1982); Piano Quintet (1983); *Tides* for Violin, Marimba, and Harp (1984); *Elegy* for Cello and Piano (1985). PIANO: *Studies in Line* (1941); Variations (1942); Sonata (1945); *Sonata Fantasy* (1947); 2 sonatinas (1951); *Mirror Study* (1952); 2-piano Sonata (1953); *Toccata* (1958); *3 Duets after Pictures by Paul Klee* (1959); *Fantasy* (1962); *Puppet Show* (1964); *Shadows* (1964); *Signs* (1964); *Suite borealis* (1966); *Space Studies* (1967); *Arctica* for Young Pianists (1971–73); *Vita brevis* (1973); *Tenebrae* (1976); *Ephemera* (1974–78); *Vincula* (1983); *Horizons* (1985); also choruses; songs.

BIBL.: S. Eastman and T. McGee, *B. P.* (Toronto, 1983).

Pépin, (Jean-Josephat) Clermont, Canadian composer; b. St.-Georges-de-Beauce, May 15, 1926. He studied piano and harmony as a child with Georgette Dionne; then studied piano with Arthur Letondal and harmony and counterpoint with Claude Champagne in Montreal (1937–41); was a scholarship student of Jeanne Behrend (piano) and Rosario Scalero (composition) at the Curtis Inst. of Music in Philadelphia (diploma, 1945); after further training from Lubka Kolessa (piano) and Arnold Walter (composition) at the Toronto Cons., he won the Prix d'Europe (1949) and went to Paris to complete his composition studies with Jolivet, Honegger, and Messiaen; subsequently was prof. of composition at the Montreal Cons. (1955–64; director, 1967–72).

WORKS: STAGE: 3 ballets: *Les Portes de l'enfer* (1953); *L'Oiseaux-Phénix* (1956); *Le Porte-rêve* (1957–58). ORCH.: 2 piano concertos (1946, 1949); *Variations symphoniques* (1947); 5 syms.: No. 1 (1948); No. 2 (Montreal, Dec. 22, 1957); No. 3, *Quasars* (Montreal, Feb. 7, 1967); No. 4, *La Messe sur le monde*, for Narrator, Chorus, and Orch. (1975); No. 5, *Implosion* (Montreal, Sept. 13, 1983); *Guernica*, symphonic poem after Picasso's painting (Quebec, Dec. 8, 1952); *Le Rite de soleil noir*, symphonic poem (Luxembourg, Sept. 1955); *Hymne au vent du nord*, cantata (1960); *Monologue* for Chamber Orch. (1961); *Nombres* for 2 Pianos and Orch. (Montreal, Feb. 6, 1963); *Monade* for String Orch. (1964); *Prismes et cristaux* for String Orch. (Montreal, April 9, 1974); *Monade* for Violin and Orch. (1972); *Chroma* (Guelph, Ontario, May 5, 1973). CHAMBER: Piano Sonata (1947); 5 string quartets (1948, 1955, 1956, 1960, 1976); *Musique pour Athalie* for Woodwinds and Brass (1956); Suite for Piano Trio (1958); *Sequences* for Flute, English Horn, Violin, Viola, and Cello (1972); *Monade IV-Réseaux* for Violin and Piano (1974); *Monade VI-Réseaux* for Violin (1974–76); *Interactions* for 7 Groups of Percussion and 2 Pianos (1977); Trio No. 2 for Violin, Cello, and Piano (1982); *Monade VII* for Violin and Piano (1986). VOCAL: *Cycle-Éluard* for Soprano and Piano (1948–49); *Paysage* for Soprano, Clarinet, Cello, and Piano (1987); *Trois incantations* for Voice and Piano (1987).

Pepöck, August, Austrian composer; b. Gmunden, May 10, 1887; d. there, Sept. 5, 1967. He studied in Vienna with Heuberger and R. Fuchs; then was active as a conductor of theater music in various provincial towns in Germany; subsequently lived mostly in Vienna. He scored great success with his operettas *Mädel ade!* (Vienna, Oct. 5, 1930) and *Der Reiter de Kaiserin* (Vienna, April 30, 1941). He also wrote some chamber music and songs.

Pepper, Art(hur Edward, Jr.), American jazz alto saxophonist; b. Gardena, Calif., Sept. 1, 1925; d. Los Angeles, June 15, 1982. His father was of German origin; his mother was Italian. He played jazz clarinet and alto saxophone in school bands; got married at 17; was drafted into the U.S. Army; after discharge, he joined Stan Kenton's band (1946–52). His darkly emotional temperament led him to develop a passionate manner of shaping music which became known as the "West Coast Style." He began making records, sometimes under the punning pseudonym **Art Salt,** but his highly promising career was ruined by his demonic addiction to heroin and other narcotic drugs. He squandered his earnings and, besotted by need of expensive drugs, he descended into thievery and brawls. He was busted in 1952 on narcotics charges, and served time

in the Los Angeles County jail; was paroled to the U.S. Public Health Service Hospital at Fort Worth (1953–54), but got in trouble again, and was sentenced to jail in Los Angeles, where he served from 1954 to 1956 and again in 1960–61. Unable to control his habits, he was arrested as a recidivist and sent to San Quentin, where he served from 1961 to 1964 and, after another transgression, in 1965–66. Finally freed, he played with Buddy Rich's Big Band (1968–69). In 1977 and 1978 he completed 2 highly successful tours of Japan. He publ. an astonishingly frank autobiography, based on his own tape recordings and ed. by his 3rd wife, Laurie, under the title *Straight Life: The Story of Art Pepper* (N.Y., 1979); it is a shocking but fascinating chronicle of the nether world of the American artistic scene. A film documentary on Pepper's life was presented at the Berlin Film Festival in 1982.

Pepping, Ernst, distinguished German composer; b. Duisburg, Sept. 12, 1901; d. Berlin, Feb. 1, 1981. He studied with Gmeindl at the Berlin Hochschule für Musik; taught at the Berlin-Spandau Church Music School (from 1934); was also a prof. at the Berlin Hochschule für Musik (1953–68). He publ. *Stilwende der Musik* (Mainz, 1934) and *Der polyphone Satz:* vol. I, *Der cantus-firmus-Satz* (Berlin, 1943; 2nd ed., 1950), and vol. II, *Übungen im doppelten Kontrapunkt und im Kanon* (Berlin, 1957). By virtue of his lifelong association with Lutheran Church culture, he acquired a profound understanding of German polyphonic music, both sacred and secular. He was a significant composer of German chorales; also produced 3 notable syms. A neo-Baroque penchant is discernible in all of his works.

WORKS: VOCAL (all for a cappella chorus unless otherwise given): SACRED: *Deutsche Choralmesse* (1928); *Choralbuch* (30 works; 1931); *Spandauer Chorbuch* (20 vols., 1935–38; rev. by G. Grote, 4 vols., 1962); *Missa "Dona nobis pacem"* (1948); *Te Deum* for Solo Voices, Chorus, and Orch. (1956); *Die Weihnachtsgeschichte des Lukas* (1959); *Aus hartem Weh die Menschheit klagt* (1964); *Psalm CXXXIX* for Alto, Chorus, and Orch. (1964); *Deines Lichtes Glanz* (1967). SECULAR: *Sprüche und Lieder* (1930); *Lob der Träne* (1940); *33 Volkslieder* for Women's or Children's Chorus (1943); *Die wandelnde Glocke* (1952); also song cycles. ORCH.: 3 syms.: No. 1 (1939); No. 2 (1942); No. 3, *Die Tageszeiten* (1944); *Prelude* (1929); *Invention* (1930); *Partita* (1934); *Lust hab ich g'habt zur Musika: Variationen zu einem Liedsatz von Senfl* (1937); *Serenade* (1944–45); *Variations* (1949); Piano Concerto (1950); 2 *Orchesterstücke über eine Chanson des Binchois* (1958). CHAMBER: String Quartet (1943); Sonata for Flute and Piano (1958). ORGAN: *Grosses Orgelbuch* (3 vols., 1939); 2 concertos (both 1941); 3 *Fugues on BACH* (1943); 3 partitas: No. 1, "Ach wie flüchtig" (1953); No. 2, "Wer weiss, wie nahe mir mein Ende" (1953); No. 3, "Mit Fried und Freud" (1953); *12 Chorale Preludes* (1958); Sonata (1958); also piano pieces, including 4 sonatas (1937–45).

BIBL.: H. Poos, ed., *Festschrift E. P.* (Berlin, 1972); K. Hüschen, *Studien zum Motettenschaffen E. P.s* (Regensburg, 1987).

Pepusch, John Christopher (actually, **Johann Christoph**), German-born English composer; b. Berlin, 1667; d. London, July 20, 1752. He was taught by Klingenberg (theory) and Grosse (organ). He had a position at the Prussian court in 1681–97; then went to Holland. He was in London by 1704, where he was active as a violist and harpsichordist at Drury Lane Theatre; later as a composer, adapting Italian airs to English operas and adding recitatives and songs. In 1710 he founded (with Needler, Gates, Galliard, and others) the Academy of Ancient Music, famous for the revival of 16th-century compositions; having received the D.Mus. degree from Oxford in 1713, he served as music director to James Brydges (later the Duke of Chandos) at Cannons. He wrote the masques *Venus and Adonis* (1715), *Apollo and Daphne* (1716), and *The Death of Dido* (1716); the ode *The Union of the Three Sister-Arts* (for St. Cecilia's Day; 1723); arranged music to the ballad-operas *The Beggar's Opera, Polly,* and *The Wedding.* In 1730 a fortune brought him by marriage with the singer **Marguerite**

de l'Epine rendered him independent. From 1737 until his death he was organist of the Charterhouse. Pepusch was a learned, though conservative, musician who enjoyed high renown in England. His various odes and cantatas and his instrumental concertos and sonatas are of slight importance, and his name is preserved in music history mainly for his original music and some arranged numbers in *The Beggar's Opera.* He publ. a *Treatise on Harmony* (London, 1730; 2nd ed., rev., 1731).

BIBL.: F. Kidson, *"The Beggar's Opera," Its Predecessors and Successors* (Cambridge, 1922); C. Hughes, "J.C. P.," *Musical Quarterly* (Jan. 1945); A. Lello, "Dr P.," *Musical Times*, XCIII (1952); H. Fred, *The Instrumental Music of J.C. P.* (diss., Univ. of North Carolina, 1961); J. Williams, *The Life, Work and Influence of J.C. P.* (diss., Univ. of York, 1976).

Perabo, (Johann) Ernst, German-American pianist, teacher, and composer; b. Wiesbaden, Nov. 14, 1845; d. Boston, Oct. 29, 1920. The family moved to N.Y. in 1852. He studied with his father; then at the Leipzig Cons. with Moscheles (piano), Reinecke (composition), and others. Returning to America in 1865, he established himself as a concert pianist, and a highly successful teacher in Boston; had nearly 1,000 pupils, among them well-known musicians (Mrs. H.H.A. Beach was one of his pupils). He publ. a number of piano pieces.

Peragallo, Mario, Italian composer; b. Rome, March 25, 1910. He was a student of Alfredo Casella, and in his early works followed the line of Italian traditionalism, characterized by modern but euphonious polyphony; later he adopted a radical quasi-dodecaphonic idiom, with frequent reversions to diatonic structures.

WORKS: OPERAS: *Ginevra degli Almieri* (Rome, Feb. 13, 1937); *Lo stendardo di S. Giorgio* (Genoa, 1941); *La collina* (Venice, 1947); *La Gita in campagna* (Milan, March 24, 1954); *La parrucca dell'imperatore* (Spoleto, 1959). ORCH.: Concerto (1939); 2 piano concertos (1949, 1951); *Fantasia* (1950); Violin Concerto (1954); *Forme sovrapposte* (1959); *Emircal* for Orch. and Tape (1980). CHAMBER: 3 string quartets (1933, 1934, 1937); *Vibrazioni* for Flute, "Tiptofono," and Piano (1960); *Perclopus,* chamber concerto for Clarinet, Wind Quintet, String Quintet, and Tape (1982); also choral works; piano pieces; organ music; songs.

Perahia, Murray, outstanding American pianist of Spanish-Jewish descent; b. N.Y., April 19, 1947. He studied piano with J. Haien (1953–64); then entered the Mannes College of Music, where he studied conducting and composition (B.S., 1969); he also continued his piano studies with Artur Balsam and Mieczyslaw Horszowski. In 1968 he made his Carnegie Hall debut in N.Y.; in 1972 he became the 1st American to win (by a unanimous vote of the jury) the Leeds International Pianoforte Competition; in 1975 he was awarded the 1st Avery Fisher Prize, sharing it with the cellist Lynn Harrell. He appeared as soloist with the leading orchs. of the U.S. and Europe; also gave many recitals in the U.S. and abroad. In 1982 he was appointed co-artistic director of the Aldeburgh Festival. He excels in Classical music; mastered all of Mozart's concertos, often conducting from the keyboard; he is praised also for his congenial interpretation of the standard concert repertoire.

BIBL.: D. Cameron, "A Conversation with M. P.," *Ovation* (Feb. 1988).

Peralta, Angela, Mexican soprano, known as "The Mexican Nightingale"; b. Puebla, July 6, 1845; d. Matzatlán, Aug. 30, 1883. She made her debut in *Il Trovatore* in Mexico City at the age of 15. In 1862, at age 17, she made her Italian debut as Lucia; she sang in Havana, N.Y., and Madrid. She then barnstormed throughout Mexico as the organizer of her own opera company, presenting operas by Donizetti, Bellini, and Verdi; she also appeared in the premieres of several Mexican operas, including Melesio Morales's *Ildegonda* (Jan. 27, 1866) and *Gino Corsini* (July 14, 1877) and Aniceto Ortega's *Guatimotzin* (Sept. 13, 1871). She made her last appearance in *Il*

Trovatore (May 23, 1883), succumbing on tour to yellow fever, but not before marrying, on her deathbed, one of her many devotees.

Peranda, Marco Gioseppe, important Italian composer; b. Rome or Macerata, c.1625; d. Dresden, Jan. 12, 1675. He was taken by Christoph Bernhard to Dresden, where he was an alto in the chapel of the heir to the electorate; sang with the chapel after it was incorporated into the court (1656); was made vice-Kapellmeister (1661), Kapellmeister (1663), and 1st Hofkapellmeister (1672). Although a Roman Catholic at a Lutheran court, he earned the greatest esteem. He was a distinguished composer of sacred concertos and motets, and influenced many of his German contemporaries.

WORKS: OPERAS: *Dafne* (Dresden, Sept. 3, 1671; in collaboration with G.A. Bontempi); *Jupiter und Io* (Dresden, Jan. 16, 1673; in collaboration with Bontempi; only libretto extant). ORATORIOS: *Historia von der Geburt des Herrn Jesu Christi* (Dresden, Dec. 25, 1668; not extant); *Historia des Leidens und Sterbens unsers Herrn . . . Jesu Christi nach dem Evangelisten St. Marcum* (Dresden, March 20, 1668); *Il sacrificio de Jefte* (Bologna, 1675; only text extant); also 4 masses; sacred concertos; motets.

BIBL.: R. Engländer, "Zur Frage der 'Dafne' (1671) von G.A. Bontempi und M.G. P.," *Acta Musicologica*, XIII (1941).

Perceval, Julio, Argentine composer; b. Brussels, July 17, 1903; d. (in a traffic accident) Santiago, Chile, Sept. 7, 1963. He studied organ at the Brussels Cons.; subsequently with Marcel Dupré in Paris. Emigrating to Argentina in 1926, he became active as an organist in Buenos Aires; then was a prof. of organ at the Univ. of Cuyo (1939–59). In 1959 he went to Chile, where he taught at the National Cons. of Santiago. He composed a number of songs and organ pieces; also some chamber music.

Pereira-Salas, Eugenio, Chilean musicologist; b. Santiago, May 19, 1904; d. there, Nov. 17, 1979. He studied at the Univ. of Chile in Santiago; in 1926 he went to Europe and took courses at the Sorbonne in Paris and at the Univ. of Berlin; later enrolled at the Univ. of Calif., Berkeley on a Guggenheim fellowship (1933–34). Returning to Chile, he was a lecturer in geography and history at the Univ. of Chile; in 1938 he organized there a dept. of Chilean folklore. He publ. a number of informative books on Chilean music, among them *Los origines del arte musical en Chile* (Santiago, 1941); *La canción nacional de Chile* (Santiago, 1941); *Juegos y alegrías coloniales de Chile* (Santiago, 1947); *Historia de la música en Chile (1850–1900)* (Santiago, 1957); *Art and Music in Contemporary Latin America* (London, 1968).

Perera, Ronald (Christopher), American composer and teacher; b. Boston, Dec. 25, 1941. He studied composition with Leon Kirchner at Harvard Univ. (B.A., 1963; M.A., 1967) and then traveled on its John Knowles Paine Traveling Fellowship to study electronic music and computer composition with Gottfried Michael Koening at the Univ. of Utrecht (1967–68); also took courses in the U.S. with Randall Thompson in choral music and electronic music with Mario Davidovsky. After teaching at Syracuse Univ. (1968–70), he served as director of the Dartmouth College Electronic Music Studio (1970–71); then taught theory, composition, and electronic music at Smith College in Northampton, Mass. (from 1971); was also active as a visiting scholar at the Columbia-Princeton Electronic Music Center (1975–76). With Appleton, he ed. *The Development and Practice of Electronic Music* (1975). He received annual ASCAP awards from 1972, and in 1978 and 1988 grants from the N.E.A.

WORKS: STAGE: *The Yellow Wallpaper,* chamber opera (Northampton, Mass., May 17, 1989). ORCH.: *Chanteys* (1976; Concord, Mass., Feb. 4, 1977; rev. 1979); Chamber Concerto for Brass Quintet, 9 Winds, Piano, and Percussion (1983; Cambridge, Mass., April 19, 1984). CHAMBER: *Reverberations* for Organ and Tape (1970); *Reflex* for Viola and Tape (1973); *Fantasy Variations* for Piano and Live Electronics (1976);

Bright Angels for Organ, Percussion, and Tape (Hartford, Conn., June 6, 1977); *Tolling* for 2 Pianos and Tape (1979; Northampton, Mass., Feb. 3, 1980); *Fanfare* for Viola and Piano (1987); *Augmented Forces* for Piano and Synthesizer (1987; Northampton, Mass., May 19, 1988). VOCAL: *Mass* for Soloists, Chorus, and Orch. (1967); *Did You Hear the Angels Sing?* for Soprano, Chorus, and Organ (1968); *3 Night Pieces* for Soprano, Alto, Women's Chorus, Cello, Piano, and Percussion (1974); *The White Whale* for Baritone and Orch. (1981; Northampton, Mass., Feb. 14, 1982); *Crossing the Meridian* for Tenor, Flute, Clarinet, Violin, Viola, Cello, Piano, and Percussion (Cambridge, Mass., Dec. 8, 1982); *Earthsongs* for Women's Chorus and Orch. (1983; Northampton, Mass., May 19, 1984); *As Freedom Is a Breakfastfood* for Women's Chorus and Piano (Rye, N.Y., May 10, 1984); *The Canticle of the Sun* for Narrator, Chorus, and Digitally Synthesized Instruments (1984; Groton, Mass., April 21, 1985); songs; also electronic pieces, including *Improvisation* for Loudspeakers (1969), *Time Machine* (1970), and *Alternate Routes* (1971).

Peress, Maurice, American conductor; b. N.Y., March 18, 1930. He studied music at N.Y. Univ. (B.A., 1951) and at the Mannes College of Music, N.Y. (1955–57); was a member of the faculty of N.Y. Univ. (1957–61) and then assistant conductor of the N.Y. Phil. (1961–62). His later engagements were as music director of the Corpus Christi (Tex.) Sym. Orch. (1962–75) and of the Austin (Texas) Sym. Orch. (1970–73). He was music director of the Kansas City Phil. from 1974 to 1980. In 1981 he became president of the Conductors' Guild of the American Sym. Orch. League. In 1971 he conducted the world premiere of Leonard Bernstein's *Mass* at the Kennedy Center in Washington, D.C.; he also conducted the 1st European performance of the work at the Vienna State Opera in 1981.

Perez, David, significant Italian composer; b. Naples (of Spanish descent), 1711; d. Lisbon, Oct. 30, 1778. He studied counterpoint and composition with Mancini, Veneziano, and Galli at the Cons. di S. Maria di Loreto in Naples (1722–33); between 1735 and 1752 he produced some 19 operas, establishing himself as a leading opera composer in his day. He served as vice-maestro di cappella of the Royal Chapel Palatine in Palermo (1738–39) and as maestro di cappella in Palermo (1741–48); then was called to Lisbon (1752) as maestro di cappella and music master to the royal princesses, duties he retained for the rest of his life. He continued to compose until his last days, even though he was stricken with blindness. He was a master of the opera seria, being acclaimed as a worthy rival of Hasse and Jommelli. WORKS: OPERAS: *La nemica amante* (Naples, Nov. 4, 1735); *Li travestimenti amorosi,* opera buffa (Naples, July 10, 1740); *Il Siroe* (Naples, Nov. 4, 1740); *L'eroismo di Scipione* (Palermo, 1741); *Demetrio* (Palermo, June 13, 1741; 2nd version, Lisbon, 1766); *Astartea* (Palermo, 1743); *Medea* (Palermo, 1744); *Alessandro nell'Indie* (Genoa, Carnival 1744; 2nd version, Lisbon, March 31, 1755); *Merope* (Genoa, Carnival 1744); *L'isola incantata* (Palermo, 1746); *Artaserse* (Florence, 1748); *La clemenza di Tito* (Naples, 1749); *Vologeso* (Vienna, 1750); *Il Farnace* (Rome, 1750); *Andromaca* (Vienna, 1750); *Semiramide* (Rome, 1750); *Ezio* (Milan, Carnival 1751); *La Didone* (Genoa, 1751); *La Zenobia* (Milan, 1751); *Demofoonte* (Lisbon, 1752); *Adriano in Siria* (Lisbon, 1752); *L'Eroe cinese* (Lisbon, June 6, 1753); *Olimpiade* (Lisbon, 1753); *L'Impermestra* (Lisbon, 1754); *Lucio Vero* (Verona, 1754); *Solimano* (Lisbon, Carnival 1757); *Enea in Italia* (Lisbon, 1759); *La Berenice* (Verona, Carnival 1762); *Giulio Cesare* (Lisbon, 1762); *L'isola disabitata* (Lisbon, 1767); *Il Cinese* (Lisbon, 1769); *Creusa in Delfo* (Lisbon, Carnival 1774); *Il ritorno di Ulisse in Itaca* (Lisbon, 1774); *L'Eroe coronato* (Lisbon, 1775); *La pace fra la Virtù e la Bellezza* (Lisbon, Dec. 17, 1777). OTHER SECULAR VOCAL: *Il trionfo di Venere,* serenata (Palermo, 1738); *L'Atlanta,* serenata (Palermo, 1739); *L'amor pittore, componimento drammatico civile* (Naples, July 24, 1740); *La vera felicità* (Lisbon, 1761). SACRED: *Mattutino de' morti* for 5 Voices and Orch. (London, 1774); *Il martirio*

di S. Bartolomeo, oratorio; 8 masses for Chorus and Orch.; Mass sections; Magnificat; antiphones; motets; etc.

BIBL.: E. Soares, *D. P., Subsidios para a biografia' do célébre mestre de musica da camera de D. José* (Lisbon, 1935); P. Jackson, *The Operas of D. P.* (diss., Stanford Univ., 1967).

Pérez Casas, Bartolomeo, Spanish conductor and composer; b. Lorca, near Murcia, Jan. 24, 1873; d. Madrid, Jan. 15, 1956. He studied at the Madrid Cons.; played the clarinet in various military bands; also was a bandmaster. He then established himself in Madrid as a teacher at the Cons.; from 1915 to 1936, conducted the Orquesta Filarmónica de Madrid. He wrote a lyric drama, *Lorenzo;* an orch. suite, *A mi tierra* (an early work, which became fairly popular); a String Quartet; pieces for band.

Perfall, Karl, Freiherr von, German composer and conductor; b. Munich, Jan. 29, 1824; d. there, Jan. 14, 1907. He took music lessons with Hauptmann in Leipzig (1848–49); became conductor of the Munich Liedertafel (1850); founded the Oratorio Society (1854); in 1864, was appointed Intendant of the court music and abandoned his activities as a conductor. From 1867 to 1893 he was Intendant of the National Theater in Munich. Of his operas (all produced in Munich), *Raimondin* (March 27, 1881; rev. as *Melusine,* 1885) and *Junker Heinz* (April 9, 1886; rev. as *Jung Heinrich,* 1901) were successful. He publ. *25 Jahre Münchener Hoftheater-Geschichte* (1892; covering the period from 1867); *Ein Beitrag zur Geschichte des königlichen Theaters in München 25 November 1867–25 November 1892* (1894); *Die Entwickelung des modernen Theaters* (1899).

Pergament, Moses, Finnish-born Swedish music critic and composer; b. Helsinki, Sept. 21, 1893; d. Gustavsberg, near Stockholm, March 5, 1977. He studied violin at the St. Petersburg Cons. and conducting at Berlin's Stern Cons. In 1915 he settled in Sweden and became a naturalized Swedish citizen (1918); from 1923 to 1966 he was active as a music critic in Swedish newspapers; he publ. 4 books on music. His musical style was initially circumscribed by Russian paradigms; later he was influenced by Sibelius; still later he adopted some modernistic procedures. Several of his compositions reflect an ancestral strain of Jewish melos.

WORKS: DRAMATIC: *Himlens hemlighet* (The Secret of Heaven), chamber opera (1952); *Eli,* radio opera (1958; Swedish Radio, March 19, 1959); *Abrams Erwachen,* opera-oratorio (1970–73); 2 ballets: *Vision* (1923) and *Krelantems and Eldeling* (1920–28). ORCH.: *Romance* for Violin and Orch. (1914); *Adagio* for Clarinet and Strings (1915); *Rapsodia ebraica* (1935); *Concerto romantico* for Strings (1935); *Dibbuk,* fantasy for Violin and Orch. (1935); *Almquistiana,* 2 suites (1936, 1938); *Nedanförmänskliga visor* (Subhuman Songs) for Narrator, Soli, Chorus, and Orch. (1936); *Swedish Rhapsody* (1941); *Den judiska sången* (The Jewish Song), choral sym. (1944); Violin Concerto (1948); *Kol Nidré* for Cello and Orch. (1949); Piano Concerto (1951); Concerto for 2 Violins and Orch. (1954); Cello Concerto (1955); *Canto lirico* for Violin and Orch. (1956); *Pezzo intimo* for 16 Solo Cellos (1957); *De sju dödssynderna* (The 7 Deadly Sins), oratorio (1963); Viola Concerto (1964–65); *4 Poems by Edith Södergran* for Soprano and Orch. (1965–66); *Årstider,* 4 songs for Baritone and Orch. (1968); *Drömmen om mullen och vindarna* (The Dream of the Earth and the Winds) for Baritone and Orch. (1969); *Fantasia differente* for Cello and Strings (1970); Sonatina for Flute and String Orch. (1973); *Biblical Cantata* for Chorus and Orch. (1974). CHAMBER: Piano Trio (1912–13; rev. 1940); Violin Sonata (1918–20); 3 string quartets (1922, 1952, 1956); Solo Violin Sonata (1961); Flute Sonata (1968); *Little Suite* for Woodwinds (1970); also over 100 solo songs; theater and film music.

Perger, Richard von, Austrian composer and conductor; b. Vienna, Jan. 10, 1854; d. there, Jan. 11, 1911. He studied cello and theory; was in the Austrian army during the campaign in Bosnia (1878); then received a stipend, and took lessons with Brahms (1880–82); was director of the Rotterdam Cons.

(1890–95); returning to Vienna, he conducted the Gesell-schaftskonzerte; from 1899 to 1907 he was director of the Vienna Cons. His music bears unmistakable evidence of the profound influence of Brahms. Among his works are the text and music of a comic opera, *Der Richter von Granada* (Cologne, 1889), a singspiel, *Die 14 Nothhelfer* (Vienna, 1891), a musical fairy tale, *Das stählerne Schloss* (Vienna, 1904), a Violin Concerto, some chamber music, and songs. He publ. a biography of Brahms (1908; new ed. by Hernried, 1934); his *Geschichte der K. K. Gesellschaft der Musikfreunde in Wien* was publ. posthumously (1912).

Pergolesi, Giovanni Battista, remarkable Italian composer; b. Jesi, near Ancona, Jan. 4, 1710; d. Pozzuoli, near Naples, March 16, 1736. The original family name was Draghi; the name Pergolesi was derived from the town of Pergola, where Pergolesi's ancestors lived. He was the only surviving child of his parents, 3 others having died in infancy. His childhood seems to have been plagued by ill health; a later caricature depicts him as having a deformed leg. He first studied music with Francesco Santi, the maestro di cappella of the Jesi Cathedral; he also studied violin with Francesco Mondini. He then was given a stipend by the Marchese Cardolo Maria Pianetti, which enabled him to enter the Conservatorio dei Poveri di Gesù Cristo in Naples; he studied violin there with Domenico de Matteis, and composition with Gaetano Greco, its maestro di cappella, Leonardo Vinci, and Francesco Durante. He became highly proficient as a violinist, playing at the Conservatorio and throughout Naples. His 1st work to be performed was the dramma sacro *Li prodigi della divina grazia nella conversione di S. Guglielmo Duca d'Aquitania*, which was given by the Conservatorio at the monastery of S. Agnello Maggiore in 1731. He graduated shortly thereafter, and received a commission for his 1st opera, *La Salustia* (Naples, Jan. 1732). He then became maestro di cappella to Prince Ferdinando Colonna Stigliano, equerry to the Viceroy of Naples, in 1732. His *Lo Frate 'nnamorato* (Naples, Sept. 27, 1732) proved highly successful. In Dec. 1732 he composed several sacred works for performance at the church of S. Maria della Stella as a votive offering following a series of severe earthquakes in Naples. He was next commissioned to write an opera seria to celebrate the birthday of the empress on Aug. 28, 1733; however, the premiere of the resulting *Il Prigionier superbo* was delayed until Sept. 5, 1733; it contained the 2-act intermezzo *La Serva padrona*, which became his most celebrated stage work. He was named deputy to the maestro di cappella of Naples in 1734. During a brief sojourn in Rome, his Mass in F major was performed at the church of S. Lorenzo in Lucina (May 16, 1734).

After returning to Naples, Pergolesi became maestro di cappella to Marzio Domenico IV Carafa, the Duke of Maddaloni. For the birthday of the king's mother, he was commissioned to write the opera *Adriano in Siria*; it was premiered, without success, in Naples on Oct. 25, 1734, with the intermezzo *La Contadina astuta* (subsequently staged under various titles). He then was commissioned to write an opera for Rome's Teatro Tordinona, resulting in his unsuccessful opera seria *L'Olimpiade* (Jan. 8 or 9, 1735). His last popular success for the stage was the commedia musicale *Il Flaminio* (Naples, 1735). By 1735 his health had seriously declined, most likely from tuberculosis. Early in 1736 he went to the Franciscan monastery in Pozzuoli, where he soon died at the age of 26. He was buried in the common grave adjacent to the Cathedral. Following his death, his fame spread rapidly through performances of *La Serva padrona* and several other stage works. The Paris revival of the work in 1752 precipitated the so-called *querelle des bouffons* between the partisans of the Italian and French factions. His fame was further increased by performances of the *Salve regina* in C minor and the *Stabat Mater* in F minor.

The chaotic entanglement of spurious, doubtful, and authentic works attributed to Pergolesi was unraveled in M. Paymer's *G.B. P.: A Thematic Catalogue of the Opera Omnia with an*

Appendix Listing Omitted Compositions (N.Y., 1976). The *Opera Omnia*, ed. by F. Caffarelli (5 vols., Rome, 1939–42), is most unreliable; it is being replaced by a critical ed., the 1st vol. of which appeared in 1985.

BIBL.: C. de Rosa, Marchese di Villarosa, *Lettera biografica intorno alla patria ed all vita di G.B. P. celebre compositore di musica* (Naples, 1831; 2nd ed., 1843); F. Villars, *La Serva padrona, Son apparition à Paris en 1752, son influence, son analyse* (Paris, 1863); G. Annibaldi, *Alcune delle notizie più importanti intorno al P. recentemente scoperte: Il P. in Pozzuoli: Vita intima* (Jesi, 1890); E. Faustini-Fasini, *G.B. P. attraverso i suoi biografi e le sue opere* (Milan, 1900); G. Radiciotti, *G.B. P.: Vita, opere ed influenza su l'arte* (Rome, 1910; 2nd ed., rev., 1935; German tr., Zürich, 1954); A. Della Corte, *G.B. P.* (Turin, 1936); R. Giraldi, *G.B. P.* (Rome, 1936); F. Schlitzer, *G.B. P.* (Turin, 1940); S. Luciani, ed., *G.B. P. (1710–1736): Note e documenti* (Siena, 1942); E. Luin, *Fortuna e influenza della musica di P. in Europa* (Siena, 1943); M. Paymer, *The Instrumental Music Attributed to G.B. P.: A Study in Authenticity* (diss., City Univ. of N.Y., 1977); A. Dunning, *Count Unico Wilhelm van Wassenaer (1692–1766); A Master Unmasked; or, The P.-Ricciotti Puzzle Solved* (Büren, 1980); H. Beckwith, *G.B. P. and the Chamber Cantata* (diss., Univ. of Maryland, 1983); F. Degrada, ed., *Studi P.ani/P. Studies* (2 vols., N.Y., 1986, 1988); M. Paymer and H. Williams, *G.B. P.: A Guide to Research* (N.Y., 1989).

Peri, Jacopo, significant Italian composer, called "Il Zazzerino" for his abundant head of hair; b. Rome, Aug. 20, 1561; d. Florence, Aug. 12, 1633. He was descended from a noble Florentine family. At an early age he went to Florence, where he entered the convent of Ss. Annunziata in 1573 and became a singer; also studied music with Cristofano Malvezzi. He was organist at the Badia (1579–1605) and a singer at S. Giovanni Battista (by 1586); entered the service of the Medici court of Grand Duke Ferdinando I (1588); was also in the service of the Mantuan court (from the early 1600s). The Florentine Camerata met at the home of Count Giovanni de' Bardi in the 1580s, and it is likely that Peri participated in its activities. As early as 1583 he collaborated with other composers in writing music for the intermedi to Giovanni Fedini's dramatic comedy *Le due Persilie*. In the 1590s the home of Jacopo Corsi became the meeting place for many Florentine musicians, poets, and philosophers, and Peri undoubtedly attended, for Corsi collaborated with him in setting Ottavio Rinuccini's pastoral *Dafne* to music. The 1st known performance of this work was a private one in Florence in 1598. Later versions were given in 1599, 1600, and 1605. *Dafne* is generally recognized as the 1st opera in monodic style (i.e., vocal soli supported by instruments), which was termed stile rappresentativo. Peri's next opera was *Euridice*, again to a text by Rinuccini; some of the music was rewritten by Caccini for the 1st performance, which was given for the wedding of Maria de' Medici and Henri IV of France at the Palazzo Pitti in Florence (Oct. 6, 1600). He composed the opera *Tetide* (libretto by Cini) for Mantua in 1608, but it was not performed. His next opera, *Adone* (libretto by Cicognini), was finished by 1611; a performance scheduled for Mantua in 1620 never took place. Another work of the period, *La liberazione di Tirreno e d'Arnea* (Florence, Feb. 6, 1617), may be by Peri; it is also possible that he collaborated with M. da Gagliano on the score, or it may be totally the work of Gagliano. Peri collaborated with Marco da Gagliano on the opera *Lo sposalizio di Medoro e Angelica*. It was given in honor of the election of Emperor Ferdinand III at the Palazzo Pitti on Sept. 25, 1619. He also composed the role of Clori for the opera *La Flora*, the remainder of the music being by Gagliano. It was first performed in honor of the wedding of Margherita de' Medici and Duke Odoardo Farnese of Parma at the Palazzo Pitti on Oct. 14, 1628. Peri also collaborated with Gagliano on 3 oratorios, *La beneditione di Jacob* (Florence, Sept. 23, 1622), *Il gran natale di Christo salvator nostro* (Florence, Dec. 27, 1622), and *La celeste guida, o vero L'Arcangelo Raffaello* (Florence, Jan. 5, 1624), but these works are not extant. In addition to individual songs publ. in various collections of the time, he also brought out *La varie musiche . . . for 1 to 3 Voices, con alcune spirituali in ultimo, per cantare, harpsichord, chitarrone, ancora la maggior parte di esse per sonare semplicemente, organ* (Florence, 1609; 2nd ed., 1619).

BIBL.: G. Corazzini, *J. P. e la sua famiglia* (Florence, 1895); A. Solerti, *Le origini del melodramma* (Turin, 1903); idem, *Gli albori del melodramma* (Milan, 1904); idem, *Musica, ballo e drammatica alle corte medicea dal 1600 all 1637* (Florence, 1905); F. Ghisi, *Alle fonti della monodia: Due nuove brani della 'Dafne'* (Milan, 1940); B. Hanning, *The Influence of Humanistic Thought and Italian Renaissance Poetry on the Formation of Opera* (diss., Yale Univ., 1969); T. Carter, *J. P. (1561–1633): His Life and Works* (diss., Univ. of Birmingham, 1980).

Peričić, Vlastimir, Serbian composer and musicologist; b. Vršac, Dec. 7, 1927. He studied in Vienna with Uhl; became active as a pedagogue in Belgrade; publ. manuals on harmony and form; compiled a valuable reference work on Serbian composers, *Muzički Stvaraoci u Srbiji* (Belgrade, 1969).

WORKS: String Quartet (1950); *Symphonic Movement* (Belgrade, Oct. 14, 1952); *Fantasia quasi una sonata* for Violin and Piano (1954); Sinfonietta for Strings (Zagreb, Nov. 13, 1957); piano pieces.

Perick (real name, **Prick**), **Christof,** German conductor; b. Hamburg, Oct. 23, 1946. He studied with Brückner-Rüggeberg in Hamburg. After serving as an assistant at the Hamburg State Opera, he conducted in Trier (1970–72) and Darmstadt (1972–74). From 1974 to 1977 he was Generalmusikdirektor in Saarbrücken, and then in Karlsruhe from 1977 to 1984; he also served as 1st conductor at the Deutsche Oper in West Berlin (1977–84). He toured in Europe and the U.S. as a guest conductor with leading orchs. and opera houses. In 1991 he was named music director of the Los Angeles Chamber Orch. and chief conductor of the Niedersächsische Staatstheater in Hannover, effective with the 1992–93 season.

Périer, Jean (Alexis), French baritone; b. Paris, Feb. 2, 1869; d. there, Nov. 3, 1954. He studied at the Paris Cons., obtaining 1st prize for singing (1892); made his debut at the Paris Opéra-Comique as Monostatos in *Die Zauberflöte* on Dec. 16, 1892; was engaged there until 1894, and again from 1900 to 1920. He created the role of Pelléas at the premiere of Debussy's opera (1902), and sang the leading tenor parts in several other premieres of French operas; sang at N.Y.'s Manhattan Opera House (1908); a talented comedian, he also appeared in variety shows in Paris. He publ. an instructive album, *Mes exercises, tirés des chansons populaires de France* (Paris, 1917).

Perkins, Carl, American country-music singer, instrumentalist, and songwriter; b. Jackson, Tenn., April 9, 1932. He began his career as an entertainer at country dances and honky-tonks with the group known as the Perkins Brothers; became a favorite at the Grand Ole Opry in Nashville, Tenn.; later toured in the U.S. and abroad with his own band, which he founded with his sons. In 1956 he wrote the song *Blue Suede Shoes,* which became a hit in various renditions by popular singers of the day.

Perkins, Henry S(outhwick), American music educator and composer; brother of **William (Oscar) Perkins;** b. Stockbridge, Vt., March 20, 1833; d. Chicago, Jan. 20, 1914. He studied voice at the Boston Music School (graduated in 1861). He filled various administrative and educational posts in Iowa, Kans., and Ill.; in 1890 he founded the Chicago National College of Music; was active as a director of music festivals and conventions across the country. He was one of the organizers of the Music Teachers National Assoc. in 1876; ed. 30 songbooks, hymnbooks, class books, etc.; composed numerous hymns and songs.

Perkins, John MacIvor, American composer; b. St. Louis, Aug. 2, 1935. He studied at Harvard Univ. (B.A., 1958), at the New England Cons. of Music in Boston (B.Mus., 1958), with Boulanger in Paris and Gerhard and Rubbra in London (1958–59), and at Brandeis Univ. (M.F.A., 1962); taught at

the Univ. of Chicago (1962–65) and Harvard Univ. (1965–70); then joined the faculty of Washington Univ. in St. Louis (1970), where he also served as chairman of its music dept. (1970–75).

WORKS: *Divertimento,* chamber opera (1958); *Andrea del Sarto,* operatic monologue for Baritone, Silent Actress, and 12 Instrumentalists, after Robert Browning (1981); *Canons* for 9 Instruments (1957); *Quartet* for String Quartet and Tape (1960–84); *Fantasy and Variations* for Orch. (1961); *Variations* for Flute, Clarinet, Trumpet, Piano, and Percussion (1962); *Music for 13 Players* (1964); *Music for Orchestra* (1965); *After a Silence-Alpha* for 12 Instruments (1976); *Canzona* for Harpsichord and Piano (1982); *Divisions* for Bass Gamba and Harpsichord (1982); choral works; songs; piano pieces.

Perkins, (David) Walton, American pianist, music educator, and composer; b. Rome, N.Y., Nov. 16, 1847; d. Chicago, Feb. 6, 1929. He was a pupil of Theodor Kullak and Anton Rubinstein in Berlin; upon his return to America, he settled in Chicago; with William H. Sherwood, organized the Sherwood Music School in Chicago (1894); was its associate director until 1901; then was president of the Chicago Cons. of Music (1907–29). He composed choral works, piano pieces, and songs.

Perkins, William (Oscar), American vocal teacher and composer, brother of **Henry S(outhwick) Perkins;** b. Stockbridge, Vt., May 23, 1831; d. Boston, Jan. 13, 1902. He studied voice in Milan; lived in Boston as a teacher; publ. about 40 collections of songs, anthems, etc., including many of his own pieces.

Perkowski, Piotr, Polish composer; b. Oweczacze, Ukraine, March 17, 1901; d. Otwock, near Warsaw, Aug. 12, 1990. He studied composition with Statkowski at the Warsaw Cons. (1923–25); then took private lessons with Szymanowski in Warsaw and with Albert Roussel in Paris. He subsequently devoted himself to teaching; was director of the Toruń Cons. (1936–39); taught composition at the Warsaw Cons. (1946–51, 1954–73); was artistic director of the Krakow Phil. (1949–51) and dean of the Music Academy in Wroclaw (1951–55); served as councilor for cultural development for the city of Warsaw (1965–74). In his earlier years he followed the fashionable cosmopolitan trend of absolute music without reference to national or general programmatic subjects, but under the influence of social changes he began introducing concrete, historic, and pictorial representations.

WORKS: STAGE: OPERA: *Garlands* (Warsaw, 1962). **BALLETS:** *Swantewit* (1930; rev. 1945–47; Poznan, June 19, 1948); *Clémentine* (1960–63); *Rhapsody* (1949); *Fantasia* (1950); *Balladyna* (1960–64; Warsaw, 1965). **ORCH.:** 2 syms.: No. 1, with Chorus (1925; lost; reconstructed 1955); No. 2 (1949); *Geometric Suite* (1930); 2 violin concertos (1933, 1960); *Warsaw Overture* (1954); *Sinfonia drammatica* (1963); *Scottish Impressions* (1968). **VOCAL:** 5 cantatas: *Wisla* (1951); *Epitaphe pour Nicos Belojannis* (1952); *Suita weselna* (Merry Suite) for Soprano, Tenor, Chorus, and Orch. (1952); *Suita epicka* (1953); *Alexiares,* with Narrator and Tape (1966–69); *Niebo w plomieniach* (The Sky in Flames), song cycle, with Orch. (1969). **CHAMBER:** 2 string quartets (1930, 1977); *Elegia* for Cello and Organ (1945); Trumpet Sonatina (1954); Flute Sonata (1954); piano pieces.

Perle, George, prominent American composer and music theorist; b. Bayonne, N.J., May 6, 1915. He studied with La Violette at DePaul Univ. in Chicago (1935–38), privately with Krenek (1939–41), at the American Cons. of Music in Chicago (M.Mus., 1942), and at N.Y. Univ. (Ph.D., 1956, with the diss. *Serial Composition and Atonality;* publ. in Berkeley, 1962; 6th ed., 1991). He taught at the Univ. of Louisville (1949–57), the Univ. of Calif., Davis (1957–61), and Queens College of the City Univ. of N.Y. (1961–84); held Guggenheim fellowships (1966–67; 1974–75); was elected a member of the Inst. of the American Academy and Inst. of Arts and Letters (1978); received the Pulitzer Prize in music for his Wind Quintet No. 4 (1985). From 1989 to 1991 he was composer-in-residence of the San Francisco Sym.; was also a master artist-in-residence at the Atlantic Center for the Arts in New Smyrna Beach,

Fla. (1990). He was one of the earliest American serialists, developing a personal and distinctive "12-tone tonality." Many of his works, not reflected in the following list, were withdrawn. In addition to his many articles in music journals, he publ. *Twelve-tone Tonality* (Berkeley, 1977) and *The Operas of Alban Berg* (2 vols., Berkeley, 1980, 1985).

WORKS: ORCH.: *Solemn Procession* for Band (1947); *3 Movements* (1960; Amsterdam, June 16, 1963); Serenade No. 1 for Viola and Chamber Orch. (N.Y., May 10, 1962); *6 Bagatelles* (1965; Riverhead, N.Y., Nov. 18, 1977); Cello Concerto (1966); Serenade No. 2 for Chamber Orch. (1968; Washington, D.C., Feb. 28, 1969); Concertino for Piano, Winds, and Timpani (Chicago, April 20, 1979); *A Short Symphony* (Tanglewood, Aug. 16, 1980); *An Anniversary Rondo for Paul* for Chamber Orch. (Chicago, Jan. 17, 1982); Serenade No. 3 for Piano and Chamber Orch. (N.Y., Dec. 14, 1983); *Lyric Intermezzo*, suite (1987); *Dance Overture* (Houston, May 17, 1987); Sinfonietta (St. Paul, Minn., Jan. 29, 1988); Piano Concerto (1990; San Francisco, Jan. 24, 1991); Sinfonietta II (1990). **CHAMBER:** 8 string quartets: Nos. 1–4 and 6 (1938–69; all withdrawn); No. 5 (1960; rev. 1967); No. 7 (1973); No. 8, *Windows of Order* (1988; Washington, D.C., April 6, 1989); Solo Partita for Violin and Viola (1965); *Sonata quasi una fantasia* for Clarinet and Piano (1972); *Sonata a quattro* for Flute, Clarinet, Violin, and Cello (1982); Cello Sonata (1985); *Sonata a cinque* for Clarinet, Violin, Cello, Piano, and Bass Trombone (1987); Sextet for Piano and Winds (1988). **SOLO INSTRUMENT:** Viola Sonata (1942); 3 clarinet sonatas (1943; orig. violin sonatas); *Hebrew Melodies* for Cello (1945); Cello Sonata (1947); 2 violin sonatas (1959, 1963). **PIANO:** *Interlude and Fugue* (1937); *Little Suite* (1939); Suite (1940); *Piano Piece* (1945; rev. 1952); *6 Preludes* (1946); Piano Sonata (1950); *Interrupted Story* (1956); *3 Inventions* (1957); *Short Sonata* (1964); *Toccata* (1969); *Suite in C: Dodecatonal Suite* (1970); *Fantasy-Variations* (1971); *6 Études* (1973–76); *Ballade* (1981); *6 New Études* (1984). **VOCAL:** *The Birds*, incidental music to Aristophanes's drama for Solo Voices, Chorus, and 7 Instruments (1961); *Sonnets of Praise and Lamentation: From the 18th Psalm* for Chorus and Orch., *Sonnets to Orpheus* for Unaccompanied Chorus, and *In eius memoriam* for Solo Voices, Chorus, and Orch. (1974); songs.

BIBL.: H. Weinberg, "The Music of G. P.," *American Composers Alliance Bulletin*, X/3 (1962); L. Kraft, "The Music of G. P.," *Musical Quarterly* (July 1971); O. Knussen, "G. P., Composer," *Tempo*, no. 137 (1981); R. Swift, "A Tonal Analog: The Tone-centered Music of G. P.," *Perspectives of New Music*, XXI/1–2 (1982–83).

Perlea, Jonel, Rumanian-born American conductor and composer; b. Ograda, Dec. 13, 1900; d. N.Y., July 29, 1970. He studied piano and composition in Munich (1918–20) and conducting in Leipzig (1920–23). He made his conducting debut in Bucharest in 1919; held posts as a conductor in Leipzig (1922–23) and Rostock (1923–25); then conducted the Bucharest Opera (1929–32; 1934–36) and the Bucharest Radio Orch. (1936–44), of which he was a founder. He led conducting classes at the Bucharest Cons. (1941–44); during the last year of World War II, he was interned in a German concentration camp. After the war, he conducted opera in Rome (1945–47); in 1950, conducted at La Scala in Milan. He made his American debut at the Metropolitan Opera in N.Y. on Dec. 1, 1949, conducting *Tristan und Isolde*; appeared at the San Francisco Opera and the Lyric Opera of Chicago; from 1955 to 1970, was conductor of the Conn. Sym. Orch. He taught conducting at the Manhattan School of Music from 1952 until shortly before his death; became a naturalized U.S. citizen in 1960. He suffered a heart attack in 1957 and a stroke in 1958, as a result of which he lost the use of his right arm, but he continued to conduct with his left hand.

WORKS: ORCH.: *2 Sketches* (1919); *Symphonic Variations on an Original Theme* (1930); *Don Quixote*, symphonic poem (1946); *Symphony Concertante* for Violin and Orch. (1968); *3 Studies* (1969). **CHAMBER:** Piano Sonata; String Quartet (1921).

Perlemuter, Vlado, esteemed French pianist and pedagogue of Polish descent; b. Kaunas, Lithuania, May 26, 1904. He was taken to Paris at age 3; entered the Paris Cons. when he was 13, taking the premier prix at 15; his principal mentors were Moszkowski and Cortot. He devoted much time to teaching while making occasional appearances principally as a recitalist; was a prof. at the Paris Cons. (1950–77); also gave master classes. He acquired a remarkable reputation for his insightful interpretations of Chopin and Ravel. In 1968 he was made a member of the Légion d'honneur. With H. Jourdan-Morhange, he publ. *Ravel d'après Ravel* (Lausanne, 1953; Eng. tr., 1988, as *Ravel According to Ravel*).

Perlman, Itzhak, brilliant Israeli-American violinist; b. Tel Aviv, Aug. 31, 1945. He was stricken with polio when he was 4, which left his legs paralyzed; for the rest of his life he had to walk on crutches. Despite this ghastly handicap, he began to play the violin and gave regular recitals at Tel Aviv. In 1958 he was discovered in Israel by Ed Sullivan, the TV producer, and appeared on his show in N.Y. on Feb. 15, 1959. Perlman's courage and good humor endeared him to the public at once. He remained in N.Y., where his parents soon joined him, and was accepted as a scholarship student in the classes of Ivan Galamian and Dorothy DeLay at the Juilliard School of Music. He made his professional American debut on March 5, 1963, playing with the National Orch. Assoc. in N.Y. In 1964 he won 1st prize in the Leventritt Competition, which carried, besides the modest purse ($1,000), a significant bonus—an appearance with the N.Y. Phil. It also brought about a lasting friendship with Isaac Stern, who promoted him with all the enthusiasm of a sincere admirer. Perlman's career was no longer a problem: he toured the U.S. from coast to coast in 1965–66 and toured Europe in 1966–67. He also began to teach, and in 1975 was appointed to the faculty of Brooklyn College. He seemed to be overflowing with a genuine love of life; he played not only so-called serious stuff but also rag music and jazz; with Isaac Stern and Pinchas Zukerman, he indulged in public charivari on television to which he furnished enjoyable commentaries like a regular stand-up (but necessarily sit-down) comedian. And he became quite a habitué of the White House, being particularly popular with President Reagan, who savored Perlman's show-biz savvy; his being a Jew and a handicapped person only added to the public appreciation of his TV appearances in the center of American power. In 1986 he was awarded the U.S. Medal of Freedom.

BIBL.: B. Schwarz, *Great Masters of the Violin* (N.Y., 1983).

Perlongo, Daniel, American composer; b. Gaastra, Mich., Sept. 23, 1942. He studied composition with Bassett and Finney at the Univ. of Michigan (M.M., 1966); then took a course in composition with Petrassi at the Accademia di Santa Cecilia in Rome (1966–68); as a winner of the American Prix de Rome, he spent useful time at the American Academy in Rome (1970–72). Returning to the U.S., he devoted himself mainly to teaching; was for many years prof. of music at Indiana Univ. of Pa.

WORKS: ORCH.: *7 Pieces* (1966); *Myriad* (Rome, June 1968); *Changes* for Wind Ensemble (1970; Indiana, Pa., April 11, 1973); *Ephemeron* (Rome, Dec. 1972); *Variations* for Chamber Orch. (Indiana, Pa., Nov. 9, 1973); *Voyage* for Chamber Orch. (1975); Concertino for Chamber Orch. (Omaha, May 2, 1981). **CHAMBER:** *Episodes* for Double Bass (1966); *Movement* for 8 Players (1967); *Intervals* for String Trio (1967); *For Bichi* for Percussion Quartet (1968); *Movement in Brass* for 12 Brasses (1969); *Process 7, 5, 3 for 6 in 12* for Flute, Oboe, Clarinet, and 3 Percussionists (1969); 2 string quartets: No. 1, *Semblance* (1969–70); No. 2 (1983); *Tre Tempi* for Flute, Clarinet, Horn, Violin, and Cello (1971); *Solo* for Violin (1971); *Fragments* for Flute and Cello (1972); *Semblance, Structure and Tune* for Tuba and Percussion (1973); *Ricercar* for Wind Trio (1976); *Summer Music* for Brass Quintet (1978); *Aureole* for Saxophone Quartet (1979); *Soliloquy* for Bass Clarinet (1980). **PIANO:** Sonata (1965); *Serenade* (1977). For Organ: *Tapestry* (1981).

Perne, François Louis, French singer, double-bass player, music historian, and composer; b. Paris, Oct. 4, 1772; d. Laon, Aisne, May 26, 1832. He studied with Abbé d'Haudimont at the maîtrise of St.-Jacques-de-la-Boucherie; was a chorus singer at the Paris Opéra from 1792, and double-bass player in the orch. there (1799–1816). His profound skill in composition was illustrated by his writing a triple fugue, to be sung backward on reversing the page; his knowledge of early music was extraordinary. In 1813 he became a prof. of harmony at the Paris Cons., as successor to Catel; he became inspector-general of the Cons. in 1816, and librarian in 1819. In 1822 he went into retirement, at an estate near Laon; returned to Paris shortly before his death. He publ. *Exposition de la séméiographie, ou Notation musicale des Grecs* (1815); *Cours d'harmonie et d'accompagnement* (1822); *Chansons du Châtelain de Coucy* (1830); and a great number of articles on Greek and medieval music publ. in vols. I–IX of the *Revue Musicale,* ed. by Fétis. He also wrote several pieces of sacred music.

Pernet, André, French bass; b. Rambervillers, Jan. 6, 1894; d. Paris, June 23, 1966. He studied at the Paris Cons. with Gresse; made his debut in 1921 in Nice; was a principal member of the Paris Opéra (1928–45); appeared there again in 1948; also sang at the Paris Opéra-Comique (1931–48). His most notable roles included Don Giovanni, Boris Godunov, and Méphistophélès; he also sang in many contemporary operas.

Perosi, Don Lorenzo, distinguished Italian composer of church music; b. Tortona, Dec. 21, 1872; d. Rome, Oct. 12, 1956. He studied at the Milan Cons. (1892–93); also took courses at Haberl's School for Church Music at Regensburg (1893); became maestro di cappella at Imola, and then at San Marco in Venice (1894–98). He was ordained a priest in 1895; in 1898 he became music director of the Sistine Chapel and leader of the papal choir; he resigned this post in 1915 owing to a severe mental disturbance; spent some time in a sanatorium (1922–23), after which he nominally held these duties again until his death, although with many relapses. Shortly after his 80th birthday, he led a performance of his oratorio *Il natale del Redentore* at the Vatican before Pope Pius XII (Dec. 28, 1952). He was a self-denying and scholarly worker for the cause of the cultivation of a pure church style, both in composition and in performance, and was esteemed above all others as a church musician at the Vatican.

WORKS: ORATORIOS: *La passione di Cristo secondo San Marco* (I, *La cena del Signore;* II, *L'orazione al monte;* III, *La morte del Redentore;* Milan, Dec. 2, 1897); *La trasfigurazione del nostro Signore Gesù Cristo* (Venice, March 20, 1898); *La risurrezione di Lazaro* (Venice, July 27, 1898); *La risurrezione di Cristo* (Rome, Dec. 13, 1898); *Il natale del Redentore* (Como, Sept. 12, 1899); *L'entrata di Cristo in Gerusalemme* (Milan, April 25, 1900); *La strage degli innocenti* (Milan, May 18, 1900); *Mosè* (Milan, Nov. 16, 1901); *Dies iste* (Rome, Dec. 9, 1904); *Transitus animae* (Rome, Dec. 18, 1907); *In patris memoriam* (1909; Naples, May 15, 1919); *Giorni di tribulazione* (Milan, Oct. 1916). He wrote further some 40 masses, with Organ; a Requiem, with Instrumental Accompaniment; a *Stabat Mater* for Solo Voices, Chorus, and Orch.; *Vespertina oratio* for Solo Voices, Chorus, and Orch.; about 150 motets, Psalms, etc.; 2 symphonic poems: *Dovrei non piangere* and *La festa del villaggio;* a series of 8 orch. pieces, each named after an Italian city: *Roma, Firenze, Milano, Venezia, Messina, Tortona, Genoa, Torina;* a Piano Concerto; 2 violin concertos; chamber music; many organ works.

BIBL.: L. Seytre, *L'Abbé P.: Sa biographie, son œuvre* (Nice, 1901); A. Damerini, *L. P.* (Rome, 1924); A. Della Corte, *L. P.* (Turin, 1936); A. Paglialunga, *L. P.* (Rome, 1952); M. Glinsky, *L. P.* (Milan, 1953); M. Rinaldi, *L. P.* (Rome, 1967); M. Bruni, *L. P., el cantore evangelico* (Turin, 1972).

Perotin (called **Perotinus Magnus** and **Magister Perotinus**), celebrated composer who flourished in the 12th century. His very identity, as well as a general outline of his life, remains open to speculation. Research by H. Tischler indicates that he was born between 1155 and 1160, may have studied with Leonin, carried out his major work on the revision of the *Magnus liber* between 1180 and 1190, was involved in the early development of the motet between 1190 and 1200, wrote his works for 4 voices at the close of the century, and died between 1200 and 1205. Another chronology has been propounded by Reckow, Rokseth, and Sanders, who maintain that he wrote the works for 4 voices in the 1190s, which were the early years of his career, worked on the *Magnus liber* during the 1st years of the new century, wrote elaborate clausulas about 1210, was instrumental in creating Latin motets between 1210 and 1220, and died about 1225.

WORKS: Compositions attributed to Perotin are as follows: **4-VOICE ORGANA:** *Viderunt omnes V. Notum fecit* (gradual for Christmas and Circumcision); *Sederunt principes V. Adiuva* (gradual for St. Stephen). **3-VOICE ORGANA:** *Sancte Germane V. O. sancte Germane* (responsory for St. Germanus); *Terribilis V. Cumque* (responsory for consecration of church); *Virgo V. Sponsus* (responsory for St. Catherine); *Exiit sermo V. Sed sic* (gradual for St. John the Evangelist); *Alleluia, Pascha nostrum* (Easter); *Alleluia, Nativitas* (Nativity of the Blessed Virgin Mary); *Alleluia, Dilexit Andream* (St. Andrew); *Alleluia, Posui adiutorium* (Confessor-Bishop); *Benedicamus Domino* (1, 2, and 3). **CLAUSULAS:** *Mors* for 4 Voices; *In odorem* for 3 Voices; *Et illuminare* for 3 Voices; *Et gaudebit* for 3 Voices; *Et exaltavi* for 3 Voices; 156 clausulas for *Magnus liber* for 2 Voices. **CONDUCTUS:** *Salvatoris hodie* for 3 Voices; *Dum sigillum summi Patris* for 2 Voices; *Beata viscera* for 1 Voice. See H. Husmann, ed., *Die drei- und vierstimmigen Notre-Dame-Organa,* Publikationen Älterer Musik, XI (Leipzig, 1940), and E. Thurston, ed., *The Works of Perotin* (N.Y., 1970).

BIBL.: R. von Ficker, ed., *Perotinus: Organum quadruplum Sederunt principes* (Vienna and Leipzig, 1930); G. Reese, *Music in the Middle Ages* (N.Y., 1940); H. Tischler, *The Motet in 13th-century France* (diss., Yale Univ., 1942); F. Gennrich, *Perotinus Magnus: Das Organum Alleluja Nativitas gloriose virgins Marie und seine Sippe,* Musikwissenschaftliche Studien-Bibliothek, XII (Darmstadt, 1955); H. Tischler, "The Dates of Perotin," *Journal of the American Musicological Society,* XVI (1961); idem, "Perotinus Revisited," *Aspects of Medieval and Renaissance Music: A Birthday Offering to Gustave Reese* (N.Y., 1966); F. Reckow, ed., *Der Musiktraktat des Anonymus 4* (Wiesbaden, 1967); E. Sanders, "The Question of Perotin's Oeuvre and Dates," *Festschrift für Walter Wiora* (Kassel, 1967); R. Flotzinger, *Der Discantussatz im Magnus liber und seine Nachfolge,* Wiener Musikwissenschaftliche Beiträge, VIII (Vienna, 1969); F. Reckow, "Das Organum," *Gattungen der Musik in Einzeldarstellungen: Gedenkschrift für Leo Schrade* (Bern and Munich, 1973).

Perrault, Michel (Brunet), Canadian composer; b. Montreal, July 20, 1925. He studied harmony, oboe, and timpani at the Montreal Cons. (1943–46); also was timpanist in the Montreal Sym. Orch. (1944–46); went to Paris, where he took lessons with Honegger and Boulanger (1946–47). Returning to Canada, he was a percussion player and assistant conductor of the Montreal Sym. Orch. (1957–60); then became associated with the Minute Opera Co. He founded in Montreal a jazz organization, La Société de Concerts de Musique de Chambre Noire, and his own publishing house, Les Publications Bonart.

WORKS: STAGE: BALLETS: *Commedia del arte* (1958); *Sea Gallows* (1958); *Suite canadienne* (1965). **ORCH.:** *Les Trois Cones* for Cello and Orch. (1949); *La Belle Rose* for Cello and Orch. (1952); *Fête et parade* for Trumpet and Orch. (1952); *Esquisses en plein air* for Soprano and String Orch. (1954); *Monologues* for String Orch. (1954); *Margoton* for Harp and Orch. (1954); *Le Saucisson canadien* for 4 Saxophones and String Orch. (1955); *Pastiche espagnol* for Trumpet and Orch. (1956); *Pastiche tzigane* for 2 Trumpets and Orch. (1957); *Berubée* for Piano and Orch. (1959); *Jeux de quartes* for Harp and Orch. (1961); *Serenata per tre fratelli* for 3 Horns and Orch. (1962); Double-bass Concerto (1962); *Homage,* overture

(1966); Concerto for Horn and Orch. without Brasses (1967). **CHAMBER:** Violin Sonata (1946); Saxophone Quartet (1953); Piano Trio (1954); Sextet for Clarinet, Harp, and String Quartet (1955); also incidental music; works for jazz ensemble; songs.

Perrin, Pierre, French poet; b. Lyons, c.1620; d. Paris, April 25, 1675. He took the title of Abbé; served as introducteur des ambassadeurs for Gaston d'Orléans (1648–60). Having written the texts to 2 of Cambert's pastorals—*Pastorale d'Issy* and *Ariane, ou Le mariage de Bacchus*—he obtained the privilege to organize académies d'opéra in 1669; the Paris academy was inaugurated with the Perrin-Cambert collaboration *Pomone* (March 3, 1671), which ran for 146 performances. However, his unscrupulous business managers took flight with the proceeds, leaving Perrin to spend time in a debtors' prison (1671); later that year he sold part of his privilege to the composer Sablières and his librettist Henri Guichard, and then turned over the full privilege to Lully in 1672 in return for a pension.

BIBL.: A. Pougin, *Les Vrais Créateurs de l'opéra français, P. et Cambert* (Paris, 1881); L. Auld, *The Lyric Art of P. P., Founder of French Opera* (3 vols., Henryville, Pa., 1986).

Perron (real name, **Pergamenter**), **Karl,** noted German bass-baritone; b. Frankenthal, June 3, 1858; d. Dresden, July 15, 1928. He studied with Hey in Berlin, Hasselbasch in Munich, and Stockhausen in Frankfurt; made his debut as Wolfram in 1884 in Leipzig, where he sang until 1891; then joined the Dresden Court (later State) Opera, remaining on its roster until 1924; during his tenure there, he created the roles of Jochanaan in *Salome*, Orest in *Elektra*, and Baron Ochs in *Der Rosenkavalier*; also appeared at the Bayreuth Festivals (1889–1904), where he was acclaimed for his fine performances of Wotan and King Marke.

Perry, Edward Baxter, blind American pianist; b. Haverhill, Mass., Feb. 14, 1855; d. Camden, Maine, June 13, 1924. He became nearly blind in childhood, but was able to go to Germany, where he took lessons with Kullak, Pruckner, Clara Schumann, and Liszt. Returning to America, he originated an innovative type of "lecture-recital," with which he traveled all over the U.S.; he also did some teaching, composed a number of semi-attractive piano pieces, and publ. *Descriptive Analyses of Piano Works* (1902) and *Stories of Standard Teaching Pieces* (1910).

Perry, George Frederick, English violinist, organist, and composer; b. Norwich, 1793; d. London, March 4, 1862. He was a choirboy at the Cathedral in Norwich; moved to London in 1822, and became director of music at the Haymarket Theatre; then organist of the Quebec Chapel; from 1832 to 1848 he served as concertmaster of the Sacred Harmonic Society Orch. and from 1846 as organist at Trinity Church, Gray's Inn Rd.

WORKS: ORATORIOS: *The Death of Abel* (Norwich, 1816); *Elijah and the Priests of Baal* (Norwich, March 12, 1819); *The Fall of Jerusalem* (London, Feb. 20, 1832); *Belshazzar's Feast* (London, Feb. 10, 1836); *Hezekiah* (1847). **OPERAS:** *Morning, Noon and Night* (London, Sept. 9, 1822); *Family Jars* (London, Aug. 26, 1822); also overture to *The Persian Hunters* (London, Aug. 3, 1817); anthems; songs; piano pieces.

Perry, Janet, American soprano; b. Minneapolis, Dec. 27, 1944. She received piano and violin lessons at home, and appeared in local young people's theater productions; then studied voice with Eufemia Giannini Gregory at the Curtis Inst. of Music in Philadelphia (B.M., 1967). In 1969 she made her operatic debut as Zerlina at the Linz Landestheater, remaining on its roster until 1971; following guest appearances at the Gärtnerplatztheater in Munich and at the Cologne Opera, she became a member of the Bavarian State Opera in Munich. She further made guest appearances in opera and concert in Hamburg, Düsseldorf, Paris, Zürich, Vienna, Berlin, Glyndebourne, and Salzburg. In 1983 she made her formal U.S. debut as Despina in Washington, D.C. Among her most successful roles are Susanna, Pamina, Constanze, Gilda, and Sophie.

Perry, Julia (Amanda), black American composer; b. Lexington, Ky., March 25, 1924; d. Akron, Ohio, April 29, 1979. After studying at the Westminster Choir College in Princeton, N.J. (M.Mus., 1948), she took a course in composition with Dallapiccola at Tanglewood in the summer of 1951; then took composition lessons, intermittently, with Nadia Boulanger in Paris and again with Dallapiccola in Italy (1952–56); she also attended classes in conducting in Siena (1956–58). She received 2 Guggenheim fellowships and an award from the National Inst. of Arts and Letters.

WORKS: OPERAS: *The Bottle* (n.d.); *The Cask of Amontillado* (N.Y., Nov. 20, 1954); *The Selfish Giant,* opera-ballet (1964); *3 Warnings* (n.d.). **ORCH.:** 12 syms. (1959–72), including No. 11, *Soul Symphony* (1972); *Short Piece* (1952); *Pastoral* for Flute and Strings (1959); 2 piano concertos (1964); Violin Concerto (1964); *Module* (1975). **VOCAL:** *Chicago,* cantata for Baritone, Narrator, Chorus, and Orch. (1948); *Ruth,* cantata for Chorus and Organ (1950); *Stabat Mater* for Alto and Strings (1951); numerous songs. **CHAMBER:** *Homunculus C.F.* for Harp and 10 Percussion (1960); Woodwind Trio; String Quartet; etc.

Persen, John, Norwegian composer; b. Porsanger, Norwegian Lapland, Nov. 9, 1941. He studied composition with Finn Mortensen at the Oslo Cons. (1968–73); from 1974 to 1976, was president of Ny Musikk, the Norwegian section of the ISCM. His music follows the lines of the cosmopolitan avant-garde, with a mixture of jazz, rock, sonorism, and special effects (ČSV requires 2 pistol shots to be heard at the end of the work). Persen is a nationalistic Lapp from the extreme Polar North; some titles of his compositions are political in their allusions.

WORKS: *Øre-Verk* for Orch. (1972; the title suggests both "earache" and "aural work"); *Orkesterwerk II* (Oslo, May 4, 1974); *Sámesiidat—ČSV* for Chorus a cappella (1976; based on a "joik," a Lapp folk song); *ČSV* for Orch. (1976; Oslo, March 22, 1977; the ambiguous acronym of the title means either "Dare to show that you are a Lapp" or "the secret Lapp host"); *Stykket har ingen tittel* (i.e., *This Piece Has No Name*), subtitled *Dreietoner for Orchestra* (1976; Trondheim, Jan. 20, 1977); *Music for Resting Marching Band* for Brass Band (1977); *Under Kors og Krone* (Under Cross and Crown), opera (1978–85; based on a revolt of the Lapp population against the authorities in the late 19th century); *TTT-Things Take Time,* electronic piece (1985); *Enn!* for Chorus, 2 Narrators, and Tape (1986); *NotaBene,* electronic piece (1988); *Fuglan Veit,* electronic pieces (1989).

Persiani, Fanny (née **Tacchinardi**), renowned Italian soprano and singing teacher, known as "La Persiani"; b. Rome, Oct. 4, 1812; d. Neuilly-sur-Seine, May 3, 1867. She studied with her father, the famous tenor **Nicola (Niccolò) Tacchinardi,** and performed at an early age in his small training theater in Florence; after marrying the composer **Giuseppe Persiani** in 1830, she made her professional debut as Fournier-Gorre's Francesca da Rimini in Livorno in 1832; following successful appearances in Venice and Milan, she gained distinction as a leading performer of roles in operas by Bellini and Donizetti, creating the title role in Donizetti's *Lucia di Lammermoor* in Naples in 1835; she also sang in her husband's operas, including *Ines de Castro.* She made her 1st appearance in Paris at the Théâtre-Italien in 1837, and continued to sing there with brilliant success until 1850; made her London debut at the King's Theatre in *La Sonnambula* in 1838; remained a favorite there, and later at Covent Garden, until 1849; also sang in Vienna (1837, 1844). After singing at the Italian Opera in St. Petersburg (1850–52) she settled in Paris as a voice teacher. Blessed with a small but beautiful coloratura voice, she had few equals in her day.

BIBL.: Chaudesaigues, *Madame P.* (Paris, 1839); G. Tebaldini, "Giuseppe Persiani e F. Tacchinardi, memorie e appunti," *Rivista Musicale Italiana,* XII (1905); P. Ciarlantini, *Giuseppe Persiani e F. Tacchinardi: Due Protagonisti del Melodramma Romantico* (Ancona and Bologna, 1988).

Persiani, Giuseppe, Italian opera composer; b. Recanati, Sept. 11, 1799; d. Paris, Aug. 13, 1869. As a youth he played violin in theater orchs. in Rome and Naples, where he studied with Zingarelli and Tritto. In 1830 he married the soprano Fanny Tacchinardi, who became famous as "La Persiani"; her illustrious name completely eclipsed his; yet he was a notable composer whose dramatic opera *Ines de Castro*, produced in Naples on Jan. 27, 1835, scored great success and was performed all over Europe; the celebrated soprano Malibran sang the title role, and Czerny wrote a piano paraphrase on themes of the opera. Persiani's other operas are *Attila* (Parma, Jan. 31, 1827); *Il Solitario* (Milan, April 26, 1829); *Il Fantasma* (Paris, Dec. 14, 1843); *Eufemio di Messina* (Lucca, Sept. 20, 1829; perf. also under the alternative titles *La distruzione di Catania* and *I Saraceni a Catania*). **BIBL.:** G. Tebaldini, "G. P. e Fanny Tacchinardi, memorie e appunti," *Rivista Musicale Italiana*, XII (1905); P. Ciarlantini, *G. P. e Fanny Tacchinardi: Due Protagonisti del Melodramma Romantico* (Ancona and Bologna, 1988).

Persichetti, Vincent (Ludwig), remarkable American composer whose finely amalgamated instrumental and symphonic music created an image of classical modernity; b. Philadelphia, June 6, 1915; d. there, Aug. 13, 1987. His father was a native of Abruzzi, Italy, who emigrated to the U.S. in 1894. His mother was of German extraction, hailing from Bonn. Persichetti's middle name was given to him not to honor Beethoven but to commemorate his maternal grandfather who owned a saloon in Camden, N.J. He studied piano, organ, double bass, tuba, theory, and composition as a youth; began his career as a professional musician when he was only 11 years old; became a church organist at 15. He took courses in composition with Russell King Miller at the Combs Cons. (Mus.B., 1936); then served as head of the theory and composition dept. there; concurrently studied conducting with Fritz Reiner at the Curtis Inst. of Music (diploma, 1938) and piano with Olga Samaroff and composition with Nordoff at the Philadelphia Cons. (M.Mus., 1941; D.Mus., 1945); also studied composition with Roy Harris at Colorado College. From 1941 to 1947 he was head of the theory and composition dept. of the Philadelphia Cons.; in 1947, joined the faculty of the Juilliard School of Music in N.Y.; in 1963, was named chairman of the composition dept. there. In 1952 he became director of music publishing of Elkan-Vogel, Inc. With F. Schreiber, he wrote a biography of William Schuman (N.Y., 1954); publ. a valuable manual, *Twentieth Century Harmony: Creative Aspects and Practice* (N.Y., 1961). His music is remarkable for its polyphonic skill in fusing the ostensibly incompatible idioms of Classicism, Romanticism, and stark modernism, while the melodic lines maintain an almost Italianate diatonicism in a lyrical manner. The skillful concatenation of ostensibly mutually exclusive elements created a style that was characteristically Persichetti's. He was not interested in program music or in any kind of descriptive tonal works (exceptionally, he wrote a piece of background music for the Radio City Music Hall organs which was performed in 1969). His significance for American music, therefore, is comprised in his 9 syms., and, most particularly, in his 12 piano sonatas and 6 piano sonatinas. Although he stood far from the turmoil of musical politics, he unexpectedly found himself in the center of a controversy when he was commissioned by the 1973 Presidential Inauguration Committee to write a work for narrator and orch. for a perf. at President Richard Nixon's inauguration. Persichetti selected the text of a speech by Abraham Lincoln, his second inaugural address, but, surprisingly, objections were raised by certain groups to the passionate denunciation of war in the narrative, at a time when the Vietnam War was very much in the news. The scheduled performance by the Philadelphia Orch. was hurriedly canceled, and the work's premiere was deferred to a performance by the St. Louis Sym. Orch. on Jan. 25, 1973. In 1987 Persichetti contracted a cancer of the lungs, but even when racked by disease he continued to work on his last opus, *Hymns and Responses for the Church Year, Vol. II.* He requested that his body be donated to medical science. His devoted wife suffered a stroke and died on Thanksgiving Day in the same year. Her monograph on her husband (1960) remains unpublished.

WORKS: OPERA: *Parable XX: The Sibyl* (1976; Philadelphia, April 13, 1985). **ORCH.:** 9 syms.: No. 1 (1942; Rochester, N.Y., Oct. 21, 1947); No. 2 (1942); No. 3 (1946; Philadelphia, Nov. 21, 1947); No. 4 (1951; Philadelphia, Dec. 17, 1954); No. 5, *Symphony for Strings* (1953; Louisville, Aug. 28, 1954); No. 6, *Symphony for Band* (St. Louis, April 16, 1956); No. 7, *Liturgical* (1958; St. Louis, Oct. 24, 1959); No. 8 (Berea, Ohio, Oct. 29, 1967); No. 9, *Sinfonia: Janiculum* (1970; Philadelphia, March 5, 1971); Concertino for Piano and Orch. (1941; Rochester, N.Y., Oct. 23, 1945); *Dance Overture* (1942; Tokyo, Feb. 7, 1948); *Fables* for Narrator and Orch. (1943; Philadelphia, April 20, 1945); *The Hollow Men* for Trumpet and String Orch. (1944; Germantown, Pa., Dec. 12, 1946); *Divertimento* for Band (N.Y., June 16, 1950); *Fairy Tale* (1950; Philadelphia, March 31, 1951); Concerto for Piano, 4-hands (Pittsburgh, Nov. 29, 1952); *Pageant* for Band (Miami, May 7, 1953); Piano Concerto (1962; Hanover, N.H., Aug. 2, 1964); *Introit* for Strings (1964; Kansas City, Mo., May 1, 1965); *Masquerade* for Band (1965; Berea, Ohio, Jan. 23, 1966); *Night Dances* (Kiamesha Lake, N.Y., Dec. 9, 1970); *A Lincoln Address* for Narrator and Orch. (1972; based on excerpts from Lincoln's 2nd inaugural address; originally scheduled for perf. at President Nixon's inaugural concert on Jan. 19, 1973, but canceled because of the ominous threat in the text of the "mighty scourge of war" to be brought down on the unyielding foe, which might have been misinterpreted in the light of the then-raging war in Vietnam; the work was eventually perf. in St. Louis, Jan. 25, 1973; also a version for Band, 1973); Concerto for English Horn and String Orch. (N.Y., Nov. 17, 1977). **OTHER:** A series of works, each entitled *Serenade*: No. 1 for 10 Wind Instruments (1929); No. 2 for Piano (1929); No. 3 for Violin, Cello, and Piano (1941); No. 4 for Violin and Piano (1945); No. 5 for Orch. (Louisville, Nov. 15, 1950); No. 6 for Trombone, Viola, and Cello (1950); No. 7 for Piano (1952); No. 8 for Piano, 4-hands (1954); No. 9 for Soprano and Alto Recorders (1956); No. 10 for Flute and Harp (1957); No. 11 for Band (1960; Ithaca, N.Y., April 19, 1961); No. 12 for Tuba (1961); No. 13 for 2 Clarinets (1963); No. 14 for Oboe (1984); a series of works, each entitled *Parable: I* for Flute (1965); *II* for Brass Quintet (1968); *III* for Oboe (1968); *IV* for Bassoon (1969); *V* for Carillon (1969); *VI* for Organ (1971); *VII* for Harp (1971); *VIII* for Horn (1972); *IX* for Band (1972; Des Moines, Iowa, April 6, 1973); *X* actually his String Quartet No. 4 (1972); *XI* for Alto Saxophone (1972); *XII* for Piccolo (1973); *XIII* for Clarinet (1973); *XIV* for Trumpet (1973); *XV* for English Horn (1973); *XVI* for Viola (1974); *XVII* for Double Bass (1974); *XVIII* for Trombone (1975); *XIX* for Piano (1975); *XXI* for Guitar (1978); *XXII* for Tuba (1981); *XXIII* for Violin, Cello, and Piano (1981); *XXIV* for Harpsichord (1982); 4 string quartets (1939; 1944; 1959; 1972, also listed as *Parable X*); 12 piano sonatas (1939–80); 6 piano sonatas (1950–54); 8 harpsichord sonatas (1951–84); Suite for Violin and Cello (1940); Sonata for Solo Violin (1940); Concertato for Piano and String Quartet (1940); Sonatine for Organ, Pedals Alone (1940); *Fantasy* for Violin and Piano (1941); *Pastoral* for Woodwind Quintet (1943; Philadelphia, April 20, 1945); *Vocalise* for Cello and Piano (1945); *King Lear*, septet for Woodwind Quintet, Timpani, and Piano (1948; perf. under the title *The Eye of Anguish* by the Martha Graham Dance Co., Montclair, N.J., Jan. 31, 1949); Sonata for Solo Cello (1952); Quintet for Piano and Strings (1954; Washington, D.C., Feb. 4, 1955); *Little Recorder Book* (1956); *Infanta Marina* for Viola and Piano (1960); *Shimah B'koli* (Psalm 130) for Organ (1962); *Masques* for Violin and Piano (1965); *Do Not Go Gentle* for Organ, Pedals Alone (1974); *Auden Variations for Organ* (1977); *Reflective Keyboard Studies* (1978); *Little Mirror Book for Piano* (1978); *4 Arabesques for Piano* (1978); *3 Toccatinas for Piano* (1979); *Mirror Etudes for Piano* (1979); *Dryden Liturgical Suite for Organ* (1980); *Song of David* for Organ (1981); *Little Harpsichord Book* (1983); many choral works, including *Proverb* for

Mixed Chorus (1948); *Hymns and Responses for the Church Year* (1955; Philadelphia, Oct. 7, 1956); *Song of Peace* for Male Chorus and Piano (1959); *Mass for Mixed Chorus*, a cappella (1960; N.Y., April 20, 1961); *Stabat Mater* for Chorus and Orch. (1963; N.Y., May 1, 1964); *Te Deum* for Chorus and Orch. (1963; Philadelphia, March 15, 1964); *Spring Cantata* for Women's Chorus and Piano (1963; Boston, April 1, 1964); *Winter Cantata* for Women's Chorus, Flute, and Marimba (1964; Troy, N.Y., April 9, 1965); *Celebrations* for Chorus and Wind Ensemble (River Falls, Wis., Nov. 18, 1966); *The Pleiades* for Chorus, Trumpet, and String Orch. (1967; Potsdam, N.Y., May 10, 1968); *The Creation* for Soprano, Alto, Tenor, Baritone, Chorus, and Orch. (1969; N.Y., April 17, 1970); *Flower Songs* (Cantata No. 6) for Mixed Chorus and String Orch. (1983; Philadelphia, April 20, 1984); a number of songs, including the major cycle for Soprano and Piano entitled *Harmonium*, after poems of Wallace Stevens (1951; N.Y., Jan. 20, 1952).

BIBL.: R. Evett, "The Music of V. P.," *Juilliard Review*, II/2 (1955); W. Simmons, "A P. Perspective," *American Record Guide*, XL/6 (1977); D. and J. Patterson, V. P.: *A Bio-Bibliography* (Westport, Conn., 1988).

Persinger, Louis, eminent American violinist and teacher; b. Rochester, Ill., Feb. 11, 1887; d. N.Y., Dec. 31, 1966. He began his violin studies at an early age in Colorado, making his public debut when he was 12; then studied with Hans Becker at the Leipzig Cons. (1900–4), with Ysaÿe in Brussels, and with Thibaud in Paris. He toured Belgium and Germany; served as concertmaster of the Berlin Phil. (1914–15) and the San Francisco Sym. Orch. (1915–16). He then led his own string quartet and served as director of San Francisco's Chamber Music Society (1916–28); then devoted himself mainly to teaching; in 1930 he joined the staff of the Juilliard School of Music in N.Y. He achieved a great reputation as a teacher who subordinated technical demands to the paramount considerations of formal balance and expressiveness of the melodic line. Among his pupils were Yehudi Menuhin, Ruggiero Ricci, and Isaac Stern.

BIBL.: M. Hart, "L. P., a Tribute on his 75th," *Juilliard Review*, IX/1 (1961–62); Y. Menuhin, "L. P.," *Juilliard Review Annual* (N.Y., 1966–67); B. Schwarz, *Great Masters of the Violin* (N.Y., 1983).

Perti, Giacomo (or **Jacopo**) **Antonio,** greatly significant Italian composer; b. Crevalcore, near Bologna, June 6, 1661; d. Bologna, April 10, 1756. He began to study music with his uncle, Lorenzo Perti, and with Rocco Laurenti; later took lessons in counterpoint with Petronio Franceschini. As early as 1678 he had a Mass performed at the church of S. Tomaso al Mercato. In 1679 he collaborated on the opera *Atide*, to which he contributed the score for the 3rd act. In 1681 he was elected a member of the Accademia Filarmonica, of which he was 5 times the *principe* (in 1719 was named *censor*). He then went to Parma, where he continued his studies with Giuseppe Corso. In 1689 he had his opera *Dionisio Siracusano* performed in Parma, and another opera, *La Rosaura*, in Venice. In 1690 he succeeded his uncle as maestro di cappella at the Cathedral of S. Pietro in Bologna. In 1696 he became maestro di cappella of S. Petronio, a position he held until his death. He also held similar positions at S. Domenico (1704–55; deputized for Alberti from 1734) and at S. Maria in Galliera (1706–50). Emperor Charles VI made him a royal councillor in 1740. His students included G.B. Martini and Giuseppe Torelli.

WORKS: OPERAS: *Atide* (Bologna, June 23, 1679; incomplete; in collaboration with others); *Marzio Coriolano* (Venice, Jan. 20, 1683); *Oreste in Argo* (Modena, Carnival 1685); *L'incoronazione di Dario* (Bologna, Jan. 13, 1686); *La Flavia* (Bologna, Feb. 16, 1686); *Dionisio Siracusano* (Parma, Carnival 1689); *La Rosaura* (Venice, 1689); *Brenno in Efeso* (Venice, 1690); *L'inganno scoperto per vendetta* (Venice, Carnival 1690 or 1691); *Il Pompeo* (Genoa, Carnival 1691); *Furio Camillo* (Venice, Carnival 1692); *Nerone fatto Cesare* (Venice, 1693); *La forza della virtù* (Bologna, May 25, 1694); *Laodicea e Berenice*

(Venice, 1695); *Penelope la casta* (Rome, Jan. 25, 1696); *Fausta restituita all'impero* (Rome, Jan. 19, 1697); *Apollo geloso* (Bologna, Aug. 16, 1698); *Ariovisto* (Milan, Sept. 1699; in collaboration with others); *La prosperità di Elio Sejano* (Milan, Carnival 1699; in collaboration with others); *Dionisio rè di Portogallo* (Pratolino, Sept. 1707); *Il fratricida innocente* (Bologna, May 19, 1708); *Ginevra principessa di Scozia* (Pratolino, Fall 1708); *Berenice regina d'Egitto* (Pratolino, Sept. 1709); *Rodelinda regina de' Longobardi* (Pratolino, Fall 1710); *Lucio vero* (Bologna, Spring 1717); *Rosinde ed Emireno* (undated). **ORATORIOS:** *S. Serafina [I due gigli porporati nel martirio de S. Serafina e S. Sabina]* (Bologna, 1679); *Abramo vincitore* (Venice, 1683); *Mosè* (Modena, 1685); *Oratorio della passione di Cristo* (Bologna, 1685); *La beata Imelde Lambertini* (Bologna, 1686); *Agar* (Bologna, 1689); *La passione del Redentore* (Bologna, 1694); *S. Galgano* (Bologna, 1694); *Cristo al limbo* (Bologna, 1698); *La sepoltura di Cristo* (Bologna, 1704); *S. Giovanni* (Bologna, 1704); *Gesù al sepolcro* (Bologna, 1707); *S. Petronio* (Bologna, 1720); *L'amor divino [I conforti di Maria vergine addolorata]* (Bologna, 1723); also several undated oratorios. Additional sacred works include *Messa e salmi concertati* for 4 Voices, Instruments, and Chorus (Bologna, 1735) and *7 canzonette in aria marmoresca sopra le 7 principali feste di Nostra Signora* (Bologna, 1780); also 120 Psalms, 54 motets, 28 masses; about 150 secular cantatas; also *Cantate morali e spirituali* for 1 and 2 Voices, with Violin (Bologna, 1688).

BIBL.: L. Mancini, *J.A. P.* (Bologna, 1813); G. Atti, *Orazione in lode di I.A. P.* (1844); an extended biography of P. is found in L. Busi's *Il Padre Giambatt. Martini* (Bologna, 1891; vol. I, p. 61 et seq.); F. Giegling, "G.A. P.," *Die Musikforschung*, IV (1955); M. Fabbri, "G.A. P.," in *Musicisti Lombardi ed Emiliani*, Chigiana, XV (1958); G. Vecchi, ed., *La musica barocca a Bologna . . . G.A. P.* (Bologna, 1961); J. Berger, "The Sacred Works of G.A. P.," *Journal of the American Musicological Society*, XVII (1964).

Pertile, Aureliano, noted Italian tenor; b. Montagnana, Nov. 9, 1885; d. Milan, Jan. 11, 1952. He studied with Orefice and Fugazzola; made his debut in *Martha* in Vicenza in 1911; then sang in Naples (1914), at Milan's La Scala (1916), and the Teatro Colón in Buenos Aires (1918); made his Metropolitan Opera debut in N.Y. as Cavaradossi in *Tosca* (Dec. 1, 1921); then returned to La Scala, where he gained renown for his portrayal of Faust in *Mefistofele* (1922); was a leading tenor there until 1937; also appeared at London's Covent Garden (1927–31); retired from the stage (1946); taught at the Milan Cons. (from 1945). He was esteemed for such roles as Andrea Chénier, Manrico, Radames, Canio, and Don Alvaro; created Boito's Nerone and Mascagni's Nerone.

Pešek, Libor, Czech conductor; b. Prague, June 22, 1933. He studied at the Prague Academy of Music (graduated, 1956); was founder-conductor of the Prague Chamber Harmony (1959) and the Prague Sebastian Orch. (1965); also conducted various orchs. in his homeland and in Holland. He was a permanent conductor of the Czech Phil. from 1983, and from 1987 was principal conductor and artistic adviser of the Royal Liverpool Phil. in England. He also appeared as a guest conductor in Japan and North America.

Peskanov, Mark, Russian-born American violinist; b. Odessa, Aug. 30, 1956. He began his violin training at age 7 in Odessa; in 1973 emigrated to the U.S., where he continued his studies with Dorothy DeLay at the Juilliard School in N.Y. (B.A., 1979). In 1985 he received an Avery Fisher Career Grant, and the 1st Isaac Stern Award presented by N.Y.'s Carnegie Hall; in 1987 he was given the 1st Frederick R. Mann Young Artist Award in Philadelphia. He appeared as a soloist with several American orchs. and gave concerts in Europe, South America, Japan, and Australia.

Peskó, Zoltán, Hungarian-born Italian conductor and composer; b. Budapest, Feb. 15, 1937. He studied at the Budapest Academy of Music (graduated, 1962); also took courses in composition with Petrassi and in conducting with Ferrara in Italy, and in conducting with Boulez in Switzerland (1963–66); was assistant conductor to Maazel and the Deutsche Oper and Berlin Radio Sym. Orch. in the Western sector (1966–69); then conducted at the Berlin State Opera in East Berlin (1969–73); also served on the faculty at the Berlin Hochschule für Musik (1969–72). From 1974 to 1976 he was chief conductor of the Teatro Comunale in Bologna; subsequently was chief conductor of Venice's Teatro La Fenice (1976–77) and Milan's Orchestra Sinfonica della RAI (1978–82). He wrote some orch. music, chamber works, and keyboard pieces.

Pesonen, Olavi, Finnish composer; b. Helsinki, April 8, 1909. He studied with Ilmari Krohn and Leevi Madetoja at the Univ. of Helsinki (M.A., 1932); also took courses with Arthur Willner in Vienna and Mátyás Seiber in London, and studied organ with Günther Ramin in Leipzig; then devoted himself to teaching and composing in Helsinki. His works follow along traditional lines.

WORKS: DRAMATIC: *Havahtuminen* (Awakening), melodrama for Narrator and Orch. (1936); *Huutokauppa* (Auction), music to A. Leinonen's play (1949). **ORCH.:** *Pieni sarja* (Little Suite; 1936); *Juhla-alkusoitto* (Festive Overture; 1938; rev. 1946); *Fuga fantastica* (1948; based on the organ piece, 1939); *Tanhusoitto* (Folk Dances; 1949); 2 syms. (1949, 1953); *Suite ancienne* (1978); Pieces for String Orch., after Finnish folk songs (1980); *In dulci jubilo* for String Orch. (1981); various works for Chorus and Orch., including the cantatas *Ah autuus suuri* (O Great Bliss; 1939; rev. 1978), *Koulukantaatti* (School Cantata; 1941), and *Silenivät pitkospuut* (The Causeway Became Smoother; 1966); a cappella choruses; songs; organ music, including *Fuga fantastica* (1939; also for Orch., 1948) and *Jesu dulcis memoria* (1981).

Pessard, Emile (-Louis-Fortuné), French composer; b. Paris, May 29, 1843; d. there, Feb. 10, 1917. He studied at the Paris Cons. with Bazin (harmony), Laurent (piano), Benoist (organ), and Carafa (composition); won the 1st harmony prize in 1862, and the Grand Prix de Rome in 1866 with the cantata *Dalila* (1866). In 1881 he was appointed prof. of harmony at the Paris Cons. He enjoyed considerable regard as a composer of fine songs. As a student, Debussy copied Pessard's song *Chanson d'un fou*, and the MS in Debussy's handwriting was publ. erroneously as Debussy's own.

WORKS: OPERAS (all 1st perf. in Paris): *La Cruche cassée* (Feb. 1870); *Don Quichotte* (Feb. 13, 1874); *Le Char* (Jan. 18, 1878); *Le Capitaine Fracasse* (July 2, 1878); *Tabarin* (Jan. 12, 1885); *Tartarin sur les Alpes* (Nov. 17, 1888); *Les Folies amoureuses* (April 15, 1891); *Une Nuit de Noël* (1893); *Mam-'zelle Carabin* (Nov. 3, 1893); *La Dame de trèfle* (May 13, 1898); *L'Armée des vierges* (Oct. 15, 1902); *L'Epave* (Feb. 17, 1903); also some orch. pieces; choral works; chamber music; songs; piano pieces.

Pestalozzi, Heinrich, Swiss composer; b. Wädenswil, near Zürich, Aug. 26, 1878; d. Zürich, Aug. 9, 1940. He studied theology and music in Berlin; was a singing teacher there (1902–12); then a pastor in Arosa, Switzerland; in 1917 he became a voice teacher at the Zürich Cons. His choral works and songs acquired great popularity in his homeland; publ. several manuals on singing.

Peter, John Frederick (actually, **Johann Friedrich**), significant American Moravian violinist, organist, and composer; brother of **Simon Peter;** b. Heerendijk, the Netherlands (of German parents), May 19, 1746; d. Bethlehem, Pa., July 13, 1813. He was educated in the Netherlands and Germany; went to America in 1770. He served the Moravian Church in various capacities in the Pa. communities of Nazareth, Bethlehem, and Lititz (until 1780); then in Salem, N.C., until 1790. He spent the rest of his life mostly in Bethlehem as organist of the church. He is widely considered the greatest of the American Moravian composers. His collection of copies of instrumental works by Stamitz, J.C.F. Bach, J.C. Bach, Abel, Boccherini, and Haydn (preserved in the Archives of the Moravian Church) proves his knowledge of contemporary music. Among his com-

positions are 105 concerted anthems (he excelled in the genre) and solo songs. While in Salem, he completed (1789) a set of 6 quintets for 2 Violins, 2 Violas, and Cello (his only secular works), which are the oldest preserved examples of chamber music composed in America. His MSS are preserved in the Archives of the Moravian Church in Bethlehem and the Moravian Foundation in Winston-Salem, N.C.

BIBL.: A. Rau, "John Frederick P.," *Musical Quarterly* (July 1937); H. David, "Musical Life in the Pennsylvania Settlements of the *Unitas Fratrum*," *Transactions of the Moravian Historical Society*, XIII (1942; publ. separately as Moravian Music Foundation Publication No. 6, 1959); E. Nolte, "The Paradox of the P. Quintets," *Moravian Music Foundation Bulletin* (Fall 1967); W. Schnell, *The Choral Music of Johann Friedrich P.* (diss., Univ. of Illinois, 1973); J. Ingram, "A Musical Pot-pourri: The Commonplace Book of Johann Friedrich P.," *Moravian Music Foundation Bulletin*, XXIV/1 (1979).

Peter, Simon, American Moravian composer, brother of **John Frederick (Johann Friedrich) Peter;** b. Heerendijk, the Netherlands (of German parents), April 2, 1743; d. Salem, N.C., May 29, 1819. With his brother, he was educated at the Moravian Brethren's schools in the Netherlands and Germany; went to America in 1770. His ministry was spent in both the Northern and Southern Provinces of the Moravian Church (i.e., both Pa. and N.C.). From 1784 to 1819 he lived in N.C. as pastor of several congregations, and was a member of the governing board of the Church. He composed only a few sacred anthems, but one of these, *O Amblick, der mirs Herze bricht,* is one of the most expressive Lenten songs written in America.

BIBL.: H. David, "Musical Life in the Pennsylvania Settlements of the *Unitas Fratrum*," *Transactions of the Moravian Historical Society*, XIII (1942; publ. separately as Moravian Music Foundation Publication No. 6, 1959).

Peters, Carl Friedrich, German music publisher; b. Leipzig, March 30, 1779; d. Sonnenstein, Bavaria, Nov. 20, 1827. In 1814 he purchased Kühnel & Hoffmeister's Bureau de Musique (founded, 1800; Hoffmeister left the firm in 1805, and Kühnel led it from 1805 until his death in 1813); it became known as Bureau de Musique C.F. Peters, but encountered difficulties as a result of the Battle of Leipzig and Peters's committal to an asylum; nevertheless, it acquired a notable reputation through its publication of the 1st collected ed. of the works of J.S. Bach and of a number of works by Beethoven. In 1828 the manufacturer Carl Gotthelf Siegmund Bohme (1785–1855) took charge of the firm; after his death, the town council took it over as a charity foundation. In 1860 it was purchased by the Berlin book and music seller Julius Friedländer, who took the lawyer Max Abraham (1831–1900) into partnership in 1863; Abraham became sole owner in 1880 and proceeded to build an international reputation for the firm. In addition to publishing works by the foremost composers of the day, the firm launched the inexpensive and reliable Edition Peters in 1867, opened its large and valuable Musikbibliothek Peters to the public in 1893, and publ. the scholarly *Jahrbuch der Musikbibliothek Peters* from 1895 (it was the *Deutsches Jahrbuch der Musikwissenschaft* from 1956 to 1977; then the *Jahrbuch Peters*). Abraham's nephew, Heinrich Hinrichsen (b. Hamburg, Feb. 5, 1868; d. in the Auschwitz concentration camp, Sept. 30, 1942), became a partner in 1894 and sole owner in 1900; his son Max Hinrichsen (b. Leipzig, July 6, 1901; d. London, Dec. 17, 1965) joined the firm in 1927 and became a full partner in 1931; another son, Walter Hinrichsen (b. Leipzig, Sept. 23, 1907; d. N.Y., July 21, 1969), joined the firm in 1931, and a third son, Hans-Joachim Hinrichsen (b. Leipzig, Aug. 22, 1909; d. in the Perpignan concentration camp, Sept. 18, 1940), joined it in 1933. Walter left the firm in 1936 and founded the C.F. Peters Corp. in N.Y. in 1948; Max left the firm in 1936, and in 1938 founded the Hinrichsen Edition in London, which became the Peters Edition in 1975; Heinrich and Hans-Joachim were deprived of their ownership by the Nazis in 1939, and Johannes Petschull took control of the firm. During and after World War II, the original Leipzig firm encountered great difficulties; the German Democratic Republic took it over in 1949–50. With the Hinrichsen heirs as partners, Petschull founded a new company in Frankfurt am Main in 1950. The Leipzig firm publishes much contemporary music while issuing rev. and updated eds. of earlier scores; the London firm has brought out much English music; the N.Y. firm has a deep commitment to modern music.

Peters (real name, **Petermann**), **Roberta,** outstanding American soprano; b. N.Y., May 4, 1930. She studied voice with William Pierce Hermann; at the age of 20 she made her operatic debut with the Metropolitan Opera in N.Y. as Zerlina in *Don Giovanni* on Nov. 17, 1950, as a substitute on short notice; she subsequently remained on its roster for more than 35 years. She also sang with the opera companies of San Francisco and Chicago, at Covent Garden in London, at the Salzburg Festivals, and at the Vienna State Opera. She was one of the leading coloratura sopranos of her generation; also appeared with success on television, films, and in musical comedies. She was briefly married to the American baritone **Robert Merrill.** With Louis Biancolli, she wrote *A Debut at the Met,* which was publ. in 1967.

Petersen, Wilhelm, German composer; b. Athens, March 15, 1890; d. Darmstadt, Dec. 18, 1957. He studied in Germany and worked as a theater conductor; served in the German army during World War I; in 1922, settled in Darmstadt as a teacher. He wrote the opera *Der goldne Topf* (Darmstadt, March 29, 1941); 5 syms. (1921, 1923, 1934, 1941, 1957); 3 violin sonatas; 3 string quartets; several sacred choruses and songs. He was highly regarded in Darmstadt as a musician and pedagogue. In 1972 a Wilhelm Petersen Society was founded to memorialize his work.
BIBL.: A. Petersen, *W. P., Skizze seines Wesens und Lebens* (Darmstadt, 1962).

Peterson, Oscar (Emmanuel), noted black Canadian jazz pianist; b. Montreal, Aug. 15, 1925. He studied piano; made appearances on Canadian radio; also played with the orch. of Johnny Holmes (1944–47). In 1949 he went to N.Y., and soon established himself as one of the finest jazz pianists of the day. He made numerous tours, often appearing with a guitarist and bass player as fellow musicians (he later replaced the guitar with drums); he also was successful as a guest artist with American orchs. He was made an Officer of the Order of Canada (1973). In 1991 he was named chancellor of York Univ. in Toronto.
BIBL.: R. Palmer, *O. P.* (Tunbridge Wells and N.Y., 1984).

Peterson, Wayne, American composer and pianist; b. Albert Lea, Minn., Sept. 3, 1927. He studied with Early Rymer (piano) and with Paul Fetler, Earl George, and James Aliferis (composition) at the Univ. of Minnesota (B.A., 1951; M.A., 1953; Ph.D., 1960); studied with Lennox Berkeley and Howard Ferguson at the Royal Academy of Music in London. He served on the music faculty of the Univ. of Minnesota (1953–54), Chico (Calif.) State College (1959–60), and San Francisco State College (later Univ.; from 1960). He held numerous N.E.A. awards; also received a Guggenheim fellowship (1989–90).
WORKS: ORCH.: *Introduction and Allegro* (1953); *Free Variations* (1954–58); *Exaltation, Dithyramb and Caprice* (1959–60); *Cataclysms* (1968); *Clusters and Fragments* for String Orch. (1969); *Transformations II* for Chamber Orch. (1985; San Francisco, April 11, 1986); *Trilogy* (1987; Saratoga, Calif., June 18, 1988); *The Widening Gyre* (1990; N.Y., Feb. 10, 1991); *The Face of the Night, the Heart of the Dark* (1990–91). **CHAMBER:** *Metamorphosis* for Wind Quintet (1967); *Phantasmagoria* for Flute, Clarinet, and Double Bass (1968); *Capriccio* for Flute and Piano (1973); *Transformations* for String Quartet (1974); *Encounters* for 9 Players (1976); *An Interrupted Serenade* for Flute, Harp, and Cello (1978); *Sextet* (1982); String Quartet (1983–84); *Ariadne's Thread* for Harp, Flute, Clarinet, Horn, Percussion, and Violin (1985); *Duodecaphony* for Viola and Cello (1986–87).

Peterson-Berger, (Olof) Wilhelm, esteemed Swedish music critic, teacher, and composer; b. Ullånger, Feb. 27, 1867; d. Östersund, Dec. 3, 1942. He studied with J. Dente and O. Bolander at the Stockholm Cons. (1886–89); then in Dresden with Scholtz (piano) and Kretzschmar (composition); eventually settled in Stockholm, where he became active as a pedagogue and music critic of *Dagens Nyheter* (1896–1908; 1910–20; 1921–30). His opera *Arnljot* was one of the finest Swedish operas in the national tradition; his other notable works included his 3rd Sym., Violin Concerto, songs, and piano pieces.
WORKS: STAGE: *Sveagaldrar,* festival play for the silver jubilee of the accession of Oscar II (1897); *Lyckan* (Luck), fairy opera (Stockholm, March 27, 1903); music dramas (all produced in Stockholm): *Ran* (1899–1900; May 20, 1903); *Arnljot* (1907–9; April 13, 1910); *Domedagsprofeterna* (The Prophets of Doom; 1912–17; Feb. 21, 1919); *Adils och Elisiv* (1921–24; Feb. 27, 1927). **ORCH.:** 5 syms.: No. 1, *Baneret* (The Banner; 1889–90; 1903; Stockholm, Feb. 23, 1904; rev. 1932–33); No. 2, *Sunnanfärd* (The Journey to the South; 1910; Göteborg, March 22, 1911); No. 3, *Same Ätnam* (Lappland; 1913–15; Stockholm, Dec. 11, 1917); No. 4, *Holmia* (1929; Stockholm, April 9, 1930); No. 5, *Solitudo* (1932–33; Stockholm, April 11, 1934); *Romans* for Violin and Orch. (1915); Violin Concerto (1928; Stockholm, Feb. 6, 1929); orch. suites: *I somras* (Last Summer; 1903); *Earina* (Spring; 1917); *Italiana* (1922). **VOCAL: CANTATAS:** *Norrbotten* (1921); *Operakantaten* (1922; rev. 1935–36); *Soluppgång* (1929); 40 songs for mixed choir; nearly 100 solo songs. **CHAMBER:** 2 violin sonatas (1887, 1910); *Suite* for Violin and Piano (1896); over 100 piano pieces.
WRITINGS: *Svensk Musikkultur* (1911); *Richard Wagner som kulturföreteelse* (Richard Wagner as a Phenomenon of Civilization; 1913; in German as *Richard Wagner als Kulturerscheinung,* 1917). A selection of his essays was publ. in Stockholm in 2 vols. (1923); another, in one vol., in Östersund (1951). His reminiscences were publ. posthumously (Uppsala, 1943).
BIBL.: B. Carlberg, *W. P.-B.* (Stockholm, 1950); S. Beite, *W. P.-B.: En känd och okänd tondiktare* (Östersund, 1965).

Petit, Raymond, French music critic and composer; b. Neuilly-sur-Seine, July 6, 1893; d. Annemasse, Haute-Savoie, Sept. 25, 1976. He studied with Tournemire in Paris; then devoted himself mainly to music criticism.
WORKS: Opera, *La Sulamithe; Suite grave* for Orch. (1920); 2 *méditations* for String Quartet (1921); *Dialogue* for 2 Violins; *Hymnus* for Voice and Flute (1924); *Il cantico del sole* for Voice and Wind Instruments (ISCM Festival, Frankfurt, July 3, 1927); songs.

Petkov, Dimiter, Bulgarian composer and conductor; b. Smolyan, May 4, 1919. He studied composition with Veselin Stoyanov at the Bulgarian State Cons. in Sofia, graduating in 1950; then went to Moscow for postgraduate studies in music theory at the Cons. (1952–54). He taught theory at the Sofia Academy of Music (1949–52; 1954–58) and was director of the National Opera Theater; served as president of the Union of Bulgarian Composers (1972–80).
WORKS: Musical comedy, *Restless Hearts* (1960; Sofia, 1976); children's operetta, *The Winding Path* (1956; Michailovgrad, Oct. 29, 1975); oratorio, *Rozhan Comes Down from Rhodopa* (1965); 5 cantatas: *September Legend* (1953); *Communists* (1956); *Requiem for a Sailor* (1967); *Cantata about Paissy* (1973); *Festive Cantata* (1974); *The Sparks of October,* suite for Soloists, Children's Chorus, and Orch. (1967); *3 Polyphonic Pieces* for Flute, Clarinet, and Bassoon (1953); choruses; arrangements of folk songs.
BIBL.: E. Pavlov, *D. P.* (Sofia, 1987).

Petra-Basacopol, Carmen, Rumanian composer; b. Sibiu, Sept. 5, 1926. She studied philosophy at the Univ. of Bucharest (1945–49); then took courses with M. Jora (composition and counterpoint), T. Rogalski (orchestration), and P. Constantinescu (harmony) at the Bucharest Cons. (1949–56); attended courses in new music in Darmstadt (1968); later completed her training at the Sorbonne in Paris (Ph.D., 1976, with the diss. *L'Originalité de la musique roumaine à travers les œuvres d'Enesco, Jora et Constantinesco*; publ. in Bucharest, 1979). She taught at the Bucharest Cons. (from 1962); received the Order of Cultural Merit (1969) and the Georges Enesco composition prize of the Rumanian Academy (1980). Her music is lyrical, with colorful and effective instrumentation.

WORKS: STAGE: BALLETS: *Fata şi masca* (The Girl and the Mask; 1970); *Ciuleandra* (1985–86). **ORCH.:** Sym. No. 1 (1956); *Tara de piatra* (Stone Country; 1959); Piano Concerto (1961); *Symphonic Triptych* (1962); 2 violin concertos (1963, 1965); Concertino for Harp, Kettledrums, and Strings (1975); Concerto for Strings (1981); Cello Concerto (1982). **CHAMBER:** Suite for Flute and Piano (1950); Cello Sonata (1952); Trio for Violin, Cello, and Piano (1959); Sonata for Flute and Harp (1961); *Divertissement* for Harp, Wind Quintet, Double Bass, and Xylophone (1969); Trio for Flute, Clarinet, and Bassoon (1974); Quartet for Flute, Violin, Cello, and Piano (1978); Suite for Cello (1981); Trio for Flute, Clarinet, and Harp (1987); also piano pieces; choral music; songs.

Petrassi, Goffredo, outstanding Italian composer and teacher; b. Zagarolo, near Rome, July 16, 1904. He worked as a clerk in a music store in Rome, and soon began private piano lessons with Bastini; then commenced the study of harmony with Donato (1925); subsequently entered the Conservatorio di Santa Cecilia (1928), where he studied composition with Bustini (diploma, 1932) and organ with Germani (diploma, 1933). He taught at the Accademia di Santa Cecilia (1934–36), where he also received instruction from Molinari; was general director of Venice's Teatro La Fenice (1937–40); after teaching composition at the Conservatorio di Santa Cecilia (1939–59), he taught again at the Accademia di Santa Cecilia (1959–74); also taught at Siena's Accademia Chigiana (1966–67). Despite the late beginning, Petrassi acquired a solid technique of composition; the chief influence in his music was that of Casella; later he became interested in 12-tone procedures.

WORKS: OPERAS: *Il Cordovano* (1944–48; Milan, May 12, 1949; rev. 1958; Milan, Feb. 18, 1959); *La morte dell'aria* (1949–50; Rome, Oct. 24, 1950). **BALLETS:** *La follia di Orlando* (1942–43; Milan, April 12, 1947); *Il ritratto di Don Chisciotte* (1945; Paris, Nov. 21, 1947). **ORCH.:** *Divertimento* (1930); *Ouverture da concerto* (1931); *Passacaglia* (1931); *Partita* (1932; Rome, April 2, 1933); 8 concertos: No. 1 (1933–34; Rome, March 31, 1935); No. 2 (1951; Basel, Jan. 24, 1952); No. 3, *Récréation concertante* (1952–53; Aix-en-Provence Festival, July 23, 1953); No. 4, for String Orch. (1954; Rome, April 28, 1956); No. 5 (Boston, Dec. 2, 1955); No. 6, *Invenzione concertata,* for Brass, Strings, and Percussion (1956–57; London, Sept. 9, 1957); No. 7 (1961–64; Bologna, March 18, 1965); No. 8 (1970–72; Chicago, Sept. 28, 1972); Piano Concerto (1936–39; Rome, Dec. 10, 1939); Flute Concerto (1960; Hamburg, March 7, 1961); *Estri,* chamber sym. for 15 Performers (Dartmouth College, Hanover, N.H., Aug. 2, 1967; as a ballet, Spoleto, July 11, 1968). **VOCAL:** *3 Choruses,* with Small Orch. (1932); *Psalm IX* for Chorus, Strings, Brass, 2 Pianos, and Percussion (1934–36); *Magnificat* for Soprano, Chorus, and Orch. (1939–40); *Coro di morti,* dramatic madrigal for Male Chorus, Brass, Double Basses, 3 Pianos, and Percussion (Venice, Sept. 28, 1941); *2 liriche di Saffo* for Voice, and Piano or 11 Instruments (1941); *Quattro inni sacri* for Tenor, Baritone, and Organ (1942; version with Orch., Rome, Feb. 22, 1950); *Noche oscura,* cantata (Strasbourg, June 17, 1951); *Nonsense,* to words by Edward Lear, for Chorus a cappella (1952); *Propos d'Alain* for Baritone and 12 Performers (1960); *Sesto non-senso,* after Lear, for Chorus a cappella (1964); *Mottetti per la Passione* for Chorus a cappella (1966); *Beatitudines,* chamber oratorio in memory of Martin Luther King, Jr., for Baritone and 5 Instruments (Fiuggi, July 17, 1969); *Orationes Christi* for Chorus, Brass, 8 Violins, and 8 Cellos (1974–75; Rome, Dec. 6, 1975); *Laudes creaturarum* for Reciter and 6 Instruments (1982); *Tre cori sacri* for Chorus a cappella (1980–83). **CHAMBER:** *Sinfo-*

nia, Siciliana e Fuga for String Quartet (1929); *Siciliana e marcetta* for 2 Pianos (1930); *Introduzione e allegro* for Violin and Piano (1933; also with 11 Instruments); *Toccata* for Piano (1933); *Preludio, Aria e Finale* for Cello and Piano (1933); *Invenzioni* for 2 Pianos (1944); *Sonata da camera* for Harpsichord and 10 Instruments (1948); *Dialogo angelico* for 2 Flutes (1948); *Musica a 2* for 2 Cellos (1952); String Quartet (1958); *Serenata* for Flute, Viola, Double Bass, Harpsichord, and Percussion (1958); String Trio (1959); *Serenata II,* trio for Harp, Guitar, and Mandolin (1962); *Musica di Ottoni* for Brass and Timpani (1963); *3 per 7* for 3 Performers on 7 Wind Instruments (1966); *Ottetto di Ottoni* for 4 Trumpets and 4 Trombones (1968); *Souffle* for 1 Performer on 3 Flutes (1969); *Elogio per un'Ombra* for Violin (1971); *Nunc* for Guitar (1971); *Ala* for Flute and Harpsichord (1972); *4 odi* for String Quartet (1973–75); *Oh les beaux jours!* for Piano (1976); *Fanfare* for 3 Trumpets (1944–76); *Petite pièce* for Piano (1976); *Alias* for Guitar and Harpsichord (1977); *Sestina d'autunno* for 6 Instruments (1981–82); *Inno* for 4 Trumpets, 4 Cornets, and Trombone (1984); *Duetto* for Violin and Viola (1985).

BIBL.: J. Weissmann, *G. P.* (Milan, 1957; in Eng.; 2nd ed., 1980); C. Annibaldi, *G. P.: Catalogo delle opere e bibliografia* (Milan, 1971); G. Zosi, *Ricerca e sintesi nell'opera di G. P.* (Rome, 1978); E. Restagno, ed., *P.* (Turin, 1986).

Petrauskas, Kipras, Lithuanian tenor, brother of **Mikas Petrauskas;** b. Vilnius, Nov. 23, 1885; d. there, Jan. 17, 1968. He studied with his brother; appeared in his brother's opera *Birute* (Vilnius, Nov. 6, 1906); then was a singer at the Imperial Opera in St. Petersburg (1911–20); also appeared in Berlin, Paris, and Milan, and made a tour of the U.S. He returned to Lithuania before World War II; in 1950 he received the Stalin Prize.

Petrauskas, Mikas, Lithuanian composer, brother of **Kipras Petrauskas;** b. Kaunas, Oct. 19, 1873; d. there, March 23, 1937. He studied organ with his father; was a church organist at the age of 15; then went to St. Petersburg, where he studied with Rimsky-Korsakov at the Cons. During the abortive revolution of 1905 he became implicated in various political activities and was imprisoned; he was briefly in Vilnius, where he produced his opera *Birute* (Nov. 6, 1906); in 1907 he emigrated to America; settled in Boston in 1914, and founded the Lithuanian Cons. in Boston; produced his operas *The Devil Inventor* (Boston, May 20, 1923) and *Egle, Queen of the Snakes* (Boston, May 30, 1924; Petrauskas himself sang the part of the King of the Snakes); cantatas; etc. He publ. arrangements of Lithuanian songs in the periodical *Kankles* (Boston, 1917–21); further publ. a brief dictionary of musical terms in Lithuanian (Boston, 1916) and an album of Lithuanian songs (Boston, 1922). In 1930 he went back to Lithuania.

Petrella, Clara, Italian soprano; b. Greco Milanese, March 28, 1918; d. Milan, Nov. 19, 1987. She studied with her sister, Micaela Oliva, and with Giannina Russ in Milan; made her debut in 1939 as Liù at the Teatro Puccini in Milan; then sang in several provincial Italian theaters. She made her 1st appearance at La Scala in Milan in 1941, becoming a principal member of the company in 1947; also sang in Rome and Naples; in addition, appeared in concerts. She was particularly noted for her performances of contemporary operas by Italian composers.

Petrella, Errico, noted Italian composer; b. Palermo, Dec. 10, 1813; d. Genoa, April 7, 1877. He studied at the age of 8 with the violinist Del Giudice in Naples and then at the Cons. there, becoming a free boarder when he was 11; his teachers included Bellini, Furno, Ruggi, and Zingarelli. While still a student, he received a commission to write his 1st opera, *Il Diavolo color di rosa* (July 1829), for Naples's Teatro della Fenice; it proved a success, but led him to be expelled from the Cons. for showing such daring at his age; nevertheless, he continued to receive private instruction from Ruggi. After producing 5 more operas during the next decade, he devoted himself mainly to teaching singing. In 1851 he was named music director of Naples's Teatro Nuovo, where he successfully produced his opera *Le precauzioni* (May 20, 1851); his next opera, *Elena di Tolosa* (Teatro del Fondo, Naples, Aug. 12, 1852), proved even more successful, prompting him to compose his 1st serious opera, *Marco Visconti* (Teatro San Carlo, Naples, Feb. 9, 1854), which scored a brilliant success and spread his name throughout Italy; it also led to the production of his best-known serious opera, *Jone* (La Scala, Milan, Jan. 26, 1858). His greatest notoriety came with his opera *I promessi sposi* (Lecco, Oct. 2, 1869). Petrella was the last representative of the old Neapolitan school. He was at his best in buffo works, for his serious operas could not compete with the dramatic masterpieces of Verdi.

BIBL.: G. Carotti, *Cenni biografici e ritratto di E. P.* (Turin, 1877); F. Guardione, *Di E. P. e della traslazion e della salma da Genova a Palermo* (Palermo, 1908); G. Cosenza, *Vita e opere di E. P.* (Rome, 1909); G. Siciliano, *Di E. P., musicista palermitano* (Palermo, 1913).

Petrelli, Eleanora (née **Wigström**), Swedish soprano; b. Simtuna, April 9, 1835; d. Chicago, Feb. 21, 1904. While touring Finland as a member of a small theatrical company, she married a wealthy Russian named Petrov, and Italianized her married name to Petrelli. She studied in Milan with Lamperti, and in Paris with Viardot-García. After her husband died in 1869, she virtually abandoned the stage, but continued to give concerts in Russia, Germany, and Scandinavian countries. In 1886 she settled in Stockholm, but soon went to Chicago, where she established a school for vocal culture. She publ. a number of songs.

Petri, Egon, eminent German pianist and pedagogue of Dutch descent; b. Hannover, March 23, 1881; d. Berkeley, Calif., May 27, 1962. His father, Henri Wilhelm Petri (1856–1914), was a Dutch violinist who served as concertmaster in Hannover and of the Leipzig Gewandhaus Orch.; his mother was a singer. He studied violin and organ as well as piano from an early age; began piano lessons with Carreño, later studying with Buchmayer, Draeseke, and Busoni; also received composition lessons from Kretzschmar. Having pursued a career as an orch. violinist and as a member of his father's string quartet, he launched his career as a piano virtuoso in 1902; subsequently toured extensively in Europe; was also active as a teacher, serving on the faculties of the Royal Manchester College of Music (1905–11) and the Berlin Hochschule für Musik (1921–26); then taught in Zakopane. On Jan. 11, 1932, he made his U.S. debut in N.Y., then performed on both sides of the Atlantic until the outbreak of World War II; also taught at Boston's Malkin Cons. (1934–35). After World War II, he resumed his extensive tours; having taught at Cornell Univ. (1940–46), he then settled in California to teach at Mills College (1947–57) and the San Francisco Cons. (1952–62). He made his farewell concert appearance in a recital in 1960. As Busoni's foremost student, he followed in his mentor's grand manner of piano virtuosity. His performances of Bach and Liszt were formidable; he also championed the works of Alkan and Medtner as well as Busoni.

Petri, Michala, gifted Danish recorder player; b. Copenhagen, July 7, 1958. She began to play at the incredible age of 3 and appeared on Danish radio when she was 5; made her concert debut as a soloist in Copenhagen in 1969. She formed a trio with her mother, a harpsichordist, and her cellist brother, and toured widely with it. She studied with Ferdinand Conrad at the Hannover Staatliche Hochschule für Musik (1970–76). In addition to chamber music performances, she toured extensively as a soloist; made her U.S. debut with N.Y.'s 92nd St. Y Chamber Orch. in 1982, and first played in Japan in 1984. Her repertoire ranges from the early Baroque era to contemporary music; she has commissioned a number of composers to write works for her.

Petrić, Ivo, Slovenian composer; b. Ljubljana, June 16, 1931. He studied composition with Škerjanc and conducting with Švara at the Ljubljana Academy of Music (1950–58). In 1962 he founded a group dedicated to the promotion of new music;

was ed.-in-chief of the publ. division of the Union of Slovenian Composers (from 1970), serving as secretary of the latter (1969–80). His compositions are Romantic in their inspiration, and agreeably modernistic in technical presentation.

WORKS: ORCH.: 3 syms. (1954, 1957, 1960); *Concerto Grosso* for Strings (1955); *Divertimento* (1956); Concerto for Flute and Chamber Orch. (1955–57); Concerto for Clarinet and Chamber Orch. (1958); *Concertante Suite* for Bassoon and Strings (1959); *Concertante Overture* (1960); *Concertante Music* for Wind Quintet, Timpani, and Strings (1962); *Croquis sonores* for Harp and Chamber Ensemble (1963); *Mosaics* for Clarinet and Chamber Ensemble (1964); *Symphonic Mutations* (1964); *Epitaph* for Harp, Clarinet, Violin, Cello, Strings, and Percussion (1965); *Integrali v barvah* (Integrals in Colors; 1968); *Burlesque pour les temps passés* for Trombone and Orch. (1969); *Music Concertante* for Piano and Orch. (1970); *Dialogues concertants* for Cello and Orch. (1972); *3 Images* for Violin and Orch. (1973); *Nocturnes and Games* (1973); *Fresque symphonique* (1973); *Episodes lyriques* for Oboe and Chamber Orch. (1974); *Gemini Concerto* for Violin, Cello, and Orch. (1975); *Thus Played Kurent,* symphonic poem for Viola and Orch. (1976); *Jeux concertants* for Flute and Orch. (1978); *Hommage à Johannes* (1978); *Toccata concertante* for 4 Percussionists and Orch. (1979); *The Song of Life* for Mezzo-soprano and Orch. (1981); *The Picture of Dorian Gray* (1984); Trumpet Concerto (1986); *Dresden Concerto* for 15 Strings (1987). **CHAMBER:** 3 wind quintets (1953, 1959, 1974); Bassoon Sonata (1954); Oboe Sonata (1955); Flute Sonata (1955); Clarinet Sonata (1956–57); *7 Movements* for 7 Instruments (1963); *Jeux à 3* for Cello, Percussion, and Harp (1965); *Jeux à 4* for Flute, Piano, Harp, and Cello (1966); *Little Chamber Concerto* for Oboe, English Horn, Bass Clarinet, Horn, Harp, Piano, and String Quartet (1966); *5 Movements* for Oboe, and Harp or String Quartet (1967); *Intarzije* (Inlaid Work) for Wind Trio, Horn, Trumpet, Trombone, Percussion, and String Quintet (1968); *Quatuor 69* for String Quartet (1969); *Capriccio* for Cello and 8 Instruments (1974); Violin Sonata (1976); Concerto for 5 Percussionists (1978); *Episodes poetiques* for Oboe and 9 Instruments (1979); *Leipzig Chamber Music* for 5 Players (1983); *Quatuor 1985* for String Quartet (1985); *Fantasies and Nocturnes* for Violin, Clarinet, and Piano (1986); also a cantata, *Pierre de la mort* (Stone of Death; 1962).

Petridis, Petros (John), eminent Turkish-born Greek composer; b. Nigdé, July 23, 1892; d. Athens, Aug. 17, 1977. He studied in Constantinople at the American Robert College; received instruction in piano from Hegey and in harmony from Selvelli; then went to Paris and read law at the Sorbonne and political science at the École Libre des Sciences Politiques (1911–14); later studied with Wolff (1914) and Roussel (1919). He became a Greek citizen (1913); subsequently was a music critic for English, American, and Greek publications, dividing his time between Paris and Athens. His use of Byzantine modalities, adorned with contemporary harmonies, reveals the influence of Greek culture.

WORKS: STAGE: Opera, *Zefyra* (1923–25; rev. 1958–64); ballet, *O pramateftis* (The Pedlar; 1941–43; Athens, May 6, 1944); incidental music to Euripides's *Iphigenia in Tauris* (Athens, Oct. 15, 1941); *Kleftikoi horoi* (Cleftic Dances; 1922); 5 syms.: No. 1, *Greek* (1928–29; Athens, Jan. 16, 1933); No. 2, *Lyric* (1941; Athens, Dec. 11, 1949); No. 3, *Parisian* (1944–46; Geneva, 1949); No. 4, *Doric* (1941–43; Athens, May 20, 1945); No. 5, *Pastoral* (1949–51; rev. 1972–73); Concerto Grosso for Winds and Timpani (c.1929); *Greek Suite* (1929–30; Athens, Nov. 27, 1932); Studies for Small Orch. (Athens, Jan. 29, 1934); 2 piano concertos (1934, rev. c.1948; 1937); *Vyzantini thyssia* (Byzantine Offering; 1934–35); *Ionian Suite* (c.1935); Cello Concerto (1936); *Dighenis Akritas* (1933–39; Athens, May 17, 1940); *Chorale and Variations on Kyrie ton dynameon* for Strings (1940; Athens, June 28, 1941); *Chorale and Variations on Christos anesti* for Strings (1941–43; Athens, May 20, 1945); *Largo* for Strings (Athens, Feb. 6, 1944); *Issagoghi pentihimi ke heroiki* (Funeral and Heroic Overture; 1944;

Athens, May 20, 1945); *Hayos Pavlos*, oratorio for Narrator, Vocal Soloists, 8 Secondary Solo Voices, Chorus, and Orch. (1950; Athens, June 29, 1951); *Requiem ya ton aftorkratora* (Requiem for the Emperor) for Vocal Soloists, Chorus, and Orch. (1952–64); Violin Concerto (1972); 2–piano Concerto (1972). **CHAMBER:** Piano Trio (c.1933); String Quartet (1951; unfinished); piano pieces; also songs.

Petrobelli, Pierluigi, prominent Italian musicologist; b. Padua, Oct. 18, 1932. He studied composition with Pedrollo at Padua's Liceo Musicale and musicology with Ronga at the Univ. of Rome (arts degree, 1957). Upon receiving a Fulbright grant, he continued his studies with Lockwood, Mendel, and Strunk at Princeton Univ. (M.A., 1961), and also took courses at Harvard Univ. and the Univ. of Calif., Berkeley. He was librarian-archivist at Parma's Istituto di Studi Verdiani (1964–69); became a lecturer (1968) and later a reader in music history at the Univ. of Parma; was named librarian of the Pesaro Cons. (1970). He received his *libera docenza* in 1972, and then served as a lecturer in music (1973–77) and reader in musicology (1977–80) at King's College, London. In 1980 he was made director of the Istituto di Studi Verdiani in Parma; from 1981 to 1983 he served as prof. of music history at the Univ. of Perugia; then was a prof. at the Univ. "La Sapienza" of Rome (from 1983). He publ. the valuable study *Giuseppe Tartini: Le fonti biografiche* (Vienna, London, and Milan, 1968); with W. Rehm, ed. the critical edition of Mozart's *Il Re pastore* for the *Neue Mozart Ausgabe*.

Petrov, Andrei (Pavlovich), Russian composer; b. Leningrad, Sept. 2, 1930. He studied composition at the Leningrad Cons. with Evlakhov, graduating in 1954. In 1957 he joined the Communist party. In his music he follows the general precepts of socialist realism, ethnic in thematic material, euphonious in harmony, energetic in rhythm, stimulating in modalities, optimistic in contemporary philosophy, realistic in treatment. **WORKS: STAGE: OPERA:** *Peter the First* (Leningrad, 1975). **BALLETS:** *The Magic Apple Tree* (Leningrad, Nov. 8, 1953); *The Station Master*, after Pushkin (Leningrad, May 9, 1955); *The Shore of Hope* (1959); *The Creation of the World* (1971); *Pushkin* (1979). **MUSICAL:** *We Want to Dance* (1967). **ORCH.:** *Pioneer Suite* (1951); *Sport Suite* (1953); *Radda and Lioko*, symphonic poem (1954); *Festive Overture* (1955); *Songs of Today*, symphonic cycle (1965); *Poem*, in memory of those fallen in the siege of Leningrad, for Strings, Organ, 4 Trumpets, 2 Pianos, and Percussion (1965). **VOCAL:** *The Poem of a Young Pioneer* for Soprano, Mezzo-soprano, and Orch. (1959); *Poème pathétique* for Baritone, Chorus, and Percussion, commemorating the centennial of Lenin's birth (1970), to words by Soviet poets; *Pushkin*, vocal-poetic sym. for Narrator, Mezzo-soprano, Chorus, 2 Harps, and Orch. (1978).
BIBL.: A. Kenigsberg, *A. P.* (Moscow, 1959); L. Markhasev, *A. P., Familiar and Unfamiliar* (Leningrad, 1974).

Petrov, Ivan (Ivanovich), prominent Russian bass; b. Irkutsk, Feb. 29, 1920. He studied with A. Mineyev at the Glazunov Music College in Moscow (1938–39); then joined the Kozlovsky opera group; became a soloist with the Moscow Phil. in 1941. In 1943 he joined the staff of the Bolshoi Theater in Moscow; his most celebrated interpretation was in the title role of *Boris Godunov*, inviting comparisons with Chaliapin. He made several tours as a member of the Opera of the Bolshoi Theater in Europe, Japan, and the U.S.
BIBL.: I. Nazarenko, *I. P.* (Moscow, 1957).

Petrov, Nikolai (Arnoldovich), outstanding Russian pianist; b. Moscow, April 14, 1943. He studied with Tatiana Kestner at the Moscow Central Music School (1951–61), then continued his training with Yakov Zak at the Moscow Cons. (graduated, 1967). He won 2nd prize in both the Van Cliburn (1962) and Queen Elisabeth of Belgium (1964) competitions; then pursued a remarkable career as a virtuoso, touring widely in the Soviet Union and Eastern Europe; also performed in Western Europe and North America. As a result of the renewed U.S.-Soviet cultural exchange program, he appeared as soloist with Yuri Termirkanov and the N.Y. Phil. at N.Y.'s Avery Fisher Hall in 1986. His repertoire ranges from Classical to contemporary Soviet music; he has given 1st performances of works by Khachaturian, Khrennikov, Shchedrin, and other Soviet composers, and also tackled the original version of the Liszt transcriptions of the Paganini études.

Petrov, Osip (Afanasievich), celebrated Russian bass; b. Elizavetgrad, Nov. 15, 1807; d. St. Petersburg, March 11, 1878. He joined the Zhurakhovsky opera troupe and made his debut in Cavos's *The Cossack Poet* in Elizavetgrad (1826); received instruction from Cavos. In 1830, Lebedev, the director of the St. Petersburg Imperial Opera, heard him sing with an inferior company at a fair in Kursk, and immediately engaged him. Petrov made his debut in St. Petersburg as Sarastro that same year. The enormous compass of his voice, its extraordinary power and beautiful quality, combined with consummate histrionic skill, secured for him recognition as one of the greatest of Russian bassos; this place he held throughout his long career (he appeared on the stage for the last time on March 10, 1878, on the eve of his death). He created the roles of Susanin in Glinka's *Life for the Tsar* (1836), Ruslan in *Ruslan and Ludmila* (1842), the Miller in Dargomyzhsky's *Rusalka* (1856), and Varlaam in Mussorgsky's *Boris Godunov* (1874).
BIBL.: *Recollections of the 50th Anniversary of O.A. P.* (St. Petersburg, 1876); V. Stasov, *O.A. P.*, in vol. III of his collected works (St. Petersburg, 1894); A. Kompaneisky, "A Great Russian Singer," *Russkaya Muzykalnaya Gazeta*, 9 (1903); E. Lastotchkina, *O. P.* (Moscow, 1950).

Petrovics, Emil, Serbian-born Hungarian composer; b. Nagybecskerek, Feb. 9, 1930. He went to Budapest (1941) and studied at the Academy of Music there with Sugár (1949–51), Viski (1951–52), and Farkas (1952–57); was director of the Petőfi Theater (1960–64); taught at the Academy of Music (from 1969); served as director of the Hungarian State Opera (1986–90).
WORKS: STAGE: OPERAS: *C'est la guerre* (Budapest Radio, Aug. 17, 1961; 1st stage perf., Budapest, March 11, 1962; awarded the Kossuth Prize, 1966); *Lysistrate*, after Aristophanes (1962; rev. 1971); *Bűn és bűnhődés* (Crime and Punishment), after Dostoyevsky (Budapest, Oct. 26, 1969). **BALLET:** *Salome* (1978). **ORATORIOS:** *Jónás könyve* (The Book of Jonah; 1966); *Ott essem el én* (Let Me Die There) for Male Chorus and Orch. (1972). **ORCH.:** Flute Concerto (1957); Sym. for String Orch. (1962). **CHAMBER:** *Cassazione* for Brass (1953); String Quartet (1958); *4 Self-Portraits in Masks* for Harpsichord (1958); Wind Quintet (1964); *Passacaglia in Blues* for Bassoon and Piano (1964; as a ballet, Budapest, 1965); *Deux mouvements* for 1 or 2 Cimbaloms (1977); *Rhapsody* No. 1 for Violin (1982) and No. 2 for Viola (1983); also cantatas and choruses.

Petrucci, Ottaviano dei, Italian music publisher; b. Fossombrone, June 18, 1466; d. Venice, May 7, 1539. He was the descendant of an impoverished family of the nobility. He went to Venice about 1490; petitioned in 1498 for the exclusive privilege of printing "canto figurato" and "intabolature d'organo e de liuto" in the Venetian dominions for a period of 20 years; the privilege was granted on May 25, 1498. His 1st vol., *Harmonice musices odhecaton A*, was issued on May 15, 1501; it contained 96 works, mostly French chansons for 3 and 4 Voices. It was followed by *Canti B* (1501) and *Canti C* (1503), which contained 49 and 137 works, respectively. In 1507 he became the 1st printer to publ. lute tablature. When the war of the League of Cambrai against the Venetian Republic made further work impossible, he returned to Fossombrone (1511), leaving his associates Amedeo Scotto and Nicolò da Rafael to oversee his affairs in Venice. He was active as a publisher in Fossombrone until about 1521, bringing out eds. of both musical and non-musical works. He received a 15-year privilege from Pope Leo X in 1513 for printing mensural music and organ tablature (the privilege to publ. keyboard music was revoked in 1516); also received a 5-year extension of his Venetian privilege in 1514; ceased publishing from 1516 to 1519, again most likely due to the unsettled times. In 1520 he built a paper mill in Acqua Santa, near Fossombrone; was recalled to Venice by the senate in 1536 to supervise the publication of Latin and Italian classical texts. His eds., printed with great neatness, are rare and highly prized specimens of early presswork. In Venice he brought out eds. of works by leading composers of the Netherlands school, as well as by Italian composers. His publications in Fossombrone continued to highlight Italian music, with the French school displacing the Netherlands masters. Modern eds. of his publications include the following: K. Jeppesen, ed., *Die mehrstimmige italienische Laude um 1500: Das 2. Laudenbuch des O. d.P. (1507)* (Leipzig and Copenhagen, 1935); R. Schwartz, ed., *O. P.: Frottole, Buch I und IV*, Publikationen Älterer Musik, VIII (Leipzig, 1935); H. Hewitt, ed., *Harmonice Musices Odhecaton A* (Cambridge, Mass., 1942; 2nd ed., rev., 1946); G. Cesari, R. Monterosso, and B. Disertori, eds., *Le frottole nell' edizione principe di O. P., I: Libri, I, II, e III*, Istituta et Monumenta, i/1 (1954); B. Disertori, ed., *Le frottole per canto e liuto intabulate da Franciscus Bossinensis*, Istituzioni e Monumenti dell'arte Musicale Italiana, new series, iii (1964); H. Hewitt, ed., *O. P.: Canti B numero cinquante (Venice, 1502)*, Monuments of Renaissance Music, II (1967).

BIBL.: A. Schmid, *O. d.P. da Fossombrone und seine Nachfolger im sechzehnten Jahrhunderts* (Vienna, 1845; Italian tr. by B. Revel in *Bollettino Bibliografico Musicale*, Milan, 1931–33); D. Vernarecci, *O. d.P. da Fossombrone* (Fossombrone, 1881; 2nd ed., 1882); J. Weckerlin, *P. Harmonice musices odhecaton* (Paris, 1885); K. Jeppesen, "Die neuentdeckten Bücher der Lauden des O. d.P.," *Zeitschrift für Musikwissenschaft*, XII (1929–30); G. Reese, "The First Printed Collection of Part-Music: The *Odhecaton*," *Musical Quarterly* (Jan. 1934); C. Boer, *Chansonvormen op het einde van de XVde eeuw: Een studie naar aanleiding van P.'s "Harmonice musices odhecaton"* (Amsterdam, 1938); C. Sartori, *Bibliografia delle opere musicali stampate da O. P.* (Florence, 1948); idem, "Nuove conclusive aggiunte alla 'Bibliografia del P.'," *Collectanea Historiae Musicae*, I (1953); K. Jeppesen, *La frottola: Bemerkungen zur Bibliographie der ältesten weltlichen Notendrucke in Italien* (Copenhagen, 1968); S. Boorman, "The 'First' Edition of the *Odhecaton A*," *Journal of the American Musicological Society*, XXX (1977); J. Noble, "O. P.," *Essays in Honor of Myron P. Gilmore* (Florence, 1977).

Petrushka, Shabtai (Arieh), German-born Israeli composer; b. Leipzig, March 15, 1903. He studied at the Inst. of Technology in Berlin-Charlottenburg, and received an engineering diploma; studied music at the Leipzig Cons.; was a violinist in various Berlin theater orchs. (1928–33); after the advent of the Nazis in 1933, he was a member of the orch. of the Jewish Kulturbund, for which he wrote incidental music. He emigrated to Palestine in 1938; served as an arranger and conductor of the Palestine Broadcasting Service (1938–48); then was assistant director of music of the Israel Broadcasting Service (1948–58) and head of the music division of the Israel Broadcasting Authority (1958–68); from 1969 to 1981 he taught at the Rubin Academy of Music in Jerusalem.

WORKS: *The Broken Blackboard*, musical for children (1969); String Trio (1939); *4 Movements* for Symphonic Band (1953); *5 Oriental Dances* for Orch. (1954); *Piccolo Divertimento* for Symphonic Band (1970); *3 Jewish Melodies* for 2 Flutes and 3 Clarinets (1972); *Hebrew Melodies* for Wind Quintet (1974); Wind Quartet (1975); *Jewish Melodies* for Brass Quintet (1974); *3 Sephardic Songs* for Female Chorus (1976); Sonatina for Horn and String Quartet (1982); *Little Suite* for Band (1986).

Petrželka, Vilém, noted Czech composer and pedagogue; b. Královo Pole, near Brünn, Sept. 10, 1889; d. Brno, Jan. 10, 1967. He studied with Janáček at the Brno Organ School (1905–8) and in 1910 became Janáček's assistant at the school; subsequently took private lessons in Prague with Vítězslav Novák; taught at the Phil. Society School in Brno (1914–19), and in 1919 became a prof. at the newly formed Brno Cons. In his compositions he continued the national tradition of modern Moravian music; he was mainly influenced by Janáček, but expanded his resources and on occasion made use of jazz rhythms, quarter-tones, and other modernistic procedures.

WORKS: DRAMATIC: Opera, *Horník Pavel* (The Miner Paul; 1935–38); cantata, *Modlitba k slunci* (A Prayer to the Sun; 1921; Brno, Feb. 13, 1922); symphonic drama, *Námořník Mikuláš* (Mariner Nicholas) for Narrator, Soli, Chorus, Organ, Jazz Band, and Orch., employing quarter-tones (1928; Brno, Dec. 9, 1930). **ORCH.:** *Věčný návrat* (Eternal Return), symphonic poem (1922–23; Brno, Feb. 10, 1924); *Suite* for String Orch. (1924–25); *Dramatic Overture* (1932; Brno, March 26, 1933); *Partita* for String Orch. (1934); *Sinfonietta* (1941; Brno, Jan. 22, 1942); Violin Concerto (1943–44; rev. 1946); *Pastoral Sinfonietta* (1951–52); Sym. (1956); 2 song cycles, with Orch.: *Živly* (The Elements; 1917) and *Cesta* (The Way; 1924; also with Piano). **CHAMBER:** 5 string quartets (1909; 1914–15; *Fantasy*, op. 19, 1927; *Suite*, 1932; 1947); *Z intimních chvil* (From Intimate Moments) for Violin and Piano (1918); *Štafeta* (The Courier), 4 songs for Voice and String Quartet (1926–27); Solo Cello Sonata (1930); Violin Sonata (1932); Piano Trio (1936–37); *4 Impromptus* for Violin and Piano (1939–40); *Divertimento* for Wind Quintet (1941); *Serenade* for Nonet or Chamber Orch. (1945); *2 Pieces* for Cello and Piano (1947); Violin Sonatina (1953); *Miniatures* for Wind Quintet (1953); *2 Pieces* for Viola and Piano (1959); *Fantasy* for String Quartet (1959); *Suite* for String Trio (1961). **PIANO:** Sonata (1908); *Songs of Poetry and Prose* (1917); *Suite* (1930); *5 nálad* (5 Moods) (1954); also choruses, including the popular patriotic part-song for Men's Chorus *To je má zem* (This Is My Land; 1940); folk-song arrangements.

BIBL.: L. Firkušný, *V. P.* (Prague, 1946).

Pettersson, Gustaf Allan, remarkable sui generis Swedish composer; b. Västra Ryd, Sept. 19, 1911; d. Stockholm, June 20, 1980. His father was a blacksmith; his mother was a devout woman who could sing; the family moved to Stockholm, and lived in dire poverty. Pettersson sold Christmas cards and bought a violin from his meager returns. He also practiced keyboard playing on a church organ. In 1930 he entered the Stockholm Cons., studying violin and viola with J. Ruthström and music theory with H.M. Melchers. From 1940 to 1951 he played viola in the Stockholm Concert Society Orch., and also studied composition with Otto Olsson, Tor Mann, and Blomdahl. In his leisure hours he wrote poetry; he set 24 of his poems to music. In 1951 he went to Paris to study with Honegger and Leibowitz. Returning to Sweden, he devoted himself to composition in large forms. His music is permeated with dark moods, and he supplied deeply pessimistic annotations to his syms. and other works. In 1963 he began suffering from painful rheumatoid arthritis; he stubbornly continued to compose while compulsively proclaiming his misfortunes in private and in public print. He described himself as "a voice crying out, drowned in the noise of the times." The Stockholm Phil. played several of his syms., but when his 7th Sym., originally scheduled for its American tour in 1968, was taken off the program, Pettersson, wrathful at this callous defection, forbade performance of any of his music in Sweden. Stylistically, Pettersson's music is related to Mahler's symphonic manner, in the grandiosity of design and in the passionate, exclamatory dynamism of utterance. Most of his syms. are cast in single movements, with diversity achieved by frequent changes of mood, tempo, meter, and rhythm. Characteristically, they all, except No. 10, are set in minor keys.

WORKS (all 1st perf. in Stockholm unless otherwise given): **ORCH.:** 16 syms.: No. 1 (1950–51; withdrawn with instructions to perform it only posthumously); No. 2 (1952–53; Swedish Radio, May 9, 1954); No. 3 (1954–55; Göteborg, Nov. 21, 1956); No. 4 (1958–59; Jan. 27, 1961); No. 5 (1960–62; Nov. 8, 1963); No. 6 (1963–66; Jan. 21, 1968); No. 7 (1966–67; Oct. 13, 1968); No. 8 (1968–69; Feb. 23, 1972); No. 9 (1970; Göteborg, Feb. 18, 1971); No. 10 (1971–72; Swedish TV, filmed Dec. 16, 1973, for delayed broadcast of Jan. 14, 1974); No. 11 (1971–

73; Bergen, Oct. 24, 1974); No. 12, *De döda på torget* (The Dead on the Square), with Mixed Chorus, to words by Pablo Neruda (1973–74; Sept. 29, 1977); No. 13 (1976; Bergen, June 7, 1978); No. 14 (1978; Nov. 26, 1981); No. 15 (1978; Nov. 19, 1982); No. 16, originally Concerto for Alto Saxophone and Orch. (Feb. 24, 1983); 3 concertos for String Orch.: No. 1 (1949–50; April 6, 1952); No. 2 (1956; Dec. 1, 1968); No. 3 (1956–57; March 14, 1958); Concerto No. 1 for Violin, String Quartet, and Orch. (1949; March 10, 1951); *Symphonic Movement* (1976; as *Poem*, Swedish TV, Dec. 24, 1976); Concerto No. 2 for Violin and Orch. (1977–78; Jan. 25, 1980). **VOCAL:** 6 songs for Voice and Piano (1935); *24 Barfotasånger* (24 Barefoot Songs) for Voice and Piano (1943–45); *Vox humana*, 18 songs for Soprano, Alto, Tenor, Baritone, Mixed Chorus, and String Orch., to texts by American Indians (1974; March 19, 1976). **CHAMBER:** 2 *Elegies* for Violin and Piano (1934); *Fantasy Piece* for Viola (1936); *4 Improvisations* for Violin, Viola, and Cello (1936); *Andante espressivo* for Violin and Piano (1938); *Romanza* for Violin and Piano (1942); *Fugue in E* for Oboe, Clarinet, and Bassoon (1948); 7 sonatas for 2 Violins (1951–52). **BIBL.:** L. Aare, *A. P.* (Stockholm, 1978); P. Rapoport, *Opus Est: 6 Composers from Northern Europe* (London, 1978); idem, *A. P.* (Stockholm, 1981); B. Nielsen, "P. and Langgaard," *Nordic Sounds* (March 1988).

Pettiford, Oscar, prominent American jazz double bass player, cellist, and bandleader of black and Indian descent; b. on an Indian reservation, Okmulgee, Okla., Sept. 30, 1922; d. Copenhagen, Sept. 8, 1960. He played in his father's band; at the age of 11 he took up the piano, then the bass at 14; left the family band in 1941 to begin his own career, making appearances with Charlie Barnet, Roy Eldridge, and Dizzy Gillespie. He also worked with Coleman Hawkins, Jimmy Blanton, and Duke Ellington. A master of the string bass, he was also a good cellist. He was one of the most significant bop figures of his era.

Petyrek, Felix, Czech composer and teacher; b. Brünn, May 14, 1892; d. Vienna, Dec. 1, 1951. He studied piano with Godowsky and Sauer; composition with Schreker at the Univ. of Vienna (graduated in 1919). He taught piano at the Salzburg Mozarteum (1919–21); then at the Berlin Hochschule für Musik (1921–23); taught composition at the Odeon Athenon in Athens (1926–30); from 1930 to 1939, taught at the Stuttgart Cons.; then at the Cons. and Univ. of Leipzig (1939–49); subsequently at the Vienna Academy of Music (1949–51). Among modern composers, he occupied a fairly advanced position; in his melodic writing, he adopted the scale of alternating whole tones and semitones as a compromise between tonality and atonality. **WORKS: STAGE:** *Der Garten des Paradieses*, opera after Andersen (1923–41; Leipzig, Nov. 1, 1942); *Die arme Mutter und der Tod*, fairy play after Andersen, with Small Orch. (Winterthur, 1923); pantomimes: *Tahi* and *Komödie*. **ORCH.:** Sym. (1919); Sinfonietta (1921); 2 concertos for 2 Pianos (1931, 1949). **CHAMBER:** Sonata for Violin and Piano (1913); String Quartet (1913); String Quintet (1914); Piano Trio (1921); Divertimento for 8 Wind Instruments (1922); Sextet for Clarinet, String Quartet, and Piano (Donaueschingen Festival, July 30, 1922); also *Die Litanei* for Boys' Chorus, 2 Trumpets, 2 Harps, and Percussion (ISCM Festival, Zürich, June 21, 1926); songs; piano pieces.

Petz (Pez), Johann Christoph, German composer; b. Munich, Sept. 9, 1664; d. Stuttgart, Sept. 25, 1716. He was a chorister in Munich (1676–86); then resided in Liège and in Bonn (until 1705); in 1706 he was appointed court composer at Stuttgart, where he remained until his death. He publ. a set of 12 sonatas (Augsburg, 1696) under the title *Duplex Genius sive Gallo-italus Instrumentorum Concentus;* also a Psalm. Two of his operas were produced in Bonn.

Petzel, Johann Christoph. See **Pezel, Johann Christoph.**

Petzet, Walter, German pianist, composer, and pedagogue; b. Breslau, Oct. 10, 1866; d. Dresden, Aug. 13, 1941. He studied with Kleffel in Augsburg; later at the Munich Academy of Music with Rheinberger and others; in 1887 he went to Minneapolis, where he taught piano until 1890; from 1891 to 1896, he taught piano at the Berlin Scharwenka Cons.; in 1896 he succeeded Busoni as a prof. at the Helsinki Cons.; from 1898 to 1910, was a prof. at the Karlsruhe Cons.; subsequently taught at the Weimar Cons. (1910–13), at the Klindworth-Scharwenka Cons. in Berlin (1913–16), and at the Dresden Cons. (1917–21). He wrote 2 piano concertos, numerous piano pieces, etc.; wrote music criticism for the *Signale für die Musikalische Welt.*

Petzold, Rudolf, English composer and teacher; b. Liverpool (of a German father and English mother), July 17, 1908. He studied composition with Jarnach at the Cologne Hochschule für Musik (1930–33); taught there in 1937–38, and at the Frankfurt Hochschule für Musik in 1941–42; then rejoined the faculty of the Cologne Hochschule für Musik (1946–70), and was its deputy director (1960–69). He wrote a number of instrumental and choral works in a compact polyphonal style, among them 3 syms. (1942, 1953, 1956); 4 string quartets (1932, 1948, 1955, 1972); Concerto for Violin and String Orch. (1960); Piano Trio (1961); Cello Sonata (1964); Sonata for Violin Unaccompanied (1965); Piano Sonata (1967); Violin Sonata (1969); several sacred cantatas and other choral music.

Petzoldt, Richard (Johannes), German musicologist; b. Plauen, Nov. 12, 1907; d. Leipzig, Jan. 14, 1974. He studied at the Univ. of Berlin, where his teachers were Abert, Schering, Moser, Sachs, Hornbostel, Schünemann, and Blume; received his Ph.D. in 1933 with the dissertation *Die Kirchenkompositionen und weltlichen Kantaten Reinhard Keisers* (publ. in Düsseldorf, 1935). He ed. the *Allgemeine Musikalische Zeitung* (1935–39) and the periodical *Musik in der Schule* (1949–59); was a prof. of music history at the Univ. of Leipzig (1952–67). His publs. include *Beethoven* (Leipzig, 1938; 2nd ed., 1947); *Schubert* (Leipzig, 1940; 2nd ed., 1947); *Schumann* (Leipzig, 1941; 2nd ed., 1947); *Mozart* (Wiesbaden, 1948; 2nd ed., 1965); *Johann Sebastian Bach und Leipzig* (Leipzig, 1950); *Die Oper in ihrer Zeit* (Leipzig, 1956); iconographies of Bach (Leipzig, 1950; 2nd ed., 1970), Verdi (Leipzig, 1951), Beethoven (Leipzig, 1952; 7th ed., rev., 1968), Schubert (Leipzig, 1953), Tchaikovsky (Leipzig, 1953), Handel (Leipzig, 1954; 2nd ed., 1960), Glinka (Leipzig, 1955), Schumann (Leipzig, 1956), Mozart (Leipzig, 1956; 3rd ed., 1961); *Beethoven* (Leipzig, 1970; 2nd ed., 1973); and *Schütz* (Kassel, 1972).

Peuerl (Peurl, Bäwerl, Bäurl, Beurlin), Paul, German organist, organ builder, and composer; b. probably in Stuttgart (baptized), June 13, 1570; d. after 1625. He was an organist at Horn, Lower Austria (from 1602), and of the Protestant church school in Steyer (1609–25). He is generally acknowledged to be the originator of the German variation-suite; following the example of the lutenists, he expanded the earlier combination of pavane and galliard into a new 4-movement suite form for strings. He was also an organ builder. He ed. the following (all publ. in Nuremberg): *Newe Padouan, Intrada, Däntz und Galliarda* (1611); *Weltspiegel, das ist: Neue teutsche Gesänger* (1613); *Ettliche lustige Padovanen, Intraden, Galliarden, Couranten und Däntz sampt zweyen Canzon zu 4 Stimmen* (1620); *Gantz neue Padouanen, Auffzüg, Balletten, Couranten, Intraden und Däntz* (1625). Selections from his works, ed. by K. Geiringer, appear in Denkmäler der Tonkunst in Österreich, LXX, Jg. XXXVI/2 (1929). **BIBL.:** P. Frankl, *P. P., ein österreichischer Vokal- und Instrumentalkomponist um 1600* (diss., Univ. of Vienna, 1915); P. Nettl, "Zur Lebensgeschichte P. P.," *Bulletin de la Société "Union Musicologique,"* V (1925); K. Geiringer, "P. P.," *Studien zur Musikwissenschaft,* XVI (1929); O. Wessely, "Neues zur Lebensgeschichte P. O.s," *Jb des Oberösterreichischen Musealvereins,* XCV (1950); R. Flotzinger, "Einige neue Daten zu P. P.," *Mitteilungen der Österreichischen Gesellschaft für Musikwissenschaft,* V (1975).

Pevernage, Andries, Flemish composer; b. Harelbeke, near Courtrai, 1543; d. Antwerp, July 30, 1591. He was a boy chorister in Courtrai. On Feb. 11, 1563, he became choirmaster at St. Salvator in Bruges; on Oct. 17, 1563, he was appointed choirmaster of Notre Dame in Courtrai; due to religious upheavals, he fled to Antwerp in 1578; he returned to Courtrai to resume his post in 1584. On Oct. 29, 1585, he took the oath as choirmaster of Notre Dame in Antwerp. He was greatly honored there, and was buried in the Cathedral.

Works: [6] *Missae* for 5 to 7 Voices (Antwerp, 1602); [39] *Cantiones aliquot sacrae* for 6 to 8 Voices, *quibus addita sunt* [29] *elogia nonnulla* (Douai, 1578); 14 motets, *Laudes vespertinae B. Mariae Virginis* (Antwerp, 1604); etc. *Chansons . . . livre premier, contenant chansons spirituelles* for 5 Voices (Antwerp, 1589); *Chansons . . . livre second* for 5 Voices (Antwerp, 1590); *Chansons . . . livre troisième* for 5 Voices (Antwerp, 1590); *Chansons . . . livre quatrième* for 6 to 8 Voices (Antwerp, 1591); *Chansons . . . tant spirituelles que prophanes* for 5 Voices (Antwerp, 1606–7); etc. His complete chansons were ed. by G. Hoekstra in Recent Researches in the Music of the Renaissance, LX–LXIV (1983).

Bibl.: J. Stellfeld, *A. P.: Zijne leven, zijne werken* (Louvain, 1943).

Peyser, Joan (née **Gilbert**), American musicologist, editor, author, and journalist; b. N.Y., June 12, 1931. She played piano in public at 13; majored in music at Barnard College (B.A., 1951); studied musicology with Paul Henry Lang at Columbia Univ. (M.A., 1956); then devoted herself mainly to musical journalism; enlivened the music pages of the Sunday *N.Y. Times* with book reviews and breezy colloquies with composers; wrote scripts for the television series "The World of Music"; acted as musical adviser to the N.Y. City Board of Education. She publ. the popular book *The New Music: The Sense Behind the Sound* (N.Y., 1971; 2nd ed., rev., 1981 as *Twentieth Century Music: The Sense Behind the Sound*); created considerable excitement in the music world with her biography *Boulez: Composer, Conductor, Enigma* (N.Y., 1976); trying to penetrate the eponymous enigma, she undertook a journey to the interior of France, where she interviewed family and friends of her subject, with a fervor suggesting that Boulez was indeed the 4th B of music. From 1977 to 1984 she was ed. of the *Musical Quarterly*, the 1st woman to occupy this position; during her tenure she attempted to veer away from the prevalent musicological sesquipedalianism toward plain diction. Among her other publs. are *The Orchestra: Origins and Transformations* (N.Y., 1986) and *Leonard Bernstein: A Biography* (N.Y., 1987).

Pezel (**Petzold, Petzel, Pezelius,** etc.), **Johann Christoph,** German bandsman and composer; b. Glatz, Dec. 5, 1639; d. Bautzen, Oct. 13, 1694. He was made 4th Kunstgeiger in the Leipzig town band in 1664, and in 1670 was promoted to Stadtpfeifer. Because of the plague, he left Leipzig in 1681 for Bautzen, where he remained until his death. He publ. several collections: *Musica vespertina Lipsicaca* (1669); *Hora decima musicorum Lipsiensium, oder Musicalische Arbeit zum Ab-blasen* (1670); *Intraden* (1676); *Delitiae musicales, oder Lust-Music* (1678); etc. His most interesting work is *Fünffstimmigte blasende Musik* (1685).

Bibl.: E. Wienandt, *J. P.: Thematic Catalogue* (N.Y., 1983).

Pfannstiehl, Bernhard, German organist; b. Schmalkalden, Dec. 18, 1861; d. Freiberg, Oct. 21, 1940. He became blind in infancy, and was educated at the Inst. for the Blind in Leipzig; studied piano at the Leipzig Cons.; was thrice winner of the Mendelssohn Prize. Following Liszt's advice, he made a specialty of the organ; was a church organist in Leipzig (1896–1903), in Chemnitz (1903–11), and at the Kreuzkirche in Dresden (1912–34). He enjoyed a great reputation as an interpreter of Bach.

Bibl.: K. Hasse, "B. P.," *Die Orgel* (1910).

Pfatteicher, Carl F(riedrichs), American organist and teacher; b. Easton, Pa., Sept. 22, 1882; d. Philadelphia, Sept. 29, 1957. He studied theology in Germany and at Harvard Univ. (Th.D., 1912); taught Latin and German at various schools; then was a prof. of music at Phillips Academy in Andover, Mass. (1912–47); from 1949 he was a lecturer in musicology at the Univ. of Pa. He publ. a number of useful school manuals and collections of sacred music, among them *The Christian Church Year in Part Songs* (1915); *The Christian Church Year in Chorals* (1917); *Thesaurus musicae sacrae* (1920); *The Oxford American Hymnal* (1930); was co-ed. of *The Office Hymns of the Church in Their Plainsong Settings* and *The Church Organist's Golden Treasury.*

Pfeiffer, Georges-Jean, French composer; b. Versailles, Dec. 12, 1835; d. Paris, Feb. 14, 1908. He began his career as a pianist; then was active as a music critic in Paris. He succeeded his father as a partner in the piano firm of Pleyel, Wolff & Cie.

Works: *Le Capitaine Roche,* operetta (1862); *L'Enclume,* opera (Paris, 1884); *Le Légataire universel,* comic opera (Paris, July 6, 1901); 3 piano concertos (1859, 1864, 1883); several symphonic works; much chamber music; songs; piano pieces.

Pfeiffer, Theodor, German pianist and pedagogue; b. Heidelberg, Oct. 20, 1853; d. Baden-Baden, Nov. 9, 1929. He studied piano with Hans von Bülow at the Hoch Cons. in Frankfurt. In 1889 he settled in Baden-Baden as a private teacher. He wrote a Mass, songs, men's choruses, and piano pieces. His recollections of Bülow's remarks in teaching specific works were publ. as *Studien bei Hans von Bülow* (1894; 6th ed., 1909).

Pfitzner, Hans (Erich), eminent German composer and conductor; b. Moscow (of German parents), May 5, 1869; d. Salzburg, May 22, 1949. He studied piano with James Kwast and composition with Iwan Knorr at the Hoch Cons. in Frankfurt; in 1899 he eloped with Kwast's daughter and took her to England, where he married her. In 1892–93 he taught piano and theory at the Cons. of Koblenz; then served as assistant conductor of the Municipal Theater in Mainz (1894–96); from 1897 to 1907 he was on the faculty of the Stern Cons. in Berlin; concurrently he conducted at the Theater Westens (1903–6). During the 1907–8 season he led the renowned Kaim Concerts in Munich. From 1908 to 1918 he was in Strasbourg as municipal music director and also served as dean at the Strasbourg Cons.; from 1910 to 1916 he conducted at the Strasbourg Opera. During the 1919–20 season he was music director of the Munich Konzertverein; from 1920 to 1929 he led a master class at the Berlin Academy of Arts; from 1929 to 1934 he taught composition at the Akademie der Tonkunst in Munich. Being of certified German stock, though born in Russia, he was favored by the Nazi authorities, and became an ardent supporter of the Third Reich; he reached the nadir of his moral degradation in dedicating an overture, *Krakauer Begrüssung,* to Hans Frank, the murderous Gauleiter of occupied Poland in 1944. After the collapse of Hitler's brief millennium, Pfitzner had to face the Denazification Court in Munich in 1948; owing to his miserable condition in body and soul, he was exonerated. He was taken to a home for the aged in Munich, and later was transferred to Salzburg, where he died in misery. Eventually, his body was honorably laid to rest in a Vienna cemetery.

In his better days, Pfitzner was hailed in Germany as a great national composer. He presented a concert of his works in Berlin on May 12, 1893, with excellent auguries. After the premiere of his opera *Der arme Heinrich* in Mainz on April 2, 1895, the critics, among them the prestigious Humperdinck, praised the work in extravagant terms. Even more successful was his opera *Palestrina,* making use of Palestrina's themes, written to his own libretto, which was conducted by Bruno Walter at its 1st performance on June 12, 1917, in Munich. The Pfitzner Society was formed in Munich as early as 1904, and a Hans Pfitzner Assoc. was established in Berlin in 1938, with Furtwängler as president. Although Pfitzner's music is traditional in style and conservative in harmony, he was regarded as a follower of the modern school, a comrade-in-arms of his close contemporary Richard Strauss. Very soon, however, his fame began to dwindle; there were fewer performances of his operas and still fewer hearings of his instrumental works; he himself bitterly complained of this lack of appreciation of his art. It was a miserable end for a once important and capable musician.

WORKS: OPERAS: *Der arme Heinrich* (1891–93; Mainz, April 2, 1895); *Die Rose vom Liebesgarten* (1897–1900; Elberfeld, Nov. 9, 1901); *Das Christ-Elflein* (Munich, Dec. 11, 1906); *Palestrina* (1911–15; Munich, June 12, 1917); *Das Herz* (Berlin and Munich, Nov. 12, 1931). **INCIDENTAL MUSIC:** *Das Fest auf Solhaug*, after Ibsen (Mainz, Nov. 28, 1890); *Das Käthchen von Heilbronn*, after Kleist (Berlin, Oct. 19, 1905); *Gesang der Barden* for *Die Hermannsschlacht*, after Kleist (1906). **ORCH.:** Scherzo in C minor (1887; Frankfurt, Nov. 8, 1888); *3 Preludes*, symphonic excerpts from the opera *Palestrina* (1917); Piano Concerto (Dresden, March 16, 1921; Walter Gieseking, soloist); Violin Concerto (1923; Nuremberg, June 4, 1924); Sym. in C-sharp minor, after the 2nd String Quartet (1932; Munich, March 23, 1933, composer conducting); Cello Concerto No. 1 (Frankfurt, 1935); *Duo* for Violin, Cello, and Chamber Orch. (Frankfurt, Dec. 3, 1937, composer conducting); *Kleine Symphonie* (Berlin, Nov. 19, 1939, Furtwängler conducting); Sym. in C (Frankfurt, Oct. 11, 1940); *Elegie und Reigen* (1940; Salzburg, April 4, 1941); *Krakauer Begrüssung* (1944; written in honor of Hans Frank, Nazi governor of Poland); Cello Concerto No. 2 (Solingen, April 23, 1944, composer conducting); *Elegie* (1947). **CHAMBER:** Cello Sonata (1890); Piano Trio (1896); 4 string quartets (1886, 1903, 1925, 1942); Piano Quintet (1908); Violin Sonata (1918); *5 Klavierstücke* (1941); *6 Studien* for Piano (1943); *Sextet* for Clarinet, Violin, Viola, Cello, Double Bass, and Piano (1945). **VOCAL:** *Von deutscher Seele*, romantic cantata after J. von Eichendorff (1921; Berlin, Jan. 27, 1922); *Das dunkle Reich* for Solo Voices and Orch. (1929; Cologne, Oct. 21, 1930); *Fons salutatis* for Chorus and Orch. (1941); *Kantate*, after Goethe (1948–49; left unfinished; completed by R. Rehan); 106 lieder (1884–1931).

WRITINGS: *Gesammelte Schriften* (2 vols., Augsburg, 1926, 1929; containing Pfitzner's vicious pamphlets against modern ideas about music, including *Futuristengefahr*, directed against Busoni [1917], and *Neue Aestetik der musikalischen Impotenz*, denouncing the critic Paul Bekker); *Über musikalische Inspiration* (Berlin, 1940); *Philosophie und Dichtung in meinem Leben* (Berlin, 1944); *Eindrücke und Bilder meines Lebens* (Hamburg, 1947); W. Abendroth, ed., *Reden, Schriften, Briefe* (Berlin, 1955).

BIBL.: P. Cossmann, *H. P.* (Munich, 1904); R. Louis, *H. P.s "Rose vom Liebesgarten"* (Munich, 1904); C. Wandrey, *H. P.* (Leipzig, 1922); E. Kroll, *H. P.* (Munich, 1924); W. Lütge, *H. P.* (Leipzig, 1924); E. Valentin, *H. P.: Werk und Gestalt eines Deutschen* (Regensburg, 1939); H. Lindlar, *H. P.s Klavier-Lied* (Würzburg, 1940); J. Müller-Blattau, *H. P.* (Potsdam, 1940; 2nd ed., rev., 1969); W. Abendroth, ed., *H. P.: Ein Bild in Widmungen anlässlich seines 75. Geburtstages* (Leipzig, 1944); H. Rutz, *H. P.: Musik zwischen den Zeiten* (Vienna, 1949); K. Müller, *In memoriam H. P.* (Vienna, 1950); D. Henderson, *H.P.: The Composer and His Instrumental Music* (diss., Univ. of Michigan, 1963); H. Rectanus, *Leitmotivik und Form in den musikdramatischen Werken H. P.s* (Würzburg, 1967); W. Dietz, *H. P.s Lieder: Versuch einer Stilbetrachtung* (Regensburg, 1968); W. Abendroth and K.-R. Danler, eds., *Festscrift aus Anlass des 100. Geburtstags und des 20. Todestags H. P.s* (Munich, 1969); E. Busse, *Die Eichendorff-Rezeption im Kunstlied: Versuch einer Typologie anhand von Kompositionen Schumanns, Wolfs, und P.s* (Würzburg, 1975); W. Osthoff, ed., *Symposium H. P.* (*1981: Berlin, Germany*) (Tutzing, 1984); R. Ermen, *Musik als Einfall: H. P.s Position im ästhetischen Diskurs nach Wagner* (Aachen, 1986); E. Wamlek-Junk, *H. P. und Wien: Sein Briefwechsel mit Victor Junk und andere Dokumente* (Tutzing, 1986); J. Williamson, "P. and Ibsen," *Music & Letters* (April 1986); J. Vogel, *H. P.* (Reinbek, 1989).

Pflughaupt, Robert, brilliant German pianist; b. Berlin, Aug. 4, 1833; d. Aachen, June 12, 1871. He studied with Dehn in Berlin, Henselt in St. Petersburg, and Liszt in Weimar, then pursued a career as a virtuoso; wrote a number of agreeable piano pieces. His wife, Sophie (née Shtchepin) Pflughaupt (b. Dvinsk, Russia, March 15, 1837; d. Aachen, Nov. 10, 1867), was also a pupil of Henselt and Liszt and won praise as a pianist.

Pfohl, Ferdinand, German writer on music, teacher, and composer; b. Elbogen, Bohemia, Oct. 12, 1862; d. Bergedorf, near Hamburg, Dec. 16, 1949. He studied law in Prague; in 1885 he went to Leipzig, where he took private lessons in music with Oscar Paul. In 1892 he became the music critic of the influential *Hamburger Nachrichten*, holding this important post until his retirement in 1932; also concurrently taught music theory at the Vogt Cons. in Hamburg. His compositions include the symphonic poems *Die versunkene Glocke*, *Pierrot lunaire*, and *Frau Holle*; a symphonic fantasy, *Das Meer*; piano pieces.

WRITINGS: *Die moderne Oper* (Leipzig, 1894); *Die Nibelungen in Bayreuth* (Dresden, 1897); *Arthur Nikisch als Mensch und Künstler* (Leipzig, 1900; 2nd ed., 1925); *Carl Grammann: Ein Künstlerleben* (Berlin and Leipzig, 1910); *Richard Wagner: Sein Leben und Schaffen* (Berlin, 1911; 4th ed., 1924); *Beethoven* (Berlin, 1922; 2nd ed., 1926).

Pfordten, Hermann Ludwig von der, German writer on music; b. Munich, July 5, 1857; d. there, Nov. 16, 1933. He was the son of a Bavarian minister; studied in Munich and in Leipzig; became a prof. of music history at the Univ. of Munich.

WRITINGS: *Handlung und Dichtung der Bühnenwerke Richard Wagners* (1893; 8th ed., 1922); *Musikalische Essays* (2 vols., 1897, 1899); *Deutsche Musik* (1917; 3rd ed., 1922); *Der Musikfreund* (1923; 8th ed., 1928); *Einführung in Wagners Werke und Schriften* (3rd ed., 1925); biographies of Beethoven (1907; 4th ed., 1922), Mozart (1908; 3rd ed., 1926), Schubert (1916; 3rd ed., 1928), Weber (1919), Schumann (1920), and Robert Franz (1923).

Pfundt, Ernst (Gotthold Benjamin), celebrated German timpanist and inventor; b. Dommitzsch, near Torgau, June 17, 1806; d. Leipzig, Dec. 7, 1871. He studied theology, and at the same time developed extraordinary expertise as a drummer; was invited by Mendelssohn in 1835 to join the Gewandhaus Orch. in Leipzig, where he achieved legendary fame for his rhythmic skill. He was the inventor of the pedal kettledrums; publ. a method for drums (1849; 3rd ed., enlarged by H. Schmidt, 1894).

Phalèse, Pierre, Flemish music publisher; b. Louvain, c.1510; d. there, c.1575. He established a music publishing business in 1545; the printing was done elsewhere, and it was not until 1553 that Phalèse began to print on the premises in Louvain. From 1570 he worked in association with Jean Bellère of Antwerp; also was assisted by his sons, Corneille and Pierre Phalèse the Younger (b. Louvain, c.1550; d. Antwerp, March 13, 1629). Corneille left the business before his father's death and settled in Antwerp as a schoolmaster; Pierre the Younger took over the enterprise, with Bellère continuing his association until his death in 1595.

BIBL.: A. Goovaerts, *Notice biographique sur P.* (1869); idem, *Histoire et bibliographie de la typographie musicale dans le Pays-Bas et les anciens Pay-Bas* (Antwerp and Brussels, 1880); idem, *De muziekdrukkers P. en Bellerus te Leuven* (Antwerp, 1882).

Phile (Fyles, Pfeil, Phyla, etc.), **Philip,** German-American violinist and composer; b. in Germany, c.1734; d. Philadelphia, between Aug. 1 and Nov. 9, 1793. He served in the Pa. German Regiment during the Revolutionary War; was transferred in July 1778 to the Invalid Regiment; was discharged on Jan. 4, 1783; a pension was granted to him on July 11, 1785. He was active in Philadelphia and N.Y.; gave concerts; played in theater orchs.; conducted the orch. of the Old American Co.

of Comedians. His only extant work is *The President's March*, which appears to have been written for George Washington's 1st inauguration (1789); Joseph Hopkinson's (son of Francis Hopkinson) text "Hail Columbia" was added to it, and it was subsequently performed for the 1st time on April 25, 1798.

BIBL.: O. Sonneck, *Report on the "Star Spangled Banner," "Hail Columbia," "America," "Yankee Doodle"* (Washington, D.C., 1909; 2nd ed., rev. and enlarged, 1914).

Philidor (real name, **Danican**), family of famous French musicians:
(1) Michel Danican; b. Dauphiné, c.1600; d. Paris, Aug. 1659. He is the earliest known member of the family, although he never used the name Philidor. He went to Paris about 1620; by 1651 he was in the service of King Louis XIII as a member of the grande écurie (military band), in which he played the oboe, cromorne, and trompette marine.
(2) Jean Danican; b. probably in Dauphiné, c.1620; d. Versailles, Sept. 8, 1679. He most likely was a younger brother or son of **Michel Danican (1)**. He adopted the name Philidor about 1659; by 1657 he was in the royal service; in 1659 he became a phiphre marine; he was also a composer.
(3) André Danican Philidor (l'aîné), son of **Jean Danican (2)**; b. Versailles, c.1647; d. Dreux, Aug. 11, 1730. In 1659 he entered the grande écurie, succeeding **Michel Danican (1)**; in it he played the cromorne, trompette marine, and drums. He subsequently played the oboe, bassoon, and bass cromorne in the royal chapel and chambre du roi. In 1684 King Louis XIV appointed him royal music librarian, a position he held until his death. During his long tenure, he acquired operas, ballets, sacred music, partbooks, etc. from various periods of French history for the collection. A large portion of this collection eventually passed to St. Michael's College, Tenbury. It was sold at auction in London in 1978, and passed to the Bibliothèque Nationale in Paris and the Bibliothèque Municipale in Versailles. The latter library already housed 35 vols. of the royal collection. The Paris Cons. library once housed 59 vols., but through various misfortunes its collection was reduced to 34 vols. Additional vols. are housed in other library collections. Philidor continued to serve as a musician in the royal chapel until 1722, and in the royal service until 1729. By his 1st wife he had 16 children, and by his 2nd, 5. His most famous son was **François-André Danican Philidor (7).**

WORKS: OPÉRAS-BALLETS: *Le Canal de Versailles* (Versailles, July 16, 1687); *Le Mariage de la couture avec la grosse Cathos* (Versailles, 1687?); *La Princesse de Crète* (Marly, 1700?); *La Mascarade du roi de la Chine* (Marly, 1700); *La Mascarade du vaisseau marchand* (Marly, Feb. 18, 1700); *La Mascarade de la noce village* (Marly, 1700); also instrumental works, including dances, marches, etc.
BIBL.: J.-B. Weckerlin, "La Collection P. au Conservatoire de musique de Paris," *Chronique musicale,* IV (1874); E.H. Fellowes, "The P. Manuscripts," *Music & Letters,* XII (1931).
(4) Jacques Danican Philidor (le cadet), son of **Jean Danican (2)** and younger brother of **André Danican Philidor (l'aîné) (3)**; b. Paris, May 6, 1657; d. Versailles, May 27, 1708. In 1668 he became a phiphre in the grande écurie, and subsequently played the cromorne and trompette marine. In 1683 he became a musicien ordinaire de la chapelle, and played the oboe and bassoon. In 1690 he became a member of the chambre du roi. He composed airs, dance music, and marches (only the last are extant). Of his 12 children, 4 became musicians.
(5) Anne Danican Philidor, son of **André Danican Philidor (l'aîné) (3)**; b. Paris, April 11, 1681; d. there, Oct. 8, 1728. In 1698 he became an oboist in the grande écurie. In 1704 he became a member of the royal chapel, and in 1712 of the chambre du roi. He founded the famous Paris concert series known as the Concert Spirituel, which was launched on March 18, 1725; it was disbanded in 1790. He also founded the short-lived Concerts Français (1727–33).

WORKS: *L'Amour vainqueur,* pastoral (Marly, Aug. 9, 1697);

Diane et Endymion, pastoral (Marly, 1698); *Danaé,* opera (Marly, 1701); also a Mass, Te Deum, motets, and instrumental pieces.
BIBL.: S. Blondel, "Origine du Concert Spirituel," *Chronique Musicale,* IV (1874); D. Tunley, "P.'s 'Concerts Français,' " *Music & Letters,* XLVII (1966); D. Pierre, *Histoire du Concert Spirituel 1725–1790* (Paris, 1975).
(6) Pierre Danican Philidor, son of **Jacques Danican Philidor (le cadet) (4)**; b. Paris, Aug. 22, 1681; d. there, Sept. 1, 1731. In 1697 he became a member of the grande écurie, in 1704 an oboist in the royal chapel, and in 1712 a flutist in the chambre du roi. A pastoral he composed in 1697 was given in Marly and Versailles. He also wrote 6 suites for Transverse Flutes (publ. in Paris, 1717–18); 6 suites for 3 Flutes, and Oboes or Violins (1718); and marches.
(7) François-André Danican Philidor, the greatest in the line of musicians in the family, the youngest son of **André Danican Philidor (l'aîné) (3)**; b. Dreux, Sept. 7, 1726; d. London, Aug. 31, 1795. He was a page boy in the royal chapel in Versailles, where he studied music with the maître de chapelle, André Campra. It was also at that time that he learned to play chess. A motet by him was performed in the royal chapel when he was 12. In 1740 he went to Paris, where he supported himself by copying and teaching. His interest in chess continued; he gained distinction as an outstanding player by defeating a number of celebrated chess masters of the day. He publ. a fundamental treatise on chess, *L'Analyze des échecs* (London, 1749; rev. ed., 1777, as *Analyse du jeu des échecs;* there were more than 100 eds. of this book and several trs.). As a member of the St. James Chess Club in London, he gave lectures and demonstrations as a master; a famous chess opening was named after him. In the meantime, he began a successful career as a composer for the theater. His 1st success was *Le Maréchal ferrant* (Paris, Aug. 22, 1761), which was accorded numerous performances. His *Le Sorcier* (Paris, Jan. 2, 1764) was also a triumph. Although *Tom Jones* (Paris, Feb. 27, 1765) was an initial failure, it enjoyed great popularity after its libretto was revised by Sedaine and performed on Jan. 30, 1766. The same fate attended his *Ernelinde, princesse de Vorvège* when it was 1st given at the Paris Opéra on Nov. 24, 1767. It was subsequently revised by Sedaine and performed most successfully as *Ernelinde* in Versailles on Dec. 11, 1773. Philidor continued to compose for the stage until his death, but he allowed his love for chess to take more and more of his time. He made frequent trips to London after 1775 to play at the St. James Chess Club. Philidor was one of the finest early composers of opéra-comique. Although his scores are often hampered by poor librettos, his orch. writing is effective. He was an inventive composer, and introduced the novelty of a vocal quartet a cappella (in *Tom Jones*). He wrote sacred music as well. His choral work, the *Carmen saeculare,* after Horace, proved most successful at its premiere in London on Feb. 26, 1779. Other vocal works include 12 ariettes périodiques.
BIBL.: G. Baretti, *The Introduction to the Carmen Seculare* (London, 1779); G. Allen, *The Life of P., Musician and Chess Player* (Philadelphia, 1858; 2nd ed., 1863; reprint, 1971; 3rd ed., 1865); G.-E. Bonnet, *P. et l'évolution de la musique française au XVIIIe siècle* (Paris, 1921); C. Carroll, *F.-A. D.-P.: His Life and Dramatic Art* (diss., Florida State Univ., 1960); J. Rushton, "P. and the Tragédie Lyrique," *Musical Times,* CXVII (1976).

Philip, Achille, French composer; b. Arles, Oct. 12, 1878; d. Béziers, Hérault, Oct. 12, 1959. He studied at the Paris Cons. with Guilmant (organ) and d'Indy (composition); from 1905 to 1950 he taught organ at the Schola Cantorum in Paris. He wrote an opera, *L'Or du Menhir* (Rouen, 1934); symphonic poems: *Les Djinns* (1913); *Dans un parc enchanté* (1917); *Nymphes et Naiades* (1920); also, a number of sacred works; chamber music; songs.

Philipp, Isidor, eminent French pianist and pedagogue of Hungarian descent; b. Pest, Sept. 2, 1863; d. Paris, Feb. 20,

1958. He was taken to Paris as an infant; studied piano with Georges Mathias at the Paris Cons., winning 1st prize in 1883; then took lessons with Saint-Saëns, Stephen Heller, and Ritter. His concert career was brief, but he found his true vocation in teaching; was a prof. at the Paris Cons. (1893–1934), where he was mentor to many notable pupils, including Albert Schweitzer. In Paris he continued to perform, mostly in chamber music groups; formed a concert trio with Loeb and Berthelier, with which he gave a number of successful concerts. After the outbreak of World War II, he went to the U.S.; arrived in N.Y. in 1941; despite his advanced age he accepted private students, not only in N.Y., but also in Montreal. At the age of 91, he played the piano part in Franck's Violin Sonata (N.Y., March 20, 1955); then returned to France. He publ. some technical studies for piano, among them *Exercises journaliers; Ecole d'octaves; Problèmes techniques; Etudes techniques basées sur une nouvelle manière de travailler; La Gamme chromatique;* made arrangements for 2 pianos of works by Bach, Mendelssohn, Saint-Saëns, and others; also brought out *La Technique de Liszt* (2 vols., Paris, 1932).
BIBL.: H. Bellamann, "I. P.," *Musical Quarterly* (Oct. 1943).

Philippe de Vitry. See **Vitry, Philippe de.**

Philippot, Michel, French composer; b. Verzy, Feb. 2, 1925. He first took courses in mathematics, then studied music at the Paris Cons. (1945–47); also took private lessons with René Leibowitz (1948–50); held various posts with the ORTF (from 1949) and became a prof. at the Cons. (1970); later was active in Brazil.
WORKS: 2 Piano Sonatas (1946, 1973); Overture for Chamber Orch. (1948); Piano Trio (1953); Variations for 10 Instruments (1957); *3 Compositions* for Piano (1958); *Composition* for String Orch. (1959); *Composition* for Double Orch. (1959); *Pièce pour 10* for Chamber Ensemble; *Transformations triangulaires* for 12 Instruments (1962); *Pieces* for Violin (1967); Organ Sonata (1971); Scherzo for Accordion (1972); *Commentariolus Copernicae* for Flute, Clarinet, Bassoon, Horn, Trumpet, Violin, Cello, Piano, and Percussion (1972; Paris, Oct. 22, 1973); *Trio inachevé* for Flute, Clarinet, and Trombone (1973); Octet (1974).

Philips, Peter, important English composer; b. 1560 or 1561; d. Brussels, 1628. His surname was also rendered as **Phillips** or **Phillipps;** after leaving England, he was known as **Petrus Philippus, Pietro Philippi,** and **Pierre Philippe.** He was born into a Roman Catholic family; his name appears in the list of choirboys at St. Paul's Cathedral in London in 1574. He was befriended by a Roman Catholic almoner of St. Paul's, Sebastian Westcote, who was in charge of the music and choirboys there. Upon Westcote's death in 1582, Philips received a bequest of "five poundes thirtene shillings fower pence." He left England in 1582, and arrived at the English College at Douai on Aug. 18; then proceeded to Rome, arriving at the English College there on Oct. 20; was its organist until 1585, and also was in the service of Cardinal Alessandro Farnese. In Feb. 1585 Lord Thomas Paget, a Roman Catholic refugee from England, arrived at the English College. Philips entered his service, and on March 19, 1585, they set out for Italy and Spain; they went to France in Sept. 1586, spending most of their time in Paris from early 1587 to June 1588. They subsequently went to Antwerp, remaining there until Feb. 1589; they then proceeded to Brussels. After Paget's death in early 1590, Philips went to Antwerp and maintained himself by teaching keyboard playing. In 1593 he went to Amsterdam, where he heard and met Sweelinck. On his return to Antwerp, he stopped in Middelburg due to illness. During his stay, he was accused by a fellow Englishman of complicity in a plan to assassinate Queen Elizabeth. He was arrested by the Dutch authorities and taken to The Hague for questioning. After inquiries were made in England, he was exonerated and released. He returned to Antwerp in late 1593; publ. his 1st book of 6-part madrigals in 1596. He entered the service of the Archduke Albert in Brussels in 1597, being employed as one of the 3 organists of the vice-regal chapel until his death. His

collection of 8-part madrigals was publ. in 1598, and it proved highly popular. In later years he held a number of appointments as canon and chaplain, but he was never ordained. On March 9, 1610, he was appointed to a canonry at the collegiate church of St. Vincent, Soignies, but continued to reside in Brussels. On Jan. 25, 1621, he exchanged his prebend at Soignies for a chaplainship at St. Germain Tirlemont; in 1623 he is also described as canon of Béthune in the title page of his *Litaniae Beatae Mariae Virginis.* His 1st extensive collection of sacred works, the *Cantiones sacrae* for 5 Voices, was publ. in 1612. Other collections followed in 1613 and 1616. His last publication was a major collection of motets, *Paradisus sacris cantionibus* (Antwerp, 1628). Philips was highly esteemed as both composer and organist, his keyboard music reflecting the English style at its finest. His outstanding madrigals and motets reflect his adoption of the Roman school as a model for his vocal music.
BIBL.: P. Bergmans, *L'Organiste des archiducs Albert et Isabelle: P. P.* (Ghent, 1903); P. Lyder, *The Latin Sacred Music of P. P.* (diss., N.Y. Univ., 1955); F. Pearson, *The Madrigals of P. P.* (diss., Univ. of Michigan, 1961); L. Pike, *The Vocal Music of P. P., Its Technique and Transcription of Selected Items* (diss., Oxford Univ., 1969–70); idem, "The First English 'Basso continuo' Publication," *Music & Letters,* LIV (1973; concerning *Gemmulae sacrae*); idem, "Marian Symbolism in P.," *Musical Times* (Aug. 1984).

Phillipps, Adelaide, English contralto; b. Stratford-on-Avon, Oct. 26, 1833; d. Karlsbad, Oct. 3, 1882. Her family took her to America as a child; she was trained as a dancer, and made her 1st appearance at the Tremont Theater in Boston on Jan. 12, 1842, in a variety show. She also displayed an early gift as a vocalist, and was introduced to Jenny Lind, who encouraged her to study singing; accordingly she was sent to London, where she took lessons with Manuel García; made her operatic debut in Brescia (1853); continued to sing in Italy under the name Signorina Filippi until 1855, when she returned to Boston to appear in light opera in English; her 1st major appearance on the grand opera stage in America was as Azucena in Verdi's *Il Trovatore* (N.Y., March 17, 1856). After a long and successful tour in Europe (1861–62), she sang with the Boston Ideal Opera Co. from 1879 to 1881. She was advised to go to Karlsbad for her health in 1882, but died shortly after her arrival there.
BIBL.: A. Waterston, *A. P.: A Record* (Boston, 1883).

Phillips, Burrill, American composer; b. Omaha, Nov. 9, 1907; d. Berkeley, Calif., June 22, 1988. He studied music with Edwin Stringham in Denver; then with Howard Hanson and Bernard Rogers at the Eastman School of Music in Rochester, N.Y. (B.M., 1932; M.M., 1933). He taught at the Eastman School of Music (1933–49; 1965–66), the Univ. of Illinois in Urbana (1949–64), the Juilliard School in N.Y. (1968–69), and Cornell Univ. (1972–73). His early music was cast in a neo-Classical style; later he incorporated free serial techniques.
WORKS: STAGE: *OPERAS: Don't We All* (1947; Rochester, N.Y., May 9, 1949); *The Unforgiven* (1981). **BALLETS:** *Katmanusha* (1932–33); *Play Ball* (Rochester, N.Y., April 29, 1938); *Step into My Parlor* (1942); *La piñata* (1969); incidental music. **ORCH.:** *Selections from McGuffey's Reader* (1933; Rochester, N.Y., May 3, 1934); *Sinfonia concertante* (Rochester, N.Y., April 3, 1935); *American Dance* for Bassoon and Strings (Rochester, N.Y., April 25, 1940); *3 Satiric Fragments* (Rochester, N.Y., May 2, 1941); Piano Concerto (1942); *Scherzo* (1944); *Tom Paine Overture* (1946; N.Y., May 15, 1947); *Perspectives in a Labyrinth* for 3 String Orchs. (1962); *Soleriana concertante* (1965); *Yellowstone, Yates, and Yosemite* for Tenor Saxophone and Symphonic Band (1972). **CHAMBER:** Trio for 3 Trumpets (1937); 2 string quartets (1939–40; 1958); Violin Sonata (1941); Partita for Piano Quartet (1947); Cello Sonata (1948); *4 Figures in Time* for Flute and Piano (1952); Oboe Quintet (1967); *Intrada* for Wind Ensemble, Percussion, Piano, Violin, and Cello (1975); *Scena da camera* for Violin and Cello (1978); *Canzona VI* for Wind Quintet (1985); also piano works, includ-

ing 4 sonatas (1942–60); *9 by 9*, a set of 9 variations, each in a meter of 9 beats (1942); *Toccata* (1944); *Commentaries* (1983). VOCAL: *Declaratives* for Women's Chorus and Chamber Orch. (1943); *The Return of Odysseus* for Baritone, Narrator, Chorus, and Orch. (1956); *Letters from Italy Hill* for Soprano, Flute, Clarinet, String Quartet, and Piano (1984).

Phillips, Harvey (Gene), outstanding American tuba player and teacher; b. Aurora, Mo., Dec. 2, 1929. He played the sousaphone in high school; after attending the Univ. of Missouri (1947–48), he joined the Ringling Brothers and Barnum & Bailey Circus Band; then took general music courses at the Juilliard School of Music (1950–54) and at the Manhattan School of Music (1956–58) in N.Y.; played in various ensembles there, including the N.Y. City Ballet Orch., the N.Y. City Opera Orch., the Goldman Band, and the Sym. of the Air; he also was a founding member of the N.Y. Brass Quintet. From 1967 to 1971 he held an administrative position at the New England Cons. of Music in Boston. In 1971 he became a prof. of music at the Indiana Univ. School of Music; was named a distinguished prof. of music there in 1979. He commissioned works for tuba from Gunther Schuller, Robert Russell Bennett, Alec Wilder, and Morton Gould.

Phillips, John, American hippie-style folk singer; b. Parris Island, S.C., Aug. 30, 1935. He played guitar and sang folk songs in his soft baritone voice in Greenwich Village. In 1965 he formed a group dubbed The Mamas and The Papas with the singers Dennis Doherty (b. Halifax, N.S., Nov. 29, 1941), Cass Elliot (real name, Ellen Cohen; b. Baltimore, Sept. 19, 1941; d. Los Angeles, July 24, 1974), and (Holly) Michelle Gilliam (b. Long Beach, Calif., April 6, 1944), who was his wife for a time. The Mamas and The Papas spawned such hits as *California Dreamin'* (1966), *Monday, Monday* (1966), and *Words of Love* (1967); Philips also wrote the hippie smash hit *San Francisco (Be Sure to Wear Flowers in Your Hair)* (1967). In 1967 Phillips, together with the music manager Lou Adler, produced the eventful Monterey Pop Festival, which catapulted into the limelight such rockers as Jimi Hendrix, Janis Joplin, and The Who. But by dint of begetting the careers of others, The Mamas and The Papas exhausted their own seminal fluid, and by 1968 gave up the ghost. They reunited briefly in 1970 to record the album *People Like Us*. Cass Elliot died of a heart attack in her Los Angeles home, and in 1980, John Phillips served 30 days in jail on drug charges in N.Y. A new version of the group arose in 1982.

Phillips, Karen, American pianist, violist, and composer; b. Dallas, Oct. 29, 1942. She studied piano at the Eastman School of Music, and theory at the Juilliard School in N.Y.; she also took lessons in viola, and gave recitals both as a violist and a pianist. She wrote 4 syms., a Cello Concerto, some chamber music, and piano pieces.

Phillips, Montague (Fawcett), English composer and pedagogue; b. London, Nov. 13, 1885; d. Esher, Jan. 4, 1969. He studied with F. Corder at the Royal Academy of Music in London; subsequently taught there. He wrote a light opera, *The Rebel Maid* (London, March 12, 1921), which enjoyed some success; also a Sym. (1911), 2 piano concertos (1907, 1919), overtures, including *In Praise of My Country* (1944), *Empire March* for Orch. (1941), and many choral works.

Phillips, Philip, American singer, hymn-tune composer, and editor; b. Chautauqua County, N.Y., Aug. 13, 1834; d. Delaware, Ohio, June 25, 1895. He sang in a choir as a child; was mainly self-taught in music; taught in singing-schools from age 19; founded Philip Phillips & Co. in Cincinnati (c.1863), which sold pianos and melodeons and publ. Sunday-school songbooks; later was music ed. of the Methodist Books Concern in N.Y. He toured widely in the U.S. as a singing evangelist, being dubbed the "Singing Pilgrim"; made an extensive tour of Europe, the Holy Land, and the Far East (1875), which he related in his book *Song Pilgrimage Around and Throughout the World* (N.Y., 1882); also publ. gospel songs and wrote the hymn-tunes *Home of the Soul* and *One Sweetly Solemn Thought*.

BIBL.: A. Clark, *P. P.: His Songs and Tours* (N.Y., c.1887); R. McCutchan, *Our Hymnody* (N.Y., 1937).

Phinot, Dominique, significant Franco-Flemish composer; b. c.1510; d. c.1555. He was mainly active in Italy; was in the service of the Urbino court, and also worked in Pesaro. He was particularly important for his contribution to the development of the 8-voice double-choir technique. Among his works are 2 masses, 2 Magnificat settings, numerous motets, and many Psalms; he also publ. 2 books of chansons (Lyons, 1548). A complete ed. of his works was prepared by J. Höfler in Corpus Mensurabilis Musicae, LIX (1972–82).

BIBL.: P. Hansen, *The Life and Works of D. P.* (diss., Univ. of North Carolina, 1939); J. Höfler, "D. P. and the Beginnings of Renaissance Polychoral Music," *Zvuk*, no. 10 (1969).

Piaf, Edith (real name, **Giovanna Gassion**), noted French chanteuse; b. Paris, Dec. 19, 1915; d. there, Oct. 11, 1963. Her childhood was tragic; she was abandoned by her mother, an Italian café singer and prostitute; traveled with her father, a circus contortionist, taking part in his act as a shill for his street-corner acrobatics. She then became a street singer in Paris, earning the nickname Piaf (Parisian argot for "sparrow") on account of her ragged and emaciated appearance. She was befriended by a cabaret owner; when he was murdered, she was held by the French police as a material witness. During World War II and the German occupation, she entertained French prisoners in Germany; as a result, she was accused of collaboration, but was exonerated. She made her 1st tour of the U.S. in 1947; sang widely in subsequent years, making appearances in films and on television. Although untutored, she developed a type of ballad singing that was infused with profound sentiment and expressive artistry, eliciting an enthusiastic response from nightclub audiences and sophisticated music critics alike. She composed chansonettes, among which *La Vie en rose* became popular. Her memoirs were publ. as *Au bal de la chance* (Paris, 1958; Eng. tr. as *The Wheel of Fortune*, 1965) and *Ma vie* (Paris, 1964). A film on the early years of her life was produced in Paris in 1982.

BIBL.: S. Berteaut, *P.* (Paris, 1969; Eng. tr., N.Y., 1972); M. Crosland, *P.* (N.Y., 1985); D. Bret, *The P. Legend* (London, 1988).

Piastro, Josef, Russian-American violinist, brother of **Michel Piastro**; b. Kerch, Crimea, March 1, 1889; d. Monrovia, Calif., May 14, 1964. He studied with Leopold Auer at the St. Petersburg Cons.; went to the U.S. in 1920; was concertmaster of the Los Angeles Phil., and conducted children's concerts in Hollywood. In America he assumed the pseudonym Borissoff, to avoid confusion with his brother. He composed *Crimean Rhapsody* for Violin and Piano (1920).

Piastro, Michel, Russian-American violinist, brother of **Josef Piastro**; b. Kerch, Crimea, July 1, 1891; d. N.Y., April 10, 1970. He studied with Leopold Auer at the St. Petersburg Cons.; in 1920, settled in the U.S.; was concertmaster of the San Francisco Sym. Orch. (1925–31) and of the N.Y. Phil. (1931–43). He was conductor of WOR radio's "Longines Symphonette," sponsored by the Longines-Wittnauer Watch Co. (1941–66).

Piatigorsky, Gregor, great Russian-born American cellist and pedagogue, brother of **Alexander Stogorsky;** b. Ekaterinoslav, April 17, 1903; d. Los Angeles, Aug. 6, 1976. He received his 1st music lessons from his father, a violinist; then took cello lessons with Alfred von Glehn at the Moscow Cons.; played in various orchs. in Moscow. In 1921 he left Russia; took cello lessons with Julius Klengel in Leipzig; after serving as 1st cellist of the Berlin Phil. (1924–28), he devoted himself to a solo career. He played the solo part in *Don Quixote* by Richard Strauss under the composer's direction many times in Europe, and was probably unexcelled in this part; Strauss himself called him "mein Don Quixote." He went to America in 1929, and made his American debut in Oberlin, Ohio, on Nov. 5, 1929; played the Dvořák Concerto with the N.Y. Phil., eliciting great praise (Dec. 29, 1929). He was regarded as the world's finest cellist after Casals; continued giving solo recitals and appearing with major European and American orchs. for many years; gave 1st performances of several cello works commissioned by him from Hindemith, Dukelsky, Castelnuovo-Tedesco, and others. He became a naturalized U.S. citizen in 1942; taught at the Curtis Inst. of Music in Philadelphia (1942–51) and at the Berkshire Music Center in Tanglewood; was a prof. at the Univ. of Southern Calif., Los Angeles (1962–76); presented a series of trio concerts with Heifetz and Pennario. He was the recipient of honorary D.Mus. degrees from Temple Univ., Columbia Univ., the Univ. of Calif., Los Angeles, etc. He publ. an autobiographical vol., *Cellist* (N.Y., 1965).

Piatti, Alfredo (Carlo), renowned Italian cellist and teacher; b. Borgo Canale, near Bergamo, Jan. 8, 1822; d. Crocetto di Mozzo, July 18, 1901. He received his primary musical education from his father, the violinist Antonio Piatti, and his great uncle, the cellist Gaetano Zenetti, whom he succeeded as cellist in the local theater orch. when he was only 8; continued his studies with Merighi at the Milan Cons. (1832–37), playing his own concerto at a public Cons. concert (Sept. 21, 1837). He made his 1st tour of Europe in 1838; perf. with Liszt in Munich in 1843; made his Paris debut in 1844; on May 31 of that year he appeared in London for the 1st time, and soon established a remarkable reputation as a master of his instrument; also taught privately and at the Royal Academy of Music. He owned an outstanding Stradivari cello of 1720, which is now known as "The Piatti." He publ. a cello method (London, 1878); also composed 2 cello concertos (1874, 1877), a Concertino for Cello and Orch. (1863), 6 sonatas for Cello and Piano, 12 caprices for Cello, and various arrangements of 18th-century music.

BIBL.: M. Latham, *A. P.* (London, 1901); F. Niecks, "Recollections of Violoncellists: Alfred P.," *Monthly Musical Record,* XLIX (1919).

Piccaver (real name, **Peckover**), **Alfred,** English tenor; b. Long Sutton, Lincolnshire, Feb. 15, 1884; d. Vienna, Sept. 23, 1958. He studied at the Metropolitan School in N.Y.; made his operatic debut as Romeo in Prague in 1907; then continued his studies there and in Milan. In 1910 he deputized at the Vienna Court (later State) Opera in the Italian season; remained in Vienna as a leading lyric tenor until 1937. His repertoire included Don José, Florestan, Walther von Stolzing, Lensky, and Andrea Chénier; he also took part in the 1st Austrian performance of *La Fanciulla del West* in 1913. He appeared in Chicago (1923–25); in 1924 he sang Cavaradossi and the Duke of Mantua at Covent Garden in London. From 1937 to 1955 he taught voice in London; then returned to Vienna to attend the opening of the new building of the Staatsoper; he remained in Vienna as a voice teacher until his death.

Picchi, Mirto, Italian tenor; b. Florence, March 15, 1915; d. there, Sept. 25, 1980. He studied in Florence; made his operatic debut as Radames in 1946 in Milan. He subsequently acquired a fine reputation as a singer in a wide repertoire, which included not only the Italian standard operas, but also modern roles, such as Peter Grimes in Britten's opera and Tom Rakewell in Stravinsky's *The Rake's Progress.* He gave his farewell performance as Mozart's Don Basilio at La Scala in 1974.

Picchi, Silvano, Argentine composer; b. Pisa, Italy, Jan. 15, 1922. His family emigrated to Argentina while he was a child; he studied composition with Constantino Gaito, Alberto Ginastera, Arturo Luzzatti, Gilardo Gilardi, and Floro Ugarte in Buenos Aires. He was the music critic of *La Prensa* in Buenos Aires.

WORKS: *Suite irreverente* for Orch. (1949); *Música para caballos* for Orch. (1952); Piano Concerto (Buenos Aires, July 23, 1967); Violin Concerto (Buenos Aires, Aug. 12, 1968); *Discantus* for Guitar and Bassoon (1968); *Euè,* funeral chant for String Orch. on an African theme (Buenos Aires, March 18,

1969); *Sinfonia breve* (1970); *Mozartiana* for Strings (1971); 2 trios for Oboe, Violin, and Piano; guitar pieces; songs.

Piccinni, (Vito) Niccolò (Nicola) (Marcello Antonio Giacomo), significant Italian composer; b. Bari, Jan. 16, 1728; d. Passy, near Paris, May 7, 1800. His father was a violinist at Bari's Basilica di San Nicola, and his maternal uncle was the composer **Gaetano Latilla.** His precocity manifested itself at an early age; thanks to Muzio Gaeta, archbishop of Bari, he was able at 14 to enter Naples's Conservatorio di S. Onofrio, where he studied with Leo and Durante; upon graduation (1754), he commenced his career as a composer for the stage with his comic opera *Le Donne dispettose* (Naples, 1754). His theatrical instinct led him to select librettos rich in dramatic content; his melodic invention was fresh, and his arias were written in a pleasing style eminently suited to the voice; he elaborated the conventional climactic scenes so that dramatic interest was sustained to the end; he varied the tempos and the harmonies in the ensembles, which further contributed to the general effect. His *Zenobia* (Naples, Dec. 18, 1756) was his 1st attempt at a serious opera. After several other operas for Naples, he received a commission to write an opera for Rome, *Alessandro nelle Indie* (Jan. 21, 1758); it was followed by his comic opera *La Cecchina, ossia La buona figliuola* (Rome, Feb. 6, 1760), which proved a great success at home and abroad. In subsequent years he wrote prolifically for the stage, producing well over 100 operas for the major Italian theaters. Making his home in Naples, he served as 2nd maestro di cappella at the Cathedral, was active as an organist in convents, and taught singing. Piccinni's fortunes in Rome declined with the rise of Anfossi, his former pupil and protégé, in 1773. However, he still found success in Naples with a 2nd *Alessandro nelle Indie* (Jan. 12, 1774) and *I Viaggiatori* (1775). In 1776 he was called to Paris by the French court, where his presence precipitated the "querelle célèbre" between the "Gluckists" and "Piccinnists." Piccinni's 1st French opera, *Roland* (Jan. 27, 1778), won considerable success. He then served as director of an Italian troupe in Paris (1778–79). Although he was promised by the Paris Opéra that his *Iphigénie en Tauride* would be produced before Gluck's masterpiece on the same subject, it was not given until Jan. 23, 1781, some 2 years after the Gluck premiere. While it was fairly successful, he gained his only major success with the opera *Didon* (Fontainebleau, Oct. 16, 1783), the same year in which he finally was granted a pension by the French court. In 1784 he was appointed maître de chant at the École Royale de Chant et de Déclamation Lyrique in Paris. In spite of their rivalry, Piccinni held the highest regard for Gluck; indeed, he suggested that an annual memorial concert be given in Gluck's memory, but financial support was not forthcoming. Upon the death of another rival, Sacchini, Piccinni spoke in homage at his funeral. With the coming of the French Revolution, Piccinni lost his post as maître de chant and his pension. In 1791 he returned to Naples; upon his daughter's marriage to a French Jacobite, he was placed under house arrest in 1794; he finally gained freedom in 1798 and returned to Paris, where he obtained a partial restoration of his pension; his appointment as 6th inspector at the Cons. came when he was too ill to pursue an active life. Piccinni demonstrated a remarkable facility in writing both comic and serious operas. His historical importance rests upon his establishment of the Italian operatic style as the model for his French and German successors. His son **Luigi (Lodovico) Piccinni** (b. 1764; d. Passy, July 31, 1827) was also a composer; studied with his father and then wrote operas for Paris and several Italian cities; was Kapellmeister to the Swedish court in Stockholm (1796–1801); then taught singing. Piccinni had another son, who in turn sired an illegitimate son, **Louis Alexandre (Luigi Alessandro; Lodovico Alessandro) Piccinni** (b. Paris, Sept. 10, 1779; d. there, April 24, 1850), who also became a composer; studied piano with Haussmann and composition with Le Sueur; also received some instruction from his grandfather; was active as an accompanist and rehearsal pianist in several Parisian theaters, and was also active as a conductor; taught in various French cities, serving as director of the Toulouse music school (1840–44); wrote numerous works for the theater.

BIBL.: P. Coquéau, *Entretiens sur l'état actuel de l'opéra de Paris* (Paris, 1779); J.-B. de La Borde, *Essai sur la musique ancienne et moderne* (Paris, 1780); P. Ginguené, *Notice sur la vie et les ouvrages de Nicolas P.* (Paris, 1801); G. le Brisoys Desnoiresterres, *La Musique française au XVIIIᵉ siècle: Gluck et P. 1774–1800* (Paris, 1872); E. Thoinan, *Notes bibliographiques sur la guerre musicale des Gluckistes et P.stes* (Paris, 1878); H. de Curzon, *Les Dernières Années de P. à Paris* (Paris, 1890); J. Popovici, *La buona figliuola von Nicola P.* (Vienna, 1920); A. della Corte, *P.: settecento italiano* (Bari, 1928); P. La Rotella, *N. P.: Commemorato nel II centenario della nascità* (Bari, 1928); N. Pascazio, *L'Uomo P. e la "Querelle célèbre"* (Bari, 1951); J. Rushton, "Iphigénie en Tauride": The Operas of Gluck and P.," *Music & Letters*, LIII (1972); idem, "The Theory and Practice of P.sme," *Proceedings of the Royal Musical Association*, XCVIII (1971–72); M. Hunter, "The Fusion and Juxtaposition of Genres in Opera Buffa 1770–1800: Anelli and P.'s 'Griselda,'" *Music & Letters* (Oct. 1986).

Pichl, Wenzel (actually **Václav**), Bohemian violinist and composer; b. Bechin, Sept. 23, 1741; d. Vienna, Jan. 23, 1805. He studied violin with the local Kantor, Jan Pokorný, and composition with Seger in Prague. He was made 1st violinist of the Vienna court theater (c.1770); served as music director and Kammerdiener (valet) to Archduke Ferdinando d'Este, the Austrian governor of Lombardy, in Milan (1777–96), and then in Vienna. He wrote some 900 works, including 13 operas, over 30 masses, more than 90 syms. or symphonie concertantes, over 30 concertos or concertinos, about 20 serenatas, minuets, dances, and a vast amount of chamber music.

BIBL.: R. Kolisko, *W. P.s Kammermusik* (diss., Univ. of Vienna, 1918).

Pick-Mangiagalli, Riccardo, Italian pianist and composer; b. Strakonice, Bohemia, July 10, 1882; d. Milan, July 8, 1949. He was of mixed Italian and Bohemian parentage; studied at the Cons. Giuseppe Verdi in Milan with Appiani (piano) and Ferroni (composition). He began his career as a successful concert pianist, but later turned exclusively to composition. In 1936 he succeeded Pizzetti as director of the Cons. Giuseppe Verdi, and held this post until his death.

WORKS: STAGE: OPERAS: *Basi e Bote* (1919–20; Rome, March 3, 1927); *Casanova a Venezia* (Milan, Jan. 19, 1929; orch. suite as *Scene carnevalesche*, Milan, Feb. 6, 1931); *L'Ospite inatteso* (Milan-Turin-Genoa Radio, Oct. 25, 1931); *Il notturno romantico* (Rome, April 25, 1936). **DANCE:** *Il salice d'oro*, ballet (1911–12; Milan, 1914); *Sumitra* (1917; Frankfurt, 1922); *Mahit*, ballet-fable with singing (Milan, March 20, 1923); *La Berceuse* (San Remo, Feb. 21, 1933); *Variazioni coreografiche* (San Remo, April 13, 1935). **ORCH.:** *Sortilegi*, symphonic poem for Piano and Orch. (Milan, Dec. 13, 1917); *Notturno e rondo fantastico* (1914; Milan, May 6, 1919); *Humoresque* for Piano and Orch. (1916); *2 preludi* (Rome, March 1, 1921); *4 poemi* (Milan, April 24, 1925); *Piccola suite* (Milan, June 12, 1927); *Preludio e fuga* (Rome, March 11, 1928); *Preludio e scherzo sinfonico* (Milan, Oct. 22, 1938); Piano Concerto (1944); also a Violin Sonata; String Quartet (1909); piano pieces; songs.

BIBL.: F. Abbiati, "Musicisti contemporanei: R. P.-M.," *Emporium*, LXXIII (Bergamo, 1931).

Picka, František, Czech organist, conductor, and composer; b. Strašice, near Hořovice, May 12, 1873; d. Prague, Oct. 18, 1918. Of a musical family, he received a solid education in Prague; held several posts as a chorus master and opera conductor. His opera, *Malíř Reiner* (The Painter Reiner), was produced in Prague (April 28, 1911); the bulk of his works consists of church music, including 9 masses and many other works in an effective contrapuntal style.

Picken, Laurence (Ernest Rowland), English zoologist, biologist, musicologist, and ethnomusicologist; b. Nottingham, July 16, 1909. He studied the natural sciences at Trinity College, Cambridge (B.A., 1931; M.A., 1935; Ph.D., 1935; D.Sc., 1952). In 1944 he became a Fellow at Jesus College, Cambridge; from 1946 to 1966 he was assistant director of research in zoology at Cambridge Univ.; from 1966 to 1976 he was engaged at the Faculty of Oriental Studies there. In 1944 he went to China as a member of the British Council Scientific Mission; studied the *ch'in* there with Hsü Yuan-Pai and Cha Fu-Hsi; in 1951 he took lessons in Turkish music from Nejdet Senvarol in Istanbul. In 1962 he became ed. of the *Journal of the International Folk Music Council;* in 1959 he was a visiting prof. of zoology at the Univ. of Washington in Seattle. He was ed. of *Musica Asiatica* (1977–84); ed. the series *Music from the Tang Court* (from 1981); contributed articles to many learned journals. He publ. the comprehensive study *Folk Musical Instruments of Turkey* (London, 1975); also ed., with E. Dal, E. Stockmann, and K. Vetterl, *A Select Bibliography of European Folk Music* (Prague, 1966), and, with K. Pont, *Ancient Chinese Tunes* (London, 1973).

Picker, Tobias, American composer; b. N.Y., July 18, 1954. He studied with Wuorinen at the Manhattan School of Music (B.M., 1976) and Carter at the Juilliard School (M.M., 1978); held various awards, including a Guggenheim fellowship (1981); was composer-in-residence of the Houston Sym. Orch. (1985–87). He pursued an interest in serial techniques without abandoning tonality. The rhythms in many of his works are co-functional with melodic progressions.

WORKS: ORCH.: 2 piano concertos: No. 1 (1980); No. 2, *Keys to the City* (1983); Violin Concerto (1981); *Nova* for Piano and Orch. (San Francisco, Dec. 19, 1981); 2 syms.: No. 1 (1982; San Francisco, April 23, 1983); No. 2 (Houston, Oct. 25, 1986); *Encantadas* for Narrator and Orch. (1983); *Dedication Anthem* for Band (1984). **CHAMBER:** 4 sextets for Various Instruments: No. 1 (1973); No. 2 (1976); No. 3 (1977); No. 4, *The Blue Hula* (1981); *Rhapsody* for Violin and Piano (1978); Octet (1978); *Romance* for Violin and Piano (1979); *Serenade* for Piano and Wind Quintet (1983); *Pian-o-rama* for 2 Pianos (1984); Piano Quintet (N.Y., May 6, 1988); solo piano pieces.

Pierce, Webb, American country-music singer, guitarist, and songwriter; b. near West Monroe, La., Aug. 8, 1926; d. Nashville, Tenn., Feb. 24, 1991. He took up the guitar in his youth and began his career as a performer on KMLB radio in Monroe, La.; in 1950 became a member of the "Louisiana Hayride" radio program on KWKH in Shreveport and also launched his recording career. His recording of *Back Street Affair* (1952) brought him national recognition, and was followed by the standard country paean to strong liquid spirits, *There Stands the Glass* (1953). In 1952 he became a member of the "Grand Ole Opry" in Nashville, Tenn. In subsequent years he made many hit recordings, including *In the Jailhouse Now* (1955) and *Why, Baby, Why?* (1955), the latter with Red Scovine. Pierce's vocal style may be most accurately described as piercing in the best honky-tonk tradition.

Pierné, (Henri-Constant-) Gabriel, noted French composer, conductor, and organist, cousin of **Paul Pierné;** b. Metz, Aug. 16, 1863; d. Ploujean, near Morlaix, July 17, 1937. He studied at the Paris Cons. (1871–82), where his teachers were Marmontel (piano), Franck (organ), and Massenet (composition); he won 1st prizes for piano (1879), counterpoint and fugue (1881), and organ (1882); was awarded the Grand Prix de Rome (1882) with the cantata *Edith;* succeeded Franck as organist at Ste.-Clotilde (1890), where he remained until 1898. He was assistant conductor (1903–10) and conductor (1910–34) of the Concerts Colonne; was elected a member of the Académie des Beaux-Arts in 1925. His music reveals the hand of an expert craftsman.

WORKS: STAGE: OPERAS: *La Coupe enchantée* (Royan, Aug. 24, 1895; rev. version, Paris, Dec. 26, 1905); *Vendée* (Lyons, March 11, 1897); *La Fille de Tabarin* (Paris, Feb. 20, 1901); *On ne badine pas avec l'amour* (Paris, May 30, 1910); *Sophie Arnould,* lyric comedy, based on episodes from the life of the famous singer (Opéra-Comique, Feb. 21, 1927). **BALLETS AND PANTOMIMES:** *Le Collier de saphirs* (1891); *Les Joyeuses*

Commères de Paris (1892); *Bouton d'or* (1893); *Le Docteur Blanc* (1893); *Salomé* (1895); *Cydalise et le chèvre-pied* (1919; Paris, Jan. 15, 1923; as an orch. suite, 1926); *Impressions de Music-Hall*, "ballet à l'Américaine" (Paris, April 6, 1927); *Giration* (1934); *Fragonard* (1934); *Images*, "divertissement sur un thème pastoral" (Paris, June 19, 1935). ORATORIOS: *La Croisade des enfants* for Mixed Choir of Children and Adults (Paris, Jan. 18, 1905); *Les Enfants à Bethléem* for Soloists, Children's Chorus, and Orch. (Amsterdam, April 13, 1907); *Les Fioretti de St. François d'Assise* (1912). ORCH.: *Suite de concert* (1883); *Première suite d'orchestre* (1883); *Ouverture symphonique* (1885); *Piano Concerto* (1887); *Marche solonnelle* (1889); *Pantomime* (1889); *Scherzo-Caprice* for Piano and Orch. (1890); *Poème symphonique* for Piano and Orch. (1901); *Ballet de cour* (1901); *Paysages franciscains* (1920); *Gulliver au pays de Lilliput* (ISCM Festival, Paris, June 23, 1937). CHAMBER: *Pastorale variée dans le style ancien* for Wind Instruments (also for Piano); *Berceuse* for Violin and Piano; *Caprice* for Cello and Piano; *Canzonetta* for Clarinet and Piano; *Solo de concert* for Bassoon and Piano; *Variations libres et Finale* for Flute, Violin, Viola, Cello, and Harp. PIANO: *15 pièces* (1883); *Etude de concert*; *Album pour mes petits amis* (containing the famous *Marche des petits soldats de plomb*); *Humoresque*; *Rêverie*; *Ariette dans le style ancien*; *Pastorale variée*; *Sérénade à Colombine*; *Sérénade vénitienne*; *Barcarolle* for 2 Pianos. SONG CYCLES: *Contes* (1897); *3 Adaptations musicales* (1902); *3 mélodies* (1904); 38 other songs. Also harp music; folk-song arrangements; etc.

BIBL.: G. Masson, *G. P., musicien lorrain* (Nancy and Metz, 1987).

Pierné, Paul, French composer, cousin of **(Henri-Constant-) Gabriel Pierné;** b. Metz, June 30, 1874; d. Paris, March 24, 1952. He studied at the Paris Cons. with Lenepveu and Caussade; wrote a number of works, which were occasionally performed in Paris: the operas *Le Diable galant* (1913), *Emilde*, and *Mademoiselle Don Quichotte*; a ballet, *Le Figurinai*; 2 syms.; several symphonic poems (*Jeanne d'Arc*, *Cléopâtre*, *De l'ombre à la lumière*, *Nuit évocatrice*, *Rapsodie Lorraine*, etc.); choral works; organ pieces; a song cycle, *Schéhérazade*; piano pieces.

Pierpont, James, American composer; b. Boston, 1822; d. Winter Haven, Fla., 1893. In 1857 he publ. a ballad entitled *One Horse Open Sleigh* (composed in 1850); in 1859 it was publ. under the title *Jingle Bells, or The One Horse Open Sleigh* (the original music is reprinted in facsimile in R. Jackson's *Popular Songs of 19th-Century America*, N.Y., 1976); however, while the original words and the music to the verse are the same as those known today, the original music to the chorus is different. This song did not acquire its wide popularity as a Christmas song until the 20th century; during the 19th century, Pierpont's most popular works were *The Little White Cottage, or Gentle Nettie Moore* (1857); *We Conquer or Die* (1861); and *Strike for the South* (1863); the last 2 of these were rallying songs for the Confederacy during the Civil War (his father, in contrast, was a fiery abolitionist minister). He was the uncle of the millionaire financier John Pierpont Morgan.

BIBL.: F. Lovering, "Jingle Bells: Its Author Was a Rover," *Musical Courier* (Dec. 1959).

Pierre, Constant (-Victor-Désiré), French writer on music; b. Passy, near Paris, Aug. 24, 1855; d. there, Feb. 12, 1918. He was a pupil at the Paris Cons.; played the bassoon in various Paris orchs.; from 1881 he devoted himself mainly to musical journalism; was for many years ed. of *Le Monde Musical*.

WRITINGS: All publ. in Paris: *La Facture instrumentale à l'Exposition universelle de 1889* (1890); *Les Facteurs d'instruments de musique, les luthiers et la facture instrumentale* (1893); *L'École de chant de l'Opéra, 1672–1807* (1895); *Bernard Sarrette et les origines du Conservatoire national de musique et de déclamation* (1895); *Le Conservatoire national de musique et de déclamation: documents historiques et administratifs* (1900); *Histoire du Concert Spirituel 1725–1790* (MS, 1900;

publ. in Paris, 1975); *Les Hymnes et chansons de la Révolution française, aperçu général et catalogue avec notices* (1904).

Pierson (real name, **Pearson**), **Henry Hugo (Hugh),** English composer; b. Oxford, April 12, 1815; d. Leipzig, Jan. 28, 1873. He was educated at Trinity College, Cambridge; in 1839, went to Germany, where he took courses in music with Rinck and Reissiger; also with Tomaschek in Prague. He entered the circle of Mendelssohn in Leipzig; after a brief term as Reid Prof. of music at the Univ. of Edinburgh (1844–45), he returned to Germany, where he remained for the rest of his life; married Caroline Leonhardt, who wrote the German librettos for his operas. He changed his name from the original form Pearson to Pierson in order to secure proper pronunciation by Germans; used the pen name Edgar Mansfeldt for his publ. music. His music reflects the profound influence of Schumann. He won wide acceptance in Germany with his incidental music to part 2 of Goethe's *Faust*, the symphonic poem *Macbeth*, works for men's choruses, and lieder.

WORKS: OPERAS: *Der Elfensieg* (Brünn, 1845); *Leila* (Hamburg, Feb. 22, 1848); *Contarini oder Die Verschwörung zu Padua* (1853; Hamburg, April 16, 1872; as *Fenice*, Dessau, April 24, 1883); incidental music to part 2 of Goethe's *Faust* (Hamburg, March 25, 1854) and to Shakespeare's *As You Like It* (Leipzig, Jan. 17, 1874) and *Romeo and Juliet* (1874); also the symphonic poem, *Macbeth* (1859). ORATORIOS: *Jerusalem* (Norwich Festival, Sept. 23, 1852) and *Hezekiah* (Norwich Festival, 1869; unfinished). Also men's choruses; lieder.

BIBL.: H. Sear, "Faust and Henry Hugh Pierson," *Music Review*, X (1949); N. Temperley, "Henry Hugo Pierson, 1815–73," *Musical Times*, CXIV (1973) and CXV (1974).

Pietri, Giuseppe, Italian composer; b. Sant'Ilario, Elba, May 6, 1886; d. Milan, Aug. 11, 1946. He studied at the Cons. of Milan, and became a successful composer of operettas, the most popular among them were *Addio giovinezza* (Livorno, 1915); *Acqua cheta* (Rome, 1920); *La Donna perduta* (Rome, 1923); *Primarosa* (Milan, 1926); and *Casa mia* (Rome, 1930).

BIBL.: R. Carli, *G. P., Cantore dei goliardi* (Livorno, 1956).

Pijper, Willem, renowned Dutch composer and pedagogue; b. Zeist, Sept. 8, 1894; d. Leidschendam, March 18, 1947. He received a rudimentary education from his father, an amateur violinist; then went to the Toonkunst School of Music in Utrecht, where he studied composition with Johan Wagenaar and piano with Mme. H.J. van Lunteren-Hansen (1911–16); from 1918 to 1923, was music critic of *Utrecht Dagblad*, and from 1926 to 1929, co-ed. of the monthly *De Muziek*. He taught theory at the Amsterdam Cons. (from 1918), and was a prof. of composition there from 1925 to 1930; served as director of the Rotterdam Cons. from 1930 until his death. In his music Pijper continued the Romantic tradition of Mahler, and also adopted the harmonic procedures of the modern French School. He postulated a "germ-cell theory," in which an opening chord or motif is the source of all succeeding harmonic and melodic development; he also cultivated the scale of alternating whole tones and semitones, regarding it as his own, not realizing that it was used abundantly by Rimsky-Korsakov (in Russian reference works it is termed the Rimsky-Korsakov scale); the "Pijper scale," as it became known in the Netherlands, was also used by Anton von der Horst and others. During the German bombardment of Rotterdam in May 1940, nearly all of Pijper's MSS were destroyed by fire, including the unpubl. reduced scoring of his large 2nd Sym. (restored in 1961 by Pijper's student Karel Mengelberg); also destroyed was the unpubl. *Divertimento* for Piano and String Orch.

WORKS: STAGE: 2 operas or symphonic dramas: *Halewijn* (1932–33; Amsterdam, June 13, 1933; rev. 1934) and *Merlijn* (1939–45; incomplete; Rotterdam, June 7, 1952); incidental music to Sophocles's *Antigone* (1920; rev. 1922 and 1926); Euripides's *Bacchantes* (1924) and *The Cyclops* (1925); Shakespeare's *The Tempest* (1930); Vondel's *Phaëton* (1937). ORCH.: 3 syms.: No. 1, *Pan* (1917; Amsterdam, April 23, 1918); No. 2, for Large Orch. (1921; Amsterdam, Nov. 2, 1922; reduced scoring by K. Mengelberg, 1961); No. 3 (Amsterdam,

Oct. 28, 1926); *Orchestral Piece with Piano* (Utrecht, Dec. 11, 1915; Pijper originally titled this "Piano Concerto No. 1," which caused confusion with his later and only Piano Concerto [Amsterdam, Dec. 22, 1927], which in turn was sometimes incorrectly referred to as "Piano Concerto No. 2"); *6 Symphonic Epigrams* (Amsterdam, April 12, 1928); Cello Concerto (Amsterdam, Nov. 22, 1936; rev. 1947); Violin Concerto (1938–39; Amsterdam, Jan. 7, 1940); *6 Adagios* (1940; Utrecht, Nov. 14, 1951). CHAMBER: 2 piano trios (1913–14, 1921); 5 string quartets (1914; 1920; 1923; 1928; 1946, unfinished); Septet for Wind Quintet, Double Bass, and Piano (1920); Sextet for Wind Quintet and Piano (1922–23); Trio for Flute, Clarinet, and Bassoon (1926–27); Wind Quintet (1928–29); 2 violin sonatas (1919, 1922); 2 cello sonatas (1919, 1924); Flute Sonata (1925); Sonata for Solo Violin (1931). PIANO: *Theme with 5 Variations* (1913); *3 Aphorisms* (1915); 3 sonatinas (1917, 1925, 1925); *3 Old Dutch Dances* (1926); Sonata (1930); 2-piano Sonata (1935). VOICE AND ORCH.: *Fêtes galantes*, after Verlaine, with Mezzo-soprano (1916; Schweningen, Aug. 2, 1917); *Romance sans paroles*, after Verlaine, with Mezzo-soprano (1919; Amsterdam, April 15, 1920); *Hymne*, after Boutens, with Bass-baritone (1941–43; Amsterdam, Nov. 1945). VOICE AND PIANO: *8 vieilles chansons de France* (1918); *8 Noëls de France* (1919); *8 Old Dutch Love Songs* (1920; rev. 1943); *8 Old Dutch Songs*, in 2 sets (1924, 1935). A CAPPELLA CHORUS: *Heer Halewijn* (1920) and *Heer Danielken* (1925). CARILLON: *Passepied* (1916).
BIBL.: M. Calvocoressi, "W. P.," *Monthly Musical Record* (1924); special issue of *Mens en melodie*, II (1947); A. Ringer, "W. P. and the Netherlands School of the 20th Century," *Musical Quarterly* (Oct. 1955); W. Kloppenburg, *Thematisch-bibliografische Catalogus van de Werken van W. P.* (Assen, 1960); J. Wouters, "W. P.," *Sonorum Spectrum* (Spring 1967); H. Ryker, *The Symphonic Music of W. P.* (diss., Univ. of Washington, 1971); M. Flothuis, "W. P.: An Unharmonious Figure in an Unharmonious Age," *Key Notes*, 3 (1976).

Piket, Frederick, Austrian-American composer; b. Constantinople (of Austrian parents), Jan. 6, 1903; d. Long Island, N.Y., Feb. 28, 1974. He studied at the Vienna Academy of Music and with Schreker in Berlin; settled in N.Y. in 1940.
WORKS: Overture, *Curtain Raiser for an American Play* (Minneapolis, Dec. 30, 1948); Piano Concerto; Violin Concerto; Saxophone Concerto; Concerto for String Orch.; orch. suite, *The Funnies* (after "Superman" and "Little Orphan Annie"); *Sea Charm* for Chorus a cappella; *Legend and Jollity* for 3 Clarinets; *Reflection and Caprice* for 4 Clarinets; Woodwind Trio; numerous choral works for the Jewish service.

Pilarczyk, Helga (Käthe), German soprano; b. Schöningen, March 12, 1925. She studied piano and aspired to a concert career; then took voice lessons and sang in operetta. She found her true vocation in opera; made her debut at Braunschweig in 1951; was a member of the Hamburg State Opera from 1953 until 1968. She made a specialty of modern music; sang Schoenberg's dramatic monologue *Erwartung*, and the leading parts in Berg's *Wozzeck* and *Lulu* as well as in works by Stravinsky, Prokofiev, Dallapiccola, Honegger, Krenek, and others. She appeared as a guest artist at the Bavarian State Opera in Munich, the Vienna State Opera, La Scala in Milan, the Paris Opéra, Covent Garden in London, and the Metropolitan Opera in N.Y. (debut, Feb. 19, 1965, as Marie in *Wozzeck*); publ. an interesting essay, *Kann man die moderne Oper singen?* (Hamburg, 1964).

Pilati, Mario, Italian composer; b. Naples, Oct. 16, 1903; d. there, Dec. 10, 1938. He studied at the Naples Cons.; was an instructor there (1930–38).
WORKS: *Notturno* for Orch. (1923); *La sera* for Women's Voices and Orch. (1926); Flute Sonata (1926); *Il battesimo di Cristo* for Soli, Chorus, and Orch. (1927); Piano Quintet (1928); Violin Sonata (1929); Cello Sonata (1929); String Quartet (1930); piano pieces.
BIBL.: G. Gavazzeni, "M. P.," *Il suono è stanco* (Bergamo, 1950).

Pilkington, Francis, English composer; b. c.1570; d. Chester, 1638. He received a B.Mus. degree at Lincoln College, Oxford, in 1595. He became a lay clerk (or conduct) at Chester Cathedral in 1602, and then a minor canon in 1612. After taking Holy Orders, he was made a "full minister" on Dec. 18, 1614. He was active in the Cathedral choir, and was precentor there from 1623 until his death. He also held other curacies in Chester, including his principal charge at St. Bridget's from 1616.
WORKS: *The First Booke of Songs or Ayres of 4. Parts: with tableture for the lute or orpherian, with the violl de gamba* (London, 1605; the versions for 4 voices with lute were publ. in *The Old English Edition*, XVIII–XX, London, 1897–98; the versions for voice and lute were publ. in E.H. Fellowes, ed., *The English School of Lutenist Song Writers*, London, 1920–32; rev. by T. Dart, 1971, in *The English Lute-Songs*); *The First Set of Madrigals and Pastorals of 3. 4. and 5. parts* (London, 1613–14; ed. by E.H. Fellowes in *The English Madrigal School, A Guide to Its Practical Use*, London, 1926; rev. by T. Dart, 1959, in *The English Madrigalists*); *The Second Set of Madrigals, and Pastorals, of 3. 4. 5. and 6. Parts: apt for violls and voyces* (London, 1624; ed. by E.H. Fellowes in *The English Madrigal School . . .*, London, 1926; rev. by T. Dart, 1958, in *The English Madrigalists*). See also B. Jeffery, ed., *Francis Pilkington: Complete Works for Solo Lute* (London, 1970). He also contributed 2 songs to Sir William Leighton's collection *The Teares or Lamentacions of a Sorrowful Soule* (1614).
BIBL.: E.H. Fellowes, *English Madrigal Verse, 1588–1632* (London, 1920; 3rd ed., rev. and enl., 1967); idem, *The English Madrigal Composers* (London, 1921; 2nd ed., 1948); R. Newton, "The Lute Music of F. P.," *Lute Society Journal*, I (1958).

Pillois, Jacques, French-American composer and pedagogue; b. Paris, Feb. 14, 1877; d. N.Y., Jan. 3, 1935. He was a student of Widor and Vierne at the Paris Cons.; upon graduation, taught at various schools in Paris. In 1927 he went to the U.S. and was on the faculty of N.Y. Univ. (1927–30) and later of Smith College. He wrote some attractive pieces of chamber music and songs, under the pen name Jacques Desky.

Pimsleur, Solomon, American pianist and composer; b. Paris (of Austrian-Jewish parents), Sept. 19, 1900; d. N.Y., April 22, 1962. He was taken to the U.S. as a child in 1903; studied piano privately; took music courses at Columbia Univ., but graduated in English literature (M.A., 1923); then was a fellowship student of Rubin Goldmark at the Juilliard School of Music (1926) and subsequently took courses at the Salzburg Mozarteum. He gave numerous piano recitals in the U.S. His compositions, in a Romantically flavored and technically competent idiom, include *Ode to Intensity*, a "symphonic ballad" (N.Y., Aug. 14, 1933); *Overture to Disillusionment*; *Meditative Nocturne* for Orch.; 3 string quartets; Piano Trio; Piano Quintet; Violin Sonata; Cello Sonata; many piano pieces with imaginative titles (*Impulsive Sonata*; *Tranquil Sonata*; *Reflective Sonata*; *Mournful Prelude and Melodious Fugue*; etc.); *Shakespearean Sonnet Symphony* for Chorus and Orch.; also an unfinished opera, *The Diary of Anne Frank*.

Pincherle, Marc, noted French musicologist; b. Constantine, Algeria, June 13, 1888; d. Paris, June 20, 1974. He studied musicology in Paris with Pirro, Laloy, and Rolland; served in both world wars; was taken prisoner of war in June 1940 and was interned in Germany until March 1941. He taught at the Paris École Normale de Musique; was artistic director of the Société Pleyel (1927–55) and president of the Société Française de Musicologie (1948–56). As a musicologist, he devoted himself mainly to the study of 17th- and 18th-century French and Italian music.
WRITINGS: *Les Violonistes compositeurs et virtuoses* (Paris, 1922); *Feuillets d'histoire du violon* (Paris, 1927; 2nd ed., 1935); *Corelli* (Paris, 1933); *Les Musiciens peints par eux-mêmes* (160 letters of famous composers from his own autograph collection; Paris, 1939); *Antonio Vivaldi et la musique instrumentale* (2 vols., Paris, 1948); *Les Instruments du quatuor* (Paris, 1948; 3rd ed., 1970); *L'Orchestre de chambre* (Paris,

1948); *Jean-Marie Leclair l'aîné* (Paris, 1952); *Petit lexique des termes musicaux d'usage courant* (Paris, 1953; 2nd ed., 1973); *Corelli et son temps* (Paris, 1954; Eng. tr. as *Corelli, His Life, His Work*, N.Y., 1956); *Vivaldi* (Paris, 1955; Eng. tr. as *Vivaldi: Genius of the Baroque*, N.Y., 1957); *Fritz Kreisler* (Geneva, 1956); *Albert Roussel* (Geneva, 1957); *Histoire illustrée de la musique* (Paris, 1959; 2nd ed.; 1962; Eng. tr., N.Y., 1959); *Le Monde des virtuoses* (Paris, 1961; Eng. tr., N.Y., 1963); *Musical Creation* (Washington, D.C., 1961); *L'orchestra da camera* (Milan, 1963); *Le Violon* (Paris, 1966; 2nd ed., 1974).

Pingoud, Ernest, Russian-born Finnish composer; b. St. Petersburg, Oct. 14, 1888; d. Helsinki, June 1, 1942. He studied piano in St. Petersburg with Siloti; then went to Leipzig, where he took courses in music history with Hugo Riemann and in composition with Max Reger. In 1918 he settled in Finland, where he served as managing director of the Helsinki Phil. (1924–42). In his music he was influenced by the Russian modern school, particularly by Scriabin, from whom he acquired his predilection for mystical titles, often in French (*La Flamme éternelle, Le Chant d'espace*, etc.).

WORKS: ORCH.: *Prologue* (1916); *Confessions* (1916); *La Dernière Aventure de Pierrot* (1916); *Diableries galantes "Le fétiche"* (1917); 3 piano concertos (1917, 1921, 1922); *Hymnejä yölle* (Hymns to the Night; 1917); *Kuolemantanssi* (Danse macabre) for Chorus and Orch. (1918); 5 *Sonnets* for Chamber Orch. (1918); *Ritari peloton ja moitteeton* (The Knight without Fear or Reproach), an "adventure" (1918); *Mysterium* (1919); *Flambeaux éleints* (1919); *Chantecler* (1919); *Le Sacrifice* (1919); 3 syms. (1920, 1920, 1923–27); *Profeetta* (The Prophet; 1921); *Cor ardens* (1927); *Narcissos* (1930); *Le Chant d'espace* (1931; rev. 1938); *Suurkaupungin kasvot* (The Face of the Big City), ballet for Piano and Orch. (1936); *La Flamme éternelle* (1938–39); *Epäjumala* (The Idol), ballet. Also chamber music; piano works; songs.

Pini-Corsi, Antonio, noted Italian baritone; b. Zara, Dalmatia, June 1858; d. Milan, April 22, 1918. He made his debut as Dandini in *La Cenerentola* in Cremona (1878); then sang throughout Italy; Verdi chose him to create the role of Ford in *Falstaff* at La Scala in Milan in 1893. He also sang at Covent Garden in London (1894–96, 1902–3). On Dec. 27, 1899, he made his Metropolitan Opera debut in N.Y. as Masetto, remaining on its roster until 1901; returned for the 1909–14 seasons. He was one of the great buffo singers of his day, being famous for his portrayals of Dr. Bartolo, Leporello, Don Pasquale, and others.

Pinkham, Daniel (Rogers, Jr.), significant American composer whose music is rooted in the neo-Classical tradition diversified by a Gallic inventive spirit; b. Lynn, Mass., June 5, 1923. He was descended from a long line of religious philosophers, educators, and commercial industrialists that included the promoter of the celebrated Vegetable Compound and other patent remedies, Lydia E. Pinkham; indeed, Pinkham's father served for a time as president of the Lydia E. Pinkham Co. It was from the latter that he inherited the spirit of organization and an almost religious adherence to certain basic laws of life and art. Believing that truth in music resided in the instrumental art of the Classical tradition, he immersed himself in the study of Baroque music, especially that for the keyboard. He found ample sources for this study at Phillips Academy (1937–40), where he was guided by the director of the glee club, the Lutheran minister Carl Pfatteicher. After completion of his studies there, he entered Harvard Univ. (A.B., 1943; M.A., 1944), where he took classes with A. Tillman Merritt and Archibald Davison; later he joined the advanced composition class of Walter Piston. When Nadia Boulanger went to the U.S. during World War II, he took private lessons with her. He also attended seminars with Arthur Honegger and Aaron Copland at the Berkshire Music Center at Tanglewood, in Lenox, Mass. Apart from his studies as a composer, he continued to work as a keyboard performer, studying harpsichord with Wanda Landowska and with Putnam Aldrich. His instructor in organ was E. Power Biggs, who introduced Pink-

ham as a composer, playing his Sonata for Organ and Strings with the Boston Pops Orch. in 1944. Pinkham subsequently devoted himself to teaching and also held a position as organist at King's Chapel in Boston. In 1957 he was appointed to the faculty of the New England Cons. of Music and was also named special lecturer in music history at Simmons College in Boston. The formal design of Pinkham's music is compact and contrapuntally cohesive; the rhythmic element is propulsive; now and then he astutely introduces modernistic devices without disrupting the tonal fabric of his music.

WORKS: ORCH.: Piano Concertino (Cambridge, Mass., May 3, 1950); Concertante No. 1 for Violin and Harpsichord Soli, Strings, and Celesta (Boston, Dec. 16, 1954); Concerto for Celesta and Harpsichord Soli (N.Y., Nov. 19, 1955); Violin Concerto No. 1 (Falmouth, Mass., Sept. 8, 1956); Concertante No. 2 for Violin and Strings (Boston, May 9, 1958); 3 syms: No. 1 (Washington, D.C., April 29, 1961); No. 2 (1962; Lansing, Mich., Nov. 23, 1963); No. 3 (1985); *Catacoustical Measures* (composed to test the acoustics at Lincoln Center's Phil. Hall, N.Y., May 28, 1962); *Signs of the Zodiac* for Orch. and Optional Narrator (Portland, Maine, Nov. 10, 1964); Violin Concerto No. 2 (1968); Organ Concerto (1970); *Serenades* for Trumpet and Symphonic Wind Orch. (1979; Cambridge, Mass., March 7, 1980); *Concerto piccolo* for Piccolo, String Orch. or Quintet, and Percussion (1989). CHORAL: *Wedding Cantata* for Optional Soprano and Tenor, Chorus, and Orch. (1956); *Christmas Cantata* for Chorus and Orch. (1957); *Easter Cantata* for Chorus and Orch. (1961); *The Conversion of Saul* for Tenor, Baritone, Chorus, Trumpet, and Organ (1961); *Requiem* for Alto, Tenor, Chorus, and Orch. (N.Y., Jan. 24, 1963); *Stabat Mater* for Soprano, Chorus, and Orch. (Lenox, Mass., Aug. 10, 1964); *St. Mark Passion* (Southboro, Mass., May 22, 1965); *Magnificat* for Soprano, Women's Chorus, and Orch. (1968); *Ascension Cantata* for Chorus and Orch. (Columbus, Ohio, March 20, 1970); *Daniel in the Lion's Den* for Narrator, Tenor, Baritone, Bass, Chorus, 5 Instrumentalists, and Tape (1972); *The Passion of Judas* for Vocal Soloists, Chorus, and 5 Instruments (Washington, D.C., June 6, 1976); *The Descent into Hell* for Soprano, Tenor, Bass, Chorus, Orch., and Tape (1979; Buckhannon, W.Va., Oct. 17, 1980); *Hezekiah* (1979; Shaker Heights, Ohio, April 8, 1981; rev. 1987); *When God Arose* (1979; Norman, Okla., Feb. 15, 1980); *Before the Dust Returns* (Lewisburg, Pa., Nov. 21, 1981); *A Curse, a Lament, and a Vision* for Chorus and Piano ad libitum (1984); *In Heaven Soaring Up* for Alto, Tenor, Chorus, Oboe, and Harp (1985); *Getting to Heaven* for Soprano, Chorus, Brass Quintet, and Harp (1987); numerous other choral works; many pieces for solo voice and accompaniment. CHAMBER: Sonata No. 1 for Organ, 2 Violins, and Cello (1943; also for Organ and String Orch.); Sonata No. 2 for Organ and String Quartet (1954; also for Organ and String Orch.); *Miracles* for Organ and Flute (1978); *Prelude and Scherzo* for Wind Quintet (1981); Brass Quintet (1983); *Psalms* for Organ and Trumpet (1983); Sonata No. 3 for Organ, 2 Violins, Cello, and Contrabass (1986; also for Organ and String Orch.); *Sonata da chiesa* for Viola and Organ (1988); several dozens of adroit instrumental arrangements of Christmas songs.

BIBL.: W. Smith, "D. P.," *American Composers Alliance Bulletin*, X/1 (1961); M. Johnson, *The Choral Works of D. P.* (diss., Univ. of Iowa, 1966); M. Corzine, *The Organ Works of D. P.* (diss., Univ. of Rochester, Eastman School of Music, 1979); L. Raver, "The Solo Organ Music of D. P.," *American Organist*, XVII/6 (1983); M. Stallings, *Representative Works for Mixed Chorus by D. P.: 1968–1983* (diss., Univ. of Miami, 1984); K. Deboer and J. Ahouse, *D. P.: A Bio-Bibliography* (Westport, Conn., 1988).

Pinnock, Trevor (David), outstanding English harpsichordist and conductor; b. Canterbury, Dec. 16, 1946. He became a chorister at Canterbury Cathedral when he was 7; after receiving instruction in piano and organ, he served as a church organist; at 19 he entered the Royal College of Music in London, where he took courses in organ and later harpsichord. While still a student, he organized the Gailliard Harpsichord Trio (1966); also toured Europe with the Academy of St. Martin-in-the Fields. In 1973 he founded the English Concert, an ensemble devoted to the performance of early music on original instruments; through numerous tours and recordings, his ensemble acquired an international reputation; toured North America with it for the 1st time in 1983. He also pursued a distinguished career as a harpsichord virtuoso. On Sept. 27, 1988, he made his Metropolitan Opera debut in N.Y. conducting *Giulio Cesare*. In 1989 he founded the Classical Band of N.Y., which he led in performances of the Classical repertoire from Haydn to Mendelssohn on period instruments until resigning unexpectedly in 1990. In 1991 he was named artistic director and principal conductor of the National Arts Centre Orch. in Ottawa.

BIBL.: A. Kozinn, "T. P.," *Ovation* (Oct. 1984); *Current Biography* (Sept. 1989).

Piños, Alois Simandl, Czech composer; b. Vyškov, Oct. 2, 1925. He studied forestry at the Univ. of Brno (graduating in 1953), music with Petrželka at the Brno Cons. (1948–49) and at the Janáček Academy of Music in Brno with Kvapil and Schaeffer (1949–53); attended the summer courses of new music at Darmstadt (1965) and an electronic music seminar in Munich (1966). In 1953 he joined the faculty of the Janáček Academy of Music in Brno. In 1967 he founded in Brno a modern music group, with which he produced a number of works by the local avant-garde, some composed collectively.

WORKS: STAGE: *CHAMBER OPERA: The Criers* (1970). **AUDIO-VISUAL:** *The Lattice* for Piano and Film (1970); *The Genesis* for Chamber Orch. and Film (1970); *Static Music for Tape,* with Slides (1970). **ORCH.:** *Czech Dances* (1951); *Wedding Suite* (1952); Horn Concerto (1953); Concertino (1963); *Abbreviations* (1963); Concerto for Orch. and Tape (1964); *Double Concerto* for Cello, Piano, Winds, and Percussion (1965–66; Prague, March 7, 1967); *Chamber Concerto* for Strings (1967); *Concerto on the Name B-A-C-H* for Bass Clarinet, Cello, Piano, Strings, and Percussion (1968); sym., *Apollo XI* (1970); *Symphonic Diptych* (1973–74); Concerto for Harp and Strings (1978); *Ballad* for Chamber Orch. and Synthesizer (1981). **CHAMBER:** Cello Sonata (1950); 2 wind quintets (1951, 1959); Sonata for Viola and Cello (1960); Piano Trio (1960); Suite for String Trio (1961); *Monologues* for Bass Clarinet (1962); *Caricatures* for Flute, Bass Clarinet, and Piano (1962); String Quartet (1962); *Hunting Music* for Baritone and 4 Horns (1963); *Conflicts* for Violin, Bass Clarinet, Piano, and Percussion (1964); 2 *Lyrical Sketches* for Narrator, Flute, and Violin (1964); 4 *Lyrical Sketches* for Narrator, Flute, Bass Clarinet, and Piano (1965); 3 *Pieces* for Bass Clarinet and Piano (1965); *Pulsus intermissi* for Percussionist (1965); *Ludus floralis,* 5 songs for Baritone, Female Chorus, Percussion, and Tape (1966); *Hyperboles,* 7 pieces for Harp (1966); *Gesta Machabaeorum* for Chorus, Flute, Trumpet, Harp, and Percussion (1967–68); 16 *January 1969* for Piano Quintet and Kettledrums (1969); *Dialogues* for Bass Clarinet (1969); 2 *campanari* for Bass Clarinet, Piano, and Ringing Instruments (1971); *Be Beaten* for Percussionist (1972); *Sonata Concertante* for Cello and Piano (1974); *Power of Love* for Baritone and String Quartet (1974); *Composition for 3* for Flute, Clarinet, and Marimbaphone (1975); *Acquaintance,* to advertising texts, for Soprano, Bass-baritone, and Guitar or Harpsichord (1975); Nonet (1982–83); *Paradoxes* for Piano (1965); 2–3–1, 3 pieces for Piano (1969); *Esca* for Prepared Piano (1971). Also several tape pieces, including *Home* (1972–73) and *Speleophony* (1976); songs; choruses.

Pinsuti, Ciro, Italian singing teacher and composer; b. Sinalunga, near Florence, May 9, 1829; d. Florence, March 10, 1888. His talent developed so rapidly that at 11 he was elected an honorary member of the Accademia Filarmonica of Rome. Taken to England soon after by Henry Drummond, he studied piano under C. Potter and violin under Blagrove; returned to Bologna in 1845, and studied at the Liceo, also privately with

Rossini, soon becoming assistant teacher of a piano class. In 1848 he went back to England; was appointed a prof. of singing at London's Royal Academy of Music in 1856. He divided his time between London and Italy; brought out an opera, *Il Mercante di Venezia,* at Bologna (Nov. 9, 1873); another, *Mattia Corvino,* at Milan (1877); and a 3rd, *Margherita,* at Venice (1882). In 1871 he represented Italy at the opening of the London Exhibition, for which he composed the hymn *O people of this favoured land.* As a recipient of the order of the Italian Crown, he was styled "Cavaliere" Pinsuti. Besides his operas, he wrote some 250 songs to Eng. and Italian texts.

Pinto, Alfredo, Italian-Argentine composer; b. Mantua, Oct. 22, 1891; d. Buenos Aires, May 26, 1968. He studied piano with Longo and composition with De Nardis in Naples; then went to Buenos Aires, where he became active as a pianist and conductor. He wrote the operas *La última esposa, o Sheherazade* and *Gualicho* (Buenos Aires, 1940); symphonic poems: *Nostalgias* (1929); *Eros* (1930); *Rebelión* (1939); numerous piano pieces, choruses, and songs.

Pinto, George Frederick, English violinist, pianist, and composer; b. Lambeth, Sept. 25, 1785; d. Chelsea, March 23, 1806. His father's name was Saunders or Sanders, but he adopted his mother's surname as his own. He began violin lessons in early childhood, and became a student of Salomon at the age of 8, making his debut as a violinist at a benefit concert for Salvini (May 4, 1796); also became active as a pianist. His early death, at the age of 20, was regretted by his older contemporaries, who ascribed it, pietistically, to sexual indulgence and general dissipation, without offering facts. He wrote works for piano, including several sonatas, violin duets, and songs, a number of which reveal great promise.

BIBL.: [M. Gordon,] *Authentic Memoirs of the late celebrated G.F. P. collected by a Friend to Genius and Merit* (Edinburgh, 1807); N. Temperley, "G.F. P.," *Musical Times,* CVI (1965).

Pinto, Octavio, Brazilian composer; b. São Paulo, Nov. 3, 1890; d. there, Oct. 31, 1950. He was trained as an architect; built apartment houses in Brazil; also studied piano with Isidor Philipp. In 1922 he married the Brazilian pianist **Guiomar Novães;** Villa-Lobos wrote his suite *Prole do bébé* for their children. Pinto publ. a number of effective piano miniatures, of which *Scenas infantis* (1932) and *Children's Festival* (1939) are best known.

Pinza, Ezio (baptized **Fortunio**), celebrated Italian bass; b. Rome, May 18, 1892; d. Stamford, Conn., May 9, 1957. The family moved to Ravenna when he was an infant; he studied engineering; also was active in sports. He began to study voice at the age of 18 with Ruzza and Vizzani at the Bologna Cons.; made his opera debut as Oroveso in *Norma* in Soncino (1914); after military service in World War I, he resumed his career, making his 1st important appearance as Comte Des Grieux in Rome (1920); then sang at La Scala in Milan (1922–24); was selected by Toscanini for the leading part in the world premiere of Boito's *Nerone* (May 1, 1924). He made his American debut at the Metropolitan Opera in N.Y. as Pontifex Maximus in Spontini's *La Vestale* (Nov. 1, 1926), and remained on its staff until 1947; appeared also in San Francisco, Chicago, etc.; sang in Europe and in South America; his most celebrated roles were Méphistophélès in Gounod's *Faust,* Don Giovanni, and Boris Godunov. In 1949 he appeared as a musical comedy star in *South Pacific,* and immediately became successful in this new career; also appeared in films.

BIBL.: R. Magidoff, ed., *Ezio Pinza; An Autobiography* (N.Y., 1958); R. Tuggle, "E. P.," *The Golden Age of Opera* (N.Y., 1983).

Pipelare, Matthaeus, Flemish composer; b. c.1450; d. c.1512. He was active in Antwerp; was engaged as master of the choristers of the Marian Brotherhood in 's-Hertogenbosch (1498–1500). His style has a certain affinity with that of Pierre de la Rue. His extant works include 9 masses and a number of motets and chansons; R. Cross ed. these in Corpus Mensurabilis Musicae, XXXII/3 (1966–67).

BIBL.: R. Cross, "The Life and Works of M. P.," *Musica Disciplina* (1963).

Pipkov, Lubomir, noted Bulgarian composer; b. Lovec, Sept. 19, 1904; d. Sofia, May 9, 1974. He studied piano and composition with his father; entered the Sofia Music School (1919); completed his training with Boulanger and Dukas (composition) and Lefébure (piano) at the Paris École Normale de Musique (1926–32). Returning to Bulgaria, he occupied several administrative posts, including the directorship of the National Theater in Sofia (1944–47). His style of composition is determined by the inherent asymmetry of Bulgarian folk songs; there is a similarity in his compositions with those of Bartók, resulting from common sources in Balkan and Macedonian music; his harmonic investiture is often polytonal or polymodal.

WORKS: DRAMATIC: *OPERAS: Yaninite devet bratya* (The 9 Brothers of Yanina; 1929–37; Sofia, Sept. 19, 1937); *Momchil* (1939–44; Sofia, April 24, 1948); *Antigone 43* (1961–62; Ruse, Dec. 23, 1963); also *Oratorio for Our Time* (1959; Plovdiv, Dec. 18, 1959); 2 cantatas: *The Wedding* (1934) and *Cantata of Friendship* (1958). **ORCH.:** Concerto for Winds, Percussion, and Piano (1930); 4 syms.: No. 1 (1939–40); No. 2 (1954); No. 3 for Strings, Trumpet, 2 Pianos, and Percussion (1965); No. 4 for String Orch. (1970); *Heroic Overture* (1950); *Journey through Albania,* variations for String Orch. (1950); Violin Concerto (1951); Piano Concerto (1954); *Symphony-Concerto* for Cello and Orch. (1963; Moscow, April 20, 1964); Concerto for Clarinet and Chamber Orch. (1966); *The Partisan's Grave* for Trombone and String Orch. (1970). **CHAMBER:** 3 string quartets (1928, 1948, 1966); 2 violin sonatas (1929, 1969); Piano Trio (1930); Piano Quartet (1939); Sonata for Solo Violin (1969); *Tableaux et études métrorythmiques* for Piano (1972); *Suggestions printanières* for Piano (1972). Also choruses; songs.

BIBL.: K. Iliev, *L. P.* (Sofia, 1958); L. Koen, *L. P.* (Sofia, 1968).

Pirani, Eugenio, Italian pianist and composer; b. Bologna, Sept. 8, 1852; d. Berlin, Jan. 12, 1939. A pupil of Colinelli at the Bologna Liceo Musicale, he graduated in 1869; then studied in Berlin with T. Kullak (piano) and Kiel (composition); taught in Kullak's Academy, 1870–80; also toured Italy (1873, 1876), England, Germany, France, and Russia. He lived in Heidelberg until 1895, then settled in Berlin. He publ. concert studies and many pieces for piano solo; songs; duets; etc.; also *Die Hochschule des Klavierspiels,* op. 88 (in Ger. and Eng.) and *Secrets of the Success of Great Musicians* (Philadelphia, 1922).

Pires, (Luis) Filipe, Portuguese composer; b. Lisbon, June 26, 1934. He studied piano with Mendes and composition with Croner de Vasconcelos at the Lisbon Cons. (1946–54), and then took courses at the Hannover Hochschule für Musik (1957–60); taught composition at the Oporto Cons. (1960–70) and at the Lisbon Cons. (1972–75); subsequently worked in an electronic studio in Paris with Pierre Schaeffer. His music hews resolutely to the tenets of the cosmopolitan avant-garde.

WORKS: String Quartet (1958); Piano Trio (1960); *Eternal Return* for Baritone and Orch. (1961); *Perspectivas* for 3 groups of Instruments (1965); *Metromonie* for Flute, Viola, and Harp (1966); *Portugaliae Genesis* for Baritone, Chorus, and Orch. (1968; Lisbon, May 21, 1969); *Homo sapiens* for Magnetic Tape (1972); *Dialogues* for 8 Instrumentalists and Tape (1975).

Pires, Maria-João, Portuguese pianist; b. Lisbon, July 23, 1944. She began piano lessons at a very early age, making her recital debut at 5 and appearing as soloist in a Mozart Concerto when she was 7; studied piano with Campos Coelho at the Lisbon Academy of Music (1953–60), and concurrently received instruction in composition, theory, and music history from Francine Benoit; then pursued piano training with R. Schmid at the Munich Staatliche Hochschule für Musik and with Karl Engel. She appeared throughout her homeland and in Spain and Germany; after winning 1st prize in the Beethoven Competition in Brussels (1970), she gave concert tours in Europe, Africa, and Japan. In 1986 she made her North American debut as a soloist with the Montreal Sym. Orch., and in 1988 she made her 1st U.S. tour. Her readings of Mozart, Beethoven,

Schubert, Schumann, and Chopin are finely etched and poetically outlined.

Pirogov, Alexander (Stepanovich), noted Russian bass; b. Novoselki, Riazan district, July 4, 1899; d. Bear's Head Island, June 26, 1964. He studied voice at the Moscow Phil. Inst., and simultaneously attended classes in history and philology at Moscow Univ. In 1924 he joined the Bolshoi Theater, remaining on its roster until 1954. He specialized in the Russian operatic repertoire; his performance of the role of Boris Godunov received a prize in 1949; also notable were his interpretations of Méphistophélès in *Faust* and Don Basilio in *Il Barbiere di Siviglia.* His 2 brothers, Grigori (1885–1931) and Mikhail (1887–1933), were also bass singers.

Pironkoff, Simeon, Bulgarian composer; b. Lom, June 18, 1927. He took courses in violin, conducting (with A. Dimitrov), and composition (with P. Khadzhiev) at the Bulgarian State Cons. in Sofia (graduated, 1952); was active as a composer and conductor at Sofia's Youth Theater (1951–61); served as secretary of the Bulgarian Composer's Union (1966–69); received the Gottfried von Herder Prize of the Univ. of Vienna (1985). His music is rhythmically animated, harmonically tense, melodically modal, and instrumentally coloristic.

WORKS: DRAMATIC: OPERAS: *A Good Woman from Szechwan* (1965), *The Motley Bird* (1979), and *Ah, You, My Dream . . .* (1985); **ORATORIO:** *The Life and the Sufferings of the Sinful Sofronii* for Narrator, Tenor, Chorus, and Orch. (1976). **ORCH.:** Sym. for String Orch. (1960); *The True Apology of Socrates* for Bass, Strings, and Percussion (1967); *Movements* for String Orch. (1967); *Night Music* (1968); *Requiem for an Unknown Young Man* for String Orch. (1968); *A Big Game* for Small Orch. (1970); *Ballet Music in Memory of Igor Stravinsky* for Small Orch. (1972); *Concerto rustico* for Cello and Orch. (1982); *Entrata and Bulgarian Folk Dance* (1983); *Lyric Suite* for String Orch. (1983); *In the Eve of the Storm* for Tenor and Orch. (1986); *Symphonic Sketch on a Popular Melody: Rum and Coca-Cola* (1986); Flute Concerto (1987). **CHAMBER:** 3 trios (1949, 1950, 1987); 3 string quartets (1951, 1966, 1985); Sonata for Solo Violin (1955); *Berceuse* for Clarinet and Piano (1983); *Thema con variationi* for Violin and Piano (1985); piano pieces; also choruses; songs; film and theater music.

Pirro, André (Gabriel Edme), distinguished French musicologist and organist; b. St.-Dizier, Haute-Marne, Feb. 12, 1869; d. Paris, Nov. 11, 1943. He first studied with his father, the local organist, then went to Paris, where he served as organist and maître de chapelle at the Collège Stanislas; also audited the organ classes given by Franck and Widor at the Paris Cons. (1889–91). He studied law at the Sorbonne and continued private studies in music; also studied in the faculty of arts in Nancy (1898–99); received his doctorat ès lettres from the Sorbonne in 1907 with the dissertation *L'Esthétique de Jean-Sébastien Bach* (publ. in Paris, 1907), which was followed that same year by the supplementary dissertation *Descartes et la musique* (publ. in Paris, 1907). When the Schola Cantorum was founded in 1896, he was made a member of its board of directors and prof. of music history and organ; was organist at St. Jean-Baptiste de Belleville (1900–1904); lectured on music history at the École des Hautes Études Sociales (1904–14); was prof. of music history at the Sorbonne (1912–37). His outstanding students included Plamenac, Machabey, Rokseth, and Pincherle. In addition to his valuable books, he wrote many important articles on various aspects of music.

WRITINGS: *L'Orgue de Jean-Sébastien Bach* (Paris, 1895; Eng. tr. by J. Goodrich, N.Y., 1902); *J.-S. Bach* (Paris, 1906; 2nd ed., 1949; Eng. tr., N.Y., 1957); *Dietrich Buxtehude* (Paris, 1913); *Schütz* (Paris, 1913); *Jean Sébastien Bach auteur comique* (Madrid, 1915); *Les Clavecinistes: Étude critique* (Paris, 1924); *La Musique à Paris sous le règne de Charles VI, 1380–1422* (Strasbourg, 1930); ed. with A. Gastoué et al., *Bibliothèque nationale: La Musique française du moyen-âge à la Révolution* (Paris, 1934); *Histoire de la musique de la fin du XIVe siècle à la fin du XVIe* (Paris, 1940); *Mélanges: Recueil* *d'articles publié sous le patronage de la Société française de musicologie* (Geneva, 1971).

BIBL.: R. Rolland et al., "Hommage à A. P.," *Information musicale*, IV (Paris, 1943).

Pirrotta, Nino (actually, **Antonino**), eminent Italian musicologist; b. Palermo, June 13, 1908. He studied at the Conservatorio Vincenzo Bellini in Palermo; then received a diploma in organ and organ composition at the Florence Cons. (1930) and a liberal arts degree at the Univ. of Florence (1931). He was a lecturer in music history and a librarian at the Palermo Cons. (1936–48); was chief librarian at the Santa Cecilia Cons. in Rome (1948–56); was also a visiting prof. at Princeton Univ. (1954–55), the Univ. of Calif., Los Angeles (summer 1955), and Columbia Univ. (1955); then was a prof. at Harvard Univ. (1956–72), where he also was chairman of the music dept. (1965–68); subsequently was prof. of music history at the Univ. of Rome (1972–83). He was made a member of the American Academy of Arts and Sciences (1967) and an honorary member of the American Musicological Soc. (1980). An erudite scholar of wide interests, he greatly distinguished himself in the study of Renaissance polyphony and Baroque opera. In addition to his important books, he ed. *The Music of Fourteenth-century Italy* in the Corpus Mensurabilis Musicae series (1954–64), and contributed valuable articles to music journals and other publications.

WRITINGS: With E. Li Gotti, *Il Sacchetti e la tecnica musicale del trecento italiano* (Florence, 1935); *Il codice estense lat.568 e la musica francese in Italia al principio del '400* (Palermo, 1946); *Li due Orfei: Da Poliziano a Monteverdi* (Turin, 1969; 2nd ed., 1975; Eng. tr., 1981); *Music and Culture in Italy from the Middle Ages to the Baroque: A Collection of Essays* (Cambridge, Mass., and London, 1984); *Musica tra Medioevo e Rinascimento* (Turin, 1984); *Scelte poetiche di musicisti: Teatro, poesia e musica da Willaert a Malipiero* (Venice, 1987).

BIBL.: F. Della Seta and F. Piperno, eds., *In Cantu et in sermone: For N. P. on His 80th Birthday* (Florence, 1989).

Pirumov, Alexander, Russian composer; b. Tiflis, Feb. 6, 1930. He studied composition with Kabalevsky at the Moscow Cons. (graduated, 1956); taught piano first at the music school attached to the Cons. (1956–62), then at the Cons. itself (1962–71; lecturer, from 1971). His Prelude and Toccata (1962) and Scherzo (1974) were required pieces for the Tchaikovsky Piano Competition.

WORKS: ORCH.: 4 syms. (1956; for Strings and Percussion, 1963; 1965; 1973); Concert Variations for Piano and Orch. (1972). **VOCAL:** *October Days*, oratorio (1967); *Requiem in Memory of My Brother* (killed in World War II; 1975). **CHAMBER:** 4 string quartets (1954, 1955, 1959, 1967). **PIANO:** Sonata (1973); 2 sonatinas (1961, 1966); *Children's Album* (24 pieces; 1968); *Variations on a Theme of Bartók* (1968). **ORGAN:** 5 Preludes (1967).

Pisa, Agostino, Italian music scholar who flourished in the early 17th century. He received a degree in law in Rome (1600); publ. the earliest known treatise on conducting, *Breve dichiaratione della battuta musicale . . .* (Rome, 1611); a 2nd augmented ed. was publ. in the same year, also in Rome, as *Battuta della musica. . . .*

Pisador, Diego, Spanish vihuelist and composer; b. Salamanca, 1509 or 1510; d. probably there, after 1557. In 1526 he took minor orders; in 1552 he publ. in Salamanca *Libro de música de vihuela*, containing madrigals, a set of Spanish ballads, and transcriptions of secular and sacred works by Josquin and others. A. Morphy ed. 14 of Pisador's works in *Les luthistes espagnols du XVIᵉ siècle* (Leipzig, 1902).

Pisano (real name, **Pagoli**), **Bernardo,** significant Italian composer; b. Florence, Oct. 12, 1490; d. Rome, Jan. 23, 1548. He studied at the Florence Cathedral school; during this time he sang in the chapel of the church of Ss. Annunziata; was ordained a priest and made master of the choristers at the cathedral school (1511); also sang in the chapels of the cathedral and baptistry and became master of the cathedral chapel (1512). He was a singer in the papal chapel in Rome (1514–

48), and was active at the Medici Chapel in Florence (1515–19). During a visit to Florence in 1529, he became embroiled in a revolt against the Medici Pope Clement VII; accused of being a papal spy, he was arrested, tortured, and expelled from the city by the republican authorities. Pisano was a master of the madrigal, honored as such in his time. He composed both sacred and secular vocal works, the latter represented by his *Musica . . . sopra le canzone del Petrarcha* (Venice, 1520). Most of his works have been ed. by F. D'Accone in *Music of the Florentine Renaissance*, Corpus Mensurabilis Musicae, XXXII/I (1966).

BIBL.: F. D'Accone, "B. P. and the Early Madrigal," *International Musicological Society Congress Report*, X (Ljubljana, 1967).

Pisari, Pasquale, esteemed Italian bass and composer; b. Rome, 1725; d. there, March 27, 1778. He was a pupil of Giovanni Biordi; in 1752 he was taken into the papal chapel, being a fine bass singer; he wrote most of his sacred works for it, and the MSS are preserved in the archives of the papal chapel; they include several masses, motets, 2 Te Deums for 8 Voices, and one Te Deum for 4 Voices (his most remarkable work); also a *Dixit* in 16 parts, for 4 Choirs, and a series of motets for the entire year, written for the Lisbon Court. Padre Martini called Pisari the "Palestrina of the 18th century."

Pischna, Josef, famous Bohemian pianist and pedagogue; b. Erdischowitz, June 15, 1826; d. Prague, Oct. 19, 1896. He was a pupil at the Prague Cons.; taught for many years in Moscow; then at the Prague Cons. His pedagogical work for piano, *60 Exercises*, became a standard method in Europe and has been reprinted in many eds.

Pisendel, Johann Georg, distinguished German violinist, teacher, and composer; b. Cadolzburg, Dec. 26, 1687; d. Dresden, Nov. 25, 1755. He entered the Ansbach court chapel as a chorister at 10; became a violinist in the Court Orch. there at 16; studied singing with Pistocchi and violin with Torelli (1709), and later was a pupil of Vivaldi in Venice (1716), becoming his close friend; completed his studies with Montanari in Rome (1717). In 1709 he appeared as a soloist in a concert by Albinoni with the Leipzig Collegium Musicum; then deputized for Melchior Hoffmann with the ensemble and in the Opera orch. In 1712 he joined the Dresden Court Orch.; traveled with the Elector of Saxony to France (1714), Berlin (1715), Italy (1716–17), and Vienna (1718); assumed the duties of Konzertmeister in Dresden (1728), a title he formally received in 1730; also took that post with the orch. of the Dresden Opera (1731). He accompanied the Elector to Berlin (1728, 1744) and Warsaw (1734). Among his outstanding pupils were J.G. Graun and Franz Benda. Albinoni, Telemann, and Vivaldi were only a few of the eminent composers who wrote works for him. Pisendel's compositions reflect German, Italian, and French characteristics; his extant works include 7 violin concertos, 4 concerti grossi, a Sinfonia, 2 sonatas for Violin and Basso Continuo, and a Sonata for Solo Violin.

BIBL.: A. Moser, *Geschichte des Violinspiels* (Berlin, 1923; 2nd ed., rev. and enlarged, 1966–67); H. Jung, *J.G. P. (1687–1755): Leben und Werk* (diss., Univ. of Jena, 1956).

Pisk, Paul A(madeus), Austrian-born American composer, pedagogue, and musicologist; b. Vienna, May 16, 1893; d. Los Angeles, Jan. 12, 1990. He studied piano with J. Epstein, composition with Schreker and Schoenberg, and orchestration with Hellmesberger in Vienna; studied musicology with Adler at the Univ. of Vienna (Ph.D., 1916, with the diss. *Das Parodieverfahren in den Messen des Jacobus Gallus*); later studied at the Vienna Cons. (graduated, 1919). From 1922 to 1934 he taught at the Volkshochschule Volksheim in Vienna; in 1925–26, was instructor in music theory at the New Vienna Cons.; from 1931 to 1933, lectured at the Austro-American Cons. in Mondsee, near Salzburg. He also wrote music criticism for the Socialist newspaper *Wiener Arbeiterzeitung*; with Paul Stefan, he founded the progressive music journal *Musikblätter des Anbruch*. He was closely associated with Schoenberg, Berg, and Webern, and espoused the tenets of the New Vienna School, adopting in many of his own works the methods of composition with 12 tones related only to one another. As the dark cloud of ignorance and barbarity fell on Germany and approached Austria, Pisk left Vienna and emigrated to the U.S. (1936); became a naturalized citizen (1941). He occupied with great honor several teaching posts in America; at the Univ. of Redlands, Calif. (1937–51), the Univ. of Texas in Austin (1951–63), and Washington Univ. in St. Louis (1963–72); he also gave courses at summer sessions at the Univ. of Calif., Los Angeles (1966), the Univ. of Cincinnati (1969), and Dartmouth College (1972). In 1973 he settled in Los Angeles; his 90th birthday was celebrated by his many disciples and admirers in 1983. He continued to compose prolifically, accumulating an impressive catalogue of works, mostly chamber music. He wrote (with Homer Ulrich) *History of Music and Musical Style* (N.Y., 1963); ed. masses by Jacobus Gallus for Denkmäler der Tonkunst in Österreich. A Festschrift, *Paul A. Pisk, Essays in His Honor*, ed. by J. Glowacki, was publ. in 1966.

WORKS: STAGE: *Schattenseite*, monodrama (1931); *American Suite*, ballet (Redlands, Calif., Feb. 19, 1948). **VOCAL:** *Die neue Stadt*, "cantata for the people" (Vienna, Nov. 1926); *Der grosse Regenmacher*, scenic ballad for Narrator and Orch. (1931); *Requiem* for Baritone and Orch. (1942); *A Toccata of Galuppi* for Soprano and Orch. (1947); songs. **ORCH.:** *Partita* (ISCM Festival, Prague, May 17, 1925); *Suite on American Folksongs* for 24 Instruments (1944); *Bucolic Suite* for String Orch. (Saratoga Springs, Sept. 10, 1946); *Rococo Suite*, for Viola and Orch. (1953); *Baroque Chamber Concerto* for Violin and Orch. (1953); *Canzona* for Chamber Orch. (1954); *3 Ceremonial Rites* (1957–58); *Elegy* for String Orch. (1958); *Sonnet* for Chamber Orch. (1960). **CHAMBER:** *3 Songs with String Quartet* (Salzburg, Aug. 10, 1922); String Quartet (1924); 4 violin sonatas (1921, 1927, 1939, 1977); *Fantasy* for Clarinet and Piano (1925); *Rondo* for Violin and Piano (1932); *Variations on a Waltz by Beethoven* for Violin, Viola, and Guitar (1933); Piano Trio (1933–35); *Moresca Figures* for Violin, Clarinet, and Piano (1934); *Berceuse slave* for Oboe and Piano (1939); *Bohemian Dance Rondo* for Bassoon and Piano (1939); *Suite* for 4 Clarinets (1939); *Shanty-Boy Fantasy* for Oboe and Piano (1940); *Variations on an Old Trumpet Tune* for Brass Sextet (1942); *Little Woodwind Music* (1945); *Cortege* for Brass Choir (1945); *Variations and Fugue on an American Theme* for Violin and Cello (1946); Clarinet Sonata (1947); *Suite* for Oboe and Piano (1947); *Introduction and Rondo* for Flute and Piano (1948); *First Suite* for Flute (1950); *Intermezzo* for Clarinet and Piano (1950); *Elegy and Scherzino* for Oboe, 2 Clarinets, and Bassoon (1951); Quartet for 2 Trumpets, Horn, and Trombone (1951); Sonata for Horn and Piano (1953); *Suite* for 2 Flutes (1953); Flute Sonata (1954); *Suite* for Oboe, Clarinet, and Piano (1955); *Eclogue* for Violin and Piano (1955); *Idyll* for Oboe and Piano (1957); String Trio (1958); Woodwind Quintet (1958); Woodwind Trio (1960); *Music* for Violin, Clarinet, Cello, and Bassoon (1962); *Envoi* for 6 Instruments (1964); Duo for Clarinet and Bassoon (1966); *Perpetuum mobile* for Organ and Brass Quartet (1968); *2nd Suite* for Flute (1969); *Suite* for Woodwind and Piano (1970); *Variables* for Clarinet and Piano (1973); *Discussions* for Oboe, Clarinet, Bassoon, Viola, and Cello (1974); Brass Quintet (1976); Sonata for Violin and Piano (1977); *Three Vignettes* for Clarinet and Bassoon (1977); *3 Movements* for Violin and Piano (1978); Trio for Oboe, Clarinet, and Bassoon (1979); *Music* for Oboe and Piano (1982); *Suite* for Solo Cello (1983); piano pieces.

BIBL.: T. Collins, *The Instrumental Music of P.A. P.* (diss., Univ. of Missouri, 1972).

Pistocchi, Francesco Antonio Mamiliano, noted Italian singer, teacher, and composer, known as **Il Pistocchino;** b. Palermo, 1659; d. Bologna, May 13, 1726. A precocious child, he sang in public at age 3 and publ. his 1st work, *Capricci puerilli*, when he was 8; made appearances as a singer in Bologna's cappella musicale at S. Petronio (from 1670), where he was permanently engaged as a soprano (1674–75); then toured as a contralto with great success in his homeland and

in Germany. He was in the service of the Parma court (1686–95), then was Kapellmeister to the Margrave of Brandenburg in Ansbach (1696–99); after a sojourn in Vienna (1699–1700), he returned to Bologna, and once more sang in the cappella musicale at S. Petronio (1701–8); was made virtuoso di camera e di cappella to Prince Ferdinando of Tuscany (1702); was active as a singing teacher, his notable pupils being Antonio Bernacchi, Annibale Pio Fabri, and G.B. Martini. Having been elected to membership in the Accademia Filarmonica (1687), he served as its principe (1708, 1710); took Holy Orders (1709); became honorary chaplain to the Elector Palatine Johann Wilhelm (1714); was made a member of the Congregation of the Oratory in Forlì (1715).

WORKS: OPERAS: *Il Leandro* (Venice, May 15, 1679; 2nd version, Venice, Jan. 1682); *Il Narciso* (Ansbach, March 1697); *Le pazzie d'amore e dell'interesse* (Ansbach, June 16, 1699); *Le risa di Democrito* (Vienna, Feb. 17, 1700); *I Rivali generosi* (Reggio Emilia, April 1710; in collaboration with C. Monari and G. Cappelli). **ORATORIOS:** *Sant'Adriano* (Modena, 1692); *Maria vergine addolorata* (Ansbach, 1698); *Il sacrificio di Gefte* (Bologna, 1720); *I Pastori al Presepe* (Bologna, Dec. 25, 1721); *Davide* (Bologna, March 19, 1721). **CANTATA:** *La pace tra l'armi, sorpresa notturna nel campo* (Ansbach, Sept. 5, 1700); also *Capricci puerili saviamente composti e passeggiati in 40 modi sopra un basso d'un balleto, per il clavicembalo ed altri instrumenti*, op. 1 (Bologna, 1667); *Duetti e terzetti*, op. 3 (Bologna, 1707); etc.

Piston, Walter (Hamor, Jr.), outstanding American composer and pedagogue; b. Rockland, Maine, Jan. 20, 1894; d. Belmont, Mass., Nov. 12, 1976. The family name was originally Pistone; his paternal grandfather was Italian. He received his primary education in Boston; took courses in architectural drawing at the Massachusetts Normal Art School, graduating in 1916; then took piano lessons with Harris Shaw, and studied violin with Fiumara, Theodorowicz, and Winternitz; played in restaurants and places of public entertainment as a youth. During World War I, he was in the U.S. Navy; after the Armistice, he entered Harvard Univ., graduating in musical subjects summa cum laude in 1924; while at Harvard, he conducted concerts of the univ. orch., the Pierian Sodality. For a time he was employed as a draftsman for Boston Elevated Railway. In 1924 he went to Paris on a John Knowles Paine Traveling Fellowship, and became a student of Nadia Boulanger; also took courses with Paul Dukas at the École Normale de Musique (1925); returning to the U.S. in 1926, he was appointed to the faculty of Harvard Univ.; in 1944, became a prof. of music; was named prof. emeritus in 1960. As a teacher he was greatly esteemed, not only because of his consummate knowledge of music and pedagogical ability, but also because of his immanent humanity in instructing students whose esthetics differed from his own; among his grateful disciples was Leonard Bernstein. As a composer, Piston followed a cosmopolitan course, adhering to classical forms while extending his harmonic structures toward a maximum of tonal saturation; he was particularly expert in contrapuntal writing. Beginning about 1965, Piston adopted a modified system of 12-tone composition, particularly in initial thematic statements; his Sym. No. 8 and *Variations* for Cello and Orch. are explicitly dodecaphonic. Piston rejected the narrow notion of ethnic Americanism in his music, and stated once that an artist could be as American working in the Library of the Boston Atheneum as roaming the Western prairie; yet he employed upon occasion the syncopated rhythms of jazz. He received Pulitzer Prizes for his Sym. No. 3 and Sym. No. 7, and N.Y. Music Critics' Circle Awards for his Sym. No. 2, Viola Concerto, and String Quartet No. 5. He held the degree of D.Mus. *honoris causa* from Harvard Univ.; was elected a member of the National Inst. of Arts and Letters (1938), the American Academy of Arts and Letters (1955), and the American Academy of Arts and Sciences (1940). He traveled little and declined invitations to go to South America and to Russia under the auspices of the State Dept., preferring to live in his house in suburban

Belmont, near Boston. His working habits were remarkably methodical; he rarely altered or revised his music once it was put on paper, and his handwriting was calligraphic. With 2 exceptions, he never wrote for voices.

WORKS: STAGE: *The Incredible Flutist,* ballet (Boston, May 30, 1938; suite, 1938; Pittsburgh, Nov. 22, 1940). **ORCH.:** *Symphonic Piece* (1927; Boston, March 23, 1928); 2 suites: No. 1 (1929; Boston, March 28, 1930) and No. 2 (1947–48; Dallas, Feb. 29, 1948); Concerto for Orch. (1933; Boston, March 6, 1934); *Prelude and Fugue* (1934; Cleveland, March 12, 1936); 8 syms.: No. 1 (1937; Boston, April 8, 1938); No. 2 (1943; Washington, D.C., March 5, 1944; received the N.Y. Music Critics' Circle Award, 1945); No. 3 (1947; Boston, Jan. 9, 1948; received the Pulitzer Prize in Music, 1948); No. 4 (1950; Minneapolis, March 30, 1951); No. 5 (1954; for the 50th anniversary of the Juilliard School of Music, N.Y., Feb. 24, 1956); No. 6 (for the 75th anniversary of the Boston Sym. Orch., Nov. 25, 1955); No. 7 (1960; Philadelphia, Feb. 10, 1961; won the Pulitzer Prize in Music, 1961); No. 8 (1964–65; Boston, March 5, 1965); Concertino for Piano and Chamber Orch. (CBS Radio, N.Y., June 20, 1937); 2 violin concertos: No. 1 (1939; N.Y., March 18, 1940) and No. 2 (Pittsburgh, Oct. 28, 1960); Sinfonietta (Boston, March 10, 1941); *Prelude and Allegro* for Organ and Strings (CBS, Cambridge, Mass., Aug. 8, 1943); *Fugue on a Victory Tune* (N.Y., Oct. 21, 1944); *Variation on a Theme by Eugene Goossens* (1944; Cincinnati, March 23, 1945); *Toccata* (Bridgeport, Conn., Oct. 14, 1948); *Fantasy* for English Horn, Harp, and Strings (1952; Boston, Jan. 1, 1954); *Serenata* (Louisville, Oct. 24, 1956); Viola Concerto (1957; Boston, March 7, 1958; received the N.Y. Music Critics' Circle Award, 1959); Concerto for 2 Pianos and Orch. (1959; Hanover, N.H., July 4, 1964); *3 New England Sketches* (Worcester, Mass., Oct. 23, 1959); *Symphonic Prelude* (Cleveland, April 20, 1961); *Lincoln Center Festival Overture* (N.Y., Sept. 25, 1962); *Capriccio* for Harp and String Orch. (1963; Madrid, Oct. 19, 1964); *Variations on a Theme by Edward Burlingame Hill* (Boston, April 30, 1963); *Pine Tree Fantasy* (Portland, Maine, Nov. 16, 1965); *Variations* for Cello and Orch. (1966; N.Y., March 2, 1967); Clarinet Concerto (Hanover, N.H., Aug. 6, 1967); *Ricercare* (1967; N.Y., March 7, 1968); *Fantasia* for Violin and Orch. (1970; Hanover, N.H., March 11, 1973); Flute Concerto (1971; Boston, Sept. 22, 1972); *Bicentennial Fanfare* (Cincinnati, Nov. 14, 1975); Concerto for String Quartet, Wind Ensemble, and Percussion (Portland, Maine, Oct. 26, 1976); also *Fanfare for the Fighting French* for Brass and Percussion (Cincinnati, Oct. 23, 1942); *Tunbridge Fair: Intermezzo* for Band (1950); *Ceremonial Fanfare* for Brass and Percussion (1969; N.Y., Feb. 10, 1970). **CHAMBER:** 3 Pieces for Flute, Clarinet, and Bassoon (1926); Flute Sonata (1930); *Suite* for Oboe and Piano (1931); 5 string quartets (1933, 1935, 1947, 1951, 1962; No. 5 received the N.Y. Music Critics' Circle Award, 1964); 2 piano trios (1935, 1966); Violin Sonata (1939); *Interlude* for Viola and Piano (1942); Quintet for Flute and Strings (1942); *Partita* for Violin, Viola, and Organ (1944); Sonatina for Violin and Harpsichord or Piano (1945); *Divertimento* for 9 Instruments (1946); Duo for Viola and Cello (1949); Piano Quintet (1949); Wind Quintet (1956); Sextet for Strings (1964); Piano Quartet (1964); *Souvenirs* for Flute, Viola, and Harp (1967); Duo for Cello and Piano (1972); *3 Counterpoints* for Violin, Viola, and Cello (1973). **VOCAL:** *Carnival Song* for Men's Chorus and 11 Brasses (1938; Cambridge, Mass., March 7, 1940); *Psalm and Prayer of David* for Chorus, Flute, Clarinet, Bassoon, Violin, Viola, Cello, and Double Bass (1958). **PIANO:** Sonata (1926); *Passacaglia* (1943); *Improvisation* (1945). **ORGAN:** *Chromatic Study on B.A.C.H.* (1940).

WRITINGS: *Principles of Harmonic Analysis* (Boston, 1933); *Harmony* (N.Y., 1944; 5th ed., rev. and enlarged by M. DeVoto, 1987); *Counterpoint* (N.Y., 1947); *Orchestration* (N.Y., 1955).

BIBL.: N. Slonimsky, "W. P.," in H. Cowell, *American Composers on American Music* (Stanford, Calif., 1933); I. Citkowitz, "W. P.—Classicist," *Modern Music* (Jan.–Feb. 1936); E. Carter, "W. P.," *Musical Quarterly* (July 1946); W. Austin, "P.'s Fourth Symphony," *Music Review* (May 1955); O. Daniel et al.,

W. P. (N.Y., 1964); K. Roy, "W. P.," *Stereo Review,* XXIV/4 (1970); H. Lindenfeld, *Three Symphonies of W. P.: An Analysis* (diss., Cornell Univ., 1975); H. Gleason and W. Becker, "W. P.," *20th-century American Composers* (Bloomington, Ind., 2nd ed., rev., 1981); H. Pollack, *W. P.* (Ann Arbor, Mich., 1981).

Pitfield, Thomas B(aron), English composer; b. Bolton, April 5, 1903. He studied at the Royal Manchester College of Music; was an instructor there from 1947 to 1973; also studied engineering and painting; was a book illustrator; wrote verse; publ. his autobiography as *No Song, No Supper* (London, 1986). In his music, he adopts a simple style, in a folk-song manner. His works include a cantata, *The Rhyming Shopman;* a Piano Concerto; various pieces of chamber music; a set of piano pieces under the general title *Ballet in Education;* also various pieces of humorous content, among them *Planibestiary,* "a zoological sequence in space" for Voices, Piano, and Percussion (1966); *Adam and the Creatures,* "Morality with Music" for Speaker, Chorus, Organ, and Percussion (1968).

BIBL.: A. Holland, "T.B. P.," *Monthly Musical Record* (May 1939); D. Ellis, "T.B. P. at 80," *Musical Times* (April 1983).

Pitoni, Giuseppe Ottavio, Italian teacher, writer on music, and composer; b. Rieti, March 18, 1657; d. Rome, Feb. 1, 1743. He began music studies at 5, under Pompeo Natali in Rome; at 8 was chorister at S. Giovanni de' Fiorentini, later at the Ss. Apostoli, and studied counterpoint under Foggia. In 1673–74 he was maestro di cappella at Monterotondo; from 1674 to 1676, at Assisi Cathedral; in 1676–77, at Rieti Cathedral; finally, in 1677, he became maestro at the collegiate church of S. Marco in Rome, retaining this post until death, though simultaneously engaged at S. Apollinare, S. Lorenzo in Damaso (1694–1721), S. Giovanni in Laterano (1708–19), and St. Peter's (1719); also in some minor Roman churches. He was an excellent teacher, and taught after the same method by which he himself rose to eminence as a composer, e.g., the writing out in score of Palestrina's works to study his style. Durante, Leo, and Feo were his greatest pupils. As a composer, he cultivated a distinct feature of the Roman school, the writing in many parts.

WORKS: Some 270 masses and Mass parts; more than 200 introits; over 230 graduals; about 800 Psalms; some 650 antiphons; about 250 hymns; around 235 motets; approximately 220 canticles; only a motet for 2 Voices (Rome, 1697) was publ. during his lifetime.

BIBL.: H. Hucke, "G.O. P. und seine Messen im Archiv der Cappella Giulia," *Kirchenmusikalisches Jahrbuch,* XXXIX (1955); S. Gmeinwieser, "G.O. P. (1657–1743)," *Allgemeine Musikzeitung,* XXXII (1975); idem, *G.O. P.: Thematisches Werkverzeichnis* (Wilhelmshaven, 1976).

Pitt, Percy, English conductor and composer; b. London, Jan. 4, 1870; d. there, Nov. 23, 1932. He studied with Jadassohn and Reinecke at the Leipzig Cons. and with Rheinberger at the Akademie der Tonkunst in Munich. Returning to England in 1893, he pursued his career in London; was musical advisor (1902–7) and musical director (1907–24) of the Grand Opera Syndicate at Covent Garden; was the 1st English conductor to appear at Covent Garden (1907), returning there in 1909–10 and 1919–20; was artistic director of the British National Opera Co. (1922–24) and musical advisor to the BBC (1922–24), serving as the latter's musical director (1924–30). He wrote stage music, a *Ballade* for Violin and Orch. (1900) for Ysaÿe, a Clarinet Concerto, and a *Sérénade du passant* for Tetrazzini.

BIBL.: J. Chamier, *P. P. of Covent Garden and the BBC* (London, 1938).

Pittaluga, Gustavo, Spanish composer; b. Madrid, Feb. 8, 1906. He studied law at the Univ. of Madrid and composition with Oscar Esplá; was a member of the Grupo de los 8 in Madrid and of the Paris group of modern musicians, Triton (1935); from 1936 to 1939, was a member of the staff of the Spanish Embassy in Washington, D.C. (for the Loyalist government); then remained in the U.S.; was in charge of the film library at the Museum of Modern Art in N.Y. (1941–43).

WORKS: *La Romería de los Cornudos,* ballet (Madrid, 1933); *El Loro,* zarzuela (Madrid, 1933); *Concerto militaire* for Violin and Orch. (Barcelona, 1933); *Petite suite* for 10 Instruments (Paris, 1935; also for Piano as *3 pièces pour une espagnolade*); *Capriccio alla romantica* for Piano and Orch. (Paris, 1936); *6 danses espagnoles en suite* for Piano (1935); *Vocalise-étude* for Voice and Piano (1932); *Berceuse* for Violin and Piano (1935); *Ricercare* for Violin, Clarinet, Bassoon, and Trumpet (1934); *5 canciones populares* for Chorus and 10 Instruments (1939); *Habanera* for Violin and Piano (1942); *Lament for Federico García Lorca* for Narrator and Orch. (1942).

Pittel, Harvey, American saxophonist; b. Great Falls, Mont., June 22, 1943. He studied with Kalman Bloch and Franklyn Stokes; then took courses at the Univ. of Southern Calif. in Los Angeles (1961–65), where he received his doctorate in music education. After studies with Frederick Hemke at Northwestern Univ. (1965–66), he played in the U.S. Military Academy Band (1966–69), during which time he continued his studies, with Joseph Allard. He won the silver medal at the Geneva International Competition (1970); made his formal debut as a soloist in Ingolf Dahl's Saxophone Concerto with the Boston Sym. Orch. (1971), and his recital debut at N.Y.'s Carnegie Recital Hall (1973); subsequently toured throughout North America and Europe, appearing as a soloist with the leading orchs., as a recitalist, and as a chamber music player.

Pittrich, George Washington, German conductor and composer; b. Dresden, Feb. 22 (Washington's birthday; hence the selection of Christian names); 1870; d. Nuremberg, April 28, 1934. He studied at the Dresden Cons. with Draeseke and others; was active as a conductor in Dresden (1890–98), Hamburg (1898), Cologne (1899–1901), Frankfurt (1901–4), Dresden (1904–12), and Berlin (from 1912). He wrote the opera *Marga* (Dresden, Feb. 8, 1894); incidental music to Shakespeare's *As You Like It* and to several classical German plays; Christmas musical plays: *Der Stern von Bethlehem, Der Zauberschleier,* and *Mäusekönigin;* Clarinet Concerto; Fantasia for Piano and String Orch.; many songs.

Pitzinger, Gertrude, Bohemian contralto; b. Mährisch-Schönberg, Aug. 15, 1904. She studied music with Joseph Marx at the Vienna Academy of Music, and voice with various teachers. After several concert tours in central Europe, she went to the U.S. and gave a N.Y. recital on Jan. 17, 1938, with excellent success; she specialized in German lieder; her repertoire included some 400 songs. She taught singing at the Hochschule für Musik in Frankfurt (1960–73) before retiring.

Piutti, Karl, German organist and composer; b. Elgersburg, April 30, 1846; d. Leipzig, June 17, 1902. He studied at the Leipzig Cons.; in 1880 he became organist at the Leipzig Thomaskirche. He wrote a great number of organ works, including a *Hochzeit Sonata;* about 200 organ preludes; Psalms and motets a cappella; songs.

Pixis, Johann Peter, German pianist, teacher, and composer; b. Mannheim, Feb. 10, 1788; d. Baden-Baden, Dec. 22, 1874. Of a musical family (his father and his brother were musicians), he received his primary education at home; after touring with his brother (1796), he returned to Mannheim to study composition; continued his studies with Albrechtsberger in Vienna (1806); went to Paris in 1823, where he established himself as a teacher. In 1840 he settled in Baden-Baden as a teacher.

WORKS: OPERAS: *Almazinde, oder Die Höhle Sesam* (Vienna, April 11, 1820); *Bibiana, oder Die Kapelle im Walde* (Aachen, Oct. 8, 1829); etc.; also a Sym.; Overture; Piano Concerto; Piano Quartet; Piano Quintet; 2 string quintets; 7 piano trios; piano sonatas, variations, and transcriptions.

BIBL.: R. Batka, "Aus J.P. P. Memoiren," *Kranz: Gesammelte Blätter über Musik* (Leipzig, 1903).

Pizzetti, Ildebrando, eminent Italian composer and teacher; b. Parma, Sept. 20, 1880; d. Rome, Feb. 13, 1968. He studied piano with his father, Odvardo Pizzetti, in Parma and composition with Tebaldini at the Parma Cons., graduating in 1901;

then devoted himself to composition and teaching; was on the faculty of the Parma Cons. (1907–8); then of the Florence Cons. (1908–24), where he became director in 1917; from 1924 to 1936, was director of the Milan Cons.; then taught at the Accademia di Santa Cecilia in Rome (1936–58); from 1947 to 1952 he was also its president. In 1914 he founded (with G. Bastianelli) in Florence a modernistic periodical, pointedly named *Dissonanza,* to promote the cause of new music. In 1930 he made a trip to the U.S. to attend the performance of his *Rondo veneziano,* conducted by Toscanini with the N.Y. Phil.; in 1931 Pizzetti conducted his opera *Fra Gherardo* at the Teatro Colón in Buenos Aires. Pizzetti's music represents the Romantic trend in modern Italy; in his many works for the theater, he created the modern counterpart of medieval mystery plays; the mystical element is very strong in his own texts for his operas. He employed astringent chromatic harmony, but the mainstream of his melody flows along pure diatonic lines.

WORKS: OPERAS: *Fedra* (1909–12; Milan, March 20, 1915); *Debora e Jaele* (1915–21; Milan, Dec. 16, 1922); *Lo straniero* (1922–25; Rome, April 29, 1930); *Fra Gherardo* (1925–27; Milan, May 16, 1928); *Orsèolo* (1931–35; Florence, May 4, 1935); *L'Oro* (1938–42; Milan, Jan. 2, 1947); *Vanna Lupa* (1947–49; Florence, May 4, 1949); *Ifigenia* (RAI, Oct. 3, 1950; 1st stage perf., Florence, May 9, 1951); *Cagliostro* (RAI, Nov. 5, 1952; 1st stage perf., Milan, Jan. 24, 1953); *La figlia di Iorio* (Naples, Dec. 4, 1954); *Assassinio nella cattedrale,* after T.S. Eliot (1957; Milan, March 1, 1958); *Il calzare d'argento* (Milan, March 23, 1961); *Clitennestra* (1961–64; Milan, March 1, 1965). INCIDENTAL MUSIC TO: G. d'Annunzio's *La nave* (1905–7; Rome, March 1908) and *La Pisanella* (Paris, June 11, 1913); F. Belcare's *La sacra rappresentazione di Abram e d'Isaac* (1915–17; Florence, June 1917; expanded into an opera, 1925; Turin, March 11, 1926); Aeschylus's *Agamemnon* (Syracuse, April 28, 1930); Sophocles's *Le trachiniae* (1932; Syracuse, April 26, 1933); Sophocles's *Edipo a Colono* (Syracuse, April 24, 1936); *La festa delle Panatenee* (1935; Paestum, June 1936); Shakespeare's *As You Like It* (Florence, May 1938). ORCH.: *Ouverture per una farsa tragica* (1911); *Concerto dell'estate* (1928; N.Y., Feb. 28, 1929); *Rondo veneziano* (1929; N.Y., Feb. 27, 1930; as a ballet, Milan, Jan. 8, 1931); Cello Concerto (Venice, Sept. 11, 1934); Sym. (1940); Violin Concerto (1944; Rome, Dec. 9, 1945); *Canzone di beni perduti* (1948; Venice, Sept. 4, 1950); Harp Concerto (1958–60). VOCAL: *Messa di requiem* (1922); *De profundis* (1937); *Epithalamium,* cantata for Soloists, Chorus, and Orch. (1939); *Oritur sol et occidit,* cantata for Brass and Orch. (1943); *Cantico di gloria "Attollite portas"* for 3 Choruses, 22 Wind Instruments, 2 Pianos, and Percussion (1948); *Vanitas vanitatum,* cantata for Soloists, Men's Chorus, and Orch. (1958); *Filiae Jerusalem, adjuro vos,* cantata for Soprano, Women's Chorus, and Orch. (1966); songs. CHAMBER: 2 string quartets (1906; 1932–33); Violin Sonata (1918–19); Cello Sonata (1921); Piano Trio (1925). PIANO: 3 pieces: *Da un autunno già lontano* (1911); Sonata 1942.

WRITINGS: *La musica dei Greci* (Rome, 1914); *Musicisti contemporanei* (Milan, 1914); *Intermezzi critici* (Florence, 1921); *Paganini* (Turin, 1940); *Musica e dramma* (Rome, 1945); *La musica italiana dell' 800* (Turin, 1947).

BIBL.: R. Fondi, *I. P. e il dramma musicale italiano d'oggi* (Rome, 1919); special issue of *Il pianoforte,* II (Turin, 1921); G. Gatti, "I. P.," *Musical Quarterly* (Jan., April 1923); G. Tebaldini, *I. P. nelle memorie* (Parma, 1931); G. Gatti, *I. P.* (Turin, 1934; 2nd ed., 1955; Eng. tr., 1951); G. Gavazzeni, *Tre studi su P.* (Como, 1937); special issue of *La Rassegna Musicale,* XIII (1940); V. Bucchi, L. Dallapiccola et al., *Firenze a I. P.* (Florence, 1947); G. Gavazzeni, *Altri studi pizzettiani* (Bergamo, 1956); M. la Morgia, ed., *La città d'annunziana a I. P.: Saggi e note* (Pescara, 1958); B. Pizzetti, ed., *I. P.: Cronologia e bibliografia* (Parma, 1980).

Pizzi, Emilio, Italian composer; b. Verona, Feb. 1, 1861; d. Milan, Nov. 27, 1940. He studied at the Istituto Musicale at

Bergamo and at the Cons. of Milan (with Ponchielli and Bazzini); received 1st prize for his opera *Lina* (1885); in 1897, was appointed director of the Istituto Musicale at Bergamo; from 1900, lived for some time in London.

WORKS: OPERAS: *Lina* (1885); *Guglielmo Ratcliff* (Bologna, Oct. 31, 1889); *Gabriella* (Boston, Nov. 25, 1893); *La Rosalba* (Turin, May 31, 1899); *Vendetta* (in Ger., Cologne, Dec. 1, 1906; in Italian as *Ivania*, Bergamo, Sept. 14, 1926); comic opera in Eng., *The Bric-à-Brac Will* (London, 1895); also *Messa solenne* for Soli, Chorus, and Orch.; Requiem; violin pieces; piano pieces; songs.

Pizzini, Carlo Alberto, Italian composer; b. Rome, March 22, 1905; d. there, Sept. 9, 1981. He studied with Respighi at the Accademia di Santa Cecilia in Rome, graduating in 1929; later was an administrator there and with the RAI.

WORKS: DRAMATIC: *Dardanio*, opera (Rome, 1928); theater, film, and radio music. **ORCH.:** *Sinfonia in istile classico* (1930); *Il poema delle Dolomiti* (1931); *Strapaese* (1932); *Al Piemonte* (1941); *Grotte di Postumia* (1941); *Concierto para tres hermanas* for Guitar and Orch. (1969); also chamber music; piano pieces.

Plaidy, Louis, famous German piano teacher; b. Wermsdorf, Nov. 28, 1810; d. Grimma, March 3, 1874. He began his professional career as a violinist, and performed in public in Dresden and Leipzig; at the same time he took piano lessons from Agthe, and became greatly proficient as a pianist, so that Mendelssohn engaged him in 1843 as a piano teacher at the Leipzig Cons. Plaidy concentrated on the technical problems of piano pedagogy; taught at the Leipzig Cons. until 1865; then continued to give private lessons. He publ. a number of instructive piano studies which were widely used; his *Technische Studien für das Pianoforte-Spiel* was a standard manual; he also publ. a booklet, *Der Klavierlehrer* (1874; British ed. as *The Pianoforte Teacher's Guide*; American ed., tr. by J.S. Dwight, as *The Piano-Teacher*).

Plakidis, Peteris, Latvian composer; b. Riga, March 4, 1947. He graduated from the Latvian Cons. in Riga (1970), where he studied composition with V. Utkins and Gederts Ramans; taught there from 1973, and also was secretary of the Latvian Composer's Union (1978–84; from 1989). In 1990 he made a tour of the U.S. as harpsichordist of the Latvian Chamber Orch.

WORKS: ORCH.: *Music* for Piano, Timpani, and Strings (1969); *The Rifleman* for Voice and Orch. (1972); Concerto for Orch., with Piano (1975); *Legend* (1976); *Interchanges* for a Group of Soloists (1977); Concerto for 2 Oboes and Chamber Orch. (1982); *Concerto-Ballad* for 2 Violins, Piano, and Strings (1984); *Canto* (1989). **CHAMBER:** *Improvisation and Burlesque* for Piano Trio (1966); *Prelude and Pulsation* for Wind Quintet (1975); 2 *Sketches* for Oboe (1975); *Fifths*, invention for 2 Pianos (1976); 2 *Retrospections* (1977); *A Short Canon and Animated Cartoon Film* for Flute, Oboe, and Piano (1979); *Romantic Music* for Piano Trio (1980); *Homage to Haydn* for Piano, Flute, and Cello (1982). Also songs; choruses.

Plamenac, Dragan, eminent Croatian-born American musicologist; b. Zagreb, Feb. 8, 1895; d. Ede, the Netherlands, March 15, 1983. He studied jurisprudence at the Univ. of Zagreb; then took courses in composition with Franz Schreker at the Vienna Academy of Music and with Vítězslav Novák in Prague. In 1919 he went to Paris and attended lectures at the Sorbonne given by André Pirro; then had a seminar with Guido Adler at the Univ. of Vienna, receiving his Ph.D. there in 1925 with the dissertation *Johannes Ockeghem als Motetten- und Chansonkomponist*. From 1928 to 1939 he taught at the Univ. of Zagreb; after the outbreak of World War II, he went to the U.S., becoming a naturalized citizen in 1946. In 1947 he received a Guggenheim fellowship; then taught at the Univ. of Illinois, Urbana (1954–63). Plamenac's chief accomplishment was his painstaking and fruitful research into the sources of the music of the Renaissance. He prepared a major ed. of the works of Ockeghem in the Publikationen älterer Musik,

Jg. I/2 (Leipzig, 1927); a 2nd ed., rev. in 1959, was publ. in N.Y. as *Masses I–VIII* in the *Collected Works*, I; *Masses and Mass Sections IX–XVI* appeared as vol. II (N.Y., 1947; 2nd ed., 1966).

BIBL.: G. Reese and R. Snow, eds., *Essays in Musicology in Honor of D. P. on his 70th Birthday* (Pittsburgh, 1969).

Planchet, Dominique-Charles, French organist, teacher, and composer; b. Toulouse, Dec. 25, 1857; d. Versailles, July 19, 1946. He studied at the École Niedermeyer in Paris; was organist at the Cathedral in Versailles; in 1898 he was appointed organist at the Ste.-Trinité in Paris; taught at the École Niedermeyer; in 1905, won the Prix Chartier for chamber music. He wrote an opera, *Le Fils du Croisé* (privately perf. in Versailles, 1885); 2 cello concertos; *Esclavage africain*, cantata for Male Voices; much sacred music; organ pieces; a Piano Trio; a Violin Sonata; songs.

Plançon, Pol (-Henri), famous French bass; b. Fumay, June 12, 1851; d. Paris, Aug. 11, 1914. He was destined by his parents for a commercial career in Paris, but showed a natural vocal ability, and began to study singing with Sbriglia and Duprez; made his operatic debut as St.-Bris in *Les Huguenots* in Lyons (1877); appeared for the 1st time in Paris as Colonna in Duprat's *Pétrarque* at the Théâtre de la Gaîté (Feb. 11, 1880); after a season in Monte Carlo, he made a highly successful appearance at the Paris Opéra as Méphistophélès in Gounod's *Faust* (June 23, 1883); sang that role more than 100 times during his 10 seasons at the Opéra, and was regarded as unrivaled in his dramatic delivery and vocal power. On June 3, 1891, he sang Méphistophélès for his debut at London's Covent Garden, singing there every subsequent season until 1904; his American debut took place at the Metropolitan Opera in N.Y. on Nov. 29, 1893, as Jupiter in Gounod's *Philemon et Baucis*. He then resigned from the Paris Opéra and remained a member of the Metropolitan Opera until his retirement in 1908. He had an imposing physique, mobile features, and an innate acting ability. His repertoire consisted of about 50 roles in French, Italian, German, and Eng. In some operas he sang more than one part, as in *Roméo et Juliette* (Capulet and Friar), *Aida* (Ramfis and the King), *Les Huguenots* (St.-Bris and Marcel), etc. Of Wagnerian roles, he sang the Landgrave, King Heinrich, and Pogner.

Planquette, (Jean-) Robert, French composer of operettas; b. Paris, July 31, 1848; d. there, Jan. 28, 1903. He studied at the Paris Cons. with Duprato; wrote chansonnettes and "saynètes" for cafés-concerts in Paris; then composed a one-act operetta, *Paille d'avoine* (Paris, March 12, 1874), and others. He achieved his 1st great success with the production of *Les Cloches de Corneville*, a comic opera in 3 acts, at the Folies-Dramatiques (Paris, April 19, 1877); it was performed for the 1,000th time there in 1886, and became one of the most popular works of its genre; in Eng., it was given as *The Chimes of Normandy* (N.Y., Oct. 22, 1877; London, Feb. 23, 1878). Other operettas were *Le Chevalier Gaston* (Monte Carlo, Feb. 8, 1879); *Rip Van Winkle* (London, Oct. 14, 1882; very successful); *Nell Gwynne* (London, Feb. 7, 1884); *Surcouf* (Paris, Oct. 6, 1887; in Eng. as *Paul Jones*, London, Jan. 12, 1889); *La Cocarde tricolore* (Paris, Feb. 12, 1892); *Le Talisman* (Paris, Jan. 20, 1893); *Panurge* (Paris, Nov. 22, 1895); *Mam'zelle Quat'Sous* (Paris, Nov. 5, 1897). A posthumous operetta, *Le Paradis de Mahomet* (orchestrated by Louis Ganne), was produced at the Variétés in Paris on May 15, 1906.

Plantade, Charles-Henri, French composer; b. Pontoise, Oct. 14, 1764; d. Paris, Dec. 18, 1839. As a child, he studied singing and the cello in the Royal School for the "pages de musique"; afterward he took lessons with Honoré Langlé (theory), Hüllmandel (piano), and Petrini (harp). In 1797 he became a singing teacher at the Campan Inst. at St.-Denis, where Hortense de Beauharnais, the future Queen of the Netherlands, was his pupil. He subsequently was in the service of Queen Hortense as her representative in Paris; was a prof. at the Paris Cons. from 1799 to 1807, and again in 1815–16 and from 1818 to 1828. From 1812 to 1815 he also held the post of singing master and stage director at the Paris Opéra. He received the ribbon of the Legion of Honor from Louis XVIII (1814); from 1816, was music master of the Royal Chapel. Losing his various positions after the revolution of 1830, he retired to Batignolles. He wrote several operas, of which *Le Mari de circonstances* (Paris, March 18, 1813) was the most successful; other operas for Paris included *Les 2 Sœurs* (May 22, 1792); *Les Souliers mordores* (May 18, 1793); *Au plus brave la plus belle* (Oct. 5, 1794); *Palma, ou Le Voyage en Grèce* (Aug. 22, 1797); *Romagnesi* (Sept. 3, 1799); *Le Roman* (Nov. 12, 1800); *Zoé, ou La Pauvre Petite* (July 3, 1800); *Lisez Plutarque* (Spring 1800); *Bayard à la ferté, ou Le Siège de Mezières* (Oct. 13, 1811). He further composed masses, motets, etc.; publ. 20 sets of romances, 3 books of vocal duets (nocturnes), and a Harp Sonata. His son, Charles-François Plantade (b. Paris, April 14, 1787; d. there, May 26, 1870), was also a composer; studied at the Paris Cons.; worked in the Ministry of Fine Arts; wrote romances, chansons, and chansonettes.

Planté, Francis, French pianist; b. Orthez, Basses-Pyrénées, March 2, 1839; d. St. Avit, near Mont-de-Marsan, Dec. 19, 1934. From 1849 he was a pupil of Marmontel at the Paris Cons.; won 1st prize after 7 months' tuition. After a course in harmony in Bazin's class (1853), he retired for private study for 10 years, and then reappeared as a pianist of finished technique and style. About 1900 he suddenly vanished from concert life, vowing that he would "never be seen again in public." He created a sensation in 1915 when he was heard again in several concerts in Paris; but, in order to keep his strange vow, he was hidden from the view of the audience by a screen. **BIBL.:** O. Comettant, *F. P.* (Paris, 1874); A. Dandelot, *F. P.: Une Belle Vie d'artiste* (Paris, 1920; 3rd ed., 1930); A. Lenoir and J. de Nahuque, *F. P.: Doyen des pianistes* (Paris, 1931).

Plantinga, Leon (Brooks), American musicologist; b. Ann Arbor, Mich., March 25, 1935. He studied at Calvin College (B.A., 1957), Michigan State Univ. (M.Mus., 1959), and Yale Univ. (Ph.D., 1964, with the diss. *The Musical Criticism of Robert Schumann in the "Neue Zeitschrift für Musik"*); taught there from 1963, being made a prof. (1974), acting chairman (1978–79), and chairman (1979–86) of its music dept. **WRITINGS:** *Schumann as Critic* (New Haven, Conn., and London, 1967); *Muzio Clementi: His Life and Music* (London, 1977); *Romantic Music: A History of Musical Style in Nineteenth-Century Europe* (N.Y. and London, 1984; won the ASCAP-Deems Taylor Award, 1985); *Anthology of Romantic Music* (N.Y. and London, 1984).

Plaschke, Friedrich (real name, **Bedřich Plaške**), Czech bass-baritone; b. Jaroměr, Jan. 7, 1875; d. Prague, Nov. 10, 1951. He studied with Leontine von Döttcher and Ottilie Sklenář-Mala in Prague, and then with Karl Scheidemantel in Dresden; made his debut with the Dresden Court (later State) Opera as the Herald in *Lohengrin* in 1900; was on its roster until 1939; during his tenure there, he created the following roles in operas by Richard Strauss: Pöschel in *Feuersnot*, the 1st Nazarene in *Salome*, Da-Ud in *Die aegyptische Helena*, Count Waldner in *Arabella*, and Sir Morosus in *Die schweigsame Frau*. He made many guest appearances at Vienna and Munich; also sang at Bayreuth, at Covent Garden in London, and in the U.S. with the German Opera Co. in 1923–24.

Plass, Ludwig, German trombonist, bandmaster, composer, and writer on music; b. Osterode, March 13, 1864; d. Berlin, Sept. 16, 1946. He studied trombone at the Hochschule für Musik in Berlin; in 1893, became solo trombonist of the Royal Chapel; in 1905, court bandmaster; collected materials on military music in Germany; wrote 28 pieces for wind instruments; publ. interesting historical essays on the German post horn; also *Bachs Clarintrompeter* (1927); *Was bliesen unsere Reiter?* (1934); etc.

Plasson, Michel, French conductor; b. Paris, Oct. 2, 1933. He studied conducting at the Paris Cons. with Bigot; in 1962

he won 1st prize at the International Conducting Competition held in Besançon; he then continued his studies with Charles Munch, Leopold Stokowski, Leonard Bernstein, and Erich Leinsdorf. In 1968 he was appointed music director of the Orch. du Capitole in Toulouse; also made guest conducting appearances in London, N.Y., Tokyo, and other music centers.

Platania, Pietro, Italian composer; b. Catania, April 5, 1828; d. Naples, April 26, 1907. He studied with P. Raimondi at the Naples Cons.; was director of the Palermo Cons. (1863–82); later maestro di cappella at Milan (from 1882), and also director of the Naples Cons. (1885–1902). Rossini and Verdi considered him an excellent contrapuntist. **WORKS: OPERAS:** *Matilde Bentivoglio* (Palermo, 1852); *Piccarda Donati* (Palermo, March 3, 1857); *La vendetta slava* (Palermo, Feb. 4, 1865); *Spartaco* (Naples, March 29, 1891); etc.; also *L'Italia,* sym.; *Sinfonia festiva* for Voices and Orch. for the coronation tour of King Umberto I (1878); *Pensiero sinfonico;* much sacred music; secular songs; pedagogical pieces. **BIBL.:** F. Guardione, *P. P.* (Milan, 1908).

Plath, Wolfgang, German musicologist; b. Riga, Latvia, Dec. 27, 1930. He studied musicology at the Free Univ. of Berlin with Gerstenberg, and later at Tübingen Univ. (Ph.D., 1958, with the diss. *Das Klavierbüchlein für Wilhelm Friedemann Bach*). In 1960 he was named co-ed. (with Wolfgang Rehm) of the *Neue Mozart-Ausgabe.* His studies of Mozart autographs and texts are valuable; he contributed important articles to the *Mozart-Jahrbuch.*

Plato, great Greek philosopher; b. probably in Athens, c.428 B.C.; d. there, 347/348 B.C. In his *Timaeus* he formulated a system of music in which he likened the movements of music to those of the soul, whose development may therefore be influenced by the art of music. **BIBL.:** T.-H. Martin, *Études sur le Timée de P.n* (Paris, 1841); J. Regner, *P.s Musik-Theorie* (Halle, 1923); E. Moutsopoulos, *La musique dans l'oeuvre de P.n* (Paris, 1959); L. Richter, *Zur Wissenschaftslehre von der Musik bei P.n und Aristoteles* (Berlin, 1961).

Platti, Giovanni Benedetto, Italian composer; b. Padua, July 9, 1697; d. Würzburg, Jan. 11, 1763. In 1722 he went to Würzburg, where he was active as an instrumentalist, tenor, singing teacher, and composer at the court of the bishops until at least 1761. **WORKS: DRAMATIC:** *Arianna,* opera (Würzburg, 1729); 2 oratorios; Requiem; 6 masses; cantatas; etc. **INSTRUMENTAL** (all publ. in Nuremberg): *6 sonates pour la clavessin sur le goût italien,* op. 1 (1742; ed. in Istituzioni e Monumenti dell'Arte Musicale Italiana, VII, 1941, and Mitteldeutsches Musikarchiv, 1st series, III–IV, Leipzig, 1957); 6 Concerti for Harpsichord and Strings, op. 1 (1742); 6 Sonate for Flute and Cello, op. 3 (1743?); 6 Sonate for Harpsichord, op. 4 (c.1746; ed. in Mitteldeutsches Musikarchiv, 1st series, III–IV, Leipzig, 1957); 5 concertos for Harpsichord and Strings; 28 cello concertos; Oboe Concerto; 21 sonatas for Violin, Cello, and Bass. **BIBL.:** F. Torrefranca, "La creazione della sonata drammatica moderna rivendicata all'Italia: G. P. il grande," *Rivista Musicale Italiana,* XVIII (1910); idem, "Prime ricognizioni dello stile violoncellistico P.ano," *International Musicological Society Congress Report,* IV, *Basle 1949;* idem, *G.B. P. e la sonata moderna* (Milan, 1963).

Playford, Henry, English music publisher, son of **John Playford;** b. London, May 5, 1657; d. there, c.1707. He worked with his father before setting up a business of his own; his most important publications were *Wit and Mirth,* a collection of Tom D'Urfey's songs (1699, 1700); and the 2nd book of Purcell's *Orpheus Britannicus* (1702).

Playford, John, English music publisher, father of **Henry Playford;** b. Norfolk, 1623; d. London, Nov. 1686. He was an apprentice (1639–47) to the publisher John Benson before setting up his own business; began publishing music (1651); his most important publication was *The English Dancing Master* (London, 1651; many rev. eds. to 1728). Among his other publications, all printed in London, were *A Musicall Banquet* (1651), *Musick's Recreation on the Lyra Viol* (1652; 4th ed., 1682), J. Hilton's *Catch That Catch Can* (1652; many eds. to c.1720), *A Catalogue of All the Musik Bookes . . . Printed in England* (1653), his own *A Breefe Introduction to the Skill of Musick* (1654; 2nd ed., enlarged, 1655, with T. Campion's "Art of Composing"; many eds. to 1730), *Court Ayres* (1655; 2nd ed., rev., 1662, as *Courtly Masquing Ayres*), his own *The Whole Book of Psalmes collected into English Meeter* (1661; many later eds.), *Apollo's Banquet for the Treble Violin* (1669; many eds. to 1701), his own *Psalms and Hymns in Solemn Musick* for 4 Voices (1671), *Choice Songs and Ayres* for Voice and Theorbo or Bass Viol (5 books, 1673, 1679, 1681, 1683, 1684), and *The Whole Book of Psalmes* (1677; many eds. to 1757).

BIBL.: F. Kidson, "J. P. and 17th-Century Music Publishing," *Musical Quarterly* (Oct. 1918); J. Pulver, "J. P.," *Music News and Herald* (May 1927); C. Day and E. Murrie, *English Song-Books, 1651–1702, and Their Publishers* (London, 1936); N. Temperley, "J. P. and the Metrical Psalms," *Journal of the American Musicological Society*, XXV (1972); idem, "J. P. and the Stationers' Company," *Music & Letters*, LIV (1973).

Plaza (-Alfonzo), Juan Bautista, Venezuelan composer and organist; b. Caracas, July 19, 1898; d. there, Jan. 1, 1964. He went to Rome in 1920 to study at the Pontifical Inst. of Sacred Music; upon returning to Venezuela, became organist of the Cathedral of Caracas. He wrote a number of sacred choral works; also symphonic poems: *El picacho abrupto, Vigilia, Campanas de Pascua, Las horas,* etc.; *Fuga criolla* for Orch.; *Sonatina venezolana* for Piano; songs.

Plé-Caussade, Simone, French pianist, pedagogue, and composer; b. Paris, Aug. 14, 1897; d. Bagnères-de-Bigorre, Aug. 6, 1985. She studied piano at the Paris Cons. with Alfred Cortot and composition with Georges Caussade, whom she later married; in 1928 she was appointed prof. of harmony and counterpoint at the Paris Cons.; among her students were Gilbert Amy and Betsy Jolas. She wrote a number of orch. and chamber music works in a fine impressionistic manner.

Pleasants, Henry, American music critic; b. Wayne, Pa., May 12, 1910. He studied at the Philadelphia Musical Academy and the Curtis Inst. of Music. In 1930 he joined the *Philadelphia Evening Bulletin* as its music critic; remained until 1942. He served in the U.S. Army during World War II; then was in the Foreign Service. In 1967 he settled in London, and wrote articles for the *International Herald Tribune*. In 1955 he publ. an acerbic book titled *The Agony of Modern Music*, in which he damned in no uncertain terms all contemporary music as an ear-rasping collection of unpleasant noises produced by arrogant people lacking musical talent. Curiously enough, he found salvation in jazz as a form of folk music. Even more astringent was his 2nd book, *Death of Music? The Decline of the European Tradition and the Rise of Jazz,* publ. in 1961. Both books aroused predictable commotion in the press, which quickly subsided, however, after the sensational element contained in them was exhausted. His subsequent publs. purported to convey information and as such were of some validity: *The Great Singers from the Dawn of Opera to Our Own Time* (N.Y., 1966; 3rd ed., rev. and enlarged, 1985); *Serious Music, and All That Jazz* (N.Y., 1969); *The Great American Popular Singers* (N.Y., 1974); *Opera in Crisis: Tradition, Present, Future* (N.Y., 1989).

Pleshakov, Vladimir, Russian-American pianist; b. Shanghai (of Russian parents), Oct. 4, 1934. He studied piano with Russian teachers in Shanghai; in 1949 he went to Sydney, where he took piano lessons with Alexander Sverjensky. In 1955 he emigrated to the U.S. and studied medicine at the Univ. of Calif., Berkeley (A.B., 1958). Turning back to music, he entered Stanford Univ. in the graduate school of music (Ph.D., 1973). He made a special study of piano manufacture in Beethoven's era, and performed on reconstructed pianos at his concerts of classical music.

Pleskow, Raoul, Austrian-born American composer and teacher; b. Vienna, Oct. 12, 1931. He went to the U.S. in 1939, and became a naturalized citizen in 1945; took courses at N.Y.'s Juilliard School of Music (1950–52), with Rathaus at Queens College (B.M., 1956), and with Luening at Columbia Univ. (M.M., 1958). He taught at C.W. Post College, Long Island Univ. (from 1959). His works combine both tonal and atonal means of expression.

WORKS: ORCH.: 2 *Movements* (1968); *Music* (1980); 4 *Bagatelles* (1981); 6 *Epigrams* (1985); *Consort* for Strings (1988). **CHAMBER:** *Movement* for Flute, Cello, and Piano (1964); *Music* for 7 Players (1966); *Movement* for 9 Players (1967); 3 *Bagatelles* for Flute, Viola, and Piano (1969); Trio for Flute, Cello, and Piano (1978); String Quartet (1979); 4 *Pieces* for Flute, Cello, and Piano (1979); *Variations on a Lyric Fragment* for Cello and Piano (1980); 4 *Short Pieces* for 7 Players (1981); *Divertimento: Sua sei canzoni* for 5 Players (1984); *Intrada* for Flute, Clarinet, Violin, and Cello (1984); *Composition* for 4 Instruments (1987); solo pieces for Violin, Viola, Cello, Brass, and Piano. **VOCAL:** Cantata for 2 Sopranos, Tenor, Chorus, and Orch. (1975); 2nd Cantata for Soprano, Tenor, Chorus, and Orch. (1979); 6 *Brief Verses* for 2 Sopranos and/or Women's Voices, Strings, and Piano (1983); *Paumanok* for Soprano, Chorus, and Chamber Ensemble (1985); *Serenade* for Chorus and Orch. (1988); also many settings for Solo Voice with a variety of accompaniments.

Plessis, Hubert du, South African composer; b. Malmesbury, Cape Province, June 7, 1922. He studied music with W.H. Bell at Gordonsbai (1942–44) and later at the Rhodes Univ. College in Cape Town; in 1951 he went to London and took courses in composition with Alan Bush and Ferguson at the Royal Academy of Music; returning to South Africa in 1955, he was a lecturer on music at the College of Music in Cape Town and, from 1958, at the Univ. of Stellenbosch. As a composer, he cultivates mainly vocal music; many of his songs are based on South African motifs; among them are the cycles *In den ronde* (1948) and *Die vrou* (1960; to words in Afrikaans, Dutch, and German); he also wrote *Suid-Afrik, Nag en daeraad* for Chorus and Orch. (1966; in Afrikaans).

Pleyel, (Joseph Stephen) Camille, French pianist, piano manufacturer, and composer, son of **Ignace (Ignaz Josef) Pleyel**; b. Strasbourg, Dec. 18, 1788; d. Paris, May 4, 1855. He was a pupil of his father and later of Desormery, Dussek, and Steibelt; in 1815 became a legal partner in his father's firm, which became Ignace Pleyel et Fils Aîné; he took complete control of the business in 1824, and was joined by Kalkbrenner in 1829. Upon Camille's death, Kalkbrenner's son-in-law, A. Wolff, took over the firm. Pleyel's works include trios, sonatas, and various piano pieces. His wife, Marie-Félicité-Denise Pleyel (née Moke; b. Paris, Sept. 4, 1811; d. St.-Josse-ten-Noode, near Brussels, March 30, 1875), was a pianist, teacher, and composer; she studied with Jacques Herz, Moscheles, and Kalkbrenner, appearing as soloist in Kalkbrenner's 1st Piano Concerto in Brussels at age 14; she created a sensation with her virtuosic tour of Belgium, Austria, Germany, and Russia in her 15th year. Berlioz fell in love with her (1830), but she married the younger Pleyel that same year, only to separate from him in 1835; then she toured Europe with great success; subsequently was prof. of piano at the Brussels Cons. (1848–72); wrote some piano pieces.

Pleyel, Ignace Joseph (actually, **Ignaz Josef**), eminent Austrian-French pianist, piano manufacturer, music publisher, and composer, father of **(Joseph Stephen) Camille Pleyel;** b. Ruppersthal, near Vienna, June 18, 1757; d. on his estate near Paris, Nov. 14, 1831. He was the 24th of 38 children in the impoverished family of a schoolteacher; however, he received sufficient education, including music lessons, to qualify for admittance to the class of Wanhal; thanks to the generosity of Count Ladislaus Erdödy, he became Haydn's pupil and lodger in Eisenstadt (c.1772–77), and then was enabled to go to Rome. In 1783 he became 2nd Kapellmeister at the

Strasbourg Cathedral; was advanced to the rank of 1st Kapell-meister in 1789, but lost his position during the turbulent times of the French Revolution. He conducted the "Professional Concerts" in London during the 1791–92 season, and honored his teacher Haydn by playing a work of Haydn at his opening concert (Feb. 13, 1792). After several years he returned to Strasbourg to liquidate his estate; in 1795 he went to Paris, where he opened a music store which was in business until 1834, and in 1807 founded a piano factory, which manufac-tured famous French pianos; the firm eventually became known as Pleyel et Cie., and continued to prosper for over a century and a half. The name Pleyel is mainly known through his piano manufacture, but he was a prolific and an extremely competent composer. His productions are so close in style to those of Haydn that specialists are still inclined to attribute certain works in Haydn's catalogues to Pleyel. He composed about 45 syms., 6 symphonies concertantes, 2 violin concertos, 5 cello concertos, other concertos, 16 string quintets, Septet, Sextet, more than 70 string quartets, many trios and duos, and some vocal music, including 2 operas, *Die Fee Urgele* for puppet theater (Eszterház, Nov. 1776) and *Ifigenia in Aulide* (Naples, May 30, 1785), and some songs.

BIBL.: L. de Fourcaud, *La Salle P.* (Paris, 1893); R. Benton, "A la recherche de P. perdu, or Perils, Problems and Procedures of P. Research," *Fontes Artis Musicae*, XVII (1970); idem, *Ignace P.: A Thematic Catalogue of His Compositions* (N.Y., 1977); idem, "P. as Music Publisher," *Journal of the American Musicological Society*, XXXII (1979).

Plishka, Paul (Peter), American bass; b. Old Forge, Pa., Aug. 28, 1941. He studied at Montclair, N.J., State College; from 1961 to 1965 he was a member of the Paterson (N.J.) Lyric Opera; in 1965 he joined the Metropolitan Opera National Co., and sang with it on tour. On June 27, 1967, he made his Metropolitan Opera debut in a concert performance at the Botanical Gardens in the Bronx as the Uncle-Priest in *Madama Butterfly*; he first sang on the Metropolitan's stage as the Monk in *La Gioconda* on Sept. 21, 1967; remained on its roster for many years, most notably in such roles as King Marke, Lepo-rello, Varlaam, Oroveso, Pimen, Gounod's Méphistophélès, and Henry VIII in *Anna Bolena*. He also appeared as a concert singer with many of the major U.S. orchs.

Plotnikov, Eugene, Russian conductor; b. Odessa, Aug. 29, 1877; d. N.Y., Sept. 28, 1951. He studied at the Moscow Cons.; was coach and assistant conductor at the Moscow Opera; also conducted at the Paris Opéra (1921). In 1922 he settled in the U.S.; conducted Russian operas in N.Y. and other American cities.

Plowright, Rosalind, English mezzo-soprano, later soprano; b. Worksop, May 21, 1949. She studied at the Royal Manchester College of Music; in 1979 she won the Sofia International Competition. She made her debut as Miss Jessel in Britten's opera *The Turn of the Screw* with the English National Opera in 1979; later sang Desdemona and Elisabeth in *Mary Stuart* there. She made her Covent Garden debut as Ortlinde in 1980; sang there again in 1983. She subsequently sang Abigaille in Sofia; Ariadne and Alceste in Bern; Aida, Amelia, and Leonora in Frankfurt; Donna Anna in Munich; and Suor Angelica at La Scala in Milan. She made her American debut with Riccardo Muti and the Philadelphia Orch. in 1982, and then sang in *Il Corsaro* in San Diego.

Plüddemann, Martin, German composer; b. Kolberg, Sept. 29, 1854; d. Berlin, Oct. 8, 1897. He studied at the Leipzig Cons.; later had vocal instruction from Julius Hey in Munich and Friedrich Schmitt in Munich, but his singing career was brief due to the loss of his voice (1880); in 1889 he was engaged as a singing teacher at the Styrian Music School in Graz. He wrote a number of popular male choruses and ballads; publ. pamphlets of a Wagnerian tendency.

BIBL.: R. Batka, *M. P. und seine Balladen* (Prague, 1896); L. Schemann, *M. P. und die deutsche Ballade* (Regensburg, 1930).

Plush, Vincent, remarkable Australian composer; b. Adelaide, April 18, 1950. He studied piano, organ, and voice before em-barking on regular courses at Adelaide Univ. (B.M., 1971), where his principal instructors in composition were Andrew McCredie and Richard Meale; taught at the Sydney Cons. (1973–80); in 1976 founded the Seymour Group, an ensemble devoted to the performance of contemporary music. In 1981 he joined the staff of the Australian Broadcasting Commission (A.B.C.) in Sydney. From his earliest independent activities as a lecturer, radio commentator, and conductor, Plush dedi-cated his efforts to the promotion of Australian music. Thanks to a generous Harkness fellowship, he was able to spend a couple of years at Yale Univ., conducting interviews with a number of American composers for its Oral History Project; also worked at the Univ. of Minnesota (1981), and participated in an Australian Arts Festival in Minneapolis (1982). He then spent a year at the Center for Music Experiment and the Com-puter Music Facility at the Univ. of Calif. in San Diego. Return-ing to Australia in 1983, he became composer-in-residence for the A.B.C., where he inaugurated a series of radio broadcasts pointedly entitled "Mainstreet U.S.A.," dedicated to new Ameri-can music. A firm believer in the authentic quality of Australian folk music, he organized in Sydney the whimsically named ensemble Magpipe Musicians, which gave performances of native music in schools and art galleries, on the radio, in the concert hall, at country festivals, citizenship ceremonies, rail-way openings, and suchlike events, public and private. Their programs were deliberately explorative, aggressive, and exhor-tatory, propagandistic of new ideas, often with a decided revolu-tionary trend. The titles of Plush's own works often pay tribute to revolutionary or heroic events, e.g., *On Shooting Stars—Homage to Victor Jara* (a Chilean folksinger murdered by the fascistic Chilean police), *Bakery Hill Rising* (memorializing the suppression of the rebellion of Australian gold miners in 1854), *Gallipoli Sunrise* (commemorating the sacrificial at-tempt at capturing the Gallipoli Straits in World War I, during which thousands of Australians perished), and *The Ludlow Lullabies* (recalling the brutal attack on striking coal miners in the region of Ludlow, Colo., in 1914). The musical setting of each of these works varies from astutely homophonic to acutely polyphonic, according to the requirements of the sub-ject.

WORKS: DRAMATIC: *Australian Folksongs*, musical theater piece for Baritone and Ensemble (in celebration of Australia's colonial history and folk heritage; Sydney, July 19, 1977); *The Maitland and Morpeth String Quartet* for Narrator and String Quartet (Sydney, April 1, 1979; rev. 1985); *Facing the Danger* for Narrator and Instruments (based on the poem *Say No* by Barbara Berman; 1982; Las Vegas, Jan. 18, 1983); *Grody to the Max* for "Val"-speaker and Trumpeter (1983); *The Wake-field Chronicles*, pageant for Narrator, Solo Trumpet and Trom-bone, and Ensemble (based on the writings of Edward Gibbon Wakefield; Adelaide, March 5, 1986); *The Muse of Fire* for Narrator, Baritone, Trumpet, Flute, Piano, Chorus, 2 Brass Bands, Children's Choir, and Organ (based on the writings of Andrew Torning; 1986–87). **ORCH.:** *Pacifica* (1986; rev. 1987; Aspen, July 10, 1988); *Concord/Eendracht* (Utrecht, May 18, 1990); *Pilbara* for String Orch. (1991). **CHAMBER:** *Aurores* for Horn, Piano, and Ensemble (from *O Paraguay!*; Kensington, New South Wales, July 31, 1979); *Bakery Hill Rising* for Solo Horn and 8 Other Horns (1980; Ballarat, Victoria, Feb. 14, 1981); *On Shooting Stars—Homage to Victor Jara* for Ensemble (Sydney, Sept. 11, 1981); *FireRaisers*, "Concertino in the Style of a Vaudeville Entertainment" for Trumpet and Ensemble (Brisbane, Queensland, Sept. 30, 1984); *Gallipoli Sunrise* for Tenor Trombone and 7 Other Trombones (1984); *Helices* for Percussion Quartet (from *The Wakefield Chronicles*; 1985); *The Wakefield Convocation* for Brass Quintet (1985); *The Wakefield Chorales* for Brass Band (1986); *The Wakefield Invo-cation* for Trumpet and Organ (1986); *March of the Dalmations* for Brass Band (1987); *The Ludlow Lullabies* for Violin and Piano (Colorado Springs, Oct. 19, 1989); *SkyFire* for 10 Pianos and Tape (Colorado Springs, Nov. 19, 1989); *Aunt Kelly's Book of Tangos* for Violin, Cello, and Piano (1990); *Florilegium I, II, and III* (Sydney, Sept. 28, 1990); *Los Dios de Los Muertos* for Percussion Quartet (1990); *The Love-Songs of Herbert Hoover* for Horn Trio (1991); also pieces for Solo Instruments, including *Franz Liszt Sleeps Alone*, piano nocturne (1985; Budapest, March 12, 1986), and *Encompassings* for Organ (Canberra, March 16, 1975). TAPE: *Estuary* (1978); *Stevie Wonder's Music* for Flute and Tape (Sydney, Nov. 4, 1979); *All Ears* (1985); *Metropolis: Sydney* (WDR, Cologne, Nov. 14, 1988). VOCAL: *Magnificat* for Soprano, Flute, and 3 Vocal Quartets (1970; Sydney, Sept. 8, 1976); *3 Carols* for Soprano, Contralto, and Children's Choir (1978, 1979, 1982); *The Hymn of the Winstanly Levellers* for Speaking/Singing Chorus a cappella (Sydney, May 23, 1981); *Ode to Knocks* for Mixed Voices and Instruments (Knox, Victoria, Sept. 6, 1981); *Letters from the Antipodes: 6 English Reflections on Colonial Australia* for Small Chorus (1984; Sydney, July 9, 1989); *Letters from the Antipodes: 6 English Reflections on Colonial Australia* for Small Chorus (1984; Sydney, July 9, 1989); *All Ears*, radiophonic composition for Voices (Radio 2MBS-FM, Sydney, March 16, 1985); *The Muse of Fire*, pageant for Voices and Instruments (Penrith, New South Wales, Oct. 17, 1987); *Cornell Ceremonial Music* for Brass Instruments and Chorus (Winter Park, Fla., Nov. 10, 1988); *Andrew Torning's March to Victory* for Small Choir and Piano (1989); *The Arraignment of Henry Lawson* for Voices and Instruments (1991); songs.

Plutarch, famous Greek writer; b. Chaeronea, Boeotia, c.46; d. after 119. His series of essays, *Ethica* (Latin *Moralia*), includes a discussion of music; see the Loeb ed. (16 vols., 1928–).

Pocci, Franz, Graf von, German writer on music and composer; b. Munich, March 7, 1807; d. there, May 7, 1876. Possessing versatile talents, he wrote plays with music for a puppet theater in Munich, for which he also designed the scenery. He was at his best in pieces for children (*Blumenlieder, Bildertöne für Klavier, Soldatenlieder, Jägerlieder, Alte und neue Kinderlieder*, etc.). His 2 piano sonatas were praised by Schumann for their poetic expression and fine Romantic spirit. An opera, *Der Alchymist*, was produced in Munich (1840); his grandson F. Pocci publ. a collection, *Franz Poccis Lustiges Komödienbüchlein* (Munich, 1921).

BIBL.: H. Holland, *Zur Erinnerung an F. P.* (Munich, 1877); L. Hirschberg, "F. P., der Musiker," *Zeitschrift für Musikwissenschaft,* I (1918–19; with complete list of works); K. Pastor, *F. P. als Musiker* (diss., Univ. of Munich, 1932).

Pochon, Alfred, Swiss violinist; b. Yverdon, July 30, 1878; d. Lutry, Feb. 26, 1959. He made his 1st public appearance at the age of 11; then went to Liège to study with César Thomson, who engaged him as 2nd violin in his string quartet. In 1902 the philanthropist E. de Coppet asked Pochon to organize a string quartet, later to become famous as the Flonzaley Quartet, so named after Coppet's summer residence near Lausanne; Pochon remained a member until it was disbanded in 1929. In 1938 Pochon returned to Switzerland; was director of the Lausanne Cons. until 1957. He publ. *A Progressive Method of String-Quartet Playing* (N.Y., 1924).

Poděšt, Ludvík, Czech composer; b. Dubňany, Dec. 19, 1921; d. Prague, Feb. 27, 1968. He studied composition with Jaroslav Kvapil at the Brno Cons. (1945–48) and musicology with J. Racek and B. Štědroň at the Univ. of Brno (Ph.D., 1949); worked at Brno Radio (1947–51); was music director of the Vit Nejedlý Army Artistic Ensemble (1953–56) and of the music dept. of the Czech Television (1958–60).

WORKS: 2 operas: *Tři apokryfy* (3 Apocryphas), to Čapek short stories (1957–58; No. 1, *Staré zlaté časy*; No. 2, *Svatá noc*; No. 3, *Romeo a Julie*), and *Hrátky s čertem* (Frolics with the Devil; 1957–60; Liberec, Oct. 12, 1963); *Smrt* (Death), cantata (1942); *Písně z koncentráku* (Songs from the Concentration Camp) for Baritone and Orch. (1946); *Měsíce* (Months) for Soprano and Orch. (1948; rev. 1957–58); Sym. (1947–48; rev. 1964); *Raymonda Dienová*, symphonic poem (1950–51);

4 suites for Orch. (1951, 1954, 1956, 1960); 2 piano concertos (1951–53, 1958–59); *Jarní Serenáda*, violin concerto (1953); *Advent Rhapsody* for Orch. (1956–57); Concertino for Cimbalom and Orch. (1963); *The Seconds of a Day*, symphonic variations (1965); Concertino for 2 Cellos and Chamber Orch. (1965); *Partita* for Strings, Guitar, and Percussion (1967); 2 string quartets (1942); *5 Spring Days* (1948); *Litanie* for String Quartet (1944); Wind Quintet (1946); Violin Sonata (1947); Cello Sonata (1947); *Hojačky* for 2 Clarinets and Piano (1947); *Suite* for Viola and Piano (1955–56); Piano Sonatina (1945); Piano Sonata (1946).

Podešva, Jaromír, Czech composer; b. Brno, March 8, 1927. He studied with J. Kvapil at Brno's Cons. (1946–47) and Janáček Academy of Music (1947–51); on an American visit, attended classes of Aaron Copland at the Berkshire Music Center in Tanglewood; then had lessons with Dutilleux in Paris; wrote a book of impressions. In 1969 he was appointed to the staff of the Ostrava Cons. His music is marked by contrapuntal density and dynamic intensity.

WORKS: STAGE: *Opuslíš-li mne* (If You Leave Me), opera (1962–63); *Bambini di Praga*, opera-buffa (1968). ORCH.: Piano Concerto (1949); 7 syms.: No. 1 (1950–51); No. 2 for Strings and Flute (1960–61); No. 3, *Kulminace—Perla na dně: Dvě symfonické paralely myšlenek M. Kundery a B. Hrabala* (Culmination—The Pearl at the Bottom: 2 Symphonic Parallels to Ideas by M. Kundera and B. Hrabal; 1966); No. 4 for Chamber Orch. (1966); No. 5, after poems by Yevtushenko and Halas, for Voices and Orch. (1967); No. 6 (1970); No. 7 (1982–83); *Cesta vlasti* (Throughout My Homeland; 1952–53), 3-part cycle of symphonic poems: *Kounicovy koleje* (Kounic College; Brno site of a Nazi concentration camp), *V kraj vešla Rudá armáda* (The Red Army Enters the Country), and *Veliký pochod* (Great March); *Setkání mládeže* (Meeting of Youth) (1956); *Triple Concerto* for Violin, Cello, Piano, and Orch. (1956–57); *Suita notturna* (1957); Sinfonietta for String Orch. (1959); *Slavnost l'Humanité*, overture for Strings and Brasses in celebration of the Paris organ of the Communist Party (1961); Flute Concerto (1965); *Dotazník srdce*, chamber cantata for Narrator, Baritone, and 9 Instruments (1965); Concerto for String Quartet and Orch. (1971); Piano Concerto (1973); *Hommage à L. Janáček* (1977); *Fêtes des perce-neige* (1979–80). CHAMBER: 5 string quartets (1950; *You Shall Live in Peace*, 1951; 1955; *From the Life of Contemporary Man*, 1959–60; 1965); Clarinet Sonatina (1947–48); 2 violin sonatas (1948, 1958); Piano Trio (1948); Sextet for 2 Violins, Viola, Cello, Clarinet, and Horn (1949); *Poetic Trio* for Violin, Cello, and Piano (1954); *O šťastných dětech* (Happy Children), nonet (1955); Cello Sonatina (1960); Cornet Sonatina (1960); *3 Sonata Studies* for Flute and Piano (1964); Sonata for Soprano and Piano (1967); *5 Pieces* for Violin and Piano (1968); *Suite* for Viola and Piano (1969); Wind Quintet No. 1 (1969–70); *How the Flood Came to Earth* for 5 Children's Choirs, Flute, Trumpet, Cello, and Piano (1971). PIANO: 2 sonatas (1951; *Březen, 1953*, (1953); *4 Miniatures* (1953); *Rhapsodiettas* (1955); also numerous a cappella choruses, including *Long Live the Universe*, a quasi sinfoniette (1959–60), and *Sinfonietta to Nature* (1962).

Poglietti, Alessandro, eminent Italian organist, teacher, and composer; place and date of birth unknown; d. at the hands of the Turks during the siege of Vienna, July 1683. He served as court and chamber organist in the Vienna Kapelle of Emperor Leopold I (from 1661). He was one of the outstanding keyboard composers of his era.

WORKS: *Endimione festeggiante*, opera (Göttweig, Jan. 12, 1677); sacred vocal works; keyboard music, including 12 ricercares (ed. in Die Orgel, II/5–6, Lippstadt, 1957), suites, canzonas, capriccios, preludes, and fugues.

BIBL.: F. Riedel, "Neue Mitteilungen zur Lebensgeschichte von A. P. und Johann Kaspar Kerll," *Archiv für Musikwissenschaft,* XIX–XX (1962–63); idem, "A. P.s oper *Endimione*," *Festschrift Hans Engel* (Kassel, 1964); idem, "Ein Skizzenbuch von A. P.," *Essays in Musicology: A Birthday Offering for Willi Apel* (Bloomington, Ind., 1968).

Pogorelich, Ivo, provocative Yugoslav pianist; b. Belgrade, Oct. 20, 1958. He commenced piano lessons in Belgrade when he was 7; when he was 11 he became a pupil of A. Timakin in Moscow; after studies at its Central Music School, he continued his training at the Moscow Cons., where he became a student of Aliza Kezeradze in 1976; they married in 1980. After winning 5 competitions in his homeland and the Casagrande Competition in Terni, Italy (1978), he captured 1st prize in the Montreal Competition in 1980; later that year he entered the Chopin Competition in Warsaw, where he became the center of a major controversy after he was eliminated from its final round; one of the jurors, Martha Argerich, resigned in protest and declared that Pogorelich was a "genius"; a group of Polish music critics were moved to give him a special prize. In 1981 he made his Carnegie Hall debut in N.Y. in a recital, and that same year he made his London debut. He subsequently toured all over the world, appearing both as a soloist with orchs. and as a recitalist. His phenomenal technical mastery is well suited to showcasing his brilliant but idiosyncratic interpretations of works ranging from Bach to Bartók.
Bibl.: N. Malitz, "Idiosyncratic—Inventive—Inimitable: I. P.," *Ovation* (Feb. 1987); *Current Biography* (Sept. 1988).

Pohl, Carl Ferdinand, German writer on music; b. Darmstadt, Sept. 6, 1819; d. Vienna, April 28, 1887. He was a pupil of Sechter in Vienna. During his stay in London (1863–66) he gathered all available facts concerning the residence there of Mozart and Haydn, embodying this information in his publ. *Mozart und Haydn in London* (2 vols., Vienna, 1867); was archivist and librarian of Vienna's Gesellschaft der Musikfreunde (1866–87). Pohl also began an extended biography of Haydn, but publ. only one vol. (in 2 parts, 1875, 1882); the work was finished by Hugo Botstiber (Leipzig, 1927). Other publs.: *International Exhibition of 1862. Cursory Notices on the History of the Glass Harmonica* (London, 1862); an interesting historical review, *Die Gesellschaft der Musikfreunde . . . und ihr Conservatorium* (1871); *Denkschrift aus Anlass des hundertjährigen Bestehens der Tonkünstler-Societät in Wien* (1871); *Bibliographie der Musiksammelwerke des 16. und 17. Jahrhunderts* (with R. Eitner and A. Lagerberg; 1877).

Pohl, Richard, German writer on music; b. Leipzig, Sept. 12, 1826; d. Baden-Baden, Dec. 17, 1896. He studied natural sciences and philosophy in Karlsruhe, Göttingen, and Leipzig; in 1854 he went to Weimar, where he established a personal friendship with Liszt, and became an ardent advocate of the new German school of music. After Liszt's temporary absence from Weimar, Pohl went to Baden-Baden, where he remained until his death. He was the joint ed. of the *Neue Zeitschrift für Musik* in Weimar (1854–64), to which he contributed a number of articles under the pseudonym Hoplit. He also publ. *Bayreuther Erinnerungen* (1877); *Autobiographisches* (1881); *Franz Liszt* (1883); *Hector Berlioz, Studien und Erinnerungen* (1884); *Die Höhenzüge der musikalischen Entwickelung* (1888). He possessed a fine literary gift and wrote some poetry; when his 1st wife, Johanna, a harpist, died in 1870, he wrote a heartfelt memoir, *Meiner theuren Gattin zum Gedächtnis;* then married again; his 2nd wife, Luise, compiled Pohl's materials on Berlioz and publ. *Hector Berlioz: Leben und Werke* (1900); also a fictional life of Wagner under the title *Richard Wiegand. Episoden aus dem Leben eines grossen Meisters* (1904).

Pohlig, Karl, German conductor; b. Teplitz, Feb. 10, 1858; d. Braunschweig, June 17, 1928. A pupil of Liszt in Weimar, Pest, and Rome, he began his career as a pianist, touring Germany, Austria, Russia, Scandinavia, and Italy; became 1st Kapellmeister at Graz, then assistant conductor to Mahler at the Vienna Court Opera, and conductor at London's Covent Garden (1897–98); was 1st Kapellmeister in Coburg and then in Stuttgart (1900–7); after serving as conductor of the Philadelphia Orch. (1907–12), he settled in Braunschweig as Generalmusikdirektor.

Bibl.: H. Kuperberg, *Those Fabulous Philadelphians: The Life and Times of a Great Orchestra* (N.Y., 1969).

Poise, (Jean Alexandre) Ferdinand, French composer; b. Nîmes, June 3, 1828; d. Paris, May 13, 1892. He studied at the Paris Cons. with A. Adam and Zimmerman, taking the 2nd Grand Prix de Rome in 1852.
Works: OPÉRAS COMIQUES (all 1st perf. in Paris): *Bonsoir, voisin* (Sept. 18, 1853); *Le Thé de Polichinelle* (March 4, 1856); *Le roi Don Pèdre* (Sept. 30, 1857); *Le Jardinier galant* (March 4, 1861); *Le corricolo* (Nov. 28, 1868); *Les deux billets* (Feb. 19, 1870); *Les trois souhaits* (Oct. 29, 1873); *La surprise de l'amour* (Oct. 31, 1877); *L'amour médicin* (Dec. 20, 1880); etc.; also *Cécile,* oratorio (Dijon, 1888) and *Les moissonneurs,* cantata (Paris, Aug. 15, 1866); men's choruses; songs.

Poissl, Johann Nepomuk, Freiherr von, German composer; b. Haukenzell, Lower Bavaria, Feb. 15, 1783; d. Munich, Aug. 17, 1865. He was educated in Straubing, Munich, and at the Univ. of Landshut (1800); settled in Munich (1805), and studied composition with Danzi and Abbé Vogler; in 1811 met Weber, who became a champion of his works. As a composer for the theater, he won his most notable successes with *Athalia* (June 3, 1814) and *Der Wettkampf zu Olympia oder Die Freunde* (April 21, 1815); nevertheless, he was dogged by poverty until being made assistant superintendent of court music in 1823; was also named director of the Court Theater (1825); his opera *Die Prinzessin von Provence* was first performed at the reopening celebrations of the rebuilt Nationaltheater (Jan. 23, 1825), and remains his best-known achievement. He was replaced as director of the Court Theater (1833), but was retained as director of court music until his dismissal in 1847, when he was made 1st chamberlain. His final years were marked by illness and poverty. Poissl was an important link in the development of German opera between the eras of Mozart and Weber.
Works: OPERAS (all first perf. in Munich unless otherwise given): *Die Opernprobe,* comic opera (Feb. 23, 1806); *Antigonus,* serious opera (Feb. 12, 1808); *Ottaviano in Sicilia,* dramma eroico (June 30, 1812); *Aucassin und Nicolette,* singspiel (March 28, 1813); *Athalia,* grand opera (June 3, 1814); *Der Wettkampf zu Olympia oder Die Freunde,* grand opera (April 21, 1815); *Die wie mir oder Alle betrügen,* comic opera (1816; not perf.); *Nittetis,* grand opera (Darmstadt, June 29, 1817); *Issipile,* grand opera (1818; not perf.); *La rappresaglia,* opera semiseria (April 7, 1820); *Die Prinzessin von Provence,* magical opera (Jan. 23, 1825); *Der Untersberg,* Romantic opera (Oct. 30, 1829); *Zaide,* Romantic-tragic opera (Nov. 9, 1843). INCIDENTAL MUSIC: To Heyden's *Renata* (Munich, Oct. 12, 1823), von Schenk's *Belisar* (Munich, Feb. 23, 1826) and *Kaiser Ludwigs Traum* (Munich, March 27, 1826), and Kleist's *Hermannschlacht* (1826). ORATORIOS: *Judith* (1824); *Der Erntetag* (Munich, April 4, 1835); 3 masses (1812, c.1816, 1817); *Stabat Mater* (1821); *Miserere* (1824); other sacred works; cantatas; choral music; also Clarinet Concerto (1812); Violin Concerto (1817).
Bibl.: E. Reipschläger, *Schubaur, Danzi und P. als Opernkomponisten* (diss., Univ. of Rostock, 1911); M. Zenger, *Geschichte der Münchener Oper* (Munich, 1923); L. Schrott, "Aus dem Ringen um die deutsche Oper," *Die Musik,* XXXII (1939–40).

Pokorný, Franz (František) Xaver (Thomas), Bohemian composer; b. Königstadt, Dec. 20, 1728; d. Regensburg, July 2, 1794. He studied with Riepel in Regensburg; became a musician in the royal Kapelle of Thurn and Taxis in Regensburg (1766). He wrote some 100 syms., about 50 harpsichord concertos, 2 clarinet concertos, 2 oboe concertos, Horn Concerto, serenades, dances, marches, a String Quartet, a Trio for 2 Violins and Bass, etc.
Bibl.: J. Barbour, "P. Vindicated," *Musical Quarterly* (Jan. 1963).

Pokrass, Dimitri, Russian composer; b. Kiev, Nov. 7, 1899; d. Moscow, Dec. 20, 1978. He studied piano at the St. Petersburg Cons. (1913–17); in 1919 he joined the Soviet cavalry during the Civil War, and wrote the song *The Red Cavalry*. This was the 1st of a series of many songs that have acquired great popularity, among them *If War Comes Tomorrow* (1938), *March of the Tank Brigade, Farewell*, etc. He also wrote music for films.

Polacco, Giorgio, Italian conductor; b. Venice, April 12, 1873; d. N.Y., April 30, 1960. He studied in St. Petersburg, at Venice's Liceo Benedetto Marcello, and at the Milan Cons.; became assistant conductor at London's Covent Garden (1890), then conducted in Europe and South America; appeared in the U.S. for the 1st time for Tetrazzini's debut in San Francisco (1905); toured the U.S. with the Savage Opera Co. (1911); made his Metropolitan Opera debut in N.Y. with *Manon Lescaut* (Nov. 11, 1912), remaining on its roster until 1917; conducted the Chicago Grand Opera (1918–19; 1921) and in Boston (1927); was principal conductor of the Chicago Civic Opera (1922–30). He was married twice to the soprano Edith (Barnes) Mason.

Polansky, Larry, American composer, music theorist, and teacher; b. N.Y., Oct. 16, 1954. He studied anthropology and music at New College in Sarasota, Fla. (1974); subsequently studied mathematics and music at the Univ. of Calif., Santa Cruz (B.A., 1976), and undertook graduate work at York Univ. in Toronto (1977); finally majored in composition at the Univ. of Illinois in Champaign-Urbana (M.A., 1978); also studied composition privately with James Tenney and Ben Johnston. He performed and arranged pieces in various styles, particularly jazz and folk, on guitar and other plectra, piano, and electronics (from 1966); he was a dance accompanist (1977–81), and composed works for the choreographers Ann Rodiger and Anita Feldman. He worked as a computer programmer, systems analyst, and studio engineer (from 1975); taught at Mills College in Oakland, Calif. (1981–90), where he also was involved with its Center for Contemporary Music (1981–87; interim director, 1988) and directed its Contemporary Performance Ensemble (1981–86); in 1990 he became a prof. at Dartmouth College. He is married to Jody Diamond (b. Los Angeles, April 23, 1952), a music publisher, performer, and composer who founded and directed the American Gamelan Inst. and also ed. its journal, *Balungan*. Together they founded and directed the publishing firm Frog Peak Music, A Composers' Collective. Polansky was music advisory ed. to the journal *Leonardo* (from 1985), associate ed. of *Perspectives of New Music* (from 1988), and co-author of HMSL, a widely used computer music language. His compositions reflect sophisticated technical concerns in acoustics, intonation, and morphological processes; they are generally in variation or canonic forms, based on single ideas worked out in textures that sometimes resemble those of minimalism. He authored 2 books: *Early Works of James Tenney* (1983) and *New Instrumentation and Orchestration* (1986).

WORKS: *4 Voice Canon no. 3* for Tape (1977); *Movement for Andrea Smith* for 4 Strings (1978); *4 Voice Canon no. 4* for Marimbas (1978); *Psaltery* for Tape (1979); *Another You* for Harp (1979–80); *V'Leem 'Shol (. . . and to rule . . .), Cantillation Study no. 2* for 5 Flutes (1984); *4 Voice Canon no. 5* for Percussion (1984); *Hensley Variations* for Flute, Viola, and Guitar (1985); *B'rey'sheet (In the Beginning), Cantillation Study no. 1* for Voice and Computer (1986); *4 Voice Canon no. 6* for Computer (1986); *Simple Actions*, computer installation (1986); *Bedhaya Sadra/Bedhaya Guthrie* for Voices, Kemanak, and Gamelan (1989–90).

Poldini, Ede (Eduard), Hungarian composer; b. Budapest, June 13, 1869; d. Corseaux, Switzerland, June 28, 1957. He studied at the Budapest Cons., and later with Mandyczewski (theory) and Julius Epstein (piano) in Vienna. In 1908 he went to live at Vevey. In 1935 he received the order of the Hungarian Cross of Merit; in 1948, was awarded the Hungarian Pro Arte Prize. He wrote the successful operas *Vagabund und Prinzessin* (Budapest, Oct. 17, 1903) and *Hochzeit im Fasching* (Budapest, Feb. 16, 1924); also orch. pieces, choral works, songs, and much piano music, some of which became very popular.

Poldowski (pen name of **Irene Regine Wieniawska;** by marriage, **Lady Dean Paul**), Polish-English composer; b. Brussels, March 18, 1879; d. London, Jan. 28, 1932. She was a daughter of **Henryk Wieniawski;** her mother was an Englishwoman. She studied at the Brussels Cons. with Gevaert, and later in London with Percy Pitt; married Sir Aubrey Dean Paul; took additional courses in composition with Gédalge and d'Indy in Paris; began writing songs to French words, in the impressionist style; set to music 21 poems by Paul Verlaine, and 8 poems by others. She also composed *Caledonian Market*, a suite of 8 pieces for Piano; *Berceuse de l'enfant mourant* for Violin and Piano; *Tango* for Violin and Piano; *Suite miniature de chansons à danser* for Woodwind Instruments; 2 symphonic sketches (*Nocturnes* and *Tenements*); and an operetta, *Laughter*.

Polgar, Tibor, Hungarian-born Canadian composer, conductor, pianist, and teacher; b. Budapest, March 11, 1907. He was a pupil of Kodály at the Budapest Academy of Music (composition diploma, 1925), and earned a degree in philosophy (1931); was active as a performer and composer with the Hungarian Radio, later serving as its artistic director (1948–50). From 1962 to 1964 he was associate conductor of the Philharmonia Hungarica in Marl kreis Recklinghausen; then emigrated to Canada and became a naturalized citizen (1969). He conducted the Univ. of Toronto Sym. Orch. (1965–66), and later was on the staff of the Univ.'s opera dept. (1970–75); also taught at the Royal Cons. of Music of Toronto (1966–68); then taught orchestration at York Univ. in Toronto (1976–77).

WORKS: *Kérök* (The Suitors), opera (1954); *Improvisazione* for 4 Horns (1962); *In Private* for Violin and Viola (1964); *A European Lover*, musical theater (1965); *The Last Words of Louis Riel*, cantata for Contralto, Baritone, Chorus, and Orch. (1966–67); *The Troublemaker*, opera (1968); *Variations on a Hungarian Folk Song* for Harp, or Harp and Orch. (1969); *Ilona's 4 Faces*, suite for Clarinet or Saxophone, and Piano or Orch. (1970); *Lest We Forget the Last Chapter of Genesis*, cantata for Low Voice, and Piano or Orch. (1970); *Rhapsody of Kallo* for Violin and Harp (1970); *Notes on Hungary* for Concert Band (1971); *The Glove*, opera (1973); *How Long Shall the Ungodly Triumph?*, Psalm for 6 Voices and Organ (1974); *Annabel Lee* for Voice, Flute, and Harp (1974); *Pentatonia* for Concert Band (Toronto, Feb. 15, 1977); *A Strange Night*, opera (1978–88); *2 Symphonic Dances in Latin Rhythm* for Trumpet and Symphonic Band (1979); *Fanfare of Pride and Joy* for Symphonic Band (1982); *Frère Jacques*, introduction and variations on a children's song for 4 Harps (1984); *Concerto romantico* for Harp and Orch. (1986); *The Voice of the Soul*, fantasy for Concert Band (1989); arrangements for Children's Choir and Orch.; songs.

Poliakin, Miron, Russian violinist and pedagogue; b. Cherkassy, Feb. 12, 1895; d. Moscow, May 21, 1941. He received his early training from his father, a noted violinist, then studied with Elena Vonsovskaya in Kiev and with Auer at the St. Petersburg Cons. (1908–18). He developed a notable international career, making his N.Y. debut on Feb. 27, 1922. Returning to Russia in 1928, he became prof. of violin at the Leningrad Cons., and in 1936 joined the faculty of the Moscow Cons. With Yampolsky and Yankelevich, he produced a pleiad of fine violinists who dominated the concert annals and competition circuits in Russia and elsewhere.

BIBL.: L. Raaben, *M. P.* (Moscow, 1963).

Poliakov, Valeri(an), Russian composer and conductor; b. Orel, Oct. 24, 1913; d. Kishinev, Jan. 17, 1970. He studied clarinet and composition in Kharkov (1928–34). In 1935 he joined the staff of the Kiev Opera; in 1937 was appointed head of the music dept. of the Moldavian Music Theater in Kishinev, and taught at a music school there until 1940; then taught in Armenia (1941–45) and Riga (1945–51). He was music ed. and conductor of the Moldavian Radio (1951–54); conducted the dance ensemble Zhok (1955–57) and the jazz band Bukuria (1965–66); also taught at the Kishinev Cons. (1961–70). In 1960 he was made an Honored Artist of the Moldavian S.S.R.

WORKS: STAGE: *Where?*, opera (1969); *Iliana, An Ancient Tale*, ballet (1936); *Legend of the Architect*, ballet (1959); *Eternity*, ballet (1961). **ORCH.:** 7 syms. (1944; 1946; 1947; 1950, *Chkalov*; 1958; 1961, *Heroic Fantasy*; 1966); *Suite on Moldavian Themes* (1938); *Moldavia*, poem (1938); *Pictures of Drinking* (1939); *Fantasia Capriccio on European Themes* (1939); *Triumphant Overture* (1947); 2 piano concertos (1948, 1955); *Ballad to the Soldier* for Voices and Orch. (1948); *Rhapsody-Poem* (1951); *Through the Flames*, poem (1952); Violin Concerto (1953); Cello Concerto (1960); *Burleska* for Trombone and Orch. (1960); *Concerto rustico* (1963); *Vernal Garden*, sinfonietta (1969). **CHAMBER:** *3 Pieces in Memory of Prokofiev* for Violin and Piano (1962); *Ballade* for Cello and Piano (1963); String Quartet (1965); *Concert études* for Clarinet and Piano (1966) *Concert études* for Bassoon and Piano (1966). Also songs.

Polignac, Armande de, French composer; b. Paris, Jan. 8, 1876; d. Neauphle-le-Vieux, Seine-et-Oise, April 29, 1962. She studied with Fauré and d'Indy; composed the operas *Morgane* and *L'Hypocrite sanctifié*; a dramatic scene, *Judith de Béthulie* (Paris Opéra, March 23, 1916); *La Source lointaine*, Persian ballet (Paris, 1913); *Les 1,001 Nuits*, Arabian ballet (Paris, 1914); *Chimères*, Greek ballet (Paris Opéra, June 10, 1923); *Urashima*, Japanese ballet; also a Chinese ballet for Small Orch., *La Recherche de la vérité*; *Petite suite pour le clavecin* (1939).

Polin, Claire, American flutist and composer; b. Philadelphia, Jan. 1, 1926. She studied flute with William Kincaid and composition with Vincent Persichetti in Philadelphia, Peter Mennin at the Juilliard School of Music in N.Y., and Roger Sessions and Lukas Foss at the Berkshire Music Center in Tanglewood; held the degrees of B.Mus. (1948), M.Mus. (1950), and D.Mus. (1955); from 1949 to 1964 taught flute playing and composition at the Philadelphia Musical Academy, and from 1958, at Rutgers Univ. A versatile scholar, she wrote and lectured on music, and traveled and played flute in distant lands, including Israel, Russia, and Japan; advanced bold theories, suggesting, for example, a link between Hebrew and Welsh legends, and composed industriously in a cogently modernistic manner, often with recursive ancient modalities.

WORKS: ORCH.: 2 syms.: No. 1 (1961) and No. 2, "Korean" (1976); *Scenes from Gilgamesh* for Flute and String Orch. (1972); *Amphion* (1978); *Mythos* for Harp and String Orch. (1982). **CHAMBER:** 3 string quartets (1953, 1959, 1969); Flute Sonata (1954); *Structures* for Flute (1964); *Consecutivo* for Flute, Clarinet, Violin, Cello, and Piano (1964); *Cader Idris* for Brass Quintet (1970); *The Journey of Owain Madoc* for Brass Quintet and Percussion (1971); *Makimono I* for Flute, Clarinet, Violin, Cello, and Piano (1972); *Makimono II* for Brass Quintet (1972); Sonata for Flute and Harp (1972); *Aderyn Pur* for Flute, Alto Saxophone, and Bird Tape (1973); *Tower Sonata* for Flute, Clarinet, and Bassoon (1974); *Death of Procris* for Flute and Tuba (1974); *Serpentine* for Viola (1974); *Telemannicon* for Oboe and Self-Tape (1975); *Klockwork* for Alto Saxophone, Horn, and Bassoon (1977); *Synaulia* for Flute, Clarinet, and Piano (1977); *Vigniatures* for Harp and Violin (1980); *Felina* for Harp and Violin (1981); *Res naturae* for Woodwind Quintet (1982); *Kuequenaku-Cambriola* for Piano and Percussion (1982); *Freltic Sonata* for Violin and Piano (1986); *Garden of Earthly Delights* for Woodwind Quintet (1987); *Regensburg* for Flute, Guitar, and Dancer (1989); piano pieces. **VOCAL:** *Welsh Bardic Odes* for Soprano, Flute, and Piano (1956); *Canticles* for Male Voices (1959); *Lorca Songs* for Voices and Piano (1965); *Infinito* for Alto Saxophone, Soprano, Chorus, and Narrator (1973); *Biblical Madrigals* for Chorus (1974); *Windsongs* for Soprano and Guitar (1977); *Isaiah Syndrome* for Chorus (1980).

Polisi, Joseph W(illiam), American bassoonist and music educator; b. N.Y., Dec. 30, 1947. He had primary lessons in bassoon with his father, William Polisi, principal bassoonist

of the N.Y. Phil.; then turned to legal studies, and took a course in political science at the Univ. of Conn. (B.A., 1969) and international relations at the Fletcher School of Law and Diplomacy at Tufts Univ. (M.A., 1970). He then resumed his musical training at the Yale Univ. School of Music (M.M., 1973; M.M.A., 1975; D.M.A., 1980); also studied bassoon with Maurice Allard at the Paris Cons. (1973–74). He performed widely as a soloist and chamber music player; taught at the Univ. of Nevada (1975–76); then was executive officer of the Yale Univ. School of Music (1976–80); subsequently was dean of faculty at the Manhattan School of Music (1980–83). After serving as dean of the Univ. of Cincinnati College-Cons. of Music (1983–84), he became president of the Juilliard School in N.Y. (1984).

Polívka, Vladimír, Czech pianist and composer; b. Prague, July 6, 1896; d. there, May 11, 1948. He studied piano at the Prague Cons., and took lessons in composition from Vitězslav Novák at the Master School there (1912–18); traveled in Europe, America, and Japan with the violinist Jaroslav Kocián; from 1923 to 1930, taught piano in Chicago. In 1938 he returned to Prague and taught at the Cons.; was chairman of Přítomnost, an association for contemporary music. He publ. several collections of children's pieces, collaborated on a book about Smetana (Prague, 1941), and wrote a book of travels, describing his world tour (Prague, 1945).

WORKS: Chiefly for piano, including *Dni v Chicagu* (Days in Chicago; 1926); *3 Impromptus* (1930); *Merry Musik* (1932–33); a tragically colored piano suite, *Krajiny z let okupace* (Landscapes in the Years of Occupation; 1941); opera, *Polobůh* (The Demi-God; 1930); melodrama, *A Ballad of a Deaf-Mute* (1936); symphonic poem, *Jaro* (Spring; 1918); *Little Symphony* (1921); *Suite* for Viola and Small Orch. (1934); Concerto for Piano and Small Orch. (1934); *Overture* (1942); 2 violin sonatas (1918, 1919); *Suite* for Viola and Wind Quintet (1934); String Quartet (1937); *Divertimento* for Wind Quintet (1939); *Giacona* for Viola and Piano (1944); Viola Sonata (1945); choruses; songs; incidental music.

Polko, Elise (née **Vogel),** German singer and writer; b. Leipzig, Jan. 13, 1822; d. Munich, May 15, 1899. She studied with Manuel García in Paris; married a railway engineer, Eduard Polko, under whose name she became professionally known. She publ. a number of semifictional stories about music which became astonishingly popular in Germany during her lifetime.

WRITINGS: *Musikalische Märchen* (3 vols., 1852; also tr. into Eng.); *Faustina Hasse*, a novel about the famous singer (2 vols., 1860); *Alte Herren*, about Bach's predecessors at the Thomaskirche in Leipzig (1865); *Verklungene Akkorde* (1868); *Erinnerungen an Felix Mendelssohn-Bartholdy* (1868; in Eng., 1869); *Nicolò Paganini und die Geigenbauer* (1876); *Vom Gesange* (1876); *Aus der Künstlerwelt* (1878); *Der Klassiker der Musik* (1880); *Meister der Tonkunst* (1897).

Pollack, Ben, American jazz drummer and bandleader; b. Chicago, June 22, 1903; d. (suicide by hanging) Palm Springs, Calif., June 7, 1971. He played in the New Orleans Rhythm Kings in Chicago (1921); in 1924 he organized his own group, with 16-year-old Benny Goodman as clarinetist and Glenn Miller as trombonist and arranger; later he engaged Harry James as trumpeter; he himself presided at the drums. With this stellar personnel he cut a deep swath through jazzland and was dubbed "The Father of Swing." When his career declined, he entered the entertainment business; ran a restaurant in Hollywood; later managed a nightclub in Palm Springs. He left a suicide note, explaining his act as prompted by despondency over personal and financial problems.

Pollak, Egon, esteemed Czech-born Austrian conductor; b. Prague, May 3, 1879; d. there (of a heart attack while conducting a performance of *Fidelio*), June 14, 1933. He studied with Knittl at the Prague Cons.; was chorus master at the Prague Deutsches Theater (1901–5); conducted opera in Bremen (1905–10), Leipzig (1910–12), and Frankfurt (1912–17); also conducted in Paris and at London's Covent Garden (1914). He led Wagner's *Ring* cycle at the Chicago Grand Opera (1915–17); was able to leave the U.S. with the Austrian diplomatic legation as the U.S. entered World War I (1917). He was Generalmusikdirektor of the Hamburg Opera (1917–31); also conducted in Rio de Janeiro and at Buenos Aires's Teatro Colón (1928); appeared at the Chicago Civic Opera (1929–32) and in Russia (1932); led performances of the ensemble of the Vienna State Opera in Cairo and Alexandria (1933). He was a distinguished interpreter of the operas of Wagner and Richard Strauss.

Pollarolo, (Giovanni) Antonio, Italian composer, son of **Carlo Francesco Pollarolo;** b. Brescia (baptized), Nov. 12, 1676; d. Venice, May 30, 1746. He studied with his father, for whom he began substituting as vice-maestro di cappella at Venice's San Marco (1702); was named to that position (1723); was acting primo maestro (1733–36) and then primo maestro (1740–46); was also maestro di coro at the Ospedale degl'Incurabili (from 1716). He wrote about 12 operas, but only *I tre voti* (Vienna, 1724) is extant; also wrote some sacred music, including oratorios, cantatas, and motets.

Pollarolo, Carlo Francesco, prominent Italian organist and composer, father of **(Giovanni) Antonio Pollarolo;** b. c.1653; d. Venice, Feb. 7, 1723. His father, Orazio Pollarolo, was organist in Brescia at the parish church of Ss. Nazaro e Celso and at the Cathedral; it is likely that Carlo Francesco studied with him. After serving as organist at the Congregazione dei Padri della Pace and substituting for his father at the Cathedral, he was named his father's successor at the latter (1676); was elected capo musico there (1680); also held a similar post with the Accademia degli Erranti (1681–89). He then went to Venice, where he was elected 2nd organist at San Marco (1690); became its vice-maestro di cappella (1692), a position he held until his son Antonio succeeded him (1702); was also music director of the Ospedale degl'Incurabili. He composed about 85 operas, many of which are not extant; among those surviving are *Il Roderico* (1686), *Onorio in Roma* (Venice, 1692), *La forza della virtù* (Venice, 1693), *Il Faramondo* (Venice, 1699), *Semiramide* (Venice, 1713), *Ariodante* (Venice, 1716), and *Astinome* (Rome, 1719). He also wrote oratorios and many other sacred works; 19 solo cantatas, with Basso Continuo or Orch.; 67 arias and 5 duets, with Basso Continuo or Orch.; etc.
BIBL.: O. Termini, *C.F. P.: His Life, Time, and Music with Emphasis on the Operas* (diss., Univ. of Southern Calif., 1970); idem, "C.F. P.: Follower or Leader in Venetian Opera?," *Studi Musicali,* VIII (1979).

Pollikoff, Max, American violinist and concert director; b. Newark, N.J., March 30, 1904; d. N.Y., May 13, 1984. He studied with Auer; made his N.Y. debut in a recital (1923); subsequently devoted himself to contemporary music; he organized the series "Music of Our Time" in 1954, giving periodic concerts at the 92nd Street Y in N.Y.; the series continued until 1974; its programs included works by Ives, Bernstein, Sessions, Dello Joio, and Cage.

Pollini, Bernhard (real name, **Baruch Pohl**), German tenor, later baritone, and operatic impresario; b. Cologne, Dec. 16, 1838; d. Hamburg, Nov. 27, 1897. He made his debut as Arturo in *I Puritani* in Cologne in 1857; later sang baritone roles in an Italian opera troupe, of which he subsequently became manager and artistic director. He then undertook the management of the Italian opera at St. Petersburg and Moscow. In 1874 he became director of the Hamburg City Theater; in 1876 he also became manager of the Altona Theater and in 1894 of the Thalia Theater in Hamburg.

Pollini, Cesare, Cavaliere de', Italian writer on music and composer; b. Padua, July 13, 1858; d. there, Jan. 26, 1912. After legal studies at the Univ. of Padua, he took a 2-year course in music with Bazzini in Milan (1881–83); from 1883 to 1885 he was director of the Padua Cons.; resigned to devote himself to writing and composition. He publ. *Terminologia musicale tedesco-italiana; Teoria generale della musica; La musica italiana nelle sue principali fasi storiche;* etc.
BIBL.: G. Sacerdoti, *C. P.* (Padua, 1912); S. Leoni, *C. P. nella vita e nell'arte* (Padua, 1917).

Pollini, Francesco (Giuseppe), Italian pianist, singer, and composer of Slovenian birth; b. Laibach, March 25, 1762; d. Milan, Sept. 17, 1846. He was a pupil of Mozart (who dedicated a violin rondo to him) at Vienna; later of Zingarelli at Milan, where he was appointed a prof. of piano shortly after the opening of the Cons. (1809). He was the 1st to write piano music on 3 staves, a method imitated by Liszt, Thalberg, and others; a specimen of this style is one of his *32 Esercizi in forma di toccata,* op. 42 (1820), a central melody surrounded by passagework for both hands. He publ. *Metodo per clavicembalo* (Milan, 1811); wrote an opera buffa, *La cassetta nei boschi* (Milan, Feb. 25, 1798), chamber music, songs, many piano pieces, and harpsichord works.

Pollini, Maurizio, famous Italian pianist and conductor; b. Milan, Jan. 5, 1942. A precocious child, he began piano studies at an early age with Lonati; made his debut at age 9, then studied with Vidusso at the Milan Cons. After sharing 2nd prize in the Geneva Competition in 1958, he took his diploma in piano at the Milan Cons. (1959); also studied with Michelangeli. After capturing 1st prize in the Chopin Competition in Warsaw (1960), he launched an acclaimed career as a virtuoso; appeared throughout Europe as a soloist with the leading orchs. and as a recitalist; made his U.S. debut at N.Y.'s Carnegie Hall (Nov. 1, 1968). In later years, he made appearances as a conductor, leading concerts from the keyboard and also mounting the podium and taking charge in the opera pit. Pollini is a foremost master of the keyboard; he has won deserved renown for making his phenomenal technical resources a means of exploring a vast repertoire, ranging from Bach to the cosmopolitan avant-garde. In 1987 he was awarded the Ehrenring of the Vienna Phil.

Pololáník, Zdeněk, Czech composer; b. Tišnov, Oct. 25, 1935. He studied organ with J. Černocký at the Brno Cons. (1952–57) and composition with V. Petrželka and T. Schaefer at the Brno Academy of Music (1957–61). Much of his music represents a curious revival of medieval polyphonic forms, made astringent by abrasive dissonance.
WORKS: STAGE: OPERA-ORATORIO: *Sheer hush-sheereem* (Song of Songs; 1969). **BALLETS:** *Mechanismus* (1964); *Popelka* (1966); *Pierot* (1976); *Sněhová královna* (1978). **ORCH.:** Sinfonietta (1958); *Toccata* for Double Bass, Brass, Percussion, 2 Harps, Harpsichord, and Piano (1959); *Divertimento* for String Orch. and 4 Horns (1960); 5 syms.: No. 1 (1961); No. 2 for 11 Wind Instruments (1962); No. 3 for Organ and Percussion Orch. (1963); No. 4 for Strings (1963); No. 5 for Chamber Orch. (1968); *Concentus resonabilis* for 19 Solo Instruments and Tape (1963); *Concerto grosso* for Flute, Guitar, Harpsichord, and String Orch. (1966); Piano Concerto (1966); *Musica giocosa* for Violin and Orch. (1980). **CHAMBER:** *Suite* for Violin and Piano (1957); String Quartet (1958); Double-bass Sonata (1959); *Scherzo contrario* for Violin, Bass Clarinet, and Xylophone (1961); *Little Mythological Exercises* for Narrator and String Quartet (1961); *Musica spingenta I* for Double Bass and Wind Quintet (1961), *II* for Harpsichord and String Quartet (1962), and *III* for Bass Clarinet and 13 Percussion Instruments (1962); *Musica concisa* for Flute, Bass Clarinet, Harpsichord, Piano, and Percussion (1963); *Sonata eccentrica* for Solo Violin (1963); *Preludii dodici* (12 Preludes) for 2 Pianos and Organ (1963); Horn Sonata (1965); *Musica transcurata* for Bass Clarinet and Harpsichord (1967); *Pulsazione* for Percussion (1967). **VOCAL:** Mass for Chorus, Brasses, Harp, and Organ (1956); *Nebuchadnezzar* for Chorus, 3 Trumpets, and 4 Timpani (1960); *Song of the Dead Children* for Chorus, 3 Trumpets, and Percussion (1963); *Vávra* for Children's Chorus and Piano (1964); *Rumor letalis* for Chorus a cappella (1966); *Cantus psalmorum* for Bass, Organ, Harp, and Percussion (1966; Evanston, Ill., April 13, 1969); *Missa brevis* for Children's Chorus and Organ (1970); songs. **PIANO:** *Preludes* (1957) and

Variations on 2 Moravian Songs (1957). ORGAN: *Sonata bravura* (1959); *Sonata gaudia* (1962); *Allegro affanato* (1963).

Polovinkin, Leonid (Alexeievich), Russian composer; b. Kurgan, Aug. 13, 1894; d. Moscow, Feb. 8, 1949. He studied at the Moscow Cons. with Glière and Vassilenko; began his career as a composer by writing theater music in Moscow after the Revolution of 1917; adopted a modernistic idiom; emphasized the element of humor. Later he devoted more time to abstract instrumental music; wrote 9 syms., 4 string quartets, 2 piano trios, several overtures on folk themes, 5 piano sonatas, 24 postludes for Piano, songs.

Pommier, Jean-Bernard, French pianist and conductor; b. Béziers, Aug. 17, 1944. He studied piano with Mini Kosloff, Yves Nat, Pierre Sancan, and Eugene Istomin; graduated from the Paris Cons. in 1961 with the 1st prize; in 1961 he received the 1st diploma of honor at the Tchaikovsky Competition in Moscow; then began an international career as a soloist with the major orchs. of the world; in later years he appeared as a conductor.

Ponc, Miroslav, Czech violinist, conductor, and composer; b. Vysoké Mýto, Dec. 2, 1902; d. Prague, April 1, 1976. He studied organ with Wiedermann at the Prague Cons. (1920–22) and composition with Alois Hába there (1922–23; 1925–27); went to Berlin and took lessons with Schoenberg. Upon returning to Prague, he studied violin with Josef Suk at the Cons., graduating in 1930, and attended the quarter-tone composition class of Alois Hába, graduating in 1935; also took lessons in conducting with Scherchen in Strasbourg (1933). After World War II, he was active mainly as a theater conductor in Prague; wrote a number of scores of incidental music for plays.

Works: 5 *Polydynamic Compositions* for Piano, Xylophone, and String Quartet (1923); song cycles: *A Bad Dream* (1925) and *A Black Swan* (1926); 3 *Merry Pieces* for Wind Quintet (1929); *Little Pieces* for Flute or Cello, and Piano (1930); Piano Concertino (1930); *Overture to an Ancient Tragedy,* with the application of quarter-tones in the Greek enharmonic mode (Prague, Feb. 18, 1931); Nonet (1932); *Osudy* (The Fates), 2 antique ballet pictures (1935); *Suite* for Piano with 2 manuals tuned in quarter-tones (1935); String Trio (1937); over 100 scores of incidental music and much music for films and radio.

Ponce, Manuel (María), distinguished Mexican composer; b. Fresnillo, Dec. 8, 1882; d. Mexico City, April 24, 1948. He studied piano with his older sister; in 1904 he went to Europe, where he took lessons in composition with Enrico Bossi at Bologna and in piano with Martin Krause in Berlin. Upon his return to Mexico, he taught piano at the Mexico City Cons. (1909–15). He gave a concert of his compositions in Mexico City on July 7, 1912, which included a Piano Concerto. During World War I, he lived in N.Y. and in Havana; then went to Paris for additional study, and took lessons with Paul Dukas. His contact with French music wrought a radical change in his style of composition; his later works are more polyphonic in structure and more economical in form. He possessed a great gift of melody; one of his songs, *Estrellita* (1914), became a universal favorite, and was often mistaken for a folk song. In 1941 he made a tour in South America, conducting his own works. He was the 1st Mexican composer of the 20th century to employ an identifiably modern musical language; his place in the history of Mexican music is a very important one. His works are often performed in Mexico; a concert hall was named after him in the Instituto de Bellas Artes.

Works: orch.: Piano Concerto (1912); *Balada mexicana* for Piano and Orch. (1914); *Estampas nocturnas* (1923); *Chapultepec,* 3 *bocetos sinfonicos* (Mexico City, Aug. 25, 1929; rev. version, Mexico City, Aug. 24, 1934); *Canto y danza de los antiguos Mexicanos* (1933); *Suite en estilo antiguo* (1935); *Poema elegiaco* for Chamber Orch. (Mexico City, June 28, 1935); *Instantáneas mexicanas* (1938); *Ferial, divertimento sinfónico* (Mexico City, Aug. 9, 1940); *Concierto del Sur* for Guitar and Orch. (Montevideo, Oct. 4, 1941); Violin Concerto (Mexico City, Aug. 20, 1943). CHAMBER: Piano Trio (1911); Cello Sonata (1922); 4 *miniaturas* for String Quartet (1929); *Pequeña suite en estilo antiguo* for Violin, Viola, and Cello (1933); Sonata for Violin and Viola (1935); numerous piano pieces, some based on Mexican rhythms; 6 guitar sonatas; about 30 songs; 34 arrangements of Mexican folk songs.

Bibl.: D. López Alonso, *M.M. P.: Ensayo biográfico* (Mexico City, 1950); J. Romero, "Efemérides de M. P.," *Nuestra Música,* V/2 (1950).

Ponchielli, Amilcare, celebrated Italian composer; b. Paderno Fasolaro, near Cremona, Aug. 31, 1834; d. Milan, Jan. 15, 1886. He studied with his father, a shopkeeper and organist at the village church; entered the Milan Cons. as a non-paying student when he was 9; his mentors included Pietro Ray (theory), Arturo Angeleri (piano), Felice Frasi (composition), and Alberto Mazzucato (music history, esthetics, and composition); while a student there he collaborated on the operetta *Il sindaco babbeo* (Milan Cons., March 1851); also wrote the sym. *Scena campestre* (1852). After his graduation (1854), he went to Cremona as a church organist; was named assistant to Ruggero Manna, director of Cremona's Teatro Concordia (1855), where he brought out his opera *I promessi sposi* (Aug. 30, 1856). He was conductor of the municipal bands in Piacenza (1861–64) and Cremona (from 1864), where he also conducted opera; continued to pursue his interest in composing for the theater. He finally achieved notable success with the revised version of his *I promessi sposi* (Milan, Dec. 4, 1872), which was subsequently performed throughout Italy; his *La Gioconda* (Milan, April 8, 1876) secured his reputation. He was prof. of composition at the Milan Cons. in 1880 and again from 1881; also served as maestro di cappella at Bergamo's S. Maria Maggiore (1881–86). He married the soprano **Teresina Brambilla** in 1874. His birthplace was renamed Paderno Ponchielli in his honor. *La Gioconda* remains his only work to have acquired repertoire status; it includes the famous ballet number *Dance of the Hours.* In addition to his numerous stage works, he composed many band pieces, vocal chamber music, chamber works, and piano pieces.

Bibl.: A. Mandelli, *Le distrazioni di A. P.* (Cremona, 1897); G. Cesari, *A. P. nell'arte del suo tempo: Ricordi e carteggi* (Cremona, 1934); special issue of *Cremona* (July 1934); U. Rolandi, *Nel centenario ponchielliano: A. P. librettista* (Como, 1935); G. De Napoli, *A. P. (1834–1886): La vita, le opere, l'epistolario, le onoranze* (Cremona, 1936); A. Damerini, *A. P.* (Turin, 1940); N. Albarosa et al., eds., *A. P. 1834–1886: Saggio e ricerche nel 150° anniversario della nascita* (Casalmorano, 1984); L. Sirch, *Catalogo tematico delle musiche di A. P.* (Cremona, 1989).

Pond, Sylvanus Billings, American music publisher and composer; b. Milford, Vt., April 5, 1792; d. Brooklyn, March 12, 1871. He was a prominent musician of his time; conducted the N.Y. Sacred Musical Society and the N.Y. Academy of Sacred Music; wrote songs for Sunday school; ed. and publ. *Union Melodies* (1838), *The U.S. Psalmody* (N.Y., 1841), and *The Book of Praise,* for the Reformed Dutch Church in America (N.Y., 1866); composed the hymn tunes *Armenia* (1835) and *Franklin Square* (1850). Early in life, he went to Albany; established a piano workshop; from 1820, was partner of the publ. house of Meacham and Pond there; in 1832 he joined Firth & Hall of N.Y., and the firm's name became Firth, Hall & Pond; in 1848 it was reorganized as Firth, Pond & Co.; it was one of the principal publishers of Stephen Foster's songs. In 1850 Pond retired, and his son, **William A. Pond,** became the owner; upon the withdrawal of Firth in 1863, the firm became known as William A. Pond & Co.; W.A. Pond's eldest son, **William A. Pond, Jr.,** was taken into partnership, but died in 1884; William A. Pond, Sr., died the following year, and his 2 other sons, **Albert Edward** and **George Warren Pond,** succeeded him. In 1934 Joseph Fletcher acquired the catalogue; in 1946 it was purchased by Carl Fischer, Inc. For the dealings of Firth, Pond & Co. with Stephen Foster, see J.T. Howard, *Stephen Foster, America's Troubadour* (N.Y., 1931; 4th ed., 1965); consult also H. Dichter and E. Shapiro,

Early American Sheet Music, Its Lure and Its Lore, 1768–1889 (N.Y., 1941).

Poné, Gundaris, Latvian-born American conductor and composer; b. Riga, Oct. 17, 1932. In 1944 his family went to Germany, where he studied violin. In 1950 he emigrated to the U.S., becoming a naturalized citizen in 1956. He studied violin and composition at the Univ. of Minnesota (B.A., 1954; M.A., 1956; Ph.D., 1962). In 1966 he made his conducting debut in N.Y., and subsequently appeared as a guest conductor in the U.S. and in Europe; served as music director of the Music in the Mountains Festivals (from 1981). His compositions captured 1st prizes in the Concorso Internazionale "Citta di Trieste" (1981), the Kennedy Center Friedheim Awards Competition (1982), the International Louisville Orch. Competition (1984), the International Hambach Prize Competition (1985), and the International Georges Enesco Competition (1988). His concern as a composer has been to develop a musical language capable of communicating with the general audience while maintaining the high intellectual standards of contemporary composition.
WORKS: OPERA: *Rosa Luxemburg* (in progress since 1968). **ORCH.:** Violin Concerto (1959); *Composizione per quattro orchestre* (1967–69); *Vivos voco, Mortuos plango* (1972); *Avanti!* (1975); Horn Concerto (1976); *La Serenissima*, 7 Venetian portraits (1979–81; Trieste, Sept. 25, 1982); *American Portraits* (1982–84); *Titzarin* (1984–86); *La bella veneziana*, overture (1987). **CHAMBER:** String Quartet, *Hetaera Esmeraldo* (1963); *Serie-Alea* for Flute, Oboe, Clarinet, Bassoon, and Piano (1965); Sonata for Solo Cello (1966); *San Michele della Laguna* for Clarinet, Violin, and Piano (1969); *De Mundo Magistri Ioanni* for Chamber Ensemble (1972); *Diletti dialettici*, concerto for 9 Virtuosos (1973); *Eisleriana*, concerto for 11 Players (1978); *Woodland Elegies*, 5 pieces for 5 Instruments (1980); *Propositions for Opus 32*, 6 pieces for Woodwind Quartet and Piano (1982); *Cyprian Sketches*, 4 pieces for Clarinet, Cello, and Piano (1983); *Gran d'vo funebre* for Viola and Cello (1987); *Pezzi del tramonto* for Violin and Piano (1989); also piano pieces, including *Oltre questa porta geme la terra* for 3 Pianos (1969) and *3 Farewell Pieces* (1984); works for solo instruments. **VOCAL:** *Quattro temperamenti d'amore* for Baritone, and Orch. or Piano (1960); *Daniel Propheta* for 3 Soloists, Chorus, and Orch. (1962); *Junius Bröschure* for 4 Speakers, 18 Women's Voices, and Instrumental Ensemble (1970); *5 American Songs* for Medium Voice and Small Orch. (1975).

Pongrácz, Zoltán, Hungarian composer; b. Diószeg, Feb. 5, 1912. He studied with Kodály at the Budapest Academy of Music (1930–35); then took lessons in conducting from Nilius in Vienna (1935–38) and Krauss in Salzburg (1941). During World War II, he served as director of the music dept. of Hungarian Radio (1943–44); after the war, conducted the Debrecen Phil. (1946–49); taught composition at the Debrecen Cons. (1947–58) and electronic composition at the Budapest Academy of Music (from 1975).
WORKS: STAGE: OPERAS: *Odysseus and Nausikaa* (1949–50; Debrecen, 1960); *The Last Station* (1983). **BALLET:** *The Devil's Present* (1936). **VOCAL:** *Christmas Cantata* (1935); *St. Stephen Oratorio* (1938); cantata, *Apollo musagètes* (1958); *Negritude* for Speaking Chorus, Chorus, and Percussion (1962); *Ispirazioni* for Chorus, Orch., and Tape (1965); *Music from Nyírség* for Soloists, Chorus, and Folk Orch. (1965). **ORCH.:** Sym. (1943); *Ballo ongaro* for Youth Orch. (1955); *3 Orchestral Etudes* (1963); *Hangok és zörejek* (Tones and Noises), aleatory music (1966); *Színek és vonalak* (Colors and Lines) for Youth Orch. (1971). **CHAMBER:** *Pastorale* for Clarinet, Organ, 6 Winds, and Percussion (1941); *Javanese Music*, on a South Asiatic motif, for Chamber Ensemble (1942); *Music* for 5 Cellos (1954); Wind Quintet (1956); *Toccata* for Piano (1957); *3 Small Pieces* for Orff Ensemble (1966); *Phonothèse* for Tape (1966); *Sets and Pairs*, electronic variations for Piano and Celesta (1968); *3 Improvisations* for Piano, Percussion, and 3 Tape Recorders (1971); *3 Bagatelles* for Percussion (1972); *Zoophonia*, concrete music synthesized from animal

sounds (1973); Concertino for Soprano Saxophone and Tape (1982); *Polar and Successive Contrasts* for Electronics (1986); Concertino for Cimbalon and Electronics (1988).

Poniatowski, Józef (Michal Xsawery Franciszek Jan), Prince of Monte Rotondo, Polish tenor and composer; b. Rome, Feb. 20, 1816; d. Chislehurst, England, July 3, 1873. He was a member of the Polish nobility; his uncle was a marshal in Napoleon's army. He studied in Florence, and appeared on the stage as a tenor; then wrote operas (to Italian and French librettos); in 1848 he went to Paris and was elevated to the rank of Senator by Napoleon III; after the fall of the 2nd Empire, he went to England.
WORKS: OPERAS: *Giovanni da Procida* (Florence, Nov. 25, 1838); *Don Desiderio, ossia Il disperato per eccesso di buon cuore* (Pisa, Dec. 26, 1840); *Ruy Blas* (Lucca, Sept. 2, 1843); *Bonifazio de' Geremei* (Rome, Nov. 28, 1843); *La sposa d'Abido* (Venice, Feb. 1845); *Malek-Adel* (Genoa, June 26, 1846); *Esmeralde* (Florence, June 26, 1847); *Pierre de Médicis* (Paris, March 9, 1860); *Au travers du mur* (Paris, May 9, 1861); *L'Aventurier* (Paris, Jan. 26, 1865); *La Contessina* (Paris, April 28, 1868); *Gelmina* (London, June 4, 1872); also the popular ballad, *The Yeoman's Wedding Song.*

Poniridis, Georges, distinguished Greek composer; b. Constantinople (of Greek parents), Oct. 8, 1892; d. Athens, March 29, 1982. He studied violin with Ysaÿe at the Brussels Cons. and composition with Vincent d'Indy and Albert Roussel at the Schola Cantorum in Paris, where he remained until the outbreak of World War II; then returned to Athens and served in the Music Division of the Greek Ministry of Education (1954–58). In his music he makes use of authentic Greek motifs, at times endeavoring to emulate the simple monody of ancient Greek chants and the rhythms of classical prosody.
WORKS: ORCH.: *Triptyque symphonique* (Athens, Nov. 22, 1937); 2 syms. (1935, 1942); *3 Symphonic Preludes* (1938); Chamber Sym. for Strings and Percussion; *Petite symphonie* (1956); Piano Concerto (1968); Violin Concerto (1969). **CHAMBER:** Flute Sonata (1956); String Quartet (1959); Clarinet Sonata (1962); Quartet for Oboe, Clarinet, Bassoon, and Xylophone (1962); Trio for Xylophone, Clarinet, and Bassoon (1962); Trio for Flute, Oboe, and Clarinet (1962); 2 violin sonatas; Viola Sonata (1967); Cello Sonata (1967); 3 piano sonatas; also scores of incidental music to ancient Greek plays; arrangements of Greek folk songs.

Ponnelle, Jean-Pierre, French opera designer and producer; b. Paris, Feb. 19, 1932; d. Munich, Aug. 11, 1988. He received his training in Paris; gained early recognition for his staging of Henze's *Boulevard Solitude* at its premiere in Hannover in 1952; worked mostly in German opera houses. In 1962 he began to produce opera. He also distinguished himself in motion picture productions.

Pons, Charles, French composer; b. Nice, Dec. 7, 1870; d. Paris, March 16, 1957. He studied organ, and earned his living as a church organist in his youth; then turned to theater music, and produced a long series of operas: *L'Epreuve* (Nice, 1904); *Laura* (Paris, 1906); *Mourette* (Marseilles, 1909); *Le Voile du bonheur* (Paris, April 26, 1911); *Françoise* (Lyons, 1913); *Loin du bal* (Paris, 1913); *Les Fauves* (Paris, 1917); *Le Drapeau* (Paris, 1918); *Le Passant de Noël* (Nice, 1935); *L'Envol de la Marseillaise* (Marseilles, 1947); overture, *Pyrrhus*; symphonic poem, *Heures vendéennes*; *Symphonie tragique*; several orch. suites; oratorio, *La Samaritaine* (Nice, 1900); other vocal works, with Orch.: *La Mort de Démosthène* (Paris, 1928) and *Dans la forêt normande* (1934); chamber music; songs.

Pons, Lily (actually, **Alice Joséphine**), glamorous French soprano; b. Draguignan, April 12, 1898; d. Dallas, Feb. 13, 1976. She studied piano as a child; took voice lessons with Alberti di Gorostiaga. She made her debut as an opera singer in Mulhouse in 1927 in the title role in *Lakmé*; sang in provincial theaters in France; then was engaged at the Metropolitan Opera in N.Y., and sang Lucia at her debut there on Jan. 3, 1931, with excellent success; she remained on its roster until

1944 (again from 1945 to 1958; on Dec. 14, 1960, made a concert appearance there). While in N.Y., she continued her vocal studies with Maria Gay and Giovanni Zenatello. Her fame as an extraordinary dramatic singer spread rapidly; she was engaged to sing at the Grand Opéra and the Opéra-Comique in Paris, at Covent Garden in London, the Teatro Colón in Buenos Aires, in Mexico, and in Cuba. She went to Hollywood and appeared in motion pictures, among them *That Girl from Paris* (1936) and *Hitting a New High* (1938). During World War II, she toured the battlefronts of North Africa, India, China, and Burma; received numerous honors. So celebrated did she become that a town in Maryland was named Lillypons in her honor. She was married twice (divorced both times), to August Mesritz, a publ., and to the conductor **André Kostelanetz**. She possessed an expressive coloratura voice, which she used with extraordinary skill.

Ponse, Luctor, Swiss-born Dutch composer; b. Geneva, Oct. 11, 1914. He studied at the Cons. in Valenciennes, France, winning the Prix d'Excellence for theory in 1930 and for piano in 1932; after further study at the Geneva Cons. (1933–35), he went to the Netherlands, and in 1964 became a member of the staff of the Inst. of Sonology at Utrecht Univ.; also taught at the Groningen Cons.

Works: ORCH.: *Divertissement* for String Orch. (1946); Piano Concerto (1951–55); 3 sinfoniettas (1952, 1959, 1961); 3 syms. (1953; 1957; 1981–85); *Feestgericht,* ballet for Orch. (1957); 2-Piano Concerto (1961–62); *Concerto da camera* for Oboe and String Orch. (1962); 2 violin concertos (1963, 1965); Concerto for Piano, Orch., and Tape (1967; rev. 1980); Harp Concerto (1986); *Suite* for Piano and Orch. (1987). CHAMBER: Trio for Flute, Clarinet, and Piano (1940–41); 2 string quartets (1941, 1947); 2 cello sonatas (1943, 1950); 2 *Pieces* for Wind Quintet (1943); Duo for Violin and Cello (1946); Violin Sonata (1948); Quintet for Flute, Oboe, Violin, Viola, and Cello (1956); 2 *Caprices* for Flute and Piano (1956); Sextet for Flute, Oboe, Violin, Viola, Cello, and Harpsichord (1958); *Variations* for Flute and Harpsichord (1962); *Euterpe Suite* for 11 Instruments (1964); *Musique concertante* for Viola, Double Bass, Piano, Percussion, and Electronics (1977); Sonata for Clarinet and Tape (1981); Suite for Piano and Percussion (1982); Toccata for Harpsichord (1985); piano pieces.

Ponselle (real name, **Ponzillo**), **Carmela,** American mezzo-soprano, sister of **Rosa (Melba) Ponselle;** b. Schenectady, N.Y., June 7, 1892; d. N.Y., June 13, 1977. She began to study singing rather late in life; made her professional debut as Amneris in N.Y. in 1923, which role she also sang at her Metropolitan Opera debut there on Dec. 5, 1925; she remained on its roster until 1928; was reengaged for the seasons 1930–35; then devoted most of her time to teaching.

Ponselle (real name, **Ponzillo**), **Rosa (Melba),** brilliant American soprano, sister of **Carmela Ponselle;** b. Meriden, Conn., Jan. 22, 1897; d. Green Spring Valley, Md., May 25, 1981. Her parents, who emigrated to the U.S. from southern Italy, gave her, with a prescient hope, the middle name Melba. Her father owned a grocery store in Meriden; she studied music with her mother, an amateur singer, and sang in a local church choir. Her older sister, Carmela, also learned to sing, and the 2 sisters, billed under their real name, **Ponzillo,** as "Italian Girls," sang in vaudeville shows in Pittsburgh and in N.Y. Later she took voice lessons in N.Y. with William Thorner, who became her manager; he introduced her to Caruso, who in turn arranged for her to audition at the Metropolitan Opera. She made a fine impression, and was engaged for a debut on Nov. 15, 1918, in the role of Leonora in *La forza del destino,* opposite Caruso, who sang the male lead of Don Alvaro. She was immediately successful, and the critics, including the usually skeptical James Huneker, praised her. She subsequently sang at the Metropolitan Opera a rich assortment of Italian opera roles. She was equally successful in London when she appeared at Covent Garden as Norma (May 28, 1929). In 1936 she was married to Carl Jackson, son of the former mayor of Baltimore, who built for her a magnificent villa at Green Spring

Valley, near Baltimore; she divorced him in 1950. She made her last appearance at the Metropolitan Opera in N.Y. as Carmen on Feb. 15, 1937. After her retirement, she became active in social affairs. Her 80th birthday was celebrated in 1977 at her estate, with a multitude of friends and itinerant celebrities in attendance.

BIBL.: O. Thompson, *The American Singer* (N.Y., 1937); T. Villella and B. Park, "R. P. Discography," *Le Grand Baton* (Sept. 1975); J. Hines, "R. P.," *Great Singers on Great Singing* (Garden City, N.Y., 1982).

Pontécoulant, Louis-Adolphe le Doulcet, Marquis de, French writer on music; b. Paris, 1794; d. Bois-Colombe, near Paris, Feb. 20, 1882. After an adventurous career, he began the study of music history and the construction of instruments; publ. *Essai sur la facture musicale considérée dans ses rapports avec l'art, l'industrie, et le commerce* (1857; 2nd ed., augmented, 1861 as *Organographie*); *Musée instrumental du Conservatoire de musique* (1864); *La Musique à l'Exposition universelle de 1867* (1868); *Les Phénomènes de la musique* (1868).

Ponti, Michael, American pianist; b. Freiburg im Breisgau (of American parents), Oct. 29, 1937. He was taken to the U.S. as a child. He studied piano with Gilmour MacDonald; in 1955 he returned to Germany to continue his studies at the Frankfurt Hochschule für Musik. In 1964 he won 1st prize in the Busoni Competition in Bolzano, which launched him on a successful career. In his programs he specialized in bringing out neglected or forgotten piano masterpieces of the sonorous Romantic past.

Pontoglio, Cipriano, Italian composer; b. Grumello del Piano, Dec. 25, 1831; d. Milan, Feb. 22, 1892. He was a pupil of Antonio Cagnoni in Milan, and P. Serrao in Naples; then opened a music school in Milan. He composed 5 operas: *Lamberto Malatesta* (Pavia, 1857); *Tebaldo Brusato* (Brescia, 1865; rewritten as *L'Assedio di Brescia,* Rome, June 15, 1872); *La Schiava greca* (Bergamo, 1868); *La notte di natale* (Bergamo, Aug. 29, 1872); *Edoardo Stuart* (Milan, May 21, 1887); publ. songs, piano pieces, etc.

Ponty, Jean-Luc, French jazz violinist; b. Arranches, Sept. 29, 1942. He studied piano and violin with his parents; continued his training at the Paris Cons. (premier prix, 1960); was a member of the Concerts Lamoureux until a successful appearance at the Antibes Jazz Festival encouraged him to embark upon a career as a jazz musician. He quickly established himself as a master of the idiom, and subsequently gained success in his appearances with rock musicians, including Frank Zappa and the Mothers of Invention.

Poole, Elizabeth, English mezzo-soprano; b. London, April 5, 1820; d. Langley, Buckinghamshire, Jan. 14, 1906. She made her debut at Drury Lane in London in 1834; sang in Italian opera in the U.S. (appearing with Malibran). Until her retirement in 1870, she was immensely popular as a ballad singer. Balfe wrote for her *'Tis gone, the past is all a dream,* which she introduced into *The Bohemian Girl.*

Poot, Marcel, remarkable Belgian composer; b. Vilvoorde, near Brussels, May 7, 1901; d. Brussels, June 12, 1988. He received his 1st musical training from his father; continued his studies with Gilson (1916); then studied at the Brussels Cons. with Sevenants, Lunssens, and de Greef (1916–20), and at the Royal Flemish Cons. of Antwerp with Lodewijk Mortelmans (1921–23). In 1925, with 7 other Gilson pupils, he founded the Groupe des Synthétistes, dedicated to propaganda of new musical ideas (the group disbanded in 1930). Also in 1925, Poot was co-founder, with Gilson, of *La Revue Musicale Belge,* to which he contributed until its dissolution in 1938. He was on the staff of the Brussels Cons. from 1938 to 1966, and was its director from 1949 until his retirement. The most striking element of his music is its rhythmic vivacity; his harmony is well within the tonal sphere.

Works: DRAMATIC: *CHAMBER OPERA:* **Moretus** (1943; Brussels, 1944). *BALLETS: Pâris et les 3 divines* (1933); *Camera* (1937); *Pygmalion* (1952). *ORATORIOS: Le Dit du routier*

(1943); *Icare* (1945); radio plays (1933–36). **ORCH.**: *Variations en forme de danses* (1923); *Charlot*, 3 sketches inspired by Charlie Chaplin films (1926); *Rondo* for Piano and Small Orch. (1928); *Capriccio* for Oboe and Orch. (1928); 7 syms. (1929; *Triptyque symphonique*, 1938; 1952; 1970; 1974; 1978; 1982); *Poème de l'espace*, symphonic poem inspired by Lindbergh's flight (1929; Liège ISCM Festival, Sept. 4, 1930); *Jazz Music* (1930; Brussels, Feb. 21, 1932); *Allegro symphonique* (1935); *Fantaisie rythmique* (1936); *Ballade* for String Quartet and Orch. (1937); *Légende épique* for Piano and Orch. (1938); *Suite* for Small Orch. (1940); *Ballade* for Clarinet and Orch. (1941); *Concertstück* for Cello and Orch. (1942); *Fantasia* (1944); Sinfonietta (Chicago, Oct. 22, 1946); *Mouvement symphonique* for Wind Orch. (1946); *Divertimento* for Small Orch. (1952); *Mouvement perpétuel* (1953); *Ballade* for Violin and Orch. (1955); Piano Concerto (1959; Brussels, May 25, 1960; compulsory work for finalists of 1960 Queen Elisabeth piano competition, won by Malcolm Frager); 2 *mouvements symphoniques* (1960); *Concertstück* for Violin and Orch. (1962); *Concerto Grosso* for 11 Strings (1962); *Music* for String Orch. (1963); *Concerto Grosso* for Piano Quartet and Orch. (1969); Trumpet Concerto (1973); Alto Saxophone Concerto (1980). **CHAMBER:** Piano Quartet (1932); *3 Pièces en trio* for Piano Trio (1935); *Scherzo* for 4 Saxophones (1941); *Divertimento* for Oboe, Clarinet, and Bassoon (1942); Octet for Winds and Strings (1948); String Quartet (1952); *Ballade* for Oboe, Clarinet, and Bassoon (1954); *Fantaisie* for 6 Clarinets (1955); Concertino for Wind Quintet (1958); *Musique* for Wind Quintet (1964); *Legende* for 4 Clarinets or Saxophones (1967); Quartet for 4 Horns (1969); *Mosaïque* for 8 Winds (1969); *Musique de chambre* for Piano Trio (1971); several *Ballades* and other pieces for Solo Instruments, with Piano; solo piano pieces. Also choral works and songs; film music.

Popov, Alexander, Bulgarian composer; b. Kolarovgrad, July 14, 1927. He studied composition with Veselin Stoyanov at the Bulgarian State Cons., graduating in 1954; played viola in the orch. of the National Opera in Sofia; is a member of the Sofia Soloists chamber ensemble.

WORKS: ORCH.: *Suite* (1956); *Native Land*, variations (1958); *The Artist*, suite for String Quartet and String Orch. (1961); Sinfonietta (1964); *Concerto Grosso* for String Orch. (1966); *Prelude and Dance* (1972); *Adagio* (1973); also 2 cantatas: *Cantata about the April Uprising* (1952) and *Land of Songs* (1969); *Variants* for 13 Strings (1973); 2 string quartets; choruses; songs.

Popov, Gavriil, outstanding and original Russian composer; b. Novocherkassk, Sept. 12, 1904; d. Repino, near Leningrad, Feb. 17, 1972. He studied at the St. Petersburg Cons. with Nikolayev (piano) and Vladimir Shcherbachev (composition). From his student days, he adopted the procedures of modern music; his Septet (Moscow, Dec. 13, 1927) was written in a system of dissonant counterpoint then fashionable in Western Europe; his 1st Sym. (1927–34) was in a similar vein. When modern music became the target of attack in Russia, Popov modified his style toward a more popular conception, following the tenets of "socialist realism"; he wrote several film scores, among them *Communist Youth Union, Leader of Electrification* (1932); other works: Sym. No. 2, subtitled *Fatherland* (Moscow, Feb. 15, 1944); Sym. No. 3 for String Orch., on Spanish themes (Moscow, Jan. 31, 1947); Sym. No. 4, *Glory Be to the Fatherland* (1949); Sym. No. 5 (1965); Sym. No. 6 (Moscow, Jan. 23, 1970); Organ Concerto (1970).

Popovici, Doru, Rumanian composer and musicologist; b. Reşiţa (Banat), Feb. 17, 1932. He studied at the Bucharest Cons. with P. Constantinescu, Negrea, Andricu, Rogalski, Jora, and Vancea (1950–55); attended the annual international summer courses in new music at Darmstadt; in 1968 was appointed director of Rumanian Radio and Television.

WORKS: OPERAS: *Prometeu* (1958; Bucharest, Dec. 16, 1964); *Mariana Pineda*, after García Lorca (Bucharest, Dec. 22, 1966); *Interogateriul din zori* (Bucharest, Feb. 6, 1975); *Noaptea cea mai lungă* (Bucharest, March 30, 1978). **CANTATAS:**

Porumbeii morţii (1957); *Noapte de August* for Baritone and Orch. (1959); *In memoriam poetae Mariana Dumitrescu* (1967); *1877* (1976–77); *Cîntec de speranţă* (1977). **ORCH.:** *Triptyque* (1955); 2 *Symphonic Sketches* (1955); Concertino for String Orch. (1956); Concerto (1960); 4 syms.: No. 1 (1962); No. 2, *Spielberg* (1966); No. 3, *Bizantina*, for Chorus and Orch. (1968); No. 4 for Chorus and Orch. (1973); *Poem bizantin* (1968); *Codex Cajoni* for String Orch. (1968); *Pastorale transilvane* for String Orch. (1979); *Pastorale din Oltenia*, suite (1982). **CHAMBER:** Cello Sonata (1952); Violin Sonata (1953); String Quartet No. 1 (1954; rev. 1964); *Fantasy "Orphée"* for String Trio (1955); Sonata for 2 Cellos (1960); Sonata for 2 Violas (1965); *Omagiu lui Tuculescu*, quintet for Piano, Violin, Viola, Cello, and Clarinet (1967); *Musique solennelle* for Violin and Piano (1969); Trio for Violin, Cello, and Piano (1969–70); *Madrigal* for Flute, Clarinet, Violin, Viola, Cello, and Trombone (1979); piano pieces; also choruses; many songs.

Popp, Lucia, esteemed Czech-born Austrian soprano; b. Uhorška Veš, Nov. 12, 1939. She studied at the Bratislava Academy of Music (1959–63) and in Prague, her principal mentor being Anna Prosenč-Hŕusková; after singing at the Bratislava Opera, she went to Vienna and appeared as Barbarina at the Theater an der Wien (1963); that same year she joined the Vienna State Opera, where she established herself as a principal member; also became a favorite at the Salzburg Festivals. In 1966 she made her 1st appearance at London's Covent Garden as Oscar; then made her Metropolitan Opera debut in N.Y. in one of her finest roles, the Queen of the Night, on Feb. 19, 1967. She sang with many of the world's leading opera houses, and also won distinction as a gifted concert and lieder artist. In 1979 she was made an Austrian Kammersängerin, and was awarded the Silver Rose of the Vienna Phil. She has won accolades for her roles in operas by Mozart and Strauss, especially Pamina, Despina, Zerlina, Susanna, Zdenka, Sophie, and the Countess, as well as the Queen of the Night.

Popper, David, famous Czech cellist and composer; b. Prague, Dec. 9, 1843; d. Baden, near Vienna, Aug. 7, 1913. He studied cello with Goltermann at the Prague Cons.; began his career with a tour in 1863; then had a highly successful appearance as a soloist at the Karlsruhe Music Festival on March 29, 1865; from 1868 to 1873 he was 1st cellist of the Vienna Court Orch. In 1872 he married the famous pianist **Sophie Menter,** but they were divorced 14 years later. From 1896 until his death he taught cello at the Budapest Cons. He wrote a number of extremely attractive and marvelously idiomatic pieces for the cello, which long remained in the international repertoire, among them 4 concertos (1871, 1880, 1880, 1900) and a *Requiem* for 3 Cellos and Orch. (perf. by him, with Delsart and Howell, in London, Nov. 25, 1891); he also publ. the tutors *Hohe Schule des Violoncello-Spiels* (Leipzig, 1901–5) and *10 mittelschwere grosse Etüdien* (Leipzig, c.1905).

Poradowski, Stefan (Boleslaw), Polish composer and pedagogue; b. Wloclawek, Aug. 16, 1902; d. Poznan, July 9, 1967. He studied composition with Opieński at the Poznan Cons. (1922–26); then took private lessons with Rezniček in Berlin (1929). Returning to Poland, he taught composition and theory at the Poznan Cons. (1930–39, 1945–67); also gave courses (from 1956) at the Wroclaw Cons. He publ. *Nauka harmonii* (Science of Harmony; Poznan, 1931; 5th ed., rev., 1964), *Ogólne wiadomości z akustyki* (General Knowledge on Acoustics; Poznan, 1947), and *Sztuka pisania kanonów* (Art of Writing Canons; Poznan, 1965).

WORKS: DRAMATIC: Opera, *Plomienie* (Flames; 1961–66); Passion play, *Odkupienie* (Redemption) for Mezzo-soprano, Chorus, and Orch. (1939–41). **ORCH.:** Sinfonietta (1925); *Concerto antico* for Viola d'Amore and Orch. (1925); *Triptych* for String Orch. (1926); 8 syms. (1928; 1930; 1932; 1934; 1937–38; 1951–52; 1961; 1967); Double-bass Concerto (1929); *Capriccio on a Theme by Kreutzer* for String Orch. (1930); *Koń Swiatowida* (The Horse of Sviatovid), fantastic poem for Tenor, Baritone, Chorus, and Orch. (1931); *Serenada klasyczna for*

String Orch. (1940); *Rapsodia polska* for Violin and Orch. (1944); *Ratusz poznański* (The Town Hall of Poznan), symphonic poem (1950); Concerto for Flute, Harp, and String Orch. (1954); Violin Concerto (1965). **VOCAL:** *Pieśń wiosenna* (Spring Song) for Soprano, Chorus, and Orch. (1926); 3 cantatas (1950, 1954, 1954); 3 masses; 4 hymns; songs; folk-song arrangements. **CHAMBER:** 4 string quartets (1923, 1923, 1936, 1947); Violin Sonata (1925); 5 trios: *I* and *II* for Violin, Viola, and Double Bass (1929, 1930); *III* for String Trio (1935); *IV* for 3 Double Basses (1952); *V* for String Trio (1955); piano pieces; organ music.

Porcelijn, David, Dutch composer; b. Achtkarspelen, Friesland, Jan. 7, 1947. He studied flute with Frans Vester (1964–68) and composition with Kees van Baaren and Jan van Vlijmen (1966–70) at the Royal Cons. of The Hague; then studied conducting with Stotijn; later took lessons in conducting and composition with Tabachnik in Geneva. A modernist par excellence, Porcelijn makes explorations in every direction; his music ranges from the infraclassical to ultramathematical.

WORKS: 4 *Interpretations* for Various Instruments (1967–69); *Continuations* for 11 Wind Instruments (1968); *Combinations* for 26 Solo Instruments (1969–70); *Requiem*, in memory of Varèse, for Percussion Ensemble (1969–70); *Zen* for Flute (1970); *1,000 Frames* for 1 + Wind Instruments and/or 1 + Pianos (1970); *Confrontation and Indoctrinations* for Jazz Band and 19 Instruments (Scheveningen, June 23, 1972); *Cybernetic Object* for Orch. (The Hague, June 18, 1971); *Amoeba* for x Flutes (1971); *Pole*, ballet for 26 Instruments (1971–72); *10-5-6-5(a)* for 2 String Quartets, Wind Quintet, and 2 Vibraphones (1972); *Pulverizations I* for 52 Strings (1972); *Pulverizations* for Wind Quintet (1972); *Pulverizations II* for Alto Saxophone, 22 Winds, 5 Percussion Groups, and 52 Strings (1973); Concerto for Flute, Harp, and Orch. (1973); Flute Concerto (1975); *Shades* for Flute, Violin, and Viola (1975); *Rhythm Song* for Male Chorus and Percussion (1976); *Into the Earth* for 14 Brass and 2 Percussionists (1976); *12 November 1819* for Wind Quintet (1976); *Terrible Power* for Orch. (1977); *Explosions* for 10 Instruments (1977); *Groupings* for 5 Groups of Instruments (1979); *Sinfonia Concertante* for Orch. (1985–86); *Unfinished Songs for an Elusive Sphinx* for Oboe, Clarinet, and Bassoon (1986); *97 Endeavors to Propitiate Ra* for Flute (1986).

Porfetye, Andreas, Rumanian composer; b. Zădăreni, July 6, 1927. He studied with Drăgoi, P. Constantinescu, Rogalski, and Vancea at the Bucharest Cons. (1948–54); was ed. of the journal *Muzica* (1954–69); taught at the Bucharest Cons. (from 1969).

WORKS: ORCH.: 3 syms. (1955; 1965; 1970, *La Dramatique*); *Partita* for String Orch. (1958); Organ Concerto (1962, rev. 1967); *Sinfonia-Serenata* (1964); Violin Concerto (1966); *Sonata* (1971). **VOCAL:** *Cantata de camera* for Mezzo-soprano, Cello, and Chamber Orch. (1959); Cantata No. 2, *Comunistul*, for Mezzo-soprano, Chorus, and Orch. (1962); *In memoriam Mihail Sadoveanu*, Requiem for Soprano, Tenor, and Orch. (1962). **CHAMBER:** Horn Sonata (1956); Wind Quintet (1957); *Piccola sonata* for Violin and Organ (1962); Sonata for Cello and Organ (1963); *6 Pieces* for Clarinet and Harp (1965); Sonata No. 1 for Violin and Piano (1967); String Quartet No. 2 (1969); Piano Sonata (1963); Piano Sonatina (1965). **ORGAN:** *Passacaglia and Fugue* (1955); *Toccata, Chorale, and Fugue* (1957); 3 sonatas (1960–68); *Toccata* (1966); *Fantasy* (1968).

Porpora, Nicola (Antonio), famous Italian composer and singing teacher; b. Naples, Aug. 17, 1686; d. there, March 3, 1768. The son of a bookseller, he entered the Cons. dei Poveri at Naples at the age of 10 and studied with Gaetano Greco, Matteo Giordano, and Ottavio Campanile. Porpora's 1st opera, *Agrippina*, was presented at the Royal Palace of Naples (Nov. 4, 1708). Cardinal Grimani attended the performance and wrote a libretto on the same subject for Handel. This episode gave rise to the incorrect statement (by Fétis and others) that Handel heard Porpora's opera in Rome in 1710. Porpora produced in Naples 2 more operas: *Flavio Anicio Olibrio* (1711)

and *Basilio, re d'oriente* (June 24, 1713). From 1711 until 1725, he held the title of maestro di cappella to Philip, Landgrave of Hesse-Darmstadt. He gained a great reputation as a singing teacher, and numbered among his pupils the famous castrati Farinelli, Caffarelli, Antonio Uberti (who called himself "Porporino" out of respect for his teacher), and Salimbeni. Metastasio, who wrote librettos for several of Porpora's operas, was also his pupil. Porpora's career as a singing teacher was divided between Naples and Venice. In Naples he taught at the conservatories of Sant' Onofrio (1715–22, 1760–61) and Santa Maria di Loreto (1739–41, 1760–61); in Venice he gave lessons at the Ospedali degli Incurabili (1726–33, 1737–38), the Ospedali della Pietà (1742–46), and the Ospedaletto (1746–47). In 1718 Porpora collaborated with Domenico Scarlatti in the writing of the opera *Berenice, regina d'Egitto*, produced in Rome (1718). At about this time he succeeded in obtaining support from the Austrian court. His opera *Temistocle* was produced in Vienna on the Emperor's birthday (Oct. 1, 1718); his next opera, *Faramondo*, was staged in Naples (Nov. 19, 1719). He continued to write operas for theaters in Naples and Rome: *Eumene* (Rome, 1721); *Adelaide* (Rome, 1723); *Semiramide, regina dell'Assiria* (Naples, 1724); *Didone abbandonata* (his 1st opera to a libretto by Metastasio; Reggio Emilia, 1725). In 1726 he settled in Venice. Among the operas he wrote during the next 8 years were *Meride e Selinunte* (Venice, 1726); *Siroe, re di Persia* (Milan, 1726); *Semiramide riconosciuta* (Venice, 1729); *Mitridate* (Rome, 1730); *Tamerlano* (Turin, 1730); *Poro* (Turin, 1731); *Germanico in Germania* (Rome, 1732); *Issipile* (Rome, 1733). In 1733 he applied for the post of maestro di cappella at San Marco in Venice, but failed to obtain it. In the same year he was engaged by the directors of the Opera of the Nobility in London (organized as a rival company to that of Handel). For this venture Porpora wrote 5 operas: *Arianna in Nasso* (Dec. 29, 1733); *Enea nel Lazio* (May 11, 1734); *Polifemo* (Feb. 1, 1735); *Ifigenia in Aulide* (May 3, 1735); *Mitridate* (Jan. 24, 1736; a different score from the earlier opera of the same title). For a while he competed successfully with Handel, but soon the Opera of the Nobility began to falter, and Porpora left London on the eve of the company's collapse. From 1747 to 1751, he was in Dresden as singing teacher to the Electoral Princess. There he became Hasse's competitor for the position of music director. Although Hasse conducted Porpora's "pastoral drama" *Filandro* (Dresden, July 18, 1747), their relationship was made difficult by the intrigues of Hasse's wife, the singer Faustina Bordoni. In 1751 Porpora left Dresden for Vienna, where he became the teacher of Haydn, who paid for his lessons by serving Porpora as accompanist and personal helper. Porpora returned to Naples in 1758. His last stage work, *Il trionfo di Camilla*, was given in Naples on May 30, 1760, with little success. In addition to his varied and numerous stage works, Porpora wrote sacred oratorios and secular cantatas and serenatas. Among his instrumental works are 6 *Sinfonie da camera* for 2 Violins and Basso Continuo (London, 1736), 6 *Sonatas* for 2 Violins, Cello, and Basso Continuo (London, 1745, in collaboration with G.B. Costanza), 12 *Sonate* for Violin and Basso Continuo (Vienna, 1754), a Cello Concerto, a Flute Concerto, and *Ouverture roiale* (1763).

BIBL.: Marchese di Villarosa, *Memorie dei compositori di musica del regno di Napoli* (Naples, 1840); F. Clément, *Les Musiciens célèbres depis le XVI*^e *siècle* (Paris, 1868); S. Fassini, *Il melodramma italiano a Londra* (Turin, 1914); S. di Giacomo, *I quattro antiche Conservatorii di musica di Napoli* (Palermo, 1925); F. Walker, *A Chronology of the Life and Works of N. P.*, Italian Studies, 6 (Cambridge, 1951); U. Prota-Giurleo, "Per una esatta biografia di N. P.," *La Scala* (Jan. 1957; establishing for the 1st time Porpora's dates of birth and death); A. Mayeda, *N.A. P. als Instrumentalkomponist* (diss., Univ. of Vienna, 1967; with thematic catalogue); F. Degrada, "Le musiche strumentali di N. P.," *Chigiana*, XXV (1968); M. Robinson, "P.'s Operas for London, 1733–1736," *Soundings*, II (1971–72); E. Sutton, *The Solo Vocal Works of N. P.: An Annotated Thematic Index* (diss., Univ. of Minnesota, 1974); C.

Vitali, "Un concerto per violoncello attribuito a P.," *Studi Musicali*, VIII (1979).

Porrino, Ennio, Italian composer; b. Cagliari, Sardinia, Jan. 20, 1910; d. Rome, Sept. 25, 1959. He studied at the Accademia di Santa Cecilia in Rome with Mulè, and later took a course with Respighi (1932–35). He subsequently taught in Rome, Venice, and Naples; in 1956, became director of the Cons. in his hometown in Sardinia.

WORKS: STAGE: OPERAS: *Gli orazi* (Milan, 1941); *L'organo di bambù* (Venice, 1955); *I shardana* (Naples, 1959). **BALLETS:** *Proserpina* (Florence, 1938); *Altair* (Naples, 1942); *Mondo tondo* (Rome, 1949); *La bambola malata* (Venice, 1959). **ORCH.:** *Tartatin de Tarascon,* overture (Rome, 1933); *Sardegna,* symphonic poem, based on Sardinian folk themes (Rome, 1933; his most popular work); Trumpet Concertino (1934); *La visione di Ezechiele* (1935); *Sinfonia per una fiaba* (1936); *Notturna e Danza* (1936); *3 canzoni italiane* for Chamber Orch. (1937); *Preludio in modo religioso e ostinato* for Orch. or Piano (1942); *Sinfonietta dei fanciulli* (1947); *Sonata drammatica* for Piano and Orch. (1947); *Ostinato* for Strings and Piano (1951; Milan, Feb. 3, 1952); *Nuraghi,* 3 primitive dances (1952); *Concerto dell'Argentarola* for Guitar and Orch. (1953); *Sonar per musici* for Harpsichord and Strings (1959); *I canti dell'esilio,* 15 songs for Voice and Chamber Orch. (1947); also an oratorio, *Il processo di Cristo* (1949); chamber pieces, including *Preludio, Aria e Scherzo* for Trumpet and Piano (1942); songs.

Porro, Pierre-Jean, famous French guitarist; b. Béziers, 1750; d. Montmorency, May 31, 1831. Through his influence the guitar became a fashionable instrument in Paris; he had a class of pupils there; also was ed. and publ. of *Journal de Guitarre* (1787–1803). He publ. a guitar method, *Tableau méthodique;* numerous divertissements, sonatas, and canzonets, for guitar solo and with other instruments; also *Collection de musique sacrée* for 4 Mixed Voices and Organ.

BIBL.: F. Donnadieu, *P., Compositeur et éditeur de musique* (Béziers, 1897).

Porsile, Giuseppe, Italian composer; b. Naples, May 5, 1680; d. Vienna, May 29, 1750. He studied in Naples at the Cons. dei Poveri di Gesù Cristo with Ursino, Giordano, and Greco. He then served as vice-maestro di cappella at the Spanish chapel in Naples. In 1695 he went to Spain to organize the music chapel of King Charles II in Barcelona; he subsequently served Charles III. When Charles III was elected Holy Roman Emperor as Charles VI, with the seat in Vienna, Porsile followed him there. On Dec. 17, 1720, he became court composer. He continued to serve the court after Charles VI died in 1740, being granted an honorary stipend; he was pensioned on April 1, 1749. Most of his stage works were written for the court of Vienna.

WORKS (all 1st perf. in Vienna unless otherwise given): **OPERAS:** *Il ritorno di Ulisse alla patria* (Naples, 1707); *Il giorno natalizio dell'imperatrice Amalia Wilhelmina* (April 21, 1717); *La Virtù festeggiata* (July 10, 1717); *Alceste,* festa teatrale (Nov. 19, 1718); *Meride e Selinunte,* dramma per musica (Aug. 28, 1721); *Il tempo fermato,* componimento da camera (Oct. 15, 1721); *La Virtù e la Bellezza in lega,* serenata (Oct. 15, 1722); *Il giorno felice,* componimento da camera (Aug. 28, 1723); *Componimento a due voci* (Aug. 28, 1725); *Spartaco,* dramma per musica (Feb. 21, 1726); *Il tempio di Giano, chiuso da Cesare Augusto,* componimento per musica (Oct. 1, 1726); *La clemenza di Cesare,* servizio di camera (Oct. 1, 1727); *Telesilla,* festa teatrale (Nov. 19, 1729); *Scipione Africano, Il maggiore,* festa di camera (Oct. 1, 1730); *Dialogo tra il Decoro e la Placidezza,* festa di camera (July 26, 1732); *Dialogo pastorale a cinque voci* (Aug. 28, 1732); *Dialogo tra la Prudenza e la Vivacità,* festa di camera (Oct. 15, 1732); *La Fama accresciuta dalla Virtù,* festa di camera (Oct. 15, 1735); *Sesostri, re d'Egitto, ovvero Le feste d'Iside,* dramma per musica (Carnival 1737); *Il giudizio rivocato,* festa di camera (Oct. 15, 1737). **ORATORIOS:** *Sisara* (March 23, 1719); *Tobia* (March 14, 1720); *Il zelo di Nathan* (1721); *L'anima immortale creata e redenta per il cielo* (Feb. 26, 1722); *Il trionfo di Giuditta* (Feb. 18,

1723); *Il sacrifizio di Gefte* (March 9, 1724); *Mosè liberato dal Nilo* (March 1, 1725); *Assalone nemico del padre amante* (March 14, 1726); *L'esaltatione de Salomone* (March 6, 1727); *L'ubbidienza a Dio* (March 9, 1730); *Due re, Roboamo e Geroboamo* (Feb. 23, 1731); *Giuseppe riconosciuto* (March 12, 1733); *La madre de' Maccabei* (March 14, 1737); also chamber cantatas, duets, and instrumental pieces.

BIBL.: U. Prota-Giurleo, "G. P. e la Real cappella di Barcellona," *Gazzetta Musicale di Napoli,* II, no. 10 (1956); O. Deutsch, "Das Repertoire der höfischen Oper, der Hof- und der Staatsoper," *Österreichische Musikzeitschrift,* XXIV (1969).

Porta, Costanzo, important Italian composer; b. Cremona, 1528 or 1529; d. Padua, May 19, 1601. He most likely began his religious training at the convent of Porta S. Luca in Cremona. He then went to Casalmaggiore, possibly to enter his novitiate. He was transferred to S. Maria Gloriosa dei Frari in Venice about 1549. He studied music with Willaert, the choirmaster of San Marco. In 1552 he became maestro di cappella of the cathedral in Osimo, near Ancona. On April 14, 1565, he became maestro di cappella in the Cappella Antoniana in Padua. In 1567 he became maestro di cappella of the cathedral in Ravenna. In 1574 he was called to the Santa Casa in Loreto. He publ. his 1st book of masses in 1578, and his *Liber motectorum* followed in 1580. He returned to Ravenna in 1580, making visits to the Este court in Ferrara and the Gonzaga court in Mantua. In 1589 he took charge of the chapel of the cathedral in Padua, but in 1592 was ordered to take up residence at the Convento del Santo. In 1595 he again became maestro di cappella at the Cappella Antoniana, a position he held until his death. Porta was one of the leading Italian composers and teachers of his time; was greatly esteemed as a contrapuntist.

WORKS: SACRED VOCAL: 37 *Motectorum . . . liber primus* for 5 Voices (Venice, 1555); *Liber primus* [28] *motectorum* for 4 Voices (Venice, 1559; 2nd ed., rev., 1591); *Musica* [44] *introitus missarum . . . in diebus dominicis* for 5 Voices (Venice, 1566; 2nd ed., rev., 1588); *Musica* [40] *introitis missarum . . . in solemnitatibus omnium sanctorum* for 5 Voices (Venice, 1566; 2nd ed., rev., 1588); *Musica* [29] *canenda . . . liber primus* for 6 Voices (Venice, 1571); *Litaniae deiparae virginis Mariae* for 8 Voices (Venice, 1575); (12) *Missarum liber primus* for 4 to 6 Voices (Venice, 1578); *Liber* [52] *motectorum* for 4 to 8 Voices (Venice, 1580); *Musica* [29] *canenda . . . liber tertius* for 6 Voices (Venice, 1585); (44) *Hymnodia sacra totius per anni circulum* for 4 Voices (Venice, 1602); *Psalmodia vespertina omnium solemnitatem decantanda cum 4 canticis beatae virginis* for 8 and 16 Voices (Ravenna and Venice, 1605); (23) *Motectorum* for 5 Voices (Venice, 1605); also various motets, Psalms, and litanies in other collections of the period. **SECULAR VOCAL:** *Il primo libro de* [29] *madrigali* for 4 Voices (Venice, 1555); *Il primo libro de* [28] *madrigali* for 5 Voices (Venice, 1559); *Il secondo libro de* [29] *madrigali* for 5 Voices (Venice, 1569); *Il terzo libro de* [29] *madrigali* for 5 Voices (Venice, 1573); *Il quarto libro de* [21] *madrigali* for 5 Voices (Venice, 1586); various other madrigals in other collections of the period. A modern ed. of his works, *Costanzo Porta: Opera Omnia,* was publ. in Padua (1964–70).

BIBL.: F. Hafkemayer, *C. P. aus Cremona: Untersuchungen über seine kirchenmusikalischen Arbeiten* (diss., Univ. of Freiburg, 1953); A. Garbelotto, *Il Padre C. P. da Cremona, OFM. Conv.* (Padua, 1955); L. Pruett, *The Masses and Hymns of C. P.* (diss., Univ. of North Carolina, 1960); idem, "Parody Technique in the Masses of C. P.," *Studies in Musicology: Essays in the History, Style and Bibliography of Music in Memory of Glen Haydon* (Chapel Hill, 1969).

Porter, Andrew (Brian), brilliant English writer on music; b. Cape Town, South Africa, Aug. 26, 1928. He studied music at Diocesan College in Cape Town; then went to England; continued his education at Univ. College, Oxford; became a proficient organist. In 1949 he joined the staff of the *Manchester Guardian;* then wrote music criticism for the *Financial Times* of London (1953–74); also served as ed. of the *Musical Times* of London (1960–67). In 1972 he became the music critic of the *New Yorker*. A polyglot, a polymath, and an uncommonly diversified intellectual, Porter expanded his interests far beyond the limited surface of purely musical studies; he mastered German, Italian, and French; made an exemplary tr. into Eng. of the entire text of *Der Ring des Nibelungen*, taking perspicuous care for the congenial rendition of Wagner's words and melodic inflections; his tr. was used to excellent advantage in the performance and recording of the cycle by the conductor Reginald Goodall with the English National Opera. Porter also tr. texts of Verdi's operas, Mozart's *Die Zauberflöte*, and some French operas. His mastery of English prose and his unostentatious display of arcane erudition make him one of the most remarkable music critics writing in the English language. Selections from his reviews have been publ. in *A Musical Season* (N.Y., 1974), *Music of Three Seasons, 1974–1977* (N.Y., 1978), *Music of Three More Seasons, 1977–1980* (N.Y., 1981), *Musical Events: A Chronicle, 1980–1983* (N.Y., 1987), and *Musical Events: A Chronicle, 1983–1986* (N.Y., 1989); also was co-ed. of *Verdi's Macbeth: A Sourcebook* (N.Y., 1983).

Porter, Cole (Albert), remarkable American composer of popular music; b. Peru, Ind., June 9, 1891; d. Santa Monica, Calif., Oct. 15, 1964. He was educated at Yale Univ. (B.A., 1913); then took academic courses at Harvard Law School, and later at the Harvard School of Music (1915–16); also received instruction in counterpoint, composition, orchestration, and harmony from d'Indy at the Paris Schola Cantorum (1919). While at Yale, he wrote football songs (*Yale Bull Dog Song, Bingo Eli Yale*, etc.); also composed music for college functions. He first gained success as a composer for the stage with his *Wake Up and Dream* (London, March 27, 1929); his 1st production in N.Y. was *See America First* (March 28, 1916). There followed a cascade of musical comedies for which he wrote both the lyrics and the music, which placed him in the front rank of the American musical theater. His greatest success came with his musical comedy *Kiss Me, Kate*, after Shakespeare's *The Taming of the Shrew* (N.Y., Dec. 30, 1948). A motion picture musical biography of Porter, starring Cary Grant, was produced by Warner Bros. in 1946 as *Night and Day*. Porter was a master of subtle expression without sentimentality, a kinetic dash without vulgarity, and a natural blend of word poetry with the finest of harmonious melodies.

Works: STAGE (all are musicals 1st perf. in N.Y. unless otherwise given): *Hands Up* (July 22, 1915); *Kitchy-koo of 1919* (revue; Oct. 6, 1919); *Fifty Million Frenchmen* (Nov. 27, 1929); *Gay Divorcee* (Nov. 29, 1932); *Anything Goes* (Nov. 21, 1934); *Jubilee* (Oct. 12, 1935); *Red Hot and Blue* (Oct. 29, 1936); *Leave It to Me* (Nov. 9, 1938); *Du Barry was a Lady* (Dec. 6, 1939); *Panama Hattie* (Oct. 30, 1940); *Let's Face It* (Oct. 29, 1941); *Something for the Boys* (Jan. 7, 1943); *Mexican Hayride* (Jan. 28, 1944); *Kiss Me, Kate* (Dec. 30, 1948); *Out of This World* (Dec. 21, 1950); *Can-can* (May 7, 1953); *Silk Stockings* (Feb. 24, 1955); etc. Of his many songs, at least half a dozen became great favorites: *Begin the Beguine; It's De-Lovely; Night and Day; My Heart Belongs to Daddy; Don't Fence Me In; Wunderbar*. He also composed numerous film scores, including *Rosalie* (1937), *You'll Never Get Rich* (1941), *Les Girls* (1957), and *Aladdin* (1958). See *The Cole Porter Song Book* (N.Y., 1959) and R. Kimball, ed., *The Complete Lyrics of Cole Porter* (N.Y., 1984). **BIBL.:** D. Ewen, *The C. P. Story* (N.Y., 1965); C. Porter and R. Hubler, *The C. P. Story* (Cleveland, 1965); G. Eells, *The Life That Late He Led* (N.Y., 1967); R. Kimball and B. Gill, *C.* (N.Y., 1971); L. Siebert, *C. P.: An Analysis of 5 Musical Comedies and a Thematic Index of the Complete Works* (diss., City Univ. of N.Y., 1975); C. Schwartz, *C. P.* (N.Y., 1977; a "candid" biography; conclusively debunks the story that Cole Porter ever served in the French army, let alone the French Foreign Legion, as was claimed for him).

Porter, (William) Quincy, significant American composer and teacher; b. New Haven, Conn., Feb. 7, 1897; d. Bethany, Conn., Nov. 12, 1966. He was brought up in an intellectual atmosphere; his father and his grandfather were profs. at Yale Univ. He studied with David Stanley Smith and Horatio Parker at the Yale Univ. School of Music (B.A., 1919; B.Mus., 1921); submitted a violin concerto for the American Prix de Rome and received an honorable mention; also won the Steinert and Osborne prizes. After graduation he went to Paris, where he took courses with Lucien Capet (violin) and d'Indy (composition). Returning to America in 1922, he earned a living as a violinist in theater orchs. in N.Y. while taking a course in composition with Ernest Bloch. He taught at the Cleveland Inst. of Music (1922–28, 1931–32); played the viola in the Ribaupierre String Quartet there; spent 3 years in Paris on a Guggenheim fellowship (1928–31); was a prof. at Vassar College and conductor of the Vassar Orch. (1932–38); in 1938 he succeeded Frederick Converse as dean of the New England Cons. of Music in Boston; from 1942 to 1946, was its director; from 1946 to 1965, was a prof. at Yale Univ. His music is built on strong contrapuntal lines, with incisive rhythms; his harmonic procedures often reach stridently polytonal sonorities, while the general idiom of his works combines elements of both the modern German and the modern French styles of composition.

Works: ORCH.: *Ukrainian Suite* for String Orch. (Rochester, N.Y., May 1, 1925); Suite in C minor (1926); *Poem and Dance* (Cleveland, June 24, 1932, composer conducting); 2 syms.: No. 1 (1934; N.Y., April 2, 1938, composer conducting); No. 2 (1961–62; Louisville, Jan. 14, 1964); *Dance in Three-Time* for Chamber Orch. (St. Louis, July 2, 1937); *Music for Strings* (1941); *Fantasy on a Pastoral Theme* for Organ and String Orch. (1942); *The Moving Tide* (1944); Viola Concerto (N.Y., May 16, 1948); *Fantasy* for Cello and Small Orch. (1950); *The Desolate City* for Baritone and Orch. (1950); *Concerto Concertante* for 2 Pianos and Orch. (1952–53; Louisville, March 17, 1954; awarded the Pulitzer Prize in music under its original title, Concerto for 2 Pianos and Orch.); *New England Episodes*, symphonic suite (Washington, D.C., April 18, 1958); Concerto for Wind Orch. (1959); Harpsichord Concerto (1959; New Haven, Jan. 19, 1960); Concerto for Wind Orch. (1960); *Ohio*, overture (1963). **CHAMBER:** 10 string quartets (1923, 1925, 1930, 1931, 1935, 1937, 1943, 1950, 1958, 1965); *In Monasterio* for String Quartet (1927); Piano Quintet (1927); Clarinet Quintet (1929); *Quintet on a Childhood Theme* for Flute and Strings (1937); *String Sextet on Slavic Folk Tunes* (1947); Divertimento for Wind Quintet (1960); Oboe Quintet (1966); 2 violin sonatas (1926, 1929); *Little Trio* for Flute, Violin, and Viola (1928); Suite for Solo Viola (1930); Horn Sonata (1946); 4 pieces for Violin and Piano (1947); Duo for Violin and Viola (1954); Duo for Flute and Harp (1957). **PIANO:** Sonata (1930); *8 Pieces for Bill* (1941–42; nos. 2 and 8 not extant); *6 Miniatures* (1943); *Day Dreams* (1957; based on *8 Pieces for Bill*); also organ pieces; choruses; songs; incidental music.

BIBL.: H. Ewell, "Q. P.," *Modern Music*, XXIII (1946); H. Boatwright, "Q. P.," *American Composers Alliance Bulletin*, VI/3 (1957); idem, "Q. P. (1897–1966)," *Perspectives of New Music*, V/2 (1967).

Portugal (Portogallo; real name, Ascenção or Assumpção), Marcos Antônio (da Fonseca), prominent Portuguese composer; b. Lisbon, March 24, 1762; d. Rio de Janeiro, Feb. 7, 1830. A pupil at the ecclesiastical seminary at Lisbon, he continued his musical education with composition lessons from João de Souza Carvalho. Between 1784 and 1791 he wrote for Lisbon 17 stage works, mostly ephemeral. His reputation was made in Italy, where, with the exception of a short visit to Lisbon, he lived from 1792 to 1800, bringing out some 21 operas for various Italian theaters. Upon his return to Lisbon (1800), he was made mestre de capela of the royal chapel and director of the Teatro San Carlos. His *Il Filosofo seducente, ossia Non irritar le donne* (Venice, Dec. 27, 1798) was selected by Napoleon for opening the Théâtre-Italien at Paris in 1801. In 1807 the royal family fled to Brazil before the French invasion; Portugal remained until the Treatro San Carlos was closed in 1810, and then followed the court to Rio de Janeiro, where he served as mestre de capela of the royal chapel and master of music to the future John VI. The royal theater of São João, after its inauguration in 1813, produced several new operas by him. In that year he became director of the new Cons. at Vera Cruz, jointly with his brother **Simão;** he visited Italy in 1815, returned to Rio de Janeiro, and passed his last years there as an invalid. His masterpiece is *Fernando nel Messico* (Venice, Jan. 16, 1798; written for the famous English singer Elizabeth Billington; produced in London, in Italian, March 31, 1803); other Italian operas that had a favorable reception were *Demofoonte* (Milan, Feb. 8, 1794) and *Le Donne cambiate* (Venice, Oct. 22, 1797); of Portuguese operas, *A Castanheira* (The Chestnut Seller), produced in Lisbon in 1787, enjoyed considerable popular success. He further wrote about 100 sacred works.

BIBL.: M. Carvalhães, *M. P. na sua musica dramatica* (Lisbon, 1910).

Porumbescu, Ciprian, Rumanian choirmaster, teacher, and composer; b. Șipote, Oct. 14, 1853; d. Stupca, Bukovina, June 6, 1883. After preliminary studies in Rumania, he went to Vienna, where he became a student of F. Krenn and Bruckner at the Cons.; publ. a collection of "social songs of Rumanian students" (Vienna, 1880); composed an operetta, *Crai nou* (The New Moon; 1882), to a Rumanian libretto, and many songs. His death at the age of 29 deprived Rumania of the country's 1st national composer, but he is greatly revered as such. The town of Stupca, where he died, has been renamed Ciprian Porumbescu, and his name is attached to the official designation of several Rumanian conservatories. V. Cosma ed. the complete works (2 vols., Bucharest, 1954, 1958).

BIBL.: V. Cosma, *C. P.* (Bucharest, 1957).

Pospíšil, Juraj, Slovak composer; b. Olomouc, Jan. 14, 1931. He first studied music in his hometown; then with Petrželka at the Janáček Academy of Music in Brno and later with Alexander Moyzes and Cikker at the Bratislava Academy of Music. **WORKS: ORCH.:** *Mountains and People,* symphonic poem (1955); *Margita and Besná,* ballad for Soloists, Chorus, and Orch. (1955); 2 syms.: No. 1 (1957) and No. 2, *Nebula in Andromeda* (1963); Sonata for Strings (1961); Trombone Concerto (1962); *Concerto Eroico* for Horn and Orch. (1975); *Fragment* (Košice, Oct. 4, 1976); *Symphonic Fresco* (1976). **CHAMBER:** Cello Sonata (1956); *Passacaglia and Fugue* for Organ (1962); *Mikropoviedky* (Micro-stories) for Soprano, Flute, Violin, and Cello (1963); *Glosy* (Marginal Notes) for Wind Quintet (1964); *Protirečenia* (Contradictions) for Piano Quartet (1964); *Music* for 12 Strings (1965); Double-bass Sonata (1966); Solo Violin Sonata (1966); *Trojveršia* (3 Verses) for 9 Instruments (1966); String Quartet (1970); Flute Quartet (1971); *Bagatelles* for Trombone and Piano (1972); *Little Pieces* for Clarinet and Piano (1976).

Posselt, Ruth, American violinist; b. Medford, Mass., Sept. 6, 1914. She studied with E. Ondříček; gave numerous recitals in America and Europe; gave the world premieres of violin concertos by Walter Piston, Vladimir Dukelsky, Edward Burlingame Hill, and others. On July 3, 1940, she married **Richard Burgin.**

Postnikova, Viktoria (Valentinovna), Russian pianist; b. Moscow, Jan. 12, 1944. She studied at the Moscow Central Music School and later at the Moscow Cons., graduating in 1967. In 1966 she received 2nd prize at the Leeds Competition; then embarked upon a major career, appearing widely in recitals and concerts. She married the Russian conductor **Gennadi Rozhdestvensky** in 1969.

Poštolka, Milan, Czech musicologist; b. Prague, Sept. 29, 1932. He studied with Očadlik and Sychra at the Univ. of Prague (1951–56), passing the state examination in musicology (1956), taking the C.Sc. (1966), and obtaining his Ph.D (1967; with the diss. *Leopold Koželuh: Život a dílo* [Leopold Kozeluh: Life and Works]; publ. in Prague, 1964). He worked in the music division of Prague's National Museum (from 1958), and also taught at the Univ. of Prague (1966–79); was director of

a research team studying 17th- and 18th-century Czech music at the Czech Academy of Sciences (1972–86). He publ. books on Czech music of the 18th century (Prague, 1961) and on the young Haydn (Prague, 1988).

Poston, Elizabeth, English pianist and composer; b. Highfield, Hertfordshire, Oct. 24, 1905; d. there, March 18, 1987. She studied piano with Harold Samuel; also took courses at the Royal Academy of Music in London; during World War II, was in charge of music in the European Service of the BBC in London. Her works follow along neo-Classical lines.

WORKS: *The Holy Child* for Chorus, Vocal Soloists, and String Orch. (1950); *Concertino da Camera on a Theme of Martin Peerson* for Ancient Instruments (1950); *The Nativity* for Chorus, Vocal Soloists, and String Orch. or Organ (1951); Trio for Flute, Clarinet or Viola, and Piano (1958); *Peter Halfpenny's Tunes* for Recorder and Piano (1959); *Lullaby* and *Fiesta,* 2 pieces for Piano (1960); *Magnificat* for 4 Voices and Organ (1961); *3 Scottish Carols* for Chorus, and Strings or Organ (1969); *Harlow Concertante* for String Quartet and String Orch. (1969); *An English Day Book* for Mixed Voices and Harp (1971); Sonatina for Cello and Piano (1972); hymn tunes; Christmas carols; music for films and radio.

Pothier, Dom Joseph, learned French music scholar; b. Bouzemont, near Saint-Dié, Dec. 7, 1835; d. Conques, Belgium, Dec. 8, 1923. He was ordained a priest (1858); became a Benedictine monk in 1860 at Solesmes; in 1862, sub-prior; in 1866, prof. of theology at the Solesmes Monastery; in 1893, prior at the Benedictine monastery of Ligugé; in 1898, abbot at St.-Wandrille. When the religious orders were banned from France, he moved to Belgium. In 1904 he was appointed by Pope Pius X president of the publ. committee of the *Editio Vaticana.*

EDITIONS: *Les mélodies grégoriennes d'après la tradition* (Tournai, 1880; 2nd ed., 1890); *Liber gradualis* (Tournai, 1883; 2nd ed., 1895); *Processionale monasticum* (Solesmes, 1888); *Varie preces* (Solesmes, 1888); *Liber antiphonarius* (Solesmes, 1891); *Liber responsorialis* (Solesmes, 1895); *Cantus mariales* (Paris, 1903; 3rd ed., 1924).

BIBL.: F. Velluz, *Étude bibiographique sur les mélodies grégoriennes de Dom J. P.* (Grenoble, 1881); N. Rousseau, *L'École grégorienne de Solesmes* (Tournai, 1911); L. David, *Dom J. P., abbé de Saint-Wandrille, et la restauration grégorienne* (St.-Wandrille, 1943); A. Le Guennant, *Précis de rythmique grégorienne d'après les principes de Solesmes* (Paris, 1948); M. Blanc, *L'Enseignement musical de Solesmes* (Paris, 1953); P. Combe, *Histoire de la restauration du chant grégorien d'après des documents inédits* (Solesmes, 1969).

Potter, A(rchibald) J(ames), Irish composer; b. Belfast, Sept. 22, 1918; d. Greystones, July 5, 1980. He studied with W. Vale at the choir school of All Saints, Margaret Street, in London (1929–33); after training with D.G.A. Fox at Clifton College in Bristol (1933–36), he returned to London to study with Vaughan Williams at the Royal College of Music (1936–38); completed his courses at the Univ. of Dublin (D.Mus., 1953). From 1955 he was prof. of composition at Dublin's Royal Irish Academy of Music. His output follows in the path of tradition, opting for Romantic qualities.

WORKS: OPERA: *Patrick,* television opera (1963). **ORCH.:** *Overture to an Irish Occasion* (1951); *Concerto da chiesa* for Piano and Orch. (1952); *Variations on a Popular Tune* (1955); *Phantasmoraggia* (1956); *Elegy* for Clarinet, Harp, and Strings (1956); *Caoine* (Dirge; 1956); *Finnegans Wake* (1957); *Fantasia Gaelach* (1957); *Fantasie concertante* for Violin, Cello, and Orch. (1959); *Irish Rhapsody* (1963); *Caprice* for Cello and Orch. (1964); *Sound the Sackbuts* for 3 Trombones and Orch. (1965); *Fantasie* for Clarinet and Orch. (1965); *Spanish Point* for Guitar and Orch. (1965); *Concerto for Orchestra* (1966); *Rapsóid deire lae* (Rhapsody at the End of Day; 1966); *Dance Fantasie* (1967); *Binneadán Bél* for Harmonica and Orch. (1967); *Sinfonia de profundis* (1968); also choral works; chamber music; songs; ballets; incidental music for radio and television; folk-song arrangements.

Potter, (Philip) Cipriani (Hambley), distinguished English pianist, teacher, and composer; b. London, Oct. 2, 1792; d. there, Sept. 26, 1871. He began his musical training with his father, **Richard Huddleston Potter** (b. London, Dec. 10, 1755; d. there [buried], June 3, 1821), a founder of the Phil. Soc. of London (1813) and a violist in its orch.; then studied with Thomas Attwood, Joseph Woelffl (1805–10), and Crotch (1808–9); was made a member of the Phil. Soc. (1815), with which he made his debut as a pianist in his own Sextet for Piano, Flute, and Strings (April 29, 1816). In 1817 he went to Vienna, where he met Beethoven; at the latter's suggestion he studied counterpoint with Aloys Förster; he returned to England in 1819. He made many appearances as a pianist in London, introducing a number of Mozart's concerti and Beethoven's 1st, 3rd, and 4th concerti; also conducted the Phil. Soc. orch., and later was music director of the Madrigal Soc. (from 1854). In 1822 he became the 1st piano teacher of the men's division of the newly opened Academy of Music; was later its principal (1832–59). Potter produced several fine syms. and concertos; Wagner conducted one of his syms. at a Phil. Soc. concert in London (1855). He also wrote a set of satirical *Enigma Variations* for Piano (c.1825), comprising "variations in the style of five eminent artists."

WORKS: ORCH.: 9 syms.: No. 1, in G minor (1819; rev. 1826); B-flat major (1821; rev. 1839); No. 6, in C minor (1826); No. 7, in F major (1826); No. 8, in E-flat major (1828; rev. 1846); No. 10, in G minor (1832); "No. 2," in D major (1833); C minor (1834); "No. 4," in D major (1834); at least 1 other not extant; at least 3 piano concertos: "No. 2," in D minor (1832); E-flat major (1833); E major (1835); 4 overtures: E minor (1815; rev. 1848); *Antony and Cleopatra* (1835); *Cymbeline* (1836); *The Tempest* (1837); *Introduction and Rondo* for Piano and Orch., "alla militaire" (1827); *Duo concertant* for Piano, Violin, and Orch. (1827?); *Bravura Variations* for Piano and Orch., on a theme by Rossini (1829); *Concertante* on "Les Folies d'Espagne" for Violin, Cello, Double Bass, Piano, and Orch. (1829); *Ricercata* "on a favorite French theme" for Piano and Orch. (1830); *March* (1854). **CHAMBER:** 3 Grand Trios for Piano Trio (c.1824); *Sonata di bravura* for Horn, or Bassoon, or Cello and Piano (c.1824); Sextet for Flute and String Quartet (c.1827); Sextet for Flute, Clarinet, Viola, Cello, Double Bass, and Piano (1836); String Quartet (n.d.); many piano works, including 3 sonatas (all 1818). Also *Medora e Corrado*, cantata for Solo Voices, Chorus, and Orch. (1830).

BIBL.: G. Macfarren, "C. P.: His Life and Work," *Proceedings of the Musical Association*, X (1884); idem, "C. P.," *RAM Magazine*, no. 1 (1901); C. Oldman, "C. P.'s Edition of Mozart's Pianoforte Works," *Festschrift Otto Erich Deutsch* (Kassel, 1963); P. Peter, *The Life and Work of C. P. (1792–1871)* (diss., Northwestern Univ., 1972); N. Temperley, "Enigma: The Composer's Solution," *Musical Times* (Sept. 1988).

Poueigh, Jean (Marie-Octave-Géraud), French composer and writer on music; b. Toulouse, Feb. 24, 1876; d. Olivet, Loiret, Oct. 14, 1958. After music study in his native city, he entered the Paris Cons. as a student of Caussade, Lenepveu, and Fauré; also received advice from d'Indy; settled in Paris. He harmonized and ed. a number of folk songs of Languedoc and Gascogne in *Les Chansons de France* (1907–9), *3 chansons des Pays d'Oc*, and *14 chansons anciennes*; also ed. the collection *Chansons populaires des Pyrénées françaises* (vol. 1, 1926). Under the pen name of Octave Séré, he publ. *Musiciens français d'aujourd'hui* (Paris, 1911; 7th ed., 1921); contributed numerous articles to various French periodicals. His original compositions include the operas *Les Lointains* (1903); *Le Meneur de louves* (1921); *Perkin*, a Basque legend (Bordeaux, Jan. 16, 1931); *Le Roi de Camargue* (Marseilles, May 12, 1948); *Bois-brûlé* (1956); ballets: *Fünn* (1906); *Frivolant* (Paris Opéra, May 1, 1922); Moroccan ballet, *Chergui*; symphonic tableau, *La Basilique aux vainqueurs*; piano pieces and songs.

Pougin (Paroisse-Pougin), (François-Auguste-) Arthur, French writer on music; b. Châteauroux, Indre, Aug. 6, 1834; d. Paris, Aug. 8, 1921. He studied with Alard (violin) and

Reber (harmony) at the Paris Cons.; began playing violin in theater orchs. when he was 13; became conductor of the Théâtre Beaumarchais (1855); was assistant conductor and répétiteur of the Folies-Nouvelles (1856–59); was a member of the Opéra-Comique orch. (1860–63); then devoted himself to writing on music. He contributed articles and reviews to leading music periodicals; was musical feuilletonist for the *Journal Officiel* (from 1878) and chief ed. of *Le Ménestrel* (from 1885); wrote the articles on music for Larousse's *Grand dictionnaire universel du XIXᵉ siècle* (1866–76); edited the supplement to Fétis's *Biographie universelle* (1878–80); revised Clément and Larousse's *Dictionnaire lyrique, ou Histoire des opéras* (1898; supplement to 1904).

WRITINGS: (all publ. in Paris unless otherwise given): *André Campra* (1861; 2nd ed., 1881); *Gresnick* (1862); *Dezèdes* (1862); *Floquet* (1863); *Martini* (1864); *Devienne* (1864); the preceding 6 were orig. publ. in *Revue et Gazette Musicale*, XXVIII (1861), XXIX (1862), XXIX (1862), XXX (1863), XXXI (1864), and XXXI (1864), respectively, and then publ. as *Musiciens français du XVIIIᵉ siècle* (1864); *Meyerbeer: Notes biographiques* (1864); *F. Halévy, écrivain* (1865); *Almanach de la musique* (1866–68); *William-Vincent Wallace: Étude biographique et critique* (1866); *De la littérature musicale en France* (1867); *De la situation des compositeurs de musique et de l'avenir de l'art musicale en France* (1867); *Bellini: Sa vie, ses œuvres* (1868); *Léon Kreutzer* (1868); *Albert Grisar: Étude artistique* (1870); *Rossini: Notes, impressions, souvenirs, commentaires* (1871); *À propos de l'exécution du "Messie" de Haendel* (1873); *Auber: Ses commencements, les origines de sa carrière* (1873); *Boieldieu: Sa vie, ses œuvres, son caractère, sa correspondance* (1875); *Figures d'opéra-comique: Madame Dugazon, Elleviou, les Gavaudan* (1875); *Adolphe Adam: Sa vie, sa carrière, ses mémoires artistiques* (1876); *Rameau: Essai sur sa vie et ses œuvres* (1876); *Les Vrais Créateurs de l'opéra français: Perrin et Cambert* (1881); *Verdi: Vita aneddotica* (Milan, 1881; annotated by Folchetto [pen name of J. Caponi; rev. version in French, 1886]; *Molière et l'opéra-comique* (1882); *Viotti et l'école moderne de violon* (1888); *Méhul: Sa vie, son génie, son caractère* (1889; 2nd ed., 1893); *L'Opéra-Comique pendant la Révolution* (1891); *Acteurs et actrices d'autrefois: Histoire anecdotique des théâtres de Paris depuis trois cents ans* (1896); *Essai historique sur la musique en Russie* (1897; 2nd ed., 1904; Eng. tr., 1915); *La Jeunesse de Mme. Desbordes-Valmore* (1898); *Jean-Jacques Rousseau musicien* (1901); *La Comédie-Française et la Révolution* (1902); *Un Ténor de l'Opéra au XVIIIᵉ siècle: Pierre Jélyotte* (1905); *Hérold: Biographie critique* (1906); *Monsigny et son temps: l'Opéra-Comique et la Comédie-Italienne* (1908); *Marie Malibran: Histoire d'une cantatrice* (1911; Eng. tr., 1911); *Madame Favart: Étude théâtrale, 1727–1772* (1912); *Marietta Alboni* (1912); *Massenet* (1914); *Un Directeur de l'Opéra au XVIIIᵉ siècle (A.P.J. de Visme): L'Opéra sous l'ancien régime: L'Opéra sous la Révolution* (1914); *Une Cantatrice "amie" de Napoléon: Giuseppina Grassini 1773–1850* (1920); *Le Violon: Les Violonistes et la musique de violon du XVIᵉ au XVIIIᵉ siècle* (1924).

Pouishnov, Lev, Russian-born English pianist; b. Odessa, Oct. 11, 1891; d. London, May 28, 1959. He made his public debut at age 5; after studies in Kiev, he received instruction in piano from Essipova and in composition from Liadov, Rimsky-Korsakov, and Glazunov at the St. Petersburg Cons. (graduated with the Gold Medal and the Rubinstein Prize, 1910); then toured while also being active as a teacher in Tiflis (1913–17). He left Russia as a result of the Bolshevik Revolution, and pursued a career in the West; toured widely in Europe and also made appearances in the U.S. (from 1923); made his home in England, becoming a naturalized subject in 1935. He became best known for his performances of works from the Romantic repertoire.

Poulenc, Francis (Jean Marcel), brilliant French composer; b. Paris, Jan. 7, 1899; d. there, Jan. 30, 1963. He was born into a wealthy family of pharmaceutical manufacturers; his mother taught him music in his childhood; at 16 he began taking formal piano lessons with Ricardo Viñes. A decisive turn in his development as a composer occurred when he attracted the attention of Erik Satie, the arbiter elegantiarum of the arts and social amenities in Paris. Deeply impressed by Satie's fruitful eccentricities in the then-shocking manner of Dadaism, Poulenc joined an ostentatiously self-descriptive musical group called the Nouveaux Jeunes. In a gratuitous parallel with the Russian Five, the French critic Henri Collet dubbed the "New Youths" Le Groupe de Six, and the label stuck under the designation Les Six. The 6 musicians included, besides Poulenc: Auric, Durey, Honegger, Milhaud, and Taille-ferre. Although quite different in their styles of composition and artistic inclinations, they continued collective participation in various musical events. Poulenc served in the French army (1918–21), and then began taking lessons in composition with Koechlin (1921–24). An excellent pianist, Poulenc became in 1935 an accompanist to the French baritone Pierre Bernac, for whom he wrote numerous songs. Compared with his fortu-itous comrades-in-six, Poulenc appears a classicist. He never experimented with the popular devices of "machine music," asymmetrical rhythms, and polyharmonies as cultivated by Honegger and Milhaud. Futuristic projections had little interest for him; he was content to follow the gentle neo-Classical formation of Ravel's piano music and songs. Among his other important artistic contacts was the ballet impresario Diaghilev, who commissioned him to write music for his Ballets Russes. Apart from his fine songs and piano pieces, Poulenc revealed himself as an inspired composer of religious music, of which his choral works *Stabat Mater* and *Gloria* are notable. He also wrote remarkable music for the organ, including a concerto that became a minor masterpiece. A master of artificial sim-plicity, he pleases even sophisticated listeners by his bland triadic tonalities, spiced with quickly passing diaphonous discords.

WORKS: STAGE: OPERAS: *Les Mamelles de Tirésias*, opéra-bouffe (1944; Paris, June 3, 1947); *Dialogues des Carmélites*, religious opera (1953–56; Milan, Jan. 26, 1957); *La Voix humaine*, monodrama for Soprano (1958; Paris, Feb. 6, 1959). **BALLETS:** *La Baigneuse de Trouville* and *Discours de Général*, 2 movements for *Les Mariés de la Tour Eiffel*, ballet-farce (Paris, June 18, 1921; other movements by members of Les Six, except for Durey); *Les Biches*, with Chorus (1923; Monte Carlo, Jan. 6, 1924); *Pastourelle*, 9th movement of an 11-movement collec-tive ballet, *L'Eventail de Jeanne* (1927; 1st perf. of orch. version, Paris, March 4, 1929; movements by Roussel, Ravel, Ibert, Milhaud, and others); *Aubade*, choreographic concerto for Piano and 18 Instruments (1929; private perf., Paris, June 18, 1929; public perf., London, Dec. 19, 1929); *Les Animaux modèles* (1940–41; Paris, Aug. 8, 1942). **ORCH.:** *Concert champêtre* for Harpsichord or Piano, and Orch. (1927–28; Paris, May 3, 1929); Concerto for 2 Pianos and Orch. (Venice, Sept. 5, 1932); *2 marches et un intermède* for Chamber Orch. (Paris, 1937); Concerto for Organ, String Orch., and Timpani (1938; private perf., Paris, June 21, 1939; public perf., Paris, June 10, 1941); Sinfonietta (1947; London, Oct. 24, 1948); Piano Concerto (1949; Boston, Jan. 6, 1950); *Matelote provençale*, movement from a collective work of 7 composers, *La Guirlande de Campra* (1952); *Bucolique*, move-ment from a collective work of 8 composers, *Variations sur la nom de Marguerite Long* (1954). **CHAMBER:** Sonata for 2 Clarinets (1918; rev. 1945); Sonata for Clarinet and Bassoon (1922); Sonata for Horn, Trumpet, and Trombone (1922; rev. 1945); Trio for Oboe, Bassoon, and Piano (1926); Sextet for Piano and Wind Quintet (1930–32; rev. 1939); *Suite française* for 9 Winds, Percussion, and Harpsi-chord (1935); Violin Sonata (1942–43; rev. 1949); Cello Sonata (1948); Flute Sonata (1956); *Elégie*, to the memory of Dennis Brain, for Horn and Piano (1957); *Sarabande* for Guitar (1960); Clarinet Sonata (1962); Oboe Sonata (1962). **CHORAL:** Chanson à boire for a cappella Male Chorus (1922); *7 chansons* for a cappella Mixed Chorus (1936); *Litanies à la vierge noire* for Female Chorus and Organ (1936); Mass in G for a cappella Mixed Chorus (1937; Paris, May 1938); *Séche-*

resses (Dryness), cantata, after texts by Edward James, for Chorus and Orch. (1937; Paris, 1938); *4 motets pour un temps de pénitence* for Mixed Chorus a cappella (1938–39); *Exultate Deo* for Mixed Chorus a cappella (1941); *Salve regina* for Mixed Chorus a cappella (1941); *Figure humaine*, cantata for Double Mixed Chorus (1943); *Un Soir de neige*, chamber cantata for 6 Voices a cappella (1944); 2 books of traditional French songs, arr. for Chorus a cappella (1945); *4 petites prières de Saint François d'Assise* for Male Chorus a cappella (1948); *Stabat Mater* for Soprano, Chorus, and Orch. (1950; Strasbourg, June 13, 1951); *4 motets pour le temps de Noël* for Chorus a cappella (1951–52); *Ave verum corpus* for Female Chorus a cappella (1952); *Laudes de Saint Antoine de Padoue* for Male Chorus a cappella (1957–59); *Gloria* for Soprano, Chorus, and Orch. (1959; Boston, Jan. 20, 1961); *7 répons des ténèbres* for Boy Soprano, Boys' and Men's Chorus, and Orch. (1961; N.Y., April 11, 1963).

VOICE AND INSTRUMENTS: *Rapsodie nègre* for Baritone, String Quartet, Flute, Clarinet, and Piano (Paris, Dec. 11, 1917; rev. 1933); *Le Bestiaire*, after Apollinaire, for Mezzo-soprano, String Quartet, Flute, Clarinet, and Bassoon (1918–19); *Cocardes*, after Cocteau, for Voice, Violin, Cornet, Trombone, Bass Drum, and Triangle (1919); *Le Bal masqué*, after surrealist verses of Max Jacob, for Voice, Oboe, Clarinet, Bassoon, Violin, Cello, Percussion, and Piano (1932); *La Dame de Monte Carlo*, mono-logue for Soprano and Orch. (Paris, Dec. 5, 1961). **VOICE AND PIANO:** *Histoire de Babar le petit éléphant* for Nar-rator and Piano (1940–45; orchestrated by Jean Francaix, 1962). **SONG CYCLES:** *Le Bestiaire* (1919; arrangement); *Co-cardes* (1919; arrangement); *Poèmes de Ronsard* (1924–25; later orchestrated); *Chansons gaillardes* (1925–26); *Airs chantés* (1927–28); *8 chansons polonaises* (1934); *4 chansons pour en-fants* (1934); *5 poèmes* after Eluard (1935); *Tel jour, telle nuit* (1936–37); *3 poèmes* after de Vilmorin (1937); *2 poèmes* after Apollinaire (1938); *Miroirs brûlants* (1938–39); *Fiançailles pour rire* (1939); *Banalités* (1940); *Chansons villageoises* (1942; orchestrated 1943); *Métamorphoses* (1943); *3 chansons* after Lorca (1947); *Calligrammes* (1948); *La Fraîcheur et le feu* (1950); *Parisiana* (1954); *Le Travail du peintre* (1956); *2 mélo-dies* (1956); *La Courte Paille* (1960). **SEPARATE SONGS:** *Toréador* (1918; rev. 1932); *Vocalise* (1927); *Epitaphe* (1930); *A sa gui-tare*, after Ronsard (1935); *Montparnasse* (1941–45); *Hyde Park* (1945); *Paul et Virginie* (1946); *Le Disparu* (1947); *Mazurka* (1949); *Rosemonde* (1954); *Dernier poème* (1956); *Une Chanson de porcelaine* (1958); others. **PIANO:** Sonata, 4-hands (1918); *3 mouvements perpétuels* (1918); *Valse* (1919); *Suite in C* (1920); *6 impromptus* (1920); *Promenades* (1921); *Napoli*, suite of 3 pieces (1921–25); *2 novelettes* (1928); *3 pièces* (1928); *Pièce brève sur le nom d'Albert Roussel* (1929); *8 nocturnes* (1929–38); *15 improvisa-tions* (1932–59); *Villageoises* (1933); *Feuillets d'album* (1933); *Les Soirées de Nazelles* (1930–36); *Mélancolie* (1940); *Inter-mezzo* (1943); *L'Embarquement pour Cythère* for 2 Pianos (1951); *Thème varié* (1951); Sonata for 2 Pianos (1952–53); *Elégie* for 2 Pianos (1959); *Novelette sur un thème de Manuel de Falla* (1959). **WRITINGS:** *Emmanuel Chabrier* (Paris, 1961); *Moi et mes amis* (Paris, 1963; Eng. tr., London, 1978 as *My Friends and Myself*); *Journal de mes mélodies* (Paris, 1964). **BIBL.:** A Schaeffner, "F. P., musicien français," *Contre-points*, 1 (1946); C. Rostand, *F. P.: Entretiens avec Claude Rostand* (Paris, 1954); H. Hell, *P., musicien français* (Paris, 1958); J. Roy, *F. P.* (Paris, 1964); P. Bernac, *F. P.: The Man and His Songs* (London, 1977); K. Daniel, *F. P.: His Artistic Development and Musical Style* (N.Y., 1982); F. Bloch, *F. P.* (Paris, 1984); M. Rosenthal, *Satie, Ravel, P.: An Intimate Mem-oir* (Madras and N.Y., 1987); G. Keck, *F. P.: A Bio-Bibliography* (Westport, Conn., 1990).

Poulet, Gaston, French violinist and conductor, father of **Gérard Poulet;** b. Paris, April 10, 1892; d. Draveil, Essonne, April 14, 1974. He studied violin at the Paris Cons., winning the premier prix (1910); made his debut as soloist in the Beethoven Concerto in Brussels (1911); organized a string quartet in 1912 and gave concerts in Europe; from 1927 to 1936 he conducted the Concerts Poulet at the Théâtre Sarah-Bernhardt in Paris; from 1932 to 1944 he served as director of the Cons. of Bordeaux and conducted the Phil. Orch. there; from 1940 to 1945 he conducted the Concerts Colonne in Paris; was a guest conductor with the London Sym. Orch. (1947) and in Germany (1948); also in South America. He played the violin in the 1st performance of Debussy's Violin Sonata, with Debussy himself at the piano (1917). He was a prof. of chamber music at the Paris Cons. from 1944 to 1962; in 1948 he founded the famous Besançon Festival.

Poulet, Gérard, French violinist, son of **Gaston Poulet;** b. Bayonne, Aug. 12, 1938. He entered the Paris Cons. at the age of 11 in the class of André Asselin, and won 1st prize at 12; in the same year (1950) he played 3 violin concertos with the Colonne Orch. in Paris, under his father's direction; then appeared with other Paris orchs.; subsequently gave concerts and played with orchs. in England, Germany, Italy, Austria, and the Netherlands. In 1956 he won 1st Grand Prix at the Paganini competition of Genoa, and was given the honor of performing on Paganini's own violin, the famous Guarneri del Jesù.

Pound, Ezra (Loomis), greatly significant American man of letters and amateur composer; b. Hailey, Idaho, Oct. 30, 1885; d. Venice, Nov. 1, 1972. He was educated at Hamilton College (Ph.B., 1905) and the Univ. of Pa. (M.A., 1906). He went to England, where he established himself as a leading experimental poet and influential critic. He also pursued a great interest in early music, especially that of the troubadours, which led him to try his hand at composing. With the assistance of George Antheil, he composed the opera *Le Testament,* after poems by François Villon (1923; Paris, June 19, 1926); it was followed by a 2nd opera, *Calvacanti* (1932), and a 3rd, left unfinished, based on the poetry of Catullus. In 1924 he settled in Rapallo. Although married to Dorothy Shakespear, daughter of one of Yeats's friends, he became intimate with the American violinist Olga Rudge; Rudge bore him a daughter in 1925 and his wife bore him a son in 1926. Through the influence of Rudge, his interest in music continued, and he became a fervent champion of Vivaldi; he also worked as a music reviewer and ran a concert series with Rudge, Inverno Musicale. A growing interest in economic history and an inordinate admiration for the Fascist dictator Benito Mussolini led Pound down the road of political obscurantism. During World War II, he made many broadcasts over Rome Radio on topics ranging from literature to politics. His condemnation of Jewish banking circles in America and the American effort to defeat Fascism led to his arrest by the Allies after the collapse of Il Duce's regime. In 1945 he was sent to a prison camp in Pisa. In 1946 he was sent to the U.S. to stand trial for treason, but was declared insane and confined to St. Elizabeth's Hospital in Washington, D.C. Finally, in 1958, he was released and allowed to return to Italy, where he died. Among his writings on music is his *Antheil and the Treatise on Harmony* (1924). He also composed several works for solo violin for Rudge, including *Fiddle Music* (1924) and *Al poco giorno* (Berkeley, March 23, 1983); he also arranged Gaucelm Faidit's *Plainte pour la mort du roi Richart Coeur de Lion.* The uncatalogued collection of Pound's musical MSS at Yale Univ. includes various musical experiments, including rhythmic and melodic realizations of his poem *Sestina: Altaforte.* Among the composers who have set his poems to music are Copland, Luytens, and Berio.

BIBL.: S. Adams, *E. P. and Music* (diss., Univ. of Toronto, 1974); R. Schafer, ed., *E. P. and Music* (N.Y., 1977; a complete collection of his writings on music).

Poupinlière. See **La Pouplinière.**

Pourtalès, Guy (Guido James) de, , French writer on music; b. Berlin, Aug. 4, 1881; d. Lausanne, June 12, 1941. He studied in Bonn, Berlin, and Paris; was in the French army during World War I; then settled in Paris as a music critic. He publ. *La Vie de Franz Liszt* (1925); *Chopin, ou Le Poète* (1927; 2nd ed., 1946; Eng. tr., London, 1930 as *Chopin: A Man of Solitude*); *Wagner, Histoire d'un artiste* (1932; 2nd ed., rev. and augmented 1942); *Berlioz et l'Europe romantique* (1939).

Pousseur, Henri (Léon Marie Thérèse), Belgian composer of the ultramodern school; b. Malmédy, June 23, 1929. He studied at the Liège Cons. (1947–52) and the Brussels Cons. (1952–53); had private lessons in composition from André Souris and Pierre Boulez; until 1959, worked in the Cologne and Milan electronic music studios, where he came in contact with Stockhausen and Berio; was a member of the avant-garde group of composers "Variation" in Liège. He taught music in various Belgian schools (1950–59); was founder (1958) and director of the Studio de Musique Electronique APELAC in Brussels, from 1970 a part of the Centre de Recherches Musicales in Liège; gave lectures at the summer courses of new music in Darmstadt (1957–67), Cologne (1966–68), Basel (1963–64), the State Univ. of N.Y. in Buffalo (1966–69), and the Liège Cons. (from 1970), where he became director in 1975. In his music he tries to synthesize all the expressive powers of which man, as a biological species, *Homo sapiens* (or even *Homo insipiens*), is capable in the domain of art (or non-art); the technological resources of the subspecies *Homo habilis* (magnetic tape, electronics/synthesizers, aleatory extensions, the principle of indeterminacy, glossolalia, self-induced schizophasia) all form part of his rich musical (or non-musical) vocabulary for multimedia (or nullimedia) representations. The influence of his methods (or non-methods) of composition (or non-composition) is pervasive. He publ. *Fragments théoriques I. Sur la musique experimentale* (Brussels, 1970).

WORKS: *3 chants sacrés* for Soprano and String Trio (1951); *Seismogrammes* for Tape (1953); *Symphonies* for 15 Solo Instruments (1954–55); *Quintet to the Memory of Webern* for Violin, Cello, Clarinet, Bass Clarinet, and Piano (1955); *Scambi* for Tape (1957); *Mobile* for 2 Pianos (1956–58); *Madrigal I* for Clarinet (1958); *Madrigal II* for Flute, Violin, Viola da Gamba, and Harpsichord (1961); *Madrigal III* for Clarinet, Violin, Cello, 2 Percussionists, and Piano (1962); *Rimes pour différentes sources sonores* for 3 Orch. Groups and Tape (1958–59; Donaueschingen, Oct. 17, 1959); *Electre,* "musical action" (1960); *Répons* for 7 Musicians (1960; rev. with Actor added, 1965); *Ode* for String Quartet (1960–61); *3 visages de Liège* and *Prospective* for Tape (1961); *Votre Faust,* an aleatory "fantasy in the manner of an opera" for 5 Actors, Vocal Quartet, 12 Musicians, and Tapes, for which the audience decides the ending (in collaboration with Michel Butor; 1961–67; Milan, 1969; concert version as *Portail de Votre Faust,* for 4 Voices, Tape, and 12 Instruments); *Trait* for 15 Strings (1962); *Miroir de Votre Faust* for Piano, and Soprano ad libitum (*Caractères II,* 1964–65); *Caractères madrigalesques* for Oboe (*Madrigal IV* and *Caractères III,* 1965); *Phonèmes pour Cathy* for Voice (*Madrigal V,* 1966); *Echoes I* for Cello (1967); *Echoes II, de Votre Faust* for Mezzo-soprano, Flute, Cello, and Piano (1969); *Couleurs croisées* for Orch., a series of crypto-musical variations on the civil rights song *We Shall Overcome* (1967; Brussels Radio, Dec. 20, 1968); *Mnemosyne I,* monody, after Hölderlin, for Solo Voice, or Unison Chorus, or one Instrument (1968); *Mnemosyne II,* an instrumental re-creation of *Mnemosyne I,* with ad libitum scoring (1969); *Croisées des couleurs croisées* (an intensified sequel to *Couleurs croisées*) for Female Voice, 2–5 Pianos, Tape Recorders, and 2 Radio Receivers dialed aleatorily, to texts from Indian and Negro materials and political speeches (N.Y., Nov. 29, 1970); *Icare apprenti* for an undetermined number of Instruments (1970); *Les Ephémerides d'Icare 2* for Piano and Instruments (Madrid, April 20, 1970); *Invitation à l'Utopie* for Narrator, 2 Female Voices, 4-voice Chorus, and Instruments (Brussels Radio, Jan. 25, 1971); *L'Effacement du Prince Igor,* scene for Orch. (Brussels, Jan. 18, 1972); *Le Temps des paraboles* (1972); *Die Erprobung des Petrus Hebraicus,* chamber opera (Berlin, Sept. 12, 1974); *Vue sur les jardins* *interdits* for Organ or Saxophone Quartet (1974); *19√8/4* for Cello (1975); *Les ruines de Jeruzona* for Chorus, Piano, Double Bass, and Percussion (1978); *Humeurs du futur quotidien* for Reciter and Orch. (Paris, March 12, 1978); *Tales and Songs from the Bible of Hell* for 4 Voices, Narrator, and Electronics (1979); *Les Îles déchaînées* for Jazz Group, Electro-acoustic Ensemble, and Orch. (Brussels, Nov. 27, 1980); *Le Seconde Apothéose de Rameau* for Chamber Orch. (Paris, Nov. 9, 1981); *La Rose des voix* for Voice, Chorus, Reciter, and Instruments (Namur, Aug. 6, 1982); *La Passion selon quignol* for Vocal Quartet and Orch. (1982; Liège, Feb. 24, 1983; in collaboration with C. Paulo); *Cinquième vue sur les jardins interdits* for Vocal Quartet (1982); *Trajets dans les arpents du ciel* for Soloists and Orch. (Metz, Nov. 18, 1983); *Cortèjes des belles ténébreuses au jardin boréal* for English Horn, Viola, Horn, Tuba, and Percussion (1984); *L'Étoile des langues* for Chamber Chorus and Speaker (1984); *Patchwork des tribus américaines* for Wind Orch. (1984); *Nuits des Nuits* for Orch. (1985); *Sur le Qui-Vive* for Female Voice, Clarinet, Cello, Tuba, Keyboards, and Percussion (1985); *Arc-en-ciel de remparts* for Student Orch. and Chorus ad libitum (1986); *Un Jardin de panacailles* for Original Orchestration Globally Organized from the works of Lully, Bach, Beethoven, Brahms, and Webern with an Original Prologue, Interlude, and Grand Finale for 12 Musicians (1987); *Traverser la forêt*, cantata for Speaker, 2 Vocal Soloists, Chorus, and 12 Instruments (1987); *Ode No. 2, Mnemosyne (doublement) obstinée* for String Quartet and Soprano ad libitum (London, June 1989).

Powell, "Bud" (Earl), black American jazz pianist; b. N.Y., Sept. 27, 1924; d. there, Aug. 1, 1966. After dropping out of school at the age of 15, he began playing with local groups in N.Y. Following the zeitgeist, he adopted the bop style, and in 1943 joined Cootie Williams and his band; he also played concerts with Dizzy Gillespie, Sid Catlett, and John Kirby, achieving recognition as a fine bop pianist. He was a frequent participant in the formative jazz sessions at Minton's Playhouse. He gradually discarded the prevalent "stride" piano style with its regular beat, and emancipated the left-hand rhythm by introducing a contrapuntal line with asymmetrical punctuation. His brief career was periodically interrupted by mental eclipses caused by immoderate use of hallucinogenic drugs.

BIBL.: F. Paudras, *La Danse des infidèles: B. P.* (Paris, 1986).

Powell, John, American pianist, composer, and ethnomusicologist; b. Richmond, Va., Sept. 6, 1882; d. Charlottesville, Va., Aug. 15, 1963. His father was a schoolteacher, his mother an amateur musician; he received his primary musical education at home; then studied piano with F.C. Hahr, a pupil of Liszt; subsequently entered the Univ. of Virginia (B.A., 1901) and then went to Vienna, where he studied piano with Leschetizky (1902–7) and composition with Navrátil (1904–7); gave successful piano recitals in Paris and London; returning to the U.S., he toured the country as a pianist, playing some of his own works. His most successful piece was *Rapsodie nègre,* inspired by Joseph Conrad's *Heart of Darkness,* for Piano and Orch.; Powell was the soloist in its 1st performance with the Russian Sym. Orch. (N.Y., March 23, 1918). The titles of some of his works disclose a whimsical propensity; perhaps his most important achievement lies in ethnomusicology; he methodically collected rural songs of the South; was the organizer of the Virginia State Choral Festivals and of the White Top Mountain Folk Music Festivals. A man of versatile interests, he was also an amateur astronomer, and discovered a comet.

WORKS: ORCH.: Piano Concerto (n.d.); Violin Concerto (1910); *Rapsodie nègre* for Piano and Orch. (1917; N.Y., March 23, 1918); *In Old Virginia,* overture (1921); *Natchez on the Hill,* 3 Virginian country dances (1932); *A Set of 3* (1935); Sym. in A (1945; Detroit, April 23, 1947; substantially rev. and subtitled *Virginia Symphony,* Richmond, Va., Nov. 5, 1951). **CHAMBER:** *Sonate Virginianesque* for Violin and Piano (1906); 2 string quartets (1907, 1922); Violin Sonata (1918); *From a Loved Past* for Violin and Piano (1930). **PIANO:** 3 sona-

tas: *Sonate psychologique,* "on the text of St. Paul's 'The wages of sin is death'" (1905), *Sonate noble* (1908), and *Sonata Teutonica* (1905–13); *In the South,* suite (1906); *At the Fair,* suite (1907); *In the Hammock* for 2 Pianos, 8-hands (1915); *Dirge,* sextet for 2 Pianos, 12-hands (1928); also vocal works, including *The Babe of Bethlehem,* folk carol (1934) and other choruses; *5 Virginian Folk Songs* for Voice and Piano (1938); other songs.

BIBL.: E. Mead, "The J. P. Collection at the University of Virginia," *University of Virginia Newsletter* (Nov. 15, 1972); R. Johnson, "J. P.'s Sonata Teutonica," *American Music Teacher* (Nov./Dec. 1978).

Powell, Laurence, English-born American organist, conductor, teacher, and composer; b. Birmingham, Jan. 13, 1899; d. Victoria, Tex., Jan. 29, 1990. He studied at Ratcliffe College, Leicester (1909–15), and Ushaw College, Durham (1915–17); was in the British army and the Royal Air Force during World War I; then studied music at the Birmingham and Midland Inst. School of Music (1919–22) under Bantock; his examiner was Tovey. While there, he won a full scholarship to Birmingham Univ., where he carried on his studies concurrently with Bantock, gaining a Mus.B. degree with 1st-class honors. In 1923 he went to the U.S.; became a naturalized citizen in 1936; took courses at the Univ. of Wisconsin (M.A., 1926); subsequently held various teaching positions: at the Univ. of Wisconsin (1924–26), the Univ. of Arkansas (1926–34), and Little Rock Junior College (1934–39); was organist at St. Mary's Church in Victoria, Tex. (1947–52); organist and choirmaster at St. Francis Cathedral in Santa Fe (1952–68); choir director and organist at Assumption Church in Albuquerque (1968–70); organist and choirmaster at Our Lady of Victory Church in Victoria, Tex. (1970–75); upon retirement in 1975, was honored by a plaque inscribed "for Laurence Powell for demonstrating beauty in God and man through music and song." As a conductor, he was the organizer and music director of the Little Rock Sym. Orch. (1934–39); conductor of the Grand Rapids (Mich.) Federal Sym. Orch. (1939–41); founder and conductor of the Santa Fe Orch., later renamed Rio Grande Sym. Orch. (1953–55).

WORKS: ORCH.: *The Ogre of the Northern Fastness* (1921); *Keltic Legend* (Bournemouth, Aug. 27, 1924; rev. version, Madison, Wis., May 20, 1931); *Charivari,* suite (1925); 2 syms. (1929, 1943); *Deirdre of the Sorrows* (1933; Little Rock, March 18, 1937); *The County Fair,* suite (1936); *Suite* for String Orch. (1931; Grand Rapids, May 9, 1940); *Picnic,* an "Arkansas pastoral" for String Orch. (Oklahoma City, March 21, 1936); *Variations* (Rochester, N.Y., Oct. 28, 1941); *Duo concertante* for Recorders and Orch. (1941); *The Santa Fe Trail* for Baritone, Narrator, and Orch. (Santa Fe, April 22, 1958); *Penny Overture* (1960); *Overture on French Folk Tunes* (1970); *Oracle* (1975); *Halcyone,* dramatic poem for Chorus and Orch. (1923); *Alleluya,* cantata for Chorus and Orch. (1926); also *The Seasons* for Chorus a cappella (1928); Piano Quartet (1933); Quartet for Clarinets (1936); 3 sonatinas for Recorders Unaccompanied, one each for Soprano, Alto, and Tenor (1977); several masses; songs.

Powell, Maud, esteemed American violinist; b. Peru, Ill., Aug. 22, 1868; d. Uniontown, Pa., Jan. 8, 1920. After studying violin and piano in Aurora, Ill., she received violin lessons from William Lewis in Chicago; then studied violin with Schraideck at the Leipzig Cons. (1881–82) and theory with Charles Dancla at the Paris Cons. (1882–83); after touring England (1883), she completed her training with Joachim at the Berlin Hochschule für Musik (1884). In 1885 she appeared as a soloist with Joachim and the Berlin Phil., and with Thomas and the N.Y. Phil.; toured Europe with the N.Y. Arion Soc. (1892); subsequently performed regularly in the U.S. and Europe. She was the 1st American woman to found a string quartet (1894); organized her own trio (1908). Powell made it a point to program works by American composers; also introduced works by Dvořák, Lalo, Saint-Saëns, Sibelius, and Tchaikovsky to the U.S. Her virtuosity won her wide recognition and praise.

BIBL.: N. Greenwood, "M. P.," *Strad,* XCI (1980–81); B.

Schwarz, *Great Masters of the Violin* (N.Y., 1983); K. Schaffer and N. Greenwood, *M. P., Pioneer American Violinist* (Arlington, Va., 1988).

Powell, Mel (real name, **Melvin Epstein**), remarkable American composer; b. N.Y., Feb. 12, 1933. He acquired an early fascination for American jazz, and was barely 14 when he was chosen as pianist for Benny Goodman's band. It was then that he changed his name to the more mellifluous Mel Powell, restructured from that of his paternal uncle, Poljanowsky. He was drafted into the Army, where he was selected for the Air Force Band led by Glenn Miller. While playing jazz, Powell also began to compose. Tragedy struck at the height of his powers as a jazz musician and composer when he suddenly contracted muscular dystrophy; the disease affected his quadriceps, and he was ultimately confined to a wheelchair. He could still play the piano, but he could no longer travel with a band. He turned to serious composition and became an excellent teacher. While he was working with the Goodman band, he took lessons with Bernard Wagenaar and Joseph Schillinger in N.Y. (1937–39); later studied composition privately with Ernst Toch in Los Angeles (1946–48). A turning point in his career occurred in 1948 when he entered the Yale Univ. School of Music in the class of the formidable German composer Paul Hindemith, from whom he acquired the matchless skill of Teutonic contrapuntal writing; he received his B.Mus. degree in 1952. From then on, Powell dedicated himself mainly to teaching; served on the faculty of Yale Univ. (1957–69), and was dean of music at the Calif. Inst. of the Arts in Valencia (from 1969), serving as provost (1972–76) and as a prof. and fellow (from 1976). As a composer of growing strength, he revealed versatile talents, being technically at home in an incisive jazz idiom, in a neo-Classical manner, tangentially shadowing Stravinsky, and in an expressionist mode of Schoenberg, occasionally paralleling the canonic processes of Webern. He also evolved a sui generis sonorism of electronic music. In all these asymptotic formations, he nevertheless succeeded in projecting his own personality in a curious and, indeed, quaquaversal way; while absorbed in atonal composition, he was also able to turn out an occasional march tune or waltz figure. In all these mutually enhanced formulas, he succeeds in cultivating the unmistakable modality of his personal style without venturing into the outer space of musical entropy. In 1990 he received the meritorious Pulitzer Prize in Music for his *Duplicates*, a concerto for 2 Pianos and Orch. Powell describes this work as a "perpetual cadenza," an expression he says was used by Debussy.

WORKS: ORCH.: *Cantilena concertante* for English Horn and Orch. (1948); *Symphonic Suite* (1949); *Capriccio* for Concert Band (1950); *Intrada and Variants* (1956); *Stanzas* (1957); *Setting* for Cello and Orch. (1961); *Immobiles I–IV* (1967); *Settings* for Jazz Band (1982); *Modules*, intermezzo for Chamber Orch. (1985); *Duplicates*, concerto for 2 Pianos and Orch. (Los Angeles, Jan. 26, 1990). **CHAMBER:** 2 string quartets: No. 1, *Beethoven Analogs* (1949); No. 2, *String Quartet 1982* (1982); Harpsichord Sonata (1952); Trio for Piano, Violin, and Cello (1954); *Divertimento* for Violin and Harp (1954); *Divertimento* for 5 Winds (1955); Quintet for Piano and String Quartet (1956); *Miniatures for Baroque Ensemble* for Flute, Oboe, Violin, Viola, Cello, and Harpsichord (1958); *Filigree Setting* for String Quartet (1959); *Improvisation* for Clarinet, Viola, and Piano (1962); *Nocturne* for Violin (1965; rev. 1985); *Cantilena* for Trombone and Tape (1981); Woodwind Quintet (1984–85); *Setting* for Guitar (1986); *Invocation* for Cello (1987); *Amy-abilities* for Percussion (1987); *3 Madrigals* for Flute (1988). **PIANO:** 2 sonatinas (1951); *Étude* (1957); *Intermezzo* (1984); *Piano Preludes* (1987). **VOCAL:** *6 Choral Songs* (1950); *Sweet Lovers Love the Spring* for Women's Voices and Piano (1953); *Haiku Settings* for Soprano and Piano (1961); *2 Prayer Settings* for Tenor, Oboe, and String Trio (1963); *Cantilena* for Voice, Violin, and Tape (1969); *Settings* for Soprano and Chamber Group (1979); *Little Companion Pieces* for Soprano and String Quartet (1979); *Strand Settings: Darker* for Soprano

and Electronics (1983); *Letter to a Young Composer* for Soprano (1987); *Die Violine* for Soprano, Violin, and Piano (1987). **ELECTRONIC:** *Electronic Setting* (1958); *2nd Electronic Setting* (1961); *Events* (1963); *Analogs I–IV* (1963); *3 Synthesizer Settings* (1970–80); *Inscape*, ballet (1976); *Variations* (1976); *Computer Prelude* (1988).

BIBL.: W. Balliett, "Whatever Happened to M. P.?," *New Yorker* (May 25, 1987); special issue of *Aperiodical, Points of Arrival: M. P. at 65* (Valencia, Calif., 1988).

Power (**Powero, Polbero,** etc.), **Leonel** (**Lionel, Leonell, Leonelle, Leonellus, Lyonel,** etc.), important English composer; place and date of birth unknown; d. Canterbury, June 5, 1445. He is first recorded as an instructor of the choristers and then as a clerk in the household chapel of Thomas, Duke of Clarence, brother of Henry V. On May 14, 1423, he was admitted to the fraternity of Christ Church, Canterbury, as a layman; also served as master of the choir for the non-monastic liturgical services there. He was a contemporary of Dunstable and one of the leading and most original representatives of the English style of the day; his style so approximated Dunstable's that it is not always possible to determine the authorship of a number of works by the two. He also was author of the treatise *Upon the Gamme* (c.1450; reprinted by S. Meech in *Speculum*, July 1935). Among his works are Mass cycles, Mass movements, and various other settings of sacred Latin texts. See the complete works as ed. by C. Hamm in Corpus Mensurabilis Musicae, I (1969–76), and *The Old Hall Manuscript* as ed. by A. Hughes and M. Bent in the same series, XLVI (1969–72). See also the complete works of Dunstable as ed. by M. Bukofzer in Musica Britannica, VIII (1953; 2nd ed., rev., 1970).

BIBL.: C. Hamm, "The Motets of Lionel Power," *Studies in Music History: Essays for Oliver Strunk* (Princeton, 1968); M. Bent, *The Old Hall Manuscript: A Paleographical Study* (diss., Cambridge Univ., 1969); R. Bowers, "Some Observations on the Life and Career of Lionel Power," *Proceedings of the Royal Musical Association*, CII (1975–76).

Powers, Harold S(tone), American musicologist and teacher; b. N.Y., Aug. 5, 1928. He received his early education at Stanford Univ. and Syracuse Univ. (B.Mus., 1950); then studied with Babbitt and Cone (theory) and Strunk and Mendel (musicology) at Princeton Univ. (M.F.A., 1952; Ph.D., 1959, with a diss. on the Indian rāga system). He also studied in India under Rangaramanuja Ayyangar, Balwant Ray Bhatt, and Prem Lata Sharma on Fulbright and Rockefeller grants (1952–54; 1960–61; 1967–68). He taught at Princeton Univ. (1955–58), Harvard Univ. (1958–60), and the Univ. of Pa. (1960–73), where he became prof. of music and South Asian studies (1971); in 1973 rejoined the faculty at Princeton Univ. as a full prof. He has written extensively on Indian music, Italian opera, and music theory.

Pownall, Mary Ann, English actress, singer, and composer; b. London, Feb. 1751; d. Charleston, S.C., Aug. 11, 1796. She was known first as **Mrs. James Wrightson** (her 1st husband was a prompter in a London theater); made her debut in 1770 in *The Recruiting Officer* in London; from 1776 to 1788, was a Vauxhall favorite. In 1792 she first appeared in Boston with the Old American Co., of which she was a leading artist; later sang in subscription concerts in N.Y., and joined John Henry's N.Y. Co. She composed the text and music of numerous songs, including *Advice to the Ladies of Boston, Washington* (in honor of George Washington), and *Primroses.* Some of her songs were publ. in *Six Songs for the Harpsichord* (in collaboration with J. Hewitt; 1794) and *Kisses Sued For* (1795).

BIBL.: J. Howard, *Our American Music* (N.Y., 1931; 4th ed., rev., 1965).

Pozdro, John (Walter), significant American composer and pedagogue; b. Chicago, Aug. 14, 1923. He was of Polish extraction on his paternal line (*po-zdro* means, approximately, "your health") and of German origin on his mother's side; his father was a master cabinetmaker and an unsung artist (he played the piano and violin). Pozdro took piano lessons with Nina Shafran; then studied music theory at the American Cons. in Chicago and Northwestern Univ.; later entered the Eastman School of Music at Rochester, N.Y., as a student in composition of Howard Hanson and Bernard Rogers, graduating in 1958 with a Ph.D. He subsequently joined the music faculty at the Univ. of Kansas in Lawrence, later becoming its director of music theory and composition in 1961; from 1958 to 1968, was chairman of the Annual Symposium of Contemporary American Music at the Univ. of Kansas. His music is inherently pragmatic, with tertian torsion resulting in the formation of tastefully enriched triadic harmony, and with asymmetric rhythms enhancing the throbbing pulse of musical continuity.

WORKS: STAGE: *Malooley and the Fear Monster,* "family opera" (1976; Lawrence, Kans., Feb. 6, 1977); *Hello, Kansas!,* musical play in observance of the 100th anniversary of the statehood of Kansas (Lawrence, June 12, 1961). **ORCH.:** *Overture* (1948; Evanston, Ill., Nov. 30, 1949); Sym. No. 1 (1949); *A Cynical Overture* (1952; Univ. of Texas, March 24, 1953); Sym. No. 2 (1957; Rochester, N.Y., May 4, 1958); Sym. No. 3 (Oklahoma City, Dec. 12, 1960); *Waterlow Park* (Lawrence, May 8, 1972); *Rondo giocoso* for String Orch. (1964); *Music for a Youth Symphony* (1969). **CHAMBER:** Quintet for Woodwinds and Piano (1947); Sextet for Flute and Strings (1948); 2 string quartets (1947, 1952); *Elegy* for Trumpet and Piano (1953); *Trilogy* for Clarinet, Bassoon, Trumpet, and Piano (1960); Sonata for Brass Instruments and Percussion (1966); Violin Sonata (1971); *Impressions* for Flute, Oboe, Clarinet, Bassoon, and Piano (1984); 2 *Movements* for Cello and Piano (1987). **PIANO:** 6 sonatas (1947, 1963, 1964, 1976, 1979, 1982); 8 preludes (1950–74); *Ballade-Fantasy* (1981); *For Nancy* (1987). **VOCAL:** *All Pleasant Things* for Chorus (1960); *They That Go Down to the Sea* for Chorus (1967); *The Creation* for Children's Voices (1967); *Alleluia* for Chorus (1979); *King of Glory* for Chorus, Organ, and Piano (1983); *Spirit of Oread* for Soloists, Chorus, and Organ (1988–89). **CARILLON:** *Landscape I* (1954); *Landscape II* (1969); *Rustic Landscape* (1981); *Variation on a Slavonic Theme* (1982); *Tryptich* (1989).

Praetorius (Latinized from **Schulz, Schulze, Schultz,** or **Schultze**), family of distinguished German musicians:
(1) Jacob Praetorius, organist and composer; b. Magdeburg, c.1530; d. Hamburg, 1586. He converted to Protestantism and settled in Hamburg, where he became clerk at St. Jacobi in 1550; became assistant organist in 1554; was 1st organist from 1558 until his death. He compiled a set of monophonic liturgical chants and German chorales in 1554. He also compiled a collection known as *Opus musicum excellens et novum* (1566), which contained 204 sacred compositions for 4, 5, 6, and 8 Voices by German and Netherlands composers (a majority of compositions are copies of pieces publ. by Georg Rhau); Praetorius's only extant work, a *Te Deum* for 4 Voices, is included.
BIBL.: J. Bolte, "Eine Choralsammlung des Jakob P.," *Monatsheft für Musikgeshichte,* XXV (1893); L. Hoffmann-Erbrecht, "Das Opus musicum des J. P. von 1566," *Acta Musicologica,* XXVIII (1956).
(2) Hieronymus Praetorius, organist and composer, son of **Jacob Praetorius;** b. Hamburg, Aug. 10, 1560; d. there, Jan. 27, 1629. He studied organ with his father, then with Hinrich thor Molen (1573); also had instruction with Albinus Walran in Cologne (1574–76). He was organist in Erfurt (1580–82). He became assistant organist to his father at St. Jacobi in Hamburg in 1582; upon his father's death in 1586, he became 1st organist, a position he held until his own death 43 years later. He composed masses, motets, and Magnificat settings, of which the 8 Magnificat settings for Organ (1611) are particularly noteworthy. He also prepared a collection of monophonic German and Latin service music for the churches of Hamburg under the title *Cantiones sacrae chorales* (1587), and the *Melodeyen Gesangbuch* (Hamburg, 1604), which includes 88 4-part German chorale settings; 21 of these are by him, the remaining by his son **Jacob Praetorius,** Joachim Decker, and David Scheidemann.

BIBL.: B. Friederich, *Der Vokalstil des H. P.* (Hamburg, 1932); F. Gable, *The Polychoral Motets of H. P.* (diss., Univ. of Iowa, 1966); J. Kite-Powell, *The Visby (Petri) Organ Tablature: Investigation and Critical Edition* (Wilhelmshaven, 1977).
(3) Jacob Praetorius, organist, pedagogue, and composer, son of **Hieronymus Praetorius;** b. Hamburg, Feb. 8, 1586; d. there, Oct. 22, 1651. He studied organ with Sweelinck in Amsterdam. From 1603 until his death he was organist of St. Petri in Hamburg. He was a noted organ teacher and composer of organ music. He contributed 19 4-part chorale settings to his father's *Melodeyen Gesangbuch* (Hamburg, 1604). See W. Brieg, ed., *J. P.: Choralbearbeitungen für Orgel* (Kassel, 1974).
(4) Johannes Praetorius, organist and composer, son of **Hieronymus Praetorius;** b. Hamburg, c.1595; d. there, July 25, 1660. He studied organ with Sweelinck in Amsterdam (1608–11). From 1612 until his death he was organist of the Nikolaikirche in Hamburg.

Praetorius, Michael, great German composer, organist, and music theorist; b. Creuzburg an der Werra, Thuringia, Feb. 15, 1571; d. Wolfenbüttel, Feb. 15, 1621. The surname of the family was Schultheiss (sometimes rendered as Schultze), which he Latinized as Praetorius. He was the son of a Lutheran pastor. He studied with Michael Voigt, the cantor of the Torgau Lateinschule; in 1582 he entered the Univ. of Frankfurt an der Oder; in 1584 he continued his studies at the Lateinschule in Zerbst, Anhalt. From 1587 to 1590 he was organist of St. Marien in Frankfurt. In 1595 he entered the service of Duke Heinrich Julius of Braunschweig-Wolfenbüttel as an organist; in 1604 he also assumed the duties of court Kapellmeister. Upon the death of his patron in 1613, the Elector Johann Georg of Saxony obtained his services as deputy Kapellmeister at the Dresden court. He retained his Dresden post until 1616, and then resumed his duties in Wolfenbüttel. Praetorius devoted only a part of his time to Wolfenbüttel, for he had been named Kapellmeister to the administrator of the Magdeburg bishopric and prior of the monastery at Ringelheim in 1614. He also traveled a great deal, visiting various German cities. These factors, coupled with a general decline in his health, led to the decision not to reappoint him to his Wolfenbüttel post in 1620. He died the following year a wealthy man. Deeply religious, he directed that the greater portion of his fortune go to organizing a foundation for the poor. Praetorius was one of the most important and prolific German composers of his era. His *Musae Sioniae,* a significant collection of over 1,200 settings of Lutheran chorales, is a particularly valuable source for hymnology.

WORKS (all publ. in Wolfenbüttel unless otherwise given): *Musae Sionae . . . geistliche Concert Gesänge über die fürnembste deutsche Psalmen und Lieder . . . erster Theil* for 8 Voices (Regensburg, 1605); *Sacrarum motectarum primitiae* for 4 to 16 Voices (Magdeburg, 1606; not extant); *Musarum Sioniarum motestae et psalmi latini* for 4 to 16 Voices (Nuremberg, 1607; this may be the 2nd ed. of the preceding); *Musaie Sioniae . . . geistliche Concert Gesänge über die fürnembste deutsche Psalmen und Lieder . . . ander Theil* for 8 and 12 Voices (Jena, 1607); *Musaie Sioniae . . . geistliche Concert Gesänge . . . dritter Theil* for 8, 9, and 12 Voices (Helmstedt, 1607); *Musaie Sionae . . . geistliche Concert Gesänge . . . vierdter Theil* for 8 Voices (Helmstedt, 1607); *Musaie Sioniae . . . geistlicher deutscher . . . üblicher Lieder und Psalmen . . . fünffter Theil* for 2 to 8 Voices (1607); *Musaie Sioniae . . . deutscher geistlicher . . . üblicher Psalmen und Lieder . . . sechster Theil* for 4 Voices (1609); *Musaie Sioniae . . . deutscher geistlicher . . . üblicher Psalmen und Lieder . . . siebender Theil* for 4 Voices (1609); *Musaie Sioniae . . . deutscher geistlicher . . . Lieder und Psalmen . . . in Contrapuncto simplici . . . gesetzt . . . achter Theil* for 4 Voices (1610; 2nd ed., 1612, as *Ferner Continuierung der geistlichen Lieder und Psalmen*); *Musaie Sioniae . . . deutscher geistlicher . . . Psalmen und Lieder . . . auf Muteten, Madrigalische und sonsten eine andere . . . Art . . . gesetzt*

. . . *neundter Theil* for 2 and 3 Voices (1610; 2nd ed., 1611, as *Bicinia und Tricinia*); *Eulogodia Sionia* for 2 to 8 Voices (1611); *Hymnodia Sionia* for 3 to 8 Voices (1611; with 4 works for Organ); *Megalynodia Sionia* for 5 to 8 Voices (1611); *Missodia Sionia* for 2 to 8 Voices (1611); *Kleine und Grosse Litaney* for 5 to 8 Voices (1613); *Urania, oder Urano-Chorodia* for 2 to 4 Choirs (1613); *Epithalamium: dem . . . Fursten . . . Friedrich Ulrichen, Herzogen zu Braunschweig* for 17 Voices and Basso Continuo (1st perf., Sept. 4, 1614); *Concertgesang . . . dem . . . Fursten . . . Mauritio, Landgrafen zu Hessen* for 2 to 16 Voices and Basso Continuo (1st perf., June 26, 1617); *Polyhymnia caduceatrix et panegyrica* for 1 to 21 Voices and Basso Continuo (1619); *Polyhymnia exercitatrix seu tyrocinium* for 2 to 8 Voices and Basso Continuo (Frankfurt am Main, 1619); *Puernicinium . . . darinne 14 teutsche Kirchenlieder und anderere Concert-Gesänge* for 3 to 14 Voices (Frankfurt am Main, 1621). He also publ. a collection of French instrumental dances under the title *Terpsichore, musarum aoniarum quinta* a 4 to 6 (1612). A complete ed. of his works was prepared by F. Blume (21 vols., Wolfenbüttel, 1928–40).

WRITINGS: *Syntagma musicum*, his major achievement, was publ. in 3 vols. as follows: *Syntagmatis musici tomus primus* (Wittenberg and Wolfenbüttel, 1614–15; reprint, 1959), a historical and descriptive treatise in Latin on ancient and ecclesiastical music, and ancient secular instruments; *Syntagmatis musici tomus secundus* (Wolfenbüttel, 1618; 2nd ed., 1619; reprint, 1958, with an appendix, *Theatrum instrumentorum*, Wolfenbüttel, 1620; reprint, 1958), in German, a most important source of information on musical instruments of the period, describing their form, compass, tone quality, etc.; the organ is treated at great length, and the appendix contains 42 woodcuts of the principal instruments enumerated; *Syntagmatis musici tomus tertius* (Wolfenbüttel, 1618; 2nd ed., 1619; reprint, 1958), a valuable and interesting account of secular composition of the period, with a treatise on solmisation, notation, etc.

BIBL.: W. Gurlitt, *M. P. (Creuzburgensis): Sein Leben und seine Werke* (Leipzig, 1915); F. Blume, *Das monodische Prinzip in der protestantischen Kirchenmusik* (Leipzig, 1925); idem, *M. P. Creuzburgensis* (Wolfenbüttel, 1929); idem, "Das Werk des M. P.," *Zeitschrift für Musikwissenschaft*, XVII (1934–35); R. Unger, *Die mehrchörige Aufführungspraxis bei M. P. und die Feiergestaltung der Gegenwart* (Wolfenbüttel, 1941); G. Ilgner, *Die lateinischen liturgischen Kompositionen von M. P. Creuzburgensis* (Kiel, 1944); R. Fay, *The Vocal Style of M. P.* (diss., Univ. of Rochester, N.Y., 1946); A. Forcherts, *Das Spätwerk des M. P.* (Berlin, 1959); L. Abraham, *Der Generalbass im Schaffen des M. P.* (Berlin, 1961); F. Blume, "M. P. Creuzburgensis: Rückblick auf einen ausserordentlichen Musiker," *Neue Zürcher Zeitung* (Sept. 21, 1971); K. Gudewill and H. Haase, *M. P. Creutzbergensis 1571 (?–1612): Zwei Beiträge su seinem und seiner Kapelle Jubilaumsjahr* (Wolfenbüttel, 1971); A. Forchert, "M. P.: Werk und Wirkung," *Sagittarius*, IV (1973); C. Dahlhaus, "Über den Motettenbegriffdes M. P.," *Beiträge zur Musikgeschichte Nordeuropas: Kurt Gudewill zum 75. Geburtstag* (Wolfenbüttel, 1978); S. Vogelsänger, *M. P. beim Wort genommen: Zur Entstehungsgeschichte seiner Werke* (Aachen, 1987).

Pratella, Francesco Balilla, Italian music critic, musicologist, and composer; b. Lugo di Romagna, Feb. 1, 1880; d. Ravenna, May 17, 1955. He studied with Ricci-Signorini, then at the Liceo Rossini in Pesaro with Cicognani and Mascagni; taught in Cesana (1908–9); was director of the Istituto Musicale in Lugo (1910–29), and of the Liceo Musicale Giuseppe Verdi in Ravenna (1927–45). He joined the Italian futurist movement in 1910 (Russolo's manifesto of 1913 was addressed to "Balilla Pratella, grande musicista futurista"), and in 1913 wrote his 1st composition in a "futurist" idiom, the choral work *Inno alla vita*. After World War I, he broke with futurism.

WORKS: OPERAS: *Lilia* (won honorable mention in the Sonzogno Contest, 1903; Lugo, Nov. 13, 1905); *La Sina d'Vargöun* (1906–8; Bologna, Dec. 4, 1909); *L'Aviatore Dro* (1911–14;

Lugo, Nov. 4, 1920); *La ninnananna della bambola*, children's opera (1920–22; Milan, May 21, 1923); *La leggenda di San Fabiano* (1928–32; Bologna, Dec. 9, 1939); *L'uomo* (1934–49; not perf.); *Dono primaverile*, comedy with music (Bologna, Oct. 17, 1923); incidental music. **ORCH.:** *Romagna*, 5 symphonic poems (1903–4); *Musica futurista* (1912; renamed *Inno alla vita*; rev. 1933). Also choral works; chamber music; songs; piano pieces.

WRITINGS: *Cronache e critiche dal 1905 al 1917* (Bologna, 1918); *L'evoluzione della musica: Dal 1910 al 1917* (Milan, 1918–19); *Saggio di gridi, canzoni, cori e danze del popolo italiano* (Bologna, 1919); *Luci ed ombre: per un musicista italiano ignorato in Italia* (Rome, 1933); *Scritti vari di pensiero, di arte, di storia musicale* (Bologna, 1933); *Autobiografia* (Milan, 1971).

BIBL.: A. Toni, "La Sina d'Vargöun di F.B. P.," *Rivista Musicale Italiana*, XVI (1910); A. Ghigi, *F.B. P.* (Ravenna, 1930); *F.B. P., Appunti biografici e bibliografici* (Ravenna, 1931); R. Payton, *The Futurist Musicians: F.B. P. and Luigi Russola* (diss., Univ. of Chicago, 1974).

Pratt, Silas Gamaliel, American composer; b. Addison, Vt., Aug. 4, 1846; d. Pittsburgh, Oct. 30, 1916. Both his parents were church singers. The family moved to Chicago when he was a child, and he received his primary music education there; at 22 he went to Berlin, where he studied piano with Kullak and theory with Kiel (1868–71). He then returned to Chicago, where he served as organist of the Church of the Messiah; in 1872, established the Apollo Club. In 1875 he went to Germany once more; studied orchestration with Heinrich Dorn, and also took some piano lessons with Liszt. On July 4, 1876, he conducted in Berlin his *Centennial Overture*, dedicated to President Grant; also conducted at the Crystal Palace in London, when President Grant was visiting there; another work that he presented in London was *Homage to Chicago March*. Returning to Chicago, he conducted his opera *Zenobia, Queen of Palmyra* (to his own libretto) in concert form, on June 15, 1882 (stage perf., Chicago, March 26, 1883; N.Y., Aug. 21, 1883). The opera was received in a hostile manner by the press, partly owing to the poor quality of the music, but mainly as a reaction to Pratt's exuberant and immodest proclamations of its merit in advance of the production. Undaunted, Pratt unleashed a vigorous campaign for native American opera; he organized the Grand Opera Festival of 1884, which had some support. The following year he visited London again, and conducted there his symphonic work *The Prodigal Son* (Oct. 5, 1885). Returning to Chicago, he revised his early lyric opera *Antonio*, renamed it *Lucille*, and produced it on March 14, 1887. In 1888 he moved to N.Y.; there he presented, during the quadricentennial of the discovery of America, his opera *The Triumph of Columbus* (in concert form, Oct. 12, 1892); also produced a scenic cantata, *America*, subtitled 4 *Centuries of Music, Picture, and Song* (Nov. 24, 1894; with stereopticon projections). Other works: *Lincoln Symphony*; symphonic poem, *The Tragedy of the Deep* (1912; inspired by the *Titanic* disaster); cantata, *The Last Inca*; he also publ. a manual, *Pianist's Mental Velocity* (N.Y., 1903). In 1906 he settled in Pittsburgh; established there the Pratt Inst. of Music and Art, and remained its director until his death. Pratt was a colorful personality; despite continuous and severe setbacks, he was convinced of his own significance. The story of his salutation to Wagner at their meeting—"Herr Wagner, you are the Silas G. Pratt of Germany"—may be apocryphal, but is very much in character.

Pratt, Waldo Selden, distinguished American music historian and pedagogue; b. Philadelphia, Nov. 10, 1857; d. Hartford, Conn., July 29, 1939. He studied at Williams College and at Johns Hopkins Univ., specializing in classical languages; was practically self-taught in music. He was assistant director of the Metropolitan Museum of Art in N.Y. (1880–82); in 1882 he was appointed to the faculty of the Hartford Theological Seminary, where he taught hymnology; remained there until his retirement in 1925; he also taught music history at Smith

College (1895–1908), and later at the Inst. of Musical Art in N.Y. He ed. the American supplement to *Grove's Dictionary of Music and Musicians* (N.Y., 1920; 2nd ed., rev., 1928) and *The New Encyclopedia of Music and Musicians* (N.Y., 1924; 2nd ed., rev., 1929). He also publ. *The History of English Hymnody* (Hartford, Conn., 1895), *Musical Ministries in the Church* (N.Y., 1901; 4th ed., rev., 1915); *The History of Music* (N.Y., 1907; 3rd ed., augmented, 1935); *The Music of the Pilgrims* (Boston, 1921); *The Music of the French Psalter of 1562* (N.Y., 1939). **BIBL.:** O. Kinkeldey, "W.S. P.," *Musical Quarterly* (April 1940).

Prausnitz, Frederik (actually, **Frederick William**), German-born American conductor; b. Cologne, Aug. 26, 1920. He went to the U.S. in his youth; studied at the Juilliard School of Music in N.Y.; later served on its faculty (1947–61); then was conductor of the New England Cons. of Music sym. orch. in Boston (1961–69). He was music director of the Syracuse (N.Y.) Sym. Orch. from 1971 to 1974. In 1976 he joined the Peabody Cons. of Music in Baltimore as conductor of its sym. orch. and opera; from 1980 he acted as director of its conducting program and conductor of its Contemporary Music Ensemble. He appeared widely as a guest conductor in the U.S. and Europe, garnering a reputation as a leading advocate of contemporary music; was awarded the Gustav Mahler Medal of Honor of the Bruckner Society of America (1974). He publ. *Score and Podium: A Complete Guide to Conducting* (1983) and *Roger Sessions: A Critical Biography* (1983).

Predieri, family of Italian musicians:
(1) Giacomo (Maria) Predieri, organist, cornett player, and composer; b. Bologna, April 9, 1611; d. there, 1695. He was active as a cornett player in Bologna's municipal instrumental ensemble; was also a singer at S. Petronio (1636–57), where he was vice-maestro di cappella (1650–57); was organist at the cathedral of S. Pietro (1679–93); was a founding member of the Accademia Filarmonica (1666), and in 1693 was made its principe. He had 2 nephews who studied with him and pursued careers in music:
(2) Antonio Predieri, singer; b. Bologna, c.1650; d. there, 1710. He began his career as a tenor in F. Bassani's *L'inganno trionfato* (1673); then sang opera in various Italian cities; was also in the service of the dukes of Mantua (1684–87) and Parma (1687–99?), and also sang at the church of the Steccata in Parma (1689–96). He was made a member of Bologna's Accademia Filarmonica in 1685.
(3) Giacomo Cesare Predieri, singer and composer; b. Bologna, March 26, 1671; d. there, 1753. He also studied with G.P. Colonna; became a member of Bologna's Accademia Filarmonica as a singer in 1688, being promoted to composer in 1690; also served as its principe (1698, 1707, 1711); was maestro di cappella at the cathedral of S. Pietro (1696–1742). He wrote many sacred works, including 11 oratorios (only 1 extant). He had a nephew who was also a musician:
(4) Luca Antonio Predieri, violinist and composer; b. Bologna, Sept. 13, 1688; d. there, 1767. He studied violin with Abondio Bini and Tommaso Vitali, and counterpoint with his uncle, as well as with Angelo Predieri (b. Bologna, Jan. 14, 1655; d. there, Feb. 27, 1731), the singer and composer, and Giacomo Antonio Perti. He was an instrumentalist at the church of S. Petronio; became a member of the Accademia Filarmonica with the rank of composer (1716), serving as its principe (1723); was maestro di cappella at S. Paolo (1725–29), Madonna della Galliera (1726), Arciconfraternità della Vita (1727), and the cathedral of S. Pietro (1728–31); went to Vienna (1737), where he served as vice-maestro (1739–41) and maestro (1741–51) at the court chapel; returned to Bologna (1765). He wrote 31 operas, of which the following are extant: *Gli auguri spiegati* (Laxenburg, May 3, 1738), *La pace tra la virtù e la bellezza* (Vienna, Oct. 15, 1738), *Perseo* (Vienna, Nov. 4, 1738), *Astrea placata, ossia La felicità della terra* (Vienna, Aug. 28, 1739), and *Zenobia* (Vienna, Aug. 28, 1740). He distinguished himself as a composer of sacred music;

of his 7 oratorios, only *Il sacrificio d'Abramo* (Vienna, 1738) and *Isacco figura del Redentore* (Vienna, Feb. 12, 1740) are extant; other extant works include masses and Mass movements, antiphons, litanies, Psalms, motets, a *Stabat Mater,* cantatas, and a Sinfonia.
BIBL.: R. Ortner, *L.A. P. und sein Wiener Opernschaffen* (Vienna, 1971).

Preger, Leo, Corsican composer; b. Ajaccio, Jan. 27, 1907; d. there, Dec. 25, 1965. He studied with Nadia Boulanger in Paris, and acquired considerable mastery of antique counterpoint; devoted himself mainly to composing sacred choral music.

Preindl, Josef, Austrian organist, music theorist, and composer; b. Marbach, Jan. 30, 1756; d. Vienna, Oct. 26, 1823. He settled in Vienna, where he studied with Albrechtsberger; served as organist at the church of Maria am Gestade (1775–78), at the Carmelite church of Vienna-Leopoldstadt (1783–87), and at St. Michael's (1787); in 1793 became Kapellmeister at St. Peter's, and later served as Vice-Kapellmeister (1795–1809) and Kapellmeister (from 1809) at St. Stephen's. He brought out a *Gesang-Lehre,* op. 33 (Vienna, 2nd ed., 1833) and *Wiener Tonschule, oder Elementarbuch zum Studium des Generalbasses, des Contrapunktes, der Harmonie- und Fugen-Lehre* (ed. by I. von Seyfried, Vienna, 1827; 2nd ed., 1832, as *Anweisung zum Generalbasse*). He composed 2 piano concertos, about 14 masses and other sacred works, chamber music, and songs, but much of his output was destroyed during World War II.

Preiss, Cornelius, Austrian writer on music and composer; b. Troppau, May 20, 1884; d. Linz, April 1, 1944. He studied in Olmütz and Graz (Ph.D., 1907); taught in Graz (1908–24) and Linz (from 1924). He wrote mainly vocal music; publ. the folk-song collection *Österreichischer Liederquell* (3 vols., 1930–32). He publ. *Zur Geschichte der Operette* (1908); also monographs on Millöcker (1905), Drechsler (1910), Volkmann (1912), Süssmayer (1933), and others.

Premru, Raymond (Eugene), American trombonist, conductor, and composer; b. Elmira, N.Y., June 6, 1934. He studied at the Oberlin College Cons. of Music, at the Eastman School of Music in Rochester, N.Y. (B.Mus., 1956), and with Peter Racine Fricker in London. From 1958 to 1988 he played in the Philharmonia Orch. in London; also was a member of the Philip Jones Brass Ensemble (1960–86) and co-director of the Bobby Lamb-Ray Premru Big Band. He gave master classes in trombone virtuosity throughout the world; taught at various institutions, including the Oberlin College Cons. of Music (from 1988). Among his works are a Concerto for Orch. (1976), 2 syms. (No. 1, 1981; No. 2, Cleveland, Nov. 23, 1988), Concerto for Trumpet and Strings (1983), *Celebrations* for Timpani and Orch. (1984), *Music* for 3 Trombones, Tuba, and Orch. (1985), other instrumental pieces, and choral works.

Preobrazhensky, Anton (Viktorovich), Russian musicologist; b. Syzran, Feb. 28, 1870; d. Leningrad, Feb. 17, 1929. He studied at the Kazan Seminary; upon graduation he went to Moscow, where he taught at the Synod School (1898–1902); then was librarian at the Court Chapel in St. Petersburg; from 1920 to his death, he taught the history of Russian church music at the Petrograd (later Leningrad) Cons. He publ. a number of valuable reference works on Russian hymnody: *Dictionary of Russian Hymns* (Moscow, 1896); *Bibliography of Hymns* (Moscow, 1900); *The Monodic Hymn in the Russian Church of the 17th Century* (St. Petersburg, 1904); *Liturgic Music in Russia* (1924); also a biography of Lvov (St. Petersburg, 1908).

Presley, Elvis (Aron), fantastically popular American rock-'n'-roll singer and balladeer; b. Tupelo, Miss., Jan. 8, 1935; d. Memphis, Tenn., Aug. 16, 1977. He was employed as a mechanic and furniture repairman in his early youth; picked up guitar playing in his leisure hours; sang cowboy ballads at social gatherings. With the advent of rock 'n' roll, he revealed himself as the supreme genius of the genre; almost effortlessly he captivated multitudes of adolescents by the hallucinogenic monotone of his vocal delivery, enhanced by rhythmic pelvic gyrations (hence the invidious appellation "Elvis the Pelvis"); made recordings that sold millions of albums. He made America conscious of the seductive inanity of rock ballads; he aroused primitive urges among his multitudinous admirers with his renditions of such songs, among them *Don't Be Cruel, Hound Dog, Love Me Tender, All Shook Up, Jailhouse Rock, Heartbreak Hotel, Rock around the Clock, It's Now or Never;* his audience responded by improvising songs about him: *My Boy Elvis, I Wanna Spend Christmas with Elvis,* and *Elvis for President.* He also appeared as an actor in sentimental motion pictures. His art was the prime inspiration for the famous Liverpudlian quartet The Beatles. An International Elvis Presley Appreciation Society was organized by 1970. Presley was indeed The King of Kings of rock. His death (of cardiac arrhythmia aggravated by an immoderate use of tranquilizers and other drugs) precipitated the most extraordinary outpouring of public grief over an entertainment figure since the death of Rudolph Valentino. His entombment in the family mausoleum in Memphis was the scene of mob hysteria, during which 2 people were run over and killed by an automobile; 2 men were arrested for an alleged plot to spirit away his body and hold it for ransom. Entrepreneurs avid for gain put out a mass of memorial literature, souvenirs, and gewgaws, sweat shirts emblazoned with Presley's image in color, Elvis dolls, and even a life-size effigy, as part of a multimillion-dollar effort to provide solace to sorrowing humanity; the only discordant note was sounded by Presley's own bodyguards, who authored a book provocatively titled *Elvis, What Happened?,* with murky insinuations that the King of Rock was a drug addict. Presley's home, turned into a sanctuary at suburban Whitehaven, in Memphis, was opened to the public on June 7, 1982, and was visited by mobs, not only by drug-besotted local rock fans, but by delegations from fan clubs in civilized nations (even the U.K.). Souvenirs included an "Always Elvis" brand of wine; license plates of out-of-town motorists bore the legend ELVIS-P. A bill was submitted in Congress for declaring Presley's nativity day, Jan. 8, a national day.

BIBL.: J. Hopkins, *E., A Biography* (N.Y., 1971); S. Dunleavy, *E.: What Happened?* (N.Y., 1977); J. Hopkins, *E.: The Final Years* (N.Y., 1980); A. Goldman, *Elvis* (a damning biography in repulsive detail; N.Y., 1981); J. Whisler, *E. P.: Reference Guide and Discography* (Metuchen, N.J., 1981); P. Hammontree, *E. P.: A Bio-bibliography* (Westport, Conn., 1985).

Presser, Theodore, American music publisher; b. Pittsburgh, July 3, 1848; d. Philadelphia, Oct. 27, 1925. He studied at the New England Cons. of Music in Boston with S. Emery, G.E. Whiting, J.C.D. Parker, and B. Lang; then at the Leipzig Cons. with Zwintscher and Jadassohn; in 1883 he founded in Philadelphia the *Etude,* a well-known music monthly of which he was ed. until 1907; James F. Cooke was its ed. from 1908 to 1949; it discontinued publication in 1957. Shortly after the foundation of the *Etude,* Presser established a publishing house, the Theodore Presser Co., for music and books about music, which has come to be one of the important firms in the U.S. It acquired the catalogues of the John Church Co. (1930), the Oliver Ditson Co. (1931), the Mercury Music Corp. (1969), Elkan-Vogel (1970), and the American Music Edition (1981). Its headquarters removed to Bryn Mawr, Pa., in 1949. In 1906 he founded the Presser Home for Retired Music Teachers, which in 1908 moved to Germantown. In 1916 he established the Presser Foundation to administer this Home, to provide relief for deserving musicians, and to offer scholarships in colleges and univs. in the U.S. Presser wrote instructive pieces and studies for piano; was a co-founder of the Music Teachers National Assoc. (1876).

BIBL.: C. Yoder, *T. P., Educator, Publisher, Philanthropist: Selected Contributions to the Music Teaching Profession in America* (diss., Univ. of Illinois, 1978).

Pressler, Menahem, German-born American pianist and teacher; b. Magdeburg, Dec. 16, 1923. He was taken to Palestine by his family after the Hitlerization of Germany; he studied piano with Eliah Rudiakow and Leo Kestenberg; then played with the Palestine Sym. Orch. In 1946 he won the Debussy Prize at the piano competition in San Francisco. In 1955 he became a member of the School of Music at Indiana Univ.; that year he became pianist in the Beaux Arts Trio, with which he made numerous tours; he also continued his career as a soloist.

BIBL.: N. Delbanco, *The Beaux Arts Trio: A Portrait* (London, 1985).

Preston, Simon (John), distinguished English organist, harpsichordist, conductor, and pedagogue; b. Bournemouth, Aug. 4, 1938. He was a chorister at King's College, Cambridge (1949–51), where he received instruction in organ from Hugh McLean; after further keyboard training from Anthony Brown at Canford School, he continued his studies with C.H. Trevor at the Royal Academy of Music in London (1956–58); subsequently was an organ scholar at King's College, Cambridge (1958–62). He made his formal debut as an organist at the Royal Festival Hall in London in 1962; was sub-organist at Westminster Abbey (1962–67); after conducting the Oxford Bach Choir (1967–68), he was organist and lecturer at Christ Church, Oxford (1970–81); then was organist and master of the choristers at Westminster Abbey (1981–87). He toured widely as an organ virtuoso and gave master classes on both sides of the Atlantic; also conducted much choral music. His repertoire ranges from Handel to Messiaen.

BIBL.: M. Buxton, "S. P. at 50," *Musical Times* (Oct. 1988).

Prêtre, Georges, prominent French conductor; b. Waziers, Aug. 14, 1924. He studied at the Douai Cons.; then at the Paris Cons.; also received instruction in conducting from Cluytens. He made his debut as a conductor at the Marseilles Opera in 1946; subsequently had guest engagements in Lille, Casablanca, and Toulouse; then was music director of the Paris Opéra-Comique (1955–59); subsequently conducted at the Paris Opéra (from 1959), where he served as music director (1970–71). In 1959 he made his U.S. debut at the Chicago Lyric Opera; in 1961 he appeared for the 1st time in London. On Oct. 17, 1964, he made his 1st appearance at the Metropolitan Opera in N.Y., conducting *Samson et Dalila.* He appeared as a guest conductor with many of the major opera houses and orchs. of the world in succeeding years; also served as principal guest conductor of the Vienna Sym. Orch. (from 1986).

Previn, André (George) (real name, **Andreas Ludwig Priwin**), brilliant German-born American pianist, conductor, and composer; b. Berlin, April 6, 1929. He was of Russian-Jewish descent. He showed an unmistakable musical gift as a child; his father, a lawyer, was an amateur musician who gave him his early training; they played piano, 4–hands, together at home. At the age of 6, he was accepted as a pupil at the Berlin Hochschule für Musik, where he studied piano with Prof. Breithaupt; as a Jew, however, he was compelled to leave school in 1938. The family then went to Paris; he continued his studies at the Paris Cons., Marcel Dupré being one of his teachers. In 1939 the family emigrated to America, settling in Los Angeles, where his father's cousin, Charles Previn, was music director at Universal Studios in Hollywood. He took lessons in composition with Joseph Achron, Ernst Toch, and Mario Castelnuovo-Tedesco. He became an American citizen in 1943. Even before graduating from high school, he obtained employment at MGM; he became an orchestrator there and later one of its music directors; he also became a fine jazz pianist. He served in the U.S. Army (1950–52); stationed in San Francisco, he took lessons in conducting with Pierre Monteux, who was music director of the San Francisco Sym. Orch. at the time. During these years he wrote much music for films; he received Academy Awards for his arrangements of *Gigi* (1958), *Porgy and Bess* (1959), *Irma la Douce* (1963), and *My Fair Lady* (1964). Throughout this period he continued to appear as a concert pianist. In 1962 he made his formal conducting debut with the St. Louis Sym. Orch., and conducting soon became his principal vocation. From 1967 to 1969 he was conductor-in-chief of the Houston Sym. Orch. In 1968 he assumed the post of principal conductor of the London Sym. Orch., retaining it with distinction until 1979; then was made its conductor emeritus. In 1976 he became music director of the Pittsburgh Sym. Orch., a position he held with similar distinction until a dispute with the management led to his resignation in 1984. He had already been engaged as music director of the Royal Phil. Orch. of London in 1982, a position he held from 1985 to 1987; then served as its principal conductor. Previn also accepted appointment as music director of the Los Angeles Phil. Orch., after resigning his Pittsburgh position; he formally assumed his duties in Los Angeles in 1985, but gave up this position in 1990 after disagreements with the management over administrative procedures. During his years as a conductor of the London Sym. Orch., he took it on a number of tours to the U.S., as well as to Russia, Japan, South Korea, and Hong Kong. He also took the Pittsburgh Sym. Orch. on acclaimed tours of Europe in 1978 and 1982. He continued to compose popular music, including the scores for the musicals *Coco* (1969) and *The Good Companions* (1974); with words by Tom Stoppard, he composed *Every Good Boy Deserves Favour* (1977), a work for Actors and Orch. His other compositions include Sym. for Strings (1962); *Overture to a Comedy* (1963); Violin Sonata (1964); Flute Quartet (1964); *Elegy* for Oboe and Strings (1967); Cello Concerto (1967); Horn Concerto (1968); Guitar Concerto (1972); *Principals* for Orch. (1980); *Reflections* for Orch. (1981); *Divertimento* for Orch. (1982); Piano Concerto (1985); piano pieces; songs. He ed. the book *Orchestra* (Garden City, N.Y., 1979); also publ. *André Previn's Guide to Music* (London, 1983). He was married four times (and divorced thrice): to the jazz singer Betty Bennett, to the jazz poet Dory Langdon (who made a career of her own as composer and singer of pop songs), to the actress Mia Farrow, and in 1982 to Heather Hales.

BIBL.: E. Greenfield, *A. P.* (N.Y., 1973); M. Bookspan and R. Yockey, *A. P.: A Biography* (Garden City, N.Y., 1981); a "profile" in the *New Yorker* (Jan. 10 and 17, 1983); H. Ruttencutter, *P.* (London, 1985).

Previtali, Fernando, prominent Italian conductor; b. Adria, Feb. 16, 1907; d. Rome, Aug. 1, 1985. He studied cello, piano, and composition at the Turin Cons.; then was Gui's assistant at the Maggio Musicale Fiorentino (1928–36). He was chief conductor of the Rome Radio orch. (1936–43; 1945–53); also conducted at Milan's La Scala and at other major Italian opera houses. From 1953 to 1973 he was chief conductor of the Orchestra Sinfonica dell'Accademia Nazionale di Santa Cecilia in Rome, which he led on tours abroad. On Dec. 15, 1955, he made his U.S. debut as a guest conductor with the Cleveland Orch. Previtali became well known for his advocacy of contemporary Italian composers, and conducted the premieres of numerous operas and orch. works. He was also a composer; wrote the ballet, *Allucinazioni* (Rome, 1945), choral works, chamber music, etc. He publ. *Guida allo studio della direzione d'orchestra* (Rome, 1951).

Prévost, (Joseph Gaston Charles) André, Canadian composer; b. Hawkesbury, Ontario, July 30, 1934. He studied harmony and counterpoint with Isabelle Delorme and Jean Papineau-Couture and composition with C. Pépin (premier prix, 1960) at the Montreal Cons.; after studying analysis with Messiaen at the Paris Cons., and receiving further instruction from Dutilleux at the Paris École Normale de Musique (1961), he returned to Canada (1962) and was active as a teacher; following studies in electronic music with Michel Phillipot at the Paris ORTF (1964), he worked with Schuller, Martino, Copland, and Kodály at the Berkshire Music Center in Tanglewood (1964); then taught at the Univ. of Montreal (from 1964). In 1986 he was made an Officer of the Order of Canada.

WORKS: *Poème de l'infini,* symphonic poem (1960); *Scherzo*

for String Orch. (1960); *Fantasmes* for Orch. (Montreal, Nov. 22, 1963; posthumously dedicated to President John F. Kennedy); *Pyknon,* pièce concertante for Violin and Orch. (1966); *Célébration* for Orch. (1966); *Terre des hommes* for 2 Narrators, 3 Choirs, and Orch. (Montreal, April 29, 1967; opening of Expo '67); *Diallèle* for Orch. (Toronto, May 30, 1968); *Evanescence* for Orch. (Ottawa, April 7, 1970); *Hommage (à Beethoven)* for 14 Strings (1970–71); *Psaume 148* for Chorus, Brass, and Organ (1971; Guelph, May 1, 1971); *Chorégraphie I* (. . . *Munich, September 1972* . . .) for Orch. (1972–73; Toronto, April 22, 1975; inspired by the Munich Olympics tragedy); *Ouverture* (1975); *Chorégraphie II* ($E = MC^2$) for Orch. (1976); *Chorégraphie III* for Orch. (1976); Cello Concerto (1976; Winnipeg, Dec. 6, 1979); *Hiver dans l'âme* for Baritone and Orch. (1978); *Choréographie IV* for Orch. (1978; London, Ontario, Jan. 10, 1979); *Paraphrase* for String Quartet and Orch. (Toronto, April 29, 1980); *Cosmophonie* for Orch. (1985); *Cantate pour cordes* for Chamber Orch. (1987); *Pastorale* for 2 Harps (1955); *Fantasie* for Cello and Piano (1956); 2 string quartets (1958; *Ad pacem,* 1971–72); *Mobiles* for Flute, Violin, Viola, and Cello (1959–60); Violin Sonata (1960–61; arr. as a ballet under the title *Primordial,* 1968); 2 cello sonatas (1962; arr. for Violin, and Piano or Ondes Martenot, 1967; 1985); *Triptyque* for Flute, Oboe, and Piano (1962); *Mouvement* for Brass Quintet (1963); *Ode au St. Laurent* for optional Narrator and String Quartet (1965); *Suite* for String Quintet (1968); *Missa de profundis* for Chorus and Organ (1973); *Improvisation II* for Cello (1976) and *III* for Viola (1976); Sonata for Violin and Piano (1979); Quintet for Clarinet and String Quartet (London, England, Oct. 26, 1988); *4 Preludes* for 2 Pianos (1961); *5 Variations sur un thème grégorien* for Organ (1956); *Variations en Passacaille* for Organ (1984); songs; choruses.

Prévost, Eugène-Prosper, French conductor and composer; b. Paris, April 23, 1809; d. New Orleans, Aug. 19, 1872. He studied at the Paris Cons. with Le Sueur, winning the Grand Prix de Rome in 1831 with the cantata *Bianca Capello.* He conducted theatrical music in Le Havre (1835–38); then went to Paris (1862–67) before returning to New Orleans as a singing master. He produced several operas in Paris, of which *Cosimo* (Opéra-Comique, Oct. 13, 1835) was the most successful; another, *Blanche et René,* was given in New Orleans in 1861; he also wrote oratorios and masses.

Prey, Claude, French composer; b. Fleury-sur-Andelle, May 30, 1925. He studied at the Paris Cons. with Milhaud and Messiaen; then with Mignone in Rio de Janeiro and with Frazzi in Siena; completed his studies at the Laval Univ. in Quebec in 1958.

WORKS: Opera, *Le Phénix* (1957); "opéra épistolaire," *Lettres perdues* (1960); *La Dictée,* lyrical monodrama (1961); chamber opera after Edgar Allan Poe, *Le Cœur révélateur* (The Tell-Tale Heart; 1962); opera in 12 variations, *L'Homme occis* (1963); *Métamorphose d'Echo,* 9 variations for Female Voice and 24 Strings (1965); *Les Mots croisés (Jeu concertante)* for Contralto, Tenor, and 2 Instrumental Groups (1965); *Donna Mobile,* theater-music piece for 8 Actresses and 3 Instrumentalists (1965; Avignon Festival, July 15, 1972); "opéra-test," *La Noirceur du lait* (Strasbourg, 1967); opera-oratorio, *Jonas* (1966; scenic version, Lyons, Dec. 2, 1969); opera-parody in 2 trials, *On veut la lumière? Allons-y!* for 5 Cast Members and 8 Instruments (1967; Angers, 1968); *Fêtes de la faim,* opera for 5 Comedians, Cello, and 2 Percussionists (Avignon, 1969); short opera, *Le Jeu de l'oie* (Paris, 1970); *Théâtrophonie* for 12 Voices and Piano (1971).

Prey, Hermann, outstanding German baritone; b. Berlin, July 11, 1929. He studied with Günther Baum and Harry Gottschalk at the Berlin Hochschule für Musik; won 1st prize in a vocal competition organized by the U.S. Army (1952), and that same year made his operatic debut as the 2nd prisoner in *Fidelio* in Wiesbaden; after appearing in the U.S., he joined the Hamburg State Opera (1953); also sang in Vienna (from 1956), Berlin (from 1956), and in Salzburg (from 1959). In 1959 he became a principal member of the Bavarian State Opera in Munich; made his Metropolitan Opera debut in N.Y. as Wolfram (Dec. 16, 1960); appeared for the 1st time in England at the Edinburgh Festival (1965), and later sang regularly at London's Covent Garden (from 1973). He also appeared as a soloist with the major orchs. and as a recitalist; likewise starred in his own Munich television show. In 1982 he became a prof. at the Hamburg Hochschule für Musik. His autobiography was publ. as *Premierenfieber* (1981; Eng. tr. as *First Night Fever: The Memoirs of Hermann Prey*, 1986). Among his finest operatic roles are Count Almaviva, Papageno, Guglielmo, and Rossini's Figaro; he also sang a number of contemporary roles. As a lieder artist, he distinguished himself in Schubert, Schumann, and Brahms.

Preyer, Carl Adolph, German-American pianist, composer, and teacher; b. Pforzheim, Baden, July 28, 1863; d. Lawrence, Kans., Nov. 16, 1947. He studied at the Stuttgart Cons.; then with Navrátil in Vienna, and with H. Urban and H. Barth in Berlin. In 1893 he settled in the U.S.; became a piano teacher at the School of Fine Arts of the Univ. of Kansas, and remained with that institution throughout his life. He publ. several instructive collections for piano; also character pieces.
BIBL.: H. Gloyne, *C.A. P.: The Life of a Kansas Musician* (Lawrence, 1949).

Preyer, Gottfried von, Austrian organist and composer; b. Hausbrunn, March 15, 1807; d. Vienna, May 9, 1901. He studied with Sechter in Vienna; in 1835, became organist of the Lutheran Church in Vienna; in 1838, prof. of music theory at the Vienna Cons., of which he was director from 1844 to 1848. In 1853 he became music director at St. Stephen's; was pensioned in 1876. He wrote 3 operas; the oratorio *Noah;* a Sym.; several masses and other church music.

Prianishnikov, Ippolit (Petrovich), Russian baritone; b. Kerch, Aug. 26, 1847; d. Petrograd, Nov. 11, 1921. He joined the Russian Imperial Navy; later began to study voice, first at the St. Petersburg Cons. (1873–75), then in Italy, where he became a student of Ronconi in Milan; made his debut in Milan in 1876. Returning to Russia, he joined the Maryinsky Theater in St. Petersburg in 1878, remaining there until 1886; then went to Tiflis (1886–89) and Moscow (1892–93), where he sang and produced opera; in later years he also taught voice. Among his students were Bolshakov, Nikolai Figner, and Mravina.

Přibyl, Vilém, Czech tenor; b. Náchod, April 10, 1925; d. Brno, July 13, 1990. After making his debut with an amateur opera company in Hradec Králové (1952), he pursued vocal instruction there with Jakoubková (1952–62); sang at the opera in Ústí nad Labem (1960) and at the Janáček Opera in Brno (1960); also received further training from Vavrdová at the Brno Academy of Music. He gained notable success with his portrayal of Dalibor with the Prague National Theater Opera during its visit to the Edinburgh Festival (1964); then appeared in various European music centers; also taught at the Janáček Academy of Arts in Brno (from 1969). In 1969 he was made an Artist of Merit and in 1977 a National Artist by the Czech government. His repertoire included Lohengrin, Radames, and Otello, as well as roles in operas by Prokofiev, Martinů, and Shostakovich; he was especially esteemed for his roles in operas by Janáček.

Price, Florence B(eatrice) (née **Smith**), black American teacher and composer; b. Little Rock, Ark., April 9, 1888; d. Chicago, June 3, 1953. She studied with Chadwick and Converse at the New England Cons. of Music in Boston, graduating in 1906. She had been publishing her compositions since she was 11 (1899); in 1928 she won a prize from G. Schirmer for *At the Cotton Gin* for Piano; around this time she was also writing musical jingles for radio commercials. Her 1st notable success came in 1932 with her 1st Sym. (winner of the Wanamaker Award; perf. by the Chicago Sym. Orch. at the Century of Progress Exhibition in 1933); she became known as the 1st black woman to write syms.

WORKS: ORCH.: 6 syms.: No. 1 (1931–32); *Mississippi River Symphony* (1934); D minor (n.d.); No. 3 (1940); G minor (n.d.); *Colonial Dance Symphony* (n.d.); *Ethiopia's Shadow in America* (1932); Piano Concerto (1934); 2 violin concertos: No. 1 (n.d.); No. 2 (1952); 2 concert overtures on Negro spirituals; Piano Concerto in 1 Movement; Rhapsody for Piano and Orch.; *Songs of the Oak,* tone poem. **CHAMBER:** *Negro Folksongs in Counterpoint* for String Quartet; 2 piano quintets; pieces for Violin and Piano; also choral music; songs; arrangements of spirituals; piano pieces; organ music.
BIBL.: B. Jackson, "F. P., Composer," *Black Perspective in Music* (Spring 1977); M. Green, "F. P.," *Black Women Composers: A Genesis* (Boston, 1983).

Price, (Mary Violet) Leontyne, remarkably endowed black American soprano; b. Laurel, Miss., Feb. 10, 1927. She was taught piano by a local woman, and also learned to sing. On Dec. 17, 1943, she played piano and sang at a concert in Laurel. She went to Oak Park High School, graduating in music in 1944; then enrolled in the College of Education and Industrial Arts in Wilberforce, Ohio, where she studied voice with Catherine Van Buren; received her B.A. degree in 1948, and then was awarded a scholarship at the Juilliard School of Music in N.Y.; there she received vocal training from Florence Page Kimball, and also joined the Opera Workshop under the direction of Frederic Cohen. Virgil Thomson heard her perform the role of Mistress Ford in Verdi's opera *Falstaff* and invited her to sing in the revival of his opera *4 Saints in 3 Acts* in 1952. She subsequently performed the role of Bess in Gershwin's *Porgy and Bess* on a tour of the U.S. (1952–54) and in Europe (1955). On Nov. 14, 1954, she made a highly acclaimed debut as a concert singer in N.Y. On Dec. 3, 1954, she sang at the 1st performance of Samuel Barber's *Prayers of Kierkegaard* with the Boston Sym. Orch., conducted by Charles Munch. On Jan. 23, 1955, she performed Tosca on television, creating a sensation both as an artist and as a member of her race taking up the role of an Italian diva. Her career was soon assured without any reservations. In 1957, she appeared with the San Francisco Opera; on Oct. 18, 1957, she sang Aida, a role congenial to her passionate artistry. In 1958 she sang Aida with the Vienna State Opera under the direction of Herbert von Karajan; on July 2, 1958, she sang this role at Covent Garden in London; and again as Aida she appeared at La Scala in Milan in 1959, the 1st black woman to sing with that most prestigious and most fastidious opera company. On Jan. 27, 1961, she made her 1st appearance with the Metropolitan Opera in N.Y. in the role of Leonora in *Il Trovatore.* A series of highly successful performances at the Metropolitan followed: Aida on Feb. 20, 1961; Madama Butterfly on March 3, 1961; Donna Anna on March 25, 1961; Tosca on April 1, 1962; Pamina on Jan. 3, 1964; Cleopatra in the premiere of Samuel Barber's opera *Antony and Cleopatra* at the opening of the new Metropolitan Opera House at Lincoln Center in N.Y. on Sept. 16, 1966. On Sept. 24, 1973, she sang Madama Butterfly at the Metropolitan once more. On Feb. 7, 1975, she appeared there in the title role of *Manon Lescaut;* and on Feb. 3, 1976, she sang Aida, a role she repeated for her farewell performance in opera in a televised production broadcast live from the Metropolitan Opera in N.Y. by PBS on Jan. 3, 1985. She then continued her concert career, appearing with notable success in the major music centers. She was married in 1952 to the baritone **William Warfield** (who sang Porgy at her performances of *Porgy and Bess*), but separated from him in 1959; they were divorced in 1973. She received many honors during her remarkable career; in 1964, President Johnson bestowed upon her the Medal of Freedom, and in 1985 President Reagan presented her with the National Medal of Arts.
BIBL.: H. Lyon, *L. P.: Highlights of a Prima Donna* (N.Y., 1973).

Price, Margaret (Berenice), outstanding Welsh soprano; b. Blackwood, near Tredegar, South Wales, April 13, 1941. She commenced singing lessons when she was 9; then won the Charles Kennedy Scott scholarship of London's Trinity College of Music at 15, and studied voice with Scott for 4 years. After singing in the Ambrosian Singers for 2 seasons, she made her operatic debut as Cherubino with the Welsh National Opera (1962); then sang that same role at her Covent Garden debut in London (1963). She made her 1st appearance at the Glyndebourne Festival as Constanze in *Die Entführung aus dem Serail* (1968); then made her U.S. debut as Pamina at the San Francisco Opera (1969); subsequently sang Fiordiligi at the Chicago Lyric Opera (1972). In 1973 she sang at the Paris Opéra, later joining its cast during its U.S. tour in 1976, eliciting extraordinary praise from the public and critics for her portrayal of Desdemona; made an auspicious Metropolitan Opera debut in N.Y. in that same role on Jan. 21, 1985. She also toured widely as a concert singer. Her other notable roles include Donna Anna, Aida, Adriana Lecouvreur, and Strauss's Ariadne. Her voice is essentially a lyric soprano, but is capable of technically brilliant coloratura. She was made a Commander of the Order of the British Empire in 1982.

BIBL.: *Current Biography* (Aug. 1986).

Price, (Noble) Ray, American county-music singer and guitarist; b. near Perryville, Tex., Jan. 12, 1926. He studied at North Texas Agricultural College in Arlington (1946–49); then embarked on a career as a country-music singer; made numerous recordings, including *Crazy Arms, Heartaches by the Number, Release Me, Danny Boy, For the Good Times,* and many others; also sang on the radio.

Pride, Charley, black American country-music singer and guitarist; b. on a cotton farm near Sledge, Miss., March 18, 1938. He learned to play the guitar but, bent on a career in baseball, he played in the minor leagues (1954–64); also tried his luck as a singer. He subsequently appeared with the Grand Ole Opry in Nashville, becoming the 1st black country-music singer to gain admission to this shrine of populist entertainment.

Priestman, Brian, English conductor; b. Birmingham, Feb. 10, 1927. He studied at the Univ. of Birmingham (B.Mus., 1950; M.A., 1952) and the Brussels Cons. (diploma, 1952); served as music director of the Royal Shakespeare Theatre, Stratford-upon-Avon (1960–63); then conducted the Edmonton Sym. Orch. in Alberta, Canada (1964–68), and the Baltimore Sym. Orch. (1968–69). From 1970 to 1978 he was music director of the Denver Sym. Orch. and was also principal conductor of the New Zealand National Orch. (1973–76). From 1977 to 1980 he was music director of the Florida Phil., and subsequently was music adviser of the Cape Town Sym. in South Africa; while there he was also appointed, in 1980, prof. at the Univ. of Cape Town and director of the South African College of Music.

Prigozhin, Lucian (Ambramovich), Russian composer; b. Tashkent, Aug. 15, 1926. His father was a legal consultant; his mother, a pharmaceutical worker; the family moved to Samarkand, where Prigozhin spent his earliest childhood; they returned to Tashkent in 1934. When Germany invaded Russia in 1941, the entire faculty of the Leningrad Cons. was evacuated to Tashkent, and Prigozhin had an opportunity to study piano and theory with its members. At the end of the war, Prigozhin went to Leningrad, and enrolled in the class of Vladimir Shcherbachev; later studied with Evlakhov and Kochurov at the Leningrad Cons. His early works followed the precepts of the Russian national school; to this period belong his oratorio *Stenka Razin* and 1st Sym. Upon his graduation from the Leningrad Cons., Prigozhin became interested in modern techniques; he introduced a concept of "supplementary tones" in the 12-tone method of composition by allowing the members of the tone-row to permutate freely. However, he preserved the basic tonality even when he no longer used the key signature.

WORKS: STAGE: *Doctor Aybolit* (Ay! It Hurts!), radio opera for children (1956); *Malchish-Kibalchish,* radio opera for children (1969); *Robin Hood,* opera (1972); ballet, *Circle of Hades* (1964); incidental music for films. **VOCAL:** *Stenka Razin,* vocal-

symphonic tableau for 2 Soloists and Orch. (1949); *Song of Bread,* cantata (1959); *Prometheus Unbound* for Chorus and Orch., after Aeschylus (1959–60); *The Chronicle of Igor's Campaign* for Mezzo-soprano, Bass, Mixed Choir, and Chamber Ensemble (1966); *Snowstorm,* chamber oratorio, after Alexander Blok's poem *The Twelve* (1968); *Precursors,* chamber cantata for 2 Soloists, Alto Flute, Clarinet, Double Bass, and Percussion (1970); *In Memory of the Great Battle* for Bass, Chorus, and Orch. (1975); *Sun and Stones,* chamber cantata for Mezzo-soprano, Flute, String Quartet, and Piano (1975); *From Horace,* chamber cantata for Baritone, Chorus, Clarinet, Trombone, and Percussion (1976). **ORCH.:** Sinfonietta (1953); Sym. No. 1 (1955; rev. 1975); Sym. No. 2 (1960; rev. 1963); Sym. No. 3 (1970); *Music for Strings and Flute* (1961); Symphonic Suite from the ballet *Circle of Hades* (1965). **CHAMBER:** Sonata No. 1 for Violin and Piano (*Sonata-burlesque;* 1967); Sonata No. 2 for Violin and Piano (1969); 2 string quartets (1970, 1979); *Musica rustica* for Wind Quintet (1973); Sonata for Horn and Piano (1974). **PIANO:** Sonatina (1973); Sonata (1973); *Calendar of Nature,* 12 pieces (1974).

BIBL.: E. Ruchyevskaya, *L. P.* (Moscow, 1977).

Příhoda, Váša, noted Czech violinist and teacher; b. Vodnany, Aug. 22, 1900; d. Vienna, July 26, 1960. He received his 1st instruction from his father, a professional violinist; made his public debut at the age of 12 in Prague; in 1920, went on an Italian tour; in 1921, appeared in the U.S., and in 1927 played in England; then gave recitals throughout Europe. He continued to concertize after the absorption of Austria and Czechoslovakia into the Nazi Reich, and was briefly charged with collaboration with the occupying powers. He eventually resumed his career, and later became a prof. at the Vienna Academy of Music.

BIBL.: J. Vratislavský, *V. P.* (Prague, 1970).

Prima, Louis, black American jazz trumpeter and bandleader; b. New Orleans, Dec. 7, 1911; d. there, Aug. 24, 1978. He played the violin and the trumpet; in 1934, went to N.Y., where he led his own band with much success. He composed the hit song *Sing, Sing, Sing* (1940) for Benny Goodman. He was married to the singer Keely Smith (1952–61).

Primrose, William, eminent Scottish-born American violist and pedagogue; b. Glasgow, Aug. 23, 1903; d. Provo, Utah, May 1, 1982. He studied violin in Glasgow with Camillo Ritter, at London's Guildhall School of Music, and in Belgium (1925–27) with Ysaÿe, who advised him to take up viola so as to avoid the congested violin field. He became the violist in the London String Quartet (1930–35), with which he made several tours. In 1937 he settled in the U.S., and was engaged as the principal violist player in the NBC Sym. Orch. in N.Y. under Toscanini, holding this post until 1942. In 1939 he established his own string quartet. In 1953 he was named a Commander of the Order of the British Empire; became a naturalized U.S. citizen in 1955. From 1954 to 1962 he was the violist in the Festival Quartet. He also became active as a teacher; was on the faculty of the Univ. of Southern Calif. in Los Angeles (1962) and at the School of Music of Indiana Univ. in Bloomington (1965–72). In 1972 he inaugurated a master class at the Tokyo Univ. of Fine Arts and Music. Returning to the U.S., he taught at Brigham Young Univ. in Provo, Utah (1979–82). Primrose was greatly esteemed as a viola virtuoso; he gave 1st performances of viola concertos by several modern composers. He commissioned a viola concerto from Béla Bartók, but the work was left unfinished at the time of Bartók's death, and the task of reconstructing the score from Bartók's sketches remained to be accomplished by Bartók's friend and associate Tibor Serly; Primrose gave its 1st performance with the Minneapolis Sym. Orch. on Dec. 2, 1949. He publ. *A Method for Violin and Viola Players* (London, 1960), *Technique in Memory* (1963), and an autobiography, *Walk on the North Side* (1978); also ed. various works for viola, and made transcriptions for the instrument.

BIBL.: D. Dalton, *Playing the Viola: Conversations with W. P.* (Oxford, 1988).

Prince (in full, **Prince Roger Nelson**), provocative black American rock singer, instrumentalist, and songwriter; b. Minneapolis, June 7, 1958. His father led a jazz group called the Prince Roger Trio, and his mother sang with it. He took up piano, guitar, and drums in his youth; before graduating from high school, he formed a soul-rock band and soon learned to play a whole regiment of instruments and to write songs. When his group, renamed Champagne, proved less than a bubbling success, he made the trek to Los Angeles to conquer the recording industry. After producing the albums *For You* (1978) and *Prince* (1979), he found a lucrative and successful métier with his sexually explicit *Dirty Mind* (1980). This sizzling tour de force featured such songs as *Head*, a joyful tribute to oral sex, and *Sister*, a hymn to incest. His next album, *Controversy* (1981), faithfully lived up to its title by including the song *Private Joy*, a glorification of masturbation. Proclaiming himself His Royal Badness, he proceeded to attain ever higher orgasmic plateaus. His hit album *1999* (1982) was followed by the sensationally acclaimed film and sound-track album *Purple Rain* (1984), which won an Oscar for best original song score in 1985. One of its songs, *Darling Niki*, incited the formation of the P.M.R.C. (Parents' Music Resource Center) and its efforts to regulate album labeling. After producing the album *Parade* (1986), he starred in the films *Sign o' the Times* (1987) and *Graffiti Bridge* (1990). His album *Lovesexy* (1988), which says it all, comes with a nude photo.
    BIBL.: *Current Biography* (Feb. 1986).

Pringsheim, Klaus, German conductor and composer; b. Feldafing, near Munich, July 24, 1883; d. Tokyo, Dec. 7, 1972. A scion of a highly cultured family, he studied mathematics with his father, a prof. at Munich Univ., and physics with Röntgen, the discoverer of X-rays. His twin sister, Katherine, was married to Thomas Mann. In Munich, Pringsheim took piano lessons with Bernhard Stavenhagen and composition with Ludwig Thuille. In 1906 he went to Vienna and was engaged as assistant conductor of the Court Opera, under the tutelage of Gustav Mahler, who took him as a pupil in conducting and composition, a relationship that developed into profound friendship. Mahler recommended him to the management of the German Opera in Prague; Pringsheim conducted there from 1909 to 1914; then was engaged as conductor and stage director at the Bremen Opera (1915–18) and music director of the Max Reinhardt theaters in Berlin (1918–25). In 1923–24 he conducted in Berlin a Mahler cycle of 8 concerts, featuring all of Mahler's syms. and songs with orch. In 1927 he became the music critic of the socialist newspaper *Vorwärts*. A turning point in Pringsheim's life came in 1931 with an invitation to teach music at the Imperial Academy of Music in Tokyo, where he taught until 1937; several of his Japanese students became prominent composers. From 1937 to 1939 Pringsheim served as music adviser to the Royal Dept. of Fine Arts in Bangkok, Thailand. In 1939 he returned to Japan; was briefly interned in 1944 as an opponent of the Axis policies. In 1946 he went to California; after some intermittent activities, he returned to Japan in 1951; was appointed director of the Musashino Academy of Music in Tokyo; continued to conduct; also wrote music reviews for English-language Tokyo newspapers. As a composer, Pringsheim followed the neo-Romantic trends, deeply influenced by Mahler. His compositions include a Concerto for Orch. (Tokyo, Oct. 13, 1935); Japanese radio opera, *Yamada Nagasama* (1953); Concertino for Xylophone and Orch. (1962); *Theme, Variations, and Fugue* for Wind Orch. (his last composition, 1971–72); and a curious album of 36 2-part canons for Piano (1959). A chapter from his theoretical work *Pythagoras, die Atonalität und wir* was publ. in *Schweizerische Musikzeitung* (1957). His reminiscences, "Mahler, My Friend," were publ. posthumously in the periodical *Composer* (1973–74). Pringsheim was a signatory of a letter of protest by surviving friends of Mahler against the motion picture *Death in Venice*, after a novelette of Thomas Mann, in which the central character, a famous writer who suffers a homosexual crisis, was made to resemble Mahler.

Printz, Wolfgang Caspar, significant German music theorist and historian; b. Waldthurn, Upper Palatinate, Oct. 10, 1641; d. Sorau, Lower Lusatia, Oct. 13, 1717. He studied in Waldthurn and at the Vohenstrauss Lateinschule, where he received instruction in music from Kilian Hammer; acquired proficiency in violin and keyboard playing; after further studies in Weiden (1654–59), he became a theological student at the Univ. of Altdorf; also continued musical training. He became a Lutheran minister in 1661, but soon turned decisively to music and served as a tenor at the Heidelberg court chapel; then entered the service of a Dutch nobleman, whom he accompanied to Italy; there he devoted himself to the study of music theory. Returning to Germany, he served as court composer and music director to Count Leopold of Promnitz in Sorau until 1664; then was Kantor in Triebel (1664–65) before taking up that position in Sorau (1665); was also made music director to Count Balthasar Erdmann of Promnitz (1682). Printz's writings on music theory and history provide a valuable source for the study of 17th-century music; they greatly influenced Mattheson and Walther. He was also a composer, but his large output seems to be entirely lost. His valuable music library was destroyed in the devastating Sorau fire of 1684.
    WRITINGS: *Compendium musicae in quo . . . explicantur . . . omnia ea quae ad Oden artificiose componendam requiruntur* (Guben, 1668); *Anweisung zur Singe-Kunst oder Kurtzer Bericht wie man einen Knaben . . . könne singen lehren* (Guben, 1672); *Phrynis Mitilenaeus, oder Satyrischer Componist* (3 vols., Quedlinburg, 1676–79); *Musica modulatoria vocalis oder Manierliche und zierliche Sing-Kunst* (Schweidnitz, 1678); *Declaration oder Weitere Erklärung der Refutation des Satyrischen Componistens* (1679); *Compendium musicae signatoriae et modulatoriae vocalis, das ist Kurtzer Begriff aller derjenigen Sachen, so einem, der die Vocal-Music lernen will, zu wissen von nöthen seyn* (Dresden, 1689; 2nd ed., 1714); *Exercitationes musicae theoretico-practicae curiosae de concordantiis singulis, das ist Musicalische Wissenschaft und Kunst-Übungen* (8 parts, Dresden, 1687–89); *Historische Beschreibung der edelen Sing- und Kling-Kunst* (Dresden, 1690).
    BIBL.: E. Schmitz, "Studien über W.C. P. als Musikschriftsteller," *Monatshefte für Musikgeschichte*, XXXVI (1904); H. Heckmann, *W.C. P. und seine Rhythmuslehre* (diss., Univ. of Freiburg, 1952).

Pritchard, Sir John (Michael), distinguished English conductor; b. London, Feb. 5, 1921; d. Daly City, Calif., Dec. 5, 1989. He studied violin with his father, and then continued his musical training in Italy, returning to England to service in the British army during World War II. In 1947 he joined the staff of the Glyndebourne Festival Opera as a répétiteur; became chorus master and assistant to Fritz Busch in 1948; conducted there regularly from 1951, serving as its music director (1969–77). He made his 1st appearance at London's Covent Garden in 1952. He was principal conductor of the Royal Liverpool Phil. (1957–63) and the London Phil. (1962–66), touring widely abroad with the latter. In 1963 he made his U.S. debut as a guest conductor with the Pittsburgh Sym. Orch.; also conducted at the Chicago Lyric Opera (1969) and the San Francisco Opera (1970). On Oct. 25, 1971, he made his Metropolitan Opera debut in N.Y. conducting *Così fan tutte*. As a guest conductor, he appeared with many of the world's leading opera houses and orchs. He was chief conductor of the Cologne Opera (1978–89). In 1979 he became chief guest conductor of the BBC Sym. Orch. in London, and subsequently was made its chief conductor in 1982. He was also joint music director of the Opéra National in Brussels (1981–89), and served as the 1st music director of the San Francisco Opera (1986–89). In 1962 he was made a Commander of the Order of the British Empire, and was knighted in 1983. Pritchard was esteemed for his unpretentious but assured command of a vast operatic and symphonic repertory, extending from the Baroque masters to the leading composers of the present era.

Proch, Heinrich, Austrian conductor and composer; b. Böhmisch-Leipa, July 22, 1809; d. Vienna, Dec. 18, 1878. He studied law and at the same time took violin lessons; became conductor of the Josephstadt Theater in Vienna in 1837; from 1840 to 1870, conducted at the Vienna Court Opera. He wrote many songs that were popular for a time; his set of variations for coloratura soprano, with flute obbligato, was particularly well known; he also brought out in Vienna a comic opera, *Ring und Maske* (Dec. 4, 1844), and 3 1-act operas: *Die Blutrache* (Dec. 5, 1846); *Zweiter und dritter Stock* (Oct. 5, 1847); *Der gefährliche Sprung* (Jan. 5, 1849).

Procházka, Rudolf von, Bohemian writer on music and composer; b. Prague, Feb. 23, 1864; d. there, March 24, 1936. He studied violin with Wittich and composition with Fibich; wrote an allegorical opera, *Das Glück* (Prague, 1898); some orch. pieces; *Deutsch-böhmische Reigen* for Piano, 4-hands; solo piano pieces; many choruses and songs. He then devoted himself mainly to music education; in 1911 he organized a commission for the licensing of music teachers in Bohemia. He publ. *Dei böhmischen Musikschulen* (1890); *Mozart in Prag* (1892; rev. and augmented ed. by P. Nettl as *Mozart in Böhmen,* 1938); *Robert Franz* (1894); *Arpeggien: Musikalisches aus alten und neuen Tagen* (1897; 2nd ed. as *Musikalische Streiflichter,* 1901); *Johann Strauss* (1900; 2nd ed., 1903); *Das romantische Musik-Prag* (1914); *Der Kammermusikverein in Prag* (1926). **Bibl.:** C. Hunnius, *R. v.P., Ein deutscher Tondichter Böhmens* (Leipzig, 1902); E. Janetschek, "R. v.P.," *Neue Zeitschrift für Musik* (Dec. 1915).

Procter, Alice McElroy, American pianist; b. Albany, N.Y., April 18, 1915; d. Newton, Mass., Dec. 20, 1987. She studied composition at Smith College and at the Eastman School of Music in Rochester, N.Y., where she received her Ph.D. Subsequently, she taught piano in Boston and its environs. She publ. some ingratiating teaching pieces for piano, among them *Jumping Cat* and *Footsteps in the Night.* She was the wife of the composer **Leland Procter.**

Procter, Leland, American composer and teacher; b. Newton, Mass., March 24, 1914. He studied composition at the Eastman School of Music in Rochester, N.Y., with Howard Hanson and Bernard Rogers, and later at the Univ. of Oklahoma. Returning to Boston, he taught at the New England Cons. of Music. He publ. some teaching pieces for piano, and wrote symphonic works. He was the husband of the pianist **Alice McElroy Procter.**

Procter, (Mary) Norma, English contralto; b. Cleethorpes, Feb. 15, 1928. She studied voice with Roy Henderson and Alec Redshaw; made her debut in Handel's *Messiah* at Southwark Cathedral in 1948; soon established herself as an outstanding concert singer; in 1961 she made her operatic debut at London's Covent Garden as Gluck's Orpheus.

Prod'homme, J(acques)-G(abriel), industrious French librarian and music critic; b. Paris, Nov. 28, 1871; d. Neuilly-sur-Seine, near Paris, June 18, 1956. He studied philology and music history at the Paris École des Hautes Études Sociales (1890–94); then became a writer on musical and other subjects in the socialist publications, among them *La Revue Socialiste, Droits de l'Homme,* and *Messidor.* An ardent believer in the cause of peace, he ed. in Munich the *Deutsch-französische Rundschau,* dedicated to the friendship between the French and German peoples (1899–1902). His hopes for peace were shattered by 2 devastating world wars within his lifetime. Back in Paris, he founded, with Dauriac and Écorcheville, the French section of the IMS (1902), serving as its secretary (1903–13); with La Laurencie, he founded the French Musicological Society (1917), serving as its secretary (1917–20) and vice-president (1929–36); was curator of the library and archivist of the museum at the Paris Opéra (1931–40); was also librarian at the Paris Cons. (1934–40); was made a Chevalier of the Légion d'honneur (1928). With others, he tr. Wagner's prose works (13 vols., 1907–25); also Wagner's music dramas (1922–27) and Beethoven's conversation books (1946).

Writings: All pub. in Paris: *Le Cycle Berlioz,* in 2 vols.: *La Damnation de Faust* (1896) and *L'Enfance du Christ* (1899); with C. Bertrand, *Guides analytiques de l'Anneau du Nibelung. Crépuscule des dieux* (1902); *Hector Berlioz 1803–1869: Sa vie et ses œuvres* (1905; 2nd ed., rev., 1913); *Les Symphonies de Beethoven (1800–1827)* (1906; 15th ed., 1938); *Paganini* (1907; 2nd ed., 1927; Eng. tr., 1911); *Franz Liszt* (1910); with A. Dandelot, *Gounod 1818–93: Sa vie et ses œuvres d'après des documents inédits* (2 vols., 1911); *Ecrits de musiciens (XVe-XVIIIe siècles)* (1912); *Richard Wagner et la France* (1921); *La jeunesse de Beethoven, 1770–1800* (1921; 2nd ed., 1927); *L'Opéra, 1669–1925* (1925); *Pensées sur la musique et les musiciens* (1926); *Beethoven raconté par ceux qui l'ont vu* (1927); *Mozart raconté par ceux qui l'ont vu 1756–1791* (1928); *Schubert raconté par ceux qui l'ont vu* (1928); with E. Crauzat, *Paris qui disparaît: Les Menus plaisirs du roi; L'Ecole royale et le Conservatoire de Paris* (1929); *Wagner raconté par ceux qui l'ont vu* (1929); *Les Sonates pour piano de Beethoven, 1782–1823* (1937; 2nd ed., rev., 1950); *L'Immortelle bien-aimée de Beethoven* (1946); *Gluck* (1948); *François-Joseph Gossec, 1734–1829* (1949).

Profe, Ambrosius, German organist, music editor, and composer; b. Breslau, Feb. 12, 1589; d. there, Dec. 27, 1661. He studied theology at Wittenburg; then was Kantor and schoolmaster in Jauer, Silesia (1617–29); from 1633 to 1649 he was a church organist in Breslau. He ed. important collections of German sacred music: *Geistliche Concerte und Harmonien* for 1 to 7 Voices (4 vols., 1641–46); *Corollarium geistlicher Collectaneorum* (a supplement to the previous vol.; 1649); a collection of Christmas pieces, *Cunis solennibus Jesuli recens-nati sacra genethliaca* (1646); also brought out Heinrich Albert's *Arien* (1657).

Profeta, Laurenţiu, Rumanian composer; b. Bucharest, Jan. 12, 1925. He studied with P. Constantinescu, A. Mendelsohn, and Chirescu at the Bucharest Cons. (1945–49); later took courses at the Moscow Cons. (1954–56). He served as director of music for the Ministry of Culture (1952–60) and secretary of the Rumanian National Committee of the International Music Council (1960–70). His music is marked by rhapsodic expansiveness in Romantically rich harmonies.

Works: STAGE: *BALLETS: Soţia căpitanului* (The Captain's Wife; 1946); *Prinţ şi cerşetor* (The Prince and the Beggar; 1963–66); *Marinarul visător* (The Dreaming Sailor; 1972). *COMIC OPERA: Povestea micului Pan* (1983; Bucharest, Oct. 30, 1984). **VOCAL:** *Cîntece de tabără* (Songs of Bivouac), suite for Soloists, Children's Chorus, and Orch. (1957); *Intîmplarea din grădină* (The Adventures of the Gardener), oratorio (1958); *Cantata patriei* (Cantata of the Fatherland) for Narrator, Mezzo-soprano, Chorus, and Orch. (1959); *Brăduţul singuratic* (The Singular Spruce Tree), musical tale (1960); *6 Humorous Pieces* for Children Soloists, Children's Chorus, and Orch. (1966); *Madrigal '75,* cantata for Voices and Chamber Orch. (1975); choruses; songs. **ORCH.:** *Suite for Marionettes* for Chamber Orch. (1951); *Poemul patriei* (1952); *Zile de vacanţă* (Vacation Days), symphonic suite (1956); also *Carnival* for 2 Pianos (1957); film music.

Prohaska, Carl, Austrian composer, father of **Felix Prohaska;** b. Mödling, near Vienna, April 25, 1869; d. Vienna, March 28, 1927. He studied piano with Anna Assmayr in Vienna and with Eugen d'Albert in Berlin; composition with Franz Krenn and musicology with Mandyczewski in Vienna. In 1908 he joined the faculty of the Vienna Academy of Music, where he taught piano and theory. He wrote an opera, *Madeleine Guinard;* an oratorio, *Frühlingsfeier* (1913); String Quartet; Piano Trio; Quintet for 2 Violins, Viola, Cello, and Double Bass; a group of piano pieces.

Prohaska, Felix, Austrian conductor, son of **Carl Prohaska;** b. Vienna, May 16, 1912; d. there, March 29, 1987. He received his primary music education at home with his father; then studied piano with Steuermann, and theory with Kornauth, Gál, and others. He served as répétiteur at the Graz Opera

(1936–39); conducted opera in Duisburg (1939–41) and in Strasbourg (1941–43); then was 1st conductor of the Vienna State Opera (1945–55) and the Frankfurt Opera (1955–61); returned to Vienna (1964–67); conducted at the opera in Hannover (1965–74), and also served as director of the Hochschule für Musik there (1961–75).

Prohaska, Jaro(slav), Austrian bass-baritone; b. Vienna, Jan. 24, 1891; d. Munich, Sept. 28, 1965. He sang in the Wiener Sängerknaben; studied voice with Otto Müller in Vienna; made his operatic debut in Lübeck in 1922; then sang in Nuremberg (1925–31). In 1932 he joined the Berlin State Opera, remaining on its roster until 1953; also made many appearances at the Bayreuth Festivals (1933–44), where he excelled in such roles as Hans Sachs, Wotan, and the Dutchman. He was director of the West Berlin Hochschule für Musik (1947–59), where he also directed its opera school (1952–59).

Prokofiev (Prokofieff), Sergei (Sergeievich), great Russian composer of modern times, creator of new and original formulas of rhythmic, melodic, and harmonic combinations that became the recognized style of his music; b. Sontsovka, near Ekaterinoslav, April 27, 1891; d. Moscow, March 5, 1953. His mother was born a serf in 1859, 2 years before the emanciation of Russian serfdom, and she assumed (as was the custom) the name of the estate where she was born, Sontsov. Prokofiev was born on that estate on April 27, 1891, although he himself erroneously believed that the date was April 23; the correct date was established with the discovery of his birth certificate. He received his 1st piano lessons from his mother, who was an amateur pianist; he improvised several pieces, and then composed a children's opera, *The Giant* (1900), which was performed in a domestic version. Following his bent for the theater, he put together 2 other operas, *On Desert Islands* (1902) and *Ondine* (1904–7); fantastic subjects obviously possessed his childish imagination. He was 11 years old when he met the great Russian master, Taneyev, who arranged for him to take systematic private lessons with Reinhold Glière, who became his tutor at Sontsovka during the summers of 1903 and 1904 and by correspondence during the intervening winter. Under Glière's knowledgeable guidance in theory and harmony, Prokofiev composed a sym. in piano version and still another opera, *Plague,* based upon a poem by Pushkin. Finally, in 1904, at the age of 13, he enrolled in the St. Petersburg Cons., where he studied composition with Liadov and piano with Alexander Winkler; later he was accepted by no less a master than Rimsky-Korsakov, who instructed him in orchestration. He also studied conducting with Nikolai Tcherepnin, and form with Wihtol. Further, he entered the piano class of Anna Essipova. During the summers, he returned to Sontsovka or traveled in the Caucasus and continued to compose, already in quite an advanced style; the Moscow publisher Jurgenson accepted his 1st work, a piano sonata, for publication; it was premiered in Moscow on March 6, 1910. It was then that Prokofiev made his 1st visit to Paris, London, and Switzerland (1913); in 1914 he graduated from the St. Petersburg Cons., receiving the Anton Rubinstein Prize (a grand piano) as a pianist-composer with his Piano Concerto No. 1, which he performed publicly at the graduation concert. Because of audacious innovations in his piano music (he wrote one piece in which the right and left hands played in different keys), he was described in the press as a "futurist," and because of his addiction to dissonant and powerful harmonic combinations, some critics dismissed his works as "football music." This idiom was explicitly demonstrated in his *Sarcasms* and *Visions fugitives,* percussive and sharp, yet not lacking in lyric charm. Grotesquerie and irony animated his early works; he also developed a strong attraction toward subjects of primitive character. His important orch. work, the *Scythian Suite* (arr. from music written for a ballet, *Ala and Lolly,* 1915), draws upon a legend of ancient Russian sun-worship rituals. While a parallel with Stravinsky's *Le Sacre du printemps* may exist, there is no similarity between the styles of the 2 works. The original performance of the *Scythian Suite,* scheduled at a

Koussevitzky concert in Moscow, was canceled on account of the disruption caused by war, which did not prevent the otherwise intelligent Russian music critic Sabaneyev, blissfully unaware that the announced premiere had been canceled, from delivering a blast of the work as a farrago of atrocious noises. (Sabaneyev was forced to resign his position after this episode.) Another Prokofiev score, primitivistic in its inspiration, was the cantata *Seven, They Are Seven,* based upon incantations from an old Sumerian religious ritual. During the same period, Prokofiev wrote his famous *Classical Symphony* (1916–17), in which he adopted with remarkable acuity the formal style of Haydn's music. While the structure of the work was indeed classical, the sudden modulatory shifts and subtle elements of grotesquerie revealed decisively a new modern art.

After conducting the premiere of his *Classical Symphony* in Petrograd on April 21, 1918, Prokofiev left Russia by way of Siberia and Japan for the U.S. (the continuing war in Europe prevented him from traveling westward). He gave concerts of his music in Japan and later in the U.S., playing his 1st solo concert in N.Y. on Oct. 29, 1918. Some American critics greeted his appearance as the reflection of the chaotic events of Russia in revolution, and Prokofiev himself was described as a "ribald and Bolshevist innovator and musical agitator." "Every rule in the realm of traditional music writing was broken by Prokofiev," one N.Y. writer complained. "Dissonance followed dissonance in a fashion inconceivable to ears accustomed to melody and harmonic laws." Prokofiev's genteel *Classical Symphony* struck some critics as "an orgy of dissonant sound, an exposition of the unhappy state of chaos from which Russia suffers." A N.Y. critic indulged in the following: "Crashing Siberians, volcano hell, Krakatoa, sea-bottom crawlers. Incomprehensible? So is Prokofiev." But another critic issued a word of caution, suggesting that "Prokofiev might be the legitimate successor of Borodin, Mussorgsky, and Rimsky-Korsakov." The critic was unintentionally right; Prokofiev is firmly enthroned in the pantheon of Russian music.

In 1920 Prokofiev settled in Paris, where he established an association with Diaghilev's Ballets Russes, which produced his ballets *Chout* (a French transliteration of the Russian word for buffoon), *Le Pas d'acier* (descriptive of the industrial development in Soviet Russia), and *L'Enfant prodigue.* In 1921 Prokofiev again visited the U.S. for the production of the opera commissioned by the Chicago Opera Co., *The Love of Three Oranges.* In 1927 he was invited to be the pianist for a series of his own works in Russia. He gave a number of concerts in Russia again in 1929, and eventually decided to remain there. In Russia he wrote some of his most popular works, including the symphonic fairy tale *Peter and the Wolf,* staged by a children's theater in Moscow, the historical cantata *Alexander Nevsky,* the ballet *Romeo and Juliet,* and the opera *War and Peace.*

Unexpectedly, Prokofiev became the target of the so-called proletarian group of Soviet musicians who accused him of decadence, a major sin in Soviet Russia at the time. His name was included in the official denunciation of modern Soviet composers issued by reactionary Soviet politicians. He meekly confessed that he had been occasionally interested in atonal and polytonal devices during his stay in Paris, but insisted that he had never abandoned the ideals of classical Russian music. Indeed, when he composed his 7th Sym., he described it specifically as a youth sym., reflecting the energy and ideals of new Russia. There were also significant changes in his personal life. He separated from his Spanish-born wife, the singer Lina Llubera, the mother of his 2 sons, and established a companionship with Myra Mendelson, a member of the Young Communist League. She was a writer and assisted him on the libretto of *War and Peace.* He made one final attempt to gain favor with the Soviet establishment by writing an opera based on a heroic exploit of a Soviet pilot during the war against the Nazis. But this, too, was damned by the servile Communist press as lacking in true patriotic spirit, and the opera was quickly removed from the repertory. Prokofiev died suddenly of heart failure on March 5, 1953, a few hours before the death of Stalin. Curiously enough, the anniversary of Proko-fiev's death is duly commemorated, while that of his once powerful nemesis is officially allowed to be forgotten.

WORKS: OPERAS: *Maddalena* (1912–13, piano score only; orchestrated by Edward Downes, 1978; BBC Radio, March 25, 1979; 1st stage perf., Graz, Nov. 28, 1981; U.S. premiere, St. Louis, June 9, 1982); *The Gambler,* after Dostoyevsky (1915–16; rev. 1927; Brussels, April 29, 1929); *Love for 3 Oranges,* after Gozzi (Chicago, Dec. 30, 1921); *The Fiery Angel* (1919; 2 fragments perf., Paris, June 14, 1928; 1st complete concert perf., Paris, Nov. 25, 1954; 1st stage perf., Venice, Sept. 14, 1955); *Semyon Kotko* (1939; Moscow, June 23, 1940); *Betrothal in a Convent,* after Sheridan's *Duenna* (1940; Leningrad, Nov. 3, 1946); *War and Peace,* after Tolstoy (1941–52; concert perf. of 8 of the original 11 scenes, Ensemble of Soviet Opera of the All-Union Theatrical Society, Oct. 16, 1944; concert perf. of 9 of the original 11 scenes with scenes 6 and 8 omitted, Moscow Phil., June 7, 1945; stage perf. of Part I [*Peace*] with new Scene 2, Maly Theater, Leningrad, June 12, 1946; "final" version of 11 scenes, Prague, June 25, 1948; another "complete" version, Leningrad, March 31, 1955; rev. version in 13 scenes with cuts, Moscow, Nov. 8, 1957; 13 scenes with a choral epigraph, Moscow, Dec. 15, 1959); *A Tale about a Real Man* (1947–48; private perf., Leningrad, Dec. 3, 1948; severely censured by Soviet critics and not produced in public until given at the Bolshoi Theater, Moscow, Oct. 8, 1960).

BALLETS: *Buffoon* (1920; Paris, May 17, 1921); *Trapeze* (1924; music used in his Quintet); *Le Pas d'acier* (1924; Paris, June 7, 1927); *L'Enfant prodigue* (1928; Paris, May 21, 1929); *Sur le Borysthène* (1930; Paris, Dec. 16, 1932); *Romeo and Juliet* (1935–36; Brno, Dec. 30, 1938); *Cinderella* (1940–44; Moscow, Nov. 21, 1945); *A Tale of the Stone Flower* (1948–50; Moscow, Feb. 12, 1954).

INCIDENTAL MUSIC TO: *Egyptian Nights* (1933); *Boris Godunov* (1936); *Eugene Onegin* (1936); *Hamlet* (1937–38; Leningrad, May 15, 1938). **FILM MUSIC:** *Lt. Kijé* (1933); *The Queen of Spades* (1936); *Alexander Nevsky* (1938); *Lermontov* (1941); *Tonya* (1942); *Kotovsky* (1942); *Partisans in the Ukrainian Steppes* (1942); *Ivan the Terrible* (1942–45).

CHORAL: 2 poems for Women's Chorus, with Orch: *The White Swan* and *The Wave* (1909); *Seven, They Are Seven,* Cantata for Tenor, Chorus, and Orch. (1917–18; Paris, May 29, 1924); Cantata for the 20th anniversary of the October Revolution, for 2 Choruses, Military Band, Accordions, and Percussion, to texts by Marx, Lenin, and Stalin (1937; perf. in Moscow, April 5, 1966, but not in its entirety; the section which used a text from Stalin was eliminated); *Songs of Our Days,* op. 76, suite for Solo Voices, Mixed Chorus, and Orch. (Moscow, Jan. 5, 1938); *Alexander Nevsky,* cantata for Mezzo-soprano, Mixed Chorus, and Orch. (Moscow, May 17, 1939); *Zdravitsa: Hail to Stalin,* cantata for Mixed Chorus and Orch. for Stalin's 60th birthday (Moscow, Dec. 21, 1939); *Ballad of an Unknown Boy,* cantata for Soprano, Tenor, Chorus, and Orch. (Moscow, Feb. 21, 1944); *Hymn to the Soviet Union* (1943; submitted to the competition for a new Soviet anthem but failed to win; a song by Alexander Alexandrov was selected); *Flourish, Powerful Land,* cantata for the 30th anniversary of the October Revolution (Moscow, Nov. 12, 1947); *Winter Bonfire,* suite for Narrators, Boys' Chorus, and Orch. (Moscow, Dec. 19, 1950); *On Guard for Peace,* oratorio for Mezzo-soprano, Narrators, Mixed Chorus, Boys' Chorus, and Orch. (Moscow, Dec. 19, 1950).

ORCH.: Sinfonietta (1914; Petrograd, Nov. 6, 1915; rev. 1929; Moscow, Nov. 18, 1930); *Rêves,* symphonic tableau (St. Petersburg, Dec. 5, 1910); *Autumn,* symphonic tableau (Moscow, Aug. 1, 1911); 1st Piano Concerto (Moscow, Aug. 7, 1912, composer, soloist); 2nd Piano Concerto (Pavlovsk, Sept. 5, 1913, composer, soloist; 2nd version, Paris, May 8, 1924, composer, soloist); 1st Violin Concerto (1916–17; Paris, Oct. 18, 1923); *Scythian Suite* (1914; Petrograd, Jan. 29, 1916); *Chout,* suite from the ballet (Brussels, Jan. 15, 1924); *Classical Symphony* (1916–17; Petrograd, April 21, 1918, composer conducting); 3rd Piano Concerto (1917–21; Chicago, Dec. 16,

1921, composer, soloist); *Love for 3 Oranges,* suite from the opera (Paris, Nov. 29, 1925); Sym. No. 2 (1924; Paris, June 6, 1925; 2nd version, not completed); *Le Pas d'acier,* suite from the ballet (1926; Moscow, May 27, 1928); Overture: *American* for Chamber Orch. (Moscow, Feb. 7, 1927; also for Large Orch., 1928; Paris, Dec. 18, 1930); *Divertissement* (1925–29; Paris, Dec. 22, 1929); Sym. No. 3 (1928; Paris, May 17, 1929); *L'Enfant prodigue,* suite from the ballet (1929; Paris, March 7, 1931); Sym. No. 4 (Boston, Nov. 14, 1930; a new version, radically rev., 1947); *4 Portraits,* suite from the opera *The Gambler* (1931; Paris, March 12, 1932); *On the Dnieper,* suite from the ballet (1933); 4th Piano Concerto, for Left Hand Alone (1931; Berlin, Sept. 5, 1956); 5th Piano Concerto (Berlin, Oct. 31, 1932, composer, soloist); *Symphonic Song* (Moscow, April 14, 1934); 1st Cello Concerto (1933–38; Moscow, Nov. 26, 1938, Lev Berezovsky, soloist; rev. and perf. as Cello Concerto No. 2, Moscow, Feb. 18, 1952, M. Rostropovich, soloist; rev. and retitled *Sinfonia Concertante,* Copenhagen, Dec. 9, 1954, Rostropovich, soloist); *Lt. Kijé,* suite from the film music (1934; Paris, Feb. 20, 1937); *Egyptian Nights,* suite (Radio Moscow, Dec. 21, 1934); 2nd Violin Concerto (Madrid, Dec. 1, 1935); *Romeo and Juliet,* 1st suite from the ballet (Moscow, Nov. 24, 1936); *Romeo and Juliet,* 2nd suite from the ballet (Leningrad, April 15, 1937); *Peter and the Wolf,* symphonic fairy tale (Moscow, May 2, 1936); *Semyon Kotko,* suite from the opera (1940); *A Summer Day,* children's suite for Chamber Orch. (1941); *Symphonic March* (1941); *The Year 1941* (1941; Sverdlovsk, Jan. 21, 1943); *March* for Military Orch. (Moscow, April 30, 1944); Sym. No. 5 (1944; Moscow, Jan. 13, 1945); *Romeo and Juliet,* 3rd suite from the ballet (Moscow, March 8, 1946); *Ode on the End of the War* for 8 Harps, 4 Pianos, Military Band, Percussion Ensemble, and Double Basses (1945; Moscow, Nov. 12, 1945); *Cinderella,* 3 suites from the ballet (1946: No. 1, Moscow, Nov. 12, 1946; No. 3, Radio Moscow, Sept. 3, 1947); *Waltzes,* suite (1946; Moscow, May 13, 1947); Sym. No. 6 (1945–47; Leningrad, Oct. 11, 1947); *Festive Poem* (Moscow, Oct. 3, 1947); *Ivan the Terrible,* suite (1942–45); *Pushkin Waltzes* (1949); *Summer Night,* suite on themes from the opera *Betrothal in a Convent* (1950); *Wedding Scene,* suite from the ballet *A Tale of the Stone Flower* (Moscow, Dec. 12, 1951); *Gypsy Fantasy,* from the ballet *A Tale of the Stone Flower* (Moscow, Nov. 18, 1951); *Ural Rhapsody,* from the ballet *A Tale of the Stone Flower* (1951); *The Mistress of the Copper Mountain,* suite from the ballet *A Tale of the Stone Flower* (incomplete); *The Meeting of the Volga with the Don River* (for the completion of the Volga-Don Canal; 1951; Moscow, Feb. 22, 1952); Sym. No. 7 (1951–52; Moscow, Oct. 11, 1952); Concertino for Cello and Orch. (1952; completed by M. Rostropovich and D. Kabalevsky); Concerto for 2 Pianos and String Orch. (1952; incomplete).

CHAMBER: *Humorous Scherzo* for 4 Bassoons (1912; London, Sept. 2, 1916); *Ballade* for Cello and Piano (1912; Moscow, Feb. 5, 1914); *Overture on Hebrew Themes* for Clarinet, 2 Violins, Viola, Cello, and Piano (N.Y., Jan. 26, 1920); Quintet for Oboe, Clarinet, Violin, Viola, and Double Bass (1924; Moscow, March 6, 1927); 1st String Quartet (Washington, D.C., April 25, 1931); Sonata for 2 Violins (Moscow, Nov. 27, 1932); 1st Violin Sonata (1938–46; BBC, London, Aug. 25, 1946); 2nd String Quartet (1941; Moscow, Sept. 5, 1942); Sonata for Flute and Piano (Moscow, Dec. 7, 1943); 2nd Violin Sonata (transcription of the Flute Sonata; Moscow, June 17, 1944); Sonata for Solo Violin (1947; Moscow, March 10, 1960); Cello Sonata (1949; Moscow, March 1, 1950).

PIANO: 9 sonatas: No. 1 (1909); No. 2 (1912); No. 3 (1917); No. 4 (1917); No. 5 (1923); No. 6 (1940); No. 7 (1942); No. 8 (1944); No. 9 (1947); No. 10 (1953; unfinished); 2 sonatinas (1931–32); 4 Etudes (1909); 4 Pieces (1911); 4 Pieces (1912); Toccata (1912); 10 Pieces (1913); *Sarcasms,* suite of 5 pieces (1912–14); *Visions fugitives,* suite of 20 pieces (1915–17); *Tales of an Old Grandmother,* 4 pieces (1918); *Schubert's Waltzes,* transcribed for 2 Pianos (1911); March and Scherzo from the opera *Love for 3 Oranges* (1922); *Things in Themselves* (1928); 6 Pieces (1930–31); 3 Pieces (1934); *Pensées* (1933–34); *Chil-*

dren's Music, 12 easy pieces (1935); *Romeo and Juliet,* 10 pieces from the ballet (1937); 3 pieces from the ballet *Cinderella* (1942); 3 Pieces (1941–42); 10 pieces from the ballet *Cinderella* (1943); 6 pieces from the ballet *Cinderella* (1944).

SONGS: 2 *Poems* (1911); *The Ugly Duckling,* after Andersen (1914); 5 *Poems* (1915); 5 *Poems* (1916); 5 *Songs without Words* (1920; also for Violin and Piano); 5 *Poems* (1921); 6 *Poems* (1935); 3 *Children's Songs* (1936); 3 *Poems* (1936); 3 songs from the film *Alexander Nevsky* (1939); 7 *Songs* (1939); 7 *Mass Songs* (1941–42); 12 transcriptions of folk songs (1944); 2 duets (1945); *Soldiers' March Song* (1950).

BIBL.: M. Montagu-Nathan, "S. P.," *Musical Times* (Oct. 1916); idem, "P.'s First Pianoforte Concerto," ibid. (Jan. 1917); idem, *Contemporary Russian Composers* (N.Y., 1917); L. Sabaneyev, *Modern Russian Composers* (N.Y., 1927); N. Slonimsky, "S. P.," *Quarterly on the Soviet Union* (N.Y., April 1939); G. Abraham, *8 Soviet Composers* (London, 1943); N. Nabokov, "S. P.," *Atlantic Monthly* (July 1943); S. Prokofiev, "The War Years," *Musical Quarterly* (Oct. 1944); I. Nestyev, *S. P.* (Moscow, 1946; in Eng., N.Y., 1946; enl. Russian ed., Moscow, 1957; in Eng. with a foreword by N. Slonimsky, Stanford, Calif., 1961); R. Moisenko, *Realist Music: 25 Soviet Composers* (London, 1949); special issue of *Tempo,* no. 20 (1949); N. Nabokov, *Old Friends and New Music* (Boston, 1951); S. Schlifstein, ed., *S. P., Materials, Documents, Reminiscences* (Moscow, 1956; of prime documentary value; contains P.'s autobiography and a complete catalogue of P.'s works, with exhaustive commentaries and dates); M. Sabinina, *S. P.* (Moscow, 1958); I. Gakkel, *Piano Works of S. P.* (Moscow, 1960); C. Samuel, *P.* (Paris, 1960; Eng. tr., 1971); F. Streller, *P.* (Leipzig, 1960); L. Berger, ed., *Traits of P.'s Style* (Moscow, 1962); I. Nestyev and G. Edelman, eds., *S. P., Articles and Materials* (Moscow, 1962); A. Porter, "P.'s Early Operas," *Musical Times,* 103 (1962); idem, "P.'s Late Operas," ibid., 108 (1962); L. Danko, *The Operas of S. P.* (Moscow, 1963); M. Hofmann, *P.* (Paris, 1963); H. Brockhaus, *S. P.* (Leipzig, 1964); L. and E. Hanson, *P., The Prodigal Son* (London, 1964); S. Slonimsky, *The Symphonies of P.* (Leningrad, 1964); M. Rayment, *P.* (London, 1965); S. Schlifstein, ed., *P.* (album of pictures annotated in Russian and Eng.; Moscow, 1965); L. Danko, *S.S. P.* (Moscow, 1966); M. Brown, *The Symphonies of P.* (diss., Florida State Univ., 1967); S. Morozov, *P.* (Moscow, 1967); V. Serov, *S. P., A Soviet Tragedy* (N.Y., 1968); R. McAllister, *The Operas of S. P.* (diss., Cambridge Univ., 1970); V. Blok, *Cello Works by P.* (Moscow, 1973); I. Martynov, *P.* (Moscow, 1974); S. Prokofiev and N. Miaskovsky, *Correspondence* (Moscow, 1973); M. Brown, "P.'s *War and Peace,*" *Musical Quarterly* (July 1977); D. Appel, ed., and G. Daniels, tr., *P. by P.: A Composer's Memoir* (Garden City, N.Y., 1979); C. Bennett, "P. and Eugene Onegin," *Musical Times* (April 1980); V. Blok, ed., *S. P.: Materials, Articles, Interviews* (London, 1980); H. Robinson, *The Operas of S. P. and Their Russian Literary Sources* (diss., Univ. of Calif., Berkeley, 1980); M. Nesteyeva, *S.S. P.* (Moscow, 1981); N. Savkina, *S. P.* (Moscow, 1982; Eng. tr., Neptune City, N.J., 1984); H. Robinson, "Dostoevsky and Opera: P.'s The Gambler," *Musical Quarterly* (Winter 1984); D. Gutman, *P.* (London, 1988); R. Taruskin, "Tone, Style, and Form in P.'s Soviet Operas: Some Preliminary Observations," *Studies in the History of Music* (Vol. 2, N.Y., 1988); B. Nissman, "P.'s Two Versions of His Fifth Piano Sonata: Facsimile and Commentary," *Musical Times* (Oct. 1989).

Proksch, Josef, Bohemian pianist, pedagogue, and composer; b. Reichenberg, Aug. 4, 1794; d. Prague, Dec. 20, 1864. He studied with Koželuch; in 1811 he lost his eyesight, but still learned Logier's system, and in 1830 founded a "Musikbildungsanstalt" (school of piano playing) in Prague. He publ. a useful piano manual, *Versuch einer rationellen Lehrmethode im Pianofortespiel;* also *Musikalisches Vademecum; Aphorismen über katholische Kirchenmusik; Allgemeine Musiklehre;* made for his pupils transcriptions, for 2, 3, 4, and even 8 pianos, of orch. works; composed a Concerto for 3 Pianos, sonatas, and other works; also vocal music. His son, **Theodor Proksch**

(1843–76), and a daughter, **Marie Proksch** (1836–1900), managed the school after his death; the last director of the Proksch school was **Robert Franz Proksch,** a great-grand-nephew of Josef Proksch; he died in 1933.

BIBL.: R. Müller, *J. P.* (Prague, 1874); H. Kraus, *Musikbibliothek J. P.* (Vienna, 1934).

Prony, Gaspard-Claire-François-Marie-Riche, Baron de, French harpist and music theorist; b. Chamelot, Rhône, July 12, 1755; d. Paris, July 29, 1839. As a member of the Académie, he was in charge of educational information; he publ. a report on Erard's double-pedal harp, *Rapport sur la nouvelle harpe à double mouvement* (1815); other reports are: *Note sur les avantages du nouvel établissement d'un professorat d'harpe à l'école royale de musique* (1825); *Instruction élémentaire sur les moyens de calculer les intervalles musicaux* (1832; employing Euler's system of logarithms).

Prošev, Toma, Yugoslav composer; b. Skopje, Nov. 10, 1931. He studied with Škerjanc at the Ljubljana Academy of Music, graduating in composition in 1960; then made a musical pilgrimage to Nadia Boulanger in Paris (1964); thus musically replenished, he returned to Zagreb and devoted himself to teaching. His music is moderately modern.

WORKS: DRAMATIC: OPERAS: *Paučina* (The Cobweb; 1957); *Mali princ* (The Little Prince; 1966). BALLETS: *Okviri i odjeci* (Frames and Echoes; 1961); *Pesma nad pesmama* (Song of Songs; 1967). ORATORIOS: *Jama* (The Pit; 1961); *Skopje* (1965); *Sunce prastare zemlje* (Sun of the Ancient Country; 1967). ORCH.: Piano Concertino (1958); *Makete* (Dummies) (1960); *Concertante Music* for Cello and String Orch. (1960); *Improvisations concertante* for Violin and String Orch. (1962); Sym. (1962); 2 violin concertos (1963, 1969); *Tempera I–IV* for Strings (1963–70); *Metastasis* (1963); Concerto for Ondes Martenot and Orch. (1964); *Relations* (1964); *Morphographie* for Chamber Orch. (1965); *Diametry* for Voice and Chamber Orch. (1966); 3 *Movements* for Clarinet and String Orch. (1966); *Tempera X* for Chamber Orch. (1974); Sym. No. 3 (1976); Sym. No. 4 (1979). CHAMBER: Violin Sonata (1953); String Quartet (1959); *Colors* for 6 Solo Voices and Ensemble (1967); *Intergrali* for Piano and Chamber Ensemble (1971); *Musandra 3* for Brass Quintet (1974).

Proske, Carl, noted German music scholar and editor; b. Gröbnig, Feb. 11, 1794; d. Regensburg, Dec. 20, 1861. He was a medical student, and served in the medical corps during the war of 1813–15; took the degree of M.D. at Halle Univ. in 1817, and practiced at Oberglogau and Oppeln. In 1823 he renounced medicine for theology, and studied at Regensburg; was ordained in 1826; became vicar-choral in 1827, and canon and Kapellmeister of the Church of Our Lady at Regensburg in 1830. After diligent research in Germany and Italy, he began his lifework, the publ. of sacred classics, the 1st being Palestrina's *Missa Papae Marcelli* (Palestrina's original version, and arrangements by Anerio *a* 4 and Suriano *a* 8), followed by the famous collection *Musica divina,* containing chiefly Italian masterworks of the 16th–17th centuries: vol. I, 12 masses *a* 4 (1853); vol. II, motets for the entire church year (1855); vol. III, fauxbourdons, Psalms, Magnificats, hymns, and antiphons (1859); vol. IV, Passions, Lamentations, responses, Te Deums, litanies (1863; ed. by Wesselack); its publication was continued by Schrems and Haberl. Proske also publ. *Selectus novus missarum a* 4–8 (1855–59). His valuable library passed into the care of the Regensburg bishopric.

BIBL.: Dom Mettenleiter, *C. P.* (Regensburg, 1868; 2nd ed., 1895); K. Weinmann, *C. P., der Restaurator der katholischen Kirchenmusik* (Regensburg, 1909); idem, "Die P.sche Musikbibliothek in Regensburg," *Riemann Festschrift* (Leipzig, 1909); A. Scharnagl, "Dr. C. P.: Leben und Werk," *Der Zwiebelturm,* XVII (1962).

Prosniz, Adolf, Austrian pianist and pedagogue; b. Prague, Dec. 2, 1829; d. Vienna, Feb. 23, 1917. He was a pupil of Proksch and Tomaschek; from 1869 to 1900, was a prof. of piano at the Vienna Cons.; then retired and lived in Vienna.

WRITINGS: *Handbuch der Klavierliteratur* (vol. I [1450–1830], 1884; 2nd ed., 1908; vol. II [1830–1904], 1907); *Kompendium der Musikgeschichte* (vol. I, 1889; 3rd ed., 1920; vol. II, 1900; vol. III, 1915).

Prota-Giurleo, Ulisse, distinguished Italian musicologist; b. Naples, March 13, 1886; d. Perugia, Feb. 9, 1966. He studied with Salvatore di Giacomo in Naples; then devoted himself to the study of Neapolitan music and theater. In addition to his valuable books, he contributed important articles to various journals, including "Breve storia del teatro di corte e della musica a Napoli nei secoli XVII e XVIII," in *Il teatro di corte del Palazzo reale di Napoli* (Naples, 1952).

WRITINGS: (all publ. in Naples unless otherwise given): *Musicisti napoletani in Russia* (1923); *La prima calcofragia musicale a Napoli* (1923); *Musicisti napoletani alla corte di Portogallo* (1924); *Alessandro Scarlatti "il Palermitano"* (1926); *La grande orchestra del Teatro San Carlo nel '700* (1927); *Nicola Logroscino "il dio dell'opera buffa"* (1927); *Francesco Cirillo e l'introduzione del melodramma a Napoli* (Grumo Nevano, 1952); *Francesco Durante nel 2° centenario della sua morte* (Frattamaggiore, 1955); *La famiglia napoletana dei Prota nella storia della musica* (Milan, 1957); *Miserere, tradotto in dialetto napoletano da Nicola Valletta* (1960); *I teatri di Napoli nel '600: la commedia e le maschere* (1962); *Gian Leonardo dell'Arpa nella storia della musica* (1964); with A. Giovine, *Giacomo Insanguine detto Monopoli, musicista monopolitano: Cenno biografici, elenco di rappresentazioni, bibliografia, indice vari e iconografia* (Bari, 1969).

BIBL.: A. Giovine, *U. P.-G.: Ricordo di un mio maestro* (Bari, 1968).

Protheroe, Daniel, Welsh-American conductor and composer; b. Cwmgiedd, near Ystradgynlais, South Wales, Nov. 5, 1866; d. Chicago, Feb. 24, 1934. From 1884 to 1886 he was conductor of the Choral Society at Ystradgynlais; in 1886–1894, a choral conductor in Scranton, Pa.; from 1894 to 1909, a singer and teacher in Milwaukee; then lived in Chicago as music director of the Central Church. He wrote a symphonic poem, *In the Cambrian Hills;* a String Quartet; works for men's chorus; songs; a *Course in Harmony and Choral Conducting.*

Prout, Ebenezer, eminent English music theorist and teacher; b. Oundle, Northamptonshire, March 1, 1835; d. Hackney, Dec. 5, 1909. Excepting some piano lessons as a boy, and later a course with Charles Salaman, he was wholly self-taught. His father had him trained to be a schoolteacher, and he took the degree of B.A. at London Univ. in 1854; but in 1859 he went over definitely to music; was organist at Union Chapel in Islington from 1861 to 1873; a prof. of piano at the Crystal Palace School of Art from 1861 to 1885; a prof. of harmony and composition at the National Training School for Music (1876–82); taught at the Royal Academy of Music (1879–1909); held the non-resident position of prof. of music at Trinity College in Dublin (from 1894); also conducted the Hackney Choral Assoc. (1876–90). He was the 1st ed. of the *Monthly Musical Record* (1871–75); also was music critic of *The Academy* (1874–79) and *The Athenaeum* (1879–89). In 1895 both Dublin and Edinburgh univs. conferred on him the degree of Mus.Doc. *honoris causa.* His theoretical works are the following: *Instrumentation* (1876; 3rd ed., 1904); *Harmony, Its Theory and Practice* (1889; 20th ed., entirely rewritten, 1903); *Counterpoint, Strict and Free* (1890); *Double Counterpoint and Canon* (1891); *Fugue* (1891); *Fugal Analysis* (1892); *Musical Form* (1893); *Applied Forms* (1895); all of these have passed through many eds. He also publ. *The Orchestra* (2 vols., 1898–99; in German, 1905–6) and *Some Notes on Bach's Church-Cantatas* (1907). He was a competent composer of useless works, among them 4 syms.; 2 overtures; 2 organ concertos; a Piano Quintet; 2 string quartets; 2 piano quartets; Clarinet Sonata; the cantatas *Hereward, Alfred,* and *The Red Cross Knight;* a considerable amount of church music; organ arrangements.

Provenzale, Francesco, noted Italian composer and teacher; b. Naples, c.1626; d. there, Sept. 6, 1704. By the early 1650s he was active as a composer of operas in Naples, and thus became the 1st major figure of the so-called Neapolitan school. In 1663 he began teaching at the Conservatorio S. Maria di Loreto; that same year was made its chief maestro, a position he retained until 1675. He then was director of the music staff at the cons. of S. Maria della Pietà dei Turchini from 1675 to 1701. He also served as maestro di cappella to the city of Naples from 1665; held a similar post to the treasury of S. Gennaro from 1686 to 1699. In 1680 he was named maestro onorario, without pay, to the viceregal court under its maestro di cappella P.A., Ziani. After Ziani's death in 1684, Alessandro Scarlatti was named his successor, and Provenzale resigned in protest at being passed over by the court authorities. He returned briefly to court service in 1688 as maestro di cappella di camera. Finally, in 1690, he was renamed maestro onorario with a salary of 19 ducats a month.

WORKS: OPERAS: *Il Ciro* (Naples, 1653); *Il Theseo, o vero L'incostanza trionfante* (Naples, 1658); *Il Schiavo di sua moglie* (Naples, 1671); *La colomba ferita,* sacred opera (Naples, Sept. 18, 1672); *La Fenice d'Avila Teresa di Giesù,* sacred opera (Naples, Nov. 6, 1672); *La Stellidaura vendicata* (Naples, Sept. 2, 1674; also known as *Difendere l'offensore, ovvero La Stellidaura vendicata*). The opera *Il martirio di S. Gennaro* (Naples, Nov. 6, 1664) may be by Provenzale. The operas *Xerse* (Naples, 1655?) and *Artemisia* (Naples, 1657?), often listed as original works by Provenzale, may be adaptations by Cavalli. He also composed cantatas, motets, and other vocal works.

BIBL.: R. Roland, *Les Origines du théâtre lyrique moderne: L'Histoire de l'opéra en Europe avant Lully et Scarlatti* (Paris, 1895; 4th ed., 1936); H. Goldschmidt, "F. P. als Dramatiker," *Sammelbände der Internationalen Musik-Gesellschaft,* VII (1905–6); G. Pannain, "F. P. e la lirica del suo tempo," *Rivista Musicale Italiana,* XXXII (1925); U. Prota-Giurleo, "F. P.," *Archivi,* XXV (1958); A. Mondolfi Bossarelli, "Vita e stile di F. P.: La questione di 'Alessandro Bala,'" *Annuario del Conservatorio S. Pietro a Maiella, Naples,* X (1962–63).

Prudent, Emile (Racine Gauthier), French pianist, teacher, and composer; b. Angoulême, Feb. 3, 1817; d. Paris, May 13, 1863. Early orphaned, he was adopted by a piano tuner; studied at the Paris Cons. with Zimmerman (piano; premier prix, 1833) and Laurent (harmony; 2nd prix, 1834). He made tours as a pianist in France, Belgium, England, and Germany; then settled in Paris, and was greatly esteemed there as a teacher. He wrote a number of piano works; contemporary critics ranked him between Thalberg and Döhler; his paraphrase of *Lucia di Lammermoor* enjoyed considerable success.

Pruett, James W(orrell), prominent American music librarian and musicologist; b. Mount Airy, N.C., Dec. 23, 1932. He studied music and comparative literature at the Univ. of North Carolina in Chapel Hill (B.A., 1955; M.A., 1957; Ph.D., 1962); was a member of its library staff (1955–61), serving as music librarian (1961–76); in 1963 he joined its music dept., serving as prof. of music (1974–87); was president of the Music Library Association (1973–75) and ed. of its journal *Notes* (1974–77). He was chief of the music division of the Library of Congress in Washington, D.C. (from 1987). He ed. *Studies in Musicology: Essays in the History, Style, and Bibliography of Music in Memory of Glen Haydon* (Chapel Hill, 1969); with T. Stevens, he publ. *Research Guide to Musicology* (Chicago, 1985).

Prüfer, (Hermann Bernhard) Arthur, German musicologist; b. Leipzig, July 7, 1860; d. Würzburg, June 3, 1944. He was a law student; then turned to music; studied at the Leipzig Cons. (1887–88), also attending the lectures on musicology of Paul and Kretzschmar at the Univ.; studied further in Berlin (1888–89) with Spitta and Bargiel; took the degree of Ph.D. (Univ. of Leipzig, 1890) with the dissertation *Über den ausserkirchlichen Kunstgesang in den evangelischen Schulen des 16. Jahrhunderts;* completed his Habilitation there in 1895; joined its faculty as a lecturer (1895) and as an associate prof. (1902). He ed. the 1st collected edition of Schein's works (7 vols., 1901–23); publ. *Die Bühnenfestspiele in Bayreuth* (1899; 2nd ed., completely rewritten and greatly enlarged, as *Das Werk von Bayreuth*, 1909; new ed., 1930, as *Tannhäuser und der Sängerkrieg auf der Wartburg*); *Johann Hermann Schein und das weltliche deutsche Lied des 17. Jahrhunderts* (1908); *Die Musik als tönende Faust-Idee* (1920); *Deutsches Leben im Volkslied und Wagners Tannhäuser* (1929).

Prumier, Antoine, French harpist, teacher, and composer; b. Paris, July 2, 1794; d. there, Jan. 20, 1868. He studied at the Paris Cons.; played the harp in the orch. of the Opéra-Comique (1835–40); succeeded Nadermann as prof. of harp at the Cons. (1835–67). He composed about 100 fantasies, rondos, and airs with variations for harp. His son, **Ange-Conrad Prumier** (b. Paris, Jan. 5, 1820; d. there, April 3, 1884), was also a harpist, teacher, and composer; studied with his father at the Cons., then succeeded him at the Opéra-Comique (1840), and also was a prof. at the Cons. (from 1870). He publ. études for harp; nocturnes for harp and horn; sacred songs.

Prunières, Henry, eminent French musicologist; b. Paris, May 24, 1886; d. Nanterre, April 11, 1942. He studied music history with Rolland at the Sorbonne (1906–13), receiving his doctorat ès lettres from the Univ. of Paris in 1913 with the dissertation *L'Opéra italien en France avant Lulli* (publ. in Paris, 1913); also wrote a supplementary dissertation in 1913, *La Ballet de cour en France avant Benserade et Lully*, publ. in Paris in 1914. From 1909 to 1914, was an instructor at the École des Hautes Études Sociales in Paris; in 1920, founded the important journal *La Revue Musicale*, of which he was ed.-in-chief until 1939; was head of the French section of the ISCM. He was general editor of a complete ed. of Lully's works (10 vols., Paris, 1930–39). **WRITINGS:** All publ. in Paris: *Lully* (1910; 2nd ed., 1927); *La Musique de la chambre et de l'écurie* (1912); *La Vie et l'oeuvre de Claudio Monteverdi* (1924; Eng. tr., 1926; 2nd French ed., 1931); *La Vie illustre et libertine de Jean-Baptiste Lully* (1929); *Cavalli et l'opéra vénitien au XVIIe siècle* (1931); *Nouvelle histoire de la musique* (2 vols., 1934, 1936; Eng. tr., 1943). **BIBL.:** Special issue of *La Revue Musicale*, no. 213 (1952–53).

Pruslin, Stephen (Lawrence), American pianist, writer on music, and composer; b. N.Y., April 16, 1940. He studied at Brandeis Univ. (B.A., 1961) and Princeton Univ. (M.F.A., 1963); also studied piano with Luise Vosgerchian and Eduard Steuermann; received a Hertz Memorial Scholarship from the Univ. of Calif. (1964), which enabled him to go to Europe; settled in London, where he made his recital debut (1970); that same year he became a founding member of the Fires of London with Peter Maxwell Davies, and subsequently appeared with it frequently; also toured widely as a soloist. He became especially known as an interpreter of and a writer on contemporary music; ed. *Peter Maxwell Davies: Studies from Two Decades* (1979); composed scores for the theater, films, and television.

Prüwer, Julius, Austrian conductor; b. Vienna, Feb. 20, 1874; d. N.Y., July 8, 1943. He studied piano with Friedheim and Moriz Rosenthal, and theory with R. Fuchs and Krenn; also profited greatly by his friendly association with Brahms. He studied conducting with Hans Richter; began his career as a conductor in Bielitz; then conducted at the Cologne Opera (1894–96) and at the Breslau Opera (1896–1923), where he distinguished himself by conducting numerous new works. From 1924 to 1933 he conducted popular concerts of the Berlin Phil. In 1933 he was compelled to leave Germany owing to the barbarous racial laws of the Nazi regime; he conducted in Russia and in Austria; eventually reached N.Y., where he remained until his death.

Pryor, Arthur (Willard), American trombonist, conductor, and composer; b. St. Joseph, Mo., Sept. 22, 1870; d. Long Branch, N.J., June 18, 1942. He began his professional career in 1889 as a performer on the slide trombone. When J.P. Sousa formed his own band in 1892, he hired Pryor as his trombone

soloist; from 1895 until he left to form his own band in 1903, Pryor was assistant conductor for Sousa. Pryor's Band gave its 1st major concert at the Majestic Theatre in N.Y. on Nov. 15, 1903, but beginning in 1904 it initiated series of summer outdoor concerts at Asbury Park, Coney Island, and other amusement parks. From 1903 to 1909 it made 6 coast-to-coast tours. Unlike Sousa, who had little to do with "canned music," Pryor was quick to take advantage of the developing recording industry; he made some 1,000 acoustic recordings before 1930. He also entered upon a series of commercial radio broadcasts. He composed about 300 works, including operettas, ragtime and cakewalk tunes, and novelties such as *The Whistler and His Dog*, Pryor's best-known work. He was a charter member of ASCAP in 1914 and of the American Bandmasters Assoc. in 1929. In 1933 he retired to Long Branch. **BIBL.:** D. Frizane, *A. P. (1870–1942) American Trombonist, Bandmaster, Composer* (diss., Univ. of Kansas, 1984).

Przybilski, Bronislaw K(azimierz), Polish composer; b. Lodz, Dec. 11, 1941. He studied theory with Franciszek Wesolowski (graduated, 1964) and composition with Tomasz Kiesewetter (graduated, 1969) at the Lodz State College of Music; after further training with Boleslaw Szabelski in Katowice, he completed his studies with Roman Haubenstock-Ramati at the Vienna Hochschule für Musik (1975–76); taught at the Lodz State College of Music (from 1964). **WORKS: ORCH.:** *Quattro studi* (1970); *Suite of Polish Dances* (1971); *In honorem Nicolai Copernici* (1972); *Concerto Polacco* (1973); *Scherzi musicali* for Strings (1973); *Guernica—Pablo Picasso in memoriam* (1974); Piano Concerto (1976); *Animato e festivo* (1978); *À Varsovie* (1980); *Cottbuser Ouvertüre* (1980); *Sinfonie-Corale* (1981); *Sinfonia-Affresco* (1982); Concerto for Accordion and 12 Instruments (1983); *Folklore I*, suite for String Orch. (1983); Concerto for Harpsichord and Strings (1983); *Return*, "quasi" symphonic poem (1984); *Midnight's Echoes Music* for String Orch. (1985); *Concerto classico* for Accordion and Orch. (1986). **VOCAL:** *The Story of the Life and Death of Karol Walter-Swierczewski*, cantata (1969); *Requiem—In Memory of the Children-Martyrs of the War* (1976); *Jagdsagen* for Speaker and Wind Quintet (1978); *The Town of Hope*, cantata (1979); *In Memoriam*, 4 songs for Voice and Chamber Ensemble (1982); *Portrait of a Lady* for Female Voice, 2 Reciters, and Chamber Ensemble (1982). **CHAMBER:** Wind Quintet (1967); String Quartet, *Quartetto del Tritono* (1969); *Permutare* for Oboe, Clarinet, and Bassoon (1971); *Variazioni sopra un tema di Paganini* for Violin and Piano (1972); *Arnold Schönberg in Memoriam* for String Quartet (1977); *Programme "S"—Hommage à Karol Szymanowski* for Piano and String Ensemble (1982); *Metamorphosen* for Accordion and String Quartet (1985); *Chromatica* for 2 Violins (1985); Trio for Violin, Cello, and Accordion (1986); *Modal Piece I* and *II* for Accordion Quintet (both 1986); *Bachanalie*, suite for 2 Pianos (1986); *Per scherzo* for 3 Cellos (1987); also a ballet, *Miriam* (1985); pieces for Solo Instrument, including piano, violin, and accordion.

Ptaszyńska, Marta, Polish composer and percussionist; b. Warsaw, July 29, 1943. She studied piano and timpani at the Music Lyceum in Warsaw (1957–62); then took courses in composition with Dobrowolski and Rudziński at the Warsaw Cons. (1962–68), and worked out problems of electronic music with Kotoński in his studio; had supplementary practice in percussion at the Poznan Cons. (1963–67); in 1969 she traveled to Paris, where she had lessons with Nadia Boulanger. In 1972 she received a grant from the Kosciuszko Foundation to travel to the U.S., and studied percussion at the Cleveland Inst. of Music (until 1974). From 1974 to 1977 she taught percussion at Bennington (Vt.) College; in 1977, became an instructor in composition at the Univ. of Calif., Berkeley. She played with the "Percussions de Strasbourg"; was a composer and percussionist at the Claremont Music Festival in California. Her music is entirely free of any strictures, whether academically traditional or fashionably modern. Being a virtuoso drummer, she naturally gives a prominent place to percussion in her scores; she also makes use of stereophony by spatial separation of players or groups of instruments.

WORKS: DRAMATIC: *Oscar from Alva*, television opera (1972); *Chant for All the People on Earth*, oratorio (1969); *Helio, centricum, musicum*, multimedia spectacle for Voices, Dancers, and Instrumentalists (1973). **ORCH.:** *Improvisations* (1968; Krakow, March 26, 1971); *Spectri sonori* (1973; Cleveland, Jan. 22, 1974); *Crystallites* (1973; Bydgoszcz, Poland, Jan. 24, 1975); Concerto for Percussion Quartet and Orch. (Bennington, Vt., Oct. 20, 1974); *Chimes, Bells, Wood, Stones* for Wind and String Instruments and Percussion (Bennington, Vt., June 9, 1977); *Conductus*, ceremonial for Symphonic Wind Ensemble (1982); *La Novella d'inverno* (Winter's Tale) for String Orch. (1984); Marimba Concerto (1985). **CHAMBER:** *Preludes* for Vibraphone and Piano (1965); *Scherzo* for Xylophone and Piano (1967; received the Polish State Prize); *A Tale of Nightingales* for Baritone and 6 Instruments (1968); *Projections sonores* for Chamber Ensemble (1970); *Madrigals*, in memory of Stravinsky, for Wind Instruments, String Quartet, Trumpet, Trombone, and Gong (1971); *Sonospheres No. 1* for Clarinet, Trombone, Cello, and Piano (1971), *No. 2* for 8 Instruments (1971), and *No. 3* for Flute, Clarinet, Trombone, Cello, Piano, and Percussion (1972); *Siderals* for 2 Percussion Quintets, with Light Projections (Urbana, Nov. 21, 1974); *Recitative, Arioso, Toccata* for Violin (1969–75); *Ornaments in Wood* for Flute, Clarinet, Bass Clarinet, and Bassoon (1975); *Classical Variations* for 4 Timpani and String Quartet (1976); *Epigrams* for 20 Women's Voices, Flute, Harp, Piano, and Percussion (1976–77); *Linear Constructions in Space* for Percussion Quartet (1977); *Un Grand Sommeil noir* for Soprano, Flute, and Harp, to words by Verlaine (1977); *Soirée snobe chez la Princesse*, instrumental theater (1979); *Dream Lands, Magic Spaces* for Violin, Piano, and Percussion (1979); *Ave Maria* for 4 Men's Voices, Brass, Percussion, and Organ (1982; also for Men's Chorus and Orch., 1987); *Moon Flowers* for Cello and Piano (1986); piano pieces; percussion music for children.

Ptolemy (in Latin **Claudius Ptolemaeus**), great Greek astronomer, geographer, mathematician, and music theorist; b. probably in Ptolemais Hermii, Egypt, c.83; d. c.161. He wrote the foremost treatise on music theory of antiquity, the 3-vol. *Harmonika* (Harmonics; J. Wallis, ed., *Klaudiou Ptolemaiou Harmonikōn biblia gamma* (Oxford, 1682) and I. Düring, ed., *Die Harmonielehre des Klaudios Ptolemaios* (Göteborg, 1930), *Porphyrios Kommentar zur Harmonielehre des Ptolemaios* (Göteborg, 1932), and *Ptolemaios und Porphyrios über die Musik* (Göteborg, 1934).

BIBL.: F. Boll, *Studien über Claudius Ptolemäus: Ein Beitrag zur Geschichte der griechischen Philosophie und Astrologie* (Leipzig, 1894); L. Schönberger, *Studien zum 1. Buch der Harmonik des Cl. Ptolemäus* (Augsburg, 1914); M. Shirlaw, "Claudius Ptolemy as Musical Theorist," *Music Review* (Aug. 1955); B. Alexanderson, *Textual Remarks on Ptolemy's Harmonica and Porphyry's Commentary* (Göteborg, 1969).

Puccini, family of Italian musicians:
(1) Giacomo Puccini, composer; b. Celle di Val di Roggia, Lucca (baptized), Jan. 26, 1712; d. Lucca, May 16, 1781. He studied with Caretti in Bologna; then pursued his career in Lucca, where he was organist at S. Martino (1739–72) and director of the Cappella Palatina (1739–81); became a member of Bologna's Accademia Filarmonica (1743). He was a talented composer of vocal music; his sacred output includes 17 masses and some Mass sections, 10 Te Deums, 11 Magnificats, 78 Psalms, 12 Lamentations, and 22 motets; he also wrote a number of dramatic pieces for the Lucca municipal elections.
(2) Antonio (Benedetto Maria) Puccini, composer, son of the preceding; b. Lucca, July 30, 1747; d. there, Feb. 10, 1832. He received financial assistance from the Lucca authorities to study in Bologna with Caretti and Zanardi; while there, he married the organist Caterina Tesei; then returned to Lucca, where he was substitute organist for his father at S. Martino (from 1772); was his father's successor as director of the Cappella Palatina (1781–1805); became a member of Bologna's

Accademia Filarmonica (1771). His output reveals a composer of solid technique and expressivity in vocal writing; among his sacred works are 4 masses and various Mass sections, 2 Te Deums, 3 Magnificats, and 20 Psalms; also wrote music for the tasche.

BIBL.: H. Handt, "A.B.M. P.," *Associazione musicale lucchese*, II (1964–65).

(3) Domenico (Vencenzo Maria) Puccini, composer, son of the preceding; b. 1772; d. Lucca, May 25, 1815. After musical training with his parents, he studied with Mattei in Bologna and Paisiello in Naples; then returned to Lucca as director of the Cappella di Camera (1806–9) and of the municipal chapel (1811–15). He was notably successful as a composer of comic operas.

WORKS: Operas: *Le frecce d'amore*, opera pastorale (c.1800); *L'Ortolanella, o La Moglie capricciosa*, farsa buffa (Lucca, 1800); *Il Quinto Fabio*, opera seria (Livorno, 1810); *La scuola dei tutori*, farsa (Lucca, 1813); *Il Ciarlatano, ossia I finti savoiardi*, atto buffo (Lucca, 1815); also 2 syms.; Concerto for Harpsichord or Piano; sacred music.

(4) Michele Puccini, teacher and composer, son of the preceding; b. Lucca, Nov. 27, 1813; d. there, Jan. 23, 1864. He studied with his grandfather Antonio Puccini and others in Lucca; completed his training with Pillotti in Bologna and Donizetti and Mercadante in Naples; then returned to Lucca as a teacher at the Istituto Musicale Pacini, serving as its director (from 1862); was also organist at S. Martino. He became well known as a teacher. Among his works are 2 operas, *Antonio Foscarini* (n.d.) and *Giambattista Cattani, o La rivoluzione degli Straccioni* (Lucca, 1844); a Sym.; Concertone for Flute, Clarinet, Horn, Trumpet, Trombone, and Orch.; and much sacred music.

(5) Giacomo (Antonio Domenico Michele Secondo Maria) Puccini, celebrated composer, son of the preceding; b. Lucca, Dec. 22, 1858; d. Brussels, Nov. 29, 1924. He was the 5th of 7 children of Michele Puccini, who died when Giacomo was only 5; his musical training was thus entrusted to his uncle, Fortunato Magi, a pupil of his father; however, Giacomo showed neither inclination nor talent for music. His mother, determined to continue the family tradition, sent him to the local Istituto Musicale Pacini, where Carlo Angeloni—its director, who had also studied with Michele Puccini—became his teacher. After Angeloni's untiring patience had aroused interest, and then enthusiasm, in his pupil, progress was rapid and he soon became a proficient pianist and organist. He began serving as a church organist in Lucca and environs when he was 14, and began composing when he was 17. After hearing *Aida* in Pisa in 1876, he resolved to win laurels as a dramatic composer. Having written mainly sacred music, it was self-evident that he needed further training after graduating from the Istituto (1880). With financial support from his granduncle, Dr. Nicolao Cerù, and a stipend from Queen Margherita, he pursued his studies with Antonio Bazzini and Amilcare Ponchielli at the Milan Cons. (1880–83). For his graduation, he wrote a *Capriccio sinfonico*, which was conducted by Faccio at a Cons. concert, eliciting unstinting praise from the critics. In the same year, Ponchielli introduced Puccini to the librettist Fontana, who furnished him the text of a 1-act opera; in a few weeks the score was finished and sent to the Sonzogno competition. It did not win the prize, but on May 31, 1884, *Le villi* was produced at the Teatro dal Verme in Milan, with gratifying success. Ricordi, who was present, considered the work sufficiently meritorious to commission the young composer to write a new opera for him; but 5 years elapsed before this work, *Edgar* (3 acts; text by Fontana), was produced at La Scala in Milan (April 21, 1889), scoring only a moderate success. By this time Puccini had become convinced that, in order to write a really effective opera, he needed a better libretto than Fontana had provided. Accordingly, he commissioned Domenico Oliva to write the text of *Manon Lescaut*; during the composition, however, Puccini and Ricordi practically rewrote the entire book, and in the publ. score Oliva's name is not mentioned. With *Manon Lescaut* (4 acts), first produced at the Teatro Regio in Turin on Feb. 1, 1893, Puccini won a veritable triumph, which was even surpassed by his next work, *La Bohème* (4 acts; text by Illica and Giacosa), produced at the same theater on Feb. 1, 1896. These 2 works not only carried their composer's name throughout the world, but also have found and maintained their place in the repertoire of every opera house. With fame came wealth, and in 1900 he built at Torre del Lago, where he had been living since 1891, a magnificent villa. His next opera, *Tosca* (3 acts; text by Illica and Giacosa), produced at the Teatro Costanzi in Rome on Jan. 14, 1900, is Puccini's most dramatic work; it has become a fixture of the standard repertoire, and contains some of his best-known arias. At its premiere at La Scala on Feb. 17, 1904, *Madama Butterfly* (2 acts; text by Illica and Giacosa) was hissed. Puccini thereupon withdrew the score and made some slight changes (division into 3 acts, and addition of the tenor aria in the last scene). This revised version was greeted with frenzied applause in Brescia on May 28 of the same year. Puccini was now the acknowledged ruler of the Italian operatic stage, his works rivaling those of Verdi in the number of performances. The 1st performance of *Madama Butterfly* at the Metropolitan Opera in N.Y. (Feb. 11, 1907) took place in the presence of the composer, whom the management had invited especially for the occasion. It was then suggested that he write an opera on an American subject, the premiere to take place at the Metropolitan. He found his subject when he witnessed a performance of Belasco's *The Girl of the Golden West;* he commissioned C. Zangarini and G. Civinini to write the libretto, and in the presence of the composer the world premiere of *La Fanciulla del West* occurred, amid much enthusiasm, at the Metropolitan on Dec. 10, 1910; while it never equaled the success of his *Tosca* or *Madama Butterfly,* it returned to favor in the 1970s as a period piece. Puccini then brought out *La Rondine* (3 acts; Monte Carlo, March 27, 1917) and the 3 1-act operas *Il Tabarro* (after Didier Gold's *La Houppelande*), *Suor Angelica,* and *Gianni Schicchi* (all 1st perf. at the Metropolitan Opera, Dec. 14, 1918). His last opera, *Turandot* (after Gozzi), was left unfinished; the final scene was completed by Franco Alfano and performed at La Scala on April 25, 1926.

BIBL.: A. Brüggemann, *Madama Butterfly e l'arte di G. P.* (Milan, 1904); W. Dry, *G. P.* (London, 1906); F. Torrefranca, *G. P. e l'opera internazionale* (Turin, 1912); D. Parker, "A View of G. P.," *Musical Quarterly* (Oct. 1917); A. Weismann, *G. P.* (Munich, 1922); A. Bonaventura, *G. P.: L'Uomo, l'artista* (Livorno, 1924); A. Coeuroy, *La Tosca* (Paris, 1924); A. Fraccaroli, *La vita di G. P.* (Milan, 1925; also in German); G. Marotti and F. Pagni, *G. P. intimo* (Florence, 1926); G. Adami, *Epistolario di G. P.* (Milan, 1928; in Eng., London, 1931); G. Gatti, "The Works of P.," *Musical Quarterly* (Jan. 1928); A. Neisser, *P.* (Leipzig, 1928); F. Salerno, *Le Donne pucciniane* (Palermo, 1928); R. Merlin, *P.* (Milan, 1930); R. Specht, *P.* (Berlin, 1931; Eng. tr., N.Y., 1933); W. Maisch, *P.s musikalische Formgebung* (Neustadt, 1934); G. Adami, *P.* (Milan, 1935; German tr., 1943); M. Carner, "The Exotic Element in P.," *Musical Quarterly* (Jan. 1936); K. Fellerer, *G. P.* (Potsdam, 1937); V. Seligman, *P. among Friends* (correspondence; N.Y., 1938); F. Thiess, *P., Versuch einer Psychologie seiner Musik* (Berlin, 1947); A. Bonaccorsi, *G. P. e i suoi antenati musicali* (Milan, 1950); G. Marek, *P.: A Biography* (N.Y., 1951); D. del Fiorentino, *Immortal Bohemian: An Intimate Memoir of G. P.* (N.Y., 1952); A. Machard, *Une Vie d'amour: P.* (Paris, 1954); L. Ricci, *P. interprete di se stesso* (Milan, 1954); V. Terenzio, *Ritratto di P.* (Bergamo, 1954); M. Carner, *P.* (London, 1958; 2nd ed., rev., 1974); E. Greenfield, *P.: Keeper of the Seal* (London, 1958); C. Sartori, *P.* (Milan, 1958); C. Paladini, *G. P.* (Florence, 1961); C. Hopkinson, *A Bibliography of the Works of G. P.* (N.Y., 1968); S. Jackson, *Monsieur Butterfly: The Story of G. P.* (1974); W. Ashbrook, *The Operas of P.* (N.Y., 1968; 2nd ed., rev., 1985); D. Amy, *G. P.* (Paris, 1970); A. Monnosi, *P. a tu per tu* (Pisa, 1970); G. Tarozzi, *P.: La fine del bel canto* (Milan, 1972); N. Galli, *P. e la sua terra* (Lucca, 1974); G. Magri, *P. e le sue rime* (Milan, 1974); I. Lombardi, *P., ancora da scoprire* (Lucca, 1976); E. Siciliani, *P.* (Milan, 1976); W. Weaver, *P.: The Man and His Music* (N.Y., 1977); C. Casini, *G. P.* (Turin, 1978); L. Pinzauti, *P.* (Milan, 1978); H. Greenfield, *P.* (N.Y., 1980); C. Osborne, *The Complete Operas of P.* (London, 1981); M. Courtin, *Tosca de G. P.* (Paris, 1983); A. Bottero, *Le Donne di P.* (Lucca, 1984); M. Carner, *Tosca* (Cambridge, 1985); E. Krause, *P.* (Leipzig, 1985); D. Martino, *Metamorfosi del femminino nei libretti per P.* (Turin, 1985); A. Groos and R. Parker, *G. P.: "La Bohème"* (Cambridge, 1986); J. DiGaetani, *P. the Thinker: The Composer's Intellectual and Dramatic Development* (Bern and N.Y., 1987); M. Kaye, *The Unknown P.: A Historical Perspective on the Songs, including Little-Known Music from "Edgar" and "La Rondine," with Complete Music for Violin and Piano* (Oxford, 1987); G. Musco, *Musica e teatro in G. P.* (vol. I, Cortona, 1989).

Puchalsky, Vladimir (Viacheslavovich), Russian pianist, teacher, and composer; b. Minsk, April 2, 1848; d. Kiev, Feb. 23, 1933. He studied at the St. Petersburg Cons. with Leschetizky (piano) and Zaremba (theory); then settled in Kiev as the director and a teacher at the music school of the Russian Musical Society (1877); later was the 1st director of the Kiev Cons. (1913–15). Among his pupils was Vladimir Horowitz. He wrote an opera, *Valeria,* piano pieces, and songs.

Puchat, Max, German composer and pianist; b. Breslau, Jan. 8, 1859; d. (killed in a fall in the Karwendel Alps) Aug. 12, 1919. He studied with Kiel in Berlin, winning the Mendelssohn Prize in 1884. From 1886 to 1903 he was active as a choral conductor in the German provinces; then went to Milwaukee, where he conducted the local Musikverein (1903–5); in 1910, settled in Breslau, where he established his own music school. He wrote several symphonic works: *Euphorion* (1888); *Leben und Ideal* (1892); *Tragödie eines Künstlers* (1894); *Ouvertüre über ein nordisches Thema;* Piano Concerto; String Quartet; songs.

Pucitta, Vincenzo, Italian composer; b. Civitavecchia, 1778; d. Milan, Dec. 20, 1861. He studied with Fenaroli in Naples; traveled through Europe; was successful as an opera composer in Italy, Austria, France, and England; wrote about 30 operas, of which the best were *La burla fortunata* (Venice, April 9, 1804) and *La Vestale* (London, May 3, 1810).

Puente, Giuseppe Del, Italian baritone; b. Naples, Jan. 30, 1841; d. Philadelphia, May 25, 1900. He first studied cello at the Naples Cons. but later began to cultivate his voice, making his operatic debut at Iaşi; was then engaged for the Teatro San Carlo in Naples, and for appearances in France, Germany, Russia, Spain, and England (made his Covent Garden debut in 1873, and became very popular there). His 1st American engagement was under Strakosch at the N.Y. Academy of Music in 1873–74; he became a member of the 1st Metropolitan Opera season in N.Y. and sang the role of Valentin in the inaugural performance of *Faust* on Oct. 22, 1883; remained on its roster for the seasons of 1883–84, 1891–92, and 1894–95. In 1885 he returned to the N.Y. Academy of Music under Mapleson's management, taking part in the American premiere of *Manon* on Dec. 23 of that year; he was also a member of the opera troupes of Patti and Hinrichs; with the latter's company, he sang in the American premiere of *Cavalleria rusticana* (Philadelphia, Sept. 9, 1891). He married the mezzo-soprano Helen Dudley Campbell.

Puget, Paul-Charles-Marie, French composer; b. Nantes, June 25, 1848; d. Paris, March 14, 1917. He studied at the Paris Cons. with Marmontel (piano) and Massé (composition); won 1st Grand Prix de Rome in 1873 with the cantata *Mazeppa;* wrote much theater music; his opera *Beaucoup de bruit pour rien,* after Shakespeare (Paris, March 24, 1899), had a moderately good reception.

Pugliese, Michael (Gabriel), American percussionist and composer; b. Buffalo, N.Y., Sept. 26, 1956. He studied with Jan Williams at the State Univ. of N.Y. at Buffalo (B.F.A., 1979) and at the Manhattan School of Music (M.M., 1981), then pursued a career as an avant-garde percussionist; in 1982 produced a 12–hour marathon of the music of John Cage at Cooper Union in N.Y.; also gave premiere performances of Cage's *Études Boreales* and *Ryoanji*, and received their dedications. He was a core member of the Bowery Ensemble, the New Music Consort, and the Michael Gordon Phil.; in 1985 he joined the Merce Cunningham Dance Co., with which he subsequently toured throughout the U.S., South America, Europe, and Asia. Among his compositions is *Peace Talks* (Berkeley, Calif., Sept. 22, 1989) for a Variety of Ethnic Percussion Instruments, based on the concept of global union of socially and politically troubled nations; percussion instruments from these nations were chosen by Pugliese to illustrate peaceful communication through primitive rhythms. His other compositions include *June 22, 1978*, for Percussion Quintet, 2 Narrators, and Tape (1978); *Suite: Father of Tree* for Electronics and Percussion (1988); *Bombardements*, electronic score (1990); *Hidden Evolution* for Percussion and Tape (1990); and *Jinxed* for 4 Marimbas and 4 Berimbau (1991). He also appeared as a rock drummer, and made numerous rock arrangements.

Pugnani, (Giulio) Gaetano (Gerolamo), celebrated Italian violinist and composer; b. Turin, Nov. 27, 1731; d. there, July 15, 1798. He studied violin with G.B. Somis; when he was 10, he was allowed to play in the last chair of the 2nd violins in the orch. of Turin's Teatro Regio; he officially became a member of the orch. on April 19, 1748. In 1749, on a royal stipend, he went to Rome to study with Ciampi; later toured in Europe as a concert violinist. Pugnani was particularly successful in London, where he played concerts with J.C. Bach; from 1767 to 1769 he also served as conductor at the King's Theatre, where he brought out his successful opera *Nanetta e Lubino* (April 8, 1769). He then returned to Turin, where he was appointed concertmaster of the King's Music and of the orch. of the Teatro Regio in 1770. He was named general director of instrumental music in 1776; in 1786 he served as supervisor of military music. He made, from 1780 to 1782, a concert tour of Europe, which included a visit to Russia. He was also active as a teacher of the violin. His students included Viotti, Conforti, Bruni, and Polledro. His style of composition approximated that of Tartini. Fritz Kreisler publ. an arrangement for violin and piano of a piece, purportedly by Pugnani, titled *Preludio e Allegro e Tempo di Minuetto*, but this proved to be by Kreisler himself.

WORKS: STAGE: *Nanetta e Lubino*, opera buffa (London, April 8, 1769); *Issea*, favola pastorale (Turin, 1771); *Tamas Kouli-Kan nell'India*, dramma per musica (Turin, Feb. 1, 1772; not extant); *Aurora*, festa per musica (Turin, 1775; not extant); *Adone e Venere*, opera seria (Naples, Nov. 1784); *Achille in Sciro*, dramma per musica (Turin, Jan. 15, 1785); *Demofoonte*, dramma per musica (Turin, Dec. 26, 1787); *Demetrio a Rodi*, festa per musica (Turin, 1789); also *Corriso e Calliroe*, balleto eroico (1792; not extant); ballet music to Gluck's *Orfeo* (not extant); oratorio, *Betulia liberata*; several cantatas. He also composed a Violin Concerto, sinfonias, overtures, etc.; 40 trio sonatas; 6 string quartets; sonatas for Violin; duets for 2 Violins; about 20 sonatas for Violin and Basso Continuo.

BIBL.: G. Rangoni, *Essai sur le goût de la musique . . . Saggio sul gusto della musica col carattere de' tre celebri sonatori di violino i signori Nardini, Lolli, e P.* (Livorno, 1790); F. Fayolle, *Notices sur Corelli, Tartini, Gaviniès, P. et Viotti* (Paris, 1810); A. Bertolotti, *G. P. e altri musici alla corte di Torino nel secolo XVIII* (Milan, 1892); D. Carutti, "Della famiglia di G. P.," *Miscellanea di storia italiana,* III/2 (Turin, 1896); A. Moser, *Geschichte des Violinspiels* (Berlin, 1923; 2nd ed., rev. and enlarged, 1966–67); S. Cordero di Pamparato, "G. P., violinista torinese," *Rivista Musicale Italiana,* XXXVII (1930); A. Della Corte, *Notizie di G. P.* (Turin, 1931); A. Della Corte, "Due inedite opere teatrali di G. P.," *Musica d'Oggi,* XIII (1931); E. von Zschinsky-Troxler, *G. P.* (Berlin, 1939; with thematic catalogue); A. Müry, *Die Instrumentalwerke G. P.s* (diss., Univ. of Basel, 1941); G. Barblan, "Ansia preromantica in G. P.," *Chigiana,* XVI (1959); W. Newman, *The Sonata in the Classic Era* (Chapel Hill, 1963; 3rd ed., rev., 1983); S. McVeigh, *The*

Violinist in London's Concert Life, 1750–1784: Felice Giardini and His Contemporaries (diss., Oxford Univ., 1980); B. Schwarz, *Great Masters of the Violin* (N.Y., 1983).

Pugni, Cesare, Italian composer; b. Genoa, May 31, 1802; d. St. Petersburg, Jan. 26, 1870. He studied violin with Alessandro Rolla and composition with Asioli at the Milan Cons.; began his career as a composer for the stage with the ballet *Elerz e Zulmida* (Milan, May 6, 1826) and the opera *Il Disertore svizzero, o La nostaligia* (Milan, May 28, 1831), followed by several other operas: *La vendetta* (Milan, Feb. 11, 1832); *Ricciarda di Edimburgo* (Trieste, Sept. 29, 1832); *Il Contrabbandiere* (Milan, June 13, 1833); *Un episodio di S. Michele* (Milan, June 14, 1834); he also wrote an ingenious *Sinfonia a canone* for 2 orchs. playing the same music, but with the 2nd orch. coming in one measure later than the 1st (this musical legerdemain amused Meyerbeer). He then lived in Paris, where he struck up a rewarding collaborative relationship with the choreographer Jules Perrot and produced some 30 ballets, many of which were premiered at Her Majesty's Theatre in London; among the most successful were *Ondine, ou La naiade* (June 22, 1843) and *La Esmeralda* (March 9, 1844). In 1851 he was appointed ballet composer for the imperial theaters in St. Petersburg, where he produced such successful ballets as *Konyok gorbunyok, ili Tsar-devista* (The Little Hump-backed Horse, or the Czar's Daughter; Dec. 15, 1864).

Pugno, (Stéphane) Raoul, celebrated French pianist and teacher; b. Montrouge, near Paris (of an Italian father), June 23, 1852; d. (while on a concert tour) Moscow, Jan. 3, 1914. He studied at the Paris Cons. with G. Mathias (piano) and Ambroise Thomas (composition). He became music director of the Paris Opéra in 1871; then served as organist (1872–92) and choirmaster (1878–92) at the church of St.-Eugène; then taught harmony at the Paris Cons. (1892–96), and subsequently was a prof. of piano there (1896–1901). In the meantime he gave numerous recitals, and gradually rose to the rank of a great virtuoso; he appeared in England in 1894; in America in 1897–98. He was equally remarkable as an ensemble player; his sonata recitals with Ysaÿe became world famous. Pugno was also a composer; he wrote several operas: *Ninetta* (Paris, Dec. 23, 1882); *Le Sosie* (Oct. 7, 1887); *Le Valet de cœur* (April 19, 1888); *Le Retour d'Ulysse* (Paris, Feb. 1, 1889); *La Vocation de Marius* (March 29, 1890); etc.; ballet, *La Danseuse de corde* (Paris, Feb. 5, 1892); piano pieces; songs. His score for *La Ville morte* (after Gabriele d'Annunzio), left incomplete at his death, was finished by Nadia Boulanger.

Pujol, Francesco, Catalan conductor and composer; b. Barcelona, May 15, 1878; d. there, Dec. 24, 1945. He studied at the Barcelona Cons. and also with Millet; was assistant conductor (1900–41), then music director (1941–45), of the Orfeó Catalá in Barcelona. He wrote many sardanas; church music; orch. works; etc.; publ. studies on Catalan songs.

Pujol, Juan (Pablo), Catalan composer and organist; b. Barcelona, c.1573; d. there, May 1626. From 1593 to 1595 he was maestro de canto at Tarragona Cathedral; from 1596 to 1612, was organist at Nuestra Señora del Pilar in Saragossa; then at the Barcelona Cathedral until his death. His masses, motets, Passions, Psalms, and villancicos are preserved in MS. A selected ed. of Pujol's works was undertaken by H. Anglès, of which 2 vols. appeared (1926, 1932).

Punto, Giovanni. See **Stich, Johann Wenzel.**

Puppo, Giuseppe, Italian violinist, teacher, and composer; b. Lucca, June 12, 1749; d. Florence, April 19, 1827. He studied at Naples's Conservatorio di S. Onofrio di Loreto. He was a successful violin virtuoso at an early age; traveled in Spain; was in England from 1777 until 1783, when he settled in Paris; was a fashionable teacher there; in 1811, abandoned his family in Paris; went to Naples and then to Florence, where he died in poverty. He publ. 2 violin concertos, 8 études for violin, and 6 piano fantasias.

Purcell, Daniel, English organist and composer, brother of **Henry Purcell;** b. London, c.1660; d. there (buried), Nov. 26, 1717. He became organist of Magdalen College, Oxford, in 1688; took his brother's place as a dramatic composer in 1695, and was organist of St. Andrew's, Holborn, from 1713. He supplied scores of incidental music to over 40 plays; also wrote many other secular vocal works, and various instrumental pieces.

Purcell, Henry, great English composer, brother of **Daniel Purcell;** b. London, 1659; d. Dean's Yard, Westminster, Nov. 21, 1659. His parentage remains a matter of dispute, since documentary evidence is lacking. His father may have been Henry Purcell (d. Westminster, Aug. 11, 1664), a singer, who was named a "singing-man" and Master of the Choristers at Westminster Abbey (1661) and a Gentleman of the Chapel Royal (1661), where he became a musician-in-ordinary for the lutes and voices (1662). It is possible that his father was Thomas Purcell (d. Westminster, July 31, 1682), a singer and composer, who most likely was the brother of the elder Henry Purcell; Thomas became a Gentleman of the Chapel Royal (1661), where he was admitted to the private music for lutes, viols, and voices (1662); with Pelham Humfrey, he served as composer for the violins (from 1672); that same year he was made marshal of the Corp. of Music and a musician-in-ordinary in the King's Private Musick. Whatever the case, the young Henry Purcell became a chorister of the Chapel Royal under Cooke and Humfrey (1669), and also received instruction from Blow; when his voice broke (1673), he was appointed Assistant Keeper of the Instruments; was named composer-in-ordinary for the violins (1677). He became Blow's successor as organist of Westminster Abbey (1679) and one of the 3 organists of the Chapel Royal (1682); was named organ maker and keeper of the king's instruments (1683). His 1st printed work was a song in Playford's *Choice Ayres* (vol. I, 1675); vol. II (1679) contains other songs and an elegy on the death of Matthew Locke. In 1680 he publ. one of his finest instrumental works, the *Fantasias* for Strings; in that same year he began writing odes and welcome songs; although their texts are almost invariably stupid or bombastic, he succeeded in clothing them in some of his finest music; his incidental music for the stage also dates from that year. He wrote the anthem *My Heart is Inditing* for the coronation of King James II (1685). With *Dido and Aeneas* (1689) he produced the 1st great English opera. In the remaining years of his life he devoted much time to composition for the theater; he also wrote some outstanding sacred music, the *Te Deum* and *Jubilate* in D; for the funeral of Queen Mary, he wrote the anthem *Thou knowest, Lord, the Secrets of our Hearts* (1695); it was performed, along with his 4 canzonas for brass and 2 elegies, at his own funeral later that year.

Purcell lies in the north aisle of Westminster Abbey, and his burial tablet well expresses contemporary estimation of his worth: "Here lyes Henry Purcell, Esq.; who left this life, and is gone to that blessed place where only his harmony can be exceeded." His church music shows him to be an original melodist, and a master of form, harmony, and all contrapuntal devices; his music for the stage is equally rich in invention, dramatic instinct, and power of characterization; his chamber works surpass those of his predecessors and contemporaries.

WORKS: STAGE: OPERA: *Dido and Aeneas* (London, 1689). *SEMI-OPERAS: The Prophetess, or The History of Dioclesian* (London, 1690); *King Arthur, or The British Worthy* (London, 1691); *The Fairy Queen* (London, 1692); *The Indian Queen* (London, 1695; final masque by D. Purcell); *The Tempest, or The Enchanted Island* (c.1695). *INCIDENTAL MUSIC:* To N. Lee's *Theodosius, or The Force of Love* (1680); T. D'Urfey's *Sir Barnaby Whigg, or No Wit Like a Woman's* (1681); Tate's *The History of King Richard II* (*The Sicilian Usurper*), after Shakespeare (1681); Beaumont and Fletcher's *The Double Marriage* (c.1682–85); Lee's *Sophonisba, or Hannibal's Overthrow* (c.1685); D'Urfey's *A Fool's Preferment, or The 3 Dukes of Dunstable*, after Fletcher's *Noble Gentleman* (1688); Dryden's

Amphitryon, or The Two Sosias (1690); E. Settle's *Distressed Innocence, or The Princess of Persia* (1690); T. Southerne's *Sir Anthony Love, or The Rambling Lady* (1690); Lee's *The Massacre of Paris* (1690); C. D'Avenant's *Circe* (c.1690); *The Gordian Knot Unty'd* (1691); Dryden and R. Howard's *The Indian Emperor, or The Conquest of Mexico* (1691); Southerne's *The Wives' Excuse, or Cuckolds Make Themselves* (1691); Dryden's *Cleomenes, the Spartan Hero* (1692); W. Mountfort and J. Bancroft's *Henry the 2nd, King of England* (1692); J. Crowne's *Regulus* (1692); Dryden's *Aureng-Zebe* (c.1692); Dryden and Lee's *Oedipus* (c.1692); T. Shadwell's *The Libertine* (c.1692); D'Urfey's *The Marriage-Hater Match'd* (1692); Shadwell's *Epsom Wells* (1693); W. Congreve's *The Double Dealer* (1693); Fletcher's *Rule a Wife and Have a Wife* (1693); T. Wright's *The Female Vertuosos*, after Molière's *Les Femmes savantes* (1693); Southerne's *The Maid's Last Prayer, or Any Rather than Fail* (1693); Congreve's *The Old Bachelor* (1693); D'Urfey's *The Richmond Heiress, or A Woman Once in the Right* (1693); Dryden's *Love Triumphant, or Nature Will Prevail* (1694); E. Ravenscroft's *The Canterbury Guests, or A Bargain Broken* (1694); Southerne's *The Fatal Marriage, or The Innocent Adultery* (1694); Crowne's *The Married Beau, or The Curious Impertinent* (1694); Shadwell's *Timon of Athens*, after Shakespeare (1694); Dryden's *Tyrannic Love, or The Royal Martyr* (1694); D'Urfey's *The Virtuous Wife, or Good Luck at Last* (c.1694); Dryden's *The Spanish Friar, or The Double Discovery* (1694–95); D'Urfey's *The Comical History of Don Quixote* (1694–95); A. Behn's *Abdelazer, or The Moor's Marriage* (1695); *Bonduca, or The British Heroine*, after Beaumont and Fletcher (1695); Southerne's *Oroonoko* (1695); Norton's *Pausanias, the Betrayer of His Country* (1695); T. Scott's *The Mock Marriage* (1695); R. Gould's *The Rival Sisters, or The Violence of Love* (1695). He also composed numerous anthems and services (c.1677–c.1693), a Magnificat and Nunc dimitiis (n.d.), Morning and Evening Service (1682), and Te Deum and Jubilate (1694), as well as other sacred works. His other vocal works include 24 odes and welcome songs, numerous songs for Solo Voice and Continuo, songs for 2 or More Voices and Continuo, and catches. **INSTRUMENTAL:** Various pieces for Winds and Strings, including 14 fantasias, 3 overtures, 5 pavans, 24 sonatas, etc.; also many harpsichord pieces. A complete ed. of Purcell's works was issued by the Purcell Soc. (London, 1878–1965; 2nd ed., rev., 1974–81).

BIBL.: W. Cummings, *P.* (London, 1881; 3rd ed., 1911; abridged ed., 1923); J. Runciman, *P.* (London, 1909); P. Scholes, "H. P.: Sketch of a Busy Life," *Musical Quarterly* (July 1916); D. Arundell, *H. P.* (London, 1927); H. Dupré, *P.* (Paris, 1927; Eng. tr., 1928); A. Holland, *H. P.: The English Musical Tradition* (London, 1932; 2nd ed., 1948); F. de Quervain, *Der Chorstil H. P.'s* (Bern, 1935); J. Westrup, *P.* (London, 1937; 4th ed., rev., 1980); S. Favre-Lingorow, *Der Instrumentalstil von P.* (Bern, 1950); W. Meinardus, *Die Technik des Basso Ostinato bei H. P.* (diss., Univ. of Cologne, 1950); S. Demarquez, *P.: La Vie, l'œuvre* (Paris, 1951); G. van Ravenzwaaij, *P.* (Haarlem and Antwerp, 1954); R. Sietz, *P.: Zeit, Leben, Werk* (Leipzig, 1956); T. Dart, "P.'s Chamber Music," *Proceedings of the Royal Musical Association*, LXXXV (1958–59); I. Holst, ed., *H. P. (1659–1695): Essays on His Music* (London, 1959); R. Moore, *H. P. and the Restoration Theatre* (London, 1961); M. Laurie, *P.'s Stage Works* (diss., Cambridge Univ., 1962); D. Schjelderup-Ebbe, *P.'s Cadences* (Oslo, 1962); F. Zimmerman, *H. P., 1659–1695: An Analytical Catalogue of His Music* (London, 1963); J. Westrup, "P.'s Parentage," *Music Review*, XXV (1964); F. Zimmerman, *H. P., 1659–1695: His Life and Times* (London, 1967; 2nd ed., rev., 1983); idem, *The Anthems of H. P.* (N.Y., 1971); R. Burkart, *The Trumpet in England in the Seventeenth Century with Emphasis on Its Treatment in the Works of H. P.* (diss., Univ. of Wisconsin, 1972); I. Spink, *English Song: Dowland to P.* (London, 1974); F. Zimmerman, *H. P. 1659–1695: Melodic and Intervallic Indexes to His Complete Works* (Philadelphia, 1975); K. Rohrer, "*The Energy of English Words*": A Linguistic Approach to H. P.'s Methods of Setting Texts* (diss., Princeton Univ., 1980);

A. Hutchings, *P.* (London, 1982); C. Price, *H. P. and the London Stage* (Cambridge, 1984); E. Harris, *H. P.'s Dido and Aeneas* (Oxford, 1987); F. Zimmerman, *H. P.: A Guide to Research* (N.Y., 1988).

Puschmann, Adam (Zacharias), German poet and Meistersinger; b. Görlitz, 1532; d. Breslau, April 4, 1600. He was a pupil of Hans Sachs; brought out *Gründtlicher Bericht des deutschen Meistergesanges* (1571; 2nd ed., 1596; ed. by R. Jonas, Halle, 1888) and a *Singebuch* (1588; ed. by G. Münzer, Leipzig, 1906), which contains some 350 melodies.

Pustet, Friedrich, German music publisher; b. Hals, near Passau, Feb. 25, 1798; d. Munich, March 6, 1882. In 1826 he founded a music publishing firm, mainly for church music, in Regensburg; for 30 years he had the exclusive right of printing, with the privilege of the Holy See, the chant books according to the Editio Medicaea, which, however, was superseded by the newer Vaticana Edition. In 1921 Pustet's firm merged with the publishing house of Kösel, retaining, however, the original name; the firm thus lasted through 5 generations of the family, and was later directed, still in Regensburg, by **Friedrich Pustet** (b. Munich, Nov. 26, 1927). Pustet publ. the *Kirchenmusikalisches Jahrbuch* (1886–1935). A Festschrift was compiled by H. Bohatta on the centenary of the foundation of the firm (Regensburg, 1926).

Putnam, Ashley (Elizabeth), American soprano; b. N.Y., Aug. 10, 1952. She studied flute at the Univ. of Michigan, eventually turning to voice (B.M., 1974; M.M., 1975). After graduating, she was an apprentice with the Santa Fe Opera Co. In 1976 she made her operatic debut in the title role of Donizetti's *Lucia di Lammermoor* with the Virginia Opera Association in Norfolk. After winning 1st prize in the Metropolitan Opera Auditions and receiving the Weyerhauser Award (1976), she made her European debut as Musetta in Puccini's *La Bohème* at the Glyndebourne Festival (1978). On Sept. 15, 1978, she won accolades as Violetta in her N.Y. City Opera debut. In later seasons she appeared with various opera houses in the U.S. and abroad.

Puyana, Rafael, Colombian harpsichordist; b. Bogotá, Oct. 14, 1931. He studied piano at the New England Cons. of Music in Boston, and harpsichord with Wanda Landowska in N.Y.; had his general musical training at the Hartt College of Music in Hartford, Conn. He made a tour of Europe (1955); made his 1st appearances in N.Y. (1957) and London (1966); thereafter toured worldwide. His extensive repertory ranges from early music to contemporary scores.

Pycard, English singer and composer who flourished c.1400. The *Old Hall Manuscript* contains 6 works by him; his contrapuntal skill was out of the ordinary, and he used complicated canonic forms in sections of the Mass.

Pylkkänen, Tauno Kullervo, Finnish composer; b. Helsinki, March 22, 1918; d. there, March 13, 1980. He studied composition with Palmgren, Madetoja, and Ranta at the Helsinki Academy of Music (1937–40); also studied musicology at the Univ. of Helsinki (M.A., 1941). He worked at the Finnish Broadcasting Co. (1942–61) and was artistic director of the Finnish National Opera (1960–70); lectured on opera history at the Sibelius Academy (from 1967). He was primarily an opera composer; his idiom was basically Romantic, with sporadic excursions into modernity.

WORKS: STAGE: OPERAS: *Bathsheba Saarenmaalla* (Bathsheba at Saarenmaa; 1940; rev. 1958); *Mare ja hänen poikansa* (Mare and Her Son; 1943); *Simo Hurtta* (1948); *Sudenmorsian* (The Wolf's Bride), radio opera (1950); *Varjo* (The Shadow; 1952); *Opri and Oleksi* (1957); *Ikaros* (1956–60); *Vangit* (The Prisoners; 1964); *Tuntematon sotilas* (The Unknown Soldier; 1967). **BALLET:** *Kaarina Maununtytär* (Kaarina, Maunu's Daughter; 1960). **ORCH.:** *Introduction and Fugue* (1940); *Lapin kesä* (Summer in Lapland; 1941); *Kullervon sotaanlähtö* (Kullervo Leaves for War; 1942); *Sinfonietta* (1944); Sym. No. 1 (1945); *Suite* for Oboe and Strings (1946); *Marathon,* overture (1947); *Symphonic Fantasy* (1948); *Ultima Thule* (1949); Cello Concerto (1950); *Symphonic Prelude* (1952). **CHAMBER:** *Notturno* for Violin and Piano (1943); String Quartet (1945); *Fantasia appassionata* for Cello and Piano (1954); *Trittico* for Clarinet, Violin, Viola, and Cello (1978); several cantatas and songs.

Pythagoras, Greek philosopher and mathematician; b. Samos, c.580 **B.C.**; d. Metapontum, c.500 **B.C.** His doctrines on the musical ratios are preserved in the writings of his followers, no books by Pythagoras having come down to us. The Pythagoreans (Archytas, Didymos, Eratosthenes, Euclid, Ptolemy, etc.) reckoned only the 5th and octave as pure consonances (the 4th being the 5th below); their system recognized only intervals reached by successive skips of pure 5ths, the major 3rd being the 4th 5th above (ratio 64:81, instead of the modern 64:80, or 4:5), their minor 3rd the 3rd 5th below; etc. Their 3rds and 6ths were, consequently, dissonant intervals.

BIBL.: K. Pringsheim, "P., die Atonalität und wir," *Schweizerische Musikzeitung* (1957); I. Focht, "La Notion pythagoricienne de la musique," *International Review of the Aesthetics and Sociology of Music,* III (1972).

Q

Quadri, Argeo, Italian conductor; b. Como, March 23, 1911. He studied piano, composition, and conducting at the Milan Cons.; then conducted opera throughout Italy. In 1956 he became a conductor at Covent Garden in London; was a regular conductor at the Vienna State Opera (1957–75).

Quagliati, Paolo, Italian organist and composer; b. Chioggia, c.1555; d. Rome, Nov. 16, 1628. Born into the nobility, he settled in Rome (c.1574); was organist at S. Maria Maggiore; was also in the service of the Ludovisi family; upon the elevation of Cardinal Alessandro Ludovisi as Pope Gregory XV (1621), he became apostolic prothonotary and the pope's private chamberlain. He publ. *Il carro di Fedeltà d'Amore con aggiunta di alcune arie dell'istesso autore,* one of the earliest music dramas, containing not only monodies, but ensemble numbers up to 5 voices (Rome, 1611; ed. in Smith College Music Archives, XIII, 1957); also motets and "dialogues" *a* 2–8 (3 vols., 1612, 1620, 1627); etc.

Bibl.: A. Cametti, "P. Q., organista e compositore," *Rassegna Dorica* (Dec. 20, 1930).

Quaile, Elizabeth, Irish-American piano pedagogue; b. Omagh, Jan. 20, 1874; d. South Kent, Conn., June 30, 1951. She went to N.Y. and studied with Franklin Robinson; then devoted herself to teaching; from 1916 to 1919 she was head of the piano dept. of the David Mannes School; then went to Paris, where she studied piano with Harold Bauer. Returning to N.Y. in 1921, she founded, with Angela Diller, the Diller-Quaile School of Music. She publ. a number of highly successful piano teaching materials, some written by her alone (*First Book of Technical Exercises, A Pre-Czerny Book,* etc.), and some

in collaboration with Diller. The books proved to be standard guides for piano students for many years.

Quantz, Johann Joachim, famous German flutist, writer on music, and composer; b. Oberscheden, Hannover, Jan. 30, 1697; d. Potsdam, July 12, 1773. His father was a village blacksmith; young Johann revealed a natural gift for music, and played the double bass at village festivals at age 8; his father died when he was 10, and he was apprenticed to his uncle, Justus Quantz, a "Stadtmusikus" in Merseburg, in 1708, and later to J.A. Fleischhack; he received instruction on string and wind instruments, becoming particularly adept on the violin, oboe, and trumpet; he also studied harpsichord with J.F. Kiesewetter. He completed his apprenticeship in 1713, but remained a journeyman under Fleischhack until 1716; then became a member of the Dresden municipal band; during a 3-month leave of absence (1717), he studied counterpoint with J.D. Zelenka in Vienna; subsequently became oboist at the Polish chapel of Augustus II (1718), being active in Dresden and Warsaw, but soon turned to the transverse flute, receiving some lessons from P.G. Buffardin. In 1724 he went to Italy in the entourage of the Polish ambassador and sought out F. Gasparini in Rome for further counterpoint training; after a sojourn in Paris (1726–27), he visited England (1727) before returning to Dresden as a flutist in the court Kapelle (also 1727). He made his 1st visit to Berlin in the entourage of Augustus II (1728), where he was engaged as teacher to Crown Prince Friedrich; he continued to visit Berlin regularly to instruct the Crown Prince while carrying out his duties in Dresden, which included the making of flutes from 1739. Friedrich

ascended the throne as King of Prussia in 1740 and the next year called Quantz to Berlin, where it was his special province to oversee the King's private evening concerts; he was granted an annual salary of 2,000 thalers, plus an honorarium for each new composition and flute he produced. Quantz was held in such high esteem by his patron that he was the only individual granted the right to criticize Friedrich's performances as a musician. His extensive output included some 300 concertos for Flute, Strings, and Basso Continuo; 7 concertos for 2 Flutes, Strings, and Basso Continuo; 2 concertos for Horn, Strings, and Basso Continuo (1 may not be by Quantz); 2 concertos for Oboe, Strings, and Basso Continuo; Concerto for Oboe d'Amore, Strings, and Basso Continuo (not extant); about 200 sonatas for Flute and Basso Continuo; some 60 trio sonatas; 12 duets for 2 Flutes or Other Instruments; 12 capriccios for Flute; 8 fantasias for Flute; 22 hymns; 6 songs; etc. On the whole, these works reveal Quantz as a transitional figure in the movement from the Baroque to the Classical style. He publ. the valuable treatise *Versuch einer Anweisung die Flöte traversiere zu spielen* (Berlin, 1752; 3rd ed., 1789; many subsequent eds. and trs., including an Eng. tr. by E. Reilly, N.Y., 1966; 2nd ed., rev., 1985). He also wrote an autobiography in F. Marpurg's *Historisch-kritische Beyträge zur Aufnahme der Musik*, I (Berlin, 1754; reprint in W. Kahl, *Selbstbiographien deutscher Musiker des XVIII. Jahrhunderts*, Cologne, 1948).
BIBL.: A. Quantz, *Leben und Werke des Flötisten J.J. Q.* (Berlin, 1877); C. Zoeller, *Thematic Catalogue of the Compositions of J.J. Q.* (MS, c.1886); A. Raskin, *J.J. Q.: Sein Leben und seine Kompositionen* (diss., Univ. of Cologne, 1923); E. Helm, *Music at the Court of Frederick the Great* (Norman, Okla., 1960); E. Reilly, *Q. and His Versuch: Three Studies* (N.Y., 1971).

Quarenghi, Guglielmo, Italian cellist and composer; b. Casalmaggiore, Oct. 22, 1826; d. Milan, Feb. 3, 1882. He was a pupil at the Milan Cons. (1839–42); from 1850, was 1st cello in the orch. at La Scala; in 1851, became a prof. of cello at the Cons.; from 1879 to 1881, was maestro di cappella at the Milan Cathedral. He publ. *Metodo di violoncello* (Milan, 1876); wrote an opera *Il dì di San Michele* (Milan, 1863), church music, chamber pieces, and works for solo cello, as well as transcriptions for the instrument.

Quatremère de Quincy, Antoine-Chrysostome, noted French archeologist, esthetician, art historian, writer on music, and political leader; b. Paris, Oct. 25, 1755; d. there, Dec. 28, 1849. He studied law, then took courses in art and history at the Collège de Louis-le-Grand; made visits to Italy (from 1776), where he pursued his interest in archeology; wrote on esthetics and art in Paris (from 1786); wrote his 1st important article on music, "De la nature des opéras bouffons italiens et de l'union de la comédie et de la musique dans ces poèmes" for the *Mercure de France* (March 1789). After the Revolution, he became an advocate for artistic freedom and the inviolability of copyright protection; was elected a deputy to the Legislative Assembly (1791), but was imprisoned for 2 years and came close to being executed during the Reign of Terror; was again spared from execution (1795). He then was named a member of the Council of the 500 (1797); became a member of the Académie des Inscriptions et Belles Lettres (1804) and the Légion d'honneur (1808); served as secretary of the Institut de France (from 1816), in which capacity he gave the funeral orations and wrote the biographical notices of the deceased members of the Académie.
WRITINGS (all publ. in Paris): *Dissertation sur les opéras bouffons italiens* (1789); *Discours . . . sur la liberté des théâtres* (1790); *Rapport . . . sur les réclamations des directeurs de théâtres et la propriété des auteurs dramatiques* (1792); *Dissertation . . . sur le système imitatif des arts et le genre poétique* (c.1804); *Institut royal de France: . . . funérailles de Paisiello* (1817); *de M. de Monsigny* (1818); *de M. Méhul* (1819), *de M. Gossec* (1829), *de M. Catel* (1820), and *de M. Boieldieu* (1834); *De l'invention et de l'innovation dans les ouvrages des beaux-arts* (c.1828); *Recueil des notices historiques lues dans*

les séances publiques de l'Académie royale des Beaux-arts à l'Institut (1834; notes on Paisiello, Monsigny, and Méhul publ. separately, see above); *Suite du Recueil* (1837; notices on Gossec, Catel, and Boieldieu publ. separately, see above).

Quef, Charles, French organist and composer; b. Lille, Nov. 1, 1873; d. there, July 2, 1931. He studied at the Lille Cons. and at the Paris Cons. with Guiraud, Théodore Dubois, Guilmant, and Widor (in 1898, won 1st prize for organ and improvisation); was organist in Paris at Ste. Marie, St. Laurent, and (from 1901) of La Trinité, succeeding Guilmant; concertized in France and England. He publ. sacred choruses and other works.

Queffélec, Anne (Tita), French pianist; b. Paris, Jan. 17, 1948. She was the daughter of Henri and sister of Yann Queffélec, both noted writers. She received her initial training at the Paris Cons. with Lélia Gousseau (premier prix in piano, 1965) and Jean Hubeau (premier prix in chamber music performance, 1966); subsequently pursued her studies with Alfred Brendel, Jörg Demus, and Paul Badura-Skoda in Vienna. After capturing 1st prize at the Munich International Competition in 1968 and 5th prize at the Leeds International Competition in 1969, she toured widely at home and abroad; was a soloist with many of the major orchs. of the world, and also was active as a recitalist and chamber music artist. In addition to the French repertoire, she became particularly known for her performances of the works of Mozart and Scarlatti.

Queler, Eve (née **Rabin**), American conductor; b. N.Y., Jan. 1, 1936. She studied with Bamberger at the Mannes College of Music, and took courses at the Hebrew Union School of Education and Sacred Music; after studying with Rosenstock on a Martha Baird Rockefeller Fund grant, she continued her training with Susskind and L. Slatkin in St. Louis and with Markevitch and Blomstedt in Europe. She made her conducting debut with *Cavalleria rusticana* in Fairlawn, N.J. (1966); then devoted herself mainly to conducting operas in concert with her own Opera Orch. of N.Y. (from 1967); led performances of rarely heard operas on both sides of the Atlantic, and also gave the U.S. premieres of many works, ranging from Donizetti to Richard Strauss. She appeared as a guest conductor with several North American orchs.; was the 1st American woman to conduct such esteemed ensembles as the Philadelphia Orch., the Cleveland Orch., and the Montreal Sym. Orch.

Querol (Gavaldá), Miguel, Spanish musicologist and composer; b. Ulldecona, Tarragona, April 22, 1912. He studied music at the Benedictine Monastery of Monserrat (1926–36) and later in Barcelona with Juan Lamote de Grignon; continued his training at the Univs. of Saragossa (1943), Barcelona (1944–45), and Madrid (Ph.D., 1948, with the diss. *La escuela estética catalana contemporánea*; publ. in Madrid, 1953). He was prof. of musicology at the Univ. of Barcelona (1957–70). He publ. *La música en las obras de Cervantes* (Barcelona, 1948) and *Breve historia de la música* (Madrid, 1955). Among his compositions are sacred music, chamber pieces, and piano works.

Quilico, Louis, Canadian baritone; b. Montreal, Jan. 14, 1925. He studied voice in Montreal and N.Y. with Martial Singher. After winning several vocal competitions, he appeared with the N.Y. City Opera in 1955; made his European debut in 1959; subsequently sang at Covent Garden in London, the Paris Opéra, and the Teatro Colón in Buenos Aires. On Feb. 10, 1972, he made his Metropolitan Opera debut in N.Y. as Golaud in Debussy's *Pelléas et Mélisande*; remained on its roster, singing mostly in French and Italian operas. He was made a Companion of the Order of Canada (1975).

Quilter, Roger, English composer; b. Brighton, Nov. 1, 1877; d. London, Sept. 21, 1953. He received his primary education at Eton College; then studied with Iwan Knorr at the Hoch Cons. in Frankfurt. He was particularly noted for his fine settings of Shakespeare's poems.
WORKS: Incidental music for Shakespeare's play *As You Like It* (1922); *The Sailor and His Lass* for Soprano, Baritone, Chorus, and Orch. (1948); numerous song cycles, among them 7

Elizabethan Lyrics, 3 Songs of the Sea, 4 Shakespeare Songs, etc.; also a light opera, *Julia* (London, Dec. 3, 1936).

BIBL.: T. Hold, *The Walled-in Garden: A Study of the Songs of R. Q.* (Rickmansworth, 1978); M. Pilkington, *Gurney, Ireland, Q. and Warlock* (London, 1989).

Quinault, Jean-Baptiste-Maurice, French singer, actor, and composer; b. Verdun, Sept. 9, 1687; d. Gien, Aug. 30, 1745. He was an actor at the Théâtre Français (1712–28) and at the Comédie Française in Paris until 1734. He set to music about 20 *intermèdes,* ballets, etc., and also produced a grand ballet, *Les Amours des déesses* (Paris, Aug. 9, 1729).

Quinault, Philippe, French dramatist, poet, and librettist; b. Paris, June 3, 1635; d. there, Nov. 26, 1688. He was Lully's librettist from 1671 to 1676.

BIBL.: G. Crapelet, *Notice sur la vie et les ouvrages de Q.* (Paris, 1824); E. Richter, *P. Q.: Sein Leben, seine Tragödien, seine Bedeutung für das Theater Frankreichs und des Auslandes* (Leipzig, 1910); E. Gros, *P. Q.: Sa vie et son œuvre* (Paris, 1926); J. Buijtendorp, *P. Q.: Sa vie, ses tragédies et ses tragicomédies* (Amsterdam, 1928).

Quinet, Fernand, Belgian cellist, conductor, and composer; b. Charleroi, Jan. 29, 1898; d. Liège, Oct. 24, 1971. He studied music theory in Charleroi; then enrolled at the Brussels Cons., where he studied cello with Edouard Jacobs and composition with Léon Dubois. After graduation he devoted his time to teaching and conducting. He served as director of the Cons. in Charleroi (1924–38) and Liège (1938–63); in 1948 he founded the Liège Sym. Orch., and was its principal conductor until 1965. He composed relatively little.

WORKS: Songs: *Recueillement, Les chevaux de bois; 4 mélodies; En bateau; La Légende de sœur Béatrice,* cantata (1920); *La Guerre,* cantata (1921; received the Belgian Grand Prix de Rome); Violin Sonata (1923); *Charade,* 4 pieces for Piano Trio (1927); Viola Sonata (1928); *Moralités-non-légendaires* for Voice and 18 Instruments (1930); *L'Ecole buissonnière* for String Quartet (1930); *3 Symphonic Movements* (ISCM Festival, London, July 28, 1931); *Suite* for 3 Clarinets (1930).

Quinet, Marcel, Belgian composer; b. Binche, July 6, 1915; d. Woluwé-St. Lambert, Brussels, Dec. 16, 1986. He studied at the conservatories of Mons and Brussels with Léon Jongen, Raymond Moulaert, and Marcel Maas (1934–43); also took private composition lessons with Jean Absil (1940–45). He was on the staff of the Brussels Cons. (1943–79) and also taught at the Chapelle Musicale Reine Elisabeth (1956–59; 1968–71; 1973–74). In 1978 he was made a member of the Académie Royale de Belgique. His music is moderately modernistic in the amiable manner of the French school, with some euphoniously dissonant excrescences.

WORKS: STAGE: *Les 2 Bavards,* chamber opera (1966); *La Nef des fous,* ballet (1969). **ORCH.:** *3 esquisses concertantes* for Violin and Orch. (1946); *Divertissement* (1946); *3 pièces* (1951; Salzburg ISCM Festival, June 21, 1952); Sinfonietta (1953); *Variations élégiaques sur un thème de Rolland de Lassus* (1955); 3 piano concertos (1955, 1964, 1966); Variations (1956); *Serenade* for String Orch. (1956); *Impressions symphoniques* (1956); *Allegro de concert* (1958); *Divertimento* for Chamber Orch. (1958); Concertino for Flute, Celesta, Harp, and Strings (1959); Sym. (1960); Concertino for Oboe, Clarinet, Bassoon, and String Orch. (1960); *Ballade* for Clarinet and String Orch. (1961); Viola Concerto (1962–63); *Concerto grosso* for 4 Clarinets and Strings (1964); *Overture for a Festival* (1967); *Music for Strings and Timpani* (1971); *Mouvements* for Chamber Orch. (1973); *Esquisses symphoniques* (1973); *Gorgone* (1974); *Séquence* (1974); *Dialogues* for 2 Pianos and Orch. (1975); *Diptyque* for Chamber Orch. (1975); *Climats* for Chamber

Orch. (1978); *Caractères* (1978; rev. 1983); *Metamorphoses* (1979); *Préludes* (1979); *Chromatismes* (1980); Concerto for Kettle Drums and Orch. (1981); *Concerto grosso* for 4 Saxophones and Orch. (1982); Concerto for 2 Pianos and Orch. (1983). **CHAMBER:** *8 petites pièces* for Wind Quintet (1946); 2 string trios (1948, 1969); Wind Quintet (1949); Violin Sonatina (1952); Piano Quartet (1957); String Quartet (1958); *Petite Suite* for 4 Clarinets (1959); *Sonate à 3* for Trumpet, Horn, and Trombone (1961); *Ballade* for Violin and Wind Quintet (1962); Wind Quartet (1964); Sonata for 2 Violins and Piano (1964); *Ballatella* for Trumpet or Horn or Trombone, and Piano (1966); *Pochades* for 4 Saxophones (1967); Trio for Oboe, Clarinet, and Bassoon (1967); Flute Sonata (1968); *Polyphonies* for 3 Performers on 8 Wind Instruments (1971); *Novelettes* for 2 Pianos (1973); *Sept tankas* for Double or Triple Vocal Quartet and Piano (1978); *Terzetto* for Flute, Violin, and Harpsichord (1981); *Ebauches* for Saxophone Quartet (1984); *Hommage à Ravel* for Female Voice, Piano, Flute, and Cello (1985); solo piano pieces. **VOCAL:** 2 cantatas, *La Vague et le Sillon* (1945; Belgian Grand Prix de Rome, 1945) and *Lectio pro Feria Sexta* (1973); songs.

Quintanar, Héctor, Mexican composer; b. Mexico City, April 15, 1936. He had lessons in music theory with Carlos Chávez, Rodolfo Halffter, and Galindo at the National Cons. in Mexico City (1959–64); also worked on problems of electronic music in N.Y. (1964), Paris (1967), and Mexico City (1968). Upon his return to Mexico, he supervised the construction of the country's 1st electronic music studio at the National Univ. (1970). In his compositions he employs traditional instruments as well as electronic sound.

WORKS: 3 syms. (1961, 1962, 1964); *Sinfonia modal* (1961–62); *El viejo y el mar,* symphonic poem after Hemingway (1963); *Fábula* for Chorus and Orch. (1964); Double Quartet for String Quartet and Wind Quartet (1964–65); String Trio (1965–66); Violin Sonata (1967); *Aclamaciones* for Chorus, Tape, and Orch. (1967); Sonata for 3 Trumpets (1967); *Galaxias* for Orch. (1968; Mexico City, July 7, 1968); *Sideral I* for Tape (1968), *Sideral II* for Orch. (1969; Mexico City, July 7, 1969), *Sideral III* for Tape (1971); *Solutio?* for Soprano and Piano (1969); *Símbolos* for Violin, Clarinet, Saxophone, Horn, Trumpet, Trombone, Piano, Tape, Optical Slides, and Lights (1969); *Ilapso* for Clarinet, Bassoon, Trumpet, Trombone, Percussion, Violin, and Double Bass (1970); *Voz* for Soprano and Tape (1971); Quintet for Piano, Violin, Double Bass, Flute, and Trumpet (1973); *Diálogos* for Piano and Tape (1973).

Quiroga, Manuel, Spanish violinist; b. Pontevedra, April 15, 1890; d. there, April 19, 1961. He studied at the Royal Cons. in Madrid and at the Paris Cons.; toured in Europe and in the U.S. with great success. He suffered a street accident in N.Y. in 1937 during one of his American tours, and was compelled to abandon public appearances; then retired to Pontevedra. He composed some violin pieces and a "sainete," *Los amos del barrio* (Madrid, Sept. 7, 1938).

Quivar, Florence, black American mezzo-soprano; b. Philadelphia, March 3, 1944. She studied at the Philadelphia Musical Academy, Salzburg Mozarteum, and with Luigi Ricci in Rome; was a member of the Juilliard Opera Theater in N.Y.; subsequently launched a successful concert career, appearing as soloist with the N.Y. Phil., the Cleveland Orch., the Philadelphia Orch., the Chicago Sym. Orch., and the Boston Sym. Orch. She made her Metropolitan Opera debut in N.Y. as Marina in *Boris Godunov* on Oct. 10, 1977; then sang there regularly, appearing in such roles as Jocasta in *Oedipus Rex,* Isabella in *L'Italiana in Algeri,* Fidès in *Le Prophète,* Eboli in *Don Carlos,* Marfa in *Khovanshchina,* and Serena in *Porgy and Bess.*

R

Raabe, Peter, German conductor and writer on music; b. Frankfurt an der Oder, Nov. 27, 1872; d. Weimar, April 12, 1945. He studied with Bargiel at the Berlin Hochschule für Musik and later continued his training at the Univ. of Jena (Ph.D., 1916); in 1894, began a career as a theater conductor; from 1899 to 1903 he conducted the Netherlands Opera in Amsterdam, and from 1903 to 1907, the Volks-Symphonie-Konzerte in Munich; in 1907 he became court conductor in Weimar; in 1910 he was appointed curator of the Liszt Museum in Weimar; from 1920 to 1934 he was Generalmusikdirektor in Aachen. In 1935 he became head of the Reichsmusikkammer and the Deutscher Tonkünstlerverein; in these offices he was called upon to perform administrative tasks for the Nazi regime, including the racial restrictions of musicians. His co-workers presented him with *Von deutscher Tonkunst: Festschrift zu Peter Raabes 70. Geburtstag* (Leipzig, 1942; 2nd ed., rev., 1944). Raabe died just before the total collapse of the 3rd Reich, which he tried to serve so well. He left some scholarly and valuable writings, among them: *Grossherzog Carl Alexander und Liszt* (Leipzig, 1918); *Franz Liszt: Leben und Schaffen* (2 vols., Stuttgart, 1931; rev. ed. by his son Felix, 1968); *Die Musik im dritten Reich* (Regensburg, 1935); *Kulturwille im deutschen Musikleben* (Regensburg, 1936); *Deutsche Meister* (Berlin, 1937); *Wege zu Weber* (Regensburg, 1942); *Wege zu Liszt* (Regensburg, 1943); *Wege zu Bruckner* (Regensburg, 1944).

Raaff, Anton, esteemed German tenor; b. Gelsdorf, near Bonn (baptized), May 6, 1714; d. Munich, May 28, 1797. He studied with Ferrandini in Munich and Bernacchi in Bologna; sang in Italy; then in Bonn, in Vienna, and at various German courts (1742–52); in Lisbon (1752–55), Madrid (1755–59), and Naples, returning in 1770 to Germany, where he was attached to the court of the Elector Karl Theodor at Mannheim. In 1778 he went to Paris with Mozart; from 1779, was in Munich. Mozart wrote the role of Idomeneo for him, and also the aria *Se al labbro mio non credi*, K. 295.

BIBL.: H. Freiberger, *A. R. (1714–1797): Sein Leben und Wirken* (Cologne, 1929); P. Petrobelli, "The Italian Years of A. R.," *Mozart Jahrbuch 1973–4.*

Raalte, Albert van, Dutch conductor; b. Amsterdam, May 21, 1890; d. there, Nov. 23, 1952. He studied at the Cologne Cons. with Bram Eldering (violin) and Waldemar von Baussnern (theory); later in Leipzig with Nikisch and Max Reger; was a theater conductor in Brussels (1911) and Leipzig (1912); conducted Wagner's operas at the Municipal Opera in Leipzig (1914–15), then at the Dutch National Opera in The Hague (1915–22); formed his own opera enterprise there. He remained in the Netherlands during the German occupation; conducted the radio orch. at Hilversum; was sent to a concentration camp as a person with Jewish associations; after the liberation in 1945, he returned to his post at Hilversum, building the radio orch. to a high degree of efficiency.

Raasted, Niels Otto, Danish organist and composer; b. Copenhagen, Nov. 26, 1888; d. there, Dec. 31, 1966. He studied at the Copenhagen Cons. (1909–12); then at the Leipzig Cons., with Max Reger, Karl Straube, and R. Teichmüller (1913–14); returning to Denmark, he became organist at Copenhagen Cathedral; also conducted the Bach Soc. (1925–46).

WORKS: 3 syms. (1914, 1938, 1944); orch. suites, among them *Pictures from Finland* (1928) and *Hans Christian Andersen Suite* (1940); *Sinfonia da chiesa* (1944); 3 string quartets (1914, 1918, 1920); 5 violin sonatas; 6 organ sonatas; an oratorio, *Saul* (1923); cantatas (all perf. on Copenhagen Radio): *Sangen om København* (June 27, 1934); *Thylands pris* (May 12, 1941); *Kong Vaar* (Oct. 20, 1947).

Rääts, Jaan, Estonian composer; b. Tartu, Oct. 15, 1932. He studied with Saar (1952–54) and Eller (1954–57) at the Tallinn Cons.; was director of the music division of the Estonian Radio (1955–66); then served as music director of Estonian Television. His music possesses firm thematic lines animated by a motoric pulse.

WORKS: ORCH.: 8 syms. (1957, 1958, 1959, 1959, 1966, 1967, 1973, 1985); Concerto for Chamber Orch. (1961); 2 concertos for Violin and Chamber Orch. (1963, 1979); 2 piano concertos (1971, 1983); Concerto for 2 Pianos and Orch. (1986). **CHORAL:** *Karl Marx*, "declamatorio" for Narrator, Chorus, and Orch. (Tallinn, June 6, 1964). **CHAMBER:** 5 string quartets; 4 piano trios; 3 piano quintets; Piano Sextet; various piano pieces, including 8 sonatas.

Rabaud, Henri (Benjamin), noted French conductor, pedagogue, and composer; b. Paris, Nov. 10, 1873; d. there, Sept. 11, 1949. His father was Hippolyte Rabaud (1839–1900), prof. of cello at the Paris Cons., where Henri studied with Gédalge and Massenet (1893–94); won the Premier Grand Prix de Rome in 1894 with his cantata *Daphné*; in 1908 he became conductor at the Paris Opéra and at the Opéra-Comique; from 1914 to 1918 he was director of the Opéra. In 1918–19 he was engaged to conduct the Boston Sym. Orch.; then was appointed director of the Paris Cons. in 1922; he held this post until 1941.

WORKS: OPERAS: *La Fille de Roland* (Paris, March 16, 1904); *Le Premier Glaive* (Béziers, 1908); *Marouf, savetier du Caire* (Paris, May 15, 1914; his most successful opera); *Antoine et Cléopâtre*, after Shakespeare (1916–17); *L'Appel de la mer* (Paris, April 10, 1924); *Le Miracle des loups* (Paris, Nov. 14, 1924); *Rolande et le mauvais garçon* (Paris, May 28, 1934); *Le Jeu de l'amour et du hasard* (1948; Monte Carlo, 1954); incidental music and film scores. **ORCH.:** 2 syms. (1893, 1900); *L'Été* for Soprano, Alto, Choir, and Orch. (1895); *La Procession nocturne*, symphonic poem (Paris, Jan. 15, 1899); *Divertissement sur des chansons russes* (1899); *Lamento* (1930); *Prelude and Toccata* for Piano and Orch. (1945); also *Job*, oratorio (1900); choral works, including *Hymne à la France éternelle* (1916); String Quartet (1898); Trio for Oboe, Clarinet, and Bassoon (1949); piano pieces; songs.

BIBL.: M. d'Ollone, *H. R.: Sa vie et son œuvre* (Paris, 1958).

Rabe, Folke (Alvar Harald Reinhold), Swedish trombonist and composer; b. Stockholm, Oct. 28, 1935. He studied composition with V. Söderholm, B. Wallner, Blomdahl, and Ligeti at the Stockholm Musikhögskolan (1957–64), where he also received training in trombone and music pedagogy. He began his career as a jazz musician while still a teenager; later was a member of the Culture Quartet (1963–73) and the New Culture Quartet (from 1983), which performed contemporary scores; was on the staff (1968–80) and served as program director (1977–80) of the Inst. for National Concerts; then was a producer with the Swedish Radio. He experimented with multimedia techniques; produced pieces of "vocal theater" with non-semantic texts.

WORKS: INTERMEDIA SHOWS: *Ship of Fools* (1983); *The World Museum* (1987); *Beloved Little Pig*, musical fairy tale for children (1986); film scores; incidental music. **ORCH.:** *Hep-Hep*, overture for Small Orch. (1966); *Altiplano* for Wind Orch. (1982). **CHAMBER:** *Suite* for 2 Clarinets (1957); *Bolos* for 4 Trombones (1962; in collaboration with J. Bark); *Impromptu* for Clarinet, Trombone, Cello, Piano, and Percussion (1962); *Pajazzo* for 8 Jazz Musicians (1964); *Polonaise* for 4 Trombones and Light (1965–66; in collaboration with J. Bark); *From the Myths of Time* for 3 Cellos, Gamelan, and Percussion (1966); *Pipe Lines* for 4 Trombones (1969); *Zug* for 4 Trombones (1970); *Shazam* for Trumpet (1984); *With Love* for Piano (1985); *Escalations* for Brass Quintet (1988). **VOCAL:** 7 *Poems by Nils Ferlin* for Chorus (1958); *Notturno* for Mezzo-soprano, Flute, Oboe, and Clarinet (1959); *Pièce* for Speaking Chorus (Swedish, German, and Eng. versions, 1961; in collaboration with L. O'Mansson); *Souvenirs* for Reciter, Electric Organ, and Rhythm Section (1963); *Rondes* for Chorus (1964); *O. D.* for Men's Chorus (1965); *Joe's Harp* for Chorus (1970); *Två Strofer* for Chorus (1980); *to love* for Chorus, after e.e. cummings (1984); songs. **OTHER:** *Eh??* for Electronics (1967); *To the Barbender* for Tape (1982); *New Construction* for Small Children, Electronics, and Various Sound Sources (1984); *Cyclone* for Electronics (1985).

Rabin, Michael, gifted American violinist; b. N.Y., May 2, 1936; d. there, Jan. 19, 1972. He was of a musical family; his father was a violinist in the N.Y. Phil., his mother a pianist. He studied with Ivan Galamian in N.Y. and made excellent progress; in his early youth, he appeared as a soloist with a number of American orchs.; made several European tours as a concert violinist, and also played in Australia. His sudden death at the age of 35 was a shock to American music-lovers.

Rabinof, Benno, esteemed American violinist; b. N.Y., Oct. 11, 1908; d. Brevard, N.C., July 2, 1975. He studied privately with Victor Küzdö, Franz Kneisel, and Leopold Auer; made his debut in 1927, playing the Tchaikovsky Violin Concerto with members of the N.Y. Phil., conducted by Leopold Auer. In 1930 he played Glazunov's Violin Concerto, with Glazunov himself leading the Boston Sym. Orch. as guest conductor. With his wife, the pianist Sylvia Smith-Rabinof, he traveled extensively in Europe and America.

Rabinovich, David, Russian musicologist; b. Kharkov, Aug. 8, 1900; d. Moscow, July 23, 1978. He studied piano at the St. Petersburg Cons. with Essipova, and first performed in public at the age of 13; then entered classes in composition with Glière and piano with Igumnov at the Moscow Cons., graduating in 1930. He subsequently abandoned his career as a concert pianist, and devoted himself to musicology, specializing in monographs on Soviet composers. He publ. *D. Shostakovich, Composer* (Moscow, 1959, in an Eng. tr.); *Portraits of Pianists* (Moscow, 1962); numerous articles in Soviet music periodicals.

Rabl, Walter, Austrian conductor and composer; b. Vienna, Nov. 30, 1873; d. Klagenfurt, July 14, 1940. He was a pupil of J.F. Hummel, and later of Navratil in Vienna; studied musicology with Guido Adler at the German Univ. in Prague (Ph.D., 1897). He conducted at the Düsseldorf Opera (1903–6), and at the municipal theaters in Essen, Dortmund, and Magdeburg (1915–24); wrote an opera, *Liane* (Strasbourg, 1903); Sym.; Quartet for Clarinet, Violin, Cello, and Piano; Violin Sonata; several song cycles.

BIBL.: A. Eccarius-Sieber, "W. R.," *Monographien moderner Musiker,* Vol. II (Leipzig, 1907).

Racek, Jan, Czech musicologist; b. Bučovice, June 1, 1905; d. Brno, Dec. 5, 1979. He studied with Helfert at the Univ. of Brno (Ph.D., 1929, with the diss. *Idea vlasti, národa a slávy v dile B. Smetany* [The Idea of the Fatherland, Nation, and Glory in the Works of B. Smetana]; publ. in Brno, 1933; 2nd ed., augmented, 1947); later received a D.Sc. degree (1957). He was director of the music archives of the Moravian Regional Museum (1930–48); also was a lecturer at the Univ. of Brno (from 1939) and prof. and director of the Brno dept. of ethnography and folk music of the Czech Academy of Sciences (1948–70). He served as ed. of the journal *Musikologie* and as general ed. of Musica Antiqua Bohemica.

WRITINGS: *Leoš Janáček* (Olomouc, 1938); *Slohové problémy italské monodie* (Problems of Style in Italian Monody; Prague and Brno, 1938; German tr., 1965); ed. with L. Firkušný, *Janáčkovy feuilletony z Lidové Noviny* (Janáček's Feuilletons in the *Lidové Noviny*; Brno, 1938; 2nd ed., rev., 1958, as *Leoš Janáček: Fejetony z Lidových Noviny*; German tr., 1962); *Leoš Janáček a současni moravští skladatelé* (Leoš Janáček and Contemporary Moravian Composers; Brno, 1940); *Česká hudba* *od nejstarších dob do počátku 19. století* (Czech Music from the Earliest Times to the Beginning of the 19th Century; Prague, 1949; 2nd ed., augmented, 1958); *Ruská hudba: Od nejstarších dob az po velkou říjnovou revoluci* (Russian Music from the Earliest Times up to the Great Revolution; Prague, 1953); *Beethoven a české země* (Beethoven in Bohemia and Moravia; Brno, 1964).

Rachmaninoff, Sergei (Vassilievich), greatly renowned Russian-born American pianist, conductor, and composer; b. Semyonovo, April 1, 1873; d. Beverly Hills, March 28, 1943. He was of a musical family; his grandfather was an amateur pianist, a pupil of John Field; his father also played the piano; Rachmaninoff's *Polka* was written on a theme improvised by his father; his mother likewise played piano, and it was from her that he received his initial training at their estate, Oneg, near Novgorod. After financial setbacks, the family estate was sold and he was taken to St. Petersburg, where he studied piano with Vladimir Demiansky and harmony with Alexander Rubets at the Cons. (1882–85); acting on the advice of his cousin, Alexander Siloti, he enrolled as a piano student of Nikolai Zverev at the Moscow Cons. (1885); then entered Siloti's piano class and commenced the study of counterpoint with Taneyev and harmony with Arensky (1888). He met Tchaikovsky, who appreciated his talent and gave him friendly advice. He graduated as a pianist (1891) and as a composer (1892), winning the gold medal with his opera *Aleko*, after Pushkin. Then followed his Prelude in C-sharp minor (1892); publ. that same year, it quickly became one of the most celebrated piano pieces in the world. His 1st Sym., given in Moscow (1897), proved a failure, however. Discouraged, Rachmaninoff destroyed the MS, but the orch. parts were preserved; after his death, the score was restored and performed in Moscow (1945). In the meantime, Rachmaninoff launched a career as a piano virtuoso; also took up a career as a conductor, joining the Moscow Private Russian Orch. (1897). He made his London debut in the triple capacity of pianist, conductor, and composer with the Phil. Soc. (1899). Although he attempted to compose after the failure of his 1st Sym., nothing significant came from his pen. Plagued by depression, he underwent treatment by hypnosis with Nikolai Dahl, and then began work on his 2nd Piano Concerto. He played the 1st complete performance of the score with Siloti conducting in Moscow (Nov. 9, 1901); this concerto became the most celebrated work of its genre written in the 20th century, and its singular charm has never abated since; it is no exaggeration to say that it became a model for piano concertos by a majority of modern Russian composers, and also of semi-popular virtuoso pieces for piano and orch. written in America. On May 12, 1902, Rachmaninoff married his cousin Natalie Satina; they spent some months in Switzerland, then returned to Moscow. After conducting at Moscow's Bolshoi Theater (1904–6), he decided to spend most of his time in Dresden, where he composed his 2nd Sym., one of his most popular works. Having composed another major work, his 3rd Piano Concerto, he took it on his 1st tour of the U.S. in 1909. His fame was so great that he was offered the conductorship of the Boston Sym. Orch., but he declined; the offer was repeated in 1918, but once again he declined. He lived in Russia from 1910 until after the Bolshevik Revolution of Oct. 1917, at which time he left Russia with his family, never to return. From 1918 until 1939 he made annual tours of Europe as a pianist; also of the U.S. (from 1918 until his death), where he spent much of his time; he also owned a villa in Lucerne (1931–39), and it was there that he composed one of his most enduring scores, the *Rhapsody on a Theme of Paganini* (1934). In 1932 he was awarded the Gold Medal of the Royal Phil. Soc. of London. After the outbreak of World War II (1939), he spent his remaining years in the U.S. He became a naturalized U.S. citizen a few weeks before his death, having made his last appearance as a pianist in Knoxville, Tenn., on Feb. 15, 1943.

Among Russian composers, Rachmaninoff occupies a very important place. The sources of his inspiration lie in the Ro-

mantic tradition of 19th-century Russian music; the link with Tchaikovsky's lyrical art is very strong; melancholy moods prevail and minor keys predominate in his compositions, as in Tchaikovsky's; but there is an unmistakable stamp of Rachmaninoff's individuality in the broad, rhapsodic sweep of the melodic line, and particularly in the fully expanded sonorities and fine resonant harmonies of his piano writing; its technical resourcefulness is unexcelled by any composer since Liszt. Despite the fact that Rachmaninoff was an émigré and stood in avowed opposition to the Soviet regime (until the German attack on Russia in 1941 impelled him to modify his stand), his popularity never wavered in Russia; after his death, Russian musicians paid spontaneous tribute to him. Rachmaninoff's music is much less popular in Germany, France, and Italy; on the other hand, in England and America it constitutes a potent factor on the concert stage.

WORKS: OPERAS: *Esmeralda* (1888; introduction to Act 1 and fragment of Act 3 only completed); *Aleko,* after Pushkin's *Tsigani* (The Gypsies; 1892; Moscow, May 9, 1893); *The Miserly Knight,* op. 24, after Pushkin (1903–5; Moscow, Jan. 24, 1906); *Francesca da Rimini,* op. 25, after Dante's *Inferno* (1900; 1904–5; Moscow, Jan. 24, 1906); *Monna Vanna,* after Maeterlinck (1907; piano score of Act 1 and sketches of Act 2 only completed; Act 1 orchestrated by I. Buketoff; concert perf., Saratoga, N.Y., Aug. 11, 1984). **ORCH.:** *Scherzo* in D minor (1887); Piano Concerto in C minor (1889; sketches only); *Manfred,* symphonic poem (1890–91; not extant); 4 piano concertos: No. 1 in F-sharp minor, op. 1 (1890–91; Moscow, March 17, 1892; rev. 1917); No. 2 in C minor, op. 18 (Moscow, Nov. 9, 1901); No. 3 in D minor, op. 30 (N.Y., Nov. 28, 1909); No. 4 in G minor, op. 40 (1926; Philadelphia, March 18, 1927; rev. 1927, 1941); Sym. in D minor (1891; 1st movement only completed); *Prince Rostislav,* symphonic poem (1891); *The Rock,* fantasy (1893; Moscow, March 20, 1896); *Capriccio on Gypsy Themes* or *Capriccio bohémien,* op. 12 (1892, 1894); 2 episodes after Byron's *Don Juan* (1894; not extant); Sym. No. 1 in D minor, op. 13 (1895; St. Petersburg, March 27, 1897); Sym. (1897; sketches only); Sym. No. 2 in E minor, op. 27 (1906–8; St. Petersburg, Feb. 8, 1908); Sym. No. 3 in A minor, op. 44 (Philadelphia, Nov. 6, 1936; rev. 1938); *The Isle of the Dead,* symphonic poem, op. 29, after Böcklin's painting (Moscow, May 1, 1909); *Rhapsody on a Theme of Paganini* for Piano and Orch., op. 43 (Baltimore, Nov. 7, 1934); *Symphonic Dances,* op. 45 (1940; Philadelphia, Jan. 3, 1941). **CHAMBER:** String Quartet (1889; 2 movements only); *Romance* in A minor for Violin and Piano (c.1880–90); *Romance* in F minor for Cello and Piano (1890); *Melodie* in D major for Cello and Piano (c.1890; arranged by M. Altschuler, 1947); String Quintet (n.d.; not extant); *Trio élégiaque* in G minor for Piano Trio (1892); 2 pieces for Cello and Piano, op. 2 (1892): *Prélude* in F major (revision of a piano piece, 1891) and *Danse orientale* in A minor; 2 *Morceaux de salon* for Violin and Piano, op. 6 (1893): *Romance* and *Danse hongroise; Trio élégiaque* in D minor for Piano Trio, op. 9, in memory of Tchaikovsky (1893; rev. 1907, 1917); String Quartet (c.1896; 2 movements only); Sonata in G minor for Cello and Piano, op. 19 (1901). **CHORAL:** *Deus meus,* motet for 6 Voices (1890); *O Mother of God Vigilantly Praying* for 4 Voices (1893); *Chorus of Spirits* and *Song of the Nightingale* from *Don Juan* (c.1894); 6 choruses for Women's or Children's Voices, op. 15 (1895–96); *Panteley the Healer* (1901); *Spring,* cantata for Baritone, Chorus, and Orch., op. 20 (Moscow, March 24, 1902); *Liturgy of St. John Chrysostom,* op. 31 (Moscow, Nov. 25, 1910); *The Bells,* choral sym. for Soprano, Baritone, Chorus, and Orch., op. 35, after Poe (St. Petersburg, Dec. 13, 1913); *All-Night Vigil,* op. 37 (1915); 3 *Russian Songs* for Chorus and Orch., op. 41 (1926; Philadelphia, March 18, 1927). **PIANO:** *Song without Words* (c.1887); 3 *Nocturnes* (1887–88); 4 pieces: *Romance, Prélude, Mélodie, and Gavotte* (1887); *Canon* (1890–91); 2 pieces for 6 Hands: *Waltz* (1890) and *Romance* (1891); *Prélude* (1891; rev. as *Prélude* for Cello and Piano, 1892); *Russian Rhapsody* for 2 Pianos (1891); *Morceaux de fantaisie* (1892; includes the famous *Prélude* in C-sharp minor); *Romance* for 4 Hands (c.1894); *Fantai-*

sie-tableaux: Suite No. 1 for 2 Pianos, op. 5 (1893); *Morceaux de salon*, op. 10 (1893–94); *Romance* for 4 Hands (c.1894); *6 Morceaux* for 4 Hands, op. 11 (1894); *6 Moments musicaux*, op.16 (1896); *Improvisations* (1896; in *4 Improvisations* in collaboration with Arensky, Glazunov, and Taneyev); *Morceaux de fantaisie* (1899); *Fughetta* (1899); *Suite No. 2* for 2 Pianos, op. 17 (1900–1901); *Variations on a Theme of Chopin*, op. 22 (1902–3); *10 Préludes*, op. 23 (1901–3); *Polka italienne* for 4 Hands (c.1906); Sonata No. 1, op. 28 (1907); *13 Préludes*, op. 32 (1910); *Études-tableaux*, op. 33 (1911); *Polka V.R.*, on a theme by the composer's father, Vasily Rachmaninoff (1911); Sonata No. 2, op. 36 (1913; rev. 1931); *Études-tableaux*, op. 39 (1916–17); *Oriental Sketch* (1917); *Prelude* (1917); Fragments in A-flat major (1917); *Variations on a Theme of Corelli*, op. 42 (1931); also 82 songs (1890–1916).

BIBL.: I. Lipayev, *S. R.* (Saratov, 1913); V. Belaiev, *S. R.* (Moscow, 1924; Eng. tr. in *Musical Quarterly*, July 1927); O. von Riesemann, *R.'s Recollections* (N.Y., 1934); W. Lyle, *R.: A Biography* (London, 1939); A. and K. Swan, "R.: Personal Reminiscences," *Musical Quarterly* (Jan. and April 1944); A. Solovtsov, *S. R.* (Moscow, 1947); J. Culshaw, *S. R.* (London, 1949); V. Seroff, *R.* (N.Y., 1950); A. Alexeyev, *S. R.* (Moscow, 1954); Z. Apetian, ed., *S.V. R.: Letters* (Moscow, 1955); S. Bertensson and J. Leyda, *S. R.: A Lifetime in Music* (N.Y., 1956; 2nd ed., 1965); Z. Apetian, ed., *Reminiscences of R.* (Moscow, 1957; 4th ed., augmented, 1974); V. Bryantseva, "Where Was S.V. R. Born?," *Muzikalnaya Zhizn*, 19 (1969); Y. Keldish, *R. and His Time* (Moscow, 1973); G. Norris, "R.'s Second Thoughts," *Musical Times*, CXIV (1973); idem, "R.'s Student Opera," *Musical Quarterly*, LIX (1973); R. Threlfall, *S. R., His Life and Music* (London, 1973); P. Piggott, *R. Orchestral Music* (London, 1974); V. Bryantseva, *S.V. R.* (Moscow, 1976); G. Norris, *R.* (London, 1976); Z. Apetian, ed., *S. R.: Literary Heritage* (Moscow, 1978–80); R. Walker, *R.: His Life and Times* (Tunbridge Wells, 1980); R. Threlfall and G. Norris, *Catalogue of the Compositions of S. R.* (London, 1982); G. Norris, "R.'s Apprenticeship," *Musical Times* (Oct. 1983); R. Palmieri, *S.V. R.: A Guide to Research* (London and N.Y., 1985); C. Poivre D'Arvor, *R., ou, La Passion au bout des doigts* (Monaco, 1986).

Račiūnas, Antanas, significant Lithuanian composer and pedagogue; b. Užliašiai, near Panevėžys, Sept. 17, 1905; d. Kaunas, April 3, 1984. He studied composition with J. Gruodis at the Kaunas Cons. (graduated, 1933) and with Nadia Boulanger and Charles Koechlin in Paris (1936–39). Returning to Lithuania, he taught at the Kaunas Cons. (1933–36; 1939–49) and the Vilnius Cons. (1949–59). In 1965 he was made a People's Artist of the Lithuanian S.S.R. He wrote and produced the 1st opera in Lithuanian.

WORKS: OPERAS: *3 Talismen* (Kaunas, March 19, 1936); *Amber Shore* (1940); *Marite* (1953); *Sun City* (1965). ORCH.: 9 syms. (1933, 1946, 1951, 1960, 1961, 1966, 1969, 1970, 1974); 4 symphonic poems: *Evening in Vilnius* (1939); *The Secret of Lake Plateliu* (1956); *Jurgenas and Ramune* (1958); *Mother Pirčiupio* (1972); suite, *Scenes of Lithuania* (1955); *3 Pieces* (1964); *Prelude and Joke* (1974); Piano Concerto (1976). CHAMBER: Sonata-Fantasy for Oboe and Piano (1963); Sonatina for Cello and Piano (1965); Sonata for 2 Pianos (1967); Sonata for Cello and Piano (1968); Suite for 2 Pianos and Percussion (1973); Triptych for Oboe and Piano (1973); Sonata for Violin and Piano (1977); also works for solo piano. CHORAL: 2 cantatas (1943, 1949); *Liberated Lithuania*, oratorio (1945); many choruses; songs.

Radecke, Robert, German conductor, pedagogue, and composer, brother of **Rudolf Radecke;** b. Dittmannsdorf, Oct. 31, 1830; d. Wernigerode, June 21, 1911. He studied at the Leipzig Cons. with Ferdinand David (violin) and Moscheles (piano); also took a course in composition with Hauptmann; appeared 1st as a violinist; then went to Berlin, where he conducted the Royal Opera (1863–87); also taught at the Royal Inst. for Church Music there (1892–1907). He wrote a "Liederspiel," *Die Mönkgüter* (Berlin, May 1, 1874); several overtures;

2 piano trios; choruses and piano works; but became known to the general public mainly for his song *Aus der Jugendzeit*, which obtained extraordinary popularity in Germany and was commonly mistaken for a folk song.

Radecke, Rudolf, German conductor, pedagogue, and composer, brother of **Robert Radecke;** b. Dittmannsdorf, Sept. 6, 1829; d. Berlin, April 15, 1893. He studied at the Leipzig Cons.; in 1859 he went to Berlin, where he organized the Radecke Choral Soc. (1868) and a music school (1869); also taught music at the Stern Cons. (1864–71). He wrote a number of part-songs.

Radford, Robert, esteemed English bass; b. Nottingham, May 13, 1874; d. London, March 3, 1933. He was educated at London's Royal Academy of Music, taking voice lessons with Alberto Randegger. He made his operatic debut at Covent Garden in London in 1904 as the Commendatore in *Don Giovanni*; later sang Hagen and Hunding in the 1st English *Ring* cycle under Richter in London (1908). In 1921 he became a founder, with Beecham, of the British National Opera Co.; later became its director. In 1929 he was appointed to the faculty of his alma mater. His fame as an opera singer was great in England; in addition to singing opera, he greatly distinguished himself as a concert artist.

Radić, Dušan, Serbian composer; b. Sombor, April 10, 1929. He studied at the Belgrade Academy of Music; then went to Paris, where he had private lessons with Milhaud and Messiaen. His music follows the cosmopolitan modernistic manner, Baroque in formal structure, dissonant in contrapuntal intricacies, and hedonistic in its utilitarian appeal.

WORKS: *Symphoniette* (1954); *Spisak* (Inventory), song cycle for 2 Female Voices and 11 Instruments (Belgrade, March 17, 1954); *Balada o mesecu lutalici* (Ballad of the Errant Moon), ballet (Belgrade, Oct. 19, 1960); Concertino for Clarinet and Strings (1956); *Sinfonia* (1965–66); Piano Quintet; several cantatas; songs; theater music; film scores.

Radica, Ruben, Croatian composer; b. Split, May 19, 1931. He studied with Kelemen in Zagreb, Frazzi in Siena, and Leibowitz in Paris. In 1963 he was appointed to the faculty of the Zagreb Academy of Music; served as its dean (1981–85). He belongs to the avant-garde of Slovenian music; in 1961 he adopted the 12-tone method of composition.

WORKS: *Concerto grosso* (1957); *4 Dramatic Epigrams* for Piano and String Quartet (1959); *Concerto abbreviato* for Cello and Orch. (1960); *Lyrical Variations* for Strings (1961); *Formacije* (Formations) for Orch. (1963); *19 and 10, Interferences* for Narrator, Chorus, and Orch. (1965); *Sustajarnje* (Prostration) for Electric Organ and Orch. (1967); *Composition* for Ondes Martenot and Chamber Orch. (Graz, Sept. 26, 1968); *Extensio* for Piano and Orch. (1973); *Per se II* for Wind Quintet (1975); *Ka* for 2 Instrumental Groups and Synthesizer (1977); *Alla madrigalesca* for Mixed Choir (1979); *Passion* for Baritone and 3 Instrumental Groups (1981); *Barocchiana* for Trumpet and Strings (1984).

Radiciotti, Giuseppe, Italian writer on music; b. Iesi, Le Marche, Jan. 25, 1858; d. Tivoli, April 4, 1931. He was a music pupil of his uncle, G. Faini; after finishing a course of studies at the Univ. of Rome, he taught in secondary schools there; in 1895 he was appointed prof. at the Liceo in Tivoli.

WRITINGS: *Teatro, musica e musicisti in Sinigaglia* (1893); *Contributi alla storia del teatro e della musica in Urbino* (1899); *Il teatro e la musica in Rome nel secondo quarto del secolo XIX* (1904); *Teatro, musica e musicisti in Recanati* (1904); *L'arte musicale dei Marchigiani* (1905); *L'arte musicale in Tivoli nei secoli XVI, XVII e XVIII* (1907); *Giovanni Battista Pergolesi: Vita, opere ed influenza sull'arte* (1910; 2nd ed., 1935; German tr., 1954); *Rossini* (1914); *La Cappella musicale del duomo di Pesaro* (1914); *Gioacchino Rossini: Vita documentata, opere ed influenza sull'arte* (3 vols., 1927–29; 2nd ed., 1941); *Aneddoti rossiniani autentici* (1929).

BIBL.: A. Belardinelli, *G. R.* (Iesi, 1933).

Radnai, Miklós, Hungarian composer; b. Budapest, Jan. 1, 1892; d. there, Nov. 4, 1935. He studied violin, piano, and composition at the Budapest Academy of Music; continued his composition studies with Mottl in Munich (1911); in 1925, was appointed director of the Budapest Opera. He wrote a textbook on harmony and contributed critical essays to publications. He wrote a ballet, *The Birthday of the Infanta*, after Oscar Wilde (Budapest, April 26, 1918); *Symphony of the Magyars* for Chorus and Orch.; Violin Concerto; some chamber music.

Radó, Aladár, Hungarian composer; b. Budapest, Dec. 26, 1882; killed in battle near Belgrade, Sept. 7, 1914. He studied in Budapest and Berlin; wrote 2 operas: *The Black Knight* (1911) and *Golem* (1912); Sym. (1909); *Hungarian Concerto* for Cello and Orch. (1909); 2 string quartets; String Quintet; publ. several albums of piano pieces and song cycles.

Radoux, Jean-Théodore, Belgian composer and pedagogue, father of **Charles Radoux-Rogier;** b. Liège, Nov. 9, 1835; d. there, March 20, 1911. He studied composition with Daussoigne-Méhul at the Liège Cons.; won the Belgian Prix de Rome with the cantata *Le Juif errant* (1859); then went to Paris for additional study with Halévy. He was prof. of bassoon at the Liège Cons. (from 1856), serving as its director (from 1872). He wrote monographs on Daussoigne-Méhul (1882) and Vieuxtemps (1891), and also *La Musique et les Écoles nationales* (1896), all publ. in Brussels.
    WORKS: 2 operas: *Le Béarnais* (Liège, March 14, 1866) and *La Coupe enchantée* (Brussels, 1872); oratorio, *Cain* (1877); symphonic poems: *Ahasvère* and *Le Festin de Balthasar;* patriotic overture, *Épopée nationale;* church music.

Radoux-Rogier (real name, **Radoux**), **Charles,** Belgian pedagogue, writer on music, and composer, son of **Jean-Théodore Radoux;** b. Liège, July 30, 1877; d. there, April 30, 1952. He studied with his father at the Liège Cons., winning the Belgian Prix de Rome with his cantata *Geneviève de Brabant* (1907); was made a prof. of harmony there (1905); wrote music criticism and was active in folk-song research; served as inspector of music education (1930–42).
    WORKS: Operas: *Les Sangliers des Ardennes* (Liège, 1905) and *Oudelette* (Brussels, April 11, 1912). Choral with orch.: *Adieu-Absence-Retour, Chanson d'Halewyn, Les Fées;* orch. sketches: *Danse tzigane, Burlesque, Vision, Triptique champêtre; Scène grecque* for Cello and Orch.; *Variations* for Violin and Orch.; *Lamentation* (on a Bach prelude) for English Horn and Piano; piano pieces; folk-song albums.

Radovanović, Vladan, Serbian composer; b. Belgrade, Sept. 5, 1932. He studied at the Belgrade Academy of Music. His early works are set in a neo-Classical style; later he annexed ultramodern techniques, including electronic effects. His *Urklang* for Mezzo-soprano and Chamber Orch. (Belgrade, March 14, 1962) deploys a counterpoint of instrumental colors, with the soloist singing wordlessly. Similarly wordless is his suite *Chorales, Intermezzi e Fuga* for Women's Chorus (Belgrade, May 16, 1962). His experimental period includes such innovative works as *Sphaeroön* in 26 vocal parts, singing detached vowels (Belgrade, March 14, 1962), and *Pentaptych,* suite for Voice and 6 Instruments (Belgrade, April 22, 1964).

Radziwill, Prince Anton Heinrich (Antoni Henryk), Polish cellist, guitarist, singer, composer, and music patron; b. near Vilnius, June 13, 1775; d. Berlin, April 7, 1833. He became widely known as a music patron, his Berlin residence becoming a gathering place for musicians; he befriended Beethoven, Goethe, Mendelssohn, Zelter, Chopin, and others; became governor of the Grand Duchy of Posen (1815). Among the works dedicated to him were Beethoven's *Namensfeier* overture, op. 115; Mendelssohn's Piano Quartet, op. 1; and Chopin's *Introduction and Polonaise* for Piano and Cello, op. 3, and Trio in G minor, op. 8. His own works include incidental music to Goethe's *Faust* (Berlin, Oct. 25, 1835), piano pieces, and songs.
    BIBL.: Z. Jachimecki and W. Pózniak, *Antoni R. i jego muzyka do Fausta* (Krakow, 1957).

Rae, Allan, Canadian composer; b. Blairmore, Alberta, July 3, 1942. He studied arranging and music theory at the Berklee School of Music in Boston (graduated, 1965) and took courses in electronic music at the Royal Cons. of Music of Toronto (1970–73); then was on its faculty (1973–74).
    WORKS: MUSIC THEATER AND MULTIMEDIA: *An Approach to Improvisation* (n.d.); *Like Gods, Like Gods among Them* for 6 Speaking Voices, Chorus, Dancers, and Orch. (1973); *Mirror Mirror* (1974). **ORCH.:** *Trip* (1970); *Wheel of Fortune* for Winds and Strings (1971); 3 syms.: No. 1, *In the Shadow of Atlantis* (1972); No. 2, *Winds of Change* (1978); No. 3, *Alam-Al-Mithal* (1980); *The Hippopotamus* (1972); *A Crack in the Cosmic Turtle* for Jazz Group and Orch. (1975); *Image* (1975); Sonata for Clarinet and String Orch. (1976); Harp Concerto (1976); 4 *Paintings of Salvador Dali,* concerto for Double Bass and String Orch. (1977); Concerto for Violin and String Orch. (1979); *Mirror of Galadriel* (1982). **CHAMBER:** 2 string quartets (1966, 1967); *A Day in the Life of a Toad* for Brass Quintet (1970); *Impressions* for Wind Quintet (1971); *Sleep Whispering* for Alto Flute, Piano, and Vibraphone (1971); 4 brass quartets for 2 Trumpets and 2 Trombones (1975); *Improvizations* for String Quartet (1977); *Whispering of the Nagual* for Flute, Clarinet, Trumpet, Trombone, Cello, Piano, and Percussion (1978); *Images No. 1* for Horn and Trumpet (1979), *No. 2* for Flute and Clarinet (1979), *No. 3* for Trumpet, Horn, and Trombone (1979), and *No. 4* for Flute, Clarinet, and Bassoon (1979); *Kiwani Owapi* (Dakota: Awakening of Earth) for Clarinet, 2 Pianos, and Percussion (1981); *Reflections* for Violin, Cello, and Piano (1981); *En passant* for 2 Marimbas (1982).

Raff, (Joseph) Joachim, greatly renowned Swiss pedagogue and composer; b. Lachen, near Zürich, May 27, 1822; d. Frankfurt am Main, June 24, 1882. He was educated at the Jesuit Gymnasium in Schwyz; was a schoolteacher in Rapperswill (1840–44), but pursued an interest in music; sent some of his piano pieces to Mendelssohn (1843), who recommended them for publication; having met Liszt in Basel (1845), he received his encouragement and assistance in finding employment; later was his assistant in Weimar (1850–56), where he became an ardent propagandist of the new German school of composition; then went to Wiesbaden as a piano teacher and composer; there he married the actress Doris Genast; subsequently was director of the Hoch Cons. in Frankfurt (1877–82), where he also taught composition; students flocked from many countries to study with him; these included Edward MacDowell. Raff was a composer of prodigious fecundity, a master of all technical aspects of composition. He wrote 214 opus numbers that were publ., and many more that remained in MS. In spite of his fame, his music fell into lamentable desuetude after his death. He publ. *Die Wagnerfrage: Wagners letzte künstlerische Kundgebung im Lohengrin* (Braunschweig, 1854).
    WORKS: OPERAS: *König Alfred* (1848–50; Weimar, March 9, 1851; rev. 1852; Weimar, 1853); *Samson* (1853–57); *Die Parole* (1868); *Dame Kobold,* comic opera (1869; Weimar, April 9, 1870); *Benedetto Marcello* (1877–78); *Die Eifersüchtigen,* comic opera (1881–82). **ORCH.:** *Grosse Symphonie* (1854; not extant); 11 numbered syms.: No. 1, *An das Vaterland* (1859–61); No. 2 (1866); No. 3, *Im Walde* (1869); No. 4 (1871); No. 5, *Leonore* (1872); No. 6 (1873); No. 7, *In den Alpen* (1875); No. 8, *Frühlingsklänge* (1876); No. 9, *Im Sommer* (1878); No. 10, *Zur Herbstzeit* (1879); No. 11, *Der Winter* (1876; unfinished; completed by M. Erdmannsdörfer); *Fest-Ouvertüre* (1851–52; not extant); *Konzert-Ouvertüre* (1862); *Jubel-Ouvertüre* (1864); *Fest-Ouvertüre* (1864); overtures to Shakespeare's *The Tempest, Macbeth, Romeo and Juliet,* and *Othello* (1879); 2 violin concertos (1870–71; 1877); Piano Concerto (1873); 2 cello concertos (1874, 1876); 4 suites (1863, 1871, 1874, 1877); various choral works with orch. and many unaccompanied choral works. **CHAMBER:** 9 string quartets (1849–74); 5 piano trios (1849–70); 5 violin sonatas (1853–68); Piano Quintet (1862); Octet (1872); Sextet (1872); Cello Sonata (1873); *Sinfonietta* for 2 Flutes, 2 Oboes, 2 Clarinets, and 2 Horns (1873); 2 piano quartets (1876); solo piano pieces; pieces for piano, 4-hands; arrangements.

BIBL.: A. Schäfer, *Chronologisch-systematisches Verzeichnis der Werke J. R.s* (Wiesbaden, 1888); H. Raff, *J. R.: Ein Lebensbild* (Regensburg, 1925); J. Kälin and A. Marty, *Leben und Werk des Komponisten J. R.* (Zürich, 1972); M. Römer, *J.J. R. (1822–1882)* (Wiesbaden, 1982).

Rago, Alexis, Venezuelan composer; b. Caracas, May 25, 1930. He studied in Caracas and at the Peabody Cons. of Music in Baltimore; then took courses in piano and composition in Vienna and Rome; subsequently was director of the Aragua Cons. in his homeland.

WORKS: *3 escenas de ritos prohibidos* for Piano (1959); *Autantepuy,* symphonic poem (1962); *5 instantes* for Orch. (1968); *Mítica de sueños y cosmogonías* for Wind Quartet (Washington, D.C., June 25, 1968); *Guri,* symphonic poem on indigenous themes (1968); *Sincronismos, audiosonorrítmicos* (1969); piano suites; songs.

Rahn, John, American composer and music theorist; b. N.Y., Feb. 26, 1944. He studied bassoon at the Juilliard School in N.Y. (diploma, 1967); played in a number of ensembles (1967–70). After military service, he studied composition with Babbitt, Boretz, and Randall at Princeton Univ. (M.F.A., 1972; Ph.D., 1974, with the diss. *Lines [Of and About Music]*). He taught at the Univ. of Michigan, Ann Arbor (1973–75); then joined the faculty of the Univ. of Washington in Seattle (1975), where he became a prof. in 1984. He was associated with the journal *Perspectives of New Music* (from 1972); in 1983, became ed. In addition to his numerous articles on music theory and computer applications, his *Basic Atonal Theory* (N.Y., 1980) has the unique distinction of being a lucid introduction to set theory.

WORKS: Sonata for Bassoon and Harpsichord (1967); *Alice* for Tape (1967); *Collaboration* for 5 Instruments (1967); *Epithalamium* for Piano (1968); *5 Forms* for Piano (1968); *Games* for Saxophone and String Quartet (1969); Quintet for Winds (1969); *Reductionist Variations* for Piano (1969); *Deloumenon* for Band (1970); *3 Titbits* for Clarinet and Cello (1970); *Counterparts* for Trumpet (1970); *Trois chants de Mère L'Oie* for Soprano and Piano (1971); *Hos Estin* for Chorus and Ensemble (1971); Trio for Clarinet, Cello, and Piano (1972); *Peanut Butter Defies Gravity* for Soprano and Piano (1973); *Breakfast* for Piano (1976); *Improvisations on a Synclavier of Corn* for Tape (1978); *Another Lecture* for Tape and Speaker (1980); *Out of Haydn* for Fortepiano (1981); *IRT 4/23* for Tape (1983); *Kali* for Computer-generated Tape (1986).

Raichev, Alexander, prominent Bulgarian composer and pedagogue; b. Lom, April 11, 1922. He studied composition with Vladigerov at the Bulgarian State Cons. in Sofia (1943–47); then took courses in composition with Kodály and Viski and in conducting with Ferencsik at the Budapest Academy of Music (1949–50); returning to Sofia, he taught at the Bulgarian State Cons. (from 1950), where he also served as rector (1972–79); was deputy to the National Assembly (from 1971) and president of the Union of Bulgarian Composers (from 1980). His music makes use of innovative techniques that breathe new life into traditional genres and forms.

WORKS: DRAMATIC: OPERAS: *The Bridge* (Ruse, Oct. 2, 1965); *Your Presence* (Sofia, Sept. 5, 1969); *Alarm* (Sofia, June 14, 1974); *Khan Asparouch* (Ruse, March 9, 1981). **OPERETTA:** *The Nightingale of Orchid* (Sofia, March 7, 1963). **BALLETS:** *A Haidouk Epic* (Sofia, Feb. 13, 1953); *The Spring of the White-legged Maiden* (Sofia, Feb. 26, 1978). **ORATORIOS:** *Friendship* (1954); *Dimitrov Is Alive* (1954); *October 50* (1967); *Bulgaria—White, Green, Red* (1977); *Oratorio Meeting* (1984). **CANTATAS:** *My Dear Lassie* (1974); *Varna* (1979); *September Requiem* for Women's Chamber Choir and Orch. (1973). **ORCH.:** 5 syms.: *He Does Not Die,* sym.-cantata (1949); No. 2, *The New Prometheus* (1958); No. 3, *Strivings* (1966); No. 4 for Strings (1972); No. 5 for Chamber Orch. (1972); Piano Concerto (1947); *Sonata-Poem* for Violin and Orch. (1955); *Leninist Generations,* symphonic glorification (1970); *Radiant Dawn,* overture (1971); *Leipzig 33* (1972); Concerto (1978); *Balkan Rhapsody* (1983); overtures, including *Jubilee Overture*

(1986) and *Levsky* (1988); chamber music, choral works, songs, piano pieces, and film scores.

Raichl, Miroslav, Czech composer; b. Náchod, Feb. 2, 1930. He studied composition with Bořkovec at the Prague Academy of Music, graduating in 1953; subsequently devoted himself mainly to teaching and administrative work in the Union of Czechoslovak Composers.

WORKS: *Fuente Ovejuna,* opera after Lope de Vega (1957; Prague, 1959); 2 syms. (1955; 1958–60); Cello Concerto (1955–56); *Revolutionary Overture* (1958); Piano Sonata No. 2 (1962); *Someone Was Playing on the Oboe* for Women's Chorus a cappella (1970); Symfonietta for Chamber Orch. (1976–77); 5 *Dance Fantasies* for Orch. (1981); *Farewell Elegy,* concertant aria for Soprano and Chamber Orch. (1981–82); 3 *Ends of Love* for Women's Chorus a cappella (1982).

Raida, Karl Alexander, German composer; b. Paris (of German parents), Oct. 4, 1852; d. Berlin, Nov. 26, 1923. He studied at the conservatories of Stuttgart and Dresden; was conductor from 1878 to 1892 at the Viktoria Theater in Berlin, where he founded the Akademie für Dramatischen Gesang (1882) and the Gesellschaft der Opernfreunde (1887); from 1895 to 1897 he served as director of the new Deutsches Theater in Munich. He was a successful composer of light operas, operettas, ballets, farces, etc.

Raimann, Rudolf, Hungarian composer; b. Veszprem, May 7, 1861; d. Vienna, Sept. 26, 1913. He entered the service of Prince Esterházy as music director; wrote an opera, *Enoch Arden,* after Tennyson (Budapest, May 8, 1894), and about 12 operettas for Vienna, including *Das Waschermädel* (April 19, 1905), *Paula macht alles* (March 27, 1909), *Die Frau Gretl* (April 7, 1911), and *Unser Stammhalter* (Nov. 15, 1912).

Raimondi, Gianni, Italian tenor; b. Bologna, April 17, 1923. He studied with Melandri and Barra-Caracciolo; made his debut in 1947 in Budrio; appeared at La Scala in Milan from 1955. In 1957 he made his 1st American tour; on Sept. 29, 1965, appeared as Rodolfo in *La Bohème* at the Metropolitan Opera in N.Y.; among his other roles were Cavaradossi in *Tosca,* the Duke in *Rigoletto,* and Faust in Gounod's opera; he remained with the Metropolitan until 1969.

Raimondi, Ignazio, Italian violinist, conductor, and composer; b. Naples, c.1735; d. London, Jan. 14, 1813. He studied violin with Emanuele Barbella; played in the orch. of the Teatro San Carlo in Naples (1759–62); then was active in Amsterdam as a violinist and conductor; settled in London (1780).

WORKS: Opera: *La Muta* (Paris, Nov. 12, 1789); 2 syms.: *Les Aventures de Télémaque dans l'isle de Calypso* (Amsterdam, Jan. 15, 1777) and *The Battle* (1785); Sinfonia concertante for 2 Violins and Orch.; 6 violin concertos; much chamber music, including 27 trios, several string quartets, and other works.

Raimondi, Pietro, inventive Italian composer; b. Rome, Dec. 20, 1786; d. there, Oct. 30, 1853. He studied with La Barbara and Tritto at the Cons. della Pietà de' Turchini in Naples; in 1807 he brought out an opera buffa, *Le bizzarie d'amore,* at Genoa; it was followed by about 60 other dramatic works and 22 ballets, for whose production he traveled from place to place (Florence, Naples, Rome, Messina, Milan, etc.); was director of the royal theaters at Naples (1824–32) and a prof. at the Palermo Cons. (1834–52); in 1852 he became maestro di cappella at St. Peter's in Rome. Raimondi was a contrapuntist of remarkable skill; he publ. 4 fugues *a 4,* which could be combined as a quadruple fugue *a 16;* 6 fugues *a 4,* to be combined as a sextuple fugue *a 24;* in the *24 fughe a 4, 5, 6 e 8 voci* publ. by Ricordi, there is one such quadruple fugue *a 16,* and a quintuple fugue *a 20;* further, 6 fugues *a 4,* performable as a sextuple fugue *a 24;* and a fugue *a 64,* for 16 choirs *a 4.* His most astounding feat in combination, however, was the sacred trilogy *Giuseppe* (Joseph), comprising 3 oratorios (*Potifar, Giuseppe, Giacobbe*), performed at the Teatro Argentina in Rome, Aug. 7, 1852, at first separately, and then simultaneously, the ensemble of 400 musicians on the stage and in the orch. presenting a most striking effect and arousing great curiosity among professional musicians.

BIBL.: F. Cicconetti, *Memorie intorno a P. R.* (Rome, 1867); C. Gray, "P. R.," *Music Review* (Jan. 1940).

Raimondi, Ruggero, Italian bass; b. Bologna, Oct. 3, 1941. He was educated at the Accademia di Santa Cecilia in Rome; made his debut as Colline in Spoleto in 1964; from 1967, sang at Milan's La Scala. On Sept. 14, 1970, he made his Metropolitan Opera debut in N.Y. as Silva in *Ernani*. His other signal appearances were at the Paris Opéra, the Bavarian State Opera in Munich, and the Deutsche Oper in Berlin. He was distinguished in the role of Don Giovanni and was also praised for his dramatic rendition of Boris Godunov.

Rainey, "Ma" (real name, **Gertrude Pridgett**), prominent black American blues, jazz, and vaudeville singer; b. Columbus, Ga., April 26, 1886; d. Rome, Ga., Dec. 22, 1939. She made her 1st appearance in public in Columbus when she was 12; after touring with the Rabbit Foot Minstrels and Tolliver's Circus, she organized her own Georgia Jazz Band; made numerous recordings before retiring to Columbus in 1935. Her style of blues singing influenced Bessie Smith.

BIBL.: D. Stewart-Baxter, *M. R. and the Classic Blues Singers* (N.Y., 1970); S. Lieb, *Mother of the Blues: A Study of M. R.* (Amherst, Mass., 1981).

Rainger (real name, **Reichenthal**), **Ralph,** American pianist, arranger, and composer; b. N.Y., Oct. 7, 1901; d. in an airplane crash near Palm Springs, Calif., Oct. 23, 1942. He studied with Gallico and Clarence Adler at N.Y.'s Damrosch Inst.; became a pianist for Broadway musicals (1926); also worked as an accompanist and arranger in vaudeville; in 1930, went to Hollywood, where he prospered as a rehearsal pianist and song composer; his song *Thanks for the Memory* was introduced by Bob Hope in the film *The Big Broadcast of 1938*; it received an Academy Award and became Hope's theme song.

Rainier, Priaulx, South African–born English composer; b. Howick, Natal, Feb. 3, 1903; d. Besse-en-Chandesse, Auvergne, Oct. 10, 1986. She studied violin at the South African College of Music; in 1920 she went to London, where she studied violin and took courses with McEwen at the Royal Academy of Music; studied briefly with Nadia Boulanger in Paris (1937); from 1943 to 1961 she was a prof. at the Royal Academy of Music.

WORKS: *Incantation* for Clarinet and Orch. (1933); *3 Greek Epigrams* for Soprano and Piano (1937); String Quartet (1939); *Suite* for Clarinet and Piano (1943); *Sinfonia da camera* for String Orch. (1947; rev. London, Feb. 21, 1958); *Dance of the Rain* for Tenor and Guitar (1948); *Barbaric Dance Suite* for Piano (1949); *Ballet Suite* for Orch. (1950); *Cycle for Declamation* for Solo Soprano, Tenor, or Baritone (1953); *6 Pieces* for Wind Quintet (1954); *Requiem* for Tenor and Chorus (1955–56); *Trio-Suite* for Piano Trio (1959); *Pastoral Triptych* for Oboe (1960); *Dance Concerto "Phala-phala"* for Orch. (1960–61; London, Jan. 17, 1961); *Quanta* for Oboe Quartet (1961–62); *Suite* for Cello (1963–65); Cello Concerto (1963–64; London, Sept. 3, 1964); String Trio (1965–66); *Aequora lunae* (The Seas of the Moon) for Double Orch., Percussion, and Solo Winds (1966–67; Cheltenham Festival, July 18, 1967); *Trios and Triads* for 10 Trios and Percussion (1969–73); *The Bee Oracles*, after Sitwell, for Tenor or Baritone Solo, Flute, Oboe, Violin, Cello, and Harpsichord (1970); *Quinque* for Harpsichord (1971); *Requiem* for Chorus and Orch. (BBC, London, Nov. 29, 1971); *Ploërmel* for Winds and Percussion (London, Aug. 13, 1973); *Prayers from the Ark* for Tenor and Harp (1976); *Canti e Finale* for Violin and Orch. (1976–77; Edinburgh Festival, Sept. 8, 1977); *Concertante* for Oboe, Clarinet, and Orch. (1977–80; London, Aug. 7, 1981); *Grand Duo* for Cello and Piano (1980–82; London, May 30, 1983); songs.

BIBL.: J. Opie, *Come and Listen to the Stars: P. R.: A Pictorial Biography* (Penzance, 1988).

Rains, Leon, American bass; b. N.Y., Oct. 1, 1870; d. Los Angeles, June 11, 1954. He studied with Saenger in N.Y.

(1891–96) and with Bouhy in Paris; made a concert tour with Melba in the U.S. (1898); then was a member of the Dresden Court Opera (1899–1917); made his 1st appearance with the Metropolitan Opera in N.Y. on Feb. 24, 1909, as Hagen in *Götterdämmerung;* he settled in Los Angeles as a teacher in 1924.

Raisa, Rosa (real name, **Raisa** or **Rose Burschstein**), outstanding Polish soprano; b. Bialystok, May 23, 1893; d. Los Angeles, Sept. 28, 1963. In order to escape the horrors of anti-Semitic persecution, she fled to Naples at the age of 14; on Lombardi's advice she entered the Cons. San Pietro a Majella, where she studied under Barbara Marchisio; made her operatic debut as Leonora in Verdi's *Oberto, Conte di San Bonifacio* in Parma on Sept. 6, 1913; then sang 2 seasons at the Teatro Costanzi in Rome; in 1913–14 (and again from 1916 to 1932 and from 1933 to 1936), with the Chicago Opera Co.; in 1914 at Covent Garden; sang with increasing success in Rio de Janeiro, Montevideo, São Paulo, and Milan. In 1920 she married the baritone Giacomo Rimini, with whom she founded a singing school in Chicago in 1937. Raisa was one of the finest dramatic sopranos of her day, excelling in the Italian repertoire; she created the title role in Puccini's *Turandot* at Milan's La Scala (April 25, 1926), her husband taking the role of Ping.

Raison, André, French composer and organist; b. before 1650; d. Paris, 1719. He received instruction at the seminary of the abbey of Ste. Geneviève in Nanterre; became organist at the royal abbey of Ste. Geneviève in Paris (c.1666); later was also organist at the convent and college of the Jacobins de St. Jacques; was the mentor of Clérambault. He publ. 2 books of organ music (Paris, 1688, 1714; ed. by A. Guilmant and A. Pirro in *Archives des maîtres de l'orgue*, Paris, 1899).

Raitio, Pentti, Finnish composer and pedagogue; b. Pieksämäki, June 4, 1930. He studied composition with Joonas Kokkonen (1961–63) and Erik Bergman (1963–66) at the Sibelius Academy in Helsinki, receiving his diploma in 1966; then was director of the Hyvinkää School of Music (from 1967). He was chairman of the Lahti Organ Festival (1981–85) and of the Assoc. of Finnish Music Schools (from 1985).

WORKS: ORCH.: *"13"* (1964); *Audiendum* (1967); 5 Pieces for String Orch. (1975); *Petandrie* (1977); *Noharmus* (1978); *Noharmus II* (1980); *Canzone d'autunno* (1982); Flute Concerto (1983); *Due figure* (1985); *Yoldia arctica* (1987). **CHAMBER:** Small Pieces for Brass Instruments (1974); Wind Quintet (1975); *Nocturne* for Violin and Piano (1977). **VOCAL:** *Joki* (The River), 7 songs for Soprano and 7 Instruments (1965); *Kuun tietä* (Along the Moonlit Path), 3 songs for Soprano and 4 Instruments (1965); *Orfilainen kuoro* (Orphean Chorus), 3 songs for Baritone and Men's Chorus (1966); 3 Songs for Baritone and String Quartet (1970); *Eräs kesäilta* (One Summer Evening) for Men's Chorus (1971); *Laulu* (Song) for Men's Chorus (1972); *Lemminkäinen kuokkavieraana Pohjolassa* for 2 Baritones and Men's Chorus (1978); *Katselen jokea* (I'm Looking at the River), 6 songs for Women's or Youth Chorus (1986).

Raitio, Väinö (Eerikki), Finnish composer; b. Sortavala, April 15, 1891; d. Helsinki, Sept. 10, 1945. He studied in Helsinki with Melartin and Furuhjelm and in Moscow with Ilyinsky; also in Berlin (1921) and Paris (1925–26). His music is programmatic in the Romantic manner, but there is a more severe strain in his pieces derived from Finnish legends. He was one of the earliest Finnish composers to embrace modern compositional techniques, being mainly influenced by Scriabin, German expressionism, and French impressionism.

WORKS: OPERAS: *Jephtan tytär* (Jephtha's Daughter; 1929; Helsinki, 1931); *Prinsessa Cecilia* (1933; Helsinki, 1936); *Väinämöinen kosinta* (Väinämöinen's Courtship; 1935); *Lyydian kuningas* (The King of Lydia; 1937; Helsinki, 1955); *Kaksi kuningatarta* (2 Queens; 1937–40; Helsinki, 1945). **BALLET:** *Vesipatsas* (Waterspout; 1929). **ORCH.:** Piano Concerto (1915); *Poem* for Cello and Orch. (1915); *Symphonic Ballad* (1916); Sym. (1918–19); *Joutsenet* (The Swans; 1919);

Fantasia estatica, symphonic poem (1921); *Antigone* (1921–22); *Kuutamo Jupiterissa* (Moonlight on Jupiter), symphonic tableau (1922); *Fantasia poetica*, symphonic poem (1923); *Pyramid* for Chorus and Orch. (1924–25); *Felis domestica*, scherzo for Orch. (1935); Concerto for Violin, Cello, and Orch. (1936); *Nocturne* for Violin and Orch. (1938); *Fantasy* for Cello, Harp, and Orch. (1942); *Le Ballet grotesque* (1943); also String Quartet; Piano Quintet; Violin Sonata; works for piano and organ.

Raitt, Bonnie, American popular-music singer and guitarist, daughter of **John (Emmet) Raitt;** b. Los Angeles, Nov. 8, 1949. She took up the guitar when she was 12; after attending Radcliffe College (1967–69), she departed the academic scene to pursue a career as a recording artist. She made a number of albums, including *Give It Up* (1972) and *Sweet Forgiveness* (1977). Her career was derailed for a time by alcoholism, but she fought her way back to sobriety and success. In 1990 she captured 4 Grammy awards, including 1 for best album of the year for her *Nick of Time* (1989).

Raitt, John (Emmet), American singer of popular music and actor, father of **Bonnie Raitt;** b. Santa Ana, Calif., Jan. 29, 1917. He studied at the Univ. of Southern Calif. and the Univ. of Redlands; began his career as a singer in light opera; also appeared in recitals. He then went to N.Y., where he sang in the Broadway productions of *Oklahoma!* and *Carousel;* subsequently starred in other musicals, including *Pajama Game* and *Annie Get Your Gun;* also appeared in films and on television. In later years he devoted much of his efforts to theatrical productions.

Rajičić, Stanojlo, Serbian composer and pedagogue; b. Belgrade, Dec. 16, 1910. He studied composition (diplomas, 1934 and 1935) with Rudolf Karel and Josef Suk and piano (diploma, 1935) with Alois Sima at the Prague Cons.; then attended piano master classes of Karel Hofmeister in Prague and of Walter Kerschbaumer in Vienna. From 1937 to 1977 he was prof. of composition at the Belgrade Academy of Music. In 1950 he was elected a corresponding member and in 1958 a fellow of the Serbian Academy of Sciences and Arts, serving as secretary of its dept. of visual and musical arts (from 1964); also was elected a member of the Slovenian Academy of Sciences and Arts (1975). He received the Serbian State Prize (1968), the Gottfried von Herder Prize of Vienna (1975), and the Vuk Prize (1986). His early compositions are set in a radical idiom of atonal music, verging on dodecaphony, but later he adopted a national style derived from melorhythms of Serbian folk songs.

Works: operas: *Simonida* (1956; Sarajevo, May 24, 1957); *Karadjordje* (1973; Belgrade, June 26, 1977); *Dnevnik jednog ludaka* (The Diary of a Madman; 1977; Belgrade, April 4, 1981); *Bele noći* (White Nights; 1983; Belgrade, April 14, 1985). **ballet:** *Pod zemljom* (Under the Earth; 1940). **orch.:** 6 syms. (1935, 1941, 1944, 1946, 1959, 1967); 3 piano concertos (1940, 1942, 1950); 3 violin concertos (1941, 1946, 1950); 2 clarinet concertos (1943, 1962); Cello Concerto (1949); Bassoon Concerto (1969). **chamber:** *Magnovenja* (Moments), song cycle for Mezzo-soprano and Orch. (1964); Piano Trio (1934); 2 string quartets (1938, 1939); piano pieces.

Rajna, Thomas, Hungarian-English pianist and composer; b. Budapest, Dec. 21, 1928. He studied composition and piano at the Franz Liszt Academy of Music in Budapest (1944–47), where his teachers were Kodály, Veress, and Weiner; in 1947 he went to London on a scholarship to study with Howells and others at the Royal College of Music, graduating in 1952. He taught at the Guildhall School of Music (1963–67) and the Univ. of Surrey (1967–70), and in 1970 was appointed a lecturer in piano at the Univ. of Cape Town in South Africa. As a pianist, he excels in performances of 20th-century music. His own works assume a classical mold, with distinctly modern contents in harmony and counterpoint.

Works: *Dialogues* for Clarinet and Piano (1947); String Quartet (1948); *Rhapsody* for Clarinet and Orch. (1948–50); *Music* for Cello and Piano (1950); *Suite* for Strings (1952–54); *Music* for Violin and Piano (1956–57); *Serenade* for 10 Winds, Percussion, Harpsichord, and Piano (1958); Piano Concerto (1960–62; London, March 18, 1966); *Movements* for Strings (1962); *Cantilenas & Interludes* for Orch. (London, Feb. 7, 1968); 2 *Hebrew Prayers* for Chorus a cappella (1972–73); 4 *Traditional African Lyrics* for Voice and Piano (1976).

Rajter, Ludovít, Slovak conductor; b. Pezinok, July 30, 1906. He studied piano and cello in Bratislava; then went to Vienna to study at the Academy of Music (1924–29); took lessons in conducting with Clemens Krauss and in Budapest with Dohnányi; in Budapest he conducted the Radio Orch. (1933–45) and taught conducting at the Academy of Music (1938–45). He then was conductor of the Radio Orch. in Bratislava (1945–49); subsequently led the Slovak Phil. there (1949–61). In 1968 he was appointed principal conductor of the Radio Orch. in Bratislava.

Rakov, Nikolai, Russian composer; b. Kaluga, March 14, 1908. He studied violin in Moscow and composition at the Moscow Cons. with Glière; in 1935, joined its staff as a teacher of orchestration. He was also active as a violinist and conductor. In his compositions he pursues the Romantic and nationalistic line of Russian music.

Works: 2 syms. (1940, 1957); Sinfonietta (1958); *Little Symphony* for Strings (1962); 2 violin concertos (1944, 1955); Concertino for Violin and String Orch. (1959); Violin Sonata (1951); Oboe Sonata (1951); Flute Sonata (1970); 2 piano sonatinas; numerous pieces for Russian folk instruments.

Bibl.: A. Solovtsov, *N. R.* (Moscow, 1958).

Raksin, David, remarkable American composer for films; b. Philadelphia, Aug. 4, 1912. He studied piano in his childhood and also learned to play woodwind instruments from his father, a performer and conductor; when barely past puberty, he organized his own jazz band. In 1931 he entered the Univ. of Pa.; also studied composition privately with Isadore Freed (1934–35). In 1935 he went to Hollywood to assist Charlie Chaplin with the music for his film *Modern Times* (which he later orchestrated with Edward Powell); this provided Raksin a wonderful companionship with the great comedian. Raksin wrote a delectable piece of reminiscences, "Life with Charlie" (*Quarterly Journal of the Library of Congress*, Summer 1983). When Chaplin was forced into exile by the Red-baiters of the U.S. Congress for his alleged radical activities, Raksin struck out on his own; also studied privately with Arnold Schoenberg. He composed more than 100 film scores, some of which attained great popularity; his greatest success was the theme song *Laura*, ingratiatingly melodious in its sinuous and convoluted pattern; it generated more than 300 different versions. Apart from his activities as a composer and conductor, he appeared as an actor and commentator on television programs. Using material from his film music, he composed several symphonic suites, among them *Forever Amber* and *The Bad and the Beautiful*. Other coruscating scores were *Force of Evil, Carrie, The Redeemer,* and *Separate Tables,* all of which are featured in *Wonderful Inventions* (Library of Congress, Washington, D.C., 1985). He also wrote incidental music for the theater, as well as purely symphonic and choral pieces, including a madrigal, *Simple Symmetries*. His orchestral *Toy Concertino* became a favorite and received many performances; at the request of Stravinsky, he made the original band instrumentation of *Circus Polka* for George Balanchine's production with the Barnum and Bailey Circus. In 1956 he joined the composition faculty of the Univ. of Southern Calif.; also taught film and television composition at the Univ. of Calif., Los Angeles, and was on the faculty of the Univ. of Southern Calif. School of Public Administration (1968–89). He received an Elizabeth Sprague Coolidge Commission from the Library of Congress; the resulting composition, *Oedipus memneitai* (Oedipus Remembers) for Bass-Baritone Narrator/Soloist, 6-part Mixed Chorus, and Chamber Ensemble, text by the composer, was conducted by him at a special Founder's Day Concert, Oct. 30, 1986, in Washington, D.C.

Ralf, Oscar (Georg), Swedish tenor, brother of **Torsten (Ivar) Ralf;** b. Malmö, Oct. 3, 1881; d. Kalmar, April 3, 1964. He studied with Forsell (1902–4) and Gillis Bratt (from 1905), and in Berlin and Munich; began his career as a singer at Stockholm's Oscarsteatern, an operetta theater (1905–15); completing his studies with Bratt, he made his operatic debut as Siegmund at the Royal Opera in 1918; was a principal member of the company until 1940; also appeared as Siegmund at Bayreuth in 1927. He was best known for his roles in operas by Wagner and Verdi. He publ. an autobiography, *Tenoren han går i Ringen* (The Tenor Goes into the Ring; Stockholm, 1953).

Ralf, Richard, German composer; b. Karlsruhe, Sept. 30, 1897; d. Los Angeles, June 22, 1977. He studied piano as a child with his father, the choirmaster at the Karlsruhe Opera; later attended the Scharwenka Cons. in Berlin, graduating in 1914. Drafted into the German army in World War I, he suffered severe shell shock at the French front; returning to Berlin, he studied composition with Hugo Kaun. In 1946 he emigrated to the U.S., eventually settling in Los Angeles. His music follows the florid and emotional trend of post-Wagnerian Romanticism.

WORKS: *Transcendental,* ballet (1921); Violin Sonata (1923); String Quartet (1924); Violin Concerto (1925); *Brothers Arise,* cantata (1959); *Symphonic Songs* for Mezzo-soprano and Orch. (1968).

Ralf, Torsten (Ivar), Swedish tenor, brother of **Oscar (Georg) Ralf;** b. Malmö, Jan. 2, 1901; d. Stockholm, April 27, 1954. He studied at the Stockholm Cons. and with Hertha Dehmlow in Berlin; made his debut as Cavaradossi in Stettin (1930); then sang in Chemnitz (1932–33) and Frankfurt (1933–35). He was a member of the Dresden State Opera (1935–44), where he created the role of Apollo in Strauss's *Daphne* in 1938; was made a Kammersänger in 1936. He sang at London's Covent Garden (1935–39; 1948) and at the Teatro Colón in Buenos Aires (1946); made his Metropolitan Opera debut in N.Y. as Lohengrin on Nov. 26, 1945, and remained on its roster until 1948. He was best known for such roles as Walther von Stolzing, Tannhäuser, Parsifal, Otello, and Radames.

Ramann, Lina, German pedagogue, writer on music, and composer; b. Mainstockheim, near Kitzingen, June 24, 1833; d. Munich, March 30, 1912. She was a pupil of Franz and Frau Brendel at Leipzig; was also briefly a pupil of Liszt; founded (1858) a music seminary for women teachers in Glückstadt, Holstein, which was moved to Nuremberg (1864) and sold to A. Göllerich (1890). She wrote some piano music but became best known for her writings on music.

WRITINGS (all publ. in Leipzig unless otherwise given): *Aus der Gegenwart* (Nuremberg, 1868); *Bach und Händel* (1868); *Die Musik als Gegenstand des Unterrichts* (1868); *Allgemeine musikalische Erziehungs- und Unterrichtslehre* (1870); *Franz Liszts Oratorium Christus* (1874); ed. *Franz Liszt: Gesammelte Schriften* (1880–83); *Franz Liszt als Künstler und Mensch* (1880–94); *Grundriss der Technik des Klavierspiels* (1885); *Liszt als Psalmensänger* (1886); *Liszt-Pädagogium* (1901).

BIBL.: M. Ille-Beeg, *L. R.* (Nuremberg, 1914).

Ramboušek, Joseph, Czech double-bass virtuoso and pedagogue; b. Mníšek, Nov. 16, 1845; d. Moscow, March 10, 1901. He studied with Josef Hrabět at the Prague Cons.; went to Moscow, where he was engaged as a double-bass player at the Opera and taught at the Phil. Inst.; among his pupils was Koussevitzky.

Rameau, Jean-Philippe, great French composer, organist, and music theorist; b. Dijon (baptized), Sept. 25, 1683; d. Paris, Sept. 12, 1764. His father was organist of St. Étienne in Dijon. He learned to play the harpsichord as a small child; from age 10 to 14 he attended the Jesuit Collège des Godrans in Dijon, where he took up singing and composition instead of concentrating on his academic studies; at 18 his father sent him to Milan, where he stayed for only a brief time before

joining the orch. of a traveling French opera troupe as a violinist. In Jan. 1702 he received a temporary appointment as organist at Avignon Cathedral; in May 1702 he became organist at Clermont Cathedral. By 1706 he was in Paris, where he publ. his 1st *Livre de pièces de clavecin;* was active there as a church organist until 1708. He succeeded his father as organist at Notre Dame Cathedral in Avignon in 1709; became organist to the Jacobins in Lyons in July 1713; then was organist at Clermont Cathedral from 1715 to 1723; there he wrote his famous *Traité de l'harmonie* (Paris, 1722). This epoch-making work, though little understood at the time, attracted considerable attention and roused much opposition, so that when he settled definitely in Paris (1723) he was by no means unknown. The fact that he failed in 1727 in a competition for the position of organist at St.-Vincent-de-Paul did not injure his reputation, for it was generally known that Marchand (probably out of jealousy) had exerted his powerful influence in favor of Daquin, who was in every respect inferior to Rameau. In 1732 he became organist at Ste.-Croix-de-la-Bretonnerie, and soon was recognized as the foremost organist in France. In 1726 appeared his *Nouveau système de musique théorique,* an introduction to the *Traité.* The leading ideas of his system of harmony are (1) chord-building by thirds; (2) the classification of a chord and all its inversions as one and the same, thus reducing the multiplicity of consonant and dissonant combinations to a fixed and limited number of root chords; and (3) his invention of a fundamental bass (*basse fondamentale*), which is an imaginary series of root tones forming the real basis of the varied chord progressions employed in a composition. The stir that these novel theories occasioned, and his reputation as the foremost French organist, by no means satisfied Rameau's ambition; his ardent desire was to bring out a dramatic work at the Opéra. He had made a modest beginning with incidental music to Alexis Piron's comedy *L'Endriague* in 1723. After contributing further incidental music to Piron's comedies *L'Enrôlement d'Arlequin* (1726) and *La Robe de dissension, ou Le Faux Prodigue* (1726), he became music master to the wife of the "fermier-général" La Pouplinière; the latter obtained from Voltaire a libretto for *Samson,* which Rameau set to music; but it was rejected on account of its biblical subject. A 2nd libretto, by Abbé Pellegrin, was accepted, and *Hippolyte et Aricie* was produced at the Opéra in 1733; its reception was cool, despite undeniable superiority over the operas of Lully and his following. Rameau considered abandoning composing any further works for the theater, but the persuasions of his friends, who also influenced public opinion in his favor, were effective; in 1735 he brought out the successful opéra-ballet *Les Indes galantes,* and in 1737 his masterpiece, *Castor et Pollux,* a work that for years held its own beside the operas of Gluck. A career of uninterrupted prosperity commenced; he was recognized as the leading theorist of the time, and his instruction was eagerly sought; for the next 30 years his operas dominated the French stage; he was named Compositeur du cabinet du roy in 1745, and was ennobled 4 months before his death.

From the beginning of his dramatic career Rameau roused opposition, and at the same time found ardent admirers. The 1st war of words was waged between the "Lullistes" and the "Ramistes." This had scarcely been ended by a triumphant revival of *Pygmalion* in 1751 when the production of Pergolesi's *La Serva padrona* (1752) caused a more prolonged and bitter controversy between the adherents of Rameau and the "Encyclopédistes," a struggle known as "La Guerre des Bouffons," in which Rameau participated by writing numerous essays defending his position. Practically the same charges were made against him as would be made a century later against Wagner: unintelligible harmony, lack of melody, preponderance of discords, noisy instrumentation, etc. But when 25 years later the war between Gluckists and Piccinnists was raging, Rameau's works were praised as models of beauty and perfection. It is a matter for regret that Rameau was indifferent to the quality of his librettos; he relied so much upon his musical inspiration that he never could be brought to a realization of the importance of a good text; hence the inequality of his operas. Nevertheless, his operas mark a decided advance over Lully's in musical characterization, expressive melody, richness of harmony, variety of modulation, and expert and original instrumentation.

WRITINGS (all publ. in Paris): *Traité de l'harmonie reduite à ses principes naturels* (1722; Eng. tr., 1737; modern ed. in Eng. tr. by P. Gossett, 1971); *Nouveau système de musique théorique* (1726); *Dissertation sur les différentes méthodes d'accompagnement pour le clavecin ou pour l'orgue* (1732); *Génération harmonique ou Traité de musique théorique et pratique* (1737; modern ed. in Eng. tr. by D. Hayes in *Rameau's "Génération harmonique,"* diss., Stanford Univ., 1974); *Mémoire où l'on expose les fondements du Système de musique théorique et pratique de M. Rameau* (1749); *Démonstration du principe de l'harmonie* (1750); *Nouvelles réflexions de M. Rameau sur sa Démonstration du principe de l'harmonie* (1752); *Observations sur notre instinct pour la musique* (1754); *Erreurs sur la musique dans l'Encyclopédie* (1755–56; reprint, 1971); *Suite des erreurs sur la musique dans l'Encyclopédie* (1756; reprint, 1971); *Prospectus, où l'on propose au public, par voye de souscription, un code de musique pratique, composé de sept méthodes* (1757); *Réponse de M. Rameau à MM. les éditeurs de l'Encyclopédie* (1757; reprint, 1971); *Nouvelles réflexions sur le principe sonore* (1758–59); *Code de musique pratique, ou Méthodes pour apprendre la musique . . . avec de nouvelles réflexions sur le principe sonore* (1760); *Lettre à M. d'Alembert sur ses opinions en musique* (1760); *Origine des sciences, suivie d'une controverse sur le méme sujet* (1762); also *Vérités intéressantes* (unfinished MS). For a complete edition, see E. Jacobi, ed., *Jean-Philippe Rameau: Complete Theoretical Writings* (Rome, 1967–72).

WORKS: STAGE (all 1st perf. at the Paris Opéra unless otherwise given): *Samson* (tragédie en musique; 1733; not perf.; not extant); *Hippolyte et Aricie* (tragédie en musique; Oct. 1, 1733); *Les Indes galantes* (opéra-ballet; Aug. 23, 1735); *Castor et Pollux* (tragédie en musique; Oct. 24, 1737); *Les Fêtes d'Hébé (Les Talents lyriques)* (opéra-ballet; May 21, 1739); *Dardanus* (tragédie en musique; Nov. 19, 1739); *La Princesse de Navarre* (comédie-ballet; Versailles, Feb. 23, 1745); *Platée (ou Junon jalouse)* (comédie-lyrique; Versailles, March 31, 1745); *Les Fêtes de Polymnie* (opéra-ballet; Oct. 12, 1745); *Le Temple de la gloire* (opéra-ballet; Versailles, Nov. 27, 1745); *Les Fêtes de l'Hymen et de l'Amour, ou Les Dieux d'Egypte* (ballet-héroïque; Versailles, March 15, 1747); *Zaïs* (ballet-héroïque; Feb. 29, 1748); *Pygmalion* (acte de ballet; Aug. 27, 1748); *Les Surprises de l'Amour* (divertissement; Versailles, Nov. 27, 1748); *Naïs* (pastorale-héroïque; April 22, 1749); *Zoroastre* (tragédie en musique; Dec. 5, 1749); *Linus* (tragédie en musique; not perf.; greater portion of music not extant); *La Guirlande, ou Les Fleurs enchantées* (acte de ballet; Sept. 21, 1751); *Acante et Céphise, ou La Sympathie* (pastorale-héroïque; Nov. 18, 1751); *Daphnis et Eglé* (pastorale-héroïque; Fontainebleau, Oct. 30, 1753); *Lysis et Délie* (pastorale; 1753; not perf.; music not extant); *Les Sybarites* (acte de ballet; Fontainebleau, Nov. 13, 1753); *La Naissance d'Osiris, ou La Fête Pamilie* (acte de ballet; Fontainebleau, Oct. 12, 1754); *Anacréon* (acte de ballet; Fontainebleau, Oct. 23, 1754; rev. version to different text, May 31, 1757); *Le Procureur dupé sans le savoir* (opéra comique en vaudevilles; private perf., 1758 or 1759; music not extant); *Les Paladins* (comédie-ballet; Feb. 12, 1760); *Abaris, ou Les Boréades* (tragédie lyrique; 1st perf. in concert form in London, April 19, 1975; 1st stage perf. in Aix-en-Provence, July 21, 1982); the ballets *Nélée et Myrthis (Les Beaux Jours de l'amour)*, *Zéphyre (Les Nymphes de Diane)*, and *Io* have not been publicly performed. He also contributed music, in collaboration with others, to the following comedies by A. Piron: *L'Endriague* (Feb. 3, 1723); *L'Enrôlement d'Arlequin* (Feb. 1726); *La Robe de dissension, ou Le Faux Prodigue* (Sept. 7, 1726); *Les Jardins de l'Hymen, ou La Rose* (1726; March 5, 1744); *Les Courses de Tempé* (Aug. 30, 1734); he likewise wrote the intermède en musique *Aruéris* (Dec. 15, 1762). **SECULAR CANTATAS:** *Thétis* (1718); *Aquilon et Orinthie* (1719); *Les Amants trahis* (1721);

Orphée (1721); *L'Impatience* (1715–21); *Le Berger fidèle* (1728); *Cantate pour la fête de Saint Louis* (1740?). **SACRED VOCAL:** 4 Psalm settings for Soloists, Mixed Chorus, and Instrumental Ensemble: *Deus noster refugium* (1716?); *In convertendo* (1718?); *Quam dilecta* (1720?); *Laboravi* (publ. in *Traité de l'harmonie,* 1722). **KEYBOARD:** *Premier livre de pièces de clavecin* (1706); *Pièces de clavecin avec une méthode sur la mécanique des doigts* (1724; rev. 1731, as *Pièces de clavecin avec une table pour les agréments*); *Nouvelles suites de pièces de clavecin* (1728?); *Cinq pièces pour clavecin seul, extraites des Pièces de clavecin en concerts* (1741); *Pièces de clavecin en concerts* for Harpsichord, Violin or Flute, and Viol or Violin (1741; 2nd ed., 1752). The so-called complete edition of Rameau's works, ed. by Saint-Saëns and C. Malherbe (after the latter's death continued by M. Emmanuel and M. Teneo), was never completed (18 vols., Paris, 1895–1924). A new critical edition, under the joint auspices of the Association pour la Publication des Oeuvres de Rameau in Paris and the Broude Trust of N.Y., with N. Zaslaw as general ed. and F. Lesure as managing ed., began publishing in 1983.

BIBL.: BIOGRAPHICAL: C. Poisot, *Notice biographique sur J.-P. R.* (Paris, 1864); T. Nisard, *Monographie de J.-P. R.* (Paris, 1867); R. Garraud, *R.* (Paris, 1876); H. Grigne, *R.* (Dijon, 1876); A. Pougin, *R.* (Paris, 1876); M. Brenet, "Notes et croquis sur J.-P. R.," *Guide Musical* (1899); idem, "La Jeunesse de R.," *Rivista Musicale Italiana,* IX (1902) and X (1903); H. Quittard, "Les Années de jeunesse de R.," *Revue d'Histoire et de Critique Musicale* (1902); L. de La Laurencie, *Quelques documents sur J.-P. R. et sa famille* (Paris, 1907); idem, *R.* (Paris, 1908); L. Laloy, *R.* (Paris, 1908); M. Mayer, *J.-P. R.; J.S. Bach* (Chambéry, 1946); Y. Tiénot, *J.-P. R., Esquisse biographique, suivie d'un tableau chronologique comprenant une liste complète des oeuvres de R.* (Paris, 1954); H. Charlier, *J.-P. R.* (Lyons, 1955); P. Berthier, *Réflexions sur l'art et la vie de J.-P. R. (1683–1764)* (Paris, 1957); C. Girdlestone, *J.-P. R.: His Life and Work* (London, 1957; 2nd ed., rev., 1969); J. Malignon, *R.* (Paris, 1960); C. Kintzler, *J.-P. R.: Splendeur et naufrage de l'esthétique du plaisir à l'age classique* (Paris, 1983); L. Miller, "R. and the Royal Society of London: New Letters and Documents," *Music & Letters* (Jan. 1985); H. Schneider, "R. et sa famille: Nouveaux documents," *Recherches sur la Musique Française Classique,* XXIII (1985). **WORKS:** G. Graf, *J.-P. R. in seiner Oper Hippolyte et Aricie: Eine musikkritische Würdigung* (Wädenswil, 1927); P.-M. Masson, *L'Opéra de R.* (Paris, 1930); Z. Klitenic, *The Clavecin Works of J.-P. R.* (diss., Univ. of Pa., 1955); E. Ahnell, *The Concept of Tonality in the Operas of J.-P. R.* (diss., Univ. of Illinois, 1958); G. Seefrid, *Die Airs de danse in den Bühnenwerken von J.-P. R.* (Wiesbaden, 1969); M. Terey-Smith, *J.-P. R.: "Abaris ou les Boréades"; A Critical Edition* (diss., Eastman School of Music, 1971); J. Anthony, *French Baroque Music from Beaujoyeulx to R.* (London, 1973; 2nd ed., rev., 1978); M. Cyrs, *R.'s "Les fêtes d'Hébé"* (diss., Univ. of Calif., Berkeley, 1975); P. Rice, *The Fontainebleau Operas of J.-P. R.: A Critical Study* (diss., Univ. of Victoria, Canada, 1981); G. Sadler, "R. and the Orchestra," *Proceedings of the Royal Musical Association,* CVIII (1981–82); M. Cyr, "Towards a Chronology of R.'s Cantatas," *Musical Times* (Sept. 1983); J. de La Gorce, ed., *J.-P. R.: Dijon 1983.*

THEORIES: P. Estève, *Nouvelle découverte du principe de l'harmonie, avec un examen de ce que M. R. a publié sous le titre de Démonstration de ce principe* (Paris, 1752); J. Le Rond d'Alembert, *Éléments de musique théorique et pratique selon les principes de M. R.* (Paris, 1752; 2nd ed., 1762); Ducharger, *Réflexions sur divers ouvrages de M. R.* (Rennes, 1761); F. Marpurg, *Versuch über die musikalische Temperatur, nebst einem Anhang über den R.- und Kirnbergerschen Grundbass* (Breslau, 1776); M. Keane, *The Theoretical Writings of J.-P. R.* (diss., Catholic Univ. of America, 1961); J. Krehbiel, *Harmonic Principles of J.-P. R. and His Contemporaries* (diss., Indiana Univ., 1964); D. Hayes, *R.'s "Génération harmonique ou Traité de musique théorique et pratique"* (diss., Stanford Univ., 1974); E. Verba, *A Hierarchic Interpretation of the Theo-*

ries and Music of J.-P. R. (diss., Univ. of Chicago, 1979); H. Schneider, *J.-P. R., "Les vérités intéressantes": Kommentierte Konkordanzedition* (Wiesbaden, 1985).

Ramey, Phillip, American composer and writer on music; b. Chicago, Sept. 12, 1939. He received instruction in composition from A. Tcherepnin in Nice (1959), continuing with him at De Paul Univ. (B.A., 1962); then pursued training from Beeson at Columbia Univ. (M.A., 1965). He held 5 MacDowell Colony fellowships (1969–76); was program ed. and annotator of the N.Y. Phil. (from 1977); also wrote numerous articles and record liner notes.

WORKS: ORCH.: *Concert Suite* for Piano and Orch. (1962; rev. 1983–84); 2 piano concertos (1969–71; 1976); Concerto for Chamber Orch. (1974). **CHAMBER:** Sonata for 3 Timpani (1961); *Capriccio* for Percussion (1966); *Toccata breve* for Percussion (1966); *Night Music* for Percussion (1967); *Commentaries* for Flute and Piano (1968); *Suite* for Violin and Piano (1971); *La Citadelle,* rhapsody for Oboe and Piano (1975); *Arabesque* for Flute (1977); *Fanfare-Sonata* for Trumpet (1981); *Phantasm* for Flute and Violin, or 2 Violins (1984). **VOCAL:** *Cat Songs* for Soprano, Flute, and Piano (1962; rev. 1965); *7, they are 7: Incantations* for Bass-baritone and Orch. (1965); other songs; numerous pieces for piano, including 5 sonatas (1961, 1966, 1968, 1968, 1974).

Ramey, Samuel (Edward), outstanding American bass; b. Colby, Kans., March 28, 1942. He attended Kansas State Univ., then studied voice with Arthur Newman at Wichita State Univ. (B.Mus., 1968); after singing with the Grass Roots Opera Co. in Raleigh, N.C. (1968–69), he continued his studies with Armen Boyajian in N.Y. He made his professional operatic debut as Zuniga in *Carmen* at the N.Y. City Opera (March 11, 1973), and within a few seasons established himself as its principal bass; also made guest appearances at the Glyndebourne Festival (1976), the Netherlands Opera in Amsterdam (1978), the Hamburg State Opera (1978), Milan's La Scala (1981), and the Vienna State Opera (1981). On Jan. 19, 1984, he made a brilliant debut at the Metropolitan Opera in N.Y. as Argante in Handel's *Rinaldo.* He subsequently appeared with leading opera houses around the world, and was engaged as a soloist with the major orchs. Among his notable roles are Leporello, Don Giovanni, Figaro, Gounod's Méphistophélès, the 4 villains in *Les Contes d'Hoffmann,* Attila, Boito's Mefistofele, and Olin Blitch; he sang the role of Figaro for the sound-track recording of the award-winning film *Amadeus* (1984).

BIBL.: B. Zakariasen, "S. R.," *Ovation* (Nov. 1984).

Ramin, Günther (Werner Hans), distinguished German organist, conductor, composer, and pedagogue; b. Karlsruhe, Oct. 15, 1898; d. Leipzig, Feb. 27, 1956. As a boy he sang in the Thomanerchor in Leipzig; he then studied organ with Karl Straube, piano with Robert Teichmüller, and theory with Stephan Krehl at the Leipzig Cons. In 1918 he was appointed organist of the Thomaskirche in Leipzig; he also was organist of the Gewandhaus concerts and a teacher at the Leipzig Cons. During the season 1933–34, he toured the U.S. as an organ virtuoso. He was also active as a conductor; he led the Lehrergesangverein in Leipzig (1922–35) and the Gewandhaus Choir (1933–34; 1945–51); from 1935 to 1943 he conducted the Phil. Choir in Berlin. In 1940 he became cantor of the Thomaskirche, where he sought to preserve the integrity of the Thomanerchor after the establishment of the German Democratic Republic. His compositions include an *Orgelchoral-Suite* and many other organ pieces, as well as chamber music and songs. He ed. several collections of organ works and publ. the manual *Gedanken zur Klärung des Orgelproblems* (Kassel, 1929; new ed., 1955). A vol. of his essays on Bach was ed. by D. Hellmann (Wiesbaden, 1973).

BIBL.: L. von Koerber, *Der Thomanerchor und sein Kantor* (Hamburg, 1954); E. Hasse, *Erinnerungen an G. R.* (Berlin, 1958); C. Ramin, *G. R.* (Freiburg, 1958); idem, *Weggefährten im Geiste Johann Sebastian Bachs: Karl Straube—G. R.; zwei Thomaskantoren 1918–1956* (Darmstadt, 1981).

Ramírez, Luis Antonio, Puerto Rican composer; b. San Juan, Feb. 10, 1923. He studied piano and harmony with Alfredo Romero in San Juan (1954–57); then studied composition with Cristóbal Halffter and Daniel Bravo, and piano with Juan Molinari at the Madrid Cons. (1957–60). Returning to San Juan, he taught at the Univ. of Puerto Rico.

WORKS: *Sonata elegiaca* for Cello and Piano (1970); *Fantasia sobre un Mito Antillano* for Double Bass, Guitar, Horn, Percussion, and Strings (1970); *3 piezas breves* for Horn, 2 Trumpets, Trombone, Piano, Percussion, and Strings (1972); *Fragmentos* for Orch. (1973).

Ramón y Rivera, Luis Felipe, Venezuelan ethnomusicologist and composer; b. San Cristóbal, Aug. 23, 1913. He studied viola pedagogy at the Caracas Escuela Superior de Música (degree, 1934); returned to his native city to teach at the Escuela de Artes y Oficios de San Cristóbal (1939) and to found and direct the Táchira Music School (1940–50). He studied folklore and ethnomusicology with Carlo Vega at the Inst. of Musicology in Buenos Aires and with Isabel Aretz and Augusto Raúl Cortázar at the Colegio Libre de Estudios Superiores (1945–47); returned to Caracas as chief of musicology of the Servicio de Investigaciones Folklóricas Nacionales (1947), and then went back to Buenos Aires to direct the Americana Orch. (1948–52). In 1953 he became director of the National Inst. of Folklore of Venezuela in Caracas. He traveled extensively in South America; taught folklore and ethnomusicology at Venezuelan and foreign univs.; was president of the Venezuelan Soc. of Authors and Composers (1972–73). Ramón y Rivera's extensive fieldwork enabled him to make a comparative study of the music of the South American continent; he contributed greatly to the study of Venezuelan indigenous, folk, and popular music.

WRITINGS: *La polifonia popular de Venezuela* (Buenos Aires, 1949); *El joropo, baile nacional de Venezuela* (Caracas, 1953); *Cantos de trabajo del pueblo venezolano* (Caracas, 1955); *La música colonial profana* (Caracas, 1966); *Música indigena, folklórica y popular de Venezuela* (Buenos Aires, 1970); *La música afrovenezolana* (Caracas, 1971); *La música popular de Venezuela* (Caracas, 1976).

Ramos de Pareia, Bartolomé, significant Spanish music theorist; b. Baeza, c.1440; d. c.1491. He studied with Juan de Monte; after lecturing at the Univ. of Salamanca, he went to Bologna in 1472; publ. in 1482 his Latin treatise *Musica practica* (modern ed. by G. Vecchi, 1969), one of the important landmarks in the science of harmony. From 1484 he was in Rome. He established the mathematical ratios 4:5 and 5:6 for the intervals of the major and minor third, thus completing the definition of the consonant triad and laying the basis of our harmonic system. He was also the 1st to set forth the theory of equal temperament, probably based on the practice of the early Spanish guitarists (*vihuelistas*), since the frets on the guitar were placed a semitone apart.

BIBL.: J. Haar, "Roger Caperon and R. d.P.," *Acta Musicologica* (1969).

Ramovš, Primož, Slovenian composer; b. Ljubljana, March 20, 1921. He studied composition with Slavko Osterc at his hometown's Academy of Music (1935–41), with Vito Frazzi in Siena (1941), and privately with Casella and Petrassi in Rome (1941–43). He was a librarian (1945–52) and chief librarian (1952–87) of the Slovene Academy of Sciences and Art; was also a prof. at the Ljubljana Cons. (1948–52; 1955–64). The framework of his style of composition is neo-Classical, distinguished by great contrapuntal skill and ingenious handling of rich, dissonant sonorities; dodecaphony and aleatorality are sometimes employed.

WORKS: ORCH.: 3 numbered syms. (1940, 1943, 1948); 3 divertimentos (1941, 1942, 1944); Piano Concerto (1946); Concertino for Piano and String Orch. (1948); Concerto for 2 Pianos and String Orch. (1949); *Suite* for 2 Violins, Cello, and String Orch. (1950); Sinfonietta (1951); *Musique funèbre* (1955); *Chorale and Toccata* (1955); *Adagio* for Cello and String Orch.

(1958); *Concerto piccolo* for Bassoon and String Orch. (1958); Trumpet Concertino (1960); 7 *Compositions* for Strings (1960); Concerto for Violin, Viola, and Orch. (1961); *Koncertantza glasba* (Concertante Music) for Percussion and Orch. (1961); *Intrada* (1962); *Profiles* (1964); *Vzporedja* (Parallels) for Piano and String Orch. (1965); *Odmevi* (Echoes) for Flute and Orch. (1965); *Antiparallels* for Piano and Orch. (1966; Zagreb, May 15, 1967); *Finale* (1966); *Portret* for Harp, Winds, Strings, and Percussion (1968); *Symphony 68* (Ljubljana, Oct. 27, 1968); *Nasprotja* (Contrasts) for Flute and Orch. (1969); Sym. for Piano and Orch. (1970); Cello Concerto (1974); Double-Bass Concerto (1976); Bassoon Concerto (1978); *Triplum* (1980); Concerto for 2 Pianos and Orch. (1981); Organ Concerto (1983); *Concerto profano* for Organ and Orch. (1984); Trumpet Concerto (1985); *Kolovrat* for String Orch. (1986). **CHAMBER:** Quartet for 4 Horns (1939); Wind Trio (1942); Trio for Flute, Trumpet, and Bassoon (1952); *Kontrasti* for Piano Trio (1961); *Eneafonia* for 9 Instruments (1963); *Fluctuations* for Chamber Ensemble (1964); *Prolog* for Flute, Clarinet, and Bassoon (1966); *Nihanja* (Oscillations) for Flute, Harp, Percussion, and Strings (1969); *Siglali* for Piano and 8 Instruments (1973); many compositions for solo instruments; piano pieces; choruses; songs.

Rampal, Jean-Pierre (Louis), celebrated French flutist, conductor, and teacher; b. Marseilles, Jan. 7, 1922. He studied flute as a child with his father, 1st flutist in the Marseilles orch. and a prof. at the Cons.; then studied medicine until being drafted for military service by the German occupation authorities in 1943; when he learned that he was to be sent to Germany as a forced laborer, he went AWOL; subsequently attended flute classes at the Paris Cons., winning the premier prix in 5 months. He played solo flute in the orch. of the Vichy Opera (1946–50); concurrently began to tour, often in duo recitals with the pianist and harpsichordist Robert Veyron-Lacroix. He was solo flutist in the orch. of the Paris Opéra from 1956 to 1962, and also became a popular artist on the Paris Radio. He subsequently toured throughout the world with phenomenal success as a virtuoso, appearing as soloist with all the major orchs. and in innumerable recitals. In later years he also appeared as a guest conductor. He taught at the Paris Cons., and gave master classes worldwide. His repertoire is vast, ranging from the Baroque masters to jazz, from the music of Japan to that of India, from arrangements to specially commissioned works. Of the last, such composers as Poulenc and Jolivet wrote pieces for him. Through his countless concerts and recordings, he did more than any other flutist of his time to bring his instrument into the mainstream of musical life. He was made a Chevalier of the Légion d'Honneur in 1966 and an Officier des Arts et Lettres in 1971. With D. Wise, he publ. *Music, My Love: An Autobiography* (N.Y., 1989).

Ramsey, Robert, English organist and composer; b. c.1595; d. after 1644. He took his B.Mus. at Cambridge in 1616; was organist of Trinity College (1628–44) and Master of the Children (1637–44). He wrote numerous church services, anthems, and madrigals, which remained in MS until 1962, when an *Evening Service* and some madrigals were publ. in England; more recently E. Thompson ed. *Robert Ramsey: English Sacred Music,* in Early English Church Music, VII (London, 1967), and *Robert Ramsey: Latin Sacred Music, I–II,* ibid., XX (1978) and XXXI (1986); see also I. Spink, ed., *English Songs 1625–1660,* in Musica Britannica, XXXIII (London, 1971).

BIBL.: E. Thompson, "R. R.," *Musical Quarterly* (April 1963); idem, "R. R.'s Latin Sacred Music," *Musical Times* (April 1986).

Ran, Shulamit, Israeli pianist and composer; b. Tel Aviv, Oct. 21, 1949. She studied piano with Miriam Boskovich and Emma Gorochov and composition with Paul Ben-Haim and Alexander Boskovich; then was a scholarship student at the America-Israel Cultural Foundation and the Mannes College of Music in N.Y. (graduated, 1967), her mentors being Nadia Reisenberg (piano) and Norman Dello Joio (composition); continued piano studies with Dorothy Taubman and composition

training with Ralph Shapey (1976). She made tours of the U.S. and Europe as a pianist; was artist-in-residence at St. Mary's Univ. in Halifax, Nova Scotia (1972–73); then taught at the Univ. of Chicago. She held a Guggenheim fellowship (1977); was a visiting prof. at Princeton Univ. (1987). In 1991 she became composer-in-residence of the Chicago Sym. Orch. and was awarded the Pulitzer Prize in Music for her 1st Sym.

WORKS: ORCH.: *Capriccio* for Piano and Orch. (N.Y., Nov. 30, 1963); *Symphonic Poem* for Piano and Orch. (Jerusalem, Oct. 17, 1967); *10 Children's Scenes* (1970; arranged from a piano work); *Concert Piece* for Piano and Orch. (Tel Aviv, July 12, 1971); Piano Concerto (1977); Concerto for Orch. (1986); Sym. No. 1 (Philadelphia, Oct. 19, 1990). **VOCAL:** *Hatzvi Israel Eulogie* for Mezzo-soprano, Flute, Harp, and String Quartet (1968); *7 Japanese Love Poems* for Voice and Piano (1968); *O the Chimneys* for Mezzo-soprano, Ensemble, and Tape (1969); *Ensembles for 17* for Soprano and 16 Instruments (Chicago, April 11, 1975); *Apprehensions* for Voice, Clarinet, and Piano (1979); *Amichai Songs* for Mezzo-soprano, Oboe or English Horn, Viola da Gamba, and Harpsichord (1985); *Adonai Malach* for Cantor, Horn, Piccolo, Oboe, and Clarinet (1985). **CHAMBER:** Quartet for Flute, Clarinet, Cello, and Piano (1967); *Double Vision* for Woodwind Quintet, Brass Quintet, and Piano (1976; Chicago, Jan. 21, 1977); *A Prayer* for Clarinet, Bass Clarinet, Bassoon, Horn, and Timpani (1981); 2 string quartets (1984; 1988–89); *Concerto da camera I* for Woodwind Quintet (1985) and *II* for Clarinet, String Quartet, and Piano (1987). **PIANO:** *Structures* (1968); *Hyperbolae* (1976); *Sonata Waltzer* (1981–82); *Verticals* (1982).

Ranczak, Hildegard, Czech soprano; b. Vitkovice, Dec. 20, 1895; d. Munich, Feb. 19, 1987. She studied at the Vienna Cons.; made her debut in Düsseldorf in 1918; remained there until 1923; then sang in Cologne (1923–25) and Stuttgart (1925–27); in 1927 she joined the Bavarian State Opera in Munich, where she appeared until 1944; sang there again from 1946 to 1949; also sang at Covent Garden in London, the Paris Opéra, the Rome Opera, and the Berlin State Opera. She created the role of Clairon in Richard Strauss's *Capriccio* in 1942.

Randall, J(ames) K(irtland), American composer; b. Cleveland, June 16, 1929. He studied at the Cleveland Inst. of Music (1934–47), Columbia Univ. (B.A., 1955), Harvard Univ. (M.A., 1956), and Princeton Univ. (M.F.A., 1958); among his teachers were Leonard Shure for piano and Elwell, Thad Jones, Sessions, and Babbitt for composition; taught at Princeton (from 1958). From 1980 he produced various improvised performance pieces under the general name *INTER/PLAY.*

WORKS: *Slow Movement* for Piano (1959); *Improvisation on a Poem by e.e. cummings* for Soprano, Clarinet, Saxophone, Trumpet, Guitar, Piano or Soprano, and Piano (1960); *Pitch-derived Rhythm: 7 Demonstrations* for Flute, Clarinet, Piano, and 2 Cellos (1961–64); *Quartets in Pairs* for Computer (1964); *Mudgett: Monologues by a Mass Murderer* for Taped Violin and Computer (1965); *Lyric Variations* for Taped Violin and Computer (1968); *Quartersines* for Computer (1969); *Music for Eakins,* film score for Computer (1972); *. . . such words as it were vain to close . . .* for Piano (1974–76); *Troubador Songs* for Voice and Percussion (1977); *Meditation on Rossignol* for Piano (1978); *Soundscroll 2* for Piano (1978); *Greek Nickel 1* and *II* for Piano (1979).

Randegger, Alberto, Jr., Italian violinist and composer, nephew of **Alberto Randegger, Sr.;** b. Trieste, Aug. 3, 1880; d. Milan, Oct. 7, 1918. He accompanied his uncle to London and appeared as a violinist at an orch. concert conducted by the latter; took courses at the Royal Cons. of Music; then lived in Milan. He composed a short opera, *L'ombra di Werther* (Trieste, 1899); a Violin Concerto; piano pieces and songs.

Randegger, Alberto, Sr., Italian conductor, organist, teacher, and composer, uncle of **Alberto Randegger, Jr.;** b. Trieste, April 13, 1832; d. London, Dec. 18, 1911. He studied piano and composition in Italy; after working as a music director in Italian theaters, he settled in London (1854) and gained distinction as a conductor, singing teacher, and composer; was also organist at St. Paul's in Regent's Park (1854–70). He conducted at the Wolverhampton (from 1868) and Norwich (1881–1905) festivals, with the Carl Rosa Opera Co. (1879–85), at Drury Lane and Covent Garden (1887–98), and at the Queen's Hall (1895–97); was a prof. of singing at the Royal Academy of Music (from 1868) and later at the Royal College of Music; publ. the manual *Singing* (London, 1893). His compositions include the operas *Bianca Capello* (Brescia, 1854) and *The Rival Beauties* (Leeds, 1864); a dramatic cantata, *Fridolin* (1873); sacred music; songs.

Randolph, David, American conductor; b. N.Y., Dec. 21, 1914. He studied at City College, N.Y. (B.S., 1936) and Teachers College, Columbia Univ. (M.A., 1941); from 1943 to 1947, was assistant director of music of the U.S. Office of War Information. In 1943 he organized the Randolph Singers, which he conducted until 1972. In 1955 he founded the Masterwork Chorus and Orch.; also led the St. Cecilia Chorus and Orch. and, beginning in 1981, the Masterwork Chamber Orch. He taught conducting at the Dalcroze School (1947–50); was a prof. of music at the State Univ. of N.Y. College at New Paltz (1970–72), at Fordham Univ. (1972–73), and at Montclair State College (from 1973). He was also active as a radio music commentator. He publ. the book *This Is Music* (N.Y., 1964); also ed. The David Randolph Madrigal Series.

Rands, Bernard, remarkable English-born American composer; b. Sheffield, March 2, 1934. He studied piano and organ at home; at the age of 18 he entered the Univ. of Wales, majoring in music and English literature. He also developed a passion for Celtic lore; in his student days he became a sort of polyglot, delving into the linguistic mysteries of Welsh, Irish, and Scottish vocables, and on the way acquiring a fluency in French, Italian, and Spanish. He also immersed himself in the hypergrammatical and ultrasyntactic glossolalia of James Joyce. After graduating from the Univ. of Wales (B.Mus., 1956; M.Mus., 1958), he took lessons in musicology with Roman Vlad in Rome and studied composition with Luigi Dallapiccola in Florence (1958–60); also attended seminars in composition and conducting given by Pierre Boulez and Bruno Maderna at the Darmstadt summer courses in new music; later consulted with Luciano Berio in Milan on problems of electronic music. He was on the faculty of the Univ. of York (1968–75); then was engaged as a prof. of music at the Univ. of Calif. at San Diego, where he found the musical atmosphere particularly congenial to his innovative ideas; was a visiting prof. at the Calif. Inst. of the Arts in Valencia in 1984–85 while retaining his San Diego post. He held a Guggenheim fellowship (1982–83); became a U.S. citizen in 1983. He was awarded the Pulitzer Prize in Music in 1984 for his *Canti del sole* for Tenor and Orch. In 1989 he became composer-in-residence of the Philadelphia Orch.

The sources of Rand's music are astonishingly variegated, drawing upon religious, mystical, mathematical, and sonoristic premises. At one time he was preoccupied with Hinduism; these interests are reflected in his work *Aum* (*Om*), a mantric word interpreted as having 3 sounds representing the triune stasis of Brahma, Vishnu, and Siva. Despite the complex nature of his compositions, he seems to encounter little resistance on the part of performers and audiences; his music possesses the rare quality of immediate communication. Each work reflects a message; thus his *Metalepsis 2* is described by him as a "non-denominational Mass for all who suffer at the hands of tyrants." Several works reflect the scientific bent of his mind, as exemplified by *Formants;* there are mundane references in the titles of such works as *Memos* and *Agenda;* other sets contain references to sports, as in *Wildtrack.* Then there are in his catalog educational pieces, such as *Sound Patterns,* designed to be interpreted by children and professional performers alike. His *Canti lunatici* penetrate the inner recesses of the human mind in a state of turbulence.

WORKS: MUSIC THEATER: *Memo 2B* for Trombone and Female Dancer (1980); *Memo 2D* for Trombone, String Quartet,

and Female Dancer (1980). **ORCH.:** *Per esempio* (1968); *Wildtrack 1* (1969) and *2* (1973); *Agenda* (1969–70); *Mésalliance* for Piano and Orch. (1972); *Aum* for Harp and Orch. (1974); *Madrigali,* after Monteverdi/Berio (1977); *Canti lunatici* for Soprano and Orch. (1981); *Canti del sole* for Tenor and Orch. (1983–84); received the Pulitzer Prize in Music, 1984); *Le Tambourin,* 2 suites (both 1984); *Ceremonial 1* (1985) and *2* (1986); *Requiescant* (1985–86); *Hiraeth* for Cello and Orch. (San Diego, Feb. 19, 1987); . . . *Body and Shadow* . . . (1988; Boston, Feb. 22, 1989). **INSTRUMENTAL ENSEMBLE:** *Actions for 6* for Flute, Harp, 2 Percussion, Viola, and Cello (1962–63); *Formants 2—Labyrinthe* for Clarinet, Trombone, Piano, 2 Percussion, Viola, and Cello (1969–70); *Tableau* for Flute, Clarinet, Piano, Percussion, Viola, and Cello (1970); *déjà* for Flute, Clarinet, Piano, Percussion, Viola, and Cello (1972); *"as all get out"* (1972); *Response—Memo 1B* for Double Bass and Tape or 2 Double Basses (1973); *Cuaderno* for String Quartet (1973), *étendre* (1974); *Scherzi* for Clarinet, Piano, Violin, and Cello (1974); *Serenata 75* (1976); *Obbligato—Memo 2C* for Trombone and String Quartet (1980); *Serenata 85* for Flute, Harp, Violin, Viola, and Cello (1986); . . . *in the receding mist* . . . for Flute, Harp, Violin, Viola, and Cello (1988). **INSTRUMENTAL SOLO:** *Tre espressioni* for Piano (1960); *Formants 1—Les Gestes* for Harp (1965); *Memo 1* for Double Bass (1971), *2* for Trombone (1972), and *5* for Piano (1975). **VOICES AND INSTRUMENTS:** *Sound Patterns 1* for Voices and Hands (1967), *2* for Voices, Percussion, and Instruments (1967), and *3* for Voices (1969); *Ballad 1* for Mezzo-soprano and 5 Instruments (1970), *2* for Voice and Piano (1970), *3* for Soprano, Tape, and Bell (1973), and *4* for Voices and 20 Instruments (1980); *Flickering Shadows* for Solo Voices and Instruments (1983–84); . . . *among the voices* . . . for Chorus and Harp (Cleveland, April 16, 1988).

Rangström, (Anders Johan) Ture, prominent Swedish conductor, music critic, and composer; b. Stockholm, Nov. 30, 1884; d. there, May 11, 1947. He studied counterpoint with Johan Lindegren in Stockholm (1903–4); then went to Berlin, where he took courses in singing with J. Hey and in composition with Pfitzner (1905–6); continued his vocal training with Hey in Munich (1906–8). He was a music critic for Stockholm's *Svenska Dagbladet* (1907–9), the *Stockholms Dagblad* (1910–14; 1927–30), and the *Nya Dagligt Allehanda* (1938–42); was conductor of the Göteborg Sym. Orch. (1922–25), and thereafter made guest conducting appearances in Scandinavia. His music is permeated with a lyrical sentiment, and his forms are rhapsodic; in his syms. he achieves great intensity by concentrated development of the principal melodic and rhythmic ideas; his songs are also notable.

WORKS: OPERAS: *Kronbruden* (The Crown Bride; 1915–16; 1st perf. in German as *Die Kronbraut,* Stuttgart, Oct. 21, 1919; 1st perf. in Swedish, Göteborg, March 25, 1936); *Middelalderlig* or *Medeltida* (1917–18; Göteborg, May 11, 1921); *Gilgamesj* (1943–44; unfinished; completed and orchestrated by J. Fernström; Stockholm, Nov. 20, 1952). **ORCH.:** *Dityramb* (1909); *Ballad* for Piano and Orch. (1909; rev. 1937); *Ett midsommarstycke* (1910); *En höstrång* (1911); *Havet sjunger* (1913); 4 syms.: No. 1, *August Strindberg in memoriam* (1914; Berlin, Jan. 4, 1922); No. 2, *Mitt Land* (My Country; Stockholm, Nov. 20, 1919); No. 3, *Sång under stjärnorna* (Song under the Stars; 1912; Stockholm, Jan. 8, 1930); No. 4, *Invocatio* (Göteborg, Nov. 20, 1936); *Intermezzo drammatico,* suite for Small Orch. (1916); *Divertimento elegiaco,* suite for String Orch. (1918); *Partita* for Violin and Orch. (1933); *Vauxhall,* miniature suite (1937); *På nordisk sträng,* prelude (1941); *Värhymn* (1942); *Festpreludium: Tempest, Youth, Poetry, and Song* (1944). **CHAMBER:** *Improvisata: Vårnätterna* for Violin and Piano (1904); *Ver sacrum* for Cello and Piano (1906–7); *String Quartet: Ein Nachtstück (Notturno) in E.T.A. Hoffmanns Manier* (1909); *Suite (No. 1) in modo antico* for Violin and Piano (1912); *Suite No. 2 in modo barocco* for Violin and Piano (1921–22); piano pieces; choral works; over 250 songs.

BIBL.: Special issue of *Musikrevy,* 25 (1970); A. Helmer and S. Jacobsson, *T. R.: Life and Work* (Stockholm, 1987).

Ránki, Dezső, Hungarian pianist; b. Budapest, Sept. 8, 1951. He studied piano with Klára Máthé at the Bartók Cons. and at the Franz Liszt Academy of Music with Pál Kadosa and Ferenc Rados. In 1969 he won the International Schumann Competition in Zwickau, and from that time toured with notable success. His repertoire encompasses the classics and the moderns; he particularly excels in the works of Béla Bartók.

Ránki, György, noted Hungarian composer; b. Budapest, Oct. 30, 1907. He studied composition with Kodály at the Budapest Academy of Music (1926–30) and ethnomusicology with Schaeffner in Paris (1938–39); then devoted himself to composition; won the Erkel (1952, 1957) and Kossuth (1954) prizes; in 1963, was made a Merited Artist by the government; received the Bartók-Pásztory award (1987). He won distinction as a composer of both serious and popular works.
WORKS: STAGE: *King Pomádé's New Clothes,* comic opera (1953–67); *The Tragedy of Man,* "mystery opera" (1970); *The Boatman of the Moon,* "opera-fantasy" (1979); *Terminal,* music drama (1988); also *3 Nights,* musical tragedy (1961), an operetta, much other theater music, and numerous film scores. **ORCH.:** *Sword Dance* (1949); *Hungarian Dances from the 16th Century* (1950); *Don Quijote y Dulcinea,* 2 miniatures for Oboe and Small Orch. (1961); *Fantasy* for Piano and Orch. after woodcuts by Gyula Derkovits (1962); *Aurora tempestuosa,* prelude (1967); *Circus,* symphonic dance drama (1965); *Raga di notte* for Violin and Orch. (1974); 2 syms.: No. 1 (1977); No. 2, *In Memoriam Zoltán Kodály* (1981); Concertino for Cimbalom, Xylophone, Timpani, Percussion, and String Quintet (1978); Viola Concerto (1979); *Aristophanes Suite* for Violin and String Orch. (1947–85); Divertimento for Clarinet and String Orch. (1986). **VOCAL:** *1944,* oratorio for Baritone, Choir, and Chamber Orch. (1967); *Cantus urbis* for 4 Soloists, Choir, and Instrumental Ensemble (1972); *Leverkühn's Abschied,* monodrama for Tenor and 10 Instruments (1979); *Overture to the 21st Century* for Choir and Orch. (1987); choruses; songs. **CHAMBER:** *Serenata all'antiqua* for Violin and Piano (1956); *Pentaerophonia,* 3 pieces for Wind Quintet (1958); *Serenade of the 7-Headed Dragon* for Brass Septet (1980); String Quartet No. 1: *In Memoriam Béla Bartók* (1985); *The Tales of Father Goose,* musical joke for Brass Septet (1987); also piano pieces, including 3 sonatas (n.d., 1947, 1980).

Rankin, Nell, American mezzo-soprano; b. Montgomery, Ala., Jan. 3, 1926. She studied voice with Jeanne Lorraine at the Birmingham Cons. of Music; continued her training with Karin Branzell in N.Y. (1945–49). In 1949 she made her operatic debut as Ortrud in *Lohengrin* at the Zürich Opera, of which she later became an active member; in 1950–51 she sang at the Basel Opera, and in 1951 appeared at La Scala, Milan. In 1951 she won the Metropolitan Opera Auditions of the Air and made her debut with it in N.Y. on Nov. 22, 1951, as Amneris; she then sang at Covent Garden in London (1953–54) and at the San Francisco Opera (1955). Subsequently she appeared at the Teatro Colón in Buenos Aires and in many other opera houses, in Mexico, in Naples, and in Vienna. Her best roles were Carmen, Azucena, Ortrud, Santuzza, and Maddalena.

Rankl, Karl, Austrian-born English conductor and composer; b. Gaaden, near Vienna, Oct. 1, 1898; d. Salzburg, Sept. 6, 1968. He was a pupil of Schoenberg and Webern in Vienna; from them he acquired a fine understanding of the problems of modern music. He occupied various positions as a chorus master and an opera coach in Vienna; served as assistant to Klemperer at the Kroll Opera in Berlin (1928–31); then conducted opera in Graz (1932–37) and at the German Theater in Prague (1937–39). At the outbreak of World War II, he went to England and later became a naturalized subject; was music director at Covent Garden in London (1946–51), the Scottish National Orch. in Glasgow (1952–57), and the Elizabethan Opera Trust in Sydney (1958–60). He composed an opera, *Deirdre of the Sorrows* (won the Festival of Britain prize,

1951, but was not perf.); 8 syms.; an oratorio, *Der Mensch;* many choral works.

Ranta, Sulho, Finnish composer and writer on music; b. Peräseinäjoki, Aug. 15, 1901; d. Helsinki, May 5, 1960. He studied at the Univ. of Helsinki (M.A., 1925); took courses in composition with Melartin at the Helsinki Cons. (1921–24), and later in Germany, France, and Italy. Returning to Finland, he taught at the Sibelius Academy in Helsinki (1934–56); was also active as a music critic. He was ed. of a comprehensive biographical dictionary of Finnish composers, *Suomen Säveltäjiä* (Helsinki, 1945), and a general biographical survey of performers, *Sävelten Taitureita* (Helsinki, 1947). As a composer, he excelled in chamber music and songs.
WORKS: 4 syms.: *Sinfonia programmatica* (1929–31); *Sinfonia piccola* (1931–32); *Sinfonia semplice* (1936); *Sinfonia dell'arte* (1947); *Oratorio volgare* for Solo Voices, Chorus, and Orch. (1951); *Tuntematon maa* (The Unknown Land) for Piano and Orch. (1930); Concertino No. 1 for Piano and Strings (1932); *Kainuun kuvia* (*Images boréales*), suite for Orch. (1933); Concertino No. 2 for Flute, Harp, Viola, and Strings (1934); Concerto for Orch. (1938); *Kansansatu* (Folk Story), symphonic variations (1940); *Sydärnen tie* (The Way of the Heart), cantata (1945–46); *Eksyneitten legioonalaisten rukous* (Prayer of the Lost Legionnaires) for 8 Soloists, Chorus, and Orch. (1956); Piano Trio (1923); *Suite symphonique* for Flute, Clarinet, Horn, String Quartet, and Piano (1926–28); Concertino for String Quartet (1935); piano pieces.

Rapchak, Lawrence, interesting American composer; b. Hammond, Ind., May 7, 1951. (His unusual name is explained by the Czech origin of his grandparents.) He studied piano in grade school and learned to read music by intelligent guesswork; from his earliest attempts at composition, he was greatly impressed by Shostakovich's 10th Sym.; he tried to write a similar work, which became his 1st symphonic composition; it was performed in Cleveland on June 3, 1967. In 1969 he entered regular classes in composition with Marcel Dick and Donald Erb at the Cleveland Inst. of Music; also had a course in conducting with James Levine. In the meantime he taught himself to play drums and other percussion instruments; also led a student orch. He describes his music as having emphasis on contrasting colors with markedly propulsive rhythms.
WORKS: Sym. for Chamber Orch. (Cleveland, June 3, 1967); *2 Short Pieces* (1967); *4 Pieces for Orchestra* (1969); *Poem* for Oboe Ensemble (Cleveland, Dec. 1980); *Bifrost* (1981); *Lanterloo* (1981); *3 Rappaccini Rhapsodies* (1982); *Sky Dancers* (1983); *Magic Box* for Oboe, English Horn, and Orch. (1984); *Mesazoa* (1985); *Mystic Promenade* (St. Louis, Oct. 7, 1987); *Il concerto vetrina* for Bass Clarinet and Small Orch. (1988; Chicago, March 17, 1991); Violin Concerto (1988); *The Lifework of Juan Diaz,* based on a Ray Bradbury story (1988; Chicago, April 21, 1990, composer conducting); *Chasing the Sunset* (N.Y., April 28, 1989); *Sinfonia antiqua* (1989; Detroit, Feb. 7, 1991); *Aubade* (1990).

Rapee, Erno, Hungarian-American conductor, arranger, and composer; b. Budapest, June 4, 1891; d. N.Y., June 26, 1945. He studied piano with Emil Sauer at the National Cons. in Budapest; gave concerts as a pianist; appeared as a conductor with various European orchs.; in 1912 he settled in N.Y. as conductor of the Hungarian Opera Co.; then became conductor for S.L. Rothafel (Roxy) at his motion picture theaters in N.Y.; after several years at the Roxy Theater (1926–31), he became music director for NBC; then at Radio City Music Hall (1932–45). He introduced classical works into his programs, mostly in the form of potpourris, but upon occasion also in full version; brought out a collection of music to accompany silent movies, *Motion Picture Moods for Pianists and Organists: A Rapid Reference Collection of Selected Pieces, Adapted to 52 Moods and Situations* (1924), containing pieces of light music by famous and obscure composers depicting the emotions and excitements of joy, melancholy, passion, frustration, and also typical movie scenes, such as love-making within permissible limits (kisses not to exceed 7 seconds in duration), costumed bacchanalia, fights to the death, etc. He also publ. *Erno Rapee's Encyclopedia of Music for Pictures* (1925).

Rapf, Kurt, Austrian composer; b. Vienna, Feb. 15, 1922. He studied piano, organ, and composition at the Vienna Academy of Music (1936–42); was founder-conductor of the chamber music ensemble Collegium Musicum Wien (1945–56); was city music director in Innsbruck (1953–60); was president of the Austrian Composers' Union (1970–83).

WORKS: ORCH.: *Aphorismen* (1968); Violin Concerto (1971); 3 concertos for Chamber Orch.: No. 1, *Imaginations* (1971); No. 2, *Contrasts* (1972); No. 3, *Remembrances* (1978); *Wiener Veduten,* 11 songs for Tenor and Orch. (1972); Piano Concerto (1973); *Concerto per viaggio* for Chamber Orch. (1975); *4 Orchestral Pieces* (1975); 2 syms. (1976, 1981); Concerto for Violin, Cello, and Orch. (1976); *Leanda,* fantasy-overture (1979); Concerto for Organ and Strings (1979); *Concerto estivo* (1982); Concerto for Violin, Piano, and Orch. (1982); Organ Concerto (1977–84); Concerto (1984). CHAMBER: *6 Pieces* for Wind Quintet (1963); *4 Impressions* for 9 Players (1966); Quintet for Harp and 4 Wind Instruments (1968); *Toccata, Adagio, and Finale* for Organ (1972); *3 Episodes* for Cello (1981–84); also an oratorio, *Passio aeterna* (1979); piano pieces.

Raphael, Günter (Albert Rudolf), German composer; b. Berlin, April 30, 1903; d. Herford, Oct. 19, 1960. His father, Georg Raphael, was music director of Berlin's St. Matthäi. He studied with Max Trapp (piano), Walter Fischer (organ), and Robert Kahn (composition) at the Berlin Hochschule für Musik (1922–25); taught theory and composition at the Leipzig Cons. and at the Kirchenmusikalisches Institut (1926–34); after his works were banned by the Nazis, he lived in Meiningen and then in Sweden; following the collapse of the 3rd Reich, he taught in Laubach (1945–48); taught theory and composition at the Duisburg Cons. (1949–53); was on the faculty of the Mainz Cons. (1956–58); served as prof. at the Cologne Hochschule für Musik (1957–60). His early works followed in the German Romantic tradition, but he later adopted a more contemporary idiom with excursions into serialism.

WORKS: ORCH.: 5 syms. (1926; 1932; 1942; 1942–47; 1953); *Theme, Variations, and Rondo* (1927); 2 violin concertos (1929, 1960); *Variations on a Scottish Folktune* (1930); Chamber Concerto for Violin and Chamber Orch. (1930); *Divertimento* (1932); Organ Concerto (1936); *Smetana Suite,* after Smetana's dances (1938); *Sinfonietta* (1938); *Symphonische Fantasie* for Violin and Strings (1940); *Jabonah,* ballet suite (1948); *Reger Suite* (1948); *Sinfonia breve* (1949); Concertino for Alto Saxophone and Chamber Orch. (1951); *Die vier Jahreszeiten* for Strings (1953); *Zoologica* (1958); much choral music, including a cantata (1926), *Requiem* (1927–28), *Te Deum* (1930), *Busskantate* (1952), *Judica Kantate* (1955), and motets. CHAMBER: String Quintet (1927); 2 clarinet quintets (1924); 4 string quartets (1926, 1926, 1930, 1945); Woodwind Quintet (1945); Trios for Piano, Violin, and Cello (1925), Flute, Cello, and Piano (1938), Flute, Violin, and Viola (1940), 2 Violins and Viola (1941), and Clarinet, Cello, and Piano (1950); Sonatas for Viola and Piano (1925, 1926), Flute and Piano (1925), Violin and Piano (1926, 1968), Cello and Piano (1926), Oboe and Piano (1933), and Violin and Organ (1934); 9 solo sonatas for various instruments (1940–46); 6 duo sonatas for various instruments (1940–46); organ music; piano pieces.

BIBL.: O. Riemer, "Prophetische Musik: Zur geistlichen Chormusik G. R.s," *Musica,* I (1947); M. Mezger, "G. R.s Kirchenmusik," *Musik und Kirche,* XXIII (1953); F. Hogner, "G. R.," *Gottesdienst und Kirchenmusik,* 6 (1960).

Raphling, Sam(uel), American composer; b. Fort Worth, Texas, March 19, 1910; d. N.Y., Jan. 8, 1988. He studied piano in Chicago and, as an exchange fellowship student, in Germany. Returning to the U.S., he was active in Chicago as a teacher and pianist; publ. a number of compositions in various genres, including operas, syms., concertos and other orch. works, chamber music, piano pieces, etc.

Rappold, Marie (née **Winterroth**), English soprano; b. London, c.1873; d. Los Angeles, May 12, 1957. The family moved to America when she was a child. She studied with Oscar Saenger in N.Y.; made her Metropolitan Opera debut there as Sulamith in *Die Königen von Saba* (Nov. 22, 1905); remained on its roster until 1909; then went to Europe. She was married to Dr. Julius Rappold, but divorced him and married the tenor **Rudolf Berger.** She had another period of singing at the Metropolitan Opera (1910–20); then settled in Los Angeles as a teacher.

Rappoldi, Eduard, Austrian violinist, teacher, and composer; b. Vienna, Feb. 21, 1831; d. Dresden, May 16, 1903. He studied at the Vienna Cons.; then played violin in opera orchs. in Vienna, Rotterdam, Lübeck, and Prague; was 2nd violinist in the Joachim Quartet in Berlin (1871–77); concertmaster of the Court Opera in Dresden (1878–98); from 1893 until his death, a prof. of violin at the Dresden Cons. He publ. chamber music; piano pieces; songs. His wife, **Laura** (née **Kahrer**) **Rappoldi** (b. Mistelbach, near Vienna, Jan. 14, 1853; d. Dresden, Aug. 2, 1925), was a pianist and teacher; began her studies when she was 10, then was a pupil of Dessoff (composition), Bruckner (counterpoint), and J. Dachs (piano) at the Vienna Cons. (1866–69); later studied with Liszt in Weimar (1870, 1873), with A. Henselt in St. Petersburg (1870–73), and with Bülow (1874). She was active in Dresden (from 1887), teaching at the Cons. (1890–1910). Their son, **Adrian Rappoldi** (b. Berlin, Sept. 13, 1876; d. Bamberg, Oct. 12, 1948), was a violinist.

Rasbach, Oscar, American composer; b. Dayton, Ky., Aug. 2, 1888; d. Pasadena, Calif., March 24, 1975. He studied academic subjects in Los Angeles; music with Ludwig Thomas, Julius Albert Jahn, José Anderson, and A.J. Stamm. He was first engaged in business; then went to Vienna, where he took piano lessons with Leschetizky and studied theory with Hans Thornton. He returned to the U.S. in 1911 and settled in San Marino, Calif. He wrote 2 operettas, *Dawn Boy* and *Open House,* and a number of songs, of which *Trees,* to Joyce Kilmer's dendrological poem, became enormously popular.

Rascher, Sigurd (Manfred), German-American saxophone virtuoso; b. Elberfeld, May 15, 1907. He studied at the Stuttgart Cons., and became proficient on the saxophone. In 1939 he went to the U.S., where he developed a fine concert career. He founded the Rascher Saxophone Quartet (1969); commissioned numerous works for his instrument, including pieces by Glazunov, Ibert, Martin, Milhaud, and Hindemith.

Raselius (Raesel), Andreas, eminent German music theorist and composer; b. Hahnbach, near Amberg, Upper Palatinate, c.1563; d. Heidelberg, Jan. 6, 1602. He was the son of a Lutheran preacher; studied at the Univ. of Heidelberg (M.A., 1584); after teaching at the Heidelberg Academy (1583–84), he was compelled for religious reasons to leave the city and went to Regensburg as assistant master and Kantor at the Gymnasium Poeticum; then returned to Heidelberg as Hofkapellmeister to the Elector Palatine Friedrich IV (1600). He greatly distinguished himself as a music theorist and composer.

WORKS: *Cantionale* (1587–88); *Psalmen und geistliche Lieder* for 5 Voices (1591); *Teutscher Sprüche auss den sontäglichen Evangelia durchs gantze Jar* for 5 Voices (Nuremberg, 1594); *Erercitationes musicae . . . et aliae cantiones* for 4 to 6 and 8 Voices, *festivitatibus nuptialibus amicorum* (1594); *Teutscher Sprüche auff die fürnemsten järlichen Fest und Aposteltage . . .* for 5, 6, and 8 to 9 Voices, *auff die 12 modos dodecachordi* (Nuremberg, 1598); *Regenspurgischer Kirchenkontrapunkt, allerley . . . geistlichen Psalmen und Lieder, D. M. Lutheri . . . also gesetzt, dass jedermann . . . ungehindert wol mit singen kann* for 5 Voices (Regensburg, 1599); *Cantica sacro pro nova paochia: geistliche Psalmen und Lieder* for 5 Voices (1599); *Lateinische und deutsche Lieder* (1605).

WRITINGS: *Dodechachordi vivi, in quo 12 modorum musicorum exempla duodena* for 4 to 6 Voices (1589); *Hexachordum seu Questiones musicae practicae . . . in welcehm viva exempla Dodechachordi Glareani in utraque scala gefunden werden* (Nuremberg, 1591).

Bibl.: J. Auer, *M.A. R.* (Leipzig, 1892); L. Roselius, *A. R. als Motettenkomponist* (Berlin, 1924).

Raskin, Judith, noted American soprano; b. N.Y., June 21, 1928; d. there, Dec. 21, 1984. She studied at Smith College, graduating in 1949; took private voice lessons with Anna Hamlin in N.Y. Her stage career received an impetus on July 7, 1956, when she sang the title role in Douglas Moore's folk opera *The Ballad of Baby Doe,* produced at Central City, Colo. In 1957 she became a member of the NBC-TV Opera; in 1959, joined the N.Y. City Opera. She made her Metropolitan Opera debut in N.Y. on Feb. 23, 1962, as Susanna in *Le nozze di Figaro;* sang there until 1972. She taught at the Manhattan School of Music and the 92nd Street "Y" School of Music in N.Y. from 1975; also at the Mannes College of Music there from 1976.

Rasmussen, Karl Aage, Danish composer, conductor, and teacher; b. Kolding, Dec. 13, 1947. He took courses in music history, theory, and composition at the Århus Cons. (graduated, 1971), where his principal mentors were Per Nørgård and Pelle Gudmundsen-Holmgreen. He taught at the Funen Cons. (1970–72); in 1971 he joined the faculty of the Århus Cons. as a lecturer, becoming a docent in 1979 and a prof. in 1988; also was a docent at the Royal Danish Cons. of Music in Copenhagen (1980–82). From 1973 to 1988 he was active with the Danish Radio; in 1975 he founded a chamber ensemble, the Elsinore Players, and in 1978 the NUMUS Festival, serving as its artistic director until 1985 and again from 1987 to 1990; in 1986 he founded the Danish Piano Theater. From 1987 to 1990 he was chairman of the Danish Arts Foundation. In addition to monographs on composers, he wrote much music criticism and contributed articles on music history to periodicals in his homeland and abroad. His music follows the cosmopolitan trends of pragmatic hedonism within neo-Classical formal structures.
    Works: dramatic: *Crapp's Last Tape,* opera (1967); *Jephta,* opera (1977); *Majakovskij,* scenic concert piece (1978); *The Story of Jonah,* musical radio play (1981); *Our Hoffmann* (1986). **orch.:** *Symphony for Young Lovers* (1966); *Recapitulations* (1967); *Symphonie classique* (1968); *Anfang und Ende,* sym. (1972; Århus, Feb. 11, 1976); *Contrafactum* for Cello and Orch. (1979); *A Symphony in Time* (1982); *Movements on a Moving Line* (1987). **chamber:** *Protocol and Myth* for Accordion, Electric Guitar, and Percussion (1971); *Genklang* (Echo) for 3 Pianos (1 prepared, 1 mistuned) and Celesta (1972); *A Ballad of Game and Dream* for Chamber Ensemble (1974); *Berio Mask* for Chamber Ensemble (1977); *Encore: I* (*Lonesome*) for Guitar (1977), *II* (*Join*) for Guitar (1985), *III* (*Encore for Frances*) for Cello (1982), *IV* (*Match*) for Cello and Piano (1983), *V* (*Ich, nur . . .*) for Voice (1983), *VI* (*Chains*) for Clarinet (1983–85), *VII* (*Strain*) for Piano (1984), *VIII* (*Fugue*) for Clarinet, Vibraphone, and Piano (1983–84), and *IX* (*Beat*) for Silenced Percussion (1985); *Italian Concerto* for Chamber Ensemble (1981); *A Quartet of 5* for 2 Trumpets, Horn, and 2 Trombones (1982); *Solos and Shadows* for String Quartet (1983); *Surrounded by Scales* for String Quartet (Lerchenborg, Aug. 4, 1985); also vocal works, including *This Moment* for 3 Sopranos, Flute, and Percussion (1966) and *Love Is in the World* for Male or Female Voice, Guitar, and Percussion (1974–75).

Rasse, François (Adolphe Jean Jules), Belgian violinist, conductor, teacher, and composer; b. Helchin, near Ath, Jan. 27, 1873; d. Brussels, Jan. 4, 1955. He studied violin with Eugène Ysaÿe at the Brussels Cons., winning the Belgian Grand Prix de Rome in 1899; from 1925 to 1938, was director of the Liège Cons.
    Works: operas: *Déidamia* (1905) and *Sœur Béatrice* (1938); ballet, *Le Maître à danser* (1908). **orch.:** *Symphonie romantique* (1901); *Symphonie mélodique* (1903); *Symphonie rythmique* (1908); tone poems: *Douleur* (1911); *Joie* (1925); *Aspiration* (1946); *Violin Concerto* (1906); *La Dryade* for Clarinet and Orch. (1943); *Lamento* for Cello and Orch. (1952). **chamber:** 2 string quartets (1906, 1950); Piano Quintet

(1914); Piano Quartet (1941); 3 piano trios (1897, 1911, 1951); also choral works; song cycles; many piano pieces.

Rastrelli, Joseph (Gioseffo or **Giuseppe),** eminent Italian conductor and composer; b. Dresden, April 13, 1799; d. there, Nov. 15, 1842. He 1st studied with his father, then received instruction in violin from Poland and in harmony from Fiedler in Dresden, and in counterpoint with Padre Mattei in Bologna (1814). Returning to Dresden (1817), he gained success with his opera *La Schiava circassa* (1820); that same year he became a violinist in the royal chapel; was made deputy music director at the Court Theater (1829); was appointed royal music director (1830).
    Works: operas (all 1st perf. in Dresden unless otherwise given): *La distruzione di Gerusalemme* (Ancona, 1816); *La Schiava circassa* (1820); *Le Donne curiose* (1821); *Velleda* (1822); *Amina* (Milan, 1824); *Salvator Rosa, oder Zwey Nächte in Rom* (July 22, 1832); *Bertha von Bretagne* (1835); *Die Neuvermählten* (1839); *Il trionfo di Nabucco il grande* (n.d.); also *Der Raub Zetulbeus,* ballet (c.1836–37); Viola Concerto; sacred works; choruses; songs; etc.

Ratez, Emile-Pierre, French composer; b. Besançon, Nov. 5, 1851; d. Lille, May 19, 1934. He studied at the Paris Cons. with Bazin and Massenet (1872–81); played the viola in the orch. of the Opéra-Comique; in 1891 was appointed director of the Lille branch of the Paris Cons.; also conducted popular concerts there (1893–1906). He wrote the operas *Lydéric* (Lille, 1895) and *Paula* (Besançon, 1904); a ballet, *La Guivre* (Paris, 1925); a cantata, *Scènes héroïques* (1899); chamber music; publ. *Traité élémentaire de contrepoint et de fugue* and *Traité d'harmonie théorique et pratique.*

Rath, Felix vom, German composer; b. Cologne, June 17, 1866; d. Munich, Aug. 25, 1905. He studied piano with Reinecke in Leipzig and composition with Thuille in Munich, where he settled. A composer of more than ordinary abilities, he publ. a Piano Concerto, a Piano Quartet, a Violin Sonata, and a number of piano pieces.

Rathaus, Karol, Polish-born American pedagogue and composer; b. Tarnopol, Sept. 16, 1895; d. N.Y., Nov. 21, 1954. He studied at the Vienna Academy of Music and the Univ. of Vienna (Ph.D., 1922) and in Berlin (1920–21; 1922–23); in 1932 he went to Paris, and in 1934 to London. In 1938 he settled in the U.S., becoming an American citizen in 1946. After a brief stay in Hollywood in 1939, during which he wrote some film scores, he settled in N.Y.; in 1940 he was appointed to the faculty of Queens College. He was highly respected as a teacher of composition. His own music, however, never attracted large audiences; always noble in purpose and design and masterly in technique, it reveals a profound feeling for European neo-Romanticism.
    Works: stage: Opera: *Fremde Erde* (Berlin, Dec. 10, 1930; also a symphonic interlude, rev. 1950); ballets: *Der letzte Pierrot* (1926; Berlin, May 7, 1927); *Le Lion amoureux* (London, 1937). **orch.:** 3 syms. (1921–22; 1923; 1942–43); *4 Dance Pieces* (1924); Piano Concertino (1925); *Overture* (1927); Suite for Violin, and Chamber Orch. or Piano (1929); *Uriel Acosta,* incidental music (1930; orch. suite, 1933; rev. 1947); Suite (Liège ISCM Festival, Sept. 6, 1930); *Allegro concertante* for Strings and Trumpet obbligato (1930); *Serenade* (1932); *Symphonic Movement* (1933); *Contrapuntal Triptych* (1934); *Jacob's Dream,* nocturne (1938; Liverpool, 1961); Piano Concerto (1939; Berkeley, Calif., ISCM Festival, Aug. 1, 1942); *Prelude and Gigue* (1939); *Music for Strings* (1941); *Polonaise symphonique* (1943; N.Y., Feb. 26, 1944); *Vision dramatique* (1945; Tel Aviv, April 4, 1948); *Salisbury Cove Overture* (1949); *Sinfonia concertante* (1950–51); *Intermezzo giocoso* for Woodwinds, Brass, and Percussion (1950–51); *Prelude* (1953; Louisville, June 5, 1954). **vocal:** *Song without Words* and *Fugue,* both for Chorus and Chamber Orch. (1928); *3 Calderon Songs* for Low Voice, and Orch. or Piano (1931); *XXIII Psalm* for Tenor, Women's Chorus, and Orch. or Piano (1945); *O Juvenes,* academic cantata (1947); *Lament from "Iphigenia in Aulis" by Euripides* for Chorus and Horn (1947); *Diapason,* after Dryden

and Milton, for Baritone, Chorus, and Orch. (1950); a cappella choruses; songs. In 1952 he rev. and ed. the orch. score to Mussorgsky's *Boris Godunov* on a commission from the Metropolitan Opera, which gave the new version on March 6, 1953. **CHAMBER:** 5 string quartets (1921, 1925, 1936, 1946, 1954); 2 violin sonatas (1924, 1938); Clarinet Sonata (1927); *Little Serenade* for Clarinet, Bassoon, Trumpet, Horn, and Piano (1927); Trio for Violin, Clarinet, and Piano (1944); Piano Quintet (1948; unfinished); *Dedication and Allegro* for Violin and Piano (1949); *Rapsodia notturna* for Viola or Cello, and Piano (1950); *Trio Serenade* for Piano Trio (1953); *Divertimento* for 10 Woodwinds (1954; unfinished). **PIANO:** 4 sonatas (1920; 1920–24, rev. 1928; 1927; 1946); numerous pieces. **ORGAN:** *Prelude and Toccata* (1933). **FILM MUSIC:** 17 scores, including those for *The Brothers Karamazov* (1931), *The Dictator* (1934), *Dame de pique* (1937), *Let Us Live* (1939), and *Out of Evil* (1950).
BIBL.: B. Schwarz, "K. R.," *Musical Quarterly* (Oct. 1955).

Rathburn, Eldon (Davis), Canadian composer; b. Queenstown, New Brunswick, April 21, 1916. He studied composition with Willan, organ with Peaker, and piano with Godden at the Toronto Cons. of Music (1938–39); from 1947 to 1976, served as staff composer for the National Film Board; also taught the art of film composition at the Univ. of Ottawa (1972–76). Among his film scores for documentaries are *The Romance of Transportation* (1952), *City of Gold* (1957), and *Labyrinth* (1967).
WORKS: ORCH.: *Symphonette* (1943; rev. 1946); 2 *Cartoons* (1944, 1946); *Images of Childhood* (1949–50); *Overture to a Hoss Opera* (1952); *Nocturne* for Piano and Small Orch. (1953); *Overture burlesca* (1953); *Milk Maid Polka* (1956); *Gray City* (1960); *City of Gold*, suite from music to the film (1967); *Aspects of Railroads* (1969); 3 *Ironies* for Solo Brass Quintet and Orch. (Hamilton, Ontario, Oct. 15, 1975); *Steelhenge*, concerto for Steel Band and Orch. (1975); *The Train to Mariposa* (1986). **CHAMBER:** 5 *Short Pieces* for differing combinations of Winds, each piece having a separate title (1949–56); *Bout in 3 rounds*, for Guitar and Double Bass (1971); *The Metamorphic 10* for Accordion, Mandolin, Banjo, Guitar, Double Bass, Harp, Piano, Celesta, and 3 Percussionists (1971); 2 *Interplays* for Saxophone Quartet (1972); *Rhythmette* for 2 Pianos and Rhythm Band (1973); *The Nomadic 5*, brass quintet (1974); *Turbo* for Brass Quintet (1978); *The Rise and the Fall of the Steam Railroad* for Chamber Ensemble (1983); *Dorion Crossing*, trio for Clarinet, Cello, and Piano (1987). **PIANO:** *Silhouette* for 2 Pianos (1936); *Black and White* (1970); *The Iron Horses of Delson* (1980); 6 *Railroad Preludes* (1987).

Rațiu, Adrian, Rumanian composer; b. Bucharest, July 28, 1928. He studied with Paul Constantinescu, Negrea, and Rogalski at the Bucharest Cons. (1950–56); attended the summer courses in new music at Darmstadt (1969). He was ed. of the Rumanian music journal *Muzica* (1959–63); in 1962, was appointed to the staff of the Bucharest Cons. His music is pleasantly atonal and euphoniously dissonant.
WORKS: ORCH.: 2 syms.: No. 1 (1956; rev. 1961); No. 2, *Independenta* (1976–77); Concerto for Oboe, Bassoon, and String Orch. (1963); *Diptych* (1965); *Studi* for Strings (1968); 6 *Images* (1971); *Poem* for Cello and Orch. (1972); Piano Concerto (1973). **CHAMBER:** 2 string quartets: No. 1 (1956); No. 2, *Convergences II* (1987); *Partita* for Wind Quintet (1966); *Concertino per la "Musica Nova"* for Clarinet, Violin, Viola, Cello, and Piano (1967; Musica Nova was a Rumanian chamber ensemble); *Impresii* for Chamber Ensemble (1969); *Sonata a 5* for 2 Trumpets, Horn, Trombone, and Tuba (1973); Sonata for Solo Violin (1983–84); Trio for Piano, Clarinet, and Vibraphone (1986); *Convergences I*, quartet for Flutes (1987); *Convergences III* for Flute, Oboe, and Bassoon (1987); also *Oda păcii* (Ode to Peace), cantata (1959); choruses; songs.

Ratner, Leonard Gilbert, American musicologist and composer; b. Minneapolis, July 30, 1916. He studied composition with Arnold Schoenberg at the Univ. of Calif., Los Angeles, and musicology with Bukofzer and Elkus at the Univ. of Calif.

at Berkeley (Ph.D., 1947). He also had composition lessons with Bloch and F. Jacobi. In 1947 he was appointed to the staff of Stanford Univ.; held a Guggenheim fellowship in 1962–63.
WORKS: *The Necklace*, chamber opera; Sym.; *Harlequin*, overture; 2 string quartets; Violin Sonata; Cello Sonata; Piano Sonata.
WRITINGS: *Music: The Listener's Art* (N.Y., 1957); *Harmony: Structure and Style* (N.Y., 1962); *Classic Music: Expression, Form, and Style* (N.Y., 1979).

Rattle, Simon (Denis), brilliant English conductor; b. Liverpool, Jan. 19, 1955. He began playing piano and percussion as a child; appeared as a percussionist with the Royal Liverpool Phil. when he was 11, and was a percussionist in the National Youth Orch.; also took up conducting in his youth, and was founder-conductor of the Liverpool Sinfonia (1970–72); concurrently studied at the Royal Academy of Music in London (1971–74). After winning 1st prize in the John Player International Conductors' Competition (1974), he was assistant conductor of the Bournemouth Sym. Orch. and Sinfonietta (1974–76); made his 1st tour of the U.S. conducting the London Schools Sym. Orch. (1976). In 1977 he conducted at the Glyndebourne Festival; then was assistant conductor of the Royal Liverpool Phil. (1977–80) and the BBC Scottish Sym. Orch. in Glasgow (1977–80). He made his 1st appearance as a guest conductor of a U.S. orch. with the Los Angeles Phil. in 1979; was its principal guest conductor (from 1981); also appeared as a guest conductor with other U.S. orchs., as well as with those in Europe. In 1980 he became principal conductor of the City of Birmingham Sym. Orch.; led it on its 1st tour of the U.S. in 1988. In 1987 he was made a Commander of the Order of the British Empire.
BIBL.: N. Wheen, "S. R.," *Ovation* (June 1985); N. Kenyon, *S. R.: The Making of a Conductor* (London, 1987).

Rauchenecker, Georg Wilhelm, German violinist, conductor, teacher, and composer; b. Munich, March 8, 1844; d. Elberfeld, July 17, 1906. He studied violin with Joseph Walter; filled various posts as a theater violinist in France; then lived in Switzerland. In 1889 he established a music school in Elberfeld, and conducted an orch. society there until his death.
WORKS: Operas (all 1st perf. in Elberfeld unless otherwise given): *Die letzten Tage von Thule* (1889); *Ingo* (1893); *Don Quixote* (1897); *Sanna* (1898); *Zlatorog* (1903); *Der Florentiner* (Strasbourg, 1910); also a Sym.; *Orientalische Fantasie* for Solo Violin and String Quintet; 6 string quartets; String Sextet; Octet for Woodwind Instruments.

Raugel, Félix, French conductor and musicologist; b. St.-Quentin, Nov. 27, 1881; d. Paris, Dec. 30, 1975. While attending the Lycée at Lille, he studied music with C. Queste and F. Lecocq; continued his studies in 1900 in Paris with H. Libert and at the Schola Cantorum with Vincent d'Indy. Together with E. Borrel, he founded in 1908 the Société Haendel for the cultivation of early music; was conductor of the Rheims Phil. (1926–62).
WRITINGS (all publ. in Paris): *Les Orgues de l'abbaye de Saint-Mihiel* (1919); *Les Organistes* (1923; 2nd ed., 1961); *Recherches sur les maîtres de l'ancienne facture française d'orgues: Les Lépine, les Cavaillé, Dom Bedos* (1925); *Les Grandes Orgues des églises de Paris et du Département de la Seine* (1926); *Palestrina* (1930); *Les Grandes Orgues de Notre-Dame* (1934); *Le Chant choral* (1948; 3rd ed., 1966); *L'Oratorio* (1948).

Raupach, Hermann Friedrich, German harpsichordist, conductor, and composer; b. Stralsund, Dec. 21, 1728; d. St. Petersburg, Dec. 1778. In 1755 he went to St. Petersburg as deputy harpsichordist in the Court Orch., and subsequently served as Kapellmeister and court composer (1758–62); then was active mainly in Hamburg and Paris until 1768; in Paris he met Mozart, who used several movements of his violin sonatas in his own early keyboard concertos (K.37, 39, and 41). Upon his return to St. Petersburg in 1768, Raupach again became deputy harpsichordist in the Court Orch.; in 1770 he was once more named Kapellmeister. His opera *Alcesta* (St. Petersburg, 1758) was one of the 1st operas on a Russian text. He also wrote the operas *The New Monastery* (1759), *Siroe* (St. Petersburg, 1760), and *The Good Soldiers* (St. Petersburg, Feb. 29, 1780); ballet scenes in operas by Traetta; 6 Sonates for Violin, op. 1 (Paris, c.1762); 4 Sonates for Violin, op. 2 (Paris, c.1765); and 4 Sonates for 2 Violins and Bass, op. 3 (Paris, 1770).

Rautavaara, Einojuhani, prominent Finnish composer and pedagogue; b. Helsinki, Oct. 9, 1928. He studied at the Sibelius Academy in Helsinki (1950–57), where he received training in composition from Aarre Merikanto; also took courses in musicology at the Univ. of Helsinki (M.A., 1953); continued his training with Persichetti at the Juilliard School of Music in N.Y. and with Copland and Sessions at the Berkshire Music Center at Tanglewood (1955–56); completed his studies with Rudolf Petzold at the Cologne Hochschule für Musik and with Wladimir Vogel in Ascona (1957). He was libarian of the Helsinki City Orch. (1959–61); in 1966 he became a lecturer at the Sibelius Academy, later serving as Artist Prof. (1971–76) and as prof. of composition (from 1976). An eclectic composer, he has employed musical techniques running the gamut from Gregorian chant to the 12-tone method and aleatory devices.
WORKS: STAGE: OPERAS: *Kaivos* (The Mine; 1957–63; Finnish TV, April 10, 1963); *Apollo contra Marsyas,* comic opera-musical (1970; Helsinki, Aug. 30, 1973); *Runo 42, "Sammon ryöstö"* (The Abduction of Sampo; 1974–81; Helsinki, April 8, 1983); *Thomas* (1982–85; Joensuu, June 21, 1985); *Vincent* (1987–88; Helsinki, May 17, 1990). **MYSTERY PLAY:** *Marjatta matala neiti* (Marjatta, the Lowly Maiden; 1975; Espoo, Sept. 3, 1977). **BALLET:** *Kiusaukset* (The Temptations; 1969; Helsinki, Feb. 8, 1973). **ORCH.:** *Pelimannit* (The Fiddlers), suite for Strings (1952; rev. 1972; Helsinki, Nov. 11, 1973); *Divertimento* for String Orch. (1953); *A Requiem in Our Time* for Wind Orch. (1953; Cincinnati, May 10, 1954); *Epitaph for Béla Bartók* for String Orch. (1955; rev. 1986; Helsinki, July 27, 1987); 5 syms.: No. 1 (1956; Helsinki, Jan. 22, 1957; rev. 1988); No. 2 (Helsinki, Oct. 11, 1957; rev. 1984); No. 3 (1961; Helsinki, April 10, 1962); No. 4, *Arabescata* (Helsinki, Feb. 26, 1963); No. 5 (Helsinki, May 14, 1986); *Praevariata* (1957); *Modificata* (Helsinki, May 30, 1958); *Canto I* and *II* for String Orch. (1960; Helsinki, March 7, 1967), and *III*, "A Portrait of the Artist at a Certain Moment," for String Orch. (Jyväskylä, June 27, 1972); *Helsinki Fanfaari* for Wind Orch. (Helsinki, June 12, 1967; rev. 1987); *Anadyomene* (Helsinki, May 30, 1968); Cello Concerto (1968; Helsinki, Feb. 26, 1969); *A Soldier's Mass* for Wind Orch. (1968); Piano Concerto No. 1 (1969; Finnish Radio, May 29, 1970); *Säännöllisiä Yksikköjaksoja Puolisäännöllisessä Tilanteessa* (Regular Sets of Elements in a Semiregular Situation; 1971; Helsinki, April 19, 1972); *Cantus arcticus,* concerto for Bird and Orch. (Oulu, Oct. 18, 1972); Flute Concerto (1973; Swedish Radio, May 4, 1974); *Ballad for Harp and String Orch.* (1973; Finnish Radio, Oct. 19, 1976; also for Harp and String Quintet); Violin Concerto (Finnish Radio, Aug. 23, 1977); *"Annunciations,"* concerto for Organ and Symphonic Wind Orch. (Stockholm, Sept. 13, 1977); *Suomalainen myytti* (A Finnish Myth) for String Orch. (1977; Jyväskylä, April 29, 1978); *Angels and Visitations* (Helsinki, Jan. 22, 1978); *Pohjalainen Polska* (Vaasa, April 11, 1980); *Angel of Dusk,* double-bass concerto (1980; Finnish Radio, May 6, 1981); *Serenade in Brass* for Wind Orch. (1982; Stockholm, March 13, 1983); *Hommage à Zoltán Kodály* for String Orch. (Helsinki, Dec. 16, 1982; also for Chamber Orch.). **CHAMBER:** 4 string quartets (1952, 1958, 1965, 1975); Quartet for Oboe and String Trio (1957; rev. 1965); Wind Octet (1962); Sonata for Bassoon and Piano (1968); *Ugrilainen dialogi* for Violin and Cello (1973); Sonata for Flutes and Guitar (1975); *Polska* for 2 Cellos and Piano (1977); *Playgrounds for Angels* for 4 Trumpets, 4 Trombones, Horn, and Tuba (Helsinki, Sept. 12, 1981); piano pieces; also choral works; songs.

Rautio, Matti, Finnish composer; b. Helsinki, Feb. 25, 1922; d. Tampere, June 22, 1986. He studied at the Univ. of Helsinki (M.A., 1945); took courses in composition and piano at the

Sibelius Academy in Helsinki (certificate, 1950), where he served on its faculty as a piano teacher (1947–64), senior theory teacher (from 1956), and director of the school music dept. (1966–70). In his works he followed a median line of modern music, programmatic and utilitarian in the use of advanced techniques.
WORKS: *Divertimento 1* for Cello and Orch. or Piano (1955); *Sininen haikara* (The Blue Heron), suite from the ballet (1957); *Tanhumusiikkia* (Folk Dance Music) for Soprano, Baritone, Chorus, and Orch. (1960); Piano Concerto (1968–71); *Divertimento 2* for Cello and Piano (1972).

Rauzzini, Venanzio, Italian castrato soprano, harpsichordist, teacher, and composer; b. Camerino, near Rome (baptized), Dec. 19, 1746; d. Bath, April 18, 1810. He studied in Rome, where he made his debut in Piccini's *Il finto astrologo* (Feb. 7, 1765); then was in the service of the Elector Max Joseph III in Munich (1766–72), during which period he commenced his career as a composer for the theater; also sang in Venice and Vienna. He was primo uomo in Mozart's *Lucio Silla* (Milan, Dec. 26, 1772) and in Paisiello's *Sismano nel Mogol* (Milan, Jan. 30, 1773); Mozart wrote his famous motet *Exsultate, jubilate* for him (1773). After singing in Venice (1773–74), Padua (1773), and Turin (1774), he went to London as a leading member of the King's Theatre (1774–77); the revised version of his most successful opera, *Piramo e Tisbe,* was produced there on March 16, 1775. He subsequently was active mainly in Bath as a performer, teacher, and concert manager; also made visits to London. Among his most famous pupils were Mrs. Billington, John Braham, Michael Kelly, and Nancy Storace.
WORKS: STAGE (all 1st perf. in London unless otherwise given): **OPERAS:** *Piramo e Tisbe* (Munich, 1769; rev. version, March 16, 1775); *L'Eroe cinese* (Munich, 1771; rev. version, March 16, 1782); *Le ali d'amore* (Feb. 29, 1776; rev. version, March 13, 1777); *L'omaggio di paesani al signore del contado* (June 5, 1781; only Act 2 by Rauzzini); *Creusa in Delfo* (April 29, 1783); *Alina, o sia La Regina di Golconda* (March 18, 1784); *La Vestale, o sia L'amore protetto dal cielo* (May 1, 1787). **PASTICCIOS:** *Armida* (Nov. 19, 1774); *La Sposa fedele* (Oct. 31, 1775); *Didone* (Nov. 11, 1775); *The Duenna or Double Elopement* (Nov. 21, 1775); *Astarto* (Nov. 2, 1776); *Ezio* (Nov. 17, 1781); *The Village Maid* (n.d.); incidental music; cantatas, including *La partenza* (July 5, 1777), *La sorpresa* (1779), and *Il tributo* (Fonthill, Sept. 29, 1781). **OTHER:** Italian duets and songs and English songs; 15 sonatas for Piano or Harpsichord, and Violin Accompaniment: 6 as op. 1 (1777), 6 as op. 8 (1781), and 3 as op. 15, nos. 1 to 3 (1786); 12 string quartets: op. 2 (c.1777) and op. 7 (c.1778); 6 Quartets for Piano or Harpsichord, 2 Violins, and Cello, op. 6 (c.1778); 4 duets for Piano or Harpsichord, 4-hands: 3 as op. 12 (1783) and 1 as op. 15, no. 4 (1786); a Sinfonia; dances; lessons; etc.
BIBL.: M. Sands, "V. R.—Singer, Composer, Traveller," *Musical Times,* XCIV (1953); J. Reindl, *V. R. als Instrumental-Komponist* (diss., Univ. of Vienna, 1961).

Ravanello, Oreste, Italian composer; b. Venice, Aug. 25, 1871; d. Padua, July 2, 1938. He studied with Agostini and Girardi in Venice; in 1893, became an organist at San Marco; in 1898 was appointed maestro di cappella at San Antonio in Padua; in 1914, became director of the Istituto Musicale. He composed about 30 masses; numerous pieces for organ; publ. several useful guides for organ playing, among them *Cento studi ed esercizi per il organo.*
BIBL.: A. Garbelotto and M. Cicogna, *O. R.* (Padua, 1939).

Ravasenga, Carlo, Italian composer; b. Turin, Dec. 17, 1891; d. Rome, May 6, 1964. He studied violin, piano, and composition in Turin; then became active as a teacher and music ed. He wrote the operas *Una tragedia fiorentina,* after Oscar Wilde (Turin, 1916), and *Il giudizio di Don Giovanni* (1916); orch. suite, *Un giorno di festa* (1916); symphonic suite, *Giuditta e Oloferno; Variazioni pittoresche* for String Quartet; *Contrasto burlesco-sentimentale* for Piano; Violin Sonata; Piano Sonata.

Ravel, (Joseph) Maurice, great French composer; b. Ciboure, Basses-Pyrénées, March 7, 1875; d. Paris, Dec. 28, 1937. His father was a Swiss engineer, and his mother of Basque origin. The family moved to Paris when he was an infant. He began to study piano at the age of 7 with Henri Ghis and harmony at 12 with Charles-René. After further piano studies with Emile Descombes, he entered the Paris Cons. as a pupil of Eugène Anthiôme in 1889; won 1st medal (1891), and passed to the advanced class of Charles de Bériot; also studied harmony with Emile Pessard. He left the Cons. in 1895 and that same year completed work on his song *Un Grand Sommeil noir,* the *Menuet antique* for Piano, and the *Habanera* for 2 Pianos (later included in the *Rapsodie espagnole* for Orch.); these pieces, written at the age of 20, already reveal great originality in the treatment of old modes and of Spanish motifs; however, he continued to study; in 1897 he returned to the Cons. to study with Fauré (composition) and Gédalge (counterpoint and orchestration); his well-known *Pavane pour une infante défunte* for Piano was written during that time (1899). On May 27, 1899, he conducted the premiere of his overture *Shéhérazade* in Paris; some elements of this work were incorporated in his song cycle of the same name (1903). In 1901 he won the 2nd Prix de Rome with the cantata *Myrrha;* but ensuing attempts to win the Grand Prix de Rome were unsuccessful; at his last try (1905) he was eliminated in the preliminaries, and so was not allowed to compete; the age limit then set an end to his further effort to enter. Since 6 prizes all went to pupils of Lenepveu, suspicion of unfair discrimination was aroused; Jean Marnold publ. an article, "Le Scandale du Prix de Rome," in the *Mercure de France* (June 1905) in which he brought the controversy into the open; this precipitated a crisis at the Cons.; its director, Théodore Dubois, resigned, and Fauré took his place. By that time, Ravel had written a number of his most famous compositions, and was regarded by most French critics as a talented disciple of Debussy. No doubt Ravel's method of poetic association of musical ideas paralleled that of Debussy; his employment of unresolved dissonances and the enhancement of the diatonic style into pandiatonicism were techniques common to Debussy and his followers; but there were important differences: whereas Debussy adopted the scale of whole tones as an integral part of his musical vocabulary, Ravel resorted to it only occasionally; similarly, augmented triads appear much less frequently in Ravel's music than in Debussy's; in his writing for piano, Ravel actually anticipated some of Debussy's usages; in a letter addressed to Pierre Lalo and publ. in *Le Temps* (April 9, 1907), Ravel pointed out that at the time of the publication of his piano piece *Jeux d'eau* (1902) Debussy had brought out only his suite *Pour le piano,* which had contained little that was novel. In Paris, elsewhere in France, and soon in England and other European countries, Ravel's name became well known, but for many years he was still regarded as an ultramodernist. A curious test of audience appreciation was a "Concert des Auteurs Anonymes" presented by the Société Indépendante de Musique on May 9, 1911; the program included Ravel's *Valses nobles et sentimentales,* a set of piano pieces in the manner of Schubert; yet Ravel was recognized as the author. Inspired evocation of the past was but one aspect of Ravel's creative genius; in this style are his *Pavane pour une infante défunte, Le Tombeau de Couperin,* and *La Valse;* luxuriance of exotic colors marks his ballet *Daphnis et Chloé,* his opera *L'Heure espagnole,* the song cycles *Shéhérazade* and *Chansons madécasses,* and his virtuoso pieces for Piano *Miroirs* and *Gaspard de la nuit;* other works are deliberately austere, even ascetic, in their pointed classicism: the piano concertos, the Piano Sonatina, and some of his songs with piano accompaniment. His association with Diaghilev's Ballets Russes was most fruitful; for Diaghilev he wrote one of his masterpieces, *Daphnis et Chloé;* another ballet, *Boléro,* commissioned by Ida Rubinstein and performed at her dance recital at the Paris Opéra on Nov. 22, 1928, became Ravel's most spectacular success as an orch. piece.

Ravel never married, and lived a life of semi-retirement,

devoting most of his time to composition; he accepted virtually no pupils, although he gave friendly advice to Vaughan Williams and to others; he was never on the faculty of any school. As a performer, he was not brilliant; he appeared as a pianist only in his own works, and often accompanied singers in programs of his songs; although he accepted engagements as a conductor, his technique was barely sufficient to secure a perfunctory performance of his music. When World War I broke out in 1914, he was rejected for military service because of his frail physique, but he was anxious to serve; his application for air service was denied, but he was received in the ambulance corps at the front; his health gave way, and in the autumn of 1916 he was compelled to enter a hospital for recuperation. In 1922 he visited Amsterdam and Venice, conducting his music; in 1923 he appeared in London; in 1926 he went to Sweden, England, and Scotland; in 1928 he made an American tour as a conductor and pianist; in the same year he received the degree of D.Mus. *honoris causa* at Oxford Univ. In 1929 he was honored by his native town by the inauguration of the Quai Maurice Ravel. Shortly afterward, he began to experience difficulties in muscular coordination, and suffered from attacks of aphasia, symptoms indicative of a cerebral malady; he underwent brain surgery on Dec. 19, 1937, but it was not successful; he died 9 days later.

WORKS: OPERAS: *L'Heure espagnole* (comédie musicale; 1907–9; Opéra-Comique, Paris, May 19, 1911); *L'Enfant et les sortilèges* (fantaisie lyrique; 1920–25; Monte Carlo, March 21, 1925). **BALLETS:** *Ma Mère l'Oye* (1911; Paris, Jan. 21, 1912; based on the piano work with additional material); *Daphnis et Chloé* (1909–12; Paris, June 8, 1912); *Adélaïde, ou Le Langage des fleurs* (Paris, April 22, 1912; based on the *Valses nobles et sentimentales*); *Le Tombeau de Couperin* (Paris, Nov. 8, 1920; based on the piano work); *La Valse* (Paris, Dec. 12, 1920); *Boléro* (Paris, Nov. 22, 1928). **ORCH.:** *Shéhérazade,* ouverture de féerie (1898; Paris, May 27, 1899); *Une Barque sur l'océan* (1906; based on the piano work); *Rapsodie espagnole* (Paris, March 15, 1908); *Pavane pour une infante défunte* (Paris, Dec. 25, 1910; based on the piano work); *Daphnis et Chloé,* 2 suites (1911, 1913); *Alborada del gracioso* (Paris, May 17, 1919; based on the piano work); *Le Tombeau de Couperin* (Paris, Feb. 28, 1920; based on the piano work); *La Valse,* poème chorégraphique (Paris, Dec. 12, 1920); *Tzigane,* rapsodie de concert for Violin and Orch. (Paris, Dec. 7, 1924; based on the work for Violin and Piano); *Menuet antique* (1929; based on the piano work); Piano Concerto in D for Left Hand Alone, written for Paul Wittgenstein (1929–30; Vienna, Nov. 27, 1931); Piano Concerto in G major (1929–31; Paris, Jan. 14, 1932). **CHAMBER:** Sonata for Violin and Piano (1897); String Quartet in F major (1902–3); *Introduction et Allegro* for Harp, Flute, Clarinet, and String Quartet (1905; Paris, Feb. 22, 1907); Piano Trio (1914); *Le Tombeau de Claude Debussy* for Violin and Cello (1920); Sonata for Violin and Cello (1920–22); *Berceuse sur le nom de Gabriel Fauré* for Violin and Piano (1922); *Tzigane,* rapsodie de concert for Violin and Piano (London, April 26, 1924); Sonata for Violin and Piano (1923–27). **VOCAL:** *Les Bayadères tournent légères* for Soprano, Chorus, and Orch. (1900); 3 cantatas, all for 3 Solo Voices and Orch.: *Myrrha* (1901), *Alcyone* (1902), and *Alyssa* (1903); *Tout est lumière* for Soprano, Chorus, and Orch. (1901); *La Nuit* for Soprano, Chorus, and Orch. (1902); *Matinée de Provence* for Soprano, Chorus, and Orch. (1903); *Manteau de fleurs* for Voice and Orch. (1903; based on the song for Voice and Piano); *Shéhérazade* for Mezzo-soprano and Orch. (1903; Paris, May 17, 1904); *Noël des jouets* for Voice and Orch. (1905; 2nd version, 1913; based on the song for Voice and Piano); *L'Aurore* for Tenor, Chorus, and Orch. (1905); *Chanson de la mariée* and *Tout gai* for Voice and Orch. (1904–6; based on songs nos. 1 and 5 from the cycle *Cinq mélodies populaires grecques* for Voice and Piano); *Trois poèmes de Stéphane Mallarmé* for Voice, Piccolo, Flute, Clarinet, Bass Clarinet, Piano, and String Quartet (1913; Paris, Jan. 14, 1914); *Trois chansons* for Mixed Chorus a cappella (1914–15); *Deux mélodies hébraïques* for Voice and Orch. (1919; based on the songs for Voice and Piano); *Chanson* hébraïque for Voice and Orch. (1923–24; based on song no. 4 from the cycle *Chants populaires* for Voice and Piano); *Chansons madécasses* for Voice, Flute, Piano, and Cello (1925–26); *Don Quichotte à Dulcinée* for Baritone and Orch. (1932–33; Paris, Dec. 1, 1934); *Ronsard à son âme* for Voice and Orch. (1935; based on the song for Voice and Piano). SONGS: *Ballade de la reine morte d'aimer* (c.1893); *Un Grand Sommeil noir* (1895); *Sainte* (1896); *Chansons du rouet* (1898); *Si morne!* (1898); *Deux épigrammes de Clément Marot* (1896–99); *Manteau de fleurs* (1903); *Shéhérazade* (1903; based on the work for Mezzo-soprano and Orch.); *Noël des jouets* (1905); *Cinq mélodies populaires grecques* (1904–6); *Histoires naturelles* (1906); *Les Grands Vents venus d'outremer* (1907); *Sur l'herbe* (1907); *Vocalise-étude en forme de habanera* (1907); *Tripatos* (1909); *Chants populaires* (1910); *Trois poèmes de Stéphane Mallarmé* (1913; based on songs for Voice and Various Instruments); *Deux mélodies hébraïques* (1914); *Trois chansons* (1914–15; based on the choral work); *Ronsard à son âme* (1923–24); *Chansons madécasses* (1926; based on the work for Voice, Flute, Piano, and Cello); *Rêves* (1927); *Don Quichotte à Dulcinée* (1932–33; based on the work for Baritone and Orch.). PIANO: *Sérénade grotesque* (c.1893); *Menuet antique* (1895); *Sites auriculaires* for 2 Pianos (1895–97): *Pavane pour une infante défunte* (1899) and *Jeux d'eau* (1901); *Sonatine* (1903–5); *Miroirs* (1904–5); *Gaspard de la nuit* (1908); *Menuet sur le nom d'Haydn* (1909); *Ma mère l'oye,* 5 "pièces enfantines" for Piano, 4-hands (written for Christine Verger, age 6, and Germaine Durant, age 10, and 1st perf. by them; Paris, April 20, 1910); *Valses nobles et sentimentales* (1911); *À la manière de . . .* (1913); *Prélude* (1913); *Le Tombeau de Couperin* (1914–17); *Frontispiece* for 2 Pianos, 5-hands (1918); *La Valse* for 2 Pianos (1921; based on the orch. work); *Boléro* for 2 Pianos (1930; based on the orch. work). He also made various arrangements, including a celebrated version of Mussorgsky's *Pictures at an Exhibition* for Orch., which was commissioned by and 1st performed by Koussevitzky (Paris, Oct. 19, 1922).

BIBL.: Roland-Manuel, *M. R. et son œuvre* (Paris, 1914; 2nd ed., rev., 1926; Eng. tr., 1941); M. Morris, "M. R.," *Music & Letters* (July 1921); Roland-Manuel, "M. R.," *La Revue Musicale,* II/6 (1921); F. Shera, *Debussy and R.* (Oxford, 1925); special issue of *La Revue Musicale,* VI/8 (1925); W.-L. Landowski, *M. R., Sa vie, son oeuvre* (Paris, 1938; 2nd ed., 1950); Roland-Manuel, *À la gloire de R.* (Paris, 1938; 2nd ed., 1948; Eng. tr., 1947); special issue of *La Revue Musicale,* 187 (1938); V. Jankélévitch, *M. R.* (Paris, 1939; 2nd ed., 1956; Eng. tr., 2nd ed., 1959); P. Landormy, "M. R.," *Musical Quarterly* (Oct. 1939); R. Wild, ed., *M. R. par quelques-uns de ses familiers* (Paris, 1939); M. Goss, *Bolero: The Life of M. R.* (N.Y., 1940); M.-D. Calvocoressi, "R.'s Letters to Calvocoressi," *Musical Quarterly* (Jan. 1941); idem, "When R. Composed to Order," *Music & Letters,* XXII (1941); K. Akeret, *Studien zum Klavierwerk von M. R.* (Zürich, 1941); H. Jourdan-Morhange, *R. et nous* (Geneva, 1945); N. Demuth, *R.* (London, 1947); A. Machabey, *M. R.* (Paris, 1947); F. Onnen, *M. R.* (Stockholm, 1947); special issue of *Melos,* XIV/12 (1947); R. Malipiero, *M. R.* (Milan, 1948); L.-P. Fargue, *M. R.* (Paris, 1949); J. Bruyr, *M. R. ou Le Lyrisme et les sortilèges* (Paris, 1950); L. La Pegna, *R.* (Brescia, 1950); W. Tappolet, *M. R.: Leben und Werk* (Olten, 1950); V. Perlemuter and H. Jourdan-Morhange, *R. d'après R.* (Lausanne, 1953; Eng. tr., 1988, as *R. according to R.*); V. Seroff, *M. R.* (N.Y., 1953); M. Gerar and R. Chalupt, eds., *R. au miroir de ses lettres* (Paris, 1956); Roland-Manuel, "Lettres de M. R. et documents inédits," *Revue de Musicologie,* XXXVIII (1956); J. van Ackere, *M. R.* (Brussels, 1957); J. Geraedts, *R.* (Haarlem, 1957); R. de Fragny, *M. R.* (Lyons, 1960); R. Myers, *R.: Life and Works* (London, 1960); H. Stuckenschmidt, *M. R.: Variationen über Person und Werk* (Frankfurt, 1966; Eng. tr., 1969); A. Orenstein, "M. R.'s Creative Process," *Musical Quarterly* (Oct. 1967); P. Petit, *R.* (Paris, 1970); A. Orenstein, "Some Unpublished Music and Letters by M. R.," *Music Forum,* III (1973); idem, *R.: Man and Musician* (N.Y., 1975); R. Nichols, *R.* (London, 1977); H. Macdonald, "R.'s Unknown Choruses," *Musical Times* (Dec. 1983); S. Bress, "Le Scandale

R. de 1905," *Revue Internationale de Musique Française,* 14 (1984); A. Orenstein, "R. and Falla: An Unpublished Correspondence, 1914–1933," *Music and Civilization: Essays in Honor of Paul Henry Lang* (N.Y., 1984); M. Marnat, ed., *M. R.: L'Hommage de La Revue musicale, décembre 1938* (Lyons, 1987); R. Nichols, *R. Remembered* (London and Boston, 1987); M. Rosenthal, *Satie, R., Poulenc: An Intimate Memoir* (Madras and N.Y., 1987); T. Hirsbrunner, *M. R.: Sein Leben, sein Werk* (Laaber, 1989); A. Orenstein, ed., *R.: Correspondance, écrits et entretiens* (Paris, 1989; Eng. tr., 1989, as *A R. Reader*).

Ravenscroft, John, English composer; b. London, date unknown; d. c.1708. In 1695 he was in Rome, where he publ. a set of "sonate a trè" under the Italianized name Giovanni Ravenscroft. He apparently was a pupil of Corelli, whose style he imitated. Also extant are his 6 da camera sonatas for 2 Violins and Basso Continuo, op. 2 (London, 1708).

BIBL.: W. Newman, "R. and Corelli," *Music & Letters* (Oct. 1957).

Ravenscroft, Thomas, English editor, music theorist, and composer; b. c.1582; d. c.1635. He was a chorister at St. Paul's Cathedral in London under Thomas Giles and Edward Pearce; studied at Gresham College, Cambridge (B.Mus., 1605); was music master at Christ's Hospital in London (1618–22). Among his works are 8 verse anthems, 3 full anthems, 3 motets, and 4 fantasias for 5 Viols.

WRITINGS: *A Briefe Discourse of the True (but Neglected) Use of Charact'ring the Degrees by their Perfection, Imperfection, and Diminution in Mensurable Musicke: Harmony of four voyces concerning the pleasure of five usuall recreations, 1. Hunting, 2. Hawking, 3. Dancing, 4. Drinking, 5. Enamouring* (London, 1614); *A Treatise of Musick* (MS).

EDITIONS (all publ. in London): *Pammelia: Musick's Miscellanie: or Mixed Varietie of Pleasant Roundelayes and Delightful Catches of 3–10 Parts in one* (1609; ed. by P. Warlock, 1928); *Deuteromelia . . . [14] Freemens Songs and . . . [17] Catches* for 3 to 4 Voices (1609); *Melismata: Musicall Phansies, fitting the Court, Citie and Countrey Humours* for 3 to 5 Voices (1611); *The Whole Booke of Psalms* (1621; ed. by W. Havergal, 1845).

BIBL.: D. Mateer, *A Critical Study and Transcription of "A Briefe Discourse" by T. R.* (diss., Univ. of London, 1970); I. Payne, "T. R.: A Biographical Note," *Musical Times* (Dec. 1986).

Ravina, Jean-Henri, French composer; b. Bordeaux, May 20, 1818; d. Paris, Sept. 30, 1906. He studied at the Paris Cons. with Zimmerman (piano) and Laurent (theory); taught at the Cons. (1834–36); then made a concert tour as pianist in Russia (1858); later traveled in Spain; lived chiefly in Paris. He wrote elegant and attractive salon pieces for piano, which enjoyed considerable vogue in their day; also a Piano Concerto. He made 4-hand arrangements of all of Beethoven's syms.

Rawls, Lou(is Allen), black American singer of popular music; b. Chicago, Dec. 1, 1936. After serving in the U.S. Army (1956–58), he joined the choral gospel group The Pilgrim Travelers; after the group disbanded in 1959, he launched a career as a nightclub entertainer in Los Angeles. From 1960 on he toured in Europe, Australia, and Japan; also appeared on special television shows and issued many recordings; his record album *Stormy Monday* was a best-seller.

Rawsthorne, Alan, important English composer; b. Haslingden, May 2, 1905; d. Cambridge, July 24, 1971. He went to a dentistry school; did not begin to study music until he was 20, when he entered the Royal Manchester College of Music; later studied piano with Egon Petri in Berlin (1930–31). After returning to England in 1932, he occupied various teaching posts; then devoted himself mainly to composition, and succeeded brilliantly in producing music of agreeable, and to some ears even delectable, music. In 1961 he was made a Commander of the Order of the British Empire. His music is essentially a revival of the contrapuntal style of the past, without much harmonic elaboration; but the rhythms are virile and the melodies fluid, emanating from a focal point of tonality.

WORKS: BALLET: *Madame Chrysanthème* (London, April 1, 1955). **ORCH.:** Concerto for Clarinet and Strings (1936); *Symphonic Studies* (1938; ISCM Festival, Warsaw, April 21, 1939); 2 piano concertos: No. 1 (originally for Strings and Percussion, 1939; rescored for Full Orch., 1942; London, 1942) and No. 2 (London, June 17, 1951); 4 overtures: *Street Corner* (1944), *Cortèges* (1945), *Hallé*, for the centennial of the Hallé Orch. (1958), and *Overture for Farnham* (1967); 2 violin concertos: No. 1 (1940; sketches lost in an air raid; reconstructed 1943–48; Cheltenham Festival, July 1, 1948) and No. 2 (London, Oct. 24, 1956); Concerto for Oboe and Strings (1947); Concerto for String Orch. (1949); 3 syms.: No. 1 (London, Nov. 15, 1950); No. 2, *Pastoral*, with Soprano (Birmingham, Sept. 29, 1959); No. 3 (Cheltenham Festival, July 8, 1964); *Concertante pastorale* for Flute, Horn, and Strings (1951); *A Canticle of Man*, chamber cantata for Baritone, Chorus, Flute, and Strings (1952); *Practical Cats*, an entertainment for children, after T.S. Eliot, for Narrator and Orch. (Edinburgh, Aug. 26, 1954); *Improvisations on a Theme of Constant Lambert* (1960); Concerto for 10 Instruments (1962); *Medieval Diptych* for Baritone and Orch. (1962); *Divertimento* for Chamber Orch. (1962); *Carmen Vitale*, cantata (London, Oct. 16, 1963); *Elegiac Rhapsody* for Strings (1964); Cello Concerto (London, April 6, 1966); *The God in the Cave* for Chorus and Orch. (1967); Concerto for 2 Pianos and Orch. (1968); *Theme, Variations and Finale* (1968); *Triptych* (1970). **CHAMBER:** Trio for Flute, Oboe, and Piano (1936); *Theme and Variations* for 2 Violins (1937); Viola Sonata (1938); *Theme and Variations* for String Quartet (1939); 3 string quartets (1939, 1954, 1965); Clarinet Quartet (1948); Cello Sonata (1949); Violin Sonata (1959); Piano Trio (1962); *Concertante* for Violin and Piano (1935–62); Quintet for Piano, Oboe, Clarinet, Horn, and Bassoon (1963); *Tankas of the 4 Seasons* for Tenor, Oboe, Clarinet, Bassoon, Violin, and Cello (1965); Quintet for Piano and Strings (1968); Oboe Quartet (1970); *Suite* for Flute, Viola, and Harp (1970); Quintet for Piano, Clarinet, Horn, Violin, and Cello (1971); *Elegy* for Guitar (1971; completed from composer's sketches by Julian Bream). **PIANO:** *Bagatelles* (1938); *The Creel* for 2 Pianos (1940); *Sonatina* (1948); *4 Romantic Pieces* (1953); *Ballade* (1967); *Theme with 4 Studies* (1971); choruses; several song cycles, to French and English words. **BIBL.:** K. Avery, "A. R.," *Music & Letters* (Jan. 1951); A. Dickinson, "The Progress of A. R.," *Music Review* (May 1951); A. Poulton, ed., *A. R.: A Catalogue of His Music* (Kidderminster, 1984); F. Routh, "R.'s Instrumental Style," *Musical Times* (March 1984); A. Poulton, ed., *A. R.* (3 vols., Hindhead, 1984–86).

Raxach, Enrique, Spanish-born Dutch composer; b. Barcelona, Jan. 15, 1932. He studied composition with Nuri Aymerich; in 1958 he moved to Paris; then lived in Zürich, Munich, and Cologne. From 1959 to 1966 he attended the summer courses in Darmstadt given by Messiaen, Boulez, Maderna, and Stockhausen. In 1962 he settled in the Netherlands; in 1969 he became a Dutch citizen. In his music he explores purely structural potentialities; the idiom of his composition is influenced by Varèse and Xenakis. **WORKS: ORCH.:** *Polifonias* for String Orch. (1953–54); *Metamorphose I* (1956); *Prometheus* (1957); *Metamorphose II* (1958); *Metamorphose III* (1959); *Fluxion* (1962–63); *Syntagma* (1964–65); *6 Movements* (1965); *Textures* (1965–66); *Equinoxial* (1967–68); *Inside Outside* (1969); *Figuren in einer Landschaft* (1974); *Ad marginem* (1975); *Erdenlicht* (1975); *Soirée musicale* for Clarinet, Women's Chorus, and Orch. (1978); *Am Ende des Regenbogens* (1980); *Opus incertum* (1985); *Calles y sueños—in memoriam Federico García Lorca* (1986). **CHAMBER:** 2 string quartets (1961, 1971); *Estrofas* for Clarinet, Violin, Cello, Double Bass, and Percussion (1962); *Summer Music* for Flute, Cello, and Piano (1967); *Imaginary Landscape* for Flute and Percussion (1968); *Scattertime* for Instruments (1971); *Chimaera* for Bass Clarinet and Stereophonic Magnetic Tape (1974); *Aubade* for Percussion Ensemble (1978); *Careful with that . . .* for Clarinet and Percussion (1982); *Vortice* for Bass Clarinet and 3 Contrabass Clarinets (1983); *Antevisperas* for 4 Saxophones (1986). **VOCAL:** Cantata for Tenor and Chamber Orch. (1952); *Paraphrase* for Mezzo-soprano and 11 Players (1969); *Interface* for Chorus, Percussion, Organ, and Double Bass (1972); *Sine nomine* for Soprano and Orch. (1973); *Soirée musicale* for Bass Clarinet, Women's Choir, and Orch. (1978); *Hub of Ambiguity* for Soprano and 8 Players (1984); songs.

Ray, Don Brandon, American conductor and composer; b. Santa Maria, Calif., June 7, 1926. He studied composition with John Vincent at the Univ. of Calif., Los Angeles (B.A., 1948), and with Ernst Kanitz at the Univ. of Southern Calif.; conducting with Roger Wagner and Richard Lert. He composed orch. pieces; Protestant church services; incidental music to theatrical plays; *Symrock* (symphonic rock) for Orch. (1978).

Ray, Johnnie (John Alvin), American singer of popular music; b. Dallas, Oreg., Jan. 10, 1927; d. Los Angeles, Feb. 24, 1990. He suffered an accident as a child that cost him half of his hearing; nevertheless, he was drawn to music and taught himself to play the piano; greatly influenced by the blues and gospel music, he developed a hard-driving singing style that won the hearts of screaming American teens with his hit recording of the song *Cry* in 1952. This success presaged the rise of rock 'n' roll; in 1956 Ray turned out the phenomenally popular ballad *Just Walkin' in the Rain*; however, his career soon waned and he was swept aside by the very rock revolution he had helped to launch.

Razumovsky, Count, later **Prince Andrei,** Russian diplomat and music patron; b. St. Petersburg, Nov. 2, 1752; d. Vienna, Sept. 23, 1836. He was the Russian ambassador at Vienna from 1793 to 1809; founded the celebrated Razumovsky Quartet (1808; 1st violin, Schuppanzigh; 2nd violin, Louis Sina, whose part was occasionally taken over by Razumovsky; viola, Weiss; cello, Lincke), later known as the Schuppanzigh Quartet (without Razumovsky). Razumovsky's name was immortalized through the dedication to him of Beethoven's 3 string quartets, op. 59, and (with Prince Lobkowitz) the 5th and 6th Syms. He was a munificent and prodigal patron of art, but after the destruction by fire of his Vienna palace (Dec. 31, 1814) he gave up the quartet, and disappeared from musical history.

Rea, John, Canadian composer and teacher; b. Toronto, Jan. 14, 1944. He studied composition with John Weinzweig and Gustav Ciamaga at the Univ. of Toronto (M.M., 1959) and with Milton Babbitt at Princeton Univ. (Ph.D., 1978); taught composition and theory at McGill Univ. in Montreal (from 1973); in 1984 he was composer-in-residence in Mannheim. **WORKS: MUSIC THEATER AND MULTIMEDIA:** *Les Jours*, ballet (1969; ballet suite, Toronto, July 11, 1974); *The Prisoner's Play*, opera (Toronto, May 22, 1973); *Jeux de scène: Fantasie-Hommage à Richard Wagner*, music theater for 6 Performers on Blacksmith's Anvil, English Horn, Oboe, Cello, Piccolo, Flute, Piano, Marimba, and 3 Glockenspiels (1976; Vancouver, Feb. 27, 1977); *Com-posession*, "daemonic afterimages in the theater of transitory states" for On- and Off-stage Instruments (1980). **ORCH.:** *Hommage à Vasarely* (1977); *Vanishing Points* (1983); *Over Time* (1987); *Time and Again* (1987). **CHAMBER:** Clarinet Sonatina (1965); *Sestina* for Flute, Clarinet, Trumpet, Cello, Harpsichord, and Percussion (1968); *Prologue, Scene and Movement* for Soprano, Viola, and 2 Pianos (1968); *Tempest* for any combination of Voices and/or Instruments (1969); *What You Will*, set of 12 single pieces of 6 polytonal duets for Piano (1969); *Fantaisies et allusions* for Saxophone Quintet (1969); 4 pieces of miscellaneous instrumentation, each named *Anaphora* (1970–75); *La Dernière Sirène* for Ondes Martenot, Piano, and Percussion (1981); *Les Raisons des Forces Mouvantes* for Flutist and String Quartet (1984); *Some Time Later* for Electronic String Quartet (1986). **VOCAL:** *Le Petit Livre des Ravalet* for 4 Narrators, Early Music Instruments, and Tape (1983); *Litaneia* for Chorus and Orch. (1984); *Offenes Lied* for 2 Sopranos and Clarinet (1986).

Read, Daniel, important American tunebook compiler and composer; b. Attleboro, Mass., Nov. 16, 1757; d. New Haven,

Conn., Dec. 4, 1836. He worked on a farm as a youth; studied mechanics, and was employed as a surveyor at 18; began to compose at 17. He served in the Continental Army as a private; at 21 he settled at New Stratford; later went to New Haven. In 1782–83 he maintained a singing school on the North River. He also was a comb maker. At his death, he left a collection of some 400 tunes by him and other composers. He publ. *The American Singing Book, or a New and Easy Guide to the Art of Psalmody, devised for the use of Singing Schools in America* (New Haven, 1785; subsequent eds., 1786, 1792, 1793, 1795); the *American Musical Magazine* (containing New England church music; compiled with Amos Doolittle; New Haven, 12 numbers, May 1786 to Sept. 1787; reprinted, Scarsdale, N.Y., 1961); *Supplement to The American Singing Book* (New Haven, 1787); *The Columbian Harmonist*, in 3 books: no. 1 (New Haven, 1793), no. 2 (New Haven, 1794; 2nd ed., with numerous additions, 1798; 3rd ed., with further additions, 1801), no. 3 (New Haven, 1795); all 3 books in 1 vol. (New Haven, 1795; 2nd ed., completely rev., Dedham, Mass., 1804; 3rd ed., Boston, 1807; 4th ed., Boston, 1810); *The New Haven Collection of Sacred Music* (New Haven, 1818).
    BIBL.: G. Hood, "D. R.," *Musical Herald* (N.Y., Oct. 1882); F. Metcalf, *American Writers and Compilers of Sacred Music* (N.Y., 1925); I. Lowens, "D. R.'s World: The Letters of an Early American Composer," *Notes* (March 1952; rev. in *Music and Musicians in Early America*, N.Y., 1964); V. Bushnell, *D. R. of New Haven (1757–1836): The Man and His Musical Activities* (diss., Harvard Univ., 1979).

Read, Gardner, outstanding American composer and erudite music scholar; b. Evanston, Ill., Jan. 2, 1913. He studied theory at the Northwestern Univ. School of Music; conducting with Bakaleinikoff; composition at the Eastman School of Music in Rochester, N.Y., with Paul White, Bernard Rogers, and Howard Hanson (B.Mus., 1936; M.M., 1937); after further studies with Pizzetti in Rome on a Cromwell Traveling Fellowship (1938–39), he completed his training with Copland at the Berkshire Music Center, Tanglewood (1941); taught composition at the St. Louis Inst. of Music (1941–43), at the Kansas City Cons. of Music (1943–45), and at the Cleveland Inst. of Music (1945–48); was appointed composer-in-residence and prof. of composition at Boston Univ. School for the Arts in 1948; retired in 1978. A composer of extraordinary fecundity, he excels in instrumental music; his idiom of composition is basically Romantic, but the harmonic and contrapuntal textures are intense and dense with polytonal encounters.
    WORKS: OPERA: *Villon* (1967). **ORCH.:** *The Lotus-Eaters* (Interlochen, Mich., Aug. 12, 1932); *Sketches of the City*, symphonic suite after Carl Sandburg (Rochester, N.Y., April 18, 1934); *The Painted Desert* (Interlochen, July 28, 1935); Sym. No. 1 (1936; N.Y., Nov. 4, 1937; awarded 1st prize in the American Composer's Contest sponsored by the N.Y. Phil.); *Fantasy* for Viola and Orch. (Rochester, April 22, 1937); *Prelude and Toccata* (Rochester, April 29, 1937); *Suite* for String Orch. (N.Y., Aug. 5, 1937); *Passacaglia and Fugue* (Chicago, June 30, 1938); *The Golden Journey to Samarkand* for Chorus, Soloists, and Orch. (1936–39); *Pan e Dafni* (1940); *American Circle* (Evanston, Ill., March 15, 1941); *1st Overture* (Indianapolis, Nov. 6, 1943); Sym. No. 2 (awarded 1st prize of the Paderewski Fund Competition, 1942; Boston, Nov. 26, 1943); *Night Flight*, tone poem after Antoine de St.-Exupéry (Rochester, April 27, 1944); *Cello Concerto* (1945); *Threnody* for Flute and Strings (Rochester, Oct. 21, 1946); *A Bell Overture* (Cleveland, Dec. 22, 1946); *Partita* for Small Orch. (Rochester, May 4, 1947); *Pennsylvaniana Suite* (Pittsburgh, Nov. 21, 1947); Sym. No. 3 (1948); *Quiet Music for Strings* (Washington, D.C., May 9, 1948); *Dance of the Locomotives* (Boston, June 26, 1948); *Sound Piece* for Brass and Percussion (Boston, May 11, 1949); *The Temptation of St. Anthony*, dance-sym. after Flaubert (Chicago, April 9, 1953); *Toccata giocosa* (Louisville, March 13, 1954); *Vernal Equinox* (Brockton, Mass., April 12, 1955); Sym. No. 4 (1951–59; Cincinnati, Jan. 30, 1970); *Jeux des timbres* for Orch. (1963); *Sonoric Fantasia No. 2* for Violin and Chamber

Orch. (1965); *Piano Concerto* (1977); *Astral Nebulae* (1983).
    VOCAL: *4 Nocturnes* for Voice and Orch. (Rochester, April 3, 1935); *From a Lute of Jade* for Voice and Orch. (Rochester, March 15, 1937); *Songs for a Rainy Night* for Voice and Orch. (Rochester, April 27, 1942); *The Prophet*, oratorio after Kahlil Gibran (1960; Boston, Feb. 23, 1977); *The Reveille* for Chorus, Winds, Percussion, and Organ (1962); *Chants d'Auvergne* for Chorus and Instruments (1962); *The Hidden Lute* for Soprano, Flute, Harp, and Percussion (1979); songs and choruses. **CHAMBER:** *Suite* for String Quartet (1936); *Piano Quintet* (1945); *Sonata brevis* for Violin and Piano (1948); *9 by 6* for Wind Sextet (1951); *String Quartet No. 1* (1957); *Sonoric Fantasia No. 1* for Celesta, Harp, and Harpsichord (1958), *No. 3* for Viola and Small Orch. (1970), and *No. 4* for Organ and Percussion (1975–76); *Los dioses aztecos*, suite of 7 movements for Percussion Ensemble (1959); *Petite suite* for Recorders and Harpsichord (1963); *Invocation* for Trombone and Organ (1977); *Galactic Novae* for Organ and Percussion (1978); *Diabolic Dialogue* for Double Bass and 4 Timpani (1978–79); *Music for Chamber Winds* for Double Wind Quintet and Percussion (1980); *Phantasmagoria* for Oboe, Oboe d'Amore, English Horn, and Organ (1985–87; rev. 1988). **ORGAN:** *Passacaglia and Fugue* (1937); *Suite* (1949); *8 Preludes on Old Southern Hymns* (1951). **PIANO:** *3 Satirical Sarcasms* (1941); *Driftwood Suite* (1943); *Dance of the Locomotives* (1944); *Sonata da chiesa* (1948); *Touch Piece* (1949); *5 Polytonal Studies* (1964); *Interior Motives* (1980).
    WRITINGS: *Thesaurus of Orchestral Devices* (N.Y., 1953); *Music Notation: A Manual of Modern Practice* (Boston, 1964); *Contemporary Instrumental Techniques* (N.Y., 1976); *Modern Rhythmic Notation* (Bloomington, Ind., 1978); *Style and Orchestration* (N.Y., 1979); *Source Book of Proposed Music Notation Reforms* (Westport, Conn., 1987); *20th-Century Microtonal Notation* (Westport, Conn., 1989).

Reading, John, English organist and composer, probably the father of the following; b. Lincoln, c.1645; d. Winchester, 1692. He was made lay vicar of Lincoln Cathedral in 1667 and Master of the Choristers in 1670; served as organist of Winchester Cathedral from 1675 to 1681, then of Winchester College, for which he composed the well-known song *Dulce Domum* (publ. in Hayes's *Harmonia Wiccamica*).

Reading, John, English organist and composer, probably the son of the preceding; b. c.1685; d. London, Sept. 2, 1764. He was a chorister of the Chapel Royal under Blow until 1699; organist of Dulwich College from 1700 to 1702; lay vicar of Lincoln Cathedral in 1702, and Master of the Choristers in 1703; later organist in several London churches (1708–64). He compiled 14 autograph vols. of various works, including 3 for organ, which remain a valuable source in English music.
    WORKS (all publ. in London): *A Book of New Songs . . . with Symphonies* (c.1710); *A Book of New Anthems . . . with Proper Ritornels* (c.1715); also organ pieces and keyboard music.

Reale, Paul, American composer and pianist; b. New Brunswick, N.J., March 2, 1943. He studied with Luening and Chou Wen-chung at Columbia Univ. (B.A., 1963; M.A., 1967) and with Rochberg and Crumb at the Univ. of Pa. (Ph.D., 1970); joined the faculty of the Univ. of Calif. at Los Angeles in 1969, becoming a prof. in 1980. His works, which are mostly based in tonality, include a series of piano sonatas (Nos. 1–3, 1985; No. 5, 1988) and a number of comic stage works, including *We All Loved You, Jenny Jo* (1981) and *Uncle Sigmund Goes to the Opera* (1986). As a pianist, he toured Europe, South America, and China; from 1970, specialized in playing 20th-century American music. He also performed numerous guest lectures at the piano on 20th-century music and philosophy. Among his other compositions are *Dancer's Dream* for 9 Strings (1980), Sonata for Cello and Piano (1982; rev. 1983), and Violin Concerto (1990).

Reaney, Gilbert, learned English musicologist; b. Sheffield, Jan. 11, 1924. He took courses in music and French at the Univ. of Sheffield (B.A., 1948; M.A., 1951, with the diss. *The*

Ballades, Rondeaux and Virelais Set to Music by Guillaume de Machaut; B.Mus., 1951); also studied at the Sorbonne in Paris on a French government grant (1950–53). He was a research fellow at the Univs. of Reading (1953–56) and Birmingham (1956–59), and then a visiting prof. at the Univ. of Hamburg (1959–60); subsequently was associate prof. (1960–63) and prof. (from 1963) at the Univ. of Calif. at Los Angeles. He served as assistant ed. of *Musica Disciplina* (from 1956) and was general ed. of the Corpus Scriptorum de Musica series. His contributions to the latter include: with A. Gilles and J. Maillard, *P. de Vitry: Ars nova*, VIII (1964); *Willemus: Breviarium regulare musicae; Anon.: Tractatus de figuris; J. Torkesey: Declaratio trianguli et scuti*, XII (1966); with A. Gilles, *Anon.: Ars musicae mensurabilis secundum Franconem*, XV (1971); with A. Gilles, *Franco of Cologne: Ars cantus mensurabilis*, XVIII (1974); 3 anonymous 14th-century mensural treatises, XXX (1982); the mensural treatises of John Hothby and Thomas Walsingham, XXXI (1983); with H. Ristory, 4 mainly anonymous mensural treatises of the 13th to 14th centuries, XXXIV (1987). He also ed. *Early Fifteenth-Century Music* in the Corpus Mensurabilis Musicae series, XI/1–7 (1955–83). Among his other writings are *Ch. Jones, the Saint Nicholas Liturgy and Its Literary Relationships* (Berkeley and Los Angeles, 1963) and *Guillaume de Machaut* (London, 1971).

Reardon, John, American baritone; b. N.Y., April 8, 1930; d. Santa Fe, N.Mex., April 16, 1988. He studied at Rollins College (B.Mus., 1952); then took voice lessons with Martial Singher and Margaret Harshaw. He made his 1st appearance with the N.Y. City Opera on Oct. 16, 1954, as Falke in *Die Fledermaus*. He made his Metropolitan Opera debut in N.Y. on Sept. 28, 1965, as Count Tomsky in Tchaikovsky's *Queen of Spades*. He mastered an extensive repertoire, which included several roles in modern operas.

Rebel, family of French musicians:
(1) Jean Rebel, singer; place and date of birth unknown; d. Versailles, before Feb. 29, 1692. He was a tenor in the private chapel of Louis XIV by 1661, singing there until his death; was also a secular singer at the court. He had 2 children who became prominent musicians:
(2) Anne-Renée Rebel, singer; b. Paris (baptized), Dec. 6, 1663; d. Versailles, May 5, 1722. She began singing at the court when she was about 10, and shortly thereafter took solo roles there; was held in high esteem by the King.
(3) Jean-Féry Rebel (le père), violinist, harpsichordist, conductor, and composer; b. Paris (baptized), April 18, 1666; d. there, Jan. 2, 1747. He began playing the violin at an early age, winning the approbation of the King and Lully when he was only 8; was 1st violin at the Académie Royale de Musique (1699–1700); joined the King's 24 Violons (1705); gained the right of succession to half of the office of chamber composer to the court (1718), which was held by his brother-in-law, Lalande; was granted the title as well (1726); also was active at the Académie Royale de Musique in various capacities, being made its maître de musique (1716); conducted at the Concert Spirituel (1734–35). He was held in high regard by his contemporaries.
WORKS: Opera, *Ulysse* (Paris, Jan. 23, 1703); *Pièces . . . divisées par* [3] *suites de tons* for Violin and Basso Continuo (1705); *Recueil de 12 sonates à II et III parties* for 2 Violins, Bass Viol, and Basso Continuo (1712); (12) *Sonates* for Violin and Basso Continuo . . . *mellées de plusieurs récits* for Bass Viol (1713); also choreographed "symphonies" for the dancers at the Académie Royale de Musique: *Caprice* for 3 Violins, Cello, and Basso Continuo (1711); *La Boutade* for 2 Violins, Viol, and Basso Continuo (1712); *Les Caractères de la danse*, fantaisie for 2 Violins and Basso Continuo (1715); *Terpsichore*, sonate for Violin, Flute, and Basso Continuo (1720); *Fantaisie* for 5 Flutes, 2 Violins, and Basso Continuo (1729); *Les Plaisirs champêtres* for 2 Violins and Basso Continuo (1734); *Les Élémens*, simphonie nouvelle for 2 Violins, 2 Flutes, and Basso Continuo (1737); songs, chansons, drinking songs, etc.
BIBL.: P. Aubry, "J.-F. R.," *Revue d'Histoire et de Critique*

Musicales, V (1905); W. Gates, "J.F. R.'s 'Sonates à violon seul mellées de plusieurs récits pour la Viole' (1713)," *Journal of the American Musicological Society*, VII (1954).
(4) François Rebel (le fils), violinist, theorbist, conductor, theater director, and composer, son of the preceding; b. Paris, June 19, 1701; d. there, Nov. 7, 1775. He began music studies at an early age; joined the orch. of the Académie Royale de Musique at age 13; gained the right of succession to his father's position in the King's 24 Violons when he was 16. He soon became a close associate of François Francoeur, who collaborated with him on several stage works. He was royal chamber composer (1727–55) and surintendant and maître of the royal chamber music (1733–75); was inspecteur général (1743–53) and co-director (with Francoeur; 1757–67) of the Académie Royale de Musique; returned as its administrateur général (1772). In all, he wrote 18 stage works with Francoeur; his other works include cantatas, motets, and songs.

Rebelo (or **Rebello, Rabello, Rabelo**), **João Soares** or **João Lourenço,** Portuguese composer; b. Caminha, 1610; d. Apelacão (now in Lisbon), Nov. 16, 1661. He was maestro to King John IV of Portugal, who dedicated to Rebelo his *Defensa de la música moderna* (1649). Psalms *a* 16, Magnificats, Lamentations, and Misereres by Rebelo were publ. in Rome (1657).

Reber, (Napoléon-) Henri, French composer; b. Mulhouse, Oct. 21, 1807; d. Paris, Nov. 24, 1880. He studied with Reicha and Le Sueur at the Paris Cons.; became a prof. of harmony there in 1851; succeeded Halévy as prof. of composition in 1862 (being succeeded in turn by Saint-Saëns in 1880), and was also inspector of the branch conservatories from 1871. He publ. *Traité d'harmonie* (Paris, 1862; 2nd ed., 1889, ed. by T. Dubois).
WORKS: COMIC OPERAS (all 1st perf. at the Opéra-Comique, Paris): *La Nuit de Noël* (Feb. 9, 1848); *Le Père Gaillard* (Sept. 7, 1852); *Les Papillotes de Monsieur Benoist* (Dec. 28, 1853); *Les Dames-capitaines* (June 3, 1857). OTHER: Ballet, *Le Diable amoureux* (Sept. 23, 1840; in collaboration with F. Benoist); 4 syms.; *Suite de morceaux* for Orch.; String Quintet; Piano Quartet; 3 string quartets; 7 piano trios; piano pieces; 55 mélodies for Voice and Piano; 18 vocalises for Soprano or Tenor and Piano; etc.
BIBL.: C. Saint-Saëns, *Notice sur N.H. R.* (Paris, 1881).

Rebikov, Vladimir (Ivanovich), Russian composer; b. Krasnoyarsk, Siberia, May 31, 1866; d. Yalta, Aug. 4, 1920. He studied at the Moscow Cons. with Klenovsky; then in Berlin and Vienna. He then went to Odessa, where his 1st opera, *In the Thunderstorm*, was produced in 1894. In 1898 he moved to Kishinev, Bessarabia, where he organized a branch of the Imperial Russian Musical Soc. In 1901 he settled in Moscow, remaining there until 1919; he spent his last year of life in the Crimea. His early works were under the influence of Tchaikovsky, but beginning with *Esquisses* for Piano he made a decisive turn toward a modern style; he became particularly fond of the whole-tone scale and its concomitant, the augmented triad; claimed priority in this respect over Debussy and other European composers; his piano piece *Les Démons s'amusent* is based entirely on the whole-tone scale. He declared that music is a language of emotion and therefore could not be confined to set forms, or to arbitrarily defined consonances. An entirely new departure is represented by his *Mélomimiques*, short lyric pieces for Piano, in which mimicry and suggestion are used in an impressionistic manner. He also wrote several vocal "melomimics," 3 "rhythmo-declamations" for Piano (op. 32), and 20 for Voice and Piano. In these compositions he abandoned cohesive form in favor of a free association of melodic and rhythmic phrases, sparingly harmonized; prevalence of esthetic theories over musical substance made his experiments ephemeral. A melodious waltz from his children's opera, *The Christmas Tree*, is his most popular composition. He publ. numerous articles on musical esthetics, particularly relating to modern music; tr. into Russian Gevaert's *Traité d'instrumentation*.
WORKS: *In the Thunderstorm*, opera (Odessa, Feb. 27,

1894); *The Christmas Tree*, children's opera (Moscow, Oct. 30, 1903); *Little Snow White*, musico-psychological pantomime (Tiflis, 1909); *Prince Charming*, fairy opera; scenic fables after Krylov: *The Grasshopper and the Ant*, *A Dinner with a Bear*, *The Ass and the Nightingale*, *The Funeral*, *The Liar* (Moscow, Dec. 27, 1903); several "musico-psychological tableaux": *Slavery and Freedom*, *Songs of the Harp*, *The Nightmare*, etc.; numerous piano pieces (*Scènes bucoliques*, *Silhouettes*, *Dans la forêt*, *Chansons blanches*, *Idylles*, *Les Danses*, *Les Démons s'amusent*, etc.).

BIBL.: W. Dale, *A Study of the Musicopsychological Dramas of V.I. R.* (diss., Univ. of Calif., Los Angeles, 1955).

Rebner, Adolf, Austrian violinist, father of **Wolfgang Eduard Rebner;** b. Vienna, Nov. 21, 1876; d. Baden-Baden, June 19, 1967. He was a pupil of Grün at the Vienna Cons.; settled in Frankfurt in 1896, and from 1904 taught violin at the Hoch Cons. In 1921 he organized the Rebner String Quartet, with Hindemith as the violist, and gave numerous concerts with it, obtaining excellent success; with the advent of the Nazi regime in Germany, he went to Vienna; after the Anschluss, lived briefly in the U.S.; eventually returned to Europe and lived in Baden-Baden.

Rebner, Wolfgang Eduard, German pianist and composer, son of **Adolf Rebner;** b. Frankfurt am Main, Dec. 20, 1910. He studied at the Hoch Cons. in Frankfurt; served as accompanist to the cellist Feuermann in the U.S. (1935–37) and South America. In 1955 he returned to Germany, and taught at the Richard Strauss Cons. in Munich. He composed some excellent chamber music and the orch. suites *Persönliche Noten* (1961) and *Aus Südamerika* (1964).

Rechberger, Herman(n), Austrian-born Finnish recorder player, conductor, and composer; b. Linz, Feb. 14, 1947. He studied classical guitar at the Bruckner Cons. in Linz; after further training in Zürich and at the Brussels Cons., he settled in Finland in 1970 and became a naturalized citizen (1974); took courses with Osmo Lindeman (electronic music), Olli Ruottinen (recorder; teacher's diploma, 1973), Ivan Putilin (guitar; teacher's diploma, 1973), and Aulis Sallinen (composition; diploma, 1976) at the Sibelius Academy in Helsinki (1971–77), where he also received instruction in piano, violin, and oboe. He was active as a music teacher (1975–79); then was a producer of contemporary music for and director of the electronic music studio at the Finnish Radio (1979–84). He toured widely as a recorder player; also appeared as a conductor. In his own music, he employs the full arsenal of contemporary resources, experimenting in multimedia spectacles, with ample use of electronics.

WORKS: STAGE, MULTIMEDIA, AND RADIOPHONIC: *Naula* (The Nail) for Bass-baritone, Actors, Dancers, Slide Projection, and Instruments (1975–76); *Pekka Mikkosen nousu* (The Rise of Jonathan Smith), radiophonic piece for Narrator, Piano, Various Sound Sources, and Non-conventional Instruments (1976–78); *Tree-O* for Stage Equipment, Slide Projection, 3 Actors, and Lute (1976); *Publico concertante* for 6 to 30 Different Instruments, Audience, and Slides (1977); *Zin Kibaru*, multimedia piece for Young Performers (1977); *. . . i$mo*, multimedia piece for Sound Objects, Actor, Slide Projectors, Light Organ, Flute, Clarinet, Violin, Cello, Videotape, and Kinetic Wall (1982); *Magnus Cordius—Entries in a Diary*, radiophonic piece for Actors, Orch., Mixed Chorus, Early Instruments, Vocal Ensemble, and Tapes (1985); *Die Nonnen* (The Nuns), chamber opera (1987); also music for plays and television. **ORCH.:** Concerto for Guitar and Strings (1971); *Kaamos* for String Orch. and Timpani (1973); *Music for Under-developed Film* (1973); *Loitsut* (Charms) for High Soprano and Chamber Orch. (1974); *La macchina capricciosa* for Double Bassoon, Chamber Orch., and Optional Slides (1974–75); *Consort Music 1* for Recorders, Chamber Orch., and Tape (1974–76); *Himojen Puutarha* (The Garden of Delights; 1976–77); *Consort Music 2* for Renaissance Instruments and Chamber Orch. (1977); *Venezia, visioni per grande orchestra, diversi soli e nastro* (1985); *Consort Music 5* (1985–86). **CHAMBER:** *Ylistyslaulu höyryvetu-rille* (Ode to a Steam Locomotive) for Flute, Clarinet, Viola, and Cello (1971); *Mayenzeit one neidt* for Flute, Violin, Cello, Double Bass, Metronome, and Live Electronics (1974); *Meccanismo* for Flute, Clarinet, Violin, Cello, and Metronomes (1978); *Fragebogen* for Double Bassoon and Pedal Sounds (1979); *Consort Music 3* for 4 Trumpets, 4 Trombones, and Tuba (1980–81); *Almost 4 Seasons* for String Quartet (1981); *Consort on an Egg* for Renaissance Instruments (1985); *NCG 7293* for 2 to 4 Instrumentalists (1986); *tympanon* for 2X5 Tambourins and Cowbells (1987); works for solo instruments; pieces for tape and for tape and instruments; much choral music; text scores; musical graphics.

Redding, Otis, black American rhythm-and-blues and soul singer and songwriter; b. Dawson, Ga., Sept. 9, 1941; d. in an airplane crash near Madison, Wis., Dec. 10, 1967. He sang in church, took part in revival meetings, and adopted the "shouting" manner of projection. His early record *Shout Bamalama* is a fair example of this technique. He then progressed toward a more refined type of gospel and soul singing, and in 1966 issued an album called *Dictionary of Soul*. His death at 26 was mourned and commemorated in a posthumous album, *The Immortal Otis Redding*. His most successful hits, sung in a powerful baritone voice, included *Respect*, *(Sittin' on) The Dock of the Bay*, and *Try a Little Tenderness*.

Redel, Kurt, German flutist and conductor; b. Breslau, Oct. 8, 1918. He studied at the Breslau Cons.; also conducting with C. Krauss; in 1939 he became a member of the Salzburg Mozarteum Orch.; in 1941 he joined the orch. of the Bavarian State Opera in Munich. From 1946 to 1953 he taught at the North West German Music Academy in Detmold. In 1953 he founded the Pro Arte Orch. of Munich, with which he toured widely.

Redford, John, English organist, composer, and poet; b. c.1485; d. London, 1547. He was one of the vicars-choral, an almoner, and Master of the Choristers at St. Paul's Cathedral in London. His works are found in D. Stevens, ed., *The Mulliner Book*, in Musica Britannica, I (1951); J. Caldwell, ed., *Early Tudor Organ Music* I: *Music for the Office*, in Early English Church Music, VI (1966); and D. Stevens, ed., *Early Tudor Organ Music* II: *Music for the Mass*, in Early English Church Music, X (1969).

BIBL.: C. Pfatteicher, *J. R.* (Kassel, 1934).

Redlich, Hans F(erdinand), Austrian-born English conductor, musicologist, and composer; b. Vienna, Feb. 11, 1903; d. Manchester, Nov. 27, 1968. He studied piano and composition, but devoted his energies mainly to writing biographical and analytical books on composers; he was only 16 when he publ. an essay on Mahler. After taking courses at the Univs. of Vienna and Munich, he obtained his Ph.D. at the Univ. of Frankfurt with the dissertation *Das Problem des Stilwandels in Monteverdis Madrigalwerk* (publ. in Berlin, 1931; 2nd ed., augmented, 1932, as *Claudio Monteverdi: I. Das Madrigalwerk*). He conducted opera in Mainz (1925–29); then lived in Mannheim. In 1939 he emigrated to England; became a naturalized British subject in 1947; from 1941 to 1955 he conducted the Choral and Orch. Soc. in Letchworth; also was a lecturer for the extra-mural depts. of the Univs. of Cambridge and Birmingham (1941–55); from 1955 to 1962 he was a lecturer at the Reid School of Music at the Univ. of Edinburgh; then was at the Univ. of Manchester.

WRITINGS: *Gustav Mahler: Eine Erkenntnis* (Nuremberg, 1919); *Richard Wagner: Tristan und Isolde, Lohengrin, Parsifal* (London, 1948; 3rd ed., 1951); *Claudio Monteverdi: Leben und Werk* (Olten, 1949; Eng. tr., 1952); *Bruckner and Mahler* (London, 1955; 2nd ed., rev., 1963); *Alban Berg: Versuch einer Würdigung* (Vienna, 1957; condensed Eng. version, 1957, as *Alban Berg: The Man and His Music*).

Redman, Don(ald Matthew), black American jazz instrumentalist, composer-arranger, and bandleader; b. Piedmont, W.Va., July 29, 1900; d. N.Y., Nov. 30, 1964. He began his studies on trumpet as a child; eventually mastered all the wind instruments; was an arranger for Fletcher Henderson's band (1924–27); then worked with Louis Armstrong; also was an arranger for Paul Whiteman, Ben Pollack, and others. He toured Europe with his own band (1946–47); then appeared on television and served as music director for Pearl Bailey. His arrangement of *Deep Purple* for Jimmy Dorsey became a major hit.

Redman, Harry N(ewton), American teacher, composer, and painter; b. Mount Carmel, Ill., Dec. 26, 1869; d. Boston, Dec. 26, 1958. He received instruction in piano, violin, and theory at the New England Cons. of Music in Boston, his principal teacher being Chadwick; then was on its faculty (1897–1937); subsequently devoted himself to painting; exhibited in Boston as late as 1957. He publ. a piano method and *A Pronouncing Dictionary of Musical Terms* (1901); wrote 4 string quartets, 2 violin sonatas, and other chamber works, songs, and piano pieces.

Rée, Anton, Danish pianist, pedagogue, and composer, cousin of **Louis Rée;** b. Århus, Oct. 5, 1820; d. Copenhagen, Dec. 20, 1886. He studied with Karl Krebs in Hamburg; had a few lessons with Chopin in Paris. In 1842 he settled in Copenhagen as a teacher. He publ. *Musikhistoriske Momenter* and a book of exercises; *Bidrag til Klavierspillets Teknik; Danses caractéristiques* for Piano; etc.

Rée, Louis, Scottish-born Austrian pianist, teacher, and composer, cousin of **Anton Rée;** b. Edinburgh, Oct. 15, 1861; d. Vienna, Feb. 28, 1939. He was a pupil of Leschetizky in Vienna; settled there as a teacher; gave duo-piano concerts with his wife, Susanne Pilz-Rée (1865–1937). He wrote a Concerto for 2 Pianos (1925); publ. transcriptions for 2 pianos and various other works.

Reed, Alfred, American conductor, composer, and arranger; b. N.Y., Jan. 25, 1921. He studied harmony with John Sacco; enlisted in the U.S. Air Force during World War II and was assigned to the Army Air Force Band; upon discharge from military service, he enrolled at the Juilliard School of Music in N.Y. as a student of Vittorio Giannini; completed his training at Baylor Univ. (B.M., 1955; M.M., 1956). In 1948 he was appointed staff composer and arranger with NBC; later served in the same capacity with ABC. From 1953 to 1966 he conducted the Baylor Univ. Sym. Orch.; in 1966 he joined the music faculty at the Univ. of Miami, where he developed a unique music merchandising program; also conducted its sym. orch. (from 1980). He composed a great number of band pieces; also wrote a multitude of 3-minute musical sequences for sound-track library recordings.

Reed, H(erbert) Owen, American composer and music educator; b. Odessa, Mo., June 17, 1910. He studied at the Univ. of Missouri, at Lousiana State Univ. (B.M., 1934; M.M., 1936), and with Howard Hanson and Bernard Rogers at the Eastman School of Music in Rochester, N.Y. (Ph.D., 1939); also studied with Roy Harris at the Berkshire Music Center at Tanglewood, and with Copland and Bernstein; held a Guggenheim fellowship (1938–39); then taught at Michigan State Univ. (1939–76).

WRITINGS: *A Workbook in the Fundamentals of Music* (N.Y., 1946); *Basic Music* (Melville, N.Y., 1954); *Composition Analysis Chart* (N.Y., 1958); with P. Harder, *Basic Contrapuntal Technique* (N.Y., 1964); with J. Leach, *Scoring for Percussion* (Melville, N.Y., 1969; 2nd ed., rev., 1979); with R. Sidnell, *The Materials of Music Composition* (3 vols., Reading, Mass., 1978–).

WORKS: STAGE: *The Masque of the Red Death,* ballet-pantomime after Poe (1936); *Peter Homan's Dream,* opera (East Lansing, Mich., May 13, 1955; arranged as a musical, 1971); *Earth Trapped,* chamber dance-opera (1960; East Lansing, Feb. 24, 1962); *Living Solid Face,* chamber dance-opera (1974; Brookings, S.Dak., Nov. 28, 1976); *Butterfly Girl and Mirage Boy,* chamber dance-opera on an Indian spirit legend (1980). **ORCH.:** *Evangeline,* symphonic poem (Rochester, N.Y., March 30, 1938); Sym. (Rochester, April 27, 1939); Cello Concerto

(1949); *La fiesta mexicana* for Band (1949; also for Orch., 1964); Overture for Strings (1961); *The Turning Mind* (1968); *Ut Re Mi* for Orch. and Men's Chorus (1979; also for Band and Men's Chorus, 1980); various choral works, including an oratorio, *A Tabernacle for the Sun* (1963); chamber music; piano pieces; songs.

Reed, Jerry, American country-music singer, guitarist, and songwriter; b. Atlanta, March 20, 1937. He labored in cotton mills as a youth while pursuing his career as a singer in local haunts in Atlanta; when he was 18, he was hired as a songwriter for Capitol Records, and wrote such hits as *Amos Moses, Georgia Sunshine,* and *Alabama Wild Man.* In 1971 he scored a signal success when he brought out the song *When You're Hot, You're Hot.*

Reed, Lou(is Alan), musically educated American rock singer, guitarist, and songwriter; b. N.Y., March 2, 1942. He studied piano in his childhood; took up the guitar in high school; after graduating from Syracuse Univ., he read books, wrote poetry, essayed journalism, vocalized to guitar accompaniment, and finally found his proper niche improvising variously with such psychedelically inclined groups as The Primitives and The Warlocks. In 1966 he recruited a British musician of a similarly educated background, John Cale, and together they formed a sodality inexplicably named The Velvet Underground, projecting bizarre stage behavior and playing sophisticated numbers in dissonant harmony. They attracted the surrealist artist Andy Warhol, who hired them for his "total environment" show "The Exploding Plastic Inevitable." Under Warhol's nihilistic influence, The Velvet Underground revived the dadaistic, surrealistic type of old European modernism, superadded with the screeching, screaming, sadomasochistic electronic sound to Reed's demoralizing anarchistic lyrics openly extolling the psychedelic advantages of narcotics and totally emancipated sex play in such songs as *Heroin* and *Venus in Furs.* Reed left the group in 1970, and put out such invitations to anarchy as *Walk on the Wild Side* and *Metal Music Machine,* in which electronic bleeps and hisses accompanied the shouted homicidal orders *Live . . . Take No Prisoners.* His later albums included *Coney Island Baby* (1976), *Street Hassle* (1978), *The Blue Mask* (1982), and *New Sensations* (1984).

BIBL.: D. Clapton, *L. R. and the Velvet Underground* (London, 1982).

Reed, Thomas German, versatile English musician; b. Bristol, June 27, 1817; d. London, March 21, 1888. Under the guidance of his father, he appeared in Bath as a child of 10 in the various capacities of singer, pianist, and actor. In 1844 he married **Priscilla Horton** (b. Birmingham, Jan. 1, 1818; d. Bexley Heath, March 18, 1895), an actress and singer. Together they started the celebrated series "Mr. and Mrs. German Reed's Entertainment" (1855), which included productions of operettas by Offenbach, Balfe, Clay, Sullivan, etc. These entertainments enjoyed great success, and were continued by his son Alfred German Reed, who died in London on March 10, 1895, a few days before the death of his mother.

Reed, William Henry, English violinist and composer; b. Frome, July 29, 1876; d. Dumfries, July 2, 1942. He studied at the Royal Academy of Music in London; was a violinist in the London Sym. Orch. at its foundation in 1904; was its concertmaster (1912–35); taught violin at the Royal College of Music in London. He was a close friend of Elgar, and publ. *Elgar as I Knew Him* (London, 1936) and *Elgar* (London, 1939). His works include the orch. sketches *The Lincoln Imp* (Hereford Festival, 1921) and *Aesop's Fables* (Hereford Festival, 1924); Violin Concerto; *Rhapsody* for Violin and Orch.; 5 string quartets; violin pieces; songs; etc.

Reed, William L(eonard), English composer, lecturer, and editor; b. London, Oct. 16, 1910. He studied at London's Guildhall School of Music (1917–26); Dulwich College, Oxford (1922–29); with Howells (composition) and Lambert (conducting) at London's Royal College of Music (1934–36), where he won the 1st Cobbett Prize in composition (1936); and at Oxford University (M.A., 1934; B.Mus., 1936; D.Mus., 1939). After World War II, he traveled widely in Europe, the U.S., and Asia; in 1961 settled in London, where he served as director of music at the Westminster Theatre Arts Centre (1967–80).

WORKS: MUSICALS: *The Vanishing Island* (Santa Barbara, Calif., 1955; in collaboration with G. Fraser); *Annie* (London, 1967); *High Diplomacy* (London, 1969; in collaboration with G. Fraser); *Love All* (London, 1978). **ORCH.:** *Idyll* for Small Orch. (1935); *Doctor Johnson's Suite* for Strings (1944); *Concert Overture* (1950); other orch. pieces in a light vein. **CHAMBER:** *Fantasy* for String Quartet (1936); *Tarantelle fantastique* for Piano and String Quartet (1943); *Waltz* for Piano and String Quartet (1944); 2 suites for Violin and Piano: No. 1 (1945) and No. 2, *On the Road* (1948); *The Top Flat*, suite for Viola and Piano (1947); *Rhapsody on Christmas Carols* for Violin and Piano (1951); piano pieces; organ works; vocal music.

WRITINGS (all publ. in London): *The Treasury of Christmas Music* (1950; 7th ed., 1978); *Music of Britain* (1952); *The Treasury of Easter Music* (1963); with G. Knight, *The Treasury of English Church Music* (5 vols., 1965); *The Second Treasury of Christmas Music* (1967); with E. Smith, *The Treasury of Vocal Music* (4 vols., 1969); *National Anthems of the World* (5th ed. with M. Cartledge, 1978; 6th and 7th eds. with M. Bristow, 1985, 1987).

Reese, Della (real name, **Delloreese Patricia Early**), black American singer of gospel and popular music; b. Detroit, July 6, 1932. She studied at Wayne State Univ. in Detroit; concurrently formed Meditations, a gospel group; later toured with Mahalia Jackson (1945–49) and other gospel singers; from 1954 she turned to popular music, and became successful as a vocalist; appeared extensively in nightclubs and on radio and television.

Reese, Gustave, eminent American musicologist; b. N.Y., Nov. 29, 1899; d. Berkeley, Calif., Sept. 7, 1977. At N.Y. Univ. he studied jurisprudence (LL.B., 1921) and music (Mus.Bac., 1930); subsequently joined its faculty, teaching there during the periods 1927–33, 1934–37, and 1945–74; concurrently worked with G. Schirmer, Inc. (1924–45; from 1940 to 1945 was director of publications); was director of publications for Carl Fischer (1944–55). From 1933 to 1944 he was associate ed., and in 1944–45 ed., of the *Musical Quarterly.* In 1934 he was a co-founder of the American Musicological Soc.; was its president from 1950 to 1952, and remained its honorary president until his death. He gave numerous lectures at American univs.; also gave courses at the Juilliard School of Music in N.Y. An entire generation of American music scholars numbered among his students; he was widely regarded as a founder of American musicology as a science. He held a chair at the Graduate School of Arts and Science at N.Y. Univ., which gave him its "Great Teacher Award" in 1972 and its presidential citation on his retirement from active teaching in 1974; he then became a visiting prof. at the Graduate Center of the City Univ. of N.Y. He died while attending the congress of the International Musicological Soc. in Berkeley. Reese contributed a great number of informative articles to various American and European publications and music encyclopedias, but his most lasting achievement lies in his books, *Music in the Middle Ages* (N.Y., 1940; also in Italian, Florence, 1960) and *Music in the Renaissance* (N.Y., 1954; 2nd ed., rev., 1959), which have become classics of American music scholarship; he also brought out an interesting book that describes selected early writings on music not available in English, *Fourscore Classics of Music Literature* (N.Y., 1957).

BIBL.: J. LaRue, ed., *Aspects of Medieval and Renaissance Music: A Birthday Offering to G. R.* (N.Y., 1966; 2nd ed., 1978).

Reeser, (Hendrik) Eduard, distinguished Dutch musicologist; b. Rotterdam, March 23, 1908. He studied art history with Vogelsang and musicology with Smijers at the Univ. of Utrecht (Ph.D., 1939). He taught music history at the Rotterdam Cons. (1930–37) and musicology at the Univ. of Utrecht (1947–73); was also president of the Donemus Foundation

(1947–57), the Maatschappij tot Bevordering der Toonkunst (1951–69), and the IMS (1972–77). He was made a member of the Royal Dutch Academy of Sciences (1961) and the Royal Academy of Sciences and Arts of Belgium (1973); was also made an honorary member of the Royal Musical Assoc. in London (1974).

WRITINGS (all publ. in Amsterdam unless otherwise given): *De musikale handscriften van Alphons Diepenbrock* (1933); *Alphons Diepenbrock* (1935); *De zonen van Bach* (1941; Eng. tr., 1946); *Musiekgeschiedenis in vogelvlucht* (1942; Eng. tr., 1946); *De Vereeniging voor Nederlandsche muziekgeschiedenis 1863–1943: Gedenboek* (1943); *De geschiedenis van de wals* (1947; Eng. tr., 1947); *Muziek in gemeenschap der Kunsten* (Rotterdam, 1947); *Een eeuw Nederlandse muziek* (1950); ed. *Verzamelde geschriften van Alphons Diepenbrock* (Utrecht, 1950); *Music in Holland* (1959); ed. *Alphons Diepenbrock: Brieven en documenten* (2 vols., The Hague, 1962, 1967); *Gustav Mahler und Holland* (Vienna, 1980); *Ein Augsburger Musiker in Paris: Johann Gottfried Eckard* (Augsburg, 1985).

Reeve, William, English organist and composer; b. London, 1757; d. there, June 22, 1815. He was a pupil of Richardson; served as organist at Totness, Devon, from 1781 to 1783; returned to London, and composed operettas, pantomimes, and incidental music for plays, for Astley's Circus, and for Covent Garden (1791–1812); in 1792 he became organist of St. Martin's, Ludgate Hill; from 1802, part-proprietor of Sadler's Wells Theatre. Besides music to some 40 plays, he composed glees and songs; the song *I am a friar in orders grey,* in the play *Merry Sherwood,* was very popular.

Reeves, David Wallis, American bandmaster and composer; b. Oswego, N.Y., Feb. 14, 1838; d. Providence, R.I., March 8, 1900. As a boy he began to play cornet in circus and minstrel bands; later was in Union Army bands; in 1866 he became the leader of the American Band of Providence, which is said to trace its roots back to the War of 1812; during its 35 years under the direction of Reeves, it became a model of excellence among American municipal bands; Reeves succeeded in standardizing the instrumentation of the ordinary parade and outdoor-concert band; he wrote some 80 marches, of which the best is *The 2nd Connecticut Regiment March,* known to have been a favorite of Charles Ives. Reeves was a great friend of Patrick Sarsfield Gilmore, conductor of the band of the N.Y. 22nd Regiment, and it was Gilmore who popularized Reeves's marches. Upon Gilmore's death, Reeves took over the 22nd Regiment Band for the 1892–93 season, but then resumed the conductorship of the American Band. Sousa called Reeves "the father of band music in America."

BIBL.: D. Stockhouse, "D.W. R. and His Music," *Journal of Band Research,* V/2 (1969) and VI/1 (1969).

Reeves, Martha, black American rhythm-and-blues singer; b. Detroit, July 18, 1941. She worked as a clerk at Motown Records, and stepped in as a substitute at a recording session. She liked singing, and the Motown mogul Berry Gordy, Jr., liked her singing, too. She recruited 2 of her high-school friends to do a trio in 1963, making a hit with the song *Heat Wave,* under the moniker Martha and the Vandellas. Adapting the kinetic Motown style, they scored again with *Nowhere to Run;* becoming raunchier in their feministic affirmative action, they put out *I'm Ready for Love* and *My Baby Loves Me.* There were personnel changes, and the Vandellas finally disintegrated. She continued to make records alone, producing such autobiographical albums as *The Rest of My Life* and *Gotta Keep Moving.*

Reeves, (John) Sims, English tenor; b. Shooter's Hill, Kent, Sept. 26, 1818; d. Worthing, London, Oct. 25, 1900. He learned to play several instruments; had lessons with J.B. Cramer (piano) and W.H. Callcott (harmony); he made his debut as a baritone in *Guy Mannering* in Newcastle upon Tyne (Dec. 14, 1838); studied further and sang minor tenor roles at London's Drury Lane, 1841–43; studied in Paris under Bordogni, and in Milan under Mazzucato, appearing at La Scala in 1846 as Edgardo (*Lucia di Lammermoor*); sang Faust in the 1st British performance of Berlioz's *La Damnation de Faust* under the composer's direction (1848); then was a member of Her Majesty's Theatre in London (from 1848); also sang at the leading festivals. He retired in 1891, but reappeared in concerts in 1893; made a successful tour of South Africa in 1896. He publ. *Sims Reeves; His Life and Recollections Written by Himself* (London, 1888); *My Jubilee, or Fifty Years of Artistic Life* (London, 1889); *Sims Reeves on the Art of Singing* (London, 1900).

BIBL.: H. Edwards, *The Life and Artistic Career of S. R.* (London, 1881); C. Pearce, *S. R.: Fifty Years of Music in England* (London, 1924).

Refardt, Edgar, eminent Swiss musicologist and bibliographer; b. Basel, Aug. 8, 1877; d. there, March 3, 1968. He studied law; obtained the degree of Dr.Jur. in 1901; in 1915, was appointed librarian and cataloguer of the musical collection of the Municipal Library of Basel; publ. valuable bibliographical works on Swiss music; also essays on various literary and musical subjects.

WRITINGS: *Verzeichnis der Aufsätze zur Musik in den nichtmusikalischen Zeitschriften der Universitätsbibliothek Basel* (Leipzig, 1925); *Historisch-biographisches Musikerlexikon der Schweiz* (Leipzig and Zürich, 1928); *Hans Huber: Leben und Werk eines schweizer Musikers* (Zürich, 1944); *Theodor Fröhlich: Ein schweizer Musiker der Romantik* (Basel, 1947); *Johannes Brahms, Anton Bruckner, Hugh Wolf: Drei Wiener Meister des 19. Jahrhunderts* (Basel, 1949); *Musik in der Schweiz: Ausgewählte Aufsätze* (1952); H. Zehntner, ed., *Thematischer Katalog der Instrumentalmusik des 18. Jahrhunderts in den Handschriften der Universitätsbibliothek Basel* (Bern, 1952).

Refice, Licinio, Italian conductor and composer; b. Patrica, near Rome, Feb. 12, 1883; d. while conducting his sacred play *Santa Cecilia* in Rio de Janeiro, Sept. 11, 1954. He studied organ and composition at Rome's Liceo di Santa Cecilia (diploma, 1910); after being ordained (1910), he taught at Rome's Scuola Pontificia Superiore di Musica Sacra (1910–50) and was maestro di cappella at S. Maria Maggiore (1911–47); toured Europe and North and South America as a conductor.

WORKS: OPERAS: *Cecilia* (1922–23; Rome, 1934); *Margherita da Cortona* (Milan, 1938). **CANTATA:** *La vedova di Naim* (1912). **ORATORIOS:** *La Cananea* (1910); *Maria Magdalena* (1914); *Martyrium S. Agnetis Virginis* (1919); *Trittico Francescano* (1926); over 40 masses; *Stabat Mater* (1917); *Te Deum* (1918); many other sacred works; some instrumental pieces and secular songs.

BIBL.: E. Mucci, *L. R.* (Assisi, 1955); T. Onofri and E. Mucci, *Le composizioni di L. R.* (Assisi, 1966).

Regamey, Constantin, Swiss pianist and composer; b. Kiev (of a Swiss father and a Russian mother), Jan. 28, 1907; d. Lausanne, Dec. 27, 1982. He went to Poland in 1920 and took piano lessons with Turczyński (1921–25); then turned to linguistics and took courses in Sanskrit at the Univ. of Warsaw and later at L'École des Hautes Études in Paris, graduating in 1936. Returning to Poland, he taught Sanskrit at the Univ. of Warsaw (1937–39); concurrently he ed. periodicals on contemporary music. He was interned by the Germans during World War II, but managed to escape to Switzerland in 1944. He received an appointment to teach Slavic and oriental languages at the Univ. of Lausanne; also gave courses in Indo-European linguistics at the Univ. of Fribourg. However, he did not abandon his musical activities; he served as co-ed. of the *Revue Musicale de Suisse Romande* (1954–62); was president of the Assoc. of Swiss Composers (1963–68) and a member of the executive board of the ISCM (1969–73). In 1978 he became partially paralyzed; he dictated the last pages of his last work, *Visions*, to Jean Balissat, a fellow composer, who also orchestrated the work. As a composer, he adopted free serial methods, without a doctrinaire adherence to formal dodecaphony. In 1963 he moderated his modernity and wrote music using free, often composite, techniques.

WORKS: STAGE: *Don Robott*, opera (1970); *Mio, mein Mio,*

fairy-tale opera, after Bächli and Lindgren (1973). **ORCH.:** *Variazioni e tema* (1948); *Music* for Strings (1953); *Autographe* for Chamber Orch. (1962–66); *4 × 5*, concerto for 4 Quintets (Basel, May 28, 1964); *Lila*, double concerto for Violin, Cello, and Chamber Orch. (1976). **CHAMBER:** Quintet for Clarinet, Bassoon, Violin, Cello, and Piano (1944); String Quartet (1948). **VOCAL:** *7 chansons persanes*, after Omar Khayyám, for Baritone and Chamber Orch. (1942); *5 études* for Female Voice and Orch. (1955–56); *5 poèmes de Jean Tardieu* for Chorus a cappella (1962); *Symphonie des Incantations* for Soprano, Baritone, and Orch. (1967); *3 Lieder des Clowns* for Baritone and Orch. (1968; from the opera *Don Robott*); *Unidentity and Infinity* for Silent Narrator, Female Voice, and an unidentified number of Instruments (1969); *Alpha*, cantata for Tenor and Orch., to a Hindu text (1970); *Visions*, after the life of the prophet Daniel, for Baritone, Chorus, Orch., and Organ (1978–79; orchestrated by Jean Balissat).

WRITINGS: *Musique du XXᵉ siècle: Présentation de 80 œuvres pour orchestre de chambre* (Lausanne and Paris, 1966).

BIBL.: H. Jaccard, *Initiation à la musique contemporaine: Trois compositeurs vaudois: Raffaele d'Alessandro, C. R., Julien-François Zbinden* (Lausanne, 1955).

Reger, (Johann Baptist Joseph) Max(imilian), celebrated German composer; b. Brand, Upper Palatinate, Bavaria, March 19, 1873; d. Leipzig, May 11, 1916. His father, a schoolteacher and amateur musician, gave him instruction on the piano, organ, and various string instruments. In 1874 the family moved to Weiden, where he studied organ and theory with Adalbert Lindner; he then attended the teacher-training college; after visiting the Bayreuth Festival in 1888, he decided on a career in music. He went to Sondershausen to study with Riemann in 1890, and continued as his pupil in Wiesbaden (1890–93); was also active as a teacher of piano, organ, and theory (1890–96). Following military service, he returned to Weiden in 1898 and wrote a number of his finest works for organ. He went to Munich in 1901, first gaining general recognition as a pianist, and later as a composer; was prof. of counterpoint at the Königliche Akademie der Tonkunst (1905–6). Prominent compositions from this period included the Piano Quintet, op. 64 (1901–2), the Violin Sonata, op. 72 (1903), the String Quartet, op. 74 (1903–4), the *Variationen und Fuge über ein Thema von J.S. Bach* for Piano, op. 81 (1904), and the Sinfonietta, op. 90 (1904–5). He went to Leipzig as music director of the Univ. (1907–8) and as prof. of composition at the Cons. (from 1907). His fame as a composer was enhanced by his successful tours as a soloist and conductor in Germany and throughout Europe. While he continued to produce major chamber works and organ pieces, he also wrote such important orch. compositions as the *Variationen und Fuge über ein lustiges Thema von J.A. Hiller*, op. 100 (1907), the Violin Concerto, op. 101 (1907–8), the *Symphonischer Prolog zu einer Tragödie*, op. 108 (1908), the Piano Concerto, op. 114 (1910), and the *Variationen und Fuge über ein Thema von Mozart*, op. 132 (1914). As a result of having been awarded an honorary Ph.D. from the Univ. of Jena in 1908, he composed his most distinguished sacred work, the *Psalm C*, op. 106 (1908–9). He was called to Meiningen as conductor of the Court Orch. in 1911, assuming the title of Hofkapellmeister; was also Generalmusikdirektor (1913–14). He settled in Jena in 1915.

Reger was an extraordinarily gifted musician, widely respected as a composer, pianist, organist, conductor, and teacher. A master of polyphonic and harmonic writing, he carried on the hallowed Classical and Romantic schools of composition. Although he wrote major works in nearly every genre, his music has not found a place of permanence in the repertoire.

WRITINGS: *Beiträge zur Modulationslehre* (Leipzig, 1903; 24th ed., 1952).

WORKS: ORCH.: *Heroide*, symphonic movement (1889); *Castra vetera*, incidental music (1889–90); *Symphoniesatz* (1890; Dortmund, 1960); *Lyrisches Andante* for Strings (1898); *Scherzino* for Horn and Strings (1899); *Elegie*, op. 26/1 (1899;

arranged from a piano work); *2 Romanzen* for Violin and Orch., op. 50 (1900); *Variationen und Fuge über ein Thema von Beethoven*, op. 86 (1915; arranged from the work for 2 Pianos, 1904); *Sinfonietta*, op. 90 (Essen, Oct. 8, 1905); *Suite im alten Stil*, op. 93 (1916; arranged from the work for Violin and Piano, 1906); *Serenade*, op. 95 (1905–6); *Variationen und Fuge über ein lustiges Thema von J.A. Hiller*, op. 100 (Cologne, Oct. 15, 1907); Violin Concerto, op. 101 (Leipzig, Oct. 13, 1908); *Aria* for Violin and Chamber Orch., op. 103a (1908; arranged from the Suite for Violin and Piano, 1908); *Symphonischer Prolog zu einer Tragödie*, op. 108 (1908); Piano Concerto, op. 114 (Leipzig, Dec. 15, 1910); *Eine Lustspielouvertüre*, op. 120 (1911); *Konzert im alten Stil*, op. 123 (1912); *Eine romantische Suite*, op. 125 (1912); *4 Tondichtungen nach Arnold Böcklin*, op. 128 (Essen, Oct. 12, 1913); *Eine Ballettsuite*, op. 130 (1913); *Variationen und Fuge über ein Thema von Mozart*, op. 132 (1914; Berlin, Feb. 5, 1915; arranged from the work for 2 Pianos, 1914); *Eine vaterländische Ouvertüre*, op. 140 (1914); *Sinfonische Rhapsodie* for Violin and Orch., op. 147 (unfinished; completed by F. von Reuter).

VOCAL: 3 Choruses for Mixed Voices and Piano, op. 6 (1892); *Tantum ergo sacramentum* for 5 Voices (1895); *Hymne an den Gesang* for Male Chorus, and Orch. or Piano, op. 21 (1898); *Gloriabuntur in te omnes* for 4 Voices (1898); 7 Male Choruses, op. 38 (1899); 3 Choruses for Mixed Voices, op. 39 (1899); *Maria Himmelsfreud!* (1899); 8 settings of *Tantum ergo*, op. 61a (1901); 4 settings of *Tantum ergo* for Women's or Men's Voices and Organ, op. 61b (1901); 4 settings of *Tantum ergo* for 4 Voices and Organ, op. 61c (1901); *8 Marienlieder*, op. 61d (1901); *4 Marienlieder* for Women's or Men's Voices and Organ, op. 61e (1901); *4 Marienlieder* for 4 Voices and Organ, op. 61f (1901); *6 Trauergesänge*, op. 61g (1901); *Palmsonntagmorgen* for 5 Voices (1902); *Gesang der Verklärten* for Mixed Voices and Orch., op. 71 (1903); 5 cantatas (1903–5); *10 Gesänge* for Male Voices, op. 83 (1904, 1909); *Weihegesang* for Chorus and Wind Orch. (1908); *Psalm C* for Chorus, Organ, and Orch., op. 106 (1908–9); *Geistliche Gesänge* for 5 Voices, op. 110 (1912); *Vater unser* for 12 Voices (1909); *3 Gesänge* for 4 Women's Voices, op. 111b (1909); *Die Nonnen* for Chorus and Orch., op. 112 (1909); *Die Weihe der Nacht* for Male Voices and Orch., op. 119 (1911); *Lasset uns den Herren preisen* for 5 Voices (1911); *Römischer Triumphgesang* for Male Voices and Orch., op. 126 (1912); *8 geistliche Gesänge* for 4 to 8 Voices, op. 138 (1914); *Abschiedslied* for 4 Voices (1914); *Requiem* for Soloists, Chorus, and Orch. (1914; 2nd movement unfinished); *2 Gesänge*, op. 144 (1915); *20 Responsorien* (1916); many works for solo voice.

CHAMBER: Scherzo for Flute and String Quartet (n.d.); String Quartet (1888–89); Sonata for Violin and Piano, op. 1 (1890); Trio for Violin, Viola, and Piano, op. 2 (1891); Sonata for Violin and Piano, op. 3 (1891); Sonata for Cello and Piano, op. 5 (1892); Piano Quintet (1897–98); Sonata for Cello and Piano, op. 28 (1898); Sonata for Violin and Piano, op. 41 (1899); 4 sonatas for Violin, op. 42 (1900); 2 sonatas for Clarinet and Piano, op. 49 (1900); 2 string quartets, op. 54 (1900); *Caprice* for Cello and Piano (1901); Piano Quintet, op. 64 (1901–2); Prelude and Fugue for Violin (1902); *Romanze* for Violin and Piano (1902); *Petite caprice* for Violin and Piano (1902); *Albumblatt* for Clarinet or Violin, and Piano (1902); *Tarantella* for Clarinet or Violin, and Piano (1902); *Allegretto grazioso* for Flute and Piano (1902); Sonata for Violin and Piano, op. 72 (1903); String Quartet, op. 74 (1903–4); *Serenade* for Flute, Violin, and Viola, op. 77a (1904); String Trio, op. 77b (1904); Sonata for Cello and Piano, op. 78 (1904); *Wiegenlied, Capriccio, and Burla* for Violin and Piano, op. 79d (1902–4); *Caprice, Kleine Romanze* for Cello and Piano, op. 79e (1904); Sonata for Violin and Piano, op. 84 (1905); *Albumblatt, romanze* for Violin and Piano, op. 87 (1905); 7 sonatas for Violin, op. 91 (1905); *Suite im alten Stil* for Violin and Piano, op. 93 (1906; orchestrated 1916); Trio for Violin, Cello, and Piano, op. 102 (1907–8); *Suite (6 Vortragstücke)* for Violin and Piano, op. 103a (1908); 2 little sonatas for Violin and Piano, op. 103b (1909); *12 kleine Stücke nach eigenen Liedern* (from op. 76)

for Violin and Piano, op. 103c (1916); Sonata for Clarinet or Viola, and Piano, op. 107 (1908–9); String Quartet, op. 109 (1909); Piano Quartet, op. 113 (1910); Sonata for Cello and Piano, op. 116 (1910); Preludes and Fugues for Violin, op. 117 (1909–12); Sextet for 2 Violins, 2 Violas, and 2 Cellos, op. 118 (1910); String Quartet, op. 121 (1911); Sonata for Violin and Piano, op. 122 (1911); Preludes and Fugues for Violin, op. 131a (1914); 3 Duos (*Canons und Fugen*) *im alten Stil* for 2 Violins, op. 131b (1914); 3 suites for Cello, op. 131c (1915); 3 suites for Viola, op. 131d (1915); Piano Quartet, op. 133 (1914); Allegro for 2 Violins (1914); Sonata for Violin and Piano, op. 139 (1915); Serenade for Flute or Violin, Violin, and Viola, op. 141a (1915); String Trio, op. 141b (1915); Clarinet Quintet, op. 146 (1915); Prelude for Violin (1915); also numerous pieces for piano and organ works.

BIBL. The *Sämtliche Werke* was publ. in Wiesbaden (38 vols., 1954–86). F. Stein ed. the *Thematisches Verzeichnis der im Druck erschienenen Werke von M. R. einschliesslich seiner Bearbeitungen und Ausgaben* (Leipzig, 1953). H. Rösner ed. a *M.-R.-Bibliographie* (Bonn, 1968). See also the following: R. Braungart, *M. R.*, Monographien Moderner Musiker, II (Leipzig, 1907); V. Junk, *M. R. als Orchesterkomponist* (Leipzig, 1910); W. Fischer, *Über die Wiedergabe der Orgelkompositionen M. R.s* (Cologne, 1911); F. Rabich, *R.lieder: Eine Studie* (Langensalza, 1914); R. Eucken, *Persönliche Erinnerungen an M. R.* (Bielefeld, 1916); H. Poppen, *M. R.* (Leipzig, 1918; 3rd ed., 1947); H. Grabner, *R.s Harmonik* (Munich, 1920); R. Würz, ed., *M. R.: Eine Sammlung von Studien* (4 vols., Munich, 1920–23); K. Hasse, *M. R.: Mit R.s Schriften und Aufsätzen* (Leipzig, 1921); A. Lindner, *M. R.: Ein Bild seines Jugendlebens und künstlerischen Werdens* (Stuttgart, 1922; 3rd ed., 1938); G. Bagier, *M. R.* (Stuttgart and Berlin, 1923); E. Gatscher, *Die Fugentechnik M. R.s in ihrer Entwicklung* (Stuttgart, 1925); S. Kallenberg, *M. R.* (Leipzig, 1929); E. Reger, *Mein Leben mit und für M. R.* (Leipzig, 1930); P. Coenen, *M. R.s Variationsschaffen* (diss., Univ. of Berlin, 1935); E. Brand, *M. R. im Elternhaus* (Munich, 1938); F. Stein, *M.R.* (Potsdam, 1939); idem, *M. R.: Sein Leben in Bildern* (Leipzig, 1941; 2nd ed., 1956); A. Kalkoff, *Das Orgelschaffen M. R.s* (Kassel, 1950); special issue of the *Zeitschrift für Musik* (March 1953); G. Wehmeyer, *M. R. als Liederkomponist*, Kölner Beiträge zur Musikforschung, VIII (Regensburg, 1955); E. Otto, *M. R.: Sinnbild einer Epoche* (Wiesbaden, 1957); G. Sievers, *Die Grundlagen Hugo Riemanns bei M. R.* (Wiesbaden, 1967); M. Stein, *Der heitere R.* (Wiesbaden, 1969); H. Wirth, *M. R.* (Hamburg, 1973); K. Röhring, ed., *M. R. 1873–1973: Ein Symposion* (Wiesbaden, 1974); S. Popp and S. Shigihara, eds., *M. R.: Am Wendepunkt zur Moderne: Ein Bildband mit Dokumenten aus den Beständen des M.-R.-Instituts* (Bonn, 1987; Eng. tr., 1988, as *M. R. at the Turning Point to Modernism: An Illustrated Volume with Documents of the M. R. Institute*); W. Grim, *M. R.: A Bio-bibliography* (N.Y., 1988).

Regis, Johannes, Netherlands composer; b. c.1430; d. probably in Soignies, c.1485. He was made "magister puerorum" of Cambrai Cathedral (1460); then of Notre Dame in Antwerp (1463); was secretary to Dufay in Cambrai (1464–74); and finally canon and scholasticus in Soignies (1481–82). He wrote 2 masses on the melody of *L'Homme armé*; a 5-part motet, *O admirabile commercium*, and other vocal pieces. His collected works were publ. in 2 vols. by the American Inst. of Musicology in Rome (1956), under the editorship of C. Lindenburg.

BIBL.: C. Lindenburg, *Het Leven en de werken van J. R.* (Amsterdam, 1939).

Regli, Francesco, Italian lexicographer; b. Milan, 1802; d. Turin, March 10, 1866. He founded a theatrical publication, *Il Pirata*, in 1835; publ. a *Dizionario biografico dei più celebri poeti ed artisti melodrammatici che fiorirono in Italia dal 1800 al 1860* (Turin, 1860); *Storia del violino in Piemonte* (Turin, 1863); *Elogio a G. Rossini* (Turin, 1864); *Elogio a Felice Romani* (Turin, 1865).

Regnart, Jacob, prominent South Netherlandish composer; b. Douai, c.1540; d. Prague, Oct. 16, 1599. He began his career as a chorister in the Prague Hofkapelle of Maximilian (from 1577), continuing in his service in Vienna when he became the emperor Maximilian; after studies in Italy (1568–70), he became music teacher of the chapel choristers; after Maximilian's death (1576), Emperor Rudolf II appointed Regnart a member of his Hofkapelle, which soon thereafter was removed to Prague, where he became its Vice-Kapellmeister (1579); was Vice-Kapellmeister (1582–85) and Kapellmeister (1585–96) to Archduke Ferdinand of Innsbruck; was again in Prague as Vice-Kapellmeister (from 1596). He had 4 brothers, all of whom were active as musicians.

WORKS: SACRED VOCAL: *Sacrae aliquot cantiones, quas moteta vulgus appellat* for 5 to 6 Voices (Munich, 1575); *Aliquot cantiones, vulgo motecta appellatae, ex veteri atque novo testamento collectae* for 4 Voices (Nuremberg, 1577); *Mariale, hoc est, Opusculum sacrarum cantionum omnibus Beatissimae Virginis Mariae festivitatibus* for 4, 6, and 8 Voices (Innsbruck, 1588); *Missae sacrae ad imitationem selectissimarum cantionum suavissima harmonia* for 5 to 6 and 8 Voices (Frankfurt am Main, 1602); *Continuatio missarum sacrarum, ad imitationem selectissimarum cantionum suavissima harmonia* for 4 to 6, 8, and 10 Voices (Frankfurt am Main, 1603); *Corollarium missarum sacrarum ad imitationem selectissimarum cantionum suavissima harmonia compositarum* (Frankfurt am Main, 1603); *Sacrarum cantionum* for 4 to 8 and 12 Voices (Frankfurt am Main, 1605); *Canticum Mariae* for 5 Voices (Dillingen, 1605); *Missarum flores illustrium numquam hactenus visi* (Frankfurt am Main, 1611); *Magnificat, ad octo modos musicos compositum cum duplici antiphona, Salve regina* for 8 and 10 Voices (Frankfurt am Main, 1614); numerous other works in contemporary collections. **SECULAR VOCAL:** *Il primo libro delle canzone italiane* for 5 Voices (Vienna, 1574); *Kurtzweilige teutsche Lieder, nach der Neapolitanen oder welschen Villanellen* for 3 Voices (Nuremberg, 1576; 2nd ed., 1578, as *Der erste Theyl schöner kurtzweiliger teutscher Lieder*); *Der ander Theyl kurtzweiliger teutscher Lieder* for 3 Voices (Nuremberg, 1577); *Der dritter Theyl schöner kurtzweiliger teutscher Lieder* for 3 Voices (Nuremberg, 1579); *Newe kurtzweilige teutsche Lieder* for 5 Voices (Nuremberg, 1580); *Il secundo libro delle canzone italiane* for 5 Voices (Nuremberg, 1581); *Teutsche Lieder . . . in ein Opus zusamendruckt* for 3 Voices (Munich, 1583); *Tricinia: Kurtzweilige teutsche Lieder* for 3 Voices (Nuremberg, 1584); *Kurtzweilige teutsche Lieder* for 4 Voices (Munich, 1591); other works in contemporary collections. W. Pass ed. *Jacob Regnart: Opera omnia* in Corpus Mensurabilis Musicae, LXII/4–6 (1972–75).

BIBL.: F. Mossler, *Jakob R.s Messen* (diss., Univ. of Bonn, 1964); W. Pass, *J. R. und seine lateinischen Motetten* (diss., Univ. of Vienna, 1967); idem, *Thematischer Katalog sämtlicher Werke J. R.s,* Tabulae Musicae Austriacae, V (1969); idem, "J. R.s 'Mariale' und die katholische Reform in Tirol," *Festschrift Walter Senn* (Munich and Salzburg, 1975).

Regt, Hendrik de, Dutch composer; b. Rotterdam, July 5, 1950. He studied composition with Otto Ketting in The Hague (1968–72).

WORKS: *Canzoni e Scherzi* for Soprano, Flute, and Harp (1972); *Proteus,* music for Flute, Viola, and Harp (1974); *Metamorfosen* for Oboe and English Horn (1974); *Silenus en Bacchanten* for Flute, Oboe, and Guitar (1974); *Pastorale* for Flute and Oboe (1974–75); *Circe* for Clarinet, Violin, and Piano (1975); *4 pezzi* for Clarinet (1978); *Poème* for Flute, Violin, and Viola (1979); *Partita* for Solo Violin (1979); *Esprit errant* for Baritone and Piano (1981); choruses; about 30 works, each entitled *Musica,* written for different instrumental combinations: for Wind Quintet (1969); Oboe, Cello, Harp, and Percussion (1970); 4 Saxophones (1971); Flute, Percussion, and Narrator (1970–72); Flute, Viola, Cello, Guitar, and Percussion (1972); 2 Trumpets, Horn, and Trombone (1971–72); Flute, Guitar, and Percussion (1972); 4 Clarinets (1972–73); 4 Horns (1974); Solo Violin (1974); Flute, Violin, Viola, and Cello (1974); Flute and Viola (1975); etc.

Rehfuss, Heinz (Julius), German-born Swiss bass-baritone; b. Frankfurt am Main, May 25, 1917; d. Buffalo, June 27, 1988. He studied with his father, Carl Rehfuss (1885–1946), a singer and teacher, and with his mother, Florentine Rehfuss-Peichert, a contralto. The family moved to Neuchâtel, Switzerland, and Rehfuss became a Swiss citizen. He made his professional debut in opera at Biel-Solothurn in 1938; then sang with the Lucerne Stadttheater (1938–39) and at the Zürich Opera (1940–52). He subsequently was active mainly in Europe and in America; became a naturalized American citizen; taught voice at the Montreal Cons. in 1961; in 1965 was on the faculty of the State Univ. of N.Y. at Buffalo; in 1970 was a visiting prof. at the Eastman School of Music in Rochester, N.Y. He also toured in Asia, giving vocal recitals in India and Indonesia. He was successful mainly in dramatic roles, such as Don Giovanni and Boris Godunov.

Rehm, Wolfgang, German musicologist; b. Munich, Sept. 3, 1929. He studied with Gurlitt and Zenck at the Univ. of Freiburg im Breisgau (Ph.D., 1952, with the diss. *Das Chansonwerk von Gilles Binchois*); also studied theory and piano at the Hochschule für Musik in Freiburg. In 1954 he joined the publishing firm of Bärenreiter in Kassel, eventually becoming chief ed.; held that position until 1982. In 1960 he was named co-ed. (with Wolfgang Plath) of the Neue Mozart-Ausgabe.

Reich, Steve (Stephen Michael), American composer; b. N.Y., Oct. 3, 1936. He studied philosophy at Cornell Univ. (B.A., 1957), where he became fascinated with the irrationally powerful theories of Ludwig Wittgenstein (a brother of the amputated pianist Paul Wittgenstein), who enunciated the famous tautological formula "Whereof one cannot speak thereof one must be silent." Reich in his music confuted this dictum by speaking loudly of tonalities and modalities which had remained in limbo for a millennium. He had a normal childhood; took piano lessons and also studied drumming with Roland Koloff, timpanist of the N.Y. Phil.; synchronously, he became infatuated with jazz and Bach by way of Stravinsky's stylizations. In N.Y. he took private composition lessons with Hall Overton and earned his living by driving a taxicab. From 1958 to 1961 he took courses with William Bergsma and Vincent Persichetti at the Juilliard School of Music; later went to California, where he entered Mills College in Oakland in the classes of Darius Milhaud and Luciano Berio (M.A., 1963); during this period he became interested in electronic composition and African music. He launched his career as a composer with scores for the underground films *The Plastic Haircut* and *Oh Dem Watermelons* in 1963, utilizing tape sounds. His subsequent works for tape included *It's Gonna Rain* (1965) and *Come Out* (1966). He returned to N.Y. and in 1966 organized his own ensemble, Steve Reich and Musicians, which began as a trio with Arthur Murphy and Jon Gibson and eventually expanded into a duo-de-viginti multitude. With his work *4 Organs* for 4 Electric Organs and Maracas (1970), he first made an impact outside his small group of devotees. In the summer of 1970 Reich traveled to Accra, Ghana, where he practiced under the tutelage of indigenous drummers; this experience bore fruit with the composition *Drumming* (1971), which became quite popular. In 1973 he studied the Balinese gamelan with a native teacher at the American Soc. for Eastern Arts Summer Program at the Univ. of Washington in Seattle. Becoming conscious of his ethnic heredity, he went to Jerusalem in 1976 to study the traditional forms of Hebrew cantillation. In 1974 he received grants from the NEA and from the N.Y. State Council on the Arts; was also invited to Berlin as an artist-in-residence. He subsequently received grants from the Martha Baird Rockefeller Foundation (1975, 1979, 1980, and 1981) and a 2nd grant from the NEA (1976). In 1978 he was awarded a Guggenheim fellowship. He publ. a book, *Writings about Music* (N.Y., 1974; French tr., Paris, 1981, as *Écrits et entretiens sur la musique*).

Slowly but surely Reich rose to fame; his group was invited to perform at the Holland Festival and at the radio stations of Frankfurt and Stuttgart. His increasing success led to a sold-out house when he presented a concert of his works at N.Y.'s Carnegie Hall on Feb. 19, 1980. In 1986 he took his ensemble on a world tour. His music was astoundingly audacious; rather than continue in the wake of obsolescent modernism, inexorably increasing in complexity, he deliberately reduced his harmonic and contrapuntal vocabulary and defiantly explored the fascinating potentialities of repetitive patterns. This kind of technique has been variously described as minimalist (for it was derived from a minimum of chordal combinations), phase music (because it shifted from one chord to another, a note at a time), modular (because it was built on symmetric modules), and pulse music (because it derived from a series of measured rhythmic units). Another definition is simply "process," suggesting tonal progressions in flux. Etiologically, this type of composition is hypnopompic, for it creates a subliminal state between a strong dream and a sudden reality. Analytically, it represents a paradox, for it is uncompromisingly modern in its use of exotic instruments, infinitely challenging in its obdurate continuity, and yet elemental in the deliberate limitations of its resources. This system of composition is akin to serialism in its application of recurrent melodic progressions and periodic silences. Despite his apparent disregard for musical convention, or indeed for public taste, Reich likes to trace his musical ancestry to the sweetly vacuous homophony of the Ars Antiqua, with particular reference to the opaque works of the great master of the Notre Dame School of Paris, Perotin. He deliberately avoids fanciful titles in his works, preferring to define them by names of instruments, or numbers of musical parts. The extraordinary aspect of Reich's career is that by rejecting the conventional way of music-making, and by thus infuriating the academics, he finds a direct avenue to the hearts, minds, and ears of the young.

Works: *Pitch Charts* for Any Instruments (1963); *Plastic Haircut,* film score for Tape (1963); *Music for 3 or More Pianos or Piano and Tape* (1964); *It's Gonna Rain* for Tape (1965); *Oh Dem Watermelons,* film score for 5 Voices and Piano (1965); *Come Out* for Tape (1966); *Melodica* for Tape (1966); *Reed Phase* for Soprano Saxophone and Tape (1966; N.Y., March 17, 1967); *My Name Is* for 3 or More Tape Recorders, Performers, and Audience (1967); *Piano Phase* for 2 Pianos and 2 Marimbas (1967); *Slow Motion Sound* for Tape (1967); *Violin Phase* for Violin and Tape or 4 Violins (1967); *Pendulum Music* for 3 or More Microphones, Amplifiers, and Loudspeakers (1968; N.Y., May 27, 1969); *4 Log Drums* for Phase Shifting Pulse Gate and 4 Log Drums (N.Y., May 27, 1969); *Pulse Music* for Phase Shifting Pulse Gate (N.Y., May 27, 1969); *4 Organs* for 4 Electric Organs and Maracas (1970); *Drumming* for 2 Women's Voices, Piccolo, 4 Pairs of Tuned Bongo Drums, 3 Marimbas, and 3 Glockenspiels (N.Y., Dec. 1971); *Clapping Music* for 2 Performers (1972); *Music for Mallet Instruments, Voices, and Organ* for 3 Women's Voices, 3 Marimbas, 3 Glockenspiels, Vibraphone, and Electric Organ (N.Y., May 12, 1973); *Music for Pieces of Wood* for 5 pairs of Tuned Claves (N.Y., May 12, 1973); *6 Pianos* (N.Y., May 12, 1973); *Music for 18 Musicians* for 4 Women's Voices, 2 Clarinets, 3 Marimbas, 2 Xylophones, Vibraphone, 4 Pianos, Maracas, Violin, and Cello (N.Y., April 24, 1976); *Music for a Large Ensemble* (1978; N.Y., Feb. 19, 1980); Octet for 2 Flutes, 2 Clarinets, 2 Bass Clarinets, 2 Pianos, 2 Violins, Viola, and Cello (Frankfurt am Main radio broadcast, June 21, 1979; rev. in collaboration with Robert Wilson as *8 Lines* for Chamber Orch., N.Y., Dec. 10, 1983); *Variations for Winds, Strings and Keyboards* (1979; N.Y., Feb. 19, 1980; orch. version, San Francisco, May 17, 1980); *My Name Is* for Tape (1980); *Tehillim* (Psalms) for 3 Sopranos, Alto, and Chamber Orch. (Houston, Nov. 21, 1981; orch. version, N.Y., Sept. 16, 1982); *Vermont Counterpoint* for Piccolo, Flute, Alto Flute, and Tape (1 performer, 10 parts on tape, N.Y., Oct. 1, 1982; also for 11 Flutes, N.Y., Dec. 10, 1983); *The Desert Music* for Small Amplified Chorus and Large Orch. (1983; Cologne, March 17, 1984); Sextet for 4 Percussion and 2 Pianos (1984–85); *Impact,* dance music (N.Y., Oct. 31, 1985); *New York Counterpoint* for Clarinet, Bass Clarinet, and Tape or Clarinets and Bass Clarinets (1985; N.Y., Jan. 20, 1986); *3 Movements* for Orch. (1985–86; St. Louis, April 3, 1986); *The 4 Sections* for Orch. (San Francisco, Oct. 7, 1987); *Electric Counterpoint* for Guitar and Tape (N.Y., Nov. 5, 1987); *Different Trains* for String Quartet and Tape (1988).

Bibl.: *Current Biography* (April 1986); M. Dery, "The R. Stuff," *Ovation* (May 1987).

Reich, Willi, Austrian-born Swiss music critic and musicologist; b. Vienna, May 27, 1898; d. Zürich, May 1, 1980. He studied at the Univ. of Vienna, receiving his Ph.D. (1934) with the dissertation *Padre Martini als Theoretiker und Lehrer;* also studied privately with Berg and Webern; ed. a modern music magazine, *23—Eine Wiener Musikzeitschrift* (1932–37). In 1938 he settled in Switzerland; in 1948, became music critic of the *Neue Zürcher Zeitung;* in 1961, took Swiss citizenship. In addition to editing numerous documentary vols., he publ. the studies *Wozzeck: A Guide to the Words and Music of Alban Berg* (N.Y., 1932), *Alban Berg* (Vienna, 1937), *Romantiker der Musik* (Basel, 1947), *Alexander Tscherepnin* (Bonn, 1961; 2nd ed., 1970), *Alban Berg: Leben und Werk* (Zürich, 1963; Eng. tr., 1965), and *Arnold Schönberg oder der konservative Revolutionär* (Vienna, 1968; Eng. tr., 1971, as *Schoenberg: A Critical Biography*).

Reicha (Rejcha), Antoine (-Joseph) (Antonín or **Anton),** distinguished Czech-born French music theorist, pedagogue, and composer; b. Prague, Feb. 26, 1770; d. Paris, May 28, 1836. His father died when he was only 10 months old, and he eventually was adopted by his uncle, who gave him lessons in violin and piano; he also studied flute. The family settled in Bonn in 1785; Antoine played violin and flute there; his fellow musicians included Beethoven and C.G. Neefe. Having acquired a knowledge of composition, he conducted his 1st Sym. in Bonn in 1787. After attending the Univ. there, in the wake of the French invasion, in 1794, he went to Hamburg; he was active there as a teacher of piano, harmony, and composition; also devoted part of his time to composing. In 1799 he went to Paris to establish himself as a composer for the theater, but found success only with 2 of his syms., an overture, and some scènes italiennes. In 1801 he went to Vienna; he had made the acquaintance of Haydn in Bonn, and the 2 now became good friends; he received instruction from Albrechtsberger and Salieri. His friendship with Beethoven grew apace, and Prince Lobkowitz commissioned Reicha to write the opera *L'Ouragan* (c.1801); the Empress Marie Therese then was moved to commission him to compose the opera *Argina, regina di Granata,* which was given at the Imperial Palace in a private performance with the Empress taking a prominent role (c.1802). In 1808 he settled in Paris; although his operas *Cagliostro* (Nov. 27, 1810), *Natalie* (July 13, 1816), and *Sapho* (Dec. 16, 1822) failed to make an impression, Reicha gained prominence as a music theorist and teacher; in 1818 he was appointed prof. of counterpoint and fugue at the Paris Cons. Among those who studied with him either privately or at the Cons. were Baillot, Habeneck, Rode, Berlioz, Liszt, and Franck. His *Cours de composition musicale, ou Traité complet et raisonné d'harmonie pratique* (Paris, c.1817) was adopted by the Cons.; his most significant publication was the *Traité de haute composition musicale* (Paris, 1824–26). In 1829 he became a naturalized French citizen. He was made Chevalier of the Légion d'Honneur in 1831. In 1835 he succeeded Boieldieu as a member of the Académie. He dictated his autobiography, *Notes sur Antoine Reicha,* to his student Henri Blanchard about 1824. As a composer, he remains best known for his chamber music. He also wrote a great deal of orch. music, including at least 17 syms. and numerous concertos.

Writings: *Practische Beispiele: Ein Beitrag zur Geistescultur des Tonsetzers . . . begleitet mit philosophisch-practischen Anmerkungen* (1803); *Sur la musique comme art purement sentimental* (c.1813); *Traité de mélodie* (Paris, 1814; ed. by C. Czerny as *Vollständiges Lehrbuch der musikalischen Composition,* II, Vienna, 1832); *Petit traité d'harmonie pratique à 2 parties,* op. 84 (Paris, c.1814); *Cours de composition musicale,* *ou Traité complet et raisonné d'harmonie pratique* (Paris, c.1817; ed. by C. Czerny as *Vollständiges Lehrbuch*, I, Vienna, 1832); *Traité de haute composition musicale* (Paris, 1824–26; ed. by C. Czerny as *Vollständiges Lehrbuch*, III–IV, Vienna, 1832); *À messieurs les membres de l'Académie des beaux-arts à l'Institut de France* (Paris, 1831); *Art du compositeur dramatique, ou Cours complet de composition vocale* (Paris, 1833; ed. by C. Czerny as *Die Kunst der dramatischen Composition*, Vienna, 1833).

BIBL.: H***** (H. Berlioz), "A. R.," *Journal des Débats* (July 3, 1836); idem, "Biographie d'A. R.," *Revue et Gazette Musicale de Paris*, V/28 (1838); E. Bücken, *Anton R.: Sein Leben und seine Kompositionen* (Munich, 1912); idem, "Beethoven und Anton R.," *Die Musik*, XII (1912–13); idem, "Anton R. als Theoretiker," *Zeitschrift für Musikwissenschaft*, II (1919–20); M. Emmanuel, *Antonin R.* (Paris, 1937); K. Blum, "Bemerkungen Anton R.s zur Aufführungspraxis der Oper," *Die Musikforschung*, VII (1954); special issue of *Hudební Věda*, VII (1970); J. Vysloužil, "Antonin Josef R.," *Opus Musicum CS*, III (1971); O. Šotolová, *Antonin Rejcha* (Prague, 1977; with thematic catalog).

Reichardt, Johann Friedrich, prominent German composer and writer on music, father of **Luise Reichardt;** b. Königsberg, Nov. 25, 1752; d. Giebichenstein, near Halle, June 27, 1814. He received his initial musical training from his father, the lutenist Johann Reichardt (c.1720–80), becoming proficient as a violinist, lutenist, and singer; also studied with J.F. Hartknoch, C.G. Richter, F.A. Veichtner, and others. After attending the Univ. of Königsberg (1768–71), he traveled widely; received some instruction from Kirnberger in Berlin and from Homilius in Dresden; also briefly attended the Univ. of Leipzig. He was active as a government official for a year, and then was appointed Kapellmeister of the Royal Opera in Berlin by Frederick the Great in 1775. In 1783 he founded the Concert Spirituel in Berlin, where he brought out several of his own compositions; traveled widely while retaining his royal appointment. After the death of Frederick the Great in 1786, Reichardt's star rose under the new king, Friedrich Wilhelm II. In collaboration with Goethe, he produced the successful singspiel *Claudine von Villa Bella* (Berlin, July 29, 1789). Dissension at the Royal Opera, however, led the King to give Reichardt a leave of absence for 3 years, with full pay, in 1790. He again traveled widely; among the cities he visited was Paris (1792). His sympathies for the French Revolution led his Berlin enemies to persuade Friedrich Wilhelm to dismiss him without pay in 1794. He then settled at his estate in Giebichenstein. In 1796 Friedrich Wilhelm pardoned him and named him director of the Halle salt mines. With the French invasion of 1806, he fled with his family to north Germany; upon his return in 1807, he found that his estate had been destroyed; shortly afterward, Jérôme Bonaparte called him to Kassel as directeur général des théâtres et de son orchestre, but he renewed his travels in 1808. In 1809 he returned to Giebichenstein, where he eked out a living by writing and composing. His most significant contribution as a composer rests upon his more than 1,500 songs. He is generally regarded as the finest lieder composer before Schubert. His stage works are important for their movement away from the opera seria conventions. As a writer on music, he was a pioneering figure in music journalism. His 1st wife was **Juliane** (née **Benda**) **Reichardt** (b. Potsdam, May 4, 1752; d. there, May 11, 1783); the daughter of Franz Benda she married Reichardt in 1776; a fine pianist, she also publ. a number of songs.

BIBL.: H. Schletter, *J.F. R.: Sein Leben und seine musikalische Tätigkeit* (Augsburg, 1865); C. Lange, *J.F. R.* (Halle, 1902); M. Faller, *J.F. R. und die Anfänge der musikalischen Journalistik* (Kassel, 1929); P. Sieber, *J.F. R. als Musikästhetiker: Seine Anschauungen über Wesen und Wirkung der Musik* (Strasbourg, 1930); F. Flössner, *Beiträge zur R.-Forschung* (Frankfurt, 1933); E. Neuss, *Das Giebichensteiner Dichterparadies: J.F. R. und die Herberge der Romantik* (Halle, 1949); W. Salmen, *J.F. R.* (Freiburg, 1963); N. Reich, *A Translation and Commentary of Selected Writings of J.F. R.* (diss., N.Y. Univ., 1973).

Reichardt, Luise, German singing teacher and composer, daughter of **Johann Friedrich Reichardt;** b. Berlin, April 11, 1779; d. Hamburg, Nov. 17, 1826. She settled about 1813 in Hamburg, where she was active as a singing teacher; also conducted a women's chorus which became the core of the Hamburg Singverein in 1819. She wrote over 90 choruses and songs, both sacred and secular. Selections of her works were publ. by G. Rheinhardt (Munich, 1922) and N. Reich (N.Y., 1978).

BIBL.: M. Brandt, *Leben der L. R.* (Karlsruhe, 1858; 2nd ed., 1865).

Reichel, Friedrich, German composer; b. Oberoderwitz, Jan. 27, 1833; d. Dresden, Dec. 29, 1889. He studied with Wieck and Rietz in Dresden. Chief among his 32 publ. works is a *Frühlingssymphonie;* he also wrote an operetta, *Die geängsteten Diplomaten;* part-songs for men's voices; and some motets.

Reicher-Kindermann, Hedwig, esteemed German soprano; b. Munich, July 15, 1853; d. Trieste, June 2, 1883. She was a daughter of the baritone **August Kindermann** (b. Potsdam, Feb. 6, 1817; d. Munich, March 6, 1891); began her career as a contralto but later sang soprano. She first sang in the chorus of the Munich Court Opera (1870–71); made her debut at Karlsruhe in 1871; appeared in Berlin (1874) and Munich (1875); sang at the opening of Bayreuth in 1876; then sang in Hamburg (1877) and Vienna (1878). The impresario Neumann engaged her for his Wagner troupe in Leipzig from 1880, and she successfully performed the roles of Fricka, Isolde, Brünnhilde, Waltraute, and Erda. She was married to the playwright Emanuel Reicher, and adopted the hyphenated name Reicher-Kindermann in her professional activities. Her early death was lamented.

BIBL.: A. Neumann, *Erinnerungen an Richard Wagner* (Leipzig, 1907; in Eng., N.Y., 1908).

Reichmann, Theodor, noted German baritone; b. Rostock, March 15, 1849; d. Marbach, May 22, 1903. He studied in Berlin and Prague; after further training with Lamperti in Milan, he made his operatic debut in Magdeburg (1869). Following appearances in Rotterdam, Strasbourg, and Hamburg, he sang in 1874 in Munich, where he became a member of the Court Opera in 1875; also sang at the Bayreuth Festivals (1882–1902), where he was esteemed for his portrayal of Amfortas, which he created. In 1882 he made his London debut as Wotan; his Covent Garden debut followed as Telramund on June 11, 1884. He was a member of the Vienna Court Opera (1883–89); made his Metropolitan Opera debut in N.Y. as the Dutchman on Nov. 27, 1889, and remained on its roster until 1893; then rejoined the Vienna Court Opera, singing there until his death. He gave his farewell performance in Munich as Hans Sachs on Aug. 11, 1902.

Reichwein, Leopold, Austrian conductor; b. Breslau, May 16, 1878; d. (suicide) Vienna, April 8, 1945. He was a theater conductor in Breslau, Mannheim, and Karlsruhe; then was on the staff of the Vienna Opera (1913–21), music director of the Gesellschaft der Musikfreunde in Vienna (1921–26), and music director in Bochum (1926–38); he returned to Vienna in 1938; conducted at the State Opera and taught conducting at the Academy of Music. He was also a composer; wrote the operas *Vasantasena* (Breslau, 1903) and *Die Liebenden von Kandahar* (Breslau, 1907); incidental music to Goethe's *Faust;* songs.

Reid, Cornelius L., American voice teacher and music scholar; b. Jersey City, N.J., Feb. 7, 1911. He was a member of the Trinity Church Choir in N.Y. (1920–25), and studied with Frederick Kurzweil and Ruth Kirch-Arndt at the N.Y. College of Music (1945–48); studied voice privately with George Mead (1929), Marie Wagner (1929–30), and Douglas Stanley (1934–37), and had coaching from Frieda Hempel (1930) and Povla Frijsh (1932–40). He taught voice privately in N.Y. (from 1934); also taught at Marymount College (1940–

41) and at the General Theological Seminary there (1946–49); conducted various performing groups (1939–45) and gave master classes and lectures throughout the U.S. Reid authored 3 books defining his Functional Vocal training: *Bel Canto: Principles and Practices* (Boston, 1950), *The Free Voice* (N.Y., 1965), and *Voice: Psyche and Soma* (N.Y., 1975); also compiled the important *Dictionary of Vocal Terminology* (N.Y., 1984).

Reid (real name, **Robertson**), **General John,** Scottish amateur flutist and composer, and music patron; b. Straloch, Perthshire, Feb. 13, 1721; d. London, Feb. 6, 1807. He studied law at the Univ. of Edinburgh; entered the army in 1745, attaining the rank of general. He was a talented flutist; wrote some 20 marches, 9 menuets, and several flute sonatas. He left £52,000 to found a chair of music at the Univ. of Edinburgh, also providing that an annual concert of his own compositions should be given. The chair was founded in 1839; among its occupants were Herbert Oakeley (1865–91) and Donald Tovey (1914–40).

Reif, Paul, Czech-American composer; b. Prague, March 23, 1910; d. N.Y., July 7, 1978. He played violin as a child; studied composition in Vienna with Richard Stöhr and Franz Schmidt, and conducting with Franz Schalk and Bruno Walter; also had lessons with Richard Strauss. In 1941 he emigrated to the U.S., and in 1942 joined the U.S. Intelligence Corps; while with the U.S. Army in North Africa he set to music the soldiers' song *Dirty Gertie from Bizerte*, which was introduced by Josephine Baker in Algiers in April 1943. Upon his discharge in 1945 he was awarded the Croix de Guerre and the Purple Heart. Returning to the U.S., he was active as an arranger in Hollywood; wrote a number of lightweight pieces (*Petticoat Waltz, Dream Concerto*, etc.); also several song cycles, among them *5 Finger Exercises*, to poems by T.S. Eliot; *Reverence for Life* and *Monsieur le Pélican* as a tribute to Albert Schweitzer; etc.

WORKS: *Triple City* for Chorus and Brass Ensemble (N.Y., April 16, 1963); *Requiem to War* for Mixed Chorus and Percussion (N.Y., May 20, 1963); *Birches*, to Robert Frost's words, for Voice and Orch. (N.Y., Feb. 2, 1965); *Letter from a Birmingham Jail* for Mixed Chorus and Piano, to words by Martin Luther King, Jr. (Washington, D.C., March 2, 1965); *Philidor's Defense* for Chamber Orch., inspired by the famous Philidor chess opening: 1. P-K4, P-K4; 2. N-KB3, P-Q3 (N.Y., April 10, 1965); operas: *Mad Hamlet* (1965) and *Portrait in Brownstone* (N.Y., May 15, 1966); *Pentagram* for Piano (1969); *The Artist* (N.Y., April 17, 1972); *The Curse of Mauvais-Air* (N.Y., May 9, 1974); *5 Divertimenti* for 4 Strings (1969); *Episodes* for String Orch. (1972); Quintet for Clarinet, Viola, Piano, Percussion, and Folksinger (1974); *Duo for 3* for Clarinet, Cello, and Mezzo-soprano (1974); *America 1776–1876–1976* for Orch., Solo Guitar, Banjo, Electric Guitar, and Vocal Quartet (N.Y., Jan. 24, 1976).

Reimann, Aribert, German pianist and composer; b. Berlin, March 4, 1936. He studied piano with Otto Rausch and composition with Boris Blacher and Ernst Pepping in Berlin (1955–60); also received training in musicology at the Univ. of Vienna (1958); later received the Rome Prize and studied at the Villa Massimo in Rome (1963). In 1957 he began his career as a pianist; became well known later as an accompanist, appearing frequently in recitals with Fischer-Dieskau. From 1974 to 1983 he was a prof. at the Hamburg Hochschule für Musik; in 1983 he became a prof. at the Berlin Hochschule für Künste. In 1971 he was made a member of the Berlin Akademie der Künste, in 1976 of the Munich Akademie der Schönen Künste, and in 1985 of the Hamburg Freien Akademie der Künste. His early compositions followed the path of the 2nd Viennese School, but in 1967 he discarded serialism.

WORKS: STAGE: OPERAS: *Ein Traumspiel,* after Strindberg (1964; Kiel, June 20, 1965); *Melusine* (1970; Schwetzingen, April 29, 1971); *Lear,* after Shakespeare (1976–78; Munich, July 9, 1978); *Die Gespenstersonate,* after Strindberg (1983; Berlin, Sept. 25, 1984); *Troades,* after Euripides (1985; Munich, July 7, 1986). **BALLETS:** *Stoffreste* (1957; rev. as *Die Vogelscheu-*

chen, Berlin, Oct. 7, 1970); *Chacun sa Chimère* (1981; Düsseldorf, April 17, 1982). **ORCH.:** Violin Concerto (1959); 2 piano concertos: No. 1 (1961; Berlin, Oct. 26, 1962); No. 2 (1972; Nuremberg, Jan. 12, 1973); Sym., after the opera *Ein Traumspiel* (1964; Darmstadt, Sept. 12, 1976); *Rondes* for String Orch. (1967; Cologne, Jan. 25, 1968); *Loqui* (Saarbrücken, Dec. 5, 1969); *Variationen* (1975; Zürich, Jan. 13, 1976); Concerto for Violin, Cello, and Orch. (1986). **VOCAL:** *Ein Totentanz* for Baritone and Chamber Orch. (1960; Berlin, Sept. 29, 1961); *Hölderlin-Fragmente* for Soprano and Orch. (1963; Mannheim, Jan. 25, 1965); *Epitaph* for Tenor and 7 Instruments (1965; Heidelberg, June 2, 1967); *Verrà la morte,* cantata for Soloists, 2 Choirs, and Orch. (1966; Berlin, Feb. 28, 1967); *Inane* for Soprano and Orch. (1968; Berlin, Jan. 8, 1969); *Zyklus* for Baritone and Orch. (Nuremberg, April 15, 1971); *Lines* for Soprano and Chamber Orch. (Schwetzingen, May 14, 1973); *Wolkenloses Christfest,* Requiem for Baritone, Cello, and Orch. (Landua, June 2, 1974); *Fragmente aus Lear* for Baritone and Orch. (Zürich, April 29, 1980); *Unrevealed* for Baritone and String Quartet (1980; Berlin, Sept. 3, 1981); *Drei Lieder* for Soprano and Orch., after Poe (1980–82; Berlin, Sept. 5, 1982); *Requiem* for Soloists, Chorus, and Orch. (1980–82; Kiel, June 26, 1982); song cycles and solo songs with piano. **CHAMBER:** Piano Sonata (1958); *Canzoni e Ricercari* for Flute, Viola, and Cello (Berlin, Sept. 30, 1961); Sonata for Cello and Piano (1963; Berlin, Jan. 11, 1965); *Nocturnos* for Cello and Harp (1965); *Reflexionen* for 7 Instruments (Berlin, May 15, 1966); *Invenzioni* for 12 Players (London, June 16, 1979); *Variationen* for Piano (1979; Berlin, Nov. 29, 1982); *Solo* for Cello (1981).

Reimann, Heinrich, German organist, teacher, writer on music, and composer, son of **Ignaz Reimann;** b. Rengensdorf, Silesia, March 14, 1850; d. Berlin, May 24, 1906. He studied music with his father; conducted singing societies in Silesia; in 1887 went to Berlin, where he was engaged as a librarian, organ teacher, and music critic. He publ. *Johannes Brahms* (Berlin, 1898; 6th ed., 1922, by B. Schrader), *Aus Hans von Bülows Lehrzeit* (posthumous; Berlin, 1909), and *Johann Sebastian Bach* (Berlin, 1912; completed by Schrader); also brought out an informative memoir, *Musikalische Rückblicke* (2 vols., Berlin, 1900); publ. the collection *Internationales Volksliederbuch* (3 vols., Berlin, 1893).

Reimann, Ignaz, German composer, father of **Heinrich Reimann;** b. Albendorf, Silesia, Dec. 27, 1820; d. Rengensdorf, June 17, 1885. He publ. 18 masses, 4 Requiems, 3 Te Deums, 48 offertories, 40 graduals; many other works, including instrumental works, in MS.

Reimers, Paul, German-American tenor; b. Lunden, Schleswig-Holstein (of Danish parents), March 14, 1878; d. N.Y., April 14, 1942. He made his stage debut as Max in *Der Freischütz* in Hamburg (1902); after further training with George Henschel in Scotland, Raimund von Zur Mühlen in London, and Jean Criticos in Paris, he devoted himself to a concert career; sang widely in Europe. In 1913 he went to America; gave programs of German lieder, and also performed songs of the modern French school.

Reina, Domenico, Italian tenor; b. Lugano, 1797; d. there, July 29, 1843. He studied with Boile in Milan; made his debut in 1829 at La Scala in Milan as Ilio in Rossini's *Zelmira;* while there, he created Arturo in Bellini's *La Straniera;* also Tamas in Donizetti's *Gemma di Vergy.* He was greatly admired for his performances of the lyrico-dramatic tenor parts in the operas of Rossini, Bellini, and Donizetti.

Reinach, (Salomon) Théodore, French musicologist; b. St. Germain-en-Laye, July 3, 1860; d. Paris, Oct. 28, 1928. He studied jurisprudence and philology in Paris; was editor in chief of the *Revue des Études Grecques* (1888–1907). He publ. *La Musique grecque* (Paris, 1926); brought out Plutarch's treatise on music (with H. Weil; Paris, 1900) and *Le Second Hymne delphique à Apollon* (with L. Boëllmann; Paris, 1897).

Reinagle, Alexander, prominent English-born American pianist, teacher, impresario, and composer; b. Portsmouth (of

Austrian parents) (baptized), April 23, 1756; d. Baltimore, Sept. 21, 1809. He studied in Edinburgh with Rayner Taylor, and in London for a time; also visited Lisbon and other continental cities. From his correspondence he appears to have been a close friend of C.P.E. Bach. He went to N.Y. early in 1786, settling in the same year in Philadelphia, where he taught, managed subscription concerts (also in N.Y.), and was active as a singer, pianist, conductor, and composer; in 1787, introduced 4-hand piano music to America; was associated, possibly as harpsichordist, with the Old American Co., and took part in its 1788–89 season in N.Y.; in 1790 he was engaged as music director of a stock company for the production of plays and comic operas, with Thomas Wignell as general director; also built the New Theatre, which opened on Feb. 2, 1793, with Reinagle acting as composer, singer, and director; also managed a company in Baltimore (from 1794).

WORKS: *A Collection of . . . Scots Tunes with Variations for Keyboard* (London, c.1782; 2nd ed., abridged, 1787, as *A Selection of the Most Favorite Scots Tunes with Variations*); 6 *Sonatas with Accompaniment for Violin* (London, c.1780); *Miscellaneous Quartets* (Philadelphia, 1791); *Concerto on the Improved Pianoforte with Additional Keys* (1794); *Preludes* (1794); accompaniments and incidental music to *The Sicilian Romance* (1795), *The Witches of the Rock*, pantomime (1796), and various English plays; *Masonic Overture* (1800); 4 piano sonatas (in Library of Congress, Washington, D.C.; Sonata No. 2 publ. in abridged form by J. Howard in *A Program of Early American Piano-Music*, N.Y., 1931; see also S. Duer, *An Annotated Edition of 4 Sonatas by Alexander Reinagle* [Peabody Cons., 1976]); *Collection of Favorite Songs*; music to Milton's *Paradise Lost* (incomplete).

BIBL.: J. Parker, "Musical Reminiscences," *Euterpeiad* (Jan. 19, 1822); O. Sonneck, *Early Concert-life in America* (Leipzig, 1907); idem, *Early Opera in America* (N.Y., 1915); E. Krohn, "A. R. as Sonatist," *Musical Quarterly* (Jan. 1932); C. Horton, *Serious Art and Concert Music for Piano in America in the 100 Years from A. R. to Edward MacDowell* (diss., Univ. of North Carolina, 1965); K. Mahan, "Hopkinson and R.: Patriot-Musicians of Washington's Time," *Music Educators Journal,* LXII/8 (1976); A. Krauss, "A. R., His Family Background and Early Professional Career," *American Music* (Winter 1986).

Reinecke, Carl (Heinrich Carsten), renowned German pianist, composer, conductor, and pedagogue; b. Altona, June 23, 1824; d. Leipzig, March 10, 1910. He was a pupil of his father, a music teacher. His 1st concert tour was to Denmark and Sweden in 1843; he then went to Leipzig, learned much through meetings with Mendelssohn and Schumann, made a 2nd tour through North Germany, and was from 1846 to 1848 court pianist to Christian VIII at Copenhagen. Then, after spending some years in Paris, he became a teacher at the Cologne Cons. in 1851; was music director at Barmen (1854–59) and Breslau (1859–60), and (1860–95) conductor of the Gewandhaus Concerts in Leipzig. At the same time he was a prof. of piano and composition at the Leipzig Cons., where he taught from 1860; was its director from 1897 until his retirement in 1902. An eminent pianist, he excelled as an interpreter of Mozart, made concert tours almost yearly, and was enthusiastically welcomed in England, the Netherlands, Scandinavia, Switzerland, and throughout Germany; among his pupils were Grieg, Riemann, Sinding, Arthur Sullivan, Karl Muck, and Cosima Wagner. As a conductor, composer, and teacher of composition, Reinecke was the leader in Leipzig for over 35 years; his numerous works, in every genre, are classic in form and of refined workmanship.

WORKS: THEATER: *König Manfred* (opera; Wiesbaden, July 26, 1867); *Ein Abenteuer Händels oder Die Macht des Liedes* (singspiel; Schwerin, 1874); *Auf hohen Befehl* (comic opera; Hamburg, Oct. 1, 1886); *Der Gouverneur von Tours* (comic opera; Schwerin, 1891); also 5 musical fairy tales for Soloists, Chorus, and Piano: *Nussknacker und Mausekönig, Schneewittchen, Dornröschen, Aschenbrödel,* and *Die wilden Schwäne;* oratorio, *Belsazar;* several choral works with Orch.; numerous

choruses for Mixed Voices. **ORCH.:** 3 syms., overtures, smaller works; 4 piano concertos; Violin Concerto; Cello Concerto; Harp Concerto; Flute Concerto. **CHAMBER:** Octet for Wind Instruments; Sextet for Wind Instruments; 5 string quartets; Piano Quintet; 2 piano quartets; 6 piano trios; Trio for Piano, Oboe, and Horn; Trio for Piano, Clarinet, and Horn; Violin Sonata; 3 violin sonatinas; 3 cello sonatas; Sonata for Flute and Piano; numerous character pieces for piano; Sonata for Piano, Left Hand; suite, *Biblische Bilder;* 3 sonatas for 2 Pianos; altogether about 300 opus numbers. He wrote cadenzas to 42 movements of piano concertos by Bach, Mozart, Beethoven, and Weber.

WRITINGS: *Was sollen wir spielen?* (1886); *Zur Wiederbelebung der Mozartschen Clavier-Concerto* (1891); *Die Beethovenschen Clavier-Sonaten: Briefe an eine Freundin* (1895; Eng. tr., 1898; 9th German ed., 1924); *Und manche liebe Schatten steigen auf: Gedenkblätter an berühmte Musiker* (1900; 2nd ed., 1910); *Meister der Tonkunst* (1903); *Aus dem Reich der Töne* (1907).

BIBL.: W. von Wasielewski, *C. R.: Ein Künstlerbild* (Leipzig, 1892); E. Segnitz, *C. R.* (Leipzig, 1900); M. Steinitzer, *Das Leipziger Gewandhaus im neuen Heim unter C. R.* (Leipzig, 1924); N. Topusov, *C. R.: Beiträge zu seinem Leben und seiner Symphonik* (Sofia, 1943).

Reiner, Fritz, eminent Hungarian-born American conductor; b. Budapest, Dec. 19, 1888; d. N.Y., Nov. 15, 1963. He studied piano with Thomán and composition with Koessler at the Royal Academy of Music in Budapest; concurrently took courses in jurisprudence. He was conductor of the Volksoper in Budapest (1911–14) and of the Court (later State) Opera in Dresden (1914–21); also conducted in Hamburg, Berlin, Vienna, Rome, and Barcelona. In 1922 he was engaged as music director of the Cincinnati Sym. Orch.; was naturalized as a U.S. citizen in 1928. In 1931 he became a prof. of conducting at the Curtis Inst. of Music in Philadelphia; among his students were Leonard Bernstein and Lukas Foss. In 1936–37 he made guest appearances at London's Covent Garden; between 1935 and 1938, was guest conductor at the San Francisco Opera; from 1938 to 1948 he was music director of the Pittsburgh Sym. Orch.; then was a conductor at the Metropolitan Opera in N.Y. until 1953. He achieved the peak of his success as a conductor with the Chicago Sym. Orch., which he served as music director from 1953 to 1962, and which he brought up to the point of impeccably fine performance in both Classical and modern music. His striving for perfection created for him the reputation of a ruthless master of the orch.; he was given to explosions of temper, but musicians and critics agreed that it was because of his uncompromising drive toward the optimum of orch. playing that the Chicago Sym. Orch. achieved a very high rank among American symphonic organizations.

BIBL.: R. Potter, *F. R., Conductor, Teacher, Musical Innovator* (diss., Northwestern Univ., 1980).

Reiner, Karel, prominent Czech composer and pianist; b. Žatec, June 27, 1910; d. Prague, Oct. 17, 1979. He studied law at the German Univ. in Prague (Dr.Jur., 1933) and musicology at the Univ. of Prague; attended Suk's master classes (1931) and A. Hába's courses in microtonal music (1934–35) at the Prague Cons. He was associated with E. Burian's improvisational theater in Prague (1934–38). Unable to leave Central Europe when the Nazis invaded Czechoslovakia, he was detained at Terezín, and later sent to the dreaded concentration camps of Dachau and Auschwitz, but survived, and after liberation resumed his activities as a composer and pianist. His earliest works were atonal and athematic; in 1935–36 he wrote a *Suite* and a *Fantasy* for quarter-tone piano, and a set of 5 quarter-tone songs; after 1945 he wrote mostly traditional music; then returned to ultramodern techniques.

WORKS: 2 operas: *Pohádka o zakleté píseň* (Tale of an Enchanted Song; 1949) and *Schustermärchen* (The Cobbler's Tale or The Horrible Dragon, the Princess and the Cobbler), fairytale opera for Puppets, 5 Singers, and Chamber Ensemble (1972); ballet, *Jednota* (Unity; 1933); cantata, *Bylo jim tisíc let* (It Was a Thousand Years since Then; 1962); Piano Concerto

(1932); Violin Concerto (1937); *Concertante Suite* for Winds and Percussion (1947); *Divertimento* for Clarinet, Harp, Strings, and Percussion (1947); *3 Czech Dances* for Orch. (1949); *Spring Prelude* for Orch. (1950); *Motýli tady nežijí* (Butterflies Don't Live Here Anymore), 6 pictures for Orch., based on music to the film (1959–60; depicts the fate of Jewish children in the Terezín concentration camp); Sym. (1960); *Symphonic Overture* (1964); Concerto for Bass Clarinet, Strings, and Percussion (1966); *Concertante Suite* for Orch. (1967); Bassoon Concertino (1969); *Promluvy* (Utterances) for Chamber Orch. (1975); *Music* for Strings (1975); *Introduction and Allegro* (*Diptych* No. 2) for Orch. (1976); *Diptych* No. 1 for Orch. (1977); 3 Symphonic Movements (1978); 3 string quartets (1931, 1947, 1951); *7 Miniatures* for Wind Quintet (1931); *Dvanáct* (The 12), suite for Piano and Wind Quintet (1931); 2 nonets (Concerto, 1933; *Preambule*, 1974); *Sonata brevis* for Cello and Piano (1946); *4 Compositions* for Clarinet and Piano (1954); *3 Compositions* for Oboe and Piano (1955); *Elegie and Capriccio* for Cello and Piano (1957); Double-bass Sonata (1957); Violin Sonata (1959); *Small Suite* for 9 Wind Instruments (1960); *6 Bagatelles* for Trumpet and Piano (1962); *2 Compositions* for Oboe and Harp (1962); *4 Compositions* for Clarinet (1963); *6 Studies* for Flute and Piano (1964); *Trio* for Flute, Bass Clarinet, and Percussion (1964); Piano Trio (1965); *Suite* for Bassoon and Piano (1965); *Music* for 4 Clarinets (1965); *Črty* (Sketches) for Piano Quartet (1966–67); *Concert Studies* for Cymbalom (1967); *2 Compositions* for Saxophone and Piano (1967); *Concertante Sonata* for Percussion (1967); *Prolegomena* for String Quartet (1968); *4 Abbreviations* for Brass Quintet (1968); *Dua*, 5 compositions for 2 Flutes, 2 Oboes, 2 Clarinets, and 2 Trumpets, in any combination (1969); *Volné listy* (Loose Leaves) for Clarinet, Cello, and Piano (1969); *Formulas* for Trombone and Piano (1970); *Recordings* for Bassoon (1970); *Drawings* for Clarinet, Horn, and Piano (1970); *Maxims* for Flute Quartet (1970); *Tercetti* for Oboe, Clarinet, and Bassoon (1971); *Talks* for Wind Quintet (1971–72); *Akrostichon a Allegro* for Bass Clarinet and Piano (1972); *Duo* for 2 Quarter-tone Clarinets (1972); *Replicas* for Flute, Viola, and Harp (1973); *Sujets* for Guitar (1973); *Overtura ritmica* for Guitar (1974); *Strophes* for Viola and Piano (1975); *Portraits*, suite for String Trio (1977); *Dialogues* for 2 Flutes (1978); *Panels*, sextet for Brasses (1979); *Talks* for Baritone, Saxophone, and Flute (1979); *9 Merry Improvisations* for Piano (1928–29); *5 Jazz Studies* for Piano (1930); 3 piano sonatas (1931, 1942, 1961); *Minda-Minda*, 7 compositions for Piano (1937); songs.

Reinhard, Kurt, German ethnomusicologist; b. Giessen, Aug. 27, 1914; d. Wetzlar, July 18, 1979. He studied musicology and composition in Cologne (1933–35), and musicology and ethnology in Leipzig and Munich under Huber, Ficker, and Ubbelohdé-Doering (1935–36); received a doctorate with a dissertation on Burmese music (1938). He worked at the Staatliche Musikinstrumentensammlung in Berlin, then was director of the Berliner Phonogramm-Archiv (1948–68) and head of the dept. of music pedagogy at the Peterson Cons. (1947–52). In 1948 he began teaching at the Free Univ. in Berlin, where he completed a Habilitation on organology (1950); subsequently became prof. and head of the ethnomusicology dept. there (1957). His most important research focused on the folk and art music of Turkey.
Writings: *Die Musik exotischer Völker* (Berlin, 1951); *Chinesische Musik* (Kassel, 1956); *Türkische Musik* (Berlin, 1962); *Einführung in die Musikethnologie* (Wolfenbüttel, 1968).

Reinhardt, Delia, German soprano; b. Elberfeld, April 27, 1892; d. Arlesheim, near Basel, Oct. 3, 1974. She studied with Strakosch and Hedwig Schako at the Hoch Cons. in Frankfurt; made her debut in Breslau in 1913. In 1916 she joined the Munich Court (later Bavarian State) Opera, where she sang until 1923. She made her debut at the Metropolitan Opera in N.Y. on Jan. 27, 1923, as Sieglinde; then sang at the Berlin State Opera (1924–33); also made guest appearances at Covent Garden in London (1924–27; 1929). She was married to the

baritone **Gustav Schützendorf,** and later to the conductor **Georges Sébastian.** Among her outstanding roles were Desdemona, Elsa, and Eva.

Reinhardt, Django (actually, **Jean Baptiste**), Belgian jazz guitarist; b. Liberchies, Jan. 23, 1910; d. Fontainebleau, May 16, 1953. He began his career in Paris in 1922; gained recognition through his recordings with the singer Jean Sablon and the violinist Stephane Grappelli; in 1934 he formed the Quintette du Hot Club de France with Grappelli. After World War II, he toured the U.S.; appeared with Duke Ellington in N.Y. He was an innovative figure in the early jazz movement in Europe; in later years he utilized electrical amplification in his performances.
Bibl.: C. Delaunay, *D. R.: Souvenirs* (Paris, 1954; Eng. tr., 1961); M. Abrams, *The Book of D.* (Los Angeles, 1973); A. Schmitz and P. Maier, *D. R.: Sein Leben, seine Musik, seine Schallplatten* (Gauting-Buchendorf, 1985).

Reinhardt, Heinrich, Austrian composer; b. Pressburg, April 13, 1865; d. Vienna, Jan. 31, 1922. He studied with Bruckner and Mocker in Vienna; was music critic for several newspapers.
Works: operettas: *Das süsse Mädel* (Vienna, Oct. 25, 1901; his greatest success); *Der liebe Schatz* (Vienna, Oct. 30, 1902); *Der General-Konsul* (Vienna, Jan. 28, 1904); *Krieg im Frieden* (Vienna, Jan. 20, 1906); *Die süssen Grisetten* (Vienna, 1907); *Ein Märchen für alles* (Munich, 1908); *Die Sprudelfee* (Vienna, 1909); *Napoleon und die Frauen* (Vienna, April 28, 1911); *Prinzessin Gretl* (Berlin, 1914); *Der Gast des Königs* (Vienna, Jan. 9, 1916); *Die erste Frau* (Munich, 1918). **operas:** *Die Minnekönigin* and *Der Schuster von Delft.*

Reinhold, Hugo, Austrian composer; b. Vienna, March 3, 1854; d. there, Sept. 4, 1935. He studied piano with Julius Epstein and composition with Bruckner at the Vienna Cons., graduating in 1874; then was a piano teacher at the Akademie der Tonkunst in Vienna. He composed a number of attractive piano pieces, a Violin Sonata, and songs.

Reining, Maria, noted Austrian soprano; b. Vienna, Aug. 7, 1903; d. Deggendorf, March 11, 1991. She studied at a business school, and was employed in the foreign exchange dept. of a Vienna bank before taking up singing. In 1931 she made her debut at the Vienna State Opera, remaining on its roster until 1933; then sang in Darmstadt (1933–35) and at the Bavarian State Opera in Munich (1935–37). In 1937 she rejoined the Vienna State Opera, continuing on its roster, with interruptions, until 1958; also appeared at the Salzburg Festivals (1937–41); Toscanini engaged her to sing Eva in *Die Meistersinger von Nürnberg* in Salzburg under his direction in 1937; she also sang the role of the Marschallin in *Der Rosenkavalier* and the title role in *Arabella* by Richard Strauss. She was equally successful in soubrette roles and as a dramatic soprano. In 1938 she appeared with the Covent Garden Opera in London and with the Chicago Opera; in 1949, as the Marschallin with the N.Y. City Opera. She also sang at La Scala in Milan, and toured as a concert singer. In 1962 she became a prof. of singing at the Mozarteum in Salzburg.

Reinken (Reincken), Jan Adams, famous organist and composer; b. April 26, 1623; d. Hamburg, Nov. 24, 1722 (at the age of 99). The place of his birth has not been determined; he may have been born in Wilshausen, Alsace, Wildeshausen near Bremen, or in a Dutch village of similar name. By 1654 he was in Hamburg, where he studied with Heinrich Scheidemann, the organist of the Katharinenkirche. In 1657 he became organist of the Berghkercke in Deventer, the Netherlands. In 1658 he returned to Hamburg as assistant organist to Scheidemann at the Katharinenkirche; in 1663 he succeeded his teacher as organist, a position he held with great distinction for 60 years. Reinken was one of the most celebrated organ virtuosos of his time. In 1720 Bach played at the Katharinenkirche, and Reinken, then 97 years old, was in attendance. He was also a consultant on organ building, and a noted teacher of the organ; his students included Andreas Kneller (later his son-in-law) and G.D. Leiding. He composed several virtuoso organ pieces, and also 6 instrumental suites publ. as *Hortus musicus.*

WORKS: **KEYBOARD:** *An den Wasserflüssen Babylon; Ballet in E minor; Fuga in G minor; Partite diverse sopra l'Aria "Schweiget mir von Weiber nehmen," altrimente chiamata "La Meyerin";* 3 suites, in C major, E minor, and G major; *Toccata* in C major; *Was kann uns kommen an für Noth.* His complete works for keyboard may be found in K. Beckmann, ed., *J.A. Reincken: Sämtliche Orgelwerke* (Wiesbaden, 1974). **CHAMBER:** *Hortus musicus,* 6 suites for 2 Violins, Viola da Gamba, and Basso Continuo (Hamburg, 1687; later ed. by J. van Riemsdijk, Amsterdam, 1888). **VOCAL:** *Geistlich Konzert "auf Michael": Und es erhub sich ein Streit* for 4 Voices, 2 Violins, Viola, 2 Trumpets, Timpani, and Basso Continuo.

BIBL.: J. Mattheson, *Critica musica,* I (Hamburg, 1722); idem, *Grundlage einer Ehren-Pforte . . .* (Hamburg, 1740; new ed. by M. Schneider, Berlin, 1910); J. van Riemsdijk, "Jean Adam Reincken," *Tijdschrift van de Vereniging voor Nederlandse Muziekgeschiedenis,* II/1 (1887); M. Houck, "J(e)an Adam(s) Reincken," *Tijdschrift van de Vereniging voor Nederlandse Muziekgeschiedenis,* VI/2 (1899); W. Stahl, "Zur Biographie J.A. Reinckens," *Archiv für Musikwissenschaft,* III (1920–21); A. Pirro, "Notes pour servir, éventuellement, à la biographie de Reincken," *Gedenkboek aangeboden aan Dr. D.F. Scheurleer* (The Hague, 1925); idem, "Reincken et la musique en Alsace au XVII siècle," in *Annuaire* of the Club Vosgien (vol. 3, Strasbourg, 1935); W. Apel, "Neu aufgefundene Clavierwerke von Scheidemann, Tunder, Froberger, Reincken und Buxtehude," *Acta Musicologica,* XXXIV (1962); G. Sharp, "J. Adam Reincken, 1623–1722," *Musical Times,* CXIV (1973).

Reinmar (real name, **Wochinz**), Hans, distinguished Austrian baritone; b. Vienna, April 11, 1895; d. Berlin, Feb. 7, 1961. He studied at the Vienna Academy of Music and in Milan; made his debut in 1919 in Olomouc as Sharpless; then sang in Nuremberg, Zürich, Dresden, and Hamburg; was a member of the Berlin Städtische Oper (1928–45; 1952–61), the Bavarian State Opera in Munich (1945–46; 1950–57), the Berlin State Opera (1948–52), and the Berlin Komische Oper (1952–61); also sang at the festivals in Bayreuth and Salzburg. He excelled in dramatic roles in Italian operas.

Reinthaler, Karl (Martin), German organist, conductor, and composer; b. Erfurt, Oct. 13, 1822; d. Bremen, Feb. 13, 1896. He studied with G.A. Ritter and Marx in Berlin, and for 3 years in Rome; taught singing at the Cologne Cons. (1853–57), then was organist at Bremen Cathedral (from 1858) and conductor of the Singakademie (1858–90); was made a member of the Berlin Academy (1882) and a Royal Prof. (1888).

WORKS: 2 operas: *Edda* (Bremen, 1875) and *Käthchen von Heilbronn* (Frankfurt, 1881); oratorio, *Jephtha* (London, 1856); Sym.; cantata, *In der Wüste; Bismarck Hymne;* songs; etc.

Reisenauer, Alfred, German pianist and composer; b. Königsberg, Nov. 1, 1863; d. (on a concert tour) Libau, Latvia, Oct. 3, 1907. He was a pupil of Liszt, with whom he was on friendly terms in Rome. He traveled as a concert pianist in almost every region of the globe, including Siberia; publ. a number of attractive songs to words by Heine, Uhland, and Goethe.

BIBL.: J. von Schwerin, *Erinnerungen an A. R.* (Königsberg, 1909).

Reisenberg, Nadia, Russian-American pianist and pedagogue, sister of **Clara Rockmore;** b. Vilnius, July 14, 1904; d. N.Y., June 10, 1983. She studied piano with Leonid Nikolayev at the St. Petersburg Cons. In 1922 she emigrated to America, and continued taking piano lessons with Alexander Lambert and later with Josef Hofmann at the Curtis Inst. of Music in Philadelphia. She began her career as a concert pianist in Russia; gave recitals in Europe and America; appeared as soloist with Barbirolli, Rodzinski, and Damrosch in N.Y. and with Koussevitzky in Boston; gave sonata recitals with the cellist Joseph Schuster; played piano parts in trios, quartets, and quintets with members of the Budapest String Quartet; made a specialty of appearing on radio hours; performed all

the piano concertos of Mozart on weekly radio broadcasts in N.Y. She was also a noted teacher; taught at the Curtis Inst. of Music, Queens College, the Mannes College of Music, and the Juilliard School; also gave master classes in Jerusalem. She possessed a faultless technique, particularly in pearly scale passages, and a fine lyrical form of expression.

BIBL.: A. Sherman and R. Sherman, eds., *N. R.: A Musician's Scrapbook* (College Park, Md., 1985).

Reiser, Alois, Czech-American composer; b. Prague, April 6, 1887; d. Los Angeles, April 4, 1977. He studied composition with Dvořák; also took cello lessons and toured Europe; later emigrated to the U.S. and played cello with the Pittsburgh Sym. and the N.Y. Sym. From 1918 to 1929 he was engaged as a theater conductor in N.Y.; in 1929 he settled in Hollywood, where he worked as a composer and conductor at film studios. His works adhere to the established style of European Romanticism; typical of these are *Slavic Rhapsody,* which he conducted in Los Angeles on March 8, 1931, and *Erewhon,* which he conducted there on Jan. 24, 1936. He composed a Cello Concerto, which he performed in Los Angeles on March 23, 1933; also a considerable amount of chamber music. He wrote an opera, *Gobi,* in which he painted in tones the great Asian desert; it had its 1st and last performance in N.Y. on July 29, 1923, and even then only in concert excerpts.

Reiss, Albert, German tenor; b. Berlin, Feb. 22, 1870; d. Nice, June 19, 1940. He was an actor before his voice was discovered by Pollini, after which he studied with Wilhelm Vilmar in Berlin, and later with Beno Stolzenburg and Julius Lieban; made his operatic debut in Königsberg as Ivanov in *Zar und Zimmermann* (Sept. 28, 1897); then sang in various German towns; on Dec. 23, 1901, he made his American debut at the Metropolitan Opera in N.Y. in the minor roles of the Sailor and the Shepherd in *Tristan und Isolde;* remained on its roster until 1920; he won distinction there as David in *Die Meistersinger von Nürnberg* and Mime in the *Ring* cycle. In 1919 he returned to Berlin; in 1938, retired from the stage and lived in Nice.

Reiss, Józef (Wladyslaw), Polish musicologist; b. Dębica, Aug. 4, 1879; d. Krakow, Feb. 22, 1956. He studied musicology with Adler at the Univ. of Vienna (Ph.D., 1910, with a diss. on the Polish composer Gomółka); completed his Habilitation at the Univ. of Krakow (1922); then taught there until 1939, and again from 1949 to 1953. Among his publications, all in Polish, were *The Problem of Content in Music* (Krakow, 1915; 2nd ed., augmented, 1922); *Musical Forms* (Leipzig, 1917; 2nd ed., 1929); *Beethoven* (Warsaw, 1920); *A Concise History of Music* (Warsaw, 1920; 3rd ed., augmented, 1931); *Henryk Wieniawski* (Warsaw, 1931; 3rd ed., 1970); *An Almanac of Music in Krakow, 1780–1914* (Krakow, 1939); *Violins and Violinists* (Krakow, 1955); *Short Encyclopedia of Music* (Warsaw, 1960).

Reisserová, Julie, Czech composer; b. Prague, Oct. 9, 1888; d. there, Feb. 25, 1938. She studied with J.B. Foerster; also with Albert Roussel in Paris. Among her works are *Pastorale maritime* for Orch. (1933); *Esquisses* for Piano; several albums of songs.

BIBL.: J. Vacková, *J. R.* (Prague, 1948).

Reissiger, Carl Gottlieb, noted German conductor and composer; b. Belzig, near Wittenberg, Jan. 31, 1798; d. Dresden, Nov. 7, 1859. His father, Christian Gottlieb Reissiger, was the Belzig organist and choirmaster. He studied piano and composition with Schicht at the Leipzig Thomasschule (1811–18); then studied theory with Salieri in Vienna (1821–22) and voice and composition with Winter in Munich (1822). Weber conducted the premiere of his opera *Didone abbandonata* at the Dresden Court Opera (Jan. 31, 1824); after teaching composition in Berlin (1825–26), he was called to Dresden as director of the Court Opera in 1826; was named Hofkapellmeister in 1828, and was in charge of sacred music and chamber music, as well as the Court Opera, until his death. He was highly esteemed by his contemporaries as a conductor; he built upon the foundation laid by Weber and made the Dresden Court Opera the premiere opera house of Germany. He was a prolific composer, writing with great facility but with little originality; he attained some success with his songs and piano pieces; his *Danses brillantes pour le pianoforte* or *Webers letzter Gedanke* (1822) was very popular, as was his melodrama *Yelva* (1827).

BIBL.: W. Neumann, *K.G. R.* (Kassel, 1854); K. Kreiser, *C.G. R.: Sein Leben nebst einigen Beitragen zur Geschichte des Konzertwesens in Dresden* (diss., Univ. of Leipzig, 1918).

Reissmann, August (Friedrich Wilhelm), German writer on music and composer; b. Frankenstein, Silesia, Nov. 14, 1825; d. Berlin, July 13, 1903. He studied in Breslau; in 1850 he went to Weimar, where he became a student and an associate of Liszt. He then devoted himself mainly to musical commentary; lived in Berlin (1863–80), where he gave lectures on music history at the Stern Cons. He publ. *Von Bach bis Wagner* (1861); *Das deutsche Lied in seiner historischen Entwicklung* (Kassel, 1861); *Robert Schumann* (1865; in Eng., 1886); *Felix Mendelssohn-Bartholdy* (1867); *Schubert* (1873); *Joseph Haydn* (1879); *J.S. Bach* (1881); *Händel* (1882); *Gluck* (1882); *Weber* (1886); also contributed to German music encyclopedias. Among his compositions were 3 operas, *Gudrun* (Leipzig, 1871), *Die Bürgermeisterin von Schorndorf* (Leipzig, 1880), and *Das Gralspiel* (Düsseldorf, 1895); a Sym.; a Violin Concerto; choral works; piano pieces; songs.

BIBL.: J. Göllrich, *A. R. als Schriftsteller und Komponist* (Leipzig, 1884).

Reiter, Josef, Austrian composer; b. Braunau, Jan. 19, 1862; d. Bad Reichenhall, June 2, 1939. He received his 1st instruction in music from his father, a town organist; in 1886 went to Vienna, where he became active as a choral conductor; then was director of the Mozarteum in Salzburg (1908–11). He wrote 4 operas: *Der Bundschuh* (Troppau, 1894); *Klopstock in Zürich* (Linz, 1894); *Der Totentanz* (Dessau, 1908); *Der Tell* (Vienna, 1917); also numerous choruses and solo songs. He was an inspired Hitlerite; composed a cantata in honor of the Anschluss in 1938; and even before the reification of the Hitler magic in concrete murderous terms, dedicated his *Goethe-Symphonie* to his beloved Führer (1931).

BIBL.: M. Morold, *J. R.* (Vienna, 1904); L. Etzmannsdorfer, *J. R.* (Vienna, 1924).

Reizenstein, Franz (Theodor), German-born English pianist and composer; b. Nuremberg, June 7, 1911; d. London, Oct. 15, 1968. He studied piano with Leonid Kreutzer and composition with Hindemith at the Hochschule für Musik in Berlin (1930–34); with the advent of the anti-Semitic Nazi regime he went to England; entered the Royal College of Music in London and studied with Lambert and Vaughan Williams (1934–36); then took private piano lessons with Solomon (1938–40). He was an instructor in piano at the Royal Academy of Music in London (1958–68), and from 1962 until his death, at the Royal Manchester College of Music. He wrote music of fine neo-Romantic quality.

WORKS: 2 radio operas: *Men against the Sea* (1949) and *Anna Kraus* (1952); *Genesis,* oratorio (1958); *Voices of Night,* cantata (1950–51); *Prologue, Variations and Finale* for Violin and Orch. (1938; originally for Violin and Piano); 2 piano concertos: No. 1 (1941) and No. 2 (1956–61; London, June 7, 1961, composer soloist); *Cyrano de Bergerac,* overture (1951); *Serenade in F* for Wind Ensemble and Double Bass, or for Small Orch. (1951); Violin Concerto (1953); Concerto for String Orch. (1966–67; London, Jan. 17, 1969); Sonata for Cello Solo (1931; rev. 1967); *Theme, Variations and Fugue* for Clarinet Quintet (1932; rev. 1960); Wind Quintet (1934); *Divertimento* for String or Brass Quartet (1936–37); Oboe Sonatina (1937); *Partita* for Flute and String Trio (1938); Violin Sonata (1945); Cello Sonata (1947); Piano Quintet (1948); Trio for Flute, Oboe, and Piano (1949); *Fantasia concertante* for Violin and Piano (1956); Trio for Flute, Clarinet, and Bassoon (1963); *Concert Fantasy* for Viola and Piano

(1956); Sonata for Viola Solo (1967); Sonata for Violin Solo (1968); 2 piano sonatas (1944, 1964).

Rekašius, Antanas, Lithuanian composer; b. Pauvandene, Telsiu, July 24, 1928. He studied composition with Juzeliunas at the Lithuanian State Cons. in Vilnius (1954–59); taught at the J. Gruodis Music School in Kaunas (1959–69). His music is cast in a highly advanced idiom incorporating aleatory and sonoristic techniques.

WORKS: OPERA-ORATORIO: *The Ballad of Light* (1969). **BALLETS:** *The Light of Happiness* (1959); *The Smouldering Cross* (1963); *Passions* (1968); *A Little Humming Fly* (1969; for children). **ORCH.:** *Dramatic Poem* (1958); 5 syms. (1962; 1968; 1969; 1970; 1981, *Segments*); Concerto for Flute and Chamber Orch. (1971); *Metafonia* for Violin and Orch. (1972); *Diafonia* for Cello and Orch. (1972); *Sonnets* for Chamber Orch. (1974); *Epitaph and Poem* for Strings (1975); *Emanations,* concerto for Electric Cello and Chamber Ensemble (1981). **CHAMBER:** 4 string quartets (1954, 1974, 1976, 1980); 4 wind quintets (1974, 1976, 1978, 1980); 2 capriccios for Flute and Oboe (1974, 1976); Solo Flute Sonata (1975); Solo Oboe Sonata (1976); Solo Clarinet Sonata (1976); Solo Horn Sonata (1976); song cycles; children's choruses.

Relfe, John, English music theorist and composer; b. Greenwich, 1763; d. London, c.1837. He was a member of the King's Band in 1810; was also an esteemed teacher of piano and harmony. He composed airs, sonatas, lessons, divertimentos, etc., for harpsichord or piano; songs; publ. *Guida armonica* (3 parts, 1798; 2nd ed. as *The Principles of Harmony,* 1817); *Remarks on the Present State of Musical Instruction* (1819); *Lucidus ordo* (1821). He proposed a reformed thoroughbass figuring, marking the root chord *r.,* and the inversions ′ and ″.

Rellstab, Johann Carl Friedrich, German music publisher, writer on music, and composer, father of **(Heinrich Friedrich) Ludwig Rellstab;** b. Berlin, Feb. 27, 1759; d. there, Aug. 19, 1813. He was a pupil of Agricola and Fasch; succeeded his father as head of a printing establishment (1779), adding a music printing and publishing dept. and a circulating library of music; founded and directed amateur concerts from 1787; lost his property in the war of 1806, and gave music lessons, lectured on harmony, and wrote criticism for the *Vossische Zeitung.* His compositions, which included a singspiel, *Die Apotheke,* cantatas, odes, songs, and piano pieces, are unimportant. His daughter, **Caroline Rellstab** (b. Berlin, April 18, 1793; d. Breslau, Feb. 17, 1813), was a prominent singer; was a member of the Breslau Opera (from 1811); was noted for her portrayal of the Queen of the Night.

WRITINGS: *Versuch über die Vereinigung der musikalischen und oratorischen Declamation, hauptsächlich für Musiker und Componisten mit erläuternden Beyspielen* (Berlin, 1786); *Anleitung für Clavierspieler, den Gebrauch der Bach'schen Fingersetzung, die Manieren und den Vortrag betreffend* (Berlin, 1790); a polemical pamphlet, *Über die Bemerkungen eines Reisenden die Berlinischen Kirchenmusiken, Concerte, Oper und königliche Kammermusik betreffend* (Berlin, 1789).

BIBL.: O. Guttmann, *J.K.F. R.: Ein Beitrag zur Musikgeschichte Berlins* (Berlin, 1910).

Rellstab, (Heinrich Friedrich) Ludwig, German poet, novelist, and writer on music, son of **Johann Carl Friedrich Rellstab;** b. Berlin, April 13, 1799; d. there, Nov. 27, 1860. He revealed a precocious talent as a keyboard player in childhood; later received keyboard instruction from L. Berger and training in theory from B. Klein (1816). He was an artillery officer and a teacher of mathematics and history in the Brigade School in Berlin; retired from the army in 1821, and lived as a writer in Berlin from 1823; was ed. and music critic of the *Vossische Zeitung* (1826–48). He publ. the satirical pamphlets *Henriette, oder Die schöne Sängerin, Eine Geschichte unserer Tage von Freimund Zuschauer* (Leipzig, 1826; on Henriette Sontag's triumphs) and *Über mein Verhältniss als Critiker zu Herrn Spontini als Componisten und General-Musikdirector in Berlin, nebst einem vergnüglichen Anhang* (Leipzig, 1827;

directed against Spohr's truckling to virtuosity in *Agnes von Hohenstaufen*), for each of which he suffered a period of imprisonment, though his opinions were eventually upheld in official circles and by the public. Between 1830 and 1841 he ed. the musical periodical *Iris im Gebiete der Tonkunst;* he also contributed to several other periodicals. His *Gesammelte Schriften* (12 vols., Leipzig, 1843–44; new ed., 24 vols., 1860–61) includes reviews of opera and concerts which came out in the *Vossische Zeitung* between 1826 and 1848. He wrote an autobiography, *Aus meinem Leben* (2 vols., Berlin, 1861).

BIBL.: L. Blengert, *L. R.* (Leipzig, 1918); W. Franke, *Der Theaterkritiker L. R.* (Berlin, 1964).

Remedios, Alberto, English tenor; b. Liverpool, Feb. 27, 1935. He studied in Liverpool with Edwin Francis and later in London with Clive Carey at the Royal College of Music; made his debut as Tinca in *Il tabarro* at the Sadler's Wells Opera in 1957; made his 1st appearance at Covent Garden as Dimitri in *Boris Godunov* in 1965; sang at the Frankfurt Opera (1968–70); made his U.S. debut with the San Francisco Opera in 1973; made his Metropolitan Opera debut in N.Y. as Bacchus in *Ariadne auf Naxos* on March 20, 1976. He was highly successful as Lohengrin, Siegfried, and Siegmund; showed fine lyrical talent as Faust in Gounod's opera, and a dramatic flair in Verdi's *Otello.*

Remenkov, Stefan, Bulgarian composer; b. Silistra, April 30, 1923. He studied piano with Nenov and composition with Pantcho Vladigerov and Veselin Stoyanov at the Bulgarian State Cons. in Sofia, graduating in 1950; later took a course with Khachaturian at the Moscow Cons.

WORKS: STAGE: Operetta, *The Errors Are Ours* (1966); 2 children's operettas: *Ghanem* (1967) and *The Prince and the Pauper* (1973); ballet, *The Unvanquished* (1960). **ORCH.:** 2 piano concertos (1953, 1970); *Prelude and Dance* for String Orch. (1957); 4 syms.: No. 1, *Children's Symphony* (1961); No. 2, *Symphony in the Classical Style* (1962); No. 3 (1965); No. 4 (1968); Cello Concerto (1964); Concertino for Flute and String Orch. (1973); *Fantasy* for Violin and Orch. (1974). **CHAMBER:** Violin Sonata (1955); Nonet; 3 piano sonatas (1944, 1948, 1949).

Reményi (real name, **Hoffmann**), **Ede (Eduard),** prominent Hungarian violinist; b. Miskolc, Jan. 17, 1828; d. San Francisco, May 15, 1898. He began his training with Eger; then studied with Böhm at the Vienna Cons. (1842–45). Banished from the Austro-Hungarian realm for his participation in the Hungarian Revolution of 1848, he began the career of a wandering violinist in America; returning to Europe, he toured Germany with Brahms as his accompanist (1853); after serving as solo violinist to Queen Victoria (1854–59), he returned to Hungary following the amnesty of 1860; then was made solo violinist to the Austrian court; in 1865 he commenced a brilliant tour, visiting Paris, Germany, Belgium, and the Netherlands; then proceeded to London in 1877, and to America in 1878, traveling in the U.S., Canada, and Mexico; in 1886 he began a new concert tour around the world, visiting Japan, China, and South Africa. Some notes on his trip to the Far East are in the N.Y. Public Library. His last years were troubled by ill health and a decline in his playing; was appearing in vaudeville houses by 1898; he collapsed suddenly while playing the pizzicato from the *Sylvia* suite of Delibes at the Orpheum Theater in San Francisco and died of apoplexy a few hours later. His technique was prodigious; in vigor, passion, and pathos he was unexcelled. He made skillful transcriptions of Chopin's waltzes, polonaises, and mazurkas, and pieces by Bach, Schubert, etc.; these are united under the title *Nouvelle école du violon.* He was also a natural performer of Gypsy music; Liszt profited very much by his help in supplying and arranging authentic Gypsy tunes. He composed a Violin Concerto and some solos for violin.

BIBL.: G. Kelly and G. Upton, *Edouard R.: Musician, Littérateur, and Man* (Chicago, 1906); E. Sas, *R.* (Budapest, 1934).

Remoortel, Edouard van, Belgian conductor; b. Brussels, May 30, 1926; d. Paris, May 16, 1977. He studied at the Brussels Cons. and at the Geneva Cons.; also took courses in conducting with Guarnieri and Galliera at the Accademia Chigiana in Siena and privately with Josef Krips. From 1951 he was the principal conductor of the Belgian National Orch.; in 1958, was appointed music director of the St. Louis Sym. Orch., retaining this post until 1962. In 1965 he went to Monte Carlo as artistic consultant to the Orch. National de l'Opéra of Monaco, retiring in 1969.

Rémusat, Jean, French flutist and composer; b. Bordeaux, May 11, 1815; d. Shanghai, Sept. 1, 1880. He studied with Tulou. After successful concert giving, he became 1st flutist at the Queen's Theatre in London; from 1853 he was flutist at the Théâtre-Lyrique in Paris. He publ. a flute method and solo pieces for flute.

Remy, Alfred, German-American writer on music and editor; b. Elberfeld, March 16, 1870; d. N.Y., Feb. 26, 1937. He emigrated to the U.S. in 1882; studied at the City College of N.Y. (B.A., 1890); received private instruction in piano, violin, and theory (1890–96); completed his education at Columbia Univ. (M.A., 1905). He was music critic of *Vogue* and music ed. of *The Looker-On* (1895–97); taught music and modern languages at various N.Y. institutions (from 1896); was music ed. of the *New International Encyclopaedia* (1901–30) and editor in chief of the 3rd ed. of *Baker's Biographical Dictionary of Musicians* (1919).

Rémy, Guillaume, Belgian violinist; b. Ougrée, Aug. 26, 1856; d. Nantes, France, June 16, 1932. He studied at the Liège Cons.; graduated in 1873, sharing the 1st prize with Ysaÿe; continued his studies under Massart at the Paris Cons.; was awarded 1st prize in 1878. Settling in Paris, he became concertmaster of the Colonne Orch., frequently appearing as a soloist; from 1885 to 1930 he was a prof. at the Cons.; played recitals with Saint-Saëns and Fauré at the piano; also formed a string quartet. During the last years of his life, he was head of the violin dept. of the American Cons. at Fontainebleau.

Renaud (real name, **Cronean**), **Maurice (Arnold),** distinguished French baritone; b. Bordeaux, July 24, 1861; d. Paris, Oct. 16, 1933. He studied at the Paris Cons. and the Brussels Cons.; then sang at the Théâtre Royal de la Monnaie in Brussels (1883–90) and at the Opéra-Comique in Paris (1890–91). He made his 1st appearance at the Paris Opéra as Nelusko on July 17, 1891; remained on its roster until 1902, and then made guest appearances there until 1914; was also a member of the Monte Carlo Opera (1891–1907). He made his U.S. debut in New Orleans on Jan. 4, 1893; sang at London's Covent Garden (1897–99; 1902–4), at the Manhattan Opera in N.Y. (1906–7; 1909–10), and again in Brussels (1908–14). He made his Metropolitan Opera debut in N.Y. as Rigoletto on Nov. 24, 1910; remained on the company's roster until 1912. His finest roles included Athanaël in *Thaïs;* Coppelius, Dapertutto, and Dr. Miracle in *Les Contes d'Hoffmann;* Nevers in *Les Huguenots;* Lescaut in *Manon;* Herod in *Hérodiade;* and Saint-Saëns's Henry VIII. His non-French roles included Don Giovanni, Wolfram, Jack Rance, Telramund, and Beckmesser. He was among the most convincing dramatic artists of his era.

Renié, Henriette, eminent French harpist and composer; b. Paris, Sept. 18, 1875; d. there, March 1, 1956. She studied with Alphonse Hasselmans at the Paris Cons.; received 1st prize for harp at the age of 11; then entered the classes of Lenepveu and Dubois in harmony and composition. She performed her own Concerto for Harp and Orch. at the Concerts Lamoureux in Paris on March 24, 1901; further wrote *Pièce symphonique* for Harp and Orch.; *Légende et Danse caprice* for Harp and Orch.; publ. numerous pieces for harp solo: *Promenades matinales, Feuilles d'automne, Ballade fantastique, Légende, Contemplation, Défile lilliputien, Danse des lutins,* etc.; Trio for Harp, Violin, and Cello; Trio for Harp, Flute, and Bassoon; several songs. She taught at the Paris Cons.; among her students was Marcel Grandjany.

Renner, Josef, German choral conductor; b. Schmatzhausen, near Landshut, Bavaria, April 25, 1832; d. Regensburg, Aug.

11, 1895. He received his primary music education from his father; was a choral conductor in Regensburg (1858–92) and organized the Regensburg Madrigal Quartet with the purpose of reviving performances of German part-songs of the Renaissance. He publ. several valuable collections of German madrigals: *Auswahl deutscher Madrigale von Meistern des 16. Jahrhundert*, *Neue Regensburger Sängerhalle*, *Regensburger Oberquartette*, *Mutter Donau*, and *Männerquartette von der Donau* (242 numbers in all).

Rennert, Günther, leading German opera producer and administrator; b. Essen, April 1, 1911; d. Salzburg, July 31, 1978. He was educated in Munich, Berlin, and Halle. From 1935 to 1939 he worked in Wuppertal, in Frankfurt (with Walter Felsenstein), and in Mainz; then was chief producer in Königsberg (1939–42), at the Berlin Städtische Oper (1942–44), and at the Bavarian State Opera in Munich (1945). In 1946 he became Intendant of the Hamburg State Opera, a post he held until 1956; then worked as a guest producer with several major opera houses, including La Scala in Milan and the Metropolitan Opera in N.Y. From 1967 to 1976 he was Intendant of the Bavarian State Opera in Munich. Through the consistent successes of his operatic productions in several cities under changing circumstances, Rennert acquired a reputation as one of the most competent members of his profession.

BIBL.: W. Schäfer, *G. R., Regisseur in dieser Zeit* (Bremen, 1962).

Renz, Frederick, American harpsichordist and conductor; b. Buffalo, July 27, 1940. He studied at the State Univ. of N.Y. at Fredonia (graduated, 1962) and at Indiana Univ. (M.M. in conducting, 1964; M.M. in harpsichord, 1966); then studied harpsichord with Gustav Leonhardt on a Fulbright fellowship in Amsterdam (1967–69). After performing as a keyboard player with the N.Y. Pro Musica (1969–74), he founded his own Ensemble for Early Music in N.Y. (1974), with which he toured widely. His repertoire extends from the 12th to the early 19th century.

Resinarius, Balthasar, significant German composer; b. Tetschen, Bohemia, c.1485; d. Böhmisch-Leipa, April 12, 1544. He sang and studied under Heinrich Isaac at the court chapel of Emperor Maximilian I; enrolled at the Univ. of Leipzig (1515); although he became a Catholic priest in Tetschen (1523), he soon espoused Lutheranism and was made bishop of Leipa. He was one of the most important early Protestant composers of sacred music. His works were commissioned by Rhau, who included them in his own publications. Among Resinarius's output are 80 responsories and the *St. John Passion* (Wittenberg, 1544), 30 chorale settings (1544), 3 motets (1545), an introit (1545), and 10 hymns.

BIBL.: I.-M. Schröder, *Die Responsorienvertonungen des B. R.* (Kassel, 1954).

Resnik, Regina, American soprano, later mezzo-soprano; b. N.Y., Aug. 30, 1922. She studied in N.Y.; made her concert debut at the Brooklyn Academy of Music (Oct. 27, 1942); sang in opera in Mexico (1943); won an annual audition at the Metropolitan Opera in N.Y. in 1944, and appeared there as Leonora in *Il Trovatore* (Dec. 6, 1944); continued to sing there regularly, turning to mezzo-soprano roles in 1955. In 1953 she appeared in Bayreuth as Sieglinde; made her Covent Garden debut in London as Carmen in 1957, and sang there until 1972. She remained on the roster of the Metropolitan Opera until 1974; was active as an opera producer from 1971.

Respighi, Ottorino, eminent Italian composer; b. Bologna, July 9, 1879; d. Rome, April 18, 1936. He studied violin with F. Sarti and composition with L. Torchi and G. Martucci at Bologna's Liceo Musicale (1891–1900). In 1900 he went to Russia, and played 1st viola in the orch. of the Imperial Opera in St. Petersburg; there he took lessons with Rimsky-Korsakov, which proved a decisive influence in Respighi's coloristic orchestration. From 1903 to 1908 he was active as a concert violinist; also played the viola in the Mugellini Quartet of Bologna. In 1913 he was engaged as a prof. of composition at

Rome's Liceo (later Conservatorio) di Santa Cecilia; in 1924, was appointed its director, but resigned in 1926, retaining only a class in advanced composition; subsequently devoted himself to composing and conducting. He was elected a member of the Italian Royal Academy on March 23, 1932. In 1925–26 and again in 1932 he made tours of the U.S. as a pianist and a conductor.

His style of composition is a highly successful blend of songful melodies with full and rich harmonies; he was one of the best masters of modern Italian music in orchestration. His power of evocation of the Italian scene and his ability to sustain interest without prolixity is incontestable. Although he wrote several operas, he achieved his greatest success with 2 symphonic poems, *Le fontane di Roma* and *I pini di Roma*, each consisting of 4 tone paintings of the Roman landscape; a great innovation for the time was the insertion of a phonograph recording of a nightingale into the score of *I pini di Roma*. His wife, **Elsa Olivieri Sangiacomo Respighi** (b. Rome, March 24, 1894), was his pupil; wrote a fairy opera, *Fior di neve*; the symphonic poem *Serenata di maschere*; numerous songs; was also a concert singer. She publ. a biography of her husband.

WORKS: OPERAS: *Re Enzo* (Bologna, March 12, 1905); *Semirama*, lyric tragedy (Bologna, Nov. 20, 1910); *Marie-Victoire* (1913–14; not perf.); *La bella dormente nel bosco* or *La bella addormentata nel bosco*, musical fairy tale (1916–21; Rome, April 13, 1922); *Belfagor*, lyric comedy (1921–22; Milan, April 26, 1923); *La campana sommersa*, after Hauptmann's *Die versunkene Glocke* (1923–27; Hamburg, Nov. 18, 1927); *Maria Egiziaca*, mystery play (1929–32; N.Y., March 16, 1932); *La fiamma* (1930–33; Rome, Jan. 23, 1934); a free transcription of Monteverdi's *Orfeo* (Milan, March 16, 1935); *Lucrezia* (1935; Milan, Feb. 24, 1937). BALLETS: *La Boutique fantasque*, on themes by Rossini (London, June 5, 1919); *Scherzo veneziano* (Rome, Nov. 27, 1920); *Belkis, Regina di Saba* (1930–31; Milan, Jan. 23, 1932). ORCH.: Piano Concerto (1902); Suite for Organ and Strings (1902–5); *Notturno* (1905); *Sinfonia drammatica* (1913–14); *Le fontane di Roma*, symphonic poem (1914–16; Rome, March 11, 1917); *Antiche arie e danze per liuto*, 3 sets, the 3rd for String Orch. (1916, 1923, 1931); *Ballata delle gnomidi* (1918–20; Rome, April 11, 1920); *Concerto gregoriano* for Violin and Orch. (1921; Rome, Feb. 5, 1922); *I pini di Roma*, symphonic poem (Rome, Dec. 14, 1924); *Concerto in modo misolidio* for Piano and Orch. (N.Y., Dec. 31, 1925, composer soloist); *Rossiniana*, suite from Rossini's piano pieces (1925); *Poema autunnale* for Violin and Orch. (1920–25); *Vetrate di chiesa*, symphonic impressions (Boston, Feb. 25, 1927); *Impressioni brasiliane*, symphonic suite (1927; São Paulo, June 16, 1928, composer conducting); *Trittico Botticelliano* for Chamber Orch. (1927); *Gli Uccelli*, suite for Small Orch. on themes by Rameau, B. Pasquini, and others (1927); *Toccata* for Piano and Orch. (1928); *Feste romane*, symphonic poem (1928; N.Y., Feb. 21, 1929); *Metamorphosen modi XII* (Boston, Nov. 7, 1930); *Concerto a 5* for Violin, Oboe, Trumpet, Double Bass, Piano, and Strings (1932). CHORAL: *La Primavera*, cantata for Soloists, Chorus, and Orch. (1918–19; Rome, March 4, 1923); *Lauda per la Natività del Signore* for Soloists, Chorus, and Orch. (1928–30). CHAMBER: 11 pieces for Violin and Piano (1904–7); String Quartet in D major (1907); *Quartetto dorico* for String Quartet (1924); *Il tramonto*, after Shelley, for Mezzo-soprano and String Quartet (1917); Violin Sonata (1917). Also *Huntingtower Ballad* for Band (Sousa memorial concert, Washington, D.C., April 17, 1932); 45 songs; 3 vocalises without words; arrangements of works by Monteverdi, Vitali, Pergolesi, Cimarosa, Marcello, etc., and of several *Études tableaux* by Rachmaninoff.

BIBL.: R. de Rensis, *O. R.* (Turin, 1935); E. Respighi, *O. R.: Dati biografici ordinati* (Milan, 1954; abridged Eng. tr., 1962); *O. R.: Catalogo delle opere* (Milan, 1965); E. Battaglia, ed., *O. R.* (Turin, 1985); D. Bryant, ed., *Il Novecento musicale italiano: Tra neoclassicismo e neogoticismo: Atti del convegno di studi promosso dalla Fondazione Giorgio Cini per il 50° anniversario della scomparsa di O. R.* (Florence, 1988).

Reszke, Edouard de. See **De Reszke, Edouard.**

Reszke, Jean de. See **De Reszke, Jean.**

Rethberg, Elisabeth (real name, **Lisbeth Sattler**), outstanding German-American soprano; b. Schwarzenberg, Sept. 22, 1894; d. Yorktown Heights, N.Y., June 6, 1976. She studied at the Dresden Cons. and with Otto Watrin; made her operatic debut as Arsena in *Der Zigeunerbaron* at the Dresden Court Opera (1915); continued to sing there when it became the State Opera in 1918. She then made her U.S. debut as Aida at the Metropolitan Opera in N.Y. on Nov. 22, 1922, remaining one of its most celebrated artists until her farewell performance there in that same role on March 6, 1942. She subsequently embarked on a grand concert tour with Ezio Pinza in the U.S., Europe, and Australia; their close association resulted in a lawsuit for alienation of affection brought by Pinza's wife against her, but the court action was not pursued. Throughout her operatic career, Rethberg sang in many of the major music centers in Italy; also appeared at the Salzburg Festivals and at London's Covent Garden (1925; 1934–39). She excelled in both the German and Italian repertoires; among her memorable roles were Mozart's Countess, Donna Anna, Pamina, Constanze, and Donna Elvira; Verdi's Aida, the 2 Leonoras, Amelia, Desdemona, and Maria Boccanegra; and Wagner's Eva, Elisabeth, Sieglinde, and Elsa; also created the title role in Strauss's *Die ägyptische Helena* (Dresden, June 6, 1928). Rethberg was married twice: first to Ernst Albert Dormann, and then to **George Cehanovsky,** whom she married in 1956.
BIBL.: H. Henschel and E. Friedrich, *E. R.: Ihr Leben und Künstlertum* (Schwarzenberg, 1928); J. Richards, "E. R.'s Recordings," *Record Collector,* VIII (1953–54); J. Steane, "E. R.," *Recorded Sound,* 66–67 (1977).

Réti, Rudolph (Rudolf), Serbian-American music theorist, pianist, and composer; b. Užice, Nov. 27, 1885; d. Montclair, N.J., Feb. 7, 1957. He studied at the Vienna Academy of Music and at the Univ. of Vienna; took an early interest in new music and was one of the founders of the ISCM (Salzburg, 1922). In 1938 he went to the U.S.; in 1943, married the Canadian pianist Jean Sahlmark; in 1950 they settled in Montclair, N.J. His compositions are marked by precise structure and fine stylistic unity. Among his works are *Symphonia mystica* (1951); *Triptychon* for Orch. (1953); Concertino for Cello and Orch. (1953); 2 piano concertos; Violin Sonata; several choruses and solo songs; piano pieces. An original music analyst, he wrote several books which contributed to the development of logical theory of modern music: *The Thematic Process in Music* (N.Y., 1952); *Tonality, Atonality, Pantonality* (N.Y., 1958); *Thematic Patterns in Sonatas of Beethoven* (ed. by D. Cooke, London, 1965).

Rettich, Wilhelm, German composer and conductor; b. Leipzig, July 3, 1892; d. Sinzheim bei Baden-Baden, Dec. 27, 1988. He studied at the Leipzig Cons. with Max Reger; was in the German army in World War I and was taken prisoner by the Russians; sent to Siberia, he made his way to China after the Russian Revolution and eventually returned to Leipzig; occupied various posts as a theater conductor; was music director of the local synagogue until 1933, when the advent of the Nazi regime forced him to leave Germany; he went to the Netherlands and became a naturalized Dutch citizen. In 1964 he returned to Germany and lived in Baden-Baden. As a composer, he excelled in symphonic and chamber music; wrote 3 syms.; Violin Concerto; Piano Concerto; much chamber music for various combinations; choral works; piano pieces and songs.

Reubke, Adolf, German organ builder; b. Halberstadt, Dec. 6, 1805; d. Hausneindorf, near Quedlinburg, March 3, 1875. He founded his firm in Hausneindorf; built organs for various German cities, including those at Magdeburg Cathedral and at the Leipzig Gewandhaus. His son Emil Reubke (1836–85) became a partner in 1860 and eventually inherited the firm. Another son, **(Friedrich) Julius Reubke** (b. Hausneindorf, March 23, 1834; d. Pillnitz, near Dresden, June 3, 1858),

was a pianist, organist, and composer; he studied with Hermann Bönicke in Quedlinburg, with T. Kullak (piano) and A.B. Marx (composition) at the Berlin Cons., and with Liszt in Weimar (1856); he wrote 2 outstanding sonatas, 1 for piano and 1 for organ (both 1857). Still another son, **Otto Reubke** (b. Hausneindorf, Nov. 2, 1842; d. Halle, May 18, 1913), was a pianist, conductor, and composer; studied organ with A.G. Ritter in Magdeburg, piano with Bülow and composition with A.B. Marx and Weitzmann at the Berlin Cons., and composition with Hauptmann in Leipzig (1864–67); subsequently settled in Halle as a pianist, organist, and conductor; was named Robert Franz's assistant at the Univ. (1877); founded his own choral society (1876), and then served as conductor of the Robert Franz Singakademie (1867–1911); was named music director (1892) and prof. (1895) at the Univ.; wrote piano pieces and songs.
BIBL.: D. Chorzempa, *J. R.: Life and Works* (diss., Univ. of Minnesota, 1971).

Reuling, (Ludwig) Wilhelm, German conductor and composer; b. Darmstadt, Dec. 22, 1802; d. Munich, April 19, 1879. He studied with Rinck and Seyfried; was a theater conductor in Vienna (1829–54). He composed 37 operas and operettas, and 17 ballets, produced mostly in Vienna; in addition, he wrote overtures, chamber music, and songs. A complete list of his operas produced in Vienna, with dates of premieres, is found in Anton Bauer, *Opern und Operetten in Wien* (Vienna, 1955).

Reusner (or **Reussner**), **Esaias,** esteemed German lutenist and composer; b. Löwenberg, Silesia, April 29, 1636; d. Cölln, Berlin, May 1, 1679. A child prodigy, he studied lute with his father; then entered the service of the Swedish general Count Wittenberg in Breslau as a page when he was about 12; after a year in the service of the household of the royal war commissioner Müllner, he became a valet at the Polish court of Princess Radziwill (1651), where he continued his lute training. After returning to Breslau in 1654, he was named lutenist to Georg III, duke of Silesia, in 1655; then taught lute at the Univ. of Leipzig (1672–73); subsequently served as a chamber musician at the court of the Elector Friedrich Wilhelm of Brandenburg in Berlin (1674–79). He was a significant figure in the development of the German lute school of composition, being the 1st German composer to adapt the French lute style. A few of his works have been ed. in Das Erbe Deutscher Musik, 1st series, XII (1939).
BIBL.: G. Sparmann, *E. Reusner und die Lauten-Suite* (diss., Univ. of Berlin, 1926); E. Koletschka, "E. Reusner der Jüngerer und seine Bedeutung für die deutsche Lautenmusik des XVII. Jahrhunderts," *Studien zur Musikwissenschaft,* XV (1928); idem, "E. Reussner Vater und Sohn und ihre Choralbearbeitungen für die Laute: Eine Parallele," *Festschrift Adolf Koczirz* (Vienna, 1930).

Reuss, August, German composer; b. Liliendorf bei Znaim, Moravia, March 6, 1871; d. Munich, June 18, 1935. He was a pupil of L. Thuille in Munich; after a brief activity as Kapellmeister in Augsburg (1906) and Magdeburg (1907), he lived in Berlin; then in Munich, where he taught at the Trapp Cons. (1927–29) and at the Akademie der Tonkunst (1929–35). His works, all in a late Romantic style, include an opera, *Herzog Philipps Brautfahrt* (Graz, 1909); orch. works, including the tone poems *Johannisnacht* (1903) and *Judith* (1903), *Sommeridylle* (1920), and a Piano Concerto (1924); and numerous chamber works, including a Piano Trio (1912), 2 string quartets (1906, 1914), and an Octet for 2 Oboes, 2 Clarinets, 2 Bassoons, and 2 Horns (1918).

Reuss-Belce, Luise, Austrian soprano; b. Vienna, Oct. 24, 1860; d. (found dead in a refugee train) Aibach, Germany, March 5, 1945. She studied voice in Vienna; made her debut as Elsa in *Lohengrin* in Karlsruhe (1881); then sang in Bayreuth (1882) and in Wiesbaden (1896–99); her subsequent appearances were at Covent Garden in London (1900) and at the Metropolitan Opera in N.Y., where she made her debut as Brünnhilde in *Die Walküre* (Feb. 11, 1902); then sang in Dresden (1903–11). In 1885 she married **Eduard Reuss** (b. N.Y., Sept. 16, 1851; d. Dresden, Feb. 18, 1911), a music pedagogue; after his death, she moved to Berlin, where she established a singing school. In 1913 she was appointed stage manager at the festival opera performances in Nuremberg; she was the 1st woman to occupy such a post in Germany.

Reuter, Florizel von, American composer and violinist; b. Davenport, Iowa, Jan. 21, 1890; d. Waukesha, Wis., May 10, 1985. He studied violin with César Thomson in Brussels and Henri Marteau in Geneva; after a brief concert career, he settled in Munich (1934). His opera *Postmaster Wynn*, after Pushkin's tale, was produced in Berlin in 1947. He eventually returned to America, where he was active as a composer and writer; among his works are a *Rumanian Rhapsody* for Orch. (1966) and some chamber music. He publ. a manual, *Führer durch die Solo-Violinmusik* (Berlin, 1926), and *Psychical Experiences of a Musician* (London).

Reuter, Rolf, German conductor; b. Leipzig, Oct. 7, 1926. He studied at the Academy for Music and Theater in Dresden. He conducted in Eisenach (1951–55); then was Generalmusikdirektor in Meiningen (1955–61). In 1961 he became a conductor at the Leipzig Opera, and subsequently served as its Generalmusikdirektor (1963–78); was chief conductor of the Weimar State Orch. (1979–81). In 1981 he was appointed chief conductor and music director of the Komische Oper in East Berlin.

Reuter, Georg (von), Austrian organist and composer, father of **(Johann Adam Joseph Karl) Georg von Reutter;** b. Vienna (baptized), Nov. 3, 1656; d. there, Aug. 29, 1738. He may have studied with J.C. Kerll, whom he succeeded as organist of St. Stephen's Cathedral in Vienna in 1686; in 1695 he was in Italy, where he was ennobled by Prince Sforza. Returning to Vienna, he was a continuo player on the theorbo at the Imperial Court Chapel (1697–1703); was made court organist in 1700; became Vice-Kapellmeister in 1712 and 1st Kapellmeister in 1715 of the Cathedral, where he remained until 1728; retired as Cathedral organist in 1720 and was succeeded by his son. He wrote a number of toccatas and many *Versetteln* (brief organ preludes); his secular works are lost. A Ricercare, 2 capriccios, and most likely the canzona on *Christ ist erstanden* attributed to him in Denkmäler der Tonkunst in Österreich, XXVII, Jg. XIII/2, are by Strungk.
      BIBL.: N. Hofer, *Die beiden R. als Kirchenkomponisten* (diss., Univ. of Vienna, 1915); G. Frotscher, *Geschichte des Orgel-Spiels und der Orgel-Komposition,* vol. I (Berlin, 1935–36; 3rd ed., augmented, 1966).

Reuter, (Johann Adam Joseph Karl) Georg von, Austrian organist and composer, son of **Georg (von) Reutter;** b. Vienna (baptized), April 6, 1708; d. there, March 11, 1772. He began his studies with his father, and then had composition lessons with Caldara; by age 14 he deputized for his father as court organist; after a sojourn in Italy (1729?–31), he returned to Vienna and was made court composer; he brought out many operas and oratorios. He was named 1st Kapellmeister at St. Stephen's Cathedral upon his father's death in 1738, having unofficially carried out those duties since about 1736; while searching for choristers in 1739–40, he recruited the youthful Haydn in Hainburg and took him into his own home in Vienna. Reutter was ennobled in 1740. After L.A. Predieri became 1st Kapellmeister in 1741, he was reduced to serving as a substitute until acquiring the post of 2nd Kapellmeister in 1747. Following Predieri's retirement in 1751, Reutter took over the court Kapelle but did not receive the title of 1st Kapellmeister until Predieri's death in 1769. In 1756 he also obtained the post of 2nd Kapellmeister at the Cathedral. The musical establishment at both the court and the Cathedral declined under his leadership, due in part to inadequate funding. Reutter produced a vast amount of music which is now totally forgotten.
      BIBL.: L. Stollbrock, "Leben und Wirken des k.k. Hofkapellmeisters und Hofkompositors J.G. R.jun.," *Vierteljahrsschrift für Musikwissenschaft,* VIII (1892); N. Hofer, *Die beiden R. als Kirchenkomponisten* (diss., Univ. of Vienna, 1915).

Reutter, Hermann, outstanding German composer; b. Stuttgart, June 17, 1900; d. Heidenheim an der Brenz, Jan. 1, 1985. He studied with Franz Dorfmüller (piano), Ludwig Mayer (organ), Karl Erler (voice), and Walter Courvoisier (composition) at the Munich Academy of Music (1920–23). He began his career as a pianist in 1923; made numerous concert tours with the singer Sigrid Onegin (1930–35), including 7 separate tours in the U.S. He also devoted much time to teaching; taught composition at the Stuttgart Hochschule für Musik (1932–36); after serving as director of the Berlin Staatliche Hochschule für Musik (1936–45), he became a teacher of lieder and composition at the Stuttgart Staatliche Hochschule für Musik (1952), serving as its director (1956–66); then was prof. of music at the Munich Academy of Music. As a composer, Reutter followed the traditional line of German neo-Classicism, in which the basic thematic material, often inspired by German folk music, is arranged along strong contrapuntal lines, wherein a dissonant intervallic fabric does not disrupt the sense of immanent tonality. He excelled particularly in stage music and songs. He brought out an anthology of contemporary art songs, *Das zeitgenössische Lied* (4 vols., Mainz, 1969).
      WORKS: OPERAS: *Saul* (Baden-Baden, July 15, 1928; rev. Hamburg, Dec. 21, 1947); *Der verlorene Sohn* (Stuttgart, March 20, 1929; rev. as *Die Rückkehr des verlorenen Sohnes,* Dortmund, 1952); *Doktor Johannes Faust* (1934–36; Frankfurt, May 26, 1936; rev. Stuttgart, 1955); *Odysseus* (1940–42; Frankfurt, Oct. 7, 1942); *Der Weg nach Freundschaft: Ballade der Landstrasse* (Göttingen, Jan. 25, 1948); *Don Juan und Faust* (Stuttgart, June 11, 1950); *Die Witwe von Ephesus* (Cologne, June 23, 1954); *Die Brücke von San Luis Rey* (Frankfurt Radio, June 20, 1954); *Hamlet* (Stuttgart, 1980); also *Der Tod des Empedokles,* scenic concerto (Schwetzingen, May 29, 1966). ORCH.: 3 piano concertos (1925, 1929, 1944); Violin Concerto (c.1930); Concerto for 2 Pianos and Orch. (1949); *Prozession* for Cello and Orch. (1956); Sym. for Strings (1960); also choral works and about 200 songs; chamber music; piano pieces; etc.
      BIBL.: H. Lindlar, ed., *H. R.: Werk und Wirken: Festschrift der Freunde* (Mainz, 1965).

Revelli, William D(onald), American band director and teacher; b. Spring Gulch, near Aspen, Colo., Feb. 12, 1902. The family moved to southern Illinois, near St. Louis, when he was an infant; he began to study the violin at the age of 5; later he was a pupil of Dominic Sarli. After graduating from the Chicago Musical College in 1922, he completed his education at the Columbia School of Music in Chicago (diploma in music education, 1925). In 1925 he became supervisor of music in Hobart, Ind., where he founded the high school band, which he in time built to national prominence, winning the high school band championship for 6 consecutive years. In 1935 he was made director of the Univ. of Michigan Band at Ann Arbor, and was also in charge of its wind instruments dept. Over the next 36 years he developed his band into 7 independent groups of players and the wind dept. into a body of 14 specialist teachers. Revelli's Sym. Band toured the country many times and made several trips abroad under State Dept. auspices, most notably a 16-week tour in early 1961 that took it to the Soviet Union, Bulgaria, Turkey, Egypt, and other countries in the Middle East. In 1971 Revelli became director emeritus of the Univ. of Michigan Bands. As an instructor and promoter of bands within the U.S. academic system, Revelli continued the tradition of Fillmore and A.A. Harding. He was active as an ed., adviser, and administrator of various undertakings in the American band field; was also founder of the College Band Directors National Assoc. (1941) and was its honorary life president; received honorary doctoral degrees from 5 American univs.
      BIBL.: G. Cavanagh, *W.D. R.: The Hobart Years* (diss., Univ. of Michigan, 1971); M. Mark, "W.D. R.: Portrait of a Distinguished Career," *Journal of Band Research,* XVI/1 (1980–81).

Revész, Géza, Hungarian psychologist; b. Siófek, Dec. 9, 1878; d. Amsterdam, Aug. 19, 1955. He studied experimental psychology at the Univ. of Göttingen (Ph.D., 1905); taught psychology at the Univ. of Budapest (1906–20). In 1921 he settled in the Netherlands, where he became director of the Psychological Inst. of the Univ. of Amsterdam.

WRITINGS: *Zur Grundlegung der Tonpsychologie* (Leipzig, 1913); *Das frühzeitige Auftreten der Begabung und ihre Erkennung* (Leipzig, 1921); *Musikgenuss bei Gehörlosen* (with Katz; Leipzig, 1926); *Inleiding tot de muziekpsychologie* (Amsterdam, 1944; in German, Bern, 1946; in Eng. as *Introduction to the Psychology of Music*, N.Y., 1953). The book that attracted the most attention, and also put in doubt the efficacy of the author's method, was *Ervin Nyiregyházi. Psychologische Analyse eines musikalisch hervorragenden Kindes* (Leipzig, 1916; in Eng. as *The Psychology of a Musical Prodigy*, London, 1925), which analyzes the case of a talented Hungarian child pianist who had perfect pitch, could transpose at sight and commit to memory short musical phrases instantly; but examples cited in the book do not go beyond the capabilities of thousands of other musically gifted children.

Revueltas, Silvestre, remarkable Mexican composer; b. Santiago Papasquiaro, Dec. 31, 1899; d. Mexico City, Oct. 5, 1940. He began violin studies when he was 8 in Colima; then entered the Juárez Inst. in Durango at age 12; after studies with Tello (composition) and Rocabruna (violin) in Mexico City (1913–16), he took courses at St. Edward College in Austin, Texas (1916–18), and with Sametini (violin) and Borowski (composition) at the Chicago Musical College (1918–20); returned to Chicago to study violin with Kochanski and Ševčik (1922–26). He was active as a violinist and conductor in Texas and Alabama (1926–28); was assistant conductor of the Orquesta Sinfónica de Mexico (1929–35); only then did he begin to compose. In 1937 he went to Spain, where he was active in the cultural affairs of the Loyalist government during the Civil War. His health was ruined by exertions and an irregular lifestyle, and he died of pneumonia. His remains were deposited in the Rotonda de los Hombres Ilustres in Mexico City on March 23, 1976, to the music of his *Redes* and the funeral march from Beethoven's *Eroica*. He possessed an extraordinary natural talent and an intimate understanding of Mexican music; he succeeded in creating works of great originality, melodic charm, and rhythmic vitality.

WORKS (all 1st perf. in Mexico City unless otherwise given): **BALLETS:** *El Renacuajo paseador* (1933; Oct. 4, 1940) and *La Coronela* (left unfinished at his death; completed by Galindo and Huízar; Nov. 20, 1941). **ORCH.:** *Cuauhnahuac* (1931–32; June 2, 1933); *Esquinas* for Small Orch. (Nov. 20, 1931; for Large Orch., 1933); *Ventanas* (Windows; 1931; Nov. 4, 1932); *Alcancías* (Penny Banks; 1932); *Colorines* for Small Orch. (Aug. 30, 1932); *Ocho por Radio* for Small Orch. (Oct. 13, 1933); *Janitzio* (Oct. 13, 1933; rev. 1936); *Caminos* (Paths; July 17, 1934); *Planos*, "geometric dance" (Nov. 5, 1934); *Redes* (Waves), concert suite from the film score, for Small Orch. (1935; Barcelona, Oct. 7, 1937); *Homenaje a Federico García Lorca* for Small Orch. (1935; Madrid, Sept. 22, 1937); *Sensemayá*, based on an Afro-Cuban legend, for Voice and Small Orch. (1937; rev. for Large Orch. alone, Dec. 15, 1938); *Música para charlar* (Music for Chatter), concert suite from the film scores *El Indio* and *Ferro-carriles de Baja California* (Dec. 15, 1938); *Hora de junio* for Narrator and Orch. (1938); *La noche de los Mayas*, concert suite from the film score (1939); *Itinerarios* (1939); *Paisajes* (1940); *Parias* for Soprano, Chorus, and Small Orch. (1940); *Troka* (1940). **CHAMBER:** 3 string quartets: No. 1 (1930); No. 2, *Magueyes* (1931); No. 3, *Música de feria* (1931); *3 Pieces* for Violin and Piano (1932); *Tocata sin fuga* for Violin and 7 Winds (1933); *Canto de guerra de los frentes leales* (War Song of the Loyalist Front) for 3 Trumpets, 3 Trombones, 2 Tubas, Percussion, and Piano (1938); *3 sonetas* for Chamber Ensemble (1940); *3 Little Serious Pieces* for Piccolo, Oboe, Trumpet, Clarinet, and Saxophone (1940). He also wrote many songs.

BIBL.: O. Mayer-Serra, "S. R. and Musical Nationalism in Mexico," *Musical Quarterly* (April 1941); N. Slonimsky, *Music*

of Latin America (N.Y., 1945); G. Contreras, *S. R.: Genio atormentado* (Mexico City, 1954).

Revutsky, Lev(ko Mikolaievich), Ukrainian composer; b. Irshavetz, near Poltava, Feb. 20, 1889; d. Kiev, March 31, 1977. He studied in Kiev with Glière; then was an instructor at the Musico-Dramatic Inst. in Kiev (1924–41). During the occupation of Kiev by the Germans, he went to Tashkent; in 1944, returned to Kiev; in 1957 he was elected to the Ukrainian Academy of Sciences. His works include 2 syms. (1916–21; 1926–27); 2 piano concertos (1914, 1934); a number of choral pieces to Ukrainian words.

BIBL.: G. Kisselev, *L.M. R.* (Kiev, 1949); V. Klein, *L.M. R., Composer, Pianist* (Kiev, 1972).

Rey, Cemal Reshid, Turkish pianist, conductor, teacher, and composer; b. Jerusalem, Sept. 24, 1904; d. Istanbul, Oct. 7, 1985. Of a distinguished family (his father was a poet and also served twice as minister of the interior in the Turkish government), he went to Paris at age 9 to study composition with Laparra; then continued his studies at the Geneva Cons.; returning to Paris, he took courses in piano with Long, composition with Fauré, and conducting with Derosse. In 1923 he settled in Constantinople and taught at the Cons.; from 1949 to 1969 he was principal conductor of the Istanbul Radio Orch. His music is imbued with Turkish melorhythms; many of his works are written on Turkish subjects.

WORKS: OPERAS: *Yann Marek* (1922); *Sultan Cem* (1923); *Zeybek* (1926); *Tchelebi* (1945); *Benli Hürmüz* (1965); operetta, *Yaygara* (1969). **ORCH.:** 3 syms. (1941, 1950, 1968); *La Légende du Bebek* (Paris, Dec. 15, 1929); *Karagueuz*, symphonic poem (Paris, Feb. 14, 1932, composer conducting); *Scènes turques* (Paris, March 6, 1932); *Concerto chromatique* for Piano and Orch. (Paris, March 12, 1933, composer soloist); Violin Concerto (1939); *L'Appel*, symphonic poem (Paris, April 3, 1952, composer conducting); *Fatih* (1956); 3 symphonic scherzos (1958); *Colloque instrumental* for Flute, 2 Horns, Harp, and Strings (1957); *Variations on an Istanbul Folksong* for Piano and Orch. (1966); numerous arrangements of Turkish folk songs for various instrumental combinations; choruses; piano pieces.

Rey, Jean-Baptiste, French conductor and composer, brother of **Louis-Charles-Joseph Rey;** b. Tarn-et-Garonne, Dec. 18, 1734; d. Paris, July 15, 1810. He studied at Toulouse and became a theater conductor in the provinces. In 1776 he settled in Paris as conductor of the Opéra, being named director of its orch. in 1781; was also made master of the musique de chambre to Louis XVI (1779); conducted at the Concert Spirituel (1781–86); served as prof. of harmony at the Cons. (1799–1801); was named maître de chapelle to Napoleon in 1804. He taught according to the principles of Rameau and became embroiled in an academic controversy with the followers of the more modern method of Catel. He played an important role in producing operas by Gluck, Grétry, and others; wrote the opera *Diane et Endymion* (Paris, 1791) and arranged operas by others.

Rey, Louis-Charles-Joseph, French composer and cellist, brother of **Jean-Baptiste Rey;** b. Lauzerte, Oct. 26, 1738; d. Paris, May 12, 1811. He was trained as a cellist, and was in the orch. of the Paris Opéra from 1767 until 1806; also played in the orch. of the royal chapel (from 1772). He composed some stage pieces and chamber music.

Reyer (real name, **Rey**), **(Louis-Etienne-) Ernest,** French composer; b. Marseilles, Dec. 1, 1823; d. Le Lavandou, near Hyères, Jan. 15, 1909. An ardent admirer of Wagner, he added the German suffix *-er* to his real name. He entered a Marseilles music school when he was 6; was sent to Algiers in 1839 to work in a government dept. with an uncle; while there, he composed a Solemn Mass (for the arrival of the French governor in Algiers; perf. 1847) and publ. several songs. He definitely embarked upon a musical career in 1848, studying in Paris with his aunt, **Louise Farrenc.** In 1866 he became librarian at the Opéra, and followed d'Ortigue as music critic of the

Journal des Débats (1866–98); his collected essays were publ. in 1875 as *Notes de musique;* also in *Quarante ans de musique* (posthumous, 1909). He was elected to David's chair in the Institut in 1876; was made a Chevalier of the Legion of Honor in 1872; received the Grande-Croix in 1906. Although Reyer was an avowed admirer of Wagner, his music does not betray specific Wagnerian influences; both in form and in harmonic progressions, Reyer adheres to the Classical French school of composition, with a certain tendency toward exoticism in his choice of librettos. His reputation as a composer for the theater was securely established with his operas *Sigurd* and *Salammbô.*

WORKS: STAGE: *Le Sélam,* "symphonie orientale," but actually an opera (Paris, April 5, 1850); *Maître Wolfram,* opera (Paris, May 20, 1854); *Sacountalâ,* ballet pantomime (Paris, July 14, 1858); *La Statue,* opera comique (Paris, April 11, 1861; rev. Paris, Feb. 27, 1903); *Érostrate,* opera (in German, Baden-Baden, Aug. 21, 1862; in French, Paris, Oct. 16, 1871); *Sigurd,* opera (Brussels, Jan. 7, 1884); *Salammbô,* opera (Brussels, Feb. 10, 1890). **SACRED:** *Messe pour l'arrivé du Duc d'Aumale à Alger* (1847) and church music; works for men's chorus; piano pieces.

BIBL.: A. Jullien, *E. R.: Sa vie et ses oeuvres* (Paris, 1909); H. Roujon, *Notice sur la vie et les travaux de E. R.* (Paris, 1911); H. de Curzon, *E. R., Sa vie et ses œuvres* (Paris, 1923).

Reynolds, Anna, English mezzo-soprano; b. Canterbury, Oct. 4, 1931. She studied piano at the Royal Academy of Music in London; then went to Italy for vocal lessons; she made her operatic debut in Parma in 1960 as Suzuki; subsequently sang in Vicenza (1961), Rome (1964), Spoleto (1966), Trieste (1967), and Venice (1969), and at La Scala in Milan (1973). She made her 1st appearance in England at Glyndebourne in 1962; sang at Covent Garden in 1967; also sang at Bayreuth (1970–76). She made her Metropolitan Opera debut in N.Y. as Flosshilde in *Das Rheingold* on Nov. 22, 1968; also sang widely as a concert artist and recitalist.

Reynolds, Roger (Lee), American composer; b. Detroit, July 18, 1934. At the Univ. of Michigan he studied engineering (B.S.E., 1957) and composition (M.M., 1961); spent a year in Cologne on a Fulbright grant for work on electronic music (1962); was in Paris in 1963, and in Italy on a Guggenheim fellowship in 1964–65. In 1961 he was one of the founders of the avant-garde festival ONCE in Ann Arbor, Mich. In 1966 he went to Japan at the invitation of the Inst. of Current World Affairs. In 1969 he staged there the Cross Talk Intermedia festival, featuring experimental works by Japanese and American composers. In 1969 he joined the faculty of the Univ. of Calif. at San Diego; was founder-director of its Center for Music Experiment (1971–77); also held guest appointments as a lecturer and composer-in-residence in the U.S. and abroad. In 1989 he won the Pulitzer Prize in Music for his *Whispers Out of Time* (1988). He publ. *A Searcher's Path: A Composer's Ways* (Brooklyn, 1987). In his works, Reynolds makes use of every resource available to the contemporary composer, including traditional instruments and voices and electronic and computer-generated sounds. Much of his early music uses graphic notation, suggesting the desired sounds by pictorial shapes.

WORKS: STAGE: *The Emperor of Ice Cream,* theater piece for 8 Soloists, Percussion, Piano, and Double Bass (1962; N.Y., March 19, 1965; rev. 1974); *I/O: A Ritual for 23 Performers,* including 9 Female Vocalists, 9 Male Mimes, 2 Performers, 2 Flutes, 2 Clarinets, Electronics, and Slides, with the I/O for the title referring to "In/Out," the entire work being based on a concept of Buckminster Fuller with relation to the synergetic antonyms of the opposite sexes (1970; Pasadena, Calif., Jan. 24, 1971); *The Tempest,* incidental music to Shakespeare's play for Actors, Instruments, Computer Synthesizer, and 4-track Tape (Lenox, Mass., July 30, 1980). **ORCH.:** *Graffiti* (1964); *Threshold* (1967); *Between* for Chamber Orch. and Electronics (1968; Chicago, March 10, 1970); *Fiery Wind* (N.Y., Feb. 13, 1978); *Archipelago* for Chamber Orch. and Computer (1982; Paris, Feb. 15, 1983); *Transfigured Wind II* for Flute,

Orch., and Computer (N.Y., June 4, 1984); *Whispers Out of Time* for String Orch. (Amherst, Mass., Dec. 11, 1988). **CHAMBER:** *Quick Are the Mouths of Earth* for Chamber Ensemble (1964–65); *Gathering* for Woodwind Quintet (1965); *Traces* for Flute, Cello, Piano, and Tape (1968); *From behind the Unreasoning Mask* for Trombone, Percussion, and 4-track Tape (1975); *The Promises of Darkness* for Chamber Ensemble (1975); *Only Now, and Again* for 20 Wind Instruments, Piano, and Percussion (1977); *Less than 2* for 2 Pianos, 2 Percussion, and Tape (1977–79); *Shadowed Narrative* for Clarinet, Violin, Cello, and Piano (1977–82); *The Serpent-snapping Eye* for Trumpet, Piano, Percussion, and Tape (1979); *"Coconino . . . a shattered landscape"* for String Quartet (London, Nov. 10, 1985); *Islands from Archipelago: I Summer Island* for Oboe and Tape (1985); *Mistral* for Chamber Ensemble (1985). **VOCAL:** *Sky* for Soprano, Alto Flute, Bassoon, and Harp (1961); *A Portrait of Vanzetti* for Speaker, Ensemble, and Tape (1962–63); *Masks* for 8-part Chorus and Orch. (1965); *Blind Men* for 24 Solo Voices and Instruments (1966); *Compass* for Tenor, Bass, Cello, and Double Bass, all amplified, and 4-track Tape and Slides (1972–73); *The Palace: Voicespace IV* for Baritone and Tape (1980); *Sketchbook* for "the unbearable lightness of being" for Amplified Female Voice and Piano (1985). **4-TRACK TAPE:** *Ping,* inspired by a story of Samuel Beckett, scored for Flute (multiphonic), Piano (motorized by agitating strings), Harmonium, Bowed Cymbal and Tam-tam, Electronic Sound Distribution, Film, Ring Modulator, 35 Slides, and Magnetic Tape (1969); *Still: Voicespace I* (1975); *A Merciful Coincidence: Voicespace II* (1976); *Eclipse: Voicespace III* (1979–80).

BIBL.: G. Chase, *R. R.: Profile of a Composer* (N.Y., 1982).

Reynolds, Verne (Becker), American horn player, teacher, and composer; b. Lyons, Kans., July 18, 1926. He studied violin, piano, and horn; took courses in composition at the Cincinnati Cons. of Music (B.M., 1950) and at the Univ. of Wisconsin as a student of Cecil Burleigh (M.M., 1951); then went to London, where he enrolled at the Royal College of Music in the class of Herbert Howells. Returning to the U.S., he taught at the Univ. of Wisconsin (1950–53) and at Indiana Univ. (1954–59). In 1959 he joined the faculty of the Eastman School of Music in Rochester, N.Y., as a teacher of horn playing. He also played horn in the Cincinnati Sym. Orch. (1947–50), and was principal horn of the Rochester Phil. (1959–68).

WORKS: Violin Concerto (1951); overture, *Saturday with Venus* (1953); *The Hollow Men* for Baritone, Male Chorus, Brass Choir, and Percussion (1954); *Serenade* for 13 Winds (1958); 48 études for Horn (1959); *Celebration Overture* for Orch. (1960); Sonata for Flute and Piano (1962); *Suite* for Brass Quintet (1963); Woodwind Quintet (1964); *Serenade* for Horn and Strings (1966); String Quartet (1967); *Concertare I* for Brass Quintet and Percussion (1968); *Concertare II* for Trumpet and Strings (1968); Sonata for Tuba and Piano (1968); *Concertare III* for Woodwind Quintet and Piano (1969); Sonata for Piano (1970); 48 études for Trumpet (1970); Violin Sonata (1970); *Concertare IV* for Brass Quintet and Piano (1971); *Scenes* for Wind Instruments and Percussion (1971); *Ventures* for Orch. (1975); *Concertare V* for Chamber Ensemble (1976); *Scenes Revisited* for Wind Ensemble (1977); *Festival and Memorial Music* for Orch. (1977); Concerto for Band (1980); Sonata for Cello and Piano (1983); *Horn Vibes* for Horn and Vibraphone (1986); Quintet for Piano and Winds (1986); Brass Quintet (1987); *Songs of the Seasons* for Soprano, Horn, and Piano (1988); *Divertimento* for Oboe, Horn, and Piano (1989).

Řezáč, Ivan, Czech composer; b. Řevnice, Nov. 5, 1924; d. Prague, Dec. 26, 1977. He studied piano with Rauch and composition with Šín, Janeček, and Dobiáš at the Prague Academy, graduating in 1953; later he joined its faculty, becoming its vice-dean in 1961. In his music he follows the type of optimistic lyricism made popular by Shostakovich.

WORKS: OPERA: *Pan Theodor Mundstock* (Mr. Theodor Mundstock; 1974). **ORCH.:** 3 piano concertos (1955, 1964, 1972); 2 syms. (1958, 1961); *Návrat* (The Return) for Cello and Orch. (1962); *Quadrature of the Heart* for String Quartet and Orch. (1975); *Vivace* for 67 Musicians (1977); *Montage* (1977). CHAMBER: 2 string quartets (1955, 1971); Cello Sonata (1956); Piano Trio (1958); *Nocturnes* for Violin and Piano (1959); *Torso of a Schumann Monument* for Viola and Piano (1963); Duo for Violin and Piano Piano (1965); 6 *Tales* for Cello and Guitar (1973); *Musica da camera* for Flute, Oboe, Violin, Viola, and Cello (1973); 2 piano sonatas (1954, 1957); 2 piano sonatinas (1959, 1966); *Dry Points* for Piano (1962); *Sisyfona Neděle* (Sisyphus Sunday) for Piano (1972).

Rezniček, Emil Nikolaus von, Austrian conductor, pedagogue, and composer; b. Vienna, May 4, 1860; d. Berlin, Aug. 2, 1945. He studied law at Graz and music with Wilhelm Mayer (W.A. Rémy); later took a brief course with Reinecke and Jadassohn at the Leipzig Cons. (1884). He was subsequently engaged as a theater conductor in Zürich, Berlin, Mainz, and other cities; was court conductor in Weimar (1896) and Mannheim (1896–99). After a short residence in Wiesbaden, he settled in Berlin, and in 1902 established there a very successful series of concerts for chamber orch., the Orchester-Kammerkonzerte; in 1906 he was appointed prof. at the Scharwenka Cons. in Berlin; conducted the Warsaw Opera from 1906 to 1909; then was the conductor of the Komische Oper in Berlin (1909–11); from 1920 to 1926, he taught at the Hochschule für Musik in Berlin. His most successful score was the opera *Donna Diana;* its overture became a popular favorite.
WORKS: OPERAS: *Die Jungfrau von Orleans* (Prague, June 19, 1887); *Satanella* (Prague, May 3, 1888); *Emmerich Fortunat* (Prague, Nov. 8, 1889); *Donna Diana* (Prague, Dec. 16, 1894; rev. 1908, 1933); *Till Eulenspiegel* (Karlsruhe, Jan. 12, 1902); *Eros und Psyche* (Breslau, 1917); *Ritter Blaubart* (Darmstadt, Jan. 29, 1920); *Holofernes* (Berlin, Oct. 27, 1923); *Tanzsymphonie* (Leipzig, Jan. 13, 1927); *Satuala* (Leipzig, 1927); *Spiel oder Ernst* (Dresden, Nov. 11, 1930); *Der Gondoliere des Dogen* (Stuttgart, Oct. 29, 1931); *Das Opfer* (1932); *Tenor und Bass* (Stockholm, 1934); also an operetta, *Die Angst vor der Ehe* (Frankfurt an der Oder, 1914). ORCH.: 4 syms.: No. 1, *Tragic* (1904); No. 2, *Ironic* (1905); No. 3 (1918); No. 4 (1919); *Nachstück* for Violin or Cello and Orch. (1905); *Serenade* for Strings (1924); 4 *Symphonic Dances* (1925); Violin Concerto (Berlin, Feb. 26, 1925); *Raskolnikoff*, overture (1932); also chamber works, including 3 string quartets (1921, 1923, 1932); choral music; songs; piano pieces; organ music.
BIBL.: O. Taubmann, *E.N. v.R.* (Leipzig, 1907); M. Chop, *E.N. v.R.: Sein Leben und seine Werke* (Vienna, 1920); R. Specht, *E.N. v.R.: Eine vorläufige Studie* (Leipzig, 1923); F. von Rezniček, *Gegen den Strom* (Vienna, 1960); T. Leibnitz, *Österreichische Spätromantiker: Studien zu E.N. v.R., Joseph Marx, Franz Schmidt, und Egon Kornauth* (Tutzing, 1986).

Rhaw or **Rhau, Georg,** German publisher and composer; b. Eisfeld an der Werre, Suhl, 1488; d. Wittenberg, Aug. 6, 1548. He studied at the Univ. of Wittenberg (B.A., 1514); was then cantor of the Thomaskirche and of the Thomasschule in Leipzig from 1518 to 1520, bringing out the *Missa de Sancto Spirito* (1519) during the disputations between Luther and Eck; then settled in Eisleben as a schoolmaster; later taught in Hildburghausen (1521–23); in 1523 he went to Wittenberg, where he established a publishing business, issuing many 1st eds. of Luther's writings and numerous collections of musical works, mostly Protestant. He wrote *Enchiridion utriusque musicae practicae* (Wittenberg, 1517; 2nd ed., 1518, as *Enchiridion musices ex variis musicorum libris depromptu*; 9th ed., 1558; facsimile ed. by H. Albrecht, Kassel, 1951) and *Enchiridion musicae mensuralis* (Leipzig, 1520; 10th ed., 1553).
BIBL.: W. Wölbing, *Der Drucker und Musikverleger G. Rhaw: Ein Beitrag zur Drucker- und Verlegstätigkeit im Zeitalter der Reformation* (diss., Univ. of Berlin, 1922); V. Mattfeld, *G. Rhaw's Publications for Vespers* (Brooklyn, 1966).

Rheinberger, Joseph (Gabriel), eminent German organist, conductor, composer, and pedagogue; b. Vaduz, Liechtenstein, March 17, 1839; d. Munich, Nov. 25, 1901. He played piano and organ as a child; then took regular lessons in organ with

J.G. Herzog, piano with J.E. Leonhard, and composition with J.H. Maier at the Munich Cons.; subsequently studied composition with Franz Lachner. From 1864 to 1877 he served as principal conductor of the Munich Choral Soc.; was named Hofkapellmeister in 1877. In 1859 he succeeded his teacher Leonhard as prof. of piano at the Munich Cons., and also taught composition there. His loyalty to the cultural and musical institutions in Munich earned him many honors from the Bavarian government; King Ludwig II made him Knight of St. Michael; in 1894 he was given the rank of "Zivilverdienstorden," the equivalent of nobility; in 1899 he was made Dr.Phil. *honoris causa* by the Univ. of Munich. Rheinberger's reputation as a teacher of organ was without equal during his lifetime; students flocked to him from all parts of the world. As a composer, he created a number of works remarkable for their dignity, formal perfection, and consummate technical mastery, if not their inventive power. His organ sonatas are unquestionably among the finest productions of organ literature.
WORKS: STAGE: *Die sieben Raben*, romantic opera (Munich, 1869); *Des Türmers Töchterlein*, comic opera (Munich, 1873); incidental music. ORCH.: 2 syms.; 2 organ concertos; Piano Concerto; other orch. works. CHAMBER: 3 string quartets; 2 violin sonatas; Cello Sonata; 4 piano sonatas and other piano music. VOCAL: Masses; 3 Requiems; cantatas; motets; hymns; sacred songs; secular choral works and songs. See H.-J. Irmen, *Joseph Rheinberger: Thematisches Verzeichnis seiner Kompositionen* (Regensburg, 1975).
BIBL.: P. Molitor, *J. R. und seine Kompositionen für die Orgel* (Leipzig, 1904); T. Kroyer, *J. R.* (Regensburg, 1916); H. Grace, *The Organ Works of R.* (London, 1925); H.-J. Irmen, *J. R. als Antipode des Cäcilianismus* (Regensburg, 1970); H. Wagner and H.-J. Irmen, eds., *J.G. R.: Briefe und Dokumente seines Leben* (Vaduz, 1982).

Rhené-Baton (real name, **René Baton**), French conductor and composer; b. Courseulles-sur-Mer, Calvados, Sept. 5, 1879; d. Le Mans, Sept. 23, 1940. He studied piano at the Paris Cons. and music theory privately with Gédalge. He began his conducting career as a chorus director at the Opéra-Comique in Paris; then conducted various concert groups in Angers and Bordeaux; from 1916 to 1932 he was principal conductor of the Concerts Pasdeloup. He composed orch. pieces, chamber music, and a number of songs.

Rhodes, Phillip (Carl), American composer; b. Forest City, N.C., June 6, 1940. He studied composition with Iain Hamilton at Duke Univ. (B.A., 1962); took courses in composition with Donald Martino and Mel Powell and in theory with Gunther Schuller and George Perle at Yale Univ. (M.M., 1963). He was composer-in-residence in Cicero, Ill. (1966–68) and Louisville (1969–72); taught at Amherst College (1968–69), the Univ. of Louisville (1969–72), and Carleton College in Northfield, Minn. (from 1974). From 1985 to 1987 he served as president of the College Music Soc.
WORKS: STAGE: OPERAS: *The Gentle Boy* (1979–80; rev. 1987; Tallahassee, June 12, 1987); *The Magic Pipe* (1989). BALLET: *About Faces* (1970). ORCH.: 4 *Movements* for Chamber Orch. (1962); *Remembrance* for Symphonic Wind Ensemble (1966–67); *Divertimento* for Small Orch. (1971); 3 *"B's"* for Youth Orch. (1971); Concerto for Bluegrass Band and Orch. (Louisville, Dec. 22, 1974); *Ceremonial Fanfare and Chorale* for 2 Brass Choirs (1977); *Adventure Fantasies for Young Players* for Wind Ensemble (1983–84); works for band. CHAMBER: String Trio (1965; rev. 1973); *Museum Pieces* for Clarinet and String Quartet (1973); Quartet for Flute, Harp, Violin, and Cello (1975); pieces for solo instruments. VOCAL: *On the Morning of Christ's Nativity*, cantata for Soprano, Tenor, Wind Quintet, and Harp (1976); *Wind Songs* for Unison Children's Choir and Orff Instruments (1979); *In Praise of Wisdom* for Chorus and Brass Choir (1982); *Nets to Catch the Wind* for Chorus and Percussion (1986).

Rhodes, Willard, distinguished American music educator and ethnomusicologist; b. Dashler, Ohio, May 12, 1901. He earned his A.B. and B.Mus. degrees from Heidelberg College in Tiffin, Ohio, both in 1922; then studied at the Mannes School of Music in N.Y. (1923–25) and at Columbia Univ. (M.A., 1925); went to Paris, where he took lessons in piano with Alfred Cortot and in composition with Nadia Boulanger (1925–27). From 1927 to 1935 he served as conductor with the American Opera Co., the Cincinnati Summer Opera Co., and with his own Rhodes Chamber Opera Co. He then turned to educational music; was director of music in the public schools of Bronxville, N.Y. (1935–37). In 1937 he was appointed to the faculty at Columbia Univ.; became prof. emeritus in 1969. He held the post of music consultant to the U.S. Bureau of Indian Affairs beginning in 1937, and was a founding member (1953) and 1st president (1956–58) of the Soc. for Ethnomusicology. It was in this connection that he accumulated a most valuable collection of Amerindian folk music, both notated and recorded (many pressings released by the Library of Congress). In 1961 he was elected president of the Soc. for Asian Music, and in 1968 of the International Folk Music Council; also was a Fellow of the African Studies Assoc. and numerous other ethnomusicological organizations. He did field work in Rhodesia and Nyasaland (1957–58) and in South India (1965–66); was visiting prof. at various institutions.

BIBL.: Special issue of *Ethnomusicology* (May 1969).

Riadis (real name, **Khu**), **Emilios,** Greek composer; b. Salonica, May 13, 1885; d. there, July 17, 1935. He studied piano and harmony with Dimitrios Lalas in Salonica; then took courses with Walbrunn, Mayer-Gschrey, Becht, and Stich at the Munich Academy of Music (1908–10); later studied with Charpentier and Ravel in Paris (1910–15), where he appeared as a composer under the name Riadis, formed from the ending of his mother's maiden name, Elefteriadis (his father's real name was Khu). In 1915 he became a piano teacher at the Salonica Cons. He wrote a number of songs, distinguished by an expressive melodic line, somewhat oriental in its intervallic pattern; his harmonizations are in the French manner. Most of his works for stage, orch., and chamber ensembles were left unfinished.

Riaño, Juan Facundo, Spanish music scholar; b. Granada, Nov. 24, 1828; d. Madrid, Feb. 27, 1901. He was the founder and director of the Museo de Reproducciones Artísticas. He publ. *Critical and Bibliographical Notes on Early Spanish Music* (London, 1887), a valuable work containing many reproductions of old Spanish instruments. He developed the theory that the neumes of the Mozarabic notation were derived from the characters of the Visigothic alphabet.

Rïbakov, Sergei Gavrilovich, Russian ethnomusicologist; b. Samara, Oct. 9, 1867; d. Moscow, Dec. 28, 1921. He studied history and philosophy at St. Petersburg Univ., where he attended Rimsky-Korsakov's classes in composition. In 1893 he joined a folk-song commission set up by the Russian Geographical Soc. and the Academy of Sciences; traveled extensively in the Urals, Sibera, and southeastern Russia. On his 1st journey (1895–97), he collected over 200 folk songs of the Bashkirs and Tatars; in 1899, using a phonograph, he collected music of the Tajiks, Turkmens, and Uzbeks.

WRITINGS (all in Russian and publ. in St. Petersburg): *The Kuray: A Bashkir Musical Instrument* (1896); *The Church Bell in Russia* (1896); *Music and Song of the Ural Moslems with an Essay on Their Way of Life* (1897).

Ribáry, Antal, Hungarian composer; b. Budapest, Jan. 8, 1924. He studied composition with Rezső Kokai at the Budapest Academy of Music (1943–47); later took lessons with Ferenc Szabó.

WORKS: STAGE: 2 operas: *Lajos Király Válik* (The Divorce of King Louis; 1959) and *Liliom* (1960); ballet, *Fortunio* (1969). **ORCH.:** Sinfonietta (1956); Cello Concerto (1958); 11 syms. (1960–89); *Musica per archi* (1961); *Pantomime* (1962); Violin Concertino (1965); *Dialogues* for Viola and Orch. (1967); 3 piano concertos (1979, 1980, 1985); Violin Concerto (1987); *Funeral Music in Memory of Bohuslav Martinů* (1988). **VO-CAL:** cantatas; *Metamorphosis* for Soprano, 3 Woodwinds, Piano, Vibraphone, 3 Bongos, 3 Gongs, and Strings (1966); oratorio,

La Paques à New York (1987); songs. **CHAMBER:** 4 violin sonatas; 5 string quartets; 2 cello sonatas (1948, rev. 1973; 1968); String Quintet (1956); Viola Sonata (1958); *9 Miniatures* for String Quartet (1966); *5 Miniatures* for Wind Trio (1969); *Chamber Music* for 5 Instruments (1970); *Dialogues* for Flute and Piano (1971); *Fantasia* or *Fantasia Concertante* for Violin, Viola, and Cello (1973); *Sonata Fantasia* for Cello and Piano (1977–78); *Rhapsodietta* for Flute and Piano (1982); piano music, including 4 sonatas.

Ribera (Maneja), Antonio, Spanish conductor; b. Barcelona, May 3, 1873; d. Madrid, March 4, 1956. He studied with Riemann and Mottl in Leipzig and Munich; conducted the Wagner Soc. in Barcelona (1901–4); then was a theater conductor in Lemberg (1905–12), again in Barcelona (1912–25), and in Madrid (from 1925).

Ribera (y Tarragó), Julián, Spanish musicologist; b. Carcagente, near Valencia, Sept. 19, 1858; d. there, May 2, 1934. He was educated at the Univs. of Valencia and Madrid (Ph.D.); taught Arabic at the Univ. of Saragossa (from 1887) and Arabian-Spanish literature at the Univ. of Madrid (from 1905). He brought out the ed. *La música andaluza medieval en las canciones de trovadors, troveros y minnesinger* (3 vols., Madrid, 1923–25).

Writings (all publ. in Madrid): *La música de las cantigas [de Santa María de Alfonso el Sabio]* (1922; 2nd ed., without music transcription, as *Historia de la música árabe medieval y su influencia en la española;* abridged Eng. tr., 1929, as *Music in Ancient Arabia and Spain*); *La música de la jota aragonesa* (1928).

BIBL.: H. Spanke, "Die Theorie R.s über Zusammenhänge zwischen frühromanisch Strophenformen und andalusisch-arabischer Lyrik des Mittelalters," *Volkstum und Kultur der Romanen,* III (Hamburg, 1930); V. Castañeda, "Don J. R.y.T.," *Boletín de la Real Academia de la Historia,* 104 (Madrid, 1934).

Ricci, Federico, Italian composer, brother of **Luigi Ricci;** b. Naples, Oct. 22, 1809; d. Conegliano, Dec. 10, 1877. He studied with Zingarelli, Bellini, and his brother Luigi at the Naples Cons. (1818–29). He gained notable success as a composer for the theater with his opera *La prigione di Edimburgo* (Trieste, March 13, 1838); it was followed by the successful operas *Luigi Rolla* (Florence, March 30, 1841) and *Corrado d'Altamura* (Milan, Nov. 16, 1841); having established his reputation, he never again was able to duplicate these successes; in subsequent years he devoted himself mainly to composing comic operas. In 1853 he was made maître de chapelle of the imperial theaters in St. Petersburg, but this post only involved supervising the vocal classes at the Cons. In 1869 he went to Paris, where he found success with his opéra bouffe *Une Folie à Rome* (Jan. 30, 1869). He retired to Conegliano in 1876.

BIBL.: F. de Villars, *Notices sur Luigi et F. R., suivies d'une analyse critique de "Crispino e la comare"* (Paris, 1866); L. de Rada, *I fratelli R.* (Florence, 1878).

Ricci, Luigi, Italian composer, brother of **Federico Ricci;** b. probably in Naples, June 8(?), 1805; d. Prague, Dec. 31, 1859. He enrolled at the Naples Cons. when he was 9, his principal teachers being Furno and Zingarelli; also studied privately with Generali. His 1st opera, *L'Impresario in angustie,* was performed at the Cons. in his 18th year; he scored a major success with his opera *Chiara di Rosembergh* (Milan, Oct. 11, 1831), composed for the diva Giuditta Grisi; his *Un avventura di Scaramuccia* proved a popular favorite when premiered there (March 8, 1834). In 1836 he was appointed maestro di cappella in Trieste, where he also became maestro concertatore at the Teatro Grande; after the twins Fanny and Lidia Stolz joined its roster in 1843, Ricci became closely associated with them—indeed, so closely that he began living with them during his tenure as director of the Odessa Opera (1844–45). Returning to Trieste, he finally married Lidia in 1849 but did not abandon his intimacy with Fanny; Lidia bore him a daughter, Adelaide (1850–71), who became a singer at the

Paris Théâtre-Italien (1868–69); Fanny bore him a son, also named Luigi (1852–1906), who became a composer. After he produced his last opera, *Il Diavolo a quattro* (Trieste, May 15, 1859), a mental derangement manifested itself, and he was sent to an asylum in Prague, where he spent the remaining months of his life.

BIBL.: V. dal Torso, *L. R.* (Trieste, 1860); F. de Villars, *Notices sur L. et Federico R., suivies d'une analyse critique de "Crispino e la comare"* (Paris, 1866); L. de Rada, *I fratelli R.* (Florence, 1878).

Ricci, Ruggiero, celebrated American violinist; b. San Bruno, Calif., July 24, 1918. His musical education was lovingly fostered by his father, along with that of 6 of his siblings, every one of whom started out as a musician, and 2 of whom, the cellist Giorgio Ricci and the violinist Emma Ricci, achieved the rank of professional performer. Ruggiero studied violin with Louis Persinger, and made a sensational appearance at a public concert in San Francisco on Nov. 15, 1928, when he was 10 years old, with his teacher accompanying him at the piano. On Oct. 20, 1929, he played in N.Y.; he embarked on an international concert tour in 1932. He successfully negotiated the perilous transition from child prodigy to serious artist; he accumulated a formidable repertoire of about 60 violin concertos, including all the violin works of Paganini; ed. the newly discovered MS of Paganini's early Violin Concerto, presumed to have been composed c.1815, and gave its 1st N.Y. perf. with the American Sym. Orch. on Oct. 7, 1977; he also gave the 1st performances of violin concertos by several modern composers, among them Alberto Ginastera (1963) and Gottfried von Einem (1970). During World War II, he served as "entertainment specialist" with the U.S. Army Air Force. After the end of the war, he returned to the concert stage; made several world tours, which included South America, Australia, Japan, and Russia; he also gave master courses at the North Carolina School of the Arts, Indiana Univ., and the Juilliard School of Music in N.Y. He owns a 1734 Guarnerius del Gesù violin. In 1978 he celebrated a "Golden Jubilee," marking half a century of his professional career.

Ricciarelli, Katia, Italian soprano; b. Rovigo, Jan. 18, 1946. She studied at the Venice Cons.; made her operatic debut as Mimi in Mantua in 1969; after winning the Giuseppe Verdi Award for Young Singers in Parma (1970) and the New Verdi Voices Contest (1971), she pursued a successful career in the major Italian music centers. She made her U.S. debut as Lucrezia in *I due Foscari* in Chicago (1972); her 1st appearance at London's Covent Garden was as Mimi (1974), a role she also chose for her Metropolitan Opera debut in N.Y. (April 11, 1975). Among her finest roles are Amelia in *Simon Boccanegra*, Suor Angelica, Desdemona, Luisa Miller, and Elisabeth de Valois. In 1985 she sang the role of Desdemona in Zeffirelli's film version of Verdi's *Otello*.

Ricciotti, Carlo, Italian violinist and operatic impresario; b. c.1681; d. The Hague, July 13, 1756. He settled in The Hague, where he became director of a French opera company. Six *Concerti armonici* long attributed to Pergolesi were later attributed to Ricciotti; later they were confirmed to be the work of Count Unico van Wassenaer.

BIBL.: A. Dunning, *Count Unico Wilhelm van Wassenaer (1692–1766); A Master Unmasked; or, The Pergolesi-R. Puzzle Solved* (Buren, 1980).

Riccitelli, Primo, Italian composer; b. Campli, Aug. 9, 1875; d. Giulianova, March 27, 1941. He was a pupil of Mascagni at the Liceo Rossini in Pesaro; wrote operas: *Maria sul Monte* (1911; Milan, July 8, 1916); *I Compagnacci* (1 act; Rome, April 10, 1923; Metropolitan Opera, N.Y., Jan. 2, 1924); *Madone Oretta* (Rome, Feb. 3, 1932); also songs.

Riccius, August Ferdinand, German conductor, music critic, and composer, uncle of **Karl August Riccius;** b. Bernstadt, Feb. 26, 1819; d. Karlsbad, July 5, 1886. He was conductor of the Euterpe Concerts in Leipzig (from 1849); then at the City Theater there (1854–64); in 1864 he went to Hamburg,

where he conducted opera and wrote music criticism for the *Hamburger Nachrichten*. He composed an overture to Schiller's *Braut von Messina;* a cantata, *Die Weihe der Kraft;* piano music; choruses; songs.

Riccius, Karl August, German violinist, conductor, and composer, nephew of **August Ferdinand Riccius;** b. Bernstadt, July 26, 1830; d. Dresden, July 8, 1893. He studied in Dresden with Wieck, and in Leipzig with Mendelssohn, Schumann, and Ferdinand David. In 1847 he became violinist in the Dresden Court Orch., and later also conductor. He wrote a comic opera, *Es spukt* (Dresden, 1871); several ballets; music to various plays; publ. piano pieces and songs.

Rich, Alan, American music critic of an uncommonly bellicose disposition tempered by prejudice toward favorites; b. Boston, June 17, 1924. He muddled through a premedical course at Harvard Univ. (A.B., 1945) but made a *salto mortale* to grab a chance at a little dinky job as a secondary music critic of the moribund *Boston Herald,* at which he served in 1944–45; moving ahead, he wrote for various insolvent papers, such as the *N.Y. Sun* (1947–48). Turning serious, he took a course in musicology with Manfred Bukofzer and Joseph Kerman at the Univ. of Calif. at Berkeley (M.A., 1952); spent a season in Vienna on an Alfred Hertz Memorial Traveling Fellowship in Music (1952–53), where he was guided musicographically by the grand man of scholarly research, Otto Erich Deutsch, and incidentally learned the rudiments of conducting with Walter Gmeindl. He wrote for the *American Record Guide* (1947–61), *Musical America* (1955–61), the *N.Y. Times* (1961–63), the *N.Y. Herald Tribune* (1963–66), and its ephemeral successor, the *N.Y. World-Journal-Tribune* (1966–67), as well as for the prosperously extant weekly *New York* magazine (1968–81). Afflicted with acute Mehtaphobia, he went back west after Zubin Mehta abandoned Los Angeles for N.Y.; became a bicoastal writer, working for *New York* and its western clone, *California* magazine (1979–83); then was contributing ed. of the latter (1983–85). In 1979 he began producing documentaries for public radio; taught music criticism at the Univ. of Southern Calif., the Calif. Inst. of the Arts, and the Univ. of Calif., Los Angeles. After holding the post of general ed. of *Newsweek* magazine (1983–87), he was music critic of the *Los Angeles Herald-Examiner* (1987–90). He won 3 ASCAP–Deems Taylor awards (1970, 1973, 1974). He publ. *Careers and Opportunities in Music* (N.Y., 1964); *Music, Mirror of the Arts* (N.Y., 1969); 3 vols. of the *Simon & Schuster Listeners Guide to Music* (1980); *The Lincoln Center Story* (1984). Virgil Thomson described Rich as "our only musical muckraker."

Rich, Buddy (Bernard), remarkable American jazz drummer and bandleader; b. N.Y., June 30, 1917; d. Los Angeles, April 2, 1987. His parents were vaudeville performers who made him a part of their act before he was 2; he was only 4 when he appeared as a drummer and tap dancer on Broadway; made his 1st tour of the U.S. and Australia at the age of 6; led his own stage band by the time he was 11. In 1937 he joined the band of Joe Marsala; after working with Bunny Berigan, Harry James, Artie Shaw, and Benny Carter, he performed with Tommy Dorsey (1939–42; 1944–45); then led his own band until 1951. He again performed with James (1953–54; 1955–57; 1961–66) and Dorsey (1954–55), and also led his own combo (1957–61); in 1966 he founded his own big band, with which he toured throughout the world until it folded in 1974. In subsequent years he made appearances at his own N.Y. club, Buddy's Place, leading a small combo; during the last years of his life, he also toured with his own jazz-rock big band. Rich was one of the outstanding swing drummers of his time.

BIBL.: W. Balliett, *Super Drummer: A Profile of B. R.* (Indianapolis, 1968); D. Meriwether, *The B. R. Orchestra and Small Groups* (Spotswood, N.J., 1974); K. Stratemann, *B. R. and Gene Krupa: A Filmo-Discography* (Lübbecke, 1980); D. Meriwether, *We Don't Play Requests: A Musical Biography/Discography of B. R.* (Chicago, 1984); J. Nesbitt, *Inside B. R.: A Study of the Master Drummer's Style and Technique* (Delevan, N.Y., 1984).

Rich, Charlie, American country-music singer; b. Colt, Ark., Dec. 12, 1932. He took up the saxophone in his youth; during service in the U.S. Air Force, he played in a jazz group; after his discharge, he made a successful career as a singer.

Richafort, Jean, eminent Flemish composer; b. probably in Hainaut, c.1480; d. probably in Bruges, c.1547. He may have been a pupil of Josquin Des Prez; was maître de chapelle at St. Rombaud in Mechelen (1507–9); later was active at the French royal chapel. He excelled as a composer of motets. Among his extant works are 2 masses, a Requiem Mass, 12 Magnificats, many motets, and a number of chansons.

BIBL.: G. van Doorslaer, "J. R., maître de chapelle-compositeur," *Bulletin de l'Académie Royale d'Archéologie de Belgique, 1929* (1930); M. Kabis, *The Works of J. R., Renaissance Composer (1480?–1548)* (diss., N.Y. Univ., 1957).

Richard (real name, **Richards**), **Keith,** English rock musician; b. Dartford, Kent, Dec. 18, 1943. He met his exact contemporary Mick Jagger in London and did some experimental jamming with him, later joining a rhythm-and-blues club circuit, eventually forming one of the most successful rock groups, The Rolling Stones. Their concerts in England and America outgrew the dimensions of mere musical events and achieved the distinction of a social movement, complete with hallucinogenic drugs, homicidal eruptions, and sexual extravagance. Richard, the most reckless of the group, was busted for possession and, much worse, trafficking in heroin, but the British law was lenient to him, and he escaped *durance vile* in a jail. He was busted again in Toronto in 1977, but was sentenced only to the penalty of giving a benefit concert. He maintained close relationships with Jagger and The Rolling Stones, weathering such blows as a boycott by a feminist organization that accused the group of violent sexism and racism in the song *Brown Sugar*, containing obscene unprintable verses. His strength as the lead guitar, combined with his lurid lyrics (composed with Jagger), provided The Rolling Stones with their most outrageous successes, including *Satisfaction, 19th Nervous Breakdown, Street Fighting Man, Sympathy for the Devil, Sister Morphine,* and *Let's Spend the Night Together.*

Richards, (Henry) Brinley, Welsh pianist, teacher, and composer; b. Carmarthen, Nov. 13, 1817; d. London, May 1, 1885. He was a pupil at the Royal Academy of Music in London; resided in London, and was highly esteemed as a concert pianist and teacher. He wrote much symphonic and vocal music; also the popular hymn *God bless the Prince of Wales* (1862).

Richie, Lionel, popular black American singer and songwriter; b. Tuskegee, Ala., June 20, 1949. He taught himself to play piano and tenor saxophone; while studying economics at Tuskegee Inst., he joined the rhythm-and-blues group the Mystics, later known as the Commodores. Richie rose to prominence as the group's leading vocalist and songwriter via the albums *Caught in the Act* (1975), *Commodores* (1977), *Midnight Magic* (1979), *Heroes* (1980), and *Share Your Love* (1981). He then went solo with his album appropriately named *Lionel Richie* (1982), which included the hit single *Truly,* which garnered him a Grammy Award as best male pop vocalist of the year. His album *Can't Slow Down* (1983) won a Grammy Award in 1984 as best album of the year. With Michael Jackson, he wrote the song *We Are the World* in support of famine relief efforts in Africa; it captured a Grammy Award as best song of 1985.

BIBL.: R. Plutzik, *L. R.* (N.Y., 1985); T. Koenig, *L. R.* (Mankato, Minn., 1986).

Richings (originally, **Reynoldson**), **(Mary) Caroline,** English-born American pianist, soprano, impresario, and teacher; b. 1827; d. Richmond, Va., Jan. 14, 1882. She was taken to the U.S. as a child and adopted by the actor Peter Richings; after appearing as a pianist in Philadelphia, she received vocal instruction and made her operatic debut there as Marie in *La Fille du régiment* (Feb. 9, 1852). Her father organized the Richings Grand Opera Co. (1859), and she appeared with it both as a pianist and as a singer; when her father retired

(1867), she assumed the position of director. After she married a tenor in the company, Peter Bernard, it was renamed the Richings-Bernard Co.; in 1870 they formed a partnership with Euphrosyne Parepa-Rosa and gave performances as the short-lived Caroline Richings-Bernard Grand Opera Combination. She served as director of her own concert organization, the Old Folks Opera Co. (1874–75), and subsequently settled in Baltimore, singing in light opera and concert; was also active as a voice teacher. She made her farewell stage appearance in her own operetta, *The Duchess* (Baltimore, Aug. 1881).

Richter, Ernst Friedrich (Eduard), eminent German music theorist, teacher, organist, and composer; b. Gross-Schönau, Oct. 24, 1808; d. Leipzig, April 9, 1879. He studied at the Zittau Gymnasium and then pursued theological studies at the Univ. of Leipzig; received instruction in music from the Kantor Weinlig; when the Leipzig Cons. was founded in 1843, he became Hauptmann's co-adjutor as teacher of harmony; conducted the Leipzig Singakademie (1843–47); was organist of the Petrikirche (from 1851) and the Neukirche (from 1862); in 1868 became music director of the Nikolaikirche and cantor of the Thomasschule. He composed several sacred cantatas, masses, Psalms, etc., and also wrote chamber music, piano pieces, and organ compositions. But he became primarily known as the compiler of practical and useful manuals on harmony, counterpoint, and fugue, which went into numerous eds. and trs. into all European languages, among them *Die Grundzüge der musikalischen Formen und ihre Analyse* (Leipzig, 1852); *Lehrbuch der Harmonie* (Leipzig, 1853; 36th ed., 1953; Eng. tr., N.Y., 1867; newly tr. by T. Baker from the 25th German ed., N.Y., 1912; also in Swedish, Russian, Polish, Italian, French, Spanish, and Dutch); *Lehrbuch der Fuge* (Leipzig, 1859; 9th ed., 1921; in Eng., London, 1878; also in French); *Katechismus der Orgel* (Leipzig, 1868; 4th ed., 1896); *Lehrbuch des einfachen und doppelten Kontrapunkts* (Leipzig, 1872; 15th ed., 1920; in Eng., London, 1874, and N.Y., 1884; also in French and Russian); his son, Alfred Richter, brought out an *Aufgabenbuch zu E.F. Richters Harmonielehre* (Leipzig, 1879; 64th ed., 1952).

Richter, Ferdinand Tobias, German-born Austrian organist and composer; b. Würzburg (baptized), July 22, 1651; d. Vienna, Nov. 3, 1711. He was court and chamber organist in Vienna from 1683; enjoyed a great reputation as a theorist and teacher. Among his compositions were 20 operas, 4 oratorios and other sacred works, music for Jesuit school plays, and various keyboard pieces.

Richter, Franz Xaver, German singer, teacher, and composer of Moravian-Bohemian descent; b. probably in Holleschau, Dec. 1, 1709; d. Strasbourg, Sept. 12, 1789. He applied himself to a thorough study of Fux's *Gradus ad Parnassum;* in 1740 he became Vice-Kapellmeister to the Prince-Abbot Anselm von Reichlin-Meldegg in Kempten, Allgäu; by 1749 he was a court musician to the Elector Palatine Carl Theodor in Mannheim, where he was active as a singer and composer; about 1768 he became chamber composer there; was Kapellmeister at Strasbourg Cathedral (from 1769). He wrote a treatise, *Harmonische Belehrung oder gründliche Anweisung zur musikalischen Ton-Kunst oder regulären Composition* (MS; ed. and tr. by C. Kalkbrenner as *Traité d'harmonie et de composition,* Paris, 1804). His extant works include about 80 syms.; overtures; 6 harpsichord concertos; 8 flute concertos; Oboe Concerto; 12 sonatas for Harpsichord, and Violin or Flute or Cello; 6 sonatas for 2 Flutes or Violin; 6 solos for Flute or Violin, and Basso Continuo; 6 sonatas for 2 Violins, Cello, and Harpsichord; 12 sonatas for 2 Violins, Cello, and Harpsichord; 6 Quartettos for 2 Violins, Viola, and Cello; various keyboard pieces; and much sacred music.

BIBL.: F. Mathias, "Thematischer Katalog der im Strassburger Münsterarchiv aufbewahrten kirchenmusikalischen Werke F.X. R.s (1709–1789)," *Riemann Festschrift* (Leipzig, 1909); W. Barth, *Die Messenkompositionen F.X. R.s (1709–89)* (diss., Univ. of Munich, 1941); W. Gässler, *Die Sinfonien von F.X.*

R. (diss., Univ. of Munich, 1942); E. Schmitt, "F.X. R.," *Caecilia*, LXXII (1964).

Richter-Haaser, Hans, respected German pianist and teacher; b. Dresden, Jan. 6, 1912; d. Braunschweig, Dec. 13, 1980. At age 13 he became a pupil of Hans Schneider at the Dresden Academy of Music, where he won the Bechstein Prize when he was 18; made his debut in Dresden (1928), and thereafter performed throughout Germany. After his career was interrupted by World War II, he settled in Detmold and conducted the municipal orch. (1946–47); then was a prof. at the North West German Music Academy there (1947–62); concurrently pursued an international career; made his U.S. debut in N.Y. (1959). He was esteemed for his performances of the Classical and Romantic repertoire, winning high praise for his Beethoven. He also composed 2 piano concertos, chamber music, piano pieces, and songs.

Richter, Hans, eminent German conductor; b. Raab, Hungary, April 4, 1843; d. Bayreuth, Dec. 5, 1916. He studied theory with Sechter, violin with Heissler, and horn with Kleinecke at the Vienna Cons. (1860–65); from 1862 to 1866 he was employed as horn player in the orch. at the Kärnthnertortheater in Vienna. The turning point in his career was his contact with Wagner at Triebschen in 1866, when Wagner asked him to make a fair copy of the score of *Die Meistersinger von Nürnberg*; obviously satisfied with Richter's work, Wagner recommended him to Hans von Bülow as a chorus master at the Munich Court Opera (1867); in 1868–69 Richter was also given an opportunity to assist von Bülow as conductor of the Court Orch. in Munich. Subsequently became a favorite conductor of Wagner and prepared rehearsals of Wagner's operas, among them the Brussels performance of *Lohengrin* (March 22, 1870). From 1871 to 1875 he was chief conductor of the Pest National Theater; then conducted at the Vienna Court Opera, becoming its 1st principal conductor in 1875; concurrently he conducted the concerts of the Vienna Phil. (1875–82; 1883–97) and the Gesellschaft der Musikfreunde (1880–90). He was selected by Wagner to conduct the entire *Ring des Nibelungen* at the Bayreuth Festival in 1876; received the Order of Maximilian from the King of Bavaria and the Order of the Falcon from the Grand Duke of Weimar. When Wagner went to London in 1877, he took Richter along with him and let him conduct several concerts of the Wagner Festival in Albert Hall. In May 1879 Richter conducted a 2nd Wagner Festival in London, which led to the establishment of an annual series of May concerts known as "Orchestral Festival Concerts" and later simply "Richter Concerts," which he conducted regularly until 1897; then he was engaged as conductor of the Hallé Orch. in Manchester. He appeared as a conductor at London's Covent Garden (1882, 1886), and later was a regular conductor of Wagner's operas there (1903–10); after conducting at Bayreuth (1912), he returned to Covent Garden. He likewise was conductor of the Birmingham Festivals (1885–1909) and of the London Sym. Orch. (1904–11). He conducted his farewell concert with the Hallé Orch. in Manchester on April 11, 1911. His popularity in England was immense; his corpulent, bearlike figure and imposing Germanic beard imparted an air of authority; his technique was flawless. Besides Wagner's music, Richter championed the works of Beethoven, Brahms, Bruckner, and Dvořák; among English composers, he favored Elgar. **BIBL.:** F. Klickmann, "Dr. H. R.," *Windsor Magazine* (Sept. 1896); L. Karpath, *Wagners Briefe an H. R.* (Vienna, 1924); H. Schonberg, *The Great Conductors* (N.Y., 1967).

Richter, Karl, distinguished German organist, harpsichordist, and conductor; b. Plauen, Oct. 15, 1926; d. Munich, Feb. 15, 1981. He studied organ, harpsichord, and conducting at the Dresden Kreuzschule; then took courses at the Leipzig Cons. with Rudolf Mauersberger, Günther Ramin, and Karl Straube. In 1946 he became choirmaster of the Christuskirche in Leipzig; in 1947 was named organist of Leipzig's Thomaskirche. In 1951 he settled in Munich; organized the Munich Bach Orch. and Choir, which brought him great acclaim; made

many tours and numerous recordings with them; also appeared as a guest conductor in Europe. On April 18, 1965, he made his U.S. debut with them at N.Y.'s Carnegie Hall. **BIBL.:** D. McIntire, "K. R. (1926–1981)," *Le Grand Baton* (March 1981).

Richter, Marga, American composer; b. Reedsburg, Wis., Oct. 21, 1926. She was prepared for a musical career by her mother, Inez Chandler-Richter, a soprano; studied at the MacPhail School of Music in Minneapolis; in 1943 entered the Juilliard School of Music in N.Y., where she studied piano with Tureck and composition with Persichetti and Bergsma, graduating in 1949 (M.S., 1951). She received 14 ASCAP awards (from 1966) and 2 grants from the NEA (1977, 1979). Her compositions reflect a pragmatic modern trend without rigid adherence to any particular doctrine or technique; the overriding concern is aural. **WORKS: STAGE:** 2 ballets: *Abyss* (1964; Cannes, Feb. 5, 1965) and *Bird of Yearning* (1967; as *Der Türm*, Cologne, Oct. 30, 1969; version for Piano, 1976). **ORCH.:** Concerto for Piano, with Violas, Cellos, and Basses (1955); *Lament* for String Orch. (1956); *Aria and Toccata* for Viola and Strings (1956–57); *Variations on a Sarabande* (1959); *8 Pieces* (1961; originally for Piano); *Landscapes of the Mind I*, Concerto No. 2 for Piano and Orch. (1968–74; Tucson, March 19, 1976, Masselos soloist); *Fragments* (1976); *Country Auction* for School Band (1976); *Blackberry Vines and Winter Fruit* (North Bennington, Vt., Oct. 17, 1976); *Music for 3 Quintets and Orchestra* (1978–80); *Düsseldorf Concerto* for Solo Flute, Solo Viola, Harp, Percussion, and String Ensemble (1981–82; Düsseldorf Ensemble, Salzburg, May 20, 1982). **CHAMBER:** *1 for 2 and 2 for 3* for Trombone Duet and Trio (1947; rev. 1974); 2 string quartets: No. 1 (1950; withdrawn) and No. 2 (1958); *Ricercare* for Brass Quartet (1958); *Darkening of the Light* for Viola (1961; version for Cello, 1976); *Suite* for Violin and Piano (1964); *Landscapes of the Mind II* for Violin and Piano (1971); *Pastorale* for 2 Oboes (1975); *Landscapes of the Mind III* for Piano Trio (1979); *Sonora* for 2 Clarinets and Piano (1981); *Seacliff Variations* for Piano, Violin, Viola, and Cello (1984). **PIANO:** Sonata (1954–55); *Melodrama* for 2 Pianos (1958); *Variations on a Theme by Latimer* for Piano, 4-hands (1964); *Remembrances* (1971); *Requiem* (1976); songs; choruses; vocal sextet, *Do Not Press My Hands* (1981).

Richter, Nico (Max), Dutch composer; b. Amsterdam, Dec. 2, 1915; d. there, Aug. 16, 1945. He studied conducting with Scherchen; directed a student orch.; in Feb. 1942 he was arrested by the Nazis as a member of the Dutch Resistance, and spent 3 years in the Dachau concentration camp, which fatally undermined his health; he died shortly after liberation. **WORKS: STAGE:** *Amorijs*, chamber opera (1937); *Kannitverstan*, ballet. **ORCH.:** *Serenade*, sinfonietta for Flute, Oboe, Guitar, and Strings (1931–34); *Sinfonia-Divertimento* for Chamber Orch. (1936). **CHAMBER:** Concertino for Clarinet, Horn, Trumpet, Piano, and 2 Violins (1935); Trio for Flute, Viola, and Guitar (1935); *Serenade* for Flute, Violin, and Viola (1945; 2 extant movements reconstructed by Lex van Delden).

Richter, Sviatoslav (Teofilovich), outstanding Russian pianist; b. Zhitomir, March 20, 1915. Both his parents were pianists; the family moved to Odessa when he was a child. He was engaged as a piano accompanist at the Odessa Opera, and developed exceptional skill in playing orch. scores at sight. He made his formal debut as a concert artist at the Odessa House of Engineers in 1934; entered the Moscow Cons. in 1937 as a student of Heinrich Neuhaus, graduating in 1947. He acquired a notable following even during his student years; in 1945 he made a stunning appearance at the All-Union Contest of Performances, and was awarded its highest prize; received the Stalin Prize in 1949. In subsequent years he played throughout the Soviet Union and Eastern Europe. During the Russian tour of the Philadelphia Orch. in 1958, Richter was soloist, playing Prokofiev's 5th Piano Concerto in Leningrad; he made several international concert tours, including visits to China (1957) and the U.S. (1960). Both in Russia and abroad he has earned a reputation as a piano virtuoso of formidable attainments; is especially praised for his impeccable sense of style, with every detail of the music rendered with lapidary perfection. His performances of the Romantic repertoire have brought him great renown, and he has made notable excursions into the works of Debussy, Ravel, and Prokofiev as well; gave the 1st performances of Prokofiev's 6th, 7th, and 9th sonatas.

Rickenbacher, Karl Anton, Swiss conductor; b. Basel, May 20, 1940. He studied at the Städtisches Cons. in West Berlin (1962–66); then was engaged as an assistant conductor at the Zürich Opera (1966–69); subsequently was a conductor in Freiburg (1969–74). He was Generalmusikdirektor of the Westphalian Sym. Orch. (1976–85); also was principal conductor of the BBC Scottish Sym. Orch. in Glasgow (1977–80).

Ricketts, Frederick J., English bandmaster and composer who used the pseudonym Kenneth J. Alford; b. London, Feb. 21, 1881; d. Reigate, Surrey, May 15, 1945. Trained 1st as an organist, Ricketts graduated from Kneller Hall, afterward serving his longest stint as bandmaster of the Royal Marines (1928–44). In Feb. 1914 he publ., under his pseudonym "Alford" (not to be confused with the American bandmaster and composer Harry L. Alford), his popular march *Col. Bogey,* epitomizing the steadily swinging and moderately paced English military march. *Col. Bogey* reached its height of fame when it was introduced into the motion picture *The Bridge on the River Kwai* (1958).

Ricordi & Co., G., famous Italian music publishing firm of Milan, founded by **Giovanni Ricordi** (b. Milan, 1785; d. there, March 15, 1853). As 1st violinist and conductor at the Fiando theater, he also earned small sums as a music copyist, and in 1807 went to Leipzig to learn music engraving in Breitkopf & Härtel's establishment. On returning, he opened a little shop and began publishing in 1808, engraving the 1st works himself. He was a close friend of Rossini, whose operas he publ.; also recognized Verdi's genius when the latter was still unknown. His son **Tito Ricordi** (b. Milan, Oct. 29, 1811; d. there, Sept. 7, 1888) succeeded to the business. In 1845 he established the *Gazzetta Musicale,* one of the most important Italian music publications; also introduced the Edizioni Economiche, and under his administration the house became the largest music publishing firm in Italy. He was on terms of intimate friendship with Verdi, whose works (especially *Aida*) made a fortune for both publisher and author. Owing to ill health, he withdrew from active management in 1887. His successor was his son **Guilio Ricordi** (b. Milan, Dec. 19, 1840; d. there, June 6, 1912), a man of extraordinary business ability, who continued the policy of expansion. In 1888 he bought, and consolidated with his own, the important firm of Francesco Lucca. It was he who discovered Puccini. A trained musician, he publ., under the pseudonym of J. Burgmein, much elegant salon music (160 opus numbers). He was ed. of the *Gazzetta Musicale* until his death, upon which the magazine ceased publication. His son **Tito** (b. May 17, 1865; d. Milan, March 30, 1933), a remarkable pianist, was the subsequent head of the house; he retired in 1919, and control of the firm left the family; it became a limited company in 1952. The catalog contains over 120,000 numbers, and in the archives are the autograph scores of more than 550 operas by the most famous Italian composers. The firm has branches in N.Y., Canada, Australia, and South America.

BIBL.: G. Adami, *G. R. e i suoi musicisti* (Milan, 1933); E. di Valperga, *R.* (Rome, 1943); G. Adami, *G. R., L'Amico dei musicisti italiani* (Milan, 1945); C. Sartori, *Casa R., 1808–1958: Profilo storico* (Milan, 1958).

Ridder, Anton de, Dutch tenor; b. Amsterdam, Feb. 13, 1929. He studied voice at the Amsterdam Cons. with Herman Mulder (1947–49) and with Jan Keyzer (1951–56). From 1956 to 1962 he was on the roster of the Karlsruhe Opera; then sang at the Gärtnerplatz Theater in Munich (1962–66). In 1965 he joined the Komische Oper in West Berlin. In 1969 he took part in the Salzburg Festival; also sang in Vienna and Hamburg. He was equally adept at lyric and dramatic tenor parts.

Ridderbusch, Karl, German bass; b. Recklinghausen, May 29, 1932. He studied at the Duisburg Cons.; then won the Rudolf Schock Competition and continued his studies at the Essen Folkwangschule. He made his debut at the City Theater in Münster in 1961; then sang in Essen, Düsseldorf, Vienna, Milan, Berlin, Hamburg, and Paris. He made his Metropolitan Opera debut in N.Y. on Nov. 21, 1967, as Hunding in *Die Walküre;* in 1971 he sang at Covent Garden in London. He excels in Wagnerian roles.

Riddle, Nelson, American composer, arranger, and conductor of popular music; b. Hackensack, N.J., June 1, 1921; d. Los Angeles, Oct. 6, 1985. He took up the trombone at the age of 14; played in the bands of Charlie Spivak and Tommy Dorsey. After military service, he studied with Mario Castelnuovo-Tedesco in Los Angeles; then became an enormously successful arranger in Hollywood, preparing scores for numerous films and television programs; worked with Judy Garland, Frank Sinatra, Nat King Cole, Ella Fitzgerald, and others. He won an Academy Award for his score for the film *The Great Gatsby* (1974).

Rider-Kelsey, Corinne (née **Rider**), American soprano and teacher; b. near Batavia, N.Y., Feb. 24, 1877; d. Toledo, Ohio, July 10, 1947. She studied with Helen Rice at the Oberlin College Cons.; then with L. Torrens in Rockford, Ill., where she made her recital debut (1897); after further training with Toedt and his wife in N.Y., she became successful as a concert singer. She made her debut as a soloist in Handel's *Messiah* in St. Louis (Nov. 24, 1904); made her operatic debut as Micaëla at London's Covent Garden (July 2, 1908), but soon abandoned the opera stage to devote herself to a concert career. In 1926 she married the violinist and composer Lynnel Reed; they settled in Toledo, where she was active as a singer and a teacher.

BIBL.: L. Reed, *Be Not Afraid: Biography of Madame R. K.* (N.Y., 1955).

Řídký, Jaroslav, eminent Czech composer and teacher; b. Františkov, near Liberec, Aug. 25, 1897; d. Poděbrady, Aug. 14, 1956. He took courses in composition at the Prague Cons. (1919–23) with K. Jirák, J. Křička, and E.B. Foerster, continuing his training in Foerster's master class there (1923–26); also studied harp. He was 1st harpist in the Czech Phil. (1924–38); also was conductor of its choir (1925–30). He taught theory at the Prague Cons. (1928–48); was named a teacher (1946) and a prof. (1955) of composition at the Prague Academy of Music.

WORKS: ORCH.: 7 syms: No. 1 (1924); No. 2, with Cello obbligato (1925); No. 3 (1927); No. 4, with Chorus (1928); No. 5 (1930–31); No. 6, *The Year 1938* (1938; unfinished); No. 7 (1955); Sinfonietta (1923); Violin Concerto (1926); *Overture* (1928–29); 2 cello concertos (1930, 1940); *Serenade* for String Orch. (1941); Chamber Sinfonietta (1944–45); Piano Concerto (1952); *Slavonic March* (1954). **CHAMBER:** 2 cello sonatas (1923; 1947–48); Clarinet Quintet (1926); 5 string quartets (1926, 1927, 1931, 1933, 1937); *Serenata appassionata* for Cello and Piano (1929); 2 nonets (1933–34; 1943); Wind Quintet (1945); *Joyous Sonatina* for Violin and Piano (1947); Piano Trio (1950–51); also 2 cantatas: *A Winter Fairytale* (1936) and *To My Fatherland* (1941); piano pieces; choruses.

Ridout, Godfrey, Canadian composer; b. Toronto, May 6, 1918; d. there, Nov. 24, 1984. He studied piano, organ, conducting, and composition at the Toronto Cons. and at the Univ. of Toronto, where he became a member of the faculty in 1948; also taught at the Toronto Cons. (from 1940); retired in 1982. His music is tuneful and winsome. In 1963–64 he reconstructed a comic opera, *Colas et Colinette,* the earliest known North American work in this form, composed by the French-Canadian musician Joseph Quesnel in 1788, for which only vocal parts and a 2nd violin part were extant.

WORKS: DRAMATIC: Television opera, *The Lost Child* (1975); melodrama, *Exile* (1984); ballet, *La Prima Ballerina* (1966; Montreal Expo '67). **ORCH.:** *Ballade* for Viola and String Orch.

(1938; Toronto, May 29, 1939); *Festal Overture* (1939); *Comedy Overture* (1941); *Dirge* (1943); 2 *Études* for String Orch. (1946; rev. 1951); *Esther*, dramatic sym. for Soprano, Baritone, Chorus, and Orch. (Toronto, April 29, 1952); *Cantiones mysticae: No. 1*, after Donne, for Soprano and Orch. (N.Y., Oct. 16, 1953); *No. 2, The Ascension*, for Soprano, Trumpet, and Strings (Toronto, Dec. 23, 1962); *No. 3, The Dream of the Rood*, for Baritone or Tenor, Chorus, Orch., and Organ (1972); *Music for a Young Prince*, suite (1959); *Fall Fair* (N.Y., Oct. 24, 1961); *4 Sonnets* for Chorus and Orch. (1964); *In Memoriam Anne Frank* for Soprano and Orch. (Toronto, March 14, 1965); *When Age and Youth Unite* for Chorus and Orch. (1966); *4 Songs of Eastern Canada* for Soprano and Orch. (1967); *Partita academica* for Concert Band (1969); *Frivolités canadiennes*, based on melodies by Joseph Vézina, for Small Orch. (1973); *Jubilee* (1973); *Concerto grosso* for Piano, Violin, and String Orch. (1974; Toronto, Jan. 18, 1975); *George III His Lament*, variations on an old British tune, for Small Orch. (1975); *Tafelmusik* for Wind Ensemble (1976); *Kids' Stuff* (1978); *Ballade II* for Viola and String Orch. (1980); *No Mean City Scenes from Childhood* (1983). **CHAMBER:** *Folk Song Fantasy* for Piano Trio (1951); *Introduction and Allegro* for Flute, Oboe, Clarinet, Bassoon, Horn, Violin, and Cello (1968); choruses; songs.

Riedel, Carl, German choral conductor and composer; b. Kronenberg, near Elberfeld, Oct. 6, 1827; d. Leipzig, June 3, 1888. He was a silk dyer by trade; owing to revolutionary perturbations of 1848, he abandoned his trade and decided to study music; took lessons with Carl Wilhelm at Krefeld; then enrolled in the Leipzig Cons. In 1854 he organized a singing society which became the Riedel'scher Verein in 1855; with it, he promoted sacred music from all periods, but became best known for his championship of Schütz and Bach, as well as of composers of the new German school. In 1868 Riedel was elected president of the Allgemeiner Deutscher Musikverein, and founded its Leipzig branch; he also became president of the Wagnerverein.

BIBL.: A. Göhler, *Der R.-Verein zu Leipzig: Eine Denkschrift zur Feier seines fünfzigjährigen Bestehens* (Leipzig, 1904).

Riedt, Friedrich Wilhelm, German flutist, writer on music, and composer; b. Berlin, Jan. 24, 1710; d. there, Jan. 5, 1783. He studied with J.G. Graun and Christoph Schaffrath; in 1741, became chamber musician to Frederick the Great; in 1749, director of the "Musikübende Gesellschaft" in Berlin. He wrote 6 trios for 2 Flutes and Continuo; sonatas for 2 Flutes; Sonata for Flute and Cello; etc.; publ. *Versuch über die musikalischen Intervallen* (Berlin, 1753); contributed various articles (critical and polemical) to Marpurg's *Historisch-kritische Beyträge zur Aufnahme der Musik.*

Riegel (later changed to **Rigel**), **Henri (Heinrich) Joseph,** French composer, father of **Henri-Jean Rigel;** b. Wertheim, Franconia, Feb. 9, 1741; d. Paris, May 2, 1799. He was of German extraction; studied with F.X. Richter in Mannheim and with Jommelli in Stuttgart. In 1767 he went to Paris; from 1783 to 1788, belonged to a group of composers associated with the Concert Spirituel. On the title page of several of his works publ. in Paris his name appears as Rigel, and this gallicized form was adopted by his son Henri-Jean, who was born in Paris. Riegel was one of the earliest composers to write ensemble music with piano, publ. as "symphonies" for 2 Violins, Cello, 2 Horns, and Piano. He was a fairly voluminous composer; wrote several short operas in the manner of the German singspiel, all of which were produced in Paris unless otherwise given: *Le Savetier et le financier* (Marly, 1778); *L'Automate* (1781); *Rosanie* (1780); *Blanche et Vermeille* (1781); *Lucas et Babet* (1787); *Les Amours du Gros-Caillou* (1786); *Alix de Beaucaire* (Montansier, 1791). His other works include 6 syms.; keyboard concertos; 6 string quartets; several *Sonates de clavecin en quattuor;* a number of piano sonatas, some with violin obbligato; and 3 *Sonates en symphonies* for Piano. During the revolutionary period in France, he composed various pieces celebrating the events.

BIBL.: G. de Saint-Foix, "Rigel," *Revue Musicale* (June 1925); R. Sondheimer, "H.J. Rigel," *Music Review* (Aug. 1956).

Riegel, Kenneth, American tenor; b. Womelsdorf, Pa., April 29, 1938. He studied at the Manhattan School of Music in N.Y. and also at the Metropolitan Opera Studio. He made his operatic debut as the Alchemist in Henze's opera *König Hirsch* with the Santa Fe Opera in 1965; then sang with the Cincinnati Opera, the Houston Opera, the N.Y. City Opera, and others. On Oct. 22, 1973, he made his debut with the Metropolitan Opera in N.Y. as Iopas in *Les Troyens*. In 1977 he appeared at the Vienna State Opera, in 1978 at the Paris Opéra, in 1979 at Milan's La Scala, in 1981 at the Hamburg State Opera, in 1983 at the Deutsche Oper in Berlin, and in 1985 at London's Covent Garden. He also toured as a concert artist.

Rieger, Fritz, German conductor; b. Oberaltstadt, June 28, 1910; d. Bonn, Sept. 29, 1978. He was educated at the Prague Academy of Music, taking courses in piano with Langer, composition with Finke, and conducting with Szell. From 1931 to 1938 he conducted at the German Opera Theater in Prague; from 1939 to 1941 was conductor of the Bremen Opera; from 1947 to 1949, at the Mannheim National Theater. From 1949 to 1966 he was Generalmusikdirektor of the Munich Phil.; also conducted at the Bavarian State Opera. In 1972–73 he was chief conductor of the Melbourne Sym. Orch.; he also gave guest performances in Japan. In his programs he gave considerable prominence to modern music.

Riegger, Wallingford (Constantin), outstanding American composer and teacher; b. Albany, Ga., April 29, 1885; d. N.Y., April 2, 1961. At an early age, he was taken by his family to Indianapolis, where he received his primary musical training at home; his father played violin, and his mother, piano. After his father took the family to N.Y. to pursue his business interests (1900), Wallingford learned to play the cello. He then began serious study with Percy Goetschius (theory) and Alwin Schroeder (cello) at the Inst. of Musical Art; after graduating in 1907, he went to Berlin, where he studied cello with Robert Hausmann and Anton Hekking and composition with Max Bruch and Edgar Stillman-Kelley at the Hochschule für Musik (1907–10). In 1910 he made his debut as a conductor with Berlin's Blüthner Orch.; then returned to the U.S. and served as a cellist in the St. Paul (Minn.) Sym. Orch. (1911–14); returning to Germany, he worked as a vocal coach and assistant conductor at the operas in Würzburg (1914–15) and Königsberg (1915–16); then was again conductor of Berlin's Blüthner Orch. (1916–17) before returning to the U.S. He taught theory and cello at Drake Univ., Des Moines (1918–22); in 1922 received the Paderewski Prize for his Piano Trio; in 1924 was awarded the E.S. Coolidge Prize for his setting of Keats's *La Belle Dame sans merci;* in 1925 was given the honorary degree of D.Mus. by the Cincinnati Cons. He taught at the Inst. of Musical Art in N.Y. (1924–25) and at the Ithaca Cons. (1926–28); then settled in N.Y., where he became active as a composer and a participant in various modern music societies; took part in the development of electronic instruments (in association with Theremin), and learned to play an electric cello. His music is of a highly advanced nature; a master craftsman, he wrote in disparate styles with an equal degree of proficiency; used numerous pseudonyms for certain works (William Richards, Walter Scotson, Gerald Wilfring Gore, John H. McCurdy, George Northrup, Robert Sedgwick, Leonard Griegg, Edwin Farell, Edgar Long, etc.). After a long period of neglect on the part of the public and the critics, Riegger began to receive recognition; his 3rd Sym. was the choice of the N.Y. Music Critics' Circle in 1948. He received further attention in 1957 when he was compelled to appear before the House Un-American Activities Committee to explain his self-proclaimed leftist and pro-Communist sympathies.

WORKS: DANCE: *Bacchanale* (1930; N.Y., Feb. 2, 1931); *Evocation* (N.Y., April 21, 1932; orchestrated 1948); *Frenetic Rhythms: 3 Dances of Daemoniacal Possession* (N.Y., Nov. 19, 1933); *New Dance* (Bennington, Vt., Aug. 3, 1935; also orch. and chamber versions); *Theater Piece* (1935; N.Y., Jan. 19,

1936); *With My Red Fires* (Bennington, Vt., Aug. 13, 1936); *Chronicle* (N.Y., Dec. 20, 1936); *The Cry* (Bennington, Vt., Aug. 7, 1936); *City Nocturne* (Bennington, Vt., Aug. 7, 1936); *4 Chromatic Eccentricities* (Bennington, Vt., Aug. 7, 1936; based on the *4 Tone Pictures* for Piano, 1932); *Candide* (N.Y., May 6, 1937); *Festive Rhythm* (Bennington, Vt., Aug. 13, 1937); *Trend* (Bennington, Vt., Aug. 13, 1937); *Case History No. . . .* (N.Y., Feb. 28, 1937); *Trojan Incident* (N.Y., April 21, 1938); *Machine Ballet* (Toronto, March 1938); *Fancy Fannie's Judgement Day* (1938; N.Y., Feb. 26, 1939); *Pilgrim's Progress* (N.Y., April 20, 1941).

ORCH.: *The Beggerman*, overture (1912; St. Paul, Minn., 1913; not extant); *Elegie* for Cello and Orch. (1916; Berlin, Feb. 6, 1917); *Triple Jazz: American Polonaise* (1922; N.Y., July 27, 1923); *Rhapsody: 2nd April* (1924–26; N.Y., Oct. 29, 1931); *Holiday Sketches* for Violin and Orch. (1927); *Study in Sonority* (Ithaca, N.Y., Aug. 11, 1927; orig. *Caprice* for 10 Violins); *Fantasy and Fugue* for Organ and Orch. (1930–31; N.Y., Dec. 5, 1932); *Dichotomy* for Chamber Orch. (Berlin, March 10, 1932); *Scherzo* for Chamber Orch. (1932; N.Y., Jan. 30, 1933; also for 2 Pianos); *Consummation* (1939; withdrawn and utilized in *Music for Orchestra*, 1952); *New Dance* (1940; Pittsburgh, Jan. 30, 1942; also for Band, N.Y., July 7, 1942; also dance and chamber versions); *Canon and Fugue* for Strings (1941; Berkeley, Calif., Aug. 1, 1942; also for Orch., 1941; N.Y., Feb. 14, 1944); *Passacaglia and Fugue* for Band (1942; N.Y., June 16, 1943; also for Orch., 1942; Washington, D.C., March 19, 1944); *Processional: Funeral March* for Band (1943; West Point, N.Y., Jan. 23, 1944; also for Orch., 1943; Moscow, July 3, 1945); 4 syms.: No. 1 (1944; N.Y., April 3, 1949; withdrawn); No. 2 (1945; withdrawn); No. 3 (1946–47; N.Y., May 16, 1948); No. 4 (1956; Urbana, Ill., April 12, 1957); *Evocation* (Vancouver, British Columbia, Nov. 27, 1948; based on the dance piece, 1932); *Music for Brass Choir* for 10 Trumpets, 8 Horns, 10 Trombones, 2 Tubas, and Percussion (N.Y., April 18, 1949); *Music for Orchestra* (1952; N.Y., March 27, 1955; includes *Consummation* for Orch., 1939); *Prelude and Fugue* for Band (Louisville, May 5, 1953); *Variations* for Piano and Orch. (1952–53; Louisville, Feb. 23, 1954); *Variations* for 2 Pianos and Orch. (1952–54; Fish Creek, Wis., Aug. 1954); *Suite for Younger Orchestras* (1953; N.Y., April 26, 1954); *Dance Rhythms* (1954; Albany, Ga., March 4, 1955); *Overture* (1955; Cincinnati, Oct. 26, 1956); *Preamble and Fugue* (1955; Oklahoma City, March 18, 1956); *Festival Overture* (Boston, May 4, 1957); *Variations* for Violin and Orch. (1958; Louisville, April 1, 1959); *Quintuple Jazz* (Iowa City, May 20, 1959); *Sinfonietta* (1959); *Introduction, Scherzo, and Fugue* for Cello, Winds, and Timpani (Rochester, N.Y., Sept. 30, 1960; a revision of *Introduction and Fugue* for 4 Cellos, 1957); *Duo* for Piano and Orch. (1960).

CHAMBER: *Reverie* for Cello and Piano (1918); Piano Trio (1919–20); *Whimsy* for Cello or Violin, and Piano (1920); *Meditation* for Cello or Violin, and Piano (1927); *Blue Voyage* for Piano (1927); *Suite* for Flute (1928–29); *3 Canons for Woodwinds* for Flute, Oboe, Clarinet, and Bassoon (1931); *Scherzo* for 2 Pianos (1932; also for Chamber Orch., 1932); *4 Tone Pictures* for Piano (1932; dance version as *4 Chromatic Eccentricities*, 1932); *Divertissement* for Flute, Cello, and Harp (1933); *New Dance* for 2 Pianos, or Piano, 4–hands, or Violin and Piano, or Solo Piano (1935; also orch. and band versions, 1940–42); *Music for Voice and Flute* (1936–37); 2 string quartets (1938–39; 1948); *Duos for 3 Woodwinds* for Flute, Oboe, and Clarinet (1943); *New and Old: 12 Pieces for Piano* (1944); Sonatina for Violin and Piano (1947); Piano Quintet (1950–51); *Nonet for Brass* for 3 Trumpets, 2 Horns, 3 Trombones, and Tuba (1951); *Canon on a Ground Bass of Purcell* for Strings (1951); woodwind quintet, *Bläserquintett* (1952); Concerto for Piano and Woodwind Quintet (1953); *Variations* for 2 Pianos (1952–53); *Variations* for Violin and Viola (1957); *Movement* for 2 Trumpets, Trombone, and Piano (1957); *Introduction and Fugue* for 4 Cellos (1957; rev. as *Introduction, Scherzo, and Fugue* for Cello, Winds, and Timpani, 1960); *Cooper Square* for Accordion (1958).

VOCAL: *La Belle Dame sans merci* for Tenor, Women's Voices, and 7 Instruments (1921–24); *Eternity* for Women's Voices and 4 Instruments (1942); *From Some Far Shore* for 4 Voices, and Piano or Organ (1946); *Easter Passacaglia: Ye Watchers and Ye Holy Ones* for 4 Voices, and Piano or Organ (1946); *Little Sam: Little Black Sambo* for Narrator and Chamber Orch. (1946); *Who Can Revoke?* for 4 Voices and Piano (1948); *In Certainty of Song*, cantata for 4 Solo Voices, 4 Voices, and Piano or Chamber Orch. (1950); *Non vincit malitia: Evil Shall Not Prevail* for Antiphonal Chorus (1951); *A Child Went Forth* for 4 Voices and Oboe (1953); *A Shakespeare Sonnet* for Baritone, Chorus, and Piano or Chamber Orch. (1956); also solo songs; more than 700 arrangements of carols, anthems, and folk songs; several vols. of pedagogical works.

BIBL.: A. Weiss, "W. R.," in H. Cowell, ed., *American Composers on American Music* (Stanford, Calif., 1933); R. Goldman, "The Music of W. R.," *Musical Quarterly* (Jan. 1950); E. Carter, "W. R.," *American Composers Alliance Bulletin*, II/1 (1952); J. Schmoll, *An Analytical Study of the Principal Instrumental Compositions of W. R.* (diss., Northwestern Univ., 1954); R. Goldman, "W. R., Composer and Pedagog," *Etude*, LXXIV/8 (1956); P. Freeman, *The Compositional Technique of W. R. as Seen in Seven Major Twelve-tone Works* (diss., Eastman School of Music, 1963); D. Garwood, *W. R.: A Biography and Analysis of Selected Works* (diss., George Peabody College for Teachers, 1970); L. Ott, *An Analysis of the Later Orchestral Style of W. R.* (diss., Michigan State Univ., 1970); N. Savage, *Structure and Cadence in the Music of W. R.* (diss., Stanford Univ., 1972); S. Spackman, *W. R.: Two Essays in Musical Biography* (Brooklyn, N.Y., 1982); idem, "W. R. and the Modern Dance," *Musical Quarterly*, 4 (1985).

Riehl, Wilhelm Heinrich von, German writer on music; b. Biebrich-on-Rhine, May 6, 1823; d. Munich, Nov. 16, 1897. He studied at the Univ. of Munich, where he became (1854) a prof. of political economy; also lectured on music history. He publ. the valuable compendium *Musikalische Charakterköpfe* (3 vols., 1853–61; 6th ed., 1879) and 2 vols. of original songs, *Hausmusik* (1856, 1877). Posthumous publications: *Zur Geschichte der romantischen Oper* (Berlin, 1928); *Musik im Leben des Volkes*, a collection of Riehl's articles, ed. by J. Müller-Blattau (Kassel, 1936).

BIBL.: H. Simonsfeld, *H. R. als Kulturhistoriker* (Munich, 1899); V. von Geramb, *W.H. R., Leben und Wirken* (Salzburg, 1954).

Riem, Friedrich Wilhelm, German organist and composer; b. Kölleda, Thuringia, Feb. 17, 1779; d. Bremen, April 20, 1857. He was a pupil of J.A. Hiller in Leipzig; was organist at the Thomaskirche (1807–14) and then in Bremen. He wrote an oratorio, *Der Erlöser*; String Quintet; Piano Quartet; 3 string quartets; 4 violin sonatas; 6 piano sonatas; also publ. a collection of organ pieces for concert and church.

Riemann, (Karl Wilhelm Julius) Hugo, eminent German musicologist; b. Gross-Mehlra, near Sondershausen, July 18, 1849; d. Leipzig, July 10, 1919. He began his training with his father, Robert Riemann, a landowner and civil servant, who was an amateur musician; then continued his study of theory in Sondershausen with Heinrich Frankenberger, August Bartel, and Theodor Ratzenberger; also took courses at the Sondershausen and Arnstadt Gymnasiums. After studying classical languages and literature at the Rossleben Klosterschule (1865–68), he took courses in law and German philology and history at the Univ. of Berlin and in philosophy at the Univ. of Tübingen. He studied harmony with Jadassohn and piano and composition with Reinecke in Leipzig (1871–72); then received his Ph.D. in 1873 from the Univ. of Göttingen with the dissertation *Über das musikalische Hören* (publ. in Leipzig, 1874; also publ. as *Musikalische Logik*, Leipzig, 1873). He taught at Bielefeld (1876–78); after qualifying as a lecturer at the Univ. of Leipzig (1878), he taught in Bromberg (1880–81); then taught piano and theoretical courses at the Hamburg Cons. (1881–90); after a brief stay in Sondershausen (1890), he taught at the Wiesbaden Cons. (1890–95). In 1895 he resumed his lectures at the Univ. of Leipzig; was made prof. in 1905, and also director of the Collegium Musicum in 1908 and of the Forschungsinstitut für Musikwissenschaft in 1914. He was honored with a Mus.Doc. from the Univ. of Edinburgh (1899) and with a Festschrift on his 60th birthday.

The mere bulk of Riemann's writings, covering every branch of musical science, constitutes a monument of indefatigable industry, and is proof of enormous concentration and capacity for work. When one takes into consideration that much of this work is the result of painstaking research and of original, often revolutionary, thinking, one must share the great respect and admiration in which Riemann was held by his contemporaries. Although many of his ideas are now seen in a different light, his works treating of harmony were considered to constitute the foundation of modern music theory. His researches in the field of music history have solved a number of vexing problems, and thrown light on others. And, finally, in formulating the new science of musicology, the labors of Riemann were of great significance. His name is indelibly linked to the *Musik-Lexikon* that bears his cognomen. He contributed innumerable articles to various journals; a collection of these was publ. as *Präludien und Studien* (3 vols., 1895, 1900, 1901).

WRITINGS (all publ. in Leipzig unless otherwise given): *Die objektive Existenz der Untertöne in der Schallwelle* (Berlin, 1877); *Studien zur Geschichte der Notenschrift* (1878); *Die Entwickelung unserer Notenschrift*, Sammlung Musikalischer Vorträge, XXVIII (1881); *Musik-Lexikon* (1882; 8th ed., 1916; A. Einstein edited the 9th to 11th eds., 1919, 1922, 1929; W. Gurlitt edited the 12th ed., 3 vols., Mainz, 1959, 1961, 1967; C. Dahlhaus edited a supplement, 2 vols., Mainz, 1972, 1975; Dahlhaus and H. Eggebrecht edited the *Brockhaus-Riemann Musik-Lexikon*, 2 vols., Wiesbaden and Mainz, 1978; supplement, 1989); *Die Natur der Harmonik*, Sammlung Musikalischer Vorträge, XL (1882); *Der Ausdruck in der Musik*, ibid., L (1883); *Musikalische Dynamik und Agogik: Lehrbuch der musikalischen Phrasierung* (Hamburg, 1884); *Opern-Handbuch* (1887; 2nd ed., 1893; reprint with supplement by F. Stieger, 1979); *Wie hören wir Musik?: Drei Vorträge* (1885; 5th ed., 1921); *Katechismus der Musikinstrumente (Instrumentationslehre)* (1888; 8th ed., 1923, as *Handbuch der Musikinstrumente*; Eng. tr., 1888); *Katechismus der Musikgeschichte* (1888; 5th ed., 1914; Eng. tr., 1892); *Katechismus der Orgel (Orgellehre)* (1888; 2nd ed., 1901; 6th ed., n.d., as *Handbuch der Orgel*); *Katechismus der Musik (Allgemeine Musiklehre)* (1888; 8th ed., 1922; Eng. tr., n.d.); *Grundlinien der Musik-Ästhetik (Wie hören wir Musik?)* (1890; 3rd ed., 1911, as *Katechismus der Musikästhetik*; Eng. tr., 1895); *Präludien und Studien: Gesammelte Aufsätze zur Ästhetik, Theorie und Geschichte der Musik* (vol. I, Frankfurt am Main, 1895; vols. II and III, Leipzig, 1900, 1901); *Geschichte der Musiktheorie im IX.–XIX. Jahrhundert* (1898; 2nd ed., 1921; Eng. tr., 1962); *Die Elemente der musikalischen Ästhetik* (Berlin, 1900); *Geschichte der Musik seit Beethoven (1800–1900)* (Berlin and Stuttgart, 1901); *Beethovens Streichquartette* (Berlin, 1903); *System der musikalischen Rhythmik und Metrik* (1903); *Handbuch der Musikgeschichte* (vol. i/I, 1904; 2nd ed., 1919; 3rd ed., 1923; vol. i/2, 1905; 2nd ed., 1920; vol. ii/I, 1907; 2nd ed., 1920; A. Einstein edited vol. ii/2, 1912; 3rd ed., 1921; and vol. ii/3, 1913; 2nd ed., 1922); *Das Problem des harmonischen Dualismus: Ein Beitrag zur Ästhetik der Musik* (1905); *Kleines Handbuch der Musikgeschichte mit Periodisierug nach Stilprinzipien und Formen* (1908; 7th ed., 1947); *Grundriss der Musikwissenschaft* (1908; 4th ed., 1928, by J. Wolf); *Die byzantinische Notenschrift im 10. bis 15. Jahrhundert* (1909); *Musikgeschichte in Beispielen* (3 vols., 1911–12; A. Schering edited the 2nd to 4th eds., 1921–29); *Neue Beiträge zur Lösung der Probleme der byzantinischen Notenschrift* (1915); *Folkloristische Tonalitätsstudien* (1916); *L. van Beethovens sämtliche Klaviersolosonaten: Ästhetische und formal-technische Analyse* (Berlin, 1918–19; 4th ed., 1920). He also wrote numerous pedagogical and other works.

BIBL.: *R.-Festschrift* (Leipzig, 1909); "H. R. zum 70. Geburtstag," *Zeitschrift für Musikwissenschaft*, I (1918–19); H. Grab-

ner, *Die Funktionstheorie H. R.s und ihre Bedeutung für die praktische Analyse* (Munich, 1923); H. Denecke, *Die Kompositionslehre H. R.s* (diss., Univ. of Kiel, 1937); G. Sievers, *Die Grundlagen H. R.s bei Max Reger* (diss., Univ. of Hamburg, 1949); W. Gurlitt, "H. R.: 1849–1919," *Abhandlungen der Akademie der Wissenschaft und der Literatur Mainz*, XXV (Wiesbaden, 1951); G. Wienke, *Voraussetzungen der "musikalischen Logik" bei H. R.: Studien zur Musikästhetik in der 2. Hälfte des 19. Jahrhunderts* (diss., Univ. of Freiburg, 1952); H. Wolff, "H. R.: Der Begründer der systematischen Musikbetrachtung," *Festschrift Max Schneider* (Leipzig, 1955); H. Federhofer, "Die Funktionstheorie H. R.s und die Schichtenlehre Heinrich Schenkers," *Kongressbericht: Wien Mozartjahr 1956*; W. Mickelsen, *H. R.'s History of Harmonic Theory with a Translation of Harmonielehre* (diss., Indiana Univ., 1971).

Riemenschneider, (Charles) Albert, American organist, conductor, and educator; b. Berea, Ohio, Aug. 31, 1878; d. Akron, July 20, 1950. He began his musical training with his father, Karl Riemenschneider, president of the Methodist Episcopal Deutsches Wallace Kollegium in Berea; then studied piano, organ, and theory with James Rogers in Cleveland (1896–1902); also taught piano and organ at his father's school (from 1896), becoming director of its music dept. (1897); subsequently studied piano with Hugo Reinhold and composition with R. Fuchs in Vienna (1902–3) and organ with Charles Clemens in Cleveland (1903); later studied organ with Guilmant and composition with Widor in Paris (1904–10). Throughout this period he continued to teach at his father's school, which merged with Baldwin-Wallace College in 1913 to form the Baldwin-Wallace Cons. of Music; thereafter he served as its president until his retirement in 1947; also conducted the Baldwin-Wallace Bach Festival from 1933. He amassed a valuable Bach collection, which was bequeathed to Baldwin-Wallace College in 1951. The Riemenschneider Bach Inst. was founded in 1969; it publishes the journal *Bach*. He ed. several of Bach's vocal works.

Riepel, Joseph, Austrian violinist, music theorist, and composer; b. Hörschlag (baptized), Jan. 22, 1709; d. Regensburg, Oct. 23, 1782. He studied philosophy at the Univ. of Graz, then music in Dresden (1740–45); was a musician in the chapel of the count of Thurn und Taxis in Regensburg from 1751. His historical importance rests upon his valuable treatises. He composed syms., 3 violin concertos with string quartet accompaniment, divertimentos, canons, etc.

WRITINGS: *Anfangsgründe zur musikalischen Setzkunst, nicht zwar nach altmathematischer Einbildungsart der Zirkel-Harmonisten, sondern durchgehends mit sichtbaren Exemplen abgefasset*, I, *De rhythmopoeia oder Von der Taktordnung* (Regensburg and Vienna, 1752; 2nd ed., 1754); II, *Grundregeln der Tonordnung insgemein* (Frankfurt and Leipzig, 1755); III, *Gründliche Erklärung der Tonordnung insbesondere, zugleich aber für die mehresten Organisten insgemein* (Frankfurt and Leipzig, 1757); IV, *Erläuterung der betrüglichen Tonordnung* (Augsburg, 1765); V, *Unentbehrliche Anmerkungen zum Kontrapunkt* (Regensburg, 1768); *Harmonisches Silbenmass, Dichtern melodischer Werke gewidmet und angehenden Singkomponisten zur Einsicht mit platten Beispielen gesprächweise abgefasst* (2 vols., Regensburg, 1776; vol. 3 in MS); *Bassschlüssel, das ist Anleitung für Anfanger und Liebhaber der Setkunst* (ed. by J. Schubarth, Regensburg, 1786).

BIBL.: W. Twittenhoff, *Die musiktheoretischen Schriften J. R.s* (Halle, 1935); E. Schwarzmaier, *Die Takt- und Tonordnung J. R.s* (Wolfenbüttel, 1936); J. Merkl, *J. R. als Komponist* (Kallmünz, 1937); A. Feil, *Satztechnische Fragen in den Kompositionslehren von F.E. Niedt, J. R., und H.Chr. Koch* (Heidelberg, 1955).

Ries, Ferdinand, noted German pianist and composer, son of **Franz (Anton)** and brother of **(Pieter) Hubert Ries;** b. Bonn (baptized), Nov. 28, 1784; d. Frankfurt am Main, Jan. 13, 1838. He studied piano and violin with his father and cello with B.H. Romberg; after further studies with Peter von Winter in Munich (1801); he continued his piano studies with

Beethoven in Vienna (1801–4); also had composition lessons with Albrechtsberger. He made his debut in Beethoven's C-minor Concerto in Vienna on Aug. 1, 1804; later made successful tours in Germany, Scandinavia, and Russia (1809–13); then went to London, where he made his debut at a Phil. Concert on March 14, 1814. He returned to Germany in 1824; settled in Frankfurt in 1827; was active as a conductor and composer with the Lower Rhine Music Festivals; served as conductor of the municipal orch. and Singakademie in Aachen from 1834. His music reflects the spirit and technique, if not the genius, of Beethoven's style. With F. Wegeler, he prepared the vol. *Biographische Notizen über Ludwig van Beethoven* (Koblenz, 1838; Nachtrag by Wegeler, Koblenz, 1845; new ed. by A. Kalischer, Berlin, 1906); although a valuable early source, it must be used with caution, since Ries dictated parts of it to Wegeler late in life.

WORKS: The operas *Die Räuberbraut* (Frankfurt, 1828), *Liska, oder Die Hexe von Gyllensteen* (perf. in London as *The Sorceress*, 1831), and *Die Nacht auf dem Libanon* (1834); also a melodrama, *Die Zigeunerin* (1835); 2 oratorios; a Requiem; 8 syms.; 5 overtures; chamber music; numerous piano sonatas and other pieces for piano; songs.

BIBL.: "Memoir of F. R.," *Harmonicon*, II (1824); L. Überfeldt, *F. R.' Jugendentwicklung* (Bonn, 1915); D. McArdle, "Beethoven and F. R.," *Music & Letters*, XLVI (1965); C. Hill, *The Music of F. R.: A Thematic Catalogue* (Armidale, New South Wales, 1977); A. Tyson, "F. R. (1784–1838): The History of His Contribution to Beethoven Biography," *19th Century Music* (April 1984).

Ries, Franz, German violinist and music publisher, son of **(Pieter) Hubert Ries;** b. Berlin, April 7, 1846; d. Naumberg, June 20, 1932. He studied violin with his father and later with Massart and Vieuxtemps in Paris. His career as a concert violinist was brief, and in 1875 he entered the music publishing business; from 1881 to 1924, was director of the firm Ries & Erler in Berlin; in 1924 his son Robert Ries (1889/1942) became the proprietor; after the death of Robert Ries, the firm was taken over by his 2 daughters.

Ries, Franz (Anton), German violinist, father of **Ferdinand** and **(Pieter) Hubert Ries;** b. Bonn, Nov. 10, 1755; d. Godesberg, Nov. 1, 1846. He studied violin as a child with J.P. Salomon; entered the Court Orch. when he was 11; after successful appearances in Vienna as a soloist and chamber music player in 1779, he was given a court appointment by the Elector Maximilian in Bonn that same year; was also active as a teacher, Beethoven being one of his students; he lost his court position when the French dissolved the electoral court in 1794, and thereafter eked out a living mainly by teaching.

Ries, (Pieter) Hubert, German violinist and composer, brother of **Ferdinand** and son of **Franz (Anton) Ries;** b. Bonn, April 1, 1802; d. Berlin, Sept. 14, 1886. He studied violin with his father, and then with Spohr; also studied composition with Hauptmann; settled in Berlin in 1824 as a member of the orch. of the Königstadt Theater; joined the Court Orch. in 1825; became director of the Phil. Soc. in 1835, and its concertmaster in 1836; was also active as a teacher until his retirement in 1872. He wrote 2 violin concertos, chamber music, and studies and duets for violin; also publ. a *Violinschule* (in Eng., 1873).

Rieti, Vittorio, Italian-born American composer; b. Alexandria, Egypt, Jan. 28, 1898. He studied with Frugatta in Milan; then took courses with Respighi and Casella in Rome, where he lived until 1940, when he emigrated to the U.S. (became an American citizen, June 1, 1944). He taught at the Peabody Cons. in Baltimore (1948–49), Chicago Musical College (1950–53), Queens College in N.Y. (1958–60), and N.Y. College of Music (1960–64). His style of composition represents an ingratiating synthesis of cosmopolitan modern tendencies.

WORKS: OPERAS: *Orfeo tragedia* (1928; withdrawn); *Teresa nel bosco* (1933; Venice, Sept. 15, 1934); *Don Perlimplin* (1949; Urbana, Ill., March 30, 1952); *Viaggio d'Europa,* radio opera (1954); *The Pet Shop* (1957; N.Y., April 14, 1958); *The Clock*

(1959–60); *Maryam the Harlot* (1966). **BALLETS:** *L'Arca di Noè* (1923; only orch. suite extant); *Robinson et Vendredi* (1924); *Barabau* (London, Dec. 11, 1925); *Le Bal* (Monte Carlo, May 1929); *David triomphant* (Paris, May 1937); *Hippolyte* (1937); *The Night Shadow* (1941; N.Y., Feb. 1946); *Waltz Academy* (Boston, Oct. 1944); *The Mute Wife* (N.Y., Nov. 1944); *Trionfo di Bacco e Arianna,* ballet-cantata (1946–47; N.Y., Feb. 1948); *Native Dancer* (1959; based on the Sym. No. 5); *Conundrum* (1961); *A Sylvan Dream* (1965; Indianapolis, Oct. 1, 1982); *Scenes Seen* (1975; Indianapolis, March 25, 1976); *Verdiana* (1983; Indianapolis, Feb. 16, 1984); *Indiana* (1984; Indianapolis, Sept. 14, 1985); *Kaleidoscope* (1987; Indianapolis, April 30, 1988). **ORCH.:** 8 syms.: No. 1 (1929; Paris, Jan. 1930); No. 2 (1930; Brussels, April 1931); No. 3, *Sinfonietta* (Paris, May 1932); No 4, *Sinfonia tripartita* (1942; St. Louis, Dec. 16, 1944); No. 5 (1945; Venice, Sept. 1947); No. 6 (1973; N.Y., Dec. 11, 1974); No. 7 (1977); No. 8, *Sinfonia breve* (Lafayette, Ind., May 2, 1987); *Concerto du Loup* (named after the Loup River in southern France) for Chamber Orch. (1938); Concerto for 5 Wind Instruments and Orch. (Prague, May 31, 1924); 3 piano concertos (1926; 1930–37; 1955); 2 violin concertos: No. 1, *Concerto napoletano* (1928; Paris, May 1930); No. 2 (1969); Harpsichord Concerto (1952–55; rev. 1972); 2 cello concertos: No. 1 for Cello and Chamber Orch. (1934); No. 2 (1953); Concerto for 2 Pianos and Orch. (1951); *La fontaine,* suite (1968; N.Y., Nov. 1, 1969); *Concerto triplo* for Violin, Viola, Piano, and Orch. (1971; N.Y., Jan. 27, 1973); Concerto for String Quartet and Orch. (1976; N.Y., Feb. 1, 1978); *Enharmonic Variations* for Piano and Chamber Orch. (N.Y., Feb. 4, 1988). **CHAMBER:** Sonata for Flute, Oboe, Bassoon, and Piano (1924); 5 string quartets (1926, 1941, 1951, 1960, 1988); Woodwind Quintet (1957); Octet for Piano and 7 Instruments (1971); Piano Trio (1972); Piano Quartet (1973); *Allegretto alla croma* for Flute, Oboe, Clarinet, Bassoon, Strings, and Piano (1981); *Romanza lidica* for Clarinet and Piano (1984); *Congedo* (Leave-Taking) for Chamber Ensemble (N.Y., Feb. 3, 1988); Piano Quintet (1989); numerous works for solo piano; 2-piano pieces.

BIBL.: F. Ricci, *V. R.* (Naples, 1987).

Rietsch (Löwy), Heinrich, Austrian musicologist and composer; b. Falkenau an der Eger, Sept. 22, 1860; d. Prague, Dec. 12, 1927. He studied in Vienna under Krenn and R. Fuchs (composition) and Hanslick (music history). In 1900 he became an instructor at the German Univ. in Prague. He ed. Muffat's *Florilegium* for Denkmäler der Tonkunst in Österreich; also J.J. Fux's *Concentus musico-instrumentalis* (ibid.). He publ. *Die Tonkunst in der 2. Hälfte des 19. Jahrhunderts* (Leipzig, 1900); *Die deutsche Liedweise* (Leipzig, 1904); *Die Grundlagen der Tonkunst* (Leipzig, 1907; 2nd ed., 1918). His autobiographical sketch was publ. in *Neue Musikzeitung* (1915).

BIBL.: P. Nettl, "Verzeichnis der wissenschaftlichen und künstlerischen Arbeiten von R. bis 1920," *Zeitschrift für Musikwissenschaft,* II (1919–20).

Rietz, (August Wilhelm) Julius, German cellist, conductor, music editor, and composer; b. Berlin, Dec. 28, 1812; d. Dresden, Sept. 12, 1877. He was of a musical family: his father was a court musician, and his brother was a friend of Mendelssohn. Julius studied cello and played in theater orchs. in Berlin. In 1834 he became 2nd conductor of the Düsseldorf Opera; from 1847 to 1854 he was chief conductor of the Leipzig Opera; from 1848 to 1860, served as chief conductor of the Leipzig Gewandhaus Orch. In 1860 he became Hofkapellmeister in Dresden, being named Generalmusikdirektor in 1874; was also artistic director of the Cons. there (from 1870). A scholarly musician and competent conductor, Rietz was also an excellent music ed.; he prepared for publication the complete edition of Mendelssohn's works for Breitkopf & Härtel (1874–77), and also ed. Mozart's operas and syms., Beethoven's overtures, etc. As a composer, he followed the musical style of Mendelssohn; among his works are 9 syms., a Cello Concerto, incidental music, and songs.

BIBL.: "Pauline Viardot-Garcia to J. R., Letters of Friendship," *Musical Quarterly* (July 1915 to Jan. 1916); H. Zimmer, *J. R.* (diss., Univ. of Berlin, 1943).

Rifkin, Joshua, American musicologist, pianist, and conductor; b. N.Y., April 22, 1944. He studied with Persichetti at the Juilliard School of Music in N.Y. (B.S., 1964), with Gustave Reese at N.Y. Univ. (1964–66); at the Univ. of Göttingen (1966–67); and later with Mendel, Lockwood, Babbitt, and Oster at Princeton Univ. (M.F.A., 1969). He also worked with Stockhausen at Darmstadt (1961, 1965). From 1970 to 1982 he was on the faculty of Brandeis Univ. He led the Bach Ensemble from 1978. He is noted for his research in the field of Renaissance and Baroque music, but he became popular as a performer and explicator of ragtime.

Rigel, Henri-Jean, French pianist, teacher, and composer, son of **Henri (Heinrich) Joseph Riegel;** b. Paris, May 11, 1772; d. Abbeville, Dec. 16, 1852. After receiving lessons in piano and composition from his father, he entered the École Royale de Chant (1784), where he was made a sous-maître de solfège (1785); his works were given at the Concert Spirituel (from 1787). He taught at the Paris Cons. (1795–97); then accompanied Napoleon on his expedition to Egypt (1798), where he served as music director of the new French Theater in Cairo (until 1800). Upon his return to Paris (1800), he became active as a piano teacher and accompanist; Napoleon made him pianiste de la musique particulière de l'Empereur et Roi; he also acquired distinction as a composer. He wrote numerous works, including 2 comic operas, *Les Deux Meuniers* (Cairo, 1799) and *Le Duel nocturne* (Paris, Dec. 23, 1805), many other vocal works, a Sym., 4 piano concertos, other orch. pieces, chamber music, and piano pieces. Many of his works are lost.
BIBL.: R. Sondheimer, "H.-J. R.," *Music Review,* XVII (1956).

Righetti-Giorgi, Geltrude, outstanding Italian contralto; b. Bologna, 1793; d. there, 1862. She studied in Bologna; made her debut there (1814) under the name Righetti. After her marriage to the lawyer Giorgi (1815), she retired from the stage, only to be convinced of her vocal gifts by Rossini; she subsequently distinguished herself in his operas, creating Rosina in his *Il Barbiere di Siviglia* (1816) and the title role in his *La Cenerentola* (1817). She continued to sing regularly until 1822; made her last appearance in 1836.

Righini, Vincenzo, Italian tenor, conductor, singing teacher, and composer; b. Bologna, Jan. 22, 1756; d. there, Aug. 19, 1812. He was a choirboy at Bologna's S. Petronio; made his debut in Parma (1775), and then became a member of Bustelli's opera company in Prague (1776); that same year he wrote for it his 1st opera, *Il Convitato di pietra,* which proved successful. He abandoned his singing career and went to Vienna as a singing master to Princess Elisabeth of Württemberg and director of the Italian Opera (1780). From 1787 to 1793 he was Kapellmeister at the Mainz electoral court; in 1788 he married the contralto Anna Maria Lehritter (1762–93). In 1793 he became court Kapellmeister and director of the Italian Opera in Berlin, where he was an influential figure; in 1793 he married the singer Henriette Kneisel (1767–1801); they were divorced in 1800. After the Italian Opera was dissolved in the wake of war in 1806, he bided his time until the royal theater was reorganized in 1811, after which he and B.A. Weber shared the duties of Kapellmeister. In 1812 he returned to his homeland. In addition to his operas, Righini wrote a number of successful instrumental works and songs.
WORKS: *Il Convitato di pietra, ossia Il Dissoluto punito,* dramma tragicomico (Prague, 1776; as *Das steinerne Gastmahl, oder Der Ruchlose,* Vienna, 1777); *La bottega del cafè,* commedia giocosa (Prague, 1778); *La Vedova scaltra,* dramma giocoso (Prague, 1778); *Armida,* dramma (Vienna, 1782; rev. Berlin, 1799); *L'incontro inaspettato,* dramma giocoso (Vienna, 1785; as *Die unvermutete Zusammenkunft,* Berlin, 1793); *Il Demogorgone, ovvero Il Filosofo confuso,* opera buffa (Vienna, 1786);

Antigono, dramma serio (Mainz, 1788); *Alcide al bivio,* azione teatrale (Koblenz, 1790; rev. as a cantata, Vienna, 1804); *Vasco di Gama,* opera (Berlin, 1792; pasticcio in collaboration with others); *Enea nel Lazio,* dramma eroi-tragico (Berlin, 1793); *Il trionfo d'Arianna,* dramma (Berlin, 1793); *Atalante e Meleagro,* festa teatrale (Berlin, 1793); *La Gerusalemme liberata, ossia Arminda al campo de' franchi,* dramma (Berlin, 1799); *Tigrane,* dramma eroico (Berlin, 1800); *Minerva belebet die Statue des Dädalus,* pantomimischer Tanz (Berlin, 1802); *La selva incantata,* opera (Berlin, 1803); also an oratorio, *Der Tod Jesu* (1790); a *Missa solemnis* (1790); a *Te Deum* (1810); masses and other sacred pieces; cantatas and occasional works; many songs; piano pieces; etc.
BIBL.: K.-J. Kleinicke, *Das kirchenmusikalische Schaffen von V. R.: Beiträge zur Biographie des Komponisten* (Tutzing, 1984).

Rignold, Hugo (Henry), English conductor; b. Kingston-upon-Thames, May 15, 1905; d. London, May 30, 1976. His father was a theatrical conductor, his mother an opera singer. He was taken to Canada as a child, and studied violin in Winnipeg; in 1920 he returned to England on a scholarship to the Royal Academy of Music in London. During World War II he was stationed in Cairo, where he trained a radio orch. in performances of symphonic music. Returning to London, he was a conductor at Sadler's Wells (1947); from 1948 to 1954, was conductor of the Liverpool Phil.; from 1957 to 1960, served as music director of the Royal Ballet; was music director of the City of Birmingham Sym. Orch. (1960–68).

Rihm, Wolfgang (Michael), German composer; b. Karlsruhe, March 13, 1952. He studied theory and composition with Eugene Velte at the Hochschule für Musik in Karlsruhe (1968–72) and also attended courses given by Humphrey Searle; then went to Cologne, where he enrolled in the seminars of Stockhausen (1972–73); also audited classes of Klaus Huber in Freiburg (1973); in addition, received counseling from Wolfgang Fortner. From 1973 to 1978 he taught at the Hochschule für Musik in Karlsruhe. His music thrives on calculated unpredictability; but he does not shrink from producing shockingly euphonious and startlingly pleasurable sounds.
WORKS: STAGE: 2 operas: *Harlekin* (1977– ; in progress) and *Die Hamletmaschine* (1983–86; Mannheim, March 30, 1987); 2 chamber operas: No. 1, *Faust und Yorick* (1976), and No. 2, *Jakob Lenz* (1977–78; Hamburg, March 8, 1979); "musical scene": *Andere Schatten* (Frankfurt, Sept. 6, 1985); music theater: *Oedipus* (Berlin, Oct. 4, 1987). **ORCH.:** 3 syms.: No. 1 (1969); No. 2 (1975); No. 3, after Nietzsche and Rimbaud, for Soprano, Baritone, Chorus, and Orch. (1976–77); *Trakt* (1971); *Morphonie, Sektor IV* for String Quartet and Orch. (1972); *Magma* (1974); *Dis-Kontur* (1974); *Sub-Kontur* (1974–75; Donaueschingen, Oct. 26, 1976); *Konzertarie,* "telepsychogramm" based on a telegram King Ludwig II sent to Wagner, for Mezzo-soprano and Orch. (1975); *O Notte* for Baritone and Small Orch. (1975); *Cuts and Dissolves,* concerto for 29 Players (1976); *Nachtordnung,* 7 pieces for 15 Strings (1976); *Lichtzwang,* music for Violin and Orch., in memory of Paul Celan (1975–76); *Hölderlin-Fragmente* for Voice, and Orch. or Piano (1977); *La Musique creuse le ciel,* music for 2 Pianos and Orch. (1977–79; Cologne, Nov. 14, 1980); *Abgesangsszene* No. 1 for Orch. (Kassel, Nov. 8, 1979), No. 2, after Nietzsche and Novalis, for Voice and Orch. (1979; Karlsruhe, Oct. 5, 1980), No. 3, after Huchel, for Baritone and Orch. (1980), No. 4, after Nietzsche, for Voice and Orch. (1979–80), and No. 5 for Orch. (1979; Kiel, Jan. 12, 1981); *Walzer* (1979–81); *Doppelgesang* No. 1 for Viola, Cello, and Orch. (1980) and No. 2 for Clarinet or Bass Clarinet, Cello, and Orch. (1981–83; Hitzacker, Aug. 7, 1983); *Lenz-Fragmente,* 5 songs for Voice, and Orch. or Piano (1980); *Tutuguri,* subtitled *Ballet nach Artaud,* series of 7 works inspired by the writings of Antonin Artaud: *I* (1981), *II* (Chicago, March 3, 1982), *III* for 6 Percussionists and Orch. (Karlsruhe, Dec. 5, 1981), *IV* (Saarbrücken, May 20, 1982), *V* (1981– ; in progress), *VI* for 6 Percussionists (1981), and *VII* for 7 Voices and Orch. (1981– ; in progress); Viola Concerto (1980–83; West Berlin, Nov. 13, 1983); *Wölfli-*

Liederbuch for Baritone and Orch. or Piano (1981–82); *Chiffre I* for Piano and 7 Instruments (1982; Saarbrücken, April 22, 1983) and *II, Silence to Be Beaten*, for Percussion and Orch. (1983); *Roter und Schwarzer Tanz*, fragment from *Tutuguri* (1982–83); *Gebild* for Piccolo Trumpet, 2 Percussionists, and 20 Strings (Zürich, May 15, 1983); *Monodram* for Cello and Orch. (Graz, Oct. 9, 1983); *Dies* for Soli, Chorus, Organ, and Orch. (1984); *Schattenstück* (1982–85); *Spur* (1984–85); *Umriss* (1985; Berlin, May 5, 1986). **CHAMBER:** 8 string quartets: No. 1 (1968); No. 2 (1970); No. 3, *Im Innersten* (1976); No. 4 (1979–81); No. 5, *Ohne Titel* (Brussels, Dec. 6, 1983); No. 6, *Blaubuch* (1984; Frankfurt, June 14, 1986); No. 7 (1985); No. 8 (1988; Milan, Jan. 17, 1989); *Paraphrase* for Cello, Piano, and Percussion (1972); *Deploration* for Flute, Cello, and Percussion (1973); *Hervorgedunkelt*, 5 songs after Celan, for Mezzo-soprano, Flute, Harp, Vibraphone, Cello, Organ, and Percussion (1974); *Music for 3 Strings* for Violin, Viola, and Cello (1977); *Erscheinung*, sketch after Schubert, for 9 Strings (1978); *Ländler* for 13 Strings or Piano (1979); *Music Hall Suite* for Clarinet, Alto and Tenor Saxophones, Trumpet, Violin, Double Bass, Piano, and Percussion (1979); *Nature morte* for 13 Strings (1979–80); *Nietzsche-Fragmente* for Mezzo-soprano, Baritone, Chorus, and Flute (1981); *Canzona* for 4 Violas (1982); *Fremde Szene* for Piano Trio (1982). **SOLO SONGS:** *Alexanderlieder* for Mezzo-soprano, Baritone, and 2 Pianos (1975–76); *Neue Alexanderlieder* for Baritone and Piano (1979). **PIANO:** *Klavierstück* No. 4 (1974), No. 5, *Tombeau* (1975), No. 6, *Bagatellen* (1977–78), and No. 7 (1980); *Ländler* (1979; also for Strings). **ORGAN:** *Contemplatio* (1967); *3 Fantasies* (1967); *Fantasy* (1968); *Siebengestalt* for Organ with Tamtam (1974); *Bann, Nachtschwärmerei* (1980).
    BIBL.: R. Urmetzer, *W. R.* (Stuttgart, 1988).

Riisager, Knudåge, prominent Danish composer; b. Port Kunda, Estonia, March 6, 1897; d. Copenhagen, Dec. 26, 1974. He attended courses in political science at the Univ. of Copenhagen (1916–21); concurrently studied music with Peder Gram, Peder Møller, and Otto Malling (1915–18); then went to Paris and took private lessons with Albert Roussel and Paul Le Flem (1921–23); subsequently studied counterpoint with Hermann Grabner in Leipzig (1932). He held a civil service position in Denmark (1925–50); was chairman of the Danish Composers' Union (1937–62) and director of the Royal Danish Cons. (1956–67). A fantastically prolific composer, he wrote music in quaquaversal genres, but preserved a remarkable structural and textural consistency while demonstrating an erudite sense of modern polyphony. He also had a taste for exotic and futuristic subjects. He publ. a collection of essays, *Det usynlige mønster* (The Unseemly Monster; Copenhagen, 1957), and a somewhat self-deprecatory memoir, *Det er sjovt at være lille* (It Is Amusing to Be Small; Copenhagen, 1967).
    WORKS (All 1st perf. in Copenhagen unless otherwise given): **STAGE:** Opera buffa, *Susanne* (1948; Jan. 7, 1950); 14 ballets: *Benzin* (1927; Dec. 26, 1930); a "ballet-bouffonnerie," *Cocktails-Party* (1929); *Tolv med Posten* (12 by the Mail), after H.C. Andersen (1939; Feb. 21, 1942); *Slaraffenland* (Fool's Paradise; 1940; Feb. 21, 1942; originally an orch. piece, 1936); *Qarrtsiluni*, on Eskimo themes (Feb. 21, 1942; originally an orch. piece, 1938); *Fugl fønix* (Phoenix; 1944–45; May 12, 1946); *Étude*, based on Czerny's studies (1947; Jan. 15, 1948); *Månerenen* (The Moon Reindeer; 1956; Nov. 22, 1957); *Stjerner* (1958); *Les Victoires de l'Amour* (1958; March 4, 1962); *Fruen fra havet* (Lady from the Sea; 1959; N.Y., April 20, 1960); *Galla-Variationer* (1966; March 5, 1967); *Ballet Royal* (May 31, 1967); *Svinedrengen* (The Swineherd; Danish Television, March 10, 1969). **ORCH.:** *Erasmus Montanus*, overture (1920; Göteborg, Oct. 15, 1924); *Suite Dionysiaque* for Chamber Orch. (1924); 5 syms.: No. 1 (1925; July 17, 1926); No. 2 (1927; March 5, 1929); No. 3 (Nov. 21, 1935); No. 4, *Sinfonia gaia* (Oct. 24, 1940); No. 5, *Sinfonia serena* for Strings and Percussion (1949–50; Nov. 21, 1950); *Introduzione di traverso*, overture (1925); *Variations on a Theme of Mezangean* (1926); *T-DOXC*, "poème mécanique" (1926; Sept. 3, 1927); *Klods Hans*

(1929); *Fastelavn* (Shrovetide), overture (1929–30); *Suite* for Small Orch. (1931); *Concerto* for Orch. (1931; Dec. 7, 1936); Concertino for Trumpet and String Orch. (1933; March 2, 1934); *Primavera*, overture (1934; Jan. 31, 1935); *Slaraffenland*, 2 suites (1936, 1940; as a ballet, 1940); *Sinfonia concertante* for Strings (1937); *Partita* (1937); *Basta* (1938); *Qarrtsiluni* (1938; as a ballet, 1940); *Torgutdans* (1939); *Tivoli-Tivoli!* (Aug. 15, 1943); *Sommer-Rhapsodi* (1943; Jan. 30, 1944); *Bellman-Variationer* for Small Orch. (1945); Sinfonietta (Stockholm, Oct. 1, 1947); *Chaconne* (1949); *Archaeopteryx* (1949); *Variations on a Sarabande of Charles, Duke of Orleans, 1415* for String Orch. (1950); Violin Concerto (1950–51; Oct. 11, 1951); *Toccata* (1952); *Pro fistulis et fidibus* for Woodwinds and String Orch. (1952; March 2, 1953); *Rondo giocoso* for Violin and Orch. (June 18, 1957); *Burlesk ouverture* (1964); *Entrada-Epilogo* (May 19, 1971); *Bourrée*, ballet-variations (Danish Radio, March 7, 1972); *Trittico* for Woodwinds, Brass, Double Bass, and Percussion (Danish Radio, March 3, 1972); *Apollon* (Nov. 11, 1973); incidental music. **VOCAL:** *Dansk Salme* for Chorus and Orch. (1942; April 13, 1943); *Sang til Solen* for Mezzo-soprano, Baritone, Chorus, and Orch. (Sept. 25, 1947); *Sangen om det Uendelige* (Canto dell'Infinito) for Chorus and Orch. (Sept. 30, 1965); *Stabat Mater* for Chorus and Orch. (1966; Danish Radio, Nov. 9, 1967); choruses; songs. **CHAMBER:** 2 violin sonatas (1917, 1923); 6 string quartets (1918; 1920; 1922; 1925–26; 1932; 1942–43); Sonata for Violin and Viola (1919); Wind Quintet (1921); *Variations* for Clarinet, Viola, and Bassoon (1923); Sinfonietta for 8 Wind Instruments (1924); *Divertimento* for String Quartet and Wind Quintet (1925); Sonata for Flute, Violin, Clarinet, and Cello (1927); *Music* for Wind Quintet (1927); *Conversazione* for Oboe, Clarinet, and Bassoon (1932); Concertino for 5 Violins and Piano (1933); *Serenade* for Flute, Violin, and Cello (1936); Quartet for Flute, Oboe, Clarinet, and Bassoon (1941); *Divertimento* for Flute, Oboe, Horn, and Bassoon (1944); Sonatina for Piano Trio (1951); 2-Violin Sonata (1951); String Trio (1955). **PIANO:** *4 épigrammes* (1921); Sonata (1931); *2 morceaux* (1933); Sonatina (1950); *4 Børneklaverstykker* (1964).
    BIBL.: S. Berg, *K. R.s Kompositioner*, annotated catalog of works (Copenhagen, 1967).

Riley, Terry (Mitchell), American composer and performer of the extreme experimental left; b. Colfax, Calif., June 24, 1935. He studied piano with Duane Hampton at San Francisco State College (1955–57) and composition with Seymour Shifrin and William Denny at the Univ. of Calif. at Berkeley (M.A., 1961); went to Europe and played piano and saxophone in cabarets in Paris and in Scandinavia. In 1970 he was initiated in San Francisco as a disciple of Pandit Pran Nath, the North Indian singer, and followed him to India. He was a creative associate at the Center for Creative and Performing Arts at the State Univ. of N.Y. at Buffalo (1967); from 1971 to 1980 he was associate prof. at Mills College in Oakland, Calif. In 1979 he held a Guggenheim fellowship. In his music, Riley explores the extremes of complexity and gymnosophistical simplicity. His astrological signs are Sun in Cancer (euphemistically known in southern California as Moon Children so as to exorcise middle-aged fear of malignancy), Scorpio Rising, and Aries Moon.
    WORKS: TAPE AND INSTRUMENTAL: Trio for Violin, Clarinet, and Cello (1957); *Spectra* for 3 Winds and 3 Strings (1959); *Concert* for 2 Pianos and Tape (1960); *Earpiece* for 2 Pianos and Tape (1960); String Quartet (1960); String Trio (1961); *I Can't Stop No, Mescalin Mix*, and *She Moves* for Tape (1962–63); *In C* for Variable Ensemble, notated in fragments to be played any number of times at will in the spirit of aleatory latitudinarianism, all within the key of C major, with an occasional F sharp providing a *trompe l'oreille* effect (San Francisco, May 21, 1965); *Cadenza on the Night Plain* for String Quartet (1984). **PIECES WITH SYNTHESIZER:** *Poppy Nogoods Phantom Band* (1966); *A Rainbow in Curved Air* (1968); *Genesis '70*, ballet (1970); *Chorale of the Blessed Day* for Voice and 2 Synthesizers or Piano and Sitar (1980); *Eastern Man* for Voice

and 2 Synthesizers (1980); *Embroidery* for Voice and 2 Synthesizers or Piano, Synthesizer, Sitar, Tabla, and Alto Saxophone (1980); *Song from the Old Country* for Voice, Piano, Sitar, Tabla, String Quartet, and Synthesizer (1980); *G-Song* for Voice, String Quartet, and Synthesizer (1981); *Remember this oh Mind* for Voice and Synthesizer (1981); *Sunrise of the Planetary Dream Collector* for Voice, Synthesizer, and String Quartet (1981); *The Ethereal Time Shadow* for Voice and 2 Synthesizers (1982); *Offering to Chief Crazy Horse* for Voice and 2 Synthesizers (1982); *The Medicine Wheel* for Voice, Piano, Sitar, Tabla, String Quartet, and Synthesizer (1983); *Song of the Emerald Runner* for Voice, Piano, String Quartet, Sitar, Tabla, and Synthesizer (1983); also various improvisational pieces.

Rilling, Helmuth, noted German organist, conductor, and pedagogue; b. Stuttgart, May 29, 1933. He studied at the Hochschule für Musik in Stuttgart and later took a course in organ with Fernando Germani at the Accademia di Santa Cecilia in Rome (1955–57); went to N.Y. to study conducting with Bernstein (1967). He founded the Stuttgart Gächinger Kantorei in 1954, which he conducted on numerous tours. He taught choral conducting and organ at the Kirchenmusikschule in Berlin-Spandau (1963–66); in 1966 he was appointed to the faculty of the Frankfurt Hochschule für Musik. In 1965 he founded the Stuttgart Bach-Collegium, an instrumental ensemble to accompany his Gächinger Kantorei; made his 1st tour of the U.S. with it in 1968; in 1969 he succeeded Kurt Thomas as conductor of the Frankfurter Kantorei. He was founder–artistic director of the Oregon Bach Festival in Eugene (from 1970). He has acquired a distinguished reputation as both a performing musician and a teacher.

Rimbault, Edward (Francis), English organist, writer on music, editor, and composer; b. London, June 13, 1816; d. there, Sept. 26, 1876. He was the son of Stephen Francis Rimbault, organist and composer (1773–1837); was a pupil of his father, Samuel Wesley, and William Crotch; was organist at various London churches. He began giving lectures on English musical history in 1838; in 1840 he founded, with E. Taylor and W. Chappell, the Musical Antiquarian Soc.; received the degree of Ph.D. from the Univ. of Göttingen. He composed various songs, of which *Happy Land* became a popular favorite.

WRITINGS: *Bibliotheca Madrigaliana* (1846); *The Organ, Its History and Construction* (1855; 3rd ed., augmented, 1877); *The Pianoforte: Its Origin, Progress and Construction* (1860); *The Early English Organ-builders and Their Works* (1864); *J.S. Bach* (after Hilgenfeldt and Forkel; 1869); etc. He ed. collections of sacred and secular music, particularly those by English composers of the 16th, 17th, and 18th centuries.

Rimsky-Korsakov, Andrei (Nikolaievich), Russian musicologist, son of **Nikolai (Andreievich) Rimsky-Korsakov;** b. St. Petersburg, Oct. 17, 1878; d. there (Leningrad), May 23, 1940. He studied philology at the Univ. of St. Petersburg and later at the Univs. of Strasbourg and Heidelberg (Ph.D., 1903); returning to Russia, he devoted his energies to Russian music history. In 1915 he began the publication of an important magazine, *Musikalny Sovremennik* (The Musical Contemporary), but the revolutionary events of 1917 forced suspension of its publication. He ed. the 1st 4 vols. of the complete biography of his father, *N.A. Rimsky-Korsakov; Life and Works* (Moscow, 1933, 1935, 1936, 1937; an additional vol., no. 5, 1946, was completed and ed. by his younger brother Vladimir Rimsky-Korsakov); also publ. *M.P. Mussorgsky, Letters and Documents* (1932); ed. and annotated his father's *Chronicle of My Musical Life* (Moscow, 1935); compiled the catalog, *Musical Treasures of the Manuscript Department of the Leningrad Public Library* (1938). He was married to the composer **Julia Weissberg.**

Rimsky-Korsakov, Georgi (Mikhailovich), Russian musicologist and composer, grandson of **Nikolai (Andreievich)** and nephew of **Andrei (Nikolaievich) Rimsky-Korsakov;** b. St. Petersburg, Dec. 26, 1901; d. there (Leningrad), Oct. 10, 1965. He studied at the St. Petersburg Cons.; in 1923, founded a society for the cultivation of quarter-tone music;

composed some works in that system; publ. the articles "Foundations of the Quarter-Tone System" (Leningrad, 1925) and "The Deciphering of the 'Luce' Part in Scriabin's Prometheus," in the Russian magazine *De Musica* (1927); then became active in work on electronic musical instruments; was co-inventor of the "Emeriton" (1930), capable of producing a complete series of tones at any pitch and of any chosen or synthetic tone color; wrote solo pieces for it; also an Octet for 2 Emeritons, 2 Clarinets, Bassoon, Violin, Viola, and Cello (1932). From 1927 to 1962 he was on the faculty of the Leningrad Cons.

Rimsky-Korsakov, Nikolai (Andreievich), great Russian composer, father of **Andrei (Nikolaievich) Rimsky-Korsakov;** b. Tikhvin, near Novgorod, March 18, 1844; d. Liubensk, near St. Petersburg, June 21, 1908. He remained in the country until he was 12 years old; in 1856 he entered the Naval School in St. Petersburg, graduating in 1862. He took piano lessons as a child with provincial teachers, and later with a professional musician, Théodore Canillé, who introduced him to Balakirev; he also met Cui and Borodin. In 1862 he was sent on the clipper *Almaz* on a voyage that lasted 2½ years; returning to Russia in the summer of 1865, he settled in St. Petersburg, where he remained most of his life. During his travels he maintained contact with Balakirev, and continued to report to him the progress of his musical composition. He completed his 1st Sym. (which was also the earliest significant work in this form by a Russian composer), and it was performed under Balakirev's direction on Dec. 31, 1865, at a concert of the Free Music School in St. Petersburg. In 1871 Rimsky-Korsakov was engaged as a prof. of composition and orchestration at the St. Petersburg Cons., even though he was aware of the inadequacy of his own technique. He remained on the faculty until his death, with the exception of a few months in 1905, when he was relieved of his duties as prof. for his public support of the rebellious students during the revolution of that year. As a music educator, Rimsky-Korsakov was of the greatest importance to the development and maintenance of the traditions of the Russian national school; among his students were Glazunov, Liadov, Arensky, Ippolitov-Ivanov, Gretchaninov, Nikolai Tcherepnin, Maximilian Steinberg, Gnessin, and Miaskovsky. Igor Stravinsky studied privately with him from 1903 on.

In 1873 Rimsky-Korsakov abandoned his naval career, but was appointed to the post of inspector of the military orchs. of the Russian navy, until it was abolished in 1884. From 1883 to 1894 he was also assistant director of the Court Chapel and led the chorus and the orch. there. Although he was not a gifted conductor, he gave many performances of his own orch. works; made his debut at a charity concert for the victims of the Volga famine, in St. Petersburg, March 2, 1874; the program included the 1st performance of his 3rd Sym. From 1886 until 1900 he conducted the annual Russian Sym. concerts organized by the publisher Belaieff; in June 1889 he conducted 2 concerts of Russian music at the World Exposition in Paris; in 1890 he conducted a concert of Russian music in Brussels; led a similar concert there in 1900. His last appearance abroad was in the spring of 1907, when he conducted in Paris 2 Russian historic concerts arranged by Diaghilev; in the same year he was elected corresponding member of the French Academy, to succeed Grieg. These activities, however, did not distract him from his central purpose as a national Russian composer. His name was grouped with those of Cui, Borodin, Balakirev, and Mussorgsky as the "Mighty 5," and he maintained an intimate friendship with most of them; at Mussorgsky's death he collected his MSS and prepared them for publication; he also revised Mussorgsky's opera *Boris Godunov;* it was in Rimsky-Korsakov's version that the opera became famous. Later some criticism was voiced against Rimsky-Korsakov's reduction of Mussorgsky's original harmonies and melodic lines to an academically acceptable standard. He had decisive influence in the affairs of the Belaieff publishing firm and helped publish a great number of works by Russian composers of the St. Petersburg group; only a small part of these sumptuously printed scores represents the best in Russian music, but culturally Rimsky-Korsakov's solicitude was of great importance. Although he was far from being a revolutionary, he freely expressed his disgust at the bungling administration of Czarist Russia; he was particularly indignant about the attempts of the authorities to alter Pushkin's lines in his own last opera, *The Golden Cockerel*, and refused to compromise; he died, of angina pectoris, with the situation still unresolved; the opera was produced posthumously, with the censor's changes; the original text was not restored until the revolution of 1917.

Rimsky-Korsakov was one of the greatest masters of Russian music. His source of inspiration was Glinka's operatic style; he made use of both the purely Russian idiom and coloristic oriental melodic patterns; such works as his symphonic suite *Scheherazade* and *The Golden Cockerel* represent Russian orientalism at its best; in the purely Russian style, the opera *Snow Maiden* and the *Russian Easter Overture* are outstanding examples. The influence of Wagner and Liszt in his music was small; only in his opera *The Legend of the Invisible City of Kitezh* are there perceptible echoes from *Parsifal*. In the art of orchestration Rimsky-Korsakov had few equals; his treatment of instruments, in solo passages and in ensemble, was invariably idiomatic. In his treatise on orchestration he selected only passages from his own works to demonstrate the principles of practical and effective application of registers and tone colors. Although an academician in his general esthetics, he experimented boldly with melodic progressions and ingenious harmonies that pointed toward modern usages. He especially favored the major scale with the lowered submediant and the scale of alternating whole tones and semi-tones (which in Russian reference works came to be termed as "Rimsky-Korsakov's scale"; in the score of his opera-ballet *Mlada* there is an ocarina part tuned in this scale); in *The Golden Cockerel* and *Kashchei the Immortal* he applied dissonant harmonies in unusual superpositions; but he set for himself a definite limit in innovation, and severely criticized Richard Strauss, Debussy, and Vincent d'Indy for their modernistic practices.

WORKS: OPERAS: *The Maid of Pskov* (1868–72; St. Petersburg, Jan. 13, 1873; 2nd version, 1876–77; 3rd version, 1891–92; St. Petersburg, April 18, 1895); *May Night* (1878–79; St. Petersburg, Jan. 21, 1880); *Snow Maiden* (1880–81; St. Petersburg, Feb. 10, 1882; 2nd version, c.1895); *Mlada*, opera-ballet (1889–90; St. Petersburg, Nov. 1, 1892); *Night before Christmas* (St. Petersburg, Dec. 10, 1895); *Sadko* (1894–96; Moscow, Jan. 7, 1898); *Mozart and Salieri*, op. 48, on Pushkin's play dealing with Salieri's supposed poisoning of Mozart (1897; Moscow, Dec. 7, 1898); *Boyarynia Vera Sheloga*, op. 54 (originally the prologue to the 2nd version of *The Maid of Pskov*; Moscow, Dec. 27, 1898); *The Tsar's Bride* (1898; Moscow, Nov. 3, 1899); *The Tale of Tsar Saltan* (Moscow, Nov. 3, 1900); *Servilia* (1900–1901; St. Petersburg, Oct. 14, 1902); *Kashchei the Immortal* (Moscow, Dec. 25, 1902); *The Commander* (1902–3; St. Petersburg, Oct. 16, 1904); *The Legend of the Invisible City of Kitezh* (1903–5; St. Petersburg, Feb. 20, 1907); *The Golden Cockerel* (1906–7; Moscow, Oct. 7, 1909).

ORCH.: Sym. No. 1, op. 1 (1st version in E-flat minor, 1861–65; St. Petersburg, Dec. 31, 1865; 2nd version in E minor; 1884); *Overture on 3 Russian Themes*, op. 28 (1st version, 1866; 2nd version, 1879–80); *Fantasia on Serbian Themes*, op. 6 (1st version, 1867; 2nd version, 1886–87); *Sadko*, op. 5 (1st version, 1867; 2nd version, 1869; 3rd version, 1892); Sym. No. 2, op. 9, *Antar* (1st version, 1868; 2nd version, 1875; 3rd version, 1897); Sym. No. 3, op. 32 (1st version, 1866–73; St. Petersburg, March 2, 1874; 2nd version, 1886); Concerto for Trombone and Military Band (1877); *Variations* for Oboe and Military Band (1878); *Concertstück* for Clarinet and Military Band (1878); *Legend*, op. 29 (original title, *Baba-Yaga*; 1879–80); *Sinfonietta on Russian Themes*, op. 31 (1880–84; based on the String Quartet of 1878–79); Piano Concerto in C-sharp minor, op. 30 (1882–83); *Fantasia on 2 Russian Themes* for Violin and Orch., op. 33 (1886–87); *Capriccio espagnol*, op. 34 (1887); *Scheherazade*, symphonic suite, op. 35 (St.

Petersburg, Nov. 3, 1888); *Souvenir de trois chants polonais* for Violin and Orch. (1888); *Russian Easter Overture*, op. 36 (1888); *Serenade* for Cello and Orch., op. 37 (1903; arranged from the *Serenade* for Cello and Piano, 1893); *The Tale of Tsar Saltan*, suite from the opera, op. 57 (1903); *The Commander*, suite from the opera, op. 59 (1903); *Mlada*, suite from the opera (1903); *Night before Christmas*, suite from the opera (1903); *At the Grave* (1904; in memory of Belaieff); *The Little Oak Stick*, op. 62 (1st version, 1905; 2nd version with Chorus ad libitum, 1906); *Greeting* (1906); *The Golden Cockerel*, symphonic arrangement of the introduction and wedding march from the opera (1907).

CHAMBER: String Quartet in F major, op. 12 (1875); Sextet in A major for 2 Violins, 2 Violas, and 2 Cellos (1876); Quintet in B-flat major for Flute, Clarinet, Horn, Bassoon, and Piano (1876); *String Quartet on Russian Themes* (1878–79); 4 variations on a chorale in G minor for String Quartet (1885); *String Quartet on B-la-f* (Belaieff; 1886; other movements by Liadov, Borodin, and Glazunov); String Quartet *Jour de fête* (1887; finale only; other movements by Glazunov and Liadov); Nocturne in F major for 4 Horns (c.1888); 2 duets in F major for 2 Horns (c.1893–94); *Canzonetta and Tarantella* for 2 Clarinets (c.1883–94); *Serenade* for Cello and Piano (1893; also for Cello and Orch., 1903); String Quartet in G major (1897); Theme and Variation No. 4 in G major for String Quartet (1898; in collaboration with others); Allegro in B-flat major for String Quartet (1899; in collaboration with others).

CHORAL: WITH ORCH.: *Poem about Alexis, the Man of God*, op. 20 (1878); *Glory*, op. 21 (1879–80); *Svitezyanka*, cantata for Soprano, Tenor, Chorus, and Orch., op. 44 (1897); *Poem of Oleg the Wise* for Tenor, Bass, Men's Chorus, and Orch., op. 58 (1899); *From Homer*, prelude-cantata for Soprano, Mezzo-soprano, Alto, Women's Chorus, and Orch., op. 60 (1901). **A CAPPELLA:** 2 choruses, op. 13 (1875); op. 14 (1875); 6 choruses, op. 16 (1875–76); 2 choruses, op. 18 (1876); 4 choruses, op. 23 (1876); 15 Russian folksongs, op. 19 (1879); etc.; also 83 solo songs; 4 duets.

PIANO: Allegro in D minor (1859–60); *Variations on a Russian Theme* (1859–60); Nocturne in D minor (1860); *Funeral March* in D minor (1860); Scherzo in C minor for Piano, 4-hands (1860); 6 fugues, op. 17 (1875); 3 pieces, op. 15 (1875–76); 4 pieces, op. 11 (1876–77); 6 *Variations on B-A-C-H*, op. 10 (1878); *Variations on a Theme by Misha* for Piano, 4-hands (1878–79); Prelude-Impromptu: Mazurka, op. 38 (1894); Allegretto in C major (1895); Prelude in G major (1896); Fugal Intermezzo for Piano, 4-hands (1897); etc.

ARRANGEMENTS AND EDITIONS: He ed. a collection of 100 Russian folk songs, op. 24 (1876); harmonized 40 folk songs. After Dargomyzhsky's death, he orchestrated his posthumous opera *Kamennyi gost* (The Stone Guest); also orchestrated Borodin's *Prince Igor*; his greatest task of musical reorganization was the preparation for publication and performance of Mussorgsky's works; he reharmonized the cycle *Songs and Dances of Death* and the symphonic picture *Night on Bald Mountain*; orchestrated the opera *Khovanshchina*; rev. *Boris Godunov* (in melody and harmony, as well as in orchestration).

WRITINGS: Among his pedagogical works, the book on harmony (St. Petersburg, 1884; numerous subsequent eds. in Russian; in Eng., N.Y., 1930) is widely used in Russian music schools; publ. *Foundations of Orchestration* (2 vols., St. Petersburg, 1913; ed. by Maximilian Steinberg; also available in French and in Eng.); collected articles were publ. in 1911, ed. by M. Gnessin. His autobiographical book, *The Chronicle of My Musical Life* (posthumous, 1909; 5th ed. by his son Andrei, supplemented and annotated, 1935), is a valuable document of the most important period of Russian music; it is publ. also in Eng. (N.Y., 1924; new ed., 1942), in French (Paris, 1938), etc. A complete ed. of Rimsky-Korsakov's works was begun in Moscow in 1946, edited by A. Rimsky-Korsakov and others; 49 vols. were publ. by 1970.

BIBL.: V. Yastrebtzev, *R.-K.* (1900; 2nd ed. with a complete list of works, 1908); N. Findeisen, *R.-K.* (1908); I. Lapshin, *Philosophical Motives in the Works of R.-K.* (1911); N. van

Gilse van der Pals, *R.-K.* (Leipzig, 1914); M. Montagu-Nathan, *R.-K.* (London, 1916); I. Glebov, *R.-K.* (1922); E. Istel, "R.-K., the Oriental Wizard," *Musical Quarterly* (July 1929); N. van Gilse van der Pals, *R.-K.s Opernschaffen* (Leipzig, 1929); A. Rimsky-Korsakov, *R.-K., Life and Works* (fundamental biography; 5 fascicles; Moscow, 1933, 1935, 1936, 1937, 1946; last vol. ed. by V. Rimsky-Korsakov); I. Markevitch, *R.-K.* (Paris, 1935); G. Abraham and M. Calvocoressi, *Masters of Russian Music* (London, 1936); A. Solovtzov, *R.-K.* (Moscow, 1948; 2nd ed., 1957); G. Abraham, *R.-K.; A Short Biography* (London, 1949); M. Yankovsky, *R.-K. and the Revolution of 1905* (Moscow, 1950); V. Kisselev, *R.-K.; Documents* (Moscow, 1951); D. Kabalevsky, ed., *R.-K., Materials and Letters* (Moscow, 2 vols., 1953 and 1954); M. Gnessin, *Reflections and Reminiscences about N.A. R.-K.* (Moscow, 1956); I. Kunin, *R.-K.* (Moscow, 1964); S. Evseyev, *R.-K. and Russian National Songs* (Moscow, 1970); I. Kunin, *N.A. R.-K.* (Moscow, 1979); G. Seaman, *N.A. R.-K.: A Guide to Research* (N.Y., 1988).

Rinaldo di (da) Capua, Italian composer; b. Capua or Rome, c.1705; d. probably in Rome, c.1780. He came from the vicinity of Naples and seems to have been active chiefly in Rome, where Burney knew him in 1770, and where most of his operas were given (others were produced in Florence, Venice, London, and Paris). His career as a dramatic composer probably began in 1737. Thereafter he produced about 30 theatrical works with varying success, among them *Ciro riconosciuto* (Rome, Jan. 19, 1737), *Vologeso re de' Parti* (Rome, Carnival 1739), and *La Zingara* (Paris, June 19, 1753; his best work). He also composed 5 syms. and many overtures which reveal an adept hand at orch. writing, numerous oratorios, cantatas, and other works.
BIBL.: C. Burney, *The Present State of Music in France and Italy* (London, 1771); P. Spitta, "R. d.C.," *Vierteljahrsschrift für Musikwissenschaft*, III (1887); R. Bostian, *The Works of R. d.C.* (diss., Univ. of North Carolina, 1961).

Rinck, Johann Christian Heinrich, famous German organist, teacher, and composer; b. Elgersburg, Thuringia, Feb. 18, 1770; d. Darmstadt, Aug. 7, 1846. He studied under Kittel in Erfurt (1786–89); was town organist at Giessen (1790–1805) before settling in Darmstadt, where he was organist and teacher at the music school (from 1805); became court organist there in 1813, and chamber musician in 1817. One of the foremost players of the time, he made frequent concert tours. In addition to much music for organ, he wrote masses, cantatas, and motets. He publ. an autobiography (Breslau, 1833).
BIBL.: M. Fölsing, *Züge aus dem Leben und Wirken des Dr. C.H. R.* (Erfurt, 1848); F. Donat, *C.H. R. und die Orgelmusik seiner Zeit* (Bad Oeynhausen, 1933).

Ringbom, Nils-Eric, Finnish violinist, music critic, music administrator, and composer; b. Turku, Dec. 27, 1907; d. Korpoström, Feb. 13, 1988. He studied at the Turku Academy (M.A., 1933) and at the Univ. of Helsinki (D.Mus., 1955, with the diss. *Über die Deutbarkeit der Tonkunst;* publ. in Helsinki and Wiesbaden, 1955; among his teachers were O. Andersson and L. Funtek. He played violin in the Turku Sym. Orch. (1927–28; 1930–33); was assistant manager (1938–42) and manager (1942–70) of the Helsinki Phil.; served as artistic director of the Sibelius Festival (1951–60) and chairman of the Helsinki Festival (1966–70); was music critic of the *Svenska Pressen* (1933–44) and the *Nya Pressen* (1945–70).
WRITINGS: *Helsingfors orkesterföretag 1882–1932* (Helsinki, 1932); *Säveltaide* (The Art of Music; Helsinki, 1945); *Sibelius* (Stockholm, 1948; German tr., 1950; Eng. tr., 1954); *Musik utan normer* (Music without Norms; 1972); *Orkesterhovdingar* (1981).
WORKS: ORCH.: 5 syms. (1938–39; 1943–44; 1948; 1962; 1970); *Little Suite* (1933; rev. 1946); *Till livet* (To Life) for Chorus and Strings (1936); *Vandrerska* (The Wanderer) for Soprano and Orch. (1942); *Hymn till Helsingfors* for Chorus and Orch. (1949). **CHAMBER:** Duo for Violin and Viola (1945); Wind Sextet (1951); String Quartet (1952); piano pieces; songs.

Ringer, Alexander L(othar), American musicologist; b. Berlin (of Dutch parents), Feb. 3, 1921. He attended the Hollander Cons. in Berlin; in 1939 went to Amsterdam, where he studied composition with Henk Badings. In 1946 he emigrated to the U.S.; continued his education at the New School for Social Research in N.Y. (M.A., 1949) and at Columbia Univ. (Ph.D., 1955). He taught at the City College of N.Y. (1948–52), the Univ. of Pa. (1952–55), the Univ. of Calif., Berkeley (1955–56), and the Univ. of Oklahoma (1956–58). In 1958 he was appointed to the faculty of the Univ. of Illinois, Urbana; also was a regular guest lecturer at the Hebrew Univ. in Jerusalem. He contributed many articles to the *Musical Quarterly;* also publ. the study *Arnold Schoenberg: The Composer as Jew* (Oxford, 1990).

Rinuccini, Ottavio, great Italian poet and librettist; b. Florence, Jan. 20, 1562; d. there, March 28, 1621. He was born into a family of the nobility and became a prominent courtier; commenced writing verses for court entertainments about 1579; was also active in the Accademia Fiorentina and the Accademia degli Alterati, taking the name "Il Sonnacchioso" ("the somnolent one"). He collaborated with Bardi in preparing intermedi for the wedding of the Grand Duke Ferdinando I (1589); Corsi and Peri then set his pastoral *Dafne* to music, which work is generally recognized as the 1st opera in the monodic style (Florence, 1598). Rinuccini's *Euridice,* with music by Peri, was performed in 1600; another setting, by Caccini, in 1602. He also wrote the libretto of Monteverdi's *Arianna* (1608). These texts were republ. by A. Solerti in vol. II of *Gli albori del melodramma* (Milan, 1905) and by A. Della Corte, *Drammi per musica dal Rinuccini allo Zeno* (Turin, 1958).
BIBL.: F. Meda, *O. R.* (Milan, 1894); A. Civita, *O. R. ed il sorgere del melodramma in Italia* (Mantua, 1900); F. Raccamadoro-Ramelli, *O. R., Studio biografico e critico* (Fabriano, 1900); A. Solerti, *Le origini del melodramma* (Turin, 1903); idem, *Musica, ballo e drammatica alla corte medicea dal 1600 al 1637* (Florence, 1905); O. Sonneck, "Dafne, the First Opera: A Chronological Study," *Sammelbände der Internationalen Musik-Gesellschaft,* XV (1913–14); A. Della Corte, *O. R. librettista* (Turin, 1925); U. Rolandi, "Didascalie sceniche in un raro libretto dell'Euridice del R.," *Rivista Musicale Italiana* (1926); M. Schild, *Die Musikdramen O. R.s* (Würzburg, 1933); B. Hanning, "Apologia pro O. R.," *Journal of the American Musicological Society,* XXVIII (1975).

Rios, Waldo de los, Argentine composer, conductor, arranger, and pianist; b. Buenos Aires, Sept. 7, 1934; d. (of a self-inflicted gunshot wound) Madrid, March 29, 1977. He studied in Argentina with his mother, Martha de los Rios, a prominent Argentine folksinger; then had piano, composition, and conducting lessons at the National Academy of Music (graduated, 1954). He served in the Argentine military; concurrently made his 1st folk recordings with Columbia Records (1955). This and subsequent recordings of indigenous folk tunes arranged for sym. orch. were not well received, since Argentina was experiencing renewed interest in its folk music and was intent upon authenticity. In 1962 he emigrated to Spain, where he subsequently made it his mission to popularize the classics for the enlightenment of the masses; this he accomplished by selecting outstanding movements from large-scale, well-known works and, after condensing them to 3–5 minutes, arranging them for symphonic forces augmented by pop ensembles which included saxophone, drums, and Spanish and/or Latin percussion instruments. His rendition of Mozart's Sym. No. 40 became particularly popular. During the 1970s he was conductor-director of the Manuel de Falla Orch. and Chorus, with which he made numerous recordings, including *Sinfonias* (1971), *Operas* (1974), *Sinfonias for the 70's* (1975), *Concertos for the 70's* (1976), and *Corales* (1978). Among his legitimately original works was *South American Suite* (1957), based upon primitive melodies and rhythms of Paraguay, Argentina, Uruguay, and Peru, and scored for orch. augmented by guitars, Indian harp, and various native wind and percussion instruments.

Riotte, Philipp Jakob, German conductor and composer; b. St. Wendel, Saar, Aug. 16, 1776; d. Vienna, Aug. 20, 1856. He studied with André in Offenbach; in 1808 he settled in Vienna, where he conducted at the Theater an der Wien; produced there 48 works of his own, including operas, ballets, and minor pieces; also wrote a Sym., 9 piano sonatas, 6 violin sonatas, etc. He was the author of the "tone picture" *Die Schlacht bei Leipzig* for Piano, which achieved extraordinary popularity in Germany.
BIBL.: G. Spengler, *Der Komponist P.J. R.* (diss., Univ. of Saarbrücken, 1973).

Ripa, Alberto da, Italian lutenist and composer, known as **Alberto da Mantovano;** b. Mantua, c.1500; d. Paris, 1551. He was in the service of Ercole Gonzaga, Cardinal of Mantua; in 1529 he entered the service of François I of France, becoming valet de chambre du roi in 1533. His *Tablature de luth* was brought out posthumously by his pupil Guillaume Morlaye (6 books, Paris, 1552–58); see J.-M. Vaccaro, ed., *Alberto da Rippe: Œuvres,* in Le Chœur des Muses, Corpus des Luthistes Français (1972–75).
BIBL.: J.-G. Prod'homme, "Guillaume Morlaye, editeur d'Albert de Ripe, et bourgeois de Paris," *Revue de Musicologie,* IX (1925); L. Nordstrom, "Albert de Rippe, joueur de luth du roy," *Early Music,* VII (1979).

Risler, Edouard, Alsatian pianist; b. Baden-Baden, Feb. 23, 1873; d. Paris, July 22, 1929. He studied piano with Diémer at the Paris Cons. and continued his studies with Klindworth, Stavenhagen, and Eugène d'Albert in Germany. In 1923 he was appointed prof. at the Paris Cons. He gave concert recitals all over Europe and acquired a high reputation as a fine musician as well as a virtuoso pianist; he made a specialty of presenting cycles of one composer's works; he played Beethoven's 32 sonatas, Chopin's complete piano works, and both books of Bach's *Well-tempered Clavier.*

Rist, Johann, German poet and composer; b. Ottensen, near Hamburg, March 8, 1607; d. Wedel-on-Elbe, Aug. 31, 1667. He studied theology, law, and poetry at the Univs. of Rinteln and Rostock; was pastor in Wedel (from 1635). In 1644 he was made poet laureate by the Emperor, and in 1653 was elevated to the rank of nobleman. He organized in Hamburg a Liederschule, for which he secured the cooperation of many important composers of the day, among them Schiedemann and Thomas Selle. He has been described as the "organizer of the German Parnassus," and indeed his role in the development of a purely national type of secular song, of German folk inspiration, was historically significant. He also wrote a number of sacred songs—*O Ewigkeit, du Donnerwort; O Traurigkeit; O Herzeleid; Werde munter, mein Gemüte;* etc.—which are still sung in Lutheran churches in Germany. He compiled valuable collections of German sacred songs; a modern ed. was brought out by E. Mannack, *J. Rist: Sämtliche Werke* (Berlin, 1967–).
BIBL.: T. Hansen, *J. R. und seine Zeit* (Halle, 1872; reprint, Leipzig, 1973); W. Krabbe, *J. R. und das deutsche Lied* (Bonn, 1910); O. Kern, *J. R. als weltlicher Lyriker* (Marburg, 1919); O. Heins, *J. R. und das niederdeutsche Drama des 17. Jahrhunderts* (1930).

Ristenpart, Karl, German conductor; b. Kiel, Jan. 26, 1900; d. Lisbon, Dec. 24, 1967. He studied music in Berlin and Vienna. In 1932 he became conductor of the Berlin Chamber Orch.; also led concerts with the Radio Orch. in Berlin. In 1946 he was named conductor of the Chamber Orch. of RIAS (Radio in the American Sector of Berlin). In 1953 he became conductor of the Chamber Orch. of the Saar, a noted ensemble of the Saarland Radio in Saarbrücken; made many tours and recordings with this group.

Ristić, Milan, Serbian composer; b. Belgrade, Aug. 31, 1908; d. there, Dec. 20, 1982. He studied in Belgrade with Slavenski and in Prague with Alois Hába. A prolific composer, he wrote mostly instrumental music; his style ranged from neo-Romantic grandiosity to economic neo-Classicism, from epically declamatory diatonicism to expressionistically atonal melos. Some of his works were written in an explicit dodecaphonic technique; in some, he made use of quarter-tones.
WORKS: ORCH.: 7 syms. (1941, 1951, 1961, 1966, 1967, 1968, 1972); Violin Concerto (1944); Piano Concerto (1954); *Suite giocosa* (1956); *Symphonic Variations* (1957); *Burleska* (1957); *7 Bagatelles* (1959); Concerto (1963); Clarinet Concerto (1964); *4 Movements* for Strings (1971). **CHAMBER:** 2 string quartets; Wind Quintet; Septet; Violin Sonata; Viola Sonata; 24 fugues for various instrumental combinations; Suite for 4 Trombones in quarter-tones.

Ristori, Giovanni Alberto, Italian composer; b. probably in Bologna, 1692; d. Dresden, Feb. 7, 1753. He received his education from his father, a violinist in an Italian opera company; with him he went to Dresden (1715) and obtained the post of director of the Polish chapel in Warsaw; then was appointed chamber organist to the court of Saxony (1733), church composer (1746), and assistant conductor (1750). He wrote a number of operas for the Italian Opera in Dresden. His *Calandro,* staged at Pillnitz, near Dresden, on Sept. 2, 1726, was one of the earliest Italian comic operas produced in Germany, and so possesses historical significance beyond its intrinsic worth; other operas produced in Dresden and in court theaters near Dresden were *Cleonice* (Aug. 15, 1718); *Un pazzo ne fà cento, ovvero Don Chisciotte* (Feb. 2, 1727); *Arianna* (Aug. 7, 1736); *Le Fate* (Aug. 10, 1736); etc. He also wrote oratorios, cantatas, and masses; some instrumental music; many of his MSS were destroyed during the siege of Dresden (1760) and the bombing of the city in World War II.
BIBL.: C. Mengelberg, *G.A. R.* (Leipzig, 1916).

Ritchie, Stanley (John), Australian violinist and teacher; b. Yenda, New South Wales, April 21, 1935. He studied violin with Florent Hoogstoel at the Sydney Conservatorium (diploma, 1956); after receiving instruction in violin and chamber music from Jean Fournier and Sandor Vegh in Paris (1958–59), he went to the U.S. and continued his training with Joseph Fuchs at Yale Univ. (1959–60), Oscar Shumsky, and Samuel Kissell. He served as concertmaster of the N.Y. City Opera orch. (1963–65) and associate concertmaster of the Metropolitan Opera orch. (1965–70); was a member of the N.Y. Chamber Soloists (1970–73), founder of the early-music ensemble Aston Magna (1974), and 1st violin in the Philadelphia String Quartet (1975–81). With his wife, harpsichordist and fortepianist Elizabeth Wright, he performed in the Duo Geminiani (from 1974); was prof. of violin and director of the Baroque orch. at Indiana Univ. (from 1982) and a prof. at the Juilliard School in N.Y. (from 1984). He has championed the performance of early music on period instruments.

Ritter, Alexander, German violinist, conductor, composer, and poet; b. Narva, Estonia (of German parents), June 27, 1833; d. Munich, April 12, 1896. He was taken to Dresden in 1841; there he studied violin with Franz Schubert (namesake of the great composer), who was concertmaster of the Dresden Opera; then studied at the Leipzig Cons. (1849–51) with Ferdinand David (violin) and E.F. Richter (theory). In 1854 he married Wagner's niece Franziska Wagner and settled in Weimar, where he entered into a close association with Liszt, Bülow, Cornelius, Raff, and others; was 2nd Konzertmeister in the orch. there (until 1856). He was conductor at the opera in Stettin (1856–58), where his wife was engaged as a soprano; he then lived in Dresden (1858–60), Schwerin (1860–62), and Würzburg (1863–82). When Bülow became conductor at the Hofkapelle in Meiningen (1882), Ritter followed him there and was made 2nd Konzertmeister of the orch.; after Bülow's departure from Meiningen in 1886, Ritter moved to Munich. He wrote 2 operas, *Der faule Hans* (Munich, Oct. 15, 1885) and *Wem die Krone?* (Weimar, June 8, 1890), to his own librettos, and several symphonic poems in an intensely Romantic manner (*Seraphische Phantasie, Erotische Legende, Karfreitag und Frohnleichnam,* and *Kaiser Rudolfs Ritt zum Grabe*); a String Quartet; about 60 songs; piano pieces. Ritter's significance derives, however, not from these well-made but ephemeral compositions, but from his profound influence on young Richard Strauss; it was Ritter who encouraged Strauss in the creation of a new type of philosophical tone poem along the lines of "Musik als Ausdruck" (music as expression), a modern development of the art of Liszt, Wagner, and Berlioz. Ritter wrote the poem printed in the score of *Tod und Verklärung.*

BIBL.: S. von Hausegger, "A. R.: Ein Bild seines Charakters und Schaffens," in R. Strauss, ed., *Die Musik* (Berlin, 1907).

Ritter, August Gottfried, German organist, writer on music, and composer; b. Erfurt, Aug. 25, 1811; d. Magdeburg, Aug. 26, 1885. He was a pupil of Fischer at Erfurt, Hummel at Weimar, and Rungenhagen at Berlin; filled various posts as organist at Erfurt, Merseburg, and Magdeburg; ed. the *Urania* (1844–48); was co-ed. of the *Orgelfreund* and *Orgelarchiv;* publ. a valuable book, *Zur Geschichte des Orgelspiels im 14. bis zum Anfange des 18. Jahrhunderts* (1884), and *Die Kunst des Orgelspiels* (2 vols.; in Eng., N.Y., 1874); also organ pieces, 4 books of chorales, a Piano Concerto, a Piano Quartet, 2 syms., 3 overtures, etc.

Ritter, Frédéric Louis, German-American conductor, teacher, writer on music, and composer; b. Strasbourg, June 22, 1826; d. Antwerp, July 4, 1891. He was of Spanish extraction, his original family name being Caballero, which was tr. into German as Ritter ("knight"). He studied in Strasbourg with Schletterer and Hauser, and then in Paris with Kastner. In 1856 he went to Cincinnati, where he organized the Phil. Orch., but left for N.Y. in 1861; was active mainly as a choral conductor; in 1867, became a prof. of music at Vassar College. He publ. several manuals and music histories, including *A History of Music in the Form of Lectures* (2 vols., Boston, 1870, 1874; 2nd ed., 1880); *Music in England* (N.Y., 1883); *Music in America* (N.Y., 1883; 3rd ed., 1893); *Music in Its Relation to Intellectual Life* (N.Y., 1891). His compositions include 3 syms.; *Stella,* symphonic poem; *Othello Overture;* Cello Concerto; Piano Concerto; various chamber works; choruses; songs. His wife, **Fanny Raymond Ritter** (b. Philadelphia, 1840; d. Poughkeepsie, N.Y., Oct. 26, 1890), was the author of *Woman as a Musician: An Art-Historical Study* (1876); *Some Famous Songs* (1878); etc.

Ritter, Hermann, German violist, inventor, teacher, writer on music, and composer; b. Wismar, Sept. 16, 1849; d. Würzburg, Jan. 22, 1926. He studied at the Hochschule für Musik in Berlin; attended courses at the Univ. of Heidelberg; turning his attention to musical instruments, he began a series of experiments for the purpose of improving the muffled tone of the ordinary viola; profiting by some practical hints in A. Bagatella's book *Regole per la costruzione di violini* (Padua, 1786), he constructed a slightly larger model possessed of better resonance and a more brilliant tone. Exhibiting this new "viola alta" in 1876, he attracted the attention of Wagner, who invited his cooperation for the Bayreuth Festival; after that engagement he made successful tours of all Europe as a viola virtuoso; from 1879, he was a prof. of viola and music history at the Musikschule in Würzburg; in 1905 he founded the "Ritterquartett" (violin, W. Schulze-Prisca; viola alta, Ritter; viola tenore, E. Cahnbley; viola bassa, H. Knöchel). He publ. numerous compositions and transcriptions for viola and piano, and *Elementartechnik der Viola alta.*

WRITINGS: *Die Geschichte der Viola alta und die Grundsätze ihres Baues* (Leipzig, 1876; 2nd ed., 1877; reprinted, Wiesbaden, 1969); *Repetitorium der Musikgeschichte* (1880); *Aus der Harmonielehre meines Lebens* (1883); *Elementartheorie der Musik* (1885); *Ästhetik der Tonkunst* (1886); *Studien und Skizzen aus Musik- und Kulturgeschichte, sowie Musikästhetik* (Dresden, 1892); *Katechismus der Musikästhetik* (2nd ed., 1894); *Katechismus der Musikinstrumente* (1894); *Volksgesang in alter und neuer Zeit* (1896); *Schubert* (1896); *Haydn, Mozart, Beethoven* (1897); *Die fünfsaitige Geige und die Weiterentwicklung der Streichinstrumente* (1898); *Allgemeine illustrierte Encyklopädie der Musikgeschichte* (6 vols., 1901–2).

BIBL.: G. Adema, *H. R. und seine Viola alta* (Würzburg, 1881; 2nd ed., 1894).

Ritter, Peter, German cellist, violinist, conductor, and composer; b. Mannheim, July 2, 1763; d. there, Aug. 1, 1846. He studied violin and cello with his father; completed his theoretical studies under Abbé Vogler. He entered the Mannheim Court Orch. as a cellist in 1783; became its concertmaster in 1801, and in 1803, conductor. He brought out in Mannheim his 1st opera, *Der Eremit auf Formentera* (Dec. 14, 1788; text by the celebrated poet A. von Kotzebue), which attained considerable vogue in Germany; some 20 more operas and singspiels followed, but were not successful. In 1787 he married the famous actress Katharina Baumann (to whom Schiller had proposed); in 1790 both were employed at the Hoftheater; his wife retired on a pension in 1819, and Ritter himself in 1823. Besides his operas, he wrote a fine chorale, *Grosser Gott dich loben wir* (1792); an oratorio, *Das verlorene Paradies* (1819); much chamber music (selections publ. by Riemann in vol. 28 [16] of Denkmäler der Tonkunst in Bayern). Twenty-four autograph scores, including 2 syms., several concertos, etc., are in the Library of Congress in Washington, D.C.

BIBL.: W. Schulze, *P. R.* (Berlin, 1895); G. Schmidt, *P. R.* (diss., Univ. of Munich, 1924); M. Gilveath, *The Violoncello Concertos of P. R.* (diss., Univ. of North Carolina, Chapel Hill, 1961).

Ritter (real name, **Bennet**), **Théodore,** French pianist and composer; b. Nantes, April 5, 1841; d. Paris, April 6, 1886. He was a pupil of Liszt; made successful European tours; publ. numerous solo pieces for piano, of which *Les Courriers* was a favorite; his operas, *Marianne* (Paris, 1861) and *La Dea risorta* (Florence, 1865), were unsuccessful.

Rivé-King, Julie, American pianist, teacher, and composer; b. Cincinnati, Oct. 30, 1854; d. Indianapolis, July 24, 1937. She received her primary instruction from her mother; then studied in N.Y. with William Mason and in Leipzig with Reinecke; also was for a time a pupil of Liszt. She played Liszt's Piano Concerto No. 1 at her American debut, with the N.Y. Phil. (April 24, 1875); this was the beginning of an active career; she gave about 4,000 concerts in the U.S., retiring only a year before her death. In 1876 she married Frank King of Milwaukee. From 1905 to 1936 she was a piano instructor at the Bush Cons. in Chicago. She wrote some attractive piano pieces (*Impromptu, Polonaise héroïque, Bubbling Spring,* etc.).

BIBL.: M. Petteys, *J. R.-K., American Pianist* (diss., Univ. of Missouri, 1987).

Rivier, Jean, French composer and pedagogue; b. Villemomble, July 21, 1896; d. La Penne sur Huveaune, Nov. 6, 1987. His early musical training was interrupted by his enlistment in the French army during World War I; his health was severely damaged as a result of mustard gas, and it was only after a long recuperation that he was able to enter the Paris Cons. as a pupil of Caussade (1922); won the premier prix for counterpoint and fugue (1926); participated in various modern-music societies in Paris; formed a style of composition that combined the elements of French Classicism and Impressionism. He was also esteemed as a teacher; was on the faculty of the Paris Cons. from 1947 to 1966.

WORKS: Opera, *Vénitienne* (Paris, July 8, 1937); 7 syms.: No. 1 (Paris, Jan. 29, 1933); No. 2 for Strings (1937); No. 3 (1937; Paris, Nov. 25, 1940); No. 4 (Paris, 1947); No. 5 (Strasbourg, June 24, 1951); No. 6, *Les Présages* (Paris, Dec. 11, 1958); No. 7, *Les Contrastes* (Paris, Jan. 9, 1962); Piano Concerto (1941); Violin Concerto (1942); *3 pastorales* (Paris, Feb. 7, 1929); *Adagio* for String Orch. (Paris, March 1, 1931); *Ouverture pour une opérette imaginaire* (Paris, Dec. 13, 1931); Concertino for Viola and Orch. (Paris, Feb. 15, 1936); *Paysages pour une Jeanne d'Arc à Domrémy,* symphonic tableau (Paris, Jan. 31, 1937); *Ballade des amants désespérés* for Orch. (1945); *Rapsodie provençale* (Aix-en-Provence, July 22, 1949); *Résonances* (1965); *Brillances* for 7 Woodwind Instruments (1971); *Triade* for String Orch. (1967); *Climats* for Celesta, Vibraphone, Xylophone, Piano, and Strings (1968); Clarinet Concerto (1960); Bassoon Concerto (1965); Oboe Concerto (1966); Trumpet Concerto (1972); Duo for Flute and Clarinet (1968);

2 string quartets; violin pieces; piano pieces; song cycles; choruses.

Roach, Max(well Lemuel), remarkable black American jazz drummer and composer; b. Elizabeth City, N.C., Jan. 10, 1924. He was taken to N.Y. as a child; after playing in a church drum-and-bugle corps, he was a drummer in his high school band; also sat in on jam sessions in various jazz haunts around the city. He began his professional career as a member of Dizzy Gillespie's quintet, becoming immersed in the bebop movement; after a stint with Benny Carter's band (1944–45), he joined Charlie Parker's quintet (1947) and became widely recognized as one of the most innovative drummers of his era. He also studied composition with John Lewis at the Manhattan School of Music. He then led his own groups (from 1949), perfecting his "hard-bop" style. With the trumpeter Clifford Brown, he was co-leader of an outstanding quintet (1953–56). In subsequent years he led various groups, including M'Boom Re, a percussion ensemble (from 1970). With his own quartet, he played throughout the U.S., Europe, and Japan (1976–77). He became a prof. of music at the Univ. of Mass. in Amherst (1972), where he instituted a jazz studies program. As a composer, he became best known for his *Freedom Now Suite* (1960), an expression of his solidarity with the U.S. civil rights movement. He also wrote and recorded the avant-garde scores *Force* (1976; dedicated to Mao Tse-tung) and *1 in 2—2 in 1* (1978). He was awarded an honorary Mus.D. degree from the New England Cons. of Music in Boston in 1982.

BIBL.: *Current Biography* (July 1986).

Robbins, Marty (real name, **Martin David Robinson**), American country-western singer; b. Glendale, Ariz., Sept. 26, 1925; d. Nashville, Tenn., Dec. 8, 1982. He enlisted in the navy in 1944, and was stationed in the Pacific; after the end of the war, he worked as a ditchdigger in Phoenix, Ariz., and began to play the guitar and sing songs of his own invention; his unassuming, happy-go-lucky way of singing country songs soon won him a following; he took part in the broadcasts from the Grand Ole Opry in Nashville, Tenn., and in 1953 produced his 1st hit, *Singin' the Blues*. Other hits followed: *El Paso, Tonight Carmen, Devil Woman, Teen-age Dream, A White Sport Coat and a Pink Carnation, Up to My Shoulders in a Headache,* etc. He became a successful country-music balladeer. In 1970 he was elected to the Nashville Songwriters' Hall of Fame. In 1979 the National Cowboy Hall of Fame gave him its Golden Trustee Award for his gunfighter ballads. He was also inducted into the Country Music Hall of Fame (1982). A passionate stock-car racer, he providentially survived a number of theoretically fatal accidents. He used to say that he was in the song business because he despised honest labor. His songs extolled the beauty of a loving heart, but when his own heart had to undergo quadruple coronary bypass surgery, he died.

Roberton, Sir Hugh (Stevenson), Scottish composer and choral conductor; b. Glasgow, Feb. 23, 1874; d. there, Oct. 7, 1952. In 1906 he founded the Glasgow Orpheus Choir, which contributed to a large extent to the cultivation of choral music in Scotland. He disbanded it in 1951, but it later was reorganized as the Glasgow Phoenix Choir by some of its members. He was knighted in 1931. He publ. about 300 vocal pieces, including *The Faux Bourdon Series of Psalm Tunes, Songs of the Isles,* and *Concert Edition of Scottish Songs;* also a pamphlet, *Prelude to the Orpheus* (London, 1947).

Roberts, Megan, American composer; b. Hempstead, N.Y., Oct. 12, 1952. She was taken to California as a babe in arms, and flourished there; took lessons with Robert Ashley at Mills College in Oakland, and with Emma Lou Diemer at the Univ. of Calif., Santa Barbara. She experimented with unimedia arts of audio, video, dance, and theater; then switched to rock 'n' roll. Her most mind-boggling contribution to the unichoreovideoelectrobiosonic School of California Calisthenics is *Suite for a Small Chamber* (1976), in which the movements of dancers trigger electronic devices and tape-loop playback machines.

In her video piece *Factory* (1976), she utilizes the technique of strobosonic photophonoscopy. On Jan. 14, 1977, she presented in San Francisco a multimedia study in violence free of moral redeeming value. Her major work, *I Could Sit Here All Day* (1976), is scored for birds, drums, and disembodied human voices, and tends to represent the ante-human and anti-human predecessors of rock 'n' roll.

Robertson, Alec (Alexander Thomas Paul), English writer on music and broadcaster; b. Southsea, June 3, 1892; d. Midhurst, Jan. 18, 1982. After studies at Bradfield College and the Royal Academy of Music in London (1910–13), he was active with the Gramophone Co. (1920–30); then entered the Collegio Beda in Rome (1930) and was ordained a priest (1934). After serving at Westminster Cathedral, he joined the Gramophone Dept. of the BBC (1940), where he was chief producer of music talks on the Home and Third Programmes, a position he held until 1952. He was also a reviewer (from 1932) and music ed. (1952–72) for the journal *Gramophone*. His autobiography was publ. as *More than Music* (London, 1961).

WRITINGS (all publ. in London unless otherwise given): *The Interpretation of Plainchant* (1937); *Brahms* (1939; 2nd ed., 1974); *Dvořák* (1945; 2nd ed., 1964); *Contrasts: The Arts and Religion* (1947); *How to Listen to Music* (1948); *Sacred Music* (1950); ed. *Chamber Music* (Harmondsworth, 1956; 4th ed., 1967); ed. with D. Stevens, *Pelican History of Music* (Harmondsworth, 1960–68); *Christian Music* (N.Y., 1961); *Music of the Catholic Church* (1961); ed. *G.B. S. on Music* (1962); *Requiem: Music of Mourning and Consolation* (1967); *Church Cantatas of J.S. Bach* (1972).

Robertson, Leroy, American composer; b. Fountain Green, Utah, Dec. 21, 1896; d. Salt Lake City, July 25, 1971. He studied in Provo; then in Boston with Chadwick and Converse at the New England Cons. of Music (diploma, 1923); subsequently went to Europe, where he took courses with Bloch in Switzerland, Leichtentritt in Berlin, and Toch. Returning to America, he studied at the Univ. of Southern Calif. in Los Angeles (Ph.D., 1954). He was a prof. and chairman of the music dept. at Brigham Young Univ. in Provo (1925–48); then was chairman of the music dept. at the Univ. of Utah (1948–63). In 1947 his symphonic work *Trilogy* received the 1st prize of $25,000 in a contest sponsored by Henry H. Reichhold of Detroit; it was performed by the Detroit Sym. Orch. on Dec. 11, 1947, but despite the attendant publicity, the work was not successful, and there were few subsequent performances. Other works: *The Book of Mormon,* oratorio (Salt Lake City, Feb. 18, 1953); *Prelude, Scherzo, Ricercare* for Orch. (1940); *Rhapsody* for Piano and Orch. (1944); *Punch and Judy Overture* (1945); Violin Concerto (1948); Piano Concerto (Salt Lake City, Nov. 30, 1966); Cello Concerto (1966); Piano Quintet (1933); String Quartet (1940; N.Y. Music Critics' Circle Award, 1944); *American Serenade* for String Quartet (1944); other chamber music; piano pieces; songs.

Robertson, Rae, Scottish pianist; b. Ardersier, Inverness, Nov. 29, 1893; d. Los Angeles, Nov. 4, 1956. He studied with F. Niecks at Edinburgh Univ.; then at the Royal Academy of Music in London with Matthay and F. Corder; married the pianist **Ethel Bartlett,** and the 2 gave numerous concerts in Europe and America as duo-pianists (from 1928). With her he ed. an Oxford Univ. Press series of works for 2 pianos.

Robeson, Paul (Bustill), great black American bass and actor; b. Princeton, N.J., April 9, 1898; d. Philadelphia, Jan. 23, 1976. He 1st studied law (B.A., 1919, Rutgers Univ.; LL.B, 1923, Columbia Univ.); when his talent for singing and acting was discovered, he appeared in plays in the U.S. and England; acted the part of Emperor Jones in Eugene O'Neill's play and of Porgy in the Negro folk play by Du Bose and Dorothy Heyward. In 1925 he gave his 1st Negro spiritual recital in N.Y.; then toured in Europe. In 1927 he scored an enormous success in the musical *Show Boat*, becoming deservedly famous for his rendition of *Ol' Man River*. In 1930 he appeared in the title role of Shakespeare's *Othello* in London. Returning to the U.S., he continued to give recitals, but his outspoken admiration for the Soviet regime from the 1940s on interfered with the success of his career. In 1952 he was awarded the International Stalin Peace Prize ($25,000). During the summer of 1958 he made an extensive European tour. He continued to sing abroad until he was stricken with ill health and returned to the U.S. in 1963. His autobiography was publ. as *Here I Stand* (London, 1958).

BIBL.: E. Robeson, *P. R., Negro* (N.Y., 1930); S. Graham, *P. R.: Citizen of the World* (N.Y., 1946); M. Seton, *P. R.* (London, 1958); E. Hoyt, *P. R.: The American Othello* (London, 1967); D. Gilliam, *P. R., All American* (N.Y., 1977); P. Dean, *P. R.* (Garden City, N.Y., 1978); S. Robeson, *The Whole World in His Hands: A Pictorial Biography of P. R.* (Secaucus, N.J., 1981); L. Davis, *A P. R. Research Guide* (Westport, Conn., 1983); C. Bell, *P. R.'s Last Days in Philadelphia* (Bryn Mawr, 1986).

Robin, Mado, French soprano; b. Yseures-sur-Creuse, near Tours, Dec. 29, 1918; d. Paris, Dec. 10, 1960. She studied voice with Giuseppe Podestà; then began her career as a concert artist; made her operatic debut in 1945 as Gilda at the Paris Opéra; also sang at the Opéra-Comique; made guest appearances in Brussels, Liège, and San Francisco. She was best known for her performances in the roles of Lakmé and Lucia.

Robinson, Earl (Hawley), American composer; b. Seattle, July 2, 1910; d. (in an automobile accident) there, July 20, 1991. He studied with George McKay at the Univ. of Washington (B.M. and teaching diploma, 1933); went to N.Y. (1934), where he completed his training with Copland and Eisler; was also active with the Workers Laboratory Theater and the Composers Collective of the Pierre Degeyter Club; it was during this period that he 1st gained notice via his topical songs. He won a Guggenheim fellowship (1942); was active in Hollywood as a composer for films until he was blacklisted during the McCarthy era; then returned to N.Y. and served as head of the music dept. at Elisabeth Irwin High School (1958–65). The film *The House I Live In* (1946) was inspired by his song of that title (1942), which won him an Academy Award in 1947.

WORKS: STAGE: MUSIC DRAMA: *Song of Atlantis* (1983). FOLK OPERAS: *Sandhog* (1951–54); *David of Sassoon* (1978). MUSICALS: *Processional* (1938); *Sing for Your Supper* (1939); *1 Foot in America* (1962); *Earl Robinson's America* (1976); *Listen for the Dolphin,* children's musical (1981). BALLET: *Bouquet for Molly* (1949). ORCH.: *Good Morning* (1949); *A Country They Call Puget Sound,* tone poem for Tenor and Orch. (1956; rev. 1961); *Banjo Concerto* (1966–67); piano concerto, *The New Human* (1973); *To the Northwest Indians* for Narrator, Folk Instruments, and Orch. (1974); also various cantatas, film scores, and songs.

Robinson, Faye, prominent black American soprano; b. Houston, Nov. 2, 1943. She studied at Bennett College in Greensboro, N.C., Texas Southern Univ. in Houston, and North Texas State Univ. in Denton. After winning 1st prize in the San Francisco Opera Auditions, she made her debut as Micaela in *Carmen* at the N.Y. City Opera on Sept. 2, 1972; was on its roster until 1979. She appeared with opera companies in Houston, Philadelphia, Pittsburgh, San Diego, and Washington, D.C.; also sang widely in Europe and appeared frequently at the Aix-en-Provence Festival from 1974; was a guest artist with the Paris Opéra, the Vienna State Opera, the Hamburg State Opera, the Frankfurt Opera, the Bavarian State Opera in Munich, and others. She was also active as a concert artist. Her operatic roles include Donna Anna, Pamina, Constanze, Elvira in *I Puritani,* Gilda, Liù, Violetta, the 4 principal soprano roles in *Les Contes d'Hoffmann,* and Gounod's Juliette; also sang in the premiere of Tippett's *The Mask of Time* (Boston, April 5, 1984).

Robinson, (Peter) Forbes, English bass; b. Macclesfield, May 21, 1926; d. London, May 13, 1987. He studied at Loughborough College; then went to Italy and took courses at the La Scala Opera School in Milan. He made his professional debut as Monterone at Covent Garden in London in 1954; later sang at the Aldeburgh Festival and the Edinburgh Festival, and with the English Opera Group, the English National Opera, the Teatro Colón in Buenos Aires, and the Zürich Opera. He had an extensive repertoire; his roles included Figaro, Boris Godunov, Don Giovanni, King Philip, Claggart in *Billy Budd,* and Tippett's King Priam, which role he created in 1962; also appeared widely as a concert artist.

Robinson, Ray, American writer on music and choral conductor; b. San Jose, Calif., Dec. 26, 1932. He learned to play the viola; studied at San Jose State College (B.A., 1956) and at Indiana Univ. in Bloomington (M.M., 1958; D.Mus.Ed., 1969, with the diss. *A History of the Peabody Conservatory*). He was subsequently an associate prof. of music and chairman of the division of fine arts at Cascade College in Portland, Oreg. (1959–63). From 1963 to 1966 he was dean of the Peabody Cons. of Music in Baltimore; then was its associate director (1966–69). From 1969 to 1987 he was president of Westminster Choir College in Princeton, N.J. His books include *The Choral Experience* (with A. Winold; 1976); *Choral Music: A Norton Historical Anthology* (1978); *Krzysztof Penderecki: A Guide to His Works* (1983); *A Study of the Penderecki St. Luke Passion* (with A. Winold; 1983); *John Finley Williamson: A Centennial Appreciation* (1987).

Robinson, "Smokey" (William, Jr.), black American soul and rhythm-and-blues singer, songwriter, and record producer; b. Detroit, Feb. 19, 1940. He grew up in a Detroit ghetto; formed a pop group dubbed the Matadors, renamed the Miracles in 1954; it produced such hits as *Bad Girl, Shop Around, The Tracks of My Tears,* and *Tears of a Clown.* In 1972 Robinson pursued a solo career, bringing out such successful albums as *A Quiet Storm* (1974), *Warm Thoughts* (1980), and *Touch the Sky* (1983). With D. Ritz, he publ. *Smokey: Inside My Life* (N.Y., 1989).

Robinson, Stanford, English conductor; b. Leeds, July 5, 1904; d. Brighton, Oct. 25, 1984. He played piano in hotel orchs. in London before entering the Royal College of Music; there he studied conducting under Boult; organized the London Wireless Chorus for the BBC in 1924; was conductor of the BBC Theatre Orch. (1932–46); then became director of music productions there; served as associate conductor of the BBC Sym. Orch from 1946 to 1949; then conducted the BBC Opera Orch. for broadcasting symphonic music (1949–52); subsequently served as a staff conductor at the BBC until 1966; later was chief conductor of the Queensland Sym. Orch. in Brisbane, Australia (1968–69). He was made an Officer of the Order of the British Empire in 1972.

Robison, Paula (Judith), gifted American flutist; b. Nashville, Tenn., June 8, 1941. Her family went to Los Angeles when she was a child; there she studied piano, but then turned to the flute. After attending the Univ. of Southern Calif., she studied flute with Julius Baker at the Juilliard School of Music in N.Y. (graduated, 1963); continued her studies with Marcel Moyse at the Marlboro (Vt.) Festival and in N.Y., where she made her recital debut (1961). After sharing 1st prize in the Munich Competition (1964), she became the 1st American to capture the 1st prize for flute in the Geneva International Competition (1966). She became a member of the Chamber Music Soc. of Lincoln Center in 1969. With her husband, the violist Scott Nickrenz, she was made co–artistic director of chamber music at the Spoleto Festival of Two Worlds in Italy and Charleston, S.C. (1977), and at the Spoleto/Melbourne (Australia) Festival of Three Worlds (1986). She was also active as a teacher. She commissioned and gave the premieres of works by Leon Kirchner, Robert Beaser, Toru Takemitsu, and Oliver Knussen.

BIBL.: J. Tassel, "P. R.," *Ovation* (June 1986).

Robles, Daniel Alomias, Peruvian composer and folk-song collector; b. Huánuco, Jan. 3, 1871; d. Chosica, near Lima, July 17, 1942. He was of Indian blood; traveled through Indian villages of Peru, Bolivia, and Ecuador and collected many hundreds of melodies, of which the *Himno al sol* was notated by him as sung by a 117-year-old Indian. From 1919 to 1934 he lived mostly in the U.S.; then returned to Lima. He had no formal education and little musical technique; his melodic and rhythmic material was arranged by various composers for performances. In this manner he brought out an operetta, *El condor pasa;* several orch. suites (*El resurgimiento de los Andes, El Indio, Danza huanca,* etc.). Five melodies collected by Robles are reproduced in *La Musique des Incas et ses survivances* by Raoul and Marguerite d'Harcourt (Paris, 1925).

BIBL.: N. Slonimsky, *Music of Latin America* (N.Y., 1945).

Robyn, Alfred George, American pianist, organist, and composer; b. St. Louis, April 29, 1860; d. N.Y., Oct. 18, 1935. He studied with his father, an organist; traveled with Emma Abbott at the age of 16 as pianist and accompanist; filled numerous posts as church organist in N.Y. He wrote light operas: *The Yankee Consul* (1903); *The Gypsy Girl* (1905); *The Yankee Tourist* (1907); *Fortune Land* (1907); *All for the Ladies* (1912); etc.; oratorios: *The Ascension; Love Unending; Praise and Thanksgiving;* symphonic poem, *Pompeii;* Piano Concerto; Piano Quintet; 4 string quartets; numerous piano pieces; songs. Some of his songs and piano pieces sold extremely well.

Rocca, Lodovico, Italian composer; b. Turin, Nov. 29, 1895; d. there, June 25, 1986. He studied with Orefice at the Milan Cons.; also attended the Univ. of Turin; from 1940 to 1966 he was director of the Turin Cons.

WORKS: OPERAS: *In terra di leggenda* (1922–23; Milan, Sept. 28, 1933); *Il Dibuk* (1928–30; Milan, March 24, 1934); *La morte di Frine* (Milan, April 24, 1937); *Monte Ivnor* (1936–38; Rome, Dec. 23, 1939); *L'uragano* (1942–51 Milan, Feb. 8, 1952). **ORCH.:** *Contrasti* (1919); *Aurora di morte* (1920); *La foresta delle samodive* (1921); *L'alba del malato* (1922); *Le luci* (1923); *La cella azzurra* (1925); *Interludio epico* (1928). **VOCAL:** *Biribù, Occhi di rana* for Voice and String Quartet (1937); *Schizzi francescani* for Tenor and 8 Instruments (1942); *Antiche iscrizioni* for Soloists, Chorus, and Orch. (1952; Rome, Feb. 6, 1953); songs.

BIBL.: F. Lunghi, "L. R.," *Santa Cecilia,* III/2 (Rome, 1954); M. Bruni, *L. R.* (Milan, 1963).

Rochberg, George, significant American composer; b. Paterson, N.J., July 5, 1918. He took courses in counterpoint and composition with Hans Weisse, George Szell, and Leopold Mannes at the Mannes College of Music in N.Y. (1939–42); after military service during World War II, he took courses in theory and composition with Rosario Scalero and Gian Carlo Menotti at the Curtis Inst. of Music in Philadelphia (B.Mus., 1947); also studied at the Univ. of Pa. (M.A., 1948). He taught at the Curtis Inst. (1948–54); was in Rome on Fulbright and American Academy fellowships (1950). In 1951 he became music ed. of the Theodore Presser Co. in Philadelphia, and soon after was made its director of publications; in 1960 he joined the faculty of the Univ. of Pa. as chairman of the music dept., a position he held until 1968; then continued on its faculty as a prof. of music, serving as Annenberg Prof. of the Humanities from 1979 until his retirement in 1983. He held 2 Guggenheim fellowships (1956–57; 1966–67); was elected to membership in the American Academy and Inst. of Arts and Letters (1985) and was made a fellow of the American Academy of Arts and Sciences (1986); was awarded honorary doctorates from the Univ. of Pa. (1985) and the Curtis Inst. of Music (1988). He publ. the study *The Hexachord and Its Relation to the Twelve-Tone Row* (Bryn Mawr, Pa., 1955). A collection of his writings was ed. by W. Bolcom as *The Aesthetics of Survival: A Composer's View of Twentieth-century Music* (Ann Arbor, 1984). In his style he pursues the ideal of tonal order and logically justifiable musical structures; the most profound influence he experienced was that of Schoenberg and Webern; many of his early works follow the organization in 12 different notes; more recently, he does not deny himself the treasures of the sanctified past, and even resorts to overt quotations in his works of recognizable fragments from music

by composers as mutually unrelated as Schütz, Bach, Mahler, and Ives, treated by analogy with the "objets trouvés" in modern painting and sculpture.

WORKS: DRAMATIC: *The Confidence Man,* opera, after Melville (Santa Fe, July 31, 1982); *Phaedra,* monodrama for Mezzo-soprano and Orch. (1974–75; Syracuse, N.Y., Jan. 9, 1976); incidental music to Ben Jonson's play *The Alchemist* (1965; N.Y., Oct. 13, 1968). **ORCH.:** *Night Music* (1948; N.Y., April 23, 1953; orig. the 2nd movement of the Sym. No. 1); *Capriccio* (1949; rev. 1957; orig. the 3rd movement of the Sym. No. 1); 6 syms: No. 1 (1st version in 3 movements, 1948–57; Philadelphia, March 28, 1958; 2nd version in 5 movements, including *Night Music* and *Capriccio,* 1971–77); No. 2 (1955–56; Cleveland, Feb. 26, 1959); No. 3 for Solo Voices, Chamber Chorus, Double Chorus, and Orch. (1966–69; N.Y., Nov. 24, 1970); No. 4 (Seattle, Nov. 15, 1976); No. 5 (1984; Chicago, March 13, 1986); No. 6 (Pittsburgh, Oct. 16, 1987); *Cantio sacra* for Small Orch. (1954); *Cheltenham Concerto* for Flute, Oboe, Clarinet, Bassoon, Horn, Trumpet, Trombone, and Strings (1958); *Time-Span I* (St. Louis, Oct. 22, 1960; withdrawn) and *II* (1962; Buffalo, Jan. 19, 1964); *Apocalyptica* for Wind Ensemble (1964; Montclair, N.J., May 19, 1965); *Zodiac* (Cincinnati, May 8, 1965; orch. version of the *12 Bagatelles* for Piano, 1952); *Music for the Magic Theater* for 15 Instruments (1965); *Fanfares* for Brass (Philadelphia, March 17, 1968); *Imago mundi* (1973; Baltimore, May 8, 1974); Violin Concerto (1974; Pittsburgh, April 4, 1975); *Transcendental Variations* for String Orch. (1975; based on the String Quartet No. 3, 1972); Oboe Concerto (1983; N.Y., Dec. 13, 1984). **CHAMBER:** 7 string quartets: No. 1 (1952; N.Y., Jan. 10, 1953); No. 2, with Soprano (1959–61; Philadelphia, April 30, 1962); No. 3 (N.Y., May 15, 1972); No. 4 (1977; Philadelphia, Jan. 20, 1979); No. 5 (1978; Philadelphia, Jan. 20, 1979); No. 6 (1978; Philadelphia, Jan. 20, 1979); No. 7, with Baritone (1979; Ann Arbor, Jan. 27, 1980); Chamber Sym. for 9 Instruments (1953); *Serenate d'estate* for Flute, Harp, Guitar, and String Trio (1955); 2 piano trios (1963, 1985); *Contra mortem et tempus* for Flute, Clarinet, Piano, and Violin (1965; N.Y., May 15, 1972); Quintet for Piano and String Quartet (1975; N.Y., March 15, 1976); *Octet: A Grand Fantasia* for Flute, Clarinet, Horn, Piano, Violin, Viola, Cello, and Double Bass (N.Y., April 25, 1980); Trio for Clarinet, Horn, and Piano (1980); String Quintet (Philadelphia, Jan. 6, 1982); Quartet for Piano, Violin, Viola, and Cello (1983; Washington, D.C., June 18, 1985); *To the Dark Wood* for Woodwind Quintet (1985; Armidale, Australia, Oct. 3, 1986); Trio for Piano, Violin, and Cello (1985; Washington, D.C., Feb. 27, 1986); Sonata for Violin and Piano (1988; Pasadena, Calif., April 10, 1989). **PIANO:** *Variations on an Original Theme* (1941); *Sonata-fantasia* (1956); *Bartókiana* (1959); *Nach Bach* (1966; also for Harpsichord); *Carnival Music* (1969); *Partita-variations* (1976); *Book of Contrapuntal Pieces* (1940–77); *4 Short Sonatas* (1984). **VOCAL:** *David, the Psalmist* for Tenor and Orch. (1954); *Blake Songs* for Soprano and 8 Instruments (1961); *Passions according to the 20th Century* for Solo Voices, Chorus, Jazz Quintet, Brass Ensemble, Percussion, Piano, and Tape (1967; withdrawn); *Tableaux* for Soprano, 2 Actors, Small Men's Chorus, and 12 Instruments (1968); *Sacred Song of Reconciliation* for Bass-baritone and Chamber Orch. (1970); also a cappella choruses; songs.

BIBL.: J. Buccheri, *An Approach to Twelve-tone Music: Articulation of Serial Pitch Units in Piano Works of Schoenberg, Webern, Krenek, Dallapiccola, and R.* (diss., Univ. of Rochester, 1975); C. Sams, *Solo Vocal Writing in Selected Works of Berio, Crumb, and R.* (diss., Univ. of Washington, 1975); J. Smith, *The String Quartets of G. R.* (diss., Eastman School of Music, 1976); J. Reise, "R. the Progressive," *Perspectives of New Music,* XIX (1980–81); *Current Biography* (Sept. 1985); J. Dixon, *G. R.: A Bio-Bibliographic Guide to His Life and Works* (Stuyvesant, N.Y., 1991).

Roche, Jerome (Lawrence Alexander), English musicologist; b. Cairo, May 22, 1942. He studied at St. John's College, Cambridge (B.A., 1962; Mus.B., 1963); received his Ph.D. from

Cambridge Univ. in 1968 with the dissertation *North Italian Liturgical Music in the Early 17th Century*. In 1967 he became a lecturer at the Univ. of Durham. He publ. the books *Palestrina* (London, 1972) and *The Madrigal* (London, 1972); with his wife, Elizabeth, he brought out a useful reference source, *A Dictionary of Early Music from the Troubadours to Monteverdi* (London, 1981); also publ. *Lassus* (Oxford, 1982) and *North Italian Church Music in the Age of Monteverdi* (Oxford, 1984).

Rochlitz, (Johann) Friedrich, German writer on music; b. Leipzig, Feb. 12, 1769; d. there, Dec. 16, 1842. A pupil of Doles at the Leipzig Thomasschule, he entered the Univ. of Leipzig as a theological student; publ. some novels and sketches; his 2 pamphlets, *Blicke in das Gebiet der Künste unter der praktischen Philosophie* (Gotha, 1796) and *Einige Ideen über die Anwendung des guten Geschmacks auf die religiösen Versammlungshäuser der Christen* (Leipzig, 1796), treat in part of music. In 1798 he founded the *Allgemeine Musikalische Zeitung*, which he ed. until 1818 and contributed to until 1835. From 1805 he was a director of the Leipzig Gewandhaus Concerts. His best-known work is *Für Freunde der Tonkunst* (4 vols., Leipzig, 1824–32; 3rd ed., 1868), which contains biographies, essays, analyses of compositions, etc.; vol. IV has an outline, *Geschichte der Gesangmusik*, which Rochlitz supplemented by a *Sammlung vorzüglicher Gesang-Stücke* in 3 vols., from Dufay to Vallotti. J. Müller-Blattau compiled Rochlitz's essays on Bach under the title *Wege zu Bach* (1926). Rochlitz composed songs for men's chorus; also a setting of the 23rd Psalm; wrote texts for operas, oratorios, cantatas, etc. **BIBL.:** H. Ehinger, *F. R. als Musikschriftsteller* (Leipzig, 1929).

Rockefeller, Martha Baird, American pianist and music patroness; b. Madera, Calif., March 15, 1895; d. N.Y., Jan. 24, 1971. She studied at Occidental College in Los Angeles and the New England Cons. of Music in Boston (graduated, 1917); received instruction in piano from Artur Schnabel in Berlin. After touring with Dame Nellie Melba (1918), she appeared as a soloist with leading orchs. and as a recitalist until her retirement in 1931. In later years she devoted herself to musical philanthropy; after the death of her 3rd husband, John D. Rockefeller, Jr., she organized the Martha Baird Rockefeller Fund for Music (1962); by the time it was dissolved in 1982, it had dispensed grants of some $9,000,000 to individuals and organizations.

Rockmore, Clara, Russian-born American theremin player, sister of **Nadia Reisenberg;** b. Vilnius, March 9, 1911. She received piano lessons as a small child, and at the age of 4 entered the Imperial Cons. of Music in St. Petersburg (1915–17); subsequently settled in N.Y., where she studied violin with Auer (1925–28) and theremin with Leon Theremin, its inventor (1932–34). She thereafter devoted herself to a career as a theremin player; gave a public demonstration of the instrument (which, incidentally, plays without being touched) in a concert at N.Y.'s Town Hall on Oct. 30, 1934, which included a rendition of Franck's formidable Violin Sonata. She subsequently appeared as a soloist with major orchs. and as a recitalist. In 1977 Rockmore made a historically significant recording, *The Art of the Theremin—Clara Rockmore*. With the rekindling of interest in the instrument in the 1980s, she became something of a celebrity; at the instigation of filmmaker and theremin enthusiast Steve Martin, her ancient instrument was repaired by Robert Moog and subsequently appeared as the subject of a CBS-TV documentary program entitled *The Art of the Theremin*.

Rockstro (real name, **Rackstraw**), **William (Smith),** English pianist, organist, teacher, writer on music, and composer; b. North Cheam, Surrey, Jan. 5, 1823; d. London, July 2, 1895. He studied at the Leipzig Cons. under Mendelssohn, Plaidy, and Hauptmann. Returning to London, he taught piano and singing; wrote a popular ballad, *Queen and Huntress;* publ. piano arrangements of numerous operas; devoted himself to a close study of ecclesiastical music, and became an acknowl-

edged authority on plainchant; became a Roman Catholic in 1876. **WRITINGS** (All publ. in London): *A History of Music for Young Students* (1879); *A Key to Practical Harmony* (1881); *The Rules of Counterpoint* (1882); *The Life of G.F. Handel* (1883); *Mendelssohn* (1884); *A General History of Music* (1886; 3rd ed., 1897); with H. Holland, *Jenny Lind the Artist* (1891); *Jenny Lind: A Record and Analysis of Jenny Lind-Goldschmidt* (1891).

Rodan (real name, **Rosenblum**), **Mendi,** Rumanian-born Israeli conductor; b. Iaşi, April 17, 1929. He studied in Bucharest at the Academy of Music (1945–47) and the Arts Inst. (1947–49), then conducted various ensembles in Rumania. He settled in Israel (1960) and became a naturalized citizen (1961); was chief conductor of the Israel Broadcasting (later Jerusalem) Sym. Orch. (1963–72) and founder-conductor of the Jerusalem Chamber Orch. (1965–69), with which he toured Europe, the U.S., and the Far East; was also made a teacher (1962) and a prof. (1973) at Jerusalem's Rubin Academy of Music, where he later was director. He was music director of the Israel Sinfonietta in Beersheba (from 1977) and chief conductor of the Orch. National de Belgique in Brussels (from 1983).

Rode, (Jacques-) Pierre (Joseph), renowned French violinist and composer; b. Bordeaux, Feb. 16, 1774; d. Château de Bourbon, near Damazan, Nov. 25, 1830. He studied violin with André-Joseph Fauvel (1780–88); made his 1st public appearance at age 12 in Bordeaux, then was taken to Paris by Fauvel and became a pupil of Viotti (1787); made his 1st appearance there as soloist in Viotti's 13th Concerto (1790), and introduced Viotti's 17th and 18th concertos to the Parisian public (1792); was a violinist in the orch. of the Théâtre de Monsieur (1789–92). In 1795 he was appointed prof. of violin at the Paris Cons., but immediately embarked on a tour of Holland and Germany; also appeared in London, but was exiled (along with Viotti) for political reasons in 1798. He returned to Paris in 1799 and resumed his duties at the Cons.; also served as solo violin at the Opéra; became solo violinist to Napoleon in 1800, and brought out his extraordinarily successful 7th Violin Concerto. While on his way to Russia in 1803, he played throughout Germany; served as solo violinist to Czar Alexander I in St. Petersburg (1804–8). He scored an enormous success in Russia, but after his return to Paris his playing declined. In 1811–12 he toured Europe; while in Vienna, he performed Beethoven's Violin Sonata, op. 96—a score written expressly for him—with Archduke Rudolph (Dec. 29, 1812). He returned to France in 1819, but made only a few unsuccessful appearances in subsequent seasons; a disastrous appearance in Paris in 1828 caused him to abandon the concert stage. At the apex of his career, Rode was acclaimed as the foremost representative of the French violin school. He was also esteemed as a composer. In addition to 13 notable violin concertos, he composed 12 string quartets (quatuors brilliants), 24 duos for 2 Violins, 24 caprices, airs variés, etc. With Baillot and Kreutzer, he wrote the violin method for the Cons. (1803).

Rode, Wilhelm, German bass-baritone; b. Hannover, Feb. 17, 1887; d. Icking, near Munich, Sept. 2, 1959. He studied in Hannover; made his debut in 1908 as the Herald in *Lohengrin* in Erfurt; then sang in Bremerhaven, Breslau, and Stuttgart; was a leading member of the Bavarian State Opera in Munich (1922–30), the Vienna State Opera (1930–32), and the Deutsches Opernhaus in Berlin (1932–45), where he also served as Intendant (1935–45); also appeared at London's Covent Garden and in other European opera houses. A member of the Nazi party, he was compelled to give up his career at the close of World War II. He became best known for his roles in Wagner's operas.

Rodeheaver, Homer A(lvan), American composer of gospel hymns and music publisher; b. Union Furnace, Ohio, Oct. 4, 1880; d. Winona Lake, Ind., Dec. 18, 1955. Taken to Jellicoe, Tenn., as a child, he grew up helping in his father's lumber business and learning to play the trombone from a local musician. During the Spanish-American War, he enlisted as trombonist in the 4th Tennessee Regimental Band. After the war, he became interested in gospel songs and evangelism; accompanied the evangelist Billy Sunday on his tours (1910–30), leading the singing with his trombone. With Bentley DeForrest Ackley, he founded the Rodeheaver-Ackley publishing firm in Chicago in 1910; it became the Rodeheaver Co. in 1911 and the Rodeheaver Hall-Mack Co. in 1936; after he removed the firm to Winona Lake, Ind., in 1941, it once again became the Rodeheaver Co. He composed the music for many gospel songs, of which the best known is *Then Jesus Came.* His theme song was *Brighten the Corner,* composed by Charles H. Gabriel. Besides editing some 80 gospel song collections, he publ. *Song Stories of the Sawdust Trail* (N.Y., 1917), *20 Years with Billy Sunday* (Nashville, 1936), and *Letter from a Missionary in Africa* (Chicago, 1936). He was one of the most influential figures in American musical evangelism of his day.

BIBL.: T. Porter, *H.A. R. (1880–1955): Evangelistic Musician and Publisher* (diss., New Orleans Baptist Theological Seminary, 1981).

Röder, Carl Gottlieb, German music publisher; b. Stötteritz, near Leipzig, June 22, 1812; d. Gohlis, Oct. 29, 1883. He founded his firm in Leipzig in 1846. A book printing dept. was added later. In 1872 Röder's sons-in-law C.L.H. Wolff and C.E.M. Rentsch became partners in the firm; Röder retired in 1876. After Rentsch's death (Feb. 19, 1889) his heirs withdrew from the firm, but a son-in-law of Wolff, Karl Johannes Reichel (b. Aug. 15, 1853; d. Leipzig, Sept. 9, 1927), became a partner, and after Wolff's death (1915), head of the firm. On the 50th anniversary of its foundation the firm issued a Festschrift, to which Hugo Riemann contributed a valuable essay, *Notenschrift und Notendruck;* a 2nd Festschrift (on the 75th anniversary) took the form of a study by W. von zur Westen entitled *Musiktitel aus 4 Jahrhunderten* (1921). The firm became a joint stock company in 1930; after World War II, it was nationalized by the German Democratic Republic.

Röder, Martin, German composer and singing teacher; b. Berlin, April 7, 1851; d. Boston, June 7, 1895. After studying music in Berlin, he went to Milan, where he organized the Società del Quartetto Corale (1875), giving performances of vocal quartets; then was a singing teacher in Berlin (1881–87), in Dublin (1887–92), and at the New England Cons. of Music in Boston (from 1892). He wrote 3 operas, including *Vera* (Hamburg, Nov. 1, 1881); 2 symphonic poems, *Azorenfahrt* and *Leonore;* the overture *Attila;* chamber music; publ. *Studi, critici, raccolti* (Milan, 1881) and *Dal Taccuino di un direttore di orchestra* (1881; in German as *Aus dem Tagebuche eines wandernden Kapellmeisters,* 1884).

Rodgers, Jimmie (James Charles), pioneering American country-music singer, guitarist, and songwriter; b. Meridian, Miss., Sept. 8, 1897; d. N.Y., May 26, 1933. He worked on the railroad until his retirement in 1925. He made his 1st recordings in 1927 and became known as the "Singing Brakeman" and "America's Blue Yodeler." His short-lived career was dogged by tuberculosis and an inability to control his spendthrift life-style. In 1961 his name was the 1st to be placed in the Country Music Hall of Fame in Nashville, and in 1977 a U.S. postage stamp was issued to commemorate the 80th anniversary of his birth. He is duly recognized as the "Father of Country Music."

BIBL.: C. Rodgers, *My Husband, J. R.* (San Antonio, 1935; 2nd ed., Nashville, Tenn., 1975); C. Comber and M. Paris, *J. the Kid* (London, 1976); C. Bond, *The Recordings of J. R.* (Los Angeles, 1978); N. Porterfield, *J. R.: The Life and Times of America's Blue Yodeler* (Urbana, Ill., 1979).

Rodgers, Richard (Charles), celebrated American composer of popular music; b. Hammels Station, Long Island, N.Y., June 28, 1902; d. N.Y., Dec. 30, 1979. He began piano lessons when he was 6; studied at Columbia Univ. (1919–21) and at the Inst. of Musical Art in N.Y. (1921–23), receiving instruction in the latter from Krehbiel and Goetschius. He collaborated with the lyricist Lorenz Hart in a series of inspired and highly popular musical comedies: *The Girl Friend* (1926); *A Connecticut Yankee* (1927); *On Your Toes* (1936); *Babes in Arms* (1937); *I Married an Angel* (1938); *The Boys from Syracuse* (1942). After Hart's death in 1943, Rodgers became associated with Oscar Hammerstein II. Together they wrote the greatly acclaimed musical *Oklahoma!* (1943; Pulitzer Prize, 1944), followed by a number of no less successful productions: *Carousel* (1945); *Allegro* (1947); *South Pacific* (1949; Pulitzer Prize, 1950); *The King and I* (1951); *Me and Juliet* (1953); *Pipe Dream* (1955); *The Flower Drum Song* (1958); *The Sound of Music* (1959). After Hammerstein's death in 1960, Rodgers wrote his own lyrics for his next musical, *No Strings* (1962); then followed *Do I Hear a Waltz?* (1965) to the lyrics of Stephen Sondheim. His autobiography was publ. as *Musical Stages* (N.Y., 1975). See *The Rodgers and Hart Song Book* (N.Y., 1951) and H. Simon, ed., *The Rodgers and Hammerstein Song Book* (N.Y., 1958; 2nd ed., rev., 1968).

BIBL.: D. Taylor, *Some Enchanted Evenings: The Story of R. and Hammerstein* (N.Y., 1953); D. Ewen, *R. R.* (N.Y., 1957; 2nd ed., rev., 1963, as *With a Song in His Heart*); *R. R. Fact Book* (N.Y., 1965; new ed. with supplement, 1968); M. Kaye, *R. R.: A Comparative Analysis of His Songs with Hart and Hammerstein Lyrics* (diss., New York Univ., 1969).

Rodio, Rocco, Italian music theorist and composer; b. Bari, Apulia, c.1535; d. Naples, after 1615. He was in the service of Sigismund August of Poland; then was active in Naples (from 1575). He publ. *Regole di musica Rocco Rodio . . . tutti i canoni sopra il canto fermo* (Naples, 1600).

WORKS: *Missarum decem liber primus* for 4 to 6 Voices (Rome, 1562); *Libro di ricercate a 4* (Naples, 1575); also 17 madrigals for 4 Voices and other works.

BIBL.: M. Kastner, *Note critiche ed illustrative di R. R., cinque ricercate, una fantasia* (Padua, 1958).

Rodolphe, Jean Joseph (Johann Joseph Rudolph), Alsatian horn player, violinist, and composer; b. Strasbourg, Oct. 14, 1730; d. Paris, Aug. 12?, 1812. He studied horn with his father, Theodor Peter Rudolph; took violin lessons with J.M. Leclair (c.1745); was also a violinist in Bordeaux and Montpellier. He was in Parma as a violinist in the ducal orch. by 1754; received instruction in counterpoint from Traetta (from 1758); as a chamber virtuoso, became a member of the Stuttgart Court Orch. (c.1760), where he completed his studies with Jommelli; with the choreographer J.G. Noverre, he brought out several ballets. He appeared in Paris as a horn virtuoso at the Concert Spirituel in 1764, but continued to work in Stuttgart until returning to Paris in 1767 as a member of Prince Conti's orch.; became a violinist and hornist in the Opéra orch. and later was active at the royal chapel. He befriended the young Mozart during the latter's visit to Paris in 1778. From 1784 until the Revolution, Rodolphe taught composition at the École Royale de Chant et de Déclamation; later was prof. of solfège at the Paris Cons. (1798–1802). He publ. *Solfège ou Nouvelle méthode de musique* (Paris, 1784; 2nd ed., rev., 1790) and *Théorie d'accompagnement et de composition* (Paris, c.1785).

WORKS: OPERAS: *Le Mariage par capitulation,* opéra-comique (Paris, Dec. 3, 1764); *L'Aveugle de Palmire,* opéra-comique (Paris, March 5, 1767); *Isménor,* opéra-ballet (Versailles, Nov. 17, 1773). **BALLETS:** *Renaud et Armide* (Stuttgart, Feb. 11, 1761); *Psyche et l'Amour* (Stuttgart, Feb. 11, 1762); *Médée et Jason* (Ludwigsburg, Feb. 11, 1763; rev. by Noverre, Paris, Jan. 30, 1780); *Apollon et Daphne* (Kassel, c.1764; in collaboration with Deller); *Télèphe et Isménie ou La Mort d'Eurite* (Kassel, 1768; in collaboration with Deller); *Apelle et Campaspe* (Paris, Oct. 1, 1776); also 2 horn concertos, 24 fanfares for 3 Horns, 3 sets of violin duos, and 2 sets of violin études.

Rodrigo, Joaquín, Spanish composer; b. Sagunto, Valencia, Nov. 22, 1901. He lost his sight as a child; revealed an innate talent for music and was sent to Paris, where he studied with Paul Dukas at the Schola Cantorum; returned to Madrid in 1939, where the Manuel de Falla chair was created for him at the Univ. in 1947. His music is profoundly imbued with

Spanish melorhythms; his *Concierto de Aranjuez* for Guitar and Orch. (1939; Barcelona, Nov. 9, 1940) became famous.
WORKS: STAGE: *Pavana real*, ballet (1955); *El hijo fingido*, zarzuela (1964); *La azuzena de Quito*, opera (1965). **ORCH.:** *Juglares* (1923); *Concierto de Aranjuez* for Guitar and Orch. (1939; Barcelona, Nov. 9, 1940); *Concierto heróico* for Piano and Orch. (1942; Lisbon, April 5, 1943); *Concierto de estío* for Violin and Orch. (1943; Lisbon, April 11, 1944); *Concierto in modo galante* for Cello and Orch. (Madrid, Nov. 4, 1949); *Concierto serenata* for Harp and Orch. (1952); *Fantasía para un gentilhombre* for Guitar and Orch. (1954); *Sones en la Giralda* for Harp and Orch. (1963); *Concierto Andaluz* for 4 Guitars (1967); *Concierto-madrigal* for 2 Guitars and Orch. (1968); *Dos danzas españoles* (1969); *Palillos y panderetas* (1982); *Concierto para una fiesta* for Guitar and Orch. (1982). **CHAMBER:** *Sonata Pimpante* for Violin and Piano (1966); *Sonata a la española* for Guitar (1969); *Pájaros de primavera* for Guitar (1972); also choruses and piano pieces.
BIBL.: F. Sopeña, *J. R.* (Madrid, 1946; 2nd ed., rev., 1970); A. Iglesias, *J. R.: Su música para piano* (Madrid, 1965); V. Vaya Pia, *J. R.: Su vida y su obra* (Madrid, 1977); V. Kamhi, *De la mano de J. R.: Historia de nuestra vida* (Madrid, 1986).

Rodrígues de Ledesma, Mariano, Spanish composer; b. Saragossa, Dec. 14, 1779; d. Madrid, March 28, 1848. He was a choirboy at Saragossa Cathedral, being a pupil of F.J. García and José Gil Palomar. He conducted at the Seville Opera (1800–1805), then at Madrid's Los Caños del Peral theater; became a supernumerary tenor at the royal chapel (1807). In 1811 he emigrated to London for political reasons; there he gained distinction as a singing teacher. He returned to Spain in 1814 and became 1st tenor of the royal chapel and singing master to the Princess Luisa Carlota. In 1823 he again went to London for political reasons, and taught singing at the Royal Academy of Music. After returning to Spain in 1831, he once more served as 1st tenor (until 1836) and choirmaster (1836–47) of the royal chapel. He wrote both sacred and secular music, and is recognized as one of Spain's earliest Romanticists.
BIBL.: R. Mitjana, *El maestro R.d.L. y sus Lamentaciones de Semana Santa: Estudio crítico-biográfico* (Málaga, 1909).

Rodríguez (Amador), Augusto (Alejandro), Puerto Rican conductor and composer; b. San Juan, Feb. 9, 1904. He studied literature at the Univ. of Puerto Rico; music at Harvard Univ. with E.B. Hill, Piston, and Leichtentritt (1933–34); returning to San Juan, he was on the faculty of the Univ. of Puerto Rico (1934–70); organized its chorus, which achieved a high degree of excellence; gave a concert with it in N.Y. in 1949. He publ. choral works, piano pieces, and songs.

Rodriguez, Felipe, Spanish composer; b. Madrid, May 1, 1759; d. there, May 1814. He was a member of the Monserrat School; in 1778 he was ordained priest; served as organist in Madrid. He wrote organ pieces, some of which are printed in *Música instrumental*, ed. by D. Pujol (vol. 2, Montserrat, 1946), and church music; his *Rondo* for Piano is printed by J. Nín in the collection *17 sonates et pièces anciennes d'auteurs espagnols* (Paris, 1929).

Rodriguez, Robert Xavier, American composer; b. San Antonio, June 28, 1946. He studied with Hunter Johnson and Kent Kennan at the Univ. of Texas in Austin (B.M., 1967; M.M., 1969), Halsey Stevens and Ingolf Dahl at the Univ. of Southern Calif. in Los Angeles (D.M.A., 1975), Jacob Druckman at the Berkshire Music Center in Tanglewood, and Nadia Boulanger in Paris; also attended master classes given by Bruno Maderna and Elliott Carter. He taught at the Univ. of Southern Calif. (1973–75) and at the Univ. of Texas in Dallas (from 1975); held a Guggenheim fellowship (1976); was composer-in-residence of the Dallas Sym. Orch. (1982–85).
WORKS: OPERAS: *Le Diable amoureux* (1978); *Suor Isabella* (1982); *Tango*, chamber opera (1985). **BALLET:** *Estampie* (1980). **ORCH.:** *Adagio* for Small Orch. (1967); *Lyric Variations* for Oboe, 2 Horns, and Strings (1970); Concerto III for Piano, 13 Wind Instruments, Percussion, and Strings (1974); *Sinfonia*

concertante (1974); *Favola concertante* for Violin, Cello, and Strings (1977); *Oktoechoes* for Octet and Orch. (1983); *7 Deadly Sins* for Wind Ensemble and Percussion (1984); *A Colorful Symphony* for Narrator, Orch., and Optional Visual Effects (Indianapolis, May 3, 1988). **CHAMBER:** 2 piano trios (1970, 1971); Concerto II for Piano and 7 Instruments (1972); Sonata for Soprano Saxophone or Clarinet and Piano (1972); Toccata for Guitar Quartet (1975); Variations for Violin and Piano (1975). **VOCAL:** *Canto*, cantata (1978); *Praline and Fudge*, to texts from cookbooks, for Bass and Piano (1979).

Rodriguez, Santiago, talented Cuban-American pianist; b. Cardenas, Feb. 16, 1952. He settled in the U.S. when he was 8 and pursued training in New Orleans, at the Univ. of Texas, and at the Juilliard School in N.Y. He made his debut at age 9 with the New Orleans Phil.; in 1975 he won 1st prize at the Univ. of Maryland Piano Competition, and in 1981 shared 2nd prize at the Van Cliburn Piano Competition. In 1982 he was awarded an Avery Fisher Career Grant, and in 1986 was honored as the 1st recipient of the Shura Cherkassky Recital Award of N.Y.'s 92nd St. Y. Rodriguez has appeared widely as a soloist with orchs. and as a recitalist, both in the U.S. and abroad. He also teaches at the Univ. of Maryland at College Park. He is a versatile virtuoso whose expansive and intriguing repertoire includes not only standard works but works by Busoni, Mrs. H.H.A. Beach, Castelnuovo-Tedesco, Hanson, Ginastera, Shchedrin, and others.
BIBL.: D. Manildi, "S. R.," *Musical America* (July 1990).

Rodríguez, Vicente, Spanish organist and composer; b. Onteniente, near Valencia, c.1685; d. Valencia (buried), Dec. 16, 1760. He was a cleric; served as interim organist (1713–15) and organist (1715–60) at Valencia Cathedral. He wrote several masses; also keyboard music.

Rodríguez de Hita, Antonio, Spanish composer; b. c.1724; d. Madrid, Feb. 21, 1787. From 1740 to 1757 he was maestro de capilla at Palencia Cathedral, where he publ. a book of advice to his pupils, *Consejos que a sus discípulos da don Antonio Rodriguez de Hita*. Then he held that title at the Convent of the Incarnation in Madrid. From 1768 he collaborated with the dramatist Ramón de la Cruz in a series of notable stage works impregnated with Spanish atmosphere; the best are the zarzuelas *Las segadoras de Vallecas* (Madrid, Sept. 13, 1768) and *Las labradoras de Murcia* (Madrid, Sept. 16, 1769). He also composed the Spanish opera *La Briseida* (Madrid, July 10, 1768); various sacred and secular choral works.
BIBL.: F. Bonastre, "Estudio de la obra teórica y práctica del compositor A.R. d.H.," *Revista de Musicología*, II (1979).

Rodzinski, Artur, eminent Polish-born conductor; b. Spalato, Dalmatia, Jan. 1, 1892; d. Boston, Nov. 27, 1958. He studied jurisprudence at the Univ. of Vienna; at the same time took piano lessons with Emil Sauer, composition with Schreker, and conducting with Schalk. He made his conducting debut in Lwow in 1920; subsequently conducted at the Warsaw Opera. In 1926 he was appointed assistant conductor to Leopold Stokowski with the Philadelphia Orch.; concurrently he was head of the opera and orch. depts. at the Curtis Inst. of Music; in 1929 he was appointed conductor of the Los Angeles Phil.; after 4 seasons there, he was engaged as conductor of the Cleveland Orch., where he introduced the novel custom of presenting operas in concert form; on Jan. 31, 1935, he conducted the American premiere of Shostakovich's controversial opera *Lady Macbeth of the District of Mtzensk*. He became a U.S. citizen in 1932. In 1943 he received his most prestigious appointment as conductor of the N.Y. Phil., but his independent character and temperamental ways of dealing with the management forced him to resign amid raging controversy in the middle of his 4th season (Feb. 3, 1947); almost immediately he was engaged as conductor of the Chicago Sym. Orch., but there, too, a conflict rapidly developed, and the management announced after a few months of the engagement that his contract would not be renewed, stating as a reason that his operatic ventures using the orch. were too costly. After these distressing American experiences, Rodzinski conducted mainly in Europe; in the autumn of 1958 he received an invitation to conduct at the Lyric Opera in Chicago, but after 3 performances of *Tristan und Isolde* (Nov. 1, 7, and 10), a heart ailment forced him to cancel his remaining appearances; he died in a Boston hospital.

BIBL.: H. Rodzinski, *Our Two Lives* (N.Y., 1976).

Roesgen-Champion, Marguerite, Swiss harpsichordist and composer; b. Geneva, Jan. 25, 1894; d. Paris, June 30, 1976. She studied composition with Ernest Bloch and Jaques-Dalcroze at the Geneva Cons., but devoted herself mainly to harpsichord playing, giving numerous recitals in Europe. Her own works are couched in the neo-Romantic vein; she wrote *Faunesques* for Orch. (Paris, 1929); *Concerto moderne* for Harpsichord and Orch. (Paris, Nov. 15, 1931, composer soloist); symphonic suite, *Aquarelles* (Paris, Nov. 26, 1933); Harp Concerto (Paris, March 28, 1954); 5 concertos for Harpsichord and Orch. (1931–59); *Concerto romantique* for Piano and Orch. (1961); a number of pieces for flute in combination with the harpsichord and other instruments; a curious piece for Piano, 4-hands, entitled *Spoutnik* (1971).

Rogalski, Theodor, Rumanian composer and conductor; b. Bucharest, April 11, 1901; d. Zürich, Feb. 2, 1954. He studied at the Bucharest Cons. with Castaldi and Cuclin; at the Leipzig Cons. with Karg-Elert (1920–23); and in Paris with d'Indy (composition) and Ravel (orchestration) (1924). Returning to Rumania, he was conductor of the Bucharest Radio Sym. Orch. (1930–51); then of the Bucharest Phil.; was also prof. of orchestration at the Bucharest Cons. (1950–54). His music is permeated with the spirit of Rumanian folklore, while his harmony and orchestration reveal impressionistic traits.

WORKS: ORCH.: *Allegro simfonic* (1923); *2 dansuri românești* (1926); *2 capricii* (1932); *3 dansuri românești* (1950; Bucharest, May 27, 1951); also String Quartet (1925); violin pieces; songs.

Rogatis, Pasqual de. See **De Rogatis, Pascual.**

Rogé, Pascal, French pianist; b. Paris, April 6, 1951. He entered the Paris Cons. at age 11 and made his debut as a soloist at the same age in Paris; his principal teacher was L. Descaves, and he graduated with premiers prix in piano and chamber music (1966); then studied with Julius Katchen (1966–69). In 1969 he made his London debut; after winning joint 1st prize in the Long-Thibaud Competition in Paris in 1971, he pursued a successful international career.

Rogel, José, Spanish composer; b. Orihuela, Alicante, Dec. 24, 1829; d. Cartagena, Feb. 25, 1901. At a very early age he was taught music by the organist J. Cascales, and at 10 composed a Mass, which he conducted himself. After he finished his law studies in Valencia, he studied counterpoint with Pascual Pérez Cascón; subsequently conducted at various theaters in Madrid, and in 1854 began his unusually successful career as a composer of zarzuelas, of which he wrote 81 (some in collaboration). Among the best are *El Joven Telémaco, Las Amazones del Tormes, El Rey Midas, Los Infiernos de Madrid, Genoveva de Brabante,* and *Pablo y Virginia.*

Roger-Ducasse, Jean (-Jules Aimable), French composer; b. Bordeaux, April 18, 1873; d. Le-Taillan-Médoc, near Bordeaux, July 19, 1954. He studied at the Paris Cons. with Fauré (composition), Pessard (harmony), Gédalge (counterpoint), and de Bériot. In 1902 he won the 2nd Prix de Rome for the cantata *Alcyone;* in 1909 was appointed inspector of singing in the Paris schools; subsequently was a prof. of ensemble at the Paris Cons.; from 1935 to 1940, taught composition there; then retired to Bordeaux. His 1st work to be played in public was a *Petite suite* for Orch. (Paris, March 5, 1898). He adopted a pleasing style of Impressionism; his symphonic pieces enjoyed considerable success, without setting a mark for originality. His autobiography was publ. in *L'Écran des musiciens* (1930).

WORKS: STAGE: Comic opera, *Cantegril* (Paris, Feb. 9, 1931); mimodrama, *Orphée* (St. Petersburg, Jan. 31, 1914).

ORCH.: *Variations plaisantes sur un thème grave* (Paris, Jan. 24, 1909); *Suite française* (1909); *Prélude d'un ballet* (1910); *Le Joli Jeu de furet,* scherzo (1911); *Nocturne de printemps* (Paris, Feb. 14, 1920); *Symphonie sur la Cathédrale de Reims* (never completed); *Le Petit Faune* (Bordeaux, May 22, 1954). **VOCAL:** *Sarabande,* symphonic poem with Voices (1911); *Au Jardin de Marguerite* for Soloists, Chorus, and Orch. (1901–5); *Sur quelques vers de Virgile* for Chorus and Orch. **CHAMBER:** Piano Quartet (1899–1912); String Quartet (1900–1909); songs (*Le Cœur de l'eau, Noëls des roses,* 7 *préludes,* études, arabesques, etc.); pedagogical works (*Solfèges,* 3 vols.; *Dictée musicale,* 4 vols.; *Exercices de piano,* 3 vols.; etc.).

BIBL.: L. Ceillier, *R.-D.* (Paris, 1920); *Catalogue de l'œuvre de R.-D.* (Bordeaux, 1955).

Roger, Gustave-Hippolyte, famous French tenor; b. La Chapelle St.-Denis, near Paris, Dec. 17, 1815; d. Paris, Sept. 12, 1879. He was a pupil of Blès Martin at the Paris Cons.; made his debut as Georges in Halévy's *L'Éclair* at the Paris Opéra-Comique in 1838; then was at the Paris Opéra (from 1848), where he created the role of the Prophète in Meyerbeer's opera (1849); later toured in Germany. While he was hunting in the fall of 1859, the accidental discharge of his gun injured his right arm so severely that it had to be amputated. An artificial arm proved ineffective, and he was obliged to retire from the stage in 1861. From 1868 until his death he was a prof. of singing at the Paris Cons. He publ. his memoirs as *Le Carnet d'un ténor* (Paris, 1880).

BIBL.: A. Lagɛt, *G.-H. R.: Notice biographique* (Paris, 1865).

Roger, Victor, French composer and music critic; b. Montpellier, July 22, 1853; d. Paris, Dec. 2, 1903. He studied at the École Niedermeyer in Paris; wrote light music; composed some 30 operettas, of which the following were brought out in Paris with considerable success: *Joséphine vendue par ses sœurs* (March 20, 1886); *Oscarine* (Oct. 15, 1888); *Le Fétiche* (March 13, 1890); *Samsonnet* (Nov. 26, 1890); *Miss Nicol-Nick* (Jan. 23, 1895); *Sa Majesté l'Amour* (Dec. 24, 1896); *L'Auberge du Tohu-Bohu* (Feb. 10, 1897); *Les Fêtards* (Oct. 28, 1897); *L'Agence Crook et Cie* (Jan. 22, 1898); *La Petite Tâche* (March 26, 1898); *Le Jockey malgré lui* (Dec. 4, 1902). After his death, 3 completely finished scores were found: *La Fille de Fra Diavolo, La Princesse de Babylone,* and *Adélaïde.*

Rogers, Bernard, distinguished American composer and pedagogue; b. N.Y., Feb. 4, 1893; d. Rochester, N.Y., May 24, 1968. He began piano lessons when he was 12; after leaving school at 15, he was employed in an architectural firm while training in architecture at Columbia Univ.; subsequently received instruction in theory from Hans van den Berg, composition from Farwell, and harmony and composition from Bloch in Cleveland; returning to N.Y., he continued his studies with Goetschius at the Inst. of Musical Art (1921); later held a Guggenheim fellowship (1927–29), which made it possible for him to train with Bridge in England and Boulanger in Paris. He 1st won recognition as a composer with his orch. work *To the Fallen* (1918; N.Y., Nov. 13, 1919), on the strength of which he received a Pulitzer Traveling Scholarship. He taught at the Cleveland Inst. of Music (1922–23), the Hartt School of Music in Hartford, Conn. (1926–27), and the Eastman School of Music in Rochester, N.Y. (1929–67), where he also served as chairman of the composition dept. In 1947 he was elected to membership in the National Inst. of Arts and Letters. He publ. a valuable manual, *The Art of Orchestration* (N.Y., 1951).

WORKS (all 1st perf. in Rochester, N.Y., unless otherwise given): **OPERAS:** *Deirdre* (1922); *The Marriage of Aude* (May 22, 1931); *The Warrior* (N.Y., Jan. 11, 1947); *The Veil* (Bloomington, Ind., May 18, 1950); *The Nightingale* (1954). **ORCH.:** *To the Fallen* (1918; N.Y., Nov. 13, 1919); *The Faithful,* overture (1922); *Soliloquy No. 1* for Flute and Strings (1922); *In the Gold Room* (1924); *Pastorale* for 11 Instruments (1924); *Fuji in the Sunset Glow* (1925); *Hamlet,* prelude (1925); 5 syms.: No. 1, *Adonais* (1926; April 29, 1927); No. 2 (1928; Oct. 24, 1930); No. 3, *On a Thanksgiving Song* (1936; Oct.

27, 1937); No. 4 (1940; May 4, 1948); No. 5, *Africa* (1958; Cincinnati, Jan. 30, 1959); *3 Japanese Dances* (1933; May 3, 1934); *2 American Frescoes* (1934); *Once upon a Time*, 5 fairy tales for Small Orch. (April 4, 1935); *The Supper at Emmäus* (April 29, 1937); *Fantasy* for Flute, Viola, and Strings (1937; April 25, 1938); *Soliloquy No. 2* for Bassoon and Strings (Oct. 18, 1938); *The Song of the Nightingale*, suite (1939; Cincinnati, March 21, 1940); *The Colors of War* (Oct. 25, 1939); *The Dance of Salome* (April 25, 1940); *The Plains* for Small Orch. (1940; N.Y., May 3, 1941); *Invasion* (N.Y., Oct. 17, 1943); *Anzacs* (1944); *Elegy in Memory of Franklin D. Roosevelt* (1945; N.Y., April 11, 1946); *Characters from Hans Christian Andersen* for Small Orch. (April 28, 1945); *Amphitryon Overture* (1946; N.Y., March 10, 1947); *Elegy* for Small Orch. (1947); *The Silver World* for Small Orch. (1949); *The Colors of Youth* (1951); *Portrait* for Violin and Orch. (1952); *Fantasy* for Horn, Timpani, and Strings (1952; Feb. 20, 1955); *Dance Scenes* (Louisville, Oct. 28, 1953); *Variations on a Song by Mussorgsky* (1960); *New Japanese Dances* (1961); *Allegory* for Small Orch. (1961); *Apparitions* (1967). **CHAMBER:** *Mood* for Piano Trio (1918); 2 string quartets (1918, 1925); *The Silver World* for Flute, Oboe, and Strings (1950); String Trio (1953); *Ballade* for Bassoon, Viola, and Piano (1959); Sonata for Violin and Piano (1962). **CHORAL, WITH ORCH.:** *The Raising of Lazarus* (1928); *The Exodus* (1931); *The Passion*, oratorio (1942; Cincinnati, May 12, 1944); *A Letter from Pete*, cantata (1947); *The Prophet Isaiah*, cantata (1950); *The Light of Man*, oratorio (1964). **OTHER CHORAL:** *Psalm XCIX*, with Organ (1945); *Response to Silent Prayer* (1945); *Hear My Prayer, O Lord*, with Soprano and Organ (1955); *Psalm XVIII* for Men's Voices and Piano (1963); *Psalm LXXXIX*, with Baritone and Piano (1963); *Faery Song* for Women's Voices (1965); *Dirge for 2 Veterans*, with Piano (1967); *Psalm CXIV*, with Piano (1968). **SOLO VOCAL AND ORCH.:** *Arab Love Songs* for Soprano and Orch. (1927); *Horse Opera* for Narrator and Orch. (1948); *Leaves from the Tale of Pinocchio* for Narrator and Orch. (1951); *Psalm LXVIII* for Baritone and Orch. (1951); *The Musicians of Bremen* for Narrator and 13 Instruments (1958); *Aladdin* for Narrator and Wind Ensemble (1965).

BIBL.: H. Hanson, "B. R.," *Modern Music*, XXII (1945); D. Diamond, "B. R.," *Musical Quarterly* (April 1947); S. Dershan, *Orchestration in the Orchestral Works of B. R.* (diss., Univ. of Rochester, 1975); D. Intili, *Text-Music Relationships in the Large Choral Works of B. R.* (diss., Case Western Reserve Univ., 1977); F. Koch, *Reflections on Composing: Four American Composers: Elwell, Shepherd, R., Cowell* (Pittsburgh, 1983).

Rogers, Clara Kathleen (née **Barnett**), English-born American soprano, teacher, and composer; b. Cheltenham, Jan. 14, 1844; d. Boston, March 8, 1931. She was the daughter of the composer **John Barnett;** studied at the Leipzig Cons. with Moscheles and Plaidy (piano), Papperitz and Richter (theory), and David and Rietz (ensemble playing); then singing with Goetz in Berlin and with Sangiovanni in Milan. She made her debut in Turin (1863) as Isabella in *Robert le Diable* (stage name, "Clara Doria"); went to America in 1871 with the Parepa-Rosa Co.; made her debut in N.Y. in *The Bohemian Girl* (Oct. 4, 1871); married a Boston lawyer, Henry M. Rogers, in 1878; later settled in Boston as a teacher; from 1902, was a prof. of singing at the New England Cons. of Music. She publ. *The Philosophy of Singing* (1893); *Dreaming True* (1899); *My Voice and I* (1910); *English Diction in Song and Speech* (1912); *The Voice in Speech* (1915); *Memories of a Musical Career* (Boston, 1919) and its sequel, *The Story of Two Lives* (Norwood, Mass., 1932); composed a String Quartet (1866), a Violin Sonata (1903), a Cello Sonata, and many songs.

Rogers, Francis, American baritone and teacher; b. Roxbury, Mass., April 14, 1870; d. N.Y., May 15, 1951. He went to Harvard (graduated, 1891), where he sang in the glee club; then studied voice with William Whitney at the New England Cons. of Music in Boston (1894–95); also received lessons from Luigi Vannuccini in Florence, Jacques Bouhy in Paris, and Isidore Luckstone in N.Y.; made his debut in Boston

(1898); after appearing with the Castle Square Opera Co. in St. Louis (1900–1901), he accepted mainly concert and oratorio engagements; taught at the Juilliard School in N.Y. (1924–47); was also on the faculty of Yale Univ. He publ. *Some Famous Singers of the 19th Century* (N.Y., 1914).

Rogers, Ginger (real name, **Virginia Katherine McMath**), American singer, dancer, and actress; b. Independence, Mo., July 16, 1911. She began her career in vaudeville, and after appearing in the Broadway musical *Top Speed* (1929), went to Hollywood to pursue a career in films. She 1st gained notable success when she appeared opposite Fred Astaire in the musical film *Flying Down to Rio* (1933); they subsequently appeared together in 9 other films before she launched out on her own as a comedienne and dramatic actress; she also made several returns to Broadway.

BIBL.: D. Richards, *G.: Salute to a Star* (Brighton, England, 1969); H. Dickens, *The Films of G. R.* (Secaucus, N.J., 1975).

Rogers, Kenny (Kenneth Ray), successful American singer in the popular music genres; b. Houston, Aug. 21, 1938. During his high school years, he made appearances with his own band called The Scholars; afer taking courses in music and commercial art at the Univ. of Houston, he dropped out of school to play bass in the Bobby Doyle Trio, a jazz outfit (1960–66); then performed with the Kirby Stone 4; following a stint with the New Christy Minstrels, the popular folk music group (1966–67), he was active with his own folk-rock band dubbed Kenny Rogers and the 1st Edition (1967–76). He subsequently embarked on a major career as a country-music singer, scoring a spectacular success with his recording of the song *Lucille* (1977), which earned him a Grammy Award. An even greater success followed with his album *The Gambler* (1978), which spawned a series of television movies under the same title (1980, 1983, 1987), which provided Rogers an outlet for his pretensions as a thespian. His rough, bearded manhood, with a touch of gray, and his carefree life-style, combined with the macho image projected on the podium and on the tube, contributed greatly to his star status among prematurely faded female fans in the subculture of California and adjacent territories.

Rogers, Nigel (David), English tenor, conductor, and teacher; b. Wellington, Shropshire, March 21, 1935. He studied at King's College, Cambridge (1953–56), in Rome (1957), in Milan (1958–59), and with G. Hüsch at the Munich Hochschule für Musik (1959–64); became a singer with the Studio der frühen Musik in Munich in 1961 and later acquired a fine reputation as an interpreter of Baroque music. He was a prof. of singing at the Royal College of Music in London (from 1978) and founded the vocal ensemble Chiaroscuro for the performance of Italian Baroque music (1979).

Rogers, Roy (real name, **Leonard Slye**), American country-music singer and actor; b. Cincinnati, Nov. 5, 1911. He learned to play the guitar and then appeared as a singer with various country-music groups in California. With Bob Nolan and Tim Spencer, he organized in 1933 the Pioneer Trio, which developed into the successful Sons of the Pioneers; Nolan wrote for the group the songs *Cool Water* and *Tumbling Tumbleweeds*, which became country standards. In 1938 Slye took the professional name of Roy Rogers and embarked on a successful career as a singing cowboy in more than 100 Western films, often appearing with **Dale Evans,** whom he married in 1947; in later years they starred in their own television series. They co-authored the song *Happy Trails to You*, by which Rogers became known.

Rogers, "Shorty" (real name, **Milton Rajonsky**), American jazz trumpeter, bandleader, composer, and arranger; b. Great Barrington, Mass., April 14, 1924. He studied the trumpet at the High School of Music and Art in N.Y.; then went to California and played with Red Norvo, Woody Herman, and Stan Kenton; was also successful as an arranger. From 1954 he led his own bands. Among the compositions he wrote for his own bands, *3 on a Row* (1954) is notable for its application of the 12-tone technique to jazz.

BIBL.: C. Hofmann and E. Bakker, *S. R.: A Discography* (Amsterdam, 1983).

Roget, Henriette, French composer and organist; b. Bastia, Corsica, Jan. 9, 1910. She studied organ with Marcel Dupré and composition with Henri Busser at the Paris Cons.; received the Premier 2nd Prix de Rome in 1933. She was director in charge of voice training at the Paris Opéra until 1959; served as organist at the Oratoire du Louvre and prof. of piano accompanying and score reading at the Paris Cons. She wrote a great number of piano books for children, among them *Adroits petits doigts* (1957), *Abécédaire* (1958), and *Méthode* (1970).

WORKS: Orch.: *Montanyas del Rosello* for Organ and Orch. (Paris, April 6, 1933, composer soloist); *Sinfonia andorrana* (1936); *3 ballades françaises* (Paris, Jan. 11, 1936); *Rythmes* (Paris, Jan. 23, 1937); *Concerto sicilien* for Piano and Orch. (1943); *Concerto classique* for Cello and Orch. (1944); *Symphonie pour rire* (1947); also *Cathérinettes*, ballet (1937); a number of effective organ pieces.

Rogg, Lionel, outstanding Swiss organist; b. Geneva, April 21, 1936. He studied organ with Pierre Segond and piano with Nikita Magaloff at the Geneva Cons. and won premiers prix for both instruments. In 1961 he gave a series of recitals in Geneva devoted to the complete works for organ by Bach; subsequently he made tours of Europe and America. In 1960 he was appointed to the faculty of the Geneva Cons.; in addition, he gave master classes in organ. As a virtuoso on the organ, he possesses a remarkable gift for improvisation.

Rogister, Jean (François Toussaint), Belgian violist, pedagogue, and composer; b. Liège, Oct. 25, 1879; d. there, March 20, 1964. He studied violin, viola, horn, and composition at the Liège Cons.; was head of the viola classes there (1900–1945) and at the Brussels Cons. (1945–48); played in various orchs.; was also founder of the Liège Quartet (1925), with which he toured extensively. His style of composition followed the precepts of César Franck, but upon occasion he introduced into his music some modernistic impressionistic sonorities.

WORKS: Lyric drama, *Lorsque minuit sonna* (1930); *Requiem* (1944; with Orch. and Full Chorus, Liège, March 24, 1946); *The Bells*, oratorio after Edgar Allan Poe, for Soprano and 8 Instruments (1924); 3 syms.: No. 1 (1927); No. 2, *Symphonie wallonne* (1931–32); No. 3, with Solo String Quartet (1942–43); *Symphonie intime* for String Quartet, Double Bass, Flute, Clarinet, and Bassoon (1929); *Fantaisie concertante* for Viola and Orch. (1910); Viola Concerto (1914); Cello Concerto (1917); Trombone Concerto (1919); *Poème* for Violin and Orch. (1920); *Impression de mai* for Violin and Orch. (1935); *Suite* for Flute and Chamber Orch. (1949); symphonic poems: *Destin* (1919); *La Fiancée du lutin* (1920); *Nuit d'Avril* (1921); *Paysage* (1923); *Fantaisie burlesque sur un thème populaire* (1928); *La Lune et les peupliers* (1932); *Jeux symphoniques* (1952); *Hommage à César Franck* (1955); *Adagio* for 2 String Ensembles (1960); 8 string quartets (1902, 1914, 1921, 1926, 1927, 1928, 1931, 1940); *Esquisse dramatique* for String Quartet (1935); Quintet for Ancient Instruments (Clavecin, 2 Quintons, Viola d'Amore, and Viola da Gamba; 1934); Wind Quintet (1947); choruses; songs.

BIBL.: J. Servais, *J. R.: Un Musicien du coeur* (1972).

Rögner, Heinz, German conductor; b. Leipzig, Jan. 16, 1929. He studied piano with Hugo Steuer, viola with Gutschlicht, and conducting with Egon Bölsche at the Hochschule für Musik in Leipzig; was a conductor at the German National Theater in Weimar (1951–54); then led the opera school at the Hochschule für Musik in Leipzig (1954–58). From 1958 to 1962 he was chief conductor of the Great Radio Orch. in Leipzig; from 1962 to 1973 he was Generalmusikdirektor of the State Opera in East Berlin. In 1973 he became chief conductor of the (East) Berlin Radio Sym. Orch.; also appeared as a guest conductor in Europe. He served as music director of the Yomiuri Nippon Sym. Orch. in Tokyo (from 1985).

Rogowski, Ludomir (Michal), Polish composer and conductor; b. Lublin, Oct. 3, 1881; d. Dubrovnik, Yugoslavia, March 14, 1954. Of a musical family, he received his early training at home; after studies with Noskowski (composition) and Mlynarski (conducting) at the Warsaw Cons., he completed his training with Nikisch and Riemann in Leipzig. Returning to Poland, he conducted the Vilnius Sym. Orch., which he founded (1910); in 1911 was in Paris; from 1912 to 1914, was a theater conductor in Warsaw. He was again in France (1917–19), then in Poland (1919–26), finally settling in Dubrovnik (1926); won the Polish State Music Prize (1938). In some of his works he made use of the so-called Slavonic scale (Lydian mode with the lowered 7th) and the scale of alternating whole tones and semitones, known as Rimsky-Korsakov's scale.

WORKS: Operas: *Tamara* (1918); *Un Grand Chagrin de la petite Ondine* (1919); *La Sérénade inutile* (1921); *Królewicz Marko* (1930); ballets: *Bajka* (1922) and *Kupala* (1925); 7 syms.: No. 1, *Offering* (1921); No. 2, *Rejoicing* (1936); No. 3 (1940); No. 4 (1943); No. 5 (1947); No. 6 (1949); No. 7 (1951); other symphonic works: *Images ensoleillées* (1918); *Villafranca* (1919); *Les Saisons* (1933); *Les Sourires* (1933); *Poème du travail* (1936); *Fantômes* (1937); 4 rhapsodies on Slavonic themes (1945); *Dubrovnik Impressions* (1950); 6 works for Violin and Orch.; 2 string quartets; short pieces for various instruments; numerous arrangements of Slavonic songs for Chorus.

Roguski, Gustav, Polish composer and pedagogue; b. Warsaw, May 12, 1839; d. there, April 5, 1921. He studied in Germany with Kiel; then went to Paris, where he became a pupil of Berlioz. Returning to Warsaw in 1873, he was appointed prof. at the Cons. He wrote a Sym., 2 string quartets, a Quintet for Wind Instruments and Piano, many piano pieces, choruses, and songs; publ. a manual of harmony (with L. Zelenski). He was greatly esteemed as a teacher of composition; Paderewski was his pupil.

Rohde, (Friedrich) Wilhelm, Danish violinist and composer; b. Altona, Dec. 11, 1856; d. Gentofte, near Copenhagen, April 6, 1928. He was a pupil at the Leipzig Cons. of H. Schradieck and F. David (violin), J. Röntgen (piano), E.F. Richter (composition), and H. Kretzschmar. He lived in Chicago (1878–85); after 1 season as violist in the Boston Sym. Orch., he returned to Germany; from 1914, lived in Copenhagen. He composed several symphonic poems; a Serenade for Strings; *Höller-Galopp* for Violin, Cello, Flute, Horn, and Piano; a number of male choruses; piano pieces.

Rohloff, Ernst, German organist and music historian; b. Graudenz, West Prussia, April 17, 1899; d. Weissenfels, Jan. 2, 1983. He studied with Reger in Leipzig and Meiningen (1909–12); then studied organ with Straube and musicology with Abert and Kroyer at the Univ. of Leipzig (Ph.D., 1925); was active in Weissenfels as an organist and teacher. He publ. *Die einstimmigen Weisen des Lochamer Liederbucher* (Halle, 1953) and *Der schöne Mai ist kommen* (Leipzig, 1955).

Röhr, Hugo, German conductor and composer; b. Dresden, Feb. 13, 1866; d. Munich, June 7, 1937. He studied composition with Wüllner at the Dresden Cons.; began his career as conductor in Augsburg; after filling several engagements in Breslau, Prague, and Mannheim, he was appointed conductor at the Court Opera in Munich (1896); from 1924 to 1934 he taught conducting at the Munich Academy of Music. He wrote several short operas: *Das Vaterunser* (Munich, 1904); *Frauenlist* (Leipzig, 1917); *Cœur-Dame* (1927); *Ekkehard*, dramatic poem for Soli, Chorus, and Orch.; chamber music; songs.

Röhrig, Emil, German violinist, conductor, and composer; b. Rettert, Oct. 31, 1882; d. Aachen, July 22, 1954. After studying violin in Chemnitz, he became engaged as violinist and conductor in Krefeld and Aachen. He wrote much music for brass; concertos for double bass, viola, trumpet, etc.; cantatas and other choral works.

Roig, Gonzalo, Cuban conductor and composer; b. Havana, July 20, 1890; d. there, June 13, 1970. He played violin in theater orchs.; in 1922 organized the Orquesta Sinfónica de la Habana. He wrote zarzuelas, among which *Cecilia Valdés* enjoyed considerable success. In 1912 he wrote the song *Quie-reme mucho*, which became a popular hit.

Rojo Olalla, Casiano, Spanish organist, choirmaster, and writer on music; b. Hacinas, Aug. 5, 1877; d. Burgos, Dec. 4, 1931. He studied at the Santo Domingo de Silos monastery in Burgos, where he became a Benedictine monk (1896); later pursued studies with Pothier in Belgium; was active as an organist and choirmaster; became an authority on Gregorian chant; publ. a valuable manual, *Método de canto gregoriano* (Valladolid, 1906); also wrote *Manual de canto gregoriano* (Silos, 1908); *Cantus Lamentationum* (Bilbao, 1917); *Antiphonarium Mozarabicum de la Catedral de León* (with G. Prado; León, 1928); and *El Canto mozárabe* (with G. Prado; Barcelona, 1929).

Rokseth, Yvonne (née **Rihouët**), eminent French musicologist; b. Maisons-Laffitte, near Paris, July 17, 1890; d. Strasbourg, Aug. 23, 1948. She studied at the Paris Cons., with d'Indy and Roussel at the Schola Cantorum, and with Pirro at the Sorbonne; received her doctorat ès lettres in 1930 with the dissertation *La Musique d'orgue au XVe siècle et au début du XVIe* (publ. in Paris, 1930). She was a librarian at the Cons. and the Bibliothèque Nationale (1934–37); then was made maître de conférences at the Univ. of Strasbourg (1937); after serving in the Resistance during World War II, she rejoined its faculty as prof. of musicology. She ed. the valuable *Polyphonies du XIIIe siècle: Le Manuscrit H 196 de la Faculté de médecine de Montpellier* (4 vols., Paris, 1935–39); also publ. a biography of Grieg (Paris, 1933) and other vols.

BIBL.: G. Thibault, "Y. R.," *Revue de Musicologie*, XXVII (1948).

Roland, Claude-Robert, Belgian composer, organist, conductor, and teacher; b. Pont-de-Loup, Dec. 19, 1935. He studied composition at the Music Academy in Châtelet and at the conservatories of Mons, Liège, Paris, and Brussels with Froidebise, C. Schmit, R. Bernier, Messiaen, and Defossez; also took a course in conducting with Scherchen. He was an organist in churches in various Belgian cities (1955–67); was director of the Music Academy at Montignies-le-Tilleul (1966–75); in 1972, was appointed to the staff of the Brussels Cons.

WORKS: *Sonance* for String Quartet (1956); 2 *sonances* for Piano (1956, 1960); *Recherche* for Orch. (1956); *Indicatif 1* for 12 Strings (1957); *Sonance* for Clavichord (1959); *Sinfonia scolastica pour les bouffons de la Reine* (1961); *Serenade* for Chamber Orch. (1961); *Chansons et reveries* for Violin and Piano (1962); Organ Concerto (1963); *Ballade* for Violin and Piano (1966); *Prelude, Fugue et Rondo a 5* for Wind Quintet (1967); *Sonancelle* for Guitar (1967); *Rossignolet du bois* for Orch. (1971); *Prélude, Fugue et Commentaires* for 4 Clarinets (1971); *Faits-divers* for Horn and Piano (1981); *Thriller* for Trumpet and Piano (1985); *De profundis* for Tuba and Piano (1985).

Roland-Manuel (real name, **Roland Alexis Manuel Lévy**), French composer and writer on music; b. Paris, March 22, 1891; d. there, Nov. 1, 1966. He was a pupil of Albert Roussel and Vincent d'Indy; also studied privately with Maurice Ravel. In 1947 he became a prof. at the Paris Cons. In his compositions he adopted the French neo-Classical style, close to Roussel's manner; however, it is not as a composer but as a perspicacious critic that he became chiefly known. He publ., in Paris, 3 vols. on Ravel: *Maurice Ravel et son œuvre* (1914; 2nd ed., rev., 1926; Eng. tr., 1941), *Maurice Ravel et son œuvre dramatique* (1928), and *À la gloire Maurice Ravel* (1938; 2nd ed., 1948; Eng. tr., 1947); also monographs on Honegger (1925) and Manuel de Falla (1930).

WORKS: *Isabelle et Pantalon*, opéra-bouffe (Paris, Dec. 11, 1922); *Le Diable amoureux*, light opera (1929); *L'Écran des jeunes filles*, ballet (Paris Opéra, May 16, 1929); *Elvire*, ballet on themes of Scarlatti (Paris Opéra, Feb. 8, 1937); Piano Concerto (1938); *Cantique de la sagesse* for Chorus and Orch. (1951); oratorio, *Jeanne d'Arc* (1937).

Rolandi, Gianna, gifted American soprano; b. N.Y., Aug. 16, 1952. Her 1st contact with opera came through her mother,

herself a singer, and by the age of 15 she had already become acquainted with much of the operatic repertoire. She then enrolled at the Curtis Inst. of Music in Philadelphia (B.M., 1975). While still a student there, she was contracted to sing at the N.Y. City Opera, with which she made an impressive debut as Olympia in *Les Contes d'Hoffmann* (Sept. 11, 1975). On Dec. 26, 1979, she made her Metropolitan Opera debut in N.Y. as Sophie in *Der Rosenkavalier*. In 1981 she made her European debut at the Glyndebourne Festival singing Zerbinetta. In 1982 she sang the title role in a televised production of *Lucia di Lammermoor* with the N.Y. City Opera, receiving flattering notices from the press. She scored an outstanding success as Bianca in Rossini's *Bianca e Falliero* at its U.S. premiere at the Greater Miami Opera in 1987.

Roldán, Amadeo, Cuban violinist, conductor, and composer; b. Paris (of Cuban parents), July 12, 1900; d. Havana, March 2, 1939. He studied violin at the Madrid Cons. with Fernández Bordas, graduating in 1916; won the Sarasate Violin Prize; subsequently studied composition with Conrado del Campo in Madrid and with Pedro Sanjuán. In 1921 he settled in Havana; in 1924, became concertmaster of the Orquesta Filarmónica; in 1925, assistant conductor; in 1932, conductor; was prof. of composition at the Cons. (from 1935). In his works he employed with signal success the melorhythms of Afro-Cuban popular music; as a mulatto, he had an innate understanding of these elements.

WORKS: *La Rebambaramba*, ballet, employing a number of Cuban percussion instruments (1927–28; suite, Havana, Aug. 12, 1928); *Obertura sobre témas cubanos* (Havana, Nov. 29, 1925); *El Milagro de Anaquillé* (Havana, Sept. 22, 1929); *Danza negra* for Voice and 7 Instruments (1929); *Motivos de son* for Voice and 9 Instruments (1930); 3 *toques* for Chamber Orch. (1931); 6 *rítmicas*: Nos. 1–4 for Piano and Wind Quintet, Nos. 5 and 6 for Percussion Ensemble.

Rolfe Johnson, Anthony, English tenor; b. Tackley, Nov. 5, 1940. He studied voice in London at the Guildhall School of Music. His 1st major role was with the English Opera Group in 1973. He subsequently established himself as a leading concert singer; also sang opera with the English National Opera and the Welsh National Opera, and periodically at the Glyndebourne Festivals. On Dec. 22, 1988, he made his debut at London's Covent Garden as Jupiter in Handel's *Semele*.

Rolla, Alessandro, Italian violinist, violist, teacher, and composer, father of **Giuseppe Antonio Rolla;** b. Pavia, April 6, 1757; d. Milan, Sept. 15, 1841. He was 1st violist (1782–92) and 1st violinist (1792–1803) in the Parma ducal orch.; then was 1st violinist and 1st prof. of violin and viola at the Milan Cons. (1808–35). Paganini was sent to Parma in 1795 to study with Rolla, but upon his arrival Rolla is reported to have told him that there was nothing left to teach him.

WORKS: Ballets: *Adelasia* (Milan, 1779); *Iserbeck* (Padua, 1802); *Eloisa e Roberto* or *Il Conte d'Essex* (Rome, 1805); *Pizzarro* (Milan, 1807); *Abdul* (Vienna, 1808); *Achilles auf Skyros* (Vienna, 1808); syms.; 10 violin concertos; 15 viola concertos; other orch. works; much chamber music.

BIBL.: G. Zampieri, *L'epoca e l'arte di A. R.* (Pavia, 1941); L. Inzaghi, *A. R.: Vita e opera del grande musicista, maestro di Niccoló Paganini* (Milan, 1984).

Rolla, Giuseppe Antonio, Italian violinist and composer, son of **Alessandro Rolla;** b. Parma, April 18, 1798; d. Dresden, May 19, 1837. He studied with his father; was concertmaster of the orch. of the Italian Opera Co. in Dresden (1823–35); composed a Violin Concerto and pieces for violin and viola.

Rolland, Romain, famous French author and musicologist; b. Clamecy, Nièvre, Jan. 29, 1866; d. Vézelay, Yonne, Dec. 30, 1944. He was educated in Paris at the École Normale Supérieure (1886–89), the École de Rome (1889–91), and the Sorbonne (doctorat ès lettres, 1895, with the diss. *Les Origines du théâtre lyrique moderne: L'Histoire de l'opéra en Europe avant Lully et Scarlatti*; publ. in Paris, 1895; 4th ed., 1936).

He then was a prof. of music history at the École Normale Supérieure until becoming the 1st prof. of music history at the Sorbonne (1903); was also director of the École des Hautes Sociales (1903–9). In 1900 he organized the 1st international congress for the history of music in Paris, and read a paper on *Les Musiciens italiens en France sous Mazarin et "l'Orfeo" de Luigi Rossi* (publ. 1901); with J. Combarieu, he ed. the transactions and the papers read as *Documents, mémoires et vœux* (1901). In 1901 he founded, with J. Combarieu (ed.), P. Aubry, M. Emmanuel, L. Laloy, and himself as principal contributors, the fortnightly *Revue d'Histoire et Critique Musicales*. From 1913 he resided in Switzerland, but in 1938 returned to France and took up his residence at Vézelay.

Rolland's writings exhibit sound scholarship, broad sympathy, keen analytical power, well-balanced judgment, and intimate acquaintance with the musical milieu of his time. The book by which he is most widely known is *Jean-Christophe*, a musical novel remarkable for its blending of historical accuracy, psychological and esthetic speculation, subtle psychological analysis, and romantic interest; it won him the Nobel Prize in literature (1915). The 1st vol. was publ. in 1905, the last (10th) in 1912 (Eng. tr., N.Y., 1910–13). Rolland's other works include *Paris als Musikstadt* (1904; in Strauss's series Die Musik; rewritten and publ. in French as *Le Renouveau* in *Musiciens d'aujourd'hui*); *Beethoven* (Paris, 1903; 3rd ed., 1927, as *La Vie de Beethoven*; Eng. tr., 1969); *La Vie de Haendel* (Paris, 1906; 2nd ed., 1910; Eng. tr., 1916; rev. and enl. by F. Raugel, 1974); *Voyage musical au pays du passé* (1920; Eng. tr., 1922); *Beethoven: Les Grandes Époques créatrices* (4 vols., Paris, 1928–45; Eng. tr., 1964); *Goethe et Beethoven* (1930; Eng. tr., 1931); *Beethoven: Le Chant de la Résurrection* (1937; on the *Missa solemnis* and the last sonatas); essays in various journals he collected and publ. in 2 vols. as *Musiciens d'autrefois* (1908; 6th ed., 1919; Eng. tr., 1915) and *Musiciens d'aujourd'hui* (1908; 8th ed., 1947; Eng. tr., 1914); D. Ewen, ed., *Essays on Music* (a selection from some of the above books; N.Y., 1948). **BIBL.:** P. Seippel, *R. R.: L'Homme et l'œuvre* (Paris, 1913); S. Zweig, *R. R.: Der Mann und das Werk* (Frankfurt, 1921; Eng. tr., N.Y., 1921); J. Bonnerot, *R. R., Sa vie, son œuvre* (Paris, 1921); E. Lerch, *R. R. und die Erneuerung der Gesinnung* (Munich, 1926); M. Lob, *Un Grand Bourguignon, R. R.* (Auxerre, 1927); C. Sénéchal, *R. R.* (Paris, 1933); M. Doisy, *R. R.* (Brussels, 1945); R. Argos, *R. R.* (Paris, 1950); W. Starr, *A Critical Bibliography of the Published Writings of R. R.* (Evanston, Ill., 1950); J. Robichez, *R. R.* (Paris, 1961); E. Bondeville, *R. R. à la recherche de l'homme dans la création artistique* (Paris, 1966).

Rolle, Johann Heinrich, German organist, violinist, violist, and composer; b. Quedlinburg, Dec. 23, 1716; d. Magdeburg, Dec. 29, 1785. He studied with his father, the Kantor and composer **Christian Friedrich Rolle** (b. Halle, April 14, 1681; d. Magdeburg, Aug. 25, 1751). He was an organist in Magdeburg (1732–36); played violin and later viola in the Berlin Court Orch. (1741–47); then returned to Magdeburg as organist at the Johanniskirche; in 1751 became his father's successor. He wrote numerous oratorios, many choral works, orch. pieces, chamber music, keyboard pieces, songs, etc. **BIBL.:** W. Kawerau, *J.H. R.: Ein musikalisches Characterbild* (Magdeburg, 1885); R. Kaestner, *J.H. R.: Untersuchungen zu Leben und Werk* (Kassel, 1932).

Röllig, Carl Leopold, German glass-harmonica player, inventor, and composer; b. Hamburg, c.1735; d. Vienna, March 4, 1804. He was music director of Ackermann's theater company in Hamburg (1764–69; 1771–72); after taking up the glass harmonica about 1780, he toured widely; invented the Orphika (c.1795) and the Xänorphika (1801), pianos with bows instead of hammers; settled in Vienna (1791). He wrote a comic opera, *Clarisse* (Hamburg, Oct. 10, 1771), and various pieces for glass harmonica, including 4 concertos. He publ. *Über die Harmonika* (Berlin, 1787), *Versuch einer musikalischen Intervallentabelle* (Leipzig, 1789), *Orphica, ein musikalisches Instrument*

erfunden von C.L. Röllig (Vienna, 1795), and *Versuch einer Anleitung zur musikalischen Modulation durch mechanische Vortheile* (Vienna, 1799); his *Miscellanea, figurierter Kontrapunkt* remains in MS.

Rollin, Jean, French composer; b. Paris, Aug. 3, 1906; d. Bayeux, Calvados, Aug. 30, 1977. He studied composition at the Paris Cons. with Noël Gallon, and musicology with Pirro and Masson. His works include a Concerto for Piano and Strings (1947); a Violin Concerto (1950); a Concerto for Double Bass and Orch. (1951); 2 syms. (1953, 1958); the opera *Gringoué* (1965); chamber music; songs.

Rollins, "Sonny" (Theodore Walter), outstanding black American jazz tenor saxophonist; b. N.Y., Sept. 7, 1929. He 1st worked with Babs Gonzales, Bud Powell, and Fats Navarro; then went to Chicago, where he studied with Ike Day. After making recordings with Miles Davis, he made appearances with Charlie Parker, Thelonious Monk, and other leading jazz musicians; also served as a member of the Modern Jazz Quartet. At the height of his career, he ranked among the foremost masters of the tenor saxophone. **BIBL.:** D. Baker, *The Jazz Style of S. R.* (Lebanon, Ind., 1980); C. Blancq, *S. R.: The Journey of a Jazzman* (Boston, 1983).

Rolón, José, Mexican composer; b. Ciudad Gusmán, Jalisco, June 22, 1883; d. Mexico City, Feb. 3, 1945. He studied in Paris with Moszkowski, and later with Nadia Boulanger and Dukas. In Mexico he was active as a teacher. He composed a symphonic poem, *Cuauhtémoc* (1929; Mexico City, Jan. 10, 1930); symphonic suite, *Zapotlán* (1895; reorchestrated, 1925; Mexico City, Nov. 4, 1932); Sym. (1918–19); Piano Concerto (1935; Mexico City, Sept. 4, 1942); chamber music; many effective piano pieces; songs.

Roman, Johan Helmich, significant Swedish composer; b. Stockholm, Oct. 26, 1694; d. Haraldsmåla, near Kalmar, Nov. 20, 1758. He was of Swedish-German descent. He mastered the violin and oboe in childhood; by 1711 he was a member of the royal chapel, where his father, Johan Roman, was also a member. With the permission of King Charles XII, he pursued his training in England (c.1715–21), where he may have received lessons from Pepusch; was also associated with Ariosti, G.B. Bononcini, Geminiani, and Handel. He returned to Stockholm in 1721; was deputy master (1721–27) and chief master (1727–45) of the royal chapel; was compelled to retire as a result of deafness and ill health, and subsequently served as hovintendent (court steward). In 1731 he organized the 1st public concerts given in Stockholm. He was elected a member of the Royal Academy of Science in 1740. Roman was the 1st Swedish composer to write instrumental and choral music that could compare favorably with German and Italian works, and was for that reason called "the father of Swedish music." His style shows the influence of Handel. Some 400 extant works are attributed to him, the majority of MSS being housed at the Royal Swedish Academy of Music in Stockholm. His most celebrated work is the orch. suite *Bilägers musiquen* (Royal Wedding Music) or *Drottningholmsmusiquen* (1744; ed. by C. Genetay, Stockholm, 1958). He also wrote 6 suites; at least 17 sinfonias; 4 overtures; 4 violin concertos; 12 sonate for Flute, Violone, and Harpsichord; 13 trio sonatas for 2 Violins and Basso Continuo; at least 11 harpsichord sonatas; violin pieces; and sacred and secular vocal works. A collected ed. of his works began appearing in 1965 in the series Monumenta Musicae Svecicae. See I. Bengtsson, ed., *Mr. Roman's Spuriosity Shop: A Thematic Catalogue of 503 Works (1213 Incipits and Other Excerpts) from ca. 1680–1750 by More Than Sixty Composers* (Stockholm, 1976). **BIBL.:** A. Sahlstedt, *Äreminne öfwer hofintendenten kongl. capellmästaren . . . J.H. R.* (Stockholm, 1767); P. Vretblad, *J.H. R. 1694–1758; Svenska musikens fader* (2 vols., Stockholm, 1914); C.-A. Moberg, "J.H. R.—den svenska musikens fader," *Svensk Tidskrift för Musikforskning, XXVI* (1944); I. Bengtsson, *J.H. R. och hans Instrumentalmusik: Käll-och stilkritiska studier* (Uppsala, 1955); I. Bengtsson and R. Danielson, *Handsti-*

lar och notpikturer i Kungl. musikaliska akademiens R.-samling (Uppsala, 1955); G. Carleberg, *Buxtehude, Telemann och R.* (Stockholm, 1965).

Roman, Stella (real name, **Florica Vierica Alma Stela Blasu**), Rumanian soprano; b. Cluj, March 25, 1904. She studied in Cluj, Bucharest, Milan, and Rome; made her debut in Piacenza in 1932; then sang at the Rome Opera and at La Scala in Milan. On Jan. 1, 1941, she made her Metropolitan Opera debut in N.Y. as Aida; she remained on its roster until 1950. She was best known for her roles in Italian operas.

Romani, Carlo, Italian composer, nephew of **Pietro Romani;** b. Avelino, May 24, 1824; d. Florence, March 4, 1875. He studied with Palafuti (piano) and Picchianti (composition); completed his studies under his uncle; set to music the recitatives of *Der Freischütz* for its 1st Italian performance (Florence, Feb. 3, 1843); wrote operas (all produced in Florence): *Tutti amanti* (1847); *Il Mantello* (1852; successful); *I Baccanali di Roma* (1854); *Ermellina ossia Le Gemme della corona* (1865); an oratorio, *San Sebastiano* (1864); various patriotic songs.

Romani, Felice, renowned Italian librettist; b. Genoa, Jan. 31, 1788; d. Moneglia, Jan. 28, 1865. He was educated at the Univ. of Pisa; wrote about 100 librettos for Mayr, Winter, Vaccai, Rossini, Bellini, Donizetti, Pacini, Ricci, etc.
BIBL.: F. Regli, *Elogio a F. R.* (Turin, 1865); L. Lianovosani, *Saggio bibliografico relativo ai melodrammi di F. R.* (Milan, 1878); E. Branca (R.'s wife), *F. R. ed i più riputati maestri di musica del suo tempo* (Turin, 1882); C. Paschetto, *F. R.* (Turin, 1907); M. Rinaldi, *F. R.* (Rome, 1965).

Romani, Pietro, Italian conductor, teacher, and composer, uncle of **Carlo Romani;** b. Rome, May 29, 1791; d. Florence, Jan. 11, 1877. He studied with Fenaroli; became conductor at the Teatro della Pergola in Florence; taught singing at the Istituto Musicale there. He wrote 2 operas, *Il Qui pro quo* (Rome, 1817) and *Carlo Magno* (Florence, 1823); also ballet music; he is remembered chiefly for his aria *Manca un foglio,* for Bartolo in *Il Barbiere de Siviglia,* which he wrote for the production of the opera in Florence in 1816 as a substitute for Rossini's original aria *A un dottor della mia sorte,* which presented some vocal difficulties. Romani's aria was long retained in many productions of the opera.

Romberg, Andreas Jakob, German violinist and composer, cousin of **Bernhard Heinrich Romberg;** b. Vechta, near Münster, April 27, 1767; d. Gotha, Nov. 10, 1821. He was the son of the clarinetist and violinist **Gerhard Heinrich Romberg** (b. Aug. 8, 1745; d. Nov. 14, 1819). He studied with his father, then made his debut at age 7 in Münster with his cousin; the 2 subsequently toured (with their fathers) to Frankfurt am Main (1782) and Paris (1784, 1785); they played in the Bonn electoral orch. from 1790 until the French invasion of 1793 compelled them to flee to Hamburg; after playing in the opera orch. at the Ackermann Theater, they set out on a tour of Italy (1795–96); they also visited Vienna in 1796 and were befriended by Haydn; then returned to Italy. After another sojourn in Paris (1801), Andreas Romberg settled in Hamburg and devoted himself mainly to composition; he was then called to Gotha as court Kapellmeister (1815). He had 2 sons: **Heinrich Maria** (b. Paris, April 4, 1802; d. Hamburg, May 2, 1859) became concertmaster of the St. Petersburg Imperial Opera orch. (1827) and later served as its music director; **Ciprian Friedrich** (b. Hamburg, Oct. 28, 1807; d. there, Oct. 14, 1865) was 1st cellist of the St. Petersburg German Opera orch. (1835–45).
WORKS: OPERAS: *Der blaue Ungeheuer* (1790–93; not perf.); *Die Macht der Musik* (1791; not perf.); *Die Nebelkappen* (1793; unfinished); *Der Rabe* (Hamburg, April 7, 1794); *Don Mendoza* (Paris, 1802; in collaboration with B.H. Romberg); *Point de bruit* (Paris, 1810); *Die Ruinen zu Paluzzi* (Hamburg, Dec. 27, 1811); *Die Grossmut des Scipio* (Gotha, 1816); various sacred vocal works; many secular choral pieces, including the popular *Lied von der Glocke* (1809); part-songs; lieder. **ORCH.:** 10 syms.; 20 violin concertos; 2 concertos for Violin and Cello;

2 concertos for 2 Violins; Concerto for Clarinet and Violin. **CHAMBER:** Many works, including 19 string quartets; Octet for Strings; Clarinet Quintet; 8 flute quartets; String Quintet; Piano Quartet; 3 violin sonatas.
BIBL.: K. Stephenson, *A. R.: Ein Beitrag zur Hamburger Musikgeschichte* (Hamburg, 1938).

Romberg, Bernhard Heinrich, German cellist and composer, cousin of **Andreas Jakob Romberg;** b. Dinklage, Nov. 11, 1767; d. Hamburg, Aug. 13, 1841. He was the son of the bassoonist and cellist **Bernhard Anton Romberg** (b. Münster, March 6, 1742; d. there, Dec. 14, 1814), who played in the orch. of the Prince-Bishop of Münster (1776–1803). Bernhard Heinrich began his career in Münster when he appeared with his cousin at age 7; they toured with their fathers thereafter, making visits to Frankfurt am Main (1782) and Paris (1784, 1785); after playing in the Bonn electoral orch. (1790–93), they fled in the face of the French invasion and went to Hamburg, where they were members of the opera orch. at the Ackermann Theater; they then toured Italy (1795–96) and visited Vienna (1796), where they became friends of Haydn. After further travels in Italy and another visit to Paris (1801), the cousins pursued separate careers. Bernhard Heinrich visited Spain in 1801; served as prof. of cello at the Paris Cons. (1801–3), then joined the Berlin Royal Court Orch. (1805). He visited Russia in 1807 and England in 1814; was Berlin Hofkapellmeister (1816–19). In 1820 he went to Hamburg, which he made his home with the exception of another Berlin sojourn (1826–31); also made extensive tours as a virtuoso. He publ. *Méthode de violoncelle* (Berlin, 1840). He had 2 children who pursued musical careers: **Bernhardine** (b. Hamburg, Dec. 14, 1803; d. there, April 26, 1878), a concert singer, and **Karl** (b. Moscow, Jan. 16, 1811; d. Hamburg, Feb. 6, 1897), a cellist in the St. Petersburg German Opera orch. (1830–42).
WORKS: STAGE: *Der Schiffbruch,* operetta (1791; not perf.); *Die wiedergefundene Statue,* opera (c.1792; not perf.); *Don Mendoza,* opera (Paris, 1802; in collaboration with A. Romberg); *Ulisse und Circe,* opera (Berlin, July 27, 1807); *Rittertreue,* opera (Berlin, Jan. 31, 1817); *Daphne und Agathokles,* ballet (Berlin, 1818); *Alma,* opera (Copenhagen, May 15, 1824); incidental music. **ORCH.:** 5 syms.; *Symphonie burlesque* for Children's Instruments and Orch.; 2 overtures; 10 cello concertos; Concertino for 2 Horns and Orch.; Double Concerto for Violin, Cello, and Orch.; many pieces for cello and orch. **CHAMBER:** 11 string quartets; cello studies; piano pieces; songs.
BIBL.: H. Schäfer, *B. R.: Sein Leben und Wirken* (diss., Univ. of Bonn, 1931).

Romberg, Sigmund, famous Hungarian-born American composer; b. Nagykanizsa, July 29, 1887; d. N.Y., Nov. 9, 1951. He studied at the Univ. of Bucharest and in Vienna (with Heuberger); in 1909, went to the U.S. as an engineer; later became a naturalized citizen; settled in N.Y. in 1913 and devoted himself to composing for the theater. He composed over 70 operettas, including *The Midnight Girl* (Feb. 23, 1914; his 1st success); *The Blue Paradise* (with E. Eysler; N.Y., Aug. 5, 1915); *Maytime* (N.Y., Aug. 16, 1917); *Blossom Time* (on Schubert's melodies; N.Y., Sept. 29, 1921); *The Rose of Stamboul* (March 7, 1922); *The Student Prince* (N.Y., Dec. 2, 1924); *The Desert Song* (N.Y., Nov. 30, 1926); *My Maryland* (N.Y., Sept. 12, 1927); *The New Moon* (Sept. 19, 1928); *Up in Central Park* (N.Y., Jan. 27, 1945).
BIBL.: E. Arnold, *Deep in My Heart* (a biography in the form of a novel, N.Y., 1949); J. Koegel, *The Film Operettas of S. R.* (thesis, Calif. State Univ., 1984).

Romero, family of famous Spanish-American guitarists constituting a quartet known as Los Romeros:
Celedonio Romero (b. Málaga, March 2, 1918) pursued a career as a soloist in Spain; he served as mentor to each of his 3 sons, **Celin** (b. Málaga, Nov. 23, 1940), **Pepe** (b. Málaga, March 8, 1944), and **Angel** (b. Málaga, Aug. 17, 1946); they eventually appeared together as a guitar quartet, playing engagements throughout Spain. The family emigrated to the U.S.

in 1958 and made their 1st tour of the country in 1961; billed as "the royal family of the guitar," they toured with great success worldwide. In addition to making their own arrangements and transcriptions, they commissioned works from various composers, including Joaquín Rodrigo and Federico Moreno Torroba.

Romero, Mateo (real name, **Mathieu Rosmarin**), Netherlands-born Spanish composer; b. Liège, 1575 or 1576; d. Madrid, May 10, 1647. He was a soldier and was often called "El Maestro Capitán." After serving with the Spanish army in Flanders, he became cantor of the Flemish chapel in Madrid (1593), and was maestro de from 1598 to 1634; in 1609 he was ordained a priest. In 1638 he went to Portugal as emissary to the Duke of Braganza (the future Emperor João IV). He enjoyed a reputation as one of the finest composers of both sacred and secular music of his time. Many of his works are lost; 22 secular compositions are found in J. Aroca, ed., *Cancionero musical y poético del siglo XVII, recogido por Claudio de la Sablonara* (Madrid, 1916).
BIBL.: R. Pelinski, *Die weltliche Vokalmusik Spaniens am Anfang des 17. Jahrhunderts, der Cancionero de la Sablonara* (Tutzing, 1971).

Romeu, Luis, Spanish composer; b. Vich, near Barcelona, June 21, 1874; d. there, Sept. 23, 1937. A priest, he was 1st choirmaster, then organist, at the Cathedral in Vich. His works, which show the influence of Catalan folk song, include a Mass for the *Mare de Deu de Nuria* and *Cants catequistics et Marianes* (3 collections). He publ. a book on Catalan church music, *La Versio auténtica dels Goigs del Roser de tot l'any* (vol. I of *Obra del Cançoner popular de Catalunya*; Barcelona, 1928). The total number of his works, secular and sacred, is 331.

Römhild or **Römhildt, Johann Theodor,** German organist and composer; b. Salzungen, Sept. 23, 1684; d. Merseburg, Oct. 26, 1756. He studied with Johann Jakob Bach in Ruhla; in 1697 entered the Thomasschule in Leipzig, where he was a pupil of Schelle and Kuhnau; later studied at the Univ. of Leipzig (1705–8). He was Kantor at Spremberg and Freystadt; in 1731, was appointed court musician in Merseburg, and in 1735 Cathedral organist there. He composed over 250 sacred cantatas, 19 secular cantatas, 2 oratorios, 2 masses, a *St. Matthew Passion* (publ. in Leipzig, 1921), motets, and some instrumental works.
BIBL.: K. Paulke, "J.T. R. (1684–1756)," *Archiv für Musikwissenschaft* I (1918–19).

Ronald, Sir Landon (real name, **Landon Ronald Russell**), English pianist, conductor, and composer; b. London, June 7, 1873; d. there, Aug. 14, 1938. He was a son of the composer **Henry Russell** and brother of the impresario **Henry Russell.** He entered the Royal College of Music, where he studied composition with Charles Parry and also attended the classes of Charles Stanford and Walter Parratt. He 1st embarked on a concert career as a pianist, but soon turned to conducting light opera and summer sym. concerts; was conductor of the New Sym. Orch. of London (1909–14) and of the Scottish Orch. in Glasgow (1916–20). He served as principal of the Guildhall School of Music and Drama (1910–38). He was knighted in 1922. He composed an operetta, *A Capital Joke;* a ballet, *Britannia's Realm* (1902; for the coronation of King Edward VII); and a scenic spectacle, *Entente cordiale* (1904; to celebrate the triple alliance of Russia, France, and England); about 300 songs. He publ. 2 autobiographical books: *Variations on a Personal Theme* (London, 1922) and *Myself and Others* (London, 1931).

Roncaglia, Gino, Italian musicologist and composer; b. Modena, May 7, 1883; d. there, Nov. 27, 1968. He studied composition with Sinigaglia; devoted himself to musical biography.
WRITINGS: *Giuseppe Verdi* (Naples, 1914; 2nd ed., rev., 1940, as *L'ascensione creatice di Giuseppe Verdi*; 3rd ed., 1951); *La Rivoluzione musicale italiana* (Milan, 1928); *Rossini l'olimpico: Vita e opere* (Milan, 1946; 2nd ed., 1953); *Invito*

alla musica (Milan, 1946; 4th ed., 1958); *Invito all' opera* (Milan, 1949; 4th ed., 1958); *La Cappella musicale del Duomo di Modena* (Florence, 1957); *Galleria verdiana: Studi e figure* (Milan, 1959).

Ronconi, family of Italian musicians:
(1) Domenico Ronconi, tenor and singing teacher; b. Lendinara, near Rovigo, July 11, 1772; d. Milan, April 13, 1839. He made his debut in Venice (1797); after singing in St. Petersburg (1801–5), he returned to Italy and appeared at Milan's La Scala (1808), where he was chosen to create roles in operas by Mosca, Orlandi, and Lamberti; then sang at the Italian Opera in Vienna (1809) and in Paris (1810); after further appearances in Italy, he was a member of the Munich Hof- und Nationaltheater (1819–29); then returned to his homeland and opened his own singing school in Milan. He had 3 sons who became musicians:
(2) Giorgio Ronconi, baritone; b. Milan, Aug. 6, 1810; d. Madrid, Jan. 8, 1890. He studied with his father; made his debut as Valdeburgo in *La Straniera* in Pavia (1831); went to Rome, where he sang in the premieres of Donizetti's *Il Furioso all'isola di San Domingo* and *Torquato Tasso* in 1833; subsequently sang in the premieres of that composer's *Il campanello* in Naples (1836), *Pia de' Tolomei* in Venice (1837), *Maria di Rudez* in Venice (1838), *Maria Padilla* in Milan (1841), and *Maria di Rohan* in Vienna (1843). From 1839 he sang at Milan's La Scala, where he was chosen by Verdi to create the title role in his *Nabucco* (1842). In 1842 he made his London debut at Her Majesty's Theatre, and later made frequent appearances at Covent Garden (1847–66); also sang in St. Petersburg (1850–60). After a sojourn in N.Y. (1866–72), he went to Granada and founded his own singing school; then was prof. of singing at the Madrid Cons. (from 1874). Although his voice was mediocre, he won distinction for his dramatic abilities.
(3) Felice Ronconi, singing teacher; b. Venice, 1811; d. St. Petersburg, Sept. 10, 1875. He received his musical training from his father; was active as a singing teacher in Würzburg, Frankfurt am Main, Milan, and St. Petersburg; wrote a method on the teaching of singing; also wrote some songs.
(4) Sebastiano Ronconi, baritone; b. Venice, May 1814; d. Milan, Feb. 6, 1900. He studied with his father; made his debut as Torquato Tasso in Lucca (1836); later sang throughout Europe and the U.S.; spent his last years teaching voice in Milan.

Ronga, Luigi, eminent Italian musicologist; b. Turin, June 19, 1901. He studied at the Univ. of Turin and in Dresden; in 1926, became a prof. at the Palermo Cons.; later joined the faculties of Rome's Accademia di Santa Cecilia and Pontificio Istituto di Musica Sacra (from 1930); became a lecturer at the Univ. of Rome in 1938, and was a prof. there from 1950 to 1971. He publ. an excellent monograph on Frescobaldi (Turin, 1930); also one on Rossini (Florence, 1939) and essays on other Italian composers; his other books include *Bach, Mozart, Beethoven; Tre problemi critici* (Venice, 1956); *Arte e gusto nella musica, dell'ars nova a Debussy* (Milan, 1956); *The Meeting of Poetry and Music* (N.Y., 1956); *La musica nell'età barocca* (Rome, 1959); *Il linguaggio musicale romantico* (Rome, 1960); *La musica europa nella seconda metà dell'Ottocento* (Rome, 1961); *Storia della musica* (Rome, 1962–63).

Rongé, Jean-Baptiste, Belgian composer and translator; b. Liège, April 1, 1825; d. there, Oct. 28, 1882. He was a pupil at the Liège Cons.; won the 2nd Belgian Prix de Rome (1851); wrote occasional cantatas and other pieces; a meeting with the poet André van Hasselt directed his interests toward literary work; in collaboration they tr. into French many standard operas. After van Hasselt's death (1874), Rongé returned to composing, producing a comic opera, *La Comtesse d'Albany* (Liège, 1877); also choruses and songs.

Ronnefeld, Peter, German composer and conductor; b. Dresden, Jan. 26, 1935; d. Kiel, Aug. 6, 1965. He studied with Blacher in Berlin and Messiaen in Paris; was assistant conductor at the Vienna State Opera (1958–61); served as chief conductor at the Theater der Stadt Bonn (1961–63); then was Generalmusikdirektor in Kiel from 1963 until his death. As a conductor, he specialized in modern music, but he also excelled in the Romantic repertoire; his own opera, *Die Ameise* (Düsseldorf, Oct. 21, 1961), had a fine reception. He also wrote a chamber opera, *Nachtausgabe* (Salzburg, 1956); 2 ballets, *Peter Schlemihl* (1955–56) and *Die Spirale* (1961); Concertino for Flute, Clarinet, Horn, Bassoon, and String Orch. (1950); *Sinfonie '52* (1952); *Rondo* for Orch. (1954); 2 *Episodes* for Chamber Orch. (1956); cantata, *Quartär* (1958); chamber music; songs.

Ronstadt, (Maria) Linda, spectacular American pop singer; b. Tucson, Ariz., July 15, 1946. She filled jobs singing with her brother Pete and sister Suzi in pizza parlors in Tucson; after a semester at the Univ. of Arizona, she went to Los Angeles, where she formed a group, The Stone Poneys (1964), and soon began singing for discs. In her song selection, she ranges from country-western through resurrected Motown classics to "new wave"; in 1972 she put out an album, ambitiously announced as *Linda Ronstadt*. In 1973 she toured with Neil Young. Several hits followed, and it became clear to her and her public that she had a magic touch; among her best-selling albums were *Heart like a Wheel* (1974), *Prisoner of Disguise* (1975), *Hasten Down the Wind* (1976; won her a Grammy Award as best female pop vocalist of the year), *Simple Dreams* (1977), *Mad Love* (1983), *What's New* (1983), and *Lush Life* (1984). She sang at President Carter's inauguration in 1977. In 1980 she hit the front pages when Gov. Jerry Brown of California took her on an African safari trip; in 1981, she expanded her repertoire to include the Broadway stage by appearing in the role of Mabel in the centennial anniversary production of Gilbert and Sullivan's *Pirates of Penzance;* also appeared in the film version (1983), and attempted grand opera as Mimi in *La Bohème* in N.Y. (1984).

Röntgen, Julius, German-born Dutch pianist, conductor, pedagogue, and composer; b. Leipzig, May 9, 1855; d. Bilthoven, near Utrecht, Sept. 13, 1932. He studied music with his father, Engelbert Röntgen (1829–97); later with Plaidy and Reinecke in Leipzig and F. Lachner in Munich. From 1877 to 1925 he taught in Amsterdam; was conductor of the Soc. for the Promotion of Music (1886–98); was a co-founder (1884) of the Amsterdam Cons., and its director from 1912 to 1924. He was a friend of Brahms and Grieg; ed. the letters of Brahms to T. Engelmann (1918); publ. a biography of Grieg (1930). An astonishingly industrious composer, he wrote an enormous amount of music in every genre, cast in an expansive Romantic style: 21 syms.; 7 piano concertos; 2 violin concertos; 2 cello concertos; 3 operas (*Agnete, Samum,* and *Der lachende Kavalier*); much chamber music; etc.

Rooley, Anthony, English lutenist; b. Leeds, June 10, 1944. He studied guitar at the Royal Academy of Music in London, but was self-taught as a lutenist. In 1969 he organized (with James Tyler) the Consort of Musicke, an ensemble devoted to the performance of Renaissance music. He was the ed. of *The Penguin Book of Early Music* (Harmondsworth, 1980).

Roos, Robert de, Dutch composer; b. The Hague, March 10, 1907; d. there, March 18, 1976. He studied composition with Johan Wagenaar at his local Royal Cons.; then went to Paris, where he studied composition with Koechlin, Roland-Manuel, and Milhaud, piano with Isidor Philipp, and conducting with Monteux (1926–34); returning to the Netherlands, he worked with Sem Dresden. He served as a cultural attaché at the Netherlands Embassy in Paris (1947–56); then was 1st Secretary for Press and Cultural Affairs in Caracas (1957–62), London (1962–67), and Buenos Aires (1967).

Works: Chamber oratorio after Omar Khayyám (1928); 5 *Études* for Piano and Small Orch. (1929); *Mouvement symphonique* (1930); ballet, *Kaartspel* (Card Game; 1934); dance pantomime, *Landelijke comedie* (Pastoral Comedy) for Orch. (1937–39); *Lyrische suite* for Chorus and Small Orch. (1938); Violin Concertino (1939); *Danses* for Flute and Small Orch.

(1940); Viola Concerto (1941–42); Sinfonietta (1943); *Sinfonia romantica (Museum-Symphonie)* for Chamber Orch. (1943); Piano Concerto (1943–44); *Adam in ballingschap* for 2 Narrators, 2 Flutes, 2 Horns, and Strings (1944); *Quo Vadis,* suite for Orch. (1947); *Variations sérieuses sur un thème ingénu* for Orch. (1947); *De getemde Mars* for Chorus and Orch. (1948); 2 violin concertos (1949–50; 1956–58); Sinfonia No. 2 (1952); *Suggestioni* for Orch. (1961); *Composizioni* for Orch. (1962); *Sinfonia in 2 moti* for String Orch. (1968); *Postrema Verba,* cantata for Baritone, Chorus, and 25 Instruments (1969); 2 *Songs* for Baritone and Instruments (1971); *Musica* for Violins, Cellos, and Double Basses (1971); *Rapsodie e Danza* for 2 Flutes and Orch. (1972–73); 3 *Romantic Songs* for Soprano and Orch. (1975); Sextet for Piano and Winds (1935); 7 string quartets (1941; 1942; 1944–45; 1945–49; 1951; 1969–70); *Quartettino,* 1971); Solo Violin Sonata (1943); *Introduction, Adagio and Allegro* for 2 Violins (1945); Violin Sonata (1946); *Capriccio* for Clarinet and Piano (1952); *Distrazioni* for Violin and Piano (1953); 3 *pezzi senza nome* for Piano Quartet (1958); Trio for 2 Violins and Cello (1965); 4 *per 2* for Oboe and Viola (1966); *Incidenze* for Flute, Cello or Viola da Gamba, and Harpsichord (1966–67); *Incontri* for Wind Quintet (1966); Piano Trio (1968); 2 *moti lenti* for 2 Violins and Cello (1970); 4 *pezzi* for Wind Trio (1970–71); incidental music for Classical dramas.

Roosevelt, J(oseph) Willard, American composer and pianist; b. Madrid, Jan. 16, 1918. His grandfather was President Theodore Roosevelt. After attending Harvard College (1936–38), he pursued studies at the Longy School of Music in Cambridge, Mass. (1936–38; 1940–41); also received instruction from Nadia Boulanger in Paris and Gargenville (1938–39). After obtaining diplomas in composition and piano at the N.Y. College of Music (1946–47), he completed his education at the Hartt College of Music in Hartford, Conn. (B.Mus., 1959; M.Mus., 1960). In addition to his appearances as a pianist, he lectured on music at Columbia Univ. (1961), Fairleigh-Dickinson Univ. (1964–67), and the N.Y. College of Music (1967–68). His compositions include an opera, *And the Walls Came Tumbling Down* (1974); a Piano Concerto (1948; rev. 1983); a Cello Concerto (1963); an overture, *Amistad, homenaje al gran Morel-Campos* (1965); *Our Dead Brothers Bid Us Think of Life* for Soprano, Narrator, Dancer, and Chamber Orch. (1976); other vocal works; and chamber music.

Root, Frederick W(oodman), American organist, singing teacher, writer on music, and composer, son of **George Frederick Root;** b. Boston, June 13, 1846; d. Chicago, Nov. 8, 1916. He was taught by his father, then by B.C. Blodgett and William Mason in N.Y. In 1863 he became organist of the 3rd Presbyterian Church in Chicago; in 1865, of the Swedenborgian Church; in 1869–70 he traveled in Europe, studying singing with Vannuccini in Florence. He publ. singing manuals and vocal collections; composed anthems, cantatas, songs.

Root, George Frederick, American music educator, music publisher, and composer, father of **Frederick W(oodman) Root;** b. Sheffield, Mass., Aug. 30, 1820; d. Bailey's Island, Maine, Aug. 6, 1895. He was a pupil of George J. Webb in Boston; then lived in N.Y.; was organist of the Church of the Strangers. Going to Chicago in 1859, he joined the music publishing firm of Root and Cady, established in 1858 by his elder brother, Ebenezer Towner Root, and Chauncey Marvin Cady; it was dissolved in 1871. He wrote many popular songs (*Battlecry of Freedom; Tramp, tramp, tramp; Just before the battle, Mother*); publ. numerous collections of church music and school songs. For some of his earlier compositions he used the German tr. of his name, Friedrich Wurzel, as a pseudonym. He wrote an autobiography, *The Story of a Musical Life* (Cincinnati, 1891).

Bibl.: D. Epstein, "Music Publishing in Chicago before 1871: The Firm of R. and Cady, 1858–1871," *Notes* (June 1944–June 1946; separately publ., Detroit, 1969); P. Carder, *G.F. R., Pioneer Music Educator: His Contributions to Mass Instruction in Music* (diss., Univ. of Maryland, 1971).

Rootham, Cyril (Bradley), English organist, teacher, and composer; b. Bristol, Oct. 5, 1875; d. Cambridge, March 18, 1938. He studied music with his father, Daniel Rootham (1837–1922); won classical and musical scholarships at St. John's College, Cambridge (B.A., 1897; Mus.B., 1900; M.A., 1901; Mus.Doc., 1910); finished at the Royal College of Music in London under Stanford, Parratt, and Barton. He was organist (from 1901) and a lecturer (from 1913) at St. John's College, Cambridge; also conductor of the Univ. Musical Soc. there (1912–36). His career as a composer was very much bound to the musical life of Cambridge. He brought out his opera, *The 2 Sisters*, there on Feb. 14, 1922; also wrote *For the Fallen* for Chorus and Orch. (1919); *Brown Earth* (London, March 14, 1923). His 2nd Sym. (with a choral ending) was performed posthumously by the BBC, March 17, 1939. Other works include *Pan*, rhapsody for Orch. (1912); String Quintet (1909); String Quartet (1914); Septet for Viola, Flute, Oboe, Clarinet, Bassoon, Horn, and Harp (1930); Piano Trio (1931).

Ropartz, Joseph Guy (Marie), French conductor, teacher, and composer; b. Guingamp, Côtes-du-Nord, June 15, 1864; d. Lanloup-par-Plouha, Côtes-du-Nord, Nov. 22, 1955. He entered the Paris Cons. as a pupil of Dubois and Massenet; then took lessons in organ and composition from César Franck, who remained his chief influence in composition; from 1894 until 1919, was director of the Cons. and conductor of the sym. concerts at Nancy; from 1919 to 1929, conducted the Municipal Orch. and was director of the Cons. in Strasbourg; after that lived in retirement in Lanloup-par-Plouha.
     WORKS: OPERA: *Le Pays* (1910; Nancy, Feb. 1, 1912). BALLETS: *Prélude dominical et 6 pièces à donner pour chaque jour de la semaine* (1929) and *L'Indiscret* (1931); incidental music to *Pêcheur d'Islande* (1891) and to *Oedipe à Colonne* (1914). ORCH.: 5 syms.: No. 1 (1894); No. 2 (1900); No. 3, with Chorus (1905); No. 4 (1910); No. 5 (1944); *La Cloche des morts* (1887); *Les Landes* (1888); *Marche de Fête* (1888); *5 pièces brèves* (1889); *Carnaval* (1889); *Sérénade* (1892); *Dimanche breton* (1893); *À Marie endormie* (1912); *La Chasse du prince Arthur* (1912); *Soir sur les Chaumes* (1913); *Divertissement* (1915); *Concerto* (1930); *Sérénade champêtre* (1932; Paris, Feb. 24, 1934); *Bourrées bourbonnaises* (1939); *Petite symphonie* for Chamber Orch. (1943). SACRED CHORAL: 5 motets a cappella (1900); 3 masses; Requiem for Soloists, Chorus, and Orch. (Paris, April 7, 1939); *De Profundis* for Solo Voice, Chorus, and Orch. (1942); etc. CHAMBER: 6 string quartets (1893, 1912, 1925, 1934, 1940, 1951); Piano Trio (1918); String Trio (1935); 3 violin sonatas (1907, 1917, 1927); 2 cello sonatas (1904, 1918). PIANO: *Dans l'ombre de la montagne* (1913); *Musiques au jardin* (1917); *Croquis d'été* (1918); *Croquis d'automne* (1929); *Jeunes filles* (1929); *3 nocturnes*; etc.; many organ pieces. SONGS: *Chrysanthèmes, La Mer, Paysage, Tes yeux, De tous les temps, Poème d'adieu, En mai, Chanson de bord, Il pleut, Au bord d'un ruisseau, Douloureux mensonge, La Vieille Maison*, etc.
     BIBL.: F. Lamy, *J. G.-R., l'homme et l'œuvre* (Paris, 1948); L. Kornprobst, *J. G.-R.* (Strasbourg, 1949); *Livre du centenaire de J. G.-R.* (Paris, 1966).

Rore, Cipriano de, celebrated Flemish composer; b. 1515 or 1516; d. Parma, Sept. 1565. He may have been born in Machelen (near Ghent), Mechelen, or Antwerp; he appears to have spent his youth in Machelen before setting out for Italy. He went to Venice, where he may have been a pupil of Willaert, the maestro di cappella at San Marco; publ. his 1st book of madrigals in 1542. He may have entered the service of the Duke of Ferrara, Ercole II, as maestro di cappella as early as 1545, although records do not list him until 1547. After the death of Ercole II in 1559, Rore entered the service of Margaret of Parma, the governor of the Netherlands, at her court at Brussels. By 1561 he was in the service of her husband, Ottavio Farnese, in Parma. In 1563 he was elected Willaert's successor as maestro di cappella at San Marco. Because of problems in the cappella, he quit his post in 1564 and returned to Parma. Rore was one of the great masters of the madrigal. He was a major influence on such composers as Lasso, Monte, and Monteverdi. He also wrote a number of outstanding sacred works.
     WORKS: SACRED: *Motectorum liber primus* for 5 Voices (Venice, 1544); *Motetta* for 5 Voices (Venice, 1545); *Il terzo libro di motetti* for 5 Voices (Venice, 1549); *Passio . . . secundum Joannem* for 2 to 6 Voices (Paris, 1557); *Motetta* for 4 Voices (Venice, 1563); *Sacrae cantiones* for 5 to 7 Voices (Venice, 1595). MADRIGALS: *I madrigali* for 5 Voices (Venice, 1542; 2nd ed., enl., 1544, as *Il primo libro de madregali cromatici*); *Il secondo libro de madregali* for 5 Voices (Venice, 1544); *Il terzo libro di madrigali* for 5 Voices (Venice, 1548); *Musica . . . sopra le stanze del Petrarcha . . . libro terzo* for 5 Voices (Venice, 1548); *Il primo libro de madrigali* for 4 Voices (Ferrara, 1550); *Il quarto libro de'i madrigali* for 5 Voices (Venice, 1557); *Il secondo libro de madregali* for 4 Voices (Venice, 1557); *Li madrigali libro quarto* for 5 Voices (Venice, 1562); *Le vive fiamme de' vaghi e dilettevoli madrigali* for 4 to 5 Voices (Venice, 1565); *Il quinto libro de madrigali* for 5 Voices (Venice, 1566). CHANSONS: *Il primo libro de madrigali* for 4 Voices (Ferrara, 1550). SECULAR LATIN MOTETS: *Motetta* for 5 Voices (Venice, 1545); *Le vive fiamme de' vaghi e dilettevoli madrigali* for 4 and 5 Voices (Venice, 1565); *Il quinto libro de madrigali* for 5 Voices (Venice, 1566). The complete works, ed. by B. Meier, in Corpus Mensurabilis Musicae, commenced publication in 1959.
     BIBL.: U. Rossi, *Sei lettere di C. d.R., con cenni biografici* (Reggio Emilia, 1888); R. van Aerde, *Notice sur la vie et les oeuvres de C. d.R.* (Mechelen, 1909); J. Musiol, *Cyprian d.R., ein Meister der venezianischen Schule* (Breslau, 1933); A. Einstein, "C. d.R. and the Madrigal," *Bulletin of the American Musicological Society,* VI (1942); A. Johnson, "The Masses of C. d.R.," *Journal of the American Musicological Society,* VI (1953); D. Harran, "R. and the *Madrigale cromatico*," *Music Review,* XXXIV (1973); J. Owens, "C. d.R. a Parma (1560–1565): Nuovi documenti," *Rivista Italiana di Musicologia,* XI (1976); A. Johnson, "The 1548 Editions of C. d.R.'s Third Book of Madrigals," *Studies in Musicology in Honor of Otto E. Albrecht* (Kassel, 1977, and Clifton, N.J., 1980); R. Luoma, "Relationship between Music and Poetry (C. d.R.'s Quandro signor lasciaste)," *Musica Disciplina,* XXXI (1977); J. Owens, "Music and Meaning in C. d.R.'s Setting of 'Donec gratus eram tibi,'" *Studies in the History of Music* (vol. 1, N.Y., 1987).

Rorem, Ned, brilliant American composer, pianist, and writer; b. Richmond, Ind., Oct. 23, 1923. His parents were distinguished in various fields; his father was a medical economist and a founder of Blue Cross; his mother was active in various peace movements. At a very young age he was inculcated with piano music, which was taught to him at home by 3 consecutive female instructors. The family moved to Chicago, where Rorem began his formal study of theory and harmony with Leo Sowerby at the American Cons. (1938–39). He then entered Northwestern Univ., where he took composition courses with Alfred Nolte (1940–42). In 1943 he received a scholarship to study at the Curtis Inst. of Music in Philadelphia; there he studied counterpoint and harmony with Rosario Scalero; he also had beneficial instruction in dramatic and vocal music with Gian Carlo Menotti. In 1944 Rorem moved to N.Y. and entered the Juilliard School of Music, where he studied composition with Bernard Wagenaar (B.S., 1946; M.S., 1948); he also took private lessons in orchestration with Virgil Thomson (1944); in the summers of 1946 and 1947 he studied modern harmony with Aaron Copland at the Berkshire Music Center at Tanglewood, in Lenox, Mass. He was fortunate in obtaining the Gershwin Memorial Award, which enabled him to travel to France. There he rapidly absorbed the musical arts of the period and also mastered the French language. From 1949 to 1951 he sojourned in Morocco. Returning to Paris, he obtained the patronage of a famous friend of the arts, the Vicomtesse Noailles, and entered the circle of modern Parisian composers. The French influence remains the most pronounced characteristic of his music, particularly in his songs. Upon his return to the U.S. in 1958, he was appointed composer-in-residence at the State Univ. of N.Y. at Buffalo (1959–60); also taught at the Univ. of Utah (1966–67) and the Curtis Inst. of Music (1980–86). He developed as a composer of substance and originality, proclaiming that music must sing, even if it is written for instruments. Between times he almost unexpectedly discovered an astonishing talent as a writer. An elegant stylist in both French and English, he publ. a succession of personal journals, recounting with gracious insouciance his encounters in Paris and N.Y. He continued to obtain commissions from such prestigious institutions as the Ford Foundation and the Elizabeth Sprague Coolidge Foundation, as well as from a number of prominent performing groups. He received 2 Guggenheim fellowships (1956–57; 1978–79), and in 1976 was the recipient of the Pulitzer Prize in Music for his *Air Music*. He proudly declared that he wrote music for an audience and that he did not wish to indulge in writing songs and symphonic poems for an indefinite, abstract group. Rorem is regarded as one of the finest song composers in America; a born linguist, he has a natural feeling for vocal line and for prosody of text.

WORKS: **OPERAS:** *A Childhood Miracle* (1952; N.Y., May 10, 1955); *The Robbers* (1956; N.Y., April 14, 1958); *Miss Julie* (N.Y., Nov. 4, 1965); *3 Sisters Who Are Not Sisters* (1968; Philadelphia, July 24, 1971); *Bertha* (1968; N.Y., Nov. 26, 1973); *Fables* (1970; Martin, Tenn., May 21, 1971); *Hearing* (1976; N.Y., March 15, 1977). **ORCH.:** 3 piano concertos: No. 1 (1948; withdrawn); No. 2 (1950; Paris, 1954); No. 3, *Concerto in 6 Movements* (1969; Pittsburgh, Dec. 3, 1970); 3 syms.: No. 1 (1950; Vienna, 1951); No. 2 (La Jolla, Calif., Aug. 5, 1956); No. 3 (1957–58; N.Y., April 16, 1959); *Design* (1953; Louisville, May 28, 1955); *Sinfonia* for Symphonic Wind Orch. (Pittsburgh, July 14, 1957); *Eagles* (1958; Philadelphia, Oct. 23, 1959); *Pilgrims* for Strings (1958; N.Y., Jan. 30, 1959); *Ideas for Easy Orchestra* (1961); *Lions* (1963; N.Y., Oct. 28, 1965); *Water Music* for Clarinet, Violin, and Orch. (1966; Oakland, Calif., April 9, 1967); *Sun* (N.Y., July 1, 1967); *Solemn Prelude* (1973); *Air Music* (1974; Cincinnati, Dec. 5, 1975; won the Pulitzer Prize in Music, 1976); *Assembly and Fall* (Raleigh, N.C., Oct. 11, 1975); *Sunday Morning* (1977; Saratoga Springs, N.Y., Aug. 25, 1978); *Remembering Tommy* for Piano, Cello, and Orch. (1979); *Double Concerto in 10 Movements* for Cello, Piano, and Orch. (Cincinnati, Nov. 13, 1981); Organ Concerto (1984; Portland, Maine, March 19, 1985); Violin Concerto (1984; Springfield, Mass., March 30, 1985); String Sym. (Atlanta, Oct. 31, 1985); *A Quaker Reader* for Chamber Orch. (N.Y., Oct. 9, 1988; orchestration from the organ piece, 1976). **CHAMBER:** 2 string quartets: No. 1 (1947; withdrawn); No. 2 (1950); *Mountain Song* for Flute, or Oboe, or Violin, or Cello, and Piano (1949); Violin Sonata (1949); *11 Studies for 11 Players* (1959–60); Trio for Flute, Cello, and Piano (1960); *Lovers* for Harpsichord, Oboe, Cello, and Percussion (1964); *Day Music* for Violin and Piano (1971); *Night Music* for Violin and Piano (1972); *Book of Hours* for Flute and Harp (1975); *Sky Music* for Harp (1976); *Romeo and Juliet* for Flute and Guitar (1977); *3 Slow Pieces* for Cello and Piano (1978); *After Reading Shakespeare* for Cello (1980); Suite for Guitar (1980); *Winter Pages* for Clarinet, Bassoon, Piano, Violin, and Cello (1981); *Dances* for Cello and Piano (1983); *Picnic on the Marne* for Saxophone and Piano (1983); *The End of Summer* for Violin, Clarinet, and Piano (1985); *Scenes from Childhood*, septet for Oboe, Horn, Piano, 2 Violins, Viola, and Cello (1985); Trio for Clarinet, Violin, and Piano (1985); *Bright Music* for Flute, 2 Violins, Cello, and Piano (1988). **PIANO:** 3 sonatas (1948, 1949, 1954); *A Quiet Afternoon* (1948); *Barcarolles* (1949); *Sicilienne* for 2 Pianos (1950); *Slow Waltz* (1956); *8 Études* (1975); *Song and Dance* (1986). **ORGAN:** *A Quaker Reader* (1976; arrangement for Chamber Orch., 1988); *Views from the Oldest House* (1981). **VOCAL:** About 25 song cycles; numerous solo songs; various choral works; *An American Oratorio* for Tenor, Chorus, and Orch. (1983; Pittsburgh, Jan. 4, 1985); *Te Deum* for Chorus, 2 Trumpets, 2 Trombones, and Organ (1987).

WRITINGS (all publ. in N.Y.): *The Paris Diary of Ned Rorem* (1966; reprint, 1983, with *The New York Diary*, as *The Paris and New York Diaries*); *The New York Diary* (1967; reprint, 1983, with *The Paris Diary of Ned Rorem*, as *The Paris and New York Diaries*); *Music from Inside Out* (1967); *Music and People* (1969); *Critical Affairs: A Composer's Journal* (1970); *Pure Contraption* (1973); *The Final Diary* (1974; reprint, 1983, as *The Later Diaries*); *An Absolute Gift* (1978); *Setting the Tone: Essays and a Diary* (1983); *Paul's Blues* (1984); *The Nantucket Diary (1973–1985)* (1987); *Setting the Score: Essays on Music* (1988).

BIBL.: A. McDonald, *N. R.: A Bio-Bibliography* (Westport, Conn., 1989).

Ros-Marbá, Antoni, Spanish conductor; b. Barcelona, April 2, 1937. He studied at the Barcelona Cons., and later with Celibidache at the Accademia Chigiana in Siena and Martinon in Düsseldorf; after making his debut in Barcelona (1962), he conducted in Europe, the U.S., Mexico, and Israel. He was conductor of the Orquesta Sinfónica de Radio Televisión Española in Madrid (1966–68) and of the Orquesta Ciudad de Barcelona (1967–68). He was chief conductor of the Orquesta Nacional de España in Madrid (1979–81); served as principal conductor of the Netherlands Chamber Orch. (1979–85) and again as conductor of the Orquesta Ciudad de Barcelona (1981–86). In 1989 he became music director of the Teatro Real in Madrid.

Rosa, Carl (real name, **Karl August Nikolaus Rose**), German violinist, conductor, and operatic impresario; b. Hamburg, March 22, 1842; d. Paris, April 30, 1889. At 12 he made tours as a violinist in England, Denmark, and Germany; studied further in the conservatories of Leipzig (1859) and Paris; was concertmaster at Hamburg (1863–65); gave a concert at the Crystal Palace in London (March 10, 1866), and toured in the U.S. with Bateman, meeting the singer **Euphrosyne Parepa** and marrying her in N.Y. in 1867. They organized an English opera company and toured America until 1871; then returned to London. After his wife's death in 1874, he produced opera in English in various London theaters, forming the Carl Rosa Opera Co. (1875), which gave regular performances at the Theatre Royal at Drury Lane (from 1883). Following Rosa's death, the company became notably successful as a touring enterprise; was granted the title of the Royal Carl Rosa Opera Co. by Queen Victoria in 1893; it remained active until 1958.

Rosa, Salvator(e), Italian painter, poet, and musician; b. Arenella, near Naples, June 21, 1615; d. Rome, March 15, 1673. He studied music and became an expert lute player; from 1635 to 1640 he divided his time between Rome and Naples, and from 1640 to 1649 was court painter to the Medici at Florence; then lived in Rome. The pieces credited to Rosa by Burney and others have been proved to be spurious; it is doubtful whether Rosa ever composed music. His satire, *La musica*, written about 1640 and containing sharp criticism of Italian church music of his day, was publ. posthumously in 1695, and was reprinted several times; Mattheson attacked Rosa's views in his *Mithridat, wider den Gift einer welschen Satyre des Salvator Rosa* (1749).

BIBL.: N. d'Arienzo, "S. R. musicista," *Rivista Musicale Italiana* (1894); D. Battesti, *Saggio sulla vita e le satire di S. R.* (Bourges, 1913); F. Gerra, *S. R. e la sua vita romana dal 1650 al 1672 . . .* (a summary of 200 letters written by Rosa; Rome, 1937); F. Walker, "S. R. and Music," *Monthly Musical Record* (Oct. 1949 and Jan.–Feb. 1950).

Rosand, Aaron, gifted American violinist; b. Hammond, Ind., March 15, 1927. A child prodigy, he made his formal debut at age 9 in a recital at Chicago's Civic Opera House, sharing the occasion with Jan Peerce, who was also making his Chicago debut. After studies with P. Marinus Paulsen (1935–39) and Leon Sametini (1940–44), he completed his training with Zimbalist at the Curtis Inst. of Music in Philadelphia (1944–48). He made his N.Y. debut in a Town Hall recital (1948); following his European debut in Copenhagen (1955), he pursued an international career as a virtuoso. He taught at the Curtis

Inst. of Music (from 1981). A charismatic performer, blessed with a singing tone supported by an extraordinary technique, he established himself as a champion of the Romantic repertoire. In addition to the standard literature, he has consistently sought out rarely heard compositions by Spohr, Godard, Wieniawski, Lalo, Vieuxtemps, and many others for performance at his concerts.

Rosbaud, Hans, eminent Austrian conductor; b. Graz, July 22, 1895; d. Lugano, Dec. 29, 1962. He studied at the Hoch Cons. in Frankfurt; was director of the Hochschule für Musik in Mainz (1921–30); also conducted the City Orch. there; served as 1st Kapellmeister of the Frankfurt Radio and of the Museumgesellschaft concerts (1928–37); then was Generalmusikdirektor in Münster (1937–41) and in Strasbourg (1941–44); subsequently was appointed Generalmusikdirektor of the Munich Phil. (1945). In 1948 he became chief conductor of the Sym. Orch. of the Southwest Radio in Baden-Baden, and in 1957, music director of the Tonhalle Orch. in Zürich. He particularly distinguished himself as a conductor of modern works. He conducted the 1st performance of Schoenberg's *Moses und Aron* (concert perf., Hamburg, 1954); also conducted its 1st stage performance (Zürich, 1957).

BIBL.: J. Evans, "The H. R. Library at Washington State University, Pullman, Washington, U.S.A.," *Notes* (Sept. 1984).

Rösch, Friedrich, German composer; b. Memmingen, Dec. 12, 1862; d. Berlin, Oct. 29, 1925. He was a law student in Munich; studied music with Rheinberger; lived in Berlin, St. Petersburg, and Munich. In 1898 he, with Hans Sommer and Richard Strauss, organized the Genossenschaft Deutscher Tonsetzer (dissolved in 1937). He wrote a book, *Musikästhetische Streitfragen* (Leipzig, 1897).

WORKS: *Antonius,* a burlesque oratorio; numerous choral pieces in a humorous vein; 4-part madrigals for Men's Chorus; songs.

Rosé, Arnold (Josef), distinguished Austrian violinist and pedagogue; b. Iaşi, Oct. 24, 1863; d. London, Aug. 25, 1946. He studied under Karl Heissler at the Vienna Cons.; made his professional debut at the Gewandhaus in Leipzig, Oct. 30, 1879; in 1881 was appointed concertmaster of the Vienna Phil. and Opera orch.; held this post for 57 years; also founded the Rosé quartet in 1882, which won a high reputation throughout Europe; the quartet made its American debut at the Library of Congress in Washington, D.C., on April 28, 1928. Rosé taught at the Vienna Academy of Music (1893–1924). In the face of the Nazi Anschluss, he fled in 1938 to London, where he made his last public appearance in 1945. In 1902 Rosé married Justine Mahler, a sister of Gustav Mahler.

Rose, Bernard (William George), English organist, conductor, musicologist, and composer; b. Little Hallingbury, Hertfordshire, May 9, 1916. He studied with Sir Walter Alcock at the Royal College of Music in London (1933–35); subsequently was an organ scholar at St. Catharine's College, Cambridge, where his principal mentors were Hubert Middleton and Edward Dent (B.A., 1938; Mus.B., 1939). He then was organist (1939–57), teacher (1946–55), and lecturer (1955–81) at Queen's College, Oxford; was also made a supernumerary Fellow (1949) and an official Fellow (1954) there, obtaining his D.Mus. (1955). He served as organist, Informator choristarum, and Fellow at Magdalen College, Oxford (1957–81), where he also was vice-president (1973–75). Throughout his career he was active as a conductor, being mainly known for his choral performances. He was president of the Royal College of Organists (1974–76). In 1980 he was made an Officer of the Order of the British Empire. He prepared numerous eds. of English works ranging from the 16th to the 18th century; also composed a number of sacred works.

Rose, Jerome, noted American pianist and teacher; b. Los Angeles, Aug. 12, 1938. He was a pupil of Adolf Baller at the San Francisco Cons. (1952–56), making his debut at the age of 15 with the San Francisco Sym. Orch.; studied piano and chamber music with Leonard Shure at the Mannes College

of Music in N.Y. (B.S., 1960; M.S., 1961); also with Rudolf Serkin at the Marlboro (Vt.) School of Music (1956, 1965). In 1961 he captured 1st prize at the Busoni Competition in Bolzano, and then pursued an international career. In 1981 he organized the International Festival of the Romantics in London. In 1986 he organized the Franz Liszt Celebration in Washington, D.C., and was also awarded the Franz Liszt Medal by the Hungarian government. He was artist-in-residence at Bowling Green (Ohio) State Univ. (from 1963); also visiting artist-in-residence at the Univ. of Michigan in Ann Arbor (1984–85). Rose has won special praise for his performances of the Romantic repertoire; in addition to his compelling readings of Liszt, he provides fine interpretations of Beethoven, Schubert, Schumann, and Chopin. He is pianist-author of the film *For the Young Virtuoso: A Piano Masterclass with Jerome Rose* (1987).

Rose, Leonard (Joseph), eminent American cellist and pedagogue; b. Washington, D.C., July 27, 1918; d. White Plains, N.Y., Nov. 16, 1984. He began to study the cello at age 10; enrolled at the Miami Cons. when he was 11, and continued his training with Walter Grossman; then went to N.Y. to study with his cousin, Frank Miller; subsequently received a scholarship to the Curtis Inst. of Music in Philadelphia, where he completed his studies with Felix Salmond (1934–38). He was assistant 1st cellist of the NBC Sym. Orch. in N.Y. (1938–39); then was 1st cellist of the Cleveland Orch. (1939–43), and also served as head of the cello depts. at the Cleveland Inst. of Music and the Oberlin Cons. In 1943 he became 1st cellist of the N.Y. Phil.; appeared at his concerto debut with it at Carnegie Hall on Jan. 29, 1944; resigned his post in 1951 and embarked upon a brilliant career as a virtuoso of the 1st rank in appearances as a soloist with the world's great orchs.; also gave recitals and appeared in numerous chamber music settings, later serving as a member of the renowned Istomin-Stern-Rose Trio (from 1961). He taught at the Juilliard School of Music (1947–51; 1962–84) and at the Curtis Inst. of Music (1951–62). Among his notable pupils were Stephan Kates, Lynn Harrell, and Yo-Yo Ma.

Rösel, Artur, German violinist and composer; b. Münchenbernsdorf, Aug. 23, 1859; d. Weimar, April 3, 1934. He studied violin and composition in Weimar; was violinist in various theater orchs. in Hamburg, Lugano, and Rotterdam. In 1888 he became concertmaster of the Weimar Court Orch. He wrote a "lyric stage play," *Halimah* (Weimar, 1895); symphonic poem, *Frühlingsstürme*; 2 violin concertos; Viola Concerto; 2 string quartets; violin pieces.

Rösel, Peter, outstanding German pianist; b. Dresden, Feb. 2, 1945. In 1963 he won 2nd prize in the International Schumann Competition in Zwickau; he was then chosen by the German Democratic Republic's Ministry of Culture for further training at the Moscow Cons., where he studied with Dmitri Bashkirov and Lev Oborin, graduating in 1969. In 1978 he made a highly successful tour of the U.S. as piano soloist with the Gewandhaus Orch. of Leipzig. He became a prof. at the Dresden Hochschule für Musik in 1985. Apart from a brilliant technique, Rösel has a Romantic sensitivity characteristic of the Russian mode of instrumental playing; his repertoire is comprehensive, ranging from Mozart to Prokofiev.

BIBL.: H.-P. Müller, *P. R.: Für Sie porträtiert* (Leipzig, 1986).

Rosell, Lars-Erik, Swedish composer and organist; b. Nybro, Aug. 9, 1944. He studied organ (1962–68) and then was a composition student of Ingvar Lidholm at the Stockholm Musikhögskolan; then taught counterpoint there (from 1973); was also active as an organist, becoming well known for his advocacy of contemporary scores. In his music, he often requires improvisation from performers.

WORKS: *Moments of a Changing Sonority* for Harpsichord, Hammond Organ, and Strings (1969); *Terry Riley* for 3 Pianos (1970); *Twilight* for Chamber Ensemble (1970); *Dorian Mode* for Piano, Vibraphone, Clarinet, Cello, and Trombone (1971); *3 Psaltarpsalmer* for Chorus and Instruments (1971); *Poem* *in the Dark*, after Sachs, for Mezzo-soprano, Flute, Trombone, Double Bass, and Percussion (1972); *Efter syndafallet*, dramatic scene after Arthur Miller's play *After the Fall*, for Soprano, Alto, Baritone, and Instrumental Ensemble (Stockholm, Feb. 15, 1973); chamber opera, *Nattesang* (Copenhagen, Dec. 15, 1974); *Visiones prophetae*, biblical scene for Soloists, 3 Choruses, Wind Orch., Harp, Organ, and 2 Double Basses (Lund, June 27, 1974); *Musik* for Cello and String Orch. (Stockholm, March 4, 1975); *Expando* for Orch. (1976); *Reflections* for Trombone and Organ (1979); *Ordens källa*, scenic cantata (Stockholm, Nov. 7, 1980); *Stages* for 7 Instruments (1980); *Tillfalligt avbrott*, chamber opera (Stockholm, Dec. 12, 1981); Organ Concerto (Stockholm, Nov. 25, 1982); *Amedée*, chamber opera (1983–85).

Rosellen, Henri, French pianist, teacher, and composer; b. Paris, Oct. 13, 1811; d. there, March 18, 1876. He studied at the Paris Cons. with Zimmerman (piano) and Halévy (composition); later became a pupil of Henri Herz, under whose influence he began to compose salon music for piano. His *Rêverie* was fantastically popular for many years; also wrote *Nocturne et Tarentelle*; 12 *études brillantes*; 76 fantasias on operatic airs; variations for piano; chamber music. He was a highly successful teacher, and publ. a *Manuel des pianistes*.

Rosen, Charles (Welles), erudite American pianist and musicologist; b. N.Y., May 5, 1927. He studied piano with Moriz Rosenthal and music theory with Karl Weigl; then took a course in music history at Princeton Univ., receiving his B.A. summa cum laude in 1947 and his M.A. in 1949; also holds the degree of Ph.D. in Romance languages (1951). He made his N.Y. debut as pianist in 1951; was assistant prof. in modern languages at the Mass. Inst. of Technology (1953–55); in 1971, was appointed prof. of music at the State Univ. of N.Y. at Stony Brook; was the Ernest Bloch Prof. of Music at the Univ. of Calif., Berkeley, in 1976–77. He is equally adept as a virtuoso pianist, particularly in the modern repertoire, and as a brilliant writer on musical, philosophical, and literary subjects. In 1972 he received the National Book Award for his vol. *The Classical Style: Haydn, Mozart, Beethoven* (N.Y., 1971); also publ. *Arnold Schoenberg* (N.Y., 1975) and *Sonata Forms* (N.Y., 1980; 2nd ed., rev., 1988).

Rosen, Jerome (William), American clarinetist, teacher, and composer; b. Boston, July 23, 1921. He studied at New Mexico State Univ. in Las Cruces, and with William Denny and Roger Sessions at the Univ. of Calif. at Berkeley (M.A.); then, as recipient of a Ladd Prix de Paris, he went to Paris, where he continued his studies with Milhaud and also obtained a diploma as a clarinetist (1950). Upon his return to the U.S., he became a teacher at the Univ. of Calif. at Davis (1952); was made an associate prof. (1957) and a prof. (1963); also served as director of its electronic music studio; was made prof. emeritus (1988). **Works:** STAGE: *CHAMBER OPERA: Calisto and Melibea* (1978; Davis, Calif., May 31, 1979). MUSICAL PLAY: *Emperor Norton Lives!* (1976). DANCE SATIRES: *Search* (1953); *Life Cycle* (1954). ORCH.: Saxophone Concerto (1957; Sacramento, Calif., Jan. 24, 1958); 5 Pieces for Band (1960); *Sounds and Movements* (1963); Concerto for Clarinet, Trombone, and Band (1964); *Synket Concerto* (1968); 3 Pieces for 2 Recorders and Orch. (1972); Clarinet Concerto (1973; Sacramento, Calif., Dec. 4, 1976); *Campus Doorways* for Chorus and Orch. (1978). CHAMBER: Woodwind Quintet (1949); Sonata for Clarinet and Cello (1950); 2 string quartets (1953, 1965); Clarinet Quintet (1959); Serenade for Clarinet and Percussion (1967); Quintet for Saxophone and String Quartet (1974); Serenade for Clarinet and Violin (1977); *Play Time* for Clarinet and Double Bass (1981); *Play Time II* for Clarinet and String Quartet (1981). VOCAL: *13 Ways of Looking at a Blackbird*, song cycle for Soprano and Piano (1951); Serenade for Soprano and Saxophone (1964); *Chamber Music* for Women's Voices and Harp (1975); *White-Haired Lover*, song cycle for Baritone, Flute, Clarinet, String Quartet, and Piano (1985); *Love Poems*, song cycle for Male

and Female Speaking Voices, Flute, Clarinet, String Quartet, and Piano (1988).

Rosen, Max, Rumanian-born American violinist; b. Dorohoi, April 11, 1900; d. N.Y., Dec. 16, 1956. He was taken to the U.S. as an infant and studied with David Mannes in N.Y. In 1912 he went to Germany, where he had lessons with Leopold Auer; made his concert debut in Dresden, Nov. 16, 1915, and his American debut as soloist with the N.Y. Phil. (Jan. 12, 1918); then made tours of the U.S. (1918–21) and Europe (1921–26); subsequently appeared as a recitalist in N.Y. until his retirement there as a teacher in 1946.

Rosen, Nathaniel (Kent), American cellist and teacher; b. Altadena, Calif., June 9, 1948. He studied at Pasadena City College (1965–67) and with Gregor Piatigorsky at the Univ. of Southern Calif. in Los Angeles (Mus.B., 1971); made his debut as a soloist with the Los Angeles Phil. in 1969, and in 1970 won the Piatigorsky Award of the Violoncello Soc. of N.Y., which led to his N.Y. debut at Carnegie Recital Hall. He was an assistant prof. at Calif. State Univ. at Northridge (1970–76); also was principal cellist of the Los Angeles Chamber Orch. (1970–76) and of the Pittsburgh Sym. Orch. (1977–79). In 1978 he became the 1st American cellist to capture the Gold Medal at the Tchaikovsky Competition in Moscow; subsequently toured throughout the globe as a soloist, as a recitalist, and as a chamber music artist; taught at the Manhattan School of Music (from 1982).

Rosenberg, Hilding (Constantin), important Swedish composer and teacher; b. Bosjökloster, Ringsjön, Skåne, June 21, 1892; d. Stockholm, May 19, 1985. He studied piano and organ in his youth, and then was active as an organist. He went to Stockholm in 1914 to study piano with Andersson; then studied composition with Ellberg at the Stockholm Cons. (1915–16), and later took a conducting course there. He made trips abroad from 1920; then studied composition with Stenhammer and conducting with Scherchen. He was a répétiteur and assistant conductor at the Royal Opera in Stockholm (1932–34); also appeared as a guest conductor in Scandinavia and later in the U.S. (1948), leading performances of his own works; likewise was active as a teacher, numbering Bäck, Blomdahl, and Lidholm among his students. Rosenberg was the foremost Swedish composer of his era. He greatly influenced Swedish music by his experimentation and stylistic diversity, which led to a masterful style marked by originality, superb craftsmanship, and refinement.

Works: STAGE: *OPERAS: Resa till Amerika* (Journey to America; Stockholm, Nov. 24, 1932; orch. suite, Stockholm, Sept. 29, 1935); *Spelet om St. Örjan*, children's opera (1937; rev. 1941); *Marionetter* (1938; Stockholm, Feb. 14, 1939; 2 suites for Small Orch., 1926; overture and dance suite, 1938); *De två konungadöttrarna* (The 2 Princesses), children's opera (Swedish Radio, Stockholm, Sept. 19, 1940); *Lycksalighetens ö* (The Isle of Bliss; 1943; Stockholm, Feb. 1, 1945; *Vindarnas musik* for Orch. from the opera, 1943); *Josef och hans bröder* (Joseph and His Brothers), opera-oratorio after the novel by Thomas Mann (1946–48; Swedish Radio, Stockholm: part 1, May 30, 1946; part 2, Dec. 19, 1946; part 3, Sept. 9, 1947; part 4, Jan. 23, 1948; Partita for Orch. from the opera-oratorio, 1948); *Kaspers fettisdag* (Kasper's Shrove Tuesday), chamber opera (1953; Swedish Radio, Stockholm, Feb. 28, 1954); *Porträtett* (The Portrait), radio opera after Gogol (1955; Swedish Radio, Stockholm, March 22, 1956; rev. 1963); *Hus med dubbel ingång* (The House with 2 Doors), lyric comedy after Calderón (1969; Stockholm, May 24, 1970). BALLETS: *Eden* (1946; based on the Concerto No. 1 for Strings, 1946); *Salome* (1963; Stockholm, Feb. 28, 1964; based on the *Metamorfosi sinfoniche* Nos. 1 and 2, 1963); *Sönerna* (The Sons; Swedish TV, Stockholm, Dec. 6, 1964; based on the *Metamorfosi sinfoniche* No. 3, 1964); *Babels torn* (The Tower of Babel; 1966; Swedish TV, Stockholm, Jan. 8, 1968; based on the Sym. for Wind and Percussion, 1966). PANTOMIME: *Yttersta domen* (The Last Judgment; 1929; not perf.; 2 preludes and 2 suites for Orch. from the pantomime, 1929). MELODRAMAS: *Prometheus och*

Ahasverus (Swedish Radio, Stockholm, April 27, 1941); *Djufars visa* (Djufar's Song; Swedish Radio, Stockholm, Dec. 18, 1942; suite for Orch. from the melodrama, 1942).

ORATORIOS: *Den heliga natten* (The Holy Night; Swedish Radio, Stockholm, Dec. 27, 1936); *Perserna* (The Persians; 1937; not perf.); *Huvudskalleplats* (Calvary), for Good Friday (Swedish Radio, Stockholm, April 15, 1938; rev. 1964–65); *Svensk lagsaga* (Swedish Radio, Stockholm, Feb. 24, 1942); *Hymnus* (1965; Swedish Radio, Stockholm, July 24, 1966).

CANTATAS: *Julhymn av Romanus* (Swedish Radio, Stockholm, Dec. 25, 1941); Cantata for the National Museum (1942; Swedish Radio, Stockholm, June 1, 1943); *Lyrisk svit* (Göteborg, Oct. 2, 1954); *Hymn to a University* (1967; Lund, June 13, 1968).

ORCH.: Syms.: No. 1 (1917; rev. 1919; Göteborg, April 5, 1921; rev. 1922–71; Stockholm, May 18, 1974); No. 2, *Sinfonia grave* (1928–35; Göteborg, March 27, 1935); No. 3 (Swedish Radio, Stockholm, Dec. 11, 1939; orig. subtitled *De fyra tidsåldrarna* [The 4 Ages of Man], with text from Rolland's novel *Jean Christoph*; rev. 1952); No. 4, *Johannes uppenbarelse* (The Revelation of St. John), with Baritone and Chorus (Swedish Radio, Stockholm, Dec. 6, 1940); No. 5, *Hortulanus* or *Örtagårdsmästaren* (The Keeper of the Garden), with Alto and Chorus (Swedish Radio, Stockholm, Oct. 17, 1944); No. 6, *Sinfonia semplice* (1951; Gavle, Jan. 24, 1952); Sym. for Wind and Percussion (1966; Göteborg, Oct. 27, 1972; music also used in the ballet *Babels torn*, 1966); No. 7 (Swedish Radio, Stockholm, Sept. 29, 1968); No. 8, *In candidum*, with Chorus (1974; Malmö, Jan. 24, 1975); *Adagio* (1915); *3 fantasistycken* (1918; Göteborg, 1919); *Sinfonia da chiesa* No. 1 (1923; Stockholm, Jan. 16, 1925; rev. 1950) and No. 2 (1924; Stockholm, Jan. 20, 1926); Concerto No. 1 for Violin and Orch. (1924; Stockholm, May 8, 1927); Suite on Swedish Folk Tunes for Strings (Swedish Radio, Stockholm, Sept. 13, 1927); Threnody for Stenhammar (*Sorgemusik*) (1927); Concerto for Trumpet and Orch. (1928; Stockholm, Jan. 16, 1929); *Overtura piccola* (1934); Symphonie Concertante for Violin, Viola, Oboe, Bassoon, and Orch. (1935; Göteborg, Jan. 1936); Concerto No. 1 for Cello and Orch. (1939); *Adagio funèbre* (1940); suite, *I bergakungens sal* (In the Hall of the Mountain King; 1940); Concerto for Viola and Orch. (1942; Swedish Radio, Stockholm, Feb. 11, 1943); Concerto No. 1 for Strings (1946; Swedish Radio, Stockholm, July 6, 1947; music used in the ballet *Eden*, 1946); *Overtura bianca-nera* (1946); Concerto No. 2 for Orch. (1949; Malmö, Jan. 12, 1950); Concerto for Piano and Orch. (1950; Göteborg, March 14, 1951); Concerto No. 2 for Violin and Orch. (1951; Stockholm, March 25, 1952); *Ingresso solenne del premio Nobel* (1952); Concerto No. 2 for Cello and Orch. (1953; Swedish Radio, Stockholm, April 25, 1954); Variations on a Sarabande (1953); Concerto No. 3, *Louisville* (1954; Louisville, Ky., March 12, 1955; rev. 1968); *Riflessioni* No. 1 for Strings (1959; Swedish Radio, Stockholm, April 24, 1965), No. 2 for Strings (1960; Swedish Radio, Stockholm, March 2, 1962), and No. 3 for Strings (1960; Lucerne, 1961); *Dagdrivaren* (The Sluggard), with Baritone (1962; Stockholm, Oct. 28, 1964); *Metamorfosi sinfoniche* Nos. 1 to 3 (1963–64; music from Nos. 1 and 2 used in the ballet *Salome*, 1963; music from No. 3 used in the ballet *Sönerna*, 1964); Concerto No. 4 for Strings (1966; Stockholm, Sept. 14, 1968); various suites, preludes, partitas, etc., from operas, pantomimes, etc.; incidental music to almost 50 plays; film scores. CHAMBER: String quartets: No. 1 (1920; Stockholm, March 6, 1923); No. 2 (1924; Stockholm, March 6, 1925); No. 3, *Quartetto pastorale* (1926; Göteborg, April 3, 1932); No. 4 (1939; Stockholm, Nov. 2, 1942); No. 5 (1949; Stockholm, May 23, 1950); No. 6 (Stockholm, May 25, 1954); No. 7 (1956; Swedish Radio, Stockholm, Nov. 13, 1958); No. 8 (1956; Swedish Radio, Stockholm, Dec. 20, 1958); No. 9 (1956; Swedish Radio, Stockholm, March 17, 1959); No. 10 (1956; Swedish Radio, Stockholm, May 12, 1959); No. 11 (1956; Swedish Radio, Stockholm, Oct. 23, 1959); No. 12, *Quartetto riepilogo* (1956; Swedish Radio, Stockholm, Dec. 11, 1959); Trio for Flute, Violin, and Viola (1921); Sonata No. 1 for Violin and Piano (1926); Trio for Oboe, Clarinet,

and Bassoon (1927); *Taffelmusik* for Piano Trio or Chamber Orch. (1939); Sonata No. 2 for Violin and Piano (1940); Wind Quintet (1959); 3 sonatas for Solo Violin (1921; 1953; 1963, rev. 1967); Sonata for Solo Flute (1959); Sonata for Solo Clarinet (1960); numerous piano works; also choral pieces; songs.

BIBL.: M. Pergament, *H. R., a Giant of Modern Swedish Music* (Stockholm, 1956); P. Lyne, *H. R.: Catalogue of Works* (Stockholm, 1970).

Rosenblum, Mathew, American composer; b. N.Y., March 19, 1954. He studied at the New England Cons. of Music in Boston (B.M., 1977; M.M., 1979) and Princeton Univ. (M.F.A., 1981); in 1980 he won the Rockefeller Foundation Contemporary American Chamber Works award; also received grants and awards from BMI (1978), the New Jersey State Council on the Arts (1981), the Inst. of Contemporary American Music (1981), the American Composers Alliance (1987), and the N.Y. Foundation for the Arts (1989); was artist-in-residence at the MacDowell Colony, the Djerassi Foundation, and Yaddo. His recent works use hybrid tuning systems which combine both just- and equal-tempered intervals.

WORKS: *Harp Quartet* for Alto Flute/Flute, Bass Clarinet/Clarinet, Viola, and Harp (N.Y., Dec. 8, 1980); *Cascades* for Violin (1982; Glassboro, N.J., April 30, 1983); *Le Jon Ra* for 2 Cellos (1983; N.Y., April 24, 1987); *Continental Drift* for Horn, Percussion, and 2 Keyboards (San Francisco, Sept. 26, 1988); *Circadian Rhythms* for Cello, Percussion, and 2 Keyboards (N.Y., June 6, 1989; also for Clarinet, Harp, Synthesizer, and 2 Percussion; Oslo, Sept. 24, 1990).

Rosenboom, David (Charles), American composer, performer, designer and maker of electronic instruments, and teacher; b. Fairfield, Iowa, Sept. 9, 1947. He took courses in composition and electronic and computer music at the Univ. of Illinois at Urbana, where his principal mentors were Gordon Binkerd, Salvatore Martirano, Kenneth Gaburo, and Lejaren Hiller; also studied theory, conducting, physics, computer science, and experimental psychology. In 1967–68 he was a creative associate at the Center for Creative and Performing Arts at the State Univ. of N.Y. at Buffalo and artistic coordinator of the Electric Circus in N.Y.; also in N.Y., was co-founder and president of the Neurona Co., a research and development firm for electronics in the arts (1969–71). From 1972 to 1979 he taught at York Univ. in Toronto; concurrently served as director of the Laboratory of Experimental Aesthetics at the Aesthetic Research Center of Canada, where he pursued studies in information processing as it relates to esthetics; his studies resulted in several musical works. With D. Buchla, he developed the Touché, a computerized keyboard instrument, during his period as a software developer with Buchla's firm in Berkeley, Calif. (1979–80). In 1979 he joined the faculty of Mills College in Oakland, Calif., where he was associate prof. of music and director of the Center for Contemporary Music (from 1983); also was head of the music dept. (from 1984), holder of the Darius Milhaud Chair in Music (from 1988), and prof. of music (1989–90) there. From 1981 to 1984 he also taught at the San Francisco Art Inst. In 1990 he became dean of music at the Calif. Inst. of the Arts. He wrote a number of articles on contemporary music for various journals and publications; ed. the book *Biofeedback and the Arts: Results of Early Experiments* (1975) and brought out the vol. *Selected Articles 1968–1982* (1984); also publ. a *Leonardo* monograph, *Extended Musical Interface with the Human Nervous System: Assessment and Prospectus* (1990). His music is generally experimental in nature, explorative of unique notation systems, improvisation, and extended instrumental techniques. He designed and co-developed H(ierarchical)M(usic)(Specification) L(anguage), a widely used programmimg language for interactive computer music systems (1987).

WORKS: *Contrasts* for Violin and Orch. (1963); *Caliban upon Setebos* for Orch. (1966); *The Brandy of the Damned*, theater piece, with Electronic Tape (1967); *How Much Better if Plymouth Rock Had Landed on the Pilgrims* for Variable Ensembles, Electronics, and Outdoor Environments (1969–72); *On Being*

Invisible for Soloist, with Computer-assisted Brain Signal Analysis and Electronic Music System, Touch Sensors, and Small Acoustic Sources (1976–77); *In the Beginning: I (Electronic)* for Soloist, with Computer-assisted Electronic Music System (1978), *II (Quartet)* for 2 or 4 Cellos and 2 Violas, Trombone, and Percussion (1979), *III (Quintet)* for Woodwind Quintet (1979), *Étude I (Trombones)* for any number of Trombones (1979), *IV (Electronic)* for Soloist, with Computer-assisted Electronic Music System (1980), *Étude II (Keyboards/Mallets/Harps)* for 2, 4, 6, or 8 Players (1980), *Étude III (Piano and 2 Oranges)* for Piano (1980), and *V (The Story)* for Chamber Orch., Film or Video, and Synthetic Speech (1980); *Future Travel* for Piano, Violin, and Computer Music System (1982; rev. 1987); *Champ Vital (Life Field)*, trio for Violin, Piano, and Percussion (1987); *Systems of Judgment*, tape collage (1987); *2 Lines*, duets for Melodic Instruments (1989); also film music; improvisational pieces; sound sculptures; many other works.

Rosenfeld, Leopold, Danish composer and writer on music; b. Copenhagen, July 21, 1850; d. there, July 19, 1909. He studied at the Copenhagen Cons. and was music critic of *Musikbladet*; wrote several choral works with orch., of which *Henrik og Else* (Copenhagen, Feb. 7, 1885) had considerable success; he also publ. a number of piano pieces and about 200 songs to German and Danish texts.

Rosenfeld, Paul (Leopold), American author and music critic; b. N.Y., May 4, 1890; d. there, July 21, 1946. He studied at Yale Univ. (B.A., 1912) and at Columbia Univ. School of Journalism (Litt.B., 1913). He then associated himself with progressive circles in literature and music; wrote music criticism for *The Dial* (1920–27); contributed also to other literary and music magazines. Although not a musician by training, Rosenfeld possessed a penetrating insight into musical values; he championed the cause of modern American music. He collected the most significant of his articles in book form: *Musical Portraits* (on 20 modern composers; 1920); *Musical Chronicle*, covering the N.Y. seasons 1917–23 (1923); *An Hour with American Music* (1929); *Discoveries of a Music Critic* (1936). Analects from his articles were publ. as *Musical Impressions* (N.Y., 1969).

BIBL.: J. Mellquist and L. Wiese, eds., *P. R., Voyager in the Arts* (N.Y., 1948); H. Leibowitz, "Remembering P. R.," *Salmagundi* (Spring 1969); B. Mueser, *The Criticism of New Music in N.Y.: 1919–1929* (City Univ. of N.Y., 1975); C. Silet, *The Writings of P. R.: An Annotated Bibliography* (N.Y., 1981).

Rosenhain, Jacob (Jakob or **Jacques),** German pianist and composer; b. Mannheim, Dec. 2, 1813; d. Baden-Baden, March 21, 1894. He was a child prodigy, making his debut in Frankfurt when he was 8; studied with Kalliwoda, Jakob Schmitt, and Schnyder von Wartensee. In 1837 he went to Paris and London; continued to travel until 1870, when he settled as a teacher in Baden-Baden. His brother **Eduard Rosenhain** (b. Mannheim, Nov. 16, 1818; d. Frankfurt am Main, Sept. 6, 1861) was also a noteworthy pianist and teacher; he wrote a Serenade for Cello and Piano, and piano pieces. **WORKS: OPERAS:** *Der Besuch im Irrenhause* (Frankfurt, Dec. 29, 1834); *Le Démon de la nuit* (Paris, March 17, 1851); *Le Volage et jaloux* (Baden-Baden, Aug. 3, 1863). **ORCH.:** 3 syms.; Piano Concerto. **CHAMBER:** 4 piano trios; 3 string quartets; 2 cello sonatas; piano pieces. **BIBL.:** E. Kratt-Harveng, *Jacques R., Komponist und Pianist; Ein Lebensbild* (Baden-Baden, 1891).

Rosenman, Leonard, American composer; b. N.Y., Sept. 7, 1924. He studied with local teachers; later took courses with Sessions, Dallapiccola, and briefly with Schoenberg. His main mundane occupation is that of a movie composer; he wrote the scores for such commercially notable films as *East of Eden, Rebel without a Cause,* and *The Chapman Report* (dealing with sexual statistics); also compiled music for television programs, among them *The Defenders* and *Marcus Welby, M.D.* But he is also the composer of a number of highly respectable and even elevated musical works, among them a Violin Concerto

and the challenging score *Foci* for 3 Orchs. His *Threnody on a Song of K. R.* (written to the memory of his wife, Kay Rosenman), a set of orch. variations on her original melody, was performed by the Los Angeles Phil., under the composer's direction, May 6, 1971. Among his later compositions are *Foci I* for Orch. (1981; rev. 1983) and *Chamber Music 5* for Piano and 6 Players (1979).

Rosenmüller, Johann, significant German composer; b. Ölsnitz, near Zwickau, c.1619; d. Wolfenbüttel (buried), Sept. 12, 1684. He studied music at the Ölsnitz Lateinschule and theology at the Univ. of Leipzig (1640); was made an assistant at the Leipzig Thomasschule to teach music in 1642, being made 1st assistant in 1650; was also named organist of the Nicolaikirche in 1651 and music director in absentia of the Altenburg court in 1654; lost these posts when he and several of the schoolboys were arrested and incarcerated as homosexuals in 1655. Rosenmüller escaped and eventually made his way to Venice, where he became a trombonist at San Marco in 1658; secured a position as a composer there by 1660, and later was composer at the Ospedale della Pietà (1678–82); then returned to Germany to serve as Kapellmeister at the Wolfenbüttel court. He was a distinguished composer of both sacred vocal works and instrumental music. His compositions were well known in Germany and helped to advance the acceptance of the northern Italian styles.

WORKS: SACRED VOCAL: *Kern-Sprüche mehrentheils aus heiliger Schrifft Altes und Neues Testaments* for 1 to 5 Voices, Strings, and Basso Continuo (Leipzig, 1648; some ed. by D. Krüger, Hohenheim, near Stuttgart, 1960–68); *Andere Kern-Sprüche* for 1 to 5 Voices, Strings, and Basso Continuo (Leipzig, 1652–53; some ed. by A. Tunger, Hohenheim, near Stuttgart, 1960–63); *8 Funeral Songs* for 5 Voices (Leipzig, 1649–54; ed. by F. Hamel in *Acht Begräbnisgesänge zu fünf Stimmen,* Wolfenbüttel, 1930); *Magnificat* for 8 Voices, 5 Strings, Brass, and Basso Continuo; *Dies irae* for 4 Voices, 6 Strings, and Basso Continuo; *Gloria in excelsis Deo* for 8 Voices, 3 Strings, Brass, and Basso Continuo; *Lamentationes Jeremiae* for Voice and Basso Continuo (ed. by F. Hamel in *Nagels Musikarchiv,* XXVII–XXVIII); *Missa* for 4 Voices and Basso Continuo; *Missa brevis* for 5 Voices, 5 Strings, Brass, and Basso Continuo; *Nunc dimittis* for Voice, 3 Strings, and Basso Continuo; *Nunc dimittis* for 4 Voices, 5 Strings, and Basso Continuo; numerous other works to Latin or German texts. **INSTRUMENTAL:** *Paduanen, Alemanden, Couranten, Balletten, Sarabanden, a 3* and Basso Continuo (Organ) (Leipzig, 1645); *Studenten-Music* for 3 and 5 Strings and Basso Continuo (Leipzig, 1654; ed. by F. Hamel in *Nagels Musikarchiv,* LXI, 1929); *11 Sonate da camera* for 5 Strings and Other Instruments (Venice, 1667; ed. by K. Nef in *Denkmäler Deutscher Tonkunst,* XVIII, 1904); *12 Sonate* for 2 to 5 Strings and Other Instruments and Basso Continuo (Nuremberg, 1682; ed. by E. Pätzold, Berlin, 1954–56); various other sonatas, canons, dances, and other pieces in MS collections.

BIBL.: A. Horneffer, *J. R. (ca. 1619–1684)* (Charlottenburg, 1898); F. Hamel, *Die Psalmkompositionen J. R.s* (Strasbourg, 1933); A. Lehmann, *Die Instrumentalwerke von J. R.* (diss., Univ. of Leipzig, 1965); K. Snyder, *J. R.'s Music for Solo Voice* (diss., Yale Univ., 1970).

Rosenshein, Neil, American tenor; b. N.Y., Nov. 27, 1947. He studied at Wilkes College in Wilkes-Barre, Pa. (1967), and with Jennie Tourel and others at N.Y.'s Juilliard School (1969); made his operatic debut as Count Almaviva in *Il Barbiere di Siviglia* in Cocoa Beach, Fla. (1972); his 1st appearance in Europe was as Tom Rakewell in *The Rake's Progress* with the Netherlands Opera in Amsterdam (1982). He made frequent appearances with the major U.S. and European opera houses thereafter, and also sang with the leading orchs. on both sides of the Atlantic. On June 2, 1986, he made his Covent Garden debut in London as Lensky in *Eugene Onegin*. He made his Metropolitan Opera debut in N.Y. as Alfredo in *La Traviata* on Nov. 19, 1987. In 1988 he sang in the premiere of Argento's *The Aspern Papers* in Dallas. Among his other roles are Belmonte in *Die Entführung aus dem Serail*, Tamino in *Die Zauberflöte*, Oberon, Werther, Alfred in *Die Fledermaus*, Alfonso in Korngold's *Violanta*, and the title role in Stravinsky's *Oedipus Rex*.

Rosenstock, Joseph, Polish-born American conductor; b. Krakow, Jan. 27, 1895; d. N.Y., Oct. 17, 1985. He studied in Krakow and at the Vienna Cons.; also received instruction from Franz Schreker. He was assistant conductor at the Stuttgart Opera (1919–20); was a conductor (1920–22) and Generalmusikdirektor (1922–25) at the Darmstadt Opera; then was Generalmusikdirektor at the Wiesbaden Opera (1927–29). On Oct. 30, 1929, he made his Metropolitan Opera debut in N.Y. conducting *Die Meistersinger von Nürnberg*; returning to Germany, he became Generalmusikdirektor at the Mannheim National Theater in 1930. As a Jew, he was removed from his post by the Nazis in 1933; he then conducted the Jüdisches Kulturbund in Berlin until 1936. He went to Tokyo to become conductor of the Nippon Phil. (1936); as an alien, he lost his post and was removed to Karuizawa with the Japanese attack on Pearl Harbor in 1941; after his liberation in 1945, he returned to Tokyo to help reorganize musical life under the U.S. occupation forces. In 1946 he settled in the U.S.; became a naturalized citizen in 1949. He became a conductor at the N.Y. City Opera in 1948, and subsequently was its general director (1952–56); after serving as music director of the Cologne Opera (1958–60), he conducted at the Metropolitan Opera in N.Y. (1960–69).

Rosenthal, Harold (David), English music editor and critic; b. London, Sept. 30, 1917; d. there, March 19, 1987. He received his B.A. degree from Univ. College, London, in 1940; served as a noncombatant in the British army during World War II; in 1950 he launched, with the Earl of Harewood, the magazine *Opera* and was its ed. (1953–86). He was archivist of the Royal Opera House (1950–56); contributed to many European and American music journals; wrote numerous biographical entries on singers for *The New Grove Dictionary of Music and Musicians* (1980); was made an Officer of the Order of the British Empire (1983). His publications, all publ. in London, included *Sopranos of Today* (1956), *Two Centuries of Opera at Covent Garden* (1958), ed. with J. Warrack, *The Concise Oxford Dictionary of Opera* (1964; 2nd ed., rev., 1979), and *Covent Garden: A Short History* (1967). He ed. *The Opera Bedside Book* (1965) and *The Mapleson Memoirs* (1966); also wrote an autobiography, *My Mad World of Opera* (1982).

Rosenthal, Manuel (actually, **Emmanuel**), French composer and conductor; b. Paris (of a French father and a Russian mother), June 18, 1904. He studied violin and composition at the Paris Cons. (1918–23); also took some lessons with Ravel. He was co-conductor of the Orch. National de la Radiodiffusion in Paris from 1934 until his mobilization as an infantryman at the outbreak of World War II in 1939; after being held as a prisoner of war in Germany (1940–41), he was released and returned to France, where he became active in the Résistance. After the liberation, he served as chief conductor of the French Radio orch. (1944–47); made his 1st tour of the U.S. in 1946; in 1948, was appointed instructor in composition at the College of Puget Sound in Tacoma, Wash. In 1949 he was engaged as conductor of the Seattle Sym. Orch.; was dismissed summarily for moral turpitude in Oct. 1951 (the soprano who appeared as soloist with the Seattle Sym. Orch. under the name of Mme. Rosenthal was not his legal wife). In 1962 he was appointed prof. of conducting at the Paris Cons.; was conductor of the Liège Sym. Orch. (1964–67). He made his belated Metropolitan Opera debut in N.Y. on Feb. 20, 1981, conducting a triple bill of Ravel's *L'Enfant et les sortilèges*, Poulenc's *Les Mamelles de Tirésias*, and Satie's *Parade*; returned there in subsequent seasons with notable success. He brought out the book *Satie, Ravel, Poulenc: An Intimate Memoir* (Madras and N.Y., 1987). He composed a number of works in an entertaining manner, expertly orchestrated, but he remains best known for his brilliant and highly successful arrangement of music from various Offenbach operettas as the ballet *Gaîté parisienne* (1938).

WORKS: STAGE: *La Poule noire*, comédie musicale (1934–37); *Gaîté parisienne*, ballet after Offenbach (Monte Carlo, April 5, 1938); *Que le diable l'emporte*, ballet (1948). **ORCH.:** *Les Petits Métiers* (1936); *La Fête du vin* (1937); *Musique de table* (1941); *2 études en camaïeu* (1969); *Aeolus* for Wind Quintet and Orch. (1970). **CHORAL:** *Saint François d'Assise* for Speaker, Chorus, and Orch. (1936–39; Paris, Nov. 1, 1944); *Cantate pour le temps de la Nativité* for Soprano, Chorus, and Orch. (1943–44); *Deo Gratias Mass* for Soloists, Chorus, and Orch. (1953). **CHAMBER:** *Saxophone-Marmelade* for Alto Saxophone and Piano (1929); *Les Soirées du petit Jesus* for String Quartet (1942); also piano pieces and songs.

Rosenthal, Moriz, famous Austrian pianist; b. Lemberg, Dec. 17, 1862; d. N.Y., Sept. 3, 1946. He studied piano at the Lemberg Cons. with Karol Mikuli, who was a pupil of Chopin; in 1872, when he was 10 years old, he played Chopin's Rondo in C for 2 Pianos with his teacher in Lemberg. The family moved to Vienna in 1875, and Rosenthal became the pupil of Joseffy, who inculcated in him a passion for virtuoso piano playing, which he taught according to Tausig's method. Liszt accepted Rosenthal as a student during his stay in Weimar and Rome (1876–78). After a hiatus of some years, during which Rosenthal studied philosophy at the Univ. of Vienna, he returned to his concert career in 1884, and established for himself a reputation as one of the world's greatest virtuosos; was nicknamed (because of his small stature and great pianistic power) "little giant of the piano." Beginning in 1888 he made 12 tours of the U.S., where he became a permanent resident in 1938. He publ. (with L. Schytte) a *Schule des höheren Klavierspiels* (Berlin, 1892). His wife, **Hedwig Kanner-Rosenthal,** was a distinguished piano teacher.

Rosetti (real name, **Rösler**), (**Francesco) Antonio** (actually, **Franz Anton** or **František Antonín**), Bohemian composer; b. Leitmeritz, c.1750; d. Ludwigslust, June 30, 1792. For many years Rosetti was confused with a Bohemian cobbler named Franz Anton Rösler, who was born in Niemes in 1746 and whose date of birth was erroneously listed as that of Rosetti; by adopting the name of Antonio Rosetti, he created further problems by being confused with 5 contemporary musicians with that name. He was a theological student; was engaged as a string player in court orchs.; in 1789 he became Kapellmeister to the Duke of Mecklenburg-Schwerin. He was a prodigiously fertile composer who wrote in the manner of Haydn and Boccherini, and was even dubbed "a German Boccherini." He wrote 3 Requiems; one of these was composed in memory of Mozart; it was performed in Prague shortly after Mozart's death in 1791; its score is unfortunately lost. His other works include *Das Winterfest der Hirten*, drama with Orch. (Ludwigslust, Dec. 10, 1789), over 40 publ. syms., 5 piano concertos, 7 violin concertos, 4 clarinet concertos, about 10 flute concertos, 15 horn concertos, 6 concertos for 2 Horns, 8 bassoon concertos, etc. He also composed works for wind instruments and numerous other chamber works, as well as songs.

BIBL.: H. Kaul, *Anton Rosetti: Sein Leben und seine Werke* (diss., Univ. of Munich, 1911); H. Fitzpatrick, "Antonio Rosetti," *Music & Letters*, XLIII (1962); S. Murray, "The Rösler-Rosetti Problem: A Confusion of Pseudonym and Mistaken Identity," ibid., LVII (1976).

Rosier, Carl, Flemish violinist and composer; b. Liège, Dec. 26, 1640; d. Cologne, before Dec. 12, 1725. He became a violinist at the Bonn electoral court about 1664, and subsequently was Vice-Kapellmeister; went to Cologne in 1675, but was also active as a violinist in Holland from about 1683 to 1699; was appointed Kapellmeister of the Cologne Cathedral in 1699 and also of the city in 1701. He was an accomplished composer of instrumental music.

BIBL.: U. Niemöller, *C. R. (1640–1725), Kölner Dom- und Ratskapellmeister, Beiträge zur rheinischen Musikgeschichte*, XXIII (Cologne, 1957).

Rosing, Vladimir, Russian-American tenor and opera director; b. St. Petersburg, Jan. 23, 1890; d. Los Angeles, Nov. 24, 1963. He studied voice with Jean de Reszke; made his debut in St. Petersburg in 1912; gave a successful series of recitals in programs of Russian songs in London between 1913 and 1921. In 1923 he was appointed director of the opera dept. at the Eastman School of Music in Rochester, N.Y.; founded an American Opera Co., which he directed in a series of operatic productions in the English language. In 1939 he went to Los Angeles as organizer and artistic director of the Southern Calif. Opera Assoc.

Roslavetz, Nikolai (Andreievich), remarkable Russian composer; b. Suray, near Chernigov, Jan. 5, 1881; d. Moscow, Aug. 23, 1944. He studied violin with his uncle and theory with A.M. Abaza in Kursk; then studied violin with Jan Hřímalý, and composition with Ilyinsky and Vassilenko, at the Moscow Cons., graduating in 1912; won the Silver Medal for his cantata *Heaven and Earth,* after Byron. A composer of advanced tendencies, he publ. in 1913 an atonal Violin Sonata, the 1st of its kind by a Russian composer; his 3rd String Quartet exhibits 12-tone properties. He ed. a short-lived journal, *Muzykalnaya Kultura,* in 1924, and became a leading figure in the modern movement in Russia. But with a change of Soviet cultural policy toward socialist realism and nationalism, Roslavetz was subjected to severe criticism in the press for persevering in his aberrant ways. To conciliate the authorities, he tried to write operettas; then was given an opportunity to redeem himself by going to Tashkent to write ballets based on Uzbek folk songs; he failed in all these pursuits. But interest in his music became pronounced abroad, and posthumous performances were arranged in West Germany.

WORKS: Sym. (1922); symphonic poems: *Man and the Sea,* after Baudelaire (1921), and *End of the World,* after Paul Lafargue (1922); Cello Sonata (1921); Violin Concerto (1925); cantata, *October* (1927); *Nocturne* for Harp, Oboe, 2 Violas, and Cello (1913); 3 string quartets (1913, 1916, 1920); 3 piano trios; 4 violin sonatas; *3 Dances* for Violin and Piano (1921); Cello Sonata (1921); 5 piano sonatas.

BIBL.: D. Gojowy, "N.A.R., ein früher Zwölftonkomponist," *Die Musikforschung,* XXII (1969; includes a detailed list of the location, dates of publication, etc., of extant works).

Rösler or **Rössler, Johann Joseph (Jan Josef),** Bohemian pianist and composer; b. Banska Stiavnica, Aug. 22, 1771; d. Prague, Jan. 28, 1813. He studied music with his father; was a composer for Prague's Nostitz Theater, where he brought out the opera *Elisene, Prinzessin von Bulgarien* (Oct. 18, 1807), the 1st original stage work to be produced there; went to Vienna (1805) and was active at the Court Theater; was also in the service of Countess Lobkowitz. His other works include keyboard sonatas, piano pieces, and the *Cantate auf Mozart's Tod* (1798). A movement from one of his piano concertos was erroneously attributed to Beethoven.

BIBL.: H. Engel, "Der angeblich Beethovensche Klavierkonzertsatz," *Neues Beethovenjahrbuch* (1925).

Rosner, Arnold, American composer; b. N.Y., Nov. 8, 1945. He studied mathematics at the State Univ. of N.Y. at Buffalo, and composition with Leo Smit, Allen Sapp, and Lejaren Hiller (Ph.D., 1972). He subsequently taught at various schools, including Kingsborough Community College (from 1983). His music is couched formally in a neo-Classical idiom, but he freely admits melodic, harmonic, and contrapuntal methods of the modern school of composition.

WORKS: OPERA: *The Chronicle of 9* (1984). **ORCH.:** 6 syms. (1961, 1961, 1963, 1964, 1973, 1976); 5 *Mystical Pieces* for English Horn, Harp, and Strings (1967; later rev. as 5 *Meditations*); 6 *Pastoral Dances* (1968); *A Gentle Musicke* for Flute and Strings (1969); *A Mylai Elegy* (1971); 2 concerti grossi (1974, 1979); 5 *Ko-ans* (1976); *Responses, Hosanna and Fugue* for Harp and String Orch. (1977); *Nocturne* (1978); *Tragedy to Queen Jane* (1982); *From the Diaries of Adam Czerniakow* for Narrator and Orch. (1986); *Trinity* for Symphonic Band (1988). **CHAMBER:** 5 string quartets (1962, 1963, 1965, 1972,

1975); Sonata for Flute and Cello (1962); 3 piano sonatas (1963, 1970, 1978); Woodwind Quintet (1964); Concertino for Harp, Harpsichord, Celesta, and Piano (1968; rev. 1988); Cello Sonata (1968); Sonata for Oboe or Violin and Piano (1972); *Musique de clavecin* for Harpsichord (1974); Brass Quintet (1978); Horn Sonata (1979); *Sonatine d'amour* for Harpsichord (1987); *A Plaintive Harmony* for Horn (1988). **VOCAL: CHORAL:** masses (1967, 1971, 1974); Requiem (1973); Magnificat (1979); *Let Them Praise* for Boys' Choir (1984). **SONGS:** 3 *Elegiac Songs* (1973); *Nightstone* (1979); *Besos sin Cuento,* 6 songs for Low Voice, Flute, Viola, and Harp (1989).

Rosowsky, Solomon, Latvian music scholar and composer; b. Riga, March 27, 1878; d. N.Y., July 30, 1962. He studied law at the Univ. of Kiev, and composition at the St. Petersburg Cons. with Liadov, Rimsky-Korsakov, and Glazunov. He was a co-founder of the Soc. for Jewish Folk Music in St. Petersburg in 1909; in 1920 he went back to Riga, and organized the 1st Jewish Cons. of Music; in 1925 he emigrated to Palestine; settled in N.Y. in 1947, devoting himself mainly to the music of biblical times, culminating in the publication of an important vol., *The Cantillation of the Bible* (N.Y., 1957). His compositions include a Piano Trio (1909) and several scores of incidental music for plays in Yiddish.

Ross, Diana, black American pop and soul singer; b. Detroit, March 26, 1944. She sang for social events in Detroit; then organized a female trio whose other members were her close contemporaries Florence Ballard and Mary Wilson, assuming the grandiose name of The Supremes. Florence Ballard dropped out in 1967 and was replaced by Cindy Birdsong, and the group thenceforth was called Diana Ross and The Supremes. Their hits included *Come See about Me, Stop! In the Name of Love, Baby Love, You Can't Hurry Love, I Hear a Symphony,* ad infinitum. The Supremes, and Ross as their top singer, broke the curse of drugs and alcohol besetting so many pop singers by campaigning for virtue and love sans narcotics. In 1969 Ross left The Supremes and started on a highly successful career as a solo singer, in cabarets, in nightclubs, on the radio, on television, in Las Vegas, on Broadway, and in the movies, where she starred in a film biography of Billie Holiday, *Lady Sings the Blues.* As a soloist she hit the top of the charts with an anti-drug number, *Reach Out and Touch,* and capped it with her logo song *Ain't No Mountain High Enough;* she recorded the eponymous album *Diana! An Evening with Diana Ross,* the generic song *Why Do Fools Fall in Love,* and a duet with Lionel Richie, *Endless Love.* She also pursued her career as an actress.

BIBL.: J. Haskins, *D. R.: Star Supreme* (N.Y., 1985).

Ross, Hugh (Cuthbert Melville), English-born American organist, choral conductor, and teacher; b. Langport, Aug. 21, 1898; d. N.Y., Jan. 20, 1990. He studied at the Royal College of Music in London and at New College, Oxford (D.Mus.); his principal mentors were Mengelberg and Vaughan Williams. In 1921 he went to Winnipeg as conductor of its Male Voice Choir; in 1922 he founded that city's Phil. Choir, and in 1923 its Orchestral Club, which later became the Winnipeg Sym. Orch. In 1927 he settled in N.Y. as conductor of the Schola Cantorum, which post he held until 1971; also appeared as a guest conductor throughout North America. He taught at the Manhattan School of Music (from 1930); was also chairman of the choral dept. at the Berkshire Music Center at Tanglewood (1941–62). In 1949 he became a naturalized U.S. citizen. He championed contemporary works.

Ross, Walter (Beghtol), American composer; b. Lincoln, Nebr., Oct. 3, 1936. He studied music at the Univ. of Nebraska, receiving an M.Mus. in 1962; then composition with Robert Palmer and conducting with Husa at Cornell Univ. (D.M.A., 1966). In 1967 he was appointed to the music faculty of the Univ. of Virginia. Much of his music is inspired by American themes.

WORKS: OPERA: *In the Penal Colony* (1972). **ORCH.:** Concerto for Brass Quintet and Orch. (1966); 2 trombone concertos (1970, 1982); *A Jefferson Symphony* for Tenor, Chorus, and

Orch. (Charlottesville, Va., April 13, 1976); Concerto for Wind Quintet and String Orch. (1977); *Nocturne* for String Orch. (1980); Concerto for Bassoon and String Orch. (1983); *Concerto* for Oboe, Harp, and String Orch. (1984); *Overture to the Virginian Voyage* (1986); Concerto for Flute, Guitar, and Orch. (1987); Sinfonietta Concertante for String Orch. (1987); Concerto for Euphonium, Symphonic Brass, and Timpani (1988); Piano Concerto (1989); many works for band. CHAMBER: *Cryptical Triptych* for Trombone and Piano (1968); *5 Dream Sequences* for Percussion Quartet and Piano (1968); *Canzona I* for 4 Trumpets, 4 Horns, 4 Trombones, 2 Euphoniums, 2 Tubas, and 3 Percussion (1969), *II* for the Same Instruments as *I* (1979), *III* for 12 Horns (1986), and *IV* for 4 Trumpets, 4 Horns, 4 Trombones, 2 Tubas, Timpani, and 2 Percussion (1989); 3 wind quintets (1974, 1985, 1989); String Trio (1978); Sonata for Violin and Piano (1981); Suite No. 1 for Chamber Ensemble (1983); 3 brass trios (1985, 1986, 1986); Brass Quintet No. 1 (1987); *Oil of Dog* for Brass Quintet and Actor (1988); also numerous vocal works.

Rosseau, Norbert (Oscar Claude), Belgian composer; b. Ghent, Dec. 11, 1907; d. there, Nov. 1, 1975. He played violin as a child; his family emigrated to Italy in 1921, and he studied piano with Silvestri and composition with Respighi at the Accademia di Santa Cecilia in Rome (1925–28). His early works are cast in a traditional style of European modernism; later he halfheartedly experimented with dodecaphony and electronics; some of his works bear pseudo-scientific titles, as, for example, the symphonic poem entitled H_2O.
WORKS: OPERAS: *Sicilenne* (1947); *Les Violons du prince* (1954). BALLET: *Juventa* (1957). VOCAL: *Inferno*, oratorio after Dante (1940); *L'An mille*, dramatic ode (1946); *Incantations*, cantata (1951); *Maria van den Kerselare*, Flemish oratorio (1952); *Zeepbellen*, chamber cantata, with Children's Chorus (1958); *Il Paradiso terrestre*, oratorio after Dante (1968). ORCH.: *Suite Agreste* (1936); *H$_2$O*, symphonic poem (1938; Liège, June 24, 1939); 2 concertos (1948, 1963); 2 syms.: No. 1 (1953) and No. 2, *Sinfonia sacra*, for Soloists, Chorus, and Orch. (1960–63); *Suite concertante* for String Quintet, Winds, Harpsichord, and Timpani (1959); Concerto for Wind Quintet and Orch. (1961); *Variations* (1963); Viola Concerto (1964); *Sonata a 4* for 4 Violins and Strings (1966); Horn Concerto (1967). CHAMBER: Violin Sonatina (1949); *3 jouets* for Oboe, Clarinet, and Bassoon (1955); Wind Quintet (1955); Clarinet Sonatina (1956); String Quartet (1956); Trio for Flute, Cello, and Piano (1956); *Rapsodie* for Flute, Bassoon, and Piano (1958); *Serenade à Syrinx* for Flute, Violin, Cello, and Harp (1959); Concertino for Piano, Double String Quartet, and Double Bass (1963); *Pentafonium* for Viola, Cello, Flute, Oboe, and Harpsichord (1964); *Diptique* for String Quartet (1971); *Dialogue* for Flute, Oboe, Viola, and Piano (1971); Piano Quartet (1975).

Rossellini, Renzo, Italian composer; b. Rome, Feb. 2, 1908; d. Monte Carlo, May 14, 1982. He studied composition in Rome with Setaccioli and Sallustio; also took courses in orchestration with Bernardino Molinari. In 1940 he was appointed prof. of composition at the Rome Cons., and in 1956 at the Accademia di Santa Cecilia. In 1973 he was named artistic director at the Opera at Monte Carlo. He publ. 2 books of autobiographical content, *Pagine di un musicista* (Bologna, 1964) and *Addio del passato* (Milan, 1968).
WORKS: OPERAS: *Alcassino e Nicoletta* (1928–30); *La guerra* (Rome, Feb. 25, 1956); *Il vortice* (Naples, Feb. 8, 1958); *Uno sguardo del ponte* (Rome, March 11, 1961); *L'Avventuriere* (Monte Carlo, Feb. 2, 1968); *La Reine morte* (Monte Carlo, 1973). BALLETS: *La danza di Dássine* (San Remo, Feb. 24, 1935); *Poemetti pagani* (Monte Carlo, 1963); *Il Ragazzo e la sua ombra* (Venice, 1966). ORCH.: *Suite in 3 tempi* (1931); *Ut unum sint* (Miami, Oct. 20, 1963); *Stornelli della Roma bassa* (1946); film music.

Rosseter, Philip, English lutenist and composer; b. 1567 or 1568; d. London, May 5, 1623. He became a lutenist to King James I in 1603; was also active in several theatrical ventures.

He publ. *A Booke of Ayres, set foorth to be song to the Lute, Orpharian, and Base Viol* (London, 1601; ed. by E. Fellowes and rev. by T. Dart in The English Lute-Songs, I, VIII, and IX, London, 2nd ed., 1966) and *Lessons for Consort* (London, 1609); also lute pieces in contemporary collections.
BIBL.: N. Fortune, "P. R. and His Songs," *Lute Society Journal*, VII (1965); I. Harwood, "R.'s *Lessons for Consort*, 1609," ibid.; R. Wells, "Ars amatoria: P. R. and the Tudor Court Lyric," *Music & Letters* (Feb. 1989).

Rossi, Abbate Francesco, Italian composer; b. Bari, c.1645; d. date unknown. He was a canon in Bari in 1680. He composed the operas *Bianca di Castiglia* (Milan, 1674); *Il Sejano moserno della Tracia* (Venice, 1680); *La pena degli occhi* and *La Clorilda* (both Venice, 1688); *Mitrane* (Venice, 1689); oratorio, *La Caduta degli angeli*; Requiem; Psalms; etc.

Rossi, Giovanni (Gaetano), Italian composer; b. Borgo S. Donnino, Parma, Aug. 5, 1828; d. Genoa, March 30, 1886. He studied at the Milan Cons.; from 1852, was maestro concertatore at the Teatro Regio in Parma; was also organist at the court chapel and deputy singing master at the Cons.; became deputy composition master (1853), composition master and vice-director (1856), and director (1864) of the Cons.; then was director of the Teatro Carlo Felice in Genoa (1874–86), and also of the Genoa Liceo Musicale (1874–86).
WORKS: Operas: *Elena di Taranto* (Parma, 1852); *Giovanni Giscala* (Parma, 1855); *Nicolò de Lapi* (Parma, 1865); *La Contessa d'Altenberg* (Borgo S. Donnino, 1871); also an oratorio, *Le sette parole*; overture, *Saulo*; a Requiem; 3 masses; etc.

Rossi, Giulio, Italian bass; b. Rome, Oct. 27, 1865; d. Milan, Oct. 9, 1931. He had a tenor voice until he was 19, when an unintentional plunge into the Tiber in Dec. induced an illness, after which his voice lowered to the range of *basso profondo*. He then began vocal study under Oreste Tomassoni; made his debut at Parma, Oct. 20, 1887. In 1889 he toured South America with Adelina Patti, and made 2 tours of Mexico and California with Luisa Tetrazzini; made his Metropolitan Opera debut in N.Y. as the King in *Aida* on Nov. 16, 1908, remaining on its roster until 1919.

Rossi, Lauro, Italian composer; b. Macerata, Feb. 19, 1810; d. Cremona, May 5, 1885. He was a pupil of Furno, Zingarelli, and Crescentini at Naples, bringing out a comic opera, *Le Contesse villane*, there (1829) with fair success. He was assistant director at the Teatro Valle in Rome (1831–33); with his 10th opera, *La casa disabitata o I falsi monetari*, produced at La Scala, Milan, Aug. 11, 1834, he won a veritable triumph; it made the rounds of Italy and was given in Paris. In 1835 he went to Mexico as conductor and composer to an Italian opera troupe; when it folded, he set up his own opera company, becoming its director in 1837, and going to Havana (1840) and New Orleans (1842), returning to Italy in 1843. He brought out a new opera, *Il Borgomastro di Schiedam* (Milan, June 1, 1844), with indifferent success; his opera *Il Domino nero* (Milan, Sept. 1, 1849) fared a little better. His most successful opera was *La Contessa di Mons* (Turin, Jan. 31, 1874). He wrote 29 operas in all. In 1850 he was given the post of director of the Milan Cons.; in 1870 he succeeded Mercadante as director of the Naples Cons.; resigned in 1878, and retired to Cremona in 1880.

Rossi-Lemeni, Nicola, Italian bass; b. Constantinople (of an Italian father and a Russian mother), Nov. 6, 1920, d. Bloomington, Ind., March 12, 1991. He was educated in Italy; studied law and planned a diplomatic career. In 1943 he decided to become a professional singer, but World War II interfered with his plans, and his debut as Varlaam in Venice did not take place until May 1, 1946. He 1st sang in the U.S. as Boris Godunov with the San Francisco Opera (Oct. 2, 1951); sang at the Metropolitan Opera in N.Y. in 1953–54. In 1980 he joined the faculty of Indiana Univ. in Bloomington. He married the soprano **Virginia Zeani.** Besides the regular operatic repertoire, he sang a number of roles in modern works, such as Wozzeck.

Rossi, Luigi, eminent Italian lutenist, keyboard player, singing teacher, and composer; b. Torremaggiore, Foggia, c.1597; d. Rome, Feb. 19, 1653. He studied in Naples with G. de Macque; then went to Rome, where his opera *Il palazzo incantato, overo La guerriera amante* was produced (Feb. 22, 1642). In 1646 he was called by Cardinal Mazarin to Paris with 20 other singers, and there staged his most important opera, *Orfeo* (March 2, 1647), the 1st Italian opera expressly written for a Paris production. He wrote besides the oratorio *Giuseppe* and some 300 chamber cantatas.

BIBL.: R. Rolland, "Notes sur l'Orfeo de L. R. et sur les musiciens italien à Paris sous Mazarin," *Revue d'Histoire et de Critique Musicales*, I (1901); A. Wotquenne, *Étude bibliographique sur le compositeur napolitain L. R.* (Brussels, 1909); H. Prunières, "Notes sur la vie de L. R.," *Sammelbände der Internationalen Musik-Gesellschaft*, XII (1910–11); A. Cametti, "Alcuni documenti inediti su la vita di L. R. compositore di musica (1597–1653)," ibid., XIV (1912–13); H. Prunières, "Notes bibliographiques sur les cantates de L. R. au Conservatoire de Naples," *Zeitschrift der Internationalen Musik-Gesellschaft*, XIV (1912–13); A. Cametti, "L. R., organista a San Luigi dei Francesi," *Critica musicale* (Florence, 1919); A. Ghislanzoni, *L. R.: Biografia e analisi delle composizioni* (Milan, 1954); E. Caluori, *The Cantatas of L. R.* (diss., Brandeis Univ., 1972).

Rossi, Mario, eminent Italian conductor; b. Rome, March 29, 1902. He studied at the Rome Cons. (graduated, 1925). He was deputy conductor of the Augusteo Orch. in Rome (1926–36) and resident conductor of the Maggio Musicale Orch. in Florence (1936–44); subsequently was chief conductor of the RAI Orch. in Turin (1946–69); also appeared as a guest conductor in Europe. He became especially well known for his performances of contemporary music.

Rossi, Michel Angelo, esteemed Italian violinist, organist, and composer, known as **Michel Angelo del Violino;** b. Genoa, 1601 or 1602; d. Rome (buried), July 7, 1656. His uncle, Lelio Rossi, was a Servite friar and principal organist at the cathedral of S. Lorenzo in Genoa; Michel Angelo served as his assistant until his own departure to Rome about 1624. There he entered the service of Cardinal Maurizio of Savoy; after studies with Frescobaldi, he won the patronage of the Barberini family in 1630; entered the service of the Este family in Modena in 1638, and also served the Sforza family in Ferrara; eventually returned to Rome. Rossi won special recognition as a violinist. His importance as a composer rests upon his output for keyboard, which included *Toccate e correnti* for Organ or Harpsichord (Rome, c.1640; 2nd ed., 1657; ed. in Corpus of Early Keyboard Music, XV, 1966). He also composed 2 operas: *Erminia sul Giordano* (Rome, Feb. 2, 1633) and *Andromeda* (Ferrara, 1638).

BIBL.: G. Rose, "Purcell, M. R. and J.S. Bach: Problems of Authorship," *Acta Musicologica*, XL (1968); J. Peterson, *The Keyboard Works of M. R.* (diss., Univ. of Illinois, 1975); A. Silbiger, "The Roman Frescobaldi Tradition, c.1640–1670," *Journal of the American Musicological Society* (Spring 1980).

Rossi, Salamone (also **Salomone, Salamon de', or Shlomo**), distinguished Italian composer of Jewish descent; b. probably in Mantua, Aug. 19, 1570; d. probably there, c.1630. He was closely associated with the Mantuan court for a number of years, being granted the privilege of not having to conform to the Mantuan law of wearing a yellow badge to acknowledge his Jewish heritage; the privilege was accorded him by Duke Vincenzo Gonzaga in 1606, and was renewed by Duke Francesco II upon his accession in 1612. In later years he devoted much time to a Jewish theatrical troupe, but continued to be associated with musical events at the court. He was a leading figure in the development of the trio sonata and the chamber duet. Among his instrumental works are *Il primo libro delle sinfonie e gagliarde . . . per sonar* for 2 Violas or Cornetts and Chitarrone or Other Instruments (1607); *Il secondo libro delle sinfonie e gagliarde, a 3, per sonar . . . con alcune delle*

dette a 4, 5, ed alcune canzoni per sonar, a 4, nel fine for Violas and Chitarrone (1608); *Il terzo libro de varie sonate, sinfonie, gagliarde, brandi e corrente* for 2 Violas da Braccio and Chitarrone or Other Instruments, op. 12 (1623); and *Il quarto libro de varie sonate, sinfonie, gagliarde, brandi e corrente* for 2 Violins and Chitarrone (1622); he also wrote sacred and secular vocal pieces.

BIBL.: S. Naumbourg, *Essai sur la vie et les œuvres de Salamon R.* (Paris, 1877); E. Birnbaum, *Jüdische Musiker am Hofe zu Mantua von 1542–1628* (Vienna, 1893; Eng. tr., rev. and augmented, 1978); J. Newman, *The Madrigals of Salamon de' R.* (diss., Columbia Univ., 1962); J. Newman and F. Rikko, *A Thematic Index to the Works of Salamon R.* (Hackensack, N.J., 1972).

Rossi, Tino, popular French chansonnier; b. Ajaccio, Corsica, April 29, 1907; d. Neuilly, Seine, Sept. 26, 1983. His father, a tailor, wanted him to continue in the same profession, but Rossi apprenticed himself in a church choir. He never studied voice formally, but rather devoted himself to singing popular ballads, accompanying himself on the guitar. He filled engagements in the provinces until 1934, when he was engaged as a featured singer at the Casino de Paris. A combination of good looks and natural talent made him a "vedette" overnight; the women of Paris flocked to hear him; some of them he married. He died peacefully in his sleep of cancer of the pancreas.

Rossignol, Felix Ludger. See **Joncières, Victorin de.**

Rossini, Gioachino (Antonio), great Italian opera composer possessing an equal genius for shattering melodrama in tragedy and for devastating humor in comedy; b. Pesaro, Feb. 29, 1792; d. Paris, Nov. 13, 1868. He came from a musical family; his father served as town trumpeter in Lugo and Pesaro, and played brass instruments in provincial theaters; his mother sang opera as *seconda donna.* When his parents traveled, he was usually boarded in Bologna. After the family moved to Lugo, his father taught him to play the horn; he also had a chance to study singing with a local canon. Later the family moved to Bologna, where he studied singing, harpsichord, and music theory with Padre Tesei; also learned to play the violin and viola. Soon he acquired enough technical ability to serve as maestro al cembalo in local churches and at occasional opera productions. He studied voice with the tenor Matteo Babbini. In 1806 he was accepted as a student at the Liceo Musicale in Bologna; there he studied singing and solfeggio with Gibelli, cello with Cavedagna, piano with Zanotti, and counterpoint with Padre Mattei. He also began composing. On Aug. 11, 1808, his cantata *Il pianto d'Armonia sulla morte d'Orfeo* was performed at the Liceo Musicale in Bologna and received a prize. About the same time he wrote his 1st opera, *Demetrio e Polibio*; in 1810 he was commissioned to write a work for the Teatro San Moisè in Venice; he submitted his opera *La cambiale di matrimonio*, which won considerable acclaim. His next production was *L'equivoco stravagante*, produced in Bologna in 1811. There followed a number of other operas: *L'inganno felice* (Venice, 1812), *Ciro in Babilonia* (Ferrara, 1812), and *La scala di seta* (Venice, 1812). In 1812 he obtained a commission from La Scala of Milan; the resulting work, *La pietra del paragone*, was a fine success. In 1813 he produced 3 operas for Venice: *Il Signor Bruschino*, *Tancredi*, and *L'Italiana in Algeri*, the last became a perennial favorite. The next 3 operas, *Aureliano in Palmira* (Milan, 1813), *Il Turco in Italia* (Milan, 1814), and *Sigismondo* (Venice, 1814), were unsuccessful. By that time Rossini, still a very young man, had been approached by the famous impresario Barbaja, the manager of the Teatro San Carlo and the Teatro Fondo in Naples, with an offer for an exclusive contract, under the terms of which Rossini was to supply 2 operas annually for Barbaja. The 1st opera Rossini wrote for him was *Elisabetta, regina d'Inghilterra*, produced at the Teatro San Carlo in Naples in 1815; the title role was entrusted to the famous Spanish soprano Isabella Colbran, who was Barbaja's favorite mistress. An important innovation in the score was Rossini's use of *recitativo stromentato* in place of the usual *recitativo secco*. His next opera, *Torvaldo e Dorliska*, produced in Rome in 1815, was an unfortunate failure. Rossini now determined to try his skill in composing an opera buffa, based on the famous play by Beaumarchais *Le Barbier de Seville*; it was an audacious decision on Rossini's part, since an Italian opera on the same subject by Paisiello, *Il Barbiere di Siviglia*, originally produced in 1782, was still playing with undiminished success. To avoid confusion, Rossini's opera on this subject was performed at the Teatro Argentina in Rome under a different title, *Almaviva, ossia L'inutile precauzione*. Rossini was only 23 years old when he completed the score, which proved to be his greatest accomplishment and a standard opera buffa in the repertoire of theaters all over the world. Rossini conducted its 1st performance in Rome on Feb. 20, 1816, but if contemporary reports and gossip can be trusted, the occasion was marred by various stage accidents which moved the unruly Italian audience to interrupt the spectacle with vociferous outcries of derision; however, the next performance scored a brilliant success. For later productions he used the title *Il Barbiere di Siviglia*. Strangely enough, the operas he wrote immediately afterward were not uniformly successful: *La Gazzetta*, produced in Naples in 1816, passed unnoticed; the next opera, *Otello*, also produced in Naples in 1816, had some initial success but was not retained in the repertoire after a few sporadic performances. There followed *La Cenerentola* and *La gazza ladra*, both from 1817, which fared much better. But the following 7 operas, *Armida, Mosè in Egitto, Ricciardo e Zoraide, Ermione, La Donna del lago, Maometto II*, and *Zelmira*, produced in Naples between 1817 and 1822, were soon forgotten; only the famous Prayer in *Mosè in Egitto* saved the opera from oblivion. The *prima donna assoluta* in all these operas was Isabella Colbran; after a long association with Barbaja, she went to live with Rossini, who finally married her on March 16, 1822. This event, however, did not result in a break between the impresario and the composer; Barbaja even made arrangements for a festival of Rossini's works in Vienna at the Kärnthnertortheater, of which he became a director. In Vienna Rossini met Beethoven. Returning to Italy, he produced a fairly successful mythological opera, *Semiramide* (Venice, 1823), with Colbran in the title role. Rossini then signed a contract for a season in London with Giovanni Benelli, director of the Italian opera at the King's Theatre. Rossini arrived in London late in 1823 and was received by King George IV. He conducted several of his operas, and was also a guest at the homes of the British nobility, where he played piano as an accompanist to singers, at very large fees. In 1824 he settled in Paris, where he became director of the Théâtre-Italien. For the coronation of King Charles X he composed *Il viaggio a Reims*, which was performed in Paris under his direction on June 19, 1825. He used parts of this *pièce d'occasion* in his opera *Le Comte Ory*. In Paris he met Meyerbeer, with whom he established an excellent relationship. After the expiration of his contract with the Théâtre-Italien, he was given the nominal titles of "Premier Compositeur du Roi" and "Inspecteur Général du Chant en France" at an annual salary of 25,000 francs. He was now free to compose for the Paris Opéra; there, on Oct. 9, 1826, he produced *Le Siège de Corinthe*, a revised French version of *Maometto II*. Later he also revised the score of *Mosè in Egitto* and produced it at the Paris Opéra in French as *Moïse et Pharaon* on March 26, 1827. There followed *Le Comte Ory* (Aug. 20, 1828). In May 1829 Rossini was able to obtain an agreement with the government of King Charles X guaranteeing him a lifetime annuity of 6,000 francs. In return, he promised to write more works for the Paris Opéra. On Aug. 3, 1829, his *Guillaume Tell* was given its premiere at the Opéra; it became immensely popular. And then, at the age of 37, Rossini stopped writing operas. The French revolution of July 1830, which dethroned King Charles X, invalidated his contract with the French government. Rossini sued the government of King Louis Philippe, the successor to the throne of Charles X, for the continuation of his annuity; the incipient litigation was settled in 1835. In 1832 Rossini met Olympe Pélissier, who became his mistress; in 1837 Rossini legally

separated from Colbran. She died in 1845, and on Aug. 16, 1846, Rossini married Pélissier. From 1836 to 1848 they lived in Bologna, where Rossini served as consultant to the Liceo Musicale. In 1848 they moved to Florence; in 1855 he decided to return to Paris, where he was to remain for the rest of his life. His home in the suburb of Passy became the magnet of the artistic world. Rossini was a charming, affable, and gregarious host; he entertained lavishly; he was a great gourmet, and invented recipes for Italian food that were enthusiastically adopted by French chefs. His wit was fabulous, and his sayings were eagerly reported in the French journals. He did not abandon composition entirely during his last years of life; in 1867 he wrote a *Petite messe solennelle*; as a token of gratitude to the government of the 2nd Empire he composed a *Hymne à Napoleon III et à son vaillant peuple*; of great interest are the numerous piano pieces, songs, and instrumental works which he called *Péchés de vieillesse* (Sins of Old Age), a collection containing over 150 pieces.

What were the reasons for Rossini's decision to stop writing operas? Rumors flew around Paris that he was unhappy about the cavalier treatment he received from the management of the Paris Opéra, and he spoke disdainfully of yielding the operatic field to "the Jews" (Meyerbeer and Halévy), whose operas captivated the Paris audiences. The report does not bear the stamp of truth, for Rossini was friendly with Meyerbeer until Meyerbeer's death in 1864. Besides, he was not in the habit of complaining; he enjoyed life too well. He was called "Le Cygne de Pesaro" ("The Swan of Pesaro," his birthplace). The story went that a delegation arrived from Pesaro with a project of building a monument to Rossini; the town authorities had enough money to pay for the pedestal, but not for the statue itself. Would Rossini contribute 10,000 francs for the completion of the project? "For 10,000 francs," Rossini was supposed to have replied, "I would stand on the pedestal myself." *Se non è vero è ben trovato*. He had a healthy sense of self-appreciation, but he invariably put it in a comic context. While his mother was still living, he addressed his letters to her as "Mother of the Great Maestro."

The circumstance that Rossini was born on a leap-year day was the cause of many a bon mot on his part. On Feb. 29, 1868, he decided to celebrate his 19th birthday, for indeed, there had been then only 19 leap years since his birth. He was superstitious; like many Italians, he stood in fear of Friday the 13th. He died on Nov. 13, 1868, which was a Friday. In 1887 his remains were taken to Florence for entombment in the Church of Santa Croce.

Rossini's melodies have been used by many composers as themes for various works: Respighi utilized Rossini's *Quelques riens* in his ballet *La Boutique fantasque*, and other themes in his orch. suite *Rossiniana*. An opera entitled *Rossini in Neapel* was written by Bernhard Paumgartner. Britten made use of Rossini's music in his orch. suites *Soirées musicales* and *Matinées musicales*. The most famous arrangement of any of Rossini's compositions is the Prayer from *Mosè in Egitto*, transcribed for violin by Paganini.

A complete ed. of the works of Rossini, the *Quaderni rossiniani, a cura della Fondazione Rossini*, began publication in Pesaro in 1954.

WORKS: OPERAS: *Demetrio e Polibio*, opera seria (1808; Teatro Valle, Rome, May 18, 1812); *La cambiale di matrimonio*, farsa (Teatro San Moisè, Venice, Nov. 3, 1810); *L'equivoco stravagante*, opera buffa (Teatro del Corso, Bologna, Oct. 26, 1811); *L'inganno felice*, farsa (1811; Teatro San Moisè, Venice, Jan. 8, 1812); *Ciro in Babilonia, ossia La caduta di Baldassare*, dramma con cori or oratorio (Teatro Municipale, Ferrara, March 1812); *La scala di seta*, farsa (Teatro San Moisè, Venice, May 9, 1812); *La pietra del paragone*, melodramma giocoso or opera buffa (Teatro alla Scala, Milan, Sept. 26, 1812); *L'occasione fa il ladro, ossia Il cambio della valigia*, burletta per musica (Teatro San Moisè, Venice, Nov. 24, 1812); *Il Signor Bruschino, ossia Il Figlio per azzardo*, farsa giocosa (1812; Teatro San Moisè, Venice, Jan. 1813); *Tancredi*, opera seria or melodramma eroico (1812–13; Teatro La Fenice, Venice, Feb. 6,

1813); *L'Italiana in Algeri,* melodramma giocoso (Teatro San Benedetto, Venice, May 22, 1813); *Aureliano in Palmira,* opera seria or dramma serio (Teatro alla Scala, Milan, Dec. 26, 1813); *Il Turco in Italia,* opera buffa or dramma buffo (Teatro alla Scala, Milan, Aug. 14, 1814); *Sigismondo,* opera seria or dramma (Teatro La Fenice, Venice, Dec. 26, 1814); *Elisabetta, regina d'Inghilterra,* dramma (Teatro San Carlo, Naples, Oct. 4, 1815); *Torvaldo e Dorliska,* dramma semiserio (Teatro Valle, Rome, Dec. 26, 1815); *Il Barbiere di Siviglia,* opera buffa or commedia (1st perf. as *Almaviva, ossia L'inutile precauzione,* Teatro Argentina, Rome, Feb. 20, 1816); *La Gazzetta, ossia Il matrimonio per concorso* (subtitle does not appear in the 1st printed libretto), opera buffa (Teatro dei Fiorentini, Naples, Sept. 26, 1816); *Otello, ossia Il Moro di Venezia,* opera seria or dramma (Teatro del Fondo, Naples, Dec. 4, 1816); *La Cenerentola, ossia La bontà in trionfo,* dramma giocoso (1816–17; Teatro Valle, Rome, Jan. 25, 1817); *La gazza ladra,* melodramma or opera semiseria (Teatro alla Scala, Milan, May 31, 1817); *Armida,* opera seria or dramma (Teatro San Carlo, Naples, Nov. 11, 1817); *Adelaide di Borgogna, ossia Ottone, re d'Italia,* dramma (Teatro Argentina, Rome, Dec. 27, 1817); *Mosè in Egitto,* azione tragico-sacra or oratorio (Teatro San Carlo, Naples, March 5, 1818); *Adina, o Il Califfo di Bagdad,* farsa (1818; Teatro São Carlos, Lisbon, June 22, 1826); *Ricciardo e Zoraide,* dramma, opera seria, or opera semiseria (Teatro San Carlo, Naples, Dec. 3, 1818); *Ermione,* azione tragica (Teatro San Carlo, Naples, March 27, 1819); *Eduardo* [later *Edoardo*] *e Cristina,* dramma (Teatro San Benedetto, Venice, April 24, 1819); *La Donna del lago,* melodramma or opera seria (Teatro San Carlo, Naples, Sept. 24, 1819); *Bianca e Falliero, ossia Il consiglio dei tre,* opera seria (Teatro alla Scala, Milan, Dec. 26, 1819); *Maometto II,* dramma or opera seria (Teatro San Carlo, Naples, Dec. 3, 1820); *Matilde Shabran* [later *Matilde di Shabran*]*, ossia Bellezza e Cuor di Ferro,* opera semiseria (1820–21; Teatro Apollo, Rome, Feb. 24, 1821); *Zelmira,* dramma or opera seria (1821–22; Teatro San Carlo, Naples, Feb. 16, 1822); *Semiramide,* melodramma tragico or opera seria (1822–23; Teatro La Fenice, Venice, Feb. 3, 1823); *Il viaggio a Reims, ossia L'albergo del Giglio d'Oro,* cantata scenica (Théâtre-Italien, Paris, June 19, 1825); *Le Siège de Corinthe,* grand opera (rev. of *Maometto II;* Opéra, Paris, Oct. 9, 1826); *Moïse et Pharaon, ou Le Passage de la Mer Rouge,* grand opera (rev. of *Mosè in Egitto;* Opéra, Paris, March 26, 1827); *Le Comte Ory,* opéra-comique (utilizing numbers from *Il viaggio a Reims;* Opéra, Paris, Aug. 20, 1828); *Guillaume Tell,* grand opera (1828–29; Opéra, Paris, Aug. 3, 1829).

CANTATAS: *Il pianto d'Armonia sulla morte d'Orfeo* (Bologna, Aug. 11, 1808); *La morte di Didone* (1811; Venice, May 2, 1818); *Dalle quete e pallid'ombre* (1812); *Egle ed Irene* (1814); *L'Aurora* (Rome, Nov. 1815); *Le nozze di Teti e di Peleo* (Naples, April 24, 1816); Cantata con cori ("Omaggio Umiliato . . ."; also known as *Corifea, Partenope,* or *Igea;* Naples, Feb. 20, 1819); *Cantata a tre voci con cori* ("Cantata . . . 9 Maggio 1819"; Naples, May 9, 1819); *La riconoscenza* (Naples, Dec. 27, 1821); *L'augurio felice* (1822); *La Santa Alleanza* (Verona, Nov. 24, 1822); *Il vero omaggio* (Verona, Dec. 3, 1822); *Il Bardo* (1822); *Omaggio pastorale* (Treviso, April 1, 1823); *Il pianto delle muse in morte di Lord Byron* (London, June 9, 1824); *Cantata per il battesimo del figlio del banchiere Aguado* (Paris, July 16, 1827); *Giovanna d'Arco* (1832; rev. 1852); *Cantata ad Onore del Sommo Pontefice Pio IX* (Bologna, Aug. 16, 1846).

OTHER VOCAL: 3 early masses (the 1st contains 3 sections only by Rossini for a composite score composed by students of the Liceo Musicale in 1808 and perf. in Bologna, June 2, 1808; 1808; 1809); *Messa solenne* (Naples, March 19, 1820); *Tantum ergo* (1824); *Soirées musicales* (1830–35); *Stabat Mater* (1st version, 1831–32; orch. version, 1841; Paris, Jan. 7, 1842); *Tantum ergo* (Bologna, Nov. 28, 1847); *O salutaris Hostia* (1857); *Laus Deo* (1861); *Petite messe solennelle* (1863; Paris, March 14, 1864; orch. version, 1867; Paris, Feb. 24, 1869).

ORCH.: Overture in D major (1808); 3 sinfonias: D major (1808); E-flat major (1809; later rev. for use as the overture

to *La cambiale di matrimonio*); A major (discovered by P. Ingerslev-Jenson and called the "Odense"); *Variazioni per più strumenti obbligati con accompagnamento di orchestra* (1809); *Variazioni in fa maggiore* (1809); *Variazioni in do maggiore per clarinetto obbligato con accompagnamento di orchestra* (1810); marches.

CHAMBER: 6 *sonate a quattro* (1804); 5 string quartets (1806–8); 5 duets (1806); *Tema con variazione per quattro strumenti a fiato* for Flute, Clarinet, Horn, and Bassoon (1812); *Rondeau fantastique* for Horn and Piano (1856).

BIBL.: A valuable source is the *Bollettino del Centro Rossiniano di Studi* (Pesaro, 1955–60; 1967–   ). Also G. Righetti-Giorgi, *Cenni di una donna già cantante sopra il maestro R.* (Bologna, 1823); G. Carpani, *Le Rossiniane, ossia Lettere musico-teatrali* (Padua, 1824); Stendhal, *Vie de R.* (Paris, 1824; many subsequent eds. and trs.; in Eng. as *Life of R.,* tr. and ed. by R. Coe, London and N.Y., 1956; 2nd ed., 1970); J.A. Wendt, *R.'s Leben und Treiben* (Leipzig, 1824); J.-L. d'Ortigue, *De la guerre des dilettanti, ou De la Révolution opérée par R. dans l'opéra français, et des rapports qui existent entre la musique, la littérature et les arts* (Paris, 1830); A. Zanolini, *Biografia di G. R.* (Paris, 1836; also later eds.); H. Blaze de Bury, "R.: Sa vie et ses œuvres," *Revue des Deux Mondes* (May–June 1854); L. and M. Escudier, *R.: Sa vie et ses œuvres* (Paris, 1854); E. de Mirecourt, *R.* (Paris, 1855); A. Aulagnier, *G. R.: Sa vie et ses œuvres* (Paris, 1864); A.-J. Azevedo, *G. R.: Sa vie ses œuvres* (Paris, 1864); F. Hiller, *Plaudereien mit R.,* vol. II of *Aus dem Tonleben unserer Zeit* (Leipzig, 1868); R. Wagner, "Eine Erinnerung an R.," *Allgemeine Zeitung* (Augsburg, Dec. 17, 1868); H. Edwards, *Life of R.* (London, 1869; reissued in a condensed version as *R. and His School,* London, 1881); C. Montrond, *R.: Étude biographique* (Lille, 1870); F. Mordani, *Della vita privata di G. R.: Memorie inedite* (Imola, 1871); A. Pougin, *R.: Notes, impressions, souvenirs, commentaires* (Paris, 1871); G. Vanzolini, *Della vera patria di G. R.* (Pesaro, 1873); L. Silvestri, *Della vita e delle opere di G. R. . . .* (Milan, 1874); C. Magnico, *R. e Wagner, o La musica italiana e la musica tedesca* (Genoa, 1875); G. de Sanctis, *G. R.: Appunti di viaggio* (Rome, 1878); J. Sittard, *G.A. R.* (Leipzig, 1882); C. Thrane, *R. og operaen* (Copenhagen, 1885); V. Camaiti, *G. R.: Notizie biografiche, artistiche e aneddotiche* (Florence, 1887); R. Gandolfi, *G. R.* (Florence, 1887); G. Mazzatinti, *Lettere inedite di G. R.* (Imola, 1890); A. Allmaÿer, *Undici lettere di G. R. pubblicate per la prima volta . . .* (Siena, 1892); A. Kohut, *R.* (Leipzig, 1892); G. Mazzatinti, *Lettere inedite e rare di G. R.* (Imola, 1892); E. Michotte, *Souvenirs: Une Soirée chez R. à Beau-Sejour (Passy) 1858 . . .* (Brussels, n.d. [after 1893]; Eng. tr. by H. Weinstock, Chicago, 1968); E. Checchi, *R.* (Florence, 1898); A. Maffei, *R.* (Florence, 1898); G. Tebaldini, "Da R. a Verdi," *Aversa a Domenico Cimarosa* (Naples, 1901); G. Mazzatinti and F. and G. Manis, *Lettere di G. R.* (Florence, 1902); L. Dauriac, *R.: Biographie critique* (Paris, 1906); E. Michotte, *Souvenirs: La Visite de R. Wagner à R. (Paris, 1860): Détails inédits et commentaires* (Paris, 1906; Eng. tr. by H. Weinstock, Chicago, 1968); E. Corradi, *G. R.* (Rome, 1909); F. Cowen, *R.* (London and N.Y., 1912); G. Fara, *Genio e ingegno musicale: G. R.* (Turin, 1915); N. Morini, *La casa di R. in Bologna* (Bologna, 1916); L. Neretti, *I due inni patriottici di G. R.* (Florence, 1918); F. Vatielli, *R. e Bologna* (Bologna, 1918); H. de Curzon, *R.* (Paris, 1920; 2nd ed., 1930); G. Radiciotti, " 'Il Signor Bruschino' ed il 'Tancredi,' " *Rivista Musicale Italiana* (1920); V. du Bled, "Le Salon de R.," *La Revue Musicale* (1921); H. Prunières, "Stendhal and R.," *Musical Quarterly* (Jan. 1921); R. Fauchois, *R.* (Lyons, 1922); G. Radiciotti, *Il Barbiere di Siviglia: Guida attraverso la commedia e la musica* (Milan, 1923); idem, "Stendhal e R.," *Il Pianoforte* (Dec. 1923); G. Pannain, "R. nel' 'Guglielmo Tell,' " *Rivista Musicale Italiana* (1924); G. Radiciotti, "R. à Londres," *La Revue Musicale* (Feb. 1, 1924; Eng. tr. in *Sackbut,* April 1924); idem, "L'Italiana in Algeri' di G. R.," *Il Pianoforte* (Nov. 1925); G. Gatti, *Le "Barbier de Séville" de R.* (Paris, 1926); G. Biamonti, "Il Barbiere di Siviglia" di G. R. (Rome, 1929); idem, *Guglielmo Tell* (Rome, 1929); J. Cooke, *R.: A Short Biography* (Philadelphia, 1929); H. Peyser, "The 'Cenerentola' of R.," *Musical Amer-*

ica (June 1929); G. Radiciotti, *G. R.: Vita documenta, opere ed influenza su l'arte* (3 vols., Tivoli, 1927–29); idem, *Aneddoti rossiniani autentici* (Rome, 1929); H. de Curzon, *Une Heure avec R.* (Paris, 1930); A. Bonaventura, *R.* (Florence, 1934); G. Derwent, *R. and Some Forgotten Nightingales* (London, 1934); H. Gerigk, *R.* (Potsdam, 1934); F. Toye, *R.: A Study in Tragi-Comedy* (London and N.Y., 1934); H. Faller, *Die Gesangskoloratur in R.s Opern und ihre Ausführung* (Berlin, 1935); G. Monaldi, *Gli Uomini illustri: G. R. nell'arte, nella vita, negli aneddoti* (Milan, n.d. [1936]); L. D'Amico, *R.* (Turin, 1939); R. Bacchelli, *G. R.* (Turin, 1941; 2nd ed., 1945); F. Bonavia, *R.* (London, 1941); A. Fraccaroli, *R.* (Milan, 1941; 4th ed., 1944); G. Pannain, "Personalità di R.," *Musica*, I (1942); L. Ronga, "Vicende del gusto rossiniano nell'Ottocento," ibid.; idem, "Svolgimento del gusto rossiniano fino al Novecento," *Musica*, II (1943); G. Roncaglia, *R. l'olimpico* (Milan, 1946; 2nd ed., 1953); G. Brigante Colonna, *Vita di R.* (Florence, 1947); K. Pfister, *Das Leben R.s: Gesetz und Triumph der Oper* (Vienna and Berlin, 1948); C. van Berkel, *G. R.* (Haarlem, 1950); P. Ingerslev-Jensen, "An Unknown R. Overture: Report of a Discovery in Odense," *Music Review* (Feb. 1950); *La Rassegna Musicale*, special issue devoted to Rossini and his works (July–Sept. 1954); F. Bonafé, *R. et son œuvre* (Le-Puy-en-Velay, 1955); U. Gozzano, *R.: Il romanzo dell'opera* (Turin, 1955); B. Riboli, "Malattia di G. R. secondo una relazione medica del 1842," *Note e Riviste di Psichiatria* (July and Dec. 1955); L. Rognoni, *R., con un'appendice comprendente lettere, documenti, testimonianze* (Parma, 1956; 3rd ed., 1977); F. Schlitzer, *Rossiniana: Contributo all'epistolario di G. R., Quaderni dell'Accademia chigiana*, XXXV (1956); idem, *R. a Siena e altri scritti rossiniani (con lettere inedite), Quaderni dell'Accademia chigiana*, XXXIX (1958); R. Bacchelli, *R. e esperienze rossiniane* (Milan, 1959); P. Ingerslev-Jensen, *R.* (Copenhagen, 1959); F. Schlitzer, *Un piccolo carteggio inedito di R. con un impresario italiano a Vienna* (Florence, 1959); A. Porter, "A Lost Opera by R.," *Music & Letters* (Jan. 1964); D. Schwartz, "R.: A Psychoanalytic Approach to the Great Renunciation," *Journal of the American Psychoanalytic Society*, XIII (1965); V. Viviani, ed., *I libretti di R.* (Milan, 1965); A. Bonaccorsi, ed., *G. R.* (Florence, 1968); F. d'Amico, *L'opera teatrale di G. R.* (Rome, 1968); H. Weinstock, *R.: A Biography* (N.Y., 1968); P. Gossett, *The Operas of R.: Problems of Textual Criticism in Nineteenth-Century Opera* (diss., Princeton Univ., 1970); idem, "The Overtures of R.," *19th Century Music* (July 1979); N. Till, *R.: His Life and Times* (Tunbridge Wells, 1983); A. Camosci, *G. R. dai ritratti e dalle scritture* (Rome, 1985); P. Mioli, *Invito all'ascolto di G. R.* (Milan, 1986); R. Osborne, *R.* (London, 1986); R. Bacchelli, *Vita di R.* (Florence, 1987); S. Balthazar, "R. and the Development of the Mid-Century Lyric Form," *Journal of the American Musicological Society* (Spring 1988).

Rössl-Majdan, Hildegard, Austrian contralto; b. Moosbierbaum, Jan. 21, 1921. She was educated at the Vienna Academy of Music. In 1946 she launched her career as a concert singer; also appeared at the Vienna State Opera, Milan's La Scala, London's Covent Garden, and other European opera houses; sang at the festivals in Salzburg, Edinburgh, and Aix-en-Provence; later was active as a voice teacher.

Rössler, Ernst Karl, German organist and composer; b. Pyritz, Pomerania, Oct. 18, 1909; d. Königsfeld, Aug. 19, 1980. He studied organ and was active mainly in organ building and church music. He lectured on composition for organ in Lübeck and Freiburg im Breisgau; publ. *Klangfunktion und Registrierung* (Kassel, 1952) and several other papers concerning organ registration. He composed some sacred choruses and numerous organ pieces.

Rossum, Frederik (Leon Hendrik) van, Belgian composer and teacher of Dutch descent; b. Elsene, Brussels, Dec. 5, 1939. He took Belgian citizenship when he was 18; studied composition with Souris and Quinet at the Brussels Cons. (1956–62); won a Premier Grand Prix de Rome for his *Cantate de la Haute Mer* (1965). He taught piano at the Brussels Cons. (1965–68); then became prof. of counterpoint at the Liège

Cons. (1968); served as prof. of analysis at the Brussels Cons. (from 1971); also was director of the Watermael-Bosvoorde Academy of Music.

WORKS: *Petite pièce* for Clarinet and Piano (1961); Piano Sonata (1963); *Capriccio* for Wind Quintet (1963); Sinfonietta (1964); *Cantata sacrée* for Chorus, Strings, and Harpsichord (1966); *12 Miniatures* for Piano or Orch. (1967); *Divertimento* for String Orch. (1967); *Sinfonie concertante* for Horn, Piano, Percussion, and Orch. (1968); *Graffiti* for Violin and Piano (1968); *Duetto* for Cello and Piano (1968); *Pyrogravures* for Wind Quintet (1968); *Threni* for Mezzo-soprano and Orch. (1969); *Der Blaue Reiter*, in homage to German expressionistic painters, for Orch. (1971); *Epitaph* for String Orch. (1972); Piano Quintet (1972); *Rétrospection* for Soprano, Contralto, Chorus, 2 Pianos, and Percussion (1973); *Réquisitoire* for Brass and Percussion (1973); Piano Concerto (1975); *Petite suite réactionnaire* for Orch. (1975); 2 violin concertos (1979; 1985–89); *Polyptyque* for Orch. (1986); piano pieces.

Rostal, Max, Austrian-born English violinist and pedagogue; b. Teschen, Silesia, Aug. 7, 1905. He studied violin with Arnold Rosé in Vienna and with Carl Flesch in Berlin, where he also took courses in composition with Emil Bohnke and Mátyás Seiber at the Hochschule für Musik; then was a prof. there (1930–33). In 1934 he left Nazi Germany; eventually went to London and became a naturalized British subject. He was a prof. at the Guildhall School of Music (1944–58), the Cologne Cons. (1957), and the Bern Cons. (1958). In 1977 he was made a Commander of the Order of the British Empire. He was especially noted for his performances of contemporary music.

Rostand, Claude, French writer on music; b. Paris, Dec. 3, 1912; d. Villejuif, Oct. 9, 1970. He studied literature and law at the Sorbonne; also received private instruction from Edouard Mignan, Marc Vaubourgoin, Jacques Février, and Norbert Dufourcq; was active as a music critic; organized a modern music society in Paris, Musique d'Aujourd'hui (1958); served as vice-president of the ISCM (from 1961).

WRITINGS: *L'Œuvre de Gabriel Fauré* (Paris, 1945); *La Musique française contemporaine* (Paris, 1952); dialogues with Milhaud, Poulenc, Markevitch, and others; biographies of Brahms (2 vols., Paris, 1954–55), Liszt (Paris, 1960), Hugo Wolf (Paris, 1967), and Webern (1969); *Dictionnaire de la musique contemporaine* (Lausanne, 1970).

Rostropovich, Leopold, Russian cellist, father of **Mstislav (Leopoldovich) Rostropovich;** b. Voronezh, March 9, 1892; d. Orenburg, July 31, 1942. He studied cello with his father, Vitold Rostropovich; gave concerts; from 1925 to 1931, was a prof. at the Azerbaijan Cons.; then lived in Moscow; after the outbreak of the Nazi-Soviet war in 1941, he moved to Orenburg.

Rostropovich, Mstislav (Leopoldovich), famous Russian cellist and conductor, son of **Leopold Rostropovich;** b. Baku, March 27, 1927. A precocious child, he began cello studies with his father at an early age; also had piano lessons from his mother. In 1931 the family moved to Moscow, where he made his debut when he was 8; continued his training at the Central Music School (1939–41); then studied cello with Kozolupov and composition with Shebalin and Shostakovich at the Moscow Cons. (1943–48); subsequently studied privately with Prokofiev. He won the International Competition for Cellists in Prague in 1950, and the next year made his 1st appearance in the West in Florence. A phenomenally successful career ensued. He made his U.S. debut at N.Y.'s Carnegie Hall in 1956, winning extraordinary critical acclaim. He became a teacher (1953) and a prof. (1956) at the Moscow Cons., and also a prof. at the Leningrad Cons. (1961). A talented pianist, he frequently appeared as accompanist to his wife, the soprano **Galina Vishnevskaya,** whom he married in 1955. In 1961 he made his 1st appearance as a conductor. As his fame increased, he received various honors, including the Lenin Prize in 1963 and the Gold Medal of the Royal Phil. Soc. of London in 1970. In spite of his eminence and official honors, however, he encountered difficulties with the Soviet authorities, owing chiefly to his spirit of uncompromising independence. He let the dissident author Aleksandr Solzhenitsyn stay at his dacha near Moscow, protesting the Soviet government's treatment of the Nobel prize winner for literature in a letter to *Pravda* in 1969. Although the letter went unpubl. in his homeland, it was widely disseminated in the West. As a result, Rostropovich found himself increasingly hampered in his career by the Soviet Ministry of Culture. His concerts were canceled without explanation, as were his wife's engagements at the Bolshoi Theater. Foreign tours were forbidden, as were appearances on radio, television, and recordings. In 1974 he and his wife obtained permission to go abroad, and were accompanied by their 2 daughters. He made a brilliant debut as a guest conductor with the National Sym. Orch. in Washington, D.C. (March 5, 1975); his success led to his appointment as its music director in 1977. Free from the bureaucratic annoyances of the U.S.S.R., he and his wife publicized stories of their previous difficulties at home in Russia. Annoyed by such independent activities, the Moscow authorities finally stripped them both of their Soviet citizenship as "ideological renegades." The Soviet establishment even went so far as to remove the dedication to Rostropovich of Shostakovich's 2nd Cello Concerto. The whole disgraceful episode ended when the Soviet government, chastened by perestroika, restored Rostropovich's citizenship in Jan. 1990, and invited him to take the National Sym. Orch. to the U.S.S.R. Besides conducting the American orch. there, Rostropovich appeared as soloist in Dvořák's Cello Concerto. His return to Russia was welcomed by the populace as a vindication of his principles of liberty. A symbolic linguistic note: the difficult-to-pronounce 1st name of Rostropovich, which means "avenged glory," is usually rendered by his friends and admirers as simply Slava, that is, "glory."

Rostropovich is duly recognized as one of the greatest cellists of the century, a master interpreter of both the standard and the contemporary literature. To enhance the repertoire for his instrument, he commissioned and premiered numerous scores, including works by Prokofiev, Shostakovich, Britten, Piston, and Foss. As a conductor, he proved himself an impassioned and authoritative interpreter of the music of the Russian national and Soviet schools of composition. He organized the 1st Rostropovich International Cello Competition in Paris in 1981 and the Rostropovich Festival in Snape, England, in 1983. He was made an Officer of the French Légion d'honneur in 1982, and received an honorary knighthood from Queen Elizabeth II of England in 1987.

Bibl.: T. Gaidamovich, *M. R.* (Moscow, 1969); N. Malitz, "Slava at Sixty," *Ovation* (March 1987); *Current Biography* (Nov. 1988).

Rosvaenge (Roswaenge), Helge, esteemed Danish tenor; b. Copenhagen (of German parents), Aug. 29, 1897; d. Munich, June 19, 1972. He studied in Copenhagen and Berlin; made his operatic debut as Don José in Neustrelitz in 1921; then sang in Altenburg (1922–24), Basel (1924–26), and Cologne (1926–29). He distinguished himself as a member of the Berlin State Opera (1929–44); also sang in Vienna and Munich. He appeared at the Salzburg (1933, 1937) and Bayreuth (1934, 1936) festivals; made his debut at London's Covent Garden as Florestan in 1938. After World War II, he again sang in Berlin and Vienna; made a concert tour of the U.S. in 1962. In his prime, he was compared to Caruso as a practitioner of bel canto. He excelled in the operas of Mozart; was also noted for his portrayals of Radames, Manrico, Huon, and Calaf. He publ. the autobiographical booklets *Skratta Pajazzo* (*Ridi, Pagliaccio*; Copenhagen, 1945); *Mach es besser, mein Sohn* (Leipzig, 1962); and *Leitfaden für Gesangsbeflissene* (Munich, 1964).

Bibl.: F. Tassie, *H. R.* (Augsburg, 1975).

Rota (real name, **Rinaldi**), **Nino,** brilliant Italian composer; b. Milan, Dec. 3, 1911; d. Rome, April 10, 1979. He was a precocious musician; at the age of 11 he wrote an oratorio which had a public performance, and at 13 composed a lyric comedy in 3 acts, *Il Principe porcaro*, after Hans Christian

Andersen. He entered the Milan Cons. in 1923, and took courses with Delachi, Orefici, and Bas; after private studies with Pizzetti (1925–26), he studied composition with Casella at the Accademia di Santa Cecilia in Rome, graduating in 1930; later went to the U.S., and enrolled in the Curtis Inst. of Music in Philadelphia, studying composition with Rosario Scalero and conducting with Fritz Reiner. Returning to Italy, he entered the Univ. of Milan to study literature, gaining a degree in 1937. He taught at the Taranto music school (1937–38); then was a teacher (from 1939) and director (1950–78) at the Bari Liceo Musicale. His musical style demonstrates a great facility, and even felicity, with occasional daring excursions into the forbidding territory of dodecaphony. However, his most durable compositions are related to his music for the cinema; he composed the sound tracks of a great number of films of the Italian director Federico Fellini covering the period from 1950 to 1979.

WORKS: OPERAS: *Il Principe porcaro* (1925); *Ariodante* (Parma, Nov. 5, 1942); *Torquemada* (1943; rev. version, Naples, Jan. 24, 1976); radio opera, *I 2 timidi* (Italian Radio, 1950; stage version, London, March 17, 1952); *Il cappello di paglia di Firenzi* (Florentine Straw Hat; 1946; Palermo, April 2, 1955); *La scuola di guida* (Spoleto, 1959); *Lo scoiattolo in gamba* (Venice, Sept. 16, 1959); opera buffa, *La notte di un nevrastenico* (concert version, Turin, July 9, 1959; stage version, Milan, Feb. 8, 1960); *Aladino e la lampada magica* (Naples, Jan. 14, 1968); *La visita meravigliosa*, after H.G. Wells (Palermo, Feb. 6, 1970); *Napoli milionaria* (Spoleto, June 22, 1977). **BALLETS:** *La rappresentazione di Adamo ed Eva* (Perugia, Oct. 5, 1957); *La strada* (after the 1954 Fellini film of the same name; Milan, 1965; rev. 1978); *La Molière imaginaire* (Paris, 1976). **ORCH.:** *Balli* (1932); *Serenata* (1932); 3 syms. (1936–39; 1938–43; 1957); *Sinfonia sopra una canzone d'amore* (1947–72); Harp Concerto (1948); *Variazioni sopra un tema gioviale* (1954); *Concerto festivo* (1958); Piano Concerto (1960); *Concerto soirée* for Piano and Orch.; *Fantasia sopra 12-note del "Don Giovanni" di Mozart* for Piano and Orch. (1961); Concerto for String Orch. (1964); Trombone Concerto (1968); *Divertimento concertante* for Double Bass and Orch. (1968–69); Cello Concerto (1973); *Castel del Monte* for Horn and Orch. (1975–76); Bassoon Concerto (1974–77); *The Godfather Suite* (from the films; Buffalo, Nov. 5, 1976); *Piccolo mondo antico*, concerto for Piano and Orch. (1979). **VOCAL:** Oratorios: *L'infanzia di S. Giovanni Battista* (1923); *Mysterium Catholicum* (1962); *La vita di Maria* (1970); *Roma capomunni* (1972); *Rabelaisiana* (1978); 3 masses (1960–62); songs. **CHAMBER:** *Invenzioni* for String Quartet (1933); Viola Sonata (1934); *Canzona* for 11 Instruments (1935); Quintet for Flute, Oboe, Viola, Cello, and Harp (1935); Sonata for Flute and Harp (1937); Trio for Flute, Violin, and Piano (1958); Nonet (1958); Elegy for Oboe and Piano (1959); Sonata for Organ and Brass (1968). **PIANO:** *Variazioni e fuga sul nome B-A-C-H* (1950); *15 Preludes* (1964). **ORGAN:** Organ Sonata (1965). **FILM SCORES:** For films by Fellini, including *Lo sceicco bianco* (The White Sheik; 1950); *I vitelloni* (1953); *La strada* (1954); *Il bidone* (1955); *Notti di Cabiria* (1957); *La dolce vita* (1959); part of *Boccaccio 70* (1962); *Otto de mezza* (8½; 1963); *Giulietta degli spiriti* (Juliet of the Spirits; 1965); *Satyricon* (1969); *The Clowns* (1971); *Fellini Roma* (1972); *Amarcord* (1974); *Casanova* (1977); *Orchestra Rehearsal* (1979). His scores for other directors include Cass's *The Glass Mountain* (1950); De Filippo's *Napoli milionaria* (1950); Vidor's *War and Peace* (1956); Visconti's *Le notti bianche* (1957), *Rocco e i suoi fratelli* (1960), and *Il gattopardo* (The Leopard; 1963); Zeffirelli's *The Taming of the Shrew* (1966) and *Romeo e Giulietta* (1968); Bondarchuk's *Waterloo* (1969); Coppola's *The Godfather I* (1972) and *II* (1974); Harvey's *The Abdication* (1974); Wertmuller's *Love and Anarchy* (1974); Guillermin's *Death on the Nile* (1978); Monicelli's *Caro Michele* (1978); and Troell's *Hurricane* (1979).

Bibl.: D. Soria, "Artist Life," *High Fidelity/Musical America* (Nov. 1975); D. Elley, "N. R.: A Tribute," *Records and Recording* (June 1979).

Roters, Ernst, German composer; b. Oldenburg, July 6, 1892; d. Berlin, Aug. 25, 1961. He studied at the Klindworth-Scharwenka Cons. in Berlin with Moritz Mayer-Mahr (piano), Hugo Leichtentritt (theory), and Georg Schumann (composition); was in the German army during World War I; then worked in film; was again in the German army during the last year of World War II (1944–45); after the cessation of hostilities, he returned to Berlin, where he conducted the Deutsches Theater (1945–47). A highly prolific composer (150 opus numbers before 1955), he wrote an opera, *Die schwarze Kammer* (Darmstadt, 1928); incidental music for 15 plays; about 50 radio works; 3 piano concertos; numerous pieces of chamber music and songs.

Roth, Daniel, distinguished French organist; b. Mulhouse, Oct. 31, 1942. He studied with Marie-Claire Alain and Maurice Duruflé at the Paris Cons., making his recital debut in Paris at the age of 20; won the Grand Prix de Chartres (1971). He was deputy organist (1963–72) and organist (1972–85) at Sacré-Coeur in Paris, prof. of organ at the Marseilles Cons. (1973–79), and artist-in-residence of the National Shrine of the Immaculate Conception and chairman of the organ dept. at the Catholic Univ. of America in Washington, D.C. (1974–76). He became organist of St.-Sulpice in Paris in 1985. He made many tours of Europe; also appeared widely in North America.
  BIBL.: M. Buxton, "D. R. and the St Sulpice Tradition," *Musical Times* (Sept. 1989).

Roth, Feri, Hungarian-American violinist; b. Zvolen, Czechoslovakia, July 18, 1899; d. Los Angeles, May 7, 1969. He studied at the Royal Academy of Music in Budapest; organized the Budapest String Quartet (1923), with which he toured Europe; then emigrated to the U.S. and formed the Roth Quartet (1928; with Jenö Antal, Ferenc Molnar, and Janos Scholz), which made an American debut at the Pittsfield Music Festival, Sept. 21, 1928. In 1946 he was appointed prof. of violin and chamber ensemble at the Univ. of Calif. at Los Angeles, a post he held until his death.

Rothenberger, Anneliese, esteemed German soprano; b. Mannheim, June 19, 1924. After vocal study in Mannheim, she made her operatic debut in Koblenz in 1943. From 1946 to 1957 and again from 1958 to 1973 she was a member of the Hamburg State Opera; also had engagements in Düsseldorf, Salzburg, Edinburgh, and Aix-en-Provence. In 1958 she joined the Vienna State Opera; also sang at La Scala in Milan and in Munich. On Nov. 18, 1960, she made a notable debut at the Metropolitan Opera in N.Y. as Zdenka in *Arabella*. She was one of the most versatile singers of her generation, capable of giving congenial renditions of soprano roles in operas of Mozart and Verdi; she also gave excellent performances of the challenging role of Marie in Berg's *Wozzeck*. She further distinguished herself in the even more demanding role of Lulu in Berg's opera. She publ. an autobiography, *Melodie meines Lebens* (Munich, 1972).

Rother, Artur (Martin), German conductor; b. Stettin, Oct. 12, 1885; d. Aschau, Sept. 22, 1972. He studied piano and organ with his father; also attended the Univs. of Tübingen and Berlin. He conducted in Wiesbaden; was an assistant at the Bayreuth Festivals (1907–14); from 1927 to 1934, was Generalmusikdirektor in Dessau; in 1938 he went to Berlin as a conductor at the Deutsches Opernhaus, where he remained until 1958; was also chief conductor of the Berlin Radio (1946–49).

Rothier, Léon, French bass; b. Rheims, Dec. 26, 1874; d. N.Y., Dec. 6, 1951. He studied at the Paris Cons. with Crosti (singing), Lhérie (opéra-comique), and Melchissedec (opera), winning 1st prizes in all 3 classes upon graduation. He made his operatic debut as Jupiter in Gounod's *Philémon et Baucis* at the Opéra-Comique in Paris in 1899, remaining there until 1903; then was active in Marseilles (1903–7), Nice (1907–9), and Lyons (1909–10). On Dec. 10, 1910, he made his American debut at the Metropolitan Opera in N.Y. as Méphistophélès; remained on its roster until 1939 and then devoted

himself to recitals. He taught at the Volpe Inst. in N.Y. (from 1916); also privately after his retirement from the stage.

Rothmüller, (Aron) Marko, Yugoslav baritone; b. Trnjani, Dec. 31, 1908. He studied in Zagreb; then took lessons in singing with Franz Steiner in Vienna, and also had lessons in composition with Alban Berg. He made his operatic debut as Ottokar in *Der Freischütz* at the Schiller Theater in Hamburg-Altona in 1932; was a member of the opera in Zagreb (1932–34) and Zürich (1935–47); was with the Covent Garden Opera in London (1939; 1948–55). He sang with the N.Y. City Opera (1948–52); also at the Glyndebourne and Edinburgh festivals (1949–52); made his debut at the Metropolitan Opera in N.Y. on Jan. 22, 1959, as Kothner in *Die Meistersinger von Nürnberg*; appeared there again in 1960 and 1964. He taught at the Indiana Univ. School of Music in Bloomington from 1955 to 1979. He was distinguished in Wagnerian roles; also sang leading roles in modern works, including Wozzeck in Berg's opera. He wrote some chamber music and songs; publ. an interesting vol., *Die Musik der Juden* (Zürich, 1951; in Eng., London, 1953; 2nd ed., rev., 1967).

Rothwell, Evelyn, English oboist; b. Wallingford, Jan. 24, 1911. She studied at the Royal College of Music in London with Leon Goossens; in 1931 she joined the Covent Garden Opera touring orch.; then was a member of the Scottish Orch. in Glasgow (1933–36) and of the London Sym. Orch. (1935–39); also played in the Glyndebourne Festival Orch. (1934–39). In 1939 she married the conductor **John Barbirolli.** In 1971 she became a prof. of oboe at the Royal Academy of Music in London. She was made an Officer of the Order of the British Empire in 1984.
  BIBL.: H. Atkins and P. Cotes, *The Barbirollis: A Musical Marriage* (London, 1983).

Rothwell, Walter Henry, English-American conductor; b. London, Sept. 22, 1872; d. Santa Monica, Calif., March 12, 1927. He studied at the Vienna Cons. with J. Epstein (piano), R. Fuchs (theory), and Bruckner (composition); took further courses in Munich with Thuille and Schillings. In 1895 he became assistant conductor to Mahler at the Hamburg Opera; then conducted the German opera in Amsterdam (1903–4) and the Savage Opera Co. in the U.S. (1904–8). He was conductor of the St. Paul Sym. Orch. (1908–14); was engaged (1919) to organize and conduct the Los Angeles Phil. Orch., which he led until his death.

Rott, Hans (actually, **Johann Carl Maria**), Austrian composer; b. Vienna, Aug. 1, 1858; d. there, June 25, 1884. He studied organ and composition with Bruckner at the Vienna Cons. (1874–77), where he also took courses with L. Landskron (piano), H. Grädener (harmony), and F. Krenn (counterpoint and composition); then was organist at the Piarist Church in Vienna (until 1878); became insane in 1880 and spent the last 4 years of his short life in the psychiatric clinic of Vienna's General Hospital. Bruckner admired his talent, as did Mahler. His works include a Sym. for Strings (1874–75), Sym. in E major (1878–80), String Quartet, String Quintet, and songs. His extant compositions are housed in Vienna's Österreichische Nationalbibliothek.
  BIBL.: M. Löhr, "H. R.: Der Lieblingsschüler Anton Bruckners," *Lebendige Stadt* (Vienna, 1958); L. Nowak, "Die Kompositionen und Skizzen von H. R. in der Musiksammlung der Österreichischen Nationalbibliothek," *Beiträge zur Musikdokumentation: Franz Grasberger zum 60. Geburtstag* (Tutzing, 1975); P. Banks, *The Early Social and Musical Environment of Gustav Mahler* (diss., Oxford Univ., 1982); P. Banks and C. Tredgett, "H. R., 1858–1884," *Musical Times* (Sept. 1984); P. Banks, "H. R. and the New Symphony," ibid. (March 1989).

Rottenberg, Ludwig, Austrian conductor and composer; b. Czernowitz, Bukovina, Oct. 11, 1864; d. Frankfurt am Main, May 6, 1932. He studied with A. Hřimalý, R. Fuchs, and E. Mandyczewski in Vienna; was Kapellmeister at the Stadttheater in Brünn (1891–92) and at the Frankfurt opera (1893–1926). In 1910 and 1913 he conducted at Covent Garden in London.

He publ. a collection of 30 songs, a Violin Sonata, and piano variations; his opera, *Die Geschwister*, was produced in Frankfurt on Nov. 30, 1915. Rottenberg was the father-in-law of **Paul Hindemith.**

Rotzsch, Hans-Joachim, German tenor and choral conductor; b. Leipzig, April 25, 1929. He studied at the Leipzig Hochschule für Musik, where his principal teachers were Günther Ramin, Amadeus Webersinke, and Johannes Weyrauch; also studied voice with Fritz Polster. In 1961 he joined the faculty of the Leipzig Hochschule für Musik; in 1963 he became director of the choral program at the Univ. of Leipzig. He was named cantor of the Thomaskirche of Leipzig in 1972; also conducted the Neues Bachisches Collegium Musicum. He distinguished himself as a soloist in Bach's passions, oratorios, and cantatas as well as in the capacity of choral conductor. During the 1984–85 and 1985–86 seasons, he conducted a series of performances. of Bach's works at Leipzig's Thomaskirche and Gewandhaus in commemoration of the 300th anniversary of the master's birth.

Rouget, Gilbert, French ethnomusicologist; b. Paris, July 9, 1916. He studied at the Sorbonne in Paris under André Schaeffner and Constantin Brăiloiu (1935–42); joined the ethnomusicology dept. at the Musée de l'Homme in 1941, succeeding Schaeffner as director in 1965; also became director of research at CNRS in 1972. During expeditions to equatorial and western Africa (1946–70), he made 3 films in collaboration with J. Rouch (*Sortie des novices de Sakpata; Batteries dogon: Éléments pour une étude des rhythmes;* and *Danses des reines à Porto-Novo*). His field of study focuses on the music of Africa, particularly that of southern Benin; he has collected many recordings and written a number of articles, the originality and scholarship of which have made substantial contributions to African ethnomusicology.

Rouget de l'Isle or Lisle, Claude-Joseph, French poet and composer; b. Lons-le-Saunier, Jura, May 10, 1760; d. Choisy-le-Roy, June 27, 1836. He composed the music to the *Chant de guerre pour l'armée du Rhin* in 1792, while stationed in Strasbourg as a military engineer; it was known for a time as the *Marseillais' Hymn* and finally acquired the popular designation of the *Marseillaise,* having been taken up by the Marseilles soldiers marching toward Paris. Rouget de l'Isle was not a revolutionary; he was in fact imprisoned for refusing to take the oath against the crown. After his release, he rejoined the army. The *Marseillaise* was then authorized as the national song in 1795. However, it fell out of favor during the years of the Empire and the Restoration. Rouget de l'Isle spent many years in poverty until the *Marseillaise* regained its place during the July Revolution of 1830 and he was granted a pension by Louis-Philippe. In 1879 it became the official French national anthem. Rouget de l'Isle was honored with reburial in the Invalides in Paris on Bastille Day (July 14, 1915). He also composed a *Hymne dithyrambique sur la conjuration de Robespierre* (1794), *Chant des vengeances* (1798), and a *Chant du combat* for the army in Egypt (1800). He publ. 50 *Chants français* in 1825; wrote several opera librettos.

BIBL.: J. Tiersot, *R. d. l'Isle: Son œuvre, sa vie* (Paris, 1892); A. Köckert, *R. d. l'Isle* (Leipzig, 1898); A. Lanier, *R. d. l'Isle* (Besançon, 1907); J. Tiersot, *Histoire de la Marseillaise* (Paris, 1915); R. Brancour, *La Marseillaise et le Chant du départ* (1916); E. Istel, "Is the Marseillaise a German Composition?," *Musical Quarterly* (April 1922); V. Helfert, "La Marseillaise," *Rivista Musicale Italiana* (1922); A. Becker, *La Marseillaise* (Braunschweig, 1930); G. de Froidcourt, *Grétry, R. d. Lisle et la Marseillaise* (Liège, 1945); F. Chailley, "La Marseillaise: Étude critique sur ses origines," *Annales Historiques de la Révolution Française,* XXXII (1960).

Rouleau, Joseph (Alfred Pierre), Canadian bass; b. Matane, near Rimouski, Quebec, Feb. 28, 1929. He studied with Édouard Woolley and Albert Cornellier; then with Martial Singher at the Montreal Cons. (1949–52). After concert and operatic appearances in Canada, he completed his studies with Mario Basiola and Antonio Narducci in Milan (1952–54). His 1st major engagement was as Colline at the New Orleans Opera (1955); then returned to Canada to appear as Philip II in *Don Carlos* in Montreal (1956). After making his debut as Colline at London's Covent Garden (April 23, 1957), he pursued a career on both sides of the Atlantic. In 1977 he was named an Officer of the Order of Canada. His operatic repertoire comprised some 70 roles, including Basilio, Oroveso, Méphistophélès, Boris Godunov, and Don Quichotte.

Rouse, Christopher (Chapman), imaginative American composer; b. Baltimore, Feb. 15, 1949. He studied with Richard Hoffmann at the Oberlin College Cons. of Music (1967–71); took private lessons with George Crumb (1971–73); then entered Cornell Univ. in the class of Karel Husa (D.M.A., 1977); subsequently taught at the Univ. of Michigan (1978–81) and at the Eastman School of Music in Rochette, N.Y.; served as composer-in-residence of the Baltimore Sym. Orch. (1986–89). As a composer, Rouse pursues the professional course, that is, writing music for predictable performance rather than for individual experimentation. Among the celebrated artists who have performed his works are Yo-Yo Ma, William Albright, Jan de Gaetani, and Bertram Turetsky; among the orchs., the N.Y. Phil., the Philadelphia Orch., the St. Louis Sym., the Houston Sym., the Los Angeles Phil., and the Cleveland Orch. His works have also been played and recorded by numerous orchs. worldwide, including those of Stockholm, Tokyo, Sydney, and Melbourne. Rouse has been the recipient of awards from the NEA, the Guggenheim Foundation, the Rockefeller Foundation, and B.M.I., among others. The enumeration alone of the organizations that have opened their golden doors to the rousing tunes of Rouse conjures up an auditory hologram of music composed to be heard. It must be added that many of Rouse's works are programmatic—descriptive of Greek myths and occult mysteries.

Works: *Mitternachtlieder* for Bass-baritone and Chamber Ensemble (1979); *Liber Daemonum* for Organ (1980); *The Infernal Machine* for Orch. (Evian, France, May 9, 1981); String Quartet No. 1 (1982); *Rotae passionis* for Chamber Ensemble (1982; Boston, April 8, 1983); *Gorgon* for Orch. (Rochester, N.Y., Nov. 15, 1984); Contrabass Concerto (1985; Buffalo, N.Y., Feb. 25, 1988); *Phantasmata* (1985; St. Louis, Oct. 25, 1986); *Phaethon* (1986; Philadelphia, Jan. 8, 1987); Sym. No. 1 (1986; Baltimore, Jan. 21, 1988); *Jagannath* (1987; Houston, Sept. 22, 1990); String Quartet No. 2 (Aspen, Colo., July 23, 1988); *Iscariot* for Chamber Orch. (St. Paul, Minn., Oct. 28, 1989); *Concerto per Corde* for String Orch. (N.Y., Nov. 28, 1990); *Karolju* for Chorus and Orch. (1990; Baltimore, Nov. 7, 1991); Trombone Concerto (1991); Violin Concerto (1991); Cello Concerto (1992).

Roussakis, Nicolas, Greek-born American composer; b. Athens, June 10, 1934. He emigrated to the U.S. in 1949 and became a naturalized citizen in 1956; attended Columbia Univ. (B.A., 1956; M.A., 1960; D.M.A., 1975), where he studied with Otto Luening, Jack Beeson, Henry Cowell, Ben Weber, Ralph Shapey, and Philipp Jarnach. To earn a living, he played the clarinet; received a Fulbright grant for study in Germany (1961–63); attended seminars of Boulez, Berio, Ligeti, and Stockhausen in Darmstadt. Upon his return to the U.S., he became active with contemporary music groups. He taught at Columbia Univ. (1968–77) and at Rutgers, the State Univ. of N.J. (from 1977). His works are marked by an aggressive modernity of idiom, but are satisfyingly playable and surprisingly pleasurable even to untutored ears. They include *Night Speech* for Chorus and Percussion (1968); *Short Pieces* for 2 Flutes (1969); *Concertino* for Percussion and Woodwinds (1973); *Ode and Cataclysm* for Orch. (1975); *Ephemeris* for String Quartet (1979); *Fire and Earth and Water and Air* for Orch. (1980–83); *Pas de deux* for Violin and Piano (1985); *Trigono* for Trombone, Vibraphone, and Drums (1986); *The God Abandons Antony,* cantata for Narrator, Chorus, and Orch. (1987); *Hymn to Apollo* for Small Orch. (1989); piano pieces; choruses.

Rousseau, Eugene, noted American saxophonist and pedagogue; b. Blue Island, Ill., Aug. 23, 1932. He studied clarinet at the Chicago Musical College (B.M.B., 1953), oboe at Northwestern Univ. (M.M., 1954), and saxophone at the Paris Cons. (1960–61); completed his academic training at the Univ. of Iowa (Ph.D., 1962, with the diss. *Clarinet Instructional Materials from 1732 to circa 1825*). In 1965 he made his Carnegie Recital Hall debut in N.Y.; was the 1st saxophonist to give solo recitals in London, Amsterdam, Vienna, and Berlin (1967) and in Paris (1968); also appeared as a soloist with orchs. in the U.S., Europe, and the Far East. In 1969 he was co-founder of the World Saxophone Congress. He taught at Luther College in Iowa (1956–59), Central Missouri State Univ. (1962–64), and the Univ. of Iowa (1964); in 1964 he joined the faculty of the Indiana Univ. School of Music, where he was chairman of the woodwind dept. (1966–73), a prof. (1972–88), and Distinguished Prof. (from 1988). He was also a guest prof. at the Vienna Hochschule für Musik (1981–82), Arizona State Univ. (1984), and the Prague Cons. (1985). He publ. a *Method for Saxophone* (2 vols., 1973, 1977).

Rousseau, Jean-Jacques, great Swiss-born French philosopher and author; b. Geneva, June 28, 1712; d. Ermenonville, near Paris, July 2, 1778. Without other musical training besides desultory self-instruction, Rousseau made his debut as a music scholar at the age of 29, reading a paper before the Académie in Paris (1724), which was received and publ. as a *Dissertation sur la musique moderne* (1743). His opera *Les Muses galantes* had only 1 private representation, at the house of La Pouplinière in 1745; his revision of the intermezzo *La Reine de Navarre* (by Voltaire and Rameau) was a failure in Paris; but his opera *Le Devin du village* (Fontainebleau, Oct. 18, 1752; Paris Opéra, March 1, 1753) was very successful and remained in the repertoire for 75 years. In the meantime, his musical articles for the *Encyclopédie* had evoked scathing criticism from Rameau and others; improved by revision and augmentation, they were republ. as his *Dictionnaire de musique* (Geneva, 1767; the existence of this ed. cannot be proved; 1st known ed., Paris, 1768). In 1752 commenced the dispute, known as the "guerre des bouffons," between the partisans of French and Italian opera; Rousseau sided with the latter, publ. a *Lettre à M. Grimm au sujet des remarques ajoutées à sa lettre sur Omphale* (1752), followed by the caustic *Lettre sur la musique française* (1753; to which the members of the Opéra responded by burning him in effigy and excluding him from the theater) and *Lettre d'un symphoniste de l'Académie royale de musique à ses camarades* (1753). He wrote 2 numbers for the melodrama *Pygmalion* (1770; Paris, Oct. 30, 1775). Publ. posthumously were 6 new arias for *Le Devin du village*, and a collection of about 100 *romances* and duets, *Les Consolations des misères de ma vie* (1781), and fragments of an opera, *Daphnis et Chloé* (1780). His writings on music are included in the *Oeuvres complètes de Jean-Jacques Rousseau* (4 vols., 1959–69); for his letters, see R. Leigh, ed., *Correspondance complète Jean-Jacques Rousseau* (18 vols., 1965–73).

BIBL.: A. Jensen, *J.-J. R. Fragments inédits, recherches biographiques* (Paris, 1882); A. Jansen, *J.-J. R. als Musiker* (Berlin, 1884); A. Pougin, *J.-J. R., Musicien* (Paris, 1901); E. Istel, *J.-J. R. als Komponist seiner lyrischen Szene "Pygmalion"* (Leipzig, 1901); F. Hellouin, "J.-J. R. et la psychologie de l'orchestre," in *Feuillets d'histoire musicale française* (Paris, 1903); E. Schütte, *J.-J. R. Seine Persönlichkeit und sein Stil* (Leipzig, 1910); J. Tiersot, *J.-J. R.* (Paris, 1912); E. Faguet, *R. artiste* (Paris, 1913); A. Sells, *The Early Life of R.: 1712–40* (London, 1929); R. Gérin, *J.-J. R.* (Paris, 1930); M. Moffat, *R. et le théâtre* (Paris, 1930); J. Tiersot, "Concerning J.-J. R., the Musician," *Musical Quarterly* (July 1931); H. Somerset, "J.-J. R. as a Musician," *Music & Letters* (1936); L. Richebourg, *Contributions à l'histoire de la "querelle des bouffons"* (Paris, 1937); A. Pochon, *J.-J. R., musiciens et le critique* (Montreux, 1940); E. Kisch, "Rameau and R.," *Music & Letters* (1941); A. Oliver, *The Encyclopaedists as Critics of Music* (N.Y., 1947); J. Senelier, *Bibliographie générale des œuvres de J.-J. R.* (Paris, 1949); J. Strauss,

"J.-J. R.: Musician," *Musical Quarterly*, LXIV (1978); P. Gülke, *R. und die Musik, oder, Von der Zuständigkeit des Dilettanten* (Wilhelmshaven, 1984).

Rousseau, Marcel (-Auguste-Louis), French composer, son of **Samuel-Alexandre Rousseau;** b. Paris, Aug. 18, 1882; d. there, June 11, 1955. He studied with his father, then entered the Paris Cons. as a student of Lenepveu; won the Deuxième Premier Grand Prix de Rome with the cantata *Maia* (1905); later added his father's 1st name to his own, and produced his works as Samuel-Rousseau. In 1947 he was elected to the Académie des Beaux-Arts.

WORKS: OPERAS (All 1st perf. in Paris): *Tarass Boulba* (Nov. 22, 1919); *Le Hulla* (March 9, 1923); *Le Bon Roi Dagobert* (Dec. 5, 1927; his most successful work); *Kerkeb* (April 6, 1951). BALLETS: *Promenade dans Rome* (Paris, Dec. 7, 1936); *Entre 2 rondes* (Paris, April 27, 1940). ORCH.: Tableaux: *Solitude triste* and *Impression dolente*; etc.

Rousseau, Samuel-Alexandre, French conductor, teacher, and composer, father of **Marcel (-Auguste-Louis) Rousseau;** b. Neuve-Maison, Aisne, June 11, 1853; d. Paris, Oct. 1, 1904. He studied at the Paris Cons. with Franck (organ) and Bazin (composition); won the Grand Prix de Rome with the cantata *La Fille de Jephté* (1878); also the Prix Cressent with the comic opera *Dianora* (Paris, Opéra-Comique, Dec. 22, 1879). His opera *Mérowig* was awarded the Prize of the City of Paris, and was performed in concert form at the Grand Théâtre there on Dec. 12, 1892. In 1892 he was appointed conductor at the Théâtre-Lyrique in Paris; was for 10 years chorus master at the Société des Concerts du Cons.; also taught harmony at the Paris Cons. On June 8, 1898, his lyric drama *La Cloche du Rhin* was staged at the Paris Opéra with considerable success, but had only 9 performances in all; this was followed by the music dramas *Milia* (Opéra-Comique, 1904) and *Léone* (Opéra-Comique, March 7, 1910).

Roussel, Albert (Charles Paul Marie), outstanding French composer; b. Tourcoing, Département du Nord, April 5, 1869; d. Royan, Aug. 23, 1937. Orphaned as a child, he was educated by his grandfather, mayor of his native town, and after the grandfather's death, by his aunt. He studied academic subjects at the Collège Stanislas in Paris; music with the organist Stoltz; then studied mathematics in preparation for entering the Naval Academy; at the age of 18 he began his training in the navy; from 1889 to Aug. 1890 he was a member of the crew of the frigate *Iphigénie*, sailing to Indochina. This voyage was of great importance to Roussel, since it opened for him a world of oriental culture and art, which became one of the chief sources of his musical inspiration. He later sailed on the cruiser *Dévastation*; received a leave of absence for reasons of health, and spent some time in Tunis; was then stationed in Cherbourg, and began to compose there. In 1893 he was sent once more to Indochina. He resigned from the navy in 1894 and went to Paris, where he began to study music seriously with Eugène Gigout. In 1898 he entered the Schola Cantorum in Paris as a pupil of Vincent d'Indy; continued this study until 1907, when he was already 38 years old, but at the same time he was entrusted with a class in counterpoint, which he conducted at the Schola Cantorum from 1902 to 1914; among his students were Erik Satie, Stan Golestan, Paul Le Flem, Roland-Manuel, Guy de Lioncourt, and Varèse. In 1909 Roussel and his wife, Blanche Preisach-Roussel, undertook a voyage to India, where he became acquainted with the legend of the queen Padmâvatî, which he selected as a subject for his famous opera-ballet. His choral sym. *Les Evocations* was also inspired by this tour. At the outbreak of World War I in 1914, Roussel applied for active service in the navy but was rejected, and volunteered as an ambulance driver. After the Armistice of 1918, he settled in Normandy and devoted himself to composition. In the autumn of 1930 he visited the U.S.

Roussel began his work under the influence of French Impressionism, with its dependence on exotic moods and poetic association. However, the sense of formal design asserted itself in his symphonic works; his *Suite en fa* (1927) signalizes a transition toward neo-Classicism; the thematic development is vigorous, and the rhythms are clearly delineated, despite some asymmetrical progressions; the orchestration, too, is in the Classical tradition. Roussel possessed a keen sense of the theater; he was capable of fine characterization of exotic or mythological subjects, but also knew how to depict humorous situations in lighter works. An experiment in a frankly modernistic manner is exemplified by his *Jazz dans la nuit* for Voice and Piano.

WORKS: STAGE: *Le Marchand de sable qui passe*, incidental music (Le Havre, Dec. 16, 1908); *Le Festin de l'araignée*, ballet-pantomime (Paris, April 3, 1913); *Padmâvatî*, opera-ballet (1914–18; Paris, June 1, 1923); *La Naissance de la lyre*, lyric opera (Paris, July 1, 1925); *Bacchus et Ariane*, ballet (Paris, May 22, 1931); *Le Testament de la tante Caroline*, opéra-bouffe (1932–33; Olomouc, Nov. 14, 1936); *Aeneas*, ballet with Chorus (Brussels, July 31, 1935). ORCH.: 4 syms.: No. 1, *Le Poème de la forêt* (1904–6; Brussels, March 22, 1908); No. 2, *Symphonie en si bémol* (1919–21; Paris, March 4, 1922); No. 3, *Symphonie en sol mineur* (Boston, Oct. 24, 1930); No. 4, *Symphonie en la majeur* (1934; Paris, Oct. 19, 1935); *Suite en fa* (Boston, Jan. 21, 1927); *Sinfonietta* for Strings (Paris, Nov. 19, 1934); *Résurrection*, symphonic poem (Paris, May 17, 1904); *Evocations*, suite (Paris, May 18, 1912); *Pour une fête de printemps* (Paris, Oct. 29, 1921); *Rapsodie flamande* (Brussels, Dec. 12, 1935); *Concert pour petit orchestre* (Paris, May 5, 1927); *Petite suite pour orchestre* (Paris, April 11, 1929); Piano Concerto (Paris, June 7, 1928); Concertino for Cello and Orch. (Paris, Feb. 6, 1937); *Le Bardit de Francs* for Male Chorus, Brass, and Percussion (Strasbourg, April 21, 1928); *Psaume LXXX* for Tenor, Chorus, and Orch. (Paris, April 25, 1929); symphonic suites from theater works: *Le Festin de l'araignée* (1912); *Padmâvatî* (1914–18); *La Naissance de la lyre* (1922–24); *Bacchus et Ariane* (1930). CHAMBER: Piano Trio (1902); *Divertissement* for Flute, Oboe, Clarinet, Bassoon, Horn, and Piano (1906); *Sérénade* for Flute, Violin, Viola, Cello, and Harp (1925); Trio for Flute, Viola, and Cello (1929); String Quartet (1932); Trio for Violin, Viola, and Cello (1937); 2 violin sonatas (1908, 1924); *Joueurs de flûte*, suite for Flute and Piano (1924); *Andante et Scherzo* for Flute and Piano (1934). PIANO: *Des heures passant*, cycle of 4 pieces (1898); *Rustiques*, cycle of 3 pieces (1904–6); suite of 3 pieces (1910); Sonatina (1912); *Petit canon perpétuel* (1913); *Prélude et fugue (Hommage à Bach)*; etc. SONGS: *Adieux* (1907); *Jazz dans la nuit* (1928); *2 idylles* (1931); 3 sets of *Poèmes chinois* (1908, 1927, 1932); etc. A complete catalog of works, with a biographical notice and annotations, was publ. in Paris in 1947 and constitutes a primary source of information.

BIBL.: Roland-Manuel, "A. R.," *Revue Musicale* (Nov. 1922); L. Vuillemin, *A. R. et son œuvre* (Paris, 1924); special issue of *Courier Musical* (April 15, 1929); special issue of *Revue Musicale*, X/3 (1929); H. Prunières, "A. R. and the 80th Psalm," *Musical Quarterly* (Jan. 1930); R. Dumesnil, "L'Œuvre symphonique de A. R.," *Musique Française* (Feb. 1933); special issue of *Revue Musicale*, 178 (1937); R. Petit, "A. R.," *Modern Music* (Nov.–Dec. 1937); A. Hoérée, *A. R.* (Paris, 1938); P. Landormy, "A. R.," *Musical Quarterly* (Oct. 1938); N. Demuth, *A. R.: A Study* (London, 1947); R. Bernard, *A. R.: Sa vie, son œuvre* (Paris, 1948); M. Pincherle, *A. R.* (Geneva, 1957); B. Deane, *A. R.* (London, 1961); J. Eddins, *The Symphonic Music of A. R.* (diss., Florida State Univ., 1967); A. Surchamp, *A. R.* (Paris, 1967); special issue of *Zodiaque*, LXXX (1969); R. Chrichton, "R.'s Stage Works," *Musical Times*, CX (1969); E. Neill, "A. R.," *Musicalia*, i/1 (1970); R. Follet, *A. R.: A Bio-Bibliography* (Westport, Conn., 1988).

Rousselière, Charles, French tenor; b. St. Nazaire, Jan. 17, 1875; d. Joue-les-Tours, May 11, 1950. He studied at the Paris Cons.; made his debut in 1900 as Samson at the Paris Opéra, where he sang until 1912; also sang with the Monte Carlo Opera (1905–14), creating roles in Mascagni's *Amica*, Saint-Saëns's *L'Ancêtre*, and Fauré's *Pénélope*; also sang the role of Julien in Charpentier's opera at its 1st performance at the

Opéra-Comique in Paris. He made his debut at the Metropolitan Opera in N.Y. as Romeo on Nov. 26, 1906, but remained on its roster for only 1 season. He made guest appearances at La Scala in Milan, the Teatro Colón in Buenos Aires, in Palermo, etc. He was at his best in the roles of Radames, Manrico, Siegmund, and Loge.

Roussier, Abbé Pierre-Joseph, French writer on music; b. Marseilles, 1716; d. Ecouis, Normandy, Aug. 18, 1792. He served as canon in Ecouis.

WRITINGS: *Observations sur différents points d'harmonie* (1765); *Traité des accords, et de leur succession* (1764; supplemented by *L'Harmonie pratique*, 1775); *Mémoire sur la musique des anciens* (1770); *Notes et observations sur le mémoire du P. Amiot concernant la musique des chinois* (1779); *Mémoire sur la nouvelle harpe de M. Cousineau* (1782); *Mémoire sur le clavecin chromatique* (1782); *Lettre sur l'acceptation des mots "basse fondamentale"* (1783; *Journal Encyclopédique*, vol. I); etc.

BIBL.: R. Osborne, *The Theoretical Writings of Abbé P.-J. R.* (diss., Ohio State Univ., 1966).

Routh, Francis (John), English pianist, organist, conductor, writer on music, and composer; b. Kidderminster, Jan. 15, 1927. He studied at King's College, Cambridge (1948–51), at the Royal Academy of Music in London (1951–53), and with Mátyás Seiber; was founder and artistic director of the Redcliffe Concerts (from 1964), with which he presented works by British composers of the past and present.

WORKS: ORCH. (all 1st perf. in London unless otherwise given): Violin Concerto (1965; April 25, 1968); *Dialogue* for Violin and Orch. (May 20, 1969); Double Concerto for Violin, Cello, and Orch. (May 11, 1970); *Spring Night*, concert aria for Mezzo-soprano and Orch. (1971; March 13, 1972); Sym. (1973; Dublin, July 22, 1975); Cello Concerto (1973; May 20, 1974); Piano Concerto (1976; Sept. 26, 1977); *Scenes for Orchestra* (1978); Oboe Concerto (1984); *Poème fantastique* (1987). CHAMBER: *Dance Suite* for String Quartet (1967); Sonata for Solo Cello (1971); Piano Quartet (1971); *Serenade* for String Trio (1972); Cello Sonata (1975); Oboe Quartet (1977); *Concerto for Ensemble I* (1981) and *II* (1983); *Dance Interludes* for Flute and Guitar (1987); piano pieces; organ works. VOCAL: *Ode to the Evening Star* for Chorus (1966); *The Death of Iphigenia* for Soprano and 13 Instruments (1972); *On a Deserted Shore* for Soloists, Chorus, 2 Pianos, and 2 Percussion (1975); *Vocalise* for Soprano, Clarinet, Violin, Cello, and Piano (1979); *Love's Fool* for Soprano, Flute, and Guitar (1980); solo songs.

WRITINGS: *The Organ* (1958); *Contemporary Music: An Introduction* (1968); *Contemporary British Music* (1972); *Early English Organ Music* (1973); with others, *Patronage of the Creative Artist* (1974); *Stravinsky* (1975).

Rovelli, Pietro, Italian violinist and composer; b. Bergamo, Feb. 6, 1793; d. there, Sept. 8, 1838. He studied with R. Kreutzer; then played in Italy; was concertmaster of the Court Orch. in Munich (1815–19); then taught and conducted in Bergamo. He publ. excellent études and caprices for Violin; also *Variazioni* for Violin and Orch.

Rovere, Agostino, Italian bass; b. Monza, 1804; d. N.Y., Dec. 10, 1865. He studied in Milan; made his debut in 1826 in Pavia; was a leading singer at La Scala in Milan (1831–44; 1846–47; 1856–57); also appeared in Vienna (1839; 1842–45), where he created the role of Boisfleury in Donizetti's *Linda di Chamounix*; also sang at Covent Garden in London (1847–48). He was most famous for his buffo roles; excelled as Leporello, Bartolo, and Dulcamara.

Rovetta, Giovanni, Italian composer; b. Venice, c.1595; d. there, Oct. 23, 1668. He pursued his career in his native city, being closely associated with San Marco; was a boy treble, and later an instrumentalist (1615–17); in 1623 he was made a bass singer, and soon thereafter a priest; after serving as assistant maestro di cappella (1627–44), he succeeded Monteverdi (in 1644) as maestro di cappella, a post he held until his death. He was a fine composer of both sacred and secular works. Among his output were the operas *Ercole in Lidia* (1645) and *Argiope* (1649), masses, motets, Psalms, and madrigals.

Rowen, Ruth Halle, American music educator; b. N.Y., April 5, 1918. She studied at Barnard College (B.A., 1939) and with Mitchell, Lang, Hertzmann, and Moore at Columbia Univ. (M.A., 1941; Ph.D., 1948); was director of the education dept. of Carl Fischer, Inc. (1954–63), then taught at the City College of N.Y. (1963–67) and at the graduate school of the City Univ. of N.Y. (from 1967). She wrote *Early Chamber Music* (N.Y., 1949; new ed., 1974) and *Music through Sources and Documents* (Englewood Cliffs, N.J., 1978).

Rowicki, Witold, Polish conductor; b. Taganrog, Russia, Feb. 26, 1914; d. Warsaw, Oct. 1, 1989. He studied violin with Malawski and composition with Piotrowski and Wallek-Walewski at the Krakow Cons. (graduated as a violinist, 1938); during World War II, he studied with Rudolf Hindemith, the brother of Paul Hindemith (1942–44). Although he made his conducting debut in 1933, he pursued a career as a violinist until the end of World War II. In 1945 he helped organize the Polish Radio Sym. Orch. in Katowice, which he conducted until 1950; then in 1950 reorganized the Warsaw Phil., which he conducted until 1955, at which time he opened the orch.'s new home and oversaw the renaming of the orch. as the National Phil. before resigning his post. From 1958 to 1977 he was again the conductor of the National Phil.; then was chief conductor of the Bamberg Sym. Orch. (1982–85). He became widely known for his promotion of contemporary Polish music. He was also a composer; wrote syms., other orch. works, chamber music, and songs.

BIBL.: L. Terpilowski, *W. R.* (Krakow, 1961).

Rowley, Alec, English pianist, teacher, and composer; b. London, March 13, 1892; d. Weybridge, Jan. 11, 1958. He studied at the Royal Academy of Music in London; upon graduation, became a teacher. Among his works are a pantomime, *The Princess Who Lost a Tune*; 2 piano concertos; *Rhapsody* for Viola and Orch.; Concerto for Oboe and Orch.; *Phyllis and Corydon* for String Quartet; *From Faerie* for String Quartet; *Little Jesus* for Voice, Piano, and String Quartet; *Water-colours* for Piano, Violin, Viola, and Cello; *Pastel Portraits* for Piano, Violin, and Cello; 3 little trios for Piano, Violin, and Cello; *The Puppet Show, 4 Contrasts, A Short Suite*; also piano pieces for children.

Roxburgh, Edwin, English composer, oboist, conductor, and teacher; b. Liverpool, Nov. 6, 1937. He studied composition with Herbert Howells at the Royal College of Music in London, with Luigi Nono and Luigi Dallapiccola in Italy, and with Nadia Boulanger in France; completed his education at St. John's College, Cambridge. He was principal oboist in the Sadler's Wells Opera orch. (1964–67), then prof. of composition and founder-director of the 20th-century performance studies dept. at the Royal College of Music (from 1967); also appeared as an oboist and was conductor of the 20th Century Ensemble of London. With L. Goossens, he publ. *The Oboe* (London, 1976). He composed a number of finely crafted orch., chamber, and vocal works, his idiomatic writing for woodwinds being particularly admirable.
WORKS: STAGE: *Abelard,* opera (in progress); *The Tower,* ballet (1964). **ORCH.:** *Variations* (1963); *Montage* (1977); *7 Tableaux,* concerto for Trumpet and Orch. (1979); *Prelude* (1981); *Saturn* (1982); *Serenata* for String Orch. (1983); *Tamesis* for Chamber Orch. (1983). **CHAMBER:** *Movements* for String Quartet (1961); Quartet for Flute, Clarinet, Violin, and Cello (1964); *Music 3* for String Trio (1966); *Dithyramb I* for Clarinet and Percussion (1972) and *II* for Piano and 3 Percussion (1972); *Nebula I* for Clarinet Choir (1974) and *II* for Wind Quintet (1974); *At the Still Point of the Turning World* for Amplified Oboe and Electronics (1978); *Hexham Tropes* for Oboe, Oboe d'Amore, Bassoon, and Harpsichord (1979); Wind Quintet No. 2 (1983) for Flute, Violin, Viola, and Cello (1984); *Voyager* for 3 Oboes, 3 English Horns, and 3 Bassoons (1989); piano pieces. **VOCAL:** *Recitative after Blake* for Contralto, and

String Quintet or String Orch. (1961); *Night Music* for Soprano and Orch. (1969); *How Pleasant to Know Mr. Lear* for Narrator and Chamber Orch. (1971); *A Scottish Fantasy* for Soprano, Violin, and String Orch. (1973); *A Portrait of e e cummings* for 2 Narrators, Violin, and Orch. (1974); *The Rock,* oratorio for Soloists, Chorus, Children's Chorus, and Orch. (1979); *et vitam venturi saeculi* for Chorus (1983); other choruses; songs.

Roy, Klaus George, Austrian-born American composer, writer, and program annotator; b. Vienna, Jan. 24, 1924. He went to the U.S. in 1940 and became a naturalized U.S. citizen in 1944; studied at Boston Univ. with Karl Geiringer (B.Mus., 1947) and at Harvard Univ. with Archibald T. Davison, Otto Kinkeldey, Arthur Tillman Merritt, and Walter Piston (M.A., 1949). In 1945–46 he served as an officer in education and information with U.S. Army General Headquarters in Tokyo. From 1948 to 1957 he was employed as a librarian and instructor at Boston Univ.; wrote music criticism for the *Christian Science Monitor* (1950–57). From 1958 to 1988 he was program annotator and ed. of the Cleveland Orch.; also taught at the Cleveland Inst. of Art (from 1975) and served as adjunct prof. at the Cleveland Inst. of Music (from 1986), which bestowed upon him an honorary doctorate in music (1987). He wrote compositions in a variety of genres, all extremely pleasing to the ear.
WORKS: Duo for Flute and Clarinet (1947); *St. Francis' Canticle of the Sun* for Chorus and Viola (Boston, Nov. 5, 1951); *The Clean Dispatch of Dying,* song cycle for Soprano and Piano (1951); *Christopher-Suite* for Piano or Harpsichord (1953); *Lie Still, Sleep Becalmed* for a cappella Chorus (1954); *Sterlingman,* chamber opera (WGBH-TV, Boston, April 18, 1957); *Inaugural Fantasia* for Organ (1965); *Chorale-Variants on an Appalachian Ballad* for Orch. (1965; Cleveland, April 3, 1966); *Serenade* for Cello (Cleveland, May 15, 1968); *Lunar Modulations* for Children's Chorus and Percussion (Cuyahoga Falls, Ohio, July 19, 1969); *7 Brief Sermons on Love* for Soprano and Organ (1972); *A New Song* for Chorus, Speaking Chorus, and Organ (1973); *Winter Death Songs,* 7 haiku for Low Voice and Piano (1982); *Songs of Alexias* for Low Voice and Piano (1982); *Cheaper by the Dozen,* 12 flute duets (1985); *Miracles Are Not Ceased,* scena for Soprano and Oboe (1985); incidental music; also some 300 shorter pieces, including canons, greetings, and Christmas cards.

Royce, Edward, American composer and teacher; b. Cambridge, Mass., Dec. 25, 1886; d. Stamford, Conn., July 7, 1963. He studied at Harvard Univ. (B.A., 1907), later at the Stern Cons. in Berlin; in 1913 founded the music dept. at Middlebury College in Vermont; was head of the theory dept. at the Ithaca Cons. (1916–21); from 1923 till 1947 was a prof. of theory at the Eastman School of Music in Rochester, N.Y. He composed 2 tone poems: *The Fire Bringers* (Rochester, April 23, 1926) and *Far Ocean* (Rochester, June 3, 1929); piano pieces; songs.

Royer, Etienne, French composer; b. Grenoble, April 12, 1882; d. Paris, March 2, 1928. He studied with d'Indy and Sérieyx at the Schola Cantorum in Paris; was a cello pupil of L. Revel; wrote music criticism and publ. pedagogical works. He composed *Danse mystique* for Orch.; *Cantus memorialis* for Violin and Orch.; *Pour le temps de la moisson* and *Pour les fêtes de mai,* for String Quartet (based on French folk tunes); songs; piano pieces; etc.

Royer, Joseph-Nicolas-Pancrace, French composer; b. Turin, c.1705; d. Paris, Jan. 11, 1755. He was a native of Burgundy, and settled in Paris in 1725. He was maître de musique at the Opéra (1730–33); became maître de musique des enfans de France (1734), serving with Matho; obtained the latter's reversion as maître de la musique de la chambre du roi (1735). In 1748 he became director of the Concert Spirituel; in 1753, obtained the reversion of maître de musique de la chambre du roi from Rebel and Bury; that same year was named director and composer at the Opéra.
WORKS: Stage (all 1st perf. in Paris unless otherwise given): *Le Fâcheux Veuvage* (opéra-comique; Aug. 1725); *Crédit est*

mort (opéra-comique; Feb. 19, 1726); *Pyrrhus* (tragédie lyrique; Oct. 26, 1730); *Zaïde, reine de Granade* (opéra-ballet; Sept. 3, 1739); *Le Pouvoir de l'amour* (opéra-ballet; April 23, 1743); *Almasis* (Versailles, Feb. 26, 1748); *Myrtil et Zélie* (pastorale-héroique; Versailles, June 20, 1750); *Prométhée et Pandore* (opera; n.d.; not perf.); other vocal works and *Pièces de clavecin, 1er livre* (Paris, 1746).

Rôze, Marie (real name **Hippolyte Ponsin**), French soprano and pedagogue, mother of **Raymond Rôze;** b. Paris, March 2, 1846; d. there, June 21, 1926. She studied at the Paris Cons. with Mocker and later with Auber, winning 2 prizes in 1865; made her debut at the Opéra-Comique in the title role of Hérold's *Marie* (Aug. 16, 1865); sang there for 3 seasons; then appeared at the Paris Opéra as Marguerite in Gounod's *Faust* (Jan. 2, 1879); made her London debut as Marguerite (1872); continued to sing in England for many years. She visited America twice, in 1877–78 and 1880–81. In 1874 she married an American bass, Julius E. Perkins, who died the following year. In 1890 she settled in Paris as a teacher.

Rôze, Raymond, English composer, son of **Marie Rôze;** b. London, 1875; d. there, March 31, 1920. He studied at the Brussels Cons., where he won 1st prize; wrote overtures and incidental music to many plays. In 1913 he organized at Covent Garden a season of opera in English, during which he conducted his own opera *Joan of Arc* (Oct. 31, 1913); another opera by him, *Arabesque*, was produced at the Coliseum in London in 1916.

Rozhdestvensky, Gennadi (Nikolaievich), eminent Russian conductor, son of **Nikolai Anosov;** b. Moscow, May 4, 1931. He studied piano with Oborin and conducting with his father at the Moscow Cons.; graduated in 1954. From 1951 to 1961 he served as assistant conductor at the Bolshoi Theater in Moscow, and from 1964 to 1970 was its principal conductor. From 1961 to 1974 he was chief conductor of the All-Union Radio and TV Sym. Orch. in Moscow; also was chief conductor of the Stockholm Phil. (1975–77), the BBC Sym. Orch. in London (1978–81), and the Vienna Sym. Orch. (1981–83). In 1982 he founded and became chief conductor of the State Sym. Orch. of the Soviet Ministry of Culture in Moscow. He married the pianist **Viktoria Postnikova** in 1969. He is distinguished by his encompassing interest in new music; he conducted notable performances of works by Soviet composers, particularly Prokofiev and Shostakovich, as well as by Stravinsky, Schoenberg, Berg, Milhaud, Honegger, and Poulenc. He publ. a technical treatise, *Technique of Conducting* (Leningrad, 1974), and a collection of essays, *Thoughts about Music* (Moscow, 1975).

Rozkošný, Josef Richard, Czech composer; b. Prague, Sept. 21, 1833; d. there, June 3, 1913. He studied painting and music in Prague; his teachers were Tomaschek (piano) and Kittl (composition). His songs and choruses became popular, and he successfully attempted the composition of operas to Czech librettos; 8 operas were produced in Prague, among them: *Svatojánské proudy* (The Rapids of St. John; Oct. 3, 1871); *Popelka* (Cinderella; May 31, 1885); *Černé jezero* (The Black Lake; Jan. 6, 1906). He also publ. a number of piano pieces.

Rózsa, Miklós, brilliant Hungarian-American composer; b. Budapest, April 18, 1907. He studied piano and composition in Leipzig with Hermann Grabner; musicology with Theodor Kroyer. In 1931 he settled in Paris, where he became successful as a composer; his works were often performed in European music centers. In 1935 he went to London; composed there for the films; in 1940 he emigrated to the U.S., and settled in Hollywood; was on the staff of MGM (1948–62); also taught at the Univ. of Southern Calif. in Los Angeles (1945–65). His autobiography was publ. as *Double Life* (London, 1982). His orch. and chamber music is cast in the advanced modern idiom in vogue in Europe between the 2 world wars; neo-Classical in general content, it is strong in polyphony and incisive rhythm; for his film music, he employs a more Roman-

tic and diffuse style, relying on a Wagnerian type of grandiloquence. He won Oscars for his film scores to *Spellbound* (1945), *A Double Life* (1947), and *Ben-Hur* (1959).

Works: orch.: *Variations on a Hungarian Peasant Song* for Violin and Orch. (1929; also for Violin and Piano); Sym. (1930); *Serenade* for Small Orch. (1932; rev. 1946 as *Hungarian Serenade*); Scherzo (1933); *Theme, Variations, and Finale* (1933; rev. 1943); Concerto for String Orch. (1943; Los Angeles, Dec. 28, 1944; rev. 1957); Violin Concerto (Dallas, Jan. 5, 1956; Jascha Heifetz, soloist); *Sinfonia concertante* for Violin, Cello, and Orch. (1966); Piano Concerto (1966; Los Angeles, April 6, 1967); Cello Concerto (1969); *Tripartita* (1973); Viola Concerto (1979; Pittsburgh, May 4, 1984; Pinchas Zukerman, soloist). **chamber:** Piano Quintet (1928); Sonata for 2 Violins (1933; rev. 1973); 2 string quartets (1950, 1981); Flute Sonata (1983); Sonata for Solo Clarinet (N.Y., Jan. 14, 1987); various works for piano. **film scores:** *Knight without Armour* (1937); *The Four Feathers* (1939); *The Thief of Bagdad* (1940); *Lydia* (1941); *That Hamilton Woman* (1941); *Jacare* (1942); *Jungle Book* (1942); *5 Graves to Cairo* (1943); *Double Indemnity* (1944); *The Lost Weekend* (1945); *Spellbound* (1945); *The Killers* (1946); *The Strange Love of Martha Ivers* (1946); *Brute Force* (1947); *A Double Life* (1947); *The Naked City* (1948); *The Secret beyond the Door* (1948); *Madame Bovary* (1949); *The Asphalt Jungle* (1950); *Quo vadis?* (1951); *Ivanhoe* (1952); *Plymouth Adventure* (1952); *Julius Caesar* (1953); *The Story of Three Loves* (1953); *Knights of the Round Table* (1954); *Lust for Life* (1956); *A Time to Love and a Time to Die* (1958); *Ben-Hur* (1959); *El Cid* (1961); *King of Kings* (1961); *The V.I.P.s* (1963); *The Green Berets* (1968); *The Private Life of Sherlock Holmes* (1970); *The Golden Voyage of Sinbad* (1974); *Providence* (1977); *Time after Time* (1979); *Eye of the Needle* (1981); *Dead Men Don't Wear Plaid* (1982). **vocal:** choral works; songs.

Bibl.: C. Palmer, *M. R.: A Sketch of His Life and Work* (N.Y., 1975).

Rozsnyai, Zoltán, Hungarian conductor; b. Budapest, Jan. 29, 1927; d. San Diego, Sept. 10, 1990. He was educated at the Franz Liszt Academy of Music, where his teachers included Bartók, Kodály, and Dohnányi; also took courses at the Technical Univ. and at the Pazmany Peter Univ. of Sciences in Budapest; completed his musical training at the Univ. of Vienna. He was conductor of the Phil. Orch. in Miskolc (1948–50); then conducted the Debrecen Opera (1950–53); later led several Hungarian orchs. He left Hungary after the abortive revolution of 1956 and went to the U.S. In 1957 he organized the Philharmonia Hungarica; toured with it in 1958. He was an assistant conductor of the N.Y. Phil. (1962–63); then was music director of the Cleveland Phil. (1965–68) and the San Diego Sym. (1967–71). In 1976 he became music director of the Golden State Opera Co. in Los Angeles; in 1978, became music director of the Knoxville (Tenn.) Sym. Orch., which post he retained until 1985.

Różycki, Ludomir, Polish composer; b. Warsaw, Nov. 6, 1884; d. Katowice, Jan. 1, 1953. He studied piano with his father, a teacher at the Warsaw Cons.; theory with Noskowski at the Cons., graduating with honors in 1903. He then went to Berlin, where he took lessons with Humperdinck; in 1908 he was appointed conductor of the opera theater in Lemberg; then undertook a European tour; settled in Berlin, where he remained through the years of World War I. In 1920 he returned to Warsaw; was a prof. at the Warsaw Cons. (1930–45) and at the Katowice Cons. (from 1945). He was highly regarded in Poland as a national composer of stature; his style of composition was a successful blend of German, Russian, and Italian ingredients, yet the Polish characteristics were not obscured by the cosmopolitan harmonic and orch. dress.

Works: operas: *Bolesław Śmiały* (Boleslaw the Bold; 1908; Lemberg, Feb. 11, 1909); *Meduza* (1911; Warsaw, Oct. 22, 1912); *Eros i Psyche* (1916; in German, Breslau, March 10, 1917); *Casanova* (1922; Warsaw, June 8, 1923); *Beatrix Cenci* (1926; Warsaw, Jan. 30, 1927); *Młyn diabelski* (The Devilish

Mill; 1930; Poznan, Feb. 21, 1931). OPERETTA: *Lili chce śpie-wac* (Lile Wants to Sing; 1932; Poznan, March 7, 1933). BAL-LETS: *Pan Twardowski* (1920; Warsaw, May 9, 1921); *Apollo i dziewczyna* (Apollo and the Maiden; 1937). ORCH.: *Stańczyk*, symphonic scherzo (1903); symphonic poems: *Anhelli* (1909); *Warszawianka* (1910); *Mona Lisa Gioconda* (1910); *Pietà* (1942); *Warszawa wyzwolona* (Warsaw Liberated; 1950); 2 piano concertos (1918, 1942); Violin Concerto (1944); Piano Quintet (1913); String Quartet (1916); Violin Sonata (1903); Cello Sonata (1906); a number of piano pieces; several song cycles; choral works.

BIBL.: A. Wieniawski, *L. R.* (Warsaw, 1928); M. Kaminski, *L. R.* (Katowice, 1951); J. Kański, *L. R.* (Krakow, 1955).

Rubbra, (Charles) Edmund, notable English composer; b. Northampton, May 23, 1901; d. Gerard's Cross, Feb. 13, 1986. His parents were musical, and he was taught to play the piano by his mother. He left school when he was 14 and was employed in various factories; at the same time he continued to study music by himself, and attempted some composition; organized a concert devoted to the works of his favorite composer, Cyril Scott (Northampton, 1917); received a scholarship to study composition at Reading Univ. in 1920, and then entered the Royal College of Music in London in 1921, taking courses with Holst (composition), R.O. Morris (harmony and counterpoint), and Evlyn and Howard Jones (piano); also received some instruction from Vaughan Williams there before completing his studies in 1925. He taught at Oxford Univ. (1947–68) and at the Guildhall School of Music and Drama in London (from 1961). In 1960 he was made a Commander of the Order of the British Empire. He compensated for a late beginning in composition by an extremely energetic application to steady improvement of his technique; finally elaborated a style of his own, marked by sustained lyricism and dynamic Romanticism; his harmonic language often verges on polytonality. He publ. the books *Holst: A Monograph* (Monaco, 1947), *Counterpoint: A Survey* (London, 1960), and *Casella* (London, 1964).

WORKS: STAGE: *Bee-Bee-Bei*, opera (1933); *Prism*, ballet (1938). ORCH.: *Double Fugue* (1924); *Triple Fugue* (1929); *Sinfonia concertante* for Piano and Orch. (1934; London, Aug. 10, 1943); 11 syms.: No. 1 (1935–37; London, April 30, 1937); No. 2 (1937; London, Dec. 16, 1938; rev. 1951); No. 3 (1939; Manchester, Dec. 15, 1940); No. 4 (1941; London, Aug. 14, 1942); No. 5 (1947–48; London, Jan. 26, 1949); No. 6 (London, Nov. 17, 1954); No. 7 (Birmingham, Oct. 1, 1957); No. 8, *Hommage à Teilhard de Chardin* (1966–68; London, Jan. 5, 1971); No. 9, *Sinfonia sacra, the Resurrection*, for Soprano, Alto, Baritone, Chorus, and Orch. (1971–72); No. 10, *Sinfonia da camera* (1974; Middlesborough, Jan. 8, 1975); No. 11 (1978–79; London, Aug. 20, 1980); *Soliloquy* for Cello and Orch. (London, Jan. 1, 1945); Viola Concerto (London, April 15, 1953); Piano Concerto (1956); Violin Concerto (1959). CHAMBER: *Fantasy* for 2 Violins and Piano (1925); 3 violin sonatas (1925, 1931, 1967); *Lyric Movement* for String Quartet and Piano (1929); 4 string quartets (1933, rev. 1956; 1952; 1962–63; 1976–77); 2 piano trios (1950, 1970); various piano pieces; also many choral works; songs.

BIBL.: E. Evans, "E. R.," *Musical Times* (Feb.–March 1945); E. Payne, "E. R.," *Music & Letters*, XXXVI (1955).

Rubens, Paul (Alfred), English composer; b. London, April 29, 1875; d. Falmouth, Feb. 5, 1917. He was educated at Oxford Univ.; in 1899 he contributed some numbers to the famous musical revue *Floradora*, and this success induced him to devote himself to the composition of light operas. The following stage works by him were produced: *Lady Madcap* (1904); *Miss Hook of Holland* (1907); *My Mimosa Maid* (1908); *Dear Little Denmark* (1909); *The Balkan Princess* (1910); *The Sunshine Girl* (1912); he also wrote numerous songs and ballads.

Rubenson, Albert, Swedish music critic, teacher, and composer; b. Stockholm, Dec. 20, 1826; d. there, March 2, 1901. He studied at the Leipzig Cons. (1844–48) with Ferdinand David (violin), Hauptmann (counterpoint), and Gade (composi-

tion). Returning to Stockholm, he wrote music criticism; in 1872 he became inspector at the Stockholm Cons., and from 1888 till his death was its director. He wrote an overture, *Julius Caesar*; a Sym.; several orch. suites; a String Quartet; many songs. His style was derived from Mendelssohn and Schumann, but he attempted to inject some elements of Swedish folk song into his music, and in doing so contributed to the rise of musical nationalism in Sweden.

Rubin, Marcel, Austrian composer; b. Vienna, July 7, 1905. He studied piano with Richard Robert, theory of composition with Richard Stöhr, and counterpoint and fugue with Franz Schmidt at the Vienna Academy of Music; simultaneously attended courses in law. In 1925 he went to Paris, where he took private lessons with Darius Milhaud. He was back in Vienna in 1931 to complete his studies in law, and in 1933 received his degree of Dr.Juris. After the Nazi Anschluss of Austria in 1938, Rubin, being a non-Aryan, fled to Paris, but was interned as an enemy alien; after France fell in 1940, he made his way to Marseilles. Convinced that only the Communists could efficiently oppose fascism, he became a member of the illegal Austrian Communist party in exile; in 1942 he went to Mexico and remained there until 1946; returned to Vienna in 1947. His music follows the modernistic models of Parisianized Russians and Russianized Frenchmen, with a mandatory hedonism in "new simplicity." Although he studied works of Schoenberg, Berg, and Webern with great assiduity and wrote articles about them, he never adopted the method of composition with 12 tones in his own music.

WORKS: STAGE: *Kleider machen Leute*, comic opera (1966–69; Vienna, Dec. 14, 1973); *Die Stadt*, dance piece (1932; rev. 1980). ORCH.: 10 syms. (1927, rev. 1957; 1937, rev. 1974; 1939, rev. 1962; 1943–45, rev. 1971; 1964–65; 1973–74, rev. 1983; 1977; 1980; 1984; 1986); *Ballade* (1948); *Rondo-Burleske* (1960); *Drei Komodianten*, little suite (1963); *Sonatine* (1965); *Sinfonietta* for Strings (1966); *Pastorale* for Strings (1970); Double-bass Concerto (1970); Trumpet Concerto (1971–72); Bassoon Concerto (1976; Vienna, Aug. 23, 1977); *Hymnen an die Nacht* (1982; Vienna, April 18, 1985). CHAMBER: String Quartet No. 1 (1926; rev. 1961); Trio for Strings (1927; rev. 1962); Sonatine for Oboe and Piano (1927); Cello Sonata (1928); Divertimento for Piano Trio (1966–67); Serenade for 5 Brass (1971); Violin Sonata (1974); Clarinet Quintet (1985). PIANO: 3 sonatas (1925, 1927, 1928). VOCAL: *Ein Heiligenstädter Psalm* for Baritone, Choir, and Orch., after Beethoven's Heiligenstädt Testament (1977; Vienna, March 7, 1978); *Licht über Damaskus*, oratorio for 4 Soloists, Choir, Organ, and Orch. (1987–88).

BIBL.: H. Krones, *M. R.* (Vienna, 1975).

Rubini, Giovanni Battista, celebrated Italian tenor; b. Romano, near Bergamo, April 7, 1794; d. there, March 3, 1854. His teacher was Rosio of Bergamo; after an auspicious debut in Pavia (1814), he appeared in Naples (1815–25), where he profited from further study with Nozzari. On Oct. 6, 1825, he sang in Paris, where he scored his 1st triumphs in Rossini's operas at the Théâtre-Italien; his performances of the leading parts in the operas of Bellini and Donizetti were also very successful, and there is reason to believe that Rubini's interpretations greatly contributed to the rising fame of both of those composers. Between 1831 and 1843 he sang in Paris and London; in 1843 he undertook a tour with Liszt, traveling with him in the Netherlands and Germany; in the same year he sang in Russia with tremendous acclaim; visited Russia again in 1844; then returned to Italy, bought an estate near his native town, and remained there until his death; for some years he gave singing lessons. He publ. *12 lezioni di canto moderno per tenore o soprano* and an album of 6 songs, *L'addio*.

BIBL.: C. Traini, *Il cigno di Romano: G.B. R.* (Romano, 1954).

Rubinstein, Anton (Grigorievich), renowned Russian pianist, conductor, composer, and pedagogue, brother of **Nikolai (Grigorievich) Rubinstein;** b. Vykhvatinetz, Podolia, Nov. 28, 1829; d. Peterhof, near St. Petersburg, Nov. 20, 1894. He was of a family of Jewish merchants who became baptized in Berdichev in July 1831. His mother gave him his 1st lessons in piano; the family moved to Moscow, where his father opened a small pencil factory. A well-known Moscow piano teacher, Alexandre Villoing, was entrusted with Rubinstein's musical education, and was in fact his only piano teacher. In 1839 Villoing took him to Paris, where Rubinstein played before Chopin and Liszt; remained there until 1841; then made a concert tour in the Netherlands, Germany, Austria, England, Norway, and Sweden, returning to Russia in 1843. Since Anton's brother Nikolai evinced a talent for composition, the brothers were taken in 1844 to Berlin, where, on Meyerbeer's recommendation, Anton studied composition, with Dehn; subsequently made a tour through Hungary with the flutist Heindl. He returned to Russia in 1848 and settled in St. Petersburg. There he enjoyed the enlightened patronage of the Grand Duchess Helen, and wrote 3 Russian operas: *Dmitri Donskoy* (1852), *The Siberian Hunters* (1853), and *Thomas the Fool* (1853). In 1854, with the assistance of the Grand Duchess, Rubinstein undertook another tour in western Europe. He found publishers in Berlin, and gave concerts of his own works in London and Paris, exciting admiration as both composer and pianist; on his return in 1858, he was appointed court pianist and conductor of the court concerts. He assumed the direction of the Russian Musical Soc. in 1859; in 1862 he founded the Imperial Cons. in St. Petersburg, remaining its director until 1867. For 20 years thereafter he held no official position; from 1867 until 1870 he gave concerts in Europe, winning fame as a pianist 2nd only to Liszt. During the season of 1872–73, he made a triumphant American tour, playing in 215 concerts, for which he was paid lavishly; appeared as a soloist and jointly with the violinist Wieniawski. He produced a sensation by playing without the score, a novel procedure at the time. Returning to Europe, he elaborated a cycle of historical concerts, in programs ranging from Bach to Chopin; he usually devoted the last concert of a cycle to Russian composers. In 1887 he resumed the directorship of the St. Petersburg Cons., resigning again in 1891, when he went to Dresden. He returned to Russia the year of his death.

In 1890 he established the Rubinstein Prize, an international competition open to young men between 20 and 26 years of age. Two prizes of 5,000 francs each were offered, 1 for composition, the other for piano. Quinquennial competitions were held in St. Petersburg, Berlin, Vienna, and Paris.

Rubinstein's role in Russian musical culture was of the greatest importance. He introduced European methods into education, and established high standards of artistic performance. He was the 1st Russian musician who was equally prominent as composer and interpreter. According to contemporary reports, his playing possessed extraordinary power (his octave passages were famous) and insight, revealed particularly in his performance of Beethoven's sonatas. His renown as a composer was scarcely less. His *Ocean Symphony* was one of the most frequently performed orch. works in Europe and America; his piano concertos were part of the standard repertoire; his pieces for Piano Solo, *Melody in F, Romance,* and *Kamennoi Ostrow,* became perennial favorites. After his death, his orch. works all but vanished from concert programs, as did his operas (with the exception of *The Demon,* which is still perf. in Russia); his Piano Concerto No. 4, in D minor, is occasionally heard.

WORKS: OPERAS: *Dmitri Donskoy* (1849–50; St. Petersburg, April 30, 1852); *The Siberian Hunters* (1852; Weimar, 1854); *Stenka Razin* (1852; unfinished); *Hadji-Abrek* (1852–53; 1st perf. as *Revenge,* St. Petersburg, 1858); *Thomas the Fool* (St. Petersburg, May 23, 1853); *Das verlorene Paradies* (1856; Düsseldorf, 1875); *Die Kinder der Heide* (1860; Vienna, Feb. 23, 1861); *Feramors* (1862; Dresden, Feb. 24, 1863); *Der Thurm zu Babel* (1869; Königsberg, 1870); *The Demon* (1871; St. Petersburg, Jan. 25, 1875); *Die Makkabäer* (1874; Berlin, April 17, 1875); *Nero* (1875–76; Hamburg, Nov. 1, 1879); *The Merchant Kalashnikov* (1877–79; St. Petersburg, March 5, 1880); *Sulamith* (1882–83; Hamburg, Nov. 8, 1883); *Unter Räubern* (Hamburg, Nov. 8, 1883); *Der Papagei* (Hamburg, Nov. 11, 1884); *The Careworn One* (1888; St. Petersburg, Dec. 3, 1889);

Moses (1885–91; Prague, 1892); *Christus* (1887–93; Bremen, 1895). **BALLET:** *The Vine* (1882). **ORCH.:** 7 piano concertos: 2 unnumbered (1847; 1849, rev. as the Octet in D major, 1856); No. 1, op. 25 (1850); No. 2, op. 35 (1851); No. 3, op. 45 (1853–54); No. 4, op. 70 (1864); No. 5, op. 94 (1874); 6 syms.: No. 1, op. 40 (1850); No. 2, op. 42, *Ocean* (1st version, 1851; 2nd version, 1863; 3rd version, 1880); No. 3, op. 56 (1854–55; originally designated as Sym. No. 4); No. 4, op. 95, *Dramatic* (1874); No. 5, op. 107 (1880); No. .6, op. 111 (1886); Concert Overture, op. 60 (1853); *Triumphal Overture,* op. 43 (1855); Violin Concerto, op. 46 (1857); *Faust,* symphonic picture, op. 68 (1864); 2 cello concertos: No. 1, op. 65 (1864); No. 2, op. 96 (1874); *Ivan the Terrible,* symphonic picture, op. 79 (1869); *Fantasia* for Piano and Orch., op. 84 (1869); *Romance and Caprice* for Violin and Orch., op. 86 (1870); *Russia* (1882); *Fantasia eroica,* op. 110 (1884); *Concertstück* for Piano and Orch., op. 113 (1889); *Antony and Cleopatra,* overture, op. 116 (1890); Suite, op. 119 (1894); Overture (1894). **CHAMBER:** Octet, op. 9 (1849; originally the Piano Concerto, 1849); 3 violin sonatas: No. 1, op. 13 (1856); No. 2, op. 19 (1853); No. 3, op. 98 (1876); 5 piano trios: No. 1, op. 15 (1851); No. 2, op. 15 (1851); 3 unnumbered: op. 52 (1857), op. 85 (1870), and op. 108 (1883); 10 string quartets (1852–80); 2 cello sonatas: No. 1, op. 18 (1852); No. 2, op. 39 (1857); Viola Sonata, op. 49 (1855); Quintet for Winds and Piano, op. 55 (1855; rev. 1860); String Quintet, op. 59 (1859); Piano Quartet, op. 66 (1864); String Sextet, op. 97 (1876); Piano Quintet, op. 99 (1876); also many piano pieces; choral works; numerous songs.

WRITINGS: *Memoirs* (St. Petersburg, 1889; in Eng. as *Autobiography of Anton Rubinstein,* Boston, 1890); *Music and Its Representatives* (Moscow, 1891; in Eng., N.Y., 1892; also publ. as *A Conversation on Music*); *Leitfaden zum richtigen Gebrauch des Pianoforte-Pedals* (Leipzig, 1896; in French, Brussels, 1899); *Gedankenkorb, Litterarischer Nachlass* (Stuttgart, 1896); *Die Meister des Klaviers* (Berlin, 1899).

BIBL.: A. McArthur, *A. R.* (London, 1889); E. Zabel, *A. R.* (Leipzig, 1892); L. Martinov, *Episodes de la vie de R.* (Brussels, 1895); J. Rodenberg, "Meine persönlichen Erinnerungen an A. R., nebst Briefen," *Deutsche Rundschau,* 21 (Berlin, 1895; in Eng. in *Music,* 8, Chicago, 1905); A. Soubies, *A. R.* (Paris, 1895); E. Wessel, *Some Explanations, Hints and Remarks of A. R. from His Lessons in the St. Petersburg Cons.* (St. Petersburg, 1901; in German, Leipzig, 1904); N. Findeisen, *A. R.* (Moscow, 1907); La Mara, *A. R., Musikalische Studienköpfe* (vol. 3, 7th ed., Leipzig, 1909; separately, Leipzig, 1911); N. Bernstein, *A. R.* (Leipzig, 1911); A. Hervey, *A. R.* (London, 1913); K. Preiss, *A. R.s pianistische Bedeutung* (Leipzig, 1914); I. Glebov, *A. R. in His Musical Activities and Opinions of His Contemporaries* (Moscow, 1929); C. Bowen, *"Free Artist": The Story of A. and Nicholas R.* (N.Y., 1939; fictionalized account, but accurate as to actual events; with a complete list of works and a detailed bibliography, compiled by O. Albrecht); O. Bennigsen, "The Brothers R. and Their Circle," *Musical Quarterly* (Oct. 1939); L. Barenboym, *A.G. R.,* vol. I (Moscow, 1957); J. Norris, "The Piano Concertos of A. R.," *Music Review* (Nov. 1985).

Rubinstein, Arthur (actually **Artur**), celebrated Polish-born American pianist; b. Lodz, Jan. 28, 1887; d. Geneva, Dec. 20, 1982. He was a product of a merchant family with many children, of whom he alone exhibited musical propensities. He became emotionally attached to the piano as soon as he saw and heard the instrument; at the age of 7, on Dec. 14, 1894, he played pieces by Mozart, Schubert, and Mendelssohn at a charity concert in Lodz. His 1st regular piano teacher was one Adolf Prechner. He was later taken to Warsaw, where he had piano lessons with Alexander Różycki; then went to Berlin in 1897 to study with Heinrich Barth; also received instruction in theory from Robert Kahn and Max Bruch. In 1900 he appeared as soloist in Mozart's A major Concerto, K.488, in Potsdam; he repeated his success that same year when he played the work again in Berlin under Joachim's direction; then toured in Germany and Poland. After further studies with Paderewski in Switzerland (1903), he went to Paris, where he played with the Lamoureux Orch. and met Ravel, Dukas, and Thibaud. He also played the G minor Piano Concerto by Saint-Saëns in the presence of the composer, who commended him. The ultimate plum of artistic success came when Rubinstein received an American contract. He made his debut at Carnegie Hall in N.Y. on Jan. 8, 1906, as soloist with the Philadelphia Orch. in his favorite Saint-Saëns concerto. His American tour was not altogether successful, and he returned to Europe for further study. In 1915 he appeared as soloist with the London Sym. Orch. During the season 1916–17, he gave numerous recitals in Spain, a country in which he was to become extremely successful; from Spain he went to South America, where he also became a great favorite; he developed a flair for Spanish and Latin American music, and his renditions of the piano works of Albéniz and Manuel de Falla were models of authentic Hispanic modality. Villa-Lobos dedicated to Rubinstein his *Rudepoema*, regarded as one of the most difficult piano pieces ever written. Symbolic of his cosmopolitan career was the fact that he maintained apartments in N.Y., Beverly Hills, Paris, and Geneva. He was married to Aniela Mlynarska in 1932. Of his 4 children, 1 was born in Buenos Aires, 1 in Warsaw, and 2 in the U.S. In 1946 he became an American citizen. On June 11, 1958, Rubinstein gave his 1st postwar concert in Poland; in 1964 he played in Moscow, Leningrad, and Kiev. In Poland and in Russia he was received with tremendous emotional acclaim. But he forswore any appearances in Germany as a result of the Nazi extermination of the members of his family during World War II. On April 30, 1976, at the age of 89, he gave his farewell recital in London.

Rubinstein was one of the finest interpreters of Chopin's music, to which his fiery temperament and poetic lyricism were particularly congenial. His style of playing tended toward bravura in Classical compositions, but he rarely indulged in mannerisms; his performances of Mozart, Beethoven, Schumann, and Brahms were particularly inspiring. In his characteristic spirit of robust humor, he made jokes about the multitude of notes he claimed to have dropped, but asserted that a worse transgression against music would be pedantic inflexibility in tempo and dynamics. He was a bon vivant, an indefatigable host at parties, and a fluent, though not always grammatical, speaker in most European languages, including Russian and his native Polish. In Hollywood, he played on the sound tracks for the motion pictures *I've Always Loved You* (1946), *Song of Love* (1947), and *Night Song* (1947). He also appeared as a pianist, representing himself, in the films *Carnegie Hall* (1947) and *Of Men and Music* (1951). A film documentary entitled *Artur Rubinstein, Love of Life* was produced in 1975; a 90-minute television special, *Rubinstein at 90*, was broadcast to mark his entry into that nonagenarian age in 1977; he spoke philosophically about the inevitability of dying. He was the recipient of numerous international honors: a membership in the French Académie des Beaux Arts and the Légion d'Honneur, and the Order of Polonia Restituta of Poland; he held the Gold Medal of the Royal Phil. Soc. of London and several honorary doctorates from American institutions of learning. He was a passionate supporter of Israel, which he visited several times. In 1974 an international piano competition bearing his name was inaugurated in Jerusalem. On April 1, 1976, he received the U.S. Medal of Freedom, presented by President Ford. During the last years of his life, he was afflicted with retinitis pigmentosa, which led to his total blindness; but even then he never lost his joie de vivre. He once said that the slogan "wine, women, and song" as applied to him was 80% women and only 20% wine and song. And in a widely publicized interview he gave at the age of 95 he declared his ardent love for Annabelle Whitestone, the Englishwoman who was assigned by his publisher to help him organize and edit his autobiography, which appeared as *My Young Years* (N.Y., 1973) and *My Many Years* (N.Y., 1980). He slid gently into death in his Geneva apartment, as in a pianissimo ending of a Chopin

nocturne, ritardando, morendo . . . Rubinstein had expressed a wish to be buried in Israel; his body was cremated in Switzerland; the ashes were flown to Jerusalem to be interred in a separate emplacement at the cemetery, since the Jewish law does not permit cremation.

BIBL.: B. Gavoty, *A. R.* (Geneva, 1955; in Eng., 1956); D. Vroon, "An Appreciation: A. R.," *Le Grand Baton* (Dec. 1983; with complete discography by D. Manildi).

Rubinstein, Beryl, American pianist, teacher, and composer; b. Athens, Ga., Oct. 26, 1898; d. Cleveland, Dec. 29, 1952. He studied piano with his father and Alexander Lambert; toured the U.S. as a child (1905–11); then went to Berlin to study with Busoni and Vianna da Motta. He was appointed to the faculty of the Cleveland Inst. of Music in 1921; became its director in 1932. He wrote an opera, *The Sleeping Beauty*, to a libretto by John Erskine (Juilliard School of Music, N.Y., Jan. 19, 1938); 32 piano studies; 3 dances for Piano; transcriptions from Gershwin's *Porgy and Bess*. He conducted his orch. *Scherzo* with the Cleveland Orch. on March 17, 1927; performed his Piano Concerto in C with the same orch. on Nov. 12, 1936.

Rubinstein, Joseph, Russian pianist; b. Starokonstantinov, Feb. 8, 1847; d. (suicide) Lucerne, Sept. 15, 1884. He studied in Vienna with Dachs; later took lessons with Liszt in Weimar. He was an ardent admirer of Wagner, whom he knew personally; in 1874 he was the pianist at the preliminary rehearsals of *Der Ring des Nibelungen* at Bayreuth; made piano transcriptions of it and also of *Parsifal*.

Rubinstein, Nikolai (Grigorievich), prominent Russian pianist, conductor, teacher, and composer, brother of **Anton (Grigorievich) Rubinstein;** b. Moscow, June 14, 1835; d. Paris, March 23, 1881. He began to study piano with his mother at the age of 4, when his brother, 6 years older than he, was already on the road to fame as a child prodigy; was taken to Berlin with his brother in 1844, studying with T. Kullak (piano) and Dehn (harmony and counterpoint). The brothers met Mendelssohn and Meyerbeer; returning to Moscow in 1846, Nikolai began to take lessons with A. Villoing. He also studied law, and received a degree from the Univ. of Moscow (1855); subsequently was a minor functionary in the government; earned his living by giving private lessons. In 1858 he began his concert career; appeared in Russia, and also in London. In 1859 he became head of the Moscow branch of the Russian Musical Soc.; in 1866 this society opened the Moscow Cons., of which he was director until his death. From 1860 he was the regular conductor of the Moscow concerts of the Imperial Russian Musical Soc. In 1878 he conducted 4 Russian concerts at the Paris Exposition; at the 1st and the 4th of the series he performed Tchaikovsky's Piano Concerto No. 1 (which he had criticized sharply when Tchaikovsky 1st submitted it to him in 1874). Anton Rubinstein declared that Nikolai was a better pianist than himself, but this generous appreciation was not accepted by the public. As an educator, however, Nikolai played perhaps a greater role than his famous brother. Among his pupils were S. Taneyev, Siloti, and Emil Sauer.

BIBL.: N. Findeisen, "N. R.," *Russkaya Muzijkalnaya Gazeta*, 10 (1901); C. Bowen, *"Free Artist": The Story of Anton and N. R.* (N.Y., 1939); O. Bennigsen, "The Brothers R. and Their Circle," *Musical Quarterly* (Oct. 1939).

Rŭbner, Cornelius. See **Rybner, Cornelius.**

Rübsam, Wolfgang, German organist; b. Giessen, Oct. 16, 1946. He studied at Southern Methodist Univ. (M.Mus., 1970); took lessons with Helmut Walcha at the Frankfurt Staatliche Hochschule für Musik, where he graduated with an artist diploma in 1971; subsequently studied with Marie-Claire Alain in Paris (1971–74). In 1974 he joined the faculty of Northwestern Univ.

Rubsamen, Walter (Howard), renowned American musicologist; b. N.Y., July 21, 1911; d. Los Angeles, June 19, 1973. He studied flute with Georges Barrère in N.Y. and musicology at Columbia Univ. with Paul Henry Lang (B.A., 1933); then went to Germany, where he attended classes of Otto Ursprung and Rudolph von Ficker at the Univ. of Munich; received his doctorate there with the dissertation *Pierre de la Rue als Messenkomponist* (1937). Returning to the U.S., he was appointed to the music faculty at the Univ. of Calif., Los Angeles, obtaining a full professorship in 1955; was chairman of the music dept. (1965–73). He ed. the *Opera omnia* of Pierre de La Rue for the American Inst. of Musicology and brought out a German 16th-century *Magnificat on Christmas Carols* (N.Y., 1971); contributed a number of informative articles on ballad opera in England and on Renaissance composers to various American and European publications.

WRITINGS: *Literary Sources of Secular Music in Italy c.1500* (Berkeley, Calif., 1943; reprint, N.Y., 1972); *Chanson and Madrigal, 1480–1530* (with D. Heartz and H.M. Brown; Cambridge, Mass., 1964).

Rückauf, Anton, Bohemian composer; b. Prague, March 13, 1855; d. Schloss Alt-Erla, Austria, Sept. 19, 1903. He studied with Proksch in Prague and with Nottebohm and Nawrátil in Vienna; publ. about 80 songs, which were made popular by the singer Gustav Walter at his recitals, with Rückauf himself at the piano; he also wrote an opera, *Die Rosenthalerin* (Dresden, 1897).

Ruckers, celebrated family of Flemish harpsichord makers. **Hans Ruckers,** "the elder" (b. Mechelen, c.1545; d. Antwerp, 1598), was the 1st instrument maker in the family. His 2nd son, **Johannes Ruckers,** also known as **Hans** or **Jan** (b. Antwerp [baptized], Jan. 15, 1578; d. there, April 24, 1643), was greatly esteemed by his contemporaries. **Andreas** or **Andries Ruckers,** "the elder" (b. Antwerp [baptized], Aug. 15, 1579; d. after 1645), built harpsichords between 1601 and 1644. **Andreas** or **Andries Ruckers,** "the younger" (b. Antwerp [baptized], March 31, 1607; d. there, before 1667), son of the elder Andreas, made instruments from 1637.

BIBL.: A. Pols, *De R.s en de klavierbouw in Vlaanderen* (Antwerp, 1942); D. Boalch, *Makers of the Harpsichord and Clavichord, 1440 to 1840* (N.Y., 1956); J. Lambrechts-Douillez and M.-J. Basschaerts-Eykens, *H. en J. R.s* (Antwerp, 1983); G. O'Brien, *R.s: A Harpsichord and Virginal Building Tradition* (Cambridge, 1990).

Rudel, Julius, Austrian-born American conductor; b. Vienna, March 6, 1921. He studied at the Vienna Academy of Music; in 1938 emigrated to the U.S. (naturalized citizen, 1944) and continued his studies at the Mannes School of Music in N.Y. On Nov. 25, 1944, he made his American debut as conductor of the N.Y. City Opera; in 1957 became its music director. He also appeared as guest conductor of several operatic companies; received numerous awards from American cultural organizations. In 1961 the Austrian government bestowed on him honorary insignia for arts and sciences. He championed the cause of American opera; gave 1st performances of several new stage works by American composers. In 1979 he resigned his post with the N.Y. City Opera and became music director of the Buffalo Phil. Orch., which post he held until 1985.

Ruders, Poul, Danish composer; b. Ringsted, March 27, 1949. He studied organ with Finn Reiff and composition with Ib Nørholm at the Royal Danish Cons. of Music in Copenhagen; later was active mostly as a church organist. In his own compositions he follows neo-Baroque techniques.

WORKS: OPERA: *Tycho* (1985–86; Århus, May 16, 1987). **ORCH.:** *Pavane* (1971); *Études* (1974); *Capriccio pian' e forte* (Odense, Sept. 5, 1978); *Recitatives and Arias,* piano concerto (1978; Buffalo, April 1, 1979); Violin Concerto (1981; Copenhagen, Oct. 16, 1982); *Manhattan Abstraction* (1982); Clarinet Concerto (1985). **CHAMBER:** 3 string quartets (1972–79); *Zerstörte Horizonten* for 2 Electric Organs, Baby Grand Piano, Flute, Guitar, and Trombone (1973); *Medieval Variations* for 8 Instruments (1974); *Bravour Studium* for Cello and Piano (1976); *Rondeau* for 7 Musicians (1976); *Wind-Drumming* for Wind Quintet and Percussion (1979); *4 Compositions* for Flute, Clarinet, Horn, Piano, and String Quintet (1980); *Greeting*

Concerto for Chamber Ensemble (1982); *Symphonic Dances* for Ensemble (1983); *Vox in Rama* for Clarinet, Electric Violin, and Piano (1983); *Corpus Cum Figuris* for Ensemble (1984); *Regime* for 3 Percussionists (1984). **VOCAL:** *Stabat Mater* for Chorus, Piano, and Organ (1973); *Pest-sange* for Soprano, Guitar, and Piano (1975); *Gloria* for Chorus and 12 Brasses (1981; Copenhagen, Nov. 12, 1982). **PIANO:** 3 *Letters from the Unknown Soldier* (1967); 2 sonatas: No. 1, *Dante Sonata* (1970), and No. 2 (1982); *Recitatives* (1977). **ORGAN:** *Requiem* (1969); *Antiquitäten* (1972); *Symphonies* (1978).

Rudhyar, Dane (real name, **Daniel Chennevière**), French-born American composer, painter, and renowned mystical philosopher; b. Paris, March 23, 1895; d. San Francisco, Sept. 13, 1985. He changed his name in 1917 to Rudhyar, derived from an old Sanskrit root conveying the sense of dynamic action and the color red, astrologically related to the zodiacal sign of his birth and the planet Mars. He studied philosophy at the Sorbonne in Paris (baccalauréat, 1911), and took music courses at the Paris Cons. In composition he was largely self-taught; he also achieved a certain degree of proficiency as a pianist; developed a technique which he called "orchestral pianism." In 1913 the publisher Durand commissioned him to write a short book on Debussy, with whom he briefly corresponded. At the same time he joined the modern artistic circles in Paris. In 1916 he went to America; became a naturalized American citizen in 1926. His "dance poems" for Orch., *Poèmes ironiques* and *Vision végétale,* were performed at the Metropolitan Opera in N.Y. (April 4, 1917). In 1918 he visited Canada; in Montreal he met the pianist Alfred Laliberté, who was closely associated with Scriabin, and through him Rudhyar became acquainted with Scriabin's theosophic ideas. In Canada he also publ. a collection of French poems, *Rapsodies* (Toronto, 1918). In 1920 he went to Hollywood to write scenic music for *Pilgrimage Play, The Life of Christ,* and also acted the part of Christ in the prologue of the silent film version of *The Ten Commandments* produced by Cecil B. DeMille. In Hollywood he initiated the project of "Introfilms," depicting inner psychological states on the screen through a series of images, but it failed to receive support and was abandoned. Between 1922 and 1930 he lived in Hollywood and N.Y.; was one of the founding members of the International Composers Guild in N.Y. In 1922 his orch. tone poem *Soul Fire* won the $1,000 prize of the Los Angeles Phil.; in 1928 his book *The Rebirth of Hindu Music* was publ. in Madras, India. After 1930 Rudhyar devoted most of his time to astrology. His 1st book on the subject, *The Astrology of Personality* (1936), became a standard text in the field; it was described by Paul Clancy, the pioneer in the publication of popular astrological magazines, as "the greatest step forward in astrology since the time of Ptolemy." A new development in Rudhyar's creative activities took place in 1938 when he began to paint, along nonrepresentational symbolistic lines; the titles of his paintings (*Mystic Tiara, Cosmic Seeds, Soul and Ego, Avatar,* etc.) reflect theosophic themes. His preoccupations with astrology left him little time for music; about 1965 he undertook a radical revision of some early compositions, and wrote several new ones; was also active as a lecturer.

The natural medium for Rudhyar's musical expression was the piano; his few symphonic works were mostly orchestrations of original piano compositions. In his writing for piano he built sonorous chordal formations supported by resonant pedal points, occasionally verging on polytonality; a kinship with Scriabin's piano music was clearly felt, but Rudhyar's harmonic idiom was free from Scriabin's Wagnerian antecedents. Despite his study of oriental religions and music, Rudhyar did not attempt to make use of Eastern modalities in his own music. He lived his last years in Palo Alto, Calif., and kept active connections with the world of theosophy; he also orchestrated his early piano works. Before his death his wife asked him whom he expected to meet beyond the mortal frame; he replied, "Myself."

WORKS: ORCH.: 3 *poèmes ironiques* (1914); *Vision végétale*

(1914); *The Warrior*, symphonic poem for Piano and Orch. (1921; Palo Alto, Dec. 10, 1976); *Sinfonietta* (1927); *Syntonies in 4 sections: To the Real* (1920); *The Surge of Fire* (1921); *Ouranos* (1927); *The Human Way* (1927); *Tripthong* for Piano and Orch. (1948; rev. 1977); *Thresholds* (1954); *Dialogues for Chamber Orch.* (1977; San Francisco, May 23, 1982); *Cosmic Cycle* (1981). CHAMBER: *3 Melodies* for Flute, Cello, and Piano (1919); *3 Poems* for Violin and Piano (1920); *Solitude* for String Quartet (1950); Piano Quintet (1950); *Barcarolle* for Violin and Piano (1955); *Alleluia* for Carillon (1976); *Nostalgia* for Flute, Piano, and Strings (1977); 2 string quartets: No. 1, *Advent* (1978), and No. 2, *Crisis and Overcoming* (1979). SONGS: *3 chansons de Bilitis* (1919); *3 poèmes tragiques* (1918); *3 invocations* (1939). PIANO: *3 poèmes* (1913); *Mosaics*, tone cycle in 8 movements on the life of Christ (1918); *Syntony* (1919–34; rev. 1967); *3 Paeans* (1925); *Granites* (1929); *9 Tetragrams* (1920–67); *Pentagrams* (1924–26); *Transmutation* (1976); *Theurgy* (1976); *Autumn* and *3 Cantos* (1977); *Epic Poem* (1979); *Rite of Transcendence* (1981).
    WRITINGS: *Claude Debussy et son oeuvre* (Paris, 1913); *Art as Release of Power* (N.Y., 1930); *The Astrology of Personality* (N.Y., 1936; 2nd ed., 1979); *The Practice of Astrology* (Amsterdam, 1967; N.Y., 1970); *The Planetarization of Consciousness* (Amsterdam, 1970; N.Y., 1972); *The Astrological Houses* (N.Y., 1972); *Culture, Crisis and Creativity* (Wheaton, Ill., 1977); *The Astrology of Transformation* (Wheaton, 1980); *The Magic of Tone and the Art of Music* (Boulder, Colo., 1982); *The Rhythm of Wholeness* (Wheaton, 1983).
    BIBL.: P. Rosenfeld, *An Hour with American Music* (N.Y., 1929); A. Morang, *D. R., Pioneer in Creative Synthesis* (N.Y., 1939); *D. R.: A Brief Biography* (Berkeley, Calif., 1972); special issue of *Human Dimensions* (Buffalo, N.Y., 1975).

Rüdinger, Gottfried, German composer; b. Lindau, Aug. 23, 1886; d. Gauting, near Munich, Jan. 17, 1946. He was a student in theology; took courses in composition with Reger at the Leipzig Cons. (1907–9); in 1910 he settled in Munich and began teaching privately; taught at the Academy of Music there from 1920. He composed industriously in many genres; brought out a "peasant play-opera," *Die Tegernseer im Himmel*, and the children's operas *Benchtesgadener Sagenspiel, Musikantenkomödie, König Folkwart*, etc.; 2 syms.; 2 violin concertos; Cello Concerto; much choral and chamber music; his pieces for small brass ensembles, in the style of old town piper music, are especially attractive; also a number of instructive piano pieces.

Rudnick, Wilhelm, German organist and composer; b. Damerkow, Dec. 30, 1850; d. there, Aug. 7, 1927. He studied at Kullak's Akademie der Tonkunst in Berlin; subsequently occupied various posts as church organist in Landsberg and Liegnitz; was also active as choral conductor. He wrote numerous organ works; a fantasy on *Ein' feste Burg, Trinitatis-Sonate, Pfingsten-Sonate, Konzert-Phantasie, Choralvorspiele*; vocal works.

Rudnicki, Marian (Teofil), Polish conductor and composer; b. Krakow, March 7, 1888; d. Warsaw, Dec. 31, 1944. He conducted operetta in Krakow (1916–19) and later at the Warsaw Municipal Opera. He wrote mostly theater music; also composed choral works and solo songs.

Rudnytsky, Antin, Polish-American pianist, conductor, and composer; b. Luka, Galicia, Feb. 7, 1902; d. Toms River, N.J., Nov. 30, 1975. He studied piano with Schnabel and Petri, composition with Schreker, and musicology with Curt Sachs in Berlin; received his Ph.D. at the Univ. of Berlin in 1926. In 1927 he went to Russia, where he conducted opera in Kharkov and Kiev; then was conductor of the Lwow Opera (1932–37). In 1937 he emigrated to the U.S.; toured with his wife, the singer Maris Sokil, as her piano accompanist. He composed 3 syms. (1936, 1941, 1942); a Cello Concerto (1942); an opera, *Dovbush* (1937); some ballet music; miscellaneous pieces for instrumental ensembles; piano works.

Rudolf, Max, eminent German-born American conductor; b. Frankfurt am Main, June 15, 1902. He studied piano with

Eduard Jung and composition with Bernhard Sekles at the Hoch Cons. in Frankfurt; was employed as a coach and a conductor in various provincial opera houses in Germany; then was active as a conductor in Prague (1929–35); subsequently was a guest conductor with the Göteborg Sym. Orch. and the Swedish Broadcasting Co., and director of the Oratorio Soc. In 1940 he emigrated to the U.S.; became naturalized as an American citizen in 1946. In 1945 he joined the staff of the Metropolitan Opera in N.Y.; served as its artistic administrator from 1950 to 1958. In 1958 he was appointed music director of the Cincinnati Sym. Orch.; took it on a world tour in 1966, and on a European tour in 1969; in 1963 and from 1967 to 1970, was the music director of the Cincinnati May Festival; in 1970 he moved to Philadelphia, where he conducted the opera class at the Curtis Inst. of Music (until 1973); then was principal conductor of the Dallas Sym. Orch. (1973–74) and music advisor of the New Jersey Sym. Orch. (1976–77). He publ. *The Grammar of Conducting* (N.Y., 1950; 2nd ed., 1980), which also appeared in a Japanese translation.

Rudorff, Ernst (Friedrich Karl), German pianist, teacher, and composer; b. Berlin, Jan. 18, 1840; d. there, Dec. 31, 1916. He studied with Bargiel in Berlin and with Moscheles, Plaidy, and Reinecke in Leipzig. After teaching in Cologne (1865–69), he was head of the piano dept. at the Hochschule für Musik in Berlin (1869–1910). He was a friend of Brahms. He composed 3 syms., a *Romantische Ouvertüre, Variations on an Original Theme* for Orch., a String Sextet, choral works, duets, songs, and piano pieces.
    BIBL.: E. Rudorff, ed., *Aus den Tagen der Romantik, Bildnis einer deutschen Familie* (Leipzig, 1938); N. Reich, "The R. Collection," *Notes*, XXXI (1974–75).

Rudziński, Witold, Polish composer; b. Siebież, Lithuania, March 14, 1913. He studied with Szeligowski at the Vilnius Cons. (1928–36) and attended the Univ. of Vilnius (1931–36); went to Paris, where he took composition lessons with Nadia Boulanger and Charles Koechlin (1938–39); upon his return, he taught at the Vilnius Cons. (1939–42) and the Lodz Cons. (1945–47); settled in Warsaw and served as director of the Opera (1948–49) and as a prof. at the Cons. (from 1957). He wrote a biography of Moniuszko (2 vols., Krakow, 1955, 1961), a study on the technique of Bartók (Krakow, 1965), and an exposition on musical rhythm (2 vols., 1987), among other works.
    WORKS: OPERAS: *Janko muzykant* (Janko the Musician; 1948–51; Bytom, June 20, 1953); *Komendant Paryza* (The Commander of Paris; 1955–58; Poznan, 1960); *Odprawa posłów greckich* (The Departure of Greek Emissaries; Krakow, 1962); *Sulamita* (The Shulamite; 1964); *The Yellow Nightcap* (1969); *Chlopi* (The Peasants; 1972; Warsaw, June 30, 1974); *The Ring and the Rose* (1982). VOCAL: 2 oratorios: *Gaude Mater Polonia* for Narrator, 3 Soloists, Chorus, and Orch. (1966) and *Lipce* for Chorus and Chamber Orch. (1968); cantata, *Chlopska droga* (Peasants' Road; 1952); *Dach świata* (The Roof of the World) for Narrator and Orch. (1960); *The Nike of the Vistula*, war ballads and scenes for Narrator, 4 Soloists, Chorus, and Orch. (1973). ORCH.: Piano Concerto (1936); 2 syms. (1938, 1944); *Divertimento* for String Orch. (1940); *Uwertura baltycka* (Baltic Overture; 1948); *Parades*, suite (1958); *Music Concertante* for Piano and Chamber Orch. (1959); *Musica profana* for Flute, Clarinet, Trumpet, and Strings (1960); *Obrazy Świętokrzyskie* (Pictures from the Holy-Cross Mountains; 1965); Concerto Grosso for Percussion and 2 String Orchs. (1970; Poznan, March 29, 1973); *Uwertura góralska* (Mountain Overture; 1970). CHAMBER: Trio for Flute, Oboe, and Piano (1934); Clarinet Sonatina (1935); 2 string quartets (1935, 1943); Violin Sonata (1937); Viola Sonata (1946); Nonet (1947); Quintet for Flute and Strings (1954); *2 portraits de femmes* for Voice and String Quartet (1960); *Variations and Fugue* for Percussion (1966); *Preludes* for Clarinet, Viola, Harp, and Percussion (1967); *Polonaise-Rapsodie* for Cello and Piano (1969); *Fantazja góralska* (Mountain Fantasia) for Guitar (1970); *To Citizen John Brown*, concertino for Soprano, Flute, Horn, Cello,

Piano, and Percussion (1972); *Proverbia latina* for Harpsichord (1974); *Duo Concertante* for Percussion (1976); *Sonata Pastorale* for Violin and Piano (1976); Harpsichord Sonata (1978); piano pieces; songs.

Rudzinski, Zbigniew, Polish composer and teacher; b. Czechowice, Oct. 23, 1935. After attending the Univ. of Warsaw (1956), he pursued training in composition with Perkowski at the Warsaw Academy of Music (diploma, 1960); completed his studies in Paris and the Netherlands. He served as chief of the music dept. of the Warsaw Documentary Film Studio (1960–67); then was a prof. (from 1973) of composition at the Chopin Academy of Music in Warsaw, where he also was vice-rector (1981–83).

WORKS: STAGE: *Manekiny* (The Mannequins), chamber opera (Wroclaw, Oct. 29, 1981). **ORCH.:** *Contra fidem* (1964); *Moments musicaux I–III* (1965–68); Sym. for Men's Chorus and Orch. (1969); *Muzyka nova* (Night Music; 1970). **CHAMBER:** Sonata for 2 String Quartets, Piano, and Kettledrums (1960); String Trio (1964); *Impromptu* for 2 Pianos, 3 Cellos, and Percussion (1966); Quartet for 2 Pianos and Percussion (1969); Piano Sonata (1975); *Campanella* for Percussion Ensemble (1977); *Trytony* (Tritons) for Percussion Ensemble (1979–80). **VOCAL:** *Epigrame* for Flute, Chorus, and Percussion (1962); *Requiem ofiarom wojen* (Requiem for the Victims of the Wars) for Chorus and Orch. (1971); *Księga godzin* (The Book of Hours), 5 Romantic songs for Mezzo-soprano and Piano Trio (1983); *To nie sa sny* (These are not dreams), 6 songs for Mezzo-soprano and Piano (1987).

Rufer, Josef (Leopold), Austrian music scholar; b. Vienna, Dec. 18, 1893; d. Berlin, Nov. 7, 1985. He studied composition with Zemlinsky, and then with Schoenberg in Vienna (1919–22); was assistant to Schoenberg at the Prussian Academy of Arts in Berlin (1925–33); from 1928, was also active as a music critic. From 1947 to 1950 he ed. (with Stuckenschmidt) the monthly music magazine *Stimmen;* then taught at the Free Univ. (from 1950) and at the Hochschule für Musik (1956–69) in Berlin. He publ. a number of valuable books dealing with 12-tone music: *Die Komposition mit zwölf Tönen* (Berlin, 1952; Eng. tr. by H. Searle as *Composition with 12 Notes Related Only to One Another,* London, 1954); *Musiker über Musik* (Darmstadt, 1955); and, most important, an annotated catalog of Schoenberg's works, *Das Werk Arnold Schönbergs* (Kassel, 1959; Eng. tr. as *The Works of Arnold Schoenberg,* London, 1962).

Rüfer, Philippe (-Barthélemy), German pianist, teacher, and composer; b. Liège (of German parents), June 7, 1844; d. Berlin, Sept. 15, 1919. He studied at the Liège Cons.; in 1871, settled in Berlin, where he taught piano at the Stern Cons., Kullak's Akademie der Tonkunst, and (from 1881) the Scharwenka Cons. He wrote the operas *Merlin* (Berlin, Feb. 28, 1887) and *Ingo* (Berlin, Feb. 1896); a Sym.; 3 overtures; piano music; songs.

BIBL.: P. Magnette, *P. R.: Étude biographique et critique* (Liège, 1910).

Ruff, Willie, American jazz horn and string bass player; b. Sheffield, Ala., Jan. 9, 1931. He studied at Yale Univ. (M.M., 1954); formed a duo with pianist Dwike Mitchell, and together they filled a series of highly successful engagements in intellectual nightclubs. In 1959 they gave a series of jazz concerts in Russia, triumphantly overriding Soviet scruples regarding the allegedly decadent nature of jazz, and scoring a popular success. They were equally triumphant as part of President Johnson's goodwill entourage to Mexico in 1966. He later taught at Yale Univ.

Ruffo, Titta (real name, **Ruffo Cafiero Titta**), famous Italian baritone; b. Pisa, June 9, 1877; d. Florence, July 5, 1953. He found it convenient to transpose his 1st and last names for professional purposes. He studied with Persichini at the Accademia di Santa Cecilia in Rome, then with Casini in Milan. He made his operatic debut in Rome as the Herald in *Lohengrin* (1898); then sang in South America; returning to Italy, he

appeared in all the principal theaters; also sang in Vienna, Paris, and London. He made his American debut in Philadelphia as Rigoletto (Nov. 4, 1912) with the combined Philadelphia-Chicago Opera Co.; his 1st appearance with the Metropolitan Opera was as Figaro in *Il Barbiere di Siviglia* (N.Y., Jan. 19, 1922). He left the Metropolitan in 1929 and returned to Rome. In 1937 he was briefly under arrest for opposing the Mussolini regime; then went to Florence, where he remained until his death. His memoirs appeared as *La mia parabola* (Milan, 1937; rev. 1977, by his son). A renowned dramatic artist, he excelled in roles from Verdi's operas; was also an outstanding Figaro, Hamlet, Tonio, and Scarpia.

BIBL.: M. Barrenechea, *T. R.: Notas de psicología artística* (Buenos Aires, 1911); A. Farkas, ed., *T. R.: An Anthology* (Westport, Conn., 1984).

Ruffo, Vincenzo, Italian composer; b. Verona, c.1508; d. Sacile, near Pordenone, Feb. 9, 1587. He was a pupil at the Scuola degli Accoliti at Verona Cathedral (1524–34). From about 1542 to 1546 he was musico to Alfonso d'Alvalos, Marquis of Vasto and governor-general of Milan; in 1544 he was made maestro di cappella at the Cathedral, and in 1551 maestro di musica at the Accademia Filarmonica in Verona; after serving as maestro di cappella at Milan Cathedral (1563–72), he was active at Pistoia Cathedral (1573–77), in Verona (1578–80), and in Sacile. He was highly regarded as a composer of both sacred and secular music. Among his works were a Magnificat, masses, motets, Psalms, and madrigals.

BIBL.: W. Wtorczyk, *Die Madrigale V. R.s* (diss., Free Univ. of Berlin, 1955); L. Lockwood, "V. R. and Musical Reform after the Council of Trent," *Musical Quarterly,* XLII (1957); idem, *The Counter-Reformation and the Masses of V. R.* (Venice, 1970).

Ruggi, Francesco, Italian composer; b. Naples, Oct. 21, 1767; d. there, Jan. 23, 1845. He studied at the Cons. di S. Loreto in Naples under Fenaroli; became a prof. of composition at the Cons. di San Pietro a Majella. He wrote the operas *L'ombra di Nino* (Naples, 1795), *La Guerra aperta* (Naples, 1796), and *Sofi tripponi* (Milan, 1804); much sacred music.

Ruggles, Carl (Charles Sprague), remarkable American composer; b. Marion, Mass., March 11, 1876; d. Bennington, Vt., Oct. 24, 1971. He learned to play violin as a child; then went to Boston, where he took violin lessons with Felix Winternitz and theory with Josef Claus; later enrolled as a special student at Harvard Univ., where he attended composition classes of John Knowles Paine. Impressed with the widely assumed supremacy of the German school of composition (of which Paine was a notable representative), Ruggles Germanized his given name from Charles to Carl. In 1907 he went to Minnesota, where he organized and conducted the Winona Sym. Orch. (1908–12). In 1917 he went to N.Y., where he became active in the promotion of modern music; was a member of the International Composers Guild and of the Pan American Assoc. of Composers; taught composition at the Univ. of Miami (1938–43). Ruggles wrote relatively few works, which he constantly revised and rearranged, and they were mostly in small forms. He did not follow any particular modern method of composition, but instinctively avoided needless repetition of thematic notes, which made his melodic progressions atonal; his use of dissonances, at times quite strident, derived from the linear proceedings of chromatically inflected counterpoint. A certain similarity with the 12-tone method of composition of Schoenberg resulted from this process, but Ruggles never adopted it explicitly. In his sources of inspiration, he reached for spiritual exaltation with mystic connotations, scaling the heights and plumbing the depths of musical expression. Such music could not attract large groups of listeners and repelled some critics; one of them remarked that the title of Ruggles's *Sun-Treader* ought to be changed to *Latrine-Treader.* Unable and unwilling to withstand the prevailing musical mores, Ruggles removed himself from the musical scene; he went to live on his farm in Arlington, Vt., and devoted himself mainly to his avocation, painting; his pictures, mostly in the manner of Abstract Expressionism, were occasionally exhibited in N.Y. galleries. In 1966 he moved to a nursing home in Bennington, where he died at the age of 95. A striking revival of interest in his music took place during the last years of his life, and his name began to appear with increasing frequency on the programs of American orchs. and chamber music groups. His MSS were recovered and publ.; virtually all of his compositions have been recorded.

WORKS: *Mood* for Violin and Piano (c.1918); *Toys* for Voice and Piano (1919); *Men and Angels* (*Men* for Orch., 1920–21; *Angels* for 6 Muted Trumpets, 1920–21; perf. as *Men and Angels*, N.Y., Dec. 17, 1922; *Angels* rev. for 4 Trumpets and 3 Trombones, 1938, and perf. in Miami, April 24, 1939); *Vox clamans in deserto* for Soprano and Chamber Orch. (1923; N.Y., Jan. 13, 1924); *Men and Mountains* for Chamber Orch. (N.Y., Dec. 7, 1924; rev. for Large Orch., N.Y., March 19, 1936; rev. 1941); *Portals* for 13 Strings (1925; N.Y., Jan. 24, 1926; rev. for String Orch., 1929; rev. 1941 and 1952–53); *Sun-Treader* for Large Orch. (1926–31; Paris, Feb. 25, 1932, N. Slonimsky conducting); *Evocations*, 4 chants for Piano (1937, 1943; N.Y., Jan. 9, 1943; rev. 1954; orch. version, N.Y., Feb. 3, 1971); *Organum* for Large Orch. (1944–47; N.Y., Nov. 24, 1949; also arranged for 2 Pianos, 1946–47); *Exaltation*, hymn tune for "congregation in unison" and Organ (1958); also several unfinished works.

BIBL.: P. Rosenfeld, *An Hour with American Music* (N.Y., 1929); C. Seeger, "C. R.," *Musical Quarterly* (Oct. 1932); L. Harrison, *About C. R.* (Yonkers, N.Y., 1946); T. Peterson, *The Music of C. R.* (diss., Univ. of Washington, 1967); J. Kirkpatrick, "The Evolution of C. R.: A Chronicle Largely in His Own Words," *Perspectives of New Music*, VI/2 (1968); N. Archabal, *C. R.: Composer and Painter* (diss., Univ. of Minnesota, 1975); J. Tenney, "The Chronological Development of C. R.' Melodic Style," *Perspectives of New Music*, XVI/1 (1977); M. Ziffrin, "Interesting Lies and Curious Truths about C. R.," *College Music Symposium*, XIX/2 (1979); D. Babcock, "C. R.: Two Early Works and 'Suntreader,'" *Tempo*, 135 (1980); S. Dombek, "A Study of Harmonic Interrelationships and Sonority Types in C. R. *Angels*," *Indiana Theory Revue*, IV/1 (1980); H. Gleason and W. Becker, "C. R.," *20th-century American Composers*, Music Literature Outlines, series IV (Bloomington, Ind., 2nd ed., rev., 1981).

Rugolo, Pete, Italian-born American jazz bandleader, arranger, and composer; b. San Pietro, Patti, Sicily, Dec. 25, 1915. He was taken to the U.S. as a child; obtained a B.A. at San Francisco State College and an M.A. at Mills College, where he studied composition with Darius Milhaud. In 1945 he became an arranger for Stan Kenton; after 1949 he pursued his career as a bandleader and composer for films and television. He wrote music in a light classical idiom touched with jazz.

Rühlmann, Frans, Belgian conductor; b. Brussels, Jan. 11, 1868; d. Paris, June 8, 1948. He studied at the Brussels Cons.; filled engagements as conductor at the Théâtre de la Monnaie in Brussels, and also in Liège, Antwerp, etc. In 1905 he was engaged at the Opéra-Comique in Paris; in 1914 conducted at the Paris Opéra; also led a series of popular concerts in Antwerp.

Rühlmann, (Adolf) Julius, German trombonist, pedagogue, and writer on music; b. Dresden, Feb. 28, 1816; d. there, Oct. 27, 1877. He played the trombone in the Court Orch. of Dresden; founded the Dresden Tonkünstlerverein (1855); taught piano and music history at the Dresden Cons. He prepared a valuable *Geschichte der Bogeninstrumente*, which was publ. posthumously by his son, Richard Rühlmann (1882); also wrote *Die Urform der Bogeninstrumente* (1874).

Ruiter, Wim de, Dutch composer and organist; b. Heemstede, Aug. 11, 1943. He studied organ with Piet Kee in Amsterdam (1963–69) and composition with Ton de Leeuw there (1968–74); taught at the Zwolle Cons. (1973–77) and the Amsterdam Cons. (from 1973). With another Dutch organist he gave successful concerts of duo-organ music, 4-hands, 4-feet.

WORKS: *Solo* for Flute (1969); *Music* for 2 Double Basses (1969); Quartet for 2 Violas and 2 Cellos (1970); Quartet for Flute, Bass Clarinet, Vibraphone, and Piano (1970); 2 *Quartets Together* (1970; a joining together of the previous 2 quartets); *Situations* for 16 Voices (1970); 3 string quartets (1972, 1974, 1984); *Hoplopoia* for Chorus and Orch. (1973); *Re* for Orch. (Utrecht, Sept. 14, 1975); *Thick & Thin* for Organ, 4-hands, 4-feet (1975); *Tall & Small* for Treble Recorder (1975); *Off & On* for 4 Bass Clarinets (1976); *To Be or Not to Be* for 12 Wind Instruments and Vibraphone (1976); Quintet for 5 Flutes and Tape (1976; in collaboration with Jacques Bank); Quartet for Recorders (1977); 3 *Pieces* for Orch. (1977); *Spectrum* for Orch. (1978); *Allegro, adagio en variaties* for Orch. (1980); *Theme, Variations, and Finale* for Orch. (1985); Flute Quartet No. 2 (1986); Accordion Concerto (1987); choral works; songs.

Rummel, family of German musicians:
(1) Christian (Franz Ludwig Friedrich Alexander) Rummel, pianist, conductor, and composer; b. Brichsenstadt, Bavaria, Nov. 27, 1787; d. Wiesbaden, Feb. 13, 1849. He went to Mannheim and studied violin with Heinrich Ritter and composition with Karl Jakob Wagner; also received advice from the Abbé Vogler. He began his career as a military bandmaster in 1806; served during the Peninsular War (1808–13) and was made a prisoner of war; later fought at the Battle of Waterloo. He settled in Wiesbaden as a teacher, and then organized and conducted the Court Orch. from 1815; after it was dissolved in 1842, it was absorbed into the theater orch., with Rummel serving as conductor; he also toured widely in Europe as a pianist. He wrote pieces for piano and orch.—a Clarinet Concerto, military-band music, chamber works, numerous pieces for solo piano, and various transcriptions for piano. Several of his children became musicians, including the following:
(2) Josephine Rummel, pianist; b. Manzanares, Spain, May 12, 1812; d. Wiesbaden, Dec. 19, 1877. She studied piano with her father, then made tours of Europe; also served as court pianist in Wiesbaden.
(3) Joseph Rummel, pianist, clarinetist, and composer; b. Wiesbaden, Oct. 6, 1818; d. London, March 25, 1880. He studied piano and clarinet with his father, then was in the service of the Duke of Oldenberg in Wiesbaden; was active in Paris (1847–70) and then in London. He wrote a vast amount of music, mainly for piano.
(4) August Rummel, pianist; b. Wiesbaden, Jan. 14, 1824; d. London, Dec. 14, 1886. He studied with his father; then settled in London, where he became well known as a pianist. Other members of the family were as follows:
(5) Franz Rummel, pianist, son of **Joseph Rummel;** b. London, Jan. 11, 1853; d. Berlin, May 2, 1901. He studied with Louis Brassin at the Brussels Cons., winning 1st prize in 1872; toured in America 4 times (1878, 1886, 1890, 1898). He married a daughter of S.F.B. Morse, inventor of the telegraph.
(6) Walter Morse Rummel, distinguished pianist, son of **Franz Rummel** and grandson of S.F.B. Morse, inventor of the telegraph; b. Berlin, July 19, 1887; d. Bordeaux, May 2, 1953. He studied piano with Leopold Godowsky and composition with Hugo Kaun. In 1908 he went to Paris; there he became acquainted with Debussy, and devoted himself to promoting his piano works, of which he became a foremost interpreter. He was married to the pianist Thérèse Chaigneau, with whom he appeared in duo-piano recitals (later divorced), and to Sarah Harrington (also divorced).

Runciman, John F., English music critic; b. 1866; d. London, April 7, 1916. He was a church organist before he joined the staff of the *Saturday Review* in London (1894) as a music critic; held this position till his death; also was ed. of the *Chord* (quarterly) and the *Musician's Library*. His critical reviews were remarkable for their unabashed violence in denouncing composers and performers whom he did not like; on some occasions he became involved in libel suits. He publ. selected essays in *Old Scores and New Readings* (1899), biographical studies of Haydn (1908) and Purcell (1909), and *Richard Wagner, Composer of Operas* (1913).

Rung, Frederik, Danish conductor, teacher, and composer, son of **Henrik Rung;** b. Copenhagen, June 14, 1854; d. there, Jan. 22, 1914. He studied with his father; succeeded him as conductor of the Cecilia Soc. (1871); founded its Madrigalkoret (1887), which won considerable renown; was also 2nd conductor (1884–1908) and chief conductor (from 1908) at the Royal Theater in Copenhagen; taught at the Copenhagen Cons. (1881–93).

WORKS: OPERAS: *Det hemmelige Selskab* (The Secret Party; Copenhagen, Feb. 9, 1888); *Den trekantede Hat* (The 3-cornered Hat; Copenhagen, Nov. 7, 1894). ORCH.: 2 syms.; Rhapsody; *Danse des papillons.* CHAMBER: Serenade for 9 Instruments; Piano Quintet; 2 string quartets; Violin Sonata; piano pieces; songs.

Rung, Henrik, Danish conductor and composer, father of **Frederik Rung;** b. Copenhagen, March 3, 1807; d. there, Dec. 13, 1871. He founded the Cecilia Soc. (1851); wrote a number of choral works and popular songs.

BIBL.: C. Thrane, *Caeciliaföreningen og dens Stifter* (Copenhagen, 1901).

Rungenhagen, Carl Friedrich, German conductor and composer; b. Berlin, Sept. 27, 1778; d. there, Dec. 21, 1851. He was a pupil of Benda; in 1815 became 2nd conductor of the Singakademie, succeeding Zelter in 1833 as 1st conductor; was a member of the Berlin Academy, and a teacher in the School of Composition. He composed 4 operas, 3 oratorios, a Te Deum, 30 motets, 30 4-part songs, over 100 sacred and 1,000 secular songs; also syms., quartets, etc.

Rúnólfsson, Karl Ottó, Icelandic trumpeter, teacher, and composer; b. Reykjavík, Oct. 24, 1900; d. there, Nov. 29, 1970. He studied in Copenhagen (1926–27) and with Mixa and Urbancic at the Reykjavík College of Music (1934–39); was active with brass bands; played 1st trumpet in the Icelandic Sym. Orch. (1950–55); taught at the Reykjavík College of Music (1939–64). He wrote a set of Icelandic songs for Voice and Orch. (1938); *Esja,* sym. (1968); choral works on Icelandic themes; Trumpet Sonata; Violin Sonata.

Ruolz-Montchal, Henri (-Catherine-Camille), Comte de, French composer; b. Paris, March 5, 1808; d. there, Sept. 30, 1887. He was a pupil of Berton, Lesueur, Paër, and Rossini; won some success as a composer, but the loss of his family fortune in 1840 induced him to abandon music and devote himself to the more practical study of chemistry.

WORKS: *Attendre et courir* (with F. Halévy; 1830); *Lara* (Naples, Nov. 22, 1835); *La Vendetta* (Paris, 1839); *La Jolie Fille de Perth; Manfred;* also a Requiem; *Cantate en honneur de Jeanne d'Arc;* String Quartet; 2 piano trios; motets; songs.

Rupnik, Ivan, Serbian composer; b. Belgrade, Aug. 29, 1911. He studied in Ljubljana; later in Vienna with Alban Berg. His early works are in a neo-Romantic vein, with expressionistic overtones; later he abjured modern devices and began writing music for the masses, in conformity with socialist ideology. His cantata, *Song of the Dead Proletarians,* which he conducted in Belgrade on Dec. 14, 1947, is an epitome of programmatic realism. He also wrote 2 syms., several overtures (*Romantic Overture, Youth Overture*), ethnic symphonic works (*Musical Impressions from Istria, A Peasant Evening Party*), and a *Hymn of Peace.*

Rusca, Francesco, Italian composer who flourished in the 2nd half of the 17th century. He was maestro di cappella at Como Cathedral from 1659 until 1699. He wrote about 100 masses, Psalms, cantatas, etc., in a highly developed polyphonic style, containing as many as 16 independent vocal and instrumental parts. His 5 keyboard toccatas are included in vol. III of *I classici* (Como, 1961).

Rusconi, Gerardo, Italian composer; b. Milan, Feb. 1, 1922; d. there, Dec. 23, 1974. He studied at the Parma Cons.; began his career as a composer by writing light music for the stage, radio, and the films; then undertook more serious genres of music. He composed *La moglie di Lot* for Soprano, Horn, and

Piano (1962); *Concerto breve* for Horn and Strings (1965); *3 musiche* for Flute and Piano (1967); *Moments* for Orch. in memory of Martin Luther King (1968); *L'appuntamento,* opera (1971); numerous transcriptions and harmonizations of popular songs.

Rush, Loren, American composer; b. Fullerton, Calif., Aug. 23, 1935. He studied piano, bassoon, and double bass; played bassoon in the Oakland Sym. and double bass in the Richmond Sym.; also was a drummer. He studied composition with Robert Erickson at San Francisco State College (B.A., 1957); upon graduation, organized the Loren Rush Jazz Quartet; enrolled at the Univ. of Calif. at Berkeley, studying composition with Andrew Imbrie, Seymour Shifrin, William Denny, and Charles Cushing (M.A., 1960), and completed his training at Stanford Univ. (D.M.A., 1960). He was active in various new-music ventures; was chairman of the composition dept. at the San Francisco Cons. (1967–69); taught at Stanford Univ. (from 1967), where he served as associate director of the Center for Computer Research in Music and Acoustics (from 1975). He applies a whole spectrum of modern techniques, including serialism, spatial distribution, controlled improvisation, and pointillistic exoticism, in his works.

WORKS: *5 Japanese Poems* for Soprano, Flute, Clarinet, Viola, and Piano (1959); *Serenade* for Violin and Viola (1960); String Quartet (1960–61); *Mandala Music,* improvisation for a group, inspired by the oriental geometrization of the cosmos and an important symbol in Jungian psychology (1962); *Hexahedron* for Piano, notated on all 6 surfaces of a large cube (1964); *Nexus 16* for Chamber Orch. (1964); *Dans le sable* for Soprano, Narrator, 4 Altos, and Chamber Orch. (1967–68; also for Large Orch., 1970); *Soft Music, Hard Music* for 3 Amplified Pianos (1969–70); *The Cloud Messenger* for Orch. (1966–70); *Oh, Susanna* for Piano (1970); *A Little Traveling Music* for Amplified Piano and 4-track Tape (1971–73); *I'll See You in My Dreams* for Amplified Orch. and Tape (1973); *Song and Dance* for Orch. and 4-track Tape (1975); *The Digital Domain* for Tape (1983; in collaboration with J. Mattox).

Rushing, Jimmy (James Andrew), black American jazz singer; b. Oklahoma City, Aug. 26, 1903; d. N.Y., June 8, 1972. He was reared in a musical family; learned to play the violin and the piano, then began to make appearances as a singer; he later worked with Bennie Moten (1929–35) and Count Basie (1935–50); subsequently appeared as a guest artist with Benny Goodman, Harry James, and Eddie Condon. He was affectionately dubbed "Mr. 5 by 5."

Rushton, Julian (Gordon), English musicologist; b. Cambridge, May 22, 1941. He studied at the Guildhall School of Music and Drama in London (1959–60), Trinity College, Cambridge (B.A., 1963), and Magdalen College, Oxford (B.Mus., 1965; M.A., 1967; Ph.D., 1970, with the diss. *Music and Drama at the Académie royale de musique, Paris, 1774–1789*); taught at the Univ. of East Anglia (1968–74) and at Cambridge Univ. (1974–81); was West Riding Prof. of Music and head of the music dept. at the Univ. of Leeds (from 1982). He ed. *W.A. Mozart: Don Giovanni* (Cambridge, 1981); publ. *The Musical Language of Berlioz* (Cambridge, 1983) and *Classical Music: A Concise History* (London, 1986).

Russell, (George) Alexander, American organist and composer; b. Franklin, Tenn., Oct. 2, 1880; d. Dewitt, N.Y., Nov. 24, 1953. The son of a Presbyterian minister, he studied at home; his mother, Felicia Putnam Russell (a direct descendant of General Israel Putnam of Revolution fame), taught him piano; the family moved to Texas, where he studied academic subjects; entered the College of Fine Arts of Syracuse Univ., studying organ with George A. Parker and composition with William Berwald; subsequently studied in Europe with Leopold Godowsky and Harold Bauer (piano), and with Widor (organ). Returning to America in 1908, he toured as accompanist to various artists; from 1910 to 1952, was associated with the Auditorium concerts at Wanamaker's department store in N.Y.; was also director of music at Princeton Univ. (1917–35). He wrote a number of organ works, piano pieces, songs, and part-songs.

BIBL.: J. Howard, *Studies of Contemporary American Composers: A. R.* (N.Y., 1925).

Russell, Charles Ellsworth "Pee Wee," American jazz clarinetist; b. Maple Wood, Mo., March 27, 1906; d. Alexandria, Va., Feb. 15, 1969. He played violin, piano, and drums; later studied clarinet with Charlie Merrill; then attended the Univ. of Missouri; eventually made his way to N.Y., where he played in the bands of Red Nichols, Bobby Hackett, Eddie Condon, and others. In later years he embarked upon an ambitious solo career; appeared at the leading jazz festivals with the Newport All Stars.

Russell, George (Allan), black American jazz pianist, music theorist, teacher, and composer; b. Cincinnati, June 23, 1923. He took up the drums in his youth; then turned to composition, and later developed a modal technique which he called the Lydian Chromatic Concept of Tonal Organization (1945–46); subsequently studied composition with Stefan Wolpe. After teaching at the Lenox (Mass.) School of Jazz (1959–60), he became active as a pianist in his own sextet (1960–61); later taught at the New England Cons. of Music in Boston (from 1969). He publ. *The Lydian Chromatic Concept of Tonal Organization* (1953; 2nd ed., 1959); composed various pieces for jazz group.

Russell, Henry, English pianist, singer and composer, father of **Henry Russell** and **Sir Landon Ronald;** b. Sheerness, Dec. 24, 1812; d. London, Dec. 8, 1900. He studied in Italy as a young boy; took a few lessons from Rossini in Naples; was in London in 1828; then in Canada (c.1834); served as organist of the 1st Presbyterian Church of Rochester, N.Y. He returned to England in 1841 and became extremely popular as a composer and singer of dramatic and topical songs, of which *Woodman! Spare That Tree* attained immense popularity; other songs were *Old Arm Chair; Oh, Weep Not!; A Life on the Ocean Wave* (official march of the Royal Marines); *Cheer! Boys, Cheer!; Ivy Green; The Gambler's Wife; Old Bell; The Maniac;* etc. He publ. a book of reminiscences, *Cheer! Boys, Cheer! Memories of Men and Music* (London, 1895), and *L'Amico dei cantanti,* a treatise on singing.

BIBL.: J. Stephens, *H. R. in America: Chutzpah and Huzzah* (diss., Univ. of Illinois, 1975).

Russell, Henry, English impresario, son of **Henry Russell** and brother of **Sir Landon Ronald;** b. London, Nov. 14, 1871; d. there, Oct. 11, 1937. He studied singing at the Royal College of Music, and devised an original method of vocal instruction, which attracted the attention of Melba, who sent him a number of her good pupils. Owing to his wide acquaintance with singers, he was invited in 1904 to manage a season of opera at Covent Garden; in 1905 he took his company to the U.S., where Boston was the principal field of his operations; his success resulted, in 1909, in the formation of the Boston Opera Co., of which he was general manager until its dissolution in 1914. Just before the outbreak of World War I, he had taken the entire Boston troupe to Paris, where he gave a successful spring season at the Théâtre des Champs-Elysées. He then lived mostly in London. He publ. a book of memoirs, *The Passing Show* (London, 1926).

Russell, Leon (real name, **Hank Wilson**), American country-rock musician; b. Lawton, Okla., April 2, 1941. He played piano and trumpet; then learned to play guitar. He moved to Los Angeles in 1958, did recording gigs with Frank Sinatra, Bobby Darin, and others, and began recording his own songs, among them *Delta Lady* and *Hummingbird.* Apart from regular pop numbers, Russell also put out an album of country-and-western songs; he toured widely and successfully. He clandestinely married the vocalist Mary McCreary in 1976 and put out *The Wedding Album.* His solo releases included the albums *Leon Russell, The Shelter People, Carney,* and *Leon Live.* His use of a honky-tonk piano imparted to his songs a distinct country-and-western flavor, which contributed to the success

of his duo with Willie Nelson, *1 for the Road.* His other hits were *A Song for You, Tight Rope,* and *Magic Mirror.*

Russell, Lillian (real name, **Helen Louise Leonard**), colorful American soprano and actress; b. Clinton, Iowa, Dec. 4, 1861; d. Pittsburgh, June 6, 1922. She studied with Leopold Damrosch in N.Y., where she sang in the chorus for a production of *H.M.S. Pinafore* in 1879; in the following year she was engaged by the entertainer and manager Tony Pastor for the vaudeville circuit, assuming the stage name of Lillian Russell. Her 1st success came in 1881, when she starred in *The Grand Mogul* (also known as *The Snake Charmer*) in N.Y.; she subsequently starred in *Polly, or The Pet of the Regiment* (1885), *Pepita, or The Girl with the Glass Eyes* (1886), *The Queen's Mate* (1888), *Poor Jonathan* (1890), *La Cigale* (1891), *Princess Nicotine* (1893), *An American Beauty* (1896), and *Whirl-i-gig* (1899). She toured England and the U.S. in a burlesque company with Joe Weber and Lew Fields (1899–1904); after her last stage appearance, in *Hokey-pokey* (1912), she remained in the limelight by writing a syndicated newspaper column and lecturing on the vaudeville circuit.

BIBL.: P. Morell, *L. R.: The Era of Plush* (N.Y., 1940); J. Burke, *Duet in Diamonds: The Flamboyant Saga of L. R. and Diamond Jim Brady in America's Gilded Age* (N.Y., 1972).

Russell, William (real name, **Russell William Wagner**), American composer; b. Canton, Mo., Feb. 26, 1905. When he began to study music he eliminated his patronymic as possibly invidious, and placed his 1st Christian name as a surname. He was fascinated with the sounds of drums, and wrote music almost exclusively for percussion instruments; his 1st important work in this category was the *Fugue for 8 Percussion Instruments* (1932). Another work of importance was *3 Dance Movements,* composed in 1933 and performed for the 1st time in N.Y. on Nov. 22, 1933. The scoring is for tone clusters and piano strings activated with a fork, and a cymbal sounded by drawing the teeth of a saw across its edge; the ensemble also includes a bottle which must be broken at the climax. His other percussion works include *Ogou Badagri* (1933; based on Voodoo rites); *3 Cuban Pieces* (1935); *Made in America* (1936; the scoring calls for firecrackers); *March Suite* (1936); Concerto for Trumpet and Percussion (1937). Giving up composition, he moved to New Orleans in 1940, and from 1944 to 1957 he recorded historic jazz on his own label; from 1958, was the jazz-archive curator at Tulane Univ. As late as age 85 he continued playing violin with the New Orleans Ragtime Orch. For a retrospective concert of his works in N.Y. on Feb. 24, 1990, he broke his compositional silence by writing a percussion *Tango* to accompany his *3 Dance Movements;* the concert included the premiere performances of his Trumpet Concerto and *Ogou Badagri.*

BIBL.: K. Gann, "The Kitchen's Winter Music Festival," *Village Voice* (March 27, 1990).

Russo, William (Joseph), American composer and teacher; b. Chicago, June 25, 1928. He studied privately with Lennie Tristano (composition and improvisation, 1943–46), John J. Becker (composition, 1953–55), and Karel B. Jirák (composition and conducting, 1955–57). He was a trombonist and chief composer-arranger with the Stan Kenton Orch. (1950–54); then worked with his own groups in N.Y. and London. He taught at the School of Jazz in Lenox, Mass. (summers, 1956–57), and at the Manhattan School of Music (1958–61). In 1965 he joined the faculty of Columbia College in Chicago; also was a Distinguished Visiting Prof. of Composition at the Peabody Inst. in Baltimore (1969–71), a teacher at Antioch College (1971–72), and composer-in-residence of the city and county of San Francisco (1975–76). He publ. *Composing for the Jazz Orchestra* (Chicago, 1961; 2nd ed., 1973), *Jazz: Composition and Orchestration* (Chicago, 1968; 2nd ed., 1974), and *Composing Music: A New Approach* (Chicago, 1988). Learned counterpoint lends distinction to his compositions even when they reach the never-never land of decibel-laden rock.

WORKS: STAGE: OPERAS: *John Hooton* (1961; BBC, London, Jan. 1963); *The Island* (1963); *Land of Milk and Honey* (1964);

Antigone (1967); *Aesop's Fables*, rock opera (N.Y., Aug. 17, 1972); *A General Opera* (1976); *The Payoff*, cabaret opera (Chicago, Feb. 16, 1984); *A Cabaret Opera* (1985; alternate forms as *The Alice B. Toklas Hashish Fudge Review*, N.Y., Dec. 8, 1977; *Paris Lights*, N.Y., Jan. 24, 1980; and *The Shepherds' Christmas*, Chicago, Dec. 1979); *Dubrovsky* (1988). BALLETS: *The World of Alcina* (1954; rev. 1962); *Les Deux Errants* (Monte Carlo, April 1956); *The Golden Bird* (Chicago, Feb. 17, 1984); other stage pieces; film music. ORCH.: *Allegro* for Concert Band (1957; N.Y., July 18, 1961); 2 syms.: No. 1 (1957); No. 2, *Titans* (1958; N.Y., April 16, 1959); *Newport Suite* (Newport, R.I., July 4, 1958; rev. for Jazz Orch., 1960); *Concerto grosso* for Saxophone Quartet and Concert Band (N.Y., July 29, 1960); Cello Concerto (1962); *3 Pieces* for Blues Band and Orch. (Ravinia Festival, July 7, 1968); *Street Music: A Blues Concerto* (1975; San Francisco, May 19, 1976); *Urban Trilogy* (1981; Los Angeles, March 13, 1982). JAZZ ORCH.: *Solitaire*, with Strings (1949); 2 suites: No. 1 (1952; rev. 1962); No. 2 (1951–54; rev. 1962); *4 Pieces* (1953–54); *The 7 Deadly Sins* for Jazz Orch. (1960); *Variations on an American Theme* (1960; Kansas City, Mo., Feb. 4, 1961); *The English Concerto*, with Violin (Bath, June 11, 1963); *America 1966* (Ravinia Festival, Aug. 3, 1966); *The New Age Suite* (1984). CHAMBER: *21 Études* for Brass Instruments (1959); Sonata for Violin and Piano (1986); *Memphis* for Alto Saxophone and 9 Instruments (Memphis, Tenn., April 21, 1988); piano pieces. VOCAL: *ROCK CANTATAS: The Civil War* (1968); *David* (1968); *Liberation* (1969); *Joan of Arc* (1970); *The Bacchae* (1972); *Song of Songs* (1972). OTHER CANTATAS: *Im Memoriam* for Jazz Orch. (Los Angeles, March 7, 1966); *Songs of Celebration* for 5 Solo Voices, Chorus, and Orch. (1971; Baltimore, Feb. 21, 1973; rev. version, San Francisco, May 18, 1975); *The Touro Cantata* (N.Y., April 4, 1988). OTHER: *Talking to the Sun*, song cycle theater piece (Chicago, March 5, 1989); choruses; songs.

Russolo, Luigi, Italian inventor, painter, and futurist composer; b. Portogruaro, April 30, 1885; d. Cerro di Laveno, Varese, Feb. 4, 1947. In 1909 he joined the futurist movement of Marinetti; formulated the principles of "art of noises" in his book, *L'arte dei rumori* (Milan, 1916); constructed a battery of noise-making instruments ("intonarumori"), with which he gave concerts in Milan (April 21, 1914) and Paris (June 18, 1921), creating such a commotion in the concert hall that on one occasion a group of outraged concertgoers mounted the stage and physically attacked Russolo and his fellow noisemakers. The titles of his works sing the glory of the machine and of urban living: *Convegno dell'automobili e dell'aeroplani, Il Risveglio di una città, Si pranza sulla terrazza dell'Hotel.* In his "futurist manifesto" of 1913 the noises are divided into 6 categories, including shrieks, groans, clashes, explosions, etc. In 1929 he constructed a noise instrument which he called "Russolophone." Soon the novelty of machine music wore out, the erstwhile marvels of automobiles and airplanes became commonplace, and the future of the futurists turned into a yawning past; Russolo gradually retreated from cultivation of noise and devoted himself to the most silent of all arts, painting. His pictures, influenced by the modern French school, and remarkable for their vivid colors, had several successful exhibitions in Paris and N.Y. The text of Russolo's manifesto is reproduced, in an Eng. tr., in N. Slonimsky's *Music since 1900.* BIBL.: M. Zanovello Russolo, *R.: L'uomo, l'artista* (Milan, 1958); M. Kirby, "R. and the Art of Noise," *Futurist Performances* (N.Y., 1971); R. Payton, *The Futurist Musicians: Francesco Balilla Pratella and L. R.* (diss., Univ. of Chicago, 1974); G. Maffina, *L. R. e l'arte dei rumori* (Turin, 1978).

Rust, family of German musicians:

(1) Friedrich Wilhelm Rust, violinist, pianist, and composer; b. Wörlitz, near Dessau, July 6, 1739; d. Dessau, Feb. 28, 1796. He was a child prodigy; studied law in Halle (1758–62), where he also received instruction in music from W.F. Bach; then found a patron in Prince Leopold III of Anhalt-Dessau and continued his studies with G.F. Müller (violin and keyboard); also studied with Karl Höckh in Zerbst; during a sojourn in Potsdam (1763–64), he took courses in violin with Franz Benda and in composition with C.P.E. Bach; after traveling in Italy with his patron (1765), he returned to Dessau to serve the prince; was his court music director (from 1775). He was esteemed as a composer of instrumental music. See R. Czach, ed., *F.W. Rust: Werke für Klavier und Streichinstrumente,* Das Erbe Deutscher Musik, 2nd series, *Mitteldeutschland,* I (1939).

BIBL.: F. Hosaeus, *F.W. R. und das Dessauer Musikleben 1766–1796* (Dessau, 1882); E. Prieger, *F.W. R.: Ein Vorgänger Beethovens* (Cologne, 1894); idem, "R.iana," *Die Musik,* XII (1912–13); R. Czach, *F.W. R.* (Essen, 1927).

(2) Wilhelm Karl Rust, pianist, organist, and teacher, son of **Friedrich Wilhelm Rust;** b. Dessau, April 29, 1787; d. there, April 18, 1855. A child prodigy, he studied with his father; then went to Halle to study philosophy (1805), and there continued his musical training with Türk; he subsequently went to Vienna (1807) and won the praise of Beethoven for his expertise as a keyboard artist; after serving as organist of the Protestant church (1819–27), he returned to Dessau as a teacher.

(3) Wilhelm Rust, organist, pianist, teacher, editor, and composer, grandson of **Friedrich Wilhelm Rust;** b. Dessau, Aug. 15, 1822; d. Leipzig, May 2, 1892. He studied piano and organ with his uncle, Wilhelm Karl Rust, then composition with F. Schneider (1840–43). He went to Berlin in 1849 as a teacher; joined the Singakademie and the Bach Soc., serving as director of the latter (1862–75); was also made the Berlin representative of the Leipzig Bach-Gesellschaft (1853) and was editor in chief of the complete works of Bach publ. under its auspices (from 1858); served as organist at the church of St. Luke (from 1861) and taught composition at the Stern Cons. (from 1870). In 1878 he settled in Leipzig as organist of the Thomaskirche and a teacher at the Cons.; was named Kantor of the Thomasschule in 1880. He wrote some choral pieces, sacred songs, and keyboard music.

Ruthardt, Adolf, German piano pedagogue, composer, and music editor; b. Stuttgart, Feb. 9, 1849; d. Leipzig, Sept. 12, 1934. He studied music with his father, Friedrich Ruthardt; then enrolled at the Stuttgart Cons.; subsequently was a piano teacher in Geneva (1868–85) and at the Leipzig Cons. (1887–1914). He wrote a number of attractive piano pieces and useful student exercises; also ed. various didactic works.

Rutini, Giovanni Marco, Italian composer; b. Florence, April 25, 1723; d. there, Dec. 22, 1797. He studied with Leo (composition), Fago (harpsichord), and Pagliarulo (violin) at the Conservatorio della Pietà dei Turchini in Naples (1739–44). In 1748 he went to St. Petersburg; served as harpsichord teacher to the future Catherine II and conductor of Count Sheremetev's private orch. After returning to his homeland in 1761, he brought out a number of operas, winning particular notice for his *I matrimoni in maschera* (Cremona, 1763) and *L'Olandese in Italia* (Florence, 1765). In 1769 he became maestro di cappella to the Duke of Modena. Although Rutini won accolades as a composer for the theater during his lifetime, his historical significance rests upon his harpsichord music. His influence on the development of keyboard music may be discerned in the works of Haydn, Mozart, Beethoven, and Clementi.

BIBL.: G. Balducci, *La figura e l'opera di G.M. R.* (diss., Univ. of Florence, 1964); F. Meinero, *Le sonate di G.M. R.* (diss., Univ. of Turin, 1975).

Rutter, John (Milford), well-known English conductor and composer; b. London, Sept. 24, 1945. He was educated at Clare College, Cambridge (B.A., 1967; Mus.B., 1968; M.A., 1970), where he was later director of music (1975–79); among his teachers was David Willcocks, with whom he co-edited several choral collections, including 3 in the Carols for Choirs series (Oxford, 1970–80); he also taught through the Open Univ. (1975–88). In 1981 he founded the Cambridge Singers, subsequently conducting them in an extensive repertoire; in 1990 he conducted their Carnegie Hall debut in N.Y.; in 1984 he established Collegium Records, a label dedicated to their performances. His compositions and arrangements are numerous and accessible, and feature an extensive catalog of choral works that are frequently performed in Britain and the U.S.

WORKS: *The Falcon* for Chorus and Orch. (1969); *Fancies* for Chorus and Chamber Orch. (1972); *Partita* for Orch. (1973); *Gloria* for Choir, Brass Ensemble, Percussion, and Organ (1974; for Orch., 1988); *Bang!*, children's opera (1975); *Canticles of America* for Chorus and Orch. (1976); *Beatles' Concerto* for 2 Pianos and Orch. (1977); *The Reluctant Dragon* for Voices and Chamber Orch. (1978); *Suite antique* for Flute, Harpsichord, and Strings (1979); *Reflections* for Piano and Orch. (1979); *The Piper of Hamelin*, children's opera (1980); *The Wind in the Willows* for Voices and Chamber Orch. (1981); *Requiem*, with Soprano Solo (1985); *Te Deum* for Choir and Various Accompaniments (1988); *Magnificat* for Soprano, Chorus, and Ensemble (1990).

Ruwet, Nicolas, French linguist and musical analyst; b. Saive, Belgium, Dec. 31, 1932. He studied Romance philology at the Univ. of Liège, with Lévi-Strauss and Benveniste at the École Pratique des Hautes Études in Paris, and with Jakobson and Chomsky at the Mass. Inst. of Technology; also studied music privately. In 1968 he became prof. of linguistics at the Univ. of Paris at Vincennes. Although not primarily a musician, he has been a fundamental thinker in the semiology of music, contributing important articles which were reprinted in his *Langage, musique, poésie* (Paris, 1972). His multi-leveled system for analyzing musical syntax, "distributional analysis," has been a central influence in the work of Nattiez and his followers.

Ruyneman, Daniel, Dutch composer; b. Amsterdam, Aug. 8, 1886; d. there, July 25, 1963. He began his study of music relatively late; took composition lessons with Zweers at the Amsterdam Cons. (1913–16); in 1918, was co-founder of the Soc. of Modern Dutch Composers; in 1930, organized the Netherlands Soc. for Contemporary Music, serving as president until 1962; ed. its journal, *Maandblad voor Hedendaagse Muziek* (1930–40), until it was suppressed during the Nazi occupation of the Netherlands; was general secretary of the ISCM (1947–51). Ruyneman made a special study of Javanese instruments and introduced them in some of his works. He was naturally attracted to exotic subjects with mystic connotations and coloristic effects; also worked on restoration of early music; in 1930 he orchestrated fragments of Mussorgsky's unfinished opera *The Marriage*, and added his own music for the missing acts of the score.

WORKS: **OPERAS:** *De gebroeders Karamasoff* (1928); *Le Mariage* (1930); also music for the "psycho-symbolic" play *De Clown*, for Vocal and Instrumental Orch. (1915). **ORCH.:** 2 syms.: No. 1, *Symphonie brève* (1927), and No. 2, *Symphony 1953* (1953; Utrecht, March 14, 1956); *Musica per orchestra per una festa Olandese* (1936); Concerto for Orch. (1937); Piano Concerto (1939); Violin Concerto (1940; Amsterdam, Feb. 23, 1943); *Partita* for String Orch. (1943); *Amphitryon*, overture (1943); *Amatarasu* (Ode to the Sun Goddess), on a Japanese melody, for Chamber Ensemble (1953); *Gilgamesj*, Babylonian epos for Orch. (1962). **VOCAL:** *Sous le pont Mirabeau* for Female Chorus, Flute, Harp, and String Quartet (1917); *De Roep* (The Call), a color spectrum of wordless vowel sounds for 5-part a cappella Mixed Chorus (1918); *Sonata*, on wordless vowel sounds, for Chamber a cappella Chorus (1931); *4 Liederen* for Tenor and Small Orch. (1937); *Die Weise von Liebe und Tod des Kornets Christoph Rilke* for Narrator and Piano (1946; orchestrated 1951); *Ancient Greek Songs* for Baritone or Bass, Flute, Oboe, Cello, and Harp (1954); *5 Melodies* for Voice and Piano (1957); *3 chansons de Maquisards condamnés* for Alto or Baritone, and Orch. (1957); *Réflexions I* for Soprano, Flute, Guitar, Viola, Vibraphone, Xylophone, and Percussion (1958–59). **CHAMBER:** *Réflexions: II* for Flute, Viola, and Guitar (1959); *III* for Flute, Violin, Viola, Cello, and Piano or Harpsichord (1960–61; reconstructed by Rob du Bois); *IV* for Wind Quintet (1961); 3 violin sonatas (No. 2, 1914; No. 3, 1956);

Klaaglied van een Slaaf for Violin and Piano (1917); *Hiëroglyphs* for 3 Flutes, Celesta, Harp, Cup-bells, Piano, 2 Mandolins, and 2 Guitars (1918; the unique cup-bells, which some claim were cast by J. Taylor & Co., Loughborough, England, and which others claim were found by the composer in a London junk shop, were destroyed in a Rotterdam air raid in 1940, and perfs. of the work since then have substituted a vibraphone); Sonata for Violin (1925); *Divertimento* for Flute, Clarinet, Horn, Violin, and Piano (1927); Clarinet Sonata (1936); *4 tempi* for 4 Cellos (1937); *Sonatina in modo antiquo* for Cello and Piano (1939); *Sonata da camera* for Flute and Piano (1942); String Quartet (1946); *Nightingale Quintet* for Winds (1949); *4 chansons Bengalies* for Flute and Piano (1950); Sonatina for Flute, and Piano or Harpsichord (1951); Oboe Sonatina (1952); *3 Fantasies* for Cello, and Piano or Harpsichord (1960). **PIANO:** *3 Pathematologieën* (1915); 2 sonatinas (1917, 1954); Sonata (1931); *Kleine Sonata* (1938); *5 sonatines mélodiques pour l'enseignement moderne du piano* (1947).

BIBL.: A. Petronio, *D. R. et son œuvre* (Liège, 1922); C. Bérard, "D. R.," *Chesterian* (1928); A. Hoérée, "D. R.," *Revue Musicale* (March 1949); W. Paap, "D. R.," *Mens en Melodie*, 5 (1962); J. Wouters, "D. R.," *Sonorum Speculum*, 11 (1962); R. du Bois, "D. R.: On the Barricades," *Key Notes* (1976).

Ruzicka, Peter, German composer and Intendant; b. Düsseldorf, July 3, 1948. He studied piano, oboe, and counterpoint at the Hamburg Cons. (1963–68); then composition with Henze in Rome and Otte in Bremen. He was Intendant of the (West) Berlin Radio Sym. Orch. (1979–88), then of the Hamburg State Opera (from 1988). In 1985 he became a member of the Bavarian Academy of Fine Arts.

WORKS: **ORCH.:** *Antifone-Strofe* for 25 Solo Strings and Percussion (1970); *Metastrofe*, "attempt at a breakout" for 87 Instruments (1971); *Sinfonia* for 25 Solo Strings, 16 Vocalists, and Percussion (1971); *In processo di tempo* . . . for 26 Instruments and Cello (1971); *Feedback* for 4 Orch. Groups (1973); *Torso* for 3 Orch. Groups (1973); *Befragung*, 5 pieces (1974); *Emanazione*, variations for Flute and 4 Orch. Groups (1975); *Abbrüche*, 9 phases (1977–78); *Annäherung und Stille*, 4 fragments of Schumann for Piano and 42 Strings (1981); . . . *Den Impuls zum Weitersprechen erst empfinge* for Viola and Orch. (1981); *Satyagraha* (1984); *Drei Bruchstücke* (1984); . . . *Der die Gesänge zerschlug* for Baritone and Chamber Ensemble (1985). **CHAMBER:** Cello Sonata (1969); *Introspezione*, documentation for String Quartet (1970); . . . *Fragment* . . . , 5 epigrams for String Quartet (1970); *Stress* for 8 Groups of Percussion (1972); *Outside-Inside*, 2 models for Musical Theater (1972); *Versuch*, 7 pieces for Strings (1970–74).

Růžička, Rudolf, Czech composer; b. Brno, April 25, 1941. He studied at the Janáček Academy of Music in Brno; then taught electronic music there. In 1967 he, along with A. Parsch and M. Štědroň, joined a composing collective group originally founded by Alois Piňos, and named, in English, "Teamwork." It was modeled after the Soviet "Production Collective" (Procoll) of 1925; together, "Teamwork" produced some pieces of utilitarian music. Růžička's individual compositions include a *Sonata aleatorica* for Organ and Percussion (1964); *Melodrama I* and *II* for 3 Narrators, Chorus, and 7 Instruments (1965); *Elektronika A* for Alto, Chamber Orch., and Electronic Sound (1965), *B* for Chamber Orch. and Electronic Sound (1966), and *C* for Tape (1967); *Musica à 5* for Viola, Bass Clarinet, Harpsichord, Flute, and Percussion (1966); *Timbres* for Wind Quintet and Tape (1968); *Deliciae* for Double Bass and *musique concrète* (1969); *Contaminationi* for Bass Clarinet and Piano (1969); *Sonata nuova* for Cello and Piano (1970); *Cantata ai ai a* (1970); 2 tape pieces, *Discordia* and *Mavors* (both 1970); *Sinfonia cosmica* for Orch. and Organ (1971); *Sonate triste* for Trombone and Piano (1971); 2 string quartets.

Růžičková, Zuzana, Czech harpsichordist; b. Plzeň, Jan. 14, 1928. She studied at the Prague Academy of Music; in 1956 she won the Munich International Competition; was a member of the Prague Chamber Soloists (1962–67), which she co-founded with the conductor Vaclav Neumann. In 1962 she joined the faculty of the Prague Academy of Music. She appeared in duo recitals with Josef Suk from 1963. In 1969 she was named an Artist of Merit. In 1952 she married **Viktor Kalabis.**

BIBL.: B. Berkovec, Z. R. (Prague, 1972).

Ryan, Thomas, Irish-American violist, clarinetist, and composer; b. in Ireland, 1827; d. New Bedford, Mass., March 5, 1903. He received instruction in violin and wind instruments in Ireland before emigrating to the U.S. in 1844; settled in 1845 in Boston, where he founded the Mendelssohn Quintette Club, playing the viola (and upon occasion the clarinet), with August Fries (1st violin), Francis Riha (2nd violin), Eduard Lehmann (viola and flute), and Wulf Fries (cello); traveled all over the U.S. with it until it was dissolved in 1895, doing missionary work in bringing good music to remote communities; he also acted as its manager; arranged Classical sonatas and other works for it; after half a century, Ryan was the sole remaining original member of the organization. He publ. his memoirs, *Recollections of an Old Musician* (N.Y., 1899).

Ryba, Jakub (Šimon) Jan, Czech choirmaster, teacher, writer on music, and composer; b. Přeštice, Oct. 26, 1765; d. (suicide) Rožmitál pod Třemšínem, April 8, 1815. He studied academic subjects in Prague; in 1788 he became school- and choirmaster in Rožmitál. He wrote about 90 masses, the most famous being *Hej, mistře* (Hail, Master!; 1796); he also composed various other sacred works, including 7 Requiems, numerous motets, over 50 pastorellas, arias, and choruses. His secular works include 6 stage pieces and songs. He was also a prolific composer of instrumental music, but little of it is extant.

BIBL.: J. Němeček, *Světské skladby J.J. R.* (Secular Works; diss., Univ. of Prague, 1945); idem, *J.J. R.: Život a dílo* (Life and Works; Prague, 1963).

Rybner (real name, **Rübner**), **(Peter Martin) Cornelius,** Danish pianist, conductor, teacher, and composer; b. Copenhagen, Oct. 26, 1855; d. N.Y., Jan. 21, 1929. He studied at the Copenhagen Cons. with Gade and J.P. Hartmann; then at the Leipzig Cons. with Ferdinand David (violin) and Reinecke (piano); finished his pianistic studies under Hans von Bülow and Anton Rubinstein. After a series of concerts in Europe as pianist, he settled in Karlsruhe; succeeded Mottl in 1892 as conductor of the Phil. Soc., and held this position until 1904, when he emigrated to the U.S., succeeding MacDowell as head of the music dept. at Columbia Univ. (1904–19). About 1920 he changed his name to Rybner. His works include a ballet, *Prinz Ador* (Munich, 1902); a symphonic poem, *Friede, Kampf und Sieg;* a Violin Concerto; numerous choruses; piano pieces; songs; also some chamber music.

Rychlík, Jan, Czech composer; b. Prague, April 27, 1916; d. there, Jan. 20, 1964. He studied with Jaroslav Řídký at the Prague Cons. (1939–45) and in his master classes there (1945–46). A practical musician, he played in dance orchs., experimented with modern techniques, and was active as a music critic; he wrote a book on jazz and one on valveless brass instruments.

WORKS: *Symphonic Overture* (1944); *Suite* for Wind Quintet (1946); *Concert Overture* (1947); *Partita giocosa* for Wind Orch. (1947); Trio for Clarinet, Trumpet, and Bassoon (1948); *Divertimento* for 3 Double Basses (1951); *Études* for English Horn and Piano (1953); String Trio (1953); *4 Partitas* for Flute (1954); *Chamber Suite* for String Quartet (1954); *Arabesques* for Violin and Piano (1955); *Burlesque Suite* for Clarinet (1956); *Serenade* for Wind Octet (1957); Wind Quintet (1960); *Hommagi gravicembalistici* for Harpsichord (1960); *African Cycle I–V* for 8 Winds and Piano (1961; Prague, June 29, 1962); *Relazioni* for Alto Flute, English Horn, and Bassoon (1964); music for 55 films and 8 plays.

Rychlík, Józef, Polish composer; b. Krakow, May 12, 1946. He graduated in composition from the Krakow State College of Music. He composed *Symphonic Music I* for 2 String Quartets and 2 Pianos (1969); *Symphonic Music II* for Chamber Ensemble (1969); *Ametrio* for Flute, Violin, and Cello (1971); *Spatial*

Sequences for 22 Players (1971); *"000"* for Chamber Group and any Wind Instrument Solo (1972); *Sketches* for Organ and Orch. (1972); *Plenitudo temporis* for Orch. (1974); *Peut-être,* graphic composition for any Solo Instrument, or Voice, or Dancer, or Ballet Group, with ad libitum Tape (1974); *Podtytul- sen Eurydyki II* for Female Voice and Tape (1982).

Rydman, Kari, Finnish composer; b. Helsinki, Oct. 15, 1936. He studied musicology at the Univ. of Helsinki; was autodidact as a composer; developed energetic activities as a composer, music critic, and schoolteacher. In his music he reveals himself as a blithe spirit, writing ultramodern pieces, but also turning out some fetching Finnish pop tunes.

WORKS: 5 string quartets (1959, 1963, 1964, 1964, 1966); Piano Quintet (1960); Trio for Violin, Cello, and Percussion (1961); *Sonata 1* for 3 Violins, Viola, Cello, Piano, and Percussion (1962); *Sonata 2* for Violin, Viola, Guitar, and Percussion (1962); *Sonata 4* for Violin, Clarinet, Guitar, and Percussion (1963); *Sonata 6* for Cello and Percussion (1964); *Khoros 1* for 3 Flutes, Oboe, Percussion, Harp, Violin, Viola, Cello, and Double Bass (1964); *Khoros 2* for Orch. (1966); *Rondeaux des nuits blanches d'été* for Orch. (1966); *Sonata 8* for Viola and Harpsichord (1967); *Symphony of the Modern Worlds,* which contains blues, beat rhythms, political songs, and the Chinese Communist anthem, *Dong Fang Hong* (The East Is Red) (1968); Sonata 9 for Small Orch. (1969); *DNA* for Orch. and Electronic Organ (1970); *Suite* for Narrator and Orch. (1971).

Ryelandt, Joseph, Belgian composer; b. Bruges, April 7, 1870; d. there, June 29, 1965. He studied composition with Edgar Tinel. Thanks to a personal fortune (he was a baron), he did not have to earn a living by his music; was director of the Bruges Cons. (1924–45) and a teacher at the Ghent Cons. (1929–39). He lived a very long life (*obiit aet. 95*) and composed much music.

WORKS: *La Parabole des vierges,* spiritual drama (1894); *Sainte Cécile,* lyrical drama (1902); 5 oratorios: *Purgatorium* (1904); *De Komst des Heren* (The Coming of the Lord; 1906–7); *Maria* (1910); *Agnus Dei* (1913–15); *Christus Rex* (1921–22); Te Deum for Soli, Chorus, and Orch. (1927); 5 syms. (1897, 1904, 1908, 1913, 1934); *Gethsemani,* symphonic poem (1908); *Patria,* overture (1917); 11 piano sonatas; 4 string quartets; Horn Sonata (1897); 2 piano quintets; 2 piano trios; 7 violin sonatas; 3 cello sonatas; Viola Sonata; 7 cantatas; organ pieces; songs.

Rysanek, Leonie, distinguished Austrian soprano; b. Vienna, Nov. 14, 1926. She studied at the Vienna Cons. with Rudolf Grossmann, whom she later married. She made her debut as Agathe in *Der Freischütz* in Innsbruck in 1949; then sang at Saarbrücken (1950–52). She 1st attracted notice when she appeared as Sieglinde at the Bayreuth Festival in 1951; became a member of the Bavarian State Opera in Munich in 1952, and went with it to London's Covent Garden in 1953, where she sang Danae; in 1954 she joined the Vienna State Opera; also sang in various other major European opera houses. On Sept. 18, 1956, she made her U.S. debut as Senta at the San Francisco Opera; later made a spectacular appearance at the Metropolitan Opera in N.Y. on Feb. 5, 1959, when she replaced Maria Callas in the role of Lady Macbeth in Verdi's opera on short notice; she remained on its staff until 1973, and sang there again in 1975–76 and subsequent seasons. She received the Lotte Lehmann Ring from the Vienna State Opera in 1979. Her younger sister **Lotte Rysanek** (b. Vienna, March 18, 1928) attained a fine reputation in Vienna as a lyric soprano.

Rytel, Piotr, Polish composer; b. Vilnius, Sept. 20, 1884; d. Warsaw, Jan. 2, 1970. He studied with Michalowski and Noskowski at the Warsaw Cons.; in 1911, was appointed a prof. of piano, and in 1918 a prof. of harmony there. He was the director of Sopot State College of Music, 1956–61.

WORKS: OPERAS: *Ijola* (1927; Warsaw, Dec. 14, 1929); *Koniec Mesjasza* (1935–36); *Krzyzowcy* (1940–41); *Andrzej z Chelmna* (1942–43). BALLETS: *Faun i Psyche* (1931); *Śląski pierścień* (The Silesian Ring; 1956). ORCH.: symphonic poems:

Grazyna (1908; rev. 1954); *Poemat* (1910); *Korsarz*, after Byron (The Corsair; 1911); *Sen Dantego* (The Dream of Dante; 1911); *Legenda o św. Jerzym* (The Legend of St. George; 1918); 3 syms.: No. 1 (1909); No. 2, *Mickiewiczowska* (in honor of the Polish poet Mickiewicz) for Tenor, Chorus, and Orch. (1949); No. 3 for Tenor and Orch. (1950–51); Piano Concerto (1907); Violin Concerto (1950); *Sinfonia concertante* for Flute, Clarinet, Horn, Harp, and Orch. (1960). **CHAMBER:** *Romance* for Clarinet and Piano (1948); *Variations* for Clarinet and Piano (1957).

Ryterband, Roman, Polish-born American pianist and composer; b. Lodz, Aug. 2, 1914; d. Palm Springs, Calif., Nov. 17, 1979. After a period of study in Poland, he lived mostly in Switzerland; eventually settled in America, becoming a naturalized citizen in 1964. His works reflect Polish motifs; his harmonic idiom is mildly modernistic. His works include an "opera grotesque," *Fantômes rebelles;* a music drama, *A Border Incident;* Sonata for 2 Flutes and Harp; Quintet for 2 Flutes, Viola, Cello, and Harpsichord; *Russian Rhapsody* for Orch.; *Suite polonaise* for Piano; and assorted pieces for various instrumental combinations.

Rzewski, Frederic (Anthony), American pianist, teacher, and avant-garde composer of Polish descent; b. Westfield, Mass., April 13, 1938. He studied counterpoint with Thompson and orchestration with Piston at Harvard Univ. (B.A., 1958) and continued his studies with Sessions and Babbitt at Princeton Univ. (M.F.A., 1960); then received instruction from Dallapiccola in Florence on a Fulbright scholarship (1960–61) and from Carter in Berlin on a Ford Foundation grant (1963–65). With Curran and Teitelbaum, other similarly futuroscopic musicians, he founded the M.E.V. (Musica Elettronica Viva) in Rome in 1966; was active as a pianist in various avant-garde settings; played concerts with the topless cellist Charlotte Moorman; also devoted much time to teaching. In 1977 he became prof. of composition at the Liège Cons. As a composer, he pursues the shimmering distant vision of optimistic, positivistic anti-music. He is furthermore a granitically overpowering piano technician, capable of depositing huge boulders of sonoristic material across the keyboard without actually wrecking the instrument.

WORKS: ORCH.: *Nature morte* for 25 Instruments (1965); *A Long Time Man* for Piano and Orch. (1979); *The Price of Oil* for 2 Speakers, Winds, and Percussion (1980); *Satyrica* for Jazz Band (River Falls, Wis., April 27, 1983); *Una breve storia d'estate* for 3 Flutes and Small Orch. (1983). **INSTRUMENTAL:** Octet for Flute, Clarinet, Trumpet, Trombone, Piano, Harp, Violin, and Double Bass (1961–62); *For Violin* (1962); *Speculum Dianae* for 8 Instruments (1964); *Les Moutons de Panurge* for Ensemble (1969); *Last Judgement* for 1 or More Trombones (1969); *Attica* for Narrator and Variable Ensemble (1972); *Coming Together* for Narrator and Variable Ensemble (1972); *What Is Freedom?* for 6 Instruments (1974); *13 Instrumental Studies* (1977); *Song and Dance* for Flute, Bass Clarinet, Vibraphone, and Electric Bass (1977); *Whang Doodles*, trio for Violin, Piano, and Percussion (Ravinia Festival, Aug. 20, 1990). **PIANO:** *Preludes* (1957); *Poem* (1959); Sonata for 2 Pianos (1960); *Study I* (1960) and *II* (1961); *Falling Music* for Amplified Piano and Tape (1971); *Variations on No Place to Go but Around* (1974); *The People United Will Never Be Defeated*, 36 variations on the Chilean song ¡El pueblo unido jamás será vencido! (1975); 4 pieces (1977); *4 North American Ballads* (1978–79); *Squares* (1979); *Winnsboro Cotton Mill Blues* for 2 Pianos (1980); *A Machine* for 2 Pianos (1984). **OTHER:** *Spacecraft* (his magnum opus; 1967; "plan for spacecraft" publ. in *Source*, 3, 1968); *Impersonation*, audiodrama (1967); *Requiem* (1968); *Symphony for Several Performers* (1968).

S

Saar, Louis Victor (Franz), Dutch pianist, teacher, and composer; b. Rotterdam, Dec. 10, 1868; d. St. Louis, Nov. 23, 1937. He studied with Rheinberger in Munich (1886–89); lived in Vienna, Leipzig, and Berlin; in 1894 he went to the U.S.; taught music at various schools in N.Y.; was a member of the faculty at the Cincinnati College of Music (1906–17), the Chicago Musical College (1917–33), and the St. Louis Inst. of Music (1934–37). He wrote the orch. pieces *From the Mountain Kingdom of the Great Northwest* (1922) and *Along the Columbia River* (1924), but became best known for his choral works, songs, and violin and piano pieces.

Saar, Mart, Estonian composer; b. Vastemõisa, Livonia, Sept. 16, 1882; d. Tallinn, Oct. 28, 1963. He was a pupil of Louis Homilius, Rimsky-Korsakov, and Liadov at the St. Petersburg Cons. (1901–11); was active as a folk-song collector, critic, and teacher in Dorpat, Reval (Tallinn), and Hüpassare; also taught composition at the Tallinn Cons. (1943–56). He was one of Estonia's leading composers; wrote orch. music, choral works, including cantatas and many songs, and much piano music.

BIBL.: K. Leichter, *M. S.* (Tallinn, 1964); V. Rumessen, ed., *M. S. sõnas ja pildis* (M. S. in Words and Pictures; Tallinn, 1973).

Saariaho, Kaija, Finnish composer; b. Helsinki, Oct. 14, 1952. She studied in Helsinki with Paavo Heininen at the Sibelius Academy (1976–81) and at the Univ. of Industrial Arts; attended the Darmstadt summer courses (1980, 1982) and studied with Brian Ferneyhough and Klaus Huber at the Freiburg Hochschule für Musik (diploma, 1983); also attended courses in computer music at IRCAM in Paris (1982). She held a Finnish government artist's grant from 1983 to 1986, and in 1986 was awarded Darmstadt's Kranichstein Prize. Her works are experimental in nature, often utilizing tape, live electronics, and computers.

WORKS: THEATER AND MULTIMEDIA: *Study for Life* for Female Voice, Dancer, Tape, and Light (1980); 3 interludes and other music for *Skotten in Helsingfors*, tape music (1983); *Kollisionen* for Percussion and Tape (1984); *Csokolom* (1985); *Collisions*, tape music (1986); *Piipää* for 2 Singers, Tape, and Live Electronics (1987); *Stilleben*, radiophonic score (1987–88). **ORCH.:** *Verblendungen* for Orch. and Tape (1982–84; Helsinki, April 10, 1984). **CHAMBER:** *Canvas* for Flute (1978); *Yellows* for Horn and Percussion (1980); *Im Traume* for Cello and Piano (1980); *. . . sah den Vögeln* for Soprano, Flute, Oboe, Cello, Prepared Piano, and Live Electronics (1981); *Laconisme de l'aile* for Flute (1982); *Jardin secret II* for Harpsichord and Tape (1984–86; Savonlinna, July 12, 1986); *Lichtbogen* for Chamber Ensemble and Live Electronics (Paris, May 13, 1986); *Io* for Chamber Ensemble, Tape, and Live Electronics (Paris, April 27, 1987); *Nymphea: Jardin secret III* for String Quartet and Live Electronics (N.Y., May 20, 1987); *Petals* for Cello (1988); *Nymphea #25'* for String Quartet (1988–89). **VOCAL:** *Bruden* (The Bride), song cycle for Soprano, 2 Flutes, and Percussion (1977); *Nej och inte* (No and Not), 3 songs for Women's Vocal Quartet or Choir (1979); *Suomenkielinen sekakuorokappale* (A Piece for Mixed Choir in the Finnish Language; 1979); *Preludi-Tunnustus-Postludi* (Prelude-Confession-Postlude) for Soprano and Prepared Grand Piano (1980); *Kolme Prelude* for Soprano and Organ (1980); *Ju lägre solen* for Soprano, Flute, and Guitar

(1982; rev. as *Adjö*, 1985). TAPE: *Study II for Life* (1981); *Vers le blanc* (1982); *Jardin secret I* (1985).

BIBL.: R. Nieminen, "A Portrait of K. S.," *Nordic Sounds* (June 1986).

Sabaneyev, Leonid (Leonidovich), Russian writer on music and composer; b. Moscow, Oct. 1, 1881; d. Antibes, May 3, 1968. He studied with Taneyev at the Moscow Cons.; also took a course in mathematics at the Univ. of Moscow. In 1920 he joined the board of the newly-organized Moscow Inst. of Musical Science. In 1926 he left Russia and eventually settled in France. He was an energetic promoter of modern music, and a friend of Scriabin, about whom he wrote a monograph, which would have been important if his account of Scriabin's life and ideology could be trusted; he compromised himself when he wrote a devastating review of Prokofiev's *Scythian Suite* at a concert that never took place.

WORKS: Ballet, *L'Aviatrice* (Paris, 1928); symphonic poem, *Flots d'azur* (1936); oratorio, *The Revelation* (1940); 2 piano trios (1907, 1924); Violin Sonata (1924); piano pieces; songs.

WRITINGS: All in Russian unless otherwise given: *Richard Wagner and the Synthesis of Arts* (1913); *The Development of the Harmonic Idea* (1913); *Medtner* (1913); *Scriabin* (1916; 2nd ed., rev., 1923); *History of Russian Music* (1924; also in Ger., 1926); *Modern Russian Composers* (in Eng., N.Y., 1927); *Sergei Taneyev* (1930); *Music for the Films* (in Eng., London, 1935).

Sabata, Victor de. See **De Sabata, Victor.**

Sabbatini, Galeazzo, Italian composer and music theorist; b. probably in Pesaro, 1597; d. there, Dec. 6, 1662. He studied with Vincenzo Pellegrini, canon of Pesaro Cathedral. Sabbatini was subsequently canon there (1626–30); then was maestro di cappella to the Duke of Mirandola (1630–39); again served as canon at Pesaro Cathedral (from 1641). He publ. the theoretical vol. *Regola facile e breve per sonare sopra il basso continuo nell'organo, manacordo o altro simile stromento* (Venice, 1628). He publ. 5 books of madrigals *a* 2–5 (Venice, 1625–36) and various sacred works.

Sabbatini, Luigi Antonio, Italian music theorist and composer; b. Albano Laziale, near Rome, Oct. 24, 1732; d. Padua, Jan. 29, 1809. He studied in Padua and with Padre Martini in Bologna, where he also entered the St. Francis monastery. He was maestro di cappella at the basilica of S. Barnaba in Marino (1767–72); in 1772 he was appointed to the Franciscan basilica of the 12 Holy Apostles in Rome; in 1786 he took over the duties of maestro di cappella at the Antonius Basilica, succeeding Agostino Ricci, who was in turn the successor of Vallotti. He composed a number of sacred vocal works but his significance rests upon his work as a music theorist. Among his publications were *Notizie sopra la vita e le opere del rev. P.F.A. Vallotti* (Padua, 1780); *Elementi teorici della musica colla pratica dei medesimi, in duetti e terzetti a canone accompagnati dal basso* (Rome, 1789–90); *La vera idea delle musicali numeriche segnature diretta al giovane studioso dell'armonia* (Venice, 1799); *Trattato sopra le fughe musicali di L.A. Sabbatini corredato da copiosi saggi del suo antecessore F.A. Vallotti* (Venice, 1802).

Sabin, Wallace Arthur, English organist and composer; b. Culworth, Dec. 15, 1860; d. Berkeley, Calif., Dec. 8, 1937. He studied with M.J. Monk at Banbury and T.W. Dodds at Oxford, where he obtained a degree at Queen's College (1890). He emigrated to the U.S. and settled in San Francisco, where he was organist at St. Luke's (1894–1906), Temple Emanu-El (1895–1937), and the First Church of Christ, Scientist (1906–37). He composed the music to the plays *St. Patrick at Tara* (1906) and *The Twilight of the Kings* (1918), many part-songs for men's voices, and sacred music.

BIBL.: R. Rinder, *Tribute to W.A. S.* (San Francisco, 1938).

Sacchetti, Liberius, Russian writer on music and pedagogue; b. Kenzar, near Tambov, Aug. 30, 1852; d. Petrograd, March 10, 1916. He studied with Rimsky-Korsakov and others at the St. Petersburg Cons.; in 1878 he was appointed to its faculty as a lecturer on musical esthetics. He publ. an *Outline of General Music History* (St. Petersburg, 1882); *A Brief Anthology of Musical History* (St. Petersburg, 1896); manuals on esthetics for use at the St. Petersburg Cons.; etc. He was highly regarded as a scholar and teacher in Russia.

Sacchi, Don Giovenale, Italian scholar; b. Barzio, Como, Nov. 22, 1726; d. Milan, Sept. 27, 1789. He was a member of the Barnabite monastic order, and an assiduous student of ancient music; also was distinguished as a biographer.

WRITINGS: *Del numero e delle misure delle corde musiche e loro corrispondenze* (1761); *Della divisione del tempo nella musica, nel ballo e nella poesia* (1770); *Della natura e perfezione dell'antica musica de' Greci* (1778); *Della quinte successive nel contrappunto e delle regole degli accompagnamenti* (1780); *Vita del Cav. Don Carlo Broschi, detto Farinelli* (1784); *Don Placido, Dialogo dove cercasi se lo studio della musica al religioso convenga o disconvenga* (1786); etc.; also tr. Cardinal Fontana's *Vita di Benedetto Marcello* (1788).

Sacchini, Antonio (Maria Gasparo Gioacchino), prominent Italian composer; b. Florence, June 14, 1730; d. Paris, Oct. 6, 1786. He entered the Cons. of Santa Maria di Loreto at Naples as a violin pupil of Nicola Fiorenza; also received instruction in singing from Gennaro Manna in harpsichord, organ, and composition from Francesco Durante. His intermezzo *Fra Donato* was performed at the Cons. in 1756; his comic opera *Olimpia* was given at the Teatro dei Fiorentini in 1758, the same year in which he became maestro di cappella straordinario at the Cons.; he was made secondo maestro in 1761. His opera seria, *Olimpiade*, scored a remarkable success at its Padua premiere on July 9, 1763; it subsequently was performed throughout Italy. During a stay in Rome, he produced several comic operas, including *Il finto pazzo per amore* (1765), *La Contadina in corte* (1766), and *L'isola d'amore* (1766). In 1768 he was named director of the Conservatorio dell'Ospedaletto in Venice; also made a visit to Germany, where he brought out the operas *Scipione in Cartagena* (Munich, Jan. 8, 1770), *Calliroe* (Stuttgart, Feb. 11, 1770), and *L'Eroe cinese* (Munich, April 27, 1770). In 1772 he went to London, where he acquired a notable reputation; among the operas produced there were *Tamerlano* (May 6, 1773), *Montezuma* (Feb. 7, 1775), *Erifile* (Feb. 7, 1778), *L'Amore soldato* (May 4, 1778), *L'Avaro deluso, o Don Calandrino* (Nov. 24, 1778), and *Enea e Lavinia* (March 25, 1779). In 1781 he received an invitation from Marie Antoinette, through the "intendant des menus-plaisirs," to go to Paris. His name was already known in France, since his opera *L'isola d'amore*, arranged as *La Colonie* ("comic opera imitated from the Italian"), had been produced in Paris on Aug. 16, 1775; upon his arrival he was forthwith commissioned to write 3 works at a fee of 10,000 francs each. For this purpose he adapted his Italian opera *Armida e Rinaldo* (Milan, 1772) to a French text as *Renaud*, "tragédie lyrique" in 3 acts (produced at the Académie Royale de Musique, Feb. 25, 1783), and his opera *Il Cidde* (Rome, 1764) as *Chimène* (Fontainebleau, Nov. 18, 1783); the 3rd opera, *Dardanus*, was a new work; it was staged at the Trianon at Versailles, Sept. 18, 1784, in the presence of Louis XVI and Marie Antoinette. In Paris Sacchini found himself in unintended rivalry with Piccinni as a representative of Italian music in the famous artistic war against the proponents of the French operas of Gluck; Sacchini's most successful opera, however, was to the French text *Œdipe à Colonne*, first presented at Versailles (Jan. 4, 1786) and produced at the Paris Opéra (Feb. 1, 1787) after Sacchini's death. It held the stage for half a century, and there were sporadic revivals later on. His last opera, also to a French libretto, *Arvire et Evelina*, was left unfinished, and was produced posth. (Paris Opéra, April 29, 1788; 3rd act added by J.B. Rey). Sacchini found his métier as a composer of serious operas, but his works were nonetheless typical products of the Italian operatic art of his time, possessing melodious grace but lacking in dramatic development. The undistinguished style of Sacchini's productions is probably the reason for the disappearance of his operas from the active repertoire; Piccinni fared much better in comparison. Among his other compositions were 8 oratorios, masses, mass movements, motets, Psalms, arias, 2 syms. (1767), 6 Trio Sonatas, op. 1 (London, c.1775), 6 String Quartets, op. 2 (London, 1778), 6 Sonatas for Harpsichord or Piano and Violin, op. 3 (London, 1779), and *A Second Set of 6 Favorite Lessons* for Harpsichord or Piano and Violin, op. 4 (London, c.1780).

BIBL.: A. Jullien, *La Cour et l'opéra sous Louis XVI: Marie Antoinette et S.* (Paris, 1878); J.-G. Prod'homme, "Un musicien napolitain à la cour de Louis XVI: Les dernières années de G. S.," *Le Ménestrel* (Dec. 11 and Dec. 18, 1925); V. Morelli, "A. S. fra i Gluckisti e i briganti di Londra," *Vita musicale italiana*, VII–VIII (1926); U. Prota-Giurleo, *S. non nacque a Pozzuoli* (Naples, 1952); F. Schlitzer, *A. S.: Schede e appunti per una sua storia teatrale* (Siena, 1955); U. Prota-Giurleo, *S. a Napoli* (Naples, 1956); idem, *S. fra Piccinisti e Gluckisti* (Naples, 1957); E. Thierstein, *Five French Operas of S.* (diss., Univ. of Cincinnati, 1974).

Sacco, P(atrick) Peter, American composer of Italian descent; b. Albion, N.Y., Oct. 25, 1928. Virtually his whole family consisted of tenors: his father, a brother, and a couple of uncles. Sacco followed the family tradition and became a tenor himself. He also studied piano and exhibited himself in public as a keyboard prodigy; he also studied trumpet and tuba. After 3 years of preparatory school in music in Rochester, N.Y., he entered Fredonia State Univ. (B.M., 1950); he was drafted into the U.S. Army, and was stationed in Frankfurt am Main (1950–52); there he studied music theory with a local teacher and also played church organ and piano programs for the officers' club. In 1953 he enrolled in the Eastman School of Music in Rochester as a student of Bernard Rogers and Howard Hanson (M.M., 1954; D.Mus., 1958). He continued to perform as a tenor; sang in various school performances of classical operas and oratorios. In 1959 he was appointed to the music faculty of San Francisco State College (later Univ.), where he taught until 1980; in 1970–71 he was a visiting prof. at the Univ. of Hawaii, where he taught composition and gave vocal recitals. As a composer, he adheres to traditional harmony, but has diversified into ingenious chromatic developments, approximating a euphonious type of dodecaphony.

WORKS: Opera, *Mr. Vinegar* (Redding, Calif., May 12, 1967); oratorio, *Jesu* (Grand Rapids, Mich., Dec. 3, 1956, composer conducting); oratorio, *Midsummer Dream Night* (San Francisco, June 25, 1961, composer conducting); *Solomon*, oratorio (San Francisco, Dec. 12, 1976, composer as tenor soloist); Sym. No. 1 (Oklahoma City, Dec. 17, 1958); Sym. No. 2, *The Symphony of Thanksgiving* (San Francisco, March 23, 1976); Sym. No. 3, *The Convocation Symphony* (Redding, June 1, 1968); *Moab Illuminations* for Orch. (1972); Piano Concerto (1964; San Francisco, April 4, 1968); Violin Concerto (1969; Walnut Creek, Calif., April 24, 1974).

Sacher, Paul, respected Swiss conductor and philanthropist; b. Basel, April 28, 1906. He studied with Weingartner (conducting) at the Basel Cons. and with Karl Nef (musicology) at the Univ. of Basel. In 1926 he founded the Basel Chamber Orch., which specialized in playing works from the pre-Classical and contemporary periods; in 1928 he also organized the Basel Chamber Choir. In 1933 he founded the Schola Cantorum Basiliensis; was also director of the Collegium Musicum in Zürich from 1941. His Schola Cantorum Basiliensis was amalgamated with Basel's Cons. and Musikschule to form the Musikakademie der Stadt Basel, which he directed from 1954 to 1969. He appeared as a guest conductor in many European cities; made his U.S. debut as a guest conductor with the Collegiate Chorale in N.Y. (April 3, 1955). In 1934 he married Maja Stehlin, widow of Emmanuel Hoffmann, whose father founded the Hoffmann-La Roche pharmaceutical firm, makers of the drugs Valium and Librium. Through his wife's fortune, Sacher was able to pursue his goal of commissioning works from the leading composers of the 20th century; in all, he commissioned over 200 works, including scores by Stravinsky, Bartók, Strauss, Honegger, Hindemith, Martin, Britten, Henze,

and Boulez, many of which received their premieres under his direction. In 1983 he purchased the entire Stravinsky archive in N.Y. for $5,250,000. In 1986 the Paul Sacher Foundation building was opened in Basel; it houses the archives of Stravinsky, Webern, Martin, and Maderna, as well as of Sacher.

BIBL.: E. Lichtenhahn and T. Seebass, eds., *Musik Handschriften aus der Sammlung P. S.: Festschrift zu P. S.s siebzigstem Geburtstag* (Basel, 1976); M. Rostropovich, ed., *Dank an P. S.* (Zürich, 1976); G. Wilkins, "A Most Extraordinary Maestro," *Musical America* (March 1988).

Sachs, Curt, eminent German musicologist; b. Berlin, June 29, 1881; d. N.Y., Feb. 5, 1959. While attending the Gymnasium in Berlin, he studied piano and composition with L. Schrattenholz and clarinet with Rausch; entered the Univ. there, where he studied music history with Oskar Fleischer, and also art history (Ph.D., 1904); was active as an art historian until 1909 while receiving instruction in musicology from Kretzschmar and Wolf; then devoted himself to musicology, specializing in the history of musical instruments. In 1919 he became director of Berlin's Staatliche Instrumentensammlung; also taught at the Univ. of Berlin, the Staatliche Hochschule für Musik, and the Akademie für Kirchen- und Schulmusik. In 1933 he was compelled to leave Germany; went to Paris as chargé de mission at the Musée de l'Homme; was a visiting prof. at the Sorbonne. In 1937 he settled in the U.S.; was a prof. of music at N.Y. Univ. (1937–53); also was consultant to the N.Y. Public Library (1937–52), adjunct prof. at Columbia Univ. (from 1953), and president of the American Musicological Society (1949–50).

WRITINGS: *Musikgeschichte der Stadt Berlin bis zum Jahre 1800* (1908); *Musik und Oper am kurbrandenburgischen Hof* (1910); *Reallexikon der Musikinstrumente* (1913); *Handbuch der Musikinstrumentenkunde* (1920; 2nd ed., 1930); *Die Musikinstrumente des alten Ägyptens* (1921); *Katalog der Staatlichen Instrumentensammlung* (1922); *Das Klavier* (1923); *Die modernen Musikinstrumente* (1923); *Geist und Werden der Musikinstrumente* (1929); *Vergleichende Musikwissenschaft in ihren Grundzügen* (1930); *Eine Weltgeschichte des Tanzes* (1933; in Eng. as *World History of the Dance*, 1937); *Les Instruments de musique de Madagascar* (1938); *The History of Musical Instruments* (1940); *The Rise of Music in the Ancient World* (1943); ed. *The Evolution of Piano Music* (1944); *The Commonwealth of Art* (1946); *Our Musical Heritage* (1948; 2nd ed., 1955); *Rhythm and Tempo: A Study in Music History* (1953).

BIBL.: E. Hertzmann, "Alfred Einstein and C. S.," *Musical Quarterly* (April 1941); G. Reese and R. Brandel, eds., *The Commonwealth of Music, in Honor of C. S.* (N.Y., 1965); S. Pollens, "C. S. and Musical Instrument Restoration," *Musical Times* (Oct. 1989).

Sachs, Hans, famous German poet and Meistersinger; b. Nuremberg, Nov. 5, 1494; d. there, Jan. 19, 1576. He was educated at the Nuremberg grammar school (1501–9); after serving his apprenticeship (1511–16), he returned to Nuremberg as a master shoemaker in 1520; joined the Meistersinger guild about 1509, where he received instruction from Linhard Nunnenbeck. Under Sachs, the Meistergesang was an active force in the Reformation movement from 1520. He wrote over 6,000 poetical works, ranging from Meisterlieder to dramatic pieces; he also wrote 13 Meistertöne. For his musical works, see E. Goetze and C. Drescher, eds., *Hans Sachs: Sämtliche Fabeln und Schwänke* (Halle, 1893–1913) and F. Ellis, ed., *The Early Meisterlieder of Hans Sachs* (Bloomington, Ind., 1974). Sachs is the central figure in Wagner's opera *Die Meistersinger von Nürnberg.*

BIBL.: C. Schweitzer, *Un Poète allemand au XVIᵉ siècle: Étude sur la vie et les œuvres de H. S.* (Nancy, 1889); K. Drescher, *Studien zu H. S.* (Marburg, 1891); R. Genée, *H. S. und seine Zeit* (Leipzig, 1894; 2nd ed., 1901); B. Suphan, *H. S.: Humanitätszeit und Gegenwart* (Weimar, 1895); K. Drescher, *Nürnberger Meistersinger-protokolle von 1575–1689* (2 vols., Tübingen, 1898); K. Mey, *Der Meistergesang* (1901); H. Holzschuher, *H. S. in seiner Bedeutung für unsere Zeit*

(Berlin, 1906); E. Mummenhoff, *Musikpflege und Musikaufführungen im alten Nürnberg* (Leipzig, 1908); H. Nutzhorn, *Meistersangeren H. S.* (Copenhagen, 1911); F. Ellis, *H. S. Studies* (Bloomington, Ind., 1941); B. Könneker, *H. S.* (Stuttgart, 1971); H. Brunner, G. Hirschmann, and F. Schnelbogl, eds., *H. S. und Nürnberg: H. S. zum 400. Todestag* (Nuremberg, 1976); N. Holzberg, *H.-S.-Bibliographie* (Nuremberg, 1976); K. Wedler, *H. S.* (Leipzig, 1976).

Sachs, Joel, American pianist, conductor, and musicologist; b. New Haven, Conn., Dec. 19, 1939. He studied piano with Ray Lev and music theory with Sam DiBonaventura and David Kraehenbuehl; in 1957, entered Harvard College, majoring in chemistry and physics, but eventually turned to music, studying with Piston, Thompson, Pirotta, and Ward; also took piano lessons with Miklos Schwalb in Boston and with Rosina Lhévinne in N.Y. In 1961 he received a fellowship for travel in Europe; after appearances as a pianist in London in 1963, he returned to the U.S. to study musicology at Columbia Univ., completing his Ph.D. in composition in 1968. He joined similarly inclined musicians and scholars to form Continuum, a group devoted to the exploration of new music; gave concerts with it in the U.S. and Europe, attaining a considerable reputation for excellence. He also taught and was active as coordinator of contemporary music (from 1985) at the Juilliard School in N.Y. Through the years he gave several hundred concerts and lectures dealing with 20th-century music; also directed radio performances in Europe dedicated to the works of Ives and Webern. In purely musicological pursuits, particularly valuable are his detailed writings on the works of J.N. Hummel, for which he had the cooperation of Hummel's descendants.

Sachs, Léo, German-born French composer; b. Frankfurt am Main, April 3, 1856; d. Paris, Nov. 13, 1930. He was active in Paris; composed several symphonic poems (*Retour des cloches; Sur l'eau; Lamento*); a Piano Quintet; 2 string quartets; a Piano Trio; 3 violin sonatas; a Viola Sonata; a Cello Sonata; *Petite suite* for String Quartet; 24 preludes for piano.

Sachse, Leopold, German-American bass, opera producer, and administrator; b. Berlin, Jan. 5, 1880; d. Englewood, N.J., April 3, 1961. He studied at the Cologne Cons.; then in Vienna; in 1902 he joined the Strasbourg Opera as a baritone; then was Intendant in Münster (1907), Halle (1914–19), and at the Hamburg Opera (1922–33), where he produced a number of contemporary works. He was forced to leave his homeland by the Nazis and settled in the U.S.; was a producer at the Metropolitan Opera in N.Y. (1935–55); was a stage director at the N.Y. City Opera (from 1945); founded his own Opera in English Co. (1951). From 1936 to 1943 he taught stage technique at the Juilliard Graduate School in N.Y.

Sack (real name, **Weber**), **Erna,** German soprano; b. Berlin, Feb. 6, 1898; d. Mainz, March 2, 1972. She studied in Prague and with O. Daniel in Berlin; made her operatic debut as a contralto at the Berlin Städtische Oper (1925); then turned to coloratura soprano roles and sang in Bielefeld (1930–32), Wiesbaden (1932–34), and Breslau (1934–35); subsequently, in 1935, joined the Dresden State Opera, where she was chosen to create the role of Isotta in Strauss's *Die schweigsame Frau;* appeared with the company as Zerbinetta under Strauss's direction during its visit to London's Covent Garden in 1936. In 1937 she sang opera in Chicago and made a concert tour of the U.S.; also appeared in opera in Milan, Paris, Vienna, Salzburg, and other major European music centers. After World War II, she made an extensive world tour as a concert singer (1947–52); again gave concerts in the U.S. (1954–55). In 1966 she settled in Wiesbaden.

Sacks, Stuart, American composer; b. Albany, N.Y., Feb. 28, 1941. He studied at Boston Univ. with Hugo Norden; developed a neo-Romantic style couched in emotional tonality. The CBS television network presented on April 11, 1965, in N.Y., performances of his *Saul* for Mezzo-soprano, Oboe, Percussion, and Strings and *Poème* for Violin and Piano. His other works include an overture; *Arioso* for Strings; *Divertissement* for Winds and Strings; *Elegy* for Cello and Orch.

Sacrati, Francesco, Italian composer; b. Parma (baptized), Sept. 17, 1605; d. probably in Modena, May 20, 1650. He was one of the earliest composers for the opera theaters that opened in Venice after 1637; was also a pioneer of opera buffa before the rise of the Neapolitan school. He wrote an opera, *La Delia,* for the opening of the Teatro Crimani dei Santi Giovanni e Paolo in Venice (Jan. 20, 1639); there followed *La finta pazza* (Teatro Novissimo, Venice; Jan. 14, 1641); this was also one of the earliest Italian operas performed in Paris (Salle du Petit Bourbon, Dec. 14, 1645); other operas by Sacrati were: *Bellerofonte* (Venice, 1642); *L'Ulisse errante* (Venice, 1644); *L'isola d'Alcina* (Bologna, 1648). All of his operas are lost. In 1649 he became maestro di cappella to the Modena court. Research by A. Curtis suggests that Sacrati played a major role in preparing the final form of Monteverdi's last opera, *L'incoronazione di Poppea.*

BIBL.: A. Curtis, "*La Poppea Impasticciata* or, Who Wrote the Music to *L'Incoronazione* (1643)?," *Journal of the American Musicological Society* (Spring 1989).

Sadai, Yizhak, Bulgarian-born Israeli composer; b. Sofia, May 13, 1935. He emigrated to Israel in 1949; studied with Haubenstock-Ramati and Boscovich at the Tel Aviv Academy of Music (1951–56); then devoted himself to teaching; in 1966 joined the music staff of the Univ. of Tel Aviv.

WORKS: *Divertimento* for Alto, Flute, Viola, and Piano (1954); 3 cantatas: *Ecclesiastes* (1956); *Hazvi Israel* (1957); *Psychoanalysis* (1958); *Ricercare symphonique* for Orch. (1956); *Serenade* for Winds (1956); *Interpolations* for Harpsichord and String Quartet (1960); *Nuances* for Chamber Orch. (1964); *Aria da Capo* for 6 Instruments and 2 Tape Recorders (1965); *Registers* for Violin and Piano (1967); *Préludes a Jérusalem* for Voice and Instruments (1968); *From the Diary of a Percussionist* for Percussion Player and Tape (1971); *The Interrupted Prayer* for Tape (1975); *Trial,* opera (1979); *Anamorphoses* for String Quartet (1982); *Antiphonies* for Chamber Ensemble (1986); *Canti Fermi* for Orch. and Synthesizer (1986); *Reprises* for Nonet (1986).

Sade (real name, **Helen Folasade Adu**), gifted Nigerian-born black English singer of popular music; b. Ibadan, Jan. 16, 1959. Her father was Nigerian and her mother English; in 1963 she went to England, where she studied fashion design at St. Martin's School of Art and opened a boutique. She sang with the group Ariva (from 1981), which evolved into the group Pride; both group and singer eventually changed to the name Sade (pronounced "shar-day"), a shortened form of Folasade. Their record *Diamond Life* (1984) included the international hit *Smooth Operator.* Sade's melancholy, chic urban songs and exquisite looks led to major stardom; her face eventually appeared on the covers of *Vogue, Cosmopolitan, Elle,* and even *Time* (April 6, 1986). Among her later albums were *Promise* (1985) and *Stronger than Pride* (1988).

Sadie, Stanley (John), eminent English writer on music and lexicographer; b. London, Oct. 30, 1930. He studied music privately with Bernard Stevens (1947–50) and then with R.T. Dart, P.A.S. Hadley, and C.L. Cudworth at Cambridge (B.A. and Mus.B., 1953; M.A., 1957; Ph.D., 1958, with the diss. *British Chamber Music, 1720–1790*). He was on the staff of Trinity College of Music in London (1957–65); from 1964 to 1981, was a music critic on the staff of the *Times* of London. In 1967 he became the ed. of the *Musical Times,* which position he retained until 1987. A distinguished scholar, he wrote the following monographs: *Handel* (London, 1962); *Mozart* (London, 1966); *Beethoven* (London, 1967; 2nd ed., 1974); *Handel* (London, 1968); and *Handel Concertos* (London, 1972); also publ. numerous articles in British and American music journals. With Arthur Jacobs, he ed. *The Pan Book of Opera* (London, 1964; rev. ed. as *Opera: A Modern Guide,* N.Y., 1972; new ed., 1984). In 1969 he was entrusted with the formidable task of preparing for publication, as ed.-in-chief, a completely new ed. of *Grove's Dictionary of Music and Musicians;* after 11 years of labor, *The New Grove Dictionary of Music and*

Musicians was publ. in London in 1980; this 6th ed., in 20 vols., reflected the contributions of more than 2,400 scholars throughout the world, and was accorded a premier place of honor among the major reference sources of its kind. He also ed. *The New Grove Dictionary of Musical Instruments* (1984) and was co-ed., with H. Wiley Hitchcock, of *The New Grove Dictionary of American Music* (4 vols., 1986). With A. Hicks, he ed. the vol. *Handel Tercentenary Collection* (Ann Arbor, 1988). He also ed. *The Grove Concise Dictionary of Music* (1988; U.S. ed., 1988, as *The Norton/Grove Concise Encyclopedia of Music*) and *The New Grove Dictionary of Opera* (4 vols., 1992). He served as ed. of the Master Musicians series from 1976. In 1981 he received the honorary degree of D.Litt. from the Univ. of Leicester and was made an honorary member of the Royal Academy of Music, London. In 1982 he was made a Commander of the Order of the British Empire.

Sadra, I Wayan, significant Indonesian composer, performer, and writer on music; b. Denpasar, Bali, Aug. 1, 1953. He attended the local high school cons., Konservatori Karawitan (KOKAR; graduated, 1972), where he specialized in traditional Balinese music, particularly *gender wayang* (music for the Balinese shadow play). In 1973–74 he worked with the well-known experimental Indonesian choreographer Sardono W. Kusumo; after touring with his group in Europe and the Middle East, Sadra settled in Jakarta, where he studied painting and taught Balinese gamelan at Institut Kesenian Jakarta (IKJ, Jakarta Fine Arts Inst.; 1975–78); also taught Balinese music at the Indonesian Univ. (1978–80), and experimental composition, Balinese gamelan, and music criticism at Sekolah Tinggi Seni Indonesia Surakarta (STSI, National College of the Arts; from 1983), where he earned a degree in composition (1988); concurrently wrote new-music criticism for various Indonesian newspapers, including *Suara Karya* and *Bali Post*. He appeared widely as a performer with traditional Indonesian ensembles; performed throughout Indonesia and Europe, and in Singapore, Japan, Hong Kong, Australia, and Seoul. In 1988 he was keynote speaker at the national Pekan Komponis (Composers' Festival) in Jakarta; in 1989, appeared in California at the Pacific Rim Festival; in 1990, was a featured participant at Composer-to-Composer in Telluride, Colo. Concurrent with the development of Indonesia's national identity has come an increase of national new-music festivals, increased interaction among artists from different regions, and the greater degree of individual freedom to create autonomous music; all have contributed to the emergence of a distinct Indonesian esthetic and a contemporary art music. Sadra is one of the outstanding young composers to emerge from this period, and his works have contributed much to the development of "musik kontemporer," "komposisi," and "kreasi baru" ("new creations"). He is also concerned with the social context of performance, considering audience development as important as the development of new works. His compositions are often scored for unusual combinations of instruments. In an experimental piece performed at the Telluride Inst., raw eggs were thrown at a heated black panel; as the eggs cooked and sizzled, they provided both a visual and sonic element for the closing of the piece. He also proposed to the mayor of Solo, Central Java, a new work entitled *Sebuah Kota Yang Bermain Musik* (A City That Plays Music), wherein the entire population of the city would make sounds together for a specified 5 minutes; the proposal was not accepted, but Sadra hopes for its realization in the future.

Works: *Nadir* for Gong Kebyar (1977); *Lanyad* for Gong Kebyar (1978); *Lad-Lud-an* for Knobbed Gongs from Reong and Terompong, 4 Kempul, Gong, 8 Kendang, 2 Suling, Gentorak, Ceng-Ceng, and Rebab (1981); *Gender* for Javanese Gender, 2 Balinese Gender, and Visual Elements, including Shadow Puppets (1982); *Sekitar 12–14 Menit* for Javanese Gamelan (1987); *Karya spontan* (Spontaneous Creation), accompaniment for Theater Perampok, for Saluang (Sumatran endblown flute), Gender, Bumbung, and Kenong (1988); *Stay a Maverick* for Javanese Gamelan, Balinese Suling, and Sunda-

nese Kecapi (1989); *Terus dan Terus* (On and On) for Balinese Drum, Javanese Drum, and Drone Instruments (1989). DANCE ACCOMPANIMENT: *Kicaka* for Gender Wayang, Suling Gambuh, Reong, Terompong, and Kendang (1976); *Gatotkaca-Sraya* for Gong Kebyar (1980); *Mecanda* (for children's improvised dance) for Genggong, Ceng-Ceng Kopyak, Tambur, and Gong Kebyar (1981); *Kusalawa* (1984); *Drebah* (1987); *Buhin*, collaborative improvisation for Triplex (Masonite board), Milk Cans Suling Gambuh, Balinese Drums, Gentorak, Knobbed Gongs, Rebab, and Slentem (1983); *O-A-E-O* for Voices, Flexotone, Kemanak, Suling, Rebab, Kendang, and Javanese Gamelan (1988); *Aku* for Street Musicians, Suling, Singers, and Drums (1990).

Saenger, Gustav, American music editor and arranger; b. N.Y., May 31, 1865; d. there, Dec. 10, 1935. He studied violin with Leopold Damrosch and others; was an orch. violinist; then conducted theater orchs. in N.Y.; in 1897 was engaged as an arranger for Carl Fischer, Inc., and in 1909 became ed.-in-chief of Fischer's publs.; also edited the Fischer periodicals *Metronome* (from 1900) and the *Musical Observer* (1904–29). Besides a vast number of arrangements, he publ. pieces for violin and piano (5 *Silhouettes*; 3 *Concert Miniatures*; etc.); also *New School of Melody*.

Saenger, Oscar, American singing teacher; b. Brooklyn, Jan. 5, 1868; d. Washington, D.C., April 20, 1929. He sang in church as a boy; studied voice with J. Bouhy at the National Cons. in N.Y., and taught there from 1889 to 1897; made his debut with the Hinrichs Grand Opera Co. in 1891; after a brief tour in Germany and Austria, he returned to America and devoted himself entirely to teaching. Among his students were many well-known singers (Marie Rappold, Paul Althouse, Mabel Garrison, etc.).

Saenz, Pedro, Argentine composer; b. Buenos Aires, May 4, 1915. He studied piano with Alberto Williams, and theory with Arturo Palma. In 1948 he went to Paris, where he took lessons with Arthur Honegger, Darius Milhaud, and Jean Rivier. Returning to Buenos Aires, he occupied numerous teaching and administrative posts in educational institutions.

Works: *Movimientos sinfónicos* for Orch. (1963); Piano Quintet (1942); String Trio (1955); *Divertimento* for Oboe and Clarinet (1959); *Capriccio* for Harpsichord and String Quartet (1966); numerous piano pieces and songs.

Saeverud, Harald (Sigurd Johan), prominent Norwegian composer, father of **Ketil Hvoslef** (real name, **Saeverud**); b. Bergen, April 17, 1897. He studied music theory at the Bergen Music Academy with B. Holmsen (1915–20) and with F.E. Koch at the Hochschule für Musik in Berlin (1920–21); took a course in conducting with Clemens Krauss in Berlin (1935). In 1953 he received the Norwegian State Salary of Art (a government life pension for outstanding artistic achievement). He began to compose very early, and on Dec. 12, 1912, at the age of 15, conducted in Bergen a program of his own symphonic pieces. His music is permeated with characteristically lyrical Scandinavian Romanticism, with Norwegian folk melos as its foundation; his symphonic compositions are polyphonic in nature and tonal in essence, with euphonious dissonant textures imparting a peculiarly somber character to the music.

Works: Ballet, *Ridder Blåskjeggs mareritt* (Bluebeard's Nightmare; Oslo, Oct. 4, 1960); 9 syms.: No. 1, in 2 symphonic fantasias (1916–20; Bergen, 1923); No. 2 (1922; Bergen, Nov. 22, 1923; rev. 1934; Oslo, April 1, 1935); No. 3 (1925–26; Bergen, Feb. 25, 1932); No. 4 (Oslo, Dec. 9, 1937); No. 5, *Quasi una fantasia* (Bergen, March 6, 1941); No. 6, *Sinfonia dolorosa* (1942; Bergen, May 27, 1943); No. 7, *Salme* (Psalm; Bergen, Sept. 1, 1945); No. 8, *Minnesota* (Minneapolis, Oct. 18, 1958); No. 9 (Bergen, June 12, 1966); *Ouverture Appassionata* (1920; retitled 2nd fantasia of his 1st Sym.); 50 *Small Variations* for Orch. (1931); *The Rape of Lucretia*, incidental music for Shakespeare's play (1935; also a *Lucretia Suite* for

Orch., 1936); Oboe Concerto (1938); *Divertimento No. 1* for Flute and Strings (1939); *Syljetone* (The Bride's Heirloom Brooch) for Chamber Orch. or Piano (1939); *Rondo amoroso* for Chamber Orch. or Piano (1939); *Gjaetlevise-Variasjoner* (Shepherd's Tune Variations) for Chamber Orch. (1941); *Siljuslåtten* (Countryside Festival Dance; 1942; also for Piano); *Galdreslåtten* (The Sorcerer's Dance; 1942); *Romanza* for Violin, and Orch. or Piano (1942); *Kjempeviseslåtten* (Ballad of Revolt; 1943; also for Piano); *Peer Gynt*, incidental music to Ibsen's drama (1947; Oslo, March 2, 1948; also exists as 2 orch. suites and as a piano suite); *Olav og Kari*, dance scene for 2 Singers, Chorus, and Orch. (1948); Piano Concerto (1948–50); Violin Concerto (1956); *Allegria* (Sinfonia concertante) (1957); Bassoon Concerto (1963); *Mozart-Motto-Sinfonietta* (1971); *5 Capricci* for Piano (1918–19); Piano Sonata (1921); *Tunes and Dances from "Siljustøl,"* 5 vols. for Piano (1943–45); 6 piano sonatinas (1948–50); *20 Small Duets* for Violins (1951); 3 string quartets (1970, 1975, 1978); *Fabula gratulatorum* for Piano (1973); *Pastorale* (Indian Summer) for Cello (1978). **BIBL.:** C. Baden, *H. S. 80 år* (Oslo, 1977).

Saeverud, Ketil. See **Hvoslef, Ketil.**

Safonov, Vasili (Ilich), eminent Russian pianist, conductor, and pedagogue; b. Ishcherskaya, Caucasus, Feb. 6, 1852; d. Kislovodsk, Feb. 27, 1918. He went to St. Petersburg to study piano with Leschetizky; entered the Cons. in 1879 and took courses in piano with Brassin and in theory with Zaremba, graduating with a gold medal; made his debut as pianist with the Imperial Russian Music Society in St. Petersburg on Nov. 22, 1880; then taught piano at the St. Petersburg Cons. (1881–85); in 1885 he was appointed to the piano faculty of the Moscow Cons., and in 1889 became its director, resigning in 1905; among his pupils were Scriabin and Medtner. He conducted the sym. concerts of the Imperial Russian Music Society in Moscow (1889–1905; 1909–11); was the 1st modern conductor to dispense with the baton; achieved international fame as a forceful and impassioned interpreter of Russian music; conducted in almost all the capitals of Europe. On March 5, 1904, he made his debut as a guest conductor with the N.Y. Phil., obtaining sensational success; as a consequence, he was invited to serve as its conductor (1906–9); at the same time, he was also director of the National Cons. in N.Y. He publ. *A New Formula for the Piano Teacher and Piano Student* (Moscow, 1916; in Eng.). **BIBL.:** Y. Ravicher, *V.I. S.* (Moscow, 1959).

Safranek-Kavić, Lujo, Croatian composer; b. Zagreb, Oct. 12, 1882; d. there, July 18, 1940. He wrote a symphonic suite for Violin and Orch., *Guslar* (inspired by the playing of the gusle, the South Slav national instrument); 2 operas (*Hasanaginica* and *The Queen of Medvedgrad*); chamber music; songs.

Sagaev, Dimiter, Bulgarian composer; b. Plovdiv, Feb. 27, 1915. He studied composition with Stoyanov and Vladigerov at the Bulgarian State Cons. in Sofia, graduating in 1940; then became an instructor there. His music is Romantic in essence and is national in its thematic resources with its rhythmical pulse derived from Bulgarian folk songs. **WORKS: DRAMATIC: OPERAS:** *Under the Yoke* (1965); *Samouil* (1975). **BALLET:** *The Madara Horseman* (1960). **ORATORIO:** *In the Name of Freedom* (1969). **CANTATA-POEM:** *The Shipka Epic* (1977; commemorating the centennial of the crucial battle between the Russian and the Turkish forces in the Balkans). **ORCH.:** *Youth Suite* (1952); *Sofia*, symphonic poem (1954); *3 Bulgarian Symphonic Dances* (1956); 2 violin concertos (1963, 1964); Viola Concerto (1963); Oboe Concerto (1964); Sym. No. 1 for Narrator, Singer, 2 Female Choruses, and Orch. (1964); Bassoon Concerto (1973; Burgas, March 26, 1974); Flute Concerto (1974). **CHAMBER:** 7 string quartets (1945, 1962, 1962, 1963, 1966, 1967, 1968); 2 wind quintets (1961, 1962); Trio for Flute, Violin, and Piano (1974); Quartet for Flute, Viola, Harp, and Piano (1975); also songs; incidental music.

Sagittarius. See **Schütz, Heinrich.**

Saikkola, Lauri, Finnish violinist and composer; b. Vyborg, March 31, 1906. He studied violin at the Viipuri (Vyborg) School of Music (1919–28) and then took private composition lessons from Akimov and Funtek (1930–34); was a violinist in the Viipuri Phil. (1923–34) and the Helsinki Phil. (1934–65). His music is rooted in the Romantic tradition. **WORKS: OPERAS:** *Ristin* (Helsinki, 1959); *The Master's Snuff Box*, chamber opera (1970). **ORCH.:** *3 Symphonic Scenes* (1932); *1500-Meter Race*, parody (1933); *Partita* (1935); *Pastorale* (1936); 5 syms.: No. 1, *Sinfonia campale* (1938); No. 2, *Sinfonia tragica* (1946); No. 3 (1949); No. 4 (1951); No. 5 (1958); *Karelian Scenes* (1940); *Karelia in Flames* (1940); *Nocturno* for Cello and Orch. (1944); *Taivaaseen menijä* (Going to Heaven), folk story for Narrator, Soloists, Chorus, and Orch. (1950); Violin Concerto (1952); *Concerto di miniatura* for Cello and Chamber Orch. (1953); *Concerto da camera* for Piano and Chamber Orch. (1957); *Pezzi* for Strings (1965); *Musica sinfonica* (1966); *The Well of Dreams* for Baritone, Chorus, and Chamber Orch. (1968); Clarinet Concerto (1969); *Raasepori fantasia* (1971). **CHAMBER:** 3 string quartets (1931–68); *Divertimento* for Wind Quartet (1949); Wind Quintet (1968); 2 suites for Clarinet and Piano (1955, 1968); *Suite* for Oboe and Piano (1968); Viola Sonatina.

Saint-Foix, (Marie-Olivier-) Georges (du Parc Poulain), Comte de, eminent French musicologist; b. Paris, March 2, 1874; d. Aix-en-Provence, May 26, 1954. He studied law at the Sorbonne and concurrently attended classes in music theory with d'Indy and had violin lessons (diploma, 1906) at the Schola Cantorum in Paris. His principal, and most important, publ. was *Wolfgang-Amédée Mozart, sa vie musicale et son œuvre, de l'enfance à la pleine maturité* (5 vols., Paris, 1912–46; vols. 1-2 with T. de Wyzewa); also publ. *Les Symphonies de Mozart* (Paris, 1932; 2nd ed., 1948; Eng. tr., London, 1947).

Saint-George, George, noted English viola d'amore player, father of **Henry Saint-George;** b. Leipzig (of English parents), Nov. 6, 1841; d. London, Jan. 5, 1924. He studied piano, violin, and theory in Dresden and Prague; his violin teacher, Moritz Mildner of Prague, had a fine viola d'amore, which he lent to Saint-George for practicing; he made such progress on this little-used instrument that he decided to adopt it as a specialty. About 1862 he settled in London and became a manufacturer of string instruments; gave performances on the Welsh crwth for the "Hon. Soc. Cymmrodorion"; also played the viola d'amore in duos with his son, who assisted him on the viola da gamba.

Saint-George, Henry, English instrumentalist and writer on music, son of **George Saint-George;** b. London, Sept. 26, 1866; d. there, Jan. 30, 1917. He studied the violin with his father, with whom he subsequently gave concerts, playing works for early instruments; was ed. of *The Strad;* publ. *The Bow: Its History, Manufacture and Use* (1895; 3rd ed., 1922); *The Place of Science in Music* (1905); *Fiddles: Their Selection, Preservation and Betterment* (1910).

Saint-Georges, Joseph Boulogne, Chevalier de, noted West Indian violinist and composer; b. near Basse Terre, Guadeloupe, c.1739; d. Paris, June 9?, 1799. He was the son of a wealthy Frenchman and a black slave; was raised in Santo Domingo; went to Paris with his father in 1749 (his mother joined them in 1760); as a youth he studied boxing and fencing, and became one of the leading fencers of Europe; he also studied music with Jean-Marie Leclair *l'aîné* and with François Gossec (1763–66); the latter dedicated his op. 9 string trios to him. In 1769 he became a violinist in the orch. of the Concert des Amateurs; became its director in 1773; after it was disbanded in 1781, he founded his own Concert de la Loge Olympique, for which Haydn composed his set of Paris syms.; it was disbanded in 1789. He also continued his activities as a fencer, and visited London in this capacity in 1785 and 1789. In 1791 he became a captain in the National Guard in Lille and soon was charged with organizing a black regiment, the Légion Nationale des Américains et du Midi (among his 1,000 troops was the father of Dumas père); when the venture proved of little success, he was relieved of his duties and later imprisoned for 18 months; after living on St. Dominique, he returned to Paris about 1797.

WORKS: OPERAS (all 1st perf. in Paris): *Ernestine* (July 19, 1777); *La Chasse* (Oct. 12, 1778); *L'Amant anonyme* (March 8, 1780); *Le Droit du seigneur* (n.d.); *La Fille garçon* (Aug. 18, 1787); *Le Marchand de marrons* (1788); *Guillaume tout cœur* (1790); also 9 symphonies concertantes; 15 violin concertos; chamber music; songs.

BIBL.: L. de La Laurencie, "The Chevalier de S.-G., Violinist," *Musical Quarterly*, 5 (1919); idem, *L'École française de violon* (vol. 2, 1923); B. Brook, *La Symphonie française dans la seconde moitié du XVIIIᵉ siècle* (Paris, 1962); E. Derr, *J. B., C. de S.-G.: Black Musician and Athlete in Galant Paris* (Ann Arbor, 1972); D.-R. de Lerma, "Two Friends within the S.-G. Songs," *Black Perspective in Music* (Fall 1973); idem, "The C. de S.-G.," *Black Perspective in Music* (Spring 1976).

Saint-Huberty, Mme. de (real name, **Antoinette Cécile Clavel**), French soprano; b. Strasbourg, Dec. 15, 1756; d. (murdered) London, July 22, 1812. She studied with J.B. Lemoyne in Warsaw; after singing in Strasbourg, she went to Paris and appeared as Melissa in Gluck's *Armide* (1777); was a leading singer at the Opéra (1781–90), where she sang in the premiere of Piccinni's *Didon* (1783); also created Hypermnestra in Salieri's *Les Danaïdes* (1784) and the title roles in Edelmann's *Ariane dans l'isle de Naxos* (1782), Sacchini's *Chimène* (1783), and Lemoyne's *Phédre* (1786). With the coming of the Revolution, she left France in the company of the Count of Antraigues; they were married in 1790. When her husband was imprisoned by Napoleon in Italy in 1797, she assisted in his rescue; they finally settled in London, where they were both murdered by a servant.

BIBL.: E. de Goncourt, *Mme. S.-H.* (1885).

Saint-Lubin, Léon de, violinist and composer; b. Turin, July 5, 1805; d. Berlin, Feb. 13, 1850. After filling various positions as a theater violinist, he pursued further studies with Spohr; was concertmaster at the Josephstadt Theater in Vienna (1823–30); then at the Königstadt Theater in Berlin (1830–47). He composed 2 operas, *König Branors Schwert* and *Der Vetter des Doctor Faust;* 5 violin concertos; 2 string quintets; 2 piano trios; Violin Sonata; 19 string quartets.

Saint-Marcoux, Micheline Coulombe, Canadian composer; b. Notre-Dame-de-la-Doré, Quebec, Aug. 9, 1938; d. Montreal, Feb. 2, 1985. She studied with François Brassard in Jonquière; then in Montreal with Claude Champagne at the Ecole Vincent d'Indy, graduating in 1962, and with Gilles Tremblay and Clermont Pépin at the Cons. (1963–67). She went to Paris in 1969 and studied composition with Gilbert Amy and Jean-Paul Guézec and electronic music with members of the Groupe de Recherches Musicale; was a co-founder of the Groupe International de Musique Electroacoustic, along with 5 other composers from different countries. She returned to Montreal in 1971; became active as a teacher.

WORKS: Flute Sonata (1964); *Kaléidoscope* for Piano, left-hand (1964); String Quartet (1965–66); *Equation I* for 2 Guitars (1967); *Modulaire* for Orch. (1967; Montreal, March 31, 1968); *Séquences* for 2 Ondes Martenots and Percussion (1968); *Assemblages* for Piano (1969); *Doréanes* for Piano (1969); *Hétéromorphie* for Orch. (Montreal, April 14, 1970); *Bernavir* for Tape (1970); *Trakadie* for Tape and Percussion (1970); *Makazoti* for 8 Voices and Instrumental Group (1971); *Arksalalartôq* for Tape (1971); *Contrastances* for Tape (1971); *Moustières* for Tape (1971); *Zones* for Tape (1972); *Alchéra* for Mezzo-soprano, Flute, Clarinet, Trombone, Violin, Cello, Percussion, Harpsichord or Hammond Organ, and Tape (1973); *Ishuma* for Soprano, Instrumental Group, Ondes Martenot, and Synthi A (1973–74); *Genesis* for Wind Quintet (1975); *Miroirs* for Tape and Harpsichord (1975); *Moments* for Soprano, Flute, Viola, and Cello (1977).

Sainton, Prosper (Philippe Cathérine), French violinist and composer; b. Toulouse, June 5, 1813; d. London, Oct. 17, 1890. He was a pupil of Habeneck at the Paris Cons., winning 1st prize for violin in 1834; made a successful tour of Europe; then was a prof. at the Toulouse Cons. (1840–44). He settled in England in 1844; was a prof. at the Royal Academy of Music (from 1845) and was concertmaster of the orchs. of the Phil. Society (1846–54), the Royal Italian Opera at Covent Garden (1847–71), the Sacred Harmonic Society (from 1848), and at Her Majesty's Theatre (1871–80); served as conductor of the state band and as violin soloist to the Queen (1848–55). He wrote 2 violin concertos and several violin solos. In 1860 he married **Charlotte (Helen,** née **Dolby) Sainton-Dolby** (b. London, May 17, 1821; d. there, Feb. 18, 1885), a contralto, teacher, and composer. She prepared a singing manual; also composed cantatas and numerous songs.

Saint-Requier, Léon, French choral conductor, teacher, and composer; b. Rouen, Aug. 8, 1872; d. Paris, Oct. 1, 1964. He went to Paris and studied with d'Indy, Guilmant, and Bordes; taught harmony at the Schola Cantorum (1900–1934) and at the École César Franck (1934–44); was active as a choral conductor at various Paris churches; ed. the collection *Palestrina* (sacred songs of the 16th, 17th, and 18th centuries). He composed a Christmas motet, *Il est né le divin enfant,* using some folk melodies (1924); the oratorio *La Mort du doux Jésus* (1932); *Messe de grande louange* (1946); *Le Sermon sur la montagne* (1949); *Messe de St. Jean Apôtre* (1957); other religious works.

Saint-Saëns, (Charles-) Camille, celebrated French composer; b. Paris, Oct. 9, 1835; d. Algiers, Dec. 16, 1921. His widowed mother sent him to his great-aunt, Charlotte Masson, who taught him to play piano. He proved exceptionally gifted, and gave a performance in a Paris salon before he was 5; at 6 he began to compose; at 7 became a private pupil of Stamaty; so rapid was his progress that he made his pianistic debut at the Salle Pleyel on May 6, 1846, playing a Mozart concerto and a movement from Beethoven's C minor Concerto, with Orch. After studying harmony with Pierre Maleden, he entered the Paris Cons., where his teachers were Benoist (organ) and Halévy (composition). He won the 2nd prize for organ in 1849, and the 1st prize in 1851. In 1852 he competed unsuccessfully for the Grand Prix de Rome, and failed again in a 2nd attempt in 1864, when he was already a composer of some stature. His *Ode à Sainte Cécile* for Voice and Orch. was awarded the 1st prize of the Société Sainte-Cécile (1852). On Dec. 11, 1853, his 1st numbered sym. was performed; Gounod wrote him a letter of praise, containing a prophetic phrase regarding the "obligation de devenir un grand maître." From 1853 to 1857 Saint-Saëns was organist at the church of Saint-Merry in Paris; in 1857 he succeeded Lefébure-Wély as organist at the Madeleine. This important position he filled with distinction, and soon acquired a great reputation as virtuoso on the organ and a master of improvisation. He resigned in 1876, and devoted himself mainly to composition and conducting; also continued to appear as a pianist and organist. From 1861 to 1865 he taught piano at the École Niedermeyer; among his pupils were André Messager and Gabriel Fauré. Saint-Saëns was one of the founders of the Société Nationale de Musique (1871), established for the encouragement of French composers, but withdrew in 1886 when d'Indy proposed to include works by foreign composers in its program. In 1875 he married Marie Truffot; their 2 sons died in infancy; they separated in 1881, but were never legally divorced; Madame Saint-Saëns died in Bordeaux on Jan. 30, 1950, at the age of 95. In 1891 Saint-Saëns established a museum in Dieppe (his father's birthplace), to which he gave his MSS and his collection of paintings and other art objects. On Oct. 27, 1907, he witnessed the unveiling of his own statue (by Marqueste) in the court foyer of the opera house in Dieppe. He received many honors: in 1868 he was made a Chevalier of the Legion of Honor; in 1884, Officer; in 1900, Grand-Officer; in 1913, Grand-Croix (the highest rank). In 1881 he was elected to the Institut de France; he was also a member of many foreign organizations; received an honorary Mus.D. degree at Cambridge Univ. He visited the U.S. for the 1st time in 1906; was a representative of the French government at the Panama-Pacific Exposition in 1915 and conducted his choral work *Hail California* (San Francisco, June 19, 1915), written for the occasion. In 1916, at the age of 81, he made his 1st tour of South America; continued to appear in public as conductor of his own works almost to the time of his death. He took part as conductor and pianist in a festival of his works in Athens in May 1920. He played a program of his piano pieces at the Saint-Saëns museum in Dieppe on Aug. 6, 1921. For the winter he went to Algiers, where he died.

The position of Saint-Saëns in French music was very important. His abilities as a performer were extraordinary; he aroused the admiration of Wagner during the latter's stay in Paris (1860–61) by playing at sight the entire scores of Wagner's operas; curiously, Saint-Saëns achieved greater recognition in Germany than in France during the initial stages of his career. His most famous opera, *Samson et Dalila*, was produced in Weimar (1877) under the direction of Eduard Lassen, to whom the work was suggested by Liszt; it was not performed in France until nearly 13 years later, in Rouen. He played his 1st and 3rd piano concertos for the 1st time at the Gewandhaus in Leipzig. Solidity of contrapuntal fabric, instrumental elaboration, fullness of sonority in orchestration, and a certain harmonic saturation are the chief characteristics of his music, qualities that were not yet fully exploited by French composers at the time, the French public preferring the lighter type of music. However, Saint-Saëns overcame this initial opposition, and toward the end of his life was regarded as an embodiment of French traditionalism. The shock of the German invasion of France in World War I made him abandon his former predilection for German music, and he wrote virulent articles against German art. He was unalterably opposed to modern music, and looked askance at Debussy; he regarded later manifestations of musical modernism as outrages, and was outspoken in his opinions. That Saint-Saëns possessed a fine sense of musical characterization, and true Gallic wit, is demonstrated by his ingenious suite *Carnival of the Animals*, which he wrote in 1886 but did not allow to be publ. during his lifetime. He also publ. a book of elegant verse (1890).

WORKS: **STAGE** (all 1st perf. in Paris unless otherwise given): **OPERAS:** *La Princesse jaune* (June 12, 1872); *Le Timbre d'argent* (Feb. 23, 1877); *Samson et Dalila* (Weimar, Dec. 2, 1877); *Étienne Marcel* (Lyons, Feb. 8, 1879); *Henry VIII* (March 5, 1883); *Proserpine* (March 16, 1887); *Ascanio* (March 21, 1890); *Phryné* (May 24, 1893); *Frédégonde* (Dec. 18, 1895); *Les Barbares* (Oct. 23, 1901); *Hélène* (Monte Carlo, Feb. 18, 1904); *L'Ancêtre* (Monte Carlo, Feb. 24, 1906); *Déjanire* (Monte Carlo, March 14, 1911); also a ballet, *Javotte* (Lyons, Dec. 3, 1896); incidental music to: *Antigone* (Nov. 21, 1893); *Parysatis* (Béziers, Aug. 17, 1902); *Andromaque* (Feb. 7, 1903); *La Foi* (Monte Carlo, April 10, 1909); *On ne badine pas avec l'amour* (Feb. 8, 1917); film score, *L'Assassinat du Duc de Guise* (Nov. 16, 1908). **ORCH.:** Overture to a comic opera (c.1850); *Scherzo* for Small Orch. (c.1850); 5 syms.: A major (c.1850); No. 1 in E-flat major, op. 2 (Paris, Dec. 18, 1853); F major, *Urbs Roma* (1856; Paris, Feb. 15, 1857); No. 2 in A minor, op. 55 (Leipzig, Feb. 20, 1859); No. 3 in C minor, op. 78, *Organ* (London, May 19, 1886); *Ouverture d'un opéra comique inachevé*, op. 140 (1854); *Tarantelle* for Flute, Clarinet, and Orch., op. 6 (1857); 5 piano concertos (all 1st perf. with Saint-Saëns as soloist): No. 1, op. 17 (1858; Leipzig, Oct. 26, 1865); No. 2, op. 22 (Paris, May 6, 1868); No. 3, op. 29 (Leipzig, Nov. 25, 1869); No. 4, op. 44 (Paris, Oct. 31, 1875); No. 5, op. 103, *Egyptian* (Paris, June 3, 1896); 3 violin concertos: No. 1, op. 20 (1859; Paris, April 4, 1867); No. 2, op. 58 (1858; Paris, Feb. 13, 1880); No. 3, op. 61 (1880; Paris, Jan. 2, 1881); *Introduction and Rondo capriccioso* for Violin and Orch., op. 28 (1863); Suite, op. 49 (1863); *Spartacus Overture* (1863); *Marche héroïque*, op. 34 (1871); *Romance* for Flute or Violin and Orch.,

op. 37 (1871); *Le Rouet d'Omphale*, op. 31 (Paris, Jan. 9, 1872); 2 cello concertos: No. 1, op. 33 (1872; Paris, Jan. 19, 1873); No. 2, op. 119 (1902; Paris, Feb. 5, 1905); *Phaéton*, op. 39 (Paris, Dec. 7, 1873); *Romance* for Horn or Cello and Orch., op. 36 (1874); *Romance* for Violin and Orch., op. 48 (1874); *Danse macabre*, op. 40 (1874; Paris, Jan. 24, 1875); *La Jeunesse d'Hercule*, op. 50 (Paris, Jan. 28, 1877); *Suite algérienne*, op. 60 (Paris, Dec. 19, 1880); *Morceau de concert* for Violin and Orch., op. 62 (1880); *Une Nuit à Lisbonne*, op. 63 (1880; Paris, Jan. 23, 1881); *Jota aragonese*, op. 64 (1880); *Rapsodie d'Auvergne*, op. 73 (1884); *Wedding Cake* for Piano and Orch., op. 76 (1885); *Le Carnaval des animaux* (1886; Paris, Feb. 26, 1922); *Havanaise* for Violin and Orch., op. 83 (1887); *Morceau de concert* for Horn and Orch., op. 94 (1887); *Rapsodie bretonne*, op. 7 bis (1891); *Africa* for Piano and Orch., op. 89 (Paris, Oct. 25, 1891); *Sarabande et Rigaudon*, op. 93 (1892); *Marche du couronnement*, op. 117 (c.1902); *Caprice andalous* for Violin and Orch., op. 122 (1904); *Trois tableaux symphoniques d'après La foi*, op. 130 (1908); *Morceau de concert* for Harp and Orch., op. 154 (1918); *Cyprès et Lauriers* for Organ and Orch., op. 156 (1919); *Odelette* for Flute and Orch., op. 162 (1920); also works for Band.

CHAMBER: 2 piano quartets (1853, 1875); Piano Quintet, op. 14 (1855); *Caprice brillant* for Piano and Violin (1859); Suite for Piano and Cello, op. 16 (1862); 2 piano trios, opp. 18 and 92 (1863, 1892); *Sérénade* for Piano, Organ, Violin, and Viola or Cello, op. 15 (1866; also for Orch.); *Romance* for Piano, Organ, and Violin, op. 27 (1868); *Les Odeurs de Paris* for 2 Trumpets, Harp, Piano, and Strings (c.1870); *Berceuse* for Piano and Violin, op. 38 (1871); 2 cello sonatas, opp. 32 and 123 (1872, 1905); *Allegro appassionato* for Cello and Piano, op. 43 (1875; also for Cello and Orch.); *Romance* for Piano and Cello, op. 51 (1877); Septet for Piano, Trumpet, and Strings, op. 65 (1881); *Romance* for Piano and Horn, op. 67 (1885); 2 violin sonatas, opp. 75 and 102 (1885, 1896); *Caprice sur des airs danois et russes* for Piano, Flute, Oboe, and Clarinet, op. 79 (1887); *Chant saphique* for Piano and Cello, op. 91 (1892); *Fantaisie* for Harp, op. 95 (1893); *Barcarolle* for Violin, Cello, Organ, and Piano, op. 108 (1897); 2 string quartets, opp. 112 and 153 (1899, 1918); *Fantaisie* for Violin and Harp, op. 124 (1907); *La Muse et le poète* for Violin, Cello, and Piano, op. 132 (1910; also for Violin, Cello, and Orch.); *Triptyque* for Piano and Violin, op. 136 (1912); *Elégie* for Piano and Violin, op. 143 (1915); *Cavatine* for Piano and Trombone, op. 144 (1915); *L'Air de la pendule* for Piano and Violin (c.1918); *Prière* for Organ and Violin or Cello, op. 158 (1919); *Élégie* for Piano and Violin, op. 160 (1920); Oboe Sonata, op. 166 (1921); Clarinet Sonata, op. 167 (1921); Bassoon Sonata, op. 168 (1921); also numerous piano pieces; sacred vocal works, including *Oratorio de Noël* for Solo Voices, Chorus, String Quartet, Harp, and Organ, op. 12 (1858), *Veni Creator* for Chorus and Organ ad libitum (1858), and *Le Déluge*, oratorio for Solo Voices, Chorus, and Orch., op. 45 (1875; Paris, March 5, 1876); secular choral works; song cycles (*Mélodies persanes* [1870], *La Cendre rouge* [1914], etc.); about 100 solo songs; also cadenzas to Mozart's piano concertos K.482 and 491, and to Beethoven's 4th Piano Concerto and Violin Concerto; made various transcriptions and arrangements.

For a complete list of his works, see the Durand *Catalogue général et thématique des œuvres de Saint-Saëns* (Paris, 1897; rev. ed., 1909).

WRITINGS: All publ. in Paris unless otherwise given: *Notice sur Henri Reber* (1881); *Harmonie et mélodie* (1885; 9th ed., 1923); *Charles Gounod et le "Don Juan" de Mozart* (1893); *Problèmes et mystères* (1894; rev. ed., augmented, 1922 as *Divagations sérieuses*); *Portraits et souvenirs* (1899; 3rd ed., 1909); *Essai sur les lyres et cithares antiques* (1902); *Quelques mots sur "Prosperpine"* (Alexandria, 1902); *École buissonnière: Notes et souvenirs* (1913; abridged Eng. tr., 1919); *Notice sur Le Timbre d'argent* (Brussels, 1914); H. Bowie, ed., *On the Execution of Music, and Principally of Ancient Music* (San Francisco, 1915); *Au courant de la vie* (1916); *Germanophile* (1916); *Les idées de M. Vincent d'Indy* (1919); F. Rothwell,

tr., *Outspoken Essays on Music* (London and N.Y., 1922).
BIBL.: C. Bellaigue, *M. C. S.-S.* (Paris, 1889); C. Kit and P. Loanda, *Musique savante. Sur la musique de M. S.-S.* (Lille, 1889); Blondel, *C. S.-S. et son cinquantenaire artistique* (Paris, 1896); O. Neitzel, *C. S.-S.* (Berlin, 1899); E. Solenière, *C. S.-S.* (Paris, 1899); P. Locard, *Les Maîtres contemporains de l'orgue* (Paris, 1900); special *S.-S.* issue of *Le Monde Musical* (Oct. 31, 1901); A. Hervey, *French Music in the 19th Century* (London, 1903); E. Baumann, *Les Grandes Formes de la musique: L'Œuvre de S.-S.* (Paris, 1905; new ed., 1923); special *S.-S.* issue of *Musica* (June 1907); L. Aubin, *Le Drame lyrique* (Tours, 1908); R. Rolland, *Musiciens d'aujourd'hui* (Paris, 1908; Eng. tr., 1914); A. Jullien, *Musiciens d'hier et d'aujourd'hui* (Paris, 1910); O. Séré, *Musiciens français d'aujourd'hui* (Paris, 1911; rev. ed., 1921); L. Augé de Lassus, *S.-S.* (Paris, 1914); J. Bonnerot, *C. S.-S.* (Paris, 1914; 2nd ed., 1922); J. Montargis, *C. S.-S.* (Paris, 1919); *Funérailles de S.-S.* (collection of speeches, Paris, 1921); J. Chantavoine, *L'Œuvre dramatique de C. S.-S.* (Paris, 1921); A. Hervey, *S.-S.* (London, 1921); W. Lyle, *C. S.-S., His Life and Art* (London, 1923); G. Servières, *S.-S.* (Paris, 1923; 2nd ed., 1930); L. Laloy, *Cinquante ans de musique française, 1874–1923* (1924); A. Dandelot, *S.-S.* (Paris, 1930); J. Handschin, *C. S.-S.* (Zürich, 1930); J. Normand, *S.-S.* (1930); L. Schneider, *Une Heure avec S.-S.* (1930); J. Langlois, *C. S.-S.* (Moulins, 1934); R. Dumanine, *Les Origines normandes de C. S.-S.* (Rouen, 1937); R. Fauchois, *La Vie et l'œuvre prodigieuse de C. S.-S.* (Paris, 1938); D. Brook, *Five Great French Composers* (London, 1946); J. Chantavoine, *C. S.-S.* (Paris, 1947); J. Harding, *S.-S. and His Circle* (London, 1965); S. Ratner, *The Piano Works of C. S.-S.* (diss., Univ. of Michigan, 1972); D. Fallon, *The Symphonies and Symphonic Poems of C. S.-S.* (diss., Yale Univ., 1973); E. Harkins, *The Chamber Music of S.-S.* (diss., N.Y. Univ., 1976); M. Stegemann, *C. S.-S. und das französische Solokonzert von 1850 bis 1920* (Mainz, 1984; Eng. tr., 1991).

Saito, Hideo, Japanese cellist, conductor, and music educator; b. Tokyo, May 23, 1902; d. there, Sept. 18, 1974. He was a cello student of Julius Klengel in Leipzig (1923–27) and of Feuermann in Berlin (1930). Returning to Japan, he played cello in the Nihon Sym. Orch., and studied conducting with Rosenstock. He was a co-founder of the Toho Music School in Tokyo, where he taught cello, conducting, and academic music courses. Among his students was Seiji Ozawa, who came to regard Saito's influence as a major factor in his own career.

Sakač, Branimir, Croatian composer; b. Zagreb, June 5, 1918; d. there, Dec. 29, 1979. He graduated in composition from the Zagreb Academy of Music in 1941; later taught there. In his music he adopted a purely structural method, using highly dissonant contrapuntal combinations within strict neo-Classical forms.

WORKS: *Serenade* for String Orch. (1947); *Simfonija o mrtvom vojniku* (Symphony of the Dead Soldiers; 1951); Chamber Sym. (1953); Solo Violin Sonata (1953); *3 sintetskim poemama* (3 Synthetic Poems; 1959); *Aleatory Prelude* for Piano and Tape (1961); *2 Miniatures* for Flute, Harp, and Percussion (1963); *Episode* for Orch. and Tape (1963); *Study I* for Piano and Percussion (1963); *Study II* for Piano (1964); *Structure I* for Chamber Ensemble (1965); *Prostori* (Spaces) for Orch; *Solo I* for Violin and Chamber Orch.; *Doppio* for String Quartet; *Canto dalla Commedia*, after Dante, for Violin, Percussion, and Chorus (1969); *Turm-Musik* (Tower Music) for Orch. (1970); *Ad litteram* for Piano (1970); *Barasou* (Ballad of Rats and Mice) for Voice and Chamber Ensemble (1971); *Matrix Symphony* for 3 Voices and Orch. (1972); *Syndrome* for Chamber Ensemble (1974); tape pieces.

Sala, Nicola, Italian teacher, music theorist, and composer; b. Tocco-Gaudio, near Benevento, April 7, 1713; d. Naples, Aug. 31, 1801. He was a pupil of Fago, Abos, and Leo at the Cons. della Pietà de' Turchini in Naples (1732–40); apparently taught there for many years, serving as secondo maestro (1787–93) and primo maestro (1793–99). He publ. the celebrated theoretical work *Regole del contrappunto prattico* (3 vols., 1794;

reprinted by Choron in Paris, 1808, as *Principii di composizione delle scuole d'Italia*). He brought out several operas: *Vologeso* (Rome, 1737); *La Zenobia* (Naples, Jan. 12, 1761); *Demetrio* (Naples, Dec. 12, 1762); *Merope* (Naples, Aug. 13, 1769); an oratorio, *Giuditta* (1780); masses; litanies; other religious works.

Salabert, Francis, French music publisher; b. Paris, July 27, 1884; d. in an airplane accident at Shannon, Ireland, Dec. 28, 1946. The Editions Salabert was founded by his father, **Edouard Salabert** (b. London, Dec. 1, 1838; d. Paris, Sept. 8, 1903), in 1896; Francis took over from his ailing father in 1901. A professional musician and composer in his own right, he made a series of practical arrangements for small orch. of numerous classical and modern works, which were widely used. Editions Salabert expanded greatly through the purchase of the stock of orch. and other music of the firms Gaudet (1927), Mathot (1930), Senart (1941), Rouart-Lerolle (1942), and Deiss (1946). On the death of Francis Salabert, his widow assumed the directorship.

Salaman, Charles (Kensington), English pianist, conductor, teacher, and composer; b. London, March 3, 1814; d. there, June 23, 1901. He studied with Charles Neate in London and with Henri Herz in Paris. In 1828 he made his debut as a pianist in Blackheath; made regular appearances in London from 1830; was a founder of the Concerti da Camera in 1835; from 1837 to 1855 was an associate of the Phil. Society; in 1849 he was a founder of an amateur choral society in London; was a co-founder, in 1858, of the Musical Society of London; was one of the founders of the Musical Assoc. in 1874. He wrote a comic opera, *Pickwick* (London, 1889); about 100 choral works for the synagogue; many anthems, part-songs, piano pieces; also many songs to Eng., Latin, Greek, and Hebrew texts.

Salas Viú, Vicente, Spanish-born Chilean musicologist; b. Madrid, Jan. 29, 1911; d. Santiago, Chile, Sept. 2, 1967. He studied piano and theory at the Madrid Cons. (1928–30); also received instruction in composition from his brother-in-law, Rodolfo Halffter, and from Falla. He wrote for various literary and musical publs. until 1939, when he emigrated to Chile; became a prof. of music history at the National Cons. in Santiago. He was founder-ed. of the *Revista Musical Chilena* (1945); was director of the Instituto de Investigaciones Musicales (from 1947). He publ. a very valuable book, *La creación musical en Chile 1900–1950* (Santiago, 1952), in 2 sections, embracing a general account of musical activities in Chile and detailed biographies of 40 Chilean composers; also *La última luz de Mozart* (Santiago, 1949) and *Momentos decisivos en la música* (Buenos Aires, 1957).

Salas y Castro, Esteban, Cuban composer; b. Havana, Dec. 25, 1725; d. Santiago de Cuba, July 14, 1803. He studied organ and theology; in 1764 became maestro de capilla in Santiago de Cuba; was also active as a conductor of a chamber ensemble; became a priest in 1790, and subsequently taught philosophy, theology, and ethics. He wrote mainly villancicos.
BIBL.: P. Hernández Balaguer, *Obras de E. S.* (Santiago de Cuba, 1960).

Salazar, Adolfo, eminent Spanish musicologist; b. Madrid, March 6, 1890; d. Mexico City, Sept. 27, 1958. He studied with Falla and Pérez Casas; then went to Paris, where he completed his training with Ravel. He was ed.-in-chief of the *Revista Musical Hispano-Americana* (1914–18) and music critic of Madrid's *El Sol* (1918–36); was founder and later secretary of the Sociedad Nacional de Música (1915–22). During the final period of the Spanish Civil War, he was cultural attaché at the Spanish embassy in Washington, D.C. (1938–39); then settled in Mexico City as a writer and teacher, serving on the faculties of the Colegio de México (from 1939) and the National Cons. (from 1946). Salazar was also a composer; wrote 3 symphonic works: *Paisajes*, *Estampas*, and *Don Juan de los Infiernos*; songs to words by Verlaine; piano pieces.
WRITINGS: *Música y músicos de hoy* (Madrid, 1928); *Sinfo-*

nía y ballet (Madrid, 1929); *La música contemporánea en España* (Madrid, 1930); *La música actual en Europa y sus problemas* (Madrid, 1935); *El siglo romántico* (Madrid, 1935; new ed. as *Los grandes compositores de la época romántica*, 1955); *La música en el siglo XX* (Madrid, 1936); *Música y sociedad en el siglo XX* (Mexico City, 1939); *Las grandes estructuras de la música* (Mexico City, 1940); *La rosa de los vientos en la música europea* (Mexico City, 1940; reissued in 1954 as *Conceptos fondamentales en la historia de la música*); *Forma y expresión en la música: Ensayo sobre la formación de los géneros en la música instrumental* (Mexico City, 1941); *Introducción en la música actual* (Mexico City, 1941); *Los grandes periodos en la historia de la música* (Mexico City, 1941); *Poesía y música en lengua vulgar y sus antecedientes en la edad media* (Mexico City, 1943); *La música en la sociedad europea* (4 vols., Mexico City, 1942–46); *La música moderna* (Buenos Aires, 1944; in Eng. as *Music in Our Time*, N.Y., 1946); *Música, instrumentos y danzas en las obras de Cervantes* (Mexico City, 1948); *La danza y el ballet* (Mexico City, 1949); *La música, como proceso histórico de su invención* (Mexico City, 1950); *J.S. Bach* (Mexico City, 1951); *La música de España* (Buenos Aires, 1953).

Saldoni, Baltasar, Spanish composer and lexicographer; b. Barcelona, Jan. 4, 1807; d. Madrid, Dec. 3, 1889. He was a pupil of Mateo Ferrer in Montserrat and of Francisco Queralt in Barcelona; completed his studies with Carnicer in Madrid (1829). In 1830 he became prof. of voice training and singing at the Madrid Cons. In 1826 he produced in Madrid his light opera *El triunfo del amor* and the Italian operas *Saladino e Clotilde* (1833), *Ipermestra* (Jan. 20, 1838), and *Cleonice regina di Siria* (Jan. 24, 1840); he also wrote the zarzuelas *La corte de Mónaco* (Feb. 16, 1857) and *Los maridos en las máscaras* (Barcelona, Aug. 26, 1864). His magnum opus as a scholar was the *Diccionario biográfico-bibliográfico de efemérides de músicos españoles*, in 4 vols. (Madrid, 1868–81), to which was added a supplementary vol. in the form of a chronology of births and deaths of Spanish musicians, day by day and year by year, with exhaustive biographical notes. This monumental compilation, upon which Saldoni worked nearly 40 years, contains (inevitably) a number of errors, but in the absence of other musicographical works on Spanish musicians, it still retains considerable documentary value.

Salerno-Sonnenberg, Nadja, gifted American violinist of Russian-Italian descent; b. Rome, Jan. 10, 1961. After violin lessons with Antonio Marchetti, her mother took her to the U.S., where she continued her training with Jascha Brodsky at the Curtis Inst. of Music in Philadelphia (1969–75). In 1975 she went to N.Y. to pursue studies with Dorothy DeLay at the Juilliard School; after winning the Naumburg Competition in 1981, she dropped out of Juilliard sans diploma to launch an independent career. On Feb. 6, 1982, she made her N.Y. recital debut at Alice Tully Hall. In 1983 she was awarded an Avery Fisher Career Grant. Her non-conformist persona, highlighted by her impassioned stage deportment and disdain for conventional attire, have made her a popular media figure. All the same, she reveals a genuine talent in her virtuosic performances of the violin literature. She publ. the vol. *Nadja, On My Way* (N.Y., 1989).

BIBL.: C. Passy, "N. S.-S.," *Ovation* (April 1987); *Current Biography* (Nov. 1987).

Sales, Franz, Netherlands composer; b. Namur, c.1550; d. Prague, July 15, 1599. After serving at the courts in Hechingen and Munich (1580), he was a tenor at the Innsbruck court chapel (1580–87); then was Kapellmeister at the collegiate foundation for the ladies of families of the nobility in Hall in the Tirol (1587–91); subsequently was a tenor at the Prague imperial court (from 1591). He excelled as a composer of Mass Propers for 5 to 6 Voices (3 vols., Prague, 1596). His brother, **Nikolaus Sales** (b. probably in Namur, before 1550; d. Stuttgart, April 5, 1606), was a composer who sang at the Stuttgart court chapel (from 1565).

Sales (de Sala), Pietro Pompeo, esteemed Italian composer; b. Brescia, c.1729; d. Hanau, Nov. 21, 1797. After attending the Univ. of Innsbruck, he began his career as a conductor of an Italian opera company; traveled with it in various European cities. He served as director of the court chapel of Prince-Bishop Joseph, Landgrave of Hessen-Darmstadt, in Augsburg and Dillingen an der Donau (1756–68); then was director of the court chapel of the Trier Elector Clemens Wenzeslaus, Prince-Bishop of Augsburg, in Ehrenbreitstein am Rhein (1768–86); subsequently was active at the elector's court in Koblenz, which was disrupted twice during the French Revolutionary wars; he fled the French for the 3rd time in 1797 and made his way to Hanau, dying shortly afterward. He was a distinguished representative of the Italian style.

WORKS: DRAMATIC: OPERAS: *Le nozze di Amore e di Norizia* (Munich, 1765); *Antigona in Tebe* (Padua, 1767); *L'Antigono* (Munich, 1769); *Achille in Sciro* (Munich, 1774); *Il Re pastore* (n.d.). **SINGSPIEL:** *L'isola disabitata* (Augsburg, 1758); also *Massanissa, oder Die obsiegende Treu*, Jesuit drama (Innsbruck, 1752), and *Le Cinesi*, componimento drammatico (Augsburg, 1757). **ORATORIOS:** *Oratorio per la festa del Santo Natale* (Augsburg, 1756); *Giefte* (Mannheim, 1762); *Passion* (Ehrenbreitstein, 1772); *Giuseppe riconosciuto* (Ehrenbreitstein, 1780); *Gioas re di Giuda* (Ehrenbreitstein, 1781); *La Betulia liberata* (Ehrenbreitstein, 1783); *Affectus amantis* (Ehrenbreitstein, 1784); *Sant'Elena* (Koblenz, 1791); also sacred vocal pieces; 3 syms.; several concertos; etc.

BIBL.: F. Collingnon, *P.P. S.* (diss., Univ. of Bonn, 1923).

Saléza, Albert, French tenor; b. Bruges, near Bayonne, Oct. 18, 1867; d. Paris, Nov. 26, 1916. He studied with Bax and Obin at the Paris Cons., making his debut as Mylio in *Le Roi d'Ys* at the Paris Opéra-Comique on July 19, 1888. After appearances in Rouen, Bordeaux, and Nice, he returned to Paris to make his debut at the Opéra as Mathôs in Reyer's *Salammbô* on May 16, 1892. He sang in the posthumous premiere of Franck's *Hulda* in Monte Carlo (March 4, 1894), and then in the premiere of Lefebvre's *Djelma* at the Paris Opéra (May 25, 1894). He made his 1st appearance at London's Covent Garden as Gounod's Romeo on May 10, 1898, and continued to sing there until 1902; made his Metropolitan Opera debut in N.Y. in the same role on Dec. 2, 1898; was on its roster until 1901, and again in 1904–5; also sang regularly in Paris until 1911, when he joined the faculty of the Cons. He was especially noted for such roles as Gounod's Faust, John of Leyden, Raoul in *Les Huguenots*, Edgardo in *Lucia di Lammermoor*, the Duke of Mantua, Rigoletto, Tannhäuser, Don José, Siegmund, and Otello.

Salieri, Antonio, famous Italian composer and teacher; b. Legnago, near Verona, Aug. 18, 1750; d. Vienna, May 7, 1825. He studied violin and harpsichord with his brother, Francesco, then continued violin studies with the local organist, Giuseppe Simoni. He was orphaned in 1765; subsequently was taken to Venice, where he studied thoroughbass with Giovanni Pescetti, deputy maestro di cappella of San Marco, and singing with Ferdinando Pacini, a tenor there. Florian Gassmann took Salieri to Vienna in 1766 and provided for his musical training and a thorough education in the liberal arts; there he came into contact with Metastasio and Gluck, the latter becoming his patron and friend. His 1st known opera, *La Vestale* (not extant), was premiered in Vienna in 1768. His comic opera, *Le Donne letterate*, was successfully performed at the Burgtheater in Jan. 1770. The influence of Gluck is revealed in his 1st major production for the stage, *Armida* (June 2, 1771). Upon the death of Gassmann in 1774, Salieri was appointed his successor as court composer and conductor of the Italian Opera. After Gluck was unable to fulfill the commission for an opera to open the Teatro alla Scala in Milan, the authorities turned to Salieri; his *L'Europa riconosciuta* inaugurated the great opera house on Aug. 3, 1778. While in Italy, he also composed operas for Venice and Rome. He then returned to Vienna, where he brought out his Lustspiel, *Der Rauchfangkehrer* (April 30, 1781). With Gluck's encouragement, Salieri set his sights on Paris. In an effort to provide him with a respectful hearing, Gluck and the directors of the Paris Opéra advertised

Salieri's *Les Danaïdes* (April 26, 1784) as a work from Gluck's pen; following a number of performances, it was finally acknowledged as Salieri's creation. Returning to Vienna, he composed 3 more stage works, including the successful *La grotta di Trofonio* (Oct. 12, 1785). His French opera *Les Horaces* (Paris, Dec. 7, 1786) proved a failure. However, his next French opera, *Tarare* (Paris Opéra, June 8, 1787), was a triumphant success. After Da Ponte revised and tr. Beaumarchais's French libretto into Italian and Salieri thoroughly recomposed the score, it was given as *Axur, re d'Ormus* (Vienna, Jan. 8, 1788); it was then performed throughout Europe to great acclaim. Salieri was appointed court Kapellmeister in Vienna in 1788, and held that position until 1824; however, he did not conduct operatic performances after 1790. He continued to compose for the stage until 1804, his last major success being *Palmira, regina di Persia* (Oct. 14, 1795).

Salieri's influence on the musical life of Vienna was considerable. From 1788 to 1795 he was president of the Tonkünstler-Sozietät, the benevolent society for musicians founded by Gassmann in 1771; he was its vice-president from 1795; he was also a founder of the Gesellschaft der Musikfreunde. He was widely celebrated as a pedagogue, his pupils including Beethoven, Hummel, Schubert, Czerny, and Liszt. He was the recipient of numerous honors, including the Gold Medallion and Chain of the City of Vienna; he was also a Chevalier of the Légion d'Honneur and a member of the French Institut. Salieri's eminence and positions in Vienna earned him a reputation for intrigue; many unfounded stories circulated about him, culminating in the fantastic tale that he poisoned Mozart; this tale prompted Pushkin to write his drama *Mozart and Salieri*, which subsequently was set to music by Rimsky-Korsakov; a contemporary dramatization of the Mozart-Salieri rivalry, Peter Shaffer's *Amadeus*, was successfully produced in London in 1979 and in N.Y. in 1980; it later obtained even wider circulation through the award-winning film version of 1984. Salieri was a worthy representative of the traditional Italian school of operatic composition. He was a master of harmony and orchestration. His many operas are noteworthy for their expressive melodic writing and sensitive vocal treatment. All the same, few held the stage for long, and all have disappeared from the active repertoire. He also composed numerous sacred works; secular works, including cantatas, choruses, and songs; and instrumental pieces.

BIBL.: I. von Mosel, *Über das Leben und die Werke des A. S.* (Vienna, 1827); W. Neumann, *A. S.* (Kassel, 1855); A. von Herrmann, *A. S.: Eine Studie zur Geschichte seines künstlerischen Wirkens* (Vienna, 1897); R. Nützlader, *S. als Kirchenmusiker* (diss., Univ. of Vienna, 1924); G. Magnani, *A. S.: Musicista legnaghese* (Legnago, 1934); A. Della Corte, *Un Italiano all'estero: A. S.* (Turin and Milan, 1937); R. Angermüller, *A. S.: Sein Leben und seine weltlichen Werke unter besonderer Berücksichtigung seiner "grossen" Opern* (diss., Univ. of Salzburg, 1970; publ. in 3 vols., Munich, 1971–74); idem, "S.s Vorbemerkungen zu seinen Opern," *Mitteilungen der Internationalen Stiftung Mozarteum*, XXV/3–4 (1977); V. Braunbehrens, *S., ein Musiker im Schatten Mozarts* (Munich, 1989).

Salinas, Francisco de, eminent Spanish organist and music theorist; b. Burgos, March 1, 1513; d. Salamanca, Jan. 13, 1590. He became blind at the age of 10; was taught organ, and studied languages at the Univ. of Salamanca. In 1538 he was taken to Rome by Cardinal Pedro Sarmiento de Salinas, where he was made a priest and was granted an annual pension by Pope Paul III; from 1553 to 1558, he was organist at the vice-regal chapel in Naples; in 1559 he became organist at Sigüenza Cathedral; later was organist at León Cathedral; from 1567 he was prof. of music at the Univ. of Salamanca. He wrote the theoretical treatise *De musica libri septem* (Salamanca, 1577), chiefly valuable for the examples of Spanish folk music it contains. It was to Salinas that Luis de León dedicated his famous *Odas a Salinas*.

BIBL.: J. Trend, "S.: A Sixteenth-Century Collector of Folk-Songs," *Music & Letters* (Jan. 1927); A. Daniels, *The De musica*

libri VII of Franciscus d.S. (diss., Univ. of Southern Calif., 1962); E. Lowinsky, "Gasparus Stoquerus and Franciscus d.S.," *Journal of the American Musicological Society*, XVI (1963); J. Álverez Pérez, "El organista F. d.S.: nuevos datos para su biografía," *Anuario Musical*, XVIII (1963).

Sallinen, Aulis, prominent Finnish composer; b. Salmi, April 9, 1935. He studied under Aarre Merikanto and Joonas Kokkonen at the Sibelius Academy in Helsinki (1955–60); was managing director of the Finnish Radio Sym. Orch. in Helsinki (1960–70); also taught at the Sibelius Academy (1963–76); held the government-bestowed title of Professor of Arts for Life (from 1981), the 1st such appointment. With Penderecki, he was awarded the Withuri International Sibelius Prize in 1983. In his music, he uses modern techniques, with a prevalence of euphonious dissonance and an occasional application of serialism.

WORKS: OPERAS: *Ratsumies* (The Horseman; 1973–74; Savonlinna, July 17, 1975); *Punainen viiva* (The Red Line; 1976–78; Helsinki, Nov. 30, 1978); *Kuningas lähtee Ranskaan* (The King Goes Forth to France; 1983; Savonlinna, June 7, 1984; in Eng., London, April 1, 1987). **BALLETS:** *Variations sur Mallarmé* (1967; Helsinki, 1968); *Midsommernatten* (Atlanta, March 29, 1984; based on the Sym. No. 3); *Himlens hemlighet* (Secret of Heavens; Swedish Television, Oct. 20, 1986; based on the syms. Nos. 1, 3, and 4). **ORCH.:** 2 *Mythical Scenes* (1956); Concerto for Chamber Orch. (1959–60); *Variations for Orchestra* (1963); *Mauermusik* (1962); *14 Juventas Variations* (1963); *Metamorphoses* for Piano and Chamber Orch. (1964); Violin Concerto (1968); *Chorali* for 32 Wind Instruments, 2 Percussion, Harp, and Celesta (1970); 6 syms.: No. 1 (Helsinki, Dec. 2, 1971); No. 2, *Symphonic Dialogue* for Percussion and Orch. (1972; Norrköping, Feb. 25, 1973); No. 3 (Helsinki, April 8, 1975); No. 4 (Turku, Aug. 9, 1979); No. 5, *Washington Mosaics* (Washington, D.C., Oct. 10, 1985); No. 6, *From a New Zealand Diary* (1989–90); *Chamber Music I* for String Orch. (1975), *II* for Alto Flute and String Orch. (1975–76), and *III: The Nocturnal Dances of Don Juanquixote* for Cello and String Orch. (Naantali, June 15, 1986); Cello Concerto (1976); *Shadows*, prelude (Washington, D.C., Nov. 30, 1982); *Fanfare* for Brass and Percussion (Houston, May 17, 1986). **CHAMBER:** 5 string quartets: No. 1 (1958); No. 2, *Canzona* (1960); No. 3, *Some Aspects of Peltoniemi Hintrik's Funeral March* (1969; also for String Orch.); No. 4, *Quiet Songs* (1971); No. 5, *Pieces of Mosaic* (1983); *Elegy for Sebastian Knight* for Cello (1964); *Quattro per quattro* for Oboe or Flute or Clarinet, Violin, Cello, and Harpsichord (1964–65); *Cadenze* for Violin (1965); *Notturno* for Piano (1966); *Quatre études* for Violin and Piano (1970); *Chaconne* for Organ (1970); Sonata for Solo Cello (1971); *Metamorfora* for Cello and Piano (1974); *Canto and Ritornello* for Violin (1975). **VOCAL:** *Suite grammaticale* for Children's Choir and Chamber Orch. (1971); 4 *Dream Songs* for Soprano and Orch. (1972); *Songs from the Sea* for Unaccompanied Children's Choir (1974); *Dies Irae* for Soprano, Bass, Men's Chorus, and Orch. (1978); *Song around a Song* for Unaccompanied Children's Choir (1980); *The Iron Age: Suite* for Soprano, Children's Choir, Mixed Choir, and Orch. (1983); *The Beaufort Scale*, humoresque for Choir (1984).

BIBL.: J. Parsons, "A. S.," *Musical Times* (Nov. 1980); R. Henderson, "A. S.: Singing of Man," ibid. (April 1987).

Salmanov, Vadim (Nikolaievich), Russian composer; b. St. Petersburg, Nov. 4, 1912; d. there (Leningrad), Feb. 27, 1978. He studied piano with his father and theory with Akimenko. He studied composition with Gnessin at the Leningrad Cons. (1936–41); was head of its composition dept. (1947–51), and a teacher (1951–65) and a prof. (from 1965). His early works are marked by broad Russian melodism, with the harmonic structure following the models of Prokofiev and Shostakovich; after 1960 he adopted more advanced techniques, including dodecaphony.

WORKS: DRAMATIC: Ballet, *The Man* (1960); oratorio, *The 12*, to the text by Alexander Blok (1957); 2 cantatas: *Ode to Lenin* (1970) and *Skify*, after Blok (The Scythians; 1973).

ORCH.: *Soja*, symphonic poem for Voice and Orch. (1951); *Little Symphony* for String Orch. (1941); *The Forest*, symphonic picture (1948); *Russian Capriccio* (1950); *Slavic Dance* (1952); 4 syms. (1952, 1959, 1963, 1976); *Children's Symphony* (1962); *Poetic Pictures*, symphonic suite (1955); Sonata for Piano and String Orch. (1961); 2 violin concertos (1964, 1974); *Nights in the Big City* for Violin and Chamber Orch. (1969); *Monologue* for Cello and Chamber Orch. (1972). **CHAMBER:** 6 string quartets (1945; 1947, rev. 1958; 1961; 1963; 1968; 1971); 2 violin sonatas (1945, 1962); 2 piano trios (1946, 1949); Piano Quartet (1947); also *Spain Is in My Heart* for Mezzo-soprano and Piano (1962) and other songs; choruses.

BIBL.: M. Aranovsky, *V.N. S.* (Leningrad, 1961).

Salmen, Walter, respected German musicologist; b. Paderborn, Sept. 20, 1926. He began musicological training with Besseler at the Univ. of Heidelberg and also took organ and composition with Poppen, Fortner, and Peterson; continued musicological study at the Univ. of Münster (Ph.D., 1949, with the dissertation. *Das deutsche Tenorlied bis zum Lochamer Liederbuch*) and completed his Habilitation at the Univ. of Saarbrücken in 1958 with his *Der fahrende Musiker in europäischen Mittelalter* (Kassel, 1960). He became a research assistant at the Deutsches Volksliedarchiv in Freiburg in 1950; then was made prof. (1963) and research fellow (1964) at the Univ. of Saarbrücken; after serving as prof. and director of the musicological inst. at the Univ. of Kiel (1966–73), he was engaged as prof. and director of the musicological inst. at the Univ. of Innsbruck. He ed. the Müller-Blattau Festschrift (Saarbrücken, 1960), *Beiträge zur Musikanschauung im 19. Jahrhundert* (Regensburg, 1965), *Kieler Schriften zur Musikwissenschaft* (Kassel, 1967–74), *Der Sozialstatus des Berufsmusikers vom 17. bis 19. Jahrhundert* (Kassel, 1971), *Innsbrucker Beiträge zur Musikwissenschaft* (Innsbruck, 1977–), *The Social Status of the Professional Musician from the Middle Ages to the 19th Century* (N.Y., 1983), and *Der musikalische Satz* (Innsbruck, 1987).

WRITINGS: *Das Lochamer Liederbuch* (Leipzig, 1951); *Die Schichtung der mittelalterlichen Musikkultur in der ostdeutschen Grenzlage* (Kassel, 1954); *Das Erbe des ostdeutschen Volksgesanges: Geschichte und Verzeichnis seiner Quellen und Sammlungen* (Würzburg, 1956); *Johann Friedrich Reichardt* (Freiburg, 1963); *Geschichte der Musik in Westfalen* (Kassel, 1963–67); *Geschichte der Rhapsodie* (Freiburg, 1966); *Haus- und Kammermusik: Privates Musizieren im gesellschaftlichen Wandel zwischen 1600 und 1900* (Leipzig, 1969); *Musikgeschichte Schleswig-Holsteins von der Frühzeit bis zur Reformation* (Neumünster, 1972); *Musikleben im 16. Jahrhundert* (Leipzig, 1976); *Bilder zur Geschichte der Musik in Österreich* (Innsbruck, 1983); *Musiker im Porträt* (Munich, 1983); *Der Spielmann im Mittelalter* (Innsbruck, 1983); *Das Konzert: Eine Kulturgeschichte* (Munich, 1988); *Tänze im 17. und 18. Jahrhundert* (Leipzig, 1988); *Tanz im 19. Jahrhundert* (Leipzig, 1989).

Salmenhaara, Erkki (Olavi), Finnish composer and musicologist; b. Helsinki, March 12, 1941. He studied at the Sibelius Academy in Helsinki with Kokkonen; then went to Vienna, where he took lessons with Ligeti (1963); then pursued his education with Tawaststjerna at the Univ. of Helsinki (Ph.D., 1970), where he taught (from 1963). He was chairman of the Society of Finnish Composers (1974–76). His music is often inspired by literary works; he favors unusual combinations of instruments, including electronics; makes use of serial techniques in dense, fastidious sonorities.

WORKS: OPERA: *Portugalin nainen* (The Woman of Portugal; 1970–72; Helsinki, Feb. 4, 1976). **ORCH.:** 4 syms.: No. 1, *Crescendi* (1962; Helsinki, Jan. 11, 1963; rev. 1963); No. 2 (1963; Helsinki, Jan. 17, 1964; rev. 1966); No. 3 (Turku, Dec. 5, 1963; rev. 1964); No. 4, *Nel mezzo del cammin di nostra vita* (1971–72; Helsinki, Oct. 13, 1972); *Le Bateau ivre* (Helsinki, June 1, 1965; rev. 1966); *Suomi—Finland*, "unsymphonic poem" (1966; Helsinki, Oct. 31, 1967); *La Fille en mini-jupe* (1967; Helsinki, Feb. 13, 1968); *Canzonetta per archi*

(1971; Savonlinna, July 10, 1972); *Illuminations* (1971); Horn Concerto (1973; Oslo, Oct. 3, 1974); *Canzona per piccola orchestra* (Kuopio, July 26, 1974); *Poema* for Violin or Viola or Cello and String Orch. (1975; Graz, May 28, 1976); *Introduction and Chorale* for Organ and Orch. (Helsinki, Dec. 1, 1978); *Lamento per orchestra d'archi* (Kokkola, Aug. 26, 1979); Concerto for 2 Violins and Orch. (1980; Helsinki, Sept. 21, 1982); *Adagio* for String Orch. (1981; Porvoo, June 13, 1982; also for Oboe and Piano or Organ); *Adagietto* (1981; Finnish Radio, Dec. 23, 1982); *Sinfonietta per archi* (1985; Kokkola, Feb. 16, 1986); Cello Concerto (1983–87; Lahti, March 25, 1988). **CHAMBER:** 2 cello sonatas (1960, rev. 1969; 1982); *Elegy I* for 3 Flutes, 2 Trumpets, and Double Bass (1963) and *II* for 2 String Quartets (1963); Quintet for Wind Instruments (1964); Quartet for Flute, Violin, Viola, and Cello (1971); Sonatine for 2 Violins (1972); String Quartet No. 1 (1977); Sonatine for Flute and Guitar (1981); Sonata for Violin and Piano (1982); *Sonatella* for Piano, 4-hands (1983); *Introduction and Allegro* for Clarinet or Viola, Cello, and Piano (1985); also various pieces for Solo Instrument; vocal works, including *Requiem profanum* (Helsinki, May 24, 1969), various choral works, and song cycles.

Salmhofer, Franz, Austrian conductor, operatic administrator, and composer; b. Vienna, Jan. 22, 1900; d. there, Sept. 22, 1975. He studied composition with F. Schreker and F. Schmidt at the Vienna Academy of Music and musicology with Guido Adler at the Univ. of Vienna. In 1929 he became conductor at the Vienna Burgtheater, for which he composed incidental music, ballets, and operas; he resigned in 1939; from 1945 to 1955, was director at the Vienna State Opera; then was director of the Vienna Volksoper (1955–63). In 1923 he married the pianist Margit Gál.

WORKS: STAGE: OPERAS: *Dame im Traum* (Vienna, Dec. 26, 1935); *Iwan Sergejewitsch Tarassenko* (Vienna, March 9, 1938); *Das Werbekleid* (Salzburg, Dec. 5, 1943); *Dreikönig* (1945; Vienna, 1970). **BALLETS:** *Das lockende Phantom* (1927); *Der Taugenichts in Wien* (1930); *Österreichische Bauernhochzeit* (1933); *Weihnachtsmärchen* (1933); incidental music to about 300 plays. **ORCH.:** *Der Ackermann und der Tod*, overture (1922); Trumpet Concerto (1922); *Kammersuite* for 16 Instruments (Vienna, May 10, 1923); *Der geheimnisvolle Trompeter*, symphonic poem for Narrator and Orch. (1924); Cello Concerto (1927); 2 syms. (1948, 1955); Violin Concerto (1950); Symphonic Prologue (1966). **CHAMBER:** 6 string quartets; Piano Quartet; String Trio; Viola Sonata; Cello Sonata; piano pieces; songs.

Salminen, Matti, Finnish bass; b. Turku, July 7, 1945. After vocal studies in Finland, he made his operatic debut at the Helsinki Opera as King Philipp in *Don Carlos* in 1969; he then toured in Europe, appearing in Cologne, Zürich, Hamburg, Munich, and Stuttgart, at Covent Garden in London, and at the Bayreuth Festival. He particularly distinguished himself in the great basso roles in operas by Mozart, Wagner, and Verdi.

Salmond, Felix (Adrian Norman), distinguished English cellist and pedagogue; b. London, Nov. 19, 1888; d. N.Y., Feb. 19, 1952. He studied at the Royal College of Music in London with W.E. Whitehouse, and in Brussels with Edouard Jacobs; made his debut in London (1909), accompanied at the piano by his mother, Mrs. Norman Salmond. He gave the world premiere of Elgar's Cello Concerto, under Elgar's direction, in London on Oct. 27, 1919; after a European tour, he settled in America (debut, N.Y., March 29, 1922); was head of the cello dept. at the Curtis Inst. of Music in Philadelphia (1925–42) and taught at the Juilliard Graduate School of Music in N.Y. (from 1924). He enjoyed a reputation as a fine chamber music player and an excellent teacher; was the mentor of Orlando Cole, Leonard Rose, Bernard Greenhouse, and many other cellists of distinction.

Salò, Gasparo da. See **Gasparo da Salò.**

Saloman, Siegfried, composer; b. Tondern, Schleswig, Oct. 2, 1816; d. Stockholm, July 22, 1899. He studied composition with J.P. Hartmann in Copenhagen, and violin with Lipinski in Dresden. He lived in Copenhagen for many years and produced 2 operas there, *Tordenskjold I Dynekilen* (May 23, 1844) and *Diamantkorset* (The Diamond Cross; March 20, 1847); toured Russia and the Netherlands (1847–50); married the singer Henriette Nissen, and traveled with her; in 1859, settled in Russia; one of his operas, to a German libretto, was produced in Russian as *Karpatskaya roza* in Moscow, Jan. 7, 1868; several other operas were produced in Stockholm, where he went in 1879 after the death of his wife. Some of his violin pieces and songs have been publ.

Salomon (Salomonis). See **Elias, Salomon.**

Salomon, Johann Peter, German violinist, impresario, and composer; b. Bonn (baptized), Feb. 20, 1745; d. London, Nov. 25, 1815. He was a member of the Electoral orch. at Bonn (1758–62); after a successful concert tour he was engaged as concertmaster and composer to Prince Heinrich of Prussia at Rheinsberg (1764). When the orch. was disbanded (c.1780), Salomon went to Paris and then to London, where he settled in 1781; made his debut at Covent Garden on March 23 of that year; began promoting concerts in 1783, introducing syms. by Haydn and Mozart in 1786. In 1790 he went to Italy to engage singers for the Italian Opera in London, and from there went to Vienna, where he saw Haydn and persuaded him to accept an engagement in London. At Salomon's behest Haydn wrote the works familiarly known as his "Salomon Symphonies"; it is through his association with Haydn's 2 visits to England, in 1790–91 and 1794–95, that Salomon's name remains in the annals of music. He was a founder of the Phil. Society in London (1813); conducted its 1st concert on March 8, 1813. His own works are of merely antiquarian interest; they include the operas *Les Recruteurs* (Rheinsberg, 1771); *Le Séjour du bonheur* (Berlin, March 5, 1773); *Titus* (Rheinsberg, 1774); *La Reine de Golconde* (Rheinsberg, 1776); *Windsor Castle,* or *The Fair Maid of Kent* (Covent Garden, London, April 6, 1795; in collaboration with R. Spofforth); he also wrote an oratorio, *Hiskias* (1779) and other vocal works, several violin concertos, string trios, string quartets, sonatas for violin and cello, etc.

BIBL.: F. Rochlitz, "J.P. S.," *Allgemeine musikalische Zeitung,* XVIII (1816); [P. Ayrton,] "Memoir of J.P. S.," *Harmonicon* (Feb. 1830); H. Unverricht, "Die Kompositionen J.P. S.s: Ein Überblick," *Studien zur Musikgeschichte des Rheinlandes,* III (Cologne, 1965).

Salonen, Esa-Pekka, Finnish conductor and composer; b. Helsinki, June 30, 1958. He entered the Sibelius Academy in Helsinki as a horn pupil of Holgar Fransman in 1973, taking his diploma in 1977; then studied composition with Rautavaara and conducting with Panula; subsequently studied with Donatoni in Siena, attended the Darmstadt summer course, and finally received instruction from N. Castiglioni in Milan (1980–81). After appearances as a horn soloist, he took up conducting; was a guest conductor throughout Scandinavia, and later extended his activities to include Europe. In 1984 he made his U.S. debut as a guest conductor with the Los Angeles Phil. He became principal conductor of the Swedish Radio Sym. Orch. in Stockholm in 1984; led it on a tour of the U.S. in 1987; also served as principal guest conductor of the Oslo Phil. (from 1984) and the Philharmonia Orch. in London (from 1985). In 1989 he was appointed music director of the Los Angeles Phil., his tenure to begin in 1992. In his music he tends toward pragmatic aural accessibility, employing fairly modern techniques while preserving the formal centrality of traditional tonality.

WORKS: ORCH.: *Aubades* for Flute, Soprano, and Strings (1977–78); *Apokalyptische Phantasie* for Brass Band and Electronic Tape (1978); *Boutade* for Violin, Cello, Piano, and Orch. (1979); . . . *auf den ersten Blick und ohne zu wissen* (a quotation from Kafka's *The Trial*) for Alto Saxophone and Orch. (1980–81); *Giro* (1981). **CHAMBER:** *Horn Music I* for Horn and Piano (1976); *Horn Music II* for 6 Horns, Percussion, and Electronic Tape (1979); Cello Sonata (1976–77); *Nachtlieder* for Clarinet

and Piano (1978); *Sets* for Brass Quintet (1978); *Prologue* for Oboe, Violin, Cello, and Percussion (1979); *Goodbye* for Violin and Guitar (1979–80); *Meeting* for Clarinet and Harpsichord (1982); Wind Quintet (1982); *YTA 1* for Flute (1982) and *YTA 2* for Piano (1985).

Salonen, Sulo (Nikolai), Finnish organist and composer; b. Pyhtää, Jan. 27, 1899; d. Porvoo, May 21, 1976. He was a pupil of Furuhjelm and Palmgren at the Helsinki Cons. (1917–22; 1926–29); then was organist in Jacobstad (1929–48) and Sibbo (1952–64).

WORKS: *Passion Cantata* (1942); *Viisauden ylistys* (In Praise of Wisdom) for Narrator, Voices, and Instruments (1961); *Requiem* (1962); Wind Quintet (1962); String Trio (1971); 2 string quartets (1971, 1972); *Cum jubilo* for Chorus, Organ, and Percussion (Helsinki, Jan. 24, 1974); about 50 motets; numerous organ pieces.

Salter, Lionel (Paul), English conductor, pianist, harpsichordist, and writer on music; b. London, Sept. 8, 1914. He studied at the Royal College of Music and at Cambridge Univ. with Dent and Ord (B.A., 1935; B.Mus., 1936); then returned to the Royal College of Music, where he studied conducting with Lambert and piano with Benjamin. He began his career working in radio and television in London; in 1945 he became assistant conductor of the BBC Theatre Orch.; from 1948 he held administrative posts with the BBC; retired in 1974. His books include *Going to a Concert* (London, 1950), *Going to the Opera* (London, 1955), *The Musician and His World* (London, 1963), and *Music and the 20th-Century Media* (with J. Bornoff; Florence, 1972); he also compiled a useful *Gramophone Guide to Classical Music and Recordings.*

Salter, Mary Elizabeth (née **Turner**), American soprano and composer; b. Peoria, Ill., March 15, 1856; d. Orangeburg, N.Y., Sept. 12, 1938. She studied in Burlington, Iowa, and in Boston; sang in Boston and N.Y. churches (1874–93); she married Sumner Salter (1856–1944) in 1881, with whom she settled in Williamstown, Mass. She composed until her 80th year; among her compositions are song cycles: *Love's Epitome, A Night in Naishapur, Lyrics from Sappho,* and *From Old Japan;* about 80 songs publ. separately (*The Cry of Rachel, The Pine Tree, Für Musik, Die stille Wasserrose,* etc.); duets; some part-songs; church music.

Saltzmann-Stevens, Minnie, American soprano; b. Bloomington, Ill., March 17, 1874; d. Milan, Jan. 25, 1950. She studied voice with Jean De Reszke in Paris; made her operatic debut as Brünnhilde in the English version of the *Ring des Nibelungen* at London's Covent Garden in 1909; she continued to sing there until 1913; also appeared at the Bayreuth Festivals of 1911 and 1913; from 1911 to 1914 she sang with the Chicago Grand Opera. Her other roles included Kundry, Isolde, and Sieglinde.

Salva, Tadeáš, Slovak composer; b. Lúčky, near Ružomberok, Oct. 22, 1937. He studied with Ján Zimmer in Bratislava; then with Cikker and A. Moyzes in Prague and with Szabelski and Lutoslawski in Warsaw (1960–65); was manager of the music dept. of the radio at Košice (1965–68); then was a dramaturgist for the television studio in Bratislava.

WORKS: Television opera, *Margita a besné* (Margaret and the Wild; 1972); radio opera, *The Weeping* (1978–79); 4 string quartets: No. 1 (1960–61); No. 2 (1962); No. 3 (1970); No. 3b (1972; reconstruction and alteration of No. 3); *Cantiliniae* for Chamber Chorus (1961); *Canticum Zachariae* (1963); Concerto for Clarinet, Narrator, 4 Voices, and Percussion (1965); *Symfónia lásky* (Symphony of Love) for Narrator, Chorus, 3 Oboes, Horn, Double Bass, Piano, and Percussion (1965); *Requiem* for 3 Narrators, 3 Choruses, Brass, 6 Kettledrums, Percussion, and Organ (1966); Concerto for Cello and Chamber Orch. (1967); *Mša glagolskaja* (Glagolitic Mass) for Solos, Chorus, 2 Harps, 3 Oboes, Brass, Percussion, and Organ (1969); *Aliquoten* for Tape (1971); Nonet (1971); *Musica per archi* (1971); *War and the World,* poem for Baritone, Women's Chorus, Double Bass, Organ, and Chamber Orch. (1972); *Ballad-*

Fantasy for Soprano, Piano, and Orch. (1972); *Burlesque* for Violin and Chamber Orch. (1972); *Elegies* for Narrator, Soprano, Chorus, and Chamber Orch. (Bratislava, Oct. 5, 1974); *Ballad* for 2 Clarinets (1974); *Music in Memoriam Arthur Honegger* for Organ, Bass Voice, Trumpet, and Strings (1977); *Rhapsody* for Violin and Orch. (1982).

Salvayre, Gaston (actually, **Gervais-Bernard**), French composer; b. Toulouse, June 24, 1847; d. St. Ague, near Toulouse, May 17, 1916. He was a pupil at the Toulouse Cons.; then entered the Paris Cons., studying organ with Benoist and composition with Ambroise Thomas. After failing to win the Prix de Rome for 5 consecutive years, he finally obtained it in 1872 with the cantata *Calypso;* subsequently devoted himself mainly to composition and also wrote music criticism for *Gil Blas;* was made a Chevalier of the Légion d'honneur in 1880.
    WORKS: STAGE: OPERAS: *Le Bravo* (Paris, April 18, 1877); *Richard III* (in Italian as *Riccardo III,* St. Petersburg, Dec. 21, 1883; in French, Nice, Jan. 29, 1891); *La Dame de Monsoreau* (Paris, Jan. 30, 1888); *Solange* (Paris, March 10, 1909); *Egmont* (Paris, Dec. 6, 1886). BALLETS: *Le Fandango* (Paris, Nov. 26, 1877); *La Fontaine des fées* (Paris, 1899); *L'Odalisque* (Paris, 1905); also *Calypso,* dramatic scene (1872). ORCH.: *Le Jugement dernier* (Paris, Dec. 3, 1876; also known as *La Résurrection* and *La Vallée de Josaphat*); *Ouverture symphonique* (Paris, March 22, 1874); *Air et Variations* for String Orch. (1877).

Salvi, Lorenzo, Italian tenor; b. Ancona, May 4, 1810; d. Bologna, Jan. 16, 1879. He made his debut at the Teatro San Carlo in Naples in 1830; then sang at La Scala in Milan (1839–42); during his tenure there, he created the title role in Verdi's *Oberto;* also the role of Riccardo in *Giorno di regno;* made guest appearances at Covent Garden in London (1847–50) and in N.Y. He became particularly known for his roles in operas by Bellini and Donizetti.

Salvini-Donatelli, Fanny (real name, **Francesca Lucchi**), Italian soprano; b. Florence, 1815; d. Milan, June 1891. She made her debut at the Teatro Apollo in Venice as Rosina in 1839; then sang throughout Italy; also appeared in Vienna (1842) and in London at Drury Lane (1858); likewise appeared in various other European music centers; she retired from the stage in 1859 but briefly resumed her career in 1865. She created the role of Violetta in *La Traviata* in 1853 in Venice and distinguished herself in other Verdi operas.

Salviucci, Giovanni, Italian composer; b. Rome, Oct. 26, 1907; d. there, Sept. 4, 1937. He studied with Respighi and Casella; also took courses in law at the Univ. of Rome; then taught at the Istituto Muzio Clementi in Rome and wrote music criticism for the *Rassegna Nazionale.* He developed a fine style of instrumental writing; his works were performed by Italian orchs. with increasing frequency, but his early death cut short his promising career. His *Ouverture* in C-sharp minor (1932) received a national prize.
    WORKS: ORCH.: *La Tentazione e la preghiera,* symphonic poem (1931); *Sinfonia italiana* (1932; Rome, Feb. 25, 1934); Overture in C-sharp minor (1932); *Sinfonia da camera* (1933); *Introduzione, Passacaglia e Finale* (1934); *Serenata* for 9 Instruments (1937); *Psalm of David* for Soprano and Chamber Orch. (Rome, 1935); *Alcesti,* after Euripides, for Chorus and Orch. (1937); also String Quartet (1932) and other chamber music; songs.
    BIBL.: F. Ballo, "Musicisti del nostro tempo: G. S.," *Rassegna Musicale* (Jan. 1937); G. Arledler, *Prospettive critiche su G. S.* (diss., Univ. of Bologna, 1974).

Salzedo (actually, **Salzédo**), **(Léon) Carlos,** eminent French-born American harpist, pedagogue, and composer; b. Arcachon, France, April 6, 1885; d. Waterville, Maine, Aug. 17, 1961. He studied at the Bordeaux Cons. (1891–94), winning 1st prize in piano; then entered the Paris Cons., where his father, Gaston Salzédo, was a prof. of singing; studied with Charles de Bériot (piano), gaining 1st prize in 1901, and with

Hasselmans (harp), also receiving 1st prize. He began his career as a concert harpist upon graduation; traveled all over Europe (1901–5); was solo harpist of the Association des Premiers Prix de Paris in Monte Carlo (1905–9); in 1909 he settled in N.Y.; was 1st harpist in the orch. of the Metropolitan Opera (1909–13). In 1913 he formed the Trio de Lutèce (from Lutetia, the ancient name for Paris), with Georges Barrère (flute) and Paul Kéfer (cello). In 1921 he was co-founder, with Edgard Varèse, of the International Composers' Guild in N.Y., with the aim of promoting modern music; this organization presented many important contemporary works; in the same year he founded a modern music magazine, *Eolian Review,* later renamed *Eolus* (discontinued in 1933). He became an American citizen in 1923; was elected president of the National Assoc. of Harpists; held teaching positions at the Inst. of Musical Art in N.Y., and the Juilliard Graduate School of Music; organized and headed the harp dept. at the Curtis Inst. of Music in Philadelphia. In 1931 he established the Salzedo Harp Colony at Camden, Maine, for teaching and performing during the summer months. Salzedo introduced a number of special effects, and publ. special studies for his new techniques; designed a "Salzedo Model" harp, capable of rendering novel sonorities (Eolian flux, Eolian chords, gushing chords, percussion, etc.). His own compositions are rhythmically intricate and contrapuntally elaborate and require a virtuoso technique. He publ. *Modern Study of the Harp* (N.Y., 1921; 2nd ed., 1948), *Method for the Harp* (N.Y., 1929), and *The Art of Modulating* (with L. Lawrence; N.Y., 1950).
    WORKS: 3 *morceaux* for Harp (1913); *Terres enchantées* or *The Enchanted Isle,* symphonic poem for Harp and Orch. (1918; Chicago, Nov. 28, 1919, composer soloist); 5 *Poetical Studies* for Harp (1918); 3 *Poems* for Soprano, 6 Harps, and 3 Wind Instruments (1919); *Bolmimerie* for 7 Harps (1919); 4 *Preludes to the Afternoon of a Telephone* for 2 Harps (1921); *Sonata* for Harp and Piano (1922); 3 *Poems by Mallarmé* for Soprano, Harp, and Piano (1924); Concerto No. 1 for Harp and 7 Wind Instruments (1925–26; N.Y., April 17, 1927, composer soloist); *Pentacle,* 5 pieces for 2 Harps (1928); *Préambule et Jeux* for Harp, 4 Wind Instruments, and 5 String Instruments (Paris, 1929); *Scintillation* for Harp (1936); *Panorama,* suite for Harp (1937); Suite for Harp (1943); 10 *Wedding Presents* for Harp (1946–52); *Prélude fatidique* for Harp (1954); Harp Concerto No. 2 (orchestration completed by R.R. Bennett); various other works; many transcriptions for Harp.
    BIBL.: Special issue of *Harp News,* III/4 (1961); S. Archambo, *C. S. (1885–1961): The Harp in Transition* (diss., Univ. of Kansas, 1984).

Salzer, Felix, distinguished Austrian-born American music theorist and pedagogue; b. Vienna, June 13, 1904; d. N.Y., Aug. 12, 1986. He studied musicology with Guido Adler at the Univ. of Vienna (Ph.D., 1926, with the diss. *Die Sonatenform bei Schubert*); concurrently studied theory and analysis with Weise and Schenker; later received a conducting diploma from the Vienna Academy of Music (1935). With O. Jonas, he was founder-ed. of the journal *Der Dreiklang* (1937–39). He emigrated to the U.S. in 1939 and became a naturalized citizen in 1945; taught at N.Y.'s Mannes College of Music (1940–56), serving as its executive director (1948–55); was again a teacher there (1962–81); was also a prof. of music at Queens College of the City Univ. of N.Y. (from 1963). He was a leading "Schenkerian" theorist and was instrumental in bringing the views of his teacher to the attention of American musicians; his own contribution was in the expansion and application of Schenker's concepts (previously restricted to a narrow range of tonal music) to Renaissance, medieval, and some 20th-century music. He publ. a number of important books on music theory: *Sinn und Wesen der abendländischen Mehrstimmigkeit* (Vienna, 1935); *Structural Hearing* (2 vols., N.Y., 1952; new ed., N.Y., 1962); *Counterpoint in Composition: The Study of Voice Leading* (with C. Schachter; N.Y., 1969); ed. (with William Mitchell) *Music Forum* (N.Y., from 1967), a hardcover periodical.

Salzman, Eric, American composer, writer on music, editor, and teacher; b. N.Y., Sept. 8, 1933. He attended the High School of Music and Art in N.Y. (1947–51) and studied composition at Columbia Univ. with Otto Luening, Vladimir Ussachevsky, William Mitchell, and Jack Beeson (B.A., 1954), and at Princeton Univ. with Roger Sessions and Milton Babbitt (M.F.A., 1956); in addition, he took courses in musicology with Oliver Strunk, Arthur Mendel, and Nino Pirotta. In 1957 he went to Rome on a Fulbright fellowship to study with Goffredo Petrassi at the Accademia di Santa Cecilia; also attended courses of Karlheinz Stockhausen at Darmstadt. Returning to the U.S., he was a music critic for the *N.Y. Times* (1958–62) and for the *N.Y. Herald Tribune* (1963–66). He taught at Queens College of the City Univ. of N.Y. (1966–68) and at N.Y. Univ. (from 1982); served as ed. of the *Musical Quarterly* (from 1984). He was director of "New Images of Sounds," a series of concerts given at Hunter College in N.Y. He founded the Quog Music Theater in 1970 with the aim of creating a new music theater for contemporary performing arts. In his compositions he follows the most advanced techniques in mixed media. His writings include *Twentieth Century Music: An Introduction* (Englewood Cliffs, N.J., 1967; 3rd ed., rev., 1988) and *Making Changes: A Practical Guide to Vernacular Harmony* (with M. Sahl; N.Y., 1977).

Works: String Quartet (1955); Flute Sonata (1956); *Partita for Solo Violin* (1958); *Inventions* for Orch. (1957–58); *In Praise of the Owl and the Cuckoo,* song cycle for Soprano, Guitar, Violin, and Viola (1963–64); *Verses and Cantos* for 4 Voices and Instruments with electronic extensions (N.Y., Nov. 30, 1967); *Larynx Music* for Soprano, Guitar, and 4-track Tape (1966–67); *Feedback,* "environment piece" for Magnetic Tape and Film (1968); *The Nude Paper Sermon* for Actor, Renaissance Consort, Chorus, and Electronics (1968–69); *The Conjurer,* multimedia spectacle (1975; with Michael Sahl); *Civilization and Its Discontents,* opera buffa for radio (N.Y., 1977; with Sahl); *Noah,* spectacle (N.Y., Feb. 10, 1978); *The Passion of Simple Simon* (N.Y., 1979; with Sahl); *Variations on Sacred Harp Hymn Tunes* for Harpsichord (1982); *Big Jim & the Small-time Investors,* music-theater piece (1984–85; with N. Jackson and Sahl); *Toward a New American Opera,* mixed-media piece (1985).

Samara, Spiro (actually, **Spyridon Filiskos),** Greek composer; b. Corfu, Nov. 29, 1861; d. Athens, March 25, 1917. He was a pupil of Enrico Stancampiano in Athens; later of Léo Delibes at the Paris Cons. He won considerable success with his 1st opera, *Flora mirabilis* (Milan, May 16, 1886), and devoted himself almost exclusively to dramatic composition. Other operas were *Medgè* (Rome, 1888); *Lionella* (Milan, 1891); *La Martyre* (Naples, May 23, 1894); *La furia domata* (Milan, 1895); *Istoria* (Milan, 1903; as *La biondinetta,* Gotha, 1906); *Mademoiselle de Belle-Isle* (Genoa, Nov. 9, 1905); *Rhea* (Florence, April 11, 1908); *La guerra in tempo di guerra* (Athens, 1914). He publ. *Scènes orientales,* suite for Piano, 4-hands; many pieces for piano solo; songs.

Samaroff, Olga (née **Hickenlooper),** American pianist and educator; b. San Antonio, Aug. 8, 1882; d. N.Y., May 17, 1948. She studied as a child with her mother and grandmother (Mrs. L. Grünewald, a former concert pianist); subsequently studied in Paris (with Delaborde), Baltimore (with Ernest Hutcheson), and Berlin (with Ernst Jedliczka). She made her concert debut in N.Y. (Jan. 18, 1905) with the N.Y. Sym. Society; appeared with other orchs. in the U.S. and Europe; gave joint recitals with Kreisler, Zimbalist, and other violinists; was music critic for the *N.Y. Evening Post* (1927–29); was on the faculties of the Philadelphia Cons. and the Juilliard School of Music in N.Y. (1924–48); among her outstanding students were Eugene List, Rosalyn Tureck, William Kapell, and Alexis Weissenberg. In 1911 she married **Leopold Stokowski;** they divorced in 1923. Her autobiography was publ. as *An American Musician's Story* (N.Y., 1939); she also publ. *The Layman's Music Book* (N.Y., 1935; 2nd ed., rev., 1947 as *The Listener's Music Book),*

The Magic World of Music (N.Y., 1936), and *A Music Manual* (N.Y., 1937).
Bibl.: D. Pucciani, *O. S. (1882–1948), American Musican and Educator* (diss., N.Y. Univ., 1979).

Samazeuilh, Gustave (Marie Victor Fernand), French writer on music and composer; b. Bordeaux, June 2, 1877; d. Paris, Aug. 4, 1967. He studied music with Chausson and at the Paris Schola Cantorum with d'Indy; also took some lessons from Dukas. In his music he absorbed the distinct style of French Impressionism, but despite the fine craftsmanship of his work, performances were few and far between. He publ. the studies *Paul Dukas* (Paris, 1913; 2nd ed., 1936) and *Ernest Chausson: Musicien de mon temps* (Paris, 1947); also ed. *Écrits de Paul Dukas sur la musique* (Paris, 1948).

Works: Orch.: *Étude symphonique* (1906); *Nuit* (Paris, March 15, 1925); *Naïades au soir* (Paris, Oct. 18, 1925); *Serenade* (1926); *Gitanes* (1931); *L'Appel de la danse* (1946). **Orch., with Chorus:** *Le Sommeil de Canope* (1908); *Chant d'Espagne* (Paris, Jan. 10, 1926); *Le Cercle des heures* (Paris, Feb. 17, 1934). **Chamber:** Violin Sonata (1903); String Quartet (1911); *Esquisse d'Espagne* for Flute and Piano (1914); *Luciole* for Clarinet and Piano (1934); *Suite en trio* for Strings (1938); *Cantabile e capriccio* for String Quartet (1948); many transcriptions for piano of orch. works by d'Indy, Debussy, Franck, and Fauré.
Bibl.: J. Poupard, *Entretiens avec G. S.* (Paris, 1962).

Saminsky, Lazare, Russian-American composer, conductor, and writer on music; b. Valegotsulova, near Odessa, Nov. 8, 1882; d. Port Chester, N.Y., June 30, 1959. He studied mathematics and philosophy at the Univ. of St. Petersburg; composition with Rimsky-Korsakov and Liadov, conducting with N. Tcherepnin at the St. Petersburg Cons. (graduated, 1910). He emigrated to the U.S. in 1920, settling in N.Y.; in 1923 he was a co-founder of the League of Composers; served as music director of Temple Emanu-El in N.Y. (1924–56), where he founded the annual Three Choirs Festival (1926). He was married to an American writer, Lillian Morgan Buck, who died in 1945; in 1948 he married the American pianist Jennifer Gandar. He wrote an autobiography, *Third Leonardo* (MS, 1959). In his compositions he followed the Romantic tradition; Hebrew subjects and styles play an important part in some of his music.

Works: Stage: *The Gagliarda of a Merry Plague,* opera ballet (1924; N.Y., Feb. 22, 1925); *The Daughter of Jephta,* opera ballet (1928); *Julian, the Apostate Caesar,* opera (1933–38). **Orch.:** 5 syms.: No. 1, *Of the Great Rivers,* in "E-Frimoll" (free minor mode) (1914; Petrograd, Feb. 25, 1917, composer conducting); No. 2, *Symphonie des sommets* (1918; Amsterdam, Nov. 16, 1922); No. 3, *Symphony of the Seas* (1924; Paris, June 1925, composer conducting); No. 4 (1926; Berlin, April 19, 1929, composer conducting); No. 5, *Jerusalem, City of Solomon and Christ,* with Chorus (1929–30; N.Y., April 29, 1958); *Vigiliae,* symphonic triptych (Moscow, Feb. 20, 1913, composer conducting); *Lament of Rachel,* ballet suite (Boston, March 3, 1922); *Litanies of Women* for Voice and Chamber Orch. (1925; Paris, May 21, 1926); *Venice,* "poem-serenade" for Chamber Orch. (Berlin, May 9, 1928); *Ausonia,* suite (1930; Florence, Feb. 24, 1935); *To a New World* (1932; N.Y., April 16, 1951); *3 Shadows* (1935; N.Y., Feb. 6, 1936); *Pueblo, A Moon Epic* (1936; Washington, D.C., Feb. 17, 1937); *Stilled Pageant* (1937; Zürich, Aug. 1938); *East and West,* suite for Violin and Orch. (1943). **Vocal:** *Eon Hours,* suite of 4 rondos for 4 Voices and 4 Instruments (1935; N.Y., Nov. 28, 1939); *Requiem,* in memory of Lillian M. Saminsky (N.Y., May 20, 1946); *A Sonnet of Petrarch* for 3 Voices and 3 Instruments (1947); several Hebrew services; also piano pieces.
Writings: *Music of Our Day* (N.Y., 1932; 2nd ed., rev. and augmented, 1939); *Music of the Ghetto and the Bible* (N.Y., 1934); *Living Music of the Americas* (N.Y., 1949); *Physics and Metaphysics of Music and Essays on the Philosophy of Mathematics* (The Hague, 1957); *Essentials of Conducting* (N.Y., 1958).

BIBL.: D. de Paoli et al., *L. S.: Composer and Civic Worker* (N.Y., 1930); A. Weisser, ed., "L. S.'s Years in Russia and Palestine: Excerpts from an Unpublished Autobiography," *Musica Judaica*, II (1977–78).

Sammarco, (Giuseppe) Mario, Italian baritone; b. Palermo, Dec. 13, 1868; d. Milan, Jan. 24, 1930. He studied singing with Antonio Cantelli, making a successful debut as Valentine in *Faust* in Palermo (1888); then sang in Brescia, Madrid, Lisbon, Brussels, Moscow, Warsaw, Berlin, and Vienna. After his London appearance as Scarpia in *Tosca* at Covent Garden in 1904, he sang there every season until the outbreak of World War I in 1914. He made his American debut as Tonio (Feb. 1, 1908) at the Manhattan Opera House in N.Y.; from 1910 to 1913 he sang with the Chicago Grand Opera; retired from the operatic stage in 1919 and later settled in Milan as a teacher. He was one of the finest verismo singers of his time.

Sammartini, Giovanni Battista, significant Italian composer and pedagogue, brother of **Giuseppe (Francesco Gaspare Melchiorre Baldassare) Sammartini;** b. probably in Milan, 1700 or 1701; d. there, Jan. 15, 1775. It is likely that he studied music with his father, Alexis Saint-Martin, a French oboist who settled in Italy. In 1728 he became maestro di cappella of the Congregation of the SS. Entierro in Milan, which met at the Jesuit church of S. Fedele; he held this position most of his life. He also held similar positions with various other churches in Milan, and was active as a composer of sacred music and as an organist. In 1768 he became maestro di cappella to the ducal chapel at S. Gottardo; was a founder-member of Milan's philharmonic society. A noted teacher, he taught at the Collegio de' Nobili from 1730. His most famous pupil was Gluck, who studied with him from about 1737 to 1741. Sammartini's historical importance rests upon his contribution to the development of the Classical style; his large body of syms. (68 in all), concertos, and other works for orch. are noteworthy for their extensive thematic development and evolution of sonata form. The earliest known dated syms., in 3–movement form, are credited to him. However, the claim that he composed a 4-movement sym. in 1734 lacks confirmation. See B. Churgin, ed., *The Symphonies of G.B. S.* (Cambridge, Mass., 1968–). Additional works for orch. include 6 violin concertos, a Concerto for 2 Violins, 2 flute concertos, a Concerto for 2 Violins and 2 Oboes, 7 orch. concertinos, etc. His chamber music includes 21 quartets, 6 quintets, about 200 trios, many sonatas and duets, etc. He composed the following works for the theater: *Memet*, opera (Lodi, 1732); *L'ambizione superata dalla virtù*, opera (Milan, Dec. 26, 1734); *L'Agrippina, moglie di Tiberio*, opera (Milan, Jan. 1743); *La gara dei geni*, introduzione e festa da ballo (Milan, May 28, 1747); *Il trionfo d'amore*, ballet (Milan, 1773); also composed a number of arias and secular cantatas, as well as sacred cantatas and other religious works, including the oratorio *Gesù bambino adorato dalli pastori* (Milan, Jan. 11, 1726). Many other works attributed to him are doubtful or spurious.

BIBL.: H. Mishkin, "Five Autograph String Quartets by G.B. S.," *Journal of the American Musicological Society*, VI (1953); idem, "The Published Instrumental Works of G.B. S.," *Musical Quarterly* (1959); B. Churgin, *The Symphonies of G.B. S.* (diss., Harvard Univ., 1963); W. Newman, *The Sonata in the Classic Era* (Chapel Hill, 1963; 3rd ed., rev., 1983); B. Churgin, "New Facts in S. Biography: The Authentic Print of the String Trios, Op. 7," *Journal of the American Musicological Society*, XX (1967); idem, "G.B. S. and the Symphony," *Musical Times*, CXVI (1975); N. Jenkins and B. Churgin, *Thematic Catalogue of the Works of G.B. S.: Orchestral and Vocal Music* (Cambridge, Mass., 1976); N. Jenkins, "The Vocal Music of G.B. S.," *Chigiana*, XXIV (1977); M. Marley, *The Sacred Cantatas of G.B. S.* (diss., Univ. of Cincinnati, 1978).

Sammartini, Giuseppe (Francesco Gaspare Melchiorre Baldassare), Italian oboist and composer, brother of **Giovanni Battista Sammartini,** called "il Londinese" after settling in London; b. Milan, Jan. 6, 1695; d. London, Nov. 1750. He most likely studied oboe with his father, Alexis Saint-Martin, who settled in Italy. By 1720 he was a member of the orch. of the Teatro Regio Ducal in Milan. In 1728 he went to London, where he established himself as a virtuoso oboist; also played in the opera orch. at the King's Theatre. From 1736 until his death he also was music master to the wife and children of the Prince of Wales. He composed a considerable number of instrumental works, including 12 concerti grossi, 16 overtures, concertos for various instruments, many sonatas, duets, etc. His vocal music includes 9 cantatas; also an aria and a sinfonia for the oratorio *La calunnia delusa* (Milan, 1724), a pasticcio by several Italian composers. He may also have composed the masque *The Judgement of Paris* (c.1740), which is usually attributed to Arne; see R. Fiske, "A Cliveden Setting," *Music & Letters*, XLVII (1966).

Sammons, Albert (Edward), esteemed English violinist and pedagogue; b. London, Feb. 23, 1886; d. Southdean, Sussex, Aug. 24, 1957. He received some instruction from his father and others in London, but was mainly autodidact; began his professional career at age 11, making his solo debut at 20. He was 1st violinist of the London String Quartet (1907–16); was also concertmaster of Beecham's Orch. (1908–13), Diaghilev's Ballets Russes orch. (from 1911), and the orch. of the Phil. Soc. (from 1913). In subsequent years he appeared as a soloist with various orchs. in England, becoming well known as a champion of the Elgar Violin Concerto; Delius dedicated his Violin Concerto to Sammons, who ed. its violin part and was soloist in its premiere (London, Jan. 30, 1919). For a quarter of a century he gave duo recitals with the pianist William Murdoch, often playing premieres of British scores. He served as a prof. at the Royal College of Music in London. In 1944 he was made a Commander of the Order of the British Empire. He also composed; his *Phantasy Quartet* for Strings was awarded the Cobbett Prize. He publ. *The Secret of Technique in Violin Playing* (London, 1916) and *Violin Exercises for Improving the Bowing Technique by Means of the Tone Perfecter* (London, 1930).

Samosud, Samuil (Abramovich), prominent Russian conductor and teacher; b. Tiflis, May 14, 1884; d. Moscow, Nov. 6, 1964. He studied cello at the Tiflis Cons. (graduated, 1906); after playing cello in various orchs., he went to St. Petersburg, where he was a conductor at the Maryinsky Theater (1917–19) and artistic director of the Maly Theater (1918–36); then settled in Moscow and was artistic director of the Bolshoi Theater (1936–43), the Stanislavsky-Nemirovich-Danchenko Music Theater (1943–50), and the Moscow Phil. and the All-Union Radio orch. (1953–57); also taught conducting at the Leningrad Cons. (1929–36), being made a prof. in 1934. In 1937 he was made a People's Artist of the U.S.S.R. He conducted premieres of a number of works by Soviet composers, including Shostakovich's opera *The Nose* (1930) and Prokofiev's 7th Sym. (1952).

Sams, Eric, English music critic; b. London, May 3, 1926. He was educated at Cambridge Univ.; became active in broadcasting and in musical journalism; publ. valuable monographs: *The Songs of Hugo Wolf* (London, 1961; 2nd ed., rev., 1983), *The Songs of Robert Schumann* (London, 1969; 2nd ed., rev., 1975), and *Brahms Songs* (London, 1972).

Samuel, Adolphe (-Abraham), Belgian composer and teacher; b. Liège, July 11, 1824; d. Ghent, Sept. 11, 1898. He was educated at the Liège Cons. and the Brussels Cons., winning the Belgian Grand Prix de Rome (1845); taught harmony at the Brussels Cons. (1850–70); in 1871 he was appointed director of the Ghent Cons. He publ. *Cours d'accompagnement de la basse chiffrée* (Brussels, 1849), *Cours d'harmonie pratique* (Brussels, 1861), and *Livre de lecture musicale* (Paris, 1886).

WORKS: 5 operas: *Il a rêvé* (1845); *Giovanni da Procida* (1848); *Madeleine* (1849); *Les Deux Prétendants* (1851); *L'Heure de la retraite* (1852); 7 syms.; overtures; string quartets; piano pieces.

BIBL.: E. Mathieu, *Notice sur A. S.* (Brussels, 1922).

Samuel, Gerhard, German-born American conductor, teacher, and composer; b. Bonn, April 20, 1924. He studied violin as a child; his family emigrated to America in 1939, where he became a naturalized citizen in 1943. He performed menial jobs as a dishwasher and shoe salesman in N.Y. before winning a scholarship at the Eastman School of Music in Rochester, N.Y.; studied conducting with Hermann Genhart (B.S., 1945); also played violin with the Rochester Phil. (1941–45). In 1945 he enrolled at Yale Univ., studying composition with Paul Hindemith (M.M., 1947); attended the conducting sessions with Koussevitzky at the Berkshire Music Center in Tanglewood (1946, 1947). From 1949 to 1959 he was a violinist and assistant conductor with the Minneapolis Sym. Orch.; from 1959 to 1971 he was music director of the Oakland (Calif.) Sym. Orch.; also was founder-director of the Oakland Chamber Orch. and the Cabrillo Music Festival (1962–66); was associate conductor of the Los Angeles Phil. (1970–73). In 1972 he became a teacher at the Calif. Inst. of the Arts; was a prof. of music and orch. director at the Univ. of Cincinnati College-Cons. of Music (from 1976). He also was music director of the Pacific Northwest Ballet (from 1982); then was chief guest conductor of the Oakland Ballet (from 1984). He composed a number of orch., chamber, and vocal works in a fine modernistic idiom.

WORKS: *12 on Death and No* for Tenor, Small Chorus, and Orch. (1968); *Looking at Orpheus Looking* for Orch. (1971); *To an End* for Chorus and Orch. (1972); *Into Flight From* for Orch. (1973); *Requiem for Survivors* for Orch. (1974); 2 string quartets (1978, 1981); *Out of Time*, sym. (1978); *Chamber Concerto for Flute in the Shape of Summer* for Flute, Strings, and 3 Percussion (1981); *AGAM*, ballet music (1983).

Samuel, Harold, distinguished English pianist and pedagogue; b. London, May 23, 1879; d. there, Jan. 15, 1937. He studied at the Royal College of Music in London with Dannreuther (piano) and Stanford (composition); later was on its faculty. He was particularly distinguished as an interpreter of Bach; in 1921 he gave 6 successive Bach recitals in London and a similar cycle in N.Y.; toured the U.S. regularly from 1924. He wrote a musical comedy, *Hon'ble Phil*, songs, and piano pieces.

Samuel, Léopold, Belgian composer; b. Brussels, May 5, 1883; d. there, March 10, 1975. He studied with Edgar Tinel at the Brussels Cons. and took courses in Berlin, winning the Belgian Prix de Rome with his cantata *Tycho-Brahé* (1911); later served as inspector of music education in Belgium (1920–45) and was made a member of the Belgian Royal Academy (1958). His works follow in a late Romantic style, with pronounced impressionistic elements.

WORKS: OPERAS: *Ilka* (1919); *La Sirène au pays des hommes* (1937). **ORCH.:** *Morceaux de concert* for Cello and Orch. (1908); *Petite suite fantasque* (1945). **CHAMBER:** String Quintet (1909); Piano Trio (1920); 3 string quartets (1941, 1942, 1948); *Pièce à 5* for Flute, String Trio, and Harp (1954); *Invocation* for Cello and Piano (1959); also songs.

Samuel-Rousseau, Marcel. See **Rousseau, Marcel.**

Sances, Giovanni Felice, Italian singer, teacher, and composer; b. Rome, c.1600; d. Vienna (buried), Nov. 12, 1679. After serving several patrons, he was called to Vienna as a singer in the court chapel in 1636; in 1649 he was named assistant Kapellmeister, and subsequently was Kapellmeister (1669–76). He played a significant role in the cultivation of Italian dramatic music at the Viennese court; composed the operas *Ermiona* (Padua, April 11, 1636), *I trionfi d'Amore* (Prague, July 2, 1648), *La Roselmina fatta canara* (Vienna, Feb. 1662), *Mercurio esploratore* (Vienna, Feb. 21, 1662), *Apollo deluso* (Vienna, June 9, 1669), and *Aristomene Messenio* (Vienna, Dec. 22, 1670), 6 sepolcri (1669–76), about 600 sacred works, and various secular vocal chamber pieces.

BIBL.: P. Webhofer, *G.F. S. (ca. 1600–1679): Biographisch-bibliographische Untersuchung und Studie über sein Motettenwerk* (Innsbruck, 1965).

Sánchez de Fuentes, Eduardo, important Cuban composer and educator; b. Havana, April 3, 1874; d. there, Sept. 7, 1944. He studied music with Ignacio Cervantes and Carlos Anckermann. He occupied an influential position in the artistic affairs of Cuba; wrote 5 operas and many other works, but is known outside Cuba chiefly by his popular song *Tú*, which he publ. at the age of 18.

OPERAS (all 1st perf. in Havana): *El náufrago*, after Tennyson's *Enoch Arden* (Jan. 31, 1901); *La dolorosa* (April 23, 1910); *Doreya* (Feb. 7, 1918); *El caminante* (1921); *Kabelia*, after a Hindu legend (June 22, 1942); also *Temas del patio*, symphonic prelude; *Bocetos cubanos* for Soprano, Women's Chorus, and Orch. (Barcelona, 1922); *Anacaona*, symphonic poem (1928); songs; piano pieces.

WRITINGS (all publ. in Havana): *El folklore en la música cubana* (1923); *Folklorismo* (1928); *Viejos ritmos cubanos* (1937).

BIBL.: M. Guiral, *Un gran musicógrafo y compositor cubano: E. S.d.F.* (Havana, 1944); O. Martínez, *E. S.d.F.: In Memoriam* (Havana, 1944).

Sandberg, Mordecai, Rumanian-born American composer and music theorist; b. in Rumania, Feb. 4, 1897; d. Toronto, Dec. 28, 1973. As a child, he studied violin with a Gypsy violinist-conductor, composing the overture *Demosthenes* while still in his teens. He pursued training in music in Vienna while attending the Univ. there as a medical student (M.D., 1921). From 1922 to 1938 he was active as both a physician and a composer in Jerusalem, where he founded the local branch of the ISCM and the Inst. of New Music; in 1930 he served as contributing ed. of the Hebrew monthly music journal *Hallel*. In 1929–30 he pursued research on acoustics in Germany; also lectured at the Berlin Hochschule für Musik and publ. an essay on his music theories as *Die Musik der Menschheit: Die Tondifferenzierung und ihre Bedeutung*. In 1938 he lectured on microtones at the Congress of Music and Life in London. He went to the U.S. in 1939 and later settled in N.Y., where several of his works were premiered, including *Ezkerah* (I Remember; 1952), an oratorio "dedicated to the memory of all victims of persecution, oppression, and hatred." From 1970 until his death he taught at York Univ. in Toronto. Sandberg was an original and prolific composer. He was one of the earliest explorers of microtonal music, originating his own "Universal Tonal System" using microtones based on a synthesis of Oriental and Western scales. To facilitate the writing and performance of microtonal music, he designed a refined notational system and several instruments, including 2 harmoniums—one bichromatic with quarter-tones (1926) and one with 12th and 16th tones (1929), both built by Straube. He composed orch. works, including 5 syms., a Concerto for Clarinet and Strings, and a Concerto for Oboe, Viola, and Orch.; much chamber music, including sextets, quintets, quartets, and sonatas for cello, piano, violin, viola, and organ; numerous sacred and secular vocal works, including 15 oratorios, among them *Ruth* (N.Y., May 22, 1949) and *Ezkerah* (N.Y., April 22, 1952); *Shelomoh*, symphonic tetralogy for Soloists, Chorus, and Orch.; *Jerusalem*, cantata (N.Y., Nov. 10, 1943); *Hebrew Spirituals* and *Prayer for Peace* (N.Y., Jan. 16, 1946). His major achievement was his *Symphonic Psalms*, settings of the entire book of *Psalms*, among them *Pilgrim Songs* (Psalms 128, 130, and 134; N.Y., Jan. 16, 1946), *Songs of Ascent* (Psalms 126, 131, and 132; N.Y., June 17, 1947), and *Psalm 51* (N.Y., May 30, 1987).

Sandberger, Adolf, eminent German musicologist; b. Würzburg, Dec. 19, 1864; d. Munich, Jan. 14, 1943. He studied composition in Würzburg and Munich (1881–87) and musicology in Munich and Berlin (1883–87); obtained his Ph.D. in 1887 at the Univ. of Würzburg with the dissertation *Peter Cornelius* (publ. in Leipzig, 1887) and completed his Habilitation in 1894 at the Univ. of Munich. In 1889 he was appointed head of the music dept. at the Bavarian Hofbibliothek in Munich; also was a reader (1900–1904) and a prof. (1904–30) at the Univ. of Munich. He was ed. of Denkmäler der Tonkunst in Bayern (1900–1931) and the *Neues Beethoven-Jahrbuch* (1924–42); with F. Haberl, he also ed. Breitkopf & Härtel's monumental edition of the complete works of Lassus (1894–1927). Sandberger was one of the most important teachers of musicology in Germany; he formulated the basic principles of 20th-century musical bibliography. Among his writings were *Emmanuel Chabriers Gwendoline* (Munich, 1898), *Über zwei ehedem Wolfgang Mozart zugeschriebene Messen* (Munich, 1907), and *Ausgewählte Aufsätze zur Musikgeschichte* (Munich, 1921–24). He was also a composer; wrote 2 operas, choral pieces, chamber works, songs, etc.

BIBL.: T. Kroyer, ed., *Festschrift zum 50. Geburtstag A. S.* (Munich, 1918); L. Schiedermair, "A. S.," *Zeitschrift für Musikwissenschaft* (Jan. 1935).

Sandby, Hermann, Danish cellist and composer; b. Kundby, near Holbaek, March 21, 1881; d. Copenhagen, Dec. 14, 1965. He studied cello with Hugo Becker and composition with Iwan Knorr in Frankfurt am Main (1895–1900); gave concerts in Scandinavia, England, and Germany; in 1912 he settled in America as 1st cellist of the Philadelphia Orch.; moved to N.Y. in 1916; returned to Denmark in 1930.

WORKS: ORCH.: 5 syms. (1930–54); Cello Concerto (Philadelphia, Feb. 5, 1916); *Pastorale d'automne* (1937); *Serenade* for Strings (1940); *Nordische Rhapsodie* (1954); Violin Concerto; Triple Concerto for Violin, Viola, Piano, and Orch. **CHAMBER:** 4 string quartets (1907–36); String Quintet (1936); Piano Quintet (1938); Piano Trio (1940); piano pieces; also songs.

Sanderling, Kurt, eminent German conductor, father of **Thomas Sanderling;** b. Arys, Sept. 9, 1912. Following private studies, he joined the Berlin Städtische Oper as a répétiteur (1931); being Jewish, he left Nazi Germany and made his way to the Soviet Union (1936); was a conductor with the Moscow Radio Orch. (1936–41) and the Leningrad Phil. (1941–60). He then was chief conductor of the (East) Berlin Sym. Orch. (1960–77). From 1964 to 1967 he was chief conductor of the Dresden State Opera. He also filled a number of engagements as a guest conductor in Western Europe and America.

BIBL.: H. Bitterlich, *K. S.: Für Sie porträtiert* (Leipzig, 1987).

Sanderling, Thomas, German conductor, son of **Kurt Sanderling;** b. Novosibirsk, Oct. 2, 1942. He was trained at the school of the Leningrad Cons. and at the Berlin Hochschule für Musik in East Berlin; in 1962 he made his debut as a guest conductor with the (East) Berlin Sym. Orch., in 1964 was made chief conductor in Reichenbach, and in 1966 became music director in Halle. From 1978 he served as permanent guest conductor at the (East) Berlin State Opera; also toured widely as a guest conductor throughout Europe, North America, Japan, Israel, and Australia.

Sanders, Paul, Dutch composer; b. Amsterdam, Dec. 21, 1891; d. North Tarrytown, N.Y., July 25, 1986. He studied with Sem Dresden and Willem Pijper; contributed to various Dutch publications; was co-founder (with Pijper) of the magazine *De Muziek.* He publ. *De piano* (Amsterdam, 1926) and *Moderne Nederlandsche componisten* (The Hague, 1933).

WORKS: *Pierrot aan de lantaarn,* ballet for Recitation and Chamber Orch. (1923); *Rataplan,* ballet for Chamber Orch. (1925); *Mara* for Chorus and Orch.; String Quartet; Sonata for Solo Violin (1933); etc.

Sanders, Robert L(evine), American organist, conductor, music educator, and composer; b. Chicago, July 2, 1906; d. Delray Beach, Fla., Dec. 26, 1974. He studied at the Bush Cons. of Music in Chicago (Mus.B., 1924; Mus.M., 1925); in 1925 he went to Rome on a fellowship of the American Academy there, and studied composition with Respighi; later was in Paris, where he took lessons with Guy de Lioncourt. Returning to America in 1929, he joined the faculty of the Chicago Cons.; was also organist at the First Unitarian Church; from 1938 to 1947 he was dean of the School of Music at Indiana Univ. in Bloomington; from 1947 to 1973 he taught at Brooklyn College of the City Univ. of N.Y.

WORKS: BALLET: *L'Ag'ya* (1943). **ORCH.:** Violin Concerto (1932–36); *Scenes of Poverty and Toil* (1934–35; perf. as *The Tragic Muse,* Chicago, Jan. 30, 1936, composer conducting); 3 Little Syms. (1936–37; 1953; 1963); Sym. for Concert Band (1942–43); *The Mystic Trumpeter* for Narrator, Baritone, Chorus, and Orch., after Walt Whitman (1939–41); also choral works, including *Song of Myself,* for Reciter, Soprano, Chorus, Brass, and Percussion, after Whitman (1966–70; N.Y., April 19, 1970); hymns. **CHAMBER:** Piano Trio (1926); Brass Quintet (1942); Brass Quartet (1949); Brass Trio (1958); various sonatas; piano pieces; organ music.

Sanders, Samuel, American pianist; b. N.Y., June 27, 1937. He attended Hunter College (B.A., 1959), and studied the art of accompaniment with Sergius Kagen and piano with Irwin Freundlich at the Juilliard School of Music in N.Y. (M.S., 1961); also pursued studies with Martin Canin and Nadia Boulanger. He made his debut as a recitalist at N.Y.'s Town Hall at age 12; after winning a prize as a piano accompanist at the Tchaikovsky Competition in Moscow (1966), he became well known as an accompanist to many major artists; was also active as a chamber music player. In 1963 he joined the faculty of the Juilliard School of Music; was also a prof. at the State Univ. of N.Y. in Purchase (1972–79). He founded the Cape and Islands Chamber Music Festival in 1980 and the Musica Camerit of N.Y.'s Hebrew Arts School in 1983.

Sanderson, Sibyl, American soprano; b. Sacramento, Calif., Dec. 7, 1865; d. Paris, May 15, 1903. She was educated in San Francisco, where her musical talent attracted attention; taken to Paris by her mother at the age 19, she studied at the Cons. with Massenet, Sbriglia, and Mathilde Marchesi. Massenet was charmed with her voice and her person; wrote the leading part in *Esclarmonde* for her; she created it at the Opéra-Comique, on May 14, 1889; the role of Thaïs (Paris Opéra, March 16, 1889) was also written by Massenet for her. Other French composers were equally enchanted with her; Saint-Saëns wrote *Phryné* for her (1893). She made her American debut at the Metropolitan Opera in N.Y. as Manon (Jan. 16, 1895), but had little success with the American public. In 1897 she married a wealthy Cuban, Antonio Terry, who died in 1899.

BIBL.: J. Massenet, *Mes souvenirs* (Paris, 1912); O. Thompson, *The American Singer* (N.Y., 1937).

Sandi, Luis, Mexican conductor, teacher, and composer; b. Mexico City, Feb. 22, 1905. He studied violin with Rocabruna (1923–30) and composition with Campa and Mejía (1925–31) at the National Cons. of Mexico City. He conducted a chorus at the Cons. (1922–35); in 1937 he founded the Coro de Madrigalistas and conducted it until 1965. He was a prof. of music in primary schools (1924–32) and chief of the Music Section of the Secretariat of Public Education (1933–65). He publ. *Introducción al estudio de la música: Curso completo* (Mexico City, 1923; 2nd ed., 1956) and a collection of articles as *De música y otras cosas* (Mexico City, 1969).

WORKS: STAGE: OPERAS: *Carlota* (Mexico City, Oct. 23, 1948); *La señora en su balcón* (1964). **BALLETS:** *Día de difuntos* (Day of the Dead, 1938); *Bonampak* (1948; Mexico City, Nov. 2, 1951); *Coatlicue* (1949). **ORCH.:** *El venado* (1932; Mexico City, Oct. 28, 1938); *Sonora* (1933); *Suite banal* for Small Orch. (1936); *Norte* (Mexico City, Aug. 15, 1941); Concertino for Flute and Orch. (1944); *Tema y Variaciones* (1944); *Esbozos sinfónicos* (1951); *4 Miniatures* (1952); *América,* symphonic poem (1965). **VOCAL:** *Las troyanas* for Chorus and Instruments (1936); *Gloria a los héroes,* cantata (1940); *La suave patria,* cantata (1951). **CHAMBER:** String Quartet (1938); *La hoja de plata* for Instruments (1939); *Fátima,* suite for Guitar (1948); *Cuatro momentos* for String Quartet (1950); *Hoja de album* for Cello and Piano (1956); Cello Sonatina (1958); Quintet (1960); Sonatina for Solo Violin (1967); Violin Sonata (1969); *4 piezas* for Recorders (1977); also numerous choruses; songs; piano pieces.

BIBL.: C. Chávez, "L. S.," *Nuestra Música* (July 1949).

Sándor, Arpád, Hungarian-born American pianist, cousin of **György Sándor;** b. Budapest, June 5, 1896; d. there, Feb. 10, 1972. He studied with Bartók and Kodály at the Royal Academy of Music in Budapest, graduating in 1914; toured the U.S. as an accompanist in 1922; wrote art and music criticism for the *Berliner Tageblatt* (1926–33); then settled in the U.S. and became a naturalized citizen (1943); toured widely as an accompanist to leading artists, including Jascha Heifetz and Lily Pons.

Sándor, György, admired Hungarian-born American pianist and teacher, cousin of **Arpád Sándor;** b. Budapest, Sept. 21, 1912. He studied at the Royal Academy of Music in Budapest with Bartók (piano) and Kodály (composition). After making his debut in Budapest (1930), he toured in Europe before settling in the U.S. (1939); became a naturalized citizen (1943). After World War II, he played in major music centers of the world; also taught at Southern Methodist Univ. in Dallas (1956–61); was director of graduate studies in piano at the Univ. of Michigan in Ann Arbor (1961–81); taught at the Juilliard School in N.Y. (from 1982). He won particular distinction as an interpreter of the music of Bartók, Kodály, and Prokofiev; was soloist in the premiere of Bartók's 3rd Piano Concerto (Philadelphia, Feb. 8, 1946). He made brilliant transcriptions of Dukas's *L'Apprenti sorcier* and Shostakovich's *Danse russe*; publ. *On Piano Playing: Motion, Sound, and Expression* (N.Y., 1981).

Sandoval, Miguel, Guatemalan-American pianist, conductor, and composer; b. Guatemala City, Nov. 22, 1903; d. N.Y., Aug. 24, 1953. He settled in the U.S. in 1925; was active as a conductor and pianist; wrote a symphonic poem, *Recuerdos en un paseo,* and publ. numerous piano works and songs in a Latin American vein.

Sandström, Sven-David, Swedish composer and teacher; b. Borensberg, Oct. 30, 1942. He studied art history and musicology at the Univ. of Stockholm (1963–67); attended composition classes with Lidholm at the Stockholm Musikhögskolan (1967–72); also took special courses in advanced techniques of composition with Nørgård and Ligeti. In 1981 he joined the faculty of the Stockholm Musikhögskolan. In his works he pursues the techniques of enhanced serialism, making use of fractional tones and occasionally resorting to aleatory procedures; some of his applications are aggressively oxymoronic and deliberately offensive; thus, his *Requiem,* dedicated to the memory of child victims of war and racism, has a text in Swedish and English by the poet Tobias Berggren, replete with sadistic obscenities and pornographic proclamations.

WORKS: STAGE: Church opera, *Stark såsom döden* (Strong like Death; Stockholm, April 18, 1978); chamber opera, *Hasta o älskade brud* (Hasta, O Beloved Bride, 1978); music drama, *Kejsaren Jones* (Emperor Jones), after O'Neill (1980); incidental music for *Ett drömspel* (The Dreamplay), after Strindberg, for Chorus, Brasses, Percussion, Organ, and String Quartet (1980); church opera, *Amos* (1981); opera, *Slottet det vita* (1981–82; Stockholm, Feb. 12, 1987); 2 ballets, *Admorica* (1985) and *Den elfte gryningen* (Stockholm, Nov. 4, 1988). ORCH.: *Bilder* (Pictures) for Percussion and Orch. (Norrköping, April 17, 1969); *Intrada* for Wind Instruments, Strings, and Percussion (1969); *17 Bildkombinationen* (17 Picture Combinations) for Wind Instruments, Percussion, and Strings (1969); *In the Meantime* for Chamber Orch. (1970); *Sounds* for 14 Strings (1970); *To You* (Arvika, Aug. 15, 1970); *Around a Line* for Wind Instruments, Piano, Percussion, and Strings (1971); *Through and Through* (1972; Stockholm, Feb. 1, 1974); *Con tutta forza* for 41 Wind Instruments and 6 Percussionists (Stockholm, Oct. 28, 1976); *Culminations* (Swedish Radio, Feb. 22, 1977); *Agitato* for Piano and Orch. (1978); *The Rest Is Dross* for String Orch. (1979); Flute Concerto (1980; Stockholm, Oct. 24, 1983); *Lonesome,* guitar concerto (Malmö, May 18, 1983); Concerto for Violin and String Orch. (1985; Orebro, Jan. 18, 1986); *A Day—The Days* (1987); Overture (Stockholm, June 18, 1987); *Invigningsfanfar* for the 50th anniversary of the Swedish Radio (Swedish Radio, Oct. 14, 1988). CHAMBER:

Music for 5 String Instruments (1968); Sonata for Flute Solo (1968); *Combinations* for Clarinet (1960); *Concertato* for Clarinet, Trombone, Cello, and Percussion (1969); String Quartet (1969); *Disturbances* for 6 Brasses (1970); *Disjointing* for Trombone (1970); *Jumping Excursions* for Clarinet, Cello, Trombone, and Cymbal (1970); *Mosaic* for String Trio (1970); *Under the Surface* for 6 Trombones (1971); *Concentration* for 8 Wind Instruments and 4 Double Basses (1971); *Closeness* for Clarinet (1973); *. . . And All the Flavors Around,* 6 pieces for Violin, Piano, Clarinet, and Flute (with variable accompaniment; 1973); *6 Character Pieces* for Flute, Oboe, Bassoon, 2 Violins, Double Bass, and Percussion (1973); *Convergence* for Bassoon (1973); *Inside* for Bass Trombone and Piano (1974); *Metal, Metal* for 4 Percussionists (1974); *In the Shadow of . . .* for Piano, Cello, and Percussion (1974); *Ratio* for Tuba and Bass Drum (1974); *Utmost* for Wind Quintet, Trumpet, Trombone, Tuba, and Percussion (London, Nov. 10, 1975); *Effort* for Cello (1977); *Break This Heavy Chain That Does Freeze My Bones Around* for 2 Bassoons (1979); *Within* for 8 Trombones and ad lib Percussion (1979); *Drums* for Timpani and 4 Percussionists (1980); *Behind* for String Quartet (1981); *The Last Fight* for Percussion (1984); *Sax Music* for Saxophone Quartet (1985); *Chained* for Percussion Ensemble (1986); *The Slumberous Mass* for 4 Trombones (1987); *Dance III* for 3 Cellos (1988). VOCAL: *Invention* for 16 Voices (1969); *Lamento* for 3 Choral Groups and 4 Trombones (1971); *Visst?* for Soprano, 2 Choruses, Wind Instruments, Pop Orch., and Violin Group (1971; Mellerud, April 23, 1972); *Just a Bit* for Soprano, Bassoon, Violin, and Harp (1972); *Birgitta-Music I* for Speaking and Singing Groups, Orch., Renaissance Ensemble, Organ, and Folk Musicians and Dancers (Vadstena, June 23, 1973); *Dilecte mi* (*Canticum canticorum*), motet for Female Choir and Male Choir (1974); *Expression* for Amplified Mezzo-soprano, Cello, Piano, 4-hands, and Tape (1976); *A Cradle Song/The Tyger,* 2 poems after Blake, for Chorus a cappella (1978); *Spring—Introduction—Earth's Answer,* 3 poems after Blake, for Chorus a cappella (1978); *Tystnaden* (Silence) for Tenor, Narrator, and 14 String Instruments (1979); *Requiem: De ur alla minnen fallna* (Requiem: Mute the Bereaved Memories Speak) for 4 Soloists, Mixed Chorus, Children's Chorus, Orch., and Tape (1979; Stockholm, Feb. 19, 1982); *Agnus Dei* for Chorus a cappella (1980); *Our Peace,* motet for 3 Choirs and 3 Organs (1983); *Missa brevis* for Chorus (1984); *Ut över slätten med en doft av hav,* cantata for Soloists, Chorus, and Orch. (1984); *Convivere* for 5 Singers and 6 Instrumentalists (1985); *Kantat till Filharmonin* for Soloists, Chorus, and Orch. (1985); *Stille etter Gud* for 3 Choirs (1986); *24 romantiska etyder* for Chorus (1988). KEYBOARD: PIANO: *Concentration II* for 2 Pianos (1972); *High Above* (1972); *5 Duets for One Piano* (1973); *Introduction—Out of Memories—Finish* for 2 Pianos (1981). ORGAN: *The Way* (1973); *Openings* (1975); *Libera me* (1980).

Sandt, Maximilian van de, Dutch pianist, teacher, and composer; b. Rotterdam, Oct. 18, 1863; d. Cologne, July 14, 1934. He was a pupil of Liszt in the last year of the master's life; toured in Europe with conspicuous success; was on the faculty of the Cologne Cons. (1896–1906); from 1910 he taught at Bonn. He composed many brilliant piano pieces in a Romantic vein.

Sandvik, Ole Mørk, respected Norwegian musicologist; b. Hedemarken, May 9, 1875; d. Holmenkollen, near Oslo, Aug. 5, 1976. He received training for careers in teaching (1895) and theology (graduated, 1902); also studied music with his father and Gudbrand Bøhn, and in Germany (1913); took his Ph.D. in 1922 at the Univ. of Christiania. He taught at Christiania's (Oslo's) Hegdehaugen School (1913–45) and gave courses in church music at the Seminary for Practical Theology at the Univ. of Christiania (Oslo; 1916–45). He was founder of the Norwegian Musicological Soc., serving as ed. of its yearbook (1937–72).

WRITINGS: *Norsk kirkenmusikk og densilder* (Christiania, 1918); *Folkemusik i Gudbrandsdalen* (Christiania, 1919; 2nd

ed., 1948); *Norsk folkemusik: Saerlig Østlandsmusikken* (Christiania, 1921); with G. Schjelderup, *Norges musikhistorie* (Christiania, 1921–22); ed. with H. Panum and W. Behrend, *Illustreret musikleksikon* (Copenhagen, 1924–26; new ed., 1940); *Graduale for den norske kirke* (Oslo, 1925; 2nd ed., 1957); with J. Gleditsch et al., *Koralbok for den norske kirke* (Oslo, 1926); *Liturgisk musikk til minnegudstjenester på 900-års-jubileet Olsok 1930* (Oslo, 1930); *Norsk koralhistorie* (Oslo, 1930); *Kingotona* (Oslo, 1941); *Vesperale for den norske kirke* (Oslo, 1941); *Gregoriansk sang* (Oslo, 1945); *Ludwig M. Lindeman og folkemelodien: Ein kilderstudie* (Oslo, 1950); *Setesdalsmelodier* (Oslo, 1952); *Norske religiose folketoner* (Oslo, 1960–64); *"Springleiker" i norske bygdier* (Oslo, 1967); ed. with O. Gaukstad, *David Monrad Johansen i skrift og tale* (Oslo, 1968).
BIBL.: *Festschrift til O.M. S.s, 70 års dagen 1875–9. Mai 1945* (Oslo, 1945).

Sangiovanni, Antonio, celebrated Italian singing teacher; b. Bergamo, Sept. 14, 1831; d. Milan, Jan. 6, 1892. He studied at the Milan Cons.; in 1854, was appointed prof. of singing there. Two generations of Italian and foreign singers were his pupils.

Sanjuán, Pedro, Spanish-born American conductor, teacher, and composer; b. San Sebastián, Nov. 15, 1886; d. Washington, D.C., Oct. 18, 1976. He studied composition with Turina; after conducting in Europe, he went to Havana, where he organized the Havana Phil. (1926); was also a teacher of composition there; Roldán, Caturla, and other Cuban composers were his pupils. After a sojourn in Madrid (1932–36), he again conducted the Havana Phil. (1939–42); in 1942 he was appointed prof. of composition at Converse College in Spartanburg, S.C.; became an American citizen in 1947.
WORKS: ORCH.: *Rondo fantástico* (Havana, Nov. 29, 1926); *Castilla,* suite (Havana, June 12, 1927); *Sones de Castilla* for Small Orch.; *La Macumba,* a "ritual sym." (St. Louis, Dec. 14, 1951, composer conducting); *Antillean Poem* for Band (N.Y., Aug. 11, 1958, composer conducting); *Symphonic Suite* (Washington, D.C., May 9, 1965); also choral works; piano pieces.

Sankey, Ira D(avid), noted American evangelistic singer, gospel hymn composer, and hymnbook compiler; b. Edinburgh, Pa., Aug. 28, 1840; d. N.Y., Aug. 13, 1908. As a youth of 17, he became choir leader in the Methodist Church of New Castle, Pa.; served for a year with the N.Y. 12th Infantry Regiment at the time of the Civil War. In 1870 he was a delegate to the YMCA convention at Indianapolis, where his forceful singing attracted the attention of the evangelist preacher Dwight L. Moody. He joined Moody as music director and remained at this post for some 30 years, until approaching blindness forced his retirement in 1903. Of his many gospel tunes, the most popular has proved to be *The Ninety and Nine* (1874), which he improvised at a moment's notice during a service in Edinburgh, Scotland. His chief publications were *Sacred Songs and Solos* (London, 1873) and 6 vols. of *Gospel Hymns and Sacred Songs* (1875–91). As president of the publ. firm of Biglow & Main (1895–1903), he brought out numerous works, including many of his own. He also publ. *My Life and the Story of the Gospel Hymns and of the Sacred Songs and Solos* (Philadelphia, 1906). He is not to be confused with another gospel song writer, Ira Allan Sankey, a lesser light than Ira D(avid) Sankey.
BIBL.: E. Goodspeed, *A Full History of the Wonderful Career of Moody and S., in Great Britain and America* (N.Y., 1876); *The I.D. S. Centenary: Proceedings of the Centenary Celebration . . . with Some Hitherto Unpublished Correspondence* (New Castle, Pa., 1941); C. Ludwig, *S. Still Sings* (Anderson, Ind., 1947); R. Stevenson, "I.D. S. and the Growth of 'Gospel Hymnody,'" *Patterns of Protestant Church Music* (Durham, N.C., 1953); A. Debus, "The Recordings of Moody and S.," *Hobbies,* LXI/3 (1956).

Sanromá, Jesús María, brilliant Puerto Rican pianist; b. Carolina (of Catalonian parents), Nov. 7, 1902; d. San Juan, Oct. 12, 1984. At the age of 14 he was sent to the U.S. by the governor of Puerto Rico; he studied piano with Antoinette Szumowska at the New England Cons. of Music in Boston; in 1920, won the Mason & Hamlin piano prize; then studied with Alfred Cortot (in Paris) and Artur Schnabel (in Berlin); from 1926 to 1944 he was pianist of the Boston Sym. Orch.; he taught at the New England Cons. of Music (1930–41); gave annual concerts in the U.S., Canada, and South America; also played in Europe. In 1951 he was appointed chairman of the music dept. at the Univ. of Puerto Rico; he was head of the piano dept. at the Puerto Rico Cons. of Music (1959–80). He excelled particularly as an interpreter of contemporary music; gave the world premieres of Piston's Concertino (1937) and Hindemith's Concerto (1947).
BIBL.: E. Belava, *El niño S.: Biografia mínima* (San Juan, 1952; 2nd ed., 1962).

San Sebastián, Padre José Antonio de. See **Donostia, Jose Antonio de.**

Santa Cruz (Wilson), Domingo, eminent Chilean composer and music educator; b. La Cruz, near Quillota, July 5, 1899; d. Santiago, Jan. 6, 1987. He studied jurisprudence at the Univ. of Chile; then entered diplomatic service; was 2nd secretary of the Chilean legation in Spain (1921–24); received his musical training with Enrique Soro in Santiago and with Conrado del Campo in Madrid. Returning to Chile, he devoted himself to musical administration, teaching, and composition; from 1928 to 1953 he served as a prof. at the National Cons. in Santiago; was acting dean (1932–33) and dean (1933–51; 1962–68) of the faculty of fine arts at the Univ. of Chile. His role in the promotion of musical culture in Chile was of great importance; in his works he followed the cosmopolitan traditions of neo-Classical music; made use of identifiable Chilean melodies in but a few of his compositions.
WORKS (all 1st perf. in Santiago unless otherwise given): *5 piezas breves* for Strings (May 31, 1937); *Cantata de los ríos de Chile* for Chorus and Orch. (1941; Nov. 27, 1942); *Variaciones* for Piano and Orch. (June 25, 1943); *Sinfonia concertante* for Flute, Piano, and Strings (Nov. 29, 1945); 4 syms.: No. 1 for Strings, Celesta, and Percussion (1945–46; May 28, 1948; rev. 1970); No. 2 for Strings (Nov. 26, 1948); No. 3, with Contralto Solo (Washington, D.C., May 9, 1965); No. 4 (1968); *Egloga* for Soprano, Chorus, and Orch. (1949; Nov. 24, 1950); *Cantares de la pascua* for Women's Voices (1949; Dec. 7, 1950); *Canciones del mar,* song cycle (1955); *Endechas* for Tenor and 8 Instruments (1957); *Oratio Ieremiae prophetae* for Chorus and Orch. (1970); 3 string quartets (1930; 1946–47; 1959); piano pieces.
BIBL.: Special issue of *Revista Musical Chilena* (Dec. 1951).

Santa María, Fray Tomás de, important Spanish organist and composer; b. Madrid, c.1510; d. Ribadavia, 1570. He publ. *Libro llamado Arte de tañer fantasía* (Valladolid, 1565), a treatise on playing fantasias on keyboard instruments and on the guitar or lute (Ger. tr., with critical and biographical introduction, by E. Harich-Schneider and R. Boadella, Leipzig, 1937).
BIBL.: W. Hultberg, *Sancta Maria's "Libro llamado Arte de tañer fantasia": A Critical Evaluation* (diss., Univ. of Southern Calif., 1964).

Santana, Carlos, Mexican-American jazz and rock guitarist; b. Jalisco, July 20, 1947. He took up clarinet and violin, switching to guitar at 14. In 1962 the family moved to San Francisco. In 1967 he formed The Santana Blues Band, and played the honky-tonk circuit. His appearance at the Woodstock Festival in 1969 was marked by a performance of a long, specially composed work, *Soul Sacrifice,* for band, which mesmerized the multitudes assembled there. His album *Abraxas* included the Latin American hits *Samba Pa Ti* and *Oye Como Va* by Tito Puente, and Peter Green's *Black Magic Woman.* The band began to disintegrate in 1972, when Santana saw the light in the bearded visage of a traveling guru, went berserk, and assumed the pseudo-Hindu name Devadip. He found other converts to the new faith among disenchanted Americans, but by 1976 returned to his Latin roots and put out several successful albums, including the hit *She's Not There*, and culminating with the exclamatory *Zebop!* in 1981.

Santelmann, William Henry, German-American violinist, bandmaster, and composer; b. Offensen, Sept. 24, 1863; d. Washington, D.C., Dec. 17, 1932. He studied at the Leipzig Cons.; in 1887 he settled in America; played the baritone in the U.S. Marine Band in Washington, D.C. (1887–95); was its conductor (1898–1927). He wrote the suite *Pocahontas* for Band; marches and dances; made numerous transcriptions.

Santi, Nello, Italian conductor; b. Adria, Sept. 22, 1931. He studied composition at the Padua Cons.; made his debut leading *Rigoletto* at the Teatro Verdi there in 1951; then conducted in leading Italian opera houses. He first conducted at the Zürich Opera in 1958 and at London's Covent Garden in 1960; made his Metropolitan Opera debut in N.Y. conducting *Un ballo in maschera* on Jan. 25, 1962. In subsequent years he made appearances as a guest conductor. He was chief conductor of the Basel Radio Sym. Orch. (from 1986).

Santini, Abbate Fortunato, Italian music scholar and composer; b. Rome, Jan. 5, 1778; d. there, Sept. 14, 1861. He studied counterpoint with Jannacconi and at the Collegio Salviati; later studied organ with Guidi; was ordained a priest in 1801. He devoted much time to acquiring a valuable library, which included about 4,500 MSS and 1,100 printed items; its holdings were enumerated in his *Catalogo della musica esistente presso Fortunato Santini in Roma nel palazzo de' principi Odescalchi incontro la chiesa de' SS. XII. Apostoli* (Rome, 1820). His original compositions include a Requiem; a *Stabat Mater*; many motets.

BIBL.: V. Stassov, *L'Abbé S. et sa collection musicale à Rome* (Florence, 1854); J. Killing, *Kirchenmusikalische Schätze der Bibliothek des Abbate F. S.* (Düsseldorf, 1910); K. Fellerer, "Verzeichnis der kirchenmusikalischen Werke der S.schen Sammlung," *Kirchenmusikalisches Jahrbuch*, XXVI (1931), XXVII (1932), XXVIII (1933), XXIX (1934), and XXXI (1936–38); R. Ewerhart, "Die Bischöfliche S.-Bibliothek," *Das Schöne Münster*, XXXV (1962).

Santini, Gabriele, Italian conductor; b. Perugia, Jan. 20, 1886; d. Rome, Nov. 13, 1964. He studied in Perugia and Bologna; then conducted opera in Rio de Janeiro, Buenos Aires, N.Y., and Chicago. From 1925 to 1929 he was Toscanini's assistant at La Scala in Milan; then was a conductor (1929–33) and artistic director (1944–47) at the Rome Opera.

Santley, Sir Charles, noted English baritone; b. Liverpool, Feb. 28, 1834; d. Hove, near London, Sept. 22, 1922. He studied with Nava in Milan; made his operatic debut as Dr. Grenville in *La Traviata* in Pavia (1857); then continued his training with Garcia in London, where he sang for the 1st time as Adam in Haydn's *Creation* on Nov. 16, 1857. His British operatic debut followed as Hoël in *Dinorah* at Covent Garden in a production mounted by the Pyne-Harrison Co. (Oct. 1, 1859); he continued to sing with the company until 1863, creating many roles in English operas under its auspices. In 1862 he appeared with the Royal Italian Opera at Covent Garden; that same year he became a member of Mapleson's company at Her Majesty's Theatre, winning renown for his portrayal of Valentine in 1863; he left the company in 1870. After singing at the Gaiety Theatre and touring in the U.S. as a concert artist (1871), he sang with the Carl Rosa Opera Co. (1875–77); subsequently devoted himself to oratorio and concert appearances. He sang in Australia (1889–90) and again in the U.S. (1891). On May 23, 1911, he made his farewell appearance at Covent Garden but came out of retirement in 1915 to sing at a concert for Belgian war refugees. In 1887 he was made a Commander of the Order of St. Gregory by Pope Leo XIII; in 1907 he was knighted by King Edward VII. He publ. some songs under the pseudonym Ralph Betterton; he also publ. *Student and Singer* (London, 1892; reminiscences); *The Singing Master* (2 parts, London, 1900); *The Art of Singing and Vocal Declamation* (London, 1908); *Reminiscences of My Life* (London, 1909).

BIBL.: J. Levien, *Sir C. S.* (London, 1930).

Santoliquido, Francesco, Italian composer; b. San Giorgio a Cremano, Naples, Aug. 6, 1883; d. Anacapri, Italy, Aug. 26, 1971. He studied at the Liceo di Santa Cecilia in Rome; graduated in 1908; in 1912 he went to live in Hammamet, a village in Tunisia, spending part of each year in Rome; in 1933 he made his home in Anacapri. Many of his compositions contain melodic inflections of Arabian popular music. He publ. *Il Dopo-Wagner, Claudio Debussy e Richard Strauss* (Rome, 1909; 2nd ed., 1922); also books of verse; wrote short stories in Eng. His 3rd wife was the pianist and teacher Ornella (née Puliti) Santoliquido (b. Florence, Sept. 4, 1906; d. there, Nov. 11, 1977); she studied with Brugnoli; after receiving her diploma at the Florence Cons., she continued her training with Casella in Rome and Cortot in Paris; was a teacher at the Rome Cons. (1939–71); played in chamber-music concerts; became an advocate of contemporary music.

WORKS: OPERAS: *La Favola di Helga* (Milan, Nov. 23, 1910); *Ferhuda* (Tunis, Jan. 30, 1919); *L'Ignota* (1921; not perf.); *La porta verde*, musical tragedy (Bergamo, Oct. 15, 1953); also a ballet, *La Bajadera dalla maschera gialla* (1917). **ORCH.:** *Crepuscolo sul mare* (Nuremberg, Jan. 19, 1909, composer conducting); *Acquarelli* (1914; Rome, April 11, 1923); *Il profumo delle oasi sahariane* (1915; Tunis, April 17, 1918); 2 syms. (1916, c.1927); *La sagra dei morti*, heroic elegy for the victims of World War I (1920); *Grotte di Capri* (1925; rev. 1943); *Preludio e Burlesca* for String Orch. (Rome, 1938); *Alba di gloria sul passo Uarièu*, symphonic prelude (1939; Rome, Nov. 13, 1940); *Santuari asiatici*, symphonic sketches (Naples, 1952). **CHAMBER:** Sonata for Violin and Piano (1924); String Quartet (1931); *Aria antica* for Cello and Piano; *Chiarità lunare* for Violin and Piano; *2 pezzi* for 5 Wind Instruments; *Piccola ballata* for Piano; *2 acquaforti tunisine* for Piano; also a cycle of songs to words by Pierre Louÿs; *Messa facile* for Chorus.

Santoro, Claudio, important Brazilian violinist, conductor, and composer; b. Manaus, Nov. 23, 1919; d. Brasília, March 27, 1989. He studied at the Cons. of Rio de Janeiro and later in Paris with Nadia Boulanger. Returning to Brazil, he taught music in various schools; conducted concerts in South America and Europe, including Russia. He wrote music in an advanced idiom as a youth, mostly in the 12-tone style; but later he decided to compose works accessible to the masses, and this attitude was strengthened by his acceptance of the Russian tenets of socialist realism in art; however, he returned to the avant-garde type of composition (including aleatory practices) in his music of the 1960s. In 1970 he went to Germany and became a prof. of composition at the Hochschule für Musik in Heidelberg; he returned to Brazil in 1978.

WORKS: BALLETS: *A fábrica* (The Factory; 1947); *Anticocos* (1951); *O café* (1953); *Icamiabas* (1959); *Zuimaaluti* (1960); *Prelúdios* (1962). **ORCH.:** *Ode to Stalingrad* for Chorus and Orch. (1947); 11 syms.: No. 1 (1940); No. 2 (1945); No. 3 (Rio de Janeiro, Dec. 20, 1949); No. 4, *Da paz* (Symphony of Peace; Rio de Janeiro, Oct. 30, 1945); No. 5 (Rio de Janeiro, March 28, 1956); No. 6 (Paris, May 1, 1963); No. 7, *Brasilia* (1960); No. 8 (1963); No. 9 (1982); No. 10 (1982); No. 11 (1984); *Variations on a 12-tone Row* (1945); *Chôro* for Saxophone and Orch. (Rio de Janeiro, June 20, 1952); *Ponteio* for String Orch. (Rio de Janeiro, June 19, 1945); *Abertura tragica* (1958); 2 violin concertos (1951, 1958); 3 piano concertos (1953, 1959, 1960); Cello Concerto (1961; Washington, D.C., May 12, 1965); *Asymptotic Interactions* (1969). **CHAMBER:** 7 string quartets (1943–65); 5 violin sonatas (1940–57); 4 cello sonatas (1943–63); String Trio (1941); Flute Sonata (1941); Oboe Sonata (1943); Trumpet Sonata (1946); *Diagrammas cíclicos* for Piano and Percussion (1966); 6 pieces for various Instruments, entitled *Mutations* (1968–72); *Anti-struktur* for Harp and Cello (1970); 25 preludes for Piano (1957–63); also an oratorio, *Berlin, 13 de agôsto* for Narrator, Chorus, and Orch. (1962); *Agrupamento à 10* for Voice and Chamber Orch. (1966); *Aleatorius I–III*, in graphic notation (1967).

Santos, (José Manuel) Joly Braga, Portuguese conductor and composer; b. Lisbon, May 14, 1924; d. there, July 18, 1988. He studied composition with Luís de Freitas Branco at the Lisbon Cons. (1934–43), conducting with Scherchen at the Venice Cons. (1948), electronic music at the Gavessano (Switzerland) Acoustic Experimental Stadium (1957–58), and composition with Mortari at the Rome Cons. (1959–60). He conducted the Oporto Radio Sym. Orch. (1955–59); subsequently was active as a guest conductor. His music represents a felicitous fusion of Portuguese Renaissance modalities and folk rhythms.

WORKS: DRAMATIC: *OPERAS: Viver ou morrer* (To Live or to Die), radio opera (1952); *Mérope* (Lisbon, May 15, 1959); *Trilogia das Barcas* (1969; Lisbon, May, 1970). BALLETS: *Alfama* (1956); *A nau Catrineta* (1959); *Encruzilhada* (1968). ORCH.: 3 symphonic overtures (1945, 1947, 1954); 6 syms.: No. 1 (1946); No. 2 (1948); No. 3 (1949); No. 4 (1950); No. 5, *Virtus Lusitaniae* (1966); No. 6, with Solo Soprano and Chorus (1972); *Nocturno* for String Orch. (1947); Concerto for String Orch. (1951); *Variações sinfónicas sobre un theme de l'Alentejano* (1952); Viola Concerto (1960); *Divertimento* for Chamber Orch. (1961); *3 esboços sinfónicos* (3 Symphonic Sketches; 1962); Sinfonietta for String Orch. (1963); *Double Concerto* for Violin, Cello, String Orch., and Harp (1965); *Variações concertantes* for String Orch. and Harp (1967); Piano Concerto (1973); *Variações* (1976). VOCAL: *Requiem à memória de Pedro de Freitas Branco* for Soloists, Chorus, and Orch. (1964); *Ode à música* for Chorus and Orch. (1965); choruses. CHAMBER: *Nocturno* for Violin and Piano (1942); 2 string quartets (1944, 1956); Violin Sonata (1945); Piano Quartet (1957).

Santucci, Marco, Italian composer; b. Camajore, Tuscany, July 4, 1762; d. Lucca, Nov. 29, 1843. He studied at the Conservatorio di Loreto in Naples; went to Lucca in 1790 and was ordained a priest in 1794; after serving as maestro di cappella at Rome's S. Giovanni in Laterano (1797–1808), he returned to Lucca as canon at the Cathedral. A motet *a* 16 for 4 choirs received a prize from the Accademia Napoleone in 1806 because of the "entirely new and original" combination of voices. Baini publ. an energetic protest against this award, pointing out that such polyphonic writing was common in works by Italian composers of the 16th and 17th centuries. Santucci also wrote masses, motets, Psalms, canons in up to 7 parts, syms., organ sonatas, etc.; publ. the treatise *Sulla melodia, sull'armonia e sul metro* (Lucca, 1828).

BIBL.: G. Rinuccini, *Biografia di M. S.* (Milan, 1851).

Sanz, Gaspar, Spanish priest, guitarist, and composer who flourished from the mid-17th century to the early 18th century. A native of Calanda, Aragón, he received the Bachelor of Theology degree at the Univ. of Salamanca; after studying music with Cristofor Caresana, Orazio Benevoli, P.A. Ziani, and Lelio Colista in Italy, he returned to Spain to pursue his career. He wrote the significant treatise *Instrucción de música sobre la guitarra española y método de sus primeros rudimentos hasta tañerla con destreza* (Saragossa, 1674; 8th ed., 1697; facsimile eds., Madrid, 1951 and Saragossa, 1966), which he dedicated to his pupil, Don Juan of Austria; it contains examples of contemporary Spanish dance music and folk songs.

BIBL.: R. de Zayas, "G. S.: A Transcription of His Complete Works for the Guitar," *The Consort*, XXXI (1975).

Sanzogno, Nino, Italian conductor and composer; b. Venice, April 13, 1911; d. Milan, May 4, 1983. He studied composition with Malipiero in Venice; took conducting lessons with Scherchen in Brussels in 1935; after playing violin in a string quartet, he was appointed conductor at the Teatro La Fenice in Venice in 1937; first conducted at La Scala in Milan in 1939; was a regular conductor there in succeeding years; also toured in South America. He became known as a conductor of modern opera in Italy; also gave courses on conducting in Darmstadt. He composed 2 symphonic poems, *I quattro cavalieri dell'Apocalisse* (1930) and *Vanitas* (1931), a Viola Concerto (1935), a Cello Concerto (1937), other orch. works, chamber music, etc.

Sapelnikov, Vasili, Russian pianist and composer; b. Odessa, Nov. 2, 1867; d. San Remo, March 17, 1941. He was a pupil of L. Brassin and Sophie Menter at the St. Petersburg Cons.; in 1888, made his debut at Hamburg with Tchaikovsky's First Piano Concerto, under the composer's direction; then made tours throughout Europe; after living in Russia (1916–22), he settled in the West. He wrote an opera, *Der Khan und sein Sohn,* and piano pieces.

Saperton, David, American pianist and teacher; b. Pittsburgh, Oct. 29, 1889; d. Baltimore, July 5, 1970. He received his 1st instruction on the piano from his grandfather, a former tenor at the Brünn Opera, while his father, a physician and former concert bass, superintended his theoretical studies. At the age of 10, he made his 1st public appearance with an orch. in Pittsburgh; in 1905 he gave a recital in N.Y.; from 1910 to 1912, toured Germany, Austria, Hungary, Italy, Russia, and Scandinavia; then returned to the U.S.; in 1924, joined the piano faculty of the Curtis Inst. of Music in Philadelphia.

Saporiti (real name, **Codecasa**), **Teresa,** Italian soprano; b. c.1763; d. Milan, March 17, 1869. She joined Pasquale Bondini's Italian company in 1782 and appeared with it in Leipzig, Dresden, and Prague, often being obliged to appear in male costume and take on castrati roles. The success of Bondini's production of *Le nozze di Figaro* in Prague in 1786 prompted him to request an opera from Mozart for the following year; the part of Donna Anna in *Don Giovanni* was written with Saporiti's voice in mind: the taxing coloratura in her aria in the 2nd act indicates that Mozart had a high opinion of her ability. She then appeared in Venice (1788–89) and at Milan's La Scala (1789); later in Bologna, Parma, and Modena. By 1795 she was prima buffa assoluta in Gennaro Astarita's company in St. Petersburg; sang in Astarita's own comic operas, as well as in revivals of Cimarosa's *Italiana in Londra* and Paisiello's *Il Barbiere di Siviglia.* She then fell into total oblivion; if the dates of her life can be verified, she lived to about the age of 105.

Sapp, Allen Dwight, American composer; b. Philadelphia, Dec. 10, 1922. After studying music with local teachers, he entered Harvard Univ., where he studied composition with Walter Piston and orchestration with E.B. Hill (A.B., 1942; A.M., 1949); he also did graduate work there with A.T. Davison, A.T. Merritt, and Randall Thompson; attended classes of Copland and Boulanger in Cambridge, Mass. (1942–43). He subsequently taught at Harvard Univ. (1949–58), Wellesley College (1958–61), the State Univ. of N.Y. at Buffalo (1961–76), and Florida State Univ. (1976–78). He was dean (1978–80) and prof. of composition (from 1980) at the Univ. of Cincinnati College-Cons. of Music. His music is cast in a neo-Classical idiom, with contrapuntal elements coalescing in a florid design.

WORKS: ORCH.: *Andante* (1941); Concertino No. 1 for Piano and Chamber Orch. (1942); 2 suites (1952, 1954); *Ricercari* for Strings (1956); *The Double Image* (1957); *The Septagon* (1957); *Colloquies I* for Piano and String Orch. (1963); *Imaginary Creatures* for Harpsichord and Chamber Orch. (1981); *Colloquies IV* (1983); *The Cheektowaga and Tonawanda Divisions* for Wind Orch. (1983). VOCAL: *Crenelations* for Tenor and Orch., after Ezra Pound's *Marvoil* (1982); *Illusions and Affirmations* for Bass Voice and Strings (1982). CHAMBER: 4 violin sonatas (1943, 1949, 1960, 1981); 7 piano sonatas (1940, 1956, 1957, 1957, 1980, 1981, 1981); 4 string quartets (1951, 1981, 1981, 1982); Viola Sonata (1949); Piano Trio (1950); String Trio (1956); 3 piano sonatas, 4-hands (1944, 1981, 1981); *Nocturne* for Cello (1978); *Colloquies III* for Piano and 10 Wind Instruments (1982); *Colloquies II* for Piano, Flute, and Viola (1983); *The Companion of Sirius: The Serious Companion* for Tuba and Piano (1984).

Sárai, Tibor, Hungarian composer and teacher; b. Budapest, May 10, 1919. He studied composition with Pál Kadosa and violin with Frigyes Sándor at the Franz Liszt Academy of Music in Budapest (diploma, 1942). In 1948 he became secretary general of the Union of Hungarian Musicians; after serving as head of the music dept. of the Hungarian Ministry of Culture (1949–50), he held that position with the Hungarian Radio (1950–53). From 1953 to 1959 he taught at the Béla Bartók Cons. in Budapest; then was a prof. at the Franz Liszt Academy of Music (1959–80). He was also secretary general of the Assoc. of Hungarian Musicians (1959–78); likewise was vice-president (1975–77) and secretary general (1980–82) of the International Music Council of UNESCO. In 1959 he was awarded the Erkel Prize and in 1975 the Kossuth Prize. In 1988 he was made a Merited Artist by the Hungarian government. In his compositions he adheres to the national Hungarian tradition, enhanced by a free use of euphonious dissonances.

WORKS: ORCH.: *Serenade* for String Orch. (1946); *Tavaszi concerto* (Spring Concerto) for Flute, Viola, Cello, and String Orch. (1955); *6 Scenes* from the dance play *János vitéz* (1956–57); 3 syms. (1965–67; 1972–73; 1987); *Musica* for 45 Strings (1970–71); *Epitaph in Memory of Ferenc Szabó* (1974); *Notturno* (1977–78); *Autumn Concerto* for Violin, Cello, Horn, Trumpet, and Orch. (1984). **CHAMBER:** 3 string quartets (1958; 1971; 1980–82); *Lassú és friss* for Violin and Piano (1958); Quartet for Flute, Violin, Viola, and Cello (1961–62); *Studio* for Flute and Piano (1964); piano pieces. **VOCAL:** *Variations on a Theme of Peace*, oratorio for Soloists, Chorus, and Orch. (1961–64); *De profundis*, cantata for Tenor and Wind Quintet (1968); *Diagnosis '69* for Tenor and Orch. (1969); *Future Questioning* for Alto, Baritone, Men's Chorus, and Orch. (1971); *Christ or Barabbas* for Tenor, Baritone, Bass, Chorus, and Orch. (1976–77); *Scena* for Soprano and Bassoon (1980); songs.

Sarasate (y Navascuéz), Pablo (Martín Melitón) de, celebrated Spanish violinist and composer; b. Pamplona, March 10, 1844; d. Biarritz, Sept. 20, 1908. He commenced playing the violin when he was 5; after making his public debut at age 8, he was granted a private scholarship to study with M. Sáez in Madrid; with the assistance of Queen Isabella, he pursued his studies with Alard at the Paris Cons. (from 1856), where he took premiers prix in violin and solfège (1857) and in harmony (1859). He launched his career as a virtuoso with a major concert tour when he was 15. In 1866 he acquired a Stradivarius violin. His playing was noted for its extraordinary beauty of tone, impeccable purity of intonation, perfection of technique, and grace of manner. In the early years of his career, his repertoire consisted almost exclusively of fantasies on operatic airs, most of which he arranged himself. He later turned to the masterpieces of the violin literature. His tours, extending through all of Europe, North and South America, South Africa, and the Orient, were an uninterrupted succession of triumphs. He bequeathed to his native city the gifts that had been showered upon him by admirers throughout the world; the collection was placed in a special museum. Among the works written for him were Bruch's 2nd Concerto and *Scottish Fantasy*, Lalo's Concerto and *Symphonie espagnole*, Saint-Saëns's 1st and 3rd concertos and *Introduction et Rondo capriccioso*, and Wieniawski's 2nd Concerto. Sarasate's compositions, pleasing and effective, include his *Zigeunerweisen* (1878), *Spanische Tänze* (4 books, 1878–82), and *Carmen* fantasy (1883).

BIBL.: M. van Vorst, "S.," *Scribner's Magazine* (March 1896); J. Altadill, *Memorias de S.* (Pamplona, 1909); A. Hartmann, "The Perfect Virtuoso," *Musical America* (March 25, 1940); L. Zárate, *S.* (Barcelona, 1945); G. Woolley, "P. S.: His Historical Significance," *Music & Letters* (July 1955); A. Sagardia, *P. S.* (Palencia, 1956); B. Schwarz, *Great Masters of the Violin* (N.Y., 1983).

Saraste, Jukka-Pekka, Finnish conductor; b. Helsinki, April 22, 1956. He studied violin and conducting at the Sibelius Academy in Helsinki, obtaining diplomas in both subjects in 1979; then made his debut as a conductor with the Helsinki Phil. in 1980. After winning the Nordic conducting competition in 1981, he appeared as a guest conductor throughout Scandinavia. In 1983 he made his 1st tour of the U.S. as co-conductor (with Okko Kamu) of the Helsinki Phil.; his British debut followed in 1984, when he appeared as a guest conductor of the London Sym. Orch. at a Promenade concert in London;

he also made his German debut as a guest conductor with the Munich Phil. In 1985 he was named principal guest conductor of the Finnish Radio Sym. Orch. in Helsinki. He toured Australia in 1986. In 1987 he took the Finnish Radio Sym. Orch. to England, during which tour he conducted all the Sibelius syms. at the Brighton Festival; that same year he was promoted to chief conductor of the orch. and became principal conductor of the Scottish Chamber Orch. in Glasgow.

Sargeant, Winthrop, prominent American music critic; b. San Francisco, Dec. 10, 1903; d. Salisbury, Conn., Aug. 15, 1986. He studied violin in San Francisco with Arthur Argiewicz and with Lucien Capet in Paris; took composition lessons with Albert Elkus in San Francisco and with Carl Prohaska in Vienna. He played the violin in the San Francisco Sym. Orch. (1922–24), the N.Y. Sym. Orch. (1926–28), and the N.Y. Phil. (1928–30). He then devoted himself to musical journalism; was on the editorial staff of *Musical America* (1931–34); was music critic of the *Brooklyn Daily Eagle* (1934–36); served as music ed. of *Time* magazine (1937–39); also wrote essays on various subjects for *Time* (1939–45); subsequently was roving correspondent for *Life* magazine (1945–49) and music critic for the *New Yorker* (1947–72), continuing as a contributor to the latter until his death. He evolved a highly distinctive manner of writing: professionally solid, stylistically brilliant, and ideologically opinionated; he especially inveighed against the extreme practices of the cosmopolitan avant-garde. He publ. *Jazz: Hot and Hybrid* (N.Y., 1938; 3rd ed., N.Y., 1975); *Geniuses, Goddesses, and People* (N.Y., 1949); *Listening to Music* (N.Y., 1958); *In Spite of Myself: A Personal Memoir* (N.Y., 1970); *Divas: Impressions of Today's Sopranos* (N.Y., 1973).

Sargent, Sir (Harold) Malcolm (Watts), eminent English conductor; b. Stamford, Lincolnshire, April 29, 1895; d. London, Oct. 3, 1967. He studied organ at the Royal College of Organists in London; then was articled to Keeton, organist of Peterborough Cathedral (1912–14); served in the infantry during World War I. He made his 1st major conducting appearance on Feb. 3, 1921, in Leicester, leading the Queen's Hall Orch. of London in his own composition, *Allegro impetuoso: An Impression on a Windy Day*. He then went to London, where he conducted the D'Oyly Carte Opera Co. and Diaghilev's Ballets Russes; from 1928 he was conductor-in-chief of the Royal Choral Society. From 1929 to 1940 he was conductor of the Courtauld-Sargent Concerts in London. He toured Australia in 1936, 1938, and 1939, and Palestine in 1937. He was conductor-in-chief and musical adviser of the Hallé Orch. of Manchester (1939–42); then was principal conductor of the Liverpool Phil. (1942–48). In 1945 he made his American debut with the NBC Sym. Orch. in N.Y.; then made appearances in Europe, Australia, and Japan. He was knighted in 1947. From 1950 to 1957 he was chief conductor of the BBC Sym. Orch.; led this ensemble on several European tours. From 1948 to 1966 he also served as chief conductor of the London Promenade Concerts. He took the London Phil. on an extensive Far Eastern tour in 1962; also led the Royal Phil. to the Soviet Union and the U.S. in 1963. His performances of the standard repertoire were distinguished for their precision and brilliance; he championed the music of Elgar, Vaughan Williams, Walton, and other English composers throughout his career. A commemorative stamp with his portrait was issued by the Post Office of Great Britain on Sept. 1, 1980.

BIBL.: C. Reid, *M. S.: A Biography* (London, 1968).

Sargon, Simon, Indian-born American pianist and composer; b. Bombay (of Sephardic, Russian-Jewish, and Indian descent), April 6, 1938. He took private piano lessons with Mieczyslaw Horszowski; studied music theory at Brandeis Univ. (B.A., 1959) and composition with Vincent Persichetti at the Juilliard School of Music in N.Y. (M.S., 1962); also took a course with Darius Milhaud at the Aspen School of Music. He was a teacher at Sarah Lawrence College (1965–68), at the Rubin Academy of Music in Jerusalem (1971–74), where he served as head of the voice dept., and at Hebrew Univ. in Jerusalem (1973–

74). In 1974 he was appointed music director at Temple Emanu-El in Dallas.

WORKS: DRAMATIC: Chamber opera, *Thirst,* after a play of Eugene O'Neill (Jerusalem, Dec. 17, 1972); opera, *Saul, King of Israel* (1990); oratorio, *Not by Might,* based on the Books of the Maccabees (Dallas, Dec. 16, 1979); 3 cantatas: *Elul: Midnight* (Dallas, Sept. 17, 1976), *Visions of Micah* (Dallas, April 30, 1980), and *Flame of the Lord* (Dallas, May 31, 1977); a musical play for children, *A Voice Still and Small* (Dallas, Dec. 6, 1981); Sym. No. 1, *Holocaust,* for Baritone, Men's Chorus, and Orch. (1985); *Questings,* horn concerto (1987); also temple services; songs.

Sari, Ada (real name, **Jadwiga Szajerowa**), Polish soprano; b. Wadowice, near Krakow, June 29, 1886; d. Ciechocinek, July 12, 1968. She studied in Milan; after appearances in Rome, Naples, Trieste, and Parma, she joined the Warsaw Opera; made extensive tours in Europe, South America, and the U.S.; later taught voice in Warsaw.

Sárközy, István, Hungarian composer; b. Pesterzsébet, Nov. 26, 1920. He studied composition with Kodály, Farkas, and Viski at the Budapest Academy of Music; in 1959 he was appointed to its faculty.

WORKS: DRAMATIC: Cantatas: *Ode to Stalin* (1949); *Julia Songs* (1958); *The Earthquake Approaches* (1958); also a comedy oratorio, *"Y" War,* for 10 Solo Voices, Vocal Quintet, and 8 Instruments (1971). **ORCH.:** *Concerto grosso* (1943–44; rev. with an added subtitle, *Ricordanze I,* 1969); *Small Suite* (1951); *Fantasy and Dance* for Gypsy Orch. (1952); *To Youth,* overture (1953); *Sinfonia concertante* for Clarinet and Orch. (1963); *Concerto semplice (Ricordanze II)* for Violin and Orch. (Budapest, Oct. 11, 1974); *Confessioni* for Piano and Orch. (1979). **CHAMBER:** *12 Variations* for Piano (1945); Sonatina for 2 Pianos (1950); *Sonata da camera* for Flute and Piano (1964); *Ciaccona* for Cello (1967); *Chamber Sonata* for Clarinet and Piano (1969); *Psaume et Jeu,* quartet for Wind Instruments (1970); *4 Etudes* for Clarinet (1972); *Ricordanze III* for String Quartet (1977); also scores of incidental music; songs.

Sarly, Henry, Belgian composer; b. Tirlemont, Dec. 28, 1883; d. Brussels, Dec. 3, 1954. He studied with his father and with Huberti, Tinel, Gilson, and Du Bois at the Brussels Cons.; in 1921 he became inspector of musical education in Belgian schools. He composed a number of attractive pieces, among them *Scènes brabançonnes* for Orch.; Piano Quintet; *Poème* for Piano Trio; Violin Sonata; numerous piano pieces and songs. He also publ. a manual, *Cours théorique et pratique d'harmonie.*

Saro, J. Heinrich, German bandmaster and composer; b. Jessen, Jan. 4, 1827; d. Berlin, Nov. 27, 1891. In 1859 he became a bandmaster in Berlin; in 1867 his band won the international competition at the Paris Exposition; in 1872 he was awarded a gold medal for his performance at the Boston Jubilee. He wrote a number of brilliant pieces of military music, and also some symphonic works; publ. *Lehre vom musikalischen Wohlklang und Tonsatz* and *Instrumentationslehre für Militärmusik.*

Sárosi, Bálint, Hungarian ethnomusicologist; b. Csíkrákos, Jan. 1, 1925. He was educated in Csolszereda, and took a doctorate in Hungarian and Rumanian philology in Budapest (1948); also received diplomas in musicology (1956) and composition (1958) at the Budapest Academy of Music, where his teachers included Kodály. He worked in Kodály's group for folk-music research at the Hungarian Academy of Sciences in 1958; in 1974 he became director of the folk-music dept. of the Academy's Inst. for Musicology. His fieldwork includes trips to Ethiopia (1965) and Armenia (1972); his most important research is in the field of instrumental folk music.

WRITINGS: *Die Volksmusikinstrumente Ungarns* (Leipzig, 1967); *Cigányzene* (Gypsy Music; Budapest, 1971; Eng. tr., 1978); *Zenei anyanyelvünk* (Our Own Musical Vernacular; Budapest, 1973).

Sarrette, Bernard, French bandmaster and pedagogue; b. Bordeaux, Nov. 27, 1765; d. Paris, April 11, 1858. A captain in the national guard at Paris, he brought together, after July 13, 1789, 45 musicians to form the nucleus of the Parisian band of the national guard. In 1790 the City of Paris assumed the expenses of this band, which was increased to 70 members, among them artists of distinction. In 1792 the financial embarrassments of the Commune led to the suspension of payment; but Sarrette held the band together and, with the aid of the municipality, established a free school of music employing all the members as teachers. From this school came the musicians employed in the 14 armies of the Republic. Its energetic principal had it converted into a national Inst. of Music, in a decree of Nov. 8, 1793; it was organized as the Paris Cons. in a decree of Aug. 3, 1795. Sarrette, having gained his end, assumed the captaincy of the 103rd Regiment; but the board of directors (5 inspectors and 4 profs.) proved so incompetent that he was recalled to the directorship of the Cons. in 1796. By introducing advanced methods of instruction and establishing the school of declamation, the concert hall, the grand library, etc., he raised the Cons. to an institution of the 1st rank. At the Restoration in 1814 he was deprived of his position; nor would he accept it after the revolution of 1830, not wishing to oust his friend Cherubini.

BIBL.: P. Constant, *B. S. et les origines du Conservatoire national de musique et de déclamation* (Paris, 1895).

Sarro (or **Sarri**), **Domenico Natale,** Italian composer; b. Trani, Apulia, Dec. 24, 1679; d. Naples, Jan. 25, 1744. He settled in Naples and studied at the Conservatorio di S. Onofrio. From 1704 to 1707 he was vicemaestro di cappella at the court; in 1725, became its vice-maestro, and in 1735, assumed the duties of maestro di cappella when Mancini fell ill; upon Mancini's death in 1737, Sarro formally assumed the post. From 1728 he was also maestro di cappella of the city. Sarro was one of the principal Neapolitan composers of his day. His output includes 28 secular operas, several sacred operas and oratorios, serenatas, cantatas, and a Flute Concerto.

Sarti, Giuseppe, noted Italian composer, nicknamed **"Il Domenichino";** b. Faenza (baptized), Dec. 1, 1729; d. Berlin, July 28, 1802. He took music lessons in Padua with Valotti; when he was 10, he went to Bologna to continue his studies with Padre Martini. Returning to Faenza, he was organist at the Cathedral (1748–52); in 1752 he was appointed director of the theater in Faenza; that same year his 1st opera, *Pompeo in Armenia,* was performed. His next opera, *Il Re pastore,* was staged in Venice in 1753 with great success. Toward the end of 1753 he went to Copenhagen as a conductor of Pietro Mingotti's opera troupe. His work impressed the King of Denmark, Frederik V, and in 1755 he was named court Kapellmeister. He subsequently was made director of the Italian Opera, but it was closed in 1763; he then was appointed director of court music. In 1765 he was sent by the King to Italy to engage singers for the reopening of the Opera, but Frederik's death aborted the project. Sarti remained in Italy, where he served as maestro di coro at the Pietà Cons. in Venice (1766–67). In 1768 he returned to Copenhagen, where he resumed his duties as director of the royal chapel; from 1770 to 1775 he was conductor of the court theater. He then returned to Italy with his wife, the singer Camilla Passi, whom he had married in Copenhagen. He became director of the Cons. dell'Ospedaletto in Venice in 1775. In 1779 he entered the competition for the position of maestro di cappella at Milan Cathedral, winning it against a number of competitors, including Paisiello. By this time his prestige as a composer and as a teacher was very high. Among his numerous pupils was Cherubini. In 1784 he was engaged by Catherine the Great as director of the Imperial chapel in St. Petersburg. On his way to Russia, he passed through Vienna, where he was received with honors by the Emperor Joseph II; he also met Mozart, who quoted a melody from Sarti's opera *Fra i due litiganti* in *Don Giovanni.* His greatest success in St. Petersburg was *Armida e Rinaldo* (Jan. 26, 1786), remodeled from an earlier opera, *Armida abbandonata,* originally performed in Copenhagen in 1759; the leading role was sung by the celebrated Portuguese mezzo-soprano

Luiza Todi, but she developed a dislike of Sarti, and used her powerful influence with Catherine the Great to prevent his reengagement. However, he was immediately engaged by Prince Potemkin, and followed him to southern Russia and Moldavia during the military campaign against Turkey; on the taking of Ochakov, Sarti wrote an ode to the Russian liturgical text of thanksgiving, and it was performed in Jan. 1789 at Jassy, Bessarabia, with the accompaniment of cannon shots and church bells. Potemkin offered him a sinecure as head of a singing school in Ekaterinoslav, but Sarti did not actually teach there. After Potemkin's death in 1791, his arrangements with Sarti were honored by the court of St. Petersburg; in 1793 he was reinstated as court composer and was named director of a conservatory. Sarti's operas enjoyed considerable success during his lifetime but sank into oblivion after his death. He was an adept contrapuntist, and excelled in polyphonic writing; his *Fuga a otto voci* on the text of a *Kyrie* is notable. He was also astute in his adaptation to political realities. In Denmark he wrote singspiels in Danish; in Russia he composed a Requiem in memory of Louis XVI in response to the great lamentation at the Russian Imperial Court at the execution of the French king (1793). He also composed an offering to the Emperor Paul, whose daughters studied music with Sarti. After Paul's violent death at the hands of the palace guard, Sarti decided to leave Russia, but died in Berlin on his way to Italy. In 1796 Sarti presented to the Russian Academy of Sciences an apparatus to measure pitch (the so-called St. Petersburg tuning fork).

WORKS: *Pompeo in Armenia*, dramma per musica (Faenza, Carnival 1752); *Il Re pastore*, dramma per musica (Venice, Carnival 1753); *Vologeso*, dramma per musica (Copenhagen, Carnival 1754); *Antigono*, dramma per musica (Copenhagen, Oct. 14, 1754; some arias by other composers); *Ciro riconosciuto*, dramma per musica (Copenhagen, Dec. 21, 1754); *Arianna e Teseo*, dramma per musica (Copenhagen, Carnival 1756); *Anagilda*, dramma per musica (Copenhagen, Fall 1758); *Armida abbandonata*, dramma per musica (Copenhagen, 1759; later version as *Armida e Rinaldo*, St. Petersburg, Jan. 26, 1786); *Achille in Sciro*, dramma per musica (Copenhagen, 1759); *Andromaca*, dramma per musica (Copenhagen, 1759?); *Filindo*, pastorale eroica (Copenhagen, 1760); *Astrea placata*, festa teatrale (Copenhagen, Oct. 17, 1760); *La Nitteti*, dramma per musica (Copenhagen, Oct. 12, 1760); *Issipile*, dramma per musica (Copenhagen, 1760?); *Alessandro nell'Indie*, dramma per musica (Copenhagen, 1761); *Semiramide*, dramma per musica (Copenhagen, Fall 1762); *Didone abbandonata*, dramma per musica (Copenhagen, Winter 1762); *Narciso*, dramma pastorale (Copenhagen, Carnival 1763); *Cesare in Egitto*, dramma per musica (Copenhagen, Fall 1763); *Il naufragio di Cipro*, dramma pastorale (Copenhagen, 1764); *Il gran Tamerlano*, tragedia per musica (Copenhagen, 1764); *Ipermestra*, dramma per musica (Rome, Carnival 1766); *La Giardiniera brillante*, intermezzo (Rome, Jan. 3, 1768); *L'Asile de l'amour*, dramatic cantata (Copenhagen, July 22, 1769); *La Double Méprise, ou, Carlile et Fany*, comédie mêlée d'ariettes (Copenhagen, July 22, 1769); *Soliman den Anden*, singspiel (Copenhagen, Oct. 8, 1770); *Le Bal*, opéra comique (Copenhagen, 1770); *Il tempio d'eternità*, festa teatrale (Copenhagen, 1771); *Demofoonte*, dramma per musica (Copenhagen, Jan. 30, 1771); *Tronfølgen i Sidon*, lyrisk tragicomedia (Copenhagen, April 4, 1771); *Il Re pastore*, dramma per musica (Copenhagen, 1771; a different score from the one of 1753); *La clemenza di Tito*, dramma per musica (Padua, June 1771); *Deucalion og Pyrrha*, singspiel (Copenhagen, March 19, 1772); *Aglae, eller Støtten*, singspiel (Copenhagen, Feb. 16, 1774); *Kierlighedsbrevene*, singspiel (Copenhagen, March 22, 1775); *Farnace*, dramma per musica (Venice, 1776); *Le gelosie villane* (*Il Feudatario*), dramma giocoso (Venice, Nov. 1776); *Ifigenia*, dramma per musica (Rome, Carnival 1777); *Medonte re di Epiro*, dramma per musica (Florence, Sept. 8, 1777); *Il Militare bizzarro*, dramma giocoso (Venice, Dec. 27, 1777); *Olimpiade*, dramma per musica (Florence, 1778); *Scipione*, dramma per musica (Mestre, Fall 1778); *I contratempi*, dramma giocoso (Venice, Nov. 1778); *Adriano*

in Siria, dramma per musica (Rome, Dec. 26, 1778); *L'ambizione delusa*, intermezzo (Rome, Feb. 1779); *Mitridate a Sinope*, dramma per musica (Florence, Fall 1779); *Achille in Sciro*, dramma per musica (Florence, Fall 1779); *Siroe*, dramma per musica (Turin, Dec. 26, 1779); *Giulio Sabino*, dramma per musica (Venice, Jan. 1781); *Demofoonte*, dramma per musica (Rome, Carnival 1782; a different score from the one of 1771); *Didone abbandonata*, dramma per musica (Padua, June 1782; a different score from the one of 1762); *Alessandro e Timoteo*, dramma per musica (Parma, April 6, 1782); *Fra i due litiganti il terzo gode*, dramma giocoso (Milan, Sept. 14, 1782; subsequently perf. under various titles); *Attalo re di Bitinia*, dramma per musica (Venice, Dec. 26, 1782); *Idalide*, dramma per musica (Milan, Jan. 8, 1783); *Erifile*, dramma per musica (Pavia, Carnival 1783); *Il trionfo della pace*, dramma per musica (Mantua, May 10, 1783); *Olimpiade*, dramma per musica (Rome, 1783; a different score from the one of 1778); *Gli Amanti consolati*, opera comica (St. Petersburg, Oct. 30, 1785); *Armida e Rinaldo*, dramma per musica (St. Petersburg, Jan. 26, 1786; based upon *Armida abbandonata* of 1759); *Castore e Polluce*, dramma per musica (St. Petersburg, Oct. 3, 1786); *Zenoclea*, azione teatrale (1786; not performed); *Alessandro nell'Indie*, dramma per musica (Palermo, Winter 1787; a different score from the one of 1761); *Cleomene*, dramma per musica (Bologna, Dec. 27, 1788); *The Early Reign of Oleg*, Russian opera to a libretto by Catherine the Great (St. Petersburg, Oct. 22, 1790; in collaboration with V. Pashkevich); *Il trionfo d'Atalanta* (1791; not performed); *Andromeda*, dramma per musica (St. Petersburg, Nov. 4, 1798); *Enea nel Lazio*, dramma per musica (St. Petersburg, Oct. 26, 1799); *La Famille indienne en Angleterre*, opera (St. Petersburg, 1799); *Les Amours de Flore et de Zéphire*, ballet anacréontique (Gatchina, Sept. 19, 1800); also several secular cantatas, masses, Requiems, Te Deums, etc.; instrumental works, including syms. and chamber music.

BIBL.: G. Pasolini, *G. S.* (Faenza, 1883); C. Thrane, "S. in Kopenhagen," *Sammelbände der Internationalen Musik-Gesellschaft*, III (1901–2); A. Untersteiner, "G. S.," *Gazzetta Musicale di Milano*, LVII (1902); C. Rivalta, *G. S., Musicista faentino del secolo XVIII* (Faenza, 1928); F. Samory, *A G. S. nel 2° centenario di sua nascita* (Faenza, 1929); G. Fesetchko, "G. S.," *Sovietskaya Muzyka* (Dec. 1950); R.A. Mooser, *Annales de la musique et des musiciens en Russie au XVIIIᵉ siècle* (vol. II, Geneva, 1951); D. Lehmann, "Zwischen S. und Rasumowski, Mozart im russischen Musikleben des 18. Jahrhunderts," *Acta Mozartiana*, II/2–3 (1955); H. O'Douwes, "De russische jaren van G. S.," *Mens en melodie*, XII (1957); M. Selden, "Laurels for Catherine the Great (The Early Reign of Oleg)," *Opera News*, XXIII/20 (1959); R. Jones, *A Performing Edition and Discussion of G. S.'s Te Deum in D* (diss., Stanford Univ., 1966); W. Mitchell, "G. S. and Mozart's Quartet K421," *Current Musicology*, no. 9 (1969).

Sartori, Claudio, eminent Italian music scholar and bibliographer; b. Brescia, April 1, 1913. He received an arts degree in 1934 from the Univ. of Pavia with a thesis in music history; then studied with Gérold at the Univ. of Strasbourg and with Vittadini at the Pavia Cons. He served as an assistant librarian at the Bologna Cons. (1938–42); in 1943 he was appointed prof. of Italian literature there; in 1967 he assumed a similar professorship at the Milan Cons. He founded and became director of the Ufficio Ricerche Musicali in 1965; its aim was to conduct a thorough codification of Italian musical sources, providing information on all MSS and publ. music in Italy before 1900, on all publ. librettos in Italy down to 1800, and on all literature on music in Italy. In addition to this invaluable compilation, he also served as ed.-in-chief of *Dizionario Ricordi della musica e dei musicisti* (Milan, 1959).

WRITINGS: *Il R. Conservatorio di Musica G.B. Martini di Bologna* (Florence, 1942); *Bibliografia delle opere musicali stampate da Ottaviano Petrucci* (Florence, 1948; later continued as "Nuove conclusive aggiunte alla 'Bibliografia del Petrucci,'" *Collectanea Historiae Musicae*, I, 1953); *Bibliografia* *della musica strumentale italiana stampata in Italia fino al 1700* (2 vols., Florence, 1952 and 1968); *Monteverdi* (Brescia, 1953); *Catalogo delle musiche della Cappella del Duomo di Milano* (Milan, 1957); *Riccardo Malipiero* (Milan, 1957); *Casa Ricordi 1808–1958* (Milan, 1958); *Dizionario degli editori musicali italiani* (Florence, 1958); *Giacomo Puccini a Monza* (Monza, 1958); *Puccini* (Milan, 1958); ed. *Puccini Symposium* (Milan, 1959); *Assisi: La Cappella della Basilica di S. Francesco: Catalogo del fondo musicale nella Biblioteca comunale di Assisi* (Milan, 1962); ed. *L'enciclopedia della musica* (Milan, 1963–64); *Commemorazione di Ottaviano de' Petrucci* (Fossombrone, 1966); *Giacomo Carissimi: Catalogo delle opere attribuite* (Milan, 1975); ed., with F. Lesure, *Bibliografia della musica italiana vocale profana pubblicata dal 1500 al 1700* (Geneva, 1978).

Sartorio, Antonio, important Italian composer; b. Venice, 1630; d. there, Dec. 30, 1680. His 1st opera, *Gl' amori infruttuosi di Pirro,* was performed in Venice on Jan. 4, 1661; his second opera, *Seleuco* (Venice, Jan. 16, 1666), established his reputation. In 1666 he went to Germany to take up the post of Kapellmeister to Duke Johann Friedrich of Braunschweig-Lüneburg, who maintained his court in Hannover. He held this post until 1675, but continued to make regular visits to Venice to oversee productions of his operas. It was in Venice that he brought out his most famous opera, *L'Adelaide,* on Feb. 19, 1672. He returned to Venice permanently in 1675; in 1676 he was appointed vice-maestro di cappella at San Marco, a position he held until his death. Sartorio was a leading representative of the Venetian school of opera; his operas are notable for their arias, which he composed in a varied and effective manner.

Works: Operas (all 1st perf. in Venice unless otherwise given): *Gl'amori infruttuosi di Pirro* (Jan. 4, 1661); *Seleuco* (Jan. 16, 1666); *La prosperità d'Elio Seiano* (Jan. 15, 1667); *La caduta d'Elio Seiano* (Feb. 3, 1667); *L'Ermengarda regina de' Longobardi* (Dec. 26, 1669); *L'Adelaide* (Feb. 19, 1672); *L'Orfeo* (Dec. 14, 1672); *Massenzio* (Jan. 25, 1673); *Alcina* (c.1674; not perf.); *Giulio Cesare in Egitto* (Dec. 17, 1676); *Antonino e Pompeiano* (1677); *L'Anacreonte tiranno* (1677); *Ercole su'l Termodonte* (1678); *I duo tiranni al soglio* (Jan. 15, 1679); *La Flora* (music completed by M.A. Ziani; Carnival 1681); a number of cantatas and sacred vocal works; publ. 23 *Salmi a due chori ma accomodati all' uso della serenissima cappella ducale di S. Marco* for 8 Voices (Venice, 1680). **BIBL.:** H. Wolff, *Die Venezianische Oper in der zweiten Hälfte des 17. Jahrhunderts* (Berlin, 1937); S. Worsthorne, *Venetian Opera in the Seventeenth Century* (Oxford, 1954).

Sartorius (real name, **Schneider**), **Paul,** German organist and composer; b. Nuremberg (baptized), Nov. 16, 1569; d. Innsbruck, Feb. 28, 1609. He studied with Lechner in Nuremberg; then went to Rome for further study; was organist at the court chapel of Archduke Maximilian II of Austria in Mergentheim, Franconia (1594–1602) and in Innsbruck (1602–9).

Works: *Missae tres* for 8 Voices (Munich, 1599); *Madrigali libro primo* for 5 Voices (1600); *Neue teutsche Liedlein, nach Art der welschen Canzonette* for 4 Voices (Nuremberg, 1601): *Sonetti spirituali* for 6 Voices (Nuremberg, 1601); *Sacrae cantiones sive motecta* for 6 to 8, 10, and 12 Voices (Nuremberg, 1602); other works in contemporary collections.

Sáry, László, Hungarian composer; b. Győr, Jan. 1, 1940. He studied at the Budapest Academy of Music with Endre Szervánszky; after graduation in 1966, he helped to found the Budapest New Music Studio (1970). His works represent various contemporary trends, ranging from the music of Christian Wolff to the American minimalists.

Works: Orch.: *Canzone solenne* (1970); *Immaginario No. 1* (1971); *Diana búcsúja* (Diana's Farewell) for Chamber Orch. (1976); *Music for 24 Strings and 24 Winds: Hommage à Szervánszky* (1977); *Párhuzamos mozgások* (Parallel Movements) for Chamber Orch. (1981); *In memoriam Igor Stravinsky* for 24 Wind Instruments (1981); *Hyperion sorsdala* (Hyperion's Song of Destiny) for 24 String Instruments (1985–86); *Tükör-képek* (Mirror Images) for 24 Strings and 24 Winds (1986); *Polyphonie* for 18 Strings and 10 Winds (1986). **Chamber Ensemble:** *Polyrhythmia* for 100 Bells and 10 Players (1979); *Discussions* (1980); *Pentagram* for 5 Percussion Groups and Prepared Piano (1982); *Előjáték és hat miniatűr* (Prelude and Six Miniatures) for 5 Percussion Groups (1982); *Hölderlin tornya* (Hölderlin's Tower; 1985); *Az ismétlődő ötös* (Fives Repeated; 1985). **Chamber:** *Variazioni* for Clarinet and Piano (1965); *Catacoustics* for 2 Pianos (1967); *Pezzo concertato* for Flute and Piano (1967); *Fluttuazioni* for Violin and Piano (1967); *Incanto* for 5 Saxophones (1969); *Versetti* for Organ and Percussion (1970); *Sonanti No. 2* for Flute and Percussion (1970); *Image* for Clarinet, Cello, and Piano (1972); *Az ég virágai* (Flowers of Heaven) for 1 to 4 Pianos (1973); *Oda egy feketerigó halálára* (Ode on the Death of a Blackbird) for Brass Quintet (1982); *Egy akkordsor forgatókönyve* (Scenario of a Series of Chords) for Piano(s) and Flute(s) (1982); *Kettős végtelen* (Double Infinity) for 2 Cimbaloms (1986); String Quartet in 4 Movements with Piano in the 4th movement (1986); *In All Eternity* for String Quartet (1986); *Az elhagyott kert éneke* (Song of the Deserted Garden) for String Quartet and Alto Flute (1986); *és a Nap?* (and the Sun?) for String Quartet (1986); Variations for String Quartet (1986–88); also works for Solo Instruments; pieces for Unspecified Instruments. **Vocal:** *Lamento* for 5 Voices (1965); *Három madrigál* (3 Madrigals) for 5 Voices or Chamber Choir (1966); *Quartetto* for Flute, Violin, Cimbalom, and Soprano (1968); *Incanto* for 5 Voices (1969); Cantata No. 1 for Chamber Choir, Soprano, and Instrumental Ensemble (1969); *Hommage aux ancêtres* for 6 Voices, 3 Trumpets, and 3 Trombones (1970); *Psalmus* for Soprano and a Melody Instrument (1972); *In sol* for 4-part Vocal Ensemble (1975); *Lied in lyd* for Chamber Choir and Alto and Bass Solo (1975); *Hangok fehérben* (Voices in White) for Chamber Choir (1975); *Variáciok 14 hang fölött* (Variations on 14 Pitches) for Soprano and Piano (1975); *Dob és tánc* (Drum and Dance) for 24-part Women's Chorus (1975); *A hangzók változásai* (Mutations of the Sounds of Speech) for Mixed Chorus and Solos and Strings (1979); *Socrates utolsó tanítása* (Socrates's Last Teaching) for Soprano and Piano (1980); *Imitatio homophona* for Soprano and 3 Identical Instruments (1982); *Hold-ének* (Moon-Song) for Mixed Chorus and Soprano and Bass Solo (1982); *Kánon a felkelő naphoz* (Canon to the Rising Sun) for 4- or 6-part Chorus of Equal Voices or Instrumental Ensemble (1982); *Magnificat* for Soprano and Melody Instrument (1982; rev. 1986); also collaborative works, including *Hommage à Dohnányi* for Chamber Ensemble (1979; with Z. Jeney, B. Dukay, and L. Vidovszky).

Sás (Orchassal), Andrés, French-born Peruvian composer; b. Paris, April 6, 1900; d. Lima, July 25, 1967. He went to Brussels, where he studied harmony at the Anderlecht Academy, violin with Marchot, chamber music with Miry, and music history with Closson at the Cons., and counterpoint and fugue privately with Imbert. In 1924 he was engaged by the Peruvian government to teach violin at the National Academy of Music in Lima; in 1928 he returned temporarily to Belgium; the following year, settled in Lima permanently; married the Peruvian pianist Lily Rosay, and with her established the Sás-Rosay Academy of Music. He became profoundly interested in Peruvian folk music, and collected folk melodies; made use of many of them in his own compositions.

Works: Stage: Incidental music to Molière's *Le Malade imaginaire* (1943). **Ballets:** *La señora del pueblo* (Viña del Mar, Chile, Jan. 20, 1946); *El hijo pródigo* (1948). **Orch.:** *Canción india* (1927); *3 estampas del Perú* (1936); *Poema indio* (1941); *Sueño de Zamba* (1943); *Danza gitana* (1944); *La patrona del pueblo* (1945); *La parihuana* (1946); *Las seis edades de la Tía Conchita* (1947); *La leyenda de la Isla de San Lorenzo* (1949); *Fantasía romántica* for Trumpet and Orch. (1950). **Chamber:** *Recuerdos* for Violin and Piano (also for Orch.; 1927); *Rapsodia peruana* for Violin and Piano (also for Orch.; 1928); *Sonata-Fantasía* for Flute and Piano (1934); String

Quartet (1938); *Cantos del Perú* for Violin and Piano (1941). PIANO: *Aires y Danzas del Perú* (2 albums, 1930 and 1945); *Suite peruana* (1931); *Himno y Danza* (1935); *Sonatina peruana* (1946); also numerous choruses and songs.

BIBL.: N. Slonimsky, *Music of Latin America* (N.Y., 1945).

Sass, Marie Constance, Belgian soprano; b. Oudenaarde, Jan. 26, 1834; d. Auteuil, near Paris, Nov. 8, 1907. She studied with Gevaert in Ghent, Ugalde in Paris, and Lamperti in Italy; made her operatic debut as Gilda in Venice (1852); then went to Paris, where she sang at the Théâtre-Lyrique (1859) and at the Opéra (from 1860), where she was the 1st Paris Elisabeth in the controversial mounting of *Tannhäuser* (1861) and where she created the roles of Selika in *L'Africaine* (1865) and Elisabeth de Valois in *Don Carlos* (1867); subsequently appeared at Milan's La Scala (1869–70). During her Paris years, she made appearances under the name Marie Sax until a lawsuit was brought against her by Adolphe Sax; thereafter she reverted to her real name, also using the name Sasse. She was married to **Castelmary** (1864–67). After retiring from the stage in 1877, she taught voice; died in abject poverty.

Sass, Sylvia, Hungarian soprano; b. Budapest, July 12, 1951. She was educated at the Franz Liszt Academy of Music in Budapest; upon graduation, she joined the Hungarian State Opera and made her debut as Gutrune (1972); later sang in Vienna, Salzburg, and Hamburg. In 1976 she made her 1st appearance at Covent Garden in London as Giselda; on March 17, 1977, she made her Metropolitan Opera debut in N.Y. as Tosca; also gave recitals.

Sassòli, Ada, Italian harpist; b. Bologna, Sept. 25, 1886; d. Rome, Dec. 3, 1946. She studied at the Bologna Cons.; then entered the class of A. Hasselmans at the Paris Cons., winning 1st prize for harp playing in 1902. She toured with Melba in England and Australia (1904–5); made several tours of the U.S.; appeared as a soloist with American orchs.; returned to Europe in 1916; was prof. of harp at the Santa Cecilia Cons. in Rome.

Satie, Erik (Alfred-Leslie), celebrated French composer who elevated his eccentricities and verbal virtuosity to the plane of high art; b. Honfleur, May 17, 1866; d. Paris, July 1, 1925. He received his early musical training from a local organist, Vinot, who was a pupil of Niedermeyer; at 13 he went to Paris, where his father was a music publisher, and received instruction in harmony from Taudou and in piano from Mathias; however, his attendance at the Cons. was only sporadic between 1879 and 1886. He played in various cabarets in Montmartre; in 1884 he publ. a piano piece which he numbered, with malice aforethought, op. 62. His whimsical ways and Bohemian manner of life attracted many artists and musicians; he met Debussy in 1891; joined the Rosicrucian Society in Paris in 1892 and began to produce short piano pieces with eccentric titles intended to ridicule modernistic fancies and Classical pedantries alike. Debussy thought highly enough of him to orchestrate 2 numbers from his piano suite *Gymnopédies* (1888). Satie was almost 40 when he decided to pursue serious studies at the Paris Schola Cantorum, taking courses in counterpoint, fugue, and orchestration with d'Indy and Roussel (1905–8). In 1898 he had moved to Arcueil, a suburb of Paris; there he held court for poets, singers, dancers, and musicians, among whom he had ardent admirers. Milhaud, Sauguet, and Desormière organized a group, which they called only half-facetiously "École d'Arcueil," in honor of Satie as master and leader. But Satie's eccentricities were not merely those of a Parisian poseur; rather, they were adjuncts to his esthetic creed, which he enunciated with boldness and total disregard for professional amenities (he was once brought to court for sending an insulting letter to a music critic). Interestingly enough, he attacked modernistic aberrations just as assiduously as reactionary pedantry, publishing "manifestos" in prose and poetry. Although he was dismissed by most serious musicians as an uneducated person who tried to conceal his ignorance of music with persiflage, he exercised a profound influ-

ence on the young French composers of the 1st quarter of the 20th century; moreover, his stature as an innovator in the modern idiom grew after his death, so that the avant-garde musicians of the later day accepted him as inspiration for their own experiments; thus "space music" could be traced back to Satie's *musique d'ameublement*, in which players were stationed at different parts of a hall playing different pieces in different tempi. The instruction in his piano piece *Vexations*, to play it 840 times in succession, was carried out literally in N.Y. on Sept. 9, 1963, by a group of 5 pianists working in relays overnight, thus setting a world's record for duration of any musical composition. When critics accused Satie of having no idea of form, he publ. *Trois Morceaux en forme de poire*, the eponymous pear being reproduced in color on the cover; other pieces bore self-contradictory titles, such as *Heures séculaires et instantanées* and *Crépuscule matinal de midi*; other titles were *Pièces froides, Embryons desséchés, Prélude en tapisserie, Préludes flasques (pour un chien), Descriptions automatiques*, etc. In his ballets he introduced jazz for the 1st time in Paris; at the performance of his ballet *Relâche* (Nov. 29, 1924), the curtain bore the legend "Erik Satie is the greatest musician in the world; whoever disagrees with this notion will please leave the hall." He publ. a facetious autobiographical notice as *Mémoires d'un amnésique* (1912); N. Wilkins tr. and ed. *The Writings of Erik Satie* (London, 1980).

WORKS: STAGE: *Geneviève de Brabant*, marionette opera (1899); *Le Piège de Méduse*, lyric comedy (1913); also 3 ballets: *Parade* (Paris, May 18, 1917), *Mercure* (Paris, June 15, 1924), and *Relâche* (Paris, Nov. 29, 1924); incidental music to *Le Fils de étoiles* (1891; prelude reorchestrated by Ravel, 1913), *Le Prince de Byzance* (1891), *Le Nazaréen* (1892), *La Porte héroïque du ciel* (1893), and *Pousse l'Amour* (1905). ORCH.: *Jack in the Box* (1900; orchestrated by Milhaud, 1920); *En habit de cheval* (1911); *Cinq Grimaces* (1914); *Trois petites pièces montées* (1919; also for Piano, 4-hands, 1920); *La belle excentrique* (1920). CHORAL: *Messe des Pauvres*, with Organ or Piano (1895; orchestrated by D. Diamond, 1960); *Socrate* for 4 Sopranos and Chamber Orch. (1918; Paris, Feb. 14, 1920). PIANO: 3 *Sarabandes* (1887–88; orch. by Caby); *Trois Gymnopédies* (1888; Nos. 1 and 3 orchestrated by Debussy, 1896; No. 2 orchestrated by H. Murrill and by Roland-Manuel); *Trois Gnossiennes* (1890; orchestrated by Lanchbery; No. 3 orch. by Poulenc, 1939); *Trois Préludes* from *Le Fils des étoiles* (1891; orchestrated by Roland-Manuel); 9 *Danses gothiques* (1893); *Quatre Préludes* (1893; Nos. 1 and 3 orchestrated by Poulenc, 1939); *Prélude de la Porte héroïque du ciel* (1894; orchestrated by Roland-Manuel, 1912); 2 *Pièces froides* (1897); *Valse, Je te veux* (c.1900; arranged for Violin and Orch.; also arranged for Orch. by C. Lambert); 3 *Nouvelles Pièces froides* (n.d.); *Le Poisson rêveur* (1901; arranged for Piano and Orch. by Caby); *Trois Morceaux en forme de poire* for 4-Hands (1903; orchestrated by Désormière); *Douze Petits Chorals* (c.1906); *Passacaille* (1906); *Prélude en tapisserie* (1906); *Aperçus désagréables* for 4-Hands (1908–12); *Deux Rêveries nocturnes* (1910–11); *En habit de cheval* for 4-Hands (1911); *Trois Véritables Préludes flasques (pour un chien)* (1912); 3 *Descriptions automatiques* (1913); 3 *Embryons desséchés* (1913); 3 *Croquis et agaceries d'un gros bonhomme en bois* (1913); 3 *Chapitres tournés en tous sens* (1913); 3 *Vieux Séquins et vieilles cuirasses* (1913); *Enfantines* (1913); 6 *Pièces de la période 1906–13*; 21 *Sports et divertissements* (1914); *Heures séculaires et instantanées* (1914); *Trois Valses du précieux dégoûté* (1914; orchestrated by Greenbaum); *Avant-dernières pensées* (1915); *Parade*, suite for 4-Hands after the ballet (1917); *Sonatine bureaucratique* (1917); 5 *Nocturnes* (1919); *Premier Menuet* (1920). VIOLIN AND PIANO: *Choses vues à droite et à gauche (sans lunettes)* (1914). VOICE AND PIANO: *Trois Mélodies de 1886; Trois Poèmes d'amour* (1914); *Trois Mélodies* (1916); *Ludions*, 5 songs (1923).

BIBL.: C. van Vechten, "E. S.," *Interpreters and Interpretations* (N.Y., 1917); R. Chennevière, "E. S. and the Music of Irony," *Musical Quarterly* (Oct. 1919); W. Roberts, "The Problem of S.," *Music & Letters* (Oct. 1923); 2 special issues of the *Revue Musicale* (March 1924; June 1925); W. Dankert, "Der Klassizismus E. S.s und seine geistesgeschichtliche Stellung," *Zeitschrift für Musikwissenschaft* (Nov. 1929); P.-D. Templier, *E. S.* (Paris, 1932); D. Milhaud, "Notes sur E. S.," *Les Œuvres nouvelles* (vol. 6, N.Y., 1946); R. Myers, *E. S.* (London, 1948); A. Rey, *E. S.* (Paris, 1974); G. Wehmeyer, *E. S.* (Berlin, 1974); M. Brendel, *E. S.* (1982); V. Lajoinie, *E. S.* (Lausanne, 1985); J.-J. Barbier, *Au piano avec E. S.* (Paris, 1986); M. Rosenthal, *S., Ravel, Poulenc: An Intimate Memoir* (Madras and N.Y., 1987); A. Gillmor, *E. S.* (Boston, 1988); R. Orledge, *S. the Composer* (Cambridge, 1990).

Satter, Gustav, Austrian pianist and composer; b. Rann, Slovenia, Feb. 12, 1832; place and date of death unknown. He studied in Vienna and Paris; undertook a pianistic tour in the U.S. and Brazil (1854–60) with surprising success; went back to Paris, where Berlioz warmly praised his music; then lived in Vienna, Dresden, Hannover, and Stockholm.

WORKS: Opera, *Olanthe;* overtures: *Lorelei, Julius Cæsar, An die Freude;* 2 syms.; symphonic poem, *George Washington;* much chamber music; 3 sonatas, studies, waltzes, etc., for piano; about 160 opus numbers in all.

BIBL.: Anonymous (most likely Satter), *The Life and Works of G. S.* (Macon, Ga., 1879).

Sattler, Heinrich, German organist, teacher, and composer; b. Quedlinburg, April 3, 1811; d. Oct. 17, 1891. He devoted himself mainly to teaching; from 1861, was on the staff of the Oldenburg Seminary. He publ. a treatise, *Die Orgel* (5 eds.); a book, *Erinnerung an Mozarts Leben und Werke* (1856); composed an oratorio, *Die Sachsentaufe;* 2 cantatas, *Triumph des Glaubens* and *Pfingstkantate;* sacred works; chamber music; many organ pieces.

Satz, Ilya, Russian composer; b. Chernobyl, Kiev Oblast, April 30, 1875; d. Moscow, Dec. 24, 1912. He studied cello in Kiev; then took lessons in composition with Taneyev in Moscow; his general education was desultory. He traveled in Europe in 1900; then made a tour as a cellist through Siberia. He returned to Moscow in 1903; in 1905 he became music director of the Studio of the Moscow Art Theater, and wrote incidental music for new plays, including Maeterlinck's *Blue Bird* and Andreyev's *A Man's Life;* also composed ballet music for Salome's dance; the ballet *The Goat-Footed (The Dance of the Satyrs)* was reorchestrated and prepared for performance by Glière. Satz had a talent for the grotesque; a lack of technique prevented his development into a major composer. A memorial vol., *Ilya Satz,* with articles by Glière and several members of the Moscow Art Theater, was publ. in Moscow in 1923.

Sauer, Emil (Georg Konrad) von, eminent German pianist and pedagogue; b. Hamburg, Oct. 8, 1862; d. Vienna, April 27, 1942. He studied with Nikolai Rubinstein in Moscow (1879–81), and Liszt in Weimar (1884–85); made numerous European tours; played in the U.S. in 1898–99 and 1908. From 1901 to 1907, and again from 1915, he was a prof. at the Meisterschule für Klavierspiel in Vienna; from 1908 to 1915 he lived in Dresden; he appeared in concerts until 1936, and then retired to Vienna. He was ennobled for his services to music. He wrote 2 piano concertos, 2 piano sonatas, and many studies for piano; ed. the complete works of Brahms and pedagogical works of Pischna, Plaidy, Kullak, and others. He publ. an autobiography, *Meine Welt* (Stuttgart, 1901).

Sauguet, Henri (real name, **Jean Pierre Poupard**), French composer; b. Bordeaux, May 18, 1901; d. Paris, June 22, 1989. He assumed his mother's maiden name as his own. He was a pupil of Joseph Canteloube; in 1922 he went to Paris, where he studied with Koechlin; became associated with Erik Satie, and formed a group designated as the École d'Arcueil (from the locality near Paris where Satie lived). In conformity with the principles of utilitarian music, he wrote sophisticated works in an outwardly simple manner; his 1st conspicuous success was the production of his ballet *La Chatte* by Diaghilev in 1927. He was elected a member of the Académie des Beaux Arts in 1975.

WORKS: STAGE: OPERAS: *Le Plumet du colonel* (Paris, April 24, 1924); *La Contrebasse* (1930; Paris, 1932); *La Chartreuse de Parme* (1927–36; Paris, March 16, 1939; rev. 1968); *La Gageure imprévue* (1942; Paris, July 4, 1944); *Les Caprices de Marianne* (Aix-en-Provence, July 20, 1954); *Le Pain des autres* (1967–74); *Boule de suif* (Lyons, 1978); *Tistou les pouces verts* (Paris, 1980). **BALLETS:** *La Chatte* (Monte Carlo, April 30, 1927); *Paul et Virginie* (Paris, April 15, 1943); *Les Mirages* (Paris, Dec. 15, 1947); *Cordelia* (Paris, May 7, 1952); *L'As de cœur* (1960); *Paris* (1964); *L'Imposteur ou Le Prince et le mendiant* (1965). **ORCH.:** 3 piano concertos (1934; 1948; 1961–63); 4 syms.: No. 1, *Expiatoire,* in memory of innocent war victims (1945; Paris, Feb. 8, 1948); No. 2, *Allégorique* (1949); No. 3, *INR* (1955); No. 4, *Du troisième âge* (1971); *Orphée* for Violin and Orch. (Aix-en-Provence, July 26, 1953); *Mélodie concertante* for Cello and Orch. (1963); *The Garden Concerto* for Harmonica and Orch. (1970); *Reflets sur feuilles* for Harp, Piano, Percussion, and Orch. (1979). **CHAMBER:** *Alentours saxophoniques* for Alto Saxophone, Wind Ensemble, and Piano (1976); *Ne moriatur in aeternum* "in memoriam André Jolivet" for Trumpet and Organ (1979); *Sonate d'église* for Organ and String Quintet (1985); *Musique pour Cendrars* for Piano and String Quintet (1986); 3 string quartets (1926, 1948, 1979); also vocal works, including an oratorio, *Chant pour une ville meurtrie* (1967) and songs; piano pieces.

BIBL.: M. Schneider, *H. S.* (Paris, 1959); F.-Y. Bril, *H. S.* (Paris, 1967).

Saunders, Arlene, American soprano and teacher; b. Cleveland, Oct. 5, 1935. She studied at Baldwin-Wallace College and in N.Y.; made her operatic debut as Rosalinde with the National Opera Co. in 1958; won the Vercelli Vocal Competition and made her European debut as Mimi at Milan's Teatro Nuovo in 1961; that same year she appeared as Giorgetta in *Il tabarro* at the N.Y. City Opera. In 1964 she joined the Hamburg State Opera, where she subsequently sang regularly and was made a Kammersängerin in 1967; also appeared as Pamina at the Glyndebourne Festival (1966), as Louise at the San Francisco Opera (1967), as the creator of the title role in Ginastera's *Beatrice Cenci* at the Opera Soc. in Washington, D.C. (Sept. 10, 1971), as Eva in her Metropolitan Opera debut in N.Y. (April 2, 1976), and as Minnie at London's Covent Garden (1980); in 1985 she made her farewell appearance in opera as the Marschallin at the Teatro Colón in Buenos Aires. She taught at Rutgers, the State Univ. of New Jersey (from 1987), and at the Abraham Goodman School in N.Y. (from 1987). Among her other roles were Sieglinde, Nedda, Desdemona, Tosca, and Santuzza.

Sauret, Emile, French violinist, pedagogue, and composer; b. Dun-le-Roi, Cher, May 22, 1852; d. London, Feb. 12, 1920. A child prodigy, he appears to have studied with Bériot at the Brussels Cons.; he also claimed to have been a pupil of Vieuxtemps and Wieniawski. He made his London debut at the age of 14; toured the U.S. in 1872, 1874, 1876, 1877, and 1895. After teaching at the Royal Academy of Music in London (1890–1903), he was on the faculty of the Chicago Musical College (1903–6); following a sojourn in Geneva and Berlin, he returned to London as a prof. at Trinity College of Music in 1908. In 1873 he married the pianist **Teresa Carreño** (divorced in 1876). He was a typical representative of the French school of violin playing, distinguished by grace, elegance, and excellent taste.

WORKS: VIOLIN AND ORCH.: *Souvenir de Moscou, Rapsodie russe, Rapsodie suédoise, Farfalla,* and *Elégie et Rondo.* **VIOLIN AND PIANO:** *Feuilles d'album, Pensées fugitives, Scènes champêtres, 20 grandes études, 12 études artistiques, 24 études-caprices;* publ. a method, *Gradus ad Parnassum du violoniste;* made about 25 transcriptions.

Sauveur, Joseph, French acoustician; b. La Flèche, March 24, 1653; d. Paris, July 9, 1716. A deaf-mute, learning to speak in his 7th year, he became a remarkable investigator in the realm of acoustics; in 1696, became a member of the Académie.

He was the 1st to calculate absolute vibration numbers, and to explain scientifically the phenomenon of overtones.

WRITINGS (all publ. in the *Mémoires* of the Académie): *Principes d'acoustique et de musique* (1700–1); *Application des sons harmoniques à la composition des jeux d'orgue* (1702); *Méthode générale pour former des systèmes tempérés . . .* (1707); *Table générale des systèmes tempérés* (1711); *Rapports des sons des cordes d'instruments de musique aux flèches des cordes* (1713).

Sauzay, (Charles-) Eugène, French violinist, teacher, and composer; b. Paris, July 14, 1809; d. there, Jan. 24, 1901. He studied with Baillot at the Paris Cons., winning the premier prix (1827); played in the orch. of the Société des Concerts du Cons. (from 1828) and in Baillot's string quartet (until 1840); then was active with his own chamber group; taught violin at the Cons. (1860–92). He publ. *Symphonie rustique; Études harmoniques* for Violin; numerous transcriptions; also the books *Études sur les quatuors de Haydn, Mozart, et Beethoven* (Paris, 1861; 2nd ed., 1884), *L'École de l'accompagnement* (Paris, 1869), and *Le Violon harmonique* (Paris, 1889).

Savage, Henry W(ilson), American impresario; b. New Durham, N.H., March 21, 1859; d. Boston, Nov. 29, 1927. He started in business as a real estate operator in Boston, where he took control of the Castle Square Opera House by default in 1894; founded his own company there to present opera in English in 1895, and subsequently gave performances in Chicago, N.Y., and other cities; with Maurice Grau, he produced opera in English at the Metropolitan Opera in N.Y. (1900). His Henry Savage Grand Opera Co. toured throughout the U.S. with an English-language production of *Parsifal* in 1904–5; subsequently made successful tours with Puccini's *Madama Butterfly* (1906) and *La fanciulla del West* (1911), and Lehár's *Die lustige Witwe* (1907).

Savard, (Marie-Gabriel-) Augustin, French music educator, father of **Marie-Emmanuel-Augustin Savard;** b. Paris, Aug. 21, 1814; d. there, June 7, 1881. He studied with Leborne and Bazin; in 1843 he was appointed prof. of solfège at the Paris Cons., and later taught harmony and thoroughbass. He was an excellent teacher; among his many foreign students was MacDowell. He publ. the manuals *Cours complet d'harmonie théorique et pratique* (2 vols., Paris, 1853, 1856) and *Principes de la musique* (Paris, 1861; very popular; 14th ed., 1913); its abridged version, *Premières notions de musique* (Paris, 1866), also went into numerous eds.

Savard, Marie-Emmanuel-Augustin, French composer and pedagogue, son of **(Marie-Gabriel-) Augustin Savard;** b. Paris, May 15, 1861; d. Lyons, Dec. 6, 1942. He studied at the Paris Cons. with Durand, Taudou, and Massenet; won the Prix de Rome in 1886 with the cantata *La Vision de Saul;* was director of the Lyons Cons. (1902–21).

WORKS: Lyric drama, *La Forêt* (Paris, 1910); 2 syms.; an overture, *Roi Lear; Poème* for Voice and Orch.; String Quartet; Violin Sonata; etc.

Savart, Félix, French acoustician; b. Mézières, June 30, 1791; d. Paris, March 16, 1841. He was a prof. of acoustics at the Collège de France; in 1821, was elected a member of the Académie.

WRITINGS: All publ. in the *Annales de Physique et de Chimie: Mémoire sur la construction des instruments à cordes et à archet* (1819, separate reprint; in German, 1844); *Sur la communication des mouvements vibratoires entre les corps solides* (1820); *Sur les vibrations de l'air* (1823); *Sur la voix humaine* (1825); *Sur la communication des mouvements vibratoires par les liquides* (1826); *Sur la voix des oiseaux* (1826); etc.

Saville, Frances, American soprano; b. San Francisco, Jan. 6, 1863; d. Burlingame, Calif., Nov. 8, 1935. She went early to Australia, where she made her debut in oratorio; continued her studies in Paris with Marchesi; in 1892 she made her operatic debut in Brussels; also appeared with the Carl Rosa Co. in England, at the Opéra-Comique in Paris, and in Vienna, Berlin, St. Petersburg, Warsaw, etc.; on Nov. 18, 1895, she made her debut as Juliette at the Metropolitan Opera in N.Y., on whose roster she remained through that season and again in 1899–1900; also sang with the Vienna Court Opera (1899–1903).

Savín, Francisco, Mexican conductor and composer; b. Mexico City, Nov. 18, 1929. He studied piano in Mexico City with José Velásquez (1944–53) and took conducting lessons with Scherchen and composition with Rodolfo Halffter (1955–56); continued his studies at the Prague Academy of Music, and also had composition lessons with Karel Janeček (1957–59). He was an assistant conductor of the Mexican National Sym. Orch. (1959–62) and principal conductor of the Xalapa Sym. Orch. (1963–67); was then director of the National Cons. of Music in Mexico City (1967–70); led conducting workshops there (from 1973).

WORKS: *Quetzalcoátl,* symphonic poem for 2 Narrators and Orch. (1957); *Metamorfosis* for Orch. (1962); *2 formas plásticas* for Wind Quintet (1964, 1965); *3 líricas* for Mezzo-soprano, Flute, Clarinet, Viola, Percussion, and Piano (1966); *Crececión* for Electronic Organ and Orch. (1969); *Monología de las Delicias* for 4 Female Voices and Orch. (1969); *Quasar 1* for Electronic Organ, Tape, and Percussion (1970).

Savine, Alexander, Serbian-American conductor, teacher, and composer; b. Belgrade, April 26, 1881; d. Chicago, Jan. 19, 1949. He studied in Belgrade with S. Mokranjac, and later studied voice at the Vienna Cons. with Pauline Lucca. He was an opera conductor in Berlin (1905–7); taught voice at the Musical Academy in Winnepeg, Canada (1908–12); settled in the U.S.; was director of the opera dept. at the Inst. of Musical Art in N.Y. (1922–24); in 1929 he moved to Chicago. He married in 1914 the soprano Lillian Blauvelt. He wrote the opera *Xenia* (Zürich, May 29, 1919); 4 symphonic poems; choruses; songs.

Sawallisch, Wolfgang, eminent German conductor; b. Munich, Aug. 26, 1923. He began piano study when he was 5; later pursued private musical training with Ruoff, Haas, and Sachse in Munich before entering military service during World War II (1942); then completed his musical studies at the Munich Hochschule für Musik. In 1947 he became répétiteur at the Augsburg Opera, making his conducting debut there in 1950; then was Generalmusikdirektor of the opera houses in Aachen (1953–58), Wiesbaden (1958–60), and Cologne (1960–63); also conducted at the Bayreuth Festivals (1957–61). From 1960 to 1970 he was chief conductor of the Vienna Sym. Orch.; made his 1st appearance in the U.S. with that ensemble in 1964; also was Generalmusikdirektor of the Hamburg State Phil. (1961–73). From 1970 to 1980 he was chief conductor of the Orch. de la Suisse Romande in Geneva; from 1971, also served as Generalmusikdirektor of the Bavarian State Opera in Munich, where he was named Staatsoperndirektor in 1982. In 1990 he was named music director of the Philadelphia Orch. effective with the 1993–94 season. He appeared as a guest conductor with a number of the world's major orchs. and opera houses. A distinguished representative of the revered Austro-German tradition, he has earned great respect for his unostentatious performances; he has also made appearances as a sensitive piano accompanist to leading singers of the day. His autobiography appeared as *Im Interesse der Deutlichkeit: Mein Leben mit der Musik* (Hamburg, 1988).

BIBL.: H. Krellmann, ed., *Stationen eines Dirigenten, W. S.* (Munich, 1983); G. Loney, "W. S.," *Musical America* (May 1989).

Sax, Adolphe (actually, **Antoine-Joseph**), Belgian inventor of the saxophone, son of **Charles-Joseph Sax;** b. Dinant, Nov. 6, 1814; d. Paris, Feb. 4, 1894. He acquired great skill in manipulating instruments from his early youth; his practical and imaginative ideas led him to undertake improvements of the clarinet and other wind instruments. He studied the flute and clarinet at the Brussels Cons.; in 1842 he went to Paris with a wind instrument of his invention, which he called the "saxophone," made of metal, with a single-reed mouthpiece and conical bore. He exhibited brass and woodwind instruments at the Paris Exposition of 1844, winning a silver medal; his father joined him in Paris, and together they continued the manufacture of new instruments; evolved the saxhorn (improved over the bugle-horn and ophicleide by replacing the keys with a valve mechanism) and the saxo-tromba, a hybrid instrument producing a tone midway between the bugle and the trumpet. Conservative critics and rival instrument makers ridiculed Sax's innovations, but Berlioz and others warmly supported him; he also won praise from Rossini. His instruments were gradually adopted by French military bands. Sax won a gold medal at the Paris Industrial Exposition of 1849. Financially, however, he was unsuccessful, and was compelled to go into bankruptcy in 1856 and again in 1873. He taught the saxophone at the Paris Cons. from 1858 to 1871, and also publ. a method for his instrument. He exhibited his instruments in London (1862) and received the Grand Prix in Paris (1867) for his improved instruments. Although Wieprecht, Červený, and others disputed the originality and priority of his inventions, legal decisions gave the rights to Sax; the saxophone became a standard instrument; many serious composers made use of it in their scores. The instrument fell into desuetude after Sax's death, but about 1918 a spectacular revival of the saxophone took place, when it was adopted in jazz bands; its popularity became worldwide; numerous methods were publ. and special schools established; and there appeared saxophone virtuosos for whom many composers wrote concertos.

BIBL.: O. Comettant, *Histoire d'un inventeur au XIXe siècle* (Paris, 1860); T. Lajarte, *Instruments S. et fanfares civiles* (Paris, 1876); J. Kool, *Das Saxophone* (Leipzig, 1931); A. Remy, *La Vie tourmentée d'A. S.* (Brussels, 1939); L. Kochnitzky, *A. S. and His Saxophone* (N.Y., 1949); M. Perrin, *Le Saxophone, Son histoire, sa technique et son utilisation dans l'orchestre* (Paris, 1955); J. Londeix, *125 ans de musique pour saxophone* (Paris, 1971); M. Haine, *A. S.: Sa vie, son œuvre, ses instruments de musique* (Brussels, 1980); W. Horwood, *A. S., 1814–1894: Life and Legacy* (Baldock, 1983).

Sax, Charles-Joseph, Belgian instrument maker, father of **Adolphe (Antoine-Joseph) Sax;** b. Dinant-sur-Meuse, Feb. 1, 1791; d. Paris, April 26, 1865. He began his career by manufacturing brass and woodwind instruments in Dinant-sur-Meuse; then established an instrument factory at Brussels in 1815, manufacturing not only wind instruments, but also pianos, harps, and guitars; his specialty, however, was brass instruments. He joined his son in Paris, and helped him to launch his revolutionary inventions.

Saxton, Robert, English composer; b. London, Oct. 8, 1953. He studied composition with Elisabeth Lutyens (1970–74), with Robin Holloway at Cambridge Univ. (1974–75), and with Robert Sherlaw Johnson at Oxford Univ. (B.Mus., 1975); then had lessons with Luciano Berio. His music reveals fine craftsmanship and harmonic invention.

WORKS: ORCH.: *Reflections of Narziss and Goldmund* (1975; also for 2 Chamber Groups); *Choruses to Apollo* (1980); *Traumstadt* (1980); *The Ring of Eternity* (London, Aug. 24, 1983); Concerto (London, Aug. 13, 1984); *In the Beginning* (London, Jan. 30, 1988). **VOCAL:** *La Promenade d'Automne* for Soprano and 7 Instruments (1972); *Where Are You Going to, My Pretty Maid?* for Soprano and 6 Instruments (1973); *What Does the Song Hope For?* for Soprano, 7 Instruments, and Tape (1974); *Brise marine* for Soprano, Piano, and Tape (1976); *Cantata on Poems of Hölderlin* for Tenor, Countertenor, and Piano (1979); Cantata No. 2 for Tenor, Oboe, and Piano (1980); *Éloge* for Soprano and 9 Instruments (1980); Cantata No. 3 for 2 Sopranos and Tape Delay (1981); *Chaconne* for Double Choir (1981); *The Child of Light,* carol (1985). **CHAMBER:** *Krystallen* for Flute and Piano (1973); *Echoes of the Glass Bead Game* for Wind Quintet (1975); *Poems for Mélisande* for Flute and Piano (1977); Sonatas for 2 Pianos (1977); *Arias* for Oboe and Piano (1977); *Study for a Sonata* for Flute, Oboe, Cello, and Harpsichord (1977); *Canzone* for 8 Instruments (1978);

Processions and Dances for 8 Instruments (1981); *Piccola musica per Luigi Dallapiccola* for 5 Instruments (1981); *The Sentinel of the Rainbow* for 6 Instruments (1984); *Circles of Light* for 15 Instruments (London, March 5, 1986). **SOLO INSTRUMENTS:** *Ritornelli and Intermezzi* for Piano (1972); 2 pieces for Piano (1976); *Toccata* for Cello (1978); Piano Sonata (1981); *Chiaroscuro* for Percussion (1981); *Fantasiestück* for Accordion (1982).

BIBL.: P. Griffiths, "A Little Light on R. S.," *Musical Times* (March 1986).

Sayão, Bidú (actually, **Balduina de Oliveira**), noted Brazilian soprano; b. Niteroi, near Rio de Janeiro, May 11, 1902. She studied with Elena Teodorini in Rio de Janeiro, and then with Jean de Reszke in Vichy and Nice. Returning to Brazil, she gave her 1st professional concert in Rio de Janeiro in 1925; in 1926 she sang the role of Rosina in *Il Barbiere di Siviglia* at the Teatro Municipal there. She made her American debut on Dec. 29, 1935, in a recital in N.Y. On Feb. 13, 1937, she sang Manon at her Metropolitan Opera debut in N.Y., earning enthusiastic reviews; remained on its roster until 1952. She retired in 1958. Her finest performances were in lyric roles in bel canto operas; especially memorable were her interpretations of Violetta in *La Traviata,* Gilda in *Rigoletto,* and Mimi in *La Bohème.* She also showed her versatility in coloratura parts, such as Lakmé; in France, she was described as "a Brazilian nightingale." She also sang vocal parts in several works of her great compatriot Villa-Lobos. She was a recipient of numerous honors from European royalty, and of the Palmes Académiques from the French government; in 1972 she was decorated a Commandante by the Brazilian government.

Saygun, Ahmed Adnan, Turkish teacher and composer; b. Izmir, Sept. 7, 1907; d. Istanbul, Jan. 6, 1991. He studied composition in Paris with E. Borrel at the Cons. and with Le Flem and d'Indy at the Schola Cantorum; returning to Turkey in 1931, he taught at the Istanbul Cons. (1936–39); accompanied Béla Bartók on a music-ethnological trip through Anatolia (1936). From 1964 he taught composition at the State Cons. in Ankara and from 1972 at the Istanbul State Cons. He wrote operas, including *Tasbebek* (Ankara, Dec. 27, 1934) and *Kerem* (1947; Ankara, March 1, 1953); also the oratorio *Yunus Emre* (Ankara, May 25, 1946), a Piano Concerto (1956), 4 syms. (1953, 1955, 1961, 1973), a Violin Concerto (1967), and chamber pieces.

Saylor, Bruce (Stuart), American composer; b. Philadelphia, April 24, 1946. He studied composition with Weisgall and Sessions at the Juilliard School in N.Y. (B.M., 1968; M.S., 1969); then took courses with Petrassi and Evangelisti at the Accademia di Santa Cecilia in Rome (1969–70); returning to the U.S., he enrolled at the City Univ. of N.Y. Graduate School as a composition student of Weisgall and Perle (Ph.D., 1978). He held teaching posts as lecturer at Queens College (1970–76) and instructor at N.Y. Univ. (1976–79). In 1979 he was appointed associate prof. at Queens College. In 1982–83 he held a Guggenheim fellowship. He publ. *The Writings of Henry Cowell* (Brooklyn, 1977).

WORKS: STAGE: OPERA: *My Kinsman, Major Molineux* (Pittsburgh, Aug. 28, 1976). **DANCE SCORES:** *Cycle* for Voice and Instruments (1978); *Inner World Out* for Clarinet, Violin, Viola, and Cello (1978); *Wildfire* for 2 Flutes and 2 Harps (1979). **ORCH.:** *Cantilena* for Strings (1965); *Notturno* for Piano and Orch. (1969); *Turns and Mordents* for Flute and Orch. (New Haven, Conn., March 6, 1977); *Paeans to Hyacinthus* (1980; Houston, Feb. 6, 1981). **CHAMBER:** Woodwind Quartet (1965); *Suite* for Viola (1967); *Conductus* for 3 Winds, 3 Strings, and Percussion (1970); Duo for Violin and Viola (1970); *Firescreen* for Flute, Cello, and Piano (1979); *St. Ulmo's Fire* for Flute and Harp (1980); *Saltarello* for Piano (1981); *Carillon Te Deum* for Bell Choir (1983); Trio for Clarinet, Viola, and Piano (Washington, D.C. June 20, 1989). **VOCAL:** *5 Songs* from "Whispers of Heav'nly Death" by Whitman for Soprano and String Quartet (1965–67); *To Autumn, To Winter* for Chorus and Orch. (1968); *Lyrics* for Soprano and Violin (1971); *Love-*

play for Mezzo-soprano, Flute, Viola, and Cello ad libitum (1974); *Songs from Water Street* for Mezzo-soprano, Viola, and Piano (1976–80); *The Waves*, dramatic monologue for Mezzo-soprano, Flute, Clarinet, Viola, and Cello, after Virginia Woolf (1981); 5 *Old Favorites* for Voice, Flute, and Piano (1983).

Sayn-Wittgenstein-Berleburg, Count Friedrich Ernst, German composer; b. Castle Sannerz, Fulda, June 5, 1837; d. Meran, April 16, 1915. He pursued a military career; also studied music with Julius Rietz in Leipzig; publ. *Szenen aus der Frithjofsage* for Voice and Orch.; also songs; wrote 2 operas: *Die Wolfenbraut* (Graz, 1879) and *Antonius und Kleopatra* (Graz, 1883).

Sayve, Lambert de, Flemish composer; b. Sayve, near Liège, 1548 or 1549; d. Linz, between Feb. 16 and 28, 1614. As a youth he went to Vienna, where he became a singer in the imperial chapel in 1562; in 1569 he became choirmaster at the monastery of Melk, near Linz, a post he retained until 1577 (made a trip to Spain in 1570–71). He was a tutor to the choirboys in the chapel of Archduke Karl in Graz (1577–82); was named choirmaster of the chapel of Archduke Matthias of Austria in 1583, and returned to Vienna; became master of the imperial chapel in 1612. He publ. *Sacrae symphoniae* for 4 to 13 and 15 to 16 Voices (Klosterbruck, 1612) and wrote several motets, masses, and other sacred works; also publ. *Primo libro delle* [24] *canzoni a la napolitana* for 5 Voices (Vienna, 1582) and (22) *Teutsche Liedlein* for 4 Voices (1602).

BIBL.: R. Bragard, *L. d.S.: étude biographique et bibliographique* (Liège, 1934); H. Federhofer, "L. d.S. an der Grazer Hofkapelle," *Revue Belge de Musicologie*, 3 (1949); G. Rebscher, *L. d.S. als Motettenkomponist* (diss., Univ. of Frankfurt, 1959).

Sbriglia, Giovanni, Italian tenor and singing teacher; b. Naples, June 23, 1829; d. Paris, Feb. 20, 1916. He made his debut at the Teatro San Carlo in Naples in 1853; was heard in Italy by Maretzek, the impresario, who engaged him for a season at the Academy of Music in N.Y., where Sbriglia appeared with Adelina Patti (1860); then made a grand tour of the U.S. with Parodi and Adelaide Phillipps; also sang in Mexico and Havana. He returned to Europe in 1875 and settled in Paris, where he became a highly successful vocal teacher. Jean, Joséphine, and Edouard de Reszke studied with him when they were already professional artists; he trained the baritone voice of Jean de Reszke, enabling him to sing tenor roles. Pol Plançon, Nordica, and Sibyl Sanderson were among his pupils.

Scacchi, Marco, eminent Italian choirmaster, pedagogue, writer on music, and composer; b. Gallese, near Viterbo, c.1600; d. there, c.1684. After studies with Giovanni Francesco Anerio, he went to Warsaw and was made a royal musician in 1626; then served as choirmaster at the court from 1628 until ill health compelled him in 1649 to retire to Gallese, where he devoted himself to teaching. He composed 10 operas for Warsaw (1628–49) and also wrote masses, sacred concertos, and madrigals. For his works, see J. Mattheson, *Der volkommene Capellmeister* (Hamburg, 1739). Scacchi was a distinguished writer on music and effectively defended modern music against the polemics of Paul Siefert. His most significant writings are *Cribrum musicum ad triticum Syferticum, seu Examinatio succinta psalmorum* (Venice, 1643), *Lettera per maggiore informatione a chi leggerà il mio "Cribrum"* (Venice, 1644), *Epistola ad Excellentissimum Dn. CS. Wernerum* (c.1648), *Judicium cribri musici* (Warsaw, c.1649), and *Breve discorso sopra la musica moderna* (Warsaw, 1649).

BIBL.: P. Syfert (Seifert), *Anticribratio musica ad avenam S.anam* (Danzig, 1645); C. Palisca, "M. S.'s Defense of Modern Music (1649)," *Words and Music: The Scholar's View . . . in Honor of A. Tillman Merritt* (Cambridge, Mass., 1972).

Scacciati, Bianca, Italian soprano; b. Florence, July 3, 1894; d. Brescia, Oct. 15, 1948. She studied in Milan; made her debut there as Marguerite in *Faust* in 1917. She rapidly asserted herself as one of the most impressive dramatic sopranos in Italy; sang for many seasons at La Scala in Milan; also made

successful appearances at Covent Garden in London, at the Paris Opéra, and at the Teatro Colón in Buenos Aires. She was particularly noted for her interpretation of the title role of Puccini's *Turandot*.

Scala, Francis (Maria), Italian-American bandmaster and composer; b. Naples, 1819 or 1820; d. Washington, D.C., April 18, 1903. Beginning his musical career on the clarinet, he enlisted in the U.S. Navy as a musician 3rd-class on the frigate *Brandywine* when it was anchored at Naples in 1841. Following the ship's return to Washington, D.C., Scala left the navy for the Marine Corps, and in 1843 was designated fife-major of the fife corps associated with Marine Corps headquarters. On Sept. 9, 1855, he became de facto the leader of the Marine Band; in 1861 he was made "Principal Musician," and on Sept. 4, 1868, was referred to, for the 1st time, as "Leader of the Band," a position he retained until 1871. John Philip Sousa was one of his apprentice bandsmen. In 1945 his son Norman P. Scala made the 1st of several gifts to the Library of Congress honoring his father; these materials contain a large amount of MSS and printed music, chiefly band arrangements made by or for Scala, that represent in essence the library of the Marine Band during the Civil War; included is a note in the hand of President Abraham Lincoln, then Scala's Commander-in-Chief.

BIBL.: D. Ingalls, *F. S., Leader of the Marine Band from 1855–1871* (thesis, Catholic Univ. of America, 1955).

Scalchi, Sofia, celebrated Italian mezzo-soprano; b. Turin, Nov. 29, 1850; d. Rome, Aug. 22, 1922. She studied with Boccabadati; made her debut at Mantua in 1866 as Ulrica in Verdi's *Un ballo in maschera*; then sang throughout Italy; appeared in concert in London (Sept. 16, 1868) and at Covent Garden (Nov. 5, 1868) as Azucena, obtaining enormous success; continued to appear there regularly until 1889; also sang in St. Petersburg (1872–81; 1889–90). On Dec. 20, 1882, she made her U.S. debut as Arsaces in *Semiramide* at N.Y.'s Academy of Music; then was engaged for the 1st performance at the Metropolitan Opera, where she sang Siebel in *Faust* on Oct. 22, 1883; was again on its roster in 1891–92 and from 1893 to 1896, and then retired from the operatic stage. Her voice had a range of 2½ octaves; it was essentially a contralto voice, but with so powerful a high register that she successfully performed soprano parts. Among her other roles were Fidès, Ortrud, Amneris, Emilia, and Mistress Quickly.

Scalero, Rosario, eminent Italian pedagogue and composer; b. Moncalieri, near Turin, Dec. 24, 1870; d. Settimo Vittone, near Turin, Dec. 25, 1954. He studied violin with Sivori in Genoa, and in London with Wilhelmj; subsequently studied general subjects with Mandyczewski in Vienna. He taught violin in Lyons (1896–1908); then went to Rome as a teacher of theory at the Accademia di Santa Cecilia; was also founder-director of the Società del Quartetto (1913–16) and a high commissioner for examinations at the conservatories of Naples, Rome, and Parma. From 1919 to 1928 he was chairman of the theory and composition dept. at N.Y.'s David Mannes School; also taught at the Curtis Inst. of Music in Philadelphia (1924–33; 1935–46), where his students included Samuel Barber, Gian Carlo Menotti, and Lukas Foss. He wrote a Violin Concerto; *Neapolitan Dances* for Violin and Piano; chamber music; sacred songs; etc.

Scandello, Antonio, distinguished Italian instrumentalist and composer; b. Bergamo, Jan. 17, 1517; d. Dresden, Jan. 15, 1580. He was born into a family of the nobility; studied in his native city and played cornett at S. Maria Maggiore there. After serving Cardinal Christoph Madruzzi in Trent (1547–49), he was called to Dresden by the Elector Moritz of Saxony as an instrumentalist in the court chapel; later became a Protestant and in 1562 was made a citizen of Dresden. When the Kapellmeister Le Maistre became ill in 1566, Scandello assumed most of his responsibilities; upon Le Maistre's retirement in 1568, Scandello was made his successor. Under his leadership, the Dresden court chapel attained notable distinction. Scandello was a particularly fine composer of sacred music. His *St. John Passion* (1561) was the 1st work of its kind in Germany to combine the chorale and motet styles. His other works include masses, motets, and Italian and German secular songs.

BIBL.: R. Kade, "Antonius Scandellus," *Sammelbände der Internationalen Musik-Gesellschaft*, XV (1913–14).

Scaria, Emil, outstanding Austrian bass; b. Graz, Sept. 18, 1838; d. Blasewitz, near Dresden, July 22, 1886. He studied with Netzer in Graz and Lewy in Vienna; made his debut as St. Bris in *Les Huguenots* in Pest (1860); following additional training with García in London, he sang in Dessau (1862–63), Leipzig (1863–65), and Dresden (from 1865), where he won notable distinction by singing both bass and baritone roles. After appearing as a guest artist at the Vienna Court Opera (1872–73), he sang there regularly as one of its leading artists until his death. He also sang with Angelo Neumann's company; while appearing in *Die Walküre* with the company in London in May 1882, he suffered a mental breakdown; however, he appeared in public 2 days later in *Siegfried*, and then sang Gurnemanz in the 1st mounting of *Parsifal* at the Bayreuth Festival on July 26, 1882. He continued to make tours with Neumann's company, returned to Bayreuth in 1883, and made a concert tour of the U.S. in 1884. In early 1886 he suffered a relapse and shortly thereafter died insane. He was hailed as one of the greatest Wagnerians of his time.

Scarlatesco, Ion, Rumanian composer; b. Bucharest, 1872; d. there, Sept. 19, 1922. A versatile musician, he began his career as a pianist; also wrote plays and was active as a music critic and harmony teacher. He composed about 50 ballads for Voice and Piano; a String Quartet; *Rumanian Rhapsody* for Orch.; several other pieces in the Rumanian style, among which *Bagatelle* for Violin became popular.

Scarlatti, (Pietro) Alessandro (Gaspare), important Italian composer, father of **(Giuseppe) Domenico Scarlatti;** b. Palermo, May 2, 1660; d. Naples, Oct. 22, 1725. Nothing is known concerning his musical training. When he was 12, he went with his 2 sisters to Rome, where he found patrons who enabled him to pursue a career in music. His 1st known opera, *Gli equivoci nel sembiante,* was performed there in 1679. By 1680 he was maestro di cappella to Queen Christina of Sweden, whose palace in Rome served as an important center for the arts. He also found patrons in 2 cardinals, Benedetto Pamphili and Pietro Ottoboni, and served as maestro di cappella at S. Gerolamo della Carità. From 1684 to 1702 he was maestro di cappella to the Viceroy at Naples. During these years he composed prolifically, bringing out numerous operas; he also composed serenatas, oratorios, and cantatas. In addition, he served as director of the Teatro San Bartolomeo, where he conducted many of his works. His fame as a composer for the theater soon spread, and many of his works were performed in the leading music centers of Italy; one of his most popular operas, *Il Pirro e Demetrio* (Naples, Jan. 28, 1694), was even performed in London. His only confirmed teaching position dates from this period, when he served for 2 months in the spring of 1689 as a faculty member of the Conservatorio di Santa Maria di Loreto. Tiring of his exhaustive labors, he was granted a leave of absence and set out for Florence in June 1702. Prince Ferdinando de' Medici had been one of his patrons for some years in Florence, and Scarlatti hoped he could find permanent employment there. When this did not materialize, he settled in Rome and became assistant maestro di cappella at S. Maria Maggiore in 1703; he was promoted to maestro di cappella in 1707. One of his finest operas, *Il Mitridate Eupatore,* was performed in Venice in 1707. Since the Roman theaters had been closed from 1700, he devoted much of his time to composing serenatas, cantatas, and oratorios. In late 1708 he was again appointed maestro di cappella to the Viceroy at Naples. His most celebrated opera from these years, *Il Tigrane,* was given in Naples on Feb. 16, 1715. His only full-fledged comic opera, *Il trionfo dell'onore,* was performed in Naples on Nov. 26, 1718. Scarlatti's interest in purely instrumental music dates from this period, and he composed a number of conservative

orch. and chamber music pieces. Having again obtained a leave of absence from his duties, he went to Rome to oversee the premiere of his opera *Telemaco* (1718). His last known opera, *La Griselda,* was given there in Jan. 1721. From 1722 until his death he lived in retirement in Naples, producing only a handful of works. Scarlatti was the foremost Neapolitan composer of the late Baroque era in Italy.

WORKS: OPERAS (all are drammas and were 1st perf. in Naples unless otherwise given): *Gli equivoci nel sembiante* (1st perf. publicly, Rome, Feb. 5, 1679; later perf. as *L'errore innocente,* Bologna, 1679, and as *L'amor non vuole inganni,* Linz, Carnival 1681); *L'honestà negli amori* (Rome, Feb. 6, 1680); *Tutto il mal non vien per nuocere,* commedia (Rome, 1681; later perf. as *Dal male il bene,* Naples, 1687); *Il Pompeo* (Rome, Jan. 25, 1683); *La Guerriera costante* (Rome, Carnival 1683); *L'Aldimiro o vero Favor per favore* (Nov. 6, 1683); *La Psiche o vero Amore innamorato* (Dec. 21, 1683); *Olimpia vendicata* (Dec. 23, 1685); *La Rosmene o vero L'infedeltà fedele,* melodramma (Rome, Carnival 1686); *Clearco in Negroponte* (Dec. 21, 1686); *La Santa Dinna,* commedia (Rome, Carnival 1687; only Act 3 by Scarlatti); *Il Flavio* (Nov. 14?, 1688); *L'Anacreonte tiranno,* melodramma (Feb. 9, 1689); *L'Amazzone corsara [guerriera] o vero L'Alvilda* (Nov. 6, 1689); *La Statira* (Rome, Jan. 5, 1690); *Gli equivoci in amore o vero La Rosaura,* melodramma (Rome, Dec. 1690); *L'humanità nelle fiere o vero Il Lucullo* (Feb. 25, 1691); *La Teodora Augusta* (Nov. 6, 1692); *Gerone tiranno di Siracusa* (Dec. 22, 1692); *L'Amante doppio o vero Il Ceccobimbi,* melodramma (April 1693); *Il Pirro e Demetrio* (Jan. 28, 1694; later perf. as *La forza della fedeltà,* Florence, 1712); *Il Bassiano o vero Il maggior impossibile,* melodramma (1694); *La santa Genuinda, o vero L'innocenza difesa dall'inganno,* dramma sacro (Rome, 1694; only Act 2 by Scarlatti); *Le nozze con l'inimico o vero L'Analinda,* melodramma (1695; later perf. as *L'Analinda overo Le nozze col nemico,* Florence, Carnival 1702); *Nerone fatto Cesare,* melodramma (Nov. 6, 1695); *Massimo Puppieno,* melodramma (Dec. 26, 1695); *Penelope la casta* (Feb. 23?, 1696); *La Didone delirante,* opera drammatica (May 28, 1696); *Comodo Antonino* (Nov. 18, 1696); *L'Emireno o vero Il consiglio dell'ombra,* opera drammatica (Feb. 2, 1697); *La caduta de' Decemviri* (Dec. 15, 1697); *La Donna ancora è fedele* (1698); *Il Prigioniero fortunato* (Dec. 14, 1698); *Gli'inganni felici* (Nov. 6, 1699; later perf. as *L'Agarista ovvero Gl'inganni felici,* with the intermezzo *Brenno e Tisbe,* Florence, Carnival 1706); *L'Eraclea* (Jan. 30, 1700); *Odoardo,* with the intermezzo *Adolfo e Lesbina* (May 5, 1700); *Dafni,* favola boschereccia (Aug. 5, 1700; later perf. as *L'amore non viene dal caso,* Jesi, Carnival 1715); *Laodicea e Berenice* (April 1701); *Il pastor[e] di Corinto,* favola boschereccia (Aug. 5, 1701); *Tito Sempronio Gracco,* with the intermezzo *Bireno e Dorilla* (Carnival? 1702); *Tiberio imperatore d'Oriente* (May 8, 1702); *Il Flavio Cuniberto* (Pratolino, Sept.? 1702); *Arminio* (Pratolino, Sept. 1703); *Turno Aricino* (Pratolino, Sept. 1704); *Lucio Manlio l'imperioso* (Pratolino, Sept. 1705); *Il gran Tamerlano* (Pratolino, Sept. 1706); *Il Mitridate Eupatore,* tragedia (Venice, Carnival 1707); *Il trionfo della libertà,* tragedia (Venice, Carnival 1707); *Il Teodosio* (Jan. 27, 1709); *L'amor volubile e tiranno* (May 25, 1709; later perf. as *La Dorisbe o L'amor volubile e tiranno,* Rome, Carnival 1711, and as *La Dorisbe,* Genoa, 1713); *La Principessa fedele* (Feb. 8, 1710); *La fede riconosciuta,* dramma pastorale (Oct. 14, 1710); *Giunio Bruto o vero La caduta dei Tarquini* (1711; not perf.; only Act 3 by Scarlatti); *Il Ciro* (Rome, Carnival 1712); *Scipione nelle Spagne,* with the intermezzo *Pericca e Varrone* (Jan. 21, 1714); *L'amor generoso,* with the intermezzo *Despina e Niso* (Oct. 1, 1714); *Il Tigrane o vero L'egual impegno d'amore e di fede* (Feb. 16, 1715); *Carlo re d'Allemagna* (Jan. 30, 1716); *La virtù trionfante dell'odio e dell'amore* (May 3, 1716); *Telemaco* (Rome, Carnival 1718); *Il trionfo dell'onore,* commedia (Nov. 26, 1718); *Il Cambise* (Feb. 4, 1719); *Marco Attilio Regolo,* with the intermezzo *Leonzio e Eurilla* (Rome, Carnival 1719); *La Griselda* (Rome, Jan. 1721). Several operas attributed to him are now considered doubtful. A complete edition of his operas began to appear in the Harvard Publications in Music series in 1974.

SERENATAS: *Diana ed Endimione* (c.1680–85); Serenata in honor of James II of England (Rome, 1688); *Il genio di Partenope, la gloria del Sebeto, il piacere di Mergellina* (Naples, Jan. 1696); *Venere, Adone e Amore* (Naples, July 15, 1696); *Il trionfo delle stagioni* (Naples, July 26, 1696); *Venere ed Amore* (c.1695–1700); *Clori, Lidia e Filli* (c.1700); *Clori, Dorino e Amore* (Naples, May 2, 1702); *Venere e Adone: Il giardino d'amore* (c.1702–5); *Endimione e Cintia* (Rome, 1705); *Amore e Virtù ossia Il trionfo della virtù* (Rome, 1706); *Clori e Zeffiro* (Rome, 1706?); *Fileno, Niso e Doralbo: Serenata a Filli* (Rome, 1706?); *Sole, Urania e Clio: Le Muse Urania e Clio lodano le bellezze di Filli* (Rome, 1706?); *Venere, Amore e Ragione: Il ballo delle ninfe: Venere, havendo perso Amore, lo ritrova fra le ninfe e i pastori dei Sette Colli* (Rome, 1706); *Cupido e Onestà: Il trionfo dell'Onestà* (Rome, Sept. 1709); *Le glorie della Bellezza del Corpo e dell'Anima* (Naples, Aug. 28, 1709); *Pace, Amore e Provvidenza* (Naples, Nov. 4, 1711); *Il genio austriaco* (Naples, June 21, 1712); *Il genio austriaco: Zefiro, Flora, il Sole, Partenope e il Sebeto* (Naples, Aug. 28, 1713); Serenata in honor of the Vicereine, Donna Barbara d'Erbenstein (Naples, Dec. 4, 1715); *La gloria di Primavera: Primavera, Estate, Autunno, Inverno e Giove* (Vienna, April 1716?); *Partenope, Teti, Nettuno, Proteo e Glauco* (Naples, 1716); *Filli, Clori e Tirsi* (Naples, 1718?); *La virtù negli amori: La Notte, il Sole, Lanso, Lisa, Toante e Agave* (Rome, Nov. 16, 1721); *Erminia, Tancredi, Polidoro e Pastore* (Naples, June 13, 1723); *Diana, Amore, Venere* (undated).

ORATORIOS AND OTHER SACRED: Oratorio (Rome, Feb. 24, 1679); Oratorio (Rome, April 12, 1680); *Passio Domini Nostri Jesu Christi secundum Joannem* (c.1680); Oratorio (Rome, Feb. 20, 1682); *Agar et Ismaele esiliati* (Rome, 1683); *Il trionfo della gratia* (Rome, 1685); *Il martirio di S. Teodosia* (Modena, 1685); *I dolori di Maria sempre vergine* (Naples, 1693); *La Giuditta* (Naples, 1693); *Samson vindicatus* (Rome, March 25, 1695); *Cantata . . . per la notte di Natale* (Rome, Dec. 24, 1695); *Il martirio di S. Orsola* (c.1695–1700); *Davidis pugna et victoria* (Rome, March 5, 1700); *La Giuditta* (1700); *L'assunzione della Beata Vergine Maria* (Rome, 1703); *S. Michaelis Arcangelis cum Lucifer pugna et victoria* (Rome, April 3, 1705); *S. Casimiro, re di Polonia* (Florence, 1705); *S. Maria Maddalena de' pazzi* (Rome, 1705); *S. Filippo Neri* (Rome, 1705); *Qual di lieti concenti* (Rome, 1705?); *Il Sedecia, re di Gerusalemme* (Urbino, 1705?); *Abramo il tuo sembiante*, Christmas cantata (Rome, Dec. 24, 1705); *Il trionfo della Ss. Vergine assunta in cielo* (Florence, 1706); *S. Francesco di Paolo* (Urbino, 1706); *Humanità e Lucifero* (1706?); *Il martirio di S. Susanna* (Florence, 1706); *Alcene, ove per queste*, Christmas cantata (Rome, Dec. 24, 1706); *Cain overo Il primo omicidio* (Venice, Lent 1707); *Il giardino di rose: La Ss. Vergine del Rosario* (Rome, April 24, 1707); *Il martirio di S. Cecilia* (Rome, Lent 1708); *La Ss. Annunziata* (Rome, March 25, 1708); *Oratorio per la Passione di Nostro Signore Gesù Cristo* (Rome, April 4, 1708); *La vittoria della fede* (Rome, Sept. 12, 1708); *Il trionfo del valore* (Naples, March 19, 1709); *La Ss. Trinità* (Naples, May 1715); *La Vergine addolorata* (Rome, 1717); *La gloriosa gara tra la Santità e la Sapienza* (Rome, June 13, 1720). An edition of his oratorios commenced publication in Rome in 1964. He also composed over 600 cantatas, a number of masses and mass movements, motets, and madrigals. His instrumental music includes 12 sinfonie di concerto grosso, toccatas for keyboard, sonatas, suites, etc.

BIBL.: E. Dent, *A. S.: His Life and Works* (London, 1905; 2nd ed., rev., 1960, by F. Walker); C. van den Borren, *A. S. et l'esthétique de l'opéra napolitain* (Brussels and Paris, 1921); P. Strüver, *Die Cantata da camera A. S.s* (diss., Univ. of Munich, 1923); U. Prota-Giurleo, *A. S. "il Palermitano"* (Naples, 1926); A. Lorenz, *A. S.s Jugendoper* (Augsburg, 1927); O. Tilby, *La Famiglia S.: Nuove ricerche e documenti* (Rome, 1947); P. Taylor Lee, *The Keyboard Style of A. S.* (diss., Yale Univ., 1959); M. Fabbri, *A. S. e il Principe Ferdinando de' Medici* (Florence, 1961); E. Hanley, *A. S.'s Cantate da Camera: A Bibliographical Study* (diss., Yale Univ., 1963); O. Henry, *The Doctrine of*

Affections in Selected Solo Cantatas of A. S. (diss., Ohio State Univ., 1963); C. Morey, *The Late Operas of A. S.* (diss., Indiana Univ., 1965); D. Poultney, *The Oratorios of A. S.: Their Lineage, Milieu, and Style* (diss., Univ. of Michigan, 1968); P. Brandvik, *Selected Motets of A. S.* (diss., Univ. of Illinois, 1969); J. Shaffer, *The Cantus Firmus in A. S.'s Motets* (diss., George Peabody College of Teachers, 1970); P. Piersall, *The Bass Cantatas of A. S.* (diss., Univ. of Oregon, 1971); R. Pagano, L. Bianchi, and G. Rostirolla, *A. S.* (Turin, 1972); M. Inkeles, *A Study, Realization, and Performance of Unpublished Cantatas for Soprano and Basso Continuo ca. 1690–1706 of A. S.* (diss., Columbia Univ. Teachers College, 1977); D. Grout, *A. S.: An Introduction to His Operas* (Berkeley, 1979); W. Holmes, *La Statira by Pietro Ottoboni and A. S.: The Textual Sources, with a Documentary Postscript* (N.Y., 1983); F. D'Accone, *The History of a Baroque Opera: A. S.'s "Gli equivoci nel sembiante"* (N.Y., 1985); R. Pagano, *S.: A. e Domenico: Due vite in una* (Milan, 1985).

Scarlatti, (Giuseppe) Domenico, famous Italian composer, harpsichordist, and teacher, son of **(Pietro) Alessandro (Gaspare) Scarlatti;** b. Naples, Oct. 26, 1685; d. Madrid, July 23, 1757. Nothing is known about his musical training. On Sept. 13, 1701, he was appointed organist and composer at the Royal Chapel in Naples, where his father was maestro di cappella. The 2 were granted a leave of absence in June 1702, and they went to Florence; later that year Domenico returned to Naples without his father, and resumed his duties. His 1st opera, *Ottavia ristituita al trono,* was performed in Naples in 1703. He was sent to Venice by his father in 1705, but nothing is known of his activities there. In 1708 he went to Rome, where he entered the service of Queen Maria Casimira of Poland; he remained in her service until 1714, and composed a number of operas and several other works for her private palace theater. He became assistant to Bai, the maestro di cappella at the Vatican, in 1713; upon Bai's death the next year, he was appointed his successor; he also became maestro di cappella to the Portuguese ambassador to the Holy See in 1714. During his years in Rome, he met such eminent musicians as Corelli and Handel. Mainwaring relates the unconfirmed story that Scarlatti and Handel engaged in a friendly contest, Scarlatti being judged the superior on the harpsichord and Handel on the organ. He resigned his positions in 1719; by 1724 he was in Lisbon, where he took up the post of mestre at the patriarchal chapel. His duties included teaching the Infanta Maria Barbara, daughter of King John V, and the King's younger brother, Don Antonio. In 1728 Maria Barbara married the Spanish Crown Prince Fernando, and moved to Madrid. Scarlatti accompanied her, remaining in Madrid for the rest of his life. In 1724 he visited Rome, where he met Quantz; in 1725 he saw his father for the last time in Naples; in 1728 he was in Rome, where he married his 1st wife, Maria Caterina Gentili. In 1738 he was made a Knight of the Order of Santiago. When Maria Barbara became queen in 1746, he was appointed her maestro de cámera. His last years were spent quietly in Madrid; from 1752 until 1756, Antonio Soler studied with him. So closely did he become associated with Spain that his name eventually appeared as Domingo Escarlatti.

Scarlatti composed over 500 single-movement sonatas for solo keyboard. Although these works were long believed to have been written for the harpsichord, the fact that Maria Barbara used pianos in her residences suggests that some of these works were written for that instrument as well; at least 3 were written for the organ. His sonatas reveal his gifts as one of the foremost composers in the "free style" (a homophonic style with graceful ornamentation, in contrast to the former contrapuntal style). He also obtained striking effects by the frequent crossing of hands, tones repeated by rapidly changing fingers, etc. During his lifetime the following collections of keyboard works were publ.: *Essercizi per gravicembalo* (London, 1738), *XLII Suites de pièces pour le clavecin* (London, 1739), and *Pièces pour le clavecin* (3 vols., Paris, 1742–46). The principal MS sources are found in the library of the Arrigo

Boito Conservatorio in Parma and the Biblioteca Marciana in Venice. Alessandro Longo, Ralph Kirkpatrick, and Giorgio Pestelli prepared chronological catalogues of his sonatas. The one by Kirkpatrick is the most widely accepted. The following editions of his sonatas should be consulted: A. Longo, ed., *Opere complete per clavicembalo di D. S.* (11 vols., Milan, 1906–8); R. Kirkpatrick, *D. S.: Sixty Sonatas* (N.Y., 1953); K. Gilbert, ed., *D. S.: Sonates,* in Le Pupitre (Paris, 1971–85); R. Kirkpatrick, ed., *D. S.: Complete Keyboard Works in Facsimile* (N.Y., 1971–); E. Fadini, ed., *D. S.: Sonate per clavicembalo* (Milan, 1978–). He composed the following operas: *Ottavia ristituita al trono,* melodramma (Naples, Carnival 1703); *Giustino,* dramma per musica (Naples, Dec. 19, 1703; in collaboration with Legrenzi); *Irene,* dramma per musica (Naples, Carnival 1704; a complete revision of the opera by Pollarolo); *Silvia,* dramma pastorale (Rome, Jan. 27, 1710); *Tolomeo e Alessandro, ovvero La corona disprezzata,* dramma per musica (Rome, Jan. 19, 1711); *Orlando, ovvero La gelosa pazzia,* dramma, Carnival 1711); *Tetide in Sciro,* dramma per musica (Rome, Jan. 10, 1712); *Ifigenia in Aulide,* dramma per musica (Rome, Jan. 11, 1713); *Ifigenia in Tauri,* dramma per musica (Rome, Feb. 15, 1713); *Amor d'un ombra e gelosia d'un'aura,* dramma per musica (Rome, Jan. 20, 1714; rev. version as *Narciso,* London, May 30, 1720); *Ambleto,* dramma per musica (Rome, Carnival 1715); *La Dirindina,* farsetta per musica (1715; intermezzo for the preceding work; not perf.); *Intermedi pastorali,* intermezzo in *Ambleto* (Rome, Carnival 1715); *Berenice, regina d'Egitto, ovvero Le gare d'amore e di politica,* dramma per musica (Rome, Carnival 1718; in collaboration with Porpora). He also composed oratorios, cantatas, a Stabat Mater, a Salve Regina for Soprano and Strings, and other sacred music.

BIBL.: A. Longo, *D. S. e la sua figura nella storia della musica* (Naples, 1913); W. Gerstenberg, *Die Klavier-Kompositionen D. S.s* (Regensburg, 1933); S. Sitwell, *A Background for D. S.* (London, 1935); C. Valabrega, *Il Clavicembalista D. S., il suo secolo, la sua opera* (Modena, 1937; 2nd ed., rev., 1955); S. Luciani, *D. S.* (Turin, 1939); R. Kirkpatrick, *D. S.* (Princeton and London, 1953; 3rd ed., rev., 1968); M. Bogianckino, *L'arte clavicembalista di D. S.* (Rome, 1956); A. Basso, *La formazione storica ed estetica della storia di D. S.* (diss., Univ. of Turin, 1957); H. Keller, *D. S., ein Meister des Klaviers* (Leipzig, 1957); G. Pestelli, *Le sonate di D. S.: Proposta di un ordinamento cronologico* (Turin, 1967); J. Sheveloff, *The Keyboard Music of D. S.: A Reevaluation of the Present State of Knowledge in the Light of the Sources* (diss., Brandeis Univ., 1970); S. Choi, *Newly Found 18th-century Manuscripts of D. S.'s Sonatas and Their Relationship to Other 18th and Early 19th-century Sources* (diss., Univ. of Wisconsin, Madison, 1974); B. Ife, *D. S.* (Sevenoaks, England, 1985); R. Pagano, S.: *Alessandro e D.: Due vite in una* (Milan, 1985); P. Williams, ed., *Bach, Handel, and S.: Tercentenary Essays* (Cambridge, 1985); M. Boyd, *D. S.: Master of Music* (London, 1986).

Scarlatti, Giuseppe, Italian composer, grandson of **(Pietro) Alessandro (Gaspare)** and nephew of **(Giuseppe) Domenico Scarlatti;** b. Naples, c.1718; d. Vienna, Aug. 17, 1777. He was in Rome in 1739, and later in Lucca, where he married Barbara Stabili, a singer (1747); went to Vienna in 1757. He wrote 31 operas, produced in Rome, Florence, Lucca, Turin, Venice, Naples, Milan, and Vienna; of these the most successful was *L'isola disabitata* (Venice, Nov. 20, 1757). Another Giuseppe Scarlatti (a nephew of Alessandro Scarlatti), whose name appears in some reference works, was not a musician.

BIBL.: H. Springer, "Das Partitur-Autograph von G. S.s bisher verschollener Clemenza di Tito," *Beiträge zum Bibliotheks- und Buchwesen* (1913); *Gli S.* (Siena, 1940); O. Tiby, *La famiglia S.: Nuove ricerche e documenti* (Rome, 1947); F. Walker, "Some Notes on the S.s," *Music Review* (Aug. 1951).

Scarmolin, (Anthony) Louis, Italian-American composer; b. Schio, July 30, 1890; d. Union City, N.J., July 13, 1969. He went to the U.S. as a boy; graduated from the N.Y. College of Music in 1907; served in the U.S. Army during World War I; then lived in Union City, N.J. He wrote 6 operas and several

symphonic poems and overtures; also *Miniature Symphony* (Cleveland, Feb. 7, 1940).

Scarpini, Pietro, Italian pianist, teacher, and composer; b. Rome, April 6, 1911. He studied at the Accademia di Santa Cecilia in Rome; made his concert debut in 1936; then gave recitals in Europe and in the U.S.; from 1940 to 1967 he taught at the Florence Cons.; in 1967 he joined the faculty of the Milan Cons. He specializes in the modern repertoire of piano music; wrote a Piano Concerto and a Piano Quintet; also made an arrangement for 2 pianos of Mahler's 10th Sym.

Scelsi, Giacinto (actually, **Conte Giacinto Scelsi di Valva),** remarkable Italian composer; b. La Spezia, Jan. 8, 1905; d. Rome, Aug. 9, 1988. He was descended from a family of the nobility. He received some guidance in harmony from Giacinto Sallustio; after studies with Egon Koehler in Geneva, he completed his formal training with Walter Klein in Vienna (1935–36), where he became interested in the Schoenbergian method of writing music outside the bounds of traditional tonality; at the same time, he became deeply immersed in the study of the musical philosophy of the East, in which the scales and rhythms are perceived as functional elements of the human psyche. As a result of these multifarious absorptions of ostensibly incompatible ingredients, Scelsi formulated a style of composition that is synthetic in its sources and pragmatic in its artistic materialization. His works began to have a considerable number of performances in Italy and elsewhere, most particularly in the U.S. A curious polemical development arose after his death, when an Italian musician named Vieri Tosatti publ. a sensational article in the *Giornale della Musica,* declaring "I was Giacinto Scelsi." He claimed that Scelsi used to send him thematic sections of unfinished compositions, usually in the 12-tone system, for development and completion, using him as a ghostwriter. So many of such "improvisations" did Scelsi send to Tosatti that the latter had 2 other musicians to serve as secondary "ghosts," who, in turn, comfirmed their participation in this peculiar transaction. The matter finally got to the court of public opinion, where it was decided that the works were genuine compositions by Scelsi, who improvised them on his electric piano, and merely ed. for better effect by secondary arrangers.

WORKS: ORCH.: *Rotative* for 3 Pianos, Wind Instruments, and Percussion (1930); *Rapsodia romantica* (1931); Sinfonietta (1932); *Preludio e fuga* (1938); *Balata* for Cello and Orch. (1945); *La nascità del verbo* (1948; Brussels I.S.C.M. Festival, June 28, 1950); *4 pezzi su una nota sola* (1959); *Hurqualia* for Orch. and Amplified Instruments (1960); *Aion* (1961); *Nomos* for 2 Orchs. and Organ (1963); *Chukrim* for String Orch. (1963); *Amahit* for Violin and 18 Instruments (1965); *Anagamin* for 12 String Instruments (1965); *Ohoi* for 16 String Instruments (1966); *Uaxuctum* for Chorus, Orch., and Ondes Martenot (1966); *Natura renovatur* for 11 String Instruments (1967); *Konx-om-pax* for Chorus, Orch., and Organ (1969); *Pfhat* for Chorus and Orch. (1974). **CHAMBER:** 4 string quartets (1944, 1961, 1963, 1964); *Piccola Suite* for Flute and Clarinet (1953); *Hyxos* for Alto Flute, Gong, and Bells (1955); String Trio (1958); *Elegia* for Viola and Cello (1958); *Rucke di Guck* for Piccolo and Oboe (1958); *I presagi* for 10 Instruments (1958); *Kya* for Clarinet and 7 Instruments (1959); *Khoom* for Soprano and 6 Instruments (1962); *Duo* for Violin and Cello (1965); *Ko-lho* for Flute and Clarinet (1966); *Okanagon* for Harp, Tam-tam, and Double Bass (1968); *Duo* for Violin and Double Bass (1977); *5 Divertimenti* for Violin (1952–56); *Pwill* for Flute (1954); *Coelocanth* for Viola (1955); *3 Studies* for Viola (1956); *Trilogy,* 3 pieces for Cello (1957–65); *Ko-Tha* for Guitar (1967); *Praham II* for 9 Instruments (1973); *3 pezzi* for Clarinet; *3 pezzi* for Trumpet; *3 pezzi* for Saxophone; *3 pezzi* for Horn; *3 pezzi* for Trombone; other pieces for Solo Instruments. **VOCAL:** *Taiagaru,* 5 invocations for Soprano (1962); *20 canti del Capricorno* for Solo Voice (1962–72); *Manto per 4* for Voice, Flute, Trombone, and Cello (1972); *Praham I* for Voice, 12 Instruments, and Tape (1972). **PIANO:** 24 preludes (1936–40); *Hispania* (1939); 10 suites; 3 sonatas.

Schaab, Robert, German organist and composer; b. Rötha, near Leipzig, Feb. 28, 1817; d. Leipzig, March 18, 1887. He studied with C.F. Becker and Mendelssohn; became organist of the Johanniskirche in Leipzig; publ. a great number of works for organ; his 60 *Choralvorspiele* (opp. 118, 119, 121) are of interest.

Schachner, Rudolf Joseph, German pianist, teacher, and composer; b. Munich, Dec. 31, 1821; d. Reichenhall, Aug. 15, 1896. He was a pupil of J.B. Cramer; appeared in concert in Vienna, Paris, Leipzig, etc.; in 1853, settled in London as a teacher; later went to Vienna. He composed 2 piano concertos and a number of pieces for piano solo.

Schacht, Matthias Henriksen, Danish scholar, writer on music, and composer; b. Visby, Gotland, April 29, 1660; d. Kerteminde, Fyn, Aug. 8, 1700. He studied at the Univ. of Copenhagen and at univs. in Germany; was a schoolmaster in Visby (1682–83), Kantor of the Odense grammar school (1683–86), and rector at the Kerteminde school (from 1686), where he was also active as a town musician. He wrote widely on scholarly subjects; also wrote the vol. *Musicus danicus eller Danske sagmester,* which includes a biographical dictionary of musicians; he completed the MS in 1687, but it was not publ., even though Gerber utilized it for his own *Lexikon* (1790–92); it was finally ed. and publ. by G. Skjerne in Copenhagen in 1928. His compositions are not extant.

Schacht, Theodor, Freiherr von, German pianist, composer, and conductor; b. Strasbourg, 1748; d. Regensburg, June 20, 1823. He studied piano with Küffner and harmony with Riepel in Regensburg (1756–66); then took lessons in composition with Jommelli in Stuttgart (1766–71). Returning to Regensburg in 1771, he became Hofkavalier; in 1773 he was appointed court music Intendant, serving as director of its Italian opera from 1774 to 1778 and again from 1784 to 1786. From 1786 to 1805 he was music director of the court orch. He then went to Vienna; in 1812 he returned to Germany. He was a prolific musician; wrote a number of operas and theater pieces to German and Italian texts, as well as competently crafted syms., concertos, and chamber music. He was a minor master of contrapuntal arts; his series of 84 canons, dedicated to members of "the fair sex," quite amusing and even daring for his time, was publ. in Baden in 1811 under the title *Divertimento del bel sesso nel soggiorno di Baden.*
Bibl.: S. Färber, *Das Regensburger fürstlich Thurn und Taxissche Hoftheater und seine Oper 1760–1786* (Regensburg, 1936); J. LaRue, "A New Figure in the Haydn Masque," *Music & Letters,* XL (1959).

Schack, Benedikt (Emanuel), Bohemian-born Austrian tenor and composer; b. Mirotitz (baptized), Feb. 7, 1758; d. Munich, Dec. 10, 1826. He began his training with his father, a school teacher; after further studies in Staré Sedlo and Svatá Hora, he continued his training as a chorister at the Prague Cathedral (1773–75); then went to Vienna, where he received lessons in singing from Karl Frieberth, and also studied medicine and philosophy. He became Kapellmeister to Prince Heinrich von Schönaich-Carolath in Silesia in 1780; became a member of Schikaneder's traveling theater troupe in 1786, and went with it to Vienna, where he was its principal tenor at the Freihaus-Theater auf der Wieden (from 1789). He was a close friend of Mozart, who wrote the role of Tamino for him; his wife, Elisabeth (née Weinhold) Schack, appeared as the 3rd Lady in the 1st perf. of *Die Zauberflöte.* If contemporary accounts are to be trusted, it was Schack who sang passages from the Mozart Requiem for the dying composer. After a sojourn in Graz (1793–96), he went to Munich as a member of the Hoftheater; having lost his voice, he was pensioned about 1814. Mozart wrote piano variations (K. 613) on an aria from Schack's opera *Die verdeckten Sachen.* Among Schack's theatrical pieces, the following were performed in Vienna: *Der dumme Gärtner aus dem Gebirge* (July 12, 1789); *Die wiener Zeitung* (Jan. 12, 1791); *Die Antwort auf die Frage* (Dec. 16, 1792); *Die beiden Nannerin* (July 26, 1794).

Schad, Joseph, German pianist, organist, teacher, and composer; b. Steinach, March 6, 1812; d. Bordeaux, July 4, 1879. He studied at the Würzburg Cons. and with Aloys Schmitt in Frankfurt. In 1834 he became an organist at Morges, Switzerland; in 1847, settled in Bordeaux, where he gained high repute as a piano teacher. He publ. a great number of melodious piano pieces which enjoyed some success during his lifetime; also wrote fantasias and transcriptions.

Schadewitz, Carl, German composer; b. St. Ingbert, Jan. 23, 1887; d. Reppendorf, near Kitzingen, March 27, 1945. He studied in Würzburg, and lived there most of his life as a choral conductor and teacher. He was a prolific composer; his works include a musical fairy tale, *Johannisnacht;* a "Romantic" oratorio, *Kreislers Heimkehr;* an opera, *Laurenca;* a tone poem, *Heldengedenken* (1943); a number of songs, of which the cycle *Die Heimat* (1934) is outstanding; much chamber music; choruses.
Bibl.: A. Maxsein, *C. S.* (Würzburg, 1954).

Schaefer, Theodor, Czech composer; b. Telč, Jan. 23, 1904; d. Brno, March 19, 1969. He studied with Jaroslav Kvapil at the Brno Cons. (1922–26) and with Novák at the Prague Cons. (1926–29). Upon graduation, he taught at the Palacký Univ. at Olomouc, the Brno Cons. (1948–59), and at the Janáček Academy of Music in Brno (1959–69). He was an advocate of a so-called diathematic principle of constructing themes using fragments of preceding thematic units.
Works: stage: Children's opera, *Maugli* (1932); ballet, *Legenda o štestí* (Legend of Happiness; 1952). **orch.:** 2 unnumbered syms. (1926, 1955–61); Violin Concerto (1932–33); *Wallachian Serenade* (1936); Piano Concerto (1937–43); *Jánošík,* balladic overture (1939); *Winter Cantata* for Soprano, Chorus, and Orch. (1943–45); *Diathema* for Viola and Orch. (1955–56); *The Barbarian and the Rose* for Piano and Orch. (1957–58); *Diathema* (1957–58); *Rhapsodic Reportage* (1960). **chamber:** 3 string quartets (1929, 1941, 1944–45); Wind Quintet (1935–36); *Divertimento mesto* for Wind Quintet and String Trio (1946); *Cikánovy housle* (Gypsy Violin), 4 movements for Violin and Piano (1960); *Etudes* for Piano (1936–37); *Theme with Variations* for Piano (1936); also choruses; songs, including *Milostné balady* (Love Ballads) for Voice and Piano, commemorating the destruction of the village of Lidice by the Nazis (1943), and *Bithematikon* for Baritone and Piano (1967).

Schaeffer, Boguslaw (Julien), outstanding Polish composer, pedagogue, writer on music, and playwright; b. Lwow, June 6, 1929. He studied violin in Opole; then went to Krakow, where he took courses in composition with Malawski at the State High School of Music and in musicology with Jachimecki at the Jagiello Univ. (1949–53); later received instruction in advanced techniques from Nono (1959). In 1963 he became prof. of composition at the Krakow Cons.; served as prof. of composition at the Salzburg Mozarteum (from 1986). In 1967 he founded the periodical *Forum Musicum,* devoted to new music; in addition to his writings on music, he was active as a playwright from 1979; he was the most widely performed playwright in Poland during the 1987–88 season, winning an award at the Wroclaw Festival of Contemporary plays in 1987. As a composer, he received many awards, and numerous concerts of his works were presented in Poland and abroad. He is married to **Mieczyslawa Janina Hanuszewska-Schaeffer.** Their son, **Piotr (Mikolaj) Schaeffer** (b. Krakow, Oct. 1, 1958), is a music journalist. Schaeffer's earliest compositions (*19 Mazurkas* for Piano, 1949) were inspired by the melorhythms of Polish folk songs, but he made a decisive turn in 1953 with his *Music for Strings: Nocturne,* which became the 1st serial work by a Polish composer; he devised a graphic and polychromatic optical notation indicating intensity of sound, proportional lengths of duration, and position of notes in melodic and contrapuntal lines, with the components arranged in binary code; he also wrote music in the "third stream" style, combining jazz with classical procedures. In 1960 he invented topophonical music in a tone-color passacaglia form in his *Topofonica* for 40 Instruments. In 1967 he introduced his own rhythmic system, built on metric-tempo proportions. In 1970 he began using synthesizers and computers. Many of his chamber scores, such as *Quartet 2+2*, utilize indeterminacy. In his music for and with actors, he uses mixed-media procedures. With his *Missa elettronica* (1975), he charted a bold course in sacred music. Schaeffer is regarded as one of the foremost composers of microtonal scores. *Three Short Pieces* for Orch. (1951) and *Music for String Quartet* (1954) are notable examples of his early microtonal works in which he uses a 24-tone row with 23 different microtonal intervals. In 1979 he introduced a new kind of instrumentation in which the disposition of instruments totally changes many times, thus utilizing various changing orchs.; in his Organ Concerto the disposition of instruments changes 53 times. Each of his orch. works and concertos follows this new disposition, sometimes very specifically, as in his *Musica ipsa*.

WORKS: Sonata for Solo Violin (1955; Warsaw, April 24, 1983); *Permutations* for 10 Instruments (1956); 12 *Models* for Piano (1954, 1957, 1961, 1963, 1965, 1970, 1971, 1972, 1976, 1977, 1981, 1984); *Extremes* for 10 Instruments, a score without notes (1957); 5 string quartets (1957, 1964, 1971, 1973, 1986); *4 movimenti* for Piano and Orch. (1957); *Tertium datur*, treatise for Harpsichord and Chamber Orch. (1958; Warsaw, Sept. 19, 1960); *Monosonata* for 6 String Quartets subdivided into 3 uneven groups (1959; ISCM Festival, Darmstadt, June 19, 1961); *Equivalenze sonore*, concerto for Percussion Chamber Orch. (1959); *Concerto breve* for Cello and Orch. (1959); Concerto for String Quartet (1959); *Joint Constructions* for Strings (1960); *Montaggio* for 6 Players (1960); *Topofonica* for 40 Instruments (1960); *Little Symphony: Scultura* (1960; Warsaw, Sept. 29, 1965); *Concerto per sei e tre* for a changing Solo Instrument (Clarinet, Saxophone, Violin, Cello, Percussion, and Piano) and 3 Orchs. (1960; Katowice, Nov. 7, 1962); *Musica* for Harpsichord and Orch. (Venice, April 25, 1961); *Kody* (Codes) for Chamber Orch. (Warsaw, Sept. 19, 1961); *Azione a due* for Piano and 11 Instruments (1961; Stuttgart, June 6, 1971); *Imago musicae* for Violin and 9 Interpolating Instruments (1961); *Course "J"* for Jazz Ensemble and Chamber Sym. Orch. (Warsaw, Oct. 28, 1962); *Musica ipsa* for an Orch. of Deep Instruments (Warsaw, Sept. 20, 1962); *TIS-MW-2*, metamusical audiovisual spectacle for Actor, Mime, Ballerina, and 5 Musicians (1962–63; Krakow, April 25, 1964); *Expressive Aspects* for Soprano and Flute (1963); *Collage and Form* for 8 Jazz Musicians and Orch. (1963; Urbana, Ill., March 19, 1967); Violin Concerto (1961–63); *TIS GK*, stage work (1963); *Music for MI* for Voice, Vibraphone, 6 Narrators, Jazz Ensemble, and Orch. (1963); *S'alto* for Saxophone and Chamber Orch. of Soloists (Zagreb, May 13, 1963); *Audiences I–V* for Actors (1964); *Collage* for Chamber Orch. (1964); Quartet for 2 Pianists and 2 Optional Performers (1965); *Przeslanie* (Transmissions) for Cello and 2 Pianos (1965); *Symphony: Electronic Music* for Tape (1964–66); *Howl*, monodrama, after Ginsberg's poem, for Narrator, 2 Actors, Ensemble of Instrumentalists, and Ensemble of Performers (1966; Warsaw, March 1, 1971); Trio for Flute, Harp, Viola, and Tape (1966); Quartet for Oboe and String Trio (1966); Quartet for 4 Actors (1966; ISCM Festival, Athens, Sept. 15, 1979); Piano Concerto No. 2 (1967); *Media* for Voices and Instruments (1967); *Symfonia: Muzyka orkiestrowa* (1967); *Jazz Concerto* for Jazz Ensemble of 12 Instruments and an Orch. of Flutes, Bassoons, Trumpets, Trombones, and Low Strings (1969; ISCM Festival, Boston, Oct. 30, 1976); Piano Trio (1969); *Heraklitiana* for 10 Solo Instruments and Tape (1970); *Texts* for Orch. (1971); *Mare*, concertino for Piano and 9 Instruments (1971); *Estratto* for String Trio (1971; Krakow, April 7, 1987); *Experimenta* for Pianist (on 2 pianos) and Orch. (1971; Poznan, April 27, 1972); *Variants* for Wind Quintet (1971); *Sgraffito* for Flute, Cello, Harpsichord, and 2 Pianos (1971); *Confrontations* for Solo Instrument and Orch. (1972); Concerto for 3 Pianos (1972); *Free Form* No. 1 for 5 Instruments (1972) and No. 2, *Evocazioni*, for Double Bass (1972); *blueS No. 1* for 2 Pianos and Tape (1972; Wroclaw, April 21, 1977); *blueS No. 2* for Instrumental Ensemble (1972); *blueS No. 3* for 2 Pianos (1978); *blueS No. 4* for 2 Pianos and Tape (audiovisual; 1980); *Bergsoniana* for Soprano, Flute, Piano, Horn, Double Bass, and Piano (1972); *Dreams of Schäffer*, after Ionesco, for an Ensemble of Performers (1972; Krakow, April 14, 1975); *Hommage à Czybzewski* for an Ensemble of Stage and Musical Performers (1972); Sym. in 9 movements for Large Orch. and 6 Solo Instruments (1973; Wroclaw, Sept. 18, 1978); *tentative music* for 159 Instruments (1973; 7 versions: for 1, 5, 9, 15, 19, 59, and 159 instruments); *Harmonies and Counterpoints* for Orch. (2 overtures: *Warsaw Overture*, 1975; Warsaw, Sept. 10, 1975; and *Romuald Traugutt*, 1975; Warsaw, Sept. 20, 1977); *Missa elettronica* for Boys' Choir and Electronic Tape (1975; Warsaw, Sept. 23, 1976; also for Mixed Choir and Tape); *Spinoziana* for an Ensemble of Performers (1977); *Gravesono* for an Orch. of Wind and Percussion Instruments (1977); *Vaniniana* for 2 Actors, Soprano, Piano, Cello, and Electronic Sources (1978; Lecce, Oct. 24, 1985); *Kesukaan* for 13 String Instruments (1978; Rzeszow, April 8, 1983); *Miserere* for Soprano, Choir, Orch., and Tape (1978); *Jangwa* for Double Bass and Orch. (1979); *Te Deum* for Solo Voices, Vocal Ensemble, and Orch. (1979); *Maah* for Orch. and Tape (1979); *Berlin '80/I (Tornerai)* for Piano, Syn-lab, Electronic Media, and Tape (West Berlin, Oct. 2, 1980); *Berlin 80/II (In jener Zeit)* for Piano, Syn-lab, Electronic Media, and Tape (West Berlin, Oct. 3, 1980); Concerto for Saxophone Quartet (1980); Octet for Wind Instruments and Double Bass (1980); *5 Introductions and an Epilogue* for Small Chamber Orch. (1981); *Entertainment Music* for an Orch. of Wind and Percussion Instruments (1981); *Addolorato* for Violin and Tape (1983; Krakow, Feb. 22, 1988); *Open Music Nos. 2, 3*, and *4* for Piano and Tape (1983); *Teatrino fantastico* for Actor, Violin, and Piano, with Multimedia and Tape (Brussels, Nov. 17, 1983); *Stabat Mater* for Soprano, Alto, Choir, Strings, and Organ (1983); *Gasab* for Gasab-violin and Piano Accompaniment (Brussels, Nov. 16, 1983); Guitar Concerto (Rzeszow, March 9, 1984); Accordion Concerto (1984); Concerto for Organ, Violin, and Orch., *B-A-C-H* (1984; Nuremberg, July 5, 1985); 4 organ sonatas: I, *Spring* (1985); II, *Summer* (1985); III, *Autumn* (1986); IV, *Winter* (1986); *Schpass* (Nonet) for 3 Oboists (1986; Krakow, Feb. 22, 1988); *Kwaiwa* for Violin and Computer (1986; Krakow, Feb. 22, 1988); *Missa sinfonica* for Orch., with Soprano Solo, Violin Solo, and Soprano Saxophone Solo (Katowice, April 25, 1986); Concerto for Flute, Harp, and Orch. (1986); Concerto for Saxophone (Soprano, Alto, and Tenor) and Orch. (1986); Concerto for Violin, Gasab-violin, English Horn, 2 Oboes, and Orch. (Krakow, June 10, 1986); *Little Concerto* for Violin and 3 Oboes (1987; Krakow, Feb. 22, 1988); *Acontecimiento* for 3 Pianos and Computer (1988); Piano Concerto No. 3 (1988); Violin Concerto (1988). **PLAYS (WITH ORIGINAL MUSIC):** *Anton Webern* (1955); *Eskimos' Paradise* (1964; the same as his *Audience III*); *Scenario* for 3 Actors (1970); *Mroki* (Darknesses; 1979); *Zorza* (Dawn; 1981); *Grzechy starosci* (Sins of Old Age; 1985); *Kaczo* for 2 Actors and an Actress (1987); *Ranek* (Daybreak; 1988).

WRITINGS: *Maly informator muzyki XX wieku* (Little Lexicon of Music of the 20th Century; Krakow, 1958; new ed., 1987); *Nowa muzyka, problemy wspolczesnej techniki kompozytorskiej* (New Music: Problems of Contemporary Technique in Composing; Krakow, 1958; new ed., 1969); *Klasycy dodekafonii* (Classics of Dodecaphonic Music; 2 vols., Krakow, 1961, 1964); *Leksykon kompozytorów XX wieku* (Lexicon of 20th-century Composers; 2 vols., Krakow, 1963, 1965); *W kręgu nowej muzyki* (In the Sphere of New Music; Krakow, 1967); *Dźwieki i znaki* (Sounds and Signs: Introduction to Contemporary Composition; Warsaw, 1969); *Muzyka XX wieku, Tworcy i problemy* (Music of the 20th Century, Composers and Problems; Krakow, 1975); *Wstęp do kompozycji* (Introduction to Composition; in Polish and Eng.; Krakow, 1976); *Dzieje muzyki* (History of Music; Warsaw, 1983); *Dzieje kultury muzycznej* (History of Music Culture; Warsaw, 1987); *Kompozytorzy XX wieku* (Composers of the 20th Century; Krakow, 1988).

BIBL.: J. Hodor and B. Pociej, *B. S. and His Music* (Glasgow,

1975); J. Hodor, "Twórczość kompozytorska B. S.a," *Miesiecznik Literacki*, IX (1979).

Schaeffer, Pierre, French acoustician, composer, and novelist; b. Nancy, Aug. 14, 1910. Working in a radio studio in Paris, he conceived the idea of arranging a musical montage of random sounds, including outside noises. On April 15, 1948, he formulated the theory of *musique concrète*, which was to define such random assemblages of sounds. When the magnetic tape was perfected, Schaeffer made use of it by rhythmic acceleration and deceleration, changing the pitch and dynamics and modifying the nature of the instrumental timbre. He made several collages of elements of "concrete music," among them *Concert de bruits* (1948) and (with Pierre Henry) *Symphonie pour un homme seul* (1950); also created an experimental opera, *Orphée 53* (1953). He incorporated his findings and ideas in the publ. *A la recherche de la musique concrète* (Paris, 1952) and in *Traité des objects sonores* (Paris, 1966). Eventually he abandoned his acoustical experimentations and turned to literature. He publ. both fictional and quasi-scientific novels, among them *Traité des objets musicaux* (1966); *Le Gardien de volcan* (1969); *Excusez-moi si je meurs* (1981); *Prélude, Chorale et Fugue* (1983).

BIBL.: M. Pierret, *Entretiens avec P. S.* (Paris, 1969); S. Brunet, *P. S.* (Paris, 1970).

Schaeffner, André, French musicologist and ethnomusicologist; b. Paris, Feb. 7, 1895; d. there, Aug. 11, 1980. He studied composition with d'Indy at the Schola Cantorum (1921–24), ethnology with M. Mauss at the Institut d'Ethnologie (1932–33), religious science at the École Pratique des Hautes Études (1934–37; diploma, 1940), and archeology with S. Reinach at the École du Louvre. In 1929 he founded the ethnological dept. at the Musée de l'Homme in Paris, which he headed until 1965. Between 1931 and 1958 he led 6 scientific excursions in Africa. From 1958 to 1961 he was president of the Société Française de Musicologie. He also took great interest in modern music and in lexicography; in addition to editing the French edition of Riemann's *Musiklexikon* (*Dictionnaire de musique*, Paris, 1931), he brought out the books *Le jazz* (with A. Cœuroy; Paris, 1926), a monograph on Stravinsky (Paris, 1931), *Origines des instruments de musique* (Paris, 1936; reprint, 1968), *Les Kissi: une Société noire et ses instruments de musique* (Paris, 1951), and *Segalen et Claude Debussy* (with A. Joly-Segalen; Monaco, 1961). A Festschrift was publ. in his memory in 1982.

Schäfer, Dirk, eminent Dutch composer, pianist, and pedagogue; b. Rotterdam, Nov. 23, 1873; d. Amsterdam, Feb. 16, 1931. He studied in Rotterdam and Cologne; after a European concert tour he settled in Amsterdam, where he was active as a pianist and teacher. I Schäfer-Dumstorff ed. his *Het klavier* (Amsterdam, 1942).

WORKS: *Suite pastorale* for Orch. (1903); *Rhapsodie javanaise* for Orch. (1904); 4 violin sonatas (1901–9); Piano Quintet (1901); Cello Sonata (1909); String Quartet (1922); many piano pieces; songs.

BIBL.: *Ter herinnering aan D. S.* (Amsterdam, 1923).

Schafer, R(aymond) Murray, Canadian composer; b. Sarnia, Ontario, July 18, 1933. He studied at the Royal Cons. of Music of Toronto with John Weinzweig (1952–55); went to Vienna in 1956 and then on to England, where he was active with the BBC (1956–61). Returning to Canada in 1961, he served as artist-in-residence at Memorial Univ. (1963–65) and taught at Simon Fraser Univ. (1965–75); held a Guggenheim fellowship in 1974. He was active with the World Soundscape project from 1972. In 1987 he received the Glenn Gould Award. He developed a sui generis system of topological transmutation, exemplified by his satire/tribute for orch. and tape *The Son of Heldenleben* (Montreal, Nov. 13, 1968), in which he systematically distorted the thematic materials of *Ein Heldenleben* by Richard Strauss, retaining the essential motivic substance of the original score.

WRITINGS: *British Composers in Interview* (London, 1963);

The Composer in the Classroom (Toronto, 1965; 3rd ed., 1972); *Ear Cleaning* (Toronto, 1967; 3rd ed., 1972); *The New Soundscape* (Toronto, 1969; 3rd ed., 1972); *The Book of Noise* (Vancouver, 1970; 2nd ed., 1973); *When Words Sing* (Toronto, 1970; 3rd ed., 1972); *The Public of the Music Theatre: Louis Riel: A Case Study* (London, 1972); *The Music of Ezra Pound* (N.Y., 1974); *E.T.A. Hoffmann and Music* (Toronto, 1975); ed. *Ezra Pound and Music: The Complete Criticism* (N.Y., 1977); *The Tuning of the World* (N.Y., 1977); *The Thinking Ear* (Toronto, 1986).

WORKS: STAGE: 2 operas: *Loving/Toi,* with Electronic Sound (stage premiere, Toronto, March 11, 1978), and *Patria,* a trilogy-in-progress, of which *Patria II* is complete (Stratford, Ontario, Aug. 23, 1972); *Jonah,* musical-dramatic work for Actors, Singers, Chorus, and Instruments (1979). **ORCH.:** *Canzoni for Prisoners* (1961–62); 2 educational works of variable duration for Youth Orch.: *Invertible Material* (1963) and *Statement in Blue,* in aleatory notation (1964); *Untitled Composition* (1963); *The Son of Heldenleben* for Tape and Orch. (Montreal, Nov. 13, 1968); *No Longer Than 10 Minutes* (1970; the title derives from the stipulation of the maximum length of the piece; Toronto, Feb. 16, 1971); *East* (1972); *North/White* for Orch. (1973; Vancouver, Aug. 17, 1973; a protest of government and industry's "rape of the Canadian North"); *Train* for Youth Orch. (1976); *Apocalypsis* for 500 Professional and Amateur Performers (1976; London, Ontario, Nov. 28, 1980); Flute Concerto (Vancouver, Oct. 26, 1985). **VOCAL:** *Minnelieder* for Mezzo-soprano and Wind Quintet (1956); *Protest and Incarceration,* 2 songs for Mezzo-soprano and Orch. (1960); *St. Jean de Brebeuf,* cantata for Baritone and Orch. (1961); *5 Studies on Texts by Prudentius* for Soprano and 4 Flutes (1962); *Requiems for the Party Girl* for Soprano and 9 Instruments (1966); *Threnody* for 5 Young Narrators, Youth Chorus, and Orch., with Tape (1966); *Gita,* piece for Chorus, Brass Ensemble, and Tape (Lenox, Mass., Aug. 10, 1967); *From the Tibetan Book of the Dead* for Soprano, Chorus, Flute, Clarinet, and Tape (1968); *Sappho* for Mezzo-soprano, Harp, Piano, Guitar, and Percussion (1970); *Enchantress* for Soprano, Flute, and 8 Cellos (1971); *In Search of Zoroaster* for Male Voice, Chorus, Percussion (played by chorus members), and Organ (1971); *Tehillah* for Chorus and Percussion (1972); *Arcana* for Voice and Instruments (1972); the trilogy *Lustro* (1969–72; premiere as a trilogy, Toronto, May 31, 1973), consisting of 3 separately composed works: *Divan i Shams i Tabriz* for 7 Singers, Tape, and Orch. (1969), *Music for the Morning of the World* for Voice and Tape (1970), and *Beyond the Great Gate of Light* for 7 Singers, Tape, and Orch. (1972); *Adieu Robert Schumann* for Contralto and Orch., derived from Clara Schumann's diaries chronicling Schumann's madness (1976; Ottawa, March 14, 1978); *Beauty and the Beast* for Voice and String Quartet (1980); *RA,* multimedia work with audience participation, based on the myth of the Egyptian sun god (Toronto, dawn-to-dusk, May 6, 1983). **CHAMBER:** Concerto for Harpsichord and 8 Wind Instruments (1954); String Quartet (1970); *Okeanos* for Tape (1971); String Quartet No. 2, *Waves* (1976); String Quartet No. 4 (Toronto, April 18, 1989).

Schäffer, August, German composer; b. Rheinsberg, Aug. 25, 1814; d. Baden-Baden, Aug. 7, 1879. He was a pupil, from 1833, of Mendelssohn in Berlin, where he spent most of his life. His humorous duets and quartets won great popularity; he also composed the operas *Emma von Falkenstein* (Berlin, 1839), *José Riccardo* (Hannover, 1857), and *Junker Habakuk* (Hannover, 1861); also syms., string quartets, and piano pieces.

Schäffer, Julius, German choral conductor, writer on music, and composer; b. Krevese, near Osterburg, Sept. 28, 1823; d. Breslau, Feb. 10, 1902. He studied theology at Halle, where friendship with Franz, and musicians in the nearby city of Leipzig, won him over to music. In 1850 he went to Berlin to study under Dehn; in 1855, to Schwerin, where he founded and conducted the Schlosskirchenchor. In 1860 he became conductor of the Singakademie in Breslau. He publ. chorale books (1866, 1880), songs, and part-songs. In defense of Franz's "additional accompaniments" to scores by Bach and Handel, Schäffer wrote, *versus* Chrysander, *Zwei Beurteiler Robert Franzs* (1863), *Fr. Chrysander in seinen Klavierauszugen zur deutschen Händel-Ausgabe* (1876), and *R. Franz in seinen Bearbeitungen älterer Vokalwerke* (1877); also *Die Breslauer Singakademie* (1875).

BIBL.: E. Bonn, *J. S.* (Breslau, 1903).

Schaffrath, Christoph, German harpsichordist, teacher, and composer; b. Hohenstein-on-Elbe, near Chemnitz, 1709; d. Berlin, Feb. 17, 1763. He was harpsichordist to the king and Polish Prince Sangusko (from 1730); entered the service of Crown Prince Freidrich (later Friedrich the Great) in Ruppin in 1734, following his patron to Rheinsberg in 1736; when Friedrich became king in 1740, Schaffrath went to Berlin as harpsichordist in the court Kapelle; was named musician to Princess Amalie, the king's sister, in 1741. He wrote some 13 syms., 6 overtures, a Flute Concerto, 2 violin concertos, 13 keyboard concertos, 2 concertos for 2 Keyboards and Strings, much chamber music, etc.

Schalk, Franz, noted Austrian conductor, brother of **Josef Schalk;** b. Vienna, May 27, 1863; d. Edlach, Sept. 2, 1931. He studied with Bruckner at the Vienna Cons.; after making his debut in Liberec (1886), he conducted in Reichenbach (1888–89), Graz (1889–95), and Prague (1895–98), and at the Berlin Royal Opera (1899–1900). He subsequently concentrated his activities in Vienna, where he conducted at the Hofoper (from 1900); when it became the Staatsoper in 1918, he was named its director; after sharing that position with R. Strauss (1919–24), he was sole director until 1929. He was a regular conductor with the Vienna Phil. from 1901 until his death; also was conductor of the Gesellschaft der Musikfreunde (1904–21). On Dec. 14, 1898, he made his Metropolitan Opera debut in N.Y. conducting *Die Walküre,* but remained on the roster for only that season. He also conducted *Ring* cycles at London's Covent Garden in 1898, 1907, and 1911; likewise conducted at the Salzburg Festivals. He devoted part of his time to teaching conducting in Vienna. A champion of Bruckner, he ed. several of his syms., even recomposing his 5th Sym. While Schalk's eds. were well-intentioned efforts to obtain public performances of Bruckner's scores, they are now totally discredited. L. Schalk ed. his *Briefe und Betrachtungen* (Vienna, 1935).

Schalk, Josef, Austrian pianist, teacher, and writer on music, brother of **Franz Schalk;** b. Vienna, March 24, 1857; d. there, Nov. 7, 1900. He studied with Bruckner and Epstein; was a piano teacher at the Vienna Cons. His arrangements of the Bruckner syms. for piano, 4-hands, did much to make these works known, and his book, *Anton Bruckner und die moderne Musikwelt* (1885), effectively upheld Bruckner's music. He was also a friend of Hugo Wolf, whom he championed.

Schall, Claus Nielsen, Danish violinist and composer; b. Copenhagen, April 28, 1757; d. there, Aug. 9, 1835. He became a dancer at the Royal Theater in 1772; was made a member of the court chapel in 1775; became répétiteur and director of the ballet at the Royal Theater in 1776. After touring in Europe, he returned to Copenhagen as Konzertmeister of the Opera in 1792; was made composer to the Royal Ballet in 1795; served as music director of the Opera (1818–34). He wrote 6 singspiels, of which the following (all 1st perf. in Copenhagen) were the most successful: *Claudine af Villa Bella* (Jan. 29, 1787); *Kinafarerne* (March 2, 1792); *Domherren i Milano* (March 16, 1802); *De tre Galninger* (March 19, 1816). He also wrote some 20 ballets, various orch. pieces, chamber music, and songs.

BIBL.: J. Friedrich, *C. S. als dramatischer Komponist* (diss., Univ. of Breslau, 1930).

Schall, Richard, German musicologist; b. Dortmund, Dec. 3, 1922. He studied at the Univ. of Marburg (Ph.D., 1946, with the diss. *Hugo Kaun: Leben und Werk, 1863–1932: Ein Beitrag zur Musik der Jahrhundertwende;* publ. in Regensburg, 1948); also received instruction in music theory from H.

Gebhard-Elsass and in conducting from H. von Waltershausen, and later attended the library school of the Bavarian State Library in Munich, where he took the senior librarian's examination (1956). From 1962 to 1986 he was musicological adviser to the Bavarian Radio, for which he prepared various publications. He contributed numerous articles to *Die Musik in Geschichte und Gegenwart;* also served as ed. of the *Quellenkataloge zur Musikgeschichte* (Wilhelmshaven, from 1966), the *Taschenbücher zur Musikwissenschaft* (Wilhelmshaven, from 1969), *Veröffentlichungen zur Musikforschung* (Wilhelmshaven, from 1972), and *Paperbacks on Musicology* (N.Y., from 1980). His writings are of value for the bibliography of German musicology.

Scharrer, August, German composer and conductor; b. Strasbourg, Aug. 18, 1866; d. Weiherhof, near Fürth, Oct. 24, 1936. He studied music in Strasbourg and Berlin; then was a theater conductor in Karlsruhe (1897–98) and Regensburg (1898–1900); from 1914 to 1931 he conducted the Phil. Society of Nuremberg. He wrote an opera, *Die Erlösung* (Strasbourg, Nov. 21, 1895); overtures; chamber music; choruses; songs.

Scharrer, Irene, English pianist and teacher; b. London, Feb. 2, 1888; d. there, Jan. 11, 1971. She studied with T. Matthay at the Royal Academy of Music in London; after making her London debut in 1904, she toured throughout England and Europe; made her 1st visit to the U.S. in 1925. In addition to appearing as a soloist with orchs., recitalist, and chamber-music artist, she gave duo recitals with her cousin, Dame Myra Hess, with whom she gave her farewell perf. in London in 1958. She also engaged in teaching.

Scharwenka, (Ludwig) Philipp, Polish-German composer and pedagogue, brother of **(Franz) Xaver Scharwenka;** b. Samter, Posen, Feb. 16, 1847; d. Bad Nauheim, July 16, 1917. He studied with Wüerst and Dorn at the Kullak Academy of Music in Berlin; in 1868 he was appointed teacher of composition there; with his brother **Xaver,** he founded in 1881 the Scharwenka Cons. in Berlin; together they made an American trip in 1891; in 1893 the Scharwenka Cons. was amalgamated with the Klindworth Cons.; the resulting Klindworth-Scharwenka Cons. acquired an excellent reputation for its teaching standards. He was an accomplished composer; among his works were 2 syms., overtures, *Arkadische Suite* for Orch. (1887), a Violin Concerto (1895), *Frühlingswogen,* symphonic poem (1891), *Dramatische Fantasie* for Orch. (1900), choral works, chamber music, piano pieces, and songs.

Scharwenka, (Franz) Xaver, Polish-German pianist, composer, and pedagogue, brother of **(Ludwig) Philipp Scharwenka;** b. Samter, Posen, Jan. 6, 1850; d. Berlin, Dec. 8, 1924. He studied with Kullak and Wüerst at the Kullak Academy of Music in Berlin, graduating in 1868; then joined its faculty. He made his debut in Berlin in 1869; made regular tours from 1874; also presented chamber music concerts in Berlin from 1881. With his brother, he founded the Scharwenka Cons. in Berlin in 1881; in 1891 he went to the U.S. and opened a N.Y. branch of his Cons.; appeared as soloist in his own Piano Concerto (N.Y., Jan. 24, 1891). Returning to Berlin in 1898, he became co-director of the newly amalgamated (1893) Klindworth-Scharwenka Cons.; in 1914 he established his own course of master classes for piano. As a composer, he was undoubtedly superior to his brother, although both were faithful imitators of Schumann and other German Romantics. He wrote an opera, *Mataswintha* (Weimar, Oct. 4, 1896); a Sym. (1885); 4 piano concertos; chamber music; numerous effective piano pieces, of which his *Polish Dances* became favorites with American piano teachers and students. He also publ. technical studies for piano, *Beiträge zur Fingerbildung; Studien im Oktavenspiel;* a collection of famous études, arranged according to progressive difficulty, under the title *Meisterschule des Klavierspiels; Methodik des Klavierspiels* (1907; with A. Spanuth); and a book of memoirs, *Klänge aus meinem Leben: Erinnerungen eines Musikers* (Leipzig, 1922).

Schat, Peter, Dutch composer; b. Utrecht, June 5, 1935. He studied with Kees van Baaren at the Utrecht Cons. (1952–

58), M. Seiber in London, and Boulez in Basel (1960–62). Upon returning to the Netherlands, he became active with the Studio for Electro-Instrumental Music in Amsterdam. From his earliest steps in composition, he adopted the serial method; also experimented with electronic sonorities. With Louis Andriessen and Misha Mengelberg, he organized in 1968 a series of Political-Demonstrative Experimental Concerts and also formed the Amsterdam Electric Circus, an itinerant troupe of musicians. His most notorious production was *Labyrinth*, a "total theater" spectacle in mixed media (1961–65; Amsterdam, June 23, 1966), which spawned a series of excerpts: *Choirs from the "Labyrinth"* for Chorus and Orch. (1962–63); *Voices from the "Labyrinth"* for 3 Voices and Orch. (1962–63); *Dances from the "Labyrinth"* for Orch. (1962); *Scenes from the "Labyrinth"* for Speaking Voices, Soprano, Tenor, Bass, Chorus, and Orch. (1961–64); *Improvisations from the "Labyrinth"* for 3 Voices, Bass Clarinet, Double Bass, Piano, and Percussion (1964); *Tapes from the "Labyrinth"* for 4 Tapes (1964–65). He also collaborated with Louis Andriessen, Reinbert de Leeuw, Misha Mengelberg, and Jan van Vlijmen on the anti-imperialist opera *Reconstructie* (Holland Festival, Amsterdam, June 29, 1969). His other works include: *Introduction and Adagio in Old Style* for String Quartet (1955); Septet for Flute, Oboe, Horn, Bass Clarinet, Piano, Cello, and Percussion (1957); *2 Pieces* for Flute, Violin, Trumpet, and Percussion (1959); Wind Octet (1959); *Inscripties* for Piano (1959); *Mosaics* for Orch. (1959); *Crytogamen* for Baritone and Orch. (1959); *Concerto da camera* for 2 Clarinets, Piano, Strings, and Percussion (1960); *Improvisations and Symphonies* for Wind Quintet (1960); *The Fall*, after James Joyce, for Chorus a cappella (1960); *Entelechie I* for 5 Instrumental Groups (1961); *Entelechie II*, scenes for 11 Musicians (1961); *Signalement* for 6 Percussionists and 3 Double Basses (1961); *Sextet*, fragment for 3 Actors and 3 Musicians (1961); *First Essay on Electrocution* for Violin, Guitar, and Metal Guitar (1966); *Clockwise and Anti-clockwise* for 16 Wind Instruments (1967); *Anathema* for Piano (1968); *On Escalation* for 6 Solo Percussionists and Orch. (Amsterdam, May 30, 1968); *Hypothema* for Recorders (1969); *Thema* for Electrified Oboe, 4 Electric Guitars, Hammond Organ, and 18 Wind Instruments (Amsterdam, July 5, 1970); *To You* for Voice, 6 Guitars, 3 Bass Guitars, 4 Pianos, 2 Hammond Organs, 6 Humming Tops, and Electronics (1970–72; Amsterdam, June 20, 1972); *Canto General*, dedicated to the memory of Salvador Allende, for Mezzo-soprano, Violin, and Piano (1974); *May 75*, a song of liberation for 2 Soloists, Chorus, and Orch. (1975; 10th scene from the opera *Houdini*); *Houdini Symphony* for 4 Soloists, Chorus, and Orch. (1976); *Houdini*, a circus opera (1974–76; Amsterdam, Sept. 29, 1977); *Kind en kraai*, song cycle for Soprano and Piano (1977); Sym. No. 1 (1978; rev. 1979); *Aap verslaat de knekelgeest* (Monkey Subdues the White-Bone Demon), opera (1980); *Polonaise* for Piano (1981).

Schaub, Hans (actually, **Siegmund Ferdinand**), German music critic, teacher, and composer; b. Frankfurt am Main, Sept. 22, 1880; d. Hanstedt, near Marburg, Nov. 12, 1965. He studied at the Frankfurt Hoch Cons. with Iwan Knorr (theory) and Carl Friedberg (piano), with Arnold Mendelssohn in Darmstadt, and with Humperdinck in Berlin; also took lessons with Richard Strauss. He taught at the Breslau Cons. (1903–6); was on the faculty of Benda's Cons. and served as ed. of the *Deutsche Musikerzeitung* in Berlin (1906–16); after working as a music critic and pedagogue in Hamburg (1916–51), he settled in Hanstedt.
    Works: *Passacaglia* for Orch. (1928); *3 Intermezzi* for Small Orch.; *Capriccio* for Violin and Piano; cantata, *Den Gefallenen* (1940); oratorio, *Deutsches Te Deum* (1942).

Schaum, John W., American piano pedagogue; b. Milwaukee, Jan. 27, 1905; d. there, July 19, 1988. He studied at Milwaukee State Teachers College, at Marquette Univ. (B.M., 1931), and at Northwestern Univ. (M.M., 1934). He established a successful piano teaching class in Milwaukee and publ. several piano methods and many collections of piano pieces that sold an enormous number of copies: *The Schaum Piano Course* (9 vols.); *The Schaum Adult Piano Course* (3 vols.); *The Schaum Duet Albums* (2 vols.); also theory books: *The Schaum Theory Lessons* (2 vols.) and *The Schaum Note Spellers* (2 vols.).

Schech, Marianne, German soprano; b. Geitau, Jan. 18, 1914. She was educated in Munich; made her operatic debut in Koblenz in 1937; then sang in Munich (1939–41), Düsseldorf (1941–44), and at the Dresden State Opera (1944–51); also sang with the Bavarian State Opera in Munich. In 1956 she was named a Kammersängerin. On Jan. 22, 1957, she made her debut at the Metropolitan Opera in N.Y. as Sieglinde in *Die Walküre;* also made guest appearances in London, Vienna, and Hamburg. She retired from the stage in 1970 and devoted herself mainly to teaching.

Scheel, Fritz, German conductor; b. Lübeck, Nov. 7, 1852; d. Philadelphia, March 13, 1907. His grandfather and father were orch. conductors, and at 9 the boy played the violin in his father's orch.; from 1864 to 1867 he was a pupil of F. David in Leipzig. At 17 he began his career as a concertmaster and conductor at Bremerhaven; in 1873 he was solo violinist and conductor of the summer concerts in Schwerin; in 1884 he became conductor of the Chemnitz municipal orch.; from 1890 to 1893 he was conductor of orch. concerts in Hamburg. He went to the U.S. in 1893, and after conducting the Trocadero concerts at the World's Columbian Exposition in Chicago (1894), he served as founder-conductor of the San Francisco Sym. Society (1895–99); subsequently was the 1st conductor of the Philadelphia Orch. (1900–1907).
    Bibl.: F. Wister, *25 Years of the Philadelphia Orchestra, 1900–1925* (Philadelphia, 1925); H. Kupferberg, *Those Fabulous Philadelphians: The Life and Times of a Great Orchestra* (N.Y., 1969).

Scheff, Fritzi, famous Austrian soprano; b. Vienna, Aug. 30, 1879; d. N.Y., April 8, 1954. She studied with her mother, the singer Anna Jäger; after further training with Schröder-Hanfstängl in Munich, she completed her studies at the Frankfurt Cons.; made her debut as Martha in Frankfurt (1896), and soon adopted her mother's maiden name of Scheff for professional purposes. After singing at the Munich Hofoper (1897–1900), she made her Metropolitan Opera debut in N.Y. as Marzellina in *Fidelio* (Dec. 28, 1900), and remained on its roster until 1903; concurrently sang at London's Covent Garden. She later shifted to light opera, and it was in this field that she became famous. She created the role of Fifi in Victor Herbert's operetta *Mlle. Modiste* (Trenton, N.J., Oct. 7, 1905); her singing of Fifi's waltz song *Kiss Me Again* became a hallmark of her career. She also found success as a dramatic actress, becoming particularly well known for her appearance in *Arsenic and Old Lace*. Her 3 marriages (to Baron Fritz von Bardeleben, the American writer John Fox, Jr., and the singer George Anderson) ended in divorce.

Scheffler, Siegfried, German composer; b. Ilmenau, May 15, 1892; d. Hamburg, June 5, 1969. He studied with his father; then took courses at the Leipzig Cons. with Max Reger, Stephan Krehl, Hans Sitt, and others; also attended classes in musicology at the Univ. of Leipzig with Hugo Riemann and Arnold Schering, and in Berlin with Humperdinck and Kretzschmar. In 1924 he settled in Hamburg; wrote music criticism and supervised music programs at the Hamburg Radio. He composed *Wunderhorn Lieder* (1914); *Rokoko-Novelle* for Orch. (1923); incidental music for various plays. He publ. *Richard Wagner* (2 vols., Hamburg, 1928) and *Melodie der Welle* (Berlin, 1933).

Scheibe, Johann Adolf, German music theorist and composer; b. Leipzig, May 3, 1708; d. Copenhagen, April 22, 1776. He was the son of the organ builder **Johann Scheibe** (b. Saxony, c.1680; d. Leipzig, Sept. 3, 1748); lost his right eye in his father's workshop when he was 8. He commenced the study of keyboard instruments at age 6; after attending the school of the Nicolaikirche, he entered the Univ. of Leipzig as a law student in 1725, but was compelled to give up his studies when the family's financial condition changed for the worse. He subsequently devoted himself to music, being mainly autodidact; failing to obtain organ posts at the Nicolaikirche in Leipzig (1729; Bach was one of the adjudicators), in Prague and Gotha (1735), and in Sondershausen and Wolfenbüttel (1736), he went to Hamburg as a music critic and composer (1736); brought out his *Der critische Musikus*, which includes his famous attack on Bach (No. 6, 1737). After serving as Kapellmeister to Margrave Friedrich Ernst of Brandenburg-Culmbach, the governor of Holstein (1739–40), he was made Kapellmeister at the court of King Christian VI in Copenhagen in 1740; with the accession of King Frederik V in 1747, Scheibe was pensioned and settled in Sønderborg, where he devoted himself to running a music school for children. In 1766 he once again resumed a relationship with the Danish court, serving as a composer for it until his death. The major portion of his compositional output, which includes the singspiel *Thusnelde* (libretto publ. in Leipzig and Copenhagen, 1749), 150 flute concertos, and some 30 violin concertos, is not extant. He is therefore primarily known as an important music theorist of his era.

WRITINGS: *Compendium musices theoretico-practicum, das ist Kurzer Begriff derer nötigsten Compositions-Regeln* (c.1730; publ. by P. Benary in *Die deutsche Kompositionslehre des 18. Jahrhunderts*, Leipzig, 1961); *Der critische Musikus* (vol. I, Hamburg, 1738; vol. II, Hamburg, 1740; complete ed., Leipzig, 1745); *Beantwortung der unparteiischen Anmerkungen über eine bedenkliche Stelle in dem sechsten Stücke des critischen Musicus* (Hamburg, 1738; reprint in *Der critische Musikus*, Leipzig, 1745); *Eine Abhandlung von den musicalischen Intervallen und Geschlechtern* (Hamburg, 1739); *Thusnelde, ein Singspiel in vier Aufzügen, mit einem Vorbericht von der Möglichkeit und Beschaffenheit guter Singspiele begleitet* (Leipzig and Copenhagen, 1749); *Abhandlung vom Ursprunge und Alter der Musik, insonderheit der Vokalmusik* (Altona and Flensburg, 1754); *Über die musikalische Composition, erster Theil: Die Theorie der Melodie und Harmonie* (Leipzig, 1773).

BIBL.: K. Storch, *S.s Anschauungen von der musikalische Historie, Wissenschaft und Kunst* (diss., Univ. of Leipzig, 1923); E. Rosenkaimer, *J.A. S. als Verfasser des Critischen Musikus* (Bonn, 1929); I. Willheim, *J.A. S.: German Musical Thought in Transition* (diss., Univ. of Illinois, 1963); G. Skapski, *The Recitative in J.A. S.'s Literary and Musical Work* (diss., Univ. of Texas, 1963).

Scheibler, Johann Heinrich, German inventor and writer on music; b. Montjoie, near Aachen, Nov. 11, 1777; d. Krefeld, Nov. 20, 1837. He studied with J.N. Wolff. A silk manufacturer at Krefeld, he became interested in acoustic phenomena and invented an apparatus, consisting of 56 tuning forks, for tuning fixed-tone instruments according to the equally tempered scale. At the Stuttgart Congress of physicists in 1834, Scheibler proposed the pitch of a¹ = 440 (vibrations) at 69° F, which was adopted (hence called the "Stuttgart pitch"). His system is more clearly explained by Töpfer (1842), Vincent (1849), and Lecomte (1856).

WRITINGS: *Der physikalische und musikalische Tonmesser* (Essen, 1834); *Anleitung, die Orgel vermittelst der Stösse (vulgo Schwebungen) und des Metronoms correct gleichschschwebend zu stimmen* (Krefeld, 1834); *Über mathematische Stimmung, Temperaturen und Orgelbaustimmung nach Vibrationsdifferenzen oder Stossen* (Krefeld, 1835); *Mitteilung über das Wesentliche des musikalischen und physikalischen Tonmessers* (Krefeld, 1836).

BIBL.: J. Löhr, *Über die S.'sche Erfindung überhaupt und dessen Pianoforte- und Orgel-Stimmung insbesondere* (Krefeld, 1836).

Scheidemann, Heinrich, important German organist, pedagogue, and composer; b. Wöhrden, Holstein, c.1595; d. Hamburg, 1663. He studied with Sweelinck in Amsterdam (1611–14); in 1629 he succeeded his father as organist at the Katharinenkirche in Hamburg, and held that post until his death. Among his students was J.A. Reinken, who became his assis-

tant in 1658 and his successor at his death. Scheidemann excelled especially as a composer of organ music. See G. Fock and W. Breig, eds., *Heinrich Scheidemann: Orgelwerke* (1967–71).

Scheidemantel, Karl, noted German baritone; b. Weimar, Jan. 21, 1859; d. there, June 26, 1923. He was a pupil of Bodo Borchers, and sang at the court theater in Weimar (1878–86); also studied voice with Julius Stockhausen in the summers of 1881–83. He was a member of the Dresden Court Opera from 1886 to 1911; also sang at the Munich Court Opera (1882), London's Covent Garden (debut as Wolfram, June 14, 1884), the Vienna Court Opera (1890), and Milan's La Scala (1892). From 1911 to 1920 he was a prof. at the Grossherzogliche Musikschule in Weimar; from 1920 to 1922 he was director of the Landestheater in Dresden. He publ. *Stimmbildung* (1907; 4th ed. as *Gesangsbildung*, 1913; in Eng., 1910); also ed. a collection of songs, *Meisterweisen* (1914). Among his finest roles were Hans Sachs, Kurwenal, Amfortas, Klingsor, Telramund, Pizarro, and Scarpia; he also created the roles of Kunrad in *Feuersnot* (Dresden, Nov. 21, 1901) and Faninal in *Der Rosenkavalier* (Dresden, Jan. 26 1911).

BIBL.: P. Trede, *K. S.* (Dresden, 1911).

Scheidt, Samuel, important German organist, teacher, and composer; b. Halle (baptized), Nov. 3, 1587; d. there, March 24, 1654. He studied at the Halle Gymnasium; from c.1603 to 1608 he was organist at the Moritzkirche in Halle, and then went to Amsterdam to study with Sweelinck. He returned to Halle in 1609, and was appointed court organist to Margrave Christian Wilhelm of Brandenburg; in 1619 he also assumed the post of court Kapellmeister; when the margrave left for Denmark in 1625 to support the Protestant cause in the Thirty Years' War, Scheidt retained his post even though without emolument, eking out a modest living by teaching. In 1628 he was named music director of the Marktkirche, the principal church in Halle, continuing in this employment until 1630. In 1638 he resumed his post as court Kapellmeister and served until his death. Scheidt was highly esteemed as an organist; was consulted on the building of organs as an inspector; was also a noted organ teacher. As a composer, Scheidt excelled in both keyboard and sacred vocal works.

WORKS: KEYBOARD: *Tabulatura nova continens variationes aliquot psalmorum, fantasiarum, cantilenarum, passamezzo et canones* (Hamburg, 1624); *Pars secunda tabulaturae continens fugarum, psalmorum, cantionum et echus, tocatae, variationes varias omnimodas pro quorumvis organistarum captu et modulo* (Hamburg, 1624); *III. et ultima pars tabulaturae continens Kyrie Dominicale, Credo in unum Deum, Psalmum de Coena Domini sub communione, hymnos praecipuorum festorum totius anni, Magnificat . . . & Benedicamus* (Hamburg, 1624); *Tabulatur-Buch hundert geistlicher Lieder und Psalmen* (Görlitz, 1650); additional instrumental works include *Paduana, galliaria, courante, alemande, intrada, canzonetto, ut vocant, in gratiam musices studiosorum, potissimum violistarum, a 4, 5,* and Basso Continuo (Hamburg, 1621); *Ludorum musicorum secunda pars continens paduan, galliard, alemand, canzon, et intrad, a 4, 5, 7,* and Basso Continuo (Hamburg, 1622); *Ludorum musicorum tertia pars continens paduanas, cour. et canzon., a 3, 4, 7, 8,* and Basso Continuo (Hamburg, 1624; not extant); *Ludorum musicorum quarta pars, a 3, 4,* and Basso Continuo (Hamburg, 1627); *LXX Symphonien auff Concerten manir: Vornemlich auff Violinen zu gebrauchen durch die gewöhnliche Tonos, und die 7 Claves, a 2* and Basso Continuo (Leipzig, 1644); also canons in *Tabulatura nova continens variationes aliquot psalmorum, fantasiarum, cantilenarum, passamezzo et canones* (Hamburg, 1624). VOCAL CHURCH MUSIC: *Cantiones sacrae* for 8 Voices (Hamburg, 1620); *Pars prima concertuum sacrorum, adiectis symphoniis et choris instrumentalibus* for 2 to 5, 8, and 12 Voices and Basso Continuo (Hamburg, 1622); *Newe geistliche Concerten . . . prima pars* for 2 and 3 Voices and Basso Continuo (Halle, 1631); *Geistlicher Concerten . . . ander Theil* for 2 to 6 Voices and Basso Continuo (Halle, 1634); *Geistlicher Concerten . . . dritter Theil* for 2 to 6 Voices and Basso Continuo (Halle, 1635); *Liebliche Krafft-Blümlein aus des Heyligen Geistes Lustgarten abgebrochen und zum Vorschmack dess ewigen Lebens im zweystimmichten Himmels-Chor versetzet* for 2 Voices and Basso Continuo (Halle, 1635); *Geistlicher Concerten . . . vierter Theil* for 2 to 6 Voices and Basso Continuo (Halle, 1640). A collected ed. of his works was begun by G. Harms and continued by others (16 vols., 1923–83).

BIBL.: C. Mahrenholz, *S. S.: Sein Leben und sein Werk* (Leipzig, 1924); R. Hünicken, *S. S.: Ein althallischer Musikus* (Halle, 1934); W. Serauky, *S. S. in seinen Briefen* (Halle, 1937); a Festschrift in honor of his 350th birthday (Wolfenbüttel, 1937); A. Adrio, "Zu S. S.s Vokalmusik," *Musik und Kirche*, XXIV (1954); C. Mahrenholz, "S. S. und die Orgel," *Musik und Kirche*, XXV (1955); E. Gessner, *S. S.s geistliche Konzerte: Ein Beitrag zur Geschichte der Gattung* (Berlin, 1961); W. Braun, "S. S.s Bearbeitungen alter Motetten," *Archiv für Musikwissenschaft*, XIX–XX (1962–63); W. Breig, "Zu den handschriftlich überlieferten Liedvariationen von S. S.," *Die Musikforschung*, XXII (1969); A. Adrio, "S. S.s Cantiones Sacrae Octo Vocum von 1620: Beobachtungen und Anmerkungen," *Kerygma und Melos: Christhard Mahrenholz 70 Jahre* (Kassel, 1970); F. Krummacher, *Die Choralbearbeitung in der protestantischen Figuralmusik zwischen Praetorius und Bach* (Kassel, 1978); P. Kenyon, " 'Imitatio violistica' in S.'s 'Tablatura Nova'," *Musical Times* (Jan. 1989).

Schein, Ann, American pianist; b. White Plains, N.Y., Nov. 10, 1939. She studied with Glenn Gunn in Washington, D.C., Mieczyslaw Munz at the Peabody Cons. in Baltimore, Artur Rubinstein (1961–63), and Dame Myra Hess (1961–65). She made her London debut in a recital in 1958; after appearing as a soloist with the N.Y. Phil. and making her Carnegie Hall recital debut in 1962, she toured widely. In 1968 she organized the People-to-People Music Committee in an effort to encourage amicable relations between nations via the art of music. She taught at the Peabody Cons. (from 1980) and the Aspen School of Music (from 1984). Her husband is the violinist Earl Carlyss. In addition to her performances of Chopin, she has won accolades for her interpretations of works by contemporary composers.

Schein, Johann Hermann, important German composer; b. Grünhain, near Annaberg, Jan. 20, 1586; d. Leipzig, Nov. 19, 1630. His father was a pastor; upon his death, Schein moved to Dresden, where he entered the Hofkapelle of the Elector of Saxony as a boy soprano; received instruction from the Kapellmeister, Rogier Michael; continued his studies in music at Pforta, an electoral school near Naumburg (1603–7); his teachers were Bartholomäus Scheer and Martin Roth. In 1607 he returned to Dresden; in 1608 he received an electoral scholarship to study jurisprudence and liberal arts at the Univ. of Leipzig, where he remained until 1612. In 1613 he became Hausmusikmeister to Gottfried von Wolffersdorff in Weissenfels, and also served as praeceptor to his children. In 1615 he was appointed Kapellmeister to Duke Johann Ernst the Younger in Weimar. In 1616 he was named cantor at the Thomasschule in Leipzig, as successor to Calvisius. His duties in Leipzig inlcuded directing the choral music at the Thomaskirche and the Nicolaikirche, and teaching singing and Latin grammar and syntax at the Thomasschule. Schein was one of the earliest German composers to introduce into Lutheran church music the Italian techniques of madrigal, monody, and concerto. In the alliterative parlance of learned German writers, Schein became known as the chronologically second of the glorious trio of near-contemporaneous German masters, Schütz (b. 1585), Schein (b. 1586), and Scheidt (b. 1587). But Schütz, the oldest of them, outlived Schein by 42 years; he visited him at his deathbed and brought him, as a friendly offering, a 6-part motet of his composition on Schein's favorite passage from the New Testament.

WORKS: SACRED VOCAL: *Cymbalum Sionium sive Cantiones sacrae,* for 5 to 12 Voices (Leipzig, 1615); *Opella nova, geistlicher Concerten . . . auff italiänische Invention componirt* for

3 to 5 Voices and Basso Continuo (Leipzig, 1618; 2nd ed., 1626); *Fontana d'Israel, Israelis Brünlein, auserlesener Krafft-Sprüchlin altes und Newen Testaments . . . aufeiner . . . Italian madrigalische Manier* for 5 and 6 Voices and Basso Continuo (Leipzig, 1623; 2nd ed., 1651); *Opella nova, ander Theil, geistlicher Concerten* for 3 to 6 Voices, Instruments, and Basso Continuo (Leipzig, 1626); *Cantional oder Gesangbuch Augspurgischer Confession* for 4 to 6 Voices (Leipzig, 1627; 2nd ed., enl., 1645). SECULAR VOCAL: Texts by Schein: *Venus Kräntzlein . . . oder Newe weltliche Lieder* for 5 Voices, *neben etzlichen Intraden, Gagliarden und Canzonen* (Wittenberg, 1609); *Musica boscareccia, oder Wald-Liederlein auff italian-villanellische Invention . . . mit lebendiger Stimm . . . auch auff musicalischen Instrumenten zu spielen* for 3 Voices (Leipzig, 1621; 6th ed., 1643; *Ander Theil* [Leipzig, 1628; 6th ed., 1641] *Dritter Theil* [Leipzig, 1628; 5th ed., 1643]; also publ. with rev. text as *Musica boscareccia sacra* [3 vols., Erfurt, 1644–51]); *Diletti pastorali, Hirten Lust* for 5 Voices and Basso Continuo, *auff Madrigal-Manier componirt* (Leipzig, 1624); *Studenten-Schmauss a 5: Einer löblischen Compagni de la Vinobiera* (Leipzig, 1626). INSTRUMENTAL: *Banchetto musicale newer . . . Padouanen, Gagliarden, Courenten und Allemanden a 5, auff allerley Instrumenten* (Leipzig, 1617); other works are found in several of his vocal collections. A collected ed. of his works, edited by A. Prüfer, was publ. by Breitkopf und Härtel (7 vols., Leipzig, 1901–23); the *Neue Ausgabe sämtlicher Werke,* ed. by A. Adrio, began publ. in Kassel in 1963 by Bärenreiter.

BIBL.: A. Prüfer, *J.H. S.* (Leipzig, 1895); A. Prüfer, "Zur Familiengeschichte des Leipziger Thomas-Kantors J.H. S.," *Monatshefte für Musikgeschichte*, XXX (1898); A. Prüfer, *J.H. S. und das weltliche deutsche Lied des 17. Jahrhunderts* (Leipzig, 1908); W. Brauer, "Jakob Regnart, J.H. S. und die Anfänge der deutschen Barocklyrik," *Deutsche Vierteljahrsschrift für Literaturwissenschaft und Geistersgeschichte*, XVII (1939); I. Hueck, *Die künstlerische Entwicklung J.H. S.s, dargestellt an seinen geistlichen Werken* (diss., Univ. of Freiburg, 1945); H. Redlich, "S. and the German Madrigal," *The Listener*, LIII (1959); A. Adrio, *J.H. S.* (Berlin, 1959); H. Rauhe, *Dichtung und Musik im weltlichen Vokalwerk J.H. S.s* (diss., Univ. of Hamburg, 1959); W. Reckziegel, *Das Cantional von J.H. S.: Seine geschichtlichen Grundlagen* (Berlin, 1963); F. Peterson, *J.H. S.'s Cymbalum Sionium: A Liturgico-musical Study* (diss., Harvard Univ., 1966); S. Sorensen, "J.H. S.s Opella nova," in *Renaissance muziek 1400–1600: Donum natalicium René Bernard Lenaerts* (Louvain, 1969); F. Krummacher, *Die Choralbearbeitung in der protestantischen Figuralmusik zwischen Praetorius und Bach* (Kassel, 1978).

Scheinpflug, Paul, German violinist, conductor, and composer; b. Loschwitz, near Dresden, Sept. 10, 1875; d. Memel, March 11, 1937. He studied violin with Rappoldi and composition with Draeseke at the Dresden Cons.; in 1898 he went to Bremen as concertmaster of the Phil. and conductor of the Liederkranz; then was conductor of the Königsberg Musikverein (1909–14); conducted the Blüthner Orch. in Berlin (1914–19); was music director in Duisburg (1920–28); in 1929 he became conductor of the Dresden Phil., holding this post until 1933.

WORKS: OPERA: *Das Hofkonzert* (1922). ORCH.: *Frühling* (1906); *Lustspiel-Ouvertüre* (1909); *Bundes-Ouvertüre* (1918); *Serenade* for Cello, English Horn or Viola, Harp, and Strings (1937); *Ein Sommertagebuch* (1937); *Nokturno* (1937). CHAMBER: Piano Quartet (1903); Violin Sonata (1908); String Quartet (1912); String Trio (1912); also men's choruses and many songs.

BIBL.: F. Dubitzky, "P. S.," *Monographien moderner Musiker*, II (Leipzig, 1907).

Schelble, Johann Nepomuk, German singer, conductor, pedagogue, and composer; b. Hüfingen, Black Forest, May 16, 1789; d. there, Aug. 6, 1837. He studied with Weisse in Donaueschingen, Volger in Darmstadt, and Krebs in Stuttgart, where he then sang as a tenor and baritone at the court and opera (1808–14); also was a teacher at the Royal Musical Inst.

(from 1812). From 1814 to 1816 he was in Vienna and became a close friend of Beethoven; settled in Frankfurt, where he founded the Cäcilien-Verein (1818), and sang at the Frankfurt theater (1817–19). His methods for teaching the musical rudiments and training the sense of absolute pitch were much admired; he enjoyed the esteem of many musicians of his time; Mendelssohn paid tribute to him in his correspondence. In addition to various didactic works, he also composed vocal and chamber music.

BIBL.: K. Lang, *Die Gehörsentwicklungs-Methode von S.* (Braunschweig, 1873); O. Bormann, *J.N. S. 1789–1837* (diss., Univ. of Frankfurt am Main, 1926).

Schelle, Johann, significant German composer; b. Geising, Thuringia (baptized), Sept. 6, 1648; d. Leipzig, March 10, 1701. He received his early musical training from his father, a schoolmaster; in 1655 he was sent to Dresden to sing in the choir of the electoral chapel, which was directed by Schütz; in 1657 he went to Wolfenbüttel, where he sang in the choir of the ducal court. In 1665 he became a student at the Thomasschule in Leipzig under Knüpfer; subsequently studied at the Univ. of Leipzig, becoming cantor in Eilenburg in 1670. In 1677 he succeeded Knüpfer as cantor of the Thomaskirche in Leipzig; also served as director chori musici for the city, and acted as director of music for the Nicolaikirche. He taught music at the Thomasschule; he was succeeded by his cousin, **Johann Kuhnau.** Schelle's importance as a composer rests upon his settings of the sacred Gospel cantata to German texts (in place of the traditional Latin texts) for Protestant liturgical use in Leipzig. He extended this practice to the chorale cantata as well. See A. Schering's ed. in the Denkmäler Deutscher Tonkunst, LVIII–LIX (1918).

BIBL.: B. Richter, "Zwei Funeralprogramme auf die Thomaskantoren Sebastian Knüpfer und Joh. S.," *Monatshefte für Musikgeschichte,* XXXIII (1901) and XXXIV (1902); F. Graupner, *Das Werk des Thomaskantors J. S.* (Berlin, 1929); R. Murray, *The German Church Music of J. S.* (diss., Univ. of Michigan, 1971).

Schelle, Michael, American composer; b. Philadelphia, Jan. 22, 1950. He studied theater at Villanova Univ. (B.A., 1971), then pursued musical training at Butler Univ. (B.M., 1974), at the Hartt School of Music of the Univ. of Hartford (M.M., 1976), and with Dominick Argento at the Univ. of Minnesota (Ph.D., 1980); also studied with Aaron Copland (1976–77). From 1979 he taught theory and composition at Butler Univ., where he was composer-in-residence from 1981; in 1981 he also became director of the univ.'s New Music Ensemble.

WORKS: STAGE: *Soap Opera,* chamber opera (1988; Indianapolis, June 9, 1989). **ORCH.:** *Lancaster Variations* (1976); *Masque—A Story of Puppets, Poets, Kings, and Clowns* (1977); *El Medico* (1977); *Pygmies* for Youth Orch. and Tape (1982); *Pygmies II* for Youth Orch. and Speaker (1983); *Golden Bells* for Orch. and Chorus (1983; completion of an unfinished work by N. Dinerstein); Oboe Concerto (Indianapolis, Jan. 6, 1984); *Swashbuckler!* (1984); Concerto for 2 Pianos and Orch. (Indianapolis, Jan. 14, 1988); *Kidspeace* for Orch. and Voices (1987). **SYMPHONIC BAND:** *King Ubu* (1980); *Cliff Hanger March* (1984); *7 Steps from Hell* (1985). **CHAMBER:** Piano Sonata No. 2 (1974); *Katzenmusik,* "4 Tales from *Old Possum's Book of Practical Cats*" by T.S. Eliot for Baritone and 6 Players (1976); *Song without Words* for Piano Trio (1977); Chamber Concerto for Solo Violin and 3 Players (1978); *Music for the Last Days of Strindberg* for 9 Players (1979); Double Quartet for 8 Winds (1980); *Cry Wolf!* for Piano, Cello, and 5 Percussionists (1981); *Music* for 2 Pianos (1982); *Rattlesnake!* for Percussionist with Auxiliary Percussionists (1982); *Blue Plate Special* for Tuba with Auxiliary Percussion (1983); *Music for the Alabama Kid* for 8 Players (1984); *Play Us Chastity on Your Violin,* chamber concerto for Violin and 13 Players (1984); *Howl!* for Clarinet and 4 Players (1986); *Daydream* for 6 Players or Actors (1988); *Musica Magnetizzare* for Piano and 4 Players (1988); *Racing with Rabbits* for Percussionist (1988). **VOCAL:** *The Wife Wrapt in Wether's Skin* for Men's Chorus (1974); *Cantus Matrimo-*

nium for Chorus, Organ, and Instruments (1976); *Caroleluia* for Chorus (1978); *Swanshite—Letters to Strindberg from Harriet Bosse,* cycle for Soprano and Piano (1980); *Deus Angelis* for Chorus and Organ (1987); *6 Seasonal Anthems* for Chorus and Organ (1987); *Oboe Darkness* for Youth Chorus, Oboe, and Percussion (1987).

Schelling, Ernest (Henry), American conductor, composer, and pianist; b. Belvidere, N.J., July 26, 1876; d. N.Y., Dec. 8, 1939. He 1st appeared in public as a child prodigy, playing the piano at the age of 4½ at the Academy of Music in Philadelphia. He was then sent to Paris in 1882, where he studied at the Cons. with Mathias until 1885; later received instruction from Moszkowski, Leschetizky, H. Huber, K. Barth, and finally Paderewski in Morges, Switzerland (1898–1902). Extended tours in Europe (from Russia to Spain) followed; he also toured in South America; returned to the U.S. in 1905, and devoted most of his energies to conducting and composing. He conducted the N.Y. Phil. young people's concerts (1924–39); was conductor of the Baltimore Sym. Orch. (1936–38); also made frequent appearances as a conductor in Europe. He was elected a member of the National Inst. of Arts and Letters in 1913.

WORKS: ORCH.: Sym. (n.d.); *Légende symphonique* (1904; Philadelphia, Oct. 31, 1913); *Suite fantastique* for Piano and Orch. (1905; Amsterdam, Oct. 10, 1907); *Impressions from an Artist's Life,* symphonic variations for Piano and Orch. (1913; Boston, Dec. 31, 1915, composer soloist); Violin Concerto (Providence, R.I., Oct. 17, 1916; Fritz Kreisler, soloist); *A Victory Ball,* symphonic poem after Noyes (Philadelphia, Feb. 23, 1923; his most successful work); *Morocco,* symphonic tableau (N.Y., Dec. 19, 1927, composer conducting). **CHAMBER:** Violin Sonata (n.d.); Divertimenti for Piano Quintet (1925); piano pieces.

BIBL.: T. Hill, *E. S. (1876–1939): His Life and Contributions to Music Education through Educational Concerts* (diss., Catholic Univ. of America, 1970).

Schemelli, Georg Christian, German musician; b. Herzberg, c.1676; d. Zeitz, March 5, 1762. He sang in the Dresden court Kapelle; was at the Leipzig Thomasschule (1695–1700), then was Kantor in Treuenbrietzen (1707–17), and court Kantor in Zeitz (1727–58). He publ. a vol. of 954 hymns as *Musicalisches Gesangbuch* (Leipzig, 1736), to which J.S. Bach contributed (see C. Terry, *The Four-part Chorales of J.S. Bach;* London, 1929; 2nd ed., 1964).

BIBL.: A. Schering, "Bach und das S.sche Gesangbuch," *Bach Jahrbuch,* XXI (1924); F. Hamel, "Die Kompositionen J.S. Bachs im S.schen Gesangbuch," *Zeitschrift für Musikwissenschaft,* XII (1929–30).

Schenck, Johannes, esteemed Dutch-born German viola da gambist and composer; b. Amsterdam (baptized), June 3, 1660; d. c.1712. He entered the service of the Elector Palatine Johann Wilhelm I of Düsseldorf about 1696; was granted the post of Kammerdiener, and later was court chamber councillor (c.1710–12). Among his instrumental works were *Uitgevondene tyd en konstoeffeningen* for Viola da Gamba and Basso Continuo, op. 2 (c. 1668), *Il giardino armonico* for 2 Violins, Viola da Gamba, and Basso Continuo, op. 3 (1691), *Scherzi musicali* for Viola da Gamba and Basso Continuo ad libitum, op. 6 (n.d.; ed. by H. Leichtentritt, Leipzig, 1906), (18) *Suonate* for Violin and Violone or Harpsichord, op. 7 (n.d.), and *L'echo du Danube,* 6 sonatas for Viola da Gamba, op. 9 (c.1705); also vocal works, including (27) *Eegine gesangen, uit de opera von Bacchus, Ceres en Venus* for Voice and Basso Continuo, op. 1 (1687), *C. van Eekes koninklyke harpliederen* for 2 Voices, 2 Viola da Gambas, and Basso Continuo, op. 4 (c. 1693), and (63) *Zangswyze uitbreiding over't Hooglied van Salomen* for Voice and Basso Continuo, op. 5 (1697).

BIBL.: K. Pauls, "Der kurpfälzische Kammermusikus J. S.," *Die Musikforschung,* XV (1962) and XIX (1966).

Schenck, Pyotr, Russian pianist, conductor, and composer; b. St. Petersburg, Feb. 28, 1870; d. Perkiarvy, Finland, July 5, 1915. He studied piano and theory at the St. Petersburg

Cons.; gave concerts as a pianist; then devoted himself to conducting; appeared in several European countries. His music was entirely under the influence of Tchaikovsky.

WORKS: OPERAS: *Acteya* (concert perf., St. Petersburg, Dec. 3, 1899, composer conducting), and *The Miracle of Roses* (St. Petersburg, Oct. 7, 1913); also ballet music; 3 syms.; orch. fantasy, *Dukhy* (Ghosts); symphonic poem, *Hero and Leander;* instrumental pieces; choruses; songs.

Schenk, Erich, eminent Austrian musicologist; b. Salzburg, May 5, 1902; d. Vienna, Oct. 11, 1974. He studied theory and piano at the Salzburg Mozarteum and musicology with Sandberger at the Univ. of Munich (Ph.D., 1925, with the diss. *Giuseppe Antonio Paganelli: Sein Leben und seine Werke;* publ. in Salzburg, 1928); completed his Habilitation at the Univ. of Rostock in 1929 with his *Studien zur Triosonate in Deutschland nach Corelli;* subsequently founded its musicology dept. (1936). From 1940 until his retirement in 1971 he was a prof. of musicology at the Univ. of Vienna. He was particularly esteemed for his studies of Baroque and Classical music. In 1947 he revived the Denkmäler der Tonkunst in Österreich series, overseeing its progress until 1972. In 1955 he also took over the valuable *Studien zur Musikwissenschaft.* Festschrifts honored him on his 60th (Vienna, 1962) and 70th (Kassel, 1975) birthdays.

WRITINGS: *Johann Strauss* (Potsdam, 1940); *Musik in Kärnten* (Vienna, 1941); *Beethoven zwischen den Zeiten* (Bonn, 1944); *950 Jahre österreichische Musik* (Vienna, 1946); *Kleine wiener Musikgeschichte* (Vienna, 1946); *W.A. Mozart: Eine Biographie* (Vienna, 1955; in Eng., 1960, as *Mozart and His Time;* 2nd Ger. ed., augmented, 1975, as *Mozart: Sein Leben, seine Welt); Ausgewählte Aufsätze: Reden und Vorträge* (Vienna, 1967); ed. *Beethoven-Studien* (Vienna, 1970).

Schenk, Johann Baptist, Austrian composer and teacher; b. Wiener-Neustadt, Nov. 30, 1753; d. Vienna, Dec. 29, 1836. He received elementary instruction in music as a small child, and then studied with the Baden choirmaster Anton Stoll; learned to play violin and keyboard instruments, and began composing in his youth. In 1773 he went to Vienna, where he took courses in counterpoint and composition with Wagenseil; in 1778 he established his reputation with the performance of a Mass; in 1780 he began composing for the theater, winning notable success with his *Der Dorfbarbier.* In 1793 Beethoven took surreptitious lessons from him while studying formally with Haydn.

WORKS: STAGE (all singspiels and 1st perf. in Vienna unless otherwise given): *Der Schatzgräber,* opera (1780; not perf.); *Der Dorfbarbier,* comedy (June 18, 1785; as a singspiel, Oct. 30, 1796); *Die Weinlese* (Oct. 12, 1785); *Die Weihnacht auf dem Lande* (Dec. 14, 1786); *Im Finstern ist nicht gut tappen* (Oct. 12, 1787); *Das unvermutete Seefest* (Dec. 9, 1789); *Das Singspiel ohne Titel,* operetta (Nov. 4, 1790); *Der Erntekranz* (July 9, 1791); *Achmet und Almanzine* (July 17, 1795); *Die Jagd* (May 7, 1799); *Der Fassbinder* (Dec. 17, 1802); other works include 5 cantatas, various sacred pieces, 10 syms., several concertos, chamber music, choruses, and songs.

BIBL.: F. Staub, *J. S. Eine Skizze seines Lebens* (Wiener-Neustadt, 1901); E. Rosenfeld (-Roemer), *J.B. S. als Opernkomponist* (diss., Univ. of Vienna, 1921); F. Rieger, *J. S.: Ein Altmeister des deutschen Singspiels* (St. Pölten, 1944).

Schenker, Heinrich, outstanding Austrian music theorist; b. Wisniowczyki, Galicia, June 19, 1868; d. Vienna, Jan. 13, 1935. He studied jurisprudence at the Univ. of Vienna (Dr.Jur., 1890); concurrently took courses with Bruckner at the Vienna Cons. He composed some songs and piano pieces; Brahms liked them sufficiently to recommend Schenker to his publisher Simrock. For a while Schenker served as accompanist of the baritone Johannes Messchaert; then returned to Vienna and devoted himself entirely to the development of his theoretical research; gathered around himself a group of enthusiastic disciples who accepted his novel theories, among them Otto Vrieslander, Hermann Roth, Hans Weisse, Anthony van Hoboken, Oswald Jonas, Felix Salzer, and John Petrie Dunn. He endeav-

ored to derive the basic laws of musical composition from a thoroughgoing analysis of the standard masterworks. The result was the contention that each composition represents a horizontal integration, through various stages, of differential triadic units derived from the overtone series. By a dialectical manipulation of the thematic elements and linear progressions of a given work, Schenker succeeded in preparing a formidable system in which the melody is the "Urlinie" (basic line), the bass is "Grundbrechung" (broken ground), and the ultimate formation is the "Ursatz" (background). The result seems as self-consistent as the Ptolemaic planetary theory of epicycles. Arbitrary as the Schenker system is, it proved remarkably durable in academia; some theorists even attempted to apply it to modern works lacking in the triadic content essential to Schenker's theories.

WRITINGS: *Ein Beitrag zur Ornamentik als Einführung zu Ph.E. Bachs Klavierwerke* (Vienna, 1904; 2nd ed., rev., 1908; Eng. tr. in *Music Forum,* IV, 1976); *Neue musikalische Theorien und Fantasien:* I. *Harmonielehre* (Stuttgart, 1906; Eng. tr., ed. by O. Jonas, Chicago, 1954); II. *Kontrapunkt* in 2 vols., *Cantus Firmus und zweistimmiger Satz* (Vienna, 1910), and *Drei- und mehrstimmiger Satz, Übergänge zum freien Satz* (Vienna, 1922); Eng. tr. of both vols. by J. Thymn, N.Y., 1987); III. *Der freie Satz* (Vienna, 1935; new ed. by O. Jonas, 1956; Eng. tr. by E. Oster, 1979); *Beethovens Neunte Sinfonie* (Vienna, 1912); *Der Tonwille* (a periodical, 1921–24); *Beethovens Fünfte Sinfonie* (Vienna, 1925); *Das Meisterwerk in der Musik* (3 vols., Vienna, 1925, 1926, 1930); *Fünf Urlinie-Tafeln* (Vienna, 1932; 2nd ed., rev., 1969 as *Five Graphic Music Analyses* by F. Salzer); *Johannes Brahms: Oktaven und Quinten* (Vienna, 1933).

BIBL.: W. Riezler, "Die Urlinie," *Die Musik* (April 1930); I. Citkowitz, "The Role of H. S.," *Modern Music,* 11 (1933); O. Jonas, *Das Wesen des musikalischen Kunstwerks* (Vienna, 1934; 2nd ed., rev., 1973 as *Einführung in die Lehre H. S.s*); A. Katz, "H. S.'s Method of Analysis," *Musical Quarterly* (July 1935); R. Sessions, "H. S.'s Contribution," *Modern Music,* 12 (1953); A. Waldeck and N. Broder, "Musical Synthesis as Expounded by H. S.," *Musical Mercury* (Dec. 1935); A. Katz, *Challenge to Musical Tradition* (N.Y., 1945); W. Mann, "S.'s Contribution to Music Theory," *Music Review,* X (1949); F. Salzer, *Structural Hearing* (N.Y., 1952; 2nd ed., 1962); F. Salzer and C. Schachter, *Counterpoint in Composition: The Study of Voice Leading* (N.Y., 1969): L. Laskowski, ed., *H. S.: An Annotated Index to His Analyses of Musical Works* (N.Y., 1978); A. Whittall, "S. and the Prospects for Analysis," *Musical Times* (Sept. 1980); A. Forte and S. Gilbert, *An Introduction to S.ian Analysis* (London, 1982); W. Pastille, "H. S., Anti-Organicist," *19th Century Music* (Summer 1984); D. Beach, "The Current State of S.ian Research," *Acta Musicologica,* LVII (1985); H. Siegel, ed., *S. Studies* (Cambridge, 1989); A. Cadwallader, ed., *Trends in S.ian Research* (N.Y., 1990).

Scherchen, Hermann, eminent German conductor, father of **Tona Scherchen;** b. Berlin, June 21, 1891; d. Florence, June 12, 1966. He was mainly self-taught in music; learned to play the viola and joined the Blüthner Orch. in Berlin at age 16; then was a member of the Berlin Phil. (1907–10). He worked with Arnold Schoenberg (1910–12), and toured as a conductor (1911–12); became conductor of the Riga Sym. Orch. in 1914, but with the outbreak of World War I that same year, he was interned in Russia. After the Armistice, he returned to Berlin and founded the Neue Musikgesellschaft in 1918; also ed. the periodical *Melos* (1920–21). He was conductor of the Frankfurt Museumgesellschaft concerts (1922–28) and Generalmusikdirektor in Königsberg (1928–33); also conducted at many contemporary-music festivals. With the advent of the Nazi regime in 1933, he settled in Switzerland, where he had conducted the concerts of the Winterthur Musikkollegium from 1922; continued in this capacity until 1947. He also conducted the Zürich Radio Orch. (from 1933), serving as its director (1944–50); was ed. of the Brussels periodical *Musica Viva* (1933–36); founded the Ars Viva Orch. (1939)

and that same year an annual summer school for conductors. After World War II, he resumed his extensive European guest conducting engagements. On Oct. 30, 1964, he made his long-awaited U.S. debut, as a guest conductor with the Philadelphia Orch. He distinguished himself as a scholarly exponent of modern music; conducted many world premieres of ultra-modern works; publ. a valuable manual, *Lehrbuch des Dirigierens* (Leipzig, 1929; in Eng. as *Handbook of Conducting*, London, 1933; 6th ed., 1949); also publ. *Vom Wesen der Musik* (Zürich, 1946; in Eng. as *The Nature of Music*, London, 1947; Chicago, 1950); *Musik für Jedermann* (Winterthur, 1950).

Scherchen, Tona, Swiss-born French composer, daughter of **Hermann Scherchen;** b. Neuchâtel, March 12, 1938. She was taken to China at age 12 by her mother, the Chinese composer Hsia Shu-sien, who was her 1st mentor in theory, composition, and classical Chinese music (from 1952). She studied basic Western music theory and the Chinese instrument P'i p'a at the conservatories in Shanghai and Peking (1957–60). Upon returning to Europe, she studied composition with Hans Werner Henze at the Salzburg Mozarteum (1961–63). She continued her training in Paris with Pierre Schaeffer at the Centre de Recherche Musicale (1963), and also received instruction in analysis from Messiaen at the Cons. (1963–64), where she won a premier prix; then had private lessons with Ligeti in Vienna (1966–67). In 1972 she settled in France and later became a naturalized French citizen. In addition to works for traditional instruments, she has produced electronic and multimedia scores. In all her works, her Eastern heritage has remained a powerful resource and inspiration.

WORKS: DRAMATIC: *Tzan-Shen,* ballet (1970–71; version of *Shen* for Percussion, 1968); *Éclats obscurs,* radiophonic piece, after St.-John Perse (1982); multimedia pieces: *Between* (1978–86), *Cancer, solstice '83* (1983–87), and *Fuite?* (1987). **ORCH.:** *Tzang* for Chamber Orch. (1966); *Khouang* (1966–68); *Tao* for Viola and Orch. (1971); *Vague-T'ao* (1974–75); "*S . . .*" for Chamber Orch. (1975); *Oeil de chat* (1976–77); *L'Invitation au voyage* for Chamber Orch. (1977); *Lô* for Trombone and 12 Strings (1978–79); *L'Illégitime* for Orch. and Tape (1985–86). **VOCAL:** *Wai* for Mezzo-soprano and String Quartet (1966–67); *Tzi* for 16-voice Chorus (1969–70); *La Larme de crocodile* for Voice (1977). **CHAMBER:** *In, Sin,* 2 pieces for Flute (1965); *Hsun* for 6 Instruments (1968); *Shen* for 6 Percussionists or Percussion Orch. (1968; ballet version as *Tzan-Shen,* 1970–71); *Tzoue,* trio for Clarinet or Flute, Cello or Double Bass, and Harpsichord (1970; also as a multimedia piece, 1980); *Yun-Yu* for Violin or Viola, and Vibraphone (1972); *Bien* for 12 Instruments (1972–73); *Tjao-Houen* for 9 Instruments (1973); *Ziguidor* for Wind Quintet (1977); *Tzing* for Brass Quintet (1979); *Tarots* for Harpsichord and 7 Instruments (1981–82); *Lustucru* for Variable Ensemble (1983).

Scheremetiev, Alexander. See **Sheremetiev, Alexander.**

Schering, Arnold, eminent German music historian; b. Breslau, April 2, 1877; d. Berlin, March 7, 1941. His father was a merchant; the family moved to Dresden, where Schering began to take violin lessons with Blumner. In 1896 he went to Berlin, where he studied violin with Joachim, hoping to start a concert career; he organized a tour with the pianist Hinze-Reinhold, but soon gave up virtuoso aspirations, and in 1898 entered classes in musicology with Fleischer and Stumpf at the Univ. of Berlin; then took courses with Sandberger at the Univ. of Munich and with Kretzschmar at the Univ. of Leipzig, obtaining his Ph.D. in 1902 with the dissertation *Geschichte des Instrumental- (Violin-) Konzerts bis A. Vivaldi* (publ. in Leipzig, 1905; 2nd ed., 1927); subsequently completed his Habilitation there in 1907 with his *Die Anfänge des Oratoriums* (publ. in an augmented ed. as *Geschichte des Oratoriums,* Leipzig, 1911). He devoted himself to teaching and musical journalism; from 1904 to 1939 he was ed. of the *Bach-Jahrbuch.* From 1909 to 1923 he taught at the Leipzig Cons.; from 1915 to 1920 he was prof. of the history and esthetics of music at the Univ. of Leipzig; then was prof. of music at the Univ. of Halle (1920–28); subsequently was prof. of musicology at the

Univ. of Berlin (1928–41). In 1928 he became president of the German Musicological Society. In his voluminous publications, he strove to erect an infallible system of aesthetic principles derived from musical symbolism and based on psychological intuition, ignoring any contradictions that ensued from his axiomatic constructions. In his book *Beethoven in neuer Deutung,* publ. in 1934 at the early dawn of the Nazi era, he even attempted to interpret Beethoven's music in terms of racial German superiority, alienating many of his admirers. But in his irrepressible desire to establish an immutable sequence of historic necessity, he compiled an original and highly informative historical tabulation of musical chronology, *Tabellen zur Musikgeschichte,* which was publ. in 1914 and went through several eds.

WRITINGS: *Musikalische Bildung und Erziehung zum musikalischen Hören* (Leipzig, 1911; 4th ed., 1924); *Tabellen zur Musikgeschichte* (Leipzig, 1914; 4th ed., 1934; 5th ed., 1962, by H.J. Moser); *Aufführungspraxis alter Musik* (Berlin, 1931); *Geschichte der Musik in Beispielen* (Leipzig, 1931; 2nd ed., 1954; Eng. tr., 1950); *Beethoven in neuer Deutung* (Berlin, 1934); *Beethoven und die Dichtung* (Berlin, 1936); *Johann Sebastian Bachs Leipziger Kirchenmusik* (Leipzig, 1936; 2nd ed., 1954); *Von grossen Meistern der Musik* (Leipzig, 1940); *Das Symbol in der Musik* (ed. by W. Gurlitt; Berlin, 1941); *Über Kantaten J.S. Bachs* (ed. by F. Blume; Berlin, 1942; 2nd ed., 1950); *Vom musikalischen Kunstwerk* (ed. by F. Blume; Berlin, 1949; 2nd ed., 1951); *Humor, Heldentum, Tragik bei Beethoven* (Strasbourg, 1955). **BIBL.:** H. Osthoff, ed., *Festschrift A. S. zum 60. Geburtstag* (Berlin, 1937).

Scherman, Thomas (Kielty), American conductor; b. N.Y., Feb. 12, 1917; d. there, May 14, 1979. He was a son of Harry Scherman, founder and president of the Book-of-the-Month Club; attended Columbia Univ. (B.A., 1937); then studied piano with Isabelle Vengerova, theory with Hans Weisse, and conducting with Carl Bamberger, Max Rudolf, and Otto Klemperer, whose assistant he became in conducting a chamber orch. composed of European refugees at The New School for Social Research in N.Y. (1939–41). He subsequently served in the U.S. Army (1941–45), reaching the rank of captain in the Signal Corps. In 1947 he became assistant conductor of the National Opera in Mexico City; that same year, he organized in N.Y. the Little Orch. Society for the purposes of presenting new works, some of them specially commissioned, and of reviving forgotten music of the past; he also gave performances of operas in concert versions. He terminated the seasons of the Little Orch. Society in 1975, but organized the New Little Orch. Society to present children's concerts; these he continued to lead until his death.

Schermerhorn, Kenneth (de Witt), American conductor; b. Schenectady, N.Y., Nov. 20, 1929. He studied conducting with Richard Burgin at the New England Cons. of Music in Boston (graduated, 1950); also took courses at the Berkshire Music Center at Tanglewood, where he won the Koussevitzky Prize. His 1st important engagement was as conductor of the American Ballet Theater in N.Y. (1957–67); also was assistant conductor of the N.Y. Phil. (1960–61). He was music director of the New Jersey Sym. Orch. in Newark (1963–68) and the Milwaukee Sym. Orch. (1968–80); then was general music director of the American Ballet Theater in N.Y. (from 1982) and also music director of the Nashville (Tenn.) Sym. Orch. (1983–88) and the Hong Kong Phil. (1984–88). In 1975 he married **Carol Neblett.**

Schetky, Johann Georg Christoph, German cellist and composer; b. Darmstadt, Aug. 19, 1737; d. Edinburgh, Nov. 29, 1824. The original family name was Von Teschky; Schetky's ancestors were from Transylvania. His father was a court official and musician in Hessen-Darmstadt. He became principal cellist in the Darmstadt court orch. in 1758; received instruction in composition from the court Vice-Kapellmeister Endler and in cello from Anton Filtz of Mannheim. After a sojourn in Hamburg (1768–69), he went to London in 1772; settled in Edinburgh, where he was principal cellist of its Musical Society. He married Maria Anna Teresa Reinagle, sister of Alexander Reinagle. He played a prominent role in Edinburgh musical life; as a composer, he won distinction for his chamber music, which included 6 string quartets; 6 string trios; 6 duos for Violin and Cello; 6 sonatas for Cello and Bass; harpsichord sonatas; and songs. He also composed syms., cello concertos, and vocal pieces. His son J(ohn) George Schetky (b. Edinburgh, June 1, 1776; d. Philadelphia, Dec. 11, 1831) was the 2nd of 11 children; he emigrated to America in 1787; was naturalized in Philadelphia on Nov. 19, 1806. He appeared as a cellist in Philadelphia; c.1800 he entered into partnership with Benjamin Carr in the music publ. business; was a co-founder of the Musical Fund Society in Philadelphia. His arrangement for military band of Koczwara's *Battle of Prague* was much played.

BIBL.: L. Schetky, *The S. Family; A Compilation of Letters, Memoirs and Historical Data* (Portland, Oreg., 1942); G. Beechey, "J.G.C. S. and his 'Observations' on Playing the Cello," *Musical Quarterly* (Oct. 1974).

Scheurleer, Daniel François, Dutch musicologist; b. The Hague, Nov. 13, 1855; d. there, Feb. 6, 1927. Although a banker, he took an active part in musical affairs; was president of the Vereeniging voor Nederlandsche Muziekgeschiedenis; founded the Union Musicologique (1921). He was the owner of a valuable musical library and instrument collection, most of which is now housed at The Hague's Gemeentemuseum. He publ. *Het muziekleven in Nederland in de tweede helft der 18ᵉ eeuw in verband met Mozart's verbliff aldaar* (The Hague, 1909) and other studies; ed. *Jan Fruytiers Ecclesiasticus* (Amsterdam, 1898), etc.

BIBL.: *Gedenkboek aangeboden aan Dr. D.F. S. op zijn 70sten Verjaardag* (The Hague, 1925).

Schibler, Armin, Swiss composer; b. Kreuzlingen, Nov. 20, 1920; d. Zürich, Sept. 7, 1986. He studied with Müller, Frey, and Burkhard in Zürich; also received instruction from Rubbra and Tippett in England (1946), and attended the Darmstadt summer courses (1949–53); served as music director of Zürich's Kanton Gymnasium (from 1944). Much of his music is cast in neo-Classical forms; some works employ a modified form of the 12-tone technique. He publ. the books *Neue Musik in dritter Generation* (Amriswil, 1953), *Zum Werk Gustav Mahlers* (Lindau, 1955), and *Zur Oper der Gegenwart* (Amriswil, 1956).

WORKS: DRAMATIC: OPERAS: *Der spanische Rosenstock* (1947–50; Bern, April 9, 1950); *Der Teufel im Winterpalais* (1950–53); *Das Bergwerk von Falun* (1953); *Die späte Sühne* (1953–54); *Die Füsse im Feuer* (Zürich, April 25, 1955; aroused considerable interest); *Urs und Flurina,* youth opera (1956–60). **BALLET:** *Der Raub des Feuers* (1954). **DANCE BURLESQUE:** *Blackwood & Co.* (1955–58; Zürich, June 3, 1962). **ORATORIO:** *Media in vita* (1956; Zürich, April 26, 1963). **ORCH.:** Concertino for Piano and Chamber Orch. (1943); *Fantasy* for Viola and Small Orch. (1945); *Fantasy* for Oboe, Harp, and Small Orch. (1946); Sym. No. 1 (1946); *Passacaglia* (1949); *Symphonic Variations* (1950); *Concertante fantasie* for Cello and Orch. (1951); Sym. No. 2 (1950); *Concerto for Amateur Orchestra* (1953); Sym. No. 3 (Winterthur, Nov. 13, 1957); *Metamorphoses Ebrietatis,* symphonic poem (Montreux, Sept. 6, 1966); Horn Concerto (1956); Trombone Concerto (1957); *Concerto breve* for Cello and Orch. (1958–59); Violin Concerto (1960); Trumpet Concerto (1960–61); *Concerto for Percussion and Orch.* (Zürich, Jan. 6, 1961); Piano Concerto (1962–68); Concerto for Piano, Percussion, and String Orch. (1963); Double Concerto for Flute, Harp, and Chamber Orch. (1966); Bassoon Concerto (1967); *6 Pieces* (1969); *Konzertante Fantasie* for Saxophone and Small Orch. (1977–78). **CANTATAS:** *Die Hochzeit* (1946); *Gefährten* (1946); *Weil alles erneut sich begibt* (1949); *Mondlicht* (1950). **CHAMBER:** Solo Sonata for Flute (1944); Suite for Cello Alone (1945); *Little Concerto* for Viola Alone (1947); 5 string quartets (1945, 1951, 1958, 1960, 1975); *Trio concertante* for Trumpet, Violin, and Piano (1948); *Duo*

concertante for Violin and Piano (1950); *Dodecaphonic Studies* for Piano; also works for Speaking and Singing Voices.

BIBL.: K. Wörner, *A. S.: Werk und Persönlichkeit* (Amriswil, 1953).

Schicht, Johann Gottfried, German keyboard player, conductor, and composer; b. Reichenau, Saxony, Sept. 29, 1753; d. Leipzig, Feb. 16, 1823. In 1776, already well trained as an organist and pianist, he matriculated at the Univ. of Leipzig as a law student; he concurrently played in Hiller's "Grosses Concert"; giving up the law, he played in Hiller's Musikübende Gesellschaft; in 1781 he became a violinist in the Gewandhaus concerts, succeeding Hiller as their conductor in 1785. He was founder-conductor of the Singakademie (1802–7); then was music director of the Univ. (from 1808) and Kantor of the Thomasschule (from 1810). He publ. *Grundregeln der Harmonie nach dem Verwechslungssystem* (Leipzig, 1812).

WORKS: ORATORIOS: *Die Feier der Christen auf Golgotha, Moses auf Sinai,* and *Das Ende des Gerechten;* masses, motets, Te Deums, the *100th Psalm;* several chorale-motets (*Nach einer Prüfung kurzer Tage, Jesus meine Zuversicht, Herzlich lieb hab' ich dich, o Herr,* etc.); 9 settings of Leo's *Miserere* a 4–8; an excellent book of chorales (1819; of 1,285 melodies, 306 are original); a concerto, sonatas, caprices, etc., for Piano.

BIBL.: P. Langer, *Chronik der Leipziger Singakademie* (Leipzig, 1902).

Schick, George, Czech-American conductor; b. Prague, April 5, 1908; d. N.Y., March 7, 1985. He studied at the Prague Cons.; was assistant conductor at the Prague National Theater from 1927 until 1938. He settled in the U.S. in 1939; was conductor of the San Carlo Opera (1943); from 1948 to 1950 he was conductor of the Little Sym. of Montreal; from 1950 to 1956 he was associate conductor of the Chicago Sym. Orch. He was a conductor at the Metropolitan Opera in N.Y. (1958–69); then served as president of the Manhattan School of Music in N.Y. (1969–76).

Schick, Margarete (Luise) (née **Hamel**), noted German soprano; b. Mainz, April 26, 1773; d. Berlin, April 29, 1809. Her father was the bassoonist J.N. Hamel; after keyboard and vocal training, the elector of Mainz ennabled her to continue her vocal studies with Dominicus Steffani in Würzburg; returning to Mainz, she sang at the electoral court while pursuing further studies with Righini; made her stage debut there in 1791. She settled in Berlin in 1793 as a court chamber and theater singer; also sang at the National Theater (from 1794). She especially excelled at operas by Gluck and Mozart; her most celebrated role was Gluck's Iphigenia, but also was admired for Mozart's Susanna and Zerlina. Her contemporaries regarded her as the equal of the famous Mara. In 1791 she married the violinist Ernst Schick.

BIBL.: K. von Levezow, *Leben und Kunst der Frau M.L. S., geboren Hamel* (Berlin, 1809).

Schickele, Peter, American composer and musical humorist; b. Ames, Iowa, July 17, 1935. He was educated at Swarthmore College (B.A., 1957); studied composition with Roy Harris in Pittsburgh (1954), Milhaud at the Aspen School of Music (1959), and Persichetti and Bergsma at the Juilliard School of Music in N.Y. (M.S.). After serving as composer-in-residence to the Los Angeles public schools (1960–61), he taught at Swarthmore College (1961–62) and at the Juilliard School of Music (from 1962). He rocketed to fame at N.Y.'s Town Hall on April 24, 1965, in the rollicking role of the roly-poly character P.D.Q. Bach, the mythical composer of such outrageous travesties as *The Civilian Barber, Gross Concerto for Divers Flutes* (featuring a Nose Flute and a Wiener Whistle to be eaten during the perf.), *Concerto for Piano vs. Orchestra, Iphigenia in Brooklyn, The Seasonings, Pervertimento for Bagpipes, Bicycles & Balloons, No-No Nonette, Schleptet, Fuga Meshuga, Missa Hilarious, Sanka Cantata, Fantasie-Shtick,* and the opera *The Abduction of Figaro* (Minneapolis, April 24, 1984). He publ. *The Definitive Biography of P.D.Q. Bach (1807–1742?)* (N.Y., 1976). In 1967 he organized a chamber-rock-jazz trio known as Open Window, which frequently presented his serious compositions; among these are several orch. works, vocal pieces, film and television scores, and chamber music.

Schidlowsky, León, Chilean composer; b. Santiago, July 21, 1931. He studied at the National Cons. (1940–47), and also took courses in philosophy and psychology at the Univ. of Chile (1948–52), and had private lessons in composition with Focke and in harmony with Allende-Blin; then went to Germany for further studies (1952–55). Returning to Chile, he organized the avant-garde group Agrupación Tonus for the propagation of new techniques of composition. He taught at the Santiago Music Inst. (1955–63); served as prof. of composition at the Univ. of Chile (1962–68); held a Guggenheim fellowship (1968). In 1969 he emigrated to Israel, where he was appointed to the faculty of the Rubin Academy of Music. In his music he adopts a serial technique, extending it into fields of rhythms and intensities; beginning in 1964, he superadded aleatory elements, using graphic notation.
WORKS: OPERA: *Die Menschen* (1970). **VOCAL AND OTHER:** *Requiem* for Soprano and Chamber Orch. (1954); *Caupolicán,* epic narrative for Narrator, Chorus, 2 Pianos, Celesta, and Percussion Orch. (1958); *Oda a la tierra* for 2 Narrators and Orch. (1958–60); *La Noche de Cristal,* sym. for Tenor, Male Chorus, and Orch., commemorating the martyrdom of Jews on the Nazi "crystal night" (1961); *Invocación* for Soprano, Narrator, Percussion, and String Orch. (1964); *Jeremías* for 8 Mixed Voices and String Orch. (1966); *Rabbi Akiba,* scenic fantasy for Narrator, 3 Soloists, Children's and Mixed Chorus, and Orch. (1972); *Amereida* (consisting of *Memento, Llaqui,* and *Ecce Homo*) for Narrator and Orch. (1965–72); *Hommage à Neruda* for Chorus and Orch. (1975); *Adieu* for Mezzo-soprano and Chamber Orch. (1982); *Amerindia,* a pentology: *I: Prologue* for Orch. (1982); *II: Los Heraldos Negros* for Narrator, Harp, Piano, Percussion, and String Orch. (1983); *III: Sacsahuaman* for Winds and Percussion (1983); *IV: Yo Vengo a Hablar* for Narrator and Orch. (1983); *V: Era e Crepusculo de la Iguana* for Narrator and Orch. (1985); *Missa in nomine Bach* for Chorus and 8 Instruments (1984); *Laude* for Chorus and Orch. (1984); *Missa-dona nobis pacem* for Chorus (1987); *Chanson* for Voice and Tam-Tam (1988). **ORCH.:** *Tríptico* (1959); *Eróstrato* for Percussion Orch. (1963); *Nueva York,* dedicated to "my brothers in Harlem" (Washington, D.C., May 9, 1965); *Kadish* for Cello and Orch. (1967); *Epitaph for Hermann Scherchen* (1967); *Babi Yar* for String Orch., Piano, and Percussion (1970); *Serenata* for Chamber Orch. (1970); *Arcanas* (1971); *Constellation II* for String Orch. (1971); *Prelude to a Drama* (1976); *Images* for String Orch. (1976); *Lux in Tenebris* (1977); *Tel Aviv* (1978–83); *Trilogy* (1986); *Ballade* for Violin and Orch. (1986); *Elegy* (1988); *Laudatio* (1988). **CHAMBER:** *Elegía* for Clarinet and String Quartet (1952); Trio for Flute, Cello, and Piano (1955); *Cuarteto mixto* for Flute, Clarinet, Violin, and Cello (1956); Concerto for 6 Instruments (1957); *In memoriam* for Clarinet and Percussion (1957); *4 Miniatures* for Flute, Oboe, Clarinet, and Bassoon (1957); *Soliloquios* for 8 Instruments (1961); *Visiones* for 12 Strings (1967); String Quartet (1967); Wind Quintet (1968); *Eclosión* for 9 Instruments (1967); *6 Hexáforos* for 6 Percussionists (1968); Sextet (1970); *Kolot* for Harp (1971); *Meshulash* (Triangle) for Piano Trio (1971); *Voices* for Harp (1972); *Invention* for Flute and Piano (1975); Piano Quartet (1988); String Quartet (1988). **PIANO:** *6 Miniatures,* to paintings by Klee (1952); *8 Structures* (1955); *5 Pieces* (1956); *Actus* (1972).
BIBL.: M. Grebe, "L. S., síntesis de su trayectoria creativa," *Revista Musical Chilena* (1968); W. Elias, *L. S.* (Tel Aviv, 1978).

Schiedermair, Ludwig, eminent German musicologist; b. Regensburg, Dec. 7, 1876; d. Bensberg, near Cologne, April 30, 1957. He studied in Munich with Sandberger and Beer-Walbrunn; received his Ph.D. at the Univ. of Erlangen in 1901 with the dissertation *Die Künstlerische Bestrebungen am Hofe des Kurfürsten Ferdinand Maria von Bayern;* studied further with Riemann at the Univ. of Leipzig and with Kretzschmar at the Univ. of Berlin; completed his Habilitation in

1906 at the Univ. of Marburg, where he then taught (1906–11); then went to the Univ. of Bonn (1911), where he was a reader (1915–20) and a prof. (1920–45). He was founder-director of the Beethoven Archives in Bonn; was made president of the Deutsche Gesellschaft für Musikwissenschaft (1937) and chairman of the music section of the Deutsche Akademie (1940). A Festschrift was publ. in honor of his 60th (Berlin, 1937) and 80th (Cologne, 1956) birthdays.
WRITINGS: *Gustav Mahler* (Leipzig, 1901); *Bayreuther Festspiele im Zeitalter des Absolutismus* (Leipzig, 1908); *Die Briefe Mozarts und seiner Familie* (5 vols., Munich, 1914; vol. 5 is an iconography); *W.A. Mozarts Handschrift* (Bückeburg, 1919; facsimiles); *Einführung in das Studium der Musikgeschichte* (Munich, 1918; new ed., Bonn, 1947); *Mozart* (Munich, 1922; 2nd ed., Bonn, 1948); *Der junge Beethoven* (Leipzig, 1925; 4th ed., 1970); *Beethoven: Beiträge zum Leben und Schaffen* (Leipzig, 1930; 3rd ed., 1943); *Die deutsche Oper* (Leipzig, 1930); *Die Gestaltung weltanschaulicher Ideen in der Vokalmusik Beethovens* (Leipzig, 1934); *Musik am Rheinstrom* (Cologne, 1947); *Musikalische Begegnungen; Erlebnis und Erinnerung* (Cologne, 1948); *Deutsche Musik im Europäischen Raum* (Münster, 1954).
BIBL.: J. Kross, "L. S.," *Bonner Gelehrte* (1968).

Schiedermayer, Johann Baptist, German organist and composer; b. Pfaffenmünster, Bavaria, June 23, 1779; d. Linz, Jan. 6, 1840. He served as Linz Cathedral organist. He wrote *Theoretisch-praktische Chorallehre zum Gebrauch beim katholischen Kirchenritus* (1828); composed the singspiels *Wellmanns Eichenstämme* (Linz, 1815), *Das Glück ist kugelrund* (Linz, 1816), and *Die Rückkehr ins Vaterhaus* (Linz, 1816); 16 masses and much other sacred music; syms.; string trios; organ pieces; etc.

Schiedmayer, the name of 2 well-known German firms of piano makers in Stuttgart: Schiedmayer & Söhne and Schiedmayer Pianofortefabrik. **Balthasar Schiedmayer** (1711–81) began manufacturing musical instruments in Erlangen c.1740; at his death, his son **Johann David Schiedmayer** (1753–1805) assumed the management; he was succeeded by his 19-year-old son, **Johann Lorenz Schiedmayer** (1786–1860), with whom he had moved (c.1800) from Erlangen to Nuremberg. Johann Lorenz ended the business at Nuremberg after 2 years, and went to Vienna for a brief time; in 1809 he was in Stuttgart, where he set up business in partnership with a young piano maker, Carl Dieudonné (d. 1825); from 1825, he carried on the business alone, until 1845, when his eldest sons, **Adolf Schiedmayer** (1819–90) and **Hermann Schiedmayer** (1820–61), entered the firm, which was then called J.L. Schiedmayer & Söhne. In 1853 Johann Lorenz Schiedmayer provided his 2 younger sons, **Julius** (1822–78) and **Paul** (1829–90), with their own separate factory, producing harmoniums. After their father's death, they turned to piano making, and their business became known as Schiedmayer Pianofortefabrik. Upon Paul Schiedmayer's death, his son **Max Julius,** became head of the firm.
BIBL.: A. Eisenmann, *S. und Söhne* (Stuttgart, 1909); *150 Jahre S. und Söhne* (Stuttgart, 1959).

Schieferdecker, Johann Christian, German organist and composer; b. Teuchern, near Weissenfels, Nov. 10, 1679; d. Lübeck, April 5, 1732. He studied at the Thomasschule (1692–97) and Univ. (1697–1702) in Leipzig. In 1706 he became Buxtehude's deputy at Lübeck's St. Marienkirche; on Jan. 23, 1707, he succeeded Buxtehude as organist and parish clerk; as the successful applicant, he was required to marry Buxtehude's daughter, Anna Margareta (Sept. 5, 1707), a requirement declined by Mattheson and Handel. The Abendmusiken, which had achieved wide respect under Tunder and Buxtehude, were continued under his supervision until 1730. His works for these concerts are lost. He also wrote several operas, other church music, and organ pieces.

Schierbeck, Poul (Julius Ouscher), distinguished Danish organist, pedagogue, and composer; b. Copenhagen, June 8, 1888; d. there, Feb. 9, 1949. He studied composition with

Nielsen and Laub; also received instruction from Paul Hellmuth, Henrik Knudsen, and Frank van der Stucken. He was organist at Copenhagen's Skovshoved Church (1916–49) and a teacher of composition and instrumentation at the Royal Danish Cons. of Music (1931–49). In 1947 he was made a member of the Royal Swedish Academy of Music.

WORKS: OPERA: *Fête galante* (1923–30; Copenhagen, Sept. 1, 1931). **ORCH.:** Sym. (1916–21; Göteborg, Feb. 15, 1922, Nielsen conducting); *Natten* (The Night), symphonic scene for Piano and Orch. (1938); *Andante doloroso* for Strings (1942). **VOCAL:** Many cantatas; numerous choral works; songs, including the sets *Nakjaelen* (1921) and *Alverden gaar omkring* (The World Goes Round; 1938); also chamber music, organ chorales, etc.

BIBL.: O. Mathisen, *P. S.* (diss., Univ. of Copenhagen, 1972).

Schiff, András, distinguished Hungarian pianist; b. Budapest, Dec. 21, 1953. He studied piano as a child with Elizabeth Vadasz in Budapest, where he made his debut at 9; then entered the Franz Liszt Academy of Music at 14, continuing his studies with Pál Kadosa; also studied with George Malcolm in London. After winning prizes at the Tchaikovsky Competition in Moscow in 1974 and at the Leeds Competition in 1975, he embarked upon an international career; made his U.S. debut at N.Y.'s Carnegie Hall as soloist with the visiting Franz Liszt Chamber Orch. of Budapest in 1978; then settled in the West (1979). He first gained recognition for his insightful and intellectually stimulating interpretations of the music of Bach; also was a distinguished interpreter of Mozart, Beethoven, Schubert, Schumann, and Chopin. On Oct. 19, 1989, he made his Carnegie Hall recital debut in N.Y.

BIBL.: M. Kimmelman, "A. S.," *Ovation* (July 1985).

Schiff, Heinrich, prominent Austrian cellist and conductor; b. Gmunden, Nov. 18, 1951. He first studied piano; then took cello lessons with Tobias Kühne in Vienna and later with André Navarra in Detmold. After winning prizes in competitions in Geneva, Vienna, and Warsaw, he was a soloist with the Vienna Phil., the Concertgebouw Orch. in Amsterdam, the Stockholm Phil., the BBC Sym., and the Royal Phil. in London; also concertized in Toronto and Montreal. He made his U.S. debut as soloist in the Dvořák Cello Concerto with Sir Colin Davis and the Cleveland Orch. at the Blossom Music Center (Aug. 21, 1981); also appeared in Australia, Israel, and Japan. He maintains a comprehensive repertory, ranging from Vivaldi to such contemporary works as Henze's concerto, written for him; also performs rarely-heard scores, including 2 concertos by Vieuxtemps, which he discovered. His playing is marked by assured technical resources and mellowness of tone. Schiff has also appeared as a conductor; in 1990 he became artistic director of the Northern Sinfonia in Newcastle upon Tyne.

Schifrin, Lalo (Boris), Argentine-American pianist, conductor, and composer; b. Buenos Aires, June 21, 1932. He studied music at home with his father, the concertmaster of the Teatro Colón orch.; subsequently studied harmony with Juan Carlos Paz; won a scholarship to the Paris Cons. in 1950, where he received guidance from Koechlin, and took courses with Messiaen. He became interested in jazz, and represented Argentina at the International Jazz Festival in Paris in 1955; returning to Buenos Aires, he formed his own jazz band, adopting the bebop style. In 1958 he went to N.Y. as arranger for Xavier Cugat; then was pianist with Dizzy Gillespie's band (1960–62); composed for it several exotic pieces, such as *Manteca, Con Alma,* and *Tunisian Fantasy,* based on Gillespie's *Night in Tunisia.* In 1963 he wrote a ballet, *Jazz Faust.* In 1964 he went to Hollywood, where he rapidly found his métier as composer for the films and television; among his scores are *The Liquidator* (1966), *Cool Hand Luke* (1967), *The Fox* (1967), *The Amityville Horror* (1978), *The Sting II* (1983), and *Bad Medicine* (1985). He also experimented with applying the jazz idiom to religious texts, as, for instance, in his *Jazz Suite on Mass Texts* (1965). He achieved his greatest popular success with the theme-motto for the television series *Mission: Impossible* (1966–73), in 5/4 time, for which he received 2 Grammy

awards. His adaptation of modern techniques into mass media placed him in the enviable position of being praised by professional musicians. His oratorio *The Rise and Fall of the Third Reich,* featuring realistic excerpts and incorporating an actual recording of Hitler's speech in electronic amplification, was brought out at the Hollywood Bowl on Aug. 3, 1967. His other works include a Suite for Trumpet and Brass Orch. (1961); *The Ritual of Sound* for 15 Instruments (1962); *Pulsations* for Electronic Keyboard, Jazz Band, and Orch. (Los Angeles, Jan. 21, 1971); *Madrigals for the Space Age,* in 10 parts, for Narrator and Chorus (Los Angeles, Jan. 15, 1976); Capriccio for Clarinet and Strings (Los Angeles, Nov. 5, 1981); Guitar Concerto (1984); Piano Concerto; *Songs of the Aztecs* for Soloist and Orch. (Teotihuacan, Mexico, Oct. 29, 1988). He served as music director of the newly-organized Paris Phil from 1988.

Schikaneder, Emanuel (actually, **Johannes Joseph**), prominent Austrian actor, singer, dramatist, theater director, and composer; b. Straubing, Sept. 1, 1751; d. Vienna, Sept. 21, 1812. He studied at Regensburg's Jesuit Gymnasium, where he was a chorister at the cathedral; became an actor with F.J. Moser's troupe about 1773, then its director (1778); met Mozart in Salzburg in 1780. In 1783 he became lessee of Vienna's Kärnthnertortheater until 1784; was a member of the National Theater (1785–86), then organized his own theater company. Following a sojourn as director of the Regensburg Court Theater (1787–89), he returned to Vienna to assume the directorship of the Freihaus-Theater; gave up his management duties in 1799, but remained the theater's artistic director until it closed in 1801. He persuaded Mozart to set his play *Die Zauberflöte* to music; with Schikaneder as Papageno, it was 1st performed on Sept. 30, 1791. In 1801 he opened the Theater an der Wien, but then sold it in 1806; after a period as director of the Brünn theater, he returned to Vienna. He suffered several financial setbacks over the years and died insane. He wrote roughly 100 plays and librettos.

BIBL.: von Komorzynski, *E. S.: Ein Beitrag zur Geschichte des deutschen Theaters* (Berlin, 1901; 2nd ed., rev., 1951); O. Deutsch, *Das Freihaus-theater auf der Wieden, 1787–1801* (Vienna, 1937); E. von Komorzynski, *Der Vater der Zauberflöte: E. S.s Leben* (Vienna, 1948); W. Senn, "S.s Weg zum Theater," *Acta Mozartiana,* IX (1962); F. Fischer, "E. S. und Salzburg," *Jahrbuch der Gesellschaft für Wiener Theaterforschung,* XV-XVI (1966).

Schiller, (Johann Christian) Friedrich von, great German man of letters; b. Marbach, Nov. 10, 1759; d. Weimar, May 9, 1805. Many musicians have turned to his works for inspiration.

BIBL.: M. Berendt, *S. bis Wagner* (Berlin, 1901); J. Baltz, *Beethoven und S.* (Arnsberg, 1905); A. Kohut, *F. S. in seinen Beziehungen zur Musik* (Stuttgart, 1905); H. Knudsen, *S. und die Musik* (diss., Univ. of Greifswald, 1908); G. Adler, *S. und Schubert* (Vienna, 1910); P. Weigand, "S.'s Dramas as Opera Texts," *Monatshefte,* XLVI (1954); R. Longyear, *S. and Music* (Chapel Hill, 1966); P. Branscombe, "S. and Music," *Forum for Modern Language Studies,* iv/4 (1968).

Schiller, Madeline, gifted English pianist; b. London, 1845; d. N.Y., July 3, 1911. She studied piano in London with Benjamin Isaacs, Benedict, and Hallé, and later with Moscheles in Leipzig; made her debut there with the Gewandhaus Orch. on Jan. 23, 1862, in Mendelssohn's 1st Piano Concerto. She became known for her extraordinary ability to learn a new work in a short time; she demonstrated this talent by learning a piano concerto by Raff in a week and repeating this feat with the 4th Piano Concerto of Saint-Saëns. She engaged in an active career as a concert pianist in Europe, Australia, and the U.S. In 1872 she married an American, Marcus Elmer Bennett, but was widowed in 1876. On Nov. 12, 1881, Schiller made history when she gave the world premiere of Tchaikovsky's 2nd Piano Concerto with the N.Y. Phil., anticipating its 1st Moscow performance by 6 months. She continued to perform as a soloist and with orchs. until 1900, when an injury forced her to retire. She died of a cerebral hemorrhage during an intense heat wave in N.Y.

BIBL.: M. Keyton, "M. S.," *Music and Musicians International* (May 1987).

Schilling, Gustav, German musical lexicographer; b. Schwiegershausen, near Hannover, Nov. 3, 1805; d. Crete, Nebr., March 1880. He studied theology and music in Göttingen and Halle; was active as a writer on theology, music, and politics; when he was prosecuted for debt in 1857, he fled to the U.S. and later settled in Nebr. His most important work was the *Enzyklopädie der gesammten musikalischen Wissenschaften oder Universal-Lexikon der Tonkunst* (6 vols., 1835–38; 2nd ed., 7 vols., 1840–42); also pub. *Versuch einer Philosophie des Schönen in der Musik* (1838); *Lehrbuch der allgemeinen Musikwissenschaft* (1840); *Geschichte der heutigen oder modernen Musik* (1841); *Die musikalische Europa* (1842); *Musikalische Dynamik; oder, Die Lehre vom Vortrage in der Musik* (1843); *Der Pianist* (1843); *Franz Liszt* (1844); *Sicher Schlüssel zur Klaviervirtuosität* (1844); *Die schöne Kunst der Töne* (1847); *Musikalische Didaktik* (1851); *Allgemeine Volksmusiklehre* (1852); *Akustik oder die Lehre vom Klange* (2nd ed., 1856).

Schillinger, Joseph (Moiseievich), Russian-born American music theorist and composer; b. Kharkov, Aug. 31, 1895; d. N.Y., March 23, 1943. He studied at the St. Petersburg Cons. with Tcherepnin, Wihtol, and others; was active as a teacher, conductor, and administrator in Kharkov (1918–22), Moscow, and Leningrad (1922–28). In 1928 he emigrated to the U.S. and became a naturalized citizen in 1936; settled in N.Y. as a teacher of music, mathematics, and art history as well as his own system of composition based on rigid mathematical principles; taught at the New School for Social Research, N.Y. Univ., and Columbia Univ. Teachers College; also gave private lessons. Among his pupils were Tommy Dorsey, Vernon Duke, George Gershwin, Benny Goodman, Oscar Levant, and Glenn Miller. Schillinger publ. a short vol. of musical patterns, *Kaleidophone: New Resources of Melody and Harmony* (N.Y., 1940). L. Dowling and A. Shaw ed. and publ. his magnum opus, *The Schillinger System of Musical Composition* (2 vols., N.Y., 1941; 4th ed., 1946); this was followed by *The Mathematical Basis of the Arts* (N.Y., 1948) and *Encyclopedia of Rhythm* (N.Y., 1966). Schillinger was also a composer; his works include *March of the Orient* for Orch. (Leningrad, May 12, 1926); *First Airphonic Suite* for Theremin and Orch. (Cleveland, Nov. 28, 1929; Leo Theremin, soloist); *North-Russian Symphony* (1930); *The People and the Prophet,* ballet (1931); piano pieces; songs; etc.

BIBL.: H. Cowell, "J. S. as Composer," *Music News,* XXXIV/3 (1947); V. Duke, "Gershwin, S., Dukelsky: Some Reminiscences," *Musical Quarterly* (Jan. 1947); F. Schillinger, *J. S.: A Memoir by His Wife* (N.Y., 1949); D. Augustine, *Four Theories of Music in the United States, 1900–1950: Cowell, Yasser, Partch, S.* (diss., Univ. of Texas, 1979); J. Burk, "S.'s Double Equal Temperament System," in E. Asmus, ed., *The Pyschology and Acoustics of Music: A Collection of Papers* (Lawrence, Kans., 1979).

Schillings, Max von, German composer and conductor; b. Düren, April 19, 1868; d. Berlin, July 24, 1933. While attending the Gymnasium at Bonn, he studied violin with O. von Königslöw, and piano and composition with K.J. Brambach. He then entered the Univ. of Munich, where he studied law, philosophy, literature, and art. He became associated with Richard Strauss, and under his influence decided to devote himself entirely to music. In 1892 he was engaged as assistant stage director at the Bayreuth Festival Theater; in 1902 he became chorus master. He went to Stuttgart in 1908 as assistant to the Intendant at the Royal Opera, and then was its Generalmusikdirektor (1911–18); upon the inauguration of its new opera theater, he was ennobled as von Schillings; was Intendant of the Berlin State Opera (1919–25). He made several visits as a conductor to the U.S. In 1923 he married the soprano **Bar-**

bara Kemp. As a composer, he trailed in the path of Wagner, barely avoiding direct imitation.

WORKS: OPERAS: *Ingwelde* (Karlsruhe, Nov. 13, 1894); *Der Pfeifertag* (Schwerin, Nov. 26, 1899; rev. 1931); *Moloch* (Dresden, Dec. 8, 1906); *Mona Lisa* (Stuttgart, Sept. 26, 1915; enjoyed considerable success). **ORCH.:** 2 Phantasiestücke: *Dem Andenken seiner Mutter* (1883) and *Aus dem Jahre* (1890); 2 symphonische Phantarien: *Meergruss* and *Seemorgen* (1895); *Ein Zwiegespräch,* tone poem for Violin, Cello, and Orch. (1896); *Symphonischer Prolog zu Sophokles Ödipus* (1900); *Musik zu Aeschylos Orestie* (1901); *Musik zu Goethes Faust,* part 1 (1908; rev. and augmented, 1915); Violin Concerto (1910); *Festlicher Marsch* for Military Band (1911); *Tanz der Blumen* for Small Orch. (1930). **CHAMBER:** String Quartet (1887; rev. 1906); Improvisation for Violin and Piano (1895); Piano Quintet (1917); piano pieces; also choral works and songs. J. Beck ed. *Max von Schillings: Gesamtverzeichnis seiner Werke* (Berlin, 1933).

BIBL.: R. Louis, *M. S.* (Leipzig, 1909); A. Richard, *M. S.* (Munich, 1922); W. Raupp, *M. v.S.: der Kampf eines deutschen Künstlers* (Hamburg, 1935); J. Geuenich and K. Strahn, eds., *Gedenkschrift M. v.S. zum 100. Geburtstag* (Düren, 1968).

Schimon, Adolf, Austrian pianist, singing teacher, and composer; b. Vienna, Feb. 29, 1820; d. Leipzig, June 21, 1887. He studied with Berton, Halévy, and others at the Paris Cons.; studied the Italian method in Florence, bringing out his opera *Stradella* there in 1846; was *maestro al cembalo* at Her Majesty's Theatre in London (1850–53), then at the Italian Opera in Paris (1854–59). In 1858 Flotow brought out Schimon's comic opera *List um List* at Schwerin. He taught singing at the Leipzig Cons. (1874–77) and in Munich (1877–86). His other works included Italian and French songs; German lieder; 2 string quartets; Piano Trio; Violin Sonata; piano music; etc. He married the soprano **Anna Regan (Schimon-Regan)** in 1872.

Schimon-Regan, Anna, distinguished German soprano; b. Aich, near Karlsbad, Sept. 18, 1841; d. Munich, April 18, 1902. In 1859 she had her 1st singing lessons from Mme. Schubert in Karlsbad; the next year her aunt, **Caroline Unger,** took her to Florence and taught her until 1864; was then engaged at the court opera in Hannover (1864–67); during the winter of 1867–68 she sang in Berlioz's concerts in St. Petersburg. She made her 1st visit to England in 1869, appearing in concerts with Unger; gave song recitals there every winter until 1875. In 1872 she married **Adolf Schimon,** and settled in Munich.

Schindelmeisser, Louis (actually, **Ludwig Alexander Balthasar**), German conductor and composer; b. Königsberg, Dec. 8, 1811; d. Darmstadt, March 30, 1864. He studied with Marx and Gährich in Berlin; then with his stepbrother, Heinrich Dorn, in Leipzig (1831), where he was befriended by Wagner. He conducted in Salzburg, Innsbruck, Graz, Berlin (1837), Pest (1838–47), Hamburg, Frankfurt, and Wiesbaden; then was Hofkapellmeister in Darmstadt (from 1853).

WORKS: STAGE: OPERAS: *Peter von Szapáry* (Budapest, Aug. 8, 1839); *Malwina* (Budapest, 1841); *Der Rächer,* after Corneille's *Le Cid* (Budapest, April 4, 1846); *Melusine* (Darmstadt, 1861). **BALLET:** *Diavolina;* also 2 orch. overtures: *Rule Britannia* and *Loreley;* numerous piano pieces and songs.

Schindler, Anton Felix, Moravian violinist, conductor, and writer on music; b. Meedl, Moravia, June 13, 1795; d. Bockenheim, near Frankfurt am Main, Jan. 16, 1864. He studied violin with his father; went to Vienna in 1813 to study law. In 1814 he met Beethoven, soon becoming his secretary, his social mediator, and, to some extent, his business manager; for some years he held the position of concertmaster of the orch. of the Josephstadttheater. Beethoven's stormy temper created inevitable difficulties; during one such outburst, Beethoven even accused his faithful helper of mishandling the financial receipts from the ticket sales for the premiere of the 9th Sym. However, Schindler had enough modesty and intelligence to disregard such personal misunderstandings, and continued to serve Beethoven. After Beethoven's death, Schindler obtained possession of valuable MSS, documents, papers, and about 400 of the biographically important conversation books, which recorded Beethoven's dialogues with friends and visitors. In a misguided attempt to protect Beethoven's reputation, Schindler apparently destroyed some of these materials, at least the parts that reflected Beethoven's pettiness and complaints. More reprehensible is the indication that some of Beethoven's conversation books, invaluable in their biographical content, were altered by Schindler, as appears from the painstaking handwriting analysis conducted on these books in 1977 by D. Beck and G. Herre. In 1846 Schindler sold most of his Beethoven collection to the Royal Library in Berlin. He served as music director in Münster (1831–35) and Aachen (1835–37). In 1848 he moved to Frankfurt and supported himself mainly by teaching. In 1856 he settled in Bockenheim, where he remained until his death. No matter what criticism can be raised against Schindler as a man of limited endowments unable to grasp the dimension of Beethoven's genius, the fact remains that it was Schindler who became the prime source of information about Beethoven's life, a witness to the musical greatness that Beethoven embodied. His fundamental book, *Biographie von Ludwig van Beethoven*, was publ. in Münster in 1840; the 2nd ed., containing the valuable supplement *Auszüge aus Beethovens Konversationsheften*, appeared in 1845; the English tr. of the original ed., made by Moscheles, was publ. in London in 1841. The 3rd ed. of Schindler's biography appeared in 1860 and was tr. into Eng. by D. MacArdle under the title *Beethoven as I Knew Him* (London, 1966). Of interest are also Schindler's diaries (1841–43), which were ed. by M. Becker (Frankfurt, 1939).

BIBL.: E. Hüffer, *A.F. S., Der Biograph Beethovens* (diss., Univ. of Münster, 1909); W. Nohl, "Die Beziehungen A. S.s zu Beethoven," *Die Musik*, XVII (1925); D. MacArdle, "A.F. S., Friend of Beethoven," *Music Review*, XXIV (1963); E. Doernberg, "A. S.," *Musical Quarterly* (April 1965); D. Beck and G. Herre, "Einige Zweifel an der Überlieferung der Konversationshefte," *Internationaler Beethoven-Kongress: Berlin 1977*; P. Stadlen, "S.'s Beethoven Forgeries," *Musical Times* (July 1977); D. Beck and G. Herre, "A. S.s fingierte Eintragungen in den Konversationsheften," in H. Goldschmidt, ed., *Zu Beethoven: Aufsätze und Annotationen* (Berlin, 1979).

Schindler, Kurt, German-American conductor, music editor, and composer; b. Berlin, Feb. 17, 1882; d. N.Y., Nov. 16, 1935. He studied piano with Ansorge and composition with Bussler and others in Berlin; took additional theory lessons in Munich with Thuille. He then was briefly assistant conductor to Richard Strauss in Berlin and to Mottl in Munich; in 1904 he emigrated to America and, after serving as an assistant chorus master at the Metropolitan Opera in N.Y., was engaged as a reader, ed., and critic for G. Schirmer (1907), remaining with the firm for about 20 years. In 1909 he founded the MacDowell Chorus, which became the Schola Cantorum of N.Y. in 1912. Schindler conducted it until 1926 in programs including his choral arrangements of folk songs of various nations. Among his valuable folk song eds. are *A Century of Russian Song from Glinka to Rachmaninoff* (N.Y., 1911); *Songs of the Russian People* (Boston, 1915); *Masters of Russian Song* (1917); *Sixty Russian Folk-Songs for One Voice* (N.Y., 1918–19); and *Folk Music and Poetry of Spain and Portugal* (N.Y., 1941); also ed. the anthology *The Development of Opera: From its Earliest Beginnings to the Masterworks of Gluck* (1913).

BIBL.: I. Katz, "K. S.'s Musicological Field Work in Soria, Spain," *American Philosophical Society Yearbook 1973*.

Schiøler, Victor, Danish pianist and conductor; b. Copenhagen, April 7, 1899; d. there, Feb. 17, 1967. He studied with his mother, Augusta Schiøler (1868–1946); then with Ignaz Friedman and Artur Schnabel; made his debut in 1914; from 1919, toured in Europe; made his 1st American tour in 1948–49. He was also active as a conductor in Denmark.

Schiørring, Nils, Danish musicologist; b. Copenhagen, April 8, 1910. He studied musicology with Abrahamsen and Larsen at the Univ. of Copenhagen (M.A., 1933); concurrently took lessons in cello from L. Jensen. He completed his musicological training at the Univ. of Copenhagen (Ph.D., 1950, with the diss. *Det 16. og 17. århundredes verdslige danske visesang*; publ. in Copenhagen, 1950). He worked at the Copenhagen Music History Museum (1932–53); also wrote music criticism and served as ed. of *Dansk musiktidsskrift* (1943–45) and *Dansk årbog for musikforskning* (with S. Sorensen; from 1961). In 1950 he joined the faculty of the Univ. of Copenhagen, retiring in 1980.

WRITINGS: (all publ. in Copenhagen): *Billeder fra 125 aars musikliv (1827–1952)* (1952); *Selma Nielsens Viser* (1956); *Allemande og fransk ouverture* (1957); *Musikkens vije* (1959; 2nd ed., 1964); ed. with S. Kragh-Jacobsen, *August Bournonville: Lettres à la maison de son enfance* (1969–70); with N. Jensen, *Deutschdänische Begegnungen um 1800: Kunst, Dichtung, Musik* (1974); *Musikkens Historie i Danmark* (1978).

Schiøtz, Aksel (Hauch), famous Danish tenor, baritone, and pedagogue; b. Roskilde, Sept. 1, 1906; d. Copenhagen, April 19, 1975. His father was an architect, and he urged Schiøtz to follow an academic career; accordingly, he enrolled at the Univ. of Copenhagen in language studies (M.A., 1929). He also studied singing, first at the Danish Royal Opera School in Copenhagen, and later with John Forsell in Stockholm. He made his concert debut in 1938; his operatic debut followed in 1939 as Ferrando in *Così fan tutte* at the Royal Danish Theater in Copenhagen, and soon gained wide recognition as a Mozartian and as a lieder artist. In 1946 he made appearances in England; in 1948 he visited the U.S. His career was tragically halted when he developed a brain tumor in 1950, which led to an impairment of his speech; however, he regained his capacities as a singer and gave concerts as a baritone. From 1955 to 1958 he taught voice at the Univ. of Minnesota; from 1958 to 1961, was a prof. of voice at the Royal Cons. of Music and the Univ. of Toronto; from 1961 to 1968, at the Univ. of Colorado; and from 1968, at the Royal Danish School of Educational Studies in Copenhagen. In 1977 a memorial fund was formed in the U.S. to preserve his memory by granting scholarships in art songs. He publ. *The Singer and His Art* (N.Y., 1969).

BIBL.: G. Schiøtz, *Kunst og Kamp: Gerd og A. S.* (Copenhagen, 1951).

Schipa, Tito (baptized **Raffaele Attilio Amadeo**), famous Italian tenor; b. Lecce, Jan. 2, 1888; d. N.Y., Dec. 16, 1965. He studied with A. Gerunda in Lecce and with E. Piccoli in Milan, and began his career as a composer of piano pieces and songs; then turned to singing, and in 1910 made his debut at Vercelli in *La Traviata*. After numerous appearences in Europe, he was engaged by the Chicago Opera (1919–32); made his 1st appearance with the Metropolitan Opera in N.Y. on Nov. 23, 1932, as Nemorino in *L'elisir d'amore*; continued to sing with the Metropolitan until 1935, then again in 1941. Schipa made extensive tours of Europe and South America, as well as in the U.S. He retired from the operatic stage in 1954, but continued to give concerts until late in life. Among his greatest roles were Des Grieux in *Manon*, the Duke of Mantua, Don Ottavio, and Werther. He wrote an operetta, *La Principessa Liana* (1935); a Mass (1929); several songs; also wrote a book, *Si confessi* (Genoa, 1961).

Schipper, Emil (Zacharias), Austrian bass-baritone; b. Vienna, Aug. 19, 1882; d. there, July 20, 1957. He studied in Vienna and with Guarino in Milan; made his debut at the German Theater in Prague in 1904 as Telramund; then sang in Linz (1911–12), at the Vienna Volksoper (1912–15), the Bavarian Court (later State) Opera (1916–22), and the Vienna State Opera (1922–28); also made guest appearances at Covent Garden in London (1924–28), in Chicago (1928–29), and in Salzburg (1930; 1935–36). His finest roles were in operas by Wagner and R. Strauss. He was married to the mezzo-soprano **Maria Olczewska.**

Schippers, Thomas, greatly gifted American conductor; b. Kalamazoo, Mich., March 9, 1930; d. N.Y., Dec. 16, 1977.

He played piano in public at the age of 6, and was a church organist at 14. He studied piano at the Curtis Inst. of Music in Philadelphia (1944–45) and privately with Olga Samaroff (1946–47); subsequently attended Yale Univ., where he took some composition lessons from Paul Hindemith. In 1948 he won 2nd prize in the contest for young conductors organized by the Philadelphia Orch. He then took a job as organist at the Greenwich Village Presbyterian Church in N.Y.; joined a group of young musicians in an enterprise called the Lemonade Opera Co., and conducted this group for several years. On March 15, 1950, he conducted the N.Y. premiere of Menotti's opera *The Consul;* also conducted the television premiere of his *Amahl and the Night Visitors* (N.Y., Dec. 24, 1951). On April 9, 1952, he made his 1st appearance at the N.Y. City Opera, conducting Menotti's *The Old Maid and the Thief,* remaining on its roster until 1954. On March 26, 1955, he led the N.Y. Phil. as guest conductor. On Dec. 23, 1955, he made his debut at the Metropolitan Opera in N.Y., conducting *Don Pasquale;* conducted there regularly in subsequent seasons. From 1958 to 1976 he was associated with Menotti at the Spoleto Festival of Two Worlds. Other engagements included appearances with the N.Y. Phil., which he accompanied in 1959 to the Soviet Union as an alternate conductor with Leonard Bernstein. In 1962 he conducted at La Scala the world premiere of Manuel de Falla's cantata *Atlantida;* in 1964 he conducted at the Bayreuth Festival. He was a favorite conductor for new works at the Metropolitan Opera; conducted the 1st performance of Menotti's opera *The Last Savage* and the opening of the new home of the Metropolitan with Samuel Barber's *Antony and Cleopatra* (Sept. 16, 1966); he also conducted the 1st production at the Metropolitan of the original version of Mussorgsky's *Boris Godunov* (1974). In 1970 he was appointed music director of the Cincinnati Sym. Orch., one of the few American-born conductors to occupy a major sym. orch. post; was also a prof. at the Univ. of Cincinnati College-Cons. of Music (from 1972). There was an element of tragedy in his life. Rich, handsome, and articulate, he became a victim of lung cancer, and was unable to open the scheduled season of the Cincinnati Sym. Orch. in the fall of 1977; in a grateful gesture the management gave him the title of conductor laureate; he bequeathed a sum of $5,000,000 to the orch. His wife died of cancer in 1973. When he conducted *La forza del destino* at the Metropolitan Opera on March 4, 1960, the baritone Leonard Warren collapsed and died on the stage.

Schirmer, family of German-American music publishers. The 1st of the family to be connected with music was **Johann Georg Schirmer,** who settled in Sondershausen. He was a cabinet and instrument maker. His son, **Ernst Ludwig Rudolf Schirmer** (b. Sondershausen, May 8, 1784), emigrated to N.Y. with his wife and children in 1840. His son **(Friedrich) Gustav (Emil) Schirmer** (b. Königsee, Thuringia, Sept. 19, 1829; d. Eisenach, Aug. 5, 1893) found employment in the music store of Scharfenberg & Luis, and later entered the employ of Kerksieg & Breusing, music dealers, becoming manager in 1854. In 1861 he took over the business with a partner, and acquired sole control in 1866, establishing the firm that was to become **G. Schirmer, Inc.** He was an enlightened and progressive publisher; entered into personal relations with noted European composers, and was among the original patrons of Wagner's Bayreuth Festival. He was an amateur pianist and had a real love for music. The diary of Tchaikovsky's visit to N.Y. in 1891 makes repeated mention of Schirmer and his family. Schirmer married an American, Mary Fairchild, by whom he had 5 daughters and 2 sons. The younger of these sons, **Gustave Schirmer** (b. N.Y., Feb. 18, 1864; d. Boston, July 15, 1907), organized in 1885 the Boston Music Co., which gained prominence especially through the publ. of Ethelbert Nevin's music. Shortly afterward, with his brother **Rudolph Edward Schirmer** (b. N.Y., July 22, 1859; d. Santa Barbara, Calif., Aug. 19, 1919), he became a partner in the firm founded by their father in N.Y., and after the latter's death in 1893, he managed the business jointly with his

brother, retaining independent control of the Boston Music Co. Rudolph was educated in N.Y. public schools, and lived in Weimar with his mother, brother, and 4 sisters (1873–75); studied violin and piano with Helene Stahl and came in contact with the Liszt circle; in 1876 he entered the College of New Jersey (later Princeton Univ.), and after graduation in 1880 studied law for 4 years at Columbia College, being admitted to the bar in 1884. In 1885 he took the place of his brother Gustave in his father's music publ. business. Later he was rejoined by Gustave, and upon their father's death in 1893, Rudolph became president of the firm, assuming sole control from 1907. In 1915 he founded the *Musical Quarterly.* **Gustave Schirmer, 3rd** (b. Boston, Dec. 29, 1890; d. Palm Beach, Fla., May 28, 1965), son of Gustave Schirmer and grandson of the founder of G. Schirmer, Inc., inherited the Boston Music Co. from his father and acquired the Willis Music Co. of Cincinnati. He was president of G. Schirmer, Inc. from 1919 to 1921 and from 1944 to 1957. Rudolph E. Schirmer's son, also named **Rudolph Edward Schirmer** (b. Santa Barbara, Calif., June 8, 1919), was vice-president from 1949 to 1965 and chairman of the board from 1965 to 1979 of G. Schirmer, Inc.

Schirmer, Ernest Charles, American music publisher; b. Mt. Vernon, N.Y., March 15, 1865; d. Waban, Mass., Feb. 15, 1958. He was a nephew of **Gustav Schirmer,** and became an apprentice in his N.Y. music store in 1878. After serving as business manager (1891–1902) and partner (1902–17) of the Boston Music Co., he founded the E.C. Schirmer Music Co. in 1921. It publishes the Concord Series, the Choral Repertory of the Harvard Univ. Glee Club, Radcliffe, Vassar, and Wellesley College Choral Music, the Polyphonic and "A Cappella" Libraries, the St. Dunstan Edition of Sacred Music, and treatises on harmonic analysis, musical theory, and music appreciation. The firm enjoys a world market for its publications, with agencies in London and Hamburg.

Schirmer, G., Inc., one of the leading American music publishing firms. It was an outgrowth of the business founded in N.Y. in 1848 by Kerksieg & Breusing, of which **Gustav Schirmer** became manager in 1854. With another employee, Bernard Beer, he took over the business in 1861, and the firm became known as "Beer & Schirmer." In 1866 he became the sole owner, establishing the house of "G. Schirmer, Music Publishers, Importers and Dealers." After his death in 1893, the firm was incorporated under the management of his sons, **Rudolph Edward Schirmer** and **Gustave Schirmer.** Rudolph Schirmer died in 1919, and was succeeded by his nephew **Gustave Schirmer, 3rd,** who was president until 1921. W. Rodman Fay was president (1921–29). Carl Engel served as president from 1929 to 1944, with the exception of 1933, when Hermann Irion held the office. Gustave Schirmer, 3rd, was again president from 1944 until 1957. He was succeeded by Rudolph Tauhert (1957–72). Until 1880, the business was located at 701 Broadway in N.Y.; then it was moved to 35 Union Square, and in 1909 was transferred to a 7-story building at 3 East 43rd St. It remained at that address until 1960, when it was moved to 609 5th Ave., and its retail store relocated at 4 East 49th St. In 1969 G. Schirmer, Inc. was acquired by Macmillan, Inc., and in 1973 the executive offices were moved to 866 3rd Ave. In 1973 Schirmer Books was founded as a division of Macmillan Publ. Co., Inc., taking over the publication of books on music for college, trade, and professional/reference markets, while G. Schirmer continued publication of musical works. In 1986 the latter was sold to Music Sales Corp. of N.Y. The N.Y. firm also maintained branches in Cleveland (until 1962) and in Los Angeles (until 1967). In 1892 the firm began publ. of the Library of Musical Classics, notable for careful editing and general typographical excellence; with its didactic Latin motto, "Musica laborum dulce lenimen," it became a familiar part of musical homes. In the same year was launched the Collection of Operas, a series of vocal scores with original text and Eng. tr.; another series, The Golden Treasury, was begun in 1905. Schirmer's Scholastic Series, containing pedagogical works, began publ. in 1917. Among other laudable initiatives was the American Folk-Song Series, offering authentic folk material. The firm entered the field of musical lexicography in 1900 when it publ. *Baker's Biographical Dictionary of Musicians,* ed. by Theodore Baker. A 2nd ed. appeared in 1905. Alfred Remy was ed. of the 3rd edition (1919). The 4th edition was ed. by Carl Engel (1940). Nicolas Slonimsky brought out a Supplement in 1949, and then ed. the 5th edition (1958) and the Supplements of 1965 and 1971; he subsequently ed. the 6th (1978), 7th (1984), and 8th (1991) editions. Theodore Baker also compiled and ed. *A Dictionary of Musical Terms* (G. Schirmer, N.Y., 1895; many reprints) and *Pronouncing Pocket-Manual of Musical Terms* (1905; more than a million copies sold). In 1915 the *Musical Quarterly* was founded under the editorship of O.G. Sonneck; its subsequent editors have been Carl Engel (1929–44), Gustave Reese (1944–45), Paul Henry Lang (1945–72), Christopher Hatch (1972–77), Joan Peyser (1977–84), and Eric Salzman (from 1984). It has publ. articles by the foremost scholars of Europe and the U.S.; beginning in 1989, it was publ. by the Oxford Univ. Press. The music catalog of G. Schirmer, Inc. comprises tens of thousands of publs., ranging from solo songs to full orch. scores. Particularly meritorious is the endeavor of the publishers to promote American music; the firm has publ. works by Ernest Bloch, Charles Loeffler, Charles Griffes, Walter Piston, Roy Harris, William Schuman, Samuel Barber, Gian Carlo Menotti, Paul Creston, Leonard Bernstein, Elliott Carter, Henry Cowell, Norman Dello Joio, Morton Gould, Virgil Thomson, Milton Babbitt, Gunther Schuller, and many others; it also took over some works of Charles Ives. Among European composers, the works of Arnold Schoenberg, Gustav Holst, and Benjamin Britten are included in the Schirmer catalogue, as well as a number of works by Soviet composers.

Schiske, Karl (Hubert Rudolf), significant Austrian composer; b. Raab, Feb. 12, 1916; d. Vienna, June 16, 1969. He studied music theory privately with Ernst Kanitz in Vienna (1932–38) and musicology with Orel and Schenk at the Univ. of Vienna (Ph.D., 1942). In 1952 he was appointed prof. of composition at the Vienna Academy of Music; in 1967 he received the Great Austrian State Prize. In 1966–67 he was a visiting prof. at the Univ. of Calif., Riverside. His technique of composition is curiously synthetic, and yet invariably logical, containing elements of medieval counterpoint and the serial methods of composition. **WORKS: ORCH.:** *Vorspiel* (1938); Piano Concerto (1938–39); 2 concertos for String Orch. (1941, 1945); 5 syms. (1941–42; 1947–48; 1950–51; 1955; 1965); *Tanzrondo* (1942); *Kammerkonzert* for Chamber Orch. (1949); Violin Concerto (1952); *Divertimento* for Chamber Orch. or 10 Instruments (1963). **CHAMBER:** 2 string quartets (1936, 1945); Sextet for Clarinet, String Quartet, and Piano (1937); Wind Quintet (1945); Violin Sonata (1943–48); *Musik* for Clarinet, Trumpet, and Viola (1948); *3 Pieces for Gloria* for Violin (1951); *Synthese* for "4 x 4" Instruments (1958). **VOCAL:** *Reitjagd,* cantata for Baritone, Chorus, and Orch. (1938); *Vom Tode,* oratorio (1946); *Candada,* 4 pieces for Soprano, Chorus, and Small Orch. (1956; Vienna, March 9, 1972); choruses. **PIANO:** Sonata, 4-hands (1949); Sonatina (1953); other piano pieces; also organ pieces.

Schiuma, Alfredo, Argentine composer; b. Buenos Aires, July 1, 1885; d. there, July 24, 1963. He studied with Romaniello in Buenos Aires, and later established his own music school there. He wrote several operas in a singable Italianate idiom for Buenos Aires: *Amy Robsart,* based on Walter Scott's novel *Kenilworth* (April 24, 1920); *La Sirocchia* (April 23, 1922); *Tabaré* (Aug. 6, 1925); *Las virgenes del sol* (June 20, 1939); *La infanta* (Aug. 12, 1941); also 4 syms. (1928–57); symphonic tableau, *Pitunga* (Buenos Aires, March 31, 1929); symphonic sketch, *Los Incas* (Buenos Aires, April 26, 1931); choruses; chamber music; songs.

Schjelderup, Gerhard (Rosenkrone), Norwegian composer and writer on music; b. Christiansand, Nov. 17, 1859; d. Benediktbeuren, Bavaria, July 29, 1933. He went to Paris in 1878, and studied with Franchomme (cello) and Massenet and Sa-

vard (composition); in 1888 he settled in Germany. He wrote music influenced partly by Wagner, partly by Grieg. **WORKS: OPERAS:** *Østenfor sol og vestenfor mane* (East of the Sun and West of the Moon; 1889–90); *Sampo Lappelill* (1890; not perf.); *Sonntagsmorgen* (1891–92; Munich, May 9, 1893); *Norwegische Hochzeit* (1894; Prague, March 17, 1900); *En hellig aften* (A Holy Evening; 1895; Christiania, 1915); *Et folk i nød* (A People in Need; n.d., not perf.); *Frühlingsnacht* (1906–7; Dresden, May 1, 1908; later perf. as *Vaarnat* [Spring Night] and *Stjernenaltter* [Starry Nights]); *Opal* (Dresden, 1915); *Die scharlachrote Blume* (n.d.; not perf.); *Sturmvögel* (Schwerin, Sept. 19, 1926); also a ballet, *Wunderhorn* (Christiania, 1905); incidental music. **ORCH.:** 2 syms. (1887, 1924); *In Baldurs Hain* (In Baldur's Grove) for Violin and Orch. (1904); 2 symphonic poems: *Eine Sommernacht auf dem Fjord* and *Brand;* also choral works; chamber music; songs; etc. **WRITINGS:** *Edvard Grieg og hans verker* (Copenhagen, 1903; 2nd ed., 1908, with Niemann); *Richard Wagner: hans liv og verker* (Copenhagen, 1907; 2nd ed., 1923); with S. Sandvik, *Norges musikhistorie* (Christiania, 1921). **BIBL.:** O. Sandvik, "G. S.," *Schweizerische Musikzeitung* (Oct. 1948).

Schläger, Hans, Austrian composer; b. Felskirchen, Dec. 5, 1820; d. Salzburg, May 17, 1885. He was a pupil of Preyer at Vienna; chorus master of the Männergesangverein (1844–61); then Kapellmeister of the Salzburg Cathedral, and director of the Mozarteum, resigning on his marriage to Countess Zichy in 1867. He wrote the operas *Heinrich und Ilse* (Salzburg, 1869) and *Hans Haidekukuk* (Salzburg, 1873); the symphonic tone picture *Waldmeisters Brautfahrt;* syms.; string quartets; etc.

Schlegel, Leander, Dutch pianist, teacher, and composer; b. Oegstgeest, near Leiden, Feb. 2, 1844; d. Overveen, near Haarlem, Oct. 20, 1913. He studied at the royal music school in The Hague; then went to Leipzig, where he was a student of Reinecke; toured with Wilhelmj as his accompanist; then returned to the Netherlands; was director of the music school in Haarlem (1870–98); in 1898 he moved to Overveen, where he continued to teach. He was a composer of solid attainments; in his music he tried to emulate Brahms; wrote a Sym., a Violin Concerto, a Piano Quartet, a String Quartet, a number of piano pieces in a Romantic mood, and many melodious songs.

Schlesinger, Adolph Martin, German music publisher, father of **Maurice (Moritz) Adolphe Schlesinger;** b. Sülz, Silesia, Oct. 4, 1769; d. Berlin, Nov. 11, 1838. He was active as a book dealer in Berlin before 1795; founded his own music publ. firm in 1810; it became Schlesinger'sche Buch- und Musikalienhandlung in 1821. He was one of Beethoven's German publishers. In 1831 his son, **Heinrich Schlesinger** (b. Berlin, 1810; d. there, Dec. 14, 1879), took charge of the firm; after his father's death, his mother shared control of the business (1838–44); thereafter he resumed sole charge. The firm publ. the influential journal *Echo* (1851–65). In 1864 the business was sold to R. Lienau (1838–1920), whose sons took it over after his death. The firm was further enlarged and enriched by the acquisition of several other music publ. firms, among them Haslinger of Vienna (1875), Krentzlin of Berlin (1919), Vernthal of Berlin (1925), and Köster of Berlin (1928). Schlesinger was the original publisher of *Der Freischütz* by Carl Maria von Weber; Beethoven's opp. 108–11, 132, 135; also works by Mendelssohn, Chopin, Liszt, and Berlioz.

Schlesinger, Kathleen, Irish musicologist; b. Hollywood, near Belfast, June 27, 1862; d. London, April 16, 1953. She was educated in Switzerland; then settled in England; became interested in musical instruments; publ. *The Instruments of the Modern Orchestra* (2 vols., London, 1910). Her chief work is *The Greek Aulos* (London, 1939), not only containing a description of ancient Greek instruments, but also propounding an original theory of the formation of Greek modes, which aroused much controversy; the weight of learned opinion inclined against her hypotheses.

Schlesinger, Maurice (Moritz) Adolphe (baptized **Mora Abraham**), German music publisher, son of **Adolph Martin Schlesinger**; b. Berlin, Oct. 3, 1797; d. Baden-Baden, Feb. 25, 1871. He moved to Paris in 1819, and was at first engaged in book selling. In 1821 he established a music publishing business, and launched the publication of the *Gazette musicale de Paris* (1834–35), which merged with the *Revue musicale* to become the *Revue et gazette musicale* (1835); the latter continued to appear until 1880. He became one of the most important Paris publishers; brought out scores by Beethoven, Donizetti, Meyerbeer, Berlioz, Liszt, Chopin, and others. In 1846 he sold the catalogue to Brandus and Dufour; later it was acquired by Joubert.
   BIBL.: A. Tyson, "M. S. as a Publisher of Beethoven, 1822–27," *Acta Musicologica*, XXXV (1963).

Schlesinger, Sebastian Benson, German composer; b. Hamburg, Sept. 24, 1837; d. Nice, Jan. 8, 1917. He went to the U.S. at the age of 13; studied music in Boston, chiefly under Otto Dresel; was for 17 years German consul in Boston; then lived for a time in London, and during his last years in Paris. He was a gifted composer; publ. about 120 songs, which received praise from Max Bruch and Robert Franz; wrote several piano pieces in a Romantic vein.

Schletterer, Hans Michel, German conductor, pedagogue, writer on music, and composer; b. Ansbach, May 29, 1824; d. Augsburg, June 4, 1893. He studied with Spohr in Kassel and Ferdinand David in Leipzig. After filling a number of teaching posts in provincial towns, he taught at the Univ. of Heidelberg (1854–58); then was a choral conductor and singing teacher in Augsburg, where he founded an oratorio society and a music school. He publ. 17 books of choral music a cappella; a selection of Lutheran church music, *Musica sacra* (2 vols., 1887; 3rd ed., 1927); *Das deutsche Singspiel* (1863); *J.Fr. Reichardt* (1865); *Geschichte der geistlichen Dichtung und kirchlichen Tonkunst* (1869); *Studien zur Geschichte der französischen Musik* (3 vols., 1884–85; mostly borrowed from Castil-Blaze); etc.

Schlick, Arnolt, eminent blind German organist and composer; b. probably in Heidelberg, c.1460; d. probably there, after 1521. He was made organist for life at the Palatine court in Heidelberg in 1509; also traveled as an organist and a consultant on the organ. He publ. *Spiegel der Orgelmacher und Organisten* (Speyer, 1511; facsimile and Eng. tr. by E. Barber, Buren, 1978). He brought out *Tablaturen etlicher lobgesang und lidlein uff die orgeln un lauten* (Mainz, 1512; ed. by G. Harms, Hamburg, 1924; 2nd ed., 1957).
   BIBL.: R. Kendall, "Notes on A. S.," *Acta Musicologica*, XI (1939); H. Lenneberg, "The Critic Criticized: Sebastian Virdung and His Controversy with A. S.," *Journal of the American Musicological Society* (Spring 1957); W. Thomas and J. Rhodes, "S., Praetorius and the History of Organ Pitch," *Organ Yearbook*, II (1971).

Schloezer, Boris de, renowned Russian-French writer on music; b. Vitebsk, Dec. 20, 1881; d. Paris, Oct. 7, 1969. He studied music in Brussels and Paris; returning to Russia, he devoted himself to a profound study of philosophy, esthetics, and music theory. His sister, Tatiana Schloezer, was the 2nd wife of Scriabin, and Schloezer became a close friend of Scriabin, who confided to him his theosophic and musical ideas. In 1920 he emigrated to France, where he continued his literary activities in the Russian émigré press and in French literary magazines. He publ. a monograph on Scriabin in Russian (vol. 1, Berlin, 1923; French tr., Paris, 1975; Eng. tr. by N. Slonimsky, Berkeley and Los Angeles, 1987; vol. II not completed); other books include *Igor Stravinsky* (Paris, 1929) and *Introduction à J.S. Bach* (Paris, 1947). He also wrote a philosophical fantasy, *Mon nom est personne* (My Name Is Nobody) and *Rapport secret*, depicting a distant planet whose inhabitants achieved immortality and divinity through science.

BIBL.: *B. d.S.*, collection of articles by 10 authors (Paris, 1981).

Schlögel, Xavier, Belgian composer; b. Brillonville, Famène, July 14, 1854; d. Ciney, near Namur, March 23, 1889. He studied with Ledent at the Liège Cons. He composed *Scènes champêtres* for Orch.; *Ballade des épées* for Voice and Orch.; *Messe solennelle* for Male Chorus, Organ, and Orch.; string quartets and piano trios.

Schlösser, (Karl Wilhelm) Adolf, German pianist, teacher, and composer, son of **Louis Schlösser**; b. Darmstadt, Feb. 1, 1830; d. Great Bookham, England, Nov. 10, 1913. He studied with his father; made his debut at Frankfurt in 1847; after concert tours in Germany, France, and England, he settled in London (1854); taught (until 1903) at the Royal Academy of Music. He composed a Piano Quartet; Piano Trio; 24 studies and many other pieces for piano.

Schlösser, Louis, German conductor and composer, father of **(Karl Wilhelm) Adolf Schlösser**; b. Darmstadt, Nov. 17, 1800; d. there, Nov. 17, 1886. He was pupil of Rinck at Darmstadt, of Seyfried, Mayseder, and Salieri at Vienna, and of Le Sueur and Kreutzer at the Paris Cons.; was court conductor in Darmstadt.
   WORKS: OPERAS: *Granada* (Vienna, 1826); *Das Leben ein Traum* (1839); *Die Jugend Karls II. von Spanien* (1847); *Die Braut des Herzogs* (1847); *Benvenuto Cellini*; operetta, *Kapitän Hector*; melodrama, *Die Jahreszeiten*; music to *Faust*; ballets; entr'actes; syms.; overtures; string quartets; Concertino for Horn, with Orch.; piano pieces; songs; etc.

Schlosser, Max, distinguished German tenor; b. Amberg, Oct. 17, 1835; d. Utting am Ammersee, Sept. 2, 1916. He sang in Zürich, St. Gallen, and Augsburg, but then decided to become a baker. Still, he did not abandon hopes for a stage career; he met Hans von Bülow, who entrusted him with the role of David at the premiere of *Die Meistersinger von Nürnberg* in Munich in 1868; he remained a member of the Munich Court Opera until his retirement in 1904. He also sang at Bayreuth and made guest appearances with Neumann's traveling opera company. He was principally known for his fine performances of the Wagnerian repertoire.

Schlottmann, Louis, German pianist, teacher, and composer; b. Berlin, Nov. 12, 1826; d. there, June 13, 1905. He studied with Taubert and Dehn; gave successful concerts in London and elsewhere, and settled in Berlin as a teacher.
   WORKS: Overtures to *Romeo and Juliet* and *Wallensteins Lager*; *Trauermarsch, Rezitativ und Finale*, symphonic scene for Orch.; *Concertstück* for Piano; chamber music; piano pieces (*3 Capricettes; Polonaise de concert; Andantino; Jugendspiegel*); choruses; songs.

Schlusnus, Heinrich, eminent German baritone; b. Braubach am Rhein, Aug. 6, 1888; d. Frankfurt am Main, June 18, 1952. He studied voice in Frankfurt and Berlin; made his operatic debut as the Herald in *Lohengrin* at the Hamburg Opera on Jan. 1, 1914; was then on its roster for the 1914–15 season; he subsequently sang in Nuremberg (1915–17), then was a leading member of the Berlin Royal (later State) Opera, remaining there until 1945; also appeared in Chicago (1927–28), Bayreuth (1933), and Paris (1937). He was renowned as a lieder artist.
   BIBL.: E. von Naso and A. Schlusnus, *H. S., Mensch und Sänger* (Hamburg, 1957).

Schmedes, Erik, Danish tenor; b. Gentofte, near Copenhagen, Aug. 27, 1868; d. Vienna, March 21, 1931. He studied with Artôt in Paris, Rothmühl in Berlin, and Ress in Vienna; made his operatic debut as a baritone in Wiesbaden (Jan. 11, 1891) as the Herald in *Lohengrin*; then sang tenor roles in Nuremberg (1894) and Dresden (1894–97). After a course of study with A. Iffert in Dresden, he developed a definite tenor voice, and appeared as Siegfried at the Vienna Opera (Feb. 11, 1898); remained on its roster until 1924. He sang at the Bayreuth Festivals (1899–1902; 1906); made his Metropolitan

Opera debut in N.Y. as Siegmund (Nov. 18, 1908), remaining on its roster for only that season.

Schmelzer, Johann Heinrich, eminent Austrian violinist and composer; b. Scheibbs, Lower Austria, c.1621; d. Prague, between Feb. 20 and March 20, 1680. He settled in Vienna, where he received his musical training; became a violinist in the court chapel (about 1635) and in the Court Orch. (1649); served as Vice-Kapellmeister (1671–79) and as Kapellmeister (1679–80). In 1673 he was ennobled and added "von Ehrenruef" to his name. He died of the plague. Schmelzer was a significant composer of instrumental music, playing a key role in the development of the suite and sonata. He had 3 sons who became musicians: **Andreas Anton Schmelzer** (b. Vienna [baptized], Nov. 26, 1653; d. there, Oct. 13, 1701) was a violinist and composer; studied with his father; played in the Court Orch. from 1671; succeeded his father as composer of ballet music (1681–93), producing about 65 ballet suites. **Georg Joseph Schmelzer** (b. Vienna [baptized], April 7, 1655; d. probably there, c.1700). **Peter Clemens (Clement) Schmelzer** (b. Vienna [baptized], June 28, 1672; d. there, Sept. 20, 1746) played in the Court Orch. from 1692 until a finger injury ended his active career in 1729; however, he did not officially retire until 1740.
BIBL.: E. Wellesz, *Die Ballett-Suiten von J.H. und A.A. S.* (Vienna, 1914); A. Koczirz, "Zur Lebensgeschichte J.H. S.s," *Studien zur Musikwissenschaft,* XXVI (1964).

Schmelzl, Wolfgang, Austrian singer, teacher, and composer; b. Kennath, c.1500; d. Steinfeld, c.1561. He was a Protestant cantor in Amberg; then, c.1540, went to Vienna as a teacher; was also a singer at the S. Salvator Chapel; settled as a Catholic priest at St. Lorenz in Steinfeld. He is known for a collection of 4- to 5-voiced quodlibets and folk songs of the period (1544).
BIBL.: E. Bienenfield, "W. S., Sein Liederbuch (1544) und das Quodlibet des XVI. Jahrhunderts," *Sammelbände der Internationalen Musik-Gesellschaft,* VI/1 (1904).

Schmid, Anton, Austrian writer on music; b. Pihl, near Leipa, Bohemia, Jan. 30, 1787; d. Salzburg, July 3, 1857. After studying singing at the monastery of the Calced Augustinians in Leipa, he went to Vienna, where he was employed as a librarian (1819) and custodian (1844) at the court library, where he compiled the collection which became the Austrian National Library.
WRITINGS: *Ottaviano dei Petrucci da Fossombrone, der erste Erfinder des Musiknotendruckes mit beweglichen Metalltypen, und seine Nachfolger im 16. Jahrhundert* (Vienna, 1845); *Joseph Haydn und Niccolò Zingarelli* (Vienna, 1847); *Christoph Willibald Ritter von Gluck: dessen leben und tonkünstlerisches Wirkens* (Leipzig, 1854).

Schmid, Erich, Swiss conductor; b. Balsthal, Jan. 1, 1907. He studied at the Hoch Cons. in Frankfurt and took composition lessons with Arnold Schoenberg in Berlin. He returned to Switzerland in 1933; was Generalmusikdirektor in Glarus until 1949, when he became chief conductor of the Zürich Tonhalle Orch. From 1957 to 1972 he was chief conductor of the Zürich Radio Orch., and served as a prof. of conducting at the Basel Music Academy (1963–73). He then went to England, and conducted the City of Birmingham Sym. Orch. (1979–81). He became known as a champion of modern music; brought to performance numerous works by Swiss composers.

Schmid, Ernst Fritz, eminent German musicologist; b. Tübingen, March 7, 1904; d. Augsburg, Jan. 20, 1960. He studied violin, viola, and viola d'amore at the Munich Academy of Music; took private lessons in music theory and conducting; then studied musicology at the univs. of Munich (with Sandberger), Freiburg (with Gurlitt), Tübingen (with Hasse), and Vienna (with Haas, Orel et al.); received his Ph.D. from the Univ. of Tübingen in 1929 with the dissertation *Carl Philipp Emanuel Bach und seine Kammermusik* (publ. in Kassel, 1931); completed his Habilitation as a Privatdozent in musicology at the Univ. of Graz in 1934 with his *Joseph Haydn: Ein Buch von Vorfahren und Heimat des Meisters* (publ. in Kassel, 1934).

He became a prof. at the Univ. of Tübingen in 1935; also founded the Schwäbisches Landesmusikarchiv; he left Tübingen in 1937 to devote himself to private research; during World War II, he served in the German army; in 1948 he founded the Mozartgemeinde, and in 1951 the German Mozartgesellschaft. In 1954 he became academic director of the Neue Mozart Ausgabe; from 1955 he oversaw the publ. of the new critical ed. of Mozart's complete works, the *Neue Ausgabe Sämtlicher Werke.* In addition to his valuable research on Mozart, he discovered the private music collection of Emperor Franz II in Graz in 1933; this important collection is now housed in Vienna's Nationalbibliothek.
WRITINGS: *Wolfgang Amadeus Mozart* (Lübeck, 1934; 3rd ed., 1955); *Die Orgeln der Abtei Amorbach* (Buchen, 1938); ed. *Ein schwäbisches Mozartbuch* (Lorch and Stuttgart, 1948); *Musik am Hofe der Fürsten von Löwenstein-Wertheim-Rosenberg, 1720–1750* (Würzburg, 1953); *Musik an den schwäbischen Zollernhöfen der Renaissance* (Kassel, 1962).
BIBL.: W. Fischer et al., eds., *In memoriam E.F. S., 1904–1960: Ein Gedenkblatt für seine Angehörigen und Freunde* (Recklinghausen, 1961).

Schmid, Heinrich Kaspar, German composer and teacher; b. Landau an der Isar, Bavaria, Sept. 11, 1874; d. Munich, Jan. 8, 1953. He studied with Thuille and Bussmeyer at the Munich Academy of Music (1899–1903); in 1903 he went to Athens, where he taught music at the Odeon; in 1905 he returned to Munich and was on the faculty of the Academy of Music until 1921; then was director of the Karlsruhe Cons. (1921–24) and of the Augsburg Cons. (1924–32). His eyesight failed him and he was totally blind during the last years of his life. As a composer, he followed the Romantic tradition of the Bavarian School; he wrote a great number of lieder, and composed singspiels in a folklike manner, as well as choruses and chamber music.
BIBL.: H. Roth, *H.K. S.* (Munich, 1921); W. Zentner, "H.K. S.," *Neue Musikzeitschrift* (Aug.–Sept. 1949).

Schmidl, Carlo, Italian music publisher and lexicographer; b. Trieste, Oct. 7, 1859; d. there, Oct. 7, 1943. He was the son and pupil of the Hungarian composer **Antonio** (actually, **Anton**) **Schmidl** (1814–80). In 1872 he entered the employ of the music publisher Vicentini, and in 1889 he established his own business at Trieste; also directed the Leipzig branch of the Ricordi Co. (1901–6). He compiled and publ. an important biographical music dictionary, *Dizionario universale dei musicisti* (Milan, 1887–89; 2nd ed., 1926–29; supplement, 1938; 3rd ed., 1938), containing scrupulously accurate data on Italian musicians, exact dates of performance of major works, and other information testifying to independent research. Schmidl also wrote biographies of Schumann (1890) and G.S. Mayr (1901).

Schmidt, Annerose, German pianist; b. Wittenberg, Oct. 5, 1936. She studied with her father for 12 years, making her debut in Wittenberg when she was 9; then completed her training with Hugo Steurer at the Leipzig Hochschule für Musik (1953–58). In 1954 she was awarded a diploma at the International Chopin Competition in Warsaw, and in 1956 captured 1st prize at the International Robert Schumann Competition in Zwickau. She toured in both Eastern and Western Europe, appearing with the Gewandhaus Orch. of Leipzig, the Dresden State Orch., the Royal Phil. of London, the Concertgebouw Orch. of Amsterdam, and the Residentie Orch. of The Hague; also appeared at festivals in Salzburg, the Netherlands, Prague, Edinburgh, Berlin, Dresden, and Warsaw. In 1980 she made her U.S. debut as soloist with Kurt Masur and the Gewandhaus Orch. at Carnegie Hall in N.Y. She became a prof. at the East Berlin Hochschule für Musik in 1986. While best known for her performances of Bach, Mozart, Beethoven, Schumann, Chopin, and Brahms, Schmidt also plays contemporary works, including those of Siegfried Matthus and Wolfgang Rihm.

Schmidt, Arthur P(aul), German-American music publisher; b. Altona, April 1, 1846; d. Boston, May 5, 1921. He settled in Boston in 1866, and entered the music firm of George D. Russell & Co. In 1876 he established a business of his own; the Arthur P. Schmidt Co. won prominence by publication of the works of MacDowell; it brought out virtually the complete output of Arthur Foote (more than 150 items); also works by Chadwick, Hadley, Paine, Mrs. Beach, and other composers of the "New England School." The firm was purchased by Summy-Birchard of Chicago in 1960.

Schmidt, Franz, important Austrian composer and pedagogue; b. Pressburg, Dec. 22, 1874; d. Perchtoldsdorf, near Vienna, Feb. 11, 1939. He began his musical training with the Pressburg Cathedral organist, Maher; in 1888 his family settled in Vienna, where he had piano lessons from Leschetizky and also studied composition with Bruckner, theory with Fuchs, and cello with Hellmesberger at the Cons. (from 1890). He was a cellist in the orch. of the Vienna Hofoper (1896–1911); also taught cello at the Cons. of the Gesellschaft der Musikfreunde (1901–8) and was prof. of piano (1914–22) and of counterpoint and composition (from 1922) at the Vienna Staatsakademie; also served as director (1925–27); subsequently was director of the Vienna Hochschule für Musik (1927–31). In 1934 he was awarded an honorary doctorate from the Univ. of Vienna. After his retirement in 1937, Schmidt received the Beethoven Prize of the Prussian Academy in Berlin. His 2nd wife, Margarethe Schmidt, founded the Franz Schmidt-Gemeinde in 1951. Schmidt's music is steeped in Viennese Romanticism; the works of Bruckner and Reger were particularly influential in his development, but he found an original voice in his harmonic writing. Although he is regarded in Austria as a very important symphonic composer, his music is almost totally unknown elsewhere. Outside his homeland, he remains best known for his orch. suite, *Zwischenspiel aus einer unvollständigen romantischen Oper* (Vienna, Dec. 6, 1903), taken from his opera *Notre Dame* (1902–4; Vienna, April 1, 1914). Among his other significant works are 4 syms.: No. 1 (1896–99; Vienna, Jan. 25, 1902); No. 2 (1911–13; Vienna, Dec. 3, 1913); No. 3 (Vienna, Dec. 2, 1928); No. 4 (1932–33; Vienna, Jan. 10, 1934); a Piano Concerto for Left Hand and Orch., for Paul Wittgenstein (1923; Vienna, Feb. 2, 1924); and the oratorio *Das Buch mit Sieben Siegeln* (1935–37; Vienna, June 15, 1938). He also composed 2 string quartets (1925, 1929) and other chamber works, 2 piano sonatas, and much organ music.

BIBL.: A. Liess, *F. S.: Sein Leben und Schaffen* (Graz, 1951); C. Nemeth, *F. S.: Ein Meister nach Brahms und Bruckner* (Vienna, 1957); R. Scholz, *F. S. als Orgelkomponist* (Vienna, 1971); N. Tschulik, *F. S.* (Vienna, 1972; Eng. tr., 1980); H. Truscott, *The Music of F. S.*: vol. I, *The Orchestral Music* (London, 1985); T. Leibnitz, *Österreichische Spätromantiker: Studien zu Emil Nikolaus von Reznicek, Joseph Marx, F. S., und Egon Kornauth* (Tutzing, 1986); T. Cornfield, "'A door was opened in heaven': Reflections on F. S.'s apocalyptic oratorio," *Musical Times* (Feb. 1989); P. Franklin, "The case of F. S.," ibid.

Schmidt, Gustav, German conductor and composer; b. Weimar, Sept. 1, 1816; d. Darmstadt, Feb. 11, 1882. He studied with Hummel, Eberwein, and Lobe in Weimar and with Mendelssohn in Leipzig; conducted opera in Brünn (1841–44), Würzburg (1845), Frankfurt (1846; 1851–61), Wiesbaden (1849), Leipzig (1864–76), and Mainz; was court Kapellmeister in Darmstadt (from 1876). He was a determined champion of Wagner and Berlioz. He wrote the operas *Prinz Eugen* (Frankfurt, 1847), *Weibertreue* or *Die Weiber von Weinsberg* (Weimar, 1858), *La Réole* (Breslau, 1863), and *Alibi* (Weimar, 1880); also songs and choruses.

Schmidt, Johann Christoph, German organist and composer; b. Hohnstein, near Pirna, Aug. 6, 1664; d. Dresden, April 13, 1728. He entered the Dresden court chapel as a chorister in 1676; there he received training from Christoph Bernhard; after serving as an instrumentalist in the Court Orch., he became master of the choristers in 1687 and 2nd organist in 1692. In 1694 he went to Italy to complete his

training. Upon his return to Dresden, he was made deputy Kapellmeister and chamber organist (1696). In 1698 he was promoted to principal Kapellmeister, pursuing his duties in Krakow and Warsaw as well as in Dresden, since he was responsible for the music for both the Saxon electoral and Polish courts. He also served as Kapellmeister for the Protestant and Catholic church music at the court, turning over his duties for the Catholic church music to J.D. Heinichen in 1717. Under Schmidt's leadership, the Dresden Court Orch. became one of the most celebrated in Europe. He wrote an opera seria, *Latona in Delo* (n.d.); a divertissement, *Les Quatre Saisons* (Dresden, Sept. 23, 1719); 4 overture-suites; 4 masses; 7 cantatas; and 4 motets.

Schmidt, Johann Philipp Samuel, German composer; b. Königsberg, Sept. 8, 1779; d. Berlin, May 9, 1853. He settled in Berlin, where he studied with J.G. Naumann and then took a government position; also devoted much time to performing, writing on music, and composing. He wrote several operas, including *Das Fischermädchen* (1818), orch. works, chamber music, sacred works, songs, etc.

Schmidt, John Henry (actually, **Johann Heinrich**), German-American organist, singing teacher, and composer who flourished in the late 18th century. He lived in Radevormwald, near Düsseldorf, until 1783, when he went to the Netherlands; was organist at the Cathedral of St. John in Schiedam (1785–90); was active as a singing teacher and piano manufacturer in Charleston, S.C., in 1796; that same year, he settled in Philadelphia, where he became organist of St. Peter's Church (1797); also announced concerts in Baltimore (1796) and Albany (1797). He composed a *Sonata for Beginners*.

BIBL.: O. Sonneck, *Bibliography of Early Secular American Music* (Washington, D.C., 1905); idem, *Early Concert Life in America* (Leipzig, 1907).

Schmidt, Joseph, Rumanian tenor; b. Bavideni, Bukovina, March 4, 1904; d. Zürich, Nov. 16, 1942. He studied at the Berlin Cons.; in 1928 began his career as a radio singer and won great popularity in Germany. In 1933 he went to Belgium; in 1938 was briefly in America; then settled in Switzerland. His voice was regarded as of great lyric expressiveness, but being almost a dwarf (he stood only 4 feet 10 inches in height), he was unable to appear in opera.

Schmidt, Ole, Danish conductor and composer; b. Copenhagen, July 14, 1928. He attended the Royal Danish Cons. of Music in Copenhagen; had conducting lessons from Albert Wolff, then from Rafael Kubelik and Sergui Celibidache. He was conductor of the Royal Danish Opera and Ballet (1959–65) and conductor of the Hamburg Sym. Orch. (1970–71); also was a guest conductor of the Danish Radio Sym. Orch. in Copenhagen (from 1971); was chief conductor of the Århus Sym. Orch. (1979–85). His music follows the vigor and lyrical sentiment of Scandinavian Romanticism, while sustaining the Classical symmetry of form.

WORKS: STAGE: *Edstillingen* (The Exhibition), opera (Copenhagen, Dec. 5, 1969); *Fever*, ballet (Copenhagen, Oct. 18, 1957). **ORCH.:** Sym. No. 1 (1955); *Chamber Concerto for Piano and Strings* (1955); *Pièce concertante* for Trumpet, Trombone, Harp, Piano, Celesta, Percussion, and Strings (1956); *Chamber Symphony* for Wind Quintet and Strings (1958); *Symphonic Fantasy and Fugue* for Accordion and Chamber Orch. (1959); *Pastel* for Chamber Orch. (1961); *Briol*, symphonic sketch (1962); Concerto No. 2 for Accordion, Wind Orch., and Percussion (1963–64); Horn Concerto (Copenhagen, Sept. 8, 1966); Violin Concerto (Dortmund, May 19, 1971); Tuba Concerto (1973). **CHAMBER:** *Divertimento* for Violin, Viola, Cello, and Piano (1957); 5 string quartets (1962–77); *Improvisation* for Piano, Double Bass, and Drums (1961); *Painting and Plugging* for Harp, Strings, and Piano (1963); Brass Quintet (1977); *Sinfonietta for 3 Quintets* for Brass, Woodwinds, and Strings (1977).

Schmidt, Trudeliese, German contralto; b. Saarbrücken, Nov. 7, 1943. She studied in her native city; made her debut there in 1965; then sang in Wiesbaden and Düsseldorf. From 1971 she made regular appearances in Munich and Hamburg; sang at the Bayreuth Festival in 1975; also made concert tours abroad.

Schmidt, William, American composer; b. Chicago, March 6, 1926. He moved to Los Angeles in 1952, and studied composition with Halsey Stevens and Ingolf Dahl at the Univ. of Southern Calif.; at the same time, was active as a jazz arranger. He composed *Concerto Breve for Brass and Band* (1957); pieces for orch. and numerous works for various chamber ensembles; 6 bassoon duets (1957); *Percussive Rondo* for Percussion Quartet (1957); *Serenade* for Tuba and Piano (1958); *Rondino* for Trombone and Piano (1959); *Viola Sonata* (1959); Woodwind Quintet (1959); etc.

Schmidt-Görg, Joseph, eminent German musicologist; b. Rüdinghausen, near Dortmund, March 19, 1897; d. Bonn, April 3, 1981. He studied musicology with Schiedermair and Schmitz at the Univ. of Bonn (Ph.D., 1926, with the diss. *Die Messen des Clemens non Papa;* completed his Habilitation there, 1930, with his *Die Mitteltontemperatur*). He became Schiedermair's assistant in the Beethoven Archives in Bonn in 1927; later served as director of the archives (1946–72); concurrently lectured on musicology at the Univ. of Bonn (1930–65). On his 70th birthday, he was presented with a Festschrift under the friendly Latin title *Colloquium amicorum* (Bonn, 1967), containing a catalogue of his writings. His publs. include *Unbekannte Manuskripte zu Beethovens weltlicher und geistlicher Gesangsmusik* (Bonn, 1928), *Katalog der Handschriften des Beethoven-Hauses und Beethoven-Archivs Bonn* (Bonn, 1935), *Nicolas Gombert: Leben und Werk* (Bonn, 1938), and *Ludwig van Beethoven* (with H. Schmidt; Bonn, 1969; Eng. tr., N.Y., 1970).

Schmidt-Isserstedt, Hans, respected German conductor; b. Berlin, May 5, 1900; d. Holm-Holstein, near Hamburg, May 28, 1973. He studied composition with Franz Schreker at the Berlin Hochschule für Musik; also took courses at the Univs. of Berlin, Heidelberg, and Münster. In 1923 he became a répétiteur at the Wuppertal Opera; after conducting opera in Rostock (1928–31) and Darmstadt (1931–33), he held the post of 1st conductor at the Hamburg State Opera (1935–43); then joined the Deutsche Oper in Berlin, where he was made Generalmusikdirektor in 1944. In 1945 he was mandated by the British occupation authorities with the direction of the music section of the Hamburg Radio; he organized the North German Radio Sym. Orch., which he led with notable distinction until his retirement in 1971; was also chief conductor of the Stockholm Phil. (1955–64). He appeared widely as a guest conductor; also conducted at Covent Garden in London and at the Bavarian State Opera in Munich. He was especially admired for his cultured performances of the Austro-German repertoire.

Schmieder, Wolfgang, noted German music librarian; b. Bromberg, May 29, 1901; d. Fürstenfeldbruck, Nov. 8, 1990. He studied musicology with Kroyer and Moser, German philology and literature with F. Panzer and F. von Waldberg, and art history with C. Neumann at the Univ. of Heidelberg (Ph.D., 1927, with the diss. *Zur Melodiebildung in Liedern von Neidhart von Reuental);* then was an assistant lecturer in its musicology dept. (1927–30); subsequently studied library science with M. Bollert at the Sächsischen Landesbibliothek in Dresden and with O. Glauning at the Univ. of Leipzig Library. He was librarian of the Technische Hochschule in Dresden (1931–33); then went to Leipzig as head of the archives of Breitkopf & Härtel (1933–42). In 1946 he founded the music dept. of the City and Univ. Library in Frankfurt, which he headed until 1963. He was presented a Festschrift on his 70th birthday in 1971, *Quellenstudien zur Musik,* ed. by K. Dorfmüller and G. von Dadelsen. Of his numerous publications, of fundamental importance is his exhaustive *Thematisch-systematisches Verzeichnis der musikalischen Werke von Johann Sebastian Bach: Bach-Werke-Verzeichnis* (Leipzig, 1950; 3rd ed., 1961; 4th ed., 1966); also valuable is *Musikalische alte Drücke bis etwa 1750* (with G. Hartweig; 2 vols., Wolfenbüttel, 1967).

Schmitt, Aloys, German pianist and composer, brother of **Jacob** and father of **Georg Aloys Schmitt;** b. Erlenbach, Aug. 26, 1788; d. Frankfurt am Main, July 25, 1866. He studied composition with André at Offenbach; in 1816 went to Frankfurt, where he remained all his life with the exception of short stays in Berlin and Hannover (1825–29). He composed 4 operas: *Der Doppelgänger* (Hannover, 1827); *Valeria* (Mannheim, 1832); *Das Osterfest zu Paderborn* (Frankfurt, 1843); *Die Tochter der Wüste* (Frankfurt, 1845); 2 oratorios: *Moses* and *Ruth;* church music; etc. But he is principally known and appreciated for his numerous piano compositions, including 4 piano concertos, several piano quartets, piano trios, a number of attractive character pieces for piano, and studies for school.

BIBL.: H. Henkel, *Leben und Wirken von Dr. Aloys Schmitt* (Frankfurt, 1873).

Schmitt, Camille, Belgian organist, pedagogue, and composer; b. Aubange, March 30, 1908; d. Limelette, May 11, 1976. He studied at the Brussels Cons. (1928–37); was an organist in France and Belgium (1923–29; 1940–48), a prof. at the Liège Cons. (1947–66), and director of the French Section of the Brussels Cons. (1966–73). His wife was the composer **Jacqueline Fontyn.**

WORKS: ORCH.: *Triptyque angevin* (1941); *Psaume* (1942); Sinfonietta (1943); *Rapsodie* (1944); *Préludes joyeux* (1945; I.S.C.M. Festival, Copenhagen, June 2, 1946); Piano Concerto (1955); *Métamorphoses* (1963); *Contrepoints* (1965); *Polyphonies* (1966); *Alternances* (1970). **CHAMBER:** Wind Quintet (1943); Trio for Oboe, Clarinet, and Bassoon (1945); String Quartet (1948); *Prélude* for Clarinet and Piano (1952); *Dialogue* for Violin and Piano (1953); *Métamorphoses* for Cello and Piano (1961); Quartet for 4 Clarinets (1964); *Burlesques* for Flute, Oboe, Clarinet, and Bassoon (1965); *Contrepoints* for Wind Quintet (1965); *Polyphonies* for Wind Quintet (1969); *Polyphonies* for Saxophone Quartet (1970). **VOCAL:** *Psautier* for Alto, Piano, Oboe, Clarinet, and Bassoon (1946); *La Halte des heures,* cantata for Solo Voice and Piano (1959); choruses. **PIANO:** *Polyphonies* (1966); *Histoire pour Pierre* (1970).

Schmitt, Florent, outstanding French composer; b. Blâmont, Meurthe-et-Moselle, Sept. 28, 1870; d. Neuilly-sur-Seine, near Paris, Aug. 17, 1958. He studied piano with H. Hess and harmony with G. Sandré at the Nancy Cons. (1887–89); then entered the Paris Cons., where he took courses in harmony with Dubois and Lavignac, fugue with Gédalge, and composition with Massenet and Fauré; won the 2nd Prix de Rome with his cantata *Frédégonde* (1897) and the Grand Prix de Rome with his cantata *Sémiramis* (1900). He spent the years 1901–4 in the Villa Medicis in Rome, sending to the Académie several important instrumental and choral works; then traveled in Germany, Austria, Hungary, and Turkey. In 1906 he returned to Paris, where he served as a member of the executive committee of the Société Musicale Indépendante from its foundation in 1909; was also a member of the Société Nationale de Musique. He became an influential music critic, writing regularly for *Le Temps* (1919–39); was also director of the Lyons Cons. (1922–24). In 1936 he was elected to Dukas's place in the Institut; also became a Commander of the Légion d'honneur. Schmitt spent his formative years in the ambience of French symbolism in poetry and Impressionism in music, and he followed these directions in his programmatically conceived orch. music; he nonetheless developed a strong, distinctive style of his own, mainly by elaborating the contrapuntal fabric of his works and extending the rhythmic design to intricate, asymmetrical combinations; he also exploited effects of primitivistic percussion, in many respects anticipating the developments of modern Russian music. The catalogue of his works is very long; he continued to compose until his death at the age of 87.

WORKS: BALLETS: *La Tragédie de Salomé* (Paris, Nov. 9, 1907); *Le Petit Elfe Ferme-l'œil,* after Hans Christian Andersen (Paris, Feb. 29, 1924); *Oriane la sans-égale* (Paris, Jan. 7, 1938); incidental music to *Antoine et Cléopâtre,* after Shakespeare

(Paris, June 14, 1920); *Reflets* (Paris, May 20, 1932). VOCAL, WITH ORCH.: *Musique sur l'eau* (1898); *Psaume XLVII* for Soprano, Chorus, Orch., and Organ (1904; Paris, Dec. 27, 1906); *Danse des Devadasis* for Solo Voice, Chorus, and Orch. (1900–1908); *Tristesse au Jardin* (1897–1908); *Chant de guerre* for Tenor, Male Chorus, and Orch. (1914); *Kerob-Shal* for Tenor and Orch. (1920–24); *Fête de la lumière* for Soprano, Chorus, and Orch. (1937); *L'Arbre entre tous* for Chorus and Orch. (1939); *A contre-voix* for Mixed Chorus (1943); motets and choruses a cappella. ORCH.: *En été* (1894); *Feuillets de voyage* (1903–13); *Reflets de l'Allemagne*, suite of waltzes (1905); *Puppazzi*, suite in 8 movements (1907); *Musiques de plein-air* (1897–99); *Sélamlik*, symphonic poem for Military Band (1906); *Le Palais hanté*, symphonic study after Poe (1900–4); *3 rapsodies* (1903–4); *Scherzo vif* for Violin and Orch. (1903–10); *La Tragédie de Salomé*, from the ballet of the same title (Paris, Jan. 8, 1911); *Légende* for Viola or Saxophone, and Orch. (1918); *Mirages: Tristesse de Pan, La Tragique Chevauchée* (1921); *Fonctionnaire MCMXII: Inaction en musique* (1924; Paris, Jan. 16, 1927); *Danse d'Abisag* (1925); *Salammbô*, 6 symphonic episodes after Flaubert, from film music (1925); *Ronde burlesque* (1927; Paris, Jan. 12, 1930); *Çhançunik* (humorous phonetic spelling of *Sens unique*, i.e., "one-way street"; Paris, Feb. 15, 1930); *Symphonie concertante* for Piano and Orch. (Boston, Nov. 25, 1932, composer soloist); *Suite sans esprit de suite* (Paris, Jan. 29, 1938); *Branle de sortie* (Paris, Jan. 21, 1939); *Janiana*, subtitled "Sym. for Strings," score entitled Sym. No. 2 (1941; Paris, May 1, 1942); *Habeyssée* for Violin and Orch. (phonetic representation of "ABC," as pronounced in French; Paris, March 14, 1947); Sym. (1957; Strasbourg, June 15, 1958). CHAMBER: *Scherzo-pastorale* for Flute and Piano (1889); *4 pièces* for Violin and Piano (1901); *Andante et Scherzo* for Harp and String Quartet (1906); Piano Quintet (1901–8); *Lied et Scherzo* for Double Wind Quintet (1910); *Sonate libre en deux parties enchaînées* for Violin and Piano (1919); *Suite en rocaille* for Flute, Violin, Viola, Cello, and Harp (1934); *Sonatine en trio* for Flute, Clarinet, and Harpsichord (1935); *Minorités* for Flute, Violin, and Piano (1938); *Hasards* for Violin, Viola, Cello, and Piano (1939); *A tours d'anches* for Flute, Clarinet, Bassoon, and Piano (1939); Quartet for Saxophones (1941); String Trio (1944); Quartet for Flutes (1944); String Quartet (1945–48). PIANO: *Soirs* (10 preludes); *Ballade de la neige* (1896); *Musiques intimes* (2 sets, 1890–1900 and 1898–1904); *Nuits romaines* (1901); *Puppazzi*, 8 pieces (1907; also for Orch.); *Pièces romantiques* (6 pieces, 1900–1908); *3 danses* (1935; also for Orch.); *Feuillets de voyage* (1903; also for Orch.); *Reflets de l'Allemagne*, 8 waltzes, 4-hands (1905; also for Orch.); *Suite sans esprit de suite* (1938; also for Orch.); *Clavecin obtempérant*, suite (1945). SONGS: *Soir sur le lac* (1898); *4 lieds*, to words by Richepin, Maeterlinck, etc.; *Kerob-Shal*, 3 songs (also for Voice and Orch.). BIBL.: M.D. Calvocoressi, "Œuvres de F. S.," *L'Art Moderne* (Jan. 6, 1907); P. Ferroud, *Autour de F. S.* (Paris, 1927); E. Blom, "F. S.," *Chesterian* (March 1932); Y. Hucher, *F. S.*, *L'homme et l'artiste* (Paris, 1953); Y. Hucher and M. Raveau, *L'Œuvre de F. S.* (Paris, 1960).

Schmitt, Georg Aloys, German pianist, conductor, and composer, son of **Aloys Schmitt;** b. Hannover, Feb. 2, 1827; d. during a rehearsal in Dresden, Oct. 15, 1902. He studied with his father; after theory training from Vollweiler in Heidelberg, he toured Europe as a pianist; subsequently devoted himself mainly to theatrical conducting; he was court conductor at Schwerin (1857–92); in 1893 he was appointed director of the Mozartverein in Dresden, which had a multitudinous choral ensemble (some 1,400 members) and its own orch. He wrote 3 operas, orch. works, chamber music, piano pieces, songs, etc.; also ed. and completed Mozart's Mass in C minor (1901).

Schmitt, Hans, German piano teacher; b. Koben, Bohemia, Jan. 14, 1835; d. Vienna, Jan. 14, 1907. He was at first an oboist at Bucharest and Vienna, but throat trouble compelled him to study piano instead with Dachs at the Vienna Cons. (1860–62), taking the silver medal, and joining its faculty. He wrote numerous didactic works for his instrument, including *300 Studies without Octave-stretches, Vademecum, Fundament der Klaviertechnik, Zirkelübungen in Skalen und Akkorden, 120 kleine Vortragsstücke, Repertoirestudien,* and *Das Pedal des Klaviers* (1875, after L. Köhler; Eng. tr., 1893).

Schmitt, Jacob, German pianist, teacher, and composer, brother of **Aloys Schmitt;** b. Obernburg, Bavaria, Nov. 2, 1803; d. Hamburg, May 24, 1853. He studied with his brother; was a reputable piano teacher; wrote about 370 piano pieces, including sonatinas for 2- and 4-hands, numerous studies, rondos, and nocturnes; especially useful is his *Musikalisches Schatzkästlein*, a collection of 133 short piano pieces.

Schmitt-Walter, Karl, German baritone; b. Gernersheim am Rhein, Dec. 23, 1900; d. Kreuth, Oberbayern, Jan. 14, 1985. He studied in Nuremberg and Munich; made his debut in 1921 in Oberhausen; then sang in Nuremberg, Saarbrücken, and Dortmund; was a member of the Wiesbaden Opera (1929–34), the Berlin Deutsche Oper (1934–50), and the Bavarian State Opera in Munich (1950–61); also sang at Bayreuth and Salzburg. In 1957 he became a prof. of voice at the Munich Academy of Music.

Schmitz, (Franz) Arnold, German musicologist; b. Sablon, near Metz, July 11, 1893; d. Mainz, Nov. 1, 1980. He took courses in musicology, history, and philosophy at the Univs. of Bonn, Munich, and Berlin; his principal mentors were Friedlaender, Kroyer, Sandberger, Schiedermair, and Wolf; received his Ph.D. in 1919 from the Univ. of Bonn with the dissertation *Untersuchungen über des jungen Schumann Anschauungen vom musikalischen Schaffen;* completed his Habilitation there in 1921. He taught there (1921–28) and at the Dortmund Cons. (1925–29), then at the Univs. of Breslau (1929–39) and Mainz (1947–61); he served as rector at the latter (1953–54; 1960–61); later taught at the Univ. of Basel (1965–67). WRITINGS: *Beethovens "zwei Prinzipe"* (Berlin, 1923); *Beethoven: unbekannte Skizzen und Entwürfe* (Bonn, 1924); *Das romantische Beethovenbild* (Berlin, 1927); *Die Bildlichkeit der wortgebundenen Musik J.S. Bachs* (Mainz, 1950).

Schmitz, Elie Robert, eminent French pianist and pedagogue; b. Paris, Feb. 8, 1889; d. San Francisco, Sept. 5, 1949. He studied at the Paris Cons. with Diémer, winning the premier prix; in 1908 he toured as accompanist of Slezak, Emma Eames, and other celebrated singers; in 1912, organized in Paris the Assoc. des Concerts Schmitz, which he led until 1914; in 1919 he toured the U.S. as a pianist; in 1920 he founded the Franco-American Music Society in N.Y. (incorporated in 1923 as Pro Musica), of which he was president from its inception; toured again in the U.S. and Europe (1921–29), and in the Orient (1929–30, 1932–33); eventually settled in San Francisco as a teacher. He publ. a book on his system of piano study, *The Capture of Inspiration* (N.Y., 1935; 2nd ed., 1944), and a valuable technical analysis with commentary, *The Piano Works of Claude Debussy* (N.Y., 1950).

Schmitz, Eugen, German musicologist; b. Neuburg an der Donau, Bavaria, July 12, 1882; d. Leipzig, July 10, 1959. He studied musicology with Sandberger and Kroyer at the Univ. of Munich (Ph.D., 1905, with the diss. *Der Nürnberger Organist Johann Staden: Beiträge zur Würdigung seiner musikgeschichtlichen Stellung;* extracts publ. in Leipzig, 1906); then completed his Habilitation there in 1909. He wrote music criticism in Dresden; taught music at the Dresden Technische Hochschule (1916–39). From 1939 to 1953 he was director of the Musikbibliothek Peters in Leipzig. WRITINGS: *Hugo Wolf* (Leipzig, 1906); *Richard Strauss als Musikdramatiker: eine ästhetische-kritische Studie* (Munich, 1907); *Richard Wagner* (Leipzig, 1909; 2nd ed., 1918); *Harmonielehre als Theorie: Aesthetik und Geschichte der musikalischen Harmonik* (Munich, 1911); *Palestrina* (Leipzig, 1914; 2nd ed., 1954); *Musikästhetik* (Leipzig, 1915; 2nd ed., 1925);

Orlando di Lasso (Leipzig, 1915; 2nd ed., 1954); *Klavier, Klavermusik und Klavierspiel* (Leipzig, 1919); *Richard Wagner: Wie wir ihn heute sehen* (Dresden, 1937).

Schmuller, Alexander, Russian violinist and teacher; b. Mozyr, Dec. 5, 1880; d. Amsterdam, March 29, 1933. He was a pupil of Ševčik, Hřimaly, and Auer; from 1908 he taught at the Stern Cons. in Berlin, and from 1914 at the Amsterdam Cons. For several years he gave concerts with Max Reger, whose music he was one of the first to champion; made many concert tours in Europe and the U.S.

Schnabel, Artur, celebrated Austrian-born American pianist and pedagogue, father of **Karl Ulrich Schnabel;** b. Lipnik, April 17, 1882; d. Axenstein, Switzerland, Aug. 15, 1951. He first studied with Hans Schmitt and made his debut at 8; then studied with Leschetizky in Vienna (1891–97). He went to Berlin in 1900; there he married the contralto Therese Behr (1905), with whom he frequently appeared in recitals; he also played in recitals with leading musicians of the day, including Flesch, Casals, Feuermann, Huberman, Primrose, and Szigeti; likewise gave solo recitals in Europe and the U.S., presenting acclaimed cycles of the Beethoven sonatas; taught at the Berlin Hochschule für Musik (from 1925). After the advent of the Nazi regime in 1933, he left Germany and settled in Switzerland; taught master classes at Lake Como and recorded the 1st complete set of the Beethoven sonatas. With the outbreak of World War II in 1939, he went to the U.S.; became a naturalized citizen in 1944; taught at the Univ. of Michigan (1940–45); then returned to Switzerland. Schnabel was one of the greatest pianists and pedagogues in the history of keyboard playing; eschewing the role of the virtuoso, he concentrated upon the masterworks of the Austro-German repertoire with an intellectual penetration and interpretive discernment of the highest order; he was renowned for his performances of Beethoven and Schubert; prepared an edition of the Beethoven piano sonatas. He was also a composer; in his works, he pursued an uncompromisingly modernistic idiom, thriving on dissonance and tracing melodic patterns along atonal lines.
WORKS: ORCH.: 3 syms.: No. 1 (1938–40; Minneapolis, Dec. 13, 1946); No. 2 (1941–42); No. 3 (1948); Piano Concerto (1901); *Rhapsody* (Cleveland, April 15, 1948); *Duodecimet* (unfinished; completed and orchestrated by R. Leibowitz). **CHAMBER:** 5 string quartets; *Notturno* for Voice and Piano (1914); Piano Quintet (1916); Sonata for Solo Violin (1919); Sonata for Solo Cello (1931); Violin Sonata (1935); also solo piano pieces and songs.
WRITINGS: *Reflections on Music* (Manchester, 1933; N.Y., 1934); *Music and the Line of Most Resistance* (Princeton, N.J., 1942); *My Life and Music* (London, 1961).
BIBL.: C. Saerchinger, *A. S.* (London, 1957); K. Wolff, *The Teaching of A. S.* (London, 1972); H. Goldsmith, "S. the pianist," *Musical Times* (June 1989); M. Swed, "S. the composer," ibid.

Schnabel, Joseph Ignaz, German organist, violinist, teacher, and composer; b. Naumburg am Queiss, Silesia, May 24, 1767; d. Breslau, June 16, 1831. He settled in Breslau in 1797, where he became organist at St. Clara and a violinist at the Vincentiuskirche and in the theater orch.; was appointed Kapellmeister of the Cathedral in 1804; from 1812, taught at the Roman Catholic Seminary and was director of the Royal Inst. for Church Music. He wrote many sacred works, including masses, graduals, offertories, and hymns; also a Clarinet Concerto, marches for military band, vocal works, and chamber music. His brother, **Michael Schnabel** (b. Naumburg, Sept. 23, 1775; d. Breslau, Nov. 6, 1842), founded a piano factory in Breslau (1814); his son, **Karl Schnabel** (b. Breslau, Nov. 2, 1809; d. there, May 12, 1881), an excellent pianist and composer of operas and piano music, carried on the business.
BIBL.: H. Guckel, "J.I. S.," *Katholische Kirchenmusik in Schlesien* (Leipzig, 1912); A. Schirdewahn, *Dommkapellmeister J. S. und sein Sohn August als Lehrer am Breslauer Schullehrer-Seminar* (Breslau, 1935).

Schnabel, Karl Ulrich, German pianist, teacher, and composer, son of **Artur Schnabel;** b. Berlin, Aug. 6, 1909. He studied piano with Leonid Kreutzer and composition with Paul Juon at the Berlin State Academy (1922–26); after a series of appearances as a soloist in Europe and Russia, he made his U.S. debut in N.Y. (Feb. 23, 1937), where he settled shortly before the outbreak of World War II. He played duo-piano recitals with his father and with his wife, Helen Fogel; devoted much time to teaching; publ. *Modern Technique of the Pedal* (N.Y., 1950).

Schnebel, Dieter, German composer and writer on music; b. Lahr, March 14, 1930. He began his musical training with Wilhelm Sibler (1942–45); after piano instruction from Wilhelm Resch in Villingen (1945–49), he took courses in theory and music history with Erich Doflein at the Freiburg im Breisgau Hochschule für Musik (1949–52); also attended courses in new music in Darmstadt, and studied theology, philosophy, and musicology (with Walter Gerstenberg) at the Univ. of Tübingen (1952–56). He was active in the Lutheran church but devoted much of his time to composition. In 1976 he was a prof. of experimental music and musicology at the Berlin Hochschule für Musik. His writings on music include highly intelligent forays into the confusing territory occupied by Bussotti, Kagel, and Metzger. He authored *Mauricio Kagel* (Cologne, 1970) and *Denkbare Musik: Schriften 1952–1972* (Cologne, 1972). His musical works are conceptually sophisticated, highly avant-garde, and employ unusual materials such as vocal noise, breath, graphics, and theater; his *mo-no: Musik zum Lesen* (1969) is purely graphic in form and does not involve sound notation.
WORKS: MUSIC THEATER: *Zeichen-Sprache* (Berlin, April 12, 1989); radiophonic scores. **ORCH.:** *Compositio* (1955–56; rev. 1964; Venice, Sept. 13, 1971); *Webern-Variationen* (1972; Paris, Oct. 20, 1973); *Canones* (Paris, Oct. 24, 1975); *In motu proprio* (1975); *Diapason* (1977); *Orchestra* (1974–77; Cologne, Jan. 20, 1978); *Schubert-Phantasie* (1977–78); *Wagner-Idyll* for Chamber Ensemble (1980); *Thanatos-Eros* (1979–82); *Sinfonie-Stücke* (Hamburg, June 23, 1985); *Beethoven-Sinfonie* for Chamber Ensemble (1984–85; Essen, April 14, 1988); *Mahler-Moment* for Strings (1984–85); *Raumklang X* for Orch. and 4 Instrumental Groups (1987–88; Cologne, May 25, 1989). **CHAMBER:** *réactions* for Instrumentalist and Audience (1960–61); *visible music I* for Conductor and Instrumentalist (1960–61); *Nostalgie* for Conductor (1962); *Espressivo*, music drama for Piano (1961–63); *Concert sans orchestre* for Piano and Audience (1964); *anschläge-ausschläge* for 3 Instrumentalists (1965–66); *Beethoven-Sonate* for Percussion (1970); Quintet (1976–77); *Pan* for Flute (1978); *Monotonien* for Piano and Live Electronics (Donaueschingen, Oct. 21, 1989); organ pieces. **VOCAL:** *Für Stimmen (. . . missa est)* for Chorus (1956–69); *glossolalie 61* for 3 to 4 Speakers and 3 to 4 Instrumentalists (1960–61); *Maulwerke* for 3 to 12 Voices (1968–74); *Bach-Contrapuncti* for Chorus (1972–76); *Jowaeglili* for 2 Speakers, Voices, and Chamber Ensemble (1983); *Lieder ohne Worte* for Voice and Instrument(s) (1980–86); *Missa: Dahlemer Messe* for 4 Solo Voices, 2 Choruses, Orch., and Organ (1984–87; Berlin, Nov. 12, 1988); tape pieces; graphic and conceptual compositions.

Schneerson, Grigori, eminent Russian musicologist; b. Eniseisk, Siberia, March 13, 1901; d. Moscow, Feb. 6, 1982. He was the son of a political exile under the tsarist regime; went to Moscow as a youth, and studied piano at the Cons. with Medtner and Igumnov. From 1939 to 1948 he was in charge of the music dept. of the Society for Cultural Relations with Foreign Nations; from 1948 to 1961, was head of the foreign section of the monthly *Sovietskaya Muzyka*, and from 1954 to 1966, ed. the bibliographic series Foreign Literature of Music. A remarkably gifted linguist, he mastered several European languages and undertook a study of Chinese. In his polemical writings he displayed wit and sarcasm in attacking the extreme manifestations of Western modernism, but preserved scholarly impartiality in analyzing the music of all genres and styles.

He was a Member Correspondent of the Academy of the Arts of the German Democratic Republic (1968), Honorary Member of the Accademia di Scienze, Lettere, Arti (1976), and a recipient of the Bernier Prize of the Académie des Beaux-Arts, Paris (1976).

WRITINGS: All publ. in Moscow: *Musical Culture in China* (1952); *Aram Khachaturian* (1957; in Eng., 1959); *Music, Living and Dead* (in praise of the state of music in the nations of the socialist bloc, and in condemnation of Western trends; 1960; rev. and mitigated, 1964); *Ernst Busch* (1962; rev. 1964); *French Music of the 20th Century* (1964; rev. 1970); *Music and Times* (1970); *Articles on Foreign Music: Essays, Reminiscences* (1974); *American Song* (1977); *Portraits of American Composers* (1977); ed. *D. Shostakovich: Articles and Materials* (1976).

Schnéevoigt, Georg (Lennart), prominent Finnish conductor; b. Vyborg, Nov. 8, 1872; d. Malmö, Nov. 28, 1947. He studied cello with Karl Schröder in Sondershausen and Julius Klengel in Leipzig; appeared as a cellist; in 1901, began his career as a conductor in Riga; from 1904 to 1908, conducted the Kaim Orch. in Munich; in 1908–9, the Kiev Sym. Orch.; from 1912 to 1914, the Riga Sym. Orch. He conducted the Helsinki Sym. Orch. (1912–14), which then merged with Kajanus's Helsinki Phil. in 1914 to form the Helsinki City Orch.; Kajanus and Schnéevoigt were joint conductors from 1916 to 1932; Schnéevoigt then succeeded Kajanus and continued until 1941; from 1915 to 1921 he also led the Konsertförening in Stockholm; in 1919 he founded the Christiania (later Oslo) Phil., and led it until 1927; also conducted in Germany; conducted the Los Angeles Phil. (1927–29); was general director of the National Opera in Riga (1929–32); then went to Malmö. In 1907 he married the pianist and teacher **Sigrid Ingeborg Sundgren** (b. Helsinki, June 17, 1878; d. Stockholm, Sept. 14, 1953); she studied at the Helsinki Music Inst. (1886–94) and with Busoni in Berlin (1894–97); taught at the Helsinki Music Inst. (from 1901); appeared as a soloist with orchs., often under the direction of her husband; also was active as a recitalist.

Schneider, family of German musicians:
(1) Johann (Gottlob) Schneider, organist, teacher, and composer; b. Alt-Waltersdorf, Saxony, Aug. 1, 1753; d. Gersdorf, May 3, 1840. He studied music with his father; took law courses at the Univ. of Leipzig, becoming its church organist in 1812. He had 3 sons who became musicians:
(2) (Johann Christian) Friedrich Schneider, organist, conductor, teacher, and composer; b. Alt-Waltersdorf, Saxony, Jan. 3, 1786; d. Dessau, Nov. 23, 1853. He commenced musical studies with his father, then received training from Schönfelder and Unger in Zittau; began composing as a youth and publ. 3 piano sonatas in 1804; entered the Univ. of Leipzig (1805) and became its organist (1807); was also organist at Leipzig's Thomaskirche (from 1812) and music director of the city theater (from 1817); brought out the extremely successful oratorio *Das Weltgericht* (1819), and then was called to Anhalt-Dessau as court Kapellmeister in 1821; was founder-director of a celebrated music school (1829–53). His son, **Theodor Schneider** (b. Dessau, May 14, 1827; d. Zittau, June 15, 1909), was a cellist and conductor; studied with his father and with Drechsler; became a cellist in the Anhalt-Dessau Court Orch. (1845); was made Kantor and choirmaster at Dessau's Schlosskirche (1853); served as Kantor and music director of Chemnitz's Jakobikirche (1860–96), and was also conductor of the Singakademie and of the Männergesangverein.
WORKS: ORATORIOS: *Die Höllenfahrt* (1810); *Das Weltgericht* (1819); *Totenfeier* (1821); *Die Sündflut* (1823); *Das verlorene Paradies* (1824); *Jesu Geburt* (1825); *Pharao* (1828); *Christus das Kind* (1828–29); *Gideon* (1829); *Absalon* (1831); *Das befreite Jerusalem* (1835); *Salomonis Tempelbau* (1836); *Bonifazius* (1837); *Christus der Erlöser* (1838); *Gethesemane und Golgotha* (1838); also 14 masses, 25 cantatas, and other sacred works; 7 operas; 23 syms.; 7 piano concertos; 20 overtures;

much chamber music; about 400 part-songs for Men's Voices; about 200 lieder.
WRITINGS: *Elementarbuch der Harmonie und Tonsetzkunst* (1820; in Eng., etc., 1828); *Vorschule der Musik* (1827); *Handbuch des Organisten* (1829–30).
BIBL.: W. Neumann, *F. S.: Eine Biographie* (Kassel, 1854); F. Kempe, *F. S. als Mensch und Künstler* (Dessau, 1859; 2nd ed. Berlin, 1864); A. Fast, *F. S. in seinen Sinfonien und Ouvertüren* (diss., Univ. of Halle, 1924); K. Hoede, *F. S. und die Zerbster Liedertafel zur Hundertjahrfeier 1927* (Zerbst, 1927); H. Lomnitzer, *Das musikalische Werk F. S.s (1786–1853), insbesondere die Oratorien* (diss., Univ. of Marburg, 1961).
(3) Johann Schneider, organist, pedagogue, and composer; b. Alt-Gersdorf, near Zittau, Oct. 28, 1789; d. Dresden, April 13, 1864. He studied jurisprudence and organ; in 1812 he became a church organist at Görlitz, and in 1825 was appointed court organist at Dresden. He was praised by Mendelssohn as one of the finest organ virtuosos of the period; was also greatly renowned as a teacher. He composed a number of organ pieces and songs with organ obbligato.
(4) (Johann) Gottlieb Schneider, organist and composer; b. Alt-Gersdorf, near Zittau, July 19, 1797; d. Hirschberg, Aug. 4, 1856. He studied with his father and at the Univ. of Leipzig; was organist at Hirschberg's Kreuzkirche (from 1825); wrote organ works and piano pieces.

Schneider, (Abraham) Alexander, Russian-American violinist, conductor, and teacher; b. Vilnius, Oct. 21, 1908. He enrolled in the Vilnius Cons. at 10 and in the Frankfurt Hochschule für Musik at 16; at the latter he studied violin with Adolf Rebner; later took lessons with Carl Flesch in Berlin. While still in his teens, he became concertmaster of the Frankfurt Museumgesellschaft Orch.; was also active in Saarbrücken and Hamburg. In 1932 he became 2nd violinist in the Budapest Quartet, with which he toured widely. He settled in the U.S. in 1938, and remained with the Budapest Quartet until 1944; then played in the Albeneri Trio and the N.Y. Quartet, and also conducted chamber orch. concerts. In 1945 he received the Elizabeth Sprague Coolidge Medal for eminent services to chamber music. In 1950 he persuaded Casals to come out of retirement and honor the 200th anniversary of Bach's death with a festival in Prades; he continued to work with Casals in subsequent years, organizing the Casals Festival in San Juan, Puerto Rico, in 1957. He founded his own quartet in 1952, and was again a member of the Budapest Quartet from 1955 until it disbanded in 1967. In later years he gave increasing attention to conducting, leading both chamber groups and major orchs.; he was also active as a teacher.
BIBL.: B. Schwarz, *Great Masters of the Violin* (N.Y., 1983); O. Roca, "A. S.," *Ovation* (Jan. 1989).

Schneider, Edward Faber, American pianist, composer, and pedagogue; b. Omaha, Nebr., Oct. 3, 1872; d. Santa Clara, Calif., July 1, 1950. He studied with X. Scharwenka (piano and composition) in N.Y., and with K.H. Barth (piano) and O.B. Boise (theory and composition) in Berlin. He taught at Mills College in Oakland, Calif. (1901–36), and also was dean of its music school (1910–19). He wrote several unnecessary symphonic pieces in a mandatory Romantic vein, including *In Autumn Time* (1909–13), *Legend of the Sargasso Sea* (1923), and *Thus Spoke the Deepest Stone* (1927–34), all perf. in San Francisco for the 1st and last time; also some quite acceptable chamber works and piano pieces, and, inevitably, songs.

Schneider, Georg Abraham, German horn player, oboist, conductor, and composer; b. Darmstadt, April 19, 1770; d. Berlin, Jan. 19, 1839. He studied with J.W. Magnold in Darmstadt, where he became a member of the court chapel in 1787; later took courses in theory and composition with J.G. Portmann. In 1795 he joined the Rheinsberg Court Orch.; then settled in Berlin and became a member of the royal chapel in 1803; founded a series of subscription concerts in 1807 and the Musikalische Übungsakademie zur Bildung der Liebhaber in 1818; also was conductor of the Reval theater (1813–

16). He was made music director of Berlin's royal theater in 1820 and then its Kapellmeister in 1825; taught at the music school of the royal theater and at the Prussian Academy of Arts.

Works: operettas: *Die Orakelspruch; Aucassin und Nicolette; Die Verschworenen; Der Traum; Der Währwolf;* also 13 ballets; music to numerous plays, melodramas, etc.; 2 oratorios; cantatas; orch. masses; 54 entr'actes for Orch.; overtures; concertos for Horn, Flute, Oboe, English Horn, Bassoon, etc.; quintets, quartets, and other chamber music.

Bibl.: A. Meyer-Hanno, *G.A. S. und seine Stellung im Musikleben Berlins* (Berlin, 1965).

Schneider, Julius, German organist, teacher, and composer; b. Berlin, July 6, 1805; d. there, April 3, 1885. He studied composition with Bernhard Klein, and organ and piano with various teachers in Berlin. In 1829 he became organist of the Friedrichwerder church in Berlin, and in 1854 was appointed teacher of organ at the Berlin Inst. of Church Music. He composed a variety of organ pieces; a Piano Concerto; some chamber music.

Schneider, Marius, distinguished German musicologist; b. Hagenau, July 1, 1903; d. Marquartstein, July 10, 1982. He studied philology and musicology at the Univs. of Strasbourg and Paris, then trained with Wolf at the Univ. of Berlin (Ph.D., 1930, with the diss. *Die Ars nova des XIV. Jahrhunderts in Frankreich und Italien*; publ. in Wolfenbüttel, 1931); his Habilitation was rejected there after Nazi intervention in 1937, but was subsequently accepted by the Univ. of Cologne after the collapse of the Third Reich (1955). He was Hornbostel's assistant at the Berlin Phonogramm-Archiv (1932–34), and then was its director; after serving in the armed forces during World War II, he went to Barcelona in 1944 as founder-director of the ethnomusicology dept. at the Spanish Inst. of Musicology; taught at the Consejo Superior de Investigaciones Cientificas at the Univ. of Barcelona (1947–55); then taught comparative musicology and ethnomusicology at the Univ. of Cologne (1955–68); subsequently was on the faculty of the Univ. of Amsterdam (1968–70). He made valuable contributions to musicology, the philosophy of music, and the history of musical structures. A Festschrift was publ. in his honor (Regensburg, 1977).

Writings: *Geschichte der Mehrstimmigkeit: Historische und phänomenologische Studien: I, Die Naturvölker; II, Die Anfänge in Europa* (Berlin, 1934–35; 2nd ed., 1968, with vol. III, *Die Kompositionsprinzipien und ihre Verbreitung*); *El origen musical de los animales-simbolos en la mitología y la escultura antiguas: Ensayo histórico-etnográfico sobre la subestructura totemística y megalítica de las altas culturas y su supervivencia en el folklore español* (Barcelona, 1946); *La danza de espadas y la tarantela: Ensayo musicológico, etnográfico y arqueológico sobre los ritos medicinales* (Barcelona, 1948); *Singende Steine: Rhythmus-Studien an drei kalantanischen Kreuzgängen romanischen Stils* (Kassel, 1955); *Die Natur des Lobgesangs* (Basel, 1964); ed. *Aussereuropäische Folklore und Kunstmusik* (Cologne, 1972); ed. *Studien zur Mittelmeermusik: I, Die tunesische Nuba ed Dhil* (Regensburg, n.d.).

Schneider, Max, eminent German musicologist; b. Eisleben, July 20, 1875; d. Halle, May 5, 1967. He studied musicology at the Univ. of Leipzig with Riemann and Kretzschmar, and harmony and composition with Jadassohn; continued his musicological training at the Univ. of Berlin (Ph.D., 1917), where he was a librarian (1904–7); then was assistant librarian at the Royal Library (1907–14). He conducted in Halle (1897–1901); also taught at the Church Music Inst. in Berlin; then was a prof. at the Univs. of Breslau (1915–28) and Halle (1928–60). He publ. *Beiträge zu einer Anleitung Clavichord und Cembalo zu spielen* (Strasbourg, 1934) and *Beiträge zur Musikforschung* (vol. I, Halle, 1935). He did useful work in compiling miscellaneous bio-bibliographical materials in music; ed. numerous important bibliographical surveys; also ed. the works of Heinrich Schütz. He enjoyed a well-merited reputation in Germany as a thorough scholar. He was honored 3 times by

Festschrifts: H. Zingel, ed., *Festschrift Max Schneider zum 60. Geburtstag* (Halle, 1935), W. Vetter, ed., *Festschrift Max Schneider zum 80. Geburtstag* (Leipzig, 1955), and W. Siegmund-Schulze, ed., *Festschrift Max Schneider zum 85. Geburtstag* (Leipzig, 1960).

Schneiderhan, Wolfgang (Eduard), noted Austrian violinist and pedagogue; b. Vienna, May 28, 1915. He studied violin mainly in Prague with Ševčik and Pisek; later with Julius Winkler in Vienna. He was concertmaster of the Vienna Sym. Orch. (1933–37); then of the Vienna Phil. (1937–51); concurrently was 1st violinist in his own Scheiderhan Quartet. From 1951 he made tours of Europe as a soloist with the major orchs. He taught at the Salzburg Mozarteum (1938–56) and at the Vienna Academy of Music (1939–50); was on the faculty of the Lucerne Cons. (from 1949). With Rudolf Baumgartner, he helped to found the Lucerne Festival Strings in 1956. He married the German soprano **Irmgard Seefried** in 1948. He was best known for his performances of the Viennese classics and contemporary music.

Bibl.: F. Fassbind, *W. S., Irmgard Seefried: Eine Künstler- und Lebensgemeinschaft* (Bern, 1960); *W. S. zum 60. Geburtstag* (Wiesbaden, 1975).

Schneider-Trnavský, Mikuláš, Slovak choral conductor and composer; b. Trnava, May 24, 1881; d. Bratislava, May 28, 1958. He studied in Budapest, Vienna, and Prague; was choirmaster of the cathedral of St. Mikuláš in Trnava (1909–58); was named a National Artist in 1956. He publ. several valuable collections of Slovak folk songs, arranged with piano accompaniment: *Sbierka slovenských ludových piesní* (2 vols., 1905–10); *Sbierka slovenských národných piesní* (5 sections, Bratislava, 1930; new ed., Prague, 1935–40); *50 Slovakische Volkslieder* (Bratislava, 1943). He publ. a book of memoirs, *Usmevy a slzy* (Smiles and Tears; Bratislava, 1959).

Works: Operetta, *Bellarosa* (Bratislava, 1941); *Dumka and Dance* for Orch. (1905); *Comedy Overture* (1930–31); *Symphony of Recollections* (1956); Violin Sonata (1905); *Slovak Sonatina* for Piano (1938); church music, including several masses; songs.

Bibl.: J. Samko, *M. S.-T.-phol'ad na život a dielo* (Bratislava, 1965).

Schneidt, Hanns-Martin, German organist, conductor, pedagogue, and composer; b. Kitzingen, Dec. 6, 1930. He studied at the Thomasschule in Leipzig with Günther Ramin; also took courses in choral music in Munich and served as a church organist there. In 1955 he became director of the Church Music School in Berlin; was also conductor of the Berlin Bach-Collegium and Choir, as well as cantor and organist at the Church of St. John the Evangelist. In 1963 he became conductor of the Wuppertal City Orch.; it became the Wuppertal Sym. Orch. in 1976, and he continued as its conductor until 1985; also held the post of Generalmusikdirektor for the city of Wuppertal (1975–85). He was prof. of conducting at the Hamburg Hochschule für Musik (from 1971). In 1984 he became conductor of the Munich Bach Choir. He wrote a number of choral works.

Schneitzhoeffer, Jean, French composer; b. Toulouse, Oct. 13, 1785; d. Paris, Oct. 4, 1852. He studied with Catel at the Paris Cons.; after serving as timpanist at the Paris Opéra (1815–23), he was appointed *chef du chant* there; from 1831 to 1850 he was in charge of choral classes at the Paris Cons. He composed several ballet scores for the Paris Opéra; of these, *La Sylphide* (1832), which he wrote for the famous dancer Maria Taglioni, became a perennial favorite. His other ballets are *Proserpine* (1818); *Zémire et Azor* (1824); *Mars et Vénus;* he also wrote *Sinfonia dei gatti*, several concert overtures, and a Requiem.

Schnitger, Arp, esteemed German organ builder; b. Schmalenfleth, Golzwarden, Oldenburg, July 2, 1648; d. Neuenfelde, July 24, 1719. He was apprenticed to his cousin, Berendt Huess, in Glückstadt, Holstein, whom he assisted in building the organ for St. Cosmae in Stade (1669–73), which he later augmented;

his finest instrument is at St. Nicolai in Hamburg (1682–87). Two of his sons followed in his profession: **Johann Georg (Jürgen) Schnitger** (b. [baptized] Sept. 4, 1690; d. after 1733) and **Franz Caspar Schnitger** (b. [baptized] Oct. 15, 1693; d. in the Netherlands, 1729); they completed their father's work at the Grote Kerk in Zwolle, and also rebuilt the large organ at St. Laurents in Alkmaar.

BIBL.: P. Rubardt, *A. S.* (Freiberg, 1928); G. Fock, *S. und seine Schule* (Kiel, 1931); W. Sumner, "A. S. and His Organs," *Organ*, XVII (1938); G. Fock, *A. S. und seine Schule* (Kassel, 1975).

Schnittke, Alfred (Garsievich), prominent Russian composer of German descent; b. Engels, near Saratov, Nov. 24, 1934. He studied piano in Vienna (1946–48), where his father was a correspondent of a German-language Soviet newspaper; then took courses in composition with Golubev and in instrumentation with Rakov at the Moscow Cons. (1953–58); after serving on its faculty (1962–72), he devoted himself fully to composition. He pursued many trips abroad, and in 1981 was a guest lecturer at the Vienna Hochschule für Musik und Darstellende Kunst. In 1981 he was elected a member of the West German Akademie der Künste. In 1985 he survived a serious heart attack. After writing in a conventional manner, he became acutely interested in the new Western techniques, particularly in serialism and "sonorism," in which dynamic gradations assume thematic significance; soon he became known as one of the boldest experimenters in modernistic composition in Soviet Russia.

WORKS: STAGE: An unfinished opera, *The 11th Commandment* (1962); ballet, *Labyrinths* (1971; Leningrad, June 7, 1978); scenic work, *Der gelbe Klang*, after Kandinsky, for Pantomime, Lights, Instrumental Ensemble, and Chorus on Tape (Saint Bomme, France, summer 1974); ballet, *Sketches*, after themes of Gogol (in collaboration with Gubaidulina, Denisov, and Rozhdestvensky; Moscow, Jan. 16, 1985); ballet, *Peer Gynt*, after Ibsen (1986; Hamburg, Jan. 1989); orch. *Epilogue from "Peer Gynt,"* with Chorus on Tape (Hamburg, April 27, 1987).

ORCH.: 4 violin concertos: No. 1 (1957; rev. 1962; Moscow, Nov. 29, 1963); No. 2, with Chamber Orch. (1966; Leningrad, Feb. 20, 1968); No. 3, with Chamber Orch. (1978; Moscow, Jan. 29, 1979); No. 4 (1982; West Berlin, Sept. 11, 1984); Piano Concerto (1960); *Poem about Cosmos* (1961); *Music for Chamber Orch.* (1964); *Music for Piano and Chamber Orch.* (1964); . . . *pianissimo* . . . (1967–68; Donaueschingen, Oct. 19, 1969); Sonata for Violin and Chamber Orch. (1968; Moscow, Feb. 5, 1986; chamber-orch. version of Sonata No. 1 for Violin and Piano); Double Concerto for Oboe, Harp, and Strings (1970–71; Zagreb, May 1972); 5 syms.: No. 1 (1969–72; Gorky, Feb. 9, 1974); No. 2, *St. Florian*, with Chamber Chorus (1979; London, April 23, 1980); No. 3 (Leipzig, Nov. 5, 1981); No. 4 for Tenor, Alto, Chorus, and Orch. or Chamber Orch. (Moscow, April 12, 1984); No. 5, *Concerto Grosso No. 4/Symphony No. 5* (Amsterdam, Nov. 10, 1988); *In memoriam* (1972–78; Moscow, Dec. 20, 1979; orch. version of Piano Quintet); 5 concerti grossi: No. 1 for 2 Violins, Prepared Piano, Harpsichord, and Strings (Leningrad, March 21, 1977); No. 2 for Violin, Cello, and Orch. (West Berlin, Sept. 11, 1982); No. 3 for 2 Violins and Chamber Orch. (Moscow, April 20, 1985); No. 4, *Concerto Grosso No. 4/Symphony No. 5* (Amsterdam, Nov. 10, 1988); No. 5 for Violin and Orch. (N.Y., May 2, 1991); Concerto for Piano and Strings (Leningrad, Dec. 10, 1979); *Passacaglia* (1979–80; Baden-Baden, Nov. 8, 1981); *Gogol Suite* (from incidental music to *The Dead Souls Register*; London, Dec. 5, 1980); *Ritual* (Novosibirsk, March 15, 1985); *(K)ein Sommernachstraum* ([Not] A Midsummer Night's Dream; Salzburg, Aug. 12, 1985); Viola Concerto (1985; Amsterdam, Jan. 6, 1986); 2 cello concertos: No. 1 (Munich, May 7, 1986); No. 2 (1989); *Quasi una Sonata* for Violin and Chamber Orch. (1987; chamber-orch. version of Sonata No. 2 for Violin and Piano); *Trio Sonata* for Chamber Orch. (1987; chamber-orch. version of String Trio); *4 Aphorisms* (West Berlin, Sept. 18,

1988); *Monologue* for Viola and String Orch. (Bonn, June 4, 1989); Concerto for Piano, 4–hands, and Chamber Orch. (1989; Moscow, April 27, 1990).

CHAMBER: 2 violin sonatas: No. 1 (1963); No. 2, *Quasi una Sonata* (1968); *Dialogue* for Cello and 7 Instruments (1965); 4 string quartets (1966, 1980, 1983, 1989); *Serenade* for Violin, Clarinet, Double Bass, Piano, and Percussion (1968); *Canon in memoriam Igor Stravinsky* for String Quartet (1971); *Suite in Old Style* for Violin, and Piano or Harpsichord (1972); Piano Quintet (1972–76; orchestrated as *In memoriam*); *Hymnus I* for Cello, Harp, and Timpani (1974), *II* for Cello and Double Bass (1974), *III* for Cello, Bassoon, Harpsichord, and Bells or Timpani (1975), and *IV* for Cello, Double Bass, Bassoon, Harpsichord, Harp, Timpani, and Bells (1976; all 4 1st perf. Moscow, May 26, 1979); *Praeludium in memoriam Dmitri Shostakovich* for 2 Violins, or 1 Violin and Tape (1975); *Cantus Perpetuus* for Keyboards and Percussion (1975); *Moz-Art* for 2 Violins (1976); *Mozart à la Haydn* for 2 Violins, 2 Small String Ensembles, Double Bass, and Conductor (1977); Cello Sonata (1978); *Stille Musik* for Violin and Cello (1979); *Polyphonic Tango* for Ensemble (1979); *Moz-Art* for Oboe, Harpsichord, Harp, Violin, Cello, and Double Bass (1980); Septet (1981–82); *Lebenslauf* for 4 Metronomes, 3 Percussionists, and Piano (1982); *A Paganini* for Violin (1982); *Schall und Hall* for Trombone and Organ (1983); String Trio (1985; new version for Chamber Orch. as *Trio-Sonata*); Piano Quartet (1988); *Klingende buchstaben* for Cello (1988); 3 × 7 for Clarinet, Horn, Trombone, Harpsichord, Violin, Cello, and Double Bass (1989).

VOCAL: 2 oratorios: *Nagasaki* (1958) and *Songs of War and Peace*, with thematic materials from contemporary Russian folk songs (1959); *3 Poems* for Mezzo-soprano and Piano (1965); *Voices of Nature* for 10 Female Voices and Vibraphone (1972); *Requiem*, after stage music to Schiller's *Don Carlos*, for Chorus, Organ, Piano, Electric Bass, Brass, Percussion, and Celesta (1975; Budapest, Oct. 8, 1977); *Der Sonnengesang des Franz von Assisi* for 2 Choruses and 6 Instruments (1976); *3 Madrigals* for Soprano, Violin, Viola, Double Bass, Harpsichord, and Vibraphone (Moscow, Nov. 11, 1980); *3 Scenes* for Soprano and Ensemble (1980); *Minnesang* for 52 Voices (1980–81); *Seid nüchtern und wachet . . .*, cantata for 4 Soloists, Chorus, and Orch., based on the version of the Faust legend publ. in 1587 under the title *Historia von D. Johann Fausten*, commissioned by the Vienna Choral Academy on the occasion of its 125th anniversary (premiered as *Faust Cantata*, Vienna, June 19, 1983); Concerto for Chorus (1984–85).

PIANO: *Prelude and Fugue* (1963); *Improvisation and Fugue* (1965); *Variations on a Chord* (1965); *4 Pieces* (1971); *Dedication to Stravinsky, Prokofiev, and Shostakovich* for Piano, 6-hands (1979); Sonata (1988); also 2 *Little Pieces* for Organ (1980); an electronic study, *Der Strom* (1969); and several cadenzas for concertos of Mozart and Beethoven.

Schnoor, Hans, distinguished German writer on music; b. Neumünster, Oct. 4, 1893; d. Bielefeld, Jan. 15, 1976. He studied with H. Riemann and A. Schering at the Univ. of Leipzig, where he received his Ph.D. with the dissertation *Das Buxheimer Orgelbuch* in 1919; was a music critic in Dresden and Leipzig (1922–26); then music ed. of the *Dresdner Anzeiger* (1926–45). He was an authority on the life and music of Weber.

WRITINGS: *Musik der germanischen Völker im XIX. und XX. Jahrhundert* (Breslau, 1926); with G. Kinsky and R. Haas, *Geschichte der Musik in Bildern* (Leipzig, 1929; Eng. tr., 1930); *Weber auf dem Welttheater* (Dresden, 1942; 4th ed., 1963); *Weber: Ein Lebensbild aus Dresdner Sicht* (Dresden, 1947); *400 Jahre deutscher Musikkultur; Zum Jubiläum der Staatskapelle und zur Geschichte der Dresdner Oper* (Dresden, 1948); *Geschichte der Musik* (1953); *Weber; Gestalt und Schöpfung* (Dresden, 1953; 2nd ed., rev., 1974); *Oper, Operette, Konzert; Ein praktisches Nachschlagsbuch* (Gutersloh, 1955); ed. *Bilderatlas zur Musikgeschichte* (Brussels, 1960; 2nd ed., 1963); *Harmonie und Chaos* (Munich, 1962); *Musik und Theater ohne eigene Dach* (Hagen, 1969); *Die Stunde des Rosenkavalier* (Munich, 1969).

Schnorr von Carolsfeld, Ludwig, greatly admired German tenor; b. Munich, July 2, 1836; d. Dresden, July 21, 1865. He was the son of the noted painter Julius Schnorr von Carolsfeld; after studies with J. Otto in Dresden and at the Leipzig Cons., he was engaged by Eduard Devrient for the Karlsruhe Opera in 1854; became its principal tenor in 1858; then was the leading tenor at the Dresden Court Opera (from 1860). Wagner chose him to create the role of Tristan in *Tristan und Isolde* (Munich, June 10, 1865); his wife, **Malvina Schnorr von Carolsfeld,** sang Isolde. He was also an outstanding Tannhäuser, and won accolades as an oratorio and lieder artist as well. His death at the age of 29 was widely lamented.

BIBL.: C. Garrigues, *Ein ideales Sängerpaar, L. S.v.C. und Malvina Schnorr von Carolsfeld* (Copenhagen, 1937).

Schnorr von Carolsfeld, Malvina (née **Garrigues**), esteemed German soprano; b. Copenhagen, Dec. 7, 1825; d. Karlsruhe, Feb. 8, 1904. She studied with García in Paris; made her operatic debut in *Robert le diable* in Breslau (1841), and sang there until 1849; after appearances in Coburg, Gotha, and Hamburg, she joined the Karlsruhe Opera in 1854. Wagner chose her to create the role of Isolde in *Tristan und Isolde* (Munich, June 10, 1865), with her husband singing Tristan. Following his untimely death at the age of 29, she quit the operatic stage and became a convert to spiritualism. She publ. a vol. of poems by her husband and herself in 1867.

BIBL.: C. Garrigues, *Ein ideales Sängerpaar, Ludwig Schnorr von Carolsfeld und M. S.v.C.* (Copenhagen, 1937).

Schnyder von Wartensee, (Franz) Xaver, significant Swiss composer; b. Lucerne, April 18, 1786; d. Frankfurt am Main, Aug. 27, 1868. He had piano lessons at age 16 with P. Heggli; then taught himself to play the double bass, cello, clarinet, viola, and timpani; in 1811 he went to Vienna, where he met Beethoven and studied composition with J.C. Kienlen; after teaching at Pestalozzi's Inst. in Yverdun (1816–17), he settled in Frankfurt; played recitals on the glass harmonica and piano, taught, composed, and founded the Liederkranz (1828). He founded the Schnyder von Wartensee Foundation in 1847, which sponsors competitions in the sciences and assists in the publ. of scientific and artistic works.

WORKS: STAGE: *Ubaldo,* opera (1811–12; only 1 chorus extant); *Heimweh und Heimkehr,* operetta (1854; Zürich, Dec. 14, 1855). **ORCH:** 5 syms., including No. 2, *Erinnerung an Joseph Haydn* (Frankfurt, Oct. 20, 1837), and No. 3, *Militärsymphonie* (Frankfurt, Jan. 18, 1850); other orch. works; chamber music; much choral music; songs; piano music.

BIBL.: *Lebenserinnerungen von X. S.v.W.* (Zürich, 1887; contains an autobiography and a complete list of works; new ed. by W. Schuh, Berlin, 1940).

Schoberlechner, Franz, Austrian pianist and composer; b. Vienna, July 21, 1797; d. Berlin, Jan. 7, 1843. He studied with Hummel in Vienna, making his debut in Hummel's 2nd Concerto (1809), written for him; continued his training with E.A. Förster. On a pianistic tour to Italy, he produced his opera *I Virtuosi teatrali* at Florence (1814), and the next year became maestro di cappella to the Duchess of Lucca, producing there a 2nd opera, *Gli Arabi nelle Gallie* (1816); in 1820 returned to Vienna, where he brought out an opera in German, *Der junge Onkel* (Jan. 14, 1823); made a trip to Russia in 1823, and there married the singer **Sophie dall'Occa** (1807–63), with whom he made further tours to Italy and Vienna. He purchased a villa in Florence in 1831, and retired to it some years later. Besides his operas, he composed overtures, string quartets, a Piano Trio, and many piano pieces.

Schobert, Johann, important composer; b. probably in Silesia, c.1735; d. Paris, Aug. 28, 1767 (with his entire family, except 1 child, from eating poisonous mushrooms). About 1760 he settled in Paris, where he entered the service of the Prince de Conti. His works show the general characteristics of the Mannheim School, although it cannot be proved that he ever was in that city. Mozart was significantly influenced by him, and reworked and incorporated movements of his scores into his own sonatas and piano concertos.

WORKS: *Le Garde-chasse et le braconnier,* opéra comique (Paris, Jan. 18, 1766); the following were publ. in Paris (1761–67), and many appeared in later eds. with different op. nos.: (2) Sonates for Harpsichord and Violin ad libitum, op. 1; (2) Sonates for Harpsichord and Violin ad libitum, op. 2; 2 Sonates for Harpsichord and Violin ad libitum, op. 3; (2) Sonates for Harpsichord, op. 4; (2) Sonates for Harpsichord and Violin ad libitum, op. 5; (3) Sonates en trio for Harpsichord and Violin and Cello ad libitum, op. 6; (3) Sonates en quatuor for Harpsichord and 2 Violins and Cello ad libitum, op. 7; 2 Sonates for Harpsichord and Violin, op. 8; (3) Sinfonies for Harpsichord and Violin and Horns ad libitum, op. 9; (3) Sinfonies for Harpsichord and Violin and Horns ad libitum, op. 10; Concerto I for Harpsichord, 2 Violins, Viola, Cello, and 2 Horns ad libitum, op. 11; Concerto II for Harpsichord, 2 Violins, Viola, Cello, 2 Oboes, and 2 Horns ad libitum, op. 12; Concerto III pastorale for Harpsichord, 2 Violins, 2 Horns ad libitum, Viola, and Cello, op. 13; 6 Sonates for Harpsichord and Violin ad libitum, op. 14; Concerto IV for Harpsichord, 2 Violins, 2 Horns ad libitum, Viola, and Cello, op. 15; 4 Sonates for Harpsichord, Violin, and Cello, op. 16; 4 Sonates for Harpsichord and Violin, op. 17; Concerto V for Harpsichord, 2 Violins, and Cello, op. 18; 2 Sonates for Harpsichord or Piano, and Violin, op. 19 (may be spurious); 3 Sonates for Harpsichord and Violin, op. 20 (probably by T. Giordani); *Morceau de musique curieux . . . menuet qui peut s'exécuter de différentes façon* for Harpsichord, Violin, and Cello. See H. Riemann, ed., *Johann Schobert: Ausgewählte Werke,* Denkmäler Deutscher Tonkunst, XXXIX (1909).

BIBL.: G. de Saint-Foix, "Les Premiers Pianistes parisiens, i: Jean S., vers 1740–1767," *Revue Musicale,* III/10 (1922); H. David, *J. S. als Sonatenkomponist* (Leipzig, 1928); K. Fischer, "S. und Schubart," *Zeitschrift für Musikwissenschaft,* XVI (1934); H. Turrentine, *J. S. and French Clavier Music from 1700 to the Revolution* (diss., Univ. of Iowa, 1962).

Schoeck, Othmar, eminent Swiss pianist, conductor, and composer; b. Brunnen, Sept. 1, 1886; d. Zürich, March 8, 1957. He was the son of the painter Alfred Schoeck; went to Zürich, where he took courses at the Industrial College before pursuing musical training with Attenhofer, Freund, Hegar, and Kempter at the Cons. (from 1905); after further studies with Reger in Leipzig (1907–8), he returned to Zürich and conducted the Aussersihl Men's Chorus (1909–15), the Harmonie Men's Chorus (1910–11), and the Teachers' Chorus (1911–17); then was conductor of the St. Gallen sym. concerts (1917–44). Schoeck was one of the most significant Swiss composers of his era; he won his greatest renown as a masterful composer of songs, of which he wrote about 400. He also was highly regarded as a piano accompanist and a conductor. Among his many honors were an honorary doctorate from the Univ. of Zürich (1928), the 1st composer's prize of the Schweizerische Tonkünstlerverein (1945), and the Grand Cross of Merit and Order of Merit of the Federal Republic of Germany (1956). In 1959 the Othmar Schoeck Gesellschaft was founded to promote the performance of his works.

WORKS: OPERAS: *Don Ranudo de Colibrados,* op. 27 (1917–18; Zürich, April 16, 1919); *Venus,* op. 32 (1919–20; Zürich, May 10, 1922); *Penthesilea,* op. 39 (1924–25; Dresden, Jan. 8, 1927); *Massimilla Doni,* op. 50 (1934–35; Dresden, March 2, 1937); *Das Schloss Dürande,* op. 53 (1938–39; Berlin, April 1, 1943); other stage works. **ORCH.:** *Serenade* for Small Orch., op. 1 (1906–7); *Eine Ratcliff-Ouvertüre* (1907); *Concerto quasi una fantasia* for Violin and Orch., op. 21 (1911–12); *Praeludium,* op. 48 (1932); *Sommernacht* for String Orch., op. 58 (1945); *Suite* for String Orch., op. 59 (1949); Cello Concerto, op. 61 (1947); *Festlicher Hymnus,* op. 64 (1951); Horn Concerto, op. 65 (1951). **CHORAL:** *'s Seeli* for Men's Chorus (1906–7); 5 Lieder (1906–15); *Sehnsucht* for Men's Chorus (1909); *Der Postillon* for Tenor, Men's Chorus, and Piano or Orch., op. 18 (1909); *Dithyrambe* for Double Chorus and Orch., op. 22 (1911); *Wegelied* for Men's Chorus, and Piano or Orch., op. 24 (1913); *Trommelschläge* for Chorus and Orch., op. 26 (1915); *Die Drei* for Men's Chorus (1930); Cantata for Baritone, Men's Chorus, and Instruments, op. 49 (1933); *Für ein Gesangfest im Frühling* for Men's Chorus and Orch., op. 54 (1942); *Nachruf* (1943); *Zimmerspruch* for Men's Chorus (1947); *Vision* for Men's Chorus, Brass, Percussion, and Strings, op. 63 (1950); *Maschinenschlacht* for Men's Chorus, op. 67a (1953); *Gestutze Eiche* for Men's Chorus, op. 67b (1953); numerous works for Solo Voice with instrumental accompaniment; about 400 songs, including cycles; also chamber works, including 3 violin sonatas (1908, 1909, 1931), 2 string quartets (1912–13; 1923), and 2 sonatas for Clarinet and Piano (1916; 1927–28); piano pieces.

BIBL.: H. Corrodi, ed., *O. S.: Festgabe . . . zum 50. Geburtstag* (Erlenbach and Zürich, 1936); special issues of *Schweizerische Musikzeitung/Revue Musicale Suisse,* LXXXIII (1943) and XCVI (1956); W. Vogel, *Wesenszüge von O. S.s Liedkunst* (Zürich, 1950); idem, *Thematisches Verzeichnis der Werke von O. S.* (Zürich, 1956); F. Kienberger, *O. S.: Eine Studie* (Zürich, 1975); S. Tiltmann-Fuchs, *O. S.s Liederzyklen für Singstimme und Orchester* (Regensburg, 1976); D. Puffet, *The Song Cycles of O. S.* (Stuttgart and Bern, 1982).

Schoelcher, Victor, French statesman and writer on music; b. Paris, July 21, 1804; d. Houilles, Dec. 24, 1893. He was educated at the Collège Louis le Grand; as a radical republican, he was expelled from France upon the accession of Napoleon II; he lived in England until his return to Paris in 1870; was elected a member of the National Assembly in 1871 and was made a life senator in 1875. He collected musical instruments, scores, and rare books; also pursued an intensive study of the life of Handel. With the assistance of Rophino Lacy, he wrote the valuable work *Haendel et son temps,* which was publ. in an Eng. tr. by J. Lowe as *The Life of Handel* (London, 1857); the 1st 4 chapters of the French MS were publ. in *La France Musicale* (1860–62), and the entire MS was purchased by the Paris Cons. in 1881. In 1873 he gave his extensive private library to the Paris Cons. He also publ. *La Modernité de la musique* (Paris, 1881).

Schoemaker, Maurice, Belgian composer; b. Anderlecht, near Brussels, Dec. 27, 1890; d. Brussels, Aug. 24, 1964. He studied harmony with Théo Ysaÿe, counterpoint with Michel Brusselmans, fugue with Martin Lunssens, and composition and orchestration with Paul Gilson; was one of 8 Gilson pupils to form, in 1925, the Groupe des Synthétistes, whose aim was to promote modern music. He held administrative posts in various Belgian musical organizations.

WORKS: DRAMATIC: OPERAS: *Swane* (1933); *Arc-en-ciel* (1937); *De Toverviool* (1954). **RADIO PLAYS:** *Sire Halewijn* (1935); *Médée la magicienne* (1936); *Philoctetes* (1942). **BALLETS:** *Breughel-Suite* (1928); *Pan* (1937). **ORCH.:** *Le Facétieux Voyage* (1914); *Récit, Aria et Final* for Violin and Orch. (1920); *Pan,* prelude (1921); *Feu d'artifice* for Wind Orch. (1922); *2 fantasques* (1924); *Sinfonia da camera* (1929); *Légende de Sire Halewijn,* symphonic poem (1930); *Rapsodie flamande* (1931); *Variations on a Popular Song* (1937); *Sinfonia breve* (1938); *Pièce concertante* for Trombone and Orch. (1939); *Variazioni* for Horn and Orch. (1941); *Mouvement symphonique* (1942); *Scènes espagnoles* (1943); *2 danses flamandes* (1944); Sym. (1946); Bassoon Concerto (1947); *Ouverture romane* (1947); *Marillac l'Epée,* dramatic prologue (1949). **CHAMBER:** Piano Trio (1934); Piano Sonata (1934); Solo Cello Sonata (1940); *Suite champêtre* for Oboe, Clarinet, and Bassoon (1940); String Quartet (1945); *Variations miniatures* for String Trio (1949); *Morceau de concert* for Trombone and Piano (1949); *Tombeau de Chopin* for 2 Pianos (1949); *Sonata du souvenir* for Cello and Piano (1953); *La Cage des oiseaux* (Birdcage) for 4 Clarinets (1961).

Schoenberg (originally, **Schönberg**), **Arnold** (**Franz Walter**), great Austrian-born American composer whose new method of musical organization in 12 different tones related only to one another profoundly influenced the entire development of modern techniques of composition; b. Vienna, Sept. 13, 1874; d. Los Angeles, July 13, 1951. He studied at the Realschule in Vienna; learned to play the cello, and also became proficient on the violin. His father died when Schoenberg was 16; he took a job as a bank clerk to earn a living; an additional source of income was arranging popular songs and orchestrating operetta scores. Schoenberg's 1st original work was a group of 3 piano pieces, which he wrote in 1894; it was also about that time that he began to take lessons in counterpoint from Alexander Zemlinsky, whose sister he married in 1901. He also played cello in Zemlinsky's instrumental group, Polyhymnia. In 1897 Schoenberg wrote his 1st String Quartet, in D major, which achieved public performance in Vienna on March 17, 1898. About the same time he wrote 2 songs with piano accompaniment which he designated as op. 1. In 1899 he wrote his 1st true masterpiece, *Verklärte Nacht,* set for string sextet, which was first performed in Vienna by the Rosé Quartet and members of the Vienna Phil. on March 18, 1902. It is a fine work, deeply imbued with the spirit of Romantic poetry, with its harmonic idiom stemming from Wagner's modulatory procedures; it remains Schoenberg's most frequently performed composition, known principally through its arrangement for string orch. About 1900 he was engaged as conductor of several amateur choral groups in Vienna and its suburbs; this increased his interest in vocal music. He then began work on a choral composition, *Gurre-Lieder,* of monumental proportions, to the translated text of a poem by the Danish writer Jens Peter Jacobsen. For grandeur and opulence of orchestral sonority, it surpassed even the most formidable creations of Mahler or Richard Strauss; it calls for 5 solo voices, a speaker, 3 male choruses, an 8-part mixed chorus, and a very large orch. Special music paper of 48 staves had to be ordered for the MS. He completed the 1st 2 parts of *Gurre-Lieder* in the spring of 1901, but the composition of the remaining section was delayed by 10 years; it was not until Feb. 23, 1913, that Franz Schreker was able to arrange its complete performance with the Vienna Phil. and its choral forces.

In 1901 Schoenberg moved to Berlin, where he joined E. von Wolzogen, F. Wedekind, and O. Bierbaum in launching an artistic cabaret, which they called Überbrettl. He composed a theme song for it with trumpet obbligato, and conducted several shows. He met Richard Strauss, who helped him to obtain the Liszt Stipendium and a position as a teacher at the Stern Cons. He returned to Vienna in 1903 and formed friendly relations with Gustav Mahler, who became a sincere supporter of his activities; Mahler's power in Vienna was then at its height, and he was able to help him in his career as a composer. In March 1904 Schoenberg organized with Alexander Zemlinsky the Vereinigung Schaffender Tonkünstler for the purpose of encouraging performances of new music. Under its auspices he conducted on Jan. 26, 1905, the 1st performance of his symphonic poem *Pelleas und Melisande;* in this score occurs the 1st use of a trombone glissando. There followed a performance on Feb. 8, 1907, of Schoenberg's *Kammersymphonie,* op. 9, with the participation of the Rosé Quartet and the wind instrumentalists of the Vienna Phil.; the work produced much consternation in the audience and among critics because of its departure from traditional tonal harmony, with chords built on fourths and nominal dissonances used without immediate resolution. About the same time, he turned to painting, which became his principal avocation. In his art, as in his music, he adopted the tenets of Expressionism, that is, freedom of personal expression within a self-defined program. Schoenberg's reputation as an independent musical thinker attracted to him such progressive-minded young musicians as Alban Berg, Anton von Webern, and Egon Wellesz, who followed Schoenberg in their own development. His 2nd String Quartet, composed in 1908, which included a soprano solo, was his last work that carried a definite key signature, if exception is made for his *Suite* for Strings, ostentatiously marked as in G major, which he wrote for school use in America in 1934. On Feb. 19, 1909, Schoenberg completed his piano piece op.

11, no. 1, which became the 1st musical composition to dispense with all reference to tonality. In 1910 he was appointed to the faculty of the Vienna Academy of Music; in 1911 he completed his important theory book *Harmonielehre,* dedicated to the memory of Mahler; it comprises a traditional exposition of chords and progressions, but also offers illuminating indications of possible new musical developments, including fractional tones and melodies formed by the change of timbre on the same note. In 1911 he went again to Berlin, where he became an instructor at the Stern Cons. and taught composition privately. In 1912 he brought out a work that attracted a great deal of attention: *5 Orchesterstücke,* which was performed for the 1st time not in Germany, not in Austria, but in London, under the direction of Sir Henry Wood, who conducted it there on Sept. 3, 1912; the critical reception was that of incomprehension, with a considerable measure of curiosity. The score was indeed revolutionary in nature, each movement representing an experiment in musical organization. In the same year Schoenberg produced another innovative work, a cycle of 21 songs with instrumental accompaniment, entitled *Pierrot Lunaire,* and consisting of 21 "melodramas," to German texts translated from verses by the Belgian poet Albert Giraud. Here he made systematic use of *Sprechstimme,* with a gliding speech-song replacing precise pitch (not an entire innovation, for Engelbert Humperdinck had applied it in his incidental music to Rosmer's play *Königskinder* in 1897). The work was given, after some 40 rehearsals, in Berlin on Oct. 16, 1912, and the reaction was startling, the purblind critics drawing upon the strongest invective in their vocabulary to condemn the music.

Meanwhile, Schoenberg made appearances as conductor of his works in various European cities (Amsterdam, 1911; St. Petersburg, 1912; London, 1914). During World War I he was sporadically enlisted in military service; after the Armistice, he settled in Mödling, near Vienna. Discouraged by his inability to secure performances for himself and his associates in the new music movement, he organized in Vienna, in Nov. 1918, the Verein für Musikalische Privataufführungen (Society for Private Musical Performances), from which critics were demonstratively excluded, and which ruled out any vocal expression of approval or disapproval. The organization disbanded in 1922. About that time, Schoenberg began work on his *Suite for Piano,* op. 25, which was to be the 1st true 12-tone piece consciously composed in that idiom. In 1925 he was appointed prof. of a master class at the Prussian Academy of Arts in Berlin. With the advent of the beastly Nazi regime, the German Ministry of Education dismissed him from his post as a Jew. As a matter of record, Schoenberg had abandoned his Jewish faith in Vienna on March 21, 1898, and in a spirit of political accommodation converted to Catholicism, which was the principal faith in Austria; 35 years later, horrified by the hideous persecution of Jews at the hands of the Nazis, he was moved to return to his ancestral faith and was reconverted to Judaism in Paris on July 24, 1933. With the rebirth of his hereditary consciousness, he turned to specific Jewish themes in works such as *Survivor from Warsaw* and *Moses und Aron.* Although Schoenberg was well known in the musical world, he had difficulty obtaining a teaching position; he finally accepted the invitation of Joseph Malkin, founder of the Malkin Cons. of Boston, to join its faculty. He arrived in the U.S. on Oct. 31, 1933. After teaching in Boston for a season, he moved to Hollywood. In 1935 he became a prof. of music at the Univ. of Southern Calif., and in 1936 accepted a similar position at the Univ. of Calif. in Los Angeles, where he taught until 1944, when he reached the mandatory retirement age of 70. On April 11, 1941, he became a naturalized American citizen. In 1947 he received the Award of Merit for Distinguished Achievements from the National Inst. of Arts and Letters. In the U.S. he changed the original spelling of his name from Schönberg to Schoenberg.

In 1924 Schoenberg's creative evolution reached the all-important point at which he found it necessary to establish a new governing principle of tonal relationship, which he called the "method of composing with 12 different notes related en-

tirely to one another." This method was adumbrated in his music as early as 1914, and is used partially in his *5 Klavierstücke,* op. 23, and in his *Serenade,* op. 24; it was employed for the 1st time in its integral form in the piano *Suite,* op. 25 (1924); in it, the thematic material is based on a group of 12 different notes arrayed in a certain pre-arranged order; such a tone row was henceforth Schoenberg's mainspring of thematic invention; development was provided by the devices of inversion, retrograde, and retrograde inversion of the basic series; allowing for transposition, 48 forms were obtainable in all, with counterpoint and harmony, as well as melody, derived from the basic tone row. Immediate repetition of thematic notes was admitted; the realm of rhythm remained free. As with most historic innovations, the 12-tone technique was not the creation of Schoenberg alone but was, rather, a logical development of many currents of musical thought. Josef Matthias Hauer rather unconvincingly claimed priority in laying the foundations of the 12-tone method; among others who had elaborated similar ideas at about the same time with Schoenberg was Jef Golyscheff, a Russian émigré who expounded his theory in a publication entitled "12 Tondauer-Musik." Instances of themes consisting of 12 different notes are found in the *Faust Symphony* of Liszt and in the tone poem *Also sprach Zarathustra* of Richard Strauss in the section on Science. Schoenberg's great achievement was the establishment of the basic 12-tone row and its changing forms as foundations of a new musical language; using this idiom, he was able to write music of great expressive power. In general usage, the 12-tone method is often termed "dodecaphony," from Greek *dodeca,* "12," and *phone,* "sound." The tonal composition of the basic row is devoid of tonality; an analysis of Schoenberg's works shows that he avoided using major triads in any of their inversions, and allowed the use of only the 2nd inversion of a minor triad. He deprecated the term "atonality" that was commonly applied to his music. He suggested, only half in jest, the term "atonicality," i.e., absence of the dominating tonic. The most explicit work of Schoenberg couched in the 12-tone idiom was his *Klavierstück,* op. 33a, written in 1928–29, which exemplifies the clearest use of the tone row in chordal combinations. Other works that present a classical use of dodecaphony are *Begleitungsmusik zu einer Lichtspielszene,* op. 34 (1929–30); Violin Concerto (1934–36); and Piano Concerto (1942). Schoenberg's disciples Berg and Webern followed his 12-tone method in general outlines but with some personal deviations; thus, Berg accepted the occasional use of triadic harmonies, and Webern built tone rows in symmetric groups. Other composers who made systematic use of the 12-tone method were Egon Wellesz, Ernst Krenek, René Leibowitz, Roberto Gerhard, Humphrey Searle, and Luigi Dallapiccola. As time went on, dodecaphony became a lingua franca of universal currency; even in Russia, where Schoenberg's theories were for many years unacceptable on ideological grounds, several composers, including Shostakovich in his last works, made use of 12-tone themes, albeit without integral development. Ernest Bloch used 12-tone subjects in his last string quartets, but he refrained from applying inversions and retrograde forms of his tone rows. Stravinsky, in his old age, turned to the 12-tone method of composition in its total form, with retrograde, inversion, and retrograde inversion; his conversion was the greatest artistic vindication for Schoenberg, who regarded Stravinsky as his most powerful antagonist, but Schoenberg was dead when Stravinsky saw the light of dodecaphony.

Schoenberg's personality was both heroic and egocentric; he made great sacrifices to sustain his artistic convictions, but he was also capable of engaging in bitter polemics when he felt that his integrity was under attack. He strongly opposed the claims of Hauer and others for the priority of the 12-tone method of composition, and he vehemently criticized in the public press the implication he saw in Thomas Mann's novel *Doktor Faustus,* in which the protagonist was described as the inventor of the 12-tone method of composition; future historians, Schoenberg argued, might confuse fiction with facts, and credit the figment of Mann's imagination with Schoenberg's own discovery. He was also subject to superstition in the form of triskaidecaphobia, the fear of the number 13; he seriously believed that there was something fateful in the circumstance of his birth on the 13th of the month. Noticing that the title of his work *Moses und Aaron* contained 13 letters, he crossed out the 2nd "a" in Aaron to make it 12. When he turned 76 and someone remarked facetiously that the sum of the digits of his age was 13, he seemed genuinely upset, and during his last illness in July 1951, he expressed his fear of not surviving July 13; indeed, he died on that date. Schoenberg placed his MSS in the Music Division of the Library of Congress in Washington, D.C.; the remaining materials were deposited after his death at the Schoenberg Inst. at the Univ. of Southern Calif. in Los Angeles. Schoenberg's centennial in 1974 was commemorated worldwide. A *Journal of the Schoenberg Institute* began publ. in 1976, under the editorship of Leonard Stein.

Schoenberg's personality, which combined elements of decisive affirmation and profound self-negation, still awaits a thorough analysis. When he was drafted into the Austrian armed forces during World War I (he never served in action, however) and was asked by the examiner whether he was the "notorious" modernist composer, he answered "someone had to be, and I was the one." He could not understand why his works were not widely performed. He asked a former secretary to Serge Koussevitzky why the Boston Sym. Orch. programs never included any of his advanced works; when the secretary said that Koussevitzky simply could not understand them, Schoenberg was genuinely perplexed. "Aber, er spielt doch Brahms!" he said. To Schoenberg, his works were the natural continuation of German classical music. Schoenberg lived in Los Angeles for several years during the period when Stravinsky was also there, but the two never made artistic contact. Indeed, they met only once, in a downtown food market, where they greeted each other, in English, with a formal handshake. Schoenberg wrote a satirical canon, *Herr Modernsky*, obviously aimed at Stravinsky, whose neo-Classical works ("ganz wie Papa Bach") Schoenberg lampooned. But when Schoenberg was dead, Stravinsky said he forgave him in appreciation of his expertise in canonic writing.

In his private life, Schoenberg had many interests; he was a fairly good tennis player, and also liked to play chess. In his early years in Vienna, he launched several theoretical inventions to augment his income, but none of them ever went into practice; he also designed a set of playing cards. The MSS of arrangements of Viennese operettas and waltzes he had made in Vienna to augment his meager income were eventually sold for large sums of money after his death. That Schoenberg needed money but was not offered any by an official musical benefactor was a shame. After Schoenberg relocated to Los Angeles, which was to be his final destination, he obtained successful appointments as a prof. at the Univ. of Southern Calif. and eventually at the Univ. of Calif., Los Angeles. But there awaited him the peculiar rule of age limitation for teachers, and he was mandatorily retired when he reached his seventieth year. His pension from the Univ. of Calif., Los Angeles, amounted to $38 a month. His difficulty in supporting a family with growing children became acute and eventually reached the press. He applied for a grant from the munificent Guggenheim Foundation, pointing out that since several of his own students had received such awards, he was now applying for similar consideration, but the rule of age limitation defeated him there as well. It was only after the Schoenberg case and its repercussions in the music world that the Guggenheim Foundation cancelled its offensive rule. Schoenberg managed to square his finances with the aid of his publishing income, however, and, in the meantime, his children grew up. His son Ronald (an anagram of Arnold) eventually became a city judge, an extraordinary development for a Schoenberg!

WORKS: STAGE: *Erwartung*, monodrama, op. 17 (1909; Prague, June 6, 1924, Gutheil-Schoder, mezzo-soprano, Zemlinsky conducting); *Die glückliche Hand*, drama with music,

to Schoenberg's own libretto, op. 18 (1910–13; Vienna, Oct. 14, 1924, Stiedry conducting); *Von Heute auf Morgen*, opera in one act, op. 32 (1928–29; Frankfurt, Feb. 1, 1930, W. Steinberg conducting); *Moses und Aron*, biblical drama, to Schoenberg's own libretto (2 acts composed 1930–32; 3rd act begun in 1951, but not completed; radio perf. of Acts 1 and 2, Hamburg, March 12, 1954, Rosbaud conducting; stage perf., Zürich I.S.C.M. Festival, June 6, 1957, Rosbaud conducting).

ORCH.: *Frülings Tod*, symphonic poem (fragment, 1898; Berlin, March 18, 1984, R. Chailly conducting); *Pelleas und Melisande*, symphonic poem after Maeterlinck, op. 5 (1902–3; Vienna, Jan. 26, 1905, composer conducting); *Kammersymphonie* No. 1, for 15 Instruments, op. 9 (1906; Vienna, Feb. 8, 1907; arranged for Orch., 1922; new version for Orch., op. 9b, 1935); *5 Orchester-Stücke*, op. 16 (1909; London, Sept. 3, 1912, Sir Henry Wood conducting; rev. 1922 and 1949); *3 Little Pieces* for Chamber Orch. (1911; Berlin, Oct. 10, 1957); *Variations*, op. 31 (1926–28; Berlin, Dec. 2, 1928, Furtwängler conducting); *Begleitungsmusik zu einer Lichtspielszene* (Accompaniment to a Cinema Scene), op. 34 (1929–30; Berlin, Nov. 6, 1930, Klemperer conducting); Suite in G major for Strings (1934; Los Angeles, May 18, 1935, Klemperer conducting); Violin Concerto, op. 36 (1934–36; Philadelphia, Dec. 6, 1940, Krasner, soloist; Stokowski conducting); 2nd Chamber Sym., op. 38a (1906–16 and 1939; N.Y., Dec. 15, 1940, Stiedry conducting; op. 38b is an arrangement for 2 Pianos, 1941–42); Piano Concerto, op. 42 (1942; N.Y., Feb. 6, 1944, Steuermann, pianist; Stokowski conducting); *Theme and Variations* for Wind Band, op. 43a (1943; arranged for Orch., op. 43b, Boston, Oct. 20, 1944, Koussevitzky conducting).

CHORAL: *Gurre-Lieder* for Soli, Mixed Chorus, and Orch. (1900–3 and 1910–11; Vienna, Feb. 23, 1913, Schreker conducting); *Friede auf Erden*, op. 13 (1907; Vienna, Dec. 9, 1911, Schreker conducting); 4 pieces for Mixed Chorus, op. 27 (1925); *3 Satires*, op. 28 (1925); 3 German folk songs (Vienna, Nov. 1929); 6 pieces for Men's Chorus, op. 35 (1929–30; Frankfurt, Nov. 29, 1931, F. Schmidt conducting); *Kol Nidre* for Speaker, Chorus, and Orch., op. 39 (Los Angeles, Oct. 4, 1938, composer conducting); *Genesis*, prelude for Orch. and Mixed Chorus (Los Angeles, Jan. 11, 1945); *A Survivor from Warsaw* for Narrator, Chorus, and Orch., op. 46 (1947; Albuquerque, Nov. 4, 1948); 3 German folk songs for Chorus a cappella, op. 49 (1948); *Dreimal tausend Jahre* for Mixed Chorus a cappella, op. 50a (Fylkingen, Sweden, Oct. 29, 1949); *De Profundis* for Chorus a cappella, to a Hebrew text, op. 50b (1950; Cologne, Jan. 29, 1954); *Modern Psalm* for Mixed Chorus, Speaker, and Chorus (text by the composer; unfinished; Cologne, May 29, 1956, Sanzogno conducting). The oratorio *Die Jakobsleiter*, begun in 1917, was left unfinished; a performing version was prepared by Winfried Zillig, and given for the 1st time in Vienna on June 16, 1961.

CHAMBER: String Quartet in D major (1897; Vienna, March 17, 1898); *Verklärte Nacht* (Transfigured Night), sextet for Strings, op. 4 (1899; Vienna, March 18, 1902; arranged for String Orch., 1917; rev. 1943; perf. as a ballet under the title *The Pillar of Fire*, Metropolitan Opera, N.Y., April 8, 1942); *Ein Stelldichein* for Oboe, Clarinet, Violin, Cello, and Piano (1905); String Quartet No. 1, in D minor, op. 7 (1904–5; Vienna, Feb. 5, 1907); String Quartet No. 2, in F-sharp minor, op. 10, with Voice (Vienna, Dec. 21, 1908, Rosé Quartet, Gutheil-Schoder, mezzo-soprano; arranged for String Orch., 1929); *Die eiserne Brigade*, march for String Quartet and Piano (1916); *Weihnachtsmusik* for 2 Violins, Cello, Harmonium, and Piano (1921); Serenade for Clarinet, Bass Clarinet, Mandolin, Guitar, Violin, Viola, and Cello, op. 24 (4th movement with a sonnet by Petrarch for Baritone; 1920–23; Donaueschingen, July 20, 1924); Quintet for Flute, Oboe, Clarinet, Horn, and Bassoon, op. 26 (Vienna, Sept. 13, 1924); Suite for 2 Clarinets, Bass Clarinet, Violin, Viola, Cello, and Piano, op. 29 (1925–26; Paris, Dec. 15, 1927); String Quartet No. 3, op. 30 (Vienna, Sept. 19, 1927; Kolisch Quartet); String Quartet No. 4, op. 37 (1936; Los Angeles, Jan. 9, 1937; Kolisch Quartet); *Ode to Napoleon*, after Byron, for String Quartet, Piano, and Reciter (1942; also in version with String Orch., N.Y., Nov. 23, 1944, Rodzinski conducting); String Trio, op. 45 (1946; Cambridge, Mass., May 1, 1947); *Phantasy* for Violin, with Piano Accompaniment (Los Angeles, Sept. 13, 1949).

SONGS: 2 songs, op. 1 (1898); 4 songs, op. 2 (1899); 7 Chansons, *Bretll-Lieder* (1901); *Nachtwandler* for Soprano, Piccolo, Trumpet, Side Drum, and Piano (1901); 6 songs, op. 3 (1899–1903); 8 songs, op. 6 (1903–5); 6 songs, op. 8 (nos. 2, 5, and 6 for Orch., Prague, Jan. 29, 1914, Zemlinsky conducting); 2 ballads, op. 12 (1907); 2 songs, op. 14 (1907–8); cycle of 15 poems from Stefan George's *Das Buch der hängenden Gärten* (1908–9; Vienna, Jan. 14, 1910); *Herzgewächse*, after Maeterlinck, for Soprano, with Celesta, Harmonium, and Harp, op. 20 (1911); *Pierrot Lunaire*, 21 poems by Albert Giraud, for Sprechstimme with Piano, Flute (interchangeable with Piccolo), Clarinet (interchangeable with Bass Clarinet), Violin (interchangeable with Viola), and Cello, op. 21 (Berlin, Oct. 16, 1912, A. Zehme, soloist, composer conducting); 4 songs, op. 22 (with Orch.; 1913–16; Frankfurt, Feb. 21, 1932, Rosbaud conducting); *Lied der Waldtaube* for Mezzo-soprano and Chamber Ensemble (1922; arranged from *Gurre-Lieder*); 3 songs, op. 48 (1933; London, June 5, 1952).

KEYBOARD: PIANO: 3 *Klavierstücke*, op. 11 (1909; Vienna, Jan. 14, 1910; rev. 1924); 6 *kleine Klavierstücke*, op. 19 (1911; Berlin, Feb. 4, 1912); 5 *Klavierstücke*, op. 23 (1920–23); *Suite*, op. 25 (1921–23); *Klavierstück*, op. 33a (1928–29; Hamburg, Jan. 30, 1931); *Klavierstück*, op. 33b (1931). **ORGAN:** *Variations on a Recitative*, op. 40 (1941; N.Y., April 10, 1944).

ARRANGEMENTS AND TRANSCRIPTIONS: 2 chorale preludes by Bach, for Large Orch.: No. 1, *Komm, Gott, Schöpfer, Heiliger Geist*, and No. 2, *Schmücke dich, O liebe Seele* (N.Y., Dec. 12, 1922); *Prelude and Fugue* in E-flat major for Organ by Bach, for Large Orch. (1928; Vienna, Nov. 10, 1929, Webern conducting); Piano Quartet No. 1, in G minor, op. 25, by Brahms, for Orch. (1937; Los Angeles, May 7, 1938, Klemperer conducting); also a Cello Concerto, transcribed from a Harpsichord Concerto by G.M. Monn (1932–33; London, Dec. 7, 1935, Feuermann, soloist); Concerto for String Quartet and Orch. after Handel's Concerto Grosso, op. 6, No. 7 (1933; Prague, Sept. 26, 1934, Kolisch Quartet); etc.

WRITINGS: *Harmonielehre* (Vienna, 1911,; 3rd ed., rev., 1922; abridged Eng. tr. as *Theory of Harmony*, N.Y., 1947; complete Eng. tr., 1978); *Models for Beginners in Composition* (N.Y., 1942; 3rd ed., rev., 1972, by L. Stein); *Style and Idea* (N.Y., 1950; enl. ed. by L. Stein, London, 1975); *Structural Functions of Harmony* (N.Y., 1954; 2nd ed., rev., 1969, by L. Stein); *Preliminary Exercises in Counterpoint*, ed. by L. Stein (London, 1963); *Fundamentals of Musical Composition*, ed. by L. Stein (London, 1967); also numerous essays in German and American publs.

BIBL.: COLLECTED WORKS, SOURCE MATERIAL: J. Rufer and his successors are preparing a complete ed. of his works, *A. S.: Sämtliche Werke* (Mainz, 1966-). Rufer also compiled an annotated catalogue, *Das Werk A. S.s* (Kassel, 1959; Eng. tr., 1962; 2nd Ger. ed., rev., 1975). I. Vojtěch ed. vol. I of the *Gesammelte Schriften* (Frankfurt, 1976).

See also the following: Special issue of *Der Merker*, II/17 (1911); *A. S.: Mit Beiträgen von Alban Berg, Paris von Gutersloh . . .* (essays by 11 admirers; Munich, 1912); E. Wellesz, "S. and Beyond," *Musical Quarterly* (Jan. 1916); idem, *A. S.* (Leipzig, 1921; Eng. tr., rev., London, 1925); C. Gray, "A. S., A Critical Study," *Music & Letters* (Jan. 1922); E. Stein, *Praktischer Leitfaden zu S.s Harmonielehre* (Vienna, 1923); P. Stefan, *A. S.: Wandlung, Legende, Erscheinung, Bedeutung* (Vienna, 1924); *A. S. zum 60. Geburtstag* (articles by friends and pupils; Vienna, 1934); H. Wind, *Die Endkrise der bürgerlichen Musik und die Rolle A. S.s* (Vienna, 1935); R. Hill, "S.'s Tone-Rows and the Tonal System of the Future," *Musical Quarterly* (Jan. 1936); M. Armitage, ed., *A. S.* (contains essays by Sessions, Krenek, E. Stein, C. Engel, Klemperer, P. Pisk, P. Stefan et al.; also 2 by Schoenberg: "Tonality and Form" and "Problems of Harmony"; N.Y., 1937); H. Jalowetz, "On the Spontaneity of S.'s Music," *Musical Quarterly* (Oct. 1944); D. Milhaud,

"To A. S. on His Seventieth Birthday: Personal Recollections," ibid.; R. Sessions, "S. in the United States," *Tempo*, no. 9 (1944; rev. in *Tempo*, no. 103, 1972); P. Gradenwitz, "The Idiom and Development in S.'s Quartets," *Music & Letters*, XXVI (1945); R. Leibowitz, *S. et son école* (Paris, 1947; Eng. tr., 1949); D. Newlin, *Bruckner, Mahler, S.* (N.Y., 1947; rev. ed., 1978); W. Rubsamen, "S. in America," *Musical Quarterly* (Oct. 1951); H. Stuckenschmidt, *A. S.* (Zürich, 1951; 2nd ed., rev., 1957; Eng. tr., 1959); G. Perle, "S.'s Later Style," *Music Review*, XIII (1952); J. Rufer, *Die Komposition mit zwölf Tönen* (Berlin, 1952; Eng. tr. as *Composition with 12 Notes Related to One Another*, London, 1954); L. Rognoni, *Espressionismo e dodecafonia* (Turin, 1954; 2nd ed., rev., 1966, as *La scuola musicale di Vienna*); H. Keller, "S.'s 'Moses and Aron,' " *Score*, no. 21 (1957); T. Tuttle, "S.'s Compositions for Piano Solo," *Music Review*, XVIII (1957); K. Wörner, *Gotteswort und Magie* (Heidelberg, 1959; Eng. tr., rev., 1963, as *S.'s "Moses and Aron"*); M. Kassler, *The Decision of A. S.'s Twelve-Note-Class-System and Related Systems* (Princeton, 1961); H. Pauli, "Zu S.s 'Jakobsleiter,' " *Schweizerische Musikzeitung/Revue Musicale Suisse*, CII (1962); G. Perle, *Serial Composition and Atonality: An Introduction to the Music of S., Berg and Webern* (Berkeley, 1962; 5th ed., rev., 1982); W. Rogge, *Das Klavierwerke A. S.s* (Regensburg, 1964); P. Friedheim, "Rhythmic Structure in S.'s Atonal Compositions," *Journal of the American Musicological Society*, XIX (1966); J. Meyerowitz, *A. S.* (Berlin, 1967); B. Boretz and E. Cone, eds., *Perspectives on S. and Stravinsky* (Princeton, 1968); G. Krieger, *S.s Werke für Klavier* (Göttingen, 1968); A. Payne, *S.* (London, 1968); W. Reich, *A. S., oder Der konservative Revolutionär* (Vienna, 1968; Eng. tr., 1971); R. Brinkmann, *A. S.: Drei Klavierstücke Op. 11* (also includes bibliography of publ. writings; Wiesbaden, 1969); R. Leibowitz, *S.* (Paris, 1969); D. Rexroth, *A. S. als Theoretiker der tonalen Harmonik* (Bonn, 1971); J. Maegaard, *Studien zur Entwicklung des dodekaphonen Satzes bei A. S.* (Copenhagen, 1972); A. Whittall, *S. Chamber Music* (London, 1972); E. Freitag, *A. S. in Selbstzeugnissen und Bilddokumenten* (Reinbek, 1973); J. Samson, "S.'s 'Atonal' Music," *Tempo*, no. 109 (1974); E. Steiner, "S.'s Quest: Newly Discovered Works from His Early Years," *Musical Quarterly* (Oct. 1974); H. Stuckenschmidt, *S.: Leben, Umwelt, Werk* (Zürich, 1974; Eng. tr. as *S.: His Life, World and Work*, London, 1976); C. Rosen, *A. S.* (N.Y., 1975); G. Schubert, *S.s frühe Instrumentation* (Baden-Baden, 1975); M. Macdonald, *S.* (London, 1976); D. Newlin, *S. Remembered: Diaries and Recollections (1938–76)* (N.Y., 1980); W. Bailey, *Programmatic Elements in the Works of A. S.* (Ann Arbor, 1983); W. Jakobik, *A. S.: die Verräumlichte Zeit* (Regensburg, 1983); J. Christensen, "The Spiritual and the Material in S.'s Thinking," *Music & Letters* (Oct. 1984); J. Hahl-Koch, ed., *A. S./ Wassily Kandinsky: Letters, Pictures and Documents* (London, 1984); P. Franklin, *The Idea of Music: S. and Others* (London, 1985); G. Bauer, *A Contextual Approach to S.'s Atonal Works: Self Expression, Religion, and Music Theory* (diss., Washington Univ., 1986); J. Brand, C. Hailey, and D. Harris, eds., *The Berg-S. Correspondence* (N.Y., 1986); E. Smaldone, *Linear Analysis of Selected Posttonal Works of A. S.: Toward an Application of Schenkerian Concepts to Music of the Posttonal Era* (diss., City Univ. of N.Y., 1986); J. Smith, *S. and His Circle: A Viennese Portrait* (N.Y., 1986); J. Straus, "Recompositions by S., Stravinsky, and Webern," *Musical Quarterly*, no.3 (1986); E. Haimo, "Redating S.'s Passacaglia for Orchestra," *Journal of the American Musicological Society* (Fall 1987); D. Lambourn, "Henry Wood and S.," *Musical Times* (Aug. 1987); M. Mäckelmann, *S.: Fünf Orchesterstücke op. 16* (Munich, 1987); J. and J. Christensen, *From A. S.'s Literary Legacy: A Catalog of Neglected Items* (Warren, Mich., 1988); W. Frisch, "Thematic Form and the Genesis of S.'s D-Minor Quartet, Opus 7," *Journal of the American Musicological Society* (Summer 1988); E. Haimo, *S.'s Serial Odyssey: The Evolution of his Twelve-Tone Method, 1914–1928* (Oxford, 1990); A. Ringer, *A. S.: The Composer as Jew* (Oxford, 1990); A. Trenkamp and J. Suess, eds., *Studies in the S.ian Movement in Vienna and the United States: Essays in Honor of Marcel Dick* (Lewiston, N.Y., 1990).

Schoenefeld, Henry, American conductor and composer; b. Milwaukee, Oct. 4, 1857; d. Los Angeles, Aug. 4, 1936. He studied at the Leipzig Cons.; went to Chicago in 1879, where he was conductor of the Germania Männerchor; settled in Los Angeles in 1904, and was conductor of the Women's Sym. Orch. and the Germania Turnverein. He was one of the earliest American composers to make use of American Indian, spiritual, minstrelsy, and other expressions of American culture in his music.

WORKS: STAGE: *Atala, or The Love of 2 Savages,* opera; *Wachicanta,* pantomime-ballet. ORCH.: *Suite caractéristique* for Strings (c.1890); 2 syms.: No. 1, *Rural* (won a $500 prize of the National Cons. in N.Y., 1892); No. 2, *Spring;* Piano Concerto; Violin Concerto; *The American Flag,* overture; *In the Sunny South,* overture; *American Caprice;* 2 *Indian Legends;* 2 *American Rhapsodies;* 2 *Impromptus; Nocturne* for Strings. CHAMBER: Piano Trio (1872–73); 2 violin sonatas; Cello Sonata; piano music; also choruses; songs.

Schoen-René, Anna, German-American singing teacher; b. Koblenz, Jan. 12, 1864; d. N.Y., Nov. 13, 1942. She studied singing with Pauline Viardot-García, and sang in opera before settling in the U.S., where she taught in Minneapolis and then at the Juilliard School of Music in N.Y. She publ. a book of memoirs, *America's Musical Heritage* (N.Y., 1941).

Schöffler, Paul, distinguished German bass-baritone; b. Dresden, Sept. 15, 1897; d. Amersham, Buckinghamshire, Nov. 21, 1977. He studied in Dresden, Berlin, and Milan; in 1925, made his debut at the Dresden State Opera as the Herald in *Lohengrin;* continued on its roster until 1938, then was a member of the Vienna State Opera until 1965. He also sang at London's Covent Garden (1934–39; 1949–53), the Bayreuth Festivals (1943–44; 1956), and the Salzburg Festivals (1938–41; 1947; 1949–65). He made his Metropolitan Opera debut in N.Y. on Jan. 26, 1950, as Jokanaan in *Salome;* continued to sing there, with interruptions, until 1956, returning there in 1963 to sing one of his finest roles, Hans Sachs; remained on its roster until 1965, when he went to England. His other notable roles included Figaro, Don Giovanni, the Dutchman, Kurwenal, Scarpia, and Hindemith's Cardillac and Mathis der Maler; he also created the role of Jupiter in the 1st stage perf. of Strauss' *Die Liebe der Danae* (1952) and Einem's Danton (1947).

BIBL.: H. Christian, *P. S.: Versuch einer Würdigung* (Vienna, 1967).

Scholes, Percy (Alfred), eminent English writer on music; b. Leeds, July 24, 1877; d. Vevey, Switzerland, July 31, 1958. (He pronounced his name "Skoles.") He took his B.Mus. at the Univ. of Oxford in 1908, and his doctorat ès lettres from the Univ. of Lausanne (1934) for his study of Puritans and music. He began his career as a church organist; in 1907, founded the Home Music Study Union, and until 1921 ed. its *Music Student* (later *Music Teacher);* also wrote for the *Evening Standard* (1913–20), *Observer* (1920–27), and the *Radio Times* (1923–29). He lived in Switzerland (1928–40); then made his home in England (1940–57) until returning to Switzerland. He received many honors, including the degrees of D.Mus. (1943) and D.Litt. (1950) from the Univ. of Oxford, and D.Litt. (1953) from the Univ. of Leeds; was made an Officer of the Order of the British Empire in 1957. A writer of great literary attainments and stylistic grace, he succeeded in presenting music "appreciation" in a manner informative and stimulating to the layman and professional alike.

WRITINGS: *Everyman and His Music* (1917); *An Introduction to British Music* (1918); *The Listener's Guide to Music* (1919; 10th ed., 1942); *Music Appreciation: Why and How?* (1920; 4th ed., 1925); *The Book of the Great Musicians* (3 vols., 1920); *New Works by Modern British Composers* (2 series, 1921, 1924); *The Beginner's Guide to Harmony* (1922); *The Listener's History of Music* (3 vols., 1923–28; 4th ed., 1933); *Crotchets* (1924); *Learning to Listen by Means of the Gramophone* (1925); *Everybody's Guide to Broadcast Music* (1925); *The Appreciation of Music by Means of the Pianola and Duo-*

Art (1925); *A Miniature History of Music* (1928); *The Columbia History of Music through Eye and Ear* (5 albums of records with accompanying booklets; 1930–39; eds. in Japanese and Braille); *Music and Puritanism* (Vevey, 1934); *The Puritans and Music in England and New England* (London, 1934); *Music: The Child and the Masterpiece* (1935; American ed., *Music Appreciation: Its History and Technics); Radio Times Music Handbook* (1935; 3rd ed., 1936; American ed. as *The Scholes Music Handbook,* 1935); *The Oxford Companion to Music* (1938; 9th ed., rev., 1955; rev. and augmented by D. Arnold as *The New Oxford Companion to Music,* 2 vols., 1983); *God Save the King: Its History and Romance* (1942; new ed. as *God Save the Queen! The History and Romance of the World's First National Anthem,* 1954); *The Mirror of Music, 1844–1944, A Century of Musical Life in Britain as Reflected in the Pages of the "Musical Times"* (1947); *The Great Dr. Burney* (2 vols., 1948); *Sir John Hawkins: Musician, Magistrate, and Friend of Johnson* (1952); *The Concise Oxford Dictionary of Music* (1952; 3rd ed., rev., 1980 by M. Kennedy; rev. and augmented ed., 1985 by Kennedy as *The Oxford Dictionary of Music); The Oxford Junior Companion to Music* (1954; 2nd ed., rev., 1979).

Schollum, Robert, Austrian composer, writer on music, and teacher; b. Vienna, Aug. 22, 1913; d. there, Sept. 30, 1987. He studied at the Vienna Academy of Music and the New Vienna Cons.; also studied privately with Marx and Lustgarten (theory and composition), Lafite (piano and organ), and Nilius (conducting). He taught voice at the Vienna Academy of Music from 1959 to 1982; received the Austrian State Prize for composition (1961) and the prize of the City of Vienna (1971); served as president of the Austrian Composers Guide (1965–70; 1983).

WRITINGS: *Musik in der Volksbildung* (Vienna, 1962); *Egon Wellesz* (Vienna, 1964); *Die Wiener Schule. Entwicklung und Ergebnis* (Vienna, 1969); with J. Fritz et al., *Das kleine Wiener Jazzbuch* (Salzburg, 1970); *Singen als menschliche Kundgebung: Einführung in die Arbeit mit den "Singblattern zur Musikerziehung"* (Vienna, 1970); *Das Österreichische Lied des 20. Jahrhunderts* (Tutzing, 1977); *Vokale Aufführungspraxis* (Vienna, 1983).

WORKS: STAGE: *Der Tote Mann,* musical comedy (1936–38); *Mirandolina,* musical comedy (1950); *Der Biedermann Elend,* opera (1962). ORCH.: 6 syms. (1954–55; 1955–59; 1962; 1966–67; *Venetianische Ergebnisse,* 1969; 1987); 3 violin concertos (1944; 1961; 1979–81); Cello Concerto (1953–55); *Seestuck* for Piano and Orch. (1974–79); *Konzertstuck, Fanfares* (Linz, Sept. 8, 1984). CHAMBER: 2 string quartets (1949; 1966–67); Octet (1959); Trio for Violin, Viola, and Harp (1971); Wind Quintet (1975); numerous chamber works with piano; solo piano pieces; organ works; vocal settings.

Scholtz, Herrmann, German pianist, teacher, and composer; b. Breslau, June 9, 1845; d. Dresden, July 13, 1918. He studied in Breslau, with Plaidy in Leipzig, and with Hans von Bülow and Rheinberger in Munich; taught at the Munich Hochschule für Musik (1870–75); then went to Dresden. He was an accomplished pianist and a fine teacher; also wrote a number of piano pieces in a fashionable style: *Albumblätter, Mädchenlieder, Lyrische Blätter, Stimmungsbilder, Ballade,* etc.

Scholz, Bernhard E., German conductor, pedagogue, and composer; b. Mainz, March 30, 1835; d. Munich, Dec. 26, 1916. He studied with H. Esser and H. Pauer in Mainz, S. Dehn in Berlin, and A. Sangiovanni in Milan; after teaching in Munich and conducting in Zürich and Nuremberg, he was assistant court Kapellmeister in Hannover (1859–65); then conducted the Cherubini Society in Florence (1865–66); led the concerts of the Breslau Orch. Society (1871–82), and in 1883 succeeded Raff as director of the Hoch Cons. in Frankfurt; retired in 1908.

WORKS: Operas: *Carlo Rosa* (Munich, 1858); *Ziethen'sche Husaren* (Breslau, 1869); *Morgiane* (Munich, 1870); *Golo* (Nuremberg, 1875); *Der Trompeter von Säkkingen* (Wiesbaden, 1877); *Die vornehmen Wirte* (Leipzig, 1883); *Ingo* (Frankfurt, 1898); *Anno 1757* (Berlin, 1903); *Mirandolina* (Darmstadt,

1907); a great many choral works, with orch.; 2 syms.; Piano Concerto; 2 string quartets; String Quintet; Piano Quartet; 2 piano trios; 3 violin sonatas; 5 cello sonatas; numerous piano pieces and songs.

WRITINGS: Ed. *S.W. Dehns Lehre vom Contrapunkt, dem Canon und der Fuge* (Berlin, 2nd ed., 1883); *Wohin treiben wir?* (Frankfurt, 1897); *Musikalisches und Persönliches* (Stuttgart, 1899); *Die Lehre vom Kontrapunkt und der Nachahmung* (Leipzig, 1904); *Verklungene Weisen* (Mainz, 1911).

Schönbach, Dieter, German composer; b. Stolp-Pommern, Feb. 18, 1931. He studied at the Freiburg Hochschule für Musik with Bialas and Fortner (1949–59); was music director of the Bochum theater (1959–73). His style of composition is quaquaversal. He wrote the 1st genuine multimedia opera, *Wenn die Kälte in die Hütten tritt, um sich bei den Frierenden zu wärmen, weiss einer "Die Geschichte von einem Feuer"* (Kiel, 1968); his other works include *Farben und Klänge*, in memory of Kandinsky, for Orch. (1958); Piano Concerto (1958); *Canticum Psalmi Resurrectionis* (ISCM Festival, Rome, June 13, 1959); *Kammermusik* for 14 Instruments (1964); *Hoquetus* for 8 Wind Instruments (1964); 4 chamber music pieces, each titled *Canzona da sonar* (1966–67); *Atemmusik* for Fifes, Whistles, and some other "breath" Instruments (1969); *Hymnus 2*, multimedia show (Munich, 1972).

Schönberg, Arnold (Franz Walter). See **Schoenberg (Schönberg), Arnold (Franz Walter).**

Schonberg, Harold C(harles), eminent American music critic; b. N.Y., Nov. 29, 1915. He studied at Brooklyn College (B.A., 1937) and at N.Y. Univ. (M.A., 1938). He served in the army (1942–46); then was on the staff of the *N.Y. Sun* (1946–50); he was appointed to the music staff of the *N.Y. Times* in 1950; was senior music critic from 1960 until 1980. In 1971 he was the 1st music critic to be honored with the Pulitzer Prize in criticism. In his concert reviews and feature articles, he reveals a profound knowledge of music and displays a fine journalistic flair without assuming a posture of snobbish aloofness or descending to colloquial vulgarity. His intellectual horizon is exceptionally wide; he is well-versed in art, and can draw and paint; he is a chess aficionado and covered knowledgeably the Spassky-Fischer match in Reykjavík in 1972 for the *N.Y. Times.* He publ. in N.Y.: *Chamber and Solo Instrument Music* (1955); *The Collector's Chopin and Schumann* (1959); *The Great Pianists* (1963; 2nd ed., rev., 1987); *The Great Conductors* (1967); *Lives of the Great Composers* (1970; 2nd ed., 1981); *Facing the Music* (1981); *The Glorious Ones: Classical Music's Legendary Performers* (1985).

Schönberg, Stig Gustav, Swedish organist and composer; b. Västra Husby, May 13, 1933. He studied at the Stockholm Müsikhogskolan (1953–60), where he graduated with diplomas as a music teacher, organist, and choirmaster; his composition mentors were Lars-Erik Larsson and Karl-Birger Blomdahl; also studied theory with Erland von Koch and Valdemar Söderholm; also organ with Flors Peeters in Belgium. He was active as a church organist and toured as a recitalist.

WORKS: BALLET: *Madeleine och Conrad* (1967; rev. 1972). **ORCH.:** *Intermezzo* (1958); *Introduktion och Allegro* for String Orch. (1958–59); Concerto for Organ and String Orch. (1962); *Sinfonia aperta* (1965); 3 concertinos for String Orch. (1966); *Fantasia* for String Orch. (1967); *Concitato* (1968); *Impromptu visionario* (1972); Concerto for 2 Flutes and String Orch. (1976); Sym. No. 2 (1977); Concerto for Organ and Orch. (1982); Concerto for Organ and Brass Orch. (1986–87). **CHAMBER:** 7 string quartets (1961–84); *Madrigaler* for 2 Trumpets and 2 Trombones (1962); *Intrada* for 2 Trumpets, 2 Trombones, and Organ (1963); Sonata for Flute and Organ (1963); Trio for Flute, Violin, and Cello (1967); 2 violin sonatas (1964, 1967); *Vad Ijus over griften,* intrada for Organ and Brass Ensemble (1971); *Liten fantasi* for 2 Trumpets (1973); Flute Sonata (1974); *Pastoral* for Horn and Organ (1979); *Air* for Viola and Organ (1982); Sonata for Cello and Organ (1984); *Poème memorial* for Viola, and Piano or Organ or Harpsichord (1985); piano pieces and organ music; various works for Soloists, Chorus, and Instrument(s), including *Regina coeli* (1973), *Cantata gloriae* (1975), *Missa coralis* (1983), and *Missa da pacem* (1985); choruses; songs.

Schönberger, Benno, Austrian pianist, teacher, and composer; b. Vienna, Sept. 12, 1863; d. Wisborough Green, Sussex, March 9, 1930. He studied piano with Anton Door and composition with Bruckner and Volkmann at the Vienna Cons.; then took lessons with Liszt. After a European concert tour, he went to London, where he taught at the Royal Academy of Music and appeared in chamber music concerts. For piano, he wrote 3 sonatas, 3 rhapsodies, a Bolero, and a Polonaise; also about 40 songs.

Schöne, Lotte (real name, **Charlotte Bodenstein**), admired Austrian-born French soprano; b. Vienna, Dec. 15, 1891; d. Paris, Dec. 22, 1977. She studied in Vienna; made her debut at the Vienna Volksoper in 1912, and continued to appear there until 1917; then sang at the Vienna Court (later State) Opera (1917–26); also at the Berlin Städtische Oper (1926–33); made many appearances at the Salzburg Festivals (1922–35). After leaving Germany in 1933, she went to Paris, became a French citizen, and made guest appearances at the Opéra and the Opéra-Comique; she was compelled to go into hiding during the Nazi occupation, but resumed her career after the liberation, and sang in Berlin in 1948; she retired in 1953. Among her many notable roles were Cherubino, Papagena, Susanna, Despina, Pamina, Zerlina, Sophie, Mimi, Liù, and Mélisande.

Schönherr, Max, Austrian conductor, musicologist, and composer; b. Marburg an der Drau, Nov. 23, 1903; d. Mödling, near Vienna, Dec. 13, 1984. He studied with Hermann Frisch in Marburg and Roderich von Mojsisovics at the Graz Cons.; later studied musicology at the Univ. of Vienna (Ph.D., 1970). After conducting at the Graz Landestheater (1924–28), he settled in Vienna as a conductor with the Theater an der Wien and Stadttheater (1929–33), the Volksoper (1933–38), and the Austrian Radio (1931–68), where he won distinction for his idiomatic readings of light Viennese scores. He composed much light music in a stylish manner, and also made effective arrangements of scores by the Viennese Strausses et al. He publ. *Carl Michael Ziehrer: Sein Werk, sein Leben, seine Zeit* (Vienna, 1974).

Schöning, Klaus, German radio producer and writer on music; b. Rastenburg, Feb. 24, 1936. After univ. studies in Munich, Göttingen, and Berlin, he worked in the theater; in 1961 he began a lengthy association with the Westdeutscher Rundfunk (WDR) of Cologne, where he is producer, director, and chief ed. of the WDR Studio for Acoustic Art, an international workshop for audio art and research that he established. He commissioned and produced over 1,000 radio broadcasts for the WDR and other international radio stations; was a pioneer in the reorientation of the German Hörspiel in the late 1960s, his main programs being "New Hörspiel," "Composers as Hörspielmakers," and "Ars Acustica." Among the composers from whom he has commissioned works are John Cage, Alvin Curran, Pauline Oliveros, Alison Knowles, Charles Amirkhanian, Jackson Mac Low, and Joan La Barbara. With support from the WDR and the Goethe Inst., he also developed a transcontinental link for acoustic art, Acustica International; in 1985 he was artistic director of the 1st Acustica International Festival (Cologne), and in 1990, of the Sound Art Festival and 2nd Acustica International Festival (N.Y. and Montreal). He has won numerous awards for his productions, including the Prix Italia, Prix Futura, Karl-Sczuka-Preis, Hörspielpreis der Kriegsblinden, and Premio Ondas; in 1983 he received the Berliner Kunstpreis for Film/Radio/TV. He also lectured extensively in Germany, France, and the U.S.; was curator of the exhibition "American Audio Art on WDR" at the Whitney Museum of Art in N.Y. (1990). Among his numerous publications are *John Cage: Roaratorio: Ein irischer Circus über Finnegans Wake* (1982), *Geschichte und Typologie des Hörspiels* (7 vols., 1988–90), and *1. Acustica International: Komponisten als Hörspielmacher* (1990).

Schönstein, Karl, Austrian singer and government official; b. Ofen, June 26, 1797; d. Vienna, July 16, 1876. Before he assumed office, he had a career as a concert singer; was one of the earliest interpreters of Schubert's songs; Schubert's song cycle *Die schöne Müllerin* is dedicated to him.

Schönzeler, Hans-Hubert, German conductor and musicologist; b. Leipzig, June 22, 1925. He went to Australia as a youth, and studied conducting with Eugene Goossens at the New South Wales Cons. of Music in Sydney; later traveled in Europe, where he received further instruction in conducting with Rafael Kubelik, with Carlo Zecchi in Hilversum, and with Paul van Kempen in Siena. He eventually made his home in London, where he led the 20th-Century Ensemble (1957–62). In 1967 he was appointed deputy chief conductor of the West Australian Sym. Orch. in Perth, while continuing his appearances as a guest conductor in Europe. He publ. *Bruckner* (London and N.Y., 1970; rev. ed., 1978), *Dvořák* (London, 1984), *Furtwängler* (London, 1987), and *Zu Bruckners IX. Symphonie: die Krakauer Skizzen/Bruckner's 9th Symphony: the Cracow Sketches* (Vienna, 1987).

Schoop, Paul, Swiss-American composer; b. Zürich, July 31, 1909; d. Los Angeles, Jan. 1, 1976. He studied piano in Paris with Cortot and Casadesus, and in Berlin with Schnabel; also composition with Dukas in Paris, and with Hindemith and Schoenberg in the U.S. He settled in Los Angeles, and wrote music for films; also composed a comic opera, *The Enchanted Trumpet*; a symphonic poem, *Fata Morgana*; ballet scores for productions of his sister, Trudi Schoop, a modern dancer.

Schopenhauer, Arthur, great German philosopher; b. Danzig, Feb. 22, 1788; d. Frankfurt am Main, Sept. 21, 1860. Although his excursions into the realm of music are neither remarkable nor very valuable, they are stimulating, and have inspired a number of valuable contributions by modern investigators, especially in the field of musical esthetics. Wagner was influenced to a considerable extent by Schopenhauer's philosophical system.

BIBL.: F. von Hausegger, *Richard Wagner und A. S.* (Leipzig, 1878; 2nd ed., 1892); M. Seydel, *A. S.s Metaphysik der Musik* (Leipzig, 1895); E. Zoccoli, *L'estetica di S.* (Milan, 1901); G. Melli, *La filosofia di S.* (Florence, 1905); T. Lessing, *S., Wagner, Nietzsche* (Munich, 1906); A. Mäcklenburg, "S. und seine Stellung zur Musik," *Die Musik* (Dec. 1908); F. Wagner, *Beiträge zur Würdigung der Musiktheorie S.s* (diss., Univ. of Bonn, 1910); A. von Gottschalk, *Beethoven und S.* (Blanckenburg, 1912); L. Dunton Green, "S. and Music," *Musical Quarterly* (April 1930); A. Huebscher, *S.: Gestern-Heute-Morgen* (1973).

Schorr, Friedrich, renowned Hungarian-American bass-baritone; b. Nagyvárad, Sept. 2, 1888; d. Farmington, Conn., Aug. 14, 1953. He studied law at the Univ. of Vienna, and also took private lessons in singing; appeared with the Chicago Grand Opera (1912); then was a member of the opera companies in Graz (1912–16), Prague (1916–18), Cologne (1918–23), and of the Berlin State Opera (1923–31); also sang Wotan at Bayreuth (1925–31), and appeared at London's Covent Garden (1925–33). He made his Metropolitan Opera debut in N.Y. as Wolfram on Feb. 14, 1924, and continued as a member until his farewell performance as the Wanderer in *Siegfried* on March 2, 1943. Schorr is generally recognized as the foremost Wagnerian bass-baritone of his era; he also sang roles in operas by Beethoven, Strauss, Verdi, and Puccini, and appeared in the U.S. premieres of Krenek's *Jonny Spielt Auf* (Daniello; 1929) and Weinberger's *Schwanda* (title role; 1931) at the Metropolitan Opera.

Schott, Anton, German tenor; b. Schloss Staufeneck, June 24, 1846; d. Stuttgart, Jan. 6, 1913. He was in the Prussian army; after the Franco-Prussian War, he sang at the Munich Opera (1871) and the Berlin Opera (1872–75); then in London and in Italy; made his U.S. debut at the Metropolitan Opera in N.Y. as Tannhäuser (Nov. 17, 1884); was on its roster until 1885, and again in 1886–87. He excelled as an interpreter of Wagnerian roles. He publ. a polemical brochure, *Hie Welf, hie Waibling* (1904).

Schott, Bernhard, prominent German music publisher; b. Eltville, Aug. 10, 1748; d. Sandholf, near Heidesheim, April 26, 1809. He studied at the Univ. of Mainz, graduating as magister artium in 1771. He was granted a privilegium exclusivum and the title of music engraver to the elector in 1780. At his death, his sons, **Johann Andreas** (1781–1840) and **Johann Joseph** (1782–1855), carried on the business as B. Schotts Söhne. The 2 sons of Johann Andreas, **Franz Philipp** (b. July 30, 1811; d. May 8, 1874) and **Peter** (d. Paris, Sept. 20, 1894), continued the business; Peter was manager of the Paris and Brussels branches, and Franz Philipp was sole owner of the Mainz firm (from 1855). Peter Schott, Jr. eventually became director, together with Franz von Landwehr and **Ludwig Strecker** (1853–1943); the latter's sons, **Ludwig Strecker** (1883–1978) and **Willy Strecker** (1884–1958), became partners in the firm in 1920. The Schott catalogue is one of the richest in the world, publishing works by the great masters as well as by leading contemporary composers; among its critical editions are the complete works of Wagner, Schoenberg, and Hindemith. It also publ. the journals *Cäcilia* (1824–48), *Süddeutsche Musikzeitung* (1852–69), and *Melos* (1920–34; 1946–74); the last was combined with the *Neue Zeitschrift für Musik* in 1974. The firm likewise publ. the famous Riemann *Musik-Lexikon*.

BIBL.: *Der Musikverlag B. S.* (Mainz, 1954); H.-C. Müller, *B. S., Hofmusikstecher in Mainz: Die Frühgeschichte seines Musikverlages bis 1797, mit einem Verzeichnis der Verlagswerke 1779–1797* (Mainz, 1977).

Schouwman, Hans, Dutch pianist and composer; b. Gorinchem, Aug. 8, 1902; d. The Hague, April 8, 1967. He was a pupil of Peter van Anrooy; developed a singing voice and gave recitals, accompanying himself on the piano.

WORKS: *3 danswijzen* (3 Dance Tunes) for Voice, 2 Flutes, Strings, and Percussion (1938); *5 Sketches* for Clarinet and Small Orch. (1942); *Friesland*, 4 songs for Voice and Orch. (1945); *Memento mori* for Alto, Chorus, and Small Orch. (1947); *Suite* for Amateur Orch. (1958); *De Prinses op de erwt* for Orch. (1965); 2 oboe sonatinas (1940, 1944); *Aubade en Barcarolle* for Clarinet and Piano (1944); Trio for Clarinet, Bassoon, and Piano (1944); *Romance en Humoreske* for Bassoon and Piano (1944); *4 Pieces* for Flute and Piano (1944); 2 *Legends* for Horn and Piano (1944); *Notturno* for Mezzo-soprano, Cello, and Piano (1949); *Nederlandse suite* for Wind Quintet (1953); *Om de kribbe* for Soprano, Contralto, Female Chorus, and Piano (1952); *3 Preludes* for Piano, left-hand (1959); 2 series of old Dutch songs, with string accompaniment; arrangements of folk songs for various instruments; vocal duets; solo songs.

Schrade, Leo, eminent German musicologist; b. Allenstein, Dec. 13, 1903; d. Spéracédès, Alpes-Maritimes, Sept. 21, 1964. He studied with Hermann Halbig at the Univ. of Heidelberg (1923–27), with Adolf Sandberger at the Univ. of Munich, and with Theodor Kroyer at the Univ. of Leipzig (Ph.D., 1927, with the diss. *Die ältesten Denkmäler der Orgelmusik als Beitrag zu einer Geschichte der Toccata*; publ. in Münster, 1928); completed his Habilitation in 1929 at the Univ. of Königsberg. He taught at the Univs. of Königsberg (1928–32) and Bonn (from 1932). In 1937 he emigrated to the U.S.; was on the faculty of Yale Univ. (1938–58), where he taught music history; in 1958 he was appointed to the music faculty of the Univ. of Basel. He was also the Charles Eliot Norton Lecturer at Harvard Univ. in 1962–63. He was founder-ed. of the Yale Studies in the History of Music and the Yale Collegium Musicum series (1947–58); was co-ed. of the *Journal of Renaissance and Baroque Music* (1946–47), *Annales musicologiques* (1953–64), and the *Archiv für Musikwissenschaft* (1958–64); served as an ed. of the series Polyphonic Music in the Fourteenth Century (vols. 1-3, 1956; vol. 4, 1958).

WRITINGS: *Beethoven in France: The Growth of an Idea* (New Haven, 1942); *Monteverdi: Creator of Modern Music* (N.Y., 1950; 2nd ed., 1964); *Bach: The Conflict Between the Sacred and the Secular* (N.Y., 1954); *W.A. Mozart* (Bern and Munich,

1964); *Tragedy in the Art of Music* (Cambridge, Mass., 1964).

BIBL.: *Musik und Geschichte: L. S. zum sechzigsten Geburtstag* (Cologne, 1963; Eng. tr., 1965, as *Music and History: L. S. on the Occasion of His 60th Birthday*); *L. S. in memoriam* (Bern and Munich, 1966); E. Lichtenhahn, ed., *L. S.: De scientia musicae studia atque orationes* (Bern and Stuttgart, 1967); W. Arlt et al., eds., *Gattungen der Musik in Einzeldarstellungen: Gedenkschrift für L. S.* (Bern and Munich, 1973).

Schrader, Barry, American composer; b. Johnstown, Pa., June 26, 1945. He received degrees at the Univ. of Pittsburgh in English literature (B.A., 1967) and in musicology (M.A., 1970); also served as an organist at Heinz Chapel. In 1969–70 he studied electro-acoustic techniques with Morton Subotnick. In 1970 he moved to Los Angeles and attended the Calif. Inst. of the Arts (M.F.A. in composition, 1971); later joined its faculty. From 1975 to 1978 he also taught at Calif. State Univ. at Los Angeles. He organized a series of electro-acoustic music programs under the name "Currents," held in Los Angeles from 1973 to 1979; also participated in many electronic music festivals in other countries. In 1984 he became the 1st president of the Society for Electro-Acoustic Music in the U.S.; publ. *Introduction to Electro-Acoustical Music* (Englewood Cliffs, N.J., 1982). Most of his music is for electronic sound; in his *Bestiary* (1972–74), Schrader explored the potentialities of synthesizing new timbres; in his *Trinity* (1976), he transmuted given timbres to more complex sonorities. In his *Lost Atlantis,* he essayed a programmatic use of electronic sound. He also experimented in combining live music with electronic resources, as in his work *Moon-Whales and other Moon Songs* (1982–83).

WORKS: *Signature for Tempo* for Soprano and Piano (1966); *Serenade* for Tape (1969); *Incantation* for Tape (1970); *Sky Ballet* for Sound Environment (1970); *Elysium* for Harp, Dancers, Tape, and Projections (1971); *Besitary* for Tape (1972–74); *Trinity* for Tape (1976); *Lost Atlantis* for Tape (1977); *Moon-whales and Other Moon Songs* for Soprano and Tape (1982–83); *Electronic Music Box I* for Sound Installation (1983), *II* (1983), and *III* (1984); *TWO: Square Flowers Red: SONGS* (1990); also many film scores, including *Death of the Red Planet* (1973), *Heavy Light* (1973), *Exploratorium* (1975), *Mobiles* (1978), *Along the Way* (1980), and *Galaxy of Terror* (1981).

Schradieck, Henry (actually, **Carl Franz Heinrich**), German-American violinist and teacher; b. Hamburg, April 29, 1846; d. N.Y., March 25, 1918. He studied violin as a child with Léonard in Brussels (1854–58), and later with Ferdinand David in Leipzig (1859–61). He then served as concertmaster of the Hamburg Phil. Society orch. (1868–74) and of the Gewandhaus Orch. in Leipzig (1874–83). After again serving as concertmaster of the Hamburg Phil. Society orch. (1889–94), he settled in the U.S.; was prof. of violin at the National Cons. in N.Y. and then at the South Broad Street Cons. in Philadelphia (1899–1912); subsequently returned to N.Y. and taught at the American Inst. of Applied Music. He publ. various pedagogical books.

Schramm, Margit, German soprano; b. Dortmund, July 21, 1935. She was educated at the Dortmund Cons., and made her debut at Saarbrücken in 1956. She sang in Koblenz (1957–58), in Munich at the Gärtnerplatz Theater (1959–64), in Berlin at the Theater des Westens (1965–66), and in the municipal theaters in Dortmund (1967). In 1968 she joined the ensemble of the State Theater in Wiesbaden. Her repertoire of German and Austrian operettas is vast and impressive.

Schramm, Melchior, esteemed German organist and composer; b. Münsterberg, Silesia, c.1553; d. Offenburg, Baden, Sept. 6, 1619. After serving as a chorister in the Hofkapelle of Archduke Ferdinand of the Tirol, he was awarded a scholarship to study with the Innsbruck court organist, Servatius Rorif. In 1571–72 he was organist at a Halle convent; after serving as organist (1574–1605) and Kapellmeister (1574–94) at the Sigmarigen court, he was civic organist at Offenburg's Heilig Kreuz Kirche (from 1605). His works include 3 vols.

of motets (1576, 1606, 1612) and a vol. of German madrigals (1579).

Schreck, Gustav, German composer and teacher; b. Zeulenroda, Sept. 8, 1849; d. Leipzig, Jan. 22, 1918. He studied at the Leipzig Cons. with Plaidy, Papperitz, and Jadassohn; he taught in Finland and at the Leipzig Cons. (from 1887). He wrote an oratorio, *Christus der Auferstandene,* and other sacred works; Sonata for Bassoon and Piano; Sonata for Oboe and Piano; *Divertimento* for 9 Woodwinds; piano pieces; songs.

Schreiber, Frederick (actually, **Friedrich**), Austrian-American organist, choirmaster, and composer; b. Vienna, Jan. 13, 1895; d. N.Y., Jan. 15, 1985. He studied piano, cello, and composition in Vienna; after teaching at the Cons. there (1927–38), he emigrated to N.Y. and was organist and choirmaster of the Reformed Protestant Church (1939–58). Among his orch. works are 7 syms. (1927–57); *The Beatitudes,* symphonic trilogy for Orch. and Chorus (1950); *Christmas Suite* (1967); *Images* (1971); *Contrasts* (1972); 2 piano concertos; Cello Concerto; 2 violin concertos; *Variations on a German Folksong* (1974); numerous choral pieces; chamber music, including 2 string quintets, 7 string quartets, Piano Quartet, and 3 piano trios; much organ music.

Schreiber, Friedrich Gustav, German organist, conductor, teacher, and composer; b. Bienstedt, Aug. 5, 1817; d. Mühlhausen, July 14, 1889. He studied with E. Kast and L. Gebhardt in Erfurt; taught organ in Prague (1840–47); settled at Erfurt in 1851 as municipal music director and cantor at St. Balsius's; founded and conducted a choral society; wrote choral works and songs.

Schreier, Peter (Max), esteemed German tenor and conductor; b. Meissen, July 29, 1935. He sang in the Dresdner Kreuzchor; gained a taste for the theater when he appeared as one of the 3 boys in *Die Zauberflöte* at Dresden's Semper Opera House (1944). He received private vocal lessons from Polster in Leipzig (1954–56), and then with Winkler in Dresden; also took courses at the Hochschule für Musik there (1956–59); concurrently worked at the studio of the Dresden State Opera, where he appeared as Paolino in *Il matrimonio segreto* (1957); made his official debut there as the 1st Prisoner in *Fidelio* (1959), and went on to become a regular member of the company in 1961. In 1963 he joined the Berlin State Opera, and became one of its principal artists; he also made guest appearances with opera houses throughout Eastern Europe and the Soviet Union; likewise sang in London (debut as Ferrando with the visiting Hamburg State Opera, 1966) and at the Salzburg Festivals (from 1967), the Vienna State Opera (from 1967), the Metropolitan Opera in N.Y. (debut as Tamino, Dec. 25, 1967), La Scala in Milan (1969), and the Teatro Colón in Buenos Aires (1969). His roles in Mozart's operas brought him critical acclaim; he was also a distinguished oratorio and lieder artist, excelling in a repertoire that ranged from Bach to Orff. In 1970 he launched a second, equally successful career as a conductor. In 1964 he was honored with the title of Kammersänger. He publ. the book *Aus meiner Sicht: Gedanken und Erinnerungen* (ed. by M. Meier; Vienna, 1983).

BIBL.: G. Schmiedel, *P. S.: Für Sie porträtiert* (Leipzig, 1976).

Schreker, Franz, eminent Austrian conductor, pedagogue, and composer; b. Monaco (of Austrian parents), March 23, 1878; d. Berlin, March 21, 1934. His father, the court photographer, died when he was 10; the family went to Vienna, where he studied with Arnold Rosé; also received instruction in composition from Robert Fuchs at the Cons. (1892–1900). He first gained notice as a composer with his pantomime *Der Geburtstag der Infantin* (Vienna, Aug. 1908); that same year he founded the Phil. Chorus, serving as its conductor until 1920. He won great distinction with his opera *Der ferne Klang* (Frankfurt am Main, Aug. 18, 1912); outstanding among his later operas were *Die Gezeichneten* (Frankfurt am Main, April 25, 1918) and *Der Schatzgräber* (Frankfurt am Main, Jan. 21,

1920). After teaching composition at the Vienna Academy of Music (1912–20), he settled in Berlin as director of the Hochschule für Musik. Being of Jewish birth, he became a target of the rising Nazi movement; in 1931 he withdrew from performance his opera *Christophorus* in the face of Nazi threats; his last opera, *Der Schmied von Gent*, was premiered in Berlin on Oct. 29, 1932, in spite of Nazi demonstrations. Schreker was pressured into resigning his position at the Hochschule für Musik in 1932, but that same year he was given charge of a master class in composition at the Prussian Academy of Arts; he lost this position when the Nazis came to power in 1933. Shortly afterward, he suffered a major heart attack, and spent the remaining months of his life in poor health and reduced circumstances. As a composer, Schreker led the neo-Romantic movement in the direction of Expressionism, emphasizing psychological conflicts in his operas; in his harmonies he expanded the basically Wagnerian sonorities to include many devices associated with Impressionism. He exercised considerable influence on the German and Viennese schools of his time, but with the change of direction in modern music toward economy of means and away from mystical and psychological trends, Schreker's music suffered a decline after his death.

WORKS: STAGE: OPERAS (all to his own libretto, the 1st excepted): *Flammen* (c.1900; concert perf., Vienna, April 24, 1902); *Der ferne Klang* (1901–10; Frankfurt am Main, Aug. 18, 1912); *Das Spielwerk und die Prinzessin* (1909–12; Frankfurt am Main and Vienna, March 15, 1913; rev. as *Das Spielwerk*, 1916; Munich, Oct. 30, 1920); *Die Gezeichneten* (1913–15; Frankfurt am Main, April 25, 1918); *Der Schatzgräber* (1915–18; Frankfurt am Main, Jan. 21, 1920); *Irrelohe* (1919–23; Cologne, March 27, 1924); *Christophorus, oder Die Vision einer Oper* (1924–27; Freiburg, Oct. 1, 1978); *Der singende Teufel* (1924–28; Berlin, Dec. 10, 1928); *Der Schmied von Gent* (1929–32; Berlin, Oct. 29, 1932). **PANTOMIME:** *Der Geburtstag der Infantin* for String Orch. (Vienna, Aug. 1908; rev. as *Spanisches Fest* for Orch., 1923). **DANCE ALLEGORY:** *Der Wind* for Clarinet and Piano Quartet (1908). **BALLET:** *Rokoko* (1908; rev. as *Ein Tanzspiel*, 1920). **ORCH.:** *Love Song* for Strings and Harp (1895; not extant); *Intermezzo* for Strings (1900; included in the *Romantische Suite*, 1902); *Romantische Suite* (1902; includes the *Intermezzo* for Strings, 1900); *Ekkehard*, overture (1902); *Phantastische Ouvertüre* (1902); *Festwalzer und Walzerintermezzo* (1908); *Vorspiel zu einem Drama* (1913; used as a prelude to his opera *Die Gezeichneten*); *Kammersymphonie* for 23 Solo Instruments (1916; Vienna, March 12, 1917); *Kleine Suite* for Chamber Orch. (1928; Breslau, Jan. 17, 1929); *4 Little Pieces* (1930); *Vorspiel zu einer grossen Oper* (1933; Baden-Baden, March 11, 1958; symphonic fragments from an unfinished opera, *Memnon*). **VOCAL:** *Der Holdstein* for Soprano, Bass, Chorus, and Orch. (c.1898); *Psalm CXVI* for Women's Chorus, Orch., and Organ (1900); *Schwanengesang* for Chorus and Orch. (1902); *Fünf Gesänge* for Alto or Bass, and Orch. (c.1921; based on the song cycle, 1909); *Vom ewigen Leben* for Voice and Orch. (1927; based on *Zwei lyrische Gesänge*, 1924); some unaccompanied choral pieces; songs. **CHAMBER:** Sonata for Violin and Piano (1897); piano pieces.

BIBL.: P. Bekker, *F. S.: Studie zur Kritik der modernen Oper* (Berlin, 1919; 2nd ed., 1983); special issue of *Musikblätter des Anbruch*, ii/1–2 (1920); R. Hoffmann, *F. S.* (Leipzig and Vienna, 1921); J. Kapp, *F. S.: Der Mann und sein Werk* (Munich, 1921); F. Bayerl, *F. S.s Opernwerk* (Erlangen, 1928); *S.-Heft* (Berlin, 1959); G. Neuwirth, *F. S.* (Vienna, 1959); H. Bures-Schreker, *El caso S.* (Buenos Aires, 1969; rev. Ger. tr. with H. Stuckenschmidt and W. Oehlmann as *F. S.*, Vienna, 1970); G. Neuwirth, *Die Harmonik in der Oper "Der ferne Klang" von F. S.* (Regensburg, 1972); F. Heller, ed., *Arnold Schönberg—F. S.: Briefwechsel* (Tutzing, 1974); O. Kolleritsch, ed., *F. S. am Beginn der neuen Musik*, Studien zur Wertungsforschung, XI (Graz, 1978); R. Ermen, ed., *F. S. (1878–1934) zum 50. Todestag* (Aachen, 1984); M. Brzoska, *F. S.s Oper "Der Schatzgräber"* (Stuttgart, 1988).

Schröder, family of German musicians:
(1) Karl Schröder, violinist and violist; b. Oberbosa, Thuringia, March 17, 1816; d. Berlin, April 21, 1890. He studied with G. Siebeck and A.B. Marx in Eisleben; after serving as a town musician in Quedlinburg, he was music director in Neuhaldensleben; also played in a family quartet with his sons:
(2) Hermann Schröder, violinist, teacher, and composer; b. Quedlinburg, July 28, 1843; d. Berlin, Jan. 30, 1909. He studied with his father, and with W. Sommer and A.G. Ritter in Magdeburg; settled in Berlin, where he was director of his own music school (from 1873); also taught at the Institut für Kirchenmusik (from 1885), where he later was assistant director. He publ. *Untersuchung über die sympathischen Klänge der Geigeninstrumente* (1891); *Die symmetrische Umkehrung in der Musik* (1902); *Ton und Farbe* (1906); chamber music for instructive purposes: 6 *instruktive Quartette, 3 kleine Trios*, etc.; a violin method, *Die Kunst des Violinspiels* (1887).
(3) Karl Schröder, cellist, conductor, teacher, and composer; b. Quedlinburg, Dec. 18, 1848; d. Bremen, Sept. 22, 1935. He studied with his father; became a member of the Sondershausen Hofkapelle when he was 14; also received instruction from Drechsler and Kiel. He played in the family quartet until it was dissolved in 1873; was Kapellmeister at Berlin's Kroll Opera (1872–73); after serving in the Braunschweig Hofkapelle (1873–74), he was solo cellist in the Gewandhaus Orch. in Leipzig (1874–81), where he also taught at the Cons. In 1881 he returned to Sondershausen as Hofkapellmeister; also was director of his own music school until 1886; then was conductor of the German Opera in Rotterdam (1886–87), in Berlin (1887–88), and in Hamburg (1888–90). In 1890 he once more returned to Sondershausen as director of the Cons. (until 1909); then taught cello at Berlin's Stern Cons. (1911–24). He wrote 2 operas: *Aspasia* (1892), and *Asket* (1893); 3 syms.; 6 cello concertos; chamber music. He compiled 3 pedagogical manuals: *Katechismus der Dirigierens und Taktierens* (1889), *Katechismus des Violinspiels* (1889), and *Katechismus des Violoncellspiels* (1890); these were also publ. in Eng. (1893, 1895, 1896). His collections of Classical works for the cello, especially *Vortragstudien* (60 pieces), are of value.
(4) Alwin Schröder, violist, cellist, and teacher; b. Neuhaldensleben, June 15, 1855; d. Boston, Oct. 17, 1928. He studied piano with his father and violin with his brother Hermann; continued violin studies with De Ahna and Tappert at the Berlin Hochschule für Musik. He was 11 when he took his father's place as violist in the family quartet; was a violinist (1872–75) and a cellist (from 1875) in Karl Liebig's orch.; in 1880 he became deputy to his brother Karl in Leipzig's Gewandhaus Orch., and then was joint principal with J. Klengel (from 1881); also taught at the Cons. In 1891 he emigrated to the U.S. and later became a naturalized citizen; played in the Boston Sym. Orch. (1891–1925); also was a member of the Kneisel Quartet. He wrote some manuals and prepared transcriptions for cello.

Schröder, Hanning, German composer; b. Rostock, July 4, 1896; d. Berlin, Oct. 16, 1987. He was a medical student; concurrently he took violin lessons with Havemann in Berlin and composition with Weismann in Freiburg im Breisgau; then took a course in musicology with W. Gurlitt. In 1929 he married the musicologist **Cornelia Auerbach** (b. Breslau, Aug. 24, 1900); they remained in Germany under the Nazi regime, but were barred from professional work for their act of human charity in giving shelter to a Jewish couple in their Berlin apartment. After the fall of the Third Reich, they resumed their careers.

WORKS: *Musik* for Recorder (1954), and similar solo works for Viola, Cello, Violin, and Bassoon; *Hänsel und Gretel*, singspiel for children (Berlin, Dec. 23, 1952); *Divertimento* for 5 Wind Instruments (1957); *Divertimento* for Viola and Cello (1963); *Metronome 80* for Violin (1969); Nonet for Wind Quintet, Violin, Viola, Cello, and Double Bass (1970); *Varianten* for Flute and Orch. (1971).

Schröder, Jaap, distinguished Dutch violinist and pedagogue; b. Amsterdam, Dec. 31, 1925. He studied violin at the Amsterdam Cons. and in Paris; also attended classes in musicology at the Sorbonne. He then served as concertmaster of the Hilversum Radio Chamber Orch., and was a member of the Netherlands String Quartet. In 1975 he founded the Quartetto Esterhazy, which gave performances of music from the Classical era on period instruments; it was dissolved in 1981. He subsequently, served as music director and concertmaster of the Academy of Ancient Music in London. In 1982 he was appointed visiting music director of the Smithsonian Chamber Players in Washington, D.C.

Schröder, Jens, Danish conductor; b. Bielsko, Poland, Nov. 6, 1909. He was educated at the Prague Academy of Music; then conducted in Copenhagen and other Danish cities; subsequently, was in Aalborg as chief conductor of the Municipal Theater (1942–75) and of the Sym. Orch. (1942–80); was also a guest conductor with the Danish Radio Sym. and the Royal Danish Orch., as well as a conductor with the Jutland Opera (from 1974). In 1980 Queen Margrethe II made him a Knight of the Dannebrog Order (First Grade) in appreciation of his many contributions to the musical life of Denmark.

Schröder-Devrient, Wilhelmine, celebrated German soprano; b. Hamburg, Dec. 6, 1804; d. Coburg, Jan. 26, 1860. She received early training for the stage from her father, Friedrich Schröder (1744–1816), a baritone, and from her mother, Antoinette Sophie Bürger, a well-known actress; she herself played children's parts and was an actress until her 17th year. After the death of her father, she followed her mother to Vienna, where she studied with Mozatti; made her operatic debut at the Kärnthnertortheater in Vienna on Jan. 20, 1821, as Pamina; then sang Agathe in *Der Freischütz* under Weber's direction (Vienna, March 7, 1822). When *Fidelio* was revived in Vienna in 1822, she sang Leonore in the presence of Beethoven (Nov. 3, 1822). In 1822 she sang in Dresden, and then was a member of its court opera from 1823 to 1847, where she received additional training from the chorus master, Aloys Mieksch. She also made guest appearances in Berlin (1828), Paris (1830–32), and London (1832–33; 1837); likewise won renown as a concert artist, continuing to make appearances in this capacity in Germany until 1856. She was one of the great singing actresses of her era; among her many fine roles were Donna Anna, Euryanthe, Norma, Rossini's Desdemona, Amina, and Lady Macbeth. Wagner held her in high esteem and chose her to create the roles of Adriano Colonna in *Rienzi* (Dresden, Oct. 20, 1842), Senta in *Der fliegende Holländer* (Dresden, Jan. 2, 1843), and Venus in *Tannhäuser* (Dresden, Oct. 19, 1845). She was married 3 times: her 1st husband was the actor Karl Devrient, whom she divorced in 1828; her 2nd husband, a Saxon officer named Von Döring, cheated her out of her earnings, and she likewise divorced him; her 3rd husband was the Livonian baron Von Bock, whom she married in 1850. A purported autobiography, publ. anonymously in many eds. since about 1870 as *Aus den Memoiren einer Sängerin* or *Memoires d'une chanteuse allemande,* is in fact a pornographic fantasy whose real author is unknown. A novel based on her life by Eva von Baudissin, *Wilhelmine Schröder-Devrient: Der Schicksalsweg einer grossen Künstlerin,* was publ. in Berlin in 1937.
BIBL.: C. von Glümer, *Erinnerungen an W. S.-D.* (Leipzig, 1862; reprint, 1905); A. von Wolzogen, *W. S.-D.* (Leipzig, 1863); G. Bonacci, "G. Schröder-Devrient e Gasparo Spontini," *Nuova Antologia* (Rome, 1903); C. Hagemann, *W. S.-D.* (Berlin, 1904; 2nd ed., 1947); E. Schuré, *Précurseurs et revoltés* (Paris, 1904); J. Bab, *Die D.s* (Berlin, 1932).

Schröder-Feinen, Ursula, German soprano; b. Gelsenkirchen, July 21, 1936. She studied voice with Maria Helm in Gelsenkirchen, and took courses at the Essen Folkwangschule. She sang in the chorus of the Gelsenkirchen Opera (1958), where she made her operatic debut as Aida in 1961, and remained on its roster until 1968; then sang with the Deutsche Oper am Rhein in Düsseldorf (1968–72). On Dec. 4, 1970, she made her Metropolitan Opera debut in N.Y. as Chrysothemis in *Elektra;* also sang at Bayreuth, Salzburg, Milan, and Berlin. She was a versatile singer whose repertoire included major dramatic roles in German and Italian opera.

Schröter, family of German musicians:
(1) Johann Friedrich Schröter, oboist and teacher; b. Eilenburg, 1724; d. Kassel, 1811. He began his career as an oboist in Count Brühl's regiment; in 1766 went to Leipzig, where he nurtured his children's musical careers; also took them on tours of Germany, the Netherlands, and England (1771–c.1773); later was a court musician and teacher in Hanau (1779–86) and Kassel. His 4 children were:
(2) Corona (Elisabeth Wilhelmine) Schröter, soprano, actress, and composer; b. Guben, Jan. 14, 1751; d. Ilmenau, Aug. 23, 1802. She began her musical training with her father, becoming proficient as a keyboard player, guitarist, and singer; continued her studies with Hiller in Leipzig, where she sang in his Grand Concerts from 1765; later became active as an actress in amateur productions there. She won the admiration of Goethe, who arranged for her to be made a Kammersängerin to the Duchess Anna Amalia in Weimar in 1776; she also appeared as an actress at the amateur court theater, frequently taking roles opposite Goethe in his own dramas. When the court theater became a professional ensemble in 1783, she devoted herself to singing, teaching, poetry, drawing, and painting. Her association with the court ended about 1788. She settled in Ilmenau about 1801. She created the title role in and wrote music for Goethe's singspiel *Die Fischerin* (1782); also wrote other stage music and publ. *25 Lieder in Musik gesetzt* for Voice and Piano (Weimar, 1786; includes one of the earliest settings of Goethe's *Der Erlkönig* from *Die Fischerin*) and (16) *Gesänge* for Voice and Piano (Weimar, 1794).
BIBL.: R. Keil, *Vor Hundert Jahren,* II: *C. S.: Ein Lebenskizze mit Beiträgen zur Geschichte der Genie-Periode* (Leipzig, 1875); H. Düntzer, *Charlotte von Stein und C. S.: Eine Vertheidigung* (Stuttgart, 1876); P. Pasig, *Goethe und Ilmenau mit einer Beigabe: Goethe und C. S.* (Ilmenau, 1902); H. Stümcke, *C. S.* (Bielefeld, 1904; 2nd ed., 1926).
(3) Johann Samuel Schroeter, pianist and composer; b. probably in Guben, c.1752; d. London, Nov. 1, 1788. He commenced musical studies with his father; about 1763, became a pupil of Hiller in Leipzig, where he sang in Hiller's concerts and later was active as a pianist (from 1767). He went to London with his family, then settled there; was organist at the German Chapel before being made music master to Queen Charlotte in 1782 in succession to J.S. Bach; eventually entered the service of the Prince of Wales (later King George IV). He publ. 12 concertos for Keyboard and Strings (London, 6 c.1774 and 6 c.1777), various sonatas and other chamber pieces, and some vocal music. His widow became attached to Haydn during Haydn's stay in London (1790–91), and sent him many impassioned letters, of which copies made by Haydn are extant.
BIBL.: K. Wolff, "J.S. S.," *Musical Quarterly* (July 1958).
(4) (Johann) Heinrich Schröter, violinist and composer; b. Warsaw, c.1760; d. probably in Paris, after 1782. He first made an impression as a soloist in a Dittersdorf violin concerto in Leipzig (1770); after appearing in concerts with his family in London, he went with his father to Hanau in 1779; gave concerts with his sister Marie in Frankfurt am Main (1780) and in Leipzig (1782) before disappearing from the musical scene. His extant works comprise 6 violin duets (London, c.1772), 6 *Duo concertans* for 2 Violins (Paris, c.1785), and 6 string trios (London and Paris, c.1786).
(5) Marie Henriette Schröter, singer; b. Leipzig, 1766; d. probably in Karlsruhe, after 1804. She studied with her father; gave concerts in Leipzig; went with her father to Hanau, where she became a court music teacher when she was only 13; was a Kammersängerin at the Darmstadt court until 1804.

Schröter, Christoph Gottlieb, German organist, music theorist, and composer; b. Hohnstein, near Schandau, Saxony, Aug. 10, 1699; d. Nordhausen, May 20, 1782. He began his musical studies with his father; in 1706 was sent to Dresden, where he became a soprano in the royal chapel and received instruction in keyboard instruments from the Kapellmeister; was made Ratsdiskantist in 1710, and later took instruction in organ and fugue at the Kreuzschule. After theological training in Leipzig (1717–18), he returned to Dresden as music copyist to Antonio Lotti; in 1719 he was made a secretary to a baron, in which capacity he traveled throughout Germany, the Netherlands, and England. He was a lecturer on music at the Univ. of Jena (1724–26); then was organist at the principal church in Minden (1726–32) and in Nordhausen (1732–82). In 1739 he became a member of Mizler's Societät der Musikalischen Wissenschaften of Leipzig. During the French occupation of Nordhausen in 1761, his home was ransacked and his library destroyed. He composed 5 cantata cycles, 4 Passions, a *Sieben Worte Jesu*, and various instrumental works, including serenades, concertos, sonatas, organ pieces, etc., almost all of which are lost. Schröter claimed priority for the invention of a hammer action for keyed string instruments, anticipating Cristofori's invention of the pianoforte; his argument is expounded with polemical passion in his paper "Umständliche Beschreibung eines neuerfundenen Clavierinstruments, auf welchem man in unterschiedenen Graden stark und schwach spielen kann," which was publ. in 1763 in Marpurg's *Kritische Briefe*; however, music historians rejected his arguments as chronologically invalid. In the field of music theory, he publ. an important paper, *Deutliche Anweisung zum General-Bass, in beständiger Veränderung des uns angebohrnen harmonischen Dreyklanges* (Halberstadt, 1772), in which he expounded the thesis that the major and minor triads are the sole fundamental chords in harmony; he also publ. *Christoph Gottlieb Schröters . . . Letzte Beschäftigung mit musicalischen Dinge, nebst sechs Temperatur-Plänen und einer Noten-Tafel* (Nordhausen, 1782) and other works in an egotistically assertive vein. **BIBL.:** R. N., "S.'s Piano Action," *Musical Opinion*, LXXXVII (1964).

Schröter, Leonhart, German composer; b. Torgau, c.1532; d. Magdeburg, c.1601. He was educated in Torgau, Annaberg, and Meissen; was town Kantor in Saalfeld (1561–71; 1573–76) and librarian at the Wolfenbüttel court (1571–73); then Kantor at Magdeburg's Alstadt Lateinschule (1576–95). His works include *55 geistliche Lieder* for 4 Voices (Wittenberg, 1562); *Der 12. und 124. Psalm Davids* for 4 Voices (Magdeburg, 1577); *Canticum sanctorum Ambrosii et Augustini Te Deum laudamus* for 8 Voices (Magdeburg, 1584); *Epithalamii cantilena . . . in honorem nuptiarum . . . Melchioris Papae* for 10 Voices (Magdeburg, 1587). **BIBL.:** G. Hofmann, *L. S.: Ein lutherischer Kantor zu Magdeburg* (diss., Univ. of Freiburg, 1932); H. Hasse, *Der erste herzogliche Bibliothekar: Ein Musiker: Bemerkungen über den Kantor und Komponisten L. S.* (Frankfurt am Main, 1972).

Schryock, Buren, American composer and conductor; b. Sheldon, Iowa, Dec. 13, 1881; d. San Diego, Jan. 20, 1974. At the age of 7, he moved to West Salem, Oreg., where he studied music and played organ in a church; occupied various teaching posts in Mich., Tex., Nebr., and Calif.; was conductor of the San Diego Sym. Orch. (1913–20) and the San Diego Opera (1920–36). **WORKS: OPERAS:** *Flavia* (1930–46); *Mary and John* (1948); *Nancy and Arthur* (1951); *Malena and Nordico* (1954); *Tanshu and Sanchi* (1955); also a Sym.; chamber music; piano pieces.

Schub, André-Michel, French-born American pianist; b. Paris, Dec. 26, 1952. He was taken to N.Y. as an infant and was taught piano by his mother; then became a pupil of Jascha Zayde. After attending Princeton Univ. (1968–69), he studied with Rudolf Serkin at the Curtis Inst. of Music in Philadelphia (1970–73). In 1974 he won 1st prize in the Naumburg competition and in 1977 the Avery Fisher Prize; after winning 1st prize in the Van Cliburn competition in 1981, he pursued an international career. His brilliant virtuoso technique is matched by a sensitive temperament; he shines in the Classic and Romantic repertoire.

Schubart, Christian Friedrich Daniel, prominent German instrumentalist, poet, journalist, writer on music, and composer; b. Obersontheim, Swabia, March 24, 1739; d. Stuttgart, Oct. 10, 1791. He revealed musical and literary gifts as a child, but his parents insisted that he pursue theological studies; he took courses in Nördlingen and Nuremberg, and also received some instruction in music from his father and G.W. Gruber; then was a student at the Univ. of Erlangen (1758–60), where he proved a contentious pupil. He served as organist and preceptor in Geisslingen (1763–69); was made court organist in Ludwigsburg in 1769, and also was harpsichordist at the opera and a music teacher before being banished for dissolute conduct in 1773; then went to Augsburg, where he brought out the periodical *Deutsche Chronik* in 1774, continuing its publication in Ulm until 1777. His journal was devoted to politics, literature, and music; his political writings won him many enemies, and in 1777 he was imprisoned by Duke Carl Eugen of Württemberg in the Hohenasperg fortress. During his imprisonment, he wrote extensively and also composed. He won particular distinction as a keyboardist and writer. As a composer, he was most successful with songs, most of which he set to his own texts. They are historically important for their contribution to the creation of the German lied of the folk type. A number of composers set his poems to music: Schubert's settings of his *Die Forelle* and *An mein Klavier* became famous. **WRITINGS:** *Ideen zu einer Ästhetik der Tonkunst* (1784–85; ed. by his son, Ludwig Schubart, Vienna, 1806); *Leben und Gesinnungen, von ihm selbst im Kerker aufgesetzt* (2 vols., Stuttgart, 1791–93). **BIBL.:** L. Schubart, *S.s Karakter* (Erlangen, 1798); idem, ed., *C.F.D. S.: Gesammelte Schriften und Schicksale* (Stuttgart, 1839–40); G. Hauff, *S. in seinen Leben und seinen Werken* (Stuttgart, 1885); E. Holzer, *S. als Musiker* (Stuttgart, 1905); D. Ossenkop, *C.F.D. S.'s Writings on Music* (diss., Columbia Univ., 1960); R. Harpster, "Genius in the 18th Century: C.F.D. S.'s 'Vom musikalischen Genie,'" *Current Musicology*, no. 15 (1973); R. Schollum, "S.s und Schuberts 'Forelle'-Vertonungen," *Musikerziehung*, XXVIII (1974–75).

Schubaur, Johann Lukas, German physician and composer; b. Lechfeld (baptized), Dec. 23, 1749; d. Munich, Nov. 15, 1815. He was the son of the painter Ignatius Schubaur; was orphaned quite young and then reared in the Zwiefalten monastery; after attending school in Augsburg, he studied at the Neuburg an der Donau theological seminary, where he received a thorough grounding in music; then went to Vienna and studied music while earning his livelihood by giving piano lessons and composing short pieces; took his medical degree in Ingolstadt, and then began his practice at the Barmherzige Brüder hospital in Neuburg an der Donau in 1775; shortly thereafter, he settled in Munich, where he became court physician and president of the medical commission. A dilettante composer, he won notable success with only one score, his singspiel *Die Dorfdeputierten* (Munich, May 8, 1783); his other singspiels, all produced in Munich, were *Melide oder Der Schiffer* Sept. 24, 1782), *Das Lustlager* (1784), and *Die treuen Köhler* (Sept. 29, 1786). **BIBL.:** E. Reipschläger, *S., Danzi und Poissl als Opernkomponisten* (diss., Univ. of Rostock, 1911).

Schubel, Max, American composer; b. N.Y., April 11, 1932. He was educated at N.Y. Univ. (graduated, 1953); his composition teachers were Charles Haubiel in N.Y. and Frank Martin. In 1960 he formed OPUS ONE, an independent recording company dedicated to producing non-commercial concert and electronic music; in 1982 its headquarters was moved to a small cabin he built on a remote mountain in the Catskills. From 1954 Schubel spent much of his time on his small island in Moosehead Lake, Maine, where he became interested in environmental protection and self-sufficient living; developed skills in recycling, composting, raising chickens, and developing non-electrical sources of power and water. As a composer, he received 2 N.E.A. awards (1974, 1982) and a Ford Foundation Recording Grant (1971); also was in residence at the Mac-Dowell Colony, the Wurlitzer Foundation, Ossabaw Island, and Wolf Trap.

WORKS: ORCH.: *Fracture* (1969); *Divertimento* for Piano, Trumpet, and Chamber Orch. (1980; rev. 1987); *Guale* (1984); *Punch and Judie* for Chamber Orch. (1980); *Scherzo* (1987); *SuperScherzo* for Chamber Orch. (1988–89). **CHAMBER:** *Insected Surfaces*, concerto for Clarinet, Cello, Bass, Harpsichord, and Piano (1965); *Exotica* for Cello and Harpsichord (1967); 2 string quartets (1968, 1980); *Zing and ZipZap* for Chamber Ensemble (1986); *The Spoors of Time* for Viola and Piano (1986); Septet (1988); *Dragondust* for Clarinet and Piano (1988); String Quintet (1989); Trio for Violin, Cello, and Piano (1989). **PIANO:** *Everybody's Favourite Rag* (1979); *Miraplex* (1979); *B Natural* for Prepared Piano (1980); *Stable Turner* (1981); *Klish Klash* for Prepared Piano (1982); *Dragonseed* (1986).

Schubert, family of German musicians:

(1) Anton Schubert, double-bass player; b. Dresden, June 28, 1766; d. there, Oct. 12, 1853. He was a member of the Dresden Court Orch. from 1790 until he retired in 1840.

(2) Franz Anton Schubert, double-bass player and composer, brother of the preceding; b. Dresden, July 20, 1768; d. there, March 5, 1827. He was named director of the Italian Opera in 1808 and royal church composer in 1814 in Dresden. He composed much church music.

(3) Franz Schubert, violinist and composer, son of the preceding; b. Dresden, July 22, 1808; d. there, April 12, 1878. He studied with his father, Rottmeier, and L. Haase; after further training with C.P. Lafont in Paris, he returned to Dresden as a member of the Court Orch. in 1823, becoming its concertmaster in 1861. With F.A. Kummer, he wrote some duos for cello; also composed 12 bagatelles, *Die Biene* being the most successful in his day. His wife was the soprano **Maschinka Schubert** (b. Reval, Aug. 25, 1815; d. Dresden, Sept. 20, 1882), the daughter of the Kapellmeister **Georg Abraham Schneider** (1770–1839) and the singer Caroline Portmann; she was a pupil of her mother and of Giulio Bordogni; made her debut in London (1832), and later was a leading singer at the Dresden Court Opera. Their daughter was the soprano **Georgine Schubert** (b. Dresden, Oct. 28, 1840; d. Strelitz, Dec. 26, 1878); she studied with her mother, and later with Jenny Lind and Manuel García; made her operatic debut in *La Sonnambula* in Hamburg (1839), and then sang widely in both opera and concert.

Schubert, Ferdinand (Lukas), Austrian teacher and composer, brother of **Franz (Peter) Schubert;** b. Lichtenthal, near Vienna, Oct. 18, 1794; d. Vienna, Feb. 26, 1859. He began his musical training with his father; after taking instruction at Vienna's Normalhauptschule (1807–8), he taught at his father's school. He was an assistant teacher (1810–16) and a teacher (1816–24) at the Alsergrund orphanage; then was headmaster (1824–51) and director (1851–59) of the Normalhauptschule. He was devoted to his brother and took charge of his MSS after his death. He wrote 2 singspiels and much sacred music, including 4 masses and a Requiem.

Schubert, Franz (Peter), great Austrian composer, a supreme melodist and an inspired master of lieder, brother of **Ferdinand (Lukas) Schubert;** b. Himmelpfortgrund (then a suburb of Vienna and now a part of that city), Jan. 31, 1797; d. Vienna, Nov. 19, 1828. He studied violin with his father, a schoolmaster, and received instruction on the piano from his brother Ignaz; in addition, he took lessons in piano, organ, singing, and theory with Holzer, the choirmaster. In 1808 he became a member of the Vienna Imperial Court chapel choir, and also entered the Stadtkonvict, a training school for court singers, where he studied music with the Imperial Court organist Wenzel Ruzicka and with the famous court composer Salieri. He played violin in the school orch. and conducted it whenever an occasion called for it. He began composing in school; wrote a *Fantasie* for Piano, 4-hands, several chamber music works, orch. overtures, and the unfinished singspiel *Der Spiegelritter.*

His 1st song, *Hagars Klage*, is dated March 30, 1811. In 1813 he left the Stadtkonvict, but Salieri, evidently impressed by his talent, continued to give him instruction. He further attended a training college for teachers in Vienna, and then became an instructor at his father's school. Although very young, he began writing works in large forms; between 1813 and 1816 he composed 5 syms., 4 masses, several string quartets, and also some stage music. He also wrote his 1st opera, *Des Teufels Lustschloss.* It was then that he wrote some of his most famous lieder. He was only 17 when he wrote *Gretchen am Spinnrade*, and only 18 when he composed the overpowering dramatic song *Erlkönig.* The prodigious facility that Schubert displayed is without equal; during the year 1815 he composed about 140 songs; on a single day, Oct. 15, he wrote 8 lieder. From his sketches, it is possible to follow his method of composition; he would write the melody 1st, indicate the harmony, and then write out the song in full; often he subjected the finished work to several revisions. He became friendly with the poets Johann Mayrhofer and Franz von Schober, and set a number of their poems to music. In 1817 he lodged with Schober and his widowed mother, arranging to pay for his keep from his meager resources. It was then that he met the noted baritone Johann Michael Vogl, who put many of Schubert's songs on his concert programs. Outstanding lieder from this period include the 3 *Harfenspieler, Der Wanderer, Der Tod und das Mädchen, Ganymed, An die Musik,* and *Die Forelle.* During the summer of 1818, he served as music tutor to the family of Count Esterházy at Zélesz in Hungary. On March 1, 1818, his Overture in C major, "in the Italian style," became his 1st orch. work to be accorded a public performance in Vienna. On June 14, 1820, his singspiel *Die Zwillingsbrüder* was performed at the Kärnthnertortheater in Vienna. On Aug. 19, 1820, a score of his incidental music for the play *Die Zauberharfe* was heard at the Theater an der Wien; this score contains an overture that became subsequently popular in concert performances under the name *Rosamunde Overture*, although it was not composed for the score to the play *Rosamunde, Fürstin von Zypern*, which was produced at the Theater an der Wien more than 3 years later, on Dec. 20, 1823. Although Schubert still had difficulties in earning a living, he formed a circle of influential friends in Vienna, and appeared as a pianist at private gatherings; sometimes he sang his songs, accompanying himself at the keyboard; he was also able to publ. some of his songs. A mystery is attached to his most famous work, begun in 1822, the Sym. in B minor, known popularly as the "Unfinished" Sym. Only 2 movements are known to exist; portions of the 3rd movement, a Scherzo, remain in sketches. What prevented him from finishing it? Speculations are as rife as they are worthless, particularly since he was usually careful in completing a work before embarking on another composition. A hundred years after Schubert's death, an enterprising phonograph company arranged a contest for the completion of the "Unfinished" Sym.; prizes were given, but the products delivered, even some signed by well-known composers, were spectacularly poor. In 1823 he completed his masterly song cycle *Die schöne Müllerin*; in 1824 he once again spent the summer as a private tutor in Count Esterházy's employ in Zélesz. In 1827 he wrote another remarkable song cycle, *Die Winterreise.* On March 26, 1828, he presented in Vienna a public concert of his works. From that year, which proved to be his last, date such masterpieces as the piano sonatas in C minor, A major, and B-flat major; the String Quintet in C major; and the 2 books of songs collectively known as the *Schwanengesang.* His health was frail, and he moved to the lodgings of his brother Ferdinand. On the afternoon of Nov. 19, 1828, Schubert died, at the age of 31. For a thorough account of his illness, see E. Sams's "Schubert's Illness Reexamined," *Musical Times* (Jan. 1980). There is no incontrovertible evidence that Schubert died of syphilis; from all accounts of his daily life, he was never promiscuous, and was not known to engage in unseemly liaisons.

Schubert is often described as the creator of the genre of strophic lieder; this summary description is chronologically untenable; Zelter wrote strophic lieder a generation before him. Goethe, whose poems were set to music by Zelter, Beethoven, and Schubert, favored Zelter's settings. What Schubert truly created was an incomparably beautiful florilegium of lieder typifying the era of German Romantic sentiment and conveying deeply felt emotions, ranging from peaceful joy to enlightened melancholy, from philosophic meditation to throbbing drama; the poems he selected for his settings were expressive of such passing moods. He set to music 72 poems by Goethe, 47 by Mayrhofer, 46 by Schiller, 44 by Wilhelm Müller, 28 by Matthison, 23 by Hölty, 22 by Kosegarten, 13 by Körtner, 12 by Schober, and 6 by Heine.

In a sense, Schubert's *Moments musicaux*, *Impromptus*, and other piano works are songs without texts; on several occasions he used musical material from his songs for instrumental works, as in the great *Wanderer Fantasia* for Piano, based on his song *Der Wanderer*, and the "Forellen" Piano Quintet, in which the 4th movement is a set of variations on the song *Die Forelle*. His String Quartet in D minor includes a set of variations on his song *Der Tod und das Mädchen* in its 2nd movement. But Schubert was not given to large theater works and oratorios. Even his extended works in sonata form are not conceived on a grand scale but, rather, are constructed according to the symmetry of recapitulations; his music captivates the listeners not by recurring variety but by the recalled felicities; time and again in his MSS, he simply indicates the repetition of a group of bars by number. Therein lies the immense difference between Schubert and Schumann, both Romantic poets of music: where Schubert was satisfied with reminding the listener of a passage already heard, Schumann variegates. Schubert was indeed the most symmetrical composer in the era of free-flowing musical prose and musical poetry.

Much confusion exists in the numbering of Schubert's syms., the last being listed in most catalogues as No. 9; the missing uncounted sym. is No. 7, which exists as a full draft, in 4 movements, of which the 1st 110 bars are fully scored; several "completions" exist, the 1st by John Francis Barnett, made in 1883; the 2nd by Felix Weingartner, manufactured in 1934; and the 3rd, and perhaps the most Schubertomorphic, constructed with artful imitation of Schubert's ways and means, by Brian Newbould, in 1977. The "Unfinished" Sym. is then No. 8. There remains the "Gmunden" or "Gastein" Sym., so named because Schubert was supposed to have written it in Gastein, in the Tirol, in 1825. It was long regarded as irretrievably lost, but was eventually identified with No. 9, the great C major Sym. Incredibly, as late as 1978 there came to light in a somehow overlooked pile of music in the archives of the Vienna Stadtsbibliothek a sketch of still another Schubert sym., composed during the last months of his life; this insubstantial but magically tempting waft of Schubert's genius was completed by Brian Newbould; it is numbered as his 10th.

The recognition of Schubert's greatness was astonishingly slow. Fully 40 years elapsed before the discovery of the MS of the "Unfinished" Sym. Posthumous performances were the rule for his sym. premieres, and the publication of his syms. was exceedingly tardy. Schumann, ever sensitive to great talent, was eager to salute the kindred genius in Schubert's syms., about whose "Heavenly length" he so admiringly complained. But it took half a century for Schubert to become firmly established in music history as one of the great Sch's (with Chopin phonetically counted in).

WORKS: In the list of Schubert's works given below, the D. numbers are those established by O. Deutsch (with D. Wakeling) in his *Schubert: Thematic Catalogue of All His Works in Chronological Order* (London, 1951; in German as *Franz Schubert: Thematisches Verzeichnis seiner Werke in chronologischer Folge . . . .*, publ. in the *Neue Ausgabe sämtlicher Werke* of Schubert in a rev. ed. in 1978).

STAGE: *Der Spiegelritter*, D.11, singspiel (1811–12; unfinished; only the Overture and Act I completed; 1st perf. by the Swiss Radio, Dec. 11, 1949); *Des Teufels Lustschloss*, D.84, opera (1813–15; 2 versions; Vienna, Dec. 12, 1879); *Adrast*,

D.137, opera (1817–19; unfinished; Vienna, Dec. 13, 1868); *Der vierjährige Posten*, D.190, singspiel (1815; Dresden, Sept. 23, 1896); *Fernando*, D.220, singspiel (1815; Vienna, April 13, 1907); *Claudine von Villa Bella*, D.239, singspiel (1815; unfinished; only the Overture and Act I completed; Vienna, April 26, 1913); *Die Freunde von Salamanka*, D.326, singspiel (1815; Halle, May 6, 1928); Die Bürgschaft, D.435, opera (1816; unfinished; only Acts I and II completed; Vienna, March 7, 1908); *Die Zauberharfe*, D.644, melodrama (1820; Theater an der Wien, Vienna, Aug. 19, 1820); *Die Zwillingsbrüder*, D.647, singspiel (1819; Kärnthnertortheater, Vienna, June 14, 1820); *Sakuntala*, D.701, opera (1820; only sketches for Acts I and II; these 1st perf. in Vienna, June 12, 1971); Duet and Aria for Hérold's *Das Zauberglöckchen (La Clochette)*, D.723 (1821; Vienna, June 20, 1821); *Alfonso und Estrella*, D.732, opera (1821–22; Weimar, June 24, 1854); *Die Verschworenen (Der häusliche Krieg)*, D.787, singspiel (1823; Vienna, March 1, 1861); *Rüdiger*, D.791, opera (1823; sketches only; these 1st perf. in Vienna, Jan. 5, 1868); *Fierabras*, D.796, opera (1823; Karlsruhe, Feb. 9, 1897); *Rosamunde, Fürstin von Zypern*, D.797, incidental music to the play by H. von Chézy (1823; Theater an der Wien, Vienna, Dec. 20, 1823); *Der Graf von Gleichen*, D.918, opera (1827; sketches only); *Der Minnesänger*, D.981, singspiel (date unknown; unfinished; not extant).

CHURCH: *Salve Regina* in F major for Soprano, Organ, and Orch., D.27 (1812); Kyrie in D minor for Soprano, Tenor, Choir, Organ, and Orch., D.31 (1812); Kyrie in B-flat major for Choir, D.45 (1813); Kyrie in D minor for Soprano, Alto, Tenor, Bass, Choir, and Orch., D.49 (1813); Kyrie in F major for Choir, Organ, and Orch., D.66 (1813); Mass No. 1, in F major, for 2 Sopranos, Alto, 2 Tenors, Bass, Choir, Organ, and Orch., D.105 (1814); *Salve Regina* in B-flat major for Tenor, Organ, and Orch., D.106 (1814); *Totus in corde langueo*, offertory in C major for Soprano or Tenor, Clarinet or Violin, Organ, and Orch., D.136 (1815); Mass No. 2, in G. major, for Soprano, Tenor, Bass, Choir, Organ, and Strings, D.167 (1815); *Stabat Mater* in G minor for Choir, Organ, and Orch., D.175 (1815); *Tres sunt*, offertory in A minor for Choir, Organ, and Orch., D.181 (1815); *Benedictus es, Domine*, gradual in C major for Choir, Organ, and Orch., D.184 (1815); *Dona nobis pacem* in F major for Bass, Choir, Organ, and Orch., D.185 (alternative movement for D.105; 1815); *Salve Regina* (offertorium) in F major for Soprano, Organ, and Orch., D.223 (2 versions, 1815 and 1823); Mass No. 3, in B-flat major, for Soprano, Alto, Tenor, Bass, Choir, Organ, and Orch., D.324 (1815); *Deutsches Salve Regina (Hymne an die heilige Mutter Gottes)* in F major for Choir and Organ, D.379 (1816); *Stabat Mater* (oratorio) in F major/F minor for Soprano, Tenor, Bass, Choir, and Orch., D.383 (1816); *Salve Regina* in B-flat major for Choir, D.386 (1816); Mass No. 4, in C major, for Soprano, Alto, Tenor, Bass, Choir, Organ, and Orch., D.452 (1816); *Tantum ergo* in C major for Soprano, Choir, Organ, and Orch., D.460 (1816); *Tantum ergo* in C major for Soprano, Alto, Tenor, Bass, Choir, and Orch., D.461 (1816); Magnificat in C major for Soprano, Alto, Tenor, Bass, Choir, Organ, and Orch., D.486 (1815); *Auguste jam coelestium* in G major for Soprano, Tenor, and Orch., D.488 (1816); *Deutsches Requiem (Deutsche Trauermesse)* in G minor for Soprano, Alto, Tenor, Bass, Choir, and Organ, D.621 (1818); *Salve Regina* (offertorium) in A major for Soprano and Strings, D.676 (1819); Mass No. 5, in A-flat major, for Soprano, Alto, Tenor, Bass, Choir, Organ, and Orch., D.678 (2 versions, 1819–22); *Tantum ergo* in B-flat major for Soprano, Alto, Tenor, Bass, Choir, Organ, and Orch., D.730 (1821); *Tantum ergo* in C major for Choir, Organ, and Orch., D.739 (1814); *Tantum ergo* in D major for Choir, Organ, and Orch., D.750 (1822); *Salve Regina* in C major for 2 Tenors and 2 Basses, D.811 (1824); *Deutsche Messe* for Choir and Organ, or Choir, Organ, and Orch., D.872 (1827); Mass No. 6, in E-flat major, for Soprano, Alto, Tenor, Bass, Choir, and Orch., D.950 (1828); Benedictus in A minor for Soprano, Alto, Tenor, Bass, Choir, Organ, and Orch., D.961 (alternative movement for D.452; 1828); *Tantum ergo* in E-flat major for Soprano,

Alto, Tenor, Bass, Choir, and Orch., D.962 (1828); *Intende voci*, offertory in B-flat major for Tenor, Choir, and Orch., D.963 (1828); etc.

OTHER VOCAL: *Quell' innocente figlio*, D.17 (many versions, 1812); *Entra l'uomo allor che nasce*, D.33 (many versions, 1812); *Te solo adoro* for Soprano, Alto, Tenor, and Bass, D.34 (1812); *Serbate, o dei custodi*, D.35 (2 versions, 1812); *Die Advokaten* for Men's Voices and Piano, D.37 (1812); *Totengräberlied* for Men's Voices, D.38 (1813); *Dreifach ist der Schritt der Zeit* for Men's Voices, D.43 (1813); *Dithyrambe*, D.47 (1813; fragment only); *Unendliche Freude* for Men's Voices, D.51 (1813); *Vorüber die stöhnende Klage* for Men's Voices, D.53 (1813); *Unendliche Freude*, canon for Men's Voices, D.54 (1813); *Selig durch die Liebe* for Men's Voices, D.55 (1813); *Hier strecket der wallende Pilger* for Men's Voices, D.57 (1813); *Dessen Fahne Donnerstürme wallte* for Men's Voices, D.58 (1813); *Hier umarmen sich getreue Gatten* for Men's Voices, D.60 (1813); *Ein jugendlicher Maienschwung*, D.61 (1813); *Thronend auf erhabnem Sitz* for Men's Voices, D.62 (1813); *Wer die steile Sternenbahn* for Men's Voices, D.63 (1813); *Majestätsche Sonnenrosse* for Men's Voices, D.64 (1813); *Schmerz verzerret ihr Gesicht*, canon, D.65 (1813; sketch only); *Frisch atmet des Morgens lebendiger Hauch* for Men's Voices, D.67 (1813); *Dreifach ist der Schritt der Zeit*, D.69 (1813); *Dreifach ist der Schritt der Zeit (Ewig still steht die Vergangenheit)*, canon for Men's Voices, D.70 (1813); *Die zwei Tugendwege* for Men's Voices, D.71 (1813); *Trinklied (Freunde, sammelt euch im Kreise)* for Bass, Men's Voices, and Piano, D.75 (1813); *Zur Namensfeier meines Vaters* for Men's Voices and Guitar, D.80 (1813); *Verschwunden sind die Schmerzen*, canon for Men's Voices, D.88 (1813); *Wer ist gross?* for Bass, Men's Voices, and Orch., D.110 (1814); *Mailied (Grüner wird die Au)* for Men's Voices, D.129 (1815); *Der Schnee zerrinnt*, canon, D.130 (1815); *Lacrimoso son io*, canon, D.131 (2 versions, 1815); *Lied beim Rundetanz*, D.132 (1815?); *Lied im Freien*, D.133 (1815?); *Klage um Ali Bey* for Men's Voices, D.140 (1815); *Bardengesang* for Men's Voices, D.147 (1816); *Trinklied (Brüder! unser Erdenwallen)* for Tenor, Men's Voices, and Piano, D.148 (1815); *Nun lasst uns den Leib begraben (Begrabnislied)* for Choir and Piano, D.168 (1815); *Osterlied* for Choir and Piano, D.168a (originally D.987; 1815); *Trinklied vor der Schlacht* for 2 Unison Choruses and Piano, D.169 (1815); *Schwertlied* for Voice, Unison Chorus, and Piano, D.170 (1815); *Trinklied (Ihr Freunde und du gold'ner Wein)* for Voice, Unison Chorus, and Piano, D.183 (1815); *An die Freude* for Voice, Unison Chorus, and Piano, D.189 (1815); *Mailied (Grüner wird die Au)* for 2 Voices, D.199 (1815); *Mailied (Der Schnee zerrinnt)* for 2 Voices, D.202 (1815); *Der Morgenstern* for 2 Voices, D.203 (1815); *Jägerlied* for 2 Voices, D.204 (1815); *Lützows wilde Jagd* for 2 Voices, D.205 (1815); *Hymne an den Unendlichen* for Choir and Piano, D.232 (1815); *Das Abendrot* for Men's Voices and Piano, D.236 (1815); *Trinklied im Winter* for Men's Voices, D.242 (1815); *Frühlingslied (Die Luft ist blau)* for Men's Voices, D.243 (1815); *Willkommen, lieber schöner Mai*, canon for 3 Voices, D.244 (2 versions, 1815); *Punschlied: Im Norden zu singen* for 2 Voices, D.253 (1815); *Trinklied (Auf! jeder sei nun froh)* for Men's Voices and Piano, D.267 (1815); *Bergknappenlied* for Men's Voices and Piano, D.268 (1815); *Das Leben*, D.269 (2 versions, 1815); *Punschlied (Vier Elemente, innig gesellt)* for Men's Voices and Piano, D.277 (1815); *Namensfeier für Franz Michael Vierthaler (Gratulations Kantate)* for Soprano, Tenor, Bass, Chorus, and Orch., D.294 (1815); *Das Grab*, D.329a (1815; sketch only); *Das Grab* for 4 Voices and Piano, D.330 (1815); *Der Entfernten* for Men's Voices, D.331 (1816?); *Die Einsiedelei* for Men's Voices, D.337 (1816?); *An den Frühling* for Men's Voices, D.338 (1816?); *Amors Macht*, D.339 (1816?); *Badelied*, D.340 (1816?); *Sylphen*, D.341 (1816?); *Trinklied (Funkelnd im Becher)* for Men's Voices, D.356 (1816); *Gold'ner Schein*, canon for 3 Voices, D.357 (1816); *Fischerlied* for Men's Voices, D.364 (1816?); *Das Grab* for Men's Voices and Piano, D.377 (1816); *Die Schlacht*, D.387 (1816; sketch only); *Beitrag zur fünfzig jährigen Jubelfeier des Herrn Salieri* for Tenor, Men's Voices, and

Piano, D.407 (1816); *Naturgenuss* for Men's Voices and Piano, D.422 (1822?); *Andenken (Ich denke dein, wenn durch den Hain)* for Men's Voices, D.423 (1816); *Erinnerungen (Am Seegestad)* for Men's Voices, D.424 (1816); *Lebensbild* for Men's Voices, D.425 (1816; not extant); *Trinklied (Herr Bacchus ist ein braver Mann)* for Men's Voices, D.426 (1816; not extant); *Trinklied im Mai* for Men's Voices, D.427 (1816); *Widerhall (Auf ewig dein)* for Men's Voices, D.428 (1816); *An die Sonne* for Choir and Piano, D.439 (1816); *Chor der Engel* for Choir, D.440 (1816); *Das grosse Halleluja* for Chorus and Piano, D.442 (1816); *Schlachtlied* for Chorus and Piano, D.443 (1816); *Prometheus*, cantata for Soprano, Bass, Chorus, and Orch., D.451 (1816; not extant); *Kantate zu Ehren von Josef Spendou* for 2 Sopranos, Bass, Choir, and Orch., D.472 (1816); *Der Geistertanz* for Men's Voices, D.494 (1816); *La pastorella al prato* for Men's Voices and Piano, D.513 (1817?); *Jagdlied* for Unison Voices and Piano, D.521 (1817); *Gesang der Geister über den Wassern* for Men's Voices, D.538 (1817); *Das Grab* for Unison Voices and Piano, D.569 (1817); *Lied im Freien* for Men's Voices, D.572 (1817); *Das Dörfchen*, D.598 (originally D.641; 1817; sketch only); *Die Geselligkeit (Lebenslust)* for Choir and Piano, D.609 (1818); *Leise, leise lasst uns singen* for Men's Voices, D.635 (1819?); *Viel tausend Sterne prangen* for Choir and Piano, D.642 (1812?); *Das Grab* for Choir, D.643a (1819); *Sehnsucht (Nur wer die Sehnsucht kennt)* for Men's Voices, D.656 (1819); *Ruhe, schönstes Gluck der Erde* for Men's Voices, D.657 (1819); *Kantate zum Geburtstag des Sängers Johann Michael Vogl (Der Frühlingsmorgen)* for Women's and Men's Voices and Piano, D.666 (1819); *Lazarus, oder Die Feier der Auferstehung*, oratorio for 3 Sopranos, 2 Tenors, Bass, Choir, and Orch., D.689 (1820; unfinished); *Der 23. Psalm* for Women's Voices and Piano, D.706 (1820); *Frühlingsgesang* for Men's Voices, D.709 (1822); *Im Gegenwärtigen Vergangenes* for Men's Voices and Piano, D.710 (1821); *Gesang der Geister über den Wassern* for Men's Voices, 2 Violas, 2 Cellos, and 2 Double Basses, D.714 (originally D.704 as a sketch; 1820–21); *Die Nachtigall* for Men's Voices and Piano, D.724 (1821); *Frühlingsgesang* for Men's Voices and Piano, D.740 (1822); *Geist der Liebe (Der Abend schleiert Flur und Hain)* for Men's Voices and Piano, D.747 (1822); *Am Geburtstag des Kaisers*, cantata for Soprano, Alto, Tenor, Bass, Choir, and Orch., D.748 (1822); *Gott in der Natur* for Women's Voices and Piano, D.757 (1822); *Des Tages Weihe* for Choir and Piano, D.763 (1822); *Ich hab' in mich gesogen*, D.778b (1823?; sketch only); *Gondelfahrer* for Men's Voices and Piano, D.809 (1824); *Gebet* for Choir and Piano, D.815 (1824); *Lied eines Kriegers* for Bass, Unison Voices, and Piano, D.822 (1824); *Wehmut* for Men's Voices, D.825 (1826); *Ewige Liebe* for Men's Voices, D.825a (1826); *Flucht* for Men's Voices, D.825b (1825); *Der Tanz* for Choir and Piano, D.826 (1828); *Bootgesang* for Men's Voices and Piano, D.835 (1825); *Coronach (Totengesang der Frauen und Mädchen)* for Women's Voices and Piano, D.836 (1825); *Trinklied aus dem 16. Jahrhundert* for Men's Voices, D.847 (1825); *Nachtmusik* for Men's Voices, D.848 (1825); *Widerspruch* for Men's Voices and Piano, D.865 (1826); *Canon* for 6 Voices, D.873 (1826?; sketch only); *Nachklänge* for Men's Voices, D.873a (1826?; sketch only); *Die Allmacht* for Choir and Piano, D.875a (1826; sketch only); *Mondenschein* for Men's Voices and Piano, D.875 (1826); *Nachthelle* for Tenor, Men's Voices, and Piano, D.892 (1826); *Grab und Mond* for Men's Voices, D.893 (1826); *Wein und Liebe* for Men's Voices, D.901 (1827); *Zur guten Nacht* for Baritone, Men's Voices, and Piano, D.903 (1827); *Schlachtlied* for Men's Voices, D.912 (1827); *Nachtgesang im Walde* for Men's Voices and 4 Horns, D.913 (1827); *Frühlingslied* for Men's Voices, D.914 (1827); *Das stille Lied* for Men's Voices, D.916 (1827; sketch only); *Ständchen*, D.920 (originally D.921; 2 versions, 1827); *Der Hochzeitsbraten* for Soprano, Tenor, Bass, and Piano, D.930 (1827); *Kantate für Irene Kiesewetter* for 2 Tenors, 2 Basses, Choir, and Piano, 4-hands, D.936 (1827); *Hymnus an den Heiligen Geist*, D.941 (now listed as D.948; 2 versions, 1828); *Mirjams Siegesgesang* for Soprano, Choir, and Piano, D.942 (1828); *Der 92. Psalm: Lied für den Sabbath* for Soprano, Alto, Tenor, Baritone, Bass, and Choir, D.953 (1828); *Glaube, Hoffnung und Liebe* for 2 Tenors, 2 Basses, Choir, and Wind Instruments or Piano, D.954 (1828); *Gott im Ungewitter* for Choir and Piano, D.985 (1827?); *Gott der Weltschopfer* for Choir and Piano, D.986 (1827?); *Liebe säuseln die Blätter,* canon for 3 Voices, D.988 (1815?).

SONGS: Sketch for a song, D.1a (no text; 1810?); *Hagars Klage,* D.5 (Schücking; 1811); *Des Mädchens Klage,* D.6 (Schiller; 1811?); *Leichenfantasie,* D.7 (Schiller; 1811?); *Der Vatermörder,* D.10 (Pfeffel; 1811); *Der Geistertanz,* D.15 and 15a (fragments only; Matthisson; 1812?); *Quell'innocente figlio,* D.17 (Metastasio; 1812); *Klaglied,* D.23 (Rochlitz; 1812); *Der Jüngling am Bache,* D.30 (Schiller; 1812); *Entra l'uomo allor che nasce,* D.33 (Metastasio; 1812); *Serbate, o dei custodi,* D.35 (Metastasio; 1812); *Lebenstraum,* D.39 (Baumberg; 1810?); *Misero pargoletto,* D.42 (several versions; Metastasio; 1813?); *Totengräberlied,* D.44 (Hölty; 1813); *Die Schatten,* D.50 (Matthisson; 1813); *Sehnsucht,* D.52 (Schiller; 1813); *Verklärung,* D.59 (Pope; Herder, tr.; 1813); *Thekla: Eine Geisterstimme,* D.73 (Schiller; 1813); *Pensa, che questo istante,* D.76 (2 versions; Metastasio; 1813); *Der Taucher,* D.77 (2 versions; 2nd version originally D.111; Schiller; 1st version, 1813–14; 2nd version, 1815); *Son fra l'onde,* D.78 (Metastasio; 1813); *Auf den Sieg der Deutschen,* D.81, with 2 Violins and Cello (Schubert?; 1813); *Zur Namensfeier des Herrn Andreas Siller,* D.83, with Violin and Harp (1813); *Don Gayseros,* D.93 (3 versions: *Don Gayseros, Don Gayseros; Nächtens klang die süsse Laute; An dem jungen Morgenhimmel;* F. de la Motte Fouqué; 1815?); *Adelaide,* D.95 (Matthisson; 1814); *Trost: An Elisa,* D.97 (Matthisson; 1814); *Erinnerungen,* D.98 (2 versions; Matthisson; 1814); *Andenken,* D.99 (Matthisson; 1814); *Geisternähe,* D.100 (Matthisson; 1814); *Erinnerung,* D.101 (Matthisson; 1814); *Die Betende,* D.102 (Matthisson; 1814); *Die Befreier Europas in Paris,* D.104 (3 versions; Mikan; 1814); *Lied aus der Ferne,* D.107 (2 versions; Matthisson; 1814); *Der Abend,* D.108 (Matthisson; 1814); *Lied der Liebe,* D.109 (Matthisson; 1814); *An Emma,* D.113 (3 versions; Schiller; 1814); *Romanze,* D.114 (2 versions; Matthisson; 1814); *An Laura, als sie Klopstocks Auferstehungslied sang,* D.115 (Matthisson; 1814); *Der Geistertanz,* D.116 (Matthisson; 1814); *Das Mädchen aus der Fremde,* D.117 (Schiller; 1814); *Gretchen am Spinnrade,* D.118 (Goethe; 1814); *Nachtgesang,* D.119 (Goethe; 1814); *Trost in Tränen,* D.120 (Goethe; 1814); *Schäfers Klagelied,* D.121 (2 versions; Goethe; 1814); *Ammenlied,* D.122 (Lubi; 1814); *Sehnsucht,* D.123 (Goethe; 1814; *Am See,* D.124 (2 versions; Mayrhofer; 1814); *Szene aus Goethes Faust,* D.126, with 4 Voices (2 versions; Goethe; 1814); *Ballade,* D.134 (Kenner; 1815?); *Rastlose Liebe,* D.138 (2 versions; Goethe; 1st version, 1815; 2nd version, 1821); *Der Mondabend,* D.141 (Kumpf; 1815); *Geistes-Gruss,* D.142 (6 versions; Goethe; 1815?); *Genügsamkeit,* D.143 (Schober; 1815); *Romanze,* D.144 (unfinished; F. Graf zu Stolberg-Stolberg; 1816); *Der Sänger,* D.149 (2 versions; Goethe; 1815); *Lodas Gespenst,* D.150 (Ossian; E. Baron de Harold, tr.; 1816); *Auf einen Kirchhof,* D.151 (Schlechta; 1815); *Minona,* D.152 (Bertrand; 1815); *Als ich sie erröten sah,* D.153 (Ehrlich; 1815); *Das Bild,* D.155 (1815); *Die Erwartung,* D.159 (2 versions; Schiller; 1816); *Am Flusse,* D.160 (Goethe; 1815); *An Mignon,* D.161 (2 versions; Goethe; 1815); *Nähe des Geliebten,* D.162 (2 versions; Goethe; 1815); *Sängers Morgenlied,* D.163 (Körner; 1815); *Liebesrausch,* D.164 (fragment only; Körner; 1815); *Sängers Morgenlied,* D.165 (Körner; 1815); *Amphiaraos,* D.166 (Körner; 1815); *Trinklied vor der Schlacht,* D.169, for 2 Unison Choruses (Körner; 1815); *Schwertlied,* D.170, with Unison Chorus (Körner; 1815); *Gebet während der Schlacht,* D.171 (Körner; 1815); *Der Morgenstern,* D.172 (fragment only; Körner; 1815); *Das war ich,* D.174 (2 versions; Körner; 1st version, 1815; 2nd version, 1816); *Die Sterne,* D.176 (Fellinger; 1815); *VergeblicheLiebe,* D.177 (Bernard; 1815); *Liebesrausch,* D.179 (Körner; 1815); *Sehnsucht der Liebe,* D.180 (2 versions; Körner; 1815; 2nd version not extant); *Die erste Liebe,* D.182 (Fellinger; 1815); *Trinklied,* D.183, with Unison Chorus (Zettler; 1815); *Die Sterbende,* D.186 (Matthisson; 1815); *Stimme der Liebe,* D.187 (Matthisson; 1815); *Naturgenuss,* D.188 (Matthisson; 1815); *An die*

Freude, D.189, with Unison Chorus (Schiller; 1815); *Des Mädchens Klage,* D.191 (2 versions; Schiller; 1815); *Der Jüngling am Bache,* D.192 (Schiller; 1815); *An den Mond,* D.193 (Hölty; 1815); *Die Mainacht,* D.194 (Hölty; 1815); *Amalia,* D.195 (Schiller; 1815); *An die Nachtigall,* D.196 (Hölty; 1815); *An die Apfelbäume, wo ich Julien erblickte,* D.197 (Hölty; 1815); *Seufzer,* D.198 (Hölty; 1815); *Auf den Tod einer Nachtigall,* D.201 (fragment only; Hölty; 1815); *Das Traumbild,* D.204a (Hölty; 1815; not extant); *Liebeständelei,* D.206 (Körner; 1815); *Der Liebende,* D.207 (Hölty; 1815); *Die Nonne,* D.208 (2 versions; Hölty; 1st version, fragment only, 1815; 2nd version, originally D.212, 1815); *Der Liedler,* D.209 (Kenner; 1815); *Die Liebe (Klärchens Lied),* D.210 (Goethe; 1815); *Adelwold und Emma,* D.211 (Bertrand; 1815); *Der Traum,* D.213 (Hölty; 1815); *Die Laube,* D.214 (Hölty; 1815); *Jägers Abendlied,* D.215 (Goethe; 1815); *Meerestille,* D.215a (Goethe; 1815); *Meerestille,* D.216 (Goethe; 1815); *Kolmas Klage,* D.217 (Ossian; 1815); *Grablied,* D.218 (Kenner; 1815); *Das Finden,* D.219 (Kosegarten; 1815); *Der Abend,* D.221 (Kosegarten; 1815); *Lieb Minna,* D.222 (Stadler; 1815); *Wandrers Nachtlied,* D.224 (Goethe; 1815); *Der Fischer,* D.225 (Goethe; 1815); *Erster Verlust,* D.226 (Goethe; 1815); *Idens Nachtgesang,* D.227 (Kosegarten; 1815); *Von Ida,* D.228 (Kosegarten; 1815); *Die Erscheinung,* D.229 (Kosegarten; 1815); *Die Täuschung,* D.230 (Kosegarten; 1815); *Das Sehnen,* D.231 (Kosegarten; 1815); *Geist der Liebe,* D.233 (Kosegarten; 1815); *Tischlied,* D.234 (Goethe; 1815); *Abends unter der Linde,* D.235 (Kosegarten; 1815); *Abends unter der Linde,* D.237 (Kosegarten; 1815); *Die Mondnacht,* D.238 (Kosegarten; 1815); *Huldigung,* D.240 (Kosegarten; 1815); *Alles um Liebe,* D.241 (Kosegarten; 1815); *Die Bürgschaft,* D.246 (Schiller; 1815); *Die Spinnerin,* D.247 (Goethe; 1815); *Lob des Tokayers,* D.248 (Baumberg; 1815); *Die Schlacht,* D.249 (Schiller; 1815; fragment only); *Das Geheimnis,* D.250 (Schiller; 1815); *Hoffnung,* D.251 (Schiller; 1815); *Das Mädchen aus der Fremde,* D.252 (Schiller; 1815); *Punschlied: Im Norden zu singen,* D.253 (Schiller; 1815); *Der Gott und die Bajadere,* D.254 (Goethe; 1815); *Der Rattenfänger,* D.255 (Goethe; 1815); *Der Schatzgräber,* D.256 (Goethe; 1815); *Heidenröslein,* D.257 (Goethe; 1815); *Bundeslied,* D.258 (Goethe; 1815); *An den Mond,* D.259 (Goethe; 1815); *Wonne der Wehmut,* D.260 (Goethe; 1815); *Wer kauft Liebesgötter?,* D.261 (Goethe; 1815); *Die Fröhlichkeit,* D.262 (Prandstetter; 1815); *Cora an die Sonne,* D.263 (Baumberg; 1815); *Der Morgenkuss,* D.264 (2 versions; Baumberg; 1815); *Abendständchen: An Lina,* D.265 (Baumberg; 1815); *Morgenlied,* D.266 (Stolberg; 1815); *An die Sonne,* D.270 (Baumberg; 1815); *Der Weiberfreund,* D.271 (Cowley; Ratschky, tr.; 1815); *An die Sonne,* D.272 (Tiedge; 1815); *Lilla an die Morgenröte,* D.273 (1815); *Tischlerlied,* D.274 (1815); *Totenkranz für ein Kind,* D.275 (Matthisson; 1815); *Abendlied,* D.276 (Stolberg; 1815); *Ossians Lied nach dem Falle Nathos,* D.278 (2 versions; Ossian; Harold, tr.; 1815); *Das Rosenband,* D.280 (Klopstock; 1815); *Das Mädchen von Inistore,* D.281 (Ossian; Harold, tr.; 1815); *Cronnan,* D.282 (Ossian; Harold, tr.; 1815); *An den Frühling,* D.283 (Schiller; 1815); *Lied,* D.284 (Schiller?; 1815); *Furcht der Geliebten (An Cidli),* D.285 (2 versions; Klopstock; 1815); *Selma und Selmar,* D.286 (2 versions; Klopstock; 1815); *Vaterlandslied,* D.287 (2 versions; Klopstock; 1815); *An sie,* D.288 (Klopstock; 1815); *Die Sommernacht,* D.289 (2 versions; Klopstock; 1815); *Die frühen Gräber,* D.290 (Klopstock; 1815); *Dem Unendlichen,* D.291 (3 versions; Klopstock; 1815); *Shilric und Vinvela,* D.293 (Ossian; Harold, tr.; 1815); *Hoffnung,* D.295 (2 versions; Goethe; 1816?); *An den Mond,* D.296 (Goethe; 1816?); *Augenlied,* D.297 (2 versions; Mayrhofer; 1817?); *Liane,* D.298 (Mayrhofer; 1815); *Der Jüngling an der Quelle,* D.300 (Salis-Seewis; 1817?); *Lambertine,* D.301 (Stoll; 1815); *Labetrank der Liebe,* D.302 (Stoll; 1815); *An die Geliebte,* D.303 (Stoll; 1815); *Wiegenlied,* D.304 (Körner; 1815); *Mein Gruss an den Mai,* D.305 (Kumpf; 1815); *Skolie,* D.306 (Deinhardstein; 1815); *Die Sternewelten,* D.307 (Jarnik; Fellinger, tr.; 1815); *Die Macht der Liebe,* D.308 (Kalchberg; 1815); *Das gestörte Glück,* D.309 (Körner; 1815); *Sehnsucht,* D.310 (2 versions; Goethe; 1815); *An den Mond,* D.311 (1815; fragment only);

Hektors Abschied, D.312 (2 versions; Schiller; 1815); *Die Sterne*, D.313 (Kosegarten; 1815); *Nachtgesang*, D.314 (Kosegarten; 1815); *An Rosa*, D.315 (Kosegarten; 1815); *An Rosa*, D.316 (2 versions; Kosegarten; 1815); *Idens Schwanenlied*, D.317 (2 versions; Kosegarten; 1815); *Schwangesang*, D.318 (Kosegarten; 1815); *Luisens Antwort*, D.319 (Kosegarten; 1815); *Der Zufriedene*, D.320 (Reissig; 1815); *Mignon*, D.321 (Goethe; 1815); *Hermann und Thusnelda*, D.322 (Klopstock; 1815); *Klage der Ceres*, D.323 (Schiller; 1815–16); *Harfenspieler*, D.325 (Goethe; 1815); *Lorma*, D.327 (Ossian; Harold, tr.; 1815; fragment only); *Erlkönig*, D.328 (4 versions; Goethe; 1815); *Die drei Sänger*, D.329 (Bobrik; 1815; fragment only); *Das Grab*, D.330 (Salis-Seewis; 1815); *An mein Klavier*, D.342 (Schubart; 1816?); *Am Tage aller Seelen (Litanei auf das Fest aller Seelen)*, D.343 (2 versions; Jacobi; 1816); *Am ersten Maimorgen*, D.344 (Claudius; 1816?); *Der Entfernten*, D.350 (Salis-Seewis; 1816?); *Fischerlied*, D.351 (Salis-Seewis; 1816); *Licht und Liebe (Nachtgesang)* D.352, for Soprano and Tenor (Collin; 1816?); *Die Nacht*, D.358 (Uz; 1816); *Sehnsucht*, D.359 (Goethe; 1816); *Lied eines Schiffers an die Dioskuren*, D.360 (Mayrhofer; 1816); *Am Bach im Frühlinge*, D.361 (Schober; 1816); *Zufriedenheit*, D.362 (Claudius; 1816?); *An Chloen*, D.363 (Uz; 1816; fragment only); *Der König in Thule*, D.367 (Goethe; 1816); *Jägers Abendlied*, D.368 (Goethe; 1816); *An Schwager Kronos*, D.369 (Goethe; 1816); *Klage*, D.371 (1816); *An die Natur*, D.372 (Stolberg-Stolberg; 1816); *Lied*, D.373 (Fouqué; 1816); *Der Tod Oskars*, D.375 (Ossian; Harold, tr.; 1816); *Lorma*, D.376 (Ossian; Harold, tr.; 1816; fragment only); *Morgenlied*, D.381 (1816); *Abendlied*, D.382 (1816); *Laura am Klavier*, D.388 (2 versions; Schiller; 1816); *Des Mädchens Klage*, D.389 (Schiller; 1816); *Entzuckung an Laura*, D.390 (Schiller; 1816); *Die vier Weltalter*, D.391 (Schiller; 1816); *Pflügerlied*, D.392 (Salis-Seewis; 1816); *Die Einsiedelei*, D.393 (Salis-Seewis; 1816); *An die Harmonie*, D.394 (Salis-Seewis; 1816); *Lebensmelodien*, D.395 (Schlegel; 1816); *Gruppe aus dem Tartarus*, D.396 (Schiller; 1816; fragment only); *Ritter Toggenburg*, D.397 (Schiller; 1816); *Frühlingslied*, D.398 (Hölty; 1816); *Auf den Tod einer Nachtigall*, D.399 (Hölty; 1816); *Die Knabenzeit*, D.400 (Hölty; 1816); *Winterlied*, D.401 (Hölty; 1816); *Der Flüchtling*, D.402 (Schiller; 1816); *Lied*, D.403 (4 versions; Salis-Seewis; 1816); *Die Herbstnacht*, D.404 (Salis-Seewis; 1816); *Der Herbstabend*, D.405 (2 versions; Salis-Seewis; 1816); *Abschied von der Harfe*, D.406 (Salis-Seewis; 1816); *Die verfehlteStunde*, D.409 (Schlegel; 1816); *Sprache der Liebe*, D.410 (Schlegel; 1816); *Daphne am Bach*, D.411 (Stolberg-Stolberg; 1816); *Stimme der Liebe*, D.412 (2 versions; Stolberg-Stolberg; 1816); *Entzückung*, D.413 (Matthisson; 1816); *Geist der Liebe*, D.414 (Matthisson; 1816); *Klage*, D.415 (Matthisson; 1816); *Lied in der Abwesenheit*, D.416 (Stolberg-Stolberg; 1816; fragment only); *Stimme der Liebe*, D.418 (Matthisson; 1816); *Julius an Theone*, D.419 (Matthisson; 1816); *Minnelied*, D.429 (Hölty; 1816); *Die frühe Liebe*, D.430 (2 versions; Hölty; 1816; 2nd version not extant); *Blumenlied*, D.431 (Hölty; 1816); *Der Leidende*, D.432 (2 versions; 1816); *Seligkeit*, D.433 (Hölty; 1816); *Erntelied*, D.434 (Hölty; 1816); *Klage*, D.436 (2 versions; Hölty; 1816; 2nd version originally D.437); *Das grosse Halleluja*, D.442 (Klopstock; 1816); *Schlachtlied*, D.443 (Klopstock; 1816); *Die Gestirne*, D.444 (Klopstock; 1816); *Edone*, D.445 (Klopstock; 1816); *Die Liebesgötter*, D.446 (Uz; 1816); *An den Schlaf*, D.447 (1816); *Gott im Frühlinge*, D.448 (2 versions; Uz; 1816); *Der gute Hirt*, D.449 (Uz; 1816); *Fragment aus dem Aeschylus*, D.450 (2 versions; Aeschylus; Mayrhofer, tr.; 1816); *Grablied auf einen Soldaten*, D.454 (Schubart; 1816); *Freude der Kinderjahre*, D.455 (Köpken; 1816); *Das Heimweh*, D.456 (Winkler; 1816); *An die untergehende Sonne*, D.457 (Kosegarten; 1816–17); *Aus Diego Manazares (Ilmerine)*, D.458 (Schlechta; 1816); *An Chloen*, D.462 (Jacobi; 1816); *Hochzeit-Lied*, D.463 (Jacobi; 1816); *In der Mitternacht*, D.464 (Jacobi; 1816); *Trauer der Liebe*, D.465 (2 versions; Jacobi; 1816); *Die Perle*, D.466 (Jacobi; 1816); *Pflicht und Liebe*, D.467 (Gotter; 1816); *An den Mond*, D.468 (Hölty; 1816); *Mignon*, D.469 (Goethe; 1816; fragments only); *Liedesend*, D.473 (2 versions; Mayrhofer;

1816); *Lied des Orpheus, als er in die Hölle ging*, D.474 (2 versions; Jacobi; 1816; 1st version unfinished); *Abschied (nach einer Wallfahrtsarie)*, D.475 (Mayrhofer; 1816); *Rückweg*, D.476 (Mayrhofer; 1816); *Alte Liebe rostet nie*, D.477 (Mayrhofer; 1816); *Harfenspieler I (Gesänge des Harfners No. 1)*, D.478 (2 versions; Goethe; 1st version, 1816; 2nd version, 1822); *Harfenspieler II (Gesänge des Harfners No. 3)*, D.479 (2 versions; Goethe; 1st version, 1816; 2nd version, 1822); *Harfenspieler III (Gesänge des Harfners No. 2)*, D.480 (3 versions; Goethe; 1st and 2nd versions, 1816; 3rd version, 1822); *Sehnsucht*, D.481 (Goethe; 1816); *Der Sänger am Felsen*, D.482 (Pichler; 1816); *Lied*, D.483 (Pichler; 1816); *Gesang der Geister über den Wassern*, D.484 (Goethe; 1816; fragment only); *Der Wanderer*, D.489 (3 versions; Lübeck; 1816; 2nd version originally D.493b; 3rd version originally D.493a); *Der Hirt*, D.490 (Mayrhofer; 1816); *Geheimnis*, D.491 (Mayrhofer; 1816); *Zum Punsche*, D.492 (Mayrhofer; 1816); *Abendlied der Fürstin*, D.495 (Mayrhofer; 1816); *Bei dem Grabe meines Vaters*, D.496 (Claudius; 1816); *Klage um Ali Bey*, D.496a (Claudius; 1816); *An die Nachtigall*, D.497 (Claudius; 1816); *Wiegenlied*, D.498 (1816); *Abendlied*, D.499 (Claudius; 1816); *Phidile*, D.500 (Claudius; 1816); *Zufriedenheit*, D.501 (2 versions; Claudius; 1816); *Herbstlied*, D.502 (Salis-Seewis; 1816); *Mailied*, D.503 (Hölty; 1816); *Am Grabe Anselmos*, D.504 (2 versions; Claudius; 1816); *Skolie*, D.507 (Matthisson; 1816); *Lebenslied*, D.508 (Matthisson; 1816); *Leiden der Trennung*, D.509 (2 versions; Metastasio; Collin, tr.; 1816; 1st version, fragment only); *Vedi quanto adoro*, D.510 (Metastasio; 1816); *Nur wer die Liebe kennt*, D.513a (Werner; 1817?; sketch only); *Die abgeblühte Linde*, D.514 (Széchényi; 1817?); *Der Flug der Zeit*, D.515 (Széchényi; 1817?); *Sehnsucht*, D.516 (Mayrhofer; 1816?); *Der Schäfer und der Reiter*, D.517 (2 versions; Fouqué; 1817); *An den Tod*, D.518 (Schubart; 1817?); *Die Blumensprache*, D.519 (Platner?; 1817?); *Frohsinn*, D.520 (2 versions; Castelli; 1817); *Jagdlied*, D.521 (Werner; 1817); *Die Liebe*, D.522 (Leon; 1817); *Trost*, D.523 (1817); *Der Alpenjäger*, D.524 (3 versions; Mayrhofer; 1817); *Wie Ulfru fischt*, D.525 (2 versions; Mayrhofer; 1817); *Fahrt zum Hades*, D.526 (Mayrhofer; 1817); *Schlaflied (Abendlied; Schlummerlied)*, D.527 (2 versions; Mayrhofer; 1817); *La pastorella al prato*, D.528 (Goldoni; 1817); *An eine Quelle*, D.530 (Claudius; 1817); *Der Tod und das Mädchen*, D.531 (Claudius; 1817); *Das Lied vom Reifen*, D.532 (Claudius; 1817; fragment only); *Täglich zu singen*, D.533 (Claudius; 1817); *Die Nacht*, D.534 (Ossian; Harold, tr.; 1817); *Lied*, D.535, with Small Orch. (1817); *Der Schiffer*, D.536 (2 versions; Mayrhofer; 1817); *Am Strome*, D.539 (Mayrhofer; 1817); *Philoket*, D.540 (Mayrhofer; 1817); *Memnon*, D.541 (Mayrhofer; 1817); *Antigone und Oedip*, D.542 (Mayrhofer; 1817); *Auf dem See*, D.543 (2 versions; Goethe; 1817); *Ganymed*, D.544 (Goethe; 1817); *Der Jüngling und der Tod*, D.545 (2 versions; Spaun; 1817); *Trost im Liede*, D.546 (Schober; 1817); *An die Musik*, D.547 (2 versions; Schober; 1817); *Orest auf Tauris*, D.548 (Mayrhofer; 1817); *Mahomets Gesang*, D.549 (Goethe; 1817; fragment only); *Die Forelle*, D.550 (5 versions; Schubart; 1817?–21); *Pax vobiscum*, D.551 (Schober; 1817); *Hänflings Liebeswerbung*, D.552 (2 versions; Kind; 1817); *Auf der Donau*, D.553 (Mayrhofer; 1817); *Uraniens Flucht*, D.554 (Mayrhofer; 1817); sketch for a song, D.555 (no text; 1817); *Liebhaber in allen Gestalten*, D.558 (Goethe; 1817); *Schweizerlied*, D.559 (Goethe; 1817); *Der Goldschmiedsgesell*, D.560 (Goethe; 1817); *Nach einem Gewitter*, D.561 (Mayrhofer; 1817); *Fischerlied*, D.562 (Salis-Seewis; 1817); *Die Einsiedelei*, D.563 (Salis-Seewis; 1817); *Gretchen im Zwinger (Gretchen; Gretchens Bitte)*, D.564 (Goethe; 1817; fragment only); *Der Strom*, D.565 (1817); *Das Grab*, D.569, for Unison Chorus (Salis-Seewis; 1817); *Iphigenia*, D.573 (Mayrhofer; 1817); *Entzückung an Laura*, D.577 (2 versions; Schiller; 1817; fragments only); *Abschied*, D.578 (Schubert; 1817); *Der Knabe in der Wiege (Wiegenlied)*, D.579 (2 versions; Ottenwalt; 1817; 2nd version, fragment only); *Vollendung*, D.579a (originally D.989; Matthisson; 1817); *Die Erde*, D.579b (originally D.989a; Matthisson; 1817); *Gruppe aus dem Tartarus*, D.583 (Schiller; 1817); *Elysium*, D.584 (Schiller; 1817); *Atys*, D.585 (Mayrhofer; 1817); *Erlaf-*

see, D.586 (Mayrhofer; 1817); *An den Frühling*, D.587 (2 versions; Schiller; 1817; 2nd version originally D.245); *Der Alpenjäger*, D.588 (2 versions; Schiller; 1817; 1st version, fragment only); *Der Kampf*, D.594 (Schiller; 1817); *Thekla: Eine Geisterstimme*, D.595 (2 versions; Schiller; 1817); *Lied eines Kindes*, D.596 (1817; fragment only); *Auf der Riesenkoppe*, D.611 (Körner; 1818); *An den Mond in einer Herbstnacht*, D.614 (Schreiber; 1818); *Grablied für die Mutter*, D.616 (1818); a vocal exercise for 2 Voices and Figured Bass, D.619 (no text; 1818); *Einsamkeit*, D.620 (Mayrhofer; 1818); *Der Blumenbrief*, D.622 (Schreiber; 1818); *Das Marienbild*, D.623 (Schreiber; 1818); *Blondel zu Marien*, D.626 (1818); *Das Abendrot*, D.627 (Schreiber; 1818); *Sonett I*, D.628 (Petrarch; Schlegel, tr.; 1818); *Sonett II*, D.629 (Petrarch; Schlegel, tr.; 1818); *Sonett III*, D.630 (Petrarch; Gries, tr.; 1818); *Blanka (Das Mädchen)*, D.631 (Schlegel; 1818); *Vom Mitleiden Mariä*, D.632 (Schlegel; 1818); *Der Schmetterling*, D.633 (Schlegel; 1819?); *Die Berge*, D.634 (Schlegel; 1821?); *Sehnsucht*, D.636 (3 versions; Schiller; 1821?); *Hoffnung*, D.637 (Schiller; 1819?); *Der Jüngling am Bache*, D.638 (2 versions; Schiller; 1819); *Widerschein*, D.639 (2 versions; Schlechta; 1819?; 2nd version originally D.949); *Abend*, D.645 (Tieck; 1819; fragment only); *Die Gebüsche*, D.646 (Schlegel; 1819); *Der Wanderer*, D.649 (Schlegel; 1819); *Abendbilder*, D.650 (Silbert; 1819); *Himmelsfunken*, D.651 (Silbert; 1819); *Das Mädchen*, D.652 (2 versions; Schlegel; 1819); *Bertas Lied in der Nacht*, D.653 (Grillparzer; 1819); *An die Freunde*, D.654 (Mayrhofer; 1819); *Marie*, D.658 (Novalis; 1819); *Hymne I*, D.659 (Novalis; 1819); *Hymne II*, D.660 (Novalis; 1819); *Hymne III*, D.661 (Novalis; 1819); *Hymne IV*, D.662 (Novalis; 1819); *Der 13. Psalm*, D.663 (M. Mendelssohn, tr.; 1819; fragment only); *Beim Winde*, D.669 (Mayrhofer; 1819); *Die Sternennächte*, D.670 (Mayrhofer; 1819); *Trost*, D.671 (Mayrhofer; 1819); *Nachtstück*, D.672 (2 versions; Mayrhofer; 1819); *Die Liebende schreibt*, D.673 (Goethe; 1819); *Prometheus*, D.674 (Goethe; 1819); *Strophe aus Die Götter Griechenlands*, D.677 (2 versions; Schiller; 1819); *Über allen Zauber Liebe*, D.682 (Mayrhofer; 1820?; fragment only); *Die Sterne*, D.684 (Schlegel; 1820); *Morgenlied*, D.685 (Werner; 1820); *Frühlingsglaube*, D.686 (3 versions; Uhland; 1st and 2nd versions; 1820; 3rd version, 1822); *Nachthymne*, D.687 (Novalis; 1820); *4 Canzonen: Non t'accostar all'urna* (Vitorelli), *Guarda, che bianca luna* (Vitorelli), *Da quel sembiante appresi* (Metastasio), *Mio ben ricordati* (Metastasio), D.688 (all 1820); *Abendröte*, D.690 (Schlegel; 1823); *Die Vögel*, D.691 (Schlegel; 1820); *Der Knabe*, D.692 (Schlegel; 1820); *Der Fluss*, D.693 (Schlegel; 1820); *Der Schiffer*, D.694 (Schlegel; 1820); *Namenstagslied*, D.695 (Stadler; 1820); *Des Fräuleins Liebeslauschen (Liebeslauschen)*, D.698 (Schlechta; 1820); *Der entsühnte Orest*, D.699 (Mayrhofer; 1820); *Freiwilliges Versinken*, D.700 (Mayrhofer; 1820); *Der Jüngling auf dem Hügel*, D.702 (Hüttenbrenner; 1820); *Der zürnenden Diana*, D.707 (2 versions; Mayrhofer; 1820); *Im Walde (Waldesnacht)*, D.708 (Schlegel; 1820); *Lob der Tränen*, D.711 (2 versions; Schlegel; 1818); *Die gefangenen Sänger*, D.712 (Schlegel; 1821); *Der Unglückliche*, D.713 (2 versions; Pichler; 1821); *Versunken*, D.715 (Goethe; 1821); *Grenzen der Menschheit*, D.716 (Goethe; 1821); *Suleika*, D.717 (1821?); *Geheimes*, D.719 (Goethe; 1821); *Suleika*, D.720 (2 versions; 1821); *Mahomets Gesang*, D.721 (Goethe; 1821; fragment only); *Linde Lüfte wehen*, D.725 (1821; fragment only); *Mignon*, D.726 (Goethe; 1821); *Mignon*, D.727 (Goethe; 1821); *Johanna Sebus*, D.728 (Goethe; 1821; fragment only); *Der Blumen Schmerz*, D.731 (Mayláth; 1821); *Ihr Grab*, D.736 (Engelhardt; 1822?); *An die Leier*, D.737 (Bruchmann; 1822?); *Im Haine*, D.738 (Bruchmann; 1822?); *Sei mir gegrüsst*, D.741 (Rückert; 1821?); *Der Wachtelschlag*, D.742 (Sauter; 1822); *Selige Welt*, D.743 (Senn; 1822); *Schwanengesang*, D.744 (Senn; 1822); *Die Rose*, D.745 (2 versions; Schlegel; 1822); *Am See*, D.746 (Bruchmann; 1822?); *Herrn Josef Spaun, Assessor in Linz (Sendschreiben an den Assessor Spaun in Linz)*, D.749 (Collin; 1822); *Die Liebe hat gelogen*, D.751 (Platen-Hallermünde; 1822); *Nachtviolen*, D.752 (Mayrhofer; 1822); *Heliopolis*, D.753 (Mayrhofer; 1822); *Heliopolis*, D.754 (Mayrhofer; 1822); *Du liebst mich nicht*,

D.756 (2 versions; Platen-Hallermünde; 1822); *Todesmusik*, D.758 (Schober; 1822); *Schatzgräbers Begehr*, D.761 (2 versions; Schober; 1822); *Schwestergruss*, D.762 (Bruchmann; 1822); *Der Musensohn*, D.764 (2 versions; Goethe; 1822); *An die Entfernte*, D.765 (Goethe; 1822); *Am Flusse*, D.766 (Goethe; 1822); *Willkommen und Abschied*, D.767 (2 versions; Goethe; 1822); *Wandrers Nachtlied*, D.768 (Goethe; 1824); *Drang in die Ferne*, D.770 (Leitner; 1823); *Der Zwerg*, D.771 (Collin; 1822?); *Wehmut*, D.772 (Collin; 1822?); *Auf dem Wasser zu singen*, D.774 (Stolberg-Stolberg; 1823); *Dass sie hier gewesen*, D.775 (Rückert; 1823?); *Du bist die Ruh*, D.776 (Rückert; 1823); *Lachen und Weinen*, D.777 (Rückert; 1823?); *Greisengesang*, D.778 (2 versions; Rückert; 1823); *Die Wallfahrt*, D.778a (Rückert; 1823?); *Der zürnende Barde*, D.785 (Bruchmann; 1823); *Viola*, D.786 (Schober; 1823); *Lied (Die Mutter Erde)*, D.788 (Stolberg-Stolberg; 1823); *Pilgerweise*, D.789 (Schober; 1823); *Vergissmeinnicht*, D.792 (Schober; 1823); *Das Geheimnis*, D.793 (Schiller; 1823); *Der Pilgrim*, D.794 (2 versions; Schiller; 1823); *Die schöne Müllerin*, song cycle, D.795 (Müller; 1823; 1, *Das Wandern*; 2, *Wohin?*; 3, *Halt!*; 4, *Danksagung an den Bach*; 5, *Am Feierabend*; 6, *Der Neugierige*; 7, *Ungeduld*; 8, *Morgengruss*; 9, *Des Müllers Blumen*; 10, *Tränenregen*; 11, *Mein!*; 12, *Pause*; 13, *Mit dem grünen Lautenbande*; 14, *Der Jäger*; 15, *Eifersucht und Stolz*; 16, *Die liebe Farbe*; 17, *Die böse Farbe*; 18, *Trockne Blumen*; 19, *Der Müller und der Bach*; 20, *Des Baches Wiegenlied*); *Romanze zum Drama Rosamunde*, D.797 (Chézy; 1823); *Im Abendrot*, D.799 (Lappe; 1824?); *Der Einsame*, D.800 (2 versions; Lappe; 1825); *Dithyrambe*, D.801 (Schiller; 1826); *Der Sieg*, D.805 (Mayrhofer; 1824); *Abendstern*, D.806 (Mayrhofer; 1824); *Auflösung*, D.807 (Mayrhofer; 1824); *Gondelfahrer*, D.808 (Mayrhofer; 1824); *Lied eines Kriegers*, D.822, with Unison Chorus (1824); *Nacht und Träume*, D.827 (2 versions; Collin; 1823); *Die junge Nonne*, D.828 (Craigher de Jachelutta; 1825); *Abschied*, D.829 (Pratobevera; 1826); *Lied der Anne Lyle*, D.830 (MacDonald; 1825); *Gesang der Norna*, D.831 (Scott; Spiker, tr.; 1825); *Des Sängers Habe*, D.832 (Schlechta; 1825); *Der blinde Knabe*, D.833 (2 versions; Cibber; Craigher, tr.; 1825); *Im Walde*, D.834 (2 versions; Schulze; 1825); *Ellens Gesang*, D.837 (Scott; Storck, tr.; 1825); *Ellens Gesang*, D.838 (Scott; Storck, tr.; 1825); *Ellens Gesang (Hymne an die Jungfrau)*, D.839 (Scott; Storck, tr.; 1825); *Totengräbers Heimwehe*, D.842 (Craigher; 1825); *Lied des gefangenen Jägers*, D.843 (Scott; Storck, tr.; 1825); *Normans Gesang*, D.846 (Scott; Storck, tr.; 1825); *Das Heimweh*, D.851 (2 versions; Felsö-Eör; 1825); *Die Allmacht*, D.852 (2 versions; Pyrker; 1825); *Auf der Bruck*, D.853 (2 versions; Schulze; 1825); *Fülle der Liebe*, D.854 (Schlegel; 1825); *Wiedersehn*, D.855 (Schlegel; 1825); *Abendlied für die Entfernte*, D.856 (Schlegel; 1825); *2 Szenen aus dem Schauspiel Lacrimas*, D.857: 1, *Lied der Delphine*; 2, *Lied des Florio* (Schütz; 1825); *An mein Herz*, D.860 (Schulze; 1825); *Der liebliche Stern*, D.861 (Schulze; 1825); *Um Mitternacht*, D.862 (2 versions; Schulze; 1st version, 1825; 2nd version, 1826); *An Gott*, D.863 (Hohlfeld; 1827; not extant); *Das Totenhemdchen*, D.864 (Bauernfeld; 1824; not extant); *Widerspruch*, D.865 (Seidl; 1826?); *4 Refrainlieder*, D.866 (Seidl; 1828): 1, *Die Unterscheidung*; 2, *Bei dir allein*; 3, *Die Männer sind méchant*; 4, *Irdisches Glück*; *Wiegenlied*, D.867 (Seidl; 1826?); *Totengräber-Weise*, D.869 (Schlechta; 1826); *Der Wanderer an den Mond*, D.870 (Seidl; 1826); *Das Zügenglöcklein*, D.871 (2 versions; Seidl; 1826); *O Quell, was strömst du rasch und wild*, D.874 (Schulze; 1826; fragment only); *Im Jänner 1817 (Tiefes Leid)*, D.876 (Schulze; 1826); *Gesänge aus Wilhelm Meister*, D.877: 1, *Mignon und der Harfner*; 2, 3, and 4, *Lied der Mignon* (Goethe; 1826); *Am Fenster*, D.878 (Seidl; 1826); *Sehnsucht*, D.879 (Seidl; 1826); *Im Freien*, D.880 (Seidl; 1826); *Fischerweise*, D.881 (2 versions; Schlechta; 1826); *Im Frühling*, D.882 (Schulze; 1826); *Lebensmut*, D.883 (Schulze; 1826); *Über Wildemann*, D.884 (Schulze; 1826); *Trinklied (Come, thou monarch of the vine)*, D.888 (Shakespeare; Grünbühel and Bauernfeld, tr.; 1826); *Standchen (Hark, hark the lark)*, D.889 (Shakespeare; Schlegel, tr.; 1826); *Hippolits Lied*, D.890 (Gerstenberg; 1826); *Gesang (An Sylvia; Who Is Sylvia?)*, D.891

(Shakespeare; Bauernfeld, tr.; 1826); *Fröhliches Scheiden*, D.896 (Leitner; 1827–28; sketch only); *Sie in jedem Liede*, D.896a (Leitner; 1827–28; sketch only); *Wolke und Quelle*, D.896b (Leitner; 1827–28; sketch only); *3 Gesänge*, D.902 (1827): 1, *L'incanto degli occhi* (*Die Macht der Augen*); 2, *Il Traditor deluso* (*Der getäuschte Verräter*); 3, *Il modo di prender moglie* (*Die Art, ein Weib zu nehmen*); *Alinde*, D.904 (Rochlitz; 1827); *An die Laute*, D.905 (Rochlitz; 1827); *Der Vater mit dem Kind*, D.906 (Bauernfeld; 1827); *Romanze des Richard Löwenherz*, D.907 (2 versions; Scott; Müller, tr.; 1826); *Jägers Liebeslied*, D.909 (Schober; 1827); *Schiffers Scheidelied*, D.910 (Schober; 1827); *Die Winterreise*, song cycle, D.911 (Müller; 1827; Book I: 1, *Gute Nacht*; 2, *Die Wetterfahne*; 3, *Gefrorne Tränen*; 4, *Erstarrung*; 5, *Der Lindenbaum*; 6, *Wasserflut* [2 versions]; 7, *Auf dem Flusse*; 8, *Rückblick*; 9, *Irrlicht*; 10, *Rast* [2 versions]; 11, *Frühlingstraum*; 12, *Einsamkeit* [2 versions]; Book II: 13, *Die Post*; 14, *Der greise Kopf*; 15, *Die Krähe*; 16, *Letzte Hoffnung*; 17, *Im Dorfe*; 18, *Der stürmische Morgen*; 19, *Täuschung*; 20, *Der Wegweiser*; 21, *Das Wirthaus*; 22, *Mut* [2 versions]; 23, *Die Nebensonnen* [2 versions]; 24, *Der Leiermann* [2 versions]; sketch for a song, D.916a (no text; 1827); *Das Lied im Grünen*, D.917 (Reil; 1827); *Frühlingslied*, D.919 (Pollak; 1827); *Heimliches Lieben*, D.922 (2 versions; 1827); *Eine altschottische Ballade*, D.923 (3 versions; 1st and 3rd for 2 Voices; Eng. author unknown; Herder, tr.; 1827); *Das Weinen*, D.926 (Leitner; 1827–28); *Vor meiner Wiege*, D.927 (Leitner; 1827–28); *Der Wallensteiner Lanzknecht beim Trunk*, D.931 (Leitner; 1827); *Der Kreuzzug*, D.932 (Leitner; 1827); *Des Fischers Liebesglück*, D.933 (Leitner; 1827); *Lebensmut*, D.937 (Rellstab; 1828; fragment only); *Der Winterabend*, D.938 (Leitner; 1828); *Die Sterne*, D.939 (Leitner; 1828); *Auf dem Strom*, D.943, with Horn or Cello obbligato (Rellstab; 1828); *Herbst*, D.945 (Rellstab; 1828); *Glaube, Hoffnung und Liebe*, D.955 (Kuffner; 1828); *Schwanengesang*, D.957 (1828; Book I: 1, *Liebesbotschaft* [Rellstab]; 2, *Kriegers Ahnung* [Rellstab]; 3, *Frühlingssehnsucht* [Rellstab]; 4, *Ständchen* [Rellstab]; 5, *Aufenthalt* [Rellstab]; 6, *In der Ferne* [Rellstab]; Book II: 7, *Abschied* [Rellstab]; 8, *Der Atlas* [Heine]; 9, *Ihr Bild* [Heine]; 10, *Das Fischermädchen* [Heine]; 11, *Die Stadt* [Heine]; 12, *Am Meer* [Heine]; 13, *Der Doppelgänger* [Heine]; 14, *Die Taubenpost* [Seidl]); *Der Hirt auf dem Felsen*, D.965, with Clarinet obbligato (Müller; 1828); *Der Graf von Habsburg*, D.990 (Schiller; 1815?); *Kaiser Maximilian auf der Martinswand*, D.990a (Collin; 1815?); *Augenblicke in Elysium*, D.990b (originally D.582; Schober; not extant); *Das Echo*, D.990c (originally D.868; Castelli); *Die Schiffende*, D.990d (Hölty; not extant); *L'incanto degli occhi*, D.990e (Metastasio); *Il Traditor deluso*, D.990f (Metastasio; not extant); *Mein Frieden*, D.AI/30 (Heine; 1815?).

ORCH.: Overture in D major, D.2a (originally D.996; 1811?; fragment only); Sym. in D major, D.2b (originally D.997; 1811?; fragment of 1st movement only); Overture in D major, to Albrecht's comedy *Der Teufel als Hydraulicus*, D.4 (1812?); Overture in D major, D.12 (1811?); Overture in D major, D.26 (1812); 3 minuets and trios, D.39a (1813; not extant); orch. fragment in D major, D.71c (originally D.966a; 1813); Sym. No. 1, in D major, D.82 (1813); orch. fragment in B-flat major, D.94a (1814?); Sym. No. 2, in B-flat major, D.125 (1814–15); Sym. No. 3, in D major, D.200 (1815); Concerto (Concertstück) in D major for Violin and Orch., D.345 (1816); Sym. No. 4, in C minor, D.417, "Tragic" (1816); Rondo in A major for Violin and Strings, D.438 (1816); Overture in B-flat major, D.470 (1816); Sym. No. 5, in B-flat major, D.485 (1816); Overture in D major, D.556 (1817); Polonaise in B-flat major for Violin and Orch., D.580 (1817); Sym. No. 6, in C major, D.589 (1817–18); Overture in D major, D.590, "im italienischen Stile" (1817); Overture in C major, D.591, "im italienischen Stile" (1817); Sym. in D major, D.615 (piano sketches for 2 movements only; 1818); Overture in E minor, D.648 (1819); Sym. in D major, D.708a (sketches only; 1821); Sym. (No. 7) in E minor/major, D.729 (1821; sketched in score; performing version realized by R.F. Barnett, Felix Weingartner, and Brian Newbould); Sym. No. 8, in B minor, D.759, "Unfinished"

(1822; 2 movements and an unfinished scherzo); "Gmunden" or "Gastein" Sym., D.849 (identical with D.944); Sym. (No. 10) in D major, D.936a (1828; sketches only; performing version realized by Brian Newbould); Sym. No. 9, in C major, D.944, "Great" (1825–26).

PIANO: Fantasie in C minor, D.2e (originally D.993; 1811); Fugue in D minor, D.13 (1812?); Overture, D.14 (1812?; sketch only; not extant); 6 variations in E-flat major, D.21 (1812; not extant); 7 variations in F major, D.24 (1812; fragment only; not extant); Fugue in C major, D.24a (1812); Fugue in G major, D.24b (1812); Fugue in D minor, D.24c (1812); Fugue in C major, D.24d (1812; fragment only); Fugue in F major, D.25c (1812; fragment only); Andante in C major, D.29 (1812); fugal sketches in B-flat major, D.37a (originally D.967; 1813?); Fugue in E minor, D.41a (1813; fragment only); Fugue in E minor, D.71b (1813; fragment only); Allegro in E major, D.154 (sketch of D.157; 1815); 10 variations in F major, D.156 (1815); Sonata in E major, D.157 (1815; unfinished); Adagio in G major, D.178 (1815); Sonata in C major, D.279 (1815); Allegretto in C major, D.346 (1816?; fragment only); Allegretto moderato in C major, D.347 (1813?; fragment only); Andantino in C major, D.348 (1816; fragment only); Adagio in C major, D.349 (1816?; fragment only); Sonata in F major, D.459 (1816; fragment only); 5 Klavierstücke, D.459a (1st 2 from preceding work; 1816?); Adagio in D-flat major, D.505 (original slow movement of D.625; 1818); Rondo in E major, D.506 (1817); Sonata in A minor, D.537 (1817); Sonata in A-flat major, D.557 (1817); Sonata in E minor, D.566 (1817); Sonata in D-flat major, D.567 (unfinished; 1st version of D.568; 1817); Sonata in E-flat major, D.568 (1826?); Scherzo in D major and Allegro in F-sharp minor, D.570 (unfinished; 1817); Sonata in F-sharp minor, D.571 (1817; fragment only); Sonata in B major, D.575 (1817); 13 variations on a theme by Anselm Hüttenbrenner, in A minor, D.576 (1817); 2 scherzos, in B-flat major and D-flat major, D.593 (1817); Andante in A major, D.604 (1816?); Fantasia in C major, D.605 (1821–23; fragment only); Fantasy in C major, D.605a, "Grazer Fantasie" (1818?); March in E major, D.606 (1818?); Adagio in E major, D.612 (1818); Sonata in C major, D.613 (2 movements; 1818); Sonata in F minor, D.625 (2 movements; 1818); Sonata in C-sharp minor, D.655 (1819; fragment only); Sonata in A major, D.664 (1819?); Variations on a Waltz by Diabelli, in C minor, D.718 (1821); Overture to *Alfonso und Estrella*, in D major, D.759a (an arrangement of the D.732 overture; 1822); Fantasy in C major, D.760, "Wanderfantasie" (1822); Sonata in E minor, D.769a (originally D.994; 1823?; fragment only); 6 *Momens musicals* [sic], in C major, A-flat major, F minor, C-sharp minor, F minor, A-flat major, D.780 (1823–28); Sonata in A minor, D.784 (1823); *Ungarische Melodie* in B minor, D.817 (1824); Sonata in C major, D.840, *Reliquie* (unfinished; 1825); Sonata in A minor, D.845 (1825); Sonata in D major, D.850 (1825); Sonata in G major, D.894 (originally known as the *Fantasie, Andante, Menuetto und Allegretto*; 1826); 4 impromptus, in C minor, E-flat major, G-flat major, and A-flat major, D.899 (1827); Allegretto in C minor, D.900 (1820?; fragment only); Allegretto in C minor, D.915 (1827); sketch for a piano piece in C major, D.916b (1827); sketch for a piano piece in C minor, D.916c (1827); 4 impromptus, in F minor, A-flat major, B-flat major, and F minor, D.935 (1827); 3 Klavierstücke, in E-flat minor, E-flat major, and C major, D.946 (1828); Sonata in C minor, D.958 (1828); Sonata in A major, D.959 (1828); Sonata in B-flat major, D.960 (1828); March in G major, D.980f (date unknown).

PIANO, 4-HANDS: Fantasie in G major, D.1 (1810); Fantasie in G major, D.1b (1810?; fragment only); Sonata in F major, D.1c (1810; unfinished); Fantasie in G minor, D.9 (1811); Fantasie in C minor, D.48, "Grande sonate" (2 versions; 1813); Overture in D major, D.592, "im italienischen Stile" (an arrangement of D.590; 1817); Overture in C major, D.597, "im italienischen Stile" (an arrangement of D.591; 1817); 4 polonaises, in D minor, B-flat major, E major, and F major, D.599 (1818); 3 *marches héroïques*, in B minor, C major, and D major, D.602 (1818?); Rondo in D major, D.608 (2 versions; 1818);

Sonata in B-flat major, D.617 (1818); Deutscher in G major, with 2 trios and 2 Ländler, in E major, D.618 (1818); Polonaise and Trio, D.618a (sketch only; 1818; orch. by Raymond Leppard; Indianapolis, Nov. 8, 1990, Leppard conducting); 8 variations on a French song, in E minor, D.624 (1818); Overture in G minor, D.668 (1819); Overture in F major, D.675 (1819); 3 *marches militaires*, in D major, G major, and E-flat major, D.733 (1818); Overture to *Alfonso und Estrella*, D.773 (an arrangement of the D.732 overture; 1823); Overture to *Fierabras*, D.798 (an arrangement of the D.796 overture; 1823); Sonata in C major, D.812, "Grand duo" (1824; orchestrated by Raymond Leppard; Indianapolis, Nov. 8, 1990, Leppard conducting); 8 variations on an original theme, in A-flat major, D.813 (1824); 4 Ländler, in E-flat major, A-flat major, C minor, and C major, D.814 (1824); *Divertissement à l'hongroise* in G minor, D.818 (1824); 6 *grandes marches*, in E-flat major, G minor, B minor, D major, E-flat minor, and E major, D.819 (1824); *Divertissement sur des motifs originaux français* in E minor, D.823: 1, *Marche brillante*; 2, *Andantino varié*; 3, *Rondeau brillant* (1825?); 6 polonaises, in D minor, F major, B-flat major, D major, A major, and E major, D.824 (1826); *Grande marche funèbre* in C minor, D.859 (on the death of Alexander I of Russia; 1825); *Grande marche héroïque* in A minor, D.885 (for the coronation of Nicholas I of Russia; 1826); 8 variations on a theme from Hérold's *Marie*, in C major, D.908 (1827); March in G major, D.928, "Kindermarsch" (1827); Fantasie in F minor, D.940 (1828); Allegro in A minor, D.947, Lebensstürme (1828); Rondo in A major, D.947 (1828); Fugue in E minor, D.952 (1828); Allegro moderato in C major and Andante in A minor (Sonatine), D.968 (1818?); Introduction, 4 variations on an original theme, and Finale, in B-flat major, D.968a (originally D.603; 1824?); 2 *marches caractéristiques* in C major, D.968b (originally D.886; 1826?).

DANCES FOR PIANO: Waltzes and March, D.19b (1812?; not extant); 12 minuets with trios, D.22 (1812; not extant); 30 minuets with trios, D.41 (1813; 10 not extant); 2 minuets, in D major and A major, both with 2 trios, D.91 (1813; 2 other minuets lost); 12 Wiener Deutsche, D.128 (1812?); Deutscher in E major, with trio, D.135 (1815); Deutscher in C-sharp minor, with trio, D.139 (1815); 12 waltzes, 17 Ländler, and 9 écossaises, D.145 (1815–21); 20 waltzes (*Letzte Walzer*), D.146 (Nos. 1 and 3–11, 1815; Nos. 2 and 12–20, 1823); Ecossaise in D minor/F major, D.158 (1815); Minuet in A minor, with trio, D.277a (1815); 12 écossaises, D.299 (1815); Minuet in A major, with trio, D.334 (1815?); Minuet in E major, with 2 trios, D.335 (1813?); 36 Originaltänze (*Erste Walzer*), D.365 (1816–21); 17 Ländler, D.366 (1816–24); 8 Ländler, D.378 (1816); 3 minuets, in E major, A major, and C major, each with 2 trios, D.380 (1816); 12 Deutsche, D.420 (1816); 6 écossaises, D.421 (1816); Ecossaise in E-flat major, D.511 (1817?); 8 écossaises, D.529 (1817); Minuet in C-sharp minor, D.600 (1814?); Trio in E major, D.610 (1818); Deutscher in C-sharp minor and Ecossaise in D-flat major, D.643 (1819); 12 Ländler, D.681 (1815?; Nos. 1–4 not extant); 6 écossaises, D.697 (1820); Deutscher in G-flat major, D.722 (1821); 16 Ländler and 2 écossaises (*Wiener-Damen Ländler*), D.734 (1822?); Galop and 8 écossaises, D.735 (1822?); 2 Deutsche, in A major and D major, D.769 (No. 1, 1824; No. 2, 1823); 34 *Valses sentimentales*, D.779 (1823?); 12 écossaises, D.781 (1823); Ecossaise in D major, D.782 (1823?); 16 Deutsche and 2 écossaises, D.783 (1823–24); 12 Deutsche (Ländler), D.790 (1823); 3 écossaises, D.816 (1824); 6 Deutsche, D.820 (1824); 2 Deutsche, in F major and G major, D.841 (1825); Waltz in G major (*Albumblatt*), D.844 (1825); 12 Grazer Walzer, D.924 (1827); Grazer Galopp in C major, D.925 (1827); Deutscher, D.944a (1828; not extant); 12 waltzes (*Valses nobles*), D.969 (1826); 6 Ländler, D.970 (date unknown); 3 Deutsche, in A minor, A major, and E major, D.971 (1822); 3 Deutsche, in D-flat major, A-flat major, and A major, D.972 (date unknown); 3 Deutsche, in E major, E major, and A-flat major, D.973 (date unknown); 2 Deutsche, both in D-flat major, D.974 (date unknown); Deutscher in D major, D.975 (date unknown); Cotillon in E-flat major, D.976 (1825); 8 écossaises, D.977 (date un-

known); Waltz in A-flat major, D.978 (1825); Waltz in G major, D.979 (1826); 2 waltzes, in G major and B minor, D.980 (1826); 2 dance sketches, in A major and E major, D.980a (originally D.640; date unknown); 2 Ländler, both in E-flat major, D.980b (originally D.679; date unknown); 2 Ländler, both in D-flat major, D.980c (originally D.680; fragment only; date unknown); Waltz in C major, D.980d (1827); 2 dance sketches, in G minor and F major, D.980c (date unknown).

CHAMBER: String Quartet, D.2c (originally D.998; 1811?; fragment only); 6 minuets, D.2d (originally D.995; 1811); sketch for a trio of a minuet, in C major, D.2f (1811); String Quartet in C minor, D.3 (1812; fragment only); Overture in C minor, D.8 (1811); Overture in C minor, D.8a (an arrangement of D.8; 1811); String Quartet in G minor/B-flat major, D.18 (1810?); String Quartet, D.19 (1810?; not extant); String Quartet, D.19a (1810?; not extant); Overture in B-flat major, D.20 (1812; not extant); Trio (Sonata in one movement) in B-flat major, D.28 (1812); String Quartet in C major, D.32 (1812); String Quartet in B-flat major, D.36 (1812–13); String Quartet in C major, D.46 (1813); String Quartet in B-flat major, D.68 (1813; 2 movements only); Wind Octet in F major, D.72 (1813); Allegro in F major, D.72a (1813; unfinished); String Quartet in D major, D.74 (1813); Wind Nonet in E-flat minor, D.79, "Franz Schuberts Begräbnis-Feyer" (*Eine kleine Trauermusik*) (1813); Minuet in D major, D.86 (1813); String Quartet in E-flat major, D.87 (1813); Andante in C major, D.87a (1813); 5 minuets and 6 trios, D.89 (1813); 5 Deutsche and 7 trios, with coda, D.90 (1813); String Quartet in D major, D.94 (1811?); 5 minuets and 6 Deutsche, with trios, D.94b (1814; not extant); Trio in G major, for Schubert's arrangement of Matiegka's *Notturno*, op. 21, D.96 (1814); String Quartet in C minor, D.103 (1814; fragments, Grave, and Allegro extant); String Trio in B-flat major, D.111a (1814; not extant); String Quartet in B-flat major, D.112 (1814); String Quartet in G minor, D.173 (1815); String Quartet in E major, D.353 (1816); 4 komische Ländler in D major, D.354 (1816); 8 Ländler in F-sharp minor, D.355 (1816); 9 Ländler in D major, D.370 (1816); 11 Ländler in B-flat major, D.374 (1816); Sonata (Sonatina) in D major, D.384 (1816); Sonata (Sonatina) in A minor, D.385 (1816); Sonata (Sonatina) in G minor, D.408 (1816); String Trio in B-flat major, D.471 (1816; unfinished); Adagio and Rondo concertante in F major, D.487 (1816); Sonata (Duo) in A major, D.574 (1817); String Trio in B-flat major, D.581 (1817); Variations in A major, D.597a (1817; not extant); Overture in B-flat major, D.601 (an arrangement of the D.470 overture; 1816?; fragment only); Piano Quintet in A major, D.667, "Die Forelle" (1819); String Quartet in C minor, D.703 (*Quartettsatz*) (1820); Introduction and variations on *Trockne Blumen* from *Die schöne Müllerin*, in E minor/E major, D.802 (1824); Octet in F major, D.803 (1824); String Quartet in A minor, D.804 (1824); String Quartet in D minor, D.810, "Der Tod und das Mädchen" (1824); Sonata in A minor, D.821, "Arpeggione" (1824); String Quartet in G major, D.887 (1826); Rondo in B minor (*Rondo brillant*), D.895 (1826); Piano Trio movement in E-flat major, D.897, "Notturno" (1828?); Piano Trio in B-flat major, D.898 (1828?); Piano Trio in E-flat major, D.929 (1827); Fantasy in C major, D.934 (1827); String Quintet in C major, D.956 (1828); Fugue in C major, D.A1/3 (1812?; fragment only).

BIBL.: COLLECTED EDITIONS, SOURCE MATERIAL: The 1st complete critical edition of his works, *F. S.s Werke: Kritisch durchgesehene Gesamtausgabe*, edited by E. Mandyczewski (assisted by Brahms, Brüll, Hellmesberger, J.N. Fuchs et al.), was publ. by Breitkopf & Härtel (40 vols. in 21 series, Leipzig, 1884–97). A new and exhaustive critical edition, *F. S.: Neue Ausgabe sämtlicher Werke*, ed. by W. Dürr, A. Feil, C. Landon et al., is being publ. under the sponsorship of the Internationalen Schubert-Gesellschaft (Kassel, 1964–). The standard thematic catalogue is by O. Deutsch and D. Wakeling, *F. S.: Thematic Catalogue of All His Works in Chronological Order* (London, 1951; in Ger. as *F. S.: Thematisches Verzeichnis seiner Werke in chronologischer Folge . . .* , publ. in the *Neue Ausgabe sämtlicher Werke* of Schubert in a rev. ed. in 1978). See also R.

van Hoorickx, "Thematic Catalogue of S.'s Works: New Additions, Corrections and Notes," *Revue Belge de Musicologie*, XXVIII–XXX (1974–76).

Other sources include the following: O. Deutsch, ed., *F. S.s Briefe und Schriften* (Munich, 1919; Eng. tr., 1928; 4th Ger. ed., 1954); *Bericht über den Internationalen Kongress für S.forschung: Wien 1928* (essays on source material and collections; Augsburg, 1929); O. Deutsch, ed., *F. S.s Tagebuch* (facsimile and transcription; Vienna, 1928; Eng. tr., 1928); R. Lachmann, "Die S.-Autographen der Staatsbibliothek zu Berlin," *Zeitschrift für Musikwissenschaft*, XI (1928); J.-G. Prod'homme, "Les Manuscrits de S. à la Bibliothèque du Conservatoire de Paris," *Revue Musicale*, XII (1928); W. Kahl, *Verzeichnis des Schrifttums über F. S.: 1828–1928* (Regensburg, 1938); H. Werlé, ed., *F. S. in seinen Briefen und Aufzeichnungen* (Leipzig, 1948; 4th ed., 1955); M.J.E. Brown, "Recent S. Discoveries," *Music & Letters*, XXXII (1951); idem, "New, Old and Rediscovered S. Manuscripts," ibid., XXXVII (1957); R. van Hoorickx, "About Some Early S. Manuscripts," *Music Review*, XXX (1969); C. Landon, "Neue S.-Funde," *Österreichische Musikzeitschrift*, XXIV (1969; Eng. tr. in *Music Review*, XXXI, 1970); R. Klein, *S.-Stätten* (Vienna, 1972); R. van Hoorickx, "Some Unknown S. Manuscripts," *Musical Times*, CXVIII (1977); E. Hilmar, *Verzeichnis der S.-Handschriften in der Musiksammlung der Wiener Stadt- und Landesbibliothek* (Kassel, 1978).

ICONOGRAPHY: A. Trost, "F. S.s Bildnisse," *Berichte und Mittheilungen des Alterthums-Vereines zu Wien*, XXXIII/2 (1898); O. Deutsch, *Die historischen Bildnisse F. S.s in getreuen Nachbildungen* (Vienna, 1922); A, Orel, *F. S., 1797–1828: Sein Leben in Bildern* (Leipzig, 1939); R. Petzoldt, *F. S.: Sein Leben in Bildern* (Leipzig, 1953); E. Hilmar and O. Brusatti, eds., *F. S.* (exhibition catalogue; Vienna, 1978); E. Badura-Skoda, "A S. Life Mask," *Musical Times*, CXX (1979).

BIOGRAPHICAL: H. Kreissle von Hellborn, *F. S., Eine biographische Skizze* (Vienna, 1861; 2nd ed., greatly enl. as *F. S.*, 1865; Eng. tr., London, 1866); A. Reissmann, *F. S.: Sein Leben und seine Werke* (Berlin, 1873); H. Frost, *F. S.* (London, 1881; 2nd ed., 1923); M. Friedlaender, *Beiträge zur Biographie F. S.s* (Berlin, 1887; new ed. as *F. S.: Skizze seines Lebens und Wirken*, Leipzig, 1928); A. Niggli, *S.* (Leipzig, 1890); H. Ritter, *F. S.* (Bamberg, 1896); R. Heuberger, *F. S.* (Berlin, 1902; 3rd ed., rev., 1920, by H. von der Pforten); M. Zenger, *F. S.s Wirken und Erdenwallen* (Langensalza, 1902); O. Deutsch, *S.-Brevier* (Berlin, 1905); W. Klatte, *S.* (Berlin, 1907); L.-A. Bourgault-Ducoudray, *S.* (Paris, 1908; new ed., 1926); H. Antcliffe, *S.* (London, 1910); W. Dahms, *S.* (Berlin, 1912); O. Deutsch, ed., *F. S.: Die Dokumente seines Lebens und Schaffens* (in collaboration, 1st with L. Scheibler, then with W. Kahl and G. Kinsky; it was planned as a comprehensive work in 3 vols. containing all known documents, pictures, and other materials, arranged in chronological order, with a thematic catalogue; only 2 vols. publ.: vol. III, *Sein Leben in Bildern*, Munich, 1913; vol. II, part 1, *Die Dokumente seines Lebens*, Munich, 1914, which appeared in an Eng. tr. by Eric Blom as *S.: A Documentary Biography*, London, 1946, and in an American ed. as *The S. Reader: A Life of F. S. in Letters and Documents*, N.Y., 1947; a 2nd German ed., enl., was publ. in the *Neue Ausgabe sämtlicher Werke* of Schubert in 1964); K. Kobald, *S. und Schwind* (Zürich, 1921); O. Bie, *F. S.: Sein Leben und sein Werk* (Berlin, 1925; Eng. tr., 1928); E. Bethge, *F. S.* (Leipzig, 1928); H. Eulenberg, *S. und die Frauen* (Hellerau, 1928); N. Flower, *F. S.* (London and N.Y., 1928; new ed., 1949); A. Glazunov, *S.* (Leningrad, 1928); K. Kobald, *F. S. und seine Zeit* (Zürich, 1928; Eng. tr., 1928; new German ed., 1948); G. Kruse, *F. S.* (Bielefeld, 1928); P. Landormy, *La Vie de S.* (Paris, 1928); J.-G. Prod'homme, *S.* (Paris, 1928); idem, *S. raconté par ceux qui l'ont vu* (Paris, 1928); P. Stefan, *F. S.* (Berlin, 1928; new ed., Vienna, 1947); A. Weiss, *F. S.* (Vienna, 1928); R. Bates, *F. S.* (London, 1934); W. Vetter, *F. S.* (Potsdam, 1934); G. Schünemann, *Erinnerungen an S.* (Berlin, 1936); A. Orel, *Der junge S.* (Vienna, 1940); A. Kolb, *F. S., Sein Leben* (Stockholm, 1941); K. Höcker, *Wege zu S.* (Regensburg, 1942); B. Paumgart-

ner, *F. S.* (Zürich, 1943; 2nd ed., 1947); R. Tenschert, *Du holde Kunst: Ein kleiner S.-Spiegel* (Vienna, 1943); A. Hutchings, *S.* (London, 1945; 4th ed., rev., 1973); W. and P. Rehberg, *F. S.* (Zürich, 1946); C. Weingartner, *F. S.* (Alten, 1947); R. Schauffler, *F. S.: The Ariel of Music* (N.Y., 1949); A. Einstein, *S.: A Musical Portrait* (N.Y., 1951; German ed., 1952); H. Rutz, *S., Dokumente seines Lebens und Schaffens* (Munich, 1952); H. Goldschmidt, *F. S.* (Berlin, 1954; 5th ed., 1964); P. Mies, *F. S.* (Leipzig, 1954); O. Deutsch, ed., *S.: Die Erinnerungen seiner Freunde* (Leipzig, 1957; Eng. tr. as *S.: Memoirs by His Friends*, N.Y., 1958; 3rd German ed., 1974); M.J.E. Brown, *S.: A Critical Biography* (London, 1958; 2nd ed., 1961); F. Hug, *F. S.: Leben und Werk eines Frühvollendeten* (Frankfurt, 1958); L. Kusche, *F. S.: Dichtung und Wahrheit* (Munich, 1962); K. Kobald, *F. S.* (Vienna, 1963); A. Kolb, *S.* (Gütersloh, 1964); J. Bruyr, *F. S.: L'Homme et son œuvre* (Paris, 1965); F. de Eaubonne and M.-R. Hofmann, *La Vie de S.* (Paris, 1965); W. Marggraf, *F. S.* (Leipzig, 1967); J. Reed, *S.: The Final Years* (London, 1972); J. Wechsberg, *S.* (N.Y., 1977); H. Fröhlich, *S.* (Munich, 1978); H. Osterheld, *F. S.: Schicksal und Persönlichkeit* (Stuttgart, 1978); O. Biba, "S.'s Position in Viennese Musical Life," *19th Century Music* (Nov. 1979); W. Dürr, "S. and Johann Michael Vogl: A Reappraisal," ibid.; M. Soloman, "S. and Beethoven," ibid.; E. Sams, "S.'s Illness Re-examined," *Musical Times* (Jan. 1980); P. Gammond, *S.* (London, 1982); A. Mann, "S.'s Lessons with Sechter," *19th Century Music* (Fall 1982); E. Hilmar, *F. S. in seiner Zeit* (Vienna, 1985); G. Marek, *S.* (N.Y., 1985); C. Osborne, *S. and his Vienna* (London, 1985); J. Reed, *S.* (London, 1987); B. Shamgar, "Three Missing Months in S.'s Biography: A Further Consideration of Beethoven's Influences on S.," *Musical Quarterly*, 73/3 (1989); F. Hilmar, *S.* (Graz, 1989); E. Krenek, *F. S.: Ein Porträt* (Tutzing, 1990).

CRITICAL, ANALYTICAL: J. Rissé, *F. S. in seinen Liedern* (2 vols., Hannover, 1872); H. de Curzon, *Les Lieder de F. S.* (Brussels, 1899); M. Gallet, *S. et le Lied* (Paris, 1907); O. Wissig, *F. S.s Messen* (Leipzig, 1909); M. Bauer, *Die Lieder F. S.s* (Leipzig, 1915); H. von der Pfordten, *S. und das deutsche Lied* (Leipzig, 1916; 2nd ed., 1920); W. Kahl, "Das lyrische Klavierstück S.s," *Archiv für Musikwissenschaft*, 3 (1921); R. Krott, *Die Singspiele S.s* (diss., Univ. of Vienna, 1921); O. Deutsch, *Die Originalausgaben von S.s Goethe-Liedern* (Vienna, 1926); H. Költzsch, *F. S. in seinen Klaviersonaten* (Leipzig, 1927); F. von Kraus, *Beiträge zur Erforschung des malenden und poetisierenden Wesens in der Begleitung von F. S.s Liedern* (Mainz, 1927); R. Capell, *S.'s Songs* (London, 1928; 3rd ed., rev., 1973, by M. Cooper); F. Damian, *F. S.s Liederkreis, Die schöne Müllerin* (Leipzig, 1928); F. Günther, *S.s Lied* (Stuttgart, 1928); K. Huschke, *Das 7 Gestirn der grossen S. 'schen Kammermusikwerke* (Pritzwalk, 1928); K. Kobald, *Der Meister des deutschen Liedes, F. S.* (Vienna and Leipzig, 1928); C. Lafite, *Das Schubertlied und seine Sänger* (Vienna, 1928); P. Mies, *S., Der Meister des Liedes* (Berlin, 1928); F. Weingartner, *S. und sein Kreis* (Zürich, 1928); H. Biehle, *S.s Lieder als Gesangsproblem* (Langensalza, 1929); H. Bosch, *Die Entwicklung des Romantischen in S.s Liedern* (Leipzig, 1930); H. Therstappen, *Die Entwicklung der Form bei S.* (Leipzig, 1931); E. Laaff, *F. S.s Sinfonien* (Wiesbaden, 1933); T. Archer, "The Formal Construction of *Die schöne Müllerin*," *Musical Quarterly* (Oct. 1934); E. Porter, *The Songs of S.* (London, 1937); E. Schaeffer, "S.'s *Winterreise*," *Musical Quarterly* (Jan. 1938); O. Deutsch, "The Chronology of S.'s String Quartets," *Music & Letters*, XXIV (1943); G. Abraham, ed., *The Music of S.* (N.Y., 1947); O. Deutsch, "The Discovery of S.'s Great C Major Symphony: A Story in 15 Letters," *Musical Quarterly* (Oct. 1952); M.J.E. Brown, "S.'s *Winterreise*, Part I," ibid. (April 1953); W. Vetter, *Der Klassiker S.* (2 vols., Leipzig, 1953); E. Schmitz, *S.s Auswirkung auf die deutsche Musik bis zu Hugo Wolf und Bruckner* (Leipzig, 1954); H. Haas, *Über die Bedeutung der Harmonik in den Liedern F. S.s* (Bonn, 1957); H.-M. Sachse, *F. S.s Streichquartette* (Munich, 1958); M. Chusid, *The Chamber Music of F. S.* (diss., Univ. of Calif., Berkeley, 1961); E. Porter, *S.'s Song-technique* (London, 1961); E. Norman-McKay, *The Stage-works of S.,*

Considered in the Framework of Austrian Biedermeier Society (diss., Oxford Univ., 1962–63); A. Bell, *The Songs of S.* (Lowestoft, 1964); R. Stringham, *The Masses of F. S.* (diss., Cornell Univ., 1964); S. Kunze, *F. S.: Sinfonie h-moll: Unvollendete* (Munich, 1965); M.J.E. Brown, *Essays on S.* (London, 1966); idem, *S. Songs* (London, 1967); T. Georgiades, *S.: Musik und Lyrik* (Göttingen, 1967); P. Radcliffe, *S. Piano Sonatas* (London, 1967); D. Weekley, *The One-piano, Four-hand Compositions of F. S.: Historical and Interpretative Analysis* (diss., Indiana Univ., 1968); J. Westrup, *S. Chamber Music* (London, 1969); M.J.E. Brown, *S. Symphonies* (London, 1970); H. Gal, *F. S. oder Die Melodie* (Frankfurt, 1970; Eng. tr. as *F. S. and the Essence of Melody*, London, 1974); M. Citron, *S.'s Seven Complete Operas: A Musico-dramatic Study* (diss., Univ. of North Carolina, 1971); R. Coolidge, "Form in the String Quartets of F. S.," *Music Review*, XXXII (1971); D. Fischer-Dieskau, *Auf den Spuren der S.-Lieder; Werden–Wesen–Wir* (Wiesbaden, 1971; Eng. tr. as *S.: A Biographical Study of the Songs*, London, 1976); R. Weber, *Die Sinfonien F. S.s im Versuch einer Strukturwissenschaftlichen Darstellung und Untersuchungen* (diss., Univ. of Münster, 1971); G. Cunningham, *F. S. als Theaterkomponist* (diss., Univ. of Freiburg, 1974); G. Moore, *The S. Song Cycles, with Thoughts on Performance* (London, 1975); J. Reed, "How the 'Great' C major Was Written," *Music & Letters*, LVI (1975); B. Newbould, "S.'s Other Unfinished," *Musical Times* (July 1978); R. Winter, "S.'s Undated Works, A New Chronology," ibid., CXIX (1978); C. Brauner, "Irony in the Heine Lieder of S. and Schumann," *Musical Quarterly* (April 1981); R. van Hoorickx, "An Unknown S. Letter," *Musical Times* (May 1981); E. Badura-Skoda and P. Branscombe, eds., *S. Studies: Problems of Style and Chronology* (Cambridge, 1982); L. Minchin, *S. in English* (London, 1982); R. Pascall, "Brahms and S.," *Musical Times* (May 1983); B. Newbould, "Completing S.'s Unfinished Orchestral Works," *Ovation* (Dec. 1984); J. Reed, *The S. Song Companion* (Manchester, 1984); W. Maser, *Armer S.!: Fälschungen und Manipulationen: Marginalien zu F. S.s Sinfonie von 1825* (Stuttgart, 1985); R. Schulz-Storck, *Tempobezeichnungen in F. S.s Liedern* (1985); B. Newbould, "S.'s Last Symphony," *Musical Times* (May 1985); W. Frisch, *S.: Critical and Analytical Studies* (Lincoln, Nebr., 1986); H. Jaskulsky, *Die lateinischen Messen F. S.s* (Mainz, 1986); S. Youens, "S., Mahler and the Weight of the Past: 'Lieder eines fahrenden Gesellen' and 'Wintereisse,'" *Music & Letters* (July 1986); A. Fehn and R. Hallmark, "Text and Music in S.'s Pentameter Lieder: A Consideration of Declamation," *Studies in the History of Music* (vol. I, N.Y., 1987); R. Kramer, "Gradus ad Parnassum: Beethoven, S., and the Romance of Counterpoint," *19th Century Music* (Fall 1987); E. McKay, *The Impact of the New Pianofortes on Classical Keyboard Style: Mozart, Beethoven, and S.* (West Hagley, West Midlands, 1987); J. Reed, "S.'s E flat Piano Sonata: a new date," *Musical Times* (Sept. 1987); B. Eckle, *Studien zu F. S.s Orchestersatz: Das obligate Accompagnement in den Sinfonien* (Stuttgart, 1988); E. Partsch, ed., *F. S.—Der Fortschrittliche? Analysen—Perspektiven—Fakten* (Tutzing, 1989).

Schubert, Louis, German violinist, singing teacher, and composer; b. Dessau, Jan. 27, 1828; d. Dresden, Sept. 17, 1884. He went to St. Petersburg at the age of 17; then was concertmaster of the City Theater in Königsberg for 6 years; eventually settled in Dresden, and became a singing teacher. He publ. a *Gesang-Schule in Liedern*, opp. 18 and 23 to 24 (Leipzig, c.1868); composed the operettas *Aus Sibirien* (Königsberg, 1856), *Die Rosenmädchen* (Königsberg, 1860), *Die Wahrsagerin* (Dresden, 1864), *Wer ist der Erbe?* (Dresden, 1865), *Die beiden Geizigen* (Altenburg, 1879), and the opera *Faustina Hasse* (Altenburg, 1879).

Schuberth, family of German musicians and music publishers:
(1) Gottlob Schuberth, clarinetist and oboist; b. Karsdorf, Aug. 11, 1778; d. Hamburg, Feb. 18, 1846. He studied in Jena and received violin lessons from Stamitz; was active as

a clarinetist and oboist in Magdeburg (from 1804); settled in Hamburg in 1833. He had 4 sons:
(2) Julius (Ferdinand Georg) Schuberth, music publisher; b. Magdeburg, July 14, 1804; d. Leipzig, June 9, 1875. He learned the music publishing business in Magdeburg; founded his own business in Hamburg in 1826; as proprietor of J. Schuberth & Co., he opened branches in Leipzig (1832) and in N.Y. (1850); his brother, Friedrich Schuberth, took over the Hamburg firm in 1853 under the name of Fritz Schuberth. Julius Schuberth ed. a *Musikalisches Fremdwörterbuch* (Hamburg, 1840; 8th ed., 1870), the *Kleine Hamburger Musik Zeitung* (1840–50), a *Musikalisches Conversationslexicon* (Leipzig, 1850; 10th ed., 1877; Eng. tr., 1895), the *New Yorker Musikzeitung* (1867), and *Schuberths kleine Musikzeitung* (1871–72). After his death, his widow and nephew ran the firm until it was sold to Felix Siegel in 1891. In 1943 the entire stock of the business was destroyed in an air raid; after World War II, it was reestablished in Wiesbaden.
(3) Ludwig Schuberth, conductor and composer; b. Magdeburg, April 18, 1806; d. St. Petersburg, May 1850. He studied with his father and Carl Maria von Weber; was only 16 when he was made music director at the Magdeburg theater; later was Hofkapellmeister in Oldenburg; subsequently settled in St. Petersburg as conductor of the German Opera (1845). He wrote operas, syms., and chamber music.
(4) Carl Schuberth, cellist, conductor, and composer; b. Magdeburg, Feb. 25, 1811; d. Zürich, July 22, 1863. He studied piano with his father and cello with L. Hesse; after touring (1828–29), he became 1st cellist in the Magdeburg theater orch.; then toured widely in Europe before settling in St. Petersburg as solo cellist at the court (1835); was also music director of the Univ. and conductor of the imperial court orch.; settled in Switzerland (1855). He publ. 2 cello concertos; Variations for Cello and Orch.; String Octet; 2 string quintets; 4 string quartets; Cello Sonata.
(5) Friedrich (Wilhelm August) Schuberth, music publisher; b. Magdeburg, Oct. 27, 1817; d. after 1890. In 1853 he took over the Hamburg firm established by his brother Julius Schuberth, under the name Fritz Schuberth.

Schubiger, Anselm (baptized **Josef Alois**), Swiss writer on music; b. Uznach, March 5, 1815; d. Einsiedeln, March 14, 1888. He took Holy Orders in 1839, and assumed the clerical name Anselm. He wrote *Die Sängerschule St. Gallens . . .* (Einsiedeln, 1858); *Die Pflege des Kirchengesanges und der Kirchenmusik in der deutschen katholischen Schweiz* (Einsiedeln, 1873); *Musikalische Spicilegien . . .* (Berlin, 1876; a collection of miscellaneous essays on medieval music); also various papers publ. in journals.

Schuch, Ernst von, eminent Austrian conductor; b. Graz, Nov. 23, 1846; d. Kötzschenbroda, near Dresden, May 10, 1914. He studied law in Graz, where he also received instruction in music from Eduard Stolz, and served as director of the Musikverein; then went to Vienna, where he completed his training in law at the Univ. and also continued his musical studies with Otto Dessoff. He began his career as a violinist; after serving as music director of Lobe's theater in Breslau (1867–68), he conducted in Würzburg (1868–70), Graz (1870–71), and Basel (1871). In 1872 he was called to Dresden as conductor of Pollini's Italian Opera; that same year he was named Royal Music Director at the Court Opera, and then Royal Kapellmeister in 1873, sharing his duties with Julius Rietz until 1879 and with Franz Wüllner until 1882, when he became sole Royal Kapellmeister. In addition to his exemplary performances at the Court Opera, he also distinguished himself as conductor of the concerts of the Königliche Kapelle from 1877. In 1889 he was named Dresden's Generalmusikdirektor, and in 1897 was ennobled by Emperor Franz Joseph of Austria-Hungary. He appeared widely as a guest conductor in Europe; his only visit to the U.S. was in 1900, when he led concerts in N.Y. During his long tenure, Schuch conducted 51 world premieres at the Dresden Court Opera, including Strauss's *Feuersnot* (Nov. 21, 1901), *Salome* (Dec. 9, 1905),

Elektra (Jan. 25, 1909), and *Der Rosenkavalier* (Jan. 26, 1911); was also the 1st conductor to perform Puccini's operas and Mascagni's *Cavalleria rusticana* in Germany. In his concert programs, he likewise conducted many works by contemporary composers. In 1875 he married the Hungarian soprano Clementine Procházka (b. Odenburg, Feb. 12, 1850; d. Kötzschenbroda, June 8, 1932); she studied with Mathilde Marchesi at the Vienna Cons., then was principal coloratura soprano at the Dresden Court Opera (1873–1904), where she took the name Schuch-Proska after her marriage. On June 4, 1884, she made her debut at London's Covent Garden as Eva in *Die Meistersinger von Nürnberg*; also sang in Vienna and Munich. Her other notable roles included Blondchen, Zerlina, Amina, Aennchen, and Violetta. Their daughter **Liesel von Schuch** (b. Dresden, Dec. 12, 1891; d. there, Jan. 10, 1990) was also a coloratura soprano at the Dresden Court (later State) Opera (1914–35); then taught voice at the Dresden Hochschule für Musik (until 1967).
  BIBL.: H. von Brescius, *Die Königliche musikalische Kapelle von Reissiger bis S. (1826–1898): Festschrift zu Feier des 350-jährigen Kapelljubiläums* (Dresden, 1898); P. Sakolowski, *E. v.S.* (Leipzig, 1901); F. von Schuch, *Richard Strauss, E. v.S. und Dresdens Oper* (Dresden, 1952; 2nd ed., 1953).

Schüchter, Wilhelm, German conductor; b. Bonn, Dec. 15, 1911; d. Dortmund, May 27, 1974. He studied conducting with Hermann Abendroth and composition with Philipp Jarnach at the Cologne Hochschule für Musik. He then conducted opera at Würzburg (1937–40), and served as assistant to Herbert von Karajan in Aachen (1940–42); also conducted at the Berlin Städtische Oper (1942–43). In 1947 he was appointed to the post of 1st conductor of the North German Radio Sym. Orch. in Hamburg. After serving as principal guest conductor of the NHK Sym. Orch. in Tokyo (1958–61), he settled in Dortmund as Generalmusikdirektor in 1962; was named artistic director of its Städtische Oper in 1965, and conducted the inaugural production at its new opera house in 1966. He acquired a fine reputation as a Wagnerian interpreter.

Schudel, Thomas, American-born Canadian composer and teacher; b. Defiance, Ohio, Sept. 8, 1937. He studied composition with Marshal Barnes, and received training in bassoon at Ohio State Univ. (B.Sc., 1959; M.A., 1961); then studied composition with Leslie Bassett and Ross Lee Finney at the Univ. of Michigan (D.M.A., 1971). In 1964 he joined the faculty of the Univ. of Regina in Saskatchewan; also was principal bassoonist in the Regina Sym. Orch. (1964–74); became a naturalized Canadian citizen in 1974. In 1972 his 1st Sym. won 1st prize in the City of Trieste International Competition for symphonic composition.
  WORKS: ORCH.: 2 syms.: No. 1 (1971; Trieste, Oct. 20, 1972); No. 2 (1983); *Variations* (1977); *Winterpiece* for Chamber Orch. and Dancers (1979); *Elegy and Exaltation* for Concert Band (1984); Concerto for Piccolo, String Orch. or String Quintet, and Percussion (1988). **CHAMBER:** *Set No. 2* for Wind and Brass Quintets (1963); Violin Sonata (1966); *String Quartet 1967* (1967); *Chanson and Minuet* for Oboe and Piano (1977); Trio for 3 Percussionists (1977); *Triptych* for Chamber Wind Ensemble (1978); *Richter 7.8* for 12 Tubas or Low Brass (1979); *4 by 2* for Horn and Marimba (1980); *Etchings* for Horn and Piano (1985); *Incantations* for Double Bass and Percussion (1986); *Intermezzo* for Flute and Clarinet (1987); *Dialogues* for Trombone and Percussion (1987); *Bagatelle* for 2 Flutes (1987); *Pentagram* for Saxophone Quartet and Percussionist (1987); *2 Images* for Alto Saxophone and Piano (1988); solo pieces; piano works. **VOCAL: CHORAL:** *Psalm 23* (1968); *Acquainted with the Night* (1980); *Fire and Ice* (1980); *Desert Places* (1980); *A Dream within a Dream* (1985); *Ale* (1985); *Eldorado* (1985); also *Queer Cornered Cap* for Mezzo-soprano, Flute, and Marimba (1982); *A.C.T.S.* for Narrator, Flute, Oboe, Clarinet, Double Bass, and Percussion (1986); *Edging Out* for Soprano, Flute, Oboe, and Vibraphone (1987); songs.

Schuecker, Edmund, Austrian-American harpist and composer; b. Vienna, Nov. 16, 1860; d. Bad Kreuznach, Nov. 9,

1911. After studying with Zamara at the Vienna Cons., he played the harp in various orchs. After playing in the Gewandhaus Orch. and teaching at the Leipzig Cons. (1884–91), he joined Theodore Thomas's newly organized Chicago Orch. as solo harpist in 1891. He was a member of the Vienna Court Opera orch. (1900), and then played in the Pittsburgh Sym. Orch. (1903–4), the Philadelphia Orch. (1904–9), and the Metropolitan Opera orch. in N.Y. (1910). He wrote various pieces for solo harp, of which a *Mazurka*, op. 12 became popular; also publ. 10 vols. of solo studies and 7 vols. of orch. studies.

Schuh, Willi, eminent Swiss music critic and musicologist; b. Basel, Nov. 12, 1900; d. Zürich, Oct. 4, 1986. He studied music in Aarau with Kutschera and Wehrli, in Bern with Papst, and in Munich with Courvoisier and Beer-Walbrunn. He took courses in art history and musicology in Munich with Sandberger and in Bern with Kurth; in 1927 he received his Ph.D. from the Univ. of Bern with the dissertation *Formprobleme bei Heinrich Schütz* (publ. in Leipzig, 1928). In 1928 he was engaged as music critic of the *Neue Zürcher Zeitung;* was its music ed. from 1944 until 1965; was also ed.-in-chief of the *Schweizerische Musikzeitung* (1941–68). He also taught music history and harmony in Winterthur, in St. Gall, and at the Zürich Cons. He was made an honorary member of the Schweizerischer Tonkünstlerverein in 1969 and of the Schweizerische Musikforschende Gesellschaft in 1971. He was an ed. of the *Schweizer Musikerlexikon* (Zürich, 1964). Several of his writings were republished in *Kritiken und Essays* (4 vols.: vol. 1, *Über Opern von Richard Strauss,* Zürich, 1947; vol. 2, *Zeitgenössische Musik,* Zürich, 1947; vol. 3, *Schweizer Musik der Gegenwart,* Zürich, 1948; vol. 4, *Von neuer Musik,* Zürich, 1955); also *Umgang mit Musik: Über Komponisten, Libretti und Bilder* (Zürich, 1970; 2nd ed., 1971). He was the ed. of *Die Briefe Richard Wagners an Judith Gautier* (Zürich, 1936); *Ferruccio Busoni: Briefe an seine Frau* (Zürich, 1936); Hugo von Hofmannsthal's *Beethoven* (Vienna, 1937; 2nd ed., 1949); with H. Ehinger and E. Refardt, *Schweizer Musikbuch* (Zürich, 1939); *Richard Strauss: Betrachtungen und Erinnerungen* (Zürich, 1949; Eng. tr., 1955; 2nd Swiss ed., rev., 1957); *Hugo von Hofmannsthal: Briefwechsel* (Zürich, 1952; Eng. tr., 1961; 4th Swiss ed., rev., 1970); *Richard Strauss: Briefe an die Eltern* (Zürich, 1954); *Igor Strawinsky: Leben und Werk, von ihm selbst* (Zürich and Mainz, 1957); *Richard Strauss und Stefan Zweig: Briefwechsel* (Frankfurt, 1957; Eng. tr. as *A Confidential Matter: The Letters of Richard Strauss and Stefan Zweig 1931–1935,* Berkeley, Calif., 1977); with G. Kende, *Richard Strauss und Clemens Krauss: Briefwechsel* (Munich, 1963; 2nd ed., 1964); *Richard Strauss und Willi Schuh: Briefwechsel* (Zürich, 1969). His publ. writings include *Othmar Schoeck* (Zürich, 1934); *In memoriam Richard Strauss* (Zürich, 1949); *Danae oder Die Vernunftheirat* (Frankfurt, 1952); *Renoir und Wagner* (Zürich, 1959); *Ein paar Erinnerungen an Richard Strauss* (Zürich, 1964); *Hugo von Hofmannsthal und Richard Strauss: Legende und Wirklichkeit* (Munich, 1964); *Der Rosenkavalier: Vier Studien* (Olten, 1968); *Richard Strauss: Jugend und frühe Meisterjahre: Lebenschronik 1864–98* (the authorized biography; Zürich, 1976; Eng. tr. as *Richard Strauss: A Chronicle of the Early Years 1864–98,* Cambridge, 1982).
  BIBL.: J. Stenzl, "W. S. zum 75. Geburtstag," *Schweizerische Musikzeitung/Revue Musicale Suisse,* CXV (1975).

Schüler, Johannes, German conductor; b. Vietz, Neumark, June 21, 1894; d. Berlin, Oct. 3, 1966. He studied at the Berlin Hochschule für Musik; conducted opera in Gleiwitz (1920–22), Königsberg (1922–24), and Hannover (1924–28); served as music director in Oldenburg (1928–32); also conducted in Halle (1932); later was music director in Essen (1933–36). In 1936 he joined the roster of the Berlin State Opera; in 1949 he became Generalmusikdirektor in Hannover, a post he held until 1960.

Schulhoff, Erwin (actually, **Ervín**), Czech pianist, teacher, and composer, great-grandnephew of **Julius Schulhoff;** b. Prague, June 8, 1894; d. in a concentration camp in Wülzbourg, Bavaria, Aug. 18, 1942. He studied music in Prague and Vienna; then went to Leipzig, where he studied piano with Teich-müller and composition with Max Reger (1908–10); continued his studies in Cologne (1910–14). Returning to Prague, he was active as a piano teacher; traveled as a concert pianist in Russia and France. He was an eager propagandist of modern music; together with Alois Hába, he worked on the problems of quarter-tone music. In 1933 he was a delegate at the International Congress of Revolutionary Musicians in Moscow. Convinced of the necessity of social revolution, he became a member of the Communist party; after the Nazi occupation of Czechoslovakia in 1939, he was granted Soviet citizenship to protect him from arrest; however, after the Nazi invasion of Russia in 1941, he was arrested and sent to the concentration camp in Wülzbourg, where he perished. As a composer, he followed the modern trends of the period between the 2 World Wars, including the European species of jazz. He was the 1st to set to music the original German text of the Communist Manifesto of 1848; the MS disappeared, but was eventually retrieved, and the work was finally performed in Prague on April 5, 1962.

Works: Stage: *Ogelala,* ballet (Dessau, Nov. 21, 1925); *La Somnambule,* ballet dance-grotesque (1925; Oxford I.S.C.M. Festival, July 24, 1931); *Bartipanu,* ballet scenes for Molière's *Le Bourgeois Gentilhomme* (1926; also an orch. suite); *Plameny (Flames),* opera (1927–28; Brno, Jan. 27, 1932). **ORCH.:** 2 piano concertos (1913, 1923); *32 Variations on an Original Theme* (1919); *Suite* for Chamber Orch. (1921); 8 syms.: No. 1 (1925); No. 2 (1932; Prague, April 24, 1935); No. 3 (1935); No. 4, *Spanish,* for Baritone and Orch. (1936–37); No. 5 (1938); No. 6, *Symphony of Freedom,* with choral finale (1940–41; Prague, May 5, 1946); No. 7, *Eroica* (1941; unfinished); No. 8 (1942; unfinished); *Double Concerto* for Flute, Piano, String Orch., and 2 Horns (Prague, Dec. 8, 1927); Concerto for String Quartet and Wind Orch. (1930; Prague, Nov. 9, 1932). **CHAMBER:** 2 violin sonatas (1913, 1927); Cello Sonata (1915); *5 Pieces for String Quartet* (1923); String Sextet (1924); 2 string quartets (1924, 1925); Duo for Violin and Cello (1925); *Concertino* for Flute, Viola, and Double Bass (1925); *Divertissement* for Oboe, Clarinet, and Bassoon (1926); Sonata for Solo Violin (1927); Flute Sonata (1927); *Hot Sonata* for Saxophone and Piano (1930). **VOCAL:** *Landschaften,* sym. for Mezzo-soprano and Orch. (1918); *Menschheit,* sym. for Alto and Orch. (1919); *H.M.S. Royal Oak,* jazz oratorio (radio perf., Brno, Feb. 12, 1935); *The Communist Manifesto,* cantata to the German text of the famous declaration of Marx and Engels (1932; Prague, April 5, 1962); *1917,* cycle of 12 songs (1933). **PIANO:** *Variations on an Original Theme* (1913); *5 Grotesken* (1917); 4 sonatas (1918, 1924, 1926, 1927); *5 Arabesken* (1919); *Ironies* (1920); *Rag Music* (1922); *Partita* (1922); *Ostinato* (1923); *5 Etudes de Jazz* (1926); *6 Esquisses de Jazz* (1927); *Hot Music* (1928); *Suite dansante en Jazz* (1931).

BIBL.: V. Stara, ed., *Erwin S., Vzpomniky, studie a dokumenty* (Prague, 1958).

Schulhoff, Julius, noted Bohemian pianist, teacher, and composer, great-granduncle of **Erwin (Ervín) Schulhoff;** b. Prague, Aug. 2, 1825; d. Berlin, March 13, 1898. He studied in Prague; proceeded to Paris, where he gave concerts under the patronage of Chopin, to whom he dedicated his 1st composition, an *Allegro brillant.* He made a long tour through Austria, England, Spain, and Southern Russia; returning to Paris, he was a successful teacher; after the outbreak of the Franco-Prussian War (1870), he settled in Dresden; moved to Berlin shortly before his death. He publ. excellent salon music for piano; his *Galop di bravura* and *Impromptu Polka* were great favorites.

Schuller, Gunther (Alexander), significant American composer, conductor, and music educator; b. N.Y., Nov. 22, 1925. He was of a musical family; his paternal grandfather was a bandmaster in Germany before emigrating to America; his father was a violinist with the N.Y. Phil. He was sent to Germany as a child for a thorough academic training; returning to N.Y., he studied at the St. Thomas Choir School (1938–

44); also received private instruction in theory, flute, and horn. He played in the N.Y. City Ballet orch. (1943); then was 1st horn in the Cincinnati Sym. Orch. (1943–45) and the Metropolitan Opera orch. in N.Y. (1945–49). At the same time, he became fascinated with jazz; he played the horn in a combo conducted by Miles Davis; also began to compose jazz pieces. He taught at the Manhattan School of Music in N.Y. (1950–63), the Yale Univ. School of Music (1964–67), and the New England Cons. of Music in Boston, where he greatly distinguished himself as president (1967–77). He was also active at the Berkshire Music Center at Tanglewood as a teacher of composition (1963–84), head of contemporary-music activities (1965–84), artistic co-director (1969–74), and director (1974–84). In 1984–85 he was interim music director of the Spokane (Wash.) Sym. Orch.; then was director of its Sandpoint (Idaho) Festival. In 1986 he founded the Boston Composers' Orch. In 1988 he was awarded the 1st Elise L. Stoeger Composer's Chair of the Chamber Music Soc. of Lincoln Center in N.Y. In 1975 he organized Margun Music to make available unpubl. American music. He founded GunMar Music in 1979. In 1980 he organized GM Recordings. He publ. the manual *Horn Technique* (N.Y., 1962) and the very valuable study *Early Jazz: Its Roots and Musical Development* (3 vols., N.Y., 1968–). A vol. of his writings appeared as *Musings* (N.Y., 1985). In his multiple activities, he tried to form a link between serious music and jazz; he popularized the style of "cool jazz" (recorded as *Birth of the Cool*). In 1957 he launched the slogan "third stream" to designate the combination of classical forms with improvisatory elements of jazz as a synthesis of disparate, but not necessarily incompatible, entities, and wrote fanciful pieces in this synthetic style; in many of these, he worked in close cooperation with John Lewis of the Modern Jazz Quartet. As part of his investigation of the roots of jazz, he became interested in early ragtime and formed, in 1972, the New England Cons. Ragtime Ensemble; its recordings of Scott Joplin's piano rags in band arrangement were instrumental in bringing about the "ragtime revival." In his own works he freely applied serial methods, even when his general style was dominated by jazz. He received honorary doctorates in music from Northwestern Univ. (1967), the Univ. of Illinois (1968), Williams College (1975), the New England Cons. of Music (1978), and Rutgers Univ. (1980). In 1967 he was elected to membership in the National Inst. of Arts and Letters, and in 1980 to the American Academy and Inst. of Arts and Letters. In 1989 he received the William Schuman Award of Columbia Univ. In 1991 he was awarded a MacArthur Foundation grant.

Works: DRAMATIC: OPERAS: *The Visitation* (Hamburg, Oct. 12, 1966); *The Fisherman and His Wife,* children's opera (Boston, May 7, 1970); *A Question of Taste* (Cooperstown, N.Y., June 24, 1989). **BALLET:** *Variants* for Jazz Quartet and Orch. (1960; N.Y., Jan. 4, 1961). **FILM SCORES:** *Automation* (1962); *Journey to the Stars* (1962); *Yesterday in Fact* (1963). **TELEVISION SCORES:** *Tear Drop* (1966); *The 5 Senses,* ballet (1967). **ORCH.:** 2 horn concertos: No. 1 (1944; Cincinnati, April 6, 1945, composer soloist); No. 2 (1976; Budapest, June 19, 1978); Cello Concerto (1945; rev. 1985); *Suite* for Chamber Orch. (1945); *Vertige d'Eros* (1945; Madison, Wis., Oct. 15, 1967); *Symphonic Study* (1947–48; Cincinnati, May 1949); *Dramatic Overture* (1951; Darmstadt, Aug. 1954); *Recitative and Rondo* for Violin and Orch. (1953; Chicago, July 16, 1967; also for Violin and Piano); *Symphonic Tribute to Duke Ellington* (1955; Lenox, Mass., Aug. 19, 1976); *Little Fantasy* (Englewood, N.J., April 7, 1957); *Contours* for Chamber Orch. (1958; Cincinnati, Dec. 31, 1959); *Spectra* (1958; N.Y., Jan. 14, 1960); *Concertino* for Jazz Quartet and Orch. (1959; Baltimore, Jan. 2, 1960); *7 Studies on Themes of Paul Klee* (Minneapolis, Nov. 27, 1959); *Capriccio* for Tuba and Orch. (1960); *Contrasts* for Wind Quintet and Orch. (1960; Donaueschingen, Oct. 22, 1961); *Journey into Jazz* for Narrator, Jazz Quintet, and Orch. (Washington, D.C., May 30, 1962); *Journey to the Stars* (Toledo, Ohio, Dec. 1, 1962); *Movements* for Flute and Strings (Dortmund, May 29, 1962); 2 piano concertos: No. 1 (Cincinnati, Oct. 29, 1962); No. 2 (1981; Mainz, Nov. 24, 1982); *Composition in 3 Parts*

(Minneapolis, March 29, 1963); *Diptych* for Brass Quintet and Band (1963; also for Brass Quintet and Orch.; Ithaca, N.Y., March 22, 1964); *Meditation* for Band (Greensboro, N.C., March 7, 1963); *Threnos* for Oboe and Orch. (Cologne, Nov. 29, 1963); *5 Bagatelles* (Fargo, N.Dak., March 22, 1964); *American Triptych: 3 Studies in Textures* (New Orleans, March 9, 1965); Sym. (Dallas, Feb. 8, 1965); 2 concertos: No. 1, *Gala Music* (Chicago, Jan. 20, 1966); No. 2 (Washington, D.C., Oct. 12, 1976); *5 Études* (1966; New Haven, March 19, 1967); *Triplum I* (N.Y., June 28, 1967) and *II* (Baltimore, Feb. 26, 1975); *Colloquy* for 2 Pianos and Orch. (Berlin, June 6, 1968); Double-bass Concerto (N.Y., Jan. 27, 1968); *Fanfare for St. Louis* (St. Louis, Jan. 24, 1968); *Shapes and Designs* (Hartford, April 26, 1969); *Consequents* (New Haven, Dec. 16, 1969); *Museum Piece* for Renaissance Instruments and Orch. (Boston, Dec. 11, 1970); *Concerto da camera* for Chamber Orch. (1971; Rochester, N.Y., April 24, 1972); *Capriccio stravagante* (San Francisco, Dec. 6, 1972); *3 Nocturnes* (Interlochen, July 15, 1973); *4 Soundscapes—Hudson Valley Reminiscences* (1974; Poughkeepsie, N.Y., March 7, 1975); Violin Concerto (Lucerne, Aug. 25, 1976); *Deaï—Encounters* for 7 Voices and 3 Orchs. (Tokyo, March 17, 1978); Contrabassoon Concerto (1978; Washington, D.C., Jan. 16, 1979); Trumpet Concerto (Jefferson, N.H., Aug. 25, 1979); *Eine kleine Posaunenmusik* for Trombone and Orch. (Norfolk, Conn., July 18, 1980); *Music for a Celebration* for Chorus, Audience, and Orch. (Springfield, Mass., Sept. 26, 1980); *In Praise of Winds* for Large Wind Orch. (Ann Arbor, Feb. 13, 1981); Alto Saxophone Concerto (1983; Pittsburgh, Jan. 18, 1984); *Concerto quarternio* for Violin, Flute, Oboe, Trumpet, and Orch. (N.Y., Nov. 21, 1984); *Concerto festivo* for Brass Quintet and Orch. (Trier, Nov. 29, 1984); *Jubilee Musik* (Dayton, March 7, 1984); Bassoon Concerto, *Eine kleine Fagottmusik* (Washington, D.C., May 17, 1985); *Farbenspiel*, concerto (Berlin, May 8, 1985); Viola Concerto (New Orleans, Dec. 17, 1985); Concerto for String Quartet and Orch. (Madison, Wis., Feb. 20, 1988); Flute Concerto (Chicago, Oct. 13, 1988); *On Winged Flight*, divertimento for Band (Tallahassee, Fla., March 4, 1989); *Chamber Symphony* (Cleveland, April 16, 1989); *Concerto for Piano 3 Hands* for 2 Pianos (3–hands) and Chamber Orch. (1989; Springfield, Ill., Jan. 19, 1990).

CHAMBER: *Romantic Sonata* for Clarinet, Horn, and Piano (1941; rev. 1983); *Suite* for Woodwind Quintet (1945); *3 hommages* for Horn or 2 Horns, and Piano (1942–46); *Fantasia concertante No. 1* for 3 Oboes and Piano (1947) and *No. 2* for 3 Trombones and Piano (1947); Quartet for 4 Double Basses (1947); *Perpetuum mobile* for 4 Horns, and Bassoon or Tuba (1948); Trio for Oboe, Horn, and Viola (1948); Oboe Sonata (1948–51); Duo Sonata for Clarinet and Bass Clarinet (1948–49); *Fantasy* for Cello (1951); *5 Pieces* for 5 Horns (1952); *Recitative and Rondo* for Violin and Piano (1953; also for Violin and Orch.); 3 string quartets (1957, 1965, 1986); Woodwind Quintet (1958); *Fantasy Quartet* for 4 Cellos (1959); *Fantasy* for Harp (1959); *Lines and Contrasts* for 16 Horns (1960); Double Quintet for Wind and Brass Quintets (1961); *Music for Brass Quintet* (1961); *Fanfare* for 4 Trumpets and 4 Trombones (1962); *Music for Carillon* (1962; also arranged for other instruments); *Studies* for Horn (1962); *Little Brass Music* for Trumpet, Horn, Trombone, and Tuba (1963); *Episodes* for Clarinet (1964); *Aphorisms* for Flute and String Trio (1967); *5 Moods* for 4 Tubas (1973); *Sonata serenata* for Clarinet, Violin, Cello, and Piano (1978); Octet (1979); Piano Trio (1983); *On Light Wings* for Piano Quartet (1984); Sextet for Bassoon, Piano, and String Quartet (1986); *The Sandpoint Rag* for Ragtime Ensemble (1986; also for Brass Sextet); *Chimeric Images* for Chamber Group (1988); *A Bouquet for Collage* for Clarinet, Flute, Violin, Cello, Piano, and Percussion (1988); Sonata for Horn and Piano (1988); *5 Impromptus* for English Horn and String Quartet (1989).

VOCAL: *O Lamb of God* for Chorus and Optional Organ (1941); *O Spirit of the Living God* for Chorus and Optional Organ (1942); *6 Renaissance Lyrics* for Tenor and 7 Instruments (1962); *5 Shakespearean Songs* for Baritone and Orch. (1964);

Sacred Cantata for Chorus and Chamber Orch. (1966); *The Power within Us*, oratorio for Baritone, Narrator, Chorus, and Orch. (1971); *Poems of Time and Eternity* for Chorus and 9 Instruments (1972); *Thou Art the Son of God*, cantata for Chorus and Chamber Ensemble (1987); songs.

BIBL.: J. Tassel, "G. S.: Composer, Conductor and Musical Conscience," *Ovation* (Nov. 1985); N. Carnovale, *G. S.: A Bio-Bibliography* (Westport, Conn., 1987).

Schulthess, Walter, Swiss conductor and composer; b. Zürich, July 24, 1894; d. there, June 23, 1971. He studied with Andreae in Zürich, Courvoisier in Munich, and Ansorge in Berlin; in 1918, settled in Zürich. As a composer, he excelled in lyric songs, in a style resembling Othmar Schoeck's. He also wrote a Violin Concertino (1921), *Serenade* for Orch. (1921), *Symphonische Variationen* for Cello and Orch. (1926), and various chamber works, including a String Quartet (1921), 2 violin sonatas (1921, 1922), and *3 Capricen nach Paganini* for Violin and Piano (1923); also wrote piano pieces, choruses, and lieder. He married the violinist **Stefi Geyer** in 1919.

Schultz, Edwin, German baritone, conductor, and composer; b. Danzig, April 30, 1827; d. Tempelhof, near Berlin, May 20, 1907. He studied singing with Brandstätter in Berlin; conducted choral societies and concerts. In 1880 the Prussian Ministry of War commissioned him to compile a book of soldiers' songs. He publ. many male choruses, songs, duets, and the collection *Meisterstücke für Pianoforte.*

Schultz, Svend (Simon), Danish pianist, conductor, and composer; b. Nykøbing, Dec. 30, 1913. He studied at the Royal Danish Cons. of Music in Copenhagen (1933–38); was music critic of *Politiken*, the Copenhagen newspaper (1942–49). He was a choral conductor with the Danish Radio (from 1949); also toured Europe as a pianist and conductor of his own compositions. In his music, he evolved a neo-Classical style characterized by simplicity of form and a cumulative rhythmic drive.

WORKS: DRAMATIC: Operas: *Bag kulisserne* (Behind the Scenes; 1946; Copenhagen, May 26, 1949); *Solbadet* (The Sunbath; 1947; Aarhus, Nov. 26, 1949); *Kaffehuset* (The Coffee House; 1948); *Høst* (Harvest; 1950); *Bryllupsrejsen* (The Honeymoon; 1951); *Tordenvejret* (The Thunderstorm; 1954); *Hosekraemmeren* (The Stocking Peddler; 1955); *Dommer Lynch* (Judge Lynch; 1959); comic television opera, *Konen i muddergrøften* (The Woman in the Muddy Ditch; 1964; Danish Television, April 18, 1965); children's opera, *Lykken og forstanden* (1973); 2 marionette operas: *Hyrdinden og skorstensfejeren* (The Shepherdess and the Chimney-Sweep; 1953) and *The Marionettes* (1957); chamber operetta, *Den kåde Donna* (Copenhagen, Aug. 30, 1957); musical church play, *Eva* (1968); oratorio, *Job* (1945). **VOCAL:** *Sankt Hans Nat* for Soloists, Chorus, and Orch. (1953); *Hymn* for Chorus and Orch. (Copenhagen, March 13, 1957); *Hr. Mortens klosterrov* (Morten's Pillage of the Monastery) for Soloists, Chorus, and Chamber Orch. (1958; Copenhagen, Oct. 13, 1960); *3 Pastorales* for Soloists, Chorus, and Orch. (Danish Radio, May 28, 1962); *The 4 Temperaments* for Female and Male Choruses and Orch. (Hillerød, Nov. 15, 1974). **ORCH.:** *Serenade* for String Orch. (1940); 7 syms.: No. 1, *Sinfonia piccola* (1941); No. 2 (1949); No. 3 (1955); No. 4 (1957); No. 5 (1960); No. 6 (1962); *Sinfonia piccola No. 2* (1973); Piano Concerto (1943); *Storstrømsbroen* (The Storstroem Bridge), symphonic vision (1951); *Introduction and Rondo* for Piano and Orch. (Danish Radio, Nov. 8, 1964); *2 Variations: Nocturne and Aubade* (1965); *Northern Overture* (1975). **CHAMBER:** 6 string quartets (1939, 1940, 1960, 1961, 1962, 1975); Flute Quartet (1961); *Romantic Trio* for Piano Trio (1961); Quartet for Flute, Violin, Viola, and Cello (1962); 2 piano trios (1942, 1963); Clarinet Quintet (1965); *Music for Wind Players* for Flute, Trumpet, Clarinet, Percussion, Vibraphone, and Piano (1966); Piano Sonata (1931); 2 piano sonatinas (1940, 1950).

Schultze, Norbert, German composer; b. Braunschweig, Jan. 26, 1911. He studied piano, conducting, and composition at the Cologne Staatliche Hochschule für Musik; after studying theatrical arts in Cologne and Munich (1931), he was active as an actor and composer in a student cabaret, *Vier Nachrichter,* in Munich (1931–32); then conducted opera in Heidelberg (1932–33) and Darmstadt (1933–34); later was a composer for stage, films, and television; was head of his own music publishing business (from 1953). He wrote the operas *Schwarzer Peter* (Hamburg, 1936) and *Das kalte Herz* (Leipzig, 1943); television opera, *Peter der dritte* (1964); operetta, *Regen in Paris* (Nuremberg, 1957); pantomimes: *Struwwelpeter* (Hamburg, 1937); *Max und Moritz* (Hamburg, 1938); *Maria im Walde* (Vienna, 1940); but his chief claim to fame was a sentimental song, *Lili Marleen,* which he wrote in 1938, and which became immensely popular during World War II among both German and Allied soldiers after it was broadcast from the German-occupied Belgrade in 1941; it was tr. into 27 languages. For some of his works he used the names Frank Norbert, Peter Kornfeld, and Henri Iversen.

Schulz, Johann Philipp Christian, German conductor and composer; b. Langensalza, Feb. 1, 1773; d. Leipzig, Jan. 30, 1827. He studied with Engel and Schicht in Leipzig; from 1810, was conductor of the Gewandhaus concerts and the Singakademie there; became music director of the Univ. of Leipzig in 1818. He wrote an overture to Klingemann's *Faust* and other orch. works, stage music, a *Salvum fac regem* for Chorus and Orch., partsongs, and lieder.

Schulz-Beuthen, Heinrich, German composer; b. Beuthen, June 19, 1838; d. Dresden, March 12, 1915. He was destined for a career as a civil engineer; while a student at the Univ. of Breslau, he learned to play the piano and attempted composition; produced a singspiel, *Fridolin* (Breslau, 1862); then went to study at the Leipzig Cons. with Moscheles (piano) and Hauptmann (composition). In 1866 he went to Zürich, where he remained until 1880; then lived in Dresden (1880–93) and Vienna (1893–95); finally settled in Dresden, where he became a prof. at the Cons. He was an ardent disciple of Liszt and Wagner; during his lifetime, he was regarded as a significant composer.

WORKS: 5 operas, including *Aschenbrödel* (Zürich, 1879); 8 syms.: No. 1, *Dem Andenken Haydns;* No. 2, *Frühlingsfeier;* No. 3, *Sinfonia maestosa;* No. 4, *Schön Elsbeth;* No. 5, *Reformationssymphonie* (with Organ); No. 6, *König Lear* (with Male Chorus); No. 7 (expanded from a string quartet); No. 8, *Siegessymphonie;* symphonic poems: *Mittelalterliche Volksszene, Des Meeres und der Liebe Wellen, Beethoven-Hymnus, Ein Pharaonenbegräbnis, Wilhelm Tell, Sturmesmythe;* overtures; orch. suites; *Symphonisches Konzert* for Piano and Orch.; String Quintet; Wind Octet; String Trio; etc.; sacred choral music; piano pieces.

    BIBL.: K. Mey, *H. S.-B.* (Leipzig, 1909); A. Zosel, *H. S.-B.* (Würzburg, 1931).

Schulze, Christian Andreas, German composer; b. Dresden, c.1660; d. Meissen, Sept. 11, 1699. He was a pupil at the Dresden Kreuzschule and the Univ. of Leipzig; in 1678 he settled in Meissen as Kantor of the municipal church and the Franciscaneum, the municipal Lateinschule; he later became Kantor of the Cathedral as well. He was a notable composer of sacred music; among his works are a *Historia resurrectionis* (1686), sacred concertos, and Protestant church cantatas.

Schulze, Hans-Joachim, distinguished German musicologist; b. Leipzig, Dec. 3, 1934. He studied musicology in Leipzig at the Hochschule für Musik (1952–54) and with Serauky, Eller, and Besseler at the Karl Marx Univ. (1954–57); completed his education at the Univ. of Rostock (Ph.D., 1979, with the diss. *Studien zur Bach-Überlieferung im 18. Jahrhundert;* publ. in Leipzig, 1984). In 1957 he became a research assistant at the Leipzig Bach Archive, where he later served as deputy director (1974–79); with C. Wolff, he was co-ed. of the *Bach-Jahrbuch* (from 1975). He was made head research fellow of the Nationale Forschungs- und Gedenkstätten Johann Sebastian Bach in Leipzig in 1979, and was appointed director of the Leipzig Bach Archive in 1986. He was a lecturer at

the Martin Luther Univ. in Halle-Wittenberg (1987–88), and has lectured as a visiting prof. in univs. in Europe and the U.S. A devoted scholar of Bach, Schulze is a respected authority in his field.

    WRITINGS: Ed. with W. Neumann, *Schriftstücke von der Hand Johann Sebastian Bachs,* Bach-Dokumente, I (Leipzig, 1963); ed. *Fremdschriftliche und gedruckte Dokumente zur Lebensgeschichte Johann Sebastian Bachs 1685–1750,* Bach-Dokumente, II (Leipzig, 1969); ed. *Dokumente zum Nachwirken Johann Sebastian Bachs 1750–1800,* Bach-Dokumente, III (Leipzig, 1972); *Johann Sebastian Bach: Leben und Werk in Dokumenten* (Leipzig, 1975); ed. with C. Wolff, *Bach Compendium: Analytisch-bibliographisches Repertorium der Werke Johann Sebastian Bachs* (5 vols., Leipzig and Dresden, 1985–).

Schulz-Evler, Andrei, Polish pianist, teacher, and composer; b. Radom, Dec. 12, 1852; d. Warsaw, May 15, 1905. He studied at the Warsaw Cons., and later with Tausig in Berlin; was a prof. of piano at the Kharkov Music School (1888–1904); publ. 52 piano pieces and songs; his transcription of the *Blue Danube Waltz* was very popular with pianists for a time.

Schulz-Schwerin, Karl, German pianist, teacher, and composer; b. Schwerin, Jan. 3, 1845; d. Mannheim, May 24, 1913. He studied at the Stern Cons. in Berlin (1862–65) with Bülow, Stern, and Weitzmann. He was court pianist to the Grand Duke of Mecklenburg; then taught at the Stern Cons. (1885–1901). He composed a sym.; overtures to *Torquato Tasso* and *Die Braut von Messina; Serenata giocosa, In Memoriam,* and *Jubiläums-Festmarsch* for Orch.; *Sanctus, Osanna, Benedictus, Ave Maria,* etc., for Soli, Chorus, and Orch.; piano pieces.

Schulz, Johann Abraham Peter, esteemed German conductor and composer; b. Lüneburg, March 31, 1747; d. Schwedt an der Oder, June 10, 1800. He studied with J.C. Schmügel in Lüneburg and Kirnberger in Berlin (1765–68); from 1768 to 1773 he was accompanist and music teacher to Princess Sapieha Woiwodin von Smolensk of Poland, with whom he traveled throughout Europe. He returned to Berlin as music director of the new French theater in 1776 and of the private theater of the Prussian crown princess Friederike Luise in 1778; then was court composer to Prince Heinrich, the brother of the king, in Rheinsberg (1780–87). In 1787 he went to Copenhagen as Hofkapellmeister and director of the Royal Danish Theater, positions he held with distinction until tuberculosis compelled him to step down in 1795. He spent his last years in Berlin and Rheinsberg, visiting Schwedt an der Oder intermittently for his health. He was known primarily for his marked ability as a lieder composer.

    WORKS: STAGE: *Das Opfer der Nymphen* (for the birthday of Friedrich the Great; 1774); *Clarissa, oder Das unbekannte Dienstmädchen* (Berlin, 1775); *Musique de l'impromptu* (c.1779); *La Fée Urgèle, ou Ce qui plaît aux dames* (1780–81; Rheinsberg, 1782; rev. version in German, Berlin, 1789); *La Vérité* (Rheinsberg, 1785); *Panomphée* (c.1785); *Athalie* (Rheinsberg, 1785; rev. version, Berlin, 1786); *Minona oder Die Angelsachsen* (Hamburg, 1786); *Aline, reine de Golconde* (Rheinsberg, 1787); *Indtoget* (1789–90; Copenhagen, Feb. 26, 1793); *Høstgildet* (Copenhagen, Sept. 16, 1790); *Peters bryllup* (Copenhagen, Dec. 12, 1793). **ORATORIOS:** *Maria og Johannes* (1787–88); *Christi død* (Christiansborg, 1792); *Frelserens sidste Stund* (Copenhagen, March 1794). **CANTATAS:** *Vater, bester lebe* for Voice and Orch. (Berlin, 1774); *Universitiets-kantata til død af H. v. Stampe* (Copenhagen, 1789); *Kantata til Kronprinds Fredericks formoeling* (Copenhagen, 1790); *Sorge-sange da Prindsesse Sophie Frederike bisattes* (Roskilde, Dec. 28, 1794); *Jesu Minde* (1794); also motets, hymns, and other sacred works; lieder, including (25) *Gesänge am Clavier* (Berlin and Leipzig, 1779), (48) *Lieder im Volkston* (3 vols., Berlin, 1782–85), *Johann Peter Uzens lyrische Gedichte religiösen Inhalts* (Hamburg, 1784; 2nd ed., 1794), and *Gedichte von Friederike Brun, geboren Münter* (Zürich, 1795); chamber music.

    WRITINGS: With J. Kirnberger, *Die wahren Grundsätze zum Gebrauche der Harmonie . . . als Zusatz zu der Kunst des reinen Satzes in der Musik* (Berlin and Königsberg, 1773; 2nd ed.,

1793; publ. as Kirnberger's); *Entwurf einer neuen und leichtverständlichen Musiktablatur* (Berlin, 1786); *Gedanken über den Einfluss der Musik auf die Bildung eines Volks* (Copenhagen, 1790; Danish tr., 1790); *Über den Choral und die ältere Literatur desselben* (2nd ed., Erfurt, 1872).

BIBL.: C. Klunger, *J.S.P. S. in seinen volkstümlichen Liedern* (Leipzig, 1909); O. Riess, *J.A.P. S.' Leben* (Leipzig, 1913); E. Schmitz, *Unverwelkter Volkslied-Stil J.A.P. S. und J.H. Voss* (Kassel and Basel, 1960).

Schuman, William (Howard), eminent American composer, music educator, and administrator; b. N.Y., Aug. 4, 1910. He began composing at 16, turning out a number of popular songs; also played in jazz groups. He took courses at N.Y. Univ.'s School of Commerce (1928–30) before turning decisively to music and taking private lessons in harmony with Max Persin and in counterpoint with Charles Haubiel (1931) in N.Y. After attending summer courses with Bernard Wagenaar and Adolf Schmid at N.Y.'s Juilliard School (1932–33), he pursued his education at Teacher's College of Columbia Univ. (B.S., 1935; M.A., 1937); also studied conducting at the Salzburg Mozarteum (summer 1935) and composition with Roy Harris, both at the Juilliard School (summer 1936) and privately (1936–38). He came to the attention of Koussevitzky, who conducted the premieres of his *American Festival Overture* (1939), 3rd Sym. (1941; received the 1st N.Y. Music Critics' Circle Award), *A Free Song* (1943; received the 1st Pulitzer Prize in Music), and the Sym. for Strings (1943); Rodzinski conducted the premiere of his 4th Sym. (1942). After teaching at Sarah Lawrence College (1935–45), he served as director of publications of G. Schirmer, Inc. (1945–52) and as president of the Juilliard School of Music (1945–62), where he acquired a notable reputation as a music educator; he subsequently was president of Lincoln Center for the Performing Arts in N.Y. (1962–69). He was chairman of the MacDowell Colony (from 1973) and the 1st chairman of the Norlin Foundation (1975–85). The recipient of numerous honors, he held 2 Guggenheim fellowships (1939–41), was elected a member of the National Inst. of Arts and Letters (1946) and the American Academy of Arts and Letters (1973), was awarded the gold medal of the American Academy and Inst. of Arts and Letters (1982), won a 2nd, special Pulitzer Prize (1985), and received the National Medal of Arts (1987). Columbia Univ. established the William Schuman Award in 1981, a prize of $50,000 given to a composer for lifetime achievement; fittingly, Schuman was its 1st recipient. His music is characterized by great emotional tension, which is maintained by powerful asymmetric rhythms; the contrapuntal structures in his works reach a great degree of complexity and are saturated with dissonance without, however, losing the essential tonal references. In several of his works, he employs American melorhythms, but his general style of composition is cosmopolitan, exploring all viable techniques of modern composition.

WORKS: DRAMATIC: OPERA: *The Mighty Casey* (1951–53; Hartford, Conn., May 4, 1953; rev. as the cantata *Casey at the Bat*, Washington, D.C., April 6, 1976). **BALLETS:** *Undertow* (N.Y., April 10, 1945); *Night Journey* (Cambridge, Mass., May 3, 1947); *Judith* (1949; Louisville, Jan. 4, 1950); *Voyage for a Theater* (N.Y., May 17, 1953; withdrawn); *The Witch of Endor* (N.Y., Nov. 2, 1965; withdrawn). **FILM SCORES:** *Steeltown* (1941); *The Earth Is Born* (1959).

ORCH.: *Potpourri* (1932; withdrawn); 10 syms.: No. 1 for 18 Instruments (1935; N.Y., Oct. 21, 1936; withdrawn); No. 2 (1937; N.Y., May 25, 1938; withdrawn); No. 3 (Boston, Oct. 17, 1941); No. 4 (1941; Cleveland, Jan. 22, 1942); No. 5, *Sym. for Strings* (Boston, Nov. 12, 1943); No. 6 (1948; Dallas, Feb. 27, 1949); No. 7 (Boston, Oct. 21, 1960); No. 8 (N.Y., Oct. 4, 1962); No. 9, *Le fosse ardeatine* (1968; Philadelphia, Jan. 10, 1969); No. 10, *American Muse* (1975; Washington, D.C., April 6, 1976); Piano Concerto (1938; rev. 1942; N.Y., Jan. 13, 1943); *American Festival Overture* (Boston, Oct. 6, 1939); *Newsreel, in 5 Shots* for Concert Band (1941; also for Orch., N.Y., July 15, 1942); *Prayer in Time of War* (Pittsburgh,

Feb. 26, 1943); *William Billings Overture* (1943; N.Y., Feb. 17, 1944; withdrawn); *Variations on a Theme by Eugene Goossens* (No. 5 of 10 variations, each by a different composer; 1944; Cincinnati, March 23, 1945); *Circus Overture: Side Show* (1944; for Small Orch., Philadelphia, July 20, 1944; for Full Orch., Pittsburgh, Jan. 7, 1945); *Undertow,* choreographic episodes from the ballet (Los Angeles, Nov. 29, 1945); Violin Concerto (1947; Boston, Feb. 10, 1950; rev. 1954; N.Y., Feb. 26, 1956; rev. 1958–59; Aspen, Colo., Aug. 9, 1959); *George Washington Bridge* for Concert Band (Interlochen, Mich., July 30, 1950); *Credendum, Article of Faith* (Cincinnati, Nov. 4, 1955); *New England Triptych* (Miami, Oct. 28, 1956); *Chester Overture* for Concert Band from *New England Triptych* (1956); *When Jesus Wept* for Concert Band from *New England Triptych* (1958); *A Song of Orpheus* for Cello and Orch. (1961; Indianapolis, Feb. 17, 1962; arranged for Cello and Chamber Orch. in collaboration with J. Goldberg, 1978); *Variations on "America"* after the organ work by Ives (1963; N.Y., May 20, 1964; also for Band, 1968); *The Orchestra Song* (1963; N.Y., April 11, 1964; also for Band as *The Band Song*); *Philharmonic Fanfare* for Concert Band (N.Y., Aug. 10, 1965; withdrawn); *Dedication Fanfare* for Concert Band (St. Louis, July 4, 1968); *To Thee Old Cause* for Oboe, Brass, Timpani, Piano, and Strings (N.Y., Oct. 3, 1968); *In Praise of Shahn,* canticle (1969; N.Y., Jan. 29, 1970); *Anniversary Fanfare* for Brass and Percussion (1969; N.Y., April 13, 1970); *Voyage for Orchestra* (Rochester, N.Y., Oct. 27, 1972); *Prelude for a Great Occasion* for Brass and Percussion (Washington, D.C., Oct. 1, 1974); *Be Glad Then, America* for Concert Band from *New England Triptych* (1975); *3 Colloquies* for Horn and Orch. (1979; N.Y., Jan. 24, 1980); *American Hymn* (1980; St. Louis, Dec. 24, 1982; also for Band).

VOCAL (all for a cappella Mixed Chorus unless otherwise given): *God's World* for Voice and Piano (1932); *4 Canonic Choruses* (1932–33; N.Y., May 3, 1935); *Pioneers!* for 8-part Chorus (1937; Princeton, N.J., May 23, 1938; withdrawn); *Choral Étude* (1937; N.Y., March 16, 1938); *Prologue* for Chorus and Orch. (N.Y., May 7, 1939); *Prelude* for Soprano and Women's or Mixed Chorus (1939; N.Y., April 24, 1940); *This Is Our Time,* secular cantata No. 1 for Chorus and Orch. (N.Y., July 4, 1940); *Requiescat* for Women's or Mixed Chorus and Piano (N.Y., April 4, 1942); *Holiday Song* for Women's Voices or Mixed Chorus, and Piano (1942; N.Y., Jan. 13, 1943; also for Voice and Piano); *A Free Song,* secular cantata No. 2 for Chorus and Orch. (1942; Boston, March 26, 1943); *Orpheus and His Lute* for Voice and Piano (1944; also for Cello and Orch. as *A Song of Orpheus,* 1961); *Te Deum* (1944; Cambridge, Mass., April 1945); *Truth Shall Deliver* for Men's Chorus (New Haven, Conn., Dec. 7, 1946); *The Lord Has a Child* for Mixed or Women's Chorus or Voice, and Piano (1956); *5 Rounds on Famous Words* (Nos. 1–4, 1956; No. 5, 1969); *Carols of Death* (1958; Canton, N.Y., March 20, 1959); *Deo ac veritati* for Men's Chorus (Hamilton, N.Y., April 19, 1963); *Declaration Chorale* (1971; N.Y., April 30, 1972); *Mail Order Madrigals* (1971; Ames, Iowa, March 12, 1972); *To Thy Love,* choral fantasy on old English rounds for 3-part Women's Chorus (1973); *Concerto on Old English Rounds* for Viola, Women's Chorus, and Orch. (Boston, Nov. 29, 1974); *The Young Dead Soldiers* for Soprano, Horn, Woodwinds, and Strings (1975; Washington, D.C., April 6, 1976); *Casey at the Bat,* cantata for Soprano, Baritone, Chorus, and Orch. (Washington, D.C., April 6, 1976; revision of the opera *The Mighty Casey*); *Time to the Old* for Voice and Piano (1979); *Esses: Short Suite for Singers on Words Beginning with S* (Ithaca, N.Y., Nov. 13, 1982); *Perceptions* (1982; Greenwich, Conn., Jan. 9, 1983); *On Freedom's Ground: An American Cantata* for Baritone, Chorus, and Orch., for the rededication of the Statue of Liberty (1985; N.Y., Oct. 28, 1986).

CHAMBER: *Canon and Fugue* for Piano Trio (1934; withdrawn); 2 pastorales: No. 1 for Alto and Clarinet, or 2 Violas, or Violin and Cello (1934); No. 2 for Flute, Oboe, and Clarinet; or Flute, Violin, and Clarinet (1934; withdrawn); 5 string quartets: No. 1 (N.Y., Oct. 21, 1936; withdrawn); No. 2 (1937); No. 3 (1939; N.Y., Feb. 27, 1940); No. 4 (Washington, D.C.,

Oct. 28, 1950); No. 5 (1987; N.Y., June 21, 1988); *Quartettino* for 4 Bassoons (1939); *Amaryllis*, variations for String Trio (Washington, D.C., Oct. 31, 1964; also for String Orch.); *In Sweet Music* for Mezzo-soprano, Flute, Viola, and Harp (N.Y., Oct. 29, 1978; based on the song *Orpheus and His Lute*, 1944); *XXV Opera Snatches* for Trumpet (1978; N.Y., Jan. 10, 1979); *Night Journey* for Various Instruments, after the ballet (1980; Albany, N.Y., Feb. 27, 1981); *American Hymn* for Brass Quintet (1980; N.Y., March 30, 1981); *Dances* for Wind Quintet and Percussion (1984; N.Y., Oct. 1, 1985); also the piano pieces *3-score Set* (1943), *Voyage* (1953), and *3 Piano Moods* (1958).

BIBL.: L. Bernstein, "W. S.," *Modern Music*, XIX (1942); A. Frankenstein, "W. S.," ibid., XXII (1944–45); N. Broder, "The Music of W. S.," *Musical Quarterly* (Jan. 1945); F. Schreiber and V. Persichetti, *W. S.* (N.Y., 1954); S. Keats, "W. S.," *Stereo Review*, XXXII/6 (1974); H. Hitchcock, "W. S.: Musical All-American," *Keynote* (Aug. 1980); C. Rouse, *W. S.: Documentary* (N.Y., 1980); P. Dickinson, "W. S.: An American Symphonist at 75," *Musical Times* (Aug. 1985); D. Hall, "A Bio-Discography of W. S.," *Ovation* (Aug. and Sept. 1985); J. Clark, "W. S. on His Symphonies: An Interview," *American Music* (Fall 1986).

Schumann, Camillo, German organist and composer, brother of **Georg (Alfred) Schumann;** b. Königstein, March 10, 1872; d. Gottleuba, Dec. 29, 1946. He learned the rudiments of music from his father; then studied with Jadassohn and Reinecke at the Leipzig Cons. After further study with Adolf Bargiel in Berlin (1894–96), he became organist at the Eisenach church. For some years before his death, he lived in retirement at Gottleuba. He was a prolific composer, especially noted for his organ works; he also wrote 6 cantatas, 3 piano trios, 5 cello sonatas, 2 clarinet sonatas, 2 violin sonatas, and 30 albums of piano pieces.

Schumann, Clara (Josephine) (née **Wieck**), famous German pianist, teacher, and composer, daughter of **Friedrich Wieck** and wife of **Robert (Alexander) Schumann;** b. Leipzig, Sept. 13, 1819; d. Frankfurt am Main, May 20, 1896. She was only 5 when she began musical training with her father; made her debut at the Leipzig Gewandhaus on Oct. 20, 1828, where she gave her 1st complete recital on Nov. 8, 1830; her father then took her on her 1st major concert tour in 1831–32, which included a visit to Paris. Upon her return to Leipzig, she pursued additional piano training as well as studies in voice, violin, instrumentation, score reading, counterpoint, and composition; she also publ. several works for piano. In 1838 she was named kk. Kammervirtuosin to the Austrian court. Schumann entered Clara's life in 1830 when he became a lodger in the Wieck home; in 1837 he asked her to marry him, a request which set off a contentious battle between the couple and Clara's father; the issue was only settled after the couple went to court, and they were finally married on Sept. 12, 1840. They went to Dresden, and then to Düsseldorf (1850). In spite of her responsibilities in rearing a large family, she continued to pursue a concert career. She also became active as a teacher, serving on the faculty of the Leipzig Cons. and teaching privately. After her husband's death in 1856, she went to Berlin in 1857; after a sojourn in Baden-Baden (1863–73), she lived intermittently in Berlin (1873–78). Throughout these years, she toured widely as a pianist; made regular appearances in England from 1856; toured Russia in 1864. In 1878 she settled in Frankfurt as a teacher at the Hoch Cons., a position she retained with distinction until 1892. She made her last public appearance as a pianist in 1891. As a pianist, she was a masterly and authoritative interpreter of Schumann's compositions; later she became an equally admirable interpreter of Brahms, her lifelong friend. She was completely free of all mannerisms, and impressed her audiences chiefly by the earnestness of her regard for the music she played. A remarkable teacher, she attracted students from many countries. As a composer, she revealed a genuine talent especially in her numerous character pieces for piano. She wrote a Piano Concerto (1836), a Piano Trio (1847), a Piano

Concertino (1847), *Drei Romanzen* for Violin and Piano (1853), and some songs. Schumann made use of her melodies in several of his works. She wrote cadenzas to Beethoven's concertos in C minor and G major; ed. the Breitkopf & Hartel edition of Schumann's works, and some of his early correspondence; also ed. finger exercises from Czerny's piano method.

BIBL.: A. von Meichsner, *Friedrich Wieck und seine leiden Töchter C. S., geb. Wieck, und Marie Wieck* (Leipzig, 1875); La Mara, *C. S.,* in vol. V of *Musikalische Studienköpfe* (Leipzig, 1882; 3rd ed., 1902); B. Litzmann, *C. S.: Ein Künstlerleben nach Tagebüchern und Briefen* (3 vols., Leipzig, 1902–8; Eng. tr. in 2 vols., abridged, London, 1913); W. Kleefeld, *C. S.* (Bielefeld, 1910); F. May, *The Girlhood of C. S.* (London, 1912); F. Schumann, "Brahms and C. S.," *Musical Quarterly* (Oct. 1916); E. Schumann, *Erinnerungen* (1925; Eng. tr., 1927); B. Litzmann, ed., *C. S.–Johannes Brahms: Briefe aus den Jahren 1853–1896* (2 vols., Leipzig, 1927; Eng. tr., n.d.); K. Höcker, *C. S.* (1938); J. Burk, *C. S.: A Romantic Biography* (N.Y., 1940); A. De Lara, "C. S.'s Teaching," *Music & Letters* (Jan. 1945); L. Henning, *Die Freundschaft C. S.s mit Johannes Brahms* (Zürich, 1952); W. Quednau, *C. S.* (Berlin, 1955); M. and J. Alley, *A Passionate Friendship: C. S. and Brahms* (London, 1956); R. Pitron, *C. S.* (Paris, 1961); K. Stephenson, *C. S.: 1819–1896* (Bonn, 1969); P. Susskind Pettler, "Johannes Brahms and C. S.: C.'s Influence as Critic, Advisor and Friend," *International Brahms Congress: Detroit 1980*; J. Chissell, *C. S.* (London, 1983); N. Reich, *C. S.: The Artist and the Woman* (London, 1985); C. Lépront, *C. S.: La vie à quatre mains* (Paris, 1988); R. Hallmark, "The Rückert Lieder of Robert and C. Schumann," *19th Century Music* (Summer 1990).

Schumann, Elisabeth, celebrated German-born American soprano; b. Merseburg, June 13, 1888; d. N.Y., April 23, 1952. She studied in Dresden, Berlin, and Hamburg; made her debut at the Hamburg Opera on Sept. 2, 1909, as the Shepherd in *Tannhäuser*; remained on its roster until 1919. In the meantime, she made her American debut at the Metropolitan Opera in N.Y. on Nov. 20, 1914, as Sophie in *Der Rosenkavalier*, one of her most famous roles; sang there only one season (1914–15). From 1919 to 1938 she was a principal member of the Vienna State Opera; in 1921 made a concert tour of the U.S. with Richard Strauss; after the Anschluss in 1938, she settled in the U.S.; taught at the Curtis Inst. of Music in Philadelphia; became a naturalized citizen in 1944. She publ. *German Song* (London, 1948). Among her finest roles were Blondchen, Zerlina, Susanna, Adele, and Sophie; she also was renowned as an incomparable lieder artist.

BIBL.: E. Puritz, *The Teaching of E. S.* (1956); D. Shawe-Taylor, "Lotte Lehmann and E. S.: A Centenary Tribute," *Musical Times* (Oct. 1988).

Schumann, Georg (Alfred), German conductor and composer, brother of **Camillo Schumann;** b. Königstein, Oct. 25, 1866; d. Berlin, May 23, 1952. He studied with his father, the town music director, and with his grandfather, a cantor; then took courses in Dresden and at the Leipzig Cons. with Reinecke and Jadassohn; received the Beethoven Prize in 1887. He conducted a choral society in Danzig (1890–96) and the Bremen Phil. (1896–99). In 1900 he settled in Berlin, where he was made conductor of the Singakademie; was made a member of the Akademie der Künste in 1907, teaching a master class in composition (1913–45); was elected its president in 1934.

WORKS: *Zur Karnevalszeit*, orch. suite; *Liebesfrühling*, overture; *Lebensfreude*, overture; 2 syms.; 2 violin sonatas; 2 piano quintets; Cello Sonata; Piano Trio; Piano Quartet; oratorio, *Ruth* (1909); other choral works, with Orch.: *Amor und Psyche, Totenklage, Sehnsucht, Das Tränenkrüglein*; numerous songs; piano pieces.

BIBL.: P. Hielscher, *G. S.,* in vol. 1 of *Monographien moderner Musiker* (Leipzig, 1906); H. Biehle, *G. S.* (Münster, 1925).

Schumann, Robert (Alexander), great German composer of surpassing imaginative power whose music expressed the deepest spirit of the Romantic era, husband of **Clara (Jose-**

phine) (neé **Wieck**) **Schumann;** b. Zwickau, June 8, 1810; d. Endenich, near Bonn, July 29, 1856. He was the 5th and youngest child of a Saxon bookseller, who encouraged his musical inclinations. At the age of 10 he began taking piano lessons from J.G. Kuntzsch, organist at the Zwickau Marienkirche. In 1828 he enrolled at the Univ. of Leipzig as *studiosus juris,* although he gave more attention to philosophical lectures than to law. In Leipzig he became a piano student of Friedrich Wieck, his future father-in-law. In 1829 he went to Heidelberg, where he applied himself seriously to music; in 1830 he returned to Leipzig and lodged in Wieck's home; he also took a course in composition with Heinrich Dorn. His family life was unhappy; his father died at the age of 53 of a nervous disease not distinctly diagnosed; his sister Emily committed suicide at the age of 19. Of his 3 brothers, only one reached late middle age. Schumann became absorbed in the Romantic malaise of Weltschmerz; his idols, the writers and poets Novalis, Kleist, Byron, Lenau, and Hölderin, all died young and in tragic circumstances. He hoped to start his music study with Carl Maria von Weber, who also died unexpectedly. Schumann wrote plays and poems in the Romantic tradition and at the same time practiced his piano playing in the hope of becoming a virtuoso pianist. He never succeeded in this ambition; ironically, it was his beloved bride, Clara, who became a famous concert pianist, and Schumann himself was often introduced to the public at large as merely her husband. His own piano study was halted when he developed an ailment in the index and middle fingers of his right hand. He tried all the fashionable remedies of the period, allopathy, homeopathy, and electrophysical therapy; in addition, he used a mechanical device to lift the middle finger of his right hand, but it only caused him harm. His damaged fingers exempted him from military service; the medical certificate issued in 1842 stated that the index and middle fingers of his right hand were affected so that he was unable to pull the trigger of a rifle. Schumann had a handsome appearance; he liked the company of young ladies, and enjoyed beer, wine, and strong cigars; this was in sharp contrast with his inner disquiet; as a youth, he confided to his diary a fear of madness. He had auditory hallucinations which caused insomnia; he also suffered from acrophobia. When he was 23 years old, he noted sudden onsets of inexpressible angst, momentary loss of consciousness, and difficulty in breathing. He called his sickness a pervasive melancholy, a popular malaise of the time. He thought of killing himself. What maintained his spirits then was his great love for Clara Wieck, 9 years his junior; he did not hesitate to confess his psychological perturbations to her. Her father must have surmised the unstable character of Schumann, and resisted any thought of allowing Clara to become engaged to him; the young couple had to go to court to overcome Wieck's objections, and were finally married on Sept. 12, 1840, the day before Clara turned 21. In 1843, when Schumann and Clara already had 2 daughters, Wieck approached him with an offer of reconciliation. Schumann gladly accepted the offer, but the relationship remained only formal.

Whatever inner torment disturbed Schumann's mind, it did not affect the flowering of his genius as a composer; some psychologists have even expressed the belief that madness is a necessary attribute of genius, and that poetry, art, and music are but external aspects of a delusion. However that might be, as a young man he wrote music full of natural beauty, harmonious and melodious in its flow; his compositions are remarkably free from the somber and dramatic qualities that characterize the music of Beethoven and his Romantic followers. One of the most extraordinary features of Schumann's artistic imagination was his fanciful way of personifying his friends and intimates through musical notes; thus his Platonic love for Ernestine von Fricken, who came from the little town of Asch in Bohemia, inspired him to use the notes A, E-flat (Es), C, and B-natural (H), or A-flat (As), C, and B (H), spelling Asch, as themes for his most famous piano pieces, *Papillons* and *Carnaval.* His very 1st opus number was a set of variations on the notes A, B, E, G, G, which spelled the name of Countess

Meta von Abegg, to whom he was also poetically attached. And, incidentally, it was Ernestine's adoptive father, an amateur flutist, who gave him the theme for his remarkable set of variations for Piano titled *Etudes symphoniques.*

As Schumann's talent for music grew and he became recognized as an important composer, he continued his literary activities. In 1834 he founded, with J. Knorr, L. Schunke, and Wieck, a progressive journal, *Neue Zeitschrift für Musik,* in which he militated against the vapid mannerisms of fashionable salon music and other aspects of musical stagnation. He wrote essays, signing them with the imaginary names of Florestan, Eusebius, or Meister Raro. (Eusebius was the name of 3 Christian saints; etymologically, it is a compound of the Greek components *eu,* "good," and *sebiai,* "to worship." Florestan is obviously "one in a state of flowering"; Raro is "rare"; he also noticed that the juxtaposition of the names Clara and Robert would result in the formation of Raro: ClaRARObert.) As early as 1831, Schumann, in the guise of Eusebius, hailed the genius of Chopin in an article containing the famous invocation "Hut ab, ihr Herren, ein Genie!" The article appeared in the *Allgemeine Musikalische Zeitung;* it was signed only by his initials; in an editorial note, he was identified merely as a young student of Prof. Wieck; but the winged phrase became a favorite quotation of biographers of both Chopin and Schumann, cited as Schumann's discovery of Chopin's talent. Actually, Chopin was a few months older than Schumann, and had already started on a brilliant concert career, while Schumann was an unknown. One of the most fanciful inventions of Schumann was the formation of an intimate company of friends, which he named Davidsbündler to describe the sodality of David, dedicated to the mortal struggle against Philistines in art and to the passionate support of all that was new and imaginative. He immortalized this society in his brilliant piano work *Davidsbündlertänze.* Another characteristically Romantic trait was Schumann's attachment to nocturnal moods, nature scenes, and fantasies; the titles of his piano pieces are typical: *Nachtstücke, Waldszenen,* and *Fantasiestücke,* the last including the poetic *Warum?* and the explosive *Aufschwung.* A child at heart himself, he created in his piano set of exquisite miniatures, *Kinderszenen,* a marvelous musical nursery which included the beautifully sentimental dream piece *Träumerei.* Parallel with his piano works, Schumann produced some of his finest lieder, including the song cycles to poems by Heine (op. 24) and Eichendorff (op. 39), *Die Frauenliebe und Leben* (op. 42), and *Dichterliebe,* to Heine's words (op. 48). In 1841, in only 4 days, he sketched out his First Sym., in B-flat major, born, as he himself said, in a single "fiery hour." He named it the *Spring* sym. It was followed in rapid succession by 3 string quartets (op. 41), the Piano Quintet (op. 44), and the Piano Quartet (op. 47). To the same period belongs also his impassioned choral work *Das Paradies und die Peri.* Three more syms. followed the *Spring* sym. within the next decade, and also a Piano Concerto, a masterpiece of a coalition between the percussive gaiety of the solo part and songful paragraphs in the orch.; an arresting hocketus occurs in the finale, in which duple meters come into a striking conflict with the triple rhythm of the solo part.

In 1843 Schumann was asked by Mendelssohn to join him as a teacher of piano, composition, and score reading at the newly founded Cons. in Leipzig. In 1844 he and Clara undertook a concert tour to Russia; in the autumn of 1844 they moved to Dresden, remaining there until 1850. To this period belong his great C major Sym. (1846), the Piano Trio (1847), and the opera *Genoveva* (1848). In 1847 he assumed the conducting post of the Liedertafel, and in 1848 organized the Chorgesang-Verein in Dresden. In 1850 he became town music director in Düsseldorf, but his disturbed condition began to manifest itself in such alarming ways that he had to resign the post, though he continued to compose. In 1853 he completed a Violin Concerto. Joachim, in whose care Schumann left the work, thought it was not worthy of his genius, and ruled that it should not be performed until the centennial of Schumann's death. In the 1930s an eccentric Hungarian violinist, Jelly d'Aranyi, declared that Schumann's ghost had appeared before her at a spiritualistic séance, revealed to her the place where the MS was kept (it was no secret, anyway; the MS was where it was supposed to be, on the shelf of the Prussian Library in Berlin), and urged her to perform it. She was cheated out of the prize, however, and the concerto was 1st performed by another violinist in Berlin, on Nov. 26, 1937. Jelly d'Aranyi had to be satisfied with giving its 1st British performance.

Schumann's condition continued to deteriorate. On Feb. 27, 1854, he threw himself into the Rhine, but was rescued. On March 4, 1854, he was placed, at his own request, in a sanatorium at Endenich, near Bonn, remaining there until the end of his life. Strangely enough, he did not want to see Clara, and there were months when he did not even inquire about her and the children. But Brahms was a welcome visitor, and Schumann enjoyed his company during his not infrequent periods of lucidity; in Feb. 1855 Brahms played piano, 4-hands, with him. The common assumption that Schumann's illness was syphilitic in origin remains moot, but cumulative symptomology and clearly observed cyclothymic sudden changes of moods point to tertiary syphilis and final general paresis. The doctor who treated him was inclined to diagnose his condition as the result of a sclerosis of the brain; other physicians described it as dementia praecox. Schumann had 7 children; 3 daughters lived to a very old age, but one son suffered from mental disease. A detailed account of Schumann's illness is contained in Dieter Kerner's *Krankheiten grossen Musiker* (Stuttgart, 1973).

WORKS: STAGE: *Der Corsar,* opera (1844; unfinished; only a chorus and sketch for an air completed); *Genoveva,* opera, op. 81 (1847–49; Leipzig, June 25, 1850); *Manfred,* incidental music to Byron's play, op. 115 (1848–49; Leipzig, June 13, 1852).

VOCAL: For various voices: *Psalm CL* for Soprano, Alto, Piano, and Orch. (1822); Overture and chorus (*Chor von Landleuten*), with Orch. (1822); 6 *Lieder* for Men's Voices, op. 33 (1840): 1, *Der träumende See* (Mosen); 2, *Die Minnesänger* (Heine); 3, *Die Lotosblume* (Heine); 4, *Der Zecher als Doktrinär* (Mosen); 5, *Rastlose Liebe* (Goethe); 6, *Frühlingsglocken* (Reinick); *Tragödie* for Chorus and Orch. (Heine; 1841); *Das Paradies und die Peri* for Solo Voices, Chorus, and Orch., op. 50 (adaptation of Moore's *Lalla Rookh;* 1843; Leipzig, Dec. 4, 1843); *Szenen aus Goethes Faust* for Solo Voices, Chorus, and Orch. (Goethe; 1844–53; Cologne, Jan. 13, 1862); 5 *Lieder* for Mixed Voices, op. 55 (R. Burns; 1846): 1, *Das Hochlandmädchen;* 2, *Zahnweh;* 3, *Mich zieht es nach dem Dörfchen hin;* 4, *Die alte, gute Zeit;* 5, *Hochlandbursch;* 4 *Gesänge* for Mixed Voices, op. 59 (1846): 1, *Nord oder Süd!* (K. Lappe); 2, *Am Bodensee* (Platen); 3, *Jägerlied* (Mörike); 4, *Gute Nacht* (Rückert); also a 5th song added later, *Hirtenknaben-Gesang* (Droste-Hulshoff); 3 *Gesänge* for Men's Voices, op. 62 (1847): 1, *Der Eidgenossen Nachtwache* (Eichendorff); 2, *Freiheitslied* (Rückert); 3, *Schlachtgesang* (Klopstock); *Ritornelle in canonischen Weisen* for Men's Voices, op. 65 (Rückert; 1847): 1, *Die Rose stand im Tau;* 2, *Lasst Lautenspiel und Becherklang;* 3, *Blüt' oder Schnee!;* 4, *Gebt mir zu trinken!;* 5, *Zürne nicht des Herbstes Wind;* 6, *In Sommertagen rüste den Schlitten;* 7, *In Meeres Mitten ist ein offener Laden;* 8, *Hätte zu einem Traubenkerne; Beim Abschied zu singen* for Chorus and Wind Instruments, op. 84 (Feuchtersleben; 1847); *Zum Anfang* for Men's Voices (Rückert; 1847); 3 *Freiheitsgesänge* for Men's Voices, with Wind Instruments ad libitum (1848): 1, *Zu den Waffen* (Ullrich); 2, *Schwarz-Rot-Gold* (Freiligrath); 3, *Deutscher Freiheitsgesang* (Furst); *Romanzen und Balladen* for Mixed Voices, op. 67, I (1849): 1, *Der König von Thule* (Goethe); 2, *Schön-Rohtraut* (Mörike); 3, *Heidenröslein* (Goethe); 4, *Ungewitter* (Chamisso); 5, *John Anderson* (Burns); *Romanzen und Balladen* for Mixed Voices, op. 75, II (1849): 1, *Schnitter Tod* (Des Knaben Wunderhorn; Brentano); 2, *Im Walde* (Eichendorff); 3, *Der traurige Jäger* (Eichendorff); 4, *Der Rekrut* (Burns); 5, *Vom verwundeten Knaben* (Herder's Volkslieder); *Romanzen* for Women's Voices and Piano ad libitum, op. 69, I (1849): 1, *Tamburinschlägerin*

(Alvaro de Ameida; Eichendorff, tr.); 2, *Waldmädchen* (Eichendorff); 3, *Klosterfräulein* (Kerner); 4, *Soldatenbraut* (Mörike); 5, *Meerfey* (Eichendorff); 6, *Die Kapelle* (Uhland); *Romanzen* for Women's Voices and Piano ad libitum, op. 91, II (1849): 1, *Rosmarien (Des Knaben Wunderhorn);* 2, *Jäger Wohlgemut (Des Knaben Wunderhorn);* 3, *Der Wassermann* (Kerner); 4, *Das verlassene Mägdelein* (Mörike); 5, *Der Bleicherin Nachtlied* (Reinick); 6, *In Meeres Mitten* (Rückert); *Verzweifle nicht im Schmerzenstal,* motet for Double Chorus and Organ ad libitum, op. 93 (Rückert; 1852; orchestrated 1852); *Requiem für Mignon* for Solo Voices, Chorus, and Orch., op. 98b (Goethe; 1849; Düsseldorf, Nov. 21, 1850); 5 *Gesänge aus H. Laubes Jagdbrevier* for Men's Voices and Piano, 4-hands, ad libitum, op. 137 (Laube; 1849): 1, *Zur hohen Jagd;* 2, *Habet acht!;* 3, *Jagdmorgen;* 4, *Frühe;* 5, *Bei der Flasche; 4 doppelchörige Gesänge* for Mixed Voices, op. 141 (1849): 1, *An die Sterne* (Rückert); 2, *Ungewisses Licht* (Zedlitz); 3, *Zuversicht* (Zedlitz); 4, *Talismane* (Goethe); *Romanzen und Balladen* for Mixed Voices, op. 145, III (1849–51): 1, *Der Schmidt* (Uhland); 2, *Die Nonne* (anonymous); 3, *Der Sänger* (Uhland); 4, *John Anderson* (Burns); 5, *Romanze vom Gänsebuben* (Malsburg); *Romanzen und Balladen* for Mixed Voices, op. 146, IV (1849–51): 1, *Brautgesang* (Uhland); 2, *Der Bänkelsänger Willie* (Burns); 3, *Der Traum* (Uhland); 4, *Sommerlied* (Rückert); *Das Schifflein,* with Flute and Horn (Uhland); *Nachtlied* for Chorus and Orch., op. 108 (Hebbel; 1849; Düsseldorf, March 13, 1851); *Der Rose Pilgerfahrt* for Solo Voices, Chorus, and Orch., op. 112 (Horn; 1851; Düsseldorf, Feb. 5, 1852); *Der Königssohn* for Solo Voices, Chorus, and Orch., op. 116 (Uhland; 1851); *Des Glockentürmers Töchterlein* for Mixed Voices (Rückert; 1851); *Fest-Ouvertüre* for Tenor, Chorus, and Orch., op. 123 (Müller and Claudius; 1852–53; Düsseldorf, May 17, 1853); *Des Sängers Fluch* for Solo Voices, Chorus, and Orch., op. 139 (Pohl, after Uhland; 1852); *Vom Pagen und der Königstochter* for Solo Voices, Chorus, and Orch., op. 140 (Geibel; 1852); *Das Glück von Edenhall* for Solo Voices, Chorus, and Orch., op. 143 (Hasenclever, after Uhland; 1853); *Bei Schenkung eines Flügels* for Mixed Voices and Piano (Schumann; 1853); *Neujahrslied* for Chorus and Orch., op. 144 (Rückert; 1849–50; Düsseldorf, Jan. 11, 1851); *Mass* for Chorus and Orch., op. 147 (1852–53); *Requiem* for Chorus and Orch., op. 148 (1852).

SONGS: *Verwandlung* (Schulze; 1827); *Lied* (Schumann; 1827); *Sehnsucht* (Schumann; 1827); *Die Weinende* (Byron; 1827); *Erinnerung* (Jacobi; 1828); *Kurzes Erwachen* (Kerner; 1828); *Gesanges Erwachen* (Kerner; 1828); *An Anna,* I (Kerner; 1828); *An Anna,* II (Kerner; 1828); *Im Herbste* (Kerner; 1828); *Hirtenknabe* (Schumann; 1828); *Der Fischer* (Goethe; 1828); *Klage* (Jacobi; 1828; not extant); *Vom Reitersmann* (date unknown); *Maultreiberlied* (1838; not extant); *Ein Gedanke* (Ferrand; 1840); *Patriotisches Lied* for Voice, Chorus, and Piano (N. Becker; 1840); *Der Reiter und der Bodensee* (Schwab; 1840; fragment only); *Die nächtliche Heerschau* (Zedlitz; 1840; fragment only); *Liederkreis,* op. 24 (Heine; 1840): 1, *Morgens steh ich auf und frage;* 2, *Es treibt mich hin;* 3, *Ich wandelte unter den Bäumen;* 4, *Lieb Liebchen;* 5, *Schöne Wiege meiner Leiden;* 6, *Warte, warte, wilder Schiffmann;* 7, *Berg und Burgen schaun herunter;* 8, *Anfangs wolit ich fast verzagen;* 9, *Mit Myrten und Rosen; Myrthen,* op. 25 (1840): 1, *Widmung* (Rückert); 2, *Freisinn* (Goethe); 3, *Der Nussbaum* (Mosen); 4, *Jemand* (Burns); 5, *Lieder aus dem Schenkenbuch im Divan,* I (Goethe); 6, *Lieder aus dem Schenkenbuch im Divan,* II (Goethe); 7, *Die Lotosblume* (Heine); 8, *Talismane* (Goethe); 9, *Lied der Suleika* (Goethe; attributed to Marianne von Willemer); 10, *Die Hochländer-Witwe* (Burns); 11, *Lieder der Braut aus dem Liebesfrühling,* I (Rückert); 12, *Lieder der Braut aus dem Liebesfrühling,* II (Rückert); 13, *Hochländers Abschied* (Burns); 14, *Hochländisches Wiegenlied* (Burns); 15, *Aus den hebräischen Gesängen* (Byron); 16, *Rätsel* (C. Fanshawe); 17, *2 Venetianische Lieder,* I (Moore); 18, *2 Venetianische Lieder,* II (Moore); 19, *Hauptmanns Weib* (Burns); 20, *Weit, weit* (Burns); 21, *Was will die einsame Träne?* (Heine); 22, *Niemand* (Burns); 23, *Im Westen* (Burns); 24, *Du bist wie eine Blume* (Heine); 25, *Aus den östlichen Rosen* (Rückert); 26, *Zum Schluss* (Rückert); *Lieder und Gesänge,* op. 27, I (1840): 1, *Sag an, o lieber Vogel* (Hebbel); 2, *Dem roten Röslein* (Burns); 3, *Was soll ich sagen?* (Chamisso); 4, *Jasminenstrauch* (Rückert); 5, *Nur ein lächelnder Blick* (G.W. Zimmermann); *3 Gedichte,* op. 29 (Geibel; 1840): 1, *Ländliches Lied* for 2 Sopranos; 2, *Lied* for 3 Sopranos; 3, *Zigeunerleben* for Soprano, Alto, Tenor, and Bass, and Triangle and Tambourine ad libitum; *3 Gedichte,* op. 30 (Geibel; 1840): 1, *Der Knabe mit dem Wunderhorn;* 2, *Der Page;* 3, *Der Hidalgo; 3 Gesänge,* op. 31 (1840): 1, *Die Löwenbraut* (Chamisso); 2, *Die Kartenlegerin* (Chamisso, after Béranger); 3, *Die rote Hanne,* with Chorus ad libitum (Chamisso, after Béranger); *4 Duette* for Soprano and Tenor, op. 34 (1840): 1, *Liebesgarten* (Reinick); 2, *Liebhabers Ständchen* (Burns); 3, *Unterm Fenster* (Burns); 4, *Familien-Gemälde* (A. Grün); *12 Gedichte,* op. 35 (Kerner; 1840): 1, *Lust der Sturmnacht;* 2, *Stirb, Lieb und Freud!;* 3, *Wanderlied;* 4, *Erstes Grün;* 5, *Sehnsucht nach der Waldgegend;* 6, *Auf das Trinkglas eines verstorbenen Freundes;* 7, *Wanderung;* 8, *Stille Liebe;* 9, *Frage;* 10, *Stille Tränen;* 11, *Wer machte dich so krank?;* 12, *Alte Laute; 6 Gedichte,* op. 36 (Reinick; 1840): 1, *Sonntags am Rhein;* 2, *Ständchen;* 3, *Nichts schöneres;* 4, *An den Sonnenschein;* 5, *Dichters Genesung;* 6, *Liebesbotschaft; 12 Gedichte aus "Liebesfrühling,"* op. 37 (Rückert; 1840; Nos. 2, 4, and 11 by Clara Schumann): 1, *Der Himmel hat ein' Träne geweint;* 3, *O ihr Herren;* 5, *Ich hab in mich gesogen;* 6, *Liebste, was kann denn uns scheiden?* for Soprano and Tenor; 7, *Schön ist das Fest des Lenzes* for Soprano and Tenor; 8, *Flügel! Flügel! um zu fliegen;* 9, *Rose, Meer und Sonne;* 10, *O Sonn, o Meer, o Rose;* 12, *So wahr die Sonne scheinet* for Soprano and Tenor; *Liederkreis,* op. 39 (Eichendorff; 1840): 1, *In der Fremde;* 2, *Intermezzo;* 3, *Waldesgespräch;* 4, *Die Stille;* 5, *Mondnacht;* 6, *Schöne Fremde;* 7, *Auf einer Burg;* 8, *In der Fremde;* 9, *Wehmut;* 10, *Zwielicht;* 11, *Im Walde;* 12, *Frühlingsnacht; 5 Lieder,* op. 40 (1840): 1, *Märzveilchen* (H.C. Andersen); 2, *Muttertraum* (Andersen); 3, *Der Soldat* (Andersen); 4, *Der Spielmann* (Andersen); 5, *Verratene Liebe* (Chamisso); *Frauenliebe und -leben,* op. 42 (Chamisso; 1840): 1, *Seit ich ihn gesehen;* 2, *Er, der Herrlichste von allen;* 3, *Ich kann's nicht fassen, nicht glauben;* 4, *Du Ring an meinem Finger;* 5, *Helft mir, ihr Schwestern;* 6, *Süsser Freund, du blickest;* 7, *An meinem Herzen, an meiner Brust;* 8, *Nun hast du mir den ersten Schmerz getan; 3 zweistimmige Lieder,* op. 43 (1840): 1, *Wenn ich ein Vöglein wär* (Des Knaben Wunderhorn); 2, *Herbstlied* (S.A. Mahlmann); 3, *Schön Blümelein* (Reinick); *Romanzen und Balladen,* op. 45, I (1840): 1, *Der Schatzgräber* (Eichendorff); 2, *Frühlingsfahrt* (Eichendorff); 3, *Abends am Strand* (Heine); *Dichterliebe,* op. 48 (Heine; 1840): 1, *Im wunderschönen Monat Mai;* 2, *Aus meinen Tränen spriessen;* 3, *Die Rose, die Lilie, die Taube, die Sonne;* 4, *Wenn ich in deine Augen seh;* 5, *Ich will meine Seele tauchen;* 6, *Im Rhein, im heiligen Strome;* 7, *Ich grolle nicht;* 8, *Und wüssten's die Blumen, die kleinen;* 9, *Das ist ein Flöten und Geigen;* 10, *Hör' ich das Liedchen klingen;* 11, *Ein Jüngling liebt ein Mädchen;* 12, *Am leuchtenden Sommermorgen;* 13, *Ich hab' im Traum geweinet;* 14, *Allnächtlich im Traume;* 15, *Aus alten Märchen;* 16, *Die alten, bösen Lieder; Romanzen und Balladen,* op. 49, II (1840): 1, *Die beiden Grenadiere* (Heine); 2, *Die feindlichen Brüder* (Heine); 3, *Die Nonne* (A. Fröhlich); *Lieder und Gesänge,* op. 51, II: 1, *Sehnsucht* (Geibel; 1840); 2, *Volksliedchen* (Rückert; 1840); 3, *Ich wandre nicht* (C. Christern; 1840); 4, *Auf dem Rhein* (K. Immermann; 1846); 5, *Liebeslied* (Goethe; 1850); *Romanzen und Balladen,* op. 53, III (1840): 1, *Blondels Lied* (Seidl); 2, *Loreley* (W. Lorenz); 3, *Der arme Peter* (Heine); *Belsatzar,* op. 57 (Heine; 1840); *Romanzen und Balladen,* op. 64, IV: 1, *Die Soldatenbraut* (Mörike; 1847); 2, *Das verlassne Mägdelein* (Mörike; 1847); 3, *Tragödie* (Heine; 1841); *Spanisches Liederspiel,* op. 74 (Geibel, after Spanish poets; 1849): 1, *Erste Begegnung* for Soprano and Alto; 2, *Intermezzo* for Tenor and Bass; 3, *Liebesgram* for Soprano and Alto; 4, *In der Nacht* for Soprano and Tenor; 5, *Es ist verraten* for Soprano, Alto, Tenor, and Bass; 6, *Melancholie* for Soprano; 7, *Geständnis* for Tenor; 8, *Botschaft* for Soprano and Alto; 9, *Ich bin geliebt* for Soprano, Alto, Tenor, and Bass; 10, *Der Kontrabandiste* for Baritone; *Lieder und Ge-*

sänge, op. 77, III: 1, *Der frohe Wandersmann* (Eichendorff; 1840); 2, *Mein Garten* (Hoffmann von Fallersleben; 1850); 3, *Geisternähe* (Halm; 1850); 4, *Stiller Vorwurf* (O. Wolff?; 1840); 5, *Aufträge* (C. L'Egru; 1850); *Soldatenlied* (Hoffmann von Fallersleben; 1844); *Das Schwert* (Uhland; 1848); *Der weisse Hirsch* (Uhland; 1848; sketches only); *Die Ammenuhr* (Des Knaben Wunderhorn; 1848); *4 Duette* for Soprano and Tenor, op. 78 (1849): 1, *Tanzlied* (Rückert); 2, *Er und Sie* (Kerner); 3, *Ich denke dein* (Goethe); 4, *Wiegenlied* (Hebbel); *Sommerruh,* duet (C. Schad; 1849); *Lieder-Album für die Jugend,* op. 79 (1849): 1, *Der Abendstern* (Hoffmann von Fallersleben); 2, *Schmetterling* (von Fallersleben); 3, *Frühlingsbotschaft* (Hoffmann von Fallersleben); 4, *Frühlingsgruss* (von Fallersleben); 5, *Vom Schlaraffenland* (von Fallersleben); 6, *Sonntag* (von Fallersleben); 7, *Zigeunerliedchen* (Geibel); 8, *Des Knaben Berglied* (Uhland); 9, *Mailied,* duet ad libitum (C. Overbeck); 10, *Das Käuzlein* (Des Knaben Wunderhorn); 11, *Hinaus ins Freie!* (von Fallersleben); 12, *Der Sandmann* (Kletke); 13, *Marienwürmchen* (Des Knaben Wunderhorn); 14, *Die Waise* (von Fallersleben); 15, *Das Glück,* duet (Hebbel); 16, *Weihnachtslied* (Andersen); 17, *Die wandelnde Glocke* (Goethe); 18, *Frühlingslied,* duet ad libitum (von Fallersleben); 19, *Frühlings Ankunft* (von Fallersleben); 20, *Die Schwalben,* duet (Des Knaben Wunderhorn); 21, *Kinderwacht* (anonymous); 22, *Des Sennen Abschied* (Schiller); 23, *Er ist's* (Mörike); *Spinnelied,* trio ad libitum (anonymous); *Des Buben Schützenlied* (Schiller); 26, *Schneeglöckchen* (Rückert); 27, *Lied Lynceus des Türmers* (Goethe); 28, *Mignon* (Goethe); *3 Gesänge,* op. 83 (1850): 1, *Resignation* (Buddeus); 2, *Die Blume der Ergebung* (Rückert); 3, *Der Einsiedler* (Eichendorff); *Der Handschuh,* op. 87 (Schiller; 1850); *6 Gesänge,* op. 89 (W. von der Neun; 1850): 1, *Es stürmet am Abendhimmel;* 2, *Heimliches Verschwinden;* 3, *Herbstlied;* 4, *Abschied vom Walde;* 5, *Ins Freie;* 6, *Röselein, Röselein!; 6 Gedichte,* op. 90 (Lenau; 1850): 1, *Lied eines Schmiedes;* 2, *Meine Rose;* 3, *Kommen und Scheiden;* 4, *Die Sennin;* 5, *Einsamkeit;* 6, *Der schwere Abend;* 7, *Requiem; 3 Gesänge,* op. 95 (Byron; 1849): 1, *Die Tochter Jephthas;* 2, *An den Mond;* 3, *Dem Helden; Lieder und Gesänge,* op. 96, IV (1850): 1, *Nachtlied* (Goethe); 2, *Schneeglöckchen* (anonymous); 3, *Ihre Stimme* (Platen); 4, *Gesungen!* (Neun; Schöpff); 5, *Himmel und Erde* (Neun; Schöpff); *Lieder und Gesänge aus Wilhelm Meister,* op. 98a (Goethe; 1849): 1, *Kennst du das Land;* 2, *Ballade des Harfners;* 3, *Nur wer die Sehnsucht kennt;* 4, *Wer nie sein Brot mit Tränen ass;* 5, *Heiss mich nicht reden;* 6, *Wer sich der Einsamkeit ergibt;* 7, *Singet nicht in Trauertönen;* 8, *An die Türen will ich schleichen;* 9, *So lasst mich scheinen; Minnespiel,* op. 101 (Rückert; 1849): 1, *Meine Töne still und heiter* for Tenor; 2, *Liebster, deine Worte stehlen* for Soprano; 3, *Ich bin dein Baum* for Alto and Bass; 4, *Mein schöner Stern!* for Tenor; 5, *Schön ist das Fest des Lenzes* for Soprano, Alto, Tenor, and Bass; 6, *O Freund, mein Schirm, mein Schutz!* for Alto or Soprano; 7, *Die tausend Grüsse* for Soprano and Tenor; 8, *So wahr die Sonne scheinet* for Soprano, Alto, Tenor, and Bass; *Mädchenlieder* for Soprano and Alto or 2 Sopranos, op. 103 (Kulmann; 1851): 1, *Mailied;* 2, *Frühlingslied;* 3, *An die Nachtigall;* 4, *An den Abendstern; 7 Lieder,* op. 104 (Kulmann; 1851): 1, *Mond, meiner Seele Liebling;* 2, *Viel Glück zur Reise, Schwalben!;* 3, *Du nennst dich armes Mädchen;* 4, *Der Zeisig;* 5, *Reich mir die Hand, o Wolke;* 6, *Die letzten Blumen starben;* 7, *Gekämpft hat meine Barke; Schön Hedwig,* declamation, op. 106 (Hebbel; 1849); *6 Gesänge,* op. 107 (1851–52): 1, *Herzeleid* (Ullrich); 2, *Die Fensterscheibe* (Ullrich); 3, *Der Gärtner* (Mörike); 4, *Die Spinnerin* (Heyse); 5, *Im Wald* (Müller); 6, *Abendlied* (Kinkel); *3 Lieder* for Women's Voices, op. 114 (1853): 1, *Nänie* (Bechstein); 2, *Triolett* (L'Egru); 3, *Spruch* (Rückert); *4 Husarenlieder* for Baritone, op. 117 (Lenau; 1851): 1, *Der Husar, trara!;* 2, *Der leidige Frieden;* 3, *Den grünen Zeigern;* 4, *Da liegt der Feinde gestreckte Schar; 3 Gedichte,* op. 119 (G. Pfarrius; 1851): 1, *Die Hütte;* 2, *Warnung;* 3, *Der Bräutigam und die Birke; 2 Balladen,* declamations, op. 122 (1852–53): 1, *Ballade vom Haideknaben* (Hebbel); 2, *Die Flüchtlinge* (Shelley); *5 heitere Gesänge,* op. 125 (1850–51): 1, *Die Meerfee* (Buddeus); 2, *Husarenabzug* (C.

Candidus); 3, *Jung Volkers Lied* (Mörike); 4, *Frühlingslied* (Braun); 5, *Frühlingslust* (Heyse); 5 *Lieder und Gesänge*, op. 127: 1, *Sängers Trost* (Kerner; 1840); 2, *Dein Angesicht* (Heine; 1840); 3, *Es leuchtet meine Liebe* (Heine; 1840); 4, *Mein altes Ross* (Moritz, Graf von Strachwitz; 1850); 5, *Schlusslied des Narren* (Shakespeare; 1840); *Frühlingsgrüsse* (Lenau; 1851); *Gedichte der Königin Maria Stuart*, op. 135 (1852): 1, *Abschied von Frankreich*; 2, *Nach der Geburt ihres Sohnes*; 3, *An die Königin Elisabeth*; 4, *Abschied von der Welt*; 5, *Gebet; Spanische Liebeslieder*, op. 138 (Geibel; 1849): 1, *Vorspiel* for Piano, 4-hands; 2, *Tief im Herzen trag ich Pein* for Soprano; 3, *O wie lieblich ist das Mädchen* for Tenor; 4, *Bedeckt mich mit Blumen* for Soprano and Alto; 5, *Flutenreicher Ebro* for Baritone; 6, *Intermezzo* for Piano, 4-hands; 7, *Weh, wie zornig ist das Mädchen* for Tenor; 8, *Hoch, hoch sind die Berge* for Alto; 9, *Blaue Augen hat das Mädchen* for Tenor and Bass; 10, *Dunkler Lichtglanz* for Soprano, Alto, Tenor, and Bass; from *Des Sängers Fluch*, op. 139 (Pohl, after Uhland; 1852): 4, *Provenzalisches Lied*; 7, *Ballade; 4 Gesänge*, op. 142 (1840): 1, *Trost im Gesang* (Kerner); 2, *Lehn deine Wang* (Heine); 3, *Mädchen-Schwermut* (Bernhard); 4, *Mein Wagen rollet langsam* (Heine); *Mailied*, duet (1851); *Liedchen von Marie und Papa*, duet (Schumann; 1852); *Glockentürmers Töchterlein* (Rückert); *Das Käuzlein* (*Des Knaben Wunderhorn*); *Deutscher Blumengarten*, duet (Rückert).

ORCH.: Piano Concerto in E-flat major (1828; unfinished); Piano Concerto in F major (1829–31; unfinished); *Introduction and Variations on a Theme of Paganini* (1831); Sym. in G minor (1832–33; 1st movement perf. Zwickau, Nov. 18, 1832; 1st complete perf., Schneeberg, Feb. 12, 1833; 3 movements only with a sketch for a 4th movement); Piano Concerto in D minor (1839; one movement only); Sym. in C minor (1840–41; sketches for 4 movements; some of the music used in Sym. No. 2, in C major, op. 61); Sym. No. 1, in B-flat major, op. 38, *Spring* (Leipzig, March 31, 1841); *Ouvertüre, Scherzo, und Finale* in E major, op. 52 (Leipzig, Dec. 6, 1841; rev. 1845); Piano Concerto in A minor, op. 54 (1st movement composed as the *Fantasie* for Piano and Orch., 1841; movements 2–3, 1845; Leipzig, Jan. 1, 1846); Sym. No. 2, in C major, op. 61 (1845–46; Leipzig, Nov. 5, 1846); *Conzertstück* in F major for 4 Horns, op. 86 (1849; Leipzig, Feb. 25, 1850); *Introduction and Allegro Appassionato, Conzertstück*, op. 92 (1849; Leipzig, Feb. 14, 1850); Sym. No. 3, in E-flat major, op. 97, *Rhenish* (1850; Düsseldorf, Feb. 6, 1851); *Die Braut von Messina*, overture in C minor, to Schiller's play, op. 100 (1850–51; Düsseldorf, March 13, 1851); Sym. No. 4, in D minor, op. 120 (originally his Sym. No. 2; Leipzig, Dec. 6, 1841; rev. as his Sym. No. 4, 1851; Düsseldorf, Dec. 30, 1852); *Julius Cäsar*, overture in F minor, to Shakespeare's play, op. 128 (1851; Düsseldorf, Aug. 3, 1852); Cello Concerto in A minor, op. 129 (1850; Leipzig, June 9, 1860); *Fantasie* in C major for Violin, op. 131 (1853; Hannover, Jan. 1854); *Introduction and Allegro* in D minor/D major for Piano, op. 134 (1853; Utrecht, Nov. 26, 1853); *Hermann und Dorothea*, overture in B minor, to Goethe's poem, op. 136 (1851); Violin Concerto in D minor (1853; 1st perf. in Berlin, Nov. 26, 1937).

CHAMBER: Quartet in C minor for Violin, Viola, Cello, and Piano (1828–30); Quartet in F minor (1829); Quartet in B major for Violin, Viola, Cello, and Piano (1831–32; unfinished); Quartet (1838; not extant); sketches for 2 string quartets: D major and E-flat major (1839); 3 string quartets, op. 41: A minor, F major, A major (1842); Quintet in E-flat major for 2 Violins, Viola, Cello, and Piano, op. 44 (1842); Quartet in E-flat major for Violin, Viola, Cello, and Piano, op. 47 (1842); *Andante and Variations* for 2 Pianos, 2 Cellos, and Horn (1843; original version of op. 46); Trio No. 1, in D minor, for Violin, Cello, and Piano, op. 63 (1847); *Adagio and Allegro* for Horn and Piano, with Violin or Cello ad libitum, in A-flat major, op. 70 (1849); *Phantasiestücke* for Clarinet and Piano, with Violin or Cello ad libitum, op. 73 (1849); Trio No. 2, in F major, for Violin, Cello, and Piano, op. 80 (1847); *Phantasiestücke* for Violin, Cello, and Piano, op. 88 (1842); 3 *Romanzen* for Oboe and Piano, with Violin or Clarinet ad libitum, op.

94 (1849); 5 *Stücke im Volkston* for Cello and Piano, with Violin ad libitum, op. 102 (1849); Sonata No. 1, in A minor, for Violin and Piano, op. 105 (1851); Trio No. 3, in G minor, for Violin, Cello, and Piano, op. 110 (1851); *Märchenbilder* for Viola and Piano, with Violin ad libitum, op. 113 (1851); Sonata No. 2, in D minor, for Violin and Piano, op. 121 (1851); *Märchenerzählungen* for Clarinet, Viola, and Piano, with Violin ad libitum, op. 132 (1853); Sonata for Violin and Piano, F. A. E. [based on the thematic motto of Joachim, *Frei aber einsam*, "Free but alone"] (1853; 2nd and 4th movements by Schumann; 1st movement by Dietrich; 3rd movement by Brahms); Sonata No. 3, in A minor, for Violin and Piano (1853; incorporates Schumann's 2 movements composed for the F. A. E. sonata); 5 *Romanzen* for Cello and Piano (1853; not extant).

PIANO: 8 polonaises for Piano, 4-hands (1828); *Variations on a Theme of Prince Louis Ferdinand of Prussia* for Piano, 4-hands (1828); *Romanze* in F minor (1829; unfinished); 6 *Walzer* (1829–30); *Thème sur le nom Abegg varié pour le pianoforte*, op. 1 (1829–30); *Variations on a Theme of Weber*, from *Preziosa* (1831); *Valse* in E-flat major (1831; unfinished); *Valse per Friedrich Wieck* (1831–32; unfinished); Sonata in A-flat major (1831–32; 1st movement and Adagio); *Andante with Variations on an Original Theme* in G major (1831–32); *Prelude and Fugue* (1832); *Papillons*, op. 2 (1829–31); 6 *Studien nach Capricen von Paganini*, op. 3, I (1832; formerly op. 2); 6 *Intermezzos*, op. 4 (1832; formerly known as *Pièces phantastiques*, op. 3); *Phantasie satyrique* (1832; fragments only); *Fandango* in F-sharp minor (1832); *Exercice fantastique* (1832; formerly op. 5; not extant); *Rondo* in B-flat major (1832; unfinished); 12 *Burlesken* (1832); *Fugue* in D minor (1832); *Fugue No. 3* (1832); 5 pieces (1832–33; 1, 4, and 5 unfinished); *Sehnsuchtswalzer Variationen: Scènes musicales sur un thème connu-* (1832–33); 10 *Impromptus über ein Thema von Clara Wieck*, op. 5 (1833); *Etüden in Form freier Variationen über ein Beethovensches Thema* (1833); *Variations sur un nocturne de Chopin* (1834); movement for a Sonata, in B-flat major (1836); Sonata No. 4, in F minor (1836–37; unfinished); *Davidsbündlertänze*, 18 character pieces, op. 6 (1837); *Toccata* in C major, op. 7 (1829–32; formerly op. 6); *Allegro* in B minor, op. 8 (1831); *Carnaval: Scènes mignonnes sur quatre notes*, op. 9 (1833–35); 6 *Konzert-Etüden nach Capricen von Paganini*, op. 10, II (1833); Sonata No. 1, in F-sharp minor, op. 11 (1832–35); *Phantasiestücke*, op. 12 (1832?–37); *Symphonische Etüden*, op. 13 (1834–37); *Concert sans orchestre* in F minor, op. 14 (1835–36; rev. as Sonata No. 3, 1853); *Scherzo* (1836; from op. 14); *Kinderszenen*, op. 15 (1838); *Kreisleriana*, op. 16 (1838; rev. 1850); *Phantasie* in C major, op. 17 (1836–38); *Arabeske* in C major, op. 18 (1838); *Blumenstück* in D-flat major, op. 19 (1839); *Humoreske* in B-flat major, op. 20 (1838); 8 *Novelletten*, op. 21 (1838); Sonata No. 2, in G minor, op. 22 (1833–38; new finale, 1838); *Nachtstücke*, 4 pieces, op. 23 (1839); *Allegro* in C minor (1839; not extant); *Faschingsschwank aus Wien: Phantasiebilder*, op. 26 (1839–40); 3 *Romanzen*, op. 28: B-flat minor, F-sharp major, B major (1839); *Klavierstücke*, op. 32 (1838–39); Sonatina in B-flat major (1840; not extant); *Andante and Variations* in B-flat major, op. 46, for 2 Pianos (1843); *Studien für den Pedal-Flügel*, op. 56 (1845); 4 *Skizzen für den Pedal-Flügel*, op. 58 (1845); 6 *Fugues on B-A-C-H*, op. 60, for Pedal Piano or Organ (1845); *Bilder aus Osten: 6 Impromptus*, op. 66, for Piano, 4-hands (1848); *Album für die Jugend*, op. 68 (1848); 4 *Fugues*, op. 72: D minor, D minor, F minor, F major (1845); 4 *Marches*, op. 76: E-flat major, G minor, B-flat major (Lager-Scene), E-flat major (1849); *Waldszenen*, op. 82 (1848–49); 12 *vierhändige Klavierstücke für kleine und grosse Kinder*, op. 85 (1849); *Bunte Blätter*, op. 99 (1838–49); *Ballszenen*, op. 109, for Piano, 4-hands (1851); *Phantasiestücke*, 3 pieces, op. 111: C minor, A-flat major, C minor (1851); 3 *Clavier-Sonaten für die Jugend*, op. 118: G major, D major, C major (1853); *Albumblätter*, op. 124 (1854); 7 *Klavierstücke in Fughettenform*, op. 126 (1853); *Kinderball*, op. 130, for Piano, 4-hands (1853); 5 *Gesänge der Frühe*, op. 133 (1853); *Canon on F. Himmel's An Alexis send ich dich*, in A-flat major (1854); *Thema* in E-flat major (1854); *Variations on an Original Theme* (1854).

BIBL.: COLLECTED WORKS, SOURCE MATERIAL: A complete edition of his works, *R. S.: Werke*, was ed. by Clara Schumann et al. and publ. by Breitkopf & Härtel (34 vols., Leipzig, 1881–93; supplement ed. by Brahms, 1893). His *Gesammelte Schriften über Musik und Musiker* is a collection of his articles from *Neue Zeitschrift für Musik* (4 vols., Leipzig, 1854; Eng. tr., London, 1877; 5th Ger. ed., rev. by M. Kreisig, 1914). A judicious selection from the complete writings, ed. by H. Simon, was publ. under the same title as the original edition (3 vols., Leipzig, 1888–89). A selection of Schumann's critical reviews, tr. into Eng. by P. Rosenfeld, was publ. in N.Y. in 1946. The R.-S.-Gesellschaft began the publication of the *Sammelbände der R.-S.-Gesellschaft* in Leipzig in 1961. See also H. Drinker, *Texts of the Vocal Works of R. S. in English Translation* (N.Y., 1947), and L. Minchin, *S. in English: Four Famous Song-Cycles in Singable English Verse* (London, 1981).

A thematic catalogue was prepared by A. Dörffel, *Thematisches Verzeichniss sämmtlicher in Druck erschienenen Werke R. S.s* (Leipzig, 1860; 4th ed., 1868). See also K. Hofmann, *Die Erstdrucke der Werke von R. S.* (Tutzing, 1979).

Other sources include: F. Kerst, *S.-Brevier* (Berlin, 1905); A. Schumann, ed., *Der junge S.: Dichtungen und Briefe* (Leipzig, 1910); E. Bienenfeld, "Die Stammtafel der Familie R. S.s: Ahnen und Nachkommen eines Genies," *Archiv für Rassen- und Gesellschaftsbiologie*, XXVI (1932); W. Boetticher, *R. S. in seinen Schriften und Briefen* (Berlin, 1942); G. Eismann, *R. S.: Ein Quellenwerk über sein Leben und Schaffen* (2 vols., Leipzig, 1956); P. Mies, "Literatur um R. S.: Ein Beitrag zu seinem 100. Todestag," *Musikhandel*, VII (1956); R. Münnich, *Aus R. S.s Briefen und Schriften* (Weimar, 1956); C. Eismann, "Bemerkenswertes zur Genealogie R. S.s," *Die Musikforschung*, XXII (1969); F. Munte, *Verzeichnis des deutschsprachigen Schrifttums über R. S. 1856–1970* (Hamburg, 1972); G. Nauhaus, *R. S.: Haushaltbücher* (2 vols., Leipzig, 1982).

CORRESPONDENCE AND DIARIES: C. Schumann, ed., *S.s Jugendbriefe. Nach den Originalen mitgeteilt* (Leipzig, 1885; Eng. tr., London, 1888; 4th Ger. ed., 1910); F. Jansen, ed., *R. S.s Briefe: Neue Folge* (Leipzig, 1886; Eng. tr., London, 1890; 2nd Ger. ed., augmented, 1904); H. Erler, *R. S.s Leben: Aus seinen Briefen geschildert* (2 vols., Berlin, 1886–87; 3rd ed., 1927); "Aus S.s Kreisen," *Die Musik*, 14 (1914; unpubl. letters from and to S.); G. Eismann, ed., *R. S.: Tagebücher, Vol. I (1827–38)* (Leipzig, 1971); E. Weissweiler, ed., *Clara Schumann and R. S.: Briefwechsel: kritische Gesamtausgabe*, vol. I (Basel, 1984).

BIOGRAPHICAL: W. von Wasielewski, *R. S.* (Dresden, 1858; Eng. tr., Boston, 1871; augmented Ger. ed., 1906); A. Reissmann, *R. S.: Sein Leben und seine Werke* (Berlin, 1865; 3rd ed., 1879; in Eng., London, 1886); A. Niggli, *R. S.* (Basel, 1879); P. Spitta, *Ein Lebensbild R. S.s* (Leipzig, 1882); W. von Wasielewski, *Schumanniana* (Bonn, 1883); J. Fuller-Maitland, *S.* (London, 1884; new ed., 1913); H. Reimann, *R. S.s Leben und Werke* (Leipzig, 1887); R. Batka, *S.* (Leipzig, 1893); H. Abert, *R. S.* (Berlin, 1903; 3rd ed., 1918); A. Paterson, *S.* (London, 1903; rev. ed., 1934); L. Schneider and M. Mareschal, *S.: Sa vie et ses œuvres* (Paris, 1905); C. Mauclair, *S.* (Paris, 1906); P. Möbius, *Über R. S.s Krankheit* (Halle, 1906); M.D. Calvocoressi, *S.* (Paris, 1912); M. Wieck, *Aus dem Kreise Wieck-S.* (Dresden, 1912; 2nd ed., 1914); W. Dahms, *S.* (Berlin, 1916); F. Nussbaum, *Der Streit um R. S.s Krankheit* (diss., Univ. of Cologne, 1923); F. Niecks, *R. S.: A Supplementary and Corrective Biography* (London, 1925); R. Pitrou, *La Vie intérieure de R. S.* (Paris, 1925); E. Schumann, *Erinnerungen* (Stuttgart, 1925; Eng. tr., London, 1927); V. Basch, *S.* (Paris, 1926); idem, *La Vie douloureuse de S.* (Paris, 1928; Eng. tr., N.Y., 1931); H. Tessmer, *R. S.* (Stuttgart, 1930); E. Schumann, *R. S.: Ein Lebensbild meines Vaters* (Leipzig, 1931); M. Beaufils, *S.* (Paris, 1932); C. Valabrega, *S.* (Modena, 1934); W. Gertler, *R. S.* (Leipzig, 1936); W. Korte, *R. S.* (Potsdam, 1937); E. Bücken, *R. S.* (Cologne, 1940); W. Boetticher, *R. S.: Einführung in Persönlichkeit und Werk* (Berlin, 1941); H. Kleinebreil, *Der kranke S.: Untersuchungen über Krankheit und Todesursache R. S.s* (diss., Univ. of Jena, 1943); R. Schauffler, *Florestan:*

The Life and Work of R. S. (N.Y., 1945); J. Chissell, *S.* (London, 1948; 5th ed., rev., 1989); R. Sutermeister, *R. S.: Sein Leben nach Briefen, Tagebüchern und Erinnerungen des Meisters und seiner Gattin* (Zürich, 1949); K. Wörner, *R. S.* (Zürich, 1949); A. Cœuroy, *R. S.* (Paris, 1950); E. Müller, *R. S.* (Olten, 1950); M. Brion, *S. et l'âme romantique* (Paris, 1954; in Eng. as *S. and the Romantic Age*, London, 1956); P. and W. Rehberg, *R. S.: Sein Leben und sein Werk* (Zürich, 1954); G. Eismann, *R. S.: Eine Biographie in Wort und Bild* (Leipzig, 1956; 2nd ed., augmented, 1964; Eng. tr., 1964); H. Moser and E. Rebling, eds., *R. S.: Aus Anlass seines 100. Todestages* (Leipzig, 1956); R. Petzold and E. Crass, *R. S.: Sein Leben in Bildern* (Leipzig, 1956); A. Boucourechliev, *S.* (Paris, 1957; Eng. tr., 1959); P. Young, *Tragic Muse: The Life and Works of R. S.* (London, 1957; 2nd ed., enl., 1961); E. Sams, "S.'s Hand Injury," *Musical Times* (Dec. 1971 and May 1972); K. Laux, *R. S.* (Leipzig, 1972); R. Henson and H. Urich, "S.'s Hand Injury," *British Medical Journal*, no. 1 (1978); T. Dowley, *S.: His Life and Times* (Tunbridge Wells, 1982); P. Sutermeister, *R. S.: eine Biographie nach Briefen, Tagebuchern und Erinnerungen von R. und Clara S.* (Tübingen, 1982); R. Taylor, *R. S.: His Life and Work* (London, 1982); H. Köhler, *R. S.: sein Leben und Wirken in den Leipziger Jahren* (Leipzig, 1986).

CRITICAL, ANALYTICAL: A. Ambros, "R. S.s Tage und Werke," *Kultur-historische Bilder aus dem Musikleben der Gegenwart* (Leipzig, 1860); H. Deiters, "S. als Schriftsteller," *Allgemeine Musikalische Zeitung*, 47–49 (1865); L. Mesnard, *Un Successeur de Beethoven: Étude sur R. S.* (Paris, 1876); S. Bagge, "S. und seine Faustszenen," *Sammlung musikalischer Vorträge*, no. 4 (Leipzig, 1879); P. Graf von Waldersee, "Über S.s *Manfred*," ibid., no. 13 (Leipzig, 1880); F. Jansen, *Die Davidsbündler. Aus R. S.s Sturm- und Drangperiode* (Leipzig, 1883); B. Vogel, *R. S.s Klaviertonpoesie* (Leipzig, 1886); M. Friedlaender, *Textrevision zu R. S.s Liedern* (Leipzig, 1887); V. Joss, *Friedrich Wieck und sein Verhältniss zu R. S.* (Dresden, 1900); H. Kretzschmar, "R. S. als Ästhetiker," *Jahrbuch der Musikbibliothek Peters 1906*; H. Abert, "R. S.s Genoveva," *Zeitschrift der Internationalen Musik-Gesellschaft*, XI (1909); M. Katz, *Die Schilderung des musikalischen Eindrucks bei S.* (Giessen, 1910); I. Hirschberg, *R. S.s Tondichtungen balladischen Charakters* (Langensalza, 1913); E. Wolff, *R. S. Lieder in ersten und späteren Fassungen* (Leipzig, 1914); O. Karsten, *Die Instrumentation R. S.s* (diss., Univ. of Vienna, 1922); F. Schnapp, *Heinrich Heine und R. S.* (Hamburg, 1924); P. Frenzel, *R. S. und Goethe* (Leipzig, 1926); G. Minotti, *Die Enträtselung des Schumannschen Sphinx-Geheimnisses* (Leipzig, 1926); J. Fuller-Maitland, *S.'s Pianoforte Works* (London, 1927); G. Minotti, "Die Enträtselung des Schumannschen Abegg-Geheimniss," *Zeitschrift für Musik* (July–Aug. 1927); M. Cohen, *Studien zur Sonataform bei R. S.* (diss., Univ. of Vienna, 1928); K. Wagner, *R. S. als Schüler und Abiturient* (Zwickau, 1928); J. Fuller-Maitland, *S.'s Concerted Chamber Music* (London, 1929); M. Ninck, *S. und die Romantik in der Musik* (Heidelberg, 1929); R. Goldenberg, *Der Klaviersatz bei S.* (diss., Univ. of Vienna, 1930); H. Rosenwald, *Geschichte des deutschen Liedes zwischen Schubert und S.* (Berlin, 1930); W. Gertler, *R. S. in seinen früheren Klavierwerken* (Wolfenbüttel, 1931); M. Schweiger, *Die Harmonik in den Klavierwerken R. S.s* (diss., Univ. of Vienna, 1931); W. Schwarz, *S. und die Variation: Mit besonderer Berücksichtigung der Klavierwerke* (Kassel, 1932); H. Kötz, *Der Einfluss Jean Pauls auf R. S.* (Weimar, 1933); G. Wilcke, *Tonalität und Modulation im Streichquartett Mendelssohns und S.s* (Leipzig, 1933); G. Minotti, *Die Geheimdokumente der Davidsbündler* (Leipzig, 1934); G. Abraham, "The Three Scores of S.'s D minor Symphony," *Musical Times*, LXXXI (1940); R. Felber, "S.'s Place in German Song," *Musical Quarterly* (July 1940); R. Hernried, "Four Unpublished Compositions by R. S.," ibid. (Jan. 1942); P. Kehm, *Die "Neue Zeitschrift für Musik" unter S.s Redaktion: 1834–44* (diss., Univ. of Munich, 1943); I. Forger, *R. S. als Kritiker: Ein Beitrag zur Geschichte der musikalischen Kritik und zum S.-Problem* (diss., Univ. of Münster, 1948); W. Edelmann, *Über Text und Musik in R. S.s Sololieder* (diss., Univ. of Münster, 1950); G.

Abraham, "S.'s 'Jugendsinfonie' in G minor," *Musical Quarterly* (Jan. 1951); G. Abraham, ed., *S.: A Symposium* (London, 1952); H. Homeyer, *Grundbegriffe der Musikanschauung R. S.s: Ihr Wesen, ihre Bedeutung und Funktion in seinem literarischen Gesamtwerk* (diss., Univ. of Münster, 1956); H. Pleasants, *The Musical World of R. S.* (N.Y., 1965); A. Zlotnik, "Die beiden Fassungen von S.s D-Moll Symphonie," *Österreichische Musikzeitschrift*, XXI (1966); L. Plantinga, *S. As Critic* (New Haven, 1967); T. Brown, *The Aesthetics of R. S.* (N.Y., 1968); A. Gebhardt, *R. S. als Symphoniker* (Regensburg, 1968); E. Sams, *The Songs of R. S.* (London, 1969; 2nd ed., rev., 1975); S. Walsh, *The Lieder of S.* (London, 1971); J. Chissel, *S. Piano Music* (London, 1972); A. Desmond, *S. Songs* (London, 1972); A. Walker, ed., *R. S.: The Man and His Music* (London, 1972; 2nd ed., rev., 1976); L. Siegel, "A Second Look at S.'s *Genoveva*," *Music Review*, XXXVI (1975); W. Boetticher, *R. S.s Klavierwerke: Entstehung, Urtext, Gestalt: Untersuchungen anhand unveröffentlicher Skizzen und biographischer Dokumente* (Wilhelmshaven, 1976-); R. Hallmark, *The Genesis of S.'s "Dichterliebe": A Source Study* (Ann Arbor, 1979); C. Becker, "A New Look at S.'s Impromptus," *Musical Quarterly* (Oct. 1981); C. Brauner, "Irony in the Heine Lieder of Schubert and S.," ibid. (April 1981); G. Moore, *"Poet's Lore" and Other S. Cycles and Songs* (London, 1981); B. Turchin, "S.'s Conversion to Vocal Music: A Reconsideration," *Musical Quarterly* (July 1981); J. Finson, "The Sketches for R. S.'s C Minor Symphony," *Journal of Musicology*, I (1982); A. Gerstmeier, *Die Lieder S.s: zur Musik des frühen 19. Jahrhunderts* (Tutzing, 1982); J. Finson, "S., Popularity, and the Ouvertüre, Scherzo, und Finale, op.52," *Musical Quarterly* (Winter 1983); H.-P. Fricker, *Die musikkritischen Schriften R. S.s: Versuch eines literaturwissenschaftlichen Zugangs* (Bern, 1983); J. Finson and R. Todd, eds., *Mendelssohn and S.: Essays on their Music and its Context* (Durham, N.C., 1984); R. Kapp, *Studien zum Spätwerk R. S.s* (Tutzing, 1984); F. Otto, *R. S. als Jean-Paul-Leser* (Frankfurt, 1984); B. Borchard, *R. S. und Clara Wieck: Bedingungen künstlerischer Arbeit in der ersten Hälfte des 19. Jahrhunderts* (Weinheim, 1985); D. Fischer-Dieskau, *R. S.: das Vokalwerk* (Munich, 1985); B. Meissner, *Geschichtsrezeption als Schaffenkorrelat: Studien zum Musikgeschichtsbild R. S.s* (Bern, 1985); P. Ostwald, *S.: Music and Madness* (London, 1985); A. Burton, "R. S. and Clara Wieck: A Creative Partnership," *Music & Letters* (April 1988); G. Dietel, *"Eine neue poetische Zeit": Musikhandschauung und stilistiche Tendenzen im Klavierwerk R. S.s* (Kassel, 1989); H. Dill, "Romantic Irony in the Works of R. S.," *Musical Quarterly*, 3/2 (1989); J. Finson, *R. S. and the Study of Orchestral Composition: The Genesis of the First Symphony* (Oxford, 1989); R. Hallmark, "The Rückert Lieder of R. and C. Schumann," *19th Century Music* (Summer 1990).

Schumann, Walter, American composer; b. N.Y., Oct. 8, 1913; d. Minneapolis, Aug. 21, 1958. He studied law and music at the Univ. of Southern Calif. in Los Angeles; became associated with radio shows, and composed music for films; wrote an opera, *John Brown's Body* (Los Angeles, Sept. 21, 1953). He contributed the famous ominously syncopated theme to the television show *Dragnet*, based on the initial 3 notes of the minor scale.

Schumann-Heink, Ernestine (née **Rössler**), famous Austrian-born American contralto and mezzo-soprano; b. Lieben, near Prague, June 15, 1861; d. Los Angeles, Nov. 17, 1936. Her father was an officer in the Austrian army; her mother, an Italian amateur singer. In 1872 she was sent to the Ursuline Convent in Prague, where she sang in the church choir; after lessons from Marietta von Leclair in Graz, she made her 1st public appearance there as soloist in Beethoven's 9th Sym. (1876); made her operatic debut at the Dresden Court Opera (Oct. 15, 1878) as Azucena, where she sang until 1882; also continued her studies with Karl Krebs, Franz Wüllner, and others. From 1883 to 1897 she was a member of the Hamburg Opera; appeared with the company on its visit to London's Covent Garden in 1892, where she sang Erda, Fricka, and Brangäne. She was a regular singer at the Bayreuth Festivals

from 1896 to 1914; appeared at Covent Garden (1897–1901); also sang with the Berlin Royal Opera. She made her U.S. debut as Ortrud in Chicago on Nov. 7, 1898, a role she chose for her Metropolitan Opera debut in N.Y. on Jan. 9, 1899; canceled her contract with the Berlin Royal Opera in order to remain a member of the Metropolitan Opera (until 1903; then appeared intermittently until 1932; created the role of Klytemnestra in *Elektra* (Dresden, Jan. 25, 1909); made her last operatic appearance as Erda at the Metropolitan on March 11, 1932. She became a naturalized U.S. citizen in 1908. During the last years of her life, she was active mainly as a teacher. Her operatic repertoire included about 150 parts; her voice, of an even quality in all registers, possessed great power, making it peculiarly suitable to Wagnerian roles. She was married in 1882 to Ernst Heink of Dresden, from whom she was later divorced; in 1893 she married the actor Paul Schumann in Hamburg; he died in 1904; she assumed the names of both Schumann and Heink. Her 3rd husband was a Chicago lawyer, William Rapp, Jr., whom she married in 1905 and then subsequently divorced (1914).

BIBL.: M. Lawton, *S.-H., The Last of the Titans* (N.Y., 1928); J. McPherson, "E. S.-H.," *Record Collector*, Nos. 5, 6, and 7 (1967).

Schünemann, Georg, eminent German musicologist and music educator; b. Berlin, March 13, 1884; d. there (suicide), Jan. 2, 1945. He studied at the Stern Cons. in Berlin; played flute in various orchs. in Berlin; then took courses in musicology with Kretzschmar, Friedländer, Wolf, and others at the Univ. of Berlin; also studied German literature and philosophy there, receiving his Ph.D. in 1907 with the dissertation *Geschichte des Dirigierens* (publ. in Leipzig, 1913). In 1919 he joined the faculty of the Univ. of Berlin; was appointed deputy director of the Berlin Hochschule für Musik in 1920, and director in 1932; later held the post of director of the State Musical Instrument Collections. In 1935 he was appointed director of the music division of the Prussian State Library. He took his own life during the darkest stages of World War II.

WRITINGS: *Das Lied der deutschen Kolonisten in Russland* (Berlin, 1923); *Die Musica des Listhenius* (Berlin, 1927); *Geschichte der deutschen Schulmusik* (Leipzig, 1928; 2nd ed., 1931); *Die Musikerziehung, I: Die Musik in Kindheit und Jugend, Schule und Volk* (Leipzig, 1930); *C.F. Zelter, der Begründer der preussischen Musikpflege* (Berlin, 1932); *Führer durch die deutsche Chorliteratur* (2 vols., Wolfenbüttel, 1935–36); ed. *Musiker-Handschriften von Bach bis Schumann* (facsimile ed., Berlin, 1936; rev. and publ. in an Eng. tr. by W. Gerstenberg and M. Hürimann, 1968); *C.F. Zelter, Der Mensch und sein Werk* (Berlin, 1937); *Die Violine* (Hamburg, 1940); *Geschichte der Klaviermusik* (Hamburg, 1940; 2nd ed., rev. by H. Gerigk, 1953; 3rd ed., 1956); *Die Singakademie zu Berlin* (Regensburg, 1941); ed. *Ludwig van Beethovens Konversationshefte* (not complete; 3 vols., Berlin, 1941–43).

BIBL.: E. Preussner, "G. S.," *Die Musikforschung*, I (1948).

Schunke, Karl, German pianist, teacher, and composer, cousin of **Ludwig Schunke;** b. Magdeburg, 1801; d. (suicide) Paris, Dec. 16, 1839. He studied music with his father, the horn player **Michael Schunke** (1778–1821); then took some lessons with Ferdinand Ries, whom he accompanied to London. In 1828 he went to Paris, where he became a fashionable piano teacher; nevertheless, he suffered from some sort of malaise and killed himself. He composed a number of brilliant salon pieces à la mode and transcriptions of operatic arias for piano.

Schunke, Ludwig, German pianist and composer, cousin of **Karl Schunke;** b. Kassel, Dec. 21, 1810; d. Leipzig, Dec. 7, 1834. He studied with his father, Gottfried Schunke (1777–1861), who was a horn player; went to Paris, where he studied piano with Kalkbrenner and Reicha; settled in Leipzig in 1833 and became a close friend of Schumann, of whom he was an exact contemporary, and with whom he became associated in founding the *Neue Zeitschrift für Musik*. His early death was greatly mourned, for his piano pieces were full of promise;

among them were a Sonata, a set of variations, 2 *Caprices,* and a set of *Charakterstücke.* Schumann wrote a heartfelt appreciation of Schunke's talent, which was reprinted in his *Gesammelte Schriften.*

Schuppanzigh, Ignaz, esteemed Austrian violinist; b. Vienna, Nov. 20, 1776; d. there, March 2, 1830. After learning to play the viola, he took up the violin about 1793; became 1st violinist in a string quartet with Kraft, Sina, and Weiss that appeared weekly at Prince Lichnowsky's residence; among the prince's guests was Beethoven, who befriended Schuppanzigh. In 1795 he became concertmaster of the Augarten orch. concerts, and about 1798, manager. During the 1804–5 season, he organized with Kraft, Mayseder, and Schreiber his own string quartet, which gave subscription concerts. In 1808 he founded the private string quartet of Count Razumovsky with Linke and Weiss; when the count did not play, Sina took his place as 2nd violinist. After a fire destroyed Razumovsky's palace in 1814, the quartet was dissolved. In 1816 Schuppanzigh went to St. Petersburg, where he proved a determined champion of the music of Beethoven. In 1823 he returned to Vienna and became a member of the court chapel; later was director of the Court Opera; also continued to be active as a quartet player. In addition to playing in premieres of works by Beethoven, he also played in premieres of works by Schubert. Although his friendship with Beethoven was frequently tested by Beethoven's moods, Schuppanzigh never wavered in his respect. He also composed; publ. a *Solo brillant* for Violin, with String Quartet; solo variations on a Russian theme; 9 variations for 2 Violins.
BIBL.: D. MacArdle, "Beethoven and S.," *Music Review,* XXVI (1965).

Schuré, Edouard, Alsatian writer on music; b. Strasbourg, Jan. 21, 1841; d. Paris, April 7, 1929. He studied law and philology in Strasbourg; in 1867, settled in Paris. He was an avowed propagandist of German music, particularly of Wagner.
WRITINGS: *Histoire du Lied; ou, La Chanson populaire en Allemagne* (Paris, 1868; new ed. with the study *Le Réveil de la poésie populaire en France,* 1903); *Le Drame musical* (Paris, 1875; 12th ed., 1914; Ger. tr. by H. von Wolzogen as *Das musikalische Drama;* 3rd ed., 1888); *Souvenirs sur Richard Wagner* (Paris, 1900); *Précurseurs et révoltés* (Paris, 1904); *The Musical Idea in Wagner* (Eng. tr. from French, Hampstead, 1910).
BIBL.: J. Mainor, *E. S.* (Angers, 1905); A. Roux and R. Veyssié, *E. S., Son œuvre et sa pensée* (Paris, 1913); R. Schuler, *E. S. à travers son écriture* (Paris, 1928); A. Roux, *In memoriam S.* (Paris, 1931).

Schürer, Johann Georg, prominent German composer; b. probably in Raudnitz, Bohemia, c.1720; d. Dresden, Feb. 16, 1786. He settled in Dresden about 1746; there he first gained notice as composer and music director of an opera troupe at the Zwinger; in 1748 he was made Kirchencompositeur to the court, a position he held with distinction until his retirement in 1780. His mastery of contrapuntal writing is revealed in his numerous sacred compositions, which include the oratorios *Il Figliuol Prodigo* (1747), *Isacco figura del Redentore* (1748), and *La Passione di Jesu Christo* (n.d.), and various masses and Psalms. He also wrote the operas *Astrea placata ovvero La felicità della terra* (Warsaw, Oct. 7, 1746), *La Galatea* (Dresden, Nov. 8, 1746), *L'Ercole sul Termodonte* (Dresden, Jan. 9, 1747), *Doris* (Dresden, Feb. 13, 1747), and *Calandro* (Dresden, Jan. 20, 1748), and 7 cantatas.
BIBL.: R. Haas, *J.G. S. (1720–1786): Ein Beitrag zur Geschichte der Musik in Dresden* (Dresden, 1915).

Schuricht, Carl, distinguished German conductor; b. Danzig, July 3, 1880; d. Corseaux-sur-Vevey, Switzerland, Jan. 7, 1967. He studied at home, his father being an organ manufacturer and his mother a pianist. He then took lessons with Humperdinck at the Hochschule für Musik in Berlin, and later in Leipzig with Reger. He began his career conducting in various provincial theaters; in 1911 he became music director in Wies-

baden, and in 1942 conductor of the Dresden Phil.; also made numerous guest conducting appearances in various European music centers, and also conducted in the U.S. for the 1st time in 1927. After falling out of favor with the Nazis in 1944, he fled to Switzerland, which remained his home until his death. In 1946 he reopened the Salzburg Festival; continued to conduct there and in France. In 1956 he took the Vienna Phil. on its 1st U.S. tour, sharing his duties with André Cluytens. In 1957 he conducted at the Ravinia Festival with the Chicago Sym. Orch. and at the Tanglewood Festival with the Boston Sym. Orch.; in subsequent years, he regularly conducted the Berlin and Vienna Phils.; also was a frequent guest conductor of the Stuttgart Radio Sym. Orch. He also composed, wrote orch. music, piano pieces, and songs. As a conductor, Schuricht was one of the last representatives of the Austro-German tradition. After concentrating on contemporary music in his early years, he turned to the great masterworks of the Austro-German repertory, his interpretations being noted for their freedom and beauty of expression
BIBL.: B. Gavoty, *C. S.* (Geneva, 1955).

Schurig, Volkmar (Julius Wilhelm), German organist and composer; b. Aue an der Mulde, March 24, 1822; d. Dresden, Jan. 31, 1899. He studied in Dresden, where he played organ in the English Church (1844–56); subsequently filled various other posts as an organist, singing teacher, and cantor. He publ. organ fantasias; organ preludes; sacred choruses to Eng. texts; children's songs; brought out a useful collection, *Liederperlen deutscher Tonkunst.*

Schürmann, Georg Caspar, eminent German composer; b. Idensen, near Hannover, 1672 or 1673; d. Wolfenbüttel, Feb. 25, 1751. He went to Hamburg, where he became a male alto at the Opera and in various churches when he was 20; after appearing with the Hamburg Opera at the Braunschweig court of Duke Anton Ulrich of Braunschweig-Lüneburg in 1697, the duke engaged him as solo alto to the court; was also active as a conductor at the Opera and at the court church; after the duke sent him to Italy for further training (1701–2?), he was loaned to the Meiningen court as Kapellmeister and composer; in 1707 he resumed his association with the Braunschweig-Wolfenbüttel court, where he was active as a composer and conductor for the remainder of his life. Schürmann was a leading opera composer during the Baroque era. He wrote over 40 operas, only 3 of which survived in their entirety after their Braunschweig premieres: *Heinrich der Vogler* (part I, Aug. 1, 1718; part II, Jan. 11, 1721), *Die getreue Alceste* (1719), and *Ludovicus Pius, oder Ludewig der Fromme* (1726; partial edition in Publikationen Älterer Praktischer und Theoretischer Musikwerke, XVII, 1890). He was also a noted composer of sacred music.
BIBL.: H. Sommer, "Die Oper Ludwig der Fromme von G.C. S.," *Monatshefte für Musikgeschichte,* XIV (1882); G. Schmid, *Die frühdeutsche Oper und die musikdramatische Kunst G.C. S.s* (2 vols., Regensburg, 1933–34); E. Rosendahl, "Wo und wann G.K. S. geboren wurde," *Archiv für Musikforschung,* VII (1942).

Schurmann (Schürmann), (Eduard) Gerard, pianist, conductor, and composer of Dutch and Hungarian descent; b. Kertosono, Dutch East Indies, Jan. 19, 1924. His father was an employee at a sugar factory in Java; his mother was a pianist who had studied with Béla Bartók at the Budapest Academy of Music. As war clouds gathered over Southeastern Asia, Schurmann was sent to England in 1937; he went to school in London, and after matriculation joined the Royal Air Force, serving in aircrews on active flying duty. While still in uniform, he gave piano recitals; studied piano with Kathleen Long and composition with Alan Rawsthorne. During his travels in Italy, he took lessons in conducting with Franco Ferrara. The government of the Netherlands offered him the position of cultural attaché at the Dutch Embassy in London; being fluent in the Dutch language, which was his mother tongue in the Dutch East Indies, he accepted. Later, he moved to the Netherlands, where he was active with the radio in

Hilversum. He developed a successful career in London as a pianist, conductor, and composer. In 1981 he settled in Hollywood, where he became active as a film composer; also traveled widely as a guest conductor, presenting a comprehensive repertory ranging from Haydn to contemporary composers, including his own works. The structure of Schurmann's music is asymptotic toward tonality; melodic progressions are linear, with the fundamental tonic and dominant often encasing the freely atonal configurations, while dodecaphony assumes the adumbrative decaphonic lines, with 2 notes missing in the tone row. The harmonic texture is acrid, acerbic, and astringent; the styptic tendency is revealed in his predilection for dissonant minor seconds and major sevenths treated as compound units; yet after the needed tension is achieved, the triadic forms are introduced as a sonic emollient. Thanks to this versatility of application, Schurmann achieves a natural felicity in dealing with exotic subjects; his proximity to gamelan-like pentatonicism during his adolescence lends authentic flavor to his use of pentatonic scales; remarkable in his congenial treatment is the set *Chuench'i*, to Eng. trs. of 7 Chinese poems. On the other hand, his intimate knowledge of Eng. music and history enables him to impart a true archaic sentiment to his opera-cantata based on the medieval poem *Piers Plowman*. Schurmann is self-critical in regard to works of his which he deems imperfect; thus, he destroyed his Piano Concerto, which he had played under prestigious auspices with the London Sym. Orch. conducted by Sir Adrian Boult in Cambridge in April 1944.

WORKS: OPERA: *Piers Plowman*, opera-cantata after William Langland (Gloucester Cathedral, Aug. 22, 1980). **ORCH.:** *6 Studies of Francis Bacon*, comprising *Figures in a Landscape*, *Popes*, *Isabel*, *Crucifixion*, *George and the Bicycle*, and *Self-Portrait* (Dublin, Jan. 7, 1969); *Variants* (Guildford Festival, March 8, 1971); *Attack and Celebration* (1971); Piano Concerto (Portsmouth, Nov. 21, 1973); Violin Concerto (Liverpool, Sept. 26, 1978). **CHAMBER:** Violin Sonata (1943); 2 string quartets (1943, 1946); *Duo* for 2 Violins (1950); Wind Quintet (1964; rev. 1976); *Fantasia* (1968); Sonatina for Flute and Piano (1968); *Serenade* for Violin (1969); *Duo* for Violin and Piano (1984). **PIANO:** Sonata (1943); *Rotterdam*, suite for 2 Pianos (1944); *Bagatelles* (1945); *Contrasts* (1973); *Leotaurus* (1975); 2 *Ballades* (1981–83). **VOCAL:** *Pacific*, 3 songs (1943); 5 *Facets* (London, Jan. 20, 1946; Peter Pears, tenor; Benjamin Britten, pianist); 9 poems of William Blake (1956); *Chuench'i*, cycle of 7 songs from the Chinese for Voice and Orch. (1966; Harrogate, Aug. 10, 1969); *Summer Is Coming*, madrigal, unaccompanied (1970); *The Double Heart*, cantata for Voices Unaccompanied (1976).

Schuster, Bernhard, German music publisher and composer; b. Berlin, March 26, 1870; d. there, Jan. 13, 1934. He studied piano, organ, and violin; then was active as a theater conductor. In 1901 he founded the fortnightly review *Die Musik*, which from its inception ranked with the foremost musical journals of Germany; was its ed.-in-chief until 1933. In 1905 he founded the publishing house "Schuster und Loeffler" (Berlin and Leipzig), which brought out a number of important works on music (the business was acquired by the Stuttgart Deutsche Verlags-Anstalt in 1922). He wrote the operas *Der Jungbrunnen* (Karlsruhe, 1920) and *Der Dieb des Glücks* (Wiesbaden, March 10, 1923); a Sym.; a String Quartet; sacred choruses; songs.

Schuster, Joseph, distinguished German conductor and composer; b. Dresden, Aug. 11, 1748; d. there, July 24, 1812. After initial training with his father, a Dresden court musician, and J.G. Schürer, he pursued his studies on a scholarship in Italy with Girolamo Pera (1765–68). After serving as a church composer in Dresden (1772–74), he returned to Italy and completed his studies with Padre Martini in Bologna; wrote operas for Venice and Naples, and was named honorary maestro di cappella to the King of Naples. Settling in Dresden in 1781, he was active as a conductor at the court church and theater; with Seydelmann, he shared the duties of Kapellmeister to the elector from 1787. Schuster assumed a leading position at the Dresden court, both as a conductor and as a composer. Of his some 20 works for the stage, the singspiel *Der Alchymist oder Der Liebesteufel* (Dresden, March 1778) won great popularity in Germany. He was an admired composer of orch. works, sacred music, chamber music, and pieces for the fortepiano. His Padua String Quartet in C major (1780) was formerly attributed to Mozart.

BIBL.: R. Engländer, "Die Opern J. S.s (1748–1812)," *Zeitschrift für Musikwissenschaft*, X (1927–28); idem, "Les Sonates de violon de Mozart et les 'Duetti' di J. S.," *Revue de Musicologie*, XX (1939); idem, "Nochmals Mozart und der Dresdner J. S.," *Svensk tidskrift för Musikforskning*, XXXIX (1957).

Schütt, Eduard, Russian-born Austrian pianist and composer; b. St. Petersburg, Oct. 22, 1856; d. Obermias, near Merano, Italy, July 26, 1933. After studying piano at the St. Petersburg Cons., he took courses with Richter, Jadassohn, and Reinecke at the Leipzig Cons.; then proceeded to Vienna, where he became a private pupil of Leschetizky. He wrote the comic opera *Signor Formica* (Vienna, Nov. 19, 1892); 2 piano concertos; Piano Quartet; 2 piano trios; numerous character pieces for piano, some of which were long popular.

Schütz, Heinrich (also **Henrich**), great German composer; b. Köstritz, Oct. 8, 1585; d. Dresden, Nov. 6, 1672. He was born into a prosperous family of innkeepers; in 1590 the family settled in Weissenfels, where his father became burgomaster. He was trained in music by Heinrich Colander, the town organist. In 1599 he became a choirboy in the court chapel of Landgrave Moritz of Hessen-Kassel; in Kassel he pursued his academic studies with Georg Otto, the court Kapellmeister. On Sept. 27, 1608, he entered the Univ. of Marburg to study law; an opportunity to continue his musical education came in 1609 when Landgrave Moritz offered to send him to Venice to take lessons with the renowned master Giovanni Gabrieli. Under Gabrieli's tutelage, he received a thorough training in composition, and he also learned to play the organ. In 1611 he brought out a book of 5-voice madrigals, which he dedicated to his benefactor, Landgrave Moritz. After Gabrieli's death in 1612 Schütz returned to Kassel, serving as second organist at the court chapel. In 1615 the Elector invited him to Dresden as Saxon Kapellmeister; Praetorius was also active at the Dresden court for special occasions at this time. In 1616 Landgrave Moritz asked the Elector to allow Schütz to return to Kassel, but the Elector declined; in 1617 Schütz assumed fully his duties as Saxon Kapellmeister, being granted an annual salary of 400 florins from 1618. In addition to providing music for court occasions, he was responsible for overseeing the functions of the court chapel. In 1619 he publ. his 1st collection of sacred music, the *Psalmen Davids sampt etlichen Moteten und Concerten*. On June 1, 1619, he married Magdalena Wildeck, the daughter of a court official in Dresden. They had 2 daughters. His wife died on Sept. 6, 1625, and Schütz remained a widower for the rest of his life. During a court visit to Torgau, Schütz produced the 1st German opera, *Dafne*, set to Opitz's translation and adaptation of Rinuccini's libretto for Peri's opera; it was presented at Hartenfels Castle on April 13, 1627, to celebrate the wedding of the Princess Sophia Eleonora of Saxony to Landgrave Georg II of Hesse-Darmstadt. In 1628 he was granted a leave of absence, and went to Italy. There he had an occasion to study the new operatic style of Monteverdi; he adopted this new style in his *Symphoniae sacrae* (publ. in Venice, 1629). He returned to his post in Dresden in 1629. When Saxony entered the Thirty Years' War in 1631, conditions at the Dresden court chapel became difficult. In 1633 Schütz accepted an invitation to go to Copenhagen, where he obtained the post of Kapellmeister to King Christian IV. In June 1634 he returned to Dresden. His *Musicalische Exequien*, composed for the interment of Prince Heinrich Posthumus, appeared in 1636. He also publ. 2 vols. of *Kleine geistliche Concerte* (1636 and 1639). He composed the music for the opera-ballet *Orpheus und Euridice*, which was performed in Dresden on Nov. 20, 1638, to celebrate the marriage of Prince Johann Georg of Saxony and Princess Magdalena Sybilla of Brandenburg. In late 1639 Schütz obtained another leave of absence to serve as Kapellmeister to Georg of Calenberg, who resided in Hildesheim. After a year's stay in Dresden, in 1641–42, he set out once more for Copenhagen, where he again served as Kapellmeister, until April 1644. Returning to Germany, he lived mostly in Braunschweig (1644–45), and was active at the court of nearby Wolfenbüttel. In 1645 he returned to Dresden; the Elector declined his request for retirement but did allow him to live a part of each year in Weissenfels. Schütz continued to compose industriously during these years. The second book of his *Symphoniae sacrae* appeared in 1647, followed by his *Geistliche Chor-Music* in 1648. In succeeding years, Schütz repeatedly asked to be pensioned, but his requests were ignored. Finally, when Johann Georg II became Elector in 1657, Schütz was allowed to retire on a pension with the title of Chief Kapellmeister. His Passions *St. Luke*, *St. John*, and *St. Matthew* all date from these last years, as does his *Christmas Oratorio*. About 1670 he returned to Dresden to settle his affairs and await his end, which came peacefully in 1672, in his 87th year.

The importance of Schütz in music history resides in his astute adaptation of the new Italian styles to German music. He was extraordinarily productive, but not all of his works survived; the majority of his extant compositions are vocal works of a sacred nature. The most important collection of Schütz's MSS is housed in the Hessische Landesbibliothek in Kassel. The 1st major edition of his works, edited by Philipp Spitta, was publ. by Breitkopf und Härtel (16 vols., Leipzig, 1885–94; supplementary vols. were publ. in 1909 and 1927). A 2nd edition of his works, *Neuen Schütz-Gesellschaft*, began to appear in 1955 in Kassel. A 3rd ed., *Stuttgarter Schütz-Ausgabe*, began publication in 1971. A catalogue of his works, ed. by W. Bittinger, is found in his *Schütz-Werke-Verzeichnis (SWV): Kleine Ausgabe* (Kassel, 1960).

Works: *Il primo libro de madrigali* (Venice, 1611); *Die Wort Jesus Syrach . . . auff hochzeitlichen Ehrentag des . . . Herrn Josephi Avenarii* (perf. in Dresden, April 21, 1618; publ. in Dresden, 1618); *Concert mit 11 Stimmen: Auff des . . . Herrn Michael Thomae . . . hochzeitlichen Ehren Tag,* (perf. in Leipzig, June 15, 1618; publ. in Dresden, 1618); *Psalmen Davids sampt etlichen Moteten und Concerten* (Dresden, 1619); *Der 133. Psalm . . . auff die hochzeitliche Ehrenfrewde Herrn Georgii Schützen* (perf. in Leipzig, Aug. 9, 1619; publ. in Leipzig, 1619; not extant); *Syncharma musicum* (perf. in Breslau, Nov. 3, 1621; publ. in Breslau, 1621; not extant); *Historia der frölichen und siegreichen Aufferstehung unsers einigen Erlösers und Seligmachers Jesu Christi* (Dresden, 1623); *Kläglicher Abschied von der churfürstlichen Grufft zu Freybergk* (perf. in Freiberg, Jan. 28, 1623; publ. in Freiberg, 1623); *Cantiones sacrae* (Freiberg, 1625); *De vitae fugacitate: Aria . . . bey Occasion des . . . Todesfalles der . . . Jungfrawen Anna Marien Wildeckin* (perf. in Dresden, Aug. 15, 1625; publ. in Freiberg, 1625); *Ultima verba psalmi 23 . . . super . . . obitu . . . Jacobi Schultes* (perf. in Leipzig, July 19, 1625; publ. in Leipzig, 1625); *Psalmen Davids, hiebevorn in teutzsche Reimen gebracht, durch D. Cornelium Beckern, und an jetzo mit ein hundert und drey eigenen Melodeyen . . . gestellet* (Freiberg, 1628; 2nd ed., 1640; 3rd ed., rev. and enl., Dresden, 1661); *Symphoniae sacrae* (Venice, 1629); *Verba D. Pauli . . . beatis manibus Dn. Johannis-Hermanni Scheinii . . . consecrata* (perf. in Leipzig, Nov. 19, 1630; publ. in Dresden, 1631; not extant); *An hoch printzlicher Durchläuchtigkeit zu Dennemarck . . . Beylager: Gesang der Venus-Kinder in der Invention genennet Thronus Veneris* (perf. in Copenhagen, Oct. 1634; publ. in Copenhagen, 1634); *Musicalische Exequien . . . dess . . . Herrn Heinrichen dess Jüngern und Eltisten Reussen* (perf. in Gera, Feb. 4, 1636; publ. in Dresden, 1636; not extant); *Erster Theil kleiner geistlichen Concerten* (Leipzig, 1636); *Anderer Theil kleiner geistlichen Concerten* (Dresden, 1639); *Symphoniarum sacrarum secunda pars* (Dresden, 1647); *Danck-Lied: Für die hocherwiesene fürstl. Gnade in Weymar* (perf. in Weimar, Feb. 12, 1647; publ. in Gotha, 1647); *Musicalia ad chorum sacrum, das ist: Geistliche Chor-Music . . . erster Theil* (Dresden, 1648); *Sym-*

phoniarum sacrarum tertia pars (Dresden, 1650); *Zwölff geistliche Gesänge* (Dresden, 1657); *Canticum B. Simeonis . . . nach dem hochseligsten Hintritt . . . Johann Georgen* (perf. in Dresden, Oct. 8, 1657; publ. in Dresden, 1657); *Historia, der freuden- und gnadenreichen Geburth Gottes und Marien Sohnes, Jesu Christi* (Dresden, 1664; includes the *Christmas Oratorio,* which was lost until discovered by Schering, 1908); *Die sieben Wortte unsers lieben Erlösers und Seeligmachers Jesu Christi* (date not determined); *Historia des Leidens und Sterbens unsers Herrn und Heylandes Jesu Christi nach dem Evangelisten S. Matheum* (perf. in Dresden, April 1, 1666); *Historia des Leidens und Sterbens . . . Jesu Christi nach dem Evangelisten St. Lucam* (perf. in Dresden, April 8, 1666); *Historia des Leidens und Sterbens . . . Jesu Christi nach dem Evangelisten St. Johannem* (perf. in Dresden, April 13, 1666); *Königs und Propheten Davids hundert und neunzehender Psalm . . . nebenst dem Anhange des 100. Psalms . . . und eines deutschen Magnificats* (Dresden, 1671).

Bibl.: *H. S.: Autobiographie (Memorial 1651)* (facsimile ed., Leipzig, 1972); M. Geier, *Kurtze Beschreibung des . . . Herrn H. S.ens . . . Lebens-Lauff* (Dresden, 1672; reprint, 1935); J. Mattheson, *Grundlage einer Ehren-Pforte . . .* (Hamburg, 1740; new ed. by M. Schneider, Berlin, 1910); M. Fürstenau, *Beiträge zur Geschichte der königlich sächsischen musikalischen Kapelle* (Dresden, 1849); W. Schäfer, "Einige Beiträge zur Geschichte der kurfürstlichen musikalischen Capelle oder Cantorei unter den Kurfürsten August, Christian I. u. II. u. Johann Georg I.," *Sachsen-Chronik,* I (1854); idem, "H. S.: Kurfürstlich sächsischer Kapellmeister, 1617 bis 1672," ibid.; M. Fürstenau, *Zur Geschichte der Musik und des Theaters am Hofe zu Dresden* (vol. I, Dresden, 1861); F. Chrysander, "Geschichte der Braunschweig-Wolfenbüttelschen Capelle und Oper vom 16. bis zum 18. Jahrhundert," *Jahrbuch für musikalische Wissenschaft* (vol. I, 1863); F. Spitta, *Die Passionen nach den vier Evangelisten von H. S.* (Leipzig, 1886); P. Spitta, "S., H.," in the *Allgemeine deutsche Biographie;* rev. as "H. S.' Leben und Werke," in *Musikgeschichtliche Aufsätze,* (Berlin, 1894); P. Spitta, "Händel, Bach und S.," *Zur Musik* (Berlin, 1892); P. Spitta, *Die Passionsmusiken von Sebastian Bach und H. S.* (Hamburg, 1893); M. Seiffert, "Anecdota S.iana," *Sammelbände der Internationalen Musik-Gesellschaft,* I (1899–1900); A. Schering, "Ein wiederaufgefundenes Werk von H. S.," *Zeitschrift der Internationalen Musik-Gesellschaft,* X (1908–9); A. Pirro, *S.* (Paris, 1913; 2nd ed., 1924); E. Müller von Asow, *H. S.: Leben und Werke* (Berlin and Dresden, 1922); J. Müller-Blattau, ed., *Die Kompositionslehre H. S.ens in der Fassung seines Schülers Christoph Bernhard* (Leipzig, 1926; 2nd ed., 1963); H. Spitta, *H. S.' Orchester- und unveröffentlichte Werke* (diss., Univ. of Göttingen, 1927); W. Schuh, *Formprobleme bei H. S.* (Leipzig, 1928); R. Gerber, *Das Passionsrezitativ bei H. S. und seine stilgeschichtlichen Grundlagen* (Gütersloh, 1929); E. Müller von Asow, ed., *H. S.: Gesammelte Briefe und Schriften* (Regensburg, 1931); M. Schneider, "Zum Weihnachtsoratorium von H. S.," in *Theodor Kroyer: Festschrift zum sechzigsten Geburtstage* (Regensburg, 1933); A. Heller, *Der Deutsche H. S. in seinen italienischen Madrigalen* (diss., Univ. of Prague, 1934); W. Kreidler, *H. S. und der Stile concitato von Claudio Monteverdi* (Kassel, 1934); A. Abert, *Die stilistischen Voraussetzungen der "Cantiones sacrae" von H. S.* (Wolfenbüttel and Berlin, 1935); F. Blume, "H. S. 1585–1672," in *Die grossen Deutschen* (vol. I, Berlin, 1935); K. Gudewill, *Das sprachliche Urbild bei H. S.* (Kassel, 1936); H. Moser, *H. S.: Sein Leben und Werk* (Kassel, 1936; 2nd ed., rev., 1954; Eng. tr. as *H. S.: His Life and Work* by C. Pfatteicher, St. Louis, 1959); L. Reitter, *Doppelchortechnik bei H. S.* (Derendingen, 1937); H. Hoffmann, *H. S. und Johann Sebastian Bach: Zwei Tonsprachen und ihre Bedeutung für die Aufführungspraxis* (Kassel, 1940); H. Moser, *Kleines H.-S.-Buch* (Kassel, 1940; 3rd ed., 1952; Eng. tr., 1967); C. Roskowski, *Die "Kleinen geistlichen Konzerte" von H. S.* (diss., Univ. of Münster, 1947); J. Piersig, *Das Weltbild des H. S.* (Kassel, 1949); G. Toussaint, *Die Anwendung der musikalisch-rhetorischen Figuren in den Werken von H. S.* (diss., Univ. of Mainz, 1949); G. Weizsäcker,

H. S.: Lobgesang eines Lebens (Stuttgart, 1952; 2nd ed., 1956); articles in *Bekenntnis zu H. S.* (Kassel, 1954); articles in *Festschrift zur Ehrung von H. S. (1585–1672)* (Weimar, 1954); L. Schrade, "H. S. and Johann Sebastian Bach in the Protestant Liturgy," *The Musical Heritage of the Church* (Valparaiso, Ind., 1954); C. Agey, *A Study of the "Kleine geistliche Konzerte" and "Geistliche Chormusik" of H. S.* (diss., Florida State Univ., 1955); J. Heinrich, *Stilkritische Untersuchungen zur "Geistlichen Chormusik" von H. S.* (diss., Univ. of Göttingen, 1956); W. Gurlitt, "H. S. 1585–1672," in *Die grossen Deutschen* (vol. V, Berlin, 2nd ed., 1957); H. Eggebrecht, *H. S.: Musicus poeticus* (Göttingen, 1959); G. Kirchner, *Der Generalbass bei H. S.* (Kassel, 1960); W. Haacke, *H. S.: Eine Schilderung seines Lebens und Wirkens* (Königstein, 1960); A. Rowley, *A Bibliography of H. S.* (diss., Univ. of London, 1960); W. Huber, *Motivsymbolik bei H. S.* (Basel, 1961); L. Schrade, *Das musikalische Werk von H. S. in der protestantischen Liturgie* (Basel, 1961); D. McCulloch, "H. S. (1585–1672) and Venice," *Church Music*, II, no. 20 (1967); H. Wichmann-Zemke, *Untersuchungen zur Harmonik in den Werken von H. S.* (diss., Univ. of Kiel, 1967); R. Tellart, *H. S.: L'Homme et son œuvre* (Paris, 1968); H. Drude, *H. S. als Musiker der evangelischen Kirche* (diss., Univ. of Göttingen, 1969); H. Eggebrecht, *S. und Gottesdienst: Versuch über das Selbstverständliche* (Stuttgart, 1969); J. Larsen, "S. und Dänemark," *Sagittarius*, II (1969); D. Manicke, "H. S. als Lehrer," ibid.; W. Breig, "Neue S.-Funde," *Archiv für Musikwissenschaft*, XXVII (1970); R. Bray, "The 'Cantiones sacrae' of H. S. Re-examined," *Music & Letters*, LIII (1971); D. Arnold, "S. in Venice," *Music and Musicians*, XXI/1 (1972); O. Brodde, *H. S.: Weg und Werk* (Kassel, 1972); R. Petzoldt and D. Berke, *H. S. und seine Zeit in Bildern* (Kassel, 1972); W. Siegmund-Schultze, ed., *H. S. 1585–1672: Festtage 1972* (Gera, 1972); R. Grunow, ed., *Begegnungen mit H. S.: Erzählungen über Leben und Werk* (Berlin, 1974); A. Skei, *H. S.: A Guide to Research* (N.Y. and London, 1981); M. Gregor-Dellin, *H. S.: sein Leben, sein Werk, seine Zeit* (Munich, 1984); H. Krause-Graumnitz, *H. S.: ein Leben im Wert und in den Dokumenten seiner Zeit* (Leipzig, 1985); B. Smallman, *The Music of H. S.* (Leeds, 1985); D. Miller and A. Highsmith, eds., *H. S.: A Bibliography of the Collected Works and Performing Editions* (N.Y., 1986); G. Spagnoli, ed., *The Letters and Documents of H. S., 1656–1672: An Annotated Translation* (Ann Arbor, 1990).

Schützendorf, family of German musicians, all brothers:

(1) Guido Schützendorf, bass; b. Vught, near 's-Hertogenbosch, the Netherlands, April 22, 1880; d. in Germany, April 1967. He studied at the Cologne Cons.; sang with the German Opera Co., with which he toured the U.S. (1929–30); also sang under the name **Schützendorf an der Mayr.**

(2) Alfons Schützendorf, bass-baritone; b. Vught, May 25, 1882; d. Weimar, Aug. 1946. He studied in Cologne and with Borgatti in Milan; sang at the Bayreuth Festivals (1910–12) and at London's Covent Garden (1910); taught at the Essen Folkwangschule (1927–31) and in Berlin (from 1932); was esteemed for such roles as Wotan, Klingsor, and Telramund.

(3) Gustav Schützendorf, baritone; b. Cologne, 1883; d. Berlin, April 27, 1937. He studied at the Cologne Cons. and in Milan; made his operatic debut as Don Giovanni in Düsseldorf (1905); after singing in Berlin, Wiesbaden, and Basel, he was a member of the Bavarian Court Opera (later State Opera) in Munich (1914–20) and the Berlin State Opera (1920–22); made his Metropolitan Opera debut in N.Y. as Faninal on Nov. 17, 1922, and remained on its roster until 1935. He married the soprano **Grete Stückgold** in 1929.

(4) Leo Schützendorf, bass-baritone; b. Cologne, May 7, 1886; d. Berlin, Dec. 31, 1931. He studied with D'Arnals in Cologne; made his operatic debut in Düsseldorf (1908); sang in Krefeld (1909–12), Darmstadt (1913–17), Wiesbaden (1917–19), and Vienna (1919–20) and at the Berlin State Opera (1920–29), where he created the role of Wozzeck (Dec. 14, 1925); among his other roles were Faninal, Beckmesser, and Boris Godunov.

Schuyler, Philippa Duke, black American pianist and composer; b. N.Y., Aug. 2, 1931; d. in a helicopter crash in Da Nang Bay, Vietnam, May 9, 1967. By the age of 12, she had written the whimsical *Cockroach Ballet* for Piano and had become the youngest member of ASCAP; at the age of 14, she appeared as piano soloist with the N.Y. Phil. at Lewisohn Stadium in a program that included the scherzo from her "fairy-tale symphony," *Rumpelstiltskin* (July 13, 1946); made her Town Hall debut in N.Y. on May 12, 1953. She traveled to Africa, Europe, South America, and Asia under the auspices of the State Dept., playing command performances for such leaders as Emperor Haile Selassie of Ethiopia and the Queen of Malaya. A product of miscegenation (her mother was from a wealthy white Texas family; her father, George Schuyler, was the black novelist and newspaper ed.), she was a founder of the Amerasian Foundation to aid children fathered by American soldiers in Vietnam. Most of her more than 60 compositions were for solo piano, many with humorous titles, some inspired by her travels; few were publ. Her last completed composition, *Nile Fantasia* for Piano and Orch., was performed posthumously (N.Y., Sept. 24, 1967). She wrote 5 books about her life and travels: *Adventures in Black and White* (N.Y., 1960); *Who Killed the Congo* (N.Y., 1963); *Jungle Saints: Africa's Heroic Catholic Missionaries* (Rome, 1962); *Kingdom of Dreams* (with her mother, Josephine Schuyler; N.Y., 1966); *Good Men Die* (N.Y., 1969). Her funeral at St. Patrick's Cathedral in N.Y. received extensive press coverage. In recognition of her musical and literary precocity, Mayor Fiorello LaGuardia declared June 19, 1940, Philippa Schuyler Day at the N.Y. World's Fair.

BIBL.: J. Schuyler, *Philippa the Beautiful American: The Travelled History of a Troubadour* (N.Y., 1969); R. Fisher, "Two Black Prodigies on the Concert Stage," *Musical Prodigies* (N.Y., 1973); K. Talalay, "P.D. S., Pianist/Composer/Writer," *The Black Perspective in Music* (1982).

Schuyt (Schuijt), Cornelis (Floriszoon), eminent Netherlands organist and composer; b. Leiden, 1557; d. there, June 9, 1616. With the exception of a visit to Italy as a young man, he spent his entire life in his native city; was named assistant town organist to his father in 1593, and was active at the Pieterskerk and the Hooglandsche Kerk; after his father's death in 1601, he was appointed his successor as 1st organist at the Pieterskerk. The influence of Italian music is revealed in his masterful madrigals.

WORKS: All publ. in Leiden: *Il primo libro de madrigali* for 5 Voices (1600); *Hollandsche madrigalen* for 5 to 6 and 8 Voices (1603); *12 padovante et altretante gagliarde . . . con 2 canzone alla francese*, a 6 (1611); *Hymneo, overo Madrigali nuptiali et altri amorosi* for 6 Voices, *con un echo doppio* for 12 Voices (1611).

BIBL.: M. Seiffert, "C. Schuijt," *Tijdschrift der Vereeniging voor Noord-Nederlands Musiekgeschiedenis*, 5 (1897); A. Annegarn, *Floris en C. Schuyt: Muziek in Leiden van de vijftiende tot het begin van de zeventiende eeuw* (Utrecht, 1973).

Schuyt, Nico(laas), Dutch composer; b. Alkmaar, Jan. 2, 1922. He studied piano and harmony with Jacob van Domselaar, piano with Eberhard Rebling, and theory with Willem Hijstek; received instruction in composition from Bertus van Lier (1949–52); was active with Donemus (from 1964).

WORKS: School opera, *De Varkenshoeder* (The Little Pig Boy) 1951); ballet, *De Kast van de oude chinees* (The Old Chinese Cupboard); a cantata for student performance, *Wij zullen een muur bouwen* (1952); Concerto for Youth Orch. (1952–53); *Sonata a tre* for Oboe, Bassoon, and Piano (1953–54); 5 *Dramatic Nocturnes* for Flute and Piano (1954); *Sonatina in due pezzi* for Piano (1955); *Réveil* for Orch. (1955); *Corteggio* for Orch. (1958); *Sinfonia divertente* for Small Orch. (1958); Sonatina for Youth Chamber Orch. (1961); *Quatuor de ballet* for Clarinet, Trumpet, Percussion, and Piano (1962); *De belevenissen van Strip-Thijs* for Clarinet, Trumpet, Percussion, and Piano (1962); Sonata for Orch. (1964); *Discorsi capricciosi* for Small Orch. (1965); *Allegro and Passacaglia* for Violin and

Piano (1965); *Arkadia* for Mezzo-soprano, Viola, and Cello (1966); *Hymnus* for Small Orch. (1966); *Naar de maan* (To the Moon) for Female Chorus, Mixed Chorus, and Orch. (1967–68); *Greetings from Holland* for Small Orch. (1970); *Alla notturna* for 2 Oboes, Oboe d'Amore, and English Horn (1971); *Quasi in modo de valzer* for Orch. (1973); *3 Preludes* for Strings and Piano (1973); *Furies for 4*, piano quartet (1975); *Discorsi, discorsi . . .* for Wind Orch. (1979); *Festa seria* for Orch. (1980); *Alla deriva* for Choir and Orch. (1982); *Down to the Shades* for Orch. (1985); *Atalanta* for Flute, Violin, Cello, and Harp (1986).

Schwalb, Miklos̆, Hungarian-American pianist and teacher; b. Budapest, Feb. 20, 1903; d. Boston, Oct. 2, 1981. He was a piano student of Dohnányi, and appeared with the Budapest Phil. as soloist at the age of 17. He settled in Boston as a teacher in 1935; also gave recitals.

Schwanenberg, Johann Gottfried, German keyboard player, music theorist, and composer; b. probably in Wolfenbüttel, c.1740; d. Braunschweig, March 29, 1804. He studied with G.C. Schürmann and Ignazio Fiorillo in Wolfenbüttel; after continuing his training in Venice on a court stipend with Hasse, Gaetano Latilla, and Giuseppe Saratelli (1756–61), he returned to the Braunschweig court as Kapellmeister (1762–1802). He was praised by his contemporaries as both a keyboard virtuoso and as a composer. In one of his theoretical papers, he argues for the deletion of H from the German musical scale. He produced 14 operas to Italian librettos, all 1st perf. in Braunschweig, including *Adriano in Siria* (Aug. 1762), *Solimano* (Nov. 4, 1762), and *Antigono* (Feb. 2, 1768); also various sacred vocal works; 23 syms.; 4 harpsichord concertos; 25 harpsichord sonatas; etc.

Schwann, William (Joseph), pioneering American discographer; b. Salem, Ill., May 13, 1913. He began his career as an organist and choir director in Louisville (Ky.) churches (1930–35); also studied at the Univ. of Louisville (B.A., 1935), Boston Univ. (1935–37), and Harvard Univ. (1937–39), where his teachers included E.B. Hill, Hugo Leichtentritt, A.T. Merritt, Walter Piston, and G. Wallace Woodworth; also received private organ instruction from E. Power Biggs. He was a music critic for the *Boston Herald* (1937–41), and also ran his own record shop in Cambridge (1939–53). In 1949 he launched his *Schwann Record Catalog,* the 1st monthly compilation of available recordings in the world; an invaluable source, it expanded over the years to include not only long-playing records but also tapes and compact discs; special compilations were also issued from time to time. In 1976 his firm, W. Schwann, Inc., was acquired by ABC Publishing Co. Among Schwann's numerous accolades are honorary D.Mus. degrees from the Univ. of Louisville (1969) and the New England Cons. of Music in Boston (1982).

Schwantner, Joseph, American composer; b. Chicago, March 22, 1943. As a youth, he studied classical guitar and wrote jazz compositions. He enrolled in the Chicago American Cons. and studied composition with Bernard Dieter (B.M., 1964); then went to Northwestern Univ., where he worked with Anthony Donato and Alan Stout (M.M., 1966; D.M., 1968), garnering 3 B.M.I. Student Composer awards. In 1970 he joined the faculty of the Eastman School of Music in Rochester, N.Y., and became prof. of composition in 1980; from 1982 to 1985 he was composer-in-residence of the St. Louis Sym. Orch. The recipient of various awards and numerous commissions, Schwantner won the Pulitzer Prize in Music in 1979 for his orch. score *Aftertones of Infinity*. His early works followed the dictates of serialism, but he eventually developed an eclectic style, incorporating tonal materials into harmonically complex works. Interested in new devices of color, texture, and timbre, he often employs tonalities produced by unusual and sometimes unorthodox musical instruments.

WORKS: ORCH.: *Modus Caelestis* (1973); *And the Mountains Rising Nowhere* (1977); *Aftertones of Infinity* (1978; N.Y., Jan. 29, 1979); *From a Dark Millennium* (1981); *New Morning for the World* (*Daybreak of Freedom*) for Speaker and Orch., after Martin Luther King, Jr. (1982); *Magabunda* (*Witchnomad*), song cycle for Soprano and Orch. (1983); *Distant Runes and Incantations* for Piano and Orch. (1984); *Dreamcaller,* song cycle for Soprano, Violin, and Orch. (1984); *Someday Memories* (1984); *A Sudden Rainbow* (1984; St. Louis, Jan. 31, 1986); *Toward Light* (1986; Canton, Ohio, March 15, 1987); Piano Concerto (N.Y., July 8, 1988); *From Afar,* fantasy for Guitar and Orch. (1988); *Freeflight* (1989); *A Play of Shadows* for Flute and Orch. (1990); Concerto for Percussionist and Orch. (1991). **CHAMBER:** *Diaphonia Intervallum* for Alto Saxophone and Chamber Ensemble (1965); *Chronicon* for Bassoon and Piano (1968); *Consortium I* for Flute, Clarinet, Violin, Viola, and Cello (1970) and *II* for Flute, Clarinet, Violin, Cello, Piano, and Percussion (1971); *Elixir* for Flute and 5 Players (1974); *Autumn Canticles* for Violin, Cello, and Piano (1974); *In Aeternum* for Cello and 4 Players (1975); *Canticle of the Evening Bells* for Flute and 12 Players (1976); *Wild Angels of the Open Hills,* song cycle for Soprano, Flute, Harp, and Chamber Ensemble (1977); *Sparrows* for Soprano and Chamber Ensemble (1979); *Wind Willow, Whisper* for Chamber Ensemble (1980); *Through Interior Worlds* for Chamber Ensemble (1981); *Music of Amber* for Flute, Clarinet, Violin, Cello, Percussion, and Piano (1981); *2 Poems of Agueda Pizarro* for Voice and Piano (1981).

Schwartz, Arthur, American composer of popular music; b. N.Y., Nov. 25, 1900; d. Kintnersville, Pa., Sept. 3, 1984. He studied English at N.Y. Univ. (B.A., 1920) and literature at Columbia Univ. (M.A., 1921), where he subsequently took a degree in law (1924). He taught himself to play the piano and began writing songs while still in college; after practicing law (1924–28), he turned to music. With the lyricist Howard Dietz, he began a successful collaboration on works for the N.Y. musical stage, such as the revues *Three's a Crowd* (Oct. 15, 1930; includes the song *Something to Remember You By*), *The Band Wagon* (June 3, 1931; includes the song *Dancing in the Dark;* the film version of 1953 includes the song *That's Entertainment*), and *Flying Colors* (Sept. 15, 1932; includes the song *Louisiana Hayride*) and the musicals *Revenge with Music* (Nov. 28, 1934; includes the songs *If There Is Someone Lovelier Than You* and *You and the Night and the Music*) and *Between the Devil* (Dec. 22, 1937; includes the song *I See Your Face Before Me*). With Dorothy Fields, he wrote the musicals *Stars in Your Eyes* (Feb. 9, 1939), *A Tree Grows in Brooklyn* (April 19, 1951), and *By the Beautiful Sea* (April 8, 1954). Again with Dietz, he produced the revue *Inside USA* (April 30, 1948) and the musicals *The Gay Life* (Nov. 18, 1961) and *Jennie* (Oct. 17, 1963). He also wrote for films (1936–55).

Schwartz, Elliott (Shelling), American composer, teacher, and writer on music; b. N.Y., Jan. 19, 1936. He studied composition with Otto Luening and Jack Beeson at Columbia Univ. (A.B., 1957; M.A., 1958; Ed.D., 1962); also had private instruction in piano from Alton Jones and in composition from Paul Creston; likewise studied composition at the Bennington (Vt.) Composers Conference (summers 1961–66). After teaching at the Univ. of Mass. in Amherst (1960–64), he joined the faculty of Bowdoin College in Brunswick, Maine (1964); was associate prof. (1970–75) and then prof. and chairman of its music dept. (from 1975); also held appointments as Distinguished Visiting Univ. Prof. (1985–86) and prof. of composition (1989–91) at Ohio State Univ. He was vice president of the American Music Center (1982–88), chairman of the American Soc. of Univ. Composers (1984–88), and president of the College Music Soc. (1989–90). In his compositions he develops the Satiesque notions of unfettered license leading to a completely unbuttoned state.

WRITINGS: *The Symphonies of Ralph Vaughan Williams* (Amherst, Mass., 1964); ed. with B. Childs, *Contemporary Composers on Contemporary Music* (N.Y., 1967); *Electronic Music: A Listener's Guide* (N.Y., 1973; 2nd ed., rev., 1976); *Music: Ways of Listening* (N.Y., 1982).

WORKS: DRAMATIC: *Elevator Music* for Any Instruments

(1967); *Areas* for Flute, Clarinet, Violin, Cello, Trombone, Piano, and 2 to 4 Dancers (1968); *Gibson Hall* for Keyboards and Synthesizer (1969); *Music for Soloist and Audience* (1970); *Telly* for 5 Woodwind or Brass, 4 Percussion, 3 Television Sets, and Tape (1972); *A Dream of Beats and Bells* for Piano and Audience (1977); *California Games* for 4 to 6 Players, Tape, and Audience (1978); *Radio Games*, duet for Performers in a Radio Studio and Audience (1980). ORCH.: *Music* for Orch. and Tape (1965); *Texture* for Chamber Orch. (1966); *Magic Music* for Piano and Orch. (1968); *Island* (1970); *Dream Overture* (1972); *The Harmony of Maine* for Synthesizer and Orch. (1974); *Eclipse III* for Chamber Orch. (1975); *Janus* for Piano and Orch. (1976); *Chamber Concerto I* for Double Bass and 15 Instruments (1977); *Chamber Concerto III* for Piano and Small Orch. (1977); *Zebra* for Youth Orch. and Tape (1981); *Celebrations/Reflections: A Time Warp* (1985); *4 Ohio Portraits* (Columbus, Ohio, April 12, 1986). CHAMBER: Oboe Quartet (1963); Trio for Flute, Cello, and Piano (1964); *Music for Napoleon and Beethoven* for Trumpet, Piano, and 2 Tapes (1969); Septet for Voice, Piano, and 5 Instruments (1969); *Eclipse I* for 10 Instruments (1971); Octet (1972); *Echo Music II* for Wind Quartet and Tape (1974); *A Bowdoin Anthology* for Narrator, Instruments, and Tape (1976); *Chamber Concerto II* for Clarinet and 9 Instruments (1977); *Bellagio Variations* for String Quartet (1980); *Chamber Concerto IV* for Saxophone and 10 Instruments (1981); *Octagon* for 8 Percussion (1984); *Purple Transformation* for Wind Ensemble (1987); *Northern Pines* for 2 Oboes, Clarinet, 2 Horns, and Piano (1988); *Palindromes* for Cello and Percussion (1989).

Schwartz, Francis, American composer, teacher, and music critic; b. Altoona, Pa., March 10, 1940. He studied piano with Lonny Epstein, music theory with Vittorio Giannini, and chamber music with Louis Persinger at the Juilliard School of Music in N.Y. (B.S., 1961; M.S., 1962) and with Daniel Charles at the Univ. of Paris (Ph.D. in musical esthetics, 1981). In 1965 he went to Puerto Rico; was music critic of the *San Juan Star* (1966–81); concurrently taught at the Univ. of Puerto Rico, where he was later chairman of the music dept. (1971–80) and Director of Cultural Affairs (1981–86); was also composer-in-residence at the Centro de Investigaciones de Comunición Masiva y Tecnología in Buenos Aires (1975) and visiting prof. of experimental music at the Univ. of Paris (1977–78). He wrote with María Luisa Muñoz the book *El mundo de la música* (1982). Schwartz was a key figure in the introduction of contemporary music in Puerto Rico and the proliferation of the avant-garde in Paris; in Puerto Rico, he was active with Grupo Fluxus and the 2nd Biennal of Contemporary Music; among his prestigious commissions was the "Commande d'État" from the French government to compose a work for the group 2E2M. In 1986 he was made a Chevalier of the Order of the Arts and Letters of France. His compositions employ a broad range of avant-garde techniques; in many, he cultivates multimedia forms, in which music, stage, and electronics are combined.

WORKS: STAGE: *Auschwitz* for Tape, Lights, Odors, and Movement (San Juan, May 15, 1968); *My Name's Caligula, What's Yours?* for 3 Actor-Instrumentalists (1970; N.Y., March 3, 1975)); *Geo-flux*, electronic ballet (1974); *Time, Sound, and the Hooded Man* for Actors, Tape, and Videotape (Buenos Aires, July 16, 1975)); *Is There Sex in Heaven?* (1976); *Hommage à K . . .* (1978); *Mon oeuf* for Tape, Videotape, Odors, Sculpture, and Audience (1979); *Musique pour Juvisi* for Tape, Videotape, and Synthesizer (1979; in collaboration with C. Miereanu); *Cosmos* (1980); *La guerra de las flores* (1982). ORCH.: *Plegaria* (1973); *Yo protesto* (San Juan, March 23, 1974); *The Tropical Trek of Tristan Trimble* (1975); *Amistad III* (1979); *Un sourire festif* (1981); *Gestos* for Orch. and Audience (1983); *Fantasía de la Libertad* (1986). CHAMBER: *Caníbal-Calibán* for Voice and Variable Ensemble (1976); *4 + 3 = Paris VIII*, didactic music for Voice, Violin, Guitar, Alto Saxophone, Trumpet, Trombone, and Percussion (1978); *Ergo sum* for Flute and Tape (1979); *Eros by Any Other Name* for Double Bass and Piano (1983);

I've Got (Poly) Rhythm for Guitar, Body Percussion, and Vocal Sounds (1984); *Quasi una Sonatina . . . devero* for Violin and Piano (1985); *Que reine la Paz* for 4 Guitars (1987); *El Trango del último momento* for Piano or Harpsichord (1988); *Trio para Edgar Allan Poe* for Violin, Cello, and Piano (1988). VOCAL: *Grimaces* for Voice, Flute, Alto Saxophone, Double Bass, Percussion, Tape, and Audience (1984); *Tres canciones para el futuro* for Flute or Oboe, Soprano or Tenor, 2 Percussion, and Audience (1985); *The night of the fiery angels* for Flute, Oboe, Clarinet, Horn, and Audience (1987); *Dos Canciones sobre textos de Schopenhauer* for Soprano and Synthesizer (1988); *Dulce Libertad* for Soprano, Violin, Cello, and Piano (1988); *El Sueño de Bolívar* for Soprano, Clarinet, Violin, and Piano (1988); other songs with Instruments or Tape.

Schwarz, Boris, distinguished Russian-born American violinist, teacher, and musicologist; b. St. Petersburg, March 26, 1906; d. N.Y., Dec. 31, 1983. He went to Berlin as a youth; at the age of 14, made his debut as a violinist in Hannover, accompanied at the piano by his father, Joseph Schwarz. He took violin lessons with Flesch in Berlin (1922–25) and Thibaud and Capet in Paris (1925–26); subsequently took courses in musicology with Sachs, Schering, and Wolf at the Univ. of Berlin (1930–36). In 1936 he emigrated to the U.S., becoming a naturalized citizen in 1943. He completed his musicological studies with Lang at Columbia Univ. (Ph.D., 1950, with the diss. *French Instrumental Music Between the Revolutions, 1789–1830;* publ. in N.Y., 1950; 2nd ed., rev., 1983). After serving as concertmaster of the Indianapolis Sym. Orch. (1937–38) and playing in the NBC Sym. Orch. in N.Y. (1938–39), he was a prof. of music at Queens College of the City Univ. of N.Y. (1941–76), where he founded (1945) the Queens College Orch. Society, conducting annual concerts of symphonic and choral music; also was chairman of its music dept. (1948–51; 1952–55). In 1959–60 he held a Guggenheim fellowship. A trilingual writer, he was fluent in Russian, German, and English; contributed numerous articles, mostly on Russian music, to *The New Grove Dictionary of Music and Musicians* (1980) and to various music journals. His valuable study, *Music and Musical Life in Soviet Russia, 1917–1970* (N.Y., 1972; 2nd ed., rev., 1983), was highly critical of certain aspects of the musical situation in Russia; it won an award from ASCAP as the best book on music criticism. His 2nd book, *Great Masters of the Violin* (N.Y., 1983), is valuable for its accuracy of documentation.

BIBL.: M. Brown, ed., *Russian and Soviet Music: Essays for B. S.* (Ann Arbor, 1984).

Schwarz, Gerard (Ralph), esteemed American conductor; b. Weehawken, N.J., Aug. 19, 1947. He commenced trumpet lessons when he was 8; after attending the National Music Camp in Interlochen, Mich. (summers, 1958–60), he studied at N.Y.'s High School of Performing Arts; also received trumpet instruction from William Vacchiano (1962–68), and completed his training at the Juilliard School (B.S., 1972). He played in the American Brass Quintet (1965–73) and the American Sym. Orch. in N.Y. (1966–72); also made appearances as a conductor. After serving as co-principal trumpet of the N.Y. Phil. (1972–75), he pursued a conducting career. He was music director of the Waterloo Festival in Stanhope, N.J., and of its music school at Fairleigh Dickinson Univ. (from 1975), of the 92nd St. Y Chamber Sym. (later N.Y. Chamber Sym.) in N.Y. (from 1977), and of the Los Angeles Chamber Orch. (1978–86). He also appeared widely as a guest conductor; one such engagement, at the Mostly Mozart Festival in N.Y. in 1980, led to his appointment as its music adviser in 1982; he then served as its music director (from 1984). He also was music adviser (1983–85) and principal conductor (from 1985) of the Seattle Sym. Orch. In 1989 he received the Alice M. Ditson Award for Conductors. Schwarz is duly recognized as one of America's outstanding conductors, and a musician of uncommon attainments. He has won especial critical accolades for his discerning and innovative programs; his vast repertoire ranges from early music to the contemporary era.

Bibl.: *Current Biography* (April 1986); H. Kupferberg, "The Bi-Coastal Baton of G. S.," *Ovation* (July 1986).

Schwarz, Hanna, German mezzo-soprano; b. Hamburg, Aug. 15, 1943. She received her vocal training in Hamburg and Essen; made her operatic debut in Hannover (1970); was a member of the Hamburg State Opera from 1973. In addition to guest appearances with other European opera houses, as well as those in the U.S., she toured as a soloist, singing with, among others, the Berlin Phil., the Vienna Phil., the Concertgebouw Orch. of Amsterdam, and the Chicago Sym. Orch. Some of her noted operatic roles are Brangäne, Erda, Fricka, and Jocasta; she also appeared as Countess Geschwitz in the 1st complete performance of *Lulu* in Paris in 1979.

Schwarz, Rudolf, Austrian-born English conductor; b. Vienna, April 29, 1905. He studied violin; joined the Düsseldorf Opera as a répétiteur (1923), and then made his conducting debut there (1924); subsequently was a conductor at the Karlsruhe Opera (1927) until being removed in 1933 by the Nazis as a Jew; after serving as music director of the Jüdischer Kulturbund in Berlin (1936–39), he was imprisoned (1939-40), and then interred at the Belsen concentration camp (1943–45). Following his liberation, he settled in England, becoming a naturalized subject in 1952. He was conductor of the Bournemouth Municipal Orch. (1947–51) and music director of the City of Birmingham Sym. Orch. (1951–57); after serving as chief conductor of the BBC Sym. Orch. in London (1957–62), he was principal conductor (1964–67) and artistic director (1967–73) of the Northern Sinfonia in Newcastle upon Tyne. He was made a Commander of the Order of the British Empire in 1973.

Schwarz, Vera, Austrian soprano; b. Zagreb, July 10, 1889; d. Vienna, Dec. 4, 1964. She studied voice and piano in Vienna; appeared in operettas there; went to Hamburg in 1914 and to Berlin in 1917; toured in South America. In 1939 she went to Hollywood, where she became a vocal instructor; in 1948 she returned to Austria; gave courses at the Mozarteum in Salzburg. Her best roles were Carmen and Tosca.

Schwarzkopf, (Olga Maria) Elisabeth (Friederike), celebrated German soprano; b. Jarotschin, near Posen, Dec. 9, 1915. She studied with Lula Mysz-Gmeiner at the Berlin Hochschule für Musik; made her operatic debut as a Flower Maiden in *Parsifal* at the Berlin Städtische Oper (April 17, 1938); then studied with Maria Ivogün while continuing on its roster, appearing in more important roles from 1941. In 1942 she made her debut as a lieder artist in Vienna, and also sang for the 1st time at the State Opera there as Zerbinetta, remaining on its roster until the Nazis closed the theater in 1944. Having registered as a member of the German Nazi Party in 1940, Schwarzkopf had to be de-Nazified by the Allies after the end of World War II. In 1946 she rejoined the Vienna State Opera and appeared as Donna Elvira during its visit to London's Covent Garden in 1947; subsequently, sang at Covent Garden regularly until 1951. In 1947 she made her 1st appearance at the Salzburg Festival as Susanna; also sang regularly at Milan's La Scala (1948–63). Furtwängler invited her to sing in his performance of the Beethoven 9th Sym. at the reopening celebrations of the Bayreuth Festival in 1951. She then created the role of Anne Trulove in Stravinsky's *The Rake's Progress* in Venice on Sept. 11, 1951. On Oct. 25, 1953, she gave her 1st recital at N.Y.'s Carnegie Hall; made her U.S. operatic debut as the Marschallin with the San Francisco Opera on Sept. 20, 1955. On Oct. 13, 1964, she made her belated Metropolitan Opera debut in N.Y. in the same role, continuing on its roster until 1966. In 1975 she made a farewell tour of the U.S. as a concert singer. She was married to Walter Legge in 1953; ed. his memoir, *On and Off the Record* (N.Y., 1982; 2nd ed., 1988). In addition to her acclaimed Mozart and Strauss roles, she was also admired in Viennese operetta. As an interpreter of lieder, she was incomparable.

Schweinitz, Wolfgang von, German music theorist and composer; b. Hamburg, Feb. 7, 1953. He studied at the Hochschule für Musik in Hamburg, taking courses in advanced composition with György Ligeti. In 1975 he went to California, where he joined the Center for Computer Research in Music and Acoustics of the Artificial Intelligence Laboratory at Stanford Univ.; also preoccupied himself with the musical aspects of digital sound systems and with the special problems of psychoacoustics. In 1976 he was awarded the Stuttgart prize for young composers. Understandably, his works reflect his extraterrestrial interests, as exemplified in his *Cosmic Harmony* (1970–72). He further wrote 2 grand syms. (1973, 1974); a Piano Concerto (1979); chamber music, including 2 *Perpetual Canons* (1973), a Wind Quintet, and a Septet for Viola and Wind Instruments; and much vocal music, including 15 songs entitled *Paper Stars* (1961), and a Mass for Soloists, Choir, and Orch. (1984).

Schweitzer, Albert, famous Alsatian theologian, philosopher, medical missionary, organist, and music scholar; b. Kaysersberg, Jan. 14, 1875; d. Lambaréné, Gabon, Sept. 4, 1965. He studied piano as a child with his father, a Lutheran pastor; then began organ studies at 8, his principal mentors being Eugen Münch in Mulhouse, Ernst Münch in Strasbourg, and Widor in Paris. He pursued training in philosophy (Ph.D., 1899) and theology (Ph.D., 1900) at the Univ. of Strasbourg; also received instruction in music theory from Jacobsthal in Strasbourg and in piano from Philipp and M. Jaëll in Paris. In 1896 he became organist of the Bach Concerts in Strasbourg; also joined the faculty of the Univ. there in 1902, where he also completed his full medical course (M.D., 1912); concurrently was organist of the Bach Society in Paris (1905–13). In 1913 he went to Lambaréné in the Gabon province of French Equatorial Africa, and set up a jungle hospital, which subsequently occupied most of his time and energy. However, he continued to pursue his interest in music, theology, and philosophy, making occasional concert tours as an organist in Europe to raise funds for his hospital work among the African natives. In 1952 he was awarded the Nobel Peace Prize, the only professional musician to hold this prestigious award. His philosophical and theological writings had established his reputation as one of the foremost thinkers of his time. In the field of music he distinguished himself as the author of one of the most important books on Bach, greatly influencing the interpretation of Bach's music, and contributing to the understanding of Bach's symbolic treatment of various musical devices. He ed. *J.S. Bach: Complete Organ Works: A Critico-practical Edition* (N.Y.; vols. I-V, 1912–14, with C. Widor; vols. VI-VIII, 1954–67, with E. Nies-Berger).

Writings: *Eugène Munch, 1857–1898* (Mulhouse, 1898); *J.S. Bach, le musicien-poète* (Paris, 1905; augmented Ger. eds., 1908, 1915; Eng. tr. by E. Newman, 2 vols., Leipzig, 1911); *Deutsche und französische Orgelbaukunst und Orgelkunst* (Leipzig, 1906; 2nd ed., 1927); *Aus meiner Kindheit und Jugendzeit* (Bern and Munich, 1924; Eng. tr., 1924, as *Memoirs of Childhood and Youth*); *Aus meinem Leben und Denken* (Leipzig, 1931; Eng. tr., 1933, as *Out of My Life and Thought*); also various theological and philosophical books. A complete German ed. of his writings was ed. by R. Grabs (5 vols., Munich, 1974).

Bibl.: C. Campion, *A. S.: Philosopher, Theologian, Musician, Doctor* (N.Y., 1928); J. Regester, *A. S.: The Man and His Work* (N.Y., 1931); M. Ratter, *A. S.* (London, 1935; rev. ed., 1950); G. Sutherland, "The S.ian Heresy," *Music & Letters,* XXIII (1942); A. Roback, ed., *The A. S. Jubilee Book* (Cambridge, Mass., 1946); H. Hagedorn, *Prophet in the Wilderness: The Story of A. S.* (N.Y., 1947); O. Kraus, *A. S.: His Work and His Philosophy* (N.Y., 1947); G. Seaver, *A. S.: The Man and His Mind* (London, 1947); R. Grabs, *A. S.: Weg und Werk eines Menschenfreundes* (Berlin, 1953); R. Sonner, *S. und die Orgelbewegung* (Colmar, 1955); W. Picht, *The Life and Thought of A. S.* (N.Y., 1965); E. Jacobi, *A. S. und die Musik* (Wiesbaden, 1975).

Schweitzer, Anton, German composer; b. Coburg (baptized), June 6, 1735; d. Gotha, Nov. 23, 1787. He was a chorister, and later played viola in Hildburghausen; after study with J.F. Kleinknecht in Bayreuth, he returned to Hildburghausen as Kammermusicus; following further training in Italy (1764–66), he returned once more to Hildburghausen as court Kapellmeister. In 1769 he became conductor of Seyler's opera troupe, which was engaged by the Weimar court in 1771; produced his successful singspiel *Die Dorfgala* there (June 30, 1772), which was followed by the successful *Alkeste* (May 28, 1773), the 1st through-composed grand opera to a German libretto, the text being by C.M. Wieland. After fire destroyed the Weimar theater in 1774, he accompanied Seyler's troupe to Gotha, where he subsequently was director of the ducal chapel from 1778 until his death. Among his other stage works were *Rosamunde* (singspiel; Mannheim, Jan. 20, 1780), *Die Wahl des Herkules* (lyric drama; Weimar, Sept. 4, 1773), and the melodrama *Pygmalion*, after Rousseau (Weimar, May 13, 1772; not extant). He also wrote many ballets, syms., and piano pieces.

BIBL.: J. Maurer, *A. S. als dramatischer Komponist* (Leipzig, 1912); I. Strohschneider-Kohrs, "Künstlerthematik und monodramatische Form in Rousseaus Pygmalion," *Poetica*, VII (1975).

Schwencke, family of German musicians:

(1) Johann Gottlieb Schwencke, bassoonist and composer; b. Breitenau, Saxony, Aug. 11, 1744; d. Hamburg, Dec. 7, 1823. He was greatly esteemed as a bassoonist; served as a town musician in Hamburg, where he was also active as a piano teacher.

(2) Christian Fredrich Gottlieb Schwencke, pianist and composer, son of the preceding; b. Wachenhausen, Harz, Aug. 30, 1767; d. Hamburg, Oct. 27, 1822. He began piano study as a child, performing one of his father's piano concertos in Hamburg in 1779; went to Berlin in 1782 to study with Marpurg and Kirnberger; after attending the Univs. of Leipzig and Halle (1787–88), he was in 1788 named C.P.E. Bach's successor as Hamburg Stadtkantor, a position he retained until his death; was also a contributor to the *Allgemeine Musikalische Zeitung* (from 1799), ran his own music business (from 1801), and was director of a music academy for private performances (from 1805). He wrote incidental music, oratorios, cantatas, 2 piano concertos, an Oboe Concerto, 3 piano sonatas, 3 violin sonatas, 6 organ fugues, and songs. He also ed. rescored versions of Handel's *Messiah* and *Alexander's Feast*, Bach's Mass in B minor and *Magnificat*, and Hasse's *Te Deum*. He had 2 sons who became musicians:

(3) Johann Friedrich Schwencke, organist, cellist, clarinetist, and composer; b. Hamburg, April 30, 1792; d. there, Sept. 28, 1852. He received instruction in theory and composition from his father; was made organist of Hamburg's Nikolaikirche in 1829. He wrote numerous cantatas, over 500 chorale preludes and postludes for organ, and a Septet for 5 Cellos, Double Bass, and Kettledrums; harmonized about 1,000 chorales and 73 Russian folk songs; publ. the popular *Choralbuch zum Hamburgischen Gesangbuch* (1832); made many transcriptions; orchestrated Beethoven's *Adelaide* and various works by other composers. His son, **Friedrich Gottlieb Schwencke** (b. Hamburg, Dec. 15, 1823; d. there, June 11, 1896), was a pianist, organist, and composer; studied with his father, whom he succeeded as organist at the Nikolaikirche in 1852; also made tours as a pianist and organist, including a successful visit to Paris (1855). He wrote 2 fantasies for Organ, Trumpet, Trombones, and Timpani; sacred songs for Women's Voices and Organ; chorale preludes; and songs. He also brought out an augmented ed. of his father's chorales (1886).

(4) Karl Schwencke, pianist and composer; b. Hamburg, March 7, 1797; d. probably in Nussdorf, near Vienna, Jan. 7, 1870. He traveled widely; in Vienna in 1824 he met Beethoven, who composed the canon *Schwenke dich* for him; his own works include a Sym. in D major (Paris, 1843), a Mass, a Violin Sonata, 3 sonatas for Piano Duet, and solo piano pieces.

Schwerké, Irving, American writer on music; b. Appleton, Wis., July 21, 1893; d. Neenah, Wis., Nov. 3, 1975. He studied at Charleston (S.C.) College and the Univ. of Wisconsin; in 1920, went to Europe, continuing his education at the Univ. of Madrid, and taking piano lessons with Rosenthal; went to Paris in 1921, where he was active as a pianist, teacher, and a music and drama critic for the Paris *Tribune* (until 1934) and a Paris correspondent for the *Musical Digest* of N.Y. (1922–29), the *Musical Courier* of N.Y. (1932–41), the *Nuova Italia musicale* of Rome, and the *Musical Times* of London; organized the 1st European festival of American music in Bad Homburg (1931). In 1941 he settled in Wisconsin as a teacher and writer. In 1954 the French government made him a Chevalier of the Légion d'honneur. He publ. *Kings Jazz and David* (Paris, 1927), *Alexandre Tansman: compositeur polonais* (Paris, 1931), and *Views and Interviews* (Paris, 1936). He contributed an account of his Paris years in H. Ford's *The Left Bank* (University Park, Pa., 1973).

Schwertsik, Kurt, Austrian composer of the avant-garde, horn player, and teacher; b. Vienna, June 25, 1935. He studied composition with Marx and Schiske, and horn with Freiberg at the Vienna Academy of Music (1949–57); then continued his composition studies with Stockhausen in Cologne and Darmstadt (1959–62), where he also worked with Kagel and Cage in 1962 and later was associated with Cardew; pursued the study of analysis with Polnauer in 1964–65. With Friedrich Cerha, he founded the contemporary music ensemble "die reihe" in Vienna in 1958. He also played horn in the Niederösterreichisches Tonkünstler-Orch. (1955–59; 1962–68) and with the Vienna Sym. Orch. from 1968. In 1966 he was a visiting prof. of composition at the Univ. of Calif. at Riverside, where he took further instruction in modern analysis from Oswald Jonas. He taught composition at the Vienna Cons. from 1979. An all-Schwertsik concert was given by Cerha and "die reihe" in Vienna in honor of his 50th birthday in 1985. Although he wore a scholarly beard, he repeatedly militated against rebarbative neo-Classicism. Indeed, his works reject the "false beards" of scholasticism, seeking a fruitful symbiosis of serialism and post-serialism with a flexibly handled, rich tonality. A skillful and imaginative composer, he explores in his works many new paths in synthesizing the experimental with the traditional.

WORKS: STAGE: *BALLET:* *Wiener Chronik 1848* (Cologne, Feb. 17, 1977; also arranged as 3 suites for Orch.). *DANCE:* *Macbeth* for Piano Duo and Percussion (Heidelberg, Feb. 10, 1988). *OPERAS:* *Der lange Weg zur grossen Mauer* (1974; Ulm, May 13, 1975); *Das Märchen von Fanferlieschen Schönefusschen* (1982; Stuttgart, Nov. 24, 1983). *ORCH.:* *Draculas Haus- und Hofmusik, Transylvanian sym. for Strings* (1968); Alphorn Concerto (1975; Vienna, May 15, 1977); Violin Concerto, *Romanzen "in Schwarztinten-Ton und der geblümten Paradies-Weis"* (Graz, Oct. 9, 1977); *Epilog zu Rosamunde* (Vienna, May 31, 1978); *Tag- und Nachtweisen* (Salzburg, Aug. 25, 1978); Guitar Concerto (1979); *Irdische Klänge,* sym. in 2 movements (Vienna, April 16, 1980); *Instant Music* for Flute and Wind Orch. (1981; Vienna, Nov. 28, 1982); *Starckdeutsche Lieder und Tänze* for Baritone and Orch. (1980–82; Vienna, Feb. 13, 1986); *Der irdischen Klänge 2. Teil, nämlich Fünf Naturstücke* (1984; Vienna, Dec. 4, 1985); *Konzert für Pauken und Orch.* for Tom-tom and Orch. (Vienna, July 5, 1988). **CHAMBER:** Piano Trio (1960); String Quartet (1961); *Solatto romano* for 12 Instruments (1961); *Liebestraume* for 7 Instruments (1963); *Eichendorff Quintet* for Winds (1964); *Proviant* for Wind Sextet (1965); *Stückwerk* for Soprano and Chamber Orch. (1966; Vienna, Jan. 30, 1967); *Querschnitt durch eine Operette* for Wind Quintet (1966); *Österreichisches Quodlibet* for 10 Instruments (Montreal, April 28, 1967); *Musik vom Mutterland Mu* for 11 Instruments (1971); *Skizzen und Entwürfe* for String Quartet (Hamburg, Sept. 13, 1974); *Twilight Music: A Celtic Serenade* for Octet (1976; Hall, Aug. 25, 1977); *Kleine Blasmusik* for 2 Trumpets and 2 Trombones (Graz, Oct. 16, 1977); *Bagatellen für Klaviertrio in stark wechseinder Laune* (Vienna, Dec. 12, 1979); *Sotto Voce (Gedämpfte Unterhaltung)* for Flute, Violin, Cello, and Guitar (Stuttgart, Oct. 3, 1980); *Blechpartite* *im neuesten Geschmack* for Brass Quintet (Innsbruck, Nov. 8, 1982); *Hornpostille*, 4 pieces for 4 Horns (1983); *Strecken und gähnen* for Trumpet (1985); *Neues von Eu-Sirius, nämentlich 3 Sonaten und 2 Fugen für Karlheinz Stockhausen zur Unterhaltung* for 2 Violins and Viola (Vienna, Oct. 2, 1988); *Ein empfindsames Konzert für Kontrabass* (Heidelberg, April 29, 1989). SONG CYCLES: *Brautigan Songbook* for Voice and Piano (1971); *Ich sein Blumenbein* for Voice and Piano, or Voice, Guitar, and Keyboards (1980); *. . . & was ist dann Friede?* for Voice and Guitar (1983); *Iba de gaunz oaman Fraun* for Soprano, Piano, Bass, and Drums (1983); *Cinq chansons cryptiques* for Voice and Piano (1985); *Gute Nacht, Guten Morgen* for Voice and Piano (1985); *Das Leben* for Mezzo-soprano and Celtic Naturehorn (1986); *Gedichte an Ljuba* for Voice and Piano (1986).

Schwieger, Hans, German-born American conductor; b. Cologne, June 15, 1906. He studied in Cologne; was assistant conductor at the Berlin State Opera (1927–30), at the Kassel Opera (1930–31), in Mainz (1932–33), and in Danzig (1936–37). In 1937 he went to Japan, where he conducted the Tokyo Sym. Orch. In 1938 he settled in the U.S.; became a naturalized citizen in 1944. He organized and conducted the Southern Sym. Orch. in Columbia, S.C. (1938–41); then was conductor of the Fort Wayne Phil. (1944–48). From 1948 to 1971 he was conductor of the Kansas City Phil.; then filled engagements as a guest conductor in Europe.

Schwindl, Friedrich, violinist and composer; b. May 3, 1737; d. Karlsruhe, Aug. 7, 1786. He was Konzertmeister to the Margrave of Wied-Runkel and virtuoso di camera to the Count of Colloredo before going to The Hague (about 1770), where he was active as a teacher and as 1st violinist to Prince William V of Orange. After a sojourn in Switzerland, he was made Konzertmeister to the Margrave of Bad Durlach in Karlsruhe in 1780. Throughout his career, he traveled widely as a virtuoso. He was greatly admired as a composer of instrumental music, which was played in Europe and even in America during his lifetime. His output includes more than 30 syms., much chamber music, and vocal pieces.
  BIBL.: A. Downs, *The Symphonies of F. S.* (diss., N.Y. Univ., 1973).

Schytte, Ludvig (Theodor), Danish pianist, teacher, and composer; b. Århus, April 28, 1848; d. Berlin, Nov. 10, 1909. He was a pharmacist as a young man; then began to study piano with Anton Rée and composition with Gade, finishing under Taubert in Berlin and Liszt in Weimar. He settled in Vienna in 1887 as a teacher; moved to Berlin in 1907; taught there at the Stern Cons. A master of the miniature forms, he wrote a number of attractive piano pieces, some of which became extremely popular; about 200 were publ.
  WORKS: Piano: *Promenades musicales, Rapsodie norwégienne, Aus froher Kinderzeit, Spanische Nächte, Valse piquante, Waldbilder, Aus der Heimat und Fremde*; numerous piano studies (6 *brillante Vortragsetüden, Melodische Spezialetüden, Studien in Ornamentik und Dynamik*); Piano, 4-hands: *Bajaderntänze, Kindersymphonie, Musikalische Wandelbilder, Reiseblätter, Kindersuite*, etc.; also an opera, *Hero* (Copenhagen, Sept. 25, 1898); operetta, *Der Mameluk* (Vienna, Dec. 22, 1903); Piano Concerto; chamber music; a song cycle, *Die Verlassene*.

Sciammarella, Valdo, Argentine composer; b. Buenos Aires, Jan. 20, 1924. He studied composition with Julián Bautista; subsequently engaged in pedagogy. In 1965 he was appointed head of the music dept. at the National School of Fine Arts in Buenos Aires. He wrote a lyric comedy, *Marianita Limena* (Buenos Aires, Nov. 11, 1957); *Variaciones concertantes* for Piano and Orch. (1952); *Scherzino* for Oboe, Clarinet, and Bassoon (1956); *Galeria humana*, chamber ballet (1962); piano pieces.

Sciarrino, Salvatore, Italian composer; b. Palermo, April 4, 1947. He was 12 when he began to compose under the tutelage of Antonino Titione; also received some guidance from Evan-

gelisti. After studies with Turi Belfiore (1964), he attended Evangelisti's electronic music sessions at the Accademia di Santa Cecilia in Rome (1969). He taught at the Milan Cons. (from 1974); also served as artistic director of the Teatro Comunale in Bologna (1977–80). His music reveals an innovative approach to traditional forms; in some works he utilizes aleatoric procedures.
  WORKS: OPERAS: *Amore e Psiche* (Milan, March 2, 1973); *Aspern* (Florence, June 8, 1978); *Cailles en sarchophage* (Venice, Sept. 26, 1979); *Vanitas* (Milan, Dec. 11, 1981); *Lohengrin* (Milan, Jan. 15, 1983). ORCH.: *Berceuse* (1967; Venice, Sept. 13, 1969); *Da a da da* (Venice, Sept. 12, 1970); *Sonata da camera* (Rome, Oct. 31, 1971); *Grande sonata da camera* (1971; Paris, Feb. 21, 1972); *Rondo* for Flute and Orch. (1972; Naples, April 6, 1973); *Romanza* for Viola d'Amore and Orch. (Florence, Oct. 20, 1973); *Variazioni* for Cello and Orch. (Saarbrücken, May 23, 1974); *Clair de lune* for Piano and Orch. (Milan, Feb. 12, 1976); *Il paese senz'alba* (Naples, June 19, 1977); *Il paese senza tramonto* for Soprano and Orch. (Montepulciano, Aug. 14, 1977); *Kindertotenlied* for Soprano, Tenor, and Small Orch. (1978; Venice, Oct. 7, 1979); *Che sai guardiano, della notte?* for Clarinet and Small Orch. (Paris, June 19, 1979); *Un'immagine di Arpocrate* for Piano, Chorus, and Orch. (Donaueschingen, Oct. 19, 1979); *Flos florum* for Chorus and Orch. (Turin, April 30, 1981); *Efebo con radio* for Voice and Orch. (Florence, May 28, 1981); *Autoritratto nella notte* (Lugano, March 17, 1983); Violin Concerto, *Allegoria della notte* (Rome, Oct. 1, 1985); *Sul poemi concentrici I, II,* and *III* (RAI, Turin, April 8, 1988); *Morte di Borromini* for Narrator and Orch. (Milan, Oct. 18, 1988). CHAMBER: *Quartetto II* for String Quartet (1967); *Aka aka to I, II,* and *III* for Soprano and 12 Instruments (1968); *. . . Da un divertimento* for 10 Instruments (1970); *Arabesque* for 2 Organs (1971); *2 Studies* for Cello (1974); 2 piano trios (1975, 1986); 2 quintets (1976, 1977); *12 canzoni da battello* for Soprano and Instruments (1977); *Ai limiti della notte* for Viola (1979; also for Cello); *Fauno che fischia a un merlo* for Flute and Harp (1980); *Introduzione all'oscuro* for Instruments (1981); *Nox apud Orpheum* for 2 Organs and Instruments (1982); *Codex purpureus I* for String Trio (1983); *Rose, Liz* for Voice and 5 Instruments (1984); *Codex purpureus II* for 2 Violins, Viola, Cello, and Piano (1984); *La canzone di ringraziamento* for Flute (1985); *Esplorazione del bianco III* for Jazz Ensemble (1986); *Il motivo degli oggetti di vetro* for 2 Flutes and Piano (1987); also piano pieces, including 3 sonatas (1976, 1983, 1986).

Scimone, Claudio, Italian conductor, musicologist, and music educator; b. Padua, Dec. 23, 1934. He studied conducting with Zecchi, Mitropoulos, and Ferrara. In 1959 he founded the noted chamber orch. I Solisti Veneti (in Padua), and made numerous tours with it, presenting works from the Baroque to the avant-garde. He also acquired a fine reputation as a scholar specializing in Italian music; supervised a modern ed. of the works of Giuseppe Tartini, and prepared a complete edition of Rossini. He taught at the Venice Cons. (1961–67) and the Verona Cons. (1967–74); then was a teacher and director of the Padua Cons. (1974–83). In addition to numerous articles for various music journals, he publ. *Segno, Significato, Interpretazione* (1970).
  BIBL.: D. Soria, "C. S. & Solisti Veneti," *Musical America* (July 1989).

Sciutti, Graziella, Italian soprano; b. Turin, April 17, 1927. She studied singing in Rome; made her debut at Aix-en-Provence in 1951. She sang at the Glyndebourne Festivals (1954–59), Milan's La Scala (from 1956), and the Salzburg Festivals (1958–66); made her U.S. debut as Susanna with the San Francisco Opera in 1961. She was particularly noted for her soubrette roles; ran her own music academy in Florence (from 1986).

Scontrino, Antonio, prominent Italian double bass player, teacher, and composer; b. Trapani, May 17, 1850; d. Florence, Jan. 7, 1922. He studied at the Palermo Cons.; was a virtuoso on the double bass, and gave concerts; went to Munich for a special study of German music at the Musikschule (1872–74); after various engagements as an orch. player and teacher, he settled in Florence in 1892, and taught composition at the Reale Istituto Musicale.

WORKS: OPERAS: *Matelda* (Milan, June 19, 1879); *Il Progettista* (Rome, Feb. 8, 1882); *Il sortilegio* (Turin, June 21, 1882); *Gringoire* (Milan, May 24, 1890); *La Cortigiana* (Milan, Jan. 30, 1896); also incidental music to Gabriele d'Annunzio's *Francesca da Rimini* (Rome, Dec. 12, 1901). **ORCH.:** *Sinfonia marinaresca* (Florence, Feb. 12, 1897); Double Bass Concerto (Hamburg, Oct. 18, 1908); *Sinfonia romantica* (Berlin, March 9, 1914); *Preludio Religioso* (1919); Bassoon Concerto (Florence, Dec. 20, 1920); Piano Concerto. **CHAMBER:** 4 string quartets (1901, 1903, 1905, 1918); pieces for Violin and Piano; piano pieces; also choral music; songs.

BIBL.: *A. S. nella vita e nell'arte* (Trapani, 1935); A. Damerini, "Ricordi di A. S.," *I grandi anniversari del 1960 e la musica sinfonica e da camera nell'ottocento in Italia*, Chigiana, XVII (1960).

Scott, Charles Kennedy, English conductor and composer; b. Romsey, Nov. 16, 1876; d. London, July 2, 1965. He studied organ at the Brussels Cons., taking 1st prize (1897). In 1898 he settled in London; in 1904 he established the Oriana Madrigal Society, in 1919 the Phil. Choir, and in 1922 the Euterpe String Players. He publ. *Madrigal Singing* (London, 1907; 2nd ed., enl., 1931), *Word and Tone: An English Method of Vocal Technique* (2 vols., London, 1933), and *The Fundamentals of Singing* (London, 1954).

Scott, Cyril (Meir), remarkable English composer; b. Oxton, Cheshire, Sept. 27, 1879; d. Eastbourne, Dec. 31, 1970. He was a scion of a cultural family; his father was a classical scholar, his mother a fine amateur musician. Having displayed a natural penchant for music as a child, he was sent to Frankfurt am Main at age 12 to study with Uzielli and Humperdinck, remaining there for a year and a half before returning to England; he once again went to Frankfurt am Main in 1895 to study piano and theory with Iwan Knorr. In 1898 he went to Liverpool as a teacher. In 1900 Hans Richter conducted Scott's *Heroic Suite*, in Liverpool and Manchester; also in 1900, his 1st Sym. was played in Darmstadt; his overture *Pelléas and Mélisande* was performed in Frankfurt am Main. His 2nd Sym. (1902) was given at a Promenade Concert in London on Aug. 25, 1903. (It was later converted into 3 *Symphonic Dances*.) His setting of Keats's *La Belle Dame sans merci* for Baritone, Chorus, and Orch. was produced in London in 1916. His opera *The Alchemist* (1917), for which he wrote his own libretto, was produced in Essen on May 28, 1925. In 1920 Scott traveled to the U.S. and played his 1st Piano Concerto with the Philadelphia Orch. under Stokowski (Nov. 5, 1920). But he acquired fame mainly as a composer of some exotically flavored piano pieces, of which *Lotus Land* became a perennial favorite; Fritz Kreisler arranged it for violin and piano, and played it repeatedly at his concerts. Other popular piano pieces were *Danse nègre, Chinese Serenade, Russian Dance, Sphinx, Autumn Idyll, Berceuse, Little Russian Suite, Indian Suite, Spanish Dance,* and most particularly the ingratiating suite *Impressions of the Jungle Book,* after Kipling. He also wrote over 100 songs. In all these pieces, Scott showed himself a master of musical miniature; he wrote in a distinctly modern idiom, very much in the style of French Impressionism; employed sonorous parallel progressions of unresolved dissonant chords; made frequent use of the whole-tone scale. His writing for piano is ingratiating in its idiomatic mastery; his harmonious modalities exude an aura of perfumed euphony. Among his other works are: 2 more operas, *The Saint of the Mountain* (1925) and *Maureen O'Mara* (1946); 3 ballets, *The Incompetent Apothecary* (1923), *Karma* (1926), and *The Masque of the Red Death* (1932); *Christmas Overture* (London, Nov. 13, 1906); *La Princesse Maleine,* symphonic poem (London, Aug. 22, 1907); 3 violin concertos (1927, c.1935, c.1935); Cello Concerto (1931); Harpsichord Concerto (1937); Sym. No. 3, *The Muses* (1939); Oboe Concerto (1946); Sinfonietta for Strings, Organ, and Harp (1954); *Neapolitan*

Rhapsody for Orch. (1960); Sinfonietta for Strings (1962); numerous overtures and suites; *Nativity Hymn* for Chorus and Orch. (1913); *The Ballad of Fair Helen of Kirkconnel* for Baritone and Orch. (1925); *Rima's Call to the Birds* for Soprano and Orch. (1933); *Let Us Now Praise Famous Men* for Chorus and Orch. (1935); *Ode to Great Men* for Tenor and Orch. (1936); *Hymn of Unity* for Solo Voices, Chorus, and Orch. (1946); more than 100 songs; 2 piano quintets (1924, 1952); Clarinet Quintet (1953); 4 string quartets (1920, 1958, 1960, 1968); Piano Quartet (1900); 2 string trios (1931, 1949); 3 piano trios (1920, 1950, 1957); Sonata for Cello and Piano (1950); Sonata for Flute and Piano (1961); 3 piano sonatas (1910, 1932, 1956); 160 other piano pieces. From his early youth, Scott was attracted to occult sciences, and was a believer in the reality of the supernatural; he publ. books and essays on music as a divinely inspired art, and inveighed violently against jazz as the work of Satan. Among his books, all publ. in London, are *The Initiate Trilogy* (1920, 1927, 1935); *My Years of Indiscretion* (1924); *The Philosophy of Modernism in Its Connection with Music* (1917); *The Influence of Music on History and Morals: A Vindication of Plato* (1928); *Music: Its Secret Influence through the Ages* (1933; augmented ed., 1958); *An Outline of Modern Occultism* (1935); *The Christian Paradox* (1942); an autobiographical vol., *Bone of Contention* (1969); also 2 books on medical matters: *Medicine, Rational and Irrational* (1946) and *Cancer Prevention* (1968).

BIBL.: A. Hull, *C. S.: Composer, Poet and Philosopher* (London, 1918; 3rd ed., 1921); C. Palmer, "C. S.: Centenary Reflections," *Musical Times,* CXX (1978).

Scott, Francis George, Scottish composer; b. Hawick, Roxburghshire, Jan. 25, 1880; d. Glasgow, Nov. 6, 1958. He studied humanities at the Univ. of Edinburgh, Moray House College of Education in Edinburgh, and the Univ. of Durham (B.M., 1909); also took theory lessons with a local organist, and later pursued training with Roger-Ducasse. After a period as a school teacher, he was a lecturer in music at Jordanhill College in Glasgow (1925–46). Scott was at his best as a composer of songs; publ. *Scottish Lyrics* for Voice and Piano (5 vols., London and Glasgow, 1922–39) and *35 Scottish Lyrics and Other Poems* (Glasgow, 1949); also wrote *The Ballad of Kynd Kittok* for Baritone and Orch. (1934), *Renaissance,* overture (1937; Glasgow, Jan. 14, 1939), *The Seven Deadly Sinnes,* dance suite for Orch. (1941), and *Lament for the Heroes* for String Orch. (1941). Scott had a number of ardent admirers in England, among them the poet Hugh MacDiarmid and the composer Kaikhosru Sorabji, who in their exuberant encomiums place him in the ranks of Schubert and Schumann as a songwriter.

BIBL.: M. Lindsay, "The Scottish Songs of F.G. S.," *Music & Letters,* XXVI (1945); H. MacDiarmid, *F.G. S.: An Essay on his 75th Birthday* (Edinburgh, 1955).

Scott, Hazel (Dorothy), Trinidad-born American jazz pianist and singer; b. Port of Spain, June 11, 1920; d. N.Y., Oct. 2, 1981. She was taken to the U.S. as a child and was musically nurtured by her mother, who led an all-female band. She enrolled at the Juilliard School of Music in N.Y., but soon abandoned all academic ambitions and effloresced in nightclubs. In 1938 she sang in the Broadway show *Sing Out the News;* she also appeared in several films, among them *Broadway Rhythm* and *Rhapsody in Blue.* From 1939 to 1945 she performed at Cafe Society Downtown, a Greenwich Village club in N.Y. In 1945 she married the black Harlem congressman Adam Clayton Powell, Jr., but divorced him in 1960 as he got into messy political, financial, and personal troubles that led to his expulsion from Congress; they had a child, who became a television executive. Her 2nd marriage also failed. She went to Paris, where she became quite a vedette at fashionable watering holes; in 1967 she returned to N.Y., remaining active as a performer until a few weeks before her death of cancer of the pancreas.

Scott, James (Sylvester), significant black American ragtime pianist and composer; b. Neosoho, Mo., Feb. 12, 1885; d. Kansas City, Kans., Aug. 30, 1938. He received music lessons from

John Coleman in Neosoho; after the family went to Carthage, Mo., he became active as a pianist in various local haunts. In 1902 he began working for the Dumars Music Co., which publ. his 1st rags; he gained his 1st success with his *Frog Legs Rag* (1906); his finest rag, *Grace and Beauty*, was publ. in 1909. About 1920, after travels as a ragtime pianist, he settled in Kansas City, where he was active as a teacher, theater musician, and bandleader. Although relatively unknown in his day, Scott is now recognized as one of the leading ragtime composers of his era.

BIBL.: P. Affeldt, "J. S., Crown Prince of Ragtime," *Jazz Report*, I/2 (1960); W. Schafter, "Grace and Beauty: The Case of J. S.," *Mississippi Rag*, II/10 (1975); M. Van Gilder, "J. S.," in J. Hasse, ed., *Ragtime: Its History, Composers, and Music* (N.Y., 1985).

Scott, Marion (Margaret), English violinist and writer on music; b. London, July 16, 1877; d. there, Dec. 24, 1953. She studied at the Royal College of Music in London. In 1911 she organized, with Gertrude Eaton, the Society of Women Musicians; was ed. of the *RCM Magazine* (1936–44). She specialized in Haydn research, giving special attention to his string quartets; also publ. *Beethoven* (London, 1934; rev. ed. by J. Westrup, 1947) and *Mendelssohn* (London, 1938).

BIBL.: R. Hughes, "M. S.'s Contribution to Musical Scholarship," *RCM Magazine*, I (1954).

Scott, Stephen, American composer and performer; b. Corvallis, Oreg., Oct. 10, 1944. He studied with Homer Keller at the Univ. of Oregon (B.A., 1967) and with Paul Nelson at Brown Univ. (M.A., 1969); also studied African music in Ghana, Tanzania, and Zimbabwe (1970). In 1969 he began teaching at Colorado College in Colorado Springs, where he founded the Pearson Electronic Sound Studio (1969) and the New Music Ensemble (1972). Scott's compositions are built around gentle repetitions and gradual rhythmic changes. In 1977 he developed a "bowed piano" technique for up to 10 players, resulting in his recording *New Music for Bowed Piano* (1984).

WORKS: Woodwind Quintet (1967); *5 Ferlinghetti Poems* for Narrator, Voices, and Tape (1969); *Traffic Jam* for Unspecified Ensemble (1970); *Baby Ben* for Ensemble (1971); *Suspended Animation* for 2 Pianos, 2 Harpsichords, and Tape Delay (1972); *Glacier Music* for Woodwind Quintet and Tape Delay (1973); *Variations on an American Folk Tune* for Orch. and Tape (1973); *Monophonies and Euphonies* for Wind Ensemble (1974); *American Pie* for Voices and Ensemble (1976); *Barney's Piece* for Ensemble (1977); *Rauschpfanpfare* for 3 Rauschpfeiffen (1979); *3-piece Suitcase*, sound sculpture (1979); *Ceremonial Music* for Brass (1979); *The Orphan*, incidental music (1980); *The Things Which Are Seen* for Tenor, Chorus, Synthesizer, and Orch. (1981); *Resonant Resources* for Bowed Piano (1983); *Ta ta logy* for Voices (1984); many works for Bowed Piano, including *Music I* (1977), *II* (1978), and *III* (1979), *Arcs* (1980; rev. 1984), and *Rainbows* (1981).

Scott, Tom (actually, **Thomas Jefferson**), American folksinger and composer; b. Campbellsburg, Ky., May 28, 1912; d. N.Y., Aug. 12, 1961. He studied violin with an uncle; played in dance bands; wrote songs; then went to Hollywood, where he took theory lessons with George Antheil; subsequently studied with Harrison Kerr and Wallingford Riegger.

WORKS: OPERA: *The Fisherman* (1956). **ORCH.:** *Song with Dance* (1932); *Plymouth Rock* (1938); *Hornpipe and Chantey* (1944); Sym. No. 1 (Rochester, N.Y., Oct. 22, 1946); *From the Sacred Harp* (1946); *Ballad of the Harp Weaver* for Narrator, Harp, Chorus, and String Quartet (N.Y., Feb. 22, 1947); *Johnny Appleseed* (N.Y., March 1, 1948); *Lento* for Saxophone and Strings (1953). **CHAMBER:** 2 string quartets (1944, 1956); *Emily Dickinson Suite* for Violin and Harp (1955); also chanteys for chorus; solo songs; arrangements of folk songs; etc.

BIBL.: J. Ringo, "Some Notes on T. S.'s Music," *American Composers Alliance Bulletin* (Winter 1957; with a list of works).

Scotti, Antonio, celebrated Italian baritone; b. Naples, Jan. 25, 1866; d. there, Feb. 26, 1936. He studied with Ester Trifari-Paganini in Naples; made his operatic debut in Naples (March 1889) as Cinna in Spontini's *La Vestale*; then sang elsewhere in Italy, Russia, Spain, and South America; made his London debut at Covent Garden on June 8, 1899, as Don Giovanni, and appeared in the same role with the Metropolitan Opera in N.Y. (Dec. 27, 1899). He remained with the Metropolitan for 33 years; made his farewell appearance on Jan. 20, 1933. He also toured in America with his own company. He possessed great histrionic ability, and was especially noted for his dramatic roles (Scarpia, Rigoletto, Falstaff, Don Giovanni, and Iago).

Scotto, Renata, famous Italian soprano; b. Savona, Feb. 24, 1933. She commenced music study in Savona at age 14; when she was 16, she went to Milan for vocal training with Emilio Ghirardini, then with Merlini, and finally with Mercedes Llopart; made her debut as Violetta in Savona in 1952. After winning a national vocal competition in 1953, she made her formal debut as Violetta at Milan's Teatro Nuovo; then joined Milan's La Scala, where she sang secondary roles until being called upon to replace Maria Callas as Amina during the company's visit to the Edinburgh Festival in 1957. She made her U.S. debut at the Chicago Lyric Opera on Nov. 2, 1960, as Mimi, a role she also chose for her Metropolitan Opera debut in N.Y. on Oct. 13, 1965. She scored a brilliant success with her portrayal of Mimi in the Metropolitan Opera production of *La Bohème* in the "Live from Lincoln Center" telecast on PBS (March 15, 1977); thereafter she was a stellar figure in the U.S. opera scene; also toured widely as a recitalist. Among her other fine roles were Lucia, Gilda, Elena in *I Vespri Siciliani*, Norma, Manon Lescaut, and Luisa Miller. She publ. the book *Scotto: More than a Diva* (with O. Riva; N.Y., 1984).

BIBL.: B. Tosi, *R. S.: Voce di due mondi* (Venice, 1990).

Scotus, John. See **Erigena, John Scotus.**

Scovotti, Jeanette, American soprano; b. N.Y., Dec. 5, 1936. She studied in N.Y. at the High School of Music and Art, and at the Juilliard School of Music. She first made appearances as a concert singer; on Nov. 15, 1962, she sang Adele in *Die Fledermaus* at her debut at the Metropolitan Opera in N.Y.; also sang in Chicago, San Francisco, Buenos Aires, Hamburg, and Munich.

Scriabin, Alexander (Nikolaievich), remarkable Russian composer whose solitary genius had no predecessors and left no disciples, father of **Marina Scriabine;** b. Moscow, Jan. 6, 1872; d. there, April 27, 1915. His father was a lawyer; his mother, Lyubov Petrovna (née Shchetinina), was a talented pianist who had studied with Leschetizky at the St. Petersburg Cons.; his mother died of tuberculosis when he was an infant, and his father remarried and spent the rest of his life in the diplomatic service abroad. Scriabin was reared by an aunt, who gave him initial instruction in music, including piano; at 11 he began regular piano lessons with Georgi Conus, and at 16 became a pupil of Zverev; in 1885 he commenced the study of theory with Taneyev. When he entered the Moscow Cons. in 1888, he continued his studies with Taneyev, and also received instruction in piano with Safonov. He practiced assiduously, but never became a virtuoso pianist; at his piano recitals, he performed mostly his own works. Graduating with a gold medal from Safonov's class, Scriabin remained at the Moscow Cons. to study fugue with Arensky, but failed to pass the required test and never received a diploma for composition. Upon leaving the Cons. in 1892, he launched a career as a concert pianist. By that time he had already written several piano pieces in the manner of Chopin; the publisher Jurgenson brought out his opp. 1, 2, 3, 5, and 7 in 1893. In 1894 Belaieff became his publisher and champion, financing his 1st European tour in 1895; on Jan. 15, 1896, Scriabin gave a concert of his own music in Paris. Returning to Russia, he completed his 1st major work, a Piano Concerto, and was soloist in its 1st performance on Oct. 23, 1897, in Odessa. In the same year, he married the pianist Vera Isakovich. They spent some time abroad; on Jan. 31, 1898, they gave a joint recital in

Paris in a program of Scriabin's works. From 1898 to 1903 Scriabin taught piano at the Moscow Cons. His 1st orch. work, *Rêverie*, was conducted in Moscow by Safonov on March 24, 1899; he also conducted the 1st performance of Scriabin's 1st Sym. (March 29, 1901). Scriabin's 2nd Sym. was brought out by Liadov in St. Petersburg (Jan. 25, 1902). After the death of Belaieff in 1904, Scriabin received an annual grant of 2,400 rubles from the wealthy Moscow merchant Morosov, and went to Switzerland, where he began work on his 3rd Sym., *Le Poème divin;* it had its 1st performance in Paris on May 29, 1905, under the direction of Arthur Nikisch. At that time Scriabin separated from Vera Isakovich and established a household with Tatiana Schloezer, sister of the music critic Boris de Schloezer, who subsequently became Scriabin's close friend and biographer. In Dec. 1906 he appeared as a soloist with Modest Altschuler and the Russian Sym. Society in N.Y.; also gave recitals of his works there and in other U.S. music centers. Tatiana Schloezer joined him in N.Y. in Jan. 1907, but they were warned by friends familiar with American mores of the time that charges of moral turpitude might be brought against them, since Scriabin had never obtained a legal divorce from his 1st wife and Tatiana Schloezer was his common-law wife. There was no evidence that such charges were actually contemplated, but to safeguard themselves against such a contretemps, they went to Paris in March 1907. Altschuler continued to champion Scriabin's music, and on Dec. 10, 1908, gave the world premiere with his Russian Sym. Orch. of Scriabin's great work *Le poème de l'extase;* the 1st Russian performance followed in St. Petersburg (Feb. 1, 1909). In the spring of 1908, Scriabin met Serge Koussevitzky, who became one of his most ardent supporters, both as a conductor and as a publisher. He gave Scriabin a 5-year contract with his newly established publishing firm Editions Russes, with a generous guarantee of 5,000 rubles annually. In the summer of 1910, Koussevitzky engaged Scriabin as soloist on a tour in a chartered steamer down the Volga River, with stopovers and concerts at all cities and towns of any size along the route. Scriabin wrote for Koussevitzky his most ambitious work, *Promethée,* or *Poème du feu,* with an important piano part, which featured the composer as soloist at its premiere in Moscow (March 15, 1911). The score also included a color keyboard (*clavier à lumière* or, in Italian, *luce*) intended to project changing colors according to the scale of the spectrum, which Scriabin devised (for at that time he was deeply immersed in the speculation about parallelism of all arts in their visual and auditory aspects). The construction of such a color organ was, however, entirely unfeasible at the time, and the premiere of the work was given without *luce.* A performance with colored lights thrown on a screen was attempted by Altschuler at Carnegie Hall in N.Y. on March 20, 1915, but it was a total failure. Another attempt was made in Moscow by Safonov after Scriabin's death, but that, too, was completely unsuccessful. The crux of the problem was that the actual notes written on a special staff in the score had to be translated into a color spectrum according to Scriabin's visualization of corresponding colors and keys (C major was red, F-sharp major was bright blue, etc.). Perhaps the nearest approximation to Scriabin's scheme was the performance of *Promethée* by the Univ. of Iowa Sym. Orch. on Sept. 24, 1975, under the direction of James Dixon, with a laser apparatus constructed by Lowell Cross; previously, the American pianist Hilde Somer made use of the laser to accompany her solo piano recitals of Scriabin's works, without attempting to follow the parallelism of sounds and colors envisioned by Scriabin, but nonetheless conveying the idea underlying the scheme. The unique collaboration between Scriabin and Koussevitzky came to an unfortunate end soon after the production of *Promethée;* Scriabin regarded Koussevitzky as the chief apostle of his messianic epiphany, while Koussevitzky believed that it was due principally to his promotion that Scriabin reached the heights in musical celebrity; to this collision of 2 mighty egotisms was added a trivial disagreement about financial matters. Scriabin left Koussevitzky's publishing firm, and in 1912 signed a contract with Jurgenson, who guaranteed

him 6,000 rubles annually. In 1914 Scriabin visited London and was soloist in his Piano Concerto and in *Prometheus* at a concert led by Sir Henry Wood (March 14, 1914); he also gave a recital of his own works there (March 20, 1914). His last public appearance was in a recital in Petrograd on April 15, 1915; upon his return to Moscow, an abscess developed in his lip, leading to blood poisoning; he died after a few days' illness. His 3 children (of the union with Tatiana Schloezer) were legitimized at his death. His son Julian, an exceptionally gifted boy, was accidentally drowned at the age of 11 in the Dnieper River at Kiev (June 22, 1919); Julian's 2 piano preludes, written in the style of the last works of his father, were publ. in a Scriabin memorial vol. (Moscow, 1940).

Scriabin was a genuine innovator in harmony. After an early period of strongly felt influences (Chopin, Liszt, and Wagner), he gradually evolved in his own melodic and harmonic style, marked by extreme chromaticism; in his piano piece *Désir,* op. 57 (1908), the threshold of polytonality and atonality is reached; the key signature is dispensed with in his subsequent works; chromatic alterations and compound appoggiaturas create a harmonic web of such complexity that all distinction between consonance and dissonance vanishes. Building chords by fourths rather than by thirds, Scriabin constructed his "mystic chord" of 6 notes (C, F-sharp, B-flat, E, A, and D), which is the harmonic foundation of *Promethée.* In his 7th Piano Sonata (1913) appears a chordal structure of 25 notes (D-flat, F-flat, G, A, and C, repeated in 5 octaves), which was dubbed "a 5-story chord." These harmonic extensions were associated in Scriabin's mind with theosophic doctrines; he aspired to a universal art in which the impressions of the senses were to unite with religious experience. He made plans for the writing of a "Mysterium," which was to accomplish such a synthesis, but only the text of a preliminary poem (*L'Acte préalable*) was completed at his death. Scriabin dreamed of having the "Mysterium" performed as a sacred action in the Himalayas, and actually made plans for going to India; the outbreak of World War I in 1914 put an end to such a project. Scriabin's fragmentary sketches for *L'Acte préalable* were arranged in 1973 by the Russian musician Alexander Nemtin, who supplemented this material with excerpts from Scriabin's 8th Piano Sonata, *Guirlandes,* and Piano Preludes, op. 74; the resulting synthetic score was performed in Moscow on March 16, 1973, under the title *Universe;* a species of color keyboard was used at the performance, projecting colors according to Scriabin's musical spectrum.

WORKS: ORCH.: Piano Concerto, op. 20 (1896; Odessa, Oct. 23, 1897, composer soloist); Symphonic Poem (1896–97); *Rêverie,* op. 24 (1898; Moscow, March 24, 1899); *Andante* for String Orch. (1899); Sym. No. 1, op. 26 (1899–1900; Moscow, March 29, 1901); Sym. No. 2, op. 29 (1901; St. Petersburg, Jan. 25, 1902); Sym. No. 3, op. 43, *Le divin poème* (1902–4; Paris, May 29, 1905); *Le poème de l'extase,* op. 54 (1905–8; N.Y., Dec. 10, 1908); *Promethée, le poème du feu,* op. 60 (1908–10; Moscow, March 15, 1911, composer soloist). **PIANO:** *Canon* (1883); *Nocturne* in A-flat major (1884); *Valse* in F minor, op. 1 (1885); *Sonate-fantaisie* (1886); *Valse* in G-sharp minor (1886); *Valse* in D-flat major (1886); *Variations on a Theme by Mlle. Egorova* (1887); 11 sonatas: in E-flat major (1887–89), op. 6 (1892), op. 19, *Sonata-Fantasy* (1892–97), op. 23 (1897–98), op. 30 (1903), op. 53 (1907), op. 62 (1911), op. 64, *Messe blanche* (1911), op. 66 (1913), op. 68, *Messe noire* (1913), and op. 70 (1913); 3 Pieces, op. 2 (1887–89); *Feuillet d'album* in A-flat major (1889); *10 Mazurkas,* op. 3 (1889); *Mazurka* in F major (1889?); *Mazurka* in B minor (1889?); *Fantasy* for 2 Pianos (1889?); *Allegro appassionato,* op. 4 (1892; based on the 1st movement of the Sonata in E-flat major); 2 *Nocturnes,* op. 5 (1890); *Deux impromptus à la Mazur,* op. 7 (1892); *Douze etudes,* op. 8 (1894); 2 Pieces for Left Hand, op. 9 (1894); 2 *Impromptus,* op. 10 (1894); 24 *Préludes,* op. 11 (1888–96); 2 *Impromptus,* op. 12 (1895); 6 *Préludes,* op. 13 (1895); 2 *Impromptus,* op. 14 (1895); 5 *Préludes,* op. 15 (1895–96); 5 *Préludes,* op. 16 (1894–95); 7 *Préludes,* op. 17 (1895–96); *Allegro de concert,* op. 18 (1896); *Polonaise,* op. 21 (1897); *4 Préludes,* op. 22 (1897); *9 Mazurkas,* op. 25 (1899); *2 Préludes,* op. 27 (1900); *Fantaisie,* op. 28 (1900); *4 Préludes,* op. 31 (1903); *Deux poèmes,* op. 32 (1903); *4 Préludes,* op. 33 (1903); *Poème tragique,* op. 34 (1903); *3 Préludes,* op. 35 (1903); *Poème satanique,* op. 36 (1903); *4 Préludes,* op. 37 (1903); *Valse,* op. 38 (1903); *4 Préludes,* op. 39 (1903); *2 Mazurkas,* op. 40 (1902–3); *Poème,* op. 41 (1903); *Huit études,* op. 42 (1903); *Deux poèmes,* op. 44 (1905); *3 Pieces,* op. 45 (1904–5); *Scherzo,* op. 46 (1905); *Quasi-valse,* op. 47 (1905); *4 Préludes,* op. 48 (1905); *3 Pieces,* op. 49 (1905); *Feuille d'album* (1905); *4 Pieces,* op. 51 (1906); *3 Pieces,* op. 52 (1906); *4 Pieces,* op. 56 (1907); *2 Pieces,* op. 57 (1907); *Feuillet d'album,* op. 58 (1910); *2 Pieces,* op. 59 (1910); *Poème-nocturne,* op. 61 (1911); *Deux poèmes,* op. 63 (1911); *Trois études,* op. 65 (1912); *2 Préludes,* op. 67 (1912–13); *Deux poèmes,* op. 69 (1913); *Deux poèmes,* op. 71 (1914); *Vers la flamme,* op. 72 (1914); *Deux danses,* op. 73 (1914); *5 Préludes,* op. 74 (1914). **CHAMBER:** *Romance* for Horn and Piano (1890); 2nd Variation for *Variations on a Russian Theme* for String Quartet (1899; in collaboration with 9 other composers).

BIBL.: L. Sabaneyev, "Prometheus von S.," *Der blaue Reiter* (Munich, 1912; 2nd ed., 1965; Eng. tr., 1974); G. Clutsam, "The Harmonies of S.," *Musical Times,* LIV (1913); I. Lipayev, *A.N. S.* (Moscow, 1913); R. Newmarch, "S. and Contemporary Russian Music," *Russian Review,* II (1913); idem, "Prometheus: The Poem of Fire," *Musical Times,* LV (1914); E. Gunst, *S. and His Work* (Moscow, 1915); V. Karatigin, *S.* (Petrograd, 1915); special issues of *Musikalnyi Sovremennik,* IV (1915) and V (1916); A. Hull, *A Great Russian Tone-poet: S.* (London, 1916; 2nd ed., 1927); idem, "The Pianoforte Works of S.," *Musical Times,* LVII (1916); idem, "S.'s Scientific Derivation of Harmony versus Empirical Methods," *Proceedings of the Musical Association,* XLIII (1916–17); idem, "A Survey of the Pianoforte Works of S.," *Musical Quarterly* (Oct. 1916); A. Koptyayev, *A.N. S.* (Petrograd, 1916); L. Sabaneyev, *S.* (Moscow, 1916; 2nd ed., 1923); M. Montagu-Nathan, *Handbook to the Piano Works of A. S.* (London, 1917; 2nd ed., 1922); I. Glebov, *S.* (Petrograd, 1921); B. de Schloezer, "S.," *La Revue Musicale,* II (1921); I. Lapshin, *S.'s Intimate Thoughts* (Petrograd, 1922); L. Sabaneyev, *A.N. S.* (Moscow, 1922; 2nd ed., 1923); B. Asafiev, *S. 1871–1915* (Petrograd, 1923); L. Sabaneyev, *Pisma A.N. S.a* (letters; Moscow,1923); B. de Schloezer, *A. S. lichnost mysteriya* (A. S., Character of Mystery; vol. I, Berlin, 1923; French tr., Paris, 1975; Eng. tr., by N. Slonimsky, Berkeley and Los Angeles, 1987; vol. II not completed); A. Swan, *S.* (London, 1923); H. Antcliffe, "The Significance of S.," *Musical Quarterly,* X (1924); L. Sabaneyev, *Reminiscences of S.* (Moscow, 1925); V. Yakovlev, *A.N. S.* (Moscow, 1925); E. von Tideböhl, "Memories of S.'s Volga Tour (1910)," *Monthly Musical Record,* LVI (1926); L. Sabaneyev, "S. and the Idea of a Religious Art," *Musical Times,* LXXII (1931); M. Cooper, "S.'s Mystical Beliefs," *Music & Letters,* XVI (1935); P. Dickenmann, *Die Entwicklung der Harmonik bei A. S.* (Bern and Leipzig, 1935); M. Metshik, *A. S.* (Moscow, 1935); A. Nikolayev, *A. S.* (Moscow, 1940); N. Rimskaya-Korsakova, "Rimsky-Korsakov i S.," *Sovetskaya musika,* No. 5 (1950); L. Danilevich, *A.N. S.* (Moscow, 1953); B. de Schloezer, "A. S.," *Musique russe,* II (Paris, 1953); H. Boegner, *Die Harmonik der späten Klavierwerke S.s* (diss., Univ. of Munich, 1955); R. Wood, "S. and His Critics," *Monthly Musical Record,* LXXXVI (1956); R. Myers, "S.: A Reassessment," *Musical Times,* XCVIII (1957); D. Blagoy, *Etyudi S.a* (Moscow, 1963); C. von Gleich, *Die sinfonischen Werke von A. S.* (Bilthoven, 1963); H. Förster, *Die Form in den symphonischen Werken von A.N. S.* (diss., Univ. of Leipzig, 1964); P. Dickinson, "S.'s Later Music," *Music Review,* XXVI (1965); O. Sakhaltuyeva, *S.'s Harmony* (Moscow, 1965); M. Mikhailov, *A.N. S.* (Moscow, 1966); V. Dernova, *S.'s Harmony* (Leningrad, 1968; Eng. tr. and commentary by R. Guenther, diss., Catholic Univ. of America, 1979); F. Bowers, *S.: A Biography of the Russian Composer* (2 vols., Palo Alto, 1969); S. Pavchinsky, *The Works of S.'s Last Period* (Moscow, 1969); V. Delson, *S.* (Moscow, 1971); V. Belaieff, *Mussorgsky, S., Stravinsky* (Moscow, 1972); W. Evrard, *S.* (Paris, 1972);

E. Kaufman, *The Evolution of Form and Technique in the Late Works of S.* (diss., Yale Univ., 1972); H. Steger, *Der Weg der Klaviersonaten bei A. S.* (Munich, 1972); F. Bowers, *The New S.: Enigma and Answers* (N.Y., 1973); S. Pavchinsky and V. Zuckerman, eds., *A.N. S.* (Moscow, 1973); H. Steger, *Materialstrukturen in den fünf späten Klaviersonaten A. S.s* (Regensburg, 1977); G. Eberle, *Zwischen Tonalität und Atonalität: Studien zur Harmonik A. S.s* (Munich, 1978); M. Kelkel, *A. S., sa vie, l'esotérisme et la langage musical dans son œuvre* (Paris, 1978); H. Macdonald, *S.* (London, 1978); M. Brown, "S. and Russian 'Mystic' Symbolism," *19th Century Music* (July 1979); E. Rudakova and A. Kandinsky, *A.N. S.* (Moscow, 1979); O. Kolleritsch, ed., *A. S.* (Graz, 1980); I. Belza, *A.N. S.* (Moscow, 1983); H. Metzger and R. Riehn, eds., *A. S. und die S.isten, Musik Konzepte,* Nos. 32–33 (Munich, 1983) and Nos. 37–38 (Munich, 1984); S. Schibli, *A. S. und seine Musik: Grenzuberschreitungen eines prometheischen Geistes* (Munich, 1983); G. Perle, "S.'s Self-Analyses," *Musical Analysis,* III (1984); M. Cooper, "A. S. and the Russian Renaissance," *Slavonic and Western Music: Essays for Gerald Abraham* (Ann Arbor and Oxford, 1985); J. Baker, *The Music of A. S.* (New Haven, 1986); A. Pople, *S. and Stravinsky 1908–1914: Studies in Theory and Analysis* (N.Y. and London, 1989).

Scriabine, Marina, Russian-French music scholar and composer, daughter of **Alexander (Nikolaievich) Scriabin;** b. Moscow, Jan. 30, 1911. After her father's death, she lived with her mother in Kiev and Moscow; when her mother died, she went to Belgium to live with her maternal grandmother; in 1927 she settled in Paris. She studied at the Ecole Nationale des Arts Décoratifs and designed art posters; studied music theory with René Leibowitz. In 1950 she joined the Radiodiffusion Française and worked in electronic techniques; composed a *Suite radiophonique* (1951); also a ballet, *Bayalett* (1952), and some chamber music. In 1967 she received a doctorate in esthetics for her thesis *Représentation du temps et de l'intemporalité dans les arts plastiques figuratifs.* She publ. *Problèmes de la musique moderne* (in collaboration with her uncle, Boris de Schloezer; Paris, 1959; also in Spanish, 1960); *Le Langage musical* (Paris, 1963); *Le Miroir du temps* (Paris, 1973). She contributed the biographical entry on Scriabin for the *Encyclopédie de la musique* (Paris, 1961); wrote an introduction to Schloezer's book on Scriabin, in French (Paris, 1975).

Scribe, (Augustin) Eugène, famous French dramatist and librettist; b. Paris, Dec. 24, 1791; d. there, Feb. 20, 1861. He was a scholarship student at the Collège Ste.-Barbe in Paris; after training in the law, he turned to the theater; was made a member of the Académie Française (1836). He was closely associated as a librettist with Meyerbeer, but also wrote librettos for Auber, Bellini, Donizetti, Gounod, Halévy, Offenbach, Verdi, and others. See *Eugène Scribe: Oeuvres complètes* (76 vols., Paris, 1874–85).

BIBL.: N. Arvin, *E. S.* (N.Y., 1924); J.-G. Prod'homme, "Wagner, Berlioz and Monsieur S.," *Musical Quarterly* (July 1926); K. Pendle, *E. S. and French Opera of the 19th Century* (Ann Arbor, 1979).

Scribner, Norman (Orville), American organist, conductor, and composer; b. Washington, D.C., Feb. 25, 1936. He studied organ with Paul Callaway and theory with Walter Spencer Huffman at the Peabody Cons. of Music in Baltimore (B.Mus., 1961). In 1960 he was appointed director of music of St. Alban's Episcopal Church in Washington, D.C.; was also a staff keyboard artist with the National Sym. Orch. (1963–67). In 1965 he founded the all-volunteer Choral Arts Society of Washington, D.C.; in 1971 he founded the Norman Scribner Choir. He served on the faculties of American Univ. (1960–63) and George Washington Univ. (1963–69). He composed a Sextet for Winds and Piano (1975); *The Nativity,* choral cantata (1975); *The Tide Pool,* song cycle for Mezzo-soprano and Orch. (1977); *Laudate Dominum,* choral cantata (1979); *I Hear America Singing,* choral suite (1979); *Nicholas,* musical show (1980).

Scruggs, Earl (Eugene), American country-music singer and banjo player; b. Flint Hill, N.C., Jan. 6, 1924. He took up the banjo as a child and developed such a mastery of the instrument that he made a hit as a member of Bill Monroe's Blue Grass Boys; he then teamed up with Lester Flatt, the guitarist, and they organized their own band, The Foggy Mountain Boys, which quickly assumed a prominent place in country-music circles. Scruggs's 3-finger banjo style was artistically complemented by Flatt's accomplished guitar playing. After they dissolved their partnership in 1969, Scruggs formed his own group, the Earl Scruggs Revue; with it he cultivated the country-rock genre. He starred in the movie *Banjo Man* in 1975. The Flatt-Scruggs partnership resulted in such successful songs as *Roll in My Sweet Baby's Arms, Old Salty Dog Blues, The Ballad of Jed Clampett* (from the insipid television comedy series "The Beverly Hillbillies"), and *Foggy Mountain Breakdown* (the theme song of the film *Bonnie and Clyde*). He publ. the book *Earl Scruggs and the 5-String Banjo* (N.Y., 1968).

Scudo, P(ietro), Italian-born French writer on music and composer; b. Venice, June 8, 1806; d. Blois, Oct. 14, 1864. He was reared in Germany; then went to Paris, where he studied at Choron's Institution Royale de Musique Classique et Religieuse (c.1824–30); was for a time an opera singer; played clarinet in military bands; then turned to journalism; publ. several political pamphlets; became music critic of the influential *Revue des Deux Mondes.* A writer of considerable talent, he held reactionary views; violently attacked Berlioz, Liszt, and Wagner. He became deranged and died in an insane asylum. He was the composer of several songs; also wrote a musical novel, *Le Chevalier Sarti* (1857; not connected with the composer Giuseppe Sarti); its sequel, *Frédérique,* was publ. in the *Revue des Deux Mondes.*

WRITINGS: All publ. in Paris: *Critique et littérature musicales* (vol. I, 1850; 3rd ed., enl., 1856; vol. II, 1859); *L'art ancienne et l'art moderne: nouveaux mélanges de critique et de littérature musicales* (1854); *L'année musicale, ou Revue annuelle des théâtres lyriques et des concerts* (1860–62); *La musique en l'année 1862* (1863).

Sculthorpe, Peter (Joshua), eminent Australian composer; b. Launceston, Tasmania, April 29, 1929. He studied at the Univ. of Melbourne Conservatorium of Music (B.Mus., 1951); then took courses from Egon Wellesz and Edmund Rubbra at Wadham College, Oxford (1958–60); returning to Australia, he became a lecturer in music at the Univ. of Sydney in 1963; was made a reader there in 1969. He also was composer-in-residence at Yale Univ. while on a Harkness Fellowship (1965–67) and a visiting prof. of music at the Univ. of Sussex (1971–72). In 1977 he was made an Officer of the Order of the British Empire. In 1980 he received the honorary degree of Doctor of Letters from the Univ. of Tasmania; later received an honorary D.Litt. degree from the Univ. of Sussex and an honorary D.Mus. degree from the Univ. of Melbourne (both 1989). In his music, Sculthorpe rejects European techniques such as serialism in favor of a typically Australian approach to music. He has looked to Asia, in particular Japan, Indonesia, and Tibet, for both literary and musical inspiration. As a result, his music is often a battleground for European Expressionism and native ritualism. He has also been influenced by the physical environment of Australia, as in *Sun Music I–IV* for Orch., and in his utilization of birdcalls and insect sounds.

WORKS: STAGE: OPERAS: *Rites of Passage* (1971–73); *Quiros,* television opera (1982). **BALLET:** *Sun Music Ballet* (Sydney, 1968; incorporates music from the 4 separate *Sun Music* pieces). **ORCH.:** *Small Town From The 5th Continent* for Speaker and Chamber Orch. (1963; rev. 1976; uses narrated selections from D.H. Lawrence's novel *Kangaroo*); *Sun Music: I* (1965), *II* (1966; rev. 1969), *III, Anniversary Music* (1967), and *IV* (1967); *Overture for a Happy Occasion* (1970); *Love 200* for 2 Singers, Rock Band, and Orch. (Sydney, Feb. 14, 1970); *Music for Japan* (1970); *Rain* (1970); *Lament for Strings* (1976); *Port Essington* for Strings (1977); *Mangrove* (Sydney, April 28, 1979); Guitar Concerto (1980); Piano Concerto (1983); *Little Suite* for String Orch. (1983); Sonata for Strings

(1983); *Sun Song* (1984); *Earth Cry* (1986); Second Sonata for Strings (1988); *Kakadu* (1988); *Nourlangie* for Guitar, Percussion, and Strings (1989); *Two Grainger Arrangements* for Strings and Percussion (1989). **CHAMBER:** 10 string quartets: No. 1 (1947); No. 2 (1948); No. 3 (1949); No. 4 (1950); No. 5, *Irkanda II* (1959); No. 6 (1964–65); No. 7, previously titled *Red Landscape* (1966); No. 8, previously titled *String Quartet Music* (1969); No. 9 (1975); No. 10 (1982); *The Loneliness of Bunjil* for String Trio (1954; rev. 1960); 4 works titled *Irkanda* (aboriginal for "a remote and lonely place"): *I* for Violin (1955), *II* (String Quartet No. 5; 1959), *III* for Piano Trio (1961), and *IV* for Solo Violin, Strings, and Percussion (1961); *Tabuh Tabuhan* for Wind Quintet and Percussion (1968); *Dream* for Any Instruments and Any Number of Performers (1970); *How the Stars Were Made* for Percussion Ensemble (1971); *The Song of Tailitnama* for Soprano, 6 Cellos, and Percussion (1974); *Sun Song* for Recorder Quartet (1976); *Landscape II* for Piano Quartet (1978); *Cantares* for Flamenco, Classical, and Jazz Guitars and String Quartet (1980); *Tailitnama Song* for Flute, Percussion, Violin, and Cello (1981; also for Cello and Piano, 1989); *Sun Song* for Percussion Ensemble (1989). **VOCAL:** *Sun Music for Voices and Percussion* (1966); *Night Piece* for Chorus and Piano (1966); *Morning Song for the Christ Child* for Chorus (1966); *The Stars Turn,* from *Love 200* for Chorus (1970; rev. 1976); *Ketjak* for 6 Male Voices and Tape Echo (1972); *Eliza Fraser Sings* for Soprano, Flute, and Piano (1978); *Child of Australia* for Soprano, Narrator, Chorus, and Orch. (1988). **PIANO:** Sonatina (1954); *Left Bank Waltz* (1957); *Five Night Pieces: Snow, Moon, and Flowers, Night,* and *Stars* (1965–71); *Landscape I* for Amplified Piano and Prerecorded Tape Loop (1971); *Koto Music I* (1973) and *II* (1976) for Piano and Prerecorded Tape Loop; *Mountains* (1981); *Djilile* (1986); *Callabona* (1986; rev. 1989); *The Rose Bay Quadrilles* (1989); also incidental music for films, plays, and radio.

BIBL.: M. Hannan, *P. S., His Music and Ideas 1929–1979* (Brisbane, 1982).

Seagle, Oscar, American baritone and singing teacher; b. Chattanooga, Tenn., Oct. 31, 1877; d. Dallas, Dec. 19, 1945. He sang in concerts in the U.S. from 1896 until 1905; then went to Paris for further study with Jean de Reszke; made his Paris debut in 1907, and also sang in England; returned to America at the outbreak of World War I in 1914, and settled in N.Y. as a singing teacher.

Seaman, Christopher, English conductor; b. Faversham, Kent, March 7, 1942. He was educated at King's College, Cambridge; studied music at the Guildhall School of Music in London; then joined the London Phil. as timpanist in 1964. In 1968 he became assistant conductor of the BBC Scottish Sym. Orch. in Glasgow; was its principal conductor from 1971 to 1977; was also principal conductor and artistic director of the Northern Sinfonia (1973–79); served as principal conductor of the Robert Mayer children's concerts in London (from 1978); was principal guest conductor and artistic advisor to the conducting course at the Guildhall School of Music and Drama in London (from 1989).

Search, Frederick Preston, American cellist, conductor, and composer; b. Pueblo, Colo., July 22, 1889; d. Carmel Valley, Calif., Nov. 1, 1959. After studying cello in Jena (from 1901), he returned to the U.S. and continued his training with Adamowski at the New England Cons. of Music in Boston (1903–4) and with Lino Mattioli and Georg Rogovoy at the Cincinnati College Cons. of Music (1904–7); then studied cello with Klengel, conducting with Nikisch, and composition with Reger, Schreck, Hofmann, and Sitt at the Leipzig Cons. (1907–11); also played cello in the Gewandhaus Orch. (1910–12). On his return to the U.S., he was conductor of the Mare Island Naval Training Station orch. and band (1918–19) and the orch. of the Hotel Del Monte in Del Monte, Calif. (1920–32); after further tours as a recitalist (1932, 1934), he served as conductor of the Federal Symphonic Band in San Francisco (1936–40). In 1923 he married the pianist and composer Opal Piontkowski Heron.

WORKS: ORCH.: *The Bridge Builders* for Soloists, Chorus, and Orch. (1937); 4 syms.: No. 1, in D major (1913); No. 2, in G minor (1938; Oakland, Calif., Feb. 23, 1940); No. 3, in B minor (1931); No. 4, in B-flat major, *Roan Stallion* (1941); Cello Concerto (1932; Monterey, Aug. 22, 1933); *Korkle* (1932; Oakland, Calif., Aug. 4, 1936); *Exhilaration,* overture (1933; San Francisco, Jan. 9, 1936); *Holly, A Jolly Suite* (1934); *Oriental Dance* for Cello and Orch. (1934); *Rhapsody* (1934; San Francisco, April 30, 1936); *Sinfonietta* (1938); *Suite* for Saxophone and Orch. (1939); *Romanze* for Cello or Viola, and Orch. (San Francisco, Sept. 20, 1939; transcription of the 3rd string quartet); *Jollity* for Trumpet and Orch. (1957); *Quicksilver* for Flute and Orch. (1957); *Polly* (1958). **BAND:** *Courageous* (1936); *Carmelita* (1938); *Kathleen* (1938); *Romantic Overture* (1938); *Sweet Dreams* (1938); *Woodland Sketch* (1938); *March militaire* (1939); *Minuet* (1939); *Reverie* (1939). **CHAMBER:** 4 string quartets (1910; 1915; 1932, rev. 1942; 1935); *Reverie of the Garda-See* for Violin or Cello, and Piano (1911); *Romance* for Cello and Piano (1912); *Étude* for Cello (1913); *Aria* for Cello and Piano (1914); Cello Sonata (1914); *Elégie* for Piano Trio (1920); *Amara* for Saxophone and Piano (1930; also for Band, 1937); Septet (1936); *Jamesburg Quintet* (1937); *Chinese Dance* for Woodwind Quintet (1957).

Searle, Humphrey, distinguished English composer, teacher, and writer on music; b. Oxford, Aug. 26, 1915; d. London, May 12, 1982. He studied classical literature at Oxford (1933–37) and music at the Royal College of Music in London (1937), where his teachers were John Ireland and R.O. Morris. In 1937 he went to Vienna, where he took private lessons with Webern; this study proved to be a decisive influence in Searle's own compositions, which are imbued with the subtle coloristic processes peculiar to the 2nd Viennese School of composition. He served in the British army during World War II, and was stationed in Germany in 1946. Returning to London, he engaged in various organizations promoting the cause of modern music. He was honorary secretary of the Liszt Society (1950–62); was an adviser on music for the Sadler's Wells Ballet (1951–57). In 1964–65 he was composer-in-residence at Stanford Univ. in California; then occupied a similar post at the Univ. of Southern Calif., Los Angeles (1976–77); from 1965 to 1976 he was a prof. at the Royal College of Music in London. In 1968 he was made a Commander of the Order of the British Empire. Although Searle's method of composing included some aspects of the 12-tone method, he did not renounce tonal procedures, and sometimes applied purely national English melodic patterns. As a writer, he became particularly well known for his writings on Liszt.

WORKS: STAGE: OPERAS: *The Diary of a Madman* (Berlin, Oct. 3, 1958); *The Photo of the Colonel* (Frankfurt am Main, June 3, 1964); *Hamlet* (1964–68; Hamburg, March 5, 1968). **BALLETS:** *Noctambules* (1956); *The Great Peacock* (1957–58); *Dualities* (1963). **ORCH.:** 2 suites for Strings (1942, 1943); 2 piano concertos (1944, 1955); *Fuga giocosa* (1948); 5 syms.: No. 1 (1953); No. 2 (1956–58); No. 3 (1958–60; Edinburgh, Sept. 3, 1960); No. 4 (Birmingham, Nov. 8, 1962); No. 5 (Manchester, Oct. 7, 1964). *Scherzi* for Small Orch. (1964); *Sinfonietta* (1968–69); *Zodiac Variations* for Small Orch. (1970); *Labyrinth* (1971); *Tamesis* (1979). **CHAMBER:** Bassoon Quintet (1945); *Intermezzo* for 11 Instruments (1946); Quartet for Clarinet, Bassoon, Violin, and Viola (1948); *Passacaglietta in nomine Arnold Schoenberg* for String Quartet (1949); *Gondoliera* for English Horn and Piano (1950); *Suite* for Clarinet and Piano (1956); *3 Movements* for String Quartet (1959); *Il penseroso e L'allegro* for Cello and Piano (1975). **CHORAL:** *Gold Coast Customs* for Speaker, Men's Chorus, and Orch. (1947–49); *The Shadow of Cain* for Speakers, Men's Chorus, and Orch. (1951); *Jerusalem* for Speakers, Tenor, Chorus, and Orch. (1970); *Kubla Khan* for Tenor, Chorus, and Orch. (1973); *Rhyme Rude to My Pride* for Men's Voices (1974); *My Beloved Spake* for Chorus and Organ (1976); *Dr. Faustus* for Solo Voices, Chorus, and Orch. (1977).

WRITINGS: All publ. in London: *The Music of Liszt* (1954; 2nd ed., 1966); *Twentieth Century Counterpoint* (1954); *Ballet Music: An Introduction* (1958; 2nd ed., rev., 1973); with R. Layton, *Twentieth-Century Composers 3: Britain, Scandinavia and the Netherlands* (1972).

Seashore, Carl Emil, Swedish-American psychologist; b. Mörlunda, Jan. 28, 1866; d. Lewiston, Idaho, Oct. 16, 1949. He was taken to the U.S. as a child; studied at Gustavus Adolphus College in Minn. (B.A., 1891), and pursued the study of psychology at Yale Univ. (Ph.D., 1895), where he was an assistant in its psychological laboratory (1895–97); joined the faculty of the Univ. of Iowa in 1902, where he was head of its psychology dept. and its psychological laboratory (from 1905). He devised a widely used method for measuring musical talent ("Seashore Test") through special measurements of his own invention (audiometer, tonoscope, chronograph, etc.).

WRITINGS: *Measures of Musical Talent* (N.Y., 1919; 2nd ed., rev., 1939 with D. Lewis and J. Saetveit as *Seashore Measures of Musical Talents;* 3rd ed., rev., 1960); ed. *Psychology of the Vibrato in Voice and Instrument* (Iowa City, 1936); *Psychology of Music* (N.Y., 1938); *In Search of Beauty in Music: A Scientific Approach to Musical Esthetics* (N.Y., 1947).

BIBL.: Special issue of *Iowa Studies in Psychology: Psychological Monographs,* XXXIX/2 (1929); W. Miles, "C.E. S., 1866–1949," *Biographical Memoirs,* National Academy of Sciences, XXIX (N.Y., 1956).

Sébastian, Georges (real name, **György Sebestyén**), Hungarian conductor; b. Budapest, Aug. 17, 1903; d. near Paris, April 12, 1989. He studied with Bartók, Kodály, and Weiner at the Budapest Academy of Music (graduated, 1921); then received instruction in conducting from Bruno Walter in Munich (1922–23). He conducted at the Hamburg Opera (1924–25) and with the Leipzig Gewandhaus Orch. (1925–27). After serving as principal conductor at Berlin's Städtische Oper (1927–31), he went to Moscow as music director of the Radio and as a conductor with the Phil. In 1938 he went to the U.S.; was conductor of the Scranton (Pa.) Phil. (1940–45); also conducted in South America. In 1946 he settled in Paris, where he conducted at the Opéra and the Opéra-Comique; also appeared with the Orch. National de France.

Sebastian, John, American pop musician; b. N.Y., March 17, 1944. His father, a classical harmonica player, taught him music. He played a variety of instruments as a child before turning to guitar. He formed a group called The Lovin' Spoonful, which began to produce one "good-time" hit after another. A crisis came in 1967 when his vocalist was busted in San Francisco on drug charges. The group folded in 1969. Sebastian embraced radical politics and counter-culture, and made a spectacular hit at the notorious gathering of acidheads at the Woodstock Festival in 1969. Among The Lovin' Spoonful's best successes were *Do You Believe in Magic* and *Summer in the City.* Also successful were *Younger Girl, Did You Ever Have to Make Up Your Mind,* and *Darling, Be Home Soon.* The band created sound-track albums for the films *What's Up, Tiger Lily* and *You're a Big Boy Now.*

Sebastiani, Johann, German composer; b. near Weimar, Sept. 30, 1622; d. Königsberg, 1683. He settled in Königsberg about 1650; was made Kantor at the Cathedral in 1661 and court Kapellmeister to the Elector of Brandenburg in 1663; was pensioned in 1679. He wrote a Passion, *Das Leyden und Sterben unsers Herrn und Heylandes Jesu Christi nach dem heiligen Matthaeo* for 5 Voices, 6 Instruments, and Basso Continuo (Königsberg, 1672; ed. in Denkmäler Deutscher Tonkunst, XVII, 1904), which is noteworthy for the devotional chorales therein introduced. He also wrote *Erster Theil der Parnass-Blumen oder* [60] *geist- und weltliche Lieder* (Hamburg and Wolfenbüttel, 1672), *Ander Theil der Parnass-Blumen* (Hamburg, 1675), various funeral songs (1663–80), and many occasional pieces.

Sebestyén, János, esteemed Hungarian harpsichordist, organist, and pedagogue; b. Budapest, March 2, 1931. He was an organ pupil of Ferenc Gergely at the Budapest Academy of Music (graduated, 1956); toured as a harpsichord and organ virtuoso in Europe, the U.S., and the Far East. He was founder-director of the harpsichord dept. at the Budapest Academy of Music (from 1970); in 1982 he was made a Merited Artist by the Hungarian government.

Sebök, György, Hungarian pianist; b. Szeged, Nov. 2, 1922. He 1st studied piano in Szeged; then went to the Franz Liszt Academy of Music in Budapest, where he studied composition with Kodály and chamber music with Leo Weiner. In 1949 he was appointed to the faculty of the Bartók Cons. in Budapest; in 1952 he won the Liszt Prize. During the Hungarian turmoil in 1956 he went to Paris, and later settled in the U.S. In 1962 he was appointed prof. of piano at the Indiana Univ. School of Music in Bloomington; continued to travel widely, visiting South Africa and Japan as a pianist and pedagogue.

Šebor, Karl, Bohemian conductor and composer; b. Brandeis, Aug. 13, 1843; d. Prague, May 17, 1903. He was a pupil of Kittl; was conductor of the National Opera (1864–67) and military bandmaster in Vienna (from 1871). He wrote Czech operas (all produced in Prague): *The Templars in Moravia* (Oct. 19, 1864); *Drahomira* (1867); *The Hussite's Bride* (Sept. 28, 1868); *Blanka* (1870); *The Frustrated Wedding* (Oct. 25, 1879); cantatas; overtures; songs.

Sechter, Simon, famous Austrian organist, pedagogue, and composer; b. Friedberg, Bohemia, Oct. 11, 1788; d. Vienna, Sept. 10, 1867. In 1804 he went to Vienna, where he studied with L. Koželuh and Hartmann; then was a piano and singing teacher at the Inst. for the Blind (1810–25); also was assistant (1824–25) and principal (from 1825) Hoforganist; likewise served as prof. of thoroughbass and counterpoint at the Cons. (1851–63). He won his greatest renown as a teacher; among his best-known pupils were Henselt, Bruckner, Vieuxtemps, and Thalberg; Schubert took a lesson from him (Nov. 4, 1828) shortly before his untimely death. Although he was a master contrapuntist, his output is unknown outside his homeland. Among his more than 8,000 works were 3 operas: *Ezzeline, die unglückliche Gegangene aus Deli-Katesse* (1843; not perf.), *Ali Hitsch-Hatsch* (1843; Vienna, Nov. 12, 1844), and *Melusine* (1851; not perf.); 2 oratorios: *Die Offenbarung Johannes* (1838–45) and *Sodoms Untergang* (1840); 35 masses; 2 Requiems; many other sacred works; choral pieces; orch. music; chamber pieces.

WRITINGS: *Die Grundsätze der musikalischen Komposition:* I, *Die richtige Folge der Grundharmonien* (Leipzig, 1853), II, *Von den Gesetzen des Taktes in der Musik; Vom einstimmigen Satz; Die Kunst, zu einer gegebenen Melodie die Harmonie zu finden* (Leipzig, 1853), and III, *Vom drei- und zweistimmigen Satze; Rhythmische Entwürfe; Vom strengen Satze, mit Kurzen Andeutungen des freien Satzes; Vom doppelten Contrapunkte* (Leipzig, 1854).

BIBL.: C. Pohl, *S. S.* (Vienna, 1868); J. Markus, *S. S.: Biographisches Denkmal* (Vienna, 1888); G. Capellen, *Ist das System S. S.s ein geeigneter Ausgangspunkt für die theoretische Wagnerforschung?* (Leipzig, 1902); E. Tittel, *S. S. als Kirchenkomponist* (diss., Univ. of Vienna, 1935).

Seckendorff, Karl Siegmund, Freiherr von, German writer and composer; b. Erlangen, Nov. 26, 1744; d. Ansbach, April 26, 1785. He studied literature and jurisprudence at the Univ. of Erlangen; was an officer in the Austrian army (1761–74), then in the diplomatic service in Weimar (1776–84); shortly before his death, he was appointed Prussian ambassador in Ansbach (1784). At Weimar he was on close terms with Goethe, who allowed him to write music for a number of his poems before their publ. (*Der Fischer, Der König in Thule,* etc.); in these songs, Seckendorff caught the characteristic inflections of folk melodies.

WORKS: STAGE: *Lila* (Liederspiel; Weimar, 1776); *Le marché* (*La foire*) *du village* (ballet comique; 1776); *Proserpina* (monodrama; Weimar, 1778); *Die Laune des Verliebten* (Weimar, May 20, 1779; not extant); *Jery und Bätely* (singspiel; Weimar, July 12, 1780; not extant); *Der Geist der Jugend* (comé-

die-ballet; Weimar, Jan. 30, 1782; not extant); *Der Blumenraub* (operetta; 1784); *Die Empfindsamkeit* (n.d.); also chamber music; *Volks- und andere Lieder* for Voice and Piano (3 vols., Weimar, 1779–82), as well as other lieder in contemporary collections; keyboard music, including 2 sonatas for 3 Pianos.

BIBL.: V. Knab, *K.S. v.S.* (1774–1785): *ein Beitrag zur Geschichte des deutschen volkstümlichen Liedes und der Musik am weimarischen Hof im 18. Jahrhundert* (diss., Univ. of Bonn, 1914).

Secunda, Sholom, Russian-born American composer; b. Alexandria, near Kherson, Sept. 4, 1894; d. N.Y., June 13, 1974. His family went to the U.S. in 1907. He took music lessons with Percy Goetschius and Ernest Bloch at the Inst. of Musical Art in N.Y., graduating in 1917; became a naturalized American citizen in 1923. In 1932 he became a founder of the Society of Jewish Composers, Publishers and Songwriters, which was absorbed by Broadcast Music, Inc. in 1940. From 1916 to 1973 he was associated with the Yiddish Theater in N.Y., for which he wrote over 40 operettas; most of these hardly made any impression outside ethnic circles, but one song, *Bei mir bist du schön,* from the operetta *I Would if I Could* (1933), made an unexpected splash even among gentiles, and was sung, in the original Yiddish, by the Andrews Sisters, Rudy Vallee, July Garland, and Kate Smith, becoming one of the most popular songs worldwide. Secunda sold the copyright in 1937 for $30; he regained it in 1961, but never made any appreciable sum of money from it; a legal hassle with the author of the lyrics, Jacob Jacobs, further depleted Secunda's income. Other songs from his operettas were often taken as traditional; among these, *Dona, Dona, Dona,* from the operetta *Esterke* (1940), was recorded by Joan Baez. He also wrote some Jewish service music.

BIBL.: V. Secunda, *Bei Mir Bist Du Schön: The Story of S. S.* (N.Y., 1982).

Seedo (Sidow or **Sydow),** German composer; b. c.1700; d. probably in Prussia, c.1754. He was active at London's Drury Lane (1731–34), where he contributed music to several stage pieces; about 1736, he went to Potsdam to work with the Royal Band.

BIBL.: W. Rubsamen, "Mr. Seedo, Ballad Opera, and the Singspiel," *Miscelánea en Homenaje a Monseñor Higinio Anglés* (vol. II, Barcelona, 1961); E. Roberts, "Mr. Seedo's London Career, and His Work with Henry Fielding," *Philological Quarterly,* XLV (1966).

Seefried, Irmgard, outstanding German soprano; b. Köngetried, Bavaria, Oct. 9, 1919; d. Vienna, Nov. 24, 1988. She received her early musical instruction from her father; then studied voice at the Augsburg Cons., graduating in 1939. She made her professional operatic debut as the Priestess in *Aida* at the Aachen Stadttheater (Nov. 8, 1940); her 1st appearance at the Vienna State Opera followed as Eva in *Die Meistersinger von Nürnberg* (May 2, 1943); Richard Strauss chose her for the role of the Composer in *Ariadne auf Naxos* at his 80th birthday celebration there (1944). She subsequently sang in Salzburg, Edinburgh, Berlin, Paris, London, and Buenos Aires. On Nov. 20, 1953, she made her Metropolitan Opera debut in N.Y. as Susanna in *Le nozze di Figaro.* She was made a Kammersängerin of the Vienna State Opera in 1947; was named an honorary member in 1969. In 1948 she married **Wolfgang Schneiderhan.**

BIBL.: F. Fassbind, *Wolfgang Schneiderhan, I. S.; Eine Künstler- und Lebensgemeinschaft* (Bern, 1960).

Seeger, Charles (Louis), eminent American musicologist, ethnomusicologist, teacher, and composer; b. Mexico City (of American parents), Dec. 14, 1886; d. Bridgewater, Conn., Feb. 7, 1979. He was educated at Harvard Univ. (graduated, 1908); after conducting at the Cologne Opera (1910–11), he returned to the U.S. as chairman of the music dept. of the Univ. of Calif. at Berkeley (1912–19), where he gave the 1st classes in musicology in the U.S. (1916); then taught at N.Y.'s Inst. of Musical Art (1921–33) and the New School for Social Research (1931–35); at the latter, he gave the 1st classes (with Henry Cowell) in ethnomusicology in the U.S. (1932); was also active in contemporary music circles, as a composer and a music critic. He served as a technical adviser on music to the Resettlement Administration (1935–38), as deputy director of the Federal Music Project of the Works Progress Administration (1938–41), and as chief of the music division of the Pan-American Union (1941–53) in Washington, D.C.; was also a visiting prof. at Yale Univ. (1949–50). He subsequently was a research musicologist at the Inst. of Ethnomusicology at the Univ. of Calif. in Los Angeles (1960–70), and then taught at Harvard Univ. (from 1972). He was a founder and chairman (1930–34) of the N.Y. Musicological Soc., which he helped to reorganize as the American Musicological Soc. in 1934; was its president (1945–46) and also president of the American Soc. for Comparative Musicology (1935) and the Soc. for Ethnomusicology (1960–61; honorary president from 1972. Seeger also was instrumental (with Cowell and Joseph Schafer) in the formation of the N.Y. Composers' Collective (1932); since he was profoundly interested in proletarian music throughout the 1930s, he wrote on the need for a revolutionary spirit in music for such publications as *The Daily Worker*; he also contributed songs under the name Carl Sands to *The Workers Song Books* (1934 and 1935). Two of his essays are of especial historical interest: "On Proletarian Music" (*Modern Music*, XI/3 [1934]), which lamented the dearth of folk songs in the work of professional musicians, and "Grassroots for American Composers" (*Modern Music*, XVI [1938–40]), which, by shedding earlier Marxist rhetoric, had wide influence on the folk movement in the 1950s. Since many of his compositions were destroyed by fire at Berkeley in 1926, his extraordinary contribution to American music rests upon his work as a scholar whose uniquely universalist vision for the unification of the field of musicology as a whole continues to challenge the various, sometimes contentious contributing factions: musicology, ethnomusicology, and comparative musicology. He was also a noted teacher; one of his most gifted students, **Ruth (Porter) Crawford**, became his 2nd wife. In addition to his son Pete(r) Seeger, 2 other of his children became musicians: **Mike (Michael) Seeger** (b. N.Y., Aug. 15, 1933) was a folksinger and instrumentalist; after learning to play various folk instruments on his own, he became active in promoting the cause of authentic folk music of the American Southeast; became widely known for his expertise as a banjo player; with John Cohen and Tom Paley, he organized the New Lost City Ramblers in 1958; then founded the Strange Creek Singers in 1968. **Peggy** (actually, **Margaret**) Seeger (b. N.Y., June 17, 1935) was a folksinger, songwriter, and song collector; studied both classical and folk music; after further training at Radcliffe College, she became active as a performer; settled in England in 1956, becoming a naturalized subject in 1959; became a leading figure in the folk-music revival. **WRITINGS:** With E. Stricklen, *Harmonic Structure and Elementary Composition* (Berkeley, 1916); *Music as Recreation* (Washington, D.C., 1940); with R. Crawford Seeger, J. Lomax, and A. Lomax, *Folk Song: USA* (N.Y., 1947; 2nd ed., rev., 1975); *Music and Society: Some New World Evidence of Their Relationship* (Washington, D.C., 1953); *Studies in Musicology, 1935–75* (Berkeley, 1977); ed. *Essays for a Humanist: An Offering to Klaus Wachsmann* (N.Y., 1977). **BIBL.:** H. Cowell, *American Composers on American Music* (Stanford, Calif., 1933; 2nd ed., 1962); D. Dunaway, "C. S. and Carl Sands: The Composers' Collective Years," *Ethnomusicology*, XXIV/2 (1980); B. Zuck, *A History of Musical Americanism* (Ann Arbor, 1980).

Seeger, Horst, German musicologist; b. Erkner, near Berlin, Nov. 6, 1926. He began his training at the Berlin Hochschule für Musik (1950–55); then studied musicology at Humboldt Univ. in Berlin, where he received his Ph.D. in 1958 with the diss. *Komponist und Folklore in der Musik des 20. Jahrhunderts*. He was chief dramaturg of the (East) Berlin Komische Oper (1960–73); from 1973 to 1983 he served as Intendant

of the Dresden State Opera. His books include *Wolfgang Amadeus Mozart* (Leipzig, 1956); *Kleines Musiklexikon* (Berlin, 1958); *Joseph Haydn* (Leipzig, 1961); *Der kritische Musikus: Musikkritiken aus zwei Jahrhunderten* (Leipzig, 1963); *Musiklexikon* (Leipzig, 1966); *Wir und die Musik* (Berlin, 1968); *Opern-Lexikon* (Berlin, 1978; 3rd ed., rev., 1987).

Seeger, Pete(r), noted American folksinger, songwriter, and political activist, son of **Charles (Louis) Seeger;** b. Patterson, N.Y., May 3, 1919. He studied sociology at Harvard Univ. before turning to folk music; taking up the banjo, he became active as a traveling musician; with Lee Hays and Millard Lampell, he organized the Almanac Singers in 1941, and subsequently appeared before union and political audiences; then joined the Weavers in 1949, with which he became well known via Leadbelly's *Goodnight Irene*. His political activism was targeted by the House Committee on Un-American Activities, which cited him for contempt of Congress in 1956; in spite of his being blacklisted, he pursued his career and his commitment to various causes. A leading figure in the folk-song revival of the late 1950s, he won notable success with his songs *Where Have All the Flowers Gone?* and *If I Had a Hammer.* In all, he wrote over 100 songs, many of which became popular via his many tours through the U.S. and abroad. He wrote manuals for the 5-string banjo (1948; 3rd ed., rev., 1961) and the 12-string guitar (with J. Lester; 1965). J. Schwartz ed. a collection of his essays as *The Incompleat Folksinger* (1972). **SONG COLLECTIONS** (all publ. in N.Y.): ed. with W. Guthrie, *The People's Songbook* (1948); ed. *The Caroler's Songbag* (1952); ed. *American Favorite Ballads* (1961); *The Goofing Off Suite* (1961); *The Bells of Rhymney* (1964); *Bits and Pieces* (1965); *Oh Had I a Golden Thread* (1968); *Pete Seeger on Record* (1971). **BIBL.:** D. Dunaway, *How Can I Keep from Singing? P. S.* (N.Y., 1981; new ed., 1990).

Seeger, Ruth Crawford. See **Crawford (Seeger), Ruth Porter.**

Seeling, Hans, Bohemian pianist and composer; b. Prague, 1828; d. there, May 26, 1862. He went to Italy in 1852; then traveled in the East, returning to Europe in 1857; was in Paris in 1859; then in Germany; finally went back to Prague. He publ. many salon pieces which were successful.

Segal, Uri, Israeli conductor; b. Jerusalem, March 7, 1944. He studied violin and conducting at the Rubin Cons. in Jerusalem; then went to London and enrolled as a conducting student at the Guildhall School of Music (1966–69); later in Siena. In 1969 he won 1st prize in the Mitropoulos Competition in N.Y.; served as Leonard Bernstein's assistant with the N.Y. Phil. (1969–70); subsequently developed a fine career conducting major orchs. in Europe and America. He was principal conductor of the Philharmonia Hungarica in Marl (1979–84) and of the Bournemouth Sym. Orch. (1980–82).

Seger (also **Seeger, Seegr, Segert, Zeckert,** etc.), **Josef (Ferdinand Norbert),** eminent Czech organist, pedagogue, and composer; b. Řepín, near Mělník (baptized), March 21, 1716; d. Prague, April 22, 1782. He studied organ with Czernohorsky, counterpoint with Jan Zach and František Tuma, and thoroughbass with Felix Benda in Prague, where he also was a graduate in philosophy from the Univ. He was active in Prague as a violinist at St. Martin's and as an organist at the Crusader's Church (1745–82); also served as organist at the church in Tyn (1741?–82). He was greatly esteemed as a teacher of composition; his most important pupils were Josef Jelínek, Karl Kopřiva, J.A. Koželuch, Jan Kuchař, Vincenc Mašek, Josef Mysliveček, and Václav Pichl. He composed many preludes, toccatas, and fugues for organ; D. Türk ed. 8 toccatas and fugues (1793; modern ed. in Musica Antiqua Bohemica); he also wrote sacred music and pedagogical works.

Segerstam, Leif (Selim), prominent Finnish conductor and composer; b. Vaasa, March 2, 1944. He studied composition with Fougstedt, Kokkonen, and Englund at the Sibelius Academy in Helsinki; also took courses in violin and conducting (diplomas in both, 1963); then continued his training at the

Juilliard School of Music in N.Y., where he received instruction in violin from Persinger, in composition from Overton and Persichetti, and in conducting from Morel (diploma, 1964; postgraduate diploma, 1965); also attended Susskind's conducting course at Aspen (summer 1964). Returning to Helsinki, he conducted at the Finnish National Opera (1965–68); concurrently taught conducting at the Klemetti Inst. of Music. In 1968 he became a conductor at the Royal Theater in Stockholm, being made its principal conductor in 1970 and its music director in 1971; then held the post of 1st permanent conductor at the Deutsche Oper in Berlin (1972–73); subsequently was general manager of the Finnish National Opera (1973–74). He was chief conductor of the Austrian Radio Sym. Orch. in Vienna (1975–82) and of the Finnish Radio Sym. Orch. in Helsinki (1977–87); also served as Generalmusikdirektor of the State Phil. in Rheinland-Pfalz (1983–89). In 1989 he became chief conductor of the Danish Radio Sym. Orch. in Copenhagen. Segerstam describes his music as being "freely pulsative."

WORKS: ORCH.: *A Legend* for String Orch. (1960); *Divertimento* for String Orch. (1963); *Pandora*, essay (1967; also a ballet); *Concerto Serioso* for Violin and Orch. (1967); *Capriccio* for Sopranino and Small Orch. (1967); *Seven Red Moments* for Trumpet and Orch. (1967); *Patria* (1973; Stockholm, April 27, 1974); *Two; onwards: inwards, outwards, (upwards, downwards). . . aroundwards . . towards . . .* for 2 Pianos and Orch., with 2 String Sections (1974; Helsinki, April 29, 1975); *Screams & Visions* (1975); *Visions of Inner Time* for Piano and String Orch. (1976); *Concerto-Fantasia* for Violin, Piano, and Small Orch. (1977); 2 piano concertos: No. 1, *Thoughts 1978* (1977); No. 2, *Orchestral Diary Sheet No. 11d* (1981); syms.: No. 1, *Orchestral Diary Sheets Nos. 33, 34 & 36* (1977–78); No. 2, *Orchestral Diary Sheet No. 22* (1980); No. 3, *Orchestral Diary Sheet No. 23* (1981); No. 4, *Orchestral Diary Sheets Nos. 24, 25 & 26* (1981); No. 5, *Orchestral Diary Sheet No. 12* (1982); No. 6, *Sinfonia piccola* or *Orchestral Diary Sheet No. 7* (1982); No. 7, *Orchestral Diary Sheet No. 15* (1982); No. 8, *Orchestral Diary Sheets Nos. 1 & 2* (1984); No. 9, *Sinfonia piccola* or *Orchestral Diary Sheet No. 3* (1985); No. 10, "Three Times . . ." (1986); No. 11, *Small Symphony* or *Orchestral Diary Sheet No. 5* (1986); No. 12, *Orchestral Diary Sheet No. 9* (1986); No. 14, *Moments of Peace III* or *Orchestral Diary Sheet No. 44* (1987); *Plays* for 2 Amplified Cellos, Percussion, and Small Orch. (1978; Vienna, Feb. 1, 1978); *Orchestral Diary Sheet No. 11a*, Cello Concerto No. 1 (1981), *11b*, Violin Concerto No. 2 (1981), *11c*, with Violin and Cello Obbligato (1981), *11d*, Piano Concerto No. 2 (1981), *11e*, with Organ Solo (1981), *11f*, with Trombone Solo (1981), *11g*, with Clarinet Solo (1981), *11h*, with Alto Saxophone Solo (1981); *Orchestral Diary Sheet No. 14a*, Cello Concerto No. 2 (1983), *14b*, Violin Concerto No. 3 (1983), *14c*, Trumpet Concerto (1983), *14d*, Concerto No. 2 for 2 Pianos and Orch. (1983), *14e*, Clarinet Concerto No. 2 (1983); Violin Concerto No. 4 (1983; also as a Flute Concerto and a Viola Concerto, 1985); *Orchestral G-A-L-A music (with B-A-S-F)* (1985); "So It Feels . . ." or Violin Concerto No. 5 (1985; also as Oboe Concerto, Cello Concerto No. 3, Viola Concerto No. 2, Piano Concerto No. 3, Concerto for 2 Pianos and Orch. No. 3, and as a chamber ensemble work); "A Last Melodioso" for Violin and Orch. (1985); Violin Concerto No. 6, "Feelings & Visions" (1986; also as Cello Concerto No. 4); *Thoughts 1987* or *Orchestral Diary Sheet No. 49* (1987); *Thoughts 1988* or *Orchestral Diary Sheet No. 19* (1988); *Thoughts 1989* or *Orchestral Diary Sheet No. 18* (1989).

CHAMBER: String quartets: No. 1 (1962); No. 2 (1964); No. 3 (1965–66); No. 4 (1966); No. 5, *Three hundred sixty Degrees*, the *Lemming Quartet* (1970); No. 6 (1974); No. 7 (1974–75); No. 8 (1975–76); No. 9 (1976); No. 10, *A Contemplation of a Serious Matter*, homage to Ives (1976); No. 11, *Voces con visione* (1977); No. 12 (1977); No. 13 (1978); No. 14 (1978); No. 15 (1978); No. 16, *A Moment of String Time* (1979); No. 17 (1979); No. 18 (1979); No. 19 (1979); No. 20 (1980); No. 21 (1980); No. 22 (1980); No. 23 (1980); No. 24 (1982); No. 25, (Another) *Mad Song* with Mezzo-soprano or Soprano (1982); No. 26, I

for "Four . . . or One & Three . . ." and II for "Two & Two mostly . . ." (1986); *Improvisation* for Violin (1965); *Myriasm* for 2 Violins (1965); *Poem* for Violin or Cello, and Piano (1966); *3 Moments of Parting* for Various Instruments and Piano (1973); *A Nnnnooooowwws* for Wind Quintet (1973); *At the Border* for a String Instrument and Piano (1974); *Another of Many Nnnnooooowwws* for Wind Quintet (1975); *Moments kept Remaining* for Flute and Cello or Violin and Clarinet, and Piano (1975); *Visions of Inner Time* for Violin, Viola, Cello, and Piano (1976); 2 piano trios (1976, 1977); *Tranquil Traumas* Nos. 1, 4 & 5 for 2 Violins (1976–77) and Nos. 2 & 3 for 2 Double Basses (1976); *Music for 4 Friends* for Violin, Trumpet, Horn, and Percussion (1976); *Epitaph* No. 1 for Cello (1977), No. 2a for Violin and Piano (1977), No. 2b for Cello and Piano (1977), No. 2c for Saxophone and Piano (1977), No. 2d for Bass Clarinet and Piano (1977), and No. 3 for Violin and Piano (1981); 3 string trios (1977–78); *8 Noëms* for Violin or Cello and Piano (1977–86); *Signature* for 3 Trumpets (1978); *A Moment of Brasstime* for 2 Trumpets and 2 Trombones (1978); *24 Episodes* for Various Instrumental Combinations (1978–85); also piano pieces, organ music, and many songs.

Seghers, François-Jean-Baptiste, Belgian violinist and conductor; b. Brussels, Jan. 17, 1801; d. Margency, near Paris, Feb. 2, 1881. He studied in Brussels with Gensse, and at the Paris Cons. with Baillot; founded in Brussels the Société Ste.-Cécile in 1848, and conducted it until 1854. Its concerts of orch. and choral works were famous; after the founder's death, it rapidly declined and was soon dissolved.

Segni, Julio, important Italian organist, harpsichordist, and composer, known as **Julio da Modena;** b. Modena, 1498; d. Rome, July 23, 1561. He studied singing with Bidon da Asti in Modena, where he sang plainchant at the Cathedral (1513), and also was a pupil of Giacomo Fogliano (1512–14). He later went to Rome, where his performances at the Vatican were acclaimed; after serving as 1st organist at San Marco in Venice (1530–32), he entered the service of Guido Ascanio Sforza, Cardinal of S. Fiore, in Rome. Segni was regarded as the foremost organist of his time. A number of his impressive ricercari have been publ. in modern eds.

BIBL.: G. Roncaglia, "Di J. Fogliani e J. S.: Documenti," *Rivista Musicale Italiana*, XLVI (1942).

Segovia, Andrés, Marquis of Salobreña, great Spanish guitarist and teacher; b. Linares, near Jaen, Feb. 21, 1893; d. Madrid, June 2, 1987. He took up the guitar at a very early age; his parents opposed his choice of instrument and saw to it that he received lessons in piano and cello instead, all to no avail; while taking courses at the Granada Inst. of Music, he sought out a guitar teacher; finding none, he taught himself the instrument; later studied briefly with Miguel Llobet. He made his formal debut in Granada at the age of 16; then played in Madrid in 1912, at the Paris Cons. in 1915, and in Barcelona in 1916; toured South America in 1919. He made his formal Paris debut on April 7, 1924; his program included a work written especially for him by Roussel, entitled simply *Segovia*. He made his U.S. debut at N.Y.'s Town Hall on Jan. 8, 1928; subsequently toured all over the world, arousing admiration for his celebrated artistry wherever he went. He did much to reinstate the guitar as a concert instrument capable of a variety of expression; made many transcriptions for the guitar, including one of Bach's *Chaconne* from the Partita No. 2 for Violin. He also commissioned several composers to write works for him, including Ponce, Turina, Castelnuovo-Tedesco, Moreno-Torroba, Villa-Lobos, and Tansman. He continued to give concerts at an advanced age; made appearances in 1984 in celebration of the 75th anniversary of his professional debut. He received many honors during his long career; a commemorative plaque was affixed in 1969 to the house where he was born, honoring him as the "hijo predilecto de la ciudad." In 1981 King Juan Carlos of Spain made him Marquis of Salobreña; that same year the Segovia International Guitar Competition was founded in his honor. In 1985 he was awarded the Gold Medal of the Royal Phil. Society of London. He wrote *Andrés*

Segovia: An Autobiography of the Years 1893–1920 (N.Y., 1976). **BIBL.:** V. Borri, *The S. Technique* (N.Y., 1972); G. Wade, *S.: A Celebration of the Man and His Music* (London, 1983); A. Kozinn, "A. S.," *Ovation* (April 1984); G. Wade, *Maestro S.* (London, 1986).

Seiber, Mátyás (György), significant Hungarian-born English composer; b. Budapest, May 4, 1905; d. (in an automobile accident) Kruger National Park, Johannesburg, South Africa, Sept. 24, 1960. Of a musical family, he learned to play the cello at home; later entered the Budapest Academy of Music, where he studied composition with Kodály (1919–24). During the following years, he traveled as a member of a ship's orch. on a transatlantic liner; visited Russia as a music journalist. From 1928 to 1933 he taught composition at the Frankfurt Hoch Cons.; was the cellist in the Lenzewski Quartet, which specialized in modern music; then was again in Budapest. The catastrophic events in Germany and the growing Nazi influence in Hungary forced him to emigrate to England in 1935, where he quickly acquired a group of loyal disciples; was co-founder of the Society for the Promotion of New Music (1942) and founder-conductor of the Dorian Singers (1945); taught at Morely College (from 1942). His early music followed the national trends of the Hungarian School; later he expanded his melodic resources to include oriental modes and also jazz, treated as folk music; by the time he arrived in England, he had added dodecaphony to his oeuvre, though he used it in a very personal, lyrical manner, as in his cantata *Ulysses* and his 3rd String Quartet. He publ. the books *Schule für Jazz-Schlagzeug* (Mainz, 1929) and *The String Quartets of Béla Bartók* (London, 1945).
WORKS: STAGE: *Eva spielt mit Puppen,* opera (1934); also 2 operettas; *The Invitation,* ballet (London, Dec. 30, 1960). **ORCH.:** *Besardo Suite* No. 1 (1940); *Besardo Suite* No. 2 for String Orch. (1941); *Transylvanian Rhapsody* (1941); *Pastorale and Burlesque* for Flute and String Orch. (1941–42); *Fantasia concertante* for Violin and String Orch. (1943–44; London, Dec. 3, 1945); *Notturno* for Horn and String Orch. (1944); Concertino for Clarinet and String Orch. (1951; London, May 11, 1954); *Elegy* for Viola and Small Orch. (1955); *3 Pieces* for Cello and Orch. (1956); *Improvisations* for Jazz Band and Sym. Orch. (in collaboration with J. Dankworth; London, June 2, 1959). **VOCAL:** Cantata, *Ulysses,* after Joyce, for Tenor, Chorus, and Orch. (1946–47; London, May 27, 1949); *4 French Folksongs* for Soprano and Strings (1948); *Faust* for Soprano, Tenor, Chorus, and Orch. (1949); *Cantata secularis* for Chorus and Orch. (1949–51); chamber cantata, *3 Fragments from "A Portrait of the Artist as a Young Man,"* after Joyce, for Narrator, Wordless Chorus, and Instrumental Ensemble (1957); also arrangements of folk songs; songs with instrumental or orch. accompaniments. **CHAMBER:** 3 string quartets (1924; 1934–35; *Quartetto Lirico,* 1948–51); *Sarabande and Gigue* for Cello and Piano (1924); *Sonata da camera* for Violin and Cello (1925); *Serenade* for 2 Clarinets, 2 Bassoons, and 2 Horns (1925); *Divertimento* for Clarinet and String Quartet (1928); *2 Jazzolettes* for 2 Saxophones, Trumpet, Trombone, Piano, and Percussion (1929, 1933); *4 Hungarian Folksongs* for 2 Violins (1931); *Fantasy* for Cello and Piano (1940); *Fantasia* for Flute, Horn, and String Quartet (1945); *Andantino and Pastorale* for Clarinet and Piano (1949); *Concert Piece* for Violin and Piano (1953–54); *Improvisation* for Oboe and Piano (1957); *More Nonsense,* after E. Lear, for Baritone, Violin, Guitar, Clarinet, and Bass Clarinet (1957); *Permutazioni a cinque* for Wind Quintet (1958); Violin Sonata (1960); piano pieces; also scores for over 25 films, including Orwell's *Animal Farm* (1954).
BIBL.: H. Keller, "M. S.," *Musical Times* (Nov. 1955); H. Wood, "The Music of M. S.," ibid. (Sept. 1970).

Seidel, Friedrich Ludwig, German organist, conductor, and composer; b. Treuenbrietzen, June 1, 1765; d. Charlottenburg, May 5, 1831. He studied with Benda in Berlin; served as organist of the Marienkirche (from 1792); became assistant conductor at the National Theater in 1801; was named music director of the royal chapel in 1808 and court Kapellmeister in 1822,

being pensioned in 1830. He composed the singspiel *Claudine von Villa Bella,* several operas, and other dramatic pieces; 3 ballets; incidental music; sacred works; chamber music; and piano pieces.

Seidel, Jan, Czech composer; b. Nymburk, Dec. 25, 1908. He was 1st attracted to architecture and graphic art; attended Alois Hába's classes in quarter-tone composition at the Prague Cons. (1936–40); then took private lessons in music theory with J.B. Foerster for a more traditional musical training. He was a composer, conductor, and pianist in E.F. Burian's Theater; acted as artistic adviser to the recording firm Esta (1938–45) and the Gramophone Corp. (1945–53); was chief of the Opera of the National Theater (1958–64); then served as dramatic adviser there. In 1976 he was made a National Artist by the Czech government. His String Quartet No. 2 is in the quarter-tone system, but most of his music is based on folksong tradition according to the doctrine of socialist realism.
WORKS: OPERA: *Tonka Šibenice* (Tonka the Gallows; 1964). **ORCH.:** Sym. No. 1, *Prologue* (1942); 2 oboe concertos (1955); 2 orch. suites from the film *The Piper of Strakonice* (1956, 1958); *Lovecká sinfonietta* (Hunting Sinfonietta) for Horn and Small Orch. (1965–66; Prague, March 14, 1973); Concerto for Flute, Strings, and Piano (1966); *Giocosa* (1972). **VOCAL:** 3 cantatas: *Call to Battle* (1946); *May Prelude* (1952); *Message to the Living* (1953); also numerous patriotic choruses and songs. **CHAMBER:** 4 string quartets: No. 1, with Solo Soprano (1930); No. 2, with Narration (1940); No. 3, *Chrysanthemums* (1943); No. 4 (1944); 2 wind quintets (1941, 1946); Violin Sonata (1950).

Seidel, Toscha, Russian-born American violinist and teacher; b. Odessa, Nov. 17, 1899; d. Rosemead, Calif., Nov. 15, 1962. He began to play the violin as a small child, and took lessons with Max Fiedelmann in Odessa; subsequently studied with Alexander Fiedelmann in Berlin, and then became a pupil of Leopold Auer at the St. Petersburg Cons. He made his U.S. debut at N.Y.'s Carnegie Hall on April 14, 1918; settled in the U.S., becoming a naturalized citizen in 1924; made many tours in Europe and the U.S.; also played in Australia. He suffered an irreversible mental illness and was confined to a sanatorium in California for several years before his death.

Seidl, Anton, famous Hungarian conductor; b. Pest, May 7, 1850; d. N.Y., March 28, 1898. He studied at the Univ. and at the Cons. in Leipzig; then was engaged by Hans Richter as chorus master at the Vienna Court Opera; Richter in turn recommended him to Wagner to assist in preparing the score and parts of the *Ring* tetralogy for the Bayreuth Festival of 1876. Returning to Leipzig, he was 1st conductor of its Opera (1879–82); in 1882 he was engaged by the impresario Angelo Neumann for a grand tour of Wagner's operas. From 1883 he conducted the Bremen Opera; in 1885 he was engaged to conduct the German opera repertoire at the Metropolitan Opera in N.Y. He made his American debut with *Lohengrin* there (Nov. 23, 1885); then conducted the American premieres of *Die Meistersinger von Nürnberg* (Jan. 4, 1886), *Tristan und Isolde* (Dec. 1, 1886), *Siegfried* (Nov. 9, 1887), and the *Ring* cycle (March 4–11, 1889). In 1891 he was engaged as conductor of the N.Y. Phil., and led it until his death (of ptomaine poisoning). Seidl was an excellent technician of the baton and established a standard of perfection rare in American orch. playing of that time; he introduced many unfamiliar works by German composers and conducted the world premiere of Dvořák's *New World Sym.* (N.Y., Dec. 15, 1893). He married the Austrian soprano Auguste Kraus (b. Vienna, Aug. 28, 1853; d. Kingston, N.Y., July 17, 1939; after vocal studies with Marchen, she made her operatic debut at the Vienna Court Opera in 1877, where she sang minor roles; then sang in Leipzig (1881–82), where she subsequently became a member of Neumann's Wagnerian company and married Seidl, it's conductor; sang at Her Majesty's Theatre in London in 1882 and then made her Metropolitan Opera debut in N.Y. as Elisabeth in *Tannhäuser* under her husband's direction, remaining on its roster until 1888. Among her best known roles were Elsa, Eva, Sieglinde, and Gutrune.

BIBL.: H. Krehbiel, *A. S.* (N.Y., 1898); H. Finck, ed., *A. S.: A Memorial by His Friends* (N.Y., 1899).

Seidl, Arthur, German writer on music; b. Munich, June 8, 1863; d. Dessau, April 11, 1928. He studied with Spitta and Bellermann in Berlin; completed his training at the Univ. of Leipzig (Ph.D., 1887, with the diss. *Vom Musikalisch-Erhabenen. Prolegomena zur Ästhetik der Tonkunst;* publ. in 1887; 2nd ed., 1907); was music critic of Munich's *Neueste Nachrichten* (1899–1903).

WRITINGS: *Zur Geschichte des Erhabenheitsbegriffs seit Kant* (1889); *Hat Richard Wagner eine Schule hinterlassen?* (1892); *Richard Strauss. Eine Charakterstudie* (with W. Klatte; 1896); *Moderner Geist in der deutschen Tonkunst* (1901; 2nd ed., 1913); *Wagneriana* (3 vols., 1901–2); *Moderne Dirigenten* (1902); *Kunst und Kultur* (1902); *Die Hellerauer Schulfeste und die "Bildungsanstalt Jaques-Dalcroze"* (1912); *Straussiana* (1913); *Ascania. Zehn Jahre in Anhalt* (1913); *Richard Wagners "Parsifal"* (1914); *Neue Wagneriana* (3 vols., 1914); *Hans Pfitzner* (1921); *Neuzeitliche Tondichter und zeitgenössische Tonkünstler* (2 vols. 1926).

BIBL.: L. Frankenstein, *A. S.* (Regensburg, 1913); B. Schuhmann, ed., *Musik und Kultur. Festschrift zum 50. Geburtstag A. S.s* (1913).

Seiffert, Max, eminent German musicologist; b. Beeskow an der Spree, Feb. 9, 1868; d. Schleswig, April 13, 1948. He studied musicology with Philipp Spitta at the Univ. of Berlin (Ph.D., 1891, with the diss. *J.P. Sweelinck und seine direkten deutschen Schüler;* publ. in Leipzig, 1891). He was ed.-in-chief of *Sammelbände der Internationalen Musik-Gesellschaft* (1903–14); with J. Wolf and M. Schneider, he ed. the *Archiv für Musikwissenschaft* (1918–26); also taught at Berlin's Hochschule für Musik and at the Akademie für Kirchen- und Schulmusik (from 1909); served as provisional director of the Fürstliches Forschungsintitut für Musikwissenschaft in Bückeburg (from 1921); after it became the Staatliches Institut für deutsche Musikforschung in Berlin in 1935, he served as its director until 1942. He publ. *Geschichte der Klaviermusik* (Berlin, 1899–1901), nominally the 3rd ed. of Weitzmann's history, but actually a new and valuable study. He contributed many editions to the Denkmäler Deutscher Tonkunst series (1892–1927); also ed. the works of Sweelinck (12 vols., 1895–1901). Festschrifts were publ. in his honor for his 70th (1938) and 80th (1948) birthdays.

Seifriz, Max, German violinist, conductor, and composer; b. Rottweil, Württemberg, Oct. 9, 1827; d. Stuttgart, Dec. 20, 1885. He served as court Kapellmeister to Prince Hohenzollern in Löwenberg (1854–69); then moved to Stuttgart as municipal music director. He publ., with E. Singer, a *Grosse theoretisch-praktische Violinschule* (2 vols., 1884–97); wrote a Sym. and choruses.

Seinemeyer, Meta, admired German soprano; b. Berlin, Sept. 5, 1895; d. Dresden, Aug. 19, 1929. She studied with Nikolaus Rothmühl and Ernst Grenzebach in Berlin; made her operatic debut there in *Orphée aux enfers* at the Deutsches Opernhaus (1918), where she continued to sing until 1925; also toured the U.S. with the German Opera Co. (1923–24); then was a member of the Dresden State Opera (from 1925); also appeared in South America (1926), at the Vienna State Opera (1927), and at London's Covent Garden (1929). She married the conductor Frieder Weissmann on her deathbed. Her voice possessed a silken quality and a natural expressiveness; she was particularly esteemed for her roles in operas by Wagner, Verdi, Puccini, and Strauss.

Seiss, Isodor (Wilhelm), German conductor, teacher, and composer; b. Dresden, Dec. 23, 1840; d. Cologne, Sept. 25, 1905. He studied piano with Friedrich Wieck and music theory with J. Otto. In 1870 he was appointed to the faculty of the Cologne Cons., where he conducted the concerts of the Musikalische Gesellschaft (1873–1900); among his students was

Willem Mengelberg. He publ. a number of useful piano studies in the bravura style (*Bravourstudien, Fantasie in Form einer Tokkata,* etc.); also an opera, *Der vierjährige Posten.*

Seixas (real name, **Vas**), **(José Antonio) Carlos de,** important Portuguese organist and composer; b. Coimbra, June 11, 1704; d. Lisbon, Aug. 25, 1742. He received his primary musical education from his father, whom he succeeded as organist at Coimbra Cathedral when he was 14; at 16 he was named organist at the royal chapel, a position he retained until his death; was knighted by John V of Portugal in 1738. He wrote a great number of keyboard sonatas (sometimes designated as "toccatas"), of which 88 are preserved. He knew Domenico Scarlatti personally, but was not demonstrably influenced by the Italian style of keyboard composition. Eighty keyboard sonatas by Seixas were ed. by S. Kastner in Portugaliae Musica (Lisbon, 1965); an overture, sinfonia, and Harpsichord Concerto were ed. in the same series (1969).

BIBL.: S. Kastner, *C. S.* (Coimbra, 1947); K. Heimes, *C. S.'s Keyboard Sonatas* (diss., Univ. of South Africa, 1967).

Séjan, Nicolas, French organist, teacher, and composer; b. Paris, March 19, 1745; d. there, March 16, 1819. He studied organ with his uncle, Nicolas-Gilles Forqueray, and harmony and improvisation with Louis Charles Bordier. In 1760 he became organist at St.-André-des-Arts; in 1764 he made his 1st appearance at the Concert Spirituel, where he earned a reputation as a virtuoso. In 1773 he was named one of the 4 organists at Notre Dame Cathedral; was also organist at the church of the Cordeliers (1773–76), St. Séverin (from 1782), St. Sulpice (1783–91), and the royal chapel (1790–91); also was the 1st prof. of organ at the École Royale de Chant (from 1789). He lost all of his posts during the Revolution, but succeeded in preventing the destruction of the organs in his care, and assisted the church musicians during the Reign of Terror. He was prof. of organ at the Paris Cons. from its founding in 1795 until 1802; was made organist at the Dôme des Invalides and at St. Sulpice in 1806, and also at the royal chapel in 1814. He publ. 6 sonates for Harpsichord and Violin ad libitum (Paris, c.1772; violin part not extant); *Recueil de pièces* for Harpsichord and Piano, *dans le genre gracieus ou gay* (Paris, 1784); 3 sonatas for Harpsichord or Piano (Paris, 1784; Nos. 1 and 3 with Violin and Cello obbligato).

BIBL.: C. Bouvet, "N. S. et Gervais François Couperin, organistes de l'Opéra," *Musique et théâtre* (1926); G. Favre, "Les Créateurs de l'école française de piano: N. S., 1745–1819," *Revue de Musicologie,* XVII/58 (1936).

Šejna, Karel, Czech conductor; b. Zálezly, Nov. 1, 1896; d. Prague, Dec. 17, 1982. He studied double bass with F. Cerný at the Prague Cons. (1914–20); also took private lessons in composition with K.B. Jirák. In 1921 he joined the Czech Phil. in Prague as principal double bass; later appeared as a conductor with it; in 1937 he was appointed its 2nd conductor; was its artistic director in 1949–50; then 2nd conductor again from 1950 until 1965; subsequently appeared with it as a guest conductor. He was particularly esteemed for his congenial interpretations of Czech music. In 1960 he was made an Artist of Merit by the Czech government.

Sekles, Bernhard, German conductor, composer, and teacher; b. Frankfurt am Main, March 20, 1872; d. there, Dec. 8, 1934. He studied with Knorr and Uzielli at the Hoch Cons. in Frankfurt, where he became a prof. of theory in 1896; from 1923 to 1933 he was director of the Cons.

WORKS: STAGE: OPERAS: *Scheherazade* (Mannheim, Nov. 2, 1917); *Die zehn Küsse* (Frankfurt, 1926). **BALLETS:** *Der Zwerg und die Infantin* (Frankfurt, 1913); *Die Hochzeit des Faun* (Wiesbaden, 1921). **ORCH.:** *Aus den Gärten der Semiramis,* symphonic poem; *Die vier Temperamente;* Sym.; *Sommergedicht; Kleine Suite; Serenade* for 11 Instruments. **CHAMBER:** *Passacaglia und Fuge* for String Quartet; Trio for Clarinet, Cello, and Piano; Violin Sonata; also songs; piano music.

Selby, Bertram Luard, English organist, composer, and teacher; b. Ightham, Kent, Feb. 12, 1853; d. Winterton, Dec.

26, 1918. He studied with Reinecke and Jadassohn at the Leipzig Cons.; filled various organ positions in London; was organist at the Rochester Cathedral.

Works: 2 operas: *The Ring* (1886) and *Adela* (1888); operetta ("duologue"), *Weather or no* (London, Aug. 10, 1896; very successful; also produced in Germany as *Das Wetterhäuschen*); 2 piano quintets; a Violin Sonata; piano pieces; organ works.

Selby, William, English organist and composer; b. in England, c.1738; d. Boston, Dec. 12, 1798. In 1760 he was appointed organist at Holy Sepulcher Church in London; from 1765 to 1770 he publ. both sacred and secular music there. He settled in the U.S. in 1771, becoming organist at King's Chapel in Boston; in 1773–74, was organist at Trinity Church in Newport, R.I.; in 1776, returned to Boston as organist at Trinity Church, and from 1778 was organist at the Stone Chapel (formerly King's Chapel). He led an extremely active musical life in Boston as an organist and conductor, giving many concerts of secular music as well as religious, and generally raising the musical standards of the area. He composed and publ. 9 Psalms and hymns for Solo Voice; 8 religious and secular choral works; 6 songs; 9 pieces for Guitar and 3 for Keyboard.
Bibl.: O. Sonneck, *Early Concert-life in America* (Leipzig, 1907); D. McKay, "W. S., Musical Emigré in Colonial Boston," *Musical Quarterly* (Oct. 1971).

Selig, Robert Leigh, American composer; b. Chicago, Jan. 29, 1939; d. Cambridge, Mass., Jan. 15, 1984. He studied at Northwestern Univ., and later (1966–67) took doctoral courses at Boston Univ., where he studied with Gardner Read. He held Guggenheim fellowships twice, in 1971 and in 1977. In 1968 he was appointed to the faculty at the New England Cons. of Music in Boston.
Works: *Mirage* for Trumpet and String Orch. (1967); *Variations* for Brass Quintet (1967); *Islands* for Chorus and Chamber Orch. (1968); Concerto for Rock Group and Orch. (1969); *Rhapsody* for Flute, Violin, and Clarinet (1970); *Orestes: Flight into Fury* for Trumpet and Piano (1970); Quartet for Voice, Flute, Cello, and Percussion (1971); Sym. for Woodwind Quintet (1971); *Chocorua*, opera for Voice, Chorus, and Chamber Orch. (1972); *Pometacomet, 1676* for Band (1974–75); *Survival Fragments* for Soprano and Piano (1976); Sonata, 3 *Cryptic Portraits* for Piano (1977); Music for Brass Instruments (1977); *Reflections from a Back Window* for Piano (1980); *After the Ice* for Soprano and Piano (1981).

Seligmann, Hippolyte-Prosper, French cellist and composer; b. Paris, July 28, 1817; d. Monte Carlo, Feb. 5, 1882. He studied at the Paris Cons., taking 1st prize in 1836; made extensive tours. He publ. 6 *études caractéristiques*, fantasies, caprices, etc., for cello, with piano; 2 albums of songs.

Sellars, Peter, provocative American theater producer; b. Pittsburgh, Sept. 27, 1957. His fascination with the stage began at age 10, when he began working with a puppet theater; he then attended Harvard Univ., where his bold theatrical experiments resulted in his expulsion from student theater groups. He gained wide notice when he produced Gogol's *The Inspector General* for the American Repertory Theater in Cambridge, Mass., in 1980. During the 1981–82 season, he staged a highly controversial mounting of Handel's *Orlando,* in which the protagonist is depicted as an astronaut. In 1983 he became director of the Boston Shakespeare Co. and in 1984 of the American National Theater Co. at the Kennedy Center in Washington, D.C. In 1987, at the Houston Grand Opera, he produced John Adam's opera *Nixon in China,* which he then mounted in other U.S. cities and at the Holland Festival in 1988; that same year he jolted the Glyndebourne Festival with his staging of Nigel Osborne's *Electrification of the Soviet Union.* He oversaw the Los Angeles Festival in 1990.
Bibl.: M. Gray, "P. S.: Opera's *Enfant Terrible* Reaches Mark Two," *Ovation* (Sept. 1988).

Selle, Thomas, German composer; b. Zörbig, near Bitterfeld, March 23, 1599; d. Hamburg, July 2, 1663. He was educated in Delitzsch and at the Univ. of Leipzig (matriculated, 1622);

was Kantor in Heide, and then rector in Wesselburen (1625–34); after serving as Kantor in Itzehoe (1634–41), he settled in Hamburg as Kantor at the Johanneum and as civic director of church music (from 1641). Selle wrote a vast amount of vocal music, both sacred and secular, including the *St. John Passion* for 5 to 6 Voices (1641; enl. 1643; ed. in Das Chorwerk, XXVI, 1934), historically important as the 1st such work to include instrumental interludes. He prepared a collected MS edition of his works, consisting of 16 partbooks and 3 books of tablature; it includes 282 compositions, 193 to German texts and 89 to Latin texts (1646–53).
Bibl.: S. Günther, *Die geistliche Konzertmusik von T. S. nebst einer Biographie* (diss., Univ. of Giessen, 1935); E. Schild, *Geschichte der protestantischen Messenkomposition im 17. und 18. Jahrhundert* (diss., Univ. of Giessen, 1935); J. Birke, *Die Passionsmusiken von T. S.* (diss., Univ. of Hamburg, 1957); idem, "Zur Geschichte der Passionsaufführungen in Hamburg bis zum Tode des Kantors T. S. (1663)," *Zeitschrift des Vereins für Hamburgische Geschichte,* XLIV (1958).

Sellner, Joseph, German oboist, conductor, teacher, and composer; b. Landau, Bavaria, March 13, 1787; d. Vienna, May 17, 1843. He played the oboe in an Austrian army regiment; then at the German Opera in Prague (1811–17); subsequently settled in Vienna, where he played at the Court Opera (from 1817) and taught at the Cons. (from 1821), conducting its student concerts (until 1838). His *Theoretischpraktische Oboen-Schule* is a fine method for oboe; he also publ. a Concerto and 3 concertinos for Oboe and Orch.; and a Concerto for 2 Oboes.

Selmer, Johan Peter, Norwegian conductor and composer; b. Christiania, Jan. 20, 1844; d. Venice, July 21, 1910. After studying law in Norway, he took a course under Ambroise Thomas at the Paris Cons. (1869–70); later studied at the Leipzig Cons. with Richter (1871–74). From 1883 to 1886 he conducted Christiania's Musikforeningen. He was greatly influenced by Berlioz, Liszt, and Wagner; his symphonic pieces bear the imprint of late Romanticism; like Grieg, he made use of Norwegian folk material.
Works: ORCH.: All 1st perf. in Christiania: *L'année terrible,* scène funèbre (Sept. 30, 1871); *Alastor* (Oct. 24, 1874); *Karneval i Flandern* (Nov. 8, 1890); *In den bergen,* suite (1892); *Prometheus,* symphonic poem (Oct. 29, 1898; his most important work). CHORAL WITH ORCH.: *Nordens aand* (The Spirit of the North; 1872); *Hilsen til Nidaros* (Greeting to Nidaros; 1883); *Selvmorderen og pilgrimene* (The Suicide and the Pilgrims; 1888); *Tyrekerne gaar nod Athen* (The Turks Go Towards Athens; c. 1893); various works for Men's Voices and Women's Voices; about 100 songs; etc.
Bibl.: P. Merkel, *Der norwegische Komponist J. S.: Ein Lebensbild* (Leipzig, 1904); S. Lind, *J. S. som komponist* (diss., Univ. of Oslo, 1950).

Selva, Blanche, French pianist and teacher; b. Brive, Jan. 29, 1884; d. St. Amand, Tallende, Puy-de-Dome, Dec. 3, 1942. She studied piano at the Paris Cons., and took courses in composition with d'Indy at the Paris Schola Cantorum. She was one of the strongest propagandists of modern French music early in the 20th century; she presented programs of piano works by Debussy, Ravel, and others; also became a proponent of Czech music. She taught at the Schola Cantorum (1901–22); then at the Strasbourg Cons. and Prague Cons. She publ. several books dealing with piano technique; her compendium, *L'Enseignement musical de la technique du piano* (4 vols., Paris, 1922) is valuable; also publ. disquisitions on musical form: *La Sonate* (Paris, 1913); *Quelques mots sur la sonate* (Paris, 1914); *Les Sonates de Beethoven* (Barcelona, 1927); also a monograph on Déodat de Sévérac (Paris, 1930).

Selvaggi, Rito, Italian composer and pedagogue; b. Noicattaro di Bari, May 22, 1898; d. Zoagli (Genoa), May 19, 1972. He studied piano and composition at the Liceo Musicale in Pesaro, and later took lessons with Busoni. He was a prof. at the Parma Cons. (1934–38), then director of the Palermo Cons. (1938–

58) and the Pesaro Cons. (1959–68). He composed the operas *Maggiolata veneziana* (Naples, 1929) and *Santa Caterina de Siena* (1947); the music drama *Eletta* (1947); the oratorio *Estasi francescana* (1926); a "trittico sinfonico," *La Natività di Gesù* (1935); *Sonata drammatica* for Viola and Piano (1954); *Elegie* for Cello, Chorus, and Orch., in memory of Toscanini (1957); numerous choruses and piano transcriptions of Classical syms.

Sembrich, Marcella (real name, **Prakseda Marcelina Kochańska;** Sembrich was her mother's maiden name), famous Polish-American soprano; b. Wiśniewczyk, Galicia, Feb. 15, 1858; d. N.Y., Jan. 11, 1935. Her father, Kasimir Kochański, was a village musician; she began studying piano with him when she was 4 and soon thereafter violin as well; at 10 she played both instruments in public; at 11 she entered the Lemberg Cons., where her principal teacher was Wilhelm Stengel (b. Lemberg, Aug. 7, 1846; d. N.Y., May 15, 1917), whom she later married (May 5, 1877). In 1874 she played and sang for Liszt, who urged her to train her voice. She then studied singing with Viktor Rokitansky in Vienna, and with G.B. Lamperti, the younger, in Milan. She made her operatic debut in Athens on June 3, 1877, as Elvira in Bellini's *I Puritani* under the stage name of Sembrich. Following training in the German repertory from Richard Lewy in Vienna, she sang Lucia di Lammermoor at the Dresden Court Opera in 1878, remaining on its roster until 1880. On June 12, 1880, she chose that role for her 1st appearance at London's Covent Garden, where she sang for 5 seasons. It was also as Lucia di Lammermoor that she made her U.S. debut at the Metropolitan Opera in N.Y. on Oct. 24, 1883. Thereafter she sang at the principal opera houses of Germany, Austria, France, Spain, Scandinavia, and Russia until 1898, then was a regular member of the Metropolitan Opera from 1898 to 1900, and again from 1901 to 1909. Her farewell appearance in opera was at the Metropolitan on Feb. 6, 1909. In subsequent years she devoted herself to lieder recitals, remaining active until her retirement in 1917. She was also active as a teacher, serving as head of the vocal depts. at both the Curtis Inst. of Music in Philadelphia and at the Inst. of Musical Art in N.Y. Her operatic repertoire included some 40 roles, the most outstanding being Susanna, Zerlina, the Queen of the Night, Rosina, Gilda, Violetta, Eva in *Die Meistersinger von Nürnberg,* Elsa in *Lohengrin,* and Mimi, as well as her incomparable Lucia.
BIBL.: G. Armin, *M. S. und Herr Prof. Julius Hey* (Leipzig, 1898); H. Owen, *A Recollection of M. S.* (N.Y., 1950).

Semet, Théophile (-Aimé-Emile), French composer; b. Lille, Sept. 6, 1824; d. Corbeil, near Paris, April 15, 1888. He studied with Halévy in Paris; was a percussionist in the Opéra orch. there; wrote popular songs before producing the following operas for Paris: *Nuits d'Espagne* (Dec. 30, 1857); *Gil Blas* (March 23, 1860); *Ondine* (Jan. 7, 1863); *La Petite Fadette* (Sept. 11, 1869).

Semkow, Jerzy, prominent Polish conductor; b. Radomsko, Oct. 12, 1928. He studied at the Univ. of Krakow (1946–50) and at the Leningrad Cons. (1951–55); after serving as assistant conductor of the Leningrad Phil. (1954–56), he conducted at Moscow's Bolshoi Theater (1956–58); also continued his training with Kleiber in Prague, Serafin in Rome, and Walter in Vienna. He was artistic director and chief conductor of the Warsaw National Opera (1959–62); then was chief conductor of the Copenhagen Royal Theater (1966–76). In 1968 he made his U.S. debut as a guest conductor of the Boston Sym. Orch. He served as music director of the St. Louis Sym. Orch. (1976–79), artistic director of the RAI orch. in Rome (1979–83), and music adviser and principal conductor of the Rochester (N.Y.) Phil. (1985–89). His guest conducting engagements took him all over the world. He is especially admired for his performances of Polish and Russian scores, particularly of works from the late Romantic era.

Senaillé (also **Senaillié, Senallié,** etc.), **Jean Baptiste,** French violinist and composer; b. Paris, Nov. 23, 1687; d. there, Oct. 15, 1730. Although the spelling "Senaillé" is widely used, he signed his name "Senaillié," as did his father; contemporary eds. of his music invariably used the form "Senaillié." He most likely studied with his father, whom he succeeded in the "24 violons du roi" in 1713; after an Italian sojourn (c.1717–19), he resumed his position in Paris in 1720; also appered at the Concert Spirituel (1728–30). His music reflects Italian influences. He publ. 50 violin sonatas (with continuo) in 5 books (1710–27).
BIBL.: L. de La Laurencie, *L'École française de violon* (vol. I, Paris, 1922); A. Moser, *Geschichte des Violinspiels* (1923; 2nd ed., rev. and enl., 1966–67); A. Kish, *J.B. Senallié: His Life, his Time and his Music* (diss., Bryn Maur College, 1964).

Sender (Barayón), Ramon, Spanish-born American poet, novelist, writer on music, and composer; b. Madrid, Oct. 29, 1934. He was sent to the U.S. in 1939 as a Spanish Civil War refugee. After studies in piano with George Copeland (1948–52) and in composition with Elliott Carter, he took courses at the Accademia di Santa Cecilia in Rome (1952–53); also had private lessons with Alexei Haieff. Returning to the U.S., he had lessons with Harold Shapero and Henry Cowell; also studied at Brandeis Univ. (1953–54) and at the San Francisco Cons. of Music (B.Mus., 1962). In 1962 he cofounded (with Morton Subotnick) the San Francisco Tape Music Center, which gave important 1st performances of works by Oliveros, Riley, Reich, and others; while serving as its co-director, he continued his composition studies with Darius Milhaud at Mills College in Oakland, Calif. (M.A., 1965), where the Tape Music Center was moved in 1966. In 1966 Sender moved to Sonoma, Calif., where he undertook research into acoustic vocalizations and comparative religions; also taught hatha-yoga, meditation, and mantric chant at the Morning Star Range, a shelter for Haight-Ashbury youth; in 1969 he became co-music director of Wheeler's Ranch; wrote a series of essays on the Open Land Movement (*The Open Land Church,* 1971; etc.); also taught courses in electronic music composition at Sonoma State Univ. (1971); traveled to South America and to India, where he studied yoga and Sanskrit. From 1976 to 1980 he served as assistant director of the Occidental Community Choir. In addition to his work as a composer, Sender devoted much time to writing essays, novels, and poetry; among his literary works are *Zero Weather* (1980) and *Death in Zamora, a Son's Search for His Mother* (1984). In 1983 he received an NEA grant for creative prose; from 1981 to 1984 he wrote book and music reviews for the *San Francisco Chronicle.*
WORKS: *Kore* for 2-channel Tape and Liquid Projections (1961); *Balances* for Amplified and Prepared String Trio and String Bass, and Mixer Console (1962); Violin Sonata (1962); *Time Fields,* study in multiple, simultaneous rhythms for Piano, Cello, String Bass, Oboe, Clarinet, and Percussion (1963); *City Scape,* a 6-hour work for approximately 10 Actor-Musicians, House, 2 Parks, and 2 Trucks (with A. Martin and K. Dewey; 1963); *Information* for 2 Pianos and Narrator (1963); *Transformation,* a collaborative theater piece (with M. Subotnick and R. Levine; 1963); *Desert Ambulance* for Accordion, 2-channel Tape, Movie, Slides, and Liquid Projections (with A. Martin; 1964); *In the Garden* for 2-channel Tape, Viola, Clarinet, and Visual Score (with A. Martin; 1965); *Loopy Gamelan on C,* "O 'C' Can You Say," for Children's Chorus and 4 Cassette Recorders loaded with Loopies (1976); *Great[10] Grandpa Lemuel's Death-Rattle Reincarnation Blues* for Amplified Accordion and Dixieland Band with Ampex PR-10 Tape Duplicator (or equivalent) (1981); *Our Mother the Earth* for Chorus, to a text by Tewa Pueblo Indians (1983); *I Have a Dream* for Chorus, to a text by Martin Luther King, Jr. (1984).

Sendrey, Albert Richard, American composer, son of **Aladár Szendrei;** b. Chicago, Dec. 26, 1911. He studied in Leipzig, Paris, and London; was an arranger for film companies in Paris (1935–37) and London (1937–44) before settling in Hollywood in 1944. Among his original works are *Oriental Suite* for Orch. (1935); 3 syms.; piano pieces; cello pieces.

Sendrey, Alfred. See **Szendrei, Aladár.**

Senesino–Serato

1684

Senesino (real name, **Francesco Bernardi**), celebrated Italian castrato alto who took his professional name from his birthplace; b. Siena, c.1680; d. probably there, c.1759. He began his career in Venice (1707–8); after singing in Bologna (1709) and Genoa (1709, 1712), he again appeared in Venice (1713–14); then sang in Naples (1715–16). In 1717 he was called to the Dresden court, where he was a prominent singer until he was dismissed for unconscionable behavior during a rehearsal in 1720. Handel heard him during a visit to Dresden, and engaged him for the Royal Academy of Music opera productions in London, where Senesino made his debut at the King's Theatre on Nov. 19, 1720. He remained with the company until 1728, although his arrogance caused bitter disputes with Handel. After singing in Venice (1729), he was reengaged by Handel and Heidegger for the new Academy opera productions in London (1730–33). Senesino's dislike for Handel prompted him to lend his support to the Opera of the Nobility, with which he was associated from 1733 to 1736. After appearances in Florence (1737–39), he retired from the operatic stage (1740). Although Senesino was personally disagreeable to many of his colleagues, there was no denying the greatness of his vocal abilities; indeed, in spite of their disagreements, Handel wrote no fewer than 17 roles for him.

BIBL.: F. Haböck, *Die Kastraten und ihre Gesangskunst* (Stuttgart, 1927); A. Heriot, *The Castrati in Opera* (London, 1956).

Senff, Barthof (Wilhelm), German music publisher and editor; b. Friedrichshall, near Coburg, Sept. 2, 1815; d. Badenweiler, June 25, 1900. As a young man he entered Kistner's music publ. house in Leipzig, advancing to the position of managing clerk; began editing the *Signale für die Musikalische Welt*, a trial number appearing in Dec. 1842; the 1st regular number was issued on Jan. 1, 1843. This was one of the most important German music periodicals of the 19th century; it includes reports of musical events, special articles, and correspondence from the music centers of the world; many celebrated musicians contributed to it. He remained ed. until his death, and publication continued (1917–18 excepted) until 1941. He founded his own publishing business in 1847; his catalogue included original publications of works by Schumann, Liszt, Anton Rubinstein, Raff, et al. His niece, Marie Senff, managed the firm until 1907, when she sold it and the *Signale* to Simrock of Berlin.

Senfl, Ludwig, important Swiss composer; b. probably in Basel, c.1486; d. Munich, between Dec. 2, 1542 and Aug. 10, 1543. He became a choirboy in Emperor Maximilian I's Hofkapelle in 1496; went with the Kapelle to Konstanz in 1507, where he was Isaac's copyist; he apparently accompanied the latter to Italy about 1509, but by 1513 he was a member of the Kapelle in Vienna as Isaac's successor; after the emperor's death in 1519, he was dismissed the following year. In 1523 he settled in Munich as composer to the Bavarian Hofkapelle of Duke Wilhelm IV; under his direction, the Hofkapelle was raised to an exalted standard. Senfl was one of the great masters of the motet and lied of his era. He ed. and completed Isaac's *Choralis Constantinus;* also ed. the historically-important *Liber selectarum cantionum* (1520), one of the earliest books with musical notation publ. in Germany.

WORKS: 5 *Salutationes Domini nostri Hiesu Christi,* motets in 4 voices (Nuremberg, 1526); *Varia carminum genera, quibus tum Horatius tum alii egreii poetae harmoniis composita* for 4 Voices (Nuremberg, 1534; 9 odes are in P. Hofhaimer's *Harmonie poeticae,* 1539); *Magnificat octo tonorum* for 4–5 Voices (Nuremberg, 1537); 81 numbers are in *121 newe Lieder* (Nuremberg, 1534), and 64 numbers in *115 guter newer Liedlein* (Nuremberg, 1544); also single compositions in various collections of the period. W. Gerstenberg et al. began ed. his complete works (Wolfenbüttel, 1937–61).

BIBL.: T. Kroyer, *L. S. und sein Motettenstil* (Munich, 1902); H. Moser, "Instrumentalismen bei L. S.," *Musikwissenschaftliche Beiträge: Festschrift für Johannes Wolf* (Berlin, 1929); idem, "Der Altmünchner Tonmeister L. S.," *Süddeutsche Monatshefte* (1930); E. Löhrer, *Die Messen von L. S.* (Lichtensteig, 1938); H. Birtner, "Sieben Messen von L. S.," *Archiv für Musikforschung,* VII (1942); H. Zenck, "L. S. zur 400. Wiederkehr seines Todesjahres," *Deutsche Musikkultur,* VIII (1943–44); W. Gerstenberg, "Bemerkungen zu S.s Motetten," ibid., IX (1944); idem, "Motetten- und Liedstil bei L. S.," *International Musicological Society Congress Report,* IV, Basel 1949; E. Dreyer, *L. S.s melodische Arbeit und ihre Tradition* (diss., Univ. of Leipzig, 1958); W. Gerstenberg, "Senfeliana," *Festschrift Helmuth Osthoff* (Tutzing, 1961); M. Bente, *Neue Wege der Quellenkritik und die Biographie L. S.s* (Wiesbaden, 1968); W. Seidel, *Die Lieder L. S.s* (Bern and Munich, 1969).

Senilov, Vladimir, Russian composer; b. Viatka, Aug. 8, 1875; d. Petrograd, Sept. 18, 1918. He was a student of jurisprudence at the Univ. of St. Petersburg; went to Leipzig, where he studied with Hugo Riemann (1895–1901); returning to Russia, he studied composition with Rimsky-Korsakov and Glazunov at the St. Petersburg Cons., graduating in 1906. His works include a lyric drama, *Vasili Buslayev;* an opera, *Hippolytus,* after Euripides; *In Autumn,* symphonic poem; *Mtziri,* symphonic poem after Lermontov; *Pan,* symphonic poem; *The Scythians,* symphonic poem; 3 string quartets; choral pieces; songs.

Serafin, Tullio, eminent Italian conductor; b. Rottanova de Cavarzere, Venice, Sept. 1, 1878; d. Rome, Feb. 2, 1968. He studied at the Milan Cons.; made his conducting debut in Ferrara in 1898. In 1901 Toscanini engaged him as one of his assistant conductors at La Scala in Milan. Later he was principal conductor of La Scala (1909–14, 1917–18); from 1924 to 1934 he was a conductor at the Metropolitan Opera in N.Y. In 1934 he became chief conductor and artistic director of the Rome Opera, a post he retained until 1943; then engaged as artistic director of La Scala (1946–47). From 1956 to 1958 he conducted at the Chicago Lyric Opera; in 1962 he was named artistic adviser of the Rome Opera. He was especially authoritative in the Italian operatic repertoire. As an artistic adviser, he helped launch the careers of Maria Callas and several other noted artists. He publ. (with A. Toni) 2 vols. on the history of Italian opera, *Stile, tradizioni e convenzioni del melodramma italiano del Settecento e del l'Ottocento* (Milan, 1958–64).

BIBL.: T. Celli and G. Pugliese, *T. S.: il patriarca del melodramma* (Venice, 1985).

Seraphin (also **Serafin, Serafino**), **Sanctus (Santo),** celebrated Italian violin maker; b. Udine, Nov. 1, 1699; d. Venice, c.1758. He was a pupil of Niccolò Amati; settled in Venice about 1720; signed his name on the labels as "Sanctus Seraphinus Nicolai Amati Cremonensis Alumnus." His instruments contained elements characteristic of Stainer and Niccolo Amati. His nephew Giorgio Seraphin (Serafino) (b. Venice, c.1726; d. there, Jan. 25, 1775) worked in Venice in the 1st half of the 18th century.

Serassi, Giuseppe, Italian organ builder, known as "il Vecchio;"b. Como, 1694; d. Crema, Aug. 1, 1760. He settled in Bergamo about 1730, and built the organs at San Pellegrino, Lodi, and the Santuario di Caraveggio. His son, Andrea Luigi Serassi (b. Bergamo, May 19, 1725; d. there, 1799), carried on the business; built the cathedral organs in Crema, Fossano, Parma, and Vigevano. His son, Giuseppe Serassi, known as "Il Giovane" (b. Bergamo, Nov. 16, 1750; d. there, Feb. 19, 1817), continued the family tradition and built about 350 organs. He publ. a description of the new organ at Como (1808), with a short history of the organ and good rules for registration; also brought out a pamphlet, *Sugli organi* (Bergamo, 1816). After his death, the family tradition was carried on by his son and grandson; the business was dissolved in 1870.

Serato, Arrigo, Italian violinist; b. Bologna, Feb. 7, 1877; d. Rome, Dec. 27, 1948. He began his training with his father, the cellist Francesco Serato (1843–1919), then studied with Federico Sarti at the Bologna Cons. (diploma, 1894). He was mainly active as a chamber music player; formed the Trio Bolognese with Sarti and Gustavo Tofano, and the Quartetto

Bolognese with Sarti, Massarenti, and Angelo Consolini; then settled in Berlin, where he took a course in violin study with Joachim, and was also a member of Joachim's string quartet. He returned to Italy in 1915, and taught master classes at the Accademia di Santa Cecilia in Rome (1926–48); also taught postgraduate courses at the Accademia Chigiana in Siena.

BIBL.: A. Della Corte, *A. S. violinista* (Siena, 1950).

Serauky, Walter (Karl-August), eminent German musicologist; b. Halle, April 20, 1903; d. there, Aug. 20, 1959. He studied musicology in Halle and with Schering at the Univ. of Leipzig (Ph.D., 1929, with the diss. *Die musikalische Nachahmungsästhetik im Zeitraum von 1700 bis 1850*; publ. in Münster, 1929); completed his Habilitation in 1932 at the Univ. of Halle, where he subsequently served as a prof. (from 1940); then was director of the musicological inst. at the Univ. of Leipzig (from 1949), which post he shared with Besseler (from 1956). He contributed valuable essays to various German publications; also publ. *Samuel Scheidt in seinen Briefen* (Halle, 1937) and *G.F. Händel: sein Leben, sein Werk* (Kassel and Leipzig, 1956–58).

Serebrier, José, Uruguayan-American conductor and composer; b. Montevideo, Dec. 3, 1938. He began to conduct at the age of 12; went to the U.S. in 1950; studied composition with Vittorio Giannini at the Curtis Inst. of Music in Philadelphia (1956–58) and conducting with Antal Dorati in Minneapolis; also took conducting lessons with Monteux at his summer residence in Maine. He subsequently conducted guest engagements in the U.S., South America, and Europe; gave the 1st performance in Poland of the 4th Sym. of Charles Ives. He was associate conductor of the American Sym. Orch. in N.Y. (1962–67), composer-in-residence of the Cleveland Orch. (1968–70), and music director of the Cleveland Phil. (1968–71). He was principal guest conductor of the Adelaide Sym. Orch. (from 1982); was founder and artistic director of the International Festival of the Americas (1984). In 1969 he married the American soprano **Carole Ann Farley.**

WORKS: Quartet for Saxophones (1955); *Pequeña música* for Wind Quintet (1955); Sym. No. 1 (1956); *Momento psicológico* for String Orch. (1957); *Suite canina* for Wind Trio (1957); Sym. for Percussion (1960); *The Star Wagon* for Chamber Orch. (1967); *Nueve* for Double Bass and Orch. (1970); *Colores mágicos,* variations for Harp and Chamber Orch., with "Synchrona" images (Washington, D.C., May 20, 1971); *Preludio fantastico y danza magica* for 5 Percussion (1973).

Sereni, Mario, Italian baritone; b. Perugia, March 25, 1928. He studied at the Accademia di Santa Cecilia in Rome; also in Siena with Mario Basiola; made his debut at the Florence May Festival in 1953, and then sang throughout Italy. In 1956 he sang at the Teatro Colón in Buenos Aires. He made his Metropolitan Opera debut in N.Y. on Nov. 9, 1957, as Gérard in *Andrea Chénier;* also sang in London, Vienna, Milan, Chicago, Houston, Dallas, and other opera centers.

Seress, Rezsö, Hungarian composer of popular songs; b. Budapest, Nov. 3, 1899; d. there, Jan. 12, 1968. He earned his living by playing piano and singing in restaurants and nightclubs; acquired fame in 1936 by his song *Gloomy Sunday,* which was banned in Hungary and several other countries because its morbid tune precipitated a wave of Sunday suicides among the young. Seress himself jumped out of a window from the 2nd floor of his Budapest apartment on Jan. 8, 1968 (a Monday, not a Sunday), and died 4 days later.

Sérieyx, Auguste (Jean Maria Charles), French teacher, writer on music, and composer; b. Amiens, June 14, 1865; d. Montreux, Feb. 19, 1949. He studied in Paris at the Schola Cantorum with Gédalge and d'Indy; taught composition there (1900–1914). He collaborated with d'Indy on his monumental *Cours de composition* (3 vols., Paris, 1897–1933); publ. *Les Trois Etats de la tonalité* (Paris, 1910) and *Cours de grammaire musicale* (Paris, 1925). His compositions include both sacred and secular vocal works, a Violin Sonata, piano pieces, and songs.

BIBL.: J. Matthey, *Inventaire de fonds musical A. S.* (Lausanne, 1974).

Serini, Giovanni Battista, Italian teacher and composer; b. Cremona, c.1724; place and date of death unknown. He studied with Galuppi; was Kapellmeister at the court of Count Wilhelm zu Schaumberg-Lippe in Bückeburg; may have also been in the service of Robert d'Arcy, 4th Earl of Holdernesse (Yorkshire). Among his extant works are sinfonies, 6 harpsichord concertos, 6 sonatas for Flute and Basso Continuo, 3 harpsichord sonatas, and vocal pieces.

BIBL.: J. Pilgrim, "A Note on G.B. S.," *Musical Times* (Aug. 1964).

Serkin, Peter (Adolf), outstanding American pianist, son of **Rudolf Serkin;** b. N.Y., July 24, 1947. At age 11 he enrolled at the Curtis Inst. of Music in Philadelphia, where he studied with M. Horszowski, L. Luvisi, and his father (graduated, 1964); made his debut as a soloist with A. Schneider and a chamber orch. at the Marlboro (Vt.) Music Festival (1958); later studied there with the flutist M. Moyse, and also received additional piano training from Karl Ulrich Schnabel. He made his N.Y. debut as a soloist with Schneider and his chamber orch. (Nov. 29, 1959); his N.Y. recital debut followed (March 27, 1965). In 1973 he formed the group Tashi ("good fortune" in Tibetan) with clarinetist Richard Stoltzman, violinist Ida Kavafian, and cellist Fred Sherry; the group toured extensively, giving performances of contemporary music in particular. After leaving the group in 1980, Serkin renewed his appearances as a soloist and recitalist. While he championed modern music, he acquired a distinguished reputation as an interpreter of both traditional and contemporary scores. He excels in works by Mozart, Beethoven, Schubert, Brahms, Stravinsky, Schoenberg, Messiaen, Takemitsu, Peter Lieberson, and others. He also made appearances as a fortepianist. In 1983 he was awarded the Premio of the Accademia Musicale Chigiana in Siena.

BIBL.: M. Kimmelman, "P. S.," *Ovation* (Jan. 1986); *Current Biography* (June 1986).

Serkin, Rudolf, eminent Austrian-born American pianist and pedagogue of Russian descent, father of **Peter (Adolf) Serkin;** b. Eger, March 28, 1903; d. Guilford, Vt., May 8, 1991. He studied piano with Richard Robert and composition with Joseph Marx and Arnold Schoenberg in Vienna; made his debut as a soloist with Oskar Nedbal and the Vienna Sym. Orch. at age 12; his career began in earnest with his Berlin appearance with the Busch Chamber Orch. in 1920; thereafter he performed frequently in joint recitals with Adolf Busch, whose daughter he married in 1935. He made his U.S. debut in a recital with Busch at the Coolidge Festival in Washington, D.C., in 1933; then made a critically acclaimed appearance as a soloist with Toscanini and the N.Y. Phil. (Feb. 20, 1936). In 1939 he became a naturalized U.S. citizen. After World War II, he pursued an international career; appeared as a soloist with all the major orchs. of the world, gave recitals in the leading music centers, and played in numerous chamber music settings. In 1939 he was appointed head of the piano dept. at the Curtis Inst. of Music in Philadelphia; was its director from 1968 to 1976. In 1950 he helped to establish the Marlboro (Vt.) Music Festival and school, and subsequently served as its artistic director. In 1985 he celebrated his 70th anniversary as a concert artist. He received the Presidential Medal of Freedom in 1963; in 1988 he was awarded the National Medal of Arts. The authority and faithfulness of his interpretations of the Viennese classics placed him among the masters of the 20th century.

Serly, Tibor, Hungarian-born American violist, conductor, teacher, music theorist, and composer; b. Losonc, Nov. 25, 1901; d. London, Oct. 8, 1978. His family moved to the U.S. in 1905, and he became a naturalized citizen in 1911. He received his early musical training from his father, Lajos Serly, founder of the 1st Hungarian theater in N.Y. and his own Hungarian-German opera company; then returned to Hungary, where he enrolled in the Royal Academy of Music in Budapest; there he took courses with Koessler, Hubay, Bartók, and Kodály (graduated, 1925). Upon his return to the U.S., he was a violist in the Cincinnati Sym. Orch. (1926–27); then was a violinist (1928–35) and assistant conductor (1933–35) with the Philadelphia Orch.; subsequently was a violinist in the NBC Sym. Orch. in N.Y. (1937–38). After studying conducting with Scherchen in Europe (1934), he led various concerts in N.Y.; was primarily active as a private teacher from 1938. When Bartók settled in the U.S. in 1940, Serly became his closest friend and adviser; after Bartók's death in 1945, Serly completed the last 17 measures of Bartók's 3rd Piano Concerto, and totally reconstructed and orchestrated Bartók's Viola Concerto from 13 unnumbered MS pages. In 1948 he devised a system of composition called Modus Lascivus. Although the medieval Modus Lascivus was synonymous with the C-major scale, Serly expanded its connotation to include enharmonic modulation. He wrote the treatises *A Second Look at Harmony* (1965), *Modus Lascivus: The Road to Enharmonicism* (1976), and *The Rhetoric of Melody* (with N. Newton; 1978). Shortly before his death, he arranged Bartók's Viola Concerto for cello and orch.

WORKS: ORCH.: *Transylvania Rhapsody* (1926); Viola Concerto (1929); 2 syms.: No. 1 (1931; Budapest, May 13, 1935, composer conducting); No. 2 for Winds, Brass, and Percussion (1932); *6 Dance Designs* (1932–33; Budapest, May 13, 1935); *Transylvanian Suite* for Chamber Orch. (1935); *Sonata concertante* for Strings (1935–36); *Colonial Pageant* and *Alarms and Excursions*, 2 suites (1936–37); *The Pagan City*, symphonic poem (1932–38; in collaboration with John Klenner); *Midnight Madrigal* for Trumpet and Orch. (1939); *American Elegy*, based on *Taps* (1945); *Rhapsody* for Viola and Orch. (1946–48; N.Y., Feb. 27, 1948); *Miniature Suite* for 12 Winds and Percussion (1947; revision of a discarded *Rhapsody* of 1927); *American Fantasy of Quodlibets* (1950); Concerto for Trombone and Chamber Orch. (1952–54); *Lament: Homage to Bartók* (1955); Concerto for 2 Pianos and Orch. (1943–58); Concerto for Violin, Winds, and Orch. (1953–58; Portland, Oreg., Nov. 30, 1978); *Symphonic Variations for Audience and Orch.* (1956); *Little Christmas Cantata* for Audience and Orch. (1957); String Sym. (1956–58); *Symphony in 4 Cycles* for Strings (1960); *Concertino 3 × 3* for Piano and Chamber Orch. (1964–65; Syracuse, N.Y., Jan. 13, 1967); *Canonic Fugue in 10 Voices on 10 Tones* for Strings (1971; Portland, Oreg., June 5, 1977); *Music for 2 Harps and Strings* (1976). **CHAMBER:** Violin Sonata (1923); String Quartet (1924); Sonata for Solo Violin (1947); Trio for Clarinet, Violin, and Piano (1949); *Chorale in 3 Harps* (1967); *Rondo Fantasy in Stringometrics* for Violin and Harp (1969); piano pieces, including *40 Piano Études in Modus Lascivus* (1946–60; 1st complete perf. by his 2nd wife, Miriam Molin, N.Y., May 4, 1977). **BALLETS:** *Mischchianza* (1937); *Ex Machina* (1943); *Cast Out* (1973). **VOCAL:** *4 Songs from Chamber Music* for Soprano and Orch., after James Joyce (1926); *Strange Story* for Mezzo-soprano and Orch., after E. Wylie (1927); *Anniversary Cantata on a Quodlibet* for Voices and Small Orch. (1966); *Consovowels 1–5*: No. 1 for Soprano (1968); Nos. 2 and 3 for Soprano and Clarinet (1970, 1971); Nos. 4 and 5 for Soprano and Violin (both 1974).

BIBL.: E. Jablonski, "T. S.," *International Musician*, LXXV/5 (1976).

Sermilä, Jarmo (Kalevi), Finnish trumpeter and composer; b. Hämeenlinna, Aug. 16, 1939. He was active as a jazz musician before studying at the Hämeenlinna School of Music; subsequently received composition instruction from Tauno Marttinen and Joonas Kokkonen at the Sibelius Academy in Helsinki (diploma, 1975) and from František Kovaříček in Prague; concurrently pursued training in musicology and literature at the Univ. of Helsinki (M.A., 1975). He was artistic director of the Finnish Radio's Experimental Music Studio in Helsinki (1973–79); also was composer-in-residence for the city of Hämeenlinna (1977–82); served as vice-president of the Soc. of Finnish Composers (from 1981). He also pursued a career as a trumpeter, performing in both classical and jazz settings. His compositions, which range from aleatory to jazz pieces, employ various contemporary means.

WORKS: STAGE: *The Wolf Bride*, electro-acoustic ballet (1980). **ORCH.:** *Early Music* for Strings (1971); *Pentagram* for Trumpet and Orch. (1972); *Mimesis 2* (1974); *Cornologia* for 24 to 44 Horns (1975); *Counterbass* for Double Bass and String Orch. (1975); *Manifesto* (1977); *Time Machine* for 4 Trumpets, 4 Trombones, 4 Horns, Baritone Horn, Tuba, and 4 Percussion (1977); *A Circle of the Moon* for Oboe and Orch. (1979); *LABOR!* (1982); *Due divertimenti* for Oboe, Trumpet, and String Orch. (1983); *Transformations* for String Orch. (1984); *La Place Revisitée* for Flute or Alto Flute, Clarinet or Bass Clarinet, 2 Percussionists, Strings, and Tape (1984); *Rilievo 4* for Small Orch. (1989). **CHAMBER:** *Monody* for Horn and Percussion (1970); *Homage to EV* for 2 Horns, 2 Trumpets, 3 Trombones, and 2 Percussionists (1971); *Crisis* for Clarinet, 2 Violins, Viola, and Cello (1972); *Colors & Contrasts* for Flute, Violin, and Piano (1976); *Thus I Saw This* for Flute, Oboe, Clarinet, Bassoon, and Horn (1977); *Invocation* for English Horn, Baritone, and Tape (1978); *Dissimilitudes* for 2 Violins, 2 Violas, and 2 Cellos (1980); *A Canonized Reflection* for 2 Flutes, 2 Oboes, 2 Clarinets, 2 Horns, 2 Trumpets, 2 Trombones, and 2 Percussionists (1980); *The Mythic Man* for 5 Percussionists (1982); *The Sermon* for Trumpet and 4 Reciters (1983); *A Prague Thoroughfare* for Electric Guitar, 2 Violins, Viola, and Cello (1983); *. . . and an elk was formed by Hiisi* for 2 Trombones, 2 Percussionists, and Tape (1984); *Jean-Éduard en face du fait accompli* for Soprano, Alto, Tenor, and Baritone Saxophones (1986); *Movimenti e ritornelli* for 2 Violins, Viola, and Cello (1986); *Ego I* for Violin, Double Bass, and Accordion (1988); *Final Conclusion* for Trumpet and Tape (1988); also vocal works, electro-acoustic music, and jazz pieces.

Sermisy, Claudin or **Claude de,** significant French composer; b. c.1490; d. Paris, Sept. 13, 1562. He served as a cleric at the Saint-Chapelle in Paris in 1508; also was a singer in the private chapel of Louis XII, and may have traveled abroad with the King's chapel. After serving as a canon at Notre-Dame-de-la-Rotonde in Rouen, he went to the parish church of Cambron in the Amiens diocese in 1524. In 1532 he returned to Paris as sous-maître at the royal chapel; also held the 11th canonry of the Saint-Chapelle from 1533. He was an outstanding composer of both sacred and secular music. A number of his chansons, masses, and motets were publ. in contemporary collections. G. Allaire and I. Cazeaux ed. a complete collection of his works in Corpus Mensurabilis Musicae, LXII/1 (1970–74).

BIBL.: G. Allaire, *The Masses of Claudin d.S.* (diss., Boston Univ., 1960); I. Cazeaux, *The Secular Music of Claudin d.S.* (diss., Columbia Univ., 1961); G. Allaire, "Les Messes de Claudin d.S. (c.1490–1562)," *Revue de Musicologie*, LIII (1967).

Serocki, Kazimierz, prominent Polish composer; b. Toruń, March 3, 1922; d. Warsaw, Jan. 9, 1981. He studied piano with Szpinalski and composition with Sikorski at the Lodz Cons. (graduated, 1946); then received further training in composition from Boulanger and in piano from Lévy in Paris (1947–48). He was active as a pianist in Poland (1946–51); formed, with Tadeusz Baird and Jan Krenz, the modernistic Group '49, dedicated to the cause of the avant-garde; in 1956 he was one of the organizers of the audaciously futuristic "Warsaw Autumn" Festivals. In the interim he toured as a concert pianist. In his early music, he fell into the fashionable neo-Classical current strewn with tolerable dissonances and spiked with bristling atonalities; experimented with Webernized dodecaphonies before molding his own style of composition, an amalgam of pragmatic serialism and permissible aleatory procedures, while maintaining an air of well-nigh monastic nominalism in formal strictures and informal structures; in some pieces, he makes incursions into the exotic field of American jazz.

WORKS: *Symphonic Scherzo* (1948); *Triptych* for Chamber Orch. (1949); *4 tańce ludowe* (4 People's Dances) for Chamber

Orch. (1949); *Romantic Concerto* for Piano and Orch. (1950); 2 syms.: No. 1 (1952) and No. 2, *Symphony of Songs*, for Soprano, Baritone, Chorus, and Orch. (Warsaw, June 11, 1953); Trombone Concerto (1953); Sinfonietta for 2 String Orchs. (1956); *Musica concertante* for Chamber Orch. (1958); *Episodes* for Strings and 3 groups of Percussion (1958–59); *Segmenti* for 12 Winds, 6 Strings, Piano, Celesta, Harpsichord, Guitar, Mandolin, and 58 Percussion Instruments (1960–61); *Symphonic Frescoes* (1963); *Forte e piano*, music for 2 Pianos and Orch. (1967; Cologne, March 29, 1968); *Dramatic Story* for Orch. (1968–71; Warsaw, Sept. 23, 1971); *Fantasia elegiaca* for Organ and Orch. (1971–72; Baden-Baden, June 9, 1972); Sonatina for Trombone and Orch. (1972–73; Strasbourg, Dec. 19, 1975); *Concerto alla cadenza* for Recorder and Orch. (1975); *Ad Libitum*, 5 pieces for Orch. (1976; Hamburg, Sept. 17, 1977); *Pianophonie* for Piano, Electronic Sound Transformation, and Orch. (1976–78; Metz, Nov. 18, 1978); *3 melodie Kurpiowskie* (3 Melodies from Kurpie) for 6 Sopranos, 6 Tenors, and Chamber Orch. (1949); 2 cantatas: *Mazowsze* (1950) and *Murarz warszawski* (1951); *Serce nocy* (Heart of the Night), cycle for Baritone and Piano (1956); *Oczy powietrza* (Eyes of the Wind), cycle for Soprano and Orch. or Piano (1957–58); *Niobe* for 2 Narrators, Chorus, and Orch. (1966); *Poezje* (Poems) for Soprano and Chamber Orch. (1968–69); *Suite* for 4 Trombones (1953); *Continuum*, sextet for 123 Percussion Instruments manipulated by 6 Multimanual Percussionists (1965–66); *Swinging Music* for Clarinet, Trombone, Cello or Double Bass, and Piano (1970); *Phantasmagoria* for Piano and Percussion (1970–71); *Impromptu fantastique* for 6 Flutes, Mandolins, Guitars, Percussionists, and Piano (1973–74); Piano Sonatina (1952); Piano Sonata (1955); *A piacere* for Piano (1963).

Seroff, Victor, Russian-born American writer on music; b. Batumi, Caucasus, Oct. 14, 1902; d. N.Y., May 10, 1979. He studied law at the Univ. of Tiflis; then took piano lessons with Moriz Rosenthal in Vienna and Theodore Szanto in Paris; eventually settled in N.Y. and became an American citizen.

Writings: All publ. in N.Y.: *Dmitri Shostakovich: The Life and Background of a Soviet Composer* (1943); *The Mighty Five: The Cradle of Russian National Music* (1948); *Rachmaninoff* (1950); *Maurice Ravel* (1953); *Debussy, Musician of France* (1956); *Hector Berlioz* (1967); *Prokofiev: A Soviet Tragedy* (1968); *Mussorgsky* (1968); *Franz Liszt* (1970).

Bibl.: M. Werner, *To Whom It May Concern: The Story of V.I.S.* (N.Y., 1931).

Serov, Alexander (Nikolaievich), important Russian music critic and composer; b. St. Petersburg, Jan. 23, 1820; d. there, Feb. 1, 1871. He studied law; also took cello lessons with Karl Schuberth; became a functionary in the Ministry of Justice and served in St. Petersburg (1840–45), Simferopol, Crimea (1845–48), and Pskov (1848–51). He never took lessons in composition, except a correspondence course in counterpoint with Joseph Hunke, but achieved a certain mastery in harmony and orchestration by studying the classics. In 1851 he began writing critical articles on music, and soon became an important figure in Russian journalism; in 1856 he became ed. of the *Musical and Theatrical Monitor*. In 1858 he made his 1st trip abroad, visiting Germany and Bohemia; the following year made another German visit, and also traveled in Austria and Switzerland; during this journey he met Wagner, whose ardent admirer he became and remained to the end of his career; expounded Wagner's ideas in Russian publications and engaged in bitter polemics with those who did not subscribe to his views, including his old friend and schoolmate Vladimir Stasov. He started very late in the field of composition; inspired by the performance of a biblical play, *Judith*, by an Italian troupe at St. Petersburg in 1861, he resolved to write an opera on this subject, essaying an Italian libretto, but later deciding on a Russian text. *Judith* was produced in St. Petersburg on May 28, 1863, with excellent success, but although Serov intended to emulate Wagner in the music, the style of *Judith* was closer to Meyerbeer. Quite different was Serov's 2nd opera,

Rogneda, written on a Russian subject, in a distinctly national idiom, with plentiful use of Russian folk songs. *Rogneda* was staged in St. Petersburg on Nov. 8, 1865, and won a spectacular success; the Tsar Alexander II attended a subsequent performance and granted Serov an annual stipend of 1,000 rubles for it. He then began the composition of another Russian opera, *Vrazhya sila* (Malevolent Power), but death (as a result of heart failure) overtook him when the 5th act was still incomplete; the opera was finished by N.T. Soloviev and produced in St. Petersburg on May 1, 1871. All 3 operas of Serov retain their popularity in Russia but are unknown elsewhere. Serov wrote further an Ave Maria for Adelina Patti (1868); a Stabat Mater; incidental music to *Nero*; *Plyaska Zaporozhtsev* (Dance of the Zaporozh Cossacks) for Orch. (1867); *Ouverture d'une comédie* for Piano, 4-hands; and a few other small pieces. A selection from his writings was publ. in 4 vols. (St. Petersburg, 1892–95). In 1863 Serov married a Cons. pupil, Valentina Bergmann (1846–1924), who was the 1st Russian woman to compose operas: *Uriel Acosta* (Moscow, 1885) and *Ilya Murometz* (Moscow, March 6, 1899; with Chaliapin in the title role). She helped to ed. and publ. Serov's posthumous works; wrote essays; publ. a number of piano pieces and a book of memoirs (St. Petersburg, 1914) under the name Valentina Serova.

Bibl.: N. Findeisen, *A.N.S.: His Life and Music* (St. Petersburg, 1900; 2nd ed., 1904); V. Serova, *A.N.S.* (St. Petersburg, 1914); G. Khubov, *The Life of A.N.S.* (Moscow, 1950); G. Abraham, "The Operas of S.," *Essays Presented to Egon Wellesz* (Oxford, 1966); R. Taruskin, "Opera and Drama in Russia: The Case of S.'s *Judith*," *Journal of the American Musicological Society*, XXXII (1979).

Serpette, (Henri Charles Antoine) Gaston, French composer and music critic; b. Nantes, Nov. 4, 1846; d. Paris, Nov. 3, 1904. He studied with Ambroise Thomas at the Paris Cons., taking the Premier Grand Prix de Rome in 1871 with the cantata *Jeanne d'Arc*. From 1874 he produced in Paris a steady progression of light operas, of which the following enjoyed a modicum of success: *La branche cassée* (Jan. 23, 1874); *Le manoir du Pic-Tordu* (May 28, 1875); *Le moulin du vert-galant* (April 12, 1876); *La petite muette* (Oct. 3, 1877); *Le petit chaperon rouge* (Oct. 10, 1885); *Adam et Eve* (Oct. 6, 1886); *Le demoiselle du téléphone* (May 2, 1891); *Shakespeare* (Nov. 23, 1899).

Serrano y Ruiz, Emilio, Spanish conductor, teacher, and composer; b. Vitoria, March 13, 1850; d. Madrid, April 8, 1939. He studied at the Madrid Cons., and taught piano and composition there (1870–1920); also conducted sym. concerts in Madrid. He wrote 5 operas: *Mitridates* (Madrid, 1882); *Doña Juana la Loca* (Madrid, 1890); *Irene de Otranto* (Madrid, Feb. 17, 1891); *Gonzalo de Córdoba* (Madrid, Dec. 6, 1898); *La Maja de Rumbo* (Buenos Aires, Sept. 24, 1910); a zarzuela, *La bejarana* (in collaboration with F. Alonso); Sym. (1887); Piano Concerto (1904); String Quartet (1908); songs.

Serrao, Paolo, Italian pedagogue and composer; b. Filadelfia, Catanzaro, 1830; d. Naples, March 17, 1907. He studied with Mercadante at the Naples Cons., and taught there from 1863. His 1st opera to be performed was *Pergolesi* (Naples, July 19, 1857), followed by *La duchessa di Guisa* (Naples, Dec. 6, 1865) and *Il figliuol prodigo* (Naples, April 23, 1868); also composed an oratorio, *Gli Ortonesi in Scio* (1869); *Omaggio a Mercadante*, funeral sym. (1871); passion, *Le tre ore d'agonia*; much church music.

Serres, Louis (Arnal) de, French composer and teacher; b. Lyons, Nov. 8, 1864; d. Néronde, Loire, Dec. 25, 1942. He studied at the Paris Cons. with Taudou (harmony) and Franck (organ); joined the faculty of the Schola Cantorum in 1900; when the institution was reorganized in 1935 as the École César Franck, he became its director. His compositions include *Les Heures claires* for Voice and Orch.; *Les Caresses* for Orch.; choruses, motets, and songs.

Servais, (Adrien-) François, famous Belgian cellist, teacher, and composer, father of **Joseph Servais;** b. Hal, near Brussels,

June 6, 1807; d. there, Nov. 26, 1866. He studied at the Brussels Cons.; played in a Brussels theater orch.; then went to Paris, where he gave a concert in 1834 with brilliant success; on May 25, 1835, he played his own Cello Concerto at a Phil. Society concert in London; subsequently made a grand tour of Europe; spent several years in Russia as a concert player, even reaching Siberia. He was appointed prof. at the Brussels Cons. in 1848, and taught many pupils who became distinguished artists. His adopted son was **François (Franz Matheiu) Servais**. He wrote 2 cello concertos, 16 fantasias for Cello and Orch., 6 études and 14 duos for Cello and Piano (with Gregoir), 6 caprices for Cello and Cello ad libitum, 3 duos for Violin and Cello (with Léonard), and a duo for Violin and Cello (with Vieuxtemps).

Servais, François (Franz Matheiu), French composer and conductor; b. St. Petersburg, c.1847; d. Asnières, near Paris, Jan. 14, 1901. It was claimed for him that he was an illegitimate son of Liszt and Princess Carolyne Sayn-Wittgenstein, but nothing in her voluminous correspondence with Liszt indicates that she was an expectant mother. However it might be, he was adopted by **(Adrien-) François Servais** and assumed his name. He studied cello with Kufferath at the Brussels Cons., and won the Belgian Prix de Rome in 1873 with the cantata *La mort du Tasse*. He founded the Concerts d'Hiver in Brussels; was a champion of Wagner, several of whose operas he introduced to Brussels. He wrote an opera, *L'Apollonide*, later titled *Ión* (Karlsruhe, 1899).

Bibl.: E. Michotte, *Au souvenir de F. S.* (Paris, 1907).

Servais, Joseph, Belgian cellist, teacher, and composer, son of **(Adrien-) François Servais;** b. Hal, near Brussels, Nov. 23, 1850; d. there, Aug. 29, 1885. He was a pupil of his father at the Brussels Cons., where he won a premier prix in cello (1866); made his debut in a joint recital with him in Warsaw (1867); then went to Weimar, where he played in the court orch. (1868–70); from 1872, served as a prof. at the Brussels Cons. He wrote a Cello Concerto (unfinished) and a String Quartet.

Sessions, Roger (Huntington), eminent American composer and teacher; b. Brooklyn, Dec. 28, 1896; d. Princeton, N.J., March 16, 1985. He studied music at Harvard Univ. (B.A., 1915); took a course in composition with Horatio Parker at the Yale School of Music (B.M., 1917); then took private lessons with Ernest Bloch in Cleveland and N.Y.; this association was of great importance for Sessions; his early works were strongly influenced by Bloch's rhapsodic style and rich harmonic idiom verging on polytonality. He taught music theory at Smith College (1917–21); then was appointed to the faculty of the Cleveland Inst. of Music, 1st as assistant to Ernest Bloch, then as head of the dept. (1921–25). He lived mostly in Europe from 1926 to 1933, supporting himself on 2 Guggenheim fellowships (1926, 1927), an American Academy in Rome fellowship (1928), and a Carnegie Foundation grant (1931); also was active with Copland in presenting the Copland-Sessions Concerts of contemporary music in N.Y. (1928–31), which played an important cultural role at that time. His subsequent teaching posts included Boston Univ. (1933–35), the New Jersey College for Women (1935–37), Princeton Univ. (1935–44), and the Univ. of Calif. at Berkeley (1944–53); returned to Princeton as Conant Professor of Music in 1953 and as co-director of the Columbia-Princeton Electronic Music Center in N.Y. in 1959; subsequently taught at the Juilliard School of Music in N.Y. (1965–85); also was Bloch Prof. at Berkeley (1966–67) and Norton Prof. at Harvard Univ. (1968–69). In 1974 he received a special citation of the Pulitzer Award Committee "for his life's work as a distinguished American composer." In 1982 he was awarded a 2nd Pulitzer Prize for his *Concerto for Orchestra*. In his compositions, Sessions evolved a remarkably compact polyphonic idiom, rich in unresolvable dissonances and textural density, and yet permeated with true lyricism. In his later works, he adopted a *sui generis* method of serial composition. The music of Sessions is decidedly in advance of his time; the difficulty of his idiom, for both performers

and listeners, creates a paradoxical situation in which he is recognized as one of the most important composers of the century, while actual performances of his works are exasperatingly infrequent.

Works: stage: operas: *Lancelot and Elaine* (1910); *The Fall of the House of Usher* (1925; unfinished); *The Trial of Lucullus* (Berkeley, April 18, 1947); *Montezuma* (1941–63; West Berlin, April 19, 1964). **incidental music to:** L. Andreyev's *The Black Maskers* (Northampton, Mass., June 1923; orch suite, 1928; Cincinnati, Dec. 5, 1930); Volkmüller's *Turandot* (Cleveland, May 8, 1925). **orch.:** Sym. in D major (1917); 9 numbered syms.: No. 1 (Boston, April 22, 1927); No. 2 (1944–46; San Francisco, Jan. 9, 1947); No. 3 (1955–57; Boston, Dec. 6, 1957); No. 4 (1958; Minneapolis, Jan. 2, 1960); No. 5 (Philadelphia, Feb. 7, 1964); No. 6 (Newark, N.J., Nov. 19, 1966); No. 7 (Ann Arbor, Mich., Oct. 1, 1967); No. 8 (N.Y., May 2, 1968); No. 9 (1975–78; Syracuse, Jan. 17, 1980); *Nocturne* (1921–22); *3 Dirges* (1933; withdrawn); Violin Concerto (1930–35; Chicago, Jan. 8, 1940); Piano Concerto (N.Y., Feb. 10, 1956); *Divertimento* (1959–60; Honolulu, Jan. 9, 1965); *Rhapsody* (Baltimore, March 18, 1970); Concerto for Violin, Cello, and Orch. (N.Y., Nov. 5, 1971); Concertino for Chamber Orch. (Chicago, April 14, 1972); *Concerto for Orchestra* (1979–81; Boston, Oct. 23, 1981; won the Pulitzer Prize in Music, 1982). **vocal:** *Romualdo's Song* for Soprano and Orch. (Northampton, Mass., June 1923); *On the Beach at Fontana* for Soprano and Piano (1930); *Turn, O Libertad* for Chorus and Piano, 4-hands or 2 Pianos (N.Y., April 1944); *Idyll of Theocritus* for Soprano and Orch. (1953–54; Louisville, Jan. 14, 1956); *Mass for Unison Choir* (1955; N.Y., April 1956); *Psalm CXL* for Soprano and Organ (Princeton, N.J., June 1963; also for Soprano and Orch., Boston, Feb. 11, 1966); *When Lilacs Last in the Dooryard Bloom'd*, cantata for Soprano, Alto, Baritone, Chorus, and Orch. (1964–70; Berkeley, Calif., May 23, 1971); *3 Choruses on Biblical Texts* for Chorus and Orch. (1971–72; Amherst, Mass., Feb. 8, 1975). **chamber:** Piano Trio (1916); 3 violin sonatas (1916; 1953; 1981, unfinished); *Pastorale* for Flute (1927; not extant); 2 string quartets: No. 1 (1936; Washington, D.C., April 1937); No. 2 (Madison, Wisc., May 28, 1951). Duo for Violin and Cello (1942); String Quintet (1957–58; N.Y., Nov. 23, 1959); 6 Pieces for Cello (1966; N.Y., March 31, 1968); *Canons (to the Memory of Igor Stravinsky)* for String Quartet (1971); Duo for Violin and Cello (1978; unfinished). **piano:** 3 sonatas: No. 1 (1927–30; N.Y., May 6, 1928); No. 2 (1946; N.Y., March 1947); No. 3 (1964–65; Berkeley, Calif., March 1969); *4 Pieces for Children* (1935–39); *Pages from a Diary*, later titled *From My Diary* (1937–39); *5 Pieces* (1975); *Waltz* (1977–78). **organ:** *3 Chorale Preludes* (1924–26); *Chorale* (1938).

Writings: *The Musical Experience of Composer, Performer, Listener* (Princeton, N.J., 1950); *Harmonic Practice* (N.Y., 1951); *Reflections on the Music Life in the United States* (N.Y., 1956); *Questions about Music* (Cambridge, Mass., 1970); E. Cone, ed., *Roger Sessions on Music: Collected Essays* (Princeton, N.J., 1979).

Bibl.: N. Slonimsky, in H. Cowell, ed., *American Composers on American Music* (Stanford, Calif., 1933); M. Brunswick, "American Composers, X: R.H. S.," *Modern Music*, X (1932–33); A. Copland, *Our New Music* (N.Y., 1941; 2nd ed., rev. and enl., 1968 as *The New Music 1900–1969*); M. Schubart, "R. S.: Portrait of an American Composer," *Musical Quarterly* (April 1946); A. Imbrie, "R. S.: In Honor of his 65th Birthday," *Perspectives of New Music*, i/1 (1962); E. Schweitzer, *Generation in String Quartets of Carter, S., Kirchner, and Schuller* (diss., Eastman School of Music, 1965); E. Cone, "In Honor of R. S.," *Perspectives of New Music*, X/2 (1972); A. Imbrie, "The Symphonies of R. S.," *Tempo*, No. 103 (1972); L. Wright and A. Bagnall, "R.H. S.: A Selective Bibliography and a Listing of His Compositions," *Current Musicology*, 15 (1973); R. Henderson, *Tonality in the Pre-serial Instrumental Music of R. S.* (diss., Eastman School of Music, 1974); A. Olmstead, "R. S.: A Personal Portrait," *Tempo*, No. 127 (1978); C. Oja, "The Copland-S. Concerts," *Musical Quarterly*, LXV (1979); H. Gleason and W. Becker, "R. S.," *20th-century American Composers* (Bloomington, Ind., 2nd ed., rev., 1981); M. Campbell, *The Piano Sonatas of R. S.: Sequel to a Tradition* (diss., Peabody Inst., 1982); C. Gagne and T. Caras, "R. S.," in *Soundpieces: Interviews with American Composers* (Metuchen, N.J., 1982); S. Kress, *R. S., Composer and Teacher: A Comparative Analysis of R. S.'s Philosophy of Educating Composers and his Approach to Composition in Symphonies Nos. 2 and 8* (diss., Univ. of Florida, 1982); C. Mason, *A Comprehensive Analysis of R. S.'s Opera Montezuma* (diss., Univ. of Illinois, Urbana, 1982); F. Prausnitz, *R. S.: A Critical Biography* (London, 1983); O. Daniel, "R. S.," *Ovation* (March 1984); R. Meckna, *The Rise of the American Composer-Critic: Aaron Copland, R. S., Virgil Thomson, and Elliott Carter in the Periodical "Modern Music," 1924–1946* (diss., Univ. of Calif., Santa Barbara, 1984); A. Olmstead, *R. S. and his Music* (Ann Arbor, 1985); idem, *Conversations with R. S.* (Boston, 1986); M. Nott, "R. S.'s Fugal Studies with Ernest Bloch: A Glimpse into the Workshop," *American Music* (Fall 1989).

Šesták, Zdeněk, Czech composer; b. Citoliby, Dec. 10, 1925. He studied composition with Hlobil and Krejčí at the Prague Cons. (1945–50) and music history at Charles Univ. (1945–49).

WORKS: ORCH.: *To Fallen Warriors,* symphonic prelude (1949); *Pantomime* (1959); *Rhapsodic Fantasy* for Cello and Orch. (1960); 6 numbered syms.: No. 1, *Epitaph* (1961); No. 2 (1970); No. 3 (1971); No. 4 for String Orch. (1973); No. 5 (1978); No. 6 (1979); *Balladic Intermezzo* (1964); *Symphonic Fantasy,* variations (1966); Concerto for String Orch. (1974); *Sonata sinfonica* for Wind Instruments (1976); *La Presentation d'un moment,* symphonic variations (1980); Concerto for Violin and Wind Instruments (1981); Violin Concerto (1981); Viola Concerto (1982); *Remembrance,* symphonic variations (1983). **VOCAL:** *Auschwitz,* melodrama to a text by Quasimodo (1959); *Vocal Symphony* for Chorus and Orch. (1962); *Hommage à Apollinaire* for 12 Mixed Choruses (1972); *The Death of Manon Lescaut,* 4 dramatic fragments for Soprano, Tenor, Chorus, Viola, and Piano (1974); *Fatum,* vocal symphonic fragment after Sophocles (1983); songs. **CHAMBER:** *Cassation* for 5 Wind Instruments (1958); *Suite* for Flute and Piano (1959); 2 *Pieces* for Violin and Piano (1960); Concertino for Wind Quintet (1964); *Divertimento concertante* for Wind Quintet (1966); 5 *Virtuoso Inventions* for Bassoon (1966); Sonata for 2 Clarinets (1967); *Music* for Oboe (1967); Concertino No. 1 for Horn and Piano (1967); 3 *Metamorphoses* for Flute (1968); *Musica partita* for Clarinet (1968); Concertino No. 2 for Horn and Piano (1972); 5 string quartets; String Quintet (1975); *Divertimento Concertante* for 5 Wind Instruments (1976); *Sonata du camera* for 8 Wind Instruments (1978); also children's pieces.

Setaccioli, Giacomo, Italian composer and teacher; b. Corneto, Tarquinia, Dec. 8, 1868; d. Siena, Dec. 5, 1925. He studied at the Accademia di Santa Cecilia in Rome; after teaching there (1922–25), he was appointed director of the Cons. Cherubini in Florence. He wrote the operas *La Sorella di Mark* (Rome, May 7, 1896), *L'ultimo degli Abenceragi* (Rome, 1893), and *Il Mantelaccio* (Rome, 1954); several symphonic pieces; a *Requiem;* chamber music; songs; piano pieces. He publ. *Debussy è un innovatore?* (Rome, 1910) and *Studi e conferenze di critica musicale* (Rome, 1923).

Seter, Mordecai, Russian-born Israeli composer; b. Novorossiysk, Feb. 26, 1916. He went to Palestine in 1926, where he studied with J. Weinberg and R. Burstein-Arber; then traveled to Paris, where he received instruction in piano from Lévy and in theory from Dandelot (1932–34), completing his training with Dukas (1934–35) and Boulanger (1935–37) at the École Normale de Musique; returning to Palestine, he taught at the Rubin Academy of Music at the Univ. of Tel Aviv (from 1951); was a prof. there from 1972 until his retirement as prof. emeritus in 1985. In 1962 he received the Prix d'Italie, in 1965 the Israel State Prize, and in 1983 the A.C.U.M.

Prize. His works are marked by the eastern Mediterranean style and techniques of composition.

WORKS: DRAMATIC: 6 ballets: *Pas de deux* or *Women in Tent* (ballet version of the 1956 *Ricercar*); *Midnight Vigil, Rhapsody on Yemenite Themes* (1958); *The Legend of Judith* (1962); *Part Real, Part Dream* (ballet version of the *Fantasia concertante,* 1964); *Jephthah's Daughter* (ballet version of sym. score, 1965); *Stone of Destiny* (1974); radiophonic oratorio, *Midnight Vigil* (1962; concert version of the ballet; Jerusalem, July 16, 1963). **ORCH.:** *Elegy* for Viola or Clarinet, and Orch. or Piano (1954); *Ricercar* for Violin, Viola, Cello, and String Ensemble (1956); *Variations* (1959); *Fantasia concertante* for Chamber Orch. (1965); Sinfonietta (1966); *Yemenite Suite* for Chamber Orch., with optional Voice (1966); *Meditation* (1967); *Rounds* for Chamber Orch. (1967–68); *Requiem* for Oboe, Piano, and String Orch. (1970). **VOCAL:** *Sabbath Cantata* for Soloists, Chorus, and String Orch. (1940); *Jerusalem* for Chorus and Orch. (1966); *Saperi,* music for Chorus, Percussion, Piano, and Strings (1968). **CHAMBER:** *Partita* for Violin and Piano (1951); Sonata for 2 Violins (1952); Sonata for Solo Violin (1953); *Diptyque* for Wind Quintet (1955); *Chamber Music 1970,* 6 works for different instrumental combinations (1970); *Concertante* for Violin, Oboe, Horn, and Piano (1973); Piano Trio (1973); Woodwind Trio (1974); Quintet for Violin, Cello, Flute, Horn, and Piano (1975); *Ensemble* for 6 Instruments (1975); *Solo and Tutti* for Clarinet and String Quartet (1976); 4 string quartets (1976–77); *The Double* for Clarinet and Piano (1986); *Post Scriptum* for String Quartet (1986). **PIANO:** 2 quartets (1973–81, 1982); Sonata (1982); *Triptyque I, II,* and *III* (all 1985); *Contrasts* (1987).

Ševčík, Otakar, noted Czech violinist and pedagogue; b. Horaždowitz, March 22, 1852; d. Písek, Jan. 18, 1934. He studied violin with his father; then at the Prague Cons. with Anton Bennewitz. From 1870 to 1873 he was concertmaster of the Mozarteum in Salzburg; held a similar post in the Theater an der Wien in Vienna. He was a prof. at the Prague Cons. (1892–1906); after teaching privately in Písek, he was prof. of violin at the Vienna Academy of Music (1909–18), and then taught at the Prague Master School (1919–21); also gave master classes in the U.S. (1920, 1924, 1931), London (1932), and elsewhere. His method, in contradistinction to the usual diatonic system, is founded on chromatic progressions, especially valuable in securing both accuracy and facility. His most famous pupils were Jan Kubelík, Efrem Zimbalist, and Erica Morini. He wrote many pieces for solo violin.

WRITINGS: *Schule der Violine-Technik* (1881); *Schule der Bogentechnik* (1895); *Lagenwechsel und Tonleiter-Vorstudien* (1895); *Triller-Vorstudien und Ausbildung des Finger-Anschlages* (1901); *Doppelgriff-Vorstudien in Terzen, Sexten, Oktaven und Dezimen* (1901); *Violine-Schule für Anfänger* (1904–8).

BIBL.: V. Nopp, *Profesor O. S.: život a dílo* (Professor O. S.: Life and Work; Brno, 1948); O. Ševl and J. Dostál, eds., *O. S.* (Prague, 1953).

Séverac, (Marie-Joseph-Alexandre) Déodat de, French composer; b. Saint Félix de Caraman en Lauragais, Haute-Garonne, July 20, 1872; d. Céret, Pyrénées-Orientales, March 24, 1921. He studied piano with his father, a painter and music lover, then in Toulouse at the Dominican College of Sorèze, at the Univ. (law) and at the Cons. (1893–96); also took courses with d'Indy and Magnard (composition), Blanche Selva and Albéniz (piano), Guilmant (organ), and Bordes (choral conducting) at the Paris Schola Cantorum; after completing his training (1907), he divided his time between Paris and his native town, devoting himself mainly to composition. His works are notable for their Gallic refinement.

WORKS: STAGE: OPERAS: *Le Cœur du moulin* (1903–8; Paris, Dec. 8, 1909); *Héliogabale* (Béziers, Aug. 21, 1910); *La Fille de la terre* (Coursan, July 1913); *Le Roi pinard* (1919). **INCIDENTAL MUSIC TO:** L. Damard's *Le Mirage* (Royan, 1905); M. Navarre's *Muguetto* (Tarn, Aug. 13, 1911); E. Verhaeren's *Hélène de Sparthe* (Paris, May 5, 1912). **ORCH.:** Symphonic poems:

L'Automne for Voice and Orch. (1900); *L'Hiver* for Voice and Orch. (1900); *Nymphes au crépuscule* (1901); *Les Grenouilles qui demandent un roi* (1909–21); *Didon et Énée,* suite (1903); *Tryptique* (1903–4). CHAMBER: *Sérénade au clair de lune* for Flute or Oboe, Piano, Harp, and String Quintet (1890; rev. 1919); Piano Quintet (1898); *Les Muses sylvestres,* suite for 5 Woodwinds and String Quartet (1908); *Le Parc aux cerfs* for Oboe, String Quintet, and Piano (1909); also choral works, piano pieces, organ music, and arrangements of early folk songs.

BIBL.: W. Roberts, "D. d.S.," *Music & Letters,* III (1922); B. Selva, *D. d.S.* (Paris, 1930); P. Landormy, "D. d.S.," *Musical Quarterly* (April 1934); E. Brody, *The Piano Works of D. d.S.: A Stylistic Analysis* (diss., N.Y. Univ., 1964); *Centenaire D. d.S.* (Paris, 1972).

Severinsen, "Doc" (Carl Hilding), American trumpeter, bandleader, and teacher; b. Arlington, Oreg., July 7, 1927. He studied cornet with his father, and later with Benny Baker; subsequently played in several jazz bands, including those of Charlie Barnet and Tommy Dorsey; later joined the band of the Johnny Carson "Tonight" television show, and eventually became its conductor. He also led other groups and appeared as a soloist with major orchs; taught brass playing in various settings.

Severn, Edmund, English-American composer and teacher; b. Nottingham, Dec. 10, 1862; d. Melrose, Mass., May 14, 1942. In 1866 his father, a violinist, settled in Hartford, Conn.; Severn studied violin with him and with Bernhard Listemann in Boston; then composition with Chadwick in Boston and with Philipp Scharwenka in Berlin. He wrote 2 symphonic poems: *Lancelot and Elaine* (1898) and *Eloise and Abelard* (1915); a suite, *From Old New England* (originally for Violin and Piano, 1912; orch. version, Springfield [Mass.] Music Festival, May 17, 1919); *Song Celestial* for Orch. (1912); Violin Concerto (N.Y., Jan. 7, 1916); choral works; songs.

Sevitzky (real name, **Koussevitzky**), **Fabien,** Russian-born American conductor, nephew of **Serge (Alexandrovich) Koussevitzky;** b. Vishny Volochok, Sept. 29, 1891; d. Athens, Feb. 2, 1967. He studied double bass at the St. Petersburg Cons., where he graduated with its gold medal (1911); then played in orchs., made appearances as a soloist, and began his conducting career. His uncle, who was already a celebrated double-bass player himself, suggested that he adopt a truncated form of the last name, and he complied to avoid a family quarrel. In 1922–23 he played in the orch. of the Warsaw Opera and in the Warsaw Phil. With his wife, the Russian singer Maria Koussevitzky, he went to Mexico in 1923; then emigrated to the U.S., becoming a naturalized citizen in 1928; played in the Philadelphia Orch. (1923–30); organized the Philadelphia Chamber String Sinfonietta in 1925, and led several ensembles in Boston from 1930. He then was music director of the Indianapolis Sym. Orch. (1937–55), the Univ. of Miami Sym. Orch. (1959–65), and the Greater Miami Phil. (1965–66). He died while on a visit to Athens to conduct the State Orch.

Seybold, Artur, German violinist, conductor, teacher, and composer; b. Hamburg, Jan. 6, 1868; d. Weissenfels, near Leipzig, Dec. 15, 1948. He studied at the Hamburg Cons.; traveled as violinist with Laube's orch. in Russia (1888); lived in Hamburg as a teacher and conductor of choral societies (from 1890). His numerous compositions for violin and piano and his male choruses won considerable popularity; he also publ. a violin method, *Das neue System,* and instructive pieces.

Seydelmann, Franz, German composer; b. Dresden, Oct. 8, 1748; d. there, Oct. 23, 1806. He was the son of Franciscus Seydelmann, a tenor in the Dresden electoral Kapelle, where he received instruction in music from J.C. Weber, J.G. Schürer, and J.G. Naumann; accompanied Naumann on a study tour of Italy (1765–68). Returning to Dresden, he was named church composer (1772) and Kapellmeister (1787) at the court. His most successful works for the theater were 2 operas buffa,

Il Mostro ossia Da gratitudine amore (1785) and *Il Turco in Italia* (1788); thereafter he devoted himself mainly to writing sacred music.

WORKS: STAGE (all 1st perf. in Dresden unless otherwise given): *La Serva scaltra* (1773); *Arsene* or *Die schöne Arsene* (March 3, 1779); *Das tartarische Gesetz* (c.1779); *Der lahme Husar* (Leipzig, July 17, 1780); *Der Kaufmann von Smyrna* (c.1780); *Der Soldat* (1783); *Il capriccio corretto* (1783); *La Villanella di Misnía* (1784; in German as *Das sächsische Bauermädchen,* Frankfurt am Main, 1791); *Il Mostro ossia Da gratitudine amore* (1785); *Il Turco in Italia* (1788); *Amore per oro* (1790). ORATORIOS: *La Betulia liberata* (1774); *Gioas rè di Giuda* (1776); *La morte d'Abele* (1801); also about 36 masses, 40 Psalms, 37 offertories, 32 antiphons, 15 vespers, etc.; cantatas; songs; 6 sonatas for Harpsichord and Flute (Nos. 1, 2, and 6 as 3 sonates, Dresden, 1785); 3 sonates for Harpsichord or Piano and Violin (Dresden, c.1786); *6 Sonaten für zwo Personen auf einem Clavier* (Leipzig, 1781); other sonatas for Harpsichord.

BIBL.: R. Cahn-Speyer, *F. S. als dramatischer Komponist* (Leipzig, 1909).

Seyffardt, Ernst (Hermann), German conductor, teacher, and composer; b. Krefeld, May 6, 1859; d. Partenkirchen, Nov. 30, 1942. He studied at the Cologne Cons. with F. Hiller and G. Jensen, and at the Berlin Hochschule für Musik with Kiel; conducted the Liedertafel in Freiburg (1887–92); in 1892 he was appointed conductor of the Neuer Singverein in Stuttgart; also taught at the Stuttgart Cons.; retired in 1929.

WORKS: Opera, *Die Glocken von Plurs* (Krefeld, 1912); *Thusnelda,* dramatic scene; Sym.; Violin Sonata; Piano Quartet; String Quartet; choral music; songs.

Seyfried, Ignaz (Xaver), Ritter von, Austrian conductor, teacher, and composer; b. Vienna, Aug. 15, 1776; d. there, Aug. 27, 1841. He was a close friend of Mozart, and had some piano lessons with him; studied also with Koželuh and Albrechtsberger. In 1797 he became conductor at Schikaneder's Freihaus-Theater in Vienna; then was conductor of the Theater an der Wien (1801–27). He was an extremely prolific composer, and some of his singspiels were very successful; one of them, *Die Ochsenmenuette,* based on Haydn's music (Vienna, Dec. 31, 1823), gave rise to the well-known anecdote about Haydn's composing an *Ox Minuet* for a butcher and receiving an ox as a gift. Seyfried also wrote the opera *Der Wundermann am Rheinfall* (Vienna, Oct. 26, 1799), which elicited praise from Haydn. He further wrote numerous melodramas, ballets, oratorios, motets, syms., quartets, etc. He publ. Albrechtsberger's *Sämmtliche Schriften* (1826), Preindl's *Wiener Tonschule* (1827), and *Ludwig van Beethoven's Studien im Generalbasse, Contrapuncte und der Compositions-Lehre* (1832).

BIBL.: A. Schmidt, *Denksteine: Biographien von I.R. v.S. . . .* (Vienna, 1848); A. Bauer, *150 Jahre Theater an der Wien* (Zürich, 1952); idem, *Opern und Operetten in Wien* (Graz, 1955).

Seymour, John Laurence, American composer; b. Los Angeles, Jan. 18, 1893; d. Feb. 2, 1986. He studied piano at the Univ. of Calif. at Berkeley (B.A. in music, 1917; M.A. in Slavic languages, 1919); received instruction in piano and theory from Fannie Charles Dillon and in violin from Leila Fagge; then took courses in composition with Pizzetti and Bohgen in Italy and with d'Indy in Paris (1923–28); later obtained his Ph.D. in English literature in 1940 from the Univ. of Calif. at Berkeley with the dissertation *Drama and Libretto;* lectured there on opera and drama (1928–36), and also served as chairman of the theater dept. of Sacramento Junior College; later was a special librarian at Southern Utah State College (from 1969).

WORKS: STAGE: OPERAS: *Les précieuses ridicules* (1920); *In the Pasha's Garden* (1934; Metropolitan Opera, N.Y., Jan. 24, 1935; won the David Bispham Memorial Award); *Ramona* (Provo, Utah, Nov. 11, 1970); *Ollanta, el Jefe Kolla* (1977); etc. OPERETTAS: *Bachelor Belles* (1922); *Hollywood Madness* (1936); *The Devil and Tom Walker* (1942). MUSICALS: *Ming Toy* (1949); *The Lure and the Promise* (1960); also a Piano

Concerto; String Quartet; 2 string trios; sonatas for various instruments; piano pieces; songs; etc.

Sgambati, Giovanni, celebrated Italian pianist, conductor, teacher, and composer; b. Rome, May 28, 1841; d. there, Dec. 14, 1914. He studied piano with Amerigo Barbieri, and appeared in public at the age of 6; in 1849 he was taken by his family to Trevi, where he studied with Natalucci; returning to Rome in 1860, he received lessons in counterpoint from Giovanni Aldega. In 1862 he became a pupil of Liszt, remaining his lifelong friend and champion; after taking his diploma di socio onorario at the Accademia di Santa Cecelia in Rome (1866), he embarked upon an outstanding career as a pianist, making tours of Europe with enormous success. In Rome he also was active as a conductor. Historically, Sgambati's concerts were important as the 1st systematic attempt to introduce to the Italian public a varied fare of symphonic music. Sgambati continued to tour as a pianist; after a concert tour in Italy and Germany, he established in 1868 a free piano class annexed to the Accademia di Santa Cecilia in Rome, which in 1877 was formally recognized by the government as the Liceo Musicale; it became the foremost music school in Italy; Sgambati taught piano there until his death. He was an ardent admirer of Wagner, whom he met in 1876; Wagner recommended Sgambati to Schott of Mainz, who subsequently brought out many of Sgambati's works. As a pianist and teacher, Sgambati enjoyed a very high reputation in Germany and Italy; his own music betrays strong Germanic influence; unlike most Italian composers of his time, he devoted his energies exclusively to instrumental music, avoiding all service to the theater.

WORKS: ORCH.: 2 syms.: No. 1 in D minor (Rome, March 28, 1881); No. 2 in E-flat major (1883); Piano Concerto (1878–80); *Epitalamio sinfonico* (1887); *Te Deum laudamus* for String Orch. and Organ (1893; also for Large Orch., 1908); also sacred music, including a Requiem for Baritone, Voices, and Orch. or Organ (1895–96; rev. 1901); chamber works, including 2 string quartets (1864; c.1882); String Nonet (1866; not extant); 2 piano quintets (1866; c.1876); songs; numerous piano pieces; transcriptions for Piano.

BIBL.: B. Walker, *My Musical Experiences* (1892); E. Segnitz, "S.s Klaviermusik," *Musikpädagogische Blätter,* 11, 12 (1911); A. de Angelis, "I musicisti italiani contemporanei: G. S.," *Rivista Musicale Italiana,* XIX (1912); A. Bonaventura, "G. S.," *Nuova Musica,* XIX (Florence, 1914); A. Casella, "G. S.," *Music & Letters* (Oct. 1925); A. Bonaventura, "G. S. (nel primo centenario della sua nascita)," *Musica d'oggi,* 1st series, XXIII (1941).

Sgouros, Dimitris, gifted Greek pianist; b. Athens, Aug. 30, 1969. He enrolled in the Athens Cons., where he found a mentor in Maria Herogiorgiou-Sigara; later took lessons with Stewart Gordon in Baltimore and Guy Johnson at the Royal Academy of Music in London; subsequently pursued training in mathematics at the Univ. of Athens. He won the UNICEF Competition in 1980. His musical prowess was evident in his youth: he was only 7 when he made his public debut in Piraeus, and at the age of 12 he appeared as soloist in the Rachmaninoff 3rd Piano Concerto with Rostropovich and the National Sym. Orch. at Carnegie Hall in N.Y. He made his London debut at 13, and subsequently performed as a soloist with many major orchs. and as a recitalist.

Sgrizzi, Luciano, Italian keyboard artist; b. Bologna, Oct. 30, 1910. He took courses in piano, organ, composition, and music theory in Bologna, Parma, and Paris; made his debut as a pianist in 1923, but also appeared as a harpsichordist and clavichordist (from 1948). He edited numerous performing eds., ranging from Monteverdi to Pergolesi.

Shafran, Daniel (Borisovich), remarkable Russian cellist; b. Petrograd, Jan. 13, 1923. He studied cello with his father, Boris Shafran, who was an eminent cellist in his own right. He received 1st prize at the 1937 All-Union competition for string players in Moscow; continued his training with Alexander Stirmer at the Leningrad Cons. (graduated, 1950); won

the Prague International Cello Competition (1950); subsequently toured with great success all over the world; was made a People's Artist of the R.S.F.S.R. (1955).

BIBL.: I. Yampolsky, *D. S.* (Moscow, 1973).

Shakespeare, William, English tenor, singing teacher, and composer; b. Croydon, June 16, 1849; d. London, Nov. 1, 1931. He studied at the Royal Academy of Music with Sterndale Bennett in London; went to Leipzig for study with Reinecke, but soon left for Milan to cultivate his voice under Lamperti's guidance. From 1875 he appeared in England as a tenor; in 1878 he was appointed prof. of singing at the Royal Academy of Music, where he was highly esteemed. His compositions are entirely in the vein of German Romanticism, his model being Mendelssohn. He publ. *The Art of Singing* (3 parts; 1898–99); *Singing for Schools and Colleges* (1907); *Plain Words on Singing* (1924); *The Speaker's Art* (1931).

Shallon, David, Israeli conductor; b. Tel Aviv, Oct. 15, 1950. He studied composition and conducting with Noam Sheriff, then completed his conducting studies with Hans Swarowsky at the Vienna Academy of Music (1973–75). He was an assistant to Leonard Bernstein in Europe (1974–79), and also made appearances as a guest conductor with many of the major European orchs. and opera houses; led the premiere of Gottfied von Einem's controversial opera *Jesu Hochzeit* in Vienna in 1980. He made his U.S. debut as a guest conductor with the San Francisco Sym. Orch. in 1980. In 1987 he became Generalmusikdirektor of the Düsseldorf Sym.

Shamo, Igor, talented Ukrainian composer; b. Kiev, Feb. 21, 1925; d. there, Aug. 17, 1982. He studied medicine in Kiev; after World War II, studied composition with Liatoshinsky at the Kiev Cons., graduating in 1951. Many of his works, numbering some 200, used native instruments such as the bayan and the bandura, and the lyrics extolled Soviet youth and the Soviet system. In 1975 he received the Shevchenko State Prize of the Ukrainian SSR and became a National Artist of the Ukraine.

WORKS: ORCH.: 3 syms. (1964, 1968, 1975); Symphonic Dances (1949); Piano Concerto (1951); *Festival Suite* (1954); *Moldavian Poem—Rad o diya* (1956); *Komsomol Overture* (1967); *Theatrical Kaleidoscope* (1968); *Evening Music* (1971); *Morning Music* (1975); Flute Concerto (1975); Concerto for Bayan and Strings (1980); Sinfonietta-Concerto for Chamber Orch. (1980); *Lenin,* cantata-oratorio (1980). **CHAMBER:** 5 string quartets (1955–80); Piano Trio (1947); Piano Quintet (1958); also solo piano works; choruses; film music.

BIBL.: L. Efremova, *I. S.* (Moscow, 1958).

Shanet, Howard, American conductor; b. N.Y., Nov. 9, 1918. He studied cello with Evsei Beloussoff; played in the National Orch. Assoc., under the direction of Leon Barzin; later studied conducting with Rudolph Thomas and Fritz Stiedry, and at the Berkshire Music Center in Tanglewood with Koussevitzky; took composition lessons with Hans Weisse, Paul Dessau, Martinu, Lopatnikoff, and Arthur Honegger. He completed his academic studies at Columbia Univ. (A.B., 1939; A.M., 1941). He served in the U.S. Army as warrant officer and bandleader (1942–46); taught at Hunter College in N.Y. (1941–42; 1946–53); was on the staff at the Berkshire Music Center in the summers of 1949 to 1952; in 1953, was appointed to the faculty of Columbia Univ. and as conductor of the Univ. Orch. and assistant (later full) prof. of music, which led to his designation as Director of Music Performance in 1978; in 1989 he was named Professor Emeritus. He served as assistant conductor of the N.Y. City Sym. (1947–48), conductor of the Huntington (W.Va.) Sym. Orch. (1951–53), and a guest conductor with the Israel Phil. (1950) and the N.Y. Phil. (1951, 1959). In 1977 he received the presidential citation of the National Federation of Music Clubs and a certificate of distinguished service from the Inst. of International Education; in 1990 he was invited by the College of Physicians and Surgeons of Columbia Univ. to give the Dean's Distinguished Lecture in the Humanities, the 1st musician to be accorded that honor. He composed

Allegro Giocoso for String Quartet (1942; also for String Orch., 1987); *A War March* for Military Band (1944); *Introduction and Fugue* for Flute, Clarinet, and Bassoon (1947); 2 *Canonic Pieces* for 2 Clarinets (1947); *Variations on a Bizarre Theme* for Orch. (1960); arr. and reconstructed the score *Night of the Tropics* by Gottschalk (1955). He publ. an "adult education book," *Learn to Read Music* (N.Y., 1956; tr. into Norwegian, 1972, Italian, 1975, and Spanish, 1981); a fundamental documentary vol., *Philharmonic: A History of New York's Orchestra* (N.Y., 1975); ed. and wrote a critical introduction for *Early Histories of the New York Philharmonic,* containing reprints of books by Krehbiel, Huneker, and Erskine (N.Y., 1978). He also publ. authoritative articles on such varied subjects as Bach's transpositions, Bizet's suppressed sym., and (in *The New Grove Dictionary of American Music*) the development of orchs. in the U.S.

Shankar (Lakshminarayana), Indian singer, composer, arranger, producer, and violinist; b. Madras, April 26, 1950. He 1st studied voice, violin, and drumming at home with his father, V. Lakshminarayana (d. Dec. 3, 1990), and mother, L. Seethlakshmi; then went to the U.S., where he earned his Ph.D. at Wesleyan Univ. in Connecticut (1974). With the English-Irish composer Caroline, he formed the pop group The Epidemics in 1980, bringing together in its performances and recordings a variety of genres, including classical Indian, folk, pop, and Western; is also active with his own Indian classical group, Shankar. He invented the Ten String Stereophonic Double Violin, a double-bodied instrument that, when both necks are played simultaneously, is capable of producing all the tones of the orch. string family; when the necks are played separately, the strings of the one not played resound sympathetically. The instrument made its debut in Shankar's *Ragam Tanam Pallavi Ragam Hemmavthi* for Double Violin and South and North Indian Drums (1980), which appeared on the album *Who's to Know;* other albums include *Palghat Mani Tyer* (2 vols.), *Pancha Nadai Pallavi,* and *Eye Catcher.* His music was also used in the film scores for *The Last Temptation of Christ* (1989) and *Jacob's Ladder* (1990). Shankar has appeared widely at festivals promoting a variety of social causes; he performed at the United Nations Peace Day Festival in N.Y. (1987), festivals in support of the Schizophrenia Research Foundation in India (1989–91), and the Tibet Alive for World Peace concert (1991). His other compositions include *Himmalaya* for Vocalists and Double Violin (1981) and the song *Never Take No for an Answer* (1985).

Shankar, Ravi, famous Indian sitarist and composer; b. Benares, April 7, 1920. He was trained by his brother, Uday Shankar, and began his career as a musician and a dancer; then engaged in a serious study of the Indian classical instrument, the sitar; in time became a great virtuoso on it. As a consequence of the growing infatuation with oriental arts in Western countries in the 1960s, he suddenly became popular, and his concerts were greeted with reverential awe by youthful multitudes. This popularity increased a thousandfold when the Beatles went to him to receive the revelation of Eastern musical wisdom, thus placing him on the pedestal usually reserved for untutored guitar strummers. As a composer, he distinguished himself by several film scores, including the famous *Pather Panchali* trilogy; he also wrote the film scores for *Kabulliwallah* and *Anuradha.* For the Tagore centenary he wrote a ballet, *Samanya Kshati,* based on Tagore's poem of the same name; it was produced in New Delhi on May 7, 1961. He also wrote 2 concertos for Sitar and Orch. (1970, 1976). He publ. a memoir, *My Music, My Life* (N.Y., 1968); E. Barnett ed. *Ravi Shankar: Learning Indian Music, A Systematic Approach* (1981).

Shapero, Harold (Samuel), American pianist, teacher, and composer; b. Lynn, Mass., April 29, 1920. He learned to play piano as a youth; was for several years a pianist in dance orchs.; began serious study in 1936 at the Malkin Cons. in Boston with Slonimsky; then studied with Krenek, with Piston at Harvard Univ., with Hindemith at the Berkshire Music Cen-

ter in Tanglewood, and with Boulanger in Cambridge, Mass. He graduated from Harvard Univ. in 1941; received the American Prix de Rome for his *9-Minute Overture* (N.Y., June 8, 1941); held 2 Guggenheim fellowships (1947, 1948) and a Fulbright fellowship (1948). In addition to appearances as a pianist, he taught at Brandeis Univ. (from 1952), where he was founder-director of its electronic music studio. He married the painter Esther Geller in 1945. In his music Shapero adheres to an austere Classical pattern, without excluding a highly emotional melodic line; his exceptional mastery of contrapuntal technique secures clarity of intermingled sonorities in his chamber music. In some of his early compositions he applied the dodecaphonic method.

WORKS: ORCH.: *9-Minuet Overture* (1940; N.Y., June 8, 1941); *Serenade* in D major for String Orch. (1945); *Symphony for Classical Orchestra* (1947; Boston, Jan. 30, 1948); *The Travelers Overture* (1948); *Credo* (Louisville, Oct. 19, 1955); *Lyric Dances* (1955); *On Green Mountain* for Jazz Ensemble (1957; for Orch., 1981); *Partita* in C major for Piano and Small Orch. (1960). **CHAMBER:** String Trio (1938); 3 *Pieces for 3 Pieces* for Flute, Clarinet, and Bassoon (1939); Trumpet Sonata (1940); String Quartet (1941); Violin Sonata (1942); 3 *Improvisations* in B major (1968), 3 *Studies* in C-sharp minor (1969), and 4 *Pieces* in B-flat major (1970), all for Piano and Synthesizer. **PIANO:** Sonata for Piano 4-hands (1941); 3 sonatas (1944); *Variations* in C minor (1947); Sonata in F minor (1948); *American Variations* (1950). **VOCAL:** 2 *Psalms* for Chorus (1952); *Hebrew Cantata* for Vocal Soloists, Chorus, Flute, Trumpet, Violin, Harp, and Organ (1954).

Shapey, Ralph, American conductor, teacher, and composer; b. Philadelphia, March 12, 1921. He studied violin with Emanuel Zeitlin and composition with Stefan Wolpe; served as assistant conductor of the Philadelphia National Youth Administration Sym. Orch. (1938–47). In 1954 he founded and became music director of the Contemporary Chamber Players of the Univ. of Chicago, with which he presented new works; in 1963–64, he taught at the Univ. of Pa., and then was made prof. of music at the Univ. of Chicago in 1964; after serving as Distinguished Prof. of Music at the Aaron Copland School of Music at Queens College of the City Univ. of N.Y. (1985–86), he resumed his duties at the Univ. of Chicago. Disappointed by repeated rejections of his works by performers and publishers, Shapey announced in 1969 that he would no longer submit his works to anyone for performance or publication. However, in 1976 he had a change of heart and once more gave his blessing to the performance and publication of his works. In 1982 he became a MacArthur Fellow and in 1989 was elected a member of the American Academy and Inst. of Arts and Letters. His music employs serialistic but uncongested procedures in acrid counterpoint, while formally adhering to neo-Classical paradigms.

WORKS: ORCH.: *Fantasy for Symphony Orchestra* (1951); Sym. No. 1 (1952); Concerto for Clarinet and Chamber Ensemble (1954; Strasbourg, June 9, 1958); *Challenge—The Family of Man* (1955); *Ontogeny* (1958; Buffalo, May 1, 1965); *Invocation,* concerto for Violin and Orch. (1958; N.Y., May 24, 1968); *Rituals* (1959; Chicago, May 12, 1966); Double Concerto for Violin, Cello, and Orch. (1983; N.Y., Jan. 24, 1984); *Groton: 3 Movements for Young Orchestra* (1984); *Symphonie concertante* (1985); Concerto for Piano, Cello, and String Orch. (1986). **CHAMBER:** 7 string quartets (1946; 1949; 1950–51; 1953; 1957–58; 1963; 1972); Piano Quintet (1946–47); Violin Sonata (1949–50); Oboe Sonata (1951–52); Quartet for Oboe, Violin, Viola, and Cello (1952); Cello Sonata (1953); Piano Trio (1953–55); *Evocation* for Violin, Piano, and Percussion (1959; N.Y., March 26, 1960); *Soliloquy* for Narrator, String Quartet, and Percussion (1959); *De Profundis* for Double Bass, Piccolo or Flute, Oboe or English Horn, Clarinet or Bassoon, and Clarinet or Alto Saxophone (1960); *Movements* for Woodwind Quintet (1960); *Chamber Symphony* for 10 Instruments (1962); *Convocation* for Chamber Ensemble (1962); Piece for Violin, 7 Instruments, and Percussion (1962); Brass Quintet

(1963); String Trio (1965; 2nd movement for Solo Violin as Sonata No. 1, 1972); *Partita* for Violin, 11 Instruments, and 2 Percussion (1966); *Partita-fantasy* for Cello, 14 Instruments, and Percussion (1966); *3 for 6* for Chamber Ensemble (1979); Concerto Grosso for Woodwind Quintet (1981); *Discourse II* for Violin, Clarinet, Cello, and Piano (1983); Concertante for Trumpet and 10 Performers (1984); *Kroslish Sonate* for Cello and Piano (1985); *Concertante II* for Alto Saxophone and 14 Performers (1987); *Variations* for Viola and 9 Performers (1987); also piano pieces and organ works. VOCAL: Cantata for Soprano, Tenor, Bass, Narrator, Chamber Orch., and Percussion (1951; rev. as String Quartet No. 5, 1957–58); *Dimensions* for Soprano and 23 Instruments (1960); *Incantations* for Soprano and 10 Instruments (1961); *Praise*, oratorio for Bass-baritone, Double Chorus, and Chamber Ensemble (1962–71; Chicago, Feb. 28, 1976); *Songs of Eros* for Soprano, Orch. and Tape (1975); *The Covenant* for Soprano, Chamber Orch. and Tape (1977); *Song of Songs* for Soprano, Chamber Orch. and Tape: *I* (1979), *II* (1980), and *III* (1980); *In Memoriam Paul Fromm* for Soprano, Baritone, and 9 Performers (1987).

Shapleigh, Bertram, American pianist, cellist, writer on music, and composer; b. Boston, Jan. 15, 1871; d. Washington, D.C., July 2, 1940. He studied composition with G.E. Whiting and Chadwick at the New England Cons. of Music in Boston (graduated, 1891); also received instruction from MacDowell; studied medicine at Vermont Medical College (M.D., 1893). After giving a series of lecture-recitals in the U.S., he went to Europe (1898); lived in England from 1902 until his return in 1917 to the U.S., where he was active as a lecturer and writer on music; became a specialist in oriental music. His compositions are in a Romantic vein. The Bertram Shapleigh Foundation was founded in Washington, D.C., after his death. WORKS: ORCH.: 2 suites: *Ramayana* and *Gur Amir* (both 1908); *Symphonic Prelude*; 2 syms.; *Poem* for Cello and Orch. VOCAL: 7 operas; various choral works, some with Orch.; some 200 songs; also chamber music and instrumental pieces.

Shaporin, Yuri (Alexandrovich), significant Russian composer; b. Glukhov, Ukraine, Nov. 8, 1887; d. Moscow, Dec. 9, 1966. He studied law, and graduated from the Univ. of St. Petersburg in 1912; also studied at the St. Petersburg Cons. with Sokolov (composition), graduating in 1918. He wrote theatrical music in Leningrad; moved to Moscow in 1936, where he served as a prof. at the Cons. (from 1939). His masterpiece is the opera *The Decembrists*, which occupied him for over 30 years. WORKS: Opera, *Polina Gyebl* (1925; rev. and enl. as *The Decembrists*, 1920–53; Moscow, June 23, 1953); about 80 theater scores; much film music; *The Flea*, comic suite for Orch. (1928); Sym. for Chorus, Orch., Band, and Piano (1928–33; Moscow, May 11, 1933); *On the Field of Kolikovo*, sym.-cantata for Solo Voices, Chorus, and Orch. (1918–39; Moscow, Nov. 18, 1939); *A Tale of the Battle for the Russian Land*, oratorio for Solo Voices, Chorus, and Orch. (Moscow, April 18, 1944); 2 piano sonatas (1924, 1926); songs. BIBL.: D. Abraham, *Eight Soviet Composers* (London, 1943); E. Grosheva, *Y. S.: i evo oratorii* (Moscow, 1947); idem, *Y.A. S.* (Moscow, 1957); S. Levit, *Y.A. S.: A Sketch of his Life and Work* (Moscow, 1964); I. Martynov, *Y. S.* (Moscow, 1966).

Sharp, Cecil (James), English folk music collector and editor; b. London, Nov. 22, 1859; d. there, June 23, 1924. He studied mathematics and music at Uppingham and Clare College, Cambridge; in 1882 he went to Australia, settling in Adelaide, where he worked in a bank and practiced law, becoming associate to the Chief Justice of Southern Australia; in 1889 he resigned from the legal profession and took up a musical career; was assistant organist of the Adelaide Cathedral, and co-director of the Adelaide College of Music. In 1892 he returned to England; was music instructor of Ludgrove School (1893–1910) and principal of the Hampstead Cons. (1896–1905). At the same time, he became deeply interested in English folk songs; publ. a *Book of British Songs for Home and School* (1902); then proceeded to make a systematic survey of English

villages with the aim of collecting authentic specimens of English songs. In 1911 he established the English Folk Dance Society; also was director of the School of Folk Song and Dance at Stratford-upon-Avon. During World War I he was in the U.S., collecting folk music in the Appalachian Mountains, with a view to establishing their English origin. In 1923 he received the degree of M.M. *honoris causa* from the Univ. of Cambridge. In 1930 the "Cecil Sharp House" was opened in London as headquarters of the English Folk Dance Society (amalgamated with the Folk Song Society in 1932). WRITINGS: All publ. in London: *English Folk-song: Some Conclusions* (1907; 2nd ed., 1936; 4th ed., 1965, by M. Karpeles); *Folk-singing in Schools* (1912); *Folk-dancing in Elementary and Secondary Schools* (1912); with A. Oppé, *The Dance: An Historical Survey of Dancing in Europe* (1924). FOLKSONG EDITIONS: All publ. in London: *Folk Songs from Somerset* (1904–9); with S. Baring-Gould et al., *Songs of the West* (1905); with S. Baring-Gould, *English Folk Songs for Schools* (1905); with H. MacIlwaine and G. Butterworth, *The Morris Book* (1907–13); with G. Butterworth, *Morris Dance Tunes* (1907–24); with G. Butterworth and M. Karpeles, *The Country Dance Book* (1909–22); *Country Dance Tunes* (1909–22); *English Folk-carols* (1911); *The Sword Dances of Northern England* (1911–13; 2nd ed., 1950–51, by M. Karpeles); with O. Campbell, *English Folk-songs from the Southern Appalachians* (1917; 2nd ed., 1932; 3rd ed., 1960, by M. Karpeles); *Folk-songs of English Origin Collected in the Appalachian Mountains* (1919–21); M. Karpeles, ed., *Cecil Sharp's Collection of English Folk Songs* (1973). BIBL.: W. Shaw, "C. S. and Folk Dancing," *Music & Letters* (Jan. 1921); A. Fox Strangways and M. Karpeles, *C. S.* (London, 1933; 2nd ed., 1955; rev. by Karpeles as *C. S.: His Life and Work*, 1967).

Sharp, Elliott, American electric guitarist and composer; b. Cleveland, March 1, 1951. He studied anthropology at Cornell Univ. (1969–71); then took degrees in music at Bard College (B.A., 1973), where he studied ethnomusicology with Roswell Rudd and composition with Elie Yarden and Benjamin Boretz, and at the State Univ. of N.Y. at Buffalo (M.A., 1977), where he studied ethnomusicology with Charles Keil and composition with Lejaren Hiller. In 1980 he formed Carbon, one of N.Y.'s most innovative "downtown" ensembles; in late 1989 its flexible instrumentation included, in addition to electric harp, keyboards, and drums, "slabs"—homemade instruments made of wood and long metal strips that produce both ethereal harmonics and percussive sounds when struck with drumsticks. Since he is well versed in both science and physics, Sharp employs mathematical formulas and relationships in his works; he tends toward micro-rhythms, what he calls "layers of resonating rhythms that groove hard and cause a certain type of turbulence," which led one reviewer to describe his music as "urban ragas." His musical aims are often political; some works utilize sampled voices of politicians, while Sharp sees the flexible organization and improvisatory performance style of Carbon itself as an implicit expression of his own social and political ideas. WORKS: *Innosense* for 3 Musicians and Tapes (N.Y., Oct. 22, 1981); *Crowds and Power* for 21 Musicians (N.Y., Oct. 15, 1982); *Haka* for 4 Musicians (Washington, D.C., Oct. 12, 1983); *Marco Polo's Argali* for 10 Musicians (N.Y., March 1, 1985); *Sili/Contemp/Tation* for 3 Musicians (N.Y., April 4, 1986); *Self-Squared Dragon* for 9 Musicians (Zürich, Feb. 5, 1986); *Re/Iterations* for Orch. (N.Y., June 23, 1986); *Tessalation Row* for String Quartet (N.Y., July 11, 1986); *20 Below* for 6 Keyboards (N.Y., April 1, 1987); *Mansereel* for 4 Musicians (Philadelphia, Oct. 2, 1987); *Larynx* for 13 Musicians (N.Y., Nov. 13, 1987); *Hammer Anvil Stirrup* for String Quartet (Pori, Finland, July 15, 1988); *Jump Cut* for 4 Musicians (Troy, N.Y., Dec. 5, 1988); *Ferrous* for 5 Musicians (N.Y., Nov. 30, 1989); *Deception* for 6 Musicians and Film (N.Y., Feb. 8, 1990).

Sharrow, Leonard, noted American bassoonist and pedagogue; b. N.Y., Aug. 4, 1915. He studied at the Inst. of Musical

Art in N.Y. (1932–35). He was 1st bassoonist in the National Sym. Orch. in Washington, D.C. (1935–37); then played in the NBC Sym. Orch. in N.Y. (1937–41); subsequently was 1st bassoonist in the Buffalo Phil. (1946), Detroit Sym. Orch. (1946–47), NBC Sym. Orch. (1947–51), Chicago Sym. Orch. (1951–64), and Pittsburgh Sym. Orch. (1977–87). He taught at the Juilliard School of Music in N.Y. (1948–51), Roosevelt College in Chicago (1952–55), the Indiana Univ. School of Music in Bloomington (1964–77), the Aspen Music School (from 1967), and the New England Cons. of Music in Boston (1986–89). He also toured as a bassoon virtuoso and chamber music player. As a teacher, he was mentor to several generations of bassoonists. He publ. eds. of works by Corelli, Vivaldi, Handel, Boismortier, Weber, Hummel, J.A. Koželuh et al.

Shaverzashvili, Alexander, Russian composer; b. Tiflis, July 8, 1919. He studied at the Tiflis Cons. with Andrei Balanchivadze; from 1955 he was a prof. there. He wrote a comic opera, *Grasshopper* (Tbilisi, March 18, 1955); Sym. (1945); 2 piano concertos (1946, 1949); Piano Quintet (1955); String Quartet; Piano Trio; Violin Sonata; songs.

Shaw (real name, **Shukotoff**), **Arnold,** American composer, writer, editor, lecturer, and music executive; b. N.Y., June 28, 1909; d. Las Vegas, Sept. 26, 1989. He was of Russian-Jewish extraction; majored in English literature at the City College of N.Y. (B.S., 1929) and Columbia Univ. (M.A., 1931). In his college years he was a campus radical, active particularly in the Anti-Fascist Association of the Staffs of the City College. As such, he was listed as "subversive" by some right-wing political organizations. He made a living by composing and teaching music at the New School for Social Research in N.Y., the Univ. of Calif. at Los Angeles, and the Univ. of Nevada in Reno and Las Vegas, where in 1985 he founded the Popular Music Research Center. In order to protect himself against would-be political factions, he changed his name from the Russian-sounding Shukotoff to the more common name Shaw. Among the various positions he occupied was that of music executive with the Dutchess Music Corp. (1950–53), Hill and Range Songs (1953–55), and the Edward B. Marks Music Corp. (1955–66); at these companies he promoted such popular singers as Rod McKuen, Burt Bacharach, and Elvis Presley. He wrote numerous articles and books; received the ASCAP–Deems Taylor Award (1968, 1979); ed., with L. Dowling, *The Schillinger System of Musical Composition* (N.Y., 1941); and publ. a novel, *The Money Song* (N.Y., 1953). His compositions include the musical *They Had a Dream* (1976), some snappy piano pieces, and songs.

WRITINGS: (all publ. in N.Y.): *Lingo of Tin Pan Alley* (1950) *Belafonte: An Unauthorized Biography* (1960); *Sinatra: Twentieth-Century Romantic* (1968); *The Rock Revolution* (1969); *The World of Soul: Black America's Contribution to the Pop Music Scene* (1970); *The Street That Never Slept: New York's Fabled 52nd Street* (1971; reprint, 1977, as *52nd Street, the Street of Jazz*); *The Rockin' 50s: The Decade That Transformed the Pop Music Scene* (1974); *Honkers and Shouters: The Golden Years of Rhythm and Blues* (1978); *Dictionary of American Pop Rock: From Blue Suede Shoes to Blondie* (1982); *Sinatra, the Entertainer* (1982).

Shaw, Artie (real name, **Arthur Jacob Arshawsky**), outstanding American jazz clarinetist, bandleader, composer, and arranger; b. N.Y., May 23, 1910. He was brought up in New Haven, Conn., where he became an alto saxophonist in Johnny Cavallaro's dance band when he was 15; took up the clarinet at 16, and then worked as music director and arranger for the Austin Wylie Orch. in Cleveland until 1929; subsequently toured as a tenor saxophonist with Irving Aaronson's band, going with it to N.Y., where he played in Harlem and found a mentor in Willie "the Lion" Smith. After a stint as a freelance studio musician (1931–35), he formed a sophisticated band that stirred excitement with its rendition of his *Interlude in B-flat* in N.Y. in 1936; in 1937 he organized a swing band that won enormous success with the hit recording of Cole Porter's *Begin the Beguine* in 1938. In 1940 he went to Holly-

wood, where he produced the hit recording *Frenesi;* toured again with his own big band, from which he drew members of the Gramercy Five, a group with which he was active off and on from 1940 until its last recording session in 1954. In the interim, he led several big bands, winning his greatest acclaim with his recording of *Little Jazz* (1945). His interest in the classical repertoire for his instrument led him to appear as a soloist with various orchs.; also performed at N.Y.'s Carnegie Hall. In 1983 he came out of retirement to lead still another big band. Shaw is a remarkable clarinetist; his superb playing is perhaps best revealed in his recording *Concerto for Clarinet* (1940). He was married 8 times, numbering among his wives the film stars Lana Turner and Ava Gardner. He publ. a quasi-autobiographical novel, *The Trouble with Cinderella: An Outline of Identity* (N.Y., 1952), and the novel *I Love You, I Hate You, Drop Dead!* (1965).

BIBL.: E. Blandford, *A. S.: A Bio-discography* (Hastings, 1973); V. Simosko, "A. S. and His Gramercy Fives," *Journal of Jazz Studies,* I/1 (1973); B. Korst and C. Garrod, *A. S. and His Orchestra* (Spotswood, N.J., 1974).

Shaw, George Bernard, famous Irish dramatist; b. Dublin, July 26, 1856; d. Ayot St. Lawrence, England, Nov. 2, 1950. Before winning fame as a playwright, he was active as a music critic in London, writing for the *Star* under the name of "Corno di Bassetto" (1888–89) and for the *World* (1890–94). In 1899 he publ. *The Perfect Wagnerite,* a highly individual socialistic interpretation of the *Ring of the Nibelung.* His criticisms from the *World* were reprinted as *Music in London* (3 vols., 1932; new ed., 1950); those from the *Star* as *London Music in 1888–89* (London and N.Y., 1937); selected criticisms were ed. by E. Bentley (N.Y., 1954). Shaw's play *Arms and the Man* was made into an operetta, *The Chocolate Soldier,* by Oskar Straus (1908); his *Pygmalion* was converted into a highly successful musical comedy under the title *My Fair Lady,* with a musical score by Frederick Loewe (1956).

BIBL.: W. Irvine, "G.B. S.'s Musical Criticism," *Musical Quarterly* (July 1946).

Shaw, Martin (Edward Fallas), English organist and composer; b. London, March 9, 1875; d. Southwold, Sussex, Oct. 24, 1958. He was a pupil at the Royal College of Music in London; played organ in various churches in London. In 1900 he founded the Purcell Operatic Society in London. He was made an Officer of the Order of the British Empire in 1955. He composed the operas *Mr. Pepys* (London, Feb. 11, 1926) and *The Thorn of Avalon* (1931); also incidental music; sacred works; some 100 songs; etc. He publ. *The Principles of English Church Music Composition* (London, 1921) and *Up to Now* (autobiography; London, 1929). Among his eds., all publ. in London, are *Songs of Britain* (with F. Kidson; 1913), *The English Carol Book* (with P. Dearmer; 1913–19), *The League of Nations Song Book* (with P. Dearmer; 1921), *Songs of Praise* (with P. Dearmer and R. Vaughan Williams; 1925; 2nd ed., augmented, 1931), and *The Oxford Book of Carols* (1928; 25th ed., rev., 1964).

BIBL.: E. Routley, *M. S.: A Centenary Appreciation* (London, 1975).

Shaw, Mary (née **Postans**), English contralto; b. Lea, Kent, 1814; d. Hadleigh Hall, Suffolk, Sept. 9, 1876. She studied at the Royal Academy of Music in London (1828–31), and then with Sir George Smart; under the name Mary Postans, she made a successful debut in London (1834); the next year she married the painter Alfred Shaw and thereafter appeard as Mary Shaw. In 1838 she sang with the Leipzig Gewandhaus Orch. under Mendelssohn's direction; her operatic debut followed as Imelda in the premiere of Verdi's 1st opera, *Oberto, conte di San Bonifacio,* at Milan's La Scala (Nov. 17, 1839); in 1842 she sang at Lodnon's Covent Garden and at Drury Lane. In 1844, at the height of her success, her husband went insane; the shock affected her vocal cords, so that she was unable to sing. Some time later she remarried and went to live in the country.

Shaw, Oliver, blind American organist, tenor, teacher, and composer; b. Middleboro, Mass., March 13, 1779; d. Providence, R.I., Dec. 31, 1848. He lost his eyesight in an accident; about 1800 he began taking music lessons with John Berkenhead, Gottlieb Graupner, and Thomas Granger. After teaching piano and organ in Dedham, Mass. (1805–7), he settled in Providence; was organist at the First Congregational Church (1809–32); was a founder of the Psallonian Society in 1809, remaining its director until it was disbanded in 1833. He was a composer of popular psalm tunes and ballads, including *Mary's Tears, The Inspiration, Sweet Little Ann,* and *The Death of Perry.* He publ. the manuals *A Plain Introduction to the Art of Playing the Pianoforte* (1811) and *O. Shaw's Instructions for the Pianoforte* (1831).

BIBL.: T. Williams, *A Discourse on the Life and Death of O. S.* (Boston, 1851); F. Denison, A. Stanley, and E. Glezen, eds., *Memorial of O. S.* (Providence, R.I., 1884); B. Degen, *O. S.: His Music and Contribution to American Society* (diss., Univ. of Rochester, 1971).

Shaw, Robert (Lawson), distinguished American conductor; b. Red Bluff, Calif., April 30, 1916. He came from a clerical family; his father and his grandfather were clergymen; his mother sang in church choirs. He studied at Pomona College (1934–38), where he conducted its Glee Club; in 1938 Fred Waring asked him to help organize the Fred Waring Glee Club, and Shaw conducted it until 1945. In 1941 he founded his own Collegiate Chorale in N.Y., which he led in diversified programs of choral music, old and new, until 1954. In 1944 he was awarded a Guggenheim fellowship. He taught choral conducting at the Berkshire Music Center at Tanglewood (1946–48), and concurrently at the Juilliard School of Music in N.Y. In 1946 he made his debut as a sym. conductor with the Naumburg Orch. in N.Y. In 1948 he founded the Robert Shaw Chorale, which he conducted with notable success for 20 seasons. Eager to acquire more experience as an orch. conductor, he studied conducting with Monteux in San Francisco and Rodzinski in N.Y. in 1950. From 1953 to 1958 he conducted summer concerts of the San Diego Sym. Orch. In 1956 he led the Robert Shaw Chorale through a tour of 15 countries of Europe, including Russia, and the Middle East, under the auspices of the State Dept. In 1964 the Robert Shaw Chorale gave concerts in South America. For his Chorale, Shaw commissioned several choral works from contemporary composers, including Béla Bartók, Darius Milhaud, Benjamin Britten, Samuel Barber, and Aaron Copland. Beginning in 1956 he was co-director of the Alaska Festival of Music in Anchorage. From 1956 to 1967 he served as associate conductor with Szell and the Cleveland Orch. In 1967 he became music director of the Atlanta Sym. Orch., and by dint of talent and perseverance brought it to a high degree of excellence. In 1977 he conducted it at the gala concert for President Carter's inauguration in Washington, D.C., and in 1988 he took it to Europe. After retiring from his post in 1988, he was accorded the titles of music director emeritus and conductor laureate. He then was active as director of the new inst. named in his honor at Emory Univ.

BIBL.: J. Mussulman, *Dear People . . . R. S.: A Biography* (Bloomington, Ind. and London, 1979); M. Shakespeare, "R. S. Remembers," *Ovation* (May 1988).

Shaw, (Harold) Watkins, English musicologist and teacher; b. Bradford, April 3, 1911. He studied history at Wadham College, Oxford (B.A., 1932); then took courses in musicology with Colles and R.O. Morris at the Royal College of Music in London (1932–33); received the D.Litt in the faculty of music from the Univ. of Oxford (1967). In 1949 he was appointed lecturer at the Worcester College of Education; from 1971 until his retirement in 1980, he served as keeper of the Parry Room Library at the Royal College of Music. In 1985 he was made an Officer of the Order of the British Empire. Among his publs. are *The Three Choirs Festival, c. 1713–1953* (1954), *The Story of Handel's "Messiah," 1741–1784* (London, 1963), *A Textual and Historical Companion to Handel's "Messiah"*

(London, 1965), and *The Organists and Organs of Hereford Cathedral* (Hereford, 1976); also ed. *Sir Frederick Ouseley and St Michael's, Tenbury* (Birmingham, 1988).

Shawe-Taylor, Desmond (Christopher), eminent Irish music critic; b. Dublin, May 29, 1907. He was educated at Oriel College, Oxford (1926–30); through the years he contributed literary and musical criticism to various newspapers and periodicals. After service in World War II, he was engaged as music critic of the *New Statesman* in 1945, retaining his post until 1958; from 1950 to 1958 he also served as phonograph record reviewer for the *Observer.* In 1958 he was named music critic of the *Sunday Times;* he retired in 1983; also was a guest critic for the *New Yorker* (1973–74). He was made a Commander of the Order of the British Empire in 1965. His writings are notable for their unostentatious display of wide learning. He publ. the vol. *Covent Garden* for the World of Music series (London, 1948); also, with Edward Sackville-West, *The Record Guide* (London, 1951, and later rev. eds.). He contributed a number of insightful biographies of singers to *The New Grove Dictionary of Music and Musicians* (1980).

Shchedrin, Rodion (Konstantinovich), brilliant Russian composer; b. Moscow, Dec. 16, 1932. His father was a music theorist and writer. After piano lessons in childhood, he attended the music and then choral schools (1948–51) attached to the Moscow Cons.; subsequently took courses in piano with Yakov Flier and composition with Yuri Shaporin at the Cons. (1951–55), where he subsequently taught (1965–69). Following graduation, he achieved great recognition within the accepted Soviet establishment; wrote about current trends in Soviet music in official publications; held several significant posts within the Composer's Union, including chairman of the Russian Federation section (from 1974); received many awards, and was made a People's Artist of the U.S.S.R. (1981). In 1964, 1968, and 1986 he visited the U.S. on cultural-exchange programs. His music has wide appeal, artfully employing numerous pseudo-modernistic devices; particularly interesting among his compositions are the aleatoric 2nd Sym., the prepared encore for the 1st Piano Concerto, and his ballets *Anna Karenina* and *Carmen Suite,* which incorporate music by earlier composers (Tchaikovsky and Bizet, respectively). He was married to the ballerina Maya Plisetskaya, for whom he wrote several ballets.

WORKS: (all 1st perf. in Moscow unless otherwise given): STAGE: OPERAS: *Not for Love Alone* (Dec. 25, 1961; version for Chamber Orch., 1971); *Dead Souls,* after Gogol (1976; June 7, 1977). BALLETS: *The Little Humpback Horse* (1955; March 4, 1960); *Carmen Suite* (April 20, 1967); *Anna Karenina* (1971; June 10, 1972); *The Seagull* (1979; rev. 1980); also incidental music to plays and films. ORCH.: 2 syms.: No. 1 (Dec. 6, 1958); No. 2, 25 *Preludes* (April 11, 1965); 2 concertos: No. 1, *The Naughty Limericks* (Warsaw, Sept. 1963); No. 2, *Ringing Bells* (N.Y., Jan. 11, 1968); 3 piano concertos: No. 1 (Nov. 7, 1954; rev. version, May 5, 1974); No. 2 (1966; Jan. 5, 1967); No. 3 (1973; May 5, 1974); 2 suites from *The Little Humpback Horse* (1955, 1965); Suite from *Not for Love Alone* (1964); *Symphonic Fanfares,* festive overture (Nov. 6, 1967); *Anna Karenina,* Romantic music (Oct. 24, 1972); *The Nursery,* transcription of Mussorgsky's song cycle (Stockholm, March 5, 1972); *Solemn Overture* (Dec. 1982); *Music for the Town of Kothen* for Chamber Orch. (1985); *Geometry of Sound* for 18 Soloists (Cologne, April 28, 1987). CHAMBER: Suite for Clarinet and Piano (1951); Piano Quintet (1952); 2 string quartets (1951, 1954); Chamber Suite for 20 Violins, Harp, Accordion, and 2 Double Basses (1961); *The Frescoes of Dionysus* for Nonet (1981); *Musical Offering* for Organ, 3 Flutes, 3 Bassoons, and 3 Trombones (Oct. 21, 1983); *Musical Offering* for Organ and Wind Instruments (1985); *Echo Sonata* for Solo Violin (Cologne, April 28, 1987). PIANO: 2 Études (1949); *Festivity on a Collective Farm* (1951); 9 Pieces (1952–61); *Variations on a Theme of Glinka* (1957); *Toccatina* (1958); Sonata (1962); 24 Preludes and Fugues (1970); *Polyphonic Book* (1972); *Notebook for Youth* (1982); numerous other solo pieces. VOCAL: *Ukrainian Night*

Is Quiet (1950); 13 Russian Folk Songs (1950); 12 Choruses (1950–70); *Song and Ditties of Varvara* (1961); *Bureaucratiade*, cantata based upon rules of a boarding house (1963; Feb. 24, 1965); 3 Solfège Exercises (1965); 2 *Laments* (1965); *Poetica*, concerto for Narrator, Female Soloist, Chorus, and Orch. (Feb. 24, 1968); *Lenin Lives in the People's Heart* (1969; Feb. 6, 1970); *The Song of Pugachev* (1981); 6 Stanzas from *Eugene Onegin* (1981); Concertino for Chorus a cappella (1982).

Shcherbachev, Vladimir (Vladimirovich), Russian composer; b. Warsaw, Jan. 24, 1889; d. Leningrad, March 5, 1952. He studied at the St. Petersburg Cons. with Maximilian Steinberg and Liadov, graduating in 1914. From 1924 to 1931 he was a prof. of composition at the Leningrad Cons. He wrote an opera, *Anna Kolosova* (1939); 5 syms.: No. 1 (1913; Petrograd, Nov. 5, 1916); No. 2 (1922–24; Leningrad, Dec. 14, 1924); No. 3 (1926–31; Leningrad, Feb. 4, 1932, composer conducting); No. 4, *History of the Izhorsky Factory* (1932–34; partial perf., Leningrad, May 28, 1934; 1st complete perf., Radio Leningrad, Dec. 23, 1935; 1st public perf., Leningrad, Jan. 21, 1936); No. 5, *Russkaya* (1942–48; Leningrad, Dec. 21, 1948; rev. version, Kiev, Oct. 21, 1950); music for films; the orch. suite from one of them, *The Thunderstorm*, became popular in Russia; he further wrote *A Fairy Tale* for Orch. (Petrograd, Dec. 20, 1915); Nonet (1917); numerous piano works.

BIBL.: G. Orlov, *V.V. S.* (Leningrad, 1959).

Shearing, George (Albert), prominent blind English-born American jazz pianist; b. London, Aug. 13, 1919. He was blind from birth; learned to read music with Braille notation; for several years, he played piano in a blind band; then transferred to the U.S. in 1947 (naturalized in 1955), and organized a quintet, with vibraphone, guitar, drums, and bass. In the early 1940s he played a typical stride style of the time; in the late 1940s, influenced by the innovations of bebop, he developed a new manner, characterized by surprising, extended harmonies, and a pianistic technique whereby both hands play thick chords in parallel motion ("locked-hand style"). He composed famous tunes, among them *Lullaby of Birdland* (1952).

BIBL.: L. Feather, "Piano Giants of Jazz: G. S.," *Contemporary Keyboard*, III/8 (1977).

Shebalin, Vissarion (Yakovlevich), Russian composer; b. Omsk, June 11, 1902; d. Moscow, May 28, 1963. He studied at the Moscow Cons. with Miaskovsky (1923–28); then began teaching there; in 1935, was appointed prof. of composition there; from 1942 to 1948, was its director. On Feb. 10, 1948, by resolution of the Central Committee of the Communist Party, he was condemned (along with Shostakovich, Prokofiev, Miaskovsky, and others) for adhering to a "decadent formalism" in composition; but these strictures were removed in a corrective declaration of May 28, 1958, "restoring the dignity and integrity of Soviet composers."

WORKS: STAGE: MUSICAL COMEDY: *Bridegroom from the Embassy* (Sverdlovsk, Aug. 1, 1942). **OPERAS:** *The Taming of the Shrew,* after Shakespeare (concert version, Oct. 1, 1955; stage premiere, Kuibishev, May 25, 1957); *Sun over the Steppe* (Moscow, June 9, 1958). **BALLETS:** *Festival* (1958; unfinished); *Reminiscences of a Bygone Day* (1961). **ORCH.:** 5 syms.: No. 1 (1925; Leningrad, Nov. 13, 1926); No. 2 (1929); No. 3 (1934; Moscow, Feb. 11, 1944); No. 4 (1935; Moscow, Feb. 27, 1936); No. 5 (Moscow, Oct. 9, 1962); *Overture on Mari Themes* (1926); Horn Concertino (1930; rev. 1959); Violin Concertino (1931); 3 suites (1935; 1935, rev. 1961; 1963); *Variations on Russian Folk Songs* (1940); Violin Concerto (Leningrad, Oct. 29, 1940); *Russian Overture* (1941); Sinfonietta (1949); Cello Concerto (1950); symphonic poem, *Lenin*, with Chorus and Soloists (1931; Leningrad, Jan. 21, 1934; rev. 1959). **CHAMBER:** 9 string quartets (1923, 1934, 1939, 1940, 1942, 1943, 1947, 1960, 1963); Piano Trio (1924); Viola Sonata (1954); Violin Sonata (1958); Cello Sonata (1960); Guitar Sonatina (1963); also several piano sonatas; vocal works, including a cantata, *Moscow* (Moscow, Dec. 14, 1946), and songs. He completed Mussorgsky's unfinished opera *The Fair at Sorochintsy*, using only

Mussorgsky's own material (Leningrad, Dec. 21, 1931; version with supplementary materials, Moscow, March 19, 1952).

BIBL.: G. Abraham, *Eight Soviet Composers* (London, 1943); I. Boelza, *V. S.* (Moscow, 1945); I. Boelza and V. Protopopov, eds., *V.Y. S.: Articles, Reminiscences, Materials* (Moscow, 1970); V. Protopopov, ed., *V.Y. S.: Literary Heritage* (Moscow, 1975).

Shedlock, J(ohn) S(outh), English pianist and writer on music; b. Reading, Sept. 29, 1843; d. London, Jan. 9, 1919. After graduating from London Univ. (1864), he studied composition with Lalo in Paris; upon his return to London, he devoted himself to writing; was music critic of the *Academy* (1879–1901) and the *Athenæum* (1898–1916); also ed. the *Monthly Musical Record*; taught piano and music history at the Royal Academy of Music in London (1901–5). He publ. a detailed description of Beethoven's sketchbook purchased by the British Museum (*Musical Times*, June 1892–Jan. 1893); this led him to further investigations of Beethoven memorabilia, and in 1893 he discovered in Berlin a copy of Cramer's studies with notations by Beethoven; publ. his findings as *The Beethoven-Cramer Studies* (1893); also publ. 2 vols. of Beethoven's letters in English translation (1909), a short biography of Beethoven (1905), and a valuable book, *The Pianoforte Sonata: Its Origin and Development* (London, 1895).

Sheinfeld, David, American composer and violinist; b. St. Louis, Sept. 20, 1906. He began violin training as a child, then studied harmony and counterpoint in Chicago; subsequently was a student of Respighi in Rome (1929–31). After pursuing his career in Chicago (1931–44), he studied conducting with Monteux; then played in the Pittsburgh Sym. Orch. (1944–45) and the San Francisco Sym. Orch. (1945–71). In his compositions from 1962, he combined tonal and atonal writing.

WORKS: *Adagio and Allegro* for Orch. (1946; San Francisco, March 14, 1947); *Concerto for Orchestra* (1949; San Francisco, Feb. 20, 1951); Sonata for Solo Violin (1950); *Fantasia* for Trumpet, Piano, Percussion, and Strings (1951); Violin Concerto (1955; Philadelphia, April 23, 1965); Concerto for Woodwinds and Chamber Orch. (1957; San Francisco, Jan. 14, 1958); *Études* for Orch. (1959; Pittsburgh, Nov. 18, 1960); *Serenade* for 6 Instruments (1961); *Patterns* for Harp (1962); *4 Pieces* for Cello (1964); Duo for Viola and Harp (1965); *Dialogues* for Chamber Orch. (Philadelphia, Oct. 26, 1966); *Confrontations* for Electric Guitar, Electric Violin, Saxophone, and Orch. (1969; Oakland, Calif., Jan. 20, 1970); *Memories of Yesterday and Tomorrow* for 3 Players (1971); *Time Warp* for Electric Instruments and Orch. (1972; San Francisco, Jan. 24, 1973); *Elegiac Sonorities* for Organ (1973); *Dualities* for Harp (1976); 2 string quartets (1978, 1990); *The Earth Is a Sounding Board* for Small Chorus and Orch. (1978); *Dreams and Fantasies* for Orch. (1981; San Francisco, May 5, 1982); *Threnody* for Violin (1981); *Polarities*, sym. (1990).

Shekhter, Boris (Semyonovich), Russian composer and teacher; b. Odessa, Jan. 20, 1900; d. Moscow, Dec. 16, 1961. He was graduated from the Odessa Cons. in 1922; then entered the Moscow Cons., studying composition with Vasilenko and Miaskovsky; graduated in 1929. In 1940 he became a prof. at the Ashkhabad Cons.

WORKS: OPERAS: *1905 god* (The Year 1905; 1935; rev. 1955; in collaboration with A. Davidenko); *Yusup i Akhmet* (1941; Ashkhabad, June 12, 1942; in collaboration with A. Kuliyev). **ORCH.:** 5 syms. (1929; 1943; 1944–45; 1947; 1951, rev. 1952–53); *Turkmenia*, suite based on Central Asian themes (1932; Florence ISCM Festival, April 4, 1934); Piano Concerto (1932); *Rhapsody* (1935); also cantatas; choruses; piano pieces; songs.

Shelley, Harry Rowe, American organist, teacher, and composer; b. New Haven, Conn., June 8, 1858; d. Short Beach, Conn., Sept. 12, 1947. He was a pupil of Dudley Buck and Dvořák in N.Y.; from 1878 he was active as a church organist and teacher. He ed. 4 organ anthologies, including *Gems for the Organ, The Modern Organist,* and *101 Interludes for Organ;* a number of his compositions were quite popular in his day.

WORKS: OPERAS: *Romeo and Juliet* (1901); *Old Black Joe* (1911). **ORCH.:** Violin Concerto (1891); Sym. (1897); *Santa Claus*, overture (1900); other orch. pieces. **CANTATAS:** *Vexilla regis* (1893); *The Inheritance Divine* (1895); *Death and Life* (1898); *Lochinvar's Ride* (1915); etc.; also partsongs; songs; organ pieces.

Shelton, Lucy (Alden), American soprano; b. Pomona, Calif., Feb. 25, 1944. She studied at Pomona College (B.A., 1965) and with Gladys Miller at the New England Cons. of Music in Boston (M.M., 1968); completed her training with Jan De-Gaetani at the Aspen School of Music. While a member of the Jubal Trio, she shared in winning the Naumburg Competition in 1977, and then won it on her own in 1980. She sang with the Waverly Consort, the N.Y. Pro Musica, and the 20th Century Consort of the Smithsonian Institution, and also pursued a career as a touring solo artist. While she has become closely associated with the performance of contemporary music, her repertoire ranges across the entire spectrum of music.

Sheng, Bright, remarkable Chinese composer; b. Shanghai, Dec. 6, 1955. He began piano lessons when he was 5; after graduating from high school, he worked as a pianist and timpanist in a dance company in Chinhai, near Tibet, where he began to study Chinese folk music. After China's Cultural Revolution, he entered the Shanghai Cons. (1976), where he earned an undergraduate degree in composition. In 1982 he followed his parents to the U.S., where he attended Queens College at the City Univ. of N.Y. and Columbia Univ.; his teachers included Chou-Wen Chung, Mario Davidovsky, George Perle, and Hugo Weisgall. Sheng received numerous awards, both in China and the U.S., including NEA grants, a Guggenheim fellowship, and awards from the American Academy and Inst. of Arts and Letters. His works have been championed by such eminent artists as Peter Serkin, who commissioned his *MY SONG* (1988), and Gerard Schwarz, who has given many premiere performances of his orch. pieces. His *H'UN (Lacerations): In Memoriam 1966–1976* was the 1st runner-up for the 1989 Pulitzer Prize in music. Sheng appeared throughout the U.S. as a lecturer; he is currently composer-in-residence of the Chicago Lyric Opera, for which he is writing an opera, *The Song of Majnun*, to a libretto by Andrew Porter on an Islamic legend. He also orchestrated Leonard Bernstein's *Arias and Barcarolles*, which received its premiere performance under the direction of Leonard Slatkin in N.Y. on Dec. 6, 1990. Like so many refugees of China's cultural upheaval, Sheng strives to find the personal means to integrate the disparate musical styles of China and the West.

WORKS: Trio for Flute, Harp, and Cello (1982); *3 Pieces* for Orch. (1981; Shanghai, July 1, 1982); *3 Pieces* for Flute (1982; N.Y., Nov. 8, 1985); *5 Pieces* for Oboe and Cello (1983; N.Y., Feb. 20, 1986); 2 string quartets: No. 1 (1984; N.Y., Nov. 11, 1985); No. 2 (1984; Tanglewood, Aug. 21, 1985); *4 Poems from the Tang Dynasty* for Mezzo-soprano and Piano (1984; Tanglewood, Aug. 23, 1985); Suite for Piano (Aspen, Aug. 23, 1984); *5 Chinese Folk Songs* for Tenor and Piano (N.Y., Sept. 21, 1985); *3 Poems from the Sung Dynasty* for Soprano and Chamber Orch. (1985; N.Y., March 26, 1986); *Shao* for Oboe, Violin, Cello, and Piano (N.Y., April 1986); *3 Pieces* for Viola and Piano (1986; N.Y., Jan. 15, 1987); *Adagio* for Chamber Orch. (N.Y., March 7, 1987); *H'UN (Lacerations): In Memoriam 1966–1976* for Orch. (1987; N.Y., April 16, 1988); *3 Chinese Love Songs* for Soprano, Viola, and Piano (Tanglewood, Aug. 26, 1988); *MY SONG* for Piano (1988; N.Y., 1989); *3 Chinhai Folk Songs* for Chorus and Orch. (Boston, Oct. 28, 1989).

BIBL.: M. Swed, "B. S.: A Long Musical March from China," *N.Y. Times* (Dec. 4, 1990).

Shenshin, Alexander (Alexeievich), Russian conductor, teacher, and composer; b. Moscow, Nov. 18, 1890; d. there, Feb. 14, 1944. He studied philology at Moscow Univ.; later took music lessons with Gretchaninoff and Glière. He subsequently taught music in Moscow, and also conducted occasional sym. concerts. His music is cast in a style reminiscent

of Liadov; the elements of exotic musical patterns are noticeable. He composed an opera, *O T'ao* (1925); ballets: *Ancient Dances* (1933) and *Story of Carmen* (1935); a song cycle, *From Japanese Anthologies;* numerous songs to German poems.

BIBL.: V. Belaiev, *A.A. S.* (Moscow, 1929).

Shepherd, Arthur, eminent American composer and pedagogue; b. Paris, Idaho, Feb. 19, 1880; d. Cleveland, Jan. 12, 1958. He studied with G. Haessel; in 1892, entered the New England Cons. of Music in Boston, where he studied piano with Dennée and Carl Faelten, and composition with Goetschius and Chadwick. In 1897 he went to Salt Lake City, where he settled as a teacher and as conductor of the Salt Lake Sym. Orch.; returned to Boston in 1908, and became a prof. of harmony and counterpoint at the New England Cons. of Music (until 1917; again in 1919–20). In 1917 he joined the U.S. Army, and was bandmaster of the 303rd Field Artillery in France. He settled in Cleveland, where he was assistant conductor (1920–26) and program annotator (1920–30) of its orch., prof. at Western Reserve Univ. (1927–50), and music critic of the *Cleveland Press* (1928–31). In 1938 he was elected to membership in the National Inst. of Arts and Letters. A composer of national tendencies, he wrote in a grand Romantic manner, derived from an intense feeling for American melos. He publ. a valuable handbook, *The String Quartets of Beethoven* (Cleveland, 1937).

WORKS: ORCH.: Overtures: *The Nuptials of Attila, Ouverture joyeuse* (Paderewski Prize, 1902); *The Festival of Youth* (1915); *Overture to a Drama* (1919; Cleveland, March 27, 1924); *Fantaisie humoresque* for Piano and Orch. (Boston, Feb. 8, 1918); *Horizons*, 1st Sym. (Cleveland, Dec. 15, 1927); *Choreographic Suite* (Cleveland, Oct. 22, 1931); 2nd Sym. (Cleveland, March 7, 1940); *Fantasy on Down East Spirituals* (Indianapolis, Nov. 2, 1946); Violin Concerto (1946–47); *Theme and Variations* (Cleveland, April 9, 1953); *Hilaritas*, overture for Concert Band (1942). **CHORAL:** *The City in the Sea* for Baritone, Double Chorus, and Orch. (1913); *Song of the Sea Wind* for Women's Voices and Piano (1915); *He Came All So Still* for Women's Voices a cappella (1915); *Deck Thyself My Soul* for Chorus and Organ (1918); *Song of the Pilgrims* for Tenor, Double Chorus, and Orch. (1932); *Ballad of Trees and the Master* for Chorus (1935); *Invitation to the Dance* for Chorus and Orch. or 2 Pianos (1936); *Grace for Gardens* for Chorus (1938); *Build Thee More Stately Mansions* for Women's Voices (1938); *Psalm XLII* for Chorus and Orch. (1944); *Drive On* for Baritone and Chorus (1946); songs. **CHAMBER:** 2 violin sonatas (1914, 1927); *Triptych* for Voice and String Quartet (1926); 5 string quartets (1926, 1933, 1936, 1944, 1955); Piano Quintet (1940); *Praeludium salutatorium* for Flute, Oboe, Horn, Bassoon, Violin, Viola, and Cello (1942); *Divertissement* for Flute, Oboe, Clarinet, Bassoon, and Horn (1943). **PIANO:** 2 sonatas in F minor (1907, 1929).

BIBL.: D. Leedy, "A. S.," *Modern Music*, XVI (1939); W. Newman, "A. S.," *Musical Quarterly* (April 1950); R. Loucks, *A. S.: American Composer* (Provo, Utah, 1980).

Sheppard, John, English composer; b. c.1515; d. c.1559. He became Informator choristarum at Magdalen College, Oxford, in 1543; by 1552 he was a Gentleman of the Chapel Royal. His distinguished output of sacred music includes Latin masses, Mass sections, Magnificats, motets, English service music, and anthems.

BIBL.: H. Lamont, *J. S.: His Life and Music* (diss., Univ. of Southern Calif., 1963).

Shere, Charles, American writer on music and composer; b. Berkeley, Calif., Aug. 20, 1935. He was reared on a small farm in Sonoma County, where he attended high school and learned to play wind instruments; after graduating from the Univ. of Calif. at Berkeley with a degree in English (1960), he studied composition with Robert Erickson privately and at the San Francisco Cons. of Music, and also studied conducting with Gerhard Samuel (1961–64); also studied art, on which he later wrote and lectured extensively. From 1964 to 1967 he was music director of Berkeley's KPFA-FM; also was active at San Francisco's KQED-TV (1967–73), an instructor at Mills College in Oakland (1973–84), and art and music critic for the Oakland *Tribune* (1972–88). He was co-founder, publisher, ed., and a major contributor to *EAR*, a monthly new-music tabloid magazine. He is married to Lindsey Remolif Shere, the famed pastry chef of Chez Panisse in Berkeley. Shere describes his early compositions, many notated in open form and scored for unspecified or variable ensembles, as "rural and contemplative rather than urban and assertive in nature"; his later works utilize more conventional notation, his shift from pen-and-ink to computer-generated notation, coinciding with a greater use of rhythmic conventions, as in the ostinatos in the finales of his *Symphony in 3 Movements* (1988), *Concerto for Violin with Harp, Percussion, and Small Orchestra* (1985), and *Sonata: Bachelor Machine* (1989).

WORKS: *Fratture* for 7 Instruments (1962; Osaka, Dec. 23, 1963); *Small Concerto* for Piano and Orch. (1964; Aptos, Calif., Aug. 22, 1965); *Ces désirs du quatuor* for any 4 Musicians (1965); *Quartet No. 2* for 3 to 5 or 6 Musicians (1966); *Ces désirs du vent des gregoriens* for Tape (1967); *Nightmusic* for Diminished Orch. (1967; Oakland, Jan. 24, 1982, K. Nagano conducting); *Screen, Quartet No. 3* for 4 to 6 Strings (1969); *Quartet No. 7, Like a piece of silvered glass,* for Flute, English Horn, Clarinet, and Bassoon (1970); *Handler of Gravity* for Organ and Optional Chimes (1971); *Soigneur de gravité (de l'orgue pour orchestre)* for Orch. (1972); *Parergon to Woodwind Quintet* for English Horn, Bass Clarinet, and Bassoon (1974); *Music for Orchestra (Symphony)* (Kensington, Calif., Oct. 28, 1976, composer conducting); *Tongues* for Poet (speaking in tongues), Chamber Orch., and Tape (San Francisco, May 6, 1978); *String Quartet No. 1* (Oakland, Calif., May 10, 1980); *The Box of 1914,* opera (1980; San Francisco, Jan. 29, 1981); *Certain Phenomena of Sound* for Soprano and Violin (1983; San Francisco, Feb. 11, 1984); *The Bride Stripped Bare by Her Bachelors, Even,* opera (partial perf., Oakland, Dec. 1, 1984); *Concerto for Violin with Harp, Percussion, and Small Orchestra* (1985; Aptos, Calif., July 21, 1990); *Requiem with Oboe* for 8 Voices or Double Chorus, and Oboe (San Francisco, June 11, 1985); *Ladies Voices,* chamber opera for 3 Sopranos and 6 Instruments (Berkeley, Oct. 30, 1987); *Symphony in 3 Movements* (1988; Berkeley, April 28, 1989, K. Nagano conducting); *I Like It to Be a Play* for Tenor, Baritone, Bass, and String Quartet (San Francisco, Feb. 6, 1989); *Sonata: Bachelor Machine* for Piano (1989; San Francisco, July 25, 1990).

Sheremetiev, Count Alexander, Russian nobleman and amateur musician; b. St. Petersburg, March 12, 1859; d. Ste.-Geneviève-des-Bois, near Paris, May 18, 1931. The private choir maintained by his father, Dmitri, attained wide celebrity in St. Petersburg. In 1882 Count Alexander founded a sym. orch. in his own name, and in 1884 a church choir under the direction of Archangelsky. In 1898 he instituted in St. Petersburg a series of sym. concerts at popular prices, conducted by himself and others. Thanks to his inherited wealth, he was able to engage excellent musicians; presented programs of Russian composers, thus contributing to the cause of national music. He also wrote some pieces himself (*Pathetische Fantasie* for Orch.; chamber music; etc.). After the Revolution of 1917 he went to Paris, and died in poverty, in a Russian charity institution near Paris.

Sheriff, Noam, Israeli composer; b. Tel Aviv, Jan. 7, 1935. He took private lessons in composition with Ben-Haim (1949–57); studied philosophy at the Hebrew Univ. of Jerusalem (1956–60); then attended classes of Boris Blacher at the Hochschule für Musik in Berlin (1960–62). Returning to Israel, he taught at the Jerusalem Academy of Music (from 1966) and at the National Academy in Tel Aviv (from 1967). Most of his works are inspired by Jewish folk rhythms and melodic patterns, arranged in modernistic atonal and asymmetrical configurations.

WORKS: ORCH.: *Festival Prelude* (1957); *Song of Degrees* (1960); *Israel Suite* (1965); *Metamorphoses on a Galliard* for Chamber Orch. (1967); 2 *Epigrams* for Chamber Orch. (1968);

A Stone in the Tower of David (1970); *Sonata* for Chamber Orch. (1973); *Song of Songs* for Flute and Orch. (1981); *Prayers* for String Orch. (1983); *La Follia,* variations (1984). **CHAMBER:** *Destination 5 Minutes* for Brass and Percussion (1962); *Confession* for Cello (1966); *Arabesque* for Flute (1966); 3 *Inventions* for Flute (1967), Horn (1968), and Harp (1968); 2 string quartets (1973, 1982); *Quintet for Harp and Strings* (1975–76); *Viola Sonata* (1976); *Mai-Ko-Mashma Ian* (What do we Understand from the Discussions of Rabbis?) for Harp and String Quartet (1976); *Trei-Assar,* dodecalogue for 12 Cellos (1978); *Mirkam for Chen* for Vibraphone (1982); *Butterflies* for 2 Flutes (1983); *A Little "Ligur,"* partita for Viola and Cello (1984). VOCAL: *Ashrei* (Blessed Is the Man) for Contralto, Flute, 2 Harps, and 2 Tom-toms (1961); *The Story of Deborah,* choreographic movement for Chorus, Brass, Percussion, and Synthesizers (1976); *Nocturnes* for Voice and Piano (1983). **BALLET MUSIC:** *Heptaprisms* (1965); *Cain,* electronic ballet music (1969); also numerous folk song arrangements.

Sherman, Norman, American bassoonist, teacher, and composer; b. Boston, Feb. 25, 1926. He studied composition in Boston with Roslyn Brogue Henning and at Boston Univ. (1946–50), where he also received instruction in bassoon from Ernst Panenka; subsequently attended Messiaen's analysis class at the Paris Cons. (1950). He was principal bassoonist with the Winnipeg Sym. Orch. (1957–61), the Residentie Orch. in The Hague (1961–69), the National Arts Centre Orch. in Ottawa (1969–73), the Israel Radio Orch. (1973–74), and the Kingston (Ont.) Sym. Orch. (from 1974); also taught bassoon and chamber music at the Queen's Univ. in Kingston (from 1974).

WORKS: BALLET: *The Red Seed* (1950). ORCH.: *Sinfonia concertante* for Bassoon and Strings (1950; Winnipeg, Jan. 19, 1961); 2 *Pieces* (1952–62); *Through the Rainbow and/or Across the Valley* (1966–67; Rotterdam, April 25, 1968); *Thesis* (Kingston, March 23, 1975); *Canadian Summer* (1976); *The Events of November 10, 1812* for Narrator and Orch. (1978); *Icthyon* for 13 Strings (1979); *The 2-Bit Dance Hall* (1980); *The Pioneers* for Band (1982); *Garden of Love* for Strings, Brass, and Percussion (1988). **CHAMBER:** Concerto for Flute, Clarinet, Horn, Bassoon, and Piano (1948); *Traditions* for Flute, Oboe, Clarinet, and Bassoon (1948); *The Reunion* for Flute, Violin, Viola, and Cello (1971; CBC, Feb. 4, 1979); *Quadron* for String Quartet (Kingston, July 15, 1976); *Quintessant* for Flute, Oboe, Clarinet, Horn, and Bassoon (Kingston, May 11, 1977); *Bouquet* for Piano or Celesta, Clarinet, and 3 Percussion (1978); *Entretien* for Flute and Bassoon (1981); *Euphoria* for Flute, Clarinet, Horn, Bassoon, and Percussion (1983); *Tango* for Flute, Horn, Viola, and Cello (1984); *La Bodega* for Flute and Guitar (1987); also piano pieces.

Sherman, Russell, American pianist; b. N.Y., March 25, 1930. He took instruction in piano with Steuermann (1941–55); earned a degree in humanities at Columbia Univ. (B.A., 1949). On Nov. 17, 1945, he made his formal debut in a recital in N.Y., and then pursued a modest concert career while devoting himself mainly to teaching. In 1967 he became chairman of the piano dept. of the New England Cons. of Music in Boston; he was active in promoting contemporary music in chamber ensembles in the Boston area. His performances won praise for their discernment and spontaneity. In 1975 a N.Y. recital attracted attention and quickened interest in his career; in 1978 he performed in Paris and London, and was a soloist with the leading orchs. of Europe. In 1986 he joined the faculty of the Juilliard School in N.Y.

BIBL.: R. Dyer, "The Searching Talent of R. S.," *Ovation* (June 1985).

Sherrington, Helen. See **Lemmens-Sherrington, Helen.**

Sherry, Fred (Richard), American cellist and conductor; b. Montrose, N.Y., Oct. 27, 1948. He studied cello with Leonard Rose and Channing Roberts, and chamber music with Felix Galimir at the Juilliard School of Music in N.Y. (1965–69); in 1968, won the Young Concert Artist competition, which led to his solo debut at N.Y.'s Carnegie Recital Hall in 1969. With Richard Fritz, he organized the new-music group Speculum Musicae in 1971, remaining with it until 1978; was also a founding member of the chamber group Tashi in 1973. In 1989 he became artistic director of the Chamber Music Soc. of Lincoln Center in N.Y., which position he resigned in 1991.

Sherwin, William F(isk), American composer; b. Buckland, Mass., March 14, 1826; d. Dorchester, Mass., April 14, 1888. He received his musical training in singing schools led by Lowell Mason, G.J. Webb et al. He taught in the public schools and at the Claverack Seminary in Hudson, N.Y.; then went to Albany about 1855 as a teacher at the Female Academy and as music director at the Pearl Street Baptist Church. After being employed with the publishers Biglow & Main and Scribner & Co. in N.Y. (1865–80), he joined the firm of John Church & Co., in Cincinnati; then was director of choral music at the New England Cons. of Music in Boston (from 1884). With C.C. Case, he also was director of music at Chautauqua (from 1874). He publ. several hymnbooks and composed hymns; among his best known are *Bread of Life* (1877) and *Chautauqua* (1877), both to texts by Mary Ann Lathbury.
  BIBL.: S. Torrey, "W.F. S.," *Choir and Choral Magazine,* V/7 (1905); F. Metcalf, "Mary A. Lathbury and W.F. S.," *Choir and Musical Journal,* X (1919).

Sherwood, William Hall, American pianist, pedagogue, and composer; b. Lyons, N.Y., Jan. 31, 1854; d. Chicago, Jan. 7, 1911. He was the son of Rev. L.H. Sherwood, the founder of the Lyons Music Academy, from whom he received his primary education; spent 5 years studying with Kullak in Berlin; also took lessons with Liszt in Weimar. He returned to the U.S. in 1876; toured widely as a pianist; gave performances of numerous works by American composers and was also soloist in the U.S. premiere of Grieg's Piano Concerto. He taught at the New England Cons. of Music in Boston, in N.Y., and at the Chicago Cons. (1889–96), where he was head of the piano dept.; in 1897 he established his own Sherwood School of Music in Chicago; also was head of piano studies at the Chautauqua Institution (from 1889). Among his publ. compositions for piano are 2 suites and 2 sets of *Gypsy Dances.*

Shibata, Minao, Japanese composer; b. Tokyo, Sept. 29, 1916. He attended Tokyo Univ., graduating from the faculty of science in 1939; took private lessons in composition with Saburo Moroi (1940–43); taught at the Tokyo Geijutsu Daigaku (National Univ. of Fine Arts and Music; 1959–69).
  WORKS: Radio opera, *Strada a Roma* (1961); Piano Sonata (1943); 2 string quartets (1943, 1947); *Classical Suite* for Violin and Piano (1947); *Symbology* for Soprano and Chamber Orch. (1953); *Black Portrait* for Soprano and Chamber Orch. (1954); *Musique concrète* for Stereo Tape (1955); 2 *Improvisations* for Piano (1957, 1968); *Black Distance* for Soprano and Chamber Orch. (1958); 3 *Poems on Katsue Kitazono* for Soprano and Chamber Orch. (1954–58); Sinfonia (1960; Tokyo, Dec. 12, 1960); *Michi* (The Street) for Chorus and 4 Percussion Instruments (1960); *Poem Recited in the Night* for Soprano and Chamber Orch. (1963); *Essay* for 3 Trumpets and 3 Trombones (1965); *Improvisation for Electronic Sounds* (1968); *Imagery* for Marimba (1969); *Display '70 I and II* for Ryûteki, Marimba, Percussion, and Tape (1969, 1970); *Concerto for 8* for 8 Flutes (1971); *Consort* for Orch. and Tape (1972–73); *Trimurti* for Flute, Violin, Keyboard, and Electronics (1973–74); *Metaphor* for 27 Japanese Instruments (1975); *Yūgaku* for Orch. and Tape (1977); *Diaphonia* for Orch. and Tape (1979).

Shicoff, Neil, American tenor; b. N.Y., June 2, 1949. He began vocal training with his father, a cantor; then studied at the Juilliard School in N.Y. After singing Narroboth in *Salome* in Washington, D.C., he appeared as Ernani at the Cincinnati May Festival in 1975. On Oct. 15, 1976, he made his Metropolitan Opera debut in N.Y. as Rinuccio in *Gianni Schicchi,* returning there in subsequent seasons as the Duke in *Rigoletto,* Rodolfo, Werther, Hoffmann, Roméo, and Massenet's Des

Grieux; also sang at London's Covent Garden (debut as Pinkerton, 1978), the Chicago Lyric Opera (debut as Rodolfo, 1979), the San Francisco Opera (debut as Edgardo, 1981), and the Paris Opéra (debut as Roméo, 1981); also toured as a concert artist. In 1978 he married the soprano Judith Haddon.

Shield, William, English violinist and composer; b. Swalwell, County Durham, March 5, 1748; d. Brightling, Sussex, Jan. 25, 1829. He was taught by his father, a singing master, on whose death he was apprenticed to a shipbuilder; then took lessons in music with Charles Avison at Newcastle upon Tyne; played violin in various small theaters in the neighborhood; in 1772 he settled in London as violinist at the King's Theatre; from 1773 to 1791 he played the viola there. He produced his 1st comic opera, *A Flitch of Bacon,* at the Haymarket Theatre on Aug. 17, 1778; it was followed by a great number of theatrical pieces; he held the post of composer to Covent Garden from 1778 to 1791; then traveled in France and Italy, returning to Covent Garden in 1792; he retained this position until 1797. He was appointed Master of the King's Music in 1817, and was the last to compose court odes in 1818. He wrote about 40 light operas, pantomines, musical farces, ballad operas, etc.; he also wrote 6 string quartets; 6 string trios; 6 duets for 2 Violins; other instrumental pieces; publ. *An Introduction to Harmony* (1800) and *The Rudiments of Thoroughbass* (1815). He had some original ideas, and was not averse to experimentation; e.g., he wrote movements in 5/4 time.
  BIBL.: W. Hauger, "W. S.," *Music & Letters* (Oct. 1950).

Shifrin, Seymour, American composer and teacher; b. N.Y., Feb. 28, 1926; d. Boston, Sept. 26, 1979. After studies at N.Y.'s High School of Music and Art, he received private instruction from Schuman (1942–45); continued his training at Columbia Univ. (B.A., 1947), where he completed his graduate study in composition with Luening (M.A., 1949); then pursued additional training with Milhaud in Paris on a Fulbright scholarship (1951–52). He held 2 Guggenheim fellowships (1956, 1960); taught at Columbia Univ. (1949–50), City College of the City Univ. of N.Y. (1950–51), the Univ. of Calif. at Berkeley (1952–66), and at Brandeis Univ. (1966–79). He wrote music of high chromatic consistency, with finely delineated contrapuntal lines often resulting in sharp dissonance.
  WORKS: ORCH.: *Music for Orchestra* (1948); *Chamber Symphony* (1952–53); *3 Pieces* (1958; Minneapolis, Jan. 8, 1960). **CHAMBER:** Cello Sonata (1948); 5 string quartets (1949; 1962; 1965–66; 1966–67; 1971–72); *Serenade* for Oboe, Clarinet, Horn, Viola, and Piano (1954); *Concert Piece* for Violin (1959); *In eius memoriam* for Flute, Clarinet, Violin, Cello, and Piano (1967–68); *Duo* for Violin and Piano (1969); Piano Trio (1974); *The Nick of Time* for Flute, Clarinet, Percussion, Piano Trio, and Double Bass (1978); also piano pieces, including 4 *Cantos* (1948), *Composition* (1950), *Trauermusik* (1956), *The Modern Temper* for Piano, 4-hands (1959), *Fantasy* (1961), *Responses* (1973), and *Waltz* (1977). **VOCAL:** *Cantata to Sophoclean Choruses* for Chorus and Orch. (1957–58; Boston, May 2, 1984); *Odes of Chang* for Chorus, Piano, and Percussion (1963); *Satires of Circumstance* for Mezzo-soprano, Flute, Clarinet, Violin, Cello, Double Bass, and Piano (1964); *Chronicles* for 3 Male Soloists, Chorus, and Orch. (1970; Boston, Oct. 27, 1976); *A Renaissance Garland* for Soprano, Tenor, Recorders, Viols, Lute, and Percussion (1975); *Five Last Songs* for Soprano and Piano (1979; also for Soprano and Chamber Orch. as completed by M. Boykan).
  BIBL.: R. Morgan, "Remembering S. S. (1926–79)," *Perspectives of New Music,* XIX/1–2 (1980–81).

Shilkret, Nat(haniel), American conductor, arranger, and composer; b. N.Y., Jan. 1, 1895; d. Franklin Square, Long Island, N.Y., Feb. 18, 1982. He studied composition with Pietro Floridia; played the clarinet in the Russian Sym. Orch. in N.Y., the N.Y. Phil., the N.Y. Sym. Orch., and the Metropolitan Opera orch., as well as in bands led by Sousa, Pryor, and E.F. Goldman. In 1916 he became music director of the Victor Talking Machine Co., and created the Victor Salon Orch. in 1924, for which he made numerous arrangements, recordings, and radio broadcasts. In 1935 he went to Hollywood, where he became active as a film score arranger and composer. He wrote a symphonic poem, *Skyward* (1928), a Trombone Concerto (1942), various descriptive pieces for orch., chamber music, and numerous songs; also commissioned Schoenberg, Stravinsky, Toch, Milhaud, Castelnuovo-Tedesco, and Tansman to write a movement each for a biblical cantata, *Genesis* (1947), to which he himself contributed a movement.

Shiloah, Amnon, Israeli ethnomusicologist; b. Lanus, Argentina (of Syrian parents), Sept. 28, 1928. He went to Israel in 1941 to study flute with Uri Toeplitz at the Rubin Academy of Music in Jerusalem; later studied flute at the Paris Cons. (1954–58), and also took courses with Corbin and Chailley at the Sorbonne Inst. of Musicology. He returned to Israel as flutist of the Israel Broadcasting Sym. Orch. (1959–60); studied Hebrew and Arab literature at Hebrew Univ. in Jerusalem (M.A., 1960); subsequently earned his Ph.D. at the Sorbonne (1963, with the diss. *La Perfection des connaissances musicales*, a study of Arab music theory; publ. in Paris, 1972). As head of the folklore dept. of the Israel Broadcasting Authority, Shiloah undertook extensive fieldwork in Jewish and Arab music (1965–69); also directed the Jewish music center at Hebrew Univ. (1967–71), where he was head of the musicology dept. (1970–75) and a prof. (from 1973). He co-edited the periodical *Yuval;* also produced records of Jewish and Eastern Christian music. His research focuses on the literature of Arab and Hebrew music theory in addition to contemporary musics of both cultures.
     WRITINGS: *Caractéristiques de l'art vocale arabe du Moyen-Âge* (Tel Aviv, 1963); *Kit'ey ham-musika baz-zohar* (Musical Passages in the Zohar; Jerusalem, 1977); *The Epistle on Music of the Ikhwan al-Safa* (Tel Aviv, 1978).

Shimizu, Osamu, Japanese composer; b. Osaka, Nov. 4, 1911. He studied traditional Japanese instruments; also took courses in music theory and composition with Hashimoto and Hosokawa at the Tokyo Music School (1936–39); was active in the music dept. of Tokyo Radio; wrote articles on music.
     WORKS: DRAMATIC: OPERAS: *The Tale of the Mask-Maker Shuzenji* (Osaka, Nov. 4, 1954); *The Charcoal Princess* (Osaka, Nov. 1, 1956); *The Man Who Shoots at the Blue Sky* (Osaka, Nov. 26, 1956); *Gauche, the Violoncellist* (Osaka, Oct. 11, 1957); *The Singing Skeleton* (Osaka, March 15, 1962); *Shunkan, the Exile* (Osaka, Nov. 18, 1964); *The Merciful Poet*, operetta (1965); *Muko Erabi* (The Marriage Contest), comic opera (Los Angeles, Oct. 3, 1968); *Daibutsu-Kaigen* (The Great Image of Buddha), historic opera on the inauguration of the bronze statue of Buddha on April 9, A.D. 752 (Tokyo, Oct. 2, 1970); *Ikuta Gawa* (The River Ikuta; Tokyo, Nov. 10, 1971). **BALLETS:** *The Sun* (1955); *The Crane* (1956); *The Earth* (1957); *Araginu* (1958); *Fire in the Field* (1962); *Love Poems* (1966); also numerous cantatas, including *Ren-nyo* (Tokyo, April 8, 1948), *La Paix* (Tokyo, April 22, 1949), and *Hymn to Dengyō-Daishi* (1966). **ORCH.:** 3 syms.: No. 1 (Tokyo, Dec. 8, 1951); No. 2 (1957); No. 3 (1961); *Dance Suite on the Themes of Flowers* (1944). *Poème* for Flute and Orch. (1950); *4 Movements on Indian Melodies* (1950); *Suite* (1953); *Taiheiraku*, gagaku (1971). **CHAMBER:** String Quartet (1940); *Ballad* for Flute and Piano (1940); *Ballad* for Violin and Orch. (1941); Quartet for Flute, Oboe, Clarinet, and Bassoon (1958); *Olympic Hymn* for the opening of the Olympic Games in Japan (Tokyo, Oct. 10, 1964); also much choral music; many songs.

Shimoyama, Hifumi, Japanese composer; b. Aomoriken, June 21, 1930. He studied violin with Hiroshi Narita and composition with Yoritsuné Matsudaira; was a member of the "Group 20.5," with the aim of promoting new music, which included works by Yori-Aki Matsudaira, Kenjiro Ezaki, and others (1956–62).
     WORKS: Violin Sonata (1956); String Quartet (1959); Piano Sonata (1960); *Structure* for 4 Players (1961); *Dialog* for Cello and Piano (1962); *Dialog 1-3* for 2 Guitarists (1963, 1971, 1984); *Reflections* for Strings in 3 groups (1967; Hamburg ISCM Festival, June 27, 1969); *Zone* for 16 Strings (1970); 2

Ceremonies for Cello (1969, 1971); *Exorcism* for 5 Strings (1970); *Breath* for Chorus, Percussion, Piano, and 3 Horns (1971; Tokyo, Nov. 9, 1972); *MSP* for Violin and Piano (1972); *Wave* for Cello, Strings, Harp, Piano, and Percussion (1972); *Transmigration 1* for Percussion and Double Bass (1973) and *2* for Shakuhachi, Cello, and Harp (1984); *Poem* for Cello, Piano, and Tape (1974); *Fumon* for Chamber Orch. and Tape (1974); *Halley's Comet* (*Fulfillment of a 76-Year Vow*), radiophonic work for Soloists, Chorus, and Orch. (1981); *Saikyo* for Orch. (1981); *Kaisho* for Organ and Percussion (1982); *Landscape* for Organ (1983); *Meditation* for Cello and Piano (1983); *Fumon IV* for Percussion and Tape (1984); Cello Concerto (1984); *Cube* for 8 Cellos and Timpani (1985); *The Da* for 4 Percussionists (1985); *Voices* for 3 Soloists and 2 Percussionists (1985); *Emanation* for Alto Saxophone and Percussion (1986); *Yugenism* for Orch. (1988).

Shinohara, Makota, Japanese composer; b. Osaka, Dec. 10, 1931. He studied composition with Ikenouchi at the Tokyo Geijitsu Daigaku (National Univ. of Fine Arts and Music; 1952–54); took lessons with Messiaen at the Paris Cons. (1954–59); subsequently took courses with Zimmermann at the Hochschule für Musik in Cologne (1962–64) and with Stockhausen in Cologne (1962–65); later worked at the Electronic Music Studio of Utrecht Univ. (1965–66) and at the Columbia-Princeton Electronic Music Studio in N.Y. (1971–72); subsequently was active in Tokyo. In 1978 he was a prof. of Japanese music at McGill Univ. in Montreal; from 1979 he lived and taught in Holland.
     WORKS: Violin Sonata (1958); *3 pièces concertantes* for Trumpet and Piano (1959); *Obsession* for Oboe and Piano (1960); *Solitude* for Orch. (1961); *Alternance* for 6 Percussionists (1961–62); *Tendance* for Piano (1962); *Vision* and *Mémoires* for Tape (1965, 1966); *Consonance* for Flute, Horn, Cello, Harp, Vibraphone, and Marimba (1967); *Personnage* for Male Voice and Stereo Tape, with optional Pantomime and Color Lighting (1968); *Visione II* for Orch. (1970); *Reflexion* for Oboe (1970); *City Visit* for Tape (1971); *Rencontre* for Percussion and Tape (1972); *Tayutai* for Koto, Percussion, and Voice (1972); *Kyudo* for Shakuhachi and Harp (1973); *Egalisation* for 25 Instruments (1975); *Elevation* for Organ (1976); *Liberation* for 20 Strings (1977); *Passage* for Stereophonically-Amplified Bass Flute (1980; rev. 1986); *Play* for 9 Winds (1982; rev. 1985); *Turns* for Violin and Koto (1983); *Tabiyuki* for Chamber Ensemble (1984); *Evolution* for Cello (1986).

Shira, Francesco, Italian conductor, singing teacher, and composer; b. Malta, Aug. 21, 1808; d. London, Oct. 15, 1883. He studied at the Milan Cons. with Basili; brought out his 1st opera, *Elena e Malvina*, at La Scala in Milan (Nov. 17, 1832); on the strength of his success, he was engaged as conductor of the Teatro San Carlos in Lisbon (1833–42); also taught at the Lisbon Cons. In 1842, after a brief sojourn in Paris, he became conductor for the English Opera at the Princess's Theatre in London; then conducted at Drury Lane in London (1844–47); in 1848 he went over to Covent Garden; returned to Drury Lane in 1852; in later years he made a high reputation as a singing teacher, without abandoning composition; wrote the operas *Niccolò de' Lapi* (London, 1863), *Selvaggia* (Venice, Feb. 20, 1875), and *Lia* (Venice, 1876).

Shirinsky, Vasili (Petrovich), Russian violinist, conductor, teacher, and composer; b. Ekaterinodar, Jan. 17, 1901; d. Mamontovka, near Moscow, Aug. 16, 1965. He studied violin with D. Krein and composition with Miaskovsky at the Moscow Cons.; then played in orchs.; in 1923 he joined the Moscow Cons. Quartet as 2nd violin. Concurrently, he was active as conductor with the Moscow Radio Orch. (1930–32) and the Opera Theater Orch. (1932–36); was a teacher (1939–49) and a prof. (1949–65) at the Moscow Cons. In 1944 he was made a People's Artist of the R.S.F.S.R. He wrote 2 operas, *Pyer i Lyus* (1943–46) and *Ivan the Terrible* (1951–54); 2 syms. (1936, 1938); Harp Concerto (1957); Violin Concerto (1921); 6 string quartets (1923, 1925, 1929, 1940, 1953, 1958); Piano

Sonata (1929); 98 fugues for Piano (1937–63); 24 piano preludes (1962); incidental music for theatrical plays; film scores; choruses. His music adheres to the principles of socialist conservatism, emphasizing playability and tonal coherence; it was met with appreciation by the Soviet critics, but its performances were few and far between. His brother, **Sergei Shirinsky** (b. Ekaterinodar, July 18, 1903; d. Moscow, Oct. 18, 1974), was a cellist, who promoted in his programs the cause of Soviet music; he also made playable arrangements of various works by Classical and Romantic composers.

Shirley, George (Irving), black American tenor and teacher; b. Indianapolis, April 18, 1934. He was educated at Wayne State Univ. in Detroit, and then received vocal training from Thelmy Georgi in Washington, D.C. and Cornelius Reid in N.Y.; made his operatic debut as Eisenstein in *Die Fledermaus* with the Turnau Opera Players in Woodstock, N.Y. (1959). In 1960 he won the American Opera Auditions and in 1961 the Metropolitan Opera Auditions; following appearances in Europe, he made his Metropolitan Opera debut in N.Y. as Ferrando on Oct. 24, 1961, and continued to sing there until 1973, as well as with other U.S. opera companies; in addition, he sang at Glyndebourne, Covent Garden in London, and La Scala in Milan. He created the role of Romilayu in Kirchner's *Lily* (N.Y., April 14, 1977); also was active as a teacher.

Shirley-Quirk, John (Stanton), distinguished English baritone; b. Liverpool, Aug. 28, 1931. (His hyphenated name is composed of the place-name Shirley, in Derbyshire, where his ancestors lived, and the Celtic appellation in the Manx language, used on the channel isle of Man.) He studied voice with Roy Henderson, and at the same time took courses in chemistry and physics at the Univ. of Liverpool; made his operatic debut as the Doctor in *Pelléas et Mélisande* at the Glyndebourne Festival (1961); then was a leading member of the English Opera Group (1964–76), where he became well known for his roles in Britten's operas; created all 7 baritone roles in Britten's *Death in Venice* (June 16, 1973). In 1973 he sang at London's Covent Garden; then made his Metropolitan Opera debut in N.Y. in *Death in Venice* on Oct. 18, 1974. On July 7, 1977, he created the role of Lev in Tippett's *The Ice Break* at Covent Garden. He also toured widely as a concert artist. In 1975 he was made a Commander of the Order of the British Empire.

Shishov, Ivan, Russian composer; b. Novocherkassk, Oct. 8, 1888; d. Moscow, Feb. 6, 1947. He studied composition with Koreshchenko at the Phil. Society in Moscow, and also took courses in choral polyphony with Kastalsky and in form and orchestration with G. Conus, graduating in 1914. He subsequently conducted choral groups and taught at the Moscow Cons. (1925–31). He wrote the opera *Painter Serf* (Moscow, March 24, 1929); 2 syms.(1925, 1933); a Requiem in memory of Lenin (1925); a symphonic poem, *In the Desert* (1920); a festive overture, *Song of Victory* (1942; anticipating the victory over Nazi Germany by 3 years); piano pieces; choruses; more than 300 songs; he also arranged Russian folk songs.

Shmueli, Herzl, Israeli musicologist; b. Constantinople, Nov. 8, 1920. He began studying violin at 7 and piano at 10; in 1933, went to Palestine, where he studied violin with P. Ginzburg (until 1934); later attended the Tel Aviv Cons. (1944–48) while studying theory and composition with Boskovich; subsequently studied musicology with A.-E. Cherbuliez, composition and history with Hindemith at the Univ. of Zürich, and acoustics at the Zürich Eidgenössische Technische Hochschule für Musik (1949–53); received his Ph.D. from the Univ. of Zürich (1953, with the diss. *Higgajon Bechinnor: Betrachtungen zum Leierspiel des Jehudaa Ben-Arie Mosscato, Rabbi zu Mantua*; publ. in Tel Aviv, 1954). He returned to Tel Aviv to teach at the Music Teachers' Seminary (from 1953), where he served as director (1955–66); concurrently taught at the Tel Aviv Academy of Music. When the dept. of musicology of Tel Aviv Univ. was founded in 1966, he joined its faculty, subsequently becoming a prof. and dept. chairman (1971);

also was chairman of the Israeli Musicological Soc. (1968–71). Shmueli directed a series of programs on music for Israeli Instructional Television, and spoke throughout Israel before many non-academic audiences; his research centers on Israeli song and art music, in addition to music of the early Romantics and of England in the 17th and 19th centuries.

WRITINGS: *Umanut harmusica* (Musical Craft; Tel Aviv, 1955); *Toldot hamak'hela* (History of the Choir; Tel Aviv, 1963); *Hazemer hayisraeli* (Israeli Song; Tel Aviv, 1971).

Shnitke, Alfred. See Schnittke, Alfred.

Shoemaker, Carolie J., American composer and multidisciplinary performance artist; b. Kennewick, Wash., April 9, 1963. She studied composition with William O. Smith and Diane Thome, and voice with Montserrat Alavedra at the Univ. of Washington (B.F.A., 1989); conducted lifelong studies in violin, voice, drama, dance, literary arts, linguistics, electronic music, and composition. Her work emphasizes the interaction of language and music and brings together such aural and visual elements as speech, narration, movement, tape, electronics, and live music into a synergistic whole. Many of her compositions are scored for variable ensemble and involve structured improvisation.

WORKS: *The Elephant's Child* for Narrator and Brass Quintet (1987); *Stitch in Time* for Voice and Tape (1988); *Classified Info* for Mixed Instruments and Newspaper (1989); *Crackdown* for Tape with Optional Live Sung/Spoken Performance (1989); *Extended Forcast* for Voice, String Quartet, and Bass Viol (1989); *Lagan Tide* for Tape, Mixed Instruments, and Voice (1989); *Bedtime Stories* for Voice over Variable Solo, or Group Ensemble with Electronics (1990); *Yo(u) Tarzan* for Voice, Sequenced Electronics, and Tape (1990).

Shore, "Dinah" (Frances Rose), American singer of popular music and actress; b. Winchester, Tenn., March 1, 1917. She studied sociology at Vanderbilt Univ. (B.A., 1938). However, she soon experienced a plenary inspiration to sing forth, and betook herself to N.Y.; there she auditioned, over radio station WNEW, with the song *Dinah*, which soon became her stage name; she often shared the honors as a radio "thrush" with the rising star Frank Sinatra. By 1940 she reached stardom in the radio polls; Eddie Cantor was so taken with her rendition of the song *Yes, My Darling Daughter*, supposedly derived from a Jewish-Ukrainian folk song, that he hired her to sing on his highly successful radio show. Her records, such as *Blues in the Night* and *Buttons and Bows*, sold into the millions. From 1951 to 1961 she starred in her own television show.

BIBL.: B. Cassiday, *D.!* (N.Y., 1979).

Shore, John, English trumpeter and lutenist; b. c.1662; d. London, Nov. 20, 1752. He was made a trumpeter-in-ordinary to James II in 1688; became a musician-in-ordinary in the court band in 1695; succeeded his uncle as Sergeant-trumpeter in 1707. He is the reputed inventor of the tuning fork. Purcell wrote for Shore trumpet obbligatos to many of his songs.

Short, "Bobby" (Robert Waltrip), black American singer and pianist of popular music; b. Danville, Ill., Sept. 15, 1926. He was self-taught in music; appeared in vaudeville as a child; later went to N.Y., where he began his career as a highly successful nightclub entertainer; also appeared in Los Angeles, London, and Paris with equal success. He ultimately garnered a reputation as the leading café singer of his time. He is the POSSLQ of Gloria Vanderbilt. His autobiography appeared under the title *Black and White Baby* (N.Y., 1971).

Shostakovich, Dmitri (Dmitrievich), preeminent Russian composer of the Soviet generation, whose style and idiom of composition largely defined the nature of new Russian music, father of **Maxim Shostakovich;** b. St. Petersburg, Sept. 25, 1906; d. Moscow, Aug. 9, 1975. He was a member of a cultured Russian family; his father was an engineer employed in the government office of weights and measures; his mother was a professional pianist. Shostakovich grew up during the most difficult period of Russian revolutionary history, when famine and disease decimated the population of Petrograd. Of frail physique, he suffered from malnutrition; Glazunov, the director of the Petrograd Cons., appealed personally to the Commissar of Education, Lunacharsky, to grant an increased food ration for Shostakovich, essential for his physical survival. At the age of 9, he commenced piano lessons with his mother; in 1919 he entered the Petrograd Cons., where he studied piano with Nikolayev and composition with Steinberg; graduated in piano in 1923, and in composition in 1925. As a graduation piece, he submitted his 1st Sym., written at the age of 18; it was 1st performed by the Leningrad Phil. on May 12, 1926, under the direction of Malko, and subsequently became one of Shostakovich's most popular works. He pursued postgraduate work in composition until 1930. His 2nd Sym., composed for the 10th anniversary of the Soviet Revolution in 1927, bearing the subtitle *Dedication to October* and ending with a rousing choral finale, was less successful despite its revolutionary sentiment. He then wrote a satirical opera, *The Nose*, after Gogol's whimsical story about the sudden disappearance of the nose from the face of a government functionary; here Shostakovich revealed his flair for musical satire; the score featured a variety of modernistic devices and included an interlude written for percussion instruments only. *The Nose* was produced in Leningrad on Jan. 12, 1930, with considerable popular acclaim, but was attacked by officious theater critics as a product of "bourgeois decadence," and quickly withdrawn from the stage. Somewhat in the same satirical style was his ballet *The Golden Age* (1930), which included a celebrated dissonant *Polka*, satirizing the current disarmament conference in Geneva. There followed the 3rd Sym., subtitled *May First* (Leningrad, Jan. 21, 1930), with a choral finale saluting the International Workers' Day. Despite its explicit revolutionary content, it failed to earn the approbation of Soviet spokesmen, who dismissed the work as nothing more than a formal gesture of proletarian solidarity. Shostakovich's next work was to precipitate a crisis in his career, as well as in Soviet music in general; it was an opera to the libretto drawn from a short story by the 19th-century Russian writer Leskov, entitled *Lady Macbeth of the District of Mtzensk*, and depicting adultery, murder, and suicide in a merchant home under the Czars. It was produced in Leningrad on Jan. 22, 1934, and was hailed by most Soviet musicians as a significant work comparable to the best productions of Western modern opera. But both the staging and the music ran counter to growing Soviet puritanism; a symphonic interlude portraying a scene of adultery behind the bedroom curtain, orchestrated with suggestive passages on the slide trombones, shocked the Soviet officials present at the performance by its bold naturalism. After the Moscow production of the opera, *Pravda*, the official organ of the Communist party, publ. an unsigned (and therefore all the more authoritative) article accusing Shostakovich of creating a "bedlam of noise." The brutality of this assault dismayed Shostakovich; he readily admitted his faults in both content and treatment of the subject, and declared his solemn determination to write music according to the then-emerging formula of "socialist realism." His next stage production was a ballet, *The Limpid Brook*, portraying the pastoral scenes on a Soviet collective farm. In this work he tempered his dissonant idiom, and the subject seemed eminently fitting for the Soviet theater; but it, too, was condemned in *Pravda*, this time for an insufficiently dignified treatment of Soviet life. Having been rebuked twice for 2 radically different theater works, Shostakovich abandoned all attempts to write for the stage, and returned to purely instrumental composition. But as though pursued by vengeful fate, he again suffered a painful reverse. His 4th Sym. (1935–36) was placed in rehearsal by the Leningrad Phil., but withdrawn before the performance when representatives of the musical officialdom and even the orch. musicians themselves sharply criticized the piece. Shostakovich's rehabilitation finally came with the production of his 5th Sym. (Leningrad, Nov. 21, 1937), a work of rhapsodic grandeur, culminating in a powerful climax; it was hailed, as though by spontaneous consensus, as a model of true Soviet art, classical in formal design, lucid in its harmonic idiom, and optimistic in its philo-

sophical connotations. The height of his rise to recognition was achieved in his 7th Sym. He began its composition during the siege of Leningrad by the Nazis in the autumn of 1941; he served in the fire brigade during the air raids; then flew from Leningrad to the temporary Soviet capital in Kuibishev, on the Volga, where he completed the score, which was performed there on March 1, 1942. Its symphonic development is realistic in the extreme, with the theme of the Nazis, in mechanical march time, rising to monstrous loudness, only to be overcome and reduced to a pathetic drum dribble by a victorious Russian song. The work became a musical symbol of the Russian struggle against the overwhelmingly superior Nazi war machine; it was given the subtitle *Leningrad Symphony,* and was performed during the war by virtually every orch. in the Allied countries. After the tremendous emotional appeal of the *Leningrad Symphony*, the 8th Sym., written in 1943, had a lesser impact; the 9th, 10th, and 11th syms. followed (1945, 1953, 1957) without attracting much comment; the 12th Sym. (1960–61), dedicated to the memory of Lenin, aroused a little more interest. But it was left for his 13th Sym. (Leningrad, Dec. 18, 1962) to create a controversy which seemed to be Shostakovich's peculiar destiny; its vocal 1st movement for solo bass and male chorus, to words by the Soviet poet Evtushenko, expressing the horror of the massacre of Jews by the Nazis during their occupation of the city of Kiev, and containing a warning against residual anti-Semitism in Soviet Russia, met with unexpected criticism by the chairman of the Communist party, Nikita Khrushchev, who complained about the exclusive attention in Evtushenko's poem to Jewish victims, and his failure to mention the Ukrainians and other nationals who were also slaughtered. The text of the poem was altered to meet these objections, but the 13th Sym. never gained wide acceptance. There followed the remarkable 14th Sym. (1969), in 11 sections, scored for voices and orch., to words by Federico García Lorca, Apollinaire, Rilke, and the Russian poet Küchelbecker. Shostakovich's 15th Sym., his last (perf. in Moscow under the direction of his son **Maxim** on Jan. 8, 1972), demonstrated his undying spirit of innovation; the score is set in the key of C major, but it contains a dodecaphonic passage and literal allusions to motives from Rossini's *William Tell Overture* and the Fate Motif from Wagner's *Die Walküre*. Shostakovich's adoption, however limited, of themes built on 12 different notes, a procedure that he had himself condemned as anti-musical, is interesting both from the psychological and sociological standpoint; he experimented with these techniques in several other works; his 1st explicit use of a 12-tone subject occurred in his 12th String Quartet (1968). Equally illuminating is his use in some of his scores of a personal monogram, D.S.C.H. (for D, Es, C, H in German notation, i.e., D, E-flat, C, B). One by one, his early works, originally condemned as unacceptable to Soviet reality, were returned to the stage and the concert hall; the objectionable 4th and 13th syms. were publ. and recorded; the operas *The Nose* and *Lady Macbeth of the District of Mtzensk* (renamed *Katerina Izmailova*, after the name of the heroine) had several successful revivals.

Shostakovich excelled in instrumental music. Besides the 15 syms., he wrote 15 string quartets, a String Octet, Piano Quintet, 2 piano trios, Cello Sonata, Violin Sonata, Viola Sonata, 2 violin concertos, 2 piano concertos, 2 cello concertos, 24 preludes for Piano, 24 preludes and fugues for Piano, 2 piano sonatas, and several short piano pieces; also choral works and song cycles.

What is remarkable about Shostakovich is the unfailing consistency of his style of composition. His entire oeuvre, from his 1st work to the last (147 opus numbers in all), proclaims a personal article of faith. His idiom is unmistakably of the 20th century, making free use of dissonant harmonies and intricate contrapuntal designs, yet never abandoning inherent tonality; his music is teleological, leading invariably to a tonal climax, often in a triumphal triadic declaration. Most of his works carry key signatures; his metrical structure is governed by a unifying rhythmic pulse. Shostakovich is equally eloquent in dramatic and lyric utterance; he has no fear of prolonging his slow movements in relentless dynamic rise and fall; the cumulative power of his kinetic drive in rapid movements is overwhelming. Through all the peripeties of his career, he never changed his musical language in its fundamental modalities. When the flow of his music met obstacles, whether technical or external, he obviated them without changing the main direction. In a special announcement issued after Shostakovich's death, the government of the U.S.S.R. summarized his work as a "remarkable example of fidelity to the traditions of musical classicism, and above all, to the Russian traditions, finding his inspiration in the reality of Soviet life, reasserting and developing in his creative innovations the art of socialist realism, and in so doing, contributing to universal progressive musical culture." His honors, both domestic and foreign, were many: the Order of Lenin (1946, 1956, 1966), People's Artist of the U.S.S.R. (1954), Hero of Socialist Labor (1966), Order of the October Revolution (1971), honorary membership in the American Inst. of the Arts (1943), honorary Doctor of Oxford Univ. (1958), Laureate of the International Sibelius Prize (1958), and Doctor of Fine Arts from Northwestern Univ. (1973). He visited the U.S. as a delegate to the World Peace Conference in 1949, as a member of a group of Soviet musicians in 1959, and to receive the degree of D.F.A. from Northwestern Univ. in 1973. A postage stamp of 6 kopecks, bearing his photograph and an excerpt from the *Leningrad Symphony*, was issued by the Soviet Post Office in 1976 to commemorate his 70th birthday. A collected edition of his works was publ. in Moscow (42 vols., 1980-).

WORKS: STAGE: OPERAS: *The Nose*, op. 15 (1927–28; Leningrad, Jan. 12, 1930); *Lady Macbeth of the District of Mtzensk*, op. 29 (1930–32; Leningrad, Jan. 22, 1934; rev. as *Katerina Izmaylova*, op. 114, 1956–63; Moscow, Jan. 8, 1963); *The Gamblers* (1941–42; unfinished; Leningrad, Sept. 18, 1978). **OPERETTA:** *Moskva, Cheryomushki*, op. 105 (1958; Moscow, Jan. 24, 1959). **BALLETS:** *The Golden Age*, op. 22 (Leningrad, Oct. 26, 1930); *Bolt*, op. 27 (Leningrad, April 8, 1931); *The Limpid Brook*, op. 39 (Leningrad, April 4, 1935). **INCIDENTAL MUSIC:** *The Bedbug*, op. 19 (Moscow, Feb. 13, 1929); *The Shot*, op. 24 (Leningrad, Dec. 14, 1929; not extant); *Virgin Soil*, op. 25 (Leningrad, May 9, 1930; not extant); *Rule, Britannia!*, op. 28 (Leningrad, May 9, 1931); *Conditionally Killed*, op. 31 (Leningrad, Oct. 20, 1931); *Hamlet*, op. 32 (Moscow, March 19, 1932); *The Human Comedy*, op. 37 (Moscow, April 1, 1934); *Hail, Spain*, op. 44 (Leningrad, Nov. 23, 1936); *King Lear*, op. 58a (1940; Leningrad, March 24, 1941); *Native Country*, op. 63 (Moscow, Nov. 7, 1942); *Russian River*, op. 66 (Moscow, Dec. 1944); *Victorious Spring*, op. 72 (1945; Moscow, May 1946). **FILM SCORES:** *New Babylon*, op. 18 (1928–29); *Alone*, op. 26 (1930–31); *Golden Mountains*, op. 30 (1931); *Counterplan*, op. 33 (1932); *The Tale of the Priest and His Worker Blockhead*, op. 36 (1933–34; unfinished; rev. as a comic opera by S. Khentova, 1980); *Love and Hatred*, op. 38 (1934); *The Youth of Maxim*, op. 41 (1934); *Girl Friends*, op. 41a (1934–35); *The Return of Maxim*, op. 45 (1936–37); *Volochayev Days*, op. 48 (1936–37); *The Vyborg District*, op. 50 (1938); *Friends*, op. 51 (1938); *The Great Citizen*, op. 52 (1937); *The Man with a Gun*, op. 53 (1938); *The Great Citizen*, op. 55 (1938–39); *The Silly Little Mouse*, op. 56 (1939; unfinished); *The Adventures of Korzinkina*, op. 59 (1940; not extant); *Zoya*, op. 64 (1944); *Simple People*, op. 71 (1945); *The Young Guard*, op. 75 (1947–48); *Pirogov*, op. 76 (1947); *Michurin*, op. 78 (1948); *Encounter at the Elbe*, op. 80 (1948); *The Fall of Berlin*, op. 82 (1949); *Belinsky*, op. 85 (1950); *The Unforgettable Year 1919*, op. 89 (1951); *Song of the Great Rivers* (*Unity*), op. 95 (1954); *The Gadfly*, op. 97 (1955); *The First Echelon*, op. 99 (1955–56); *Five Days—Five Nights*, op. 111 (1960); *Hamlet*, op. 116 (1963–64); *A Year is a Lifetime*, op. 120 (1965); *Sofia Perovskaya*, op. 132 (1967); *King Lear*, op. 137 (1970).

ORCH.: 15 syms.: No. 1, op. 10 (1924–25; Leningrad, May 12, 1926); No. 2, with Bass and Chorus in the finale, op. 14, *To October* (Leningrad, Nov. 5, 1927); No. 3, with Chorus in the finale, op. 20, *The First of May* (1929; Leningrad, Jan. 21, 1930); No. 4, op. 43 (1935–36; Moscow, Dec. 30, 1961); No. 5, op. 47 (Leningrad, Nov. 21, 1937); No. 6, op. 54 (Leningrad, Nov. 5, 1939); No. 7, op. 60, *Leningrad* (1941; Kuibishev, March 1, 1942); No. 8, op. 65 (Moscow, Nov. 3, 1943); No. 9, op. 70 (Leningrad, Nov. 3, 1945); No. 10, op. 93 (Leningrad, Dec. 17, 1953); No. 11, op. 103, *The Year 1905* (Moscow, Oct. 30, 1957); No. 12, op. 112, *The Year 1917*, dedicated to the memory of Lenin (Leningrad, Oct. 1, 1961); No. 13, with Bass and Men's Chorus, op. 113, *Babiy Yar* (Moscow, Dec. 18, 1962); No. 14 for Soprano, Bass, Strings, and Percussion, op. 135 (Leningrad, Sept. 29, 1969); No. 15, op. 141 (1971; Moscow, Jan. 8, 1972); *Scherzo*, op. 1 (1919); *Theme and Variations*, op. 3 (1921–22); *Scherzo*, op. 7 (1923–24); 2 *Pieces for E. Dressel's opera Der arme Columbus*, op. 23 (1929); 2 piano concertos: No. 1 for Piano, Trumpet, and Strings, op. 35 (Leningrad, Oct. 15, 1933); No. 2, op. 102 (Moscow, May 10, 1957); 5 *Fragments*, op. 42 (1935); *Solemn March* for Military Band (1942); 2 violin concertos: No. 1, op. 77 (1947–48; Leningrad, Oct. 29, 1955); No. 2, op. 129 (Moscow, Sept. 13, 1967); 3 *Pieces for Orchestra* (1947–48); *Festive Overture*, op. 96 (1954); 2 cello concertos: No. 1, op. 107 (Leningrad, Oct. 4, 1959); No. 2, op. 126 (Moscow, Sept. 25, 1966); *Novorossiisk Chimes: The Flame of Eternal Glory* (1960); *Overture on Russian and Khirghiz Folk Themes*, op. 115 (1963; Moscow, Oct. 10, 1965); *Funeral-Triumphal Prelude in Memory of the Heroes of the Battle of Stalingrad*, op. 130 (1967); *October*, symphonic poem, op. 131 (Moscow, Sept. 26, 1967); *March of the Soviet Militia* for Military Band, op. 139 (1970); also 27 suites from various works (1927–65).

VOCAL: CHORAL: *The Oath to the People's Commissar* for Bass, Chorus, and Piano (1941); *Poem of the Motherland*, cantata for Mezzo-soprano, Tenor, 2 Baritones, Bass, Chorus, and Orch., op. 74 (1947); *Song of the Forests*, oratorio for Tenor, Bass, Boys's Choir, Chorus, and Orch., op. 81 (Leningrad, Nov. 15, 1949); 10 *Poems for Chorus and Boys's Choir*, op. 88 (1951); 10 *Russian Folksong Arrangements for Soloists, Chorus, and Piano* (1951); *The Sun Shines on our Motherland*, cantata for Boys's Choir, Chorus, and Orch., op. 90 (1952); 2 *Russian Folksong Arrangements for Chorus*, op. 104 (1957); *Little Paradise*, cantata for 4 Basses, Small Chorus, and Piano (c.1960; Washington, D.C., Jan. 12, 1989); *The Execution of Stepan Razin* for Bass, Chorus, and Orch., op. 119 (Moscow, Dec. 28, 1964); *Loyalty*, 8 ballads for Men's Chorus, op. 136 (1970). **SOLO VOICE:** 2 *Fables of Krilov* for Mezzo-soprano and Orch., op. 4 (1922; Moscow, Sept. 16, 1981); 6 *Romances on Texts of Japanese Poets* for Tenor and Orch., op. 21 (1928–32); 4 *Romances* for Bass and Piano, op. 46 (1936–37; Nos. 1 to 3 orchestrated); 6 *Romances* for Bass and Piano, op. 62 (1942; orchestrated as opp. 62a and 140); *Patriotic Song* (1943); *Song About the Red Army* (1943; in collaboration with A. Khachaturian); *From Jewish Folk Poetry* for Soprano, Alto, Tenor, and Piano, op. 79 (1948; orchestrated as op. 79a); 2 *Romances* for Male Voice and Piano, op. 84 (1950); 4 *Songs* for Voice and Piano, op. 86 (1951); 4 *Monologues* for Bass and Piano, op. 91 (1952); *Greek Songs* for Voice and Piano (1952–53); 5 *Romances: Songs of our Days* for Bass and Piano, op. 95 (1954); *There Were Kisses* for Voice and Piano (1954); *Spanish Songs* for Mezzo-soprano and Piano, op. 100 (1956); *Satires: Pictures of the Past* for Soprano and Piano, op. 109 (1960); 5 *Romances* for Bass and Piano, op. 121 (1965); *Preface to the Complete Collection of My Works and Reflections on this Preface* for Bass and Piano, op. 123 (1966); 7 *Romances on Poems of A. Blok* for Soprano, Violin, Cello, and Piano, op. 127 (1967); *Spring, Spring* for Bass and Piano, op. 128 (1967); 6 *Romances* for Bass and Chamber Orch., op. 140 (1971); 6 *Poems of Marina Tsvetayeva* for Alto and Piano, op. 143 (1973; orchestrated as op. 143a); *Suite* for Bass and Piano, op. 145 (1974; orchestrated as op. 145a); 4 *Verses of Captain Lebyadkin* for Bass and Piano, op. 146 (1975).

CHAMBER: 2 piano trios: No. 1, op. 8 (1923); No. 2, op. 67 (Leningrad, Nov. 14, 1944); 3 *Pieces for Cello and Piano*, op. 9 (1923–24; not extant); 2 *Pieces for String Octet*, op. 11 (1924–25); Cello Sonata, op. 40 (Leningrad, Dec. 25, 1934); 15 string quartets: No. 1, op. 49 (Leningrad, Oct. 10, 1938); No. 2, op. 68 (Leningrad, Nov. 14, 1944); No. 3, op. 73 (Moscow, Dec. 16, 1946); No. 4, op. 83 (1949; Moscow, Dec. 3, 1953); No. 5, op. 92 (1952; Moscow, Nov. 13, 1953); No. 6, op. 101 (Leningrad, Oct. 7, 1956); No. 7, op. 108 (Leningrad, May 15, 1960); No. 8, op. 110 (Leningrad, Oct. 2, 1960); No. 9, op. 117 (Moscow, Nov. 20, 1964); No. 10, op. 118 (Moscow, Nov. 10, 1964); No. 11, op. 122 (Leningrad, May 28, 1966); No. 12, op. 133 (Moscow, Sept. 14, 1968); No. 13, op. 138 (Leningrad, Dec. 13, 1970); No. 14, op. 142 (Leningrad, Nov. 12, 1973); No. 15, op. 144 (Leningrad, Nov. 15, 1974); 3 Pieces for Violin (1940); Piano Quintet, op. 57 (Moscow, Nov. 23, 1940); Violin Sonata, op. 134 (1968; Moscow, May 3, 1969); Viola Sonata, op. 147 (Leningrad, Oct. 1, 1975).

PIANO: *Minuet, Prelude, and Intermezzo* (1919–20; unfinished); *Murzilka* (n.d.); 8 *Preludes*, op. 2 (1918–20); 5 *Preludes* (1919–21); 3 *Fantastic Dances*, op. 5 (1920–22); Suite for 2 Pianos, op. 6 (1922); 2 sonatas: No. 1, op. 12 (Leningrad, Dec. 12, 1926); No. 2, op. 61 (Moscow, June 6, 1943); *Aphorisms*, op. 13 (1927); 24 *Preludes*, op. 34 (1932–33); *Children's Notebook*, op. 69 (1944–45); *Merry March* for 2 Pianos (1949); 24 *Preludes and Fugues*, op. 87 (1950–51; Leningrad, Dec. 23, 1952); Concertino for 2 Pianos, op. 94 (1953).

Also orchestrations of several works, including Mussorgsky's *Boris Godunov* (1939–40), *Khovanshchina* (1958), and *Songs and Dances of Death* (1962).

BIBL.: N. Slonimsky, "D.D. S.," *Musical Quarterly* (Oct. 1942); V. Seroff, *D. S.: The Life and Background of a Soviet Composer* (N.Y., 1943); M. Sahlberg-Vatchnadze, *S.* (Paris, 1945); I. Martinov, *D. S.* (Moscow, 1946; 2nd ed., 1956; Eng. tr., 1947); L. Danilevich, *D. S.* (Moscow, 1958); D. Rabinovich, *D. S., Composer* (Moscow and Leningrad, 1959); M. Sabinina, *D. S.* (Moscow, 1959); L. Mazel, *D.D. S.'s Symphonies* (Moscow, 1960); V. Bobrovsky, *S.'s Instrumental Chamber Music* (Moscow, 1961); G. Orlov, *Simfonii S.s* (Moscow, 1961–62); H. Brockhaus, *D. S.* (Leipzig, 1962; 2nd ed., abr., 1963); I. Martinov, *D. S.: A Study of His Life and Works* (Moscow, 1962); R.-M. Hofmann, *D. S.: l'homme et son oeuvre* (Paris, 1963); S. Khentova, *S.—pianist* (Leningrad, 1964); L. Danilevich, *Our Contemporary: The Work of S.* (Moscow, 1965); A. Dolzhansky, *D. S.'s Instrumental Chamber Music* (Moscow, 1965); M. Sabinina, *Simfonizm S.a* (Moscow, 1965); K. Laux, *D. S., Chronist seines Volkes* (Berlin, 1966); G. Orlov, *D. S.* (Leningrad, 1966); V. Vanslov, *The Work of S.* (Moscow, 1966); L. Berger, ed., *D. S.'s Stylistic Traits* (Moscow, 1967); L. Danilevich, ed., *D. S.* (Moscow, 1967); G. Ordzhonokidze, ed., *D. S.* (Moscow, 1967); V. Delson, *The Piano Works of S.* (Moscow, 1971); N. Kay, *S.* (London, 1971); P. Buske, *D. S.* (Berlin, 1975); S. Khentova, *S.'s Youthful Years* (vol. I, Moscow, 1975; vol. II, Leningrad, 1980); special issues of *Sovetskaya Musika* (1976, 1981); M. Sabinina, *S. as Symphonist: Dramaturg, Aesthetics, Style* (Moscow, 1976); G. Schneerson, ed., *D. S.: Articles and Materials* (Moscow, 1976); L. Tretyakova, *D. S.* (Moscow, 1976); M. MacDonald, *D. S.: A Complete Catlogue* (London, 1977); H. Ottaway, *S. Symphonies* (London, 1978); R. Blokker *The Music of D. S.: The Symphonies* (London, 1978); A. Bogdanova, *S.'s Operas and Ballets* (Moscow, 1979); S. Khentova, *D.D. S. in the Years of World War II* (Leningrad, 1979); idem, *S. v Petrograde-Leningrade* (Leningrad, 1979; 2nd ed., 1979); G. Norris, "S.'s The Nose," *Musical Times*, CXX (1979); M. Shaginyan, *D. S.* (On S.; Moscow, 1979); S. Volkov, ed., *Testimony: The Memoirs of D. S.* (London and N.Y., 1979; a highly controversial report of the author's numerous interviews with Shostakovich, seemingly approved by the latter, with the notation after each interview, "*Chital*," meaning "read." The book aroused a great deal of criticism in the Soviet press as inaccurate and unfair to Soviet society); L. Danilevich, *D. S.: Life and Works* (Moscow, 1980); L. Fay, "S. Versus Volkov: Whose *Testimony*?," *Russian Review*, XXXIX (1980); N. Lukyanova, *D.D. S.* (Moscow, 1980); G. Norris, "Bitter Memories: The S. Testimony," *Musical Times*, CXXI (1980); D. and L. Sollertinsky, *Pages from the Life of D. S.* (N.Y., 1980); D. Hulme, *D. S.: Catalogue, Bibliography and Discography* (Muir of Ord, 1982);

S. Khentova, *D.D. S.: The Thirty Years 1945–1975* (Leningrad, 1982); C. Norris, ed., *S.: The Man and His Music* (London, 1982); E. Roseberry, *S.: His Life and Times* (Tunbridge Wells and N.Y., 1982); F. Streller, *D. S.* (Leipzig, 1982); J. Devlin, *S.* (Borough Green, 1983); D. Gojowy, *D. S. mit Selbstzeugnissen und Bilddokumenten* (Reinbek bei Hamburg, 1983); J. Hubard, *The First Five Symphonies of D. S.* (diss., Ball State Univ., 1984); B. Schwarz, "S., Soviet Citizen and Anti-Stalinist," *Music and Civilization: Essays in Honor of Paul Henry Lang* (N.Y., 1984); J. Braun, "The Double Meaning of Jewish Elements in D. S.'s Music," *Musical Quarterly*, LXXI, No. 1 (1985); D. Fanning, *The Breath of a Symphonist: S.'s Tenth* (London, 1988); I. MacDonald, *The New S.* (Boston, 1990).

Shostakovich, Dmitri, Russian pianist, son of **Maxim** and grandson of **Dmitri (Dmitrievich) Shostakovich;** b. Moscow, Aug. 9, 1961. He studied piano with Elena Khoven; made his debut as a soloist with the State Academy Sym. Orch. in 1978 in Moscow; also toured Italy in 1979. In April 1981 he was soloist with the U.S.S.R. State Radio Orch. during its tour of West Germany, conducted by his father, who then decided not to return to Russia; both applied for resident visas for the U.S., which were granted. In Sept. 1981 he joined his father and Mstislav Rostropovich in a series of concerts with the National Sym. Orch. of Washington, D.C., in celebration of the 75th anniversary of the birth of his grandfather. He also appeared with other U. S. and European orchs.

Shostakovich, Maxim, Russian conductor, son of **Dmitri (Dmitrievich)** and father of **Dmitri Shostakovich;** b. Leningrad, May 10, 1938. He studied piano at the Moscow Cons. with Yakov Flier, and conducting with Gauk and Rozhdestvensky. In 1963 he became assistant conductor of the Moscow Sym. Orch., and in 1966, of the U.S.S.R. State Orch., which he accompanied on its U.S. tour in 1969; then was its principal conductor from 1971 until he defected during the orch.'s tour of West Germany in 1981. He and his son then settled in the U.S. On Memorial Day 1981, he conducted the National Sym. Orch. of Washington, D.C., in a special concert on the West Lawn of the U.S. Capitol; subsequently appeared as a guest conductor throughout North America, Europe, and the Far East. He was principal conductor of the Hong Kong Phil. (1983–85), artistic director of the Hartford (Conn.) Sym. Orch. (1985–86), and music director of the New Orleans Sym. Orch. (1986–91). He has become best known for his obviously authentic interpretations of his father's works.

BIBL.: *U.S. News & World Report* (Nov. 9, 1981); D. Hendricks, "M. S.," *Ovation* (June 1984).

Shtogarenko, Andrei (Yakovlevich), Ukrainian composer; b. Noviye Kaidaki, near Ekaterinoslav, Oct. 15, 1902. He studied with S. Bogatyrev at the Kharkov Cons., graduating in 1936. During World War II, he worked in Turkmenia. From 1954 to 1968 he was director of the Kiev Cons.; was a prof. of music there from 1960; was made a People's Artist of the U.S.S.R. in 1972. Virtually all of his music is devoted to Ukrainian subjects.

WORKS: 3 syms. (1947, rev. 1958; 1965, rev. 1970; 1971); symphonic cantata, *My Ukraine* (1943); cantata, *Moscow*, for the 800th anniversary of its foundation (1948); *Partisan Sketches* for Orch. (1957); *The Dawn of Communism Has Come* for Chorus, Vocal Soloists, and Orch. (1957); choral sym., *Lenin Walks the Planet* (1958); Violin Concerto (1969); Piano Concertino (1972); Violin Concertino (1972); choruses; chamber music; piano pieces; songs; film scores.

BIBL.: A. Znosco-Borovsky, *A. S.* (Kiev, 1947; 2nd ed., 1951); M. Borvoyk, *A.Y. S.* (Kiev, 1961); G. Vynogradov, *A. S.* (Kiev, 1973).

Shudi or **Tschudi, Burkhard.** See **Broadwood & Sons.**

Shulman, Alan, American cellist, teacher, and composer; b. Baltimore, June 4, 1915. He studied cello with F. Salmond at the Peabody Cons. of Music in Baltimore, and composition with B. Wagenaar at the Juilliard School of Music in N.Y., graduating in 1937; was a member of the NBC Sym. Orch.

in N.Y. (1937–42; 1945–54); during World War II, was in the U.S. Maritime Service; also was a teacher at Sarah Lawrence College and at the Juilliard School of Music.

WORKS: ORCH.: *A Laurentian Overture* (N.Y., Jan. 7, 1952); *Waltzes* (1949); *Popocatepetl*, symphonic picture (1952); *Theme and Variations* for Viola and Orch. (N.Y., Feb. 17, 1941); *Pastorale and Dance* for Violin and Orch. (N.Y., July 15, 1944); Cello Concerto (1948; N.Y., April 13, 1950). **CHAMBER:** *Rendezvous* for Clarinet and Strings (1946); *Threnody* for String Quartet (1950); *Suite Miniature* for Octet of Cellos (1956); *Suite* for Solo Cello (1950); *Top Brass* for 12 Brass Instruments (Portland, Oreg., April 25, 1958); *4 Diversions* for a Pride of Cellos (Philadelphia, April 6, 1975); numerous short works for Violin, for Cello, for Piano, etc.

Shumsky, Oscar, esteemed American violinist, conductor, and pedagogue; b. Philadelphia, March 23, 1917. He commenced violin lessons at an early age and made his debut with Stokowski and the Philadelphia Orch. as a soloist in Suk's Fantasy for Violin and Orch. when he was only 8 (March 27, 1925); that same year he began private lessons with Auer, and then continued training with him at the Curtis Inst. of Music in Philadelphia (1928–30), where he subsequently studied with Zimbalist (1930–36); after further private studies with Zimbalist (1936–38), he played in the NBC Sym. Orch. in N.Y. (1939–42); also was 1st violinist in the Primrose Quartet, and appeared as a soloist with the leading U.S. orchs.; later was solo violinist with the Bach Aria Group. In 1959 he made his debut as a conductor with the Canadian National Festival Orch.; then was music director of the Canadian Stratford Festival (1959–67). In 1942 he became a teacher at the Peabody Cons. of Music in Baltimore; in 1953 he joined the staff of the Juilliard School of Music in N.Y.; also taught at the Curtis Inst. of Music (1961–65) and at the Yale School of Music (from 1975); gave up teaching in 1981 to concentrate on his performance activities. His son, Eric Shumsky (b. Port Chester, N.Y., Dec. 7, 1953), is a violist who appeared frequently with his father in chamber music concerts.

BIBL.: D. Henry, "O. S.: A Profile," *Strad*, XCII (1981–82); B. Schwarz, *Great Masters of the Violin* (N.Y., 1983).

Shure, Leonard, respected American pianist and teacher; b. Los Angeles, April 10, 1910. He was a pupil of Artur Schnabel at the Berlin Hochschule für Musik (graduated, 1928); made his recital debut in Berlin in 1927; after serving as Schnabel's teaching assistant (1928–33), he made his U.S. debut in Boston in 1933; subsequently appeared as soloist with many U.S. orchs., as a recitalist, and as a chamber music artist. He served on the faculties of the Longy School of Music in Cambridge, Mass., the New England Cons. of Music in Boston, the Mannes College of Music in N.Y., the Cleveland Inst. of Music, the Univ. of Texas in Austin, and Boston Univ., numbering among his pupils David del Tredici, Gilbert Kalisch, Gary Karr, Ursula Oppens, and Pinchas Zukerman. He was particularly admired for his performances of Beethoven, Schubert, and Brahms.

Siagian, Rizaldi, significant Indonesian performer, composer, and ethnomusicologist; b. Medan, North Sumatra, early 1950s. He played drums and guitar, and also sang in urban pop groups in the late 1960s, then became interested in traditional Sumatran music; studied at the Univ. of North Sumatra (B.A., 1982) and at San Diego State Univ. (M.A., 1985, with a thesis on South Indian drumming); then returned to Indonesia to head the ethnomusicology program at Universitas Sumatera Utara (U.S.U., Univ. of North Sumatra). He participated in various independent music groups; in 1981 he appeared at London's Royal Albert Hall with the group Ansambel Bukit Barisan, and in 1989 directed a performance at the National Palace in Jakarta. In 1987 he served as artistic director for the performance of North Sumatran music for the Cultural Festival Celebration of North Sumatra and in The Hague. In 1991 he was engaged to lead a group of Batak musicians from the Lake Toba area of North Sumatra on a tour of the U.S. as part of its "Festival of Indonesia." As a composer, Siagian was first active as an arranger of popular music (1970–80); in 1986

he began composing works that combined modern and traditional musical elements, his intent being to reintegrate North Sumatran traditional instruments into the musical life of North Sumatra and Indonesia. An example of such compositional "conservation" is his resurrection of the Gambus (plucked lute), as in his *Gambus Menjelang Magrib* for Gambus, Voice, Frame Drum, Harmonium, and Violin, and in his *Gambus Kehendak in 7* and *Gambus Binal*, both for Gambus, Malaysian Drum, Taganing, Gong, Lonceng, Harmonium, Violin, Hasapi, Tube Zither, and Voice. He also composed *Lebah*, a dance accompaniment for Tube Zither, Drum, Shawm, Slit Drum, Cymbal, and Voice.

Sibelius, Jean (actually, **Johan Julius Christian**), great Finnish composer whose music, infused with the deeply felt modalities of national folk songs, opened a modern era of Northern musical art; b. Hämeenlinna, Dec. 8, 1865; d. Järvenpää, Sept. 20, 1957. The family name stems from a Finnish peasant named Sibbe, traced back to the late 17th century; the Latin noun ending was commonly added among educated classes in Scandinavia. Sibelius was the son of an army surgeon; from early childhood, he showed a natural affinity for music. At the age of 9, he began to study piano; then took violin lessons with Gustaf Levander, a local bandmaster. He learned to play violin well enough to take part in amateur performances of chamber music. In 1885 he enrolled at the Univ. of Helsingfors (Helsinki) to study law, but abandoned it after the 1st semester. In the fall of 1885 he entered the Helsingfors Cons., where he studied violin with Vasiliev and Csillag; he also took courses in composition with Wegelius. In 1889 his String Quartet was performed in public, and produced a sufficiently favorable impression to obtain for him a government stipend for further study in Berlin, where he took lessons in counterpoint and fugue with Albert Becker. Later he proceeded to Vienna for additional musical training, and became a student of Robert Fuchs and Karl Goldmark (1890–91). In 1892 he married Aino Järnefelt. From then on, his destiny as a national Finnish composer was determined; the music he wrote was inspired by native legends, with the great Finnish epic *Kalevala* as a prime source of inspiration. On April 28, 1892, his symphonic poem *Kullervo*, scored for soloists, chorus, and orch., was 1st performed in Helsingfors. There followed one of his most remarkable works, the symphonic poem entitled simply *En Saga*, that is, "a legend"; in it he displayed to the full his genius for variation forms, based on a cumulative growth of a basic theme adorned but never encumbered with effective contrapuntal embellishments. From 1892 to 1900 he taught theory of composition at the Helsingfors Cons. In 1897 the Finnish Senate granted him an annual stipend of 3,000 marks. On April 26, 1899, he conducted in Helsingfors the premiere of his 1st Sym. He subsequently conducted the 1st performances of all of his syms., the 5th excepted. On July 2, 1900, the Helsingfors Phil. gave the 1st performance of his most celebrated and most profoundly moving patriotic work, *Finlandia*. Its melody soon became identified among Finnish patriots with the aspiration for national independence, so that the Czarist government went to the extreme of forbidding its performances during periods of political unrest. In 1901 Sibelius was invited to conduct his works at the annual festival of the Allgemeiner Deutscher Tonkünstlerverein at Heidelberg. In 1904 he settled in his country home at Järvenpää, where he remained for the rest of his life; he traveled rarely. In 1913 he accepted a commission for an orch. work from the American music patron Carl Stoeckel, to be performed at the 28th annual Festival at Norfolk, Conn. For it he contributed a symphonic legend, *Aalotaret* (*Nymphs of the Ocean;* it was later rev. as *The Oceanides*). He took his only sea voyage to America to conduct its premiere on June 4, 1914; on that occasion he received the honorary degree of Mus.D. from Yale Univ. Returning to Finland just before the outbreak of World War I, Sibelius withdrew into seclusion, but continued to work. He made his last public appearance in Stockholm, conducting the premiere of his 7th Sym. on March 24, 1924. He wrote 2 more works after that, including a score for Shakespeare's *The Tempest* and a symphonic poem, *Tapiola;* he practically ceased to compose after 1927. At various times, rumors were circulated that he had completed his 8th Sym., but nothing was forthcoming from Järvenpää. One persistent story was that Sibelius himself decided to burn his incomplete works. Although willing to receive journalists and reporters, he avoided answering questions about his music. He lived out his very long life as a retired person, absorbed in family interests; in some modest ways he was even a *bon vivant;* he liked his cigars and his beer, and he showed no diminution in his mental alertness. Only once was his peaceful life gravely disrupted; this was when the Russian army invaded Finland in 1940; Sibelius sent an anguished appeal to America to save his country, which by the perverse fate of world politics became allied with Nazi Germany. But after World War II, Sibelius cordially received a delegation of Soviet composers who made a reverential pilgrimage to his rural retreat.

Honors were showered upon him; festivals of his music became annual events in Helsinki; in 1939 the Helsinki Cons. was renamed the Sibelius Academy in his honor; a postage stamp bearing his likeness was issued by the Finnish government on his 80th birthday; special publications—biographical, bibliographical, and photographic—were publ. in Finland. Artistically, too, Sibelius attained the status of greatness rarely vouchsafed to a living musician; several important contemporary composers paid him homage by acknowledging their debt of inspiration to him, Vaughan Williams among them. Sibelius was the last representative of 19th-century nationalistic Romanticism. He stayed aloof from modern developments, but he was not uninterested in reading scores and listening to performances on the radio of works of such men as Schoenberg, Prokofiev, Bartók, and Shostakovich.

The music of Sibelius marked the culmination of the growth of national Finnish art, in which Pacius was the protagonist, and Wegelius a worthy cultivator. Like his predecessors, he was schooled in the Germanic tradition, and his early works reflect German lyricism and dramatic thought. He opened a new era in Finnish music when he abandoned formal conventions and began to write music that seemed inchoate and diffuse but followed a powerful line of development by variation and repetition; a parallel with Beethoven's late works has frequently been drawn. The thematic material employed by Sibelius is not modeled directly on known Finnish folk songs; rather, he re-created the characteristic melodic patterns of folk music. The prevailing mood is somber, even tragic, with a certain elemental sweep and grandeur. His instrumentation is highly individual, with long songful solo passages, and with protracted transitions that are treated as integral parts of the music. His genius found its most eloquent expression in his syms. and symphonic poems; he wrote relatively little chamber music, and only in his earlier years. His only opera, *The Maid in the Tower* (1896), to a text in Swedish, was never publ. He wrote some incidental music for the stage; the celebrated *Valse triste* was written in 1903 for *Kuolema,* a play by Arvid Järnefelt, brother-in-law of Sibelius.

WORKS: STAGE: *Jungfrun i tornet* (The Maid in the Tower), opera (1896; Helsinki, Nov. 7, 1896); incidental music: Overture, op. 10, and Suite, op. 11, to *Karelia* (1893; Helsinki, Nov. 13, 1893); *King Kristian II,* op. 27, for a play by A. Paul (1898; Helsinki, Feb. 28, 1898, composer conducting); *Kuolema* (Death) for Strings and Percussion, op. 44, for a play by Arvid Järnefelt (1903; Helsinki, Dec. 2, 1903, composer conducting); *Pelléas et Mélisande,* op. 46, for Maeterlinck's play (1905; Helsinki, March 17, 1905, composer conducting); *Belshazzar's Feast,* op. 51, for a play by H. Procopé (1906; Helsinki, Nov. 7, 1906, composer conducting); *Svanevhit* (Swanwhite), op. 54, for Strindberg's play (1908; Helsinki, April 8, 1908, composer conducting); *Ödlan* (The Lizard) for Solo Violin and String Quintet, op. 8, for a play by M. Lybeck (1909; Helsinki, April 6, 1910, composer conducting); *Jedermann* for Mixed Chorus, Piano, Organ, and Orch., op. 83, for Hofmannsthal's play (1916; Helsinki, Nov. 5, 1916); *The*

Tempest, op. 109, for Shakespeare's play (1925; Copenhagen, March 16, 1926); also *Näcken* (The Watersprite), 2 songs with Piano Trio, for a play by Wennerberg (1888); *The Language of the Birds,* a wedding march for A. Paul's play *Die Sprache der Vögel* (1911); *Scaramouche,* op. 71, a "tragic pantomime" after the play by P. Knudsen and M. Bloch (1913; Copenhagen, May 12, 1922).

ORCH.: 7 syms.: No. 1, in E minor, op. 39 (Helsinki, April 26, 1899, composer conducting); No. 2, in D major, op. 43 (Helsinki, March 8, 1902, composer conducting); No. 3, in C major, op. 52 (1904–7; Helsinki, Sept. 25, 1907, composer conducting); No. 4, in A minor, op. 63 (Helsinki, April 3, 1911, composer conducting); No. 5, in E-flat major, op. 82 (Helsinki, Dec. 8, 1915, Kajanus conducting; rev. 1916; Helsinki, Dec. 14, 1916; rev. 1919; Helsinki, Nov. 24, 1919); No. 6, in D minor, op. 104 (Helsinki, Feb. 19, 1923, composer conducting); No. 7, in C major, op. 105 (Stockholm, March 24, 1924, composer conducting); *Andantino* and *Menuetto* for Clarinet, 2 Cornets, 2 Horns, and Bassoon (1890–91); Overture in E minor (1890–91); *Scène de ballet* (1891); *Menuetto* (1894); *Skogsrået* (The Wood Nymph), tone poem, op. 15 (1894); *Vårsång* (Spring Song), tone poem, op. 16 (Vaasa, June 21, 1894); 4 *Legends,* op. 22 (all 4 1st perf. in Helsinki, April 13, 1896, composer conducting): 1, *Lemminkäinen and the Maidens of the Island* (1895; rev. 1897 and 1939); 2, *The Swan of Tuonela* (1893; rev. 1897 and 1900); 3, *Lemminkäinen in Tuonela* (1895; rev. 1897 and 1939); 4, *Lemminkäinen's Home-ward Journey* (1895; rev. 1897 and 1900); *King Kristian II,* suite from the incidental music, op. 27 (1898); *Scènes historiques,* op. 25, I (1899; rev. 1911); *Finlandia,* tone poem, op. 26 (1899; rev. 1900; Helsinki, July 2, 1900, Kajanus conducting); *Björneborgarnas March* (1900); *Cortège* (1901); Overture in A minor (Helsinki, March 3, 1902, composer conducting); *Romance* in C major for Strings, op. 42 (1903; Turku, March 1904, composer conducting); Concerto in D minor for Violin and Orch., op. 47 (1903; Helsinki, Feb. 8, 1904; Viktor Nováček, soloist; composer conducting; rev. 1905; Berlin, Oct. 19, 1905; Karl Halir, soloist; R. Strauss conducting); *Cassazione,* op. 6 (1904); *Pelléas et Mélisande,* suite from the incidental music, op. 46 (1905); *Pohjola's Daughter,* symphonic fantasia, op. 49 (St. Petersburg, Dec. 29, 1906, composer conducting); *Belshazzar's Feast,* suite from the incidental music, op. 51 (1906; Helsinki, Sept. 25, 1907); *Pan and Echo,* dance intermezzo, op. 53 (1906); *Nightride and Sunrise,* tone poem, op. 55 (1907; St. Petersburg, Jan. 1909); *Svanevhit* (Swanwhite), suite from the incidental music, op. 54 (1908); *In Memoriam,* funeral march, op. 59 (1909; Helsinki, April 3, 1911); *The Dryad,* tone poem (1910), and *Dance Intermezzo* (1907), op. 45; *Rakastava* (The Lover) for Strings and Percussion, op. 14 (1911); *Scènes historiques,* op. 66, II (1912); 2 serenades for Violin and Orch., op. 69: No. 1, in D major (1912), and No. 2, in G minor (1913); *The Bard,* tone poem, op. 64 (1913; rev. 1914); *Aallottaret* (Nymphs of the Ocean), tone poem, op. 73 (1914; 2nd version as *The Oceanides,* 1914; the latter 1st perf. at the Norfolk [Conn.] Festival, June 4, 1914, composer conducting); 2 pieces for Violin or Cello, and Orch., op. 77 (1914); 2 *Humoresques* for Violin and Orch., op. 87 (1917); 4 *Humoresques* for Violin and Orch., op. 89 (also numbered as 3–6 in continuation of the preceding; 1917); *Promotiomarssi* (Academic March) (1919); 3 pieces, op. 96: 1, *Valse lyrique* (1920); 2, *Autrefois, Scène pastorale* for 2 Voices and Orch. (1919); 3, *Valse chevaleresque* (1920); *Suite mignonne* for 2 Flutes and Strings, op. 98a (1921); *Suite champêtre* for Strings, op. 98b (1921); *Andante festivo* for Strings and Percussion (1922; also for String Quartet); *Suite caractéristique* for Harp and Strings, op. 100 (1922); *The Tempest,* concert version of the incidental music, op. 109 (1925); *Tapiola,* tone poem, op. 112 (N.Y., Dec. 26, 1926, W. Damrosch conducting); Suite for Violin and String Orch., op. 117 (n.d.; Lahti, Dec. 8. 1990).

CHAMBER: *Vattendroppar* (Water Drops) for Violin and Cello (1875–76); Quartet in E minor for Piano, 2 Violins, and Cello (1881–82); Piano Trio in A minor (1881–82); Sonata in D minor for Violin and Piano (1881–82); *Andantino* for Cello and Piano (1884); Quartet for Violin, Cello, Harmonium, and Piano (1884?); String Quartet in E-flat major (1885); Suite in G minor for String Trio (1885); Duo for Violin and Viola (1886); *Andante cantabile* for Violin and Piano (1887); Piano Trio, *Korpo* (1887); Piano Trio in C major, *Loviisa* (1888); *Romance and Epilogue* for Violin and Piano, op. 2 (1888; rev. 1912); *Fugue* for String Quartet (1888); *Theme and Variations* in C-sharp minor for String Quartet (1888); String Quartet in A minor (1889); Sonata in F major for Violin and Piano (1889); Suite in A major for String Trio (1889); Quintet in G minor for Piano and Strings (1889–90); String Quartet in B-flat major, op. 4 (1890); Octet for Flute, Clarinet, and Strings (1891); Quartet in C major for Piano, 2 Violins, and Cello (1891); Rondo for Viola and Piano (1893); *Kehtolaulu* (Lullaby) for Violin and Kantele (1899); Fantasia for Cello and Piano (1899–1900); *Malinconia* for Cello and Piano, op. 20 (1901); String Quartet in D minor, op. 56, *Voces intimae* (1909); 4 pieces for Violin or Cello, and Piano, op. 78: 1, *Impromptu* (1915); 2, *Romance* (1915); 3, *Religioso* (1919); 4, *Rigaudon* (1915); 6 pieces for Violin and Piano, op. 79: *Souvenir, Tempo di menuetto, Danse caractéristique, Sérénade, Danse idyll,* and *Berceuse* (1915); Sonatina in E major for Violin and Piano, op. 80 (1915); 5 pieces for Violin and Cello, op. 81: *Mazurka, Rondino, Waltz, Aubade,* and *Menuetto* (1915); *Novelette* for Violin and Piano, op. 102 (1923); 5 *danses champêtres* for Violin and Piano, op. 106 (1925); 4 pieces for Violin and Piano, op. 115: *On the Heath, Ballade, Humoresque,* and *The Bells* (1929); 3 pieces for Violin and Piano, op. 116: *Scène de danse, Danse caractéristique,* and *Rondeau romantique* (1929); also *Adagio* for String Quartet (date unknown). **PIANO:** Over 25 works composed between 1893 and 1929, including Sonata in F major, op. 12 (1893). **ORGAN:** 2 pieces, op. 111: *Intrada* (1925) and *Surusoitto* (Mournful Music; 1931).

VOCAL: *Kullervo,* symphonic poem for Soprano, Baritone, Male Chorus, and Orch., op. 7 (1892; Helsinki, April 28, 1892); *Rakastava* (The Lover) for Male Chorus a cappella, op. 14 (1893; Helsinki, April 28, 1894); *Laulu Lemminkäiselle* (A Song for Lemminkäinen) for Male Chorus and Orch., op. 31, No. 1 (1900); *Har du mod?* (Have You Courage?) for Male Chorus and Orch., op. 31, No. 2 (1904); *Atenarnes sång* (The Song of the Athenians) for Male Voices, with Wind Instruments and Percussion, op. 31, No. 3 (Helsinki, April 26, 1899); *Tulen synty* (The Origin of Fire) for Baritone, Male Chorus, and Orch., op. 32 (Helsinki, April 9, 1902; composer conducting; rev. 1910); *Vapautettu kuningatar* (The Liberated Queen), cantata for Mixed Chorus and Orch., op. 48 (Helsinki, May 12, 1906); *Luonnotar* (Spirit of Nature), tone poem for Soprano and Orch., op. 70 (1910; Gloucester, Sept. 10, 1913); *Oma maa* (Our Native Land), cantata for Mixed Chorus and Orch., op. 92 (1918); *Jordens sång* (Song of the Earth), cantata for Mixed Chorus and Orch., op. 93 (1919); *Maan virsi* (Hymn of the Earth), cantata for Mixed Chorus and Orch., op. 95 (Helsinki, June 1920, composer conducting; *Väinön virsi* (Väinö's Song) for Mixed Chorus and Orch., op. 110 (Helsinki, June 28, 1926, Kajanus conducting); *Masonic Ritual Music* for Male Voices, Piano, and Organ, op. 113 (1927–46; rev. 1948); also numerous other choral works, and 95 songs composed between 1891 and 1917.

BIBL.: K. Flodin, *Finska musiker* (Helsinki, 1900); R. Newmarch, *J. S.: A Finnish Composer* (Leipzig, 1906); E. Furuhjelm, *J. S.: Hans tondikting och drag ur hans liv* (Borgå, 1916); W. Niemann, *J. S.* (Leipzig, 1917); C. Gray, *S.* (London, 1931; 2nd ed., 1945); K. Ekman, *J. S.: En konstnärs liv och personlighet* (Stockholm, 1935; Eng. tr. as *J. S.: His Life and Personality,* Helsinki, 1935; 4th Swedish ed., 1959); C. Gray, *S.: The Symphonies* (London, 1935); A. Meyer, "*S.:* Symphonist," *Musical Quarterly* (Jan. 1936); B. de Törne, *S.: A Close-Up* (London, 1937); R. Newmarch, *J. S.: A Short History of a Long Friendship* (Boston, 1939; 2nd ed., 1945); H. Askeli, "A Sketch of S. the Man," *Musical Quarterly* (Jan. 1940); B. Sandberg, *J. S.* (Helsinki, 1940); E. Arnold, *Finlandia: The Story of S.* (N.Y., 1941; 2nd ed., 1951); E. Roiha, *Die Symphonien von J. S.: Eine formanalytische Studie* (Jyväskylä, 1941); I. Krohn, *Der Formen-*

bau in den Symphonien von J. S. (Helsinki, 1942); E. Tanzberger, *Die symphonischen Dichtungen von J. S. (Ein inhalt-sund formanalytische Studie)* (Würzburg, 1943); S. Levas, *J. S. ja hänen Ainolansa* (Helsinki, 1945; 2nd ed., 1955); M. Similä, *Sibeliana* (Helsinki, 1945); B. de Törne, *S., i närbild och samtal* (Helsinki, 1945; 2nd ed., 1955); G. Abraham, ed., *S.: A Symposium* (London, 1947; 2nd ed., 1952); I. Hannikainen, *S. and the Development of Finnish Music* (London, 1948); N.-E. Ringbom, *S.* (Stockholm, 1948; Eng. tr., Norman, Okla., 1954); V. Helasvuo, *S. and the Music of Finland* (Helsinki, 1952; 2nd ed., 1957); O. Anderrson, *J. S. i Amerika* (Åbo, 1955); S. Parmet, *S. symfonier* (Helsinki, 1955; Eng. tr. as *The Symphonies of S.: A Study in Musical Appreciation,* London, 1959); L. Solanterä, *The Works of J. S.* (Helsinki, 1955); H. Johnson, *J. S.* (N.Y., 1959); E. Tanzberger, *J. S.: Eine Monographie* (Wiesbaden, 1962); F. Blum, *J. S.: An International Bibliography on the Occasion of the Centennial Celebrations, 1965* (Detroit, 1965); R. Layton, *S.* (London, 1965; 3rd ed., rev., 1983); E. Tawaststjerna, *J. S.* (5 vols., Helsinki, 1965–88; Eng. tr. by R. Layton, 1976-); R. Layton, *The World of S.* (London, 1970); B. James, *The Music of J. S.* (East Brunswick, N.J.; London; and Mississauga, Ontario; 1983); E. Salmenhaara, *J. S.* (Helsinki, 1984); F. Dahlström, *The Works of J. S.* (Helsinki, 1987); special issue of *Finnish Music Quarterly,* 3–4 (1990).

Siboni, Erik (Anthon Valdemar), Danish organist, teacher, and composer of Italian parentage; b. Copenhagen, Aug. 26, 1828; d. Frederiksberg, Feb. 11, 1892. He was the son of the tenor **Giuseppe Siboni** (b. Forli, Jan. 27, 1780; d. Copenhagen, March 28, 1839, as director of the Opera and Cons.); studied with J.P.E. Hartmann; then with Moscheles and Hauptmann at Leipzig and with Sechter at Vienna; returned to Copenhagen, and in 1865 became organist and prof. of piano at the Søro Academy; retired in 1883.

WORKS: 2 operas: *Loreley* (Copenhagen, 1859) and *Carl den Andens flugt* (Flight of Charles II; Copenhagen, 1861); 2 syms.; Piano Concerto (1864); *Otello,* overture (1881); choral works; Piano Quartet (1862); piano pieces.

Sicilianos, Yorgos, Greek composer; b. Athens, Aug. 29, 1922. He studied harmony with Varvoglis at the Hellenic Cons. and with Sklavos at the Athens Cons. (until 1943); then went to Rome, where he took a course with Pizzetti at the Accademia di Santa Cecilia (1951–53); supplemented his music education at the Paris Cons. (1953–54), where he studied with Milhaud and Aubin. He received a Fulbright scholarship to continue his training with Piston at Harvard Univ., Blacher at the Berkshire Music Center at Tanglewood, and Persichetti at the Juilliard School of Music in N.Y. (1955–56). Upon his return to Greece, he occupied various educational and administrative posts; was head of music services for the National Broadcasting Inst. (1960–61; 1979); taught at Pierce College in Athens (from 1967). His style of composition is classical in format, pandiatonic in harmony, and intricately polyphonic in contrapuntal and fugal developments.

WORKS: BALLETS: *The Pearl* (1957); *Tanagra* for 2 Pianos and Percussion (Athens, April 21, 1958; orch. version, Athens, Feb. 5, 1962); *Bacchantes* (Athens, Jan. 11, 1960). **ORCH.:** Sym. (1941–47); Sym. No. 1 (1955–56; N.Y., March 1, 1958); *Prelude and Dance* (Athens Radio, Sept. 1, 1948); *The Revelation of the Fifth Seal,* symphonic poem (1951; Athens, May 11, 1952); Concertino for 5 Winds and Strings (Rome, June 9, 1953); Concerto (Athens, Nov. 28, 1954); *Synthesis* for 2 String Orchs. and Percussion (Athens, Nov. 26, 1962; based on the String Quartet No. 3, 1957–62); Cello Concerto (1963); *Variations on 4 Rhythmical Themes* (1963); *Perspectives* for 4 Orch. Groups (1966); *Episodia* for 17 Instruments (1964–67); *Antiphona* for Strings, Brass, and Percussion (1976). **CHAMBER:** 4 string quartets (1951; 1954–55; 1957–62; 1967); *Study* for Tuba (1974); *Schemata* for 6 Percussion (1976). **PIANO:** 3 sonatas (1939); 8 *Children's Miniatures* (1963); (8) *Études compositionnelles* (1972–73; rev. as 6 études for Piano and Orch., 1975). **VOCAL:** *Stasimon II* for Mezzo-soprano, Women's

Voices, and Orch. (1965); *Episodes II* for Double Chorus, Piano, Double Bass, Percussion, and Tape (1971); *Epitaphion: in memoriam Nikos Marangopoulos* for Chorus, Children's Voices, Narrator, and Orch. (1971); *Parable* for Chorus, Flute, Tuba, Percussion, and Tape (1973); *6 Songs* for Mezzo-soprano or Baritone and Piano (1975); *Moonlight Sonata*, cantata for Mezzo-soprano, Clarinet, Viola, and Guitar (1976–77).

Sidarta, Otok Bima, active Indonesian composer, teacher, dancer, painter, and journalist; b. Yogyakarta, Java, May 18, 1960. He was born into an artistic family; his father, Bagong Kussudiarja, is a famous choreographer and painter, and his brother, Djaduk Ferianto, a well-known composer. Sidarta studied dance at his father's Pusat Latihan Tari (PLT, Center for Dance Study; 1967) and at Pamulangan Beksa Nyayogyakarta (PBN, 1979), founded by the important choreographer/dancer Romo Sasminta Mardawa; also studied music at the Yogyakarta high school cons., Sekolah Menengah Karawitan Indonesia (SMKI). From 1980 to 1984 he was active in California; appeared at World Music Festivals at the Calif. Inst. of the Arts in Valencia (1981) and in San Diego (1982); also participated in the Asian Pacific Culture Festival at Loyola Marymount Univ. (1983) and in the activities of the Indonesian Cultural Center, both in Los Angeles. In 1984 he returned to Indonesia, where he founded the group Kelompok Musik Sempu (KMS), which took 1st place in the "best creativity" category at the Acoustic Music Competition (1984); taught dance and music in Sumatra (1985) and in Kuala Lumpur (1986), following a tour to Malaysia; also was active at his father's Padepokan Seni Bagong Kussudiarja (PSBK, Residential Art Center) in Yogyakarta. In 1987 he participated in the ASEAN workshop on Liturgy and Music in Manila; also performed his own *Meja, meja* (Table, table) at a PSBK concert, "Experimental Arts I," and collaborated on and performed in the collective composition *Antara Tugu Ngejaman* with his brother at the national Pekan Komponis (Composers Festival) in Jakarta. He also founded a group that specialized in children's songs, Sanggar Dolanan Anak-anak Among Siswa. After touring with his father's group in Seoul, Japan, Hong Kong, Singapore, and Malaysia (1988), he founded Pusat Latihan Karawitan Yogyakarta (PLK, Center for the Study of [Javanese] Music). In 1989 he founded and coordinated the 1st composition festival in Yogyakarta for new music using Javanese gamelan, "Lomba Komposisi Karawitan I," in cooperation with PSBK and the Yogyakarta Arts Council. Sidarta's musical innovations include the addition to the gamelan of hand-held percussion instruments (such as bells, triangles, and claves), as well as the development of new percussion techniques, including placing hanging gongs horizontally on cloth and striking them muted. He also created a personal drumming style that combines Javanese, Sundanese, and original elements. He composed for various venues; from 1984 he created pieces for dance accompaniment, alone and collectively, which included *Kebangkitan Nasional, Lintasan Sejarah (ABRI)* (Armed Forces) and *Sendratari Kelahiran;* also created works for folk theater, known as *ketoprak,* which were performed in art centers and on Indonesian National TV (TVRI) in Yogyakarta and Jakarta. His compositions for Javanese gamelan include *Meja, meja* (1987), *Antara Tugu Ngejaman* (with Djaduk Ferianto), and *Sang Pahlawan, Lesehan, Sibab,* and *511* (all 1988). Among his popular songs is *Kemuning* (1983). He was also active as a choreographer, numbering among his dance works *Sasap* (1978); *GothakGathuk* (1979); *Kelahiran* (1981); *Gerka Suara Nusantara* (1981); *Gaung Kaputren, Santyang,* and *Kasonangane* (all 1985); and *Lima Alit* (1988). From 1975 he was active as a painter; his works have been exhibited in Bali and at the Indonesian Consulate in Los Angeles.

Sidlin, Murry, American conductor; b. Baltimore, May 6, 1940, of Russian-Latvian parents. He studied theory with Elliott Galkin and Louis Cheslock, and trumpet with Harold Rherig, at the Peabody Cons. in Baltimore (B.A., 1962; M.M., 1968). During the summers of 1961 and 1962 he traveled to Italy and studied conducting with Sergiu Celibidache at the Accademia Chigiana in Siena. Returning to the U.S., he took courses with Donald Grout and Karel Husa at Cornell Univ. (1963–65). He was assistant conductor of the Aspen Music Festival (1970–71); after working with Barzin and the National Orchestral Association in N.Y. (1971), he was assistant conductor of the Baltimore Sym. Orch. (1971–73); then was resident conductor of the National Sym. Orch. in Washington, D.C. (1973–77). He was music director of the New Haven Sym. Orch. (1977–88), the Tulsa Phil. (1978–80), and the Long Beach (Calif.) Sym. Orch. (1980–1988), which he brought to a considerable degree of excellence.

Sieber, Ferdinand, Austrian singing teacher and composer; b. Vienna, Dec. 5, 1822; d. Berlin, Feb. 19, 1895. He studied with Ronconi; after a brief period of singing in opera, he was a singing teacher in Dresden (1848–54) and in Berlin. He publ. the treatises *Die Kunst des Gesangs* (with a supplement, *50 Vocalisen und Solfeggien*); *Vollständiges Lehrbuch der Gesangskunst für Lehrer und Schüler* (1858; 3rd ed., 1878); *Katechismus der Gesangskunst* (1862 and many subsequent eds.); *Die Aussprache des Italienischen im Gesang* (1860; 2nd ed., 1880); *Handbuch des deutschen Liederschatzes* (1875), containing a catalogue of 10,000 songs arranged according to vocal range; also wrote many songs.

Siebert, Wilhelm Dieter, German composer; b. Berlin, Oct. 22, 1931. He studied with Rufer in Berlin and with Fortner in Freiburg im Breisgau. About 1957 he devoted himself mainly to experimental music, incorporating the rhythmic resources of jazz and the unlimited sonorities of electronics; in 1963 he joined the Neue Musik group in Berlin.

WORKS: Trio for Flute, Harp, and Percussion (1967); *Paganini Variations* for Flute, Piano, String Trio, and Magnetic Tape (1968); choral music with tape; opera, *The Sinking of the Titanic* (1979).

Siegel, Carl F.W., German music publisher; d. Leipzig, March 29, 1869. He founded his firm in 1846, making a specialty of choral music. He was succeeded by Richard Linnemann (b. Leipzig, April 14, 1845; d. there, Dec. 1, 1909), who studied at the Leipzig Cons. and in 1871 acquired control of *Die Sängerhalle* (organ of the German singing society), which continued publ. until 1916. His sons, Carl Linnemann (b. Leipzig, Sept. 25, 1872; d. there, Dec. 14, 1945) and Richard Linnemann, Jr. (b. Leipzig, Nov. 5, 1874; d. there, April 5, 1932), entered the business in 1901; bought the stock of E.W. Fritzsch in 1901 and that of K.F. Kistner in 1919.

Siegel, Janis, American popular vocalist; b. N.Y., July 23, 1952. She was a member of the all-girl folk groups Young Generation and Laurel Canyon; later sang with Jon Hendricks and Bobbie McFerrin, and recorded the albums *Experiment in White* (1982), *At Home,* and *Short Stories* (1989); also recorded Ilhan Mimaroglu's Prelude No. 16 and String Quartet No. 4 (1978), both written for her. Siegel became best known as a member of Manhattan Transfer, a spirited vocal quartet devoted to the performance of harmonic arrangements of jazz and popular music; formed originally in 1969, the group was reconstructed in 1972 by its only surviving member, bass Tim Hauser (b. Troy, N.Y., Dec. 12, 1941), to include Siegel, tenor Alan Paul (b. Newark, N.J., Nov. 23, 1949), and alto Laurel Massé (b. 1954); their early recordings include *Manhattan Transfer* (1975; with the songs *Tuxedo Junction* and *Java Live*), *Coming Out* (1976), *Pastiche* (1978), and *Manhattan Transfer Live* (1978). After Massé was replaced by Cheryl Bentyne (b. Jan. 17, 1954) in 1979, the group produced such critically acclaimed recordings as *Extensions* (1979; with the songs *Birdland* and *Twilight Zone*), *Mecca for Moderns* (1981; with the songs *Boy from New York City* and *Until I Met You*), *Bodies and Souls* (1983), *Bop Doo-Wop* (1984), *Vocalese* (1985; dedicated to the music of jazz vocalist Jon Hendricks), and *Brazil* (1988). They also created an experimental television miniseries (1975) and a video, *Vocalese Live 1986* (1987). Manhattan Transfer has become the prototype for sophisticated and imaginative jazz vocal performance.

Siegel, Jeffrey, American pianist; b. Chicago, Nov. 18, 1942. He studied piano with Rudolph Ganz at the Chicago Musical College and later with Rosina Lhévinne and Ilona Kabos at the Juilliard School of Music in N.Y. He won the silver medal at the Queen Elisabeth of Belgium Competition in Brussels (1968); then was a soloist with many of the leading orchs. of the U.S. and Europe, including the Chicago Sym., Boston Sym., N.Y. Phil., London Sym., and London Phil.

Siegl, Otto, Austrian violinist, conductor, teacher, and composer; b. Graz, Oct. 6, 1896; d. Vienna, Nov. 9, 1978. He received his 1st music lessons from his mother, an amateur pianist; then studied composition with Mojsisovics, Kroemer, Künzel, and Kornauth at the Graz Schule des Steiermärkischen Musikvereins (1901–15; 1918–20); was drafted into the Austro-Hungarian army and served as a Tirol rifleman in World War I. While still in the service, he met the musicologist Max Auer, who gave him instruction in the classics. After the Armistice, he was a violinist in the Vienna Sym. Orch. (1921–22) and assistant conductor at the Graz Opera (1922–24); also wrote music criticism. In 1926 he went to Germany, where he worked as a choral conductor from 1933 to 1948 he was on the staff of the Cologne Hochschule für Musik; from 1948 to 1967 he taught at the Vienna Academy of Music. In 1957 he was awarded the Great State Prize for Music. A pragmatic musician, he was a master of polyphony; his choral writing is especially meritorious. **WORKS:** 2 syms. (1958, 1959); Cello Concerto (1957); Flute Concerto (1955); Chamber Concerto for Piano and Orch. (1960); Clarinet Concerto with String Orch. (1968); 2 string quintets (1940, 1954); *Quintet-Serenade* for Clarinet, Bassoon, Violin, Viola, and Cello (1961); 5 string quartets (1924–56); Trio for Clarinet, Cello, and Piano (1959); 4 cello sonatas (1923, 1923, 1924, 1967); 2 violin sonatas (1925, 1940); 2 viola sonatas (1925, 1938); 2 clarinet sonatas (1965, 1968); Flute Sonata (1968); Sonata for Clarinet and Cello (1965); oratorio, *Stern des Lebens* (1959); several cantatas; 4 masses; numerous choruses; about 80 lieder. **BIBL.:** W. Trienes, *O. S.* (Mülheim, 1956); W. Suppan, *O. S.* (Vienna, 1966).

Siegmeister, Elie, significant American composer and teacher, whose works reflect the national moods and preoccupations from early social trends to universal concepts; b. N.Y., Jan. 15, 1909; d. Manhasset, N.Y., March 10, 1991. He took piano lessons as a youth with Emil Friedberger; in 1925 he entered Columbia Univ. and studied theory and composition with Seth Bingham (B.A., 1927); also took private lessons in counterpoint with Riegger; after training with Boulanger in Paris (1927–32), he received instruction in conducting from Stoessel at the Juilliard School of Music in N.Y. (1935–38). He was active with the Composers Collective of N.Y., for which he wrote songs under the name L.E. Swift; was a founder of the American Composers Alliance in 1937; was founder-conductor of the American Ballad Singers (1939–46), which he led in performances of American folk songs. He felt strongly that music should express the social values of the people; in his early songs, he selected texts by contemporary American poets voicing indignation at the inequities of the modern world; he also gave lectures and conducted choruses at the revolutionary Pierre Degeyter (composer of the *Internationale*) Club in N.Y. As a result of his multiple musical experiences, Siegmeister developed an individual style of composition ranging from the populist American manner to strong modernistic sonorities employing a sort of euphonious dissonance with intervallic stress on minor seconds, major sevenths, and minor ninths. In his syms. and chamber music, he organized this dissonant idiom in self-consistent modern formulations, without, however, espousing any of the fashionable doctrines of composition, such as dodecaphony. The subject matter of his compositions, especially in the early period, was marked by a strongly national and socially radical character, exemplified by such works as *American Holiday, Ozark Set, Prairie Legend, Wilderness Road,* and *Western Suite,* the last achieving the rare honor of being performed by Toscanini. Siegmeister did not ignore the homely vernacular; his Clarinet Concerto is a brilliant realization of jazz, blues, and swing in a classically formal idiom. Siegmeister achieved an important position as an educator; he taught at Brooklyn College (1934), the New School for Social Research (1937–38), the Univ. of Minnesota (1948), and Hofstra Univ. (1949–76), where he also was composer-in-residence (from 1966); in 1976 he became prof. emeritus. He received numerous commissions and awards; held a Guggenheim fellowship in 1978 and in 1990 was elected a member of the American Academy and Inst. of Arts and Letters. In accepting this honor, he stated his *profession de foi* as 1st formulated in 1943: "My aim is to write as good music as I can that will at the same time speak the language of all our people."

WORKS: OPERAS: *Darling Corie* (1952; Hempstead, N.Y., Feb. 18, 1954); *Miranda and the Dark Young Man* (1955; Hartford, Conn., May 9, 1956); *The Mermaid of Lock No. 7* (Pittsburgh, July 20, 1958); *Dublin Song* (St. Louis, May 15, 1963; rev. as *The Plough and the Stars,* Baton Rouge, La., March 16, 1969); *Night of the Moonspell* (Shreveport, La., Nov. 14, 1976); *Marquesa of O* (1982); *Angel Levine* (N.Y., Oct. 5, 1985); *The Lady of the Lake* (N.Y., Oct. 5, 1985); also *Doodle Dandy of the USA,* play with music (N.Y., Dec. 26, 1942); *Sing Out, Sweet Land,* musical (Hartford, Conn., Nov. 10, 1944); *Fables from the Dark Woods,* ballet (Shreveport, April 25, 1976); incidental music; film scores, including *They Came to Cordura* (1959). **ORCH.:** 8 syms.: No. 1 (N.Y., Oct. 30, 1947; rev. 1972); No. 2 (1950; N.Y., Feb. 25, 1952; rev. 1971); No. 3 (1957; Oklahoma City, Feb. 8, 1959); No. 4 (1967–70; Cleveland, Dec. 6, 1973); No. 5, *Visions of Time* (1971–75; Baltimore, May 4, 1977); No. 6 (1983; Sacramento, Nov. 4, 1984); No. 7 (1986); No. 8 (1989; Albany, N.Y., March 30, 1990); *American Holiday* (1933); *Abraham Lincoln Walks at Midnight* (1937); *Ozark Set* (1943; Minneapolis, Nov. 7, 1944); *Prairie Legend* (1944; N.Y., Jan. 18, 1947); *Wilderness Road* (1944; Minneapolis, Nov. 9, 1945); *Western Suite* (N.Y., Nov. 24, 1945); *Sunday in Brooklyn* (N.Y., July 21, 1946); *Lonesome Hollow* (1946; Columbus, Ohio, 1948); *Summer Night* (1947; N.Y., Sept. 27, 1952); *From My Window* (1949; also for Piano); *Divertimento* (1953; Oklahoma City, March 28, 1954); Clarinet Concerto (Oklahoma City, Feb. 3, 1956); Flute Concerto (1960; Oklahoma City, Feb. 17, 1961); *Theater Set,* after the film score *They Came to Cordura* (1960; Rochester, N.Y., May 8, 1969); *Dick Whittington and His Cat* for Narrator and Orch. (1966; Philadelphia, Feb. 10, 1968); *5 Fantasies of the Theater* (1967; Hempstead, N.Y., Oct. 18, 1970); Piano Concerto (1974; Denver, Dec. 3, 1976; rev. 1982); *Shadows and Light: Homage to 5 Paintings* (Shreveport, La., Nov. 9, 1975); *Double Concerto: An Entertainment* for Violin, Piano, and Orch. (Columbia, Md., June 25, 1976); Violin Concerto (1977–83; Oakland, Calif., Jan. 29, 1985); *Fantasies in Line and Color: 5 American Paintings* (1981); *From These Shores: Homage to 5 American Authors* (1986; Merillville, Ind., Feb. 13, 1990); *Figures in the Wind* (1990); also works for Band. **VOCAL: CHORAL:** *Heyura, Ding, Dong, Ding* (1935–70); *John Henry* (1935); *American Ballad Singers Series* (1943); *American Folk Song Choral Series* (1953); *I Have a Dream,* cantata for Baritone, Narrator, Chorus, and Orch., after Martin Luther King, Jr. (1967; Omaha, Oct. 7, 1968); *A Cycle of Cities* for Soprano, Tenor, Chorus, and Orch. (Wolf Trap, Va., Aug. 8, 1974); *Cantata for FDR* for Baritone, Chorus, and Wind Ensemble (1981; Denver, May 5, 1982); *Sing Unto the Lord a New Song* for Chorus and Organ (1981). **SONGS AND SONG CYCLES:** (all for Solo Voice and Piano unless otherwise given): *Cortège for Rosenbloom* (1926); *4 Robert Frost Songs* (1930); *The Strange Funeral in Braddock* (1933; also for Baritone and Orch., 1938); *3 Elegies for García Lorca* (1938); *Johnny Appleseed* for Solo Voice (1940; also for Chorus, 1940); *Nancy Hanks* (1941); *For My Daughters* (1952); *Madam to You* (1964); *The Face of War* (1966; also for Voice and Orch., 1967–68; N.Y., May 24, 1968); *Songs of Experience* (1966; rev. for Alto or Bass, Viola, and Piano, 1977); 11 songs to words by e.e. cummings (1970); *Songs of Innocence* (1972); *City Songs* (1977); *3 Minute Songs* (1978); *Brief Introduction to the Problems of Philosophy* (1979); *Ways of Love* for Voice and Chamber Orch. (1983; N.Y., Jan. 15, 1984); *Bats in My Belfry* (1990); *4 Langston Hughes Songs* (1990); *Outside My Window* (1990).

CHAMBER: *Nocturne* for Flute and Piano (1927); *Prelude* for Clarinet and Piano (1927); *Contrasts* for Bassoon and Piano (1929); 3 string quartets (1935, 1960, 1973); *Down River* for Alto Saxophone and Piano (1939); 6 violin sonatas (1951, 1965, 1965, 1971, 1975, 1988); *Song for a Quiet Evening* for Violin and Piano (1955); *Fantasy and Soliloquy* for Cello (1964); Sextet for Brass and Percussion (1965); *American Harp* for Harp (1966); *Declaration* for Brass and Timpani (1976); *Summer* for Viola and Piano (1978); *Ten Minutes for 4 Players* for Wind Quartet (N.Y., Jan. 15, 1989). **PIANO:** *Theme and Variations No. 1* (1932) and *No. 2* (1967); *Toccata on Flight Rhythms* (1937); 5 sonatas: No. 1, *American* (1944), No. 2 (1964), No. 3 (1979), No. 4, *Prelude, Blues, and Toccata* (1980), and No. 5 (1987; N.Y., Jan. 15, 1988); *Sunday in Brooklyn* (1946); *3 Moods* (1959); *On This Ground* (1971); *3 Studies* (1982); also 4 vols. of educational pieces (1951–77).

WRITINGS: Ed. with O. Downes, *A Treasury of American Song* (N.Y., 1940; 3rd ed., 1984); *The Music Lover's Handbook* (N.Y., 1943; rev., 1973, as *The New Music Lover's Handbook*; new ed., 1983); *Work and Sing* (N.Y., 1944); *Invitation to Music* (Irvington-on-Hudson, 1961); *Harmony and Melody* (2 vols.; Belmont, Calif., 1965–66).

BIBL.: G. Schneerson, *Portraits of American Composers* (Moscow, 1977); J. Gallagher, *Structural Design and Motivic Unity in the 2nd, 3rd, and 4th Symphonies of E. S.* (diss., Cornell Univ., 1982); C. Oja, "Composer with a Conscience: E. S. in Profile," *American Music* (Summer 1988).

Siegmund-Schultze, Walther, German musicologist; b. Schweinitz, July 6, 1916. He studied musicology with Arnold Schmitz at the Univ. of Breslau (Ph.D., 1940, with the dissertation *Mozarts Vokal- und Instrumentalmusik in ihren motivisch-thematischen Beziehungen*); he completed his Habilitation at the Univ. of Halle with his *Untersuchungen zum Brahms Stil und Brahms Bild* in 1951. In 1954 he became a lecturer at the Univ. of Halle; in 1956 he was made a prof. of musicology, director of the musicological faculty, and dean of the philosophy faculty. He is noted for his studies of 18th-century music; his analysis of the styles of Bach, Handel, and Mozart is interesting as an example of Marxist theories applied to music.

WRITINGS: *Die Musik Bachs* (Leipzig, 1953); *Georg Friedrich Händel: Leben und Werk* (Leipzig, 1954; 3rd ed., 1962); *Mozarts Melodik und Stil: Eine Studie* (Leipzig, 1957); *Lehrbriefe für das Fernstudium: Die Musik der Klassik* (Halle, 1964); *Georg Friedrich Händel: Thema mit 20 Variationen* (Halle, 1965); *Die Hauptvertreter der bürgerlichen Musikkultur im 20. Jahrhundert* (Halle, 1966–67); *Johannes Brahms: Eine Biographie* (Leipzig, 1966; 2nd ed., 1974); *Die Musik der sozialistischen Länder (ausser DDR)* (Halle, 1967); *Ziele und Aufgaben der sozialistischen Musikerziehung* (Leipzig, 1967; 3rd ed., 1975); *Die Bach-Händel-Epoche* (Halle, 1968); *Das Musikschaffen der DDR* (Halle, 1969); *Ludwig van Beethoven: Eine Biographie* (Leipzig, 1975; 2nd ed., 1977); *Johann Sebastian Bach* (Leipzig, 1976).

Siehr, Gustav, noted German bass; b. Arnsberg, Sept. 17, 1837; d. Munich, May 18, 1896. He studied with Heinrich Dorn and Julius Krause; made his debut in 1863 in Neustrelitz; then sang in Prague (1865–70), Wiesbaden (1870–81), and at the Munich Court Opera (1881–96); also sang at the Bayreuth Festivals, where he created the role of Hagen in *Götterdämmerung* (Aug. 17, 1876). He was particularly distinguished as a Wagnerian interpreter.

Siems, Margarethe, outstanding German soprano; b. Breslau, Dec. 30, 1879; d. Dresden, April 13, 1952. She studied with Orgeni; made her debut at the Prague May Festival in 1902, and that same year joined the Prague Opera; in 1908 she joined the Dresden Court (later State) Opera, where she was a leading dramatic coloratura soprano until 1920; Strauss chose her to create the roles of Chrysothemis in *Elektra* (Jan. 25, 1909) and the Marschallin in *Der Rosenkavalier* (Jan. 26, 1911) there, and also Zerbinetta in *Ariadne auf Naxos* in Stuttgart (Oct. 25, 1912). In 1913 she made her London debut in Covent Garden. She retired from the operatic stage in Breslau in 1925 but continued to sing in concerts; taught at the Berlin Cons. (1920–26), and then in Dresden and Breslau. In addition to her roles in Strauss's operas, she gained renown for her performances in the operas of Bellini, Donizetti, Verdi, and Wagner.

Siepi, Cesare, admired Italian bass; b. Milan, Feb. 10, 1923. He studied at the Milan Cons. He made his operatic debut as Sparafucile in Schio, near Vicenzo (1941); appeared as Zaccaria in *Nabucco* in Verona (1945) and at his La Scala debut in Milan (1946), where he was a principal artist until 1958; also appeared with the company during its 1950 visit to London's Covent Garden, where he was a regular singer from 1962 to 1973. On Nov. 6, 1950, he made his Metropolitan Opera debut in N.Y. as Philip II in *Don Carlos*, remaining on its roster until 1973; also sang in other major opera houses on both sides of the Atlantic. An esteemed *cantante* artist, he excelled in the operas of Mozart and Verdi.

Sierra, Roberto, Puerto Rican composer; b. Vega Baja, Oct. 9, 1953. He began musical training at the Puerto Rico Cons. of Music and at the Univ. of Puerto Rico (graduated, 1976); then pursued studies in London at the Royal College of Music and the Univ. (1976–78), at the Inst. of Sonology in Utrecht (1978), and with György Ligeti at the Hamburg Hochschule für Musik (1979–82). He was assistant director (1983–85) and director (1985–86) of the cultural activities dept. at the Univ. of Puerto Rico, then dean of studies (1986–87) and chancellor (from 1987) at the Puerto Rico Cons. of Music. In 1989 he became composer-in-residence of the Milwaukee Sym. Orch.

WORKS: STAGE: *El Mensajero de Plata,* chamber opera (1984); *El Contemplado,* ballet (1987). **ORCH.:** *Jubilo* (1985); *Cuatro ensayos orquestales* (1986); *Glosas* for Piano and Orch. (1987); *Deascargo* (1988; also for Chamber Ensemble); *Sasima* (San Antonio, Feb. 22, 1990). **CHAMBER:** *Tiempo Muerto* for String Quartet (1978; London, Feb. 7, 1986); *Salsa on the C String* for Cello and Piano (1981); *Seis piezas fáciles* for 2 Violins (1982); *Bongo-O* for Percussion (1982); *Salsa* for Wind Quintet (1983); *Cinco bocetos* for Clarinet (1984); *Concierto Nocturnal* for Harpsichord, Flute, Clarinet, Oboe, Violin, and Cello (1985); *Memorias Tropicales* for String Quartet (1985); *El sueño de Antonia* for Clarinet and Percussion (1985); *Toccata y Lamento* for Guitar (1987); *Essays* for Wind Quintet (1987); *Mano a mano* for 2 Percussionists (1987); *Introducción y Descarga* for Piano, Brass Quintet, and Percussion (1988); *Tributo* for Harp, Flute, Clarinet, and String Quartet (1988). **PIANO:** *Descarga en sol* (1981); *Vestigios Rituales* for 2 Pianos (1984); *Tres inventos* (1987). **HARPSICHORD:** *Tres miniaturas* (1982); *Con salsa* (1984). **VOCAL:** *Cantos populares* for Chorus (1983); *Doña Rosita* for Mezzo-soprano and Wind Quintet (1985); *Invocaciones* for Voice and Percussion (1986); *Glosa a la sombra . . .* for Mezzo-soprano, Viola, Clarinet, and Piano (1987); also *entre terceras* for 2 Synthesizers and Computer (1988).

Sieveking, Martinus, Dutch pianist and teacher; b. Amsterdam, March 24, 1867; d. Pasadena, Calif., Nov. 26, 1950. He studied piano with his father; began his career as an accompanist; traveled with Adelina Patti on her tour of England (1891–92); then settled in the U.S.; in 1915 he established his own piano school in N.Y. and announced a new method which guaranteed to achieve virtuosity in 24 months; not very successful in N.Y., he went to California, where he found a fertile field for his quick road to virtuosity for everybody.

Siface (real name, **Giovanni Francesco Grossi**), famous Italian castrato soprano; b. Uzzanese Chiesina, Feb. 12, 1653; d. (murdered) near Ferrara, May 29, 1697. He was a member of Rome's Papal Chapel (1675–77); appeared in Venice as Syphax in Cavalli's *Scipione Africano* (1678), from which opera he took his stage name; was in Modena from 1679 to 1687;

also sang in London (from 1679). Purcell, one of his many admirers, wrote the harpsichord piece *Sefauchi's Farewell* upon Siface's departure from England. The singer was murdered by the postillion during his travels from Bologna to Ferrara.

Sigismondi, Giuseppe, Italian librarian, historian, singing teacher, and composer; b. Naples, Nov. 13, 1739; d. there, May 10, 1826. He studied law (degree, 1759); received instruction in singing, figured bass, and counterpoint, taking lessons with Durante and later with Porpora (1761–67). He wrote comedies for an amateur theater company; also composed 2 stage pieces, sacred and secular vocal works, and pieces for organ and for harpsichord, but became best known as a singing teacher; served as archivist-librarian at the Pièta dei Turchini Cons. (from 1794). He prepared a 4 vol. MS, *Apoteosi della musica del regno di Napoli in tre ultimi transundati secoli* (1820), which was reworked and publ. by Villarosa as *Memorie dei compositori di musica del regno di Napoli* (Naples, 1840).

Sigtenhorst-Meyer, Bernhard van den, Dutch composer; b. Amsterdam, June 17, 1888; d. The Hague, July 17, 1953. He studied at the Amsterdam Cons.; later in Vienna and Paris; settled in The Hague as a composer and writer.

Writings: *Jan Pieterszoon Sweelinck en zijn instrumentale muziek* (The Hague, 1934; 2nd ed., 1946); *De vocale muziek van Jan Pieterszoon Sweelinck* (The Hague, 1948).

Works: 2 string quartets (1919, 1944); Sonata for Cello Solo (1926); 2 violin sonatas (1926, 1938); 6 *Miniatures* for Oboe and Piano (1926–46); 2 piano sonatas (1922, 1925); 3 piano sonatinas (1928, 1930, 1948); other piano pieces: *La Vieille Chine* (1916), *Les Oiseaux* (1917); 2 albums, *Le Monde de contesbleus* (1926–28).

Bibl.: H. Antcliffe, "S. M.: A Personal Impression," *Monthly Musical Record* (Dec. 1953).

Sigurbjörnsson, Thorkell, prominent Icelandic composer, pedagogue, and administrator; b. Reykjavík, July 16, 1938. He studied at the Reykjavík College of Music (1948–57); then had lessons in composition with R.G. Harris at Hamline Univ. in St. Paul, Minn. (B.A., 1959), and in electronic music with Lejaren Hiller and composition with Kenneth Gaburo at the Univ. of Illinois in Urbana (M.M., 1961); also attended sessions in Nice and Darmstadt (1962). Returning to Reykjavík, he founded the modern group Musica Nova; taught at the Reykjavík College of Music (from 1962), becoming a full prof. in 1969; also was active with the Icelandic State Radio (1966–69). In 1973 he was a creative associate at the State Univ. of N.Y. at Buffalo, and in 1975 was a research musician at the Univ. of Calif. in La Jolla. He served as secretary (1969–85) and president (1985–88) of the Icelandic Soc. of Composers. In addition to his work as a composer, pedagogue, and broadcaster, he also appeared as a pianist and conductor.

Works: STAGE: *Composition in 3 Scenes,* chamber opera (1964); *Apaspil,* children's opera (1966); *Rabbi,* children's opera (1968); *Thorgeirsboli* (The Bull-man), ballet (1971). ORCH.: *Flökt* (Fluctuations; 1961); *Cadenza and Dance* for Violin and Orch. (1967); *Ymur* (1969); *Ys og Thys* (Much Ado), overture (1970); *Laeti* for Orch. and Orch. on Tape (1971); *Mistur* (1972); *Haflög* (1973); *Nidur,* concerto for Double Bass and Orch. (1974); *Búkolla,* concerto for Clarinet and Orch. (1974); *Albumblatt* (1975); *Eurydice* for Flute and Orch. (1978); *Sequences,* concerto for Violin and Orch. (1981); *Ulisse ritorna,* concerto for Cello and Orch. (1981); *Columbine,* divertimento for Flute and Strings (Falun, Sweden, Dec. 5, 1982); *Diaphony* (1984); Triple Concerto for Violin, Cello, Piano, and Orch. (1984). VOCAL: *Ballade* for Tenor, Flute, Viola, and Guitar (1960); *Leikar* for Chorus and Orch. (1961); *Solstice* for Soprano, Alto, Baritone, Flute, Marimba, and Double Bass (1976). CHAMBER: *Víxl* (Rotation) for Violin, Clarinet, Cello, and Duplicate Instruments on Tape (1962); *Hässelby-Quartet,* string quartet (1968); *Kisum* for Clarinet, Viola, and Piano (1970); *Intrada* for Clarinet, Viola, and Piano (1970); *Happy Music* for Brass Ensemble (1971); *Dáik* for Clarinet, Cello, and Synthesizer (1973); *Hylling* (Homage) for Flute, Cello, Piano, Percussion, Tape, and Audience (1974); *4 Better or Worse* for

Flute, Clarinet, Cello, and Piano (1975); *Copenhagen Quartet* for String Quartet (1977); *The Pied Piper* for Flute and String Trio (1978); *Bergabesk* for Woodwind Quintet (1979); *Ra's Dozen* for 12 Flutes (1980); *Tema senza variazioni* for Clarinet, Cello, and Piano (1981); *Saman* for 2 Flutes, 2 Oboes, 2 Clarinets, 2 Bassoons, 2 Horns, and Piano (1983); *Drift* for Clarinet and Piano (1984); *Hot Spring Birds* for Flute, Guitar, and Cello (1984); *Hoquetus minor* (Minor Hiccups) for Harpsichord and Percussion (1987); 6 *Icelandic Folksongs* for Flute, Violin, and Cello (1988).

Bibl.: G. Bergendal, "A Portrait of T. S.," *Nordic Sounds* (March 1987).

Sigwart, Botho (real name, **Sigwart Botho, Count of Eulenburg**), German pianist, musicologist, and composer; b. Berlin, Jan. 10, 1884; d. from wounds received in battle, Galicia, June 2, 1915. He was the son of the German diplomat and poet Count Phillip of Eulenburg. He studied piano in Vienna and musicology at the Univ. of Munich (Ph.D., 1907, with the diss. *Erasmus Widmann*); completed his studies with Reger in Leipzig (1908–9). In 1909 he married the concert singer Helene Staegemann. He wrote a number of piano pieces, a String Quartet, and several melodramas.

Siki, Béla, distinguished Hungarian pianist and teacher; b. Budapest, Feb. 21, 1923. He studied with Dohnányi and Leo Weiner at the Budapest Academy of Music; later took lessons with Dinu Lipatti in Geneva. In 1945 he made his debut in Budapest; in 1947 he won the Concours International d'Exécutions Musicales in Geneva; then made tours of Australia, Japan, South America, and the U.S. In 1965 he became a prof. of piano at the Univ. of Washington in Seattle, and in 1980 at the Univ. of Cincinnati College-Cons. of Music. He wrote *Piano Repertoire: A Guide to Interpretation and Performance* (N.Y., 1981). He became especially known for his authoritative performances of the works of Liszt and Bartók.

Siklós (real name, **Schönwald**), **Albert,** Hungarian cellist, musicologist, pedagogue, and composer; b. Budapest, June 26, 1878; d. there, April 3, 1942. He changed his name to Siklós in 1910. He studied law, and later took courses with Koessler at the Budapest Academy of Music, graduating in 1901; he taught at the Academy from 1910, and gradually became one of its most respected teachers. He was a prolific composer, but few of his works were publ., and there were virtually no performances outside Hungary. He publ. a number of instructive books; also a music dictionary (1923).

Works: STAGE: OPERAS: *Knight Fulkó* (1896); *The House of Moons* (1926; Budapest, Dec. 21, 1927). BALLET: *The Mirror* (Budapest, March 28, 1923); also 2 cello concertos (1895, 1902); 3 sym. (1896; *Anlauf,* 1896; 1901); *Symphonie aethérique* for 12 Double Basses (1899); Violin Concerto (1899); overtures; suites; chamber music; vocal works; piano music; organ music.

Sikorski, Kazimierz, Swiss-born Polish composer and pedagogue, father of **Tomasz Sikorski;** b. Zürich (of Polish parents), June 28, 1895; d. Warsaw, June 23, 1986. He studied composition with Szopski at the Chopin Music High School in Warsaw (graduated, 1919); took courses in philosophy at the Univ. of Warsaw (graduated, 1921) and then pursued musicology training with Chybiński at the Univ. of Lwow; completed his musical studies in Paris (1925–27; 1930). He taught at the Lodz Cons. (1947–54) and the Warsaw Cons. (1951–57), serving as director of the latter (1957–66). Among his many students were Bacewicz, Panufnik, Palester, Serocki, and his own son. He publ. *Instrumentoznawstwo* (The Study of Instruments; Warsaw, 1932; 3rd ed., 1975), *Harmonia* (Harmony; 3 vols., Krakow, 1948–49; 4th ed., 1972), and *Kontrapunkt* (Counterpoint; 3 vols., Krakow, 1953–57).

Works: 6 syms. (1918; 1921; 1953; 1969; 1978–79; 1983); *Suite* for String Orch. (1917); Clarinet Concerto (1947); Concerto for Horn and Small Orch. (1948); *Popular Overture* (1954); Flute Concerto (1957); Concerto for Trumpet, String Orch., 4 Timpani, Xylophone, and Tam-tam (1959); 6 *Old*

Polish Dances for Small Orch. (1963); *Concerto Polyphonique* for Bassoon and Orch. (1965); Oboe Concerto (1967); Trombone Concerto (1973); 3 string quartets; String Sextet; choruses.

Sikorski, Tomasz, Polish composer and pianist, son of **Kazimierz Sikorski;** b. Warsaw, May 19, 1939. He studied piano with Drzewiecki and composition with his father at the Warsaw Cons.; then took lessons with Boulanger in Paris. As a pianist, he emphasizes new music in his programs. His own compositions are also in the advanced idiom.

WORKS: Radio opera, *Przygody Sindbada zeglarza* (The Adventures of Sinbad the Sailor, 1971); *Echoes 2 quasi improvvisazione* for 1 to 4 Pianos, Percussion, and Tape (1961–63); *Antyfony* for Soprano without Text, Piano, Horn, Chimes, 2 Gongs, 2 Tam-tams, and Tape (1963); *Prologues* for Female Chorus, 2 Pianos, 4 Flutes, 4 Horns, and 4 Percussionists (1964); *Architectures* for Piano, Winds, and Percussion (1965); *Concerto breve* for Piano, 24 Winds, and 4 Percussionists (1965); *Sequenza I* for Orch. (1966); *Sonant* for Piano (1967); *Intersections* for 36 Percussion Instruments (1968); *Homophony* for 4 Trumpets, 4 Horns, 4 Trombones, Piano, and 2 Gongs (1968); *Diafonia* for 2 Pianos (1969); *For Strings* for 3 Violins and 3 Violas (1970); *Vox humana* for Chorus, 12 Brasses, 2 Pianos, 4 Gongs, and 4 Tam-tams (1971); *Zerstreutes Hinausschauen* for Piano (1971); *Holzwege* for Orch. (1972); *Étude* for Orch. (1972); *Bez tytulu* (Untitled) for Piano, Clarinet, Trombone, and Cello (1972); *Listening Music* for 2 Pianos (1973); *Music from Afar* for Chorus and Orch. (1974); *Other Voices* for Winds and Percussion (1975); *Sickness Unto Death* for Narrator, 2 Pianos, 4 Trumpets, and 4 Horns (1976); *Music in Twilight* for Piano and Orch. (1978); *Strings in the Earth* for 15 String Instruments (1979–80); *Self-portrait* for Orch. (1983); *Autoritratto* for 2 Pianos and Orch. (1983); *La Notte* for String Orch. (1984); *Das Schweigen der Sirenen* for Cello (1986); *Omaggio per quattro pianoforti ed orchestra in memoriam Borges* (1987).

Silas, Edouard, Dutch organist, pianist, teacher, and composer; b. Amsterdam, Aug. 22, 1827; d. London, Feb. 8, 1909. He first studied music with Neher; then received instruction in piano from Lacombe in Frankfurt (1839–42) and Kalkbrenner in Paris, where he later was a Cons. pupil in organ of Benoist (premier prix, 1849) and in composition of Halévy. In 1850 he settled in England; was organist at the Roman Catholic chapel in Kingston upon Thames and a teacher of harmony at the Guildhall School of Music and the London Academy of Music. Among his works are 3 syms., including No. 1 (1852) and the burlesque sym., *Mr. Punch's Musical Recollections* (1856–66); 3 piano concertos; 2 string quintets; 2 piano trios; numerous piano pieces; oratorio, *Joash* (Norwich Festival, 1863); Mass (1866).

Silbermann, family of eminent German organ and piano makers.

(1) **Andreas Silbermann,** b. Klein-Bobritzsch, Saxony, May 16, 1678; d. Strasbourg, March 16, 1734. He worked with the organ builder Friedrich Ring in Alsace before going to Strasbourg in 1702; was in Paris, 1704–6, then returned to Strasbourg; built the Münster organ there (1713–16) and 33 others.

(2) **Gottfried Silbermann,** brother of the preceding; b. Klein-Bobritzsch, Jan. 14, 1683; d. Dresden, Aug. 4, 1753. Apprenticed to a bookbinder, he ran away and joined his brother in Strasbourg about 1702 as his helper; during his brother's sojourn in Paris (1704–6), he ran the family business; upon his brother's return to Strasbourg, they worked as partners. After working on his own there and in other cities, he went to Freiberg in 1711. His finest organ was the instrument built for the Katholische Hofkirche in Dresden (3 manuals, 44 stops), begun in 1750 and completed after his death by his pupil Zacharias Hildebrandt. He owed his fame, however, mainly to the manufacture of pianos in Germany, in which field he was a pioneer; the hammer action in his instruments was practically identical with that of Cristofori, the piano inventor. Silbermann also invented the "cembal d'amour," a clavichord

with strings of double length, struck in the middle by the tangents, thus yielding the duplicated octave of the tone of the entire string. He supplied 3 pianos to Frederick the Great for Potsdam, and Bach played on them during his visit there in 1747.

(3) **Johann Andreas Silbermann,** son of **Andreas Silbermann;** b. Strasbourg, May 26, 1712; d. there, Feb. 11, 1783. He received his training from his father; built 54 organs; publ. *Geschichte der Stadt Strassburg* (1775).

(4) **Johann Daniel Silbermann,** brother of the preceding; b. Strasbourg, March 31, 1717; d. Leipzig, May 9, 1766. He worked with his uncle Gottfried at Freiberg, and continued the manufacture of pianos after the latter's death.

(5) **Johann Heinrich Silbermann,** brother of the 2 preceding; b. Strasbourg, Sept. 24, 1727; d. there, Jan. 15, 1799. He made pianos at Strasbourg, similar to those of his uncle Gottfried, and introduced them into France. His son, **Johann Friedrich Silbermann** (b. Strasbourg, June 21, 1762; d. there, March 8, 1817), was an organist and composer; during the Revolution, he wrote a *Hymne à la Paix;* also composed songs.

BIBL.: L. Mooser, *G. S.* (Langensalza, 1857); G. Zschaler, *G. S.* (1898); E. Flade, *Der Orgelbauer G. S.* (Leipzig, 1926); H. Hullemann, *Die Tätigkeit des Orgelbauers G. S. im Reussenland* (Leipzig, 1937); E. Flade, "S.iana," *Musik und Kirche,* X (1938); R. Gärtner, *G. S. der Orgelbauer* (Dresden, 1938); J. Wörsching, *Die Orgelbauer Familie S. in Strassburg im Elsass* (Mainz, 1941; 2nd ed., 1960); U. Dähnert, *Die Orgeln G. S.s in Mitteldeutschland* (Leipzig, 1953); E. Flade, *G. S. Ein Beitrag zur Geschichte des deutschen Orgel- und Klavierbau im Zeitalter Bachs* (Leipzig, 1953); D. Boalch, *Makers of the Harpsichord and Clavichord 1440–1840* (London, 1956); W. Müller, *Auf den Spuren von G. S.* (Kassel, 1968); idem, *G. S.: Persönlichkeit und Werk: Eine Dokumentation* (1983).

Silcher, (Philipp) Friedrich, German composer; b. Schnait, Württemberg, June 27, 1789; d. Tübingen, Aug. 26, 1860. He studied with his father and with Auberlen, an organist in Fellbach; in 1815 he went to Stuttgart to study piano and composition with K. Kreutzer and Hummel; in 1817 he was appointed music director at the Univ. of Tübingen, receiving an honorary Ph.D. in 1852. He was an influential promoter of German popular singing; publ. several collections of German folk songs, in which he included his own compositions; of the latter, *Lorelei (Ich weiss nicht, was soll es bedeuten,* to words by Heinrich Heine) became so popular that it was often mistaken for a folk song; in all, he wrote about 250 songs. He also publ. *Choralbuch* for 3 voices; 3 books of hymns for 4 voices; *Tübinger Liedertafel* (male choruses). A critical ed. of his output was publ. in 1960. He wrote the books *Geschichte des evangelischen Kirchengesanges* (1844); *Harmonie- und Kompositionslehre* (1851; 2nd ed., 1859).

BIBL.: A. Köstlin, *F. S. und Weber* (Stuttgart, 1877); H. Weber, *F. S., Neujahrsgeschenk an die Zürcherische Jugend von der Allgemeinen Musik-Gesellscaft Zürich,* LXVII (Zürich, 1879); A. Prümers, *P.F. S.* (Stuttgart, 1910); A. Bopp, *F. S.* (Stuttgart, 1916); idem, *Liederbuch aus Schwaben* (1918); H. Kleinert and H. Rauschnabel, eds., *F. S.* (Stuttgart, 1935); A. Lämmle, *F. S.* (Mühlacker, 1956); J. Müller-Blattan, "F. S. zu seinem 100. Todestag," *Hausmusik,* VI-VII (1960); H. Dahmen, *F. S.: Komponist und Demokrat: eine Biographie* (Stuttgart, 1989); M. Schmid, ed., *F. S., 1789–1860: Studien zu Leben und Nachleben* (Stuttgart, 1989).

Silja, Anja, remarkable German soprano; b. Berlin, April 17, 1935. Her grandmother was the singer Paula Althof; at the age of 8 she began vocal training with her grandfather, Egon van Rijn; gave a solo recital in Berlin at the age of 10. In 1956 she sang Rosina at the Berlin Städtische Opera; after appearing at the Braunschweig State Theater (1956–58), she sang at the Württemberg State Theater in Stuttgart (1958), at the Frankfurt Opera (1960–63), and at the Bayreuth Festivals (from 1965). In 1968 she made her U.S. debut as Senta with the Chicago Lyric Opera; her Metropolitan Opera debut followed in N.Y. as Leonore in *Fidelio* on Feb. 26, 1972. In subsequent years she made appearances with leading North American and European opera houses; also sang in concerts with major orchs. The breadth of her repertoire is commanding. Wagner's grandson Wieland coached her in the Wagnerian roles, among them Elisabeth, Elsa, Eva, and Senta, which she performed at Bayreuth. She also sang the roles of Salome and Elektra in Strauss's operas, of Marie and Lulu in Berg's operas, and of the sole character in Schoenberg's *Erwartung*. As a matter of course, she mastered the majority of standard soprano roles. She married the conductor **Christoph von Dohnányi**, under whose baton she sang in both operatic and concert settings.

Sills, Beverly (real name, **Belle Miriam Silverman**), celebrated American soprano and operatic administrator; b. N.Y., May 25, 1929. Her father was an insurance salesman from Rumania and her mother a rather musical person from Odessa. At the age of 3 she appeared on the radio under the cute nickname "Bubbles," and won a prize at a Brooklyn contest as "the most beautiful baby of 1932." At 4, she joined a Saturday morning children's program, and at 7 she sang in a movie. At 10 she had a part on the radio show "Our Gal Sunday." Her natural thespian talent and sweet child's voice soon proved to be valuable financial assets. She did a commercial advertising Rinso White soap, and appeared on an early television program, "Stars of the Future." She began formal vocal studies with Estelle Liebling when she was 7; also studied piano with Paolo Gallico; in Public School 91 in Brooklyn she was voted most "likely to succeed." In 1947 she made her operatic debut as Frasquita in *Carmen* with the Philadelphia Civic Opera; then toured with several operas companies, and sang with the San Francisco Opera (1953) and the N.Y. City Opera (1955), quickly establishing herself at the latter as one of its most valuable members. She extended her repertoire to embrace modern American operas, including the title role of Douglas Moore's *The Ballad of Baby Doe*; she also sang in the American premiere of Luigi Nono's avant-garde opera *Intolleranza 1960*. She was a guest singer at the Vienna State Opera and in Buenos Aires in 1967, at La Scala in Milan in 1969, and at Covent Garden in London and the Deutsche Oper in Berlin in 1970. She made her 1st appearance with the Metropolitan Opera as Donna Anna in a concert production of *Don Giovanni* on July 8, 1966, at the Lewisohn Stadium in N.Y.; her formal debut with the Metropolitan took place at Lincoln Center in N.Y. as Pamira in *Le Siège de Corinthe* on April 7, 1975. At the height of her career, she received well-nigh universal praise, not only for the excellence of her voice and her virtuosity in coloratura parts, but also for her intelligence and erudition, rare among the common run of operatic divas. She became general director of the N.Y. City Opera in 1979, and made her farewell performance as a singer in 1980. She showed an uncommon administrative talent; during her tenure with the N.Y. City Opera, she promoted American musicians and broadened the operatic repertoire; retired in 1988; also produced television shows dealing with opera and concert singing. In her personal life, she suffered a double tragedy; one of her 2 children was born deaf, and the other was mentally retarded. In 1972 she accepted the national chairmanship of the Mothers' March on Birth Defects. She publ. *Bubbles: A Self-portrait* (N.Y., 1976; 2nd ed., rev., 1981, as *Bubbles: An Encore*) and *Beverly: An Autobiography* (N.Y., 1987). She received (deservedly so) honorary doctorates from Harvard Univ., N.Y. Univ., and the Calif. Inst. of the Arts. On Nov. 22, 1971, she was the subject of a cover story in *Time*. In 1980 she was awarded the U.S. Presidential Medal of Freedom. Her most notable roles included Cleopatra in Handel's *Giulio Cesare*, Lucia, Elisabeth in *Roberto Devereux*, Anna Bolena, Elvira in *I puritani*, and Maria Stuarda.

BIBL.: M. Kerby, *B. S.: America's Own Opera Star* (N.Y., 1989).

Siloti, Alexander, eminent Russian pianist, pedagogue, and conductor; b. near Kharkov, Oct. 9, 1863; d. N.Y., Dec. 8, 1945. He studied piano with Zverev and Nikolai Rubinstein

at the Moscow Cons., and music theory there with Tchaikovsky (1876–81), winning the gold medal. He made his debut as a pianist in Moscow in 1880; then made a tour in Germany; Liszt accepted him as a student in 1883, and Siloti continued his study with Liszt in Weimar until Liszt's death in 1886. Returning to Russia, he was a prof. of piano at the Moscow Cons. (1888–91); among his students was Rachmaninoff (his 1st cousin). Between 1891 and 1900 he lived in Germany, France, and Belgium; returned to Russia in 1901 and conducted the concerts of the Moscow Phil. Society during the season 1901–2; in 1903 he organized his own orch. in St. Petersburg; these concerts acquired great cultural importance; Siloti invited Mengelberg and Mottl as guest conductors, and Rachmaninoff, Casals, and Chaliapin as soloists. In 1915 he began a series of popular free concerts, and in 1916 started a Russian Musical Fund to aid indigent musicians. In 1919 he left Russia; in 1922 he settled in N.Y., where he was active principally as a teacher but continued to appear as a soloist with American orchs.; from 1925 to 1942 he was on the faculty of the Juilliard School of Music. He publ. a collection of piano pieces which he ed., with indications of fingering and pedaling; also arranged and ed. concertos by Bach and Vivaldi. He publ. a book of reminiscences of Liszt (St. Petersburg, 1911; Eng. tr., Edinburgh, 1913).

Silva, Francisco Manuel da, Brazilian conductor and composer; b. Rio de Janeiro, Feb. 21, 1795; d. there, Dec. 18, 1865. He began his musical training with José Maurício Nunes Garcia; later studied counterpoint and composition with Sigismund Neukomm in Rio de Janeiro. He was a singer and then a cellist in the orch. of the royal chapel and chamber until it was disbanded when Emperor Dom Pedro I abdicated in 1831; that same year he wrote the abdication hymn *Hino ao 7 de Abril*, which was adopted as the Brazilian national anthem (with new text) upon the establishment of the Republic in 1889. In 1833 he founded the Sociedade Beneficência Musical; became conductor of the Sociedade Filarmônica in 1834; served as composer of the imperial chamber (from 1841) and as master composer of the imperial chapel (from 1842); founded the Rio de Janeiro Cons. (1847). He wrote an opera, *O prestigio da lei*, and much sacred music.

BIBL.: A. de Albuquerque, *Ouviram do Ypiranga, Vida de F.M. d.S.* (Rio de Janeiro, 1959); A. de Andráde, *F.M. d.S. e seu tempo, 1808–65. Uma fase do pássado musical do Rio de Janeiro á luz de novos documentos* (2 vols., Rio de Janeiro, 1967).

Silva, Luigi, Italian-born American cellist and pedagogue; b. Milan, Nov. 13, 1903; d. N.Y., Nov. 29, 1961. He was of a musical family; his father was a vocal teacher; his mother a singer. He studied music at home; then took cello lessons with Arturo Bonucci in Bologna and composition with Respighi in Rome. He played in the Quartetto di Roma (1930–39); in 1939 he emigrated to the U.S.; became a naturalized citizen in 1945. On April 5, 1941, he made his N.Y. debut in a joint recital with Leopold Mannes; with the latter and Vittorio Brero, he performed with the Mannes Trio (from 1949). He served as chairman of the cello and chamber music depts. at the Eastman School of Music in Rochester, N.Y. (1941–49); then taught at the Mannes College of Music (1949–61), the Yale Univ. School of Music (1951–58), the Juilliard School of Music (1953–61), and the Hewitt School (1956–61). He made transcriptions for cello of works by Paganini, Boccherini, and other Italian composers; ed. Bach's unaccompanied cello suites.

Silva, Oscar da, Portuguese pianist, teacher, and composer; b. Paranhos, near Oporto, April 21, 1870; d. Oporto, March 6, 1958. He studied at the Lisbon Cons.; in 1892 he went to Leipzig, where he had lessons with Reinecke and Clara Schumann. Returning to Portugal in 1910, he devoted himself mainly to teaching, acquiring a very high reputation as a piano pedagogue. From 1932 to 1952 he lived in Brazil; then returned to Portugal. He wrote an opera, *Dona Mecia* (Lisbon, July 4, 1901); a symphonic poem, *Alma crucificada*; chamber music; songs; effective piano pieces.

BIBL.: A. Pinto, *Musica moderna portuguesa e os seus representantes* (Lisbon, 1930).

Silva, (David) Poll da, French composer; b. St.-Esprit, near Bayonne, March 28, 1834; d. Clermont, Oise, May 9, 1875. He went to Paris as a youth, and was encouraged by Halévy to study music and compose despite his incipient blindness; his mother, who was an educated musician, wrote out his compositions from dictation. Despite his handicap, he wrote 3 operas, 2 oratorios, 2 syms., and various other works.

Silver, Charles, French composer; b. Paris, April 16, 1868; d. there, Oct. 10, 1949. He studied with Dubois and Massenet at the Paris Cons., winning the Grand Prix de Rome in 1891 with the cantata *L'Interdit*. He wrote the operas *La Belle au bois dormant* (Marseilles, 1902); *Le Clos* (Paris, 1906); *Myriane* (Nice, 1913); *La Mégère apprivoisée* (Paris, Jan. 30, 1922); *La Grand'-mère* (Oct. 7, 1930); *Quatre-vingt-treize* (Paris, Jan. 24, 1936); also orch. works, songs, etc.

Silver, Horace (Ward Martin Tavares), black American jazz pianist, bandleader, and composer; b. Norwalk, Conn., Sept. 2, 1928. He studied saxophone and piano in high school; served as a member of Stan Getz's quintet (1950–51); then was music director of Art Blakey's Jazz Messengers; in 1956 he organized his own quintet. He was a leading proponent of "funky" jazz, which combined elements of swing and gospel music; he composed several pieces in this style that attained classic status among jazz aficionados.

BIBL.: L. Lyons, "H. S.: Father of Funk," *Contemporary Keyboard*, ii/1 (1976); L. Feather, "Piano Giants of Jazz: H. S.," ibid., V/9 (1979).

Silver, Sheila, talented, prolific, and original American composer; b. Seattle, Wash., Oct. 3, 1946. She studied at the Univ. of Wash. in Seattle (1964–65), then went to Paris for a course at the Inst. for European Studies (1966–67); returned to the U.S. to earn her B.A. degree at the Univ. of Calif. at Berkeley (1968), and then enrolled at the Paris Cons. (1968). She further took courses at the Hochschule für Musik in Stuttgart, where her mentors were György Ligeti and Erhard Karkoschka. Shuttling back to the U.S. once more, she studied with Seymour Shifrin, Arthur Berger, and Harold Shapero at Brandeis Univ., completing her Ph.D. in composition there in 1976; she also attended lectures in modern music at the festival sessions in Darmstadt (summer 1970), and in 1972 studied with Jacob Druckman at the Berkshire Music Center at Tanglewood. There followed a number of grants that enabled her to travel to London and to Italy, where she was awarded the Prix de Rome at the American Academy. The list of awards she has received is most impressive. In 1979 she was appointed instructor in composition at the State Univ. of N.Y. at Stony Brook. During all of her peregrinations, she continued to compose productively; her mature style may be described as enlightened dissonance devoid of ostensible disharmonies.

WORKS: OPERA: *The Thief of Love*, after a Bengali tale (1986). **ORCH:** *Galixidi* (Seattle, Wash., March 1977); *Chariessa* for Soprano and Orch., after Sappho (Rome, June 1980; also for Soprano and Piano, 1978); *Shirat Sarah* (Song of Sarah) for String Orch. (Hartford, Conn., Jan. 1987); *Dance of Wild Angels* for Chamber Orch. (1990). **CHAMBER:** String Quartet (Boston, Dec. 1977); *Dynamis* for Horn (Rome, May 1979); *Theme and Variations for Bowed Vibraphone* (N.Y., April 1981); *Dance Converging* for Viola, Horn, Piano, and Percussion (1987); *G Whiz*, étude for 2 Violins and Marimba (N.Y., May 1988); *Window Waltz* for Bass Clarinet, Horn, Strings, Harpsichord, Piano, and Percussion (N.Y., May 1988); Sonata for Cello and Piano (N.Y., Nov. 1988). **PIANO:** *Fantasy Quasi Theme and Variations* (Washington, D.C., April 1981); *Oh, Thou Beautiful One* (1989). **VOCAL:** *Chariessa* for Soprano and Piano (1978; also for Soprano and Orch., 1980); *Canto* for Baritone and Chamber Ensemble, after Ezra Pound's "Canto XXXIX" about Ulysses (1979); 2 *Elizabethan Songs* for Chorus (N.Y., Sept. 1982); *Ek Ong Kar* for Chorus (N.Y., Feb. 1983).

Silverstein, Joseph, distinguished American violinist and conductor; b. Detroit, March 21, 1932. He received his early instruction in violin from his father; then studied with V. Reynolds and Zimbalist at the Curtis Inst. of Music in Philadelphia (1945–50) and later with Gingold and Mischakoff. He played in the Houston Sym. Orch., Denver Sym. Orch., and Philadelphia Orch. before joining the Boston Sym. Orch. in 1955, where he was concertmaster (1962–83) and assistant conductor (1971–83). Having won the Queen Elisabeth of Belgium competition (1959) and the Naumburg Foundation Award (1960), he made solo appearances while retaining his Boston posts; was also chairman of the violin faculty of the Berkshire Music Center and a teacher at Boston Univ. He appeared as guest conductor with various U.S. orchs.; served as interim music director of the Toledo (Ohio) Sym. Orch. (1979–80) and principal guest conductor of the Baltimore Sym. Orch. (1981–83). He then was music director of the Utah Sym. Orch. in Salt Lake City (from 1983) and the Chautauqua (N.Y.) Sym. Orch. (from 1987). As both a violinist and conductor, he impressed his auditors by his technical expertise and musical integrity.

Silvestri, Constantin, esteemed Rumanian-born English conductor and composer; b. Bucharest, June 13, 1913; d. London, Feb. 23, 1969. He studied piano as a child, making his debut at age 10; after taking courses in piano and composition (with Jora) at the Bucharest Cons., he was active as a pianist. In 1930 he made his debut as a conductor with the Bucharest Radio Sym. Orch.; was a conductor with the Bucharest Opera (from 1935) and music director of the Bucharest Phil. (1947–53); also taught conducting at the Bucharest Cons. (from 1948). In 1956 he went to Paris, and in 1957 settled in England, becoming a naturalized subject in 1967. In 1961 he became principal conductor of the Bournemouth Sym. Orch., which he led with distinction until his death; took it on a European tour in 1965. In 1963 he made his debut at London's Covent Garden conducting *Khovanshchina*. He was an impassioned if sometimes willful interpreter of the classics. He composed mostly in small forms in an unpretentious, neo-Baroque manner.

WORKS: Concerto Grosso (1941); 2 string quartets (1935, 1947); *Sonatina a 2 voci* for Clarinet and Cello (1938); Oboe Sonata (1939); 2 violin sonatas (1939); piano pieces; songs.

Silvestrov, Valentin (Vasilievich), Russian composer; b. Kiev, Sept. 30, 1937. He studied with Liatoshinsky at the Kiev Cons. (1958–64); began to compose in a boldly experimental idiom of Western provenance; wrote piano pieces in the strict 12-tone technique. Although severely reprimanded in the press, he was not forcibly restrained from continuing to write music in a modernistic manner.

WORKS: ORCH.: 4 syms.: No. 1 (1963); No. 2 for Flute, Percussion, Piano, and Strings (1965); No. 3 (1966); No. 4 for Brass Instruments and Strings (1976); *Monodia* for Piano and Orch. (1965); *Spectrum* for Chamber Orch. (1965); *Meditation* for Cello and Chamber Orch. (1972). **CHAMBER:** Piano Quintet (1961); *Quartetto piccolo* for String Quartet (1961); Trio for Flute, Trumpet, and Celesta (1962); *Mysteries* for Alto Flute and Percussion (1964); *Projections* for Harpsichord, Vibraphone, and Bells (1965); *Drama* for Violin, Cello, and Piano (1971); String Quartet (1974). **PIANO:** *Variations* (1958); Sonatina (1959); Sonata (1960); *Signals* (1962); *Serenade* (1962); also songs.

Simai, Pavol, Czech composer; b. Levice, June 29, 1930. He studied with Pál Kadosa in Budapest, with Alexander Moyzes and Jan Cikker in Bratislava, and with Paul Dessau in East Berlin. In 1968 he settled in Sweden.

WORKS: Flute Sonatina (1952); *Zuzuka*, ballet (1954–60); *Mother Speaks*, melodrama for Female Speaker, Flute, Clarinet, Bassoon, Guitar, and Percussion (1959); *Victory* for Orch. (1963); *Meditation* for Contralto and String Quartet (1965); *5:10* for Clarinet, Violin, Cello, and Piano (1972); Piano Trio (1974); *Violoncellen* for Mezzo-soprano, Cello, and Piano (1975).

Simandl, Franz, Bohemian double-bass player, pedagogue, and composer; b. Blatna, Aug. 1, 1840; d. Vienna, Dec. 13,

1912. He was a double-bass player in the Vienna Court Opera orch. and the Vienna Phil. (1869–1904); also taught at the Vienna Cons. (from 1869). He publ. *Neueste Methode des Kontrabass-Spiels* (in 3 parts) and *30 Etüden für Kontrabass; Die hohe Schule des Kontrabass-Spiels*, a collection of concertos, studies, solo pieces, etc. His original compositions include a *Konzertstück, Konzert-Etude*, Concerto, fantasias, and minor pieces for his instrument.

Simeonov, Konstantin (Arsenievich), Russian conductor; b. Koznakovo, June 20, 1910; d. Kiev, Jan. 3, 1987. He began a career as a singer; then studied conducting at the Leningrad Cons. with Alexander Gauk; subsequently appeared as a guest conductor throughout the Soviet Union. He served as chief conductor of the Ukrainian Theater of Opera and Ballet in Kiev (1961–66); then occupied a similar post at the Kirov Theater of Opera and Ballet in Leningrad (1966–75); he resumed his Kiev post in 1975. He also filled engagements abroad; conducted opera at La Scala in Milan in 1964.

Similä, Martti, Finnish conductor and composer; b. Oulu, April 9, 1898; d. Lahti, Jan. 9, 1958. He studied in Finland, then in Paris and London; conducted the Helsinki Opera (1927–44) and the Municipal Orch. of Lahti. He made 2 tours in the U.S. as a pianist, in 1923 and 1926; was again in the U.S. in 1957 to lead a memorial concert of the music of Sibelius with the N.Y. Phil. (Dec. 8, 1957). He wrote the book, *Sibeliana* (Helsinki, 1945); also composed orch. music.

Simionato, Giulietta, outstanding Italian mezzo-soprano; b. Forlì, May 12, 1910. She studied with Locatello and Palumbo in Rovigo; won the bel canto competition in Florence in 1933, and then returned there to sing in the premiere of Pizzetti's *Orsèolo* (May 5, 1935). In 1939 she joined Milan's La Scala, remaining on its roster as one of its principal artists until 1966. In 1947 she made her British debut as Cherubino at the Edinburgh Festival; her 1st appearance at London's Covent Garden followed, as Adalgisa in 1953. In 1954 she made her U.S. debut at the Chicago Lyric Opera. On Oct. 26, 1959, she made her 1st appearance at the Metropolitan Opera in N.Y. as Azucena; sang there again in 1960 and 1962. She gave her farewell stage performance as Servilia in *La clemenza di Tito* at Milan's Piccola Scala in 1966. A distinguished coloratura artist, she excelled in the operas of Rossini, Donizetti, Bellini, and Verdi.

Bibl.: J.-J. Hanine Vallaut, *G. S.: Come Cenerentola divenne regina* (n.p., 1987).

Simmons, Calvin (Eugene), gifted black American conductor; b. San Francisco, April 27, 1950; d. (drowned) Connery Pond, east of Lake Placid, N.Y., Aug. 21, 1982. He was the son of a longshoreman and a gospel singer. He joined the San Francisco Boys' Choir at age 11, where he received conducting lessons from its conductor, Madi Bacon; then went to the Cincinnati College-Cons. of Music, where he studied conducting with Max Rudolf (1968–70); when Rudolf was appointed to the faculty of the Curtis Inst. of Music in Philadelphia, Simmons joined him there (1970–72); he also took piano lessons with Serkin. He served as a rehearsal pianist and assistant conductor under Kurt Herbert Adler at the San Francisco Opera (1968–75), where he made his formal debut conducting *Hänsel und Gretel* in 1972. In 1975 he made his British debut at the Glyndebourne Festival. He was assistant conductor of the Los Angeles Phil. and music director of the Young Musicians Foundation orch. (1975–78). In 1979 he was appointed music director of the Oakland (Calif.) Sym. Orch. Before his tragic death in a canoeing accident, he appeared as a guest conductor with increasing success throughout North America; made his Metropolitan Opera debut in N.Y. in 1978 and his N.Y. City Opera debut in 1980.

Simon, Abbey, distinguished American pianist and teacher; b. N.Y., Jan. 8, 1922. He studied with David Saperton and Josef Hofmann at the Curtis Inst. of Music in Philadelphia (1932–41); also took lessons with Leopold Godowsky in N.Y. In 1941 he won the Naumberg Award and then launched a major career, appearing as a soloist with the leading U.S. orchs.;

made his 1st tour of Europe in 1949, and subsequently traveled all over the world. He taught at the Indiana Univ. School of Music in Bloomington (1960–74), the Juilliard School in N.Y. (from 1977), and the Univ. of Houston (from 1977). A master of the repertory from Beethoven to Rachmaninoff, he evolved a grand bravura style of pianistic virtuosity in which no technical difficulties seem to exist, no tempi are too fast, no nuance is too subtle.

Simon, Alicja, Polish musicologist; b. Warsaw, Nov. 13, 1879; d. Lodz, May 23, 1957. She studied in Warsaw, Berlin, and Zürich; then received instruction in musicology from Kretzschmar and Wolf at the Univ. of Berlin (1904–9), where she also took courses in philosophy, psychology, and history; subsequently completed her training at the Univ. of Zürich (Ph.D., 1914). She worked in Berlin (1920–23) and Geneva (1923–24); went to the U.S., and worked on the staff of the Library of Congress in Washington, D.C. (1924–28); then returned to Poland. She was a reader (1945–54) and a prof. (1954–57) at the Univ. of Lodz. She publ. the study *The Polish Songwriters* (Warsaw, 1936; 2nd ed., enl., 1939).

Simon, Anton, French pianist, conductor, and composer; b. Paris, Aug. 5, 1850; d. St. Petersburg, Feb. 1, 1916. He studied piano at the Paris Cons.; in 1871 he went to Moscow, where he became active as a piano teacher. He wrote the operas *Rolla* (Moscow, April 29, 1892); *The Song of Triumphant Love* (Moscow, Dec. 14, 1897); *The Fishermen* (Moscow, March 7, 1899); a mimodrama, *Esmeralda* (1902); 2 ballets: *The Stars* (1898) and *Living Flowers* (1900 c. 1910); Piano Concerto; Clarinet Concerto; 22 pieces for Brass Instruments; numerous piano compositions and songs.

Simon, James, German musicologist and composer; b. Berlin, Sept. 29, 1880; d. in the Auschwitz concentration camp, about Oct. 14, 1944. He studied piano with Ansorge and composition with Bruch in Berlin. From 1907 to 1919 he taught at the Klindworth-Scharwenka Cons. in Berlin. He left Germany shortly after the advent of the Nazi regime in 1933, and lived in Zürich; then moved to Amsterdam, where the Hitlerite wave engulfed him after the Nazi invasion of the Netherlands. He was deported to Theresienstadt on April 5, 1944, and from there, on Oct. 12, 1944, was sent to Auschwitz, where he was put to death a few days later. His opera, *Frau im Stein*, was produced in Stuttgart in 1925; he also wrote a Sym.; Piano Concerto; Sextet for Piano and Wind Instruments; choruses; many songs.

Simon, Paul, popular American singer, guitarist, and songwriter; b. Newark, Oct. 13, 1941. While in high school in N.Y. City, he got together with the singer Art Garfunkel; as Tom and Jerry, they recorded the rock-'n'-roll song *Hey, Schoolgirl* in 1957, and appeared on Dick Clark's "American Bandstand." He then studied English literature at Queens College at the City Univ. of N.Y.; also was active as a promoter and songwriter for various N.Y. music publishers. After appearing in N.Y. clubs, he teamed up with Garfunkel again and, as Simon and Garfunkel, brought out the album *Wednesday Morning 3 A.M.* (1964), which included the song *The Sound of Silence*, issued as a hit single in 1965. In 1966 they brought out an album entitled *The Sounds of Silence*, which secured their reputation. Among their subsequent albums were *The Graduate* (1968; from the film of the same title; includes the hit song *Mrs. Robinson*), *Bookends* (1968), and *Bridge over Troubled Water* (1970). Simon and Garfunkel became a hyphenated entity as far as the public was concerned, but the difference between them was great. Simon was an introspective intellectual who wrote poetry of surprising excellence, while Garfunkel was adept in practical endeavors, composing little but singing and acting in films. Simon's solo albums included *Paul Simon* (1972), *There Goes Rhymin' Simon* (1973), *Still Crazy after All These Years* (1975), *One-Trick Pony* (1980; from his own film of the same title), *Hearts and Bones* (1983), and the controversial, Grammy award-winning *Graceland* (1986).

Bibl.: S. Leigh, *P. S. Then and Now* (Liverpool, 1973).

Simon, Stephen (Anthony), American conductor; b. N.Y., May 3, 1937. He studied piano with Joel Rosen; then enrolled at the Yale Univ. School of Music; also took courses in choral conducting with Hugh Ross and Julius Herford. In 1963 he became music director of the Westchester Orch. Society; from 1970 to 1974 he was music director of the Handel Society in N.Y., and then of the Handel Festival in Washington, D.C. (from 1977).

Simonds, Bruce, American pianist and pedagogue; b. Bridgeport, Conn., July 5, 1895; d. Hamden, Conn., June 2, 1989. After studying at Yale Univ. (A.B., 1917), he attended the Schola Cantorum in Paris (1919–20) and the Matthay School in London (1920–21). He made his debut as a pianist in Europe in 1921; that same year he became a teacher at the Yale Univ. School of Music, where he was made a prof. (1938) and served as dean (1941–54); also continued to give concerts until 1973, the year he retired from Yale.

Simone, Nina (real name, **Eunice Kathleen Waymon**), black American singer, pianist, and composer of popular music; b. Tryon, N.C., Feb. 21, 1933. After completing her high school training, her hometown residents raised the money to send her to the Juilliard School of Music in N.Y., where she studied piano and theory with Carl Friedberg; then continued her studies with Vladimir Sokoloff at the Curtis Inst. of Music in Philadelphia. In 1954 she began singing at an Atlantic City, N.J., nightclub, and subsequently devoted herself to popular music genres, appearing as a jazz, pop, and soul artist. She also composed some instrumental music and over 50 songs.
BIBL.: P. Garland, "N. S.: High Priestess of Soul," *Sound of Soul* (Chicago, 1969).

Simoneau, Léopold, distinguished Canadian tenor; b. St. Flavien, near Quebec City, May 3, 1918. He 1st studied with Émile Larochelle, and then with Salvator Issaurel in Montreal, where he made his debut at the Variétés Lyriques as Hadji in *Lakmé* (1941); subsequently continued his studies with Paul Althouse in N.Y. (1945–47) while singing throughout the U.S. He made his European debut as Mireille at the Opéra-Comique in Paris in 1948; then sang at the Paris Opéra, Milan's La Scala, the Vienna State Opera, and major festivals, gaining renown as a Mozartian; also made appearances in the U.S. and Canada as a soloist with major orchs. and as a recitalist. He made his Metropolitan Opera debut in N.Y. on Oct. 18, 1963, as Ottavio in *Don Giovanni*. In later years he taught voice in Canada and the U.S.; was on the faculty of the San Francisco Cons. (from 1972). In 1946 he married the soprano **Pierrette Alarie.** In 1971 he was made an Officer of the Order of Canada.

Simonetti, Achille, Italian-English violinist and composer; b. Turin, June 12, 1857; d. London, Nov. 19, 1928. He began violin lessons with Francesco Bianchi; after training with Eugenio Cavallini at the Milan Cons. (1872–73), he returned to Turin to study violin with Giuseppe Gamba and composition with Carlo Pedrotti; then continued his violin training with Sivori in Genoa, and finally studied violin with Danda and composition with Massenet at the Paris Cons. (1881–83). In 1887 he settled in England, where he toured with Maria Rôze and Benno Schönberger; lived in London from 1891; was a member of the London Trio (1901–12) and a prof. of violin at the Irish Royal Academy of Music (1912–19). He was greatly esteemed as both a soloist and chamber music artist. An early champion of the Brahms Violin Concerto, he wrote a cadenza for the work, which he introduced in Dresden (Dec. 11, 1896). He composed numerous pieces for solo violin; his *Madrigale* became world famous.

Simon-Girard, Juliette, French soprano; b. Paris, May 8, 1859; d. Nice, Dec. 1959, at the age of 100. She made her debut at the Folies-Dramatiques in Paris, where she created the principal role in *Les Cloches de Cornevilles* on April 19, 1877; then sang at the premieres of *La Fille du Tambour-major* (1879), *Fanfan la tulipe* (1882), and many other operettas; she became particularly successful in Offenbach's repertoire. She married the tenor **Nicolas Simon,** known as **Simon-Max** (1855–1923); divorced him in 1894, and married the comedian Huguenet; then retired to Nice.

Simonis, Jean-Marie, Belgian composer; b. Mol, Nov. 22, 1931. He studied composition with Stekke, Souris, Louel, and Quinet, and conducting with Defossez at the Brussels Cons.; taught there (from 1969) and at the Uccles Academy of Music (from 1971).
WORKS: RADIO OPERA: *Gens de maison* (1962). **ORCH.:** *3 Motets* for Soprano, Chorus, and Orch. (1961); *Introduction et Danse* for Chamber Orch. (1963); *3 esquisses symphoniques* (1964); *Sinfonia da camera* for String Orch. (1966); *L'Automne,* symphonic poem (1967); *Scherzetto* for Chamber Orch. (1968); *Évasions* (1982); *Cantilène* for Violin and Orch. (1985); *Espressioni* (1988). **CHAMBER:** *3 Pieces* for 4 Clarinets (1965); *Duetti* for Viola and Piano (1968); *Impromptu* for Cello (1968–69); *Séquences* for Clarinet and Piano (1969); *3 Lagu Dolanan* for Soprano and Percussion (1969); *Suggestions* for Flute and 4 Percussionists (1970); *Boutades* for 4 Saxophones (1971); *Mouvements* for 2 Pianos (1971); *Résonances* for Percussion and Piano (1979); *Introit et Graduel* for String Quartet and Organ (1984); *Fantasia a due* for Violin and Piano (1986). **PIANO:** *Étude de Concert* (1963); *Historiettes* (1972); *Impromptu* (1973); *2 animations* (1973); *2 pastourelles* (1973); *Évocations* (1974); *Incantations* (1974).

Simonov, Yuri (Ivanovich), Russian conductor; b. Saratov, March 4, 1941. He studied viola and conducting at the Leningrad Cons.; then was conductor of the Kislovodsk Phil. (1967–69). In 1969 he won 1st prize at the international competition of conductors at the Accademia di Santa Cecilia in Rome; returning to Moscow, he was appointed a conductor of the Bolshoi Theater, and in 1970 was named its chief conductor; subsequently toured with it in Europe, North America, and Japan; also was active as a sym. conductor. He particularly distinguished himself as a proponent of contemporary Soviet music.

Simonsen, Rudolph (Hermann), eminent Danish music historian and composer; b. Copenhagen, April 30, 1889; d. there, March 28, 1947. He studied piano with Agnes Adler and theory with Otto Malling at the Copenhagen Cons. (1907–9), completing his piano studies with Teresa Carreño and Anders Rachlew; also earned a law degree from the Univ. of Copenhagen (1912). He taught at the Copenhagen Cons. from 1916, succeeding Nielsen as director in 1931. Although his compositions reveal the influence of Nielsen, he succeeded in producing works of distinction and individuality, but it is as a compiler of books on music culture and philosophy that he is best known.
WORKS: 4 syms.: No. 1, *Zion* (Göteborg, Feb. 4, 1920); No. 2, *Hellas* (Berlin, Sept. 23, 1921); No. 3, *Roma* (1923; Copenhagen, March 5, 1928); No. 4, *Danmark* (1925; Copenhagen, April 4, 1931); Piano Concerto (Copenhagen, Nov. 15, 1915); works for Chorus and Orch.; Piano Quintet (1908); 2 string quartets (1923, 1925); Clarinet Quintet (1929); songs. **WRITINGS:** *Musikkultur* (Copenhagen, 1927); *Musikhistoriske hovedstrømninger* (Copenhagen, 1930); *Alenmenneskelige vaerdier: Plato-Spinoza-Goethe* (Copenhagen, 1940); *Sub specie aeternitatis* (Copenhagen, 1942); *Musikhistorisk kompendium* (Copenhagen, 1946).
BIBL.: *Mindeskrift om R. S.* (Copenhagen, 1949).

Simovich, Roman, outstanding Ukrainian composer; b. Sniatin, Feb. 28, 1901; d. Lwow, July 30, 1984. He studied piano and composition with Novák at the Prague Cons. (1933–36); then taught at the Lisenko Institutes in Drogobych and Stanislav (1936–44) and at the Lwow Cons. (from 1944), where he became a prof. in 1963. He was made an Honored Artist of the Ukraine in 1954. His compositions were firmly rooted in the history and lore of the western Ukraine.
WORKS: BALLET: *Sopilka Dovbusha* (1948). **ORCH.:** 7 syms. (*Gutsulska,* 1945; *Lemkovsk,* 1947; *Springtime,* 1951; *Heroic,*

1954; *Celestial*, 1955; 1965; 1972); 3 suites; 6 symphonic poems; 4 overtures: *Carnival* (1936), *Youth* (1958), *Ceremonial* (1966), and *Bombastic* (1967); Flute Concerto (1953); Piano Concerto (1971). **CHAMBER:** 2 piano trios (1929, 1935); 2 string quartets (1929, 1950); also solo piano pieces; vocal works, including 4 vocal symphonic poems: *The Shawl* (1933), *The Word* (1946), *In the Carpathians* (1949), and *The Flowers of Happiness and Freedom* (1959).
BIBL.: A. Tereshchenko, *R. S.* (Kiev, 1973).

Simpson (Sympson), Christopher, eminent English viol player, music theorist, and composer; b. probably in Westonby, near Egton, Yorkshire, c.1605; d. probably in Holborn, London, between May 5 and July 29, 1669. He fought on the Royalist side in the English Civil War (1643–44) and later entered the service of Sir Robert Bolles as music tutor to the latter's son. His playing, writings, and compositions won him great esteem.
WRITINGS: *The Division-violist, or, An Introduction to the Playing Upon a Ground* (London, 1659; 2nd ed., rev., 1665 as *Chelys minuritionum artificio exornata/The Division-viol, or the Art of Playing Extempore upon a Ground;* 3rd ed., 1712); *The Principles of Practical Musick* (London, 1665; 2nd ed., rev. and augmented, 1667 as *A Compendium of Practical Musick;* ed by P. Lord, Oxford, 1970); also annotations to T. Campion in J. Playford, *A Brief Introduction to the Skill of Musick* (London, 2nd ed., 1655).
WORKS: Airs in *The Principles of Practical Musick* (see Writings above); various other airs in MS; divisions in *The Division-violist* (see Writings above); various other divisions in MS; fantasias and fantasia-suites in MS.
BIBL.: M. Meredith, *C. Simpson and the Consort of Viols* (diss., Univ. of Wales, Cardiff, 1969).

Simpson, Robert (Wilfred Levick), English composer and writer on music; b. Leamington, March 2, 1921. He studied composition with Howells in London (1942–46); received his Mus.D. from the Univ. of Durham in 1951; joined the staff of the BBC as a music producer in 1951, resigning in 1980. He was awarded the Carl Nielsen Gold Medal of Denmark in 1956 and the Bruckner Medal in 1962.
WORKS: ORCH.: 10 syms.: No. 1 (1951; Copenhagen, June 11, 1953); No. 2 (1955; Cheltenham Festival, July 16, 1957); No. 3 (1962; Birmingham, March 14, 1963); No. 4 (1970–72; Manchester, April 26, 1973); No. 5 (1972; London, May 3, 1973); No. 6 (1976; London, April 8, 1980); No. 7 (1977); No. 8 (1981; London, Nov. 10, 1982); No. 9 (1985; Poole, April 8, 1987); No. 10 (1988); Violin Concerto (1959; Birmingham, Feb. 25, 1960); Piano Concerto (Cheltenham Festival, July 14, 1967). **CHAMBER:** 12 string quartets (1952, 1953, 1954, 1973, 1974, 1975, 1977, 1979, 1982, 1983, 1984, 1987); *Canzona* for Brass (1958); *Variations and Fugue* for Recorder and String Quartet (1958); Trio for Clarinet, Cello, and Piano (1967); Quartet for Clarinet and Strings (1968); Quartet for Horn, Violin, Cello, and Piano (1975); *Media morte in vita sumus*, motet for Chorus, Brass, and Timpani (1975); Quintet for Clarinet, Bass Clarinet, and String Trio (1981); Trio for Horn, Violin, and Piano (1984); Sonata for Violin and Piano (1984); String Trio (1987); String Quintet (1987); Trio for Violin, Cello, and Piano (1988–89). **PIANO:** Sonata (1946); *Variations and Finale on a Theme by Haydn* (1948); 2-piano Sonata (1980).
WRITINGS: *Carl Nielsen, Symphonist* (London, 1952; 2nd ed., rev., 1979); *Bruckner and the Symphony* (London, 1963); *Sibelius and Nielsen* (London, 1965); *The Essence of Bruckner* (London, 1966); ed. *The Symphony* (Harmondsworth, vol. I, 1966; 2nd ed., 1972; vol. II, 1967); *Beethoven Symphonies* (London, 1970); *The Proms and Natural Justice* (London, 1981).
BIBL.: R. Johnson, *R. S.: 50th Birthday Essays* (London, 1971); S. Johnson, "R. S.'s Ninth," *Musical Times* (April 1987).

Simpson, Thomas, English viol player, music editor, and composer; b. Milton next Sittingbourne, Kent (baptized), April 1, 1582; d. probably there, after 1630. He went to Germany as a youth; served as a viol player at the Heidelberg court from 1608; then was at the court of the Count of Holstein-Schaumburg in Bückeburg (c.1615–21), and subsequently was employed in the royal chapel of Copenhagen as a court musician to King Christian IV (1622–25). An excellent composer of court dances and songs, he brought out *Opusculum* [30] *newer Pavanen, Galliarden, Couranten und Volten, a 5* (Frankfurt am Main, 1610; includes 24 pieces by Simpson), *Opus* [22] *newer Paduanen, Galliarden, Intraden, Canzonen, Ricercaren, a 5* (Frankfurt am Main, 1611; not extant; 2nd ed., Hamburg, 1617), and (50) *Taffel-Consort, a 4* and Basso Continuo (Hamburg, 1621; includes 7 pieces by Simpson).

Simrock, Nikolaus, famous German music publisher; b. Mainz, Aug. 23, 1751; d. Bonn, June 12, 1832. He played the horn in the Electoral Orch. in Bonn until 1794. He began dealing in printed music and instruments in 1780; in 1785, opened a music shop in Bonn, selling musical instruments; in 1793 he established a music publ. house with its own printing press. During Beethoven's lifetime, Simrock's catalogue listed 85 of his works, including the *Kreutzer Sonata* and opus nos. 17, 31, 81b, 102, and 107. His son **Peter Joseph Simrock** (b. Bonn, Aug. 18, 1792; d. Cologne, Dec. 13, 1868) succeeded him and greatly increased the prestige of the house by acquiring the early works of Brahms. He was succeeded by his son **"Fritz" (Friedrich August) Simrock** (b. Bonn, Jan. 2, 1837; d. Ouchy, near Lausanne, Aug. 20, 1901), who transferred the firm to Berlin in 1870, publ. the works of Brahms, and, at the suggestion of Brahms, added the works of Dvořák to his catalogue. His nephew **"Hans" (Johann Baptist) Simrock** (b. Cologne, April 17, 1861; d. Berlin, July 26, 1910) reorganized the firm in 1902 as a stock company and established branches in London and Paris. A grandson of Fritz Simrock, **Fritz Auckenthaler Simrock** (b. Zürich, Nov. 17, 1893; d. Basel, April 19, 1973), headed the firm (1920–29) when it was sold to A.J. Benjamin in Hamburg; in 1951 the Hamburg firm, which also had a branch in London, resumed its original name, N. Simrock Co.
BIBL.: *Verzeichnis des Musikalien-Verlages N. S.* (Berlin, 1893; 3 suppls., 1902–27); W. Ottendorf-Simrock, *Das Haus S.* (Ratingen, 1954); K. Stephenson, *Johannes Brahms und Fritz S., Weg einer Freundschaft. Briefe des Verlegers an den Komponisten* (Hamburg, 1961).

Sims, Ezra, American composer of innovative music; b. Birmingham, Ala., Jan. 16, 1928. His education was highly diversified; he took courses in mathematics at Birmingham Southern College, obtaining a B.A. in 1947, and concurrently studied with Hugh Thomas and B. Ackley Brower at the Birmingham Cons. (1945–48). He entered Yale Univ. as a student of Quincy Porter (B.M., 1952), and then enrolled in the U.S. Army Language School, where he earned a degree in Mandarin Chinese in 1953. Returning to music, he studied with Darius Milhaud and Leon Kirchner at Mills College (M.A., 1955). He attended Aaron Copland's seminar at the Berkshire Music Center at Tanglewood, Mass., in 1960. To earn a living, he took all kinds of menial jobs, as a mail clerk, steelworker, and display designer. From 1958 to 1962 and again from 1965 to 1974, he was employed as a cataloguer at the music library of Harvard Univ. In 1962 he received a Guggenheim fellowship, and had an opportunity to go to Tokyo, where he put together the electronic portion of the background score for the Japanese play *Sakoku*. In 1978 he again traveled to Japan. He made his permanent home in Cambridge, Mass.; there he founded the whimsically named New England Dinosaur Dance Theatre (1968–78) and Annex (1977–81); however, there was nothing extinct about his concerts there; on the contrary, the Dinosaur programs were projections into a distant future rather than a retrospection into a fossilized past. The music Sims writes is microtonal, based on a scale of 18 tones within a larger complex of 72 degrees in equal temperament. Amazingly enough, he found string players in Boston and elsewhere who could perform his microtonal pieces with spectacular ease. In 1977 he developed a polyphonic keyboard providing any tuning whatsoever, in Pythagorean, or just, intonation, as well as in equal temperament that divides the octave into fewer than 37 intervals.

WORKS: *Chamber Cantata on Chinese Poems* (1954); Cello Sonata (1957); String Quartet No. 1 (1959); String Quartet No. 2, in *Sonate concertante* (1961); String Quartet No. 3 (1962); Octet for Strings in quarter-tones and sixth-tones (1964); *Antimatter* for Magnetic Tape Collage (1968); *A Frank Overture: 4 Dented Interludes and Coda* (1969); *Real Toads,* musique concrète (1970); *Dreams for Sale* for Mezzo-soprano, Baritone, and Piano (1970); Quartet for Oboe and Strings (1971); *Second Thoughts* for Double Bass, microtonal music with quarter-tones and sixth-tones (1974); Quintet for Flute, Clarinet, Violin, Viola, and Cello (1974); *Slow Hiccups* for 2 Recorders (1975); *Elegie nach Rilke* for Soprano, Flute, Clarinet, Violin, and Cello, microtonal music including *Sprechstimme* (Cambridge, Mass., Nov. 16, 1976); *Yr obedt servt* for Small Ensemble (1977); *Aeneas on the Saxophone* for Voices, Clarinet, Horn, Trombone, Viola, and Double Bass, microtonal music to 18-note scale (perf. on Sims's 50th birthday, Boston, Jan. 16, 1978); *And, As I Was Saying* for Viola or Violin, microtonal music (1979); *All Done from Memory* for Violin, microtonal music in an 18-tone scale or equal temperament in 72-tone scale (1980; Boston, Jan. 18, 1981); Sextet for Clarinet, Saxophone, Horn, Violin, Viola, and Cello (1981); *This Way to the Egress—or—Manners Makyth Man* for String Trio (1984); String Quartet No. 4 (1984).

Sims, Jon Reed, American conductor; b. Smith Center, Kans., May 6, 1947; d. (of AIDS) San Francisco, July 16, 1984. He studied piano and horn, and was drum major of his high school band; later attended Wichita State Univ. (B.Mus. and B.A., 1969) and Indiana Univ. (M.Mus., 1972). He studied eurhythmics at the Dalcroze School in N.Y.; arts administration at San Francisco's Golden Gate Univ.; dance in N.Y., Chicago, and San Francisco; and horn and composition (with Milhaud). He taught in Chicago (1972–74) and San Francisco (1974–78). In 1978 he founded the San Francisco Gay Freedom Day Marching Band & Twirling Corps, which made its debut performance at the Gay Pride Day parade that same year; founded in rapid succession the San Francisco Gay Men's Chorus (Nov. 1978), the Golden Gate Performing Arts (an administrative organization, March 1979), Lambda Pro Musica, and the San Francisco Lesbian & Gay Men's Community Chorus; directed the San Francisco Band & Corps until early 1982. Sims's dream was to create a nationwide network of gay and lesbian instrumental and choral ensembles; the San Francisco chorus toured the U.S. in 1981, a public gesture that caused the founding of ensembles nationwide. Gay and lesbian choruses appeared in quick succession in Los Angeles (July 12, 1979), Seattle (Nov. 1979), and Chicago. The 1st meeting of what was to become GALA (Gay and Lesbian Assoc. [of choruses]; Chicago, June 1981) included directors and ensemble founders Jerry Carlson (Chicago Gay Men's Chorus; later director of the Los Angeles Gay Men's Chorus; d. of AIDS, Nov. 1987), Dennis Coleman (Seattle Men's Chorus), Richard Garrin (Chicago's Windy City Gay Chorus), Dick Kramer (San Francisco Gay Men's Chorus), Gary Miller (N.Y. City Gay Men's Chorus), and Susan Schleef (Chicago's Artemis Singers). The 1st West Coast conference of GALA included 9 choruses (1982); the 1st national conference, with 11 choruses (N.Y., 1983), was followed by conferences with 17 (Minneapolis, 1986) and 43 choruses (Seattle, 1989); in 1990 GALA boasted a membership of 88 choruses situated throughout North America and Europe. Most GALA choruses are made up of gay men, although there are a number of lesbian and mixed-voice ensembles; many additional lesbian groups are not GALA members. Following Sims's example, gay and lesbian musical organizations have grown remarkably in number, size, and sophistication; they are important examples of communal expression in American gay and lesbian culture.

Sims, "Zoot" (John Haley), noted American jazz tenor, alto, and soprano saxophonist; b. Inglewood, Calif., Oct. 29, 1925;

d. N.Y., March 23, 1985. He began to study clarinet as a child; later mastered the tenor and alto saxophones. He played with Bobby Sherwood's band; then joined Benny Goodman in 1943, with whom he worked on and off for many years; gained renown as one of the "Four Brothers" saxophone section of Woody Herman's orch. (1947–49); subsequently appeared with Stan Kenton (1953) and with Gerry Mulligan (1954–56; 1960); also led a quintet with Al Cohn (from 1957).

BIBL.: A. Astrup, *The J.H. S. (Z. S.) Discography* (Lyngby, Denmark, 1980).

Šín, Otakar, eminent Czech music theorist and composer; b. Rokytno, Moravia, April 23, 1881; d. Prague, Jan. 21, 1943. He studied composition with Vítězslav Novák at the Prague Cons., where he was appointed a prof. of theory in 1920. He publ. the textbooks *A Complete Harmony Course on the Basis of Melody and Rhythm* (Prague, 1922; 6th ed., rev., 1949), *Counterpoint, Imitation and Fugue* (Prague, 1936; 2nd ed., 1945), and *A General Music Course* (Prague, 1949; completed by F. Bartoš and K. Janeček).

WORKS: 2 symphonic poems: *Tillotama* (1908) and *King Menkera* (1916–18); *Radio Overture* (1936); *3 Czech Dances* for Orch. (1939; also for Nonet); 2 string quartets (1923, 1926–28); Cello Sonata (1934); *Small Suite* for Violin and Piano (1937); *Hunting,* festive greeting for Horns (1938); numerous piano pieces; choruses; songs.

BIBL.: K. Janeček, *O. S.* (Prague, 1944).

Sinatra, Frank (Francis Albert), popular American singer and actor; b. Hoboken, N.J., Dec. 12, 1915, of immigrant Italian parents. He had no training as a singer and could not read music; after singing in a school glee club and on amateur radio shows, he appeared on N.Y. radio shows. In 1939 he became a singer with Harry James, and then gained fame as a vocalist with Tommy Dorsey (1940–42). Inspired by the tone production of Dorsey's trombone playing, he evolved, by convex inhalation from a corner of the mouth, a sui generis "mal canto" in *sotto voce* delivery, employing a Caruso-like *coup-de-glotte* at climactic points. This mode of singing, combined with an engagingly slender physique, stirred the young females of the World War II era to fainting frenzy at his performances. Sinatra's press agents were quick to exploit the phenomenon, dubbing him "Swoonlight Sinatra." He eventually overcame his anesthetic appeal and became a successful baritone crooner. In 1952 he revealed an unexpected dramatic talent as a movie actor, eliciting praise from astonished cinema critics and an Academy Award for his appearance in *From Here to Eternity.* Other successful films followed, and his singing career gained momentum as he toured throughout the globe. He also made numerous recordings and television appearances. A fixture on the nightclub circuit, the Univ. of Nevada at Las Vegas conferred on him the honorary degree of Literarum Humanitarum Doctor, in appreciation of his many highly successful appearances in the hotels and gambling casinos of Las Vegas (1976). President Reagan was so moved to present him with the U.S. Presidential Medal of Freedom in 1985.

BIBL.: E. Kahn, *The Voice: The Story of an American Phenomenon* (N.Y., 1947); A. Shaw, *S.: 20th-Century Romantic* (N.Y., 1965); A. Lonstein and V. Marino, *The Compleat S. Discography, Filmography, Television Appearances, Motion Picture Appearances, Radio, Concert, Stage Appearances* (Ellenville, N.Y., 1970; 2nd ed., rev. and enl., 1979); E. Wilson, *S.: An Unauthorized Biography* (N.Y., 1976; Sinatra instituted a suit for $3 million against the publishers for alleged distortion of his life as "boring and uninteresting"); J. Rockwell, *S.: An American Classic* (N.Y., 1984); K. Kelley, *His Way: The Unauthorized Biography of F. S.* (Toronto and N.Y., 1986); B. Adler, *S., the Man and the Myth: An Unauthorized Biography* (N.Y., 1987).

Sinclair, George Robertson, English organist and conductor; b. Croydon, Oct. 28, 1863; d. Birmingham, Feb. 7, 1917. He received his musical education in Dublin; in 1889 he was appointed organist of Hereford Cathedral; also conducted the Three Choirs Festivals (1891–1912) and the Birmingham Festival Choral Society (1899–1917). He acquired a reputation as a master organist; the 11th variation of Elgar's *Enigma Variations* is inscribed to Sinclair ("G.R.S.") and vividly portrays Sinclair's virtuosity in the use of the organ pedals.

Sinding, Christian (August), celebrated Norwegian composer; b. Kongsberg, Jan. 11, 1856; d. Oslo, Dec. 3, 1941. He studied 1st with L. Lindeman in Norway, then at the Leipzig Cons. (1874–78) with Schradieck (violin), Jadassohn (theory), and Reinecke (orchestration); a government stipend enabled him to continue his studies in Germany, and he spent 2 years (1882–84) in Munich, Berlin, and Dresden; there he wrote his 1st opera, *Titandros*, much influenced by Wagner. On Dec. 19, 1885, he gave a concert of his works in Oslo; during another stay in Germany, his Piano Quintet was played in Leipzig, with Brodsky and Busoni among the performers (Jan. 19, 1889); Erika Lie-Nissen played his Piano Concerto in Berlin (Feb. 23, 1889). He publ. a number of piano pieces in Germany; of these, *Frühlingsrauschen* became an international favorite. His opera to a German text, *Der heilige Berg* (1914), was not successful. In 1915 he received a life pension of 4,000 crowns "for distinguished service"; on his 60th birthday (1916), the Norwegian government presented him with a purse of 30,000 crowns, a mark of appreciation for "the greatest national composer since Grieg." He was invited by George Eastman to teach at the Eastman School of Music in Rochester, N.Y., during the academic season 1921–22; after this journey, he lived mostly in Oslo. He continued to compose, and toward the end of his life wrote in larger forms; his 3rd Sym. was conducted by Nikisch with the Berlin Phil. in 1921, and his 4th Sym. was performed on his 80th birthday in Oslo (1936). His works aggregate to 132 opus numbers. Most of his music is of a descriptive nature; his lyric pieces for piano and his songs are fine examples of Scandinavian Romanticism, but the German inspiration of his formative years is much in evidence; he was chiefly influenced by Schumann and Liszt.

WORKS: OPERAS: *Titandros* (1884; not perf); *Der heilige Berg* (1912; Dessau, April 19, 1914). **ORCH.:** 4 syms.: No. 1 (1880–82; Christiania, March 25, 1882); No. 2 (1903–4; Berlin, March 22, 1907); No. 3 (1920; Berlin, Jan. 10, 1921); No. 4, *Vinter og vår* (1921–36; Oslo, Jan. 11, 1936); *Episodes chevaleresques* (1888); *Rondo infinito* (1886; rev. 1897); Piano Concerto (Berlin, Feb. 23, 1889); 3 violin concertos (1898, 1901, 1917); *Legende* for Violin and Orch. (1900); *Romanze* for Violin and Orch. (1910); *Abendstimmung* for Violin and Orch. (1915). **CHAMBER:** 2 string quartets (1884, 1904); Piano Quintet (1882–84); 3 piano trios (1893, 1902, 1908); 4 violin sonatas (1894, 1895, 1905, 1909); *Scènes de la vie* for Violin and Piano (1900); *Cantus doloris*, variations for Violin and Piano (1906); *Nordische Ballade* for Cello and Piano (1911); etc. **PIANO:** Sonata (1909); *Fatum*, variations (1909); 5 *Stücke*, op. 24 (1894); 7 *Stücke*, op. 25 (1895); 6 *Stücke*, op. 31 (1896); 6 *Stücke*, op. 32 (1896; No. 3 is the celebrated *Frühlingsrauschen*); 6 *Charakterstücke*, op. 33 (1896; contains *A la Menuetto* and *Ständchen*); 6 *Charakterstücke*, op. 34 (1896; contains *Chanson*); 6 *Klavierstücke* (1899; contains *Humoresque*); *Mélodies mignonnes* (1900); 4 *morceaux de salon* (1900; contains *Sérénade*); etc. **VOCAL:** Songs: *Alte Weisen* (1886); *Lieder und Gesänge* (1888; contains *Viel Träume* and *Ein Weib*); *Galmandssange* (1893; contains *Mainat*); *Nyinger* (1908); etc.; about 250 in all; several cantatas and other choral works. A complete list of Sinding's works was publ. by Ö. Gaukstad in *Norsk Musikkgranskning arbok* (Oslo, 1938).

Singelée, Jean-Baptiste, Belgian violinist and composer; b. Brussels, Sept. 25, 1812; d. Ostend, Sept. 29, 1875. He publ. 144 works (2 concertos, many solos for violin, fantasias on operatic airs, etc.).

Singer, Edmund, Hungarian violinist, teacher, and composer; b. Totis, Oct. 14, 1830; d. Stuttgart, Jan. 23, 1912. He studied in Budapest, and later at the Paris Cons.; was a concertmaster in Weimar (1853–61); later was a prof. at the Stuttgart Cons. He publ. a number of attractive violin pieces; wrote cadenzas for the violin concertos of Beethoven and Brahms; ed. the

études of Rode, Kreutzer, Fiorillo, Rovelli, and Gaviniés; with M. Seifriz, compiled the *Grosse theoretisch-praktische Violinschule* (2 vols., 1884).

Singer, George, Czech-born Israeli conductor and composer; b. Prague, Aug. 6, 1908; d. Tel Aviv, Sept. 30, 1980. He studied piano at the Prague Academy of Music with Schulhoff and composition with Zemlinsky; made his 1st appearance as an opera conductor in Prague in 1926. In 1930 he received an engagement at the Hamburg Opera, returning to Prague in 1934. When the Nazis invaded Czechoslovakia in 1939, he, being Jewish, was compelled to take refuge in Tel Aviv, where he established himself favorably as a conductor. He also accepted engagements as a conductor in Russia and in the U.S., where he led the N.Y. City Opera in 1968. Back in Israel, he gave performances of several works of local composers. He was known for his phenomenal facility in sight-reading, performing works perfectly at 1st reading on the piano and conducting every nuance of an orch. score. He composed some orch pieces.

Singer, Peter (Alkantara) (actually, **Josef Anton**), Austrian organist, music theorist, teacher, instrument maker, and composer; b. Unterhäselgehr, North Tirol, July 18, 1810; d. Salzburg, Jan. 25, 1882. He became a Franciscan monk in 1830, and was made a priest in 1837; served as organist and choirmaster in Bolzano and Innsbruck (1837–40), and then at the Salzburg Franciscan convent. He wrote over 100 masses, some 40 motets, 15 litanies, numerous Marian hymns, many offertories, etc. In 1839 he invented the "Pansymphonikon," a kind of orchestrion with reeds; publ. *Metaphysische Blicke in die Tonwelt, nebst einem neuen System der Tonwissenschaft* (Munich, 1847).

BIBL.: Pater Hartmann, *P. S.* (Innsbruck, 1910); V. Keldorfer, *Der Spielmann des Herrn Pater P. S.* (Salzburg, 1952).

Singher, Martial (Jean-Paul), noted French baritone and pedagogue; b. Oloron-Ste. Marie, Aug. 14, 1904; d. Santa Barbara, Calif., March 10, 1990. He received his education as a public-school teacher in Dax, and at the École Normale de Toulouse and the École Normale Supérieure de St. Cloud. He then studied voice with André Gresse at the Paris Cons. (premier prix for singing, 1929; premier prix for opera and opéra-comique singing, 1930; Grand Prix Osiris de l'Institute de France, 1930); also studied voice with Juliette Fourestier. He made his operatic debut in Amsterdam as Orestes in *Iphigénie en Tauride* on Nov. 14, 1930; then joined the Paris Opéra, remaining with it until 1941; also sang at the Opéra-Comique. On Jan. 10, 1940, he married Margareta Busch, daughter of the conductor Fritz Busch. He went to the U.S. in 1941; made his Metropolitan Opera debut in N.Y. on Dec. 10, 1943, as Dapertutto in *Les Contes d'Hoffmann;* subsequently sang the roles of the Count in *Le nozze di Figaro,* Lescaut in *Manon,* and all 4 baritone roles in *Les Contes d'Hoffmann;* remained on the roster, with some interruptions, until 1959. He also sang with the leading orchs. of the U.S., and appeared widely in song recitals. He was on the faculty of the Mannes College of Music in N.Y. (1951–62) and the Curtis Inst. of Music in Philadelphia (1955–68); then was director of the voice and opera dept., and was the opera producer at the Music Academy of the West in Santa Barbara (1962–81). His students included Donald Gramm, John Reardon, James King, Louis Quilico, Judith Blegen, Benita Valente, and Jeannine Altmeyer. He was a particularly distinguished interpreter of the French operatic and song repertoire. He wrote a book useful to vocalists aspiring to an operatic career entitled *An Interpretive Guide to Operatic Arias: A Handbook for Singers, Coaches, Teachers, and Students* (1983).

Singleton, Alvin (Elliot), black American composer; b. N.Y., Dec. 28, 1940. He took courses in composition and music education at N.Y. Univ. (B.M., 1967), then continued his study of composition with Powell and Wyner at Yale Univ. (M.M.A., 1971). He received a Fulbright fellowship to study with Petrassi in Rome at the Accademia di Santa Cecilia (1971–72), and in 1981 was awarded an NEA grant. From 1985 to 1988 he served as composer-in-residence of the Atlanta Sym. Orch.; in 1988 he was appointed composer-in-residence at Spelman College in Atlanta.

WORKS: OPERA: *Dream Sequence '76* (1976). **ORCH.:** *Kwitana* for Piano, Double Bass, Percussion, and Chamber Ensemble (1974); *Again* for Chamber Orch. (1979); *A Yellow Rose Petal* (1982); *Shadows* (1987); *After Fallen Crumbs* (1988). **CHAMBER:** Woodwind Quintet (1969); *Argoru I* for Piano (1970), *II* for Cello (1970, *III* for Flute (1971), *IV* for Viola (1978), *V* for Bass Clarinet (1984), and *VI* for Marimba (1989). **VOCAL:** *Messa* for Soprano, Chorus, Flute, 2 Guitars, Electric Organ, Cello, and Double Bass (1975); also a wordless drama, *Necessity Is a Mother* (1981).

Singleton, "Zutty" (Arthur James), prominent black American jazz drummer; b. Bunkei, La., May 14, 1898; d. N.Y., July 14, 1975. He began his career in New Orleans in 1915; in 1929 he went to N.Y., where he played with Louis Armstrong, Sidney Bechet, and others; also formed his own jazz groups. He was especially esteemed for his work as a sideman, being a notable representative of the New Orleans-Chicago jazz styles.

BIBL.: M. Williams, "Z. S., the Pioneer Jazz Forgot," *Down Beat*, XXX/30 (1963); idem, "Z.," *Jazz Masters of New Orleans* (N.Y., 1967).

Sinico, Francesco, Italian organist, choirmaster, teacher, and composer; b. Trieste, Dec. 12, 1810; d. there, Aug. 18, 1865. He studied with G. Farinelli; was an organist and conductor in various churches; in 1843, established his own singing school in Trieste, providing excellent training for choral singing. He produced his opera *I Virtuosi di Barcellona* in 1841. His son, **Giuseppe Sinico** (b. Trieste, Feb. 10, 1836; d. there, Dec. 31, 1907), continued the popular singing classes at the Sinico School in Trieste; wrote several operas, which he produced there: *Marinella* (Aug. 26, 1854), *I Moschettieri* (March 26, 1859), *Aurora di Nevers* (March 12, 1861), *Alessandro Stradella* (Lugo, Sept. 19, 1863), and *Spartaco* (Nov. 20, 1886). He publ. *Breve metodo teoricopratico di canto elementare.*

BIBL.: *Una famiglia triestina di musicisti "I S."* (Trieste, 1932).

Sinigaglia, Leone, Italian composer; b. Turin, Aug. 14, 1868; d. there, May 16, 1944. He was a pupil at the Turin Cons., studying with Giovanni Bolzoni; later studied in Vienna (1894–1900) with Mandyczewski, and in Prague with Vysoka and Dvořák (1900–1901). His 1st successful work was a violin concerto (1900) dedicated to Arrigo Serato, who played it with considerable success in the principal cities of Germany. His early works were much influenced by Brahms and Dvořák; then he turned for inspiration to the music of his native Piedmont, and in this field achieved a lasting reputation. Toscanini conducted in Turin the premiere of Sinigaglia's suite *Danze piemontesi*, on popular themes (May 14, 1905); later Sinigaglia publ. a collection of songs (6 albums), *Vecchie canzoni popolari del Piemonte;* another work in the folk-song manner is the symphonic suite *Piemonte* (1909; Utrecht, Feb. 16, 1910); he further wrote *Le Baruffe Chiozzotte*, an overture to Goldoni's comedy (Utrecht, Dec. 21, 1907); *Rapsodia piemontese* for Violin and Orch. (1900); *Romanze* for Violin and Orch. (1899); *Variations on a Theme of Brahms* for String Quartet (1901); *Serenade* for String Trio (1906); Cello Sonata (1923).

BIBL.: E. Desderi, "L. S.," *Rivista Musicale Italiana*, XLVII (1946); L. Rognoni, "L. S.," *Musicisti piemontesi e liguri*, Chigiana, XVI (1959); C. Mosso and E. Bassi, eds., *L. S., Torino, 1868–1944: Primo centenario della nascita* (Turin, 1968).

Sinopoli, Giuseppe, distinguished Italian conductor and composer; b. Venice, Nov. 2, 1946. He studied organ and harmony as a youth in Messina, then took courses in harmony and counterpoint at the Venice Cons.; also studied medicine at the Univ. of Padua (degree in psychiatry, 1971) while concurrently studying composition privately with Donatoni in Paris; then took a course in conducting with Swarowsky at the Vienna

Academy of Music. He organized the Bruno Maderna Ensemble in 1975, and conducted it in performances of contemporary music; was also active as a teacher. After a successful engagement as a guest conductor at the Teatro La Fenice in Venice in 1976, he appeared at the Deutsche Oper in Berlin (1980), the Hamburg State Opera (1980), and the Vienna State Opera (1982). On May 3, 1983, he made his Covent Garden debut in London, conducting *Manon Lescaut;* his Metropolitan Opera debut followed in N.Y. on March 11, 1985, when he led a performance of *Tosca*. He served as chief conductor of the Orchestra dell'Accademia Nazionale di Santa Cecilia in Rome (1983–87); also was principal conductor of the Philharmonia Orch. of London (from 1984). In 1990 he became Generalmusikdirektor of the Deutsche Oper in Berlin, but abruptly resigned that same year after disagreements with its Intendant, Götz Friedrich. He then accepted the post of chief conductor of the Dresden Staatskapelle. His training as a psychiatrist led him to probe deeply into the scores he conducted, often resulting in startlingly revealing but controversial interpretations. As a composer, he pursues contemporary modes of expression.

WORKS: OPERA: *Lou Salome* (Munich, May 10, 1981; also 2 suites: No. 1 for Soli, Chorus, and Orch., 1981, and No. 2 for Orch., 1985). **ORCH.:** *Opus Daleth* (1970); *Opus Ghimel* for Chamber Orch. (1971); Piano Concerto (1974–75); *Tombeau d'Armor I* (1975) and *II* (1977). **CHAMBER:** String Quintet (1970); *Numquid* for Chamber Ensemble (1972); Chamber Concerto for Piano and Instrumental Ensemble (1977–78); *Numquid et unum* for Flute and Harpsichord (1970); also a Piano Sonata (1973–75). **VOCAL:** *Symphonie imaginaire* for Soloists, Choir, Piano, and Orch. (1973); *Souvenirs à la Mémoire* for Solo Voices and Chamber Orch. (1973–74); *Opus Shir*, cantata (1971); *Requiem Hashshirim* for Chorus (1975–76).

BIBL.: D. Stearns, "The Psychodynamics of S.," *Ovation* (March 1989).

Siohan, Robert (-Lucien), French conductor, composer, and writer on music; b. Paris, Feb. 27, 1894; d. there, July 16, 1985. He studied at the Paris Cons. (1909–22); in 1929 he founded the Concerts Siohan, which he conducted until 1936; was chorus master at the Paris Opéra (1931–46); from 1948 to 1962 he was an instructor in solfège and sight-reading at the Paris Cons.; subsequently served as inspector-general of music in the Ministry of Culture. He received his doctorate at the Sorbonne in Paris in 1954 with the dissertation *Théories nouvelles de l'homme* (publ. as *Horizons sonores*, Paris, 1956). Among his compositions are the opera *Le saut dans les etoiles* (1926–27); *Cantique au frère soleil* for Soloists, Chorus, and Orch. (1926); Violin Concerto (1928); Piano Concerto (1939); String Quartet (1922); *Gravitations* for Viola and Piano (1952). He publ. *Stravinsky* (Paris, 1959; Eng. tr., London, 1966) and *Histoire du public musical* (Lausanne, 1967); also numerous articles in French and German publs.

Sipilä, Eero (Aukusti), Finnish composer; b. Hailuoto, July 27, 1918; d. Kajaani, May 18, 1972. He studied in Helsinki at the Church Music Inst. (graduated, 1943) and the Sibelius Academy (organ diploma, 1945); then taught at the Kajaani training college (1945–72).

WORKS: String Trio (1952); *Partita* for Wind Quartet (1955); *Super flumina Babylonis* and *Miserere*, 2 motets for Chorus (1963); *Te Deum Laudamus* for Alto, Baritone, Chorus, and Orch. (1969); *Fugue and Chaconne* for String Orch. (1969); *Lux aeterna* for String Quartet (1972); *Composition* for Orch. (Kajaani, May 8, 1973); song cycles; organ music.

Siqueira, José (de Lima), Brazilian composer and conductor; b. Conceição, June 24, 1907. He played saxophone and trumpet, taking instruction from his father; then entered the National School of Music in Rio de Janeiro, where he studied with Burle Marx and Francisco Braga. He founded the Orquesta Sinfónica Brasileira (1940), which he conducted until 1948; in 1949 he organized the Orquesta Sinfónica de Rio de Janeiro; he also filled engagements as a conductor in the U.S. (1944) and Russia (1955).

WORKS: Opera, *A compadecida* (1959; Rio de Janeiro, Dec. 20, 1961); symphonic drama, *Gimba* (1960); *O carnaval Carioca*, festive theater piece to commemorate the centennial of the city of Rio de Janeiro (1965); *Alvorada brasileira*, symphonic poem (1936); *4 poemas indígenas* for Orch. (1944); 4 syms. (1933, 1951, 1954, 1956); 6 orch. pieces, each entitled *Dança brasileira* (1955–70); 5 symphonic suites on Brazilian themes (1955–70); *Candomblé*, oratorio on folkloric texts (Rio de Janeiro, Dec. 20, 1957); *Encantamento da Magia Negra*, a fetishist motet on native themes (1957); Cello Concerto (1952); 3 piano concertos (1955, 1965, 1966); Violin Concerto (1957); 3 string quartets (1933, 1963, 1963); 2 violin sonatas (1949, 1952); Wind Quintet (1962); numerous songs and piano pieces.

Širola, Božidar, Croatian musicologist and composer; b. Žakanj, Dec. 20, 1889; d. Zagreb, April 10, 1956. He studied composition with Ivan Zajc, then musicology with Robert Lach at the Univ. of Vienna (Ph.D., 1921). Returning to Yugoslavia, he was on the faculty of the Zagreb Academy of Music (1935–41); then was director of the Ethnographic Museum. With the advent of the Tito regime, he devoted himself to private research. He was an authority on Croatian folk music; among his books, all publ. in Zagreb, are *Survey of the History of Croatian Music* (1922) and *Croatian Folk Music* (1940; 2nd ed., 1942). As a composer, he became best known for his operas and songs.

WORKS: STAGE: OPERAS: *Stanac* (1915); *The Cittern and the Drum* (1929); *The Student of the Black Arts* (1935); *The Young Gentleman* (1940); *The Stone Wedding Guests* (1954); also ballets and melodramas; incidental music. **ORCH.:** *The Story of Stanac*, overture (1912); *Symphonic Scherzo* (1912); *Festival Overture* (1920); *Concerto da Camera* for 2 Flutes and Chamber Orch. (1927); *Koncertna uvertira* (1927); *Romanca* for Violin and Strings (1939); Sym. (1945); *Sinfonia concertante* for Piano and Orch. (1952); Violin Concerto (1953); also numerous oratorios; other sacred works; choruses; song cycles. **CHAMBER:** 13 string quartets (*Medimurski*, 1920; *Bodulski*, 1933; 1946; 1946; 1951; 1951; 1951; 1952; *Nizozemski*, 1953; 1955; 1955; 1955; 1955); 3 piano trios (1934, 1937, 1939); other chamber works; piano pieces.

BIBL.: A. Goglia, "Hrvatski skladatalj i muzikolog dr. B. S.: život i djelo" (The Croatian Composer and Musicologist B. S.: Life and Work), *Sveta Cecilija*, XXXIII (Zagreb, 1939).

Sissle, Noble (Lee), black American singer, bandleader, lyricist, and composer; b. Indianapolis, July 10, 1889; d. Tampa, Dec. 17, 1975. He became a singer in Edward Thomas's Male Quartet (1908) and then in Hann's Jubilee Singers (1912); subsequently attended DePauw Univ. and Butler Univ. After conducting a hotel orch. in Indianapolis, he sang with Bob Young's band in Baltimore (1915), where he met Eubie Blake; the two then worked with James Reese Europe's Society Orch. in N.Y. Following service as a drum major in the 369th Regimental Infantry Band in France during World War I, Sissle returned to the U.S. and teamed up with Blake as a vaudeville duo (1919). After success with their musicals *Shuffle Along* (1921) and *Chocolate Dandies* (1924), they performed in Europe. Sissle remained in Europe to work with his own band and as a solo performer from 1927 until returning to the U.S. to resume his association with Blake in 1933; they then produced the show *Shuffle Along of 1933*. He was subsequently active with his own bands, making regular appearances at Billy Rose's Diamond Horseshoe in N.Y. (1938–50); later operated his own nightclub, dubbed Noble's.

BIBL.: W. Bolcom and R. Kimball, *Reminiscing with S. and Blake* (N.Y., 1973).

Sistermans, Anton, Dutch bass; b. 's-Hertogenbosch, Aug. 5, 1865; d. The Hague, March 18, 1926. He studied with Stockhausen in Frankfurt; from 1895 gave concerts in Europe; his only appearance in opera was as Pogner (Bayreuth, 1899); taught singing at Berlin's Klindworth-Scharwenka Cons. (1904–15).

Sitkovetsky, Dmitry, Russian-born American violinist; b. Baku, Sept. 27, 1954. His father, Julian Sitkovetsky, was a

well-known Russian violinist; his mother, **Bella Davidovich,** is the famous pianist. He studied at the Moscow Cons. with Yankelevich and Bezrodny. In 1977 he went to the U.S., where he took lessons with Galamian at the Juilliard School in N.Y. In 1979 he received the 1st prize at the prestigious Fritz Kreisler Competition in Vienna. He maintains a dual residence in Wiesbaden and in N.Y. City, pursuing a concert career in Europe and the U.S., often joining his mother in duo recitals. He is married to the opera singer Susan Roberts.

Sitsky, Larry, Australian pianist, teacher, and composer; b. Tientsin, China (of Russian parents), Sept. 10, 1934. He was improvising on the piano and writing music by the age of 10; in 1951 his family went to Australia, where he studied piano with Winifred Burston and composition with Raymond Hanson at the New South Wales State Conservatorium in Sydney (1951–55); after further piano training with Petri in San Francisco (1958–61), he taught piano at the Queensland State Conservatorium (1961–65); then was head of keyboard studies (1966–78) and composition and musicology (from 1981) at the Canberra School of Music. He undertook official exchange visits as a composer to Russia (1977) and to the People's Republic of China (1983), where he was the 1st composer from the West to make an official visit since the 1950s; also appeared as a pianist in China (1945–51). He specializes in late Romantic and early 20th-century scores, showing preference for the music of Busoni. He publ. *Busoni and the Piano: The Music, the Writings, the Recordings: A Complete Survey* (Westport, Conn., 1986) and *The Classical Reproducing Piano Roll: A Catalogue-Index* (2 vols., Westport, Conn., 1990); also made transcriptions and ed. some of Busoni's scores for publication. Sitsky's own music is advanced, although it makes no systematic use of particular devices.

WORKS: OPERAS: *Fall of the House of Usher* (Hobart Festival, Aug. 1965); *Lenz* (1969–70; Sydney, March 1974); *The Fiery Tales*, after Chaucer and Boccaccio (1975); *Voices in Limbo*, radio opera (1977); *The Golem* (1980; orch. extracts as *Songs and Dances* and *9 Orchestral Interludes*, 1984). **ORCH.:** *4 Orchestral Pieces*, cycle of individually titled works that may be performed separately (1966–74); 3 violin concertos: No. 1, with Women's Voices, *Mysterium Cosmographicum* (1971); No. 2, *Gurdjieff* (1983); No. 3, *I Ching: The 8 Trigrams* (1987); Concerto for Wind Quintet and Orch. (Sydney, April 3, 1971); Concerto for Trombone, Keyboards, and Percussion, *Kundalini* (1981–82); Concerto for Clarinet and Strings, *Santana* (1981); Guitar Concerto (1984); Concerto for Orch. (completion and realization of Busoni's *Fantasia Contrappuntistica*; 1984). **CHAMBER:** Sonata for Solo Violin (1959); 2 sonatas for Solo Flute: No. 1 (1959); No. 2, *The 14 Days of Bardo Thodol* (1979). Wind Quartet (1963); *Sinfonia* for 10 Players (1964; also as a TV ballet, *The Dark Refuge*); Sonata for 2 Guitars (1968); 2 string quartets: No. 1 (1969); No. 2, *13 Concert Studies* (1981); *Fantasia No. 3* for Trumpet and String Ensemble, in memory of Don Banks (1980); *Zugerq* for Clarinet and Bongos (1984); 5 trios (1969–86); *Diabolus in Musica* for 4 Percussionists (1986); *The Secret Gates of the House of Osiris* for Flute, Viola, Cello, and Piano (1987); other chamber works; various piano pieces. **VOCAL:** *Concert Aria* for Low Voice, Ensemble, Tape, and Synthesizer (1972); *7 Orchestral Songs* for Low Voice and Orch. (1979); *De Profundis* for Baritone, 2 String Quartets, and Percussion (1982); *Deep in My Hidden Country*, cantata for Soprano, Flute, Cello, Piano, and Percussion (1983–84); solo songs.

BIBL.: "L. S.: Interview," *Musica Viva Bulletin* (Sept./Dec. 1984).

Sitt, Hans, Bohemian violinist, violist, conductor, teacher, and composer; b. Prague, Sept. 21, 1850; d. Leipzig, March 10, 1922. He studied violin at the Prague Cons.; held various positions as a violinist and conductor of theater orchs. in Breslau, Prague, and Chemnitz. In 1881 he settled in Leipzig; organized a series of popular concerts there; was violist in the Brodsky Quartet; conducted the Bachverein (1885–1903) and other musical societies. He wrote 3 violin concertos, a

Viola Concerto, 2 cello concertos; publ. valuable studies for the violin; also *Praktische Violaschule*; *Schulausgabe neuerer Violinlitteratur* (5 books); and (with Reinecke) *Lyrica*, a collection of 30 Classical and Romantic pieces for violin and piano.

Sivori, (Ernesto) Camillo, renowned Italian violinist and composer; b. Genoa, Oct. 25, 1815; d. there, Feb. 19, 1894. At a very early age he began violin lessons with Restano and then with Giacomo Costa, Paganini's former teacher; after further training with Agostino Dellepiane, he received instruction from Paganini himself (1824). In 1827 he made his debut in Genoa, then performed in London and Paris. Returning to Genoa, he took lessons in composition with Giovanni Serra (1829); played 1st violin in the theater orch., and taught at the Cons. He made an extensive tour of Europe in 1841–42, and then toured throughout the world during the next 14 years with great success; won notable acclaim during his tours of North and South America (1846–50). From 1855 his career was centered in Europe, where he made regular appearances in France, Italy, Germany, and England. He resided in Paris (1863–92), and then retired to Genoa. Many honors were bestowed upon him, including the French Légion d'honneur in 1886. He was one of the great violin virtuosos of the 19th century; his demanding compositions include 2 violin concertos (both 1841) and numerous solo violin pieces, including the greatly admired *Études-caprices* (1867).

BIBL.: E. James, *C. S.: A Sketch of His Life, Talent, Travels and Successes* (London, 1845; 2nd ed., 1846); G. Da Fieno, *Die due chiarissimi genovesi: Cav. C. S., violinista e comm. F. Romani, poeta lirico* (Milan, 1871); A. Pierrottet, *C. S.* (Milan, 1896); B. Schwarz, *Great Masters of the Violin* (N.Y., 1983).

Sixt, Johann Abraham, German organist, harpsichordist, and composer; b. Gräfenhausen, Baden-Württemberg, Jan. 3, 1757; d. Donaueschingen, Jan. 30, 1797. He was the son of a schoolmaster and organist, Johann Michael Sixt, who gave him his 1st music lessons; later attended the Stuttgart Karlsschule; was in Vienna in 1784, and received a recommendation from Mozart. After holding minor posts as an organist, he was active in Stuttgart; became a harpsichordist and composer at the Donaueschingen court in 1784. He wrote piano trios, sonatas, and other instrumental works; of particular interest are his lieder, with long introductions in the accompaniment, setting the mood of the text.

BIBL.: F. Baser, "J.A. S.," *Musica*, XII (1958); idem, "J.A. S.," *Schwäbische Heimat*, X (1959).

Sixta, Jozef, Slovak composer; b. Jičín, May 12, 1940. He studied with Očenaš at the Cons. in Bratislava (1955–60) and with Alexander Moyzes at the Music Academy there (1960–64); then went to Paris, where he had lessons with Messiaen and Jolivet. Returning to Bratislava, he taught at the Academy of Music there.

WORKS: Quintet for Piano and Winds (1961); *Fantasia* for Piano (1962); Sym. (1964); String Quartet (1965); *Variations* for 13 Instruments (1967); *Synchronia* for String Orch. (1968); *Asynchronia* for String Orch. (1970); Nonet (1970); Quartet for 4 Flutes (1976).

Sjöberg, Svante Leonard, Swedish organist, conductor, and composer; b. Karlskrona, Aug. 28, 1873; d. there, Jan. 18, 1935. He studied at the Stockholm Cons. with Nordquist and Dente, and in Berlin with Bruch; was organist at the Stadskyrka in Karlskrona and conductor of the Musikförening (1901–34). He wrote an overture to *Gustaf Vasa* (1901); some chamber music; songs.

Sjögren, (Johan Gustaf) Emil, Swedish organist and composer; b. Stockholm, June 16, 1853; d. there, March 1, 1918. He studied composition at the Stockholm Cons. with H. Berens, in Berlin with Kiel, and in Vienna with Grädener. In 1891 he was appointed organist at St. John's Church in Stockholm. His importance as a composer rests chiefly on his songs, of which he wrote about 200, to texts in Swedish, French, and German; he also wrote a *Festspel* for Orch. (1892); several choruses; 5 violin sonatas; a Cello Sonata; 2 piano sonatas; several groups of lyric pieces for piano.

BIBL.: C. Nyblom, *E. S.* (Stockholm, 1916); G. Norlen, W. Peterson-Berger, T. Rangström et al., *E. S. in memoriam* (Stockholm, 1918); S. Svensson, "E. S.s vokala lyrik," *Svensk Tidskrift för Musikforskning*, XVIII (1935).

Skaggs, Ricky, American country-music singer and instrumentalist; b. Cordell, Ky., July 18, 1954. He took up the mandolin in early childhood and began performing regularly in his teens; then was a member of the Stanley Brothers' band (1970–72) and subsequently of several bluegrass groups. He organized his own Boone Creek band (1975); after he appeared as a singer and instrumentalist with Emmylou Harris, his career blossomed in 1981. He toured widely and made many successful recordings. His fine tenor voice and mastery on the mandolin, fiddle, and acoustic guitar made him one of the most potent figures in traditional country-music circles.

Skalkottas, Nikos (actually **Nikolaos**), greatly talented Greek composer; b. Chalkis, island of Euboea, March 8, 1904; d. Athens, Sept. 19, 1949. He studied violin with his father, with his uncle, and with a nonrelated violinist at the Athens Cons. (1914–20). In 1921 he went to Berlin, where he continued his violin studies at the Hochschule für Musik (until 1923); then took lessons in music theory with Philipp Jarnach (1925–27). But the greatest influence on his creative life was Schoenberg, with whom he studied in Berlin (1927–31); Schoenberg, in his book *Style and Idea*, mentions Skalkottas as one of his most gifted disciples. Skalkottas eagerly absorbed Schoenberg's instruction in the method of composition with 12 tones related only to one another, but in his own music applied it in a very individual manner, without trying to imitate Schoenberg's style. In Berlin, Skalkottas also received some suggestions in free composition from Kurt Weill (1928–29). He returned to Athens and earned his living by playing violin in local orchs., but continued to compose diligently, until his early death from a strangulated hernia. His music written between 1928 and 1938 reflects Schoenberg's idiom; later works are tonally conceived, and several of them are in the clearly ethnic Greek modalities, set in the typical asymmetric meters of Balkan folk music. After his death, a Skalkottas Society was formed in Athens to promote performances and publications of his works; about 110 scores of various genres are kept in the Skalkottas Archives in Athens.

WORKS: ORCH.: Symphonic Suite, op. 3 (1928; not extant); Concerto for Winds and Orch., op. 6 (1929; Berlin, May 20, 1930; not extant); *Little Suite* for Violin and Chamber Orch., op. 23 (1929; Berlin, April 6, 1930; not extant); Concerto for Piano, Violin, and Chamber Orch., op. 21 (Berlin, April 6, 1930; not extant); Piano Concerto No. 1, op. 16 (1931); Concertino for 2 Pianos and Orch., op. 20 (1935; Geneva, June 15, 1952); Symphonic Suite No. 1, op. 3a (1935; London, April 28, 1973); *36 elliniki choriie (36 griechische Tänze)*, op. 11 (1931–36; reorchestrated, 1948–49); Piano Concerto No. 2, op. 17 (1937–38; Hamburg, Oct. 12, 1953); Violin Concerto, op. 22 (1937–38; Hamburg, May 14, 1962); *The Maiden and Death*, ballet, op. 12 (1938; Athens, May 10, 1940; rev. version, Athens, March 23, 1947); Cello Concerto, op. 26 (1938; not extant); Piano Concerto No. 3, with 10 Winds and Percussion, op. 18 (1938–39; London, July 9, 1969); Concerto for Violin, Viola, Winds, and Double Basses, op. 25 (1939–40; London, July 7, 1969); *10 Musical Sketches* for String Orch., op. 8 (1940; Athens, Nov. 6, 1952; also for String Quartet); *Little Suite* for Strings, op. 7 (1942; Zürich, Aug. 30, 1953); *The Return of Ulysses*, overture, op. 5 (1942–43; London, June 23, 1969; also for 2 Pianos, 1943–44); Double Bass Concerto, op. 27 (1942–43); Symphonic Suite No. 2, op. 4 (1944; orchestrated, 1946–49; London, Jan. 31, 1966); Concerto for 2 Violins and Orch., op. 24 (1944–45); *Klassiki symphonia* for Winds and Double Basses, op. 9 (1947); *Henry V*, incidental music to Shakespeare's play, op. 2 (1947–48; not extant); Sinfonietta, op. 10 (1948); Piano Concertino, op. 19 (1948); *Kleine Tanz-Suite: 4 Tänze für Ballett*, op. 13 (Athens, May 2, 1949); *Dance Suite*, op. 15 (1948–49); *Nocturne-divertimento* for Xylophone and Orch., op. 29 (1949); *The Sea*, op. 14 (1949). **CHAMBER:**

String Trio, op. 40b (1924; not extant); String Quartet, op. 31 (1924; not extant); 2 suites for 2 Pianos, op. 79e-f (1924–25); Sonata for Solo Violin, op. 69 (1925); String Quartet No. 1, op. 32 (1928; Berlin, June 19, 1929); Sonata No. 1 for Violin and Piano, op. 49a (1928; not extant); String Quartet No. 2, op. 33 (1929; Athens, Nov. 27, 1930; not extant); *Easy Music* for String Quartet, op. 32a (1929; Athens, Nov. 27, 1930; not extant); Sonatina No. 1 for Violin and Piano, op. 46 (1929; only 2nd movement extant); Octet for Flute, Clarinet, Bassoon, Trumpet, Trombone, and Piano Trio (1929; not extant); Sonatina No. 2 for Violin and Piano, op. 47 (1929); Octet for Woodwind Quartet and String Quartet, op. 30 (Berlin, June 2, 1931); String Quartet No. 3, op. 34 (1935; Oxford, July 3, 1965); String Trio, op. 41 (1935; Athens, March 20, 1954); Sonatina No. 3 for Violin and Piano, op. 48 (1935); Sonatina No. 4 for Violin and Piano, op. 49 (1935); Piano Trio, op. 42 (1936); *March of the Little Soldiers Rondo, Nightpiece, Little Chorale, and Fugue* for Violin and Piano, opp. 53–56 (1937–38); Suite for Cello and Piano, op. 61 (1937–38; not extant); Duo for Violin and Viola, op. 44 (1938); *8 Variations on a Greek Folk Tune* for Piano Trio, op. 43 (1938; Athens, March 31, 1950); *Gavotte, Scherzo, Menuetto cantato* for Violin and Piano, opp. 57–58 (1939); Concertino for Oboe and Piano, op. 28 (1939); *Scherzo* for Piano Quartet, op. 39 (1939–40); Sonata No. 2 for Violin and Piano, op. 50 (1940); String Quartet No. 4, op. 35 (1940; London, July 13, 1969); 2 quartets for Oboe, Bassoon, Trumpet, and Piano, opp. 40-40a (1940–42; Bamberg, June 15, 1968); Concertino for Trumpet and Piano, op. 68 (1940–42); *Largo* for Cello and Piano, op. 66 (1941–42); *Sonata concertante* for Bassoon and Piano, op. 67 (1943); *Little Serenade* for Cello and Piano, op. 64 (1945); *Bolero* for Cello and Piano, op. 63 (1945); *9 Greek Dances* for String Quartet, op. 37 (1938–47); Cello Sonatina, op. 62 (1949); *Tender Melody* for Cello and Piano, op. 65 (1949); also many vocal works, including *The Spell of May*, incidental music for Mezzo-Soprano, Orch., and Chorus ad libitum, op. 1 (1943–44; orchestrated 1949; London, May 30, 1961); numerous piano pieces.

BIBL.: J. Papaioannou, "Nikos S.," H. Hartog, ed., *European Music in the Twentieth Century* (London, 1957).

Škerjanc, Lucijan Marija, Slovenian pianist, conductor, teacher, writer on music, and composer; b. Graz, Dec. 17, 1900; d. Ljubljana, Feb. 27, 1973. He studied composition in Vienna with Marx and in Paris with d'Indy. He became a music teacher in Ljubljana in 1922, where he was a teacher of composition at the Cons. (1926–40) and at the Academy of Music (1940–70), serving as rector of the latter (1945–47). He was conductor of the Glasbena Matica orch. society (1925–45), and director of the Slovene Philharmonia (1950–55). Much of his music reflects neo-Romantic trends, with some impressionistic colors; in later works he also utilized 12-note techniques. **WORKS: ORCH.:** 2 violin concertos (1927, 1944); 5 syms. (1931, 1938, 1940, 1941, 1943); Piano Concerto (1940); Bassoon Concerto (1953); Harp Concerto (1954); Concerto for Clarinet, Strings, Percussion, and Harp (1958); Flute Concerto (1962); Concerto for Piano, Left Hand (1963). **CHAMBER:** 5 string quartets (1917, 1921, 1925, 1935, 1945); Wind Quintet (1925); Piano Trio (1935); String Quintet (1945); Concertone for 4 Cellos (1954); other chamber works; piano pieces; songs.

Škerl, Dane, Slovenian composer; b. Ljubljana, Aug. 26, 1931. He studied with Škerjanc at the Ljubljana Academy of Music, graduating in 1952; then took courses in electronic music in Cologne. He taught at the Sarajevo Academy of Music (1960–70); in 1970 he was appointed to the faculty of the Ljubljana Academy of Music. **WORKS:** 2 ballets: *Kontrasti* (Contrasts; 1967) and *Grozdanin kikot* (1969); Concertino for Violin and String Orch. (1948); *Prelude and Scherzo* for Clarinet and Strings (1948); Concertino for Piano and Strings (1949); 5 syms. (1951, 1963, 1965, 1970, 1972); *Serenade* for Strings (1952); Concerto for Orch. (1956); *Rolo* for Orch. (1959); *Inventions* for Violin and Strings (1960); *18 Etudes* for Strings (1960); *5 Compositions* for Clarinet and Strings (1961); *Contrasts* for Orch. (1962); Clarinet Concerto (1963); *Little Suite* for Orch. (1965); *7 Bagatelles* for Strings (1966); *Improvvisazione concertante* for Horn, Viola, and Chamber Orch. (1968); Trombone Concerto (1970); cantata, *Moj dom* (My House; 1962); *4 Miniatures* for Flute, Bassoon, and Piano (1957); *Prelude and Scherzo* for Violin, Clarinet, and Piano (1959); *Skica* (Sketch) for Violin and Piano (1964); *3 Improvisations* for Flute, Cello, and Piano (1966); piano pieces.

Skilton, Charles Sanford, American composer and teacher; b. Northampton, Mass., Aug. 16, 1868; d. Lawrence, Kans., March 12, 1941. He first studied in Germany; after graduating from Yale Univ. (B.A., 1889), he studied in N.Y. with Harry Rowe Shelley (organ) and Dudley Buck (composition); then at the Berlin Hochschule für Musik with Bargiel (1891–93). From 1893 to 1896 he was director of music at the Salem (N.C.) Academy and College, and conducted the local orch. there; then filled a similar post at the State Normal School in Trenton, N.J. (1897–1903); in 1903 he was engaged as a prof. of organ and theory at the Univ. of Kansas, Lawrence, where he remained most of his life. He made a detailed study of Indian music, and introduced Indian motifs into the traditional forms of the suite and fantasy. **WORKS: OPERAS:** *Kalopin* (1927; received the David Bispham Memorial Medal, 1930; not perf.); *The Sun Bride* (NBC, April 17, 1930); *The Day of Gayomair* (1936; not perf.). **ORCH.:** *Suite Primeval*, on Indian melodies, in 2 parts: 2 *Indian Dances* (originally for String Quartet, 1915; Minneapolis, Oct. 29, 1916) and part II (Minneapolis, Nov. 13, 1921); *Autumn Night* (Detroit, Dec. 11, 1930); *Shawnee Indian Hunting Dance* (Detroit, Dec. 11, 1930); *A Carolina Legend*, symphonic poem; *Mt. Oread*, overture. **VOCAL:** *The Witch's Daughter*, cantata (1918); *The Guardian Angel*, oratorio (1925); *From Forest and Stream* for Women's Chorus (1930). **CHAMBER:** 2 *Indian Dances* for String Quartet (1915; orchestrated as part 1 of *Suite Primeval*); Sonatina for Violin and Piano (1923); String Quartet (1938); also piano pieces, including *3 Indian Sketches* (1919) and *Shawnee Indian Hunting Dance* (1929); organ music, including *American Indian Fantasy* (1926; also arranged for Orch., 1932).

BIBL.: J. Howard, *C.S. S.* (N.Y., 1929); J. Smith, *C.S. S. (1868–1941)*, Kansas Composer (thesis, Univ. of Kansas, 1979).

Skinner, Ernest M(artin), American organ builder; b. Clarion, Pa., Jan. 15, 1866; d. Duxbury, Mass., Nov. 27, 1960. He was the founder of the Ernest M. Skinner Co., organ builders, originally of Dorchester, later of Methuen, Mass. Until 1905 the business was carried on by Skinner himself; it was then incorporated, with Skinner as president. From 1917 to 1932 he was technical director of the Skinner Organ Co., which in 1932 was merged with the Aeolian Co. of Garwood, N.J., and became the Aeolian-Skinner Organ Co. He was especially successful in the construction of organ pipes reproducing the exact tone color of the various woodwind instruments and the French horn; among several important inventions is the "duplex windchest," by means of which the stops of 2 manuals are made interchangeable, and the arrangement of placing the stops on swinging sides. The Skinner Co. built the organ in the National Cathedral at Washington, D.C. He publ. *The Modern Organ* (1915; 6th ed., 1945) and *The Composition of the Organ* (1947).

BIBL.: D. Holden, *The Life and Work of E.M. S.* (Richmond, Va., 1985).

Sklavos, George, Greek composer and teacher; b. Brailov, Rumania (of Greek parents), Aug. 20, 1888; d. Athens, March 19, 1976. He studied with Armand Marsick at the Athens Cons.; was instructor there from 1913 to 1968. He devoted himself chiefly to the musical theater. **WORKS: OPERAS:** *Niovi* (1919); *Lestenisa* (1923; Athens, March 14, 1947); *Kassiani* (1929–36; Athens, Oct. 30, 1959); *Krino st' akroyali* (Lily at the Seashore; 1937–41); *Amphitryon* (1955–60); *St' Ai Yorghi to panyghiri* (At St. George's Fair; 1961–62). **ORCH.:** *Aetos* (Eagle; 1922); *Arcadian Suite* (1922);

Cretan Fantasy (1922); *Heroiko poiema* (1926); 2 idylls (1928); *Nissiotikos gamos* (Marriage on a Greek Island; 1937); also choruses; songs; incidental music.

Sköld, (Karl) Yngve, Swedish composer; b. Vallby, April 29, 1899. He studied piano and composition in Stockholm (1915–18), then in Brno (1920–22) and Prague (1922). From 1938 to 1964 he was librarian of the Swedish Composers' Society. His music blends Nordic Romanticism with subdued modernity.
WORKS: 4 syms. (1915, 1937, 1949, 1968); 3 piano concertos (1917, 1946, 1968); Cello Sonata (1927); 4 string quartets (1930, 1955, 1965, 1974); *Suite concertante* for Viola and Orch. (1936); *Sinfonia di chiesa* for Orch. (1939); Violin Concerto (1941); Cello Concerto (1947); *Double Concerto* for Violin, Cello, and Orch. (1950); *Divertimento* for Orch. (1951); Quintet for 2 Flutes, Cello, and Piano (1958); Sonata for Viola and Organ (1962); Concertino for 5 Winds, Timpani, and Strings (1963); 2 piano sonatas (1963); Piano Sonatina (1970); *Divertimento* for Violin, Viola, and Cello (1971); *Trio domestico* for Piano Trio (.1974).

Skriabin, Alexander (Nikolaievich). See Scriabin, Alexander (Nikolaievich).

Škroup, František Jan, prominent Bohemian conductor and composer, brother of **Jan Nepomuk Škroup;** b. Osice, near Pardubice, June 3, 1801; d. Rotterdam, Feb. 7, 1862. He received his musical training from his father, the teacher and composer **Dominik Josef Škroup** (1766–1830). He studied law in Prague. In 1827 he became assistant conductor, and in 1837 principal conductor, at the Estates Theater, Prague, and remained at that post until 1857; he put into performance several Wagner operas for the 1st time in Prague. He wrote several operas to Czech librettos, which he conducted in Prague: *Dráteník* (The Tinker; Feb. 2, 1826); *Oldřich a Božena* (Dec. 14, 1828); *Libušin snatek* (Libusa's Marriage; April 11, 1835; rev. 1849; April 11, 1850); *Die Geisterbraut* (Nov. 17, 1836); *Drahomira* (Nov. 20, 1848); *Der Mergeuse* (Nov. 29, 1851). In 1860 he went to Rotterdam as conductor of a German opera troup. He also scored a success as a composer with his incidental music to Josef Tyl's play *Fidlovačka* (Prague, Dec. 21, 1834), which includes the song *Kde domov můj?* (Where Is My Home?); the latter became so famous that it was mistaken for a folk song and the 1st part of it was made into the Czech national anthem in 1918. He also wrote sacred music, cantatas, choruses, chamber music, and songs.
BIBL.: J. Plavec, *F. S.* (Prague, 1946).

Škroup, Jan Nepomuk, Bohemian conductor, teacher, and composer, brother of **František Jan Škroup;** b. Osice, near Pardubice, Sept. 15, 1811; d. Prague, May 5, 1892. He studied at the Prague Gymnasium; conducted various orch. concerts and theater productions and served as choirmaster in churches and monasteries in Prague; was choirmaster at St. Vitus Cathedral (1848–87). He wrote the operas *Svédové v Praze* (The Swedish Girl in Prague; 1844), *Der Liebesring* (1860), and *Vineta* (1861); also *Festive Overture* (1842); incidental music; choral works; partsongs; songs.

Skrowaczewski, Stanislaw, eminent Polish-born American conductor and composer; b. Lwow, Oct. 3, 1923. His father was a brain surgeon; his mother, a fairly good pianist. A precocious *wunderkind* even for a fabled land of child prodigies, he composed an orch. overture at the age of 8, played a piano recital at 11, and performed Beethoven's 3rd Piano Concerto at 13, conducting the orch. from the keyboard. He studied composition and conducting at the Lwow Cons. and also physics, chemistry, and philosophy at the Univ. of Lwow. The oppressive Nazi occupation of Poland interrupted his studies, and an unfortunate bomb exploded in the vicinity of his house, causing an injury to his hands that interfered with his further activities as a concert pianist. After World War II, he went to Krakow to study composition with Palester and conducting with Bierdiajew. In 1947 he received a French government scholarship which enabled him to study composition with Bou-langer and conducting with Kletzki in Paris. He then conducted the Wroclaw Orch. (1946–47), the State Silesian Phil. in Katowice (1949–54), the Krakow Phil. (1954–56), and the National Phil. in Warsaw (1956–59). In 1956 he won 1st prize in the international conducting competition in Rome. On Dec. 4, 1958, he made his American debut as a guest conductor of the Cleveland Orch., scoring an impressive success. In 1960 he was named music director of the Minneapolis Sym. Orch. (renamed the Minnesota Orch. in 1968), and asserted his excellence both as a consummate technician of the baton and a fine interpreter of the classic and modern repertoire. In 1966 he became a naturalized American citizen. In the interim, he appeared as a guest conductor in Canada, Mexico, South America, Israel, Hawaii, Australia, and New Zealand. As an opera conductor, he made his Metropolitan Opera debut in N.Y. on Jan. 8, 1970, with *Die Zauberflöte*. In 1979 he resigned as music director of the Minnesota Orch., and was made its conductor emeritus. He was principal conductor and musical adviser of the Hallé Orch. in Manchester from 1984 to 1990; also served as music adviser of the St. Paul (Minn.) Chamber Orch. (1987–88).
WORKS: BALLET: *Ugo and Parisina* (1949). ORCH.: 4 syms.: No. 1 (1936); No. 2 (1945); No. 3, *Symphony for Strings* (1947); No. 4 (1954); *Overture 1947* (1947); *Music at Night*, extracts from *Ugo and Parisina* (1949–51); Concerto for English Horn and Orch. (Minneapolis, Nov. 21, 1969); *Ricercari notturni* for Saxophone and Orch. (1977; Minneapolis, Jan. 19, 1978); Concerto for Clarinet and Orch. (1981); Violin Concerto (Philadelphia, Dec. 12, 1985). CHAMBER: 4 string quartets; Trio for Clarinet, Bassoon, and Piano (1982–84); *Fantasie per quattro* for Clarinet, Violin, Cello, and Piano (1984); *Fantasie per sei* for Oboe, Violin, Viola, Cello, Bass, and Piano (Atlanta, April 16, 1989); String Trio (1990); also 6 piano sonatas; songs; theater and film music.

Skuherský, František Zdeněk (Xavier Alois), Bohemian conductor, teacher, music theorist, and composer; b. Opočno, July 31, 1830; d. Budweis, Aug. 19, 1892. He 1st studied medicine; then had music lessons with Kittl in Prague; from 1854 to 1866 he was in Innsbruck, where he conducted the Musikverein. In 1866 he went to Prague as director of the Organ School; also was choirmaster at St. Hastal's and at the Holy Trinity, was director of the court chapel, and was a teacher of music theory at the Czech Univ. (from 1882). In 1890 he retired. Among his outstanding pupils were J. F. Foerster and Janáček. Skuherský was a leading figure in the reform of church music in his homeland. He publ. several texts on music theory (in Prague): *O formách hudebních* (Musical Form; 1873; 2nd ed., 1884); *Nauka o hudební komposici* (Theory of Musical Composition; 4 vols., 1880–84); *Nauka o harmonii na vědeckém základě ve formě nejjednodušší* (Theory of Harmony on a Scientific Basis in the Simplest Form; 1885).
WORKS: OPERAS: *Samo* (1854; unfinished); *Der Apostat* (rev. as *Vladimir, bohů zvolenec* [Vladimir, the Gods's Chosen One], Prague, Sept. 27, 1863); *Der Liebesring* (Innsbruck, 1861; Czech version as *Lora*, Prague, April 13, 1868); *Der Rekrut* (Czech version as *Rektor a generál* [Rector and General], Prague, March 28, 1873); *Smrt krále Václava* (King Wenceslas's Death; 1868; unfinished). ORCH.: Sym. (n.d.); *Máj* (May), symphonic fantasia (1874; Brünn, April 22, 1877); 3 *Fugues* (1883–84). CHAMBER: Piano Quintet (1871); String Quartet (1871); Piano Trio (1871–72); also much sacred vocal music; choruses; songs; piano pieces; organ music.

Slatkin, Felix, American violinist and conductor, father of **Leonard (Edward) Slatkin;** b. St. Louis, Dec. 22, 1915; d. Los Angeles, Feb. 8, 1963. He studied violin with Zimbalist and conducting with Reiner at the Curtis Inst. of Music in Philadelphia; was a member of the St. Louis Sym. Orch. (1931–37). In 1937 he went to Los Angeles, where he played in film studio orchs. In 1947 he organized the Hollywood String Quartet, which gave regular performances until it was dissolved in 1961. He also was active as a conductor, especially in programs of light music.

Slatkin, Leonard (Edward), prominent American conductor, son of **Felix Slatkin;** b. Los Angeles, Sept. 1, 1944. He received musical training in his youth, studying violin, viola, piano, and conducting; after attending Indiana Univ. (1962) and Los Angeles City College (1963), he received valuable advice from Susskind at the Aspen Music School (1964); then studied conducting with Morel at the Juilliard School of Music in N.Y. (Mus.B., 1968). In 1968 he joined the St. Louis Sym. Orch. as assistant conductor to Susskind, and was successively named associate conductor (1971), associate principal conductor (1974), and principal guest conductor (1975). He made his European debut in London as a guest conductor with the Royal Phil. in 1974. He was music adviser of the New Orleans Phil. (1977–80); also music director of the Minnesota Orch. summer concerts (from 1979). In 1979 he became music director of the St. Louis Sym. Orch.; took it on a major European tour in 1985. In 1990 he also became music director of the Great Woods Performing Arts Center in Mansfield, Mass., the summer home of the Pittsburgh Sym. Orch., and in 1991 of the Blossom Music Center, the summer home of the Cleveland Orch. He appeared widely as a guest conductor of major orchs., both in North America and Europe, demonstrating particular affinity for works of the 19th and 20th centuries.

BIBL.: *Current Biography* (Feb. 1986).

Slavenski (real name, **Štolcer**), **Josip,** outstanding Yugoslav composer and teacher; b. Čakovec, May 11, 1896; d. Belgrade, Nov. 30, 1955. He studied with Kodály in Budapest and with Novák in Prague. He taught at the Zagreb Cons. (1923–24); then settled in Belgrade, where he taught at the Stankovič Music School; subsequently was a teacher (1937–45) and a prof. (1945–55) at the Academy of Music. About 1930 he adopted the name Slavenski, which he used exclusively in his publ. works. A musician of advanced ideas, he attempted to combine Slavic melodic and rhythmic elements with modern ingredients; he experimented with nontempered scales and devised a "natural" scale of 53 degrees to the octave. His significance was only fully recognized in his homeland after his death.

WORKS: ORCH.: *Nocturne* (1916; rev. 1920); *Chaos* (1918–32); *Prasimfonia* ("protosymphony") for Organ, Piano, and Orch. (1919–26); *Balkanophonia,* suite (Berlin, Jan. 25, 1929); Violin Concerto (1927); *Religiophonia (Simfonija orijenta)* for Solo Voices, Chorus, and Orch. (1934); *4 balkanske igre* (4 Balkan Dances; 1938); *Simfonijski epos* (1944–46); Piano Concerto (1951; unfinished). **CHAMBER:** 4 string quartets (1923; *Lyric,* 1928; 1938; c.1949, arr. from the *4 Balkan Dances* for Orch., 1938); *Slavenska,* sonata for Violin and Piano (1924); *Sonata religiosa* for Violin and Organ (1925); Wind Quintet (1930); Piano Trio (1930); *Pesme moje majik* (Songs of My Mother) for Alto and String Quartet (1944); also choral pieces; piano music; incidental scores; film music.

Slavický, Klement, Czech composer; b. Tovačov, Sept. 22, 1910. He studied composition with Jirák and Suk, and conducting with Dědeček and Talich at the Prague Cons. (1927–31) and then at its Master School there (1931–33); was music director of the Czech Radio in Prague (1936–51); then taught privately.

WORKS: ORCH.: *Fantasia* for Piano and Orch. (1931); 4 sinfoniettas (1940; 1962; 1972–80; 1982); *Moravian Dance Fantasies* (1951); *Rhapsodic Variations* (1953; Prague, Feb. 17, 1954). **CHAMBER:** 2 string quartets (1932, 1972); *2 Compositions* for Cello and Piano (1936); Trio for Oboe, Clarinet, and Bassoon (1937); *Suite* for Oboe and Piano (1959); *Partita* for Violin (1962); *Intermezzi mattutini* for Flute and Harp (1965); *Trialogo* for Violin, Clarinet, and Piano (1966); *Capricci* for Horn and Piano (1967); *Musica monologica* for Harp (1968); *Poema a rondo* for Cello and Piano (1973); *Přátelstí* (Friendship), violin sonata (1974); *Sentenze* for Trumpet and Piano (1976). **PIANO:** *3 Compositions* (1947); *Zamyšlení nad životem* (Contemplation of Life), sonata 1957–58; *In Black and White* (1958); *12 Little Etudes* (1964); *Etudes and Essays,* 7 pieces

(1965); *Suite* for Piano, 4-hands (1968); *Cycle* (1970); also organ pieces; choruses; songs.

Slavík, Josef, Bohemian violinist and composer; b. Jince, March 26, 1806; d. Budapest, May 30, 1833. He studied violin with Pixis and theory and composition with B. Weber at the Prague Cons. (1816–23); went to Vienna in 1826; then went on a concert tour; in 1829 he was appointed to the court chapel in Vienna, and became a friend of Schubert, who dedicated to him his Fantasia in C major, D.934, which Slavík performed for the 1st time on Jan. 20, 1828. Among his own compositions are a Violin Concerto (1823) and *Grand Potpourri* for Violin and Orch. (1826).

BIBL.: J. Pohl, *J. S.: Český houslista* (J. S.: Czech Violinist; Prague, 1906); S. Klíma, *J. S.* (Prague, 1956); L. Ginzburg, *J. S.* (Moscow, 1957).

Slawson, Wayne, American composer and music theorist; b. Detroit, Dec. 29, 1932. He studied at the Univ. of Michigan (B.A. in mathematics, 1955; M.A. in composition, 1959) and Harvard Univ. (Ph.D. in psychoacoustics, 1965); was a computer programmer and systems analyst with the U.S. Air Force, the Rand Corp. in Santa Monica, Calif. (1955–57), and the Mitre Corp. in Bedford, Mass. (1959–62), specializing in speech synthesis. He taught at Yale Univ. (1967–72), the Univ. of Pittsburgh (1972–86; prof. from 1984), and the Univ. of Calif. in Davis (from 1986), where he directed the Computer and Electronic Music Studio. He composed *MUCH*, electronic music from various sources, with Robert Morris (1971–74); developed the music and speech synthesis programs MUSE (1961) and SYNTAL (1969–89); publ. numerous articles on theory and psychoacoustics, his monograph *Sound Color* (Berkeley, 1985) seeking to systematize timbre for analytical and compositional purposes.

WORKS: *Music for an Ordination* for Organ and Choir (1963); *Wishful Thinking about Winter* for Tape (1967); *5 Turns for 10* for Variable Ensemble (1970); *Pieces* for String Quartet (1970; rev. and augmented as *Limits,* 1977); *Motions* for Orch. (1973); *Pity . . . Not* for Choir (1974); *Reflections* for Cello and Piano (1975; rev. and augmented as *Rereflections,* 1988); *Death, Love, and the Maiden* for Tape (1975); *Omaggio a Petrarca* for Choir (1975); *Minglings* for Men's Chorus (1976); *poor flesh and trees, poor stars and stones* for Tape (1977); Variations for 2 Violins (1977); *Colors,* computer music (1981); *Triad* for Clarinet, Horn, and Cello (1984); *Greetings,* computer music (1985); *Quatrains Miniature I, II, III,* computer music (1985); *Quatrains Miniature IV, V,* computer music (1985); *Quick Trick* for String Quartet (1987); *Swapper I,* computer music (1989; rev. and augmented as *If These 2 Tolled,* 1990).

Sleeper, Henry Dike, American organist, music educator, and composer; b. Patten, Maine, Oct. 9, 1865; d. Winter Park, Fla., Jan. 28, 1948. He studied at Harvard Univ. and the Hartford Theological Seminary (graduated, 1891); although ordained as a Congregational minister, he turned to music and studied with J.K. Paine, Clarence Eddy, and Frederick Root; after teaching at various colleges and at the Univ. of Wisconsin, he was a teacher (1898–1924) and head of the music dept. (1902–24) at Smith College; also was active as a church organist (from 1895). He wrote orch. pieces, partsongs, and an organ suite.

Slenczynska, Ruth, American pianist of precocious talent; b. Sacramento, Calif., Jan. 15, 1925. Her father, a violinist, subjected her to severe discipline when her musical talent was revealed in early childhood; she was only 4 when she began piano lessons with Alma Schmidt-Kennedy; played in public in Berlin at 6 years and with an orch. in Paris at 11. She made a sensation and was acclaimed by European critics as a prodigy of nature; she took lessons with Egon Petri, Artur Schnabel, Alfred Cortot, and others in Europe and America, and even played for Rachmaninoff, who became interested in her destiny. However, she developed psychological difficulties with her father, whose promotion of her career became obsessive, and had to cease public appearances; when she played concerts at the age of 15, the critics characterized her performances as mechanical reproductions of the music, seemingly without any personal projection. She then withdrew from public performances; after taking a degree in psychology at the Univ. of Calif. at Berkeley (1954), she resumed her career; also taught at Southern Illinois Univ. at Edwardsville (1964–90). She publ. a book of memoirs (with L. Biancolli), *Forbidden Childhood* (N.Y., 1957), in which she recounted the troubles of a child prodigy's life; she also brought out a pedagogical ed., *Music at Your Fingertips. Aspects of Pianoforte Technique* (with A. Lingg; N.Y., 1961).

Slezak, Leo, famous Austrian tenor; b. Mährisch-Schönberg, Moravia, Aug. 18, 1873; d. Egern am Tegernsee, Bavaria, June 1, 1946. He studied with Adolf Robinson; as a youth, sang in the chorus of the Brünn Opera, making his operatic debut there as Lohengrin (March 17, 1896), one of his finest roles. He appeared with the Berlin Royal Opera (1898–99); in 1901 he became a member of the Vienna Opera, where he was active until 1926; also performed frequently in Prague, Milan, and Munich. Not satisfied with his vocal training, he went to Paris, where he studied with Jean de Reszke in 1907. He made his London debut with marked acclaim as Lohengrin, May 18, 1900, at Covent Garden; appeared in America for the 1st time as Otello, with the Metropolitan Opera in N.Y. (Nov. 17, 1909); remained with the company until 1913. He returned to the Vienna Opera as a guest artist, making his farewell appearance in *Pagliacci* on Sept. 26, 1933. Slezak also toured widely as a recitalist of impeccable taste; also made some appearances in films. He was a man of great general culture, and possessed an exceptionally sharp literary wit, which he displayed in his reminiscences, *Meine sämtlichen Werke* (1922) and *Der Wortbruch* (1927); both were later combined in a single vol. (1935; Eng. tr. as *Songs of Motley: Being the Reminiscences of a Hungry Tenor*, London, 1938); he also publ. *Der Rückfall* (1940). A final book of memoirs, *Mein Lebensmärchen*, was publ. posthumously (1948). His son, the film actor Walter Slezak, publ. Slezak's letters, *Mein lieber Bub. Briefe eines besorgten Vaters* (Munich, 1966), and *What Time's the Next Swan?* (N.Y., 1962), alluding to the possibly apocryphal story of the swan failing to arrive in time during one of his father's performances as Lohengrin, thus prompting the non-Wagnerian query from the hapless hero.

BIBL.: L. Kleinenberger, *L. S.* (Munich, 1910); J. Dennis, "L. S.," *Record Collector*, XV (1964).

Slick, Grace, American rock singer and songwriter; b. Chicago, Oct. 30, 1939. She attended Finch College and the Univ. of Miami; then moved to San Francisco and soon became a part of the radical milieu there. With her husband, Jerry Slick, and others, she formed the rock group The Great Society in 1965. In 1966 she joined The Jefferson Airplane, which airlifted her to the stratosphere of rock fame; she rose even higher with its successor, The Jefferson Starship, in 1974; in 1978 she struck out on her own, only to return to it in 1981. Among her most successful songs were *Somebody to Love* (1967) and *White Rabbit* (1967).

Slobodianik, Alexander, brilliant Russian pianist; b. Kiev, Sept. 5, 1941. He studied at the Moscow Cons. with Gornostaeva, graduating in 1964. In 1966 he received 4th prize at the Tchaikovsky Competition in Moscow. He subsequently undertook numerous concert tours in Russia and abroad. He was particularly successful during his American tours in the 1970s. Like most Russian pianists who venture abroad, he astounds by his unlimited technical resources, but he is also appreciated for the romantic élan of his playing.

Slobodskaya, Oda, esteemed Russian soprano; b. Vilnius, Dec. 10, 1888; d. London, July 29, 1970. She studied at the St. Petersburg Cons.; made her operatic debut as Lisa in *The Queen of Spades* at the Maryinsky Theater there in 1917. She also sang the regular repertoire there, including the roles of Marguerite in *Faust* and Aida. She emigrated in 1922; sang in Paris, at La Scala in Milan, and in Buenos Aires; eventually settled in London; sang Venus in *Tannhäuser* at Covent Garden

in 1932. She developed an active career in England, establishing herself as an authoritative interpreter of Russian songs in recital; she also joined the faculty of the Guildhall School of Music and proved a sympathetic and effective voice teacher.
BIBL.: M. Leonard, *S.: A Biography of O. S.* (London, 1978).

Slonimsky, Nicolas (actually, **Nikolai Leonidovich**), legendary Russian-born American musicologist of manifold endeavors, uncle of **Sergei (Mikhailovich) Slonimsky;** b. St. Petersburg, April 27, 1894. A self-described failed wunderkind, he was given his 1st piano lesson by his illustrious maternal aunt **Isabelle Vengerova,** on Nov. 6, 1900, according to the old Russian calendar. Possessed by inordinate ambition, aggravated by the endemic intellectuality of his family of both maternal and paternal branches (novelists, revolutionary poets, literary critics, university professors, translators, chessmasters, economists, mathematicians, inventors of useless artificial languages, Hebrew scholars, speculative philosophers), he became determined to excel beyond common decency in all these doctrines; as an adolescent, wrote out his future biography accordingly, setting down his death date as 1967, but survived. He enrolled in the St. Petersburg Cons. and studied harmony and orchestration with 2 pupils of Rimsky-Korsakov, Kalafati and Maximilian Steinberg; also tried unsuccessfully to engage in Russian journalism. After the Revolution he made his way south; was a rehearsal pianist at the Kiev Opera, where he took some composition lessons with Glière (1919); then was in Yalta (1920), where he earned his living as a piano accompanist to displaced Russian singers, and as an instructor at a dilapidated Yalta Cons.; thence proceeded to Turkey, Bulgaria, and Paris, where he became secretary and piano-pounder to Serge Koussevitzky. In 1923 he went to the U.S.; became coach in the opera dept. of the Eastman School of Music in Rochester, N.Y., where he took an opportunity to study some more composition with the visiting prof. Selim Palmgren, and conducting with Albert Coates; in 1925 he was again with Koussevitzky in Paris and Boston, but was fired for insubordination in 1927. He learned to speak polysyllabic English and began writing music articles for the *Boston Evening Transcript* and the *Christian Science Monitor;* ran a monthly column of musical anecdotes of questionable authenticity in *Etude* magazine; taught theory at the Malkin Cons. in Boston and at the Boston Cons.; conducted the Pierian Sodality at Harvard Univ. (1927–29) and the Apollo Chorus (1928–30). In 1927 he organized the Chamber Orch. of Boston with the purpose of presenting modern works; with it he gave 1st performances of works by Charles Ives, Edgar Varèse, Henry Cowell, and others. He became a naturalized U.S. citizen in 1931. In 1931–32 he conducted special concerts of modern American, Cuban, and Mexican music in Paris, Berlin, and Budapest under the auspices of the Pan-American Assoc. of Composers, producing a ripple of excitement; he repeated these programs at his engagements with the Los Angeles Phil. (1932) and at the Hollywood Bowl (1933), which created such consternation that his conducting career came to a jarring halt. From 1945 to 1947 he was, by accident (the head of the dept. had died of a heart attack), lecturer in Slavonic languages and literatures at Harvard Univ. In 1962–63 he traveled in Russia, Poland, Yugoslavia, Bulgaria, Rumania, Greece, and Israel under the auspices of the Office of Cultural Exchange at the U.S. State Dept., as a lecturer in native Russian, ersatz Polish, synthetic Serbo-Croatian, Russianized Bulgarian, Latinized Rumanian, archaic Greek, passable French, and tolerable German. Returning from his multinational travels, he taught variegated musical subjects at the Univ. of Calif., Los Angeles; was irretrievably retired after a triennial service (1964–67), ostensibly owing to irreversible obsolescence and recessive infantiloquy; but, disdaining the inexorable statistics of the actuarial tables, continued to agitate and even gave long-winded lecture-recitals in institutions of dubious learning. As a composer, he cultivated miniature forms, usually with a gimmick, e.g., *Studies in Black and White* for Piano (1928) in "mutually exclusive consonant counterpoint," a song cycle, *Gravestones*, to texts from tombstones in an old cemetery in Hancock, N.H. (1945), and *Minitudes,* a collection of 50 quaquaversal piano pieces (1971–77). His only decent orch. work is *My Toy Balloon* (1942), a set of variations on a Brazilian song, which includes in the score 100 colored balloons to be exploded *f f f* at the climax. He also conjured up a *Möbius Strip-Tease,* a perpetual vocal canon notated on a Möbius band to be revolved around the singer's head; it had its 1st and last performance at the Arrière-Garde Coffee Concert at UCLA, on May 5, 1965, with the composer officiating at the piano non-obbligato. A priority must be conceded to him for writing the earliest singing commercials to authentic texts from the *Saturday Evening Post* advertisements, among them *Make This a Day of Pepsodent, No More Shiny Nose,* and *Children Cry for Castoria* (1925). More "scholarly," though no less defiant of academic conventions, is his *Thesaurus of Scales and Melodic Patterns* (1947), an inventory of all conceivable and inconceivable tonal combinations, culminating in a mind-boggling "Grandmother Chord" containing 12 different tones and 11 different intervals. Beset by a chronic itch for novelty, he coined the term "pandiatonicism" (1937), which, *mirabile dictu,* took root and even got into reputable reference works, including the 15th ed. of the *Encyclopædia Britannica.* In his quest for trivial but not readily accessible information, he blundered into the muddy field of musical lexicography; publ. *Music Since 1900,* a chronology of musical events, which actually contains some beguiling serendipities (N.Y., 1937; 4th ed., 1971; supplement, 1986); took over the vacated editorship (because of the predecessor's sudden death during sleep) of Thompson's *International Cyclopedia of Music and Musicians* (4th to 8th eds., 1946–58) and accepted the editorship of the 5th, 6th, 7th, and 8th eds. of the prestigious *Baker's Biographical Dictionary of Musicians* (N.Y., 1958, 1978, 1984, 1991). He also abridged this venerable vol. into *The Concise Baker's Biographical Dictionary of Musicians* (N.Y., 1988). In 1978 he mobilized his powers of retrospection in preparing an autobiography, *Failed Wunderkind,* subtitled *Rueful Autopsy* (in the sense of self-observation, not dissection of the body); the publishers, deeming these titles too lugubrious, renamed it *Perfect Pitch* (N.Y., 1988). He also translated Boris de Schloezer's biography of Scriabin from the original Russian (Berkeley and Los Angeles, 1987), which was followed by his *Lectionary of Music,* a compendium of articles on music (N.Y., 1988). His other writings include *Music of Latin America* (N.Y., 1945; several reprints; also in Spanish, Buenos Aires, 1947); *The Road to Music,* ostensibly for children (N.Y., 1947); *A Thing or Two about Music* (N.Y., 1948; inconsequential; also lacking an index); *Lexicon of Musical Invective,* a random collection of pejorative reviews of musical masterpieces (N.Y., 1952); numerous articles for encyclopedias; also a learned paper, *Sex and the Music Librarian,* valuable for its painstaking research; the paper was delivered by proxy, to tumultuous cachinnations, at a symposium of the Music Library Assoc., at Chapel Hill, N.C., Feb. 2, 1968.

BIBL.: H. Cowell, "N. S.," *American Composers on American Music* (Stanford, Calif., 1933; cf. reciprocally, N. Slonimsky, "Henry Cowell," ibid.); C. Nott, "The Many-Sided Musical Mind of N. S.," *Ovation* (July 1984); L. Weschler, "N. S.," *The New Yorker* (Nov. 17 and 24, 1986); R. Kostelanetz, "Conversation with N. S. about His Composing," *Musical Quarterly,* No. 3 (1990).

Slonimsky, Sergei (Mikhailovich), greatly talented Russian composer, nephew of **Nicolas (Nikolai Leonidovich) Slonimsky;** b. Leningrad, Aug. 12, 1932. A member of a highly intellectual family (his father was a well-known Soviet author; his paternal grandfather, an economist, the author of the 1st book on Karl Marx in the Russian language; his father's maternal uncle was a celebrated Russian ed. and literary critic; his father's maternal aunt was the noted piano teacher Isabelle Vengerova), he studied at the Leningrad Cons., taking composition with Boris Arapov and Orest Evlakhov (graduated, 1955) and piano with Vladimir Nilsen (graduated, 1956); he also took courses in musicology with F. Rubtzov (folk music) and

N. Uspensky (polyphonic analysis). While a student, he wrote a fairy-tale suite, *Frog-Princess,* and in 1951 composed a string quartet on Russian folk motifs. In 1959 he was appointed to the faculty of the Leningrad Cons. For further study of folk music he traveled into the countryside, in the rural regions of Pskov and Novgorod. Concurrently, he explored the technical modalities of new music, in the tradition of Soviet modernism, evolving a considerable complexity of texture in a framework of dissonant counterpoint, while safeguarding the tonal foundation in triadic progressions. Some of his works, such as his opera *Virineya,* represent a contemporary evolution of the Russian national school of composition, broadly diatonic and spaciously songful; his other works tend toward ultramodern practices, including polytonality, microtonality, dodecaphony, tone-clusters, amplified sound, prepared piano, electronic sonorism, aleatory proceedings, and spatial placement of instruments. His Concerto for Orch. employs electronically amplified guitars and solo instruments; even more advanced is his *Antiphones* for String Quartet, employing non-tempered tuning and an "ambulatory" setting, in which the players are placed in different parts of the hall and then walk, while playing, en route to the podium; the piece is especially popular at modern music festivals. A prolific composer, he has written 9 syms. and a remarkably varied catalogue of chamber music pieces which he produces with a facility worthy of Rossini. He also has an easy hand with choral works. Although his natural impulse tends towards the newest sound elements, he proves remarkably successful in gathering and transforming folk motifs and rhythms, as in his *Novgorod* choruses, composed for the American Festival of Soviet Music of 1988. The most unusual subject, for a Soviet composer, was an opera based on the life and death of the Catholic Queen of Scotland, Mary Stuart. *Mary Stuart* was 1st produced in Kuibyshev on Oct. 1, 1983, and then subsequently performed in Leningrad and in Leipzig (1984). It was then selected for a gala production at the Edinburgh Festival in Scotland, where it was given on Aug. 22, 1986, by the Leningrad Opera in a performance in the Russian language. The score utilizes authentic Scottish folk songs, suitably arranged in modern harmonies, as well as original themes in the pentatonic scale. The opera received the prestigious Glinka Prize in 1983. Slonimsky encountered considerable difficulties in producing his chamber opera, *The Master and Margarita,* after a novel by Bulgakov, because the subject had to do with mystical religious events. The Soviet authorities delayed its production for nearly 15 years. Finally, with a liberal change in the political climate, the opera was produced, 1st in East Germany, and, eventually and to considerable acclaim, in Leningrad, on Dec. 1, 1989. Practically all of his music, including the operas, has been publ. Apart from his work as a composer and teacher, Slonimsky contributes music criticism to Soviet magazines; he also publ. a valuable analytic survey, *The Symphonies of Prokofiev* (Leningrad, 1976).

WORKS: OPERAS: *Virineya* (Leningrad, Sept. 30, 1967); *The Master and Margarita,* chamber opera after a novel by Bulgakov (1973; Leningrad, Dec. 1, 1989); *Mary Stuart,* opera-ballad (1978–80; Kuibyshev, Jan. 31, 1981).

BALLET: *Icarus* (1962–69; Moscow, May 29, 1971).

ORCH.: 9 syms.: No. 1 (1958; Leningrad, March 11, 1962); No. 2 (1977; Leningrad, Sept. 21, 1979); No. 3 (Leningrad, Dec. 15, 1982); No. 4, dedicated to the memory of his father (Kuibyshev, Oct. 1, 1983); No. 5 (1983; Kuibishev, Oct. 1, 1984); No. 6 (1983; Leningrad, June 21, 1986); No. 7 (1984; Leningrad, June 21, 1986); No. 8 for Chamber Orch. (Vilnius, Sept. 30, 1985); No. 9 (Leningrad, Feb. 18, 1989); No. 9 (Leningrad, Feb. 18, 1989); *Carnival Overture* (1957); *Choreographic Miniatures* (1964); *Concerto buffo* (1964–65; Leningrad, April 28, 1966); Concerto for Sym. Orch., 3 Electric Guitars, and Solo Instruments (1973; Leningrad, Feb. 9, 1974); *Dramatic Song* (1974); *Festive Music* for Balalaika, Castanets, and Orch. (1975); *Symphonic Motet* (1976); *Quiet Music* (1981; Leningrad, March 7, 1982); *Concerto primaverile* for Violin and String Orch. (Vilnius, Oct. 8, 1983; Sergei Stadler, soloist).

CHAMBER: String Quartet on Russian Themes (1951); 2 Pieces for Viola and Piano (1956); Suite for Viola and Piano (1959); Sonata for Violin Solo (1960); *Chromatic Flute and Humoresque* for Flute (1961); 3 Pieces for Cello (1964); *Dialogues* for Wind Quintet (1964); *Antiphones* for String Quartet (1968); *Sonatina allegro* for Horn and Piano (1974); *Monologue and Toccata* for Clarinet and Piano (1974); *Solo espressivo* for Oboe (1975); *Exotic Suite* for 2 Violins, 2 Electric Guitars, Saxophone, and Percussion (1976; Leningrad, Nov. 3, 1978); *Legend* for Domra and Piano (1976); *Merry Rondo* for Domra and Piano (1976); *Novgorod Dance* for Clarinet, Trombone, Cello, Piano, and Percussion (1980); *Rondo*, on a theme by Gounod, for Trumpet and Piano (1980); *Musica lirica* for Flute, Violin, and Harpsichord (1981); *Dithyramb* for Cello Ensemble and Piano (1982); *In the World of Animals*, children's suite for Cello and Piano (1982); *Suite* (Seattle, July 1990). **VOCAL:** *Songs of Freedom*, on Russian folk motifs, for Mezzo-soprano, Baritone, and Piano (1957); *Spring has arrived*, vocal cycle on verses by Japanese poets, for Voice and Piano (1958); *Polish Stanzas*, vocal cycle on works by the Polish poet Anthoni Slonimski, 1st cousin of the composer's father (1963); *Lyric Stanzas*, vocal cycle for Voice and Piano (1964); *Voice from the Chorus*, cantata to words by Alexander Blok (1964); *Farewell to a Friend* for Voice and Piano (1966); *Monologues* for Soprano, Oboe, Horn, and Harp (1967); 2 *Russian Songs* for Chorus a cappella (1968); 6 *Songs* to words by Anna Akhmatova (1969); *Northern Landscapes* for Chorus a cappella (1969); *Merry Songs* for Voice and Piano (1971); *Choral Games* for Children's Chorus, Boy Soloist, and 2 Percussion Instruments (1972); *Evening Music* for Chorus a cappella (1973); 4 *Songs* to words by Osip Mandelstam (1974); 10 *Songs* to words by Anna Akhmatova (1974); 4 *Russian Songs* for Chorus a cappella (1974); *Virineya*, suite-oratorio from the opera of the same name (1974); *Pesnohorka* (Sing-Chorus) for Contralto, Flute, Oboe, Trumpet, Balalaika, Accordion, 3 Electric Guitars, Castanets, and Vibraphone, on Russian folk songs (1975); *Songs of the Troubadours*, vocal cycle on old French ballads for Soprano, Tenor, 4 Recorders, and Lute (1975); *Songs of Songs* for Soprano, Tenor, Chorus, Oboe, French Horn, and Harp (1975); *Bashkir Girl's Song* for Voice, Flute, and 2 Bongos (1977); *Quiet Flows the Don* for Mixed Choir, to words of old Cossack chants, after Sholokhov's novel (1977); 2 *Poems* to words by Pushkin, for Chorus a cappella (1979); Suite from the opera *Mary Stuart* for Chorus and Orch. (1980); 2 *Songs* to words by Alexander Blok, for Mezzo-soprano and Piano (1980); *White Night* for Chorus a cappella (1980); *Morning Song* for Children's Chorus and Snare Drum (1981); *Strophes of Dhammapada*, after the classic Buddhist epic, for Soprano, Harp, and Percussion (1983; Leningrad, Feb. 21, 1984); *Song of Leningrad* for Bass, Chorus, and Orch. (1983); *Little Triptych* for Chorus a cappella (1983); 2 *Vocalises* for Soprano and Mezzo-soprano (1983); *Railroad* for Chorus, Trumpet, Piano, and Percussion (1983); *White Night in Leningrad* for Chorus a cappella (1983); 4 *Strophes* from *Oedipus Colonus* of Sophocles, for Chorus (1983). **PIANO:** Sonata (1962); *Three Graces*, suite in the form of variations (1964); *Children's Pieces* (1970); *Coloristic Fantasy* (1972); *Tiny Pieces* for children (1973); *Serenade from a Musical*, street song (1976); *Round Dance and Merry Rumba* (1977); *Charlie Chaplin Whistles On* (1978); *Cat's Lullaby* (1978); *Hungarian March* for Piano, 4-hands (1980); *Intermezzo in Memory of Brahms* (1980); *Travel Suite* (1981); *Romantic Waltz* (1982); *Variations on a Theme by Mussorgsky* (1984); 3 pieces: *Jump Rope; Blues; Metro* (1984). **ORGAN:** *Pastorale and Toccata* (1961); *Chromatic Poem* (1969); *Round Dance and Fugue* (1976); *Rondo-Humoresque* (1979); also incidental music for theatrical plays; film music. **BIBL.:** A. Milka, *S. S.* (Leningrad, 1976).

Slonimsky, Yuri, eminent Russian writer on ballet; b. St. Petersburg, March 13, 1902; d. there (Leningrad), April 23, 1978. He studied law at the Univ. of St. Petersburg; at the same time, attended the Inst. of Art History; was a co-founder, with Georgi Balanchivadze (George Balanchine), of Young Bal-

let, a group organized to promote modern dance. A brilliant ballet critic, Slonimsky achieved a fine reputation for his penetrating analysis of current productions and historical essays on ballet. He publ. *Giselle* (Leningrad, 1926; rev. 1969); *Masters of Ballet* (Moscow, 1937); *The Soviet Ballet* (in Eng., N.Y., 1947); *Tchaikovsky and the Ballet Theater of His Time* (Moscow, 1956). He was the author of several ballet librettos, among them *Icarus* by Sergei Slonimsky (no relation).

Slonov, Mikhail, Russian folk-song collector and composer; b. Kharkov, Nov. 16, 1869; d. Moscow, Feb. 11, 1930. He collected Russian folk songs and composed a number of songs, some of them popularized by Chaliapin, such as *Farewell*.

Sloper, (Edward Hugh) Lindsay, English pianist, teacher, and composer; b. London, June 14, 1826; d. there, July 3, 1887. He studied with Moscheles in London, A. Schmitt in Frankfurt, and Rousselot in Paris; made his debut in London (1846); became a popular concert pianist and teacher there. He wrote many piano pieces; studies and textbooks for piano; songs.

Slovák, Ladislav, Slovak conductor; b. Bratislava, Sept. 9, 1919. He studied organ and conducting at the Bratislava Cons. (1938–45) and conducting with Talich at the Bratislava Academy of Music (1949–53). He was music director of Bratislava Radio (from 1949), where he founded and conducted its choir; after serving as an assistant to Mravinsky and the Leningrad Phil. (1953–55), he returned to Bratislava as conductor of the Radio Orch. (1955–61); then was chief conductor of the Slovak Phil. there (1961–81) and of the Prague Sym. Orch. (1972–76). In 1964 he was made an Artist of Merit and in 1977 a National Artist by the Czech government.

Smallens, Alexander, Russian-born American conductor; b. St. Petersburg, Jan. 1, 1889; d. Tucson, Ariz., Nov. 24, 1972. He was taken to the U.S. as a child; became a naturalized citizen in 1919. He studied at the Inst. of Musical Art and the College of the City of N.Y. (B.A., 1909); then took courses at the Paris Cons. (1909). He was assistant conductor of the Boston Opera (1911–14); accompanied the Anna Pavlova Ballet Co. on a tour of South America (1915–18); then was on the staff of the Chicago Opera (1919–23) and of the Philadelphia Civic Opera (1924–31); from 1927 to 1934 he was assistant conductor of the Philadelphia Orch., and from 1947 to 1950, was music director at Radio City Music Hall in N.Y. In 1934 he conducted the premiere of Gershwin's *Porgy and Bess* in Boston; conducted it on a European tour in 1956. He retired in 1958.

Smalley, Roger, English pianist, composer, and teacher; b. Swinton, Manchester, July 26, 1943. He studied piano with Antony Hopkins and composition with Peter Racine Fricker and John White at the Royal College of Music in London (1961–65); also took private composition lessons with Goehr and attended Stockhausen's Cologne course for new music (1965). With Tim Souster, he founded the contemporary music ensemble Intermodulation, with which he toured extensively in Europe until 1976. In 1968 he became the 1st artist-in-residence at King's College, Cambridge; in 1974 he was named musician-in-residence at the Univ. of Western Australia, where he became a research fellow (1976) and then senior lecturer. As a pianist, he consistently champions avant-garde music. His compositions are steeped in electronic and aleatory techniques. **WORKS: MUSIC THEATER:** *William Derrincourt*, entertainment for Baritone, Male Chorus, and Instrumental Ensemble (1978; Perth, Aug. 31, 1979); *The Narrow Road to the Deep North*, "journey" for Baritone and 6 Players (London, Nov. 29, 1983). **ORCH.:** *Variations* for Strings (1964); *Gloria Tibi Trinitas* (1965; rev. 1969; Liverpool, Sept. 30, 1969); *Beat Music* for Percussion, Electric Organ, Viola, Soprano Saxophone, and Orch. (London, Aug. 13, 1971); *Strata* for 15 Solo Strings (1971; London, Feb. 19, 1973); *Konzertstuck* for Violin and Orch. (Perth, Feb. 23, 1980); Sym. (1981; London, Aug. 25, 1982); Piano Concerto (Swansea, Aug. 11, 1985); *Strung Out* for 13 Solo Strings (Perth, Feb. 20, 1988). **CHAMBER:** String

Sextet (1964); *Missa Parodia II*, nonet (1967); *Pulses* for Brass, Percussion, and Live Electronics (1969; rev. 1986); *Zeitebenen* for Live Electronic Ensemble and Tape (1973); *Echo II* for Cello and Stereo Tape-delay System (1978); *Echo III* for Trumpet and Stereo Tape-delay System (1978); String Quartet (1979); *Movement* for Flute and Piano (1976–80); *Echo IV* for Horn and Stereo Tape-delay System (1986); *Impulses* for Flute, Trombone, Percussion, Piano, Synthesizer, and Cello (1986); *Ceremony I* for Percussion Quartet (1987); various piano pieces; also choral music.

Smallwood, Williams, English organist and composer; b. Kendal, Dec. 31, 1831; d. there, Aug. 6, 1897. He studied with Dr. Camidge and H. Phillips; was organist of the Kendal Parish Church (1847–97). He composed didactic piano pieces and salon music; also anthems, hymns, songs, etc. His *Pianoforte Tutor* had an immense sale.

Smareglia, Antonio, talented Italian composer; b. Pola, Istria, May 5, 1854; d. Grado, Istria, April 15, 1929. He was trained in engineering before turning to music; studied composition with Franco Faccio at the Milan Cons. (1873–77), who became an early champion of his works. He 1st attracted notice with his opera *Preziosa* (Milan, Nov. 19, 1879); wrote his finest opera for Trieste, *Nozze istriane* (March 28, 1895). In 1903 he was stricken with blindness and was soon reduced to poverty; through the intervention of the Tartini Cons. in Trieste, which made him honorary artistic director in 1921, and the local industrialist Carlo Sai, his fortunes were mended and he was able to present several of his operatic and orch. works. He also engaged in private teaching. After the onset of his blindness, he continued to compose with the assistance of an amanuensis.

WORKS: OPERAS: *Preziosa* (Milan, Nov. 19, 1879); *Bianca di Cervia* (Milan, Feb. 7, 1882); *Re Nala* (Venice, Feb. 9, 1887; destroyed by the composer); *Il vassallo di Szigeth* (1st perf. as *Der Vasall von Szigeth*, Vienna, Oct. 4, 1889; 1st perf. in Italian, Pola, Oct. 4, 1930); *Cornil Schut* (1st perf. as *Cornelius Schut*, Prague, May 20, 1893; 1st perf. in Italian, Trieste, Feb. 17, 1900; rev. as *Pittori fiamminghi*, Trieste, Jan. 21, 1928); *Nozze istriane* (Trieste, March 28, 1895); *La falena* (Venice, Sept. 4, 1897); *Oceàna* (Milan, Jan. 22, 1903); *Abisso* (Milan, Feb. 9, 1914). ORCH.: *Leonora, ballata di Bürger,* "descriptive sym." (1877); *Oceàna Suite* (1902). VOCAL: *Caccia lontana,* melodramatic scene (Milan, Aug. 10, 1875); *Inno a Tartini* for Voices and Band (1896); *Salve regina* for Voices and Piano or Harmonium (1930).

BIBL.: G. Zuccoli, *A. S.* (Trieste, 1922); G. Nacamuli, *A. S.* (Trieste, 1930); A. Smareglia, *Vita ed arte di A. S.: un capitolo di storia del teatro lirico italiano* (Lugano, 1932; 2nd ed., 1936); M. Smareglia, *A. S. nella storia del melodramma italiano: accolta di critiche musicali e di altri documenti* (Pola, 1934); V. Levi, *Nozze istriane: nel centenario della nascita di A. S.* (Trieste, 1954); S. Benco, *Ricordi di A. S.* (Duino, 1968).

Smart, family of prominent English musicians:
(1) Sir George (Thomas) Smart, organist, conductor, and composer; b. London, May 10, 1776; d. there, Feb. 23, 1867. He was a chorister in the Chapel Royal under Aryton until 1791; studied organ with Cupuis and composition with Arnold. In 1791 he became organist at St. James's Chapel, Hampstead Road, and also was a violinist in Salomon's concert series. In 1811 he conducted a series of Dublin concerts and was knighted. He was a founder in 1813 of the Phil. Soc. of London, where he was active as a conductor until 1844, leading the 1st British performance of Beethoven's 9th Sym. in 1826. He also conducted the Lenten oratorio concerts at Covent Garden and Drury Lane (1813–25) and the City Amateur Concerts (1818–22), at which he introduced many works of Mozart and Beethoven. In 1822 he was named organist at the Chapel Royal, and in 1838 was made one of its composers. He toured widely in Europe; his valuable journal relates his conversations with Beethoven in Vienna. He also befriended Weber, who died in his house during his visit to London. His works include 6 anthems, 8 glees, Kyries, Psalm tunes, and chants. He also

ed. Gibbons's madrigals (1841) and Handel's *Dettingen Te Deum* (1846–47).

BIBL.: H. and C. Cox, *Leaves from the Journals of Sir G. S.* (London, 1907); C. Maclean, "Sir G. S., Musician-Diarist," *Sammelbände der Internationalen Musik-Gesellschaft,* X (1909); A. King, "The Importance of Sir G. S.," *Musical Times* (Dec. 1950).

(2) Henry Smart, violinist, brother of **Sir George (Thomas) Smart;** b. London, 1778; d. Dublin, Nov. 27, 1823. He studied violin with W. Cramer, beginning his career at age 14 at the Opera, the Concert of Ancient Music, and the Academy of Ancient Music. He served as concertmaster of the orch. at the Lyceum Theatre (1809–12) and at the Drury Lane Theatre (1812–21); also was active with the Phil. Soc. (from 1813). He opened a piano factory in 1821. He wrote a ballet, *Laurette* (1803).

(3) Henry Thomas Smart, organist and composer, son of **Henry Smart;** b. London, Oct. 26, 1813; d. there, July 6, 1879. He was educated at Highgate and received instruction in instrumentation from W.H. Kearns. After serving as organist of the Blackburn parish church (1831–36), he returned to London as organist of St. Philip's Church, Regent Street, in 1836; also was active as a music critic for the *Atlas* and engaged in teaching; then was organist at St. Luke's, Old Street (1844–64), and at St. Pancras, Euston Road (1864–79). In 1864 he became blind and in 1879 was awarded a government pension, but died without its benefits. His partsongs and organ pieces were especially admired. He also wrote an opera, *Berta, or The Gnome of the Hartzberg* (London, May 26, 1855); an oratorio, *Jacob* (Glasgow, 1873); cantatas; services; anthems; hymn tunes; songs; etc.

BIBL.: J. Broadhouse, *H. S.'s Compositions for Organ* (London, 1880); W. Spark, *H. S.* (London, 1881); D. Hill, *H. S.: Neglected Nineteenth Century Organ Master* (Schagen, 1988); idem, "H. S.'s Contribution to Victorian Hymnody," *Musical Times* (April 1989).

Smend, Friedrich, eminent German musicologist; b. Strasbourg, Aug. 26, 1893; d. Berlin, Feb. 10, 1980. He studied theology at the Univs. of Strasbourg, Tübingen, Marburg, and Münster (Ph.D., 1921, with the diss. *Die Acta-Berichte über Bekehrung des Paulus nach ihrem Quellenwert*). He was employed at the Univ. of Münster Library (1921–23) and at the Prussian State Library in Berlin (1923–45); was a teacher (1945–46), director of the library (1946–58), a prof. (1949–58), and rector (1954–57) at the Kirchliche Hochschule in Berlin. In 1951 he received an honorary doctorate in theology from the Univ. of Heidelberg and in 1954 an honorary doctorate in philosophy from the Univ. of Mainz. He was an authority on the life and music of Bach.

WRITINGS: *Luther und Bach* (Berlin, 1947); *J.S. Bachs Kirchen-Kantaten* (Berlin, 1947–49; 2nd ed., 1950); *Johann Sebastian Bach bei seinem Namen gerufen* (Kassel and Basel, 1950); *Bach in Köthen* (Berlin, 1951); *Goethes Verhältnis zu Bach* (Berlin and Darmstadt, 1955); *Bach Studien: Gesammelte Reden und Aufsätze* (Kassel, 1969).

BIBL.: *Festschrift für F. S. zum 70. Geburtstag dargebracht von Freunden und Schülern* (Berlin, 1963); A. Dürr, "F. S. (1893–1980)," *Die Musikforschung,* XXXIII (1980); R. Tatlow, "J.S. Bach and the Baroque Paragram: A Reappraisal of F. S.'s Number Alphabet Theory," *Music & Letters* (May 1989).

Smetáček, Václav, noted Czech oboist, conductor, and teacher; b. Brünn, Sept. 30, 1906; d. Prague, Feb. 18, 1986. He studied oboe with Ladislav Skuhrovský, composition with Jaroslav Křička, and conducting with Metod Doležil and Pavel Dědeček at the Prague Cons. (1922–30); also took courses in musicology and esthetics at the Charles Univ. in Prague (Ph.D., 1933). In 1928 he founded the Prague Wind Quintet, remaining with it until 1955; was also oboist in the Czech Phil. (1930–33). He conducted the Radio Orch. (1934–43) and the Hlahol Choir (1934–46) in Prague; became chief conductor of Prague's FOK Sym. Orch. in 1942; it became the Prague Sym. Orch. in 1952, and he continued to lead it until 1972; he also appeared widely as a guest conductor. He taught at Prague's Cons. and Academy of Music (1945–66). In 1962 he was made an Artist of Merit and in 1976 a National Artist by the Czech government. He was best known for his performances of Czech music, both traditional and contemporary.

BIBL.: L. Šíp, *V. S.* (Prague, 1957).

Smetana, Bedřich, great Bohemian composer; b. Leitomischl, March 2, 1824; d. Prague, May 12, 1884. His talent manifested itself very early, and although his father had misgivings about music as a profession, he taught his son violin; Bedřich also had piano lessons with a local teacher, making his 1st public appearance at the age of 6 (Oct. 14, 1830). After the family moved to Jindrichův Hradec in 1831, he studied with the organist František Ikavec; continued his academic studies in Jihlava and Německý Brod, then entered the Classical Grammar School in Prague in 1839; also had piano lessons with Jan Batka, and led a string quartet for which he composed several works. His lack of application to his academic studies led his father to send him to the gymnasium in Plzeň, but he soon devoted himself to giving concerts and composing. He met a friend of his school days there, Kateřina Kolářová, whom he followed to Prague in 1843; he was accepted as a theory pupil of Kolářová's piano teacher, Josef Proksch, at the Music Inst. To pay for his lessons, Bedřich Kittl, director of the Prague Cons., recommended Smetana for the position of music teacher to the family of Count Leopold Thun. He took up his position in Jan. 1844, and for 3½ years worked earnestly in the count's service; also continued to study theory and to compose. Bent on making a name for himself as a concert pianist, Smetana left the count's service in the summer of 1847 and planned a tour of Bohemia; however, his only concert in Plzeň proved a financial disaster, and he abandoned his tour and returned to Prague, where he eked out a meager existence. He wrote to Liszt, asking him to find a publisher for his op. 1, the *6 Characteristic Pieces* for piano; Liszt was impressed with the score, accepted Smetana's dedication, and found a publisher. In 1848 Smetana established a successful piano school, and on Aug. 27, 1849, he married Kolářová. In 1850 he became court pianist to the abdicated Emperor Ferdinand. His reputation as a pianist, especially as an interpreter of Chopin, grew, but his compositions made little impression. The death of his children and the poor health of his wife (who had tuberculosis) affected him deeply; he set out for Sweden in 1856; gave a number of successful piano recitals in Göteborg, where he remained. He soon opened his own school, and also became active as a choral conductor. His wife joined him in 1857, but the cold climate exacerbated her condition; when her health declined, they decided to return to Prague (1859), but she died en route, in Dresden, on April 19, 1859. Stricken with grief, Smetana returned to Göteborg. Before his wife's death, he had composed the symphonic poems *Richard III* and *Valdštýnův tábor* (Wallenstein's Camp); he now began work on a 3rd, *Hakan Jarl*. On July 10, 1860, he married Betty Ferdinandi, which proved an unhappy union. During Smetana's sojourn in Sweden, Austria granted political autonomy to Bohemia (1860), and musicians and poets of the rising generation sought to establish an authentic Bohemian voice in the arts. Agitation for the erection of a national theater in Prague arose; although earlier attempts to write operas in a Bohemian vein had been made by such composers as František Škroup and Jiří Macourek, their works were undistinguished. Smetana believed the time was ripe for him to make his mark in Prague, and he returned there in May 1861. However, when the Provisional Theater opened on Nov. 18, 1862, its administration proved sadly unimaginative, and Smetana contented himself with the conductorship of the Hlahol Choral Soc., teaching, and writing music criticism. In his articles he condemned the poor musical standards prevailing at the Provisional Theater. In 1862–63 he composed his 1st opera, *Braniboři v Čechách* (The Brandenburgers in Bohemia), conducting its successful premiere at the Provisional Theater on Jan. 5, 1866. His next opera, *Prodaná nevěsta* (The Bartered Bride),

proved a failure at its premiere in Prague under his direction on May 30, 1866, but eventually it was accorded a niche in the operatic repertoire at home and abroad. Smetana became conductor of the Provisional Theater in 1866. He immediately set out to reform its administration and to raise its musical standards. For the cornerstone laying of the National Theater on May 16, 1868, he conducted the 1st performance of his tragic opera *Dalibor*, which was criticized as an attempt to Wagnerize the Bohemian national opera. In 1871, when there was talk of crowning Emperor Franz Josef as King of Bohemia, Smetana considered producing his opera *Libuše* for the festivities; however, no coronation took place and the work was withheld. Hoping for a popular success, he composed the comic opera *Dvě vdovy* (The 2 Widows), which proved to be just that at its premiere under his direction on March 27, 1874. Smetana's success, however, was short-lived. By the autumn of 1874 he was deaf and had to resign as conductor of the Provisional Theater. In spite of the bitter years to follow, marked by increasingly poor health, family problems, and financial hardship, he continued to compose. Between 1874 and 1879 he produced his 6 orch. masterpieces collectively known as *Má Vlast* (My Country): *Vyšehrad* (referring to a rock over the river Vltava, near Prague, the traditional seat of the ancient kings of Bohemia), *Vltava* (The Moldau), *Šárka* (a wild valley, near Prague, depicting the legendary story of the maiden Šárka), *Z Českých luhů a hájů* (From Bohemia's Woods and Fields), *Tábor* (the medieval town in southern Bohemia, the seat of the Hussites, and thus the traditional symbol of freedom and religion; the work is based on the chorale *Ye Who Are God's Warriors*), and *Blaník* (the mountain that served as a place of refuge for the Hussites; the previously mentioned chorale serves as the foundation of the work). From 1876 dates his famous String Quartet in E minor, subtitled *Z mého života* (From My Life), which he described as a "remembrance of my life and the catastrophe of complete deafness." His opera *Hubička* (The Kiss) was successfully premiered in Prague on Nov. 7, 1876. It was followed by the opera *Tajemství* (The Secret), which was heard for the 1st time on Sept. 18, 1878. For the opening of the new National Theater in Prague on June 11, 1881, his opera *Libuše* was finally given its premiere performance. The ailing Smetana attended the opening night and was accorded sustained applause. His last opera, *Čertova stěna* (The Devil's Wall), was a failure at its 1st hearing in Prague on Oct. 29, 1882. By this time Smetana's health had been completely undermined by the ravages of syphilis, the cause of his deafness. His mind eventually gave way and he was confined to an asylum. A detailed account of his illness and death is found in D. Kerner's *Krankheiten grosser Musiker* (Vol. II, Stuttgart, 1969); see also B. Large's *Smetana* (N.Y., 1970). At his death in 1884, the nation was plunged into a state of mourning. The funeral cortège passed the National Theater as Smetana was carried to his final resting place in the Vyšehrad cemetery.

Smetana was the founder of the Czech national school of composition, and it was through his efforts that Czech national opera came of age. Although the national element is predominant in much of his music, a highly personal style of expression is found in his String Quartet No. 1 and in many of his piano pieces. Outside his homeland, he remains best known for *The Bartered Bride*, *Má Vlast*, and the aforementioned string quartet. The centenary of his death in 1984 was marked by numerous performances of his music in Czechoslovakia and a reaffirmation of his revered place in the history of his nation.

WORKS: **OPERAS** (all 1st perf. in Prague): *Braniboři v Čechách* (The Brandenburgers in Bohemia; 1862–63; Jan. 5, 1866, composer conducting); *Prodaná nevěsta* (The Bartered Bride; 1863–66; May 30, 1866, composer conducting; 2 revs., 1869; final version, 1869–70; Sept. 25, 1870, composer conducting); *Dalibor* (1865–67; May 16, 1868, composer conducting; rev. 1870); *Libuše* (1869–72; June 11, 1881, A. Čech conducting); *Dvě vdovy* (The 2 Widows; March 27, 1874, composer conducting; final version, 1877; March 15, 1878, Čech conducting); *Hubička* (The Kiss; Nov. 7, 1876, Čech conducting);

Tajemství (The Secret; Sept. 18, 1878, Čech conducting); *Čertova stěna* (The Devil's Wall; 1879–82; Oct. 29, 1882, Čech conducting); *Viola* (sketches begun in 1874; fragment from 1883–84 only).

ORCH.: Minuet (1842); *Galop bajadérek* (Bajader's Galop; 1842); *Pochod Pražké studentské legie* (March for the Prague Students' Legion; 1848; arranged for Military Band by J. Pavlis); *Pochod Národní gardy* (March for the National Guard; 1848; arranged for Military Band by J. Pavlis); Polka (1849; later known as *Našim devám* [To Our Girls]); Overture (1849); Prelude (1849; 3 unconnected fragments only); *Frithjof* (1857; unfinished fragment only); *Slavnostní Symfonie* (Festival or Triumphal Sym.; 1853–54; Prague, Feb. 26, 1855, composer conducting); *Plavba vikingů* (The Viking's Voyage; 1857; unfinished fragment only); *Richard III*, symphonic poem after Shakespeare (1857–58; 1st perf. in an arrangement for 4 Pianos, Göteborg, April 24, 1860; 1st orch. perf., Prague, Jan. 5, 1862, composer conducting; *Valdštýnův tabor* (Wallenstein's Camp), symphonic poem after Schiller (1858–59); *Hakon Jarl*, symphonic poem after Oehlenschläger (1860–61; Prague, Feb. 24, 1864, composer conducting; *Doktor Faust*, prelude to a puppet play by M. Kopecký for Chamber Orch. (1862); *Oldřich a Božena*, prelude to a puppet play by M. Kopecký for Chamber Orch. (1863); *Pochod k slavnostl Shakespearove* (March for Shakespeare Festival; 1864); *Fanfáry k Shakespearovu dramatu Richard III* (Fanfares for Shakespeare's Drama *Richard III*; 1867); *Slavnostní predehra* (Ceremonial Prelude; 1868); *Prodaná nevěsta* (The Bartered Bride), tableau vivant for Chamber Orch. (1869); *Rybar* (The Fisherman), tableau vivant after Goethe's *Der Fischar* for Chamber Orch. (1869); *Libušin soud* (Libuše's Judgment), tableau vivant for Chamber Orch. (1869); *Divertissement na slovanské napevy* (Divertissement on Slavonic Songs) for Solo Flügelhorn and Military Band (1869; not extant); *Má Vlast* (My Country), cycle of 6 symphonic poems: 1, *Vyšehrad* (1872–74; Prague, March 14, 1875); 2, *Vltava* (The Moldau; 1874; Prague, April 4, 1875); 3, *Šárka* (1875; Prague, March 17, 1877); 4, *Z Českych luhů a hájů* (From Bohemia's Woods and Fields); 1875; Prague, Dec. 10, 1876); 5, *Tábor* (1878; Prague, Jan. 4, 1880); 6, *Blaník* (1878–79; Prague, Jan. 4, 1880) (1st complete perf. of the entire cycle, Prague, Nov. 5, 1882, Čech conducting); *Venkovanka* (The Peasant Woman), polka (1879); *Pražský karneval* (Prague Carnival), introduction and polonaise (1883; Prague, March 2, 1884); *Grosse Sinfonie* (1883–84; sketch for part of the 1st movement only).

CHORAL: *Jesu meine Freude*, chorale (1846); *Ich hoffe auf den Herrn*, fugue (1846); *Lobet den Herrn*, introduction and fugue (1846); *Heilig, Heilig, ist der Herr Zabaoth* for Double Chorus (1846); *Scapulis suis obumbrabit tibi Dominus*, offertory for Chorus, Horns, Strings, and Organ (1846); *Meditabitur in mandatis tuis* (*Offertorium à la Händel*) for Chorus, Horns, Strings, and Organ (1846); *Píseň svobody* (Song of Freedom) for Unison Voices and Piano (1848); *Česká píseň* (Song of the Czechs) for Men's Voices (1860); *Tři jezdci* (The 3 Riders) for Men's Voices (1862); *Odrolilec* (The Renegade) for Double Chorus of Men's Voices (1863); *Rolnická* (Farming) for Men's Voices (1868); *Slavností sbor* (Ceremonial Chorus) for Men's Voices (1870); *Píseň na moři* (Song of the Sea) for Men's Voices (1877); *Má hvězda* (My Star) for Women's Voices (1878); *Přiletěly vlaštorvičky* (The Swallows Have Gone) for Women's Voices (1878); *Za hory slunce zapadá* (The Sun Sets behind the Mountain) for Women's Voices (1878); *Věno* (Dedication) for Men's Voices (1882); *Modlitba* (Prayer) for Men's Voices (1880); *Dvě hesla* (2 Slogans) for Men's Voices (1882); *Naše píseň* (Our Song) for Men's Voices (1883).

CHAMBER: Polka for String Quartet (1839–40; not extant); *Osmanen Polka* for String Quartet (1839–40; not extant); String Quartet (1839–40; not extant); Waltz for String Quartet (1839–40; 1st violin part only extant); Overture for String Quartet (1839–40; not extant); Fantasia on motifs from Bellini's *Il Pirata* for String Quartet (1840); Fantasia on *Sil jsem proso* (I Sowed Millet) for Violin and Piano (1842–43); Trio for Piano, Violin, and Cello (1855; rev. 1857); String Quartet (No. 1), *Z mého života* (From My Life; 1876); *Z domoviny*, 2 duets for

Violin and Piano (1880); String Quartet (No. 2) (1882–83); also numerous piano pieces.

BIBL.: K. Teige, *Přispěvky k životopisu a umělecké činnosti mistra B.a Smetany*, I: *Skladby Smetanovy* (S.'s Works; Prague, 1893) and II: *Dopisy Smetanoy* (S.'s Letters; Prague, 1896); O. Hostinský, *B. S. a jeho boj o moderni českou hudbu* (S. and His Struggle for Modern Czech Music; Prague, 1901; 2nd ed., 1941); W. Ritter, *S.* (Paris, 1907); Z. Nejedlý, *Zpěvohry Smetanovy* (S.'s Operas; Prague, 1908; 3rd ed., 1954); V. Balthasar, *B. S.* (Prague, 1924); V. Helfert, *Tvůrci rozvoj B.a Smetany* (S.'s Creative Development; Prague, 1924; 3rd ed., 1953; German tr., 1956); Z. Nejedlý, *B. S.* (the standard Czech biography, although incomplete; 4 vols., Prague, 1924–33; 2nd ed., 7 vols., 1950–54; additional vol. as *S.: Dobá zrání* [S.: The Period of Maturity], Prague, 1962); J. Tiersot, *S.* (Paris, 1926); F. Bartoš, *S. ve vzpomínkách a dopisech* (S. in Reminiscences and Letters; Prague, 1939; 9th ed., 1954; German tr., 1954; Eng. tr., 1955); idem, *B. S.* (Prague, 1940); J. Teichman, *B. S.: Život a dilo* (S.: Life and Work; Prague, 1944); O. Šourek, *Komorni skladby B.a Smetany* (S.'s Chamber Music: Prague, 1945); P. Pražák, *Smetanovy zpěvohry* (S.'s Operas; Prague, 1948); M. Malý, *B. S.* (Prague, 1954; Eng. tr., 1956); J. Plavec, *Smetanova tvorba skorova* (S.'s Choral Works; Prague, 1954); H. Boese, *Zwei Urmusikanten: S.—Dvořák* (Zürich, 1955); M. Očadlík, *Klavirni dilo B.a Smetany* (S.'s Piano Works; Prague, 1961); J. Plavec, *B. S. v obrazech* (S. in Pictures; Prague, 1964); B. Karásek, *B. S.* (Prague, 1966; Eng. tr., 1967); C. Thörnqvist, *S. in Göteborg, 1856–1862* (in Eng.; Göteborg, 1967); B. Large, *S.* (N.Y., 1970); J. Clapham, *S.* (London, 1972); K. Janeček, *Smetanova komorni hudba* (S.'s Chamber Music; Prague, 1979); J. Clapham, "S.: A Century After," *Musical Times* (April 1984); H. Séguardtová, *B. S.* (Leipzig, 1985); C. Fifield, "S. and 'The Devil's Wall,'" *Musical Times* (Feb. 1987).

Smeterlin, Jan, Polish-born English pianist; b. Bielsko, Feb. 7, 1892; d. London, Jan. 18, 1967. He was a child prodigy; made his public debut at 8; after studies with Godowsky in Vienna, he toured throughout Europe and the U.S. (from 1930), eventually settling in London just before the outbreak of World War II; became a naturalized British subject. He was praised for his congenially Romantic interpretations of Chopin's music; celebrated his 50th anniversary as a concert artist at London's Wigmore Hall in 1951.

Smijers, Albert(us Antonius), eminent Dutch musicologist; b. Raamsdonksveer, July 19, 1888; d. Huis ter Heide, near Utrecht, May 15, 1957. He studied music with Averkamp at the Amsterdam Cons.; was trained for the priesthood; was ordained in 1912; then entered the school for church music at Klosterneuburg; took a course in musicology with Guido Adler at the Univ. of Vienna (Ph.D., 1917, with the diss. *Karl Luython als Motettenkomponist*; publ. in Amsterdam, 1923). He taught at Beekvliet Seminary in Amsterdam until 1929, then at the Amsterdam Cons. (1929–33); in 1930 he was appointed prof. of musicology at the Univ. of Utrecht; formed the Inst. of Musicology there. He brought out 7 vols. of the anthology *Van Ockeghem tot Sweelinck* (Amsterdam, 1939–56); in collaboration with C. Van den Borren and others, he publ. *Algemeene Muziekgeschiedenis* (Utrecht, 1938; 4th ed., 1947); ed. the collected works of Josquin Des Prez (Amsterdam, 1921–56) and Obrecht (Vols. I-III, Amsterdam, 1953–56).

Smirnov, Dmitri (Alexeievich), outstanding Russian tenor; b. Moscow, Nov. 19, 1882; d. Riga, April 27, 1944. He sang in a church choir as a youth; then studied voice with Dodonov and others in Moscow. On Feb. 3, 1903, he made his debut as Gigi in Esposito's *Camorra* at Moscow's Hermitage Theater. In 1904 he was accepted as a member of the Bolshoi Theater there, but interrupted his career by traveling to Paris and Milan for further voice training. Returning to Moscow in 1906, he sang again at the Bolshoi Theater; from 1910 he appeared also with the Maryinsky Opera Theater in St. Petersburg. During the same period, he took part in the famous Russian Seasons in Paris. On Dec. 30, 1910, he made his debut at the Metropolitan Opera in N.Y. in the role of the Duke of Mantua in *Rigoletto,* remaining with the company until 1912; then sang with the Boston Opera (1911); after a tour of Latin America, he appeared at London's Drury Lane (1914) and other European theaters. Although he lived mostly abroad, he revisited Russia in 1926 and 1928 as a guest artist. He later appeared mostly in solo recitals; was also active as a voice teacher; taught at the Athens Cons. and in Riga. In Russia he was regarded as one of the finest lyric tenors of his time, often compared to Caruso; as a *bel canto* singer, he was praised by Russian and European critics. Apart from the Russian repertoire, in which he excelled, he made a deep impression in such lyrico-dramatic roles as Faust, Don José, Canio, and Rodolfo.

BIBL.: J. Stratton, "D. S.," *Record Collector*, XIV (1962).

Smirnov, Dmitri, Russian composer; b. Minsk, Nov. 2, 1948. He studied composition with Edison Denisov at the Moscow Cons. Upon graduation in 1972, he was ed. of the Leningrad publication *Soviet Composer* (1973–79). His wife, **Elena Firsova** (b. Leningrad, March 21, 1950), is also a composer.

WORKS: ORCH.: 2 piano concertos: No. 1 (1971) and No. 2, with Strings (1978); *Pastorale* (1975); Clarinet Concerto (1974–77); *Triple Concerto* for Saxophone, Piano, Double Bass, Strings, and Percussion (1977); *The 4 Seasons*, sym. (1980). **CHAMBER:** *Monolog* for Clarinet (1968); 2 violin sonatas (1969, 1979); String Trio (1970); *2 Fugues* for Violin (1970); String Quartet (1973); *Lyrical Composition* for Flute, Oboe, Violin, Cello, and Harpsichord (1975); *Solo* for Harp (1976); Bassoon Sonata (1977); Piano Trio (1977); Cello Sonata (1978); *Mirages*, 5 pieces for Saxophone Quartet (1979). **VOCAL:** *6 Songs after Blok* for Voice and Orch. (1972); *6 Haiku* for Voice, Flute, and Piano (1973); *Cantata in Memory of Pablo Neruda* for 2 Solo Voices, Chorus, Strings, and Percussion (1974); *5 songs after Pushkin* for Voice, Flute, Violin, Cello, and Percussion (1976); *Eternal Calm* for Voice, Strings, Organ, and Percussion (1972–77). **PIANO:** 2 sonatas (1966–67, 1980); *2 Little Pieces* (1968).

Smit, Leo, Dutch composer; b. Amsterdam, May 14, 1900; d. in the Auschwitz concentration camp, 1943. He studied piano (diploma, 1922) and took courses in composition (diploma, 1924) with Zweers and Dresden at the Amsterdam Cons., where he taught analysis and harmony (1924–27); after a sojourn in Paris (1927–33), he returned to Amsterdam as a music teacher. He was arrested by the Nazi occupiers in 1943 and sent to the concentration camp at Westerbork in the Netherlands, and eventually perished in Asuchwitz. His music was greatly influenced by the contemporary French school.

WORKS: *Introduction to Teirlinck's play "De Vertraagde Film"* for Chamber Orch. (1923); Quintet for Flute, Violin, Viola, Cello, and Harp (1928); *Schemselnihar*, ballet (1929); *Silhouetten*, suite for Orch.; *2 hommages* (Sherlock Holmes and Remington) for Piano (1928–30); Harp Concertino (1933); Sextet for Piano and Wind Quintet (1933); Sym. (1934–36); Concerto for Piano and Wind Orch. (1937); *Forlane en Rondeau* (orch. by Godfried Devreese); Concertino for Cello and Small Orch. (1937); *Suite* for Oboe and Cello (1938); Trio for Clarinet, Viola, and Piano (1938); Concerto for Viola and Strings (1940); *Divertimento* for Piano, 4-hands (1940); Flute Sonata (1943).

Smit, Leo, American pianist and composer; b. Philadelphia, Jan. 12, 1921. He studied piano with Isabelle Vengerova at the Curtis Inst. of Music in Philadelphia (1930–32); took lessons in composition with Nicolas Nabokov (1935). He made his debut as a pianist at Carnegie Hall in N.Y. in 1939; then made tours of the U.S.; also taught at Sarah Lawrence College (1947–49), at the Univ. of Calif. in Los Angeles (1957–63), and at the State Univ. of N.Y. at Buffalo (from 1962); likewise served as director of the Monday Evening Concerts in Los Angeles (1957–63) and as composer-in-residence at the American Academy in Rome (1972–73) and at Brevard Music Center (1980). His style of composition is neo-Classical, marked by a strong contrapuntal fabric; the influence of Stravinsky, with whom he had personal contact, is particularly pronounced here.

WORKS: STAGE: OPERAS: *The Alchemy of Love* (1969); *Magic Water* (1978). **MELODRAMA:** *A Mountain Eulogy* (1975). **BAL-**

LETS: *Yerma* (1946); *Virginia Sampler* (N.Y., March 4, 1947; rev. 1960). **ORCH.:** 3 syms.: No. 1 (1956; Boston, Feb. 1, 1957); No. 2 (1965); No. 3 (1981); *The Parcae*, overture (Boston, Oct. 16, 1953); *Capriccio* for Strings (Ojai, Calif., May 23, 1958; rev. 1974); Piano Concerto (1968; rev. 1980); *4 Kookaburra Marches* for Orch. and Tape (1972); *Symphony of Dances and Songs* (1981); *Variations* for Piano and Orch. (1981). **CHAMBER:** Sextet for Clarinet, Bassoon, and Strings (1940); *Invention* for Clarinet and Piano (1943); *In Woods* for Oboe, Harp, and Percussion (1978); *Delaunay Pochoirs*, 3 pieces for Cello and Piano (1980); Sonata for Solo Cello (1982); *Flute of Wonder*, 3 pieces for Flute and Piano (1983); *Tzadik* for Saxophone Quartet (1983), 12 Instruments (1984), String Quartet (1984), and Piano Trio (1985); *Exequy* for String Trio (1985); also numerous piano pieces, including a Sonata for Piano, 4-hands (1987); vocal works, including *Academic Graffiti* for Voice, Clarinet, Cello, Piano, and Percussion, to a text by W.H. Auden (1959), various choruses, songs, and song cycles; etc.

Smith, Ada (Beatrice Queen Victoria Louise Virginia), black American singer of popular music, known as **Bricktop;** b. Alderson, W.Va., Aug. 14, 1894; d. N.Y., Jan. 31, 1984. Fascinated with saloons, she danced and sang in Chicago's cabarets. In 1924 she went to Paris and opened her own club on Rue Pigalle, which she called Chez Bricktop, dispensing chic informality. She met celebrities and taught the Prince of Wales, the future King Edward VIII, the Black Bottom; she was on friendly terms with Hemingway, Evelyn Waugh, Steinbeck, and other habitués of her boîte. Her admirers called her Brickie. Returning to N.Y. in 1939, she became a hostess in café society; Cole Porter wrote a song for her, *Miss Otis regrets, she's unable to lunch today.* In 1951 she opened a club on the Via Veneto in Rome; also had a club in Mexico. In 1964 she returned to N.Y. In 1973 she made a documentary film, *Honeybaby, honeybaby!* On her last birthday in 1983, when she turned 89, she was presented by N.Y.'s Mayor Koch with a seal of the city and a certificate of appreciation for her "extraordinary talent and indomitable spirit." In 1983 she publ. (with professional assistance) an autobiography, *Bricktop by Bricktop.*

Smith, Alice Mary (Mrs. Meadows White), English composer; b. London, May 19, 1839; d. there, Dec. 4, 1884. She was a pupil of Sterndale Bennett and G.A. Macfarren; married M. White in 1867.

WORKS: 2 syms.; 4 overtures: *Endymion, Lalla Rookh, Masque of Pandora,* and *Jason;* Clarinet Concerto; *Introduction and Allegro* for Piano and Orch.; Cantatas: *Rüdesheim* (1865); *Ode to the Northeast Wind* (1878); *Ode to the Passions* (1882); *Song of the Little Baltung* (1883); *The Red King* (1884); part-songs; 4 piano quartets; 3 string quartets; Piano Trio.

Smith, Bernard (real name, **Bernhard Schmidt**), German-born English organ builder, known as **"Father Smith;"** b. c.1630; d. London, Feb. 20, 1708. He was trained in his homeland and was active in Holland before settling in London in 1666; was organ maker to the king from 1671, a title formally bestowed upon him in 1681. He built or rebuilt some 70 organs.

BIBL.: A. Freeman, *Father S.* (London, 1926).

Smith, Bessie (actually, **Elizabeth**), famous black American blues, jazz, and vaudeville singer; b. Chattanooga, Tenn., April 15, 1894; d. Clarksville, Miss., Sept. 26, 1937 (as a result of injuries sustained in an automobile accident near Coahana, Miss.). Born in a wretchedly poor family, she joined Rainey's Rabbit Foot Minstrels (blues pioneer Ma Rainey was her teacher) in 1912 and developed a style of singing that rapidly brought her fame. Her 1st record, *Down Hearted Blues*, sold 800,000 copies in 1923, and she was subsequently billed as the "Empress of the Blues." In all, she made over 200 recordings; also appeared in the film *St. Louis Blues* (1929). Her last years were marred by alcoholism. She was a large, impressive woman—5' 9" and weighing over 200 pounds—and had a powerful voice to match; the excellence of her vocal equipment, along with her natural expressive qualities and improvisatory abilities, combined to make her the consummate blues singer of her time.

BIBL.: P. Oliver, *B. S.* (London, 1959); C. Moore, *Somebody's Angel Child* (N.Y., 1969); C. Albertson, *B.* (N.Y., 1973); C. Albertson and G. Schuller, *B. S.: Empress of the Blues* (N.Y., 1975); E. Brooks, *The B. S. Companion* (St. Albans, 1982); E. Feinstein, *B. S.* (N.Y., 1985).

Smith, Carleton Sprague, distinguished American musicologist; b. N.Y., Aug. 8, 1905. He was educated at Harvard Univ. (M.A., 1928) and at the Univ. of Vienna (Ph.D., 1930, with the diss. *Die Beziehungen zwischen Spanien und Oesterreich im 17. Jahrhundert*). Returning to the U.S., he was an instructor in history at Columbia Univ. (1931–35), then at N.Y. Univ. (1939–67); he also served as chief of the Music Division at the N.Y. Public Library (1931–43; 1946–59). A linguist, he lectured in South America, in Spanish and Portuguese, on the social history of the U.S.; a skillful flutist, he often took part in concerts of early and new music.

Smith, Chas, American composer and performer; b. West Brookfield, Mass., March 15, 1948. He began playing piano at the age of 8; played guitar in rock bands (1964–69), and attended N.Y.'s Utica College (1967) and studied jazz composition and arranging at the Berklee School of Music in Boston (1969–70). He studied composition with Powell, Subotnick, Budd, Brown, and Tenney at the Calif. Inst. of the Arts in Valencia (B.F.A., 1975; M.F.A., 1977), where he performed with Michael Le Donne-Bhennet, Michael Jon Fink, and William Hawley at galleries and performance spaces under such ensembles as Ronin, C33, 100 Miles of Sheep Jokes, and Stilllife (1975–80). The Chas Smith Ensemble, formed in 1985, made appearances in various Los Angeles venues. His recordings include *Stilllife* (1981), *Santa Fe* (1982), and *Nakadai* (1987); also played on records by Harold Budd, Jim Fox, and Carole Caroompas and appeared in several rock videos that feature his extensive tattoos, of which he is justly proud; also performed in a number of film soundtracks, including *The Lost Boys* and *Less than Zero*. Smith performs chiefly on the pedal steel guitar, but also plays other stringed instruments, keyboards, and electronics; his music consists of austere meditations on very slowly evolving chords in the Lydian mode. He is a certified welder.

WORKS: *Ontolosis* for Electronics (1974); *Triactus* for Electronics (1975); *Mirage* for Voices, Bells, and Mallet Instruments (1977); *Santa Fe, October 68,* and *After,* all for Pedal Steel Guitar (1979–82); *Scicura* for 2 Pianos, 3 Vibraphones, Marimba, and Wind Instruments (1975; also arranged for Dobro and Pedal Steel Guitar, 1982); *Beatrix* for Pedal Steel Guitar (1983); *James Tenney* for Pedal Steel Guitar (1984); *Nakadai* for Multitrack Pedal Steel Guitar (1985); *A Judas Within: Seduction and Betrayal* for Vibraphone, Marimba, Hammer Dulcimer, Pedal Steel Guitar, Microtonal Chimes, Bowed Rods, and Small Metal Objects (1985–86); *Hollister* for Pedal Steel Guitar (1986).

Smith, Clarence "Pine Top", black American blues singer and pianist; b. Troy, Ala., June 11, 1904; d. (accidentally shot during a disturbance in a dance hall) Chicago, March 14, 1929. After playing in clubs in Pittsburgh, he served as accompanist to Ma Rainey; went to Chicago, where he became a pioneering figure as a pianist in the boogie-woogie style; his 1928 recording of *Pine Top's Boogie Woogie* secured his fame among jazz enthusiasts.

Smith, Curtis O(tto) B(ismarck) Curtis-. See **Curtis-Smith, Curtis O(tto) B(ismarck).**

Smith, Cyril (James), English pianist and teacher; b. Middlesbrough, Aug. 11, 1909; d. London, Aug. 2, 1974. He was a pupil of Herbert Fryer at the Royal College of Music in London; made his formal debut as a soloist in the Brahms 2nd Piano Concerto in Birmingham (1929). In 1937 he married the pianist Phyllis Sellick, with whom he often appeared in works for 2 pianos from 1941; during a visit to the Soviet Union in 1956, he suffered a stroke that incapacitated his

left arm; they subsequently gave concerts for piano, 3–hands (from 1957). He taught at the Royal College of Music (1934–74). In 1971 he was made an Officer of the Order of the British Empire. His autobiography was appropriately titled *Duet for Three Hands* (London, 1958). At the apex of his career, he won particular distinction for his performances of Rachmaninoff; he later commissioned new works and arrangements for piano, 3–hands.

Smith, David Stanley, American conductor, music educator, and composer; b. Toledo, Ohio, July 6, 1877; d. New Haven, Conn., Dec. 17, 1949. He studied with Horatio Parker at Yale Univ., graduating in 1900. He then went to Europe, where he took courses in composition with Thuille in Munich and Widor in Paris. Upon his return to the U.S., he obtained a Mus.B. degree at Yale (1903) and was appointed an instructor at the Yale Univ. School of Music; in 1916 he became a prof. there; in 1920 was appointed dean of the School of Music, retiring in 1946. He was conductor of the New Haven Sym. Orch. from 1920 to 1946. In 1910 he was elected a member of the National Inst. of Arts and Letters. His compositions were cast in a conservative mold.

WORKS: OPERA: *Merrymount* (1914). **ORCH.:** 4 syms.: No. 1 (1910); No. 2 (1917); No. 3 (1928; Cleveland, Jan. 8, 1931, composer conducting); No. 4 (1937; Boston, April 14, 1939, composer conducting); *Prince Hal,* overture (New Haven, Dec. 1912); *Impressions,* suite (1916); *Fête galante,* fantasy for Flute and Orch. (N.Y., Dec. 11, 1921); *Epic Poem* (1926; Boston, April 12, 1935, composer conducting); *Sinfonietta* for String Orch. (1931); *1929: A Satire* (1932; N.Y., Nov. 15, 1933); *Requiem* for Violin and Orch. (1939); *Credo,* symphonic poem (1941); 4 Pieces for String Orch. (1943); *The Apostle,* symphonic poem (1944). **CHORAL:** *Rhapsody of St. Bernard* for Solo Voices, Chorus, and Orch. (1915); *The Vision of Isaiah* for Soprano, Tenor, Chorus, and Orch. (1927); *The Ocean* for Bass, Chorus, and Orch. (1945). **CHAMBER:** 10 string quartets (1899–1938); *Sonata Pastorale* for Oboe and Piano (1918); Violin Sonata (1923); *Flowers* for 10 Instruments (1924); Piano Quintet (1927); String Sextet (1931); piano pieces, including a sonata (1929); also song cycles.

BIBL.: B. Tuthill, "D.S. S.," *Musical Quarterly* (Jan. 1942); E. Goode, *D.S. S. and his Music* (diss., Univ. of Cincinnati, 1978).

Smith, Gregg, American conductor and composer; b. Chicago, Aug. 21, 1931. He studied composition with Leonard Stein, Lukas Foss, and Ray Moreman and conducting with Fritz Zweig at the Univ. of Calif. at Los Angeles (M.A., 1956). In 1955 in Los Angeles he founded the Gregg Smith Singers, a chamber choir, with which he toured and recorded extensively; from 1970, was active with it in N.Y. He also taught at Ithaca College, the State Univ. of N.Y. at Stony Brook, the Peabody Cons. of Music in Baltimore, Barnard College, and the Manhattan School of Music in N.Y. His repertoire extends from early music to works by contemporary American composers. He ed. the Gregg Smith Choral Series; wrote much vocal music, including 2 operas, choral works, songs, and pieces for chamber orch.

Smith, Hale, black American composer; b. Cleveland, June 29, 1925. He studied piano with Dorothy Price and composition with Marcel Dick at the Cleveland Inst. of Music (B.Mus., 1950; M.Mus., 1952); went to N.Y. in 1958 and was active as a music ed. for publishers, as a jazz arranger, and as a teacher; later was a prof. at the Univ. of Connecticut in Storrs (1970–84). His output is remarkable for its utilization of serial procedures with jazz infusions; wrote musical scores for Dizzy Gillespie, Ahmad Jamal, Eric Dolphy, and Abby Lincoln, and worked in various capacities for Quincy Jones, Clark Terry, Oliver Nelson, Miriam Makeba, and Hugh Masekela.

WORKS: CHAMBER OPERA: *Blood Wedding* (Cleveland, 1953). **ORCH.:** *Orchestral Set* (1952; rev. 1968); *Contours* (Louisville, Oct. 17, 1961); *By Yearning and By Beautiful* for String Orch. (1964); *Music* for Harp and Orch. (1972); *Ritual and Incantations* (1974); *Innerflexions* (N.Y., Sept. 2, 1977). **CHAMBER:**

Duo for Violin and Piano (1953); Cello Sonata (1955); *Epicedial Variations* for Violin and Piano (1956); *3 Brevities* for Flute (1960); *Introductions, Cadenzas and Interludes* for 8 Players (1974); *Variations* for 6 Players (1975); *Variations a due* for Cello, Alto Saxophone, and Flute or Saxophone, or Clarinet ad libitum (1984); also the piano pieces *Evocation* (1966) and *Anticipations, Introspections and Reflections* (1971). VOCAL: *5 Songs* for Voice and Violin (1956); *2 Love Songs of John Donne* for Soprano and 9 Instruments (1958); *Comes Tomorrow*, jazz cantata for Chorus and Accompaniment (1972; rev. 1977); *Toussaint L'Ouverture 1803* for Chorus and Piano (1977); *Symphonic Spirituals* for Soprano and Orch. (1979); *Meditations in Passage* for Soprano, Baritone, and Piano or Orch. (1980). BIBL.: M. Breda, *H. S.: Biographical and Analytical Study of the Man and His Music* (diss., Univ. of Southern Mississippi, Harrisburg, 1975).

Smith, Jabbo (actually, **Cladys**), black American jazz trumpeter, trombonist, and singer; b. Pembroke, Ga., Dec. 24, 1908; d. St. Louis, Jan. 16, 1991. He received his musical training while living at the Jenkins's Orphanage in Charleston, S.C., where he played in its band. At age 16 he began his professional career as a member of Harry Marsh's band in Philadelphia; then played with Charlie Johnson's band (1925–28). He gained wide recognition as a sideman on Duke Ellington's recording of *Black and Tan Fantasy* (1927); subsequently led his own band in Milwaukee. In 1978 he toured in his own show, *One Mo' Time*, and in 1981 appeared at N.Y.'s West End Café.

Smith, Joe (Joseph), black American jazz trumpeter; b. Ripley, Ohio, June 28, 1902; d. N.Y., Dec. 2, 1937. He played with jazz groups in St. Louis; then went to N.Y., where he worked with Fletcher Henderson's orch. (1925–28); also acted as accompanist to Bessie Smith, Ma Rainey, and Ethel Waters; subsequently played in Bennie Moten's band and McKinney's Cotton Pickers until ill health cut short his career.

Smith, John Christopher (real name, **Johann Christoph Schmidt**), German-born English organist and composer; b. Ansbach, 1712; d. Bath, Oct. 3, 1795. His father, Johann Christoph Schmidt, went to London in 1716 as Handel's treasurer and chief copyist; the son followed in 1720, and received a few lessons from Handel about 1725; after lessons from Pepusch, he studied with Thomas Roseingrave. He wrote his 1st opera, *Ulysses*, in 1733; after its failure, he gave up the theater; following a sojourn abroad (1746–48), he became organist at the Foundling Hospital in London in 1754, where he directed the annual performance of *Messiah* (1759–68). He scored a success with his opera *The Enchanter of Love and Magic* (1760), but thereafter devoted himself to composing oratorios; with Stanley, he oversaw the Lenten performances of oratorios at Covent Garden (1760–74). He settled in Bath, where he was active as a teacher; upon his father's death in 1763, he was bequeathed his father's large Handel collection; after being granted a royal pension by King George III (1772), he in turn bequeathed the collection to the king; it is now housed in the Royal Music Library at the British Museum. WORKS: (all 1st perf. in London unless otherwise given): OPERAS: *Ulysses* (April 16, 1733); *Rosalinda* (Jan. 4, 1740); *The Seasons* (1740; not perf.); *Issipile* (1743; not perf.); *Il ciro riconosciuto* (1745; not perf.); *Dario* (1746; not perf.); *Artaserse* (1748; unfinished); *The Fairies* (Feb. 3, 1755); *The Tempest* (Feb. 11, 1756); *The Enchanter of Love and Magic* (Dec. 13, 1760); *Medea* (1760–61; unfinished). ORATORIOS: *David's Lamentation over Saul and Jonathan* (1738; Feb. 22, 1740); *Paradise Lost* (1757–58; Feb. 29, 1760); *Judith* (1758; not perf.); *Feast of Darius* (1761–62; not perf.; based on the opera *Dario*); *Rebecca* (March 16, 1764); *Nabal* (March 16, 1764); *Jehosaphat* (1764; not perf.); *Gideon* (Feb. 10, 1769; based on the *Feast of Darius* and works by Handel); *Redemption* (1774; not perf.). OTHER VOCAL: *The Mourning Muse of Alexis*, funeral ode (1729); *Thamesis, Isis and Proteus*, cantata; *Daphne*, cantata (1744); *The Foundling Hymn* (1763); *Funeral Service for the Dowager Princess of Wales* (1772); songs. HARPSICHORD (all publ. in London): 6 suites, op. 1 (1732); 6 suites, op. 2 (c.1735); 6 *Suites of Lessons*, op. 3 (c.1755); 6 *Lessons*, op. 4 (c.1758); 12 *Sonatas*, op. 5 (1763).

BIBL.: [W. Coxe], *Anecdotes of George Frederick Handel and J.C. S.* (London, 1799); J. Hall, "J.C. S.: Handel's Friend and Secretary," *Musical Times*, XCVI (1955); A. McCredie, "J.C. S. as a Dramatic Composer," *Music & Letters*, XLV (1964); A. Williams, "Stanley, S. and Teraminta," *Music & Letters*, LX (1979).

Smith, John Stafford, English music scholar, organist, and composer; b. Gloucester (baptized), March 30, 1750; d. London, Sept. 21, 1836. He studied with his father, Martin Smith, organist at Gloucester Cathedral, and later with Boyce and Nares. In 1784 he was made a Gentleman of the Chapel Royal, and in 1802 was made one of its organists; from 1785 he served as lay-vicar at Westminster Abbey; also served as Master of the Children at the Chapel Royal (1805–17). His importance to music history rests upon his work as a music scholar; he acquired an invaluable collection of early music MSS and editions, which included the Mulliner Book and the Old Hall MS. In all, he acquired 2,191 vols. of music, of which 578 were in MS. After his death, the collection was sold at auction and dispersed without a trace. As a composer, he became best known for his glees. In the 5th collection of his glees (1799), he included an arrangement of the tune *To Anacreon in Heaven*, to which Francis Scott Key wrote *The Star-Spangled Banner* (1814); but there were several reasons for questioning whether he was the composer; his authorship was doubted by many reputable American scholars. William Lichtenwanger, in his "The Music of *The Star-Spangled Banner:* From Ludgate Hill to Capitol Hill," *Quarterly Journal of the Library of Congress* (July 1977), seems to have dispelled these doubts by publ. excerpts from the "Recollections" of Richard John Samuel Stevens, an active member of the Anacreontic Society of London, who states in the rubric for 1777: "The president was Ralph Tomlinson. . . . He wrote the Poetry of the Anacreontic Song; which Stafford Smith set to Music." Smith was an excellent musician; he transcribed into modern notation early MSS for the *History of Music* by Sir John Hawkins; ed. *Musica antiqua*, containing compositions "from the commencement of the 12th to the 18th century" (2 vols., 1812); publ. *A Collection of Songs of Various Kinds for Different Voices* (1785).

BIBL.: B. Frith, *J.S. S., 1750–1836, Gloucester Composer* (Gloucester, 1950); E. Cole, "S. S.'s Burney," *Music & Letters*, XL (1959); F. Grameny, *J.S. S., 1750–1836: An Early English Musicologist* (diss., Boston Univ., 1987).

Smith (real name, **Vielehr**), **Julia (Frances),** American pianist, composer, and writer on music; b. Denton, Tex., Jan. 25, 1911; d. N.Y., April 27, 1989. She studied at North Texas State Univ. (graduated, 1930), then took courses in piano with Carl Friedberg and received instruction in composition at the Juilliard School of Music in N.Y. (diploma, 1939); also studied at N.Y. Univ. (M.A., 1933; Ph.D., 1952). She was the pianist of the all-women Orchestrette of N.Y. (1932–39); made tours of the U.S., Latin America, and Europe; taught at the Hartt School of Music in Hartford, Conn. (1941–46). WRITINGS: *Aaron Copland: His Work and Contribution to American Music* (N.Y., 1955); *Master Pianist: The Career and Teaching of Carl Friedberg* (N.Y., 1963); *Directory of American Women Composers* (Indianapolis, 1970). WORKS: OPERAS: *Cynthia Parker* (1938; Denton, Feb. 16, 1940; rev. 1977); *The Stranger of Manzano* (1943; Dallas, May 6, 1947); *The Gooseherd and the Goblin* (1946; N.Y., Feb. 22, 1947); *Cockcrow* (1953; Austin, Tex., April 22, 1954); *The Shepherdess and the Chimney Sweep* (1963; Fort Worth, Tex., Dec. 28, 1967); *Daisy* (Miami, Nov. 3, 1973). ORCH.: *Episodic Suite* (1936); Piano Concerto (1938; rev. 1971; Dallas, Feb. 28, 1976; arr. for 2 Pianos, 1971); *Folkways Symphony* (1948); *Remember the Alamo* for Symphonic or Full Band and Optional Narrator and Chorus (1965; in collaboration with C. Vashaw). CHAMBER: Piano trio, *Cornwall* (1955); String Quartet (1964); Suite for Wind Octet (1980); piano pieces; also vocal works, including *Our Heritage* for Double Chorus and Orch. (1958)

and *Prairie Kaleidoscope*, song cycle for Soprano and String Quartet (1982).

Smith, Kate (Kathryn Elizabeth), famous American singer of popular music; b. Greenville, Va., May 1, 1907; d. Raleigh, N.C., June 17, 1986. As a child, she sang in church socials and later for the troops in Army camps in the Washington, D.C., area during World War I. Although she had no formal training in music, she landed a part in the musical *Honeymoon Lane* in Atlantic City, N.J., in 1926, and then appeared in it on Broadway; subsequently sang in the Broadway musicals *Hit the Deck* (1927) and *Flying High* (1930). She began singing on her own radio show in 1931, opening her 1st broadcast with *When the Moon Comes over the Mountain*, which thereafter served as her theme song. In 1938 she introduced Irving Berlin's *God Bless America*, which she immortalized in innumerable subsequent performances; when the original MS for the song was discovered in Las Vegas in 1990, the Kate Smith God Bless America Foundation of N.Y. put it up for sale for $295,000. Thanks to her enormous popularity, she raised more money for U.S. War Bonds during World War II than any other artist. She starred in her own television show (1950–55; 1960), and continued to make guest appearances until 1975. President Reagan awarded her the U.S. Medal of Freedom in 1982. Smith was one of the most successful singers of popular music in her time. During her lengthy career, she made over 15,000 radio broadcasts, introducing over 1,000 songs; also recorded nearly 3,000 songs. She publ. the autobiographical vol. *Upon My Lips a Song* (N.Y., 1960).

BIBL.: M. Pitts, *K. S.: A Bio-bibliography* (N.Y., 1988).

Smith, Lawrence Leighton, American conductor and pianist; b. Portland, Oreg., April 8, 1936. He studied piano with Ariel Rubstein in Portland and then with Leonard Shure in N.Y.; enrolled in Portland State Univ. (B.S., 1956) and at the Mannes College of Music in N.Y. (B.M., 1959). In 1964 he received 1st prize at the Mitropoulos International Conducting Competition in N.Y.; was then assistant conductor at the Metropolitan Opera in N.Y. (1964–67). He was music director of the Westchester (N.Y.) Sym. Orch. (1967–69) and principal guest conductor of the Phoenix (Ariz.) Sym. Orch. (1971–73); also was music director of the Austin (Tex.) Sym. Orch. (1972–73). He served as music director of the Oregon Sym. Orch. in Portland (1973–80) and of the San Antonio Sym. Orch. (1980–85); also was artistic adviser and principal guest conductor of the North Carolina Sym. Orch. in Raleigh (1980–81) and music director of the Louisville Orch. (from 1983) and of the Music Academy of the West in Santa Barbara (from 1985). In addition to his appearances as a conductor in the U.S. and abroad, he continued to perform as a pianist, especially as an accompanist.

Smith, Leland (Clayton), American bassoonist, clarinetist, teacher, and composer; b. Oakland, Calif., Aug. 6, 1925. He studied composition at Mills College with Milhaud (1941–43; 1946–47); also took courses in composition with Sessions and in musicology with Bukofzer at the Univ. of Calif. at Berkeley (M.A., 1948); completed his training with Messiaen at the Paris Cons. (1948–49). He taught at the Univ. of Calif. at Berkeley (1950–51), Mills College (1951–52), the Univ. of Chicago (1952–58), and Stanford Univ. (from 1958), where he was a prof. (from 1968); held a Fulbright scholarship (1964–65). He was also active as a bassoonist and clarinetist. He publ. *Handbook of Harmonic Analysis* (Stanford, 1963). His style of composition is that of liberal modernism marked by a discriminate application of eclectic idioms, not excluding triadic usages.

WORKS: Sonata for Trumpet and Piano (1947); Trio for Flute, Cello, and Piano (1947); Trio for Violin, Trumpet, and Clarinet (1948); *Divertimento No. 1* for 5 Instruments (1949); Sym. No. 1 (1951); Woodwind Quintet (1951); Sonata for Heckelphone (or Viola) and Piano (1954); *Santa Claus*, opera in 5 scenes on the libretto by e.e. cummings (Chicago, Dec. 9, 1955); Concerto for Orch. (1956); Quintet for Bassoon and Strings (1956); *Divertimento No. 2* for Chamber Orch. (1957);

3 Pacifist Songs (1960); Wind Trio (1960); Quartet for Horn, Violin, Cello, and Piano (1961); *Dona nobis pacem* for Chorus and Chamber Ensemble (1964); *Orpheus* for Guitar, Harp, and Harpsichord (1967); *Machines of Loving Grace* for Computer, Bassoon, and Narrator (1970).

Smith, Moses, American music critic; b. Chelsea, Mass., March 4, 1901; d. Boston, July 27, 1964. He studied law at Harvard Univ. (graduated, 1924) and also music. He was music critic of the *Boston American* (1924–34) and of the *Boston Evening Transcript* (1934–39); then was music director of the Columbia Phonograph Co. (1939–42). In 1947 he publ. a controversial biography of Koussevitzky, who brought a libel suit for $1,000,000 against Smith and his publisher, claiming that the book described him as "generally incompetent, brutal to the musicians and a poseur." The suit, however, was dismissed.

BIBL.: K. DeKay, "Koussevitzky and His Biographers," *Koussevitzky Recordings Society*, newsletter, Vol. II, No. 1 (1988).

Smith, Patrick J(ohn), American music critic, author, and editor; b. N.Y., Dec. 11, 1932. He was educated at Princeton Univ. (A.B., 1955); then pursued a career as a music critic, contributing articles to *High Fidelity*, *Musical America*, the *Musical Quarterly*, and the *Musical Times*. From 1965 to 1985 he was book ed. of *Musical America*; also served as N.Y. music correspondent to the *Times* of London. He was president of the Music Critics Association (1977–81); was director of the Opera-Musical Theater Program of the NEA (from 1985). In 1988 he was appointed ed.-in-chief of *Opera News*. He publ. *The Tenth Muse, A Historical Study of the Opera Libretto* (N.Y., 1970) and *A Year at the Met* (N.Y., 1983).

Smith, Ronald, English pianist; b. London, Jan. 3, 1922. He studied at the Royal Academy of Music in London; made his debut at a Promenade concert in London in 1942. He became best known for his interpretations of the massive, programmatic works of Alkan, about whom he publ. in London the studies *Alkan, The Man and His Music* (1975), *Alkan, Vol. I: The Enigma* (1976) and *Alkan, Vol. II: The Music* (1987), and *Alkan in Miniature* (1978). He toured Australia as a lecturer and gave talks on the BBC and French Radio. He also composed a number of works, including a Sym. and a Violin Concerto.

Smith, William O(verton), American clarinetist, teacher, and composer; b. Sacramento, Calif., Sept. 22, 1926. He began playing clarinet at the age of 10, and at 12 started a grade-school dance band. He then enrolled at the Juilliard School of Music in N.Y. (1945–46) while earning a living by playing in jazz groups. Returning to California, he took courses with Milhaud at Mills College in Oakland (1946–47) and attended sessions with Sessions at the Univ. of Calif. at Berkeley (M.A., 1952). He taught at the San Francisco Cons., at the Univ. of Southern Calif. in Los Angeles (1954–60), and at the Univ. of Washington in Seattle (from 1966). Intermittently, he played in Dave Brubeck's jazz octet in California (1947–52). In 1957 he was awarded the American Prix de Rome and in 1960 a Guggenheim fellowship. His scholarly interests were certainly insular in the great mass of innocent jazz practitioners; his own music is omnivorous, ingesting dodecaphony, inhaling electronics, and absorbing by osmosis a variety of quaquaversal elements, while maintaining a dignified formality of organized musical structure.

WORKS: Suite for Clarinet, Flute, and Trumpet (1947); *Serenade* for Flute, Violin, Trumpet, and Clarinet (1947); *Schizophrenic Scherzo* for Clarinet, Trumpet, Alto and Tenor Saxophones, and Trombone (1947); Clarinet Sonata (1948); *"anyone,"* cantata for Soprano, Women's Chorus, and Chamber Orch. (1948); Concertino for Trumpet and Jazz Instruments (1948); Clarinet Quintet (1950); String Quartet (1952); *Suite* for Violin and Clarinet (1952); *"my father moved through dooms of love,"* cantata for Chorus and Small Orch. (1955); *Divertimento* for Violin, Cello, Clarinet, Bassoon, and Horn (1955); *Divertimento* for Flute, Clarinet, Guitar, Vibraphone, Bass, and Drums (1956); Concerto for Clarinet and Jazz Combo (1957); Trio for Clarinet, Violin, and Piano (1957); Quintet for Clarinet,

Violin, Cello, and Piano (1958); Concerto for Jazz Soloist (Clarinet) and Orch. (1962); *Explorations* for Jazz Combo and Tape (1963); *Interplay* for Jazz Combo and Orch. (1964); *Mosaic* for Clarinet and Piano (1964); *Elegy for Eric* for Jazz Combo (1964; in memory of Eric Dolphy); *Tangents* for Clarinet and Orch. (Rome Radio, July 3, 1965); *Explorations II* for 5 Instruments (1966); *Quadi* for Jazz Quartet and Orch. (N.Y., Oct. 6, 1968); *Songs for Myself Alone* for Soprano and Percussion (1970); *Quadrodram* for Clarinet, Trombone, Piano, Percussion, Dancer, and Film (Seattle, Dec. 9, 1970); *Chamber Muse* for Percussion, Clarinet, and Dancer (1970); *Straws* for Flute and Bassoon (1974); *Jazz Set* for Flute and Clarinet (1974); *Agate* for Soloist and Jazz Orch. (1974); *Theona* for Jazz Ensemble and Orch. (1975; Seattle, March 15, 1978); *Chrones* for String Quartet (1975); *Elegia* for Clarinet and String Orch. (Seattle, Nov. 14, 1976); *5* for Brass Quintet (1975); *Ilios* for Chorus and Wind Instruments (1977); *Janus* for Trombone and Jazz Orch. (1977; Seattle, March 2, 1978); *Ecco!* for Clarinet and Orch. (Seattle, March 15, 1978); *Intermission* for Soprano, Chorus, and Instruments (1978); *Webster's Story* for Soprano, Clarinet, and Trombone (1978); *Twelve* for Clarinet and Strings (1979); *Eternal Truths* for Woodwind Quintet (1979); *Five for Milan* for Clarinet and Jazz Orch. (1980); *Reflections* for Voices and Clarinet (1980); *Morning Incantation* for Voices and Horn (1981); *Quiet Please* for Jazz Orch. (1982); *Mandala III* for Large Flute Ensemble (1982); *Thirteen* for Flute, 2 Clarinets, Horn, 2 Trombones, Cello, and Piano (1982); *Musing* for 3 Clarinets and 3 Dancers (1983); *Pente* for Clarinet and String Quartet (1983).

Smith, Willie "the Lion"(William Henry Joseph Bonaparte Bertholoff), remarkable black American jazz pianist and composer; b. Goshen, N.Y., Nov. 24, 1897; d. N.Y., April 18, 1973. He attended Howard Univ. in Washington, D.C., and studied music privately with Hans Steinke. After serving in the U.S. Army in World War I, he settled in Harlem, where he established himself as one of the great "stride" pianists. He toured Europe several times, and toured in Africa in 1949–50. His own compositions (*Fingerbuster, Echoes of Spring, Portrait of the Duke,* etc.) had an authenticity that described perfectly the atmosphere of Harlem. His autobiography, *Music on My Mind,* is a personal impression of the Harlem jazz scene (with G. Hoefer; N.Y., 1964). Duke Ellington dedicated his *Portrait of a Lion* to him.
BIBL.: L. Feather, "Piano Giants of Jazz: W. 'the Lion' S.," *Contemporary Keyboard,* III/10 (1977).

Smith Brindle, Reginald, English composer and writer on music; b. Bamber Bridge, Jan. 5, 1917. After studying architecture and serving in World War II, he turned to music and pursued his training at the Univ. College of North Wales in Bangor (1946–49); then went to Italy, where he was a composition pupil of Pizzetti at the Accademia di Santa Cecilia in Rome (1949–52). He also studied with Dallapiccola in Florence (1949; 1952–53) and was active with the RAI (1956–61) before returning to Bangor to teach at the Univ. College (1967–70); subsequently was prof. of music at the Univ. of Surrey (from 1970). Among his books are *Serial Composition* (1966), *Contemporary Percussion* (1970), *The New Music* (1975), and *The Avant-Garde since 1945* (rev. ed., 1987).
WORKS: OPERA: *Antigone* (1969). **ORCH.:** Sym. (1954); *Variations on a Theme of Dallapiccola* (1955); *Epitaph for Alban Berg* for String Orch. (1955); *Symphonic Variations* (1957); *Cosmos* (1959); *Via Crucis* for String Orch. (1960); *Homage to H.G. Wells* (1960); Clarinet Concerto (1960); *Creation Epic* (1964); *Apocalypse* (1970); *Interface* (1972); *Fons bonitatis II* (1973). **CHAMBER:** *String Quartet Music* (1958); Concerto for 5 Instruments and Percussion (1960); *Tre dimensione* for Harp, Vibraphone, and Harpischord (1965); *Segments and Variants* for Wind Quintet (1965); *In memoriam Jan Palach* for Electric Organ (1969); *Tubal Cain's Legacy* for Trombone and Piano (1973); *The Walls of Jericho* for Tuba and Tape (1975); *Concerto on Cum Jubilo* for Brass Quintet (1975). **GUITAR:** *Variants* (1970); Trio for 3 Guitars (1970); *Concerto breve* for 8 Guitars

and Percussion (1970); *Memento* (1973); *Concerto de Angelis* for 4 Guitars (1973; also for 3 Guitars, 1974); *November Memories* (1974); *Do not go gentle* (1974); *4 Poems of Lorca* (1975); *Guitar Cosmos* (1976); also choral works and electronic pieces.

Smither, Howard E(lbert), distinguished American musicologist; b. Pittsburg, Kans., Nov. 15, 1925. He studied at Hamline Univ. in St. Paul, Minn. (A.B., 1950), and at Cornell Univ. with Grout and Austin (M.A., 1952; Ph.D., 1960, with the diss. *Theories of Rhythm in the Nineteenth and Twentieth Centuries, with a Contribution to the Theory of Rhythm for the Study of Twentieth Century Music*); also attended classes of Rudolf von Ficker at the Univ. of Munich (1953–54). He taught at the Oberlin Cons. of Music (1955–60), the Univ. of Kansas (1960–63), and Tulane Univ. (1963–68); in 1968 he was appointed a prof. of music at the Univ. of North Carolina at Chapel Hill; served as president of the American Musicological Society (1981–82). His major work is the valuable study *A History of the Oratorio* (3 vols., Chapel Hill, 1977–87); also contributed to *The New Grove Dictionary of Music and Musicians.*

Smits van Waesberghe, Jos(eph Maria Antonius Franciscus), prominent Dutch musicologist; b. Breda, North Brabant, April 18, 1901; d. Amsterdam, Oct. 9, 1986. He studied at several Jesuit seminaries; became a priest; in addition to his training in philosophy (1922–26) and theology (1930–35), he also studied music with Louis van Tulder, Marius Monnikendam, and Johan Winnubst. He taught at Canisius College in Nijmegen (1935–37), Ignatius College in Amsterdam (1937–43), the Rotterdam Cons. (1939–43), the Amsterdam Cons. (1944–46), and the Univ. of Amsterdam, where he was a Privatdozent in music and medieval theory (1945–57) and a prof. (1957–71). He served as general secretary of the Koninklije Nederlandse Toonkunstenaars Vereniging (1945–48), founder-secretary of the Nederlandse Toonkunstenaars Raad (from 1948), and president of the Gregoriusvereniging (1958–67).
WRITINGS: *Klokken en klokkengieten in de middeleeuwen* (Tilburg, 1937); *Muziekgeschiedenis der middeleeuwen* (Tilburg, 1936–42); *Het Gregoriaans* (Amsterdam, 1943; Eng. tr., 1946); *Muziek en drama in de middeleeuwen* (Amsterdam, 1943; 2nd ed., 1954); *De uitzonderlijke plaats van de Ars Musica in de ontwikkeling der wetenschappen gedurende de eeuw der Karolingers* (The Hague, 1947); *Handleiding voor het lezen der neumletters van St. Gallen* (Tilburg, 1947); *School en muziek in de Middeleeuwen* (Amsterdam, 1949); *Melodieleer* (Amsterdam, 1950; Eng. tr., 1954); *Cymbala: Bells in the Middle Ages* (Rome, 1951); *De musico et musico-paedogogico Guidone Aretino* (Florence, 1953); *Oud-Nederlands paasspel* (Bussum, 1953); *Het toonkunstenaarsboek van Nederland* (Amsterdam, 1956); with P. Fischer and C. Maas, *The Theory of Music from the Carolingian Era up to 1400* (1961); *Musikerziehung* (Leipzig, 1969); *De muzische mens: Zijn motoriek* (Amsterdam, 1971).
BIBL.: *Organicae voces: Festschrift J. S.v.W. angeboten anlässlich seines 60. Geburtstages* (Amsterdam, 1963); *Dia-pason, de omnibus: Ausgewählte Aufsätze von J. S.v.W.: Festgabe zu seinem 75. Geburtstag* (Buren, 1976).

Smolensky, Stepan (Vasilievich), Russian music scholar; b. Kazan, Oct. 20, 1848; d. Vasilsursk, near Nizhny-Novgorod, Aug. 2, 1909. He studied law and philology while active as a choral conductor; then taught at the Kazan Seminary (1875–89) and pursued research in early church music; went to Moscow as prof. of church music history at the Cons. (1891), and was also director of the Synodal School of Church Music, where he compiled a collection of over 1,000 musical MSS; subsequently was director of the St. Petersburg imperial court chapel (1901–3). He devoted much study to Russian chant, especially to neumatic notation. N. Findeisen ed. a memorial vol. in *Muzykalnaya starina,* V (1911; includes a list of his writings).

Smulders, Charles, Belgian composer; b. Maastricht, May 8, 1863; d. Liège, April 21, 1934. He studied at the Liège

Cons.; won the Belgian Prix de Rome in 1889; taught at the Liège Cons. He wrote the symphonic poems *Adieu-Absence-Retour*; *Chant d'amour*; *Le Jour*; *Le Crépuscule*; 2 piano concertos; *Hebrew Melodies* for Cello and Orch.; Violin Sonata; Piano Sonata; choruses; songs.

BIBL.: W. Paap, "C. S. en A. Diepenbrock," *Mens en Melodie*, 1 (1946).

Smyth, Dame Ethel (Mary), eminent English composer; b. London, April 22, 1858; d. Woking, Surrey, May 8, 1944. She became a pupil of Reinecke and Jadassohn at the Leipzig Cons. in 1877, but soon turned to Heinrich von Herzogenberg for her principal training, following him to Berlin; her String Quintet was performed in Leipzig in 1884. She returned to London in 1888; presented her orchestral *Serenade* (April 26, 1890) and an overture, *Antony and Cleopatra* (Oct. 18, 1890). Her prestige as a serious woman composer rose considerably with the presentation of her Mass for Solo Voices, Chorus, and Orch. at the Albert Hall (Jan. 18, 1893). After that she devoted her energies to the theater. Her 1st opera, *Fantasio*, to her own libretto in German, after Alfred de Musset's play, was produced in Weimar on May 24, 1898; this was followed by *Der Wald* (Berlin, April 9, 1902), also to her own German libretto; it was produced in London in the same year, and in N.Y. by the Metropolitan Opera on March 11, 1903. Her next opera, *The Wreckers*, was her most successful work; written originally to a French libretto, *Les Naufrageurs*, it was 1st produced in a German version as *Strandrecht* (Leipzig, Nov. 11, 1906); the composer herself tr. it into Eng., and it was staged in London on June 22, 1909; the score was revised some years later, and produced at Sadler's Wells, London, on April 19, 1939. She further wrote a comic opera, *The Boatswain's Mate* (London, Jan. 28, 1916); a one-act opera, described as a "dance-dream," *Fête galante* (Birmingham, June 4, 1923); and the opera *Entente cordiale* (Bristol, Oct. 20, 1926). Other works are a Concerto for Violin, Horn, and Orch. (London, March 5, 1927); *The Prison* for Soprano, Bass Chorus, and Orch. (London, Feb. 24, 1931); 2 string quartets (1884; 1902–12); Sonata for Cello and Piano (1887); Sonata for Violin and Piano (1887); 2 trios for Violin, Oboe, and Piano (1927); choral pieces, including *Hey Nonny No* for Chorus and Orch. (1911) and *Sleepless Dreams* for Chorus and Orch. (1912); songs; etc. Her music never overcame the strong German characteristics, in the general idiom as well as in the treatment of dramatic situations on the stage. At the same time, she was a believer in English national music and its potentialities. She was a militant leader for woman suffrage in England, for which cause she wrote *The March of the Women* (1911), the battle song of the WSPU After suffrage was granted, her role in the movement was officially acknowledged; in 1922 she was made a Dame Commander of the Order of the British Empire. She publ. a number of books in London, mostly autobiographical in nature: *Impressions That Remained* (2 vols., 1919; new ed., 1945); *Streaks of Life* (1921); *As Time Went On* (1936); *What Happened Next* (1940); also some humorous essays and reminiscences, *A Three-legged Tour in Greece* (1927); *A Final Burning of Boats* (1928); *Female Pipings in Eden* (1934); *Beecham and Pharaoh* (1935); *Inordinate (?) Affection* (1936).

BIBL.: K. Dale, "D. E. S.," *Music & Letters*, XXV (1944); C. St. John, *E. S.: A Biography* (N.Y., 1959); L. Collis, *Impetuous Heart: The Story of E. S.* (London, 1984).

Snel, Joseph-François, Belgian violinist, conductor, teacher, and composer; b. Brussels, July 30, 1793; d. Koekelberg, near Brussels, March 10, 1861. He studied violin with Corneille Vander Nicolas in Brussels; continued his training with Baillot and Dourlen at the Paris Cons. In 1818 he founded in Brussels the Académie de Musique et de Chant (with Mees); he popularized in Belgium the instructional singing methods of Galin and Wilhem; was an inspector of army music schools (1829). He conducted at the Théâtre Royal de la Monnaie (1831–34); was made conductor of the Société Royale de la Grande-harmonie (1831), maître de chapelle at the Church of St. Michel

et Ste. Gudule (1835), and head of the music of the Civic Guard (1837). In 1847 he became a member of the Classe des Beaux-arts of the Belgian Royal Academy.

WORKS: BALLETS (all 1st perf. in Brussels): *Frisac, ou La double noce* (Feb. 13, 1825); *Le page inconstant* (June 27, 1825); *Le cinq juillet* (July 9, 1825; in collaboration with C.-L. Hanssens, Jr.); *Pourceaugnac* (Feb. 3, 1826); *Les enchantements de Polichinelle* (March 8, 1829); *Les barricades* (Feb. 3, 1830); also a Symphonic concertante; Violin Concerto; 2 clarinet concertos; Clarinet Concertino; various pieces for Wind Band; chamber music; sacred and secular vocal works; piano pieces.

Snetzler (Schnetzler), Johann, Swiss organ builder; b. Schaffhausen, April 6, 1710; d. there, Sept. 28, 1785. He was apprenticed to the Passau organ builder Egedacher, with whom he worked on the Passau Cathedral organ (1731–33); after serving as assistant to Müller in Haarlem, he went to England and settled in London about 1746 as an organ builder; constructed the organ for St. Margaret's, King's Lynn (1753–54); retired about 1781 and returned to his homeland.

BIBL.: A. Freeman, "J. S. and his Organs," *The Organ*, XIV (1934–35); W. Sumner, *The Organ: Its Evolution, Principles of Construction and Use* (London, 1952; 4th ed., rev. and enl., 1973).

Snow, Hank (actually, **Clarence Eugene**), Canadian-born American country-music singer, guitarist, and songwriter; b. Liverpool, Nova Scotia, May 9, 1914. He began his singing career on a radio station in Halifax in 1935; also made recordings and toured extensively throughout Canada and the U.S. as The Singing Ranger. He settled in the U.S. in 1948; became an American citizen in 1957. In 1950 he joined the "Grand Ole Opry" radio program in Nashville, Tenn.; also made tours of Europe and the Far East. He was elected to the Country Music Hall of Fame in 1979.

Sobinov, Leonid (Vitalievich), celebrated Russian tenor; b. Yaroslavl, June 7, 1872; d. Riga, Oct. 14, 1934. He was an offspring of a middle-class family with peasant roots (his grandfather was an emancipated serf). He studied law at the Univ. of Moscow, where he also sang in a student choir. In 1892 he began to study voice with Dodonov and appeared professionally in a traveling Italian opera company in Moscow without interrupting his univ. study (1893–94); he graduated in law in 1894, and was appointed assistant advocate to a Moscow lawyer. Turning decisively to singing, he made his debut at the Bolshoi Theater in Moscow in 1897, and retained his connection with it during almost his entire career. In 1901 he also joined the Imperial Maryinsky Theater in St. Petersburg. His successes on the European stage were no less outstanding; he sang at La Scala in Milan (1904–6); from 1909 he also appeared in London, Paris, and Berlin. He was eloquent in the roles of Alfredo in *La Traviata*, Des Grieux in *Manon*, and Faust in Gounod's opera. His performance of Lensky in *Eugene Onegin* remained an unsurpassed model of Russian operatic lyricism. In his solo recitals he could squeeze the last fluid ounce out of Tchaikovsky's melancholy songs. No wonder that he was idolized by Russian audiences, particularly among the young and female; a whole tribe of "Sobinovites" appeared, and long queues formed before his concerts, willing to stand in line for hours in the hope of obtaining scarce tickets. He served as director of the Bolshoi Theater in 1917–18. In 1918–19 he gave recitals in and around Kiev, N. Slonimsky serving occasionally as his accompanist. He retired from the stage in 1924.

BIBL.: Y. Boyarsky, ed., *L. S.: Life and Creative Work* (Moscow, 1937); M. Lvov, *L. S.* (Moscow, 1951); A. Orfenov, *Creative Work of L. S.* (Moscow, 1965).

Sobolewski, Edward (actually, **Johann Friedrich Eduard**), German-born American violinist, conductor, and composer of Polish descent; b. Königsberg, Oct. 1, 1804; d. St. Louis, May 17, 1872. He was a composition pupil of Zelter in Berlin and of Weber in Dresden (1821–24); became an opera conductor in Königsberg (1830); was founder-conductor of the orch. of the Philharmonische Gesellschaft (from 1838) and conductor of the choir of the Academy of Music (from 1843); subsequently was director of music at the Bremen Theater (from 1854). In 1859 he emigrated to the U.S., settling in Milwaukee, then a center of German musical immigrants; was founder-conductor of the Milwaukee Phil. Society Orch. (1860); then settled in St. Louis, where he conducted the Phil. Society (1860–66); was prof. of vocal music at Bonham's Female Seminary (from 1869).

WORKS: OPERAS: *Imogen* (1833); *Velleda* (1836); *Salvator Rosa* (1848); *Komala* (Weimar, Oct. 30, 1858); *Mohega, die Blume des Waldes* (Milwaukee, Oct. 11, 1859, to his own libretto, in German, on an American subject dealing with an Indian girl saved by Pulaski from death); *An die Freude* (Milwaukee, 1859); also symphonic poems, oratorios and other choral works, songs, etc. **BIBL.:** R. Laudon, "E. S., Frontier Kapellmeister: From Königsberg to St. Louis," *Musical Quarterly,* 73/1 (Nov. 1989).

Socor, Matei, Rumanian composer; b. Iaşi, Sept. 28, 1908; d. Bucharest, May 30, 1980. He studied theory with Castaldi at the Bucharest Cons. (1927–29) and composition with Karg-Elert at the Leipzig Cons. (1930–33); then was active as a composer and teacher in his homeland.

WORKS: OPERA: *Conu Leonida faţă cu reacţiunea* (1976; Bucharest, Dec. 28, 1978). **ORCH.:** Concerto for Clarinet, Horn, Cello, and Orch. (1939); *Passacaglia* for Cello and Chamber Orch. (1944; also for Violin or Cello and Piano); Violin Concerto (1955). **VOCAL:** *Mama,* poem for Mezzo-soprano, Chorus, and Orch. (1949); choruses; songs. **CHAMBER:** Piano Sonata (1932); Concerto for Oboe, Clarinet, Bassoon, Violin, Viola, Cello, and Piano (1936); Wind Sextet (1968).

Söderblom, Ulf, Finnish conductor; b. Turku, Feb. 5, 1930. He studied conducting with Hans Swarowsky at the Vienna Academy of Music, graduating in 1957; then joined the Finnish National Opera in Helsinki as a conductor; he became its chief conductor in 1973; took it to N.Y. for performances at the Metropolitan Opera in 1983.

Soderini, Agostin, esteemed Italian organist and composer who flourished in the late 16th and early 17th centuries. He was organist of Milan's S. Maria della Rosa in 1608. He publ. in Milan *Sacrarum cantionum 8 et 9 Vocibus liber primus* (1599) and *Canzoni a 4 et 8 voci libro primo* (1608).

Söderlind, Ragnar, Norwegian composer; b. Oslo, June 27, 1945. He studied in Oslo with Baden (counterpoint), Hukvari (conducting), and Ulleberg (horn); then studied at the Sibelius Academy in Helsinki with Erik Bergman and Joonas Kokkonen; later studied conducting with Arvid Fladmoe at the Oslo Cons. (graduate degree, 1976).

WORKS: STAGE: *Esther and the Blue Serenity,* opera (1973); *Hedda Gabler,* choreographic poem (1978); *Kristin Lavransdatter,* ballet (1982). **ORCH.:** *Nocturne* (1963); *Preludium per orchestra: Alban Berg in Memoriam* (1964–65); *Pietà* for Mezzo-soprano and String Orch. (1965); *Rokkomborre,* symphonic poem (1967; rev. 1973); *Polaris,* symphonic visions (1967–70); *Trauermusik* (1968); *Fantasia borealis* (1969); *Sinfonia minimale* (1971); *International Rhapsody* for Small Orch. (1971; for Full Orch., 1977); 3 syms.: No. 1 for Soprano and Orch. (1975); No. 2, *Sonfonia breve* (1981); No. 3, *Les illuminations symphoniques* (1983–84); *Hedda Gabler,* symphonic/choreographic drama (1978); *Amor et labor,* symphonic poem (1979); *Come, Sea Winds, Come!,* symphonic poem (1982); *Olavs Hymne* for Mezzo-soprano, Chorus, and Orch., for King Olav's 80th birthday (1983); *September Light* for Mezzo-soprano, Chorus, and Orch. (1983); *Toccata brillante* (1984); *Eystradalir* (1984). **CHAMBER:** *Elegia I* for Cello and *II* for Violin (1966; when played simultaneously, *Elegia III*); *Dithyrambe,* sketch for Bassoon and Harp (1967); *Körsbärblommor* (Cherry Blossom), 5 Japanese love poems for Baritone, Flute, English Horn, Cello, and Percussion (1967); *Intermezzo* for Percussionist (1968); *La Mort des pauvres* for Male Chorus,

4 Trombones, and Percussion (1969); *La poema battutta* for 8 Percussionists (1973); *2 Pieces from the Desert* for Oboe and Piano (1973; orch. 1974); String Quartet (1975); Quintet for 2 Trumpets, Horn, Trombone, and Tuba (1982); *Consolation* for Piano (1969); also choruses; songs.

Soderlund, Gustav Frederic, Swedish-American music scholar, teacher, and composer; b. Göteborg, Jan. 25, 1881; d. Rochester, N.Y., Nov. 28, 1972. He studied piano and theory in Sweden; after teaching at the Valparaiso Cons. in Chile (1908–16), he settled in the U.S.; taught at the Univ. of Kansas (1919–27) and at the Eastman School of Music in Rochester, N.Y. (1928–47).

WORKS: ORCH.: *Nocturne* (1918); *Svithiod,* symphonic poem (1928); *Serenade* (1929); *Festival Symphony* (1942); *Suite* for Small Orch. (1965); also chamber music; piano pieces. **WRITINGS:** *Examples Illustrating the Development of Melodic Line and Contrapuntal Style from Greek Melody to Mozart* (Rochester, N.Y., 1932); *Examples of Gregorian Chant and Works by Orlandus Lassus and Giovanni Pierluigi Palestrina* (Rochester, 1937; 3rd ed., 1946); *Direct Approach to Counterpoint in 16th Century Style* (N.Y., 1947).

Söderman, (Johan) August, Swedish composer; b. Stockholm, July 17, 1832; d. there, Feb. 10, 1876. He studied piano and composition at the Stockholm Cons. (1847–50); then joined Stjernstrom's theater company as director of music and toured with it in Sweden and Finland; following further studies with E.F. Richter in Leipzig (1856–57), he resumed his post with the Stjernstrom company; later was chorusmaster and deputy director at Stockholm's Royal Theater. He was particularly influenced by the lyric works of Schumann, Wagner, and Liszt, an influence that is combined with Swedish national elements in his theater music.

WORKS: OPERETTAS: *Urdur, eller Neckens dotter Zigenarhöfdingen Zohrab* (Zohrab, the Gypsy Chief; Helsinki, 1852) and *Hin Ondes första lärospan* (The Devil's First Lesson; Stockholm, Sept. 14, 1856); incidental music to some 80 plays; orch. pieces; choral works; chamber music; many ballads and songs. **BIBL.:** G. Jeanson, *A. S.: En svensk tondiktares liv och verk* (Stockholm, 1926; includes a complete list of his works).

Sodero, Cesare, Italian-American conductor and composer; b. Naples, Aug. 2, 1886; d. N.Y., Dec. 16, 1947. He studied with Alessandro Longo (piano) and Martucci (composition) at the Naples Cons.; in 1907 he emigrated to the U.S. and settled in N.Y.; was a music director of the Edison Phonograph Co., the National Broadcasting Co., and the Mutual Broadcasting Co.; conducted the San Carlo Grand Opera Co. and the Philadelphia Grand Opera. He wrote an opera, *Ombre russe* (Venice, June 19, 1930); ballets; chamber music.

Söderström (-Olow), (Anna) Elisabeth, prominent Swedish soprano; b. Stockholm, May 7, 1927. She studied voice with Andreyeva von Skilondz in Stockholm; also took courses in languages and literary history at the Univ. of Stockholm, and received a thorough musical education at the Stockholm Royal Opera School; made her operatic debut as Bastienne in Mozart's *Bastien und Bastienne* at the Drottningholm Court Theater in Stockholm in 1947; became a member of the Royal Opera there in 1950. She made her 1st appearance in Salzburg as Ighino in Pfitzner's *Palestrina* in 1955; then at the Glyndebourne Festival as the Composer in *Ariadne auf Naxos* in 1957, becoming one of its most noted singers. She made her Metropolitan Opera debut in N.Y. as Susanna in *Le nozze di Figaro* on Oct. 30, 1959, and remained on its roster until 1964; subsequently pursued her career mainly in Europe until returning to the U.S. in 1977 to sing the title role in *Kát'a Kabanová* at the San Francisco Opera; returned to the Metropolitan Opera in 1983 as Ellen Orford in *Peter Grimes.* In 1988 she sang in the premiere of Argento's *The Aspern Papers* in Dallas. In 1990 she was appointed artistic director of the Drottningholm Court Theater. Her extraordinary command of languages made her an outstanding concert and lieder artist, both in Europe and in North America. Among her notable roles were Fiordiligi, Tatyana, Sophie, Marie in *Wozzeck*, the Countess in *Capriccio*, Jenůfa, Emilia Marty in *The Makropoulos Affair*, and the Governess in *The Turn of the Screw*. She publ. a lighthearted autobiography, *I Min Tonart* (1978; in Eng., 1979, as *In My Own Key*).

BIBL.: *Current Biography* (Nov. 1985).

Soffredini, Alfredo, Italian writer on music, teacher, and composer; b. Livorno, Sept. 17, 1854; d. Milan, March 12, 1923. He studied with Mazzucato and Sangalli at the Milan Cons.; ed. Milan's influential *Gazzetta Musicale* (1896–1912); also taught composition; among his students was Mascagni. He composed 8 operas to his own librettos: *Il Saggio* (Livorno, Feb. 3, 1883); 2-act children's opera, *Il piccolo Haydn* (Faenza, Nov. 24, 1889); *Salvatorello* (Pavia, March 25, 1894); *Tarcisio* (Milan, Nov. 23, 1895); *Aurora* (Pavia, April 21, 1897); *La coppa d'oro* (Milan, Jan. 27, 1900); *Graziella* (Pavia, Nov. 15, 1902); *Il leone* (Cesena, 1914).

Sofronitzky, Vladimir (Vladimirovich), esteemed Russian pianist and teacher; b. St. Petersburg, May 8, 1901; d. Moscow, Aug. 29, 1961. He studied with A. Lebedeva-Geshevich and A. Mikhailovsky in Warsaw, where he began his career while still a child; completed his training with Nikolayev at the Petrograd Cons. (graduated, 1921); then toured throughout Europe; also was a prof. at the Leningrad Cons. (1936–42) and the Moscow Cons. (1942–61). He was greatly praised for his interpretations of Chopin and Scriabin; his performances of Liszt, Schumann, and Rachmaninoff were also notable.

BIBL.: V. Delson, *V. S.* (Moscow, 1959); Ya. Milstein, ed., *Vospominaniya o Sofronitskom* (Reminiscences of S.; Moscow, 1970).

Sohal, Naresh (Kumar), Indian composer; b. Harsipind, Punjab, Sept. 18, 1939. He took courses in science and mathematics at Punjab Univ. In 1962 he settled in England and pursued training in harmony and counterpoint at the London College of Music (1965) and in composition with Jeremy Dale Roberts (1965–66); then conducted research on micro-intervals under Alexander Goehr.

WORKS: ORCH.: *Asht Prahar* (1965; London, Jan. 17, 1970); Concerto for Harmonica, Percussion, and Strings (1966); *Aalaykhyam I* (1970; London, Nov. 27, 1971) and *II* (1972; London, Feb. 5, 1973); *Indra-Dhanush* (1973); *Dhyan I* for Cello and Small Orch. (1974); *Tandavva Nritya: Dance of Destruction and Re-creation* (1984). **CHAMBER:** *Hexand* for 8 Players (1971); *Octal* for 8 Players (1972); *Hexahedron* for 6 Players (1975); 2 brass quintets (1981, 1983). **VOCAL:** *Kavita I* for Soprano and 8 Players (1970), *II* for Soprano, Flute, and Piano (1972), and *III* for Soprano and Electric Double Bass (1972); *Surya* for 5 Soloists, Chorus, Flute, and 3 Percussion (1970); *Inscape* for 6 Solo Voices, Flute, Percussion, and Electronics (1979); *The Wanderer* for Baritone, Chorus, and Orch. (1981; London, Aug. 23, 1982); *From Gitanjali* for Bass-baritone and Orch. (N.Y., Sept. 12, 1985).

Söhngen, Oskar, learned German theologian and musicologist; b. Hottenstein, Dec. 5, 1900; d. Berlin, Aug. 28, 1983. He studied philosophy and theology (Ph.D., 1922) at the Univ. of Bonn; took courses in philosophy and theology (licentiate, 1924) at the Univ. of Marburg, where he also received instruction in musicology from Stephani. He was a priest in Cologne (1926–32), then an adviser to the Evangelical Church Synod (1932–33; 1935–69); also taught at the Berlin Hochschule für Musikerziehung und Kirchenmusik (1935–59). He devoted his efforts to the study and promotion of liturgical music; was an ed. of the journal *Kunst und Kirche*.

WRITINGS: *Pfarrer und Kirchenmusiker: Sinn und Richtlinien einer Arbeitsgemeinschaft* (Kassel, 1933); *Die neue Kirchenmusik: Wandlungen und Entscheidungen* (Berlin, 1937); ed. with C. Mahrenholz, *Handbuch zum Evangelischen Kirchengesangbuch* (Berlin, 1953); *Kämpfende Kirchenmusik: Die Bewährungsprobe der evangelischen Kirchenmusik im Dritten Reich* (Kassel and Basel, 1954); *Theologische Grundlagen der*

Kirchenmusik (Kassel, 1958); *Wandel und Beharrung* (Berlin, 1965); *Theologie der Musik* (Kassel, 1967); *Erneuerte Kirchenmusik: Eine Streitschrift* (Göttingen, 1975).

Sojo, Vicente Emilio, Venezuelan conductor, pedagogue, ethnomusicologist, and composer; b. Guatire, Dec. 8, 1887; d. Caracas, Aug. 11, 1974. He studied music at the Academia de Bellas Artes in Caracas (1910); in 1921 he became a prof. of music theory at the Escuela Superior de Música in Caracas. In 1937 he founded the Orquesta Sinfónica Venezuela and the choral ensemble Orfeón Lamas, which became of prime importance in the musical culture of Venezuela. Sojo was also active in national ethnomusicology; he collected and harmonized several hundred Venezuelan folk songs and church hymns of the colonial period. He composed mainly sacred music, motets, and organ pieces.

BIBL.: R. Fernández, *V.E. S.* (Caracas, 1968)).

Sokalsky, Pyotr (Petrovich), Russian writer on music and composer; b. Kharkov, Sept. 26, 1832; d. Odessa, April 11, 1887. He studied science and taught school. His significance in Russian music lies in his being an ardent collector of Russian folk songs; his chief work, *Russian Folk Music, Great Russian and Ukrainian, its Melodic and Rhythmic Structure and its Difference from the Principles of Contemporary Harmonic Music*, was publ. in Kharkov in 1888. He composed the operas *May Night* (1876), *The Siege of Dubno* (1878), and *Mazeppa* (unfinished); also orch. works; a cantata; songs; piano pieces.

Sokola, Miloš, Czech composer; b. Bučovice, Moravia, April 18, 1913; d. Malé Kyšice, Sept. 27, 1976. He studied composition with Petrželka and violin with O. Vávra at the Brno Cons. (1929–38); had further composition studies at the Prague Cons. with V. Novák (1938–40) and J. Křička (1942–44). From 1942 to 1973 he was a violinist in the Prague National Theater orch.

WORKS: OPERA: *Marnotratný syn* (The Prodigal Son; 1948; Olomouc, 1963). **ORCH.:** *9 Variations on a Theme by Vítězslava Kaprálová* (1952; Prague, Feb. 17, 1957; from Kaprálová's *April Preludes*); Violin Concerto (1952); *Devátý květen* (The Ninth of May), symphonic poem (1960); Concerto for Organ and String Orch. (1971); Piano Concertino (1972). **CHAMBER:** 5 string quartets (1944; with Solo Tenor, 1946; 1955; 1964; 1971); Violin Sonata (1972); Wind Quintet (1973). **PIANO:** 5 Miniatures (1931); Sonata (1946); *Valses* (1953); *12 Preludes* (1954); *Suite* for Left Hand (1972). **ORGAN:** *Toccata quasi Passacaglia* (1964); *B-A-C-H Studies* (1972); *Andante cantabile* (1973).

Sokoloff, Nicolai, Russian-born American conductor; b. near Kiev, May 28, 1886; d. La Jolla, Calif., Sept. 25, 1965. He was taken to the U.S. as a child, and studied violin with Loeffler in Boston; played violin in the Boston Sym. Orch. In 1907 he went to Europe to complete his studies. After serving as concertmaster of the Russian Sym. Orch. in N.Y., he decided to settle in the U.S. in 1914 and became a naturalized citizen; became music director of the San Francisco Phil. in 1914, then served as the 1st music director of the Cleveland Orch. (1918–33). He was director of the Federal Music Project (1935–38) and music director of the Seattle Sym. Orch. (1938–40); later was music director of the La Jolla Arts Association.

Sokolov, Nikolai Alexandrovich, Russian composer and pedagogue; b. St. Petersburg, March 26, 1859; d. there (Petrograd), March 27, 1922. He was a pupil of Rimsky-Korsakov at the St. Petersburg Cons. (graduated, 1884); taught harmony there from 1896 until his death; was a mentor to Shostakovich. He was also a prolific composer in the traditional Russian manner; among his works were the ballets *The Wild Swans* (1900), *The Flowers of Little Ida*, and *The Winter's Tale* (1915); *Elégie* for String Orch. (c.1880–90); *Divertissement* for Orch.; 3 string quartets (1890, 1894, 1895); 2 string trios; songs.

Solano, Francisco Ignacio, Portuguese music theorist; b. probably in Coimbra, c.1720; d. Lisbon, Sept. 18, 1800. He studied with Giovanni Giorgi at the S. Catharina de Ribamar music school; was director of his own Lisbon music school (from 1779).

WRITINGS (all publ. in Lisbon): *Nova instrucção musical, ou Theorica pratica* (1764); *Nova tratado de musica metrica, e rythmica* (1779); *Dissertação sobre a caracter, qualidades, e antiguidades da musica* (1780); *Vindicias do tono* (1793).

Solares, Enrique, Guatemalan pianist and composer; b. Guatemala City, July 11, 1910. He studied piano with Salvador Ley in Guatemala and composition with Raymond Moulaert in Brussels, Jaroslav Křička in Prague (1936–39), and Alfredo Casella in Rome (1939–42). He returned to Guatemala in 1943 and taught piano; then was a consular officer in Guatemalan embassies in Rome, Brussels, Madrid, and Paris. His compositions are set in Baroque forms; later he experimented with serial techniques.

WORKS: *Ricercare sobre el nombre de BACH* for String Orch. (1941); *Toccatina* for Guitar (1946); *Partita* for String Orch. (1947); Sonata for Solo Violin (1958); *Fantasia* for Guitar (1959); *Idea con 15 Deformaciones* for Piano (1962); *7 Traversuras* for Piano (1969); *12 Microtransparencias* for Piano (1970).

Soldat, Marie, Austrian violinist; b. Graz, March 25, 1863; d. there, Sept. 30, 1955. She studied in Graz and with Joachim at the Berlin Hochschule für Musik (1879–82), graduating with the Mendelssohn Prize. She made a specialty of the Brahms Violin Concerto, which she performed with great authority. In 1887 she formed in Berlin her own string quartet (all women); in 1899 she married the lawyer Röger, and settled in Vienna, where she formed a new string quartet; also continued to appear as a soloist.

Soler (Ramos), Antonio (Francisco Javier José), important Catalan composer and organist; b. Olot, Gerona (baptized), Dec. 3, 1729; d. El Escorial, near Madrid, Dec. 20, 1783. He entered the Montserrat monastery choir school in 1736, where his mentors were the maestro Benito Esteve and the organist Benito Valls. About 1750 he was made maestro de capilla in Lérida; in 1752, was ordained a subdeacon and also became a member of the Jeronymite monks in El Escorial, taking the habit, and then being professed in 1753; was made maestro de capilla in 1757. He also pursued studies with José de Nebra and Domenico Scarlatti. Soler was a prolific composer of both sacred and secular vocal music, as well as instrumental music. Among his works are 9 masses, 5 Requiems, 60 Psalms, 13 Magnificats, 14 litanies, 28 Lamentations, 5 motets, and other sacred works; 132 villancicos (1752–78); 120 keyboard sonatas (100 sonatas and a *Fandango* ed. by F. Marvin, N.Y., 1958–59); 6 quintets for 2 Violins, Viola, Cello, and Organ (1776; ed. by R. Gerhard, Barcelona, 1933); *6 conciertos de dos organos obligados* (ed. in Musica Hispana, series C, 1952–62, and by S. Kastner, Mainz, 1972); liturgical organ pieces. His writings include *Llave de la modulación, y antigüedades de la música en que se trata del fundamento necessario para saber modular: Theórica, y prática para el más claro conocimiento de qualquier especie de figuras, desde el tiempo de Juan de Muris, hasta hoy, con albunos cánones enigmáticos, y sus resoluciones* (Madrid, 1762; ed. and tr. by M. Crouch, diss., Univ. of Calif., Santa Barbara, 1978), *Satisfacción a los reparos precisos hechos por D. Antonio Roel del Rio, a la Llave de la modulación* (Madrid, 1765), *Carta escrita a un amigo en que le da parte de un diálogo ultimamente publicado contra su Llave de la modulación* (Madrid, 1766), and *Combinación de Monedas y Cálculo manifiesto contra el Libro anónimo intitulado: Correspondencia de la Moneda de Cataluña a la de Castilla* (Barcelona, 1771).

BIBL.: F. Carroll, *An Introduction to A. S.* (diss., Univ. of Rochester, 1960); S. Rubio, "El Padre Fray A. S.: Vida y obra," *Monasterio de San Lorenzo el Real El Escorial* (Madrid, 1964); T. Espinosa, *Selected Unpublished Villancicos of Padre Fray A. S.* (diss., Univ. of Southern Calif., 1969); K. Heimes, *A. S.'s Keyboard Sonatas* (Pretoria, 1969); S. Rubio, "Música del P. A. S. que se conserva en el Monasterio de El Escorial," *Tesoro Sacro Musical*, LV (1972); idem, "El Padre S., compositor de música vocal," ibid., LVI (1973); idem, "A. S., carta escrita a un amigo," *Revista de Musicologia*, II (1979).

Soler, Josep, Catalan composer; b. Barcelona, March 25, 1935. He studied composition with René Leibowitz in Paris (1959)

and with Cristòfor Taltabull in Barcelona (1960–64). In 1977 he was appointed to the staff of the Barcelona Cons.

WORKS: Operas: *Agamemnon* (1960); *Edipo y Iocasta* (1972; Barcelona, Oct. 30, 1974); *Jesús de Nazaret* (1974–78); *Danae* for String Orch. (1959; rev. 1969; Lisbon, June 23, 1977); *Cantata Ioel Prophetae,* chamber cantata (1960); Trio for 2 Violins and Piano (1961); Piano Trio (1964); *Orpheus* for Piano and Orch. (1965; rev. 1974); *Quetzalcoatl* for Flute and Chamber Orch. (1966); 2 syms.: *The Solar Cycle I* and *The Solar Cycle II* (1967; 1969, rev. 1977); *Lachrymae* for 11 Instruments (1967); *Diaphonia* for 17 Wind Instruments (1968); String Trio (1968); *Música triste* for Guitar (1968); Piano Concerto (1969); Concerto for Harpsichord, Oboe, English Horn, Bass Clarinet, Viola, and Cello (1969); *Sounds in the Night* for 6 Percussionists (1969); *Inferno* for Chamber Ensemble (1970); 3 string quartets (1966, 1971, 1975); *Tañido de Falsas* for Guitar and Percussion (1971); *Noche oscura* for Organ and Percussion (1971); Cello Concerto (1973); *Requiem* for Solo Percussion and Orch. (1974–75; Kassel, Sept. 18, 1977); *Apuntava l'alba* for Orch. (1975; Barcelona, Feb. 5, 1976); *3 Erotic Songs* for Chorus a cappella (1976); *Shakespeare Lieder* for Tenor and Orch. (1976–77); *Harmonices mundi,* in 3 vols.: No. 1 for Piano, and Nos. 2 and 3 for Organ (1977); songs.

Solerti, Angelo, Italian philologist and music scholar; b. Savona, Sept. 20, 1865; d. Massa Carrara, Jan. 10, 1907. He studied at the Istituto di Studi Superiori in Florence and at the Univ. of Turin (arts degree, 1887). His contributions to the early history of opera are valuable: *Le origini del melodramma: testimonianze dei contemporanei* (a collection of contemporary documents and prefaces to the earliest operas; Turin, 1903); *Gli albori del melodramma* (3 vols., Milan, 1904–5); *Musica, ballo e drammatica alla corte medicea dal 1600 al 1637: notizie tratte da un diario (tenuto da Cesare Tinghi), con appendice di testi inediti e rari* (Florence, 1905); *Ferrara e la Corte Estense nella second metà del secolo XVI* (contains a chapter on *Musica e canto;* Città di Castello, 1891).

Sollberger, Harvey (Dene), American flutist, conductor, teacher, and composer; b. Cedar Rapids, Iowa, May 11, 1938. He studied composition with Philip Bezanson and Eldon Obrecht at the Univ. of Iowa (B.A., 1960) and also received instruction in flute from Betty Bang Mather; completed his training in composition with Jack Beeson and Otto Luening at Columbia Univ. (M.A., 1964); held 2 Guggenheim fellowships (1969, 1973). With Charles Wuorinen, he founded the Group for Contemporary Music in N.Y. in 1962; appeared regularly with it as a flutist and conductor; also toured as a flutist and conductor in the U.S. and Europe. He served on the faculties of Columbia Univ. (1965–83), the Manhattan School of Music (1971–83), the Philadelphia College of the Performing Arts (1980–82), C.W. Post College of Long Island Univ. (from 1981), and the Indiana Univ. School of Music (from 1983), where he also directed its new-music ensemble. His music reveals an imaginatively applied serial method.

WORKS: *Grand Quartet* for Flutes (1962); *2 Oboes Troping* (1963); *Chamber Variations* for 12 Players and Conductor (1964); *Music for Sophocles' Antigone,* electronic music (1966); *Fanfare Mix Transpose,* electronic music (1968); *As Things Are and Become* for String Trio (1969; rev. 1972); *Musica transalpina,* 2 motets for Soprano, Baritone, and 9 Players (1970); *Elegy for Igor Stravinsky* for Flute, Cello, and Piano (1971); *The 2 and the 1* for Amplified Cello and 2 Percussionists (1972); *Folio,* 11 pieces for Bassoon (1974–76); *Sunflowers* for Flute and Vibraphone (1976); *Flutes and Drums* for 8 Flutes, 8 Percussionists, and 4 Double Basses (1977); *Music for Prepared Dancers* for Dancers, Flute, Violin, and Percussion (1978); *6 Quartets* for Flute and Piano (1981); *The Humble Heart/CAT Scan* for Woodwind Quintet (1982); *Interrupted Night* for 5 Instruments (1983); *Killapata/Chaskapata* for Flute and Flute Choir (1983); *Double Triptych* for Flute and Percussion (1984); *3 or 4 Things I Know about the Oboe,* chamber concerto for Oboe and 13 Players (1986); *original substance/manifests/ traces* for Flute, Harp, Guitar, Piano, and Percussion (1987);

Persian Golf for String Orch. (1987); *Quodlibetudes* for Flute (1988).

Sollertinsky, Ivan (Ivanovich), brilliant Russian musicologist and music critic; b. Vitebsk, Dec. 3, 1902; d. Novosibirsk, Feb. 11, 1944. He studied Hispanic philosophy at the Univ. of Petrograd (1919–24) and drama at the Inst. for the History of the Arts (graduated, 1923), subsequently pursuing postgraduate courses (1926–29); also took conducting lessons with Malko. He was active as a lecturer and music critic in Leningrad, where he later taught at the Cons. (from 1936). He showed profound understanding of the problems of modern music and was one of the earliest supporters of Shostakovich; publ. numerous articles dealing with Soviet music in general; M. Druskin ed. 4 vols. of his writings (Leningrad, 1946; 1956, 2nd ed., 1963; 1973; 1973).
    BIBL.: L. Mikheeva, *I.I. S.* (Leningrad, 1988).

Solomon (actually, **Solomon Cutner**), outstanding English pianist; b. London, Aug. 9, 1902; d. there, Feb. 2, 1988. He studied with Mathilde Verne, making a sensational debut as a child prodigy as soloist in Tchaikovsky's 1st Piano Concerto in London (June 30, 1911); later studied in Paris with Lazare Lévy and Marcel Dupré, and then resumed his career in 1923, adopting his 1st name for his concert engagements. In 1926 he made his U.S. debut, and in subsequent years toured all over the world as a soloist with orchs., recitalist, and chamber music artist. His remarkable career was cut short at the height of his interpretative powers when he was stricken by an incapacitating illness in 1955. In 1946 he was made a Commander of the Order of the British Empire. His performances of the classics were particularly esteemed; he eschewed virtuosity for its own sake, opting instead for intellectually insightful and unmannered interpretations of the highest order.

Solomon, Izler, American conductor; b. St. Paul, Minn., Jan. 11, 1910; d. Fort Wayne, Ind., Dec. 6, 1987. He took violin lessons with Myron Poliakin in Philadelphia and Michael Press in N.Y.; then studied at Michigan State College (1928–31). He made his debut as a conductor with the Lansing (Mich.) Civic Orch. on March 17, 1932; led that orch. until 1936; then conducted the Illinois Sym. Orch. (1936–42) and the Columbus (Ohio) Phil. (1941–49); was guest conductor of the Israel Phil. during its American tour in 1951. His major post, which established his reputation, was as music director of the Indianapolis Sym. Orch. (1956–75), which he brought to a level of excellence. In his programs he included many modern American works. In 1976 he suffered a stroke, which ended his career.

Solomon, Maynard (Elliott), American recording executive and writer on music; b. N.Y., Jan. 5, 1930. He was educated in N.Y. at the High School of Music and Art and at Brooklyn College (A.B., 1950); then pursued postgraduate studies at Columbia Univ. (1950–51). He was co-founder and co-owner of the Vanguard Recording Society, Inc., of N.Y. (1950–86); was on the faculty of the City Univ. of N.Y. (1979–81) and served as a visiting prof. at the State Univ. of N.Y. at Stony Brook (1988–89). He contributed many articles on Beethoven, Schubert, and other composers to the *Musical Quarterly, Music & Letters, 19th Century Music, Beethoven Studies,* the *Beethoven-Jahrbuch,* the *Journal of the American Musicological Society,* and other publications, and also served as associate ed. of *American Imago.* He ed. "Beethoven's Tagebuch 1812–1818," in *Beethoven Studies 3* (London, 1982).
    WRITINGS: *Marxism and Art* (1973); *Beethoven* (1977); *Myth, Creativity and Psychoanalysis* (1978); *Beethoven Essays* (1988).

Soloviev-Sedoy, Vasili (Pavlovich), Russian composer; b. St. Petersburg, April 25, 1907; d. Moscow, Dec. 2, 1979. He learned to play the balalaika, guitar, and piano before pursuing studies at the Mussorgsky Music School (1929–31) and the Leningrad Cons. (1931–36). He was active as a pianist, playing improvisations on the radio and accompanying exercises in the Leningrad Studio of Creative Gymnastics. During World War II, he organized a series of theatrical productions for the Soviet army. He was a member of the Supreme Soviet in the 3rd, 4th, and 5th congresses. In 1975 he was awarded the order of Hero of Socialist Labor. He was regarded in Russia as one of the most expert composers of Soviet songs, some of which acquired immense popularity; one of them, *Evenings at Moscow,* became a musical signature of daily news broadcasts on the Soviet radio. In all, he wrote over 700 songs. He was able to synthesize the melos of Russian folk songs with revolutionary ballads and marching rhythms. His other works include an opera, several operettas, the ballet *Taras Bulba* (Leningrad, Dec. 12, 1940; rev. 1953), a few orch. pieces, film scores, and piano music.
    BIBL.: A. Sokhor, *V.P. S.-S.* (Leningrad and Moscow, 1952; 2nd ed., 1967); Yu. Kremlyov, *V.P. S.-S. ocherk zhizni i tvorchestva* (V.P. S.-S.: Outline of His Life and Work; Leningrad, 1960).

Soloviev, Nikolai (Feopemptovich), Russian music critic, teacher, and composer; b. Petrozavodsk, May 9, 1846; d. Petrograd, Dec. 27, 1916. After completing his studies in composition at the St. Petersburg Cons. (1868–72), he joined its faculty as a teacher of theory (1874–85) and a prof. of composition (1885–1909); also was active as a music critic (from 1870), acquiring a reputation as a determined opponent of the contemporary scene and being highly critical of Tchaikovsky and the national school of composers. He composed the operas *Vakula the Smith* (1875; concert perf., St. Petersberg, 1880), *Cordelia* (St. Petersburg, Nov. 24, 1885; rev. as *Vengeance,* 1898), and *The House at Kolomna* (n.d.); also *Russia and the Mongols,* symphonic picture (1870); *Ey, ukhnem,* orch. fantasy (1882); *Samson,* cantata (1870), and other cantatas; choral pieces; chamber music; piano pieces; songs. He also orchestrated Act 5 and part of Act 1 of Serov's opera *The Evil Power.*

Solti, Sir Georg (actually, **György),** eminent Hungarian-born English conductor; b. Budapest, Oct. 21, 1912. He began to study the piano when he was 6, making his 1st public appearance in Budapest when he was 12; at 13 he enrolled there at the Franz Liszt Academy of Music, studying piano with Dohnányi and, briefly, with Bartók; took composition courses with Kodály. He graduated at the age of 18, and was engaged by the Budapest Opera as a répétiteur; also served as an assistant to Bruno Walter (1935) and Toscanini (1936, 1937) at the Salzburg Festivals. On March 11, 1938, he made a brilliant conducting debut at the Budapest Opera with Mozart's *Le nozze di Figaro;* the wave of anti-Semitism in Hungary under the reactionary military rule forced him to leave Budapest (he was Jewish). In 1939 he went to Switzerland, where he was active mainly as a concert pianist; in 1942 he won the Concours International de Piano in Geneva; finally, in 1944, he was engaged to conduct concerts with the orch. of the Swiss Radio. In 1946 the American occupation authorities in Munich invited him to conduct *Fidelio* at the Bavarian State Opera; his success led to his appointment as its Generalmusikdirektor, a position he held from 1946 to 1952. In 1952 he became Generalmusikdirektor in Frankfurt, serving as director of the Opera and conductor of the Museumgesellschaft Concerts. He made his U.S. debut with the San Francisco Opera on Sept. 25, 1953, conducting *Elektra;* later conducted the Chicago Sym. Orch., the N.Y. Phil., and at the Metropolitan Opera in N.Y., where he made his 1st appearance on Dec. 17, 1960, with *Tannhäuser.* He was then engaged as music director of the Los Angeles Phil., but the project collapsed when the board of trustees refused to grant him full powers in musical and administrative policy. In 1960–61 he was music director of the Dallas Sym. Orch. In the meantime, he made his Covent Garden debut in London in 1959; in 1961 he assumed the post of music director of the Royal Opera House there, retaining it with great distinction until 1971. In 1969 he became music director of the Chicago Sym. Orch., and it was in that capacity that he achieved a triumph as an interpreter and orch. builder, so that the "Chicago sound" became a synonym for excellence. He showed himself an enlightened disciplinarian and a master of orch.

psychology, so that he could gain and hold the confidence of the players while demanding from them the utmost in professional performance. Under his direction the Chicago Sym. Orch. became one of the most celebrated orchs. in the world. He took it to Europe for the 1st time in 1971, eliciting glowing praise from critics and audiences; subsequently led it on a number of acclaimed tours there; also took it to N.Y. for regular appearances at Carnegie Hall. He held the additional posts of music adviser of the Paris Opéra (1971–73) and music director of the Orch. de Paris (1972–75), which he took on a tour of China in 1974; he served as principal conductor and artistic director of the London Phil. from 1979 to 1983; was then accorded the title of conductor emeritus. During all these years, he retained his post with the Chicago Sym. Orch., while continuing his appearances as a guest conductor with European orchs. In 1983 he conducted the *Ring* cycle at the Bayreuth Festival, in commemoration of the 100th anniversary of the death of Richard Wagner. Solti retained his prestigious position with the Chicago Sym. Orch. until the close of the 100th anniversary season in 1990–91, and subsequently held the title of Laureate Conductor. In 1992 he was scheduled to assume the post of artistic director at the Salzburg Music Festival. In 1968 he was made an honorary Commander of the Order of the British Empire; in 1971 he was named an honorary Knight Commander of the Order of the British Empire. In 1972 he became a British subject and was knighted, assuming the title of Sir Georg. Solti is generally acknowledged as a superlative interpreter of the symphonic and operatic repertoire. He is renowned for his performances of Wagner, Verdi, Mahler, Richard Strauss, and other Romantic masters; he also conducts notable performances of Bartók, Stravinsky, Schoenberg, and other composers of the 20th century. His recordings received innumerable awards.

BIBL.: W. Furlong, *Season with S.: A Year in the Life of the Chicago Symphony* (N.Y. and London, 1974); P. Robinson, *S.* (London, 1979); J. von Rhein, "S. at Seventy-five," *Ovation* (Nov. 1987).

Soltys, Adam, Polish pedagogue and composer, son of **Mieczyslaw Soltys;** b. Lemberg, July 4, 1890; d. there (Lwow), July 6, 1968. He studied with his father, and later with Georg Schumann in Berlin; also took courses in musicology at the Univ. of Berlin with Kretzschmar and Johannes Wolf (Ph.D., 1921). Returning to Poland, he served as director of the Lwow Cons. (1930–39) and again after World War II. His compositions include 2 syms. (1927, 1946); the symphonic poems *Slowanie* (1949), *O pokoj* (About Peace; 1953), and *Z gór i dolin* (From Mountains and Valleys; 1960); numerous teaching pieces for violin and for piano.

Soltys, Mieczyslaw, Polish conductor, teacher, and composer, father of **Adam Soltys;** b. Lemberg, Feb. 7, 1863; d. there (Lwow), Nov. 12, 1929. He studied in Lemberg and Paris; returning to Lemberg in 1899, he was director of the Cons. and of the Musical Society; also wrote music criticism.

WORKS: OPERAS: *Rzeczpospolita Babińska* (Republic of Babin; 1894; Lemberg, April 27, 1905); *Panie Kochanku* (1890; Lwow, May 3, 1924) *Opowieść kresowa* or *Opowieść ukraińska* (A Ukraine Story; 1909; Lemberg, March 8, 1910); *Nieboska komedia* (1925); also 2 syms.; 3 symphonic poems; *Concerto religioso* for Piano and Orch.; oratorios; choruses; piano pieces; songs; organ music.

Somary, Johannes, American organist, conductor, and composer; b. Zürich (of American parents), April 7, 1935. He was taken to the U.S. as a child, and received his musical training at Yale College (B.A., 1957) and with Quincy Porter and Keith Wilson at the Yale Univ. School of Music (M.M., 1959). In 1961 he founded the Amor Artis Chorale and Orch., which he conducted in much Baroque music; led the U.S. premieres of Handel's *Esther* in 1961, *Theodora* in 1963, and *Susanna* in 1965; also was a guest conductor in the U.S. and Europe. He composed orch. works, choral pieces, songs, and chamber music.

Somer, (Ruth) Hilde, Austrian-born American pianist; b. Vienna, Feb. 11, 1922; d. Freeport, Bahamas, Dec. 24, 1979. She studied with her mother; in 1938 the family went to the U.S. and she enrolled at the Curtis Inst. of Music in Philadelphia as a student of Rudolf Serkin; also took private lessons with Claudio Arrau. She cultivated modern works; commissioned piano concertos from John Corigliano, Jr. (San Antonio, April 7, 1968) and Antonio Tauriello (Washington, D.C., June 29, 1968), the 2nd Piano Concerto by Alberto Ginastera (Indianapolis, March 22, 1973), and a "spatial concerto" by Henry Brant (Tucson, Ariz., Nov. 16, 1978). She also gave a series of concerts of piano music by Scriabin, with color images projected upon the screen to suggest Scriabin's own ideas of a synthesis of sounds and colors.

Somers, Harry Stewart, outstanding Canadian composer and pianist; b. Toronto, Sept. 11, 1925. He studied piano with Dorothy Hornfelt (1939–41), Reginald Godden (1942–43), Weldon Kilburn (1945–48), and E.R. Schmitz (1948) in Toronto; also attended classes in composition with John Weinzweig (1941–43; 1945–49); then studied with Milhaud in Paris (1949–50). Returning to Canada, he eked out a meager living as a music copyist, finally receiving commissions in 1960; also became active as a broadcaster. In 1972 he was made a Companion of the Order of Canada. His historical opera, *Louis Riel,* was performed at the Kennedy Center in Washington, D.C., on Oct. 23, 1975, as part of America's Bicentennial celebration. His musical idiom is quaquaversal, absorbing without prejudice ancient, national, and exotic resources, from Gregorian chant to oriental scales, from simple folkways to electronic sound, all handled with fine expertise.

WORKS: STAGE: *The Fool,* one-act chamber opera for 4 Soloists and Chamber Orch. (1953; Toronto, Nov. 15, 1956); *The Homeless Ones,* television operetta (Canadian Television, Toronto, Dec. 31, 1955); *The Fisherman and His Soul,* ballet (Hamilton, Nov. 5, 1956); *Ballad,* ballet (Ottawa, Oct. 29, 1958); *The House of Atreus,* ballet (1963; Toronto, Jan. 13, 1964); *Louis Riel,* historical opera (Toronto, Sept. 23, 1967; uses electronic sound); *Improvisation,* theater piece for Narrator, Singers, Strings, any number of Woodwinds, 2 Percussionists, and Piano (Montreal, July 5, 1968); *And,* choreography for Dancers, Vocal Soloists, Flute, Harp, Piano, and 4 Percussionists (Canadian Television, Toronto, 1969); *Enkidu,* chamber opera after the epic of Gilgamesh (Toronto, Dec. 7, 1977). **ORCH.:** *Scherzo* for Strings (1947); 2 piano concertos: No. 1 (Toronto, March 2, 1949) and No. 2 (Toronto, March 12, 1956); *North Country* for String Orch. (Toronto, Nov. 10, 1948); *Suite* for Harp and Chamber Orch. (Toronto, Dec. 11, 1952); *The Case of the Wayward Woodwinds* for Chamber Orch. (1950); Sym. No. 1 (1951; Toronto, April 27, 1953); *Passacaglia and Fugue* (1954); *Little Suite for String Orchestra on Canadian Folk Songs* (1955); *Fantasia* (Montreal Orch., April 1, 1958); *Lyric* (Washington, D.C., April 30, 1961); *5 Concepts* (1961; Toronto, Feb. 15, 1962); *Movement* (Canadian Television, Toronto, March 4, 1962); *Stereophony* (Toronto, March 19, 1963); *The Picasso Suite,* light music for Small Orch. (1964; Saskatoon, Feb. 28, 1965); *Those Silent Awe-filled Spaces,* from a saying by the Canadian artist Emily Carr, for Orch. (Ottawa, Feb. 2, 1978). **VOCAL:** *5 Songs for Dark Voice* for Contralto and Orch. (Stratford, Ontario, Aug. 11, 1956); *At the Descent from the Cross* for Bass Voice and 2 Guitars (1962); *12 Miniatures* for Soprano, Recorder or Flute, Viola da Gamba, and Spinet (1963); *Crucifixion* for Chorus, English Horn, 2 Trumpets, Harp, and Percussion (1966); *Kuyas* for Soprano, Flute, and Percussion (1967; adapted from *Louis Riel*); *Voiceplay* for Male or Female Singer/ Actor (Toronto, Nov. 14, 1972; Cathy Berberian, soloist); *Kyrie* for Soloists, Chorus, Flute, Oboe, Clarinet, Cello, 3 Trumpets, Piano, and 6 Percussionists (1970–72); *Zen, Yeats and Emily Dickinson* for Female Narrator, Male Narrator, Soprano, Flute, Piano, and Tape (1975); choruses; songs. **CHAMBER:** 3 string quartets (1943, 1950, 1959); *Suite* for Percussion (1947); *Mime* for Violin and Piano (1948); *Rhapsody* for Violin and Piano (1948); Wind Quintet (1948); Trio for Flute, Violin, and Cello

(1950); 2 violin sonatas (1953, 1955); *Movement* for Wind Quintet (1957); Sonata for Solo Guitar (1959); *Theme and Variations* for any combination of Instruments (1964); *Music for Violin* (1974). PIANO: *Strangeness of Heart* (1942); *Flights of Fancy* (1944); 5 sonatas (*Testament of Youth*, 1945; 1946; 1950; 1950; 1957); *3 Sonnets* (1946); *Solitudes* (1947); *4 Primitives* (1949); *12 × 12*, fugues (1951).

BIBL.: B. Cherney, *H. S.* (Toronto, 1975).

Somervell, Sir Arthur, English music educator and composer; b. Windermere, June 5, 1863; d. London, May 2, 1937. He studied the classics at King's College, Cambridge (B.A., 1883), where he also took courses in music with Stanford; after further training at the Berlin Hochschule für Musik (1883–85), he studied at the Royal College of Music in London (1885–87); then received private instruction from Parry. He taught at the Royal College of Music (1893–1901); then was active as an inspector of music. He was knighted in 1929. He was at his best as a composer of vocal music.

WORKS: ORCH.: *Normandy*, symphonic variations (1912); *Thalassa*, sym. (1912); *Highland Concerto* for Piano and Orch. (1921); Violin Concerto (1932). CHORAL: 2 Masses (1891, 1907); *Joan of Arc* (1893); *Ode to the Sea* (1897); *Ode on the Intimations of Immortality* (1907); *Christmas*, cantata (1926); also song cycles; piano pieces; numerous educational pieces for schools; etc.

Somfai, László, Hungarian musicologist; b. Jászladány, Aug. 15, 1934. He studied at the Budapest Academy of Music as a student of Szabolcsi and Bartha; received his Ph.D. there in 1959; served as a music librarian at the National Széchényi Library (1958–62); in 1963 he joined the staff of the Bartók Archives (from 1969 known as the Inst. of Musicology of the Hungarian Academy of Sciences); became its director in 1972. He also taught at the Budapest Academy of Music (from 1969) and was ed. of the archive series Documenta Bartókiana (from 1972).

WRITINGS: *Haydn als Opernkapellmeister: Die Haydn-Dokumente der Esterházy-Opernsammlung* (with D. Bartha; Budapest and Mainz, 1960); *Joseph Haydn: Sein Leben in zeitgenössischen Bildern* (Budapest and Kassel, 1966; Eng. tr., 1969); *Anton Webern* (Budapest, 1968).

Somis, Giovanni Battista, eminent Italian violinist, teacher, and composer, brother of **Lorenzo Giovanni Somis;** b. Turin, Dec. 25, 1686; d. there, Aug. 14, 1763. He studied violin with his father, **Francesco Lorenzo Somis** (1663–1736), a violinist in the Turin ducal orch. known as "Ardy" or "Ardito." About 1696 he joined his father in the ducal orch., then studied with Corelli in Rome (1703–6) under the patronage of the Duke of Savoy; returning to Turin in 1707, he served as solo violinist and director of the ducal chapel until his death. He scored a brilliant success as a soloist at the Concert Spirituel in Paris (April 2 and May 14, 1733). He was the mentor of Pugnani, J.M. Leclair, Guignon, and Guillemain. He was a distinguished composer of chamber music, his solo sonatas being of particular historical interest. Much of his output is not extant.

WORKS: (12) *Sonate da camera* for Violin, and Cello or Harpsichord (Amsterdam, c.1717; 2nd ed., 1725); (12) *Sonate da camera* for Violin, and Cello or Harpsichord, op. 2 (Turin, 1723; ed. in Monumenti Musicali Italiani, II, Milan, 1976); (12) *Sonates* for Violin, and Cello or Harpsichord, op. 4 (Paris, 1726); (6) *Sonate a tre* for 2 Violins, and Cello or Harpsichord, op. 5 (Paris, 1733); (12) *Sonate da camera* for Violin, Cello, and Harpsichord, op. 6 (Paris, 1733); *Ideali trattenimenti da camera* for 2 Violins or Flutes or Descant Viols, op. 7 (Paris, n.d.); 6 *sonata a tre* for 2 Violins and Cello, op. 8 (n.p., n.d.); *12 sonate* for Cello and Bass (Paris, c.1740); many concertos: 150 for Violin, 3 for 2 Violins, 3 for Flute, 1 for Oboe, and 4 for Trumpet; also 75 sonatas for Violin and Basso Continuo.

BIBL.: G. Fino, "Un grande violinista torinese ed una famiglia di violinisti, G.B. S.," *Il Momento* (Turin, Oct. 25–26, 1927); F. Ghisi, "Giovanbattista e Lorenzo S.: Musicisti Piemontesi,"

Chigiana, XX (1963); B. Schwarz, *Great Masters of the Violin* (N.Y., 1983).

Somis, Lorenzo Giovanni, Italian violinist, teacher, and composer, brother of **Giovanni Battista Somis;** b. Turin, Nov. 11, 1688; d. there, Nov. 29, 1775. He studied in Bologna, where he was made a member of the Accademia Filarmonica; after a sojourn in Paris, he returned to Turin as 2nd violin in the ducal chapel (1724–70); his most distinguished student was Felice Giardini. He composed (12) *Sonate* for Violin and Cello or Harpsichord, op. 1 (Rome, 1722), (8) *Sonate* for Violin and Cello or Harpsichord, op. 2 (Paris, c.1740; ed. in Monumenti musicali italiani, III, Milan, 1976), and 6 *sonate a 2* for Violin and Cello or Harpsichord, op. 3 (Paris, c.1740); also several violin concertos.

Sommer, Hans (real name, **Hans Friedrich August Zincke**), German teacher, writer on music, and composer; b. Braunschweig, July 20, 1837; d. there, April 26, 1922. He studied mathematics at the Univ. of Göttingen (Ph.D., 1858), where he became a prof. of physics; taught mathematics at Braunschweig's Technische Hochschule (1859–84), serving as its director (from 1875). He then devoted himself to music. In 1898 he helped to found the Genossenschaft Deutscher Komponisten, which became the Genossenschaft Deutscher Tonsetzer in 1903. His lyric songs were greatly appreciated in Germany and England.

WORKS: OPERAS: *Der Nachtwächter* (Braunschweig, Nov. 22, 1865); *Der Vetter aus Bremen* (1865; not perf.); *Loreley* (Braunschweig, April 11, 1891); *Saint Foix* (Munich, Oct. 31, 1894); *Der Meermann* (Weimar, April 19, 1896); *Augustin* (1898; not perf.); *Münchhausen* (1896–98; not perf.); *Rübezahl und der Sackpfeifer von Neisse* (Braunschweig, May 15, 1904); *Riquet mit dem Schopf* (Braunschweig, April 14, 1907); *Der Waldschratt* (Braunschweig, March 31, 1912); also orch. pieces, choruses for Men's Voices, and songs.

BIBL.: E. Stier, "H. S.," in vol. 1 of *Monographien moderner Musiker* (Leipzig, 1906); E. Valentin, *H. S.* (Braunschweig, 1939).

Sommer, Vladimír, Czech teacher and composer; b. Dolní Jiřetín, near Most, Feb. 28, 1921. He studied composition with K. Janeček at the Prague Cons. (1942–46) and with Bořkovec at the Prague Academy of Music (1946–50). He was music ed. of foreign broadcasts of Radio Prague (1953) and then was creative secretary of the Czech Composers Union (1953–56); taught at the Prague Academy of Music (1953–60) and then at the Charles Univ. in Prague, where he was named prof. of music theory in 1968. His music is crafted in a fine, expressive manner.

WORKS: Sonata for 2 Violins (1948; also for Violin and Viola); *Cantata on Gottwald* for Baritone, Chorus, and Orch. (Prague, Nov. 20, 1949); Violin Concerto (Prague, June 13, 1950); 3 string quartets (1950; 1955; 1960–66); Piano Sonata (1954–56); *Antigone*, overture (1956–57); 3 syms.: No. 1, *Vokální symfonie*, for Narrator, Mezzo-soprano, Chorus, and Orch., to texts by Dostoyevsky, Kafka, and Cesare Pavese (1957–59; rev. 1963; Prague, March 12, 1963); No. 2, *Anno mundi ardenti*, for String Orch., Piano, and Timpani (1968); No. 3, *Sinfonia concertante*, for 2 Violins, Viola, Cello, and Chamber Orch. (1968); Cello Concerto (1956–59); *Černý Muž* (The Black Man), symphonic poem for Tenor, Bass, and Orch. (1964); *Sinfonia da Requiem: Vokální symfonie No. 2* for Soli, Chorus, and Orch. (1978); songs.

Sommerfeldt, Øistein, Norwegian composer; b. Christiania, Nov. 25, 1919. He studied piano, bassoon, theory, and composition in Paris with Boulanger (1950–56); was active as a music critic and composer in Oslo.

WORKS: ORCH.: 3 suites (1956; based on Grieg's *Dances* for Piano, op. 72); *Miniature Suite* (1958; rev. 1972); *Miniature Overture* (1960); *Adagio, Scherzo, and Finale* (1969);'*Hafrsfjord* for Narrator and Orch. (1972); *3 Lyrical Scenes* for Tenor or Soprano and Orch. (1973); *Sinfonia "La Betulla"* (1974); *Mot en Lengsel: Piano Concerto in 1 Movement* (1976–77); *Intrada*, symphonic prelude (1980); *Eika*, symphonic prelude (1981–

83). **CHAMBER:** *Divertimento* for Flute (1960; rev. 1969); *Divertimento* for Bassoon (1960; rev. 1973); *Transformation*, audiovisual score for Chamber Group and Tape (1970); *Divertimento* for Trumpet (1971); *Violin Sonata* (1971); *Elegy* for Trumpet and Organ (1971); *Suite* for Piano Trio (1973); *Divertimento* for Oboe (1974); also 5 piano sonatinas (1956, 1960, 1968, 1970, 1972).

Somogi, Judith, American conductor; b. N.Y., May 13, 1937; d. Rockville Centre, N.Y., March 23, 1988. She studied violin, piano, and organ at the Juilliard School of Music in N.Y. (M.M., 1961); attended courses at the Berkshire Music Center in Tanglewood; later was an assistant to Thomas Schippers at the Spoleto Festival and to Leopold Stokowski at the American Sym. Orch. in N.Y. In 1974 she made a successful appearance with the N.Y. City Opera conducting *The Mikado*, and subsequently conducted in San Francisco, San Diego, San Antonio, and Pittsburgh. She made her European debut in Saarbrücken in 1979. After conducting *Madama Butterfly* at the Frankfurt Opera in 1981, she held its position of 1st conductor from 1982 to 1987.

Somogyi, László, Hungarian conductor; b. Budapest, June 25, 1908. He took courses with Kodály and Weiner at the Budapest Academy of Music; played violin in the Budapest Concert Orch. (1932–36). After conducting studies with Scherchen in Brussels (1935), he made his debut as a conductor at the Budapest Academy of Music in 1936; then appeared as a guest conductor in Europe. Returning to Budapest, he conducted the Omike Orch. (1939–42), the Hungarian State Sym. Orch. (1945–52), and the Sym. Orch. of the Hungarian Radio and Television (1952–56). In 1956 he left his homeland and appeared as a guest conductor throughout Western Europe, Israel, and North and South America. He served as music director of the Rochester (N.Y.) Phil. from 1964 to 1969; then pursued his career in Europe.

Sondheim, Stephen (Joshua), brilliant American composer and lyricist; b. N.Y., March 22, 1930. Of an affluent family, he received his academic education in private schools; composed a school musical at the age of 15. He then studied music at Williams College, where he wrote the book, lyrics, and music for a couple of college shows; graduated magna cum laude in 1950. In quest of higher musical learning, he went to Princeton Univ., where he took lessons in modernistic complexities with Milton Babbitt, and acquired sophisticated techniques of composition. He made his mark on Broadway when he wrote the lyrics for Bernstein's *West Side Story* (1957). His 1st success as a lyricist-composer came with the Broadway musical *A Funny Thing Happened on the Way to the Forum* (1962), which received a Tony award. His next musical, *Anyone Can Whistle* (1964), proved unsuccessful, but *Company* (1970), for which he wrote both lyrics and music, established him as a major composer and lyricist on Broadway. There followed *Follies* (1971), for which he wrote 22 pastiche songs; it was named best musical by the N.Y. Drama Critics Circle. His next production, *A Little Night Music*, with the nostalgic score harking back to the turn of the century, received a Tony, and its leading song, "Send in the Clowns," was awarded a Grammy in 1976. This score established Sondheim's characteristic manner of treating musicals; it is almost operatic in conception, and boldly introduces dissonant counterpoint *à la moderne*. In 1976 he produced *Pacific Overtures*, based on the story of the Western penetration into Japan in the 19th century, and composed in a stylized Japanese manner, modeled after the Kabuki theater; he also wrote the score to the musical *Sunday in the Park with George*, inspired by the painting by Georges Seurat entitled "Sunday Afternoon on the Island of La Grande Jatte" (1982; N.Y., May 1, 1984), which received the Pulitzer Prize for drama in 1985. In 1987 his musical *Into the Woods*, based on 5 of the Grimm fairytales, scored a popular success on Broadway. It was followed by the musical *Assassins* in 1990.
BIBL.: C. Zadan, *S. & Co.* (N.Y., 1974); T. Adler, "The Musical Dramas of S. S.: Some Critical Approaches," *Journal of Popular Culture*, XII (1978–79); M. Adams, *The Lyrics of S. S.: Form and Function* (diss., Northwestern Univ., 1980); D. Cartmell, *S. S. and the Concept Musical* (diss., Univ. of Calif., Santa Barbara, 1983); S. Wilson, *Motivic, Rhythmic, and Harmonic Procedures of Unification in S. S.'s "Company" and "A Little Night Music"* (diss., Ball State Univ., 1983); T. Sutcliffe, "S. and the Musical," *Musical Times* (Sept. 1987); J. Gordon, *Art Isn't Easy: The Achievement of S. S.* (Carbondale, Ill., 1990).

Sonneck, Oscar G(eorge) T(heodore), eminent American musicologist; b. Jersey City, N.J., Oct. 6, 1873; d. N.Y., Oct. 30, 1928. He attended the Gelehrtenschule in Kiel (1883–89) and the Kaiser Friedrich Gymnasium in Frankfurt (1889–93), where he also took piano lessons with James Kwast; attended the Univ. of Heidelberg and received instruction in musicology from Sandberger at the Univ. of Munich (1893–97); studied composition privately with Melchior and Ernest Sachs in Munich; took courses in composition and orchestration with Iwann Knorr in Frankfurt and in conducting with Carl Schröder at the Sondershausen Cons. (1897–98). After doing research in Italy in 1899, he returned to the U.S. to pursue his interest in early American music. From 1902 to 1917 he was chief of the Music Division of the Library of Congress in Washington, D.C. He then became director of the Publishing Dept. of G. Schirmer in N.Y., managing ed. of the *Musical Quarterly* (of which he had been ed. since its foundation in 1915), and personal representative of the president, Rudolph E. Schirmer; in 1921 he became vice-president of G. Schirmer. He took a leading part in the formation of the Society for the Publication of American Music, and of the Beethoven Assoc. in N.Y. Under Sonneck's administration, the Music Division of the Library of Congress became one of the largest and most important music collections in the world. His writings, exhibiting profound and accurate scholarship and embodying the results of original research, laid a real foundation for the scientific study of music in the U.S.; his elaborate catalogues, issued by the Library of Congress, are among the most valuable contributions to musical bibliography. The Sonneck Society, an organization designed to encourage the serious study of American music in all its aspects, was established in 1975 and named after Sonneck in recognition of his achievements in this area. He was also a composer and a poet; wrote symphonic pieces; a String Quartet; *Rhapsody* and *Romanze* for Violin and Piano; some vocal works and piano pieces. He publ. 2 vols. of poems: *Seufzer* (1895) and *Eine Totenmesse* (1898).
WRITINGS: *Protest gegen den Symbolismus in der Musik* (Frankfurt, 1897); *Classification: Class M, Music: Class ML, Literature of Music: Class MT, Musical Instruction: Adopted December, 1902: as in force April, 1904* (Washington, D.C., 1904; 2nd ed., rev., 1917; 3rd ed., 1957); *A Bibliography of Early Secular American Music* (Washington, D.C., 1905; 2nd ed., rev. and enl., 1945 by W. Upton); *Francis Hopkinson, the First American Poet-Composer (1737–1791) and James Lyon, Patriot, Preacher, Psalmodist (1735–1794): Two Studies in Early American Music* (Washington, D.C., 1905); *Early Concert-life in America (1731–1800)* (Leipzig, 1907); *Dramatic Music: Catalogue of Full Scores in the Collection of the Library of Congress* (Washington, D.C., 1908; 2nd ed., 1917); *Report on "The Star-Spangled Banner," "Hail Columbia," "America," "Yankee Doodle"* (Washington, D.C., 1909; 2nd ed., rev. and enl., 1914); *Orchestral Music Catalogue: Scores* (Washington, D.C., 1912); with J. Gregory, *Catalogue of Early Books on Music (before 1800)* (Washington, D.C., 1913); *Catalogue of Opera Librettos Printed before 1800* (Washington, D.C., 1914); with W. Whittlesey, *Catalogue of First Editions of Stephen C. Foster (1826–1864)* (Washington, D.C., 1915); *Early Opera in America* (N.Y., 1915); *Suum cuique: Essays in Music* (N.Y., 1916); *Catalogue of First Editions of Edward MacDowell (1861–1908)* (Washington, D.C., 1917); *Miscellaneous Studies in the History of Music* (N.Y., 1921); *Beethoven: Impressions of Contemporaries* (N.Y., 1926); *Beethoven Letters in America* (N.Y., 1927).
BIBL.: H. Putnam and R. Goldmark, "Remarks at the Funeral Services for O.G. S.," *Musical Quarterly* (Jan. 1929);

C. Engel, "O.G. S.," ibid. (Jan. 1939); O. Kinkeldey, "O.G.T. S.," *Notes*, XI (1953–54); G. Chase, "The Significance of O. S.: A Centennial Tribute," *Yearbook for Inter-American Musical Research*, IX (1973); H. Wiley Hitchcock, *After 100 [ ] Years: The Editorial Side of S.* (Washington, D.C., 1974; with complete list of writings and compositions compiled by I. Lowens); W. Lichtenwanger, ed., *O. S. and American Music* (Urbana, Ill., 1983).

Sonninen, Ahti, Finnish composer; b. Kuopio, July 11, 1914; d. Helsinki, Aug. 27, 1984. Following graduation from the Kajaani training college, he took courses in theory and composition with Palmgren, Merikanto, Ranta, and Funtek at the Sibelius Academy in Helsinki (1939–47). He taught elementary school (1936–43), then taught in the school music dept. of the Sibelius Academy (from 1957). He followed the tenets of international musical modernism in his technique of composition, but also adhered to subjects from Finnish folklore.

WORKS: STAGE: *Merenkuninkaan tytär* (Daughter of Neptune), opera (1949); *Pessi and Illusia*, ballet (1952); *Ruusu-solmu* (Wreath of Roses), ballet (1956); *Karhunpeijaiset* (Feast to Celebrate the Killing of a Bear), ritual opera (1968); *Se* (It), ballet farce (Helsinki, Feb. 24, 1972); *Haavruuva* (Lady of the Sea), opera (1971). **VOCAL:** *7 Songs to Hungarian Folk Poems* for Soprano and Orch. (1939–41); *Midsummer Night* for Soprano and Orch. (1946); *El amor pasa* for Soprano, Flute, and Orch. (1953); *Smith of the Heavens* for Baritone and Orch. (1957); *The Karelian Wedding* for Voice, Chorus, Flute, Accordion, Percussion, Harpsichord, and Tape (1965); *Highway Requiem* for Soprano, Baritone, Chorus, and Orch. (1970); *Forging of the Golden Virgin* for Voices, 2 Percussionists, and Tape (1971); *Finnish Messiah* for Soloists, Mixed and Children's Choruses, and Orch. (1972); *In the Court of the Lamb*, suite for Soloists, Chorus, and Orch. (1972); about 15 cantatas and 100 choruses a cappella. **ORCH.:** *East Karelian Suite* (1942); Violin Concerto (1943–45); Piano Concerto (1944–45); *Symphonic Sketches* (1947); *Preludio festivo* (1953); *Under Lapland's Sky*, suite (1954); *Pezzo pizzicato* (1954–55); *Rhapsody* (1957); *4 Partitas* for Strings (1958); *Prelude and Allegro* for Trumpet, Trombone, and Orch. (1961); *Reactions* for Chamber Orch. (1961). **CHAMBER:** *Conference* for Clarinet, Horn, Trumpet, and Trombone (1954); *Theses* for String Quartet (1968); *Divertimento* for Wind Quintet (1970). **PIANO:** Suites: *In the Big City* (1954); *White Pepper* (1970); *Black Pepper* (1970); *Koli* (1970); *3 Characters* (1971); about 70 songs with piano; music for films.

Sonnleithner, family of Austrian musicians and writers: **(1) Christoph Sonnleithner,** composer; b. Szegedin, May 28, 1734; d. Vienna, Dec. 25, 1786. He was 2 when he was taken to Vienna, where he received his musical training from his uncle, Leopold Sonnleithner, a choirmaster; he took courses in law and served as a barrister in the employ of Prince Esterházy, becoming associated with Haydn. His works include syms., sacred pieces, and 36 string quartets. His daughter Anna was the mother of the famous poet Grillparzer. He also had 2 sons who were active in music: **(2) Joseph Sonnleithner,** librettist and archivist; b. Vienna, March 3, 1766; d. there, Dec. 25, 1835. He acquired material for the emperor's private library; was ed. of the *Wiener Theater-Almanach* (1794–96); served as secretary of the Court theaters (1808–14), and also was manager of the Theater an der Wien (until 1807); was one of the founders of the Gesellschaft der Musikfreunde (1812). He wrote some librettos and adapted others, including *Fidelio* for Beethoven and *Faniska* by Cherubini. In 1827 he discovered the famous Antiphonary of St. Gall of the 9th century, in neume notation, probably a copy of the one sent there by Charlemagne in 790. He bequeathed his collection of opera librettos to the Vienna Cons. and his instrument collection and library to the Gesellschaft der Musikfreunde. He was a close friend of Schubert and Grillparzer. **(3) Ignaz (von) Sonnleithner,** bass, doctor, and scientist; b. Vienna, July 30, 1770; d. there, Nov. 27, 1831. He appeared

as principal bass with the Gesellschaft der Musikfreunde; held musical soirees in his home (1815–24), at which Schubert tried out several of his vocal works. His son was **Leopold von Sonnleithner** (b. Vienna, Nov. 15, 1797; d. there, March 4, 1873). A barrister, he was a staunch friend of Schubert and enabled him to publ. the *Erlkönig* (Schubert's 1st publ. work); was a great lover of music; was active with the Gesellschaft der Musikfreunde, to which he left his musical papers.

BIBL.: A. Fareanu, "L. v.S.s Erinnerungen an Franz Schubert," *Zeitschrift für Musikwissenschaft*, I (1919); O. Deutsch, "L. v.S.s Erinnerungen an des Musiksalons der vormarzlichen Wien," *Österreichische Musikzeitschrift*, XVI (1961).

Sontag, Henriette (real name, **Gertrude Walpurgis Sonntag**), celebrated German soprano; b. Koblenz, Jan. 3, 1806; d. Mexico City, June 17, 1854. Her father was the actor Franz Sonntag and her mother the actress and singer Franziska (née Martloff) Sonntag (1798–1865); she studied with her mother, and began appearing in stage plays and operas at age 5. In 1815 she was admitted to the Prague Cons., where she received instruction in singing from Anna Czegka, in theory from Josef Triebensee, and in piano from Pixis. In 1821 she made her formal operatic debut as the princess in Boieldieu's *Jean de Paris* in Prague; in 1822 she went to Vienna, where she appeared in German and Italian opera; was chosen by Weber to create the title role in his *Euryanthe* (Oct. 25, 1823); then was chosen by Beethoven to sing in the 1st performances of his 9th Sym. and *Missa solemnis* (May 7 and 13, 1824, respectively). She sang in Dresden in 1825, and that same year made her Berlin debut at the Königstädter Theater as Isabella in *L'Italiana in Algeri* (Aug. 3). On May 15, 1826, she made a stunning debut at the Théâtre-Italien in Paris as Rosina in *Il Barbiere di Siviglia*; following engagements in Germany, she returned to Paris in 1828 to win further accolades as Donna Anna and Semiramide. During a visit to Weimar, she won the approbation of Goethe, who penned the poem *Neue Siren* for the "fluttering nightingale" of the operatic stage. On April 19, 1828, she chose the role of Rosina for her British debut at the King's Theatre in London; during her British sojourn, she married Count Carlo Rossi, a Sardinian diplomat, secretly (so as not to jeopardize his career); after the King of Prussia ennobled her as Henriette von Lauenstein, she was able to publicly join her husband in The Hague, her low birth no longer a matter of concern; however, she quit the stage in 1830, and then appeared only in private and concert settings in the cities where her husband was stationed. After her husband lost his diplomatic post at the abdication of the King of Sardinia in 1849, she resumed her stage career with appearances at Her Majesty's Theatre in London; toured England that same year, and then created the role of Miranda in Halévy's *La tempesta* at Her Majesty's Theatre on June 8, 1850; after further appearances in London and Paris in 1851, she toured with great success in Germany; then appeared in the U.S. in 1852. In 1854 she toured Mexico as a member of an Italian opera company; on June 11 of that year she made her last appearance as Lucrezia Borgia; the next day she was stricken with cholera and died 5 days later. Her beautiful voice, which ranged from a to e^3, her striking physical appearance, and her natural acting abilities led to her reputation as the equal or superior to all other divas of the age. She was a matchless interpreter of roles in operas by Mozart, Rossini, Donizetti, and Bellini.

BIBL.: T. Gautier, *L'Ambassadrice, Biographie de la comtesse Rossi* (Paris, 1850); J. Gundling, *H. S.* (2 vols., Leipzig, 1861); W. Berger, *Berühmte Frauen* (Berlin, 1904); H. Stümcke, *H. S.* (Berlin, 1913); F. Rogers, "H. S. in New York," *Musical Quarterly* (Jan. 1942); E. Pirchan, *H. S.: Die Sängerin des Biedermeier* (Vienna, 1946); F. Russell, *Queen of Song, The Life of H. S., Countess de Rossi* (N.Y., 1964).

Sonzogno, Edoardo, Italian music publisher; b. Milan, April 21, 1836; d. there, March 14, 1920. He inherited a printing plant and bookstore founded by his grandfather, and in 1874 began to publ. popular eds. of French and Italian music with marked success. In 1883 he inaugurated a series of contests for new operas; the 2nd contest, in 1889, was won by Mascagni (then unknown) with *Cavalleria rusticana*. Sonzogno established his own theater (the Lirico Internazionale) at Milan in 1894. From 1861 until his retirement in 1909 he was sole proprietor of the newspaper *Il Secolo;* was also published of the journals *Il teatro illustrato* (1881–92) and *La musica popolare* (1882–92). He was succeeded by his son, **Riccardo Sonzogno** (1871–1915); upon his death, his cousin, **Renzo** (1877–1920), who had run his own firm from 1910, took over the business. In 1923 the firm became known as Società Anonima Sonzogno, and is now known as the Società per Azioni Sonzogno.

Sonzogno, Giulio Cesare, Italian composer; b. Milan, Dec. 24, 1906; d. there, Jan. 23, 1976. He was related to the family of the music publishers Sonzogno. He studied cello and composition in Milan; composed mostly for the stage.
    WORKS: Ballet, *L'amore delle tre melarancie* (La Scala, Milan, Feb. 1, 1936); operas: *Regina Uliva* (Milan, March 17, 1949); *I Passeggeri* (Trieste, 1961); *Il denaro del Signor Arne* (1968); *Boule de suif,* after Maupassant (Bergamo, 1970); *Mirra* (1970).

Soot, Fritz (actually, **Friedrich Wilhelm),** distinguished German tenor; b. Wellesweiler-Neunkirchen, Saar, Aug. 20, 1878; d. Berlin, June 9, 1965. He 1st pursued a career as an actor in Karlsruhe (1901–7); then studied voice with Scheidemantel in Dresden; made his debut with the Dresden Court Opera as Tonio in *La Fille du régiment* in 1908, remaining on its roster until 1918; during his tenure there, he sang in the 1st performance of *Der Rosenkavalier* as the Italian Singer. His subsequent engagements were in Stuttgart (1918–22), at the Berlin State Opera (1922–44, 1946–52), and at the Berlin Städtische Oper (1946–48). He sang in the premieres of Berg's *Wozzeck,* as well as in works by Pfitzner and Schreker; he excelled in such Wagnerian roles as Tristan, Siegmund, and Siegfried.

Sopeña (Ibáñez), Federico, noted Spanish musicologist; b. Valladolid, Jan. 25, 1917. He studied in Bilbao and Madrid; later obtained a doctorate in theology at the Università Gregoriana in Rome. He was active as a music critic; from 1951 to 1956, was director of the Madrid Cons.; was also the founder and publisher of the music magazine *Música*. He publ. (in Madrid) a number of useful monographs of Spanish composers, including *Joaquín Turina* (1943; 2nd ed., 1952) and *Joaquín Rodrigo* (1946; 2nd ed., rev. 1970); also *Historia de la música* (1946; 5th ed., 1974); *La música europea contemporánea* (1952); *Historia de la música española contemporánea* (1958; 2nd ed., 1967); *Música y literatura* (1974).

Sopkin, Henry, American conductor; b. N.Y., Oct. 20, 1903; d. Stanford, Calif., March 1, 1988. He was reared in Chicago, where he earned degrees in violin at the American Cons. of Music; was head of its instrumental dept. and also taught at Woodrow Wilson College; in 1944 he became conductor of the Atlanta Youth Sym. Orch., which served as the foundation of the Atlanta Sym. Orch. in 1945, which he conducted until 1966; then taught briefly at the Calif. Inst. of the Arts in Valencia.

Soproni, József, Hungarian composer; b. Sopron, Oct. 4, 1930. He was a pupil of János Viski at the Budapest Academy of Music (1949–56); then taught at the Béla Bartók Cons. from 1957 and at the Academy from 1963, where he served as rector from 1988. His music is marked by a strong polyphonic art, but he also employs the technique of sonorism, or sound for sound's sake.
    WORKS: Concerto for String Orch. (1953); *4 Bagatelles* for Piano (1957); *Partita* for Harpsichord (1957); Viola Sonatina (1958); 4 string quartets (1958, 1960, 1965, 1971); *Meditatio con Toccata* for Organ (1959); *Requiem on the Death of a Poet* (1960); *Carmina polinaesiana,* cantata for Female Chorus and Chamber Ensemble (1963); *Musica da camera* No. 1 for Piano Trio (1963); *7 Pieces* for Piano (1963); *Ovidii metamorphoses,*

cantata for Soprano, Chorus, and Orch., with Solo Violin (1965); Violin Concerto (1967); 2 cello concertos (1967, 1984); *De aetatibus mundi carmina,* cantata after Ovidius for Soprano, Baritone, Chorus, and Orch. (1968); *Eklypsis* for Orch. (1969); *Incrustations* for Piano (1970); *Invenzioni sul B-A-C-H* for Piano (1971); Flute Sonata (1971); *Concerto da camera* for 12 Performers (1972); 3 syms: No. 1 (1975); No. 2, *The Seasons* (1977); No. 3, *Sinfonia da Requiem,* for Soloists, Chorus, and Orch. (1979–80); *Musica da camera* No. 2 for Clarinet, Violin, Cello, and Piano (1976); Horn Sonata (1976); 2 violin sonatas (1979, 1980); Violin Concerto (1982–83); *Comments on a Theme by Handel* for Orch. (1985); *Antigone,* opera (1987); *3 Pieces* for Orch. (1987–88); songs.

Sor (real name, **Sors), (Joseph) Fernando (Macari),** celebrated Catalan guitarist and composer; b. Barcelona, Feb. 13, 1778; d. Paris, July 10, 1839. At the age of 11 he entered the school of the monastery of Montserrat, where he studied music under the direction of Anselmo Viola; wrote a Mass; then attended the Barcelona military academy. In 1799 he went to Madrid; subsequently held administrative sinecures in Barcelona (from 1808), and also was active in the battle against France, but about 1810 accepted an administrative post under the French. When Bonapartist rule was defeated in Spain in 1813, he fled to Paris. There he met Cherubini, Méhul, and others, who urged him to give concerts as a guitarist, and he soon acquired fame. His ballet *Cendrillon* (London, 1822) became quite popular and was given more than 100 times at the Paris Opéra; it was heard at the gala opening of the Bolshoi Theater in Moscow in 1823. Sor was active in Russia from 1823; wrote funeral music for the obsequies of Czar Alexander I in 1825. He returned to Paris via London in 1826, and subsequently devoted himself to performing and teaching. An outstanding guitar virtuoso, he also garnered recognition as a composer; in all, he wrote over 65 works for the guitar, including a number of standard pieces. He also wrote the most important guitar method ever penned.
    WORKS: STAGE: OPERAS: *Telemaco nell'isola de Calipso* (Barcelona, Aug. 25, 1797); *Don Trastullo* (unfinished; not extant). **BALLETS:** *La Foire de Smyrne* (London, 1821; not extant); *Le Seigneur généreux* (London, 1821; not extant); *Cendrillon* (London, 1822); *L'Amant peintre* (London, 1823); *Hercule et Omphale* (Moscow, 1826); *Le Sicilien* (Paris, 1827); *Hassan et le calife* (London, 1828; not extant). **OTHER:** Various vocal works, including 25 *boleros or seguidillas boleras* for 1 to 3 Voices and Guitar or Piano, 33 ariettas for Voice and Piano, Spanish, Italian, and English songs and duets, and some sacred music; also over 65 guitar pieces, including 3 sonatas, fantasias, variations, divertimentos, studies, etc.; piano pieces; also 2 syms., 3 string quartets, a Concertante for Guitar and String Trio, and a march for Military Band, all of which are lost.
    BIBL.: M. Rocamora, *F. S.* (Barcelona, 1957); W. Sasser, *The Guitar Works of F. S.* (diss., Univ. of North Carolina, Chapel Hill, 1960); G. Marini, "La música per chitarra di F. S.," *Il Convegno Musicale,* I (Jan. 1964); B. Jeffery, *F. S.: Composer and Guitarist* (London, 1977).

Sorabji, Kaikhosru Shapurji (actually, **Leon Dudley),** remarkable English pianist, writer on music, and composer of unique gifts; b. Chingford, Aug. 14, 1892; d. Wareham, Dorset, Oct. 14, 1988. His father was a Parsi, his mother of Spanish-Sicilian extraction. He was largely self-taught in music; after appearing with notable success as a pianist in London, Paris, Vienna (1921–22), Glasgow, and Bombay, he gave up the concert platform and began writing on music. Through sheer perseverance and an almost mystical belief in his demiurgic powers, he developed an idiom of composition of extraordinary complexity, embodying within the European framework of harmonies the Eastern types of melodic lines and asymmetrical rhythmic patterns, and creating an enormously intricate but architectonically stable edifice of sound. His most arresting work is his magisterial *Opus Clavicembalisticum,* completed in 1930, taking about 5 hours to play and comprising 3 parts with 12 subdivisions, including a theme with 49 variations and a passacaglia with 81 variations; characteristically, the score is dedicated to "the everlasting glory of those few men blessed and sanctified in the curses and execrations of those many whose praise is eternal damnation." Sorabji gave its premiere in Glasgow under the auspices of the Active Society for the Propagation of Contemporary Music on Dec. 1, 1930. Wrathful at the lack of interest in his music, Sorabji issued in 1936 a declaration forbidding any performance of his works by anyone anywhere; since this prohibition could not be sustained for works actually publ., there must have been furtive performances of his piano works in England and the U.S. by fearless pianists. Sorabji eventually mitigated his ban, and in 1975 allowed the American pianist Michael Habermann to perform some of his music; in 1976 he also gave his blessing to the English pianist Yonty Solomon, who included Sorabji's works in a London concert on Dec. 7, 1976; on June 16, 1977, Solomon gave in London the 1st performance of Sorabji's 3rd Piano Sonata. Gradually, Sorabji's music became the cynosure and the lodestone of titanically endowed pianists. Of these, the most Brobdingnagian was the Australian pianist Geoffrey Madge, who gave the second complete performance in history of *Opus Clavicembalisticum* at the 1982 Holland Festival in Utrecht; he repeated this feat at the 1st American performance of the work at the Univ. of Chicago on April 24, 1983; 2 weeks later he played it in Bonn. True to his estrangement from the human multitudes and music officials, Sorabji took refuge far from the madding crowd in a castle he owned in England; a notice at the gate proclaims: Visitors Unwelcome. Yet as he approached his 90th birthday, he received at least 2 American musicians who came to declare their admiration, and allowed them to photocopy some of his MSS.

Works: orch.: 8 indefinitely numbered piano concertos (1915–16; 1916–17; 1917; 1918; 1922; *Simorg-Anka*, 1924; 1924–25; 1927); *Chaleur* (1920); Sym. No. 1 for Orch., Chorus, Organ, and Piano (1921–22); *Opusculum* (1923); *Jāmī*, sym. for Orch., Baritone, Chorus, Organ, and Piano (1942–51); *Symphonic Variations* for Piano and Orch. (1951–55); *Symphonic High Mass* for Orch., Solo Voices, Chorus, Organ, and Piano (1955–61); *Opus Clavisymphonicum* for Piano and Orch. (1957–59); *Opusculum Claviorchestrale* for Piano and Orch. (1973–75). **chamber:** 2 piano quintets: No. 1 (1920); No. 2 (1949–53); *Concertino non Grosso* for 4 Violins, Viola, 2 Cellos, and Piano (1968); *Il tessuto d'Arabeschi* for Flute and String Quartet (1979; Philadelphia, May 2, 1982). **piano:** 6 sonatas: No. 0 (1917); No. 1 (1919); No. 2 (1920); No. 3 (1922); No. 4 (1928–29); No. 5, *Opus Archimagicum* (1934–35); 2 pieces: *In the Hothouse* and *Toccata* (1918, 1920); *Fantaisie espagnole* (1919); *Prelude, Interlude and Fugue* (1920–22); 3 *Pastiches:* on Chopin, Bizet, and Rimsky-Korsakov (1922); *Le Jardin parfumé* (1923); *Variations and Fugue on "Dies Irae"* (1923–26); *Valse-Fantaisie (Hommage à Johann Strauss)* (1925); *Fragment* (1926; rev. 1937); *Djâmî*, noctourne (1928); 4 toccatas: No. 1 (1928); No. 2 (1933–34); No. 3 (1937); No. 4 (1964–67); *Opus Clavicembalisticum* (Glasgow, Dec. 1, 1930, composer at the keyboard); *Symphonic Variations* (1935–37); 6 solo syms.: No. 1, *Tantrik* (1938–39); No. 2 (1954); No. 3 (1959–60); No. 4 (1962–64); No. 5, *Symphonia Brevis* (1973–75); No. 6, *Symphonia Magna* (1975–76); *Gulistan*, nocturne (1940); *100 Transcendental Studies* (1940–44); *St. Bertrand de Comminges: "He Was Laughing in the Tower"* (1941); *Concerto per suonare da me solo* (1946); *Sequentia Cyclica on "Dies Irae"* (1949); *Un nido di scatole* (1954); *Passeggiata veneziana* (1956); *Rosario d'arabeschi* (1956); *Fantasiettina* (1961); *Symphonic Nocturne* (1977–78); *Il grido del gallino d'oro* (1978–79); *Evocazione nostalgicaVilla Tasca* (1979); *Opus secretum* (1980–81); *Passeggiata arlecchinesca* (1981–82). **vocal:** 5 sonetti del Michelangelo Buonarroti for Voice and Chamber Orch. (1923; Toronto, Feb. 2, 1980); songs. **organ:** 3 solo syms.: No. 1 (1924); No. 2 (1929–32); No. 3 (1949–53).

Writings: *Around Music* (London, 1932); *Mi contra fa: The Immoralisings of a Machiavellian Musician* (London, 1947).

Bibl.: A. Browne, "The Music of K. S.," *Music & Letters* (Jan. 1930); E. Rubbra, "S.'s Enigma," *Monthly Musical Record*

(Sept. 1932); B. Posner, *S.* (diss., Fordham Univ., N.Y., 1975); P. Rapoport, "S. and the Computer," *Tempo*, no. 117 (1976); idem, *Opus Est: 6 Composers from Northern Europe* (London, 1978, and N.Y., 1979).

Sørensen, Søren, distinguished Danish musicologist, organist, and harpsichordist; b. Copenhagen, Sept. 20, 1920. He studied organ with F. Viderø at the Royal Danish Cons. of Music in Copenhagen (diploma, 1943) and musicology with Abrahamsen and Larsen at the Univ. of Copenhagen (M.A., 1943; Ph.D., 1958, with the diss. *Diderich Buxtehudes vokale kirkemusik*; publ. in Copenhagen, 1958). In 1943, with L. Friisholm, he founded Copenhagen's Collegium Musicum, a chamber ensemble with which he made frequent appearances as an organist and harpsichordist; also was organist at Holmens Church (1947–58). He was prof. of musicology and chairman of the musicologial inst. at the Univ. of Århus (from 1958); was co-ed. of the *Dansk Årbog for Musikforskning* (from 1961). Among his many administrative positions were the chairmanships of the Danish Soc. of Organists and Choirmasters (1953–59), the Carl Nielsen Soc. (from 1966), the Danish Council for Research in the Humanities (from 1974), and the State Council of Music Education (from 1986). In 1982 he was awarded Hungary's Bartók Medal. He won notable distinction as an authority on 17th-century music, most particularly that of Buxtehude.

Writings: *Kirkens liturgi* (Copenhagen, 1952; 2nd ed., 1969); ed. with B. Hjelmbor, *Natalicia musicologica Knud Jeppesen* (Copenhagen, 1962); *Renaissancebegrebet i musikhistorien* (Århus, 1964); *Das Buxtehudebild im Wandel der Zeit* (Lübeck, 1973); *Kobenhavns Drengekor gennem 50 år* (Copenhagen, 1974); ed. *Gads musikleksikon* (Copenhagen, 1976; 2nd ed., 1987).

Sörenson, Torsten, Swedish organist, teacher, and composer; b. Grebbestad, April 25, 1908. He studied at the Stockholm Musikhögskolan, where he obtained diplomas as a music teacher and church musician (1934) and as an organist (1936); after training in counterpoint from Torsten Ahlberg in Göteborg (1936–39), he studied composition with Hilding Rosenberg (1942) and Carl Orff (1949). He was mainly active as a church organist in Göteborg (from 1935), where he later served at the Oscar Fredrik Church (1946–75); also taught theory at the Musikhögskolan there (1954–76). He wrote a number of fine vocal works.

Works: *Den underbara Kvarnan* for Baritone and Orch. (1936; rev. 1958); *Sinfonietta* for String Orch. (1946; rev. 1957); 2 trios for Flute, Clarinet, and Oboe (1949, 1959); *Hymn om Kristus*, cantata (1950); Concerto for Organ and String Orch. (1952); Sym. for Chamber Orch. (1956); Sonata for Viola Solo (1956); *Sinfonia da chiesa* Nos. 1 and 2 for String Orch. (1958, 1964–69); 3 sonatas for Flute Solo (1962, 1964, 1966); *Hymnarium*, 56 motets for One to 6 Voices, and Instruments (1957–62); *Per quattro archi*, string quartet (1970); Brass Quintet (1970); *Laudate nomen Domini* for Chorus, 17 Winds, and Percussion (1972); *En sang om Herrens boninger* for Soprano, 2 Choruses, and Orch. (1975); *Divertimento* for Flute, Oboe, Violin, and Viola (1976); Concerto for Flute, String Orch., and Percussion (1976); *Gud är här tillstädes*, cantata (1978); *Quintafonia* for 5 Instrumentalists (1979); *Due contrasti*, String Quartet No. 2 (1983); Violin Sonata (1985); Sonata for Solo Cello (1985); *Pezzo d'amore* for Viola d'amore and 4 Violas (1986); numerous piano pieces, including a Sonata (1956), *Svart-Vitt* (Black and White), 24 pieces (1975), and *Två sånger* (1988).

Soresina, Alberto, Italian composer; b. Milan, May 10, 1911. He studied with Paribeni and Bossi at the Milan Cons., graduating in 1933; then took a course in composition in Siena with Frazzi; subsequently was on the faculty of the Milan Cons. (1947–60) and the Turin Cons. (1963–66); then again at the Milan Cons. (from 1967).

Works: operas: *Lanterna rossa* (Siena, 1942); *Cuor di cristallo* (Bergamo, 1942); *L'amuleto* (Bergamo, Oct. 26, 1954); *Tre sogni per Marina* (Lecco, 1967). **orch.:** *Trittico Wildiano*

(1939); *Il Santo*, symphonic poem (1940); 2 *notturni* for Harp and String Orch. (1946); *Divertimento* (1956). CHAMBER: Concertino for Viola, Cello, and Piano (1953); *Sonatina serena* for Violin and Piano (1956); also several works for Voice and Orch., including *La Fanciulla mutata in rio* (1939); piano pieces.

Sorge, Georg Andreas, eminent German organist, music theorist, and composer; b. Mellenbach, Schwarzburg, Thuringia, March 21, 1703; d. Lobenstein, Thuringia, April 4, 1778. He began his music training in Mellenbach with Nicolas Walter, the local Kantor and organist, and his assistant, Caspar Tischer; then continued his studies with Tischer in Schney (Franconia) from 1714 to 1716; returned to Mellenbach to study academic subjects and composition with Pastor Johann Wintzern. After serving as a private tutor in Burg (Vogtland), he was made court and civic organist in Lobenstein when he was 19; he remained there until his death. In 1747 he was elected to membership in Mizler's Societät der Musikalischen Wissenschaften of Leipzig. He won distinction as an authority on organ building, as a music theorist, and as a composer. Although his keyboard music was widely disseminated during his lifetime, his importance now rests upon his contributions to music theory. In his masterwork, *Vorgemach der musicalischen Composition* (Lobenstein, 1745–47), he places prime importance on the triad as the foundation upon which all musical composition is based.

WRITINGS: *Genealogia allegorica intervallorum octavae diatono-chromaticae* (Hof, 1741); *Anweisung zur Stimmung und Temperatur sowohl der Orgelwerk, als auch anderer Instrumente, sonderlich aber des Claviers* (Hamburg, 1744); *Vorgemach der musicalischen Composition, oder: Ausführlich, ordentliche und vor heutige Praxin hinlängliche Anweisung zum General-Bass* (Lobenstein, 1745–47); *Gespräch zwischen einem Musico theoretico und einem Studioso musices von der Prätorianischen, Printzischen, Werckmeisterischen, Neidhardtischen, und Silbermannischen Temperatur wie auch von dem neuen Systeme Herrn Capellmeister Telemanns, zu Beförderung reiner Harmonie* (Lobenstein, 1748); *Ausführliche und deutliche Anweisung zur Rational-Rechnung, und der damit verknüpfften Ausmessung und Abteilung des Monochords* (Lobenstein, 1749); *Gründliche Untersuchung, ob die ... Schröterischen Clavier-Temperaturen für gleichschwebend passieren können oder nicht* (Lobenstein, 1754); *Ausweichungs-Tabellen in welchen auf vierfache Art gezeiget wird wie eine jede Tonart in ihre Neben-Tonarten ausweichen könne* (Nuremberg, 1753); *Georg A. Sorgens ... zuverlässige Anweisung Claviere und Orgeln behörig zu temperiren und zu stimmen* (Leipzig and Lobenstein, 1758); *Compendium harmonicum oder Kurzer Begriff der Lehre von der Harmonie* (Lobenstein, 1760; also publ. as *Herrn G.A. Sorgens Anleitung zum Generalbass und zur Composition*, Berlin, 1760); *Die geheim gehaltene Kunst von der Mensuration von Orgel-Pfeiffen* (MS, c.1760; facsimile ed. and Eng. tr. in Bibliotheca Organologica, XXIII, Busen, 1977); *Kurze Erklärung des Canonis Harmonici* (Lobenstein, 1763); *Anleitung zur Fantasie oder: Zu der schönen Kunst das Clavier wie auch andere Instrumente aus dem Kopfe zu spielen* (Lobenstein, 1767); *Bei der Einweihung ... über die Natur des Orgel-Klangs* (Hof, 1771); *Der in der Rechen-und Messkunst wohlerfahrne Orgelbaumeister* (Lobenstein, 1773); *Die Melodie aus der Harmonie ... hergeleitet* (MS). BIBL.: M. Frisch, *G.A. S. und seine Lehre von der musikalischen Harmonie* (diss., Univ. of Leipzig, 1954).

Soriano, Alberto, Uruguayan composer and musicologist; b. Santiago del Estero, Argentina, Feb. 5, 1915. He studied violin in Bahia, Brazil; in 1937 he went to Montevideo, where he was prof. of ethnomusicology at the Univ. (1953–69). In his music he makes use of South American melorhythms, while retaining fundamental classical forms. From 1953 to 1969 he was a prof. of enthnomusicology at the Univ. of Montevideo. Among his scholarly publications is *Algunas de las inmanencias etnomusicológicas* (Montevideo, 1967). WORKS: Piano Concerto (1952); Guitar Concerto No. 1

(1952); *Sinfonietta* for Guitar, Cello, Bassoon, and Flute (1952); 4 *rituales sinfónicos* (1953); *Divertimento* for Bassoon and String Orch. (1954); Cello Sonata (1955); Violin Concerto (1956); Guitar Concerto No. 2 (1957); Violin Sonata (1959); Piano Trio (1961); *Canticos sinfónicos a la Revolución de Cuba* (1961); Concertino for Cello and Orch. (1961); *Pastoral de Sibiu* for Flute and Orch. (1962); *Tríptico de Praga* for Orch. (1962); *Tiempo sinfónico para los caidos en Buchenwald* (1962).

Soriano, Francesco, outstanding Italian composer; b. Soriano, near Viterbo, 1548 or 1549; d. Rome, July 19, 1621. He went to Rome, where he was a choirboy at St. John Lateran; received instruction from Annibale Zoilo, Bartolomeo Roy, G.B. Montanari, and Palestrina. About 1574 he entered the priesthood; was maestro di cappella at S. Luigi dei Francesi by 1580. After serving in a similar capacity to the Gonzaga court in Mantua (1581–86), he returned to Rome as maestro di cappella at S. Maria Maggiore (1587–99; 1601–3), St. John Lateran (1599–1601), and the Cappella Giulia at St. Peter's (1603–20). With Felice Anerio, he was named by a papal commission to complete the revision of the chant books started by Palestrina and Zoilo in 1577; the *Editio medicaea* was finished in 1612 and publ. in 1614. Soriano was a masterful polyphonist.

WORKS: SACRED: *Motectorum* for 8 Voices (Rome, 1597); *Missarum liber primus* for 4 to 6 and 8 Voices (Rome, 1609); *Psalmi et motecta* for 8, 12, and 16 Voices and Basso Continuo (organ) (Venice, 1616); *Passio D. N. Jesu Christe secundum quatuor Evangelistas, Magnificat, sequentia fidelium defunctorum, una cum responsoria* for 4 Voices (Rome, 1619). SECULAR: *Il primo libro di madrigali* for 5 Voices (Venice, 1581); *Il secondo libro di madrigali* for 5 Voices (Rome, 1592); *Il primo libro di madrigali* for 4 to 6 Voices (Rome, 1601); *Il secondo libro di madrigali* (n.p., 1602); *Canoni et oblighi di 110 sorte, sopra l'Ave maris stella* for 3 to 8 Voices (Rome, 1610); other works in contemporary collections. BIBL.: S. Kniseley, *The Masses of F. S.: A Style-critical Study* (Gainesville, Fla., 1967).

Soriano, Gonzalo, Spanish pianist; b. Alicante, March 14, 1913; d. Madrid, April 14, 1972. He studied with Cabiles in Madrid, and later with Cortot and Landowska at the Paris Cons. He made his debut in Alicante in 1929; pursued an active career in Europe; also gave concerts in the U.S. and the Far East. He was particularly noted for his congenial performances of Spanish music.

Soriano Fuertes y Piqueras, Mariano, Spanish music historian and composer; b. Murcia, March 28, 1817; d. Madrid, March 26, 1880. He was a pupil of his father, Indalecio Soriano Fuertes (1787–1851), who served as maestro de capilla at Madrid's royal chapel. In 1843 he became a prof. at the Madrid Cons.; from 1844, he was director, successively, of music schools at Córdoba, Seville, and Cádiz; was appointed director of the Gran Teatro del Liceo in Barcelona in 1852; also founded the journal *Gaceta musical barcelonesa* (1861). He publ. *Música árabe-española y conexíon de la música con la astronomia, medicina y arquitectura* (Barcelona, 1853); *Historia de la música española desde la venida de los fenicios hasta el año de 1850* (4 vols., Madrid and Barcelona, 1855–59; a pioneering work, but quite unscientific and unreliable); *Memoria sobre las sociedades corales en España* (1865); *Calendario histórico musical ...* (1872). His compositions are undistinguished.

Sormann, Alfred (Richard Gotthilf), German pianist and composer; b. Danzig, May 16, 1861; d. Berlin, Sept. 17, 1913. He studied at the Hochschule für Musik in Berlin with Barth, Spitta, and Bargiel; in 1885, studied with Liszt. He made his debut in 1886, giving successful concerts in the chief German towns. He composed the operas *Die Sibylle von Tivoli* (Berlin, 1902) and *König Harald* (Stettin, 1909); a Piano Concerto; 2 string quartets; a Piano Trio; concert études and other piano pieces; songs.

Soro (Barriga), Enrique, significant Chilean composer; b. Concepción, July 15, 1884; d. Santiago, Dec. 2, 1954. He was a son of the Italian composer José Soro Sforza, with whom he studied piano and theory; played in public as a small child. He was granted a stipend by the government of Chile for study in Italy; entered the Milan Cons. at 14; graduated in 1904 with a grand prize in composition. Returning to Chile in 1905, he was appointed inspector of musical education in primary schools; in 1906 he joined the faculty of the Santiago Cons.; from 1919 to 1928 he was its director. He traveled as a pianist; gave concerts in Europe and South America; also publ. a number of works. In 1948 he was awarded the Premio Nacional de Arte.

WORKS: ORCH.: *Andante appassionato* (1915); *Danza fantástica* (1916); *Suite sinfónica*, No. 1, *Pensamientos intimos* (1918) and No. 2 (Santiago, May 9, 1919, composer conducting); *Impresiones líricas* for Piano and Strings (1919); Piano Concerto (1919); *Sinfonía romántica* (1920); *3 preludios sinfónicos* (Santiago, July 18, 1936); *Aires chilenos* for Orch. (Santiago, 1942); *Suite en estilo antiguo* (Santiago, May 28, 1943). CHAMBER: Piano Quintet (1919); String Quartet (1904); Piano Trio (1926); Violin Sonata; Cello Sonata; 3 piano sonatas (1920, 1923, 1942); a number of piano pieces in a salon genre, some of them based on Chilean melorhythms.

BIBL.: L. Giarda, *Analytische Studie über S. 2. Sonate für Violine und Klavier A moll, das Quartett A dur und das Klavierquintett* (Santiago, 1919); V. Salas Viú, *La creación musical en Chile 1900–1951* (Santiago, 1953).

Sotin, Hans, German bass; b. Dortmund, Sept. 10, 1939. He studied at the Dortmund Cons.; made his debut with the Essen Opera in 1962; from 1964 he sang with the Hamburg State Opera; also at the Bayreuth Festivals from 1971. He made his debut at the Metropolitan Opera in N.Y. on Oct. 26, 1972, as Sarastro in *Die Zauberflöte*; in 1973 he joined the Vienna State Opera. In 1974 he sang at Covent Garden in London; also appeared in concerts. He commended himself as a dramatic singer in operas of Mozart as well as in those of Wagner. He also toured widely as a concert singer.

Soto de Langa, Francisco, Spanish singer, music editor, and composer; b. Langa, Soria province, 1534; d. Rome, Sept. 25, 1619. He spent most of his life in Rome, where he was a member of the Papal Choir (1562-1611); also was a member of the oratory of St. Filippo Neri (1566-75). In 1575 he became a priest and went to S. Maria in Vallicella. In 1590 he served as interim maestro di cappella of the Papal Choir in Rome. He has been credited with compiling 5 significant vols. of laude spirituale (Rome, 1583-98), which includes several of his own pieces.

BIBL.: R. Mitjana, "El Padre F.S. d.L. (1534–1619)," *Música sacrohispana*, IV-V (1911–12).

Soubies, Albert, French writer on music; b. Paris, May 10, 1846; d. there, March 19, 1918. He studied law and was admitted to the bar; about the same time he became a pupil of Savard, Bazin, and Guilmant at the Paris Cons. In 1876 he became music critic for *Le Soir* and in 1885 began to write for the *Revue de l'Art Dramatique*. In 1874 he revived the famous old *Almanach Duchesne* (publ. between 1752 and 1815), reissuing it as *Almanach des Spectacles* (43 vols. publ. to 1914). His articles were publ. under the name B. de Lamange.

WRITINGS (all publ. in Paris): with C. Malherbe, *L'oeuvre dramatique de Richard Wagner* (1886); with H. de Curzon, *Précis de l'histoire de l'Opéra-Comique* (1887); *Une première par jour: causeries sur le théâtre* (1888); with C. Malherbe, *Wagner et Meyerbeer: documents inedits* (1891); with C. Malherbe, *Histoire de l'Opéra-Comique: la seconde Salle Favart* (1892); with C. Malherbe, *Mélanges sur Richard Wagner* (1892); *Soixante-sept ans à l'Opéra en une page* (1893); *Musique russe et musique espagnole* (1894); *La Comédie-Française depuis l'époque romantique* (1895); *Histoire de la musique dans les différents pays d'Europe* (1895); *Histoire du théâtre-lyrique 1851–1870* (1899); with H. de Curzon, *Documents inédits sur le Faust de Gounod* (1912); *Massenet historien* (1913).

Soubre, Etienne-Joseph, Belgian composer; b. Liège, Dec. 29, 1813; d. there, Sept. 8, 1871. He studied at the Liège

Cons., and became its director (1862). He composed the opera *Isoline, ou Les chaperons blancs* (Brussels, 1855); 2 cantatas; a Requiem; *Stabat Mater* and *Ave Verum; Hymne à Godefroid de Bouillon* for Male Chorus and Orch.; choruses, overtures, syms., etc.

Souhaitty, Jean-Jacques, French music theorist who flourished in the mid 17th century. He was active in Paris as a Franciscan monk. He was the 1st to employ number notation, indicating by the numerals 1 to 7 the degrees of the scale, and used this system for popular teaching. He publ. *Nouvelle méthode pour apprendre le plain-chant et la musique* (Paris, 1665; 2nd ed. as *Nouveaux éléments de chant, ou L'essay d'une nouvelle découverte quón a fait dans l'art de chanter*, 1677) and *Essai du chant de l'église par la nouvelle méthode des chiffres* (Paris, 1679).

Soukupová, Věra, Czech mezzo-soprano; b. Prague, April 12, 1932. She studied voice in Prague; joined the Pilsen Opera in 1957; then was a member of the National Theater in Prague (1960–63); from that time she began to make regular appearances with many of the leading opera houses of both Eastern and Western Europe; also sang at the major festivals; likewise toured widely as a concert singer.

Souliotis, Elena, Greek soprano; b. Athens, May 28, 1943. She was educated in Milan; made her debut at the Teatro San Carlo in Naples in 1964 as Santuzza; then made appearances at La Scala in Milan, Covent Garden in London, and the Teatro Colón in Buenos Aires.

Šourek, Otakar, Czech writer on music; b. Prague, Oct. 1, 1883; d. there, Feb. 15, 1956. He was trained as an engineer; was employed in the Prague City Council works dept. (1907–39); music was his avocation. He wrote music criticism for several publications, including Prague's *Venkov* (1918–41). However, it was as an authority on the life and music of Dvořák that he gained distinction; he devoted fully 40 years to Dvořák research, and served as the 1st ed. of the composer's collected works.

WRITINGS: *Život a dilo Antonína Dvořáka* (The Life and Works of Dvořák; 4 vols., Prague, 1916–33; vols. I–II, 3rd ed., 1955–56; vols. III–IV, 2nd ed., 1957–58; in German as *Dvořák: Leben und Werk*, one vol., abr. by P. Stefan, Vienna, 1935; Eng. tr. by Y. Vance as *Anton Dvořák*, N.Y., 1941); *Dvořák's Werke: Ein völlstandiges Verzeichnis in chronologischer, thematischer und systematischer Anordnung* (Berlin, 1917; rev. Czech ed., Prague, 1960); *Výlety pana Broučka* (Mr. Brouček's Excursions; Prague, 1920); *Dvořákovy symfonie* (Prague, 1922; 3rd ed., 1948; abr. ed. in Ger. in *Antonín Dvořák Werkanalysen I, Orchesterwerke*, Prague, 1954, and in Eng. in *The Orchestral Works of Antonín Dvořák*, Prague, 1956); *Antonín Dvořák* (Prague, 1929; 4th ed., 1947; Eng. tr. as *Antonín Dvořák: His Life and Work*, Prague, 1952); *Dvořákova citanka* (A Dvořák Reader; Prague, 1929; 3rd ed., 1946; in Eng., Prague, 1954); *Dvořák ve vzpomínkach a dopisech* (Prague, 1938; 9th ed., 1951; in Eng. as *Dvořák: Letters and Reminiscences*, Prague, 1954; in German, 1955; in Russian, 1964); *Smetanova Má vlast* (Prague, 1940); *Antonín Dvořák přátelům doma* (Dvořák to His Friends at Home; 395 letters; Prague, 1941); *Antonín Dvořák a Hans Richter* (letters to Richter; Prague, 1942); *Dvořákovy skladby komorni* (Prague, 1943; 2nd ed., 1949; abr. ed. in Ger. in *Antonín Dvořák Werkanalysen II, Kammermusik*, Prague, 1954, and in Eng. in *The Chamber Music of Antonín Dvořák*, Prague, 1956); *Dvořákovy skladby orchestralni* (2 vols., Prague, 1944 and 1946; abr. ed. in Ger. in *Antonín Dvořák Werkanalysen I, Orchesterwerke*, Prague, 1954, and in Eng. in *The Orchestral Works of Antonín Dvořák*, Prague, 1956); *Komorni skladby Bedřicha Smetany* (Smetana's chamber works; Prague, 1945); *Rudolf Karel* (Prague, 1947).

BIBL.: F. Oeser, "O. Š.," *Musica* (April 1956).

Souris, André, prominent Belgian conductor, musicologist, and composer; b. Marchienne-au-Pont, Hainaut, July 10, 1899; d. Paris, Feb. 12, 1970. He studied at the Brussels Cons. (1911–

18) with M. Lunssens (harmony) and Closson (music history), and privately with Gilson (composition). In 1925 he began teaching at the Royal Cons. in Brussels; in 1927 he won the Prix Rubens, and traveled to Italy, France, and Austria; conducted the Belgian Radio Orch. (1937–46); from 1949 to 1964 he was a prof. of harmony at the Royal Cons. in Brussels. He was the founder of the quarterly music review *Polyphonie* (1947–54). He collaborated with R. Vannes on the *Dictionnaire des musiciens (compositeurs)* (Brussels, 1947); also ed. works by various composers. His compositions reflect the influence of the French avant-garde of the period between the 2 World Wars; in a few of his later works he adopted serialism.

WORKS: ORCH.: *Scherzo* (1923); *Danceries de la Renaissance* (1932); *Hommage à Babeuf* for Wind Orch. and Percussion (1934); *Symphonies* (1939); *Pastorales Wallonnes* for Vocal Quartet and Small Orch. (1942); *Le Marchand d'images,* rustic cantata on popular Walloon songs, for Soli, Chorus, and Orch. (3 versions, 1944, 1954, and 1965); 5 *Laude* for Vocal Quartet, Chorus, and Small Orch. (1961); *Ouverture pour une arlequinade* (1962); 7 pieces, after Isaac (1963). **CHAMBER:** *3 poèmes japonais* for Soprano, String Quartet, and Piano (1916); *Berceuse* for Violin and Piano (1924); *Choral, Marche et Galop* for 2 Trumpets and 2 Trombones (1925); *Avertissement* for 3 or 5 Narrators and Percussion (1926); *Quelques airs de Clarisse Juranville* for Mezzo-soprano and 8 Instruments or Piano Quintet (1928); *Fatrasie* for Violin and Harp or Piano (1934); *Rengaines* for Wind Quintet (1937); *Comptines pour enfants sinistres* for Soprano, Mezzo-soprano, Violin, Clarinet, and Piano (1942); *Triptyque pour un violon* for Narrator, Soli, Organ, and Percussion (1963); *Concert flamand,* suite for 4 Winds (1965); *3 pièces anciennes* for Violin and Viola (1969); also theater, film, and radio scores; songs.

BIBL.: L. van Deuren, "Les oeuvres d'A. S.," *Revue Belge de Musicologie,* XX (1966); A. Fraiken, "Necrologies: A. S.," *La Vie Musicale Belge* (Jan.–Feb. 1970).

Sousa, John Philip, famous American bandmaster and composer; b. Washington, D.C., Nov. 6, 1854; d. Reading, Pa., March 6, 1932. He was the son of a Portuguese father and a German mother. He studied violin and orchestration with John Esputa, Jr., and violin and harmony with George Felix Benkert in Washington, D.C.; also acquired considerable proficiency on wind instruments. After playing in the Marine Band (1868–75), he was active in theater orchs.; in 1876 he was a violinist in the special orch. in Philadelphia conducted by Offenbach during his U.S. tour. In 1880 he was appointed director of the Marine Band, which he led with distinction until 1892. He then organized his own band and led it in its 1st concert in Plainfield, N.J., on Sept. 26, 1892. In subsequent years he gave successful concerts throughout the U.S. and Canada; played at the Chicago World's Fair in 1893 and at the Paris Exposition in 1900; made 4 European tours (1900, 1901, 1903, and 1905), with increasing acclaim, and finally a tour around the world, in 1910–11. His flair for writing band music was extraordinary; the infectious rhythms of his military marches and the brilliance of his band arrangements earned him the sobriquet "The March King"; particularly celebrated is his march *The Stars and Stripes Forever,* which became famous all over the world; in 1987 a bill was passed in the U.S. Congress and duly signed by President Ronald Reagan making it the official march of the U.S.. During World War I, Sousa served as a lieutenant in the Naval Reserve. He continued his annual tours almost to the time of his death. He was instrumental in the development of the Sousaphone, a bass tuba with upright bell, which has been used in bands since the 1890s.

WORKS (in alphabetical order): **OPERETTAS:** *The American Maid* (1909; Rochester, N.Y., Jan. 27, 1913); *The Bride Elect* (New Haven, Conn., Dec. 28, 1897); *El Capitan* (1895; Boston, April 13, 1896); *The Charlatan* (Montreal, Aug. 29, 1898); *Chris and the Wonderful Lamp* (New Haven, Conn., Oct. 23, 1899); *Desiree* (1883; Washington, D.C., May 1, 1884); *The Free Lance* (1905; Springfield, Mass., March 26, 1906); *The Irish Dragoon* (1915; unfinished); *Katherine* (1879); *The Queen*

of Hearts (1885; Washington, D.C., April 12, 1886); *The Smugglers* (Washington, D.C., March 25, 1882); also incidental music.

MARCHES: *Across the Danube* (1877); *America First* (1916); *Anchor and Star* (1918); *Ancient and Honorable Artillery Company* (1924); *The Atlantic City Pageant* (1927); *The Aviators* (1931); *The Beau Ideal* (1893); *The Belle of Chicago* (1892); *Ben Bolt* (1888); *The Black Horse Troop* (1924); *Bonnie Annie Laurie* (1883); *Boy Scouts of America* (1916); *The Bride Elect* (1897); *Bullets and Bayonets* (1918); *El Capitan* (1896); *A Century of Progress* (1931); *The Chantyman's March* (1918); *The Charlatan* (1898); *The Circumnavigators Club* (1931); *Circus March* (n.d.); *Columbia's Pride* (1914); *Comrades of the Legion* (1920); *Congress Hall* (1882); *Corcoran Cadets* (1890); *The Crusader* (1888); *Daughters of Texas* (1929); *The Dauntless Battalion* (1922); *The Diplomat* (1904); *The Directorate* (1894); *Esprit de Corps* (1878); *The Fairest of the Fair* (1908); *The Federal* (1910); *Flags of Freedom* (1918); *La Flor de Sevilla* (1929); *Foshay Tower Washington Memorial* (1929); *The Free Lance* (1906); *From Maine to Oregon* (1913); *The Gallant Seventh* (1922); *George Washington Bicentennial* (1930); *The Gladiator* (1886; the 1st work to sell a million copies); *Globe and Eagle* (1879); *The Glory of the Yankee Navy* (1909); *Golden Jubilee* (1928); *The Golden Star* (1919); *The Gridiron Club* (1926); *Guide Right* (1881); *Hail to the Spirit of Liberty* (1900); *Hands Across the Sea* (1899); *Harmonica Wizard* (1930); *The High School Cadets* (1890); *Homeward Bound* (n.d.); *The Honored Dead* (1876); *Imperial Edward* (1902); *In Memoriam* (1881; for the assassinated President Garfield); *The Invincible Eagle* (1901); *Jack Tar* (1903); *Kansas Wildcats* (1931); *Keeping Step with the Union* (1921); *King Cotton* (1895); *The Lambs' March* (1914); *The Legionnaires* (1930); *The Liberty Bell* (1893); *Liberty Loan* (1917); *The Loyal Legion* (1890); *Magna Carta* (1927); *The Man Behind the Gun* (1899); *Manhattan Beach* (1893); *March of the Mitten Men* (1923); *March of the Pan-Americans* (1915); *March of the Royal Trumpets* (1892); *Marquette University March* (1924; on receiving an honorary D.M., Nov. 16, 1923); *Mikado March* (1885); *The Minnesota March* (1927); *Mother Goose* (1883); *Mother Hubbard March* (1885); *National Fencibles* (1888); *The National Game* (1925; for the 50th anniversary of the National League of baseball); *The Naval Reserve* (1917); *New Mexico* (1928); *The New York Hippodrome* (1915); *Nobles of the Mystic Shrine* (1923); *The Northern Pines* (1931); *The Occidental* (1887); *Old Ironsides* (1926); *On Parade* (1892); *On the Campus* (1920); *On the Tramp* (1879); *Our Flirtations* (1880); *The Pathfinder of Panama* (1915); *Pet of the Petticoats* (1883); *The Phoenix March* (1875); *The Picador* (1889); *Powhatan's Daughter* (1907); *President Garfield's Inauguration March* (1881); *The Pride of Pittsburgh* (1901); *The Pride of the Wolverines* (1926); *Prince Charming* (1928); *The Quilting Party March* (1889); *Recognition March* (c.1880); *Resumption March* (1879); *Review* (1873; his 1st publ. march); *Revival March* (1876); *Riders for the Flag* (1927); *The Rifle Regiment* (1886); *Right Forward* (1881); *Right—Left* (1883); *The Royal Welch Fusiliers* (No. 1, 1929; No. 2, 1930); *Sable and Spurs* (1918); *Salutation* (1873); *The Salvation Army* (1930); *Semper Fidelis* (1888); *Sesquicentennial Exposition March* (1926); *Solid Men to the Front* (1918); *Sound Off* (1885); *The Stars and Stripes Forever* (1896; made the official march of the U.S. by act of Congress, 1987); *The Thunderer* (1889); *Transit of Venus* (1883); *The Triton* (1892); *Triumph of Time* (1885); *Universal Peace* (probably 1925); *University of Illinois* (1929); *University of Nebraska* (1928); *USAAC March* (1918); *U.S. Field Artillery* (1917); *The Victory Chest* (1918); *The Volunteers* (1918); *The Washington Post* (1889); *Wedding March* (1918); *The White Plume* (1884); *The White Rose* (1917); *Who's Who in Navy Blue* (1920); *The Wildcats* (1930 or 1931); *Wisconsin Forward Forever* (1917); *The Wolverine March* (1881); *Yorktown Centennial* (1881); also suites for Band; overtures; descriptive pieces; instrumental solos; orch. works; about 76 songs, ballads, hymns; many arrangements and transcriptions.

WRITINGS: AUTOBIOGRAPHICAL: *Through the Years with*

Sousa (1910); *Marching Along* (1928). MANUALS: *The Trumpet and Drum* (1886); *National Patriotic and Typical Airs of All Lands* (1890). NOVELS: *The Fifth String* (1902); *Pipetown Sandy* (1905); *The Transit of Venus* (1919).

BIBL.: M. Simon, *J.P. S., the March King* (N.Y., 1944); A. Lingg, *J.P. S.* (N.Y., 1954); K. Berger, *The March King and His Band* (N.Y., 1957); R. Goldman, "The Great American Composers: J.P. S.," *HiFi Stereo Review* (July 1967); J. Smart, *The S. Band: A Discography* (Washington, D.C., 1970); W. Stacy, *J.P. S. and His Band Suites: An Analytic and Cultural Study* (diss., Univ. of Colorado, 1972); P. Bierley, *J.P. S.: American Phenomenon* (N.Y., 1973; 2nd ed., rev., 1986); idem, *J.P. S.: A Descriptive Catalog of His Works* (Urbana, Ill., 1973; 2nd ed., rev. and augmented, 1984, as *The Works of J.P. S.*); J. Newsom, ed., *Perspectives on J.P. S.* (Washington, D.C., 1983); W. Mitziga, *The Sound of S.: J.P. S. Compositions Recorded* (Chicago, 1986).

Souster, Tim(othy Andrew James), English composer of the extreme avant-garde; b. Bletchley, Buckinghamshire, Jan. 29, 1943. He studied with Rose, Lumsden, and Wellesz at the Univ. of Oxford (B.A., 1964; B.Mus., 1965); in 1964 he attended courses in new music given by Stockhausen and Berio in Darmstadt; received private instruction from Bennett (1965). He was a music producer for the BBC (1965–67); after serving as composer-in-residence at King's College, Cambridge (1969–71), he was a teaching assistant to Stockhausen in Cologne (1971–73); later was a research fellow in electronic music at the Univ. of Keele (1975–77); in 1988–89 he was chairman of the Association of Professional Composers. He became one of the most articulate exponents of serial, aleatory, and combinatorial ideas, in which electronic media are employed in conjunction with acoustical performances by humans; he expounded these ideas in his writings in the *Listener, Tempo,* and other progressive publications. In 1969 he was a co-founder (with Roger Smalley) of the Intermodulation Group, with the aim of presenting works by congenial composers and experimenters; it disbanded in 1976 and he then formed a new group, OdB.

WORKS: *Songs of the Seasons* for Soprano and Viola (1965); *Poem in Depression* for Soprano, Flute, Viola, Cello, and Piano (1965); *Parallels* for 2 Percussion Players (1966); *Metropolitan Games* for Piano Duet (1967); *Titus Groan Music* for Wind Quintet, Electronics, and Magnetic Tape (1969); *Chinese Whispers* for Percussion and 3 Electronic Synthesizers (1970); *Waste Land Music* for Soprano Saxophone, Modulated Piano, Modulated Organ, and Electronic Synthesizer (London, July 14, 1970); *Triple Music II* for 3 Orchs. (London, Aug. 13, 1970); *Song of an Average City* for Small Orch. and Tape (1974); *Afghan Amplitudes* for Keyboards and Synthesizers (1976); Sonata for Cello and Ensemble (1979); *Mareas* for 4 Amplified Voices and Tape (1981); *Paws 3D* for Orch. (1984); *Le Souvenir de Maurice Ravel* for Septet (1984); *Hambledon Hill* for Amplified String Quartet (1985); Concerto for Trumpet, Live Electronics, and Orch. (1988).

Southern, Eileen, black American musicologist; b. Minneapolis, Feb. 19, 1920. The Norwegian pianist Meda Zarbell Steele supervised her studies at Chicago Musical College and helped her obtain scholarships at the Univ. of Chicago, where she studied with Scott Goldwaite and Sigmund Levarie (B.A., 1940; M.A., 1941, with the thesis *The Use of Negro Folksong in Symphonic Music*). She then taught at Prairie View State College (1941–42), Southern Univ. (1943–45, 1949–51), Alcorn State College (1945–46), Claflin Univ. (1947–49), and secondary schools in N.Y. (1954–60). Simultaneously she pursued her own studies of medieval and Renaissance music; enrolled at N.Y. Univ. in the classes of Gustave Reese and Martin Bernstein, and wrote her diss., *The Buxheim Organ Book* (Ph.D., 1961; publ. 1963). She gave courses in Renaissance music at Brooklyn College (1960–68) and York College (1968–75); also founded the journal *Black Perspective in Music* (1973). She was prof. of music and chairman of the dept. of Afro-American studies at Harvard Univ. (from 1976). In addition

to her articles in journals, she was a contributor to *The New Grove Dictionary of Music and Musicians* (1980) and *The New Grove Dictionary of American Music* (1986).

WRITINGS: *The Music of Black Americans: A History* (N.Y., 1971; 2nd ed., 1984); *Readings in Black American Music* (N.Y., 1971; 2nd ed., 1983); *Biographical Dictionary of Afro-American and African Musicians* (Westport, Conn., 1982).

Souzay, Gérard (real name, **Gérard Marcel Tisserand**), distinguished French baritone; b. Angers, Dec. 8, 1918. He studied voice with Pierre Bernac, Claire Croiza, Vanni Marcoux, and Lotte Lehmann; was a student at the Paris Cons. (1940–45); made his recital debut in Paris in 1945, his U.S. debut in a recital at N.Y.'s Town Hall in 1950, and his operatic debut as Count Robinson in Cimarosa's *Il Matrimonio segreto* at the Aix-en-Provence Festival in 1957. He made his Metropolitan Opera debut in N.Y. as Count Almaviva in *Le nozze di Figaro* on Jan. 21, 1965. In subsequent years he toured extensively, mainly as a recitalist. In 1985 he joined the faculty of the Indiana Univ. School of Music in Bloomington; taught at the Univ. of Texas in Austin (from 1986). Souzay won renown as a concert artist; after Bernac, he was esteemed as the foremost interpreter of French art songs; equally acclaimed were his performances of German lieder, which received encomiums from German critics and audiences.

Sowande, Fela (actually, **Olufela**), Nigerian composer; b. Oyo, May 29, 1905; d. Ravenna, Ohio, March 13, 1987. He studied music in Lagos; then went to London, where he played in a combo in nightclubs; at the same time he took courses at London Univ. and the Trinity College of Music. He served in the Royal Air Force during World War II. In 1944 he composed an *African Suite* for Strings; returned to Nigeria in 1953; in 1957 he received a grant from the State Dept. to travel in the U.S.; was again in the U.S. in 1961, on a Rockefeller grant, and on June 1, 1961, conducted a group of members of the N.Y. Phil. in Carnegie Hall in a program of his own compositions, among them *Nigerian Folk Symphony*. Upon returning to Nigeria, he joined the staff of the Univ. College at Ibadan. In his music he pursued the goal of cultural integration of native folk material with Western art forms.

Sowerby, Leo, remarkable American composer and organist; b. Grand Rapids, Mich., May 1, 1895; d. Fort Clinton, Ohio, July 7, 1968. He studied piano with Calvin Lampert and music theory with Arthur Andersen in Chicago; also had sporadic lessons with Percy Grainger. He learned to play the organ without a teacher, and yet developed a virtuoso technique that enabled him to hold prestigious appointments as a church organist. He was extremely precocious; on Jan. 17, 1917, he presented himself in Chicago in a program grandiloquently billed "Leo Sowerby: His Music," which included such ambitious works as a Piano Concerto, with the composer at the keyboard; a Cello Concerto; and symphonic pieces. During World War I, he served as a bandmaster in the U.S. Army. He completed his musical studies at the American Cons. in Chicago (M.M., 1918). In 1921 he received the American Prix de Rome, the 1st of its kind to be awarded for composition; he spent 3 years at the American Cons. in Rome. Returning to Chicago, he served as a teacher of composition at the American Cons. (1925–62); also was organist and choirmaster at the Episcopal Cathedral of St. James (1927–62); then was founder-director of the College of Church Musicians at the National Cathedral in Washington, D.C. (1962–68). In 1935 he was elected to membership in the National Inst. of Arts and Letters. In 1946 he won the Pulitzer Prize for his *Canticle of the Sun.* Sowerby never attempted to discover new ways of making music; his style was eclectic in the positive sense of the word, selecting what appeared to be the best in various doctrines and styles. Hindemith's invidious reference to Sowerby as the 4th B in music, a "sour B," is not appropriate, for Sowerby's music is anything but sour; he certainly knew how to build up sonorous masses, particularly in his vocal compositions.

WORKS: ORCH.: Violin Concerto (1913; rev. 1924); *The Sor-*

row of *Mydath*, symphonic poem (1915); *Rhapsody on British Folk Tunes* (1915); *Comes Autumn Time*, overture (Chicago, Jan. 17, 1917); Cello Concerto No. 1 in A major (Chicago, Jan. 17, 1917); Piano Concerto, with Soprano obbligato (Chicago, Jan. 17, 1917; rev., 1919, without soprano); *The Irish Washerwoman*, transcription (Chicago, Jan. 17, 1917); *Money Musk*, transcription (1917); *A Set of 4: Suite of Ironics* (Chicago, Feb. 15, 1918); Concerto for Harp and Small Orch. (1919); 5 syms.: No. 1 (Chicago, April 7, 1922); No. 2 (Chicago, March 29, 1929); No. 3 (Chicago, March 6, 1941); No. 4 (Boston, Jan. 7, 1949, Koussevitzky conducting); No. 5 (1964); *King Estmere*, ballad for 2 Pianos and Orch. (Rome, April 8, 1923); *Rhapsody* for Chamber Orch. (1922); *From the Northland* (Rome, May 27, 1924); *Synconata* and *Monotony* for Jazz Orch. (1924, 1925; Chicago, Oct. 11, 1925); *Medieval Poem* for Organ and Orch. (Chicago, April 20, 1926); *Prairie*, symphonic poem (Interlochen, Mich., Aug. 11, 1929); Cello Concerto No. 2, in E minor (1929–34; N.Y., April 2, 1935); *Passacaglia, Interlude and Fugue* (1931–32); 2nd Piano Concerto (1932; Boston, Nov. 30, 1936); Sinfonietta for String Orch. (1933–34); *Theme in Yellow*, after Sandburg (1937); Concerto in C for Organ and Orch. (Boston, April 22, 1938; E. Power Biggs, soloist); *Concert Overture* (1941); *Poem* for Viola, and Orch. or Organ (1941); *Fantasy on Hymn Tunes* (1943); *Classic Concerto* for Organ and String Orch. (1944); *Portrait: Fantasy in Triptych* (1946; Indianapolis, Nov. 21, 1953); *Concert Piece* for Organ and Orch. (1951); *All on a Summer's Day* (1954; Louisville, Ky., Jan. 8, 1955); untitled work (Concerto No. 2) for Organ and Orch. (1967–68). VOCAL: *A Liturgy of Hope* for Soprano, Male Chorus, and Organ (1917); an untitled oratorio in 5 parts based on the Book of Psalms (1924); *The Vision of Sir Launfal*, cantata after James Lowell (1925); *Great Is the Lord* for Chorus, Orch., and Organ (1933); *Forsaken of Man* for Chorus and Organ (1939); *Song for America* for Chorus and Orch. (1942); *The Canticle of the Sun*, after St. Francis, for Chorus and Orch. (1944; N.Y., April 16, 1945; won the 1946 Pulitzer Prize); *Christ Reborn*, cantata for Chorus and Organ (1950; Philadelphia, Nov. 1, 1953); *The Throne of God* for Chorus and Orch. (1956; Washington, D.C., Nov. 18, 1957); *The Ark of the Covenant*, cantata for Chorus and Organ (1959); *Solomon's Garden*, cantata for Tenor, Chorus, and Chamber Orch. (1964); *La Corona* for Chorus and Orch. (1967); numerous anthems, songs, etc. CHAMBER: Quartet for Violin, Cello, Horn, and Piano (1911); 3 unnumbered piano trios (in D, undated; 1911; 1953); 5 unnumbered violin sonatas (in E, 1912, rev. 1916; in G, undated; in B-flat, 1922; in A, *Fantasy Sonata*, 1944; in D, 1959); 2 unnumbered cello sonatas (1912; in E minor, 1920); Sonata for Solo Violin (1914); Serenade for String Quartet (1916); Wind Quintet (1916); Trio for Flute, Viola, and Piano (1919); 2 string quartets (1923–24, 1934–35; both MSS lost); *Pop Goes the Weasel* for Wind Quintet (1927); *Chaconne* for Trombone and Piano (1936); Clarinet Sonata (1938); *Poem* for Viola and Organ (1941); Trumpet Sonata (1945); *Ballade* for English Horn and Organ (1949); *Fantasy* for Trumpet and Organ (1962); *Suite* for Oboe and Piano (1963); *Triptych of Diversions* for Organ, 2 Violins, Double Bass, Oboe, and Percussion (1962); *Dialog* for Organ and Piano (1967); an undated Horn Trio. ORGAN: Sonata (1914–17); Sym. in G major (1930); *Suite* (1934); Church Sonata (1956); *Sinfonia brevis* (1965); *Bright, Blithe and Brisk* (1967); *Passacaglia* (1967); pieces. PIANO: Sonata in E-flat major (1912); *Florida*, suite (1929); Sonata in D (1948; rev. 1964); *Suite* (1959); *Suite* for Piano, 4-hands (1959); pieces.

BIBL.: "L. S.: A Symposium of Tribute," *Music: the A.G.O. and R.C.C.O. Magazine*, II/10 (1968); M. Guiltinan, *The Absolute Music for Piano Solo by L. S.* (diss., Univ. of Rochester, 1977); *L. S.: A Short Biography and a Complete List of His Compositions* (Chicago, 1979); D. Bading, *L. S.'s Works for Organ with Orchestra or Ensemble* (thesis, Univ. of Kansas, 1983).

Sowinski, Wojciech (Albert), Polish pianist, teacher, writer on music, and composer; b. Lukaszówka, Podolia, c.1803; d.

Paris, March 5, 1880. He was a pupil of Czerny, Gyrowetz, Leidersdorf, and Seyfried in Vienna, where he made his debut as a pianist in 1828; after touring Italy, France, and England, he settled in Paris as a music teacher in 1830. He publ. the 1st dictionary of Polish musicians in a Western language, *Les Musiciens polonais et slaves, anciens et modernes. Dictionnaire biographique des compositeurs, chanteurs, instrumentistes, luthiers* (Paris, 1857; in Polish, Paris, 1874), and it is through this publication that his name is remembered. He wrote the operas *Lenore, ou Les morts vont vite, Le Modèle, Une Scène sous la ligne*, and *Zlote gody*; an oratorio, *Saint Adalbert*; several motets; a Sym.; overtures on Polish subjects; 2 piano concertos; a Piano Quartet; a Piano Trio; numerous piano pieces in the salon genre.

Soyer, Roger (Julien Jacques), French bass; b. Paris, Sept. 1, 1939. He studied at the Paris Cons.; made his debut at the Paris Opéra in 1962; then sang at La Scala in Milan, the Salzburg Festival, the Vienna State Opera, and the Bavarian State Opera in Munich. He made his Metropolitan Opera debut in N.Y. as Don Giovanni on Nov. 16, 1972; also appeared as a concert artist.

Spadavecchia, Antonio (Emmanuilovich), Russian composer of Italian descent; b. Odessa, June 3, 1907; d. Moscow, Feb. 7, 1988. He studied with Shebalin at the Moscow Cons. (graduated, 1937); also with Prokofiev (1944).

WORKS: OPERAS: *The Magic Steed* (Ufa, Nov. 7, 1942; rev. 1952; in collaboration with Zaimov); *The Inn Hostess*, after Goldoni (Moscow, April 24, 1949); *Pilgrimage of Sorrows*, after A. Tolstoi (Perm, Dec. 29, 1953); *The Gadfly* (Perm, Nov. 8, 1957); *Yukki* (1970); *Ordeal by Fire* (1971). BALLETS: *Enemies* (Moscow, May 20, 1938); *The Shore of Happiness* (Moscow, Nov. 6, 1948; rev. 1955); also musical comedies; incidental music; film scores; symphonic suite, *Dzangar* (1940); *Heroic Overture on Bashkir Songs* (Ufa, Nov. 6, 1942); Piano Concerto (1944); *Romantic Trio* for Violin, Cello, and Piano (1937); String Quartet (1937); *Elegie* for Cello and Piano (1955); songs.

Spaeth, Sigmund, American writer on music; b. Philadelphia, April 10, 1885; d. N.Y., Nov. 11, 1965. He studied piano and violin with A. Bachmann; then attended Haverford College (B.A., 1905; M.A., 1906) and Princeton Univ. (Ph.D., 1910, with the diss. *Milton's Knowledge of Music*; publ. in Princeton, N.J., 1913). He was music ed. of the *N.Y. Evening Mail* (1914–18); education director of the American Piano Co. (1920–27); president of the National Assoc. of American Composers and Conductors (1934–37); lectured widely on music; gave popular talks on the radio; was active in musical journalism; held various posts in educational organizations. He ed. the valuable collections *Read 'em and Weep* (1926; rev. 1945) and *Weep Some More, My Lady* (1927).

WRITINGS: (all publ. in N.Y. unless otherwise given): *The Common Sense of Music* (1924); *The Art of Enjoying Music* (1933; rev. 1949); *Music for Everybody* (1934); *Great Symphonies* (Garden City, N.Y., 1936; 2nd ed., rev., 1952); *Stories behind the World's Great Music* (1937); *Music for Fun* (1939); *Great Program Music* (1940); *A Guide to Great Orchestral Music* (1943); *At Home with Music* (Garden City, N.Y., 1945); *A History of Popular Music in America* (1948); *Dedication: The Love Story of Clara and Robert Schumann* (N.Y., 1950); *Opportunities in Music Careers* (1950; 2nd ed., rev., 1966); *Fifty Years with Music* (1959); *The Importance of Music* (1963).

Spalding, Albert, esteemed American violinist; b. Chicago, Aug. 15, 1888; d. N.Y., May 26, 1953. He studied violin with Ulpiano Chiti in Florence and with Juan Buitrago in N.Y. before entering the Bologna Cons. at the age of 14; subsequently received further violin training from Augustin Lefort at the Paris Cons., and studied composition with Antonio Scontrino in Florence. He made his public debut in Paris on June 6, 1905, and his American debut as a soloist with the N.Y. Sym. Orch. on Nov. 8, 1908. Beginning in 1919, he made annual tours of the U.S. and acquired the reputation of a fine artist, even though not necessarily a contagiously flamboyant one.

He also made appearances in Europe. On June 20, 1950, he gave his farewell performance in N.Y. In 1926 he was elected to the National Inst. of Arts and Letters and in 1937 to the American Academy of Arts and Letters. He gave the U.S. premieres of the violin concertos of Dohnányi, Elgar, and Barber. His own works include an orch. suite, 2 violin concertos, a String Quartet, a Violin Sonata, various violin pieces, songs, and piano pieces. He publ. an autobiography, *Rise to Follow* (N.Y., 1943), and a fictionalized biography of Tartini, *A Fiddle, a Sword, and a Lady* (N.Y., 1953).

BIBL.: W. Timblin, "A. S. as a Teacher and Composer," *School Musician*, XLIX/6 (1978); B. Schwarz, *Great Masters of the Violin* (N.Y., 1983).

Spangenberg, Heinrich, German composer; b. Darmstadt, May 24, 1861; d. there, Sept. 27, 1925. He studied at the Hoch Cons. in Frankfurt; in 1881, was a pupil of N. Rubinstein (piano) in Moscow; then studied with Leschetizky (piano) and Grädener (composition) in Vienna. In 1884 he became Kapellmeister at the Opera and instructor at the Cons. in Mainz; in 1886 he became an instructor at Fredenberg's Cons. in Wiesbaden; was founder-director of his own cons. there (1890?–1914). He composed 3 operas; piano pieces; songs; numerous choruses for men's voices.

Spani, Hina (real name, **Higinia Tuñon**), Argentine soprano; b. Puán, Feb. 15, 1896; d. Buenos Aires, July 11, 1969. She studied in Buenos Aires and Milan; made her operatic debut at La Scala in Milan in 1915 as Anna in Catalani's *Loreley;* also sang in Turin, Naples, and Parma; made many appearances at the Teatro Colón in Buenos Aires (1915–40). From 1946 she taught voice in Buenos Aires, and from 1952 served as director of the School of Music at the Univ. of Buenos Aires. She was highly regarded as a dramatic soprano; her repertoire included more than 70 roles.

Spanier, "Muggsy" (Francis Joseph), American jazz cornetist; b. Chicago, Nov. 9, 1906; d. Sausalito, Calif., Feb. 12, 1967. He began his professional career in 1921 in Chicago, where he worked with several bands; he played with Ted Lewis (1929–36) and Ben Pollack (1936–38); later played with Earl Hines; eventually made his home in California.

Sparnaay, Harry, prominent Dutch bass-clarinetist; b. Amsterdam, April 14, 1944. He played tenor saxophone in the Bohemia Jazz Quintet and later in the Theo Deken Orch.; studied clarinet at the Amsterdam Cons., where he eventually turned to the bass clarinet. He had over 100 works written for him (as a soloist or for his chamber duo, Fusion Moderne, which was formed in 1971 with the pianist Polo de Haas) by Berio, Goeyvaerts, Hrisanidis, Kunst, Logothetis, Raxach, Straesser, and others; played in contemporary music festivals.

Spasov, Ivan, Bulgarian composer; b. Sofia, Jan. 17, 1934. He studied composition with Vladigerov at the Bulgarian State Cons. (1951–56) and later with Sikorski and Wislocki at the Warsaw Cons.; subsequently devoted himself mainly to teaching and composing. He is one of the few Bulgarian composers to make use of advanced techniques.

WORKS: ORCH.: *Sonata concertante* for Clarinet and Orch. (1959); 3 syms. (1960, 1975, 1978); *Micro-Suite* for Chamber Orch. (1963); *Dances* (1964); *2 Bulgarian Melodies* (1968, 1970); *Competition* for 22 Winds (1969; Plovdiv, May 10, 1973); Cello Concerto (1974); Piano Concerto (1976); *Firework* (1980); Violin Concerto (1980). **VOCAL:** *Plakat,* oratorio (1958); *Monologues of a Lonely Woman,* monodrama for Soprano, Female Choir, Chamber Ensemble, and Tape (1976); *Canti lamentosi* for 2 Sopranos and Chamber Orch. (1979). **CHAMBER:** Clarinet Sonata (1959); Viola Sonata (1960); *Bagatelles* for Flute and Harp (1964); *Episodes* for 4 Instrumental Groups (1965); *Movements I* for 12 Strings (1966) and *II* for 12 Strings and 3 Bagpipes (1968); *10 Groups* for Hunting Horn and Piano (1965); *Musique pour des amis* for String Quartet and Jazz Quartet (1966); String Quartet No. 1 (1973); Cello Sonata (1980); Piano Trio (1981). **PIANO:** *Games* (1964); *The Art of the Seria* in 3 notebooks (1968, 1969, 1970).

Spataro, Giovanni, Italian music theorist and composer; b. Bologna, c.1458; d. there, Jan. 17, 1541. He studied with Bartolomeo Ramos de Pareia while the latter was in Bologna in 1482. Ramos publ. his *Musica pratica* in 1482, which resulted in an attack from Niccolo Buzio. Spataro countered on his teacher's behalf with his *Honesta defensio* (1491). Gaffurius entered the fray with his *Apologia* (1520), which Spataro answered in his *Errori* (1521). Spataro championed what he saw as the progressive ideas of his teacher. He was active as a member of the choir at S. Petronio from at least 1505; was installed as maestro di canto in 1512. His only extant works are 6 motets and 1 laude; they are publ. in the Antiquae Musicae Italicae series *Monumenta Bononiensa,* II (1967).

WRITINGS: *Honesta defensio in Nicolai Burtii parmensis opusculum* (Bologna, 1491; ed. in the Antiquae Musicae Italicae series *Monumenta Bononiensa,* II/1, 1967); *Dilucide, et probatissime demonstratione . . . contra cert frivole et vane excusatio[n]e, da Fra[n]chino Gafurio (maestro de li errori)* (Bologna, 1521); *Errori di Franchino Gafurio da Lodi, da maestro Joanne Spatario, musico bolognese, in sua defensione, e del suo precettore mro. Bartolomeo Ramis hispano subtilmente dimonstrati* (Bologna, 1521); *Tractato di musica, nel quale si tracta de la perfectione de la sesquialtera producta in la musica mensurata* (Venice, 1531).

BIBL.: L. Frati, "La musica di G. S.," *L'Archiginnasio,* XI (Bologna, 1916); G. Vecchi, "Le utili e brevi regule dello S.," *Quadrivium,* V (1961).

Spazier, Johann Gottlieb Karl, German pedagogue, writer on music, and composer; b. Berlin, April 20, 1761; d. Leipzig, Jan. 19, 1805. He was a student of philosophy at the Univ. of Halle; was a prof. of philosophy at the Univ. of Giessen; settled in Leipzig in 1800. He composed many songs, some of which became great favorites. Among his writings are *Freymüthige Gedanken über die Gottesverehrung der Protestanten* (Gotha, 1788), *Carl Pilger's Roman seines Lebens von ihm selbst geschrieben: ein Beitrag zur Erziehung und Kultur des Menschen* (Berlin, 1792–96), and *Etwas über Gluckische Musik und die Oper Iphigenia in Tauris auf dem Berlinischen Nationaltheater* (Berlin, 1795).

BIBL.: M. Friedlaender, *Das deutsche Lied im 18. Jahrhundert* (Stuttgart and Berlin, 1902); E. Wege, "Der Liederkomponist und Musikschriftsteller J.G.K. S.," *Beiträge zur Musikwissenschaft,* V (1963).

Speaks, Oley, American baritone and song composer; b. Canal Winchester, Ohio, June 28, 1874; d. N.Y., Aug. 27, 1948. He studied singing with Emma Thursby and composition with Max Spicker and W. Macfarlane; sang at various churches in N.Y. (1898–1906); then devoted himself entirely to concert singing and composition. He wrote some of the most popular songs in the American repertoire of his day: *On the Road to Mandalay* (1907), *Morning* (1910), *To You* (1910), *Sylvia* (1914), and *The Prayer Perfect* (1930).

Speer, Daniel, noted German composer, music theorist, and writer; b. Breslau, July 2, 1636; d. Göppingen, Oct. 5, 1707. He studied at the Maria-Magdalenen-Gymnasium in Breslau, then traveled throughout southeastern Europe, obtaining practical experience in music. After serving as a church musician in Stuttgart (1664–66), he was a schoolteacher and church musician in Göppingen (1667–68); then was active in Gross Bottwar and Leonberg, near Stuttgart. In 1673 he settled in Göppingen as a teacher at the Lateinschule. In 1689 he publ. a pamphlet criticizing the Württemberg authorities for their lack of adequate response to the French invasion; for this he was arrested and imprisoned at the Hohenneuffen fortress. Upon his release, he was sent to Waiblingen, near Stuttgart. In 1694 he returned to Göppingen as Kollaborator at the Lateinschule, where he later became Kantor. His most significant work was the treatise *Grund-richtiger . . . Unterricht der musicalischen Kunst* (Ulm, 1687; 2nd ed., rev. and enl., 1697, as *Grund-richtiger . . . Unterricht der musicalischen Kunst, oder Vierfaches musicalisches Kleeblatt;* see H. Howery, *A Comprehensive Performance Project in Trombone Literature with an*

Essay Consisting of a Translation of Daniel Speer's "Vierfaches Musikalisches Kleeblatt," diss., Univ. of Iowa, 1971). He composed sacred vocal works and 3 valuable quodlibet collections (1685, 1687, 1688). Among his other works are novels and various political writings.

Speidel, Wilhelm, German pianist, conductor, teacher, and composer; b. Ulm, Sept. 3, 1826; d. Stuttgart, Oct. 13, 1899. He was a pupil at Munich of Wänner and W. Kuhe, and of Ignaz Lachner (composition); in 1854, became music director at Ulm; in 1857, became conductor of the Liederkranz at Stuttgart; he was co-founder, with Lebert and others, of the Stuttgart Cons., and a teacher of piano there until he founded his Künstler- und Dilettantenschule für Klavier in 1874. On Lebert's death (1884), Speidel rejoined the Cons., uniting with it his own school.

Spelman, Timothy (Mather), American composer; b. Brooklyn, Jan. 21, 1891; d. Florence, Italy, Aug. 21, 1970. He studied with H.R. Shelley in N.Y. (1908), W.R. Spalding and E.B. Hill at Harvard Univ. (1909–13), and Walter Courvoisier at the Munich Cons. (1913–15); he returned to the U.S. in 1915 and was active as director of a military band. After 1918 he went back to Europe with his wife, the poetess Leolyn Everett, settling in Florence. He returned to the U.S. in 1935; in 1947 he went back to Florence. His music was performed more often in Europe than in America; indeed, his style of composition is exceedingly European, influenced by Italian Romanticism and French Impressionism.

WORKS: STAGE: *Snowdrop,* pantomime (Brooklyn, 1911); *The Romance of the Rose,* "wordless fantasy" (Boston, 1913; rev., St. Paul, Minn., Dec. 4, 1915); *La Magnifica,* short music drama to a libretto by Leolyn Everett-Spelman (1920); *The Sea Rovers,* opera (1928); *The Sunken City,* opera (1930); *Babakan,* fantastic comedy (1935); *The Courtship of Miles Standish,* opera after Longfellow (1935). ORCH.: *Saint's Days,* suite in 4 movements, including *Assisi, the Great Pardon of St. Francis* (Boston, March 26, 1926); *The Outcasts of Poker Flat,* symphonic poem after Bret Harte (1928); Sym. (1935; Rochester, N.Y., Oct. 29, 1936); *Jamboree,* "pocket ballet" (1945); Oboe Concerto (1954). CHAMBER: 5 *Whimsical Serenades* for String Quartet (1924); *Le Pavillion sur l'eau* for Flute, Harp, and Strings (1925); *Eclogue* for 10 Instruments (1926); String Quartet (1953); piano pieces, including a sonata (1929). VOCAL: *Pervigilium Veneris* for Soprano, Baritone, Chorus, and Orch. (1929; Paris, April 30, 1931); *I Love the Jocund Dance* for Women's Voices and Piano (1938); choruses; songs.

Spencer, Émile-Alexis-Xavier, French composer; b. Brussels, May 24, 1859; d. Nanterre, Seine, May 24, 1921. He studied piano in Brussels; in 1881 he went to Paris, where he found his métier as a composer for vaudeville; he was credited with about 4,000 chansonettes, which were popularized by famous singers, among them Yvette Guilbert. His chanson *Jambes de bois* was used by Stravinsky in *Pétrouchka* under the impression that it was a folk song; when Spencer brought an action for infringement on his authorship, Stravinsky agreed to pay him part of the royalties for performances.

Spendiarov, Alexander (Afanasii), significant Armenian composer; b. Kakhovka, Crimea, Nov. 1, 1871; d. Erevan, May 7, 1928. He studied violin as a child; in 1896 he went to St. Petersburg and took private lessons with Rimsky-Korsakov. In his works, he cultivated a type of Russian orientalism in which the elements of folk songs of the peripheral regions of the old Russian Empire are adroitly arranged in the colorful harmonies of the Russian national school. His best work in this manner was an opera, *Almast,* the composition of which he undertook a decade before his death. It was completed and orchestrated by Maximilian Steinberg, and performed posthumously in Moscow on June 23, 1930. Other works are: *The 3 Palm Trees,* a symphonic tableau (1905); *Crimean Sketches* for Orch. (1903–12); 2 *Songs of the Crimean Tatars* for Voice and Orch. (1915; Moscow, Dec. 25, 1927); *Études d'Eriwan,* on Armenian melodies (1925). A complete ed. of his works was publ. in Erevan (1943–71).

BIBL.: A. Shaverdian, *A. S.* (Moscow, 1929); G. Tigranov, *A. S.* (Erevan, 1953); idem, *A. S.* (Moscow, 1959; 2nd ed., 1971); R. Atadjan, *A. S.* (Erevan, 1971).

Sperontes (real name, **Johann Sigismund Scholze**), German poet and musical anthologist; b. Lobendau, Silesia, March 20, 1705; d. Leipzig, Sept. 27, 1750. He was educated in Liegnitz and then settled in Leipzig, where he was active as a poet and amateur musician. His most important work was the collection of strophic songs publ. as *Singende Muse an der Pleisse* (4 vols., Leipzig, 1736, 1742, 1743, 1745; ed. in Denkmäler Deutscher Tonkunst, XXXV-XXXVI, 1909). It contained 250 poems with 248 musical settings, the latter being almost wholly from pre-existing instrumental and vocal works adapted by Sperontes. Many of these songs were popular in his day, and several entered the standard repertoire.

BIBL.: P. Spitta, "S. 'Singende Muse an der Pleisse': Zur Geschichte des deutschen Hausgesanges im 18. Jahrhundert," *Vierteljahrsschrift für Musikwissenschaft,* I (1885); H. von Hase, "S., Singende Muse an der Pleisse," *Zeitschrift der Internationalen Musik-Gesellschaft,* XIV (1912–13); A. Schering, "Zwei Singspiele des S.," *Zeitschrift für Musikwissenschaft,* VII (1924–25).

Sperry, Paul, American tenor; b. Chicago, April 14, 1934. He studied psychology at Harvard Univ., then attended the Sorbonne in Paris; returning to the U.S., he took courses at the Harvard Business School. He then decided upon a career in music, and proceeded to take vocal lessons from a number of coaches, among them Olga Ryss, Michael Trimble, Randolph Mickelson, Martial Singher, Pierre Bernac, Jennie Tourel, and Hans Hotter. He made his debut at Alice Tully Hall in N.Y. on Oct. 8, 1969, then toured throughout the U.S. and Europe. He became chiefly known for his performances of contemporary scores. In 1989 he was elected president of the American Music Center.

Speyer, Wilhelm, German violinist and composer; b. Frankfurt am Main, June 21, 1790; d. there, April 5, 1878. He studied in Offenbach with F. Fränzl (violin) and A. André (composition); later in Paris with Baillot (violin). After extensive travels as a concert violinist, he returned to Frankfurt and embraced a mercantile career, but continued his association with eminent musicians (Spohr, Mendelssohn, etc.) and began to compose. He wrote a great deal of chamber music; his violin pieces were often played, but he achieved lasting popularity with his ballads written in a characteristically Romantic style; of these, *Der Trompeter, Die drei Liebchen,* and *Rheinsehnsucht* were particularly famous. His son **Edward** (actually **Eduard**) **Speyer** (b. Frankfurt am Main, May 14, 1839; d. Shenley, Hertfordshire, Jan. 8, 1934) settled in England in 1859, where he organized the Classical Concerts Society; his 2nd wife was the soprano Antonia Kufferath, whom he married in 1885.

BIBL.: E. Speyer, *W. S., der Liederkomponist* (Munich, 1925); idem, *My Life and Friends* (London, 1937).

Spialek, Hans, Austrian-American orchestrator, arranger, and composer; b. Vienna, April 17, 1894; d. N.Y., Nov. 20, 1983. He took courses at the Vienna Cons. He was drafted into the Austrian army during World War I and taken prisoner by the Russians. In Russia his musical abilities were duly appreciated, and after the Russian Revolution he was given a job at the Bolshoi Theater in Moscow as assistant stage manager (1918–20); later he conducted sym. orchs. in Bessarabia (1920–22). He married a Russian singer, Dora Boshoer. In 1923 he went to Germany, and in 1924 reached the U.S. He earned his living as a music copyist; he also supplied orch. interludes and entr'acte music, showing such expertise at organizing the raw materials of American musicals that even before he could master the American tongue he intuitively found the proper instrumentation for the text; and he could work fast to meet the deadlines. Altogether he orchestrated 147 shows, among them 5 by Cole Porter and 11 by Richard Rodgers and Lorenz Hart. With Robert Russell Bennett, he became one of the most reliable arrangers on Broadway. He also composed some orch.

works in the approved Broadway style, with such idiosyncratic titles as *The Tall City* (1933) and *Manhattan Watercolors* (1937).

Spicker, Max, German-American composer and music editor; b. Königsberg, Aug. 16, 1858; d. N.Y., Oct. 15, 1912. He studied with Louis Köhler (piano), then at the Leipzig Cons. with Reinecke and Richter. In 1882 he settled in N.Y., where he became a reader for G. Schirmer, Inc. He wrote many songs; ed. various collections.

Spiegel, Laurie, American composer, innovator in computer-music technology, computer artist, and writer on music; b. Chicago, Sept. 20, 1945. She took up guitar, lute, and mandolin in her youth; majored in social sciences at Shimer College in Mt. Carroll, Ill. (B.A., 1967), before studying composition with Jacob Druckman at the Juilliard School in N.Y. (1969–72) and then at Brooklyn College of the City Univ. of N.Y. (M.A., 1975), where she also studied American music with H. Wiley Hitchcock and Richard Crawford; received additional training in philosophy at Oxford Univ., in classical guitar from John W. Duarte in London, in Renaissance and Baroque lute from Oscar Ghiglia, and in computer music from Emmanuel Ghent and Max Mathews at Bell Labs (1973–79). She taught composition and/or directed electronic- and computer-music studios at Bucks County Community College in Newton, Pa. (1971–75), Aspen (Colo.) Music School (summers, 1971–72), the Cooper Union for the Advancement of Science and Art in N.Y. (1979–81), and N.Y. Univ. (1982); throughout the 1970s, worked as a composer and music ed. for film and television and also created computer-generated visual art and computer-animation software based on her music software. She served as a consultant to firms involved in information- and signal-processing technology, being a designer of computer systems and software for musical composition and performance; her program Music Mouse—An Intelligent Instrument is widely known and used. In addition to her electronic and computer scores, she has composed works for traditional media. Her realization of Kepler's *Harmony of the Planets* was sent into space as the 1st cut in the recording *Sounds of Earth* on each of the 2 *Voyager* spacecrafts in 1977. Her articles on such topics as music and computers, software design and applications, analogies between the musical and visual arts, and music in the media have appeared in a variety of publications; in 1977–78 she served as co-ed. (with Beth Anderson) of *EAR* magazine, a monthly tabloid devoted to the promulgation of new musical ideas. Spiegel has most recently been associated with the revival of Romanticism, tonality, and folk modalities and with the development of visual music, interactive process composition, algorithmic composition, logic-based intelligent instruments, and the use of the computer as a performance instrument.

WORKS: COMPUTER OR ELECTRONIC: *Orchestras* (1971); *A Tombeau* (1971); *Sojourn* (1971); *Before Completion* (1971); *Mines* (1971); *Harmonic Spheres* (1971); *Return to Zero* (1972); *Sediment* (1972); *Rāga* (1972); *Sunsets* (1973); *Introit* (1973); *2 Fanfares* (1973); *Purification* (1973); *Water Music* (1974); *A Meditation* (1974); *Appalachian Grove* (1974); *The Unquestioned Answer* (1974; also for Harp, 1981); *The Orient Express* (1974); *Pentachrome* (1974); *Patchwork* (1974; rev. 1976); *The Expanding Universe* (1975); *Drums* (1975); *Clockworks* (1975); *Voyages* (1976; rev. with video, 1978); *Music for a Garden of Electronic Delights* (1976); *A Folk Study* (1976); *Kepler's Harmony of the Planets* (1977); Concerto for Digital Synthesizer (1977); *5 Short Visits to Different Worlds* (1977); *An Acceleration* (1978); *Voices Within* (1979); *2 Nocturnes* (1980); *Modes* (1980); *A Quadruple Canon* (1980); *A Canon* (1980); *Phantoms* (1980); *Nomads* (1981); *A Harmonic Algorithm* (1981); *A Cosmos* (1982); *Progression* (1982); *Idea Pieces* (1983); *Harmonic Rhythm* (1983); *Immersion* (1983); *3 Modal Pieces* (1983); *Over Time* (1984); *Cavis Muris* (1986); *Passage* (1987). OTHER: *A Deploration* for Flute and Vibraphone (1970); *An Earlier Time* for Guitar (1972); *Waves*, dance piece (1975); *Music for Dance*, dance-video piece (1975); *East River*, dance piece

(1976); *Escalante*, ballet (1977); *Evolutions*, music with video (1977); *A Living Painting*, silent visual study (1979); *Hearing Things* for Chamber Orch. (1983); *Over Time*, dance piece (1984); *A Stream* for Mandolin (1984); *Gravity's Joke*, dance piece (1985); *Rain Pieces*, dance suite (1985); *All Star Video*, music for videotape by Nam June Paik (1985); *Song without Words* for Guitar and Mandolin (1986); *Cavis Muris* (1986); *Passage* (1987); *A Harmonic Algorithm* (1988; from the projected *A Musical Offering*); *3 Sonic Spaces* (1989); *Returning East* and *After the Mountains* (N.Y., Oct. 10, 1990); *3 Movements for Harpsichord* (1990); also computer versions of pieces for Piano or Guitar; incidental music; film and video scores.

BIBL.: P. Lehrman, "L. S.: Esthetic Engineer," *Keyboard* (Nov. 1986).

Spiegelman, Joel (Warren), American pianist, harpsichordist, conductor, and composer; b. Buffalo, N.Y., Jan. 23, 1933. He studied at the Yale School of Music (1949–50), the Univ. of Buffalo (B.A., 1953), the Longy School of Music at Cambridge, Mass. (1953–54), and Brandeis Univ., where he attended the classes of Harold Shapero, Irving Fine, and Arthur Berger (1954–56; 1960–61; M.F.A.); also studied with Nadia Boulanger privately in Paris and took courses at the Cons. there (1956–57). He taught at the Longy School of Music (1961–62), Brandeis Univ. (1961–66), and Sarah Lawrence College (from 1966), where he was director of its Studio for Electronic Music and Sound Media. He made tours as a harpsichordist; was director of the N.Y. Electronic Ensemble (1970–73) and conductor of the Russian Orch. of the Americas (1976–79). His output as a composer reveals an eclectic bent.

WORKS: *Ouverture de Saison 1958* for 2 Harps, 2 Flutes, Piano, and Celesta (1958); *Kusochki* (Morsels) for Piano, 4-hands (1966); *3 Miniatures* for Clarinet and Piano (1972); *Chamber Music* for Piano Quartet and Percussion (1973); *2 Fantasies* for String Quartet (1963, 1974); *Midnight Sun* for Oboe and 4-track Tape (1976); *A Cry, a Song, a Dance* for Strings (1978); *How Lovely is Thy Dwelling Place* for Bass, Chorus, and Organ (1982); *Astral Dimensions II—Metamorphosis* for Piano, Violin, and Cello (1983; rev. 1984); *Cicada Images: Moltings* for Soprano, Flute, Piano, Pipa, Erhu, and Percussion (1983).

Spies, Claudio, Chilean-born American teacher, conductor, and composer; b. Santiago, March 26, 1925. He settled in the U.S. in 1942 and became a naturalized U.S. citizen in 1966; in 1942 he entered the New England Cons. of Music in Boston and in 1943 became a pupil of Boulanger at the Longy School of Music in Cambridge, Mass.; received private instruction from Harold Shapero (1944–45) and attended the conducting class at the Berkshire Music Center in Tanglewood (summer 1946); pursued his musical training with Fine, Hindemith, A. Tillman Merritt, Piston, and Thompson at Harvard Univ. (A.B., 1950), completing his graduate studies there under Piston and Otto Gombosi (M.A., 1954). He was an instructor at Harvard Univ. (1954–57) and a lecturer at Vassar College (1957–58); was assistant prof. (1958–64), associate prof. (1964–69), and prof. (1969) at Swarthmore College, where he also conducted its orch. (1958–69); was visiting associate prof. at Princeton Univ. (1966–67), returning there as prof. in 1970. In 1950–51 he held a John Knowles Paine Traveling Fellowship and in 1956 received the Lili Boulanger Memorial Fund Award; also received the Brandeis Univ. Creative Arts Award (1967) and an NEA fellowship (1975).

WORKS: ORCH.: *Music for a Ballet* (1955); *Tempi* for 14 Instrumentalists (1962); *LXXXV, Eights and Fives* for Strings and Clarinets (1967). CHAMBER: *Canon* for 4 Flutes (1959); *Canon* for Violas (1961); *Viopiacem*, duo for Viola and Keyboard Instruments (1965); *Times 2* for Horns (1968); *Half-time* for Clarinet and Trumpet (1981). PIANO: *Impromptu* (1963); *Bagatelle* (1970); *A Between-Birthdays Bagatelle* for Roger Sessions's 80th–81st (1977); *Ein Aggregats-Walzer* (1978); *Bagatelle* (1979); *Verschieden* (1980); *Jahrhundertwalzer* (1981). VOCAL: *Il cantico de frate solo* for Bass and Orch. (1958); *Proverbs on Wisdom* for Men's Voices, Organ, and Piano (1964); *7 En-*

zensberger-Lieder for Baritone, Clarinet, Horn, Cello, and Percussion (1972); *Rilke: Rühmen* for Soprano, Clarinet, Trumpet, and Piano (1981); *7 Sonnets* for Soprano, Bass, Clarinet, Bass Clarinet, and String Trio (1989).

Spies, Hermine, eminent German contralto; b. Löhneberger Hütte, near Weilburg, Feb. 25, 1857; d. Wiesbaden, Feb. 26, 1893. She was a pupil of Stockhausen in Frankfurt; in 1883, began to give song recitals in Germany; in 1889, made an appearance in England with excellent success; also sang in Austria, Denmark, and Russia. She excelled as an interpreter of songs by Brahms, who had a high regard for her.

BIBL.: M. Spies, *H. S.: Ein Gedenkbuch für ihre Freunde* (Stuttgart, 1894).

Spies, Leo, German conductor and composer; b. Moscow, June 4, 1899; d. Ahrenshoop an der Ostsee, May 1, 1965. He studied with Oskar von Riesemann (1913–15), then continued his training with Schreyer in Dresden and with Kahn and Humperdinck at the Berlin Hochschule für Musik (1916–17). He worked as a répétiteur and conductor in German theaters and with the Universum Film AG; then was in Berlin as conductor of the ballet at the State Opera (1928–35) and the Deutsche Opernhaus (1935–44); subsequently was director of studies and conductor at the Komische Oper (1947–54). In 1956 he was awarded the National Prize of the German Democratic Republic. His compositions follow Romantic lines.

WORKS: BALLETS: *Apollo und Daphne* (1936); *Der Stralauer Fischzug* (1936); *Seefahrt* (1937); *Die Sonne lacht* (1942); *Pastorale* (1943); *Die Liebenden von Verona* (1944); *Don Quijote* (1944). ORCH.: *Saltabile* for Strings (1929); Cello Concerto (1940); *Divertimento notturno* for Piano and Orch. (1941); *Fröhliche Ouvertüre* (1951); *Trauermusik* (1951); Violin Concerto (1953); *Orchesterfantasie "Friedrich Engels"* (1955); 2 syms. (1957, 1961); Viola Concerto (1961); *Festmusik* (1964). CHAMBER: 2 string quartets (1939, 1961); *Divertimento goldoniano* for 9 Instruments (1939); *Serenade* for 6 Winds, Harp, Percussion, and Double Bass (1946); Sonata for 3 Violins (1958); Trio for 2 Cellos and Piano (1959); 2 sonatas for Wind Quintet (1959, 1963); *Rustikale Fantasien* for 9 Instruments (1962); piano pieces, including 3 sonatas (1917, 1938, 1963); much vocal music, including cantatas, choruses, lieder, mass songs, etc.; incidental music for theater.

Spiess, Meinrad, German music theorist and composer; b. Honsolgen, Aug. 24, 1683; d. Irsee, June 12, 1761. In 1701 he entered the Irsee Benedictine abbey, where he was ordained a priest in 1708; after musical training with Giuseppe Antonio Bernabei in Munich (1708–12), he returned to the abbey as music director (until 1749); later served as its prior. In 1743 he was made a member of Mizler's Societät der musikalischen Wissenschaften in Leipzig. He wrote mainly sacred music, much of which is lost. He remains best known for his treatise *Tractatus musicus compositorio-practicus. Das ist, musicalischer Tractat, in welchem alle gute und sichere Fundamenta zur musicalischen Composition aus denen alt- und neuesten besten Autoribus herausgezogen, zusammen getragen, gegen einander gehalten, erkläret, und mit untersetzten Exemplen dermassen klar und deutlich erläutert werden* (Augsburg, 1745).

BIBL.: E. Federl, "Der Tractatus Musicus der Pater M. S. (1683–1761)," *Festschrift Bruno Stäblein* (Kassel, 1967).

Spilka, František, Czech composer; b. Štěken, Nov. 13, 1887; d. Prague, Oct. 20, 1960. He studied at the Prague Cons. with Stecker, Knittl, and Dvořák; in 1918 he was appointed administrative director of the Prague Cons. He established the Prague Teachers' Choral Society in 1908, of which he remained choirmaster until 1921, and gave concerts with it in France and England; later directed the Prague singing ensemble Smetana. Spilka developed, together with Ferdinand Vach, a new approach to choral performance, emphasizing sound color.

WORKS: 2 operas: *Stará práva* (Ancient Rights; 1915; Prague, June 10, 1917) and *Cain or The Birth of Death* (1917); oratorio, *Jan Hus at the Stake* (1907); cantata, *Miller's Journey-*

man (1947); *Rhapsody* for Orch. (1896); *Overture* (1897); *6 Sonnets* for Violin and Piano (1944); *Rhapsodic Sonata* for Cello and Piano (1946); numerous piano pieces; songs and choruses.

Spindler, Fritz, German pianist, teacher, and composer; b. Wurzbach, Nov. 24, 1817; d. Lössnitz, near Dresden, Dec. 26, 1905. He studied with Friedrich Schneider at Dessau; settled in 1841 at Dresden, where he had great success as a teacher. Most of his works (over 400 opus numbers) are salon pieces and characteristic pieces for piano; also publ. instructive sonatinas and a 4-hand Sonatina.

Spinelli, Nicola, Italian pianist, conductor, and composer; b. Turin, July 29, 1865; d. Rome, Oct. 17, 1909. He studied with Sgambati in rome and at the Naples Cons. under Serrao. In 1889 his opera *Labilia* took the 2nd prize in the famous competition instituted by the publisher Sonzogno, when Mascagni won the 1st prize with *Cavalleria rusticana*; Spinelli's opera was produced in Rome on May 7, 1890, with indifferent success. His next opera, *A basso porto*, was more fortunate; after its initial production in Cologne on April 18, 1894 (in a German version), it was staged in Rome, in Italian (March 11, 1895), and then in Budapest, St. Petersburg, etc.; it was also produced in the U.S. (St. Louis, Jan. 8, 1900; N.Y., Jan. 22, 1900). He toured widely as a pianist from 1889 to 1894; then was active as a conductor until becoming mentally ill.

Spink, Ian (Walter Alfred), noted English musicologist; b. London, March 29, 1932. He studied at London's Trinity College of Music (B.Mus., 1952) and pursued postgraduate studies at the Univ. of Birmingham (diss., 1957–58, *The English Declamatory Ayre, c. 1620–60*). He served as an overseas examiner for Trinity College of Music (1958–60), then was senior lecturer at the Univ. of Sydney (1962–69); subsequently was head of the music dept. of Royal Holloway College at the Univ. of London (from 1969), where he was a reader (1971–74) and a prof. (from 1974); also was dean of the Faculty of Arts (1973–75) and of the Faculty of Music (from 1974). A learned authority on English lute songs, he ed. the valuable collection *English Songs, 1625–1660* for the Musica Britannica series, XXXIII (1971); also authored *An Historical Approach to Musical Form* (London, 1967) and *English Song: Dowland to Purcell* (London, 1974).

Spinner, Bob (Robert Channing), American dulcimer player; b. Elk Rapids, Mich., Oct. 25, 1932; d. (in an automobile accident) near there, Oct. 1, 1990. He was born with perfect pitch and built his 1st hammer dulcimer at the age of 12; as a teen, was known as an exceptional player throughout northern Michigan, one of the traditional homes of the instrument, where he performed at community venues. He played banjo, fiddle, piano, and the cymbalom, and performed Hungarian music on both the dulcimer and the cymbalom; played at the Indiana State Fair in 1952, whereupon he was invited to Indiana Univ. to assist with research and restoration of its dulcimer collection. He appeared on the recorded collection *The American Hammer Dulcimer* (1977) and was taped for the Univ. of Michigan video archive. Spinner was a mentor to numerous dulcimer players, among them Michael Masley, Thomas Bauer, and Paul Gifford; also was co-founder of the Everett Dulcimer Club. He owned more than 20 instruments; a favorite was an unusual and partly damaged instrument made by John Brown of Torch Lake Village in 1880, which went with him to his grave.

Spinner, Leopold, Austrian composer; b. Lemberg (Galicia), April 26, 1906; d. London, Aug. 12, 1980. He studied at the Univ. of Vienna with Adler, von Ficker, and Lach (Ph.D., 1931, with the diss. *Das Rezitativ in der romantischen Oper bis Wagner*); also studied composition with Pisk (1930) and Webern (1935–38). He settled in London in 1938. He received the Hertzka Prize (1933) and the Henri-le-Boeuf Prize (1936) for his compositions. Most of his works are set in the serial mode. His paper "The Abolition of Thematicism" was publ. posthumously in *Tempo* (Sept. 1983).

WORKS: ORCH.: Sym. for Small Orch. (1933); *Passacaglia*

for Winds and Piano Trio (1934; Brussels, April 29, 1936); Concerto for Piano and Chamber Orch. (1948; Paris, May 13, 1949); Violin Concerto (1955); Concerto (1957); *Ricercata* (1965); Chamber Sym. (1979; BBC, April 15, 1985). CHAMBER: 3 string quartets (1935, 1941, 1952); Violin Sonata (1936); Piano Quintet (1937); Piano Trio (1950); Suite for Clarinet and Piano (1956); Clarinet Sonata (1961); Quintet for Clarinet, Horn, Bassoon, Guitar, and Double Bass (1963). PIANO: Fantasy (1954); 5 Inventions (1958). VOCAL: *Die Sonne sinkt*, cantata (1952); 6 Canons on Irish Folk Songs for Chorus (1963); many songs.

BIBL.: D. Drew and L. S., "12 Questions for L. S.," *Tempo* (Dec. 1971); M. Graubart, "The Music of L. S.," ibid. (June 1974); idem, "L. S.'s Later Music," ibid. (Sept. 1974); idem, "L. S.: The Final Phase," ibid. (Sept. 1981); R. Bush, "L. S.," *Österreichische Musik Zeitschrift*, No. 10 (1982); D. Drew, "S., 'Die Reihe,' and Thematicism," *Tempo* (Sept. 1983); R. Bush, "L. S.: A List of His Works," ibid. (Sept. 1985).

Spisak, Michal, eminent Polish composer; b. Dąbrowa Górnicza, Sept. 14, 1914; d. Paris, Jan. 29, 1965. He studied music in Katowice; then took composition with Sikorski in Warsaw and with Boulanger in Paris, where he lived from 1937 until his death. He was greatly influenced by Boulanger and by the music of Stravinsky.

WORKS: OPERA: *Marynka* (1955). ORCH.: *Serenade* (1939); Concertino for String Orch. (1942); *Aubade* for Small Orch. (1943); *Allegro de Voiron* (1943); Bassoon Concerto (1944; Copenhagen ISCM Festival, June 2, 1947); *Toccata* (1944); *Suite* for String Orch. (1945); Piano Concerto (1947); 2 *Symphonies concertante* (1947, 1956); *Etudes* for Strings (1948); *Divertimento* for 2 Pianos and Orch. (1948); Sonata for Violin and Orch. (1950); Trombone Concertino (1951); *Divertimento* (1951); *Andante and Allegro* for Violin and Orch. (1954); *Concerto giocoso* for Chamber Orch. (1957); Oboe Concerto (1962); Violin Concerto (Katowice, Jan. 30, 1976). CHAMBER: Quartet for Oboe, 2 Clarinets, and Bassoon (1938); Sonatina for Oboe, Clarinet, and Bassoon (1946); Violin Sonata (1946); Wind Quintet (1948); *Duetto concertante* for Viola and Bassoon (1949); String Quartet (1953); *Suite* for 2 Violins (1957); *Improvvisazione* for Violin and Piano (1962); Concerto for 2 Solo Pianos (1942); also choruses; piano pieces; songs.

Spitalny, Phil(ip), Russian-American conductor and composer of popular music; b. Odessa, Nov. 7, 1889; d. Miami, Oct. 11, 1970. He studied clarinet, violin, and piano at the Odessa Cons; emigrated to the U.S. in 1905; played clarinet in various bands. In 1934 he conceived the idea of organizing an instrumental ensemble consisting only of girls of nubile age and engaging exterior; dubbed Phil Spitalny and his All-girl Orch., they had their own "Hour of Charm" radio program (1935–48). In 1937 he won the award of merit of the Radio Committee of the Women's National Exposition of Arts and Industries. With the advent of television, Spitalny's radio program fell into terminal desuetude, and he went to Florida. He was also an amateur composer; wrote a number of popular songs, including *Madelaine, Save the Last Dance for Me*, and *This Kiss I Can't Forget*.

Spitta, (Julius August) Philipp, eminent German music scholar; b. Wechold, near Hoya, Dec. 27, 1841; d. Berlin, April 13, 1894. He studied piano, organ, and composition in his youth; in 1860 he entered the Univ. of Göttingen as a student of theology, where he later studied classical philology (Ph.D., 1864). He taught Greek and Latin at Reval's Ritter und Domschule (1864–66), at Sondershausen's Gymnasium (1866–74), and at Leipzig's Nikolai-Gymnasium (1874–75), where he was co-founder of the Bach-Verein (1874). In 1875 he settled in Berlin as prof. of music history at the Univ., life-secretary to the Royal Academy of Arts, and a teacher at, and vice-director of, the Hochschule für Musik. As a teacher, he had extraordinary success; among his pupils were O. Fleischer, A. Sandberger, M. Freidlaender, R. Schwartz, M. Seiffert, E. Vogel, K. Krebs, J. Combarieu, and J. Wolf. He was one of the leading spirits in organizing the publication of Denkmäler Deutscher

Tonkunst in 1885. With Chrysander and G. Adler, he founded the journal *Vierteljahrsschrift für Musikwissenschaft* in 1884; also contributed to various other journals. He ed. Buxtehude's organ works (2 vols., 1875–76) and the complete works of Schütz (16 vols., 1885–94; supp. vols., 1909, 1927).

WRITINGS: *Ein Lebensbild Robert Schumanns* (Leipzig, 1862); *Johann Sebastian Bach* (the standard source; although in error concerning some details, it remains an essential study; 2 vols., Leipzig, 1873–80; Eng. tr. by C. Bell and J. Fuller Maitland, with many additions, 3 vols., London, 1884–85; 2nd ed., 1899; reprint, 2 vols., N.Y., 1951); *Zur Musik* (Berlin, 1892; essays); *Musikgeschichtliche Aufsätze* (Berlin, 1894; collected essays).

BIBL.: H. Riemann, *P. S. und seine Bach-Biographie* (Berlin, 1900); W. Gurlitt, "Der Musikhistoriker P. S.," *Musik und Kirche*, XIV (1942); C. Wolff, "From Berlin to Lödz: The S. Collection Resurfaces," *Notes* (Dec. 1989).

Spitzmüller (-Harmersbach), Alexander, Freiherr von, Austrian composer; b. Vienna, Feb. 22, 1894; d. Paris, Nov. 12, 1962. His father was the last finance minister of Austria-Hungary. He studied law at the Univ. of Vienna (D.Jur., 1919); later took lessons in composition with Alban Berg and Hans Apostel. In 1928 he went to Paris, where he taught at the Schola Cantorum; also was active in radio broadcasting and as a music critic. In 1959 he was awarded the music prize of the city of Vienna. His early works are in the neo-Classical vein; eventually he followed the method of composition with 12 tones, following its usage by Berg and Webern.

WORKS: STAGE: OPERA: *Der Diener zweier Herren* (1958). BALLETS: *Le premier amour de Don Juan* (1954); *Die Sackgasse* (1957); *Construction humaine* (1959). ORCH.: *Sinfonietta ritmica* (1933); 2 piano concertos (1937, 1953); Sym. (1939); *Der 40. Mai*, suite for Chamber Orch. (1941; Amsterdam ISCM Festival, June 12, 1948); 3 *hymnes à la Paix* (1947); Sym. for Strings (1954); also chamber music; choral works.

Spivacke, Harold, eminent American musicologist and librarian; b. N.Y., July 18, 1904; d. Washington, D.C., May 9, 1977. He studied at N.Y. Univ. (B.A., 1923; M.A., 1924) and at the Univ. of Berlin (Ph.D., 1933, with the diss. *Über die objektive und subjektive Tonintensität*); while in Berlin, he took private lessons with Eugen d'Albert and Hugo Leichtentritt as an American-German Students Exchange Fellow and an Alexander von Humboldt Stiftung Fellow. Returning to the U.S., he joined the staff of the Music Division of the Library of Congress in Washington, D.C., 1st as assistant chief (1934–37), then as chief (1937–72). He also held numerous advisory positions with the Dept. of State, UNESCO, etc. As chief of the Music Division of the Library of Congress, he was responsible for the acquisition of many important MSS by contemporary composers, including a large collection of Schoenberg's original MSS. He also commissioned works from contemporary composers for the Coolidge Foundation at the Library of Congress. He publ. some valuable bibliographical papers, among them *Paganiniana* (Washington, D.C., 1945). In 1939 he was chairman of the Organizing Committee of the National Music Council, and until 1972 was Archivist and a member of the Executive Committee of the Council.

BIBL.: C. Sprague Smith, "H. S. (1904–1977)," *Musical Quarterly*, LXIII (1977).

Spivak, Charlie, Russian-born American trumpet player and bandleader; b. Trilsey, Feb. 17, 1905; d. Cleveland, March 1, 1982. After settling in the U.S., he played trumpet in the bands of Tommy and Jimmy Dorsey, Jack Teagarden, and Ray Noble; during the big-band era of the early 1940s he became a popular bandleader in his own right, and enjoyed popularity until the advent of bebop.

BIBL.: C. Garrod, *C. S. and His Orch.* (Zephyrhills, Fla., 1986).

Spivakov, Vladimir, Russian violinist and conductor; b. Ufa, Sept. 12, 1944. He studied with Veniamin Sher at the music school of the Leningrad Cons. (1956–60), and with Yankelevich at the Moscow Cons. (graduated, 1967); also received instruction in conducting. He won prizes in various competitions, including the prestigious Long-Thibaud in Paris (3rd, 1965), the Paganini in Genoa (2nd, 1967), the Montreal (1st, 1969), and the Tchaikovsky in Moscow (2nd, 1970). On Feb. 2, 1975, he made his N.Y. debut. In 1979 he made his debut as a conductor with the Chicago Sym. Orch. at the Ravinia Festival; that same year he founded the Moscow Virtuosi, with which he appeared both as violinist and conductor.

Spivakovsky, Tossy, outstanding Russian-American violinist; b. Odessa, Feb. 4, 1907. He studied with Arrigo Serato and Willy Hess at the Berlin Hochschule für Musik; made his concert debut there at the age of 10; toured Europe (1920–33) and Australia (1933–39). In 1940 he settled in the U.S. and made his N.Y. debut that same year at N.Y.'s Town Hall; then appeared with major American orchs. He taught at the Juilliard School in N.Y. (from 1974). A brilliant virtuoso, his repertory ranged from the classics to contemporary works. As a teacher, he advocated new bowing techniques which proved controversial.

BIBL.: G. Yost, *The S. Way of Bowing* (Pittsburgh, 1949); S. and S. Applebaum, "T. S.," *The Way They Play* (Vol. I, Neptune City, N.J., 1972).

Spohr, Louis (actually, **Ludewig**), celebrated German violinist, composer, and conductor; b. Braunschweig, April 5, 1784; d. Kassel, Oct. 22, 1859. His name is entered in the church registry as Ludewig, but he used the French equivalent, Louis. The family moved to Seesen in 1786; his father, a physician, played the flute, and his mother was an amateur singer and pianist. Spohr began violin lessons at the age of 5 with J.A. Riemenschneider and Dufour, a French émigré. In 1791 he returned to Braunschweig, where he studied with the organist Carl August Hartung and the violinist Charles Louis Maucourt; also composed several violin pieces. Duke Carl Wilhelm Ferdinand admitted him to the ducal orch. and arranged for his further study with the violinist Franz Eck. In 1802 Eck took him on a tour to Russia, where he met Clementi and Field; returned to Braunschweig in 1803 and resumed his post in the ducal orch. The violin technique and compositional traits of Pierre Rode, whom Spohr met on his return, were major influences on both his compositions and his violin technique. In 1804 Spohr made his 1st official tour as a violinist to Hamburg (his 1st actual tour to Hamburg in 1799 proved a failure, and a 2nd, early in 1804, was aborted when his Guarnerius violin was stolen); gave concerts in Berlin, Leipzig, and Dresden. In 1805 he became concertmaster in the ducal orch. at Gotha. On Feb. 2, 1806, he married the harpist Dorette (Dorothea) Scheidler (1787–1834); wrote many works for violin and harp for them to perform together, and also toured with her in Germany (1807). His reputation as a virtuoso established, he began writing compositions in every genre, all of which obtained excellent success. In 1812 he gave a series of concerts in Vienna and was acclaimed both as a composer and as a violinist; was concertmaster in the orch. of the Theater an der Wien until 1815. He then made a grand tour of Germany and Italy, where Paganini heard him in Venice. In 1816 Spohr's opera *Faust*, skillfully employing many devices that foreshadowed developments in later German operas, was performed by Weber in Prague. After a visit to Holland in 1817, he became Kapellmeister of the Frankfurt Opera, where he produced one of his most popular operas, *Zemire und Azor*. In 1820 he and his wife visited England and appeared at several concerts of the London Phil. Soc.; this was the 1st of his 6 visits to England, where he acquired an immense reputation as a violinist, composer, and conductor; his works continued to be performed there long after his death. On his return trip to Germany, he presented concerts in Paris; his reception there, however, failed to match his London successes, and he proceeded to Dresden, where Weber recommended him for the Kapellmeistership at the court in Kassel; attracted by the lifetime contract, Spohr accepted the post and settled there in 1822, producing his operatic masterpiece, *Jessonda*, which remained popular throughout the rest of the 19th century, in 1823. Following this success were performances of his oratorio *Die letzten Dinge* (1826) and his 4th Sym., *Die Weihe der Töne* (1832), both of which elicited great praise. The *Violinschule*, a set of 66 studies covering every aspect of his violin style, was publ. in 1831. Spohr's wife died on Nov. 20, 1834; on Jan. 3, 1836, he married the pianist Marianne Pfeiffer, the sister of his friend Carl Pfeiffer, librettist of *Der Alchymist*. In 1837 Spohr began having difficulties with the Electoral Prince of Kassel, who caused the cancellation of a festival in Kassel and forbade Spohr from making a trip to Prague, which the composer made nevertheless to conduct *Der Berggeist*; on his return, he visited Mozart's widow and birthplace in Salzburg. He traveled to England in 1839 for the Norwich Festival, but could not obtain permission from the Prince to return for the performance of his *Fall of Babylon* in 1842. In 1841, returning from the Lucerne Festival, he received the suggestion from his wife to use 2 orchs. for his 7th Sym. in 3 parts, portraying the mundane and divine elements in life. In 1843, in England, his success was so great that a special concert was given by royal command; it was the 1st time a reigning English monarch attended a Phil. Concert. In 1844 he received the silver medal from the Société des Concerts in Paris, and a festival honoring him was held in Braunschweig. Spohr never visited the U.S., in spite of the fact that his daughter lived in N.Y. and an invitation to hold a festival in his honor was issued. In 1845 he received a golden wreath from the Berlin Royal Opera. In 1847 he visited England for the 3rd time, then went to Frankfurt for the German National Assembly. Returning to Kassel, he found himself in an increasingly difficult position because of his dissident political views; the Elector of Hesse refused him further leaves of absence; Spohr ignored the ban, however, traveling to Switzerland and Italy. In the litigation that followed with the Kassel court, Spohr was ordered to forfeit part of his yearly income. He was retired from Kassel on Nov. 22, 1857, on a pension despite his lifetime contract. In 1853 he appeared at the New Phil. Concerts in London. Although he fractured his left arm in a fall on Dec. 27, 1857, he conducted *Jessonda* in Prague in July 1858; he conducted his last performance in Meiningen (1859).

Spohr's compositional style was characteristic of the transition period between Classicism and Romanticism. He was technically a master; while some of his works demonstrate a spirit of bold experimentation (*The Historical Symphony*; Sym. for 2 Orchs.; Quartet Concerto; Nonet; etc.), in his esthetics he was an intransigent conservative. He admired Beethoven's early works but confessed total inability to understand those of his last period; he also failed to appreciate Weber. It is remarkable, therefore, that he was an early champion of Wagner; in Kassel he produced *Der fliegende Holländer* (1843) and *Tannhäuser* (1853), despite strenuous opposition from the court. He was a highly esteemed teacher; among his students were Ferdinand David and Moritz Hauptmann. His memoirs were publ. posthumously as *Louis Spohrs Selbstbiographie* (2 vols., Kassel, 1860–61; abridged version in Eng., London, 1865, 1878, and 1969; different tr. by H. Pleasants as *The Musical Journeys of Louis Spohr*, Norman, Okla., 1961). A new ed., edited by F. Göthel using the autograph, was publ. as *Lebenserinnerungen* (Tutzing, 1968). The Spohr Soc. was founded in Kassel in 1908, disbanded in 1934, and revived in 1952. A new ed. of his works, *Neue Auswahl der Werke*, edited by F. Göthel, was begun in 1963 (Kassel, Verlag der Spohr-Gesellschaft). A *Thematisch-bibliographisches Verzeichnis der Werke von Louis Spohr*, compiled by F. Göthel, was publ. in Tutzing in 1981.

WORKS: DRAMATIC (all 1st perf. in Kassel unless otherwise given): OPERAS: *Die Prüfung* (1806); *Alruna, die Eulenkönigin* (1808); *Der Zweikampf mit der Geliebten* (Hamburg, Nov. 15, 1811); *Faust* (1813; Prague, Sept. 1, 1816; rev. 1852; London, July 15, 1852); *Zemire und Azor* (Frankfurt am Main, April 4, 1819); *Jessonda* (July 28, 1823); *Der Berggeist* (March 24, 1825); *Pietro von Abano* (Oct. 13, 1827); *Der Alchymist* (July 28, 1830); *Die Kreuzfahrer* (Jan. 1, 1845). ORATORIOS: *Das jüngste Gericht* (Erfurt, Aug. 15, 1812); *Die letzten Dinge* (March 25, 1826); *Des Heilands letzte Stunden* (Easter 1835); *Der Fall Babylons* (Norwich Festival, Sept. 14, 1842). **OTHER VOCAL:** *Das befreite Deutschland,* dramatic cantata (Frankenhausen, Oct. 1815); Mass for Double 5–part Chorus; 6 Psalms; Requiem (unfinished); hymns; partsongs; 7 duets; 64 songs; *An sie am Klavier,* sonatina for Voice and Piano (1848).

ORCH.: 10 Syms: No. 1 (Leipzig, June 11, 1811); No. 2 (London, April 10, 1820); No. 3 (Kassel, April 6, 1828); No. 4, *Die Weihe der Töne* (London, Feb. 23, 1835); No. 5 (Vienna, March 1, 1838); No. 6, *Historische Symphonie* (London, April 6, 1840); No. 7, *Irdisches und Göttliches im Menschenleben* (London, May 30, 1842); No. 8 (Kassel, Dec. 22, 1857); No. 9, *Die Jahreszeiten* (London, Nov. 25, 1850); No. 10 (1847). *OVERTURES:* C minor (1807); F major (1820); *Macbeth* (1825); *Die Tochter der Luft,* phantasie in the form of an overture (1836); *Der Matrose* (1838); Concert Overture "im ernsten Styl" (1842). *SOLO INSTRUMENTS AND ORCH.:* 18 violin concertos (c.1799–1844); Concerto for String Quartet (1845); 4 clarinet concertos; 2 Concertantes for 2 Violins; 2 Concertantes for Harp and Violin.

CHAMBER: Nonet (1814); Octet (1815); 4 double quartets for Strings; Septet (1854); Sextet (1848); 7 string quintets; Piano Quintet; Quintet for Piano and Winds; 34 string quartets; 5 piano trios; 14 duets for 2 Violins; 3 duets for Piano and Violin; 3 sonatas for Harp and Violin; Piano Sonata; etc.

BIBL.: W. Neumann, *L. S.* (Kassel, 1854); H. Giehne, *Zur Erinnerung an L. S.* (Karlsruhe, 1860); A. Malibran, *L. S.* (Frankfurt, 1860); L. Stierlin, *L. S.* (2 vols., Zürich, 1862–63); M. Hauptmann, *Briefe von M. Hauptmann an L. S. und andere* (Leipzig, 1876; Eng. tr., London, 1892); H. Schletterer, *L. S.* (Leipzig, 1881); L. Nohl, *S.* (Leipzig, 1882); C. Robert, *L. S.* (Berlin, 1883); R. Wassermann, *L. S. als Opernkomponist* (diss., Univ. of Rostock, 1910); H. Glenewinckel, *L. S. Kammermusik für Streichinstrumente* (diss., Univ. of Munich, 1912); F. Göthel, *Das Violinspiel L. S.s* (diss., Univ. of Berlin, 1934); E. von Salburg, *L. S.* (Leipzig, 1936); H. Heussner, *Die Symphonien L. S.s* (diss., Univ. of Marburg, 1956); F. Göthel, *L. S.: Briefwechsel mit seiner Frau Dorette* (Kassel, 1957); D. Mayer, *The Forgotten Master: The Life and Times of L. S.* (London, 1959); D. Greiner, *L. S. Beitrage zur deutschen romantischen Oper* (diss., Univ. of Kiel, 1960); H. Homburg, *L. S.: Bilder und Dokumente seiner Zeit* (Kassel, 1968); S. Johnston, *The Clarinet Concertos of L. S.* (diss., Univ. of Maryland, 1972); C. Brown, *The Popularity and Influence of S. in England* (diss., Oxford Univ., 1980); P. Katow, *L. S.: Persönlichkeit und Werk* (Luxembourg, 1983); C. Brown, *L. S.: A Critical Biography* (Cambridge, 1984); H. Peters, *Der Komponist, Geiger, Dirigent und Pädagoge L. S. (1784–1859) mit einer Auswahlbibliographie zu Leben und Schaffen* (Braunschweig, 1987).

Spontini, Gaspare (Luigi Pacifico), significant Italian opera composer; b. Majolati, Ancona, Nov. 14, 1774; d. there, Jan. 24, 1851. His father, a modest farmer, intended him for the church and gave him into the charge of an uncle, a priest at Jesi, who attempted to stifle his musical aspirations. Spontini sought refuge at Monte San Vito with another relative, who not only found a competent music teacher for him, but effected a reconciliation so that, after a year, he was able to return to Jesi. In 1793 he entered the Cons. della Pietà de' Turchini in Naples, where his teachers were Tritto (singing) and Sala (composition). When he failed to obtain the position of maestrino there in 1795, he quit the Cons. without permission. He rapidly mastered the conventional Italian style of his time; some of his church music performed in Naples came to the attention of a director of the Teatro della Pallacorda in Rome, who commissioned him to write an opera. This was *Li puntigli delle donne,* produced during Carnival in 1796. He served as maestro di cappella at Naples's Teatro del Fondo during Carnival in 1800, and that same year went to Palermo to produce 3 operas. Returning to the mainland in 1801, he produced operas for Rome and Venice before going to Paris in 1803. After eking out an existence as a singing teacher, he found a

patron in Joséphine. He 1st gained success as a composer in Paris with a revised version of his *La finta filosofa* (Feb. 11, 1804); it was followed by *La Petite Maison* (May 12, 1804), which proved unsuccessful. All the same, the poet Etienne de Jouy now approached Spontini to write the music to his libretto *La Vestale,* a task previously turned down by Boieldieu, Cherubini, and Méhul. In the meantime, Spontini brought out 2 more operas without much success: *Milton* (Nov. 27, 1804) and *Julie, ou Le Pot de fleurs* (March 12, 1805). However, he won appointment as composer of Joséphine's private music in 1805; for her he wrote several occasional pieces, including the cantata *L'eccelsa gara* (Feb. 8, 1806), celebrating the battle of Austerlitz. Thanks to Joséphine's patronage, *La Vestale* won a triumphant success at its premiere on Dec. 15, 1807, in spite of virulent opposition. Spontini's next opera, *Fernand Cortez* (Nov. 28, 1809), failed to equal his previous success, although the 2nd version (May 8, 1817) won it a place in the repertoire. In 1810 he was awarded the prix décennal for having composed the finest grand opera of the preceding decade; that same year he married Céleste Erard, daughter of Jean-Baptiste Erard, and accepted the post of director of the Théâtre-Italien. Although his artistic policies were successful, his personality clashed with those of his superiors and he was dismissed in 1812. On Aug. 23, 1814, his opera *Pélage, ou Le Roi et la paix,* celebrating the Restoration, was successfully produced. The following month he was named director of Louis XVIII's private music and of the Théâtre-Italien, although soon after he sold his privilege to the latter to Catalani. Having become a favorite of the Bourbons, he was made a French citizen by the king in 1817 and was granted a pension in 1818. In spite of his favored position, his grand opera *Olimpie* proved a dismal failure at its premiere on Dec. 22, 1819. The next year he went to Berlin as Generalmusikdirektor, scoring an initial success with the revised version of *Olimpie* on May 14, 1821. However, his position of eminence quickly waned. He had been placed on an equality with the Intendant of the Royal Theater, and there were frequent misunderstandings and sharp clashes of authority, not mitigated by Spontini's jealousies and dislikes, his overweening self-conceit, and his despotic temper. Partly through intrigue, partly by reason of his own lack of self-control, he was formally charged in criminal court with lèse-majesté in Jan. 1841. On April 2, 1841, while he was conducting the overture to *Don Giovanni,* a riot ensued and Spontini was compelled to leave the hall in disgrace. In July 1841 he was sentenced to 9 months in prison, and soon thereafter was dismissed as Generalmusikdirektor by the king, although he was allowed to retain his title and salary. In May 1842 his sentence was upheld by an appeals court, but the king pardoned him that same month. He then went to Paris, where illness and growing deafness overtook him. In 1844 he was raised to the papal nobility as the Conte di San Andrea. In 1850 he retired to his birthplace to die. Spontini's importance to the lyric theater rests upon his effective blending of Italian and French elements in his serious operas, most notably in *La Vestale* and *Fernand Cortez.* His influence on Berlioz was particularly notable.

WORKS: Operas: *Li puntigli delle donne,* farsetta (Rome, Carnival 1796); *Il finto pittore* (Rome?, 1797 or 1798); *Adelina Senese, o sia L'amore secreto,* dramma giocoso (Venice, Oct. 10, 1797); *L'eroismo ridicolo,* farsa (Naples, Carnival 1798); *Il Teseo riconosciuto,* dramma per musica (Florence, 1798); *La finta filosofa,* commedia per musica (Naples, 1799; rev. as a dramma giocoso per musica, Paris, Feb. 11, 1804); *La fuga in maschera,* commedia per musica (Naples, Carnival 1800); *I quadri parlante,* melodramma buffo (Palermo, 1800); *Gli Elisi delusi,* melodramma serio (Palermo, Aug. 26, 1800); *Gli amanti in cimento, o sia Il Geloso audace,* dramma giocoso (Rome, Nov. 3, 1801); *Le metamorfosi di Pasquale, o sia Tutto è illusione nel mondo,* farsa giocosa (Venice, Carnival 1802); *La Petite Maison,* opéra comique (Paris, May 12, 1804); *Milton,* opéra comique (Paris, Nov. 27, 1804); *Julie, ou Le Pot de fleurs,* opéra comique (Paris, March 12, 1805); *La Vestale,* tragédie lyrique (Paris, Dec. 15, 1807); *Fernand Cortez, ou La Conquête* *du Mexique*, tragédie lyrique (Paris, Nov. 28, 1809; 2nd version, Paris, May 8, 1817; 3rd version, Berlin, Feb. 1832); *Pélage, ou Le Roi et la paix*, opéra (Paris, Aug. 23, 1814); *Les Dieux rivaux ou Les Fêtes de Cythère*, opéra-ballet (Paris, June 21, 1816; in collaboration with Kreutzer, Persuis, and Berton); *Olimpie*, tragédie lyrique (Paris, Dec. 22, 1819; rev. as a grosse Oper, Berlin, May 14, 1821); *Nurmahal, oder Das Rosenfest von Caschmir*, lyrisches Drama (Berlin, May 27, 1822); *Alcidor*, Zauberoper (Berlin, May 23, 1825); *Agnes von Hohenstaufen*, lyrisches Drama (Act 1 only, Berlin, May 28, 1827; 2nd version as a grosse historisch-romantische Oper, Berlin, June 12, 1829; rev. version, Berlin, Dec. 6, 1837); other dramatic pieces include *L'eccelsa gara*, cantata (Paris, Feb. 8, 1806), *Tout le monde a tort*, vaudeville (Malmaison, March 17, 1806), and *Lalla Rûkh*, Festspiel (Berlin, May 27, 1822); also arias and duets; etc. He further wrote many songs, some choral music, and several instrumental pieces.

BIBL.: L. Rellstab, *Über mein Verhältnis als Kritiker zu Herrn S. als Componist und General Musikdirektor* (Leipzig, 1827); idem, "S.s Oper *Agnes von Hohenstaufen*," *Berliner allgemeine musikalische Zeitung*, IV (1828); *Des dramatischen Leib-Compositeurs, kgl.-preuss. General-Musikdirectors . . . Herrn Ritters G. S. Klagen über den Verfall der dramatischen Musik: Aus dem Französischen übersetzt und mit erläuternden Anmerkungen begleitet von einer Gesellschaft von Kunstfreunden und Verehren des grossen Meisters* (Leipzig, 1837); E. Oettinger, *S.* (Leipzig, 1843); D. Raoul-Rochette, *Notice historique sur la vie et les oeuvres de M. S.* (Paris, 1852); C. Robert, *S.: Eine biographische Skizze* (Berlin, 1883); P. Spitta, "S. in Berlin," *Zur Musik* (Berlin, 1892); W. Altmann, "S. an der Berliner Opera," *Sammelbände der Internationalen Musik-Gesellschaft*, IV (1902–3); C. Bouvet, *S.* (Paris, 1930); K. Schubert, *S.s italienische Schule* (Strasbourg, 1932); A. Ghizlanzoni, *G. S.* (Rome, 1951); P. Fragapane, *S.* (Bologna, 1954); A. Belardinelli, *Documenti s.ani inediti* (Florence, 1955); H. Engel, "Wagner und S.," *Archiv für Musikwissenschaft*, XII (1955); F. Schlitzer, *Frammenti biografici di G. S. con lettere inedite*, Accademia Musicale Chigiana: Settimane Musicali Senesi, XXXIII (Siena, 1955); idem, *La finta filosofa di G. S.* (Naples, 1957); idem, *Circonstanze della vita di G. S. con lettere inedite*, Accademia Musicale Chigiana: Settimane Musicali Senesi, XXXVII (Siena, 1958); F. Schnapp, "E.T.A. Hoffmanns Textbearbeitung der Oper 'Olimpia' von S.," *Jahrbuch des Wiener Goethe-Vereins*, LXVI (1962); A. Van der Linden, "Notes de Madame G. S. sur la vie et l'œuvre de son mari," *Revue Belge de Musicologie*, XXVIII-XXX (1974–76); P. Fragapane, *S.* (Florence, 1983).

Spoorenberg, Erna, Dutch soprano; b. Yogyakarta, Java, April 11, 1926. She studied in Hilversum and Amsterdam; made her debut in an appearance with Radio Hilversum in 1947. In 1958 she became a leading member of the Netherlands Opera in Amsterdam. She made occasional appearances at various European music centers, but principally was associated with the musical life of the Netherlands; made her 1st appearance at the Vienna State Opera in 1949 and her U.S. debut in N.Y. in 1967. She was esspecially esteemed for her roles in operas by Mozart and for her portrayal of Mélisande.

Sporck, Georges, French composer; b. Paris, April 9, 1870; d. there, Jan. 17, 1943. He studied with Guiraud and Dubois at the Paris Cons., and later with d'Indy; was Officer of Public Instruction; wrote a number of symphonic works of a programmatic nature, often with regional color: *Symphonie vivaraise; Islande; Boabdil; Kermesse; Paysages normandes; Esquisses symphoniques; Préludes symphoniques; Méditation; Orientale;* Violin Sonata; piano pieces.

Spratlan, Lewis, American composer; b. Miami, Sept. 5, 1940. He studied composition with Yehudi Wyner, Gunther Schuller, and Mel Powell at Yale Univ. (B.A., 1962; M.M., 1965); then studied with George Rochberg and Roger Sessions at the Berkshire Music Center in Tanglewood (1966); held a Guggenheim fellowship (1980–81). He taught at Bay Path Junior College (1965–67), Pennsylvania State Univ. (1967–70), and at Am-

herst College (from 1970), where he was made a prof. in 1980; also served as chairman of its music dept. (1977–80; 1984; 1985–88).

WORKS: STAGE: *Life is a Dream*, opera (1975–77); *Unsleeping City*, dance music (1967). **ORCH.:** 2 Pieces (1971); *Penelope's Knees*, double concerto for Alto Saxophone, Double Bass, and Chamber Orch. (1986); *Apollo and Daphne Variations* (1987; Kislovodsk, Russia, Oct. 4, 1989). **CHAMBER:** *Flange* for 14 Instruments (1965); *Serenade* for 6 Instruments (1970); *Trope-Fantasy* for Oboe, English Horn, and Harpsichord (1970); *Summer Music* for Oboe, Horn, Violin, Cello, and Piano (1971); Woodwind Quintet (1971); *Dance Suite* for Clarinet, Violin, Guitar, and Harpsichord (1973); *Fantasy* for Piano and Chamber Ensemble (1973); *Coils* for Flute, Clarinet, Violin, Viola, Cello, Percussion, and Piano (1980); *Diary Music II* for Chamber Ensemble (1981); String Quartet (1982); *When Crows Gather* for 3 Clarinets, Violin, Cello, and Piano (1986); *A Fanfare for the Tenth* for String Quartet (1988). **VOCAL:** *Missa brevis* for Men's Chorus and Winds (1965); *Cantata Domine* for Men's Chorus, Winds, and Tape (1968); *Structures after Hart Crane* for Tenor, Piano, and Tape (1968); *Moonsong* for Chorus and Ensemble (1969); *3 Carols on Medieval Texts* for Chorus and Ensemble (1971); *3 Ben Jonson Songs* for Soprano, Flute, Violin, and Cello (1974); *Night Songs* for Soprano, Tenor, and Orch. (1976); *Celebration* for Chorus and Orch. (1984); *Wolves* for Soprano, Flute, Clarinet, and Piano (1988); also electronic pieces.

Springer, Max, German writer on music and composer; b. Schwendi, Württemberg, Dec. 19, 1877; d. Vienna, Jan. 20, 1954. He attended the Univ. of Prague, and studied music with Klička. In 1910 he was appointed prof. of Gregorian choral singing and organist in the section for church music of the Klosterneuburg Academy, retiring shortly before his death. He publ. *Die Kunst der Choralbegleitung* (1907; Eng. tr., 1908) and manuals on liturgical choral singing; *Graduale Romanum* in modern notation (1930); *Kontrapunkt* (Vienna, 1936). He composed 4 syms. and a great deal of church music, including 8 masses.

Springsteen, Bruce, seeded American rock singer, guitarist, and songwriter; b. Freehold, N.J., Sept. 23, 1949. He sang and played guitar in honky-tonks in Newark and in Greenwich Village in N.Y. He began recording songs of personal discontent and societal alienation with such titles as *It's Hard to Be a Saint in the City*. He recruited several similarly dissident rock musicians to form the E-Street Band, and in 1975 produced the album *Born to Run*, which struck a sympathetic chord with disillusioned youth, and soon made Springsteen a cult figure. The title song received a certified gold award. His next release was *Darkness on the Edge of Town* (1978), further exploiting the general malaise of American youth. In 1980 he produced his greatest hit, *The River*, an album that glorified, with bitter irony, the automobile as a symbol of the age, with titles such as *Stolen Car, Drive All Night*, and *Wreck on the Highway*. In 1981 he made an extraordinarily successful tour of Europe. He won a Grammy Award as best male vocalist in 1984. After bringing out the hit album *Born in the U.S.A.* (1984), he made a triumphant world tour. He subsequently brought out the albums *Bruce Springsteen & the E-Street Band Live/1975–1985* (1985) and *Tunnel of Love* (1987), the latter winning him a Grammy Award in 1987. In 1988 he was active with the Amnesty International Human Rights Now! Tour; in 1990 he ended his 16-year affiliation with the E-Street Band.

BIBL.: L. Goldsmith, *S.* (N.Y., 1984); P. Gambaccini, *B. S.* (N.Y., 1985); T. Koenig, *B. S.* (Mankato, Minn., 1986); D. Marsh, *Glory Days: B. S. in the 1980's* (N.Y., 1987).

Sprongl, Norbert, Austrian composer; b. Obermarkersdorf bei Retz, April 30, 1892; d. Mödling, near Vienna, April 26, 1983. He studied at the Vienna Cons. (graduated, 1933) with J. Marx (composition), N. Kahrer (piano), and R. Lach (theory). Following the development of a style of "free dissonance" modeled after Bartók and Hindemith, he wrote 166 works.

WORKS: ORCH.: 4 syms. (1941, 1956, 1964, 1969); 4 symphonic dances (1956); 2 partitas (1962, 1966); 5 piano concertos (1935, 1938, 1952, 1953, 1975); 2 violin concertos (1955, 1968); Concerto for Mandolin, Lute, and Guitar (1953); Concerto for Viola and Piano (1960); Concerto for Flute and Guitar (1965); Passacaglia for Piano and Strings (1945); etc. **CHAMBER:** 4 string quartets (1936, 1941, 1944, 1945); 2 double-bass sonatas (1944, 1960); Cello Sonata (1937); 2 clarinet sonatas (1948, 1960); Viola Sonata (1955); Viola d'Amore Sonata (1957); Oboe Sonata (1960); Trio for Violin, Guitar, and Double Bass (1964); etc.

BIBL.: R. Stockhammer, *N. S.* (Vienna, 1977).

Spross, Charles Gilbert, American pianist, organist, and composer; b. Poughkeepsie, N.Y., Jan. 6, 1874; d. there, Dec. 23, 1961. He studied piano with X. Scharwenka in N.Y.; also studied organ with various teachers; for nearly 40 years was an organist at various churches in Poughkeepsie, Paterson, N.J., N.Y., etc.; was accompanist to celebrated singers (Fremstad, Schumann-Heink, Nordica, Emma Eames, et al.). He wrote some 450 works, including 250 songs, 5 sacred cantatas, and chamber music.

Squarcialupi, Antonio, renowned Italian organist, known as **Antonio degli Organi, Antonio de Bartolomeo,** and **Antonio del Bessa;** b. Florence, March 27, 1416; d. there, July 6, 1480. He was the son of a butcher, Bartolomeo di Giovanni, and adopted the name of the prominent Squarcialupi family of Tuscany about 1457. He pursued his career in Florence; was organist of Orsanmichele (1431–33) and at the cathedral of S. Maria del Fiore (1432–80). His name is immortalized through the 15th century MS of Florentine polyphonic music known as the "Squarcialupi Codex," which was once in his possession; it was ed. by J. Wolf (1955).

BIBL.: O. Kade, "Biographisches zu A. S., dem Florentiner Organisten im XV. Jahrhundert," *Monatshefte für Musikgeschichte,* XVII (1885); B. Becherini, "A. S. e il codice Mediceo-Palatino 87," *L'ars nova italiana del trecento I: Certaldo 1959;* F. D'Accone, "A. S. alla luce di documenti inediti," *Chigiana,* XXIII/3 (1966).

Squire, W(illiam) Barclay, English music librarian; b. London, Oct. 16, 1855; d. there, Jan. 13, 1927. He received his education in Frankfurt am Main and at Pembroke College, Cambridge (B.A., 1879; M.A., 1902). In 1885 he was placed in charge of the printed music in the British Museum, retiring as Assistant Keeper in 1920; compiled catalogues of music for the British Museum (publ. in 1899 and 1912); also the catalogue of the King's Music Library (3 vols., 1927–29). He ed. (with J. Fuller Maitland) *The Fitzwilliam Virginal Book* (2 vols., London, 1899; reprint, N.Y., 1963); ed. Byrd's masses, Purcell's music for harpsichord, and Elizabethan madrigals.

Šrámek, Vladimír, Slovak composer; b. Košice, March 10, 1923. He graduated from the Prague Cons.; was active in the music dept. of the National Museum (1953–63).

WORKS: Chamber opera, *Jezdci* (1955); Trio for 2 Violins and Viola (1957); *3 Serious Compositions* for Flute and Piano (1958); *Astronauts,* overture (1959); *Exercises* for Flute, Oboe, and Clarinet (1959); *Tempi* for String Quartet (1959); 2 wind quintets (1959, 1960); *Variabilité* for String Trio (1960); *Metamorphoses I–VII* for Variable Ensemble (1961–63); *Metra symmetrica* for Wind Quintet (1961); *Rondo* for 8 Winds (1961); *Smích* (Laughter) for Voice, Tape, Flute, Piano, and Percussion (1962); *Spectrum I–III,* musical theater (1963–65); *Die Grube,* solo pantomime, with Bass Clarinet, Guitar, and Percussion (1963); *Kobaltová květina* (The Cobalt Flower), television play for Soprano, Alto, Female Chorus, and Orch. (1964); *Kaleidoscope* for String Trio (1965); *Anticomposizione* for String Trio (1966); *Bericht über eine Katastrophe* for Chamber Ensemble (1966); *Anderer Bericht über eine Katastrophe* for Nonet (1969).

Srebotnjak, Alojz, Slovene composer; b. Postojna, April 27, 1931. He studied with Škerjanc at the Ljubljana Academy of Music (1953–58), in Siena (1954–57), with Porrena in Rome (1958–59), with Fricker in London (1960–61), and in Paris

(1963); taught in Ljubljana at the Pedagogical Academy (1964–70); then was a prof. of composition and theory at the Academy of Music (from 1970).

WORKS: BALLET: *The Trumped and the Devil* (1983; orch. suite, 1983). **ORCH.:** *Music* for Strings (1955); *Sinfonietta* (1959); *Monologues* for Flute, Oboe, Horn, Timpani, and Strings (1962); *Kraska Suite* (1964); *Antifona* (1964); *Episodes* (1967); *Harp Concerto* (1971); *Violin Concerto* (1975); *Slovenica* (1976); *Ballads* (1977); *Naturae vox* (1981); *Slovene Folk Dances* for Strings (1982). **CHAMBER:** *Serenata* for Flute, Clarinet, and Bassoon (1961); *Diary* for Piano Trio (1972); *Slovene Folk Dances* for Violin and Piano (1982); also collage works for a Group of Different Musical Instruments, including *Naif* (1977), *Macedonica* (1978), and *Spray* (1981). **PIANO:** *Invenzione variata* (1961); *Macedonian Dances* (1976); *Variations on a Theme by Marij Kogoj* (1984); *The Folk-Music Player,* folk melodies (1988). **VOCAL:** *Mother* for Voice and Strings (1955); *War Pictures* for Tenor, Viola, Piano, and Percussion (1957); *Requiem for a Hostage* for Chorus, Harp, Timpani, and Tam-tam (1963); *Micro-Songs* for Voice and Chamber Ensemble (1964); *Ecstasy of Death* for Baritone, Chorus, and Orch. (1965); *A Naive Orpheus* for Chorus and Chamber Ensemble (1973).

Srnka, Jiří, Czech composer; b. Písek, Aug. 19, 1907; d. Prague, Jan. 31, 1982. He took violin lessons at the Prague Cons. under A. Mařák and J. Feld (1922–24); then studied composition there with Otakar Šín (1924–28) and V. Novák (1928–32); had instruction in quarter-tone music with Alois Hába (1927–28, 1934–37). He was an assistant conductor and violinist with J. Ježek's Liberated Theater in Prague (1929–35); then became interested in film music; produced over 120 film scores. From 1950 to 1953 he taught classes in film music at the Academy of Musical Arts in Prague.

WORKS: ORCH.: *Symphonic Fantasy* (1932); Violin Concerto (1957; Olomouc, Sept. 23, 1958); *Historical Pictures from the Písek Region* for Amateur String Orch. (1961); *Partita* for Violin and Chamber Orch. (1962); Piano Concerto (1968); Concerto for Flute, String Orch., and Piano (1974; Prague, March 8, 1975); *Nocturne* for Strings (1975); *Echo of Songs of the Prácheň Region* (1976); *Sinfonietta* (1977); *Mater Dolorosa* for Flute, Harp, and String Orch. (1977); *Lyrical Symphony* (1979). **CHAMBER:** 2 string quartets (1928, 1936); Wind Quartet (1928); *Suite* for Violin and Piano (1929); String Quintet (1930); *3 Pieces* for Violin and Piano (1961); *Léto budiž pochváleno* (Summer Be Thou Praised) for String Quartet (1980); *Byl tichý letní večer* (There Was a Quiet Summer Evening) for String Quartet (1980); *Nonet* (1981). **PIANO:** *Suite* (1933); *Fantasy* (1934); 2 *Quarter-Tone Pieces* (1936); *3 Pieces* (1936); also songs.

Šrom, Karel, Czech composer, writer on music, and administrator; b. Pilsen, Sept. 14, 1904; d. Prague, Oct. 21, 1981. He studied composition with Jan Zelinka and Karel Hába in Prague (1919–25); also took courses in law at the Univ. (Jur.Dr., 1927); wrote music criticism (1928–45) and served as head of the music dept. of the Czech Radio (1945–51).

WRITINGS (all publ. in Prague): *Orchestr a dirigent* (1960); *Záhudbi* (Beyond Music; 1965); *Karel Ančerl* (1968).

WORKS: ORCH.: 2 syms. (1930, 1951); *Plivník* (The Gnome), scherzo (1953); *Vzdech na bruslích* (A Sigh on Skates), symphonic allegretto (1957); *Hayaya,* suite for adults and children (1961); Piano Concerto (1961); *Etudes* (1970); *Malá* for Chamber Orch. (1972). **CHAMBER:** Violin Sonata (1920); 3 string quartets (1923, 1941, 1966); *Scherzo Trio* for String Trio (1943); *Vynajitka* (Fairytale) for Nonet (1952); *Etudes* for Nonet (1959); Concertino for 2 Flutes, and String Quintet or String Orch. (1971). **PIANO:** *Whiles,* trifles (1942); 7 *Pieces* (1942); *Black Hour,* cycle (1965).

Stabile, Mariano, prominent Italian baritone; b. Palermo, May 12, 1888; d. Milan, Jan. 11, 1968. He studied voice at the Accademia di Santa Cecilia in Rome; made his debut as Amonasro in Palermo (1909). For a number of seasons he sang in provincial opera houses in Italy. The turning point in his career came when he was engaged by Toscanini to sing Falstaff in Verdi's opera at La Scala (Dec. 26, 1921). He triumphed and the role became his major success; he sang it more than 1,000 times. His guest engagements took him to London's Covent Garden (1926–31), the Salzburg Festivals (1935–39), the Glyndebourne Festivals (1936–39), again in London (1946–49), and the Edinburgh Festival (1948). He retired in 1960. Among his other notable roles were Don Giovanni, Mozart's and Rossini's Figaro, Don Alfonso, Dr. Malatesta, Iago, Rigoletto, and Scarpia.

Stabinger, Mathias, German flutist, clarinetist, conductor, and composer; b. c.1750; d. Venice, c.1815. He was a flutist and clarinetist in Lyons in 1772, and then made his 1st appearance in Paris that same year. In 1777 he went to Italy, where he brought out the highly successful opera buffa *Le astuzie di Bettina* (Genoa, 1780), which subsequently was performed throughout Europe. In 1781 he was maestro al cembalo at the Warsaw Opera; in 1782 he was active with the Mattei-Orecia opera troupe in St. Petersburg, and then was associated with the Petrovsky Theater in Moscow. After another Italian sojourn (1783–85), he returned to Moscow as director of the orch. at the Petrovsky Theater, where he produced such successful stage works as *Schastlivaya Tonia* (Lucky Tonia; Jan. 14, 1786), *Baba Yaga* (Dec. 2, 1786), *Zhenitba neudachnaya* (The Unfortunate Marriage; Feb. 19, 1788), and *Orphée traversant l'enfer à la recherche d'Eurydice* (Feb. 22, 1792). About 1800 he returned once more to Italy, finally settling in Venice in 1814. He also wrote an oratorio, *Betulia liberata* (Moscow, March 26, 1783), and publ. much chamber music.

Stäblein, Bruno, distinguished German musicologist; b. Munich, May 5, 1895; d. Erlangen, March 6, 1978. He studied musicology with Sanderberger and Kroyer at the Univ. of Munich (Ph.D., 1918, with the diss. *Musicque de Joye: Studien zur Instrumentalmusik des 16. Jahrhunderts*); later completed his Habilitation at the Univ. of Erlangen in 1946 with his *Hymnestudien*. He was a theater conductor in Innsbruck, Coburg, and Regensburg, where he was also active as an adviser in musical studies. He was a prof. and chairman of the seminars in musicology at the Univ. of Erlangen (1956–63); in 1967 he was appointed director of the Society for Bavarian Music History; he ed. the important collection Monumenta Monodica Medii Aevi (Kassel, 1956–70); contributed a number of informative articles on the music of the Middle Ages and the Renaissance; ed. reprints of documentary materials pertaining to these epochs. A Festschrift in his honor, issued for his 70th birthday, contains a complete list of his publs. (Kassel, 1967).

Stäbler, Gerhard F., German organist and composer; b. Wilhelmsdorf, near Ravensburg, July 20, 1949. He studied in Detmold (1968–70) and Essen (1970–76), then had lessons in composition with Huber and in organ with Zacher; taught at the Essen Folkwang Hochschule für Musik (1982–84). He produced music programs for radio; founded the Essen Eisler Choir and served as ed. of the journal *linkskurve*. As an organist, he toured Europe and the U.S. with a repertoire including works by Ligeti, Cage, Gesualdo, and himself, as well as revised versions of works by J.S. Bach and John Bull. Stäbler's early works are avant-garde, often featuring involved improvisations; works dating from 1980 are political and dialectical in concept, involving various media. In 1986 he co-founded (with pianist Ivan Popovic) Aktive Musik, a touring concert/lecture series on new music and sociopolitical consciousness. Their Essen festival (1986) included workshops and performances in unusual geographic contexts in an effort to reestablish a working relationship with the public.

Works: *Dämpfe,* 5-fold chamber music (1968–70); *Mo-ped* for Organ and Motorcycle (1970–71); *drüber . . .* for 8 Active Screamers, Cello, Synthesizer, and Tape (1972–73); *Gehörsmassage* for Active Audience (1973); *Cage-Mix,* arrangement with Animal Voices (1973–74); *Suchen nach . . . ,* experiments with historical materials for Various Ensembles (1976–80); *Drei Lieder zu Gedichten von Gert Udo Jerns* for Voice, Drum, and Piano (1979–82); *Hitlerchoräle IV-VI* for Choir and Elec-

tronic Organ (1980); *. . . fürs Vaterland,* 3 songs for Instruments, Voices, and Speech Choir (1981–82); *Reisegepäck,* traveling works (1981–84); *Den Toten von Sabra und Chatila* for Flute, Oboe, Clarinet, Piano, and Voice (1982); *Das Sichere ist nicht sicher,* spiraling rondo for 8 Instruments and Tape (1982); *Windows: Elegien* for Chamber Ensemble (1983; various other versions, 1983–85); *Schatten wilder Schmerzen* for Orch. (1984–85); *Die Spieldose* for Percussion, Tape, and Visual Media (1984–85); *Hart auf Hart,* improvisatory music for Ensemble (1986); *rasend still* for Euphonium or Trumpet (1986); *Warnung mit Liebeslied* for Harp, Accordion, and Percussion (1986); *Mit wachen Sinnen* for Choir and Drums (1986–87); *Ruck—VERSCH^{ei}BEN Zuck* for Accordion and Orch. (1986–88); *. . . strike the ear . . .* for String Quartet (Essen, Nov. 16, 1988); *auf dem Seil, auf scharf gespanntem Seil* for Flute, Violin, Trombone, and Piano (1988); *fallen, fallen . . . und liegen und fallen* for Alto, Accordion, Tuba, and Tape (1988–89); *Oktober* for Flute, Violin, and Contrabass (1989); *Affiliert* for Ensemble (1989–90); *Den Müllfahrern von San Francisco* for 17 Instruments (1989–90); *. . . Im Spalier . . .* for Brass Quintet (1990); *Zeitsprünge* for Accordion and Percussion (1990); *Co—wie Kobalt* for Contrabass Solo and Orch. (1989–91); *Gloriette,* music-theater work (1990–91); also songs; piano pieces.

Stachowski, Marek, Polish composer; b. Piekary Śląskie, March 21, 1936. He studied theory and composition with Penderecki at the Krakow Cons. (1963–66); then taught there and at the Jagiellonian Univ. in Krakow, remaining on the faculty of the latter until 1979. His music is both constructivistically impressionistic and sonoristically coloristic.

Works: *Pieć zmysłów i rósa* (5 Senses and the Rose) for Voice, Flute, Horn, Trombone, and Marimbaphone (1964); *Chamber Music* for Flute, Harp, and Percussion (1965); 2 string quartets (1965, 1972); *Musica con una battuta del tam-tam* for String Orch. and Tam-tam (1968); *Lines of Dylan Thomas* for 2 Choruses and Orch. (1967); *Sequenze concertanti* for Orch. (1968); *Neusis II* for 2 Choral Groups, Percussion, Cello, and Double Bass (1968); *Chant de l'espoir,* after Eluard, for Narrator, Soprano, Baritone, Chorus, Boys' Chorus, and Orch. (1969); *Irisation* for Orch. (Graz, Oct. 23, 1970); *Audition* for Flute, Cello, and Piano (1970); *Words* for Soprano, Bass, Chorus, and Orch. (1971); *Solemn Music* for Orch. (1973; Warsaw, Sept. 27, 1974); *Extensions,* 3 pieces in sequence for One, 2, or 3 Performers on Piano (1971–74); *Thakurian Songs* for Chorus and Orch. (1974); *Poème sonore* for Orch. (1975; Mönchengladbach, June 24, 1976); *Birds* for Soprano and Ensemble (1976); *Divertimento* for String Orch. (1978); *Quartetto da ingresso* for String Quartet (1980); *Choreia* for Orch. (1980); *Capriccio* for Orch. (1983); *Sapphic Odes* for Mezzo-soprano and Orch. (1985); *Musique en quatre scènes pour clarinette et quatuor à cordes* (1987).

Stacy, Thomas, American English-horn player; b. Little Rock, Ark., Aug. 18, 1938. He studied at the Eastman School of Music in Rochester, N.Y., graduating in 1960; made his solo debut with the Minneapolis Sym. Orch., with which he served as solo English horn; since 1972, has served the same role with the N.Y. Phil. He premiered 2 of the principal works for the instrument, the concertos by Skrowaczewski (Minneapolis, 1970) and Persichetti (N.Y., 1977).

Stade, Frederica von. See **Von Stade, Frederica.**

Staden, Johann, eminent German organist and composer, father of **Sigmund Theophil Staden;** b. Nuremberg (baptized), July 2, 1581; d. there (buried), Nov. 15, 1634. He spent most of his life in his native city; won particular distinction as an organist by the time he was 18; served as court organist in Bayreuth (1604–5) and then went with the court to Kulmbach following a disastrous fire; returned to Nuremberg as organist at the Spitalkirche (1616), St. Lorenz (1616–18), and St. Sebald (from 1618); also was active as a teacher, Kindermann being his most celebrated pupil. Only about half of Staden's extant output has survived in complete form; these include distinguished sacred and secular vocal works as well as instrumental pieces. He was one of Germany's 1st exponents of the concertato style.

BIBL.: R. Eitner, "J. S.: Eine Bio- und Bibliographie," *Monatshefte für Musikgeschichte,* XV (1883); W. Nagel, "Zur Biographie J. S.s und seiner Söhne," ibid., XXIX (1897).

Staden, Sigmund Theophil, esteemed German organist, instrumentalist, music theorist, and composer, son of **Johann Staden;** b. Kulmbach (baptized), Nov. 6, 1607; d. Nuremberg (buried), July 30, 1655. He studied organ, violin, and composition with his father; after receiving instruction in keyboard instruments, cornett, trombone, bassoon, viola, and composition from Jakob Paumann in Augsburg (1620–23), he was active in Nuremberg as a city musician; then completed his training with Walter Rowe in Berlin (1627). He returned to Nuremberg in 1627; was made organist at St. Lorenz in 1634. On many occasions he was called upon to act as Kapellmeister to the city. His *Seelewig* (1644; publ. in *Frauenzimmer Gesprächspiele,* vol. IV, 1644; ed. in *Monatshefte für Musikgeschichte,* XIII, 1881) is the earliest extant singspiel, which he wrote in the Italian manner; he also composed incidental music; about 50 lieder; etc.

BIBL.: G. Narciss, *Studien zu den Frauenzimmergesprächspielen* (Leipzig, 1928); H. Druener, *S.T. S. 1607–1655* (diss., Univ. of Bonn, 1946); P. Keller, *S.s Oper "Seelewig"* (diss., Univ. of Zürich, 1970).

Stader, Maria, noted Hungarian-born Swiss soprano; b. Budapest, Nov. 5, 1911. She studied voice with Keller in Karlsruhe, Durigo in Zürich, Lombardi in Milan, and T. Schnabel in N.Y.; won the Geneva International Competition (1939). After a brief career as an opera singer, she devoted herself to a distinguished concert career after World War II; toured extensively in Europe, North America, and the Far East; following her retirement in 1969, she was active as a teacher. She was particularly esteemed as an interpreter of Mozart, in both operatic and concert settings.

Stadler, Abbé Maximilian (actually, **Johann Karl Dominik**), prominent Austrian keyboard player, music historian, and composer; b. Melk, Aug. 4, 1748; d. Vienna, Nov. 8, 1833. He began his musical training with Johann Leuthner, a bass at the Melk Benedictine abbey; then went as a choirboy in 1758 to Lilienfeld, where he received instruction in violin, clavichord, and organ; concurrently took music lessons with Albrechtsberger in Melk; completed his education at the Jesuit College in Vienna in 1762. In 1766 he returned to Melk and became a novice; took his vows in 1767 and was made a priest in 1772; then was made head of the abbey's theological studies. After being made chaplain in Wullersdorf in 1783, he was elected prior of Melk in 1784. In 1786 he became abbot of Lilienfeld and in 1789 in Kremsmünster. After a sojourn in Linz (1791–96), he settled in Vienna. In 1803 he was secularized and was given the titular canonry of Linz; was parish priest in Alt-Lerchenfeld (1803–10) and Grosskrut (1810–15); then was again active in Vienna. He was esteemed as a keyboard player and composer by his contemporaries; his oratorio *Die Befreyung von Jerusalem* (1813) was widely performed in his day. His *Materialen zur Geschichte der Musik unter den österreichischen Regenten* (c.1816–25) is duly recognized as the 1st Austrian history of music. He was a friend of Mozart, and took care of Mozart's MS of the Requiem, which he copied at Mozart's death. When the authenticity of the work was called into question by Gottfried Weber and others, Stadler publ. a pamphlet in its defense, *Vertheidigung der Echtheit des Mozartschen Requiems* (Vienna, 1825; supplement, 1826). His own compositions include, in addition to the above-cited oratorio, a singspiel, *Das Studenten-Valete* (Melk, Sept. 6, 1781), incidental music, numerous sacred works, secular cantatas, lieder, orch. and chamber music pieces, keyboard works, and completions and arrangements of works by other composers.

WRITINGS: *Anleitung zur musikalischen Composition durch Würfelspiel* (MS, c.1780); *Erklärung, wir man aus . . . Ziffer- und Notentabellen eine Menuet herauswürfeln könne* (Vienna,

1781); *Priorats-Ephemeriden* (MS, 1784–86); *Beschreibung der Fragmente aus Mozart's Nachlass* (MS, c.1798); *Fragmente von Singstücken* (MS, c.1798); *Fragmente einiger Mozartischen Klavierstücke, die von einem Liebhaber der Musik vollendet worden* (MS; ed. in *Österreichische Musikzeitschrift,* XXI, 1966); *Materialen zur Geschichte der Musik unter den österreichischen Regenten* (MS, c.1816–25; ed. by K. Wagner, Kassel, 1974); *Eigenhändig geschriebene Selbst-Biographie des Hochwürdigen Herrn Maximilian Stadler* (MS, c.1816–26; ed. in *Mozart-Jahrbuch 1957*); *Vertheidigung der Echtheit des Mozartschen Requiems* (Vienna, 1825; supplement 1826); *Nachtrag zur Vertheidigung* (Vienna, 1827); *Zweyter und letzter Nachtrag zur Vertheidigung . . . sammt Nachbericht über die Ausgabe . . . durch Herrn André in Offenbach, nebst Ehrenrettung Mozart's und vier fremden Briefen* (Vienna, 1827); *Biographische Notizen über Abbé Maximilian Stadler von ihm selbst aufgezeichnet* (MS, c.1833; ed. in *Mozart Jahrbuch 1964*).

BIBL.: H. Sabel, *M. S.s weltliche Werke und seine Beziehungen zur Wiener Klassik* (diss., Univ. of Cologne, 1941); idem, "M. S. und Wolfgang Amadeus Mozart," *Neues Mozart-Jahrbuch,* III (1943); K. Wagner, *A.M. S.* (Kassel, 1974).

Stadler, Anton (Paul), famous Austrian clarinetist and basset-horn player; b. Bruck an der Leitha, June 28, 1753; d. Vienna, June 15, 1812. With his brother, **Johann (Nepomuk Franz) Stadler** (b. Vienna, May 6, 1755; d. there, May 2, 1804), a clarinetist and basset-horn player, he first attracted attention as a soloist with the Vienna Tonkünstler-Sozietät in 1773; after serving Count Dimitri Golitsin, the Russian ambassador to Vienna, they entered the service of the imperial wind band in 1782; entered the Court Orch. as clarinetists in 1787, Johann taking 1st position and Anton 2nd. Anton became one of Mozart's closest friends; the composer wrote his Quintet, K.581, and Clarinet Concerto, K.622, for him. After accompanying Mozart to Prague in 1791, where he played the clarinet and basset-horn obbligatos in *La clemenza di Tito* to great applause, he toured widely in Europe as a virtuoso. In 1796 he finally returned to his post in Vienna, being pensioned in 1799; then played for several seasons in the opera orch. In 1806 he made his farewell appearance as a solo artist with the Tonkünstler-Sozietät. Anton was also a competent composer; among his works are 10 sets of variations for Clarinet (Vienna, 1810), 12 ländlerische Tänze for 2 Clarinets (Vienna, c.1823), 3 caprices for Clarinet (Vienna, c.1825), 6 progressive duets for 2 Clarinets (Vienna, c.1827), 18 trios for 3 Basset Horns, partitas for 6 Wind Instruments, and other pieces.

BIBL.: M. Kingdon-Ward, "Mozart's Clarinetist," *Monthly Musical Record,* LXXXV (1955); W. Maynard, "A. S., Composer," *Woodwind World,* VIII (1968); G. Croll and K. Birsak, "A. S.s 'Bassettklarinette' und das 'S.-Quintet' KV 581," *Österreichische Musikzeitschrift,* XXIV (1969); P. Weston, *Clarinet Virtuosi of the Past* (London, 1971); P. Poulin, "A Little-Known Letter of A. S.," *Music & Letters* (Jan. 1988); idem, "A View of Eighteenth-Century Musical Life and Training: A. S.'s 'Musick Plan,'" ibid. (May 1990).

Stadlmair, Hans, Austrian conductor and composer; b. Neuhofen an der Krems, May 3, 1929. He received his musical training in Linz and Vienna; eventually settled in Munich. In 1956 he founded the Munich Chamber Orch., with which he traveled on numerous tours in Europe, the U.S., South America, Africa, and Asia. As a composer, he wrote mostly instrumental works, in a neo-Baroque manner, among them a Toccata for Strings and Harpsichord (1966), a Trumpet Concerto with Strings (1967), and *Sinfonia serena* for Strings (1970); he also wrote some choral pieces.

Stadlmayr, Johann, eminent German composer; b. probably in Freising, Bavaria, c.1575; d. Innsbruck, July 12, 1648. He went to Salzburg, where he entered the service of the Archbishop in 1603; in 1604 he was made Vice-Kapellmeister, and soon thereafter Kapellmeister. In 1607 he was called to Innsbruck as Kapellmeister at the Habsburg court of Archduke Maximilian II of the Tirol. After the latter's death, the new archduke, Leopold V, disbanded the Innsbruck court chapel in favor of his Alsatian establishment in 1618. Stadlmayr petitioned Leopold to retain his services, but it was not until 1624 that he was reappointed to his Innsbruck position, which subsequently flourished under his direction. Stadlmayr was a leading composer of music for the Catholic church. Among his works were 4 vols. of Magnificats (1603–18), 7 vols. of masses (1596–1643), hymns, motets, Psalms, etc.

BIBL.: J. Peregrinus (J. Hupfauf), *J. S.* (Salzburg, 1885); F. Daniel, *Die konzertanten Messen J. S.s* (diss., Univ. of Vienna, 1928); B. Hinterleitner, *Die Vokalmessen S.s* (diss., Univ. of Vienna, 1930); K. Gress, *Die Motetten J. S.s im Lichte der Entwicklung der Motette im beginnenden siebzehnten Jahrhundert* (diss., Univ. of Vienna, 1931); H. Junkermann, *The Magnificats of J. S.* (diss., Ohio State Univ., 1966).

Stadtfeld, Alexandre, composer; b. Wiesbaden, April 27, 1826; d. Brussels, Nov. 4, 1853. He studied with Fétis at the Brussels Cons., winning the Belgian Prix de Rome in 1849. He composed the operas *Hamlet* (Darmstadt, 1857), *Abu Hassan*, *L'Illusion*, and *La Pedrina*; 4 syms.; overtures; 2 concertinos for Piano and Orch.; String Quartet; Piano Trio; a Mass; a Te Deum; etc.

BIBL.: M. Weber, *A. S., Leben und Werk* (Bonn, 1969).

Staempfli, Edward, Swiss composer; b. Bern, Feb. 1, 1908. He studied composition with Jarnach in Cologne and Dukas in Paris. He returned to Switzerland at the outbreak of World War II; in 1954 he went to Berlin. In his music he was influenced chiefly by the French School of composition; later he adopted the Schoenbergian method of composition with 12 tones.

WORKS: 2 operas: *Ein Traumspiel* (1943) and *Medea* (1954); 3 syms. (1938, 1942, 1945); 4 ballets: *Le pendu* (1935); *Choreographisches divertimento* (1942), *Die Prinzessin und der Schweinehirt* (1943), and *Spannungen* (1961); 3 oratorios (1950, 1970, 1972); 4 piano concertos (1932–63); 3 violin concertos (1936–41); *Ornamente* for 2 Flutes, Celesta, and Percussion (1960); 6 string quartets (1926–62); Quartet for Clarinet, Violin, Cello, and Harp (1965); Duo for Clarinet and Piano (1970); several choral works.

Stagno, Roberto (real name, **Vincenzo Andriolo**), Italian tenor; b. Palermo, Oct. 11, 1840; d. Genoa, April 26, 1897. He studied with Giuseppe Lamperti in Milan; made his operatic debut as Rodrigo in Rossini's *Otello* in Lisbon (1862); then sang with notable success in Madrid (from 1865), Moscow (1868), and Buenos Aires (from 1879), and throughout Italy. While in Buenos Aires, he became the mentor of the soprano Gemma Bellincioni; their teacher-pupil relationship developed into intimacy, and they subsequently toured widely together. Their daughter, Bianca Stagno-Bellincioni (b. Budapest, Jan. 23, 1888; d. Milan, July 26, 1980), became a singer. Stagno was engaged for the 1st season of the Metropolitan Opera in N.Y., making his debut there as Manrico in *Il Trovatore* on Oct. 26, 1883; remained there for only that season. In 1884 he appeared at the Paris Théâtre-Italien. He was chosen to create the role of Turiddu in *Cavalleria rusticana* opposite Bellincioni's Santuzza in Rome (1890).

BIBL.: B. Stagno-Bellincioni, *R. S. e Gemma Bellincioni, intimi* (Florence, 1943).

Stählin, Jacob von, German music historian; b. Memmingen, May 10, 1709; d. St. Petersburg, July 6, 1785. He was educated at the Memmingen Lateinschule, the Zittau Gymnasium, and the Univ. of Leipzig; while in Leipzig, he became a friend of Bach. In 1735 he went to Russia, where he worked as a fireworks director and as a teacher of poetry and rhetoric; he held various posts at the imperial court in St. Petersburg. His valuable *Nachrichten von der Musik in Russland* (publ. in J. Haigold's *Beylagen zum neuveränderten Russland*, Riga and Leipzig, 1769–70) was the 1st study of Russian music, theater, and dance.

BIBL.: K. Stählin, "J. v.S.: Ein biographischer Beitrag zur deutsch-russischen Kulturgeschichte des 18. Jahrhunderts," *Quellen und Aufsätze zur Russischen Geschichte*, I (Leipzig, n.d.).

Stahlman, Sylvia, American soprano; b. Nashville, Tenn., March 5, 1933. She studied voice at the Juilliard School of Music in N.Y.; then went to Europe and pursued her budding career under a suitably Italianate pseudonym, Giulia Bardi; made her debut in Brussels in 1951; then sang regularly in Frankfurt am Main (1954–72). In 1956, under her own name, she joined the N.Y. City Opera; then sang at San Francisco (1958) and Chicago (1960). She also toured as a concert artist.

Stainer, Jacob (or **Jakob**), esteemed Austrian violin maker; b. Absam, near Hall, Tirol, July 14, 1617?; d. there, Oct. or Nov. 1683. He was trained as a chorister, then apprenticed to a German violin maker who lived in Italy. After traveling to Salzburg, Munich, Venice, and other cities to sell his instruments, he settled in Absam; was named archprince's servant (purveyor to the court) by Ferdinand Karl, prince of Tirol, in 1656. His fortunes suffered an adverse turn when, in 1669, he was accused of Lutheran leanings, and spent several months in prison; was stricken with bouts of mental instability from 1675, although he continued to make instruments during periods of remission. His instruments were made between 1638 and 1682. He also made alto and tenor viols, cellos, and double basses. His violins were especially admired for their expert craftsmanship and beauty of tone. He was no relation to Markus (Marcus) Stainer (b. Hallein, Salzburg, c.1633; d. Laufen, Upper Bavaria, Nov. 27, 1693), who was also a fine Austrian violin maker; settled in Laufen, where he was made a citizen in 1656; his instruments are highly prized.

BIBL.: S. Ruf, *Der Geigenmacher Jacobus S. von Absam im Tirol* (Innsbruck, 1872; 2nd ed., 1892); F. Lentner, *J. S.s Lebenslauf im Lichte archivarischer Forschung* (Leipzig, 1898); E. Heron-Allen, "A Pilgrimage to the House of J. S.," *Musical Times* (Aug. 1900); Princesse de la Tour et Taxis, *Le Violon de J. S.* (Paris, 1910); W. Senn, *J. S., der Geigenmacher zu Absam: Die Lebesgeschichte nach urkundlichen Quellen* (Innsbruck, 1951); W. Salmen, ed., *J. S. und seine Zeit: Bericht über die J.-S.-Tagung Innsbruck 1983* (Innsbruck, 1984); W. Senn and K. Roy, *J. S.: Leben und Werk des Tiroler Meisters, 1617–1683* (Frankfurt am Main, 1986).

Stainer, Sir John, English organist, music scholar, and composer; b. London, June 6, 1840; d. Verona, March 31, 1901. He received organ lessons at an early age from his father, William Stainer, the parish schoolmaster at St. Thomas, Southwark; although he was blinded in the left eye in an accident when he was 5, he persevered in his musical training. He was a probationer (1848–49) and a chorister (1849–54) at St. Paul's Cathedral in London; then served as organist at St. Benedict and St. Peter, Paul's Wharf (1854–56), and subsequently at the College of St. Michael, Tenbury. He continued his education at Christ Church, Oxford (B.Mus., 1860; B.A., 1864; D.Mus., 1865; M.A., 1866); served as organist at St. Paul's Cathedral (1872–88) and at the National Training School of Music (1876–89), where he also was its principal (1881–89). From 1889 until his death he was a prof. at Oxford Univ. In 1888 he was knighted. He wrote much liturgical music, which has not withstood the test of time. His reputation rests upon his scholarly pursuits.

WORKS: ORATORIOS: *Gideon* (Oxford, 1865) and *The Crucifixion* (London, Feb. 24, 1887). **CANTATAS:** *The Daughter of Jarius* (Worcester, 1878); *St. Mary Magdalen* (Gloucester, 1887); *Jubilee* (1887); *The Story of the Cross* (1893); also services; anthems; hymn tunes; madrigals; partsongs; songs; organ music.

EDITIONS: With H. Bramley, *Christmas Carols, New and Old* (London, 1871); with S. Flood et al., *The Cathedral Psalter* (London, 1874); *Six Italian Songs* (London, 1896); *The Church Hymnary* (Edinburgh, 1898); with J. and E. Stainer, *Early Bodleian Music* (London and N.Y., 1901); with W. Frere and H. Briggs, *A Manual of Plainsong* (London, 1902).

WRITINGS (all publ. in London): *A Theory of Harmony* (1871); with W. Barrett, *A Dictionary of Musical Terms* (1876); *The Organ* (1877); *Music of the Bible, with an Account of the Development of Modern Musical Instruments from Ancient Types*

(1879; 2nd ed., 1914, with supplement by F. Galpin); *Music in Relation to the Intellect and Emotions* (1892); *Dufay and His Contemporaries* (1898).

BIBL.: F. Edwards, "J. S.," *Musical Times*, XLII (1901); E. Fellowes, "Sir J. S.," *English Church Music*, XXI (1951); P. Carlton, *The Life and Influence of Sir J. S.* (diss., Univ. of East Anglia, 1976); idem, *J. S. and the Musical Life of Victorian Britain* (Newton Abbot, 1984).

Stainlein, Comte Louis Charles Georges Corneille de, cellist and composer; b. Hungary, July 3, 1819; d. Angleur-lez-Liège, Belgium, Nov. 22, 1867. A talented cellist, he appeared with success in Germany and France; with Sivori, Ney, and others he gave concerts of chamber music in Paris.

WORKS: Violin Sonata; Piano Trio; 2 string quartets; String Quintet; String Sextet; pieces for cello and piano; male choruses; songs.

Stainov, Petko, Bulgarian composer; b. Kazanluk, Dec. 1, 1896; d. Sofia, June 25, 1977. Despite an almost complete loss of sight at age 5, he learned to play piano by ear; studied composition with Wolf and piano with E. Münch in Braunschweig and Berlin (1920–24). Returning to Sofia, he taught piano at the Inst. for the Blind (1927–41); then was director of the National Opera (1941–44) and of the Inst. for Music of the Bulgarian Academy of Sciences (from 1948).

WORKS: ORCH.: *Thracian Dances* (1925–26); *Legend,* symphonic poem (1927; Sofia, Jan. 1, 1928); *Balkan,* overture (1936); 2 syms. (1945, 1948); *Youth Concert Overture* (1952); also numerous choruses and choral ballads.

BIBL.: V. Krastev, *P. S.* (Sofia, 1957).

Stair, Patty, American organist, teacher, and composer; b. Cleveland, Nov. 12, 1869; d. there, April 26, 1926. She studied at the Cleveland Cons. (1882–89); was on its faculty (1889–1926) and also taught at the Univ. School (1892–1926); likewise was organist in Cleveland. She wrote the light operas *The Fair Brigade* and *Sweet Simplicity; Woodland Scene* for Orch. of Toy Instruments; *Berceuse* for Violin and Piano; anthems; partsongs; songs.

Stalvey, Dorrance, American composer; b. Georgetown, S.C., Aug. 21, 1930. He studied clarinet and general music subjects at the College of Music in Cincinnati (M.M., 1955). Prior to his late twenties, his interest was primarily in jazz improvisation. In composition he was wholly self-taught, and thanks to that developed an independent style marked by quaquaversal contrapuntal and harmonic techniques vivified by asymmetrical rhythms. He embraced a variegated career of teaching, composing, and management. He lectured on music history, theory, and analysis, off and on, at various schools; was an assistant prof. in composition at the Immaculate Heart College in Los Angeles (1972–77) and full prof. (1977–80). In 1971 he assumed the post of artistic director of the Monday Evening Concerts in Los Angeles, and since 1981 has been music director for the Los Angeles County Museum of Art; also served as a radio commentator. He had numerous conducting engagements; received several awards from ASCAP and other musical organizations. His compositions had frequent performances, and astonishingly good reviews from habitually fatigued critics for his special spatial effects in multifarious multimedia productions.

WORKS: *Celebration-Principium* for Brass and Percussion (1967); *Points-Lines-Circles* for Clarinet, Double Bass, Harp, Guitar, and Percussion (1968); *In Time and Not* for Multimedia Ensembles (1970); *Togethers:* I for Guitar and Tape (1970); II for Percussion and Tape (1970); III for Clarinet and Tape (1970); *Celebration-Sequents* for Various Instruments: I (1973); II (1976); IV (1980); *Agathlon* for Modern Dance and Instruments (1978); *Ex Ferus* for 6 Cellos or String Sextet (1982); *Pound Songs* for Soprano and Instruments (1985); *Dualities* for Guitar, Soprano, and Instruments (1986–87); *String Quartet 1989* (1989); *Exordium/Genesis/Dawn* for 6 Players (1990). Also theatrical multi-lectures; chamber works (with and without tape); piano solos; composite compositions compounded of combinations of original numbers.

Stam, Henk (actually, **Hendrikus Gerardus**), Dutch composer, conductor, teacher, and writer on music; b. Utrecht, Sept. 26, 1922. He studied instrumentation with Hendrik Andriessen and piano with Jan Wagenaar and André Jurres at the Utrecht Cons.; later studied musicology at the Univ. of Utrecht and composition with Fortner in Germany. He taught at the music school in Deventer (1948–54); was director at the music schools in Zeeland (1954–61) and Rotterdam (1962–72).

WORKS: 5 piano sonatinas (1943, 1946, 1946, 1947, 1953); 2 *Rispetti* for Baritone and String Orch. (1944); 3 string quartets (1947, 1948, 1949); *Histoire de Barbar,* 8 pieces for Piano (1949); *Cassation,* pantomime for 3 Dancers, Violin, Flute, Cello, Trombone, Mezzo-soprano, Baritone, Speaking Voice, and Chamber Orch. (1949); Violin Sonata (1950); Sonata for Solo Violin (1951); *Suite* for Violin and Piano (1953); *Ouverture Michiel de Ruyter* (1957); Cello Sonata (1966); *Tropic* for Flute, Oboe, and Piano (1972); Flute Sonata (1972); *Klachte der Prinsesse van Oranjen* for Chorus and 3 Trumpets ad libitum (1973); *Sonata concertante* for Cello and Piano (1982); *Berceuse pour B.* for Cello and Piano (1983); choruses.

Stamaty, Camille (-Marie), Graeco-French pianist, teacher, and composer; b. Rome, March 13?, 1811; d. Paris, April 19, 1870. He was of Greek-French origin; his mother, a Frenchwoman, educated him after the death of his father in 1818, and took him to Paris, where he became a pupil of Kalkbrenner; in 1836 he went to Leipzig, where he studied with Mendelssohn. He returned to Paris the next year and remained there as a pianist and teacher; among his students were Saint-Saëns and Gottschalk. He became well known as a champion of the music of Bach, Mozart, and Beethoven. In 1862 he was made a Chevalier of the Légion d'honneur. He wrote a Piano Concerto, which won the approbation of Schumann; his other works include a Piano Trio, various works for piano, including a Sonata, variations, and solo pieces, and a number of didactic works.

Stamitz, family of distinguished Bohemian musicians:

(1) Johann (Wenzel Anton) (Jan Waczlaw or **Václav Antonín) Stamitz,** eminent violinist, teacher, and composer; b. Deutsch-Brod, June 19, 1717; d. Mannheim, March 27, 1757. He most likely began his musical training with his father in Deutsch-Brod; after studies at the Iglau Jesuit Gymnasium (1728–34), he attended the Univ. of Prague (1734–35). About 1741 he entered the service of the Mannheim court, where his 1st patron was Carl Philipp, margrave of Pfalz. His playing at the coronation of the Emperor Charles VII on Feb. 12, 1742, created a sensation, and Prince Carl Theodor, who in 1743 became Palatine Elector, engaged him as a chamber musician; the court journals reported on his virtuosity in extravagant terms, extolling his ability to perform his own concerto on several different instruments—violin, viola d'amore, cello, and contra-violin solo. In 1743 the Elector made him "1st court violinist" in Mannheim; the next year, he married Maria Antonia Lüneborn. So widespread was his fame that Baron Grimm publ. in Paris a satirical pamphlet, *Le Petit Prophète de Boehmisch-Broda,* ridiculing Stamitz's innovations. By 1746 he was Konzertmeister, and then was promoted to the newly created position of director of instrumental music in 1750, being charged with composing orch. and chamber music for the Mannheim court. On Sept. 8, 1754, he made his debut at the Paris Concert Spirituel; also was engaged as director of La Poupelinière's private orch. and made some appearances at the Concert Italien. In 1755 he returned to his duties in Mannheim, where the Court Orch. became the finest in Europe under his discerning leadership. Among his outstanding students were Cannabich, W. Cramer, and I. Fränzl, as well as his own sons, Carl and Anton. Stamitz's major contribution to music rests upon his skillful adaptation and expansion of the overture style of Jommelli and his Italian compatriots to the Mannheim school of composition. His most important works are his 58 extant syms. and 10 orch. trios. Among his other extant works are violin concertos, 11 flute concertos, 2 harpsichord concertos, an Oboe Concerto, a Clarinet Concerto, much chamber music, and some sacred vocal pieces. For a selection of his orch. and chamber music, see H. Riemann, ed., Denkmäler der Tonkunst in Bayern, IV, Jg. III/1 (1902), XIII, Jg. VII/2 (1906), and XXVII, Jg. XVI (1915).

BIBL.: P. Gradenwitz, *J. S.: Das Leben* (Brno, 1936; 2nd ed., greatly augmented, as *J. S.: Leben, Umwelt, Werke*, 2 vols., Wilhelmshaven, 1984); idem, "The Symphonies of J. S.," *Music Review*, I (1940); idem, "The S. Family: Some Errors, Omissions and Falsifications Corrected," *Notes* (Dec. 1949); P. Nettl, *Der kleine "Prophète von Böhmisch-Broda"* (Esslingen, 1953); P. Gradenwitz, "J. S. als Kirchenkomponist," *Die Musikforschung*, XI (1958); H.-R. Dürrenmatt, *Die Durchführung bei J. S.* (Bern, 1969); E. Wolf, *The Symphonies of J. S.: Authenticity, Chronology and Style* (diss., N.Y. Univ., 1972); H. Scharschuch, "J. S.," *Archiv für Musikwissenschaft*, XXXIII (1976); E. Wolf, "Authenticity and Stylistic Evidence in the Early Symphony: A Conflict in Attribution between Richter and S.," *A Musical Offering: Essays in Honor of Martin Bernstein* (N.Y., 1977); idem, "On the Origins of the Mannheim Symphonic Style," *Studies in Musicology in Honor of Otto E. Albrecht* (Kassel, 1977, and Clifton, N.J., 1980); idem, *The Symphonies of J. S., A Study in the Formation of the Classic Style* (Utrecht, 1981).

His 2 sons were also distinguished musicians:

(2) Carl (Philipp) Stamitz, violinist, violist, viola d'amorist, and composer; b. Mannheim (baptized), May 8, 1745; d. Jena, Nov. 9, 1801. He commenced his musical training with his father, then studied with Cannabich, Holzbauer, and Richter at the Mannheim court, where he played 2nd violin in the Court Orch. (1762–70). With his brother, Anton, he went to Strasbourg in 1770; by 1771 he was in Paris as court composer and conductor to Duke Louis of Noailles. On March 25, 1772, Carl and Anton made their 1st appearance at the Concert Spirituel, where Carl performed regularly until 1777; he also made tours as a virtuoso to Vienna in 1772, Frankfurt in 1773, and Augsburg, Vienna, and Strasbourg in 1774. After a London sojourn (1777–79), he went to The Hague, where he made appearances at the court as a violist (1782–84); then toured extensively in Germany, including appearances in Hamburg, Leipzig, and Berlin in 1786 and in Dresden and Halle in 1787; also performed in Prague in 1787. He served as director of Kassel's Liebhaber concerts (1789–90). In 1795 he settled in Jena as city Kapellmeister and as a music teacher at the Univ. He was a significant composer of orch. music. He wrote at least 51 syms. (28 are extant), some 38 syms. concertantes, and more than 60 concertos, including 15 for Violin, 10 for Clarinet, 7 for Flute, and 7 for Bassoon; many of his concertos are lost. Among his other works are chamber music pieces and vocal music. Some of his works are found in H. Riemann, ed., Denkmäler der Tonkunst in Bayern, XV, Jg. VIII/2 (1907), XXVII, Jg. XV (1914), and XXVIII, Jg. XVI (1915).

BIBL.: F. Kaiser, *C. S. (1745–1801): Biographische Beiträge, das symphonische Werk, thematischer Katalog der Orchesterwerke* (diss., Univ. of Marburg, 1962); D. Thomason, *A Discussion of the Viola d'Amore Music of K. S.* (n.p., 1979).

(3) Anton (actually, **Thadäus Johann Nepomuk) Stamitz,** violinist, violist, and composer; b. Deutsch-Brod (baptized), Nov. 27, 1750; d. probably in Paris or Versailles, after 1789. He studied violin with his brother, Carl, and with Cannabich in Mannheim, where he was 2nd violinist in the Court Orch. (1764–70); then accompanied his brother to Strasbourg, moving on to Paris with him by 1771; appeared regularly at the Concert Spirituel (from 1772). He was active in Versailles from 1778, and was the teacher of Rodolphe Kreutzer until 1780; then was a member of the musique du roi from 1782 until disappearing from the musical scene without a trace in 1789. Among his extant compositions are 12 syms., 2 syms. concertantes, over 22 violin concertos, several other concertos, 66 string quartets, many trios, numerous duos, etc.

Standage, Simon, English violinist; b. High Wycombe, Buckinghamshire, Nov. 8, 1941. He studied at Bryanston School

and Cambridge Univ.; subsequently took private lessons with Ivan Galamian in N.Y. (1967–69). Upon his return to England, he became an associate member of the London Sym. Orch. and sub-concertmaster of the English Chamber Orch. In 1973 he was appointed principal violin of the English Concert and concertmaster of the Richard Hickox Orch. and City of London Sinfonia. In 1981 he founded the Salomon String Quartet. In 1983 he was appointed teacher of Baroque violin at the Royal Academy of Music. In 1990 he founded with Richard Hickox the Collegium Musicum 90 of London.

Standford, Patric (actually, **John Patric Standford Gledhill**), English composer; b. Barnsley, Feb. 5, 1939. He was a student of Edmund Rubbra and Raymond Jones at the Guildhall School of Music in London (1961–63); after receiving the Mendelssohn Scholarship in 1964, he continued his studies with Gian Francesco Malipiero in Italy and with Witold Lutoslawski. He taught at the Guildhall School of Music (1968–80) and also served as chairman of the Composer's Guild of Great Britain (1977–79); then was head of music at Bretton Hall College (from 1980). In 1983 he was awarded the Ernest Ansermet prize of Geneva for his 3rd Sym.

WORKS: STAGE: OPERA: *Villon* (1972–85). **BALLETS:** *Celestial Fall* (1968; orch. suite, 1971); *Reflections* (1980). **ORCH.:** 5 syms: No. 1, *The Seasons* (1971–72); No. 2, *Christus-Requiem* for 4 Soloists, Narrator, Chorus, Children's Chorus, and Orch. (1971–72; rev. 1980); No. 3, *Toward Paradise* for Chorus and Orch. (1982; Geneva, June 11, 1986); No. 4, *Taikyoku* for 2 Pianos and Percussion (1975–79); No. 5, with Soprano Solo (Manchester, Jan. 24, 1986); *Saracinesco*, symphonic poem (1966); *Notte*, poem for Chamber Orch. (1968); *Antitheses* for 15 Strings (1971); Cello Concerto (1974); Violin Concerto (1975); *Variations* (1977; arranged from the Piano Variations, 1969); Piano Concerto (1979); *Dialogues* for Cimbalom and Chamber Orch. (1981); *Folksongs* for String Orch. (3 sets, 1982, 1985, 1986). **CHAMBER:** 2 string quartets (1965, 1973); *Suite française*, 4 pieces for Wind Quintet (1964); Piano Sonata (1979–80); *4 Cartoons* for Oboe, Clarinet, and Bassoon (1984); Concertino for Piano, Oboe, and String Trio (1986); *Suite humoresque* for Piano, Oboe, Clarinet, and Bassoon (1987); Piano Quartet (1988). **VOCAL:** 3 motets: *In memoriam Benjamin Britten* for Chorus (1976–77); *Mass* for Chorus and Brass Band (1980); *O sacrum convivium* for Chorus (1985); *Mass of Our Lady and St. Rochus* for Chorus (1988).

BIBL.: L. East, "S. and His Fifth Symphony," *Musical Times* (Jan. 1986).

Stanford, Sir Charles Villiers, eminent Irish organist, conductor, pedagogue, and composer; b. Dublin, Sept. 30, 1852; d. London, March 29, 1924. Brought up in an intellectual atmosphere, he was a diligent student in his early youth; studied piano, organ, violin, and composition with Michael Quarry at St. Patrick's Cathedral, and with Robert Stewart and Joseph Robinson at the Royal Irish Academy of Music in Dublin; in 1862, was sent to London, where he studied piano with Ernst Pauer and composition with Arthur O'Leary. In 1870 he entered Queen's College, Cambridge, as a choral scholar (B.A., 1874); then studied composition with Reinecke in Leipzig (1874–76) and with Kiel in Berlin (1876); was awarded the M.A. degree from Cambridge (1877). In 1883 he was appointed prof. of composition at the Royal College of Music and conductor of the orch. there; in 1887 he also became a prof. of music at Cambridge, holding both positions until his death; he was conductor of the Leeds Festivals from 1901 to 1910, and appeared as guest conductor of his own works in Paris, Berlin, Amsterdam, and Brussels; from 1885 to 1902 he conducted the London Bach Choir. He was knighted in 1902. He was an extremely able and industrious composer in a distinctly Romantic style, yet unmistakably national in musical materials, both Irish and English. His music, however, remains virtually unknown outside Great Britain, and his significance to British music rests largely upon his importance as a pedagogue.

WORKS: OPERAS: *The Veiled Prophet of Khorassan* (1877; Hannover, Feb. 6, 1881); *Savonarola* (Hamburg, April 18,

1884); *The Canterbury Pilgrims* (London, April 23, 1884); *Lorenza* (c.1894; not perf.); *Shamus O'Brian* (London, March 2, 1896); *Christopher Patch (The Barber of Bath)* (c.1897; not perf.); *Much Ado about Nothing* (London, May 30, 1901); *The Critic, or An Opera Rehearsed* (London, Jan. 14, 1916); *The Traveling Companion* (1919; amateur perf., Liverpool, April 30, 1925; professional perf., Bristol, Oct. 25, 1926); also incidental music. ORCH.: 7 syms.: No. 1 (1875); No. 2, *Elegiac* (Cambridge, 1882); No. 3, *Irish* (London, May 17, 1887); No. 4 (Berlin, Jan. 14, 1889); No. 5, *L'allegro ed il penseroso* (1894; London, 1895); No. 6, *Im memoriam G.F. Watts* (c.1905); No. 7 (1911); *Suite* for Violin and Orch. (Berlin, Jan. 14, 1889; Joachim, soloist); 3 piano concertos (1896, 1915, 1919); 6 *Irish Rhapsodies* (1901–c.1923); *Overture in the Style of a Tragedy* (1904); 2 violin concertos (1904, 1918); *Irish Concertino* for Violin, Cello, and Orch. (1919); Variations for Violin and Orch. (1921; also for Violin and Piano). CHAMBER: 4 sonatas for Violin and Piano (c.1880, 1893, c.1898, 1919); 3 piano trios (1889, 1899, 1918); 8 string quartets (c.1891–c.1919); 2 string quintets (1903, c.1903); various piano pieces, including 5 sonatas (1917–21); organ music. VOCAL: *Eden*, oratorio (Birmingham, 1891); Mass (London, 1893); *Requiem* (Birmingham, 1897); *Te Deum* (Leeds, 1898); *Stabat Mater* (Leeds, 1907); numerous other works, including 2 *Magnificats* (1872, 1873), anthems, services, choruses, song cycles, and solo songs.

WRITINGS: *Studies and Memories* (London, 1908); *Musical Composition: A Short Treatise for Students* (London, 1911; 6th ed., 1950); *Brahms* (London, 1912); *Pages from an Unwritten Diary* (London, 1914); *Interludes: Records and Reflections* (London, 1922).

BIBL.: J. Porte, *Sir C.V. S.* (London and N.Y., 1921); T. Dunhill, "C.V. S.: Some Aspects of his Life and Works," *Proceedings of the Musical Association*, LIII (1927–28); J. Fuller Maitland, *The Music of Parry and S.* (Cambridge, 1934); H. Plunket Greene, *C.V. S.* (London, 1935); F. Hudson, "C.V. S.: nova bibliographica," *Musical Times*, CIV (1963); idem, "A Catalogue of the Works of C.V. S. (1852–1924)," *Music Review*, XXV (1964); idem, "C.V. S.: nova bibliographica II," *Musical Times*, CV (1964); idem, "C.V. S.: nova bibliographica III," ibid., CVIII (1967); idem, "A Revised and Extended Catalogue of the Works of C.V. S. (1852–1924)," *Music Review*, XXXVII (1976); G. Norris, *S., the Cambridge Jubilee and Tchaikovsky* (Newton Abbot, 1980).

Stanislav, Josef, Czech composer; b. Hamburg, Jan. 22, 1897; d. Prague, Aug. 5, 1971. He went in his youth to Prague, where he took lessons in composition with Jeremiáš and Foerster and in piano with Mikeš and Veselý; completed his training in the Cons. master classes of Novák in composition (1922) and of Hoffmeister in piano (1929); also studied with Nejedlý at the Univ. He joined the Czech Communist party and was active in various left-wing organizations. His music was banned during the German occupation, but after the liberation in 1945, he played a prominent role in Czech musical life; was a prof. at the Prague Academy of Music (from 1948) and director of the ethnographical and folklore inst. of the Czech Academy of Sciences (from 1953).

WORKS: *Symfonické vypravovani* (Symphonic Narration; n.d.); *Rudoarmějská symfonie* (Red Army Sym.; 1942); Viola Sonata (1920); 3 piano sonatas (1921, 1929, 1944); Viola Sonata (1933); String Quartet (1935); several cantatas; choruses; songs; incidental music.

WRITINGS: *O té lidové a vážné hudbě a lidových hudebnících* (Folk Music, Art Music, and Folk Musicians; Prague, 1939); *Hudebni kultura, umění a život* (Musical Culture, Art, and Life; Prague, 1940); *Ludvík Kuba* (Prague, 1963).

Stanislavsky (real name, **Alexeiev**), **Konstantin (Sergeievich),** famous Russian actor and theater and opera director; b. Moscow, Jan. 17, 1863; d. there, Aug. 7, 1938. He received practical experience by performing in and directing operettas in his family's private theater; studied voice with Komisarzhevsky, but gave up all hope of a career in opera when his voice proved inadequate. Then, with Nemirovich-Danchanko,

he founded the Moscow Art Theater in 1898; it became an innovative setting for both stage plays and operas. In 1918 he founded the Bolshoi Theater Opera Studio, which became an independent studio in 1920; it was named the Stanislavsky Opera Theater in his honor in 1926. The Stanislavsky method as applied to opera concentrates upon the musical score as the guiding force of a production, allowing all elements to evolve naturally to present a realistic work of art. He wrote several books on his theater methods.

BIBL.: G. Kristi, *Rabota Stanislavskovo v opernom teatre* (S.'s Work in the Opera Theater; Moscow, 1952); I. Vinogradskaya, ed., *Zhizn i tvorchestvo K.S. Stanislavskovo: Letopis* (The Life and Work of K.S. S.: A Chronicle; Moscow, 1973); E. Hapgood, ed., *S. on Opera* (N.Y., 1975).

Stankovich, Evgeny, Russian composer; b. Sbaliava, Ukraine, Sept. 19, 1942. He studied composition at the Kiev Cons. with Liatoshinsky, graduating in 1970. In 1975 he joined the Communist Party. In his music he follows the doctrine of socialist realism, with an emphasis on Ukrainian folk motifs. He wrote 3 syms.: *Sinfonia larga* for 15 String Instruments (1973); No. 2 (1975); No. 3, *I Commit Myself*, with Chorus (1976); his most popular work); Cello Concerto (1970); *Sinfonietta* (1971); Chamber Sym. (1973); cantata, *Lenin* (1980); numerous choruses and songs; chamber music; film scores.

Stanley, John, prominent English organist and composer; b. London, Jan. 17, 1712; d. there, May 19, 1786. Blind from early childhood, he studied organ with Maurice Greene, and soon was able to fill church positions; composed theater music, and publ. a number of instrumental works. He was the youngest individual ever to take the B.Mus. degree at the Univ. of Oxford in 1729. In 1779 he succeeded Boyce as Master of the King's Band of Musicians. He enjoyed the friendship and esteem of Handel, after whose death he conducted performances of Handel's oratorios with J.C. Smith. He especially distinguished himself as a composer of keyboard music and cantatas.

WORKS: DRAMATIC: OPERA: *Teraminta* (not perf.). MASQUE: *The Tears and Triumphs of Parnassus* (London, Nov. 17, 1760). PASTORAL: *Arcadia, or The Shepherd's Wedding* (London, Oct. 26, 1761). INCIDENTAL MUSIC: to J. Hawkesworth's *Oroonoko* (London, Dec. 1, 1759). ORATORIOS: *Jephtha* (c.1751–52); *Zimri* (London, March 12, 1760); *The Fall of Egypt* (London, March 23, 1774); also cantatas; various court odes; anthems and hymns; songs; much instrumental music.

BIBL.: G. Finzi, "J. S.," *Tempo*, no. 27 (1953); T. Frost, "The Cantatas of J. S. (1713–86)," *Music & Letters* LIII (1972); G. Williams, *The Life and Works of J. S. (1712–86)* (diss., Univ. of Reading, 1977); A. Williams, "S., Smith and 'Teraminta'," *Music & Letters*, LX (1979).

Stapp, Olivia, American soprano; b. N.Y., May 30, 1940. She studied voice in N.Y.; subsequently appeared at the N.Y. City Opera, San Francisco Opera, Chicago Lyric Opera, Hamburg State Opera, and Vienna State Opera. She scored an excellent success in the role of Lady Macbeth in Verdi's opera at the Metropolitan Opera in N.Y. on Dec. 7, 1982. Her other roles were Norma, Tosca, Aida, Elektra, and Turandot.

Starczewski, Felix, Polish composer; b. Warsaw, May 27, 1868; d. there, Nov. 29, 1945. He studied in Berlin and Paris; returning to Poland, he was engaged in various activities as a teacher, composer, and music critic. He wrote an opera, *Taniec kwatów* (Warsaw, April 28, 1918); a Violin Sonata; songs.

Starer, Robert, Austrian-born American composer; b. Vienna, Jan. 8, 1924. He studied at the Vienna Academy of Music (1937–38); after the Anschluss in 1938, went to Jerusalem and studied at the Cons. with Rosowsky, Tal, and Partos (until 1943). After service in the British Royal Air Force (1943–46), he emigrated to the U.S. and became a naturalized citizen in 1957; took courses at the Juilliard School of Music in N.Y. (1947–49) and also studied with Copland at the Berkshire Music Center in Tanglewood (1948); held 2 Guggenheim fellowships (1957, 1963). He taught at the Juilliard School of Music (1949–74); also taught at the N.Y. College of Music (1959–60) and the Jewish Theological Seminary (1962–63); in 1963 he was appointed associate prof. of music at Brooklyn College, where he later was made a full prof. (1966) and a Distinguished Prof. (1986). He wrote the book *Rhythmic Training* (1969); his autobiography appeared as *Continuo: A Life in Music* (N.Y., 1987). Starer's output reflects his grounding in the 20th-century Viennese tradition; in some of works he utilized aleatory techniques, but he is best known for his use of collage.

WORKS: OPERAS: *The Intruder* (N.Y., Dec. 4, 1956); *Pantagleize* (1967; N.Y., April 7, 1973); *Apollonia* (Minneapolis, 1978); *The Last Lover* (1974; Katonah, N.Y., Aug. 2, 1975). **BALLETS:** *The Story of Esther* (1960); *The Dybbuk* (Berlin, 1960); *Samson Agonistes* (N.Y., 1961); *Phaedra* (N.Y., 1962); *The Sense of Touch* (1967); *The Lady of the House of Sleep* (N.Y., 1968); *Holy Jungle* (N.Y., April 2, 1974). **ORCH.:** 3 piano concertos (1947, 1953, 1972); 3 syms. (1950, 1951, 1969); *Concerto à tre* for Clarinet, Trumpet, Trombone, and Strings (1954); Concerto for Viola, Strings, and Percussion (1958; Geneva, July 3, 1959); Concerto for Violin, Cello, and Orch. (1967; Pittsburgh, Oct. 11, 1968); Violin Concerto (1979–80; Boston, Oct. 16, 1981); *Concerto a quattro* for Solo Woodwind and Chamber Orch. (1983); *Hudson Valley Suite* (1984); *Serenade for Trombone, Vibraphone, and Strings* (1984); *Symphonic Prelude* (1984); Cello Concerto (N.Y., May 7, 1988). **CHAMBER:** String Quartet (1947); *5 Miniatures* for Woodwinds (1948); Trio for Clarinet, Cello, and Piano (1964); *Profiles in Brass* for Brass (1974); *Annapolis Suite* for Harp and Brass Quintet (1982); Piano Trio (1985); *Kaaterskill Quartet* (1987); *Duo for Violin and Piano* (Washington, D.C., Nov. 18, 1988); piano pieces, including 2 sonatas (1949, 1965); many vocal works, including several cantatas on biblical subjects; songs.

Stark, Robert, eminent German clarinetist; b. Klingenthal, Sept. 19, 1847; d. Würzburg, Oct. 29, 1922. He studied at the Dresden Cons.; began his career as an orch. player at Chemnitz; from 1873 to 1881 played the clarinet in Wiesbaden; then was a prof. at the Hochschule für Musik in Würzburg. He publ. valuable and practical pieces for his instrument: 3 concertos; *Romanze* for Clarinet and Orch.; also a *Ballade* for Trombone and Orch.; *Quintett concertante* for Flute, Oboe, Clarinet, Horn, and Bassoon; *Serenade* for Oboe and Piano; instructive works: *Die Kunst der Transposition auf der Klarinette, Grosse theoretisch-praktische Klarinett-Schule*, in 2 parts, followed by part III, *Die hohe Schule des Klarinett-Spieles* (24 virtuoso studies).

Starker, János, renowned Hungarian-born American cellist and pedagogue; b. Budapest, July 5, 1924. He made his 1st public appearance when he was only 6 and at 7 studied cello with Adolf Cziffer at the Budapest Academy of Music; made his solo debut there at the age of 11. After graduating, he served as 1st cellist of the Budapest Opera orch. (1945–46), but decided to leave Hungary; he emigrated to the U.S. in 1948; became a naturalized citizen in 1954; held the positions of 1st cellist in the Dallas Sym. Orch. (1948–49), the Metropolitan Opera Orch. (1949–53), and the Chicago Sym. Orch. (1953–58); subsequently he embarked upon a solo career. In 1958 he was appointed a prof. of music at the Indiana Univ. School of Music in Bloomington, where he was named Distinguished Prof. of Music in 1965. As a soloist, he achieved renown in performances of Bach's unaccompanied-cello suites; also devoted much attention to modern music; promoted cello works of Kodály and gave 1st performances of works by Messiaen, Peter Mennin, Miklós Rozsa, and others. He publ. *An Organized Method of String Playing* (1961).

BIBL.: S. and S. Applebaum, *The Way they Play* (Vol. II, Neptune, N.J., 1973).

Starokadomsky, Mikhail, Russian composer; b. Brest-Litovsk, June 13, 1901; d. Moscow, April 24, 1954. He studied composition with Miaskovsky at the Moscow Cons., graduating in 1928. He remained in Moscow, where he became a prof.

of orchestration. His works follow the traditional line of Russian nationalism, but several of his early orch. scores are purely neo-Classical, and in this respect parallel the European developments.

WORKS: Opera, *Sot* (1933); operettas: *3 Encounters* (1942); *The Gay Rooster* (1944); *The Sun Flower* (1947); Concerto for Orch. (Paris ISCM Festival, June 22, 1937); Violin Concerto (Moscow, March 20, 1939); some chamber music; numerous songs for children, by which he is best known in Russia.

Starr, "Ringo" (real name, **Richard Starkey**), English rock 'n' roll drummer, member of the celebrated Liverpudlian group The Beatles; b. Liverpool, July 7, 1940 (delivered by forceps on account of his enormous puerperal bulk). His nickname, "Ringo," originated from his ostentatious habit of wearing several rings on each of his fingers. As an adolescent he performed menial jobs as a messenger boy for British railways, a barman on a boat, etc. A sickly boy, he spent several years in hospitals to cure an effusion on the lung, but he played drums in ward bands. He spontaneously evolved a rhythmic technique of an overwhelming animal vitality. In 1962 he joined The Beatles; his association with them continued until the dissolution of the group in 1970. His histrionic ability in handling the drums became the most striking visual feature in the beatlophonic ritual, contributing much to the mass frenzy that attended their shows wherever The Beatles went.

BIBL.: H. Davies, *The Beatles* (N.Y., 1968); N. Rorem, "The Beatles," *N.Y. Review of Books* (Jan. 18, 1968); E. Davies, "The Psychological Characteristics of Beatle Mania," *Journal of the History of Ideas* (April–June 1969); P. McCabe and R. Schonfeld, *Apple to the Core: The Unmaking of the Beatles* (N.Y., 1972); W. Mellers, *Twilight of the Gods: The Music of the Beatles* (N.Y., 1973); T. O'Grady, *The Beatles: A Musical Evolution* (Boston, 1983).

Staryk, Steven, Canadian violinist and teacher; b. Toronto, April 28, 1932. He studied at the Royal Cons. of Music of Toronto and with Mischakoff, Shumsky, and Schneider in N.Y. (1950–51). He played in the Toronto Sym. Orch. (1950–52) and the CBC Sym. Orch. (1952–56); in 1956 he took 2nd prizes in the Geneva Competition and the Carl Flesch Competition in London. He was concertmaster of the Royal Phil. in London (1956–60) and of the Concertgebouw Orch. in Amsterdam (1960–63), where he concurrently taught at the Amsterdam Cons.; then was concertmaster of the Chicago Sym. Orch. (1963–67) and a teacher at Northwestern Univ. and the American Cons. He was a prof. at the Oberlin College Cons. of Music (1968–72) and then at the Univ. of Washington in Seattle, before returning to Canada to teach at the Royal Cons. of Music of Toronto (from 1975) and the Univ. of Western Ontario (from 1976); also was concertmaster of the Toronto Sym. (1982–87) and a teacher at the Univ. of Washington in Seattle (from 1987).

Starzer, Josef, outstanding Austrian composer; b. 1726 or 1727; d. Vienna, April 22, 1787. By about 1752 he was a violinist in Vienna's Burgtheater orch., where he began his career as a composer of ballets. During the winter of 1758–59, he went to Russia, where he was active at the Imperial court in St. Petersburg; gave concerts and later was made Konzertmeister and then deputy Kapellmeister and composer of ballet music; served as maître de chapelle et directeur des concerts in 1763. Returning to Vienna about 1768, he composed several notable ballets; with Gassmann, he helped in 1771 to organize the Tonkünstler-Sozietät, for which he wrote a number of works. In 1779 he retired as a violinist and in 1785 gave up his duties with the society. Starzer was one of the leading Austrian composers of his day, winning distinction not only for his ballets but for his orch. and chamber music; his string quartets have been compared favorably with those of Haydn.

WORKS: BALLETS: *Diane et Endimione* (Vienna, c.1754); *Les Bergers* (Laxenburg, 1755); *Le Misantrope* (Vienna, 1756); *L'Amour venge* (Laxenburg, 1759); *L'Asile de le vertu* (St. Petersburg, 1759; in collaboration with H. Raupach); *Les Nouveaux Lauriers* (St. Petersburg, c.1759; in collaboration with

H. Raupach); *La Victoire de Flore su Borée* (St. Petersburg, 1760); *Siroe* (St. Petersburg, 1760); *Le Jugement de Paris* (St. Petersburg, 1761); *Prométhée et Pandore* (St. Petersburg, 1761); *Le Pauvre Yourka* (Moscow, 1762); *Le Seigneur de village moqué* (Moscow, 1762); *Le Vengeance du dieu de l'amour* (Moscow, 1762); *Apollon et Daphne, ou Le Retour d'Apolon au Parnasse* (St. Petersburg, 1763); *Apollon et Diane* (Vienna, 1763); *Le Retour de la déesse du printemps en Arcadie* (Moscow, 1763); *Les Fêtes hollandoises* (Vienna, 1763); *Pygmalion, ou La Statue animée* (St. Petersburg, 1763); *Acis et Galatée* (St. Petersburg, 1764); *Le Triomphe du printemps* (St. Petersburg, 1766); *Don Quichotte* (Vienna, c.1768); *Les Moissonneurs* (Vienna, 1770); *Agamemnon* (Vienna, 1771); *Atlante* (Vienna, 1771); *Les Cinque Soltanes* (Vienna, 1771); *Roger et Bradamante* (Vienna, 1771); *Adèle de Ponthieu* (Vienna, 1773); *El Cid* (Vienna, 1774); *Le Ninfe* (Vienna, 1774); *Les Horaces et les Curiaces* (Vienna, 1774); *Les Moissonneurs* (Vienna, 1775); *Montezuma* (Vienna, 1775); *Teseo in Creta* (Vienna, 1775); etc. **ORCH.:** 7 syms.; Violin Concerto (ed. in Diletto Musicale, LXXXII, Vienna, 1964); Concerto for 2 Orchs. (Vienna, March 23, 1779); Concerto for 2 Clarinets, 2 Horns, Bassoon, and Orch. (Vienna, March 14, 1780); *Die Belagerung Wiens*, overture (1799); 6 menuetti; Menuetto e contradanze. **CHAMBER:** About 25 string quartets (2 ed. in Denkmäler der Tonkunst in Österreich, XXXI, Jg. XV/2, 1908); 3 string trios; *Musica da camera*, 5 pieces for Chalumeaux or Flutes, 3 C-clarinos, 2 D-clarinos, and Timpani; *Le Matin et le soir*, octet for 2 Oboes, 2 English Horns or Clarinets, 2 Horns, and 2 Bassoons; etc. **VOCAL:** *La passione di Gesù Christo*, oratorio (Vienna, 1778); *Die drei Pächter*, singspiel; arrangements.

BIBL.: C. Pohl, *Denkschrift aus Anlass des hundertjährigen Bestehens der Tonkünstler-Sozietät* (Vienna, 1871); K. Riedel, "J. S.," *Wiener Instrumentalmusik vor und um 1750 I*, Denkmäler der Tonkunst in Österreich, XXXI, Jg. XIX/2 (1908); L. Braun, "Die Ballettkomposition von Joseph S.," *Studien zur Musikwissenschaft*, XIII (1926); E. Schmid, "Gluck-S.-Mozart," *Zeitschrift für Musikwissenschaft*, CIV (1937).

Stasny, Ludwig, popular Bohemian bandmaster and composer; b. Prague, Feb. 26, 1823; d. Frankfurt am Main, Oct. 30, 1883. He studied at the Prague Cons.; was bandmaster in the Austrian army; settled in Frankfurt in 1871. He produced 2 operas in Mainz: *Liane* (1851) and *Die beiden Grenadiere* (1879). He was noted for his popular dances (211 opus numbers) and for his potpourris from Wagner's music dramas.

Stasov, Vladimir (Vasilievich), famous Russian writer on music; b. St. Petersburg, Jan. 14, 1824; d. there, Oct. 23, 1906. He studied foreign languages and art; received instruction in music from Antoni Gerke and then continued his training with Adolf Henselt at the so-called Law School for civil servants (1836–43). From 1847 he was active as a book and music reviewer; after an Italian sojourn as secretary to Prince A.N. Demidov (1851–54), he became active at the St. Petersburg Public Library; was made personal assistant to the director in 1856 and then head of the art dept. in 1872. Stasov played a very important role in the emergence of the Russian national school, and was to the end of his days an ardent promoter of Russian music. It was Stasov who 1st launched the expression "Moguchaya Kuchka" ("mighty little company," in an article publ. on May 24, 1867, in a St. Petersburg newspaper); although he did not specifically name the so-called "Five" (Balakirev, Borodin, Cui, Mussorgsky, and Rimsky-Korsakov), these composers became identified with the cause championed by Stasov. When young Glazunov appeared on the scene, Stasov declared him a natural heir to the Five. His numerous writings, including biographies of Glinka, Mussorgsky, and others, have the value of authenticity. Those publ. between 1847 and 1886 were reissued in book form in honor of his 70th birthday (3 vols., St. Petersburg, 1894); a 4th vol. was brought out in 1905, containing essays written between 1886 and 1904; among them, "Russian Music during the Last 25 Years" and "Art in the 19th Century" are particularly important. His collected works, including articles on art and other subjects, were

publ. in Moscow in 1952. Some of his *Selected Essays on Music* were publ. in English (London, 1968).

BIBL.: V. Komarova (his niece), *V.V. S.* (2 vols., Leningrad, 1927); A. Ogolovets, *V.V. S.: On the 50th Anniversary of his Death* (Moscow, 1956); A. Lebedev and A. Solodovnikov, *V. S.* (Moscow, 1966); Y. Olkhovsky, *V. S. and Russian National Culture* (Ann Arbor, 1983).

Statkowski, Roman, Polish composer and pedagogue; b. Szczpiorna, Jan. 5, 1860; d. Warsaw, Nov. 12, 1925. He studied law at the Univ. of Warsaw, graduating in 1886; received instruction in music from Zeleński at the Warsaw Music Inst. and then was a pupil of Soloviev (composition) and Rimsky-Korsakov (orchestration) at the St. Petersburg Cons., graduating in 1890. After teaching in Kiev, he became a prof. at the Warsaw Cons. in 1904; was founder-ed. of the *Kwartalnik muzyczny* (from 1911). His style represents a blend of German and Russian influences. He wrote the operas *Filenis* (1897; Warsaw, Sept. 14, 1904; won 1st prize at the London International Opera Contest, 1903) and *Maria* (1903–4; Warsaw, March 1, 1906); also *Polonaise* for Orch. (1900); *Symphonic Fantasy* (1900); 5 string quartets; many solo piano works.

BIBL.: J. Reiss, *S.-Melcer-Mylnarski-Stojowski* (Warsaw, 1949).

Staudigl (I), Joseph, distinguished Austrian bass, father of **Joseph Staudigl (II);** b. Wöllersdorf, April 14, 1807; d. Michaelbeueangrund, near Vienna, March 28, 1861. He was admitted in 1816 to the Wiener Neustadt Gymnasium, where he made his mark as a boy soprano; after studying at the Krems philosophical college (1823–25), he entered the Melk monastery to commence his novitiate; then went to Vienna as a medical student in 1827, but lack of funds soon compelled him to join the chorus of the Kärnthnertortheater; he subsequently sang minor roles before assuming a position as its principal bass; was a member of the Theater an der Wien (1845–48) and the Court Opera (1848–54); appeared at London's Drury Lane (1841), Covent Garden (1842), and Her Majesty's Theatre (1847). He also had a notable career as an oratorio and concert singer, both at home and abroad; sang Elijah in the premiere of Mendelssohn's oratorio (1846). He died insane.

Staudigl (II), Joseph, Austrian baritone, son of **Joseph Staudigl (I);** b. Vienna, March 18, 1850; d. Karlsruhe, April 1916. He studied with Rokitansky at the Vienna Cons.; sang at the Karlsruhe Court Theater (1875–83); made his Metropolitan Opera debut in N.Y. as Fernando in *Fidelio* on Nov. 19, 1884; there he also sang Pogner in the U.S. premiere of *Die Meistersinger von Nürnberg* (Jan. 4, 1886); appeared as Don Giovanni in Salzburg in 1886, then sang in opera and oratorio in Germany. In 1885 he married the Austrian contralto **Gisela** (née **Koppmayer) Staudigl** (b. Vienna, date unknown; d. 1929); she studied with Marchesi in Vienna, where she made her debut in a concert in 1879; sang opera in Hamburg (1882–83) and Karlsruhe (1883–84) and at Bayreuth (1886–92), where she appeared as Brangäne and Magdalene; also toured as Adriano and the Queen of Sheba with the Metropolitan Opera of N.Y. in 1886; later made another U.S. tour with the Damrosch-Ellis Opera Co. in 1897–98.

Stavenhagen, Bernhard, German pianist, conductor, and composer; b. Greiz, Nov. 24, 1862; d. Geneva, Dec. 25, 1914. He was one of the last pupils of Liszt, with whom he studied in 1885–86. After a tour as a pianist in Europe and the U.S., he became court conductor at Weimar in 1895; in 1898 he obtained a similar position in Munich. In 1907 he went to Geneva, where he conducted the municipal orch. He wrote 2 piano concertos and other piano works.

Stebbins, George C(oles), noted American evangelistic singer, composer, and editor; b. East Carlton, N.Y., Feb. 26, 1846; d. Catskill, N.Y., Oct. 6, 1945. He received instruction in singing schools and learned to play the piano in his youth; then studied singing in Rochester, N.Y., where he sang in a church choir. In 1870 he joined the Lyon & Healy Co. in Chicago, where he also was music director in several Baptist churches; then held similar posts in Boston (1874–76). In 1876 he began appearing as an evangelistic singer with Dwight L. Moody, and became active as a composer of gospel songs and hymns. With Sankey and McGranahan, he ed. vols. 3 to 6 of the *Gospel Hymns and Sacred Songs* series (1878–91; reprinted as *Gospel Hymns nos. 1–6 Complete*, 1894). Among his best-known hymns are *Jesus Is Tenderly Calling Today* (1883), *Take Time to Be Holy* (1890), and *Have Thine Own Way, Lord* (1907).

Steber, Eleanor, eminent American soprano; b. Wheeling, W.Va., July 17, 1914; d. Langhorne, Pa., Oct. 3, 1990. She studied singing with her mother; then with William Whitney at the New England Cons. of Music in Boston (Mus.B., 1938) and with Paul Althouse in N.Y. She won the Metropolitan Opera Auditions of the Air in 1940; made her debut with the Metropolitan Opera as Sophie in *Der Rosenkavalier* on Dec. 7, 1940, and remained with the company until 1962; altogether she appeared 286 times in N.Y. and 118 times on tour; she sang 28 leading roles in an extremely large repertoire. She performed brilliantly in the roles of Donna Anna in *Don Giovanni*, Pamina in *Die Zauberflöte*, and the Countess in *Le nozze di Figaro*, as well as in other Mozart operas; her other roles were Violetta, Desdemona, Marguerite, Manon, Mimi, and Tosca; in Wagner's operas she sang Eva in *Die Meistersinger von Nürnberg* and Elsa in *Lohengrin*; she also performed the challenging part of Marie in Berg's opera *Wozzeck*. She sang the title role in the premiere of Samuel Barber's opera *Vanessa* on Jan. 15, 1958. After several years of absence from the Metropolitan Opera, she took part in the final gala performance in the old opera building on April 16, 1966. Her European engagements included appearances at Edinburgh (1947), Vienna (1953), and the Bayreuth Festival (1953). After partial retirement in 1962, she was head of the voice dept. at the Cleveland Inst. of Music (1963–72); taught at the Juilliard School in N.Y. and at the New England Cons. of Music (both from 1971); also at the American Inst. of Music Studies in Graz (1978–80; 1988). She established the Eleanor Steber Music Foundation in 1975 to assist young professional singers. With R. Beatie, she publ. the study *Mozart Operatic Arias* (N.Y., 1988).

Stecker, Karel, Czech pedagogue, writer on music, and composer; b. Kosmanos, near Mladá Boleslav, Jan. 22, 1861; d. Mladá Boleslav, March 13, 1918. He studied law and esthetics at the Univ. of Prague; then entered the Prague Organ School, joining its faculty in 1885; when it became a part of the Prague Cons. in 1890, he was made a prof. He composed mostly sacred music and organ pieces; also publ. a history of music in the Czech language (2 vols., 1892, 1902), a treatise on musical form (1905), and an interesting essay on nonthematic improvisation (1903).

BIBL.: C. Sychra, *K. S.* (Prague, 1948).

Štědroň, Bohumír, eminent Czech musicologist, brother of **Vladimír** and uncle of **Miloš Štědroň;** b. Vyškov, Oct. 30, 1905; d. Brno, Nov. 24, 1982. He studied theory with Josef Blatný (1925–28) and piano with Vilém Kurz (1926–28); also took courses in history and geography at the Univ. of Brno (graduated, 1929), where he attended Helfert's lectures in musicology; after further training in Italy (1931), he returned to the Univ. of Brno to take his Ph.D. in 1934 with the dissertation *Sólové chrámové kantáty G. B. Bassaniho* (G.B. Bassani's Solo Church Cantatas) and to complete his Habilitation in 1945 with his *Chrámová hudba v Brně v XVIII. století* (Church Music in Brno in the XVIIIth Century). He taught music education at a teacher-training college (1931–39), and also was an assistant to Helfert (1932–38); then taught music history at the Brno Cons. (1939–45; 1950–52); in 1945 became a teacher at the Univ. of Brno, where he subsequently was made assistant lecturer in 1950, lecturer in 1955, and prof. in 1963. He was an authority on the life and music of Janáček. In addition to his important books, he contributed many articles to scholarly journals.

WRITINGS: *Leoš Janáček a Luhačovice* (Leoš Janáček and

Luhačovice; Luhačovice, 1939); *Leoš Janáček ve vzpomínkách a dopisech* (Prague, 1945; rev. German tr., 1955; rev. Eng. tr., 1955, as *Leoš Janáček: Letters and Reminiscences*); *Josef Bohuslav Foerster a Moravia* (Brno, 1947); ed. with G. Černušák and Z. Nováček, *Československý hudební slovník osob a institucí* (Czechoslovak Music Dictionary of Places and Institutions; Prague, 1963–65); *Vitežlav Novák v obrazech* (Vitežlav Novák in Pictures; Prague, 1967); *Zur Genesis von Leoš Janáček's Oper Jenůfa* (Brno, 1968; 2nd ed., rev., 1971); *Leoš Janáček: K jeho lidskému a uměleckému profilu* (Leoš Janáček: Personal and Artistic Profile; Prague, 1976).

BIBL.: *Sborník prací filosofické fakulty brněnské univerzitě* (1967; dedicated to S. on his 60th birthday).

Štědroň, Miloš, significant Czech composer and musicologist, nephew of **Bohumír** and **Vladimír Štědroň;** b. Brno, Feb. 9, 1942. He studied musicology with Racel, Vysloužil, and his uncle Bohumír at the Univ. of Brno (Ph.D., 1967); also studied composition at the Janáček Academy of Music in Brno (1965–70). After working in the music dept. of Brno's Moravian Museum (1963–72), he taught theory at the Univ. of Brno (from 1972). Among his books is a monograph on Monteverdi (Prague, 1985). He contributed important articles to various journals, many of which deal with the music of Janáček. His own works range from traditional scores to pieces utilizing jazz and pop elements or tape.

WORKS: STAGE: OPERAS: *Aparát* (The Apparatus), chamber opera after Kafka's *In the Penal Colony* (1967); *Kychyňské starosti* (1977); *Josef Fouché-Chameleon* (1984). BALLETS: *Justina* (1969); *Ballet macabre* (1986). ORCH.: *Moto balladico* (1968); *Quiet Platform* (1969); Concerto for Double Bass and Strings (1971); *To the Memory of Gershwin* for Piano and Jazz Orch. (1971); *Diagram* for Piano and Jazz Orch. (1971); *Music for Ballet* for Chamber Orch. (1972); *Kolo* (Wheel), sym. in memory of Yugoslav partisans of World War II (1971–72); Cello Concerto (1975); *Sette Villanelle* for Cello and Strings (1981); *Musica concertante* for Bassoon and Strings (1986); *Lammento* for Viola and Orch. (1987). CHAMBER: *Via crucis* for Flute, Bass Clarinet, Piano, Harpsichord, and Percussion (1964); *Dyptich* for Bass Clarinet, Piano, Strings, and Percussion (1967); *Lai* for Bass Clarinet and Timpani (1967); *Utis II* for Bass Clarinet and Tape (1967); *Util II* for Bass Clarinet, Piano, and Tape (1968); *O, Sancta Caecilia* for Double Bass and Tape (1968); *Musica ficta* for Wind Quintet (1968); *Duplum* for Bass Clarinet and Double Bass (1968); *Free Landino Jazz* for Bass Clarinet and Piano (1968); *Affeti graziosi* for Violin and Piano (1969); *Saluti musicali* for Bass Clarinet and Piano (1969); *4 Together (Everyman for Himself)* for Bass Clarinet, Piano, and Jazz Combo (1969); String Quartet (1970); *Seikilos z Moravy* (Seikilos from Moravia) for Bass Clarinet and Piano (1978; in collaboration with A. Parsch); *Old and New Renaissance Poems* for Bass Clarinet, Piano, Strings, and Drums (1980); *Trium vocum* for Flute, Cello, and Drums (1984); *Danze, Canti e lamenti* for String Quartet (1986); solo pieces; piano works. VOCAL: *Agrafon* for Madrigal Choir, Renaissance Instruments, and Jazz Ensemble (1968); *Mourning Ceremony*, cantata for Chorus, Trumpet, Oboe, and Church Bell (Czech Radio, Feb. 21, 1969); Vocal Sym. for Soprano, Bass-baritone, and Orch. (1969); *Verba*, cantata for Chorus and 2 Trumpets (1969); *Jazz trium vocum*, free jazz for Chorus and Jazz Ensemble (1972); *Dolorosa gioia*, madrigal-cantata (1975); *Attendite, populi*, cantata for Chorus and Drums (1982); *Conversations, Tunes, Desires* for Tenor, Lute, and Viola da Gamba (1986); *Ommaggio a Gesualdo: Death of Dobrovský*, cantata-oratorio for 2 Solo Voices, Chorus, and Orch. (1988).

Štědroň, Vladimír, Czech composer, brother of **Bohumír** and uncle of **Miloš Štědroň;** b. Vyškov, March 30, 1900; d. Brno, Dec. 12, 1982. He studied law in Prague; simultaneously took lessons in composition with Foerster, Novák, and Suk at the Prague Cons. (1919–23); then studied musicology with Helfert at the Univ. of Brno. He served for many years as a judge, but found time to compose; later was in Prague as a teacher at the Academy of Music, the Univ., and the Cons.

(1951–60). His music is couched in an unassuming style inspired by native folk songs.

WORKS: *Fidlovačka*, overture (1916); *Fantastic Scherzo* for Orch. (1920); 2 string quartets (1920, 1940–45); *Variation Fantasy* for String Quartet (1923); *Illusions*, symphonic poem (1936); *Little Domestic Suite* for 2 Violins and Viola (1937); *Janka*, polka for Orch. (1962); *Moto balladico* for Orch. (1967); *Monologe* for Flute (1967); *Monologe* for Horn (1969).

Steel, (Charles) Christopher, English composer; b. London, Jan. 15, 1939. He studied composition with John Gardner at the Royal Academy of Music in London (1957–61) and with Harald Genzmer at the Staatliche Hochschule für Musik in Munich (1961–62); taught at Cheltenham College Junior School (1963–66); was assistant director (1966–68) and director (1968–81) of music at Bradfield College, also serving as an instructor; taught at North Hennepin Community College in Brooklyn Park, Minn. (1977–78); accepted private students from 1982.

WORKS: OPERAS: *The Rescue*, chamber opera (1974); *The Selfish Giant* for Baritone and Children (Westclife-on-Sea, July 1981); *The Angry River*, chamber opera for 7 Soloists, Chorus, and Orch. (Chelmsford Festival, May 1989). **ORCH.:** 7 syms., including No. 3, *A Shakespeare Symphony* for Baritone, Chorus, and Orch. (1967), No. 4 (Manchester, Nov. 2, 1983), No. 5, *Romantic Symphony* (Manchester, Oct. 21, 1986), and No. 6, *Sinfonia sacra* for Soprano, Baritone, Chorus, and Orch. (Sheffield, Nov. 22, 1985); Concerto for Organ and Chamber Orch. (1967); Concerto for String Quartet and Orch. (1968); *Overture Island* (1968); *Odyssey*, suite for Concert Brass Band (1973); *6 Turner Paintings*, suite (1974); *Apollo and Dionysus* (1983); *The City of God and the Garden of Earthly Delights* (Reading, April 12, 1986). **VOCAL:** Cantatas: *Gethsemane* (1964); *Mary Magdalene* (1967); *Paradise Lost* (1972); *Jerusalem* (1972); also *Mass* (1968); *Piping Down the Valleys Wild*, song cycle for Baritone and Piano (1971); *Passion and Resurrection According to St. Mark* for Soloists, Chorus, and Chamber Orch. (1978); *The Path of Creation* for Baritone, Oboe, Soloists, Chorus, and Orch. (1984); anthems; also chamber music, piano pieces, and organ works.

Stefan (actually, **Stefan-Grünfeldt**), **Paul,** Austrian writer on music; b. Brünn, Nov. 25, 1879; d. N.Y., Nov. 12, 1943. He settled in Vienna, where he studied law (doctorate, 1904), philosophy, and art history at the Univ.; also received instruction in theory with Hermann Grädener and Schoenberg. He was employed as a municipal functionary, and at the same time became associated with the modern group of musicians in Vienna; ed. the progressive music periodical *Musikblätter des Anbruch* (1921–38), and was a founder of the Ansorge-Verein (1903) and the ISCM (1922). After the Anschluss in 1938, he went to Switzerland, and later to Lisbon, eventually emigrating to the U.S. in 1941.

WRITINGS: *Gustav Mahler* (Munich, 1910; 7th ed., 1921; in Eng., N.Y., 1913); *Das neue Haus: ein Halbjahrhundert Weiner Opernspiel* (Vienna, 1919); *Die Feindschaft gegen Wagner* (Regensburg, 1919); *Neue Musik und Wien* (Leipzig, 1921); *Arnold Schönberg: Wandlung, Legende, Erscheinung, Bedeutung* (Vienna, 1924); *Franz Schubert* (Berlin, 1928); *Geschichte der Wiener Oper* (Vienna, 1932); *Arturo Toscanini* (Vienna, 1936; in Eng., N.Y., 1936; in Italian, Milan, 1937); *Bruno Walter* (Vienna, 1936); *Georges Bizet* (Zürich, 1952).

Stefani, Jan, significant Polish composer of Bohemian descent, father of **Józef Stefani**; b. Prague, 1746; d. Warsaw, Feb. 24, 1829. He studied at Prague's Benedictine school; after an Italian sojourn, he went to Vienna about 1765 as a violinist in Count G. Kinski's orch.; in 1779 he settled in Warsaw as a violinist and conductor in King Stanislaw August Poniatowski's Court Orch.; also was Kapellmeister at the Cathedral and a conductor at the National Theater; later was a violinist in its orch. (1799–1811). Stefani's importance rests upon his notable contribution to Polish opera; his masterpiece is *Cud mniemany czyl; Krakowiacy i Górale* (The Supposed Mira-

cle or Krakovians and Highlanders; Warsaw, March 1, 1794). He also was a fine composer of polonaises.

WORKS: STAGE (all 1st perf. in Warsaw): **OPERAS:** *Król w kraju rozkoszy* (The King of Cockaigne; Feb. 3, 1787); *Cud mniemany czyli Krakowiacy i Górale* (The Supposed Miracle or Krakovians and Highlanders; March 1, 1794); *Wdięczni poddani czyli Wesele wiejskie* (Thankful Serfs or The Country Wedding; July 24, 1796; also known as *Przjazd pana czyli Szczęśliwi wieśniacy* [The Arrival of the Lord or Happy Country Folk]); *Drzewo zaczarowane* (The Magic Tree; 1796); *Frozyna czyli Siedem razy jedna* (Frozine or 7 Times Dressed Up; Feb. 21, 1806); *Rotmistrz Górecki czyli Oswobodzenie* (Captain Górecki or The Liberation; April 3, 1807); *Polka czyli Oblężnie* (The Polish Woman or The Siege of Trembowla; May 22, 1807); *Stary myśliwy* (The Old Huntsman; Jan. 31, 1808); *Papirius czyli Ciekawość dawnych kobiet* (Papyrus or The Curiosity of Women in Ancient Times; May 15, 1808). **BALLET:** *Miłość każdemu wiekowi przstoi* (Love Becomes Every Age; Nov. 4, 1785); also a cantata, *Niechaj wiekom wiek podawa* (May This Age Survive in History; Nov. 25, 1791); some 100 polonaises for Orch.; sacred music; songs.

Stefani, Józef, Polish composer and conductor, son of **Jan Stefani**; b. Warsaw, April 16, 1800; d. there, March 19, 1867. He was a pupil of his father and of Elsner in Warsaw (1821–24); conducted ballet at the Warsaw Opera, and wrote a number of light operas, which enjoyed a modicum of success during his lifetime: *Dawne czasy* (April 26, 1826); *Lekcja botaniki* (March 15, 1829); *Figle panien* (Aug. 6, 1832); *Talizman* (Dec. 7, 1849); *Żyd wieczny tulacz* (Jan. 1, 1850); *Piorun* (May 21, 1856); *Trwoga wieczorna* (posthumous, July 25, 1872). He also wrote church music, which was often performed in religious services in Poland. Many of his works are lost.

Stefánsson, Fjölnir, Icelandic composer; b. Reykjavik, Oct. 9, 1930. He studied cello and took theory lessons with Jón Thórarinsson at the Reykjavik Music School, graduating in 1954; then went to England, where he studied composition with Mátyás Seiber (1954–58). Returning to Iceland, he taught at his alma mater (1958–68); later was headmaster of the Kópavogur School of Music. He composed a Trio for Flute, Clarinet, and Bassoon (1951); Violin Sonata (1954); Duo for Oboe and Clarinet (1974); *Koplon* for Orch. (1979); Sextet for Flute, Clarinet, Bassoon, Horn, Violin, and Cello (1983); numerous arrangements of Icelandic folk songs for chorus.

Steffan, Joseph Anton (Josef Antonín Štepán), important Czech composer, harpsichordist, and teacher; b. Kopidlno, Bohemia (baptized), March 14, 1726; d. Vienna, April 12, 1797. His father was organist and schoolmaster in Kopidlno, and Joseph Anton most likely began his musical training under his father's tutelage; when the Prussian army invaded Bohemia in 1741, he fled to Vienna, where he found a patron in Count František Jindřich Šlik, lord of the Kopidlno estate; received instruction in violin from Hammel, his patron's Kapellmeister, whom he later succeeded, and in harpsichord and composition from G.C. Wagenseil, the court composer. He soon established himself as an outstanding harpsichord virtuoso, teacher, and composer; was made Klaviermeister to the princesses Maria Carolina (later Queen of Naples) and Maria Antonia (later Queen of France) in 1766, remaining active at the court until 1775. In subsequent years he taught privately and composed; he died in obscurity. Steffan was a major figure in the development of the Classical style. His keyboard works, including concertos and sonatas, reveal him as a worthy compatriot of Haydn and Mozart. He was the 1st to publ. lieder collections in Vienna.

WORKS: ORCH.: 10 sinfonie, 4 of which are lost; 6 concertos for Harpsichord or Harp, op. 10 (Paris, c.1773; nos. 3–6 lost); 37 concertos for Harpsichord or Piano, 1 of which is lost; 2 concertos for 2 Harpsichords, 1 of which was for long attributed to Haydn. **CHAMBER:** Concertino for Harpsichord, Flute, Violin, and Cello; Concertino for Harpsichord, Flute, Violin, Bass, and 2 Horns; 7 trios for Violin, Cello, and Harpsichord or Piano; Sonata for Violin and Piano; Variations for

Violin and Piano; several pieces for Wind Instruments. **KEY-BOARD:** *6 divertimenti* (Vienna, 1756; ed. in Musica Antiqua Bohemica, LXIV, 1964); *6 sonate*, op. 2 (Vienna, c.1759–60); *40 preludi per diversi tuoni* (Vienna, 1762); *Parte 1 a del op. 3 continente 3 sonate* (Vienna, 1763); *Parte 2a . . . continente 3 sonate* (Vienna, 1771); *Parte 3a* (lost) (Parts 1–2 ed. in Musica Antiqua Bohemica, LXIV [1964]); *Sonata I* (Vienna, 1771), *II* (Vienna, c.1771), and *III* (Vienna, 1776) (all ed. in Musica Antiqua Bohemica, LXIV [1964]); *6 sonates choisies* for Harpsichord or Piano, *par . . . Steffann et Rutini* (Paris, 1773–74); *Parte 2a continente 90 cadenze, fermade, e capricci* for Harpsichord or Piano (Vienna, 1783); *25 variationi* for Piano (Vienna, 1785–92); also various other keyboard works, including 21 divertimentos and sonatas (8 of the latter ed. in Musica Antiqua Bohemica, LXX, 1968); several single-movement sonatas; minuets; 5 sets of variations; etc. **SACRED:** *Stabat mater* for Voice and Piano (Prague and Vienna, 1782); 2 masses; 2 Christmas pastorellas (1 in collaboration with J.G. Zechner); various hymns. **SECULAR VOCAL:** *Sammlung [24] deutscher Lieder*, I (Vienna, 1778); *Sammlung [25] deutscher Lieder*, II (Vienna, 1779); *Gesang bei dem Beschlusse der . . . Prüfung der 31 Unteroffiziere und Gemeinen* (Vienna, 1780); *Sammlung [24] deutscher Lieder*, IV (Vienna, 1782); also a singspiel, *Der Doktor Daunderlaun*.

BIBL.: W. Newman, *The Sonata in the Classic Era* (Chapel Hill, 1963; 3rd ed., rev., 1983); D. Šetková, *Klavírní dílo Josefa Antonína Štěpána* (The Keyboard Works of J.A. S.; Prague, 1965); H. Picton, *The Life and Works of J.A. S. (1726–1797)* (2 vols., N.Y. and London, 1989).

Steffani, Agostino, eminent Italian composer, churchman, and diplomat; b. Castelfranco, near Venice, July 25, 1654; d. Frankfurt am Main, Feb. 12, 1728. He most likely received his early musical training in Padua, where he was probably a choirboy; in 1667 Elector Ferdinand Maria of Bavaria took him to his court in Munich, where Steffani became a ward of Count von Tattenbach; he sang in *Le pretensioni del sole* (1667) by J.K. Kerll, the court Kapellmeister, who gave him organ lessons (1668–71); then studied composition with Ercole Bernabei, maestro di capella at St. Peter's in Rome (1672–74). In 1674 he returned to Munich with Bernabei, who assumed the post of Kapellmeister; Steffani appears to have taken on the duties of court and chamber organist in 1674, although the court records only list him as such from 1678. In 1680 he became a priest. With the accession of the Elector Maximilian II Emanuel in 1680, he found great favor at the court. In 1681 the position of director of the court chamber music was especially created for him; that same year his 1st opera, *Marco Aurelio*, to a libretto by his brother Ventura Terzago, was premiered; it was also about this time that he became active as a diplomat for the court. He was made Abbot of Lepsingen in 1683. In 1688 he was called to Hannover by Duke Ernst August to serve as court Kapellmeister; he was in charge of the 1st permanent Italian opera company there (1689–97); he subsequently was mainly active as a diplomat for the Hannoverian court. In 1691 he was sent to Vienna to assist in creating Hannover as the 9th electorate. In 1693 he was made envoy extraordinary to the Bavarian court in Brussels, where he worked diligently to persuade the Elector Maximilian to support the Emperor rather than Louis XIV as the War of the Spanish Succession loomed in the background; however, his mission failed, and he returned to Hannover in 1702. In 1703 he entered the service of Johann Wilhelm, Palatine Elector, in Düsseldorf; since he had virtually given up composing, a number of his works were circulated from 1709 under the name of one of his copyists, Gregorio Piva. He began his duties in Düsseldorf in 1703 as privy councillor and president of the Spiritual Council for the Palatinate and the duchies of Jülich and Berg; later that year he was named general president of the Palatine government; also was the 1st rector magnificus (1703–5) and then a curator (from 1705) of the Univ. of Heidelberg. In 1706 he was elected Bishop of Spiga in *partibus infedelium* (Asia Minor). In 1708–9 he was in Rome to

mediate the war between the Pope and the Emperor, which resulted in the Pope making him a Domestic Prelate and Assistant to the Throne. In 1709 he was appointed Apostolic Vicar in northern Germany, and later that year settled in Hannover. He continued to be active at the court there as well, having served as minister and Grand Almoner to the Elector Johann Wilhelm from 1706. His ecclesiastical duties were particularly onerous, but he carried them out faithfully until retiring to Padua in 1722. However, at the insistence of Rome, he returned to Hannover in 1725. In 1727 he received the honor of being elected president of the Academy of Vocal Music in London, the forerunner of the Academy of Ancient Music. This honor renewed his interest in composing, but ill health soon intervened. He died while on his way to Italy. Steffani was an important composer of operas, notably influential in the development of the genre in northern Germany. All the same, his most significant achievement was as a composer of outstanding chamber duets for 2 Voices and Continuo, which had a major impact on Handel.

WORKS: DRAMATIC (all operas unless otherwise given): *Marco Aurelio* (Munich, 1691); Serenata for the wedding of Countess von Preysing (Munich, 1682); *Solone* (Munich, 1685); *Audacia e rispetto* (Munich, 1685); *Servio Tullio* (Munich, 1686); *Alarico il Baltha, cioè L'audace rè de' gothi* (Munich, 1687); *Niobe, regina di Tebe* (Munich, 1688); *Henrico Leone* (Hannover, 1689; German version by G. Schürmann, Braunschweig, 1716); *La lotta d'Hercole con Acheloo*, divertimento drammatico (Hannover, 1689); *La superbia d'Alessandro* (Hannover, 1690); *Orlando generoso* (Hannover, 1691); *Le Rivali concordi* (Hannover, 1692); *La libertà contenta* (Hannover, 1693); *Baccanali*, favola pastorale (Hannover, 1695); *I trionfi del fato* or *Le glorie d'Enea* (Hannover, 1695); *Arminio*, pasticcio (Düsseldorf, 1707); *Amor vien del destino* (Düsseldorf, 1709); *Il Tassilone* (Düsseldorf, 1709). **SACRED VOCAL:** *Psalmodia vespertina* for 8 Voices and Organ (Rome, 1674); *Sacer Ianus quadrifons* for 3 Voices and Basso Continuo (Munich, 1685); other works, including a *Stabat mater* for 6 Voices, Strings, and Basso Continuo (1727). **SECULAR VOCAL:** About 75 chamber duets for 2 Voices and Basso Continuo; many cantatas; arias; etc. **INSTRUMENTAL:** *Sonata da camera* for 2 Violins, Viola, and Basso Continuo (Amsterdam, c.1705).

BIBL.: (J. Hawkins), *Memoirs of the Life of A. S.* (London, c.1749–52); F. Woker, *Aus den Papieren des kurpfälzischen Ministers A. S., Bischofs von Spiga, spätern apostolischen Vicars von Norddeutschland . . . 1703–1709: Erste Vereinsschrift der Görresgesellschaft* (Cologne, 1885); idem, *A. S., Bischof von Spiga, i.p.i., apostolischer Vikar von Norddeutschland 1709–28: Dritte Vereinsschrift der Görresgesellschaft* (Cologne, 1886); A. Neisser, *Servio Tullio: Eine Oper aus dem Jahr 1685 von A. S.* (Leipzig, 1902); W. Baxter, Jr., *A. S.: A Study of the Man and His Work* (diss., Eastman School of Music, 1957); G. Croll, *A. S. (1654–1728): Studien zur Biographie, Bibliographie der Opern und Turnierspiele* (diss., Univ. of Münster, 1960); C. Timms, *The Chamber Duets of A. S. (1654–1728): With Transcriptions and Catalogue* (diss., Univ. of London, 1976); idem, "S. and the Academy of Ancient Music," *Musical Times*, CXIX (1978); idem, "Gregorio Piva and S.'s Principal Copyist," *Source Materials and the Interpretation of Music: A Memorial Volume to Thurston Dart* (London, 1981).

Steffek, Hanny, Austrian soprano; b. Biala, Galicia, Dec. 12, 1927. She studied at the Vienna Academy of Music and at the Salzburg Mozarteum; made her operatic debut in Wiesbaden in 1951; then sang in Graz, Frankfurt, and Munich; made guest appearances with the Vienna State Opera, the Salzburg Festival, and Covent Garden in London, etc. A fine interpreter of roles in Mozart's operas, she also excelled in Viennese operetta.

Steffen, Wolfgang, German composer; b. Neuhaldensleben, April 28, 1923. He studied at the Berlin Cons. (1946–49) and with Tiessen at the Hochschule für Musik there (1949–53); after graduation, he devoted himself principally to the promotion of new music. He was active as a conductor (1947–59);

was an honorary and guest prof. at the Berlin Staatliche Hochschule der Kunst (from 1974). In 1978 he won the Australian composition prize and in 1979 the Johann Wenzel Stamitz Prize.

WORKS: ORCH.: *Serenade* for Flute and String Orch. "im alten Stil" (1948); Sinfonietta for String Orch. (1949); *Tänzerische Impression I* for Piano and Orch. (1950) and *II* for Piano, Percussion, and Orch. (1970); *Intrada seria* (1953); *Méditations de la nuit* (1954); *Aus dem Lebensbuch eines Tänzers* (1954); Piano Concerto (1955); Violin Concerto (1966); *Polychromie* for Piano and 10 Instruments (1970; also for Piano and Orch., 1971); *Klangsegmente* for Cymbal, Harp, Harpsichord, and Orch. (1973–74); *Sinfonia da camera* (1976); *Chamber Concerto* (1978); Concerto for 6 Flutes and Orch. (1979–83); Concertino for Piano and 9 Instruments or Chamber Orch. (1984). **VOCAL:** *Nachtwachen* for Chorus, Flute, Oboe, Clarinet, and String Quintet (1954); *Hermann-Hesse-Zyklus* for Chorus, Clarinet, Viola, and Piano (1955); *Botschaft*, oratorio (1975–76); *Augenblicke* for Chorus (1986); *Kantate nach Gedichten von Gertrud Kolmar* for Soprano, Chorus, and 6 Instruments (1987); songs. **CHAMBER:** Trio for Oboe, Flute, and Bassoon (1947); *Theme with 8 Variations* for String Quartet (1948); Trio for Clarinet, Cello, and Piano (1959); *Diagram* for Viola or Cello and Piano (1965); Wind Quintet (1966); *Jeu* for Violin and Piano (1967); Trio for Flute, Cello, and Piano (1970); *Triplum 72* for Flute, Piano, and Percussion (1972); *Tetraphonie* for Flute Ensemble (1974); *Trilogie 75* for Bandoneon, Flute, and Percussion (1975); *Music* for Piano and 7 Players (1975); *Meditation* for Violin (1981); Duo for Cello and Accordion (1982); *Piece* for Clarinet (1983); String Trio (1983). **PIANO:** *Fantasy* (1947); Sonata (1955); *Reihenproportionen* (1961); *Notturno* for 4-hands (1968); *Les Spirales* (1969); *Introversion* (1982); *Music* (1985).

Steggall, Charles, English organist and composer; b. London, June 3, 1826; d. there, June 7, 1905. He was a pupil of Sterndale Bennett at the Royal Academy of Music in London, where he subsequently was a prof. (1851–1903). He wrote anthems and other religious music; ed. *Church Psalmody* (1848), *Hymns Ancient and Modern* (1889), etc. His son **Reginald Steggall** (b. London, April 17, 1867; d. there, Nov. 16, 1938) was also a pupil at the Royal Academy of Music, where he taught organ from 1895. He wrote a number of organ pieces; a Mass; a Sym.; orch. variations and overtures.

Steglich, Rudolf, eminent German musicologist; b. Rats-Damnitz, Feb. 18, 1886; d. Scheinfeld, July 8, 1976. He studied musicology with Hugo Riemann at the Univ. of Leipzig (Ph.D., 1911, with the diss. *Die Quaestiones in Musica und ihr mutmasslicher Verfasser Rudolf von St. Trond (1070–1138)*; publ. in Leipzig, 1911); completed his Habilitation in 1930 at the Univ. of Erlangen with his *Die elementare Dynamik des musikalischen Rhythmus* (publ. in Leipzig, 1930). He was in the German army during World War I; then was active as music critic of the Hannover *Anzeiger* (1919–29); in 1929 he was appointed to the faculty of the Univ. of Erlangen; retired in 1956. He was ed. of the *Händel-Jahrbuch* (1928–33) and of the *Archiv für Musikforschung* (1936–40); ed. the Hallische Händel-Ausgabe (with M. Schneider; from 1955), works by Bach's sons, early German song collections, etc.; was an authority on music of the 18th and 19th centuries.

WRITINGS: *J.S. Bach* (Potsdam, 1935); *Mozarts Flügel klingt wieder* (Nuremberg and Salzburg, 1937); *Robert Schumanns Kinderszenen* (Kassel, 1949); *Wege zu Bach* (Regensburg, 1949); *Über die 'kantable Art' der Musik J.S. Bachs* (Zürich, 1958); *Georg Friedrich Händel* (Wilhelmshaven, 1960); *Tanzrhythmus in der Musik J.S. Bachs* (Wolfenbüttel and Zürich, 1962).

Stegmann, Carl David, German tenor, harpsichordist, conductor, and composer; b. Staucha, near Meissen, 1751; d. Bonn, May 27, 1826. He studied with the Staucha organist, and then went to Dresden to study with J.F. Zillich; also attended the Kreuzschule there (1766–70) and received instruction from Homilius and H. Weisse. He was active at theaters in Breslau

(1772) and Königsberg (1773); after serving as court harpsichordist to the Bishop of Ermeland in Heilsberg (1774), he was active again in Königsberg and then in Gotha. From 1778 to 1783 he won success as a harpsichordist in Hamburg; then went to Bonn as a member of the Grossmann theater company and later was active at the Mainz Court Theater. Stegmann was a skillful composer of both vocal and instrumental works.

WORKS: STAGE: OPERAS: *Sultan Wampum oder Die Wünsche* (Mainz, March 7, 1791); *Der Roseninsel* (Hamburg, Nov. 24, 1806). **COMIC OPERAS:** *Der Kaufmann von Smirna* (Königsberg, 1773); *Die Rekruten auf dem Lande* (Danzig, 1775); *Das redende Gemahlde* (Königsberg, 1775). **SINGSPIELS:** *Heinrich der Löwe* (Frankfurt am Main, July 15, 1792); *Der Triumph der Liebe oder Das kühne Abentheuer* (Hamburg, Feb. 27, 1796). **OPERETTA:** *Der Deserteur* (Danzig, 1775). **BALLET:** *Die herrschaftliche Küche* (Danzig, 1775); incidental music. He also composed a Concerto for Piano, Oboe, Horn, and Orch., a Concerto for 2 Pianos, Violin, and Strings, other concertos, chamber music, piano pieces, and songs.

Stegmayer, Ferdinand, Austrian pianist, conductor, and composer, son of **Matthäus Stegmayer;** b. Vienna, Aug. 25, 1803; d. there, May 6, 1863. He studied with Seyfried; was chorus master in Linz and Vienna; in 1825 he was made music director of Berlin's Königstädtisches Theater; then was conductor of a German opera troupe in Paris (1829–30). After filling various engagements as a theater conductor in Leipzig, Bremen, and Prague, he settled in Vienna in 1848; was a teacher of singing at the Vienna Cons.; co-founded, with August Schmidt, the Vienna Singakademie (1858). He wrote church music, piano pieces, and songs.

Stegmayer, Matthäus, Austrian singer, poet, actor, and composer, father of **Ferdinand Stegmayer;** b. Vienna, April 29, 1771; d. there, May 10, 1820. He was a chorister in the Dominican church in Vienna; about 1792 he became a member of the Theater in der Josefstadt, where he assumed major roles and was active as a composer; in 1796 he joined Schikaneder's Freihaus-Theater. He joined the court theater in 1800, where he was active as chorus director and producer; in 1804 he became an actor, chorus master, and composer at the Theater an der Wien, for which he wrote the text to the enormously successful quodlibet *Rochus Pumpernickel* (Jan. 28, 1809) with music provided by Haibel and Seyfried; it was widely performed in German-speaking countries, and was followed by at least 3 sequels.

BIBL.: F. Blitzenetz, *M. S.* (diss., Univ. of Vienna, 1929).

Stehle, Adelina, outstanding Austrian soprano; b. Graz, 1860; d. Milan, Dec. 24, 1945. She studied in Milan; made her debut in Broni in 1881 as Amina; then sang in Bologna, Florence, and Venice; in 1890 she joined La Scala in Milan, where she created roles in *Falstaff* as Nanetta, in *Guglielmo Ratcliff* as Maria, and others; also sang in Berlin, Vienna, St. Petersburg, South America, and the U.S. After her marriage to the Italian tenor **Edoardo Garbin,** she appeared under the name of Stehle Garbin.

Stehle, J. Gustav Eduard, German organist, choirmaster, and composer; b. Steinhausen, Feb. 17, 1839; d. St. Gallen, Switzerland, June 21, 1915. He was organist in Rorschach (1869–74); in 1874 he settled in Switzerland as music director at the St. Gallen Cathedral. His Cathedral choir of 140 voices was regarded as one of the finest in Europe. For 25 years he also was ed. of the *Chorwächter*. He wrote a great deal of religious music: an oratorio, *Legende von der heiligen Cäcilia;* a cantata, *Lumen de Coelo* (to words by Pope Leo XIII); *Die Nonnen von Compiègne* for Double Chorus; *Frithjofs Heimkehr* for Solo, Male Quartet, and Chorus; *Die Heinzelmännchen,* humorous choral ballad for Double Chorus; a symphonic poem for Organ, *Saul;* 438 preludes in the church modes; etc.

BIBL.: A. Locher, *J.-G.-E. S.* (Strasbourg, 1928).

Stehle, Sophie, German soprano; b. Hohenzollern-Sigmaringen, May 15, 1838; d. Schloss Harterode, near Hannover, Oct. 4, 1921. She made her operatic debut as Emmeline in Weigl's *Schweizerfamilie* in Munich (1860); was a prominent member of the Munich Court Opera, where she created the roles of Fricka in *Das Rheingold* (Sept. 22, 1869) and Brünnhilde in *Die Walküre* (June 26, 1870). She also distinguished herself in other Wagnerian parts (Elisabeth, Elsa, Eva).

Stehman, Jacques, Belgian composer and music critic; b. Brussels, July 8, 1912; d. Heist-aan-Zee, May 20, 1975. He studied piano with Del Pueyo, composition with Jean Absil, and orchestration with Paul Gilson at the Brussels Cons.; then was active as music critic for *Le soir;* was made a prof. of practical harmony (1954) and of music history (1968) at the Brussels Cons.; also taught at the Chapelle Musicale Reine Elisabeth. His music is cautiously modernistic, with engaging touches of obsolescent jazz.

WORKS: *Symphonie de poche* (1950); *Musique de mai* for Strings (1961); *Dialogues* for Harp and Small Orch. (1964); *Melos* for Mezzo-soprano, Flute, and Strings (1968); *Escapades* for Piano and String Orch. (1968); Piano Concerto (1965–72); *Lamento* for Cello and Piano (1947); *Burlesques en 6 formes* for Piano (1934); *Colloque* for 2 Pianos (1943); *3 rythmes* for 2 Pianos (1955); *Montmartre* for 2 Pianos (1975); songs.

Steibelt, Daniel, renowned German pianist and composer; b. Berlin, Oct. 22, 1765; d. St. Petersburg, Oct. 2, 1823. He studied with Kirnberger (piano and theory); then joined the Prussian Army only to desert and flee his homeland in 1784. He publ. sonatas for Piano and Violin, as opp. 1 and 2 (Munich, 1788); then gave concerts in Saxony and Hannover before proceeding to Paris in 1790. There he found himself in strong competition with Ignaz Pleyel, but won out, and became a favorite piano teacher. His opera *Roméo et Juliette* was produced at the Théâtre Feydeau on Sept. 10, 1793, and, despite the revolutionary turmoil of the time, achieved excellent success. After defrauding his publisher, he left Paris in 1796, going to the Netherlands and then to London; became a soloist at Salomon's Concerts; played the solo part of his 3rd Piano Concerto (March 19, 1798), with its rousing finale *L'Orage, précédé d'un rondeau pastoral,* which as a piano solo became as popular as Koczwara's *Battle of Prague;* then produced the pasticcio *Albert and Adelaide, or The Victim of Constancy* at Covent Garden (Dec. 11, 1798), to which Attwood also contributed. After returning to Germany in 1799, he was granted an official pardon for his army desertion. In 1800 he visited Dresden, Prague, Berlin, and Vienna, where he challenged Beethoven to a contest of skill, but was easily bested. His next destination was Paris, where he produced Haydn's *Creation* (Dec. 24, 1800), with an orch. of 156 players, in an arrangement by Steibelt himself; Napoleon was present at that performance. A ballet by Steibelt, *Le retour de Zéphire,* was produced at the Paris Opéra on March 3, 1802; he then went to London, where he staged 2 ballets, *Le jugement du berger Paris* (May 24, 1804) and *La belle laitère* (Jan. 26, 1805). Returning once more to Paris, he wrote a festive intermezzo, *La fête de Mars,* to celebrate Napoleon's victory at Austerlitz; it was produced at the Opéra on March 4, 1806. In 1808–9 he presented concerts in Frankfurt, Leipzig, Breslau, and Warsaw on his journey to St. Petersburg to assume his appointment as director of the French Opera. In 1810 he was made maître de chapelle to the Czar. He composed several works for the French Opera, but devoted himself mainly to teaching and giving occasional concerts. On March 16, 1820, he gave the premiere of his 8th Piano Concerto in St. Petersburg. His last years were marked by ill health. Although he acquired greath wealth during his career, he squandered his money and died in relative poverty. Much of his large output is now of little interest, although several of his piano concertos and his 3 quintets for Piano and Strings are worthy of note.

BIBL.: G. Müller, *D. S.: sein Leben und seine Klavierwerke* (Leipzig and Zürich, 1933); K. Hagberg, *D. S.'s Cendrillon: A Critical Edition with Notes on S.'s Life and Works* (diss., Eastman School of Music, 1975).

Steiger, Rand, American composer and conductor; b. N.Y., June 18, 1957. He attended N.Y.'s High School of Music and Art (1972–75), then studied percussion and composition (with Tanenbaum) at the Manhattan School of Music (B.Mus., 1980); attended the Calif. Inst. of the Arts, where he studied with Brown, Mosko, Powell, and Subotnick (M.F.A., 1982); also studied at Yale Univ. with Carter, Druckman, Jolas, and Martino (1981) and at IRCAM in Paris (1982). He taught at the Univ. of Costa Rica (1984–85), the Calif. Inst. of the Arts (1982–87), and the Univ. of Calif. at San Diego (from 1987). He was the 1st Composer Fellow of the Los Angeles Phil. (1987–88). His works include *Dialogues II* for Marimba and Orch. (1979–80); *Brave New World* for Voices and Electronics (1980); *Quintessence* for 6 Instruments (1981); *Currents Caprice,* electronic film score (1982); *Kennedy Sketches* for Marimba and Vibraphone (1982); *In Nested Symmetry* for 15 Instruments and Electronics (1982); *Hexadecathlon* for Horn and 7 Instruments (1984); *Fanfare erafnaF* for Double Chamber Orch. (1985); *Tributaries* for Chamber Orch. (1986); *Tributaries for Nancarrow* for 6 Computer-controlled Pianos (1987); *Double Concerto* for Piano, Percussion, and Double Chamber Orch. (1987); *Druckman Tributary* for 11 Instruments (1988); *ZLoops* for Clarinet, Piano, and Percussion (1989); *Mozart Tributary* for Clarinet Quintet (1991); *The Burgess Shale* for Orch. (1991). Steiger has conducted and directed new-music performances by SONOR of the Univ. of Calif. at San Diego and the Los Angeles Phil. New Music Group. He is perhaps best known as a member of the Calif. E.A.R. Unit, a highly respected new-music ensemble established at the Calif. Inst. of the Arts in 1981. Other members include cellist Erika Duke-Kirkpatrick (b. Los Angeles, Aug. 1, 1956), who studied with Cesare Pascarella (1971–82) and at the Calif. Inst. of the Arts (B.F.A., 1978; M.F.A., 1982), where she later taught (from 1987); among composers who have written works for her are Subotnick, La Barbara, Powell, and Mosko; she performed as a soloist and in ensembles in the U.S., South America, and Europe. Pianist Lorna Ellen Eder (b. Aberdeen, Wash., April 2, 1953) studied at the Univ. of Puget Sound in Tacoma, Wash. (1971–73), Wash. State Univ. in Pullman (B.Mus., 1975), with Leonid Hambro at the Calif. Inst. of the Arts (M.F.A., 1980), and with Bruno Seidlhofer in Vienna (1975–77). She was a staff accompanist at the Calif. Inst. of the Arts (1980–84); played with the Santa Clarita Chamber Players (1985–90) and in duo recitals with Eugene Fodor (1984–86). Composer, percussionist, and performance artist Art(hur) Jarviven (b. Ilwaco, Wash., Jan. 27, 1956) studied at Ohio Univ. (B.Mus., 1978) and the Calif. Inst. of the Arts (M.F.A., 1981); had percussion lessons from Guy Remonko, John Bergamo, Karen Ervin, and Ruth Underwood, and composition lessons with Subotnick, Brown, and Mosko. He performed with the Los Angeles Phil. New Music Group and the performance-art ensemble Le Mômo; also worked with Steve Reich and Frank Zappa. His satiric works, which involve poetry, theater, visual media, and various musical styles, have been performed throughout the U.S.; these include *Vote of Confidence* for Percussion Trio (1979); *Through Birds, through Fire, but Not through Glass* for Percussion Quartet (1979); *Soluble Furniture* for Piano (1980); *Mercury at Right Angles* for Celesta (1980); *Viscous Linings* for Celesta, Viola, Bass Clarinet, and Percussion (1981); *Prosthesis,* false piece for anything or nothing (1981); *Raison d'être* for Marimba and Vibraphone (1981); *Carbon* for Bass Clarinet (1982); *Deductible Rooms* for Marimba (1982); *Adult Party Games from the Leisure Planet* for Various Ensembles (1985); *Ivan, Where Are You Running To* for 9 Players and Tape (1985); *Electric Jesus* for Juvenile Pianist and Large Ensemble (1985); *Mass Death of a School of Small Herring* for Chamber Orch. (1986); *A Book of 5 Rings* for Pianos and Percussion (1986); *Egyptian 2–Step* for Ensemble (1986); *The 7 Golden Vampires* for 2 Pianos (1987); *35½ Minutes for Gaylord Mowrey* for Piano, Video, and Refreshments (1987); *Goldbeater's Skin* for Clarinet (1987; other versions, 1988); *The 15 Fingers of Doctor Wu* for Oboe (1987); *Murphy-Nights* for Ensemble (1989); *The Vulture's Garden* for 4 Players (1990); *The Queen of Spain, parts I–III* for 2 Electronic Harpsichords and Percussion (1988–90). Percussionist Amy Knoles (b. Milwaukee, Sept. 10, 1959) studied at the Univ. of Wisconsin

(1977–79) and at the Calif. Inst. of the Arts (B.F.A., 1982), where she later taught. Among the composers whose works she has premiered are Powell, Subotnick, Chatham, and Tower. Violinist and vocalist Robin Lorentz (b. Seattle, Dec. 19, 1956) studied at the Cornish School of Music, the Univ. of Wash. (1977–78), and with Emanuel Zetlin and Yoko Matsuda at the Calif. Inst. of the Arts (B.F.A., 1980); taught at the Kirk Cons. of Music in Pasadena, Calif., and at the Aspen Music Festival (1989, 1990). She was concertmaster for the Ojai Festival (1986, 1988), and associate concertmaster for both the San Diego Chamber Players (1988) and the Los Angeles Phil. New Music Group (1987, 1988, 1990). She has performed with the Sterling Consort (1987–90) and the Ensemble of Santa Fe (from 1985). Her solo recording credits include works for television and film, in Irish, Cajun, bluegrass, jazz, and pop-rock styles. She joined the E.A.R. Unit in 1983. Clarinetist and saxophonist Jim Rohrig (b. Long Beach, Calif., Nov. 30, 1954) studied at the Univ. of Southern Calif. (B.A., 1977) and at the Calif. Inst. of the Arts (M.F.A., 1981; advanced certificate, 1983), where he also taught (1982–83); his teachers included Mitchell Lurie, Michelle Zukovsky, and Douglas Masek. He was a co-founder of the E.A.R. Unit. He has recorded works by Subotnick, La Barbara et al., and is an active member of the performance-art ensemble Le Mômo. He has composed incidental music for the stage and has directed and ed. film and video, including those of E.A.R. Unit performances. His in-progress projects include a film documentary of Nicolas Slonimsky. Flutist Dorothy Stone (b. Kingston, Pa., June 7, 1958) studied at the Manhattan School of Music (B.Mus., 1980) and at the Calif. Inst. of the Arts (M.F.A., 1982), her teachers including Harold Bennett, Harvey Sollberger, Thomas Nyfenger, Julius Baker, and Ann Deiner Giles; gave 1st performances of works by Boulez, Cage, Ferneyhough, and Carter; numerous composers have composed works for her, including Babbitt, Steiger, and Mosko. She composed *Wizard Ball* for Flute and Electronics, which won several awards. Stone is artistic director and administrative manager of the E.A.R. Unit. She is married to the conductor **Stephen Mosko.**

Steigleder, family of German musicians:
(1) Utz Steigleder, organist and composer; place and date of birth unknown; d. Stuttgart, Oct. 7 or 8, 1581. He was in the service of Duke Ulrich of Württemberg in Stuttgart from at least 1534, holding the posts of court and abbey organist. His only known work is *Veni Sancte Spiritus* for 6 Voices (ed. in *Die Motette,* no. 457, Stuttgart, 1963).
(2) Adam Steigleder, organist and composer, son of the preceding; b. Stuttgart, Feb. 19, 1561; d. there, Nov. 8, 1633. He studied with S. Lohet (1575–78) and in Rome (1580–83); was organist at the Stuttgart abbey church (1583–92), the Michaeliskirche in Schwäbisch Hall (1592–95), and at Ulm Minster (1595–1625); then returned to Stuttgart. His extant works consist of a *Passa e mezo* and a *Toccata primi toni.*
(3) Johann Ulrich Steigleder, organist and composer, son of the preceding; b. Schwäbisch Hall, March 22, 1593; d. Stuttgart, Oct. 10, 1635. He was a pupil of his father; although lame, he served as organist at Lindau's Stephanskirche on Lake Constance (1613–17); in Stuttgart, was organist at the abbey church (1617–35) and the ducal court (1627–35). He died of the plague. His extant works comprise *Ricercar tabulatura, organis et organoedis* (Stuttgart, 1624) and *Tabulatur-Buch* (Strasbourg, 1627), both ed. in the Corpus of Early Keyboard Music, XIII/1 (1968).
Bibl.: W. Tappert, "J.U. S.s 'Tabulaturbuch,'" *Monatshefte für Musikgeschichte,* XIX (1887); E. Emsheimer, *J.U. S.: Sein Leben und seine Werke* (Kassel, 1928).

Stein, Erwin, Austrian conductor and editor; b. Vienna, Nov. 7, 1885; d. London, July 19, 1958. He studied composition with Schoenberg in Vienna (1906–10) and became Schoenberg's early champion. From 1910 to 1914 he conducted various theater orchs. in Austria and Germany; returning to Vienna, he was a member, with Schoenberg, Berg, and Webern, of the famous Verein für musikalische Privataufführungen (So-

ciety for Musical Private Performances), which excluded music critics from attendance (1920–22). He then became an ed. for Universal Edition in Vienna, where he was instrumental in bringing out works by the composers of the Second Viennese School. He also conducted a tour with a Vienna group named Pierrot Lunaire Ensemble. After the Anschluss in 1938, he went to London and joined the music publ. firm of Boosey & Hawkes. He contributed a fundamental paper on Schoenberg's method of composition with 12 tones, "Neue Formprinzipien," publ. in *Anbruch* (1924). He publ. a selective collection of Schoenberg's letters (Mainz, 1958; in Eng., London, 1964); a collection of essays, *Orpheus in New Guises* (London, 1953); his theoretical monograph *Musik, Form und Darstellung* was publ. posthumously, 1st in Eng. as *Form and Performance* (London, 1962) and later in German (Munich, 1964).

Stein, Fritz (actually, **Friedrich Wilhelm**), German musicologist; b. Gerlachsheim, Baden, Dec. 17, 1879; d. Berlin, Nov. 14, 1961. He studied theology in Karlsruhe, then took courses in musicology with P. Wolfrum in Heidelberg; subsequently went to Leipzig, where he studied various subjects with Krehl, Nikisch, Riemann, and Straube; completed his musicological training at the Univ. of Heidelberg (Ph.D., 1910, with the diss. *Zur Geschichte der Musik in Heidelberg;* publ. in 1912; new ed., 1921, as *Geschichte des Musikwesens in Heidelberg bis zum Ende des 18. Jahrhunderts*). He went to Jena in 1906 as music director of the Univ. and city organist; in 1913 he was appointed prof. of musicology at the Univ.; was in the German army during World War I and directed a male chorus for the troops at the front. He became a reader in musicology at the Univ. of Kiel in 1920, then was a prof. from 1928 to 1933; in 1933 he became director of the Hochschule für Musik in Berlin, holding this position to the end of World War II in 1945. He achieved notoriety when he discovered in the library of the Univ. of Jena the parts of a sym. marked by an unknown copyist as a work by Beethoven. The sym. became famous as the "Jena Symphony" and was hailed by many as a genuine discovery; the score was publ. by Breitkopf & Härtel in 1911, and performances followed all over the world; Stein publ. his own exegesis of it as "Eine unbekannte Jugendsymphonie Beethovens?" in the *Sammelbände der Internationalen Musik-Gesellschaft* (1911). Doubts of its authenticity were raised, but it was not until 1957 that H.C. Robbins Landon succeeded in locating the original MS, proving that the "Jena Symphony" was in reality the work of Friedrich Witt (1770–1837). Stein publ. a monograph on Max Reger (Potsdam, 1939) and *Max Reger: Sein Leben in Bildern* (a pictorial biography; Leipzig, 1941; 2nd ed., 1956); brought out a thematic catalogue of Reger's works (Leipzig, 1934; definitive ed., 1953); ed. works by Johann Christian Bach, Telemann, Handel, Beethoven, etc.; contributed essays to numerous learned publs. A Festschrift was publ. in his honor on his 60th birthday (1939).

Stein, Horst (Walter), German conductor; b. Elberfeld, May 2, 1928. He studied at the Hochschule für Musik in Cologne, and at age 23 was engaged as a conductor at the Hamburg State Opera; then was on the staff of the State Opera in East Berlin (1955–61). He was deputy Generalmusikdirektor at the Hamburg State Opera (1961–63); after serving as Generalmusikdirektor of the Mannheim National Theater (1963–70), he returned to the Hamburg State Opera as Generalmusikdirektor (1972–77); also was Generalmusikdirektor with the Hamburg State Phil. (1973–76). He subsequently was chief conductor of the Orchestre de la Suisse Romande in Geneva (1980–85), the Bamberg Sym. Orch. (from 1985), and the Basel Sym. Orch. (from 1987). He made many guest conducting appearances in Europe and in North and South America.

Stein, Johann (Georg) Andreas, German keyboard instrument maker; b. Heidelsheim, Palatinate, May 6, 1728; d. Augsburg, Feb. 29, 1792. He worked under Johann David Stein in Strasbourg (1748–49), then was associated with F.J. Späth in Regensburg (1749–50). In 1750 he settled in Augsburg, where he built the organ of the Barfüsserkirche; was appointed organist there in 1757. He spent a few months in Paris in

1758 before returning to Augsburg. He experimented with various types of keyboard instruments; invented a "polytoniclavichordium" (1769), a "melodika" (1772), a "vis-à-vis Flügel" (1777), and a "Saitenharmonika" (1789). The business was carried on by his daughter, Nannette (b. Augsburg, Jan. 2, 1769; d. Vienna, Jan. 16, 1833), and his son, Matthäus Andreas (b. Augsburg, Dec. 12, 1776; d. Vienna, May 6, 1842). In 1794 Nannette married the pianist J.A. Streicher, and the firm was moved to Vienna, where her brother remained a partner until 1802 when he founded his own firm of André Stein. His son, Carl Andreas (b. Vienna, Sept. 4, 1797; d. there, Aug. 28, 1863), carried on his father's business while also pursuing a career as a pianist and composer.

BIBL.: F. Luib, *Biographische Skizze des J.A. S.* (1886); T. Bolte, *Die Musikerfamilien S. und Streicher* (Vienna, 1917); K. Fischer, "J.A. S., der Augsburger Orgel- und Klavierbauer," *Zeitschrift des historichen Vereins für Schwaben und Neuburg,* I (1932); E. Hertz, *J.A. S. (1728–1792): Ein Beitrag zur Geschichte des Klavierbaues* (Berlin, 1937); D. Boalch, *Makers of the Harpsichord and Clavichord, 1440 to 1840* (London, 1956).

Stein, Leon, American composer and conductor; b. Chicago, Sept. 18, 1910. He studied violin at the American Cons. in Chicago (1922–27), and theory at Crane Junior College in Chicago (1927–29); took private lessons in composition with Leo Sowerby, in orchestration with Eric DeLamarter, and in conducting with Frederick Stock and Hans Lange (1937–40); also studied at De Paul Univ. (M.M., 1935; Ph.D., 1949; diss. publ. as *The Racial Thinking of Richard Wagner,* 1951), where he served on its faculty (1931–78); served as dean of its school of music (1966–76); also was director of the Inst. of Music of the College of Jewish Studies (1952–59) and was a conductor of various community orchs. He publ. *Structure and Style: The Study and Analysis of Musical Form* (Evanston, Ill., 1962; 3rd ed., rev. and enl., 1979) and *Anthology of Musical Forms* (Evanston, Ill., 1962). In 1982 he was inducted into the city of Chicago's Hall of Fame. His music is academic, but not devoid of occasional modernities.

WORKS: OPERAS: *The Fisherman's Wife* (1953–54; St. Joseph, Mich., Jan. 10, 1955); *Deirdre,* after Yeats (1956; Chicago, May 18, 1957). **BALLETS FOR PIANO:** *Exodus* (Chicago, Jan. 29, 1939); *Doubt* (Chicago, Jan. 21, 1940). **ORCH.:** *Prelude and Fugue* (1935); *Passacaglia* (1936); *Sinfonietta* for String Orch. (1938); Violin Concerto (1938–39; Chicago, Dec. 3, 1948); 4 syms.: No. 1 (1940); No. 2 (1942); No. 3 (1950–51); No. 4 (1975); *3 Hassidic Dances* (1940–41; Chicago, April 13, 1942); *Triptych on 3 Poems of Walt Whitman* (1943; Chicago, March 29, 1949); *Great Lakes Suite* for Small Orch. (1943–44); *Rhapsody* for Flute, Harp, and String Orch. (1954; Chicago, Nov. 8, 1955); *Adagio and Rondo Ebraico* (1957); *Then Shall the Dust Return* (1971); Cello Concerto (1977; Chicago, June 11, 1983); Concerto for Clarinet and Percussion Ensemble (1979); *Nexus* for Wind Ensemble (1983); *Aria Hebraique* for Oboe and String Orch. (1984); Concerto for Oboe and String Orch. (1986; Chicago, Jan. 29, 1988). **CHAMBER:** Sonata for 2 Violins (1931); Violin Sonata (1932); 5 string quartets (1933, 1962, 1964, 1964, 1967); Woodwind Quintet (1936); *12 Preludes* for Violin and Piano (1942–49); Trio for 3 Trumpets (1953); Quintet for Saxophone and String Quartet (1957); Sextet for Alto Saxophone and Wind Quintet (1958); solo sonatas for Violin (1960), Flute (1968), Horn (1969), Trombone (1969), Trumpet (1969), Bassoon (1969), Oboe (1969), Bass (1970), and Cello (1970); Trio Concertante for Saxophone, Violin, and Piano (1961); Suite for Saxophone Quartet (1962); Tenor Saxophone Sonata (1967); Trio for Alto Saxophone, Clarinet, and Piano (1969); Quintet for Harp and String Quartet (1976); Suite for Woodwind Quintet (1978); Suite for Violin, Viola, and Cello (1980); *Dance ebraico* for Cello and Piano (1982); Duo Concertante for Bassoon or Violin and Marimba (1988); numerous solo works and various piano pieces.

Stein, Leonard, eminent American music scholar; b. Los Angeles, Dec. 1, 1916. He attended Los Angeles City College

(1933–36) and studied piano privately with Richard Buhlig (1936–39); enrolled in the class of composition and musical analysis with Arnold Schoenberg at the Univ. of Southern Calif. (1935–36) and at the Univ. of Calif. at Los Angeles (1936–42); from 1939 to 1942 he was Schoenberg's teaching assistant; received the degrees of B.A. (1939) and M.M. (1941) from the Univ. of Calif. at Los Angeles, and his D.M.A. from the Univ. of Southern Calif. (1965); was the recipient of a Guggenheim fellowship (1965–66). He taught at Occidental College (1946–48); Los Angeles City College (1948–60); Pomona College (1961–62); Univ. of Calif. at Los Angeles (1962–64); Claremont Graduate School (1963–67); Univ. of Calif. at San Diego (1966); Calif. State College at Dominguez Hills (1967–70); in 1970 he was appointed a member of the music faculty of the Calif. Inst. of the Arts; in 1975 he became adjunct prof. in the School of Music at the Univ. of Southern Calif. In 1975 he was elected director of the Arnold Schoenberg Inst. of the Univ. of Southern Calif., Los Angeles, and editorial director of the *Journal of the Arnold Schoenberg Institute.* He contributed a number of articles on the proper performance of piano works by Schoenberg; was a member of the editorial board of the complete works of Schoenberg. He ed. Schoenberg's *Nachtwandler* (1969); Piano Concerto (1972); *Ode to Napoleon Bonaparte* (1973); *Brettl-Lieder* (1974); ed. and completed Schoenberg's pedagogical works: *Preliminary Exercises in Counterpoint* (1963); *Models for Beginners in Composition* (rev. of the text, 1972); *Structural Functions of Harmony* (rev., 1969); *Style and Idea. Selected Writings of Arnold Schoenberg* (London, 1975; received the 1976 ASCAP award).

Stein, Richard Heinrich, German music theorist and composer; b. Halle, Feb. 28, 1882; d. Santa Brigida, Canary Islands, Aug. 11, 1942. He studied law and music; received his Ph.D. from the Univ. of Erlangen in 1911 with the dissertation *Die psychologischen Grundlagen der Wundtschen Ethik.* From 1914 to 1919 he lived in Spain; from 1920 to 1932 he taught in Berlin. In 1933 he settled in the Canary Islands. He was a composer of experimental tendencies; his 2 *Konzertstücke* for Cello and Piano, op. 26 (1906), was the 1st composition containing quarter-tones to be publ. In 1909 he wrote a brochure giving a detailed exposition of his quarter-tone system, and in 1914 he built a quarter-tone clarinet. He composed about 100 piano pieces and about 50 songs; *Scherzo fantastico* for Orch.; publ. the books *La música moderna* (Barcelona, 1918; in Spanish and German), *Grieg* (1921), and *Tschaikowsky* (1927).

Steinbach, Fritz, eminent German conductor; b. Grünsfeld, June 17, 1855; d. Munich, Aug. 13, 1916. He began his musical training with his brother, Emil Steinbach, then studied at the Leipzig Cons., with V. Lachner in Karlsruhe, and with G. Nottebohm in Vienna. After serving as 2nd conductor in Mainz (1880–86), he was appointed Hofkapellmeister in Meiningen in 1886; later was promoted to Generalmusikdirektor in recognition of his efforts to carry forward Bülow's tradition of excellence; in 1902 he took the Meiningen Orch. to London, where he conducted the Brahms syms. to critical acclaim. In 1903 he went to Cologne as director of the Cons. and as Kapellmeister of the Gürzenich Orch. He retired to Munich in 1914.

Steinbauer, Othmar, Austrian violinist, conductor, teacher, instrument maker, and composer; b. Vienna, Nov. 6, 1895; d. Altenburg, Sept. 5, 1962. He studied violin at the Vienna Academy of Music; founded the Chamber Concert Society of Vienna, playing and conducting works of the modern Viennese School. He publ. a theoretical treatise, *Das Wesen der Tonalität* (Munich, 1928). In 1938 he founded the Musikschule der Stadt Wien. After 1945 he devoted himself mainly to manufacturing new instruments; constructed a violin specially adapted for easy performance by amateurs. His own music is quite conservative.

Steinberg, Maximilian (Osseievich), significant Russian composer and pedagogue; b. Vilnius, July 4, 1883; d. Leningrad, Dec. 6, 1946. He studied at the Univ. of St. Petersburg (graduated, 1907); also took courses with Glazunov, Liadov, and Rimsky-Korsakov (whose daughter he married on June 17, 1908). In 1908 he was appointed teacher of theory and composition there. In 1934 he was appointed director of the Leningrad Cons., and maintained the high standards established before him by Rimsky-Korsakov and Glazunov. Among his pupils were Shostakovich, Shaporin, and other prominent composers of the Soviet period. His early compositions reflected the influence of his teachers, but gradually he evolved a more personal style distinguished by rhapsodic eloquence and somewhat touched with procedures of French Impressionism.

WORKS: Sym. No. 1 (1907); Sym. No. 2 (St. Petersburg, Nov. 27, 1909); *Metamorphoses*, ballet (2nd part perf. Paris, June 2, 1914); *La Princesse Maleine*, after Maeterlinck, for Orch. and Women's Chorus (1916); *Heaven and Earth*, dramatic poem for 6 Soloists and Orch. (1918); Sym. No. 3 (Leningrad, March 3, 1929, composer conducting); Sym. No. 4, *Turksib*, to celebrate the opening of the Turkestan-Siberian railroad (Leningrad, Dec. 2, 1933); *In Armenia*, symphonic picture (Leningrad, Dec. 24, 1940); Violin Concerto (1946); 2 string quartets; piano pieces; songs; arrangements of works by other composers, including a Cello Sonata by Gaillard (1924).

BIBL.: A. Rimsky-Korsakov, *M. S.* (Moscow, 1928); V. Bogdanov-Berezovsky, *M. S.* (Moscow, 1947).

Steinberg, (Carl) Michael (Alfred), German-born American music critic; b. Breslau, Oct. 4, 1928. He went to England in 1939 and to the U.S. in 1943; studied music at Princeton Univ. (A.B., 1949; M.F.A., 1951); then was in Italy (1952–54). Returning to America, he taught at Princeton Univ., Hunter College, Manhattan School of Music, Univ. of Saskatchewan, Smith College, Brandeis Univ., Boston Univ., and (from 1968) the New England Cons. of Music in Boston. In 1964 he was appointed music critic of the Boston *Globe*. His criticisms, utterly disrespectful of the most sacrosanct musical personalities, aroused periodic outbursts of indignation among outraged artists, aggrieved managers, and chagrined promoters. In 1969 several Boston Sym. Orch. players petitioned the management to banish him from their concerts. Then, in a spectacular peripeteia, he left the Boston *Globe* in 1976 and was appointed director of publs. for the Boston Sym. In 1979 he assumed the position of artistic adviser and publications director of the San Francisco Sym.

Steinberg, Pinchas, American conductor; b. N.Y., Feb. 12, 1945. He studied violin in N.Y., then pursued musical training at Tanglewood and at Indiana Univ. In 1967 he became a conductor at the Chicago Lyric Opera; in 1971 he conducted in Berlin; subsequently conducted opera in Frankfurt, Stuttgart, Hamburg, London, Paris, and San Francisco. From 1985 to 1989 he was Generalmusikdirektor in Bremen. In 1989 he became chief conductor of the Austrian Radio Sym. Orch. in Vienna.

Steinberg, William (actually, **Hans Wilhelm**), eminent German-born American conductor; b. Cologne, Aug. 1, 1899; d. N.Y., May 16, 1978. He studied piano and violin at home; conducted his own setting for chorus and orch. of a poem from Ovid's *Metamorphoses* in school at the age of 13; then took lessons in conducting with Hermann Abendroth, in piano with Lazzaro Uzielli, and in music theory with Franz Bölsche at the Cologne Cons., graduating in 1920, with the Wüllner Prize for conducting; subsequently became assistant to Otto Klemperer at the Cologne Opera, and in 1924 became principal conductor. In 1925 he was engaged as conductor of the German Theater in Prague; in 1929 he was appointed Generalmusikdirektor of the Frankfurt Opera, where he brought out several modern operas, including Alban Berg's *Wozzeck*. With the advent of the Nazi regime in 1933, he was removed from his position and became conductor for the Jewish Culture League, restricted to Jewish audiences. In 1936 he left Germany and became one of the conductors of the Palestine Orch., which he rehearsed and prepared for Toscanini, who subsequently engaged him as an assistant conductor of the NBC Sym. Orch. in N.Y. in 1938. His career as an orch. conductor was then connected with major American orchs. He became an American citizen in 1944. He was music director of the Buffalo Phil. (1945–52); in 1952 he was appointed music director of the Pittsburgh Sym. Orch.; concurrently, he served as music director of the London Phil. (1958–60) and of the Boston Sym. Orch. (1969–72); he retired from his Pittsburgh post in 1976. He also made many guest conducting appearances with major U.S. and European orchs. His performances were marked by impeccable taste and fidelity to the music; in this respect he was a follower of the Toscanini tradition.

Steinberg, Ze'ev (Wolfgang), German-born Israeli violist and composer; b. Düsseldorf, Nov. 27, 1918. He studied with Eldering in Cologne (1933). In 1934 he emigrated to Palestine, where he studied viola and composition with Partos (1940–42); then became a violist in the Palestine Sym. Orch. (later the Israel Phil.) in Tel Aviv; in 1957, became the violinist in the New Israeli String Quartet; from 1969 to 1972, was a lecturer at the Tel Aviv Academy of Music. His compositions present an agreeable blend of oriental melos, asymmetrical rhythms, and sharp atonal progressions in dissonant counterpoint.

WORKS: Sonata for 2 Violas (1955–56); 3 string quartets (1959; 1969; 1981–82); 6 *Miniatures* for Cello and Piano (1961); 4 *Bagatelles* for 2 Recorders (1962); 2 *concerti da camera:* No. 1 for Viola and String Orch. (1962) and No. 2 for Violin and 8 Instruments (1966); *Purim Variations* on a nursery song for Horn and String Trio (1963); *The Story of Rahab and the Spies*, biblical cantata (1969); *Festive Prologue* for Flute, Oboe, and String Trio (1969); 2 *Songs without Words* for Viola, String Quartet, and String Orch. (1970); *a little suite for a big flute* for Bass Flute in C (1972); *Variations and Dance* for Violin (1976); *Prelude and Fughetta* for Flute, Viola, and Harp (1977); 4 *Pieces* for Orch. (1985); 7 *Pieces* for 11 Instruments (1987); arrangements of works by Vivaldi, Bach, Schubert, and others.

Steiner, Emma, American composer and conductor; b. 1850; d. N.Y., Feb. 27, 1928. Her grandfather led the Maryland 16th Brigade, which won the battle of North Point (near Fort McHenry, Baltimore) on Sept. 13, 1814, enabling Francis Scott Key to finish the last stanza of *The Star-Spangled Banner*. She wrote 7 light operas, plus ballets, overtures, and songs; purportedly she was also the 1st woman ever to receive payment for conducting. Conried, the manager of the Metropolitan Opera, is said to have declared that he would have let her conduct a performance had he dared to put a woman armed with a baton in front of a totally male orch. According to unverifiable accounts, she conducted 6,000 performances of 50 different operas. She also organized an Emma R. Steiner Home for the Aged and Infirm Musicians at Bay Shore, Long Island. On Feb. 28, 1925, she conducted a concert at the Metropolitan Opera to commemorate the 50th anniversary of her 1st appearance as conductor. Her works, of different genres and light consistency, aggregate more than 200 opus numbers.

Steiner, Max(imilian Raoul Walter), Austrian-born American composer; b. Vienna, May 10, 1888; d. Los Angeles, Dec. 28, 1971. He studied at the Vienna Cons. with Fuchs and Grädener, and also had some advice from Mahler. At the age of 14 he wrote an operetta. In 1904 he went to England; in 1911 he proceeded to Paris. In 1914 he settled in the U.S.; after conducting musical shows in N.Y., he moved in 1929 to Hollywood, where he became one of the most successful film composers. His music offers a fulsome blend of lush harmonies artfully derived from both Tchaikovsky and Wagner, arranged in a manner marvelously suitable for the portrayal of psychological drama on the screen. Among his film scores, of which he wrote more than 200, are *King Kong* (1933), *The Charge of the Light Brigade* (1936), *Gone with the Wind* (1939), and *The Treasure of Sierra Madre* (1948).

BIBL.: G. Lazarou, *M. S. and Film Music: An Essay* (Athens, 1971).

Steinert, Alexander Lang, American pianist, conductor, composer, and arranger; b. Boston, Sept. 21, 1900; d. N.Y.,

July 7, 1982. He was the son of a piano manufacturer; studied at Harvard Univ., graduating in 1922; then took private lessons in composition with Loeffler in Boston, and with Koechlin and d'Indy in Paris. He lived much of his time in Europe; was active as a conductor and arranger in Hollywood. His music bears the imprint of the French modern school.

WORKS: ORCH.: *Nuit méridionale* (Boston, Oct. 15, 1926); *Leggenda sinfonica* (Rome, 1930); *Concerto sinfonico* for Piano and Orch. (Boston, Feb. 8, 1935, composer soloist); *Rhapsody* for Clarinet and Orch. (1945); *The Nightingale and the Rose* for Speaker and Orch. (Philadelphia, March 31, 1950); also a Violin Sonata; Piano Trio; piano pieces; songs.

Steingruber, Ilona, Austrian soprano; b. Vienna, Feb. 8, 1912; d. there, Dec. 10, 1962. She studied piano before taking up vocal training at the Vienna Academy of Music; sang in performances broadcast by the Austrian Radio (1939–42); made her operatic debut in Tilsit (1942); after World War II, she toured as a concert artist; also sang at the Vienna State Opera (1948–51); then taught in Darmstadt. In 1946 she married the composer **Friedrich Wildgans.**

Steinhardt, Milton, American musicologist; b. Miami, Okla., Nov. 13, 1909. After preliminary study at the Univ. of Kansas, he took courses at the Akademie der Tonkunst in Munich, and had violin lessons with Maurice Hewitt in Paris. Returning to the U.S., he enrolled in the Eastman School of Music in Rochester, N.Y. (B.M., 1936; M.M., 1937); then attended courses of Otto Kinkeldey at Cornell Univ. and Curt Sachs and Gustave Reese at N.Y. Univ. (Ph.D., 1950, with the diss. *Jacobus Vaet and His Motets;* publ. in East Lansing, Mich., 1951). He was a lecturer at Michigan State Univ. (1948–50), Ohio Univ. (1950–51), and the Univ. of Kansas (1951–75). He ed. the works of Jacobus Vaet for Denkmäler der Tonkunst in Österreich (vols. 98, 100, 103/104, 108/109, 113/114, 116) and the motets of P. de Monte in 7 vols. (1975–86) for the New Complete Edition publ. in Louvain.

Steinitz, (Charles) Paul (Joseph), English organist and conductor; b. Chichester, Aug. 25, 1909; d. Oxted, April 22, 1988. He studied at the Royal Academy of Music in London, and also privately with George Oldroyd. He then served as church organist in Ashford, Kent (1933–42). In 1947 he organized the South London Bach Society; this choral group later became noteworthy under the name of the London Bach Society. He also served as organist and choirmaster at the Church of St. Bartholomew-the-Great in London (1949–61). In 1969 he founded the Steinitz Bach Players, which he conducted on tours. In 1945 he became a prof. at the Royal Academy of Music in London; also taught at Goldsmiths' College, Univ. of London (1948–76). He publ. *Bach's Passions* (London, 1979). In 1985 he was made a member of the Order of the British Empire.

Steinpress, Boris (Solomonovich), erudite Russian musicologist; b. Berdyansk, Aug. 13, 1908; d. Moscow, May 21, 1986. He studied piano with Igumnov at the Moscow Cons., graduating in 1931, and took a postgraduate course there in musicology with Ivanov-Boretsky, completing it in 1936; was a member of its faculty (1931; 1933–36); in 1938 he received the title of candidate of fine arts for his dissertation on Mozart's *Le nozze di Figaro.* He taught at the Urals Cons. in Sverdlovsk (1936–37; 1942–43); served as head of the music history dept. of the Central Correspondence Inst. for Musical Education (1939–41), and was senior lecturer and dean of the faculty of history and theory (from 1940). In 1942 he joined the Communist Party. Although engaged primarily in musical encyclopedic work, Steinpress also composed; his patriotic songs were popular in the U.S.S.R. during World War II. From 1938 to 1990 and from 1943 to 1959 he was chief contributor to the music section of the *Great Soviet Encyclopedia.* His publcations are particularly important in musical biography; he decisively refuted the legend of Salieri's poisoning Mozart. His biography of Aliabiev clarifies the story of Aliabiev's life and his internal exile on the false charge of murder in a duel.

With I. Yampolsky, he ed. the extremely valuable and accurate one-vol. *Encyclopedic Musical Dictionary* (Moscow, 1959; 2nd ed., 1966); also with Yampolsky he compiled a useful *Brief Dictionary for Music Lovers* (Moscow, 1961; 2nd ed., 1967). In 1963 he publ. a partial vol. of a monumental work on opera premieres covering the period 1900–40, giving exact dates and names of theaters for all opera productions worldwide.

WRITINGS: *Problems of Material Culture in Music* (Moscow, 1931); *A History of So-Called Gypsy Songs in Russia* (Moscow, 1934; a critical dissection of spurious Gypsy songs); *Pages from the Life of Aliabiev* (Moscow, 1956); *Aliabiev in Exile* (Moscow, 1959); *Classicism and Romanticism* (Moscow, 1968); *Sketches and Studies* (Moscow, 1980).

Steinway & Sons, celebrated family of German-American piano manufacturers. The founder of the firm was **Heinrich Engelhard Steinweg** (b. Wolfshagen, Germany, Feb. 15, 1797; d. N.Y., Feb. 7, 1871; in 1864 he Anglicized his name to Henry E. Steinway). He learned cabinetmaking and organ building at Goslar, and in 1818 entered the shop of an organ maker in Seesen, also becoming church organist there. From about 1820 he became interested in piano making and worked hard to establish a business of his own. He built his 1st piano in 1836. In 1839 he exhibited one grand and 2 square pianos at the Braunschweig State Fair, winning the gold medal. The Revolution of 1848 caused him to emigrate to America with his wife, 2 daughters, and 4 of his 5 sons: **Charles** (actually, **Christian Karl Gottlieb;** b. Seesen, Jan. 4, 1829; d. there, March 31, 1865); **Henry** (actually, **Johann Heinrich Engelhard;** b. Seesen, Oct. 29, 1830; d. N.Y., March 11, 1865); **William** (actually, **Johann Heinrich Wilhelm;** b. Seesen, March 5, 1835; d. N.Y., Nov. 30, 1896); and **(Georg August) Albert** (b. Seesen, June 10, 1840; d. N.Y., May 14, 1877). The management of the German business at Seesen was left in charge of the eldest son, **(Christian Friedrich) Theodore** (b. Seesen, Nov. 6, 1825; d. Braunschweig, March 26, 1889). The family arrived in N.Y. on June 29, 1850, and for about 2 years father and sons worked in various piano factories there. On March 5, 1853, they established a factory of their own under the above firm name, with premises on Varick St. In 1854 they won a gold medal for a square piano at the Metropolitan Fair in Washington, D.C. Their remarkable prosperity dates from 1855, when they took 1st prize for a square over-strung piano with cast-iron frame (an innovation then) at the N.Y. Industrial Exhibition. In 1856 they made their 1st grand, and in 1862 their 1st upright. Among the numerous honors subsequently received may be mentioned 1st prize at London, 1862; 1st grand gold medal of honor for all styles at Paris, 1867 (by unanimous verdict); diplomas for "highest degree of excellence in all styles" at Philadelphia, 1876. In 1854 the family name (Steinweg) was legally changed to Steinway. In 1865, upon the death of his brothers Charles and Henry, Theodore gave up the Braunschweig business and became a full partner in the N.Y. firm; he built Steinway Hall on 14th St., which, in addition to the offices and retail warerooms, housed a concert hall that became a leading center of N.Y. musical life. In 1925 headquarters were established in the Steinway Building on 57th St. Theodore was especially interested in the scientific aspects of piano construction and made a study of the acoustical theories of Helmholtz and Tyndall, which enabled him to introduce important improvements. He returned to Germany in 1870. On May 17, 1876, the firm was incorporated and William was elected president; he opened a London branch in 1876, and established a European factory at Hamburg in 1880. In the latter year he also bought 400 acres of land on Long Island Sound and established there the village of Steinway (now part of Long Island City), where since 1910 the entire manufacturing plant has been located. Control and active management of the business, now the largest of its kind in the world, has remained in the hands of the founder's descendants. **Theodore E. Steinway** (d. N.Y., April 8, 1957), grandson of Henry E. Steinway, was president from 1927; also a stamp collector, he was honored by Liechtenstein with his portrait on a postage stamp on Sept. 7, 1972; in 1955 he was succeeded by his son, **Henry Steinway.** The firm was sold to CBS in 1972, although the Steinway family continued to be closely associated with the business. In 1988 Steinway & Sons celebrated its 135th anniversary with a special concert in N.Y. and the unveiling of its 500,000th piano.

BIBL.: O. Floersheim, *W. S.* (Breslau, 1894); E. Hubbard, *The Story of the S.s* (East Aurora, N.Y., 1911); T. Steinway, *People and Pianos* (N.Y., 1953; 2nd ed., 1961); C. Ehrlich, *The Piano: A History* (London, 1976); C. Hoover, "The S.s and their Pianos in the Nineteenth Century," *Journal of the American Musical Instrument Society,* VII (1981).

Steinweg, original name of the Steinway family of piano manufacturers. **(Christian Friedrich) Theodore Steinway** continued the piano-making business established by his father at Seesen until 1852, when he transferred it to Wolfenbüttel; in 1859 he moved it to Braunschweig, carrying it on there until 1865, when he left for America. The business was then taken over by his partners, Grotrian, Helfferich, and Schulz, under the name "Theodore Steinweg Nachfolger." In 1886 Grotrian became sole owner, and the business was carried on by his sons Willi and Kurt, the firm name being "Grotrian-Steinweg."

Stekke, Léon, Belgian composer; b. Soignies, Oct. 12, 1904; d. Anderlecht, near Brussels, Jan. 24, 1970. He studied with Joseph Jongen and Paul Gilson in Brussels; from 1942 until his death he taught at the Royal Cons. in Brussels.

WORKS: Opera, *Les Cornes du Croissant* (Brussels, 1952); 2 cantatas: *Héro et Léandre* (1931) and *La Légende de St.-Hubert* (1933); *Fantaisie-rapsodie* for Orch.; *Burlesco* for Oboe and Orch.; Trumpet Concerto (Brussels, 1948); *Fantaisie élégiaque* for English Horn and Orch.; *Poème sylvestre* for French Horn and Orch.; *Impression de cinéma* for Bassoon and Orch.; *Variations* for Trombone and Orch.; songs; piano pieces.

Stella, Antonietta, Italian soprano; b. Perugia, March 15, 1929. She studied voice with Aldo Zeetti in Perugia; made her operatic debut in Rome as Leonore in *La forza del destino* in 1951; in 1953 she sang at La Scala in Milan; further engagements were at Covent Garden in London (1955) and at the Vienna State Opera. She made her American debut at the Metropolitan Opera in N.Y. on Nov. 13, 1956, in *Aida;* after remaining on its roster until 1960, she pursued her career in Europe.

Stemper, Frank, American pianist and composer; b. Milwaukee, Oct. 19, 1951. He studied at the Univ. of British Columbia in Vancouver (B.Mus., 1975), the State Univ. of N.Y. at Stony Brook (M.A., 1978), and the Univ. of Calif. at Berkeley (Ph.D., 1981); also with Betsy Jolas at the Paris Cons. (1981, 1983). He was a studio technician at the Univ. of Calif. at Berkeley's Electronic Music Studio (1979–81) and guest composer at the Computer Music Project at the Univ. of Illinois at Urbana (1987; 1988); also appeared as a pianist in classical, jazz, and big-band settings. His music fuses postwar serial techniques with jazz elements.

WORKS: ORCH.: Violin Concerto (1978); *Seamaster* for Soprano and Chamber Orch. (1981; Milwaukee, May 13, 1983); *Hoye's Tribute* for Winds (Carbondale, Ill., Oct. 1, 1988). **CHAMBER:** Trio for Oboe, Clarinet, and Bassoon (1974; Vancouver, March 27, 1975); *Off Center to the Left* for Percussion Quartet (1977; Stony Brook, N.Y., Oct. 19, 1978); *Humble Cake* for Flute, Clarinet, Bass Clarinet, Violin, and Cello (1977; Stony Brook, N.Y., April 24, 1978); String Quartet (1982; Carbondale, Ill., March 29, 1988); Double Wind Trio for Oboe, Bassoon, and Piano (1983); *Chameleon* for Clarinet, String Trio, and Piano (Los Angeles, May 13, 1984); *Dreams* for Woodwind Quintet (1984; Bucharest, Feb. 17, 1987); *Memories from Euphoria* for Guitar and Harpsichord (1986); *2nd Diary* for Clarinet and Piano (1986; Urbana, Ill., April 3, 1988); *Some Things* for Flute, Clarinet, Violin, Cello, and Piano (1987; St. Louis, March 25, 1988); works for Solo Instruments; also vocal music, including *Written in Response to a Request for a Manifesto*

on Music, 1952 for Chorus (1980; Berkeley, April 15, 1981) and *My Breakfast with Ronald* for Soprano, Clarinet, and Piano (Raleigh, N.C., March 10, 1985).

Stenberg, Jordan, American avant-garde composer; b. Fresno, Calif., May 31, 1947. He studied music theory with Robert Moran at the San Francisco Cons. and worked on electronic problems with Robert Ashley at Mills College. In his compositions, he aims at creating an organic expression of cosmic philosophy as formalized by his deep reading of Russian theosophists and Indian psychologists. His zodiacal parameters are sun in Gemini, moon in Scorpio, with Libra rising.

WORKS: *88 Fog-Horn Seconds,* a recording of actual Fog-horns on Electronic Tape (1967); *A Snail's Progress in a Gold-fish Bowl* for Strings glissandi within a definite integral of white noise (1968); *Music for 4 Horse-Drawn Carriages,* a literal equestrian exercise (1968); *Mind over Matter,* film opera for Voices and Instruments (1969); *Extension Chords,* to be perf. by nomadic bands on the desert floor during a lunar eclipse or at the winter solstice (1970); *A Stitch in Time* for 11 Acoustical Sources (1970); *The Clock Struck One,* opera-play for Voices, Instruments, and Dervish Dancers (1970); *Circles, Lines, Planes,* a choreographed acoustical dance notated in the form of an enneagram, to be produced in a canyon by 9 Bagpipers and 9 × 9 Buglers (1970). He has also written music for flower conservatories to stimulate the growth of timid plants.

Stenborg, Carl, Swedish tenor, impresario, and composer; b. Stockholm, Sept. 25, 1752; d. Djurgarden, Aug. 1, 1813. His father, Petter Stenborg, was a theater manager. He began appearing in concerts in Stockholm when he was 14; studied vocal and instrumental music with F. Zellbel, the court Kapellmeister; appeared as Peleus in F. Uttini's *Thetis och Pelée* for the opening of the Royal Swedish Opera in 1773; was made a court singer and a member of the Academy of Music in 1782; also was active as a conductor and composer at his father's theater, which he managed from 1780 until it was closed in 1799; after leaving the court in 1806, he ran his own theater. His major work was the singspiel *Gustaf Ericsson i Dalarna* (1784); also wrote incidental music to the dramas *Caspar och Dorothea* (1775) and *Konung Gustaft Adolfs jagt* (1777).

BIBL.: J. Flodmark, *S.ska skadebanorna* (Stockholm, 1893); idem, *Elisabeth Olin och C. S.* (Stockholm, 1903).

Stendhal (real name, **Marie-Henri Beyle**), famous French writer; b. Grenoble, Jan. 23, 1783; d. Paris, March 23, 1842. He received some lessons in singing, violin, and clarinet; served as a military official under Napoleon, taking part in the German and Russian campaigns; from 1815 he lived in Milan, Paris, and Rome; in 1830 he became French consul at Trieste, and from 1831 in Civitavecchia. He became best known as a novelist (*Le Rouge et le noir, La Chartreuse de Parme,* etc.), but also wrote on music; under the name César Bombet, he publ. *Lettres écrites de Vienne, en Autriche, sur le célèbre compositeur Haydn, suivies d'une vie de Mozart, et de considérations sur Métastase et l'état présent de la musique en France et en Italie* (Paris, 1814; Eng. tr., London, 1817; new ed., 1817, as *Vies de Haydn, Mozart et Métastase,* by Stendhal; republ., 1914, by R. Rolland). The life of Haydn is in part tr. from Carpani's *Le Haydine;* the 1st 4 chapters of the life of Mozart are taken from Schlichtegroll's *Necrology* (1791), the last 3 from Cramer's *Anecdotes sur Mozart.* In Jan. 1824 Stendhal's life of Rossini was publ. in London as *Memoirs of Rossini,* in a tr. made from the original MS (republ. as *The Life of Rossini,* London, 1956); the French version, considerably expanded, was publ. in Paris as *Vie de Rossini* (1824; 2nd ed., rev., 1922 by H. Prunières; Eng. tr., 1956; 2nd ed., rev., 1970).

BIBL.: A. Paupe, *Histoire des œuvres de S.* (Paris, 1903); H. Prunières, "S. et la musique," *Revue Hebdomadaire* (1921); A. Beau, *Das Verhältnis S.s zur Musik* (diss., Univ. of Hamburg, 1930); D. Maurice, *S.* (Paris, 1931); P. Jourda, *S., L'Homme et l'œuvre* (Paris, 1934); F. Green, *S.* (Cambridge, 1939); J. Klein, "S. as a Music Critic," *Musical Quarterly* (Jan. 1943).

Stenhammar, Per Ulrik, Swedish composer, father of **(Karl) Wilhelm (Eugen) Stenhammar;** b. Törnvalla, Feb. 20, 1828; d. Stockholm, Feb. 8, 1875. He received his primary musical education from A.F. Lindblad; became interested in sacred music, and wrote choral works in Mendelssohn's style; also many solo songs. His oratorio, *Saul och David* (1869), was orchestrated by his son.

Stenhammar, (Karl) Wilhelm (Eugen), eminent Swedish pianist, conductor, and composer, son of **Per Ulrik Stenhammar;** b. Stockholm, Feb. 7, 1871; d. there, Nov. 20, 1927. He began to play the piano and to compose in childhood; attended Richard Andersson's music school and then studied theory with Joseph Dente and organ with Heintze and Lagergren (1888–89); passed the organists' examination privately (1890); later pursued theory lessons with Emil Sjögren and Andreas Hallén; completed his piano training with Heinrich Barth in Berlin (1892–93). He subsequently toured as a pianist, appearing as a soloist and frequently with the Aulin Quartet. His 1st large work for Solo Voices, Chorus, and Orch., *I rosengård* (In a Rose Garden; 1888–89; after K.A. Melin's collection of fairy tales, *Prinsessan och svennen*), was performed in Stockholm on Feb. 16, 1892, attracting considerable attention; his love for the theater prompted him to compose 2 music dramas, *Gildet på Solhaug* (1892–93) and *Tirfing* (1897–98), neither of which was successful; he did, however, compose much outstanding incidental music. He made his conducting debut with a performance of his overture *Excelsior!* in 1897. After serving as artistic director of the Phil. Soc. (1897–1900), the Royal Theater (1 season), and the New Phil. Soc. (1904–6) in Stockholm, he went to Göteborg as artistic director of the Orch. Soc.; during his tenure (1906–22), he elevated the musical life of the city; then returned to Stockholm, where he again took charge of the Royal Theater (1924–25) before ill health compelled him to retire. Stenhammar's early compositions reflect his preoccupation with the Romantic movement; the influence of Wagner and Liszt is quite perceptible, but he later developed an individual style based on his detailed study of Classical forms. His ability to absorb and transmute authentic folk melodies is a notable characteristic of many of his works. Among his most outstanding scores are the 2nd Sym., the 2nd Piano Concerto, the Serenade for Orch., several of his string quartets, his choral pieces, and a number of his songs.

Works: operas: *Gildet på Solhaug* (The Feast at Solhaug), op. 6, after Ibsen (1892–93; 1st perf. in German as *Das Fest auf Solhaug*, Stuttgart, April 12, 1899; 1st perf. in Swedish, Stockholm, Oct. 31, 1902); *Tirfing*, op. 15 (Stockholm, Dec. 9, 1898); incidental music to Strindberg's *Ett drömspel*, H. Bergman's *Lodolezzi sjunger*, Tagore's *Chitra*, and Shakespeare's *Romeo and Juliet*. **orch.:** 2 piano concertos: No. 1 (1893; Stockholm, March 17, 1894) and No. 2, op. 23 (1904–7; Göteborg, April 15, 1908); *Excelsior!*, overture, op. 13 (1896); 2 syms.: No. 1 (Stockholm, Dec. 1903) and No. 2, op. 34 (1911–15; Göteborg, April 22, 1915); 2 *sentimentala romanser* for Violin and Orch., op. 28 (1910); Serenade, op. 31 (1911–13; rev. 1919). **chamber:** 6 string quartets: No. 1, op. 2 (1894); No. 2, op. 14 (1896); No. 3, op. 18 (1897–1900); No. 4, op. 24 (1905–9); No. 5, op. 29 (1910); No. 6, op. 35 (1916); Violin Sonata, op. 19 (1899–1900). **piano:** 2 sonatas (1890, 1895); *3 fantasier*, op. 11 (1895); *Sensommarnätter*, op. 33 (1914). **choral: with orch.:** *I rosengård* with Solo Voices (1888–89); *Norrland* for Men's Voices; *Snöfrid* with Solo Voices, op. 5 (1891); *Ett folk* with Baritone, op. 22 (1904–5); *Midvinter*, op. 24 (1907); *Folket i Nifelhem Vårnatt*, op. 30 (1911–12); *Sangen* with Solo Voices, op. 44 (1921). **a cappella:** *3 körvisor till dikter av J.P. Jacobsen* (c.1890). **songs:** Voice and orch.: *Florez och Blanzeflor* for Baritone and Orch., op. 3 (1891); *Ur idyll och epigram av J.L. Runeberg* for Mezzo-soprano and Orch., op. 4a (1893); *Ithaka* for Baritone and Orch., op. 21; *4 Stockholmsdikter*, op. 38; other songs.

Bibl.: S. Broman, "W. S.: A Survey," *Music Review* (May 1947); B. Wallner, "W. S. och kammarmusiken," *Svensk Tidskrift för Musikforskning*, XXXIV (1952), XXXV (1953), and XLIII (1961); J. Rabe, "En musikalisk dagbok av W. S.," ibid., XL (1958); special issue of *Musikrevy*, XXVI/6 (1971); H. Connor, "W. S.," in A. Aulin and H. Connor, *Svensk musik* (Stockholm, 1974).

Stenzl, Jürg (Thomas), prominent Swiss musicologist; b. Basel, Aug. 23, 1942. He began instruction in recorder and violin in 1949 in Bern; then studied the oboe with Huwiler at the Bern Cons. in 1961; attended the Univ. of Bern as a student of musicology with Geering and Dickenmann (Ph.D., 1968, with the diss. *Die vierzig Clausulae der Handschrift Paris, Bibliothèque Nationale, latin 15139 [Saint Victor-Clauselae]*; publ. in Bern, 1970); he also worked with Chailley at the Univ. of Paris (1965) and later completed his Habilitation at the Univ. of Fribourg (1974), where he became a prof. in 1980. He was engaged as a visiting prof. at the Univs. of Geneva (1976–77; 1979–80), Neuchâtel (1982), Bern (1986–87), and Basel (1987–88); subsequently served at the Technical Univ. in Berlin (1988–89). He was secretary of the Société Suisse de Musicologie (1972–80) and ed. of the *Schweizerische Musikzeitung* (1975–83); contributed valuable articles and music criticism to various publications, including *Sohlmans Musiklexikon* (1975–79) and *The New Grove Dictionary of Music and Musicians* (1980). His expertise ranges from the Middle Ages to contemporary music.

Štěpán, Václav, Czech pianist and writer on music, father of **Pavel Štěpán;** b. Pečky, near Kolín, Dec. 12, 1889; d. Prague, Nov. 24, 1944. He studied musicology with Nejedlý at the Univ. of Prague (graudated, 1913), and then took courses at the German Univ. of Prague and in Berlin; also studied piano with Josef Čermák in Prague (1895–1908), and later with James Kwast in Berlin and Blanche Selva in Paris. He was active as a pianist from 1908; also taught esthetics (from 1919) and later piano at the Prague Cons. He was an authority on Suk and Novák; a collection of his major articles on these composers appeared as *Novak á Suk* (Prague, 1945); also publ. *Symbolika z přibuzé zjevy v programni hudbě* (Symbolism and Related Phenomena in Program Music; Prague, 1915). He composed some vocal, chamber, and piano pieces but abandoned composition when he was 30.

Stepanian, Aro (Levoni), Armenian composer; b. Elizavetpol, April 24, 1897; d. Erevan, Jan. 9, 1966. He studied with Gnessin in Moscow (1923–27) and with Shcherbachev and Kushnarian at the Leningrad Cons. (1926–30); then settled in Erevan, where he served as president of the Armenian Composers' Union (1938–48). He was one of the leading Armenian composers of his generation.

Works: operas: *Brave Nazar* (1934; Erevan, Nov. 29, 1935); *David of Sasun* (1936); *At the Dawn* (1937); *Nune* (1947); *Heroine* (1950); also 3 syms. (1943, 1945, 1953); 2 piano concertos (1947, 1955); Viola Concerto (1955); *Rhapsody* for Piano and Orch. (1962); 4 string quartets; 2 violin sonatas; Cello Sonata; numerous choruses and songs.

Bibl.: M. Kazakhian, *A. S.* (Erevan, 1962); G. Tigranov, *A. S.* (Moscow, 1967).

Stepanov, Lev, Russian composer; b. Tomsk, Siberia, Dec. 26, 1908. He studied with Miaskovsky at the Moscow Cons., graduating in 1938. He wrote several operas on Russian subjects, among them *Dunia's Happiness* (1937); *The Guards* (Tashkent, Nov. 8, 1947); *Ivan Bolotnikov* (Perm, Dec. 17, 1950); a ballet, *The Native Shore* (1941); 2 piano concertos (1947, 1955); Viola Concerto (1955); chamber music; choruses; many songs.

Stephan, Rudi, German composer; b. Worms, July 29, 1887; d. in battle near Tarnopol, Galicia, Sept. 29, 1915. He studied counterpoint with Bernhard Sekles at the Hoch Cons. in Frankfurt (1905), then went to Munich, where he received instruction in composition from Rudolf Louis and in piano from Heinrich Schwartz (1906–8); also studied philosophy at the Univ. His output is marked by a secure command of harmony and counterpoint with a fine feeling for orch. color. Stephan's tragic death was greatly lamented.

WORKS: *Die ersten Menschen*, opera (1911–14; Frankfurt, July 1, 1920); *Liebeszauber* for Tenor and Orch. (1909–10; Munich, Jan. 16, 1911; withdrawn; rev. for Baritone and Orch., 1913); *Musik für sieben Saiteninstrumente* (2 violins, viola, cello, double bass, harp, and piano; 1911; Danzig, May 30, 1912); *Musik für Orchester* (1912; Jena, June 6, 1913); *Musik für Geige und Orchester* (Berlin, Oct. 10, 1913); 18 songs (1908–14).

BIBL.: K. Holl, *R. S.: Studie zur Entwicklungsgeschichte der Musik am Anfang des 20. Jahrhunderts* (Saarbrücken, 1920; 2nd ed., 1922); A. Machner, *R. S.s Werk* (diss., Univ. of Breslau, 1943); idem, "Zwischen gestern und heute: Ein Wort für R. S.," *Musica*, VIII (1954); A. McCredie, "The Munich School and R. S. (1887–1915): Some Forgotten Sources and Byways of Musical Jugendstil and Expressionism," *Music Review*, XXIX (1968); R. Blackburn, "R. S.: An Unfulfilled Talent?," *Musical Times* (July 1987).

Stephan, (Gustav-Adolf Carl) Rudolf, learned German musicologist; b. Bochum, April 3, 1925. He studied in Heidelberg, receiving instruction in violin at the Cons., in music theory with Fortner at the Inst. of Protestant Church Music, and in musicology with Besseler and in philosophy with Jaspers and Hofmann at the Univ. He subsequently studied at the Univ. of Göttingen, where he took courses in philosophy with Hartmann and in musicology with Gerber (Ph.D., 1950, with the diss. *Die Tenores der Motetten Ältesten Stils*); completed his Habilitation there in 1963 with his *Antiphonar-Studien*, and then served on its faculty as a lecturer (1966–67). He was engaged as a prof. at the Free Univ. of Berlin (from 1967); was a visiting prof. at the Univ. of Vienna in 1981. He became ed. of the Schoenberg Gesamtausgabe in 1968; was president of the Institut für Neue Musik und Musikerziehung in Darmstadt (1970–76) and of the Gesellschaft für Musikforschung from 1980. He has written valuable articles on topics ranging from medieval music to Hindemith for a variety of publications.

WRITINGS: *Musik* (Frankfurt am Main, 1957); *Neue Musik* (Göttingen, 1958; 2nd ed., 1973); *Gustav Mahler: Vierte Symphonie G-Dur* (Munich, 1966); *Alexander Zemlinsky: Ein unbekannter Meister der Wiener Schule* (Kiel, 1978); *Gustav Mahler: Zweite Symphonie C-Moll* (Munich, 1979); *Gustav Mahler: Werk und Interpretation* (Cologne, 1979); *Vom musikalischen Denken* (Mainz, 1985); *Alban Berg: Violinkonzert* (Munich, 1988); *Die Wiener Schule* (Darmstadt, 1989).

Stephănescu, George, noted Rumanian conductor, teacher, and composer; b. Bucharest, Dec. 13, 1843; d. there, April 25, 1925. He studied harmony and piano with Wachmann at the Bucharest Cons. (1864–67); then pursued his training at the Paris Cons. (1867–71), where he studied harmony with Réber, composition with Auber and Thomas, piano with Marmontel, and singing with Delle; returning to Bucharest, he taught singing and opera at the Cons. (1872–1904); was a conductor of the Rumanian Opera at the National Theater (from 1877), for which he wrote several works in an effort to produce native scores for the stage; also was active as a music critic. Stephănescu was one of the foremost figures in Rumanian musical life of his era. He composed the 1st Rumanian sym. (1869). His output reflects his interest in Rumanian folk tunes, although he did not directly quote from such sources.

WORKS: OPERA: *Petra* (1902). **OPERETTAS:** *Peste Dunăre* (Across the Danube; 1880); *Scaiul bărbaţilor* (Men's Burr; 1885); *Cometa* (1900). **MUSICAL FAIRY TALE:** *Sînziana şi Pepelea* (1880). **ORCH.:** Sym. (1869); *Uverta naţionala* (1876); Symphonic poems: *In munţi* (In the Mountains; 1888); *In cring* (In the Meadow; 1889); *Intre flori* (1890); *In alte timpuri* (In Old Times; 1895); *Idilă* (1902). **CHAMBER:** Piano Sonata (1863); Cello Sonata (1863); Octet (1866); Septet (1870); String Quartet (1870); also choruses and songs.

BIBL.: V. Tomescu, "Un înaintaş al muzicii noastre" (A Forefather of Our Music), *Muzica*, I (Bucharest, 1954); G. Stephănescu, *G. S.: Viaţa în imagini* (G. S.: Life in Pictures; Bucharest, 1962).

Stephani, Hermann, German musicologist and composer; b. Grimma, June 23, 1877; d. Marburg, Dec. 3, 1960. He studied at the Leipzig Cons. with Jadassohn and Reinecke, and at the Univ. of Munich with Lipps and Sandberger; obtained his Ph.D. there in 1902 with the dissertation *Das Erhabene, insonderheit in der Tonkunst, und das Problem der Form* (publ. in Leipzig, 1903; 2nd ed., 1907). In 1921 he was appointed to the faculty of the Univ. of Marburg; taught musicology there until 1946. His scholarly publications include: *Der Charakter der Tonarten* (Habilitationsschrift, Univ. of Marburg, 1921; publ. in Regensburg, 1923); *Grundfragen des Musikhörens* (Leipzig, 1925); *Das Vierteltonproblem* (Leipzig, 1925); *Polare Harmonik bei Beethoven* (Leipzig, 1927); *Das Problem des Orgelstils* (Essen, 1942). He advocated a reform in score notation through the exclusive use of the G clef with octave indications ("Einheitspartitur") and ed. Schumann's *Manfred* overture using this system (1905). He wrote about 100 opus numbers, mostly vocal works; also contrapuntal pieces for various combinations of instruments; ed. works by Handel, Weber, etc. A Festschrift was presented to him on his 70th birthday (Regensburg, 1947).

Stephens, Catherine, noted English soprano and actress; b. London, Sept. 18, 1794; d. there, Feb. 22, 1882. She studied voice with Gesualdo Lanza; after appearing in the English provinces, she sang minor roles with an Italian opera company at London's Pantheon (1822); following additional vocal training with Thomas Welsh, she made her debut at London's Covent Garden as Mandane in Arne's *Artaxerxes* (Sept. 23, 1813); she sang there with much success until 1822; after singing at Drury Lane (1822–28), she returned to Covent Garden and appeared there until her retirement in 1835. In 1838 she married the Earl of Essex. She was highly successful as a concert and oratorio singer, as well as a singer and actress in the theater; sang Susanna in the 1st performance in English of *Le nozze di Figaro* (1819); Weber's last work, the song *From Chindara's warbling fount I come* (1826), was written for her.

Stephens, John (Elliott), American conductor and composer; b. Washington, D.C., Nov. 6, 1929. He studied at the Catholic Univ. of America in Washington, D.C. (B.M., 1959; M.M., 1962; D.M.A., 1972); also had lessons in 20th-century conducting with Boulez at the Basel Academy of Music (certificate, 1969), and studied composition privately with Wuorinen, Shapey, and Brant. He founded and was music director of the American Camerata for New Music in Washington, D.C., with which he appeared widely and made numerous recordings; taught at George Washington Univ. (1963–74), Catholic Univ. (1967–68), American Univ. (1976–83), and the Univ. of the District of Columbia (from 1983). He produced for radio the acclaimed educational series "New Sounds for Young Ears."

WORKS: String Quartet (1959); Concert Piece for Jazz Band (1960); Sym. in 1 Movement (1962); Sextet for Woodwind Quintet and Piano (1963); Chamber Sym. (1964); *Inventions* for Treble Instruments (1965); *Concert Music* for Flutes and Piano (1970); Cantata for Narrator, Chamber Chorus, Baritone, Boy's Choir, and Chamber Ensemble (1972); Songs for Soprano, Flute, Harp, and Strings (1975); *Inventions* for Clarinet (1978); *Creations* for Trombone and String Quartet (1982); *3 for 4* for Harp, Flute/Piccolo, Viola, and Trombone (1984); Double Concerto for Flute, Oboe, Strings, Percussion, and Harp (1988).

Steptoe, Roger (Guy), English composer and pianist; b. Winchester, Hampshire, Jan. 25, 1953. He studied at the Univ. of Reading (B.A., 1974) and received training in composition from Alan Bush at the Royal Academy of Music in London (1974–76). After serving as composer-in-residence at Charterhouse School, Surrey (1976–79), he was a prof. of composition at the Royal Academy of Music (from 1981). He also was active as a pianist.

WORKS: OPERA: *King of Macedon* (Surrey, Oct. 18, 1979). **ORCH.:** *2 Miniatures* for String Orch. (1977; Oxford, May 29, 1982); *Sinfonia concertante* for Violin, Viola, Cello, and Strings (1981; London, June 26, 1982); Concerto for Oboe and Strings

(1982; Crewe, Jan. 10, 1984); Concerto for Tuba and Strings (1983; London, Oct. 27, 1986); *Rapsodia sinfonica*, concerto for Violin and Orch. (1987); Sym. (1988). **CHAMBER:** 2 string quartets: No. 1 (1976; London, Jan. 5, 1977); No. 2 (1985; Aberystwyth, May 5, 1986); Suite for Solo Cello (1977); Study for Violin (1978); 2 *Impromptus* for Clarinet (1978); Quintet for Clarinet and Strings (1980); Study for Guitar (1981); *The Knight of the Sun* for Brass Quintet (1982); 3 *Pieces* for Viola and Piano (1982); 2 violin sonatas (1983, 1986); 2 *Studies* for Bassoon and Piano (1983); 4 *Sonnets* for Brass Quintet (1984); Quartet for Oboe and Strings (1988; Berlin, April 18, 1989); also piano pieces, including 3 *Preludes* (1976), 2 sonatas (1979, 1988), and *Equinox* (1981). **VOCAL:** 2 *Madrigals* for Choir (1976); 2 *Introits* for Choir and Organ (1977, 1985); *The Looking Glass* for Soprano, Oboe, and Piano (1980); *Chinese Lyrics*: set 1 for Soprano and Piano (1982) and set 2 for Mezzo-soprano or Countertenor and Piano (1983); *Another Part of the Forest*, scena for 4 Voices and Piano (1983); *In Winter's Cold Embraces Dye*, cantata for Mezzo-soprano, Tenor, Chorus, and Orch. (1985); *Elegy on the Death and Burial of Cock Robin* for Countertenor and 11 Solo Strings (1988).

Sterkel, Johann Franz Xaver, prominent German pianist, teacher, and composer; b. Würzburg, Dec. 3, 1750; d. there, Oct. 12, 1817. He received a thorough training in music from A. Kette, the court organist, and from Weismandel in Würzburg; also attended the Univ. there. In 1768 he was tonsured and named organist in the collegiate chapter of Neumünster, where he subsequently was made subdeacon (1772), deacon (1773), and priest (1774). In 1778 he was called to Mainz to serve the Liebfrauen chapter and as court chaplain; the Elector then sent him to Italy, where he toured widely as a pianist (1779–82) and produced the opera *Il Farnace* (Naples, Jan. 12, 1782); subsequently returned to Mainz to serve as a canon of his chapter. Beethoven heard him play in Aschaffenburg in 1791 and was greatly impressed by him as a pianist and composer. The French invasion of 1792 wreaked havoc with the Mainz court, but when the city was regained in 1793, Sterkel was named court Kapellmeister; however, continued warfare led to the closing of the royal chapel in 1797 and Sterkel returned to Würzburg, where he was active at the court. About 1802 he went to Regensburg, where he found a patron in Karl Theodor von Dalberg; he founded his own choir school. When his patron was made Grand Duke of Frankfurt in 1810, Sterkel went with him to Aschaffenburg as his music director. The court was disbanded in 1814 and he returned once more to Würzburg in 1815. Sterkel was a prolific composer; his most important works are his chamber music and keyboard pieces.
WORKS: OPERA: *Il Farnace* (Naples, Jan. 12, 1782). **ORCH.:** 22 syms.; 4 overtures; 6 piano concertos. **CHAMBER:** 43 piano or harpsichord trios; 28 piano or harpsichord sonatas; Grand Quintette for 2 Violins, 2 Violas, and Cello; Piano Quartet; 6 duos for Violin and Viola; numerous solo piano pieces, including 13 sonatas, 6 of which are for 4–hands; other works include 4 festival masses, 2 Te Deums, and other sacred music, and numerous lieder.
BIBL.: A. Scharnagl, *J.F.X. S.: Ein Beitrag zur Musikgeschichte Mainfrankens* (Würzburg, 1943); W. Newman, *The Sonata in the Classic Era* (Chapel Hill, 1963; 3rd ed., rev., 1983).

Sterling, Antoinette, American contralto; b. Sterlingville, N.Y., Jan. 23, 1850; d. London, Jan. 9, 1904. She studied with Abella in N.Y., Mathilde Marchesi in Cologne, and Pauline Viardot-Garcia in Baden; also took lessons with Manuel García in London. Returning to America (1871), she sang in Henry Ward Beecher's church in Brooklyn; then went to London, where she made her debut at a Covent Garden Promenade Concert (Nov. 5, 1873). She introduced many favorite songs (most of which were composed especially for her), such as Arthur Sullivan's *Lost Chord* (Jan. 31, 1877) and Barnby's *When the Tide Comes In*. In 1875 she toured the U.S.; her permanent home was in London.

BIBL.: M. MacKinlay (her son), *A. S. and Other Celebrities* (London, 1906).

Stern, Isaac, outstanding Russian-born American violinist; b. Kremenetz, July 21, 1920. He was taken to the U.S. as an infant and was trained in music by his mother, who was a professional singer. He studied the violin at the San Francisco Cons. (1928–31), then with Louis Persinger; also studied with Naoum Blinder (1932–37). On Feb. 18, 1936, he made his orch. debut as soloist in Saint-Saëns's 3rd Violin Concerto with the San Francisco Sym. Orch.; his N.Y. debut followed on Oct. 11, 1937. After further training in San Francisco, he returned to N.Y. and gave a notably successful concert on Feb. 18, 1939; his Carnegie Hall debut there on Jan. 8, 1943, was a triumph. In 1947 he toured Australia; made his European debut at the Lucerne Festival in 1948; subsequently appeared regularly with American and European orchs.; in 1956 he made a spectacularly successful tour of Russia. In 1961 he organized a trio with the pianist Eugene Istomin and the cellist Leonard Rose, which toured widely until Rose's death. In 1986 he celebrated the 50th anniversary of his orch. debut. He received various honors; in 1979 he was made an Officer of the Légion d'honneur of France, in 1984 he received the Kennedy Center Honors Award, and in 1987 was given the Wolf Prize of Israel. Stern belongs to the galaxy of virtuoso performers to whom fame is a natural adjunct to talent and industry; he is also active in general cultural undertakings, and is an energetic worker for the cause of human rights.
BIBL.: J. Wechsberg, "Profiles: I. S.," *New Yorker* (June 5, 1965); B. Schwarz, *Great Masters of the Violin* (N.Y., 1983); *Current Biography* (Feb. 1989).

Stern, Julius, eminent German music pedagogue; b. Breslau, Aug. 8, 1820; d. Berlin, Feb. 27, 1883. He studied violin with Lüstner, and later took courses with Maurer, Ganz, and Rungenhagen in Berlin; then studied singing in Dresden (1843) and subsequently in Paris, where he conducted the German Gesangverein. In 1846 he settled in Berlin, where he was founder-conductor of the Sternscher Gesangverein (1847–74); also conducted the Sinfonie-Kapelle (1869–71) and the Reichshalle concerts (1873–75). In 1850 he founded the Berlin Cons. with Kullak and Marx; Kullak withdrew in 1855, and Marx in 1857; thenceforth Stern became the sole head of the institution, now known as the Julius Stern Staatliche Hochschule für Musik; it prospered and acquired the reputation of one of the greatest music schools in Europe. He was also a composer, and received commendation from Mendelssohn for his songs; publ. *Barcarolle* for Voice, Cello, and Piano; *Les Adieux* for Violin and Piano; male choruses; songs. His opera, *Ismene*, was not produced. He also wrote singing exercises which were long in use.
BIBL.: R. Stern, *Erinnerungsblätter an J. S.* (Berlin, 1886).

Stern, Leo(pold Lawrence), noted English cellist; b. Brighton, April 5, 1862; d. London, Sept. 10, 1904. His father was a violinist and his mother a pianist; he played drum in the Brighton Sym. Soc. orch. conducted by his father; in 1877 he went to London to study chemistry, but also had cello lessons with Hugo Daubert; then studied with Pezze and Piatti at the Royal Academy of Music (1883–85); completed his training with Klengel and Davidov in Leipzig (1885–86). In 1886 he performed in London and other English cities; after touring with Adelina Patti in 1888, he gave concerts with Sauret, Paderewski, Albani, Godard, and Massenet. He was the soloist in the premiere of Dvořák's Cello Concerto (London, March 19, 1896, composer conducting), which he later performed in Leipzig, Prague, and Berlin; after touring North America (1897–98), he returned to London, but ill health compelled him to give up his career. He composed pieces for cello and songs. His 2nd wife was **Suzanne Adams.**

Sternberg, Constantin, Russian-American pianist, teacher, and composer; b. St. Petersburg, July 9, 1852; d. Philadelphia, March 31, 1924. He studied piano with Moscheles at the Leipzig Cons., and later had lessons with Theodor Kullak;

also visited Liszt at Weimar. He toured Russia as a concert pianist; in 1880 he emigrated to the U.S. In 1890 he established the Sternberg School of Music in Philadelphia, and was its director until his death. He was greatly esteemed as a piano teacher. He wrote some 200 salon pieces for piano, and *Danses cosaques* for Violin; publ. *Ethics and Esthetics of Piano Playing* (N.Y., 1917) and *Tempo Rubato and Other Essays* (N.Y., 1920).

Sternberg, Erich Walter, German-born Israeli composer; b. Berlin, May 31, 1891; d. Tel Aviv, Dec. 15, 1974. He studied composition with Hugo Leichtentritt in Berlin; emigrated to Palestine, and taught at the Tel Aviv Cons. He was co-founder of the Palestine Sym. Orch. (now the Israel Phil.). As a composer, he was inspired by biblical subjects.
WORKS: Children's opera, *Dr. Dolittle* (Jerusalem, 1939); opera "for children and others," *Pacificia, the Friendly Island* (1972–74); 2 string quartets (1924, 1926); *The Story of David and Goliath* for Baritone and Orch. (1927); *Joseph and His Brothers,* suite for String Orch. (1938); *The 12 Tribes of Israel,* variations for Orch. (1941; Tel Aviv, May 3, 1942); *My People,* 5 songs for Soprano or Tenor and Orch. (1945); *Höre Israel* for Orch. (1948); *The Raven,* after Poe, for Baritone and Orch. (1949); Violin Sonata (1955); *Contrapuntal Study* for Orch. (1955); *Sichot Haruach* (Conversations with the Wind) for Contralto and Orch. (1956); *The Distant Flute,* 3 songs for Voice and Flute (1958); oratorio, *Techiat Israel* (The Resurrection of Israel; 1959); *Tewat Noah* (Noah's Ark), 4 movements for Orch. in the form of a sym. (1960); *Tefilot* (Prayers of Humility) for Contralto and Chamber Orch. (1962); *The Sacrifice of Isaac* for Soprano and Orch. (1965); *Love Songs* for Chorus and Orch. (1968); *The Wretched* for Baritone and String Orch. (1969); *My Brother Jonathan* for Chorus and String Orch. (1969); Piano Trio; Wind Quintet; songs.

Sternberg, Jonathan, American conductor; b. N.Y., July 27, 1919. He studied at the Juilliard School of Music (1929–31), N.Y. Univ. (B.A., 1939; graduate study, 1939–40), and the Manhattan School of Music (1946); took conducting lessons with Monteux at his summer school (1946, 1947). In 1947 he made his conducting debut with the Vienna Sym. Orch.; then toured extensively as a guest conductor in Europe, North America, and the Far East. He was music director of the Royal Flemish Opera in Antwerp (1961–62), the Harkness Ballet in N.Y. (1966–68), and the Atlanta Opera and Ballet (1968–69); then was a visiting prof. of conducting at the Eastman School of Music in Rochester, N.Y. (1969–71), and prof. of music at Temple Univ. (from 1971).

Sternefeld, Daniël, Belgian conductor and composer; b. Antwerp, Nov. 27, 1905; d. Brussels, June 2, 1986. He studied flute and music theory at the Antwerp Cons. (1918–24); then composition with Gilson and conducting with van der Stucken (1928); subsequently took lessons in conducting with Paumgartner, Krauss, and Karajan at the Mozarteum in Salzburg. He was a flutist in the orch. of the Royal Flemish Opera in Antwerp (1929–38); then was its 2nd conductor (1938–44) and principal conductor (1944–48); subsequently was chief conductor of the Belgian Radio and Television Orch. in Brussels (1948–72); also appeared as a guest conductor in Europe and South America. He taught conducting at the Antwerp Cons. (1949–71).
WORKS: STAGE: *Mater Dolorosa,* opera (1934; Antwerp, 1935); 3 ballets: *Pierlala* (1937), *Antverpia* (1975), and *Rossini-azata* (1982); incidental music to various plays. **ORCH.:** *Variations symphoniques* (1928); *Elégie* (1931); *Suite de vieilles chansons flamandes et wallonnes* for Chamber Orch. (1934); 2 syms.: No. 1 (1943) and No. 2, *Bruegelsymfonie* (1981–83); *Frère Jacques,* variations for Brass and Percussion (1955); Divertimento for Wind Orch. (1980); *Waaier* (1984); also some chamber music, including *Étude-passacaglia* for Harp (1979) and a Quintet for Flute, Oboe, Clarinet, Bassoon, and Horn (1986).

Sternfeld, F(riedrich) W(ilhelm), Austrian-born English musicologist; b. Vienna, Sept. 25, 1914. He took courses with Lach and Wellesz at the Univ. of Vienna (from 1933); then pursued his training with Schrade at Yale Univ. (Ph.D., 1943, with the diss. *Goethe and Music*); held a Guggenheim fellowship (1954). He taught at Wesleyan Univ. (1940–46) and Dartmouth College (1946–56); also was a member of the Inst. for Advanced Studies at Princeton Univ. (1955). In 1956 he joined the faculty of Oxford Univ., where he served as a reader in music history (from 1972). He also became a British subject. He was ed. of *Renaissance News* (1946–54) and of the *Proceedings of the Royal Musical Association* (1957–62); publ. the books *Goethe's Relationship to Music: A List of References* (N.Y., 1954), *Music in Shakespearean Tragedy* (London, 1963; 2nd ed., 1967), and *Songs from Shakespeare's Tragedies* (London, 1964). He also ed. *A History of Western Music* (London, 1973); with Wellesz, the 7th vol. of *The New Oxford History of Music: The Age of Enlightenment 1745–1790* (Oxford, 1973); and with others, *Essays on Opera and English Music in Honour of Sir Jack Westrup* (Oxford, 1975).

Steuerlein, Johann, German organist, poet, and composer; b. Schmalkalden, Thuringia, July 5, 1546; d. Meiningen, May 5, 1613. He studied at the Magdeburg grammar school (1559–62) and at the Univ. of Wittenberg; concurrently served as a chancery clerk in Burgbreitungen; then was town clerk, organist, and Kantor in Wasungen, near Mainingen (1569–89); subsequently was chancellery secretary to the Elector of Saxony in Meiningen (from 1589), where he was made public notary and mayor in 1604; also was crowned poet laureate. He remains best known for the celebrated song *Das alte Jahr vergangen ist* for 6 Voices. He also publ. many vols. of vocal music.
BIBL.: G. Kraft, "J. S. (1546–1613)," *Zeitschrift für Musikwissenschaft,* XIII (1930–31).

Steuermann, Edward (actually, **Eduard**), eminent Polish-American pianist, pedagogue, and composer; b. Sambor, near Lemberg, June 18, 1892; d. N.Y., Nov. 11, 1964. He studied piano with Ferruccio Busoni in Berlin (1911–12), and theory with Schoenberg (1912–14); also took some composition lessons with Engelbert Humperdinck. Returning to Poland, he taught at the Paderewski School in Lwow, and concurrently at the Jewish Cons. in Krakow (1932–36). In 1936 he emigrated to the U.S.; taught piano at the Juilliard School of Music in N.Y. (1952–64); also was on the faculty of the Philadelphia Cons. (1948–63); gave summer classes at the Mozarteum in Salzburg (1953–63) and Darmstadt (1954, 1957, 1958, 1960). As a concert pianist and soloist with major orchs., Steuermann was an ardent champion of new music, particularly of Schoenberg; gave the 1st performance of Schoenberg's Piano Concerto (1944); made excellent arrangements for piano of Schoenberg's operatic and symphonic works, among them *Erwartung, Die glückliche Hand, Kammersymphonie* No. 1, and the Piano Concerto; received the Schoenberg Medal from the ISCM in 1952. Although he did not follow Schoenberg's method of composition with 12 tones with any degree of consistency, his music possesses an expressionistic tension that is characteristic of the 2nd Viennese School.
WORKS: *Variations* for Orch. (1958); *Music for Instruments* (1959–60); *Suite* for Chamber Orch. (1964); 7 *Waltzes* for String Quartet (1946); Piano Trio (1954); *Improvisation and Allegro* for Violin and Piano (1955); string quartet, *Diary* (1960–61); *Dialogues* for Unaccompanied Violin (1963); Piano Sonata (1926); *Piano Suite* (1952); 3 *Choirs* (1956); *Cantata,* after Franz Kafka, for Chorus and Orch. (1964); *Brecht-Lieder* for Contralto (1945); a number of other songs to Polish and German texts.

Stevens, Bernard (George), English composer; b. London, March 2, 1916; d. there, Jan. 2, 1983. He studied composition with Dent and Rootham at Cambridge (1934–37) and with Morris and Jacob at the Royal College of Music in London (1937–40), where he was named a prof. of composition in 1948; received his Mus.D. from Cambraidge Univ. in 1968. He wrote a number of works for various instrumental combinations; his music adheres to traditional concepts of harmony, while the programmatic content is often colored by his radical political beliefs.

WORKS: ORCH.: Violin Concerto (1943); *Ricercar* for Strings (1944); *A Symphony of Liberation* (1945); Cello Concerto (1952); Piano Concerto (1955); Sym. No. 2 (1964); *Choriamb* (1968); *Introduction, Variations and Fugue on a Theme of Giles Farnaby* (1972). **VOCAL:** Cantatas: *The Harvest of Peace* (1952); *The Pilgrims of Hope* (1956); *Et resurrexit* (1969); *The Turning World* for Baritone, Chorus, and Orch. (1971). **CHAMBER:** Trio for Violin, Horn, and Piano (1966); *Suite* for 6 Instruments (1967); *The Bramble Briar* for Guitar (1974); piano pieces.

BIBL.: B. Stevens, ed., *B. S. and His Music: A Symposium* (White Plains, N.Y., 1989).

Stevens, Denis (William), distinguished English violinist, musicologist, and conductor; b. High Wycombe, Buckinghamshire, March 2, 1922. He studied music with R.O. Morris, Egon Wellesz, and Hugh Allen at Jesus College, Oxford (M.A., 1947); played violin and viola in the Philharmonia Orch. of London (1948–49); then was a program planner in the music dept. of the BBC (1949–54). He served as a visiting prof. of music at Cornell Univ. (1955) and Columbia Univ. (1956), and taught at the Royal Academy of Music in London (1956–61). He subsequently was a visiting prof. at the Univ. of Calif. at Berkeley (1962) and at Pa. State Univ. (1963–64). He was prof. of musicology at Columbia Univ. (1964–76). He was also a visiting prof. at the Univ. of Calif. at Santa Barbara (1974) and at the Univ. of Washington at Seattle (1976–77). As a conductor, he was co-founder of the Ambrosian Singers in 1952 and served as president and artistic director of the Accademia Monteverdiana from 1961; in his programs, he emphasized early polyphonic works. He ed. several important collections, including *The Mulliner Book*, vol. I in the Musica Britannica series (1951; 3rd ed., rev., 1962); *Early Tudor Organ Music*, in the Early English Church Music series (1969); and works by Monteverdi. He was made a Commander of the Order of the British Empire in 1984.

WRITINGS: *The Mulliner Book: A Commentary* (London, 1952); *Tudor Church Music* (N.Y., 1955; 3rd ed., 1966); *Thomas Tomkins 1572–1656* (London, 1957; 2nd ed., 1967); ed. *A History of Song* (London, 1960; 2nd ed., 1970); co-ed., with A. Robertson, *The Pelican History of Music* (3 vols., Harmondsworth, 1960–68); *Plainsong Hymns and Sequences* (London, 1965); *Claudio Monteverdi: Sacred, Secular and Occasional Music* (N.Y., 1977); ed. and tr. *The Letters of Claudio Monteverdi* (London, 1980); ed. *Ten Renaissance Dialogues* (Seven Oaks, 1981); T. Lewis, ed., *Musicology in Practice: Collected Essays, Vol. I, 1948–1970* (N.Y., 1987).

Stevens, Halsey, significant American composer, teacher, and writer on music; b. Scott, N.Y., Dec. 3, 1908; d. Long Beach, Calif., Jan. 20, 1989. He studied composition with William Berwald at Syracuse Univ. (B.M., 1931; M.M., 1937) and with Ernst Bloch at the Univ. of Calif. at Berkeley (1944). He taught at Syracuse Univ. (1935–37) and Dakota Wesleyan Univ. (1937–41); was a prof. and director of the College of Music at Bradley Polytechnic Inst. in Peoria, Ill. (1941–46), and then a prof. at the Univ. of Redlands (1946). In 1946 he joined the faculty of the Univ. of Southern Calif. in Los Angeles, serving in various capacities until his retirement as prof. emeritus in 1976. He was a visiting prof. at Pomona College (1954), the Univ. of Washington (1958), Yale Univ. (1960–61), the Univ. of Cincinnati (1968), and Williams College (1969). His music is above all a monument of sonorous equilibrium; melodies and rhythms are coordinated in a fine melorhythmic polyphony; dissonances are emancipated and become natural consorts of triadic harmony. Tonality remains paramount, while a stream of coloristic passages contributes to the brilliance of the instrumental texture. Stevens wrote only "absolute" music, without resort to the stage; there are no operas or ballets in his creative catalog. He does not apply conventional modernistic devices in his music, designed at its culmination to please the aural sense. Apart from composition, Stevens took great interest in the autochthonous music of the

peoples of the earth; he was particularly fascinated by the fieldwork that Béla Bartók undertook in gathering authentic folk songs of southeastern Europe. He mastered the Hungarian language, retraced Bartók's travels, and assembled materials on Bartók's life; the result was his exemplary biography, *The Life and Music of Béla Bartók* (N.Y., 1953; 2nd ed., rev., 1964). Stevens received numerous grants and honors; he held 2 Guggenheim fellowships (1964–65; 1971–72), a grant from the NEA (1976), and the Abraham Lincoln Award of the American Hungarian Foundation (1978).

WORKS: ORCH.: 3 syms.: No. 1 (1945; San Francisco, March 7, 1946, composer conducting; rev., Los Angeles, March 3, 1950); No. 2 (1945; N.Y., May 17, 1947); No. 3 (1946); *A Green Mountain Overture* (Burlington, Vt., Aug. 7, 1948; rev. 1953); *Triskelion* (a figure with 3 branches; 1953; Louisville, Feb. 27, 1954); *Sinfonia breve* (Louisville, Nov. 20, 1957); *Symphonic Dances* (San Francisco, Dec. 10, 1958); Cello Concerto (1964; Los Angeles, May 12, 1968); *Threnos: In Memoriam Quincy Porter* (1968); Concerto for Clarinet and String Orch. (Denton, Texas, March 20, 1969); Double Concerto for Violin, Cello, and String Orch. (Los Angeles, Nov. 4, 1973); Viola Concerto (1975). **CHAMBER:** Piano Trio No. 2 (1945); Quintet for Flute, Violin, Viola, Cello, and Piano (1945; Middlebury, Vt., Aug. 30, 1946); *Suite* for Clarinet and Piano (1945; rev. 1953); Bassoon Sonata (1949); String Quartet No. 3 (1949); *3 Hungarian Folk Songs* for Viola and Piano (1950); Viola Sonata (1950); Horn Sonata (1953); Trumpet Sonata (1956); Piano Trio No. 3 (1954); *Sonatina piacevoloe* for Flute and Harpsichord (1956); Septet for Clarinet, Bassoon, Horn, 2 Violas, and 2 Cellos (Urbana, Ill., March 3, 1957); *Divertimento* for 2 Violins (1958–66); Suite for Viola and Piano (1959); Sonatina for Bass Tuba and Piano (1960); *12 Slovakian Folk Songs* for 2 Violins (1962); Cello Sonata (1965); Oboe Sonata (1971); *Quintetto "Serbelloni"* for Woodwinds (1972); also works for solo instruments. **PIANO:** 3 sonatas (1933–48); *Partita* (1954); 6 preludes (1956); *Ritratti* (1960); *Fantasia* (1961); numerous other pieces. **VOCAL:** *The Ballad of William Sycamore* for Chorus and Orch. (Los Angeles, Oct. 6, 1955); *2 Shakespeare Songs* for Voice, Flute, and Clarinet (1959); *A Testament of Life* for Tenor, Bass, Chorus, and Orch. (1959); *4 Canciones* for Voice and Piano (1961); *Magnificat* for Chorus and String Orch. (1962); *7 Canciones* for Voice and Piano (1964); *Campion Suite* for Chorus (1967); *Te Deum* for Chorus, Brass Septet, Organ, and Timpani (1967); *Chansons courtoises* for Chorus (1967); *Songs from the Paiute* for Chorus, 4 Flutes, and Timpani (1976).

BIBL.: P. Pisk, "The Music of H. S.," *American Composers Alliance Bulletin*, IV/2 (1954); J. Murphy, *The Choral Music of H. S.* (diss., Texas Tech Univ., 1980); P. Vanderkoy, *A Survey of the Choral Music of H. S.* (diss., Ball State Univ., 1981).

Stevens, John (Edgar), distinguished English musicologist; b. London, Oct. 8, 1921. He studied classics (1940–41) and English (B.A., 1948) at Magdalene College, Cambridge; then pursued training with Dart at the Univ. there (Ph.D., 1953, with the diss. *Early Tudor Song Books*); served on the univ. faculty as a teacher of English (1952–74), reader in English and music history (1974–78), and prof. of medieval and Renaissance English (from 1978). He was made a Commander of the Order of the British Empire in 1980. An erudite scholar, he contributed greatly to the understanding of music from the medieval and Renaissance periods. In addition to his books and articles, he ed. works for the Musica Britannica series. His writings include *Music and Poetry in the Early Tudor Court* (London, 1961; 2nd ed., rev., 1979), *Medieval Romance* (London, 1973), and *Words and Music in the Middle Ages* (London, 1986).

Stevens, Richard John Samuel, English organist and composer; b. London, March 27, 1757; d. there, Sept. 23, 1837. He was a chorister at St. Paul's Cathedral in London; from 1786 to 1810 he served as organist at the Inner Temple; from 1801 he was a prof. of music at Gresham College; ed. *Sacred Music . . . from the Works of the Most Esteemed Composers, Italian and English* (c.1798–1802). Stevens was one of the finest glee composers of his day. His most celebrated glees were *Ye Spotted Snakes* (1782; rev. 1791), *Sigh No More, Ladies* (1787), *Crabbed Age and Youth* (1790), *Blow, Blow, Thou Winter Wind* (1792), and *The Cloud-Cap't Towers* (1795). He also wrote an opera; *Emma*, an oratorio, *The Captivity;* various keyboard pieces, including 3 sonatas, church music, and songs.

BIBL.: J. Trend, "R.J.S. S. and His Contemporaries," *Music & Letters,* XIV (1934); C. Cudworth, "R.J.S. S. 1757–1837," *Musical Times,* CIII (1962).

Stevens, Risë, noted American mezzo-soprano; b. N.Y., June 11, 1913. The original family surname was Steenberg. She studied voice with Orry Prado; after graduating from high school, she sang minor roles with the N.Y. Opera-Comique Co. The enterprise soon went bankrupt, and for a while she had to earn her living by dress modeling, before she was offered free singing lessons by Anna Schoen-René at the Juilliard School of Music. She was subsequently sent to Salzburg to study with Marie Gutheil-Schoder at the Mozarteum, and later entered classes in stage direction with Herbert Graf. In 1936 she was engaged by Szell for the Prague Opera as a contralto; she prepared several roles from standard operas, coaching with George Schick. She went on a tour to Cairo, Egypt, with a Vienna opera group, and then sang at the Teatro Colón in Buenos Aires. She made her American debut as Octavian in *Der Rosenkavalier* with the Metropolitan Opera in Philadelphia on Nov. 22, 1938. She greatly extended her repertoire, and added Wagnerian roles to her appearances with the Metropolitan. On Jan. 9, 1939, she married in N.Y. the Czech actor Walter Surovy, who became her business manager. In 1939 she sang at the Glyndebourne Festival in England; on Oct. 12, 1940, she appeared with the San Francisco Opera as Cherubino; in 1941 she joined Nelson Eddy in a film production of the operetta *The Chocolate Soldier,* and in 1944 acted in the movie *Going My Way,* in which she sang the Habanera from *Carmen;* on Dec. 28, 1945, she appeared as Carmen at the Metropolitan Opera, scoring a fine success. Carmen became her most celebrated role; she sang it 75 times with the Metropolitan. She remained with the Metropolitan until 1961. On March 24, 1954, she appeared for the 1st time at La Scala in Milan. She retired from the stage in 1964. In 1975 she joined the teaching staff at the Juilliard School in N.Y. She also served as president of the Mannes College of Music in N.Y. (1975–78).

BIBL.: K. Crichton, *Subway to the Met: R. S.' Story* (N.Y., 1959).

Stevenson, Robert (Murrell), erudite and brilliant American musicologist, educator, composer, and pianist; b. Melrose, N.Mex., July 3, 1916. He studied at the Univ. of Texas, El Paso (A.B., 1936); then went to N.Y. to study piano with Ernest Hutcheson at the Juilliard School of Music; subsequently entered Yale Univ., studying composition with David Stanley Smith and musicology with Leo Schrade (M.Mus., 1939). In 1939 he had 23 private lessons in composition (at $25 a session) with Stravinsky in Cambridge, Mass., and in 1940 he took private piano lessons (at $40 a lesson) with Artur Schnabel in N.Y.; then attended classes in composition with Howard Hanson at the Eastman School of Music in Rochester, N.Y. (Ph.D., 1942); he later had regular music courses at Harvard Univ. (S.T.B., 1943). He also took graduate degrees in theology from the Harvard Divinity School and the Theological Seminary at Princeton Univ. (Th.M., 1949). He served as chaplain with the U.S. Army (1942–46); received the Army Commendation Ribbon; remained in service as a reserve officer until 1953. He then went to Oxford Univ. in England, where he took courses in musicology with Jack Allan Westrup (B.Litt., 1954). While thus occupied, he pursued an active career as a concert pianist; gave his 1st N.Y. recital on Jan. 5, 1942; gave another recital there on March 20, 1947; in both he included his own compositions; he played in London on Oct. 7, 1953. He taught music at the Univ. of Texas at El Paso from 1941 to 1943 and in 1949; lectured on church music at Westminster Choir College in Princeton, N.J., from 1946 to 1949. In 1949 he

was appointed to the music faculty at the Univ. of Calif., Los Angeles; was made a prof. of music in 1961; was named faculty research lecturer in 1981. In 1955–56 he was a visiting assistant prof. at Columbia Univ.; also was a visiting prof. at Indiana Univ. in Bloomington (1959–60) and at the Univ. of Chile in Santiago (1965–66). A widely informed musical scientist, he gave courses at the Univ. of Calif. on music appreciation, special seminars on individual composers, and a highly popular course in 1983 on rock-'n'-roll music. He also presented piano recitals as part of the curriculum. A master of European languages, he concentrated his scholarly energy mainly on Latin American, Spanish, and Portuguese music, both sacred and secular, and his publications on these subjects are of inestimable value; he is also an investigative explorer of Italian Renaissance music. He contributed more than 400 articles to *The New Grove Dictionary of Music and Musicians,* and numerous articles on the Baroque period and on American composers to *Die Musik in Geschichte und Gegenwart;* was its American ed. from 1967 to the completion of the last fascicle of its supplement. He held numerous grants, fellowships, and awards from learned societies; was the recipient of Fulbright research awards (1958–59; 1964; 1970–71); a Carnegie Foundation Teaching Award (1955–56); a Gulbenkian Foundation fellowship (1953–54); a Guggenheim fellowship (1962); a Ford Foundation fellowship (1966 and 1981); a National Endowment for Humanities fellowship (1974); and one from the American Philosophical Soc. He was a contributor, beginning in 1976, to the *Handbook of Latin American Studies* at the Library of Congress; from 1978 was ed. of and principal contributor to *Inter-American Music Review.* The versatility of his contributions on various subjects is indeed extraordinary. Thus, he publ. several articles containing materials theretofore unknown about Liszt's piano concerts in Spain and Portugal. He ed., transcribed, and annotated *Vilancicos portugueses* for *Portugaliae Musica XXIX* (Lisbon, 1976); contributed informative articles dealing with early American composers, South American operas, sources of Indian music, and studies on Latin American composers to the *Musical Quarterly, Revista Musical Chilena, Journal of the American Musicological Society, Ethnomusicology, Inter-American Music Review.* His avowed mission in his work is "to rescue the musical past of the Americas." The honors bestowed upon him, especially in the Spanish-speaking world, are many. In 1988 the Organization of American States created the Robert Stevenson Prize in Latin American Musicology. In April 1990 he was awarded a gold medal in ceremonies at the Prado Museum in Madrid, presided over by the King of Spain, and in Dec. of that year was inducted as an honorary member into the Sociedad Española de Musicologica. Also in 1990, the Sociedad Argentina de Musicologia made him an honorary member, and he was honored by the Comisión Nacional de Cultura de Venezuela. In coordination with the quincentennial of the discovery of America in 1992, Stevenson's book *La música en las catedrales de España durante el siglo do oro* was publ. in Madrid. In 1992 he was scheduled to address the 15th Congress of the International Musicological Soc., to be held in Madrid, concerning Mediterranean musical cultures and their influences. Among other assorted distinctions, the mayor of El Paso, Texas (where Stevenson had resided from age 2 to 18), presented him with a scroll making him an honorary citizen. Stevenson's compositions are marked by kinetic energy and set in vigorous and often acrid dissonant counterpoint. His symphonic 2 *Peruvian Preludes* were performed by Stokowski with the Philadelphia Orch. on June 28, 1962; the score was later expanded into 3 *preludias peruanos* and 1st performed in Mexico City, on July 20, 1963, with Luis Herrera de la Fuente conducting. Other works include *Nocturne in Ebony* and *A Texas Suite* for Orch.; Sonata for Clarinet and Piano; 3 piano sonatas: *A Cambridge Sonata, A Manhattan Sonata,* and *A New Haven Sonata.* He also wrote *Coronation Concerto* for Organ and *A Sandburg Cantata* for Chorus.

WRITINGS: *Music in Mexico. A Historical Survey* (N.Y., 1952); *Patterns of Protestant Church Music* (Durham, N.C.,

1953); *La musica en la catedral de Sevilla, 1478–1606; Documentos para su estudio* (Los Angeles, 1954; Madrid, 1985); *Music before the Classic Era* (London, 1955; 2nd ed., 1958; reprint, Westport, Conn., 1973); *Cathedral Music in Colonial Peru* (Lima, 1959); *The Music of Peru: Aboriginal and Viceroyal Epochs* (Washington, D.C., 1960); *Juan Bermudo* (The Hague, 1960); *Spanish Music in the Age of Columbus* (The Hague, 1960); *Music Instruction in Inca Land* (Baltimore, 1960); *Spanish Cathedral Music in the Golden Age* (Berkeley, Calif., 1961; publ. in Spanish, Madrid, 1992); *Mexico City Cathedral Music, 1600–1750* (Washington, D.C., 1964); *Protestant Church Music in America* (N.Y., 1966); *Music in Aztec and Inca Territory* (Berkeley, 1968); *Renaissance and Baroque Musical Sources in the Americas* (Washington, D.C., 1970); *Foundations of New World Opera, with a Transcription of the Earliest Extant American Opera, 1701* (Lima, 1973); *Christmas Music from Baroque Mexico* (Berkeley, 1974); *Latin American Colonial Music Anthology* (Washington, D.C., 1975); *A Guide to Caribbean Music History* (Lima, 1975); *Antologia de la musica postuguesa 1490–1680* (Lisbon, 1984).

Stevenson, Ronald, English pianist and composer; b. Blackburn, Lancashire, March 6, 1928. He studied piano as a child; began to compose at 14; took courses in composition at the Royal Manchester College of Music (1945–48); later studied at the Accademia di Santa Cecilia in Rome on an Italian government scholarship (1955). Returning to England, he was appointed lecturer at the Univ. of Edinburgh (in the Extra-Mural Dept.) in 1962; was on the music staff at the Univ. of Cape Town (South Africa) from 1963 to 1965. A fervent intellectual, he contributed cultured articles to the *Listener* and other publications; engaged in a thoroughgoing bio-musical tome on Busoni, with whose art he felt a particular kinship; publ. a book, *Western Music: An Introduction* (London, 1971). He adheres to neo-Baroque polyphony; a formidable exemplar is his *Passacaglia on DSCH* for Piano, a Brobdingnagian set of variations in 3 parts, 80 minutes long, derived from the initial D of the 1st name and the 1st 3 letters of the last name of Dmitri Shostakovich, in German notation (D; S = Es = E-flat; C; H = B), 1st performed by Stevenson himself in Cape Town, Dec. 10, 1963. Other works include: *Anger Dance* for Guitar (1965); *Triptych,* on themes from Busoni's opera *Doktor Faust,* for Piano and Orch. (Piano Concerto No. 1; Edinburgh, Jan. 6, 1966, composer soloist); *Scots Dance Toccata* for Orch. (Glasgow, July 4, 1970); *Peter Grimes Fantasy* for Piano, on themes from Britten's opera (1971); *Duo-Sonata* for Harp and Piano (1971); Piano Concerto No. 2 (1972); numerous settings for voice and piano and for chorus of Scottish folk songs; transcriptions of works of Purcell, Bach, Chopin, Berlioz, Busoni, Paderewski, Delius, Britten, Berg, Pizzetti, Grainger, and many others.

BIBL.: M. MacDonald, *R. S.: A Musical Biography* (Edinburgh, 1989).

Stewart, Humphrey John, English-American organist and composer; b. London, May 22, 1856; d. San Diego, Dec. 28, 1932. He studied privately in England; in 1886, emigrated to the U.S. and settled in San Francisco as a church organist; was one of the founders of the American Guild of Organists. His 3 operas were produced in San Francisco: *His Majesty* (1890); *The Conspirators* (1900); *King Hal* (1911). The scores of the 1st 2 were lost in the San Francisco earthquake and fire of 1906. His most successful work was the sacred music drama *The Hound of Heaven* (San Francisco, April 24, 1924); he also wrote the orch. suites *Montezuma* and *Scenes in California;* a Mass; organ pieces; songs.

Stewart, Reginald, Scottish-American pianist and conductor; b. Edinburgh, April 20, 1900; d. Montecito, near Santa Barbara, Calif., July 8, 1984. He was a boy soprano in a church choir; then took piano lessons with Mark Hambourg and Arthur Friedheim in London and with Isidor Philipp in Paris, where he also studied composition with Nadia Boulanger. He made his London debut as a concert pianist in 1924; in 1933 he went to Canada, where he was founder-conductor of the summer

series of Promenade Sym. Concerts (1934–41), which proved an auspicious opening of his career as a conductor. In 1941 he moved to the U.S.; became head of the Peabody Cons. in Baltimore, occupying this post until 1958; concurrently, he was conductor of the Baltimore Sym. Orch. (1942–52). In 1962 he went to California, where he was named head of the piano dept. and artist-in-residence at the Music Academy of the West in Santa Barbara.

Stewart, Sir Robert (Prescott), Irish organist, conductor, teacher, and composer; b. Dublin, Dec. 16, 1825; d. there, March 24, 1894. He received his musical training as a chorister at Christ Church Cathedral in Dublin, where he became organist, and at Trinity College in 1844; was made conductor of the Univ. Choral Soc. in 1846, and then took the Mus.B. and Mus.D. degrees in 1851; in 1852 became organist at St. Patrick's Cathedral, where he also served as vicar-choral; was named prof. of music at the Univ. in 1861 and at the Irish Academy of Music in 1871; served as conductor of the Dublin Phil. (from 1873); was knighted in 1872. He wrote orch. pieces, instrumental music, cantatas, services, anthems, odes, glees, and songs.

BIBL.: O. Vignoles, *Memoir of Sir R.P. S.* (London, 1899); J. Culwick, *The Works of Sir R. S.* (Dublin, 1902).

Stewart, Thomas (James), distinguished American baritone; b. San Saba, Texas, Aug. 29, 1928. He studied electrical engineering in Waco; later went to N.Y., where he became a student of Mack Harrell at the Juilliard School of Music; made his debut there in 1954 as La Roche in *Capriccio* by Richard Strauss; then sang with the N.Y. City Opera and the Chicago Opera in bass roles. In 1957 he received a Fulbright grant and went to Berlin; was engaged as a baritone with the Städtische Oper; made his debut there as the Minister in *Fidelio* (1957); remained on its roster until 1964; also sang regularly at London's Covent Garden (1960–78) and at the Bayreuth Festivals (1960–75). He made his Metropolitan Opera debut in N.Y. on March 9, 1966, as Ford in Verdi's *Falstaff;* in 1981 he sang the title role in the American premiere of Reimann's *Lear* with the San Francisco Opera. His other roles were Don Giovanni, Count di Luna in *Il Trovatore,* Escamillo in *Carmen,* Iago in *Otello,* and Wotan. In 1955 he married **Evelyn Lear,** with whom he often appeared in opera and concert settings.

Stibilj, Milan, Slovenian composer; b. Ljubljana, Nov. 2, 1929. He studied composition with Karol Pahor at the Ljubljana Academy of Music (1956–61) and with Kelemen at the Zagreb Academy of Music (1962–64); took courses in electronic music at the Univ. of Utrecht (1966–67). He composes in an advanced idiom, exploring the techniques of integral serial organization of musical parameters.

WORKS: *Anekdote* for Piano (1957); *Koncertantna glasba* (Concertante Music) for Horn and Orch. (1959); *Skladbe* (Composition) for Horn and Strings (1959); *Sarabanda* for 4 Clarinets (1960); *Slavček v vrtnica* (The Nightingale and the Rose), symphonic poem (1961); *Skladja* (Congruences) for Piano and Orch. (1963); *Impressions* for Flute, Harp, and String Quintet or String Orch. (1963); *Epervier de ta faiblesse, Domine* for Narrator and 5 Percussionists (1964); *Verz* for Orch. (1964); *Assimilation* for Violin (1965); *Contemplation* for Oboe and String Quintet (1966); *Apokatastasis,* Slovenian Requiem for Tenor, Chorus, and Orch. (1967); *Condensation* for Trombone, 2 Pianos, and Percussion (1967); *Zoom* for Clarinet and Bongos (1970); *Indian Summer* for Chamber Orch. (1974).

Stich, Johann Wenzel (actually, **Jan Václav**), Bohemian horn player, violinist, and composer who assumed the name Giovanni Punto; b. Žehušice, near Čáslav, Sept. 28, 1746; d. Prague, Feb. 16, 1803. He was sent by Count Thun to study horn with Josef Matiegka in Prague, Schinderlarž in Munich, and Hampel and Haudek in Dresden; was in the service of Count Thun in Žehušice (1763–66), and then ran away, eventually making his way to the Holy Roman Empire, where he took the name Giovanni Punto. He toured in Europe from 1768; also was in the service of the Prince of Hechingen and then of the Mainz court (1769–74). In 1778 in Paris he met Mozart, who was impressed with his virtuosity. In 1781 he played in the band of the Prince-Archbishop of Würzburg; then went to Paris to serve the Comte d'Artois (later Charles X) in 1782; during the Reign of Terror, he was active as a violinist and conductor at the Théâtre des Variétés Amusantes. In 1799 he went to Munich and in 1800 to Vienna; there he made the acquaintance of Beethoven, who was enchanted by his playing, wrote for him a Sonata for Horn and Piano (op. 17), and played it with him at a concert (April 18, 1800). After touring with J.L. Dussek in 1802, he settled in Prague. His extant works comprise 11 horn concertos (Prague, c.1787–1806), 3 quintets for Horn, Flute or Oboe, Violin, Viola, and Bassoon (Prague, c.1799), 21 quartets for either Horn, Violin, Viola, and Bassoon, or Horn, Violin, Bassoon, and Cello (Prague, c.1785–96), 20 trios for 3 Horns (Prague, c.1800), 56 duos for 2 Horns (Prague, c.1793–1803), and 6 trios for Flute, Violin and Bassoon (London, c.1773). He publ. a horn method that was a revision of Hampel's (Paris, c.1798; 3rd ed., 1798) and a book of horn exercises (Paris, 1795; 2nd ed., 1800).

BIBL.: H. Kling, "Giovanni Punto, célèbre corniste," *Bulletin Français de la Société Internationale de Musique,* IV (1908); R. Morley-Pegge, *The French Horn* (London, 1960; 2nd ed., rev., 1973); H. Fitzpatrick, *The Horn & Horn-Playing and the Austro-Bohemian Tradition 1680–1830* (London, 1970).

Stich-Randall, Teresa, American soprano; b. West Hartford, Conn., Dec. 24, 1927. She studied voice at the Hartt School of Music and Columbia Univ.; then sang in N.Y., where she appeared with Toscanini and the NBC Sym. Orch. In 1951 she won the singing competition held in Lausanne; in 1952 she made her Vienna State Opera debut; in 1962 she was made a Kammersängerin. On Oct. 24, 1961, she made her debut at the Metropolitan Opera in N.Y. as Fiordiligi in *Così fan tutte;* also appeared as a soloist with European and American orchs.

Stiedry, Fritz, eminent Austrian-born American conductor; b. Vienna, Oct. 11, 1883; d. Zürich, Aug. 9, 1968. He studied jurisprudence in Vienna and took a course in composition with Eusebius Mandyczewski. Mahler recommended him to Ernst von Schuch in Dresden, and he became his assistant conductor (1907–8); he subsequently was active as a theater conductor in the German provinces, and in Prague. He conducted at the Berlin Opera (1916–23); then led the Vienna Volksoper (1923–25). After traveling as a guest conductor in Italy, Spain, and Scandinavia (1925–28), he returned to Berlin as conductor of the Städtische Oper (1929–33). With the advent of the Nazi regime in 1933, he went to Russia, where he conducted the Leningrad Phil. (1934–37). In 1938 he emigrated to the U.S. and became a naturalized citizen; conducted the New Friends of Music Orch. in N.Y.; on Nov. 15, 1946, he made his Metropolitan Opera debut in N.Y. conducting *Siegfried,* remaining on its roster as one of its most distinguished conductors until 1958. As a conductor, he championed the 2nd Viennese School of composition. He was a close friend of Schoenberg; conducted 1st performances of his opera *Die glückliche Hand* in Vienna (1924) and his 2nd Chamber Sym. in N.Y. (1940). But he also gave fine performances of the operas of Wagner and Verdi.

Stiehl, family of German musicians:

(1) Johann Dietrich (Diedrich) Stiehl, organist; b. Lübeck, July 9, 1800; d. there, June 27, 1873. He studied organ in Lübeck with M. Bauck, whom he succeeded as organist of the Jakobikirche in 1835. He had 2 sons who became musicians:

(2) Carl (Karl) Johann Christian Stiehl, organist, conductor, teacher, and writer on music; b. Lübeck, July 12, 1826; d. there, Dec. 1, 1911. He 1st studied with his father, and then with Lobe in Weimar; completed his training at the Leipzig Cons. He taught organ and singing and served as a church organist in Jever (1848–58) and Eutin (1858–77); also was music director to the Grand Duke of Oldenburg (1860–77). He returned to Lübeck as a singing teacher in 1877; he conducted the Singakademie there until 1901; also was conductor of the Musikverein, and then founder-director of the Phil. Concerts (1886–96); likewise wrote music criticism.

WRITINGS: *Zur Geschichte der Instrumentalmusik in Lübeck* (1885); *Lübeckisches Tonkünstler-Lexikon* (1887); *Musikgeschichte der Stadt Lübeck* (1891); *Geschichte des Theaters in Lübeck* (1901).

BIBL.: J. Hennings, "Unsere Künstler—K. S.," *Neue Musik-Zeitung,* XXVII (1906); W. Stahl, "C. S.," *Vaterstädtische Blätter* (Lübeck, 1911).

(3) Heinrich (Franz Daniel) Stiehl, organist, conductor, and composer; b. Lübeck, Aug. 5, 1829; d. Reval, May 1, 1886. He studied with Lobe in Weimar, and later with Moscheles, Gade, and Hauptmann at the Leipzig Cons.; in 1853 he went to St. Petersburg as organist at the Lutheran Church and conductor of a German choral society. He was subsequently active in Vienna (1867–69), Italy (1869–72), London (1872–73), and Belfast (1874–77). In 1880 he was engaged as organist at St. Olai's Church in Reval. He wrote in all 172 opus numbers, including 2 light operas: *Der Schatzgräber* and *Jery und Bätely; Die Vision* for Orch.; 2 piano quartets; 3 piano trios; Violin Sonata; Cello Sonata; numerous piano pieces of programmatic content.

BIBL.: W. Niemann, "Meister der Klaviermusik: H. S.," *Neue Musik-Zeitung,* XXXIII (1912); W. Stahl, "H. S.," *Lübeckisches Jahrbuch der Vaterstädtischen Blätter 1929–30* (Lübeck, 1930).

Stigelli, Giorgio (real name, **Georg Stiegele**), celebrated German tenor; b. 1815; d. Boschetti, near Monza, July 3, 1868. He made extensive concert tours in Europe, and appeared in America in 1864–65. He composed many songs, among them the popular *Die schönsten Augen.*

Stignani, Ebe, esteemed Italian mezzo-soprano; b. Naples, July 11, 1904; d. Imola, Oct. 6, 1974. She studied voice with Agostino Roche at the Naples Cons.; made her operatic debut as Amneris at the Teatro San Carlo there (1925); then joined Milan's La Scala in 1926, winning great distinction for her roles in Italian operas as well as Gluck's Orfeo, Brangäne, and Ortrud. She made guest appearances at London's Covent Garden, winning success as Amneris (1937, 1939, 1955), Azucena (1939, 1952), and Adalgisa (1952, 1957); also sang in San Francisco (1938, 1948). In 1958 she made her operatic farewell as Azucena at London's Drury Lane.

Still, Robert, English composer; b. London, June 10, 1910; d. Bucklebury, Reading, Jan. 13, 1971. He was educated at Eton College (1923–28); Trinity College, Oxford (1929–32); and the Royal College of Music in London (1932–34). He served with the Royal Artillery during World War II; began to compose in earnest only after the war. He was also interested in psychoanalysis and publ. an essay on Mahler from the Freudian point of view. His works include an opera, *Oedipus* (1954–56); 4 syms. (1954, 1956, 1960, 1964); Violin Concerto (1969); Piano Concerto (1970); 5 string quartets; Clarinet Quintet; Oboe Quartet; choral music; songs; part-songs.

Still, William Grant, eminent black American composer; b. Woodville, Miss., May 11, 1895; d. Los Angeles, Dec. 3, 1978. His father was bandmaster in Woodville; after his death when Still was in infancy, his mother moved the family to Little Rock, Ark., where she became a high school teacher. He grew up in a home with cultured, middle-class values, and his stepfather encouraged his interest in music by taking him to see operettas and buying him operatic recordings; he was also given violin lessons. He attended Wilberforce College in preparation for a medical career, but became active in musical activities on campus; after dropping out of college, he worked with various groups, including that of W.C. Handy (1916); then attended the Oberlin College Cons. During World War I, he played violin in the U.S. Army; afterward returned to work with Handy, and became oboist in the Shuffle Along orch. (1921); then studied composition with Varèse, and at the New England Cons. of Music in Boston with Chadwick; held a Guggenheim fellowship in 1934–35; was awarded honorary doctorates by Howard Univ. (1941), Oberlin College (1947), and Bates College (1954). Determined to develop a symphonic type of Negro music, he wrote an *Afro-American Symphony* (1930). In his music he occasionally made use of actual Negro folk songs, but mostly he invented his thematic materials. He married the writer Verna Arvey, who collaborated with him as librettist in his stage works.

Works: operas: *Blue Steel* (1934); *Troubled Island* (1941); *A Bayou Legend* (1940; PBS, 1981); *A Southern Interlude* (1943); *Costaso* (1950); *Mota* (1951); *The Pillar* (1956); *Minette Fontaine* (1958); *Highway 1, U.S.A.* (1962; Miami, May 13, 1963). **ballets:** *La Guiablesse* (1927); *Sahdji* (1930); *Lennox Avenue* (1937); *Miss Sally's Party* (1940); also incidental music, *The Prince and the Mermaid* (1965). **orch.:** 5 syms.: No. 1, *Afro-American Symphony* (1930; Rochester, N.Y., Oct. 29, 1931); No. 2 in G minor, *Song of a New Race* (Philadelphia, Dec. 19, 1937); No. 3 (1945; discarded; new No. 3, *The Sunday Symphony;* 1958); No. 4, *Autochthonous* (1947; Oklahoma City, March 18, 1951); No. 5, *Western Hemisphere* (revision of discarded No. 3, 1945; Oberlin, Ohio, Nov. 9, 1970); *Darker America* (1924; Rochester, N.Y., Nov. 21, 1927); *From the Black Belt* (1926); *From the Journal of a Wanderer* (Rochester, N.Y., May 8, 1929); *Africa* (1930); *A Deserted Plantation* (1933); *Kaintuck (Kentucky)* for Piano and Orch. (1935; Rochester, N.Y., Jan. 16, 1936); *Dismal Swamp* (Rochester, N.Y., Oct. 30, 1936); *Beyond Tomorrow* (1936); *Ebon Chronicle* (Fort Worth, Nov. 3, 1936); *Can'tcha Line 'em* (1940); *Old California* (1941); *Pages from Negro History* (1943); *In Memoriam: The Colored Soldiers Who Died for Democracy* (1943; N.Y., Jan. 5, 1944); *Fanfare for American War Heroes* (1943); *Poem* (Cleveland, Dec. 7, 1944); *Festive Overture* (1944; Cincinnati, Jan. 19, 1945); *Fanfare for the 99th Fighter Squadron for Winds* (1945); *Archaic Ritual* (1946); *Wood Notes* (1947; Chicago, April 22, 1948); *Danzas de Panama* for String Orch. (1948; also for String Quartet); *Ennanga* for Harp and Orch. or Flute and Strings (1956); *The American Scene* (1957); *Little Red Schoolhouse* (1957); *The Peaceful Land* (1960); *Patterns* (1960); *Los alnados de España* (1962); *Preludes* for Strings, Flute, and Piano (1962); *Threnody in Memory of Jan Sibelius* (1965); *Miniature Overture* (1965); *Choreographic Prelude* for Strings, Flute, and Piano (1970). **chamber:** *Suite* for Violin and Piano (1943); *Pastorela* for Violin and Piano (1946); *4 Folk Suites* for Flute, Clarinet, Oboe, Bassoon, Strings, and Piano (1962); *Vignettes* for Oboe, Bassoon, and Piano (1962); also vocal works, including *Plain Chant for Americans* for Baritone and Orch. (N.Y., Oct. 23, 1941), *Caribbean Melodies* for Chorus, Piano, and Percussion (1941), and *Wailing Woman* for Soprano and Chorus (1946), and many songs; piano pieces; works for band; arrangements of spirituals.

Bibl.: V. Arvey, *W.G. S.* (N.Y., 1939); R. Simpson, *W.G. S.: The Man and His Music* (diss., Michigan State Univ., 1964); M. Hudgins, "An Outstanding Arkansan: W.G. S.," *Arkansas Historical Quarterly* (Winter 1965); R. Haas, ed., *W.G. S. and the Fusion of Cultures in American Music* (Los Angeles, 1972); F. Douglass, "A Tribute to W.G. S.," *Black Perspective in Music* (Spring 1974); "A Birthday Offering to W.G. S. upon the Occasion of His 80th Anniversary," ibid. (May 1975); A. Arvey, *In One Lifetime* (Fayetteville, Ark., 1984).

Stillman-Kelley, Edgar. See Kelley, Edgar Stillman.

Stillman, Mitya, Russian-American violist and composer; b. Ilyintza, near Kiev, Jan. 27, 1892; d. N.Y., April 11, 1936. He studied composition with Glière and violin and viola with Pulikovsky at the Kiev Cons.; after the Russian Revolution, he emigrated to the U.S. (1920); played viola in the Detroit Sym. Orch. and in the CBS Sym. Orch. As a composer, he developed a strong individual style in a peculiarly compact contrapuntal technique. He wrote 8 string quartets, of which No. 7 received a posthumous 1st-prize award from the NBC Guild as the best chamber music work for 1936 (N.Y., Jan. 1, 1937). He also wrote some programmatic orch. pieces, among them *Dnieprostroy* (1933); *Yalta Suite* for String Trio; *Cyprus* for Strings, Woodwinds, and Percussion; etc.

Stilwell, Richard (Dale), outstanding American baritone; b. St. Louis, May 6, 1942. After studying English at Anderson (Ind.) College, he appeared as Silvio in *Pagliacci* with the St. Louis Grand Opera (1962); then studied voice with F. St. Leger and P. Mathen at the Indiana Univ. School of Music in Bloomington (B.A., 1966) and with D. Ferro in N.Y. On April 7, 1970, he made a successful debut as Pelléas with the N.Y. City Opera; in 1973, made his British debut as Ulysses in *Il ritorno d'Ulisse in Patria* at the Glyndebourne Festival. He was chosen to create the role of Constantine in Pasatieri's *The Seagull* (Houston, 1974) and the title role in Pasatieri's *Inés de Castro* (Baltimore, 1976). On Oct. 15, 1976, he made his Metropolitan Opera debut in N.Y. as Guglielmo in *Così fan tutte;* scored a major success there as Billy Budd in 1978; also appeared at the Paris Opéra, the Netherlands Opera, the Chicago Lyric Opera, the Washington (D.C.) Opera Soc., and the Berlin Deutsche Oper; likewise sang in concerts with the major U.S. orchs. In 1988 he sang in the premiere of Argento's *The Aspern Papers* in Dallas. In addition to his remarkable portrayal of Pelléas, he also excels as Papageno, Don Giovanni, Figaro in *Il Barbiere di Siviglia*, Don Pasquale, Eugene Onegin, Rodrigo in *Don Carlos*, and Ford in *Falstaff*.

Bibl.: *Current Biography* (Feb. 1986).

Sting (real name, **Gordon Matthew Sumner**), propulsive English rock singer and songwriter; b. Wallsend, Northumberland, Oct. 2, 1951. He attended Jesuit parochial schools; autodidact in music, he took up the guitar and bass in his teens; then obtained a degree in education from Warwick College in Newcastle (1973), after which he taught history. He continued his musical activities, and became active in jazz circles; acquired his smarting sobriquet of Sting as a result of his fondness for yellow and black pullovers. In 1977 he joined forces with drummer Stewart Copeland and guitarist Andry Summers to form the group Police; in 1978 they made their 1st tour of the U.S., which propelled their hit single *Roxanne* to the top of the charts. Subsequent albums included *Regatta de Blanc* (1979), *Zenyatta Mondatta* (1980), *The Ghost in the Machine* (1981), and *Synchronicity* (1983). In 1991 their song *Every Breath You Take* received a British Music Industry award for what amounted to roughly 17 years of continuous radio play (2 million plays). In 1985 Sting branched out as a solo artist; he gathered a band of collaborators that included saxophonist Brandon Marsalis to make several albums with a strong jazz inflection: *The Dream of the Blue Turtles, Nothing Like the Sun* (1987), and *Bring On the Night*, which won him a Grammy Award in 1988. His mother and father died within 6 months of each other while he was working on *Nothing Like the Sun*. This personal loss precipitated a creative dry spell and time of reassessment, out of which came the album *The Soul Cages* (1990), a multifaceted look at birth, death, and transition. Consonant with his thoughtful lyrics, Sting gave time and energy to projects outside rock and roll. He is a longtime supporter of Amnesty International (reflected in the song *Dancing with the Dead*, about the Chileans who disappeared during the long years of the Pinochet dictatorship) and a dedicated worker for the preservation of the Brazilian rain forest; he mediated between the native Indians and the presidents of Brazil, Sarney and Collor de Mello, in negotiations to establish a substantial preserve of rain forest to benefit both the Indians and the world ecosystem.

Bibl.: *Current Biography* (July 1985).

Stirling, Elizabeth, English organist and composer; b. Greenwich, Feb. 26, 1819; d. London, March 25, 1895. She studied organ and piano with Edward Holmes, and harmony with G.A. Macfarren. She was organist of All Saints', Poplar (1839–59), and at St. Andrew's, Undershaft (1859–80). In 1856 she passed the examination for the degree of Mus.Bac. at Oxford (her work was *Psalm 130* for 5 Voices, with Orch.), but, ironically, her earned degree could not be granted to a woman. She made many organ transcriptions from classical works; publ. *6 Pedal-Fugues* and other organ pieces; also part-songs, of which *All among the Barley* won great popularity.

Stitt, "Sonny" (Edward), black American jazz tenor and alto saxophonist; b. Boston, Feb. 2, 1924; d. Washington, D.C., July 22, 1982. He took up the clarinet and alto saxophone; made his way to N.Y., where he played with Dizzy Gillespie (1946); then led his own band and combo for several years. He became one of the leading tenor and alto saxophonists of his generation.

Stivori, Francesco, noted Italian organist and composer; b. Venice, c.1550; d. probably in Graz, 1605. He was a pupil of Claudio Merulo. After serving as municipal organist in Montagna (1579–1601), he was organist to Archduke Ferdinand of Inner Austria at his Graz court (from 1602). Stivori was a significant figure in the movement to introduce multiple choral writing to Austria. He publ. 7 vols. of madrigals (1583–1605), 6 vols. of motets (1579–1601), and 3 vols. of instrumental pieces (1589–99).

Stobaeus, Johann, eminent German composer; b. Graudenz, July 6, 1580; d. Königsberg, Sept. 11, 1646. In 1595 he went to Königsberg, where from 1599 to 1608 he was a pupil of J. Eccard; also attended the Univ. (from 1600); in 1602 he became a bass in the Electoral Kapelle; served as Kantor at the Cathedral church and school in Kneiphof, Königsberg (1603–26); then was Kapellmeister at the Königsberg court. His extant works comprise *Cantiones sacrae harmoniae* for 4 to 10 Voices, *Item aliquot Magnificat* for 5 to 6 Voices (Frankfurt am Main, 1624), compositions in other collections of the era, and many pieces in MS; see G. Teschner, ed., *J. Eccard und J. Stobaeus: Preussische Festlieder* for 5 to 8 Voices (Leipzig, 1858).

BIBL.: R. Eitner, "S. oder Stoboeus," *Monatshefte für Musikgeschichte,* III (1871); L. Fischer, "Biographisches über J. S.," ibid., XV (1883); idem, "J. S. ein Mitglied Königsberger Dichterkreise," ibid., XVI (1884); A. Mayer-Reinach, "Zur Geschichte der Königsberger Hofkapelle," *Sammelbände der Internationalen Musik-Gesellschaft,* VI/1 (1904); L. Kamieński, *J. S. z Grudziadz* (Poznan, 1928); H. Haase, "Eine wichtige Quelle für J. S. Grudentinus: 6 Sammelbände aus Königsberger Beständen in Göttingen," *Festschrift Friedrich Blume* (Kassel, 1963).

Stock, David (Frederick), American composer and conductor; b. Pittsburgh, June 3, 1939. He studied composition with Nikolai Lopatnikoff and Alexei Haieff, musicology with Frederick Dorian, and trumpet at Carnegie-Mellon Univ. (B.F.A., 1962; M.F.A., 1963); took courses with Nadia Boulanger, Jean Fournet, and Andree Vaurebourg-Honegger at the École Normale de Musique in Paris (1960–61); attended the Berkshire Music Center at Tanglewood (summer 1964); engaged in advanced studies with Arthur Berger at Brandeis Univ. (M.F.A., 1973). He played trumpet in several orchs.; taught at the Cleveland Inst. of Music (1964–65), Brandeis Univ. (1966–68), and the New England Cons. of Music in Boston (1968–70). From 1970 to 1974 he taught at Antioch College and conducted its chamber orch., and also served as chairman of its music dept. (1971–74). In 1974 he held a Guggenheim fellowship. In 1975 he became conductor of the Pittsburgh New Music Ensemble. He also taught at Carnegie-Mellon Univ. (1976–77) and conducted the Carnegie Sym. Orch. (1976–82); taught at the Univ. of Pittsburgh (1978–86) and Duquesne Univ. (1987–88). In 1987–88 he was composer-in-residence of the Pittsburgh Sym. Orch. He received NEA fellowships (1974, 1976, 1978, 1983) and various commissions. His compositions are written in a gratefully accessible style.

WORKS: ORCH.: *Divertimento* (1957); *Capriccio* for Small Orch. (1963); *Symphony in 1 Movement* (1963); *Flashback* (1968); *Inner Space* (1973); *Triflumena* (1978); *Zohar* (1978); *The Philosopher's Stone* for Violin and Chamber Orch. (1980); *A Joyful Noise* (1983; Pittsburgh, May 23, 1985); *Parallel Worlds* for Chamber Orch. (1984); *American Accents* for Chamber Orch. (1984; Los Angeles, Oct. 12, 1985); *Back to Bass-ics* for String Orch. (1985); *On the Shoulders of Giants* (1986); *Rockin' Rondo* (1987); *Quick Opener* for Chamber Orch. (1987); *Tekiah* for Trumpet and Chamber Orch. (1987); *Fast Break* (1988). **WIND ENSEMBLE:** *Nova* for Band (1974); *The Body Elec-*

tric for Amplified Contrabass, Winds, and Percussion (1977); *The 'Slibert Stomp* (1985); *Evensong* for English Horn and Wind Orch. (1985); *No Man's Land* for Wind Sym. (1988); *The Winds of Summer* for Saxophone and Band (1989). **CHAMBER:** String Quartet (1962); *Shadow Music* for 5 Percussion and Harp (1964; rev. 1979); *Serenade for 5 Instruments* for Flute, Clarinet, Horn, Viola, and Cello (1964); Quintet for Clarinet and Strings (1966); *Triple Play* for Piccolo, Contrabass, and Percussion (1970); *Dreamwinds* for Woodwind Quintet (1975); *Night Birds* for 4 or More Cellos (1975); *Icicles* for Piccolo, Oboe, and Clarinet (1976); *Brass Rubbing* for 6 Trumpets (1976); *Pentacles* for Brass Quintet (1978); *Starlight* for Clarinet and Percussion (1979); *Night* for Clarinet, Violin, and Cello (1980); *Persona* for Clarinet, Violin, Cello, Piano, and Percussion (1980); *Keep the Change* for Any 5 Treble Clef Instruments (1981); *Speaking Extravagantly* for String Quartet (1981); *Sulla Spiaggia* for Alto Flute, English Horn, Bass Clarinet, Electric Piano, and Percussion (1985); *Yerusha* for Clarinet and 7 Players (1986); *Partners* for Cello and Piano (1988); *Sunrise Sarabande* for Recorder Quartet (1988). **VOCAL:** *Scat* for Soprano, Flute, Bass Clarinet, Violin, and Cello (1971); *Spirits* for Chorus or Soloists, Harp and/or Electric Piano, and Percussion (1976); *Upcountry Fishing* for Voice and Violin (1982).

Stock, Frederick (actually, **Friedrich August**), respected German-born American conductor; b. Jülich, Nov. 11, 1872; d. Chicago, Oct. 20, 1942. He was 1st trained in music by his father, a bandmaster; then studied violin with G. Japha and composition with Wüllner, Zöllner, and Humperdinck at the Cologne Cons. (1886–91); subsequently played the violin in the Municipal Orch. there (1891–95). In 1895 he was engaged as a violist in Theodore Thomas's newly organized Chicago Orch., becoming his assistant conductor in 1901; following Thomas's death in 1905, he inherited the orch., which took the name of the Theodore Thomas Orch. in 1906; it became the Chicago Sym. Orch. in 1912, with Stock serving as its conductor until his death, the 1918–19 season excepted. In 1919 he became a naturalized U.S. citizen. As a conductor, Stock was extremely competent, even though he totally lacked that ineffable quality of making orch. music a vivid experience in sound; but he had the merit of giving adequate performances of the classics, of Wagner, and of the German Romantic school. He also programmed several American works, as long as they followed the Germanic tradition. The flowering of the Chicago Sym. Orch. was to be accomplished by his successors Fritz Reiner and Georg Solti. Stock was also a composer; wrote 2 syms., a Violin Concerto (Norfolk Festival, June 3, 1915, E. Zimbalist soloist, composer conducting), and some chamber music.

BIBL.: P. Otis, *The Chicago Symphony Orchestra* (Chicago, 1925); W. Holmes, "F. S.," *Le Grand Baton,* VI/2 (1969).

Stock, Larry, American pianist and composer of popular music; b. N.Y., Dec. 4, 1896; d. Lakehurst, N.J., May 4, 1984. He studied at N.Y.'s Inst. of Musical Art with Percy Goetschius. He started his career as a concert pianist; then joined dance bands, and wrote songs in the jazz manner, later switching to swing and rock music. Among the lyricists who wrote words to his tunes were Al Lewis and Vincent Rose. Many famous men and women of the era performed and recorded his songs, among them Louis Armstrong, Elvis Presley, Frank Sinatra, Perry Como, Ella Fitzgerald, Nat King Cole, Bing Crosby, and Guy Lombardo. His hit songs included *Raindrop Serenade, Adoration Waltz, Song of Devotion,* and *I Sent a Letter to Santa.*

Stockhausen, family of prominent German musicians:

(1) Franz (Anton Adam) Stockhausen, harpist, teacher, and composer; b. Cologne, Sept. 1, 1789; d. Colmar, Sept. 10, 1868. He went to Paris about 1812; from 1825, toured Europe in concerts with his wife, the soprano **Margarethe** (née **Schmuck**) **Stockhausen** (b. Gebweiler, March 29, 1803; d. Colmar, Oct. 6, 1877), who had been a pupil of Gioseffo Catrufo at the Paris Cons. In 1840 they settled in Alsace. He composed harp pieces, some vocal music, and various arrangements for his instrument. They had 2 sons who became musicians:

(2) Julius (Christian) Stockhausen, esteemed baritone, conductor, and pedagogue; b. Paris, July 22, 1826; d. Frankfurt am Main, Sept. 22, 1906. He began his musical training at an early age with his parents; studied piano with Karl Kienzl and also received instruction in organ, violin, and cello; in 1843 he went to Paris to study with Cramer; then continued his training at the Cons. (from 1845), and also received private lessons in harmony from Matthäus Nagillers and in singing from Manuel García. In 1848 he sang in *Elijah* in Basel, and in the next year sang before Queen Victoria in London; then toured widely in Europe as a concert singer. He was 2nd baritone at the Mannheim Court Theater (1852–53); then was a member of the Paris Opéra-Comique (1856–59). In 1863 he became conductor of the Hamburg Phil. Soc. and Singakademie, which positions he held until 1867; then was conductor of the Berlin Sternscher Gesangverein (1874–78). Settling in Frankfurt, he taught voice at the Hoch Cons. (1878–80; 1883–84); also taught at his own school (from 1880). He publ. *Gesangs-methode* (2 vols., 1886–87; also in Eng.). He was a distinguished interpreter of the lieder of Schubert and Brahms; the latter was a close friend.

BIBL.: E. Friebel, "Der Sänger J. S.," *Neue Zeitschrift für Musik,* XLIV (1856); J. Wirth-Stockhausen, *J. S.: Der Sänger des deutschen Liedes* (Frankfurt am Main, 1927); idem, *Unverlierbare Kindheit* (Stuttgart, 1949); A. Fox Strangways, "J. S.," *Monthly Musical Record* (March–April 1949).

(3) Franz Stockhausen, pianist, conductor, and teacher; b. Gebweiler, Jan. 30, 1839; d. Strasbourg, Jan. 4, 1926. He began his musical studies with his parents; after piano lessons from Alkan in Paris, he pursued training with Moscheles, Richter, Hauptmann, and Davidov at the Leipzig Cons. (1860–62). He was music director in Thann, Alsace (1863–66); then went to Strasbourg, where he was conductor of the Société de Chant Sacré (1868–79), music director at the Cathedral (from 1868), and director of the Cons. and city concerts (1871–1908).

Stockhausen, Karlheinz, outstanding German composer; b. Mödrath, near Cologne, Aug. 22, 1928. He was orphaned during World War II and was compelled to hold various jobs to keep body and soul together; all the same, he learned to play the piano, violin, and oboe; then studied piano with Hans Otto Schmidt-Neuhaus (1947–50), form with H. Schröder (1948), and composition with Frank Martin (1950) at the Cologne Staatliche Hochschule für Musik; also took courses in German philology, philosophy, and musicology at the Univ. of Cologne; after studies in Darmstadt (1951), he received instruction in composition from Messiaen in Paris (1952); subsequently studied communications theory and phonetics with Werner Meyer-Eppler at the Univ. of Bonn (1954–56). He was active at the electronic music studio of the West German Radio in Cologne (from 1953); also was a lecturer at the Internationalen Ferienkurse für Musik in Darmstadt (until 1974) and was founder-artistic director of the Cologne Kurse für Neue Musik (1963–68); likewise served as prof. of composition at the Cologne Hochschule für Musik (1971–77). He was made a member of the Swedish Royal Academy (1970), the Berlin Academy of Arts (1973), and the American Academy and Inst. of Arts and Letters (1979); also was made a Commandeur dans l'Ordre des Arts et des Lettres of France (1985) and an honorary member of the Royal Academy of Music in London (1987). He investigated the potentialities of *musique concrète* and partly incorporated its techniques into his own empiric method of composition, which from the very first included highly complex contrapuntal conglomerates with uninhibited applications of non-euphonious dissonance as well as recourse to the primal procedures of obdurate iteration of single tones; all this set in the freest of rhythmic patterns and diversified by constantly changing instrumental colors with obsessive percussive effects. He further perfected a system of constructivist composition, in which the subjective choice of the performer determines the succession of given thematic ingredients and their poly-

phonic simultaneities, ultimately leading to a totality of aleatory procedures in which the ostensible application of a composer's commanding function is paradoxically reasserted by the inclusion of prerecorded materials and by recombinant uses of electronically altered thematic ingredients. He evolved energetic missionary activities in behalf of new music as a lecturer and master of ceremonies at avant-garde meetings all over the world; having mastered the intricacies of the English language, he made a lecture tour of Canadian and American univs. in 1958; in 1965, was a visiting prof. of composition at the Univ. of Pa.; was a visiting prof. at the Univ. of Calif. at Davis in 1966–67; in 1969, gave highly successful public lectures in England that were attended by hordes of musical and unmusical novitiates; publ. numerous misleading guidelines for the benefit of a growing contingent of his apostles, disciples, and acolytes. Stockhausen is a pioneer of "time-space" music, marked by a controlled improvisation, and adding the vectorial (i.e., directional) parameter to the 4 traditional aspects of serial music (pitch, duration, timbre, and dynamics), with performers and electronic apparatuses placed in different parts of the concert hall; such performances, directed by himself, are often accompanied by screen projections and audience participation; he also specifies the architectural aspects of the auditoriums in which he gives his demonstrations; thus, at the world's fair in Osaka, Japan, in 1970, he supervised the construction of a circular auditorium in the German pavilion; these demonstrations continued for 183 days, with 20 soloists and 5 lantern projections in live performances of his own works, each session lasting 5½ hours; the estimated live, radio, and television audience was 1,000,000 listeners. His annotations to his own works were publ. in the series entitled *Texte* (6 vols., Cologne, 1963–88). See also R. Maconie, ed., *Stockhausen on Music: Lectures and Interviews* (London and N.Y., 1989).

WORKS: *Chöre für Doris* (1950); *Drei Lieder* for Contralto and Chamber Orch. (1950); *Choral* (1950); *Sonatine* for Violin and Piano (1951); *Kreuzspiel* for Oboe, Bass Clarinet, Piano, and 3 Percussion (1951); *Formel* for Orch. (1951); *Etude,* concrete music (1952); *Spiel* for Orch. (1952); *Schlagtrio* for Piano and Kettledrums (1952); *Punkte* for Orch. (1952; rev. 1962); *Kontra-Punkte* for 10 Instruments (Cologne, May 26, 1953); *Klavierstücke I–IV* (1952–53); *Studie I,* electronic music (1953); *Studie II,* electronic music (1954); *Klavierstücke V–X* (1954–55); *Zeitmasse* for 5 Woodwinds (1955–56); *Gruppen* for 3 Orchs. (1955–57; Cologne, March 24, 1959); *Klavierstücke XI* (1956); *Gesang der Jünglinge,* electronic music, to a text composed of disjected verbal particles from the Book of Daniel, dealing with the ordeal of 3 monotheistic Hebrew youths in the Babylonian fiery furnace, scored for 5 groups of loudspeakers surrounding the audience (Cologne, May 30, 1956); *Zyklus* for Percussion (1959); *Carré* for 4 Orchs. and Choruses (Hamburg, Oct. 28, 1960); *Refrain* for 3 Performers (1959); *Kontakte* for Electronics (1959–60); *Kontakte* for Electronics, Piano, and Percussion (Cologne, June 11, 1960); *Originale,* music theater (1961); *Momente* for Soprano, 4 Choruses, and 13 Instrumentalists (1962–64); *Plus-Minus* for Clarinet, Trombone, Cello, and 3 Pianos (1963; Warsaw, Sept. 25, 1968); *Mikrophonie I* for 6 Performers (1964); *Mixtur* for Orch., Sinus Generator, and Ring Modulator (1964); *Mikrophonie II* for 12 Singers, Hammond Organ, 4 Ring Modulators, and Tape (1965); *Stop* for Orch. (1965); *Solo* for Melody Instrument (1965–66); *Telemusik,* electronic music (1966; Warsaw, Sept. 23, 1968); *Adieu* for Wind Quintet (1966); *Hymnen,* electronic and concrete music (Cologne, Nov. 30, 1967); *Prozession* for Ensemble (1967); *Stimmung* for 6 Vocalists (1968); *Kurzwellen* for 6 Performers (1968); *Aus den Sieben Tagen,* 15 pieces in graphic notation for various ensembles, with such verbal instructions as "play a tone in the certainty that you have plenty of time and space" (1968); *Spiral* for Soloist and Short-wave Transmitter (1968); *Dr. K.-Sextett* (1969); *Fresco* for 4 Orchs. (1969); *Pole* for 2 Performers or Singers, and Short-wave Transmitter (1969–70); *Expo* for 3 Instrumentalists or Singers, and Short-wave Transmitter (1969–70); *Mantra* for 2 Pianos (Donaueschingen, Oct. 18, 1970); *Für kommende Zeiten,* "17 texts of intuitive music" (1968–70); *Sternklang,* "park music" for 5 Groups (1971); *Trans* for Orch. (1971); *Alphabet für Liège,* 13 musical pictures for Soloist and Duo Performers (1972); *"Am Himmel wandre ich . . . ,"* Indian lieder for 2 Soloists and Orch. (Donaueschingen, Oct. 20, 1974); *"Atmen gibt das Leben . . . ,"* choral opera with Orch. or Tape (1975–77); *Herbstmusik* for 4 Performers (1974); *Musik im Brauch* for Percussion and Musical Clocks (1975); *Tierkreis* for Various Instruments and Voices (4 versions, 1975–81); *Harlekin* for Clarinet (1975); *Sirius,* electronic music, dedicated to American pioneers on earth and in space (1975–77; 1st demonstrated at the National Air and Space Museum, Smithsonian Institution, Washington, D.C., July 18, 1976); *Amour,* 5 pieces for Clarinet (1976); *Jubiläum* for Orch. (1977; N.Y., Sept. 10, 1981); *In Freundschaft* for 11 Solo Instruments (1977); *Licht,* projected cycle of 7 operas, 1 for each day of the week: *Donnerstag aus Licht* (1978–80; Milan, April 3, 1981); *Samstag aus Licht* (1981–83; Milan, May 25, 1984); *Montag aus Licht* (1985–88; Milan, May 7, 1988).

BIBL.: K. Wörner, *K. S., Werk und Wollen* (Cologne, 1963; Eng. tr. as *S., Life and Work,* London, 1973); C. Cardew, *S. Serves Imperialism,* a rambling diatribe by a disenchanted follower who became a militant Maoist (London, 1974); J. Cott, *S., Conversations with the Composer* (N.Y., 1973, and London, 1974); J. Harvey, *The Music of S.* (London, 1975); R. Maconie, *S.* (London, 1976); B. Sullivan and M. Manion, *S. in Den Haag* (The Hague, 1983); H.-J. Nagel, ed., *S. in Calcutta* (Calcutta, 1984); P. Britton, "S.'s Path to Opera," *Musical Times* (Sept. 1985); M. Tannenbaum, *Intervisto sul genio musicale* (Rome, 1985; Eng. tr. as *Conversations with S.,* Oxford, 1987); *S.: 60. Geburtstag: 22. August 1988* (n.p., 1988); M. Kurtz, *S.: Eine Biographie* (Kassel and Basel, 1988).

Stockhoff, Walter William, American composer; b. St. Louis, Nov. 12, 1876; d. there, April 1, 1968. He was largely autodidact, and began to compose early in life. In his music he was influenced mainly by German Romantic composers, but his thematic material was distinctly American. In some of his early piano music he made use of modernistic devices, such as the whole-tone scale, cadential triads with the added sixth, etc. Busoni wrote an enthusiastic article about him (1915) in which he described him as one of America's most original composers. The orch. version of his piano suite *To the Mountains* was premiered under the title *American Symphonic Suite* (Frankfurt am Main, Dec. 10, 1924). Several of his piano works and some chamber music were publ. Other works include 5 *Dramatic Poems* for Orch. (1943); Piano Sonata; *Metamorphoses* for Piano; etc.

Stockmann, (Christine) Doris, German ethnomusicologist; b. Dresden, Nov. 3, 1929. She studied piano, opera production, and music theory at the Dresden Hochschule für Musik (1947–49) and musicology with Dräger, Meyer, and Vetter at Humboldt Univ. in Berlin; then studied ethnography, folklore, and linguistics with Steinitz there, taking her doctorate in 1958 with the dissertation *Der Volksgesang in der Altmark* (publ. in Berlin, 1962). She became scientific assistant in ethnomusicology at the Inst. for German Folklore of the Academy of Sciences in Berlin (1953); lectured at Humboldt Univ. (1967–68) and at the univs. in Uppsala (1965) and Göteborg (1969). She publ. extensively, alone and with her husband, **Erich Stockmann,** on German and European folk music, particularly in their medieval and contemporary forms.

Stockmann, Erich, German ethnomusicologist; b. Stendal, March 10, 1926. He studied musicology and German at the Univ. of Greifswald (1946–49) and musicology with Dräger, Meyer, and Vetter at Humboldt Univ. in Berlin (Ph.D., 1953, with the diss. *Der musikalische Sinn der elektro-akustischen Musikinstrumente*). After serving as ethnomusicologist at the Inst. for German Folklore of the Academy of Sciences in Berlin, he became a lecturer in ethnomusicology and organology at Humboldt Univ. (1957). He was largely responsible for the development of the ethnomusicological research center of the Berlin Academy of Sciences, leading its 1st expedition to collect

folk music in Albania (1957). He ed. several series, including the Handbüchern der Europäischen Volksmusikinstrumente (Leipzig, 1967–), Annual Bibliography of European Ethnomusicology (Bratislava, 1967–), and Studia Instrumentorum Musicae Popularis (Stockholm, 1969–); also publ. extensively, alone and with his wife, **Doris Stockmann,** on European folk music and instruments.

Stoeckel, Carl, American music patron, son of **Gustave J(acob) Stoeckel;** b. New Haven, Conn., Dec. 7, 1858; d. Norfolk, Conn., Nov. 1, 1925. His contribution to American musical culture was the establishment in 1902 of the summer festivals on his estate in Norfolk. He offered cash prizes to composers who appeared at the festival in performances of their own works. Sibelius composed his tone poem *Aallottaret* especially for the Norfolk Festival, and conducted its world premiere there in its 2nd version as *The Oceanides* in 1914. Among other composers represented were J.A. Carpenter, G.W. Chadwick, S. Coleridge-Taylor, H.F. Gilbert, P. Grainger, H.K. Hadley, E.S. Kelly, C.M. Loeffler, H. Parker, D.S. Smith, C.V. Stanford, and Deems Taylor.

Stoeckel, Gustave J(acob), German-American organist, pedagogue, and composer, father of **Carl Stoeckel;** b. Maikammer, Bavarian Palatinate, Nov. 9, 1819; d. Norfolk, Conn., May 14, 1907. He studied in Speyer and Kaiserslauten; after serving as a school principal in Landstuhl and as organist at Speyer Cathedral, he left his homeland in the wake of the 1848 revolution and settled in Norfolk as a private teacher; then was "Instructor of Vocal Art, Organist, and Chapelmaster" at Yale Univ. (1855–96), where he also was the 1st Battell Prof. of Music (1890–96). He founded the New Haven Phil. Soc. and was co-founder of the Mendelssohn Soc.; also was active with male glee clubs, becoming known as the father of the American glee-club tradition. He wrote many fine glee-club arrangements; his other works include 6 operas, a Sym., choral works, songs, and piano pieces.

BIBL.: D. Smith, *G.J. S., Yale Pioneer in Music* (New Haven, 1939).

Stoessel, Albert (Frederic), distinguished American violinist, conductor, teacher, and composer; b. St. Louis, Oct. 11, 1894; d. (fatally stricken while conducting the premiere of Walter Damrosch's *Dunkirk*) N.Y., May 12, 1943. He began his musical studies in St. Louis; then received training in violin with Willy Hess and in theory with Kretzschmar at the Berlin Hochschule für Musik, where he also studied conducting. In 1914 he appeared as a violin soloist in Berlin; after touring in Europe, he returned to St. Louis and performed as a soloist there. During World War I he was a military bandmaster in the U.S. Army (1917–19), serving as director of the school for bandmasters of the American Expeditionary Force in France. Returning to the U.S., he appeared as a violin soloist with the Boston Sym. Orch. and toured with Caruso in 1920. He settled in N.Y. in 1921 as Walter Damrosch's successor as conductor of the Oratorio Soc.; also was named director of music at the Chautauqua Institution (1923) and conductor of the Worcester (Mass.) Music Festival (1925); likewise appeared widely as a guest conductor. In 1923 he founded the music dept. at N.Y. Univ., which he headed until 1930; was director of the opera and orch. depts. at the Juilliard Graduate School (from 1927), where he conducted a number of premieres of American works. He was elected a member of the National Inst. of Arts and Letters in 1931. He publ. *The Technic of the Baton* (N.Y., 1920; 2nd ed., rev. and enl., 1928).

WORKS: Opera, *Garrick* (1936; N.Y., Feb. 24, 1937); *5 Miniatures* for Violin and Piano (1917); *Suite antique* for 2 Violins and Piano (1917; arranged for 2 Violins and Chamber Orch.); Violin Sonata (1919); *Hispania Suite* for Piano (1920; arranged for Orch., 1927); *Cyrano de Bergerac,* symphonic portrait (1922); *Flitting Bats* for Violin and Piano (1925); Concerto Grosso for Piano obbligato and Strings (1935); *Early Americana,* orch. suite (1935); choral works; songs; piano pieces; transcriptions.

BIBL.: C. McNaughton, *A. S., American Musician* (diss., N.Y. Univ., 1957).

Stoeving, (Carl Heinrich) Paul, German-American violinist, teacher, and composer; b. Leipzig, May 7, 1861; d. N.Y., Dec. 24, 1948. He studied violin in Leipzig and in Paris; toured as a soloist in Russia and Scandinavia; taught at the Guildhall School of Music in London (from 1896). In 1914 he emigrated to the U.S. and was employed as a violin teacher in New Haven and N.Y. He wrote the "song-play" *Gaston and Jolivette* and some violin music of considerable insignificance, but his publications on violin technique have a certain pragmatic value; among them are *The Art of Violin Bowing* (London, 1902); *The Story of the Violin* (London, 1904); *The Mastery of the Bow and Bowing Subtleties* (N.Y., 1920); *The Violin, Cello and String Quartet* (N.Y., 1927); *The Violin: Its Famous Makers and Players* (Boston, 1928).

Stogorsky, Alexander, Russian cellist, brother of **Gregor Piatigorsky;** b. Ekaterinoslav, Feb. 26, 1910. *Piat* is "5" in Russian and *sto* is "100." A story goes that when Gregor Piatigorsky became world famous, his lesser brother changed his name to Stogorsky to avoid confusion, but observed that he was 20 times as good since 100 is 20 times 5. He studied cello at the Moscow Cons. with Mark Yampolsky; subsequently taught at the Gorky Cons. (1946–54) and at the Minsk Cons. (1954–62). As a solo cellist, he gave 1st performances of concertos by Mosolov and Zolotarev.

Stöhr, Richard, Austrian-American pedagogue and composer; b. Vienna, June 11, 1874; d. Montpelier, Vt., Dec. 11, 1967. He studied medicine in Vienna (M.D., 1898), but then turned to music and studied with Robert Fuchs and others at the Vienna Cons. In 1903 he was appointed instructor in theory there, and during his long tenure he had many pupils who later became celebrated (Artur Rodzinski, Erich Leinsdorf et al.). In 1938 he was compelled to leave Vienna; settled in the U.S., where he taught at the Curtis Inst. of Music in Philadelphia (1939–42); then taught music and German at St. Michael's College in Winooski, Vt. (1943–50). He wrote 4 operas; 4 syms.; *Vermont Suite* for Orch. (1954); much chamber music; piano pieces. He publ. a popular manual, *Praktischer Leitfaden der Harmonielehre* (Vienna, 1909; 21st ed., 1963); also *Praktischer Leitfaden des Kontrapunkts* (Hamburg, 1911); *Musikalische Formenlehre* (Leipzig, 1911; rev. 1933, as *Formenlehre der Musik*); *Modulationslehre* (1932).

BIBL.: H. Sittner, *R. S., Mensch, Musiker, Lehrer* (Vienna, 1965).

Stoin, Elena, Bulgarian ethnomusicologist, daughter of **Vassil Stoin;** b. Samokov, April 12, 1915. She graduated from the State Academy of Music in Sofia (1938), then taught music in various schools until 1945; became research assistant at the Ethnographical Museum in Sofia (1946) and also worked in the folk-music dept. of the Music Inst. of the Bulgarian Academy of Sciences (from 1950), becoming a senior research fellow (1970). She lectured widely in Eastern Europe on Bulgarian folk music; her folk-song collections include *Sbornik narodni pesni ot Samokov i Samokovsko* (Collection of Folk Songs from Samokov and the Samokov Region; Sofia, 1975), to which her father had contributed.

Stoin, Vassil, Bulgarian ethnomusicologist, father of **Elena Stoin;** b. Samokov, Dec. 5, 1880; d. Sofia, Dec. 5, 1938. He taught himself violin at the age of 10; after graduating from the seminary in Samokov (1897), he taught in neighboring villages until 1907, meanwhile recording folk songs. He studied at the Brussels Cons. (1907–10) and taught music in Sofia, Samokov, and other regions (1911–22), organizing and conducting choirs and orchs. He taught in several schools in Sofia (1922–25), and began lecturing on folk music at the State Academy of Music, becoming a prof. in 1927 and director in 1931. He founded the folk-music dept. of the National Ethnographic Museum (1926). Stoin was one of the 1st ethnomusicologists to study Bulgarian folk song, transcribing over 9,000 songs and publishing several collections; he laid a foundation

for future studies, particularly those of his daughter. His books include *Hypothèse sur l'origine bulgare de la diaphome* (Sofia, 1925), *Balgarskata narodna muzika, metrika i ritmika* (Bulgarian Folk Music, Meter, and Rhythm; Sofia, 1927), and *Bulgarska narodna muzika* (Bulgarian Folk Music; Sofia, 1956).

Stojanović, Peter Lazar, Yugoslav violinist, teacher, and composer; b. Budapest, Sept. 6, 1877; d. Belgrade, Sept. 11, 1957. He studied violin with Hubay at the Budapest Cons. and with J. Grün at the Vienna Cons.; in 1913 he established his own school for advanced violin playing in Vienna. In 1925 he settled in Belgrade and became a prof. at the Stanković Music School; was its director from 1925 to 1928; from 1937 to 1945 he was a prof. of violin at the Belgrade Academy of Music. He publ. *Schule der Skalentechnik* for Violin. His works include the operas *A Tigris* (The Tiger; Budapest, Nov. 14, 1905), *Das Liebchen am Dache* (Vienna, May 19, 1917), and *Der Herzog von Reichsstadt* (Vienna, Feb. 11, 1921); 2 ballets; 2 symphonic poems: *Heldentod* (1918) and *Sava* (1935); 7 violin concertos; 2 cello concertos; 2 viola concertos; Flute Concerto; Horn Concerto; chamber music, including a Piano Trio, a Piano Quartet, and a Piano Quintet.

Stojowski, Sigismund (actually, **Zygmunt Denis Antoni**), noted Polish-born American pianist, pedagogue, and composer; b. Strzelce, May 14, 1869; d. N.Y., Nov. 5, 1946. He was a pupil of Żeleński in Krakow and of Diémer (piano) and Delibes (composition) at the Paris Cons. (1887–89), winning 1st prize for piano playing and composition; later he took a course with Paderewski. He remained in Paris until 1906, when he emigrated to the U.S. as head of the piano dept. at the Inst. of Musical Art in N.Y. (until 1912); later held a similar position at the Von Ende School of Music in N.Y.; taught at the Juilliard Summer School for several years. He became a naturalized American citizen in 1938. In his prime he was extremely successful as a concert pianist, and in his later years was greatly esteemed as a pedagogue.

WORKS: 2 piano concertos: No. 1 (Paris, 1891, composer soloist); No. 2, *Prologue, Scherzo and Variations* (London, June 23, 1913, composer soloist); Sym. (1899); Violin Concerto (1900); *Romanza* for Violin and Orch. (1901); *Rapsodie symphonique* for Piano and Orch. (1904); Cello Concerto (1922); choral pieces; Piano Quintet; 2 violin sonatas; 2 cello sonatas; piano pieces.

Stoker, Richard, English composer and teacher; b. Castleford, Yorkshire, Nov. 8, 1938. He studied composition with Eric Fenby and later with Lennox Berkeley at the Royal Academy of Music in London (1958–62), where he won the Mendelssohn scholarship; then completed his studies with Nadia Boulanger in Paris. He was prof. of composition at the Royal Academy of Music (from 1963); ed. the journal *Composer* (from 1969); publ. the book *Open Window—Open Door* (London, 1985). In his music he cultivates the 12-tone technique, but derives it tonally from the quintal cycle of scales. As a believer in the universality of the arts, he writes utilitarian music for dilettantes, amateurs, musicasters, and children.

WORKS: OPERAS: *Johnson Preserv'd* (London, July 4, 1967); *Thérèse Raquin* (1975). **ORCH.:** *Petite Suite* (1962); *Antic Hay,* overture (1962); *Little Symphony* (1969); *Feast of Fools,* overture (1969). **CHAMBER:** 3 string quartets (1960, 1966, 1969); Trio for Flute, Oboe, and Clarinet (1960); *Festival Suite* for Trumpet and Piano (1961); Clarinet Sonata (1961); Wind Quintet (1962); *Miniature String Trio* (1963); Sextet for Wind and Strings (1963); Violin Sonata (1964); Piano Trio (1965); *3 Miniature Quartets* (1969); Oboe Quartet (1970).

Stokes, Eric (Norman), iconoclastic American composer and teacher; b. Haddon Heights, N.J., July 14, 1930. He studied at Lawrence College (B.Mus., 1952) and with Carl McKinley and F. Judd Cooke at the New England Cons. of Music (M.Mus., 1956); completed his education with Argento and Fetler at the Univ. of Minnesota (Ph.D., 1964), where he taught (from 1961; prof. from 1977); founded its electronic music laboratory and contemporary music ensemble, 1st Minnesota Moving and

Storage Warehouse Band (1971). Stokes has been variously described as a crusty, eccentric, wonderfully humorous, very healthy and resourceful American composer of gentle, witty, lyrically accessible music, with a taste for folkloric Americana and a "Whitmanesque" ear. Some of his works (i.e., the series *Phonic Paradigms*) call for unusual instruments that produce unforeseen effects; his *Rock & Roll (Phonic Paradigm I)* (1980) is executed by 5 players hitting rocks together and rolling them across the floor.

WORKS: OPERAS: *Horspfal* (1969); *Happ or Orpheus in Clover* (1977); *The Jealous Cellist & Other Acts of Misconduct* (1979); *Itaru the Stonecutter* (1982); *The Further Voyages of the Santa Maria* (1984); *Apollonia's Circus* (1984); also musicals and theater pieces, including *The Shake of Things to Come (Phonic Paradigm V)* for Mime and 3 Percussionists (1983) and *We're Not Robots, You Know* for Vocal Quintet and Optional Matching Vocal Quintet and Instrumental Ensemble (1986; Banff, Canada, Dec. 1990). **ORCH.:** *A Center Harbor Holiday* (1963); *On the Badlands—Parables* for Chamber Orch. (1972); *5 Verbs of Earth Encircled* for Chamber Orch. (1973); *The Continental Harp and Band Report* (1974–75); *The Spirit of Place among the People* for Chamber Orch. (1977); Syms.: Book I (1979), Book II (1981), and Book III, *Captains on the War against Earth* (Kansas City, Mo., Jan. 5, 1990); *Prairie Drum* for Chamber Orch. (1981); *Concert Music* for Piano and Orch. (1982); *The Greenhouse Effect* (1983); *Stages* (Homage to Kurt Weill) (Wales, Aug. 27, 1988). **CHAMBER:** Trio for Clarinet, Cello, and Piano (1955; rev. 1963); *Expositions on Themes by Henry David Thoreau* for Flute, Oboe, Trumpet, Horn, Violin, Cello, Piano, Accordion or Organ, and Percussion (1970); *Circles in a Round* for Piano and Optional Tape (1972); *Rock & Roll (Phonic Paradigm I)* for 5 Performers, Rocks, and Found Objects (1980); *Spring Song (Phonic Paradigm II)* for 5 Performers, Springs, and Found Objects (1980); Wind Quintet No. 2 (1981); *Tintinnabulary (Phonic Paradigm IV)* for Tape (1983); *Brazen Cartographies* for Brass Quintet (Philadelphia, Nov. 6, 1988); *The Lyrical Pickpocket* for Flute (Piccolo and Alto), Oboe (English Horn), Bassoon, and Piano (Toy Piano) (Minneapolis, March 25, 1990). **VOCAL:** *Smoke and Steel* for Tenor, Men's Chorus, and Orch. (Boston, May 14, 1958; rev. 1989); *The River's Minute by the Far Brook's Year* for Narrator, Chorus, and Orch. (1981); *Peppercorn Songs* for Chorus, Piano, and Optional Instrumental Ensemble (1984); *Firecho* for 5 or More Voices and Optional Percussion (Minneapolis, Aug. 23, 1987); solo songs.

Stokowski, Leopold (Anthony), celebrated, spectacularly endowed, and magically communicative English-born American conductor; b. London (of a Polish father and an Irish mother), April 18, 1882; d. Nether Wallop, Hampshire, Sept. 13, 1977. He attended Queen's College, Oxford, and the Royal College of Music in London, where he studied organ with Stevenson Hoyte, music theory with Walford Davies, and composition with Sir Charles Stanford. At the age of 18 he obtained the post of organist at St. James, Piccadilly. In 1905 he went to America and served as organist and choirmaster at St. Bartholomew's in N.Y.; became a U.S. citizen in 1915. In 1909 he was engaged to conduct the Cincinnati Sym. Orch.; although his contract was for 5 years, he obtained a release in 1912 in order to accept an offer from the Philadelphia Orch. This was the beginning of a long and spectacular career as a sym. conductor; he led the Philadelphia Orch. for 24 years as its sole conductor, bringing it to a degree of brilliance that rivaled the greatest orchs. in the world. In 1931 he was officially designated by the board of directors of the Philadelphia Orch. as music director, which gave him control over the choice of guest conductors and soloists. He conducted most of the repertoire by heart, an impressive accomplishment at the time; he changed the seating of the orch., placing violins to the left and cellos to the right. After some years of leading the orch. with a baton, he finally dispensed with it and shaped the music with the 10 fingers of his hands. He emphasized the colorful elements in the music; he was the creator of the famous "Philadelphia

sound" in the strings, achieving a well-nigh *bel canto* quality. Tall and slender, with an aureole of blond hair, his figure presented a striking contrast with his stocky, mustachioed German predecessors; he was the 1st conductor to attain the status of a star comparable to that of a motion picture actor. Abandoning the proverbial ivory tower in which most conductors dwelt, he actually made an appearance as a movie actor in the film *One Hundred Men and a Girl*. In 1940 he agreed to participate in the production of Walt Disney's celebrated film *Fantasia*, which featured both live performers and animated characters; Stokowski conducted the music and in one sequence engaged in a bantering colloquy with Mickey Mouse. He was lionized by the Philadelphians; in 1922 he received the Edward Bok Award of $10,000 as "the person who has done the most for Philadelphia." He was praised in superlative terms in the press, but not all music critics approved of his cavalier treatment of sacrosanct masterpieces, for he allowed himself to alter the orchestration; he doubled some solo passages in the brass, and occasionally introduced percussion instruments not provided in the score; he even cut out individual bars that seemed to him devoid of musical action. Furthermore, Stokowski's own orch. arrangements of Bach raised the pedantic eyebrows of professional musicologists; yet there is no denying the effectiveness of the sonority and the subtlety of color that he succeeded in creating by such means. Many great musicians hailed Stokowski's new orch. sound; Rachmaninoff regarded the Philadelphia Orch. under Stokowski, and later under Ormandy, as the greatest with which he had performed. Stokowski boldly risked his popularity with the Philadelphia audiences by introducing modern works. He conducted Schoenberg's music, culminating in the introduction of his formidable score *Gurrelieder* on April 8, 1932. An even greater gesture of defiance of popular tastes was his world premiere of *Amériques* by Varèse on April 9, 1926, a score that opens with a siren and thrives on dissonance. Stokowski made history by joining the forces of the Philadelphia Orch. with the Philadelphia Grand Opera Co. in the 1st American performance of Berg's masterpiece *Wozzeck* (March 31, 1931). The opposition of some listeners was now vocal; when the audible commotion in the audience erupted during his performance of Webern's Sym., he abruptly stopped conducting, walked off the stage, then returned only to begin the work all over again. From his earliest years with the Philadelphia Orch., Stokowski adopted the habit of addressing the audience, to caution them to keep their peace during the performance of a modernistic score, or reprimanding them for their lack of progressive views; once he even took to task the prim Philadelphia ladies for bringing their knitting to the concert. In 1933 the board of directors took an unusual step in announcing that there would be no more "debatable music" performed by the orch.; Stokowski refused to heed this proclamation. Another eruption of discontent ensued when he programmed some Soviet music at a youth concert and trained the children to sing the Internationale. Stokowski was always interested in new electronic sound; he was the 1st to make use of the Theremin in the orch. in order to enhance the sonorities of the bass section. He was instrumental in introducing electrical recordings. In 1936 he resigned as music director of the Philadelphia Orch.; he was succeeded by Eugene Ormandy, but continued to conduct concerts as co-conductor of the orch. until 1938. From 1940 to 1942 he took a newly organized All-American Youth Orch. on a tour in the U.S. and in South America. During the season 1942–43 he was associate conductor, with Toscanini, of the NBC Sym. Orch.; he shared the season of 1949–50 with Mitropoulos as conductor of the N.Y. Phil.; from 1955 to 1960 he conducted the Houston Sym. Orch. In 1962 he organized in N.Y. the American Sym. Orch. and led it until 1972; on April 26, 1965, at the age of 83, he conducted the orch. in the 1st complete performance of the 4th Sym. of Charles Ives. In 1973 he went to London, where he continued to make recordings and conduct occasional concerts; he also appeared in television interviews. He died in his sleep at the age of 95; rumor had it that he had a contract signed for a gala performance on his 100th birthday in 1982. Stokowski was married 3 times: his 1st wife was the pianist **Olga Samaroff,** whom he married in 1911; they were divorced in 1923; his 2nd wife was Evangeline Brewster Johnson, heiress to the Johnson and Johnson drug fortune; they were married in 1926 and divorced in 1937; his 3rd marriage, to Gloria Vanderbilt, produced a ripple of prurient newspaper publicity because of the disparity in their ages; he was 63, she was 21; they were married in 1945 and divorced in 1955. Stokowski publ. *Music for All of Us* (N.Y., 1943), which was translated into the Russian, Italian, and Czech languages.

BIBL.: H. Schonberg, *The Great Conductors* (N.Y., 1967); H. Kupferberg, *Those Fabulous Philadelphians* (N.Y., 1969); E. Johnson, ed., *S.: Essays in Analysis of His Art* (London, 1973); P. Robinson, *S.* (N.Y., 1977); A. Chasins, *L. S.: A Profile* (N.Y., 1979); O. Daniel, *S.: A Counterpoint of View* (N.Y., 1982); P. Opperby, *L. S.* (Tunbridge Wells and N.Y., 1982); W. Smith, "L. S.: A Re-Evaluation," *American Music,* i/3 (1983).

Stoliarsky, Piotr (Solomonovich), significant Russian violin pedagogue; b. Lipovets, near Kiev, Nov. 30, 1871; d. Sverdlovsk, April 29, 1944. He began his violin training with his father, then studied with S. Barcewica at the Warsaw Cons. and with E. Mlynarski and Josef Karbulka at the Odessa Music School (graduated, 1898). He played violin in the Odessa Opera orch. (1898–1914); also taught in his own music school (from 1911); in 1920 he joined the faculty of the Odessa Cons., where he was made a prof. in 1923; opened another school for talented youths that was the 1st of its kind in the Soviet Union (1933). His role in musical pedagogy was similar to that of Auer in training students from limited backgrounds to attain international stature as virtuosi; among his notable pupils were Oistrakh, Gilels, and Milstein.

Stolpe, Antoni, gifted Polish pianist and composer; b. Pulawy, near Lublin, May 23, 1851; d. Merano, Sept. 7, 1872. He studied piano with his father, Eduard Stolpe, then pursued composition studies with Freyer and Moniuszko at the Warsaw Music Inst., graduating with 1st prize in 1867; subsequently studied composition with Kiel and piano with Kullak in Berlin, and then taught piano there at the Stern Cons. until ill health forced him to abandon his career. His early death was lamented as a major loss for Polish music.

WORKS: Sym. (1867); Symphonic Overture (1868); Concerto Overture (1869); Piano Concerto (1869); 2 string quartets (1866, 1869); Piano Sextet (1867); 2 piano sonatas (1867, 1872); String Quintet (1868); Piano Trio (1869); *Variations for String Quartet* (1872); various piano pieces; *Credo* for Mixed Voices, Organ, and String Quintet (1867); songs.

Stolz, Rosine (real name, **Victoire Noël**), famous French mezzo-soprano; b. Paris, Feb. 13, 1815; d. there, July 28, 1903. She was the daughter of a janitor; was sent by Duchess de Berri to a convent, and in 1826 to the Choron School, which she entered under the name of Rosine Niva; it was under that name that she began her career as a concert artist; then used the name of Mlle. Ternaux, and later Mlle. Héloise Stoltz (the latter being derived from her mother's maiden name, Stoll). In 1832 she made her stage debut as Victoire Ternaux at the Théâtre Royal de la Monnaie in Brussels; after appearances in Spa, Antwerp, Amsterdam, and Lille, she obtained her 1st important engagement as Alice in *Robert le diable* at the Théâtre Royal de la Monnaie in Brussels in 1835; the next year she sang Rachel in *La Juive* there, and in 1837 married Alphonse Lescuyer, the theater's director. She made her debut at the Paris Opéra as Rachel on Aug. 25, 1837; subsequently appeared there in many premieres, including operas by Halévy; also created the roles of Ascanio in Berlioz's *Benvenuto Cellini* (Sept. 3, 1838), and Léonore in *La Favorite* (Dec. 2, 1840) and Zaida in *Dom Sébastien* (Nov. 13, 1843), both by Donizetti. She became intimate with Leon Pillet, manager of the Opéra from 1844, and through him wielded considerable influence on appointments of new singers; after a series of attacks in the press, accusing her of unworthy intrigues, she resigned in March 1847; fought for vindication through 3 obviously inspired pamphlets (C. Cantinjou, *Les Adieux de*

Madame Stoltz; E. Pérignon, *Rosine Stoltz;* and J. Lemer, *Madame Rosine Stoltz*), all publ. in 1847. At the invitation of the Brazilian Emperor Don Pedro (who was romantically attached to her) she made 4 tours of Brazil between 1850 and 1859, at a salary of 400,000 francs a season. In 1854 and 1855 she once again sang at the Paris Opéra. In 1860 she made her farewell operatic appearance in Lyons, and then sang in concerts for several seasons before retiring. Ernst II of Württemberg named her Baroness Stoltzenau and Countess of Ketschendorf in 1865; she subsequently was made Duchess of Lesignano upon her marriage to Duke Carlo Lesignano in 1872; then married the Spanish prince Manuel Godoi Bassano de la Paix in 1878. She publ. 6 songs (not composed by her, in all probability), and her name (as Princesse de Lesignano) was used as author of a learned vol., *Les Constitutions de tous les pays civilisés* (1880), which was written in her behalf. The mystifying aspects of her private life and public career are recounted by G. Bord in *Rosine Stoltz* (Paris, 1909) and by A. Pougin in "La Vérité sur Madame Stoltz," *Le Ménestrel* (Aug. 28, 1909, et seq.).

Stoltzer, Thomas, important German composer; b. Schweidnitz, Silesia, c.1480; d. (drowned in the Taja) near Znaim, Moravia, Feb. (?) 1526. He may have studied with Heinrich Finck, whose works he knew well; in 1519 became a priest in Breslau, where he held a benefice at St. Elisabeth's and was vicarius discontinuus at the Cathedral; was named magister capellae at the Hungarian royal court in Ofen by Ludwig II in 1522; he composed his most important works there. Stoltzer was one of the leading composers of sacred music of his era; his 14 Latin and 4 German Psalm motets are of a very high order. His *Octo tonorum melodiae,* 8 5-part instrumental fantasias arranged according to the church modes, is most likely the earliest motet-style cycle for instruments. Among his other works are masses, Magnificats, antiphons, hymns, Psalms, introits, sequences, responsories, and sacred and secular lieder. A number of his works were publ. in collections of his day; see also H. Albrecht and O. Gombosi, eds., *Thomas Stoltzer: Sämtliche lateinische Hymnen und Psalmen,* Denkmäler Deutscher Tonkunst, LXV (1931), and H. Albrecht and L. Hoffmann-Erbrecht, eds., *Thomas Stoltzer: Ausgewählte Werke,* I–II, ibid., XXII (1942) and LXVI (1969).

BIBL.: R. Eitner, "Briefe von T. S., Adrian Rauch und Sylvester Raid," *Monatshefte für Musikgeschichte,* VIII (1876); L. Hoffmann-Erbrecht, *T. S.: Leben und Schaffen* (Kassel, 1964).

Stoltzman, Richard (Leslie), outstanding American clarinetist; b. Omaha, July 12, 1942. He began clarinet lessons when he was 8 and gained experience playing in local jazz settings with his father, an alto saxophonist. He then studied mathematics and music at Ohio State Univ. (B.Mus., 1964); also studied clarinet with Robert Marcellus; after studies at Yale Univ. (M.Mus., 1967), he completed his clarinet training with Harold Wright at the Marlboro Music School and with Kalman Opperman in N.Y.; pursued postgraduate studies at Columbia Univ.'s Teachers College (1967–70). He played in many concerts at Marlboro; also founded the group Tashi ("good fortune" in Tibetan) with pianist Peter Serkin, violinist Ida Kavafian, and cellist Fred Sherry in 1973, and toured widely with the group; likewise taught at the Calif. Inst. of the Arts (1970–75). He made his N.Y. solo recital debut in 1974; after being awarded the Avery Fisher Prize in 1977, he pursued an international career as a virtuoso; appeared as soloist with many of the major orchs., as a chamber music artist, and as a solo recitalist. In 1982 he became the 1st clarinetist ever to give a solo recital at N.Y.'s Carnegie Hall. In 1986 he received the Avery Fisher Artist Award. He maintains an extensive repertoire, ranging from the classics to the avant-garde, and including popular music genres; he has also commissioned works and made his own transcriptions.

Stolz, Robert (Elisabeth), noted Austrian conductor and composer; b. Graz, Aug. 25, 1880; d. Berlin, June 27, 1975. His father was the conductor and pedagogue Jacob Stolz and his mother the pianist Ida Bondy; after initial studies with them, he was a pupil of R. Fuchs at the Vienna Cons. and of Humperdinck in Berlin. He became a répétiteur in Graz in 1897; after serving as 2nd conductor in Marburg an der Drau (1898–1902), he was 1st conductor in Salzburg (1902–3) and at the German Theater in Brünn (1903–5). From 1905 to 1917 he was chief conductor of the Theater an der Wien, where he conducted the premieres of many Viennese operettas. He became successful as a composer of popular songs in the Viennese tradition; his 1st success as an operetta composer came with his *Der Tanz ins Glück* (Vienna, Oct. 18, 1921). In 1924 he went to Berlin, where he eventually won success as a composer for film musicals. His disdain for the Nazi regime led him to leave Germany in 1936 and then Austria in 1938, but not before he helped to smuggle numerous Jews out of the clutches of the Nazis prior to leaving for Paris in 1938. In 1940 he went to the U.S. and was active as a conductor and as a composer for Hollywood films. In 1946 he returned to Vienna, where he conducted and composed until his last years. He possessed an extraordinary facility for stage music and composed about 65 operettas and musicals in a typical Viennese manner; of these the most famous is *2 Herzen im ³/₄ Takt* (Zürich, Sept. 30, 1933). Other operettas are: *Die lustigen Weiber von Wien* (Munich, 1909); *Das Glücksmädel* (1910); *Das Lumperl* (Graz, 1915); *Lang, lang, ist's her* (Vienna, March 28, 1917); *Die Tanzgräfin* (Vienna, May 13, 1921); *Mädi* (Berlin, April 1, 1923); *Ein Ballroman oder Der Kavalier von zehn bis vier* (Vienna, Feb. 29, 1924); *Eine einzige Nacht* (Vienna, Dec. 23, 1927); *Peppina* (1931); *Wenn die kleinen Veilchen blühen* (The Hague, April 1, 1932); *Venus im Seide* (Zürich, Dec. 10, 1932); *Der verlorene Walzer* (Zürich, Sept. 30, 1933); *Grüzi* (Zürich, 1934); *Frühling im Prater* (Vienna, Dec. 22, 1949); *Karneval in Wien* (1950); *Trauminsel* (Bregenz, July 21, 1962); *Frühjahrs-Parade* (Vienna, March 25, 1964). He wrote about 100 film scores and nearly 2,000 lieder. His other works include waltzes, marches, and piano pieces. After he was forced to leave Austria, he composed a funeral march for Hitler (at a time when Hitler was, unfortunately, very much alive). **BIBL.:** G. Holm, *Im Dreivierteltakt durch die Welt* (Linz, 1948); W.-D. Brümmel and F. van Booth, *R. S.: Melodie eines Lebens* (Stuttgart, 1967); O. Herbrich, *R. S.: König der Melodie* (Vienna and Munich, 1975).

Stolz, Teresa (real name, **Teresina Stolzová**), renowned Bohemian soprano; b. Elbekosteletz, June 5, 1834; d. Milan, Aug. 23, 1902. She was born into a musical family; her twin sisters, Francesca and Ludmila, also became sopranos; they were intimate with the composer Luigi Ricci, who had a child by each of them; Ludmila later became his wife. Teresa studied at the Prague Cons. and then with Ricci in Trieste (1856); made her operatic debut in 1857 in Tiflis, where she sang regularly during the next 5 seasons; also appeared in Odessa and Constantinople. In 1863 she sang in Turin, and thereafter appeared with brilliant success in the major Italian opera centers; she was closely associated with Verdi from 1872 to 1876, leading some writers to speculate that she was his mistress. She was without question one of the greatest interpreters of Verdi's heroines, excelling particularly as Aida and Leonora; she also sang in the premiere of his Requiem (1874). After singing in St. Petersburg (1876–77), she made her farewell appearance as a soloist in the Requiem at Milan's La Scala on June 30, 1879. Her vocal gifts were extraordinary and her range extended from g to c#³. **BIBL.:** G. Cenzato, "Verdi e la S.," *Corriere della Sera* (Oct. 30, 1932); J. Šolín, *T. S.ová: První a nejslavější Aida* (T. S.: The 1st and Most Celebrated Aida; Mělník, 1944; 2nd ed., 1946); U. Zoppi, *Mariani, Verdi e la S.* (Milan, 1947); F. Walker, *The Man Verdi* (London, 1962).

Stolze, Gerhard, German tenor; b. Dessau, Oct. 1, 1926; d. Garmisch-Partenkirchen, March 11, 1979. He studied voice in Dresden and Berlin; made his operatic debut as Augustin Moser in *Die Meistersinger von Nürnberg* at the Dresden State Opera in 1949. From 1951 he made regular appearances at

the Bayreuth Festivals; also sang at the Vienna State Opera, and from 1953 to 1961 at the Berlin Staatsoper. He established his reputation as a Wagnerian singer, but also sang leading parts in German contemporary operas, including Satan in Martin's *Le Mystère de la Nativité* (1960).

Stölzel (also **Stözl, Stöltzel**), **Gottfried Heinrich,** eminent German composer; b. Gründstädtl, near Schwarzenberg, Erzegebirge, Jan. 13, 1690; d. Gotha, Nov. 27, 1749. He began his musical training with his father; at age 13 he entered the Schneerberg grammar school, where he received musical instruction from the Kantor, Christian Umlaufft; after attending the Gera Gymnasium, where he was encouraged by the Kapelle director, Emanuel Kegel, he went to Leipzig to study at the Univ. (1707); however, he soon turned to music and found a mentor in Melchior Hofmann, whom he served as copyist; his 1st compositions were performed under his teacher's name. He went to Breslau in 1710 and taught singing and keyboard; also brought out his 1st stage work there, *Narcissus*. After traveling throughout Italy (1713–15), he was active as a composer in Prague (1715–17) and in Bayreuth (1717–18). In 1718 he became Kapellmeister at the Gera court; in 1719 he went to the Saxe-Gotha court, where he then held the post of Kapellmeister from 1720 until his death. In addition to composing, he devoted much time to teaching; also wrote the 1st significant treatise on recitative, *Abhandlung vom Recitativ* (MS; ed. by W. Steger, *Gottfried Heinrich Stölzel's 'Abhandlung vom Recitativ,'* diss., Univ. of Heidelberg, 1962). In 1739 he was elected to membership in Mizler's Societät der Musikalischen Wissenschaften. A great portion of his music, including his stage and sacred vocal works, is lost. **BIBL.:** E. Böhme, "G.H. S. in Gera," *Zeitschrift für Musikwissenschaft,* XIII (1930–31); W. Schmidt-Weiss, *G.H. S. als Instrumentalkomponist* (diss., Univ. of Munich, 1938); F. Neumann, "G.H. S.s musiktheoretische Schriften," *Sammlung musikwissenschaftlicher Abhandlungen: Festschrift für Rudolf Gerber* (MS, Göttingen, 1952); W. Steger, *G.H. S.s "Abhandlung vom Recitativ"* (diss., Univ. of Heidelberg, 1962); F. Hennenberg, *Das Kantatenschaffen von G.H. S.* (diss., Univ. of Leipzig, 1965; publ. in a rev. and abridged ed., Leipzig, 1976).

Stone, Carl, innovative American composer and performer; b. Los Angeles, Feb. 10, 1953. He studied with James Tenney and Morton Subotnick at the Calif. Inst. of the Arts in Valencia (B.F.A., 1975); served as music director of KPFK Radio in Los Angeles (1978–81) and director of Meet the Composer/California (from 1981); in 1985, was co–artistic director of the 7th New Music America Festival. Among his awards are an NEA grant (1981–82), tour support awards from the Calif. Arts Council (1984–90), and annual ASCAP awards (from 1985); in 1989 he was funded by the Asian Cultural Council for 6 months' residence in Japan. Stone composes exclusively electro-acoustic music, employing natural sounds and occasional fragments of familiar pieces, as in his *Sonali* (1988; *Die Zauberflöte*), *Hop Ken* (1987; Mussorgsky's *Pictures at an Exhibition*), and *Shing Kee* (1986; recording of a Japanese pop star singing a Schubert lied); Stone inscrutably manipulates his Macintosh computer in solo performances to create sensuous, playful, and often enigmatic real-time compositions. He is also an ethnic foods enthusiast (see J. Gold, "Carl Stone: Between Bytes," in *Los Angeles Times*, Aug. 19, 1990), naming many of his pieces after favorite restaurants. He has performed extensively in the U.S., Canada, Europe, Asia, Australia, South America, and the Near East; among choreographers who have used his music are Bill T. Jones and Ping Chong. **WORKS: TAPE:** *Chao Praya* (1972); *LIM* (1973); *Maneeya* (1975); *Sukothai* (1979); *Unthaitled* (1979); *A Tip* (1980); *Thoughts in Stone* (1980); *Woo Lae Oak* (1981); *Jang* (1984). **ELECTRONICS:** *Busogong* (1980); *Kuk Il Kwan* (1981); *Green Card March* (1982); *Dong Il Jang* (1982); *Woo Lae Oak* (1982); *Audible Structure* (1983); *Torung* (1983); *Ho Ban* for Piano and Electronics (1984; also for Solo Piano, 1990); *Spalding Gray's Map of LA,* sound track (1984); *Mae Yao* (in 2 parts; 1984; also for Electronics and Percussion, 1989); *Se Jong*

(1984); *Shibucho* (1984); *Wave Heat* (1984); *Hama* (1985); *Fanfare for Pershing Square* (1985); *Kappa* (1985); *Phô Bác* (1986); *Vim* (1986); *Chia Heng* (1986); *Everett & Jones* (1986); *Imae* (1986); *Samanalung* (1986); *Shing Kee* (1986); *Thanh My* (1986); *Hop Ken* (1987; also for Electronics, Percussion, and Bass, 1989); *Wall Me Do* (1987); *Amaterasu* (1988); *Amaterasu's Dance* (1988); *Jang Toh* (1988); *Mae* (1988); *Nekai* (1988); *Sonali* (1988); *Zang* (1988); *Zhang Toh* (1988); *Gadberry's* (1989; also version for Electronics, Percussion, and Bass); *Jakuzure* (1989; also *Jakuzure II* for Koto and Electronics); *Keika* (1989); *Kokami* (1989); *Kong Joo* (1989; also for Electronics, Percussion, and Bass); *She Gol Jib* (1989); *Chao Nue* (1990); *Mom's* (1990).
BIBL.: K. Gann, "C. S.: Free Samples," *Village Voice* (May 24, 1988).

Stone, Kurt, German-American musicologist; b. Hamburg, Nov. 14, 1911; d. Wilmington, N.C., June 15, 1989. He studied music in Hamburg and Copenhagen; went to N.Y. in 1938 as a teacher at the Dalcroze School of Music; also worked for various music publishers from 1942; contributed knowledgeable articles on modern music and composers to various periodicals. With his wife, he ed. *The Writings of Elliott Carter* (1977); publ. *Music Notation in the Twentieth Century: A Practical Guide* (1980).

Stör, Carl, German violinist and composer; b. Stolberg, June 29, 1814; d. Weimar, Jan. 17, 1889. He was a pupil of Götze and Lobe at Weimar; was appointed court conductor in 1857, but in a few years failing eyesight compelled him to resign. He composed the opera *Die Flucht* (Weimar, 1843); *Tonbilder zu Schillers "Lied von der Glocke"* for Orch.; Violin Concerto; several ballets; a *Ständchen* for Cello, with Orch.; songs.

Storace, family of Italian-English musicians (there is no evidence to substantiate the claim that the original family name was Sorace, which would have been pronounced in England as the offensive "sore-ass"):
(1) Stephen (Stefano) Storace, double-bass player; b. Torre Annunziata, c.1725; d. c.1781. By 1748 he was in Dublin, where he played in the Smock Alley Theatre band; by 1758 was in London, where he tr. several works for performance at Marylebone Gardens; he played in the band at the King's Theatre, and also at the 3 Choirs Festival (1759–70); then took his family to Italy in 1778. He had 2 children who became musicians:
(2) Stephen (John Seymour) Storace, noted composer; b. London, April 4, 1762; d. there, March 19, 1796. He entered the Conservatorio di S. Onofrio in Naples about 1776; he studied violin there, then followed his sister to Vienna, where he became acquainted with Mozart. Two of his operas to Italian librettos were produced in Vienna with satisfying success: *Gli sposi malcontenti* (June 1, 1785) and *Gli equivoci* (Dec. 27, 1786). In 1787 he returned to London, where he produced another Italian opera, *La Cameriera astuta* (March 4, 1788), and a number of English operas, among which *The Haunted Tower* (Nov. 24, 1789) became extremely successful. His finest work for the stage, *The Pirates,* was premiered at the King's Theatre on Nov. 21, 1792. During the 1792–93 season, he was in charge of the Italian opera productions at the Little Theatre and at Drury Lane. In addition to his many stage works, he also composed other vocal works and instrumental pieces.
BIBL.: R. Graves, "The Comic Operas of S. S.," *Musical Times* (Oct. 1954); R. Fiske, "The Operas of S. S.," *Proceedings of the Musical Association,* LXXXVI (1959–60).
(3) Nancy (Ann or Anna Selina) Storace, celebrated soprano; b. London, Oct. 27, 1765; d. there, Aug. 28, 1817. She studied in London with Sacchini and Rauzzini; began her career singing in concerts as a child, and appeared at Hereford's 3 Choirs Festival in 1777; the following year she was taken by her parents to Italy, where she began her operatic career in Florence in 1780; then sang in Parma (1781) and Milan (1782). In 1783 she went to Vienna as prima donna, excelling in the performance of comic operas; married the English composer **John Abraham Fisher,** but the marriage did not last; created the role of Susanna in Mozart's *Le nozze di Figaro* (May 1, 1786). In 1787 she returned to London and sang at the King's Theatre until it was destroyed by fire in 1789; then sang at Drury Lane until 1796; also appeared in Handel's oratorios and sang at the King's Theatre in 1793. In 1797 she toured Europe with the tenor John Braham, who became her lover; continued to sing in London playhouses until her retirement from the stage in 1808. She and Braham lived together until 1816.
BIBL.: M. Ward, "N. S.," *Musical Times* (Nov. 1949); B. Matthews, "The Childhood of N. S.," ibid. (July 1969); idem, "N. S. and the Royal Society of Musicians," ibid. (June 1987).

Storch, M. Anton, Austrian conductor and composer; b. Vienna, Dec. 22, 1813; d. there, Dec. 31, 1888. He was conductor at the Carl and Josephstadt theaters in Vienna, and produced several of his operettas and opera-burlesques there: *Romeo und Julie* (Oct. 31, 1863); *Das Festkleid* (April 1, 1865); *Löwen im Dorfe* (Sept. 27, 1866); *Wiener Zugstücke* (April 26, 1868); *Prinz Taugenichts* (March 8, 1870; successful); wrote many favorite male quartets.

Storchio, Rosina, Italian soprano; b. Venice, May 19, 1876; d. Milan, July 24, 1945. She studied at the Milan Cons.; then made her debut at Milan's Teatro del Verme as Micaela in *Carmen* in 1892. In 1895 she made her 1st appearance at Milan's La Scala as Sophie in *Werther*; in 1897 she sang in the premiere of Leoncavallo's *La Bohème* in Venice; returning to Milan, she appeared in the title role of Leoncavallo's *Zazà* at the Teatro Lirico in 1900; then appeared at La Scala (from 1902), where she sang in the premieres of several operas, including the title role of *Madama Butterfly* (Feb. 7, 1904); continued to appear there until 1918. After a series of tours in South America and in Europe, she was briefly engaged at N.Y.'s Manhattan Opera House and at the Chicago Grand Opera (1920–21); then retired from the stage. She was paralyzed during the last years of her life as a result of an apoplectic stroke.
BIBL.: R. Celletti, "R. S.," *Musica e Dischi,* 91 (1954); T. Hutchinson, "R. S.," *Record Collector,* XII (1958); R. Celletti, "R. S.," *Record News,* IV (1960).

Storck, Karl G(ustav) L(udwig), Alsatian writer on music; b. Dürmenach, April 23, 1873; d. Olsberg, Westphalia, May 9, 1920. He studied at the Univs. of Strasbourg and Berlin (Ph.D., 1895); wrote music criticism for the *Deutsche Zeitung* (Berlin). He publ. a unique ed., *Musik und Musiker in Karikatur und Satire* (Oldenburg, 1911), richly illustrated by numerous reproductions of caricatures on musical subjects; other publications include: *Der Tanz* (1903); *Geschichte der Musik* (1904; 6th ed., 1926); *Das Opernbuch* (1905; 44th printing, 1946); *Die Kulturelle Bedeutung der Musik* (1906); *Mozart: Sein Leben und Schaffen* (1908; 2nd ed., 1923); *Musik-Politik* (1911); *Emil Jaques-Dalcroze: Seine Stellung und Aufgabe in unserer Zeit* (1912).

Storer, John, English organist and composer; b. Hulland, near Derby, May 18, 1858; d. Berwick-on-Tweed, May 1, 1930. He was a chorister at various churches before entering Oxford Univ. (Mus.Bac., 1878). In 1891 he became music director of the old Globe Theatre in London, and later filled similar positions in London; settled in Waterford, Ireland, as organist of the Roman Catholic Cathedral, and prof. of plainchant at St. John's Ecclesiastical College; left Waterford in 1916. He composed the operas *The Punchbowl* (London, 1887) and *Gretna Green* (London, 1889); an oratorio, *Deborah and Barak* (1881); 2 syms.: *The Holiday* (1909) and *Vita* (1914); several masses; church services; songs; organ pieces.

Story, Liz, American pianist and composer; b. Los Angeles, Oct. 28, 1956. She began playing piano at an early age, tackling Mozart's 11th concerto at the age of 11; when she was in high school, her family moved to Germany, where she studied languages, philosophy, and poetry. On returning to the U.S., she studied at Hunter College (1977) and the Juilliard School in N.Y. (1978–79); heard jazz pianist Bill Evans, and recognized her own interest in improvisation. She began studying with Sanford Gold, returning to Los Angeles to study at the Univ. of Calif. and at the Dick Grove Music Workshops (1980–81). Her compositions are in reality new-age improvisations with impassioned gestures; among her recordings are *Solid Colors* (1982), *Unaccountable Effect* (1985), *Part of Fortune* (1986), and *Escape of the Circus Ponies* (1990).

Stout, Alan (Burrage), significant American composer and teacher; b. Baltimore, Nov. 26, 1932. He studied composition with Henry Cowell at the Peabody Cons. in Baltimore and took courses at Johns Hopkins Univ. (B.S., 1954); sporadically had composition lessons with Riegger in N.Y. (1951–56); pursued postgraduate studies at the Univ. of Copenhagen (1954–55); then had lessons with John Verrall at the Univ. of Washington (1958–59), acquiring an M.A. in music and in Swedish language; from 1959 to 1962 he was employed in the music dept. of the Seattle Public Library; in 1963 he was appointed to the music faculty of Northwestern Univ.; in 1973 he was a visiting lecturer at the Stockholm Musikhögskolan. Besides his primary activities as a composer and a teacher, he also performed valuable service in editing (with some conjectural reconstruction) fragmentary pieces by Ives, to prepare them for practical performance.
    WORKS: ORCH.: 4 syms.: No. 1 (1959); No. 2 (1951–66; Chicago, Aug. 4, 1968); No. 3 for Soprano, Male Chorus, and Orch. (1959–62); No. 4 (1962–71; Chicago, April 15, 1971); *3 Hymns* (1953–54); *Intermezzo* for English Horn, Percussion, and Strings (1954); *Pietà* for String or Brass Orch. (1957); *Serenity* for Solo Cello or Bassoon, Percussion, and Strings (1959); *Ricercare and Aria* for Strings (1959); *Movements* for Violin and Orch. (1962; Fish Creek, Wis., Aug. 17, 1966); *Fanfare for Charles Seeger* (1972); *Pulsar* for 3 Brass Choirs and Timpani (1972); *Nimbus* for 18 Strings (1979); *Pilvia* (1983). **VOCAL:** *2 Hymns* for Tenor and Orch. (1953); *Die Engel* for Soprano, Flute, Piano, Percussion, and Brass (1957); *2 Ariel Songs* for Soprano and Chamber Ensemble (1957); *Laudi* for Soprano, Baritone, and Small Orch. (1961); *Elegiac Suite* for Soprano and Strings (1959–61); *Canticum canticorum* for Soprano and Chamber Ensemble (1962); *George Lieder* for High Baritone and Orch. (1962; rev. 1965 and 1970; Chicago, Dec. 14, 1972); *Christmas Poem* for Soprano and Chamber Ensemble (1962); *Prologue,* oratorio (1963–64); *Nattstycken* (Nocturnes) for Narrator, Contralto, and Chamber Ensemble (Chicago, Nov. 10, 1970); *Dialogo per la Pascua* for Soloists, Chorus, and 8 Instruments (1973); *O Altitudo* for Soprano, Women's Chorus, Solo Flute, and Instrumental Ensemble (1974); *Passion,* oratorio (1953–75; Chicago, April 15, 1976); *5 visages de Laforgue* for Voice and Chamber Orch. (1978); *Triptych* for Soloists, Children's Chorus, and Orch. (1981); choruses, including *The Great Day of the Lord* (with Organ, 1956). **CHAMBER:** 10 string quartets (1952–53; 1952; 1954; 1954; 1957; 1959; 1960; 1960; 1962; 1962); *Solemn Prelude* for Trombone and Organ (1953); Quintet for Clarinet and String Quartet (1958); *Triptych* for Horn and Organ (1961); *Suite* for Flute and Percussion (1962); *Toccata* for Saxophone and Percussion (1965); Cello Sonata (1966); *Music* for Oboe and Piano (1966); *Music* for Flute and Harpsichord (1967); *2 Movements* for Clarinet and String Quartet (1968); *Recitative, Capriccio and Aria* for Oboe, Harp, and Percussion (1970); *Suite* for Saxophone and Organ (1973); Concertino for Clarinet and Chamber Ensemble (1978); *Meditation* for Tenor Saxophone and Organ (1982); Brass Quintet (1984). **PIANO:** *Varianti* (1962); *Fantasia* (1962); *Suite* (1964–67); 2-piano Sonata (1975); *Waltz* (1977). **ORGAN:** A set of 8 *Chorales* (1960); set of 3 *Chorales* (1967); *Study in Densities and Durations* (1966–67); *Study in Timbres and Interferences* (1977); *Study in Timbres and Interferences* for Fully Mechanical Organ (1978).

Stoutz, Edmond de, Swiss conductor; b. Zürich, Dec. 18, 1920. He studied law at the Univ. of Zürich; then took courses in piano, cello, oboe, percussion, and composition at the Zürich Hochschule für Musik; later pursued training in Salzburg and

Vienna. He began his career as a cellist in various ensembles in Zürich; then founded the Zürich Chamber Orch. (1954), with which he toured widely as a conductor; in 1962 he also founded the Zürich Concert Choir. In his programs he invariably included works by contemporary composers.

Stoyanov, Pencho, Bulgarian composer; b. Sofia, Feb. 9, 1931. He studied composition with Vladigerov at the Bulgarian State Cons. in Sofia, graduating in 1954, then took courses at the Moscow Cons.; returning to Bulgaria, he taught at the Cons. in Sofia. He publ. theoretical texts, including *Interaction between the Musical Forms* (Sofia, 1975).
    WORKS: ORCH.: 4 syms. (1958, 1971, 1971, 1975); *Divertimento* for String Orch. (1959); 2 violin concertinos (1961, 1965); 2 *Rhapsodies* (1963, 1969). **CHAMBER:** 2 violin sonatas (1953, 1970); 3 string quartets (1953, 1959, 1977); Concertino for Flute, Clarinet, and Bassoon (1969); Piano Quintet (1975); Piano Sonata (1965).

Stoyanov, Veselin, Bulgarian composer; b. Shumen, April 20, 1902; d. Sofia, June 29, 1969. He studied piano with his brother Andrei Stoyanov at the Sofia Cons, graduating in 1926; then went to Vienna, where he studied with Joseph Marx and Franz Schmidt. In 1937 he was appointed prof. at the Cons. in Sofia; was director of the Cons. in 1943–44 and from 1956 to 1962.
    WORKS: OPERAS: *Jensko zarstwo* (Kingdom of Women; Sofia, April 5, 1935); *Salambo* (Sofia, May 22, 1940); *Hitar Petar* (The Wise Peter; 1952; Sofia, 1958). **BALLET:** *Papessa Joánna* (1966; Sofia, Oct. 22, 1968); also a cantata, *Da bade den* (Let There Be Day; 1952). **ORCH.:** *Capriccio* (1934); *Bai Ganju* (Uncle Ganju), grotesque suite (1941); 3 piano concertos (1942, 1953, 1966); *Karwawa péssen* (Bloody Song; 1947); Violin Concerto (1948); Cello Concerto (1960); 2 syms.: No. 1 (1962) and No. 2, *Weliki Preslaw* (The Great Preslaw; 1969). **CHAMBER:** 3 string quartets (1933, 1934, 1935); Violin Sonata (1934); also piano works, including a Sonata (1930), a *Suite* (1931), and *3 Pieces* (1956); choral works.

Stracciari, Riccardo, Italian baritone; b. Casalecchio di Reno, near Bologna, June 26, 1875; d. Rome, Oct. 10, 1955. He studied with Ulisse Masetti in Bologna; then made his debut there as Marcello in 1898; was a member of La Scala in Milan (1904–6); also sang at Covent Garden in London (1905). He made his debut at the Metropolitan Opera in N.Y. on Dec. 1, 1906, as Germont *père;* remained on the roster until 1908; then returned to Europe, continuing his career there and in South America. He returned to the U.S. to sing with the Chicago Opera (1917–19) and in San Francisco (1925); continued to make appearances in Italy until 1944; also was active as a teacher from 1926, his most eminent student being Boris Christoff. He sang all the major baritone roles in the operatic repertoire, his most famous being Rossini's Figaro, which he sang more than 900 times.

Strada, Anna Maria, famous Italian soprano who flourished in the 1st half of the 18th century, also known under her married name as **Anna Maria Strada del Pò.** She was born in Bergamo; after serving Count Colloredo, governor of Milan, and singing in Venice (1720–21), she appeared in Naples (1724–26). She then was engaged by Handel for his opera and oratorio seasons in England; made her debut in London as Adelaide in the premiere of his *Lotario* in 1729, remaining as his principal soprano until 1737. Handel also composed the following roles for her: Partenope (1730), Cleofide in *Poro* (1731), Fulvia in *Ezio* (1732), Elmira in *Sosarme* (1732), Angelica in *Orlando* (1733), Deborah (1733), Josabeth in *Athalia* (1733), Arianna (1734), Erato in *Terpsicore* (1734), Ginevra in *Ariodante* (1735), Alcina (1735), the soprano part in *Alexander's Feast* (1736), Atalanta (1736), Tusnelda in *Arminio* (1737), Arianna in *Giustino* (1737), Berenice (1737), and Bellezza in *Il trionfo del tempo* (1737). In 1738 she was called to Breda to sing for the Princess of Orange; after appearances with Senesino in Naples (1739–40), she retired to Bergamo.

Stradal, August, Bohemian pianist; b. Teplitz, May 17, 1860; d. Schönlinde, Germany, March 13, 1930. He studied composition with Bruckner at the Vienna Cons. and piano with Door; was a pupil of Liszt in 1884, and became an ardent propagandist for Liszt's piano music; gave concerts in Germany, Austria, France, and England; made arrangements of Liszt's orch. works; also of works by Bach, Frescobaldi, etc. His original compositions consist of piano pieces (*Ungarische Rhapsodie*, etc.) and songs. He wrote *Erinnerungen an Franz Liszt* (Bern, 1929).

BIBL.: H. Stradal, *A. S.s Lebensbild* (Bern, 1934).

Stradella, Alessandro, important Italian composer; b. Nepi, near Viterbo, 1639; d. (murdered) Genoa, Feb. 25, 1682. He was a scion of nobility; received his early training in Bologna. In 1667 he went to Rome, where he composed oratorios, prologues, intermezzos for opera, etc. He led a tempestuous life, replete with illicit liaisons, flights from personal vendettas, and some criminal acts. In Rome he attempted to embezzle funds from the Roman Catholic church, and in 1669 fled the city to avoid exposure. He returned to Rome after the affair calmed down, but again got in trouble when he aroused the enmity of Cardinal Alderan Cibo. In 1677 he was forced to flee Rome again, and he went to Venice, where he became involved in a torrid affair with the fiancée of the Venetian nobleman Alvise Contarini; he persuaded the lady to accompany him to Turin, and the outraged bridegroom and a band of assassins followed in hot pursuit. Stradella escaped and fled to Genoa. There he became entangled with a married woman, a sister of the Lomellini brothers, who had a high social standing in the town. This time Stradella failed to evade the vengeful brothers, who hired an experienced murderer to kill him; the bloody deed was done on Feb. 25, 1682. A rather successful opera, *Alessandro Stradella* by Flotow (Hamburg, 1844), dramatized his stormy life and death; other operas on Stradella were composed by Niedermeyer (Paris, 1837) and Sinico (Lugo, 1863).

As a composer, Stradella left an important legacy, both in opera and in instrumental writing. His operas *La forza dell'amor paterno*, *Le gare dell'amore eroico*, and *Il Trespole tutore* were staged in Genoa (1678–79); he also composed the oratorio *La Susanna* and a wedding serenade, *Il barcheggio*, for Duke Francesco d'Este of Modena (1681). Other operas were *Il moro per amore*, *Il Corispero*, and *Doriclea*. His oratorios include *S. Giovanni Battista* and *S. Giovanni Crisostomo*; another oratorio, *S. Editta, vergine e monaca, regina d'Inghilterra*, remained unfinished. He wrote about 25 sinfonias (sonatas), most of them for violin, with basso ostinato; motets; arias; and canzonettas. An ed. of Stradella's oratorios was begun in 1969, under the editorship of L. Bianchi.

BIBL.: P. Bourdelot and P. Bonnet-Bourdelot, *Histoire de la musique et de ses effets depuis son origine jusqu'à présent* (Paris, 1715); A. Catelani, *Delle opere di A. S. esistenti nell'archivio musicale della R. Biblioteca Palatina di Modena* (Modena, 1866); P. Richard, "S. et les Contarinis," *Le Ménestrel*, XXXII/51–52 (1865) and XXXIII/1–5 (1866); H. Hess, *Die Opern A. S.'s*, in *Publicationen der Internationalen Musik-Gesellschaft*, supplement, II/3 (1906); F. Crawford, *S.* (London, 1911); A. Einstein, "Ein Bericht über den Turiner Mordanfall auf A. S.," in *Festschrift zum 50. Geburtstag Adolf Sandberger* (Munich, 1918); E. Dufflocq, "A. S.," *Bollettino Bibliografico Musicale*, IV (1929); A. Gentili, *A. S.* (Turin, 1936); G. Roncaglia, "Le composizioni strumentali di A. S. esistenti presso la R. Biblioteca Estense di Modena," *Revista Musicale Italiana*, XLIV (1940) and XLV (1941); idem, *Il genio novatore di A. S.* (Modena, 1941); idem, "Le composizioni vocali di A. S.," *Rivista Musicale Italiana*, XLV (1941) and XLVI (1942); E. Allam, "A. S.," *Proceedings of the Royal Musical Association*, LXXX (1953–54); E. Krohn, "Some Solo Cantatas of A. S.," *Manuscripta*, II (1958); O. Jander, *A Catalogue of the Manuscripts of Compositions by A. S. Found in European and American Libraries* (Wellesley, Mass., 1960; 2nd ed., rev., 1962); R. Giazotto, *Vita di A. S.* (2 vols., Milan, 1962); O. Jander, *A. S. and His Minor Dramatic Works* (diss., Harvard Univ., 1962); L. Bianchi, *Carissimi, S., Scarlatti e l'oratorio musicale* (Rome,

1969); O. Jander, "The Prologues and Intermezzos of A. S.," *Analecta Musicologica*, 7 (1969); H. Dietz, "Musikalische Struktur und Architektur im Werke A. S.s," ibid., 9 (1970); C. Gianturco, *The Operas of A. S.* (1644–1682) (diss., Oxford Univ., 1970); E. McCrickard, *A. S.'s Instrumental Music* (diss., Univ. of North Carolina, 1971); C. Gianturco, "Caratteri stilistici delle opere teatrali di S.," *Rivista Italiana di Musicologia*, VI (1972); idem, "Corelli e A. S.," *Studi corelliani: 2° congresso internazionale: Fusignano 1974*; K. Chaikin, *The Solo Soprano Cantatas of A. S.* (diss., Stanford Univ., 1975); C. Gianturco, "The Oratorios of A. S.," *Proceedings of the Royal Musical Association*, CI (1974–75); E. McCrickard, "Temporal and Tonal Aspects of A. S.'s Instrumental Music," *Analecta Musicologica*, 19 (1979); N. O'Loughlin, "Stradella's 'Santa Pelagia,'" *Musical Times* (May 1981); C. Gianturco, "A. S.: A True Biography," *Musical Times* (Nov. 1982); idem, ed., *A. S. e Modena* (Modena, 1983); C. Gianturco and E. McCrickard, *A. S.* (1639–1682) (thematic catalog; Stuyvesant, N.Y., 1990).

Stradivari (Latinized as **Stradivarius**), **Antonio,** celebrated Italian violin maker; b. probably in Cremona, 1644; d. probably there, Dec. 18, 1737. He was a pupil of Niccolò Amati in the early 1660s; his earliest known violin dates from 1666; he may have worked for Amati and others from 1666 before purchasing the house which contained his workshop from 1680. His finest instruments were made in the period from 1700 to 1725, but he still worked up to the year of his death; he made his last instrument at the age of 92. His label reads: "Antonius Stradivarius Cremonensis. Fecit Anno . . . (A × S)." His cellos command even higher prices than the violins, and violas the highest of all, for he made very few of them. Stradivari had 11 children; of them **Francesco** (b. Feb. 1, 1671; d. May 11, 1743) and **Omobono** (b. Nov. 14, 1679; d. July 8, 1742) were his co-workers. Stradivari also made viols of early types, guitars, lutes, mandolins, etc.

BIBL.: F.J. Fétis, *A. S., Luthier célèbre* (Paris, 1856; Eng. tr., London, 1864); P. Lombardini, *Cenni sulla celebre scuola Cremonense degli stromenti ad arco e sulla famiglia del sommo A. S.* (Cremona, 1872); A. Reichers, *The Violin and the Art of Its Construction; A Treatise on S.* (1895); H. Petherick, *A. S.* (London, 1900); W.H., A.F., and A.E. Hill, *A. S. His Life and Work* (London, 1902); A. Mandelli, *Nuove indagini su A. S.* (Milan, 1903); H. Herrmann, *Geschichte und Beschreibung von zwei Meisterwerken des A. S.* (N.Y., 1929); R. Bacchetta, *S.* (1937); G. Hoffmann, *S. l'enchanteur* (Paris, 1938); W. Orcutt, *The S. Memorial at Washington, D.C.* (Washington, D.C., 1938); M. Boger, *Das Geheimnis des S.* (Berlin, 1944); D. Balfoort, *A. S.* (Amsterdam, 1945; also in Eng.); E. Doring, *How Many Strads? . . . A Tabulation of Works Believed to Survive, Produced in Cremona by A. S. between 1666 and 1737* (Chicago, 1945); G. Ottani, *S.* (Milan, 1945); H. Goodkind, *Violin Iconography of A. S. 1644–1737* (Larchmont, N.Y., 1972); S. Sacconi, *I "segreti" di S.* (Cremona, 1972); E. Santoro, *A. S.* (Cremona, 1987).

Straesser, Joep, Dutch composer; b. Amsterdam, March 11, 1934. He studied musicology at the Univ. of Amsterdam (1952–55); then took organ lessons with Van der Horst (1956–59) and theory lessons with Felderhof (1959–61) at the Amsterdam Cons.; also received instruction in composition from Ton de Leeuw (1960–65). He was a church organist (1953–61); in 1962 he was appointed to the faculty of the Utrecht Cons.

WORKS: 5 *Close-ups* for Piano (1960–61; rev. 1973); *Music for Oboe Quartet* (1962); *Psalmus* for Male Chorus, Winds, and Percussion (1963); *22 Pages*, after a text of John Cage essays, for Wind Orch., Percussion, and 3 Male Voices (Hilversum, Sept. 14, 1965); String Quartet No. 2 (1966); *Chorai for 48 String Instruments and Percussion* (1966; Hilversum, Sept. 14, 1967; re-composed in 1974 for Full Orch. and retitled *Chorai Revisited*); *Duet* for 2 Cellos (1967); *Seismograms* for 2 Percussionists (1967; rev. 1979); *Adastra*, music for ballet (1967); *Summer Concerto* for Oboe and Chamber Orch. (1967; Styrian Autumn Festival, Graz, Austria, Oct. 24, 1969); *Ramasasiri* (Traveling Song), on texts in the Papuan language, for

Soprano, Flute, Vibraphone, Piano, and 2 Percussionists (1967–68); *Musique pour l'homme* for Soprano, Alto, Tenor, Bass, and Orch. (1968; Amsterdam, Dec. 9, 1968); *Missa* for Chorus and Wind Instruments (1969); *Intersections I* for Wind Quintet and 5 Instrumental Groups spatially positioned (1969), *II* for 100 or More Musicians (1970; Amsterdam, April 3, 1971; except for percussionists, all orch. members improvise freely), *III* for Piano (1971), *IV* for Oboe, Violin, Viola, and Cello (1972), *V* (*A Saxophone's World*) for 4 Saxophones (1974; rev. 1979), and *V-2* for Bass Clarinet and Piano (1975); *Sight-Seeing I, II, III* for Flute and Prepared Piano, *IV* for Double Bass (1970), and *V* (*Spring Quartet*) for String Quartet (1971); *Emergency Case* for Flute, Piano, and Percussion (1970); *Enclosures* for Winds and Percussion (1970; perf. as a ballet, Rotterdam, Oct. 3, 1971); *Eichenstadt und Abendstern*, 6 songs for Soprano and Piano (1972); *Encounters* for Bass Clarinet and 6 Percussionists (1973); *Chorai Revisited* for Orch. (1975); *Intervals I* for Chamber Chorus, Flute, Cello, and Harp (1975–76), *II* for Chorus and Instruments (1979), and *III: Longing for the Emperor*, 5 songs on old Japanese texts for Soprano, Clarinet, Mandolin, Guitar, Percussion, Viola, and Double Bass (1981); *3 Psalms* for Chorus and Organ (1976); "Just a moment. . ." for Piano Trio (1978); "Just a moment again. . ." for Piano, 2 Percussion, and Strings (1978); *Fusian à six*, symphonic music (1980); *Signals and Echoes* for Bass Clarinet and Orch. (1982); *Winter Concerto* for Soprano Saxophone and Orch. (1984); *Ueber Erich M.*, singspiel (1985–86); *Verzauberte Lieder* for Chorus and Orch. (1986); *Triplum* for Violin, Viola, and Cello (1986); *Faites vos jeux* for Organ (1986); *Motetus* for Chorus (1987).

Strakosch, Maurice, Bohemian pianist and impresario; b. Gross-Seelowitz, near Brünn, Jan. 15, 1825; d. Paris, Oct. 9, 1887. He studied with Sechter at the Vienna Cons.; traveled as a pianist in Europe; went to N.Y. in 1848 as a teacher; from 1856 he was active mainly as an impresario. He was the brother-in-law of **Adelina Patti,** and managed her concerts; he, his wife, and Ole Bull toured the U.S. (1852–54); returning to N.Y., he, his brother **Max Strakosch** (b. Gross-Seelowitz, Sept. 27, 1835; d. N.Y., March 17, 1892), and Bull organized a brief opera season at the Academy of Music in 1855. He then ran his own company (1856–57), which merged with Bernard Ullman's company in 1857; their partnership lasted until 1860, when he again became Adelina's manager; in 1861 he went to Europe with the Pattis, and remained Adelina's manager until 1868; also continued to work with his brother, who remained in the U.S. Maurice remained active as a pianist, making tours of Europe and the U.S. with Bull; also composed, producing the opera *Giovanna di Napoli* and salon pieces for piano; publ. *Ten Commandments of Music for the Perfection of the Voice* (posthumous; 1896) and *Souvenirs d'un impresario* (Paris, 2nd ed., 1887).

Strang, Gerald, inventive American composer; b. Claresholm, Canada, Feb. 13, 1908; d. Loma Linda, Calif., Oct. 2, 1983. He studied at Stanford Univ. (B.A., 1928) and at the Univ. of Southern Calif. in Los Angeles (Ph.D., 1948); also took private lessons in composition with Toch and Schoenberg, and served as Schoenberg's assistant at the Univ. of Calif. at Los Angeles (1936–38). He taught at Long Beach City College (1938–43; 1945–58); in 1958 he founded the music dept. at San Fernando Valley State College (later Calif. State Univ.) at Northridge, where he taught until 1965; then was chairman of the music dept. at Calif. State Univ. at Long Beach (1965–69); subsequently taught electronic music at the Univ. of Calif. (1969–74); interrupted his musical pursuits during World War II, when he was employed as an engineer at Douglas Aircraft Co. His music is strongly formal, with a unifying technical idea determining the content. An intelligent, energetic, and astute musical technician, he experimented successfully with the new resources available in the fields of acoustics, electronics, and computers; he was also active as an ed. of modern works and was for many years an associate of Henry Cowell in editing Cowell's *New Music Quarterly*. The titles of his compositions give clues to their formative semiotics; thus his piano piece *Mirrorrorrim* is an obvious palindrome or cancrizans. His series of 4 *Synclavions* is an electronic synthesis of keyboard variations. Similarly suggestive are his various pieces bearing such titles as *Compositions* (= computerized compositions) and *Synthions* (= synthetic ions). Strang was also active in the field of acoustics, and served as a consultant on some 25 newly built auditoriums in California and elsewhere.

WORKS: ORCH.: Suite for Chamber Orch. (1934–35); 2 syms. (1938–42; 1946–47); *Canzonet* for Strings (1942); *Overland Trail* (1943); Overture (1943); Concerto Grosso (1950); Cello Concerto (1951). **CHAMBER:** Clarinet Sonatina (1932); Quintet for Clarinet and Strings (1933); String Quartet (1934); *Percussion Music* for 3 Percussion (1935); Divertimento for 4 Woodwinds or Strings (1948); Violin Sonata (1949); Flute Sonata (1951); Variations for 4 Woodwinds or Strings (1956); also piano pieces; tape and electronic works.

BIBL.: M. Berman, *G. S.: Composer, Educator, Acoustician* (thesis, Calif. State Univ., Long Beach, 1977); L. Stein, "G. S. (1908–1983)," *Journal of the Arnold Schoenberg Institute,* VII (1983).

Stransky, Josef, Bohemian conductor; b. Humpoletz, near Deutschbrod, Sept. 9, 1872; d. N.Y., March 6, 1936. While studying medicine (M.D., Univ. of Prague, 1896), he also studied music in Leipzig with Jadassohn and in Vienna with R. Fuchs, Bruckner, and Dvořák. In 1898 he was engaged by A. Neumann as 1st Kapellmeister at the Landestheater in Prague; in 1903 he went in a similar capacity to the Stadttheater in Hamburg; in 1910 he resigned from the Hamburg opera to devote himself to concert work; in the autumn of 1911 became Mahler's successor as conductor of the N.Y. Phil. Soc.; a position he held until 1923. A bequest of $1,000,000 to the society (by Joseph Pulitzer, 1912) enabled Stransky to carry out successfully the sweeping reforms instituted by his illustrious predecessor (chief of which was a system of daily rehearsals during the season of 23 weeks). In 1924 he gave up his musical career and spent the rest of his life as an art dealer. He wrote an operetta, *Der General,* which was produced in Hamburg; orch. works; instrumental pieces; songs.

BIBL.: H. Shanet, *Philharmonic. A History of New York's Orchestra* (Garden City, N.Y., 1975).

Straram, Walther, French conductor; b. London (of French parents), July 9, 1876; d. Paris, Nov. 24, 1933. He was educated in Paris; played violin in Paris orchs.; then was choirmaster at the Opéra-Comique; later traveled to America as assistant to André Caplet at the Boston Opera Co. Returning to Paris, he established the Concerts Straram, which enjoyed a fine reputation. He conducted the 1st performance of Ravel's *Boléro* for Ida Rubinstein (dance recital, Nov. 22, 1928).

Strassburg, Robert, American conductor, teacher, and composer; b. N.Y., Aug. 30, 1915. He studied composition with Marion Bauer at N.Y. Univ.; then enrolled at Harvard Univ. (M.A., 1950). He was conductor and founder of the All-Miami Youth Sym. (1957–60). In 1961 he joined the faculty of the Univ. of Judaism in Los Angeles; from 1966 he was on the faculty of Calif. State College. His works include *4 Biblical Statements* for String Orch. (1946); *Fantasy and Allegro* for Violin and Orch. (1947); *Torah Sonata* for Piano (1950); folk opera, *Chelm* (1956); *Tropal Suite* for String Orch. (1967). He is the author of a monograph, *Ernest Bloch, Voice in the Wilderness* (Los Angeles, 1977).

Strässer, Ewald, German composer; b. Burscheid, June 27, 1867; d. Stuttgart, April 4, 1933. He studied with Wüllner at the Cologne Cons.; taught theory there until 1921; from 1922 to his death, was a prof. at the Stuttgart Hochschule für Musik. He wrote 6 syms., 5 string quartets, piano pieces, and songs.

BIBL.: A. Strässer, *E. S.* (Stuttgart, 1936).

Stratas, Teresa (real name, **Anastasia Stratakis**), outstanding Canadian soprano of Greek extraction; b. Toronto, May 26, 1938. Her father owned a restaurant in a town near Toronto,

and she was allowed from her earliest childhood to sing for customers. She also sang in concert with her brother, a violinist, and her sister, a pianist. In 1954 she entered the Royal Cons. of Music of Toronto, where she studied voice with Irene Jessner; she graduated with an Artist Diploma in 1959. She made her professional operatic debut with the Toronto Opera Festival as Mimi on Oct. 13, 1958. In 1959 she was a co-winner of the Metropolitan Opera Auditions, which led to her formal debut with the company in N.Y. on Oct. 28, 1959, as Poussette in *Manon*. She soon established herself as a singer of great versatility. She sang virtually all the standard soprano parts, and demonstrated her particular mettle and fettle in the complete version of Berg's opera *Lulu*, which was given for the 1st time in Paris on May 28, 1979. She won international acclaim for her dramatic portrayal of Violetta in Zeffirelli's film version of *La Traviata* (1983). In 1972 she was made an Officer of the Order of Canada. A film portrait of Stratas was made by Harry Rasky as *StrataSphere*.
BIBL.: H. Rasky, *S.: An Affectionate Tribute* (Oxford, 1989).

Strategier, Herman, Dutch organist and composer; b. Arnhem, Aug. 10, 1912; d. Doorwerth, Oct. 26, 1988. He studied music with his father, a church organist, and with H. Andriessen; succeeded his father as organist at St. Walpurgis at Arnhem in 1935, but the church was destroyed in war action in 1944. He taught at the Inst. for Catholic Church Music in Utrecht (1939–63); also taught there at the Cons. and at the Univ., and likewise at the Univ. of Rotterdam. He was notable mainly as a composer of liturgical music of the Roman Catholic rite.
WORKS: VOCAL: *Stabat Mater* for Chorus and Small Orch. (1939); *Septem cantica* for Mezzo-soprano and Piano (1941); *4 Drinkliederen* for Baritone and Orch. (1945); *Van der mollenfeeste,* old ballad for Chorus and Small Orch. (1947–48); *Henric van Veldeke* for Narrator, Baritone, and Orch. (1952); *5 Minneliederen* for Middle Voice, Flute, and Small String Orch. (1952); *Koning Swentibold,* oratorio (1955); *Arnhemsche Psalm* for Narrator, Soloists, Chorus, and Orch. (1955); *Rembrandt Cantata* (1956); *Requiem* for Chorus, Wind Quintet, and Strings (1961); *Ballade van de Maagd van Wognum* for Chorus and Orch. (1965); *Plaisanterie* for Chorus and Orch. (1966); *Te Deum* for Soprano, Alto, Chorus, and Orch. (1967); *Colloquia familiaria* for Soprano, Chorus, and String Orch. (1969); *Zoo, Buddingh'zoo* for Baritone, Chorus, and Small Orch. (1970); *Ligeia or The Shadow Out of Time* for Chorus, Flute, 6 Percussionists, Organ, and Harp (1973); *De hond (De Schoolmeester)* for Children's Chorus and Orch. (1979); *Hasseltsch meilied* for Chorus and Orch. (1981); *Lof van Walcheren* for Chorus and Orch. (1982); *Hazerswoude* for Chorus and Orch. (1984); choruses and songs. **ORCH.:** *Divertimento* for String Orch. and 4 Winds (1937); *Flute Concerto* (1943); *Haarlem-suite* (1945–47); *Ramiro-suite* (1946); *Piano Concerto* (1947–48); Sym. No. 1 (1949); *Clarinet Concertino* (1950); *Musique pour faire plaisir* for Strings (1950); *Intrada sinfonica* (1954); *Rondo giocoso* (1955); *Rapsodia elegiaca* (1956); *Turandot-suite* (1956); *Kadullen Varieties* for Flute, Bassoon, and Strings (1958); *Triptych* for Piano and Wind Orch. (1960); *Accordion Concerto* (1969); *Concertante Speelmuziek* for Flute, Bassoon, and Orch. (1970); *Intrada festiva* (1976); *Sonatine* (1978); Basset Horn Concerto (1981); *Cassation* (1983). **CHAMBER:** 3 string quartets (1935, 1936, 1937); *3 pièces* for Oboe and String Quartet (1937); Sextet for Piano and Wind Quintet (1951); *Suite* for Harp (1961); Quartet for Flute, Violin, Viola, and Cello (1968); *Curven* for Accordion and String Quartet (1970); *Divertissement* for Oboe, Clarinet, and Bassoon (1970); Piano Trio (1974); *Sonata da camera* for Flute, Oboe, Violin, Viola, Cello, and Piano (1978). **PIANO:** *Suite* for 4-hands (1945); Sonata (1948); Sonatina (1951); *Tema con variazioni* for 4-hands (1952); *Élégie* (1954); *4 pièces brèves* for 4-hands (1973); *Suite* for Piano and Harpsichord (1973); *3 Speelmuziekjes* (1974); *6 études* (1974); *Zes preludes* (1986). **ORGAN:** *Preludium, Intermezzo and Theme with Variations* (1939); *Ritornello capriccioso* (1944); *Toccatina* (1951); *Chaconne* (1955); *Voluntary* (1975).

Stratton, George (Robert), English violinist and pedagogue; b. London, July 18, 1897; d. there, Sept. 4, 1954. He studied in London; was concertmaster of the London Sym. Orch. (1933–52); also organized the Stratton String Quartet (1925–42), which became the Aeolian String Quartet, and was a founding member of the Reginald Paul Piano Quartet (1932–42); served as prof. of violin at the Royal College of Music in London (from 1942). With A. Frank, he publ. *The Playing of Chamber Music* (London, 1935).

Stratton, Stephen Samuel, English organist, writer on music, and composer; b. London, Dec. 19, 1840; d. Birmingham, June 25, 1906. He was a pupil of C. Gardner (organ) and C. Lucas (composition); settled in 1866 in Birmingham, where he held various posts as organist, the last being at the Church of the Saviour (1878–82). He was the author (with J.D. Brown) of a valuable work, *British Musical Biography* (1897); also publ. *Mendelssohn* (1901; 2nd ed., rev., 1934) and *Nicolo Paganini: His Life and Work* (1907). His compositions include chamber music, piano pieces, part-songs, and songs.

Straube, (Montgomery Rufus) Karl (Siegfried), prominent German organist, choral conductor, and pedagogue; b. Berlin, Jan. 6, 1873; d. Leipzig, April 27, 1950. He was a scion of an ancient ecclesiastical family; his father was an organist and instrument maker in Berlin; his mother was an Englishwoman who was a piano student of Sir Julius Benedict. He studied organ with his father, Dienel, Reimann, and others in Berlin, where he became deputy organist at the Kaiser-Wilhelm-Gedächtniskirche in 1895. From 1897 to 1902 he was organist at the Cathedral of Wesel; in 1902 he became organist at the Thomaskirche in Leipzig; in 1903 he was appointed conductor of the Bachverein there, and in 1907 became a prof. at the Cons. and organist *ex officio* at the Gewandhaus. In 1918 he became cantor at the Thomaskirche. At his suggestion the Gewandhaus Chorus and the Bachverein were united in 1919, and he conducted the combined choir until 1932. He conducted the Handel Festival in 1925, leading to the formation of the Handel Soc. In his teaching, he followed the great tradition of Leipzig organists, traceable to Bach. Among Straube's numerous collections of organ and choral pieces are *Alte Orgelmeister* (1904); *45 Choralvorspiele alter Meister* (1907); *Alte Meister des Orgelspiels* (2 vols., 1929); *Ausgewählte Gesänge des Thomanerchors* (1930); he brought out eds. of several works of Bach, Handel, and Liszt. His *Briefe eines Thomaskantors* was publ. posthumously (Stuttgart, 1952).
BIBL.: J. Wolgast, *K. S.* (Leipzig, 1928); *K. S. zu seinem 70. Geburtstag* (Leipzig, 1943).

Straus, Oscar, noted Austrian operetta composer and conductor; b. Vienna, March 6, 1870; d. Bad Ischl, Jan. 11, 1954. (His name was spelled "Strauss" on his birth certificate; he cut off the 2nd *s* to segregate himself from the multitudinous musical Strausses.) He studied privately in Vienna with A. Prosnitz, and H. Grädener, and with Max Bruch in Berlin. From 1893 to 1900 he conducted at various theaters in Austria and Germany; in 1901 he became conductor of the artistic cabaret Überbrettl in Berlin, and wrote a number of musical farces for it. He remained in Berlin until 1927; then lived in Vienna and Paris; on Sept. 3, 1939, he became a French citizen. In 1940 he went to America; lived in N.Y. and Hollywood until 1948, when he returned to Europe. He was one of the most successful composers of Viennese operettas. His most celebrated production was *Der tapfere Soldat*, based on G.B. Shaw's play *Arms and the Man* (Vienna, Nov. 14, 1908; in N.Y. as *The Chocolate Soldier*, Nov. 13, 1909; London, Sept. 10, 1910; numerous perfs. all over the world). Other operettas are: *Die lustigen Nibelungen* (Vienna, Nov. 12, 1904); *Hugdietrichs Brautfahrt* (Vienna, March 10, 1906); *Ein Walzertraum* (Vienna, March 2, 1907; rev. 1951); *Didi* (Vienna, Oct. 23, 1909); *Das Tal der Liebe* (Berlin and Vienna, simultaneously, Dec. 23, 1909); *Mein junger Herr* (Vienna, Dec. 23, 1910); *Die kleine Freundin* (Vienna, Oct. 20, 1911); *Love and Laughter* (London, 1913); *Rund um die Liebe* (Vienna, Nov. 9, 1914;

in N.Y. as *All around Love*, 1917); *Die himmelblaue Zeit* (Vienna, Feb. 21, 1914); *Die schöne Unbekannte* (Vienna, Jan. 15, 1915; in N.Y. as *My Lady's Glove*, 1917); *Der letzte Walzer* (Berlin, Feb. 12, 1920); *Mariette, ou Comment on écrit l'histoire* (Paris, Oct. 1, 1928); *Eine Frau, die weiss was sie will* (Berlin, Sept. 1, 1932); *Drei Walzer* (Zürich, Oct. 5, 1935); *Die Musik kommt* (Zürich, 1948; rev. as *Ihr erster Walzer*, Munich, May 16, 1952). Among his other works were ballets, film scores, orch. music, chamber pieces, choruses, about 500 cabaret songs, and piano pieces.

BIBL.: B. Grun, *Prince of Vienna: The Life, the Times, and the Melodies of O. S.* (London, 1955); F. Mailer, *Weltburger der Musik: Eine O.-S.-Biographie* (Vienna, 1985).

Strauss, family of celebrated Austrian musicians:

(1) Johann (Baptist) Strauss (I), violinist, conductor, and composer, known as "The Father of the Waltz"; b. Vienna, March 14, 1804; d. there, Sept. 25, 1849. He was born into a humble Jewish family of Hungarian descent; called "black Schani," he made a concerted effort to conceal his Jewish origins (when the ancestry of the family was realized by the chagrined Nazis a century later, they falsified the parish register at St. Stephen's Cathedral in 1939 to make the family racially pure). His father was an innkeeper who apprenticed him to a bookbinder, but his musical talent revealed itself at an early age; after Strauss ran away, his parents consented to his becoming a musician. He studied the violin under Polyschansky and harmony under Seyfried; at 15 he became a violist in Michael Pamer's dance orch., where he found a friend in Josef Lanner; in 1819 he became a member of the latter's small band, and later served as 2nd conductor of Lanner's orch. (1824–25). In 1825 he organized his own orch., which quickly became popular in Viennese inns; composed his 1st waltz, *Täuberln-Walzer*, in 1826; his reputation was secured with his appearances at the Sperl, where Pamer served as music director. His renown spread, and his orch. increased rapidly in size and efficiency; from 1833 he undertook concert tours in Austria, and in 1834 was appointed bandmaster of the 1st Vienna militia regiment. His tours extended to Berlin in 1834, and to the Netherlands and Belgium in 1836; in 1837–38 he invaded Paris with a picked corps of 28, and had immense success both there and in London. In 1846 he was named k.k. (i.e., *kaiserlich und königlich*, or imperial and royal) Hofballmusikdirektor. After catching scarlet fever from one of his children, he died at the age of 45. Among his publ. waltzes, the *Lorelei-, Gabrielen-, Taglioni-, Cäcilien-, Victoria-, Kettenbrücken-,* and *Bajaderen-Walzer* are prime favorites; also popular are his *Elektrische Funken, Mephistos Höllenrufe,* and the *Donau-Lieder*. He also wrote 33 galops; 14 polkas; 33 quadrilles; cotillions and contredances; 23 marches; and 9 potpourris. He had 3 sons who carried on the family musical tradition:

(2) Johann (Baptist) Strauss (II), greatly renowned violinist, conductor, and composer, known as "The Waltz King"; b. Vienna, Oct. 25, 1825; d. there, June 3, 1899. His father intended him for a business career, but his musical talent manifested itself when he was a mere child; at 6 he wrote the 1st 36 bars of waltz music that later was publ. as *Erster Gedanke*. While he was still a child, his mother arranged for him to study secretly with Franz Amon, his father's concertmaster; after his father left the family in 1842, he was able to pursue violin training with Anton Kohlmann; also studied theory with Joseph Drechsler until 1844. He made his 1st public appearance as conductor of his own ensemble at Dommayer's Casino at Hietzing on Oct. 15, 1844. His success was instantaneous, and his new waltzes won wide popularity. Despite his father's objections to this rivalry in the family, Johann continued his concerts with increasing success; after his father's death in 1849, he united his father's band with his own; subsequently made regular tours of Europe (1856–86). From 1863 to 1871 he was k.k. Hofballmusikdirektor in Vienna. In 1872 he accepted an invitation to visit the U.S., and directed 14 "monster concerts" in Boston and 4 in N.Y. He then turned to the theater. His finest operetta is *Die Fledermaus*, an epitome of the Vien-

nese spirit that continues to hold the stage as one of the masterpieces of its genre. It was 1st staged at the Theater an der Wien on April 5, 1874, and within a few months was given in N.Y. (Dec. 29, 1874); productions followed all over the world. It was performed in Paris with a new libretto as *La Tzigane* (Oct. 30, 1877); the original version was presented there as *La Chauve-souris* on April 22, 1904. Also very successful was the operetta *Der Zigeunerbaron* (Vienna, Oct. 24, 1885). All his operettas were 1st produced in Vienna, with the exception of *Eine Nacht in Venedig* (Berlin, Oct. 3, 1883). A complete list of the Vienna productions includes: *Indigo und die vierzig Räuber* (Feb. 10, 1871); *Der Carneval in Rom* (March 1, 1873); *Cagliostro in Wien* (Feb. 27, 1875); *Prinz Methusalem* (Jan. 3, 1877); *Blindekuh* (Dec. 18, 1878); *Das Spitzentuch der Königin* (Oct. 1, 1880); *Der lustige Krieg* (Nov. 25, 1881); *Simplicius* (Dec. 17, 1887); *Ritter Pázmán* (Jan. 1, 1892); *Fürstin Ninetta* (Jan. 10, 1893); *Jabuka, oder Das Apfelfest* (Oct. 12, 1894); *Waldmeister* (Dec. 4, 1895); *Die Göttin der Vernunft* (March 13, 1897). Although Strauss composed extensively for the theater, his supreme achievement remains his dance music. He wrote almost 500 pieces of it (498 opus numbers); of his waltzes the greatest popularity was achieved by *An der schönen blauen Donau*, op. 314 (1867), whose main tune became one of the best known in all music. Brahms wrote on a lady's fan the opening measures of it, and underneath: "Leider nicht von Brahms" ("Alas, not by Brahms"); Wagner, too, voiced his appreciation of the music of Strauss. He contracted 3 marriages: to the singer Henriette Treffz, the actress Angelika Dittrich, and Adele Strauss, the widow of the banker Anton Strauss, who was no relation to Johann's family. Strauss also composed numerous quadrilles, polkas, polka-mazurkas, marches, galops, etc.; also several pieces in collaboration with his brothers. F. Racek began editing a complete ed. of his works in Vienna in 1967.

(3) Josef Strauss, conductor and composer; b. Vienna, Aug. 22, 1827; d. there, July 21, 1870. He studied theory with Franz Dolleschal and violin with Franz Anton. He was versatile and gifted, and at various times wrote poetry, painted, and patented inventions. He 1st appeared in public conducting in Vienna a set of his waltzes (July 23, 1853); later regularly appeared as a conductor with his brother Johann's orch. (1856–62); their younger brother Eduard joined them in 1862, but Johann left the orch. in 1863 and Josef and Eduard continued to conduct the family orch. He wrote 283 opus numbers, many of which reveal a composer of remarkable talent. Among his outstanding waltzes are *Perlen der Liebe*, op. 39 (1857), *5 Kleebald'ln*, op. 44 (1857), *Wiener Kinder*, op. 61 (1858), *Schwert und Leier*, op. 71 (1860), *Friedenspalmen*, op. 207 (1867), and *Aquarellen*, op. 258 (1869); he also wrote polkas, quadrilles, marches, and other works.

(4) Eduard Strauss, conductor and composer; b. Vienna, March 15, 1835; d. there, Dec. 28, 1916. He studied theory and composition with Gottfried Preyer and Simon Sechter, violin with Amon, and harp with Parish-Alvars and Zamara. After playing harp in his brother Johann's orch., he made his debut as a conductor and composer with it at the Wintergarten of the Dianabad-Saal on April 6, 1862; after Johann left the orch. in 1863, Eduard and his other brother Josef shared the conductorship of the orch. until the latter's death in 1870. From 1870 to 1878 he was k.k. Hofballmusikdirektor; subsequently made annual tours of Europe as a guest conductor, and also with his own orch.; in 1890 and 1900–1901 he toured throughout the U.S. In 1901 he retired. He wrote some 300 works, but they failed to rival the superior works of his brothers. His memoirs were publ. in 1906. His son, **Johann (Maria Eduard) Strauss (III)** (b. Vienna, Feb. 16, 1866; d. Berlin, Jan. 9, 1939), was also a conductor and composer; after working as an accountant in the education ministry, he won success as a composer with the operetta *Katze und Maus* (Vienna, Dec. 1898); from 1900 he was active as a conductor, serving as k.k. Hofballmusikdirektor (1901–5); subsequently pursued his career mainly in Berlin. He also wrote some waltzes, the most popular being *Dichterliebe*. His nephew, **Eduard (Leo-**

pold Maria) Strauss (b. Vienna, March 24, 1910; d. there, April 6, 1969), was a conductor and the last representative of the great family tradition; studied at the Vienna Academy of Music; made his conducting debut in Vienna in 1949, and subsequently led concerts there regularly; also toured with the Vienna Johann Strauss Orch. and as a guest conductor.

BIBL.: L. Scheyrer, *Johann S.'s musikalische Wanderung durch das Leben* (Vienna, 1851); L. Eisenberg, *Johann S.: Ein Lebensbild* (Vienna, 1894); C. Flamme, *Verzeichnis der sämtlichen im Druck erschienenen Kompositionen von Johann S. (Vater), Johann S. (Sohn), Josef S. und Eduard S.* (Leipzig, 1898); R. von Procházka, *Johann S.* (Berlin, 1900; 2nd ed., 1903); F. Lange, *Joseph Lanner und Johann S.: Ihre Zeit, ihr Leben und ihre Werke* (Vienna, 1904; 2nd ed., 1919); R. Specht, *Johann S.* (Berlin, 1909; 2nd ed., 1922); F. Lange, *Johann S.* (Leipzig, 1912); E. Neumann, *Die Operetten von Johann S.: Ihre Formen und das Verhältnis von Text und Musik* (diss., Univ. of Vienna, 1919); J. Schnitzer, *Meister Johann: Bunte Geschichten aus der Johann S.-Zeit* (Vienna, 1920); E. Decsey, *Johann S.* (Stuttgart, 1922; 2nd ed., rev., 1948, by E. Rieger); K. Kobald, *Johann S.* (Vienna, 1925); S. Loewy, *Rund um Johann S.: Momentbilder aus einen Künstlerleben* (Vienna, 1925); H. Jacob, *Johann S. und das neunzehnte Jahrhundert: Die Geschichte einer musikalischen Weltherrschaft* (Amsterdam, 1937; 3rd ed., rev., 1962); H. Sündermann, *Johann S.: Ein Vollender* (Brixlegg, 1937; 3rd ed., 1949); W. Jaspert, *Johann S.: Sein Leben, sein Werk, seine Zeit* (Vienna, 1939; 2nd ed., 1949); M. Kronberg, *Johann S.* (Paris, 1939); A. Witeschnik, *Die Dynastie S.* (Vienna and Leipzig, 1939; 3rd ed., 1958); E. Schenk, *Johann S.* (Potsdam, 1940); D. Ewen, *Tales from the Vienna Woods: The Story of Johann S.* (N.Y., 1944); P. Ruff, *Johann-S.-Festschrift: Juni–September 1949* (Vienna, 1949); W. Reich, ed., *Johann S.-Brevier: Aus Briefen und Erinnerungen* (Zürich, 1950); J. Pastene, *Three-quarter Time: The Life and Music of the S. Family of Vienna* (N.Y., 1951); H. Jacob, *Johann S. Vater und Sohn* (Hamburg, 1953); M. Schönherr and K. Reinöhl, *Johann S. Vater: Ein Werkverzeichnis* (Vienna, 1954); A. Weinmann, *Verzeichnis sämtlicher Werke von Johann S. Vater und Sohn* (Vienna, 1956); F. Grasberger, *Die Walzer-Dynastie S.: Eine Ausstellung zum Neujahrskonzert der Wiener Philharmoniker* (Vienna, 1965–66); H. Jäger-Sustenau, *Johann S.: Der Walzerkönig und seine Dynastie, Familiengeschichte, Urkunden* (Vienna, 1965); A. Weinmann, *Verzeichnis sämtlicher Werke von Josef und Eduard S.* (Vienna, 1967); H. Fantel, *Johann S.: Father and Son, and Their Era* (Newton Abbot, 1971); O. Schneidereit, *Johann S. und die Stadt an der schönen blauen Donau* (Berlin, 1972); J. Wechsberg, *The Waltz Emperors* (London, 1973); F. Endler, *Das Walzer-Buch: Johann S.: Die Aufforderung zum Tanz* (Vienna, 1975); F. Mailer, *Das kleine Johann S. Buch* (Salzburg, 1975); M. Prawy, *Johann S.: Weltgeschichte im Walzertakt* (Vienna, 1975); F. Racek, *Johann S. zum 150. Geburtstag: Ausstellung der Wiener Stadtbibliothek 22. Mai bis 31. Oktober 1975* (Vienna, 1975); F. Mailer, *Joseph S.: Genie wider Willen* (Vienna and Munich, 1977; Eng. tr. as *Joseph S.: Genius against His Will*, Oxford, 1985); P. Kemp, *The S. Family: Portrait of a Musical Dynasty* (Tunbridge Wells, 1985); N. Linke, *Musik erobert die Welt, oder, Wie die Wiener Familie S. die "Unterhaltungsmusik" revolutionierte* (Vienna, 1987).

Strauss, Christoph, eminent Austrian organist and composer; b. probably in Vienna, c.1577; d. there, June 1631. He was born into a musical family long associated with the Hapsburg court. In 1594 he entered its service, becoming organist of the court church of St. Michael in 1601. After serving as administrator of the imperial estate of Kattenburg (1614–17), he was director of the court music from 1617 until he was removed in 1619 by the new Emperor, Ferdinand II. In 1626 he finally obtained the post of director of music at St. Stephen's Cathedral, where he remained until his death. He was one of the foremost Austrian composers of his time. He publ. *Nova ac diversimoda sacrarum cantionum compositio seu* [36] *motettae* for 5 to 10 Voices and Instruments (Vienna, 1613) and

Missae for 8 to 20 Voices, Instruments, and Basso Continuo (organ) (Vienna, 1631).

BIBL.: K. Geiringer, "C. S.: Ein Wiener Künstlerdasein am Beginn des 17. Jahrhunderts," *Zeitschrift für Musikwissenschaft*, XIII (1930–31).

Strauss, Franz (Joseph), German horn player and composer, father of **Richard (Georg) Strauss;** b. Parkstein, Feb. 26, 1822; d. Munich, May 31, 1905. Until his retirement in 1889 he was solo hornist at the Hofoper in Munich; although a violent opponent of Wagner, the master valued him highly, and entrusted to him at the premieres of *Tristan und Isolde, Die Meistersinger von Nürnberg,* and *Parsifal* the important solo passages; until 1896 he was a prof. of his instrument at the Akademie der Tonkunst, and from 1875 to 1896 conducted an excellent amateur orch., the Wilde Gungl, in Munich. He wrote a Horn Concerto in C minor (op. 8); *Nocturne* (op. 7) and *Empfindungen am Meere* (op. 12) for Horn and Piano; 17 *Konzertetüden* and *Übungen für Naturhorn* (2 books).

BIBL.: F. Trenner, "Der Vater: F. S.," *Zeitschrift für Musik* (June 1955).

Strauss, Richard (Georg), great German composer and distinguished conductor, one of the most inventive music masters of the modern age, son of **Franz (Joseph) Strauss;** b. Munich, June 11, 1864; d. Garmisch-Partenkirchen, Sept. 8, 1949. Growing up in a musical environment, he studied piano as a child with August Tombo, harpist in the Court Orch.; then took violin lessons from Benno Walter, its concertmaster, and later received instruction from the court conductor, Friedrich Wilhelm Meyer. According to his own account, he began to improvise songs and piano pieces at a very early age; among such incunabula was the song *Weihnachtslied,* followed by a piano dance, *Schneiderpolka.* On March 30, 1881, his 1st orch. work, the Sym. in D minor, was premiered in Munich under Hermann Levi. This was followed by the Sym. in F minor, premiered on Dec. 13, 1884, by the N.Y. Phil. under Theodore Thomas. Strauss also made progress as a performing musician; when he was 20 years old, Hans von Bülow engaged him as assistant conductor of his Meiningen Orch. About that time Strauss became associated with the poet and musician Alexander Ritter, who introduced him to the "music of the future," as it was commonly called, represented by orch. works of Liszt and operas by Wagner.

In 1886 Strauss received an appointment as the 3rd conductor of the Court Opera in Munich. On March 2, 1887, he conducted in Munich the 1st performance of his symphonic fantasy, *Aus Italien.* This was followed by the composition of his 1st true masterpiece, the symphonic poem *Don Juan,* in which he applied the thematic ideas of Liszt; he conducted its premiere in Weimar on Nov. 11, 1889; it became the 1st of a series of his tone poems, all of them based on literary subjects. His next tone poem of great significance in music history was *Tod und Verklärung;* Strauss conducted it for the 1st time in Eisenach on June 21, 1890, on the same program with the premiere of his brilliant *Burleske* for Piano and Orch., featuring Eugen d'Albert as soloist. There followed the 1st performance of the symphonic poem *Macbeth,* which Strauss conducted in Weimar on Oct. 13, 1890. In these works Strauss established himself as a master of program music and the most important representative of the nascent era of musical modernism; as such, he was praised extravagantly by earnest believers in musical progress and damned savagely by entrenched traditionalists in the press. He effectively adapted Wagner's system of leading motifs (leitmotifs) to the domain of symphonic music. His tone poems were interwoven with motifs, each representing a relevant programmatic element. Explanatory brochures listing these leading motifs were publ. like musical Baedekers to guide the listeners. Bülow, ever a phrasemaker, dubbed Strauss "Richard the 2nd," thus recognizing him as the rightful heir of Richard the 1st, Wagner.

Turning to stage music, Strauss wrote his 1st opera, *Guntram,* for which he also composed the text; he conducted its premiere in Weimar on May 10, 1894, with the leading soprano role performed by Pauline de Ahna; she was married to Strauss on Sept. 10, 1894, and remained with him all his life; she died on May 13, 1950, a few months after Strauss himself. While engaged in active work as a composer, Strauss did not neglect his conducting career. In 1894 he succeeded Bülow as conductor of the Berlin Phil., leading it for a season. Also in 1894 he became assistant conductor of the Munich Court Opera; he became chief conductor in 1896. In 1896–97 he filled engagements as a guest conductor in European music centers. His works of the period included the sparkling *Till Eugenspiegels lustige Streiche* (Cologne, Nov. 5, 1895), *Also sprach Zarathustra*, a philosophical tone poem after Nietzsche (Frankfurt am Main, Nov. 27, 1896, Strauss conducting), and *Don Quixote*, variations with a cello solo, after Cervantes (Cologne, March 8, 1898). In 1898 Strauss became a conductor at the Berlin Royal Opera; in 1908 he was made its Generalmusikdirektor, a position he held until 1918. He conducted the 1st performance of his extraordinary autobiographical tone poem *Ein Heldenleben* in Frankfurt am Main on March 3, 1899; the hero of the title was Strauss himself, while his critics were represented in the score by a cacophonous charivari; for this exhibition of musical self-aggrandizement, he was severely chastised in the press. There followed his 1st successful opera, *Feuersnot* (Dresden, Nov. 21, 1901).

In June 1903 Strauss was the guest of honor of the Strauss Festival in London. It was also in 1903 that the Univ. of Heidelberg made him Dr.Phil., *honoris causa*. For his 1st visit to the U.S., he presented to the public the premiere performance of his *Symphonia domestica* at Carnegie Hall in N.Y. on March 21, 1904. The score represented a day in the Strauss household, containing an interlude describing, quite literally, the feeding of the newly born baby. The reviews in the press reflected an aversion to such a musical self-exposure. There followed his opera *Salome*, to the German tr. of Oscar Wilde's play. Schuch led its premiere in Dresden on Dec. 9, 1905. *Salome* had its American premiere at the Metropolitan Opera in N.Y. on Jan. 22, 1907; the ghastly subject, involving intended incest, 7-fold nudity, and decapitation followed by a labial necrophilia, administered such a shock to the public and the press that the Metropolitan Opera took it off the repertoire after only 2 performances. Scarcely less forceful was Strauss's next opera, *Elektra*, to a libretto by the Austrian poet and dramatist Hugo von Hofmannsthal, in which the horrors of matricide were depicted with extraordinary force in unabashedly dissonant harmonies. Schuch conducted its premiere in Dresden on Jan. 25, 1909.

Strauss then decided to prove to his admirers that he was quite able to write melodious operas to charm the musical ear; this he accomplished in his next production, also to a text of Hofmannsthal, *Der Rosenkavalier*, a delightful opera-bouffe in an endearing popular manner; Schuch conducted its premiere in Dresden on Jan. 26, 1911. Turning once more to Greek mythology, Strauss wrote, with Hofmannsthal again as librettist, a short opera, *Ariadne auf Naxos*, which he conducted for the 1st time in Stuttgart on Oct. 25, 1912. In June 1914 Strauss was awarded an honorary D.Mus. degree from Oxford Univ. His next work was the formidable, and quite realistic, score *Eine Alpensinfonie*, depicting an ascent of the Alps, and employing a wind machine and a thunder machine in the orch. to illustrate an alpine storm. Strauss conducted its 1st performance with the Dresden Court Orch. in Berlin on Oct. 28, 1915. Then, again with Hofmannsthal as librettist, he wrote the opera *Die Frau ohne Schatten* (Vienna, Oct. 10, 1919), using a complex plot, heavily endowed with symbolism.

In 1919 Strauss assumed the post of co-director with Franz Schalk of the Vienna State Opera, a position he held until 1924. In 1920 he took the Vienna Phil. on a tour of South America; in 1921 he appeared as a guest conductor in the U.S. For his next opera, *Intermezzo* (Dresden, Nov. 4, 1924), Strauss wrote his own libretto; then, with Hofmannsthal once more, he wrote *Die ägyptische Helena* (Dresden, June 6, 1928). Their last collaboration was *Arabella* (Dresden, July 1, 1933).

In 1917 Strauss helped to organize the Salzburg Festival and appeared there in subsequent years as conductor.

When Hitler came to power in 1933, the Nazis were eager to persuade Strauss to join the official policies of the 3rd Reich. Hitler even sent him a signed picture of himself with a flattering inscription, "To the great composer Richard Strauss, with sincere admiration." Strauss kept clear of formal association with the Führer and his cohorts, however. He agreed to serve as president of the newly organized Reichsmusikkammer on Nov. 15, 1933, but resigned from it on July 13, 1935, ostensibly for reasons of poor health. He entered into open conflict with the Nazis by asking Stefan Zweig, an Austrian Jew, to provide the libretto for his opera *Die schweigsame Frau*; it was duly produced in Dresden on June 24, 1935, but then taken off the boards after a few performances. His political difficulties grew even more disturbing when the Nazis found out that his daughter-in-law was Jewish. Zweig himself managed to escape Nazi horrors, and emigrated to Brazil, but was so afflicted by the inhumanity of the world that he and his wife together committed suicide.

Strauss valiantly went through with his tasks; he agreed to write the *Olympische Hymne* for the Berlin Olympic Games in 1936. On Nov. 5, 1936, he was honored with the Gold Medal of the Royal Phil. Soc. in London; the next day he conducted the visiting Dresden State Opera in a performance of his *Ariadne auf Naxos* at Covent Garden. For his next opera, he chose Joseph Gregor as his librettist; with him Strauss produced *Daphne* (Dresden, Oct. 15, 1938), which was once more a revival of his debt to Greek mythology. For their last collaboration, Strauss and Gregor produced the opera *Die Liebe der Danaë*, also on a Greek theme. Its public dress rehearsal was given in Salzburg on Aug. 16, 1944, but by that time World War II was rapidly encroaching on devastated Germany, so that the opera did not receive its official premiere until after Strauss's death. The last opera by Strauss performed during his lifetime was *Capriccio*. Its libretto was prepared by the conductor Clemens Krauss, who conducted its premiere in Munich on Oct. 28, 1942. Another interesting work of this period was Strauss's Horn Concerto No. 2, 1st performed in Salzburg on Aug. 11, 1943.

During the last weeks of the war, Strauss devoted himself to the composition of *Metamorphosen*, a symphonic work mourning the disintegration of Germany; it contained a symbolic quotation from the funeral march from Beethoven's *Eroica* Sym. He then completed another fine score, the Oboe Concerto. In Oct. 1945 he went to Switzerland.

In Oct. 1947 Strauss visited London for the Strauss Festival and also appeared as a conductor of his own works. Although official suspicion continued to linger regarding his relationship with the Nazi regime, he was officially exonerated of all taint on June 8, 1948. A last flame of creative inspiration brought forth the deeply moving *Vier letzte Lieder* (1948), for Soprano and Orch., inspired by poems of Herman Hesse and Eichendorff. With this farewell, Strauss left Switzerland in 1949 and returned to his home in Germany, where he died at the age of 85. Undeniably one of the finest master composers of modern times, Strauss never espoused extreme chromatic techniques, remaining a Romanticist at heart. His genius is unquestioned as regards such early tone poems as *Don Juan* and *Also sprach Zarathustra*; some of his operas have attained a permanent place in the repertoire, while his *Vier letzte Lieder* stand as a noble achievement of his Romantic inspiration.

WORKS: STAGE: OPERAS: *Guntram*, op. 25 (1892–93; Hoftheater, Weimar, May 10, 1894, composer conducting; rev. version, with score cut by one 3rd, 1934–39; Deutsches Nationaltheater, Weimar, Oct. 29, 1940); *Feuersnot*, op. 50 (1900–1901; Hofoper, Dresden, Nov. 21, 1901, Ernst von Schuch conducting); *Salome*, op. 54 (1903–5; Hofoper, Dresden, Dec. 9, 1905, Schuch conducting); *Elektra*, op. 58 (1906–8; Hofoper, Dresden, Jan. 25, 1909, Schuch conducting); *Der Rosenkavalier*, op. 59 (1909–10; Hofoper, Dresden, Jan. 26, 1911, Schuch conducting); *Ariadne auf Naxos* "zu spielen nach dem *Bürger als Edelmann* des Molière," op. 60 (1911–12; Hoftheater, Stuttgart, Oct. 25, 1912, composer conducting; rev. version, with prologue, 1916; Hofoper, Vienna, Oct. 4, 1916, Franz Schalk conducting); *Die Frau ohne Schatten*, op. 65 (1914–18; Staatsoper, Vienna, Oct. 10, 1919, Schalk conducting); *Intermezzo*, op. 72 (1918–23; Staatsoper, Dresden, Nov. 4, 1924, Fritz Busch conducting); *Die ägyptische Helena*, op. 75 (1923–27; Staatsoper, Dresden, June 6, 1928, Fritz Busch conducting; rev. version, 1932–33; Festspielhaus, Salzburg, Aug. 14, 1933); *Arabella*, op. 79 (1929–32; Staatsoper, Dresden, July 1, 1933, Clemens Krauss conducting; rev. version, Munich, July 16, 1939); *Die schweigsame Frau*, op. 80 (1933–34; Staatsoper, Dresden, June 24, 1935, Karl Böhm conducting); *Friedenstag*, op. 81 (1935–36; Nationaltheater, Munich, July 24, 1938, Krauss conducting); *Daphne*, op. 82 (1936–37; Staatsoper, Dresden, Oct. 15, 1938, Böhm conducting); *Die Liebe der Danaë*, op. 83 (1938–40; public dress rehearsal, Festspielhaus, Salzburg, Aug. 16, 1944, Krauss conducting; official premiere, Festspielhaus, Salzburg, Aug. 14, 1952, Krauss conducting); *Capriccio*, op. 85 (1940–41; Bayerische Staatsoper, Munich, Oct. 28, 1942, Krauss conducting). *BALLETS AND OTHER STAGE WORKS:* *Romeo und Julia*, incidental music to Shakespeare's drama (Nationaltheater, Munich, Oct. 23, 1887); *Josephslegende*, op. 63 (1912–14; Opéra, Paris, May 14, 1914, composer conducting); *Der Bürger als Edelmann*, incidental music to Hofmannsthal's version of Molière's drama, op. 60 (1917; Deutsches Theater, Berlin, April 9, 1918); *Schlagobers*, op. 70 (1921–22; Staatsoper, Vienna, May 9, 1924, composer conducting); *Verklungene Feste*, after Couperin (1940; Nationaltheater, Munich, April 5, 1941, Krauss conducting); *Des Esels Schatten*, comedy for music (1949; Hellbrunn Castle, near Salzburg, July 31, 1982, Ernst Märzendorfer conducting).

ORCH.: Overture for the singspiel *Hochlands Treue* (1872–73); *Festmarsch* in E-flat major, op. 1 (1876; Munich, March 26, 1881, Franz Strauss conducting); Concert Overture in B minor (1876); Serenade in G major (1877); Overture in E major (1878); *Romanze* in E-flat major for Clarinet and Orch. (1879); Overture in A minor (1879); Sym. in D minor (1880; Munich, March 30, 1881, Hermann Levi conducting); Violin Concerto in D minor, op. 8 (1880–82; Vienna, Dec. 5, 1882, Benno Walter violinist, composer pianist; official premiere, Leipzig, Feb. 17, 1896, Alfred Krasselt violinist, composer conducting); Serenade in E-flat major for 13 Wind Instruments, op. 7 (1881; Dresden, Nov. 27, 1882, Franz Wüllner conducting); Horn Concerto No. 1 in E-flat major, op. 11 (1882–83; Meiningen, March 4, 1885, Gustav Leinhos soloist, Hans von Bülow conducting); Overture in C minor (Munich, Nov. 28, 1883, Levi conducting); *Romanze* in F major for Cello and Orch. (1883); *Lied ohne Worte* in E-flat major (1883); Sym. in F minor, op. 12 (1883–84; N.Y., Dec. 13, 1884, Theodore Thomas conducting); Suite in B-flat major for 13 Wind Instruments, op. 4 (Munich, Nov. 18, 1884, composer conducting); *Der Zweikampf—Polonaise* in B-flat major for Flute, Bassoon, and Orch. (1884); *Festmarsch* in D major (1884; Munich, Jan. 8, 1885, Franz Strauss conducting; rev. 1888); *Burleske* in D minor for Piano and Orch. (1885–86; Eisenach, June 21, 1890, Eugen d'Albert soloist, composer conducting); *Aus Italien*, symphonic fantasy, op. 16 (1886; Munich, March 2, 1887, composer conducting); *Macbeth*, tone poem after Shakespeare's drama, op. 23 (1886–88; rev. 1889–90; Weimar, Oct. 13, 1890, composer conducting; rev. 1891); *Don Juan*, tone poem after Lenau, op. 20 (1888–89; Weimar, Nov. 11, 1889, composer conducting); *Tod und Verklärung*, tone poem, op. 24 (1888–89; Eisenach, June 21, 1890, composer conducting); *Festmarsch* in C major (Munich, Feb. 1, 1889, Franz Strauss conducting); Fanfare for A.W. Iffland's drama *Der Jäger* (1891); *Festmusik* "Lebende Bilder" for the golden wedding anniversary of the Grand Duke and Duchess of Weimar (Weimar, Oct. 8, 1892, composer conducting); *Till Eulenspiegels lustige Streiche, nach alter schelmenweise—in Rondeauform*, op. 28 (1894–95; Cologne, Nov. 5, 1895, Wüllner conducting); *Also sprach Zarathustra*, tone poem after Nietzsche, op. 30 (1895–96; Frankfurt am Main, Nov. 27, 1896, composer conducting); *Don Quixote, fantastische Variationen über ein Thema ritterlichen Charak-*

ters for Cello and Orch., op. 35 (1896–97; Cologne, March 8, 1898, Wüllner conducting); *Ein Heldenleben*, tone poem, op. 40 (1897–98; Frankfurt am Main, March 3, 1899, composer conducting); *Symphonia domestica*, op. 53 (1902–3; N.Y., March 21, 1904, composer conducting); *Zwei Militärmärsche*, op. 57 (1906; Berlin, March 6, 1907, composer conducting); *Feierlicher Einzug der Ritter des Johanniter-Ordens* for Brass and Timpani (1909); *Festliches Präludium* for Orch. and Organ, op. 61 (for the dedication of the Konzerthaus, Vienna, Oct. 19, 1913, Ferdinand Löwe conducting); *Eine Alpensinfonie*, op. 64 (1911–15; Berlin, Oct. 28, 1915, composer conducting); *Der Bürger als Edelmann*, suite, op. 60 (1918; Vienna, Jan. 31, 1920, composer conducting); *Tanzsuite aus Klavierstücken von François Couperin* for Small Orch. (Vienna, Feb. 17, 1923, Krauss conducting); *Wiener Philharmoniker Fanfare* for Brass and Timpani (Vienna, March 4, 1924); *Fanfare zur Eröffnung der Musikwoche der Stadt Wien im September 1924* for Brass and Timpani (Vienna, Sept. 14, 1924); *Parergon zur Symphonia domestica* for Piano, Left Hand, and Orch., op. 73 (1924; Dresden, Oct. 16, 1925, Paul Wittgenstein soloist, Fritz Busch conducting); *Militärmarsch* in F major for the film *Der Rosenkavalier* (1925; Dresden, Jan. 10, 1926, composer conducting); *Panathenäenzug, symphonische Etüden in Form einer Passacaglia* for Piano, Left Hand, and Orch., op. 74 (1927; Vienna, March 11, 1928, Wittgenstein soloist, Schalk conducting); *Vier sinfonische Zwischenspiele aus Intermezzo* (BBC, London, May 24, 1931); *München*, "ein Gelegenheitswalzer" (for the film *München*, 1939; Munich, May 24, 1939; rev. 1945 as *München*, "ein Gedächtniswalzer"; Vienna, March 31, 1951); *Festmusik zur Feier des 2600jährigen Bestehens des Kaiserreichs Japan*, op. 84 (Tokyo, Dec. 7, 1940); *Divertimento, Klavierstücke von Couperin* for Small Orch., op. 86 (1940–41; Vienna, Jan. 31, 1943, Krauss conducting); Horn Concerto No. 2 in E-flat major (1942; Salzburg, Aug. 11, 1943, Gottfried Freiberg soloist, Böhm conducting); *Festmusik der Stadt Wien* for Brass and Timpani (1943; 2nd version as *Fanfare der Stadt Wien*, 1943; Vienna, April 9, 1943, composer conducting); Sonatina No. 1 in F major, "Aus der Werkstatt eines Invaliden," for 16 Wind Instruments (1943; Dresden, June 18, 1944, Karl Elmendorff conducting); *Erste Walzerfolge aus Der Rosenkavalier* (1944; London, Aug. 4, 1946, Erich Leinsdorf conducting); *Metamorphosen* for 23 Solo Strings (1945; Zürich, Jan. 25, 1946, Paul Sacher conducting); Sonatina No. 2 in E-flat major, "Fröhliche Werkstatt," for 16 Wind Instruments (1944–45; Winterthur, March 25, 1946, Hermann Scherchen conducting); Oboe Concerto in D major (1945–46; Zürich, Feb. 26, 1946, Marcel Saillet soloist, Volkmar Andreae conducting); *Symphonische Fantasie aus Die Frau ohne Schatten* (1946; Vienna, June 26, 1947, Böhm conducting); Duett-Concertino for Clarinet, Bassoon, Strings, and Harp (1947; Radio Svizzera Italiana, Lugano, April 4, 1948); *Symphonisches Fragment aus Josephslegende* (1948; San Antonio, Feb. 26, 1949, Max Reiter conducting).

CHAMBER: String Quartet in A major, op. 2 (1880; Munich, March 14, 1881); Cello Sonata in F major, op. 6 (1880–83; Nuremberg, Dec. 8, 1883); Piano Quartet in C minor, op. 13 (1883–84; Weimar, Dec. 8, 1885); Violin Sonata in E-flat major, op. 18 (1887; Munich, Oct. 3, 1888); Allegretto in E major for Violin and Piano (1948).

CHORAL: Chorus for *Elektra* of Sophocles (1881); *Wanderers Sturmlied* for Chorus and Orch., op. 14 (1884; Cologne, March 8, 1887, composer conducting); *Taillefer* for Soprano, Tenor, Baritone, Chorus, and Orch., op. 52 (Heidelberg, Oct. 26, 1903, composer conducting); *Bardengesang* for Male Chorus and Orch., op. 55 (1905; Dresden, Feb. 6, 1906); *Deutsche Motette* for Soprano, Alto, Tenor, Bass, and Unaccompanied Chorus, op. 62 (Berlin, Dec. 2, 1913); *Die Tageszeiten* for Male Chorus and Orch., op. 76 (Vienna, July 21, 1928); *Olympische Hymne* for Chorus and Orch. (1934; Berlin, Aug. 1, 1936, composer conducting); *Die Göttin im Putzzimmer* for Unaccompanied Chorus (1935; Vienna, March 2, 1952, Krauss conducting); *An dem Baum Daphne*, epilogue to *Daphne*, for Unaccompanied Chorus (1943; Vienna, Jan. 5, 1947, Felix Prohaska conducting).

SONGS (source of text precedes date of composition): *Weihnachtslied* (C. Schubart; 1870); *Einkehr* (Uhland; 1871); *Winterreise* (Uhland; 1871); *Waldkonzert* (J. Vogel; 1871?); *Der böhmische Musikant* (O. Pletzsch; 1871?); *Herz, mein Herz* (E. Geibel; 1871); *Der müde Wanderer* (A. Hoffman von Fallersleben; 1873?); *Husarenlied* (von Fallersleben; 1873?); *Der Fischer* (Goethe; 1877); *Die Drossel* (Uhland; 1877); *Lass ruhn die Toten* (A. von Chamisso; 1877); *Lust und Qual* (Goethe; 1877); *Spielmann und Zither* (T. Körner; 1878); *Wiegenlied* (von Fallersleben; 1878); *Abend- und Morgenrot* (von Fallersleben; 1878); *Im Walde* (Geibel; 1878); *Der Spielmann und sein Kind* (von Fallersleben; 1878; orchestrated); *Nebel* (Lenau; 1878?); *Soldatenlied* (von Fallersleben; 1878?); *Ein Röslein zog ich mir im Garten* (von Fallersleben; 1878?); *Waldegesang* (Geibel; 1879); *In Vaters Garten heimlich steht ein Blümchen* (Heine; 1879); *Die erwachte Rose* (F. von Sallet; 1880); *Begegnung* (O. Gruppe; 1880); *John Anderson, mein Lieb* (Burns; F. Freiligrath, tr.; 1880); *Rote Rosen* (K. Stieler; 1883); *Acht Lieder aus Letzte Blätter*, op. 10 (H. von Gilm; 1885): *Zueignung* (orchestrated, 1940), *Nichts, Die Nacht, Die Georgine, Geduld, Die Verschwiegenen, Die Zeitlose, Allerseelen; Wer hat's gethan?* (Gilm; 1885); *Fünf Lieder*, op. 15 (1884–86): *Madrigal* (Michelangelo), *Winternacht* (Schack), *Lob des Leidens* (Schack), *Aus den Liedern der Trauer (Dem Herzen ähnlich)* (Schack), *Heimkehr* (Schack); *Sechs Lieder*, op. 17 (Schack; 1885–87): *Seitdem dein Aug' in meines schaute, Ständchen, Das Geheimnis, Aus den Liedern der Trauer (Von dunklem Schleier umsponnen), Nur Muth!, Barkarole; Schlichte Weisen, Sechs Lieder aus Lotusblättern*, op. 19 (Schack; 1885–88): *Wozu noch, Mädchen, soll es frommen; Breit über mein Haupt dein schwarzes Haar; Schön sind, doch kalt die Himmelssterne; Wie sollten wir geheim sie halten; Hoffen und wieder versagen; Mein Herz ist stumm, mein Herz ist kalt; Schlichte Weisen*, op. 21 (F. Dahn; 1887–88): *All' mein Gedanken, mein Herz und mein Sinn; Du meines Herzens Krönelein; Ach Lieb, ich muss nun scheiden; Ach weh, mir unglückhaften Mann; Die Frauen sind oft fromm und still; Mädchen-blumen*, op. 22 (Dahn): *Kornblumen* (1888), *Mohnblumen* (1888), *Efeu* (1886–88), *Wasserrose* (1886–88); *Zwei Lieder*, op. 26 (Lenau; 1891): *Frühlingsgedränge, O wärst du mein; Vier Lieder*, op. 27 (1894): *Ruhe, meine Seele* (K. Henckell; orchestrated, 1948); *Cäcilie* (Hart; orchestrated, 1897); *Heimliche Aufforderung* (J. Mackay); *Morgen* (Mackay); orchestrated, 1897); *Drei Lieder*, op. 29 (Bierbaum; 1895): *Traum durch die Dämmerung, Schlagende Herzen, Nachtgang*; *Wir beide wollen springen* (Bierbaum; 1896); *Drei Lieder*, op. 31: *Blauer Sommer* (Busse; 1896), *Wenn* (Busse; 1895), *Weisser Jasmin* (Busse; 1895); added song, *Stiller Gang* (Dehmel; 1895); *Fünf Lieder*, op. 32 (1896): *Ich trage meine Minne* (Henckell), *Sehnsucht* (Liliencron), *Liebeshymnus* (Henckell); orchestrated, 1897), *O süsser Mai* (Henckell), *Himmelsboten* (*Des Knaben Wunderhorn*); *Vier Gesänge*, op. 33, for Voice and Orch.: *Verführung* (Mackay; 1896), *Gesang der Apollopriesterin* (E. von und zu Bodman; 1896), *Hymnus* (1896), *Pilgers Morgenlied* (Goethe; 1897); *Vier Lieder*, op. 36: *Das Rosenband* (Klopstock; orchestrated, 1897), *Für funfzehn Pfennige* (*Des Knaben Wunderhorn*; 1897), *Hat gesagt—bleibt's nicht dabei* (*Des Knaben Wunderhorn*; 1898), *Anbetung* (Rückert; 1898); *Sechs Lieder*, op. 37: *Glückes genug* (Liliencron; 1898), *Ich liebe dich* (Liliencron; 1898; orchestrated, 1943), *Meinem Kinde* (Falke; 1897; orchestrated, 1897), *Mein Auge* (Dehmel; 1898; orchestrated, 1933), *Herr Lenz* (Bodman; 1896), *Hochzeitlich Lied* (A. Lindner; 1898); *Fünf Lieder*, op. 39 (1898): *Leises Lied* (Dehmel), *Junghexenlied* (Bierbaum), *Der Arbeitsmann* (Dehmel), *Befreit* (Dehmel; orchestrated, 1933), *Lied an meinen Sohn* (Dehmel); *Fünf Lieder*, op. 41 (1899): *Wiegenlied* (Dehmel; orchestrated, 1916), *In der Campagna* (Mackay), *Am Ufer* (Dehmel), *Bruder Liederlich* (Liliencron), *Leise Lieder* (Morgenstern); *Drei Lieder*, op. 43 (1899): *An Sie* (Klopstock), *Muttertändelei* (G. Bürger; orchestrated, 1900), *Die Ulme zu Hirsau* (Uhland); *Zwei grössere Gesänge*, op. 44, for Voice and Orch. (1899): *Notturno* (Dehmel), *Nächtlicher Gang* (Rückert); *Weihnachtsgefühl* (Greif; 1899); *Fünf Lieder*, op. 46 (Rückert): *Ein Obdach gegen Sturm und Regen* (1900), *Gestern war ich* *Atlas* (1899), *Die sieben Siegel* (1899), *Morgenrot* (1900), *Ich sehe wie in einem Spiegel* (1900); *Fünf Lieder*, op. 47 (Uhland; 1900): *Auf ein Kind, Des Dichters Abendgang* (orchestrated, 1918), *Rückleben, Einkehr, Von den sieben Zechbrüdern; Fünf Lieder*, op. 48 (1900): *Freundliche Vision* (Bierbaum; orchestrated, 1918), *Ich schwebe* (Henckell), *Kling!* (Henckell), *Winterweihe* (Henckell; orchestrated, 1918), *Winterliebe* (Henckell; orchestrated, 1918); *Acht Lieder*, op. 49: *Waldseligkeit* (Dehmel; 1901; orchestrated, 1918); *In goldener Fülle* (P. Remer; 1901); *Wiegenliedchen* (Dehmel; 1901); *Das Lied des Steinklopfers* (Henckell; 1901); *Sie wissen's nicht* (O. Panizza; 1901); *Junggesellenschwur* (*Des Knaben Wunderhorn*; 1900); *Wer lieben will* (C. Mündel; 1901); *Ach, was Kummer, Qual und Schmerzen* (Mündel; 1901); *Zwei Gesänge*, op. 51, for Voice and Orch.: *Das Thal* (Uhland; 1902), *Der Einsame* (Heine; 1906); *Sechs Lieder*, op. 56: *Gefunden* (Goethe; 1903), *Blindenklage* (Henckell; 1903–6), *Im Spätboot* (Meyer; 1903–6), *Mit deinen blauen Augen* (Heine; 1903–6), *Frühlingsfeier* (Heine; 1903–6; orchestrated, 1933), *Die heiligen drei Könige aus Morgenland* (Heine; 1903–6; orchestrated, 1906); *Der Graf von Rom* (no text; 1906); *Krämerspiegel*, op. 66 (A. Kerr; 1918): *Es war einmal ein Bock; Einst kam der Bock als Bote; Es liebte einst ein Hase; Drei Masken sah ich am Himmel stehn; Hast due ein Tongedicht vollbracht; O lieber Künstler sei ermahnt; Unser Feind ist, grosser Gott; Von Händlern wird die Kunst bedroht; Es war mal eine Wanze; Die Künstler sind die Schöpfer; Die Händler und die Macher; O Schöpferschwarm, o Händlerkreis; Sechs Lieder*, op. 67 (1918): 1, *Lieder der Ophelia* (Shakespeare; K. Simrock, tr.): *Wie erkenn ich mein Treulieb vor andern nun?; Guten Morgen, 's ist Sankt Valentinstag; Sie trugen ihn auf der Bahre bloss*; 2, *Aus den Büchern des Unmuts der Rendsch Nameh* (Goethe): *Wer wird von der Welt verlangen; Hab' ich euch denn je geraten; Wanderers Gemütsruhe; Sechs Lieder*, op. 68 (Brentano; 1918): *An die Nacht; Ich wollt' ein Sträusslein binden; Säusle, liebe Myrthe; Als mir dein Lied erklang; Amor* (all 5 orchestrated, 1940); *Lied der Frauen* (orchestrated, 1933); *Fünf kleine Lieder*, op. 69 (1918): *Der Stern* (A. von Arnim), *Der Pokal* (Arnim), *Einerlei* (Arnim), *Waldesfahrt* (Heine), *Schlechtes Wetter* (Heine); *Sinnspruch* (Goethe; 1919); *Drei Hymnen von Friedrich Hölderlin*, op. 71, for Voice and Orch. (1921): *Hymne an die Liebe, Rückkehr in der Heimat, Die Liebe; Durch allen Schall und Klang* (Goethe; 1925); *Gesänge des Orients*, op. 77 (Bethge, tr.; 1928): *Ihre Augen* (Hafiz), *Schwung* (Hafiz), *Liebesgeschenke* (*Die chinesische Flöte*), *Die Allmächtige* (Hafiz), *Huldigung* (Hafiz); *Wie etwas sei leicht* (Goethe; 1930); *Vom künftigen Alter*, op. 87 (Rückert; 1929); *Erschaffen und Beleben* (Goethe; 1922); *Und dann nicht mehr* (Rückert; 1929); *Im sonnenschein* (Rückert; 1935); *Zugemessne Rhythmen* (Goethe; 1935); *Das Bachlein*, op. 88 (1933; orchestrated, 1935); *Blick vom oberen Belvedere* (J. Weinheber; 1942); *Sankt Michael* (Weinheber; 1942); *Xenion* (Goethe; 1942); *Vier letzte Lieder* for Voice and Orch. (1948): *Frühling* (Hesse), *September* (Hesse), *Beim Schlafengehen* (Hesse), *Im Abendrot* (Eichendorff) (London, May 22, 1950, Kirsten Flagstad soloist, Wilhelm Furtwängler conducting); *Malven* (B. Knobel; 1948; N.Y., Jan. 10, 1985).

SPEAKER AND PIANO: *Enoch Arden*, after Tennyson, op. 38 (Munich, March 24, 1897); *Das Schloss am Meer*, after Uhland (Berlin, March 23, 1899).

SOLO PIANO: 5 *Klavierstücke*, op. 3 (1880–81); Sonata in B minor, op. 5 (1880–81); 5 *Stimmungsbilder*, op. 9 (1882–84).

ARRANGEMENTS, ETC.: Strauss prepared a cadenza for Mozart's C-minor Piano Concerto, K.491 (1885); arranged Gluck's *Iphigénie en Tauride* (1899; Hoftheater, Weimar, June 9, 1900); made a new version of Beethoven's *Die Ruinen von Athen* with Hugo von Hofmannsthal (Staatsoper, Vienna, Sept. 20, 1924, composer conducting); made a new version of Mozart's *Idomeneo* with Lothar Wallerstein (1930; Staatsoper, Vienna, April 16, 1931, composer conducting).

BIBL.: WORKS, SOURCE MATERIAL: There is no complete ed. of Strauss's works. The standard thematic catalog was prepared by E.H. Mueller von Asow, *R. S.: Thematisches Verzeichnis* (3 vols., Vienna, 1954–74). Many of his writings may be found in W. Schuh, ed., *R. S.: Betrachtungen und Erinnerungen* (Zürich, 1949; Eng. tr., N.Y., 1953; 2nd German ed., rev., 1957). The major bibliographical source is *R.-S.-Bibliographie* (2 vols., Vienna; Vol. I, 1882–1944, ed. by O. Ortner, 1964; Vol. II, 1944–1964, ed. by G. Brosche, 1973). Other sources include the following: R. Specht, *R. S.: Vollständiges Verzeichnis der im Druck erschienen Werke* (Vienna, 1910); J. Kapp, *R. S. und die Berliner Oper* (Berlin, 1934–39); E. Wachten, *R. S., geboren 1864: Sein Leben in Bildern* (Leipzig, 1940); R. Tenschert, *Anekdoten um R. S.* (Vienna, 1945); idem, *R. S. und Wien: Eine Wahlverwandtschaft* (Vienna, 1949); E. Roth, ed., *R. S.: Bühnenwerk* (text in German, Eng., and French; London, 1954); W. Schuh, *Das Bühnenwerke von R. S. in den unter Mitwirkung des Komponisten geschaffenen letzten Münchner Inszenierungen* (Zürich, 1954); F. Trenner, *R. S.: Dokumente seines Lebens und Schaffens* (Munich, 1954); R. Petzoldt, *R. S.: Sein Leben in Bildern* (Leipzig, 1962); F. Dostal, ed., *Karl Böhm: Begegnung mit R. S.* (Vienna, 1964); F. Grasberger and F. Hadamowsky, eds., *R.-S.-Ausstellung zum 100. Geburtstag* (Vienna, 1964); F. Hadamowsky, *R. S. und Salzburg* (Salzburg, 1964); W. Schuh, *Ein paar Erinnerungen an R. S.* (Zürich, 1964); W. Schuh and E. Roth, eds., *R. S.: Complete Catalogue* (London, 1964); W. Thomas, *R. S. und seine Zeitgenössen* (Munich, 1964); F. Grasberger, *R. S.: Höhe Kunst, erfülltes Leben* (Vienna, 1965); W. Deppisch, *R. S. in Selbstzeugnissen und Bilddokumenten* (Reinbek, 1968); F. Grasberger, *R. S. und die Wiener Oper* (Vienna, 1969); A. Jefferson, *R. S.* (London, 1975); F. Trenner, *Die Skizzenbücher von R. S. aus dem R.-S.-Archiv in Garmisch* (Tutzing, 1977); idem, *R. S. Werkverzeichnis* (Vienna, 1985).

CORRESPONDENCE: F. Strauss, ed., *R. S.: Briefwechsel mit Hugo von Hofmannsthal* (Berlin, 1925; Eng. tr., N.Y., 1927); *R. S. et Romain Rolland: Correspondance, fragments de journal* (Paris, 1951; Eng. tr., 1968); F. von Schuch, *R. S., Ernst von Schuch und Dresdens Oper* (Leipzig, 1952; 2nd ed., 1953); W. Schuh, ed., *R. S. und Hugo von Hofmannsthal: Briefwechsel: Gesamtausgabe* (Zürich, 1952; 2nd ed., rev., 1955; in Eng. as *A Working Friendship: The Correspondence between R. S. and Hugo von Hofmannsthal*, London, 1961); idem, ed., *R. S.: Briefe an die Eltern 1882–1906* (Zürich, 1954); W. Schuh and F. Trenner, eds., "Hans von Bülow/R. S.: Briefwechsel," *R. S. Jahrbuch 1954* (Eng. tr. publ. separately in London, 1955); R. Tenschert, ed., *R. S. und Joseph Gregor: Briefwechsel 1934–1949* (Salzburg, 1955); W. Schuh, ed., *R. S., Stefan Zweig: Briefwechsel* (Frankfurt, 1957; in Eng. as *A Confidential Matter: The Letters of R. S. and Stefan Zweig 1931–1935*, Berkeley, Calif., 1977); D. Kämper, ed., *R. S. und Franz Wüllner im Briefwechsel* (Cologne, 1963); G. Kende and W. Schuh, eds., *R. S., Clemens Krauss: Briefwechsel* (Munich, 1963; 2nd ed., 1964); A. Ott, ed., *R. S. und Ludwig Thuille: Briefe der Freundschaft 1877–1907* (Munich, 1969); W. Schuh, ed., *R. S.: Briefwechsel mit Willi Schuh* (Zürich, 1969).

BIOGRAPHICAL: A. Seidl and W. Klatte, *R. S.: Eine Charakterskizze* (Prague, 1896); G. Brecher, *R. S.: Eine monographische Skizze* (Leipzig, 1900); E. Urban, *R. S.* (Berlin, 1901); R. Batka, *R. S.* (Charlottenburg, 1908); E. Newman, *R. S.* (London, 1908); M. Steinitzer, *R. S.* (Berlin, 1911; final ed., enl., 1927); H. Finck, *R. S.: The Man and His Works* (Boston, 1917); R. Specht, *R. S. und sein Werk* (2 vols., Leipzig, 1921); R. Muschler, *R. S.* (Hildesheim, 1924); S. Kallenberg, *R. S.: Leben und Werk* (Leipzig, 1926); J. Cooke, *R. S.: A Short Biography* (Philadelphia, 1929); W. Hutschenruyter, *R. S.* (The Hague, 1929); E. Gehring, ed., *R. S. und seine Vaterstadt: Zum 70. Geburtstag am 11. Juni 1934* (Munich, 1934); F. Gysi, *R. S.* (Potsdam, 1934); W. Brandl, *R. S.: Leben und Werk* (Wiesbaden, 1949); E. Bücken, *R. S.* (Kevelaer, 1949); K. Pfister, *R. S.: Weg, Gestalt, Denkmal* (Vienna, 1949); C. Rostand, *R. S.* (Paris, 1949; 2nd ed., 1965); O. Erhardt, *R. S.: Leben, Wirken, Schaffen* (Olten, 1953); E. Krause, *R. S.: Gestalt und Werk* (Leipzig, 1955; 3rd ed., rev., 1963; Eng. tr., 1964); I. Fabian, *R. S.* (Budapest, 1962); H. Kralik, *R. S.: Weltbürger der Musik* (Vienna, 1963); W. Panofsky, *R. S.: Partitur eines Lebens* (Munich, 1965); G. Marek, *R. S.: The Life of a Non-Hero* (N.Y.,

1967); H. Schonberg, *The Great Conductors* (N.Y., 1967); A. Jefferson, *The Life of R. S.* (Newton Abbot, 1973); M. Kennedy, *R. S.* (London, 1976; 2nd ed., rev., 1983); W. Schuh, *R. S.: Jugend und Meisterjahre: Lebenschronik 1864–98* (Zürich, 1976; in Eng. as *R. S.: A Chronicle of the Early Years 1864–98*, Cambridge, 1982); K. Wilhelm, *R. S. persönlich: Eine Bildbiographie* (Munich, 1984).

CRITICAL, ANALYTICAL: G. Jourissenne, *R. S.: Essai critique et biographique* (Brussels, 1899); E. Urban, *S. contra Wagner* (Berlin, 1902); O. Bie, *Die moderne Musik und R. S.* (Berlin, 1906); L. Gilman, *S.' Salome: A Guide to the Opera* (N.Y., 1906); J. Manifarges, *R. S. als Dirigent* (Amsterdam, 1907); E. Schmitz, *R. S. als Musikdramatiker: Eine aesthetisch-kritische Studie* (Munich, 1907); E. von Ziegler, *R. S. und seine dramatischen Dichtungen* (Munich, 1907); P. Bekker, *Das Musikdrama der Gegenwart* (Stuttgart, 1909); E. Fischer-Plasser, *Einführung in die Musik von R. S. und Elektra* (Leipzig, 1909); G. Gräner, *R. S.: Musikdramen* (Berlin, 1909); F. Santoliquido, *Il dopo-Wagner: Claude Debussy e R. S.* (Rome, 1909); O. Hübner, *R. S. und das Musikdrama: Betrachtungen über den Wert oder Unwert gewisser Opernmusiken* (Leipzig, 1910); E. Hutcheson, *Elektra by R. S.: A Guide to the Opera with Musical Examples from the Score* (N.Y., 1910); M. Steinitzer, *S.iana und Anderes* (Stuttgart, 1910); H. Daffner, *Salome: Ihre Gestalt in Geschichte und Kunst* (Munich, 1912); A. Seidl, *S.iana: Aufsätze zur R.S.—Frage auf drei Jahrzehnten* (Regensburg, 1913); F. Dubitzky, "R. S.' Kammermusik," *Die Musik*, XIII (1913–14); E. Thilo, "R. S. als chorkomponist," ibid.; M. Steinitzer, *R. S. in seiner Zeit, mit einem Abdruck der auf der S.woche zu Stuttgart im. Kgl. Hoftheater gehaltenen Rede und einem Bildnis* (Leipzig, 1914; 2nd ed., 1922); O. Bie, *Die neuere Musik bis R. S.* (Leipzig, 1916); L. Gilman, "R. S. and His Alpine Symphony," *North American Review*, XXIV (1919); H. Scherchen, "Tonalitäts-prinzipund die Alpen-Symphonie von R. S.," *Melos*, 1 (1920); H. von Waltershausen, *R. S.: Ein Versuch* (Munich, 1921); R. Rosenzweig, *Zur Entwicklungsgeschichte des S.'schen Musikdramas* (diss., Univ. of Vienna, 1923); H. Windt, "R. S. und die Atonalität," *Die Musik*, XVI (1923–24); W. Schrenk, *R. S. und die neue Musik* (Berlin, 1924); K. Westphal, "Das musikdramatische Prinzip bei R. S.," *Die Musik*, XIX (1926–27); E. Blom, *The Rose Cavalier* (London, 1930); T. Armstrong, *S.' Tone Poems* (London, 1931); G. Röttger, *Die Harmonik in R. S.' Der Rosenkavalier: Ein Beitrag zur Entwicklung der romantische Harmonik nach Richard Wagner* (diss., Univ. of Munich, 1931); M. Steinitzer, "R. S.' Werke für Klavier," *Die Musik*, XXIV (1931–32); E. Wachten, *Das psychotechnische Formproblem in den Sinfonischen Dichtungen von R.S. (mit besonderer Berücksichtigung seiner Bühnenwerk)* diss., Univ. of Munich, 1932; publ. in an abridged ed., Berlin, 1933); K.-J. Krüger, *Hugo von Hofmannsthal und R. S.: Versuch einer Deutung des künstlerissischen Weges Hugo von Hofmannsthals, mit einem Anhang; erstmalige Veröffentlichung der bischer ungedruckten einzigen Vertonung eines Hofmannsthalschen Gedichtes durch R. S.* (Berlin, 1935); H. Röttger, *Das Formproblem bei R. S. gezeigt an der Oper Die Frau ohne Schatten, mit Einschluss von Guntram und Intermezzo* (diss., Univ. of Munich, 1935; publ. in an abridged ed., Berlin, 1937); J. Gregor, *R. S.: Der Meister der Oper* (Munich, 1939; 2nd ed., 1942); G. Becker, *Das Problem der Oper an Hand von R. S.' Capriccio* (diss., Univ. of Jena, 1944); R. Tenschert, *Dreimal sieben Variationen über das Thema R. S.* (Vienna, 1944; 2nd ed., 1945); O. Gatscha, *Librettist und Komponist: Dargestellt an den Opern R. S.'* (diss., Univ. of Vienna, 1947); A. Pryce-Jones, *R. S.: Der Rosenkavalier* (London, 1947); W. Schuh, *Über Opern von R. S.* (Zürich, 1947); F. Trenner, *Die Zusammenarbeit von Hugo von Hofmannsthal und R. S.* (diss., Univ. of Munich, 1949); D. Lindner, *R. S./Joseph Gregor: Die Liebe der Danae: Herkunft, Inhalt und Gestaltung eines Opernwerkes* (Vienna, 1952); R. Schopenhauer, *Die antiken Frauengestalten bei R. S.* (diss., Univ. of Vienna, 1952); G. Hausswald, *R. S.: Ein Beitrag zur Dresdener Operngeschichte seit 1945* (Dresden, 1953); W. Wendhausen, *Das stilistische Verhältnis von Dichtung und Musik in der Entwicklung der musikdramatischen*

Werke R. S.' (diss., Univ. of Hamburg, 1954); G. Kende, *R. S. und Clemens Krauss: Eine Künstlerfreundschaft und ihre Zusammenarbeit an Capriccio (op. 85): Konversationsstück für Musik* (Munich, 1960); N. Del Mar, *R. S.: A Critical Commentary on His Life and Works* (3 vols., London, 1962, 1969, and 1972; reprint with corrections, 1978); A. Jefferson, *The Operas of R. S. in Britain, 1910–1963* (London, 1963); A. Natan, *R. S.: Die Opern* (Basel, 1963); A. Berger, *R. S. als geistige Macht: Versuch eines philosophischen Verständnisses* (Gisch, 1964); L. Lehmann, *Five Operas and R. S.* (N.Y., 1964; publ. in London, 1964, as *Singing with R. S.*); W. Mann, *R. S.: A Critical Study of the Operas* (London, 1964); K. Pörnbacher, *Hugo von Hofmannsthal/R. S.: Der Rosenkavalier* (Munich, 1964); W. Schuh, *Hugo von Hofmannsthal und R. S.: Legende und Wirklichkeit* (Munich, 1964); A. Goléa, *R. S.* (Paris, 1965); R. Gerlach, *Tonalität und tonale Konfiguration im Oeuvre von R. S.: Analysen und Interpretationen als Beiträge zum Verständnis von tonalen Problemen und Formen in sinfonischen Werken und in der "Einleitung" und ersten Szene des Rosenkavalier* (diss., Univ. of Zürich, 1966; publ. as *Don Juan und Rosenkavalier*, Bern, 1966); R. Schäfer, *Hugo von Hofmannsthals Arabella* (Bern, 1967); W. Gruhn, *Die Instrumentation in den Orchesterwerken von R. S.* (diss., Univ. of Mainz, 1968); W. Schuh, *Der Rosenkavalier: 4 Studien* (Olten, 1968); J. Knaus, *Hugo von Hofmannsthal und sein Weg zur Oper Die Frau ohne Schatten* (Berlin, 1971); W. Schuh, ed., *Hugo von Hofmannsthal, R. S.: Der Rosenkavalier: Fassungen, Filmszenarium, Briefe* (Frankfurt, 1971); A. Abert, *R. S.: Die Opern: Einführung und Analyse* (Hannover, 1972); A. Jefferson, *The Lieder of R. S.* (London, 1972); W. Colson, *Four Last Songs by R. S.* (diss., Univ. of Illinois, 1974); D. Daviau and G. Buelow, *The "Ariadne auf Naxos" of Hugo von Hofmannsthal and R. S.* (Chapel Hill, 1975); B. Peterson, *Ton und Wort: The Lieder of R. S.* (Ann Arbor, 1979); K. Forsyth, *Ariadne auf Naxos by Hugo von Hofmannsthal and R. S.: Its Genesis and Meaning* (Oxford, 1982); R. Hartmann, *R. S.: The Staging of His Operas and Ballets* (Oxford, 1982); R. Schlötter, *Musik und Theater im "Rosenkavalier" vom R. S.* (Vienna, 1985); H. Wajemann, *Die Chorkompositionen von R. S.* (Tutzing, 1986); G. Splitt, *R. S. 1933–1935: Ästhetik und Musikpolitik zu Beginn der nationalsozialistischen Herrschaft* (Pfaffenweiler, 1987); C. Osborne, *The Complete Operas of R. S.* (London, 1988); A. Garlington, Jr., "R. S.'s *Vier letzte Lieder*: The Ultimate *opus ultimum*," *Musical Quarterly*, 73/1 (1989).

Stravinsky, Feodor (Ignatievich), distinguished Russian bass of Polish descent, father of **Igor (Feodorovich) Stravinsky;** b. Noviy Dvor, near Rechitza, June 20, 1843; d. St. Petersburg, Dec. 4, 1902. While pursuing the study of law, he appeared in concerts with such success that he decided to study voice; in 1869 he became a student at the St. Petersburg Cons., where he received vocal training from Camillo Everardi (1871–73). On Sept. 3, 1873, he made his formal operatic debut as Count Rodolpho in *La Sonnambula* in Kiev, where he continued to sing until 1876. He became a member of the Russian Imperial Opera at St. Petersburg in 1876 and established himself as one of the greatest Russian basses before Chaliapin; his interpretation of heroic and comical characters in Russian operas evoked unbounded praise from the critics. He was famous as Méphistophélès in Gounod's *Faust*, and was distinguished not only for the power of his voice, but also for his dramatic talent on the stage. Altogether, he made 1,235 appearances in 64 operatic roles.

Stravinsky, Igor (Feodorovich), great Russian-born French, later American composer, one of the supreme masters of 20th-century music, whose works exercised the most profound influence on the evolution of music through the emancipation of rhythm, melody, and harmony, son of **Feodor (Ignatievich)** and father of **Sviatoslav Soulima Stravinsky;** b. Oranienbaum, near St. Petersburg, June 17, 1882; d. N.Y., April 6, 1971 (his body was flown to Venice and buried in the Russian corner of the cemetery island of San Michele). He was brought up in an artistic atmosphere; he often went to opera rehearsals when his father sang, and acquired an early love for the musical theater. He took piano lessons with Alexandra Snetkova, and later with Leokadia Kashperova, who was a pupil of Anton Rubinstein; but it was not until much later that he began to study music theory, 1st with Akimenko and then with Kalafati (1900–1903). His progress in composition was remarkably slow; he never entered a music school or a cons., and never earned an academic degree in music. In 1901 he enrolled in the faculty of jurisprudence at St. Petersburg Univ., and took courses there for 8 semesters, without graduating; a fellow student was Vladimir Rimsky-Korsakov, a son of the composer. In the summer of 1902 Stravinsky traveled to Germany, where he met another son of Rimsky-Korsakov, Andrei, who was a student at the Univ. of Heidelberg; Stravinsky became his friend. He was introduced to Rimsky-Korsakov, and became a regular guest at the latter's periodic gatherings in St. Petersburg. In 1903–4 he wrote a piano sonata for the Russian pianist Nicolai Richter, who performed it at Rimsky-Korsakov's home. In 1905 he began taking regular lessons in orchestration with Rimsky-Korsakov, who taught him free of charge; under his tutelage Stravinsky composed a Sym. in E-flat major; the 2nd and 3rd movements from it were performed on April 27, 1907, by the Court Orch. in St. Petersburg, and a complete performance of it was given by the same orch. on Feb. 4, 1908. The work, dedicated to Rimsky-Korsakov, had some singularities and angularities that showed a deficiency of technique; there was little in this work that presaged Stravinsky's ultimate development as a master of form and orchestration. At the same concert, his *Le Faune et la bergère* for Voice and Orch. had its 1st performance; this score revealed a certain influence of French Impressionism. To celebrate the marriage of Rimsky-Korsakov's daughter Nadezhda to the composer Maximilian Steinberg on June 17, 1908, Stravinsky wrote an orch. fantasy entitled *Fireworks*. Rimsky-Korsakov died a few days after the wedding; Stravinsky deeply mourned his beloved teacher and wrote a funeral song for Wind Instruments in his memory; it was 1st performed in St. Petersburg on Jan. 30, 1909. There followed a *Scherzo fantastique* for Orch., inspired by Maeterlinck's book *La Vie des abeilles*. As revealed in his correspondence with Rimsky-Korsakov, Stravinsky had at 1st planned a literal program of composition, illustrating events in the life of a beehive by a series of descriptive sections; some years later, however, he gratuitously denied all connection of the work with Maeterlinck's book.

A signal change in Stravinsky's fortunes came when the famous impresario Diaghilev commissioned him to write a work for the Paris season of his company, the Ballets Russes. The result was the production of his 1st ballet masterpiece, *The Firebird*, staged by Diaghilev in Paris on June 25, 1910. Here he created music of extraordinary brilliance, steeped in the colors of Russian fairy tales. There are numerous striking effects in the score, such as a glissando of harmonics in the string instruments; the rhythmic drive is exhilarating, and the use of asymmetrical time signatures is extremely effective; the harmonies are opulent; the orchestration is coruscating. He drew 2 orch. suites from the work; in 1919 he reorchestrated the music to conform to his new beliefs in musical economy; in effect he plucked the luminous feathers off the magical firebird, but the original scoring remained a favorite with conductors and orchs. Stravinsky's association with Diaghilev demanded his presence in Paris, which he made his home beginning in 1911, with frequent travels to Switzerland. His 2nd ballet for Diaghilev was *Pétrouchka*, produced in Paris on June 13, 1911, with triumphant success. Not only was the ballet remarkably effective on the stage, but the score itself, arranged in 2 orch. suites, was so new and original that it marked a turning point in 20th-century music; the spasmodically explosive rhythms, the novel instrumental sonorities, with the use of the piano as an integral part of the orch., the bold harmonic innovations in employing 2 different keys simultaneously (C major and F-sharp major, the "Pétrouchka Chord") became a potent influence on modern European composers. Debussy voiced his enchantment with the score, and young Stravinsky, still in his 20s, became a Paris celebrity. Two years later, he brought out a work of even greater revolutionary import, the ballet *Le Sacre du printemps* (Rite of Spring; Russian title, *Vesna sviashchennaya*, literally Spring the Sacred); its subtitle was "Scenes of Pagan Russia." It was produced by Diaghilev with his Ballets Russes in Paris on May 29, 1913, with the choreography by Nijinsky. The score marked a departure from all conventions of musical composition; while in *Pétrouchka* the harmonies, though innovative and dissonant, could still be placed in the context of modern music, the score of *Le Sacre du printemps* contained such corrosive dissonances as scales played at the intervals of major sevenths and superpositions of minor upon major triads with the common tonic, chords treated as unified blocks of sound, and rapid metrical changes that seemingly defied performance. The score still stands as one of the most daring creations of the modern musical mind; its impact was tremendous; to some of the audience at its 1st performance in Paris, Stravinsky's "barbaric" music was beyond endurance; the Paris critics exercised their verbal ingenuity in indignant vituperation; one of them proposed that *Le Sacre du printemps* should be more appropriately described as *Le Massacre du printemps*. On May 26, 1914, Diaghilev produced Stravinsky's lyric fairy tale *Le Rossignol*, after Hans Christian Andersen. It too abounded in corrosive discords, but here it could be explained as "Chinese" music illustrative of the exotic subject. From 1914 to 1918 he worked on his ballet *Les Noces* (Russian title, *Svadebka*; literally, Little Wedding), evoking Russian peasant folk modalities; it was scored for an unusual ensemble of chorus, soloists, 4 pianos, and 17 percussion instruments.

The devastation of World War I led Stravinsky to conclude that the era of grandiose Romantic music had become obsolete, and that a new spirit of musical economy was imperative in an impoverished world. As an illustration of such economy, he wrote the musical stage play *L'Histoire du soldat*, scored for only 7 players, with a narrator. About the same time he wrote a work for 11 instruments entitled *Ragtime*, inspired by the new American dance music. He continued his association with Diaghilev's Ballets Russes in writing the ballet *Pulcinella*, based on themes by Pergolesi and other 18th-century Italian composers. He also wrote for Diaghilev 2 short operas, *Renard*, to a Russian fairy tale (Paris, May 18, 1922), and *Mavra*, after Pushkin (Paris, June 3, 1922). These 2 works were the last in which he used Russian subjects, with the sole exception of an orch. *Scherzo à la russe*, written in 1944. Stravinsky had now entered the period usually designated as neo-Classical. The most significant works of this stage of his development were his Octet for Wind Instruments and the Piano Concerto commissioned by Koussevitzky. In these works, he abandoned the luxuriant instrumentation of his ballets and their aggressively dissonant harmonies; instead, he used pandiatonic structures, firmly tonal but starkly dissonant in their superposition of tonalities within the same principal key. His reversion to old forms, however, was not an act of ascetic renunciation but, rather, a grand experiment in reviving Baroque practices, which had fallen into desuetude. The Piano Concerto provided him with an opportunity to appear as soloist; Stravinsky was never a virtuoso pianist, but he was able to acquit himself satisfactorily in such works as the Piano Concerto; he played it with Koussevitzky in Paris on May 22, 1924, and during his 1st American tour with the Boston Sym. Orch., also under Koussevitzky, on Jan. 23, 1925. The Elizabeth Sprague Coolidge Foundation commissioned him to write a pantomime for string orch.; the result was *Apollon Musagète*, given at the Library of Congress in Washington, D.C., on April 27, 1928. This score, serene and emotionally restrained, evokes the manner of Lully's court ballets. He continued to explore the resources of neo-Baroque writing in his *Capriccio* for Piano and Orch., which he performed as soloist, with Ansermet conducting, in Paris, on Dec. 6, 1929; this score is impressed by a spirit of hedonistic entertainment, harking back to the *style galant* of the 18th century; yet it is unmistakably modern in its polyrhythmic collisions of pandiatonic harmonies. Stravin-

sky's growing disillusionment with the external brilliance of modern music led him to seek eternal verities of music in ancient modalities. His well-nigh monastic renunciation of the grandiose edifice of glorious sound to which he himself had so abundantly contributed found expression in his opera-oratorio *Oedipus Rex*; in order to emphasize its detachment from temporal aspects, he commissioned a Latin text for the work, even though the subject was derived from a Greek play; its music is deliberately hollow and its dramatic points are emphasized by ominous repetitive passages. Yet this very austerity of idiom makes *Oedipus Rex* a profoundly moving play. It had its 1st performance on May 30, 1927; its stage premiere took place in Vienna on Feb. 23, 1928. A turn to religious writing found its utterance in Stravinsky's *Symphony of Psalms*, written for the 50th anniversary of the Boston Sym. and dedicated "to the glory of God." The work is scored for chorus and orch., omitting the violins and violas, thus emphasizing the lower instrumental registers and creating an austere sonority suitable to its solemn subject. Owing to a delay of the Boston performance, the world premiere of the *Symphony of Psalms* took place in Brussels on Dec. 13, 1930. In 1931 he wrote a Violin Concerto commissioned by the violinist Samuel Dushkin, and performed by him in Berlin on Oct. 23, 1931. On a commission from the ballerina Ida Rubinstein, he composed the ballet *Perséphone*; here again he exercised his mastery of simplicity in formal design, melodic patterns, and contrapuntal structure. For his American tour he wrote *Jeu de cartes*, a "ballet in 3 deals" to his own scenario depicting an imaginary game of poker (of which he was a devotee). He conducted its 1st performance at the Metropolitan Opera in N.Y. on April 27, 1937. His concerto for 16 instruments entitled *Dumbarton Oaks*, named after the Washington, D.C., estate of Mr. and Mrs. Robert Woods Bliss, who commissioned the work, was 1st performed in Washington, on May 8, 1938; in Europe it was played under the noncommittal title *Concerto in E-flat*; its style is hermetically neo-Baroque. It is germane to note that in his neo-Classical works Stravinsky began to indicate the key in the title, e.g., Concerto in D for Violin and Orch. (1931), Concerto in E-flat (*Dumbarton Oaks*, 1938), Sym. in C (1938), Concerto in D for String Orch. (1946), and Serenade in A for Piano (1925).

With World War II engulfing Europe, Stravinsky decided to seek permanent residence in America. He had acquired French citizenship on June 10, 1934; in 1939 he applied for American citizenship; he became an American citizen on Dec. 28, 1945. To celebrate this event he made an arrangement of the *Star-Spangled Banner*, which contained a curious modulation into the subdominant in the coda. He conducted it with the Boston Sym. on Jan. 14, 1944, but because of legal injunctions existing in the state of Massachusetts against intentional alteration, or any mutilation, of the national anthem, he was advised not to conduct his version at the 2nd pair of concerts, and the standard version was substituted. In 1939–40 Stravinsky was named Charles Eliot Norton lecturer at Harvard Univ.; about the same time he accepted several private students, a pedagogical role he had never exercised before. His American years form a curious panoply of subjects and manners of composition. He accepted a commission from the Ringling Bros. to write a *Circus Polka* "for a young elephant." In 1946 he wrote *Ebony Concerto* for a swing band. In 1951 he completed his opera *The Rake's Progress*, inspired by Hogarth's famous series of engravings, to a libretto by W.H. Auden and C. Kallman. He conducted its world premiere in Venice, on Sept. 11, 1951, as part of the International Festival of Contemporary Music there. The opera is a striking example of Stravinsky's protean capacity for adopting different styles and idioms of composition to serve his artistic purposes; *The Rake's Progress* is an ingenious conglomeration of disparate elements, ranging from 18th-century British ballads to cosmopolitan burlesque. But whatever transmutations his music underwent during his long and productive career, he remained a man of the theater at heart. In America he became associated with the brilliant Russian choreographer Balanchine, who produced a number of ballets to Stravinsky's music, among them his *Apollon Musagète*, Violin Concerto, Sym. in 3 movements, *Scherzo à la russe*, *Pulcinella*, and *Agon*. It was in his score of *Agon* that he essayed for the 1st time to adopt the method of composition with 12 tones as promulgated by Schoenberg; *Agon* (the word means "competition" in Greek) bears the subtitle "ballet for 12 tones," perhaps in allusion to the dodecaphonic technique used in the score. Yet the 12-tone method had been the very antithesis of his previous tenets. In fact, an irreconcilable polarity existed between Stravinsky and Schoenberg even in personal relations. Although both resided in Los Angeles for several years, they never met socially; Schoenberg once wrote a canon in which he ridiculed Stravinsky as Herr Modernsky, who put on a wig to look like "Papa Bach." After Schoenberg's death, Stravinsky became interested in examining the essence of the method of composition with 12 tones, which was introduced to him by his faithful musical factotum Robert Craft; Stravinsky adopted dodecaphonic writing in its aspect of canonic counterpoint as developed by Webern. In this manner he wrote his *Canticum sacrum ad honorem Sancti Marci nominis*, which he conducted at San Marco in Venice on Sept. 13, 1956. Other works of the period were also written in a modified 12-tone technique, among them *The Flood*, for Narrator, Mime, Singers, and Dancers, presented in a CBS-TV broadcast in N.Y. on June 14, 1962; its 1st stage performance was given in Hamburg on April 30, 1963.

Stravinsky was married twice; his 1st wife, Catherine Nosenko, whom he married on Jan. 24, 1906, and who bore him 3 children, died in 1939; on March 9, 1940, Stravinsky married his longtime mistress, Vera, who was formerly married to the Russian painter Serge Sudeikin. She was born Vera de Bosset in St. Petersburg, on Dec. 25, 1888, and died in N.Y. on Sept. 17, 1982, at the age of 93. An ugly litigation for the rights to the Stravinsky estate continued for several years between his children and their stepmother; after Vera Stravinsky's death, it was finally settled in a compromise, according to which 2/9 of the estate went to each of his 3 children and a grandchild and 1/9 to Robert Craft. The value of the Stravinsky legacy was spectacularly demonstrated on Nov. 11, 1982, when his working draft of *Le Sacre du printemps* was sold at an auction in London for the fantastic sum of $548,000, higher than any MS by any composer. The purchaser was Paul Sacher, the Swiss conductor and philanthropist. Even more fantastic was the subsequent sale of the entire Stravinsky archive, consisting of 116 boxes of personal letters and 225 drawers containing MSS, some of them unpubl. Enormous bids were made for it by the N.Y. Public Library and the Morgan Library, but they were all outbid by Sacher, who offered the overwhelming purse of $5,250,000, which removed all competition. The materials were to be assembled in a specially constructed 7-story Sacher Foundation building in Basel, to be eventually opened to scholars for study.

In tribute to Stravinsky as a naturalized American citizen, the U.S. Postal Service issued a 2-cent stamp bearing his image to mark his centennial in 1982, an honor theretofore never granted to a foreign-born composer (the possible exception being Victor Herbert, but his entire career was made in America).

Few composers escaped the powerful impact of Stravinsky's music; ironically, it was his own country that had rejected him, partly because of the opposition of Soviet ideologues to modern music in general, and partly because of Stravinsky's open criticism of Soviet ways in art. But in 1962 he returned to Russia for a visit, and was welcomed as a prodigal son; as if by magic, his works began to appear on Russian concert programs, and Soviet music critics issued a number of laudatory studies of his works. Yet it is Stravinsky's early masterpieces, set in an attractive colorful style, that continue to enjoy favor with audiences and performers, while his more abstract and recursive scores are appreciated mainly by specialists.

WORKS: STAGE: *L'Oiseau de feu* (The Firebird), ballet (Paris Opéra, June 25, 1910; 3 suite versions: 1911, 1919, and 1945; 2 sections arranged for Violin and Piano, 1926); *Pétrouchka*, ballet (Paris, June 13, 1911, Monteux conducting; rev. 1946; excerpts officially designated as a "suite" in 1946); *Le Sacre du printemps*, ballet, "scenes of pagan Russia" (1911–13; Paris, May 29, 1913, Monteux conducting; 1st concert perf., Moscow, Feb. 18, 1914, Serge Koussevitzky conducting; 1st Paris concert perf., April 5, 1914, Monteux conducting); *Le Rossignol*, "lyric tale" in 3 acts, after Hans Christian Andersen (1908–14; Paris Opéra, May 26, 1914, Monteux conducting; in 1917 the 2nd and 3rd acts were scored as a ballet, *Le Chant du rossignol*; Paris Opéra, Feb. 2, 1920; also, in 1917, fragments from the 2nd and 3rd acts were used for a symphonic poem under the same title); *Renard*, burlesque chamber opera (1915–16; Paris, May 18, 1922); *L'Histoire du soldat*, ballet with Narrator and 7 Instrumentalists (Lausanne, Sept. 28, 1918; concert suite with original instrumentation, London, July 20, 1920, Ansermet conducting; also *Petite suite* for Violin, Clarinet, and Piano extracted from the score, 1919); *Pulcinella*, ballet "after Pergolesi" with solos, trios, and a duet for Soprano, Tenor, and Bass (Paris Opéra, May 15, 1920; an orch. suite was extracted from it in 1922, and 1st perf. in Boston, Dec. 22, 1922, rev. 1947; 2 chamber pieces, *Suite italienne*); *Mavra*, comic opera, after Pushkin (Paris Opéra, June 3, 1922); *Les Noces* (The Wedding), ballet-cantata, subtitled "choreographic Russian scenes," revision for Soloists, Chorus, 4 Pianos, and 17 Percussion Instruments (1921–23; Paris, June 13, 1923; orig. scored with Full Orch., 1914–17); *Oedipus Rex*, opera-oratorio, after Sophocles (concert perf., Paris, May 30, 1927; 1st stage perf., Vienna, Feb. 23, 1928; rev. 1948); *Apollon Musagète*, classic ballet for String Orch. (Washington, D.C., April 27, 1928; rev. 1947); *Le Baiser de la fée*, ballet on themes of Tchaikovsky (Paris Opéra, Nov. 27, 1928; in 1934 several sections were collected for an independent symphonic piece called *Divertimento*; entire ballet rev. 1950); *Perséphone*, melodrama in 3 parts for Female Narrator, Tenor, Chorus, and Orch., to a text by André Gide (1933; Paris Opéra, April 30, 1934; rev. 1949); *Jeu de cartes* (Card Game), "ballet in 3 deals" (1935–37; N.Y., April 27, 1937); *Orpheus*, ballet (1946–47; N.Y., April 28, 1948); *The Rake's Progress*, opera after Hogarth's engravings, with libretto by W.H. Auden and C. Kallman (1948–51; Venice, Sept. 11, 1951, composer conducting); *Agon*, ballet for 12 Dancers (1954–57; Los Angeles, June 17, 1957); *Noah and the Flood*, also called *The Flood*, biblical spectacle narrated, mimed, sung, and danced (CBS-TV, N.Y., June 14, 1962; 1st stage perf., Hamburg, April 30, 1963).

ORCH.: Sym. in E-flat major, op. 1 (1905–7; 1st partial perf., 2nd and 3rd movements only, St. Petersburg, April 27, 1907; 1st complete perf., St. Petersburg, Feb. 4, 1908; rev. version, Montreux, Switzerland, April 2, 1914); *Scherzo fantastique*, op. 3 (1907; St. Petersburg, Feb. 6, 1909); *Fireworks*, op. 4 (St. Petersburg, June 17, 1908; reorchestrated and 1st perf. in St. Petersburg, Jan. 22, 1910); *Chant funèbre* for Wind Instruments, on the death of Rimsky-Korsakov (1908; St. Petersburg, Jan. 30, 1909; score lost); *Le Chant du rossignol*, symphonic poem (from the opera *Le Rossignol*; Geneva, Dec. 6, 1919); *Symphonies of Wind Instruments*, in memory of Debussy (1918–20; London, June 10, 1921; rev. 1945–47); Suite No. 1 for Small Orch. (1917–25; orch. arrangement of Nos. 1–4 of the *5 pièces faciles* for Piano, 4-hands: Andante, Napolitana, Española, Balalaika); Suite No. 2 for Small Orch. (1921; orch. arrangement of *3 pièces faciles* and No. 5 of *5 pièces faciles* for Piano, 4-hands: March, Waltz, Polka, Galop); Concerto for Piano, with Wind Instruments, Double Basses, and Percussion (Paris, May 22, 1924; rev. 1950); Capriccio for Piano and Orch. (Paris, Dec. 6, 1929; rev. 1949); 4 études for Orch.: Danse, Excentrique, Cantique, Madrid (1928; orch. arrangement of 3 pieces for String Quartet, and Étude for Pianola; Berlin, Nov. 7, 1930; rev. 1952); Concerto in D for Violin and Orch. (Berlin, Oct. 23, 1931; adapted in 1940 for Balanchine's ballet *Balustrade*); *Divertimento* (sections of the ballet *Le Baiser de la fée*, combined in 1934); Praeludium for Jazz Ensemble (1936–37; rev. 1953; Los Angeles, Oct. 19, 1953); Concerto in E-flat, *Dumbarton Oaks*, for Chamber Orch. (Washington, D.C., May 8, 1938); Sym. in C

(1938–40; Chicago, Nov. 7, 1940); Tango, arrangement by Felix Günther of the piano piece (Philadelphia, July 10, 1941, Benny Goodman conducting; Stravinsky's own orchestration, 1953; Los Angeles, Oct. 19, 1953); *Danses concertantes* for Chamber Orch. (Los Angeles, Feb. 8, 1942); Circus Polka for Piano (commissioned by the Ringling Bros. Circus, to accompany the elephant numbers; arranged for Band by David Raksin, 1942; arranged by Stravinsky for sym. orch. and conducted by him with the Boston Sym. Orch., Cambridge, Mass., Jan. 13, 1944); 4 *Norwegian Moods* (1942; Cambridge, Mass., Jan. 13, 1944, composer conducting); *Ode,* in 3 parts (Boston, Oct. 8, 1943); *Scènes de ballet* (orig. composed for Billy Rose's Broadway show *The Seven Lively Arts,* which opened in Philadelphia, Nov. 24, 1944; rev. for concert performance and 1st perf. in N.Y., Feb. 3, 1945); *Scherzo à la russe* (1944; San Francisco, March 22, 1946; orig. for Big Jazz Band); Sym. in 3 movements (1942–45; N.Y., Jan. 24, 1946); *Ebony Concerto* for Clarinet and Swing Band (1945; N.Y., March 25, 1946); Concerto in D for String Orch., *Basler* (1946; Basel, Jan. 21, 1947); *Greeting Prelude* ("Happy Birthday," written for Monteux's 80th birthday; Boston, April 4, 1955); *Tres Sacrae Cantiones,* after Gesualdo, for Chamber Orch. (1957–59); *Movements* for Piano and Orch. (1958–59; N.Y., Jan. 10, 1960); *Monumentum pro Gesualdo di Venosa ad CD Annum,* instrumental surrealization of 3 madrigals by Gesualdo for 4 Wind Instruments, 8 Brass, and Strings (Venice, Sept. 27, 1960); *Variations: Aldous Huxley, In Memoriam* (1963–64; Chicago, April 17, 1965; as a ballet, N.Y., March 31, 1966); *Canon,* from finale of *The Firebird,* in memory of Monteux (Toronto, Dec. 16, 1965).

CHAMBER: 3 pieces for String Quartet (1914); *Ragtime* for 11 Instruments (1918; London, April 27, 1920); *Petite suite* for Violin, Clarinet, and Piano (1919; arranged from *L'Histoire du soldat*); 3 pieces for Clarinet (Lausanne, Nov. 8, 1919); Concertino for String Quartet (1920; rev. for 12 Instruments, 1952); Octet for Wind Instruments (Paris, Oct. 18, 1923); *Duo concertant* for Violin and Piano (Berlin, Oct. 28, 1932); *Russian Dance* for Violin and Piano, from *Pétrouchka* (1932); *Suite italienne* No. 1 for Cello and Piano, and No. 2 for Violin and Piano (both from *Pulcinella*; 1932, 1934); *Pastorale* for Violin, Oboe, English Horn, Clarinet, and Bassoon (1933; arrangement of vocal *Pastorale*); *Divertimento* for Violin and Piano, based on material from *Le Baiser de la fée* (1934); *Élégie* for Unaccompanied Violin and Viola (1944); Septet for Piano, and String and Wind Instruments (1952; Washington, D.C., Jan. 24, 1954); *Epitaphium for Prince Max of Fürstenberg* for Flute, Clarinet, and Harp (Donaueschingen, Oct. 17, 1959); *Double Canon* for String Quartet (1959); 8 instrumental miniatures for 15 Players (Toronto, April 29, 1962; instrumentation of *Les Cinq Doigts* for Piano); *Fanfare for a New Theater* for 2 Trumpets (N.Y., April 19, 1964).

VOCAL: *Le Faune et la bergère* for Mezzo-soprano and Orch. (1906; St. Petersburg, Feb. 4, 1908); *Pastorale,* "song without words" for Soprano and Piano (1908; version for Soprano, Oboe, English Horn, Clarinet, and Bassoon, 1923); 2 *Poems of Verlaine* for Baritone and Piano (1910; with Orch., 1951); 2 *Poems of Balmont* for High Voice and Piano (1911; with Chamber Orch., 1954); *Le Roi des étoiles (Zvezdoliki),* cantata for Male Chorus and Orch. (1912; Brussels Radio, April 19, 1939); 3 poems from the Japanese for Soprano, 2 Flutes, 2 Clarinets, Piano, and String Quartet (1912–13); *Pribaoutki* (Peasant Songs) for Voice and 8 Instruments (1914; Vienna, June 6, 1919); *The Saucer,* 4 Russian songs for Women's Voices (1914–17; as 4 *Russian Peasant Songs,* with 4 Horns added, 1954); *Berceuses du chat,* suite of 4 songs for Female Voice and 3 Clarinets (1915–16; Vienna, June 6, 1919); *Paternoster* for Chorus (1926); *Symphony of Psalms* for Chorus and Orch. (Brussels, Dec. 13, 1930; Boston, Dec. 19, 1930); *Credo* for Chorus (1932); *Ave Maria* for Chorus (1932); Tango for Wordless Voice and Piano (1940); *Babel* for Male Narrator, Male Chorus, and Orch. (1944; Los Angeles, Nov. 18, 1945; 7th and final movement of *Genesis Suite,* a collaborative effort, with Schoenberg, Shilkret, Tansman, Milhaud, Castelnuovo-

Tedesco, and Toch, each contributing a movement); Mass for Men's and Boys' Voices and 10 Wind Instruments (1944–48; Milan, Oct. 27, 1948); Cantata on 4 poems by anonymous English poets of the 15th and 16th centuries, for Soprano, Tenor, Female Chorus, and 5 Instruments (Los Angeles, Nov. 11, 1952); 3 songs from William Shakespeare for Mezzo-soprano, Flute, Clarinet, and Viola (1953; Los Angeles, March 8, 1954); *In Memoriam Dylan Thomas* for Tenor, String Quartet, and 4 Trombones (Hollywood, Sept. 20, 1954); 4 *Russian Songs* for Soprano, Flute, Guitar, and Harp (1954); *Canticum sacrum ad honorem Sancti Marci nominis* for Tenor, Baritone, Chorus, and Orch. (Venice, Sept. 13, 1956, composer conducting); arrangement for Chorus and Orch. of J.S. Bach's *Choral-Variationen über das Weihnachtslied "Vom Himmel hoch da komm' ich her"* (Ojai, May 27, 1956, Robert Craft conducting); *Threni,* on Lamentations of Jeremiah from the Vulgate, for 6 Solo Voices, Chorus, and Orch. (Venice ISCM Festival, Sept. 23, 1958); *A Sermon, a Narrative and a Prayer,* cantata for Speaker, Alto, Tenor, Chorus, and Orch. (1960–62; Basel, Feb. 23, 1962); anthem, *The Dove Descending Breaks the Air,* after T.S. Eliot (Los Angeles, Feb. 19, 1962, Craft conducting); *Elegy for J.F.K.* for Mezzo-soprano or Baritone, 2 Clarinets, and Corno di Bassetto (Los Angeles, April 6, 1964); *Abraham and Isaac,* sacred ballad for Baritone and Chamber Orch., to Hebrew texts (1962–64; Jerusalem, Aug. 23, 1964); *Introitus (T.S. Eliot in Memoriam)* for 6 Male Voices, Harp, Piano, Timpani, Tamtams, Viola, and Double Bass (Chicago, April 17, 1965); *Requiem Canticles* for 4 Vocal Soloists, Chorus, and Orch. (Princeton, N.J., Oct. 8, 1966); *The Owl and the Pussycat,* after Lear, for Voice and Piano (Los Angeles, Oct. 31, 1966).

PIANO: Sonata in F-sharp minor (1903–4; recovered from Leningrad library, 1962; publ. in Russia, 1973); 4 Études, op. 7 (1908); *Le Sacre du printemps* for Piano, 4-hands (1912); 3 *pièces faciles* for Piano, 4-hands (1915); 5 *pièces faciles* for Piano, 4-hands (1917); Étude for Pianola (1917); Piano-Rag-Music (1919); 3 movements from *Pétrouchka* (1921); *Les Cinq Doigts* (1920–21); Sonata (1924); Serenade in A (1925); Concerto for 2 Solo Pianos (1931–35; Paris, Nov. 21, 1935); Tango (1940); Circus Polka (1942); Sonata for 2 Pianos (Edgewood College of the Dominican Sisters, Madison, Wis., Aug. 2, 1944).

NONDESCRIPT: *Do Not Throw Paper Towels in Toilet* for Treble Voice Unaccompanied, to text from poster in men's room at Harvard Univ. (dated Dec. 16, 1939).

WRITINGS: *Chroniques de ma vie* (2 vols., Paris, 1935; in Eng. as *Chronicles of My Life,* London, 1936); *Poétique musicale,* the Charles Eliot Norton Lectures at Harvard Univ. (Paris, 1946; in Eng. as *Poetics of Music,* Cambridge, Mass., 1948); with Robert Craft, 6 vols. of revelatory autobiographical publications: *Conversations with Igor Stravinsky* (N.Y., 1958); *Memories and Commentaries* (N.Y., 1959); *Expositions and Developments* (N.Y., 1962); *Dialogues and a Diary* (N.Y., 1963); *Themes and Episodes* (N.Y., 1967); and *Retrospections and Conclusions* (N.Y., 1969); *Themes and Conclusions,* amalgamated and ed. from *Themes and Episodes* and *Retrospections and Conclusions* (1972); also R. Craft, ed., *Stravinsky: Selected Correspondence* (2 vols., N.Y., 1982 and 1984).

A sharp debate raged, at times to the point of vitriolic polemical exchange, among Stravinsky's associates as to the degree of credibility of Craft's reports in his dialogues, or even of the factual accounts of events during Stravinsky's last years of life. Stravinsky was never a master of the English language; yet Craft quotes him at length as delivering literary paragraphs of impeccable English prose. Craft admitted that he enhanced Stravinsky's actual words and sentences (which were never recorded on tape), articulating the inner, and at times subliminal, sense of his utterances. Craft's role was made clear beyond dispute by Stravinsky himself, who, in a letter to his publishing agent dated March 15, 1958, urged that the title of the book be changed to *Conversations with Igor Stravinsky by Robert Craft,* and emphatically asserted that the text was in Craft's language, and that in effect Craft "created" him.

BIBL.: C. Wise, "Impressions of I. S.," *Musical Quarterly*

(April 1916); R. Chennevière, "The Two Trends of Modern Music in S.'s Works," *Musical Quarterly* (April 1919); B. de Schloezer, *I. S.* (Paris, 1926); A. Casella, *S.* (Rome, 1926); J. Vainkop, *I. S.* (Leningrad, 1927); V. Belaiev, *I. S.'s Les Noces: An Outline* (London, 1928); I. Glebov, *S.* (Leningrad, 1929); C. Ramuz, *Souvenirs sur I. S.* (Paris, 1929; rev. ed., Lausanne, 1946); P. Collaer, *S.* (Brussels, 1930); E. White, *S.'s Sacrifice to Apollo* (London, 1930); H. Fleischer, *S.* (Berlin, 1931); A. Schaeffner, *I. S.* (Paris, 1931); J. Handschin, *I. S.* (Zürich, 1933); E. Evans, *The Firebird and Pétrouchka* (London, 1933); D. de Paoli, *I. S.* (Turin, 1934); M. Blitzstein, "The Phenomenon of S.," *Musical Quarterly* (July 1935); M. Armitage, ed., *S.*, a compendium of articles (N.Y., 1936); S., special issue of *La Revue Musicale* (May–June 1939); A. Kall, "S. in the Chair of Poetry," *Musical Quarterly* (July 1940); S. Babitz, "S.'s Symphony in C," *Musical Quarterly* (Jan. 1941); M. Fardell, *S. et les Ballets Russes* (Nice, 1941); G. Malipiero, S. (Venice, 1945); A. Casella, *S.* (Brescia, 1947, a different work from his book publ. in 1926); E. White, *S.: A Critical Survey* (London, 1947; N.Y., 1948); T. Stravinsky, *Le Message d'I. S.* (Lausanne, 1948; in Eng. as *The Message of I. S.*, London, 1953); A. Tansman, *I. S.* (Paris, 1948; in Eng., 1949); E. Corle, ed., *I. S.* (N.Y., 1949, a compendium of articles, some of them reprinted from M. Armitage's collection of 1936); M. Lederman, ed., *S. in the Theater* (N.Y., 1949); F. Onnen, *S.* (Stockholm, 1949; in Eng.); R. Myers, *Introduction to the Music of S.* (London, 1950); W.H. Auden et al., *I. S.* (Bonn, 1952); H. Strobel, *I. S.* (Zürich, 1956; in Eng. as *S.: Classic Humanist*, N.Y., 1956); special issue of *Score* for S.'s 75th birthday (London, 1957); *I. S.: A Complete Catalogue of His Published Works* (London, 1957); H. Kirchmeyer, *I. S.: Zeitgeschichte im Persönlichkeitsbild* (Regensburg, 1958); R. Vlad, S. (Rome, 1958; in Eng., London, 1960; 3rd ed., 1979); R. Siohan, *S.* (Paris, 1959; in Eng., London, 1966); F. Herzfeld, *I. S.* (Berlin, 1961); special issue of the *Musical Quarterly* on S.'s 80th birthday (July 1962); *S. and the Dance: A Survey of Ballet Productions, 1910–1962* (N.Y. Public Library, 1962); P. Lang, ed., *S.: The Composer and His Works* (London, 1966); E. White, *S.: The Composer and His Works* (Berkeley, Calif., 1966; 2nd ed., 1979); special S. issue of *Tempo* (Summer 1967); A. Boucourechliev, ed., *S.* (Paris, 1968); *The Rite of Spring: Sketches, 1911–1913* (London, 1969); A. Dobrin, *I. S.: His Life and Time* (London, 1970); B. Boretz and E. Cone, eds., *Perspectives on Schoenberg and S.* (N.Y., 1972); P. Horgan, *Encounters with S.* (N.Y., 1972; rev. ed., 1989); L. Libman, *And Music at the Close: S.'s Last Years, A Personal Memoir* (N.Y., 1972); D. De Lerma, *I. S., 1882–1971, A Practical Guide to Publications of His Music* (N.Y., 1974); T. Stravinsky, *Catherine and I. S.: A Family Album* (N.Y., 1973); B. Yarustovsky, ed., *I. S.: Articles and Materials* (Moscow, 1973); V. Stravinsky and R. Craft, *S.* (N.Y., 1975); idem, *S. in Pictures and Documents* (N.Y., 1976); L. Morton, "Footnotes to S.'s Studies: *Le Sacre du printemps*," *Tempo* (1979); R. Taruskin, "Russian Folk Melodies in *The Rite of Spring*," *Journal of the American Musicological Society* (1980); A. Boucourechliev, *I. S.* (Paris, 1982; Eng. tr., 1987); P. Griffiths, *I. S.: The Rake's Progress* (Cambridge, 1982); H. Keller and M. Cosman, *S. Seen and Heard* (London, 1982); A. Schouvaloff and V. Borovsky, *S. on Stage* (London, 1982); C. Joseph, *S. and the Piano* (Ann Arbor, 1983); S. Karlinsky, "S. and Russian Pre-Literate Theater," *19th Century Music* (Spring 1983); M. Ruskin, *I. S.: His Personality, Works and Views* (Cambridge, 1983); V. Scherliess, *I. S. und seine Zeit* (Laaber, 1983); P. van den Toorn, *The Music of I. S.* (London, 1983); J. Pasler, ed., *Confronting S.: Man, Musician, and Modernist* (Berkeley, 1986); J. Straus, "Recompositions by Schoenberg, S., and Webern," *Musical Quarterly*, 3 (1986); E. Haimo and P. Johnson, eds., *S. Retrospectives* (Lincoln, Nebr., 1987); J. Kobler, *Firebird: A Biography of S.* (N.Y., 1987); R. Craft, "The Rite: Counterpoint and Choreography," *Musical Times* (April 1988); P. van den Toorn, *S. and The Rite of Spring: The Beginnings of a Musical Language* (Oxford, 1988); S. Walsh, *The Music of S.* (London and N.Y., 1988); L. Andriessen and E. Schönberger, *The Apollonian Clockwork: On S.* (Oxford, 1989);

A. Pople, *Skryabin and S. 1908–1914: Studies in Theory and Analysis* (N.Y. and London, 1989).

Stravinsky, Sviatoslav Soulima, Russian pianist, son of **Igor (Feodorovich) Stravinsky;** b. Lausanne, Sept. 23, 1910. He studied in Paris with Isidor Philipp and Nadia Boulanger; then gave piano recitals in Europe and America; appeared frequently with his father, playing his works for 2 pianos.

Strayhorn, Billy (William Thomas), black American jazz pianist, composer, and arranger; b. Dayton, Ohio, Nov. 29, 1915; d. N.Y., May 31, 1967. He studied music in Pittsburgh; joined Duke Ellington's band as lyricist and arranger in 1939. Many songs credited to Ellington (*Chelsea Bridge, Perfume Suite, Such Sweet Thunder, A Drum Is a Woman,* etc.) are in fact products of a mutually beneficial musical symbiosis, with Ellington suggesting the initial idea, mood, and character and Strayhorn doing the actual writing, often using Ellington's quasi-impressionistic techniques (modal harmonies, whole-tone scales, etc.). Strayhorn's own acknowledged songs, *Lush Life, Take the "A" Train,* and others, are jazz standards.

Streatfeild, Richard Alexander, English writer on music; b. Edenbridge, June 22, 1866; d. London, Feb. 6, 1919. He studied at Pembroke College, Cambridge; in 1889 became an assistant in the Dept. of Printed Books in the British Museum; was music critic of the *Daily Graphic* (1898–1912).

WRITINGS (all publ. in London unless otherwise given): *Masters of Italian Music* (1895); *The Opera* (1897; 5th ed., rev. and enl., 1925, by E. Dent); *Modern Music and Musicians* (1906); *Handel* (1909; 2nd ed., rev., 1910); *Life and Stories of Great Composers* (Philadelphia, 1910); *Handel Autographs at the British Museum* (1912); *Musiciens anglais contemporains* (French tr., Paris, 1913; Eng. original not publ.); *Handel, Canons and the Duke of Chandos* (1916).

Street, Tison, American composer; b. Boston, May 20, 1943. He studied composition with Kirchner and Del Tredici at Harvard Univ.; received his B.A. (1965) and M.A. (1971) there; also studied violin with Einar Hansen (1951–59); was a composer-in-residence at the Marlboro Music Festival (1964, 1965, 1966, 1972) and a visiting lecturer at the Univ. of Calif., Berkeley (1971–72); taught at Harvard Univ. (1979–82). He was the recipient of an award from the National Inst. of the American Academy of Arts and Letters (1973), the Rome Prize Fellowship (1973), and grants from the NEA (1978) and the Guggenheim Foundation (1981).

WORKS: String Trio (1963); *Variations* for Flute, Guitar, and Cello (1964); *6 Odds and Ends from "So Much Depends"* for Voices and Diverse Instruments (1964–73); String Quartet (1972); String Quintet (1974; rev. 1976); *Piano Phantasy* (1975); *3 Pieces* for consort of Viols and Harpsichord (1977); *John Major's Medley* for Guitar (1977); *Adagio in E-flat* for Oboe and Strings (1977); *Arias* for Violin and Piano (1978); *Montsalvat* for Orch. (1980); *Variations on a Ground* for Organ and Orch. (1981).

Streich, Rita, noted German soprano; b. Barnaul, Russia, Dec. 18, 1920; d. Vienna, March 20, 1987. She studied with Erna Berger, Maria Ivogün, and Willi Domgraf-Fassbänder; made her debut as Zerbinetta in Aussig in 1943; from 1946 she sang with the Berlin State Opera; in 1951 she joined the Berlin Städtische Oper. She also appeared in Vienna, Bayreuth, Salzburg, and Glyndebourne; made her U.S. debut as Zerbinetta with the San Francisco Opera in 1957. In 1974 she became a prof. at the Folkwang-Hochschule in Essen. She was a leading interpreter of parts in Mozart operas.

Streicher, Johann Andreas, German-born Austrian pianist, teacher, piano maker, and composer; b. Stuttgart, Dec. 13, 1761; d. Vienna, May 25, 1833. During a stay in Augsburg in 1793, he married **Nannette (Maria Anna) Stein** (b. Augsburg, Jan. 2, 1769; d. Vienna, Jan. 16, 1835), daughter of the piano maker Johann Andreas Stein, and then moved the business to Vienna; later it became known as Nannette Streicher geb. Stein und Sohn when their son, **Johann Baptist Streicher** (b. Vienna, Jan. 3, 1796; d. there, March 28, 1871), entered the business; following his parents' death, he took complete control of the firm. He invented the piano action in which the hammer strikes from above. He was on friendly terms with Beethoven. In 1857 Streicher's son, Emil (1836–1916), became his partner; the business was dissolved when the latter retired. His son, **Theodor** (b. Vienna, June 7, 1874; d. Wetzelsdorf, near Graz, May 28, 1940), was a composer. He studied elocution with Ferdinand Gregori, counterpoint and composition with Heinrich Schulz-Beuthen, voice with Ferdiana Jäger, and piano and instrumentation with Ferdinand Löwe (1895–1900). He attracted wide notice as a song composer with his *30 Lieder aus Des Knaben Wunderhorn* (1903); he wrote numerous other songs in a Romantic vein, but he was unable to sustain his early success; he also composed choral pieces and a String Sextet (1911).

BIBL.: P. Klanert, *Theodore S. in seinen Liedern* (Leipzig, 1911); T. Bolte, *Die Musiker-Familien Stein und S.* (Vienna, 1917); R. Wursten, *Theodor S.: His Life and Music* (diss., Univ. of Wisconsin, 1977).

Streisand, Barbra (Barbara Joan), popular American singer and actress; b. N.Y., April 24, 1942. She studied acting for a short time in N.Y.; also learned to sing in Greenwich Village. In 1962 she made her Broadway debut in *I Can Get It for You Wholesale;* then made a hit in *Funny Girl* in 1964, a musical she filmed in 1968, and for which she received an Academy Award. Her other films include *On a Clear Day You Can See Forever* (1970), *A Star Is Born* (1976), and *Yentl* (1983). As a recording artist, she received Gold Record awards for her albums *People* (1965), *My Name Is Barbra* (1965), *Color Me Barbra* (1966), *Stony End* (1971), *Barbra Joan Streisand* (1972), *The Way We Were* (1974), *A Star Is Born* (1976), *Superman* (1977), and others.

BIBL.: R. Jordan, *The Greatest Star: The B. S. Story* (N.Y., 1975); J. Spada, *S.: The Woman and the Legend* (Garden City, N.Y., 1981); S. Considene, *B. S.: The Woman, the Myth, the Music* (N.Y., 1985).

Strelezki, Anton, English pianist and composer; b. Croydon, Dec. 5, 1849; d. after 1911. According to some sources, his real name was Burnand. He studied with Clara Schumann; settled in London, where he was very popular. He publ. a great deal of piano music (more than 225 opus numbers), some of which was widely known: *Valse-Souvenir; Jagdstück; Valsette; Sérénade espagnole; Menuet à l'antique; Barcarolle;* also songs; publ. *Personal Recollections of Chats with Liszt* (1895).

Strelnikov, Nikolai, Russian composer; b. St. Petersburg, May 14, 1888; d. there (Leningrad), April 12, 1939. He studied composition with Liadov in St. Petersburg; in 1922 he became music director of the Young People's Theater in Leningrad. He wrote 2 operas, *A Fugitive* (Leningrad, May 26, 1933) and *Count Nulin,* after Pushkin (1935); but he is chiefly remembered for his operettas: *The Black Amulet* (Leningrad, 1927); *Luna-Park* (Moscow, 1928); *The Heart of a Poet* (Leningrad, 1934); *Presidents and Bananas* (1939). Other works include a Piano Concerto, choruses, and chamber music. He also publ. monographs on several Russian composers.

Strens, Jules, Belgian organist and composer; b. Ixelles, near Brussels, Dec. 5, 1892; d. there, March 19, 1971. He studied with Paul Gilson; in 1925 was one of 8 founders of the Group des Synthétistes (all Gilson pupils), endeavoring to establish a modern style of composition within the formal categories of early music; was active mainly as an organist.

WORKS: OPERAS: *Le Chanteur de Naples* (1937); *La Tragédie d'Agamemnon* (1941). **ORCH.:** *Gil Blas,* symphonic variations (1921); *Les Elfes,* symphonic poem (1923); *Danse funambulesque* (1925); *Rapsodie tzigane* (1927); *Fantaisie concertante* for Piano and Orch. (1938); *Symphonie Sylvestre* for Soli, Chorus, and Orch. (1939); Violin Concerto (1951); Concerto for Organ and String Orch. (1958). **CHAMBER:** Piano Trio (1920); 4 string quartets (1925, 1929, 1933, 1935); Cello Sonata (1926); String Sextet (1935); Wind Quintet (1943); Quartet for 4 Horns (1950); *Suite* for 4 Horns (1951); Viola Sonata (1954); Trio

for Oboe, Clarinet, and Bassoon (1954); Piano Quartet (1955); also piano pieces; organ pieces; songs.

Strepponi, Giuseppina (actually, **Clelia Maria Josepha**), prominent Italian soprano, 2nd wife of **Giuseppe Verdi;** b. Lodi, Sept. 8, 1815; d. Sant' Agata, near Busseto, Nov. 14, 1897. She was the daughter of Felician Strepponi (1797–1832), organist at Monza Cathedral and a composer of operas. She studied piano and singing at the Milan Cons. (1830–34), taking 1st prize for bel canto; after making her operatic debut in Adria (Dec. 1834), she scored her 1st success in Rossini's *Matilda di Shabran* in Trieste (1835); that same year she sang Adalgisa and the heroine in *La Sonnambula* in Vienna, the latter role becoming one of her most celebrated portrayals. She subsequently toured widely with the tenor Napoleone Moriani, who became her lover. In 1839 she made her debut at Milan's La Scala; created Donizetti's Adelia in Rome in 1841; returning to La Scala, she created Verdi's Abigaille on March 9, 1842, but by then her vocal powers were in decline; all the same, she continued to sing in Verdi's operas, having become a favorite of the composer. In 1846 she retired from the opera stage; from 1847 she lived with Verdi, becoming his wife in 1859.

BIBL.: E. de Amicis, "G. Verdi-S.," *Nuovi ritratti letterari ed artistici* (Milan, 1902); M. Mundula, *La Moglie di Verdi: G. S.* (Milan, 1938); C. Sartori, "La S. e Verdi a Parigi nella morsa quarantottesca," *Nuova Rivista Musicale Italiana,* VIII (1974).

Stresemann, Wolfgang, German conductor and orchestral Intendant; b. Dresden, July 20, 1904. His father, Gustav Stresemann, was the distinguished chancellor and foreign minister of the Weimar Republic. He was educated in Berlin, Heidelberg, and Erlangen (Dr.Jur., 1928); also studied music in Berlin. After the Nazis came to power (1933), he left Germany and eventually settled in the U.S. He served as assistant conductor of the National Orch. Assoc. in N.Y. (1939–45); then conducted the Toledo (Ohio) Orch. (1949–55). He returned to Germany and held the post of Intendant of the (West) Berlin Radio Sym. Orch. (1956–59). In 1959 he assumed the prestigious post of Intendant of the Berlin Phil., with Herbert von Karajan as its artistic director. He retired in 1978, only to be recalled to his post in 1984 during the so-called Karajan affair, when the chief conductor and the musicians of the orch. locked horns in a bitter artistic dispute. After serving as mediator, Stresemann continued as Intendant until retiring for a second time in 1986. He wrote an informative history of the Berlin Phil., *The Berlin Philharmonic from Bülow to Karajan: Home and History of a World-Famous Orchestra* (in German and Eng.; Berlin, 1979); likewise publ. *Eine Lanze für Felix Mendelssohn* (Berlin, 1984). He also composed some orch. music and songs.

Strickland, Lily (Teresa), American composer; b. Anderson, S.C., Jan. 28, 1887; d. Hendersonville, N.C., June 6, 1958. She studied at Converse College in Spartanburg, S.C. (1901–4) and then with Albert Mildenberg, William Henry Humiston, Daniel Gregory Mason, and Percy Goetschius at the Inst. of Musical Art in N.Y.; also received private lessons from Alfred John Goodrich. She married J. Courtney Anderson of N.Y. in 1912; traveled in the Orient between 1920 and 1930, and spent several years in India; then returned to the U.S. Among her works were several operettas, including *Jewel of the Desert* (1933) and *Laughing Star of Zuni* (1946), orch. suites, the sacred cantata *St. John the Beloved* (1930), numerous songs (*Mah Lindy Lou, Dreamin' Time, Songs of India, Song from High Hills,* etc.), and many piano suites (*Moroccan Mosaics, Egyptian Scenes, Himalayan Idylls,* etc.).

BIBL.: A. Howe, *L. S.: Her Contribution to American Music in the Early Twentieth Century* (diss., Catholic Univ. of America, 1968).

Strickland, William, American conductor; b. Defiance, Ohio, Jan. 25, 1914. He studied organ and singing; then devoted himself to conducting; founded the National Youth Administration Sinfonietta in N.Y. in 1940; entered the U.S. Army in 1941; was appointed warrant officer and instructor at the Army Music School at Fort Myer, Va., in 1942; organized the Army Music School Choir, which he conducted in Washington, D.C., including a performance at the White House. After discharge from the army, he founded the Nashville (Tenn.) Sym. Orch. and led it from 1946 to 1951. In 1953 he conducted in Austria; returning to the U.S., he was music director of the Oratorio Soc. of N.Y. (1955–59); also made guest appearances as a radio conductor. In 1958 he went on a tour of Asia; conducted in Manila, Tokyo, and Seoul; in 1962 he went on a European trip; conducted guest engagements in Scandinavia, in Poland, and in Germany (until 1969). He devoted himself mainly to conducting American music.

Striegler, Kurt, German conductor, teacher, and composer; b. Dresden, Jan. 7, 1886; d. Wildthurn, near Landau, Aug. 4, 1958. He studied with Draeseke at the Dresden Cons. He became répétiteur at the Dresden Opera in 1905, and then conductor there in 1912; was associated with the company until 1945, and also taught at the Dresden Hochschule für Musik (1905–45). In 1945 he became director of the Coburg Cons. He went to Munich in 1950. He wrote the operas *Der Thomaskantor* and *Hand und Herz* (Dresden, 1924); 4 syms.; Violin Concerto; Cello Concerto; *Scherzo* for 7 Kettledrums, with Orch.; much chamber music; numerous choruses; songs and piano pieces.

Striggio, Alessandro, eminent Italian instrumentalist and composer; b. Mantua, c.1540; d. there, Feb. 29, 1592. By the 1560s he was the major composer at the court of Cosimo I de' Medici, Duke of Florence; in 1584 he was active at the court of Alfonso II d'Este in Ferrara, but that same year went to Mantua as court composer; all the same, he remained associated with the courts in Ferrara and Florence until his death; also wrote works for the Munich court. His importance rests upon his music for intermedi, stage works, and madrigals, including the 3 musical intermezzi *Psiche ed Amore* (1565). He publ. several books of madrigals and *Il cicalamento delle donne* (1567; descriptive songs in the manner of Janequin); many compositions by Striggio are found in collections of the period. His son, **Alessandro,** known as **Alessandrino** (b. Mantua, c.1573; d. Venice, June 15, 1630), was a librettist, musician, diplomat, and nobleman; studied law in Mantua and then was a diplomat in the service of the Gonzaga family there; was made secretary to Duke Vincenzo I in 1611 and later was ambassador to Milan; died of the plague while on a diplomatic mission to Venice. He wrote the librettos to Monteverdi's *Orfeo* (Mantua, 1607), *Lamento d'Apollo* (not extant), and probably *Tirsi e Clori* (1615).
BIBL.: O. Sonneck, "A Description of A. S. and Francesco Corteccia's Intermedi 'Psyche and Amor', 1565," *Miscellaneous Studies in the History of Music* (N.Y., 1921); R. Tadlock, "A. S., Madrigalist," *Journal of the American Musicological Society,* XI (1958); idem, *The Early Madrigals of A. S.* (diss., Univ. of Rochester, 1958).

Strimer, Joseph, Russian-American pianist, teacher, and composer; b. Rostov-on-the-Don, Oct. 21, 1881; d. N.Y., Jan. 1962. He studied with Rimsky-Korsakov, Liadov, Steinberg, Tcherepnin, and Glazunov at the St. Petersburg Cons.; then conducting with Nikisch in Germany; settled in N.Y. as a piano and composition teacher. He publ. a number of piano pieces; paraphrases of works by Rimsky-Korsakov, Borodin, Liadov, etc.; arrangements of folk songs.

Stringfield, Lamar (Edwin), American flutist, conductor, and composer; b. Raleigh, N.C., Oct. 10, 1897; d. Asheville, N.C., Jan. 21, 1959. He served in the U.S. Army during World War I; after the Armistice, he studied music theory with Goetschius and flute with Georges Barrère at the Inst. of Musical Art in N.Y.; also took lessons in conducting with Chalmers Clifton. In 1930 he organized the Inst. of Folk Music at the Univ. of North Carolina, and conducted its orch.; was conductor of the Knoxville Sym. Orch. (1946–47), then of the Charlotte

Sym. Orch. (1948–49). The source material of his compositions is largely derived from the folk songs of the U.S. South. He learned the trade of printing and was able to publ. his own works. He wrote *America and Her Music* (Chapel Hill, 1931) and a *Guide for Young Flutists* (MS, c.1945; included in the Nelson diss. listed in the bibliography below).
WORKS: STAGE: Opera, *The Mountain Song* (1929); musical folk-drama, *Carolina Charcoal* (1951–53); ballet, *The 7th Queue* (1928). **ORCH.:** *Indian Legend* (1923); suite, *From the Southern Mountains* (1928; contains his best-known piece, *Cripple Creek*); *A Negro Parade* (1931); *Moods of a Moonshiner* (1934); *Mountain Dawn* for Flute and String Orch. (1945). **CHAMBER:** *Chipmunks* for Flute, Clarinet, and Bassoon; *From a Negro Melody* for 12 Instruments; *Indian Sketches* for Flute and String Quartet; *Virginia Dare Dance* for Wind Quintet; also vocal works, including *About Dixie* for Chorus and Orch. (1950); songs.
BIBL.: D. Nelson, *The Life and Works of L. S. (1897–1959)* (diss., Univ. of North Carolina, 1971).

Stringham, Edwin John, American music educator and composer; b. Kenosha, Wis., July 11, 1890; d. Chapel Hill, N.C., July 1, 1974. He studied at Northwestern Univ. and at the Cincinnati Cons.; in 1920 he went to Italy, where he took lessons in composition with Respighi. Returning to the U.S., he occupied teaching posts at the Denver College of Music (1920–29), Teachers College of Columbia Univ. (1930–38), Juilliard School of Music in N.Y. (1930–45), and Queens College of the City Univ. of N.Y. (1938–46). In 1948 he settled in Chapel Hill. He publ. the books *Listening to Music Creatively* (N.Y., 1943; rev. ed., 1959) and *Creative Harmony and Musicianship* (with H.A. Murphy, N.Y., 1951).
WORKS: Orch.: *Visions,* symphonic poem (1924); *The Ancient Mariner,* after Coleridge (Denver, March 16, 1928); Sym. No. 1 (Minneapolis, Nov. 15, 1929); *Fantasy on American Folk Tunes* for Violin and Orch. (1942); chamber music; songs.

Strobel, Heinrich, eminent German musicologist, music critic, and administrator; b. Regensburg, May 31, 1898; d. Baden-Baden, Aug. 18, 1970. He studied musicology with Sandberger and Kroyer and theory with H.K. Schmidt at the Univ. of Munich (Ph.D., 1922, with the diss. *Johann Wilhelm Hässlers Leben und Werke*). He was music critic of the *Thüringer Allgemeine Zeitung* in Erfurt (from 1921) and of the *Börsenkurier* (1927–33) and *Tageblatt* (1934–38) in Berlin; also was the ed. of *Melos* (1933–34) and of the *Neue Musikblatt* (1934–39). In 1939 he went to Paris; in 1946 he returned to Germany and again became ed. of *Melos;* that same year he also was made director of music at the South-West German Radio in Baden-Baden; in 1956 he became chairman of the ISCM He devoted himself energetically to the cause of modern music; wrote numerous articles on the subject; promoted programs of avant-garde composers on the radio and at various festivals in Germany.
WRITINGS: *Paul Hindemith* (Mainz, 1928; 3rd ed., enl., 1948); *Claude Debussy* (Zürich, 1940; 5th German ed., 1961; French ed., Paris, 1942); *Igor Stravinsky* (Zürich, 1956; in Eng. as *Stravinsky: Classic Humanist,* N.Y., 1956).

Strobel, Otto, German musicologist; b. Munich, Aug. 20, 1895; d. Bayreuth, Feb. 23, 1953. He studied at the Univ. of Munich (Ph.D., 1924, with the diss. *Richard Wagner über sein Schaffen: Ein Beitrag zur "Künstlerästhetek"*; publ. in Munich, 1924). After working as an archivist at the Wahnfried Archives in Bayreuth (from 1932), he was director of the short-lived Richard Wagner Forschungsstätte (1938). He publ. *Richard Wagner: Skizzen und Entwürfe zur Ring-Dichtung* (Munich, 1930); *Genie am Werk: Richard Wagners Schaffen und Wirken im Spiegel eigenhandschriftlicher Urkunden: Führer durch die einmalige Ausstellung einer umfassenden Auswahl von Schätzen aus dem Archiv des Hauses Wahnfried* (Bayreuth, 1933; 2nd ed., rev., 1934); *Richard Wagner: Leben und Schaffen: Eine Zeittafel* (Bayreuth, 1952).

Stroe, Aurel, Rumanian composer; b. Bucharest, May 5, 1932. He studied harmony with Negrea, composition with Andricu, and orchestration with Rogalski at the Bucharest Cons. (1951–56); had a course in electronic music in Munich (1966) and attended the annual summer courses in new music given in Darmstadt (1966–69) by Kagel, Ligeti, and Stockhausen; in 1962 he joined the faculty of the Bucharest Cons.; also worked at the Bucharest Computing Center (1966–69). His early music is rooted in folklore, but in his later period he experimented with sonoristic constructions, some of which were put together by computerized calculations.

WORKS: OPERAS: *Ça n'aura pas le Prix Nobel* (*Anceastă piesă nu va primi premiul Nobel*; 1969; Kassel, Nov. 28, 1971); *De Ptolemaeo*, mini-opera for Tape (1970); *Aristophane: La Paix* (1972–73); *Orestia II* (*Purtatoarele de prinoase*), chamber opera (1974–77; Bucharest, Nov. 14, 1978). **MUSIC THEATER:** *Agamemnon* (*Orestia I*) (1979–81; Bucharest, March 1, 1983). **ORCH.:** Concerto for String Orch. (1956; Bucharest, Dec. 22, 1957); *Uvertură burlescă* (1961); *Arcade* for 11 Instrumental Formations (1962); *Muzică de concert* for Piano, Percussion, and Brass (1964–65; Cluj, April 2, 1966); *Laudes I* for 28 Strings (1966) and *II* for 12 Instrumental Formations (1968); *Canto I* (1967) and *II* (1971) for 12 Instrumental Formations; Clarinet Concerto (1974–75). **CHAMBER:** Trio for Oboe, Clarinet, and Bassoon (1953); Piano Sonata (1955); *Rêver, c'est desengrener les temps superposés II* for Clarinet, Cello, and Harpsichord (1970); String Quartet (1972); *Quintandre*, quintet for Flute, Oboe, Clarinet, Bassoon, and Horn (1984); Piano Sonata No. 2 (1984); *Anamorphoses canoniques* for 3 Flutes, Clarinet, Clavichord, Trombone, Cello, and Tape (1984). **VOCAL:** *Chipul păcii*, chamber cantata for Mezzo-soprano, Chorus, and Chamber Orch. (1959); *Monumentum* for Men's Voices and Orch. (1961); *Numai prin timp poate fi timpul cucerit* (Only through Time, Time Is Conquered) for Baritone, Organ, 4 Trombones, and 4 Gongs, after T.S. Eliot (1965); *Il giardino delle Strutture + Rime de Michelangelo* for Baritone, Trombone, Violin, Viola, Cello, Harpsichord, and Tape (1975); *Monumentum II* for Mezzo-soprano, Percussion, Double Bass, and Tape (1982); various solo songs.

Strohm, Reinhard, German musicologist; b. Munich, Aug. 4, 1942. He studied with Georgiades at the Univ. of Munich and Dahlhaus at Berlin's Technical Univ. (Ph.D., 1971, with the diss. *Italienische Opernarien des frühen Settecento [1720–1730]*, 2 vols., Cologne, 1976); was assistant ed. of the Richard-Wagner-Ausgabe (1970–81); also lectured on music at King's College, Univ. of London (1975–83); then was prof. of music history at Yale Univ. (from 1983). He publ. several valuable books, among them *Music in Late Medieval Bruges* (1985), *Essays on Handel and Italian Opera* (1985), and *Music in Late Medieval Europe* (1987).

Strong, George Templeton, American composer; b. N.Y., May 26, 1856; d. Geneva, June 27, 1948. He was the son of the N.Y. lawyer G.T. Strong, who was also a music-lover, and whose diary, expressing his dislike of Liszt and Wagner, was publ. in 1952. From him, and from his mother, who was an amateur pianist, Strong received his 1st training. In 1879 he went to Leipzig, where he studied with Jadassohn. He entered the Liszt circle at Weimar, and became an adherent of program music; from 1886 to 1889 he lived in Wiesbaden, where he became friendly with MacDowell; he returned briefly to America, and taught theory at the New England Cons. in Boston (1891–92); then went back to Europe and settled in Switzerland. He expressed his indignation at the lack of recognition of American composers in their own country; most performances of his works took place in Switzerland. In 1930 he donated many of his original MSS to the Library of Congress in Washington, D.C. Toscanini performed his orch. suite *Die Nacht* with the NBC Sym. Orch. in N.Y. on Oct. 21, 1939; his other symphonic suite, *Une Vie d'artiste* for Violin and Orch., was presented at the 20th festival of the Assoc. des Musiciens Suisses at Zürich in June 1920; he also wrote 3 syms.: No. 1, *In den Bergen*; No. 2, *Sintram*; No. 3, *An der See*; and the symphonic poems *Undine* and *Le Roi Arthur*.

BIBL.: P. Scholes, "An American Composer: G.T. S.," *Music Student*, VII (1915); J. Matthey, *Inventaire du fonds musical G.T. S.* (Lausanne, 1973); V. Lawrence, *S. on Music: The New York Music Scene in the Days of G.T. S., 1836–1875: Vol. I: Resonances, 1836–1850* (Oxford and N.Y., 1988).

Strouse, Charles (Louis), American composer; b. N.Y., June 7, 1928. He studied at the Eastman School of Music in Rochester, N.Y., and later took private lessons in composition with Aaron Copland and Nadia Boulanger, under whose guidance he wrote some ambitious instrumental music. He was mainly active as a composer for Broadway and films; with the lyricist Lee Adams (b. Mansfield, Ohio, Aug. 14, 1924), he wrote the musicals *Bye Bye Birdie* (N.Y., April 16, 1960) and *Applause* (N.Y., March 30, 1970), both of which won Tony awards. His other musicals include *Golden Boy* (N.Y., Oct. 20, 1964), after a play by Clifford Odets, and *Annie* (N.Y., April 21, 1977). He also composed a Piano Concerto and other orch. pieces and a String Quartet.

Strozzi, Piero, amateur Italian composer; b. Florence, c.1550; d. there, after Sept. 1, 1609. He was a nobleman; was a member of the Bardi circle in Florence, and one of the creators of the "stile rappresentativo," leading to the development of opera. With Caccini, Merulo, and Striggio, he wrote the festival music for the wedding of Francesco de' Medici in 1579; in 1596 he set to music Rinuccini's libretto *La mascherata degli accecati*; 2 madrigals by Strozzi are in Luca Bati's *Secondo libro di madrigali* (Venice, 1598).

Strube, Gustav, German-American composer and music educator; b. Ballenstedt, March 3, 1867; d. Baltimore, Feb. 2, 1953. He was taught the violin by his father, and later by Brodsky at the Leipzig Cons.; was a member of the Gewandhaus Orch. there until 1891, when he emigrated to America; was a violinist in the Boston Sym. Orch. from 1891 to 1913; also conducted the Boston Pops Orch. (1898; 1900–1902; 1905–12); then taught theory and conducting at the Peabody Cons. in Baltimore (from 1913), where he also was its director (1916–46). In 1916 he was appointed conductor of the newly organized Baltimore Sym. Orch., which he led until 1930. He publ. a useful manual, *The Theory and Use of Chords: A Textbook of Harmony* (Boston, 1928).

WORKS: OPERA: *Ramona* (1916; later renamed *The Captive*). **ORCH.:** Sym., "Lanier," after Sidney Lanier (Washington, D.C., March 17, 1925, composer conducting); *Sinfonietta* (1922); *Symphonic Prologue* (Baltimore, April 24, 1927, composer conducting); 2 violin concertos (1924, 1930); *Americana* (1930); *Harz Mountains*, symphonic poem (1940); *Peace Overture* (1945). **CHAMBER:** 2 string quartets (1923, 1936); 2 violin sonatas (1923); Viola Sonata (1924); Cello Sonata (1925); Piano Trio (1925); Quintet for Wind Instruments (1930).

BIBL.: G. Klemm, "G. S.: The Man and the Musician," *Musical Quarterly* (July 1942).

Strungk, Delphin, esteemed German organist and composer, father of **Nicolaus Adam Strungk**; b. 1600 or 1601; d. Braunschweig (buried), Oct. 12, 1694. He was organist at Wolfenbüttel's principal church (1630–32), the Celle court (1632–37), and Braunschweig's Marienkirche (from 1637) and other churches. He wrote vocal works and organ music.

BIBL.: M. Seiffert, "Zur Biographie D. Strunck's," *Archiv für Musikwissenschaft*, II (1919–20).

Strungk, Nicolaus Adam, prominent German violinist, organist, and composer, son of **Delphin Strungk**; b. Braunschweig (baptized), Nov. 15, 1640; d. Dresden, Sept. 23, 1700. He studied with his father, whose assistant he became at the age of 12 at the Church of St. Magnus in Braunschweig; studied violin at Lübeck under Schnittelbach while attending Helmstedt Univ. At 20 he became 1st violinist in the Wolfenbüttel court chapel; a short time later, he went to the Celle court. After appearing as a violinist at the Vienna court chapel in 1661 he decided to pursue his career there until 1665; then was in the service of the Hannover court chapel. In 1678 Strungk became music director of Hamburg's Cathedral and of the city; wrote and produced operas in German (in keeping with the nationalist trend of the time), among them *Der glück-lich-steigende Sejanus* and its sequel, *Der unglücklich-fallende Sejanus* (1678), *Alceste* (1680), *Die Liebreiche, durch Tugend und Schönheit erhöhete Esther* (1680), *Doris, oder der königliche Sklave* (1680), *Semiramis* (1681), *Theseus* (1681), and *Floretto* (1683). From 1682 to 1686 he was court organist and composer in Hannover; also visited Italy in 1685, meeting Corelli in Rome. In 1688 he became Vice-Kapellmeister and chamber organist in Dresden, succeeding Carlo Pallavicino, whose unfinished opera *L'Antiope* he completed and produced there in 1689. In this post he was beset with difficulties arising from friction with Italian musicians, and only managed to maintain his authority through the intervention of his patron, the Elector Johann Georg III; when Bernhard, Kapellmeister in Dresden, died in 1692, Strungk was appointed to succeed him. In 1693 he organized an opera company in Leipzig; between 1693 and 1700 he wrote 16 operas for it, among them *Alceste* (perf. at the inauguration of the Leipzig opera house, May 18, 1693), *Nero* (1693), *Syrinx* (1694), *Phocas* (1696), *Ixion* (1697), *Scipio und Hannibal* (1698), *Agrippina* (1699), and *Erechtheus* (1700). Financially, the enterprise was a failure, but Strungk continued to receive his salary from Dresden until his retirement on a pension in 1697. He publ. the important manual *Musicalische Übung auf der Violine oder Viola da Gamba in etlichen Sonaten über die Festgesänge, ingleichen etlichen Ciaconen mit 2 Violinen bestehend* (1691). A selection of airs from his operas was publ. in Hamburg under the title *Ein hundert auserlesenen Arien zweyer Hamburgischen Operen, Semiramis und Esther. Mit beigefügten Ritornellen* (1684). Among his instrumental works, a Sonata for 2 Violins and Viola da Gamba and several other sonatas are extant; MS No. 5056 of the Yale Univ. Music Library (Lowell Mason Collection) contains capriccios and ricercari by Strungk, among them the *Ricercar sopra la Morte della mia carissima Madre Catherina Maria Stubenrauen* (Venice, 1685). Six capriccios and a Ricercare by Strungk, included in Denkmäler der Tonkunst in Österreich, 17 (13.ii), are wrongly ascribed to Georg Reutter (Senior).

BIBL.: F. Zelle, *J. Theile und N.A. S.* (Berlin, 1891); F. Berend, *N.A. S., 1640–1700: Sein Leben und seine Werke. Mit Beiträgen zur Geschichte der Musik und des Theater in Celle, Hannover, und Leipzig* (Freiburg, 1915); G. Frotscher, *Geschichte des Orgelspiels* (Vol. I, Berlin, 1934).

Strunk, (William) Oliver, distinguished American musicologist; b. Ithaca, N.Y., March 22, 1901; d. Grottaferrata, Italy, Feb. 24, 1980. He studied at Cornell Univ. (1917–19); in 1927 took a course in musicology with Otto Kinkeldey there; then entered the Univ. of Berlin to study musicology with J. Wolf (1927–28). Returning to America, he served as a member of the staff of the Music Division at the Library of Congress in Washington, D.C. (1928–34), and then was head of its music division (1934–37). In 1937 he was appointed to the faculty of Princeton Univ.; after retirement in 1966, he lived mostly in Italy. He was a founding member of the American Musicological Soc., serving as the 1st ed. of its journal (1948) and as its president (1959–60); he was director of Monumenta Musicae Byzantinae (1961–71). He publ. *State and Resources of Musicology in the U.S.* (Washington, D.C., 1932) and the extremely valuable documentary *Source Readings in Music History* (N.Y., 1950). Collections of his writings were publ. as *Essays on Music in the Western World* (N.Y., 1974) and *Essays on Music in the Byzantine World* (N.Y., 1977).

BIBL.: H. Powers, ed., *Studies in Music History: Essays for O. S.* (Princeton, N.J., 1968).

Stuart, Leslie (real name, **Thomas Augustine Barrett**), English organist and composer; b. Southport, March 15, 1864; d. Richmond, Surrey, March 27, 1928. He was a church organist in various provincial towns in England; settled in London in 1895, and soon became known as a composer of popular songs. He achieved enormous success with his operetta *Floradora*, produced in London on Nov. 11, 1899, and subsequently performed in England and America for many seasons, but failed to duplicate this success in any of his later works, which included *The Silver Slipper* (1901); *The School Girl* (1903); *The Belles of Mayfair* (1906); *Havana* (1908); *Captain Kidd* and *The Slim Princess* (1910); *Peggy* (1911).

Stuck, Jean-Baptiste, distinguished Italian-born French cellist and composer of German descent; b. probably in Livorno, 1680; d. Paris, Dec. 8, 1755. He began his career as a cellist in Italy, then went to France in the service of the Prince of Carignam. He was in the service of Elector Max Emanuel of Bavaria about 1714; returning to France, he was ordinaire de la musique du Roy until being pensioned in 1748; also appeared at the Concert Spirituel. In 1733 he became a naturalized French citizen. He won great renown as a cellist; was also a notable composer of cantatas, of which he publ. 4 books (1706, 1708, 1711, 1714); his other works include 3 insignificant operas: *Méléagre* (Paris, May 24, 1709); *Manto la fée* (1709; Paris, Jan. 29, 1711); *Polidore* (Paris, Feb. 15, 1720); also ballets for the Versailles court; airs in contemporary collections.

BIBL.: M. Barthélemy, "Les Cantates de J.-B. S.," *Recherches sur la Musique Française Classique,* II (1962); S. Milliot, "J.-B. S.," ibid., XI (1969).

Stucken, Frank Van Der. See Van Der Stucken, Frank.

Stuckenschmidt, Hans Heinz, eminent German music critic and writer on music; b. Strasbourg, Nov. 1, 1901; d. Berlin, Aug. 15, 1988. He studied violin, piano, and composition; was chief music critic of Prague's *Bohemia* (1928–29) and of the *Berliner Zeitung am Mittag* (1929–34); also was active as a lecturer on contemporary music. In 1934 he was forbidden to continue journalism in Germany, and went to Prague, where he wrote music criticism until 1941, when his activities were stopped once more by the occupation authorities; was drafted into the German army; in 1946 he became director of the dept. for new music of the radio station RIAS in Berlin; also was a lecturer (1948–49), reader (1949–53), and prof. (1953–67) of music history at the Technical Univ. there. With Josef Rufer, he founded and ed. the journal *Stimmen* (Berlin, 1947–49).

WRITINGS: *Arnold Schönberg* (Zürich and Freiburg, 1951; 2nd ed., 1957; Eng. tr., 1960); *Neue Musik zwischen den beiden Kriegen* (Berlin and Frankfurt am Main, 1951); *Strawinsky und sein Jahrhundert* (Berlin, 1957); *Schöpfer der neuen Musik* (Frankfurt am Main, 1958); *Boris Blacher* (Berlin, 1963); *Oper in dieser Zeit* (Velber, 1964); *Johann Nepomuk David* (Wiesbaden, 1965); *Maurice Ravel: Variationen über Person und Werk* (Frankfurt am Main, 1966; Eng. tr., 1968); *Ferruccio Busoni. Zeittafel eines Europäers* (Zürich, 1967; Eng. tr., 1970); *Twentieth Century Music* (London, 1968; German original, 1969); *Twentieth Century Composers* (London, 1970; German original, 1971); *Schönberg: Leben, Umwelt, Werk* (Zürich, 1974; Eng. tr., 1976); *Die Musik eines halben Jahrhunderts: 1925–1975* (Munich, 1976); *Schöfer klassischer Musik: Bildnisse und Revisionen* (Berlin, 1983).

BIBL.: W. Burde, ed., *Aspekte der neuen Musik: Professor H.H. S. zum 65. Geburtstag* (Kassel, 1968).

Stückgold, Grete (née **Schneidt**), German soprano; b. London (of a German father and an English mother), June 6, 1895; d. Falls Village, Conn., Sept. 13, 1977. She studied voice with **Jacques Stückgold,** whom she married (divorced in 1928); later married **Gustav Schützendorf.** She commenced her career as a concert and oratorio singer; made her operatic debut in Nuremberg in 1917; joined the Berlin State Opera in 1922. On Nov. 2, 1927, she made her Metropolitan Opera debut in N.Y. as Eva in *Die Meistersinger von Nürnberg*; she continued to make appearances there until 1939; also sang in San Francisco, Philadelphia, and Chicago. She later taught voice at Bennington (Vt.) College.

Stückgold, Jacques, Polish singing teacher; b. Warsaw, Jan. 29, 1877; d. N.Y., May 4, 1953. He studied in Venice; taught voice in Germany (1899–1903), where **Grete** (née **Schneidt**) Stückgold became his pupil and wife (divorced, 1928); settled in N.Y. in 1933. He publ. *Der Bankrott der deutschen Gesangskunst* and *Über Stimmbildungskunst.*

Stucky, Steven (Edward), American composer; b. Hutchinson, Kans., Nov. 7, 1949. He studied composition with Richard Willis at Baylor Univ. (B.M., 1971) and with Husa, Phillips, and Palmer at Cornell Univ. (M.F.A., 1973; D.M.A., 1978). He was a visiting faculty member at Lawrence Univ. in Appleton, Wis. (1978–80); in 1980 he joined the faculty of Cornell Univ., where he became a prof. in 1991; also served as composer-in-residence of the Los Angeles Phil. (1988–91). In 1986 he held a Guggenheim fellowship. He publ. the study *Lutoslawski and His Music* (Cambridge, 1981), which won the ASCAP–Deems Taylor Award. His music is tonal and brightly colored.

WORKS: ORCH.: *Prelude and Toccata* (1969); 4 syms.: No. 1 (1972); No. 2 (1974); No. 3 (1976); No. 4, *Kennigar* (1978); *Transparent Things: In Memoriam V. N.* (1980); *Voyages* for Voice and Wind Orch. (New Haven, Conn., Dec. 7, 1984); Double Concerto for Violin, Oboe/Oboe d'Amore, and Chamber Orch. (1982–85; rev. 1989); *Dreamwaltzes* (Minneapolis, July 17, 1986); *Concerto for Orchestra* (1986–87; Philadelphia, Oct. 27, 1988); *Son et lumière* (1986; Baltimore, May 18, 1988); *Angelus* (1990). CHAMBER: *4 Bagatelles,* string quartet (1969); *3 Songs* for Soprano, Clarinet, Viola, and Piano (1969); *Duo* for Viola and Cello (1969); *Movements* for Cello Quartet (1970); *Divertimento* for Clarinet, Piano, and Percussion (1971); Quartet for Clarinet, Viola, Cello, and Piano (1973); *Sappho Fragments* for Soprano and 6 Instruments (1982); *Boston Fancies* for Chamber Ensemble (1985); *Threnos* for Wind Ensemble (1987–88); Woodwind Quintet (1990).

Studer, Cheryl, American soprano; b. Midland, Mich., Oct. 24, 1955. After training in Ohio and at the Univ. of Tennessee, she studied voice with Hans Hotter at the Vienna Hochschule für Musik. She appeared in concerts in the U.S. before singing at the Bavarian State Opera in Munich in 1980; then was a member of the Darmstadt Opera (1983–85). In 1984 she made her U.S. operatic debut as Micaëla at the Chicago Lyric Opera. In 1985 she joined the Deutsche Oper in West Berlin. She also sang at the Bayreuth Festivals (from 1985), at the Paris Opéra (from 1986), and at La Scala in Milan (from 1987). Among her prominent roles are Pamina, Donna Anna, Elsa, Eva, Sieglinde, and Chrysothemis.

Stumpf, (Friedrich) Carl, eminent German psychologist, acoustician, and musicologist; b. Wiesentheid, Lower Franconia, April 21, 1848; d. Berlin, Dec. 25, 1936. He studied philosophy and theology at the Univ. of Würzburg, and philosophy and natural sciences at the Univ. of Göttingen, where he took his Ph.D. (1870) and completed his Habilitation (1873). He was a prof. of philosophy at the Univs. of Würzburg (1873–79), Prague (1879–84), Halle (1884–89), Munich (1889–93), and Berlin (1893–1928). In 1893 he founded the Psychological Inst. in Berlin; its purpose was a scientific analysis of tonal psychology as it affected musical perception; but, realizing the utterly speculative and arbitrary premises of his theories, he revised them, and proposed the concepts of Konkordanz and Diskordanz to describe the relative euphony of triads and chords of several different notes. With his pupils Hornbostel and Abraham, he founded the Berlin Phonogrammarchiv in 1900. Stumpf publ. *Beiträge zur Akustik und Musikwissenschaft* (1898–1924), which incorporated his evolving theories, and, with Hornbostel, issued the *Sammelbände für vergleichende Musikwissenschaft* (1922–23); also contributed numerous articles to scholarly publications.

WRITINGS: *Tonpsychologie* (2 vols., Leipzig, 1883, 1890; reprint, Hilversum, 1965); *Geschichte des Konsonanzbegriffs* (Munich, 1901); *Die Anfänge der Musik* (Leipzig, 1911); *Die Sprachlaute. Experimentell-phonetische Untersuchungen nebst einem Anhang über Instrumentalklänge* (Berlin, 1926).

BIBL.: *Festscrift für C. S.* (Berlin, 1919); *C. S. zum 75. Geburtstag* (Berlin, 1923); E. Schumann, "Die Förderung der Musikwissenschaft durch die akustisch-psychologische Forschung C. S.s," *Archiv für Musikwissenschaft,* V (1923); C. Sachs, "Zu C. S.s achtzigstem Geburtstag," *Zeitschrift für Musikwissenschaft,* 10 (1927–28); N. Hartmann, *Gedächtnisrede C. S.* (Berlin, 1937).

Stuntz, Joseph Hartmann, Swiss conductor and composer of German descent; b. Arlesheim, near Basel, July 23, 1793; d. Munich, June 18, 1859. He studied with Peter von Winter in Munich (1808–12) and with Salieri in Vienna (1813–16); then returned to Munich as conductor of the Italian Opera, where he produced his successful opera *La rappresaglia* (composed 1818–20); in 1825 he was named conductor of the German Opera, but shortly afterward assumed the conductorship of the Court Orch., a position he retained for the rest of his life. He wrote the singspiel *Heinrich IV zu Givry* (Munich, 1820), the tragic opera *Maria Rosa* (Munich, n.d.), many ballets, cantatas, masses, choruses, and songs.

BIBL.: K. Gross, *J.H. S. als Opernkomponist* (diss., Univ. of Munich, 1934).

Stupka, František, Czech conductor; b. Tedrazice, Jan. 18, 1879; d. Prague, Nov. 24, 1965. He studied violin with Ševčik at the Prague Cons., graduating in 1901; then went to Russia, where he became a violin teacher at the Odessa Cons. He left Russia after the Revolution; served as 2nd conductor of the Czech Phil. in Prague (1919–39); also was a guest conductor with various European orchs. He specialized in the repertoire of Czech composers.

Sturgeon, Nicholas, English divine and composer; place and date of birth unknown; d. between May 31 and June 8, 1454. He was elected a scholar at Winchester College in 1399; held several canonries, including 1 at St. Paul's Cathedral in London (from 1432), where he was precentor (from 1442); also was a member of the royal household chapel. He was the owner, and possibly the scribe, of the MSS found in Old Hall, near Ware; 7 works by Sturgeon (2 not complete) are part of the Old Hall MS collection, including a curious isorhythmic motet, *Salve mater Domini,* for 3 Voices, which was probably written for the journey of Henry V to France (1416), on which Sturgeon accompanied him. A. Hughes and M. Bent, eds., publ. *The Old Hall Manuscript,* in Corpus Mensurabilis Musicae, XLVI (1969–72).

Stürmer, Bruno, German conductor, teacher, and composer; b. Freiburg im Breisgau, Sept. 9, 1892; d. Bad Homburg, May 19, 1958. He studied piano at the Karlsruhe Cons.; then organ and composition with Wolfrum at the Univ. of Heidelberg, and musicology with Sandberger and Kroyer at the Univ. of Munich. He taught piano in Karlsruhe (1917–22); was theater conductor in Remscheid, Essen, and Duisburg (1922–27); in 1927 he founded a music school in Homburg; then was a conductor of choral societies in Kassel and elsewhere (until 1945). He was a prolific composer (about 150 opus numbers) in a distinctly modern manner; was particularly adept at choral writing. He publ. the book *Frisch fröhlich woll'n wir singen* (Cologne, 1956).

WORKS: *Die Messe des Maschinenmenschen* for Baritone, Male Chorus, and Orch. (1932); dance drama, *Die Maske der Katze;* cantatas with Orch.: *Von der Vergänglichkeit, Vom Tod zum Leben, Aus Liebe, Gott in der Natur;* for Voice, with Chamber Groups: *Erlösungen, Marienlieder, Lieder der Geischa, Lieder aus den Lüften, Musikantenleben, Das Lied vom Kinde,* etc.; *Der Zug des Todes* for 8-part Chorus and Percussion; *Der Rattenfänger von Hamelin* for Baritone, Children's Chorus, and Chamber Orch.; Requiem; many choruses; several instrumental concertos; much chamber music.

Sturzenegger, (Hans) Richard, Swiss cellist, teacher, and composer; b. Zürich, Dec. 18, 1905; d. Bern, Oct. 24, 1976. He studied cello with F. Reitz at the Zürich Cons. and later had lessons with Alexanian and Casals; took a course in composition with Boulanger at the École Normale de Musique in Paris (1924–27); then studied cello with Feuermann and composition with Toch in Berlin (1929–33); returning to Switzerland, he was a member of the Bern String Quartet (1935–49); taught cello at the Bern Cons. (1935–63) and chamber music at the Zürich Cons. (1954–63). In 1963 he became director of the Bern Cons.

WORKS: OPERA: *Atalante* (1963–68). ORCH.: 4 cello concertos (1933, 1937, 1947, 1974); *Triptychon* (1951); *3 Gesänge Davids* for Violin and Orch. (1963); *Fresco* for String Orch. (1965); *Chorale Fantasy* for Contralto, Strings, Trumpet, and Drums (1941); *Cantico di San Francesco* for Chorus, Strings, and Harp (1945); *Richardis*, festival music for Chorus, Wind Orch., and Organ (1949). **CHAMBER:** Sonata for Solo Cello (1934); String Trio (1937); 2 string quartets (1940, 1974); Cello Sonata (1950); *Elegie* for Cello, Oboe, Harp, Viola, Cello, and Double Bass (1950); Piano Trio (1964).

BIBL.: R. S., *Werkverzeichnis* (Zürich, 1970); E. Hochuli, ed., *Variationen: Festgabe für R. S. zum siebzigsten Geburtstag* (Bern, 1975).

Stutschewsky, Joachim, Russian-born Israeli cellist, pedagogue, ethnomusicologist, and composer; b. Romny, Feb. 7, 1892; d. Tel Aviv, Nov. 14, 1982. He received his early education at a music school in Kherson; as a youth, played cello in various orchs. in southern Russia; then studied cello with J. Klengel and orch. playing with H. Sitt at the Leipzig Cons. (1909–12). After playing in the Jena Quartet, he was active as a performer, teacher, and editor in Zürich (1914–24) and Vienna (1924–38), where he entered the circle of Schoenberg, Berg, and Webern. Together with the violinist Rudolf Kolisch, he formed the Wiener Streichquartett (later known as the Kolisch String Quartet). With the usurpation of Austria by the Nazi hordes in 1938, Stutschewsky emigrated to Palestine, and eventually became an Israeli citizen. From 1939 to 1948 he served as inspector of music in the cultural section of the Jewish National Council. In his early compositions, he followed median modern techniques; then began a study of Jewish folklore in diaspora, and wrote music of profound racial feeling, set in the framework of advanced harmonies. He also contributed to the study of cello techniques and to ethnomusicology.

WRITINGS: *Die Kunst des Cellospiels* (Vols. 1–2, Mainz, 1929; Vols. 3–4, Vienna, 1938); *Mein Weg zur jüdischen Musik* (Vienna, 1935); *Musika yehudit* (Jewish Music; Tel Aviv, 1946); *The Cello and Its Masters: History of Cello Playing* (MS, 1950); *Klezmerim* (Tel Aviv, 1959); *Musical Folklore of Eastern Jewry* (Tel Aviv, 1959); *Korot hayav shel musikai yehudi* (The Life of a Jewish Musician; Tel Aviv, 1975).

WORKS: *Dreykut* for Cello and Piano (1924); *Palestinian Sketches* for Piano (1931); Duo for Violin and Cello (1940); *Hassidic Suite* for Cello and Piano (1946); *Israeli Landscapes* for Piano (1949); *Legend* for Cello and Piano (1952); *Israeli Dances* for Flute, Cello, and Piano (1953); *Verschollene Klänge* for Flute, String Quartet, and Percussion (1955); *Hassidic Fantasy* for Clarinet, Cello, and Piano (1956); Piano Trio (1956); *5 Pieces* for Flute (1956); String Quartet (1956); *Songs of Radiant Sadness*, cantata for Soloists, Chorus, Speaking Chorus, and Orch. (1958); Concertino for Clarinet and Strings (1958); *Terzetto* for Oboe, Clarinet, and Bassoon (1959); *Fantasy* for Oboe, Harp, and Strings (1959); String Trio (1960); Wind Sextet (1960); symphonic poem, *Safed* (1960); chamber cantata, *Jemama baschimscha* (24 Hours in the Looking Glass) for Narrator, 2 Sopranos, and 6 Instruments (1960); *Israeli Suite* for Cello and Piano (1962); *Monologue* for Clarinet (1962); *3 Pieces* for Bassoon (1963); *Moods* for Oboe (1963); *Impressions* for Clarinet and Bassoon (1963); *Soliloquy* for Viola (1964); *3 Miniatures* for 2 Flutes (1964); symphonic suite, *Israel* (1964; Tel Aviv, May 7, 1973); *Kol Kore* (Calling Voice) for Horn (1965); *Fragments* for 2 Clarinets (1966); *4 Movements* for Wind Quintet (1967); *3 for 3*, 3 pieces for 3 Cellos (1967); *4 Inattendus* for Piano (1967); Woodwind Quintet (1967); *Visions* for Flute (1968); *Thoughts and Feelings* for Violin (1969); *Prelude and Fugue* for 2 Trumpets and 2 Trombones (1969); *Monologue* for Trombone (1970); *Dialogues variés* for 2 Trumpets (1970); *Imaginations* for Flute, Violin, Cello, and Piano (1971); *Kol Nidrei* for Cello and Piano (1972); *The Rabbi's Nigun* for Cello and Piano (1974); *Sine nomine* for Cello (1975); *Splinters* for Piano (1975); *2 Pieces* for Double Bass (1975); numerous arrangements for cello of works by Mozart, Tartini, and Boccherini.

BIBL.: *J. S.'s 70th Anniversary: Catalogue of Works* (Tel Aviv, 1971).

Styne, Jule (real name, **Julius Kerwin Stein**), English-born American composer of popular music; b. London, Dec. 31, 1905. He was taught piano by his parents; was taken to the U.S. at the age of 8; appeared with the Chicago Sym. Orch. as a child pianist, but did not pursue a concert career; won a scholarship to the Chicago College of Music at 13; after playing piano in jazz groups and dance bands, he went to Hollywood (1940) and rapidly established himself as a successful song composer for films; also was notably successful as a composer of Broadway musicals (from 1947), which include *High Button Shoes* (Oct. 9, 1947), *Gentlemen Prefer Blondes* (Dec. 8, 1949; rev. as *Lorelei*, 1974), *Bells Are Ringing* (Nov. 29, 1956), *Gypsy*, to the life story of the striptease artist Gypsy Rose Lee (May 21, 1959), *Do Re Mi* (Dec. 26, 1960), *Funny Girl*, to the life story of the singer Fanny Brice (March 26, 1964), *Hallelujah, Baby!* (April 26, 1967), and *Sugar* (April 9, 1972).

BIBL.: T. Taylor, J. (N.Y., 1979).

Subirá (Puig), José, eminent Spanish musicologist; b. Barcelona, Aug. 20, 1882; d. Madrid, Jan. 5, 1980. He studied piano and composition at the Madrid Cons. and simultaneously qualified for the practice of law (Dr.Jur., 1923); then held various government posts in Madrid while pursuing musicological research. In 1952 he was elected a member of the Real Academia de Bellas Artes de San Fernando in Madrid. Apart from his scholarly pursuits, he publ. a novel, *Su virginal pureze* (1916), and a historical account, *Los Españoles en la guerra de 1914–1918* (4 vols.).

WRITINGS: *Enrique Granados* (Madrid, 1926); *La música en la Casa de Alba* (Madrid, 1927); *La participación musical en el antiguo teatro español* (Barcelona, 1930); *Tonadillas teatrales inéditas: Libretos y partituras* (Madrid, 1932); *"Celos aun del aire matan": Opera del siglo XVII, texto de Calderón y música de Juan Hidalgo* (Barcelona, 1933); *La tonadilla escénica: Sus obras y sus autores* (Barcelona, 1933); *Historia de la música teatral en España* (Barcelona, 1945); with H. Anglés, *Catálogo musical de la Biblioteca Nacional de Madrid* (Barcelona, 1946–51); *La ópera en los teatros de Barcelona* (Barcelona, 1946); *Historia de la música Salvat* (Barcelona, 1947; 3rd ed., enl., 1958); *Historia y ancedotario del Teatro Real* (Madrid, 1949); *El compositor Iriarte (1750–1791) y el cultivo español del melólogo (melodrama)* (Barcelona, 1949–50); *La música, etapas y aspectos* (Barcelona, 1949); *El teatro del Real palacio (1849–1851), con un bosquejo preliminar sobre la música palatina desde Felipe V hasta Isabel II* (Madrid, 1950); *Historia de la música española e hispanoamericana* (Barcelona, 1958); *Temas musicales madrileños* (Madrid, 1971).

Subono, Blacius, popular Indonesian composer and dhalang (shadow puppet master), brother of **Yohanes Subowo**; b. Klaten, Central Java, Feb. 3, 1954. He was born into an artistic family, the 7th of 9 children who all became successful artists. He began his music studies at 6, often accompanying his father, the shadow puppet master Yusuf Kiyatdiharjo; at 12, began to perform alone. While at the high school cons. Konservatori Karawitan (KOKAR), he helped to create a new form of puppet theater, *wayang kancil*, featuring a cast of animal characters and new musical arrangements; at the college cons. Akademi Seni Karawiten Indonesia (A.S.K.I., later Sekolah Tinggi Seni Indonesia [S.T.S.I.]) Surakarta, he was encouraged by its director, S.D. Humardani, to try his hand at musical experimentation. He composed several new works, including another wayang innovation, *wayang sandosa*; in 1983 he attended the national Pekan Komponis Muda (Young Composer's Festival) in Jakarta. He received numerous commissions and invitations to perform the 9-hour *wayang kulit*; performed and lectured in France (1982), Singapore (1982), England and Spain (1984), and Canada and the U.S. (1986); in 1990 he lectured at Simon Fraser Univ. in Vancouver, where he composed his 1st work with an English text. Subono's output includes popular songs with gamelan accompaniment as well as experimental scores, i.e., 1 for a chamber ensemble made up of only very high-pitched instruments (*griting rasa*), 1 for a wide range of knobbed gongs (*swara pencon*), and several unrealized pieces for very large chorus. His publications concerning musical accompaniment for the new, intensified style of *wayang kulit* called *pakeliran padat* include *Iringan Pakeliran Dewasa Ini* (1981), *Kuliah Letihan Tabuh Iringan Pakeliran Padat di ASKI Surakarta* (1984), and *Evaluasi Garap Iringan Pakeliran Padat* (1987).

WORKS (all scored for Central Javanese gamelan): **EXPERIMENTAL:** *Swara Pencon* (1983); *Swara Pencon II* (1986); *Griting Rasa* (1989). **DANCE:** *Komposisi Hitam Putih* (1980); *Rudrah* (1981); *Bisma Gugur* (1982); *Ronggolawe Gugur* (1982); *Kusumo Asih* (1983); *Anila Prahastho* (1985); *Bhagawatgita* (1985); *Gathutkaca Burisrawa* (1985); *Jemparingan* (1985); *Anoman Kataksini* (1986); *Rahwana Gandrung* (1987). **SHADOW PUPPET THEATER (PAKELIRAN PADAT):** *Kangsa Lena* (1983); *Kilat Buana* (1984); *Duryudana Gugur* (1985); *Gandamana Tundhung* (1985). **DANCE OPERA (WAYANG ORANG):** *Seno Kridho* (1984). **MODERN SHADOW PUPPET THEATER (WAYANG SANDOSA):** *Karna Tandhing* (1982); *Dewa Ruci* (1983); *Ciptaning* (1984). **SONGS:** *Pungjir* (1974); *Kidang Kencana* (1980); *Surakarta Lejer Budaya* (1982); *Solo Berseri* (1985); *Gotong Royong* (1985); *Bingung* (1986); *Air Minum* (1987); *Palinglih* (1987); *Sukaharja Papanku* (1987); *Urip Prasaja* (1987); also scripts for puppet theater with animal characters only (*wayang kancil*) and for dance opera (*wayang orang*).

Subotnick, Morton, American composer and teacher; b. Los Angeles, April 14, 1933. He studied at the Univ. of Denver (B.A., 1958) and with Milhaud and Kirchner at Mills College in Oakland, Calif. (M.A., 1960); then was a fellow of the Inst. for Advanced Musical Studies at Princeton Univ. (1959–60). He taught at Mills College (1959–66), N.Y. Univ. (1966–69), and the Calif. Inst. of the Arts (from 1969); also held various visiting professorships and composer-in-residence positions. In 1979 he married **Joan La Barbara.** His compositions run the gamut of avant-garde techniques, often with innovative use of electronics.

WORKS: ORCH.: *Play! No. 2* for Orch. and Tape (1964); *Lamination* for Orch. and Tape (1968); *Lamination No. 2* for Chamber Ensemble and Electronics (1969); *Before the Butterfly* for 7 Solo Instruments and Orch. (1975; Los Angeles, Feb. 26, 1976); *2 Butterflies* for Amplified Orch. (1975); *Place* (1978); *Axolotl* for Cello, Chamber Orch., and Electronics (1982); *Liquid Strata* for Piano, Orch., and Electronics (1982); *The Key to Songs* for Chamber Orch. and Synthesizer (1985); *In 2 Worlds,* concerto for Saxophone, Electronic Wind Controller, and Orch. (1987–88); *And the Butterflies Began to Sing* for YCAMS and Chamber Ensemble (1988). **MIXED MEDIA:** *Mr. and Mrs. Discobolos* for Clarinet, Violin, Cello, Narrator-Mime, and Tape (1958); *Sound Blocks* for Narrator, Violin, Cello, Xylophone, Marimba, Tape, and Lights (1961); *Mandolin* for Viola, Tape, and Film (1963); *Play! No. 1* for Wind Quintet, Tape, and Film (1963); *Play! No. 3* for Piano, Tape, and Film (1964); *Play! No. 4* for 4 Actors, Performers, Piano, Vibraphone, Cello, and 2 Films (1965); *4 Butterflies* for Tape and 3 Films (1973); *The Double Life of Amphibians,* theater piece (1984). **VOCAL:** *2 Life Histories* for Male Voice, Clarinet, and Electronics (1977); *Last Dream of the Beast* for Female Voice and Electronics (1978); *Jacob's Room* for Voice and String Quartet (1984; San Francisco, Jan. 11, 1985). **INCIDENTAL MUSIC TO:** Genet's *The Balcony* (1960); Shakespeare's *King Lear* (1960); Brecht's *Galileo* (1964) and *The Caucasian Chalk Circle* (1965); Büchner's *Danton's Death* (1966). **INSTRUMENTAL:** *Prelude No. 1* (*The Blind Owl*) for Piano (1956); *Prelude No. 2* (*The Feast*) for Piano (1956); *Viola Sonata* (1959); *String Quartet* (1960); *Sonata for Piano, 4-hands* (1960); *Serenade No. 1* for Flute, Clarinet, Vibraphone, Mandolin, Cello, and Piano (1960) and *No. 2* for Clarinet, Horn, Percussion, and Piano (1962); *10 for 10 Instruments* (1963–76); *The Tarot* for Chamber Ensemble (1965); *The Fluttering of Wings* for String Quartet (1982). **INSTRUMENTAL AND ELECTRONICS:** *Preludes Nos. 3–4* for Piano and Tape (1962–65); *Serenade No. 3* for Flute, Clarinet, Violin,

Piano, and Tape (1963); *Liquid Strata* for Piano and Electronics (1977); *Parallel Lines* for Piccolo, 9 Instruments, and Electronics (1978); *Passages of the Beast* for Clarinet and Electronics (1978); *The Wild Beasts* for Trombone, Piano, and Electronics (1978); *After the Butterfly* for Trumpet, 7 Instruments, and Electronics (1979); *The 1st Dream of Light* for Tuba, Piano, and Electronics (1979); *Ascent into Air* for 10 Instruments and Electronics (1981); *An Arsenal of Defense* for Viola and Electronics (1982); *Tremblings* for Violin, Piano, and Electronics (1983). **TAPE:** *The 5-legged Stool* (1963); *Parades and Changes* (1967); *Silver Apples of the Moon* (1967); *Realty I and II* (1968); *The Wild Bull* (1968); *Touch* (1969); *Sidewinder* (1971); *Until Spring* (1975); *Ice Floe* (1978); *A Sky of Cloudless Sulphur* (1978); *Sky with Clouds* (1978).

BIBL.: H. Whipple, "Beasts and Butterflies: M. S.'s Ghost Scores," *Musical Quarterly* (Oct. 1983).

Subowo, Yohanes, Indonesian dancer and composer, brother of **Blacius Subono;** b. Klaten, Central Java, Jan. 1, 1960. He was born into an artistic family (his 8 older siblings were professional artists), and although he wanted to join the army, he was persuaded by his father, the shadow puppet master (dhalang) Yusuf Kiyatdiharjo, to pursue a career in the arts. After studying dance and composition at Institute Seni Indonesia (I.S.I., National Arts Inst.; graduated, 1986), he joined its dance faculty. In 1982 he began experimenting with instruments other than those of the Javanese gamelan; made small instruments from bamboo, tuning them to the gamelan, using cowbells, tin roofing sheets, and whistles made from bamboo and coconut leaves; also transposed music using techniques from Javanese gamelan to such Western instruments as electronic keyboards. In some compositions he imposes strict limitations on pitch and/or instrumentation and also experiments with such extended vocal techniques as having singers sing into bamboo tubes or bronze pot-gongs. His compositions borrow their structures from jazz, rock, and Western Classical styles, while drawing on African and popular Indonesian music; these include *Orak-Arik, Lesung* (1981), *Gobyog* (1982), *Kentongan, Patmo* (1982), and *Tanggung* (1984), variously scored for Javanese gamelan, found objects, farm tools, and electronic and original instruments. His current project is a piece wherein all sounds are made by devices attached to a dancer's body. In 1985 he toured England as both a dancer and a musician.

Sucher, Josef, Hungarian conductor and composer, husband of **Rosa** (née **Hasselbeck**) **Sucher;** b. Döbör, Nov. 23, 1843; d. Berlin, April 4, 1908. He studied in Vienna with Sechter; was made a répétiteur (1870) and an assistant conductor (1873) at the Court Opera there, and then was conductor at the city's Komische Theater (1874–76). He was conductor of the Leipzig City Theater (1876–78), where he married Rosa Hasselbeck in 1877; they were at the Hamburg Stadttheater from 1878 to 1888; Sucher then became conductor of the Berlin Royal Opera, his wife being engaged there as prima donna; he left the Berlin post in 1899. He was especially distinguished as an interpreter of the Wagnerian repertoire. He composed several vocal works: *Aus alten Märchen* for Women's Voices, with Orch.; *Waldfräulein* for Soprano Solo, Chorus, and Orch.; *Seeschlacht bei Lepanto* for Male Chorus and Orch.; songs.

Sucher, Rosa (née **Hasselbeck**), German soprano, wife of **Josef Sucher;** b. Velburg, Feb. 23, 1849; d. Eschweiler, April 16, 1927. She received her early musical training from her father, a chorus master; sang in provincial operas, then in Leipzig, where she married Josef Sucher in 1877; they subsequently were engaged at the Hamburg Stadttheater (1878–88). In 1882 she made her London debut as Elsa in *Lohengrin*; in 1886 she appeared in Vienna. She made regular visits to the Bayreuth Festivals (1886–96) and was a principal member of the Berlin Royal Opera (1888–98). On June 8, 1892, she made her Covent Garden debut in London as the *Siegfried* Brünnhilde; on Feb. 25, 1895, she made her American debut as Isolde at the Metropolitan Opera in N.Y., under the sponsorship of the Damrosch Opera Co. In 1903 she gave her farewell operatic performance in Berlin as Sieglinde. In 1908 she settled in Vienna as a voice teacher. She publ. her memoirs, *Aus meinem Leben* (Leipzig, 1914). Among her other fine roles were Euryanthe, Elisabeth, and Senta.

Suchoff, Benjamin, distinguished American music educator and musicologist; b. N.Y., Jan. 19, 1918. He studied at Cornell Univ. (B.S., 1940), then took courses in composition with Vittorio Giannini at the Juilliard School of Music in N.Y. (1940–41). After serving in the U.S. Army in Europe and Asia in World War II, he resumed his studies, 1st at Juilliard (1946–47) and then at N.Y. Univ. (M.A., 1949; Ed.D., 1956, with the diss. *Guide to Bartók's Mikrokosmos*; publ. in London, 1957; 3rd ed., N.Y., 1982). From 1950 to 1978 he was administrator of music at Hewlett-Woodmere Union Free School on Long Island, where he also taught electronic music. From 1973 to 1984 he was adjunct prof. of arts and letters at the State Univ. of N.Y. at Stony Brook; also was director of its special collections and of the Center for Contemporary Arts and Letters, where he guided the fortunes of the COMMPUTE Program, a consortium of institutions active in research and development of computer-oriented music studies. In 1953 he became curator of the N.Y. Bartók Archive; in 1968 was made successor-trustee of the Bartók estate. He is the ed. of the N.Y. Bartók Archive edition of Bartók's writings in English trs. in its Studies in Musicology series; also is ed. of its edition of Bartók's compositions, known as *The Archive Edition*.

Suchoň, Eugen, significant Slovak composer; b. Pezinok, Sept. 25, 1908. He studied piano and composition with Kafenda at the Bratislava School of Music (1920–28); then took a course in advanced composition with Vítězslav Novák at the Master School of the Prague Cons. (1931–33). He taught composition at the Bratislava Academy of Music (1933–48) and music education at the Univ. of Bratislava (1949–60); was a prof. of music theory there from 1959 to 1974; in 1971 he was appointed prof. at the College of Music and Dramatic Art in Bratislava. In 1958 he was named National Artist of the Republic of Czechoslovakia. He is one of the creators of the modern Slovak style of composition, based on authentic folk motifs and couched in appropriately congenial harmonies. **WORKS: OPERAS:** *Krútňava* (The Whirlpool; 1941–49; Bratislava, Dec. 10, 1949); *Svätopluk* (1952–59; Bratislava, March 10, 1960). **ORCH.:** *Fantasy and Burlesque* for Violin and Orch. (originally a *Burlesque*, 1933; the *Fantasy* was added in 1948); *Balladic Suite* for Orch. or Piano (1935); *Metamorphoses*, symphonic variations (1951–52); *Sinfonietta rustica* (1956); *6 Pieces* for String Ensemble or String Quartet (1955–63); *Rhapsodic Suite* for Piano and Orch. (1965); *Kaleidoscope*, 6 cycles for String Orch., Percussion, and Piano (1967–68); *Symphonic Fantasy on B-A-C-H* for Organ, Strings, and Percussion (1971); *Clarinet Concertino* (1975); *Prielom Symphony* (1976). **VOCAL:** *Nox et solitudo* for Soprano, and Small Orch. or Piano (1933); *Carpathian Psalm*, cantata (1937–38); *Ad astra*, 5 songs for Soprano and Small Orch. (1961); *Contemplations* for Narrator and Piano (1964). **CHAMBER:** Violin Sonata (1930); String Quartet (1931; rev. 1939); *Serenade* for Wind Quintet (1931); Piano Quartet (1932–33); Violin Sonatina (1937); *Poème macabre* for Violin and Piano (1963); piano pieces, including a *Toccata* (1973). **BIBL.:** E. Zavarský, *E. S.* (Bratislava, 1955); J. Kresánek, *Národný umelec E. S.* (National Artist E. S.; Bratislava, 1961).

Suchý, František, Czech composer; b. Březové Hory u Příbrami, April 21, 1891; d. Prague, June 13, 1973. He studied at the local teaching inst. (1906–10); after studies with Horník and Stecker at the Prague Cons. (1913–14), he received lessons in conducting from Nikisch in Leipzig (1914–16); subsequently was active as a teacher, conductor, and composer. **WORKS:** Operas: *Lásky div* (The Wonder of Love; 1923); *Havéři* (The Miners; 1947–57); ballet: *Porcelánové království* (The Porcelain Kingdom; 1922); also *Rokoková suita* (Rococo Suite) for Small Orch. (1931); *Stříbrné město* (The Silver Town), sym. (1935); choruses; songs; piano pieces.

Suchý, František, Czech oboist and composer; b. Libina u Šumperka, April 9, 1902; d. Brno, July 12, 1977. He studied

oboe with Wagner and composition with Kvapil at the Brno Cons. (graduated, 1927); then attended Novák's master classes at the Prague Cons. (until 1937); was 1st oboist in the Brno Radio Orch. (1927–47); then was a prof. of oboe at the Cons. and a prof. of oboe and theory at the Academy in Brno. **WORKS:** *Maryla*, opera (1956); Flute Concerto (1939); *Baroque Concerto* for Violin and Orch. (1944); 4 syms. (1946, 1950, 1957, 1962); Oboe Concerto (1948); *Vysočina* (Uplands), symphonic suite (1957); *V. Gethsemané*, oratorio (1933); cantatas; songs; Sonatina for Oboe and Piano (1927); 2 wind quintets (1928, 1958); Wind Sextet (1960); various sonatas.

Suckling, Norman, English pianist, teacher, writer on music, and composer; b. London, Oct. 24, 1904. He received his academic education at Queen's College, Oxford, specializing in French literature; was assistant master at Liverpool Collegiate School (1925–43); then was a lecturer in French language and literature at King's College, Newcastle upon Tyne, in the Federal Univ. of Durham (1943–70). While thus occupied, he developed sufficient mastery of the piano to give concerts, at which he presented programs of modern French music. He publ. a monograph on Gabriel Fauré (London, 1946) and several books on French literature; also contributed articles on English and French composers to the *Listener* and other literary publications. His compositions are mostly in small forms; his songs are particularly fine. **WORKS:** *Introduction and Scherzo* for String Quartet (1923); *Ode* for Violin and Piano (1925); *A Vision of Avalon*, chamber opera (1928); *A Cycle of Shakespeare Sonnets* for Tenor, Violin, and Piano (1928); Violin Sonata (1928); *Man in the Beginning*, ballet (1934); *Berceuse élégiaque* for Clarinet and Piano, to commemorate a pet kitten, and written for the composer's 1st wife (1943); *Pastorale saugrenue* for Flute and Bassoon (1944); *Variations on a Theme of Rameau* for Flute and Piano (1947); many songs to words by English poets.

Suda, Stanislav, blind Czech flutist and composer; b. Starý Plzenec, April 30, 1865; d. Plzen, Sept. 2, 1931. He was brought up at the Prague Inst. for the Blind, and developed his innate musical abilities to the point where he could give concerts and compose operas, 3 of which were produced at Plzen: *U Božích Muk* (March 22, 1897); *Lešetínský Kovář* (April 4, 1903); *Il divino Boemo* (Dec. 30, 1927). He also wrote an autobiographical symphonic poem, *Život ve tmách* (The Life in Darkness).

Sudds, William, English-American composer; b. London, March 5, 1843; d. Gouverneur, N.Y., Sept. 25, 1920. He was taken to America as a child; was a bandmaster during the Civil War; studied violin with Eichberg in Boston; wrote over 100 piano pieces, about 75 pieces of church music, many songs, etc. He publ. 2 albums of organ music, *Organ Gems* and *50 Organ Voluntaries*; also guides to violin playing.

Suesse, Dana, American composer of popular music; b. Kansas City, Dec. 3, 1911; d. N.Y., Oct. 16, 1987. She took piano lessons with Siloti and composition with Rubin Goldmark in N.Y.; traveled to Paris for lessons with Nadia Boulanger. She played piano in Paul Whiteman's band; wrote *Symphonic Waltzes* and *Jazz Concerto* for him. Her most famous popular song was *You Oughta Be in Pictures*.

Sugár, Rezső, Hungarian composer; b. Budapest, Oct. 9, 1919; d. there, Sept. 22, 1988. He was a pupil of Kodály at the Budapest Academy of Music (1937–42); taught in Budapest at the Béla Bartók Cons. (1949–68); from 1968 to 1980 he taught at the Academy of Music. **WORKS: BALLET:** *Acisz és Galatea* (Acis and Galatea; 1957; rev. 1961 as *A tenger lánya* [The Daughter of the Sea]). **ORCH.:** *Divertimento* for String Orch. (1948); *Rondo* for Piano and String Orch. (1952); *Concerto in Memoriam Béla Bartók* (1962); *Metamorfosi* (1966); *Partita* for String Orch. (1967); *Variation Symphony* (1970); *Epilogue* (1974); Concertino for Chamber Orch. (1976); *Pastorale e rondo* (1978). **VOCAL: ORATORIOS:** *Hunyadi: Hősi ének* (Hunyadi: Heroic Song; 1951); *Paraszti háború* (Peasant War; 1976); *Savonarola* (1979). **CANTATA:** *Kőmíves Kelemen* (Kelemen, the Mason; 1958); numerous choral pieces; songs. CHAMBER: *Serenade* for 2 Violins and Viola (1943); Violin Sonata (1946); 3 string quartets (1947, 1950, 1969); *Frammenti musicali*, sextet for Piano and Wind Quintet (1958); *Rhapsody* for Cello and Piano (1959); also *Baroque Sonatina* for Piano (1943–46).

Suggia, Guilhermina, gifted Portuguese cellist; b. Oporto, June 27, 1888; d. there, July 31, 1950. She was a child prodigy and made her 1st public appearance at age 7; became 1st cellist in the Oporto Orch. when she was 12. Under the patronage of the Queen of Portugal, she was sent to Leipzig in 1904 to study with Julius Klengel; in 1905 she joined the Gewandhaus Orch. there. In 1906 she began studies with Casals; they subsequently lived and toured together, although they were never legally married; she appeared in concerts as Mme. Casals-Suggia until they parted company in 1912. Shortly afterward she settled in London, where she continued to appear in concerts until 1949, when she went back to Portugal. She was greatly appreciated for her fine musicianship as well as virtuosity. In 1923 Augustus John painted her portrait, which became famous.

Suitner, Otmar, Austrian conductor; b. Innsbruck, May 16, 1922. He studied piano at the Innsbruck Cons. and then piano with Ledwinka and conducting with Krauss at the Salzburg Mozarteum (1940–42). In 1945 he conducted at the Innsbruck Landestheater; was then music director in Remscheid (1952–57) and Generalmusikdirektor in Ludwigshafen (1957–60). From 1960 to 1964 he served as Generalmusikdirektor of the Dresden State Opera and Dresden State Orch.; from 1964 to 1971, conducted at the East Berlin State Opera, and from 1974 to 1991 was its Generalmusikdirektor. He also conducted in America; was a guest conductor with the San Francisco Opera.

Suk (I), Josef, eminent Czech violinist, pedagogue, and composer, grandfather of **Josef Suk (II);** b. Křečovice, Jan. 4, 1874; d. Benešov, near Prague, May 29, 1935. He received training in piano, violin, and organ from his father, Josef Suk (1827–1913), the Křečovice school- and choirmaster; then took courses in violin with Bennewitz, in theory with Foerster, Knittl, and Stecker, and in chamber music with Wihan at the Prague Cons. (1885–91); after graduating in 1891, he pursued additional training in chamber music with Wihan and in composition with Dvořák at the Cons. (1891–92). In 1898 he married Dvořák's daughter Otilie. He began his career playing 2nd violin in Wihan's string quartet, which became known as the Czech Quartet in 1892; he remained a member of it until his retirement in 1933. He also was a prof. of composition at the Prague Cons. (from 1922), where he was head of its master classes; also served as its rector (1924–26; 1933–35). Suk's early works were greatly influenced by Dvořák; in later years his lyrical Romantic style evolved into an individual style characterized by polytonal writing and harmonic complexity bordering on atonality.

WORKS: ORCH. (all 1st perf. in Prague unless otherwise given): *Fantasie* for Strings (1888; Jan. 29, 1940); *Smueteční pochod* (Funeral March; 1889; rev. 1934; June 3, 1935); *Dramatická overtura*, op. 4 (1891–92; July 9, 1892); *Serenade* for Strings, op. 6 (1892; Feb. 25, 1894); *Pohádka zimního večera* (Tale of a Winter's Evening), overture after Shakespeare, op. 9 (1894; April 7, 1895; rev. 1918, 1925); 2 syms.: No. 1 in E major, op. 14 (1897–99; Nov. 25, 1899); No. 2, *Asrael*, op. 27 (1905–6; Feb. 3, 1907); *Pohádka* (Fairy Tale), suite from *Radús a Mahulena*, op. 16 (1899–1900; Feb. 7, 1901); *Fantasie* for Violin and Orch., op. 24 (1902–3; Jan. 9, 1904); *Fantastické scherzo*, op. 25 (1903; April 18, 1905); *Praga*, symphonic poem, op. 26 (Pilsen, Dec. 18, 1904); *Pohádka léta* (A Summer Fairy Tale), symphonic poem, op. 29 (1907–9; Jan. 26, 1909); *Zráni* (The Ripening), symphonic poem, op. 34 (1912–17; Oct. 30, 1918); *Meditace na staročeský chorál "Svatý Vaclave"* (Meditation on an Old Czech Chorale "St. Wenceslas") for Strings, op. 35a (1914; also for String Quartet); *Legenda o mrtvých vítězich* (Legend of the Dead Victors), op. 35b (1919–20; Oct. 24, 1924); *V nozý zivot* (Toward a New Life), march, op. 35c

(June 27, 1920); also for Piano Duet); *Epilog* for Soprano, Baritone, Bass, 2 Choirs, and Orch., op. 37 (1920–33; Dec. 20, 1933); *Pod Blanikem* (Beneath Blanik), march (1932; orchestrated by J. Kalaš; Jan. 26, 1934).

INCIDENTAL MUSIC: *Radúz a Mahulena* for Alto, Tenor, Reciters, Choir, and Orch., op. 13 (Prague, April 6, 1898; rev. 1912); *Pod jabloní* (Beneath the Apple Tree) for Alto, Reciters, Choir, and Orch., op. 20 (1900–1901; rev. 1911, 1915; Prague, Jan. 31, 1934).

CHAMBER: *Polka* for Violin (1882); String Quartet (1888); *Fantasy* for String Quartet and Piano ad libidum (1888); Piano Quartet, op. 1 (1891); Piano Trio, op. 2 (1889; rev. 1890–91); *Balada* for String Quartet (1890); *Balada* for Cello and Piano, op. 3/1 (1890); *Serenade* for Cello and Piano, op. 3/2 (c.1898); *Balada* for Violin and Piano (1890); *Melodie* for 2 Violins (1890); Piano Quintet, op. 8 (1893); String Quartet, op. 11 (1896; last movement rev. 1915 and left as an independent work); 4 Pieces for Violin and Piano, op. 17 (1900); *Elegie: Pod dojmen Zeyerova Vyšehradu* (Under the Impression of Zeyer's Vyšehrad) for Violin, Cello, String Quartet, Harmonium, and Harp, op. 23 (1902; also for Piano Trio); String Quartet, op. 31 (1911); *Meditace na staročeský chorál "Svatý Václave"* (Meditation on an Old Czech Chorale "St. Wenceslas") for String Quartet, op. 35a (1914; also for String Orch.); *Bagatelle: S kyticí v ruce* (Carrying a Bouquet) for Flute, Violin, and Piano (1917); *Sousedská* for 5 Violins, Double Bass, Cymbals, Triangle, and Large and Small Drums (1935).

PIANO: Sonata (1883); *Overture* (1884–85); *Polonaise* (1886–87); *Jindřichohradecký cyklus* (Jindřichův Hradec Suite; 1886–87); *Fugue* (1888); *Tři pisně beze slov* (3 Songs without Words; 1891); *Fantaisie-polonaise*, op. 5 (1892); 6 pieces, op. 7 (1891–93); *Capriccietto* (1893); *Humoreska* (1894); *Lístek do památníku* (Album Leaf; 1895); *Nálady* (Moods), op. 10 (1895); 8 pieces, op. 12 (1895–96); Sonatina, op. 13 (1897; rev. as Suite, op. 21, 1900); *Vesnická serenáda* (Village Serenade; 1897); *Jaro* (Spring), op. 22a (1902); *Letní dojmy* (Summer Moods), op. 22b (1902); *O matince* (About Mother), op. 28 (1907); *Psina španělská* (Spanish Joke; 1909); *Životem a snem* (Things Lived and Dreamt), op. 30 (1909); *Ukolébavky*, op. 33 (1910–12); *O přátelství* (Friendship), op. 36 (1920).

VOCAL: *Křečovická mše* (Křečovice Mass) for Choir, Strings, and Organ (1888–89); men's choruses; songs.

BIBL.: J. Květ, ed., *J. S.: Život a dilo: Studie a vzpomínsky* (J. S.: Life and Works: Studies and Reminiscences; Prague, 1935); idem, *J. S.* (Prague, 1936); J. Šach, ed., *J. S.: Vzpomínková mozaika* (J. S.: A Mosaic of Reminiscences; Prague, 1941); V. Štěpán, *Novak a S.* (Prague, 1945); J. Květ, ed., *Živá slova J.a S.a* (In J. S.'s Own Words; Prague, 1946); O. Filipovský, *Klavirni tvorba J.a S.a* (J. S.'s Piano Works; Plzen, 1947); J. Květ, *J. S.* (Prague, 1947); J. Berkovec, *J. S. (1874–1935): Život a dilo* (J. S. [1874–1935]: Life and Works; Prague, 1956; 2nd ed., 1962; rev. and abridged ed., 1968, as *J. S.*; Eng., German, French, and Russian trs., 1968); J. Květ, *J. S. v obrazech* (J. S. in Pictures; Prague, 1964); Z. Sádecký, *Lyrismus v tvorbě J.a S.a* (Lyricism in J. S.'s Works; Prague, 1966).

Suk (II), Josef, outstanding Czech violinist, grandson of **Josef Suk (I)** and great-grandson of **Antonín Dvořák;** b. Prague, Aug. 8, 1929. He was only a child when he commenced violin lessons with Jaroslav Kocián, who remained his teacher until the latter's death in 1950; Suk also studied at the Prague Cons. (until 1951) and then with M. Hlouňová and A. Plocek at the Prague Academy of Music (1951–53). He made his public debut in 1940; later played in the orch. of the Prague National Theater; also was a member of the Prague Quartet (1951–52). In 1952 he founded the Suk Trio with the pianist Jan Panenka and the cellist Josef Chuchro, and toured widely with it; his interest in chamber music led him to form a duo with Zuzana Růžičková in 1963; he was also a member of a trio with Julius Katchen and Janos Starker (1967–69). In 1959 he made a grand tour as soloist to 3 continents with the Czech Phil. On Jan. 23, 1964, he made his U.S. debut with the Cleveland Orch., and subsequently appeared as soloist with other

American orchs. In 1964 he received a Czech State Prize; in 1970 he was made an Artist of Merit and in 1977 was named a National Artist of Czechoslovakia.

Suk, Váša (Václav; Viacheslav Ivanovich), noted Russian conductor and composer of Czech parentage; b. Kladno, Nov. 16, 1861; d. Moscow, Jan. 12, 1933. He studied violin at the Prague Cons. and composition privately with Fibich; was concertmaster of the Kiev Opera orch. (1880–82) and a violinist in the Bolshoi Theater orch. in Moscow (1882–87); in 1885 he launched a conducting career, and subsequently appeared throughout Russia; was a conductor of the Bolshoi Theater (1906–32) and principal conductor of the Stanislavsky Opera Theater in Moscow (from 1927). He was appreciated in Russia for his thoroughness in drilling the singers and the orch.; achieved a fine reputation as an operatic conductor. He wrote an opera, *Lord of the Forests*, which he conducted in Kharkov on Feb. 16, 1900; also composed a symphonic poem, *Jan Huss* (Moscow, March 12, 1933); a Serenade for String Orch.; piano pieces; songs.

BIBL.: I. Remezov, *V.I. S.* (Moscow and Leningrad, 1951).

Sukegawa, Toshiya, Japanese composer; b. Sapporo, July 15, 1930. He studied with Ikenouchi from 1951; graduated in composition from the Univ. of Arts in Tokyo in 1957.

WORKS: DRAMATIC: Television opera, *Pôra no Hiroba* (1959). **ORCH.:** *Passacaglia* (1954); *Partita* (1960); *Legend* (1965). **CHAMBER:** String Quartet (1956); *Music* for Flute, Clarinet, Violin, Cello, Percussion, and Piano (1958); Wind Quintet (1962); 5 *Metamorphoses* for Viola and Piano (1966); 3 *Parts for 5 Flute Players* (1967); 3 *Scenes* for Jushichigen, 3 Violins, and Viola (1969); *A Projection* for Marimba, Piccolo, Trombone, Piano, and Percussion (1969); 5 *Pieces after Paul Klee* for Marimba (1973); *Song of the Wind* for Tape (1980); *Les Jours passants*, trio for Flute, Violin, and Harpsichord (1982); *Eternal Morning* for Tape (1983); *Mirror* for 2 Flutes (1984); *The Berin Strait* for Tape (1986); *Blue Mountain* for Synthesizer and Tape (1987); *La Folia 2 (From the Galaxy Far Away)* for Synthesizer (1988). **VOCAL:** *The White World* for Chorus and Piano (1971); *Eika* for Chorus and Japanese Percussion (1972). **PIANO:** Sonata (1958); *Divertimento* for 2 Pianos (1958); *Tapestry* (1966–68); 5 *Symbolic Pictures* (1972); *Sequenza* (1985); *Komoriuta* (1986).

Sukerta, Pande Made, innovative Indonesian composer, writer on Balinese music, and teacher; b. Tekakula, Singaraja, Bali, 1953. He studied at the high school music cons. in Denpasar, specializing in the rebab (bowed double-stringed fiddle); in 1973 he entered the Akademi Seni Karawitan Indonesia (A.S.K.I.) Surakarta, where he was founding director of various Balinese gamelan groups; also was active as a performer of *eksperimen karawitan baru*, a style of experimental music played on traditional instruments. After graduating in 1979, he joined the faculty at A.S.K.I. (later Sekolah Tinggi Seni Indonesia [S.T.S.I.]), where he led improvisation workshops wherein students explored the sonic potential of both gamelan and "found" instruments. He participated in Jakarta's Young Choreographers' Festival (1978) and at the national Pekan Komponis Muda (Young Composers' Festival; 1979, 1981, 1984); his *Asanawali* for Balinese Gamelan and Chorus was heard at EXPO '86 in Vancouver as part of the 1st International Gamelan Festival on a program of the Vancouver Sym. Orch., which included works by Debussy and Colin McPhee. In 1989 he was one of 7 composers commissioned to create new works for a recording project of the American Gamelan Inst. in Hanover, N.H. He toured in France, Denmark, Italy, Switzerland, Iran, Australia, Canada, and the U.S. Sukerta's works are variously scored for Balinese and Javanese gamelans and "found" instruments and often include improvisatory aspects; his *Mana 689* (1989) makes use of drums from Java, Sunda, and Sumatra, as well as bottles, marbles, a chanting priest, and screaming children (2 of his own 4). Other works include *Malam, Demung, Gora Suara* (1981), and *Saik 789* (1989). He is also a prolific writer, numbering among his publications an extended essay on the process of composition, an encyclopedia of Balinese

instruments, and transcriptions of melodies from the archaic Balinese ensemble Gambuh.

WRITINGS (all publ. in Surakarta): *Gending-gending Semar Pegulingan Saih Pitu* (1977); *Rebaban Karawitan Bali* (1979); *Gending-gending Gong Gede; Gamelan Gong Gede di Desa Batur* (1986; notation and drawings of instruments and cases).

Šulek, Stjepan, prominent Croatian violinist, conductor, teacher, and composer; b. Zagreb, Aug. 5, 1914; d. there, Jan. 16, 1986. He studied violin with Huml at the Zagreb Academy of Music; was largely self-taught in composition; yet he succeeded in becoming a composer of considerable merit. He was active as a violinist; became best known as a conductor; conducted the Zagreb Radio Chamber Orch. on many tours of Europe; was prof. of composition at the Zagreb Academy of Music (from 1945). His compositions reveal a strong individual profile.

WORKS: OPERAS: *Koriolan*, after Shakespeare (Zagreb, Oct. 12, 1958); *Oluja* (The Tempest), after Shakespeare (Zagreb, Nov. 28, 1969). **ORCH.:** 6 syms. (1944, 1946, 1948, 1954, 1963, 1966); festive prologue, *Scientiae et arti* (1966); 4 piano concertos (1949, 1951, 1963, 1970); Cello Concerto (1950); Violin Concerto (1951); Bassoon Concerto (1958); Viola Concerto (1959); Clarinet Concerto (1967); Horn Concerto (1972); Organ Concerto (1974); also vocal works, including a cantata, *Zadnji Adam* (The Last Adam; 1964), and songs; piano pieces.

BIBL.: K. Šipuš, *S. Š.* (Zagreb, 1961).

Sullivan, Sir Arthur (Seymour), famous English composer and conductor; b. London, May 13, 1842; d. there, Nov. 22, 1900. His father, Thomas Sullivan, was bandmaster at the Royal Military College, Sandhurst, and later prof. of brass instruments at the Royal Military School of Music, Kneller Hall; his musical inclinations were encouraged by his father, and in 1854 he became a chorister in the Chapel Royal, remaining there until 1858 and studying with the Rev. Thomas Helmore; in 1855 his sacred song *O Israel* was publ. In 1856 he received the 1st Mendelssohn Scholarship to the Royal Academy of Music in London, where he studied with Sterndale Bennett, Arthur O'Leary, and John Goss; then continued his training at the Leipzig Cons. (1858–61), where he received instruction in counterpoint and fugue from Moritz Hauptmann, in composition from Julius Rietz, in piano from Ignaz Moscheles and Louis Plaidy, and in conducting from Ferdinand David. He conducted his overture *Rosenfest* in Leipzig (May 25, 1860), and wrote a String Quartet and music to *The Tempest* (Leipzig, April 6, 1861; rev. version, London, April 5, 1862). His cantata *Kenilworth* (Birmingham Festival, Sept. 8, 1864) stamped him as a composer of high rank. In 1864 he visited Ireland and composed his "Irish Symphony" (London, March 10, 1866). In 1866 he was appointed prof. of composition at the Royal Academy of Music in London. About this time he formed a lifelong friendship with Sir George Grove, whom he accompanied in 1867 on a memorable journey to Vienna in search of Schubert MSS, leading to the discovery of the score of *Rosamunde*. The year 1867 was also notable for the production of the 1st of those comic operas upon which Sullivan's fame chiefly rests. This was *Cox and Box* (libretto by F.C. Burnand), composed in 2 weeks and performed on May 13, 1867, in London. Less successful were *The Contrabandista* (London, Dec. 18, 1867) and *Thespis* (London, Dec. 26, 1871); but the latter is significant as inaugurating Sullivan's collaboration with Sir W.S. Gilbert, the celebrated humorist, who became the librettist of all Sullivan's most successful comic operas, beginning with *Trial by Jury* (March 25, 1875). This was produced by Richard D'Oyly Carte, who in 1876 formed a company expressly for the production of the "Gilbert and Sullivan" operas. The 1st big success obtained by the famous team was *H.M.S. Pinafore* (May 25, 1878), which had 700 consecutive performances in London, and enjoyed an enormous vogue in "pirated" productions throughout the U.S. In an endeavor to protect their interests, Gilbert and Sullivan went to N.Y. in 1879 to give an authorized performance of *Pinafore*, and while there they also produced *The Pirates of Penzance* (Dec. 30,

1879). On April 23, 1881, came *Patience*, a satire on exaggerated esthetic poses exemplified by Oscar Wilde, whose American lecture tour was conceived as a "publicity stunt" for this work. On Nov. 25, 1882, *Iolanthe* began a run that lasted more than a year. This was followed by the comparatively unsuccessful *Princess Ida* (Jan. 5, 1884), but then came the universal favorite of all the Gilbert and Sullivan operas, *The Mikado* (March 14, 1885). The list of these popular works is completed by *Ruddigore* (Jan. 22, 1887), *The Yeomen of the Guard* (Oct. 3, 1888), and *The Gondoliers* (Dec. 7, 1889). After a quarrel and a reconciliation, the pair collaborated in 2 further works, of less popularity: *Utopia Limited* (Oct. 7, 1893) and *The Grand Duke* (March 7, 1896). Sullivan's melodic inspiration and technical resourcefulness, united with the delicious humor of Gilbert's verses, raised the light opera to a new height of artistic achievement, and his works in this field continue to delight countless hearers. Sullivan was also active in other branches of musical life. He conducted numerous series of concerts, most notably those of the London Phil. Soc. (1885–87) and the Leeds Festivals (1880–98). He was principal of, and a prof. of composition at, the National Training School for Music from 1876 to 1881. He received the degree of Mus.Doc. *honoris causa* from Cambridge (1876) and Oxford (1879); was named Chevalier of the Legion of Honor (1878); was grand organist to the Freemasons (1887); etc. He was knighted by Queen Victoria in 1883. Parallel with his comic creations, he composed many "serious" works, including the grand opera *Ivanhoe* (Jan. 31, 1891), which enjoyed a momentary vogue. Among his cantatas the most successful was *The Golden Legend*, after Longfellow (Leeds Festival, Oct. 16, 1886); he also wrote the famous hymn *Onward, Christian Soldiers*, to words by Rev. Sabine Baring-Gould (1871). His songs were highly popular in their day, and *The Lost Chord*, to words by Adelaide A. Proctor (publ. 1877), is still a favorite. Among his oratorios, *The Light of the World* (Birmingham Festival, Aug. 27, 1873) may be mentioned. Other stage works (all 1st perf. in London unless otherwise given) include *The Zoo* (June 5, 1875); *The Sorcerer* (Nov. 17, 1877; rev. version, Oct. 11, 1884); *Haddon Hall* (Sept. 24, 1892); *The Chieftain* (Dec. 12, 1894); *The Martyr of Antioch* (Edinburgh, Feb. 15, 1898; a stage arrangement of the cantata); *The Beauty-Stone* (May 28, 1898); romantic opera, *The Rose of Persia* (Nov. 29, 1899); *The Emerald Isle* (completed by E. German, April 27, 1901); 2 ballets: *L'Île enchanté* (May 14, 1864) and *Victoria and Merrie England* (May 25, 1897).

BIBL.: A. Lawrence, *Sir A. S.: Life Story, Letters and Reminiscences* (London, 1899); W. Wells, *Souvenir of Sir A. S., Mus.Doc., M.V.O.* (London, 1901) B. Findon, *Sir A. S.: His Life and Music* (London, 1904; 2nd ed., rev., 1908, as *Sir A. S. and His Operas*); F. Cellier and C. Bridgeman, *Gilbert, S., and D'Oyly Carte* (London, 1914; 2nd ed., 1927); H. Walbrook, *Gilbert and S. Opera* (London, 1922); S. Fitz-Gerald, *The Story of the Savoy Opera* (London, 1924); A. Godwin, *Gilbert and S.* (London, 1926); H. Wyndham, *A.S. S.* (London, 1926); N. Flower and H. Sullivan, *Sir A. S.: His Life, Letters and Diaries* (London, 1927; 2nd ed., 1950); T. Dunhill, *S.'s Comic Operas: A Critical Appreciation* (London, 1928); I. Goldberg, *The Story of Gilbert and S.* (London, 1929); H. Pearson, *Gilbert and S.* (London, 1935); G. Dunn, *A Gilbert and S. Dictionary* (N.Y., 1936); C. Purdy, *Gilbert and S.: Masters of Mirth and Melody* (N.Y., 1947); W. Darlington, *The World of Gilbert and S.* (N.Y., 1950); A. Jacobs, *Gilbert and S.* (London, 1951); L. Bailey, *The Gilbert and S. Book* (N.Y., 1952; 3rd ed., 1966); A. Williamson, *Gilbert and S. Operas: A New Assessment* (N.Y., 1953); A. Powers-Waters, *The Melody Maker: The Life of Sir A. S.* (N.Y., 1959); M. Green, *Treasury of Gilbert and S.* (London, 1961); R. Mander and J. Mitchenson, *A Picture History of Gilbert and S.* (London, 1962); N. Wymer, *Gilbert and S.* (London, 1962); C. Bulla, *Stories of Gilbert and S. Operas* (N.Y., 1968); J. Helyar, ed., *Gilbert and S. International Conference: Kansas 1970* (Lawrence, Kans., 1971); P. Young, *Sir A. S.* (London, 1971); L. Ayre, *The Gilbert & S. Companion* (N.Y., 1972); M. Hardwick, *The Osprey Guide to Gilbert and S.* (Reading,

1972); P. Kline, *Gilbert and S. Production* (N.Y., 1972); L. Baily, *Gilbert & S. and Their World* (London, 1973); R. Allen and G. D'Luhy, *Sir A. S.: Composer & Personage* (N.Y., 1975); I. Bradley, ed., *The Annotated Gilbert and S.* (2 vols., London, 1982, 1984); A. Williamson, *Gilbert & S. Opera* (London, 1983); A. Jacobs, *A. S.: A Victorian Musician* (Oxford, 1984); J. Wolfson, *S. and the Scott Russells* (Chichester, 1984); D. Eden, *Gilbert & S.: The Creative Conflict* (Rutherford, N.J., 1986); C. Hayter, *Gilbert and S.* (N.Y., 1987); I. Asimov, ed., *Asimov's Annotated Gilbert & S.* (N.Y., 1988).

Sultan, Grete, German-born American pianist; b. Berlin, June 21, 1906. She was reared in a musical family; studied with Leonid Kreutzer at the Berlin Hochschule für Musik (1922–25) and later with Edwin Fischer, Claudio Arrau, and Richard Buhlig. She established herself as a pianist of both Classical and contemporary works in Berlin before going to the U.S. in 1941; she toured widely, giving all-Bach, all-Beethoven, all-Schubert, and all-contemporary programs; made her N.Y. debut in 1947. She became associated with Henry Cowell, with whom she gave performances of works by Schoenberg and Stravinsky; settling in N.Y., she met John Cage, who became a lifelong friend and associate; they often appeared in concerts together, and Cage wrote his *Études australes*, a chance-determined set of 32 études based on star maps, for her; she performed it throughout the U.S. and Europe and in Japan. In 1968–69 she gave a series of programs at N.Y.'s Town Hall under its Jonathan Peterson Lectureship Fund. Sultan's performances, which continue well into her 80s, are always critically acclaimed, her alacrity, sensitivity, and uncompromising directness uniquely enhancing the disparate works she programs; most recently she has championed the works of Ben Weber and Tui St. George Tucker. In the words of Arrau, "Sultan follows in the footsteps of the greatest women keyboard masters—Landowska, Haskil, Hess—blessed with musical purity and inwardness, reinforced by mind as well as soul."

Sulzer, Julius Salomon, Austrian violinist and conductor, son of **Salomon Sulzer;** b. Vienna, 1834; d. there, Feb. 13, 1891. He served as music director of the Hofburgtheater in Vienna from 1875.

Sulzer, Salomon, important Austrian composer, father of **Julius Salomon Sulzer;** b. Hohenems, Vorarlberg, March 30, 1804; d. Vienna, Jan. 17, 1890. He was only 16 when he was appointed cantor at the chief synagogue in his hometown. He studied music with Seyfried in Vienna; from 1825 to 1881 he was cantor of the new Vienna synagogue. He undertook a bold reform of liturgical music by the introduction of musical form and actual compositions from the Classical period, setting Schubert's songs as a model. By so doing, he succeeded in bringing traditional Jewish cantillation together with Western modes. He brought out an anthology, *Schir Zion* (The Heart of Zion; 2 vols., 1838–40; 1865–66), and *Denkschrift an die hochgeehrte Wiener israelitische Cultus-Gemeinde zum fünfzigjährigen Jubiläum des alten Bethauses* (Vienna, 1876).

BIBL.: M. Steiner, *S. S.* (Vienna, 1904); P. Minkowski, *Der S.ismus* (Vienna, 1905); E. Mandell, "*S. S.*, 1804–1890," *Journal of Synagogue Music,* 1 (1968).

Sumac, Yma (real name **Emperatriz Chavarri**), Peruvian-born American singer of a phenomenal diapason, whose origin is veiled in mystical mist; b. Ichocan, Sept. 10, 1927. She was reared in the Andes; it is credible that she developed her phenomenal voice of 5 octaves in range because her lungs were inflated by the necessity of breathing enough oxygen at the high altitude. However that might be, she married Moises Vivanco, who was an arranger for Capitol Records and who launched her on a flamboyant career as a concert singer; with him and their cousin, Cholito Rivero, she toured South America as the Inca Taky Trio (1942–46); then settled in the U.S. and became a naturalized citizen in 1955. She was billed by unscrupulous promoters as an Inca princess, a direct descendant of Atahualpa, the last emperor of the Incas, a Golden

Virgin of the Sun God worshiped by the Quechua Indians. On the other hand, some columnists spread the scurrilous rumor that she was in actuality a Jewish girl from Brooklyn whose real name was Amy (retrograde of Yma) Camus (retrograde of Sumac). But Sumac never spoke with a Brooklyn accent. She exercised a mesmeric appeal to her audiences, from South America to Russia, from California to Central Europe; expressions such as "miraculous" and "amazing" were used by Soviet reviewers during her tour of Russia in 1962; "supersonic vocal skill" was a term applied by an American critic. Her capacity did not diminish with age; during her California appearances in 1984 and again in 1988 she still impressed her audiences with the expressive power of her voice.

BIBL.: M. Leonard, "The Legendary S.," *Records and Recordings,* XXIII/2 (1979).

Sumera, Lepo, esteemed Estonian composer; b. Tallinn, May 8, 1950. He was educated at the Tallinn State Cons. (1968–73), where he subsequently was a prof. (from 1976) and chairman of its composition dept. (1988–89); also studied at the Darmstadt Summer Inst. (1988–89). He was a recording supervisor for Estonian Radio (1973–78). From 1989 to 1990 he was deputy minister of culture and from 1990 minister of culture for the Republic of Estonia. He received many Estonian Music Prizes for best composition of the year, including those for his film scores (1978), his Sym. No. 1 (1982), his Sym. No. 2 (1985), and his *Saare Piiga laul merest* (The Island Maiden; 1989).

WORKS: STAGE: *Anselmi lugu,* ballet (1977–78); *Saare Piiga laul merest* (The Island Maiden), *Linda matab Kalevit* (Linda Buries Kalev), and *Linda soome Tuuslar* (Linda Becomes Stone), multimedia dance drama for Chamber Choir, Actors, and Shaman Drum (1988); *Ja'st'eritsa,* ballet (1986–88). ORCH.: *In Memoriam* (1972); *Music for Chamber Orchestra* (1977–78; Tallinn, June 30, 1979); *Olümpiamuusika* (Olympic Music; 1981); Sym. No. 1 (1980; Tallinn, Oct. 10, 1981); *Pikseloits* (Thunder Incantation; 1983); Sym. No. 2 (Tallinn, April 4, 1984); Sym. No. 3 (Tallinn, Oct. 9, 1988); Piano Concerto (1989); *Open(r)ing* (1989); *Music for Glasgow* for Synthesizers and Chamber Orch. (1989); *Musik für Karlsruhe im Barockstil* for String Orch. and Harp (1989). CHAMBER: *Mäng punkpillidele* for Wind Quintet (1976); *Malera Kasuku,* trio for Violin, Cello, and Piano (1977); *Pantomiim* for Renaissance Instruments (1980); *Quasi improvisata* for Violin and Piano (1983); *Valss* for Violin and Piano (1985); *For Boris Björn Bagger and Friend* for Flute and Guitar (1988); *From 59'22" to 42'49"* for Guitar and Prerecorded Tape (1989); *The Borders* for Acoustic and Amplified Instruments (1990). VOCAL: *Elust ja surmast,* cantata for Choir and Orch. (1975); *Seenekantaat* (Mushroom Cantata), Part II, *Timor* (Dangerous; 1980; Tallinn, Feb. 7, 1981), Part III, *Carmen autumnus* (Tallinn, April 23, 1982), Part IV, *Luxuria* (1983); *Laulupea tuli,* cantata (1985); *Kui tume veel kauaks ka sinu maa* for Choir (1985). SOLO INSTRUMENTS: *Kaks pala sooloviiulile* for Violin (1977); *Sarvelugu* for Horn (1977); 2 capriccios for Clarinet (1984). PIANO: *Ostinato-variations* (1967); *Fughetta and Postludium* (1972); *Pianissimo* (1976); *2 Pieces from the Year 1981:* No. 1 and No. 2, *Pardon, Fryderyk!* (1980); *The Butterfly Who Woke Up in Winter* (1982); *The Sad Toreador* or *The One Who Is Wiser Concedes* (1984); also more than 40 scores for film, television, animation, and theater.

Sumner, Gordon Matthew. See **Sting.**

Sundelius (Sandtvig), Marie, Swedish-American soprano and vocal teacher; b. Karlsbad, Feb. 4, 1884; d. Boston, June 26, 1958. She was taken to America at the age of 8, and studied singing in Boston; made her debut as an opera singer with the Metropolitan Opera in N.Y. on Nov. 25, 1916; was on its roster, with interruptions, until 1928; made a tour of Sweden in 1924; then returned to Boston as a vocal teacher.

Sundgrén-Schnéevoigt, Sigrid Ingeborg, Finnish pianist; b. Helsinki, June 17, 1878; d. Stockholm, Sept. 14, 1953. She studied at the Helsinki Cons., and then with Busoni in Berlin

(1894–97). In 1907 she married the conductor **Georg Schnée-voigt,** with whom she made several tours of Scandinavia and Germany; also taught at the Helsinki Cons.

Suñol (y Baulenas), Gregoria María, learned Spanish ecclesiastic and music scholar; b. Barcelona, Sept. 7, 1879; d. Rome, Oct. 26, 1946. He became a Benedictine monk at Montserrat Abbey in 1895; was ordained a priest in 1902, and then served as choirmaster there (1907–28); in 1930 he went to Rome as director of the Istituto Pontifico di Musica Sacra; was made abbot of Ste. Cecilia in Montserrat in 1943. He publ. the valuable books *Método completo de canto gregoriano según la escuela de Solesmes* (8 eds., 1905–43; also in French, German, Eng., Italian, and Portuguese) and *Introducctió a la paleografía musical gregoriana* (Montserrat, 1925; rev. French ed., Tournai, 1935, with R. Renaudin).

Sun Ra (real name, **Herman Blount**), innovative black American jazz pianist, electric keyboardist, bandleader, and composer; b. Birmingham, Ala., May 1914. He learned to play the piano and 1st gained notice as a member of Fletcher Henderson's orch. (1946–47); then went to Chicago, where he became a prominent figure in the avant-garde jazz scene; in 1956 founded his own band, which was variously known as Solar Arkestra, Intergalactic Myth-Science Arkestra, Space Arkestra, etc.; later was active in N.Y. and Philadelphia; also toured through the U.S. and Europe; was a featured artist on the "Saturday Night Live" television show (1976). Compositionally, he developed an abrasive and complex style in which avant-garde techniques are combined with electronic resources.

Suolahti, Heikki, Finnish composer; b. Helsinki, Feb. 2, 1920; d. there, Dec. 27, 1936. He studied at the Helsinki Cons. His tragically premature death at the age of 16 moved Sibelius to say that "Finland lost one of her greatest musical talents." Suolahti composed a few fine works, including a Violin Concerto, written at the age of 14, and a *Sinfonia piccola,* which he composed at 15 and which was performed in Helsinki after his death; also left some songs.

Supervia, Conchita, famous Spanish mezzo-soprano; b. Barcelona, Dec. 9, 1895; d. London, March 30, 1936. She studied at the Colegio de las Damas Negras in Barcelona; made her debut with a visiting opera company at the Teatro Colón in Buenos Aires on Oct. 1, 1910, in Stiattesi's opera *Blanca de Beaulieu.* She then sang in the Italian premiere of *Der Rosenkavalier* in Rome in 1911, as Carmen in Bologna in 1912, and as a member of the Chicago Opera (1915–16). She appeared frequently at La Scala in Milan from 1924; also sang in other Italian music centers, and at London's Covent Garden (1934–35). She endeared herself to the Italian public by reviving Rossini's operas *L'Italiana in Algeri* and *La Cenerentola;* she also attracted favorable critical attention by performing the part of Rosina in *Il Barbiere di Siviglia* in its original version as a coloratura contralto. In 1931 she married the British industrialist Sir Ben Rubenstein. She died as a result of complications following the birth of a child.

BIBL.: H. Barnes and V. Girard, "C. S.," *Record Collector,* VI (1951); D. Shawe-Taylor, "C. S. (1895–1936)," *Opera,* XI (1960); I. Newton, "C. S.," *Recorded Sound,* 52 (1973).

Supičić, Ivo, Yugoslav musicologist; b. Zagreb, July 18, 1928. He studied piano at the Zagreb Academy of Music, graduating in 1953; worked with C.N.R.S. in Paris (1960–63) while studying musicology at the Sorbonne (Ph.D., 1962, with the diss. *Elementi sociologije muzike;* publ. in an augmented ed., N.Y., 1987, as *Music in Society: A Guide to the Sociology of Music*). He taught at the musicology dept. of the Zagreb Academy of Music (from 1964) and then at Harvard Univ. (1967–68); served on the editorial board of the journals *Acta Musicologica* and *Arti Musices;* also was ed. of the *International Review of the Aesthetics and Sociology of Music.* His numerous publications focus on sociological aspects of music, especially that of the 20th century. In addition to his valuable dissertation, he also publ. *La Musique expressive* (Paris, 1957).

Suppan, Wolfgang, Austrian musicologist; b. Irdning, Aug. 5, 1933. He studied clarinet, violin, piano, and music theory at the Graz Hochschule für Musik and musicology with Federhofer and Marx at the Univ. of Graz (Ph.D., 1959, with the diss. *Heinrich Eduard Joseph von Lannoy [1787–1853]: Leben und Werke*). He worked in Freiburg at the East German Folklore Inst. (1961–63) and as director of the music dept. of the Folk Song Archive (1963–71); completed his Habilitation at the Univ. of Mainz in 1971. He became a prof. and director of the Ethnomusicological Inst. of the Graz Hochschule für Musik in 1974. His research focuses on European folk music and music education.

WRITINGS: *Hanns Holenia: Eine Würdigung seines Lebens* (Graz, 1960); *Steirisches Musiklexikon* (Graz, 1962–66); *Volkslied: Seine Sammlung und Erforschung* (Stuttgart, 1966; 2nd ed., 1974); *Lexikon des Blasmusikwesens* (Freiburg, 1971; 2nd ed., 1976).

Suppé, Franz (von) (real name, **Francesco Ezechiele Ermenegildo, Cavaliere Suppé-Demelli**), famous Austrian composer; b. Spalato, Dalmatia (of Belgian descent), April 18, 1819; d. Vienna, May 21, 1895. At the age of 11 he played the flute, and at 13 wrote a Mass. He was then sent by his father to study law at Padua; on his father's death, he went with his mother to Vienna in 1835, and continued serious study at the Cons. with Sechter and Seyfried. He conducted at theaters in Pressburg and Baden; then at Vienna's Theater an der Wien (1845–62), Kaitheater (1862–65), and Carltheater (1865–82). All the while, he wrote light operas and other theater music of all degrees of levity, obtaining increasing success rivaling that of Offenbach. His music possesses the charm and gaiety of the Viennese genre, but also contains elements of more vigorous popular rhythms. His most celebrated single work is the overture to *Dichter und Bauer,* which still retains a firm place in the light repertoire. His total output comprises about 30 comic operas and operettas and 180 other stage pieces, most of which were brought out in Vienna; of these the following obtained considerable success: *Dichter und Bauer* (Aug. 24, 1846); *Das Mädchen vom Lande* (Aug. 7, 1847); *Dame Valentine, oder Frauenräuber und Wanderbursche* (Jan. 9, 1851); *Paragraph 3* (Jan. 8, 1858); *Das Pensionat* (Nov. 24, 1860); *Die Kartenaufschlägerin* (April 26, 1862); *Zehn Mädchen und kein Mann* (Oct. 25, 1862); *Die flotten Burschen* (April 18, 1863); *Das Corps der Rache* (March 5, 1864); *Franz Schubert* (Sept. 10, 1864); *Die schöne Galatea* (Berlin, June 30, 1865); *Die leichte Kavallerie* (March 24, 1866); *Die Tochter der Puszta* (March 24, 1866); *Die Freigeister* (Oct. 23, 1866); *Banditenstreiche* (April 27, 1867); *Die Frau Meisterin* (Jan. 20, 1868); *Tantalusqualen* (Oct. 3, 1868); *Isabella* (Nov. 5, 1869); *Cannebas* (Nov. 2, 1872); *Fatinitza* (Jan. 5, 1876; extremely popular); *Der Teufel auf Erden* (Jan. 5, 1878); *Boccaccio* (Feb. 1, 1879; very popular); *Donna Juanita* (Feb. 21, 1880); *Der Gascogner* (March 21, 1881); *Das Herzblättchen* (Feb. 4, 1882); *Die Afrikareise* (March 17, 1883); *Des Matrosen Heimkehr* (Hamburg, May 4, 1885); *Bellmann* (Feb. 26, 1887); *Die Jagd nach dem Glücke* (Oct. 27, 1888); *Das Modell* (Oct. 4, 1895); *Die Pariserin, oder Das heimliche Bild* (Jan. 26, 1898). Other works include syms., overtures, a Requiem, 3 masses, and other sacred works, choruses, dances, string quartets, and songs.

BIBL.: G. Sabalich, *F. S. e l'operetta* (Zara, 1888); O. Keller, *F. v.S., der Schöpfer der deutschen Operette* (Leipzig, 1905); E. Rieger, *Offenbach und seine Wiener Schule* (Vienna, 1920).

Suratno, Nano, prolific Indonesian composer, known as Nano S.; b. Pasar Kemis Tarogong, West Java, April 4, 1944. He earned degrees from the Akademi Seni Tari Indonesia (A.S.T.I.) Bandung (1978) and Sekolah Tinggi Seni Indonesia (S.T.S.I.) Surakarta (1989); also studied with Daeng Sutikna (music), Syafei (literature), Tjetje Somantri (choreography and dance), and, especially, Mang Koko (music); formed his own dance company and then performed with Koko's group, Ganda Mekar. He began composing experimental works for degung, a traditional Sundanese chamber ensemble of tuned gongs, drums, and bamboo flute; in 1979 his *Sangkuriang* was performed at the important national festival Pekan Komponis Muda (Young Composers' Festival); he also began composing highly expressive instrumental music ("karawitan total"), and in 1985 mounted *Umbul-umbul,* involving 75 players in a mixture of over 15 Sundanese styles, on Indonesian TV. Nano S. sees many of his songs as a means of making traditional music more accessible to Sundanese youths; he often recasts classical melodies in forms that conform to popular music styles of the West. Even in his more experimental instrumental works, which he calls "musik total" or "musik murni" (i.e., "absolute" music), he neither borrows from foreign sources nor uses diatonic tuning; while such works have not yet found a place in the standard repertoire of Sunda, audiences abroad have been receptive; in 1989, on a commission from the American Gamelan Inst. in Hanover, N.H., he composed and recorded *Jemplang Polansky,* inspired by his confusion upon listening to the computer music of Larry Polansky, and *Galura* (Emotion; 1988), an instrumental solo piece for kecapi (plucked zither). In 1986 he toured in Canada and the U.S.; after appearing in Japan (1988), he became a guest lecturer and composer at the Univ. of Calif. at Santa Cruz (1989). In 1990 he directed the touring program "Sunda: From Village to City," presented in the U.S. at its Festival of Indonesia. Nano S. is best known in Indonesia as a song composer; his texts are often about young love, cast in the regional language of Sundanese, modern Indonesian, or English. More than 200 audiotapes of his works have been released, several of them distributed by the American Gamelan Inst. Among his publications are a book of songs, *Haleuang Tondang* (Bandung, 1975), and *Mengolah Seni Pertunjukan Sebagai Media Penergangan* (Development of the Performing Arts as an Information Medium; 1989); also some 15 operetta librettos. In 1978 he married the Indonesian singer Dheniarsah; their home in Bandung is a fertile international meeting ground for artists of all disciplines.

WORKS: *Ki Lagoni,* operetta (1967); *Raja Kecit,* operetta (1974); *Bubat* for Degung (1978); *Sangkuriang* for Gamelan (1979); *Sekar Manis* for 4 Kecapi (1980); *Anjeun* for Degung (1986); *Kalangkang* for Degung (1986); *Kangen* for Degung (1987); *Kalangkang* for Jaipongan (1987; also for Western Band [1987] and *Kliningan Wanda Anyar* [1988]); *Tibelat* for Pop Sunda (1988); *Cinta* for Pop Degung (1988); *Galura* for Kecapi (1988); *Jemplang Polansky* for Mixed Ensemble (1989); *Love Smir/Parkir* for Gamelan (1990); *Warna* for Gamelan (1990); *Karesman* for Gamelan (1990); many songs.

Surdin, Morris, Canadian composer; b. Toronto, May 8, 1914; d. there, Aug. 19, 1979. He learned to play piano, violin, cello, horn, and trombone; studied composition with Gesensway in Philadelphia (1937) and with Henry Brant in N.Y. (1950); worked as a music arranger for the CBC and CBS. From 1954 he worked in Canada, primarily in scoring for musicals, radio, television, and films.

WORKS: STAGE: Opera-musical, *Wild Rose* (1967); musical comedy, *Look Ahead* (1962); ballet, *The Remarkable Rocket,* after Oscar Wilde (1960–61). **ORCH.:** *4 X Strings* for Strings (1947); *Credo* (1950); *Inheritance* for Wind Quartet and Strings (1951); *Concert Ballet* (1955); *Incident I* for Strings (1961); Concerto for Mandolin and Strings (1961–66); *5 Shades of Brass* for Trumpet and Orch. (1961); 2 concertos for Free-bass Accordion: No. 1 (1966; Toronto, Jan. 29, 1967) and No. 2, with Strings, Electric Guitar, and Percussion (1977); *2 Solitudes* for Horn or English Horn, and Strings (1967); *Formula I and II* for Concert Band (1968–69); *Horizon* for String Orch. (1968); *Short!* (No. 1) for Piano and Strings (1969) and *Short!* (No. 2) for Piano, Wind Quartet, and Strings (1969); *Alteration I* for Piccolo and Strings (1970) and *II* for Strings (1970); *Terminus* for Oboe, Bassoon, and Strings (1972); *B'rasheet* (In the Beginning) for Mandolin, Clarinet, and String Orch. (Toronto, June 15, 1974); *Eine kleine "Hammer-Klapper" Musik* for Chamber Orch. (1976); *Berceuse* for Horn and Chamber Orch. (1977); *A Group of 6* for Strings in 1st position (1977); *5 for 4* for Strings in 1st position (1977); *Who's on Bass?* for Strings (1977); *6 Pieces in Search of a Sequence* for Solo Instruments and String Orch. (1969–78); Violin Concerto (1978). **VOCAL:** *A Spanish Tragedy* for Soprano and Orch. (1955); *Suite canadienne* for Chorus and Orch. (1970); *Feast of Thunder* for Soloists, Male Chorus, and Orch. (1972); *Music Fair* for Soprano, Cello, and Harp (1975); *Quartet for Trio* for Low Voice, Cello, and Harp (1976); *Pegleg's Fiddle* for Male Chorus, Solo Violin, Mandolin Orch., Piano, and Percussion (1977); *Leave It Be* for Bass, Chorus, and Orch. (1977; based on the musical comedy *Look Ahead*). **CHAMBER:** *Suite* for Viola and Piano (1954); *Carol Fantasia* for Brass (1955); *Incident II* for Woodwinds, Horns, and Harp (1961); *Elements* for 2 Violins, Double Bass, and Harpsichord (1965); *Matin* for Wind Quartet (1965); *Arioso* for 4 Cellos (1966); String Quartet (1966); Trio for Saxophones (1968); *Piece* for Wind Quintet (1969); *Serious I–XVI* for Accordion (1969–73); *Trinitas in Morte* for 3 Oboes, Bassoon, 3 Horns, Timpani, 8 Cellos, and 2 Double Basses (1973); *Heritage I–IV* for varying Brass Quartets (1975–79); *Sly'd Trombones I & II* for Trombone and Bass Trombone, or Trombone Ensemble (1975); *Landscapes*, sonatina for Harp (1978); 2 *fabliaux* for Cello (1979). **PIANO:** *Naïveté*, 6 pieces (1962); *Poco Giocoso Variations* (1966); *In Search of Form I and II* (1970); *Fragmentations I–III* (1972).

BIBL.: M. Schulman, "At Last, Recognition for M. S.'s Music," *Canadian Composer* (March 1978).

Surette, Thomas Whitney, American music educator; b. Concord, Mass., Sept. 7, 1861; d. there, May 19, 1941. He studied piano with Arthur Foote and composition with J.K. Paine at Harvard Univ. (1889–92), but failed to obtain a degree. Deeply interested in making musical education accessible and effective in the U.S., he founded the Concord Summer School of Music in 1915, which continued to operate until 1938; with A.T. Davison, he ed. The Concord Series of educational music, which found a tremendously favorable acceptance on the part of many schools, particularly in New England; the series provided an excellent selection of good music which could be understood by most music teachers and performed by pupils. He was also largely responsible for the vogue of music appreciation courses that swept the country and spilled over into the British Isles. He publ. *The Appreciation of Music* (with D.G. Mason; 5 vols., of which vols. 2 and 5 were by Mason alone; N.Y., 1907; innumerable subsequent printings), and, on a more elevated plane, *Course of Study on the Development of Symphonic Music* (Chicago, 1915) and *Music and Life* (Boston, 1917); he also publ. popular articles on music and musicians, notable for their lack of discrimination and absence of verification of data. He was also a composer of sorts; wrote 2 light operas, *Priscilla, or The Pilgrim's Proxy*, after Longfellow (Concord, March 6, 1889; had more than 1,000 subsequent perfs. in the U.S.), and *The Eve of Saint Agnes* (1897), and a romantic opera, *Cascabel, or The Broken Tryst* (Pittsburgh, May 15, 1899).

BIBL.: C. Heffernan, *T.W. S.: Musician and Teacher* (diss., Univ. of Michigan, 1962).

Suriano, Francesco. See **Soriano, Francesco.**

Surinach, Carlos, Spanish-born American composer and conductor; b. Barcelona, March 4, 1915. He studied in Barcelona with Morera (1936–39) and later with Max Trapp in Berlin (1939–43). Returning to Spain in 1943, he was active mainly as a conductor. In 1951 he went to the U.S.; became an American citizen in 1959; was a visiting prof. of music at Carnegie-Mellon Inst. in Pittsburgh in 1966–67. He won particular success as a composer for the dance.

WORKS: OPERA: *El Mozo que casó con mujer brava* (Barcelona, Jan. 10, 1948). **BALLETS:** *Monte Carlo* (Barcelona, May 2, 1945); *Ritmo jondo* (1953); *Embattled Garden* (1958); *Acrobats of God* (1960); *David and Bathsheba* (1960); *Apasionada* (1962); *Los renegados* (1965); *Venta quemada* (1966); *Agathe's Tale* (1967); *Suite española* (1970); *Chronique* (1974); *The Owl and the Pussycat* (1978); *Blood Wedding* (1979). **ORCH.:** 3 syms.: No. 1, *Passacaglia-Symphony* (Barcelona, April 8, 1945, composer conducting); No. 2 (Paris Radio, Jan. 26, 1950, composer conducting); No. 3, *Sinfonía chica* (1957); *Sinfonietta*

flamenca (1953; Louisville, Jan. 9, 1954); *Feria mágica*, overture (Louisville, March 14, 1956); *Symphonic Variations* (1962); *Drama Jondo*, overture (1964); *Melorhythmic Dramas* (1966); *Las trompetas de los serafines*, overture (1973); Piano Concerto (1973); Harp Concerto (1978); Concerto for String Orch. (1978); Violin Concerto (1980); also choral works, songs, chamber music, piano pieces, guitar music, etc.

Surzyński, Józef, Polish theologian, conductor, music scholar, and composer; b. Szrem, near Posen, March 15, 1851; d. Kościan, March 5, 1919. He studied theory with O. Paul in Leipzig (1872–74), where he also took courses at the Cons. and was a violist at the Thomaskirche; studied theology in Rome (doctorate, 1880) and then at the Regensburg school of church music. He was in Posen as Cathedral organist (1881–87), and also conducted its choir; served in Kościan as curate (1894–1919); also was active as a conductor in various Polish cities. He was engaged in the movement to reform church music along Caecilian lines; served as ed. of the journal *Muzyka Kościelna* (Church Music; 1884–1902). His compositions include sacred works and organ music. His publications include *Directorium chori* (Posen, 1885), *Monumenta musices sacrae in Polonia* (Posen, 1885–89), and *Matka Boska w muzyce polskiej* (The Mother of God in Polish Music; Krakow, 1905). He had 2 brothers who were also musicians: **Stefan** (b. Środa, Aug. 31, 1855; d. Lwow, April 6, 1919) was an organist, conductor, teacher, and composer; **Mieczyslaw** (b. Środa, Dec. 22, 1866; d. Warsaw, Sept. 11, 1924) was an organist, conductor, teacher, and composer.

BIBL.: K. Winowicz, *J. S.* (diss., Univ. of Poznan, 1964).

Susa, Conrad, American composer; b. Springdale, Pa., April 26, 1935. He studied theory with Nicolai Lopatnikoff, musicology with Frederick Dorian, counterpoint with Roland Leich, flute with Bernard Goldberg, and cello with Leonard Eisner at the Carnegie Inst. of Technology in Pittsburgh (B.F.A., 1957); completed his training in composition with Bergsma and Persichetti at the Juilliard School of Music in N.Y. (M.S., 1961). In 1959 he became composer-in-residence at the Old Globe Theatre in San Diego, where he was active for over 30 years; also was music director of the APA-Phoenix Repertory Co. in N.Y. (1961–68) and the American Shakespeare Festival in Stratford, Conn. (1969–71); also was dramaturge at the Eugene O'Neill Center in Connecticut (from 1986).

WORKS: Operas: *Transformations* (Minnesota Opera, May 5, 1973); *Black River* (Minnesota Opera, Nov. 1, 1975); *The Love of Don Perlimplin* (1983); also incidental music; television scores; *A Sonnet Voyage*, sym. (1963); chamber music; numerous choral works, including *Dawn Greeting* (1976), *The Chanticleer's Carol* (1982), and *Earth Song* (1988); keyboard pieces.

Susato, Johannes de (real name, **Johannes Steinwert von Soest),** German singer and composer; b. Unna, 1448; d. Frankfurt am Main, May 2, 1506. He was a chorister in Cleve; after serving as succentor in Maastricht, he was made music director at the Heidelberg court (1472); also studied medicine there and later at the Univ. of Padua, where he took his M.D. about 1490; became town physician in Worms in 1495 and in Frankfurt am Main in 1500.

Susato, Tylman, German music publisher and composer; b. c.1500; d. probably in Antwerp, c.1562. He may have been born in Antwerp, where he pursued his career; was a calligrapher at the Cathedral (1529–30), becoming a trumpeter there in 1531; then was a town musician (1532–49). After serving as a partner in a printing venture (1541–43), he set up his own press in 1543 and remained active until at least 1561. His press produced 25 books of chansons, 3 books of masses, 19 books of motets, and 11 *Musyck boexken*. He was a fine composer of cantus firmus chansons for 2 to 3 Voices (1544; c.1552).

BIBL.: P. Bergmans, "Un Imprimeur musicien: Tilman S.," *Bulletin de la Société Bibliophile Anversoise* (Antwerp, 1923);

U. Meissner, *Der Antwerpener Notendrucker T. S.* (Berlin, 1967); L. Bernstein, "The Cantus-Firmus Chansons of T. S.," *Journal of the American Musicological Society* (Summer 1969).

Susskind (originally, **Süsskind**), **(Jan) Walter**, distinguished Czech-born English conductor; b. Prague, May 1, 1913; d. Berkeley, Calif., March 25, 1980. He studied composition with Josef Suk and Karel Hába and piano with Karl Hoffmeister at the Prague Cons.; also studied conducting with Szell at the German Academy of Music in Prague, where he made his debut as a conductor in 1934 with *La Traviata* at the German Opera; also was pianist with the Czech Trio (1933–38). After the German occupation in 1938, he went to London, where he continued to serve as pianist with the exiled Czech Trio until 1942; became a British citizen in 1946. He was music director of the Carl Rosa Opera Co. in London (1943–45); then went to Glasgow in that capacity with the Scottish Orch. in 1946, remaining with it after it became the Scottish National Orch. in 1950. After serving as music director of the Victorian Sym. Orch. in Melbourne (1953–55), he was music director of the Toronto Sym. Orch. (1956–65), the Aspen (Colo.) Music Festival (1962–68), the St. Louis Sym. Orch. (1968–75), and the Mississippi River Festival in Edwardsville, Ill. (1969–75); also taught at the Univ. of Southern Illinois (1968–75). His last position was that of music adviser and principal guest conductor of the Cincinnati Sym. Orch. from 1978 until his death. Susskind was a highly accomplished conductor, being a technically secure and polished musician. He also composed; among his works are 4 songs for Voice and String Quartet (Prague ISCM Festival, Sept. 2, 1935); *9 Slovak Sketches* for Orch.; *Passacaglia* for Timpani and Chamber Orch. (St. Louis, Feb. 24, 1977).

Süssmayr, Franz Xaver, Austrian composer; b. Schwanenstadt, 1766; d. Vienna, Sept. 17, 1803. He studied composition with Maximilian Piessinger and Georg von Pasterwiz; went to Vienna in 1788 as a music teacher; about 1790 he was befriended by Mozart, who gave him composition lessons; Mozart utilized his talents, employing him as a composer and collaborator. After Mozart's death, he took lessons in vocal composition from Salieri; then was a harpsichordist and acting Kapellmeister at the National Theater (1792–94); from 1794 until his death he was Kapellmeister of the National Theater's German opera productions. His most successful stage works were the singspiel *Der Spiegel von Arkadien* (1794) and the ballet *Il noce di Benevento* (1802). After Mozart's death, his widow entrusted the completion of his Requiem to Süssmayr; he was clever in emulating Mozart's style of composition, and his handwriting was so much like Mozart's that it is difficult to distinguish between them. Süssmayr wrote a number of operas and operettas, which he produced in Vienna, among them: *Moses oder Der Auszug aus Ägypten* (May 4, 1792); *L'incanto superato* or *Der besiegte Zauber* (July 8, 1793); *Idris und Zenide* (May 11, 1795); *Die edle Rache* (Aug. 27, 1795); *Die Freiwilligen* (Sept. 27, 1796); *Der Wildfang* (Oct. 4, 1797); *Der Marktschreyer* (July 6, 1799); *Soliman der Zweite, oder Die drei Sultaninnen* (Oct. 1, 1799); *Gülnare oder Die persische Sklavin* (July 5, 1800); *Phasma oder Die Erscheinung im Tempel der Verschwiegenheit* (July 25, 1801). He wrote *secco* recitatives for Mozart's opera *La clemenza di Tito* (Prague, Sept. 6, 1791); composed several numbers for the Vienna production of Grétry's *La Double Épreuve*, given there under the title *Die doppelte Erkenntlichkeit* (Feb. 28, 1796). Other works include 2 clarinet concertos; divertimentos; cassations; some chamber music; sacred works, including a Missa solemnis, 2 German Requiems, and 4 masses; etc. **BIBL.:** G. Sievers, *Mozart und S.* (Mainz, 1829); W. Lehner, *F.X. S. als Opernkomponist* (diss., Univ. of Vienna, 1927; extracts in *Studien zur Musikwissenschaft*, XVIII, 1931); J. Winterberger, *F.X. S.: Leben, Umwelt und Gestalt* (diss., Univ. of Innsbruck, 1946); F. Beyer, "Mozarts Komposition zum Requiem. Zur Frage der Ergänzung," *Acta Mozartiana*, XVIII/2 (1971); R. Angermüller, "S.: Ein Schüler und Freund Salieris," *Mitteilungen der Internationalen Stiftung Mozarteum*, XXI/1–

2 (1973); W. Wlcek, *F.X. S. als Kirchenkomponist* (Tutzing, 1978).

Sutanto, Indonesian composer with radical tendencies; b. Magelang, Central Java, Feb. 5, 1954. He studied with Jack Body at the Akademi Musik Indonesia (A.M.I., a Western music cons. in Yogyakarta), and appeared with him in piano concerts; also studied psychology and literature. He founded a cultural center, Ritus Paguyuban (Inst. of Arts and Cultural Studies), in his native Magelang, and later initiated construction of a center near Candi Mendhut (on the road to Borododur), where he resides. Sutanto calls himself a "social engineer" rather than a composer; arranges day-long conglomerations of performing groups (martial arts, folk music, and trance dance) from neighboring villages and from the more urban Magelang (experimental ensembles). In 1989 he created *Wayang Imaginasi*, a shadow puppet play without shadows or puppets—as the puppet master tells the story and the gamelan plays, a painter stands at intervals and paints characters onto the screen. His works have been played in Indonesia as well as in England, Australia, and New Zealand; his *Sketsa Ide* (1979) was performed at the national festival, Pekan Komponis Muda. He is also active as a journalist and critic. **Works:** *Proses* (1977); *Apa* (1979); *Sketsa Ide* for Chamber Orch., Percussion, and Pumps (1979); *Musik Opera*, consisting of *Blues in My Shoes* for 2 Guitars, Piano, and Vocalists, *Waras Vs Gila*, *Pegawai Sinting* (1981), and *Suara Orang-orang Luka dan Lebaran '82* for Tape (musique concrète) and 50 Dancers (July 23, 1982); *Ritus Paguyban* for 9 Ensembles totaling 74 Players; *Senam Flute* (1986); *Wayang Imaginasi* (1989).

Suter, Hermann, distinguished Swiss conductor, pedagogue, and composer; b. Kaiserstuhl, April 28, 1870; d. Basel, June 22, 1926. He was a pupil of his father, an organist and precentor in Laufenberg; then studied with Hans Huber and Alfred Glaus in Basel; also took courses at the Stuttgart Cons. with Faisst and at the Leipzig Cons. (1888–91) with Reinecke and Homeyer. From 1892 to 1902 he conducted various Swiss choral groups; then settled in Basel as conductor of the Gesangverein (1902–25), the Liedertafel (1902–25), and the Allgemeine Musikgesellschaft sym. concerts (1902–26). He taught at the Zürich Cons. (1896–1902) and was director of the Basel Cons. (1918–21). He wrote a Sym., a Violin Concerto (1924), an oratorio, *Le Laudi di S. Francesco d'Assisi* (1925), 3 string quartets (1901, 1910, 1921), a String Sextet (1921), songs, piano pieces, and organ music. **BIBL.:** W. Merian, *H. S.: Der Dirigent und der Komponist* (Basel, 1936).

Suter, Robert, Swiss composer and teacher; b. St. Gallen, Jan. 30, 1919. In 1937 he entered the Basel Cons., where he received instruction in piano from Paul Baumgartner, in theory from Gustav Güldenstein, Walter Müller von Kulm, and Ernst Mohr, and in composition from Walther Geiser; later took private composition lessons with Wladimir Vogel (1956). He taught at the Bern Cons. (1945–50) and at the Basel Academy of Music (1950–84). **Works: DRAMATIC:** *Konrad von Donnerstadt*, musical fairy tale (1950; Basel, May 5, 1954); *Der fremde Baron*, musical comedy (1951; Basel, March 23, 1952). **ORCH.:** *Kleines konzert* for Piano and Chamber Orch. (St. Gallen, Nov. 17, 1948); *Suite* for Strings (Basel, Sept. 13, 1949); *Petite suite* (1953; Geneva, Dec. 8, 1956); *Impromptu* (1956; Basel, May 11, 1957); *Variationssatz über Schnitter Tod* (1958; Basel, Dec. 2, 1959); *Lyrische Suite* for Chamber Orch. (1959; Lugano, April 29, 1960); *Fantasia* for Clarinet, Harp, and String Orch. (Zürich, Oct. 6, 1965); *Sonata* (1967; Basel, Feb. 22, 1968); *Epitaffio* for Winds, Strings, and Percussion (Lucerne, Sept. 7, 1968); *Trois nocturnes* for Viola and Orch. (1968–69; Basel, March 19, 1970); *Airs et Ritournelles* for Percussion and Instrumental Group (1973; Basel, April 17, 1974); *Jour de fête* for Winds (Grenchen, Dec. 7, 1975); *Musik* (1975–76; Basel, May 25, 1977); *Sinfonia facile* (Basel, Aug. 26, 1977); *Conversazioni concertanti* for Saxophone, Vibraphone, and String Orch. (1978; Zürich, March 2, 1979); *L'Art pour l'art* (1979; Basel,

June 6, 1980); *Marcia funèbre* for 3 Sopranos, Tape, and Orch. (1980–81; Zürich, Sept. 1982); *Vergänglichkeit der Schoenheit* for Countertenor, Tenor, Baritone, and 18 Baroque Instruments (1982–83); Concerto Grosso (1984; Lugano, March 7, 1985); *Mouvements* for Winds (1985; Bern, April 3, 1986); *Gruezi* for Winds (Geneva, May 29, 1987). **CHAMBER:** *Musikalisches Tagebuch* No. 1 for Alto and 6 Instruments (1946) and No. 2 for Baritone and 7 Instruments (1950); 2 string quartets (1952, 1988); Flute Sonata (1954); *Estampida* for Percussion and 7 Instruments (1960); *Heilige Leier, sprich, sei meine Stimme*, chamber cantata for Soprano, Flute, and Guitar (1960); *Serenata* for 7 Instruments (1963–64); *Fanfares et Pastorales* for 2 Horns, Trumpet, and Trombone (1965); *Pastorale d'hiver* for 5 Instruments (1972); Sonata for Violin, Cello, and Piano (1975); *Jeux à quatre* for Saxophone Quartet (1976); *Music for Brass* (1980–81); *Small Talk* for Flute and Guitar (1984); *Ceremonie* for 6 Percussion (1984); Sextet for 2 Violins, 2 Violas, and 2 Cellos (1987); also piano works. **CHORAL:** *Geisha-Lieder* for Soprano, Chorus, and 6 Instruments (1943); *Ballade von den Seeraeubern* for Men's Chorus and Instruments (1952); *Jedem das Seine* for Women's Chorus (1955); *Ballade von des Cortez Leuten* for Speaker, Chorus, Speaking Chorus, and Chamber Orch. (1960); *Ein Blatt aus Sommerlichen Tagen* for Women's Chorus (1965–66); *Die sollen loben den Namen des Herrn*, motet (1971); *. . . Drei Geistliche Sprüche* (1971); *. . . aber auch lobet den Himmel* for Tenor, Baritone, Bass, Men's Chorus, Children's Chorus, and Instrumental Ensemble (1976); *Der abwesende Gott* for Soprano, Tenor, Speaker, 2 Choruses, Speaking Chorus, and Orch. (1978); *Bhalt du mi Allewyyl lieb* for Children's Chorus and Wind Ensemble (1986).

BIBL.: D. Larese and J. Wildberger, *R. S.* (Amriswil, 1967); J. Wildberger, "R. S.: Schweizer Komponist," *Schweizerische Musikzeitung/Revue Musicale Suisse* (Nov.–Dec. 1967).

Sutermeister, Heinrich, important Swiss composer; b. Feuerthalen, Aug. 12, 1910. He studied philology in Basel and at the Sorbonne in Paris (1930–31); then was a pupil of Orff, Courvoisier, and Röhr at the Munich Academy of Music (1932–34). Subsequently he devoted himself mainly to composition; also taught at the Hannover Hochschule für Musik (1963–75). His main endeavor is to create a type of modern opera that is dramatically effective and melodically pleasing; in his musical philosophy he follows the organic line of thought, with the natural impulses of the human body determining the rhythmic course of a composition; discordant combinations of sounds are legitimate parts of modern harmony in Sutermeister's works, but he rejects artificial doctrines such as orthodox dodecaphony. **WORKS: OPERAS:** *Die schwarze Spinne*, radio opera (1935; Bern Radio, Oct. 15, 1936; stage premiere, St. Gall, March 2, 1949); *Romeo und Julia*, after Shakespeare (1938–40; Dresden, April 13, 1940; his 1st and greatest success); *Die Zauberinsel*, after Shakespeare's *The Tempest* (Dresden, Oct. 31, 1942); *Niobe* (1943–45; Zürich, June 22, 1946); *Raskolnikoff*, after Dostoyevsky's *Crime and Punishment* (1946–48; Stockholm, Oct. 14, 1948); *Der rote Stiefel* (1949–51; Stockholm, Nov. 22, 1951); *Titus Feuerfuchs*, burlesque opera (1956–58; Basel, April 14, 1958); *Seraphine*, opera-buffa after Rabelais (Zürich Radio, June 10, 1959; stage premiere, Munich, Feb. 25, 1960); *Das Gespenst von Canterville*, television opera after Oscar Wilde (1962–63; German television, Sept. 6, 1964); *Madame Bovary*, after Flaubert (Zürich, May 26, 1967); *La Croisade des Enfants*, television opera (1969); *Der Flaschenteufel*, television opera after R.L. Stevenson (1969–70; German television, 1971); radio ballad, *Füsse im Feuer* (stage premiere, Berlin, Feb. 12, 1950); radio melodrama, *Fingerhütchen* (stage premiere, St. Gall, April 26, 1950). **BALLETS:** *Das Dorf unter dem Gletscher* (1936; Karlsruhe, May 2, 1937); *Max und Moritz* (1951; St. Gall, 1963). **VOCAL:** 8 numbered cantatas: No. 1, *Andreas Gryphius*, for Chorus (1935–36); No. 2 for Contralto, Chorus, and 2 Pianos (1943–44); No. 3, *Dem Allgegenwärtigen*, for Soloists, Chorus, and Orch. (1957–58); No. 4, *Das Hohelied*, for Soloists, Chorus, and Orch. (1960); No. 5, *Der Papagei aus Kuba*, for Chorus

and Chamber Orch. (1961); No. 6, *Erkennen und Schaffen* (in French, *Croire et créer*), for Soloists, Chorus, and Orch. (1963); No. 7, *Sonnenhymne des Echnaton*, for Male Chorus, 2 Horns, 3 Trumpets, 2 Trombones, Tuba, Piano, and Percussion (1965); No. 8, *Omnia ad Unum*, for Baritone, Chorus, and Orch. (1965–66); also *Missa da Requiem* for Soloists, Chorus, and Orch. (1952; Basel, June 11, 1954); *Ecclesia* for Soloists, Chorus, and Orch. (1972–73; Lausanne, Oct. 18, 1975); *Te Deum* for Soprano, Chorus, and Orch. (1974). **ORCH.:** *Divertimento No. 1* for String Orch. (1936) and *No. 2* for Orch. (1959–60); 3 piano concertos (1943; 1953; 1961–62); 2 cellos concertos (1954–55; 1971); *Sérénade pour Montreux* for 2 Oboes, 2 Horns, and String Orch. (1970); Clarinet Concerto (1974); *Quadrifoglio* for 4 Wind Instruments and Orch. (1977); also chamber pieces.

BIBL.: D. Larese, *H. S.* (Amriswil, 1972).

Suthaus, (Heinrich) Ludwig, eminent German tenor; b. Cologne, Dec. 12, 1906; d. Berlin, Sept. 7, 1971. He studied voice in Cologne; made his operatic debut in Aachen in 1928 as Walther von Stolzing in *Die Meistersinger von Nürnberg*; sang in Essen (1931–33) and Stuttgart (1933–41); in 1941 he joined the Berlin State Opera, where he made many appearances until 1948; then sang with the Berlin Städtische Oper until 1965. He made his U.S. debut with the San Francisco Opera in 1953 as Aegisthus. He was one of the outstanding Heldentenors of his time and was engaged at the Bayreuth Festivals in Wagnerian roles (1943–44; 1956–57).

Sutherland, Dame Joan, celebrated Australian soprano; b. Sydney, Nov. 7, 1926. She 1st studied piano and voice with her mother; at age 19 she commenced vocal training with John and Aida Dickens in Sydney, making her debut there as Dido in a concert performance of *Dido and Aeneas* in 1947; then made her stage debut there in the title role of *Judith* in 1951; subsequently continued her vocal studies with Clive Carey at the Royal College of Music in London; also studied at the Opera School there. She made her Covent Garden debut in London as the 1st Lady in *Die Zauberflöte* in 1952; attracted attention there when she created the role of Jenifer in *The Midsummer Marriage* (1955) and as Gilda (1957); also appeared in the title role of Alcina in the Handel Opera Soc. production (1957). In the meantime, she married **Richard Bonynge** (1954), who coached her in the *bel canto* operatic repertoire. After making her North American debut as Donna Anna in Vancouver (1958), she scored a triumph as Lucia at Covent Garden (Feb. 17, 1959). From then on she pursued a brilliant international career. She made her U.S. debut as Alcina in Dallas in 1960. Her Metropolitan Opera debut in N.Y. as Lucia on Nov. 26, 1961, was greeted by extraordinary acclaim. She continued to sing at the Metropolitan and other major opera houses on both sides of the Atlantic; also took her own company to Australia in 1965 and 1974; during her husband's music directorship with the Australian Opera in Sydney (1976–86), she made stellar appearances with the company. On Oct. 2, 1990, she made her operatic farewell in *Les Huguenots* in Sydney. Sutherland was universally acknowledged as one of the foremost interpreters of the *bel canto* repertoire of her time. She particularly excelled in roles from operas by Rossini, Bellini, and Donizetti; was also a fine Handelian. In 1961 she was made a Commander of the Order of the British Empire and in 1979 was named a Dame Commander of the Order of the British Empire. With her husband, she publ. *The Joan Sutherland Album* (N.Y., 1986).

BIBL.: R. Braddon, *J. S.* (London, 1962); E. Greenfield, *J. S.* (London, 1972); B. Adams, *La Stupenda: A Biography of J. S.* (London, 1981); Q. Eaton, *S. & Bonynge: An Intimate Biography* (N.Y., 1987); N. Major, *J. S.* (London, 2nd ed., 1988).

Sutherland, Margaret (Ada), Australian pianist, teacher, and composer; b. Adelaide, Nov. 20, 1897; d. Melbourne, Aug. 12, 1984. She studied piano with Edward Goll and composition with Fritz Hart at the Marshall Hall Cons. (1914); then continued her training at the Univ. of Melbourne Conservatorium. She launched her career as a pianist in 1916; also was active as a teacher of theory and piano. In 1923 she went to Europe to pursue the study of composition and orchestration; received instruction in Vienna and briefly with Bax in London. In 1925 she returned to her homeland; was active as a pianist, teacher, and composer from 1935. In 1970 she was made an Officer of the Order of the British Empire for her services to Australian music. Her compositions are marked by Classical restraint; most of them follow Baroque forms.

WORKS: STAGE: *Dithyramb*, ballet (1941); *The Young Kabbarli*, chamber opera (1964). **ORCH.:** *Suite on a Theme of Purcell* (1935); *Pavane* (1938); *The Soldier* for Chorus and Strings (1938); *Prelude and Jig* for Strings (1939); Concerto for Strings (1945); *Adagio* for 2 Solo Violins and Orch. (1946); *Haunted Hills*, tone poem (1953); Violin Concerto (1954); *4 Symphonic Studies* (1954); Concerto Grosso (1955); *3 Temperaments* (1958); *Fantasy* for Violin and Orch. (1960); *Concertante* for Oboe, Percussion, and String Orch. (1962). **CHAMBER:** Violin Sonata (1925); Trio for Clarinet, Viola, and Piano (1934); *House Quartet* for Clarinet or Violin, Viola, Horn or Cello, and Piano (1936); 2 string quartets (1939, 1967); Sonata for Clarinet and Piano (1944); Trio for Oboe and 2 Violins (1951); *Contrasts* for 2 Violins (1944); Quartet for English Horn and String Trio (1955); *6 Bagatelles* for Violin and Viola (1956); *Divertimento* for String Trio (1958); Sonatina for Oboe and Piano (1958); Quartet for Clarinet and Strings (1967). **PIANO:** Sonatina (1958); *Extension* (1967); *Chiaroscuro 1* and *2* (1968); *Voices 1* and *2* (1968).

Sutro, Rose Laura (b. Baltimore, Sept. 15, 1870; d. there, Jan. 11, 1957) and **Ottilie** (b. Baltimore, Jan. 4, 1872; d. there, Sept. 12, 1970), American duo-pianists. They were the daughters of Otto Sutro, a patron of art and founder of the Baltimore Oratorio Soc. Both began piano lessons with their mother, and in 1889 were sent to Berlin to continue their studies. They made a spectacular debut in London on July 13, 1894; their 1st American appearance took place in Brooklyn on Nov. 13, 1894, followed by a tour of the U.S. Returning to Europe, they won fresh laurels, and were invited to play before Queen Victoria. Max Bruch wrote his Concerto for 2 Pianos and Orch. expressly for them, and they gave its premiere with the Philadelphia Orch. on Dec. 29, 1916.

Suwardi (Soewardi), Aloysius, respected Indonesian composer, performer, teacher, and experimental-instrument maker; b. Sukoharjo, Central Java, June 21, 1951. He studied in Surakarta at the Konservatori Karawitan (KOKAR, high school cons.), then at the Akademi Seni Karawitan Indonesia (A.S.K.I., college cons.), graduating in 1981 with the thesis *The Construction of Suling in Central Java*; subsequently taught classical music there (Sekolah Tinggi Seni Indonesia/S.T.S.I.). In 1974 he became involved in new music circles and subsequently participated in new music festivals throughout Indonesia. He developed a fine reputation as a player of traditional gamelan music and as a gamelan tuner and restorer; he is often called upon to repair and/or retune Javanese gamelan throughout Indonesia, Europe, and the U.S. In 1986–87 he was a Fulbright visiting scholar to the U.S., teaching at several Midwest univs. As a composer, Suwardi is best known for works that make use of his own experimental instruments; his instrument innovations include placing the bronze keys of the gender on motor-driven resonators, developing a giant-sized gambang (wooden xylophone) inspired by the log xylophones of Africa, and designing and building a kind of water suling wherein the air goes through a tube and into a tin can of water before passing, modified, into a bamboo tube with finger holes. Among his compositions are *Ngalor-Ngidul* (1982; with Rustopo and Suparno), *Gender* (1984), *Sebuah Process* (1984), and *Sak-sake* (1988). He is one of the few Indonesian composers to have been invited twice (1984, 1988) to the Pekan Komponis Muda, a national young composers' festival held annually in Jakarta.

Suzuki, Shin'ichi, influential Japanese music educator and violin teacher; b. Nagoya, Oct. 18, 1898. He was the son of Masakichi Suzuki (1859–1944), a maker of string instruments

and the founder of the Suzuki Violin Seizo Co. He studied violin with Ko Ando in Tokyo and with Karl Klinger in Berlin (1921–28); upon his return to Japan, he formed the Suzuki Quartet with 3 of his brothers; also made appearances as a conductor with his own Tokyo String Orch. He became president of the Teikoku Music School in 1930; subsequently devoted most of his time to education, especially the teaching of children. He maintained that any child, given the right stimuli under proper conditions in a group environment, could achieve a high level of competence as a performer. In 1950 he organized the Saino Kyoiku Kenkyu-kai in Matsumoto, where he taught his method most successfully. In subsequent years his method was adopted for instruction on other instruments as well. He made many tours of the U.S. and Europe, where he lectured and demonstrated his method. See K. Selden, translator, *Where Love Is Deep: The Writings of Shin-ichi Suzuki* (St. Louis, 1982).

BIBL.: C. Cook, *S. Education in Action* (N.Y., 1970); E. Mills and T. Murthy, eds., *The S. Conception: An Introduction to a Successful Method for Early Music Education* (Berkeley, 1973).

Suzuki, Yukikazu, Japanese composer; b. Tokyo, Feb. 11, 1954. He studied with Hara Hoiroshi, Shishido Mutsuo, Matsumura Teizō, and Mayuzumi Toshiro at the Tokyo National Univ. of Fine Arts and Music (degree, 1984). In 1978 he was awarded 1st prize in the Japan Music Competition, and in 1979 5th prize in the International Contemporary Composer's Conference.

WORKS: Sonata for Oboe and Piano (1976); *Kyō-in* for 6 Players (1977); *Climat* for Orch. (1978); *Symphonic Metamorphoses* for Piano (1980); *Kundarini* for Contrabass (1981); *Utsukushi i mono nitsuite*, suite for Chorus (1982); *Quintet* for Piano, 2 Violins, Viola, and Cello (1987); *Sound of Sea*, suite for Chorus (1989).

Svanholm, Set (Karl Viktor), noted Swedish tenor; b. Vasterås, Sept. 2, 1904; d. Saltsjö-Duvnäs, near Stockholm, Oct. 4, 1964. He served as a church organist in Tillberga and Säby; studied voice with John Forsell at the Opera School of the Stockholm Cons. He made his operatic debut as a baritone as Silvio at the Royal Theater in Stockholm in 1930; in 1936 he began singing tenor roles. In addition to his appearances at the Royal Theater in Stockholm, he also sang at the Salzburg Festival and the Vienna State Opera (1938), the Berlin State Opera, La Scala in Milan (1941–42), and the Bayreuth Festival (1942). In 1946 he appeared as Tristan in Rio de Janeiro and as Lohengrin in San Francisco; on Nov. 15, 1946, he made his Metropolitan Opera debut in N.Y. as Siegfried; remained on its roster until his farewell appearance as Parsifal on March 24, 1956; also sang at London's Covent Garden (1948–57). He was director of the Royal Theater in Stockholm (1956–63). Among his best roles were Radames, Tannhäuser, Otello, and Siegmund; he was equally successful in operas of Wagner and Verdi.

Švara, Danilo, Yugoslav conductor and composer; b. Ricmanje, near Trieste, April 2, 1902; d. Ljubljana, April 25, 1981. He studied piano with Troste in Vienna (1920–22); pursued training in politics and law at the Univ. of Frankfurt am Main (1922–25) and concurrently took piano lessons from Malata and studied conducting with Scherchen; attended the Frankfurt Hochschule für Musik (1927–30), where he took courses in composition with Sekles, in conducting with von Schmiedel and Rottenberg, and in stage direction with Wallerstein. He began his career as répétiteur and conductor at the Ljubljana Opera in 1925; later conducted there regularly, serving as its director (1957–59); also wrote music criticism and taught conducting at the Ljubljana Academy of Music. His compositions are cast in a modern idiom.

WORKS: OPERAS: *Kleopatra* (1937); *Veronika Deseniška* (1943); *Slovo od mladosti* (Farewell to Youth; 1952); *Ocean* (1963). **BALLET:** *Nina* (1962). **ORCH.:** 3 syms. (1933, 1935, 1947); *Valse interrompue* (1948); *Sinfonia da camera in modo istriano* (1954); *Concerto grosso dodecafono* (1961); 2 suites (1962); *Dodekafonia: I, Duo concertante* for Flute, Harpsichord, and Orch. (1967), II, Violin Concerto (1966), III, Oboe Concerto (1966), IV, *Symposium* for Oboe, Viola, Harp, and Orch. (1968), and V, Clarinet Concerto (1969); also chamber music; choral pieces; songs; piano pieces.

Svéd, Sándor, Hungarian baritone; b. Budapest, May 28, 1904; d. Vienna, June 9, 1979. He studied violin at the Budapest Cons.; then went to Milan for vocal studies with Sammarco and Stracciari. He made his operatic debut as Count Luna in Budapest in 1930; was a member of the Vienna State Opera (1936–39); also sang at Covent Garden in London and the Salzburg Festival. On Dec. 2, 1940, he made his debut under the name of Alexander Sved at the Metropolitan Opera in N.Y. as Renato in *Un ballo in maschera;* he remained on its roster until 1948, and then returned for the 1949–50 season. He subsequently sang in Rome, in Paris, and at the Bayreuth Festival; also made appearances with the Budapest Opera, and later toured as a concert singer. In 1956 he went to Stuttgart as a vocal teacher.

Sveinbjörnsson, Sveinbjörn, Icelandic pianist and composer; b. near Reykjavík, June 28, 1847; d. Copenhagen, Feb. 23, 1927. After theological training, he went to Copenhagen to pursue musical studies with V.C. Ravn (1868–70). Following further studies with Reinecke in Leipzig (1872–73), he settled in Edinburgh, where he taught piano and was active as a concert pianist, making 2 major tours of North America (1911–13; 1919–22). He was an accomplished composer of choral works, songs, and piano pieces; his hymn in celebration of the millennium anniversary of the Norse settlement in Iceland (1874) was adopted as the Icelandic national anthem.

Bibl.: J. Thorarinsson, *S. S.* (Reykjavík, 1969).

Sveinsson, Atli Heimir, Icelandic composer; b. Reykjavík, Sept. 21, 1938. He studied piano with Sigurbjónsson at the Reykjavík College of Music and piano, conducting, and composition at the Cologne Staatliche Hochschule für Musik (1959–62), where his principal mentors were Raphael, Zimmermann, and Petzold; also attended the Darmstadt (1959–61) and Cologne new music courses given by Stockhausen, Pousseur et al. and the electronic music courses in Bilthoven presented by Koenig. He was active as a teacher in Reykjavík and served as president of the Icelandic Composers' Soc. (1972–83).

Works: *Hlými* (Sonant) for Chamber Orch. (1963); *Fönsun I–III* for Singers, Actors, Tape, and Chamber Ensemble; *Klif* (Tautology) for Flute, Cello, and Piano (1968); *Seimur* (Soundings) for 1 or 2 Pianos, and any number of Instruments (1968); *Spectacles* for Percussion and Tape (1969); *Tengsl* (Connections) for Orch. (1970); *Bizzarreries I* for Flute, Piano, and Tape (1970); *Könnun,* Viola Concerto (1971); Flute Concerto (1973); *Flower Shower* for Orch. (1974); *I Call It* for Contralto, Piano, Cello, and 2 Percussionists (1974); *Trobar Clus* for Bassoon and Orch. (1980); chamber opera, *The Silken Drum* (Reykjavík, June 6, 1982); *Infinitesimal Fragments of Eternity* for Chamber Orch. (St. Paul, Oct. 7, 1982); *Kurt Weill, in memoriam* for Chamber Orch. (Reykjavík, Feb. 26, 1983); *Jubilus* for Trombone and Orch. (1983; rev. as *Jubilus II,* 1987); *Recitation* for Piano and Orch. (1984); *Centennial* for String Quartet (1985); *The Night on Our Shoulders* for Alto, Women's Chorus, and Orch. (1986); *Dreamboat* for Violin, Harpsichord, and String Orch. (1987); *Fenja og Menja* for Men's Chorus, Oboe, Clarinet, Bassoon, and Horn (1989).

Svendsen, Johan (Severin), eminent Norwegian composer and conductor; b. Christiania, Sept. 30, 1840; d. Copenhagen, June 14, 1911. His father, a military musician, taught him to play various instruments; by his early teens he was performing in local dance orchs. and composing dances and marches. After joining the army at age 15, he became solo clarinetist in the regimental band. He then received violin lessons from F. Ursin and played in the Norwegian Theater orch. in Christiania; subsequently studied with Carl Arnold. Receiving a stipend from the King, he pursued his musical training at the Leipzig Cons. (1863–67) with Ferdinand David, Moritz Hauptmann, E.F. Richter, and Carl Reinecke, graduating with a 1st prize in composition. In 1867 he conducted a concert of

his works in Christiania; although an anonymous review written by Grieg was full of praise, the public showed little interest and Svendsen returned to Leipzig. In 1868 he went to Paris, where he became acquainted with young progressive French composers. In 1871 he married the American Sarah Levett in N.Y., and then returned to Leipzig to become concertmaster and 2nd conductor of the Euterpe concerts. He went to Bayreuth in 1872 to play in the special concert of Beethoven's 9th Sym. under Wagner's direction for the laying of the cornerstone of the Festspielhaus. Svendsen subsequently became a close friend to Wagner. In 1872 he returned to Christiania to become co-conductor with Grieg of the Music Soc. concerts; in 1874 he became sole conductor and was granted an annual government composer's salary. After sojourns in Rome (1877–78) and London (1878), he again went to Paris. In 1880 he returned to Christiania and resumed his position as conductor of the Music Soc. concerts. In 1882 he conducted 2 concerts of his own music in Copenhagen, the success of which led to his appointment as principal conductor of the Royal Opera there in 1883, but the loss of his composer's salary from his native country. All the same, he retained his Norwegian citizenship while transforming the musical life of Copenhagen, conducting both operatic and orch. performances of great distinction. He also appeared as a guest conductor in Vienna, St. Petersburg, Moscow, London, Paris, Brussels, and other cities with brilliant success. In 1901 he divorced his 1st wife and married Juliette (Vilhelmine) Haase, a ballerina. In 1908 he retired from the Royal Opera and was granted an honorary pension by the Danish government; not to be outdone, the Norwegian government restored his annual composer's salary. With Grieg, Svendsen represents the full flowering of the national Romantic movement in Norwegian music. Unlike his famous compatriot, he proved a master of large orch. forms; he was unquestionably the foremost Nordic symphonist of his time, and during the last quarter of the 19th century enjoyed an international reputation equal to that of Grieg.

Works: Orch.: *Caprice* for Violin and Orch. (1863; Leipzig, Dec. 1864); 2 syms.: No. 1, op. 4 (1865–67; Christiania, Oct. 12, 1867); No. 2, op. 15 (Christiania, Oct. 14, 1876); Violin Concerto, op. 6 (1868–70; Leipzig, Feb. 6, 1872); Cello Concerto, op. 7 (1870; Leipzig, March 16, 1871); Symphonic Introduction to Bjørnson's *Sigurd Slembe,* op. 8 (Leipzig, Dec. 12, 1871); *Karneval i Paris,* op. 9 (Christiania, Oct. 26, 1872); Funeral March for King Carl XV, op. 10 (1872); *Zorahayda,* op. 11 (Christiania, Oct. 3, 1874; rev. 1879; Christiania, May 11, 1880); *Festival Polonaise,* op. 12 (Christiania, Aug. 6, 1873); Coronation March for Oscar II, op. 13 (1873); *Norsk kunstner-karneval,* op. 14 (Christiania, March 17, 1874); 4 *Norwegian Rhapsodies:* No. 1, op. 17 (1876; Christiania, Sept. 25, 1877); No. 2, op. 19 (1876; Munich, 1880); No. 3, op. 21 (1876; Paris, Jan. 1879); No. 4, op. 22 (1877; Paris, Feb. 1, 1879); *Romeo og Julie,* fantasy, op. 18 (Christiania, Oct. 14, 1876); *Romance* for Violin and Orch., op. 26 (Christiania, Oct. 30, 1881); *Polonaise,* op. 28 (1882); *Foraaret kommer* (Coming of Spring), ballet, op. 33 (Copenhagen, May 26, 1892); *Andante funèbre* (Copenhagen, June 30, 1894); *Prelude* (Copenhagen, Dec. 18, 1898). Chamber: String Quartet, op. 1 (1864; Leipzig, May 21, 1865); String Octet, op. 3 (Leipzig, Feb. 24?, 1866); String Quintet, op. 5 (Leipzig, May 17, 1867). Vocal: 2 partsongs for Men's Voices, op. 2 (1865); 5 songs for Voice and Piano, op. 23 (1879); 4 songs for Voice and Piano, op. 24 (1879); 2 songs, op. 25 (1878, 1880); 4 cantatas, op. 29 (1881, 1881, 1884, 1892). Piano: *Anna,* polka (1854); *Til saeters* (At the Mountain Pasture), waltz (1856). Also several arrangements for String Orch.

Bibl.: H. Ende, "J. S. S.," *Musikalisches Wochenblatt* (Leipzig, March 31 and April 7, 1871); "Two Afternoons with S., the Composer," *Watson's Art Journal* (N.Y., Aug. 12, 1871); "J.S. S.," *American Art Journal* (N.Y., May 8, 1880); C. Nielsen, "J. S.," *Politiken* (Copenhagen, Sept. 30, 1900); idem, "Tale til J. S., 12. november 1907," *Tilskueren,* XXV (1908); G. Hauch, ed., "Breve fra J. S.," *Samtiden,* XXIV (1913); F. Benestad, "J. S.s Violinkonsert," *Norsk musikkgranskings årbok*

1956–8; Ø. Eckhoff, "Noen saerdrag ved J. S.s instrumental-stil," *Festkrift til Olav Gurvin* (Drammen and Oslo, 1968); B. Kortsen, *J. S.'s Cellokonsert, op. 7. En analyse* (Bergen, 1970).

Svetlanov, Evgeny (Feodorovich), prominent Russian conductor and composer; b. Moscow, Sept. 6, 1928. He studied composition with Mikhail Gnessin and piano with Mariya Gurvich at the Gnessin Inst. in Moscow (graduated, 1951); took courses in composition with Shaporin and in conducting with Gauk at the Moscow Cons. (graduated, 1955). In 1953 he made his debut as a conductor with the All-Union Radio orch. in Moscow; was a conductor at the Bolshoi Theater there from 1955, serving as its chief conductor (1962–64). In 1965 he was appointed chief conductor of the State Sym. Orch. of the U.S.S.R.; from 1979 he was a principal guest conductor of the London Sym. Orch. He also made appearances as a pianist. In 1968 he was named a People's Artist of the U.S.S.R.; in 1972 he was awarded the Lenin Prize and in 1975 the Glinka Prize. He has won particular distinction for his compelling performances of the Russian repertoire. He wrote a Sym. (1956); *Siberian Fantasy* for Orch. (1953); Piano Concerto (1951); incidental music for plays; film scores. He is married to the Russian soprano **Larissa Avdeyeva.**

BIBL.: L. Krylova, *E. S.* (Moscow, 1986).

Sviridov, Georgi (Vasilevich), significant Russian composer and pianist; b. Fatezh, near Kursk, Dec. 16, 1915. He studied at the Leningrad Cons. with Shostakovich (graduated, 1941); made tours as a pianist from 1945 while devoting much time to composition. In 1970 he was made a People's Artist of the U.S.S.R. In his music, Sviridov adheres to the ideals of socialist realism, seeking inspiration in Russian folk songs; the texts of his vocal works are usually taken from Russian literature. His *Oratorio pathétique* (1959), to words by Mayakovsky, composed in a grandly songful "optimistic" style, became one of the most successful scores by a Soviet composer.

WORKS: Music for Shakespeare's *Othello* (1944); *Twinkling Lights,* operetta (1951); music for films: *Blizzard* (1964) and *Time Forge Ahead!* (1966); Sym. for String Orch. (1940); *Little Triptych* (1964); Piano Quintet (1945); Piano Trio (1945); String Quartet (1945); *Music for Chamber Orchestra* (1964); choral works: *The Decembrists,* oratorio (1955); *Poem to the Memory of Sergei Essenin* (1956); *Poem about Lenin* for Bass, Chorus, and Orch. (1960); *5 Songs about Our Fatherland* for Voices, Chorus, and Orch. (1967); numerous piano pieces and songs.

BIBL.: D. Frishman, ed., *G. S.* (Moscow, 1971); A. Sokhor, *G. S.* (Moscow, 1972).

Svoboda, Tomáš, Czech-American composer; b. Paris (of Czech parents), Dec. 6, 1939. His father was the renowned mathematician Antonín Svoboda. After the outbreak of World War II, his family went to Boston, where he began piano lessons as a child; in 1946 he went with his family to Prague and studied at the Cons. with Hlobil, Kabeláč, and Dobiáš (1954–62), graduating with degrees in composition, conducting, and percussion; he was only 17 when his 1st Sym. was premiered by the Prague Sym. Orch. Following further training at the Prague Academy of Music (1962–64), he settled in the U.S. and pursued graduate studies with Dahl and Stevens at the Univ. of Southern Calif. in Los Angeles (1966–69). In 1971 he became a teacher of composition, theory, and percussion at Portland (Oreg.) State Univ. His music is marked by broad melodic lines in economically disposed harmonies; there are elements of serialism in chromatic episodes.

WORKS: THEATER: Incidental music to D. Seabrook's play *The Clockmaker* (1986). **ORCH.:** 5 syms.: No. 1, *of Nature* (1956; Prague, Sept. 7, 1957; rev. 1984; Portland, Oreg., March 10, 1985); No. 2 (1964); No. 3 for Organ and Orch. (1965); No. 4, *Apocalyptic* (1975; Portland, Oreg., Feb. 19, 1978); No. 5, *in Unison* (1978; Portland, Oreg., Nov. 13, 1988); *Scherzo* for 2 Euphonias and Orch. (1955; Prague, Sept. 3, 1958); *In a Linden's Shadow,* symphonic poem for Organ and Orch. (1958); *Dramatic Overture* (Prague Radio, Sept. 18, 1959); *6 Variations* for Violin and String Orch. (1961); *Christmas Con-*

certino for Harp and Chamber Orch. (1961); *Suite* for Bassoon, Harpsichord, and String Orch. (1962; Prague, April 11, 1963); *Étude* for Chamber Orch. (1963); *3 Pieces* (1966; Sacramento, Calif., March 30, 1967); Concertino for Oboe, Brass Choir, and Timpani (1966; Los Angeles, March 21, 1968); *Reflections* (1968; Toronto, March 21, 1972); *Sinfoniette (à la Renaissance)* (Jacksonville, Oreg., Aug. 14, 1972); *Labyrinth* for Chamber Orch. (1974); *Prelude and Fugue* for String Orch. (1974); 2 piano concertos: No. 1 (Portland, Oreg., Nov. 17, 1974); No. 2 (1989); Violin Concerto (1975; Jacksonville, Oreg., Aug. 15, 1976); *Overture of the Season* (Bend, Oreg., Oct. 6, 1978); *Nocturne (Cosmic Sunset)* (Sunriver, Oreg., Aug. 20, 1981); *Eugene Overture (Festive)* (Eugene, Oreg., Sept. 24, 1982); *Ex libris* (Louisville, Dec. 3, 1983); *Serenade* (Sarasota, Fla., March 24, 1984); Concerto for Chamber Orch. (1986; Portland, Oreg., Sept. 9, 1988); *Dance Suite* (Jacksonville, Oreg., Aug. 8, 1987). **CHAMBER:** *Evening Negro Songs and Dances* for Piano and 2 Percussionists (1956); String Quartet (1960); *Baroque Quintet* for Flute, Oboe, Clarinet, Cello, and Piano (1962); Trio for Oboe, Bassoon, and Piano (1962); Septet for Bassoon, Harpsichord, and String Quintet (1962); Divertimento for 7 Instruments (1967); *Parabola* for Clarinet, Violin, Viola, Cello, and Piano (1971); Trio for Flute, Oboe, and Bassoon (1979); *Passacaglia and Fugue* for Violin, Cello, and Piano (1981); Trio for Electric Guitar, Piano, and Percussion (1982); Trio Sonata for Electric Guitar, Vibraphone, and Piano (1982); Brass Quintet (N.Y., Nov. 22, 1983); Violin Sonata (1984); Trio for Violin, Cello, and Piano (1984); Chorale in E-flat ("homage to Aaron Copland") for Clarinet, Violin, Viola, Double Bass, and Piano (N.Y., May 10, 1985); *Legacy* for Brass Septet (1988); also piano music, including 2 sonatas (1967, 1985); vocal works, including *Celebration of Life,* cantata on Aztec poetry for Soprano, Tenor, Chorus, Instruments, and Tape (Portland, Oreg., Oct. 31, 1976), *Festival* for Men's Chorus (1987), and songs; organ pieces.

Swan, Alfred (Julius), Russian-born English-American musicologist, educator, and composer; b. St. Petersburg (of English parents), Oct. 9, 1890; d. Haverford, Pa., Oct. 2, 1970. After attending a German-language school in St. Petersburg, he studied at Oxford Univ. (B.A., 1911; M.A., 1934); also took courses in composition at the St. Petersburg Cons. (1911). During the Russian Civil War, he served with the American Red Cross in Siberia (1918–19); then emigrated to the U.S.; taught at the Univ. of Virginia (1921–23) and was head of the music depts. at Swarthmore College and Haverford College (1926–58). His specialty was Russian music. Swan wrote a Trio for Flute, Clarinet, and Piano (1932); 2 violin sonatas (1913, 1948); 4 piano sonatas (1932–46); several albums of songs. He ed. *Songs from Many Lands* (1923) and *Recueil de chansons russes* (1936); also contributed articles to many journals.

WRITINGS: *Scriabin* (London, 1923); *Music 1900–1930* (N.Y., 1930); *The Music Director's Guide to Musical Literature* (N.Y., 1941); *Russian Music and Its Sources in Chant and Folksong* (N.Y., 1973).

Swan, Timothy, American composer and tunebook compiler; b. Worcester, Mass., July 23, 1758; d. Northfield, Mass., July 23, 1842. His only musical training consisted of 3 weeks at a singing school, and while serving in the Continental Army he also learned to play the fife. From 1783 he lived in Suffield, Conn., and in 1807 moved to Northfield, Mass. His fuging tunes *Bristol, Montague,* and *Rainbow* and his hymn tune *China* were widely known. He publ. a vol. of secular duets as *The Songster's Assistant* (c.1786) and the tunebook *New England Harmony* (1801).

BIBL.: F. Metcalf, *American Writers and Compilers of Sacred Music* (N.Y., 1925); G. Webb, *T. S.: Yankee Tunesmith* (diss., Univ. of Illinois, 1972); S. Murray, "T. S. and Yankee Psalmody," *Musical Quarterly,* LXI (1975).

Swann, Frederick (Lewis), American organist; b. Lewisburg, W.Va., July 30, 1931. He studied at the Northwestern Univ. School of Music in Evanston, Ill. (Mus.B., 1952), and at the School of Sacred Music of the Union Theological Seminary

(M. of Sacred Mus., 1954). He was organist (1958–82) and director of music (1966–82) at the Riverside Church in N.Y.; also was chairman of the organ dept. at the Manhattan School of Music (1972–82); then was director of music and organist at the Crystal Cathedral in Garden Grove, Calif. (from 1983). He made many recital tours of the U.S., Canada, and Europe.

Swanson, Howard, black American composer; b. Atlanta, Aug. 18, 1907; d. N.Y., Nov. 12, 1978. He grew up in Cleveland, where he began piano lessons at 9. As a youth, he earned a living by manual labor on the railroad and as a postal clerk. He entered the Cleveland Inst. of Music at the age of 20, enrolling in evening courses with Herbert Elwell (graduated, 1937); obtained a stipend to go to Paris, where he studied composition with Nadia Boulanger (1938–40). Returning to the U.S., he took a job with the Internal Revenue Service (1941–45). In 1952 he received a Guggenheim fellowship that enabled him to go back to Paris, where he lived until 1966 before settling permanently in N.Y. Swanson's songs attracted the attention of such notable singers as Marian Anderson and William Warfield, who sang them on tours. He achieved signal success with his *Short Symphony* (Sym. No. 2, 1948), a work of simple melodic inspiration, which received considerable acclaim at its 1st performance by the N.Y. Phil., conducted by Mitropoulos (Nov. 23, 1950). In 1952 it won the Music Critics' Circle Award.
WORKS: ORCH.: 3 syms.: No. 1 (1945); No. 2, *Short Symphony* (1948; N.Y., Nov. 23, 1950); No. 3 (N.Y., March 1, 1970); *Night Music* for Chamber Orch. (1950); *Music for Strings* (1952); *Concerto for Orchestra* (1954; Louisville, Jan. 9, 1957); Piano Concerto (1956); *Fantasy Piece* for Soprano Saxophone or Clarinet and Strings (1969). **CHAMBER:** *Nocturne* for Violin and Piano (1948); *Suite* for Cello and Piano (1949); *Soundpiece* for Brass Quintet (1952); *Vista No. 2* for String Octet (1969); Cello Sonata (N.Y., May 13, 1973); Trio for Flute, Oboe, and Piano (1975). **PIANO:** 3 sonatas (1948, 1976, 1976); *2 Nocturnes* (1967). **VOCAL:** *Songs for Patricia* for Soprano and Strings or Piano (1951); *Nightingales* for Men's Voices (1952); *We Delighted, My Friend* for Chorus (1977); 30 songs for Voice and Piano, including *The Negro Speaks of Rivers* (1942), *The Junk Man* (1946), *Ghosts in Love* (1950), and *The Valley* (1951).
BIBL.: E. Ennett, *An Analysis and Comparison of Selected Piano Sonatas by Three Contemporary Black Composers: George Walker, H. S., and Roque Cordero* (diss., N.Y. Univ., 1973); D. Baker, L. Belt, and H. Hudson, eds., *The Black Composer Speaks* (Metuchen, N.J., 1978); R. Spearman, "The *Joy* of Langston Hughes and H. S.," *Black Perspective in Music,* IX (1981).

Swarowsky, Hans, noted Austrian conductor and pedagogue; b. Budapest, Sept. 16, 1899; d. Salzburg, Sept. 10, 1975. He studied in Vienna with Schoenberg and Webern, with whom he formed a friendly association; he also was in close relationship with Richard Strauss. He devoted himself mainly to conducting; occupied posts as opera conductor in Hamburg (1932), Berlin (1934), and Zürich (1937–40); after conducting the Krakow orch. (1944–45), he was conductor of the Vienna Sym. Orch. (1946–48) and the Graz Opera (1947–50); from 1957 to 1959 he was conductor of the Scottish National Orch. in Glasgow; from 1959, appeared mainly as guest conductor of the Vienna State Opera. He became especially well known as a pedagogue; was head of the conducting class at the Vienna Academy of Music from 1946, where his pupils included Claudio Abbado and Zubin Mehta. As a conductor, he demonstrated notable command of a large symphonic and operatic repertoire, ranging from Haydn to the 2nd Viennese School. He was also a highly competent ed. of music by various composers; also tr. a number of Italian librettos into German. M. Huss ed. his book *Wahrung der Gestalt* (Vienna, 1979).

Swarthout, Gladys, American mezzo-soprano; b. Deepwater, Mo., Dec. 25, 1900; d. Florence, July 7, 1969. She studied at the Bush Cons. in Chicago, also opera with L. Mugnone; made her debut in a minor part with the Chicago Civic Opera in 1924; and then made regular appearances with the Ravinia

Opera Co. in Chicago. On Nov. 15, 1929, she made her Metropolitan Opera debut in N.Y. as La Cieca, and appeared there regularly until 1945; also sang in films; in 1954 she settled in Florence. She married the singer Frank Chapman in 1932; publ. an autobiography, *Come Soon, Tomorrow* (N.Y., 1945). Her finest roles were Carmen and Mignon.

Swayne, Giles (Oliver Cairnes), English composer; b. Stevenage, June 30, 1946. He began composing as a teenager, receiving encouragement from his cousin, Elizabeth Maconchy; then pursued training with Raymond Leppard and Nicholas Maw at Cambridge Univ. (1963–68); subsequently studied piano with Gordon Green and composition with Harrison Birtwistle, Alan Bush, and Maw at the Royal Academy of Music in London (1968–71); later attended Messiaen's classes in composition in Paris (1976–77). In 1982 he visited West Africa to study the music of the Jola people of Senegal and The Gambia. In common with many other British composers of his generation, he resolutely eschewed musical gourmandise in favor of writing music in an avant-garde, yet accessible style.
WORKS: STAGE: Opera, *Le Nozze di Cherubino* (1984; London, Jan. 22, 1985); ballet, *A World Within* for Tape (Stoke-on-Trent, June 2, 1978). **ORCH.:** *Orlando's Music* (1974; Liverpool, Feb. 3, 1976); *Charades* for School Orch. (1975); *Pentecost Music* (1977; Manchester, April 8, 1981); Sym. for Small Orch. (London, June 1, 1984); *Naaotwa Lala* (Manchester, Dec. 4, 1984); *The Song of Leviathan* (London, Oct. 10, 1988). **CHAMBER:** *4 Lyrical Pieces* for Cello and Piano (1970; Aldeburgh, June 16, 1971); 2 string quartets: No. 1 (1971) and No. 2 (1977; Manchester, Oct. 30, 1978); *Paraphrase on a Theme of Tallis* for Organ (1971); *Canto* for Guitar (1972); *Canto* for Piano (1973); *Canto* for Violin (1973); *Synthesis* for 2 Pianos (1974); *Canto* for Clarinet (1975); *Duo* for Violin and Piano (1975); *Suite* for Guitar (1976); *Freewheeling* for Viola, Baryton, and Cello (Kuhmo Festival, Finland, July 25, 1980); *Canto* for Cello (1981); *Rhythm-Study I* for 2 Xylophone Players and 2 Marimba Players (1982) and *II* for Percussion Group (1982); *A Song for Haddi* for Flute, Clarinet, Viola, Cello, Double Bass, and Percussion (Bath Festival, June 4, 1983); *into the light* for 7 Players (1986); *PP* for 14 Players (1987); *Tonos* for Flute, Harp, Violin, Viola, and Cello (1987). **VOCAL:** *The Good Morrow,* cycle of 5 settings of John Donne for Mezzo-soprano and Piano (1971); *Cry* for 28 Amplified Solo Voices (1979; The Hague, Oct. 22, 1982); *Count-Down* for 16-part Choir and 2 Percussion Players (1981; Merton Festival, Yorkshire, May 23, 1982); *Magnificat* for Choir (1982); *god-song* for Mezzo-soprano, Flute, Trombone, Cello, and Piano (1985–86); *Nunc Dimittis* for Choir and Organ (1986); *O Magnum Mysterium* for Boys' Voices and Organ (1986).

Sweelinck (real name, **Swybbertszoon**), **Jan Pieterszoon,** great Dutch organist, pedagogue, and composer; b. Deventer, May? 1562; d. Amsterdam, Oct. 16, 1621. He was born into a musical family; his father, paternal grandfather, and uncle were all organists. He went as a youth to Amsterdam, which was to be the center of his activities for the rest of his life. Jacob Buyck, pastor of the Oude Kerk, supervised his academic education; he most likely commenced his musical training under his father, then studied with Jan Willemszoon Lossy. He is believed to have begun his career as an organist in 1577, although 1st mention of him is in 1580, as organist of the Oude Kerk, a position his father held until his death in 1573. Sweelinck became a celebrated master of the keyboard, so excelling in the art of improvisation that he was called the "Orpheus of Amsterdam." He was also greatly renowned as a teacher, numbering among his pupils most of the founders of the so-called north German organ school. His most famous pupils were Jacob Praetorius, Heinrich Scheidemann, Samuel and Gottfried Scheidt, and Paul Siefert. The output of Sweelinck as a composer is now seen as the culmination of the great Dutch school of his time. Among his extant works are about 250 vocal pieces (33 chansons, 19 madrigals, 39 motets, and 153 Psalms) and some 70 keyboard works. Sweelinck was the 1st to employ the pedal in a real fugal part, and originated the organ fugue built up on 1 theme with the gradual addition of counter-themes leading to a highly involved and ingenious finale—a form perfected by Bach. In rhythmic and melodic freedom, his vocal compositions show an advance over the earlier polyphonic style, though replete with intricate contrapuntal devices. His son and pupil, **Dirck Janszoon Sweelinck** (b. Amsterdam [baptized], May 26, 1591; d. there, Sept. 16, 1652), was an organist, music editor, and composer; he was his father's successor as organist at the Oude Kerk (from 1621), where he acquired a notable reputation as an improviser.

WORKS: PSALMS AND CANTICLES: *50 pseaumes de David, mis en musique* for 4 to 7 Voices (Amsterdam, 1604; 2nd ed., 1624, as *Premier livre des pseaumes de David, mis en musique . . . seconde edition); Rimes françoises et italiennes . . . for 2 to 3 Voices, avec une chanson* for 4 Voices (Leiden, 1612); *Livre second des pseaumes de David, nouvellement mis en musique* for 4 to 9 Voices (Amsterdam, 1613); *Livre troisieme des pseaumes de David, nouvellement mis en musique* for 4 to 8 Voices (Amsterdam, 1614); *Sechs-stimmige Psalmen, auss dem ersten und andern Theil seiner aussgangenen frantzösischen Psalmen* for 6 Voices (Berlin, 1616); *Vierstimmige Psalmen, auss dem ersten, andern und dritten Theil seiner aussgangenen frantzösischen Psalmen* for 4 Voices (Berlin, 1618); *Livre quatriesme et conclusionnal des pseaumes de David, nouvellement mis en musique* for 4 to 8 Voices (Haarlem, 1621). **MOTETS:** *Canticum in honorem nuptiarum . . . Iohannis Stoboei et . . . Reginae . . . Davidis Mölleri . . . relicta vidua* for 8 Voices (Königsberg, 1617); *Cantiones sacrae* for 5 Voices and Basso Continuo (Antwerp, 1619); *Melos fausto quondam thalamo . . . conjugum Paris dicatum . . . studio et cura Iohannis Stobaei* for 5 Voices (Danzig, 1638). **CHANSONS:** *Chansons . . . de M. Iean Pierre Svvelingh organiste, et Cornille Verdonq nouvellement composées . . . accomodées tant aux instruments, comme à la voix* for 5 Voices (Antwerp, 1594); *Rimes francoises et italiennes . . . for 2 to 3 Voices, avec une chanson* for 4 Voices (Leiden, 1612). **MADRIGALS:** *Rimes françoises et italiennes . . . for 2 to 3 Voices, avec une chanson* for 4 Voices (Leiden, 1612). Many other works, including his keyboard pieces, were preserved in copies made by his pupils and were widely circulated. M. Seiffert ed. a complete edition of his works (12 vols., The Hague and Leipzig, 1894–1901). A new edition of his works, ed. by R. Lagas et al., commenced publication in Amsterdam in 1957.

BIBL.: B. van Sigtenhorst Meyer, *J.P. S. en zijn instrumentale muziek* (The Hague, 1934; 2nd ed., enl., 1946); idem, *J.P. S.* (Amsterdam, 1941); idem, *De vocale muziek van J.P. S.* (The Hague, 1948); A. Voigt, *Die Toccaten J.P. S.s: Ein Beitrag zur frühen Instrumentalmusik* (diss., Univ. of Münster, 1955); G. Gerdes, *Die Choralvariationen in J.P. S.s und seiner Schüler* (diss., Univ. of Freiburg, 1956); R. Tusler, *The Organ Music of J.P. S.* (Bilthoven, 1958); A. Curtis, *S.'s Keyboard Works: A Study of English Elements in Dutch Secular Music of the "Gouden Eeuw"* (diss., Univ. of Illinois, 1963); F. Noske, *S.* (Oxford, 1988).

Swert, Jules de, eminent Belgian cellist, pedagogue, and composer; b. Louvain, Aug. 15, 1843; d. Ostend, Feb. 24, 1891. He commenced his musical training with his father, the Louvain Cathedral choirmaster; by the time he was 10 he was performing in public; then pursued studies with Servais at the Brussels Cons., where he graduated with the premier prix in 1858. After touring as a virtuoso, he became Konzertmeister in Düsseldorf in 1865, appearing there in trio recitals with Clara Schumann and Auer; then went to Weimar as soloist in the Hofkapelle in 1868; subsequently was royal Kapellmeister in Berlin, where he taught at the Hochschule für Musik (1869–73). He was active in Wiesbaden (1873–76), and also made occasional tours; made his London debut with notable acclaim in 1875. In 1876 Wagner called him to Bayreuth to engage the musicians for his new orch. During the next few years, he devoted much time to composition; in 1881 he went to Leipzig. He settled in Ostend in 1888 as director of its

music school; also was a prof. at the conservatories in Ghent and Bruges. He wrote 2 operas, *Die Albigenser* (Wiesbaden, Oct. 1, 1878) and *Graf Hammerstein* (Mainz, 1884), a Sym., *Nordseefahrt,* 3 cello concertos, romances, fantasias, duos, and solo pieces for cello. His brother, **Isidore (Jean Gaspar) de Swert** (b. Louvain, Jan. 6, 1830; d. Brussels, Sept. 1896), was a cellist and teacher; he studied with François de Munck at the Brussels Cons., where he graduated with the premier prix in 1846; went to Bruges in 1850 as a teacher at its music school and solo cellist at the theater; then became solo cellist at the Théâtre Royal de la Monnaie in Brussels in 1856; was named a teacher at the Louvain Cons. in 1866, and that same year joined the faculty of the Brussels Cons.

Swieten, Gottfried (Bernhard), Baron van, Dutch-born Austrian diplomat, music patron, librettist, and composer; b. Leiden, Oct. 29, 1733; d. Vienna, March 29, 1803. His father was appointed personal physician to Empress Maria Theresa in 1745 and settled in Vienna. After attending the Theresianum Jesuit school, Gottfried entered the Austrian civil service; subsequently was active in the foreign diplomatic service from 1755 to 1777, serving as ambassador to Berlin from 1770 to 1777. Upon his return to Vienna, he was made Prefect of the Imperial Library. In his early years he wrote some opéras comiques and at least 10 syms., 3 of which were printed under Haydn's name. Van Swieten's significance rests upon his activities as a music patron; he did much to promote the music of J.S. Bach, C.P.E. Bach (commissioned his 6 Syms. for Strings, W. 182), and Handel. He founded a group of aristocratic patrons, the Associierte, which supported private performances of oratorios. This group commissioned Mozart to prepare his arrangements of Handel oratorios and also sponsored Haydn's *7 Last Words* (choral version, 1796), *The Creation* (1798), and *The Seasons* (1801), the latter 2 works utilizing librettos by van Swieten. Beethoven also found a patron in van Swieten and dedicated his 1st Sym. to him.

BIBL.: M. Friedlander, "V.S. und das Textbuch zu Haydns Jahreszeiten," *Jahrbuch der Musikbibliothek Peters* 1909; R. Bernhardt, "Aus der Umwelt der Wiener Klassiker, Freiherr G. v.S.," *Der Bär: Jahrbuch von Breitkopf & Härtel* 1929–30; E. Schmid, "G. v.S. als Komponist," *Mozart Jahrbuch* 1953; A. Holschneider, "Die musikalische Bibliothek G. v.S.s," *Gesellschaft für Musikforschung Kongressbericht* (Kassel 1962); E. Olleson, "G. v.S., Patron of Haydn and Mozart," *Proceedings of the Royal Musical Association,* LXXXIX (1962–63); M. Stern, "Haydns 'Schöpfung': Geist und Herkunft des v.S.schen Librettos," *Haydn-Studien,* I (1966); D. Olleson, *G., Baron v.S. and His Influence on Haydn and Mozart* (diss., Oxford Univ., 1967); H. Walter, "G. v.S.s handschriftliche Textbücher zu 'Schöpfung' und 'Jahreszeiten,'" *Haydn-Studien,* I (1967); E. Olleson, "The Origin and Libretto of Haydn's 'Creation,'" *Haydn Yearbook,* IV (1968).

Swift, Richard, American composer, teacher, and writer on music; b. Middlepoint, Ohio, Sept. 24, 1927. He studied with Grosvenor Cooper, Leonard Meyer, and Leland Smith at the Univ. of Chicago (M.A., 1956). In 1956 he joined the faculty of the Univ. of Calif. at Davis, where he became a prof. of music; also was chairman of the music dept. (1963–71); in 1977 he was a visiting prof. at Princeton Univ. He served as associate ed. (from 1981) and as co-ed. (1982–83) of the journal *19th Century Music;* also contributed articles to various other journals and to reference works. In his compositions he applies a variety of functional serial techniques, including electronic and aleatory devices.

WORKS: OPERA: *The Trial of Tender O'Shea* (Davis, Calif., Aug. 12, 1964); also incidental music to various plays. **ORCH.:** *A Coronal* (1954; Louisville, Ky., April 14, 1956); 2 concertos for Piano and Chamber Ensemble (1961, 1980); *Extravaganza* (1961); Concerto for Violin and Chamber Orch. (Oakland, Calif., May 28, 1968); *Tristia* (1967; Oakland, Calif., April 20, 1968); Sym. (1970); *Prime* for Alto Saxophone and Chamber Ensemble (1973); *Some Trees* (1982). **CHAMBER:** String Trio (1954–55); *Study* for Cello (1955); 5 string quartets (1955;

1958; 1964; 1973; 1981–82); *Serenade concertante* for Piano and Wind Quintet (1956) and *II* for Clarinet, Violin, Cello, and Piano (1985); *Stravaganza I–X* for various instrumentations (1956–85); Sonata for Clarinet and Piano (1957); Trio for Clarinet, Cello, and Piano (1957); Sonata for Solo Violin (1957); *Music for a While I* for Violin, Viola, and Harpsichord (1965), *II* for 3 Instruments (1969), and *III* for Violin and Harpsichord (1975); *Thrones* for Alto Flute and Contrabass (1966); Trio for Violin, Cello, and Piano (1976); *Some Versions of Paraphrase* for Violin, Clarinet, and Piano (1987); *In the Country of the Blue*, piano trio No. 2 for Violin, Cello, and Piano (1988); *A Stitch in Time* for Guitar (1989); also many vocal works; piano pieces.

Swoboda, Henry, Czech conductor; b. Prague, Oct. 29, 1897; d. Rossiniere, Switzerland, Aug. 13, 1990. He studied at the Cons. (with Talich) and at the German Univ. (Ph.D.) in Prague, and with Richard Robert in Vienna. He was an assistant conductor at the Opera (1921–23) and a conductor of the Radio (1931–38) in Prague; then went to the U.S., where he conducted for record companies and eventually devoted himself to teaching.

Syberg, Franz (Adolf), Danish organist and composer; b. Kerteminde, July 5, 1904; d. there, Dec. 11, 1955. His father was the painter Fritz Syberg. He took courses with Karg-Elert in Leipzig (1923–28) and studied organ with Peter Thomson in Copenhagen (organists' examination, 1932); then returned to Kerteminde as an organist. His small but finely crafted output was influenced by Nielsen.
WORKS: ORCH.: Concertino for Oboe and Strings (1932); Sinfonietta (1934); *Adagio* for Strings (1938); Sym. (1939). **CHAMBER:** String Quartet (1930–31); Quintet for Flute, Clarinet, and String Trio (1931); String Trio (1933); Wind Quintet (1940); also incidental music and organ pieces.

Sychra, Antonín, Czech esthetician; b. Boskovice, June 9, 1918; d. Prague, Oct. 21, 1969. He studied musicology with Helfert at the Univ. of Brno; then continued his training at the Univ. of Prague (Ph.D., 1946); subsequently completed his Habilitation (1952) and received his D.Sc. (1959) there. After lecturing at the Education Research Inst. in Prague, he was made a lecturer (1948), dean (1950), and prof. (1951) at the Prague Academy of Music; also lectured on esthetics and music history at the Univ. of Prague (from 1952), where he was director of the esthetics dept. (from 1959). His work, which reveals his preoccupation with a Marxist approach to music and esthetics, was productive for its contribution to musical semantics. Among his publications are *Stranická hudební kritika: Spolutvůrce nove hudby* (Party Music Criticism: A Co-creator of New Music; Prague, 1951; German tr., 1953), *O hudbu zítřka* (The Music of Tomorrow; Prague, 1952), *Oestetické vychově* (Esthetic Education; with O. Chlup; Prague, 1956), and *Hudba a slovo z experimentálního hlediska* (Music and Word—an Experimental Approach; with K. Sedláček; Prague, 1962).

Sydeman, William (Jay), American composer; b. N.Y., May 8, 1928. He studied at the Mannes College of Music in N.Y. with Salzer and Travis (B.S., 1955) and with Franchetti at the Hartt School of Music in Hartford, Conn. (M.M., 1958); also had sessions with Sessions and Petrassi. He taught at the Mannes College of Music (1959–70) and at Rudolph Steiner College in Fair Oaks, Calif. (1980–82). His early style of composition tended toward atonal Expressionism invigorated by spasmodic percussive rhythms in asymmetrically arranged meters. In his later works he moved toward tonal scores with elements of folk, pop, and jazz infusions.
WORKS: OPERA: *Aria da capo* (1982). **INCIDENTAL MUSIC:** *Encounters* (1967); *Anti-Christ* (1981); *A Winter's Tale* (1982). **ORCH.:** *Orchestral Abstractions* (1958; N.Y., Jan. 10, 1962); *Study Nos. I, II,* and *III* (1959, 1963, 1965); *Oecumenicus,* concerto (1964); *In memoriam: J.F. Kennedy* for Narrator and Orch. (1966); Concerto for Piano, 4-hands, and Orch. (1967); *5 Movements* for Winds (1973). **CHAMBER:** Woodwind Quintet

(1959–61); Quartet for Flute, Clarinet, Piano, and Violin (1963); Duo for Trumpet and Percussion (1965); *Trio montagnana* for Clarinet, Cello, and Piano (1972); *Fugue* for String Quartet or Ensemble with Optional Soprano (1975); 18 duos for 2 Violins (1976); *Long Life Prayer* for Violin and Speaker (1978); many other chamber works. **VOCAL:** *Lament of Elektra* for Alto, Chorus, and Chamber Orch. (1964); *Full Circle* for 3 Solo Voices, Clarinet, Trombone, Percussion, Organ, and Cello (1971); *Love Songs Based on Japanese Poems* for Soprano, Flute, and Violin (1978); *Calendar of the Soul* for Multi-chorus (1982).

Sygiètynski, Tadeusz, Polish conductor and arranger; b. Warsaw, Sept. 24, 1896; d. there, May 19, 1955. He studied in Lwow with Roman Statkowski and Henryk Melcer; later took courses with Reger in Leipzig and with Schoenberg in Vienna. In 1949 he organized the Mazowsze State Song and Dance Ensemble for the purpose of popularizing Polish folk music; toured with it in the Far East and in Western Europe with considerable acclaim. He made numerous arrangements of Polish folk songs for this group; in 1951 he received a state prize, and later was awarded the Banner of Labor by the State Council of Poland.

Sykes, James (Andrews), American pianist and pedagogue; b. Atlantic City, N.J., July 10, 1908; d. Hanover, N.H., July 26, 1985. He studied at Princeton Univ. (A.B., 1930) and at the Eastman School of Music in Rochester, N.Y. (M.A., 1933); also took courses at the Dalcroze School of Music in N.Y. and at the Austro-American Cons. in Mondsee, Austria. On Feb. 20, 1938, he made his Town Hall debut in N.Y.; made a world tour in 1945 under the sponsorship of the USO, and later performed in West Germany (1954), Central and South America (1960), and the Far and Middle East (1965) under the auspices of the U.S. State Dept. He was dean of the Lamont School of Music in Denver (1933–35); after serving as chairman of the music depts. at Colorado College (1935–46) and Colgate Univ. (1947–53), he was prof. of music at Dartmouth College (1953–73). He specialized in the performance of modern American music.

Sylvester (born **Sylvester James**), black American pop vocalist; b. Los Angeles, Sept. 6, 1947; d. (of AIDS) San Francisco, Dec. 16, 1988. He began singing at 5, appearing on the national gospel circuit; in his teens he moved to San Francisco with his grandmother, who encouraged his flamboyant side. Sylvester became an openly gay transvestite disco star at a time when both gay liberation and disco were receiving their greatest publicity; in the late 1960s and early 1970s, he sang with the Cockettes; also sang in a drag show for 8 years under the name Ruby Blue at San Francisco's Rickshaw Lounge; made a film appearance as a drag "Diana Ross" in Bette Midler's *The Rose* (1979). Sylvester's 1st album was *Sylvester and the Hot Band* (1972), a glitter-rock album on the Blue Thumb label with Sylvester in drag on the cover, which included the song *Why Was I Born*. His 1st backup singers were the Pointer Sisters, an Oakland-based quartet who also moved stylistically from gospel to disco. In 1976 Sylvester met Izora Rhodes and Martha Wash, 2 large women with equally large voices who sang backup for him as 2 Tons o' Fun. They worked with Sylvester until 1983, and then produced the single *It's Rainin' Men* (1984) as the Weather Girls. Until 1981, Sylvester's songs were written by Victor Orsborn (b. Los Angeles, Aug. 15, 1953; d. [of AIDS] Los Angeles, Dec. 9, 1990) and Eric Robertson. He later established a contract with Fantasy Records of Berkeley, Calif., producing the albums *Step II* (1977), with the long-term hits *Dance (Disco Heat)* and *You Make Me Feel Mighty Real, Living Proof* (1979), *Sell My Soul* (1980), and *Too Hot to Sleep* (1981); although his contract ended in 1981, the company produced a compilation album, *Sylvester's Greatest Hits* (1983). Sylvester then met Patrick Cowley of Megatone Records in San Francisco, a songwriter/producer who assisted him in making a comeback in the post-disco era; recorded *All I Need* (1982), *Call Me* (1984), and *M-1015* (1985), which included the songs *Rock the Box* and *Take Me to Paradise*. His last album, *Mutual Attraction* (1986), recorded for Warner/Elektra, included the highly successful duet with Stevie Wonder *Living for the City*. Megatone later produced various posthumous collections and singles, of which the most important is *Immortal* (1989).

Symonds, Norman, Canadian composer; b. Nelson, British Columbia, Dec. 23, 1920. He studied clarinet and piano at the Royal Cons. in Toronto (1945–47); took lessons in composition privately with Gordon Delamont in Toronto (1947–50). In 1953 he organized his own jazz octet, which continued in action until 1957. Most of his compositions are in the "3rd stream" idiom, combining jazz and symphonic styles.
Works: DRAMATIC: *Opera for 6 Voices*, jazz opera (1961); *The Spirit of Fundy*, opera (1972); *The Canterville Ghost*, music theater (1975); *Episode at Big Quill*, radio score (1979); *The Fall of the Leaf*, oratorical music drama (1982). **ORCH.:** Concerto Grosso for Jazz Quintet and Orch. (1957); *Autumn Nocturne* for Tenor Saxophone and String Orch. (1960); *Pastel Blue* for String Orch. (1963); *The Nameless Hour* for Improvising Soloist and String Orch. (1966); *The Democratic Concerto* for Jazz Quintet and Orch. (Winnipeg, Dec. 14, 1967); *Impulse* (Toronto, March 18, 1969); *3 Atmospheres* (1970); *Maya* (1973); *Forest and Sky* (1977); *Sylvia*, "an adult fairy tale" for 2 or 3 Jazz Soloists and Variable Instrumental Ensemble (1982); *On an Emerald Sea* (1983); *The Eyes of Bidesuk* for Amplified Accordion and Jazz Orch. (1987); *From the Eye of the World* (1987; Toronto, Jan. 1, 1988); also chamber music, including *A Diversion* for Brass Quintet (1972); vocal music, including *4 Images of Nature* for Chorus and Percussion (1976) and solo songs; electronic music, including a Quintet for Clarinet and Synthesizers (1977).

Synowiec, Ewa (Krystyna), Polish pianist, composer, painter, and writer; b. Krakow, April 12, 1942. She studied piano with Ludwik Stefanski at the Krakow Academy of Music (graduated, 1967) and with Susanne Roche and Vlado Perlemuter in Paris (1967–68); later studied composition with Boguslaw Schaeffer in Krakow. She toured widely as a pianist from 1948 to 1978. After serving on the faculty of the Krakow Academy of Music (1966–75), she taught piano and composition at the Gdansk Academy of Music; also was a member of the Grupa Krakowska from 1985. A versatile artist, she won recognition for both her musical and her non-musical gifts; in addition to composing in traditional forms, she has produced over 100 musical graphics that have been performed or exhibited in many European cities.
Works: ORCH.: *Schizofonia* (1971); *72 for 72 Instruments* (1972); *Fantasy* for Trumpet and Orch. (1973); *Syntonia* for 58 String Instruments (1976); Concerto for Strings (1978); *Spiegelspiel* (1981); *Trivium* for Flute or Marimba, and Orch. (1983). **CHAMBER:** String Quartet No. 1 (1966); *Little Wind Quintet* (1967); String Trio (1967); *1 + 11* for Cello and 11 Saxophones (1968); *Quartettino* for Strings (1969); *Play* for 3 to 6 Trumpets (1972); *Serial* for Flute (1973); *Plus ça change—plus c'est la même chose* for String Sextet (1973); *Natura morta I* for 3 Instruments (1974), *II* for 9 Instruments (1974), *III, UDMSW* for 6 Instruments (1975), and *IV* for 3 Instruments (1976); *Da camera* for Flute, Violin, and Cello (1977); *Sinfonietta da camera* for 10 to 15 Players (1980); *Arboretum* for 2 Violins, 2 Violas, and 2 Cellos (1980); Sonata for Solo Violin (1980); Concertino for 3 Solo Instruments and 12 Strings (1980); *Abra . . .* for Oboe and English Horn (1986). **PIANO:** *Open Form* (1966); 2 sonatas (1969, 1981); *Change* for Piano, 4-hands (1972); *Alternative I* for 1 or 2 Pianos (1978) and *II* for Harpsichord or Piano (1979); *Pianoptikum* (1986); also *Quasimodo* for Harpsichord (1985). **VOCAL:** *Psalm XXII* for Voice, Flute, Violin, and Celesta (1967); *Dedication*, 5 songs for Chorus (1983); song cycle on the 12 months of the year for Alto and Piano, to words by the composer (French version, Zürich, Dec. 6, 1987; Polish version, 1988); also more than 100 musical graphic scores.

Syukur, Slamet Abdul, important Indonesian composer, performer, and teacher; b. Surabaya, East Java, June 30, 1935.

He studied piano (1944–52), then attended the Sekolah Musik Indonesia (S.M.I.) Yogyakarta (1952–56). He was a founding member (1957–61) and president (1961–62) of Pertemuan Musik Surabaya, the 1st music society formed by the Indonesians after the liquidation of the former Dutch Muziek-Kunstkring; then went to Paris and studied organology with Chambure and analysis with Messiaen at the Cons. (1962–63); also earned degrees in piano (1965) and composition (1967) at the École Normale de Musique; in 1967–68, took part in Schaffer's Group de Recherches Musicales de l'ORTF. Syukur is among the many Indonesian composers who, after training in Europe, returned to play an important role in the development of contemporary music in Indonesia while remaining internationally active. From 1976 to 1987 he was a lecturer at the Institut Kesenian Jakarta (I.K.J., Jakarta Arts Inst.), where he also served as head of its music dept. (1981–83); from 1977 to 1981 he was head of the music committee of the Jakarta Arts Council, for which he organized a Festival of Contemporary French Music, the 1st such series given in Southeast Asia. In 1987 he joined the faculty at the Institut Seni Indonesia (I.S.I., National Arts Inst.); also lectured throughout Java, and from 1975 participated in workshops organized by Eduard van Beinum Stichting and the Gaudeamus Foundation on the problems of geographic and historical musical acculturation. In 1989 he received a grant from the French government to conduct research on the influence of the Javanese gamelan on the esthetic of Debussy. Syukur lives in Jakarta, where he founded in 1990 the Forum Musik Jakarta, an Indonesian Soc. for Contemporary Music that also serves as an information and educational center.
Works: *Point-Contre* for Vocalizing Trumpet, Percussion, and Harp (1969); *Parenthesis I–II* for Dancer, Prepared Piano, Suspended Chair, and Lighting; *Parenthesis IV* for 2 Electric Guitars, Percussion, Organ, Prepared Piano, 2 Dancers, Painter, Flute, Violin, and Cello (1973); *Laticrak*, electro-acoustic music for Dancers (1974); *Angklung* for Voices and Angklung (1975); *Parentheses VI* for 2 Guitars, Percussion, Children's Toys, Flute, Comedian (with a deep voice), Choreography, and Dancer's Voice; *Kangen* for 3 Shakuhachi, Kokyu, and Traditional Japanese Percussion (1986); *Cucuku-Cu* for Guitar (1989); *Ji-Lala-Ji* for Flute and Percussion (1989); *Suara* for Piano (1990).

Szabados, Béla Antal, Hungarian pedagogue and composer; b. Pest, June 3, 1867; d. there (Budapest), Sept. 15, 1936. He studied with Erkel and Volkmann; became an accompanist and coach at the Academy of Music and Dramatic Art (1888); in 1893 he was made a piano teacher and coach at the reorganized Academy of Music, where he was promoted to prof. of singing in 1920; in 1922 he became director of the dept. for the training of profs. of singing; served as head of the National Cons. from 1927. He wrote 2 operas: *Maria* (Budapest, Feb. 28, 1905; in collaboration with Árpád Szendy) and *Fanny* (Budapest, Feb. 16, 1927); 11 musical comedies; 4 string quartets; a Psalm; several song cycles; also publ. several vocal manuals. His brother, **Károly Szabados** (b. Pest, Jan. 28, 1860; d. there [Budapest], Jan. 25, 1892), was a pianist, conductor, and composer who studied with Liszt, Erkel, and Volkmann; became conductor at the Klausenburg National Theater (1880) and then assistant conductor at the Royal Hungarian Opera in Budapest. His most successful score was the ballet *Vióra* (1891).

Szabelski, Boleslaw, Polish organist, teacher, and composer; b. Radoryz, near Lublin, Dec. 3, 1896; d. Katowice, Aug. 27, 1979. After studies with Lysakowski in Kiev (1915), he took courses in organ with Surzyński and in composition with Szymanowski and Statkowski at the Warsaw Cons.; made tours as an organist; also was prof. of organ and composition at the Krakow Cons. (1929–39; 1954–57). He wrote in a traditional style until turning to serial techniques in 1958.
Works: 5 syms. (1926; 1934, with Soprano and Chorus; 1951; 1956; 1968, with Chorus and Organ); *Suite* for Orch. (1938); Organ Sonata (1943); Sinfonietta for String Orch. and

Percussion (1946); *Poemat bohaterski* (Heroic Poem) for Chorus and Orch. (1952); *Solemn Overture* (1953); *Concerto grosso* for Orch. (1954); Piano Concertino (1955); 2 string quartets (1935, 1956); *3 Sonnets* for Orch. (1958); *Improvisations* for Chorus and Chamber Orch. (1959); *Wiersze* (Verses) for Piano and Orch. (1961); *Aphorisms "9"* for Chamber Ensemble (1962); *Preludes* for Chamber Orch. (1963); Flute Concerto (1964); *Nicolaus Copernicus*, oratorio (Poznan, April 2, 1976); *The Wola Redoubt* for 3 Vocal Soloists and Orch. (Warsaw, Nov. 5, 1976); Piano Concerto (1978).

Szabó, Ferenc, distinguished Hungarian composer; b. Budapest, Dec. 27, 1902; d. there, Nov. 4, 1969. He studied with Kodály, Siklós, and Leo Weiner at the Budapest Academy of Music (1922–26); in 1926 he became aligned with the labor movement in Hungary and joined the outlawed Communist party in 1927; in 1932 he went to Russia, where he became closely associated with the ideological work of the Union of Soviet Composers. In 1944 he returned to Hungary as an officer in the Red Army; then was prof. of composition (1945–67) and director (1958–67) of the Budapest Academy of Music. He was awarded the Kossuth Prize in 1951 and 1954, and in 1962 was named an Eminent Artist of the Hungarian People's Republic. His music initially followed the trends of Central European modernism, with strong undertones of Hungarian melorhythms, but later he wrote music in the manner of socialist realism; his choruses are permeated with the militant spirit of the revolutionary movement.

Works: DRAMATIC: 3-act opera, *Légy jó mindhalálig* (Be Faithful until Death; 1968–69; Budapest, Dec. 5, 1975; score completed by his pupil András Borgulya); ballet, *Lúdas Matyi* (Budapest, May 16, 1960); oratorio, *Föltámadott a tenger* (In Fury Rose the Ocean; Budapest, June 15, 1955); cantata, *Meghalt Lenin* (Lenin Is Dead; 1933). ORCH.: *Suite* for Chamber Orch. (1926; rev. as *Sérénade oubliée*, 1964); *Class Struggle*, symphonic poem (Moscow, April 27, 1933); *Sinfonietta* for an ensemble of Russian National Instruments (1935); *Lyrical Suite* for String Orch. (1936); *Moldavian Rhapsody* (1940); Concerto, *Hazatérés* (Homecoming; 1948); *Számadás* (Summary), symphonic poem (1949); *Emlékeztető* (Memento), sym. (1952). CHAMBER: 2 string quartets (1926, 1962); Trio for 2 Violins and Viola (1927); Sonata for Solo Cello (1929); 2 sonatas for Solo Violin (1930); *Sonata alla rapsodia* for Clarinet and Piano (1964). PIANO: *Toccata* (1928); *8 Easy Piano Pieces* (1933); 3 sonatas (1940; 1947; 1957–61); *Felszabadult melódiák* (Melodies of Liberation), cycle of pieces (1949); also a cappella choruses, including *Song of the Wolves* (1929); *Work and Bread* (1930); *Liberty Be the Watchword* (1932); *November 7th* (1932); *Song at Dawn* (1953); *Vallomás* (Declaration) for Chorus, Brass, and Percussion (1967).
Bibl.: A. Pernye, *S. F.* (Budapest, 1965); J. Maróthy, *S. F. indulása* (Budapest, 1970).

Szabolcsi, Bence, eminent Hungarian music scholar; b. Budapest, Aug. 2, 1899; d. there, Jan. 21, 1973. He studied jurisprudence at the Univ. of Budapest; concurrently took music courses with Kodály at the Budapest Academy of Music (1917–21) and with Abert at the Univ. of Leipzig, where he received his Ph.D. in 1923 with the dissertation *Benedetti und Saracini: Beiträge zur Geschichte der Monodie.* He was a prof. of music history at the Budapest Academy of Music from 1945 until his death. He was ed. of the Hungarian music periodical *Zenei Szemle* (with D. Bartha) from 1926 to 1929. With A. Tóth, he brought out a music dictionary in the Hungarian language (1930–31); publ. a history of music (Budapest, 1940), a monograph on Beethoven (Budapest, 1948), and a number of valuable papers in various European magazines. His greatest contribution as a scholar is found in his valuable study *A melódia története* (A History of Melody; Budapest, 1950; 2nd ed., 1957; Eng. tr., 1965); also made valuable contributions to research on the life and works of Béla Bartók. On his 70th birthday he was presented with a Festschrift, ed. by Bartha, *Studia musicologica Bence Szabolcsi septuagenario* (Budapest, 1969). Of his writings on Bartók, the most important are *Bartók: Sa*

vie et son œuvre (Budapest, 1956; 2nd ed., 1968); *Béla Bartók* (Leipzig, 1968); *Béla Bartók, Musiksprachen* (Leipzig, 1972). Two of his books were publ. in Eng.: *The Twilight of Ferenc Liszt* (Budapest, 1959) and *A Concise History of Hungarian Music* (Budapest, 1964).
Bibl.: F. Bónis, "The Magnum Opus of B. S.," *New Hungarian Quarterly,* XV/53 (1974).

Szalonek, Witold (Jozef), Polish composer; b. Czechowice, March 2, 1927. He studied with Woytowicz at the Katowice State College of Music (1949–56); attended summer courses in new music at Darmstadt (1960) and had a course in musical analysis with Nadia Boulanger in Paris (1962–63). Returning to Poland, he taught at the Katowice State College of Music (from 1967); also was on the faculty of the West Berlin Hochschule für Musik (from 1973).
Works: *Pastorale* for Oboe and Orch. or Piano (1952); Trio for Flute, Clarinet, and Bassoon (1952); *Toccata polyphonica* for String Orch. (1954); *Suite kurpienne* for Contralto and 9 Instruments (1955); *Symphonic Satire* (1956); Cello Sonata (1958); *Wyznania* (Confessions), triptych for Narrator, Chorus, and Chamber Orch. (1959); Flute Concertino (1962); *Arabesques* for Violin and Piano (1964); *Les Sons* for Orch., without Violins and Cellos (1965); *4 Monologues* for Oboe (1966); *Mutations* for Chamber Orch. (1966); *Proporzioni* for Flute, Viola, and Harp (1967); *Improvisations sonoristiques* for Clarinet, Trombone, Cello, and Piano (1968); *Mutanza* for Piano (1968); *1 + 1 + 1 + 1* for 1, 2, 3, or 4 String Instruments (1969); cantata, *Ziemio mila* (O, Pleasant Earth) for Voice and Orch. (1969); *Proporzioni II* for Flute, Cello, and Piano or Harp (1967–70); *Aarhus Music* for Wind Quintet (1970); *3 Sketches* for Harp (1972); *Connections* for Wind Quintet, 4 Strings, and Piano (1972); Concerto for Strings (1971–75); *Musica concertante* for Double Bass and Orch. (1977); *Proporzioni III* for Violin, Cello, and Piano (1977); *Piernikiana* for Tuba (1977); Trio for Oboe, Clarinet, and Bassoon (1978); *Take the game . . .* for 6 Percussionists (1981); *Alice's Unknown Adventures in the Fairy Land of Percussion* for 1 Percussionist (1981); *Little B-A-C-H Symphony* for Piano and Orch. (1981); *D. P.'s 5 Ghoulish Dreams* for Alto Saxophone (1985); *Inside? Outside?* for Bass Clarinet and String Quartet (1988).

Szalowski, Antoni, Polish-born French composer; b. Warsaw, April 21, 1907; d. Paris, March 21, 1973. He studied composition (with K. Sikorski) and conducting at the Warsaw Cons., graduating in 1930; continued his studies with Boulanger in Paris (1931–36), where he then lived until his death, becoming a French citizen in 1968. His finely crafted works follow in the neo-Classical tradition with a diverting infusion of French elegance.
Works: 4 string quartets (1928, 1934, 1936, 1956); *Symphonic Variations* (1928); Piano Concerto (1930); Piano Sonata (1933); *Overture* (1936); Clarinet Sonatina (1936); Sym. (1939); Sinfonietta (1940); Concerto for Strings (1942); ballet, *Zaczarowana oberza* (The Enchanted Inn; 1943–46; Warsaw, Feb. 7, 1962); Oboe Sonatina (1946); *Tryptyk* for Orch. (1950); Concertino for Flute and String Orch. (1951); Suite for Orch. (1952); Wind Quintet (1954); Violin Concerto (1949–54); Partita for String Orch. (1954); Divertimento for Oboe, Clarinet, and Bassoon (1955); *La Danse* for Orch. (1957); television ballet, *La Femme têtue* (Paris, 1958); *Moto perpetuo* for Orch. (1958); Concerto for Oboe, Clarinet, Bassoon, and Orch. (1958); *The Resurrection of Lazarus*, symphonic poem (1960); *Intermezzo* for Orch. (1961); *Allegretto* for Bassoon and Orch. (1962); *Berceuse pour Clemantine* for Orch. (1964); *2 Pieces* for Ondes Martenot (1967); *Music for Strings* (1970); *6 Sketches* for Orch. (1972); piano pieces; songs.
Bibl.: Special issue of *Ruch Muzyczny,* XVII/10 (1973).

Szamotul, Waclaw z, significant Polish composer; b. Szamotuly, near Poznan, c.1524; d. probably in Pińczów, near Kielce, c.1560. He studied at Poznan's Collegium Lubranscianum and at the Univ. of Krakow; after serving as secretary to Hieronim Chodkiewicz, governor of Troki in Lithuania (1545–47), he became a composer at the court of King Sigismund II August;

about 1550 he espoused the Protestant cause, and from 1555 until his death he was active at the Lithuanian court of Duke Mikolaj Radziwill. He composed several outstanding a cappella sacred works.

Bibl.: A. and Z. Szweykowski, "W. a S.—renesansowy muzyk i poeta," *Muzyka,* IX/1–2 (1964).

Szántó, Theodor, Hungarian pianist and composer; b. Vienna, June 3, 1877; d. Budapest, Jan. 7, 1934. He studied with Dachs (piano) and Fuchs (composition) at the Vienna Cons., and later with Busoni in Berlin (1898–1901). He wrote an opera on a Japanese story, *Typhoon* (Mannheim, Nov. 29, 1924), *Japanese Suite* for Orch. (1926), other orch. works, chamber music, and piano pieces.

Szász, Tibor, Rumanian-born American pianist; b. Cluj (of Hungarian parents), June 9, 1948. He began formal study at 13 with Elisa Ciolan and made his public orch. debut at 16; a laureate of the Georges Enesco International Piano Competition (1967), he subsequently appeared with leading orchs. throughout Rumania. He was sentenced to prison during the Ceauşescu regime but was granted refugee status; emigrated to the U.S. in 1970, obtaining citizenship in 1980. He made his N.Y. solo debut at Carnegie Recital Hall in 1977; subsequently studied with Leon Fleisher and Theodore Lettvin at the Univ. of Michigan (D.M.A., 1983). He taught at the Univ. of Dayton (1984–87), and in 1987 became pianist-in-residence at Duke Univ. in Durham, N.C. A musician of extraordinary sensitivity and intelligence, Szász has appeared as a recitalist, chamber artist, and soloist with orchs. throughout the U.S. and Europe in a repertoire ranging from Couperin to Messiaen; he has also lectured widely, given master classes, and publ. articles on Liszt and Beethoven.

Sze, Yi-Kwei, Chinese bass-baritone; b. Shanghai, June 1, 1919. He received his musical training at the Shanghai Cons.; then emigrated to the U.S., where he studied with Alexander Kipnis. He toured widely in Europe, South America, and Asia.

Székely, Endre, Hungarian composer; b. Budapest, April 6, 1912; d. there, April 14, 1989. He studied with Siklós at the Budapest Academy of Music (1933–37), then joined the outlawed Communist party, and was active as a conductor and composer with various workers' choral groups; ed. the periodicals *Éneklö Munkás* (The Singing Worker) and *Éneklö Nép* (The People Sing). In 1960 he was appointed to the faculty of the Budapest Training College for Teachers.

Works: stage: Operas: *Vizirózsa* (Water Rose; 1959; Budapest Radio, 1962); *Közene* (Stone Music; 1981); operetta, *Aranycsillag* (The Golden Star; Budapest, 1951). **orch.:** 3 suites: No. 1 for Small Orch. (1947); No. 2 for String Orch. (1961); No. 3 for Full Orch. (1965); Sym. (1956); *Rhapsody* for Violin and Orch. (1956); *Partita* for Strings (1957); Concerto for Piano, Percussion, and Strings (1958); *Sinfonia concertante* for Violin, Piano, and Chamber Orch. (1960–61); Concerto for 8 Solo Instruments and Orch. (1964); *Partita* (1965); *Fantasma* (1969); Trumpet Concerto (1971); *Riflessioni,* concerto for Cello and Orch. (1973); *Humanisation* for Chamber Ensemble and Tape (1974); *Concerto in memoriam Weber* for Horn and Orch. (1976); Violin Concerto (1979; rev. 1987); *Rapsodia* for Piano and Orch. (1985); *Wave Motions* (1987); Concerto Grosso for Harpsichord and Strings (1987). **vocal:** Oratorios: *Dózsa György* (1959; rev. 1974); *Nenia* (1968–69); *Justice in Jerusalem* (1986); also *Meditations* for Tenor and Orch. (1961–62); *Maqamat* for Soprano and Chamber Ensemble (1970); choruses; songs. **chamber:** String Trio (1943); 3 wind quintets (1952, 1961, 1966); 5 string quartets (1953, 1958, 1962, 1972, 1981); *Rhapsody* for Viola and Piano (1956); 2 wind trios (1958, 1959); *Capriccio* for Flute and Piano (1961); *Chamber Music for 8* (1963); *Chamber Music for 3* (1965); *Musica notturna* for Piano, Wind Quintet, and String Quintet (1967); *Trio* for Percussion, Piano, and Cello (1968–69); *Musica da camera* for Double Bass, Flute, Percussion, and Piano (1978); Horn Sonata (1980); *HaBem Music* for Saxophone and

Percussion (1983); Clarinet Sonata (1984); *Quartetto per tromboni* (1988); also 4 piano sonatas (1952, 1962, 1972, 1988).

Székely, Mihály, noted Hungarian bass; b. Jászberény, May 8, 1901; d. Budapest, March 6, 1963. He studied in Budapest; made his operatic debut at Weber's Hermit at the Budapest Municipal Theater in 1923; that same year he made his 1st appearance at the Budapest Opera as Ferrando in *Il Trovatore,* remaining on its roster until his death; also made guest appearances throughout Europe. On Jan. 17, 1947, he sang the role of Hunding in *Die Walküre* at his Metropolitan Opera debut in N.Y.; continued on the roster until 1948, and then returned for the 1949–50 season. He subsequently sang in Europe, appearing at the Glyndebourne Festival, the Holland Festival, the Bavarian State Opera in Munich, etc. He was renowned for such roles as Sarastro, Osmin, King Marke, Boris Godunov, Rocco, and Bluebeard.

Bibl.: P. Várnai, *S. M.* (Budapest, 1967).

Szelényi, István, Hungarian composer and musicologist; b. Zólyom, Aug. 8, 1904; d. Budapest, Jan. 31, 1972. He studied at the Budapest Academy of Music with Kodály; toured as a concert pianist (1928–30); returning to Budapest, he taught at the Cons. (from 1945), later serving as its director; also taught at the Academy of Music (1956–72); ed. the journal *Új Zenei Szemle* (1951–56). In 1969 he was awarded the Erkel Prize.

Writings (all publ. in Hungarian, in Budapest): *Methodical Theory of Modulation* (1927; 2nd ed., 1960); *The Interrelations of the History of Music and That of Philosophy* (1944); *Liszt's Life in Pictures* (1956); *The Harmonic Realm of Romantic Music* (1959); *The History of Hungarian Music* (1965); *Principles of Folk-Song Harmonization* (1967).

Works: dramatic: 2 pantomimes: *A tékozló fiú* (The Prodigal Son; 1931) and *Babiloni vásár* (The Fair at Babylon; 1931); operetta, *Hidavatás* (1936); oratorios: *Virata* (1935); *Spartacus* (1960); *10 Days That Shook the World* (1964); *Pro Pace* (1968); etc. **orch.:** Sym. No. 1 (1926); Violin Concerto (1930); *Ouverture activiste* (1931); Triple Concerto for Violin, Cello, Piano, and Wind Orch. (1933); *Géptánc—Munkatánc* (Machine Dance—Work Dance; 1942); *Az ösök nyomában* (In the Footsteps of the Ancestors), sym. for String Orch. (1946); *Egy gyár szimfóniája* (Symphony for a Factory; 1946–47); *Hommage à Bartók* (1947); Violin Concertino (1947–48); *Suite* for String Orch. (1952); *Summa vitae* for Piano and Orch. (1956); *Concerto da camera* (1963); *Dance Suite* for String Orch. (1964); Piano Concertino (1964); *Variations concertants* for Piano and Orch. (1965); Piano Concerto (1969). **chamber:** 2 solo violin sonatas (1925, 1934); Flute Sonata (1926); 4 string quartets (1927, 1928, 1929, 1964); 2 piano trios (1934, 1962); Sonata for 4 Violins (1946); 2-violin Sonatina (1963); *Sinfonietta a tre* for 3 Violins (1964); *3 Dialogues* for Violin and Cello (1965); *Chamber Music* for 2 Trumpets, 2 Horns, and 2 Trombones (1966). **piano:** 7 sonatas (1924–69); Sonatina (1960); *Toccata* (1964); *Musical Picture Book* (1967); also choral works; songs.

Szeligowski, Tadeusz, notable Polish composer and pedagogue; b. Lemberg, Sept. 12, 1896; d. Poznan, Jan. 10, 1963. He studied piano with Kurz in Lemberg (1910–14) and composition with Wallek-Walewski in Krakow, where he also took a doctorate in law at the Univ.; after further studies with Boulanger in Paris (1929–31), he taught in Poznan (1932–39) and in Warsaw (1951–62); was also president of the Polish Composers' Union (1951–54).

Works: operas: *Bunt Żaków* (Rebellion of Clerks; Wroclaw, July 14, 1951); *Krakatuk,* after E.T.A. Hoffmann (1955; Gdansk, Dec. 30, 1956); *Theodor gentleman* (1960; Wroclaw, 1963). **ballets:** *Paw i dziewczyna* (The Peacock and the Maiden; 1948; Wroclaw, Aug. 2, 1949); *Mazeppa* (1957; Warsaw, 1959). **orch.:** *Kaziuki,* suite (1928); Concerto (1932); Clarinet Concerto (1932); *Epitaph for Karol Szymanowski* for String Orch. (1937); Piano Concerto (1941; Krakow, May 17, 1946); *Suita lubelska* for Small Orch. (1945); *Nocturne* (1947); *Burlesque Overture* (1952). **vocal:** *Triptych* for Soprano and Orch. (1946); *Kantata o sporcie* for Voice, Chorus, and Orch.

(1947); *Wesele lubelskie* (Lublin Wedding), suite for Soprano, Chorus, and Small Orch. (1948); *Rapsod* for Soprano and Orch. (1949); *Panicz i dziewczyna* (The Young Squire and the Country Girl), musical dialogue for Soprano, Baritone, Chorus, and Orch. (1949); cantata, *Karta serc* (The Charter of Hearts; 1952); *Renegade*, ballad for Bass and Orch. (1953); songs. **CHAMBER:** 2 string quartets (1929, 1934); *Nocturne* for Cello and Piano (1945); *Orientale* for Cello and Piano (1945); Wind Quintet (1950); Flute Sonata (1953); *Air grave et air gai* for English Horn and Piano (1954). **PIANO:** Trio (1956); Sonatina (1940); Sonata (1949).

BIBL.: T. S.: *W 10 rocznice śmierci* (T. S.: On the 10th Anniversary of His Death; Gdansk, 1973).

Szell, George (actually, **György**), greatly distinguished Hungarian-born American conductor; b. Budapest, June 7, 1897; d. Cleveland, July 30, 1970. His family moved to Vienna when he was a small child. He studied piano with Richard Robert and composition with Mandyczewski; also composition in Prague with J.B. Foerster. He played a Mozart piano concerto with the Vienna Sym. Orch. when he was 10 years old, and the orch. also performed an overture of his composition. At the age of 17 he led the Berlin Phil. in an ambitious program which included a symphonic work of his own. In 1915 he was engaged as an assistant conductor at the Royal Opera of Berlin; then conducted opera in Strasbourg (1917–18), Prague (1919–21), Darmstadt (1921–22), and Düsseldorf (1922–24). He held the position of 1st conductor at the Berlin State Opera (1924–29); then conducted in Prague and Vienna. He made his U.S. debut as guest conductor of the St. Louis Sym. Orch. in 1930. In 1937 he was appointed conductor of the Scottish Orch. in Glasgow; he was also a regular conductor with the Residentie Orkest in The Hague (1937–39). He then conducted in Australia. At the outbreak of war in Europe in 1939 he was in America, which was to become his adoptive country by naturalization in 1946. His American conducting engagements included appearances with the Los Angeles Phil., NBC Sym., Chicago Sym., Detroit Sym., and Boston Sym. In 1942 he was appointed a conductor of the Metropolitan Opera in N.Y., where he received high praise for his interpretation of Wagner's music dramas; remained on its roster until 1946. He also conducted performances with the N.Y. Phil. in 1944–45. In 1946 he was appointed conductor of the Cleveland Orch., a post which he held for 24 years; he was also music adviser and senior guest conductor of the N.Y. Phil. from 1969 until his death. He was a stern disciplinarian, demanding the utmost exertions from his musicians to achieve tonal perfection, but he was also willing to labor tirelessly at his task. Under his guidance, the Cleveland Orch. rose to the heights of symphonic excellence, taking its place in the foremost rank of world orchs. Szell was particularly renowned for his authoritative and exemplary performances of the Viennese classics, but he also was capable of outstanding interpretations of 20th-century masterworks.

BIBL.: R. Marsh, *The Cleveland Orchestra* (Cleveland and N.Y., 1967); H. Schonberg, *The Great Conductors* (N.Y., 1967); H.C. Robbins Landon, "In Memoriam: G. S., 1897–1970," *Ovation* (July 1985).

Szeluto, Apolinary, fecund Russian-Polish composer; b. St. Petersburg, July 23, 1884; d. Chodziez, Aug. 22, 1966. He studied with Exner at the Saratov Cons. and with Statkowski and Noskowski at the Warsaw Cons. (1902–5); then received instruction in piano from Godowsky in Berlin (1905–8); also took courses in law in Warsaw and Dorpat. He was active as a pianist (1909–31), then devoted himself to composition. In association with Szymanowski, Fitelberg, and Różycki, he formed a progressive musical group, Young Poland. He wrote a number of syms. in piano score; only 10 were orchestrated. His music is ultra-Romantic in its essence; most of his works bear descriptive titles. Several of them are inspired by contemporary political and military events.

WORKS: 28 syms., of which 18 exist without complete orchestration: No. 1, *Academic* (1920); No. 2, *Spontaneous*

(1938); No. 3, *Impressionistic* (1942); No. 4, *Romantic* (1942); No. 5, *Majestic Room* (1942); No. 6, *Birth of Stalingrad* (1943); No. 7, *Revolutionary* (1943); No. 8, *Resurrection* (1942); No. 9, *Elegiac* (1943); No. 10, *Oriental* (1944); No. 11, *Iberian* (1944); No. 12, *Nordic* (1944); No. 13, *Samurai* (1943–46); No. 14, *Neapolitan* (1943); No. 15, *Los Angeles American* (1944); No. 16, *Fate* (1946); No. 17, *Kujawska Region* (1946); No. 18, *Litewska*; No. 19, *Slaska*; No. 20, *Kupiowska*; No. 21, *Podhalanska*; No. 22, *To the Building of a Communist People's Union*; Nos. 23–28 without titles; 5 piano concertos (1937, 1939, 1940, 1943, 1948); Violin Concerto (1942–48); Cello Concerto (1942); some 32 other orch. works; 9 ballets; 14 chamber music pieces; 18 choral works; an utterly unbelievable number (purportedly 78) of operas; conservatively counting, 205 piano pieces and maybe 165 songs.

BIBL.: J. Kański, "A. S.: 1884–1966," *Ruch Muzyczny* (1967); J. Dobrowoski, "Katalog utworow fortepianowych Apolinarego Szeluty," *Muzyka* (1973).

Szendrei, Aladár, Hungarian-American conductor, musicologist, and composer who Americanized his name to Alfred Sendrey; b. Budapest, Feb. 29, 1884; d. Los Angeles, March 3, 1976. He studied with Hans Koessler at the Budapest Academy of Music (1901–5) and later took courses in musicology at the Univ. of Leipzig (Ph.D., 1932); after serving as a theater conductor in Germany, he went to the U.S., where he conducted opera in Philadelphia and Chicago (1911–12); appeared with N.Y.'s Century Co. (1913–14). He returned to Europe in 1914; served in the Austrian army during World War I; after the Armistice, conducted opera in Leipzig (1918–24) and sym. concerts there (1924–32). In 1933 he left Germany and went to Paris, where he conducted at Radiodiffusion Française; he also taught conducting; Charles Munch took private lessons in conducting with him (1933–40); after the fall of Paris, Szendrei emigrated to the U.S. and settled in Los Angeles. He was prof. of Jewish music at the Univ. of Judaism in Los Angeles (1962–73).

WORKS: 1-act opera, *Der türkisenblaue Garten* (Leipzig, Feb. 7, 1920); ballet, *Danse d'odalisque*; *Hungarian Overture* for Orch. (1904); Sym. in B-flat major (1923); Piano Quintet (1925); *Stabat Mater* for 8 Solo Voices and Chorus (1905).

WRITINGS: *Rundfunk und Musikpflege* (Leipzig, 1931); *Dirigierkunde* (Leipzig, 1932; 3rd ed., 1956); *Bibliography of Jewish Music* (N.Y., 1951); *David's Harp: A Popular History of the Music in Biblical Times* (N.Y., 1964); *Music in Ancient Israel* (N.Y., 1969); *The Music of the Jews in the Diaspora (up to 1800)* (N.Y., 1969); *Music in the Social and Religious Life of Antiquity* (Canbury, N.J., 1974).

BIBL.: I. Katz, "Alfred Sendrey (1884–1976): In Memoriam," *Musica Judaica*, i (1975–76).

Szendy, Árpád, Hungarian pianist, pedagogue, and composer; b. Szarvas, Aug. 11, 1863; d. Budapest, Sept. 10, 1922. He studied in Budapest at the Cons. and the Academy of Music; then became a student of Liszt (1881). In 1890 he was appointed to the faculty of the Academy of Music; was prof. of the piano master classes there from 1911; enjoyed great esteem in Hungary as a piano teacher. He publ. numerous eds. of piano classics; wrote an opera, *Mária* (with Béla Szabados; Budapest, Feb. 28, 1905); a String Quartet; much piano music; songs.

Szenkar, Eugen (actually, **Jenő**), Hungarian conductor; b. Budapest, April 9, 1891; d. Düsseldorf, March 28, 1977. He studied music with his father, a prominent organist; later attended classes at the Academy of Music in Budapest. He conducted at the German Theater in Prague (1911–13), the Budapest Volksoper (1913–15), the Salzburg Mozarteum (1915–16), in Altenburg (1916–20), the Frankfurt Opera (1920–23), the Berlin Volksoper (1923–24), and the Cologne Opera (1924–33). With the advent of the Nazi regime, as a Jew he was forced to leave Germany in 1933; lived in Russia until 1937; subsequently conducted the Brazilian Sym. Orch. in Rio de Janeiro (from 1944). He returned to Germany in 1950; was Generalmusikdirektor in Düsseldorf from 1952 to 1960.

Szervánszky, Endre, Hungarian composer; b. Kistétény, Dec. 27, 1911; d. Budapest, June 25, 1977. Of a musical family, he learned to play the clarinet as a child; studied composition with Siklós and clarinet with F. Förster at the Liszt Academy of Music in Budapest (1922–27; 1931–36); taught at the National Cons. (1942–48), and from 1948 at the Liszt Academy of Music. His music follows the modern Hungarian school of composition of Kodály and Bartók; he was the recipient of the Kossuth Prize in 1951 and 1955 and of the Erkel Prize in 1953 and 1954; in 1972 he was awarded the title Merited Artist of the Hungarian People's Republic.

Works: *Napkeleti mese* (Oriental Tale), dance play (1948–49); cantatas: *Három körösztény játék* (3 Christian Plays; 1940); *Honvéd cantata* (Home Guard Cantata; 1949); *Tavasi szél* (Spring Breeze; 1950); a Requiem, *Sötét mennyország* (Dark Heaven; 1963); *Divertimento I* for Strings (1939), *II* for Small Orch. (1942), and *III* for Strings (1942–43); 2 suites for Orch. (1944–45; 1946); Sym. No. 1 (1946–48); *Serenade* for Strings (1947–48); *Rhapsody* for Orch. (1950); *Serenade* for Clarinet and Orch. (1950–51); Flute Concerto (1953); *Variations* for Orch. (1964); Clarinet Concerto (1965); 2 string quartets (1936–37; 1956–57); 20 *Little Duets* for 2 Violins (1942); Violin Sonata (1945); 25 *Duos* for 2 Violins (1946); Clarinet Quintet (1948); Trio for Oboe, Clarinet, and Bassoon (1950); Trio for Flute, Violin, and Viola (1951); Flute Sonatina (1951); 2 wind quintets (1953, 1957); 5 *Concert Études* for Flute (1956); *Suite* for 2 Flutes (1956); 2 *Duos* for 2 Flutes (1972); Piano Sonatina (1940); Sonatina for Piano Duet (1950); songs; choruses; incidental music to films and plays.

Bibl.: I. Barna, *S. E.* (Budapest, 1965).

Szeryng, Henryk, celebrated Polish-born Mexican violinist and pedagogue; b. Zelazowa Wola, Sept. 22, 1918; d. Kassel, March 3, 1988. He commenced piano and harmony training with his mother when he was 5, and at age 7 turned to the violin, receiving instruction from Maurice Frenkel; after further studies with Carl Flesch in Berlin (1929–32), he went to Paris to continue his training with Jacques Thibaud at the Cons., graduating with a premier prix in 1937. On Jan. 6, 1933, he made his formal debut as soloist in the Brahms Concerto with the Warsaw Phil. With the outbreak of World War II in 1939, he became official translator of the Polish prime minister Wladyslaw Sikorski's government-in-exile in London; later was made personal government liaison officer. In 1941 he accompanied the prime minister to Latin America to find a home for some 4,000 Polish refugees; the refugees were taken in by Mexico, and Szeryng, in gratitude, settled there himself, becoming a naturalized citizen in 1946. Throughout World War II, he appeared in some 300 concerts for the Allies. After the war, he pursued a brilliant international career; was also active as a teacher. In 1970 he was made Mexico's special adviser to UNESCO in Paris. He celebrated the 50th anniversary of his debut with a grand tour of Europe and the U.S. in 1983. A cosmopolitan fluent in 7 languages, a humanitarian, and a violinist of extraordinary gifts, Szeryng became renowned as a musician's musician by combining a virtuoso technique with a probing discernment of the highest order.

Bibl.: B. Schwarz, *Great Masters of the Violin* (N.Y., 1983).

Szidon, Roberto, Brazilian pianist of Hungarian descent; b. Porto Alegre, Sept. 21, 1941. He gave a concert in his native city at the age of 9; later studied in N.Y. with Claudio Arrau; then toured in the U.S., South America, and Europe as soloist with the leading orchs. and in recitals.

Szigeti, Joseph, eminent Hungarian-born American violinist; b. Budapest, Sept. 5, 1892; d. Lucerne, Feb. 19, 1973. He began his studies at a local music school; while still a child, he was placed in the advanced class of Hubay at the Budapest Academy of Music; then made his debut in Berlin at age 13. He made his 1st appearance in London when he was 15; subsequently toured England in concerts with Busoni; then settled in Switzerland in 1913; was a prof. at the Geneva Cons. (1917–25). He made an auspicious U.S. debut playing the Beethoven Concerto with Stokowski and the Philadelphia Orch. at N.Y.'s

Carnegie Hall (Dec. 15, 1925); thereafter he toured the U.S. regularly while continuing to appear in Europe. With the outbreak of World War II, he went to the U.S. (1940), becoming a naturalized citizen in 1951. After the end of the war, he resumed his international career; settled again in Switzerland in 1960, and gave master classes. Szigeti was an artist of rare intellect and integrity; he eschewed the role of the virtuoso, placing himself totally at the service of the music. In addition to the standard repertoire, he championed the music of many 20th-century composers, including Stravinsky, Bartók, Ravel, Prokofiev, Honegger, Bloch, and Martin. He wrote the books *With Strings Attached* (N.Y., 1947), *A Violinist's Notebook* (London, 1965), and *Szigeti on the Violin: Improvisations on a Violinist's Themes* (N.Y., 1969).

Bibl.: B. Schwarz, *Great Masters of the Violin* (N.Y., 1983).

Szokolay, Sándor, Hungarian composer and teacher; b. Kunágota, March 30, 1931. He studied with Szabó (1950–52) and Farkas (1952–56) at the Budapest Academy of Music (graduated, 1957), concurrently teaching at the Municipal Music School (1952–55); then was music reader and producer for the Hungarian Radio (1955–59) and a teacher (1959–66) and prof. (from 1966) at the Budapest Academy of Music. He received the Erkel Prize (1960, 1965) and the Kossuth Prize (1966); in 1976 he was made a Merited Artist and in 1986 an Outstanding Artist by the Hungarian government. In 1987 he received the Bartók-Pásztory Award.

Works: STAGE: *OPERAS:* *Vérnász* (Blood Wedding; Budapest, Oct. 30, 1964); *Hamlet* (1965–68; Budapest, Oct. 19, 1968); *Sámson* (Budapest, Oct. 23, 1973); *Ecce homo,* passion opera (1984); *Szávitri* (1987–89); also 2 children's operas. *BALLETS:* *Orbán és as ördög* (Urban and the Devil; 1958); *Az iszonyat balladája* (The Ballad of Terror; 1960); *Tetemrehivás* (Ordeal of the Bier; 1961–71); *Az áldozat* (The Victim; 1971). ORCH.: *Concert Rondo* for Piano and String Orch. (1955); Violin Concerto (1956–57); Piano Concerto (1958); *Ballata sinfonica* (1967–68); Trumpet Concerto (1968); *Archaikus nyitány* (Archaic Overture; 1977); *Rapszódia* for Chamber Orch. (1978); Concertino for Alto Flute, Flute, Piccolo, String Orch., and Harpsichord (1981); Concerto (1982). CHAMBER: *Gyermek-kvartett* (Quartet for Children) for 2 Violins, Cello, and Piano (1954); Sonata for Solo Violin (1956); 2 string quartets (1972, 1982); *Sirató és kultikus tánc* (Lament and Ritual Dance) for Cimbalom, Celesta, Piano, and Harp (1974); *Miniature per ottoni* for Brass Sextet (1976); *Alliterációk* (Alliterations) for Brass Quintet (1977); *Játek a hangközökkel* (Playing with Intervals) for 5 Cimbalom Duos (1978); Sonata for Solo Cello (1979); *Polimorfia* (Polymorphy) for Violin, Cello, and Harpsichord or Piano (1980); *Hommage à Bartók,* divertimento for Brass Quintet (1981); *Gregorián változatok* (Gregorian Variations), 5 miniatures for Brass Quintet (1983); *Variáció egy sirató-dallamra* (Variations on a Lament Melody) for 6 Percussionists (1986). VOCAL: *Vizimesék* (Water Tales), children's cantata for Soprano, Children's Chorus, and Chamber Orch. (1957); *Világok vetélkedése* (Rivalry of Worlds), cantata for Soprano, Alto, Baritone, Choir, and Orch. (1959); *Istár pokoljárása* (Isthar's Descent to Hell), oratorio for Soprano, Alto, Baritone, Bass, Chorus, and Orch. (1960–61); *Néger kantáta* (Negro Cantata) for Alto, Chorus, and Orch. (1962); *Deploration: Concerto da requiem* for Piano, Chorus, and Orch. in memory of Francis Poulenc (1964); *Vitézi ének* (Song of Heroes), cantata for Alto, Bass, Men's Chorus, and Orch. (1970); *Ódon ének* (Ancient Song), cantata for Chorus, Woodwind, Horns, Kettledrum, Harp, and Strings (1972); *Kantáta a gályarabok emlékére* (Cantata in Memory of Galley Slaves) for Narrator, Baritone, Chorus, Organ, and Orch. (1975); *Libellus ungaricus,* cantata for Soprano, Alto, Tenor, Baritone, Bass, Chorus, Organ, and Orch. (1979); *Confessio Augustana,* cantata for Baritone, Chorus, and Orch. (1980); *Luther-Kantate* for Baritone, Chorus, Chamber Orch., and Organ (1983).

Szöllösy, András, Hungarian composer and musicologist; b. Szászváros, Transylvania, Feb. 27, 1921. He studied with Kodály and Viski at the Budapest Academy of Music (1939–44)

and took courses in musicology at the Univ. of Budapest (Ph.D., 1943); completed his training in composition with Petrassi at the Accademia di Santa Cecilia in Rome (1947–48). He was a prof. of music history and theory at the Budapest Academy of Music (from 1950). In 1971 he received the Erkel Prize, in 1985 the Kossuth Prize, and in 1986 the Bartók-Pásztory Award. He was made an Artist of Merit (1972) and an Outstanding Artist (1982) of the Hungarian People's Republic; in 1987 the French government made him a Commandeur de l'Ordre des Arts et Lettres. His music draws upon modern resources cast along traditional lines. He publ. a study on Honegger (Budapest, 1960) and ed. the writings of Bartók.

WORKS: BALLETS: *Oly korban éltem* (Improvisations on Fear; 1963); *Pantomime* (1965); *A tűz fiai* (Sons of Fire; 1977); *Diminuendo* (1977). **ORCH.:** Concerto No. 1 for Strings, Brass, Piano, and Percussion (1957); Concerto No. 2 (destroyed); Concerto No. 3 for 16 Strings (1968); Concerto No. 4 (1970); *Transfigurazioni* (1972; Budapest, June 1, 1973); *Musica per orchestra* (1972; Vienna, Sept. 26, 1973); *Musica concertante* for Chamber Orch. (1973); *Preludio, Adagio e Fuga* (1973); *Sonorità* (1974; Budapest, Sept. 29, 1975); Concerto No. 5, *Lehellet* (1975; Budapest, May 27, 1976); *Concerto per clavicembalo ed 16 archi* (1978); *Pro somno Igoris Stravinsky quieto* for Chamber Orch. (1978); *Tristia: Maros-sirató* (Maros Lament) for 16 Strings (1983); *Canto d'autunno* (1986; Swansea, Jan. 16, 1987). **CHAMBER:** *Tre pezzi per flauto e pianoforte* (1964); *100 Bars for Tom Everett* for Bass Trombone and 3 Bongos (1981); Quartetto di tromboni (1986); String Quartet (1988). **VOCAL:** *Nyugtalan ősz* (Restless Autumn), cantata for Baritone and Piano (1955); *Kolozsvári éjjel* (Night at Kolozsvár), elegy for Voice and Wind Quintet (1955); *Fabula Phaedri* for Vocal Sextet (1982); *Töredékek* (Fragments) for Mezzo-soprano, Flute, and Viola (1985).

Szönyi, Erzsébet, Hungarian composer and music educator; b. Budapest, April 25, 1924. She studied piano and composition at the Budapest Academy of Music, graduating in 1947; then went to Paris, where she took courses at the Cons. with Aubin and Messiaen; also took private lessons in composition with Boulanger. Returning to Budapest, she joined the faculty of the Academy of Music in 1948. In 1959 she was awarded the Erkel Prize. She played a major role in promoting Kodály's educational methods in Hungary and elsewhere. Her writings include *A zenei írás-olvasás módszertana* (Methods of Musical Reading and Writing; 4 vols., Budapest, 1953–65; Eng. tr., 1972) and a study on Kodály's teaching methods (Budapest, 1973; numerous trs.).

WORKS: OPERAS: *Dalma* (1952); *The Stubborn Princess* (1955); *Firenzei tragédie* (1957); *The Little Bee with the Golden Wing* (1974); *A Gay Lament* (1979); *The Truth-telling Shepherd* (1979); *Break of Transmission* (1980); *Elfrida* (1985). **ORCH.:** 2 divertimentos (1948, 1951); Organ Concerto (1958); *Musica festiva* (1964); *3 Ideas in 4 Movements* for Piano and Orch. (1980). **CHAMBER:** Trio for Oboe, Clarinet, and Bassoon (1958); Trio Sonata for Violin, Cello, and Piano (1965); Sonata for Double Bass and Piano (1982); *Evocatio* for Piano and Organ (1985); also 2 piano sonatinas (1944, 1946); Piano Sonata (1953); choral works.

Szulc, Józef Zygmunt, Polish pianist and composer; b. Warsaw, April 4, 1875; d. Paris, April 10, 1956. He studied at the Warsaw Cons. with Noskowski; then took piano lessons in Paris with Moszkowski. He remained in Paris as a piano teacher; then turned to composition of light operas. His 1st work in this genre, *Flup* (Brussels, Dec. 19, 1913), was successful and had numerous performances in Europe; he continued to produce operettas at regular intervals; the last one was *Pantoufle* (Paris, Feb. 24, 1945). He also wrote a ballet, *Une Nuit d'Ispahan* (Brussels, Nov. 19, 1909), overtures, chamber music, and piano pieces.

Szumowska, Antoinette, Polish-American pianist and teacher; b. Lublin, Feb. 22, 1868; d. Rumson, N.J., Aug. 18, 1938. She studied at the Warsaw Cons. with Michalowski,

and later took lessons with Paderewski in Paris (1890–95). In 1895 she emigrated to the U.S., settling in Boston, where she taught at the New England Cons. of Music. In 1896 she married the cellist **Josef Adamowski,** and with him and his brother Timothée, a violinist, formed the Adamowski Trio, which presented numerous concerts in New England.

Szweykowski, Zygmunt M(arian), eminent Polish musicologist; b. Krakow, May 12, 1929. He was a pupil of Chybiński at the Univ. of Poznan (graduated, 1951) and of Chomiński at the Univ. of Krakow (Ph.D., 1964, with the diss. *Technika koncertująca w polskiej muzyce wokalnmo-instrumentalnej okresu baroku* [Concerto Technique in Polish Vocal-Instrumental Music of the Baroque]; Eng. tr. in *Studia Hieronymo Feicht septuagenario dedicata*, Krakow, 1967, and in *Polish Musicological Studies*, I, 1977); completed his Habilitation at the latter in 1976 with his *Musica moderna w ujęciu Marka Scacchiego* (Musica Moderna as Conceived by Marco Scacchi; publ. in Krakow, 1977, with Eng. summary). After serving as Chybiński's assistant at the Univ. of Poznan (1950–53), he went to Krakow as ed. of Polskie Wydawnictwo Muzyczne (1954–61); also taught at the Univ. (from 1954), becoming head of its musicological dept. (1971–74; from 1979); was made a prof. in 1988. Szweykowski is a respected scholar of the Baroque era in Polish music history. He founded *Zródła do Historii Muzyki Polskiej* in 1960 and ed. various works in Wydawnictwo Dawnej Muzyki Polskiej; also contributed valuable articles to Polish and foreign journals and other publications.

WRITINGS: *Kultura wokalna XVI-wiecznej Polski* (The Vocal Culture of XVI-century Poland; Krakow, 1957); ed. *Z dziejów polskiej kultury muzycznej* (From the History of Polish Musical Culture; Krakow, 1958); *Katalog tematyczny rekopísmiennych zabytków dawnej muzyki w Polsce* (Thematic Catalog of Early Music Manuscripts in Poland; Krakow, 1969).

Szymanowska, Maria Agate (née **Wolowska**), prominent Polish pianist and composer; b. Warsaw, Dec. 14, 1789; d. St. Petersburg, July 24, 1831. She studied piano with local teachers in Warsaw, and began to play in public as a child. In 1810 she married a Polish landowner, Theophilus Joseph Szymanowski (divorced, 1820). In 1822 she toured in Russia, and was appointed court pianist; in 1823, played in Germany; in 1824, in France; then in England, the Netherlands, and Italy (1824–25), returning to Warsaw in 1826. In 1828 she settled in St. Petersburg as a pianist and teacher, and remained there until her death (of cholera). Goethe held her in high esteem and wrote his *Aussöhnung* for her; she also won the admiration of Glinka and Pushkin. She distinguished herself as a composer for the piano, presaging the genius of Chopin in her studies, nocturnes, and dances. Among her finest works for piano are *20 exercices et préludes* (Leipzig, 1820), *18 Danses* (Leipzig, 1820), *Nocturne: Le Murmure* (Paris, 1825), and *24 Mazurkas* (Leipzig, 1826). She also wrote some chamber music and vocal pieces.

BIBL.: I. Boelza, *M. S.* (Moscow, 1956); M. Iwanejko, *M. S.* (Krakow, 1959).

Szymanowski, Karol (Maciej), eminent Polish composer; b. Timoshovka, Ukraine, Oct. 6, 1882; d. Lausanne, March 28, 1937. The son of a cultured landowner, he grew up in a musical environment. He began to play the piano and compose very early in life. His 1st teacher was Gustav Neuhaus in Elizavetgrad; in 1901 he went to Warsaw, where he studied harmony with Zawirski and counterpoint and composition with Noskowski until 1904. With Fitelberg, Rózycki, and Szeluto, he founded the Young Polish Composer's Publishing Co. in Berlin, which was patronized by Prince Wladyslaw Lubomirski; the composers also became known as Young Poland in Music, publishing new works and sponsoring performances for some 6 years. Among the works the group publ. was Szymanowski's op. 1, 9 Piano Preludes (1906). He was greatly influenced by German Romanticism, and his 1st major orch. works reveal the impact of Wagner and Strauss. His 1st Sym. was premiered in Warsaw on March 26, 1909; however, he was dissatisfied with the score, and withdrew it from further performance. In 1911 he completed his 2nd Sym., which demonstrated a stylistic change from German dominance to Russian influences, paralleling the harmonic evolution of Scriabin; it was played for the 1st time in Warsaw on April 7, 1911. After a Viennese sojourn (1911–12) and a trip to North Africa (1914), he lived from 1914 to 1917 in Timoshovka, where he wrote his 3rd Sym.; he appeared in concert with the violinist Paul Kochański in Moscow and St. Petersburg, giving 1st performances of his violin works; it was for Kochański that he composed his violin triptych, *Mythes* (*La Fontaine d'Aréthuse* in this cycle is one of his best-known compositions). About this time, his music underwent a new change in style, veering toward French Impressionism. During the Russian Revolution of 1917, the family estate at Timoshovka was ruined, and Szymanowski lost most of his possessions. From 1917 to 1919 he lived in Elizavetgrad, where he continued to compose industriously, despite the turmoil of the Civil War. After a brief stay in Bydgoszcz, he went to Warsaw in 1920. In 1920–21, he toured the U.S. in concerts with Kochański and Rubinstein. Returning to Warsaw, he gradually established himself as one of Poland's most important composers. His international renown also was considerable; his works were often performed in Europe, and figured at festivals of the ISCM. He was director of the Warsaw Cons. (1927–29) and reorganized the system of teaching along more liberal lines; was rector of its successor, the Warsaw Academy of Music (1930–32). His *Stabat Mater* (1925–26) produced a profound impression, and his ballet-pantomime *Harnasie* (1923–31), based on the life and music of the Tatra mountain dwellers, demonstrated his ability to treat national subjects in an original and highly effective manner. In 1932 he appeared as soloist in the 1st performance of his 4th Sym., *Symphonie concertante* for Piano and Orch., at Poznan, and repeated his performances in Paris, London, and Brussels. In April 1936, greatly weakened in health by chronic tuberculosis, he attended a performance of his *Harnasie* at the Paris Opéra. He spent his last days in a sanatorium in Lausanne. Szymanowski developed into a national composer whose music acquired universal significance.

WORKS: STAGE: *Loteria na mezós* (The Lottery for Men), operetta (1908–9; not perf.); *Hagith*, op. 25, opera (1913; Warsaw, May 13, 1922); *Mandragora*, op. 43, pantomime (Warsaw, June 15, 1920); *Król Roger* (King Roger), op. 46, opera (1918–24; Warsaw, June 19, 1926); *Kniaź Patiomkin* (Prince Potemkin), op. 51, incidental music to T. Miciński's play (Warsaw, March 6, 1925); *Harnasie*, op. 55, ballet-pantomime (1923–31; Prague, May 11, 1935). **ORCH.:** *Salome* for Soprano and Orch., op. 6 (c.1907; reorchestrated 1912); *Concert Overture*, op. 12 (1904–5; Warsaw, Feb. 6, 1906; reorchestrated 1912–13); 4 syms.: No. 1, op. 15 (1906–7; Warsaw, March 26, 1909); No. 2, op. 19 (1909–10; Warsaw, April 7, 1911; reorchestrated with the collaboration of G. Fitelberg, 1936; rev. version by S. Skrowaczewski, Minneapolis, Oct. 14, 1967); No. 3, *Pieśń o nocy* (Song of the Night) for Tenor, Soprano, Chorus, and Orch., op. 27 (1914–16; London, Nov. 24, 1921); No. 4, *Symphonie concertante* for Piano and Orch., op. 60 (Poznan, Oct. 9, 1932, composer soloist); *Penthesilea* for Soprano and Orch., op. 18 (1908; Warsaw, March 18, 1910; reorchestrated 1912); *Pieśni miłosne Hafiza* (Love

Songs of Hafiz) for Voice and Orch., op. 26 (1914; Paris, June 23, 1925; arranged from the op. 24, 1911); *Pieśni księżnicki z baśni* (Songs of a Fairy-Tale Princess) for Voice and Orch., op. 31 (Warsaw, April 7, 1933; arranged from the songs of 1915); 2 violin concertos: No. 1, op. 35 (1916; Warsaw, Nov. 1, 1922); No. 2, op. 61 (Warsaw, Oct. 6, 1933); *Demeter* for Alto, Women's Chorus, and Orch., op. 37b (1917; reorchestrated 1924; Warsaw, April 17, 1931); *Agave* for Alto, Women's Chorus, and Orch., op. 39 (1917); *Pieśni muezina szalonego* (Songs of the Infatuated Muezzin) for Voice and Orch., op. 42 (1934; arranged from the songs of 1918); *Słopiewnie* for Voice and Orch., op. 46b (1928; arranged from the version for Voice and Piano of 1921); *Stabat Mater* for Soprano, Alto, Baritone, Chorus, and Orch., op. 53 (1925–26; Warsaw, Jan. 11, 1929); *Veni Creator* for Soprano, Chorus, Orch., and Organ, op. 57 (Warsaw, Nov. 7, 1930); *Litania do Marii Panny* (Litany to the Virgin Mary) for Soprano, Women's Chorus, and Orch., op. 59 (1930–33; Warsaw, Oct. 13, 1933). **CHAMBER:** Violin Sonata, op. 9 (1904; Warsaw, April 19, 1909); Piano Trio, op. 16 (1907; destroyed); *Romance* for Violin and Piano, op. 23 (1910; Warsaw, April 8, 1913); *Nocturne and Tarantella* for Violin and Piano, op. 28 (1915); *Mity* (Myths) for Violin and Piano, op. 30 (1915); 2 string quartets: No. 1, op. 37 (1917; Warsaw, April 1924); No. 2, op. 56 (1927; Paris, 1929); *3 Paganini Caprices* for Violin and Piano, op. 40 (Elizavetgrad, April 25, 1918); *Kołysanka* (Lullaby): *La Berceuse d'Aïtacho Enia* for Violin and Piano, op. 52 (1925). **PIANO:** *9 Preludes*, op. 1 (1900); *Variations*, op. 3 (1903); *4 Studies*, op. 4 (1902); 3 sonatas: No. 1, op. 8 (1904; Warsaw, April 19, 1907); No. 2, op. 21 (Berlin, Dec. 1, 1911); No. 3, op. 36 (1917); *Wariacje na polski temat ludowy* (Variations on a Polish Theme), op. 10 (1904; Warsaw, Feb. 6, 1906); *Fantasy*, op. 14 (1905; Warsaw, Feb. 9, 1906); *Prelude and Fugue* (1905–9); *Metopy* (Metopes), op. 29 (1915); *12 Studies*, op. 33 (1916); *Maski* (Masques), op. 34 (St. Petersburg, Oct. 12, 1916); *20 Mazurkas*, op. 50 (1924–25); *Valse romantique* (1925); *4 Polish Dances* (1926); *2 Mazurkas*, op. 62 (1933–34; London, Nov. 1934); also about 100 songs.

WRITINGS: *Wychowawcza rola kultury muzycznej w spoleczenstwie* (The Educational Role of Musical Culture in Society; Warsaw, 1931); T. Bronowicz-Chylińska, ed., *Z pism* (From the Writings; Krakow, 1958; selected essays).

BIBL.: Z. Jachimecki, "K. S.," *Musical Quarterly* (Jan. 1922); A. Tansman, "K. S.," *Revue Musicale* (May 1922); Z. Jachimecki, *K. S.: Zarys dotychczasowej twórczości* (K. S.: An Outline of His Output; Krakow, 1927); special issue of *Muzyka Polska* (1937); S. Golachowski, *K. S.* (Warsaw, 1948; 2nd ed., 1956); S. Lobaczewska, *K. S.: Zycie i twórczośc (1882–1937)* (K. S.: Life and Work [1882–1937]; Krakow, 1950); T. Bronowicz-Chylińska, ed., *S. K.: Z listów* (S. K.: From the Letters; Krakow, 1957); J. Chomiński, *Studia nad twórczóscia K.a S.ego* (Krakow, 1969); A. Wightman, *The Music of K. S.* (diss., Univ. of York, 1972); J. Samson, *The Music of S.* (London, 1980); A. Wightman, "S. and Joyce," *Musical Times* (Oct. 1982); C. Palmer, *S.* (London, 1983); M. Bristiger et al., eds., *K. S. in seiner Zeit* (Munich, 1984); Z. Sierpiński, ed., and E. Harris, tr., *K. S.: An Anthology* (Warsaw, 1986); A. Wightman, "S. and Islam," *Musical Times* (March 1987); J. Samson, "S. and Polish Nationalism," ibid. (March 1990).

T

Tabachnik, Michel, Swiss conductor and composer of Russian descent; b. Geneva, Nov. 10, 1942. He studied theory and conducting at the Geneva Cons.; attended the Darmstadt summer courses in new music (1964); after studying with Boulez at the Basel Academy of Music (1965), he served as his assistant until 1971. He was conductor of the Gulbenkian Foundation Orch. in Lisbon (1973–75), the Lorraine Phil. in Metz (1975–81), and the Ensemble Européen de Musique Contemporaine in Paris (1976–77); subsequently conducted regularly with the Toronto and Montreal operas; gave master classes in conducting at the Univ. of Toronto.

WORKS: *Supernovae* for 19 Instruments (1967); *Frise* for Piano (1968); *Pastel I* for Flute, Horn, Celesta, Harp, 2 Percussion, and Cello (1968); *Pastel II* for Orch. (1969); *Fresque* for 33 Instruments (1970); *Mondes* for 2 Orchs. (1970–72); *Sillages* for 32 Strings (1972); *D'autres sillages* for 8 Timpani and Tape (1972); *Invention à 16 voix* for 23 Instruments (1972); *Movimenti* for 51 Instruments (1973); *Eclipses* for Piano (1974); *Les Imaginaires* for Orch. (1974); *Argile* for 4 Percussion (1975); *Les Perséides* for Orch. (1975); *Cosmogonie pour une rose* for Orch. (1981); *Sept rituels atlantes* for Chorus (1985); *La Légende de Hajha* for Soloists, Chorus, and Orch. (1989).

Tabakov, Mikhail, Ukrainian trumpeter and pedagogue; b. Odessa, Jan. 6, 1877; d. Moscow, March 9, 1956. He studied at the Odessa Cons.; then went to Moscow and was engaged as a member of the Bolshoi Theater Orch. (1897–1938, with interruptions); also played in Koussevitzky's orch. (1910–17). In 1922 he became a member and manager of the conductorless orch. Persimfans (abbreviation of the Russian words Pervyí Symfonicheskii Ansambl, i.e., 1st Symphonic Ensemble), remaining with it until 1932. He devoted himself to teaching trumpet; publ. the book *Progressivnaya shkola dlya trubi* (Progressive School for Trumpet; Moscow, 1946).

Tabourot, Jehan. See **Arbeau, Thoinot.**

Tabuteau, Marcel, outstanding French oboist and pedagogue; b. Compiègne, July 2, 1887; d. Nice, Jan. 4, 1966. He studied oboe with Georges Gillet at the Paris Cons.; won a premier prix at the age of 17; in 1905 he went to the U.S., where he played in the N.Y. Sym. Orch.; also was a member of the orch. of the Metropolitan Opera (from 1908). In 1915 Stokowski engaged him as 1st oboist in the Philadelphia Orch., where he remained until 1954; he was also on the faculty of the Curtis Inst. of Music in Philadelphia (from 1924).

Tacchinardi, Nicola (Niccolò), famous Italian tenor and singing teacher; b. Livorno, Sept. 3, 1772; d. Florence, March 14, 1859. He played cello in the orch. of Florence's Teatro della Pergola (1789–97); after vocal studies, he began his operatic career with appearances in Livorno, Pisa, Florence, and Venice in 1804; in 1805 sang at Milan's La Scala, where he participated in the coronation performances for Napoleon as King of Italy. He scored a triumph in Zingarelli's *La distruzione di Gerusalemme* at the Paris Odéon on May 4, 1811; until 1814 he sang at the Théâtre-Italien, where his performances in Paisiello's *La bella molinara* were particularly acclaimed. After appearances in Spain (1815–17) and Vienna (1816), he returned to Italy; was made primo cantante of the Florence Grand Ducal Chapel in 1822, while continuing his appearances in Italian opera houses; he also revisited Vienna in 1823. He retired in 1831 and devoted himself to teaching; one of his students was his daughter, **Fanny** (née **Tacchinardi**) **Persiani.** His most celebrated role was that of Othello in Rossini's *Otello.* He composed vocal exercises and publ. *Dell'opera in musica sul teatro italiano e de' suoi difetti* (Florence, 2nd ed., 1833). His son, **Guido Tacchinardi** (b. Florence, March 10, 1840; d. there, Dec. 6, 1917), was a conductor, music critic, and composer; was director of the Florence Istituto Musicale (1891–1917).

Tacchino, Gabriel, French pianist; b. Cannes, Aug. 4, 1934. He studied at the Paris Cons. and made his concert debut in 1953. After winning 1st prizes in competitions held in Vercelli (1953), Geneva (1955), and Naples (1956), he launched an international career; distinguished himself in refined interpretations of the Classical and Romantic repertoire.

Tachezi, Herbert, Austrian organist and harpsichordist; b. Wiener Neustadt, Feb. 12, 1930. He studied organ with Alois Forer, composition with Alfred Uhl, and musicology with Otto Siegl at the Vienna Academy of Music; also attended the Univ. of Vienna. In 1958 he joined the faculty of the Vienna Academy of Music, where he taught organ and composition; in 1972 he was made a prof. there (it became the Hochschule für Musik in 1970). He appeared regularly as an organist and harpsichordist with the Concentus Musicus in Vienna from 1964; was named organist of Vienna's Hofmusikkapelle in 1974. He toured widely as a recitalist in Europe and the U.S.

Taddei, Giuseppe, noted Italian baritone; b. Genoa, June 26, 1916. He studied in Rome, where he made his debut at the Teatro Reale dell'Opera as the Herald in *Lohengrin* in 1936; sang there until he was drafted into the Italian army in 1942. After World War II, he appeared at the Vienna State Opera (1946–48); made his London debut at the Cambridge Theatre in 1947 and his Salzburg Festival debut in 1948. He sang at Milan's La Scala (1948–51; 1955–61) and at London's Covent Garden (1960–67); also appeared in San Francisco, Chicago, and other music centers. On Sept. 25, 1985, at the age of 69, he made his long-awaited debut at the Metropolitan Opera in N.Y. as Falstaff. He excelled in both lyrico-dramatic and buffo roles, including Figaro, Leporello, Papageno, Dulcamara, Falstaff, Rigoletto, Scarpia, Iago, and Macbeth.

Tadolini, Eugenia (née **Savonari**), noted Italian soprano, wife of **Giovanni Tadolini;** b. Forlì, 1809; d. Naples, after 1851. She received vocal training from her husband; after making her operatic debut in Florence in 1828, she made her 1st appearance outside her homeland at the Paris Théâtre-Italien in Rossini's *Ricciardo e Zoraide* on Oct. 23, 1830; continued to sing in Paris until 1833. On Oct. 1, 1833, she made her debut at Milan's La Scala in Donizetti's *Il furioso all'isola di San Domingo;* in 1834 she sang as his Adina in Vienna, returning there as his Antonina in 1836; Donizetti chose her to sing in the premiere of his *Linda di Chamounix* there on May 19, 1842, and she returned to create the title role in his *Maria di Rohan* on June 5, 1843. She was an early champion of Verdi, creating the title role in his *Alzira* in Naples (Aug. 12, 1845); returned there to sing Lady Macbeth in 1848. Verdi found her voice beautiful but was dubious about her dramatic talent. On May 20, 1848, she made her London debut in *Linda di Chamounix* at Her Majesty's Theatre. She retired from the operatic stage in 1851.

Tadolini, Giovanni, Italian composer and singing teacher, husband of **Eugenia** (née **Savonari**) Tadolini; b. Bologna, Oct. 18, 1785; d. there, Nov. 29, 1872. He studied composition with Mattei and singing with Babini; from 1811 to 1814 he was on the staff of the Théâtre-Italien in Paris; then returned to Italy, where he produced a succession of operas: *La fata Alcina* (Venice, 1815); *Le Bestie in uomini* (Venice, 1815); *La principessa di Navarra ossia Il Gianni di Parigi* (Bologna, 1816); *Il credulo deluso* (Rome, 1817); *Tamerlano* (Bologna, 1818); *Moctar, Gran Visir di Adrianopoli* (Bologna, 1824); *Mitridate* (Venice, 1826); *Almanzor* (Trieste, 1827); from 1829 to

1839 he was again at his post at the Théâtre-Italien. He also wrote 2 sinfonie, Concertone for Oboe, Horn, and Orch., chamber music, many sacred vocal works, and songs. He settled in Bologna in 1848 and founded his own singing school.

Taffanel, (Claude-) Paul, eminent French flutist, conductor, and pedagogue; b. Bordeaux, Sept. 16, 1844; d. Paris, Nov. 22, 1908. He was a pupil of Dorus (flute) and Reber (composition). From 1864 to 1890 he was a flutist in the Paris Opéra orch.; from 1867 to 1890, flutist of the Cons. concerts in Paris, which he conducted from 1890 to 1903; from 1892 until his death he was one of the "chefs d'orchestre" at the Paris Opéra; in 1893 he succeeded Altès as prof. of flute at the Cons. In 1879 he founded the Société des Instruments à Vent in Paris, which was active until 1892. Taffanel is considered as the father of the modern French school of flute playing. With Gaubert, he wrote *Méthode complète de flûte.* He also composed some fine chamber music for wind instruments and prepared effective arrangements for flute and piano.

Tag, Christian Gotthilf, German organist and composer; b. Beierfeld, April 2, 1735; d. Niederzwönitz, near Zwönitz, June 19, 1811. From 1749 to 1755 he studied at the Kreuzschule in Dresden; from 1755 to 1808, was cantor at Hohenstein-Ernstthal. He wrote a large body of Kantorenmusik; won especial esteem for his lieder and keyboard pieces.

Works: 6 chorale preludes for Organ (1783); 12 preludes and a Sym. for Organ (1794); songs (1783, 1785, 1793, 1798); 70 variations for Piano on an Andantino (1784); *Der Glaube,* melody with Organ (1793); *Urians Reise um die Welt* and *Urians Nachricht von der Aufklärung* (1797); *Naumann, ein Todtenopfer* (1803; Voice with Piano); *Melodie zum Vaterunser und den Einsetzungsworten* (1803; with Organ); *Wörlitz, an ode* (1803; Voice with Piano); many sacred and instrumental works are in MS.

Bibl.: H. Vieweg, *C.G. T. (1735–1811) als Meister der nachbachischen Kantate* (Leipzig, 1933).

Tagliabue, Carlo, noted Italian baritone; b. Mariano Comense, Jan. 12, 1898; d. Monza, April 5, 1978. He studied with Gennai and Guidotti; then made his debut as Amonasro in 1922 in Lodi. After singing in Italian provincial opera houses, he joined La Scala in Milan in 1930; continued to appear there regularly until 1943, and again from 1946 to 1953; also sang in Florence and Rome, at the Teatro Colón in Buenos Aires, and at Covent Garden in London (1938, 1946). On Dec. 2, 1937, he made his Metropolitan Opera debut in N.Y. as Amonasro; continued on its roster until 1939. He retired in 1960. He was a distinguished interpreter of Verdi and a fine Wagnerian.

Tagliaferro, Magda, Brazilian pianist and pedagogue; b. Petropolis, Jan. 19, 1893; d. Rio de Janeiro, Sept. 9, 1986. She studied at the São Paulo Cons. before going to Paris to continue her training at the Cons. there (graduated with a premier prix, 1907); also received private lessons from Cortot. In 1908 she launched her concert career and also was active as a teacher; after teaching a master class at the Paris Cons. (1937–39), she pursued her career in the Americas; from 1949 she was again active in Paris. Her concert career lasted for over 75 years; she made numerous appearances in recitals in the U.S., the last one in 1980; gave a London recital in 1983 at the age of 90. In her prime, she was known for her sensitive readings of the French repertoire; she also gave the premiere of Villa-Lobos's *Momoprecoce* for Piano and Orch. (1929).

Tagliafico, (Dieudonné) Joseph, distinguished French bass-baritone; b. Toulon, Jan. 1, 1821; d. Nice, Jan. 27, 1900. He studied with Piermarini and Lablache in Paris; made his debut there in 1844 at the Théâtre-Italien; in 1847 he joined the new Royal Italian Opera company at Covent Garden in London, remaining on its roster until 1876; then was its stage manager until 1882. He appeared as a guest artist in France, Russia, and the U.S. He was best known for his French and Italian roles.

Tagliapietra, Gino, Italian pianist, teacher, and composer; b. Ljubljana, May 30, 1887; d. Venice, Aug. 8, 1954. He studied piano with Julius Epstein in Vienna and with Busoni in Berlin; in 1906, was appointed to the faculty of the Liceo Benedetto Marcello in Venice; retired in 1940. His compositions include a fiaba musicale, *La bella addormentata* (Venice, March 11, 1926); Piano Concerto (1913); *Variazioni a fantasia* for Piano and Strings (1930); *Requiem* (1923), and various choral works; Violin Sonata (1937); songs; many piano pieces and various didactic works. He ed. *Antologia di musica antica e moderna per il pianoforte* (Milan, 1931–32) and *Raccolta di composizioni dei secoli XVI e XVII* (Milan, 1937).

BIBL.: F. Vadala, *G. T.* (diss., Univ. of Messina, 1976).

Tagliapietra, Giovanni, Italian baritone; b. Venice, Dec. 24, 1846; d. N.Y., April 11, 1921. He studied naval architecture and graduated from the Univ. of Padua. After a study of singing with Giovanni Corsi, he appeared in various Italian opera houses; made a tour of South America; in 1874, was engaged as member of Max Strakosch's company and sang in the U.S. In 1876 he married the famous pianist **Teresa Carreño,** but they were divorced; his brother Arturo was married to her in 1902.

Tagliavini, Ferruccio, prominent Italian tenor; b. Reggio Emilia, Aug. 14, 1913. After studying at the Parma Cons., he won 1st prize for singing at the May Festival in Florence (1938); made his opera debut there as Rodolfo in *La Bohème* (Oct. 1938); later sang at La Scala in Milan, and other opera houses in Italy; in 1946 he toured South America; on Jan. 10, 1947, he made a very successful 1st appearance, as Rodolfo, at the Metropolitan Opera, N.Y.; remained on its roster until 1954; sang there again in 1961–62. In 1965 he made his operatic farewell in Venice as Werther. In 1941 he married the soprano Pia Tassinari. Among his other distinguished roles were Elvino, Cavaradossi, Nemorino, and the Duke of Mantua.

BIBL.: C. Tedeschi, *F. T.* (Rome, 1942).

Tagliavini, Luigi Ferdinando, distinguished Italian organist, harpsichordist, and musicologist; b. Bologna, Oct. 7, 1929. He studied organ at the Bologna Cons. and with Marcel Dupré at the Paris Cons. (1947–52); also studied at the Univ. of Padua, receiving his Ph.D. there in 1951 with the dissertation *Studi sui testi delle cantate sacre J.S. Bach* (publ. in Padua, 1956); he taught organ at the G.B. Martini Cons. in Bologna (1952–54); also was head of its library (1953–60); concurrently he served as a prof. of organ at the Monteverdi Cons. in Bolzano (1954–64); from 1964 he was on the faculty of the Parma Cons. In 1959 he joined the staff of the Univ. of Bologna; from 1965 he taught music history at the Univ. of Fribourg. With R. Lunelli, he founded the journal *L'organo* in 1960; also served as ed. of Monumenti di Musica Italiana. He is an authority on organ restoration. With O. Mischiati, he ed. *Un anonimo trattato francese di arte organaria del sec. XVIII* (Bologna, 1974).

Täglichsbeck, Thomas, German violinist and composer; b. Ansbach, Dec. 31, 1799; d. Baden-Baden, Oct. 5, 1867. He became a violinist in the Isarthortheater orch. in 1817, and in 1819 its music director. In 1822 he was made solo violinist to the Munich court; also toured in Switzerland and Italy. He was named Kapellmeister to Prince Hohenlohe-Hechingen in 1827, and continued to serve his successor Prince Constantine (1838–48); when the latter reorganized his Court Orch. in Löwenberg in 1852, Täglichsbeck resumed his duties, retiring in 1857; then taught at the Dresden Cons. until 1859.

WORKS: OPERAS: *Webers Bild* (Munich, Aug. 24, 1823); *König Enzio* (Karlsruhe, May 14, 1843); *Guido oder Das Jägerhaus im Walde Sila* (not perf.); also 2 syms.; 2 concertinos for Violin and Orch.; Fantasia for Violin and Orch.; Quintet for Clarinet and Strings; 3 string quartets; Piano Trio; 3 sonatas for Violin and Piano; Concert Piece for Viola and Piano; 5 duets for 2 Violins; Mass for Solo Voices, Chorus, Orch., and Organ; songs.

BIBL.: E. Burmester, *T. T. und seine Instrumental-Kompositionen* (diss., Univ. of Munich, 1936).

Tagore, Sir Surindro Mohun (actually, **Rajah Saurindramohana Thäkura**), Hindu musicologist; b. Calcutta, 1840; d.

there, June 5, 1914. At the age of 17 he began to study Hindu music under Luchmi Prasad Misra and Kshetra Mohun Goswami, and European music under 2 European mentors; he founded and endowed from his personal fortune the Bengal Music School (1871) and the Bengal Academy of Music (1882), continuing to preside over both until his death. A connoisseur of Eastern instrumentation, he was at various times commissioned by the principal museums of Europe to procure for them instruments of Asiatic nations. He wrote nearly 60 books on an amazing variety of subjects; those concerning music (publ. in Calcutta, in Bengali, and some in Eng.) include: *Yantra Kosha, or A Treasury of the Musical Instruments of Ancient and Modern India* (1875); *Hindu Music, from Various Authors* (1875; 2nd ed., in 2 vols., 1882); *Six Principal Rāgas, with a Brief View of Hindu Music* (1876; 3rd ed., 1884); *Short Notices of Hindu Musical Instruments* (1877); *The 8 Principal Rāgas of the Hindus* (1880); *The Five Principal Musicians of the Hindus, or A Brief Exposition of the Essential Elements of Hindu Music* (1881); *The Musical Scales of the Hindus with Remarks on the Applicability of Harmony to Hindu Music* (1884); *The 22 Musical Srutis of the Hindus* (1886); *Universal History of Music, together with Various Original Notes on Hindu Music* (1896).

BIBL.: F. Chrysander, "Verzeichnis der Werke und Publikationen von Dr. S.M. T.," *Allgemeine Musikalische Zeitung,* XIV (1879); F. Vogt, "S.M. T., ein indischer Dichter-Componist," ibid., XVII (1882); *Viśvapati Caudhur: Songs and Addresses in Memory of the Late Raja Sir Saurindramohana Thākura* (Calcutta, 1919).

Tailleferre (real name, **Taillefesse**), **(Marcelle) Germaine,** fine French composer; b. Parc-St.-Maur, near Paris, April 19, 1892; d. Paris, Nov. 7, 1983. She altered her name to dispel the unwanted anatomical association in the second syllable. She studied harmony and solfège with H. Dallier (premier prix, 1913), counterpoint with G. Caussade (premier prix, 1914), and accompaniment with Estyle at the Paris Cons.; also had some informal lessons with Ravel. She received recognition as the only female member of the group of French composers known as Les Six (the other members were Honegger, Milhaud, Poulenc, Auric, and Durey). Her style of composition was pleasingly, teasingly modernistic and feministic (Jean Cocteau invoked a comparison with a young French woman painter, Marie Laurencin, saying that Tailleferre's music was to the ear what the painter's pastels were to the eye). Indeed, most of her works possess a fragile charm of unaffected *joie de jouer la musique.* She was married to an American author, Ralph Barton, in 1926, but soon divorced him and married a French lawyer, Jean Lageat. She visited the U.S. in 1927 and again in 1942. In 1974 she publ. an autobiographical book, *Mémoires à l'emporte pièce.*

WORKS: *Image* for Piano, Flute, Clarinet, String Quartet, and Celesta (1918); *Jeux de plein air* for 2 Pianos (1918); String Quartet (1918); Piano Concerto (1919); 2 violin sonatas (1921, 1951); *Pastorale* for Violin and Piano (1921); ballet, *Le Marchand d'oiseaux* (Paris, May 25, 1923); Concertino for Harp and Orch. (1926; Cambridge, Mass., March 3, 1927); *Chansons françaises* for Voice and Instruments (ISCM Festival, Liège, Sept. 2, 1930); Overture for Orch. (Paris, Dec. 25, 1932); Concerto for 2 Pianos, Voice, and Orch. (Paris, May 3, 1934); *Cantate du Narcisse* for Voice and Orch. (1937); *Pastorale* for Flute and Piano (1939); ballet, *Paris-Magie* (Paris, June 3, 1949); *Dolores,* operetta (Paris, 1950); lyric satire, *Il était un petit navire* (Paris, March 1951); musical comedy, *Parfums* (Monte Carlo, 1951); *La Guirlande de Campra* for Orch. (1952); comic opera, *Parisiana* (Copenhagen, 1955); *Concerto des vaines paroles* for Baritone and Orch. (1956); opera, *La Petite Sirène* (1958); opera-buffa, *Mémoires d'une bergère* (1959); chamber opera, *Le Maître* (1959).

Tajčević, Marko, Serbian choral conductor, music critic, teacher, and composer; b. Osijek, Jan. 29, 1900; d. Belgrade, July 19, 1984. He studied in Zagreb, Prague, and Vienna; in 1945 he was appointed a prof. at the Belgrade Academy of

Music, retiring in 1966. He was primarily a folklore composer and was at his best in his sacred and secular choral works derived from regional folk songs. He also wrote songs and piano pieces, including 7 *Balkan Dances* for Piano (1927), a set of brilliant stylizations of Serbian melorhythms.

BIBL.: D. Despić, *M. T.* (Belgrade, 1972).

Tajo, Italo, Italian bass; b. Pinerolo, April 25, 1915. He studied at the Turin Cons.; made his operatic debut as Fafner at the Teatro Regio in Turin in 1935; then was a member of the Rome Opera (1939–48) and of La Scala in Milan (1940–41; 1946–56). He made his U.S. debut in Chicago in 1946. On Dec. 28, 1948, he appeared at the Metropolitan Opera in N.Y. as Don Basilio in *Il barbiere di Siviglia*; remained on its roster until 1950; also sang with the San Francisco Opera (1948–50; 1952–53; 1956); then appeared on Broadway and in films. In 1966 he was appointed prof. at the Univ. of Cincinnati College-Cons. of Music; returned to the Metropolitan Opera after an absence of 30 years in 1980, and delighted audiences in buffo roles; made his operatic farewell there as the Sacristan in *Tosca* on April 20, 1991. He was equally adept in dramatic and buffo roles from the standard repertory, and also proved himself an intelligent interpreter in contemporary operas by Milhaud, Malipiero, Pizzetti, and even Nono.

Takács, Jenő, Hungarian pianist, ethnomusicologist, teacher, and composer; b. Siegendorf, Sept. 25, 1902. He studied composition with Marx and Gal at the Vienna Cons.; taught at the Cairo Cons. (1927–32) and at the Univ. of the Philippines (1932–34); pursued ethnological research in the Philippines before again teaching in Cairo (1934–36). From 1940 to 1942 he taught at the Music School at Szombathely; then was director of the Pécs Cons. (1942–48); after teaching piano at the Univ. of Cincinnati College-Cons. of Music (1952–71), he retired to his birthplace. In 1962 he was awarded the Austrian State Prize. Reflecting his background of travel and residence in many different countries, his music contains elements of Hungarian, oriental, American, and cosmopolitan idioms.

WORKS: BALLETS: *Nile Legend* (1937–39; Budapest, May 8, 1940); *Narcissus* (1939); *The Songs of Silence* (1967). **ORCH.:** 2 piano concertos (1932, 1937); *Philippine Suite* (1934); *Antiqua Hungarica* (1941); Partita for Guitar and Orch. (1950). **CHAMBER:** *Gumbri,* oriental rhapsody for Violin and Piano (1930); Sonata for Trombone and Piano (1957); *Homage to Pan* for 4 Pianos (1968); *Essays in Sound* for Clarinet (1968); *2 Fantastics* for Alto Saxophone and Piano (1969); *Musica reservata* for Double Bass and Piano (1969); *Tagebuch-Fragmente* for 2 Pianos (1973); Octet (1974–75).

Takagi, Tôroku, Japanese composer and pianist; b. Okayama, July 7, 1904. He graduated from the Tokyo Academy of Music in 1928; later studied in Paris. His opera *Shunko-Den* was produced in Tokyo on Nov. 20, 1948. His other works include a ballet, *Crane* (1939); *Korean Dance,* suite for Orch. (1940); 2 piano concertos (1942, 1944); Cello Concerto (1943); *Japanese Dance Music* for 2 Pianos (1941, 1943); songs.

Takahashi, Aki, innovative Japanese pianist, sister of **Yuji Takahashi;** b. Kakamura, Sept. 6, 1944. She studied 1st with her mother, then with Yutaka Ito, (Miss) Ray Lev, and George Vásárhelyi at the Tokyo Univ. of the Arts (M.A., 1969); made her public debut in Tokyo in 1970; her European debut followed in 1972. While acknowledged for her classical musicianship, she is particularly lauded for her imaginative interpretations of contemporary music; among the composers who have written works for her are Cage, Rzewski, Yuasa, Feldman, and Satoh. Her recording career is also distinguished; her *Aki Takahashi Piano Space* (20 works, including those by Berio, Boulez, Cage, Stockhausen, Webern et al.) earned her the Merit Prize at the Japan Art Festival in 1973. Her series of Satie concerts performed in Tokyo (1975–77) heralded the so-called "Satie Boom" in Japan and resulted in her editing and recording the composer's complete piano works; other noteworthy recordings include *Triadic Memories* (Feldman), *Planetary Folklore* (Mamoru Fujieda), *Eonta* (Xenakis), and *L'Histoire de Babar*

(Poulenc). Her most current recording project, *Hyper Beatles* (1990–), features arrangements of Beatles songs by internationally recognized composers. In addition to performing throughout Europe, Japan, and the U.S., Takahashi also devoted time to teaching; she was artist-in-residence at the State Univ. of N.Y. at Buffalo (1980–81) and a guest prof. at the Calif. Inst. of the Arts in Valencia (1984). She received the 1st Kenzo Nakajima prize (1982) and the 1st Kyoto Music Award (1986). In 1983 she became director of the "New Ears" concert series in Yokohama.

Takahashi, Yuji, Japanese composer and pianist, brother of **Aki Takahashi;** b. Tokyo, Sept. 21, 1938. He studied composition with Shibata and Ogura at the Toho School of Music in Tokyo (1954–58); then went to Berlin and was trained in electronics as a student of Xenakis (1963–65); also studied computer music in N.Y. and attended the summer courses at the Berkshire Music Center at Tanglewood (1966–68); was a member of the Center for Creative and Performing Arts at the State Univ. of N.Y. in Buffalo (1968–69). In his music he follows the stochastic procedures as practiced by Xenakis. He also has acquired considerable renown as a pianist in programs of avant-garde music.

WORKS: *Phonogène* for 2 Instruments and Tape (1962); *Chromamorphe I* for Violin, Double Bass, Flute, Trumpet, Horn, Trombone, and Vibraphone (1963); *Chromamorphe II* for Piano (1964); *6 Stoicheia (Elements in Succession)* for 4 Violins (1965); *Bridges I* for Electric Harpsichord or Piano, Amplified Cello, Bass Drum, and Castanets (1967); *Bridges II* for 2 Oboes, 2 Clarinets, 2 Trumpets, and 3 Violas (1968); *Rosace I* for Amplified Violin (1967); *Rosace II* for Piano (1967); *Operation Euler* for 2 or 3 Oboes (1967); *Metathèse* for Piano (1968); *Prajna Paramita* for 4 Voices, each in one of 4 Instrumental Ensembles (1969); *Orphika* for Orch. (Tokyo, May 28, 1969); *Yé Guèn* for Tape (1969); *Nikité* for Oboe, Clarinet, Trumpet, Trombone, Cello, and Double Bass (1971); *Kagahi* for Piano and 30 Instruments (Ojai, Calif., May 30, 1971); *Michi-Yuki* for Chorus, 2 Percussionists, and Electric Cello (1971); *Corona Borealis* for Piccolo, Oboe, Clarinet, Bassoon, and Horn (1971); *Tadori* for Tape (1972).

Takata, Saburô, Japanese composer; b. Nagoya, Dec. 18, 1913. He studied with Nobutkoki and Pringsheim at the Tokyo Music School (graduated, 1939); was a prof. at the Kunitachi Music College in Tokyo (from 1953); also served as president of the Japanese Society for Contemporary Music (1963–68).

WORKS: DRAMATIC: OPERA: *Aoki-ōkami* (The Dark Blue Wolf; 1970–72; Tokyo, Oct. 15, 1972). **CANTATA:** *Wordless Tears,* for Narrator, Soprano, Baritone, Chorus, and Orch. (Tokyo, March 27, 1964). **ORCH.:** *Ballade Based on a Folk Song from Yamagata (Fantasy and Fugue)* (Tokyo, Nov. 15, 1941; rev. 1965); *Seasons,* suite (1942); *Ballade* for Violin and Orch. (1943; Tokyo, Jan. 13, 1945); *The New Earth and Man* (1944); *2 Rhapsodies* (both 1945). **CHAMBER:** Octet for Clarinet, Bassoon, Horn, Trumpet, and String Quartet (1939); *Prelude and Fugue* for String Quartet (1940); Violin Sonata (1948–49); Cello Sonatina (1949–50); *Suite* for Flute, Oboe, 2 Clarinets, and Bassoon (1951); *Marionette,* suite for String Quartet (1954); *Fantasy* for String Quartet (1968); 2 piano sonatas (1935, 1941); *5 Preludes* for Piano (1947); organ pieces. Also choruses; songs.

Takata, Shin-ichi, Japanese composer; b. Tokyo, Jan. 24, 1920. He studied at the Tokyo Academy of Music; wrote a symphonic poem, *In Praise of Peace* (Tokyo, Nov. 25, 1948), the style of which reveals the influence of Richard Strauss.

Takeda, Yoshimi, Japanese conductor; b. Yokohama, Feb. 3, 1933. He was educated at the Tokyo Univ. of the Arts; then went to the U.S. on a fellowship to work with George Szell and the Cleveland Orch. (1962–64). In 1964 he became associate conductor of the Honolulu Sym. Orch.; in 1970 he was appointed music director of the Albuquerque (later New Mexico) Sym. Orch., a position he held until 1985; in addition, he was music director of the Kalamazoo Sym. Orch. (from

1974). He also appeared as a guest conductor with major orchs. in North America, Europe, and Japan.

Takemitsu, Tōru, prominent Japanese composer; b. Tokyo, Oct. 8, 1930. He studied composition privately with Yasuji Kiyose. In 1951, jointly with Yuasa and others, he organized in Tokyo the Jikken Kōbō (Experimental Workshop), with the aim of creating new music that would combine traditional Japanese modalities with modernistic procedures. In 1970 he designed the "Space Theater" for Expo '70 in Osaka, Japan. In 1975 he was a visting prof. at Yale Univ. In 1981 he served as regent lecturer at the Univ. of Calif. at San Diego. He lectured at Harvard Univ., Boston Univ., and Yale Univ. in 1983, and also was composer-in- residence of the Colorado Music Festival that same year. In 1984 he was composer-in-residence at the Aldeburgh Festival. He received numerous honors; in 1979 he was made an honorary member of the Akademie der Künste of the German Democratic Republic, in 1984 he was elected an honorary member of the American Academy and Inst. of Arts and Letters, and in 1985 he received the Ordre des Arts et des Lettres of the French government. His music belies Kipling's famous asseveration that East is East and West is West, and never the twain shall meet, for Takemitsu performed through music just this kind of interpenetration; in an oriental way, it is often formed from short motifs played out as floating dramas, subtle and exotic, through which Takemitsu seeks "to achieve a sound as intense as silence"; and on the Western side, he employs every conceivable technique developed by the European and American modernists.

Works: Orch.: Requiem for String Orch. (1957; Tokyo, June 20, 1958); Solitude sonore (1958); Ki No Kyoku (Music of Trees; 1961); Arc, Part I (1963) and Part II (1964–66) for Piano and Orch.; Arc for Strings (1963; from the 3rd movement of Arc, Part I); Textures for Piano and Orch. (1964; 1st movement of Arc, Part II); The Dorain Horizon for 17 Strings in 2 groups (1966; San Francisco, Feb. 1967, Copland conducting); November Steps for Biwa, Shakuhachi, and Orch. (N.Y., Nov. 9, 1967); Green (November Steps II; Tokyo, Nov. 3, 1967); Asterism for Piano and Orch. (1968; Toronto, Jan. 14, 1969); Eucalypts I for Flute, Oboe, Harp, and Strings (Tokyo, Nov. 16, 1970); Winter (Paris, Oct. 29, 1971); Corona for 22 Strings (1971); Cassiopeia for Solo Percussion and Orch. (Chicago, July 8, 1971); Gemeaux for Oboe, Trombone, and 2 Orchs. with separate conductors (1971–72); Autumn for Biwa, Sha-kuhachi, and Orch. (1973); Gitimalya (Bouquet of Songs) for Marimba and Orch. (Rotterdam, Nov. 1975); Quatrain for Violin, Cello, Clarinet, Piano, and Orch. (Tokyo, Sept. 1, 1975); Marginalia (Tokyo, Oct. 20, 1976); A Flock Descends into the Pentagonal Garden (San Francisco, Nov. 30, 1977); In an Autumn Garden for Gagaku Orch. (1979); Far Calls. Coming Far! for Violin and Orch. (Tokyo, May 24, 1980); Dreamtime (1981; ballet version, The Hague, May 5, 1983); Toward the Sea II for Alto Flute, Harp, and String Orch. (1981); Star-Isle (1982); Rain Coming for Chamber Orch. (1982); To the Edge of Dream for Guitar and Orch. (Liège, March 12, 1983); Orion and Pleiades for Cello and Orch. (1984); Vers, l'arc-en-ciel, Palma for Guitar, Oboe d'amore, and Orch. (Birmingham, England, Oct. 2, 1984); riverrun for Piano and Orch. (1984; Los Angeles, Jan. 10, 1985); Dream/Window (1985); Gemeaux for Oboe, Trombone, 2 Orchs., and 2 Conductors (1971–86); I Hear the Water Dreaming for Flute and Orch. (Indianapolis, April 3, 1987); Nostalgia—In Memory of Andrei Tarkovsky for Violin and String Orch. (1987); Twill by Twilight—In Memory of Morton Feldman (1988); Tree Line for Chamber Orch. (1988); Viola Concerto (1989); From Me Flows What You Call Time for Percussion Quintet and Orch. (N.Y., Oct. 19, 1990). **vocal:** Tableau noir for Narrator and Orch. (1958); Coral Island for Soprano and Orch. (1962); Wind Horse for Female Chorus (1962); Crossing for 12 Female Voices, Guitar, Harp, Piano, Vibraphone, and 2 Orchs. (1969); Grass for Male Chorus (1982); Uta for Chorus (1983); Handmade Proverbs—4 pop songs for 6 Male Voices (1987). **chamber:** Son calligraphie I–III for Double String Quartet (1958, 1958, 1963); Mask for 2 Flutes

(1959); Landscape 1 for String Quartet (1961); Ring for Flute, Terz-guitar, and Lute (1961); Sacrifice for Flute, Lute, and Vibraphone (1962); Valeria for Violin, Cello, Guitar, Electric Organ, and 2 Piccolos obbligato (1962); Hika for Violin and Piano (1966); Cross Talk for 2 Bandoneons and Tape (1968); Stanza I for Piano, Guitar, Harp, Vibraphone, and Female Voice (1968), II for Harp (1971), and III for Solo Oboe, or Oboe and Shō (1971); Eucalypts II for Flute, Oboe, and Harp (1970); Seasons in versions for 1 or 4 Percussionists (1970); Voice for Flute (1971); Munari by Munari for Percussion (1972); Distance for Solo Oboe, or Oboe and Shō (1972); Voyage for 3 Biwas (1973); Folios for Guitar (1973); Garden Rain for 4 Trumpets, 3 Trombones, Bass Trombone, Horn, and Tuba, separated into 2 groups (1974); Waves for Clarinet, Horn, 2 Trumpets, and Percussion (1976); Bryce for Flute, 2 Harps, Marimba, and Percussion (1976); Quatrain II for Clarinet, Violin, Cello, and Piano (1976); Waterways for Piano, Clarinet, Violin, Cello, 2 Harps, and 2 Vibraphones (1978); String Quartet No. 1, A Way a Lone (1980); Toward the Sea for Alto Flute and Guitar (1981); Rain Tree for 3 Percussionists or 3 Keyboard Players (1981); Rain Spell for Flute, Clarinet, Harp, Piano, and Vibraphone (1982); Rocking Mirror Daybreak for Violin Duo (1983); From far beyond Chrysanthemums and November fog for Violin and Piano (1983); Entre-temps for Oboe and String Quartet (1986); Rain Dreaming for Harpsichord (1986); All in Twilight for Guitar (1987); Signals from Heaven: I, Day Signal and II, Night Signal for Chamber Ensemble (1987). **piano:** 2 Lentos (1950); Undisturbed Rest (1952–59); Piano Distance (1961); Corona for Pianist(s) (1962); For Away (1973); Les Yeux clos (1979); Rain Tree Sketch (1981). **tape alone:** Sky, Horse and Death (1954); Static Relief (1955); Vocalism A-1 (1956); Water Music (1960); Quiet Design (1960); Kwaidan (1966; rev. of music from the film); Toward (1970); also music for a number of films including Hara-Kiri (1962); Woman in the Dunes (1964); Kwaidan (1964); Empire of Passion (1978).

Bibl.: B. Rands, " 'I sing only for myself. . .'," Musical Times (Sept. 1987); R. Reynolds, " 'Rarely sudden, never abrupt'," ibid.

Taktakishvili, Otar (Vasilievich), Russian composer and teacher; b. Tiflis, July 27, 1924; d. there (Tbilisi), Feb. 22, 1989. He studied at the Tbilisi Cons., graduating in 1947; was on its faculty as a teacher of choral literature (from 1947) and of counterpoint and instrumentation (from 1959), serving as its rector (1962–65); was a prof. (from 1966). In 1974 he was made a People's Artist of the U.S.S.R. In 1982 he was awarded the Lenin Prize. His music is imbued with the characteristic melorhythms of the Caucasus; he had a natural knack for instrumental color.

Works: operas: Mindia (Tbilisi, July 23, 1961); Sami novela (3 Stories; 1967); Chikor (1972); Mtvaris Motatseba (The Abduction of the Moon; 1976). **orch.:** Cello Concerto (1947); 2 syms. (1949, 1953); 3 overtures (1950, 1951, 1955); symphonic poems: Samgori (1950) and Mtsyri (1956); 2 piano concertos: No. 1 (Tbilisi, Nov. 15, 1951); No. 2 (1973); Trumpet Concerto (1954); Humoresque for Chamber Orch. (1963). Also oratorios; cantatas; choruses; film scores; songs; piano pieces.

Bibl.: L. Polyakova, O. T. (Moscow, 1956); L.V. Polyakova, O. T. (Moscow, 1979).

Taktakishvili, Shalva (Mikhailovich), Russian conductor, teacher, and composer; b. Kvemo-Khviti, Aug. 27, 1900; d. Tiflis, July 18, 1965. He studied at the Tbilisi Cons.; then taught music theory at the Batumi Music School, of which he was a co-founder; then served as conductor at Tbilisi Radio; from 1952 to his death, conducted the Georgian State Orch.

Works: operas: Rassvet (Sunrise; 1923); Deputat (The Delegate; 1939); Otarova vdnova (1942). **orch.:** symphonic poem, The Year 1905 (1931); Cello Concerto (1932); 2 overtures (1944, 1949). **chamber:** 2 string quartets (1930, 1933); Violin Sonata (1952); also numerous piano pieces, choruses and songs.

Bibl.: P. Hukua, S. T. (Tbilisi, 1962).

Taku, Koji, Japanese composer; b. Sakai-City (Osaka), March 10, 1904. He studied piano with Alfred Cortot and composition with Nadia Boulanger at the École Normale de Musique in Paris; then taught at the Tokyo Academy of Music. He composed 2 ballets: *White Flower* (1942) and *Journey* (1954); String Quartet (1933); Piano Sonata (1942); *Variations on a Theme of Poulenc* for Piano (1952); *Suite* for Harpsichord and Chamber Ensemble (1953); several albums of piano pieces for children.

Tal, Josef (real name, **Joseph Gruenthal**), prominent German-born Israeli composer, pianist, and pedagogue; b. Pinne, near Posen, Sept. 18, 1910. He took courses with Tiessen, Hindemith, Sachs, Trapp, and others at the Berlin Staatliche Hochschule für Musik (1928–30). In 1934 he emigrated to Palestine, settling in Jerusalem as a teacher of piano and composition at the Cons. in 1936; when it became the Israel Academy of Music in 1948, he served as its director (until 1952); also lectured at the Hebrew Univ. (from 1950), where he was head of the musicology dept. (1965–70) and a prof. (from 1971); likewise was director of the Israel Center of Electronic Music (from 1961). He appeared as a pianist and conductor with the Israel Phil. and with orchs. in Europe. In 1971 he was awarded the State of Israel Prize and was made an honorary member of the West Berlin Academy of Arts; in 1975 he received the Arts Prize of the City of Berlin, and in 1982 he became a fellow of its Inst. for Advanced Studies. A true musical intellectual, he applies in his music a variety of techniques, being free of doctrinal introversion and open to novel potentialities without fear of public revulsion. Patriotic Hebrew themes often appear in his productions.
WORKS: DRAMATIC: *Saul at Ein Dor*, opera concertante (1957); *Amnon and Tamar*, opera (1961); *Ashmedai*, opera (1968; Hamburg, Nov. 9, 1971); *Massada 967*, opera (1972; Jerusalem, June 17, 1973); *Die Versuchung*, opera (1975; Munich, July 26, 1976); *Else-Hommage*, chamber scene for Mezzo-soprano, Narrator, and 4 Instruments (1975); Scene from Kafka's diaries for Soprano or Tenor Solo (1978); *Der Turm*, opera (1983; Berlin, Sept. 19, 1987) *Der Garten*, chamber opera (1987; Hamburg, May 29, 1988); *Die Hand*, dramatic scene for Soprano and Cello (1987). **ORCH.:** 3 piano concertos: No. 1 (1944); No. 2 (1953); No. 3, with Tenor (1956); *Reflections for Strings* (1950); 4 syms.: No. 1 (1953); No. 2 (1960); No. 3 (Tel Aviv, July 3, 1978); No. 4, *Hayovel* (Jubilee; 1985; Tel Aviv, Jan. 3, 1987; for the 50th anniversary of the Israel Phil.); Viola Concerto (1954); *Hizayon Hagigi* (Festive Vision; 1959); Concerto for Cello and Strings (1961); Double Concerto for Violin, Cello, and Chamber Orch. (1970); *Dmut* (Shape) for Chamber Orch. (1975); Concerto for Flute and Chamber Orch. (1977); Concerto for 2 Pianos and Orch. (1980); Concerto for Clarinet and Chamber Orch. (1980); *Dance of the Events* (1981; rev. 1986); *Imago* for Chamber Orch. (1982); *Symphonic Fanfare* (1986). **CHAMBER:** *Kina* (Lament) for Cello and Harp (1950); Violin Sonata (1952); Oboe Sonata (1952); 3 string quartets (1959, 1964, 1976); Viola Sonata (1960); Woodwind Quintet (1966); *Fanfare* for 3 Trombones and 3 Trumpets (1968); Trio for Violin, Cello, and Piano (1974); Piano Quartet (1982); *Chamber Music* for Soprano Recorder, Marimba, and Harpsichord (1982); works for Solo Instruments; piano pieces; organ works. **VOCAL:** *Yetsi'at Mitsrayim* (Exodus), choreographic poem for Baritone and Orch. (1946); *The Mother Rejoices*, symphonic cantata for Chorus, Piano, and Orch. (1949); *Succoth Cantata* for Soloists, Choir, and Chamber Orch. (1955); *Mot Moshe* (The Death of Moses), Requiem for Soloists, Choir, Orch., and Tape (1967); *Misdar hanoflim* (Parade of the Fallen), cantata for Soprano, Baritone, Choir, and Orch. (1968); *Song* for Baritone or Alto, Flute, Horn, 2 Tom-toms, and Piano (1971) for Soloists, Choir, and Electronic Music (1976); *Bechol nafshecha* (With All Thy Soul), cantata for 3 Sopranos, Baritone, Boys' Choir, Mixed Choir, Brass, and Strings (1978); *Halom ha'igulim* (Dream of the Circles) for Baritone, Choir, and 4 Instruments (1985); *Laga'at makom* (Touch a Place) for Voice and Choir (1987); songs. **TAPE:** *Exodus II*, ballet (1954); Piano Concerto No. 4

(1962); *Ranges of Energy*, ballet (1963); *From the Depth of the Soul*, ballet (1964); Piano Concerto No. 5 (1964); Harpsichord Concerto (1964; rev. 1977); *Ashmedai*, overture to the opera (1970); *Variations*, choreographic piece (1970); Piano Concerto No. 6 (1970); Harp Concerto (1971; rev. 1980); *Min Hametsar Karati Yah* (I Called Upon the Lord in My Distress; 1971); *Frequencies 440–462: Hommage à Boris Blacher* (1972); *Backyard*, choreographic piece (1977).
BIBL.: Kaufman, "J. T.: A Composer of His Time," *Tarbut*, XXVI (1973); W. Elias, *J. T.* (Tel Aviv, 1987).

Talbot (real name, **Munkittrick**), **Howard**, English conductor and composer; b. Yonkers, N.Y., March 9, 1865; d. Reigate, Sept. 12, 1928. He was taken to England at the age of 4, and studied at the Royal College of Music in London under Parry, Bridge, and Gladstone; from 1900, was active as a conductor in various London theaters. He was a prolific composer of light operas, all produced in London; his greatest success was *A Chinese Honeymoon* (1899); his last work was *The Daughter of the Gods* (1929). Other operettas: *Monte Carlo* (1896); *3 Little Maids* (1902); *The Blue Moon* (1905); *The White Chrysanthemum* (1905); *The Girl behind the Counter* (1906); *The 3 Kisses* (1907); *The Belle of Brittany* (1908); *The Arcadians* (1909); *A Narrow Squeak* (1913); *The Pearl Girl* (1913); *A Lucky Miss* (1914); *A Mixed Grill* (1914); *The Light Blues* (1915); etc.

Talich, Václav, eminent Czech conductor; b. Kroměříž, May 28, 1883; d. Beroun, March 16, 1961. He received his early musical training from his father, Jan Talich (1851–1915), a choirmaster and music teacher; then studied violin with Mařák and Ševčik and chamber music with Kàan at the Prague Cons. (1897–1903). He was concertmaster of the Berlin Phil. (1903–4) and of the orch. of the Odessa Opera (1904–5); then taught violin in Tiflis (1905–6). He conducted the Slovenian Phil. in Ljubljana (1908–12); also took courses in composition with Reger and Sitt and in conducting with Nikisch at the Leipzig Cons.; also studied with Vigna in Milan. He was then opera conductor at Pilsen (1912–15) and chief conductor of the Czech Phil. (1919–31); in 1931–33 he was conductor of the Konsertforeningen in Stockholm; then in 1933 returned as chief conductor of the Czech Phil. (until 1941), which he brought to a high degree of excellence. He was director and conductor of the National Theater in Prague from 1935 to 1944, when the theater was closed by the Nazis; with the defeat of the Nazis, he resumed his activities there but was dismissed in 1945 after disagreements with the state authorities; he was recalled in 1947, but was dismissed once more in 1948 after conflicts with the new Communist regime. He then moved to Bratislava, where he conducted the Slovak Phil. (1949–52); returned as guest conductor of the Czech Phil. (1952–54); retired from concert appearances in 1954. He also taught conducting in Prague and Bratislava; among his pupils were Ančerl and Mackerras. He was renowned for his idiomatic performances of the Czech repertory. He was made a National Artist in 1957.
BIBL.: O. Šourek, ed., *V. T.* (Prague, 1943); V. Pospíšil, *V. T.: několik kapitol o díle a životě českého umělce* (V. T.: Some Chapters on the Life and Work of a Czech Artist; Prague, 1961); H. Masaryk, ed., *V. T.: dokument života a díla* (V. T.: A Document of His Life and Work; Prague, 1967); M. Kuna, *V. T.* (Prague, 1980).

Talley, Marion, American soprano; b. Nevada, Mo., Dec. 20, 1906; d. Los Angeles, Jan. 3, 1983. She sang in churches in Kansas City, and at the age of 16 appeared in a performance of *Mignon* there, producing such an explosion of local pride that the community raised funds to send her to N.Y. to study voice with Frank La Forge; later she went to Italy in quest of further musical enlightenment. She was then given a chance to appear at the Metropolitan Opera in N.Y. on Feb. 17, 1926, as Gilda in *Rigoletto*. She was only 19 years old at the time, and she became an instant *rara avis*, a genuine American warbler, an authentic, native thrush, and newspapers went wild over her. She sang the part of the nightingale in Stravinsky's opera *Le Rossignol* at the Metropolitan on March 6, 1926, and performed the role of the Queen of the Night in *Die Zauberflöte* there on Nov. 6, 1926. In 1928 she made a U.S. tour as a concert singer; in 1933 she sang Gilda at the Chicago Opera, with meager success; she was no longer a young American nightingale. From then on she made little music before sinking into impenetrable oblivion in darkest Hollywood; even her death went unrecorded in the daily journals.

Tallis (Tallys, Talys, Talles), Thomas, eminent English organist and composer; b. c.1505; d. Greenwich, Nov. 23, 1585. He was organist at the Benedictine Priory in Dover (1532); was in the employ of London's church of St. Mary-at-Hill (1537–38), most likely as organist; served as organist at Walthem Abbey (c.1538–40), and then was a lay clerk at Canterbury Cathedral (1541–42); from about 1543, he served as Gentleman of the Chapel Royal during the reigns of Henry VIII, Edward VI, Mary, and Elizabeth I, and as joint organist with Byrd. With Byrd, he obtained in 1575 letters patent for the exclusive privilege of printing music and ruled music paper, the 1st work issued by them being 34 *Cantiones quae ab argumento sacrae vocantur, 5 et 6 partium,* in 1575 (includes 17 pieces by each). Tallis's most famous work is *Spem in alium non habui,* a "song of 40 parts" for 8 5-part choirs. A composer of great contrapuntal skill, he was among the 1st to set Eng. words to music for the rites of the Church of England. Surviving are 3 masses, 2 Magnificats, 2 Lamentations, 52 motets and other pieces with Latin text, over 20 Eng. anthems, 9 psalm tunes, etc., as well as some keyboard music. Modern editions of his music are included in D. Stevens, ed., *T. Tallis: Complete Keyboard Works* (London, 1953); L. Ellinwood, ed., *T. Tallis: English Sacred Music,* I, *Anthems;* II, *Service Music,* in the Early English Church Music series, XII and XIII (rev. by P. Doe, 1974). **BIBL.:** H. Collins, "T. T.," *Music & Letters,* X (1929); L. Ellinwood, "T.'s Tunes and Tudor Psalmody," *Musica Disciplina,* II (1948); B. Schofield, "The Manuscripts of T.'s Forty-Part Motet," *Musical Quarterly* (April 1951); D. Stevens, "The Keyboard Music of T. T.," *Musical Times* (July 1952); J. Kerman, "Byrd, T., and the Art of Imitation," *Aspects of Medieval and Renaissance Music: A Birthday Offering to Gustave Reese* (N.Y., 1966); R. Illing, "T.'s Psalm Tunes," *Miscellanea Musicologica,* II (1967); P. Doe, *T.* (London, 1968; 2nd ed., 1976); J. Milsom, "A New T. Contrafactum," *Musical Times* (June 1982); idem, "A T. Fantasia," ibid. (Nov. 1985); idem, "T.'s First and Second Thoughts," *Journal of the Royal Musical Association,* 113/2 (1988).

Talma, Louise (Juliette), American composer and teacher; b. Arcachon, France, Oct. 31, 1906. She studied at the Inst. of Musical Art in N.Y. (1922–30) and took courses at N.Y. Univ. (B.M., 1931) and at Columbia Univ. (B.Mus., 1933); took piano lessons with Isidor Philipp and composition with Nadia Boulanger in Fontainebleau (summers 1926–39). She taught at Hunter College (1928–79); was the 1st American to teach at the Fontainebleau School of Music (summers 1936–39; 1978; 1981–82). She received 2 Guggenheim fellowships (1946, 1947); was the 1st woman composer to be elected to the National Inst. of Arts and Letters in 1974. In her music she adopts a strongly impressionistic style. She publ. *Harmony for the College Student* (1966) and *Functional Harmony* (with J. Harrison and R. Levin, 1970). **WORKS: OPERA:** *The Alcestiad* (1955–58; Frankfurt am Main, March 1, 1962). **ORCH.:** *Toccata* (1944; Baltimore, Dec. 20, 1945); *Dialogues* for Piano and Orch. (1963–64; Buffalo, Dec. 12, 1965). **CHAMBER:** String Quartet (1954); Violin Sonata (1962); *Summer Sounds* for Clarinet, 2 Violins, Viola, and Cello (1969–73); *The Ambient Air* for Flute, Violin, Cello, and Piano (1980–83); *Studies in Spacing* for Clarinet and Piano (1982). **PIANO:** 2 sonatas (1943; 1944–55); *Passacaglia and Fugue* (1955–62); *Textures* (1977). **CHORAL:** *The Divine Flame,* oratorio (1946–48); *La corona,* 7 sonnets (1954–55); *A Time to Remember* for Mixed Choir and Orch. (1966–67); *Voices of Peace* for Mixed Choir and Strings (1973); *Mass for the Sundays*

of the Year (1984). **SOLO VOCAL:** *Terre de France,* song cycle for Soprano and Piano (1943–45); *All the Days of My Life,* cantata for Tenor, Clarinet, Cello, Piano, and Percussion (1963–65); *The Tolling Bell* for Baritone and Orch. (1967–69); *Diadem,* song cycle for Tenor and Piano or 5 Instruments (1978–79); *Variations on 13 Ways of Looking at a Blackbird* for Soprano or Tenor and Flute or Oboe or Violin and Piano (1979). **BIBL.:** M. Goss, *Modern Music-Makers* (N.Y., 1952); R. Ericson, "Celebrating L. T.," *N.Y. Times* (Feb. 4, 1977); S. Teicher, "L. T.: Essentials of her style as seen through the Piano Works," *The Musical Woman: An International Perspective 1983* (Westport, Conn., 1984).

Talmi, Yoav, Israeli conductor; b. Kibbutz Merhavia, April 28, 1943. He studied at the Rubin Academy of Music in Tel Aviv (diploma, 1965) and at the Juilliard School of Music in N.Y. (1965–68); also studied conducting with Susskind at the Aspen (Colo.) School of Music (summer 1966), Maderna in Salzburg (summer 1967), Fournet in Hilversum (summer 1968), and Leinsdorf at the Berkshire Music Center at Tanglewood (summer 1969), where he won the Koussevitzky Memorial Conducting Prize. He was associate conductor of the Louisville Orch. (1968–70), music director of the Kentucky Chamber Orch. (1969–71), and co-conductor of the Israel Chamber Orch. (1970–72). After serving as artistic director of Arnhem's Het Gelders Orch. (1974–80) and as principal guest conductor of the Munich Phil. (1979–80), he returned to the Israel Chamber Orch. as its music director in 1984; also appeared widely as a guest conductor. He was music director-designate (1989–90) and music director (from 1990) of the San Diego Sym. Orch.

Taltabull, Cristòfor, Catalan composer and pedagogue; b. Barcelona, July 28, 1888; d. there, May 1, 1964. He studied piano with Granados and composition with Felipe Pedrell. In 1908 he went to Germany, where he took lessons with Max Reger. In 1912 he went to Paris, where he was an accompanist to singers, a proofreader for the publisher Durand, and a music copyist; he also composed popular songs for vaudeville and wrote film music. After the outbreak of World War II in 1939, he returned to Barcelona, where he became a teacher of composition. Many important Spanish composers of the younger generation were his pupils. As a composer, he was particularly successful in songs to French and Catalan texts. His style of composition is impressionistic, mainly derived from Debussy; he had a delicate sense of color and rhythm; thematically, most of his music retains Spanish, or Catalan, melorhythmic characteristics.

Talvela, Martti (Olavi), remarkable Finnish bass; b. Hiitola, Feb. 4, 1935; d. Juva, July 22, 1989. He received training at the Lahti Academy of Music (1958–60). After winning the Finnish lieder competition in 1960, he studied voice with Carl Martin Öhmann in Stockholm; made his operatic debut there at the Royal Theater as Sparafucile in *Rigoletto* in 1961. He made his 1st appearance at the Bayreuth Festival in 1962 as Titurel; that same year, joined the Deutsche Oper in Berlin, where he sang leading bass roles. In 1968 he made his U.S. debut in a recital at Hunter College in N.Y. He made his Metropolitan Opera debut in N.Y. as the Grand Inquisitor in *Don Carlos* on Oct. 7, 1968; appeared there in succeeding years with increasing success, being especially acclaimed for his dramatic portrayal of Boris Godunov. From 1972 to 1980 he served as artistic director of the Savonlinna Festival. He was to have assumed the post of artistic director of the Finnish National Opera in Helsinki in 1992.

Tamagno, Francesco, famous Italian tenor; b. Turin, Dec. 28, 1850; d. Varese, near Turin, Aug. 31, 1905. He studied with Pedrotti in Turin and Vannuccini in Milan; made his debut in Palermo in 1869; after appearances in Turin, he scored a major success with his portrayal of Riccardo in *Un ballo in maschera* in Palermo in 1874. He made his debut at Milan's La Scala as Vasco da Gama in *L'Africaine* in 1877, establishing himself as its leading tenor; created the role of Azaele in Ponchielli's *Il Figliuol prodigo* (1880), appeared as Gabriele Adorno in the revised version of Verdi's *Simone Boccanegra* (1881), and was the 1st Didier in Ponchielli's *Marion Demore* (1885); then won international acclaim when Verdi chose him to create the title role in *Otello* (1887), a role he sang in London in 1889 and in Chicago and N.Y. in 1890; also chose it for his Covent Garden debut in London on May 13, 1895. He made his Metropolitan Opera debut in N.Y. as Arnold in Rossini's *Guillaume Tell* on Nov. 21, 1894, remaining on the company's roster for a season. In 1901 he returned to Covent Garden and also sang at La Scala. He made his final stage appearance at Milan's Teatro dal Verme in 1904; his last appearance as a singer took place in Ostend that same year. Tamagno was one of the greatest tenors in the history of opera; in addition to his Othello, he was celebrated for his portrayals of Don Carlos, Radames, Alfredo, Manrico, Don José, John of Leyden, Faust, Ernani, and Samson.

BIBL.: E. de Amicis, *F. T.* (Palermo, 1902); M. Corsi, *T.* (Milan, 1927); E. Gara, "*F. T.,*" *La Scala* (Jan. 1954).

Tamberg, Eino, Estonian composer and pedagogue; b. Tallinn, May 27, 1930. He studied composition with E. Kapp at the Tallinn Cons., graduating in 1953; then was a music supervisor with the Estonian Radio; was a teacher (from 1967) and a prof. (from 1983) at the Tallinn Cons.; in 1975 he was made a People's Artist of the Estonian SSR.

WORKS: STAGE: OPERAS: *The House of Iron* (Tallinn, July 15, 1965); *Cyrano de Bergerac* (1974; Tallinn, July 2, 1976); *Flight* (1982; Tallinn, Dec. 30, 1983). **BALLETS:** *Ballet-Symphony* (1959; Schwerin, March 10, 1960); *The Boy and the Butterfly* (Tallinn, Nov. 30, 1963); *Joanna tentata* (1970; Tallinn, Jan. 23, 1971). **ORCH.:** Concerto Grosso (1956; Moscow, July 10, 1957); *Symphonic Dances* (Riga, Dec. 22, 1957); *Toccata* (1967); Trumpet Concerto (Tallinn, Nov. 21, 1972); 3 syms.: No. 1 (1978; Tallinn, Jan. 27, 1979); No. 2 (Tallinn, Oct. 23, 1986); No. 3 (Tallinn, Nov. 12, 1989); Violin Concerto (Tallinn, Oct. 17, 1981); Concerto for Mezzo-soprano and Orch. (1985; Tallinn, Sept. 15, 1986); Alto Saxophone Concerto (1987; Tallinn, May 6, 1988). **VOCAL:** *Moonlight Oratorio* for 2 Narrators, Soprano, Baritone, Chorus, and Orch. (1962; Tartu, Feb. 17, 1963); *Fanfares of Victory,* cantata for Bass, Chorus, and Orch. (1975); *Amores,* oratorio for Vocal Soloists, Chorus, and Orch. (1981; Tallinn, March 27, 1983); songs. **CHAMBER:** String Quartet (1958); *5 Pieces* for Oboe and Piano (1970); 2 wind quintets (1975, 1984); piano pieces.

Tamberlik, Enrico, celebrated Italian tenor; b. Rome, March 16, 1820; d. Paris, March 13, 1889. He studied singing with Zirilli in Rome and with Guglielmi in Naples, where he made his stage debut in 1841 as Tybalt in *I Capuleti e i Montecchi.* On April 4, 1850, he made his 1st London appearance, as Masaniello in Auber's *La Muette de Portici,* at the Royal Italian Opera, Covent Garden, and sang annually in London until 1864, with the exception of 1857, when he undertook an extensive European tour, including Spain and Russia. In 1860 he settled in Paris, and lived there most of his life. Verdi admired him, and wrote the part of Don Alvaro in *La forza del destino* for him; Tamberlik sang in its world premiere in St. Petersburg on Nov. 22, 1862, and this role became one of his most famous interpretations. He appeared at the Academy of Music in N.Y. on Sept. 18, 1873, but his American season was a brief one; later toured the U.S. with Maretzek's company. He excelled in many Italian, French, and German roles; he was especially renowned as Florestan, John of Leyden, Manrico, Arnold, and Rossini's Otello.

Tamburini, Antonio, esteemed Italian baritone; b. Faenza, March 28, 1800; d. Nice, Nov. 8, 1876. He was a pupil of A. Rossi and B. Asioli; made his operatic debut in Generali's *La Contessa di colle* in Cento in 1818. In 1822 he 1st sang at Milan's La Scala in Rossini's *Matilde di Shabran,* returning there that same year to take part in the premiere of Donizetti's *Chicara e Serafin.* Following engagements in Trieste and Vienna, he went to Rome and sang in the 1st performance of Donizetti's *L'ajo nell'imbarazzo* (1824). After singing in Naples and Venice, he appeared in Palermo, where he sang in the premiere of Donizetti's *Alahor di Granata* (1826). Returning to La Scala, he created Ernesto in Bellini's *Il Pirata* (Oct. 27, 1827); after appearing in the 1st performance of Donizetti's *Alina, regina di Golconda* in Genoa (1828), he went to Naples and sang in the premieres of Donizetti's *Gianni di Calais* (1828), *Imelda de' Lammbertazzi* (1830), *Francesca di Foix* (1831), *La Romanziera* (1831), and *Fausta* (1832). On Feb. 14, 1829, at La Scala, he created Valdeburgo in Bellini's *La Straniera,* a role he repeated at the King's Theatre in London on June 23, 1832; that same year he made his 1st appearance at the Théâtre-Italien in Paris, and subsequently appeared regularly in London and Paris during the next 11 years. On Jan. 24, 1835, he created the role of Sir Richard Forth in Bellini's *I Puritani* at the Théâtre-Italien; returned there to create Israele in Donizetti's *Marino Failiero* (March 12, 1835) and Malatesta in his *Don Pasquale* (Jan. 3, 1843). After singing in St. Petersburg, he returned to London to appear as Assur in *Semiramide* in the 1st production mounted by the Royal Italian Opera at Covent Garden. In 1855 he retired from the operatic stage; however, in 1860 he sang Rossini's Figaro in Nice. In 1822 he married the mezzo-soprano Marietta Goja (1801–66).

BIBL.: J. de Biez, *T. et la musique italienne* (Paris, 1877); H. Gelli-Ferraris, *A. T. nel ricordo d'una nipote* (Livorno, 1934).

Tamkin, David, Russian-American composer; b. Chernigov, Aug. 28, 1906; d. Los Angeles, June 21, 1975. He was taken to the U.S. as an infant; the family settled in Portland, Oreg., where he studied violin with Henry Bettman, a pupil of Ysaÿe; took lessons in composition with Ernest Bloch. In 1937 he settled in Los Angeles; from 1945 to 1966 he was principal composer at Universal Pictures in Hollywood. His music is deeply permeated with the melodic and rhythmic elements of the Hassidic Jewish cantillation. His magnum opus is the opera *The Dybbuk* (1928–31; N.Y., Oct. 4, 1951); also wrote the opera *The Blue Plum Tree of Esau* (1962), 2 string quartets, a Woodwind Sextet, and several choruses.

Tan, Margaret Leng, Malaysian-born American pianist; b. Penang, Dec. 12, 1945. She was educated in Singapore; at 16 went to N.Y., where she later studied at the Juilliard School, becoming the 1st woman to graduate with the D.Mus. degree (1971). She specializes in new Asian and American music, evolving a highly individual approach to performance wherein sound, choreography, and drama assume equal significance; became widely known for her interpretive command of the works of John Cage in particular, giving performances throughout Europe and the U.S.; also appeared in PBS American Masters documentaries on Cage and on the American painter Jasper Johns (1990); during the 1990–91 season, presented retrospective performances of Cage's music in conjunction with retrospective exhibitions of Johns's paintings at the Walker Art Center in Minneapolis, the Whitney Museum of American Art in N.Y., the Hayward Gallery in London, and the Center for Fine Arts in Miami. Her critically acclaimed recordings include *Litania: Margaret Leng Tan Plays Somei Satoh* (1988) and *Sonic Encounters* (1989; with works ranging from Cage to Ge Gan-ru, China's 1st avant-garde composer); also a recording devoted to Cage's music, *4 Walls/The Perilous Night* (1990). She received an NEA grant; also an Asian Cultural Council grant to study contemporary music in Japan. She appeared with the Brooklyn (1987) and N.Y. (1991) Phils. Tan currently resides in Brooklyn with 3 dogs and 3 Steinways.

Tan, Melvyn, talented Singaporean fortepianist and harpsichordist; b. Singapore, Oct. 13, 1956. He went to England, where he entered the Yehudi Menuhin School in Surrey when he was 12; later pursued training at the Royal College of Music in London. His principal mentors were Vlado Perlemuter and Nadia Boulanger. After commencing his career as a pianist, he took up the fortepiano and harpsichord in 1980; he subsequently appeared in the major British music centers, and in 1985 made his 1st tour of the U.S. In 1987 he won critical accolades as soloist in a series of Beethoven concerts, with Roger Norrington conducting the London Classical Players.

Tanabe, Hisao, Japanese musicologist and composer; b. Tokyo, Aug. 16, 1883; d. there, March 5, 1984. His mother played and taught Japanese instruments; he began learning the violin at Tokyo Music School in 1903. While studying physics at Tokyo Univ. (1904–7), he took courses in composition with Noël Peri; also had postgraduate studies in acoustics (1907–10) and studied Japanese music and dance with Shōhei Tanaka. He taught acoustics, music history, and theory at Toyo Music School (1907–35) and the Imperial Music Bureau (1919–23); also taught Japanese music history at Kokugakuin Univ. (1923), Tokyo Univ. (1930), Waseda Univ. (1947), and Musashino College of Music (1949). In 1936 Tanabe founded and served as the 1st president of the Soc. for Research in Asiatic Music; his field studies included collections of music from Korea (1921), Formosa and the Ryūkū Islands (1922), northern China (1923), and the Pacific Islands (1934). He was a pioneer among modern Japanese musicologists; his writings and lectures on European music were important for its introduction into Japan in the early 20th century. He publ. nearly 50 books on a variety of musical subjects, especially oriental music and acoustics. He also performed widely, both European and Japanese music, and composed a number of works. He publ. his autobiography as *Tanabe Hisao jijoden* (2 vols., 1981, 1982). After his death, the Soc. for Research in Asiatic Music instituted the Tanabe Hisao Prize.

Writings: *Nippon ongaku kōwa* (Lectures on Japanese Music; 1919); *Toyō ongakushi* (History of Oriental Music; 1930); *Ongaku riron* (Theories of Music; 1929; rev. 1956); *Ongaku onkyogaku* (Acoustics of Music; 1951); also ed. *Nihon ongakushū* (Collection of Japanese Music in Staff Notation; 1931) and *Kinsei Nihon ongakushū* (Collection of Modern Japanese Music in Staff Notation; 1931).

Tanaka, Toshimitsu, Japanese composer; b. Aomori, July 17, 1930. He studied music at the Kunitani Music College in Tokyo; after graduation in 1951, he joined its staff. His music is based on the melorhythmic patterns of Japanese folk songs.

Works: 2 dance suites: *Tamanna* for 2 Pianos and Percussion (1967) and *Magic Festival in the Mountain Crease* for Chorus, Ryūteki, and various types of Wadaiko (1968); *Epic "Wolf Boy" for Shamisen* for Soprano, Shamisen, Shakuhachi, Wadaiko, and Strings (Tokyo, Nov. 27, 1968); Requiem, *The Grave,* for Chorus and Orch. (Radio Tokyo, Nov. 5, 1972); Violin Sonata (1957); String Quartet (1962); *Suite* for Marimba, 7 Strings, and 2 Percussionists (1971); *Gunzo* for Orch. (1979); *Pathos* for Orch. (1981); *Earthen Vessel* for Percussion Ensemble (1982); *Locus* for Percussion (1983); *Blue Ladder* for Synthesizer (1984); *Aoi Kizahashi* for Synthesizer (1984); *Dōshō* for Piano (Vol. 1, 1986–87); *Kodai Sanka* for Chorus and Percussion Ensemble (1987); String Quartet No. 2 (1988); choruses; songs.

Tanev, Alexander, Bulgarian composer and teacher; b. Budapest (of Bulgarian parents), Oct. 23, 1928. He studied law at the Univ. of Sofia (1946–50) and composition with Veselin Stoyanov at the Bulgarian State Cons. in Sofia (graduated, 1957); at the latter, was a teacher of composition (from 1970), and dean of the faculty of composition and conductor (from 1986); also served as secretary of the Union of Bulgarian Composers (1972–76).

Works: stage: Musical drama, *Gramada* (1977); ballet, *Prasnik v Tsaravets* (Festival of Tsaravets; 1968). **orch.:** Sinfonietta (1959); *Youth Concerto* for Violin and Strings (1969); *Rondo concertante* for Trombone and Orch. (1971); Concerto for Brass and Percussion (1972); *Builder's Music* for 2 Pianos, and Orch. or Percussion (1974); *Divertimento concertante* for Piano and Orch. (1976); *The Way Is Fearful but Glorious,* symphonic poem for Bass-baritone and Orch. (1979); *Capriccio* for Symphonic and Wind Orchs. (1986); Concerto for String Orch. (1988). **vocal: oratorios:** *Annals of Freedom* for Soloists, Choir, and Orch. (1975–76); *Testament* for Bass, Reader, Choir, Children's Choir, and Orch. (1977–78); *Native Land* for Bass,

Reader, Choir, Children's Choir, and Orch. (1984–85). **cantatas:** *In Praise of the Song about Damiancho* for Women's Choir and 2 Pianos (1981); *In Praise of the Rila Monastery* for Bass, Men's Choir, and Orch. (1982); *The Song of Songs* for Tenor, Bass, and Orch. (1983). Also many song cycles; chamber music; piano pieces.

Taneyev, Alexander (Sergeievich), Russian composer; b. St. Petersburg, Jan. 17, 1850; d. there (Petrograd), Feb. 7, 1918. He was educated at the Univ. of St. Petersburg; also studied composition with F. Reichel in Dresden; upon his return to St. Petersburg, he took lessons with Rimsky-Korsakov. Music was his avocation; he followed a government career, advancing to the post of head of the Imperial Chancellery. The style of his music is Romantic, lapsing into sentimentalism; the main influence is that of Tchaikovsky.

Works: operas: *Cupid's Revenge* (concert perf., St. Petersburg, May 19, 1899); *The Snowstorm* (Petrograd, Feb. 11, 1916). **orch.:** 3 syms. (1890, 1903, 1908); 2 suites; *Alyosha Popovich,* ballade; *Festival March;* 2 mazurkas; *Reverie* for Violin and Orch.; *Hamlet,* overture. **chamber:** *Bagatelle and Serenade* for Cello and Piano; *Arabesque* for Clarinet and Piano; 3 string quartets; *Feuillet d'album* for Viola and Piano; piano pieces; songs.

Taneyev, Sergei (Ivanovich), greatly significant Russian composer and pedagogue; b. Vladimir district, Nov. 25, 1856; d. Dyudkovo, Zvenigorodsk district, June 19, 1915. He began taking piano lessons at the age of 5; was only 9 when he entered the Moscow Cons.; after academic training for a year, he re-entered the Cons. in 1869 as a piano pupil of Eduard Langer; also received instruction in theory from Nikolai Hubert and in composition from Tchaikovsky, who became his lifelong friend; in 1871 Nikolai Rubinstein became his piano mentor. On Jan. 29, 1875, he made his formal debut as a pianist as soloist in the Brahms D-minor Concerto in Moscow; on Dec. 3, 1875, he was soloist in the Moscow premiere of the Tchaikovsky 1st Concerto, and subsequently was soloist in all of Tchaikovsky's works for piano and orch. He graduated from the Cons. in 1875 as the 1st student to win the gold medal in both performance and composition. In 1876 he toured his homeland with Leopold Auer. In 1878 he succeeded Tchaikovsky as prof. of harmony and orchestration at the Moscow Cons.; after the death of Nikolai Rubinstein in 1881, he took over the latter's piano classes there; in 1883 he succeeded Hubert as prof. of composition; after serving as its director (1885–89), he taught counterpoint (1889–1905). Taneyev was a 1st-class pianist; Tchaikovsky regarded him as one of the finest interpreters of his music. His position as a composer is anomalous: he is one of the most respected figures of Russian music history, and there is a growing literature about him; his correspondence and all documents, however trivial, concerning his life are treasured as part of the Russian cultural heritage; yet outside Russia his works are rarely heard. He wrote a treatise on counterpoint, *Podvizhnoi kontrapunkt strogavo pisma* (1909; in Eng. as *Convertible Counterpoint in the Strict Style;* Boston, 1962). The style of his compositions presents a compromise between Russian melos and Germanic contrapuntal writing; the mastery revealed in his syms. and quartets is unquestionable. His most ambitious work was the trilogy *Oresteia,* after Aeschylus, in 3 divisions: *Agamemnon, Choëphorai,* and *Eumenides,* 1st performed in St. Petersburg on Oct. 29, 1895. After his death, an almost-completed treatise *Ucheniye o kanone* (The Study of Canon) was found and was ed. for publ. by V. Velaiev (Moscow, 1929).

Works: stage: *Oresteya* (The Oresteia), musical trilogy (1887–94; St. Petersburg, Oct. 29, 1895). **orch.:** Quadrille for Small Orch. (1972–73); 4 syms.: No. 1 (1873–74); No. 2 (1877–78); No. 3 (1884; Moscow, Jan. 1885); No. 4 (1896–97; St. Petersburg, April 2, 1898); Piano Concerto (1876); Sym. for Children's Instruments (c.1897); *Suite de concert* for Violin and Orch. (1909). **chamber:** 5 unnumbered string quartets (1874–76; 1880; 1882–83; 1883; 1911); 5 numbered string quartets (1890; 1895; 1886, rev. 1896; 1899; 1903); March for 10 Instruments (1877); 2 string trios (1879–80; n.d.); 2 string quintets (1901, rev. 1903; 1904); Piano Quartet (1906); Trio for Violin, Viola, and Tenor Viola (1910); Piano Quintet (1911); Violin Sonata (1911); other chamber works; also various piano pieces, choral works, and songs.

Bibl.: K. Kuznetzov, ed., *S.I. T.* (Moscow and Leningrad, 1925); V. Yakovlev, *S.I. T.: evo muzikalnaya zhizn* (S.I. T.: His Musical Life; Moscow, 1927); V. Protopopov, ed., *Pamyati S.I. T.a 1856–1946: sbornik statey i materialov k 90-letiyu so dnya rozhdeniya* (In Memory of S.I. T.: A Collection of Articles and Materials for the 90th Anniversary of His Birth; Moscow and Leningrad, 1947); G. Bernandt, *S.I. T.* (Moscow and Leningrad, 1950); V. Kiselyov et al., eds., *S.I. T.: materiali i dokumenti* (Moscow, 1952); J. Weinberg, "S.I. T.," *Musical Quarterly* (Jan. 1958); F. Arzamonov, *S.I. T.: prepodavatel kursa muzikalnikh form* (S.I. T.: Teacher of a Course in Musical Form; Moscow, 1963); T. Khoprova, *S.I. T.* (Leningrad, 1968); N. Bazhanov, *T.* (Moscow, 1971); L. Korabelnikova, *S.I. T. v Moskovskoy konservatorri* (S.I. T. at the Moscow Conservatory; Moscow, 1974).

Tango, Egisto, Italian conductor; b. Rome, Nov. 13, 1873; d. Copenhagen, Oct. 5, 1951. He 1st studied engineering; then entered the Naples Cons.; made his debut as an opera conductor in Venice (1893); conducted at La Scala in Milan (1895); then at Berlin (1903–8). He conducted at the Metropolitan Opera in N.Y. (1909–10), in Italy (1911–12), and in Budapest (1913–19), where he gave the earliest performances of stage works by Béla Bartók. From 1920 to 1926 he was active in Germany and Austria. In 1927 he settled in Copenhagen. He was distinguished for the technical precision and interpretative clarity of his performances.

Tannenberg, David, German-American organ builder; b. Berthelsdorf, Upper Lusatia, March 21, 1728; d. York, Pa., May 19, 1804. He went with a group of Moravian church colonists to Bethlehem, Pa., in 1749; was assistant to the organ builder Johann Gottlob Klemm (1757-62); then was active as an organ builder on his own, moving to Lititz, Pa., in 1765, where most of his organs were built; also made some clavichords and virginals.

Bibl.: P. Beck, "D. T., Organ Builder," *Papers Read before the Lancaster, Pa. Historical Society* (Jan. 1926); D. McCorkle, "The Moravian Contribution to American Music," *Notes* (Sept. 1956; reprinted as Moravian Music Foundation Publication No. 1, Winston-Salem, N.C., 1956); idem, "Musical Instruments of the Moravians of North Carolina," *American German Review* (Feb.–March 1955); T. McGreary, "D. T. and the Clavichord in Eighteenth-century America," *Organ Yearbook*, XIII (1982).

Tannhäuser, Der, German Minnesinger; b. c.1205; d. c.1270. He was of noble lineage; was active in the 5th Crusade to the Holy Land (1228–33) and the Cypriot war; later was at the court of Friedrich II "der Streitfare" in Vienna and at the court of Otto II of Bavaria in Landshut, among others. His name became legendary through the tale of the Venusberg, pagan intimacy with Venus, penitence, pilgrimage to Rome, and the miracle of the flowering of his pilgrim's staff. Wagner's *Tannhäuser* is based on this legend, which is unconnected with the life of the real Tannhäuser. A complete ed. of his works has been edited by H. Lomnitzer and U. Müller, *Tannhäuser* (Göppingen, 1973).

Bibl.: F. Zander, *Die T.sage und der Minnesinger T.* (1858); J. Siebert, *Der Dichter T.: Leben-Gedichte-Sage* (Hall, 1934); M. Wis, "Ursprünge der deutschen T.legende," *Neuphilologische Mitteilungen*, LXI (1966); R. Taylor, *The Art of the Minnesinger* (Cardiff, 1968).

Tansman, Alexandre, Polish-born French pianist, conductor, and composer; b. Lodz, June 12, 1897; d. Paris, Nov. 15, 1986. He studied at the Lodz Cons. (1902–14); then pursued training in law and philosophy at the Univ. of Warsaw; also received instruction in counterpoint, form, and composition from Rytel in Warsaw. In 1919 he went to Paris, where he appeared as

a soloist in his own works (Feb. 17, 1920). In 1927 he appeared as a soloist with the Boston Sym. Orch., and then played throughout Europe, Canada, and Palestine. He later took up conducting; made a tour of the Far East (1932–33). After the occupation of Paris by the Germans in 1940, he made his way to the U.S.; lived in Hollywood, where he wrote music for films; returned to Paris in 1946. His music is distinguished by a considerable melodic gift and a vivacious rhythm; his harmony is often bitonal; there are some impressionistic traits that reflect his Parisian tastes.

Works: Stage: Operas: *La Nuit kurde* (1925–27; Paris Radio, 1927); *La toisson d'or*, opéra bouffe (1938); *Sabbatat Levi, le faux Messie*, lyric fresco (1953; Paris, 1961); *Le serment* (1954; Brussels, March 11, 1955); *L'usignolo di Boboli* (1962); *Georges Dandin*, opéra comique (1974). **Ballets:** *Sextuor* (Paris, May 17, 1924); *La Grande Ville* (1932); *Bric-à-Brac* (1937); *Train de nuit* for 2 Pianos (London, 1950); *Les Habits neufs du roi* (Venice, 1959); *Resurrection* (Nice, 1962). **Orch.:** 7 syms.: No. 1 (1925; Boston, March 18, 1927); No. 2 (1926); No. 3, *Symphonie concertante* (1931); No. 4 (1939); No. 5 (1942; Baltimore, Feb. 2, 1943); No. 6, *In memoriam* (1943); No. 7 (1944; St. Louis, Oct. 24, 1947); *Danse de la sorcière* (Brussels, May 5, 1924); *Sinfonietta* (Paris, March 23, 1925); *Ouverture symphonique* (Paris, Feb. 3, 1927); Piano Concerto No. 1 (Paris, May 27, 1926, composer soloist); Piano Concerto No. 2 (Boston, Dec. 28, 1927, composer soloist); *Suite* for 2 Pianos and Orch. (Paris, Nov. 16, 1930); Viola Concerto (1936); Violin Concerto (1937); *Fantaisie* for Violin and Orch. (1937); *Fantaisie* for Cello and Orch. (1937); *Rapsodie polonaise* (St. Louis, Nov. 14, 1941); *Etudes symphoniques* (1943); Concertino for Guitar and Orch. (1945); *Ricercari* (St. Louis, Dec. 22, 1949); Concerto (1954); *Capriccio* (Louisville, March 6, 1955); Clarinet Concerto (1958); Cello Concerto (1963); *Dyptique* for Chamber Orch. (1969); *Elégie (à la mémoire de Darius Milhaud)* (1976). **Chamber:** 8 string quartets (1917–56); Violin Sonata (1919); *Danse de la sorcière* for Woodwind Quintet and Piano (1925; a version of the ballet); Flute Sonata (1925); Cello Sonata (1930); String Sextet (1940); *Divertimento* for Oboe, Clarinet, Trumpet, Cello, and Piano (1944); *Suite baroque* (1958); *Symphonie de chambre* (1960); *Stèle: In memoriam Igor Stravinsky* for Voice and Instruments (1972); *Musique à six* for Clarinet, String Quartet, and Piano (1977). **Piano:** *20 pièces faciles polonaises* (1924); 5 sonatas; mazurkas, and other Polish dances; *Sonatine transatlantique* (1930; also for Orch., Paris, Feb. 28, 1931; used by Kurt Jooss for his ballet *Impressions of a Big City*, Cologne, Nov. 21, 1932); *Pour les enfants*, 4 albums. **Writings:** *Stravinsky* (Paris, 1948; Eng. tr., 1949, as *Igor Stravinsky: The Man and His Music*).

Bibl.: R. Petit, "A. T.," *Revue Musicale* (Feb. 1929); I. Schwerké, *A. T., compositeur polonais* (Paris, 1931).

Tans'ur (real name, **Tanzer**), **William,** English organist, composer, and writer on music; b. Dunchurch, 1700 (baptized, Nov. 6, 1706); d. St. Neots, Oct. 7, 1783. He was a church organist and taught music in various provincial towns in England.

Works and Writings (all publ. in London unless otherwise given): *The Compleat Melody: or, The Harmony of Sion* (1734); *Heaven on Earth, or the Beauty of Holiness* (1738); *Sacred Mirth, or the Pious Soul's Daily Delight* (1739); *A New Musical Grammar: or, The Harmonical Spectator, with Philosophical Demonstrations on the Nature of Sound* (1746; various subsequent eds.); *The Royal Psalmodist: or, the New Universal Harmony* (1748); *The Royal Melody Compleat: or, the New Harmony of Sion* (1754–55; 3rd ed., 3 parts, 1764–66; later ed. as *The American Harmony*, Newburyport, 1771); *The Psalm-Singer's Jewell: or, Useful Companion to the Singing-psalms* (1760); *The Life of Holy David* (Cambridge, 1770); *Melodia sacra: or, The Devout Psalmist's New Musical Companion* (3rd ed., 1772); *The Beauties of Poetry* (Cambridge, 1776).

Bibl.: J. Rix, "W. T.," *Notes & Queries*, 4th series, ii (1868); E. Rimbault, "W. T.," ibid.

Tapper, Thomas, American music educator; b. Canton, Mass., Jan. 28, 1864; d. White Plains, N.Y., Feb. 24, 1958. He studied in the U.S. and Europe; ed. the *Music Record and Review* (1901–7) and the *Musician* (1905–7); then taught at N.Y. Univ. (1908–12); was lecturer at the Inst. of Musical Art (1905–24); also filled other editorial and educational positions. He publ. *The Music Life* (1891); *The Education of the Music Teacher* (1914); *Essentials in Music History* (1914; with Percy Goetschius); *The Melodic Music Course* (28 vols.; with F.H. Ripley); *Harmonic Music Course* (7 vols.); *The Modern Graded Piano Course* (19 vols.); *Music Theory and Composition* (6 vols.); *From Palestrina to Grieg* (Boston, 1929; 2nd ed., 1946). His wife, **Bertha Feiring Tapper** (b. Christiania, Norway, Jan. 25, 1859; d. N.Y., Sept. 2, 1915), was a good pianist; she studied with Agathe Backer-Gröndahl in Norway and with Leschetizky in Vienna; went to America in 1881; taught piano at the New England Cons. in Boston (1889–97) and at the Inst. of Musical Art in N.Y. (1905–10); she ed. 2 vols. of Grieg's piano works; publ. piano pieces and songs. She married Tapper on Sept. 22, 1895.

Tappert, Wilhelm, German music scholar; b. Ober-Thomaswaldau, Silesia, Feb. 19, 1830; d. Berlin, Oct. 27, 1907. He was a schoolmaster until 1856, when he entered Kullak's Academy of Music in Berlin; studied theory privately with Dehn; settled in Berlin. He was ed. of the *Allgemeine Deutsche Musikzeitung* (1866–80); collected a large assemblage of old tablatures, including unique specimens; after his death this collection and his entire valuable library were acquired by the Royal Library of Berlin. An ardent admirer of Wagner, he publ. a curious vol., *Ein Wagner-Lexikon: Wörterbuch der Unhöflichkeit, enthaltend grobe, höhnende, gehässige und verläumderische Ausdrücke welche gegen den Meister Richard Wagner, seine Werke und seine Anhänger von den Feinden und Spöttern gebraucht worden sind. Zur Gemütsergötzung in müssigen Stunden gesammelt,* a collection of anti-Wagner reviews (Leipzig, 1877; 2nd ed., enlarged, 1903 as *Richard Wagner im Spiegel der Kritik*). Other publs.: *Musik und musikalische Erziehung* (1866); *Musikalische Studien* (1868); *Das Verbot der Quintenparallelen* (1869); *Richard Wagner* (1883); *Wandernde Melodien* (2nd ed., 1889); *54 Erlkönig-Kompositionen* (1898; 2nd ed., 1906); *Katalog der Spezialausstellung von Wilhelm Tappert: die Entwicklung der Notenschrift* (1898); *900 bis 1900: tausend Jahre Entwicklungsgeschichte der musikalischen Zeichenschrift* (MS, 1901; enlarged, 1903); *Sang und Klang aus alter Zeit* (1906); also arrangements of old German songs. He composed 50 left-hand studies for piano; other piano pieces.

Tappolet, Willy, Swiss writer on music; b. Lindau, near Zürich, Aug. 6, 1890; d. Chêne-Bongeries, Feb. 24, 1981. He studied at the Univ. of Zürich (Ph.D., 1917, with the diss. *Heinrich Weber*; publ. in Zürich, 1918); completed his Habilitation at the Univ. of Geneva in 1938 with his *La Notation musicale et son influence sur la pratique de la musique du moyen-âge a nos jours* (publ. in Neuchâtel, 1945); was a reader on its faculty (1955–60). He wrote articles for various music journals; further publ. monographs on Honegger (in German, Zürich and Leipzig, 1933; in Fr., Neuchâtel, 1939; rev. ed., in Ger., 1954; in Fr., 1957) and on Ravel (Olten, 1950).

Tǎranu, Cornel, Rumanian composer; b. Cluj, June 20, 1934. He studied with Todutǎ and Muresianu at the Cluj Cons. (1951–57); in 1957 he was named senior lecturer at the Cluj Cons.; traveled to Paris and took lessons with Nadia Boulanger and Messiaen (1966–67); attended the seminars of Ligeti and Maderna at Darmstadt (1968–69; 1972); then returned to Cluj. His music is austerely formal, with atonal sound structures related through continuous variation, with permissible aleatory interludes from performers. **Works: OPERA:** *Secretul lui Don Giovanni* (The Secret of Don Juan; Cluj, July 8, 1970). **CANTATAS:** *Cîntare unui ev aprins* (1959–62; rev. 1970); *Stejarul lui Horia* (1963; Cluj, May 27, 1964); *Sub steanau Partidului* (1966; rev. Cluj, June 21, 1974); *Cortegiu* (1973; Cluj, Dec. 19, 1974); *Odǎ în metru antic* (1975). **ORCH.:** Sym. for String Orch. (1957); *Secvenţe* (Sequences) for String Orch. (1960); *Sinfonia brevia* (1962); *Simetrii* (Symmetries) (1964; Cluj, May 14, 1965); *Incantaţii* (Incantations) (1965; Cluj, Jan. 15, 1966); Piano Concerto (1966; Cluj, May 29, 1967); *Intercalǎri* (Intercalations) for Piano and Orch. (1967–69; Cluj, Dec. 13, 1969); *Sinfonietta giocosa* for String Orch. (1968; Bucharest, May 29, 1969); *Racorduri* (Transitions) for Chamber Orch. (1971); *Cîntec lung* for Clarinet, Piano, and String Orch. (1974; Bern, April 18, 1975). **CHAMBER:** String Trio (1952); *Poem-Sonata* for Clarinet and Piano (1954); Cello Sonata (1960); Flute Sonata (1961); Oboe Sonata (1963); *3 Pieces* for Clarinet and Piano (1964); *Dialogues for 6* for Flute, Clarinet, Trumpet, Vibraphone, Percussion, and Piano (1966); *Ebauche* for Voice, Clarinet, Violin, Viola, Cello, and Piano (1966–68); *Le Lit de Procruste* (The Bed of Procrustes) for Baritone, Clarinet, Viola, and Piano (1968–70); piano pieces; songs.

Tarchi, Angelo, Italian composer; b. Naples, c.1755; d. Paris, Aug. 19, 1814. He studied at the Cons. dei Turchini in Naples with Fago and Sala; was music director and composer at the King's Theatre in London in 1787–88 and again in 1789; subsequently was active in Italy until settling in Paris in 1797. He wrote about 45 operas in Italian, and 6 in French; of these the following were produced at La Scala in Milan: *Ademira* (Dec. 27, 1783); *Ariarte* (Jan. 1786); *Il Conte di Saldagna* (June 10, 1787); *Adrasto rè d'Egitto* (Feb. 4?, 1792); *Le Danaidi* (Dec. 26, 1794); *L'impostura poco dura* (Oct. 10, 1795). In Paris he produced the French version of *Il Conte di Saldagna* as *Bouffons de la foire St. Germain* (1790); *D'Auberge en auberge* (Opéra-Comique, April 26, 1800); etc. He acquired a certain notoriety by his attempt to rewrite the 3rd and 4th acts of Mozart's *Le nozze di Figaro* (1787); regarding this episode, see A. Einstein, "Mozart e Tarchi," *Rassegna Musicale* (July 1935); also C. Sartori, "Lo *Zeffiretto* di Angelo Tarchi," *Rivista Musicale Italiana* (July 1954).

Tarditi, Giovanni, Italian bandleader and composer; b. Acqui, March 10, 1857; d. Rome, Sept. 19, 1935. He traveled as a bandleader in Europe and America; publ. manuals for band playing such as *Segnalofono* for trumpet calls; wrote the operettas *Monte Carlo* (Genoa, March 1, 1897) and *L'isola degli antropofagi* (Rome, June 1, 1925), military marches, etc.

Tarditi, Orazio, esteemed Italian organist and composer; b. Rome, 1602; d. Forlì, Jan. 31, 1677. After entering the Camaldolite order, he was an organist at Arezzo Cathedral (1624–28), at S. Michele in Murano, near Venice (1629), and at Volterra Cathedral (1637); then was maestro di cappella at Forlì Cathedral (1639), Jesi Cathedral (1644–45), and Faenza Cathedral (1647–70). He was a notable composer of sacred music, producing many masses and motets; also composed madrigals and canzonets. His large output was publ. mainly in Venice, between 1622 and 1652.

Tardos, Béla, Hungarian composer; b. Budapest, June 21, 1910; d. there, Nov. 18, 1966. He studied with Kodály at the Budapest Academy of Music (1932–37); upon graduation was active as a concert manager and music publisher. He composed much choral music for mass singing employing the modalities of Hungarian folk songs. **Works: DRAMATIC:** *Laura*, comic opera (1958, rev. 1964; Debrecen, Dec. 11, 1966). **CANTATAS:** *A város peremén* (At the Outskirts of the City; 1944; 2nd version, 1958); *Rolád susog a lomb* (The Leaves Whisper About You; 1949); *Májusi kantáta* (May Cantata; 1950); *A béke napja alatt* (Under the Sun of Peace; 1953); *Hajnali dal* (Morning Song; 1953); *Dózsa feje* (Dózsa's Head; 1958); *Szabadság született* (Liberty Has Been Born; 1960); *Az új Isten* (The New Gold, 1966). **ORCH.:** *Overture* (1949); *Suite* (1950); Piano Concerto (1954); *Overture to a Fairy Tale* (1955); Sym., in memory of the victims of fascism (1960); *Fantasy* for Piano and Orch. (1961); Violin Concerto (1962); *Evocatio* (1964). **CHAMBER:** Wind Octet (1935); Piano Quartet (1941); 3 string quartets (1947, 1949,

1963); *Improvisations* for Clarinet and Piano (1960); *Prelude and Rondo* for Flute and Piano (1962); *Quartettino-Divertimento* for 4 Wind Instruments (1963); *Cassazione* for Harp Trio (1963); Violin Sonata (1965); piano pieces; also choruses; songs.

BIBL.: P. Várnai, *T. B.* (Budapest, 1966).

Tariol-Baugé, Anne, French singer; b. Clermont-Ferrand, Aug. 28, 1872; d. Asnières, near Paris, Dec. 1, 1944. She made her opera debut in Bordeaux; then went to Russia; returning to France, she sang in Toulouse and Nantes; then settled in Paris, where she appeared mainly in light opera; she sang the title role at the premiere of Messager's opera *Véronique* at the Bouffes-Parisiens (Dec. 10, 1898); distinguished herself especially in Offenbach's operettas. She was married to the baritone Alphonse Baugé.

Tarisio, Luigi, Italian violin maker and trader; b. Fontanetto, near Milan, c.1795; d. Milan, Oct. 1854. He was a carpenter by trade, and in his leisure hours acquired sufficient skill to play the violin at country fairs. He also began collecting old violins, which he repaired and sold at a profit. In 1827 he made his 1st trip to Paris, and in 1851 visited London; soon he became known as a reliable trader, and obtained many rich clients. He left a collection of about 200 violins, which were later purchased by Vuillaume in Paris.

BIBL.: G. Hart, *The Violin: Famous Makers and Their Imitators* (London, 1875); H. Haweis, *Old Violins* (London, 1898); W. Silverman, *The Violin Hunter* (N.Y., 1957).

Taronov, Gleb (Pavlovich), Ukrainian composer; b. Kiev, June 15, 1904. He studied composition with Mikhail Chernov at the Petrograd Cons. (1917–19); at the Kiev Cons., studied composition with Glière and Liatoshinsky and conducting with Blumenfield and Malko (1920–25); served on the faculty of the Kiev Cons. (1925–41; 1944–74). In 1957 he was named Honored National Artist of the Ukraine. His works are cast in the accepted Soviet mold, with emphasis on the celebration of historical events.

WORKS: OPERA: *The Battle on the Ice*, depicting the victory of Alexander Nevsky over the Teutonic Knights at Lake Peipus on April 5, 1242 (1943; rev. 1979). **ORCH.:** 9 syms. (1943; 1947; 1949, for Orch. of Native Instruments; 1957; 1963, *Antifascism;* 1964, "In Memory of Prokofiev" for Strings; 1967, *Heroic;* 1969, *Shushenskaya;* 1974, *The Banner of Victory*); Concerto Grosso (1936; rev. 1976); 5 suites (1950, 1955, 1961, 1964, 1965); 2 symphonic poems: *David Guramishvili* (1953) and *Fire in the Hangar* (1958); *The 1st in Outer Space*, scherzo-poem (1961); *Overture to Memory* (1965); *New Express* (1977). **CHAMBER:** 2 string quartets (1929, 1945); *Enthusiastic Sextet* for Piano and Strings (1945); Woodwind Quintet (1959); works for Solo Instruments; also choruses and songs.

BIBL.: M. Mikhailov, *G.P. T.* (Kiev, 1963); S. Miroshnichenko, *G. T.* (Kiev, 1976).

Tarp, Svend Erik, Danish composer; b. Thisted, Jutland, Aug. 6, 1908. He studied theory with Jeppesen and music history with Simonson at the Copenhagen Cons. (1929–31); then was on its faculty (1936–42); concurrently lectured at the Univ. of Copenhagen (1939–47) and the Royal Theater Opera School (1936–40); occupied various administrative and editorial posts; was an administrator with Edition Dania (1941–60).

WORKS: STAGE: Operas: *Princessen i det Fjerne* (The Princess at a Distance, 1952; Copenhagen, May 18, 1953); *9,90*, burlesque television opera (Copenhagen, Aug. 12, 1962). Ballets: *Skyggen* (The Shadow, after Hans Christian Andersen, 1941–44; Copenhagen, April 1, 1960); *Den detroniserede dyretoemmer* (The Dethroned Tamer; Copenhagen, Feb. 5, 1944). **ORCH.:** Sinfonietta for Chamber Orch. (1931); Violin Concertino (1931); Flute Concertino (1937); *Orania*, suite (1937); *Mosaïque*, miniature suite (1937); *Comedy Overture No. 1* (1939); *Comedy Overture No. 2* (1950); Piano Concerto (1943); 7 syms.: No. 1, *Sinfonia devertente* (1945); No. 2 (1948); No. 3, *Sinfonia quasi una fantasia* (1958); No. 4 (1975); No. 5

(1975); No. 6 (1976); No. 7 (1977); *Pro defunctis*, overture (1945); *Partita* (1947); *The Battle of Jericho*, symphonic poem (1949); *Preludio patetico* (1952); *Divertimento* (1954); *Scandinavian Design* (1955); *Lyrical Suite* (1956); *Little Dance Suite* (1964); *Little Festival Overture* (1969). **VOCAL:** *Te Deum* for Chorus and Orch. (1938); *Christmas Cantata* for Narrator, Baritone, Chorus, Organ, and Orch. (1946); songs. **CHAMBER:** *Serenade* for Flute, Clarinet, and String Trio (1930); *Serenade* for Flute and String Trio (1936); Duet for Flute and Viola (1941); String Quartet (1973); Piano Sonata (1950); other piano pieces; also music for about 40 films and 15 radio and television dramas.

Tarr, Edward H(ankins), distinguished American trumpeter, teacher, and musicologist; b. Norwich, Conn., June 15, 1936. He studied the trumpet in Boston with Roger Voisin (1953) and in Chicago with Adolph Herseth (1958–59); then studied musicology with Schrade in Basel (1959–64). He subsequently was active both as a trumpet virtuoso and a musicologist; in 1967 he organized the Edward H. Tarr Brass Ensemble, with which he performed Renaissance and Baroque music on original instruments and on modern replicas. From 1968 to 1970 he taught at the Rheinische Musikschule in Cologne; in 1972 he was appointed to the faculty of the Schola Cantorum Basiliensis in Basel as a teacher of cornett and natural trumpet; also taught trumpet at the Basel Cons. (from 1974) and served as conservator of the Trumpet Museum in Bad Säckingen (from 1985). He contributed numerous articles on trumpet playing to various publications, and publ. the book *Die Trompete* (Bern, 1977; 2nd ed., 1978; in Eng., 1988). He also ed. a number of trumpet works, including a complete edition of the trumpet music of Torelli.

Tárrega (y Eixea), Francisco, celebrated Spanish guitarist, pedagogue, and composer; b. Villarreal, Castellón, Nov. 21, 1852; d. Barcelona, Dec. 15, 1909. He began piano studies in childhood; in 1862 commenced classical guitar training with Julian Arcas; then pursued courses in theory, harmony, and piano at the Madrid Cons. (1874–77); subsequently taught music while establishing himself as a guitar virtuoso. His recital appearances in Paris and London in 1880 secured his reputation outside his homeland; he was acclaimed as the "Sarasate of the guitar." He performed throughout Spain (1885–1903), then toured Italy (1903). His remarkable career was cut short by paralysis of his right arm in 1906. He composed about 80 pieces, and prepared some 120 transcriptions for solo guitar and 21 for 2 guitars.

BIBL.: F. Buek, "Franzisko T.," *Der Gitarrefreund*, XXV (1924); M. Llobert, E. Pujol et al., "T. als Mensch und Künstler im Urteil siner Zeitgenossen," *Die Gitarre*, XI (1930); E. Schwarz-Reiflingen, "T.s Gitarrentechnik," ibid.; E. Pujol, *T., Ensayo biográfico* (Lisbon, 1960); T. Heck, "Historical notes to a T. recital of 1888," *Guitar News*, No. 107 (1970).

Tartini, Giuseppe, famous Italian violinist, teacher, music theorist, and composer; b. Pirano, Istria, April 8, 1692; d. Padua, Feb. 26, 1770. His parents prepared him for a monastic life by entrusting his education to clerics in Pirano and Capodistria, where he received some violin instruction. In 1708 he renounced the cloister but remained a nominal candidate for the priesthood. In 1709 he enrolled at the Univ. of Padua as a law student, and at the age of 19 contracted a secret marriage to the 21-year-old Elisabetta Premazore, a protégée of the powerful Cardinal Cornaro, who vengefully brought a charge of abduction against him. Tartini had to take refuge from prosecution at the monastery of the Friars Minor Conventual in Assisi, where he joined the opera orch. He was pardoned by the Paduan authorities in 1715; then lived in Venice and Padua, being made primo violino e capo di concerto at the basilica of S. Antonio in Padua in 1721. He also was allowed to travel as a virtuoso, and soon acquired a distinguished reputation. From 1723 to 1726 he served as chamber musician to Count Kinsky in Prague; then resumed his residence in Padua, where he organized a music school in 1728; among his students there were Nardini and Pugnani. He subsequently developed a brilliant career as a violinist, making numerous concert tours in Italy. He retained his post at S. Antonio until 1765, and also remained active at his school until at least 1767. In 1768 he suffered a mild stroke which effectively ended his career. His style of playing, and in particular his bowing, became a model for other concert violinists. Tartini was a prolific composer of violin music, including concertos, sonatas, and chamber combinations. An ed. of his collected works was initiated in Milan in 1971 under the editorship of E. Farina and C. Scimone as *Le opere di Giuseppe Tartini.*

Although Tartini lacked scientific training, he made several acoustical discoveries, the most important of which were the summation and differential tones; Tartini observed these effects in 1714 and summarized his findings in his *Trattato di musica secondo la vera scienza dell'armonia* (Padua, 1754); the differential tone became known also as Tartini's tone, or "terzo suono." Tartini's tones were actually described in an earlier German publ., *Vorgemach der musicalischen Composition* by G. Sorge (1745–47). These tones were also known, rather misleadingly, as "beat tones." They are in fact produced by the interference of frequencies of higher overtones. The "wolf tones" of string instruments are different in origin, and are produced by vibrations of the body of the instrument. Violinists are usually aware of interferences from differential tones and also from the less audible summation tones resulting from added frequencies; they correct them experimentally by a slight alteration of tuning. Among Tartini's compositions the most famous is his violin sonata known under the sobriquet *Trillo del Diavolo,* supposedly inspired by Tartini's dream in which the Devil played it for him; the eponymous diabolical trill appears in the last movement of the sonata.

Works: instrumental: About 135 violin concertos, as well as concertos for several other instruments; a Sinfonie; 4 sonatas *a 4* for String Quartet and Basso Continuo; some 40 trio sonatas for 2 Violins and Basso Continuo; about 135 sonatas for Violin and Basso Continuo; some 30 sonatas for Solo Violin or with Basso Continuo ad libitum. The following instrumental works were publ. during his lifetime although some are now considered dubious (all publ. in Amsterdam unless otherwise given): *Sei concerti a 5,* op. 1, lib.1 (1728); *Sei concerti a 5 del. . .Tartini a G. Visconti,* op. 1, lib.3 (c.1728); *Sei concerti a 5,* op. 1, lib.2 (1730); *VI sonate for Violin and Basso Continuo,* op. 1 (1732); (12) *Sonate e una pastorale,* op. 1 (1734); *VI concerti a 8,* op. 2 (c.1734); *VI concerti. . .d'alcuni famosi maestri,* lib.2 (c.1740); *VI Sonate* for Violin and Basso Continuo, op. 2 (1743); (12) *Sonate* for Violin and Basso Continuo, op. 2 (Rome, 1745; also publ. as op. 3, Paris, c.1747); *Nouvelle étude. . .par Mr. Pétronio Pinelli* (Paris, c.1747); (6) *Sonates,* op. 4 (Paris, 1747); (6) *Sonates,* op. 5 (Paris, c.1747); *Sei sonate,* op. 6 (Paris, c.1748); (6) *Sonate,* op. 7 (Paris, 1748); *Sei sonate a tre,* op. 8 (Paris, 1749); *XII Sonatas* for 2 Violins and Bass (London, 1750); *VI sonate* for 2 Violins and Basso Continuo (c.1755; also publ. as op. 3, London, 1756); *L'arte del arco* (Paris, 1758); *Sei sonate,* op. 9 (Paris, c.1763). His famous *Le trille du diable* was 1st publ. in J. Cartier's *L'art du violon* (Paris, 1798). He also wrote some sacred vocal music, including *Canzoncine sacre* for 1 to 3 Voices, a *Stabat mater* for 3 Voices, 2 *Tantum ergo* for 3 Voices, 3 *Miserere* for 3, 4, and 5 Voices, a *Salve regina* for 4 Voices, and a *Pange lingua* for 3 Voices. A complete ed. of his works commenced publication in Milan in 1971.

Writings: *Regole per arrivare a saper ben suonar il violino* (ed. by E. Jacobi, *Musical Quarterly,* XLVII, 1961; various other versions); *Trattato di musica secondo la vera sienza dell'armonia* (Padua, 1754; reprint, 1966 and 1973); *De' principi dell'armonia musicale contenuta nel diatonico genere* (Padua, 1767; reprint, 1970); *Risposta di Giuseppe Tartini alla critica del di lui trattato di musica di Mons. Le Serre di Ginevra* (Venice, 1767).

Bibl.: F. Fanzago, *Orazione. . .delle lodi di G. T.* (Padua, 1770; 2nd ed., enlarged, 1792); F. Fayolle, *Notices sur Corelli, T., Gaviniés, Pugnani et Viotti* (Paris, 1810); G. Benedetti, "G. T.," *Archeografo triestino,* new series, XXI (1896); A. Bachmann, *Les grands violinistes du passé* (Paris, 1913); M. Dou-

nias, *Die Violinkonzerte G. T.s* (Wolfenbüttel, 1935; 2nd ed., 1966); H. Schökel, *G. T.* (Berlin, 1936); A. Capri, *G. T.* (Milan, 1945); M. Elmer, *T.'s Improvised Ornamentation* (diss., Univ. of Calif., Berkeley, 1962); P. Petrobelli, *G. T.: le fonti biografiche* (Vienna, Milan, and London, 1968); P. Brainard, *Le sonate per violino di G. T.: catalogo tematico* (Milan, 1975); B. Schwarz, *Great Masters of the Violin* (N.Y., 1983).

Taskin, (Emile-) Alexandre, French baritone, grandson of **Henri-Joseph Taskin;** b. Paris, March 8, 1853; d. there, Oct. 5, 1897. He was a pupil of Ponchard and Bussine at the Paris Cons.; made his debut at Amiens in 1875. He sang in Lille and Geneva; returned to Paris in 1878; was engaged at the Opéra-Comique in 1879, and created important parts in many new operas. He retired in 1894, and from then until his death was prof. of lyrical declamation at the Cons. On the night of the terrible catastrophe of the burning of the Opéra-Comique (May 25, 1887) he was singing in *Mignon;* through his calmness and bravery many lives were saved, and the government decorated him with a medal.

Taskin, Pascal (-Joseph), French manufacturer of keyboard instruments; b. Theux, near Liège, 1723; d. Paris, Feb. 9, 1793. He went to Paris at an early age and entered Blanchet's atelier, later marrying Blanchet's widow and succeeding to the business in 1766; was named court instrument maker and keeper of the king's instruments in 1774. He became highly celebrated as an instrument maker; invented the leather plectra for the harpsichord (1768), replacing the crow quills previously in use. He built his 1st piano in 1776. His nephew **Pascal-Joseph Taskin** (b. Theux, Nov. 20, 1750; d. Versailles, Feb. 5, 1829) was Keeper of the King's Instruments from 1772 until the Revolution; his son **Henri-Joseph Taskin** (b. Versailles, Aug. 24, 1779; d. Paris, May 4, 1852) was an organist and composer.

Bibl.: D. Boalch, *Makers of the Harpsichord and Clavichord, 1440–1840* (London, 1956; 2nd ed., rev., 1974).

Tassinari, Pia, Italian soprano and mezzo-soprano; b. Modigliana, Sept. 15, 1909. She received her musical training in Bologna and Milan; made her debut as Mimi at Castel Monferrato in 1929; then sang at La Scala in Milan (1931–37; 1945–46) and at the Rome Opera (1933–44; 1951–52). She made her American debut at the Metropolitan Opera in N.Y. on Dec. 26, 1947, as Tosca. Although she began her career as a soprano, in later years she preferred to sing mezzo-soprano parts. Her repertoire included both soprano and mezzo-soprano roles, e.g., Mimi, Tosca, Manon, and Marguerite, and also Amneris and Carmen. She married the noted tenor **Ferruccio Tagliavini.**

Tate, Jeffrey, talented English conductor; b. Salisbury, April 28, 1943. Although a victim of spina bifida, he pursued studies at Cambridge Univ. and at St. Thomas's Medical School; then attended the London Opera Centre (1970–71). He was subsequently a member of the music staff at the Royal Opera, Covent Garden (1971–77); served as an assistant conductor at the Bayreuth Festivals (1976–80). In 1978 he made his formal conducting debut with *Carmen* at the Göteborg Opera; on Dec. 26, 1980, he made his 1st appearance at the Metropolitan Opera in N.Y. conducting Berg's *Lulu;* his debut at Covent Garden followed, with *La clemenza di Tito* on June 8, 1982. He appeared as a guest conductor at the Cologne Opera (1981), the Geneva Opera (1983), the Paris Opéra (1983), the Hamburg State Opera (1984), the San Francisco Opera (1984), the Salzburg Festival (1985), and the Vienna State Opera (1986). In 1983 he made his 1st appearance with the English Chamber Orch., being named its principal conductor in 1985; led it on tours abroad, including one to the U.S. in 1988. In 1986 he also became principal conductor at Covent Garden. In 1990 he was made a Commander of the Order of the British Empire. He became chief conductor of the Rotterdam Phil. in 1991. His extensive operatic and concert repertoire encompasses works from the Classical to the contemporary era.

Tate, Phyllis (Margaret Duncan), English composer; b. Gerrards Cross, Buckinghamshire, April 6, 1911; d. London,

May 27, 1987. She studied composition with Harry Farjeon at the Royal Academy of Music in London (1928–32); composed a Sym., a Cello Concerto, and several other works, but withdrew them as immature. In her music she follows the zeitgeist of the modern era; her music bristles with abrasive dissonances and asymmetrical rhythms, while the form retains its Classical purity. She married the music scholar and publishing official **Alan Frank** in 1935.

WORKS: Cello Concerto (1933); *Valse lointaine* for Small Orch. (1941); *Prelude, Interlude and Postlude,* for Chamber Orch. (1942); Saxophone Concerto (1944); Sonata for Clarinet and Cello (1947; Salzburg ISCM Festival, June 23, 1951); String Quartet (1952); *Occasional Overture* (1955); *The Lady of Shalott,* after Tennyson, cantata for Tenor, Viola, Percussion, 2 Pianos, and Celesta (1956); *The Lodger,* opera (London, July 14, 1960); television opera, *Dark Pilgrimage* (1963); *A Victorian Garland,* after Matthew Arnold, for Soprano, Contralto, Horn, and Piano (1965); *Secular Requiem* for Chorus and Orch. (1967); *Christmas Ale* for Soloists, Chorus, and Orch. (1967); *Apparitions,* ballad sequence for Tenor, Harmonica, String Quartet, and Piano (1968); *Illustrations* for Brass Band (1969); *Variegations* for Viola (1971); *Prelude-Aria-Interlude-Finale* for Clarinet and Piano (1981); music for schools and amateur musicians: *Twice in a Blue Moon,* fantasy operetta (1968); *Serenade to Christmas* for Mezzo-soprano, Chorus, and Orch. (1972); *Lyric Suite* for 2 Pianos (1973); *The Rainbow and the Cuckoo* for Oboe, Violin, Viola, and Cello (1974); *Sonatina Pastorale* for Harmonica and Harpsichord (1974); *St. Martha and the Dragon* for Narrator, Soloists, Chorus, and Orch. (1976); *Seasonal Sequence* for Viola and Piano (1977); *Panorama* for Strings (1977); *All the World's a Stage* for Chorus and Orch. (1977); *Scarecrow,* operetta (1982).

BIBL.: M. Carner, "The Music of P. T.," *Music & Letters* (April 1954); H. Searle, "P. T.," *Musical Times* (May 1955).

Tatum, Art(hur), noted black American jazz pianist; b. Toledo, Ohio, Oct. 13, 1910; d. Los Angeles, Nov. 5, 1956. He was blind in one eye and had limited vision in the other; he attended a school for the blind in Columbus, Ohio, and learned to read Braille music notation; at the age of 16, began to play in nightclubs. In 1932 he went to N.Y. and became successful on the radio. In 1938 he made a spectacular tour of England; then pursued his career in N.Y. and Los Angeles; organized his own trio in 1943. In 1947 he appeared in the film *The Fabulous Dorseys.* His art as a jazz improviser was captured on more than 600 recordings. He brought "stride" piano playing to a point of perfection, scorning such academic niceties as proper fingering, but achieving small miracles with ornamental figurations in the melody while throwing effortless cascades of notes across the keyboard; he also had a knack of improvising variations on popular pieces by defenseless deceased classical composers; his audiences adored Art's art, while professional musicians knitted their brows in wild surmise.

BIBL.: J. Howard, *The Improvisational Techniques of A. T.* (diss., Case Western Reserve Univ., 1978); special issue of *Keyboard,* VII/10 (1981); J. Distler, *A. T.* (N.Y., 1981); A. Laubick and R. Spencer, *A. T.: A Guide to His Recorded Music* (Metuchen, N.J., 1982); F. Howlett, *An Introduction to A. T.'s Performance Approaches: Composition, Improvisation and Melodic Variation* (diss., Cornell Univ., 1983).

Tauber, Richard, eminent Austrian-born English tenor; b. Linz, May 16, 1891; d. London, Jan. 8, 1948. He was the illegitimate son of the actor Richard Anton Tauber; his mother was a soubrette singer. He was christened Richard Denemy after his mother's maiden name, but he sometimes used the last name Seiffert, his mother's married name. He took courses at the Hoch Cons. in Frankfurt am Main and studied voice with Carl Beines in Freiburg; made his debut at Chemnitz as Tamino in *Die Zauberflöte* (March 2, 1913) with such success that he was engaged in the same year at the Dresden Court Opera; made his 1st appearance at the Berlin Royal Opera as Strauss's Bacchus in 1915, and later won particular success in Munich and Salzburg for his roles in Mozart's operas.

About 1925 he turned to lighter roles, and won remarkable success in the operettas of Lehár. He made his U.S. debut on Oct. 28, 1931, in a N.Y. recital. In 1938 he settled in England, where he appeared as Tamino and Belmonte at London's Covent Garden. In 1940 he became a British subject. He wrote an operetta, *Old Chelsea,* taking the leading role at its premiere (London, Feb. 17, 1943). He made his last American appearance at Carnegie Hall in N.Y. on March 30, 1947.

BIBL.: H. Ludwigg, ed., *R. T.* (Berlin, 1928); D. Napier-Tauber (his 2nd wife), *R. T.* (Glasgow, 1949); W. Korb, *R. T.* (Vienna, 1966); C. Castle and D. Napier-Tauber, *This Was R. T.* (London, 1971).

Taubert, (Carl Gottfried) Wilhelm, German pianist, conductor, teacher, and composer; b. Berlin, March 23, 1811; d. there, Jan. 7, 1891. He was a piano pupil of Neithardt, later of L. Berger, and for composition, of Bernhard Klein. He appeared early as a concert player; taught music in Berlin; became assistant conductor of the court orch. in 1831; was Generalmusikdirektor of the Royal Opera, Berlin, from 1845 to 1848; also court Kapellmeister from 1845 to 1869; continued to conduct the court orch. until 1883. He conducted his 1st Sym. in Berlin at the age of 20 (March 31, 1831).

WORKS: OPERAS (all 1st perf. in Berlin): *Die Kirmes* (Jan. 23, 1832); *Marquis und Dieb* (Feb. 1, 1842); *Der Zigeuner* (Sept. 19, 1834); *Joggeli* (Oct. 9, 1853); *Macbeth* (Nov. 16, 1857); *Cesario,* after Shakespeare's *Twelfth Night* (Nov. 13, 1874); incidental music to 8 plays. ORCH.: 4 syms.; 3 overtures; 2 piano concertos; Cello Concerto; Concertino for Violin. CHAMBER: 4 string quartets; 2 piano trios; violin sonatas; also choral music; piano pieces, including *Minnelieder,* op. 16; some 300 songs, including the successful *Kinderlieder,* opp. 145, 160.

BIBL.: W. Neumann, *W. T. und Ferdinand Hiller* (Kassel, 1857); E. Glusman, "T. and Mendelssohn: Opposing Attitudes towards Poetry and Music," *Musical Quarterly* (Oct. 1971).

Taubman, Howard, American music and drama critic; b. N.Y., July 4, 1907. He studied at Cornell Univ. (A.B., 1929); joined the staff of the *N.Y. Times* in 1929, where he was its music ed. (1935–55), music critic (1955–60), drama critic (1960–66), and critic-at-large (1966–72).

WRITINGS: *Opera: Front and Back* (N.Y., 1938); *Music as a Profession* (N.Y., 1939); *Music on My Beat* (N.Y., 1943); *The Maestro: The Life of Arturo Toscanini* (N.Y., 1951); *How to Build a Record Library* (N.Y., 1953; new ed., 1955); *How to Bring Up Your Child to Enjoy Music* (Garden City, N.Y., 1958); *The Making of the American Theater* (N.Y., 1965; rev. in *Musical Comedy,* XII, 1967); *The New York Times Guide to Listening Pleasure* (N.Y., 1968).

BIBL.: L. Weldy, *Music Criticism of Olin Downes and H. T. in "The New York Times," Sunday Edition, 1924–29 and 1955–60* (diss., Univ. of Southern Calif., 1965).

Taubmann, Otto, German conductor, music critic, and composer; b. Hamburg, March 8, 1859; d. Berlin, July 4, 1929. After graduation from school, he followed a commercial career for 3 years; then studied music under Wüllner, Rischbieter, Nicodé, and Blassmann at the Dresden Cons.; traveled a year for further study, and began his career as a theater conductor; from 1886 to 1889 he was director of the Wiesbaden Cons.; in 1891–92, theater conductor in St. Petersburg; from 1892 to 1895, conductor of the Cäcilienverein in Ludwigshafen; then settled in Berlin, where from 1898 he was music critic of the *Börsen-Courier;* also taught at the Hochschule für Musik (1920–25).

WORKS: *Porzia,* opera (Frankfurt am Main, 1916); Sym.; String Quartet; *Eine deutsche Messe* for Soli, Double Chorus, Organ, and Orch. (1896); *Sängerweihe,* choral drama (1904); *Kampf und Friede,* cantata (1915).

Taucher, Curt, German tenor; b. Nuremberg, Oct. 25, 1885; d. Munich, Aug. 7, 1954. He studied with Heinrich Hermann in Munich; made his debut as Faust in Augsburg in 1908; then sang in Chemnitz (1911–14) and Hannover (1915–20). In 1920 he joined the Dresden State Opera, remaining there until 1934; during his tenure there he created the role of Menelaus in Strauss's opera *Die Ägyptische Helena*. On Nov. 23, 1922, he sang the role of Siegmund in *Die Walküre* at his Metropolitan Opera debut in N.Y.; continued on its roster until 1927. He made guest appearances at Covent Garden in London (1932), at the Berlin State Opera, and at the Bavarian State Opera in Munich. He was noted for his roles in Wagner's operas.

Taudou, Antoine (-Antonin-Barthélemy), French violinist and composer; b. Perpignan, Aug. 24, 1846; d. St.-Germain-en-Laye, July 6, 1925. He studied at the Paris Cons., winning the Grand Prix de Rome in 1869 with the cantata *Francesca da Rimini*; in 1883, became prof. of harmony at the Cons. He publ. *Marche-Ballet, Chant d'automne,* and *Marche nocturne* for Orch.; Violin Concerto; String Quartet; Piano Trio; Trio for Flute, Viola, and Cello; etc.

Tauriello, Antonio, Argentine conductor and composer; b. Buenos Aires, March 20, 1931. He studied piano with Walter Gieseking and composition with Alberto Ginastera; in 1958, he was engaged to conduct opera and ballet at the Teatro Colón; appeared with the Chicago Lyric Opera in 1965 and then conducted other U.S. opera companies. His music is neo-Classical in its general mold.

WORKS: *Serenade* for Orch. (1957); *Ricercare* for Orch. (1963); *Transparencies* for 6 Instrumental Groups (Washington, D.C., May 12, 1965); Piano Concerto (Washington, D.C., June 29, 1968); *Mansión de Tlaloc* for Piano, Percussion, and Strings (1969); *Signos de los tiempos* for Flute, Clarinet, Violin, Cello, and Piano (1969).

Tausch, Franz (Wilhelm), celebrated German clarinetist, basset-horn player, and composer; b. Heidelberg, Dec. 26, 1762; d. Berlin, Feb. 9, 1817. He studied with his father, a member of the Mannheim Court Orch.; joined that orch. when he was only 8, then played in the Munich Court Orch. (1777–89), establishing himself as an outstanding virtuoso. In 1789 he went to Berlin as a member of the Court Orch.; there he founded a school for wind players in 1805; among his pupils were Heinrich Bärmann and Bernhard Crusell. He wrote several clarinet concertos, 3 concertantes for 2 Clarinets, Andante and Polonaise for Clarinet, clarinet duos, trios for 2 Clarinets with Bassoon, 6 quartets for 2 Basset Horns and 2 Bassoons (with 2 Horns ad libitum), 6 military marches, etc.

BIBL.: P. Weston, *Clarinet Virtuosi of the Past* (London, 1971).

Tausch, Julius, German conductor and composer; b. Dessau, April 15, 1827; d. Bonn, Nov. 11, 1895. He studied with Friedrich Schneider in Dessau, and at the Leipzig Cons. (1844–46); settled in Düsseldorf in 1846 as conductor of the Künstlerliedertafel; was Schumann's deputy from 1853, and in 1855 his successor as conductor of the Music Society and Subscription Concerts, retiring in 1890. He composed a *Festouvertüre* (1875), cantatas, men's choruses, and piano pieces.

Tausig, Carl (actually, **Karol**), celebrated Polish pianist and composer; b. Warsaw, Nov. 4, 1841; d. Leipzig, July 17, 1871. He began his training with his father, **Aloys Tausig** (b. Prague, 1820; d. Warsaw, March 14, 1885), who was a pupil of Thalberg and wrote brilliant piano music. Carl was 14 when his father took him to Liszt in Weimar, where he became Liszt's premier pupil; he received instruction in piano, counterpoint, composition, and instrumentation from him, whom he accompanied on his concert tours. He made his debut in 1858, at an orch. concert conducted by Hans von Bülow at Berlin. During the next 2 years he gave concerts in German cities, making Dresden his headquarters; then went to Vienna in 1862, giving orch. concerts with "advanced" programs similar to Bülow's at Berlin. He settled in Berlin in 1865, and opened the Schule des Höheren Klavierspiels. He gave concerts in the principal towns of Germany, and at St. Petersburg and other Russian centers. He died of typhoid fever at the age of 29. Although his career was lamentably brief, he acquired a brilliant reputation for his technical mastery.

WORKS: PIANO: 2 études de concert; *Ungarische Zigeunerweisen; Nouvelles soirées de Vienna; Valses-Caprices* on themes from Strauss; *Tägliche Studien* (transposing chromatic exercises; ed. by Ehrlich); also transcriptions and arrangements.

BIBL.: C. Weitzmann, *Der Letzte der Virtuosen* (Leipzig, 1868); W. von Lenz, *Die grossen Pianoforte-Virtuosen unserer Zeit* (Berlin, 1872; in Eng., N.Y., 1899).

Tausinger, Jan, Rumanian-born Czech conductor, teacher, and composer; b. Piatra Neamt, Nov. 1, 1921; d. Prague, July 29, 1980. He studied composition with Cuclin, Jora, and Mendelsohn at the Bucharest Cons., graduating in 1947; then went to Prague, where he had lessons in conducting with Ančerl; concurrently took courses in advanced harmony with Alois Hába and Bořkovec at the Prague Academy of Music (1948–52). He was active as a conductor of radio orchs. in Bucharest, Ostrava, and Plzeň; also taught at the Ostrava Cons., where he was director (1952–58); after working for the Czech Radio in Prague (1969–70), he served as director of the Prague Cons. His music is greatly diversified in style, idiom, and technique, ranging from neo-Classical modalities to integral dodecaphony; he made use of optical representational notation when justified by the structure of a particular piece.

WORKS: STAGE: *Ugly Nature*, opera, after Dostoyevsky (1971); *Dlouhá noc* (The Long Night), ballet (1966). **ORCH.:** *Suite in the Old Style* (1946–47); Sym. No. 1, *Liberation* (1952); Violin Concerto (1962–63); *Confrontazione I* and *II* (1964); *Concertino meditazione* for Viola and Chamber Ensemble (1965); *A Prayer* for Soprano and Chamber Orch. (1965); *Praeludium, Sarabande and Postludium* for Winds, Piano, and Percussion (1967); *Noc* (The Night), musical collage, after a poem by Pushkin, for Soprano, Chorus, Orch., and Guitar (1967); *Správná věc* (The Right Thing), symphonic picture to words of Mayakovsky, for Tenor, Baritone, Chorus, and Orch. (1967); *Musica evolutiva* for Chamber Orch. (1967; Zagreb, Nov. 24, 1971); *Improvisations*, in honor of Bach, for Piano and Orch. (1970); *Ave Maria* for Narrator, Soprano, and Orch. (Prague, Oct. 17, 1972); *Sinfonia bohemica* for Bass, Male Chorus, Trumpet, Harpsichord, and Orch. (1973–75); *Sinfonia slovacca* (1979). **CHAMBER:** Violin Sonata (1954); *Partita* for Viola and Piano (1957–58); 2 string trios (1960, 1965); 4 string quartets (1961; 1966; 1970; *Structures*, 1972); *Colloquium* for 4 Wind Instruments (1964); Trio for Violin, Viola, and Guitar (1965); *Le avventure* for Flute and Harp (1965); *Canto di speranza* for Piano Quartet (1965); *Happening* for Piano Trio, based on proclamation of J. Shweik (1966); *De rebus musicalibus* for Flute, Bass Clarinet, Vibraphone, Piano, and Percussion (1967); *Čmáranice po nebi* (Scrawling in the Sky), to a poem by an early Russian futurist, Khlebnikov, for Soprano, Flute, Bass Clarinet, Piano, and Percussion (1967); *Sonatina emancipata* for Trumpet and Piano (1967); Brass Quintet (1968); *Hommage à Ladislav Černý* for Viola and Piano (1971); "*On revient toujours . . . ,*" suite for Violin and Piano (1974); "*Comme il faut,*" sonatina for Oboe and Piano (1974); *Hukvaldy Nonet* (1974); "*Au dernier amour . . . ,*" suite-sonata for Cello and Piano (1974–75); *Non-isosceles* for Flute, Cello, and Piano (1975); Clarinet Sonata (1975); 4 *Evocations* for Flute, Viola, Cello, and Piano (1976); *Sketches*, 2nd nonet (1976); *Reminiscences*, 3rd nonet (1976); Sextet for Wind Quintet and Piano (1976); 7 *Microchromophonies* for Clarinet, Viola, and Piano (1977); 4 *Nuances* for Flute, Harp, Violin, Viola, and Cello (1978); Piano Sonata (1948–50); 10 *Dodecaphonic Studies* for Piano (1972); songs, including *Duetti compatibili* (*Zero Point*) for Soprano and Viola (1971) and *Starting Point* for Soprano and 2 Violins (1979–80). Also choruses.

Tauwitz, Eduard, German conductor and composer; b. Glatz, Silesia, Jan. 21, 1812; d. Prague, July 25, 1894. He was made Kapellmeister at theaters in Vilnius (1837), Riga (1840), Breslau (1843), and Prague (1846); was pensioned in 1863. He wrote more than 1,000 compositions, including 3 operas: *Trilby* (Vilna, 1836); *Bradamante* (Riga, 1844); *Schmolke und Bakel* (Breslau, 1846); church music; songs; part-songs.

Tavares, Hekel, Brazilian composer; b. Rio de Janeiro, Sept. 16, 1896; d. there, Aug. 8, 1969. He was the son of a wealthy plantation owner and, working in the fields, acquired intimate knowledge of native folk songs. Without benefit of formal education, he wrote instrumental and vocal music in large forms; his works include a Piano Concerto, based on urban and rural dance forms; another significant work on Brazilian themes is a Violin Concerto. The bulk of his compositions consists of popular songs.

Tavener, John (Kenneth), English organist, teacher, and composer; b. London, Jan. 28, 1944. He studied with Lennox Berkeley at the Royal Academy of Music in London (1961–65) and privately with David Lumsdaine (1965–67); was organist at St. John's, Kensington (from 1960); taught composition at Trinity College of Music in London (from 1969). Among the formative influences of his creative evolution were medieval hymnology and Indian transcendentalism; his technical equipment is, by contrast, ultramodern, including combinatorial serialism and electronic generation of sound.

WORKS: Piano Concerto (London, Dec. 6, 1963); *3 Holy Sonnets* for Baritone and Chamber Orch., to poems by John Donne (1962; London, July 1964); *3 Sections from T.S. Eliot's Four Quartets* for Tenor and Piano (1964); *The Cappemakers*, dramatic cantata (Charleston Manor, Sussex, June 14, 1964; rev. for the stage, 1965); *Cain and Abel*, dramatic cantata for Soloists and Chamber Orch. (1965; London, Oct. 22, 1966); Chamber Concerto (1965; rev. 1968; London, June 12, 1968); *The Whale*, dramatic cantata for Narrator, Soloists, Chorus, and Orch. (1966; London, Jan. 24, 1968); *Grandma's Footsteps* for Chamber Group (London, March 14, 1968); *Introit for the Feast of St. John Damascene* for Soprano, Contralto, Chorus, and Orch. (London, March 27, 1968); Concerto for Orch. (1968); *3 Surrealist Songs* for Mezzo-soprano, Piano, Bongos, and Tape (BBC, March 21, 1968); *In Alium* for Soprano, Orch., and Tape (London, Aug. 12, 1968); *A Celtic Requiem*, dramatic cantata for Soloists, Children's Choir, Chorus, and Orch. (London, July 16, 1969); *Ultimos ritos* for Soloists, 5 Choruses, Brass Ensemble, and Orch. (1972; Haarlem, June 22, 1974); *Coplas* for Soloists, Chorus, and Tape (Cheltenham, July 9, 1970); *Nomine Jesu* for 5 Male Speaking Voices, Mezzo-soprano, Chorus, 2 Alto Flutes, Organ, and Harpsichord (Dartington, South Devon, Aug. 14, 1970); *Canciones españolas* for 2 Countertenors or Sopranos, 2 Flutes, Organ, and Harpsichord (London, June 8, 1972); *In memoriam Igor Stravinsky* for 2 Alto Flutes, Organ, and Bells (1971); *Ma fin est mon commencement* for Tenor Chorus, 4 Trombones, Piano, and 4 Cellos (London, April 23, 1972); *Little Requiem for Father Malachy Lynch* (Winchester Cathedral, July 29, 1972); *Variations on 3 Blind Mice* for Chamber Orch. (1972); *Requiem for Father Malachy* for 6 Soloists and Chamber Orch. (London, June 10, 1973); *Thérèse*, opera (1973–76; London, Oct. 1, 1979); *Canticle of the Mother of God* for Soprano and Chorus (1976); *A Gentle Spirit*, chamber opera after the story by Dostoyevsky (Bath, June 6, 1977); *Kyklike Kinesis* for Soprano, Cello, Chorus, and Orch. (1977; London, March 8, 1978); *Lamentation, Last Prayer and Exaltation* for Soprano and Handbells (1977); *Palintropos* for Piano and Orch. (1977; Birmingham, March 1, 1979); *The Last Prayer of Mary Queen of Scots* for Soprano and Handbells (1977); *6 Russian Folk Songs* for Soprano and Ensemble (1978); *The Liturgy of St. John Chrysostom* for Chorus a cappella (London, May 6, 1978); *The Immurement of Antigone*, monodrama for Soprano and Orch. (1978; London, March 30, 1979); *6 Abbasid Songs* for Tenor and 3 Flutes (1979); *Akhmatova: Requiem* for Soprano, Baritone, and Ensemble (1980; Edinburgh, Aug. 20, 1981); *Sappho, Lyric Fragments* for 2 Sopranos and Strings (1980); *Risen!* for Chorus and Ensemble (1980); *Prayer for the World* for 16 Solo Voices (1981); *Funeral Ikos* for Chorus (1981); *Towards the Son: Ritual Procession* for Orch. (London, Nov. 15, 1983); *Vigil Service* for Chorus (1984); *Ikon of Light* for Chorus (1984); *Elis Thanaton*, dramatic cantata (1987); *Ikon of St. Serafim* for Baritone, Countertenor, Chorus, and Instruments (1988); *Let not the*

Prince be Silent for Chorus (1988); *Akathist of Thanksgiving: Glory to God for Everything* for Soloists, Chorus, and Orch. (Westminster Abbey, London, Nov. 21, 1988).

BIBL.: I. Moody, "J. T.'s 'Akathis of Thanksgiving'," *Musical Times* (Oct. 1988).

Taverner, John, important English composer; b. South Lincolnshire, c.1490; d. Boston, Lincolnshire, Oct. 18, 1545. He was a lay clerk of the choir at the collegiate church of Tattershall (1524–25). In 1526 he was appointed master of the choristers at Cardinals' College in Oxford. In 1530 he became lay clerk of the choir of the parish church of St. Botolph, in Boston, Lincolnshire, where he served until 1537. In the latter year he was elected a member of the Guild of Corpus Christi there, serving as one of its 2 treasurers from 1541 to 1543. In 1545 he was appointed a town alderman, but died soon afterward. The widely circulated stories of his imprisonment for heresy and of his serving as an agent for Cromwell are totally unfounded. Taverner was a prolific composer of church music; among his works are 8 masses, 9 mass sections, 3 Magnificats, about 25 motets, 4 part-songs, and 2 instrumental pieces. His church music is found in vols. I and III of *Tudor Church Music* (1923–24) and in H. Benham, ed., *John Taverner: The Six-part Masses*, Early English Church Music, XX (1978).

BIBL.: H. Collins, "J. T.'s Masses," *Music & Letters*, V (1924); idem, "J. T.—Part II," ibid., VI (1925); F. Harrison, "J. T.," *The New Oxford History of Music* (Vol. III, Oxford, 1960); D. Josephson, "J. T.: An English Renaissance Master," *American Choral Review*, IX/2 (1967); D. Stevens, "J. T.," *Essays in Musicology in Honor of Dragon Plamenac* (Pittsburgh, 1969); H. Benham, *The Music of J. T.: A Study and Assessment* (diss., Univ. of Southampton, 1970); D. Josephson, "In Search of the Historical T.," *Tempo*, no.101 (1972); C. Hand, *J. T.: His Life and Music* (London, 1978); D. Josephson, *J. T., Tudor Composer* (Ann Arbor, Mich., 1979).

Tawaststjerna, Erik (Werner), eminent Finnish musicologist; b. Mikkeli, Oct. 10, 1916. He studied piano with Hannikainen and Bernhard at the Helsinki Cons. (1934–44), with Leygraf in Stockholm, with Neuhaus in Moscow (1946), and with Cortot and Gentil in Paris (1947); later pursued musicological studies at the Univ. of Helsinki (Mag.Phil., 1958; Ph.D., 1960). After a brief career as a concert pianist, he devoted himself to musicology; was a prof. at the Univ. of Helsinki (from 1960).

WRITINGS (all publ. in Helsinki): *Sibeliuksen pianosävellykset ja muita esseitä* (Sibelius's Piano Works; 1955; Eng. tr., 1957); *Sergei Prokofjevin ooppera Sota ja rauha* (Sergei Prokofiev's *War and Peace*; 1960); *Jean Sibelius* (5 vols., 1965–88; Eng. tr. by R. Layton, 1976–); *Esseitä ja arvosteluja* (Essays and Criticism; 1976).

BIBL.: E. Salmenhaara, ed., *Juhlakirja E. T.lle* (Helsinki, 1976).

Taylor, "Billy" (William), black American jazz pianist; b. Greenville, N.C., July 24, 1921. He studied piano with Henry Grant; pursued his education at Virginia State College in Petersburg (B.Mus., 1942) and at the Univ. of Mass. (D.Ed., 1975). In 1951 he formed the Billy Taylor Trio; served as a radio disc jockey and program director; was host of the NPR "Jazz Alive" radio series. He was also active as a teacher; was on the staff of the Manhattan School of Music and Howard Univ. His image became an intaglio of jazz, so that he was popularly dubbed "Mr. Jazz."

Taylor, Cecil (Percival), black American jazz pianist and composer; b. N.Y., March 15, 1933. He began piano lessons at age 5; was improvising and composing by the age of 8; later studied percussion. He studied harmony and composition at the N.Y. College of Music; subsequently studied composition at the New England Cons. of Music in Boston; also immersed himself in the Boston jazz scene. He then worked with his own combos in N.Y.; 1st appeared at the Newport Jazz Festival (1957); gained a name for himself as a performer in the off-Broadway production of Jack Gelber's *The Connection* (1959).

He made his 1st tour of Europe in 1962, and then played in many jazz centers on both sides of the Atlantic; performed at N.Y.'s Carnegie Hall in 1977. He made a number of remarkable recordings, including the albums *Into the Hot* (1961), *Unit Structures* (1966), *Silent Tongues* (1975), *The Cecil Taylor Unit* (1978), and *3 Phasis* (1978). His digitally agile piano style and penchant for extended improvisation made him an important figure in avant-garde jazz circles in his time.

BIBL.: *Current Biography* (March 1986).

Taylor, Clifford, American composer; b. Avalon, Pa., Oct. 20, 1923; d. Abington, Pa., Sept. 19, 1987. He studied composition with Lopatnikoff at the Carnegie-Mellon Univ. in Pittsburgh, and with Irving Fine, Hindemith, Piston, and Thompson at Harvard Univ. (M.A., 1950). He taught at Chatham College in Pittsburgh (1950–63); in 1963 he joined the faculty of Temple Univ. in Philadelphia.

WORKS: OPERA: *The Freak Show* (1975). **ORCH.:** *Theme and Variations* (1951); *Concerto Grosso* for String Orch. (1957); 3 syms.: No. 1 (1958); No. 2 (1965; Philadelphia, Dec. 16, 1970); No. 3 (1978); Concerto for Organ and Chamber Orch. (1963); *Sinfonia Seria* for Concert Band, Flute, and Baritone Horn (1965); Piano Concerto (1974). **CHAMBER:** Violin Sonata (1952); String Quartet for Amateurs (1959); Trio for Clarinet, Cello, and Piano (1959–60); 2 string quartets (1960, 1978); *Concert Duo* for Violin and Cello (1961); Duo for Saxophone and Trombone (1965); *Movement for 3* for Violin, Cello, and Piano (1967); *Serenade* for Percussion Ensemble (1967); 5 *Poems* for Oboe and 5 Brasses (1971). **PIANO:** 2 sonatas (1952, 1978); *Fantasia and Fugue* (1959); 30 *Ideas* (1972); 36 *More Ideas* (1976). **VOCAL:** numerous a cappella choruses, including choral settings of Western Pennsylvania folk songs (1958) and *A Pageant of Characters from William Shakespeare* for Chorus and Soloists (1964); songs.

Taylor, (Joseph) Deems, greatly popular American composer and writer on music; b. N.Y., Dec. 22, 1885; d. there, July 3, 1966. He graduated from N.Y. Univ. (B.A., 1906); studied harmony and counterpoint with Oscar Coon (1908–11). After doing editorial work for various publishers and serving as war correspondent for the *N.Y. Tribune* in France (1916–17), he was music critic for the *N.Y. World* (1921–25), ed. of *Musical America* (1927–29), and music critic for the *N.Y. American* (1931–32). He was an opera commentator for NBC (from 1931); was intermission commentator for the N.Y. Phil. national broadcasts (1936–43); also served as director (1933–66) and president (1942–48) of ASCAP. In 1924 he was elected a member of the National Inst. of Arts and Letters and in 1935 of the American Academy of Arts and Letters. In 1967 the ASCAP-Deems Taylor Award was created in his memory for honoring outstanding writings on music. Following the success of his orch. suite *Through the Looking-Glass*, after Lewis Carroll's tale (1923), he was commissioned by Walter Damrosch to compose a symphonic poem, *Jurgen* (1925). Meanwhile, 2 widely performed cantatas, *The Chambered Nautilus* and *The Highwayman*, had added to his growing reputation, which received a strong impetus when his opera *The King's Henchman* (libretto by Edna St. Vincent Millay), commissioned by the Metropolitan Opera, was produced in that house on Feb. 17, 1927. Receiving 14 performances in 3 seasons, it established a record for American opera at the Metropolitan Opera, but it was surpassed by Taylor's next opera, *Peter Ibbetson* (Feb. 7, 1931); this attained 16 performances in 4 seasons. These successes, however, proved ephemeral, and the operas were allowed to lapse into unmerited desuetude.

WORKS: STAGE: Operas: *The King's Henchman* (1926; N.Y., Feb. 17, 1927); *Peter Ibbetson* (1929–30; N.Y., Feb. 7, 1931); *Ramuntcho* (Philadelphia, Feb. 10, 1942); *The Dragon* (N.Y., Feb. 6, 1958); also a comic opera, *Cap'n Kidd & Co.* (1908), a musical play, *The Echo* (1909), an operetta, *The Breath of Scandal* (1916), and incidental music. **ORCH.:** *The Siren Song,* symphonic poem (1912; N.Y., July 18, 1922); *Through the Looking-Glass* for Chamber Orch. (1917–19; N.Y., Feb. 18, 1919; for Full Orch., 1921–22; N.Y., March 10, 1923);

Jurgen, symphonic poem (N.Y., Nov. 19, 1925; rev. 1926 and 1929); *Circus Day* for Jazz Orch. (1925; orchestrated by F. Grofé for Full Orch., 1933); *Marco Takes a Walk* (N.Y., Nov. 14, 1942); *A Christmas Overture* (N.Y., Dec. 23, 1943); *Elegy* (1944; Los Angeles, Jan. 4, 1945); *Restoration Suite* (Indianapolis, Nov. 18, 1950); also several chamber works, including *The Portrait of a Lady,* rhapsody for 10 Instruments (1919); piano pieces. **VOCAL:** *The Chambered Nautilus,* cantata for Chorus and Orch. (1914); *The Highwayman,* cantata for Baritone, Mixed Voices, and Orch. (1914); also solo songs and song cycles.

WRITINGS: *Of Men and Music* (N.Y., 1937); *The Well Tempered Listener* (N.Y., 1940); *Walt Disney's Fantasia* (N.Y., 1940); ed., *A Treasury of Gilbert and Sullivan* (N.Y., 1941); *Music to My Ears* (N.Y., 1949); *Some Enchanted Evenings: The Story of Rodgers and Hammerstein* (N.Y., 1953).

BIBL.: J. Howard, *D. T.* (N.Y., 1927; 2nd ed., 1940).

Taylor, Franklin, English pianist, organist, and teacher; b. Birmingham, Feb. 5, 1843; d. London, March 19, 1919. He was a pupil of C. Flavell (piano) and T. Bedsmore (organ); also studied (1859–61) at the Leipzig Cons.; received further piano training from Clara Schumann in Paris (1861). Returning to London in 1862, he established himself as a successful pianist and teacher; also was active as a church organist; taught at the National Training School for Music (from 1876); when it was incorporated into the Royal College of Music in 1882, he remained on its faculty and was prof. of piano until 1916. He ed. the series *Progressive Studies for the Pianoforte* (London, 1893–94); publ. *Primer of Pianoforte Playing* (London, 1877) and *Technique and Expression in Pianoforte Playing* (London, 1897).

BIBL.: T. Dunhill, "F. T.," *Musical Times,* XI (1899).

Taylor, James (Vernon), American singer and songwriter of popular music; b. Boston, March 12, 1948. He studied cello and learned to play folk guitar; at 17, he committed himself to Mclean Psychiatric Hospital in Belmont, Mass.; his 10-month experience there led him to write the song *Knockin' Round the Zoo.* In 1970 he scored a hit with his recording of the song *Fire and Rain;* however, he proved most successful in subsequent years recording songs by others, among them *You've Got a Friend* (1971), *How Sweet It Is to Be Loved by You* (1975), and *Handy Man* (1977); made a comeback in 1986 with the popular *That's Why I'm Here.* Taylor's own songs tend to reflect a contemplative, somewhat bitter view of the contemporary scene. In 1972 he married the singer and songwriter Carly Simon; they were divorced in 1982. His brother Livingston Taylor is also a singer and songwriter, whose career has been highlighted by the album *Livingston Taylor.* Another brother, Hugh, is a performer as well, and Taylor also has a sister, Kate, who appears with the family and in solo performances.

Taylor, Raynor, English-American singer, organist, teacher, and composer; b. London, 1747; d. Philadelphia, Aug. 17, 1825. He received his early training as a chorister in the Chapel Royal, and in 1765 became organist of a church in Chelmsford; that same year he was also appointed music director at Marylebone Gardens and at Sadler's Wells Theatre, London. In 1792 he emigrated to the U.S.; presented musical entertainments in Richmond, Va., Baltimore, and Annapolis, where he was organist at St. Anne's Church. Moving to Philadelphia in 1793, he was organist of St. Peter's Church (1795–1813); in 1820 he was one of the founders of the Musical Fund Society. A gifted singer, he gave humorous musical entertainments which he called "olios," and in 1796 conducted an orch. concert that included several of his own compositions. In collaboration with A. Reinagle, who had been his pupil in London, he composed a monody on the death of Washington (Philadelphia, Dec. 23, 1799), and a ballad opera, *Pizarro, or the Spaniards in Peru* (1800); some of his song MSS are in the N.Y. Public Library.

BIBL.: L. Madeira, *Annals of Music in Philadelphia and History of the Musical Fund Society from its Organization in 1820* *to the Year 1858* (Philadelphia, 1896); J. Cuthbert, *R. T. and Anglo-American Musical Life* (diss., West Virginia Univ., 1980); V. Yellin, "R. T.," *American Music*, i/3 (1983).

Tchaikovsky, Boris (Alexandrovich), Russian composer; b. Moscow, Sept. 10, 1925. He studied at the Moscow Cons. with Shostakovich, Shebalin, and Miaskovsky (1941–49). He is not related to Piotr Ilyich Tchaikovsky. His later works make use of expanded tonality.

WORKS: DRAMATIC: Opera, *The Star* (1949; unfinished); much music for films, radio, and plays. ORCH.: *Procession* (1946); 3 syms.: No. 1 (1947; Moscow, Feb. 7, 1962); No. 2 (Moscow, Oct. 17, 1967); No. 3, *Sevastopol* (1980; Moscow, Jan. 25, 1981); *Slavonic Rhapsody* (1951); *Sinfonietta* for Strings (1953); *Fantasia on Russian Folk Themes* (1954); *Capriccio on English Themes* (1954); Clarinet Concerto (1957); Overture (1957); Cello Concerto (1964); Chamber Sym. (Moscow, Oct. 27, 1967); Violin Concerto (1969; Moscow, April 25, 1970); Concerto for Piano, with 2 Horns, Side Drum, Bass Drum, and Strings (Kaunas, Oct. 17, 1971); *Theme and 8 Variations* (1973; Dresden, Jan. 23, 1974); *6 Studies* for Strings and Organ (1976; Leningrad, Jan. 30, 1979). VOCAL: *Signs of the Zodiac*, cantata for Soprano, Harpsichord, and Strings (1974; Leningrad, Jan. 29, 1976); *The Last Spring*, cycle for Mezzo-soprano, Flute, Clarinet, and Piano (1980); songs. CHAMBER: Piano Trio (1953); 6 string quartets (1954, 1961, 1967, 1972, 1974, 1976); String Trio (1955); Cello Sonata (1957); Violin Sonata (1959); Suite for Solo Cello (1960); Piano Quintet (1962); *Partita* for Cello and Chamber Ensemble (1966). PIANO: 2 sonatas (1944, 1952); Sonatina (1946); Sonata for 2 Pianos (1973).

Tchaikovsky, Modest, Russian playwright and librettist, brother of **Piotr Ilyich Tchaikovsky;** b. Alapaevsk, Perm district, May 13, 1850; d. Moscow, Jan. 15, 1916. He was the closest intimate of Tchaikovsky, and the author of the basic biography. His plays had only a passing success, but he was an excellent librettist; he wrote the librettos of Tchaikovsky's last 2 operas, *The Queen of Spades* and *Iolanthe*.

Tchaikovsky, Piotr Ilyich, famous Russian composer, brother of **Modest Tchaikovsky;** b. Votkinsk, Viatka district, May 7, 1840; d. St. Petersburg, Nov. 6, 1893. The son of a mining inspector at a plant in the Urals, he was given a good education; had a French governess and a music teacher. When he was 10, the family moved to St. Petersburg and he was sent to a school of jurisprudence, from which he graduated at 19, becoming a government clerk; while at school he studied music with Lomakin, but did not display conspicuous talent as either a pianist or composer. At the age of 21 he was accepted in a musical inst., newly established by Anton Rubinstein, which was to become the St. Petersburg Cons. He studied with Zaremba (harmony and counterpoint) and Rubinstein (composition); graduated in 1865, winning a silver medal for his cantata to Schiller's *Hymn to Joy.* In 1866 he became prof. of harmony at the Moscow Cons. As if to compensate for a late beginning in his profession, he began to compose with great application. His early works (a programmatic sym. subtitled *Winter Dreams*, some overtures and small pieces for string quartet) reveal little individuality. With his symphonic poem *Fatum* (1868) came the 1st formulation of his style, highly subjective, preferring minor modes, permeated with nostalgic longing and alive with keen rhythms. In 1869 he undertook the composition of his overture-fantasy *Romeo and Juliet;* not content with what he had written, he profited by the advice of Balakirev, whom he met in St. Petersburg, and revised the work in 1870; but this version proved equally unsatisfactory; Tchaikovsky laid the composition aside, and did not complete it until 1880; in its final form it became one of his most successful works. The Belgian soprano, Désirée Artôt, a member of an opera troupe visiting St. Petersburg in 1868, took great interest in Tchaikovsky, and he was moved by her attentions; for a few months he seriously contemplated marriage, and so notified his father (his mother had died of cholera when he was 14 years old). But this proved to be a

passing infatuation on her part, for soon she married the Spanish singer Padilla; Tchaikovsky reacted to this event with a casual philosophical remark about the inconstancy of human attachments. Throughout his career Tchaikovsky never allowed his psychological turmoil to interfere with his work. Besides teaching and composing, he contributed music criticism to Moscow newspapers for several years (1868–74), made altogether 26 trips abroad (to Paris, Berlin, Vienna, N.Y.), and visited the 1st Bayreuth Festival in 1876, reporting his impressions for the Moscow daily *Russkyie Vedomosti*. His closest friends were members of his own family, his brothers (particularly Modest, his future biographer), and his married sister Alexandra Davidov, at whose estate, Kamenka, he spent most of his summers. The correspondence with them, all of which was preserved and eventually publ., throws a true light on Tchaikovsky's character and his life. His other close friends were his publisher, Jurgenson, Nikolai Rubinstein, and several other musicians. The most extraordinary of his friendships was the epistolary association with Nadezhda von Meck, a wealthy widow whom he never met but who was to play an important role in his life. Through the violinist Kotek she learned about Tchaikovsky's financial difficulties, and commissioned him to write some compositions, at large fees; then arranged to pay him an annuity of 6,000 rubles. For more than 13 years they corresponded voluminously, even when they lived in the same city (Moscow, Florence); on several occasions she hinted that she would not be averse to a personal meeting, but Tchaikovsky invariably declined such a suggestion, under the pretext that one should not see one's guardian angel in the flesh. On Tchaikovsky's part, this correspondence had to remain within the circumscribed domain of art, personal philosophy, and reporting of daily events, without touching on the basic problems of his existence. On July 18, 1877, he contracted marriage with a conservatory student, Antonina Milyukova, who had declared her love for him. This was an act of defiance of his own nature; Tchaikovsky was a homosexual, and made no secret of it in the correspondence with his brother Modest, who was also a homosexual. He thought that by flaunting a wife he could prevent the already rife rumors about his sexual preference from spreading further. The result was disastrous, and Tchaikovsky fled from his wife in horror. He attempted suicide by walking into the Moskva River in order to catch pneumonia, but suffered nothing more severe than simple discomfort. He then went to St. Petersburg to seek the advice of his brother Anatol, a lawyer, who made suitable arrangements with Tchaikovsky's wife for a separation. (They were never divorced; she died in an insane asylum in 1917.) Von Meck, to whom Tchaikovsky wrote candidly of the hopeless failure of his marriage (without revealing the true cause of that failure), made at once an offer of further financial assistance, which he gratefully accepted. He spent several months during 1877–78 in Italy, Switzerland, Paris, and Vienna. During these months he completed one of his greatest works, the 4th Sym., dedicated to von Meck. It was performed for the 1st time in Moscow on Feb. 22, 1878, but Tchaikovsky did not cut short his sojourn abroad to attend the performance. He resigned from the Moscow Cons. in the autumn of 1878, and from that time dedicated himself entirely to composition. The continued subsidy from von Meck allowed him to forget money matters. Early in 1878 he completed his most successful opera, *Evgeny Onegin* ("lyric scenes," after Pushkin); it was 1st produced in Moscow by a cons. ensemble, on March 29, 1879, and gained success only gradually; the 1st performance at the Imperial Opera in St. Petersburg did not take place until Oct. 31, 1884. A morbid depression was still Tchaikovsky's natural state of mind, but every new work sustained his faith in his destiny as a composer, despite many disheartening reversals. His Piano Concerto No. 1, rejected by Nikolai Rubinstein as unplayable, was given its world premiere (somewhat incongruously) in Boston, on Oct. 25, 1875, played by Hans von Bülow, and afterward was performed all over the world by famous pianists, including Nikolai Rubinstein. The Violin Concerto, criticized by Leopold Auer (to whom the score was originally dedicated) and attacked by Hanslick with sarcasm and virulence at its world premiere by Brodsky in Vienna (1881), survived all its detractors to become one of the most celebrated pieces in the violin repertoire. The 5th Sym. (1888) was successful from the very first. Early in 1890 Tchaikovsky wrote his 2nd important opera, *The Queen of Spades*, which was produced at the Imperial Opera in St. Petersburg in that year. His ballets *Swan Lake* (1876) and *The Sleeping Beauty* (1889) became famous on Russian stages. But at the peak of his career, Tchaikovsky suffered a severe psychological blow; von Meck notified him of the discontinuance of her subsidy, and with this announcement she abruptly terminated their correspondence. He could now well afford the loss of the money, but his pride was deeply hurt by the manner in which von Meck had acted. It is indicative of Tchaikovsky's inner strength that even this desertion of one whom he regarded as his staunchest friend did not affect his ability to work. In 1891 he undertook his only voyage to America. He was received with honors as a celebrated composer; he led 4 concerts of his works in N.Y. and one each in Baltimore and Philadelphia. He did not linger in the U.S., however, and returned to St. Petersburg in a few weeks. Early in 1892 he made a concert tour as a conductor in Russia, and then proceeded to Warsaw and Germany. In the meantime he had purchased a house in the town of Klin, not far from Moscow, where he wrote his last sym., the *Pathétique*. Despite the perfection of his technique, he did not arrive at the desired form and substance of this work at once, and discarded his original sketch. The title *Pathétique* was suggested to him by his brother Modest; the score was dedicated to his nephew, Vladimir Davidov. Its music is the final testament of Tchaikovsky's life, and an epitome of his philosophy of fatalism. In the 1st movement, the trombones are given the theme of the Russian service for the dead. Remarkably, the score of one of his gayest works, the ballet *The Nutcracker*, was composed simultaneously with the early sketches for the *Pathétique*. Tchaikovsky was in good spirits when he went to St. Petersburg to conduct the premiere of the *Pathétique*, on Oct. 28, 1893 (which was but moderately successful). A cholera epidemic was then raging in St. Petersburg, and the population was specifically warned against drinking unboiled water, but apparently he carelessly did exactly that. He showed the symptoms of cholera soon afterward, and nothing could be done to save him. The melodramatic hypothesis that the fatal drink of water was a defiance of death, in perfect knowledge of the danger, since he must have remembered his mother's death of the same dread infection, is untenable in the light of publ. private letters between the attendant physician and Modest Tchaikovsky at the time. Tchaikovsky's fatalism alone would amply account for his lack of precaution. Almost immediately after his death a rumor spread that he had committed suicide, and reports to that effect were publ. in respectable European newspapers (but not in Russian publications), and repeated even in some biographical dictionaries (particularly in Britain). After the grim fantasy seemed definitely refuted, a ludicrous paper by an émigré Russian woman was publ., claiming private knowledge of a homosexual scandal involving a Russian nobleman's nephew (in another version a member of the Romanov imperial family) which led to a "trial" of Tchaikovsky by a jury of his former school classmates, who offered Tchaikovsky a choice between honorable suicide or disgrace and possible exile to Siberia; a family council, with Tchaikovsky's own participation, advised the former solution, and Tchaikovsky was supplied with arsenic; the family doctor was supposed to be a part of the conspiracy, as were Tchaikovsky's own brothers. Amazingly enough, this outrageous fabrication was accepted as historical fact by some biographers, and even found its way into the pages of *The New Grove Dictionary of Music and Musicians* (1980). In Russia, the truth of Tchaikovsky's homosexuality was totally suppressed, and any references to it in his diary and letters were expunged.

As a composer, Tchaikovsky stands apart from the militant national movement of the "Mighty Five." The Russian element is, of course, very strong in his music, and upon occasion he made use of Russian folk songs in his works, but this national spirit is instinctive rather than consciously cultivated. His personal relationship with the St. Petersburg group of nationalists was friendly without being close; his correspondence with Rimsky-Korsakov, Balakirev, and others was mostly concerned with professional matters. Tchaikovsky's music was frankly sentimental; his supreme gift of melody, which none of his Russian contemporaries could match, secured for him a lasting popularity among performers and audiences. His influence was profound on the Moscow group of musicians, of whom Arensky and Rachmaninoff were the most talented. He wrote in every genre, and was successful in each; besides his stage works, syms., chamber music, and piano compositions, he composed a great number of lyric songs that are the most poignant creations of his genius. By a historical paradox, Tchaikovsky became the most popular Russian composer under the Soviet regime. His subjectivism, his fatalism, his emphasis on melancholy moods, even his reactionary political views (which included a brand of amateurish anti-Semitism), failed to detract from his stature in the new society. In fact, official spokesmen of Soviet Russia repeatedly urged Soviet composers to follow in the path of Tchaikovsky's aesthetics. His popularity is also very strong in Anglo-Saxon countries, particularly in America; much less so in France and Italy; in Germany his influence is insignificant.

WORKS: STAGE: OPERAS: *Voyevoda*, op. 3 (1867–68; Moscow, Feb. 11, 1869; destroyed by Tchaikovsky; reconstructed by Pavel Lamm); *Undine* (destroyed by Tchaikovsky; only fragments extant); *Oprichnik* (1870–72; St. Petersburg, April 24, 1874); *Kuznets Vakula* (Vakula the Smith; 1874; St. Petersburg, Dec. 6, 1876); *Evgeny Onegin* (1877–78; Moscow, March, 29, 1879); *Orleanskaya deva* (The Maid of Orleans; 1878–79; St. Petersburg, Feb. 25, 1881; rev. 1882); *Mazepa* (1881–83; Moscow, Feb. 15, 1884); *Cherevichki* (The Little Shoes; 1885; Moscow, Jan. 31, 1887; rev. version of *Kuznets Vakula*); *Charodeyka* (The Sorceress; 1885–87; St. Petersburg, Nov. 1, 1887); *Pikovaya dama* (The Queen of Spades), op. 68 (St. Petersburg, Dec. 19, 1890); *Iolanta*, op. 69 (1891; St. Petersburg, Dec. 18, 1892). **BALLETS:** *Lebedinoye ozero* (Swan Lake), op. 20 (1875–76; Moscow, March 4, 1877); *Spyashchaya krasavitsa* (The Sleeping Beauty), op. 66 (1888–89; St. Petersburg, Jan. 15, 1890); *Shchelkunchik* (The Nutcracker), op. 71 (1891–92; St. Petersburg, Dec. 18, 1892).

ORCH.: 6 numbered syms.: No. 1, op. 13, *Winter Dreams* (1st and 2nd versions, 1866; 2nd version, Moscow, Feb. 15, 1868; 3rd version, 1874; Moscow, Dec. 1, 1883); No. 2, op. 17, *Little Russian* or *Ukrainian* (1st version, 1872; Moscow, Feb. 7, 1873; 2nd version, 1879–80; St. Petersburg, Feb. 12, 1881); No. 3, op. 29, *Polish* (Moscow, Nov. 19, 1875); No. 4, op. 36 (1877–78; Moscow, Feb. 22, 1878); No. 5, op. 64 (St. Petersburg, Nov. 17, 1888); No. 6, op. 74, *Pathétique* (St. Petersburg, Oct. 28, 1893); also *Manfred Symphony*, op. 58 (1885; Moscow, March 23, 1886) and Sym. in E-flat Major (1892; unfinished; sketches utilized in Piano Concerto No. 3, op. 75, and in *Andante and Finale* for Piano and Orch., op. 79; sym. reconstructed and finished in 1957 by S. Bogatyrev, and publ. as Sym. No. 7); *Allegro ma non tanto* for Strings (1863–64); *Little Allegro* for 2 Flutes and Strings (1863–64); *Andante ma non troppo* for Small Orch. (1863–64); *Agitato and Allegro* for Small Orch. (1863–64); *Allegro vivo* (1863–64); *The Romans in the Coliseum* (1863–64; not extant); *Groza* (The Storm), overture to Ostrovsky's play, op. 76 (1864; St. Petersburg, March 7, 1896); Overture (1st version for Small Orch., 1865; St. Petersburg, Nov. 26, 1865; 2nd version for Large Orch., 1866; Moscow, March 16, 1866); Concerto Overture (1865–66; Voronezh, 1931); *Festival Overture* on the Danish national anthem, op. 15 (1866; Moscow, Feb. 11, 1867; *Fatum*, symphonic poem, op. 77 (1868; Moscow, Feb. 27, 1869; destroyed by Tchaikovsky; reconstructed, 1896); *Romeo and Juliet*, fantasy overture (1st version, 1869; Moscow, March 16, 1870; 2nd version, 1870; St. Petersburg, Feb. 17, 1872; 3rd version, 1880; Tiflis, May 1, 1886); *Serenade for Nikolai Rubinstein's*

Name Day for Small Orch. (Moscow, Dec. 18, 1872); *Burya* (The Tempest), symphonic fantasia, op. 18 (Moscow, Dec. 19, 1873); Piano Concerto No. 1, op. 23 (Boston, Oct. 25, 1875); *Sérénade mélancolique* for Violin with Orch., op. 26 (1875; Moscow, Jan. 28, 1876); *Slavonic March*, op. 31 (Moscow, Nov. 17, 1876); *Francesca da Rimini*, symphonic fantasia, op. 32, after Dante (1876; Moscow, March 9, 1877); *Variations on a Rococo Theme* for Cello and Orch., op. 33 (1876; Moscow, Nov. 30, 1877); *Valse-Scherzo* for Violin and Orch., op. 34 (1877; Paris, Sept. 20, 1878); Violin Concerto, op. 35 (1878; Vienna, Dec. 4, 1881); Suite No. 1, op. 43 (Moscow, Nov. 23, 1879); Piano Concerto No. 2, op. 44 (1879–80; N.Y., Nov. 11 [public rehearsal], Nov. 12 [official premiere], 1881); *Italian Capriccio*, op. 45 (Moscow, Dec. 18, 1880); *Serenade* for Strings, op. 48 (1880; St. Petersburg, Oct. 30, 1881); *1812 Overture*, op. 49 (1880; Moscow, Aug. 20, 1882); *Festival Coronation March* (Moscow, June 4, 1883); Suite No. 2, op. 53 (1883; Moscow, Feb. 16, 1884); Suite No. 3, op. 55 (1884; St. Petersburg, Jan. 28, 1885); Concert Fantasia for Piano and Orch., op. 56 (1884; Moscow, March 6, 1885); *Elegy* for Strings (Moscow, Dec. 28, 1884); *Jurists' March* (1885); Suite No. 4, op. 61, *Mozartiana* (Moscow, Nov. 26, 1887); *Pezzo capriccioso* for Cello with Orch., op. 62 (1887; Moscow, Dec. 7, 1889); *Hamlet*, fantasy overture, op. 67 (St. Petersburg, Nov. 24, 1888); *Voyevoda*, symphonic ballad, op. 78 (Moscow, Nov. 18, 1891); *Shchelkunchik* (The Nutcracker), suite from the ballet, op. 71a (St. Petersburg, March 19, 1892); Piano Concerto No. 3, op. 75 (1893; St. Petersburg, Jan. 19, 1895); *Andante and Finale* for Piano and Orch., op. 79 (1893; unfinished; finished and orchestrated by Taneyev; St. Petersburg, Feb. 20, 1896).

CHAMBER: 3 string quartets: No. 1, op. 11 (1871); No. 2, op. 22 (1874); No. 3, op. 30 (1876); Piano Trio, op. 50 (Moscow, Oct. 30, 1882); *Adagio* for 4 Horns (1863–64); Adagio for 2 Flutes, 2 Oboes, 2 Clarinets, English Horn, and Bass Clarinet (1863–64); *Adagio molto* for String Quartet and Harp (1863–64); *Allegretto* for String Quartet (1863–64); *Allegretto molto* for String Trio (1863–64); *Allegro* for Piano Sextet (1863–64); *Allegro vivace* for String Quartet (1863–64); *Andante ma non troppo*, prelude for String Quartet (1863–64); *Andante molto* for String Quartet (1863–64); String Quartet (1865; 1 movement only); *Souvenir d'un lieu cher* for Violin and Piano, op. 42 (1878); *Souvenir de Florence* for String Sextet, op. 70 (1890; rev. 1891–92; St. Petersburg, Dec. 7, 1892)).

PIANO: *Allegro* (1863–64; unfinished); *Theme and Variations* (1863–64); Sonata, op. 80 (1865); 2 pieces, op. 1 (1867); *Souvenir de Hapsal*, op. 2 (1867); *Valse caprice*, op. 4 (1868); *Romance*, op. 5 (1868); *Valse-Scherzo*, op. 7 (1870); *Capriccio*, op. 8 (1870); *Trois morceaux*, op. 9 (1870); *Deux morceaux*, op. 10 (1871); *6 morceaux*, op. 19 (1873); *6 morceaux, composés sur un seul thème*, op. 21 (1873); *Les Quatre Saisons*, 12 characteristic pieces for each month of the year (1875–76); *March for the Volunteer Fleet* (1878); *Album pour enfants: 24 pièces faciles (à la Schumann)*, op. 39 (1878); *Douze morceaux (difficulté moyenne)*, op. 40 (1878); Sonata, op. 37 (1878); *6 morceaux*, op. 51 (1882); *Impromptu-Caprice* (1884); *Dumka: Russian Rustic Scene*, op. 59 (1886); *Valse-Scherzo* (1889); *Impromptu* (1889); *Aveu passioni* (c.1892); Military march (1893); *Dix-huit morceaux*, op. 72 (1893); *Impromptu (Momento lirico)* (c.1893; unfinished; finished by Taneyev).

VOCAL: CHORAL: *K radosti* (Ode to Joy), cantata for Soloists, Chorus, and Orch. (1865; St. Petersburg, Jan. 10, 1866); Cantata for the bicentenary of the birth of Peter the Great for Tenor, Chorus, and Orch. (Moscow, June 12, 1872); Cantata for Tenor, Chorus, and Orch. (1875; St. Petersburg, May 6, 1876); *Liturgy of St. John Chrysostom* for Unaccompanied Chorus, op. 41 (1878); Vesper Service for Unaccompanied Chorus, op. 52 (1881–82); *Moskva* (Moscow), coronation cantata for Soloists, Chorus, and Orch. (Moscow, May 27, 1883); 9 sacred pieces for Unaccompanied Mixed Chorus (1884–85); Hymn in honor of Saints Cyril and Methodius for Unaccompanied Chorus (Moscow, April 18, 1885); *Legenda* for Unaccompanied Chorus, op. 54/5 (1889); etc.; also about 100 songs, among

them such favorites as *Nur wer die Sehnsucht kennt* (after Goethe) and *Berceuse.*

BIBL.: COLLECTED WORKS, SOURCE MATERIAL: An exhaustive ed. of his compositions was publ. in Moscow and Leningrad (1940–71). His diaries for the years 1873–91 were publ. in Moscow and Petrograd (1923; Eng. tr., 1945). He wrote a treatise which was publ. in an Eng. tr. as *Guide to the Practical Study of Harmony* (Leipzig, 1900). A complete ed. of his literary works and correspondence commenced publ. in Moscow in 1953.

BIOGRAPHICAL, ANALYTICAL, AND CRITICAL: H. Laroche, *Na pamyat o P.I. T.* (In Memory of P.I. T.; St. Petersburg, 1894); idem, *Pamyati T.* (Memories of T.; St. Petersburg, 1894); V. Baskin, *P.I. T.* (St. Petersburg, 1895); R. Newmarch, *T.: His Life and Works* (London, 1900); M. Tchaikovsky, *Zhizn P.I. T.* (The Life of P.I. T.; 3 vols., Moscow, 1900–2; abr. Eng. tr. by R. Newmarch as *The Life and Letters of P.I. T.*, London, 1906); E. Evans, *T.* (London, 1906; 2nd ed., rev., 1935); A. Tchaikovskaya, "Vospominaniya vdovi P.I. T.," (Reminiscences of T.'s Widow), *Russkaya Musikalnaya Gazeta* (1913); I. Glebov, *P.I. T.: evo zhizn i tvorchestvo* (P.I. T.: Life and Works; Petrograd, 1922); idem, *Instrumentalnoye tvorchestvo T.* (The Instrumental Works of T.; Petrograd, 1922); idem, *T.: opit kharakteristiki* (T: An Attempt at a Characterization; Petrograd, 1923); E. Blom, "The Early T. Symphonies," *The Stepchildren of Music* (London, 1925); idem, *T.: Orchestral Works* (London, 1927); N. Findeisen, *Kamernaya muzika T.* (T.'s Chamber Music; Moscow, 1930); G. Abraham and M.D. Calvocoressi, *Masters of Russian Music* (London, 1936; includes G. Abraham, "T."; rev. and publ. separately as *T.: A Short Biography*, 1944); J. Westrup, "T. and the Symphony," *Musical Times*, LXXXI (1940); G. Abraham, ed., *T.: A Symposium* (London, 1945); H. Weinstock, *T.* (N.Y., 1946); D. Shostakovich et al., *Russian Symphony: Thoughts About T.* (N.Y., 1947); B. Yarustovsky, *Opernaya dramaturgiya T.* (T.'s Operatic Dramatury; Moscow and Leningrad, 1947); E. Orlova, *Romansi T.* (T's Songs; Moscow and Leningrad, 1948); A. Nikolayev, *Fortepiaovye naslediye T.* (T.'s Piano Legacy; Moscow and Leningrad, 1949; 2nd ed., 1958); D. Zhitmorsky, *Baleti P. T.* (P. T.'s Ballets; Moscow and Leningrad, 1950; 2nd ed., 1958); A. Nikolayev, *Fortepiannoye proizvedeniya P.I. T.* (P.I. T.'s Piano Works; Moscow, 1957); V. Protopopov and N. Tumanina, *Opernoye tvorchestvo T.* (T.'s Operas; Moscow, 1957); N. Nikolayeva, *Simfonii P.I. T.* (P.I. T.'s Symphonies; Moscow, 1958); L. Raaben, *Skripichniye i violonchel niye proizvedeniya P.I. T.* (P.I. T.'s Violin and Cello Works; Moscow, 1958); A. Alshvang, *P.I. T.* (Moscow, 1959); A. Dolzhansky, *Simfonicheskaya muzika T.* (T.'s Symphonic Music; Moscow, 1961; 2nd ed., 1965); G. Krauklis, *Skripichniye proizvedeniya P.I. T.* (P.I. T.'s Violin Works; Moscow, 1961); N. Tumanina, *T.* (Moscow, 1962–68); A. Alshvang, *P.I. T.* (Moscow, 1967); J. Warrack, *T: Symphonies and Concertos* (London, 1969); E. Garden, *T.* (London, 1973; 2nd ed., rev., 1984); J. Warrack, *T.* (London, 1973); V. Volkoff, *T.* (Boston and London, 1974); D. Brown, *T.: A Biographical and Critical Study;* Vol. I: *The Early Years (1840–1874)* (London, 1978); Vol. II: *The Crisis Years (1874–1878)* (London, 1982); Vol. III: *The Years of Wandering (1878–1885)* (London, 1986); J. Warrack, *T. Ballet Music* (London, 1979); A. Orlova, "T.: the Last Chapter," *Music & Letters* (April 1981); W. Strutte, *T.* (Sydney, 1983); D. Brown, "T.'s Mazeppa," *Musical Times* (Dec. 1984); R. Wiley, "The Symphonic Element in Nutcracker," ibid.; idem, *T.'s Ballets* (Oxford, 1985); E. Yoffe, *T. in America: The Composer's Visit to Celebrate the Opening of Carnegie Hall in New York City* (N.Y., 1986); H. Zajaczkowski, *T.'s Musical Style* (Ann Arbor, 1987); N. John, ed., *T.: Eugene Onegin* (London, 1988); A. Kendall, *T.: A Biography* (London, 1988); A. Orlova, *T. Day by Day: A Biography in Documents* (ed. by M. Brown and tr. by F. Jonas; Ann Arbor, 1988).

Tchaikowsky, André, Polish pianist and composer; b. Warsaw, Nov. 1, 1935; d. Oxford, June 26, 1982. Most of his family fell victim to the Nazis, but he and his grandmother were hidden by a Catholic family in Warsaw (1942–45). After the liberation, he studied piano at the Lodz State Music School (1945–47) and with Emma Tekla Altberg at the Warsaw Cons. (1947–48); then took an advanced piano course with Lazare Lévy at the Paris Cons. (premier prix, 1950); subsequently studied piano with Stanislaw Szpinalski and composition with Kazimierz Sikorski at the Warsaw Cons. (1950–55); made his debut as a pianist in 1955. He went to Paris to study composition with Nadia Boulanger (1957), and then to England to continue his studies with Thea Musgrave and later with Hans Keller. Although he continued to make appearances as a pianist, he gave increasing attention to his work as a composer from 1960. An eccentric to the end, he bequeathed his skull to the Royal Shakespeare Co. for use in the graveside scene in *Hamlet* ("Alas, poor André, A fellow of infinite jest"); it made its debut in 1984.

WORKS: OPERA: *The Merchant of Venice* (1960–82). **ORCH.:** Violin Concerto (1950); Flute Concerto (1950); 2 piano concertos (1953, 1971); Clarinet Concerto (1953); Sym. (1958). **CHAMBER:** Sonata for Viola and Clarinet (1954); *Concerto classico* for Violin (1957); Clarinet Sonata (1959); Octet (1961); 2 string quartets (1967, 1975); *Trio notturno* (1978); vocal works; piano pieces.

BIBL.: D. Ferré, "A Note on A. T.," *Musical Times* (Nov. 1985).

Tchakarov, Emil, Bulgarian conductor; b. Burgas, June 29, 1948. He studied at the Bulgarian State Cons. in Sofia, where he conducted the youth orch. (1965–72); then directed the Bulgarian Television Chamber Orch. (1968–70). In 1971 he won 3rd prize at the Karajan Competition; in 1972 he studied conducting with Franco Ferrara and in 1974 with Eugen Jochum. While still in his 20s he filled engagements as a guest conductor all over the world. In 1974 he was appointed permanent conductor of the State Phil. in Plovdiv. He made his debut at the Metropolitan Opera in N.Y. on Sept. 27, 1979. In 1985–86 he was chief conductor of the Flanders Phil. in Antwerp.

Tcherepnin, Alexander (Nikolaievich), distinguished Russian-born American pianist, conductor, and composer, son of **Nikolai (Nikolaievich)** and father of **Serge (Alexandrovich)** and **Ivan (Alexandrovich) Tcherepnin;** b. St. Petersburg, Jan. 20, 1899; d. Paris, Sept. 29, 1977. (The name is pronounced with the stress on the last syllable.) He studied piano as a child with his mother; was encouraged by his father in his 1st steps in composition, but did not take formal lessons with him. He composed a short comic opera when he was 12, and a ballet when he was 13; then produced a number of piano works; composed 14 piano sonatas before he was 19. In 1917 he entered the Petrograd Cons., where he studied music theory with Sokolov, and piano with Kobiliansky, but remained there only one school year; then joined his parents in a difficult journey to Tiflis during the Civil War; he took lessons in composition there with Thomas de Hartmann. In 1921 the family went to Paris, where he continued his studies, taking piano lessons with Isidor Philipp and composition with Paul Vidal. In 1922 he played a concert of his own music in London; in 1923 he was commissioned by Anna Pavlova to write a ballet, *Ajanta's Frescoes,* which she produced in London with her troupe. Tcherepnin progressed rapidly in his career as a pianist and a composer; he played in Germany and Austria; made his 1st American tour in 1926. Between 1934 and 1937 he made two journeys to the Far East; gave concerts in China and Japan; numerous Chinese and Japanese composers studied with him; he organized a publishing enterprise in Tokyo for the publication of serious works by young Japanese and Chinese composers. He married a Chinese pianist, Lee Hsien-Ming. Despite his wide travels, he maintained his principal residence in Paris, and remained there during World War II. He resumed his concert career in 1947; toured the U.S. in 1948. In 1949 he and his wife joined the faculty of De Paul Univ. in Chicago, and taught there for 15 years. In the meantime his music became well known; he appeared as a soloist in his piano concertos with orchs. in the U.S. and Europe.

He became a U.S. citizen in 1958. In 1967 he made his 1st visit to Russia after nearly a half century abroad. He was elected a member of the National Inst. of Arts and Letters in 1974. In his early works he followed the traditions of Russian Romantic music; characteristically, his Piano Sonata No. 13, which he wrote as a youth, is entitled *Sonatine romantique.* But as he progressed in his career, he evolved a musical language all his own; he derived his melodic patterns from a symmetrically formed scale of 9 degrees, subdivided into 3 equal sections (e.g. C, D, E-flat, E, F-sharp, G, G-sharp, A-sharp, B, C); the harmonic idiom follows a similar intertonal formation; his consistent use of such thematic groupings anticipated the serial method of composition. Furthermore, he developed a type of rhythmic polyphony, based on thematic rhythmic units, which he termed "interpunctus." However, he did not limit himself to these melodic and rhythmic constructions; he also explored the latent resources of folk music, both oriental and European; he was particularly sensitive to the melorhythms of Russian national songs. A composer of remarkable inventive power, he understood the necessity of creating a communicative musical language, and was primarily concerned with enhancing the lyric and dramatic qualities of his music. At the same time he showed great interest in new musical resources, including electronic sound.

WORKS: DRAMATIC: OPERAS: *Ol-Ol* (1925; Weimar, Jan. 31, 1928; rev. 1930); *Die Hochzeit der Sobeide* (1930; Vienna, March 17, 1933); *The Farmer and the Nymph* (Aspen, Colo., Aug. 13, 1952). **BALLETS:** *Ajanta's Frescoes* (London, Sept. 10, 1923); *Training* (Vienna, June 19, 1935); *Der fahrende Schüler mit dem Teufelsbannen* (1937; score lost during World War II; reconstructed, 1965); *Trepak* (Richmond, Va., Oct. 10, 1938); *La Légende de Razine* (1941); *Le Déjeuner sur l'herbe* (Paris, Oct. 14, 1945); *L'Homme à la peau de léopard* (with Arthur Honegger and Tibor Harsányi; Monte Carlo, May 5, 1946); *La Colline des fantômes* (1946); *Jardin persan* (1946); *Nuit kurde* (Paris, 1946); *La Femme et son ombre* (Paris, June 14, 1948); *Aux temps des tartares* (Buenos Aires, 1949); *Le gouffre* (1953). **CANTATAS:** *Vivre d'amour* (1942); *Pan Kéou* (Paris, Oct. 9, 1945); *Le Jeu de la Nativité* (Paris, Dec. 30, 1945); *Les Douze* for Narrator, Strings, Harp, Piano, and Percussion (Paris, Nov. 9, 1947); *Vom Spass und Ernst,* folk-song cantata for Voice and Strings (1964); *The Story of Ivan the Fool,* with Narrator (London, Dec. 24, 1968); *Baptism Cantata* for Chorus and Orch. (1972). **ORCH.:** 6 piano concertos: No. 1 (1919–20; Monte Carlo, 1923); No. 2 (1923; Paris, Jan. 26, 1924); No. 3 (1931–32; Paris, Feb. 5, 1933); No. 4 (1947; retitled *Fantasia*); No. 5 (Berlin, Oct. 13, 1963); No. 6 (1965; Lucerne, Sept. 5, 1972); Overture (1921); *Rhapsodie georgienne* for Cello and Orch. (1922); *Concerto da camera* for Flute, Violin, and Chamber Orch. (1924); 4 syms.: No. 1 (Paris, Oct. 29, 1927); No. 2 (1947–51; Chicago, March 20, 1952); No. 3 (1952; Indianapolis, Jan. 15, 1955); No. 4 (1957; Boston, Dec. 5, 1958); *Mystère* for Cello and Chamber Orch. (Monte Carlo, Dec. 8, 1926); *Magna mater* (1926–27; Munich, Oct. 30, 1930); *Concertino* for Violin, Cello, Piano, and Strings (1931); *Russian Dances* (Omaha, Feb. 15, 1934); *Suite georgienne* for Piano and Strings (1938; Paris, April 17, 1940); *Evocation* (1948); Harmonica Concerto (1953; Venice, Sept. 11, 1956); *Suite* (1953; Louisville, May 1, 1954); *Divertimento* (Chicago, Nov. 14, 1957); *Symphony-Prayer* (1959; Chicago, Aug. 19, 1960); *Serenade* for String Orch. (1964); *Russian Sketches* (1971); *Musica sacra* for String Orch. (Lourdes, April 28, 1973). **CHAMBER:** *Ode* for Cello and Piano (1919); 2 string quartets (1922, 1926); Violin Sonata (1922); 3 cello sonatas (1924, 1925, 1926); Piano Trio (1925); Piano Quintet (1927); *Elegy* for Violin and Piano (1927); *Le Violoncelle bien tempéré,* 12 preludes for Cello with Piano, 2 of them with a Drum (Berlin, March 23, 1927); *Mouvement perpétuel* for Violin and Piano (1935); Sonatina for Kettledrums and Piano (1939); *Sonatine sportive,* for Bassoon or Saxophone, and Piano (1939); *Andante* for Tuba and Piano (1939); Trio for Flutes (1939); Quartet for Flutes (1939); *Marche* for 3 Trumpets (1939); *Suite* for Solo Cello (1946); *Sonata da chiesa* for Viola da Gamba and Organ (1966); Quintet

for 2 Trumpets, Horn, Trombone, and Tuba (1972); Woodwind Quintet (1976); Duo for 2 Flutes (1977). **PIANO:** *Scherzo* (1917); *10 bagatelles* (1913–18); *Sonatine romantique* (1918); *2 sonatas* (1918, 1961); *Toccata* (1921); *Feuilles libres* (1920–24); *5 arabesques* (1921); *9 inventions* (1921); *2 novelettes* (1922); *4 préludes nostalgiques* (1922); *6 études de travail* (1923); *Message* (1926); *Entretiens* (1930); *Etudes de piano sur la gamme pentatonique* (1935); *Autour des montagnes russes* (1937); *Badinage* (1942); *Le Monde en vitrine* (1946); *12 Preludes* (1952); *8 Pieces* (1954); also *Suite* for Harpsichord (1966). **VOCAL:** *Lost Flute*, 7 songs on poems tr. from the Chinese, for Narrator and Piano (1954); several albums of songs to poems in Russian, French, and Chinese.
    BIBL.: W. Reich, *A. Tscherepnine* (Bonn, 1959; 2nd ed., rev., 1970); N. Slonimsky, "Al. T., Septuagenarian," *Tempo* (Jan. 1969); C.-J. Chang, *A. T., His Influence on Modern Chinese Music* (diss., Columbia Univ. Teachers College, 1983); P. Ramey, "A. T.," *Ovation* (May 1984); E. Arias, *A. T.: A Bio-Bibliography* (Westport, Conn., 1988).

Tcherepnin, Ivan (Alexandrovich), French-born American composer of Russian descent, son of **Alexander (Nikolaievich)** and brother of **Serge (Alexandrovich) Tcherepnin;** b. Issy-les-Moulineaux, near Paris, Feb. 5, 1943. He studied composition with his father at home and at the Académie Internationale de Musique in Nice; also had piano lessons with his mother. He went to the U.S. and became a naturalized citizen (1960); continued his studies with Randall Thompson and Leon Kirchner at Harvard Univ. (B.A., 1964; M.A., 1969); received the John Knowles Paine Travelling Fellowship to pursue training in electronic music with Stockhausen and Pousseur in Cologne and in conducting with Boulez (1965); likewise studied electronic techniques in Toronto (1966). He taught at the San Francisco Cons. and at Stanford Univ. (1969–72), where he served as co-director, with Chowning, of its new-music ensemble, Alea II; then was associate prof. and director of the electronic music studio at Harvard Univ. (from 1972). In 1989 he traveled to China, where he performed and gave lectures in Shanghai and Beijing. From 1984 his work has been evenly divided between electronic and instrumental pieces; his *Rhythmantics* series uses digital sampling techniques and temporal displacement to explore areas of rhythmic pattern formation. His instrumental works, generally more referential, draw on musical resources ranging from gagaku and gamelan to Western tonal structures.
    WORKS: ORCH.: *Le Va et le vient* (1978); Concerto for Oboe and Orch., or Wind Orch. (1980; rev. 1988); *New Consonance* for String Orch. (1983); *Solstice* for Chamber Orch. (1983); *Status* for Wind Orch. (1986); *Constitution* for Narrator and Wind Orch. (1987); *Concerto for 2 Continents* for Synthesizer and Wind Orch. (1989). **CHAMBER:** *Suite progressive* for Flute, Cello, and Timpani (1959); *Deux entourages pour un thème russe* for Horn or Ondes Martenot, Piano, and Percussion (1961); *Suite Mozartienne* for Flute, Clarinet, and Bassoon (1962); *Cadenzas in Transition* for Clarinet, Flute, and Piano (1963); *Sombres lumières* for Flute, Guitar, and Cello (1965); *Wheelwinds* for 9 Wind Instruments (1966); *Explorations* for Flute, Clarinet, String Trio, Piano, and Optional Live Electronics (1985); *Trio Fantasia* for Violin, Cello, and Piano (1985). **PIANO:** *4 Pieces from Before* (1959–62); *Beginnings* (1963); *2 Reminiscences* (1968); *Silent Night Mix* for 2 Pianos (1969); *3 Pieces* for 2 Pianos (1970–72); *12 Variations on Happy Birthday* (1970–80); *Fêtes* (1975); *Valse éternelle: "The 45 R.P.M."* (1977); *Summer Nights* (1980). **WITH ELECTRONICS:** *AC-DC (Alternating Currents)* for 8 Percussionists and Tape (1967); *Rings* for String Quartet and Ring Modulators (1969); *Light Music* for 4 Instrumental Groups, 4 Sound-activated Strobe Lights, Photocells, Electronics, and Tape (1970); *Les Adieux* for 3 Voices, 14 Instruments, Electronics, Tape, and Colored Lights (1971); *Globose Floccose* for Brass Quintet, String Quartet, Electronics, and Tape (1973); *Set, Hold, Clear, and Squelch* for Oboe, Frequency Follower, Electronics, and Tape (1976); *Santur Opera* for Santur, Electronics, Actors, and Projections

(1977); *Flores musicales* for Oboe, Violin, Cello, Psalter, and Electronics (1979); *5 Songs* for Contralto, Flute, and Electronics (1979); *Cantilenas/Hybrids* for Violin and Electronics (1983); *New Rhythmantics* for String Quartet and Electronics (1985); *Explorations* for Flute, Clarinet, String Trio, Piano, and Optional Electronics (1985); *New Rhythmantics IV* for String Quartet, Trumpet, and Electronics (1987); also solo pieces for Tape.

Tcherepnin, Nikolai (Nikolaievich), noted Russian conductor, pedagogue, and composer, father of **Alexander (Nikolaievich) Tcherepnin;** b. St. Petersburg, May 15, 1873; d. Issy-les-Moulineaux, near Paris, June 26, 1945. He was a student of Rimsky-Korsakov at the St. Petersburg Cons. (1895–98); in 1905 he was appointed to its faculty; taught orchestration and conducting; Prokofiev was among his students. In 1908 he became a conductor at the Marinsky Theater and the Imperial Opera in St. Petersburg; was conductor of the initial season of the Ballets Russes in Paris in 1909. After the Russian Revolution in 1917, he served as director of the Tiflis Cons. (1918–21); then settled in Paris, where he was director of the Russian Cons. (1925–29; 1938–45). His music embodies the best elements of the Russian national school; it is melodious and harmonious; lyrical and gently dynamic; in some of his works there is a coloristic quality suggesting French impressionistic influence.
    WORKS: STAGE: OPERAS: *Svat* (1930); *Vanka* (1932; Belgrade, 1935). **BALLETS:** *Le pavillon d'Armide* (St. Petersburg, Nov. 25, 1907); *Narcisse et Echo* (Monte Carlo, April 26, 1911); *Le Masque de la Mort Rouge* (Petrograd, Jan. 29, 1916); *Dionysus* (1922); *Russian Fairy Tale* (1923); *Romance of the Mummy* (1924); realization and completion of Mussorgsky's opera *The Fair at Sorochinsk* (Monte Carlo, March 17, 1923). **ORCH.:** *Prelude* to Rostand's play *La Princesse lointaine* (1897); *Fantaisie dramatique* (1903); *Le Royaume enchanté*, symphonic tableau (1904); Piano Concerto (1907). **CHAMBER:** *Poème lyrique; Cadence fantastique; Un Air ancien* for Flute and Piano; *Pièce calme* for Oboe and Piano; *Pièce insouciante* for Clarinet and Piano; *Variations simples* for Bassoon and Piano; *Fanfare* for Trumpet and Piano; String Quartet; Quartet for Horns; *Divertissement* for Flute, Oboe, and Bassoon. **PIANO:** *14 esquisses sur les images d'un alphabet russe* (orch. version of 8, Boston, Nov. 27, 1931); *Primitifs; Pièces de bonne humeur; Pièces sentimentals.* **VOCAL:** Liturgical music of the Russian Orthodox rite, including masses a cappella; *Pilgrimage and Passions of the Virgin Mary* (Paris, Feb. 12, 1938); over 200 songs, some of them perennial favorites in Russia.

Tcherepnin, Serge (Alexandrovich), French-born American composer and electronic musical instrument inventor of Russian descent, son of **Alexander (Nikolaievich)** and brother of **Ivan (Alexandrovich) Tcherepnin;** b. Issy-les-Moulineaux, near Paris, Feb. 2, 1941. He studied violin as a child; was taken to the U.S. in 1949 and became a naturalized citizen in 1950; studied theory with his father and received instruction in harmony from Boulanger; took courses with Billy Jim Layton and Kirchner at Harvard Univ. (B.A., 1965), attended Princeton Univ. (1963–64), and completed his training with Eimert, Stockhausen, Nono, Earle Brown, and Boulez in Europe. He was director of the electronic music studio at N.Y. Univ. (1968–70), and was a teacher of composition at the Valencia (Calif.) School of Music (from 1970) and at Dartington Hall in England (summers, 1979–80). He invented the Serge, a modular synthesizer, which was manufactured by his own company (from 1974).
    WORKS: *Inventions* for Piano (1960); String Trio (1961); *Kaddish* for Narrator, Flute, Oboe, Clarinet, Piano, 2 Percussion, and Violin (1962); *Figures-grounds* for 7 to 77 Instruments (1964); *2 Tapes: Giuseppe's Background Music I-II* for 4-track Tape (1966); *2 More Tapes: Addition and Subtraction* for 2-track Tape (1966); *Morning After Piece* for Saxophone and Piano (1966); *Quiet Day at Bach* for Solo Instrument and Tape (1967); *Piece of Wood* for Performers, Actor, and Composer (1967); *Piece of Wood with Weeping Woman* for Musicians,

Women, Stagehand, and Tape (1967); *Film* for Mixed Media (1967); *"Hat" for Joseph Beuys* for Actor and Tape (1968); *For Ilona Kabós* for Piano (1968); *Definitive Death Music* for Amplified Saxophone and Instrumental Ensemble (1968); *Paysages électroniques*, film score (1977); *Samba in Aviary*, film score (1978).

Tchesnokov, Pavel, Russian composer; b. near Voskresensk, Oct. 24, 1877; d. Moscow, March 14, 1944. He studied at the Moscow Cons. with Vasilenko, graduating in 1917; also took courses with Sergei Taneyev and Ippolitov-Ivanov. He devoted himself exclusively to choral composition, both secular and sacred; from 1920, was prof. of choral conducting at the Moscow Cons. He publ. a manual for choral singing (Moscow, 1940).

Teagarden, Jack (actually, **Weldon Leo**), remarkable American jazz trombonist and singer; b. Vernon, Tex., Aug. 29, 1905; d. New Orleans, Jan. 15, 1964. He began to play the piano as a child; took up the trombone at 10; after playing with bands in Texas, he appeared in N.Y., Chicago, and other cities; was a member of Paul Whiteman's Orch. (1933–38). He led his own big bands (1939–46); played in Louis Armstrong's All Stars (1947–51); then formed his own All Stars, which he led until his death. One of the great jazz trombonists, he also doubled as a singer.
    Bibl.: J. Smith and L. Guttridge, *J. T.:The Story of a Jazz Maverick* (London, 1960); H. Waters, *J. T.'s Music: His Career and Recordings* (Stanhope, N.J., 1960); W. Balliett, "Profiles: J. T.," *New Yorker* (April 2, 1984).

Tear, Robert, distinguished Welsh tenor; b. Barry, Glamorgan, March 8, 1939. He was a choral scholar at King's College, Cambridge, where he graduated in English (1957–61); received vocal instruction from Julian Kimbell. He became a lay vicar at St. Paul's Cathedral in London in 1960; also was active with the Ambrosian Singers; in 1963 made his operatic debut as Quint in Britten's *The Turn of the Screw* with the English Opera Group in London, where he made regular appearances until 1971; also sang at London's Covent Garden, where he created the role of Dov in Tippett's *The Knot Garden* in 1970; was chosen to sing the role of the Painter in the 1st complete performance of Berg's *Lulu* in Paris in 1979. He made guest appearances with various opera houses at home and abroad; also won particular renown as a concert artist. In 1986 he was appointed to the International Chair of Vocal Studies at the Royal Academy of Music in London. In 1984 he was made a Commander of the Order of the British Empire. His autobiography was publ. as *Tear Here* (London, 1990).

Tebaldi, Renata, celebrated Italian soprano; b. Pesaro, Feb. 1, 1922. Her mother, a nurse, took her to Langhirano after the breakup of her marriage to a philandering cellist. Renata was stricken with poliomyelitis when she was 3; after initial vocal training from Giuseppina Passani, she studied with Ettore Campogaliani at the Parma Cons. (1937–40) and with Carmen Melis at the Pesaro Cons. (1940–43). She made her operatic debut in Rovigo as Elena in Boito's *Mefistofele* in 1944. In 1946 Toscanini chose her as one of his artists for the reopening concert at La Scala in Milan, and she subsequently became one of its leading sopranos. She made her 1st appearance in England in 1950 with the visiting La Scala company at London's Covent Garden as Desdemona; also in 1950 she sang Aida with the San Francisco Opera. On Jan. 31, 1955, she made her Metropolitan Opera debut in N.Y. as Desdemona in Verdi's *Otello*; she continued to appear regularly there until 1973. She toured Russia in 1975 and 1976. Her repertoire was almost exclusively Italian; she excelled in both lyric and dramatic roles; was particularly successful as Violetta, Tosca, Mimi, and Madame Butterfly. She also sang the role of Eva in *Die Meistersinger von Nürnberg*. On Nov. 3, 1958, she was the subject of a cover story in *Time* magazine.
    Bibl.: K. Harris, *R. T.: An Authorized Biography* (N.Y., 1974).

Tebaldini, Giovanni, Italian conductor, music scholar, and composer; b. Brescia, Sept. 7, 1864; d. San Benedetto del Tronto, May 11, 1952. He studied with Ponchielli, Panzini, and Amelli at the Milan Cons. (1883–85) and with Haller and Haberl at the Regensburg School for Church Music (1888); served as maestro of the Schola Cantorum at San Marco in Venice (1889–93), maestro di cappella at the Basilica of S. Antonio in Padua (1894–97), and director of the Parma Cons. (1897–1902). After teaching at the Cons. di San Pietro a Majella in Naples (1925–30), he went to Genoa, where he was appointed director of the Ateneo Musicale (1931). His specialty was Italian sacred music, but he gained sensational prominence when he publ. an article provocatively entitled "Telepatia musicale" (*Rivista Musicale Italiana*, March 1909), in which he cited thematic similarities between the opera *Cassandra* (1905) by the relatively obscure Italian composer Vittorio Gnecchi and *Elektra* by Richard Strauss, written considerably later, implying a "telepathic" plagiarism on the part of Strauss. However, the juxtaposition of musical examples from both operas proved specious and failed to support Tebaldini's contention.
    Writings: *La musica sacra in Italia* (Milan, 1894); *Gasparo Spontini* (Recanati, 1924); *Ildebrando Pizzetti* (Parma, 1931); also *Metodo teorico pratico per organo* (with Enrico Bossi; Milan, 1897).
    Bibl.: M. Horwath, "T., Gnecchi and Strauss," *Current Musicology*, No. 16 (1970).

Tedesco, Ignaz (Amadeus), Bohemian pianist and composer, called the "Hannibal of octaves"; b. Prague, 1817; d. Odessa, Nov. 13, 1882. He studied with Triebensee and Tomaschek; made successful concert tours, especially in southern Russia; settled in Odessa. He composed for piano in a salon style; made transcriptions.

Teed, Roy (Norman), English pianist, organist, teacher, and composer; b. Herne Bay, Kent, May 18, 1928. He studied composition with Lennox Berkeley, piano with Virginia McLean, and harmony and counterpoint with Paul Steinitz at the Royal Academy of Music in London (1949–53); in 1966 he joined its faculty; also taught at the Colchester Inst. Music School (1966–79).
    Works: OPERA: *The Overcoat*, after Gogol (1988). **ORCH.:** Piano Concerto (1952); *Festival Suite* for Cello and String Orch. (1958); *Around the Town*, comedy march (1962); *Music for a Ballet*, suite (1975); *A Celebration Overture*, for Sir Lennox Berkeley's 80th birthday (1983); Concertino for Treble Recorder and Strings (1984); Overture (1989). **CHAMBER:** *Introduction and Scherzo* for Flute, Oboe, and Piano (1960); Quartet for Flute and Strings (1961); Serenade for 10 Winds (1982); Trio for Violin, Cello, and Piano (1985); *Sextet Variations* for Clarinet, Bassoon, Horn, Violin, Viola, and Cello (1987); *Elegy, Scherzo, and Trio* for Trumpet and Piano (1988); organ works. **VOCAL:** 5 *Funny Songs* for Medium Voice and Clarinet, or Piano, or Orch. (1954); *So Blest a Day*, Christmas cantata (1960); *The Pied Piper* for Soloists, Chorus, and Orch. (1961); *The Jackdaw of Rheims*, narrative cantata (1964); *The Pardoner's Tale* for Baritone, Chorus, and Orch. (1966); 2 sets of 5 *Epitaphs*, humorous song cycles (1969, 1978); *Music of the Seasons* for Baritone, Chorus, and Orch. (1980); *Music Fills the Air* for Chorus (1984); *A Trip to the Zoo*, 23 songs for Very Young Singers, and Piano or Orch. (1987); choruses; carols; songs.

Teichmüller, Robert, German pianist and teacher; b. Braunschweig, May 4, 1863; d. Leipzig, May 6, 1939. He studied piano with his father and with Reinecke at the Leipzig Cons., where from 1897 until his death he taught piano; was made a prof. in 1908. With K. Hermann, he publ. *Internationale moderne Klaviermusik* (Leipzig, 1927).
    Bibl.: A. Baresel, *R. T. als Mensch und Künstler* (Leipzig, 1922); idem, *R. T. und die Leipziger Klaviertradition* (Leipzig, 1934).

Teike, Carl (Albert Hermann), German composer of band music; b. Altdamm, Feb. 5, 1864; d. Landsberg an der Warthe, May 22, 1922. He studied wind instruments in his early youth; at 19, joined the band of the 123rd König Karl Regiment, stationed at Ulm on the Danube. He soon began writing marches that were to become perennial favorites with German bands; at 25 he composed *Alte Kameraden,* one of the best known of German military marches, marked by a typically stolid square rhythm, with heavily accented downbeats. He subsequently was a member of the Royal German Police at Potsdam (1895–1908); then served with the postal service at Landsberg; he continued, however, to compose marches; during World War I, he wrote the march *Graf Zeppelin* (known in English eds. as *Conqueror*) which, despite its narrow militaristic nature, enjoyed international fame.

BIBL.: K. Döll, *Alte Kameraden* (Bad Homburg, 1965; Eng. tr., 1971).

Te Kanawa, Dame Kiri, brilliant New Zealand soprano; b. Gisborne, March 6, 1944. Her father was an indigenous Maori who traced his ancestry to the legendary warrior Te Kanawa; her mother was Irish. She attended Catholic schools in Auckland, and was coached in singing by a nun. She was sent to Melbourne to compete in a radio show; won 1st prize in the Melbourne *Sun* contest. In 1966 she received a grant for study in London with Vera Rozsa. She made her operatic debut at the Camden Festival in 1969, in Rossini's *La Donna del Lago;* 1st appeared at London's Covent Garden in a minor role that same year, and then as the Countess in *Le nozze di Figaro* in 1971. She made her U.S. debut in the same role with the Santa Fe Opera in 1971; it became one of her most remarkable interpretations. She sang it again with the San Francisco Opera in 1972. A proverbial *coup de théâtre* in her career came on Feb. 9, 1974, when she was called upon to substitute at a few hours' notice for the ailing Teresa Stratas in the part of Desdemona in Verdi's *Otello* at the Metropolitan Opera in N.Y.; it was a triumphant achievement, winning for her unanimous praise. She also sang in the film version of *Le nozze di Figaro.* In 1977 she appeared as Pamina in *Die Zauberflöte* at the Paris Opéra. On Dec. 31, 1977, she took the role of Rosalinde in a Covent Garden production of *Die Fledermaus,* which was televised to the U.S. She excelled equally as a subtle and artistic interpreter of lyric roles in Mozart's operas and in dramatic representations of Verdi's operas. Among her other distinguished roles were the Marschallin and Arabella. She also won renown as a concert artist. In later years she expanded her repertoire to include popular fare, including songs by Cole Porter and Leonard Bernstein's *West Side Story.* Hailed as a prima donna assoluta, she pursued one of the most successful international operatic and concert careers of her day. In 1981 she sang at the royal wedding of Prince Charles and Lady Diana Spencer in London, a performance televised around the globe. In 1973 she was made an Officer of the Order of the British Empire; in 1982 she was named a Dame Commander of the Order of the British Empire.

BIBL.: D. Fingleton, *K. T.K.* (N.Y., 1983).

Tekeliev, Alexander, Bulgarian composer; b. Svilengrad, June 3, 1942. He studied composition with Veselin Stoyanov at the Bulgarian State Cons. in Sofia, graduating in 1968; then became head of the music dept. of the Committee for Television and Radio in Sofia; also assumed music teaching duties at the Inst. for Musical and Choreographical Training.

WORKS: Oratorio-requiem, *The Year 1923* (1971); Clarinet Concerto (1968); *Ode to the USSR* for Narrator, Chorus, and Orch. (1970); *Adagio and Scherzo* for String Orch. (1972); *Poem* for Viola and Orch. (1973); 2 chamber syms. (1974, 1976); choral music and songs.

Telemann, Georg Michael, German composer and writer on music, grandson of **Georg Philipp Telemann;** b. Plon, April 20, 1748; d. Riga, March 4, 1831. He was reared and trained in music by his grandfather in Hamburg; matriculated at the Univ. of Kiel (1768); was a teacher at the Nicolaischule in Hamburg before settling in Riga as Kantor and teacher at the cathedral school (1773–1828), where he oversaw performances of many of his grandfather's works in his own eds.

WORKS: *Beytrag zur Kirchenmusik,* 10 choral anthems for 2 to 4 Voices, Oboes, 2 Trumpets, Horn, Timpani, Strings, and Basso Continuo, and 10 chorale preludes and 2 fugues

for Organ (Königsberg and Leipzig, 1785); *Sammlung alter und neuer Choralmelodien für das seit 1810 in . . . Riga eingeführte Neue Gesangbuch* (Mitau, 1811–12); a few occasional choral works, including the cantata *Deutschlands Pflegerin* for the installation of C.P.E. Bach as Hamburg Kantor (1768).

WRITINGS: *Unterricht im Generalbass-Spielen, auf der Orgel oder sonst einem Clavier-Instrumente* (Hamburg, 1773); *Beurteilung der im 23. Bande der Allgemeinen deutschen Bibliothek befindlichen Recension seines Unterrichts* (Riga, 1775); *Über die Wahl der Melodie eines Kirchenliedes* (Riga, 1821).

BIBL.: H. Miesner, "Die Lebensskizze des jüngeren T. und seine Werke," *Zeitschrift des Vereins für Hamburgische Geschichte,* XXXIII (1932).

Telemann, Georg Philipp, greatly significant German composer, grandfather of **Georg Michael Telemann;** b. Magdeburg, March 14, 1681; d. Hamburg, June 25, 1767. He received his academic training at a local school; also learned to play keyboard instruments and the violin; he acquired knowledge of music theory from the cantor Benedict Christiani. He subsequently attended the Gymnasium Andreanum in Hildesheim, where he became active in student performances of German cantatas. In 1701 he entered the Univ. of Leipzig as a student of jurisprudence; in 1702 he organized a collegium musicum there; later was appointed music director of the Leipzig Opera, where he used the services of his student singers and instrumentalists. In 1705 he went to Sorau as Kapellmeister at the court of Count Erdmann II of Promnitz. In 1708 he was appointed Konzertmeister to the court orch. in Eisenach; later he was named Kapellmeister there. In 1709 he married Louise Eberlin, a musician's daughter, but she died in 1711 in childbirth. In 1712 Telemann was appointed music director of the city of Frankfurt; there he wrote a quantity of sacred music as well as secular works for the public concerts given by the Frauenstein Society, of which he served as director. In 1714 he married Maria Katharina Textor, the daughter of a local town clerk. They had 8 sons and 2 daughters, of whom only a few survived infancy. His wife later abandoned him for a Swedish army officer. In 1721 he received the post of music director of 5 churches in Hamburg, which became the center of his important activities as composer and music administrator. In 1722 Telemann was appointed music director of the Hamburg Opera, a post he held until 1738. During his tenure he wrote a number of operas for production there, and also staged several works by Handel and Keiser. In 1737–38 he visited France. His eyesight began to fail as he grew older; his great contemporaries Bach and Handel suffered from the same infirmity. An extraordinarily prolific composer, Telemann mastered both the German and the Italian styles of composition prevalent in his day. While he never approached the greatness of genius of Bach and Handel, he nevertheless became an exemplar of the German Baroque at its grandest development. According to Telemann's own account, he composed about 20 operas for Leipzig; wrote about 4 for Weissenfels, 2 for Bayreuth, and 3 operettas for Eisenach. He lists 35 operas for Hamburg, but included in this list are preludes, intermezzi, and postludes.

WORKS: OPERAS (all 1st perf. in Hamburg): *Der gedultige Socrates* (Jan. 28, 1721); *Ulysses* (1721; with Vogler); *Sieg der Schönheit* (1722; later performed as *Gensericus*); *Belsazar* (July 19, 1723; 2nd version, Sept. 30, 1723); *Der Beschluss des Carnevals* (1724; with Campara and Conti); *Omphale* (1724); *Der neu-modische Liebhaber Damon* (June 1724); *Cimbriens allgemeines Frolocken* (Feb. 17, 1725); *Pimpinone oder Die ungleiche Heyrath,* intermezzo (Sept. 27, 1725); *La Capricciosa e il Credula,* intermezzo (1725); *Adelheid* (Feb. 17, 1727); *Buffonet und Alga,* intermezzo (May 14, 1727); *Calypso* (1727); *Sancio* (1727); *Die verkehrte Welt* (1728); *Miriways* (May 26, 1728); *Emma und Eginhard* (1728); *Aesopus* (Feb. 28, 1729); *Flavius Bertaridus, König der Langobarden* (Nov. 23, 1729); *Margaretha, Königin in Castilien* (Aug. 10, 1730); *Die Flucht des Aeneas* (Nov. 19, 1731); *Judith, Gemahlin Kayser Ludewig* *des Frommen* (Nov. 27, 1732; with Chelleri); *Orasia oder Die rachgierige Liebe* (Oct. 1736).

SACRED: ORATORIOS: *Der königliche Prophete David als ein Fürbild unseres Heilands Jesu* (1718; not extant); *Freundschaft geget über Liebe* (1720; not extant); *Donnerode* (1756–60); *Sing, unsterbliche Seele, an Mirjam und deine Wehmut,* from Klopstock's *Der Messias* (1759); *Das befreite Israel* (1759); *Die Hirten bei der Krippe zu Bethlehem* (1759); *Die Auferstehung und Himmelfahrt Jesu* (1760); *Der Tag des Gerichts* (1762). **CANTATAS:** He publ. the following sets of cantatas, each set containing 72 works: *Harmonischer Gottes-Dienst, oder Geistliche Cantaten zum allgemeinen Gebrauche* (Hamburg, 1725–26); *Auszug derjenigen musicalischen und auf die gewöhnlichen Evangelien gerichteten Arien* (Hamburg, 1727); *Fortsetzung des Harmonischen Gottesdienstes* (Hamburg, 1731–32); *Musicalisches Lob Gottes in der Gemeine des Herrn* (Nuremberg, 1744); more than a thousand other cantatas; 46 Passions; masses; Psalms; motets; wedding music; pieces for special church occasions.

INSTRUMENTAL: One of his most important collections was his *Musique de table* (Hamburg, 1733); it contained 3 orch. suites, 3 concertos, 3 quartets, 3 trios, and 3 sonatas. His orch. output was prodigious, comprising numerous overtures, concertos, sonatas, quartets, quintets, etc. A complete ed. of his works, *Georg Philipp Telemann: Musikalische Werke,* began publication in Kassel and Basel in 1950.

BIBL.: Telemann's autobiography of 1718 was publ. in J. Mattheson, *Grosse Generalbassschule* (Hamburg, 1731); his autobiography of 1739 was publ. in J. Mattheson, *Grundlage einer Ehren-Pforte* (Hamburg, 1740; new ed. by M. Schneider, Berlin, 1910); both of these, plus his autobiographical letter to Walther of 1729, have been republ. in W. Kahl, *Selbstbiographien deutscher Musiker des XVIII. Jahrhunderts* (Cologne, 1948). See also the following: B. Schmid, ed., *Herr G.P. T.: Lebenslauf* (Nuremberg, c.1745; in Ger. and Fr.); J. Winckler, "G.P. T.," *Nachrichten von niedersächsischen berühmten Leuten und Familien,* I (Hamburg, 1768); R. Rolland, *Voyage musical au pays du passé* (Paris, 1919; Eng. tr., 1922); M. Frey, *G.P. T.s Singe-, Spiel- und Generalbass-Übungen* (Zürich, 1922); H. Graeser, *G.P. T.s Instrumental-Kammermusik* (diss., Univ. of Munich, 1924); E. Valentin, *G.P. T.* (Burg, 1931; 3rd ed., 1952); H. Hörner, *G.P. T.s Passionsmusiken* (Leipzig, 1933); K. Schäfer-Schmuck, *G.P. T. als Klavierkomponist* (diss., Univ. of Kiel, 1934); H. Büttner, *Das Konzert in den Orchestersuiten G.P. T.s* (Wolfenbüttel and Berlin, 1935); W. Menke, *Das Vokalwerk G.P. T.s* (Kassel, 1942); F. Funk, *The Trio Sonatas of G.P. T.* (diss., George Peabody College for Teachers, 1954); C. Rhea, *The Sacred Oratorios of G.P. T.* (diss., Florida State Univ., 1958); E. Valentin, *T. in seiner Zeit* (Hamburg, 1960); R. Petzoldt, *T. und seine Zeitgenossen* (Magdeburg, 1966); W. Bergmann, "T. in Paris," *Musical Times,* CVIII (1967); C. Gilbertson, *The Methodical Sonatas of G.P. T.* (diss., Univ. of Kentucky, 1967); R. Petzoldt, *G.P. T.: Leben und Werk* (Leipzig, 1967; in Eng., 1974); K. Zauft, *T.s Liedschaffen und seine Bedeutung für die Entwicklung des deutschen Liedes in der 1. Hälfte des 18. Jahrhunderts* (Magdeburg, 1967); *G.P. T., Leben und Werk: Beiträge zur gleichnamigen Ausstellung* (Magdeburg, 1967); A. Hoffmann, *Die Orchestersuiten G.P. T.s* (Wolfenbüttel and Zürich, 1969); S. Kross, *Das Instrumentalkonzert bei G.P. T.* (Tutzing, 1969); M. Peckham, *The Operas of G.P. T.* (diss., Columbia Univ., 1969); K. Grebe, *G.P. T. in Selbstzeugnissen und Bilddokumenten* (Reinbeck bei Hamburg, 1970); I. Allihn, *G.P. T. und J.J. Quantz* (Magdeburg, 1971); H. Grosse and H. Jung, eds., *G.P. T., Briefwechsel* (Leipzig, 1972); *T.-Renaissance: Werk- und Wiedergabe* (Magdeburg, 1973); W. Maertens, *T. Kapitänsmusiken* (diss., Univ. of Halle, 1975); J. Wenzel, *Geschichte der Hamburger Oper, 1678–1978* (Hamburg, 1978); *G.P. T.: Leben—Werk—Wirkung* (Berlin, 1980); E. Klessmann, *T. in Hamburg* (Hamburg, 1980); M. Ruhnke, ed., *G.P. T.: thematisch-systematisches Verzeichnis seiner Werke: Instrumentalwerke,* Vol. I (Kassel, 1984); B. Stewart, *G.P. T. in Hamburg: Social and Cultural Background and Its Musical Expression* (diss., Stanford Univ., 1985); W. Hirschmann, *Studien zum Konzertschaffen von G.P. T.* (Kassel and

N.Y., 1986); W. Menke, *G.P. T.: Leben, Werk und Umwelt in Bilddokumenten* (Wilhelmshaven, 1987).

Tellefsen, Thomas (Dyke Acland), Norwegian pianist and composer; b. Trondheim, Nov. 26, 1823; d. Paris, Oct. 6, 1874. He began his training in Trondheim with his father, Johan Christian Tellefsen, an organist, and with O. Lindeman; made his debut there at age 18; then went to Paris in 1842, where he continued his studies with Charlotte Thygeson, and also received some lessons from Kalkbrenner; in 1844 he became a pupil of Chopin, and accompanied him to England and Scotland in 1848. In later years he gave frequent concerts in Paris, London, and Scandinavia; about 1861 ill health compelled him to concentrate his energies on teaching and composing. His early works were greatly influenced by Chopin; he wrote 2 piano concertos (1852, 1854), a Piano Trio (1861), 2 violin sonatas (1856), a Sonata for 2 Pianos (1870), 16 mazurkas, and a number of Norwegian dances. He also made use of Norwegian folk songs in many of his works, and thus became an early proponent of national music in Norway.

Telmányi, Emil, Hungarian violinist, conductor, and teacher; b. Arad, June 22, 1892; d. June 12, 1988. He studied with Hubay at the Royal Academy of Music in Budapest. In 1911 he began an active career as a violinist; in 1918 he married Ann Marie Nielsen, a daughter of Carl Nielsen; his 2nd wife, whom he married in 1936, was the pianist Annette Schiöler, who appeared with him and their 3 children in a quintet from 1956. He taught at the Århus Cons. (1940-69). He supervised the devising of a curved bow for the playing of Bach's violin works which became known as the Vega bow (1954); transcribed and arranged scores by Handel, Beethoven, Chopin, Schumann, and Brahms for violin.

Telva (real name, **Toucke**), **Marian,** American contralto; b. St. Louis, Dec. 26, 1897; d. Norwalk, Conn., Oct. 23, 1962. She changed her name to Telva for the sake of euphony. She sang in church in her hometown; then went to N.Y. for further study, and soon was engaged at the Metropolitan Opera, where she sang minor roles between 1920 and 1933 (1931–32 season excepted). In the meantime she married a wealthy banker and afterward made only sporadic appearances as a concert singer.

Temianka, Henri, distinguished Polish-born American violinist, conductor, and pedagogue; b. Greenock, Scotland (of Polish parents), Nov. 19, 1906. He studied violin with Blitz in Rotterdam (1915–23), W. Hess at the Berlin Hochschule für Musik (1923–24), and Boucherit in Paris (1924–26); completed his training with Flesch (violin) and Rodzinski (conducting) at the Curtis Inst. of Music in Philadelphia (graduated, 1930). In 1932 he made his N.Y. recital debut at Town Hall, and then gave recitals in Paris and London; was concertmaster of the Scottish Orch. in Glasgow (1937–38) and of the Pittsburgh Sym. Orch. (1941–42). In 1945 he became a naturalized U.S. citizen. In 1946 he founded the Paganini String Quartet, which he served as 1st violinist until it disbanded in 1966; in 1961 he founded the Calif. Chamber Sym. Orch., with which he toured extensively; in 1982 organized the Baroque Virtuosi from its ranks. He served as a prof. at the Univ. of Calif. at Santa Barbara (1960–64) and at Calif. State Univ. at Long Beach (1964–76); also gave master classes. In addition to articles on violin technique, he publ. a book of reminiscences of *Facing the Music* (N.Y., 1973). He was equally esteemed as a violin soloist and chamber player, conductor, and teacher.

BIBL.: B. Schwarz, *Great Masters of the Violin* (N.Y., 1983).

Temirkanov, Yuri, noted Russian conductor; b. Nalchik, Dec. 10, 1938. He studied at the Leningrad Cons., graduating as a violinist in 1962 and as a conductor in 1965; made his conducting debut with the Leningrad Opera in 1965. In 1966 he won 1st prize in the U.S.S.R. All-Union Conductors' Competition, which energized his career. From 1968 to 1976 he conducted the Leningrad Sym. Orch.; then served as chief conductor of the Kirov Opera and Ballet in Leningrad. He then went on an American tour; conducted in Philadelphia, Cincinnati,

San Francisco, and Minneapolis. In 1979 he became principal guest conductor of the Royal Phil. in London. In 1988 he became chief conductor of the Leningrad Phil. As is to be expected, he shines most glitteringly in the Russian repertoire, and he invariably programs Soviet works.

Temperley, Nicholas, English-born American musicologist; b. Beaconsfield, Aug. 7, 1932. He studied at Eton College (1945–51), at the Royal College of Music in London (1951–52), and at King's College, Cambridge (B.A., 1955; Mus.B., 1956; Ph.D., 1959, with the diss. *Instrumental Music in England, 1800–1850*); then was a postdoctoral fellow at the Univ. of Illinois (1959–61). He was an assistant prof. at Cambridge Univ. (1961–66); after serving as an assistant prof. at Yale Univ. (1966–67), he was an associate prof. (1967–72) and a prof. (from 1972) at the Univ. of Illinois, where he also was chairman of the musicology dept. (1972–75). In 1977 he became a naturalized U.S. citizen. He served as ed. of the *Journal of the American Musicological Society* (1978–80); also ed. the *Symphonie fantastique* for the New Berlioz Edition, XVII (Kassel, 1972), *English Songs, 1800–1860* in Musica Britannica, XLIII (1979), *The London Pianoforte School (1766–1860)* (with G. Bush; 20 vols., N.Y., 1984–87), and Haydn's *The Creation* (London, 1987; with authentic Eng. text). His books include *The Music of the English Parish Church* (2 vols., 1979); *The Romantic Age*, vol. 5 of *The Athlone History of Music in Britain* (1981); and *Fuguing Tunes in the Eighteenth Century* (with C. Manns; 1983).

Templeton, Alec (Andrew), blind Welsh-born American pianist and composer; b. Cardiff, July 4, 1909; d. Greenwich, Conn., March 28, 1963. He studied at Worcester College and in London at the Royal College of Music and the Royal Academy of Music; was only 12 when he began to appear on the BBC, remaining with it until 1935. He went to the U.S. in 1935 as a member of Jack Hylton's jazz band; became a naturalized U.S. citizen in 1941. He was extremely successful as a radio pianist, especially with his humorous musical sketches, parodies, etc., such as *Bach Goes to Town, Mozart Matriculates,* etc. He also wrote some more ambitious works, including *Concertino lirico* (1942) and *Gothic Concerto* for Piano and Orch (N.Y., Dec. 19, 1954, composer soloist). With R. Baumel, he publ. *A. T.'s Music Boxes* (N.Y., 1958).

Templeton, John, Scottish tenor; b. Riccarton, near Kilmarnock, July 30, 1802; d. New Hampton, near London, July 2, 1886. He sang in various churches in Edinburgh; then went to London, where he took lessons in singing with Welch, De Pinna, and Tom Cooke. On Oct. 13, 1831, he made his London debut at Drury Lane as Belville in Sheild's *Rosina;* subsequently was a regular member there. Maria Malibran selected him as tenor for her operatic appearances in London (1833–35). In 1842 he was in Paris; during the season of 1845–46, he made an American tour announced as "Templeton Entertainment," singing folk songs of Great Britain; his commentaries and reminiscences were publ. as *A Musical Entertainment* (Boston, 1845). He retired in 1852.
BIBL.: W. Husk, ed., *T. and Malibran. Reminiscences* (London, 1880).

Tenducci, Giusto Ferdinando, celebrated Italian castrato soprano, nicknamed "Triorchis" (triple-testicled); b. Siena, c.1735; d. Genoa, Jan. 25, 1790. He made appearances in Venice and Naples before going to London in 1758; there he sang at the King's Theatre until 1760; after a stay in a debtor's prison, he resumed his career and secured a notable success as Arbaces in the premiere of Arne's *Artaxerxes* in 1762; was again active at the King's Theatre (1763–66). He then went to Ireland, where he contracted a marriage with his 16-year-old pupil Dora Maunsell in Cork; outraged members of her family had him jailed and his new bride spirited away; shortly afterward, however, the 2 were reunited and allegedly produced 2 children. After a sojourn in Edinburgh, he returned to England in 1770 and sang at the Worcester Three Choirs Festival; then was a featured artist in the Bach-Abel Concerts in London.

By 1778 he was in Paris; sang again in London in 1785. He adapted 4 operas for the Dublin stage, and also wrote English, French, and Italian songs. His wife is reputed to have been the author of the book *A True Genuine Narrative of Mr and Mrs Tenducci* (1768).
BIBL.: A. Heriot, *The Castrati in Opera* (London, 1956); C. Oldman, "Mozart's scena for T.," *Music & Letters,* XLII (1961).

Tenney, James (Carl), highly influential American pianist, conductor, teacher, and composer; b. Silver City, N.Mex., Aug. 10, 1934. He studied engineering at the Univ. of Denver (1952–54) before devoting himself to music; received instruction in piano from Steuermann at the Juilliard School of Music in N.Y. (1954–55), took courses in piano and composition at Bennington (Vt.) College (B.A., 1958), and worked with Gaburo, Hiller, and Partch at the Univ. of Illinois (M.Mus., 1961); was also associated with Chou Wen-chung, Ruggles, and Varèse (1955–65). He was active as a performer with the Steve Reich and Philip Glass ensembles; concurrently conducted research at the Bell Laboratories (with Max Matthews; 1961–64), Yale Univ. (1964–66), and the Polytechnic Inst. of Brooklyn (1966–70). He taught at the Calif. Inst. of the Arts (1970–75), the Univ. of Calif. at Santa Cruz (1975–76), and York Univ. in Toronto (from 1976). As both a performer and a scholar, he is a prominent advocate of contemporary music; is also a notable authority on Ives and Nancarrow. He publ. *A History of Consonance and Dissonance* (N.Y., 1988).

WORKS: ORCH.: *Essay* for Chamber Orch. (1957); *Quiet Fan for Erik Satie* (1970); *Clang* (1972); *Chorales* (1974). **CHAMBER:** *Seeds* for Flute, Clarinet, Bassoon, Horn, Violin, and Cello (1956; rev. 1962); *13 Ways of Looking at a Blackbird* for Tenor, 2 Flutes, Violin, Viola, and Cello, or for Bass, Alto, Flute, Oboe, Viola, Cello, and Double Bass (1958; rev. 1971); *String Complement* for Strings (1964); *Quintext* for String Quartet and Double Bass (1972); *In the Aeolian Mode* for Prepared Piano and Variable Ensemble (1973); *3 Pieces* for Drum Quartet (1974–75); *Harmonia* Nos. 1 to 6 for Various Ensembles (1976–81); *Saxony* for Saxophones and Tape Delay (1978); *3 Indigenous Songs* for 2 Piccolos, Alto Flute, Bassoon, and Percussion (1979); *Septet* for 6 Electric Guitars and Double Bass (1981); *Glissade* for Viola, Cello, Double Bass, and Tape Delay (1982); *Voice(s)* for Female Voice(s), Instrumental Ensemble, and Multiple Tape Delay (1982); *Koan* for String Quartet (1984); *Water on the mountain . . . Fire in heaven* for 6 Electric Guitars (1985); *Changes: 64 Studies* for 6 Harps (1985); numerous works for Solo Instruments, including *Spectral Canon for Conlon Nancarrow* for Player Piano (1974). **COMPUTER OR TAPE:** *Collage No. 1: Blue Suede* for Tape (1961); *Analog No. 1: Noise Study* for Computer (1961); *Stochastic Quartet:* String Quartet for Computer or Strings (1963); *Dialogue* for Computer (1963); *Ergodos II* for Computer (1964); *Fabric for Ché* for Computer (1967); *For Ann (rising)* for Computer (1969); also various vocal and theater works.

Tennstedt, Klaus, brilliant German conductor; b. Merseburg, June 6, 1926. He studied piano, violin, and theory at the Leipzig Cons.; in 1948 he became concertmaster in Halle an der Saale, beginning his career as a conductor there in 1953; after serving as a conductor at the Dresden State Opera (1958–62), he was conductor in Schwerin (1962–71); also appeared as a guest conductor throughout East Germany, Eastern Europe, and the Soviet Union. In 1971 he settled in the West; after guest engagements in Sweden, he served as Generalmusikdirektor of the Kiel Opera (1972–76). In 1974 he made a remarkable North American debut as a guest conductor with the Toronto Sym. Orch., and also appeared with the Boston Sym. Orch., which led to numerous engagements with other major U.S. orchs. In 1976 he made his British debut as a guest conductor of the London Sym. Orch. He was chief conductor of the North German Radio Sym. Orch. in Hamburg (1979–81); was also principal guest conductor of the Minnesota Orch. in Minneapolis (1979–83). From 1980 to 1983 he was principal guest conductor of the London Phil., and then served as its principal conductor from 1983 until a diagnosis of throat cancer com-

pelled him to give up his duties in 1987. He continued to make guest appearances in subsequent seasons. On Dec. 14, 1983, he made his Metropolitan Opera debut in N.Y. conducting *Fidelio*. His appearances around the globe elicited exceptional critical acclaim; he was ranked among the foremost interpreters of the Austro-German repertoire of his day.

Tenschert, Roland, Austrian musicologist; b. Podersam, Bohemia, April 5, 1894; d. Vienna, April 3, 1970. He studied at the Leipzig Cons. (1913–15) and received instruction in musicology from Adler at the Univ. of Vienna (Ph.D., 1921); also studied composition with Schoenberg and conducting with L. Kaiser. He was librarian at the Salzburg Mozarteum (1926–31) and prof. of music history at the Vienna Academy of Music (from 1945).

WRITINGS: *Mozart: Ein Künstlerleben in Bildern und Dokumenten* (Leipzig, 1931); *Mozart* (Leipzig, 1931); *Joseph Haydn* (Berlin, 1932); *Musikerbrevier* (Vienna, 1940); *Mozart: Ein Leben für die Oper* (Vienna, 1941); *Dreimal sieben Variationen über das Thema Richard Strauss* (Vienna, 1944; 2nd ed., 1945); *Frauen um Haydn* (Vienna, 1946); *Salzburg und seine Festspiele* (Vienna, 1947); *Vater Hellmesberger: ein Kapitel Wiener Musikerhumor* (Vienna, 1947); *Richard Strauss und Wien, Eine Wahlverwandtschaft* (Vienna, 1949); *Wolfgang Amadeus Mozart* (Salzburg, 1951; Eng. tr., 1952); *Christoph Willibald Gluck: der grosse Reformer der Oper* (Olten and Freiburg, 1951).

BIBL.: E. Tenschert, *Musik als Lebensinhalt* (Vienna, 1971; contains a list of writings).

Teodorini, Elena, Rumanian soprano; b. Craiova, March 25, 1857; d. Bucharest, Feb. 27, 1926. She studied piano with Fumagalli and singing with Sangiovanni at the Milan Cons.; also received vocal instruction from G. Stephănescu at the Bucharest Cons. In 1877 she commenced her career with appearances in Italian provincial theaters as a contralto, but her voice gradually changed to a mezzo-soprano of wide range. She made her debut at Milan's La Scala as Gounod's Marguerite on March 20, 1880; subsequently sang in various South American music centers; was particularly associated with the Italian Opera and the National Opera in Bucharest. In 1904 she retired from the operatic stage and became a teacher in Paris; after teaching in Buenos Aires (1909–16) and Rio de Janeiro (1916–23), she settled in Bucharest. Her most notable pupil was Bidú Sayão. Among her prominent roles were Rosina, Donna Anna, Amelia, Lucrezia Borgia, Amneris, and Gioconda. In 1964 the Rumanian government issued a postage stamp in her honor bearing her stage portrait.

BIBL.: V. Cosma, *Cîtăreata E. T.* (Bucharest, 1962).

Terényi, Ede, Rumanian composer of Hungarian descent; b. Tîrgu-Mureş, March 12, 1935. He studied at the Tîrgu-Mureş music college (1942–52) and with Jodál and Demian at the Cluj Cons. (1952–58); was on the latter's faculty from 1960. In his compositions he applies a variety of modernistic resources.

WORKS: ORCH.: Concertino for Strings, Organ, and Electronics (1958; rev. 1969); *Pasărea măiastră* (The Wonderful Bird), symphonic variations (1965; Cluj, June 11, 1967); 5 syms.: No. 1, *Brâncuşiană* (1965; rev. 1986); No. 2 for String Orch., *In memoriam Bakfark* (1978); No. 3 for 2 Percussionists (1978); No. 4, *Hofgreff* (1982; rev. 1986); No. 5 for Strings and Timpani (1984); Piano Concerto (1969); *Musică în Do*, concerto grosso (Cluj, Dec. 11, 1979); 6 neo-Baroque concertos: No. 1 for Flute and Chamber Orch., *Vivaldiana* (Cluj, May 27, 1983); No. 2 for Oboe and Chamber Orch., *Suită franceză* (1984); No. 3 for Trumpet and Chamber Orch., clarino concerto (1984); No. 4 for Cello and Chamber Orch., *Rapsodi barocă* (1984; Cluj, March 20, 1985); No. 5 for Harp and Chamber Orch., *Capriccio grazioso* (Cluj, Oct. 10, 1985); No. 6 for Viola and Chamber Orch., *Rapsodisme händeliene* (1985). CHAMBER: 2 preludes for Flute (1962, 1966); *Sonatina burletta* for Cello and Piano (1975); *Dansuri galante*, suite for Flute, Oboe, Harpsichord, and Cello (1977); piano pieces; organ music. VOCAL: Cantata No. 1: *In memoriam* for Tenor or Soprano, and Piano (1964; rev. and orchestrated as *In memoriam József Attila*,

Cluj, May 19, 1968); *Terzine de Dante*, scenic cantata for Baritone, Trombone, and Piano (1971–72).

Terhune, Anice (née **Potter**), American pianist and composer; b. Hampden, Mass., Oct. 27, 1873; d. Pompton Lakes, N.J., Nov. 9, 1964. She studied in Cleveland, in Rotterdam (with Louis Coenen), and in N.Y. (with E.M. Bowman). In 1901 she married Albert Payson Terhune, the author. She publ. several books of songs for children (*Dutch Ditties, Chinese Child's Day, Colonial Carols, Our Very Own Book*, etc.) and a number of separate songs; also many piano pieces for children; the operas *Hero Nero* (1904) and *The Woodland Princess* (1911); a book, *Music-Study for Children* (1922), and an autobiography, *Across the Line* (N.Y., 1945).

Ternina, Milka, outstanding Croatian soprano; b. Doljnji, Moslavina, Dec. 19, 1863; d. Zagreb, May 18, 1941. She studied with Ida Winterberg in Zagreb and then with Gansbacher at the Vienna Cons. (1880–82); made her operatic debut as Amelia in *Un ballo in maschera* in Zagreb (1882); then sang in Leipzig (1883–84), Graz (1884–86), and Bremen (1886–89). In 1889 she appeared as a guest artist at the Hamburg Opera, joining its roster in 1890; also was a member of the Munich Court Opera (1890–99), where she distinguished herself as a Wagnerian singer. She was engaged by Walter Damrosch for his German Opera Co. in N.Y., and made her American debut as Elsa in *Lohengrin* in Boston on March 4, 1896; also appeared at Covent Garden, London, as Isolde (June 3, 1898); after a series of successes at the Bayreuth Festivals (1899), she made her Metropolitan Opera debut in N.Y. as Elisabeth on Jan. 27, 1900, and sang there until 1904 (1902–3 season excepted); she sang Tosca at the American premiere (Feb. 4, 1901) and Kundry in *Parsifal* (Dec. 24, 1903). She made her farewell stage appearance as Sieglinde in Munich on Aug. 19, 1906. In subsequent years she was active as a teacher, giving instruction at the Inst. of Musical Art in N.Y. and later in Zagreb, where she was the mentor of Zinka Milanov. She was renowned for her portrayals of Isolde and Beethoven's Leonore.

Terrabugio, Giuseppe, Italian composer; b. Fiera di Primiero, May 13, 1842; d. there, Jan. 8, 1933. He studied in Padua, and then in Munich under Rheinberger. In 1883 he settled in Milan, where, as ed. of Musica Sacra, he exerted a strong influence on reforming Italian church music. His publ. works (about 100 opus numbers) are almost exclusively for the church (12 masses, a Requiem, litanies, motets, etc.); he also publ. *L'organista pratico* (3 vols.).

Terradellas, Domingo (Miguel Bernabe), distinguished Spanish composer who became best known via his Italianized name of Domenico Terradeglias; b. Barcelona (baptized), Feb. 13, 1713; d. Rome, May 20, 1751. He began his musical training in Barcelona, then studied at the Cons. dei Poveri di Gesù Cristo in Naples (1732–38); while still a student, he produced his 1st significant score, the oratorio *Giuseppe riconosciuto* (1736). He gained an outstanding success with his opera *Merope* (Rome, Jan. 3, 1743). From 1743 to 1745 he was active at the Spanish church of Santiago y S. Ildefonso in Rome, and devoted much time to writing sacred music. During the 1746–47 season, he composed 2 operas for the King's Theatre in London; then returned to the Continent; was again in Italy by 1750. His last opera, *Sesostri re d'Egitto*, scored a major success at its premiere in Rome (Carnival 1751).

WORKS: OPERAS: *Astarto* (Rome, Carnival 1739); *Gli intrighi delle cantarine* (Naples, 1740); *Issipile* (Florence, 1741 or 1742); *Merope* (Rome, Jan. 3, 1743); *Artaserse* (Venice, Carnival 1744); *Semiramide riconosciuta* (Florence, Carnival 1746); *Mitridate* (London, Dec. 2, 1746); *Bellerofonte* (London, March 24, 1747); *Didone abbandonata* (Turin, Carnival 1750); *Imeneo in Atene* (Venice, May 6, 1750); *Sesostri re d'Egitto* (Rome, Carnival 1751); other stage works; also sacred vocal works, including 2 oratorios (Naples, 1736 and 1739), Missa Solemnis, masses, Te Deum, etc.

BIBL.: J. Roca, "La producció musical de Domènec Terradellas, deixeble de Durante," *Revista Musical Catalana*, XXXI (1934).

Terrasse, Claude (Antoine), French composer; b. Grand-Lemps, near Grenoble, Jan. 27, 1867; d. Paris, June 30, 1923. He studied at the Lyons Cons. and at the École Niedermeyer in Paris; from 1888 to 1895, was church organist in Arcachon; then in Paris until 1899, when he began to write for the stage, producing a series of successful operettas; the best known are *Les Travaux d'Hercule* (March 7, 1901); *Le Sire de Vergy* (April 16, 1903); *Monsieur de la Palisse* (Nov. 2, 1904); *La Marquise et le marmiton* (Dec. 11, 1907); *Le Coq d'Inde* (April 6, 1909); *Le Mariage de Télémaque* (May 4, 1910); *Les Transatlantiques* (May 20, 1911); *Cartouche* (March 9, 1912). His other works include the ballet *Les lucioles* (Dec. 28, 1910), 2 masses, a motet, songs, and piano pieces.

Terry, Charles Sanford, eminent English music scholar; b. Newport Pagnell, Buckinghamshire, Oct. 24, 1864; d. Westerton of Pitfodels, near Aberdeen, Nov. 5, 1936. He studied history at Clare College, Cambridge, 1883–86; in 1890, became a lecturer in history at Durham College of Science, Newcastle upon Tyne; joined the faculty of the Univ. of Aberdeen, 1898; from 1903 to 1930, held the Burnett-Fletcher chair of history there, and occupied himself with historical research; at the same time, he devoted much of his energy to the study of Bach and his period. His biography of Bach (London, 1928; 2nd ed., rev., 1933; 6th ed., 1967) places Bach's life within historical perspective with a fine discernment; it has become a standard in the literature on Bach in English. Other books and eds. dealing with Bach include: *Bach's Chorals* (Cambridge, 1915–21); *Joh. Seb. Bach: Cantata Texts, sacred and secular, with a Reconstruction of the Leipzig Liturgy of his Period* (London, 1926); *The Origin of the Family of Bach Musicians* (London, 1929); *Bach: The Historical Approach* (1930); *Bach's Orchestra* (1932; 4th ed., 1966); *The Music of Bach: An Introduction* (1933). To the Musical Pilgrim series he contributed analyses of the B-minor Mass (1924), the cantatas and oratorios (1925), the Passions (1926), and the Magnificat, Lutheran masses, and motets (1929). He also ed. *Coffee and Cupid (The Coffee Cantata): An Operetta by Johann Sebastian Bach* (London, 1924) and *The Four-part Chorals of J.S. Bach* (London, 1929; 2nd ed., 1964). He also wrote a biography of Johann Christian Bach (1929; 2nd ed., rev., 1967 by H.C. Robbins Landon).

Terry, Clark, black American jazz trumpet and flügelhorn player and scat singer; b. St. Louis, Dec. 14, 1920. He worked with Charlie Barnet (1947) and Count Basie (1948–51); in 1951, joined Duke Ellington's band and enjoyed a richly rewarding 8-year association. During his collaborations with Oscar Peterson, Terry evolved his trademark "Mumbles" style of scat singing, which he described as sounding like an old man storytelling while drifting into incoherence; he also evolved a style of musical monologues, made up of wittily juggled fragments of musical thought. He played as a regular in the orch. of the "Johnny Carson Show" until it was relocated to Los Angeles; also taught at various jazz clinics. In 1990 he was appointed a director for the new Thelonious Monk Inst. of Jazz at Duke Univ. in Chapel Hill, N.C.

Terry, Sir R(ichard) R(unciman), noted English organist, choirmaster, and music scholar; b. Ellington, Northumberland, Jan. 3, 1865; d. London, April 18, 1938. In 1890 he was appointed organist and music master at Elstow School; from 1892 to 1896, was organist and choirmaster at St. John's Cathedral, Antigua, West Indies; from 1896 to 1901, was at Downside Abbey. There he attracted attention by his revival of the Catholic church music of early English masters (Byrd, Tallis, Tye, Morley, Mundy, White, Fayrfax, etc.); from 1901 to 1924, he was organist and director of music at Westminster Cathedral. He was chairman of the committee appointed to prepare the Eng. supplement of the Vatican Antiphonary, and music ed. of the *Westminster Hymnal* (London, 1912; 3rd ed., rev., 1916; 7th ed., 1937), the official Roman Catholic hymnal for England. He was knighted in 1922. Besides masses, motets, and other

church music, he composed 48 *Old Rhymes with New Tunes* (1934). He ed. *The Shanty Book* (2 vols.; 1921; 1926); *Old Christmas Carols* (1923); *Hymns of Western Europe* (with Davies and Hadow; 1927); *Salt Sea Ballads* (1931); *A Medieval Carol Book* (1932); *200 Folk Carols* (1933); *Calvin's First Psalter* [1539], harmonized (1932); also the collections of 16th-century music *Downside Masses* and *Downside Motets*, *Motets Ancient and Modern*, and many separate works by early Eng. composers. He wrote the books *Catholic Church Music* (1907), *On Music's Borders* (1927), *A Forgotten Psalter and Other Essays* (1929), *The Music of the Roman Rite* (1931), *Voodooism in Music and Other Essays* (1934).

BIBL.: H. Andrews, *Westminster Retrospect: A Memoir of Sir R. T.* (London, 1948); E. Roche, "'Great Learning, fine scholarship, impeccable taste': a fiftieth anniversary tribute to Sir R. T. (1865–1938)," *Early Music* (May 1988).

Terry, Sonny (real name, **Saunders Teddell**), innovative black American virtuoso of the harmonica, singer, and songwriter; b. Greensboro, Ga., Oct. 24, 1911; d. Mineola, N.Y., March 11, 1986. He lost his sight in childhood accidents on the farm where he lived; at the age of 8, learned to play the harmonica and became a street musician in order to earn a living. In 1934 he went to North Carolina, where he worked in partnership with the singer Blind Boy Fuller, evolving remarkable techniques for the mouth harp such as cross-note playing. He met guitarist Brownie McGhee in 1939 and began a partnership that lasted 40 years. They toured continuously and recorded more than 30 albums, which included *Key to the Highway* (1959) and *What a Beautiful City* (1960). Terry's songs include *Mean Woman Blues, These Women Are Killing Me, Hootin' the Blues* (overture to the Broadway musical *Finian's Rainbow*), *I'm a Burnt Child, Jet Plane Blues, Motorcycle Blues*, and *Long Way from Home*.

Terschak, Adolf, Hungarian flutist and composer; b. Hermannstadt, Transylvania, April 6, 1832; d. Breslau, Oct. 3, 1901. He studied at the Vienna Cons.; made long tours, as far west as London, and as far east as Siberia. He wrote numerous pieces for the flute with orch. or piano; also character pieces for orch.; publ. *Ecole de mécanisme* for the flute.

Tertis, Lionel, eminent English violist and teacher; b. West Hartlepool, Dec. 29, 1876; d. London, Feb. 22, 1975. He studied violin at the Leipzig Cons. and at the Royal Academy of Music in London; took up the viola at 19 and became active as a chamber-music artist; eventually became one of the most renowned violists in Europe. In 1901 he became prof. of viola at the Royal Academy of Music, where he was director of its ensemble class (1924–29). In 1936 he retired from his concert career, but in later years made occasional appearances; his farewell performance was given at the age of 87. In 1950 he was made a Commander of the Order of the British Empire. He prepared many transcriptions for his instrument and also commissioned various works from noted English composers. He wrote *Beauty of Tone in String Playing* (London, 1938) and the autobiographical *Cinderella No More* (London, 1953; 2nd ed., rev. and enlarged, 1974, as *My Viola and I: A Complete Autobiography*). He designed the Tertis viola (16 3/4"), which is described in *Music & Letters* (July 1947).

Tervani, Irma, Finnish mezzo-soprano; b. Helsinki, June 4, 1887; d. Berlin, Oct. 29, 1936. She received her primary training with her mother, the soprano Emmy Strömer-Ackté; then studied voice in Paris and Dresden; made her debut with the Dresden Court Opera in 1908 as Dalila, remaining on its roster until 1932. She gained renown through her appearance in the role of Carmen opposite Caruso in Frankfurt am Main in 1910.

Terzakis, Dimitri, Greek composer and teacher; b. Athens, March 12, 1938. He studied composition with Iannis Papaioannou at the Hellenic Cons. in Athens (1957–64); also pursued studies with Bernd Alois Zimmermann at the Cologne Hochschule für Musik (diploma, 1970); also studied Byzantine music and at Mount Athos. He was co-founder of the Greek

Society for Contemporary Music (1966). He lectured on Byzantine music and instrumentation at the Robert Schumann Inst. in Düsseldorf (from 1974, where he taught composition at the Hochschule für Musik (from 1987); also was a visiting prof. of composition at the Berlin Hochschule für Musik (1985–86). In 1980 he founded the International Inst. of Research on the Relations Between Occidental and Southeast-European Music in Nauplia, Greece. Terzaki's music steers a resolute course in the cosmopolitan avant-garde, leaving no tonal stone unturned; ancestral Grecian ethos is present, however, both in the titles and in the modalities of his output.

WORKS: OPERAS: *Torquemada* (1974–76); *Circus Universal*, chamber opera (1975); *Hermes* (1983–84). ORCH.: *Chroai* (1970); *Transcriptions télégraphiques* (1971); *Kosmogramm* (1974); *Tropi* (1975); *Prooimion in Ethods C* for Chamber Orch. (1979); *Lachesis* (1984–85); Violin Concerto (1985–86). CHAMBER: Septet for 7 Flutes (1965–66); Trio for Guitar, Cello, and Percussion (1966); 3 string quartets (1969; 1976; 1981–82); *Stixis II* for Clarinet (1973); Brass Quintet (1983); Saxophone Quartet (1986); Octet (1988). VOCAL: *Okeaniden* for Choir and Orch. (1967); *Ikos* for Choir (1968); *Nuances* for Soprano and Tape (1970); *X* for Baritone and Ensemble (1971); *Karawassia* for 6 Singers (1971–72); *Ethos B* for Soprano and 3 Instruments (1972); *Stichiron* for Choir and Brass (1972); *Passionen*, oratorio (1978–79); *Erotikon* for Soprano and 3 Instruments (1979); *6 Monologe* for Soprano and Orch. (1985); *Das sechste Siegel* for Choir and Ensemble (1987); also *Ichochronos I*, electronic music (1967).

Terziani, Eugenio, Italian conductor, teacher, and composer; b. Rome, July 29, 1824; d. there, June 30, 1889. He studied with Mercadante at the Naples Cons. and later with Baini in Rome. At the age of 19 he produced an oratorio, *La caduta di Gerico* (Rome, March 31, 1844), followed by the operas *Giovanna regina di Napoli* (Ferrara, 1844) and *Alfredo* (Rome, Feb. 21, 1852); was conductor in Rome at the Teatro Apollo (1847–69), at La Scala in Milan (1867–71), and again in Rome (1871–75), where he then taught composition and singing at the Liceo Musicale di S. Cecilia (from 1875). He also wrote the opera *L'assedio di Firenze* (Rome, Feb. 24, 1883), 2 ballets, including *Una Silfide a Pechino* (Rome, Dec. 26, 1859), an *Inno sinfonico* (1882), and much sacred music.

Tesi-Tramontini, Vittoria, famous Italian contralto, known as **La Moretta;** b. Florence, Feb. 13, 1700; d. Vienna, May 9, 1775. She received her instruction in Florence and Bologna; appeared on the stage at the age of 16 in Parma in *Dafni*; then was engaged in Venice (1718–19). She sang in Italy every year, and also appeared in Madrid (1739). In 1748 she sang the title role in Gluck's *Semiramide riconosciuta* in Vienna, where she continued to appear until 1751; then devoted herself to teaching. She was married to one Tramontini, a barber by trade, and adopted the professional name Tesi-Tramontini. She was remarkably free in her morals, and many stories, in which it is impossible to separate truth from invention, were circulated about her life. Her letters to a priest were publ. by Benedetto Croce in his book *Un Prelato e una cantante del secolo XVIII* (Bari, 1946).

BIBL.: A. Ademollo, "Le cantanti italiane celebri del secolo decimottavo: V. T.," *Nuova antologia di scienze, lettere ed arti,* 32nd series, XXII (1889).

Tess (real name, **Tesscorolo**), **Giulia,** noted Italian mezzo-soprano, later soprano; b. Verona, Feb. 9, 1889; d. Milan, March 17, 1976. She studied with Bottagisio in Verona; made her debut as a mezzo-soprano in 1904 in Prato; later sang soprano roles after being encouraged by Battistini. In 1922 she was invited by Toscanini to sing at La Scala in Milan, where she created the role of Jaele in Pizzetti's *Debora e Jaele*. She continued to sing there with great distinction until 1936; then was director of stage craft at the Florence Centro di Avviamento al Teatro Lirico (1940–42), at the Bologna Cons. (1941–46), and at the La Scala opera school (from 1946). Her students included Tagliavini and Barbieri; she also produced opera at La Scala and other Italian opera houses. She was married to

the conductor Giacomo Armani (1868–1954). In addition to the Italian repertoire, she gained distinction as an interpreter of roles by Richard Strauss, excelling as Salome and Elektra.

Tessarini, Carlo, Italian violinist and composer; b. Rimini, c.1690; d. probably in Amsterdam, after 1766. He was a follower, if not actually a pupil, of Corelli; by 1720 he was a violinist at San Marco in Venice; was concertmaster of the concerts of the Cons. Ss. Giovanni e Paolo (from 1729); was active at the chapel of Urbino Cathedral (from c.1733). After a sojourn at the court of Cardinal Wolfgang Schrattenbach in Brünn (c.1735–38), he was again active at Urbino Cathedral until 1744; also made tours as a concert artist in 1739; appeared in the Netherlands in 1747. He was once more active at Urbino Cathedral (1750–57) although he continued to pursue his concert career; subsequently settled in Holland. His violin sonatas, generally in 3 movements, contributed to the establishment of a 3-movement sonata as a norm. He publ. many trio sonatas, duets, concertinos, and concerti grossi; also the interesting treatise, *Gramatica di musica: insegna il modo facile e breve per bene imparare di sonae il violino sù la parte* (Rome, 1741; Eng. tr., 1765).

BIBL.: W. Newman, *The Sonata in the Baroque Era* (Chapel Hill, 1959; 4th ed., rev., 1983); A. Dunning, "Some Notes on the Biography of C. T. and His Musical Grammar," *Studien zur Musikwissenschaft,* XXV (1962).

Tessier, André, French musicologist; b. Paris, March 8, 1886; d. there, July 2, 1931. He studied law, history of art, and other subjects; then devoted himself to musicology; took his diploma at the École du Louvre, 1921; was archivist in the Ministry of Fine Arts; also ed. of the *Revue de Musicologie.* He ed. the complete works of Chambonnières (with P. Brunold; 1925), and Denis Gaultier's *Rhétorique des Dieux* (facsimile, 1932; transcription, 1933). He was the author of a book on Couperin (Paris, 1926); prepared materials for the complete ed. of Couperin's works, but died before his work was finished. A complete list of his writings was publ. by A. Schaeffner in *Revue de Musicologie* (Dec. 1953).

BIBL.: P. Brunold, "Quelques souvenirs sur A. T.," *Revue de Musicologie* (Aug. 1931).

Tessier, Charles, French lutenist and composer who flourished in the late 16th and early 17th centuries. He was chamber musician to Henri IV; his book *Premier livre de chansons et airs de cour tant en français qu'en italien et en gascon à 4 et 4 parties* was publ. in London (1597), and dedicated to Lady Penelope Riche (Sir Philip Sidney's "Stella"); his *Airs et villanelles français, espagnols, suices et turcqs. . .à 3, 4, et 5 parties* was publ. in Paris (1604; 2nd ed., 1610).

BIBL.: G. Ungerer, "The French Lutenist C. T. and the Essex Circle," *Renaissance Quarterly,* XXVIII (1975); J. Ward, "T. and the Essex Circle," ibid., XXIX (1976); N. McBride, *The Chansons of C. T.: A Transcription and Commentary* (diss., Queen's Univ., Belfast, 1977); F. Dobbins, "The Lute Airs of C. T.," *Lute Society Journal,* XX (1978).

Testore, Carlo Giuseppe, Italian instrument maker; b. Novara, c.1660; d. c.1720. He was a pupil of Grancino and worked in Milan (1690–1715); made mostly cellos and double basses, and only a few violins. His son, Paolo Antonio (1690–1760), made violins on the model of Guarneri.

BIBL.: O. Mansfield, "C.G. T.," *British Musician* (1927).

Testori, Carlo Giovanni, Italian music theorist, violin pedagogue, and composer; b. Vercelli, March 24, 1714; d. there, May 20, 1782. He studied violin and composition in Milan, then taught violin in Vercelli. He publ. *La musica raggionata* (Vercelli, 1767), a theoretical treatise based on the system of Rameau; it was followed by 3 supplements (1771, 1773, 1782).

BIBL.: C. Negri, *Brevi considerazioni sull'evoluzione storica ed estetica della musica: Biografie di musicisti vercellesi* (Vercelli, 1909); R. Allorto, "*La musica raggionata* di C.G. T.," *Rivista Musicale Italiana* (July–Sept. 1951).

Tetrazzini, Eva, Italian soprano, sister of **Luisa Tetrazzini;** b. Milan, March, 1862; d. Salsomaggiore, Oct. 27, 1938. She

studied with Ceccherini in Florence, and made her debut there in 1882 as Marguerite in *Faust*. She sang Desdemona in Verdi's *Otello* at its 1st American production (N.Y., April 16, 1888). On May 15, 1887, she married the conductor **Cleofonte Campanini.** She sang with the Manhattan Opera in N.Y. in 1908; then returned to Italy.

Tetrazzini, Luisa (actually, **Luigia**), celebrated Italian soprano, sister of **Eva Tetrazzini;** b. Florence, June 28, 1871; d. Milan, April 28, 1940. She learned the words and music of several operas by listening to her sister; then studied at the Liceo Musicale in Florence with Ceccherini. She made her debut as Inez in *L'Africaine* in Florence (1890); then sang in Europe and traveled with various opera companies in South America. In 1904 she made her U.S. debut at the Tivoli Opera House in San Francisco. She made her London debut at Covent Garden as Violetta on Nov. 2, 1907. She was then engaged by Hammerstein to sing with his Manhattan Opera House in N.Y., where she sang Violetta on Jan. 15, 1908; she remained with the company until it closed in 1910; subsequently appeared for a single season at the Metropolitan Opera (1911–12), making her debut there on Dec. 27, 1911, as Lucia. After singing at the Chicago Grand Opera (1911–13), she toured as a concert artist. She made the 1st broadcast on the British radio in 1925; her last American appearance was in N.Y. in 1931. She then taught in Milan. Her fame was worldwide, and her name became a household word, glorified even in food, as in Turkey Tetrazzini. She publ. *My Life of Song* (London, 1921) and *How to Sing* (N.Y., 1923). She acquired a great fortune, only to die in poverty.
BIBL.: D. Shawe-Taylor, "A Gallery of Great Singers: L. T.," *Opera*, XIV (1963).

Teyber, family of Austrian musicians:
(1) Matthäus Teyber, violinist; b. Weinzettel, c.1711; d. Vienna, Sept. 6, 1785. He settled in Vienna, where he entered the Kapelle of the Empress Elisabeth Christine in 1741; was a court musician from 1757. His family, who became friendly with the Mozart family, included 4 children who distinguished themselves as musicians:
(2) Elisabeth Teyber, soprano; b. Vienna (baptized), Sept. 16, 1744; d. there, May 9, 1816. She was a pupil of Haase and Tesi; appeared in Haase's *Partenope* in Vienna in 1767; then was successful in Naples, Bologna, Milan, Turin, and other Italian opera centers; also sang in Russia.
(3) Anton Teyber, pianist, organist, cellist, and composer; b. Vienna, Sept. 8, 1754; d. there, Nov. 18, 1822. He studied in Vienna and with Padre Martini in Bologna; after touring with his sister in Italy, and appearing in Spain and Portugal, he returned to Vienna about 1781. He was 1st organist at the Dresden Hofkapelle (1787–91); then went again to Vienna as Weigl's deputy at the National-Hoftheater, a position that was soon abolished; however, he petitioned the emperor and was named court composer and keyboard teacher to the imperial children in 1793. His compositions include a melodrama, *Zermes (Zerbes) und Mirabelle* (Vienna, July 15, 1779); 36 syms.; 6 violin concertos; 4 keyboard concertos; 2 horn concertos; a Double Concerto for Violin and Keyboard; 3 octets for 4 Strings, 2 Oboes, and 2 Horns; 2 sextets for 4 Strings and 2 Oboes; 29 string quartets; 2 oratorios, *Gioas, rè di Giuda* (1786) and *La Passione di Gesu Cristo* (c.1790); also 11 masses, graduals, antiphons, and motets.
(4) Franz Teyber, organist, conductor, cellist, bass singer, and composer; b. Vienna, Nov. 15, 1756; d. there, Oct. 22, 1810. He studied with his father and with Wagenseil; after touring in Swabia, Switzerland, and Baden, he became a conductor and composer with Schikaneder's itinerant opera troupe in 1786. After pursuing his career in Karlsruhe (1788–89), in Cologne (1791–93), and in Regensburg, Augsburg, and Bern (1796–98), he returned to Vienna; he wrote the successful opera *Alexander* for the opening of the Theater an der Wien (June 13, 1801), where he was active until 1805; composed for the Leopoldstadt Theater (1807–10); was made organist at St. Stephen's Cathedral in 1809 and court organist in 1810.

WORKS: Dramatic (all 1st perf. in Vienna unless otherwise given): *Laura Rosetti*, opera (Pressburg, Aug. 1785); *Die Dorfdeputierten*, comic opera (Dec. 18, 1785); *Abelheid von Veltheim*, singspiel (Karlsruhe, 1788); *Fernando und Jariko oder Die Indianer*, singspiel (Sept. 5, 1789); *Alexander*, grand opera (June 13, 1801); *Der Schlaftrunk*, singspiel (Nov. 12, 1801); *Der Neuigkeitskrämer oder Der Telegraph*, singspiel (May 12, 1802); *Pfändung und Personalarrest*, singspiel (Dec. 7, 1803); *Der Zerstreute*, comic opera (Jan. 29, 1805); *Andrassek und Jurassek*, pantomime (Feb. 20, 1807); *Ruthards Abenteuer oder Die beiden Sänger*, comic opera (July 26, 1808); *Pumphia und Kulikan*, caricature opera (Oct. 8, 1808); *Der bezauberte Blumenstrauss*, pantomime (Aug. 29, 1809); *Der lebendige Postillonstiefel oder Die Luftreise des Arlequin und der Columbina*, pantomime (July 7, 1810); also sacred vocal works; 6 string quartets; 3 quartets for Keyboard and Strings; Sonata for Piano, Violin, and Cello; 3 piano sonatas; organ music; etc.
(5) Therese Teyber, soprano; b. Vienna (baptized), Oct. 15, 1760; d. there, April 15, 1830. She studied with Bonno and Tesi, making her operatic debut as Fiametta in Ulbrich's *Frühling und Liebe* at the Vienna Court Theater (Sept. 8, 1778); continued to sing there regularly and also in concerts of the Tonkünstler-Sozietät; created the role of Blondchen in *Die Entführung aus dem Serail* (July 16, 1782); retired in 1791. Her husband was the tenor Ferdinand Arnold.

Teyte (real name, **Tate**), **Dame Maggie,** distinguished English soprano; b. Wolverhampton, April 17, 1888; d. London, May 26, 1976. She studied in London; then was a pupil of Jean de Reszke in Paris (1903–7). In 1906 she made her debut at a Mozart Festival in France under her real name. In order to ensure correct pronunciation of her name in France, she changed the original spelling *Tate* to *Teyte*. She made her operatic debut as Tyrcis in Offenbach's *Myriame et Daphné* in Monte Carlo in 1907; was very successful as a concert singer in Paris, and appeared with Debussy at the piano; Debussy also selected her as successor to Mary Garden in the role of Mélisande (1908). She sang at the Paris Opéra-Comique (1908–10), with Beecham's Opera Co. in London (1910–11), with the Chicago Opera Co. (1911–14), and with the Boston Grand Opera Co. (1914–17). She made appearances at London's Covent Garden (1922–23; 1930; 1936–38); then sang in operetta and musical comedies in London; later devoted herself mainly to French song recitals there. In 1951 she made her farewell appearance in opera as Purcell's Belinda in London; gave her last concert there in 1955. She was made a Chevalier of the French Légion d'honneur in 1957 and a Dame Commander of the Order of the British Empire in 1958. In addition to her famous portrayal of Mélisande, she won notable distinction for such roles as Cherubino, Blondchen, Marguerite, Nedda, Madama Butterfly, and Mimi; she also created the Princess in Holst's *The Perfect Fool*. She had 2 indifferent husbands and 2 prominent lovers: Sir Thomas Beecham in London and Georges Enesco in Paris. She publ. a book of memoirs, *Star on the Door* (London, 1958).
BIBL.: C. Wallis, "M. T.," *Opera*, II (1952); G. O'Connor, *The Pursuit of Perfection, A Life of M. T.* (N.Y., 1979).

Thadewaldt, Hermann, German conductor and composer; b. Bodenhagen, April 8, 1827; d. Berlin, Feb. 11, 1909. He was bandmaster at Düsseldorf (1850–51) and Dieppe (1853–55); from 1857 to 1869, was conductor of his own orch. in Berlin, and in 1871 of the concerts at the Zoological Gardens there. In 1872 he founded the Allgemeiner Deutscher Musikerverband, of which he was the 1st president, and to whose interests he devoted his entire time until his death. He publ. a symphonic poem, *Das Rätsel der Sphinx; Im Walde* for Orch.; *Meermusik* for String Orch.; *Herbstlied* for String Quintet; etc.

Thalberg, Sigismond (Fortuné François), celebrated Swiss-born pianist and composer; b. Pâquis, near Geneva, Jan. 8, 1812; d. Posillipo, near Naples, April 27, 1871. His parents were Joseph Thalberg of Frankfurt am Main and Fortunée Stein, also of Frankfurt, but resident in Geneva. Thalberg, however, pretended to be the natural son of Count Moritz

Dietrichstein and Baroness von Wetzlar, who took charge of his education. At age 10 he was sent to Vienna to prepare himself for a career as a diplomat; however, he also received instruction in music from Mittag, 1st bassoonist in the orch. of the Court Opera; he subsequently studied piano with Hummel and theory with Sechter. He played as a precocious pianist in the aristocratic salons of Vienna, and began to compose. In 1830 he made a successful concert tour of England and Germany. After further training with J. Pixis and F. Kalkbrenner in Paris and with Moscheles in London, he returned to Paris in 1836 and set himself up as a serious rival to Liszt; the 2 eventually became friends, and Thalberg went on to pursue a brilliant career as a virtuoso, performing mostly his own works. In 1843 he married the widow of the painter Boucher. In 1855 he set out on a concert tour through Brazil and then visited the U.S. (1856); made a 2nd Brazilian tour in 1863, and in 1864 retired to Naples. Thalberg was unexcelled as a performer of fashionable salon music and virtuoso studies. He possessed a wonderful legato, eliciting from Liszt the remark, "Thalberg is the only artist who can play the violin on the keyboard." His technical specialty was to play a central melody with the thumb of either hand, surrounding it with brilliant arpeggios and arabesques. To present this technique graphically in notation, he made use of the method initiated by Francesco Pollini of writing piano music on 3 staves. He wrote 2 operas, *Florinda* (London, July 3, 1851) and *Cristina di Suezia* (Vienna, June 3, 1855), which were not successful; but his brilliant piano pieces were the rage of his day, easily eclipsing in popular favor those of Chopin, his close contemporary. Among them are a group of nocturnes; several *Caprices*; 2 *Romances sans paroles*; *Grandes valses brillantes*; *Le Départ, varié en forme d'étude*; *Marche funèbre variée*; *Barcarole*; *Valse mélodique*; *Les Capricieuses*; *Tarentelle*; *Souvenir de Vienne*; *La Cadence* (very popular); *Les Soirées de Pausilippe* (6 albums); *Célèbre Ballade*; *La Napolitaine*; several sonatas, many pianistic studies; fantasies on operas by Rossini, Bellini, Meyerbeer, Weber, Verdi, and others.

BIBL.: H. Schonberg, *The Great Pianists* (N.Y., 1963; 2nd ed., rev., 1987); G. Puchelt, *Verlorene Klänge. Studien zur deutschen Klaviermusik 1830–1880* (Berlin, 1969); D. Hitchcock, "S. T., 1812–1871: An Evaluation of the Famous Composer-Pianist, on the 100th Anniversary of his Death," *Piano Quarterly*, No. 77 (1971); V. Vitale, "S. T. a Posillipo," *Nuova Rivista Musicale Italiana* (Oct.–Dec. 1972); R. Lott, *The American Concert Tours of Leopold de Meyer, Henri Herz, and S. T.* (diss., City Univ. of N.Y., 1986).

Thayer, Alexander Wheelock, eminent American music scholar; b. South Natick, Mass., Oct. 22, 1817; d. Trieste, July 15, 1897. He was educated at Harvard Univ. (B.A., 1843; M.A., 1846; LL.B., 1848); was an assistant at the Harvard College library (1845–47), where he pursued valuable research in American psalmody that resulted in his *World of Music* (1846–47); also contributed to the *Philharmonic Journal, Boston Musical Gazette,* and *Musical Times* (1848–52). He went to Germany in 1849 to study German; wrote a detailed and trustworthy biography of Beethoven. In 1852 he returned to the U.S. and became a leading contributor to *Dwight's Journal;* also was on the staff of the *N.Y. Tribune* (1852–54). He was again in Europe to pursue Beethoven research (1854–56); after cataloguing the Lowell Mason private library in Boston (1856–57), he settled in Europe. In 1862 he was attached to the American embassy in Vienna; then was the American consul in Trieste (1866–82). He publ. a *Chronologisches Verzeichniss der Werke Ludwig van Beethoven* (Berlin, 1865); in 1866, vol. I of his lifework, *Ludwig van Beethovens Leben,* appeared in German, tr. from the Eng. MS by Deiters; vol. II was publ. in 1872, and vol. III in 1879. Deiters completed vols. IV and V from Thayer's material, but died before their publication. Riemann then took charge of the project, bringing out revised versions of Deiters's vols. IV (1907) and V (1908); he then revised and enlarged vols. II (1910) and III (1911), completing his task by reediting vol. I (1917). Krehbiel ed. the Eng. version

(3 vols., 1921). A redaction, titled *Thayer's Life of Beethoven,* prepared by Elliot Forbes, was publ. in 1964 (2nd ed., rev., 1967). Thayer also publ. *Ein kritischer Beitrag zur Beethoven-Literatur* (Berlin, 1877; Eng. version in *Dwight's Journal of Music,* XXXVII, 1877–78).

BIBL.: H. Krehbiel, "A.W. T. and His *Life of Beethoven*," *Musical Quarterly* (Oct. 1917); C. Hatch, "The Education of A.W. T.," ibid. (July 1956).

Thayer, (Whitney) Eugene, American organist and composer; b. Mendon, Mass., Dec. 11, 1838; d. Burlington, Vt., June 27, 1889. He began to study the organ at 14; in 1862, assisted at the opening of the great organ in the Music Hall, Boston, where he became regular organist after study with Haupt and Wieprecht in Berlin (1865–66); later played in various Boston churches and was active as a choral conductor; subsequently was organist at the Fifth Ave. Presybterian Church in N.Y. (1881–86); also gave recitals and was active as a teacher. He publ. 2 organ methods and composed various choral pieces and organ works.

Thebom, Blanche, American mezzo-soprano; b. Monessen, Pa., Sept. 19, 1918. She studied singing with Margaret Matzenauer and Edyth Walker in N.Y.; made her concert debut there in 1941 and her operatic debut, with the Metropolitan Opera, as Fricka on Dec. 14, 1944; remained on its roster until 1959, and sang there again from 1960 to 1967; also sang in various opera houses in America and Europe, with increasing success. In 1967 she was appointed head of the Southern Regional Opera Co. in Atlanta; it folded in 1968; in 1980 she was appointed director of the opera workshop of San Francisco State Univ. Among her best roles were Ortrud in *Lohengrin,* Azucena in *Il Trovatore,* Amneris in *Aida,* Laura in *La Gioconda,* and Carmen.

Theil, Johann, distinguished German composer, teacher, and music theorist; b. Naumburg, July 29, 1646; d. there (buried), June 24, 1724. He began his musical training with Johann Scheffler, Kantor in Magdeburg, then pursued the study of law at the Univ. of Leipzig; also received musical instruction from Schütz. In 1673 he was appointed Kapellmeister to Duke Christian Albrecht in Gottorf; after the Duke lost his position in 1675, Theile followed him to Hamburg, where he was chosen to compose the inaugural opera for the new opera house in the Gänsemarkt in 1678. He was Kapellmeister in Wölfenbuttel (1685–91), where he also acquired a fine reputation as a teacher; then held that position at the court of Duke Christian I in Merseburg (1691–94), where he continued to be active as a teacher. About 1718 he settled with his son in Naumburg. Theil was a notable composer of sacred music, known by his contemporaries as "the father of contrapuntists." His theoretical works are also of value.

WORKS (all 1st perf. in Hamburg): STAGE: *Adam und Eva, oder Der erschaffene, gefallene und auffgerichtete Mensch* (Jan. 2, 1678); *Orontes* (1678); *Die Geburth Christi* (1681). SACRED: *Pars prima* [6] *missarum* for 4 Voices and Basso Continuo (Wismar, 1673); *Passio nach dem Heiligen Evangelisten Matthäo* for 4 Voices, 4 Viols, and Basso Continuo (Lübeck, 1673; ed. in Denkmäler Deutscher Tonkunst, XVII, 1904); other masses; 7 Psalms; various motets. SECULAR: *Weltlicher Arien und Canzonetten erstes, anderes und drittes Zehen* for 1, 2, and 4 Voices, 4 Viols, and Basso Continuo (Leipzig, 1667); Sonata for 2 Violins, Trombone, Bassoon, and Basso Continuo; Sonata for Violin, 2 Viols, Violone, and Basso Continuo.

WRITINGS (all in MS): *Musikalisches Kunst-Buch; Curieuser Unterricht von den gedoppelten Contrapuncten; Contrapuncta praecepta; Von den dreifachten Contrapuncten; Gründlicher Unterricht von den gedoppelten Contrapuncten; Von dem vierfachen Contrapunct alla octava.*

BIBL.: J. Mattheson, *Critica musica* (vol. II, Hamburg, 1725); idem, *Grundlage einer Ehren-Pforte* (Hamburg, 1740; ed. by M. Schneider, Berlin, 1910); F. Zelle, *J. T. und N.A. Trungk* (Berlin, 1891); W. Maxton, *J. T.* (diss., Univ. of Tübingen, 1926); J. Mackey, *The Sacred Music of J. T.* (diss., Univ. of Michigan, 1968).

Theodorakis, Mikis (actually, **Michael George**), Greek composer; b. Chios, July 29, 1925. He studied at the Athens Cons. During the German occupation of his homeland, he was active in the resistance; after the liberation, he joined the Left but was arrested and deported during the civil war. In 1953 he went to Paris and studied with Messiaen; soon after he began to compose. After returning to Greece in 1961, he resumed his political activities and served as a member of Parliament in 1963. Having joined the Communist Party, he was arrested after the military coup in 1967 and incarcerated. During this period, he wrote the music for the film Z, dealing with the police murder of the Socialist politician Gregory Lambrakis in Salonika in 1963. The film and the music were greatly acclaimed in Europe and America, and the fate of Theodorakis became a cause célèbre. Yielding to pressure from international public opinion, the military Greek government freed Theodorakis in 1970. In 1972 he quit the Communist Party and was active in the United Left; returning to the Communist Party, he served in Parliament in 1981 and again in 1985–86 before quitting it once more. In 1989 he became an ambassador of conservatism in Greece, going so far as to enter the race for the legislature on the New Democracy ticket; with 416 like-minded painters, writers, musicians, singers, and actors, Theodorakis signed his name to a manifesto (Nov. 3, 1989) condemning the divisive policies of the former Socialist government of Andreas Papandreou; he also ended 4 years of musical silence by appearing on an Athens stage before a crowd of 70,000 people, singing songs of protest and love in the name of national unity. His 4-vol. autobiography was publ. in Athens (1986–88).

WORKS: STAGE: OPERAS: *Kostas Kariotakis* (1985); *Zorbas*, ballet-opera (1988). BALLETS: *Carnaval* (1953; rev. as *Le Feu aux Poudres*, 1958); *Les Amants de Teruel* (1958); *Antigone* (1958); *Antigone II* (1971); *Elektra* (1976); *Mythologie* (1976); *Zorba* (1976); *7 danses grecques* (1982); also incidental music to various dramas; film scores, including *Zorba the Greek* (1962) and *Z* (1973). ORCH.: *Assi-Gonia* (1945–50); *Oedipus Tyrannus* (1946; also for Strings, 1955); 7 syms., including No. 1 (1948–50), No. 2 for Piano, Children's Choir, and Orch. (1958), No. 3 for Soprano, Choir, and Orch. (1980), No. 4 for 2 Soloists, Choir, and Orch. (1986), and No. 7 for 4 Soloists, Choir, and Orch. (1983); 3 suites: No. 1 for Piano and Orch. (1954); No. 2 for Choir and Orch. (1956); No. 3 for Soprano, Choir, and Orch. (1956); Piano Concerto (1957). VOCAL: *L'Amour et la mort* for Mezzo-soprano and String Orch. (1948); *Axion Esti* for 2 Baritones, Speaker, Choir, and Orch. (1960); *Épiphanie Averof* for Soloist, Choir, and Piano (1968); *Canto General*, oratorio for 2 Soloists, Choir, and Orch. (1971–74); *Sadoukeon Passion*, cantata for Tenor, Baritone, Bass, Speaker, Choir, and Orch. (1982); *Phaedra*, 12 songs for 2 Soloists, Choir, and Orch. (1983); *Requiem* for 4 Soloists, Choir, and Children's Choir (1984); *Dionysos*, religious drama for Voice, Choir, and Chamber Ensemble (1984); also choruses and songs. CHAMBER: Trio for Violin, Cello, and Piano (1947); Flute Sextet (1948); 2 sonatinas for Violin and Piano (1955, 1958); various piano pieces.

BIBL.: J. Coubard, *M. T.* (Paris, 1969); G. Giannaris, *M. T.: Music and Social Change* (London, 1973); G. Host, *T.: Myth and Politics in Modern Greek Music* (Amsterdam, 1981).

Theremin (real name, **Termen;** pronounced in Russian with the accent on the last syllable; Gallicized as Thérémin; Anglicized as Theremin, with the accent on the 1st syllable), **Leon**, Russian inventor of the space-controlled electronic instrument that bears his name; b. St. Petersburg, Aug. 15, 1896. He studied physics and astronomy at the Univ. of St. Petersburg; also cello and music theory. He continued his studies in physics at the Petrograd Physico-Technical Inst.; in 1919 he became director of its Laboratory of Electrical Oscillators. On Aug. 5, 1920, he gave a demonstration there of his Aetherophone, which was the prototype of the Thereminovox; also gave a special demonstration of it for Lenin, who at the time was convinced that the electrification of Russia would ensure the

success of communism. In 1927 he demonstrated his new instruments in Germany, France, and the U.S., where, on Feb. 28, 1928, he obtained a patent for the Thereminovox. On April 29, 1930, at Carnegie Hall in N.Y., he presented a concert with an ensemble of 10 of his instruments, also introducing a space-controlled synthesis of color and music. On April 1, 1932, in the same hall, he introduced the 1st electrical sym. orch., conducted by Stoessel and including Theremin fingerboard and keyboard instruments. He also invented the Rhythmicon, for playing different rhythms simultaneously or separately (introduced by Henry Cowell), and an automatic musical instrument for playing directly from specially written musical scores (constructed for Percy Grainger). With the theorist Joseph Schillinger, Theremin established an acoustical laboratory in N.Y.; also formed numerous scientific and artistic associations, among them Albert Einstein, who was himself an amateur violinist. Einstein was fascinated by the relationships between music, color, and geometric and stereometric figures; Theremin provided him a work space to study these geometries, but he himself took no further interest in these correlations, seeing himself "not as a theorist, but as an inventor." More to Theremin's point were experiments made by Stokowski, who tried to effect an increase in sonority among certain instrumental groups in the Philadelphia Orch., particularly in the double basses. These experiments had to be abandoned, however, when the players complained of deleterious effects upon their abdominal muscles, which they attributed to the electronic sound waves produced by the Thereminovox. In 1938 Theremin decided to return to Russia. He soon had difficulties with the Soviet government, which was suspicious of his foreign contacts; he was detained for a period, and speculations and rumors abounded as to his possible fate. Whatever else may have happened, he worked steadily in electronic research for the Soviet government, continuing his experiments with sound as a sideline. Upon his retirement from his work in electronics, he became a prof. of acoustics at the Univ. of Moscow (1964). With the advent of new liberal policies in the U.S.S.R., he was able to travel abroad, appearing in Paris and in Stockholm in 1989. Among his American students from the 1930s, he especially commended Clara Rockmore, a well-known Thereminist.

BIBL.: H. Schonberg, "Music: L. T.," *N.Y. Times* (April 26, 1967); O. Mattis, "Entretien inédit avec Lev Termin," *La Revue Musicale* (Feb. 1991).

Thern, Károly, Hungarian composer of German birth; b. Iglau, Aug. 13, 1817; d. Vienna, April 13, 1886. After studies at the Univ. of Pest, he worked as assistant conductor at the National Theater (1841); taught at the National Cons. (1853–64); later settled in Vienna. He wrote the operas *Giyul* (1841), *Tihany ostroma* (The Siege of Tihany; 1845), and *A képzelt beteg* (The Imaginary Invalid; 1855); also a Sym. (1871), chamber music, songs, and piano pieces. His sons, **Vilmos** (1847–1911) and **Lajos** (1848–1920), studied with Reinecke and Moscheles at the Leipzig Cons., and later with Liszt; after winning distinction as a duo-piano team in Europe, they settled in Vienna as teachers.

Thibaud, Jacques, celebrated French violinist; b. Bordeaux, Sept. 27, 1880; d. (in an airplane crash near Mt. Cemet, in the French Alps, en route to French Indochina) Sept. 1, 1953. He began his training with his father and made his debut at age 8 in Bordeaux; at 13 he entered the Paris Cons. as a pupil of Martin Marsick, graduating with the premier prix in 1896. Obliged to earn his living, he played the violin at the Café Rouge, where he was heard by the conductor Colonne, who offered him a position in his orch.; in 1898 he made his debut as a soloist (with Colonne) with such success that he was engaged for 54 concerts in Paris in the same season. Subsequently he appeared in all the musical centers of Europe, and from 1903 visited America numerous times. With his 2 brothers, a pianist and a cellist, he formed a trio, which had some success; but this was discontinued when he joined Alfred Cortot and Pablo Casals in a famous trio (1930–35). With

Marguerite Long, he founded the renowned Long-Thibaud competition in 1943. His playing was notable for its warmth of expressive tone and fine dynamics; his interpretations of Beethoven ranked very high, but he was particularly authoritative in French music.

BIBL.: J.-P. Dorian, ed., *Un Violon parle; Souvenirs de J. T.* (Paris, 1947); B. Schwarz, *Great Masters of the Violin* (N.Y., 1983).

Thibaudet, Jean-Yves, talented French pianist; b. Lyons, Sept. 7, 1961. When he was 5, he entered the Lyons Cons., where he was a pupil of Herrenschmidt and Bossard; after winning its gold medal in 1974, he pursued training with Descaves, Gianoli, Hubeau, and Ciccolini at the Paris Cons. (1974–81), taking premiers prix in piano and chamber music (1977). In 1978 he won the silver medal at the Busoni Competition in Bolzano; then took 2nd prize at the Casadesus Competition in Cleveland (1979) and at the Tokyo Competition (1980); in 1981 he won the Young Concert Artists International Auditions in N.Y., and subsequently pursued a fine international career. In 1989 he gave a recital at N.Y.'s Lincoln Center. His brilliance as a technician is complemented by his Gallic sensitivity; in addition to his notable interpretations of the French repertoire, he has won accolades for his performances of the masterworks of the 19th and 20th centuries.

Thibault, Geneviève (La Comtesse Hubert de Chambure), French musicologist; b. Neuilly-sur-Seine, May 20, 1902; d. Strasbourg, Aug. 31, 1975. She went to Paris and studied piano with L. Lévy (1919–20), harmony and counterpoint with Eugène Cools (1915–20), and fugue and organ with Nadia Boulanger (1917–23); also took courses at the Sorbonne (diplôme d'Etudes Supérieurs, 1920); later completed her musicological training with Pirro at the École des Hautes Études (diploma, 1952). She became engaged in business, but continued her great interest in musical research; assembled a fine private library, containing rare eds. of Renaissance music, which she opened to research scholars; initiated the Société de Musique d'Autrefois, for the purpose of presenting concerts of early music performed on early instruments; from 1955 she lectured at the Sorbonne. Her contributions to musicology include: with L. Perceau, *Bibliographie des poésies de P. de Ronsard mises en musique au XVIe siècle* (Paris, 1941); with F. Lesure, *Bibliographie des éditions d'Adrien Le Roy et Robert Ballard (1551–1598)* (Paris, 1955; supplement in *Revue de Musicologie*, XL, 1957); with A. Berner and J. van der Meer, *Preservation and Restoration of Musical Instruments* (London, 1967).

BIBL.: J. Jenkins, "G. T., Madame H. d.C.: An Appreciation," *Early Music*, IV (1976).

Thibaut, Anton Friedrich Justus, German music scholar and collector; b. Hameln, Jan. 4, 1772; d. Heidelberg, March 28, 1840. He studied law, and from 1805 was a prof. of jurisprudence at the Univ. of Heidelberg; was also director of a singing club there; wrote *Über Reinheit der Tonkunst* (1825; 7th ed. by R. Heuler, 1907; in Eng. as *On Purity in Musical Art*, 1877). His valuable music library (catalogue publ. in 1842) was acquired by the Hofbibliothek in Munich.

BIBL.: E. Baumstark, *A.F.J. T.* (Leipzig, 1841).

Thibaut IV, Count of Champagne and Brie and King of Navarre, famous French trouvère; b. Troyes, May 30, 1201; d. Pamplona, July 7, 1253. He became king of Navarre in 1234; led the crusade of 1239–40. Some 47 of his works, along with 14 others of joint authorship, have been identified. See H. Anglès, ed., *Las canciones del Rey Teobaldo* (Pamplona, 1973), and K. Brahney, translator, *The Poetry of Thibaut de Champagne* (N.Y., 1988).

BIBL.: A. Wallenskold, *Les Chansons de T. de Champagne, roi de Navarre* (Paris, 1925).

Thienen, Marcel van, French composer and sculptor; b. Paris, Oct. 3, 1922. He studied in Paris, receiving instruction in violin at the École Normale de Musique and at the Cons. (graduated, 1940); also studied composition at the Cons. Russe. After serving as director of the Haiti Cons. (1954–57), he re-

turned to Paris and founded an electronic music studio; in the mid-1960s he turned to sculpture.

WORKS: Opera-farce, *Le Ferroviaire* (1951); *Petite symphonie sur le temps* (1944); *Petite suite digestive* (1951); several pieces for various instruments under the generic title *Amusette*; *Le Damné* for Soprano, Baritone, Men's Chorus, Electronic Music, and Orch. (1962); songs with orch. accompaniment.

Thill, Georges, distinguished French tenor; b. Paris, Dec. 14, 1897; d. Draguignan, Oct. 17, 1984. He studied at the Paris Cons. and with Fernando De Lucia in Naples; returning to Paris, he sang at the Opéra-Comique; made his 1st appearance at the Opéra as Nicias in *Thaïs* (Feb. 4, 1924), and continued to sing there regularly until 1940. He appeared at London's Covent Garden (1928, 1937); made his Metropolitan Opera debut in N.Y. as Roméo (March 20, 1931), remaining on the company's roster until 1932. His farewell appearance was as Canio at the Opéra-Comique in 1953. His outstanding roles included Don José, Roméo, Julien in *Louise*, Aeneas, and Samson; he was also a fine singer of Italian and German roles.

BIBL.: R. Mancini, *G. T.* (Paris, 1966).

Thilman, Johannes Paul, German composer and pedagogue; b. Dresden, Jan. 11, 1906; d. there, Jan. 29, 1973. He was a pupil of Hindemith, Grabner, and Scherchen; also studied at the Dresden Technical Univ. During the Nazi era (1933–45) he was declared an unacceptable composer, and it was only after the fall of the 3rd Reich that he was permitted to pursue his career in earnest. He was founder-director of the "New Music in Dresden" concert series (1947–51); he also taught at the Univ. of Dresden, and later was prof. of composition at the Dresden Hochschule für Musik (from 1965). He publ. *Probleme der neuen Polyphonie* (1949), *Neue Musik: Polemische Beiträge* (1950), and *Musikalische Formenlehre* (1952). Among his compositions are 7 syms. and other orch. works, much chamber music, choral works, piano pieces, and numerous works for school and domestic use.

Thiriet, Maurice, French composer; b. Meulan, May 2, 1906; d. Puys, near Dieppe, Sept. 28, 1972. He studied with Charles Koechlin and Roland-Manuel; then became engaged in radio work in Paris. His music reflects his preoccupation with the theater.

WORKS: Opera-bouffe, *Le Bourgeois de Falaise* (Paris, June 21, 1937); *Rapsodie sur des thèmes incas* for Orch. (Lyons, Jan. 20, 1936); *Afriques* for Orch. (1949); 16 ballets, including *La Nuit vénitienne* (Paris, March 17, 1938); *La Précaution inutile*, on themes by Rossini (1946); *Bonaparte à Nice* (Nice, 1960); *Le More de Venise* (Monte Carlo, 1960); *Les Amants de Mayerling* (Nice, 1961); *La Chambre noire* (Toulouse, 1969); film scores; chamber music; choral works; songs; piano pieces.

BIBL.: J. Solar, *M. T.* (Paris, 1958).

Thoinan, Ernest (real name, **Antoine-Ernest Roquet**), French writer on music; b. Nantes, Jan. 23, 1827; d. Paris, May 26, 1894. He was a merchant by trade, but also an ardent student of music; during his extensive travels in Italy, England, and Russia, he collected a fine music library.

WRITINGS: (all publ. in Paris): With A. de Lasalle, *La Musique à Paris* (1863); *L'Opéra "Les Troyens" au "Père Lachaise"* (1863; a satire); *Les Origines de la chapelle-musique des souverains de France* (1864); with C. Nuitter, *Les Origines de l'opéra français* (1886); *Déploration de Guillaume Crétin sur le trépas de Jean Ockeghem* (1864); *Maugars, célèbre joueur de viole* (1865); *Antoine de Cousu et les singulières destinées de son livre rarissime "La Musique universelle"* (1866); *Curiosités musicales et autres trouvées dans les œuvres de Michel Coyssard* (1866); *Un Bisaïeul de Molière; Recherches sur les Mazuel, musiciens des XVIe et XVIIe siècles* (1878); *Louis Constantin, roi des violons* (1878); *Notes bibliographiques sur la guerre musicale des Gluckistes et Picinistes* (1878); *Les Hotteterre et les Chédeville* (1894); also an annotated ed. of *Entretien des Musiciens* [1643] by Annibal Gantez (1878).

Thomán, István, Hungarian pianist and pedagogue; b. Homonna, Nov. 4, 1862; d. Budapest, Sept. 22, 1940. He studied with Erkel and Volkmann in Budapest (1882–85); then was a pupil of Liszt there and in Weimar and Rome; taught at the Royal Academy of Music in Budapest (1888–1906). He was greatly esteemed as a teacher; among his students were Dohnányi and Bartók. He publ. a collection of technical piano studies in 6 vols., and also composed songs and piano pieces. His wife, **Valerie Thomán** (b. Budapest, Aug. 16, 1878; d. there, Sept. 8, 1948), was a renowned concert singer, who gave early performances of works by Kodály and Bartók; their daughter **Mária Thomán** (b. Budapest, July 12, 1899; d. there, Feb. 25, 1948), a pupil of Hubay, Vecsey, and Flesch, was a fine violinist who toured throughout Europe.

Thomas, (Charles Louis) Ambroise, noted French composer and teacher; b. Metz, Aug. 5, 1811; d. Paris, Feb. 12, 1896. He entered the Paris Cons. in 1828; his teachers there were Zimmerman (piano) and Dourlen (harmony and accompaniment); he studied privately with Kalkbrenner (piano) and Barbereau (harmony); subsequently studied composition with Le Sueur at the Cons., where he won the Grand Prix de Rome with his cantata *Hermann et Ketty* (1832). After 3 years in Italy, and a visit to Vienna, he returned to Paris and applied himself with great energy to the composition of operas. In 1851 he was elected to the Académie; in 1856 he became a prof. of composition at the Paris Cons.; in 1871 he became director there. As a composer of melodious operas in the French style, he was second only to Gounod; his masterpiece was *Mignon*, based on Goethe's *Wilhelm Meister* (Paris, Nov. 17, 1866); this opera became a mainstay of the repertoire all over the world; it had nearly 2,000 performances in less then 100 years at the Opéra-Comique alone. Equally successful was his Shakespearean opera *Hamlet* (Paris, March 9, 1868). In 1845 he was made a Chevalier of the Légion d'honneur, being the 1st composer to receive its Grand Croix in 1894.

WORKS (all 1st perf. in Paris): **STAGE** (all opéras comiques unless otherwise given): *La double échelle* (Aug. 23, 1837); *Le perruquier de la régence* (March 30, 1838); *Le panier fleuri* (May 6, 1839); *Carline* (Feb. 24, 1840); *Le comte de Carmagnola* (April 19, 1841); *Le guerillero* (June 22, 1842); *Angélique et Médor* (May 10, 1843); *Mina, ou Le Ménage à trois* (Oct. 10, 1843); *Le caïd* (Jan. 3, 1849); *Le songe d'une nuit d'été* (April 20, 1850); *Raymond, ou Le secret de la reine* (June 5, 1851); *La Tonelli* (March 30, 1853); *La cour de Célimène* (April 11, 1855); *Psyché* (Jan. 26, 1857); *Le carnaval de Venise* (Dec. 9, 1857); *Le roman d'Elvire* (Feb. 4, 1860); *Mignon* (Nov. 17, 1866); *Hamlet* (opera; March 9, 1868); *Gille et Gillotin* (opera; April 22, 1871); *Françoise de Rimini* (opera; April 14, 1882). **BALLETS:** *La gipsy* (Jan. 28, 1839; in collaboration with F. Benoist and M. Marliani); *Betty* (July 10, 1846); *La tempête* (June 26, 1889). **ORCH.:** *Fantaisie brillante* for Piano and Orch. (n.d.; also for Piano and String Quartet); *Marche religieuse* (March 25, 1865); *Chant de psaume laudate* for Violin and Orch. (n.d.). **CHAMBER:** String Quartet (1833); Piano Trio (c.1835); String Quintet (1835); piano pieces; organ music; also sacred vocal works, including *Requiem Mass* for Chorus and Orch. (c.1840) and *Messe solennelle* for Chorus and Orch. (Nov. 22, 1857); secular vocal works. **BIBL.:** H. Delaborde, *Notice sur la vie et les œuvres de M.A. T.* (Paris, 1896); H. de Curzon, *A. T.* (Paris, 1921); M. Cooper, "C.L.A. T.," in A. Bacharach, ed., *The Music Masters* (Vol. II, London, 1950; also publ. separately, London, 1957–58).

Thomas, Arthur Goring, English composer; b. Ratton Park, Sussex, Nov. 20, 1850; d. (suicide) London, March 20, 1892. He was a pupil of Émile Durand in Paris (1873–75), and of Arthur Sullivan and Ebenezer Prout at the Royal Academy of Music in London (1877–80); later studied orchestration in Berlin with Max Bruch. He was mainly interested in creating English operas in the best German tradition; his operas were performed in England and Germany, and he had many important supporters for his art in England, but his music totally lacked vitality, and became of only antiquarian interest after his death. In the last years of his life he suffered from a mental illness.

WORKS: OPERAS: *The Light of the Harem* (partial perf., London, Nov. 7, 1879); *Esmeralda* (London, March 26, 1883; rev. version, London, July 12, 1890); *Nadezhda* (London, April 16, 1885); *The Golden Web* (Liverpool, Feb. 15, 1893); also a choral ode, *The Sun-worshippers* (Norwich Festival, 1881); cantata, *The Swan and the Skylark* (completed and orchestrated by C. Stanford; Birmingham Festival, 1894); chamber music; songs.

BIBL.: J. Klein, "Tragic, Forgotten Pioneer: A.G. T.," *Music Review*, XXXVI (1975).

Thomas, Augusta Read, American composer; b. Glen Cove, N.Y., April 24, 1964. She studied with Alan Stout at Northwestern Univ. (B.M., 1987) and with Jacob Druckman at Yale Univ. (M.M., 1988); completed postgraduate work at the Royal Academy of Music in London (1988–89). She received numerous awards and honors, including a Guggenheim fellowship (1989), NEA grants (1988–90), and prizes from ASCAP (1987–89) and BMI (1989).

WORKS: ORCH.: *Glow in the Light Darkness* for Chamber Orch. (1983); *Tunnel at the End of Light* for Piano and Orch. (1984); *Sonnet from the Daybreak Moon* (1986); *Moon and Light* for Trumpet and Orch. (1987); *Under the Sun* (1987); *Glass Moon* (1988); *Sunset of Empire* (1988); *Crystal Planet* (1989); *. . . to the light unseen . . .* for Flute and String Orch. (1989); *Echoes* for Soprano, Mezzo-soprano, and Chamber Orch. (1989); *Wind Dance* (1990). **CHAMBER:** *Le Radeau de la Méduse* for Piano Quartet (1985); *Trinity* for Piano and Chamber Ensemble (1986); Partita for Brass Quintet (1987); *Red Moon* for Flute, Clarinet, Violin, Cello, Piano, and 2 Percussion (1988); *Wheatfield with Lark on the Painting of Van Gogh* for Flute and 17 Winds (1988); Sonata for Solo Trumpet (1988); *Streams of Illusion* for String Quartet (1989); *Aria* for Flute, Oboe, Violin, Cello, and Piano (1989). **VOCAL:** *Tranquil Image* for Chorus (1986); *Cantata III* for Chorus and 13 Players (1987); *Folk Song* for Children's Chorus (1990); also numerous works for Solo Instruments; piano pieces, including *tqtama* (1983), *psalm* (1987), *Ballade* (1988), and *whites* (1988).

Thomas, Christian Gottfried, German horn player, music publisher, impresario, writer on music, and composer; b. Wehrsdorf, near Bautzen, Feb. 2, 1748; d. Leipzig, Sept. 12, 1806. He studied law at the Univ. of Leipzig (1770–71) before devoting himself to music. In 1771 he was made 1st horn player of the Leipzig Grosses Konzert; in 1776 he organized a music copying and MS storehouse enterprise in Leipzig, where he became an influential impresario; also toured as a horn player. Among his works, most of which are lost, were syms.; 2 double concertos for Waldhorn; *Gloria* for 3 Choirs and 24 Instruments (Hamburg, Aug. 18, 1789); *Psalm CXLIX* for Double Choir (1789–94); Cantata for 2 Choirs and 24 Instruments (Prague, Aug. 13, 1792); (2) *Gedichte* for Soprano, Tenor, and 18 Instruments (1792); *Schlachtgesang* for 2 Choirs and 30 Instruments (1795); (4) *Volksgesänge* for Choir and 20 Instruments (1797); and *Psalm CXVII* for 7 Choirs and Orch. His writings include *Praktische Beyträge zur Geschichte der Musik, musikalischen Litteratur und gemeinen Besten* (Leipzig, 1778); *Kurzgefasster Entwurf des Plan's des zuerrichtenden öffentlichen Musik-Conservatoriums und Musikalienhandlung zu N.N. (nach der neuesten vorsunehmende Einrichtung)* (Leipzig, 1781); *Unpartheiische Kritik* (Leipzig, 1798–1800?; continued as *Musikalische kritische Zeitschrift*, 1800?–1806); *Nachtricht an ein verehrungswürdiges Publikum: Die Herausgabe einer kritischen musicalischen Zeitschrift in Vergleichung mit einem andren ähnlichen Unternehmen betreffend* (Leipzig, July 11, 1798); and *Musikalisch-litterarische Anzeige* (Leipzig, Aug. 15, 1798).

Thomas, David (Lionel Mercer), English bass; b. Orpington, Kent, Feb. 26, 1943. He was educated at St. Paul's Cathedral Choir School, King's School, Canterbury, and King's College, Cambridge. He 1st gained recognition as a soloist with Rooley's Consort of Musicke, Hogwood's Academy of Music, and other early-music groups in England; subsequently appeared throughout Europe. In 1982 he made his U.S. debut at the Hollywood Bowl. In later years he pursued an international career, specializing in the Baroque and Classical concert and operatic repertoires. He won particular distinction for his performances of works by Monteverdi, Purcell, Bach, Handel, and Mozart.

Thomas, Gustav Adolf, German organist and composer; b. Reichenau, near Zittau, Oct. 13, 1842; d. St. Petersburg, May 27, 1870. He studied at the Leipzig Cons.; was organist at the Reformed Church in Leipzig; then at St. Peter's in St. Petersburg. He wrote excellent works for organ: *Konzert-Fantasie; Sechs Trios über bekannte Choralmelodien; Fuga eroica;* études; piano pieces.

Thomas, Jess (Floyd), American tenor; b. Hot Springs, S.Dak., Aug. 4, 1927. After studying psychology at the Univ. of Nebraska and at Stanford Univ., he turned to singing; had formal study with Otto Schulman; made his formal debut as Malcolm at the San Francisco Opera in 1957, then continued his training with Emmy Seiberlich; was a member of the Karlsruhe Opera (1958–61); sang Parsifal at the Bayreuth Festival (1961) and appeared in other German music centers. On Dec. 11, 1962, he made his Metropolitan Opera debut in N.Y. as Walter von Stolzing. In 1963 he joined the Bavarian State Opera in Munich, and was honored with the title of Kammersänger; also made guest appearances in Salzburg, Vienna, London's Covent Garden, and other major opera centers.

Thomas, John, celebrated Welsh harpist and composer; b. Ogmore, Glamorgan, March 1, 1826; d. London, March 19, 1913. He received instruction in harp from his father; in 1840, entered the Royal Academy of Music in London and studied harp with Chatterton. In 1871 he was made Harpist to the Queen. He gave in London a series of annual concerts of Welsh music; the 1st took place at St. James's Hall, July 4, 1862, with a chorus of 400, and 20 harps. He was also a leader of the Eisteddfod festivals. He wrote a Sym., 2 harp concertos, the cantatas *Llewelyn* (Aberdare, 1863) and *The Bride of Neath Valley* (1863), pieces for Solo Harp, and various transcriptions for his instrument; also ed. *Welsh Melodies* (1862–74). His brother, **Thomas Thomas** (1829–1913), was also a harpist.

Thomas, John Charles, American baritone; b. Meyersdale, Pa., Sept. 6, 1891; d. Apple Valley, Calif., Dec. 13, 1960. He studied at the Peabody Cons. in Baltimore; from 1913, sang in musical comedy in N.Y. He made his operatic debut as Amonasro in Washington, D.C. (March 3, 1924). In 1925 he made his European operatic debut as King Herod in Massenet's *Hérodiade* at the Théâtre Royal de la Monnaie in Brussels, where he sang until 1928; made his Covent Garden debut in London as Valentin in *Faust* (June 28, 1928). He then sang opera in Philadelphia (1928), San Francisco (1930, 1943), and Chicago (1930–32; 1934–36; 1939–42); made his Metropolitan Opera debut in N.Y. as the elder Germont on Feb. 2, 1934, and remained on the company's roster until 1943. Throughout these years he toured widely in the U.S. as a concert artist; also appeared regularly on the "Bell Telephone Hour" radio program. Among his other roles were Rossini's Figaro, Scarpia, and Strauss's Jokanaan.

Thomas, John Rogers, Welsh-American baritone and composer; b. Newport, March 26, 1829; d. N.Y., April 5, 1896. He was a lawyer's clerk in London; settled in N.Y., where he made his debut as a soloist in Haydn's *The Creation* (Dec. 3, 1849); acquired considerable success as an oratorio singer. A number of his songs enjoyed tremendous popularity in their day (*The Mother's Prayer, The Cottage by the Sea, Beautiful Isle of the Sea, Must we then meet as strangers, The Rose of Killarney,* etc.). He publ. an operetta, *Diamond Cut Diamond* (1876); a children's cantata, *The Picnic;* and much sacred music.

Thomas (Sabater), Juan María, Spanish organist and composer; b. Palma, Majorca, Dec. 7, 1896; d. there, May 4, 1966. He studied with Daniel, Mas y Serracant, and Huré; was organist at the Palma Cathedral (from 1914); founded the Capella Classica (1932), with which he toured worldwide. He publ.

the study *Don Manuel de Falla en la isla* (Palma, 1947); composed choral works, songs, organ music, and piano pieces.

BIBL.: G. Bourgligueux, "J.M. T. (1896–1966)," *L'Orgue,* No. 128 (1968).

Thomas, (Georg Hugo) Kurt, prominent German choral conductor, pedagogue, and composer; b. Tönning, May 25, 1904; d. Bad Oeynhausen, March 31, 1973. He studied organ with Straube, piano with Teichmuller, and composition with Grabner at the Leipzig Cons., and composition with A. Mendelssohn in Darmstadt. He taught theory and composition at the Leipzig Cons. (1925–34), and was conductor of the choir at the Inst. of Church Music in Leipzig (1928–34); then was a prof. at the Berlin Hochschule für Musik (1934–39). He went to Frankfurt am Main as director of the Musisches Gymnasium (1939–45) and as Kantor of the Dreikönigskirche (1945–56); also was a prof. at the North West German Music Academy in Detmold (1947–55). After serving as director of the Leipzig Thomaskantorei and of the Thomasschule (1955–61), he resumed his post with the Frankfurt Dreikönigskirche and also became conductor of the Cologne Bach Soc.; taught choral conducting at the Lübeck Academy of Music (from 1969). He publ. the important manual *Lehrbuch der Chorleitung* (3 vols., Leipzig, 1935–48; Eng. tr., 1971, as *The Choral Conductor*). Among his compositions are many choral works, including a Mass (1925), *Passionsmusik nach den Evangelisten Markus, Weihnachts-Oratorium, Auferstehungs-Oratorium,* cantatas, Psalms, and motets; several orch. works, including a Piano Concerto; chamber music, organ pieces, and songs.

BIBL.: J. Mehl, "K. T. 60 Jahre," *Gottesdienst und Kirchenmusik* (1964); M. Kluge, ed., *Choreziehung und neue Musik: Für K. T. zum 65. Geburtstag* (Wiesbaden, 1969).

Thomas, Michael Tilson, greatly talented American conductor; b. Los Angeles, Dec. 21, 1944. A grandson of Boris and Bessie Thomashefsky, founders of the Yiddish Theater in N.Y., he was brought up in a cultural atmosphere; he studied at the Univ. of Southern Calif., where he received instruction in composition with Ingolf Dahl; he also studied with the pianist John Crown and the harpsichordist Alice Ehlers; concurrently took courses in chemistry. He acquired his conductorial skill by practical work with the Young Musicians Foundation Debut Orch., which he led from 1963 to 1967. He served as pianist in the master classes of Heifetz and Piatigorsky at the Univ. of Southern Calif. in Los Angeles; also conducted at the Monday Evening Concerts, where he presented 1st performances of works by Stravinsky, Copland, Boulez, and Stockhausen; in 1966 he attended master classes at the Bayreuth Festival; in 1967 he was assistant conductor to Boulez at the Ojai Festival; he conducted there also in 1968, 1969, and 1973. As a conducting fellow at the Berkshire Music Center at Tanglewood in 1968, he won the Koussevitzky Prize. The crowning point of his career was his appointment in 1969 as assistant conductor of the Boston Sym. Orch.; he was the youngest to receive such a distinction with that great ensemble. He was spectacularly catapulted into public notice on Oct. 22, 1969, when he was called upon to conduct the 2nd part of the N.Y. concert of the Boston Sym. Orch., substituting for its music director, William Steinberg, who was taken suddenly ill. In 1970 he was appointed associate conductor of the Boston Sym. Orch., and then was a principal guest conductor there with Colin Davis from 1972 to 1974. From 1971 to 1979 he was music director of the Buffalo Phil. Orch.; served as music director of the N.Y. Phil. Young People's Concerts (1971–76). He was a principal guest conductor of the Los Angeles Phil. Orch. (1981–85). From 1986 to 1989 he was music director of the Great Woods Performing Arts Center in Mansfield, Mass., the summer home of the Pittsburgh Sym. Orch.; served as artistic advisor of the New World Sym. Orch. in Miami (from 1987). In 1988 he became principal conductor of the London Sym. Orch. He has also appeared widely as a guest conductor throughout North America and Europe. His repertoire is exhaustive, ranging from the earliest masters to the avant-garde. He is also an excellent pianist. Above all, he is a modern musician, energetic, pragmatically proficient, and able to extract the maximum value of the music on hand.

BIBL.: M. Sigman, "M.T.T., American Explorer," *Symphony Magazine*, XXVI/2 (1985); D. Stearns, "M.T. T.: 'Let 'Em Sing Gershwin'," *Ovation* (Dec. 1987).

Thomas, Theodore (Christian Friedrich), renowned German-American conductor; b. Esens, East Friesland, Oct. 11, 1835; d. Chicago, Jan. 4, 1905. Taught by his father, a violinist, he played in public at the age of 6. In 1845 the family went to N.Y., where Thomas soon began to play for dances, weddings, and in theaters, helping to support the family; in 1851 he made a concert tour as a soloist, and in 1853 he joined Jullien's orch. on its visit to N.Y., later touring the country with Jenny Lind, Grisi, Sontag, Mario, et al. He became a member of the N.Y. Phil. Society in 1854. With the pianist William Mason, he founded a series of monthly matinee chamber concerts at N.Y.'s Dodworth Hall in 1855, which remained a vital force until it was disbanded in 1869. He 1st gained notice as a conductor when he led a performance of *La favorite* at the N.Y. Academy of Music on April 29, 1859. In 1862 he led his 1st orch. concerts at N.Y.'s Irving Hall, which became known as Symphonic Soirées in 1864; they were continued at Steinway Hall (1872–78); in 1865 he began a series of summer concerts in Terrace Garden, relocating these in 1868 to Central Park Garden. The influence of these enterprises on musical culture in N.Y. was enormous; Thomas's programs attained European celebrity. The 1st concert tour with the Theodore Thomas orch. was made in 1869, and in subsequent years he led it on many tours of the U.S. and Canada. In 1873 he established the famous Cincinnati Biennial May Festival, which he conducted until his death. He also founded the Cincinnati College of Music, of which he was president and director from 1878 to 1880, having given up his own orch. in N.Y. and the conductorship of the N.Y. Phil. Society (1877–78) to accept this post. After his resignation, he returned to N.Y., where he immediately reorganized his own orch. and was reelected conductor of the Phil. Society Orch. and the Brooklyn Phil. Orch. (having been conductor of the latter in 1862–63, 1866–68, and 1873–78). Besides conducting these orch. bodies, he was at different times director of several choruses; from 1885 to 1887 he was conductor and artistic director of the American Opera Co. In 1891 he settled permanently in Chicago as conductor of the Chicago Orch. In recognition of Thomas's distinguished services, a permanent home, Orch. Hall, was built by popular subscription, and formally opened in Dec. 1904, with a series of festival concerts, which were the last directed by him. After his death, the name of the orch. was changed to the Theodore Thomas Orch. in 1906; it became the Chicago Sym. Orch. in 1912.

The influence of Thomas upon the musical development of the U.S. has been strong and lasting. An ardent apostle of Wagner, Liszt, and Brahms, he also played for the 1st time in America works of Tchaikovsky, Dvořák, Rubinstein, Bruckner, Goldmark, Saint-Saëns, Cowen, Stanford, Raff, and Richard Strauss. He likewise programmed many works by American composers.

BIBL.: G. Upton, ed., *T. T.: A Musical Autobiography* (2 vols.; Chicago, 1905); R. Thomas (his 2nd wife), *Memoirs of T. T.* (N.Y., 1911); P. Otis, *The Chicago Symphony Orchestra* (Chicago, 1925); C. Russell, *The American Orchestra and T. T.* (N.Y., 1927); E. Rice, "T. and Central Park Garden," *Musical Quarterly* (April 1940); A. Loft, "Richard Wagner, T. T., and the American Centennial," ibid. (April 1951); T. Russell, *T. T.: His Role in the Development of Musical Culture in the United States, 1835–1905* (diss., Univ. of Minnesota, 1969); E. Schabas, *T. T.: America's Conductor and Builder of Orchestras, 1835–1905* (Champaign-Urbana, 1989).

Thomas Aquinas, Saint, famous Italian theologian, philosopher, and poet; b. Roccasecca, near Aquino, 1224 or 1225; d. Fossanova, March 7, 1274. In 1263 Pope Urban IV commissioned him to compose a communion service, which contains the memorable numbers *Lauda Sion* (Corpus Christi sequence)

and *Pange lingua, Sacra solemnis, Verbum supernum,* and *Adoro te* (hymns). An extended chapter on music is contained in his *Summa Theologica* (II, *quaestio XLI*).

BIBL.: G. Amelli, *S. Tomaso e la musica* (1876); D. *Thomas Aquinatis de arte musica nunc primum ex codice bibl. univ. Ticinensis ed. illustr. Sac. Guarinus Amelli* (1880); C. Bellet, *St. Th. d'Aquin* (Paris, 1902); J. Callahan, *A Theory of Esthetics According to the Principles of St. Th. Aquinas* (diss., Catholic Univ., Washington, D.C., 1927).

Thomas-San-Galli, Wolfgang Alexander, German violist and writer on music; b. Badenweiler, Sept. 18, 1874; d. Baden-Baden, June 14, 1918. He studied philosophy, history, and law in Freiburg, Bonn, Munich, and Marburg (Dr. Jur., 1898); from 1899 to 1908, was the violist of the Süddeutsches Streich-Quartett in Freiburg; from 1908 to 1911, ed. of the *Rheinische Musikund Theaterzeitung* in Cologne; then lived in Berlin as a writer. In 1898 he married the pianist Helene San-Galli.

WRITINGS: *Sein oder Nichtsein? Aphorismen über Ethisches und Ästhetisches* (1905); *Johannes Brahms. Eine musikpsychologische Studie* (1905); *Musik und Kultur* (1908); *Musikalische Essays* (1908); *Die "unsterbliche Geliebte" Beethovens, Amalie Sebald* (1909); *Beethoven und die unsterbliche Geliebte. Amalie Sebald, Goethe, Therese Brunswick, und Anderes* (1910); *Mozart-Schatzkästlein* (1911); *Johannes Brahms* (1912; 5th ed., 1922); *Ludwig van Beethoven* (1913). He ed. *Beethovens Briefe* (1910; selection with commentary) and *Beethovens Briefe an geliebte Frauen* (1913).

Thomé, Francis (baptized **François Luc Joseph**), French composer and teacher; b. Port Louis, Mauritius, Oct. 18, 1850; d. Paris, Nov. 16, 1909. He went to Paris as a youth, and studied at the Cons. with Marmontel (piano), Duprato (harmony), and A. Thomas (composition), winning a premier prix for counterpoint and fugue (1870); then was active as a composer and teacher. He wrote the operas: *Le Caprice de la Reine* (Cannes, April 1892) and *Le Château de Königsberg* (Paris, April 22, 1896); the ballets *Djemmah* (1886), *La Folie parisienne* (1900), etc.; the religious mystery play *L'Enfant Jésus* (1891); 2 symphonic odes, *Hymne à la nuit* and *Vénus et Adonis*; Piano Trio (1893); Violin Sonata (1901); numerous songs; much piano music.

Thommessen, Olav Anton, imaginative Norwegian composer and teacher; b. Oslo, May 16, 1946. He studied composition with Bernhard Heiden at the Indiana Univ. School of Music in Bloomington (B.M., 1969), where he also attended the lectures of Iannis Xenakis; continued his training in Warsaw, and then pursued studies in electronic music with Werner Kaegi and Otto Laske at the Instituut voor Sonologie at the Univ. of Utrecht; in 1973 he joined the faculty of the Norwegian State Academy of Music in Oslo. In his compositions he utilizes Western and non-Western elements in a contemporary style mainly within the tonal tradition.

WORKS: STAGE: *Hermaphroditen* (The Hermaphrodite), chamber opera comprising the following 6 works: *Det Hemmelige Evangeliet* (The Secret Gospel; Bergen, May 24, 1976); *Hermaphroditen* (1975; Vadstena, Sweden, July 28, 1976); *Et Konsert-Kammer* (A Concert-Chamber; 1971; Warsaw, Feb. 6, 1972); *Ekko av et ekko* (Echo of an Echo; Malmö, Oct. 26, 1980); *Gjensidig* (Mutually; 1973; Luleå, Sweden, July 4, 1974); *Overtonen* (The Overtone; Bergen, May 31, 1977); *Melologer og Monodramaer* (Wordless Chamber Opera; Vadstena, July 20, 1982); incidental music. **ORCH.:** *Vårlosning* (Thaw; Bloomington, Ind., May 8, 1969); *Opp-Ned* (Up-Down; 1972–73; Oslo, March 23, 1973); *Stabsarabesk* (1974; orchestrated by A. Bukkvoll as *Barbaresk*, 1974–77; Trondheim, March 24, 1977); *Et Glassperlespill* (A Glass Bead Game), comprising the following 6 works: *Pedagogisk Ouverture* (Pedagogical Overture) for Narrator and Strings (1979–80; Oslo, Feb. 13, 1981); *Makrofantasi over Griegs a-moll Konsert* (Macrofantasy on Grieg's A-minor Concerto; 1980; Bergen, Jan. 14, 1982); *Hinsides neon* (Beyond Neon), post-commercial sound sculptures for Horn and Orch. (1981; Minneapolis, Sept. 22, 1982); *Korsymfoni over Beethoven Åttende* for Chorus and Orch. (1980);

Gjennom prisme (Through a Prism), double concerto for Cello, Organ, and Orch. (1984; Norwegian Radio, Jan. 1989); *Ekstranummer over Verdis Dies Irae: Apotheose* (Encore on Verdi's Dies Irae: Apotheosis) for Chorus and Orch. (1979–80); *Fra Oven* (From Above), concerto for Synthesizer and Orch. (1986; Stavanger, Sept. 16, 1987); *Trusselen mot lyset* (The Threat Toward the Light; 1986); *The Great Attractor*, "cadenza accompagnata" for Violin and Orch. (Oslo, Aug. 4, 1988); *The 2nd Creation*, orch. drama for Trumpet and Orch. (Oslo, Sept. 15, 1988). CHAMBER: Sonata for Violin and Piano (1966); Duo Sonata for Cello and Piano (1968); 2 string quartets (1969, 1970); *Kvadratspill I* (1972) and *II* (1974) for 4 Percussionists; *Stanza* for Clarinet (1975); *S 15* for Vihuela, Renaissance Lute or Guitar, Alto Guitar, and Small Percussion (1976); *Nok en til* (Yet Another) for Woodwind Quintet (1977); *Vennligst godta min hørsel* (Please Accept My Ears) for Violin and Piano (1981); *Blokkfuglen* (The Block-bird) for Alto or Tenor Recorder (1981); *Scherzofonia/Scherzofrenia* for Violin, Cello, and Piano (Bergen, March 6, 1982); *Gratias Agimus* for Trumpet and Piano (1983); *Minia-Teks-Tur* for Tuba and Percussion (1985); *Rhapsodia improvizata* for 2 Cellos (1985); *Smaragd tavlen* (The Emerald Tablet) for 2 Pianos and 2 Percussion (1985); *L'Éclat approchant* for Piano, Harpsichord, and Synthesizer (1986); *Tibil* for Organ and Synthesizer (1986); Piano Sonata (1986). VOCAL: *Maldoror/Hunhaien* for 2 Vocal Actors and 4 Percussionists (1974); *Stabat Mater speciosa* for Chorus (1977); *Elfuglen* (The Electric Bird) for Soprano and Electronics (1980); *Sjelen, Lyttende—En gnostisk kantate* (The Ears of the Mind—A Gnostic Cantata) for Soprano, Reciter, 2 Cellos, Double Bass, Organ, and 2 Percussion (1984).

Thompson, John Winter, American organist, teacher, and composer; b. Leland, Mich., Dec. 21, 1867; d. St. Charles, Ill., March 8, 1951. After graduating from the Oberlin Cons. (1890), he studied at the Leipzig Cons. with Schreck (1893–94); returned to Europe to study with Bonnet and Sinding (1921–22). He taught at Knox College, Galesburg, Ill. (from 1890), serving as a prof. (1909–38); also was organist at the Central Congregational Church in Galesburg (1890–1926) and toured as a recitalist. He publ. textbooks on harmony (1923) and counterpoint (1925); composed organ works, motets, and anthems.

Thompson, Oscar, American music critic and editor; b. Crawfordsville, Ind., Oct. 10, 1887; d. N.Y., July 3, 1945. He was educated at the Univ. of Washington, Seattle; studied music with G. Campanari and others; took up journalism and in 1919 joined the staff of *Musical America*, later becoming associate ed. and finally ed. (1936–43). He was music critic for the N.Y. *Evening Post* (1928–34); from 1937 to his death he was music critic for the N.Y. *Sun*. In 1928 he established the 1st class in music criticism in the U.S. at the Curtis Inst. of Music in Philadelphia; he also gave courses at Columbia Univ. and the N.Y. College of Music. In 1939 he brought out *The International Cyclopedia of Music and Musicians* in one vol. of more than 2,000 pages, with feature articles by eminent authorities; it went through 11 eds. and reprints. He wrote the books *Practical Musical Criticism* (1934); *How to Understand Music* (1935; 2nd ed., enlarged, 1958); *Tabulated Biographical History of Music* (1936); *The American Singer* (1937); *Debussy, Man and Artist* (1937); ed. *Plots of the Operas* (1940) and *Great Modern Composers* (1941), both vols. being extracts from the *Cyclopedia*.

Thompson, Randall, eminent American composer and pedagogue; b. N.Y., April 21, 1899; d. Boston, July 9, 1984. He was a member of an intellectual New England family; studied at Lawrenceville School in N.J., where his father was an English teacher; began taking singing lessons and received his rudimentary music training from the organist Francis Cuyler Van Dyck. When he died, Thompson took over his organ duties in the school. Upon graduation, he went to Harvard Univ., where he studied with Walter Spalding, Edward Burlingame Hill, and Archibald T. Davison (B.A., 1920; M.A., 1922). In 1920–21, he had some private lessons in N.Y. with Ernest

Bloch. In 1922 he submitted his orch. prelude *Pierrot and Cothurnus*, inspired by the poetical drama *Aria da Capo* by Edna St. Vincent Millay, for the American Prix de Rome, and received a grant for residence in Rome; he conducted it there at the Accademia di Santa Cecilia on May 17, 1923. Encouraged by its reception, he proceeded to compose industriously, for piano, for voices, and for orch. He returned to the U.S. in 1925. From 1927 to 1929 he taught at Wellesley College, and again from 1936 to 1937; in 1929 he was appointed a lecturer in music at Harvard Univ.; in 1929–30 he held a Guggenheim fellowship. On Feb. 20, 1930, his 1st Sym. had its premiere in Rochester, N.Y., with Howard Hanson conducting, and on March 24, 1932, Hanson conducted in Rochester the 1st performance of Thompson's 2nd Sym., which was destined to become one of the most successful symphonic works by an American composer; it enjoyed repeated performances in the U.S. and also in Europe. Audiences found the work distinctly American in substance; the unusual element was the inclusion of jazz rhythms in the score. Equally American and equally appealing, although for entirely different reasons, was his choral work *Americana*, to texts from Mencken's satirical column in his journal, the *American Mercury*. There followed another piece of Americana, the nostalgic a cappella choral work *The Peaceable Kingdom*, written in 1936, and inspired by the painting of that name by the naturalistic fantasist Edward Hicks; for it, Thompson used biblical texts from the Prophets. Another piece for a cappella chorus, deeply religious in its nature, was *Alleluia* (1940), which became a perennial favorite in the choral literature; it was 1st performed at Tanglewood, Mass., at the inaugural session of the Berkshire Music Center, on July 8, 1940. In 1942 Thompson composed his most celebrated piece of choral writing, *The Testament of Freedom*, to words of Thomas Jefferson; it was 1st performed with piano accompaniment at the Univ. of Virginia on April 13, 1943. A version with orch. was presented by the Boston Sym. Orch. on April 6, 1945. With this work Thompson firmly established his reputation as one of the finest composers of choral music in America. But he did not limit himself to choral music. His 1st String Quartet in D minor (1941) was praised, as was his only opera, *Solomon and Balkis*, after Kipling's *The Butterfly That Stamped*, a parody on Baroque usages, broadcast over CBS on March 29, 1942. In 1949 Thompson wrote his 3rd Sym., which was presented at the Festival of Contemporary American Music at Columbia Univ. in N.Y., on May 15, 1949. Thompson's subsequent works were an orch. piece, *A Trip to Nahant* (1954), a *Requiem* (1958), an opera, *The Nativity According to St. Luke* (1961), *The Passion According to St. Luke* (1965), *The Place of the Blest*, a cantata (1969), and *A Concord Cantata* (1975). During all this time he did not neglect his educational activities; he taught at the Univ. of Calif. at Berkeley (1937–39); the Curtis Inst. of Music in Philadelphia, where he served as director from 1939 to 1941; the School of Fine Arts at the Univ. of Virginia (1941–46); Princeton Univ. (1946–48); and Harvard Univ. (1948–65), where he retired as prof. emeritus in 1965. He also publ. a book, *College Music* (N.Y., 1935). In 1938 he was elected a member of the National Inst. of Arts and Letters; in 1959 he was named "Cavaliere ufficiale al merito della Repubblica Italiana." In his compositions, Thompson preserved and cultivated the melodious poetry of American speech, set in crystalline tonal harmonies judiciously seasoned with euphonious discords, while keeping resolutely clear of any modernistic abstractions.

WORKS: STAGE: *Solomon and Balkis*, opera after Kipling's *The Butterfly That Stamped* (CBS, N.Y., March 29, 1942; stage premiere, Cambridge, Mass., April 14, 1942); *The Nativity According to St. Luke*, opera (Cambridge, Mass., Dec. 13, 1961); ballet, *Jabberwocky* (1951); incidental music to *Torches* (1920), *Grand Street Follies* (N.Y., June 25, 1926; not extant), *The Straw Hat* (N.Y., Oct. 14, 1926), and *The Battle of Dunster Street* (1953). **ORCH.:** *Pierrot and Cothurnus* (1922; Rome, May 17, 1923); *The Piper at the Gates of Dawn*, symphonic prelude (Rome, May 27, 1924); *Jazz Poem* for Piano and Orch. (Rochester, N.Y., Nov. 27, 1928); 3 syms.: No. 1 (1929; Rochester,

N.Y., Feb. 20, 1930); No. 2 (1931; Rochester, N.Y , March 24, 1932); No. 3 (1947–49; N.Y., May 15, 1949); *A Trip to Nahant,* symphonic fantasy (1953–54; Philadelphia, March 18, 1955). CHAMBER: Septet for Flute, Clarinet, String Quartet, and Piano (1917); *Scherzino* for Piccolo, Violin, and Viola (1920); Quintet for Flute, Clarinet, Viola, Cello, and Piano (1920); Suite for Oboe, Violin, and Viola (1940); Trio for 3 Double Basses, a dinner-piece in honor of Koussevitzky (1949); 2 string quartets (1941, 1967). VOCAL: *5 Odes of Horace* for Chorus and Piano or Orch. (1924); *Pueri hebraeorum* for 8 Women's Voices (1928); *Rosemary* for Women's Chorus a cappella (1929); *Americana* for 4 Voices and Piano or Orch., to texts from Mencken's journal, the *American Mercury* (N.Y., April 3, 1932); *The Peaceable Kingdom* for Chorus a cappella, inspired by a painting of Edmund Hicks (Cambridge, Mass., March 3, 1936); *Tarantella* for Men's Voices and Piano (1937); *The Lark in the Morn* for Chorus a cappella (1938); *Alleluia* for Chorus a cappella, to the single word "Alleluia" of the text (Tanglewood, Mass., July 8, 1940); *The Testament of Freedom* for Male Voices with Piano or Orch., to words culled from the writings of Thomas Jefferson (CBS, April 13, 1943; orch. version, Boston, April 6, 1945); *The Last Words of David* for Chorus, and Piano or Orch. (orch. version, Tanglewood, Aug. 12, 1949); *Mass of the Holy Spirit* for Chorus a cappella (1955–56); *Ode to the Virginian Voyage* for Chorus and Piano or Orch. (Jamestown, Va., April 1, 1957); *Requiem,* dramatic dialogue in 5 parts for Double Chorus and String Ensemble (Berkeley, Calif., May 22, 1958); *Frostiana,* to words by Robert Frost, for Chorus with Piano Accompaniment (1959; orch. version, 1965); *A Feast of Praise,* cantata for Chorus and Instrumental Ensemble (1963); *The Best of Rooms* for Chorus a cappella (1963); *The Passion According to St. Luke,* oratorio (Boston, March 28, 1965); *A Psalm of Thanksgiving,* cantata for Mixed Chorus, Children's Chorus, and Orch. (Boston, Nov. 15, 1967); *The Place of the Blest,* cantata (N.Y., March 2, 1969); *Bitter-Sweet* for Chorus a cappella (1970); *Antiphon* for Chorus a cappella (1971); *A Hymn for Scholars and Pupils* for Women's Voices, Chamber Orch., and Organ (1973); *A Concord Cantata for 4 Voices and Orch.,* written for the bicentennial of Concord, Mass. (Concord, May 2, 1975); *The Morning Stars* for Chorus and Orch. (Lexington, Ky., March 18, 1976). SONGS FOR VOICE AND PIANO: *Spring* (1920); *The Ship Starting* (1922); *Tapestry* (1925); *The Heavens Declare* (1926); *Discipleship* (1926); *Southwind* (1926); *Velvet Shoes* (1927); *The Wild Home Pussy* (1927); *The Echo Child* (1927); *My Master Hath a Garden* (1927); *Doubts* (1929); *Prairie Home* (1951); *Veritas* (1954). PIANO: *The Boats Were Talking* (1925); *Little Prelude* (1935); *Jabberwocky* (1951). BIBL.: Q. Porter, "American Composers, XVIII, R. T.," *Modern Music,* XIX (1942); E. Forbes, "The Music of R. T.," *Musical Quarterly* (Jan. 1949); E. Forbes, J. Haar, A. Mann, and R. Thompson, "The Choral Music of R. T.," *American Choral Review,* XVI/4 (1974); B. McGilvray, *The Choral Music of R. T., an American Eclectic* (diss., Univ. of Missouri, Kansas City, 1979); M. Meckna, *R. T.: A Bio-Bibliography* (Westport, Conn., 1986).

Thompson, Will L(amartine), American music publisher and composer; b. Beaver County, Pa., Nov. 7, 1847; d. N.Y., Sept. 20, 1909. He studied at the Boston School of Music, the Boston Cons. of Music, and the Leipzig Cons. (1870–75); settled in East Liverpool, Ohio, where he founded his own music publishing firm. He wrote some 100 songs, both sacred and secular; perhaps his best-known song is the hymn *Softly and Tenderly Jesus Is Calling.* He ed. and publ. *Thompson's Popular Anthems* (1894), *The New Century Hymnal* (1904), and *Enduring Hymns* (1908). BIBL.: R. McCutchan, *Our Hymnody* (N.Y., 1937; 2nd ed., 1942).

Thomson, Bryden, Scottish conductor; b. Ayr, July 16, 1928. He studied at the Royal Scottish Academy of Music in Glasgow and at the Hochschule für Musik in Hamburg, his principal mentors being Hans Schmidt-Isserstedt and Igor Markevitch.

He was assistant conductor of the BBC Scottish Orch. (1958–62) and associate conductor of the Scottish National Orch. (1966–68) in Glasgow. From 1968 to 1973 he was principal conductor of the BBC Northern Sym. Orch. in Manchester; then was music director of the Ulster Orch. in Belfast (1977–85); also was principal conductor of the BBC Welsh Sym. Orch. in Cardiff (1978–82) and the R(adio) T(elefis) E(ireann) Sym. Orch. in Dublin (1984–87). In 1988 he returned to the Scottish National Orch. as its principal conductor, becoming well known for his championship of British music.

Thomson, César, eminent Belgian violinist and teacher; b. Liège, March 17, 1857; d. Bissone, near Lugano, Aug. 21, 1931. He entered the Liège Cons. at the age of 7, where he began his training with Dupuis; won the Gold Medal at 11; he subsequently studied with Vieuxtemps, Léonard, Wieniawski, and Massart. In 1873 he entered the service of Baron Paul von Derwies in Lugano; in 1879 he became concertmaster of Bilse's orch. in Berlin; in 1882 he became prof. of violin at the Liège Cons.; then in 1898 at the Brussels Cons., where he founded a celebrated string quartet (with Lamoureux, Vanhout, and Jacobs). In 1914 he settled in Paris as a prof. at the Cons. In 1924 he visited America; taught at the Cons. of Ithaca, N.Y., and at the Juilliard School of Music, N.Y., returning to Europe in 1927. He was a famous violin teacher, emphasizing perfection of technical and expressive performance, rather than bravura. He made arrangements for the violin of various works by early Italian composers. BIBL.: H. Timerman, *How to Produce a Beautiful Tone on the Violin. . .in Accordance with the Principles of C. T.* (N.Y., 1923).

Thomson, George, Scottish collector of folk songs; b. Limekilns, Dunfermline, March 4, 1757; d. Leith, Feb. 18, 1851. For 59 years (1780–1839) he was secretary to the Board of Trustees for the Encouragement of Arts and Manufactures in Scotland; from 1780, was active as a violinist in the orch. and as a singer in the choir of the Edinburgh Musical Society. An ardent collector of Scotch, Welsh, and Irish melodies, he issued a series of vols. containing authentic melodies, with piano accompaniments and instrumental arrangements by the most celebrated musicians of his time, including Beethoven, Haydn, Pleyel, and Koželuh. Each song had, in accordance with his plan, a prelude, coda, and ad libitum parts throughout (for violin, or flute, or cello). The collections are: *A Select Collection of Original Scottish Airs* (6 vols., London; vol. I, 1793; vol. II, 1798; vol. III, 1799; vol. IV, 1802; vol. V, 1818–26; vol. VI, 1841); *Collection of the Songs of R. Burns, Sir W. Scott, etc.* (6 vols., London, 1822); *Select Collection of Original Welsh Airs* (3 vols., London, 1809); *Select Collection of Original Irish Airs* (2 vols., London, 1814–16); *20 Scottish Melodies* (Edinburgh, 1839). BIBL.: J. Hadden, *G. T., the Friend of Burns. His Life and Correspondence* (London, 1898); R. Aldrich, "Beethoven and G. T.," *Music & Letters* (April 1927); C. Hopkinson and C. Oldman, "T.'s Collection of National Song," *Transactions of the Edinburgh Bibliographical Society,* II (1940); K. Geiringer, "Haydn and the Folksong of the British Isles," *Musical Quarterly* (April 1949); C. Oldman, "Beethoven's Variations on National Themes," *Music Review,* XII (1951).

Thomson, John, Scottish composer and writer on music; b. Sprouston, Roxburgh, Oct. 28, 1805; d. Edinburgh, May 6, 1841. He studied in Leipzig with Schnyder von Wartensee, and became a friend of Mendelssohn, Schumann, and Moscheles. In 1839 he was appointed the 1st Reid Prof. of Music at the Univ. of Edinburgh. At the 3rd concert given by the Edinburgh Professional Society (Feb. 1837), an analytical program was issued by Thomson, then conductor; this is the 1st recorded instance of the use of such programs. He composed the opera *Hermann, or The Broken Spear* (London, Oct. 27, 1834), the drama *The House of Aspen* (Edinburgh, Dec. 19, 1829), and the musical play *The Shadow on the Wall* (London, April 20, 1835); also orch. works, including Overture in C minor (1830) and *Allegro maestroso and allegro grazioso for*

Flute and Orch. (c.1830); *Benedictus and Osanna* for Voices and Instruments (1829); chamber music; piano pieces; songs.

Thomson, Virgil (Garnett), many-faceted American composer of great originality and a music critic of singular brilliance; b. Kansas City, Mo., Nov. 25, 1896; d. N.Y., Sept. 30, 1989. He began piano lessons at age 12 with local teachers; received instruction in organ (1909–17; 1919) and played in local churches; took courses at a local junior college (1915–17; 1919), then entered Harvard Univ., where he studied orchestration with E.B. Hill and became assistant and accompanist to A.T. Davison, conductor of its Glee Club; also studied piano with Heinrich Gebhard and organ with Wallace Goodrich in Boston. In 1921 he went with the Harvard Glee Club to Europe, where he remained on a John Knowles Paine Traveling Fellowship to study organ with Nadia Boulanger at the Paris École Normale de Musique; also received private instruction in counterpoint from her. Returning to Harvard in 1922, he was made organist and choirmaster at King's College; after graduating in 1923, he went to N.Y. to study conducting with C. Clifton and counterpoint with R. Scalero at the Juilliard Graduate School. In 1925 he returned to Paris, which remained his base until 1940; he established friendly contacts with cosmopolitan groups of musicians, writers, and painters; his association with Gertrude Stein was particularly significant in the development of his esthetic ideas. In his music he refused to follow any set of modernistic doctrines; rather, he embraced the notion of popular universality, which allowed him to use the techniques of all ages and all degrees of simplicity or complexity, from simple triadic harmonies to dodecaphonic intricacies; in so doing he achieved an eclectic illumination of astonishing power of direct communication, expressed in his dictum "jamais de banalité, toujours le lieu commun." Beneath the characteristic Parisian persiflage in some of his music there is a profoundly earnest intent. His most famous composition is the opera *Four Saints in Three Acts*, to the libretto by Gertrude Stein, in which the deliberate confusion wrought by the author of the play (there are actually 4 acts and more than a dozen saints, some of them in duplicate) and the composer's almost solemn, hymn-like treatment, create a hilarious modern opera-buffa. It was 1st introduced at Hartford, Conn., on Feb. 8, 1934, characteristically announced as being under the auspices of the "Society of Friends and Enemies of Modern Music," of which Thomson was director (1934–37); the work became an American classic, with constant revivals staged in America and Europe. In 1940 Thomson was appointed music critic of the *N.Y. Herald-Tribune*; he received the Pulitzer Prize in Music in 1948 for his score to the motion picture *Louisiana Story*. Far from being routine journalism, Thomson's music reviews are minor masterpieces of literary brilliance and critical acumen. He resigned in 1954 to devote himself to composition and conducting. He received the Légion d'honneur in 1947; was elected to membership in the National Inst. of Arts and Letters in 1948 and in the American Academy of Arts and Letters in 1959. In 1982 he received an honorary degree of D.Mus. from Harvard Univ. In 1983 he was awarded the Kennedy Center Honor for lifetime achievement. He received the Medal of Arts in 1988.

WORKS: STAGE: OPERAS: *Four Saints in Three Acts* (1927–28; orchestrated 1933; Hartford, Conn., Feb. 8, 1934); *The Mother of Us All*, to a libretto by Gertrude Stein on the life of the American suffragist Susan B. Anthony (N.Y., May 7, 1947); *Lord Byron* (1961–68; N.Y., April 13, 1972). **BALLETS:** *Filling Station* (1937; N.Y., Feb. 18, 1938); *The Harvest According* (N.Y., Oct. 1, 1952; based on the *Symphony on a Hymn Tune*, the Cello Concerto, and the Suite from *The Mother of Us All*); *Parson Weems and the Cherry Tree* (Amherst, Mass., Nov. 1, 1975). **ORCH.:** *Symphony on a Hymn Tune* (1928; N.Y., Feb. 22, 1945); Sym. No. 2 (1931; rev. 1941; Seattle, Nov. 17, 1941); *The John Moser Waltzes* (1935; orchestrated 1937); *The Plow that Broke the Plains*, suite from the film score (1936; Philadelphia, Jan. 2, 1943); *The River*, suite from the film score (1937;

N.Y., Jan. 12, 1943); *Filling Station*, suite from the ballet (1937; WNYC Radio, N.Y., Feb. 2, 1941); *Canons for Dorothy Thompson* (N.Y., July 23, 1942); *The Major LaGuardia Waltzes* (Cincinnati, May 14, 1942); *Bugles and Birds: Portrait of Pablo Picasso* (1940; orchestrated 1944; Philadelphia, Nov. 17, 1944); *Cantabile for Strings: Portrait of Nicolas de Chatelain* (1940; orchestrated 1944; Philadelphia, Nov. 17, 1944); *Fanfare for France: Portrait of Max Kahn* (1940; Cincinnati, Jan. 15, 1943); *Fugue: Portrait of Alexander Smallens* (1940; orchestrated 1944; Philadelphia, Nov. 17, 1944); *Meditation: Portrait of Jere Abbott* (1935; orchestrated 1944; Vancouver, Nov. 21, 1948); *Aaron Copland: Persistently Pastoral* (1942; orchestrated as *Pastorale*, 1944; N.Y., March 15, 1945); *Percussion Piece: Portrait of Jessie K. Lasell* (1941; orchestrated 1944; Philadelphia, Nov. 17, 1944); *Tango Lullaby: Portrait of Mlle Alvarex de Toledo* (1940; orchestrated 1944; Philadelphia, Nov. 17, 1944); *Fugue and Chorale on Yankee Doodle*, suite from the film score *Tuesday in November* (1945; Atlanta, April 16, 1969); *The Seine at Night* (1947; Kansas City, Mo., Feb. 24, 1948); *Acadian Songs and Dances* from the film score *Louisiana Story* (1948; Philadelphia, Jan. 11, 1951); *Louisiana Story*, suite from the film score (Philadelphia, Nov. 26, 1948); *Wheat Field at Noon* (Louisville, Dec. 7, 1948); *At the Beach*, concert waltz for Trumpet and Band (1949; N.Y., July 21, 1950; based on *Le bains-bar* for Violin and Piano, 1929); *The Mother of Us All*, suite from the opera (1949; Knoxville, Tenn., Jan. 17, 1950); *A Solemn Music* for Band (N.Y., June 17, 1949; also for orch., 1961; N.Y., Feb. 15, 1962); Cello Concerto (Philadelphia, March 24, 1950); *Sea Piece with Birds* (Dallas, Dec. 10, 1952); *Concerto: Portrait of Roger Baker* for Flute, Harp, Strings, and Percussion (Venice, Sept. 14, 1954; also for Flute and Piano); *Eleven Chorale Preludes* (1956; New Orleans, March 25, 1957; arr. from Brahms's op. 122); *The Lively Arts Fugue* (1957); *Fugues and Cantilenas* from the film score *Power among Men* (Ann Arbor, May 2, 1959); *A Joyful Fugue* (1962; N.Y., Feb. 1, 1963; also for Band); *Autum*, concertino for Harp, Strings, and Percussion (Madrid, Oct. 19, 1964; based on the *Homage to Marya Freund and to the Harp* and the Piano Sonata No. 2); *Pilgrims and Pioneers* from the film score *Journey to America* (1964; N.Y., Feb. 27, 1971; also for Band); *Ode to the Wonders of Nature* for Brass and Percussion (Washington, D.C., Sept. 16, 1965); *Fantasy in Homage to an Earlier England* (Kansas City, Mo., May 27, 1966); *Edges: Portrait of Robert Indiana* (1966; also for Band, 1969); *Study Piece: Portrait of a Lady* for Band (1969; originally *Insistences: Portrait of Louise Crane*, 1941); *Metropolitan Museum Fanfare: Portrait of an American Artist* for Brass and Percussion (N.Y., Oct. 16, 1969; originally *Parades: Portrait of Florine Stettheimer*, 1941); Sym. No. 3 (1972; N.Y., Dec. 26, 1976); *Thoughts for Strings* for String Orch. (1981); *A Love Scene* (1982; originally *Dead Pan: Mrs. Betty Freeman*); *Intensely Two: Karen Brown Waltuck* (1981; orchestrated 1982); *Loyal, Steady, and Persistent: Noah Creshevsky* (1981; orchestrated 1982); *Something of a Beauty: Ann-Marie Soullière* (1981; orchestrated 1982); *David Dubal in Flight* (1982).

CHAMBER: *Sonata da chiesa* for Clarinet, Trumpet, Horn, Trombone, and Viola (Paris, May 5, 1926; rev. 1973); (8) *Portraits for Violin Alone* (1928–40); *Five Portraits for Four Clarinets* for 2 Clarinets, Alto Clarinet, and Bass Clarinet (1929); *Le bains-bar* for Violin and Piano (1929; arr. as *At the Beach*, concert waltz for Trumpet and Band, 1949; N.Y., July 21, 1950); *Portraits for Violin and Piano* (1930–40); Violin Sonata (1930; Paris, Jan. 24, 1931); *Serenade* for Flute and Violin (1931); 2 string quartets: No. 1 (Paris, June 15, 1931; rev. 1957); No. 2 (1932; Hartford, Conn., April 14, 1933; rev. 1957); *Sonata for Flute Alone* (1943); *Barcarolle for Woodwinds: A Portrait of Georges Hugnet* for Flute, Oboe, English Horn, Clarinet, Bass Clarinet, and Bassoon (1944; Pittsburgh, Nov. 29, 1946; based on a piano piece); *Lamentations: Étude for Accordion* (1959); *Variations* for Koto (1961); *Étude for Cello and Piano: Portrait of Frederic James* (1966); *Family Portrait* for 2 Trumpets, Horn, and 2 Trombones (1974; N.Y., March 24, 1975); *For Lou Harrison and his Jolly Games of 16 Measures* (*count 'em*), theme without instrumentation (1981); *A Short Fanfare* for 2 Trumpets or 3 Trumpets or 3 Trumpets and 2 Drums (1981); *Bell Piece* for 2 or 4 Players (1983); *Cynthia Kemper: A Fanfare* (1983); *Lili Hasings* for Violin and Piano (1983); *A Portrait of Two* (1984); *Jay Rosen: Portrait and Fugue* for Bass Tuba and Piano (1984–85); *Stockton Fanfare* for 3 Trumpets and 2 Drums (1985); also numerous solo piano pieces, choral works, and solo vocal music.

FILM SCORES: *The Plow that Broke the Plains* (N.Y., May 25, 1936; orch. suite, Philadelphia, Jan. 2, 1943); *The River* (New Orleans, Oct. 29, 1937; orch. suite, N.Y., Jan. 12, 1943); *The Spanish Earth* (1937; in collaboration with M. Blitzstein); *Tuesday in November* (1945); *Louisiana Story* (Edinburgh, Aug. 22, 1948; orch. suite as *Acadian Songs and Dances*, Philadelphia, Jan. 11, 1951); *The Goddess* (1957; Brussels, June 1958); *Power among Men* (1958; N.Y., March 5, 1959; orch. suite as *Fugues and Cantilenas*, Ann Arbor, May 2, 1959); *Journey to America* (N.Y., July 1964; orch. suite as *Pilgrims and Pioneers*, N.Y., Feb. 27, 1971).

WRITINGS (all publ. in N.Y.): *The State Of Music* (1939; 2nd ed., rev., 1961); *The Musical Scene* (1945); *The Art of Judging Music* (1948); *Music Right and Left* (1951); *Virgil Thomson* (1966); *Music Reviewed, 1940–1954* (1967); *American Music Since 1910* (1971); *A Virgil Thomson Reader* (1981); *Music with Words: A Composer's View* (1989).

BIBL.: P. Glanville-Hicks, "V. T.," *Musical Quarterly*, XXXV (1949); M. Field, "V. T. and the Maturity of American Music," *The Chesterian*, XXVIII (1953–54); K. Hoover and J. Cage, *V. T.: His Life and Music* (N.Y., 1959); K. Ward, *An Analysis of the Relationship between Text and Musical Shape and an Investigation of the Relationship between Text and Surface Rhythmic Detail in "Four Saints in Three Acts" by V. T.* (diss., Univ. of Texas, Austin, 1978); H. Gleason and W. Becker, "V. T.," *20th-century American Composers* (Bloomington, Ind., 2nd ed., rev., 1981); M. Meckna, *The Rise of the American Composer-critic: Aaron Copland, Roger Sessions, V. T., and Elliott Carter in the Periodical Modern Music, 1924–1946* (diss., Univ. of Calif., Santa Barbara, 1984); A. Tommasini, *The Musical Portraits of V. T.* (N.Y., 1985); M. Meckna, *V. T.: A Biography* (Westport, Conn., 1986); T. and V. Page, eds., *Selected Letters of V. T.* (N.Y., 1988).

Thooft, Willem Frans, Dutch composer; b. Amsterdam, July 10, 1829; d. Rotterdam, Aug. 27, 1900. He studied with A. Dupont in Brussels and with Hauptmann at the Leipzig Cons.; then went to Rotterdam, where he organized the German Opera.

WORKS: Opera, *Aleida von Holland* (Rotterdam, 1866); *Gevonden* for Baritone, Male Chorus, and Orch.; 3 syms. (including one with Chorus, *Kaiser Karl V*); *In Leid und Freud*, fantasy for Orch.; *Die Jungfrau von Orleans*, overture; Psalms; piano pieces; songs.

Thórarinsson, Leifur, Icelandic composer; b. Reykjavík, Aug. 13, 1934. He studied with Jón Thórarinsson at the Reykjavík College of Music; then in Vienna with Hans Jelinek (1954); finally with Wallingford Riegger and Gunther Schuller in N.Y. Returning to Iceland, he became a music critic and member of the modern group Musica Nova; later moved to Denmark.

WORKS: MUSICAL COMEDY: *Hornakórallinn* (1966). ORCH.: *Epitaph (Wallingford Riegger in Memoriam)* (1961); 2 syms. (1963, 1975); Violin Concerto (1969; rev. 1976); *Rent* for Strings (1976); Oboe Concerto (1982); *Autumn Play* (1983); *Styr*, concerto for Piano and Chamber Orch. (1988); *Journey* (1988). CHAMBER: Piano Sonata (1957); *Mosaic* for Violin and Piano (1960); Piano Trio (1961); *Kadensar* for Harp, Oboe, Clarinet, Bass Clarinet, and Bassoon (1962); String Quartet (1969); *A Small Trio* for Flute, Cello, and Piano (1975); *Per Voi* for Flute and Piano (1975); *The Coming of Summer* for Flute and Harpsichord (1978); *Terms* for Clarinet, Violin, and Piano (1979); *Capriccio* for Horn and Harpsichord (1982); also vocal works, including Cantata for Soloists, Chorus, and Organ (1979), various choruses, and songs.

Thorborg, Kerstin, noted Swedish contralto; b. Venjan, May 19, 1896; d. Falun, Dalarna, April 12, 1970. She studied at the Royal Cons. in Stockholm; made her operatic debut there as Ortrud at the Royal Theater in 1924, remaining on its roster until 1930; sang in Prague (1932–33), at the Berlin Stadtische Oper (1933–35), at the Salzburg Festivals (1935–37), at the Vienna State Opera (1935–38), and at London's Covent Garden (1936–39). On Dec. 21, 1936, she made her Metropolitan Opera debut in N.Y. as Fricka, remaining on the company's roster until 1946; sang there again from 1947 to 1950; also appeared in concerts. In 1944 she was made a Swedish court singer; taught voice in Stockholm from 1950. She was particularly esteemed as a Wagnerian; also excelled as Gluck's Orfeo, Saint-Saëns's Delilah, and Strauss's Herodias and Clytemnestra.

Thorne, Edward Henry, English organist, pianist, and composer; b. Cranbourne, Dorset, May 9, 1834; d. London, Dec. 26, 1916. He was a chorister at St. George's Chapel; served as a church organist in London; gave organ and piano recitals in London and elsewhere; was especially noted for his Bach programs. He was made a Mus.D. by the Archbishop of Canterbury in 1913. He wrote a number of sacred choral works; an overture, *Peveril of the Peak* (after Walter Scott); 2 piano trios; violin sonatas; cello sonatas; publ. 7 books of organ pieces.

Thorne, Francis, American composer; b. Bay Shore, Long Island, N.Y., June 23, 1922. Of a cultural heritage (his maternal grandfather was **Gustav Kobbé**) he absorbed musical impressions crouching under the grand piano while his father, a banker, played ragtime; received instruction in composition from Donovan and Hindemith at Yale Univ. (B.A., 1942). After working in banking and stock brokerage (1946–54), he was active as a jazz pianist in the U.S. and Italy (1955–61); also studied with David Diamond in Florence. Impressed, depressed, and distressed by the inhumanly impecunious condition of middle-aged atonal composers, he established the eleemosynary Thorne Music Fund (1965–75), drawing on the hereditary wealth of his family, and disbursed munificent grants to those who qualified, among them Stefan Wolpe, Ben Weber, Lou Harrison, Lester Trimble, John Cage, and David Diamond. He served as executive director of the Lenox Arts Center (1972–76) and of the American Composers' Alliance (1975–85); in 1976 he co-founded the American Composers' Orch. in N.Y., subsequently serving as its president. In 1988 he was elected to membership in the American Academy and Inst. of Arts and Letters. Thorne's music shares with that of his beneficiaries the venturesome spirit of the cosmopolitan avant-garde, with a prudently dissonant technique serving the conceptual abstractions and titular paronomasia of many modern compositions.

WORKS: STAGE: *Fortuna*, operetta (N.Y., Dec. 20, 1961); *Opera buffa for Opera Buffs* (1965); *After the Teacups*, ballet (N.Y., July 31, 1974); *Echoes of Spoon River*, ballet (N.Y., June 20, 1976). ORCH.: 5 syms. (1961, 1964, 1969, 1977, 1984); *Elegy* (1963); *Burlesque Overture* (1964); *Rhapsodic Variations* for Piano and Orch. (1964); 3 piano concertos (1965, 1974, 1990); Double Concerto for Viola, Double Bass, and Orch. (1967–68); *Sonar Plexus* for Electric Guitar and Orch. (1968); *Liebesrock* for 3 Electric Guitars and Orch. (1969); *Fanfare, Fugue and Funk* for 3 Trumpets and Orch. (1972); Violin Concerto (1976); *Pop Partita* for Piano and Chamber Orch. (1976); *Divertimento No. 1* for Flute and Strings (1979); *Divertimento No. 2* for Bassoon and Strings (1980); *Humoresque*, overture (1985); *Concerto Concertante* for Flute, Clarinet, Violin, Cello, and Orch. (1985); *Rhapsodic Variations No. 3* for Oboe and Strings (1986). CHAMBER: 4 string quartets (1960, 1967, 1975, 1983); *Music for a Circus* for 7 Instruments (1963); *Lyric Variations II* for Woodwind and Percussion (1972); Piano Sonata (1972); *Evensongs* for Flute, Harp, Guitar, Celesta, and Percussion (1972); *Lyric Variations III* for Piano, Violin, and Cello (1972); *Prufrock Ballet Music* for 7 Instruments (1974); *Chamber Concerto* for Cello and 10 Instruments (1975); *5 Set Pieces* for Saxophone Quartet (1977); *Grand Duo* for Oboe and Harpsichord (1977); *Eine Kleine Meyermusik* for Clarinet and Cello (1980); *Burlesk Pit Music* for Clarinet and Cello (1983); *Divertimento No. 3* for Woodwind Quintet (1983); *Rhapsodic Variations No. 2* for Clarinet, Violin, and Cello (1985). VOCAL: *De profundis* for Soprano, Chorus, and Organ (1959); *Nocturnes* for Voice and Piano or String Quartet (1962); *Song of the Carolina Low Country* for Chorus and Orch. (1968); *A Mad Wriggle*, madrigal (1970); *Cantata Sauce* for Mezzo-soprano, Baritone, and 8 Players (1973); *Love's Variations* for Flute, Soprano, and Piano (1977); *La Luce Eterna* for High Voice and Orch. (1978); *Praise and Thanksgiving* for Chorus and Orch. (1983).

Thornhill, Claude, American pianist, bandleader, and composer; b. Terre Haute, Ind., Aug. 10, 1909; d. Caldwell, N.J., July 1, 1965. He studied piano and composition at the Cincinnati Cons. and at the Curtis Inst. of Music in Philadelphia; was an arranger for Benny Goodman and others; in 1940, organized a band of his own. Because of his uncommon musical literacy, he was able to make use of plausible novelties in his arrangements.

Thorpe Davie, Cedric, Scottish composer and teacher; b. London, May 30, 1913; d. Kirkcudbrightshire, Jan. 18, 1983. He began his training at the Royal Scottish Academy of Music in Glasgow; then studied in London with Craxton, Thiman, and A. Brain at the Royal Academy of Music and with R.O. Morris, Vaughan Williams, and G. Jacob at the Royal College of Music, where he won the Cobbett and Sullivan prizes in composition (1935); subsequently received instruction in piano from Petri, and also in composition from Kodály in Budapest and from Kilpinen in Helsinki. He taught theory and composition at the Royal Scottish Academy of Music (1936–45); then was master (1945–73) and prof. (1973–78) of music at St. Andrews Univ. In 1955 he was awarded the Order of the British Empire. He publ. *Musical Structure and Design* (London, 1953) and ed. the *Oxford Scottish Song Book* (London, 1968).

WORKS: DRAMATIC: *Gammer Gurton's Needle*, opera (1936); comic operas; operettas; music for theater, films, and broadcasting. ORCH.: *Elegy* (1932); *Concert Overture* (1934); *Concerto for Piano and Strings* (1943); *Sym.* (1945); *The Beggar's Benison* (1949); *Festival Overture* (1950); *Royal Mile*, march (1952); *Diversions on a Tune by Dr. Arne* (1964); *New Town*, suite (1966). CHAMBER: *Piano Trio* (1932); *Fantasy-Quartet* for Strings (1935); *Violin Sonata* (1939). CHORAL: *Dirge for Cuthullin*, with Orch. (1935); 3 anthems, with Organ (1937); *Ode for St. Andrew's Night*, with Tenor and Orch. (1950); part-songs; arrangements; solo songs.

BIBL.: C. *T.D.: Catalogue of Works* (Fife, 1988).

Thrane, Waldemar, Norwegian violinist, conductor, and composer; b. Christiania, Oct. 8, 1790; d. there, Dec. 30, 1828. He studied violin with Henrik Groth in Christiania, and then with Claus Schall in Copenhagen (1814–15); then went to Paris, where he was a pupil of Baillot (violin) and of Reicha and Habeneck (composition). Returning to Christiania in 1818, he was made conductor of the orchs. of the Dramatical Society and of the Musical Lyceum; also toured as a violinist throughout his homeland and made appearances in Stockholm. He is historically important as the composer of the 1st Norwegian opera, *Fjeldeventyret* (A Mountain Adventure; 1824; Christiania, Feb. 9, 1825); he also wrote a Concert Overture (1818), a Finale for Orch. (1818; not extant), a cantata (1827; not extant), and some piano music.

BIBL.: J. Conradi, *Musikkens Udvikling i Norge* (Christiania, 1878); F. Benestad, *W. T.: En pioner i norsk musikk* (Oslo, 1961).

Thuille, Ludwig (Wilhelm Andreas Maria), renowned Austrian composer and pedagogue; b. Bozen, Tirol, Nov. 30, 1861; d. Munich, Feb. 5, 1907. He studied theory, piano, and organ with Joseph Pembaur in Innsbruck; then went to Munich, where he was a pupil of Karl Bärmann (piano) and Joseph Rheinberger (composition) at the Königliche Musikschule, graduating with honors in 1882; in 1883 he joined its faculty and was promoted to prof. in 1890. Encouraged by Alexander

Ritter, he began to compose music in the grand Wagnerian manner; wrote 3 operas, chamber music, song cycles, and choral works. But he made his mark chiefly as a fine pedagogue; with Rudolf Louis he publ. the well-known manual *Harmonielehre* (1907; abr. ed. as *Grundriss der Harmonielehre*, 1908; 10th ed., rev., 1933 by W. Courvoisier and others).

WORKS: OPERAS: *Theuerdank* (1893–95; Munich, Feb. 12, 1897), *Lobetanz* (1896; Karlsruhe, Feb. 6, 1898); *Gugeline* (1898–1900; Bremen, March 4, 1901); also a melodrama, *Die Tanzhexe* (1899–1900). ORCH.: *Sym.* (1886); *Romantische Ouvertüre*, overture to *Theuerdank* (1896). CHAMBER: Sextet for Flute, Oboe, Clarinet, Bassoon, Horn, and Piano (1886–88); Piano Quintet (1897–1901); Cello Sonata (1901–2); Violin Sonata (1903–4); also choral works; 78 songs; piano pieces.

BIBL.: F. Munter, *L. T.* (Munich, 1923); E. Istel, "*L. T.,*" *Musical Quarterly* (July 1932); J. Lachner, "*L. T.: ein Müncher aus Tirol,*" *Süddeutsche Zeitung* (Nov. 30, 1961).

Thuren, Hjalmar Lauritz, Danish folklorist; b. Copenhagen, Sept. 10, 1873; d. there, Jan. 13, 1912. From 1899 to 1907 he taught at the Fredericksberg Folk-School and was secretary of the Danish Folklore Society. He made valuable studies of folk music in Denmark, in the Faroe Islands, and among the Eskimos.

WRITINGS (all publ. in Copenhagen): *Dans og Kvaddigtning på Faer øerne* (1901); *Folkesangen på Faer øerne* (1908); with W. Thalbitzer, *The Eskimo Music—meddelelser fra Grønland* (1911); *Melodies from East Greenland* (1914).

Thurner, Frédéric Eugène de, French oboist and composer; b. Montbéliard, Dec. 9, 1785; d. Amsterdam, March 21, 1827. He wrote 3 syms., an overture, 4 oboe concertos, 4 quartets for oboe and strings, rondos and divertissements for oboe with string quartet, Trio for Oboe with 2 Horns, duos for oboe and piano, piano music, etc.

Thursby, Emma (Cecilia), prominent American soprano; b. Williamsburg, N.Y., Feb. 21, 1845; d. N.Y., July 4, 1931. She was trained in the U.S. and Italy, her principal mentors being Julius Meyer, Achille Errani, Francesco Lamperti, Sangiovanni, and Erminie Rudersdorff. After beginning her career with solo appearances in churches in Brooklyn and N.Y., she sang with Theodore Thomas and his orch., with Patrick Gilmore and his band, and in Leopold Damrosch's oratorio concerts. She won extraordinary success touring as a concert singer in Europe (1878–82); then gave concerts and recitals in the U.S. until her farewell in Chicago in 1895. She subsequently was active as a teacher; was a prof. at the Inst. of Musical Art in N.Y. (1905–11). Her most celebrated pupil was Geraldine Farrar. Although she declined to appear in operatic productions, she included numerous arias in her concert repertoire, winning acclaim for her coloratura gifts.

BIBL.: E. Kennedy, "*E. T.: Speranza,*" *Musical Digest,* XV/9 (1930); R. Gipson, *The Life of E. T., 1845–1931* (N.Y., 1940).

Thybo, Leif, Danish organist, teacher, and composer; b. Holstebro, June 12, 1922. He studied in Copenhagen at the Cons. (1940–45) and the Univ. (1945–48). He taught harmony and counterpoint at the Univ. of Copenhagen, 1949–65; taught theory (from 1952) and organ (from 1960) at the Copenhagen Cons.; was also active as a church organist.

WORKS: CHAMBER OPERA: *Den odödliga berättelsen* (The Immortal Story; Vadstena, Sweden, July 8, 1971). ORCH.: Concerto for Chamber Orch. (1947); 2 organ concertos (1954, 1956); Concerto for Strings (1957); *Philharmonic Variations* (1958); Concertino for Organ, Chamber Orch., and Mezzo-soprano (Copenhagen, Oct. 19, 1960); Cello Concerto (1961); Piano Concerto (1961–63); Concerto for Flute and Chamber Orch. (1966); Violin Concerto (1969); Viola Concerto (1972). VOCAL: *Markus-passionen* (Passion According to St. Mark) for Soloists, Chorus, and Orch. (Copenhagen, March 19, 1964); *Te Deum* for Chorus and Winds (Copenhagen, Nov. 18, 1965); *Prophetia* for Soprano, Bass, Chorus, and Orch. (Copenhagen, Feb. 28, 1965); *In dieser Zeit* for Solo Voice, Vocal Quartet, and Instruments (1967); *Dialogue* for Soloists, Chorus, and Instruments (Copenhagen, May 27, 1968); *The Ecstacy* for Soprano, Narrator, Recorder, Oboe, Viola da Gamba, and Spinet (1972). CHAMBER: Cello Sonata (1950); 2 violin sonatas (1953, 1960); Sonata for Violin and Organ (1955); Trio for Clarinet, Cello, and Piano (1963); String Quartet (1963); Flute Quintet (1965); *Concerto breve* for Piano, Flute, Violin, Viola, and Cello (1966); *Hommage à Benjamin Britten* for Flute Quartet (1968); Trio for Oboe, Horn, and Bassoon (1970); *Engels nachtegaltje* for Recorder, Flute, and Organ (1974); Concertino for 2 Trumpets and Organ (1976); Piano Trio (1976); also solo piano works, including 2 sonatas (1947, 1956); organ pieces; songs.

Tibaldi Chiesa, Maria, Italian writer on music; b. Milan, April 28, 1896; d. there, June 21, 1968. She studied at the Univ. of Rome; wrote opera librettos, and publ. books of verse. Her musical publications include: *Schubert* (1932; 2nd ed., 1936); *Ernest Bloch* (1933); *Mussorgsky* (1935); *Vita romantica di Liszt* (1937); *Cimarosa e il suo tempo* (1939); *Paganini* (3rd ed., 1944); *Ciaikovsky* (1943).

Tibbett (real name, **Tibbet**), **Lawrence,** outstanding American baritone; b. Bakersfield, Calif., Nov. 16, 1896; d. N.Y., July 15, 1960. His real name was accidentally misspelled when he appeared in opera, and he retained the final extra letter. His ancestry was connected with the California Gold Rush of 1849; his great-uncle was reputed to be a pioneer in the navel orange industry; Tibbett's father was a sheriff of Bakersfield who was shot dead by one of the outlaws he had hunted. His mother ran a hotel in Long Beach. Tibbett led a typical cowboy life, but dreamed of a stage career; he played parts in Shakespearian productions. During World War I, he served in the U.S. Navy; after the Armistice, he earned a living by singing at weddings and funerals in a male quartet. He also took vocal lessons with Joseph Dupuy, Basil Ruysdael, Frank La Forge, and Ignaz Zitomirsky. He made his operatic debut in N.Y. with the Metropolitan Opera on Nov. 24, 1923, in the minor role of Lovitsky in *Boris Godunov*; then sang Valentin in *Faust* (Nov. 30, 1923); achieved a striking success as Ford in Verdi's *Falstaff* (Jan. 2, 1925), and thereafter was one of the leading members on its roster. Among his roles were Tonio in *Pagliacci*, Wolfram in *Tannhäuser*, Telramund in *Lohengrin*, Marcello in *La Bohème*, Scarpia in *Tosca*, Iago in *Otello*, and the title roles in *Rigoletto* and *Falstaff*. He also sang important parts in modern American operas, such as Colonel Ibbetson in Taylor's *Peter Ibbetson*, Brutus Jones in Gruenberg's *The Emperor Jones*, and Wrestling Bradford in Hanson's *Merry Mount*. During his 1st European tour in 1937 he sang the title role in the world premiere of *Don Juan de Mañara* by Eugene Goossens (Covent Garden, London, June 24, 1937); he also sang in Paris, Vienna, and Stockholm. A sincere believer in musical democracy, he did not disdain the lower arts; he often appeared on the radio and in films, among them *The Rogue Song*, *The Southerner*, and *Cuban Love Song*. During World War II, he sang in army camps. He made his farewell appearance at the Metropolitan Opera as Ivan in *Khovanshchina* on March 24, 1950. His last stage appearance was in the musical comedy *Fanny* in 1956. He publ. an autobiography entitled *The Glory Road* (Brattleboro, Vt., 1933; reprint, 1977, with discography by W. Moran). BIBL.: A. Farkas, ed., *L. T.: Singing Actor* (Portland, Maine, 1989).

Tibbits, George (Richard), Australian composer and architect; b. Boulder, Nov. 7, 1933. He studied architecture and urban planning at the Univ. of Melbourne; music was his avocation, which he plied off and on at leisure hours. His compositions often follow pictorial and literary images; a number of his instrumental pieces bear titles related to passages from the writings of James Joyce; their technical idiom oscillates quaquaversally from a Dorian columnar manner to lapidary dodecaphony. In 1968 he was appointed lecturer in architectural history at the Univ. of Melbourne.
WORKS: ORCH.: *Neuronis Nephronicus and His Lowly Queen* (1968); *Fanfare for the Great Hall* (1968); *I thought*

you were all glittering with the noblest of carriage, after James Joyce (1969); *Serenade* (1969); *Beside the rivering waters of,* after Joyce (1970); *Where oranges have been laid to rest upon the green,* after Joyce (1971); *Antediluvia* for String Orch. (1971); *The Rose Garden of the Queen of Navarre* (1975); Violin Concerto (1975). VOCAL: 5 *Songs* for Contralto and Piano (1969); *Golden Builders* for Soprano, Small Chorus, and Chamber Ensemble (1972); 5 *Bells,* after Kenneth Slesson, for Soprano and String Quartet (1972); *Shadows,* after Slesson, for Soprano, Harpsichord, and Small String Orch. (1974); *The Ice Fisherman—Lake Erie* for Soprano and Orch. (1974). CHAMBER: *Silop* for Flute and Celesta (1963); Quintet for Flute, Clarinet, Viola, Cello, and Piano (1964); String Sextet (1964); Trio for Flute, Viola, and Harpsichord (1964); *Ziz, King of Birds* for Flute, Clarinet, English Horn, French Horn, Violin, and Piano (1966); *Quashq* for Flute, Clarinet, Horn, and Piano (1966); *Pili* for 13 Instruments (1966); String Quartet (1968); *Macrame* for Flute, Bassoon, and Guitar (1974); *Gâteau* for Wind Quintet (1975). PIANO: *Variations,* 4-hands (1969); *Stasis,* 12 pieces (1970). ORGAN: *Fantasy on the ABC* (1975).

Tiby, Ottavio, Italian musicologist; b. Palermo, May 19, 1891; d. there, Dec. 4, 1955. He studied at the Palermo Cons., graduating in composition in 1921; later studied in Rome. Returning to Palermo, he devoted himself to collecting Sicilian songs; was also an authority on Byzantine music.
WRITINGS: *Acustica musicale e organologia degli strumenti musicali* (Palermo, 1933); *Antichi musicisti siciliani* (Palermo, 1933); *La musica bizantina: Teoria e storia* (Milan, 1938); *Vincenzo Bellini* (Turin, 1938); *Carl Maria von Weber* (Turin, 1941); *Claudio Monteverdi* (Turin, 1942); *La musica in Grecia e a Roma* (Florence, 1942); *I polifonisti siciliani del XVI e XVII secolo* (Palermo, 1969).

Tichatschek, Joseph (real name, **Josef Aloys Ticháček**), noted Bohemian tenor; b. Ober-Weckelsdorf, July 11, 1807; d. Blasewitz, Jan. 18, 1886. He was the son of a poor weaver; in 1827 he went to Vienna as a medical student, but then joined the chorus at the Kärnthnertortheater, and had vocal instruction from Ciccimara; was engaged at Graz in 1837; then sang in Vienna (1837). His career received a new impetus after his highly successful appearance as Auber's Gustavus III in Dresden (Aug. 11, 1837); in 1838 he joined the Dresden Court Opera, where he remained one of its leading members until he was pensioned in 1861; continued to make appearances there until 1870. He created the roles of Rienzi (Oct. 20, 1842) and Tannhäuser (Oct. 19, 1845) in Wagner's operas. Wagner mentions him often and with great praise in his autobiography.
BIBL.: M. Fürstenau, *J. T.* (Dresden, 1868); E. Kloss, "J. T.," *Neue Zeitschrift für Musik,* LXXIV (1907).

Tieffenbrucker, Gaspar. See **Duiffoprugcar, Gaspar.**

Tiehsen, Otto, German composer; b. Danzig, Oct. 13, 1817; d. Berlin, May 15, 1849. He studied at the Royal Academy in Berlin, where he settled as a teacher. He wrote the comic opera *Annette* (Berlin, 1847); *Christmas Cantata; Kyrie* and *Gloria a 6*; songs of high merit.

Tiensuu, Jukka, prominent Finnish harpsichordist, pianist, conductor, teacher, and composer; b. Helsinki, Aug. 30, 1948. He was a pupil of Paavo Heininen at the Sibelius Academy in Helsinki (1967–72), where he received diplomas in piano and composition (1972); after attending the Juilliard School in N.Y. (1972–73), he pursued studies in harpsichord and Baroque chamber music at the Freiburg im Breisgau Staatliche Hochschule für Musik (diplomas, 1976); then was active as a researcher and composer at IRCAM in Paris (1978–82); pursued computer music research at the Univ. of Calif. at San Diego and at the Mass. Inst. of Technology (1989). He toured widely as a performer in Europe, North America, and Asia; served as director of the Helsinki Biennale in 1981 and 1983; was founder-director of the International Festival and Summer Academy of Contemporary Music in Viitasaari (1982); taught at the Sibelius Academy and gave master classes on Baroque and avant-garde music. In 1988 his *Tokko* was awarded 1st prize at the UNESCO International Composers Rostrum in Paris. As a performing musician, he has won accolades for his insightful interpretations of both contemporary and Baroque scores. His own compositions utilize various avant-garde techniques.

WORKS: ORCH.: *Largo* for String Orch. (1971); *Tanka* for High Voice and Orch. (1973); *Threnos* (1973); *Fiato* for Wind Orch. (1974); *Re-Bah-Beil* for Amateur Orch. (1976); *Mxpzkl* (1977); *M* (1980); *Puro* for Clarinet and Orch. (1989). **CHAMBER:** *Concerto da camera* (1972); *preLUDI, LUDI, postLUDI* for Guitar (1974); *Lyric Trio* for Flute, Voice, and Piano (1975); *Sinistro* for Accordion and Guitar (1977); *Yang 1* and *2* for 8 Instruments (1978, 1979); *Prélude mesuré* for Microtonally Tuned Harpsichord (1983); *Tango lunaire* for Small Ensemble (1985); , *mutta* for 3 Accordions (1987); *Manaus* for Kantele (1988); Quintet for Harpsichord and String Quartet (1990); piano pieces. **ELECTRO-ACOUSTIC:** *Solo* for Piano and Live Electronics (1976); *Passage* for Soprano, 7 Instruments, and Live Electronics (1980); *P=Pinocchio?* for Soprano, 5 Instruments, Computer-generated Tapes, and Computer in Real Time (1980–82); *4 Interludes* for Tape (1987); *Tokko* for Men's Choir and Computer-generated Tape (1987).

Tierney, Harry (Austin), American composer of popular music; b. Perth Amboy, N.J., May 21, 1890; d. N.Y., March 22, 1965. He studied piano and planned a concert career; then turned to composition of popular music; wrote many numbers for the Ziegfeld Follies. His musical shows *Irene* (N.Y., Nov. 18, 1919), *Up She Goes* (N.Y., Nov. 6, 1922), and *Kid Boots* (N.Y., Dec. 31, 1923) were quite successful, but were eclipsed by the fame of his *Rio Rita* (N.Y., Feb. 2, 1927). His early song *M-i-s-s-i-s-s-i-p-p-i* (1916) flooded the nation. From 1930 until the early 1940s he composed for Hollywood films.

Tiersot, (Jean-Baptiste-Elisée-) Julien, French musicologist; b. Bourg-en-Bresse, July 5, 1857; d. Paris, Aug. 10, 1936. He was a pupil of Savard, Massenet, and Franck at the Paris Cons.; in 1883, was appointed assistant librarian at the Cons., and in 1909, chief librarian, retiring in 1921. He was also a prof. at the École des Hautes Études Sociales and president of the Société Française de Musicologie. His compositions include a Mass on the tercentenary of the death of Roland de Lassus (1894); *Danses populaires françaises* for Orch. (1900); *Hellas* (after Shelley) for Chorus and Orch.; etc.

WRITINGS (all publ. in Paris): *Histoire de la chanson populaire en France* (1889); *Musiques pittoresques: promenades musicales à l'Exposition de 1889* (1889); *Rouget de Lisle, Son œuvre, sa vie* (1892); *Le messe Douce mémoire de Roland de Lassus* (1894); *Les Types mélodiques dans la chanson populaire française* (1894); *Étude sur les Maîtres-Chanteurs de Nuremberg de Richard Wagner* (1899); *Hector Berlioz et la société de son temps* (1904); *Les Fêtes et les chants de la Révolution française* (1908); *Gluck* (1910); *Beethoven, musicien de la Révolution* (1910); *Jean-Jacques Rousseau* (1912; 2nd ed., 1920); *Histoire de la Marseillaise* (1915); *Un Demi-siècle de musique française: entre deux guerres 1870–1917* (1918; 2nd ed., 1924); *La Musique dans la comédie de Molière* (1921); *La Damnation de Faust de Berlioz* (1924); *Les Couperin* (1926; 2nd ed., 1933); *Smetana* (1926); *La Musique aux temps romantiques* (1930); *La Chanson populaire et les écrivains romantiques* (1931); *Don Juan de Mozart* (1933); *J.-S. Bach* (1934).

FOLKSONG EDITIONS: *Mélodies populaires des provinces de France* (1888–1928); *Noëls français* (1901); *Chansons populaires recueillies dans les Alpes françaises* (1903); *Chants populaires, pour les écoles* (1896–1902); *44 French Folksongs and Variants from Canada, Normandy, and Brittany* (1910); *60 Folksongs of France* (1915); *Chansons populaires françaises* (1921); *Chansons nègres* (1933).

BIBL.: L. de La Laurencie, *Un musicien bressan: J. T.* (Bourg-en-Bresse, 1932); C. Engel, "J. T.," *Musical Quarterly*, XXIII (1937).

Tiessen, (Richard Gustav) Heinz, German conductor, music critic, teacher, and composer; b. Königsberg, April 10, 1887; d. Berlin, Nov. 29, 1971. He studied music with Rüfer and Klatte in Berlin; was music critic of the *Allgemeine Musikzeitung* (1911–17); led Der Jungen Chor for children of workers (1922–32). In 1925 he was appointed to the faculty of the Hochschule für Musik in Berlin; from 1946 to 1949, was director of the Berlin Cons., returning in 1949 to the Hochschule. He left the Hochschule in 1955 to become director of the music division at the West Berlin Academy of the Arts. He publ. an autobiography, *Wege eines Komponisten* (Berlin, 1962). He composed in both traditional and modern idioms; birdcalls played a prominent role in a number of his works. His compositions include 2 syms. (1911, 1912); *Totentanz-Suite* for Violin and Orch. (1918; rev. as *Visionen*, 1954); *Konzertante Variationen über eine eigene Tanzmelodie* for Piano and Orch. (1962); *Amsel-Septett* for Flute, Clarinet, Horn, and String Quartet (1915; rev. 1957); String Quintet (1919–22); piano pieces, including a Sonata (1910); choruses; musical plays; songs.

BIBL.: E. Kroll, "H. T.," *Musica*, XI (1957).

Tietjen, Heinz, noted German conductor and opera producer; b. Tangier, June 24, 1881; d. Baden-Baden, Nov. 30, 1967. He studied conducting with Nikisch; was then active as an opera producer in Trier (1904–22); later was administrator of the Berlin City Opera (1925–27); from 1931 to 1944, was artistic director of the Bayreuth Festivals, where he also conducted. He was again administrator of the Berlin City Opera (1948–55) and also of the Hamburg State Opera (1956–59); then retired in Baden-Baden.

Tietjens, Therese (Carolina Johanna Alexandra), famous German soprano; b. Hamburg, July 17, 1831; d. London, Oct. 3, 1877. She was trained in Hamburg and Vienna; in 1849 made her operatic debut in Altona, as Donizetti's Lucrezia Borgia, which became her most celebrated role. After singing in Frankfurt (1850–51), Brünn, and Vienna, she made her London debut as Valentine in *Les Huguenots* at Her Majesty's Theatre on April 13, 1858; subsequently appeared in London every season until her death, making her Covent Garden debut as Lucrezia Borgia on Oct. 24, 1868. She also sang opera in Paris (1863), at the Teatro San Carlo in Naples (1862–63; 1868–69), and in the U.S. (1874, 1876); also became well known as an oratorio singer in England. Stricken with cancer, she made her farewell appearance at Covent Garden as Lucrezia Borgia on May 19, 1877, collapsing on the stage at the close of the performance. Among her other outstanding roles were Mozart's Countess, Pamina, and Donna Anna, Cherubini's Medea, Beethoven's Leonore, Bellini's Norma, Verdi's Leonora, and Wagner's Ortrud.

Tigranian, Armen (Tigran), Armenian composer and teacher; b. Alexandropol, Dec. 26, 1879; d. Tbilisi, Feb. 10, 1950. He studied flute and theory in Tiflis; returned to Alexandropol in 1902 and organized a choral society, specializing in Armenian music; in 1913 he settled in Tiflis, where he became an esteemed music pedagogue; received the Order of Lenin in 1939. He composed the operas *Anush* (1908–12; Alexandropol, Aug. 17, 1912) and *David-bek* (1949; Erevan, Dec. 3, 1950); *Dance Suite* for Orch. (1946); cantata, *The Bloody Night* (1936); *Suite of Armenian Dances* for Piano (1938); numerous other piano pieces; songs; theater music.

BIBL.: K. Melik-Wrtanessian, *A. T.* (Moscow, 1939); R. Atanian and M. Muradian, *A. T.* (Moscow, 1966).

Tijardović, Ivo, Croatian composer; b. Split, Sept. 18, 1895; d. Zagreb, March 19, 1976. He studied in Zagreb; began his professional career by conducting theater orchs.; wrote operettas of the Viennese type; of these, *Little Floramy* (1924) became successful in Yugoslavia. His opera *Dimnjiaci uz Jadran* (The Chimneys of the Adriatic Coast; Zagreb, Jan. 20, 1951), depicts the patriotic uprising of Yugoslav partisans during World War II; he also wrote the opera *Marco Polo* (Zagreb, Dec. 3, 1960).

BIBL.: I. Plamenac, *I. T.* (Split, 1954).

Tikka, Kari (Juhani), Finnish conductor and composer; b. Siilinjärvi, April 13, 1946. He received training in oboe (diploma, 1968), in conducting from Jorma Panula (diploma, 1979), and in composition from Einar Englund, Joonas Kokkonen, and Einojuhani Rautavaara at the Sibelius Academy in Helsinki; also studied conducting with Arvid Jansons in Leningrad and with Luigi Ricci in Rome. He played oboe in the Helsinki Phil. (1965–67) and the Finnish National Opera Orch. in Helsinki (1967–68). In 1968 he made his conducting debut in Helsinki; subsequently conducted at the Finnish National Opera there (1970–72), then was a conductor of the Finnish Radio Sym. Orch. (1972–76) and director of the Ensemble for Modern Music of the Finnish Radio. From 1975 to 1977 he was a conductor of the Royal Opera in Stockholm; then again was a conductor at the Finnish National Opera (from 1979); also appeared as a guest conductor throughout Europe. His works include a Cello Concerto (1984) and other orch. pieces; *The Prodigal Son*, an oratorio for 3 Soloists, Chorus, and Orch. (1985); cantatas; accompanied and unaccompanied choral works; chamber music; and solo songs.

Tikotsky, Evgeni (Karlovich), Russian composer of Polish descent; b. St. Petersburg, Dec. 25, 1893; d. Minsk, Nov. 24, 1970. He studied composition with Volkova-Bonch-Bruievich in St. Petersburg (1912–14) before pursuing the study of physics and mathematics at the Univ. there (1914–15). He taught in a music school in Bobruysk (1927–34); then settled in Minsk, where he taught at the music school (1934–41); was artistic director of the Belorussian State Phil. (1944–45; 1953–57). In 1944 he received the Order of Lenin and in 1955 was made a People's Artist of the U.S.S.R.
WORKS: OPERAS: *Mihas Podhorny* (Minsk, March 10, 1939); *Alesya* (Minsk, Dec. 24, 1944; rev. 1952–53). ORCH.: 5 syms. (1927; 1941; 1948–59; 1958; 1963); Trombone Concerto (1934); Concerto for Piano and Belorussian Folk Orch. (1953; also for Piano and Sym. Orch., 1954); *Slava* (Glory), overture (1961); also chamber works; choruses; songs; incidental music; film scores; folksong arrangements.
BIBL.: I. Gusin, *E.K. T.* (Moscow and Leningrad, 1965).

Till, Johann Christian, American Moravian teacher, organist, and composer; b. Gnadenthal, near Nazareth, Pa., May 18, 1762; d. Bethlehem, Pa., Nov. 19, 1844. From 1793 to 1808 he was a teacher and organist at Hope, N.J.; from 1813 to 1844, was organist of the Bethlehem congregation. In his later years he also made pianos. His compositions are listed in A. Rau and H. David, *A Catalogue of Music by American Moravians* (Bethlehem, 1938).

Tilles, Nurit, American pianist; b. N.Y., May 29, 1952. She studied at the preparatory division of the Juilliard School in N.Y. (1961–68) and at the Oberlin College Cons. of Music (B.Mus., 1973); after taking courses in tabla and gamelan at the Center for World Music (1974), she attended the State Univ. of N.Y. at Stony Brook (M.Mus., 1976), where she studied piano with Gilbert Kalish and chamber music with Arthur Weisberg. She performed and recorded with Steve Reich and Musicians (from 1975), Laura Dean Dancers & Musicians (1980–82), the Mother Mallard Band, a.k.a. the David Borden Music Co. (1980–87), and the Meredith Monk Ensemble (from 1984); collaborated with Monk on *Fayum Music* for Voice and Hammered Dulcimer and frequently toured with her. In 1978 she formed the piano duo Double Edge with Edmund Niemann, giving premiere performances in the U.S. and Europe of works specially composed for them by Borden, John Cage, "Blue" Gene Tyranny et al. Her solo recording *Ragtime: Here and Now* received high critical praise.

Tillis, Mel, American country-music singer and songwriter; b. Pahokee, Fla., Aug. 8, 1932. He began writing songs while still in school; eventually settled in Nashville, Tenn., where he became one of the leading songwriters of country music. His popular songs include *Ruby, Don't Take Your Love to Town; One More Time; Heart over Mind;* and *Take Time.* With W. Wager, he wrote the memoir *Stutterin' Boy* (N.Y., 1984).

Tillyard, H(enry) J(ulius) W(etenhall), English musicologist; b. Cambridge, Nov. 18, 1881; d. Saffron Walden, Jan. 2,

1968. He studied at Gonville and Caius College, Cambridge (1900–1904); then studied Greek church music with J. Sakellarides in Athens (1904–7). From 1908 to 1917 he taught Greek at the Univ. of Edinburgh; from 1919 to 1921, was a prof. of classics at the Univ. of Johannesburg, South Africa; prof. of Russian at the Univ. of Birmingham, 1921–26; prof. of Greek, Univ. of Cardiff, 1926–44; and lecturer in classics, at Rhodes Univ. in Grahamstown, South Africa, 1946–49. Tillyard was an authority on Byzantine chant. He publ. *Byzantine Music and Hymnography* (London, 1923) and *Handbook of the Middle Byzantine Notation* in Monumenta Musicae Byzantinae, *Subsidia*, I (1935).

Tilman, Alfred, Belgian composer; b. Brussels, Feb. 3, 1848; d. Schaerbeck, near Brussels, Feb. 20, 1895. He studied at the Brussels Cons. (1866–71); wrote the cantata *La Sirène;* also 24 vocal fugues for 2 and 3 voices.

Tilmant, Théophile (Alexandre), noted French violinist and conductor; b. Valenciennes, July 8, 1799; d. Asnières, near Paris, May 7, 1878. He studied violin with Rodolphe Kreutzer at the Paris Cons. (premier prix, 1819); was a member of the orchs. at the Théâtre-Italien (from 1819) and of the Opéra (from 1825); was deputy conductor of the Société des Concerts du Conservatoire (1818–60), and then its chief conductor (1860–63); also was deputy conductor (1834–38) and chief conductor (1838–49) of the Théâtre-Italien, as well as conductor of the Opéra-Comique (1849–68). With his brother, the cellist Alexandre Tilmant (b. Valenciennes, Oct. 14, 1808; d. Paris, June 13, 1880), he was active in a chamber music society.

Tilney, Colin, English harpsichordist; b. London, Oct. 31, 1933. He studied modern languages and music at King's College, Cambridge; then took lessons in harpsichord with Mary Potts and with Gustav Leonhardt in Amsterdam; subsequently became engaged as a soloist and ensemble player in England and on the Continent; made his 1st tour of the U.S. in 1971. His extensive repertoire covers the harpsichord literature of the 16th, 17th, and 18th centuries; it is his preference to use historical instruments or modern replicas of harpsichords, clavichords, and fortepianos in his concerts.

Timm, Henry Christian, German-American pianist, organist, conductor, and composer; b. Hamburg, July 11, 1811; d. Hoboken, N.J., Sept. 5, 1892. After study in Germany, he settled in the U.S. in 1835; was employed as a church organist in N.Y., Boston, etc.; appeared as a conductor with the Phil. Society in N.Y. at its inaugural concert (Dec. 7, 1842) and later was its president (1848–63); retired as a performing musician in 1882. He wrote choral works, organ pieces, and some piano music; made numerous transcriptions for 2 pianos of various classical works.

Timmermans, Ferdinand, Dutch organist and carillonneur; b. Rotterdam, Sept. 7, 1891; d. Oostenrijk, July 8, 1967. He studied organ with J.H. Besselaar and H. de Vries. In 1924 he became the municipal carillonneur at Rotterdam, and in 1926, at Schiedam. He subsequently gave exhibitions in Belgium, France, and England; soon he won the reputation of being one of the world's greatest carillonneurs. On May 5, 1954 he gave a concert in Washington, D.C., playing on the 50-bell carillon presented to the U.S. by the people of the Netherlands. He publ. *Luidklokken en beiaarden in Nederland* (Amsterdam, 1944).

Tinayre, Yves (Jean), French singer and music scholar; b. Paris, April 25, 1891; d. N.Y., July 12, 1972. He studied voice in London and Milan; gave recitals in France, England, Austria, etc., specializing in early songs; also revived some medieval French, German, and Italian sacred songs.

Tinctoris, Johannes, renowned Franco-Flemish music theorist and lexicographer; b. Braine l'Alleud, near Nivelles, c.1435; d. before Oct. 12, 1511. He matriculated at the German Nation of Orleans Univ. (April 1, 1463). About 1472 he became tutor to the daughter of King Ferdinand I of Naples. In 1487 Ferdinand dispatched him to the courts of Charles VIII of France and Maximilian of Rome to recruit singers for his chapel. At the time of his death, Tinctoris was a canon and prebendary in Nivelles. About 1472 he compiled a dictionary of musical terms, *Terminorum musicae diffinitorium* (Treviso, 1495), which was the 1st of its kind. The only other work known to have been publ. in his lifetime was *De inventione et usu musicae* (Naples, c.1487). Tinctoris also wrote poetry, and served as a cleric. For editions of his writings, see C.E.H. de Coussemaker, ed., *Johannes Tinctoris tractatus de musica* (Lille, 1875) and A. Seay, *Johannes Tinctoris: Opera theoretica*, in Corpus scriptorum de musica, XXII (1975).

WRITINGS: *Terminorum musicae diffinitorium* (Treviso, 1495; Ger. tr. in *Jahrbuch für Musikwissenschaft*, I, 1863; French tr., Paris, 1951; Eng. tr., London, 1964); *Complexus effectuum musices* (written c.1473–74; Italian tr., Bologna, 1979); *Proportionale musices* (written c.1473–74: Eng. tr. in *Journal of Music Theory*, I, 1957); *Liber imperfectionum notarum musicalium* (written c.1474–75); *Tractatus de regulari valore notarum* (written c.1474–75); *Tractatus de notis et pausis* (written c.1474–75); *Liber de natura et proprietate tonorum* (dated Nov. 6, 1476; Eng. tr., Colorado Springs, 1967; 2nd ed., rev., 1976); *Liber de arte contrapuncti* (dated Oct. 11, 1477; Eng. tr. in Musicological Studies and Documents, V, 1961); *Tractatus alterationum* (written after 1477); *Scriptum super punctis musicalibus* (written after 1477); *Expositio manus* (written after 1477); *De inventione et usu musicae* (Naples, c.1487).

WORKS: SACRED VOCAL: *Missa "Cunctorum plasmator summus"* for 4 Voices; *Missa "Nos amis"* for 3 Voices; *Missa sine nomine* (2 for 3 Voices; one for 4 Voices); *Alleluia* for 2 Voices; *Fecit potentiam* for 2 Voices; *Lamentationes Jeremie* for 4 Voices; *O virgo miserere mei* for 3 Voices; *Virgo Dei throno digna* for 3 Voices; also various secular chansons. For a modern edition of his works, see W. Melin, ed., *Johannes Tinctoris: Opera omnia*, in Corpus Mensurabilis musicae, XVIII (1976).

BIBL.: U. Kornmüller, "Die alten Musiktheoretiker: J. T.," *Kirchenmusikalisches Jahrbuch*, XVIII (1903); K. Weinmann, "Ein unbekannter Traktat des J. T.," *Riemann-Festschrift* (Leipzig, 1909); G. Pannain, *La teoria musicale di Giovanni T.* (Naples, 1913); K. Weinmann, *J. T. und sein unbekannter Traktat "De inventione et usu musicae"* (Regensburg, 1917); C. van den Borren, "T., J.," in *Biographie nationale (belge)* (Brussels, 1931); L. Balmer, *Tonsystem und Kirchentöne bei J. T.* (diss., Univ. of Bern, 1935); E. Krenek, *A Discussion of the Treatment of Dissonances in Ockeghem's Masses as Compared with the Contrapuntal Theory of J. T.* (St. Paul, Minn., 1947); E. Ferand, "What is Res facta?," *Journal of the American Musicological Society*, X (1957); W. Melin, *The Music of J. T. (c.1435–1511): A Comparative Study of Theory and Practice* (diss., Ohio State Univ., 1973); G. Gerritzen, *Untersuchungen zur Kontrapunktlehre des J. T.* (diss., Univ. of Cologne, 1974); R. Strohm, "Die Missa super 'Nos amis' von J. T.," *Die Musikforschung*, XXXII (1979); B. Blackburn, "A Lost Guide to T.'s Teachings Recovered," *Early Music History*, I (1981).

Tinel, Edgar (Pierre Joseph), Belgian pianist, pedagogue, and composer; b. Sinaii, East Flanders, March 27, 1854; d. Brussels, Oct. 28, 1912. He was taught at 1st by his father, a schoolmaster and organist, then entered the Brussels Cons. in 1863 as a pupil of Brassin, Dupont, Gevaert, Kufferath, and Mailly; in 1873 he took 1st prize for piano playing; won the Belgian Prix de Rome in 1877 with the cantata *De Klokke Roeland*. In 1881 he became director of the Malines Inst. of Religious Music; was appointed to the staff of the Brussels Cons. in 1896, and in 1908 became its director. He publ. *Le Chant grégorien, Théorie sommaire de son exécution* (Mechelen, 1890).

WORKS: OPERAS: *Godelieve* (Brussels, July 22, 1897); *Katharina* (Brussels, Feb. 27, 1909); also orch. music; many choral pieces, including the oratorio *Franciscu* (Mechelen, 1888); 2 Te Deums (1883, 1905), cantatas, and psalms; keyboard music; songs.

BIBL.: A. van der Elst, *E. T.* (Ghent, 1901); P. Tinel, *E.*

T.: Le récit de sa vie et l'exégèse de son œuvre de 1854 à 1886 (Brussels, 1922); idem, *E. T.* (Brussels, 1946); F. van der Mueren, "E. T.," *Musica sacra*, LXIII (1962).

Tinsley, Pauline (Cecilia), English soprano; b. Wigan, March 27, 1928. She studied at the Northern School of Music in Manchester; then with Joan Cross at the National School of Opera in London; made her operatic debut in London in 1951 as Desdemona in Rossini's *Otello*; sang with the Welsh National Opera (from 1962) and the Handel Opera Society. She joined the Sadler's Wells Opera in 1963; sang at Covent Garden from 1965. In 1969 she made her U.S. debut as Anna Bolena at the Santa Fe Opera, and later sang with other U.S. opera companies. Among her prominent roles were Mozart's Countess and Fiordiligi, Aida, Lady Macbeth, Elektra, and Turandot.

Tiomkin, Dimitri, Ukrainian-born American composer of film music; b. Poltava, May 10, 1894; d. London, Nov. 11, 1979. He studied composition with A. Glazunov and piano with F. Blumenfeld and I. Vengerova at the St. Petersburg Cons.; in 1921 went to Berlin, where he studied with Busoni, Petri, and Zadora; was soloist in Liszt's 1st Piano Concerto with the Berlin Phil. (June 15, 1924), and that same year gave several concerts with Michael Khariton in Paris. He appeared in vaudeville in the U.S. (1925); became a citizen (1937); made his conducting debut with the Los Angeles Phil. (Aug. 16, 1938), and later conducted his music with various U.S. orchs.; married Albertina Rasch, a ballerina, for whose troupe he wrote music. From 1930 to 1970 he wrote over 150 film scores, including several for the U.S. War Dept. Among his most notable scores were *Alice in Wonderland* (1933), *Mr. Smith Goes to Washington* (1939), *The Corsican Brothers* (1942), *The Moon and Sixpence* (1943), *The Bridge of San Luis Rey* (1944), *Duel in the Sun* (1946), *Champion* (1949), *High Noon* (1952; Academy Award), *Dial M for Murder* (1954), *The High and the Mighty* (1954; Academy Award), *Giant* (1956), *The Old Man and the Sea* (1958; Academy Award), *The Alamo* (1960), *The Guns of Navarone* (1961), *55 Days at Peking* (1963), *The Fall of the Roman Empire* (1964), and *Tchaikovsky* (1970). His film music betrayed his strong Russian Romantic background, tempered with American jazz. He received an honorary LL.D. from St. Mary's Univ., San Antonio, Texas; was made a Chevalier and an Officer of the French Légion d'honneur; also received awards of merit, scrolls of appreciation, plaques of recognition, and a Golden Globe. With P. Buranelli, he publ. the autobiography *Please Don't Hate Me* (N.Y., 1959).

BIBL.: C. Palmer, *D. T.: A Portrait* (London, 1984).

Tipo, Maria (Luisa), Italian pianist and pedagogue; b. Naples, Dec. 23, 1931. She studied in Naples before completing her training with Casella and Agosti; in 1948 she won 2nd prize (no 1st prize was given) at the Geneva International Competition, and returned in 1949 to capture its 1st prize; after winning 3rd prize at the Queen Elisabeth of Belgium Competition in Brussels in 1952, she toured in Europe and abroad; she eventually devoted much time to teaching, giving courses at the Bolzano Cons. and in Florence and Geneva. She championed the cause of traditional Italian keyboard music, most notably the works of Scarlatti and Clementi.

Tippett, Sir Michael (Kemp), greatly renowned English composer; b. London, Jan. 2, 1905. His family was of Cornish descent, and Tippett never refrained from proclaiming his pride of Celtic ancestry. He was equally emphatic in the liberal beliefs of his family. His father was a free thinker, which did not prevent him from running a successful hotel business. His mother was a suffragette who once served a prison term. Her last name was Kemp, which Tippett eventually accepted as his own middle name. He took piano lessons as a child and sang in his school chorus but showed no exceptional merit as a performer. He studied in London at the Royal College of Music (1923–28), where his teachers in composition were

Charles Wood and C.H. Kitson; took piano lessons there with Aubin Raymar and attended courses in conducting with Boult and Sargent; studied counterpoint and fugue with R.O. Morris (1930–32). He subsequently held several positions as a teacher and conductor; from 1933 to 1940 he led the South London Orch. at Morley College; then served as director of music there (1940–51). Socially Tippett had difficulties even early in life. He openly proclaimed his extremely liberal political views, his overt atheism, and his strenuous pacifism. His oratorio *A Child of Our Time* was inspired by the case of Henschel Grynsban, a Jewish boy who assassinated a member of the German embassy in Paris in 1938. As a conscientious objector, he refused to serve even in a non-combatant capacity in the British military forces; for this intransigent attitude he was sentenced to prison for 3 months; he served his term in a Surrey County gaol with the suggestive name Wormwood Scrubs (June 21–Aug. 21, 1943). He regained the respect of the community after the end of the war. In 1951 he initiated a series of broadcasts for the BBC; from 1969 to 1974 he directed the Bath Festival. He received high honors from the British government; in 1959 he was named a Commander of the Order of the British Empire; in 1966 he was knighted; in 1979 he was made a Companion of Honour. He visited the U.S. in 1965, and thereafter was a frequent guest in America; his symphonic works were often performed by major American orchs. Tippett's works have a grandeur of Romantic inspiration that sets them apart from the prevalent type of contemporary music; they are infused with rhapsodic eloquence and further enhanced by a pervading lyric sentiment free from facile sentimentality. He excelled in large-scale vocal and instrumental forms; he was a consummate master of the modern idioms, attaining heights of dissonant counterpoint without losing the teleological sense of inherent tonality. Yet he did not shun special effects; 3 times in his 4th Sym. he injects episodes of heavy glottal aspiration, suggested to him by viewing a film depicting the dissection of fetuses of pigs. A man of great general culture, Tippett possesses a fine literary gift; he writes his own librettos for his operas and oratorios. He publ. *Moving into Aquarius* (London, 1958; 2nd ed., 1974). M. Bowen ed. *Music of the Angels: Essays and Sketchbooks of Michael Tippett* (London, 1980).

WORKS: OPERAS: *The Midsummer Marriage* (1946–52; London, Jan. 27, 1955); *King Priam* (1958–61; Coventry, May 29, 1962); *The Knot Garden* (1966–69; London, Dec. 2, 1970); *The Ice Break* (1973–76; London, July 7, 1977); *New Year* (1985–88; Houston, Oct. 27, 1989). **ORCH.:** Concerto for Double String Orch. (1938–39; London, April 21, 1940, composer conducting); *Fantasia on a Theme by Handel* for Piano and Orch. (1939–41; London, March 7, 1942); Sym. No. 1 (Liverpool, Nov. 10, 1945); *Little Music* for String Orch. (London, Nov. 9, 1946); Suite in D major, for the birthday of Prince Charles (BBC, London, Nov. 15, 1948); *Ritual Dances*, from *The Midsummer Marriage* (Basel, Feb. 13, 1953); *Fantasia Concertante on a Theme by Corelli* for String Orch. (Edinburgh, Aug. 29, 1953, composer conducting); *Divertimento on Sellinger's Round* for Chamber Orch. (Zürich, Nov. 5, 1954); Concerto for Piano and Orch. (1953–55; Birmingham, Oct. 30, 1956); Sym. No. 2 (1956–57; London, Feb. 5, 1958); *Praeludium* for Brass, Bells, and Percussion (London, Nov. 14, 1962); Concerto for Orch. (Edinburgh, Aug. 28, 1963); Sym. No. 3 for Soprano and Orch. (1970–72; London, June 22, 1972); Sym. No. 4 (Chicago, Oct. 6, 1977); Triple Concerto for Violin, Viola, Cello, and Orch. (1979; London, Aug. 22, 1980); *Water Out of Sunlight* for String Orch. (London, June 15, 1988; arr. from the String Quartet No. 4 by M. Bowen). **VOCAL:** *A Child of Our Time*, oratorio with text by the composer, inspired by the case of the Jewish boy Henschel Grynsban, who assassinated in 1938 a Nazi member of the German embassy in Paris (1939–41; London, March 19, 1944); *Boyhood's End*, cantata to a text by W.H. Hudson, for Tenor and Piano (London, June 5, 1943); *The Heart's Assurance*, song cycle to poems by Sidney Keyes and Alun Lewis, for High Voice and Piano (London, May 7, 1951); *Dance, Clarion Air*, madrigal for 5 Voices, with

text by Christopher Fry (1952; June 1, 1953); *Crown of the Year,* cantata for Chorus and Instrumental Ensemble, with text by Christopher Fry (Bristol, July 25, 1958); *Music for Words Perhaps* for Speaking Voices and Chamber Ensemble, to love poems by W.B. Yeats (BBC, London, June 8, 1960); *Music,* unison song to the poem by Shelley, for Voices, Strings, and Piano (April 1960); *Magnificat and Nunc Dimittis* for Chorus and Organ (1961; Cambridge, March 13, 1962); *Songs for Ariel* for Medium Voice and Instrumental Ensemble (1962); *The Vision of Saint Augustine* for Baritone, Chorus, and Orch. (1963–65; London, Jan. 19, 1966; Dietrich Fischer-Dieskau, soloist; composer conducting); *The Shires Suite* for Chorus and Orch. (1965–70; Cheltenham, July 8, 1970, composer conducting); *The Mask of Time* for Chorus and Orch. (1981–84; Boston, April 5, 1984); *Byzantium* for Soloist and Orch. (Chicago, April 11, 1991). **CHAMBER:** 4 string quartets (1935, rev. 1944; 1943; 1946; 1979, arr. for String Orch. by M. Bowen as *Water Out of Sunlight,* London, June 15, 1988); *4 Inventions* for Descant and Treble Recorders (1954); Sonata for 4 Horns (1955); *Wolf Trap Fanfare* for 3 Trumpets, 2 Trombones, and Tuba (1980); *The Blue Guitar* for Guitar (1983). **PIANO:** 5 sonatas: No. 1 (1938; rev. 1942 and 1954); No. 2 (1962); No. 3 (1973); No. 4 (1979); No. 5 (1984); also *Preludio al Vespro di Monteverdi* for Organ (1946).

BIBL.: I. Kemp, ed., *M. T.: A Symposium on His 60th Birthday* (London, 1965); A. Milner, "The Music of M. T.," *Musical Quarterly* (Oct. 1974); M. Hurd, *T.* (London, 1978); E. White, *T. and His Operas* (London, 1979); D. Matthews, *M. T.: An Introductory Study* (London, 1980); M. Bowen, *M. T.* (London, 1982); A. Whittall, *The Music of Britten and T.: Studies in Themes and Techniques* (Cambridge, 1982; 2nd ed., 1990); R. Dyer, "Sir M. T.," *Ovation* (Dec. 1984); I. Kemp, *T.: the Composer and his Music* (London, 1984); P. Dennison, "Reminiscence and Recomposition in T.," *Musical Times* (Jan. 1985); P. Driver, "T. at 80: A Personal Tribute," ibid.; G. Lewis, "T.: The Breath of Life; An Approach to Formal Structure," ibid.; N. John, ed., *Operas of M. T.* (London, 1985); G. Lewis, ed., *M. T. O. M.: A Celebration* (Tunbridge Wells, 1985); idem, "Behind T.'s Mask," *Musical Times* (Feb. 1988); M. Bowen, "Sir M. T.," *Musical America* (Nov. 1989); G. Lewis, " 'New Year' in the New World," *Musical Times* (Nov. 1989); G. Theil, *M. T.: a Bio-Bibliography* (Westport, Conn., 1989).

Tipton, Billy, transvestite American jazz pianist and saxophonist; b. Oklahoma City, Dec. 29, 1914; d. Spokane, Wash., Jan. 21, 1989. It was not until the autopsy conducted by the funeral director took place that it was discovered that Billy Tipton was a woman, not a man. She grew up in Kansas City, Mo., and early decided to forego a normal life in order to play jazz. She loved jazz and played the saxophone and piano, but believed that a woman could never succeed in the profession. She dressed as a man, contracted a nominal marriage, and adopted 3 sons. She performed with the Jack Teagarden, Russ Carlyle, and Scott Cameron bands; then in the 1950s formed the Billy Tipton Trio, with which she played in nightclubs throughout the western U.S. Only her theoretical wife knew her secret; in an interview accompanying Tipton's obituary notice, she was quoted as saying, "He gave up everything. There were certain rules and regulations in those days if you were going to be a musician."

Tirindelli, Pier Adolfo, Italian violinist, teacher, and composer; b. Conegliano, May 5, 1858; d. Rome, Feb. 6, 1937. He studied violin at the Milan Cons., then in Vienna with Grün and in Paris with Massart. He taught violin at the Liceo Benedetto Marcello in Venice (1885–95) and at the Cincinnati Cons. (1896–1920). He wrote an Italian opera, *Atenaide* (Venice, Nov. 19, 1892) and a French opera, *Blanc et noir* (Cincinnati, Dec. 15, 1897); also composed some attractive songs to Italian and French words, among them *Mistica, Vaticinio, Je ne t'aime plus* and *Une Existence.*

BIBL.: E. Montanaro, *P.A. T. e la sua musica* (Rome, 1933).

Tischhauser, Franz, Swiss composer; b. Bern, March 28, 1921. He studied at the Zürich Cons.; in 1951, joined the staff of the Zürich Radio and in 1971 was appointed director of its music dept., which post he retained until 1983. **WORKS: DRAMATIC:** *Die Hampeloper* (1985–86). **BALLET:** *Birthday of the Infanta* (1941). **ORCH.:** Concertino for Piano and Small Orch. (1945); *Divertimento* for 2 Horns and String Orch. (1948); *Punctus contra punctum* for Tenor, Baritone, and Small Orch. (1962); *Omaggi a Mälzel* for 12 Stringed Instruments (1963); *Mattinata* for 23 Wind Instruments (1965); *Kontertänze* for 2 Orchs. (1968); *Eve's Meditation on Love* for Soprano, Tuba, and String Orch. (1972); *The Beggar's Concerto* for Clarinet and String Orch. (1975–76); *Dr. Bircher und Rossini* for Harpsichord and String Orch. (1978–79); also chamber works, including *Die Bremer Stadtmusikanten* for Bassoon, Clarinet, Oboe, Flute, and Piano (1982–83) and *Das Vierklaklavier* for 4 Clarinets (1984); choral works, including *Antiphonarium profanum* for 2 Men's Choruses a capella (1967).

Tischler, Hans, distinguished Austrian-American musicologist; b. Vienna, Jan. 18, 1915. He studied piano with Paul Wittgenstein and Bertha Jahn-Beer, composition with Richard Stöhr and Franz Schmidt, and musicology with Robert Lach, Robert Haas, and Egon Wellesz at the Univ. of Vienna (Ph.D., 1937, with the dissertation *Die Harmonik in den Werken Gustav Mahlers*). He left Austria in 1938, settling in the U.S.; continued his musicological studies with Leo Schrade at Yale Univ. (Ph.D., 1942, with the dissertation *The Motet in 13th-Century France*). He taught music history at West Virginia Wesleyan College (1945–47) and at Roosevelt Univ. in Chicago (1947–65). In 1965 he was appointed prof. of musicology at Indiana Univ. in Bloomington, where he remained until his retirement in 1985. **WRITINGS:** *The Perceptive Music Listener* (N.Y., 1955); *Practical Harmony* (Boston, 1964); *A Structural Analysis of Mozart's Piano Concertos* (Brooklyn, N.Y., 1966); the Eng. ed. of Willi Apel's *History of Keyboard Music to 1700* (Bloomington, Ind., 1973); *A Medieval Motet Book* (N.Y., 1973); *The Montpellier Codex* (3 vols., Madison, Wis., 1978); *Chanter m'estuet: Songs of the Trouvères* (with S. Rosenberg; Bloomington, 1981); *The Earliest Motets: A Complete Comparative Edition* (New Haven, Conn., 1982); *The Earliest Motets: Their Style and Evolution* (Henryville, Pa., 1985); *The Parisian Two-Part Organa: A Complete Comparative Edition* (N.Y., 1987); *The Monophonic Songs in the Roman de Fauvel* (Toronto, 1988).

Tishchenko, Boris (Ivanovich), Russian composer; b. Leningrad, March 23, 1939. He studied composition at the Leningrad Cons. with Salmanov, Voloshinov, and Evlakhov, graduating in 1962; also took lessons with Shostakovich (1962–65); then taught at the Leningrad Cons. (from 1965). In his works he demonstrates a strong rhythmic power and polyphonic mastery; his musical idiom is greatly advanced without overstepping the bounds of tonality. **WORKS: DRAMATIC: OPERA:** *The Stolen Sun* (1968). **BALLETS:** *The 12,* after the poem of Alexander Blok (Leningrad, Dec. 31, 1964); *Yaroslavna* (1974). **CANTATA:** *Lenin Lives* (1959). **ORCH.:** 6 syms. (1960, 1964, 1966, 1970, 1974, 1988); 2 violin concertos (1958, 1981); 2 cello concertos (1963, 1969); Piano Concerto (1962); Flute Concerto (1972); Harp Concerto (1977); *Concerto allamarcia* for 16 Performers (1989). **CHAMBER:** 5 string quartets (1957, 1959, 1969, 1980, 1984); 2 sonatas for Solo Violin (1957, 1976); 2 sonatas for Solo Cello (1960, 1979); *Capriccio* for Violin and Piano (1965); 8 piano sonatas (1957–87). **VOCAL:** *Sad Songs* for Soprano and Piano (1962); *Suzdal,* to folk texts from the Suzdal region, for Soprano, Tenor, and Chamber Orch. (1964); *Hard Frost,* aria for Mezzo-soprano and Orch. (1975).

Tisné, Antoine, French composer; b. Lourdes, Nov. 29, 1932. He studied with Darius Milhaud and Jean Rivier at the Paris Cons., obtaining the Premier Second Grand Prix de Rome in 1962. His works utilize various modern techniques. **WORKS: ORCH.:** 2 syms. (1960, 1963); 3 piano concertos (1958, 1961, 1963); *Cosmogonies* for 3 Orchs. (Paris, Dec. 10, 1968); *A une ombre* for Piano and Orch. (1972); *Impacts* for Ondes Martenot and 2 String Orchs. (1973); *Dolmen* (1978).

CHAMBER: Wind Quintet (1961); *Visions des temps immémoriaux* for Ondes Martenot, Piano, and Percussion (1964); Piano Trio (1968); *Les muses inquiétantes* for Wind Septet and Percussion (1975); *Isomorphoies* for String Sextet (1975); *Dolmen* for 7 Wind Instruments and Piano (1976); *3 études* for String Quartet (1978); keyboard pieces. Also vocal works, including *Célébration* for 3 Choruses and 3 Orchs. (1975).

Titelouze, Jean or **Jehan,** eminent French organist and composer; b. St. Omer, c.1562; d. Rouen, Oct. 24, 1633. He is believed to have received his academic and musical training in St. Omer, where he was a priest and substitute organist at the Cathedral by 1585; that same year he settled in Rouen as organist at St. Jean; served as organist at Rouen Cathedral from 1588 until his death; also was made canon by the cathedral chapter there in 1610. He was the pioneering figure of the French organ school; publ. 2 major collections, *Hymnes de l'Église pour toucher sur l'orgue, avec les fugues et recherches sur leur plain-chant* (Paris, 1623) and *Le Magnificat, ou Cantique de la Vierge pour toucher sur l'orgue, suivant les huit tons de l'Église* (Paris, 1626), versets based on plainsong. His vocal music is lost. He was also a poet and won awards from the Académie des Palinods (1613, 1630); won the title of Prince des Palinods in 1630. For his extant music, see A. Guilmant and A. Pirro, *J. Titelouze: Œuvres complètes d'orgue,* Archives des Maîtres de l'Orgue, vol. I (Paris, 1898), and N. Dufourcq, ed., *J. Titelouze: Œuvres complètes d'orgue* (Paris, 1965–67). **BIBL.:** A. Pirro, *Les Organistes français du XVIIe siècle: Jean T.* (Paris, 1898); N. Dufourcq, *La Musique d'orgue française de Jehan T. à Jehan Alain* (Paris, 1941; 2nd ed., 1949); M. Vanmackelberg, "Autour de Jehan T.," *Recherches sur la musique française classique,* IV (1964); idem, "Jehan T., prix littéraire," ibid.; E. Higginbottom, "Jehan T., c.1563–1633," *Musical Times* (Sept. 1983).

Titl, Anton Emil, Bohemian conductor and composer; b. Pernstein, Oct. 2, 1809; d. Vienna, Jan. 21, 1882. He took counterpoint lessons with Gottfried Rieger in Brünn; in 1840 he went to Vienna as conductor of the Theater in der Josefstadt; from 1850 to 1870, was conductor at the Burgtheater there. He wrote 2 operas: *Die Burgfrau* (Brünn, 1832) and *Das Wolkenkind* (Vienna, March 14, 1845); many singspiels, including the successful *Zauberschleier* (Vienna, 1842); incidental music; orch. pieces, including the popular *Serenade* for Violin and Orch.; sacred choral music; songs.

Titov, Alexei Nikolaievich, Russian violinist and composer, brother of **Sergei Nikolaievich** and father of **Nikolai Alexeievich Titov**; b. St. Petersburg, June 24, 1769; d. there, Nov. 20, 1827. He served in the cavalry, reaching the rank of major general at his retirement; was an amateur violinist, and wrote operas in the traditional Italian style; of these, the following were produced in St. Petersburg: *Andromeda and Perseus* (1802); *The Judgment of Solomon* (1803); *Nurzadakh* (June 7, 1807); *The Wedding of Filatka* (April 25, 1808); *Errant Moment* (July 10, 1812); *Emmerich Tekkely* (Dec. 13, 1812); *Intrigue in the Basket* (May 12, 1817); *Valor of the People of Kiev, or These Are the Russians* (May 12, 1817); *The Feast of the Mogul* (Sept. 15, 1823); also *The Brewer, or The Hidden Ghost of Evil* (Moscow, 1788); a ballet-pantomime, *Le Nouveau Werther,* was 1st given in St. Petersburg, on Jan. 30, 1799.

Titov, Nikolai Alexeievich, Russian composer, son of **Alexei Nikolaievich Titov**; b. St. Petersburg, May 10, 1800; d. there, Dec. 22, 1875. He received a military upbringing; like his father, he reached the rank of major general before retiring in 1867. He had no formal musical education; took some singing lessons, and studied a manual of thoroughbass; he was a typical dilettante, but possessed a gift of melodic invention; he knew Glinka and Dargomyzhsky, who helped him to develop his ability. He wrote about 60 songs, which were extremely popular in his time; his early song *Sosna* (The Pine) was erroneously believed to be the 1st Russian art song, but it had precursors; other of his songs that were popular include *Sharf goluboy* (The Blue Scarf; 1830) and *Kovarniy drug* (Treacherous Friend; 1831). He wrote a curious *Quadrille* for Piano, 3-hands, the treble part to be played by a beginner; another interesting project was a "musical romance in 12 waltzes" (under the general title *When I Was Young*), which remained incomplete.

Titov, Sergei Nikolaievich, Russian violinist, cellist, and composer, brother of **Alexei Nikolaievich Titov;** b. St. Petersburg, 1770; d. 1825. He rose to major general in the army. His best known works were the opera *Krestyane, ili Vstrecha nezvanikh* (The Peasants, or the Party for the Uninvited; 1814) and the ballet *Noviy Verter* (The New Werther). His son, Nikolai Sergeievich Titov (b. probably in St. Petersburg, 1798; d. 1843), also pursued a military career; also was a fine composer of songs; his most popular song was *Talisman* (1829).

Titta, Ruffo Cafiero. See **Ruffo, Titta.**

Titus, Alan (Wilkowski), American baritone; b. N.Y., Oct. 28, 1945. He studied at the Juilliard School of Music in N.Y.; made his debut in Washington, D.C., in *La Bohème* in 1969; then sang with the N.Y. City Opera; subsequently appeared in Amsterdam, Aix-en-Provence, Strasbourg, and other European cities. He made his debut with the Metropolitan Opera as Harlekin in *Ariadne auf Naxos* in N.Y. on March 20, 1976; also sang in San Francisco and Chicago.

Titus, Hiram, American pianist and composer; b. Minneapolis, Jan. 28, 1947. He studied piano with Guy Duckworth and composition with Dominick Argento (1957–63); had lessons with Walter Hartley at Interlochen (1963, 1964); also attended Oberlin College (B.A., 1958), where he studied piano with Emil Dananberg and composition with Richard Hoffman. In addition to concert and stage works, he composed a number of scores for television and theater productions, winning DramaLogue awards for music (1979, 1980). Among his compositions are *Bach Abashed* for Chamber Ensemble (1968), the opera *Rosina* (Minneapolis, 1980), Concerto for Guitar and Orch. (1984), and *The Sand Hills*, oratorio for Soloists, Men's Chorus, Tape, and Ensemble (Los Angeles, 1987).

Tizol, Juan, Puerto-Rican jazz trombonist; b. San Juan, Jan. 22, 1900; d. Inglewood, Calif., April 23, 1984. He studied trombone with his uncle, Manual Tizol, a member of the Municipal Band in San Juan; he used a valve trombone, which was generally adopted in Puerto Rico. He went to the U.S. in 1920 and joined Duke Ellington's orch. in 1929, remaining with it until 1944, when he became a member of the orch. led by Harry James, alternating with repeat engagements with Duke Ellington; he also appeared on television with Frank Sinatra and Nat King Cole. He was instrumental in introducing the Cuban type of jazz, of which his song *Caravan* became a popular specimen.

Tobani, Theodore Moses, German-American composer and arranger; b. Hamburg, May 2, 1855; d. N.Y., Dec. 12, 1933. He studied in Germany; his family emigrated to the U.S. c.1870, where Tobani earned his living as a youth playing violin at theaters and drinking emporia; then became associated with the music publ. firm of Carl Fischer in N.Y.; he is said to have composed or arranged over 5,000 pieces for piano or organ that enjoyed gratifying commercial success; the best known of these works, and one epitomizing the sentimental popular tastes of the time, was *Hearts and Flowers* (op.245), which he claimed to have tossed off in an hour in the late summer of 1893. Since he publ. so much music, he used a number of pseudonyms, among which Florence Reed and Andrew Herman were his favorites.

Tobias, Rudolf, Estonian organist and composer; b. Käina, May 29, 1873; d. Berlin, Oct. 29, 1918. He studied organ with L. Homilius and composition with Rimsky-Korsakov at the St. Petersburg Cons., graduating in 1897. He was an organist in St. Petersburg (1898–1904) and Tartu (1905–8); in 1910, settled in Berlin. In several of his compositions, he made use of national Estonian subjects.

Works: Oratorio, *Des Jonah Sendung* (1909); *Black Raven,*

Harbinger of War for Voices and Orch. (1909); *The Virgin of Light,* after an Estonian epic, for Soprano and Orch. (1911); 2 melodramas for Narrator and Orch.: *Kalevipoeg's Dream* (1906) and *Kalevipoeg at the Gate of the Kingdom of Death* (1912); choruses; chamber music; songs.

Bibl.: *R. T.* (Tallinn, 1973).

Tocchi, Gian-Luca, Italian composer; b. Perugia, Jan. 10, 1901. He studied in Rome with Respighi; his early works were written in a Romantic and impressionist manner: a symphonic poem, *Il Destino,* after Maeterlinck; *Rapsodia romantica* (1929); *3 canzoni alla maniera popolare italiana* (1931); he then changed to contemporary subjects, exemplified by such works as *Record* (1933), *Film* (1936), and a Concerto for Jazz Band.

Tocco, James, American pianist and teacher; b. Detroit, Sept. 21, 1943. He studied to study at the summer academy of the Salzburg Mozarteum; also studied in Paris. In 1973 he won 1st prize in the Munich Competition; subsequently made extensive tours of Europe, Russia, South America, and the Middle East. In 1977 he joined the faculty of the Indiana Univ. School of Music.

Toch, Ernst, eminent Austrian-born American composer and teacher; b. Vienna, Dec. 7, 1887; d. Los Angeles, Oct. 1, 1964. His father was a Jewish dealer in unprocessed leather, and there was no musical strain in the family; Toch began playing piano without a teacher in his grandmother's pawnshop; he learned musical notation from a local violinist, and then copied Mozart's string quartets for practice; using them as a model, he began to compose string quartets and other pieces of chamber music; at the age of 17 he had one of them, his 6th String Quartet, op. 12 (1905), performed by the famous Rose Quartet in Vienna. From 1906 to 1909 he studied medicine at the Univ. of Vienna. In 1909 he won the prestigious Mozart Prize and a scholarship to study at the Frankfurt Cons., where he studied piano with Willy Rehberg and composition with Iwan Knorr. In 1910 he was awarded the Mendelssohn Prize; also won 4 times in succession the Austrian State Prize. In 1913 he was appointed instructor in piano at Zuschneid's Hochschule für Musik in Mannheim. From 1914 to 1918 he served in the Austrian army. After the Armistice he returned to Mannheim, resumed his musical career, and became active in the modern movement, soon attaining, along with Hindemith, Krenek, and others, a prominent position in the new German school of composition. He also completed his education at the Univ. of Heidelberg (Ph.D., 1921, with the diss. *Beiträge zur Stilkunde der Melodie;* publ. in Berlin, 1923, as *Melodielehre*). In 1929 he went to Berlin, where he established himself as a pianist, composer, and teacher of composition. In 1932 he made an American tour as a pianist playing his own works; he returned to Berlin, but with the advent of the Nazi regime was forced to leave Germany in 1933. He went to Paris, then to London, and in 1935 emigrated to the U.S.; gave lectures on music at The New School for Social Research in N.Y.; in 1936, moved to Hollywood, where he wrote music for films. He became an American citizen on July 26, 1940; in 1940–41, he taught composition at the Univ. of Southern Calif., Los Angeles; subsequently taught privately; among his students were many, who, like André Previn, became well-known composers in their own right. From 1950 until his death, Toch traveled frequently and lived in Vienna, Zürich, the MacDowell Colony in New Hampshire, and Santa Monica, Calif.

Toch's music is rooted in the tradition of the German and Austrian Romantic movement of the 19th century, but his study of the classics made him aware of the paramount importance of formal logic in the development of thematic ideas. His early works consist mostly of chamber music and pieces for piano solo; following the zeitgeist during his German period, he wrote several pieces for the stage in the light manner of sophisticated entertainment; he also composed effective piano works of a virtuoso quality, which enjoyed considerable popularity among pianists of the time. Toch possessed a fine wit and a sense of exploration; his *Geographical Fugue* for speaking chorus, articulating in syllabic counterpoint the names of exotic places on earth, became a classic of its genre.

It was not until 1950 that Toch wrote his 1st full-fledged sym., but from that time on, until he died of stomach cancer, he composed fully 7 syms., plus sinfoniettas for Wind and String Orch. He was greatly interested in new techniques; the theme of his last String Quartet (No. 13, 1953) is based on a 12-tone row. In the score of his 3rd Sym. he introduced an optional instrument, the Hisser, a tank of carbon dioxide that produced a hissing sound through a valve.

Among the several honors Toch received were the Pulitzer Prize for his 3rd Sym. (1956), membership in the National Inst. of Arts and Letters (1957), and the Cross of Honor for Sciences and Art from the Austrian government (1963). An Ernst Toch Archive was founded at the Univ. of Calif., Los Angeles, in 1966, serving as a depository for his MSS.

WORKS: STAGE: OPERAS: *Wegwende* (1925; unfinished; sketches destroyed); *Die Prinzessin auf der Erbse* (Baden-Baden, July 17, 1927); *Der Fächer* (Königsberg, June 8, 1930); *The Last Tale* (1960–62).

ORCH.: *Scherzo* (1904); Piano Concerto (1904; not extant); *Phantastische Nachtmusik* (1920; Mannheim, March 22, 1921); *Tanz-Suite* for Chamber Orch. (1923); *5 Pieces* for Chamber Orch. (1924); Concerto for Cello and Small Orch. (1924; Kiel, June 17, 1925); Piano Concerto (Düsseldorf, Oct. 8, 1926; Gieseking, soloist); *Spiel für Blasorchester* (Donaueschingen, July 24, 1926); *Narziss* (1927; not extant); *Gewitter* (1927; not extant); *Komödie für Orchester* (Berlin, Nov. 13, 1927); *Vorspiel zu einem Märchen* (for *Die Prinzessin auf der Erbse;* 1927); *Fanal* for Organ and Orch. (1928); *Bunte Suite* (1928; Frankfurt, Feb. 22, 1929); *Kleine Theater-Suite* (1930; Berlin, Feb. 9, 1931); *Tragische Musik* (1931; not extant); 2 kultische Stücke (1931; not extant); Sym. for Piano and Orch. (Piano Concerto No. 2, 1932; London, Aug. 20, 1934); *Miniature Overture* for Winds (1932); *Variations on Mozart's Unser dummer Pöbel meint* (1933); *Big Ben*, variation fantasy on the Westminster Chimes (Cambridge, Mass., Dec. 20, 1934; rev. 1955); *Pinocchio*, "a merry overture" (1935; Los Angeles, Dec. 10, 1936); *Musical Short Story* (1936; not extant); *Orchids* (1936; not extant); *The Idle Stroller*, suite (1938); "The Covenant," 6th movement of 7-movement, collaborative *Genesis Suite* (Los Angeles, Nov. 18, 1945; not extant); *Hyperion*, dramatic prelude after Keats (1947; Cleveland, Jan. 8, 1948); 7 syms.: No. 1 (1949–50; Vienna, Dec. 20, 1950); No. 2, dedicated to Albert Schweitzer (1950–51; Vienna, Jan. 11, 1952); No. 3 (Pittsburgh, Dec. 2, 1955; won Pulitzer Prize in music, 1956); No. 4 (Minneapolis, Nov. 22, 1957); No. 5, *Jephta, Rhapsodic Poem* (1961–62; Boston, March 13, 1964); No. 6 (1963; Zürich Radio, Jan. 22, 1967); No. 7 (1964; Bavarian Radio, 1967); *Circus Overture* (1953; Ravinia Festival, July 8, 1954); *Notturno* (1953; Louisville, Jan. 2, 1954); *Peter Pan*, fairy tale (Seattle, Feb. 13, 1956); *Epilogue* (1959); *Intermezzo* (1959); *Short Story* (1961); *Capriccio* (1963); *Puppetshow* (1963); *The Enamoured Harlequin* (1963); Sinfonietta for String Orch. (1964; Philadelphia, Feb. 13, 1967); Theme with Variations "Muss i denn zum Städle hinaus" (1964).

CHAMBER: 13 string quartets: Nos. 1–5 (1902–3; not extant); No. 6 (1905); No. 7 (1908); No. 8 (1910); No. 9 (1919); No. 10, on the name "Bass" (1921); No. 11 (1924); No. 12 (1946); No. 13 (1953); *Kammersymphonie* (1906); Duos for Violins (1909; for open strings only in the pupil's part); Serenade for 3 Violins (1911); Violin Sonata (1913); *"Spitzweg" Serenade* for 2 Violins and Viola (1916): *Tanz Suite* for Flute, Clarinet, Violin, Viola, Bass, and Percussion (1923; excerpts choreographed as *Der Wald*, Mannheim, Nov. 19, 1923; Münster, Oct. 29, 1924); 2 *Divertimenti* for String Duos (1926); *Studie* for Mechanical Organ (1927); Violin Sonata (1928); Cello Sonata (1929); 2 *Études* for Cello (1930); String Trio (1936); Piano Quintet (1938); *Dedication* for String Quartet or String Orch. (1948); *Adagio elegiaco* for Clarinet and Piano (1950); *5 Pieces* for Flute, Oboe, Clarinet, Bassoon, 2 Horns, and Percussion (1959); *Sonatinetta* for Flute, Clarinet, and Bassoon (1959); *3 Impromptus* for Solo Violin, Solo Viola, and Solo Cello (1963); Quartet for Oboe, Clarinet, Bassoon, and Viola (1964).

PIANO: *Melodische Skizzen* (1903); *3 Preludes* (1903); *Impromptu* (1904; not extant); *Capriccio* (1905; not extant); Sonata in C-sharp minor (1905; not extant); Sonata in D major (1905; not extant); *Stammbuchverse* (1905); *Begegnung* (1908); *Reminiszenzen* (1909); *4 Klavierstücke* (1914; not extant); *Canon* (1914); *3 Burlesken* (1923; includes the popular *Der Jongleur*, publ. separately); *3 Klavierstücke* (1924); *5 Capriccetti* (1925); *3 Originalstücke für das Welte-Mignon Klavier* (1926); *Tanz- und Spielstücke* (1926?); Sonata (1928); *Kleinstadtbilder* (1929); *Fünfmal Zehn Etüden*, 50 études (1931); *Profiles* (1946); *Ideas* (1946); *Diversions* (1956); *Sonatinetta* (1956); *3 Little Dances* (1961); *Reflections*, 5 pieces (1961); Sonata for Piano, 4-hands (1962).

VOCAL: *An mein Vaterland*, sym. for Soprano, Mixed and Boys' Choruses, Orch., and Organ (1913); *Die chinesische Flöte*, chamber sym. for Soprano and 14 Solo Instruments (1921; Frankfurt, June 24, 1923; rev. 1949); 9 songs for Soprano and Piano (1926); *Der Tierkreis* for Chorus (1930); *Das Wasser*, cantata for Tenor, Baritone, Narrator, Flute, Trumpet, Percussion, and Strings (Berlin, June 18, 1930); *Gesprochene Musik* for Speaking Chorus (Berlin, June 17, 1930; includes the famous *Fuge aus der Geographie*, publ. separately in Eng. and Ger. eds.); *Music for Orchestra and Baritone Solo on Poems by Rilke* (1931); *Cantata of the Bitter Herbs* for Soloists, Narrator, and Chorus (1938); *Poems to Martha* for Voice and String Quintet (1942); *The Inner Circle*, 6 a cappella choruses (1947–53); *There Is a Season for Everything* for Soprano, Flute, Clarinet, Violin, and Cello, to words from Ecclesiastes (1953); *Vanity of Vanities, All Is Vanity* for Soprano, Tenor, Flute, Clarinet, Violin, and Cello, to words from Ecclesiastes (1954); *Phantoms* for Solo Voices and Chorus (1958); *Lange schon haben meine Freunde versucht* for Soprano and Baritone (1958); *Song of Myself* for Chorus, after Whitman (1961); *Valse* for Speaking Chorus (1961; in separate Eng. and German eds.); folk-song arrangements.

FILM SCORES: *Peter Ibbetson* (1935); *Outcast* (1937); *The Cat and the Canary* (1939); *Dr. Cyclops* (1940); *The Ghost Breakers* (1940); *Ladies in Retirement* (1941); *First Comes Courage* (1943); *None Shall Escape* (1944); *Address Unknown* (1944); *The Unseen* (1945). He also wrote incidental music for stage and radio plays.

WRITINGS: *The Shaping Forces in Music* (N.Y., 1948; new ed. by L. Weschler, 1977); M. Hood, ed., *Placed as a Link in this Chain: A Medley of Observations by Ernst Toch* (Los Angeles, 1971).

BIBL.: E. Beninger, "Pianistische Probleme, im Anschluss an die Klavierwerke von E. T.," *Melos* (1928); P. Pisk, "E. T.," *Musical Quarterly* (Oct. 1938); C. Johnson, *The Unpublished Works of E. T.* (diss., Univ. of California, Los Angeles, 1973); L. Weschler, *E. T., 1887–1964: A Biographical Essay Ten Years after His Passing* (Los Angeles, 1974); B. Barclay and M. Cole, "The T. and Zeisl Archives at UCLA," *Notes*, XXXV (1978–79); J. Diane, *The Musical Migration and E. T.* (Ames, Iowa, 1989).

Toczyska, Stefania, Polish mezzo-soprano; b. Gdansk, Feb. 19, 1943. She was a pupil of Barbara Iglikovska at the Gdansk Cons.; won prizes at competitions in Toulouse (1972) and Paris (1973). In 1973 she made her operatic debut as Carmen at the Gdansk Opera, and then sang throughout Poland. In 1977 she made her Western European debut at the Basel Opera singing the role of Amneris; later that year she appeared at the Vienna State Opera as Ulrica. She also sang at the Bavarian State Opera in Munich, the Hamburg State Opera, and the San Francisco Opera. In 1983 she appeared at London's Covent Garden and in 1986 at the Chicago Lyric Opera.

Toda, Kunio (actually, **Morikuni**), Japanese composer and teacher; b. Tokyo, Aug. 11, 1915. He studied at the Univ. of Heidelberg (1938–39); following diplomatic service in Moscow (1939–41), he returned to Tokyo to study with Saburo Moroi. He was sent to Indochina in 1944; when World War II ended in 1945, he was detained until 1948. Upon his return to Tokyo, he became active in contemporary-music circles; introduced 12-note serialism to his homeland. He remained active as a diplomat until 1964; taught at the Toho Gakuen School of Music (from 1955), remaining on its faculty as a prof. when it became a college in 1961; also was director and a prof. at the Senzolku Gakuen Academy of Music (from 1975); he retired in 1988.

WORKS: STAGE: OPERAS: *Akemi* (Tokyo, 1956); *Kyara monogatari* (History of the City of Kyara; Tokyo, 1973). **BALLETS:** *Atorie no Salome* (Salome in Studio; Tokyo, Nov. 23, 1951); *Akai tenmaku* or *Le Cirque rouge* (Tokyo, Nov. 4, 1953); *Dōkutsu* (The Cave; Tokyo, Nov. 7, 1954); *Miranda* (Tokyo, Oct. 26, 1968). **SCENIC ORATORIO-MYSTERY:** *Shito Paolo* (St. Paul; 1961–64; concert perf., Tokyo, Feb. 15, 1973). **ORCH.:** *Overture* (1943); *Densetsu* (Legend), symphonic fantasy (1944); 2 piano concertos (1944, 1955); *Passacaglia and Fugue* (1949); *Overtura buffa* (1950); Sym. in G (1956); *Concerto grosso* for 6 Solo Instruments and Orch. (Tokyo, Jan. 25, 1968). **CHAMBER:** Piano Trio (1947); *Amoroso* for Violin and Piano (1951); Violin Sonata (1957; rev. 1959); Music for 2 Koto (1959); Bassoon Sonata (1966). **PIANO:** *3 intermezzi* (1942); *Koto no ne ni yoru gensōkyoku* (Fantasy on the Sound of the Koto; 1965); Sonatina (1966); *Yottsu no yuganda kyoku* or *4 pezzi deformati* (1968). **VOCAL:** *Jochû no Anna* (Anna la Bonne), monodrama for Soprano, 2 Violas, and Tape (Tokyo, Nov. 17, 1978); *Kesa to Moritô* (Kesa and Morito), dramatic cantata for Soprano, Baritone, and String Quintet (Tokyo, Nov. 16, 1979); *Toraware no O'Shichi* (O'Shichi, the Prisoner), mono-cantata for Soprano, Flute, and Marimba (Tokyo, Sept. 16, 1981); *Ô-kawa no Uta* (Song of River) for Mezzo-soprano, Baritone, and Orch. (Tokyo, March 6, 1989); choruses; songs.

Todi, Luisa (actually, **Luiza Rosa,** née **d'Aguiar**), famous Portuguese mezzo-soprano; b. Setubal, Jan. 9, 1753; d. Lisbon, Oct. 1, 1833. She made her debut as a comic actress at age 14 in Lisbon; married the violinist Francesco Saverio Todi, concertmaster of the theater orch., when she was 16. She studied with David Perez; made her opera debut in 1770 in Scolari's *Il Viaggiatore ridicolo* in Lisbon; during the 1777–78 season, she sang comic opera at the King's Theatre in London, then established herself as a serious artist with her debut at the Paris Concert Spirituel (Nov. 1, 1778). After appearances in Germany, Austria, and Italy, she returned to Paris in 1783 and became a rival of Gertrud Elisabeth Mara at the Concert Spirituel; 2 hostile factions squared off, the Todistes and the Maratistes. After singing at Berlin's Royal Opera, she went to St. Petersburg in 1784; won great acclaim for her appearances in Sarti's *Armida e Rinaldo* (Jan. 1786) and *Castore e Polluce* (Sept. 22, 1786); after singing in Moscow in *Pollinia* (April 23, 1787), she returned to Berlin (1788–89); also sang in Mainz, Hannover, and Venice (1790–91). After further engagements in Italy and in Prague (1791), she appeared at the Madrid Opera (1792–93; 1794–95); then sang at the Teatro San Carlo in Naples (1797–99). In 1803 she retired to Lisbon, where she spent her final years in total blindness.

BIBL.: J. Ribeiro Guimarães, *Biographia de Luiza de Aguiar T.* (Lisbon, 1872); J. de Vasconcellos, *Luiza T.: Estudo critico* (Oporto, 1873; 2nd ed., 1929); M. de Sampayo Ribeiro, *Luisa de Aguiar T.* (Lisbon, 1934).

Toduţă, Sigismund, Rumanian composer; b. Simeria, May 30, 1908. He studied with Negrea at the Cons. in Cluj (1931–33), and later at the Accademia di Santa Cecilia in Rome (1936–38) with Pizzetti (composition) and Casella (piano); also took courses in musicology at the Pontificio Istituto di Musica Sacra in Rome (Ph.D., 1938, with a diss. on G.F. Anerio). In 1946 he was appointed to the faculty of the Cluj Cons. (he was its director from 1962 to 1964); in 1971 he became managing director of the Cluj State Phil. His music is distinguished by a flowing Romantic melody in large rhapsodic sonorities.

WORKS: OPERA: *Meşterul Manole* (Master-builder Manole; 1943–47; as an opera-oratorio, 1977–82; Cluj, Oct. 1, 1985).

ORCH.: *Eglogă* (1933); *Symphonic Variations* (1940); Piano Concerto (1943); 4 concertos for String Orch. (1951; 1972–73; 1974; 1980); *Divertisement* for String Orch. (1951); 5 syms.: No. 1 (1954); No. 2, "in memoria lui George Enesco" (1954–56); No. 3, *Ovidiu* (1957); No. 4 (1961); No. 5 (1963–76; Cluj, Feb. 7, 1976); *Uvertură festivă* (1959); *Simfonietă* (1966; Cluj, Jan. 21, 1977); Concerto for Winds and Percussion (1975–76; Cluj, Sept. 4, 1976); Concerto for Flute and String Orch. (Sibui, April 3, 1984); *Simfonia B—A—C—H* (1984); Concerto for Oboe and String Orch. (1986). **VOCAL: ORATORIOS:** *Miorița* (1958–68; Bucharest, Oct. 7, 1968); *Balada steagului* (1961); *Pe urmele lui Horea* (1976–78; Cluj, Dec. 2, 1978); choruses; songs. **CHAMBER:** Cello Sonata (1952); Flute Sonata (1952); Violin Sonata (1953); Oboe Sonata (1956); *Ioko,* 4 pieces for Harp (1975); *6 Pieces* for Oboe (1981); piano pieces, including *Passacaglia* (1943), Sonatina (1950), *Preludiu, Coral, Toccata* (1973–75), and *3 Pieces* (1980).

Toebosch, Louis, Dutch organist, conductor, teacher, and composer; b. Maastricht, March 18, 1916. He studied at the School of Church Music in Utrecht, the Music Lyceum in Maastricht, and then the Royal Cons. in Liège (1934–39); was active as a church organist in Breda (1940–65); conducted the Tilburg Sym. Orch. (1946–52); was founder-conductor of the Orlando di Lasso Choir (from 1953). He taught at the conservatories of Tilburg and Maastricht (1944–65); was director of the Brabant Cons. (1965–74). His music combines the polyphonic style of the Renaissance with modern techniques; he applies the 12-tone method of compostion in both secular and sacred music.

WORKS: ORCH.: 2 suites (1939, 1948); *Allegro* for Organ and Orch. (1941); *Tema con variazioni* (1945); *Het Lied van Hertog Jan* (1949); *Carnavalsige Ouverture* (1955); *Concertante Ouverture* (1956); *Variaties* (1957); *Feestelijke Ouverture* (1960); Sinfonietta No. 2 (1961); *Agena* (1966); *Changements* for Organ and Orch. (1968); Organ Concerto (1983). **VOCAL:** *Cantatorium carnevale* for Tenor, Baritone, and Orch. (1957); *Philippica-moderata* for Solo Voices, Choir, and Orch. (1963); *De vier seizoenen,* cantata-oratorio for Choir and Orch. (1981); *Cantata alfabetica* for Choir and Organ (1982). **CHAMBER:** *Sarabande en allegro* for Wind Quintet (1959); *The King's Quartet* for String Quartet (1968); *Toccata, aria e finale* for Viola (1969); *Bilingua* for Recorder and Harpsichord (1977); *Muziek voor 3 barokinstrumenten* for Recorder, Viola da Gamba, and Harpsichord (1980). **PIANO:** Sonata (1947); *Suite polyphonica* for 2 Pianos (1962); *Pasticcio di Rofena* for Piano, 4-hands (1973); *Zes speelstukken* for 3 Pianos (1983). **ORGAN:** *Tryptique* (1939; rev. 1980); *Praeludium et Fuga super Te Deum laudamus* (1954); 2 postludia (1964); *Toccana* (1973); *Orgelspiegel* (1975); *3 Movements* (1986).

BIBL.: W. Paap, "L. T.," *Sonorum speculum,* No. 21 (1964).

Toeschi, family of prominent German musicians of Italian descent, originally named **Toesca:**
(1) Alessandro Toeschi, violinist and composer; b. probably in Rome, before 1700; d. Mannheim (buried), Oct. 15, 1758. He was descended from a family of the nobility. After touring in England and Germany, he served as court musician to the Landgrave Ernst Ludwig of Hesse in Darmstadt (1719–24); then was 2nd maître des concerts at the Württemberg court in Stuttgart (1725–37); subsequently settled in Mannheim as Konzertmeister about 1742, and was director of instrumental church music at the Palatine court there from about 1750. His extant works consist of a Concerto for 2 Violins, Strings, and Continuo, and a Sonata for Violin and Continuo. He had 2 sons who became musicians:
(2) Carl Joseph Toeschi, violinist and composer, the most outstanding member of the family; b. Ludwigsburg (baptized), Nov. 11, 1731; d. Munich, April 12, 1788. He studied with Johann Stamitz and Anton Filtz; in 1752 he became a violinist in the Mannheim Court Orch., and was made its Konzertmeister in 1759; in 1774 he was named music director of the electoral cabinet; followed the court to Munich in 1778. He was one of the leading composers of the Mannheim school.

Among his output were over 66 syms., some 30 ballets, and much chamber music.

(3) Johann (Baptist) (Maria) Christoph Toeschi, violinist and composer, known as **Toesca de Castellamonte;** b. Stuttgart (baptized), Oct. 1, 1735; d. Munich, March 3, 1800. He studied with Johann Stamitz and Christian Cannabich; in 1755 became a violinist in the Mannheim Court Orch., and was also director of the Court Ballet there (from 1758); was named Konzertmeister in 1774; in 1778 followed the court to Munich, where he was music director (from 1793); also was director of the court chapel in 1798; that same year his family was granted hereditary Italian nobility and the right to use the title "de Castellamonte." He wrote a melodrama, *Dirmel und Laura* (Munich, 1784), at least 4 ballets, and various instrumental works, but his only extant compositions are 6 trio sonatas (Paris, 1768), a Sonata for Viola d'Amore and Continuo (ed. by D. Newlin and K. Stumpf, Vienna, 1963), and 3 viola d'amore pieces. His son, **Karl Theodor Toeschi** (b. Mannheim, April 17, 1768; d. Munich, Oct. 10, 1843), was also a composer; was active at the Munich court (1780–89); was named Bavarian chamber composer in 1801. He wrote an opera, a ballet, syms., overtures, a Violin Concerto, and other works, most of which are lost.

BIBL.: R. Münster, *Die Sinfonien T.s* (diss., Univ. of Munich, 1956); W. Lebermann, "Biographische Notizen über Johann Anton Fils, Johann Anton Stamitz, C.J. und J.B. T.," *Die Musikforschung,* XIX (1966); idem, "Zur Genealogie der T.," ibid., XXII (1969).

Tofft, Alfred, Danish organist, music critic, and composer; b. Copenhagen, Jan. 2, 1865; d. there, Jan. 30, 1931. He studied with J. Nebelong (organ) and G. Bohlmann (theory); was music critic for the *Berlinske Tidende* in Copenhagen, and president of the Danish Composers' Society. He was a fine organist and a talented composer of songs (op.2, *Heine-Album;* op.4, *Jacobsen-Album;* etc.). Two operas were produced in Copenhagen: *Vifandaka* (Jan. 1, 1898) and *Anathema* (May 10, 1928).

Togi, Suenobu, Japanese performer and ethnomusicologist; b. Tokyo, Jan. 1, 1932. He attended the Imperial Court Music School in Tokyo (1943–52), where he learned Japanese court music and dance as well as Western music (cello and violin); also studied Western music at the Tokyo Fine Arts Univ. (1950–52). He taught and performed in the Imperial Court Music Dept. in both the Japanese Court Orch. (gagaku and bugaku) and the Imperial Court Orch. (Western music) from 1952 to 1961; then went to the U.S., where he taught Japanese court music and dance at the Univ. of Calif., Los Angeles (1961). He returned to Tokyo in 1964; in 1968, joined the faculty at the Univ. of Calif. at Los Angeles; also gave concerts and lectures throughout the U.S. Togi is the only former court musician teaching gagaku outside of Japan. He employs the strictest court tradition (which determines gagaku practice throughout Japan); revisited Tokyo in 1973 and 1985 to remain current with changes in Imperial practice.

Togni, Camillo, Italian composer; b. Gussago, Oct. 18, 1922. He studied with Alfredo Casella in Siena and Rome (1939–42); received his diploma from the Parma Cons. (1946); took courses in philosophy at the Univ. of Pavia (graduated, 1948); then devoted himself entirely to music. His early works follow the neo-Classical style of the Italian Baroque; later he adopted the 12-tone method of composition.

WORKS: *Variations* for Piano and Orch. (1946); *Psalmus CXXVII* for Solo Voices, Violin, Viola, and Cello (ISCM Festival, Brussels, June 24, 1950); *Ricercar* for Baritone and 5 Instruments, to a text from *La Nausée* by Sartre (1953); *Fantasia concertante* for Flute and String Orch. (Cologne, March 25, 1958); *Recitativo* for Electronic Sound (1961); *Gesang zur Nacht* for Contralto and Chamber Orch. (1962); *3 rondeaux per dieci* for Soprano and 9 Instruments (1964); *Aubade* for 6 Instruments (1965); *3 Pieces* for Chorus and Orch. (Venice, Sept. 17, 1972); *Für Herbert* for 2 Violins, Viola, and Harpsichord (1976); *Some Other Where* for Orch. (Naples, June 16, 1977); String Trio (1978); *3 Preludes* for Piccolo (1980).

Tokatyan, Armand, Bulgarian tenor of Armenian descent; b. Plovdiv, Feb. 12, 1896; d. Pasadena, Calif., June 12, 1960. He was educated in Alexandria, Egypt; then studied voice with Cairone in Milan and Wolf in Vienna. He made his operatic debut in Milan in 1921; then went to the U.S., where he toured with the Scotti Opera Co. He made his debut at the Metropolitan Opera in N.Y. on Nov. 19, 1922, as Turiddu in a concert performance of *Cavalleria rusticana,* and remained a member of the company, with interruptions, until 1946. He also made appearances in London, Berlin, and Vienna.

Tolbecque, family of Belgian-French musicians:
(1) Jean-Baptiste-Joseph Tolbecque, violinist, conductor, and composer; b. Hanzinne, Namur, April 17, 1797; d. Paris, Oct. 23, 1869. He studied violin with Kreutzer and counterpoint and fugue with Reicha at the Paris Cons.; was a violinist in the orch. of the Opéra Italien (1820–25), and then was conductor of the Tivoli gardens orch. in Paris; subsequently oversaw the court dances for Louis Philippe I; helped to organize the Société des Concerts du Conservatoire, where he was a violist. With Gilbert and Guiraud, he wrote the opéra-comique *Charles V et Duguesclin* (1827), and with Deldevez, the ballet *Vert-Vert* (Paris, 1851), but he became best known as a composer of waltzes, galops, quadrilles, polkas, and other popular dances. Three of his brothers were also musicians:
(2) Isidore-Joseph Tolbecque, conductor and composer; b. Hanzinne, April 17, 1794; d. Vichy, Allier, May 10, 1871. He pursued a career as a conductor and composer of dance music.
(3) August-Joseph Tolbecque, violinist; b. Hanzinne, Feb. 28, 1801; d. Paris, May 27, 1869. He was a pupil of Kreutzer at the Paris Cons., where he won the premier prix (1821); was a member of the Opéra orch. (1824–31); also played in the Société des Concerts du Conservatoire; subsequently performed at Her Majesty's Theatre in London.
(4) Charles-Joseph Tolbecque, violinist, conductor, and composer; b. Paris, May 27, 1806; d. there, Dec. 29, 1835. He studied with Kreutzer at the Paris Cons., taking the premier prix in violin (1823); after playing in the Société des Concerts du Conservatoire, he became conductor at the Théâtre des Variétées (1830). He wrote incidental music for theater productions and songs.
(5) Auguste Tolbecque, cellist, instrument maker, and composer, son of **Auguste-Joseph Tolbecque;** b. Paris, March 30, 1830; d. Niort, Deux Sèvres, March 8, 1919. He studied cello (premier prix, 1849) with Vaslin and harmony with Reber at the Paris Cons.; after playing in the orch. of the Grand Théâtre and teaching at the Cons. in Marseilles (1865–71), he returned to Paris and played with the Société des Concerts du Conservatoire, the Lamoureux Quartet, and the Maurin Quartet; received instruction in instrument making from Victor Rambaux and then settled in Niort, where he devoted himself to restoring early instruments and making copies of same. He ed. *Monde Musical* and publ. the exercise vol. *La Gymnastique du violoncelle* (Paris, 1875). His works include the opéra-comique *Après la valse* (Niort, 1894) and many cello works. His son, Jean Tolbecque (b. Niort, Oct. 7, 1857; d. probably in Paris, 1890), was also a cellist; was a pupil of Alexandre Chevillard at the Paris Cons. (premier prix, 1873); then was a member of the Opéra-Comique orch.

WRITINGS: *Quelques considérations sur la lutherie* (Paris, 1890); *Souvenirs d'un musicien en province* (Niort, 1896); *Notice historique sur les instruments à cordes et à archet* (Paris and Niort, 1898); *L'Art du luthier* (Niort, 1903).

Toldrá, Eduardo, Catalan violinist, conductor, and composer; b. Villanueva y Geltrú, Catalonia, April 7, 1895; d. Barcelona, May 31, 1962. He studied violin and composition at Barcelona's municipal music school; made his debut as a soloist at the Barcelona Ateneo (1912); was founder-1st violinist of the Quartet Renaixement (1912-21). In 1921 he became a prof. of violin at Barcelona's municipal music school; in 1944 was appointed conductor of the Municipal Orch. He composed the comic opera *El giravolt de Maig* (Barcelona, 1928), orch. pieces, chamber music, and songs.

BIBL.: M. Capdevila Massana, *E. T.* (Barcelona, 1964; 2nd ed., rev., 1972).

Tollefsen, Carl H(enry), English-American violinist and teacher; b. Hull, Aug. 15, 1882; d. N.Y., Dec. 10, 1963. He went to N.Y. as a youth, and studied at the National Cons. (1898–1902) and at the Inst. of Musical Art (1906–8), where his teachers were Franz Kneisel (violin), and Goetschius and Rubin Goldmark (composition); was a violinist in various orchs. in N.Y. On Aug. 7, 1907, he married the pianist **Augusta Schnabel** (b. Boise, Idaho, Jan. 5, 1885; d. N.Y., April 9, 1955), and formed the Tollefsen Trio with her and with Paul Kéfer in 1909; this trio toured the U.S. for more than 30 years (succeeding cellists were M. Penha, P. Gruppe, R. Thrane, and W. Durieux). In 1939 he founded the Brooklyn Chamber Music Society. He formed a large collection of autographs of famous musicians and MS biographies (including the biographical archives gathered by Alfred Rémy, editor of the 3rd ed. of *Baker's Biographical Dictionary of Musicians*). In 1947 the cellist Yuri Bilstin bequeathed to him a collection of old instruments. His entire collection was turned over to the Southern Illinois Univ. Lovejoy Library at Edwardsville in 1969.

Tolonen, Jouko (Paavo Kalervo), Finnish musicologist and composer; b. Porvoo, Nov. 2, 1912; d. Turku, July 23, 1986. He studied piano with Linko, composition with Krohn, Madetoja, and Fougestedt, and conducting in Helsinki; pursued training in musicology at the Univ. there (Ph.D., 1969). He was director of the music dept. of the Finnish Broadcasting Co. (1946–55) and general director of the Finnish National Opera (1956–60); taught at the Sibelius Academy in Helsinki (1960–66) and at the Univ. of Turku (from 1965), where he was prof. of musicology (1972–77). He composed *Andante and Rondo alla burla* for Orch. (1948); *Andante* for Piano and Strings (1950); Sym. (1952); *3 Arabesques* for Orch. (1953); *Les Fanfares* for Brass (1970); incidental music for plays and films; vocal pieces.

Tolstoy, Dmitri, Russian composer, son of the writer Alexei Tolstoy; b. Berlin, Jan. 20, 1923. He went to Russia with his father after the latter's temporary emigration; studied at the Leningrad Cons., graduating in 1947; took courses in composition with Shebalin in Moscow and Shostakovich in Leningrad. **WORKS:** *Poem on Leningrad* for Orch. (1953); *Spring Victory,* cantata (1946); *Masquerade,* opera (Moscow, Jan. 17, 1956); *Mariuta,* opera (Perm, Dec. 30, 1960); 3 piano sonatas; 12 preludes for Piano; many songs.

Tomaschek (Tomášek), Wenzel Johann (Václav Jan Křtitel), important Bohemian composer and pedagogue; b. Skutsch, April 17, 1774; d. Prague, April 3, 1850. He was the youngest of 13 children; learned the rudiments of singing and violin playing from P.J. Wolf and studied organ with Donat Schuberth. In 1787 he became an alto chorister at the Minorite monastery in Iglau; in 1790 he went to Prague, supporting himself by playing piano in public places; also took law courses at the Univ. of Prague. From 1806 to 1822 he was attached to the family of Count Georg Bucquoy de Longeval as music tutor. In 1824 he established his own music school in Prague. Among his many pupils were J.H. Woržischek (Voříšek), Dreyschock, Hanslick, and Schulhoff. Tomaschek was the 1st to use the instrumental form of the rhapsody systematically in a number of his piano pieces, although it was anticipated by W.R. Gallenberg in a single composition a few years earlier; he also adopted the ancient Greek terms "eclogue" and "dithyramb" for short character pieces. He wrote an autobiography, publ. in installments in the Prague journal *Libussa* (1845–50); a modern ed. was prepared by Z. Němec (Prague, 1941); excerpts appeared in the *Musical Quarterly* (April 1946). **WORKS: OPERAS:** *Seraphine, oder Grossmut und Liebe* (Prague, Dec. 15, 1811); *Alvaro* (unfinished). **CHORAL:** Requiem (1820); *Krönungsmesse* (1836); Te Deum. **ORCH.:** 3 syms. (1801, 1805, 1807); 2 piano concertos (1805, 1806). **CHAMBER:** 3 string quartets (1792–93); Piano Trio (1800); Piano Quartet (1805); also works for Solo Piano, including 7

sonatas (1800–6), 42 eclogues (1807–23), 15 rhapsodies (1810), 6 *allegri capricciosi* (1815, 1818), and 6 dithyrambs (1818–23).

BIBL.: M. Tarantová, *Václav Jan Tomášek* (Prague, 1946); P. Nettl, *Forgotten Musicians* (N.Y., 1951); M. Postler, *V.J. Tomášek: Bibliografie* (Prague, 1960); T. Straková, "V.J. Tomášek a jeho klavírní eklogy," *Časopis Moravského musea,* XLV (1960); A. Simpson and S. Horsfall, "A Czech Composer Views His Contemporaries," *Musical Times,* CXV (1974); T. Volek and S. Jareš, "Portréty V.J. Tomáška," *Hudebni veda,* XII (1975).

Tomášek, Jaroslav, Czech composer; b. Koryčany, Moravia, April 10, 1896; d. Prague, Nov. 26, 1970. He studied music with Vítězslav Novák; also attended a course in musicology at the Univ. of Prague. He composed mostly in small forms; wrote 2 song cycles: *To Woman* for High Voice (1919–20; with Orch., 1944–46) and *Grief* for Tenor, Soprano, Bass, and Orch. (1958–59); *Rondo* for Piano, left hand (1924); Piano Sonata for left hand (1925); 2 string quartets; *Symphonic Rondo* for Piano and Orch. (1962); songs. His wife, **Jaromíra Tomášková-Nováková** (b. Jaroměř, May 23, 1892; d. Prague, April 25, 1957), was a soprano; she taught singing at the Prague Cons. (from 1920).

Tomasi, Henri (Frédien), French composer; b. Marseilles, Aug. 17, 1901; d. Paris, Jan. 13, 1971. He studied with Paul Vidal at the Paris Cons.; won the 2nd Grand Prix de Rome for his cantata *Coriolan* (1927). He served in the French army (1939–40); was awarded the Grand Prix de Musique Française in 1952. His music is marked by impressionistic colors; he was particularly attracted to exotic subjects, depicting in fine instrumental colors scenes in Corsica, Cambodia, Laos, Sahara, Tahiti, etc. He also wrote music inspired by Gregorian chant and medieval religious songs. During his last period he was motivated in his music by political events, and wrote pieces in homage to the Third World and Vietnam.

WORKS: STAGE: OPERAS: *Miguel de Manâra* (1942; Munich, March 29, 1956); *L'Altantide* (1952; Mulhouse, Feb. 26, 1954); *La triomphe de Jeanne* (1955; Rouen, 1956); *Sampiero Corso* (Bordeaux, May 1956); *Il Poverello* (1957); *Le silence de la mer* (1959); *Ulysse* (1961); *L'élixir du révérend père Gaucher* (1962). **BALLETS:** *La Grisi* (Paris, Oct. 7, 1935); *La Rosière de village* (Paris, May 26, 1936); *Les Santons* (Paris, Nov. 18, 1938); *La Féerie cambodgienne* (Marseilles, Jan. 31, 1952); *Les Folies mazarguaises* (Marseilles, Oct. 5, 1953); *Noces de cendre* (Strasbourg, Jan. 19, 1954); choreographic poem, *Dassine, sultane du Hoggar,* for 2 Speakers, Chorus, and Orch. (1959); *Les Barbaresques* (Nice, 1960); *Nana,* after Émile Zola (1962). **ORCH.:** *Chants de Cyrnos,* symphonic poem (Paris, Nov. 30, 1929); *Mélodies corses* (1931); *Vocero,* symphonic poem (Paris, Feb. 5, 1933); *Scènes municipales* (1933); *Tam-Tam,* symphonic poem (Paris, June 13, 1933); *Chants laotiens* (1934); *2 danses cambodgiennes* (1934); *Chant des geishas* (1936); *Impressions sahariennes* (1938); Sym. (Paris, May 4, 1943); *Concert asiatique* for Percussion and Orch. (1939); Flute Concerto (1947); Trumpet Concerto (1949); Viola Concerto (1951); Saxophone Concerto (1951); Horn Concerto (1955); Clarinet Concerto (1956); Trombone Concerto (1956); Bassoon Concerto (1958); Oboe Concerto (1958); *Jabadao,* symphonic poem (Paris, Jan. 10, 1960); Violin Concerto (1962); *Taïtienne de Gauguin* (1963); *Symphonie du tiers monde* (Paris, Feb. 18, 1968); *Chant pour le Vietnam,* symphonic poem for Wind Band and Percussion (Paris, Dec. 7, 1969); Cello Concerto (1970). **CHAMBER:** *Concerto champêtre* for Oboe, Clarinet, and Bassoon (1939); String Trio (1943); *Divertimento Corsica* for Woodwind Trio (1952); Wind Quintet (1952); *Danseuses de Degas* for Harp and String Quartet (1964); *Concerto de printemps* for Flute, Strings, and Percussion (1965); *La Moresca* for 8 Wind Instruments (1965); *Sonatine attique* for Clarinet (1966); many piano pieces; song cycles.

Tomasini, Alois Luigi, Italian violinist and composer; b. Pesaro, June 22, 1741; d. Eisenstadt, April 25, 1808. In 1757 he became a manservant to Prince Paul Anton Esterházy, who sent him to Venice to complete his musical instruction in

1759; by 1761 he was back in the Esterházy service as 1st violinist in the Hofkapelle, where he became a friend of Haydn; later served as its Konzertmeister until his death (1790–94 excepted); also was director of the Esterházy chamber music (from 1802). He wrote at least 2 syms. (both lost), 3 violin concertos (1 lost), and much chamber music, of which the 3 String Quartets, op. 8 (Vienna, 1807?), are particularly noteworthy; in all, he composed 30 string quartets (6 lost), 24 divertimentos (Nos. 1–6 and 13–24 for Baryton, Violin, and Cello, and Nos. 7–12 for Baryton, Viola, and Cello), 9 duo concertants for 2 Violins, 6 sonatas for Violin and Bass, and other works. See E. Schenck, ed., *Luigi Tomasini: Ausgewählte Instrumentalwerke*, Denkmäler der Tonkunst in Österreich, CXXIV (1972). He had 2 sons who became musicians: **Anton (Edmund) Tomasini** (b. Eisenstadt, Feb. 17, 1775; d. there, June 12, 1824) was a violinist and violist; studied with his father; in 1796 joined the Esterházy Kapelle, where he was made deputy director (1805) and then director (1818) of the orch. **Alois (Basil Nikolaus) (Luigi) Tomasini** (b. Esteráz, July 10, 1779; d. Neustrelitz, Feb. 19, 1858) was a violinist and composer; received his music training from his father; about 1793 he entered the Esterházy Kapelle as a violinist, winning the high commendation of Haydn; after marrying the singer Sophie Croll (1785–1847) in 1808, he went with her to Neustrelitz, where he later served as Konzertmeister. He was succeeded by his son, Carlo Tomasini (1813–80). Their daughter, Friederike (1810–86), a singer, studied in Munich and then appeared at the Neustrelitz Court Theater.

Bibl.: E. Fruchtman, *The Baryton Trios of T., Burgksteiner, and Neumann* (diss., Univ. of North Carolina, 1960); G. Croll, "L. T. the Younger and 'Demoiselle Croll,'" *Haydn International Musicological Conference: Washington 1975*.

Tómasson, Jónas, Icelandic composer, teacher, and conductor; b. Ísafjördur, Nov. 21, 1946. He studied theory with Jón Thórarinsson and counterpoint and composition with Thorkell Sigurbjörnsson at the Reykjavík College of Music (graduated, 1967); received training in flute from Simon Hunt, David Evans, and Josef Magnusson; studied composition with Ton de Leeuw and Jos Kunst, orchestration with Leon Ortel, and flute with Pieter Ode in Amsterdam (1969–72); then took courses in musicology at the Univ. of Munich (1976). He was a conductor of the Ísafjördur Chamber Orch. (1973–76); in 1978 he became a teacher at the Ísafjördur School of Music, where he also conducted its choir and orch.

Works: orch.: 2 syms. (1969, 1973); *1,41* (1970); *Play, Play* (1971–72); *11 Meditations on the Settlement* (1974); Concerto for Violin and Small Orch. (1974–75); *Orgia* (1975); *Notturno IV* (1981–82); *Skerpla II* (1983); *Concerto trittico* (1985); *Midi* for 2 Pianos and Orch. (1985); also chamber works, including 17 pieces entitled Sonata for various instruments; piano pieces; vocal music.

Tombelle, Fernand de la. See **La Tombelle, Fernand de.**

Tomilin, Victor, Russian composer; b. Berdichev, May 15, 1908; d. in combat near Leningrad, Dec. 9, 1941. He was a pupil of Vladimir Shcherbachev at the Leningrad Cons., graduating in 1932. He wrote 2 symphonic suites, *Episodes of Civil War* (1936) and *Crimean Suite* (1939); a number of songs and piano pieces.

Tomkins, family of English musicians:
(1) Thomas Tomkins, organist and composer; b. St. Davids, Pembrokeshire, 1572; d. Martin Hussingtree, Worcester (buried), June 9, 1656. He was the son of Thomas Tomkins, vicar choral of the Cathedral of St. Davids and later master of the choristers and organist there. He was a pupil of William Byrd; in 1596 he became instructor choristarum at Worcester Cathedral; was made a member of the Chapel Royal, becoming a Gentleman in Ordinary by 1620; was one of its organists (from 1621), becoming senior organist about 1625; continued to be active at Worcester Cathedral until parliamentary forces took the city in 1646; was allowed to live in the cathedral precincts, where he remained until settling at his son Nathaniel's home

in Martin Hussingtree in 1654. Tomkins was the last representative of the followers of William Byrd. He wrote 29 madrigals, 28 of which were publ. in *Songs of 3. 4. 5. & 6. parts* (London, 1622; ed. by E. Fellowes in The English Madrigalists, 2nd ed., rev., 1960, by T. Dart); 1 other madrigal has been ed. in The English Madrigalists, 2nd ed., 1962. While his importance as a madrigalist remains in dispute among contemporary scholars, his sacred works are generally admired; these include 5 services, about 120 anthems, and other works, most of which were publ. in *Musica Deo sacra et ecclesiae anglicanae* (London, 1668; ed. by B. Rose in Early English Church Music, V, 1965, IX, 1968, and XIV, 1973). He was a fine composer of keyboard music, his consort music being of very high quality; see S. Tuttle, ed., *Thomas Tomkins: Keyboard Music*, Musica Britannica, V (1955; 2nd ed., 1964). His son, **Nathaniel Tomkins** (b. Worcester, 1599; d. Martin Hussingtree, Oct. 20, 1681), was a musician; was educated at Balliol College, Oxford (B.D., 1629); served as a canon at Worcester Cathedral (from 1629).

Bibl.: S. de B. Taylor, *T. T.* (London, 1933); R. Cavanaugh, *The Anthems in "Musica Deo Sacra" by T. T.* (diss., Univ. of Michigan, 1953); D. Stevens, *T. T.* (London, 1957; 2nd ed., 1967).

(2) John Tomkins, organist and composer, half-brother of **Thomas Tomkins;** b. St. Davids, 1586; d. London, Sept. 27, 1638. He was a scholar at King's College, Cambridge, where he became organist in 1606 and took the Mus.B. degree in 1608; settled in London in 1619 as organist at St. Paul's Cathedral; became a Gentleman Extraordinary (1625) and a Gentleman in Ordinary (1627) of the Chapel Royal. A few of his sacred works are extant. Two of his brothers were also musicians:

(3) Giles Tomkins, organist and composer; b. St. Davids, after 1587; d. Salisbury, before Nov. 30, 1688. He was named organist of King's College, Cambridge, in 1624 and of Salisbury Cathedral in 1629; in 1630 was made Musician for the Virginals in the King's Musick, a post he held until Cromwell's rise to power; was again in the royal service after the Restoration. Two of his verse anthems are extant.

(4) Robert Tomkins, instrumentalist and composer who flourished in the last half of the 17th century. He was active as a court musician from 1633. Only a handful of his anthems are extant.

Tomlinson, John (Rowland), English bass; b. Accrington, Sept. 22, 1946. He studied civil engineering at the Univ. of Manchester (B.Sc.) and received his musical training at the Royal Manchester College of Music. In 1970 he 1st attracted notice at the Glyndebourne Opera; in succeeding years he appeared with many opera companies at home and abroad, singing regularly at the English National Opera (from 1974) and at Covent Garden (from 1977) in London. His extensive operatic repertoire includes some 100 roles.

Tommasini, Vincenzo, Italian composer; b. Rome, Sept. 17, 1878; d. there, Dec. 23, 1950. He studied violin with Pinelli; theory with Falchi at the Liceo di Santa Cecilia in Rome; then went to Berlin, where he took lessons with Max Bruch; after sojourns in Paris, London, and N.Y., he returned to Rome. He wrote music in the poetic tradition of Italian Romanticism; his operas, symphonic works, and chamber music obtained immediate performances and favorable receptions; however, his most successful piece, *Le Donne di buon umore*, was not an original work but a comedy-ballet written on music from sonatas by Domenico Scarlatti, arranged in a series of tableaux and brilliantly orchestrated; this was a commission for the Ballets Russes of Diaghilev, who staged it at Rome in April 1917, and kept it in the repertoire during his tours all over the world. He publ. *La luce invisibile* (1929) and *Saggio d' estetica sperimentale* (1942).

Works: stage: operas: *Medea* (1902–4; Trieste, April 8, 1906); *Amore di terra lontana* (1907–8); *Uguale fortuna* (1911; Rome, 1913); *Dielja* (c.1935); *Il tenore sconfitto, ovvero La presunzione punita* (Rome, 1950). **ballets:** *Le donne di buon umore* (1916; Rome, April 1917; suite, 1920; based on sonatas

by D. Scarlatti); *Le diable s'amuse* (1936; N.Y., 1937); *Tiepolesco* (Naples, 1945). ORCH.: *La vita è un sogno* (1901); *Poema erotico* (1908–9); *Inno alla beltà* (1911); *Ciari di luna* (1914–15; Rome, 1916); *Il beato regno* (1919–20; Rome, 1922); *Paesaggi toscani* (1922; Rome, 1923); *Il carnevale di Venezia* (1928; N.Y., Oct. 10, 1929); *Nápule* (1929–30; Freiburg, Dec. 7, 1931); Concerto for Violin and Small Orch. (1932); *4 pezzi* (1931–34); Concerto for String Quartet and Orch. (1939); *La tempesta* (1941); *Duo concertante* for Piano and Orch. (1948). CHAMBER: 4 string quartets (1898; 1908–9; 1926; 1943); Violin Sonata (1916–17); 2 piano trios (1929, 1946); Harp Sonata (1938); also choral works, including *Messa da requiem* for Chorus and Organ (1944); songs; piano pieces.
BIBL.: M. Zanotti-Bianco, "V. T.," *The Chesterian,* new series, IV (1922–23); A. Casella, "V. T.," *Revue Musicale,* VIII/2 (1927); M. Rinaldi, "V. T.," *Rivista Musicale Italiana,* LIII (1951).

Tomotani, Kōji, Japanese composer; b. Hiroshima, Sept. 26, 1947. He studied at the Kunitachi Music College in 1974; then went to France, where he had lessons with M. Bitsch and Messiaen (1974–76) and also studied at the École Normale de Musique de Paris (degree, 1975). His *Cosmic Landscape* trilogy is rooted in the concept of "eternal return," the "wheel of time symbolizing an intimate link between boundless space (the cosmos) and boundless time (eternity); each of the three works variously contrasts the elements of 'sound-space,' represented by tone-clusters and time relationships, and 'spaces,' which punctuate the elements comprising the 'sound-space.'"
WORKS: Concerto for Biwa and Orch. (1977); *Gyō* for Fué and Biwa (1978); *Livre de Shura* for Percussion Ensemble (1980); *Kâla-Cakra I* for Flute and Piano (1981); *Torana* for Soprano, Oboe d'Amore, and Piano (1982); *Kâla-Cakra II* for Shakuhachi and Percussion (1983); *Cosmic Landscape* for Flute and Harpsichord (1985); *Cosmic Landscape* for Orch. (1987); *Spectrum* for Flute and Piano (1988); *Spectrum II* for Piano (1989); *Cosmic Landscape* for Clarinet (1990).

Tomowa-Sintow, Anna, Bulgarian soprano; b. Stara Zagora, Sept. 22, 1941. She studied at the Bulgarian State Cons. in Sofia; made her operatic debut as Tatiana in Stara Zagora in 1965. In 1967 she joined the Leipzig Opera; in 1971 she won the international singers' competition held in Rio de Janeiro. In 1973 Herbert von Karajan chose her for the world premiere of Carl Orff's *De temporum fine comedia,* which was given at the Salzburg Festival. In subsequent seasons she sang in Munich (1974), in San Francisco (1974), at Covent Garden in London (1975), and in Vienna (1977). On April 3, 1978, she sang Donna Anna in Mozart's *Don Giovanni* in her debut at the Metropolitan Opera in N.Y. In 1984 she appeared as Wagner's Elisabeth at the Paris Opéra.

Tone, Yasunao, Japanese multimedia artist and experimental composer; b. Tokyo, March 31, 1935. He graduated with a degree in literature from the Japanese National Univ. in Chiba (1957); then studied at the Tokyo Univ. of Arts, where he co-founded the group Ongaku, dedicated to "event music." In 1962 he joined the American modern movement FLUXUS, which presented his 1st works in a Tokyo program under the title "One Man Show by a Composer"; also joined other modernistic groups that encompassed experimental happenings. His tape pieces *Days, Number,* and *Clapping Piece* won special prizes in the 1964 Nova Consonanza Festival in Rome. He further wrote works for theater and dance scenarios, among them 4 for the Merce Cunningham Dance Co., of which *Geography and Music* became one of the company's most popular productions under the title *Roadrunners* (1979). He publ. a book of collected essays, *Gendai Bijutsu no Iso* (Can Art Be Thought; 1970), and pursued his multiplicity of artistic interests as an ed. for the leading Japanese art magazine, the *Bijutsu Shihyo.* In 1972 he settled in N.Y. while continuing to travel widely as a guest of several New Wave music events. Beginning in 1976, Tone produced musical compositions as compounds of cultural studies, using visual materials compiled in combination with ancient oriental texts and electronic sounds. He con-

tributed numerous works to ultramodern media groups, among them *Dinner Happening* (1962), *Miniature Restaurant* (1963), *Metropolitan Scavening Movement* (1964), *Dance Concert with 2 Titles* (1966), *Intermedia Art Festival* (1969), *Multi Performance* (1972), *Voice and Phenomenon* (1976), *The Wall and the Books* (1982), and *Word of Mouth* (1988). From 1979 he received a steady stream of commissions for multimedia works; received a N.Y. Foundation for the Arts Fellowship (1987; performance art/emergent forms). He has been a regular participant in festivals of avant-garde art, including the Annual Avant-Garde Festival (1973–77; 1980), FLUXUS festivals (1975, 1979, 1984, 1987), Dharma Music Festival (1985), Pioneer Performance Artists (1985), Japon des Avantgardes (1986), Miami New Wave Media Festival (1988), Venice Biennale (1990), and the 2nd Acoustic International Festival (1990).
WORKS: STAGE: *Anti-Dance and Anti-Music* (1961); *Ki* and *Waranin* (for Kaoru Kawana; 1962); *Kimigayo Electronic* and *Dictionary Music* (for Yoshie Aotsu and Mika Suzuki; 1963); *Theater Piece for Computer* (1966); *Kin no Sai Sarushima Dairi,* electronic music for a Kabuki play (1968); *Clockwork Video* (for Merce Cunningham's Dance Co. as *Events #82* and *#83;* 1973); *Theatrum Philosophicum* (for Cunningham's Dance Co. as *Events #151* and *#152;* 1975); *Genealogy, Music* (for Cunningham's Dance Co. as *Event #201;* 1978); *Geography and Music* (for Cunningham's Dance Co. as *Roadrunners;* 1979); *Blind Dates* (for Blondel Cummings and Senga Nengudi; 1982); *Personal Documents* (for Susana Heyman-Chaffey; 1984); *Caught in the Fringe* (for Nancy Zendora; 1985); *Econologos* (with Nancy Zendora and Barbara Held; 1986); *Techno Eden* (for Kay Nishikawa; 1986); *Setsubun, Day of Chance* (with Alison Knowles; 1990); *Spectaclum Lyrictronica,* "anarchic flight in paramedia space" (with Barbara Held; 1990). INSTRUMENTAL: *Improvisation and Object Sonore* (Ongaku collaboration; 1961); *Piano sound with magnetic tape* (1962); *Tone Work* (1963); *Mono Tone* (1963); *Ready-made Prohibition* (1965); *Kinegraphia* (1967); *815 Catch passage* (1968); *A 2nd Music* (1972); *One day Wittgenstein. . .* (1973); *Communication with Mr.* (1974); *Geodesy* for Harpsichord (1975); *Harpsichord for 50 Fingers* (1975); *Voice and phenomenon* (1976); *Fruits for towers* (1977); *Trio for a flute player* (1985); *Piano for Taoists* (1985); *Aletheia* (1987); *Lyrictron* for Flute (1988); *What is left from a Rembrandt . . .* (1989); also tape pieces, including *T.V. is a chewing gum for eyes* (1984), *This is not a condom* (for Vernita Nemec; 1984), and *Music for 2 C.D. Players* (1986; rev. 1989); graphic scores, including *Music for Reed Organ* (1962); the film scores *An event for film projector* (for Taka Imura; 1962) and *Gingakei . . . Galaxy* (for Masao Adachi; 1967).

Toni, Alceo, Italian musicologist and composer; b. Lugo, May 22, 1884; d. Milan, Dec. 4, 1969. He was a pupil of L. Torchi and E. Bossi in Bologna; was director of the Rovereto Cons. (1908–10), technical director of D'Annunzio's Raccolta Nazionale delle Musiche Italiane (1918–21), a critic for the *Popola d'Italia* (1922–43), and president of the Milan Cons. (1936–40). He ed. numerous works by Corelli, Locatelli, Torelli, Monteverdi, Carissimi, and other early Italian composers. His own compositions include the opera *Su un cavallin di legno* (1914), the ballet *I Fantocci ribelli* (1930), a Sym., choral works, chamber music, and songs. Some of his many articles were collected in a book, *Studi critici di interpretazione* (Milan, 1923; 2nd ed., 1955). With Tullio Serafin, he publ. *Stile, tradizioni e convenzioni del melo dramma italiano del Settecento e dell'Ottocento* (2 vols., Milan, 1958–64).

Tonning, Gerard, Norwegian-American choral conductor and composer; b. Stavanger, May 25, 1860; d. N.Y., June 10, 1940. He studied in Munich with Rheinberger and others; in 1887 he emigrated to America, settling in Duluth, Minn., where he organized several choral societies; in 1905 he moved to Seattle, where he remained until 1917; then went to N.Y.
WORKS: 2 operas: *Leif Erikson* (in Norwegian; Seattle, Dec. 10, 1910) and *All in a Garden Fair* (Seattle, Nov. 1, 1913);

pantomime, *Woman's Wiles, or Love Triumphant;* Piano Trio; *Suite moderne* for Violin and Piano; *Rapsodie norvégienne* for Violin and Piano; piano pieces (*Norwegian Dances,* 3 nocturnes, etc.); songs (*Arabian Love Songs* for 4 Solo Voices); etc.

Töpfer, Johann Gottlob, famous German organist, teacher, and writer on organ building; b. Niederrossla, Dec. 4, 1791; d. Weimar, June 8, 1870. He studied with the cantor Schlömilch; then at Weimar with Destouches and A.E. Müller; also attended the Weimar Seminary, where he became a teacher of music in 1817; from 1830 he was town organist of Weimar. An expert on organ construction, he wrote *Die Orgelbaukunst* (Weimar, 1833–34); *Die Scheibler'sche Stimm-Methode* (Erfurt, 1842); *Theoretisch-praktische Orgelschule* (Erfurt, 1845); *Lehrbuch der Orgelbaukunst* (4 vols., Weimar, 1855; 2nd ed., rev., 1888 by M. Allihn as *Die Theorie und Praxis des Orgelbaus;* 3rd ed., rev., 1936 by P. Smets). He composed *Orgelweihe* for Organ, Chorus, and Tenor, various preludes, fugues, chorale preludes, and choral fantasias for Organ, a Piano Trio, and a Piano Sonata.
BIBL.: A. Gottschalg, *J.G. T.* (Berlin, 1870).

Töpper, Hertha, Austrian mezzo-soprano; b. Graz, April 19, 1924. She received her musical training in Graz, studying violin with her father at the Cons. and voice with Franz Mixa at the opera school; made her operatic debut in 1945 as Ulrica at the Graz Landestheater, where she sang until 1952. In 1951 she appeared at the Bayreuth Festival; after singing as a guest artist at the Bavarian State Opera in Munich in 1951–52, she joined its roster; was made a Bavarian Kammersängerin in 1955. In 1953 she made her 1st appearance at London's Covent Garden as Clairon with the visiting Bavarian State Opera, and later returned for guest appearances. She made her U.S. debut at the San Francisco Opera in 1960 as Octavian, a role she repeated for her Metropolitan Opera debut in N.Y. on Nov. 19, 1962. From 1971 to 1981 she was a prof. at the Munich Hochschule für Musik. In 1980 she retired from the operatic stage. Her operatic repertoire included many roles by Wagner, Verdi, and Strauss; as a concert artist, she was particularly noted for her performances of the music of Bach.

Toradze, Alexander (David), Russian-American pianist, son of **David (Alexandrovich) Toradze;** b. Tbilisi, May 30, 1952. He was a pupil at the Central Music School (1958–69) and Cons. (1969–71) in Tbilisi; later studied at the Moscow Cons. with Yakov Zak, Boris Zemlyansky, and Lev Naumov. He began his career at the age of 9 with an appearance with the Tbilisi Sym. Orch., and subsequently toured widely in his homeland; he attracted wide notice in the West when he won the Silver Medal at the Van Cliburn Competition in 1977, which led to engagements in the U.S. In 1983 he settled in the U.S. but continued to pursue an international career in his many tours.

Toradze, David (Alexandrovich), noted Russian composer, father of **Alexander (David) Toradze;** b. Tiflis, April 14, 1922; d. there (Tbilisi), Nov. 7, 1983. He studied composition with Barkhudarian and piano with Virsaladze at the Tbilisi Cons.; after pursuing composition studies with Glière at the Moscow Cons., he completed postgraduate work at the Tbilisi Cons. (1948–51); then in 1952 joined its faculty; was made a reader in 1966 and a prof. in 1973. He received various honors, including the State Prize (1951), People's Artist of the Georgian S.S.R. (1961), and the Order of Lenin.
WORKS: STAGE: OPERAS: *The Sumarmi Fortress* (1942); *The Call of the Mountains* (Tbilisi, Nov. 20, 1947); *The Bride of the North* (Tbilisi, 1958). **BALLETS:** *Gorda* (Tbilisi, 1949); *For Peace* (Tbilisi, June 17, 1953; rev. as *The Unsubdued,* 1970). **MUSICAL COMEDIES:** *Natel* (1948); *The Avengers* (1952). **ORCH.:** *Festival,* overture (1944); 2 syms. (1946, 1968); *Afrikanskiye eskizï,* symphonic poem for Soloists, Chorus, and Orch. (1962); *Georgian Folk Refrains,* choral sym. (1972). Also chamber music; songs; film scores.

Torchi, Luigi, eminent Italian musicologist; b. Mondano, near Bologna, Nov. 7, 1858; d. Bologna, Sept. 18, 1920. He studied composition at the Accademia Filarmonica in Bologna, with

Serrao at the Naples Cons., with Jadassohn and Reinecke at the Leipzig Cons., and in France; was prof. of music history and librarian at the Liceo Musicale Rossini in Pesaro (1885–91); from 1895 to 1916 he held similar positions at the Bologna Cons., also teaching composition there. From its foundation (1894) until 1904 he was ed. of the *Rivista Musicale Italiana,* for which he wrote many valuable essays. In 1890 he publ. *Riccardo Wagner: Studio critico* (2nd ed., 1913). Besides a collection of *Eleganti canzoni ed arie italiane* of the 17th century (Milan, 1894) and *A Collection of Pieces for the Violin Composed by Italian Masters of the 17th and 18th Centuries* (London; both with piano accompaniment by Torchi), from 1897 to 1907 he publ. the important anthology *L'arte musicale in Italia.*

Torelli, Gasparo, Italian composer and poet; b. Borgo S. Sepolcro, near Lucca, date unknown; d. probably in Padua, c.1613. He entered the clergy; by 1593 he was active in Padua, where he was associated with the Accademia degli Avveduti (from 1601). He set a number of his own texts to music. Among his works are a favola pastorale for 4 Voices, *I fidi amanti* (Venice, 1600; ed. by B. Somma and L. Bianchi in Capolavori Polifonici del Secolo XVI, vol. VII, 1967), as well as *Canzonette* for 3 Voices (Venice, 1593), *Il secondo libro delle canzonette* for 3 to 4 Voices (Venice, 1598), *Brevi concetti d'amore: Il primo libro de madrigali* for 5 Voices (Venice, 1598), and *Amorose faville: Il quarto libro delle canzonette* for 3 Voices (Venice, 1608).

Torelli, Giuseppe, famous Italian violinist, pedagogue, and composer; b. Verona, April 22, 1658; d. Bologna, Feb. 8, 1709. He was the brother of the noted painter Felice Torelli. After going to Bologna about 1682, he was made a member of the Accademia Filarmonica as suonatore di violino in 1684; received instruction in composition from G.A. Perti; in 1686 he entered the cappella musicale at S. Petronio as a viola player; later played tenor viol there (1689–96); he also toured as a violinist. After further travels as a violinist, he served as maestro di concerto to the Margrave of Brandenburg in Ansbach (1698–99). From 1699 until at least 1700 he was active in Vienna; by 1701 he was again in Bologna, where he became a violinist in the cappella musicale at S. Petronio. He had many pupils, most notably Francesco Manfredini. Torelli was an important figure in the development of the instrumental concerto, excelling in concerto grosso and solo concerto writing.
WORKS: (10) *Sonate a 3,* with Basso Continuo, op. 1 (Bologna, 1686); (12) *Concerto da camera* for 2 Violins and Basso Continuo, op. 2 (Bologna, 1686); (12) *Sinfonie* for 2 to 4 Instruments, op. 3 (Bologna, 1687); (12) *Concertino per camera* for Violin and Cello, op. 4 (Bologna, 1688); (6) *Sinfonie a 3 e* [6] *concerti a 4,* op. 5 (Bologna, 1692); (12) *Concerti musicali,* op. 6 (Augsburg, 1698; no. 1 ed. by G. Piccioli, Rome, 1952, and by W. Kolneder, Mainz, 1958; no. 10 ed. in Nagels Musikarchiv, LXX, 1931); op. 7 (unknown; not extant); (12) *Concerti grossi con una pastorale per il Ss. Natale,* op. 8 (Bologna, 1709; nos. 1, 3, 7, and 9 ed. by P. Santi, Milan, 1959; no. 6 ed. by D. Stevens, London, 1957; no. 8 ed. by E. Praetorius, London, 1950); other instrumental works in contemporary collections; also a few vocal works, including the oratorio *Adam auss dem irrdischen Paradiess verstossen* (music not extant), other sacred pieces, and arias.
BIBL.: A. Schering, *Geschichte des Instrumentalkonzerts* (Leipzig, 1905; 2nd ed., 1927); A. Moser, *Geschichte des Violinspiels* (Berlin, 1923; 2nd ed., rev. and enlarged, 1966–67); F. Vatielli, *Arte e vita musicale a Bologna* (Bologna, 1927); R. Brenzoni, "G. T., musicista veronese," *Note d'Archivio per la Storia Musicale,* XIII (1936); F. Giegling, *G. T., Ein Beitrag zur Entwicklungsgeschichte des italienischen Konzerts* (Kassel, 1949); R. Norton, *The Chamber Music of G. T.* (diss., Northwestern Univ., 1967); E. Enrico, *G. T.'s Music for Instrumental Ensemble with Trumpet* (diss., Univ. of Michigan, 1970); B. Schwarz, *Great Masters of the Violin* (N.Y., 1983).

Torjussen, Trygve, Norwegian composer and teacher; b. Drammen, Nov. 14, 1885; d. Oslo, Feb. 12, 1977. He studied in Christiania, Rome, and Stuttgart; was on the staff of the Christiania Cons. (1911–17) and the Barratt-Due Music Inst. (1931–41). Among his works are various suites for small orch.; *Kark* for Tenor, Bass, Female Chorus, and Orch. (Oslo, 1939); *A Musical Bridge-Evening* for String Quartet (Oslo, 1935); over 70 piano pieces, including a sonata; 30 songs.

Torkanowsky, Werner, German-born American conductor; b. Berlin, March 30, 1926. He studied music with his mother; went to Palestine after 1933; emigrated to the U.S. in 1948; in 1952 he became a naturalized citizen and also violinist in the Pittsburgh Sym. Orch.; studied conducting with Pierre Monteux (1954–59). He conducted at the Spoleto Festival (1959–62); then was music director of the New Orleans Phil. Sym. Orch. (1963–77); subsequently taught at Carnegie-Mellon Univ. (from 1982).

Torke, Michael, American composer and pianist; b. Milwaukee, Sept. 22, 1961. He studied composition with Joseph Schwantner and piano at the Eastman School of Music in Rochester, N.Y. (graduated, 1984); then completed composition studies with Martin Bresnick and Jacob Druckman at the Yale Univ. School of Music (1984–85); won the Prix de Rome and held a residency at the American Academy in Rome. His output reveals an effective blend of serious music, jazz, and rock elements.

WORKS: *Laetus* for Piano (1982); *Ceremony of Innocence* for Flute, Clarinet, Violin, Cello, and Piano (1983); *The Yellow Pages* for Flute, Clarinet, Violin, Cello, and Piano (1984); *Vanada* for Brass, Keyboards, and Percussion (1984); *Ecstatic Orange* for Orch. (N.Y., May 10, 1985; *Bright Blue Music* for Orch. (N.Y., Nov. 23, 1985; also for Piano Trio as *The Harlequins Are Looking at You*, 1985); *The Directions,* chamber opera (Iraklion, Crete, Aug. 6, 1986); *Verdant Music* for Orch. (Milwaukee, Nov. 20, 1986); *Purple* for Orch. (N.Y., June 11, 1987); *Adjustable Wrench* for Chamber Ensemble (1987); *Black & White,* ballet (N.Y., May 7, 1988); *Copper* for Brass Quintet and Orch. (Midland, Mich., June 3, 1988); *Ash* for Orch. or Chamber Orch. (St. Paul, Minn., Feb. 3, 1989); *Slate* for Concertante Group and Orch. (as the ballet *Echo,* N.Y., June 15, 1989); *Rust* for Piano and Winds (1989); Mass for Baritone Solo, Chorus, and Chamber Orch. (N.Y., June 27, 1990); Piano Concerto (N.Y., Jan. 6, 1991).

Tormé (actually, **Torme**), **Mel(vin Howard),** American singer and composer of popular music; b. Chicago, Sept. 13, 1925. He was only 4 when he began singing with the Coon-Sanders band at a Chicago restaurant; studied piano and drums, then sang with various bands and acted in radio soap operas (1934–40). After touring as a singer, drummer, and arranger with the Chico Marx band (1942–43), he appeared in films and with his own vocal swing ensemble, the Mel-Tones. Following World War II army service, he launched a prominent career as a pop and jazz vocalist; performed on radio, in nightclubs, on television, and on recordings. He won 2 successive Grammy awards for Best Male Jazz Vocalist for his albums *An Evening with George Shearing and Mel Tormé* (1983) and *Top Drawer* (also with Shearing, 1984); appeared as soloist and conductor with a variety of sym. orchs., including those of San Francisco and Dallas. In 1980 Mayor Tom Bradley proclaimed Mel Tormé week in Los Angeles in commemoration of his 50th anniversary in show business. His association with Judy Garland is recounted in his book *The Other Side of the Rainbow* (N.Y., 1970); he publ. an autobiography, *It Wasn't All Velvet* (N.Y., 1988), and also wrote *Traps, the Drum Wonder* (1990), a biography of Buddy Rich. Among his more than 300 songs, *The Christmas Song* (1946) has become a holiday favorite.

Törne, Bengt (Axel) von, Finnish composer; b. Helsinki, Nov. 22, 1891; d. Turku, May 4, 1967. He studied composition with Furuhjelm at the Helsinki Inst. of Music (1910–16) and orchestration with Sibelius (1916–17). He wrote 6 syms. (1935–66); 3 sinfoniettas; *Sinfonia da camera* for Strings (1951); Piano Concerto; Piano Quintet; 2 string quartets; 2 violin sonatas; Piano Trio; publ. a monograph on Sibelius (London, 1937; in Italian, Florence, 1943; in Finnish, Helsinki, 1945; in Swedish, Stockholm, 1945) and an autobiography (Borgå, 1945).

Torner, Eduardo Martínez, Spanish writer on music and literature; b. Oviedo, April 8, 1888; d. London, Feb. 17, 1955. He was a pupil of Vincent d'Indy at the Schola Cantorum in Paris; returned to Spain in 1914 and settled in Madrid. He was director of research of Spanish folk song at the Centro de Estudios Históricos (from 1916); also taught at the Cons.; at the close of the Civil War (1939), he went to London. He publ. the folk song collections *Cancionero musical de la lírica popular asturiana* (Madrid, 1920), *Cuarenta canciones españolas* (1924), and *Cancionero musical* (1928); also the book *Temas folklóricos; música y poesía* (Madrid, 1935); ed. and arr. for piano selected pieces from tablature books of the 16th century, and publ. them under the title *Colección de vihuelistas españoles del siglo XVI* (Madrid, 1923).

BIBL.: A. Muñiz Tocas, *Vida y obra de E.M. T.* (Oviedo, 1961).

Torrance, George William, Irish clergyman, organist, and composer; b. Rathmines, near Dublin, 1835; d. Kilkenny, Aug. 20, 1907. He was a chorister at Christ Church Cathedral, Dublin; was organist at St. Andrew's and St. Anne's; studied music at Leipzig in 1856–57; was ordained a priest in 1865; in 1869 he emigrated to Melbourne, Australia, where he remained till 1897. He was appointed chaplain to the bishop of Ossory in 1897; in 1900 was made Prebendary of Killamery, canon of St. Canice's Cathedral, and librarian of St. Canice's Library, Kilkenny. Torrance's madrigal *Dry be that tear* won the medal of the Madrigal Society in 1903. His other works include the opera *William of Normandy* (Dublin, 1858), the oratorios *Abraham* (1855), *The Captivity* (1864), and *The Revelation* (1882), services, and hymn tunes.

Torrefranca, Fausto (Acanfora Sansone dei duchi di Porta e), eminent Italian musicologist; b. Monteleone Calabro, Feb. 1, 1883; d. Rome, Nov. 26, 1955. Trained as an engineer, he took up music under E. Lena in Turin (harmony and counterpoint) and also studied by himself. It was through his initiative that the 1st chair of musicology was established in Italy; in 1913, he became a lecturer at the Univ. of Rome; from 1914 to 1924, was a prof. of music history at the Cons. di S. Pietro in Naples, and from 1915, also librarian there; from 1924 to 1938, was librarian of the Milan Cons. From 1907 he was ed. of the *Rivista Musicale Italiana.* In 1941 he was appointed a prof. of music history at the Univ. of Florence.

WRITINGS: *La vita musicale dello spirito: la musica, le arti, il dramma* (Turin, 1910); *Giacomo Puccini e l'opera internazionale* (Turin, 1912); *Le origine italiane del romanticismo musicale: i primitivi della sonata moderna* (Turin, 1930); *Il segreto del quattrocento: musiche ariose e poesia popularesca* (Milan, 1939).

Torres-Santos, Raymond, Puerto Rican-born American composer, keyboardist, and arranger; b. San Juan, June 19, 1958. He grew up in a musical family; one of his grandfathers was a violinist, and the other played the German accordion. He was educated in Puerto Rico at the Univ. (B.A. in humanities, 1980) and the Cons. of Music (B.A. in music, 1980); also had lessons with Ginastera (summers, 1977–78); continued his studies at the Univ. of Calif. in Los Angeles (M.A., 1982; Ph.D., 1986), where his mentors were Henri Lazarof, Paule Reale, and David Raksin; also attended new music courses in Darmstadt (1982). He was a visiting composer at the Center for Computer Research in Music and Acoustics at Stanford Univ. (1984) and the Centro di Sonologia Computazionale at the Univ. of Padua (1988); in 1986, joined the faculty at the Calif. State Univ. in San Bernardino, where he also directed the Electronic Music and Commercial Music programs. His compositional style is eclectic and inclusive, and his craftsmanship applicable to virtually any genre; in some of his works, he makes effective use of indigenous Puerto Rican instruments. His more than 60 popular songs and over 300 arrangements have been performed by singers and orchs. throughout Latin America and in Los Angeles.

WORKS: ORCH.: Sinfonia Concertante (1980); *Exploraciones* for String Orch. (1980); *Areytos: a Symphonic Picture* (1985); *El pais de los cuatro pisos* (1988); *La cancion de las Antillas* (San Juan, Sept. 8, 1990). **CHAMBER:** Flute Sonata (1975); Violin Sonata (1977); *Un jibarito en N.Y.* for String Quartet (1977); *Music for Brass and Percussion* (1977); String Quartet (1978); *Cordillera central* for Clarinet and Cuatro (Puerto Rican stringed instrument; 1980); *La guaracha del macho camacho* for Acoustic Piano and Electronically Modified Electric Piano (1983); Brass Quintet (1985); *Epitafio* for 6 Horns (1988); *Descarga* for Percussion Ensemble (1988); *Danzas tropicales* for Chamber Ensemble (1988). **VOCAL:** *Esta es mi vida: A Cantata* for Chorus and Orch. (1979); *Elegia de Reyes: A Christmas Cantata* for Narrator, Soprano, Chorus, Symphonic Band, and "Rondalla" (an ensemble of Spanish Guitars, Mandolins, Cuatros, etc.; 1981); *Gwakia Baba* for Chorus (1988); also numerous solo pieces; electronic and computer music; dance pieces; film scores; commercials; arrangements and orchestrations; popular songs; stage works.

Torri, Pietro, Italian composer; b. Peschiera, c.1650; d. Munich, July 6, 1737. He served as court organist and later Kapellmeister at the court in Bayreuth (until 1684); in 1689 he became organist at the court of Max Emanuel II, Elector of Bavaria, in Munich; when the elector became governor of the Spanish Netherlands in 1692, he took Torri with him to Brussels as his maître de chapelle. In 1696 he was conductor for the carnival season at Hannover; in 1701 he was appointed court chamber music director at Munich, following the Elector to Brussels upon the latter's exile in 1704; he fled Brussels with the Elector (1706). In Brussels he produced the oratorio *La vanitá del mondo* (March 5, 1706); from 1715 he was again in Munich, where he was made Hofkapell-Direktor; later he was named Hofkapellmeister (1732). He composed about 20 operas, 2 of which were produced at the Munich court: *Lucio Vero* (Oct. 12, 1720) and *Griselda* (Oct. 12, 1723); also some chamber duets. Torri became best known in his lifetime for his vocal chamber pieces.

BIBL.: K. Kremer, *P. T. und seine kammermusikalische Werke* (diss., Univ. of Munich, 1956).

Torrington, Fredrick Herbert, English-born Canadian organist, pianist, violinist, conductor, and composer; b. Dudley, Worcestershire, Oct. 20, 1837; d. Toronto, Nov. 19, 1917. He went to Canada in 1856; served as a church organist in Montreal (1857–69); then was music director at King's Chapel, Boston; in 1873, was appointed organist at the Metropolitan Church, Toronto, and conductor of the Toronto Phil. Society (until 1894). In 1888 he founded the Toronto College of Music; in 1892 he was made president of the Canadian Soc. of Musicians. Among his compositions are choruses, services, songs, and organ music.

Tort, César, Mexican composer; b. Puebla, Sept. 4, 1929. He studied piano with Ramón Serratos in 1946; composition with Conrado del Campo at the Madrid Cons. (1950–53). Returning to Mexico, he dedicated himself to a reform of children's musical education. He wrote mostly for piano: *Impresiones* (1954), *El orador* (1955), *El piano mágico* (1972), etc.; also a symphonic poem, *Estirpes* (1958), and a cantata, *La espada* (1966).

Tortelier, Paul, noted French cellist, pedagogue, composer, and political idealist, father of **Yan Pascal Tortelier;** b. Paris, March 21, 1914; d. Villarçeaux, near Paris, Dec. 18, 1990. He studied cello with Gérard Hekking at the Paris Cons., winning 1st prize at the age of 16; made his debut with the Lamoureux Orch. at the age of 17; from 1935 to 1937 he was 1st cellist of the orch. in Monte Carlo; from 1937 to 1939 he was a member of the Boston Sym. Orch. He was subsequently 1st cellist of the Paris Cons. Orch. (1946–47). In 1947 he was a soloist at the Festival of Richard Strauss in London. Tortelier inherited his progressive ideals from his father, a cabinetmaker by profession and a Marxist by political persuasion. He participated in a number of organizations destined to create a better world-at-large; he was quite serious in his work to prevent aggression or injustices to countries governed by repressive rules. Although not a Jew, he saw great hope in the formation of individual communes in Israel and spent a year there working in a kibbutz (1955–56). He then resumed his career as a professional musician; also was a prof. at the Paris Cons. (1957–59) and at the Nice Cons. (1978–80). He made some appearances as a conductor. His wife, Maud Martin Tortelier, was also a cellist, and his daughter, Maria de la Pau, was a pianist; both appeared in performances of Tortelier's works, which included *Israel Symphony*, several cello concertos, a Cello Sonata, and a Suite for Solo Cello. He publ. *How I Play, How I Teach* (London, 1975) and *Paul Tortelier, Self-Portrait* (with D. Blum; London, 1984).

Tortelier, Yan Pascal, French conductor, son of **Paul Tortelier;** b. Paris, April 19, 1947. At the age of 12 he began studying harmony and counterpoint with Nadia Boulanger; after winning the premier prix for violin at the Paris Cons. when he was 14, he made his debut as a soloist in the Brahms Double Concerto in London (1962). Following conducting studies with Franco Ferrara at the Accademia Chigiana in Siena (1973), he served as associate conductor of the Orch. du Capitole in Toulouse (1974–83); also conducted opera there and appeared as a guest conductor in other French cities. In 1978 he made his British debut as a guest conductor with the Royal Phil. of London. In 1985 he made his U.S. debut as a guest conductor with the Seattle Sym. Orch., and subsequently appeared with other North American orchs. In 1989 he became principal conductor and artistic director of the Ulster Orch. in Belfast. In 1990 he also was named chief conductor of the BBC Phil. in Manchester, effective in 1992.

Tosar Errecart, Héctor, Uruguayan composer; b. Montevideo, July 18, 1923. He studied piano and composition in Montevideo; after receiving a Guggenheim scholarship (1946), he went to the U.S. to study composition with Copland and Honegger and conducting with Koussevitzky; also took courses at Columbia Univ.; subsequently went to Paris on a French government scholarship, where he studied composition with Rivier and Milhaud at the Cons. and composition with Honegger and conducting with Bigot and Fournet at the École Normale de Musique. He was a prof. at the Montevideo Cons. (1951–54); served as prof. of the history of instruments at the Univ. of Montevideo before becoming chairman of the composition dept. of the Puerto Rico Cons. in 1974. His music is neo-Classical in facture, with a considerable influx of Latin American melorhythms.

WORKS: ORCH.: Piano Concertino (1941); 3 syms. (1945, 1950, 1973); *Oda a amigas* (1951); *Sinfonia concertante* (1957); *Naves Errantes* (1964); *Recitativo y variaciones* (1967); *A 13* (1970); choral works; chamber music; songs; piano pieces.

Tosatti, Vieri, Italian composer; b. Rome, Nov. 2, 1920. He studied piano on his own; also composition with Dobici, Ferdinandini, Jachino, and Petrassi at the Rome Cons. (diploma, 1942) and with Pizzetti. In his compositions he often exploits sensational or morbid subjects, setting them to pungent music, with a liberal application of special effects.

WORKS: DRAMATIC: Music drama, *Dionisio* (1947); "paradoxical drama," *Il sistema della dolcezza* (1949); "boxing opera," *La partita a pugni* (ISCM Festival, Venice, Sept. 8, 1953). **OPERAS:** *Il giudizio universale* (Milan, 1955); *L'isola del tesoro* (Bologna, 1958); *La fiera della Meraviglie* (Rome, 1963); *Il paradiso e il poeta* (RAI, Turin, 1971). **ORCH.:** Piano Concerto (1945); *Il concerto della demenza* for Narrator, 2 Pianos, and Chamber Orch. (1946); Viola Concerto (1966); *Concerto ipercilico* for Clarinet and Orch. (1970). **CHAMBER:** Concerto for Wind Quintet and Piano (1945); *Introduzione fiabesca* for Piano Trio (1943); *Piccola sonata* for Violin and Piano (1945). **VOCAL:** *Sinfonia corale* for Chorus and Orch. (1944); *Requiem* (1963); *2 coretti* for 3 Women's Voices (1970); songs; also a variety of whimsical piano pieces.

Toscanini, Arturo, great Italian conductor; b. Parma, March 25, 1867; d. N.Y., Jan. 16, 1957. He entered the Parma Cons. at the age of 9, studying the cello with Carini and composition with Dacci; graduated in 1885 as winner of the 1st prize for cello; received the Barbacini Prize as the outstanding graduate of his class. In 1886 he was engaged as cellist for the Italian opera in Rio de Janeiro; on the evening of June 30, 1886, he was unexpectedly called upon to substitute for the regular conductor, when the latter left the podium at the end of the introduction after the public hissed him; the opera was *Aida*, and Toscanini led it without difficulty; he was rewarded by an ovation and was engaged to lead the rest of the season. Returning to Italy, he was engaged to conduct the opera at the Teatro Carignano in Turin, making his debut there on Nov. 4, 1886, and later conducted the Municipal Orch. there. Although still very young, he quickly established a fine reputation. From 1887 to 1896 he conducted opera in the major Italian theaters. On May 21, 1892, he led the premiere of *Pagliacci* in Milan, and on Feb. 1, 1896, the premiere of *La Bohème* in Turin. He also conducted the 1st performance by an Italian opera company, sung in Italian, of *Götterdämmerung* (Turin, Dec. 22, 1895) and *Siegfried* (Milan, 1899); he made his debut as a sym. conductor on March 20, 1896, with the orch. of the Teatro Regio in Turin. In 1898 the impresario Gatti-Casazza engaged him as chief conductor for La Scala, Milan, where he remained until 1903, and again from 1906 to 1908. In the interim, he conducted opera in Buenos Aires (1903–4; 1906). When Gatti-Casazza became general manager of the Metropolitan Opera (1908), he invited Toscanini to be principal conductor; Toscanini's debut in N.Y. was in *Aida* (Nov. 16, 1908). While at the Metropolitan, Toscanini conducted Verdi's *Requiem* (Feb. 21, 1909), as well as 2 world premieres, Puccini's *The Girl of the Golden West* (Dec. 10, 1910) and Giordano's *Madame Sans-Gêne* (Jan. 25, 1915); he also brought out for the 1st time in America Gluck's *Armide* (Nov. 14, 1910), Wolf-Ferrari's *Le Donne curiose* (Jan. 3, 1912), and Mussorgsky's *Boris Godunov* (March 19, 1913). On April 13, 1913, he gave his 1st concert in N.Y. as a sym. conductor, leading Beethoven's 9th Sym. In 1915 he returned to Italy; during the season of 1920–21, he took the La Scala Orch. on a tour of the U.S. and Canada. From 1921 to 1929 he was artistic director of La Scala; there he conducted the posthumous premiere of Boito's opera *Nerone*, which he completed for performance (May 1, 1924). In 1926–27 he was a guest conductor of the N.Y. Phil., returning in this capacity through the 1928–29 season; then was its associate conductor with Mengelberg in 1929–30; subsequently was its conductor from 1930 to 1936; took it on a tour of Europe in the spring of 1930. He conducted in Bayreuth in 1930 and 1931. Deeply touched by the plight of the Jews in Germany, he acceded to the request of the violinist Huberman, founder of the Palestine Sym. Orch., to conduct the inaugural concert of that orch. at Tel Aviv (Dec. 26, 1936). During this period he also filled summer engagements at the Salzburg Festivals (1934–37), and conducted in London (1935; 1937–39). He became music director of the NBC Sym. Orch. in 1937, a radio orch. that had been organized especially for him; he conducted his 1st broadcast on Dec. 25, 1937, in N.Y. He took it on a tour of South America in 1940, and on a major tour of the U.S. in 1950. He continued to lead the NBC Sym. Orch. until the end of his active career; he conducted his last concert from Carnegie Hall, N.Y., on April 4, 1954 (10 days after his 87th birthday), and then sent a doleful letter of resignation to NBC, explaining the impossibility of further appearances. He died a few weeks before his 90th birthday.

Toscanini was one of the most celebrated masters of the baton in the history of conducting; undemonstrative in his handling of the orch., he possessed an amazing energy and power of command. He demanded absolute perfection, and he erupted in violence when he could not obtain from the orch. what he wanted (a lawsuit was brought against him in Milan when he accidentally injured the concertmaster with a broken violin bow). Despite the vituperation he at times poured on his musicians, he was affectionately known to them as "The Maestro" who could do no wrong. His ability to communicate his desires to singers and players was extraordinary, and even the most celebrated opera stars or instrumental soloists never dared to question his authority. Owing to extreme nearsightedness, Toscanini committed all scores to memory; his repertoire embraced virtually the entire field of Classical and Romantic music; his performances of Italian operas, of Wagner's music dramas, of Beethoven's syms., and of modern Italian works were especially inspiring. Among the moderns, he conducted works by Richard Strauss, Debussy, Ravel, Prokofiev, and Stravinsky, and among Americans, Samuel Barber, whose *Adagio for Strings* he made famous; he also had his favorite Italian composers (Catalani, Martucci), whose music he fondly fostered. In his social philosophy, he was intransigently democratic; he refused to conduct in Germany under the Nazi regime. He militantly opposed Fascism in Italy, but never abandoned his Italian citizenship, despite his long years of residence in America. In 1987 his family presented his valuable private archive to the N.Y. Public Library.

BIBL.: G. Ciampelli, *A. T.* (Milan, 1923); E. Cozzani, *A. T.* (Milan, 1927); T. Nicotra, *A. T.* (tr. from the Italian, N.Y., 1929); D. Bonardi, *T.* (Milan, 1929); P. Stefan, *A. T.* (Vienna, 1936; in Eng., N.Y., 1936); L. Gilman, *T. and Great Music* (N.Y., 1938); S. Hoeller, *A. T.* (N.Y., 1943); G. Ciampelli, *T.* (Milan, 1946); A. Della Corte, *T.* (Vicenza, 1946); D. Nives, *A. T.* (Milan, 1946); A. Segre, "T.: The First Forty Years," and H. Taubman, "T. in America," *Musical Quarterly* (April 1947); F. Sacchi, *T.* (Milan, 1951; Eng. tr. as *The Magic Baton: T.'s Life for Music*, N.Y., 1957); H. Taubman, *The Maestro: The Life of A. T.* (N.Y., 1951); S. Chotzinoff, *T.: An Intimate Portrait* (N.Y., 1956); R. Marsh, *T. and the Art of Orchestral Performance* (Philadelphia, 1956); B. Haggin, *Conversations with T.* (N.Y., 1959; 2nd ed., enlarged, 1979); S. Hughes, *The T. Legacy: A Critical Study of A. T.'s Performances of Beethoven, Verdi, and Other Composers* (London, 1959); L. Frassati, *Il Maestro A. T. e il suo mondo* (Turin, 1967); H. Schonberg, *The Great Conductors* (N.Y., 1967); A. Armani, ed., *T. e La Scala* (Milan, 1972); G. Marek, *T.* (N.Y., 1975); H. Sachs, *T.* (Philadelphia, 1978); D. Matthews, *A. T.* (Tunbridge Wells and N.Y., 1982); J. Freeman and W. Toscanini, *T.* (N.Y., 1987); J. Horowitz, *Understanding T.: How He Became an American Culture-God and Helped to Create a New Audience for Old Music* (N.Y., 1987); H. Sachs, *A. T. dal 1915 al 1946: l'arte all'ombra della politica: omaggio al maestro nel 30° anniversario della scomparsa* (Turin, 1987).

Toselli, Enrico, Italian pianist, teacher, and composer; b. Florence, March 13, 1883; d. there, Jan. 15, 1926. He studied with Sgambati and Martucci; gave concerts in Italy as a pianist. He wrote the operettas *La cattiva Francesca* (1912) and *La principessa bizzarra* (1913), the symphonic poem *Il fuoco*, and various salon pieces for Voice and Piano, the most celebrated being *Serenata* (1900). In 1907 he married the former Crown Princess Luise of Saxony, creating an international furor; following their separation in 1912, he recounted this affair in his book *Mari d'altessee: 4 ans de mariage avec Louise de Toscane, ex-princesse de Saxe* (Paris, 1913; Eng. tr., 1913).

Tosi, Pier Francesco, prominent Italian castrato contralto, teacher, diplomat, and composer; b. Cesena, c.1653; d. Faenza, April 1732. He studied with his father, then sang successfully in Italy and throughout Europe; in 1692, settled in London, where he gave regular concerts, and was highly esteemed as a vocal teacher. He was a composer at the Viennese court (1705–11), while concurrently serving as an emissary to Count Johann Wilhelm of the Palatinate. About 1723 he returned to London, where he remained until 1727; later returned to Italy and took holy orders in Bologna in 1730; finally settled in Faenza. He wrote the valuable treatise *Opinioni de' cantori antichi e moderni, o sieno Osservazioni sopra il canto figurato* (Bologna, 1723; in Eng., 1742, as *Observations on the Florid Song*; in German as *Anleitung zur Singkunst*, 1757; in French as *L'Art du chant*, 1774; the Eng. ed. was republ. in London in 1967). He composed some chamber cantatas.

BIBL.: R. Celletti, "La vocalita al tempo del T.," *Nuova rivista musicale italiana*, IV (1967); E. Casselman, "T. Reconsidered," *National Association of Teachers of Singing Bulletin*, XXIV (1968).

Tosti, Sir (Francesco) Paolo, Italian-born English singing teacher and composer; b. Ortano sul Mare, April 9, 1846; d. Rome, Dec. 2, 1916. He was a pupil, from 1858, of the Collegio di S. Pietro a Majella, Naples, and was appointed sub-teacher (maestrino) by Mercadante (until 1869). He visited London in 1875; had great success in concerts and settled there as a teacher, becoming singing master to the royal family in 1880, and prof. of singing at the Royal Academy of Music in 1894; became a British subject in 1906 and was knighted in 1908; retired to Rome in 1912. Besides many original songs, in both English and Italian, he publ. a collection of *Canti popolari abruzzesi*. His songs were highly popular; some of the best known are *Goodbye Forever and Forever, Mattinata,* and *Vorrei morire.*

BIBL.: *Onoranze a F.P. T.* (Pescara, 1927); E. Mario, *F.P. T.* (Siena, 1947); A. Piovano, *Ommagio a F.P. T.* (Ortona, 1972); J. Little, *Romantic Italian Song in the Works of F.P. T. and some of his Contemporaries* (diss., Univ. of Illinois, 1977).

Totenberg, Roman, Polish-born American violinist and pedagogue; b. Lodz, Jan. 1, 1911. He studied violin with Mieczyslaw Michalowicz in Warsaw, Carl Flesch in Berlin, and Georges Enesco in Paris. In 1932 he won the Mendelssohn Prize in Berlin. In 1935–36 he toured Europe with Karol Szymanowski, giving violin-piano recitals; then emigrated to the U.S.; became an American citizen in 1943. He was head of the violin dept. at the Aspen (Colo.) School of Music (1950–60) and a teacher at the Mannes College of Music in N.Y. (1951–57) before serving as prof. of music and chairman of the string dept. at Boston Univ. (1961–78); then was director of the Longy School of Music (1978–85).

Tough, "Dave" (David Jarvis), versatile American jazz drummer; b. Oak Park, Ill., April 26, 1908; d. Newark, N.J., Dec. 6, 1948. He began his career in Chicago; then played with Bud Freeman, Eddie Condon, and Red Nichols. In 1936 he joined Tommy Dorsey's orch.; subsequently worked with Benny Goodman, Jack Teagarden, Artie Shaw, and Charlie Spivak. He gained renown as a jazz drummer during his stint with Woody Herman's band in 1944–45; however, his career was cut short by ill health and alcoholism.

Toulmouche, Frédéric (Michel), French composer; b. Nantes, Aug. 3, 1850; d. Paris, Feb. 20, 1909. He studied with Victor Massé in Paris; in 1894, became director of the Menus-Plaisirs theater. He composed several opéras-comique: *Le Moûtier de S.-Guignolet* (Brussels, 1885); *La Veillée des noces* (Paris, 1888; in London, 1892, as *The Wedding Eve*); *L'Ame de la patrie* (St. Brieuc, 1892); *La Perle du Cantal* (Paris, 1895); *La St.-Valentin* (Paris, 1895); about a dozen operettas and some ballets.

Touma, Habib Hassan, Arab composer and ethnomusicologist; b. Nazareth, Dec. 12, 1934. He studied at the Haifa Cons. and the Rubin Academy of Music in Tel Aviv (1956–62); then went to the Free Univ. of Berlin, where he received a Ph.D. with a dissertation on Arab music theory (1968). He went on to teach there, and to work at the Internationale Institut für Vergleichende Musikstudien und Dokumentation. His studies of Arab music theory and history greatly influenced his compositions, which include *Oriental Rhapsody* for 2 Flutes and Percussion (1958), *Reflexus I* for 23 Strings (1965), and *Maqam for Natalie* for Piano (1974). He publ. *Die Musik der Araber* (Wilhelmshaven, 1975).

Tourangeau, (Marie Jeannine) Huguette, Canadian mezzo-soprano; b. Montreal, Aug. 12, 1938. She studied voice at the Montreal Cons. with Ruzena Herlinger, repertoire with Otto-Werner Mueller, and declamation with Roy Royal. In 1962 she made her debut in Monteverdi's *Vespro della Beata Virgine*

at the Montreal Festival; her operatic debut followed as Mercedes in *Carmen* in Montreal in 1964. She toured in the U.S. as a member of the Metropolitan Opera National Co. (1964–65); then appeared in Seattle, London, San Francisco, and Hamburg. On Nov. 28, 1973, she made her formal Metropolitan Opera debut in N.Y. as Nicklausse in *Les Contes d'Hoffmann,* and returned in later seasons as a guest artist. In 1974 she sang at the Sydney Opera and made her debut at London's Covent Garden as Elisabetta in *Maria Stuarda* in 1977. Her repertory included roles from French, German, and Italian operas.

Tourel (real name, Davidovich), Jennie, prominent Russian-born American mezzo-soprano; b. Vitebsk, June 22, 1900; d. N.Y., Nov. 23, 1973. She played flute; then studied piano. After the Revolution, her family left Russia and settled temporarily near Danzig; they later moved to Paris, where she continued to study piano and contemplated a concert career; she then began to take voice lessons with Anna El-Tour, and decided to devote herself to professional singing; she changed her last name to Tourel by transposing the syllables of her teacher's name. She made her opera debut at the Opéra Russe in Paris in 1931; then her debut at the Metropolitan Opera in N.Y. on May 15, 1937, as Mignon. In 1940, just before the occupation of Paris by Nazi troops, she went to Lisbon, and eventually emigrated to the U.S.; appeared on the Metropolitan Opera roster in 1943–45 and 1946–47; became a naturalized citizen in 1946. In 1951 she created the role of Baba the Turk in Stravinsky's *The Rake's Progress* in Venice. In later years she devoted herself to recitals and orch. engagements, excelling particularly in the French repertoire. She also taught at the Juilliard School of Music in N.Y. and at the Aspen (Colo.) School of Music.

Tourjée, Eben, American music educator; b. Warwick, R.I., June 1, 1834; d. Boston, April 12, 1891. While working in a cotton factory in Harrisville, R.I., he played the organ in church; then studied with Carl August Haupt in Berlin. Returning to America, he settled in Boston, and in 1867 founded (with R. Goldbeck) the New England Cons. of Music, which he directed until his death; also was dean of the college of music at Boston Univ. (from 1873). He was the 1st president of the Music Teachers National Assoc. (1876).

BIBL.: E. Nason, *The Lives of the Eminent American Evangelists. . .also a Sketch of the Lives of Philip P. Bliss and E. T.* (Boston, 1877); E. Samuel, "A Life Sketch of Dr. E. T.," *New England Conservatory Review,* III/2 (1913); L. Tourjée, *For God and Music: The Life Story of E. T.* (Los Angeles, 1960).

Tournemire, Charles (Arnould), distinguished French organist and composer; b. Bordeaux, Jan. 22, 1870; d. Arachon, Nov. 3, 1939. He began his training as a child in Bordeaux; was only 11 when he became organist at St. Pierre, and later was organist at St. Seurin; then went to Paris, where he studied piano with Bériot, harmony with Taudou, and organ (premier prix, 1891) with Widor and Franck at the Cons.; also studied composition with d'Indy at the Schola Cantorum; was organist at Ste. Clotilde (from 1898) and a prof. at the Cons. (from 1919); also toured Europe. His major achievement as a composer was *L'Orgue mystique,* comprising 51 Offices for the Roman Catholic liturgy.

WORKS: OPERAS: *Nittetis* (1905–7); *Les Dieux sont morts* (1910–12; Paris, March 19, 1924); *La Légende de Tristan* (1925–26); *Il Poverello di Assisi* (1936–38). **ORCH.:** 8 syms.: No. 1, *Romantique* (1900); No. 2, *Ouessant* (Paris, April 4, 1909); No. 3, *Moscou* (Amsterdam, Oct. 19, 1913); No. 4, *Pages symphoniques* (1912–13; Paris, 1914); No. 5, *Dans les Alpes* (1913–14; The Hague, March 10, 1920); No. 6 for Soloist, Chorus, Organ, and Orch. (1915–18); No. 7, *Les Danses de la vie* (1918–22); No. 8, *La Symphonie du triomphe de la mort* (1920–24); *Poème* for Organ and Orch. (1909–10). **CHORAL:** *Le Sang de la sirène* for Soloists, Chorus, and Orch. (1902–3; Paris, Nov. 17, 1904); *Psalm LVII* for Chorus and Orch. (1908–9); *Psalm XLVI* for Chorus and Orch. (1913); *Trilogie: Faust-Don Quichotte–St. François d'Assise* for Soloists, Chorus, and

Orch. (1916–29); *La Quête Saint Graal* for Soloists, Chorus, and Orch. (1926–27; Lyons, Jan. 1930); *Apocalypse de St. Jean* for Soloists, Chorus, Organ, and Orch. (1932–35); *La Douloureuse Passion du Christ* for Soloists, Chorus, and Organ (1936–37); also songs. **CHAMBER:** Violin Sonata (1892–93); 3 pièces for Oboe and Piano (1894); Cello Sonata (1895); *Andante* for Horn and Piano (1896); *Suite* for Viola and Piano (1897); Piano Quartet (1897–98); Piano Trio (1901); *Poème* for Cello and Piano (1908); *Pour une épigramme de Théocrite* for 3 Flutes, 2 Clarinets, and Harp (1910); *Musique orante* for String Quartet (1933); *Sonate-poème* for Violin and Piano (1935). **PIANO:** *Sérénade* (1896); Sonata (1899); *Sarabande* (1901); *Rhapsodie* (1904); *Poème mystique* (1908); (12) *Préludes-poèmes* (1932); *Cloches de Châteauneuf-du-Faou* (1933); *Études de chaque jour* (1936). **ORGAN:** *Andantino* (1894); *Sortie* (1894); *Offertoire* (1894–95); *Pièce symphonique* (1899); *Suite de morceaux* I (1901) and II (1902); *Triple choral* (1901); *L'Orgue mystique* (1927–32); *3 poèmes* (1932); *6 firetti* (1932); *Fantaisie symphonique* (1933–34); *Petites fleurs musicales* (1933–34); *7 chorals-poèmes* (1935); *Postludes libres* (1935); *Symphonie-choral* (1935); *Symphonie sacrée* (1936); *Suite évocatrice* (1938); *2 fresques symphoniques sacrées* (1938–39). **WRITINGS:** *César Franck* (Paris, 1931); *Précis d'exécution, de registration et d'improvisation à l'orgue* (Paris, 1936); *Petite méthode d'orgue* (Paris, 1949). **BIBL.:** F. Peeters, "L'Œuvre d'orgue de C. T.," *Musica Sacra* (Bruges, 1940); idem, "In memoriam C. T.," *Orgue*, No. 113 (1965); G. Beechey, "C. T., 1870–1939," *Musical Times*, CXI (1970); B. Lespinard, "'L'Orgue mystique' de C. T.: 'Impressions plain-chantesques,'" *Orgue*, No. 139b (1971); J.-M. Fauquet, *Catalogue de l'œuvre de C. T.* (Geneva, 1979).

Tours, Berthold, Dutch-born English organist, violinist, and composer, father of **Frank E(dward) Tours;** b. Rotterdam, Dec. 17, 1838; d. London, March 11, 1897. He received his initial musical training from his father, the organist **Barthélemy Tours** (1797–1864), and from Verhulst; went to London in 1861; in 1878 he became musical adviser and ed. for Novello & Co. He was an accomplished composer of Anglican hymn tunes, anthems, and services; also had success as a composer of instrumental pieces and songs.

Tours, Frank E(dward), English-American composer, son of **Berthold Tours;** b. London, Sept. 1, 1877; d. Santa Monica, Calif., Feb. 2, 1963. He studied with Stanford, Parratt, and Bridge at the Royal College of Music in London; went to N.Y. in 1904 and conducted light opera productions. Later he entered the motion picture field. He wrote many successful songs, among them *Mother o' Mine, Beyond the Sunset, Red Rose,* and *In Flanders Fields.*

Tourte, François (Xavier), celebrated French bow maker; b. Paris, 1747; d. there, April 26, 1835. He was born into a family of bow makers; after being apprenticed to a clockmaker in childhood, he took up the family profession; about 1785 he perfected the Tourte bow, which has since remained the standard. His mastery of workmanship led him to be hailed as the "Stradivari of the bow." **BIBL.:** W. Retford, *Bows and Bow Makers* (London, 1964); H. Whistler, "F. T.—Bow Maker Supreme," *Music Journal*, Nos. 5 and 9, XXIII (1965).

Tovey, Sir Donald (Francis), eminent English music scholar, pianist, and composer; b. Eton, July 17, 1875; d. Edinburgh, July 10, 1940. He studied privately with Sophie Weisse (piano), Sir W. Parratt (counterpoint), and James Higgs and Parry (composition) until 1894, when he won the Nettleship scholarship at Balliol College, Oxford; graduated with Classical Honors (B.A., 1898). In 1894 he appeared as a pianist with Joachim, and subsequently performed regularly with his quartet; in 1900–1901, he gave a series of chamber music concerts in London, at which he performed several of his own works; in 1901–2, he gave similar concerts in Berlin and Vienna; played his Piano Concerto in 1903 under Henry Wood and in 1906 under Hans Richter; then was an active participant in the concerts of the Chelsea Town Hall and of the Classical Concert Society. In 1914 he succeeded Niecks as Reid Prof. of music at the Univ. of Edinburgh; founded the Reid Orch. in 1917. He made his U.S. debut as a pianist in 1925; presented a series of concerts with renowned guest artists in Edinburgh in 1927–28. In 1935 he was knighted. Though highly esteemed as a composer, he was most widely known as a writer and lecturer on music, his analytical essays being models of their kind. Besides much chamber music and several piano pieces (a sonata, *Balliol Dances* for 4-hands, etc.), he composed an opera, *The Bride of Dionysus* (Edinburgh, April 23, 1929); a Sym. (1913); Cello Concerto (Edinburgh, Nov. 22, 1934; Casals soloist, composer conducting); etc. **WRITINGS** (all publ. in London): *A Companion to the Art of the Fugue* (1931); *Essays in Musical Analysis* (6 vols., 1935–39); with G. Parratt, *Walter Parratt: Master of Music* (1941); *A Musician Talks* (1941); H. Foss, ed., *Essays in Musical Analysis: Chamber Music* (1944); idem, ed., *Musical Articles from the Encyclopædia Britannica* (1944); idem, ed., *Beethoven* (1944); *A Companion to Beethoven's Piano Sonatas* (1948); H. Foss, ed., *Essays and Lectures on Music* (1949). **BIBL.:** M. Grierson, *D.F. T.* (London, 1952).

Tower, Joan (Peabody), American composer, pianist, and teacher; b. New Rochelle, N.Y., Sept. 6, 1938. She took courses in composition with Brant and Calabro and studied piano at Bennington (Vt.) College (B.A., 1961); completed her training with Luening, Beeson, Ussachevsky, and others at Columbia Univ. (M.A., 1964; D.M.A., 1978). In N.Y. in 1969 she co-founded the Da Capo Chamber Players, which became known for its promotion of contemporary music; she served as its pianist until 1984. She taught at Bard College in Annandale-on-Hudson (from 1972) and was composer-in-residence of the St. Louis Sym. Orch. (1985–87). In 1976 she held a Guggenheim fellowship; held NEA fellowships in 1974, 1975, 1980, and 1984; received a Koussevitzky Foundation grant in 1982, and an American Academy and Inst. of Arts and Letters award in 1983. In 1990 she received the Grawemeyer Award. **WORKS: ORCH.:** *Composition* (1967); *Amazon II* (Poughkeepsie, N.Y., Nov. 10, 1979; orchestrated from the work for Flute, Clarinet, Viola, Cello, and Piano); *Sequoia* (N.Y., May 18, 1981); *Amazon III* for Chamber Orch. (1982); Cello Concerto (1984); *Island Rhythms*, overture (1985); piano concerto, *Homage to Beethoven* (1985; Annandale-on-Hudson, Jan. 31, 1986); *Silver Ladders* (1986; St. Louis, Jan. 9, 1987); *Island Prelude* (St. Louis, May 4, 1989). **CHAMBER:** *Pillars* for 2 Pianos and Percussion (1961); *Study* for 2 Strings and 2 Winds (1963); Percussion Quartet (1963; rev. 1969); *Brimset* for 2 Flutes and Percussion (1965); *Opa eboni* for Oboe and Piano (1968); *Movements* for Flute and Piano (1968); *Prelude* for 5 Players (1970); *Breakfast Rhythms I* and *II* for Clarinet and 5 Instruments (1974–75); *Black Topaz* for Piano and 6 Instruments (1976); *Amazon I* for Flute, Clarinet, Viola, Cello, and Piano (1977; orchestrated as *Amazon II*, Poughkeepsie, N.Y., Nov. 10, 1979); *Petroushskates* for Flute, Clarinet, Violin, Cello, and Piano (1980); *Noon Dance* for Flute, Clarinet, Violin, Cello, Piano, and Percussion (1982); *Fantasy* for Clarinet and Piano (1983); *Snow Dreams* for Flute and Guitar (1983); piano pieces; various works for Solo Instruments.

Townsend, Douglas, American composer and musicologist; b. N.Y., Nov. 8, 1921. He studied at the High School of Music and Art in N.Y.; then received lessons in composition from Serly, Wolpe, Copland, Luening, Greissle, and others. He taught at Brooklyn College of the City Univ. of N.Y. (1958–69), Lehman College of the City Univ. of N.Y. (1970–71), the Univ. of Bridgeport, Conn. (1973–75), and the State Univ. of N.Y. in Purchase (1973–76); served as ed. of the *Musical Heritage Review* (1977–80). **WORKS: STAGE:** 3 4-minute operas (1947); 3 folk operettas (1947); *Lima Beans*, chamber opera (1954; N.Y., Jan. 7, 1956); *The Infinite*, ballet (1951; N.Y., Feb. 13, 1952). **ORCH.:** *Divertimento* for Strings and Winds (1949); *Fantasy* for Chamber Orch. (1951); *Adagio* for Strings (1956); 2 chamber syms.

(1958, 1961); Sym. for Strings (N.Y., Nov. 29, 1958); 3 chamber concertos: No. 1 for Violin and Strings (1959); No. 2 for Trombone and Strings (1962); No. 3 for Flute, Horns, Piano, and Strings (1971); 2 suites for Strings (1970, 1974); *Fantasy on Motives of Burt Bacharach* (1979); String Sym. No. 2 (1984); *Gentlewoman's Polka* for Band (1985); *Ridgefield Rag* for Band (1985). **CHAMBER:** Septet for Brass (1945); *Ballet Suite* for 3 Clarinets (1953); Duo for 2 Violas (1957); *Tower Music* for Brass Quintet (1959); *Dr. Jolly's Quickstep* for Brass Quintet (1974); piano pieces; also choral works; scores for film and television; folk-song arrangements.

Townshend, Pete(r Dennis Blandford), seeded English rock artist; b. Chiswick, May 19, 1945. He began playing banjo in a Dixieland jazz group, in which another English musician, John Entwhistle (b. Chiswick, Oct. 9, 1946), blew the trumpet. They teamed with the guitarist and vocalist Roger Daltrey (b. Hammersmith, March 1, 1944) and organized a group to which they gave the mysterious-sounding pronominal moniker The Who. The drummer Keith Moon (b. Wembley, Aug. 23, 1947; found dead in his London flat of a sedative overdose, Sept. 7, 1978) joined the group in 1964. Anxious to project a mod image in an alien world, they sported odd clothes, cultivated bizarre behavior, and indulged in maniacal conduct on the stage, which included physical destruction of their instruments in front of the public in the manner of punk rock. Their habit of flaunting loud obscenities and invitations to mayhem aroused the destructive instincts of their audiences. A murderous climax of their career was reached in Cincinnati at their concert of Dec. 3, 1979, when 11 young people were trampled to death in a mad rush for seats. Professing deep sorrow at the loss of life, The Who and their managers did not overlook the commercial advantages of wide publicity attending the incident. In the meantime, Townshend turned to fashionable oriental philosophy, worshiping at the feet of a transient guru, and producing a devotional album, *Who Came First*, with the rock hymns *Pure and Easy* and *Nothing Is Everything*. The Who took part in such media extravaganzas as the outrageous movies *Tommy* and *Quadrophenia*; Daltrey also acted in *Lisztomania*, a film that depicted Liszt as a human attachment to an immense penis used as a seesaw by a bevy of naked females; and Moon tripped around in Frank Zappa's video-movie *200 Motels*. Other influential works by The Who included the song *My Generation*, the psychedelic *I Can See for Miles*, and their album *Who's Next*.

Toyama, Yuzo, Japanese composer; b. Tokyo, May 10, 1931. He graduated from the Tokyo Academy of Music in 1952; studied in Vienna (1958–60); in 1953 he organized (with Mamiya and Hayashi) the group Yagi no Kai with the purpose of promoting Japanese music.

WORKS: STAGE: Chamber opera, *Such a Long Absence* (Osaka, April 3, 1972); musical, *Gion Festival*, for Soloists, Chorus, and Orch. (1966); ballet, *Yugen* (1965). **ORCH.:** *Little Symphony* (1953); *Rhapsody* (1960); *Divertimento* (1961; Prague, Jan. 2, 1962); 2 piano concertos (1962, 1963); 2 violin concertos (1963, 1966); *Fantasy* for Clarinet and String Orch. (1963); *Rhapsody on an Okinawan Melody* (1961); *Toki (War Cry) No. 1* and *Toki No. 2* (1965, 1966); sym., *Homeward* (1966); Cello Concerto (1967); *Kaleidoscope* (1968); *Ofukuro* for Chorus and Strings (1968); *Response*, suite for Chorus and String Orch. (1968–69); sym., *Song of Flame*, for Chorus and Orch. (1970). **CHAMBER:** Trio for Flute, Cello, and Piano (1958); *Chamber Concerto* for Wind Quintet, Piano, Double Bass, Vibraphone, and Percussion (1958); Violin Sonata (1964); *Divertimento* for String Ensemble (1965); *Guzai* for String Quartet (1965); *Meditation* for Violin and Piano (1970). Also vocal works, including a cantata, *Kyoto*, for Soprano, Chorus, Harp, and Orch. (1970); choruses.

Toye, (John) Francis, English writer on music, brother of **(Edward) Geoffrey Toye;** b. Winchester, Jan. 27, 1883; d. Florence, Oct. 31, 1964. He was a pupil of S.P. Waddington and E.J. Dent; became a critic for various newspapers in London; in 1923 he lectured on modern music in the U.S.; from

1939 to 1946, lived in Rio de Janeiro; from 1946, in Florence. **WRITINGS** (all publ. in London unless otherwise given): *The Well-Tempered Musician* (1925); *Giuseppe Verdi: His Life and Works* (1931; 2nd ed., 1962); *Rossini: A Study in Tragi-comedy* (1934; 2nd ed., 1954); *For What We Have Received: An Autobiography* (Melbourne, 1950); *Italian Opera* (1952); *Truly Thankful? A Sequel to an Autobiography* (1957).

Toye, (Edward) Geoffrey, English conductor and composer, brother of **(John) Francis Toye;** b. Winchester, Feb. 17, 1889; d. London, June 11, 1942. He studied at the Royal College of Music in London; became a conductor at various theaters there. He wrote an opera, *The Red Pen* (London, Feb. 7, 1927); a ballet; and some other works.

Tozzi, Giorgio (actually, **George**), gifted American bass of Italian descent; b. Chicago, Jan. 8, 1923. His father was a day laborer. He studied biology at De Paul Univ.; also took vocal lessons in Chicago with Rosa Raisa, Giacomo Rimini, and John Daggett Howell. He made his professional debut in N.Y. in the American premiere of Britten's *The Rape of Lucretia* as the rapist Tarquinius (Dec. 29, 1948). In 1949 he went to Europe, and sang in a musical comedy, *Tough at the Top*, in London. With the earnings obtained through this employment, he financed a trip to Italy, where he took lessons with Giulio Lorandi in Milan. He sang at the Teatro Nuovo in Milan in 1950, and in 1953 appeared at La Scala. He then returned to the U.S.; on March 9, 1955, he made his Metropolitan Opera debut in N.Y. as Alvise in *La Gioconda;* continued to sing at the Metropolitan in a variety of parts, among them Don Giovanni in Mozart's opera, Figaro in *Le nozze di Figaro*, Don Basilio in *Il barbiere di Siviglia*, Méphistophélès in Gounod's *Faust*, Hans Sachs in *Die Meistersinger von Nürnberg*, King Marke in *Tristan und Isolde*, and the title role in *Boris Godunov*. He also made regular appearances with the San Francisco Opera, where he sang for the 1st time on Sept. 15, 1955. He was a guest artist at the Salzburg Festival, and sang at Munich, Hamburg, and other European music centers. A true modern man, he did not spurn the world of musical commerce, and even sang a commercial for the Fiat automobile co., putting on an ancestral Italian accent, albeit of dubious authenticity in his generation.

Trabaci, Giovanni Maria, eminent Italian organist and composer; b. Monte Pelusio, c.1575; d. Naples, Dec. 31, 1647. He settled in Naples, where he was made a tenor at the church of the Annunziata in 1594; later was organist at the Oratorio dei Filippini; was named organist of the royal chapel of the Spanish viceroys in 1601; was maestro di cappella there from 1614 until the end of his life. During the rebellion of the Neapolitan populace against the fruit tax of 1647, Trabaci fled to the monastery of the Trinità degli Spagnuoli, where he died. He is known to have composed 169 sacred vocal works, 60 secular vocal compositions, and 165 keyboard pieces. His greatest contribution was to the keyboard genre; among his works were *Ricercate, canzone francese, capricci, canti fermi, gagliarde, patite diverse, toccate, durezze e ligature, et un madrigale passagiato nel fine* (Naples, 1603; 12 ed. in Monumenti di Musica Italiana, I/3, 1964) and *Il secondo libro de ricercate & altri varij capricci* (Naples, 1615). His canzonas include examples of rhythmic variants of a single theme ("variation canzonas"), anticipating Frescobaldi in this respect. **BIBL.:** W. Apel, "Neapolitan Links between Cabezón and Frescobaldi," *Musical Quarterly* (Oct. 1938); U. Prota-Giurleo, "G.M. T. e gli organisti della real cappella di palazzo di Napoli," *L'organo*, I (1960); R. Jackson, *The Keyboard Music of G.M. T.* (diss., Univ. of Calif., Berkeley, 1964).

Tracy, Hugh (Travers), South African ethnomusicologist; b. Willand, Devon, Jan. 29, 1903; d. Krugersdorp, Transvaal, Oct. 23, 1977. He emigrated to Southern Rhodesia in 1921; in 1929 began to record indigenous songs; from 1930, on advice from Holst and Vaughan Williams, devoted himself to recording folk music from sub-Saharan Africa; also began a career as a broadcaster. He was regional director for Natal of the South

African Broadcasting Corp. (1935–47); was co-founder of the African Music Soc. (1947), serving as its secretary and ed. of its newsletter (1948–53); also ed. the journal *African Music* (1955–71). He established the International Library of African Music in Roodepoort (1953); under his direction, it acquired an important collection of instruments and recordings, largely through his own fieldwork; he also ed. a series of more than 200 commercial recordings from its holdings. Tracey lectured at more than 50 univs. in Africa, Britain, and the U.S., and was awarded an honorary doctorate by the Univ. of Cape Town (1965). His publications and broadcasts were largely concerned with the role of African music in African education, and in the growth and understanding of modern African society.

WRITINGS: *Nyoma: An Introduction to Music for Southern Africans* (London, 1941); *Chopi Musicians: Their Music, Poetry, and Instruments* (London, 1948; 2nd ed., 1970); *African Dances of the Witwatersrand Gold Mines* (Johannesburg, 1952); *The Lion on the Path* (London, 1967).

Traetta, Filippo, Italian-American teacher and composer, son of **Tommaso (Michele Francesco Saverio) Traetta;** b. Venice, Jan. 8, 1777; d. Philadelphia, Jan. 9, 1854. He was a pupil of Fenaroli and Perillo at Venice, later of Piccinni at Naples. Becoming a soldier in the patriot ranks, he was captured and cast into prison; he escaped 6 months afterward, and sailed to Boston, arriving there in 1799; with Mallet and Graupner, he founded Boston's American Conservatorio in 1801. Shortly after he went to Charleston, S.C.; was active in N.Y. as a performer and teacher (1808–17); settled in Philadelphia in 1822 and founded the American Conservatorio. Among his compositions are an opera, *The Venetian Maskers* (n.d.) and 3 oratorios, *Peace* (N.Y., Feb. 21, 1815), *Jerusalem in Affliction* (1828), and *The Daughters of Zion* (1829); also cantatas; piano pieces; songs.

WRITINGS (all publ. in Philadelphia): *An Introduction to the Art and Science of Music* (n.d.); *Rudiments of the Art of Singing, written and composed . . . A. D. 1800* (1841–43); *Trajetta's Preludes for the Piano Forte . . . Introductory to his System of Thorough Bass* (1857).

BIBL.: "F. Trajetta," *Dwight's Journal of Music,* IV (1854).

Traetta, Tommaso (Michele Francesco Saverio), esteemed Italian composer, father of **Filippo Traetta;** b. Bitonto, near Bari, March 30, 1727; d. Venice, April 6, 1779. He entered the Conservatorio di S. Maria di Loreto in Naples at the age of 11, where he studied with Porpora and Durante. After leaving the Cons. in 1748, he wrote his 1st known opera, *Il Farnace,* which was produced at the Teatro San Carlo with fine success, on Nov. 4, 1751; there followed several more operas in Naples, and later in other Italian cities. In 1758 he was appointed maestro di cappella to the Duke of Parma; his *Armida* was staged in Vienna (Jan. 3, 1761) with excellent success, and he was commisioned to write another opera for Vienna, *Ifigenia in Tauride,* which was produced there on Oct. 4, 1763. He settled in Venice in 1765, and was director of the Cons. dell'Ospedaletto S. Giovanni for 3 years. In 1768 he was engaged for the court of Catherine the Great as successor to Galuppi, and arrived in St. Petersburg in the autumn of that year. He staged several of his operas there (mostly versions of works previously performed in Italy); also arranged music for various occasions (anniversary of the coronation of Catherine the Great; celebration of a victory over the Turkish fleet; etc.). He left Russia in 1775 and went to London, where he produced the opera *Germondo* (Jan. 21, 1776), without much success. By 1777 he had returned to Venice, where he produced his last 2 operas, *La disfatta di Dario* (Feb. 1778) and *Gli eroi dei campi Elisi* (Carnival 1779). In many respects, he was an admirable composer, possessing a sense of drama and a fine melodic gift. In musical realism, he adopted certain procedures that Gluck was to employ successfully later on; he was highly regarded by his contemporaries. Besides operas, he wrote an oratorio, *Rex Salomone* (Venice, 1766), a Stabat Mater, and other church music, 3 sinfonie, an overture, etc.

BIBL.: V. Capruzzi, *T. e la musica* (Naples, 1873); A. Nuovo,

T. T. (Rome, 1922); A. Bonaventura, "T. T.," *Pensiero Musicale* (April–May 1927); A. Damerini, "Un precursore italiano di Gluck: T. T.," *Il Pianoforte* (July 1927); idem, "T. T.," *Bollettino Bibliografico Musicale* (July 1927); V. Raeli, "T. T.," *Rivista Nazionale di Musica* (March 1927); idem, "The Bicentenary of T. T.," *Chesterian* (1927); A. Mooser, *Annales de la musique et des musiciens en Russie au XVIIIe siècle* (Vol. II, Geneva, 1951); F. Schlitzer, ed., *T. T., Leonardo Leo, Vincenzo Bellini: Notizie e documenti, Chigiana,* IX (1952); E. Saracino, *T. T.: cenni biografico-artistici* (Bitonto, 1954); F. Casavola, *T. T. di Bitonto (1727–1779): la vita e le opere* (Bari, 1957); D. Binetti, *T. T. nella vita e nell'arte* (1972); S. Martinotti, "T., o il musicista di un'impossibile 'riforma',"*Chigiana,* XXIX-XXX (1975).

Tragó, José, Spanish pianist and pedagogue; b. Madrid, Sept. 25, 1856; d. there, Jan. 3, 1934. He studied at the conservatories of Madrid and Paris, winning 1st prizes for piano at both; was for many years a prof. at the Madrid Cons. He was the teacher of Manuel de Falla and Joaquín Turina.

Trambitsky, Victor (Nikolaievich), Russian pianist, conductor, teacher, and composer; b. Brest-Litovsk, Feb. 12, 1895; d. Leningrad, Aug. 13, 1970. He went to Petrograd, where he began training with Kalafati in 1915, and then became his pupil at the Cons. in 1917. In 1930 he moved to Sverdlovsk; he taught at the Cons. from 1933. He composed the operas *Gadfly* (Sverdlovsk, 1929), *Orlena* (1934; rev. as *For Life,* 1937), *The Storm* (1941; rev. 1957), and *The Laceworker Nastia* (Leningrad, 1963); also Violin Concerto (1921); Sym. (1945); *Symphonic Pictures* (1955); piano pieces; songs; folk-song arrangements.

Trampler, Walter, eminent German-American violist and pedagogue; b. Munich, Aug. 25, 1915. He received his early musical training from his father; later enrolled at the Munich State Academy of Music; made his debut in Munich as a violinist in 1933 and in Berlin as a violist in 1935; from 1935 to 1938, served as 1st violist in the Deutschlandsender orch.; then emigrated to America. From 1947 to 1955 he was a member of the New Music String Quartet; also made appearances with the Yale, Emerson, Budapest, Juilliard, and Guarneri quartets and with the Beaux Arts Trio; was a member of the Chamber Music Society of Lincoln Center (from 1969). In 1962 he was appointed prof. of viola and chamber music at the Juilliard School of Music in N.Y.; in 1971, was named prof. at the Yale Univ. School of Music; in 1972, became a member of the faculty at Boston Univ. One of the foremost masters of the viola, he appeared as a soloist with many of the leading orchs. of North America and Europe. He premiered works by several composers, including Henze, Berio, and Persichetti.

Trần, Van Khê, Vietnamese ethnomusicologist; b. Binh Hoa Dong, July 24, 1921. He studied medicine in Hanoi (1941–43), then went to Paris to attend the Institut d'Études Politiques (1949–51). He studied organology with Schaeffner and musicology with Chailley of the Faculté des Lettres (1952–58), and historical research with Gaspardone at the Collège de France (1954–57); received his doctorate with the dissertation *La Musique vietnamienne traditionelle* (1958; publ. in Paris, 1962). In 1960 he joined the CNRS, where he became director of research in 1973. In 1964 he became director of the Centre d'Études de Musique Orientale, where he taught Vietnamese instrumental performance. He began teaching at the Institut de Musicologie of the Univ. of Paris in 1968. His research focuses on the systematic and comparative study of Asian musical languages. He publ. *Viêt-Nam: Les Traditions musicales* (Paris, 1967).

Tranchell, Peter (Andrew), English composer and teacher; b. Cuddalore, India, July 14, 1922. He studied at King's College, Cambridge (B.A., 1946; Mus.B., 1949; M.A., 1950); taught at the Univ. from 1950 to 1989; was made a Fellow and director of music at Gonville and Caius College, Cambridge, in 1960.

WORKS: STAGE: OPERAS: *The Mayor of Casterbridge* (Cambridge, July 30, 1951); *Zuleika* (1954); *Bacchae* (1956); *Troades* (1957); *Antigone* (1959). **BALLETS:** *Falstaff* (1950); *Fate's Re-*

venge (1951); *Euridice* (1952); *Spring Legend* (1957); *Images of Love* (1964). CONCERT ENTERTAINMENTS: *Daisy Simpkins* for Solo Voices, Chorus, and 2 Pianos (1954); *Murder at the Towers* for Solo Voices, Chorus, and 2 Pianos (1955; rev. 1986); *Aye, aye, Lucian!* for Men's Voices, Men's Chorus, and Piano (1960); *The Mating Season* for Solo Voices, Men's Chorus, and Piano (1962; rev. 1969); *His 1st Mayweek* for Solo Voices, Men's Chorus, and 2 Pianos (1963); *The Robot Emperor* for Men's Voices, Men's Chorus, and Orch. (1965). ORCH.: *Decalogue* for Brass, Percussion, and Organ (1956); *Scherzetto* (1960); *Eclogue* (1962); *Festive Overture* (1966); Concerto Grosso (1972). CHAMBER: Organ Sonata (1958); Organ Sonatina (1968); *Movements* for Flute, Viola, Bassoon, Harpsichord, and Piano (1987); piano pieces. CHORAL: *The Joyous Year* for Chorus and Orch. (1961); *3 Poems of Po Chü-i* for Baritone, Men's Chorus, and Orch. (1964); *Saul's Successor*, cantata for Soloists, Men's Voices, Organ, Percussion, and Timpani (1969); *Te Deum* for Chorus, 2 Violins, Piano, and Organ (1975); choral songs; anthems and carols; Psalms.

Trapp, (Hermann Emil Alfred) Max, German composer and teacher; b. Berlin, Nov. 1, 1887; d. there, May 29, 1971. He studied piano with Ernst von Dohnányi and composition with Paul Juon at the Berlin Hochschule für Musik (1905–11), where he later was on its faculty as a teacher of piano (1920–34); also gave a master class in composition at the Dortmund Cons. (1924–30); in 1929, became a member of the Prussian Academy of Arts in Berlin, where he taught a master class in composition (1934–45); from 1951 to 1953 he taught at the Berlin Cons.; in 1955 he was elected to membership in the Berlin Academy of Arts. His style is neo-Classical with a strong polyphonic texture, in the tradition of Max Reger. He was also active as a landscape painter. **WORKS: ORCH.:** 7 syms., including No. 1, *Sinfonia giocosa* (1915); No. 2 (1918); No. 3 (1924); No. 4 (1931); No. 5 (1936); No. 6 (1946); 3 concertos for Orch. (1934, 1940, 1946); Violin Concerto (1922); Piano Concerto (1930); Cello Concerto (1935); *Allegro deciso* (1942); *Kleine Spielmusik* for Chamber Orch. (1944); *Symphonischer Prolog* (1944). CHAMBER: 2 piano quintets; 3 piano quartets; String Quartet (1935); Violin Sonata; piano pieces; also choral works, including *Vom ewigen Licht* for Soprano, Baritone, Chorus, and Orch. (1942); songs. **BIBL.:** W. Matthes, "M. T.," *Zeitschrift für Musik* (Oct. 1937).

Traubel, Helen (Francesca), noted American soprano; b. St. Louis, June 20, 1899; d. Santa Monica, Calif., July 28, 1972. She studied with Vetta Karst; made her concert debut with the St. Louis Sym. Orch. on Dec. 13, 1923. On May 12, 1937, she made her Metropolitan Opera debut in N.Y. as Mary Rutledge in Damrosch's *The Man without a Country;* her 1st major role there was Sieglinde on Dec. 28, 1939; subsequently became the leading American Wagnerian soprano on its roster, excelling especially as Isolde, Elisabeth, Brünnhilde, Elsa, and Kundry. In 1953 she made appearances in N.Y. nightclubs; this prompted objections from the Metropolitan Opera management, and as a result she resigned from the Metropolitan. She also appeared on Broadway in *Pipe Dream* (1955), in films, and on television. She publ. the mystery novels *The Ptomaine Canary* and *The Metropolitan Opera Murders* (N.Y., 1951), and an autobiography, *St. Louis Woman* (N.Y., 1959).

Traugott, Rohner, Swiss-born American music magazine publisher and music educator; b. St. Gallen, Dec. 23, 1906. His family moved to the U.S. in 1914. He was educated at Central Wesleyan College (degree, 1928) and Northwestern Univ. (M.A., 1932); held teaching positions in Marshall, Minn., and Asheville, N.C., then joined the faculty at Northwestern Univ. (1933–60). He was the founding ed. of 2 important music publications, *The Instrumentalist* (1946) and *Clavier* (1962); also was founding president of the National School Orch. Assoc. at Interlochen, Mich. (1958), and in 1960 organized the National Band Assoc.

Trautwein, Friedrich (Adolf), German electrical engineer; b. Würzburg, Aug. 11, 1888; d. Düsseldorf, Dec. 20, 1956.

He was trained in electrical engineering; then was active in radio work; became a lecturer (1930) and a prof. of musical acoustics (1935) at the Berlin Hochschule für Musik; founded his own composition school in Düsseldorf after World War II, which was made part of the Robert Schumann Cons. in 1950. In 1930 he constructed an electronic musical instrument which became known, after the 1st syllable of his name, as the Trautonium. Hindemith wrote a concerto for it. Trautwein publ. a Trautonium method as *Trautoniumlehre* (1936); also wrote numerous articles on acoustics and electronic music. **BIBL.:** F. Winckel, "F. T.," *Musica*, XI (1957).

Travers, John, English organist and composer; b. probably in Windsor, c.1703; d. London, June 1758. He was probably a chorister of St. George's Chapel, Windsor; was apprenticed to Maurice Greene in 1719; also was a pupil of J.C. Pepusch; was an organist at the Royal Chapel (1737–58). He publ. *The Whole Book of Psalms* for 1 to 5 Voices and Harpsichord (London, c.1746–50) and *18 Canzonets* for 2 to 3 Voices and Harpsichord (London, 1746); also various other sacred and secular works; *12 Voluntaries* for Organ or Harpsichord (London, c.1769).

Travis (real name, **Traywick**), **Randy,** American country-music singer and songwriter; b. Marshville, N.C., May 4, 1959. He received music lessons as a child and began appearing in public at age 10; he dropped out of school when he was 15 to sow his wild oats, which led to various scrapes with the law; all the while, he performed in Charlotte night spots. In 1981 he went to Nashville, where he found employment as a cook and singer in a supper club; taking the stage name of Travis, he 1st attracted favorable notice with his recording of *Prairie Rose,* which was featured on the sound-track album of the film *Rustler's Rhapsody* (1985). As a champion of traditional country music, he hit his stride with the notably successful albums *Storms of Life* (1986), *Always & Forever* (1987), and *Old 8 × 10* (1988). In 1987 he became the youngest member in the history of the Grand Ole Opry in Nashville. In 1989 he toured Europe and Australia. **BIBL.:** *Current Biography* (Sept. 1989); D. Cusic, *R. T.: King of the New Country Traditionalists* (N.Y., 1991).

Travis, Merle (Robert), American country–music singer, guitarist, and songwriter; b. Rosewood, Ky., Nov. 29, 1917; d. Tahlequah, Okla., Oct. 20, 1983. He sang at various clubs and hotels; eventually became a regular performer on WLW radio in Cincinnati. After serving in the Marine Corps during World War II, he went on tour, gaining success with his popular songs *Old Mountain Dew, Dark as a Dungeon, Double Talking Baby,* and *16 Tons.* In 1974 he received the Pioneer of Country Music Award, and in 1977 he was inducted into the Country Music Hall of Fame. He also appeared in several Western movies, among them *Honky Tonk Man* (1982).

Travis, Roy (Elihu), American composer and teacher; b. N.Y., June 24, 1922. He studied with William J. Mitchell and Otto Luening at Columbia Univ. (B.A., 1947; M.A., 1951); also studied privately with Felix Salzer (1947–50), with Bernard Wagenaar at the Juilliard School of Music in N.Y. (B.S., 1949; M.S., 1950), and with Darius Milhaud on a Fulbright scholarship in Paris (1951–52). Returning to the U.S., he held a Guggenheim fellowship (1972–73). He taught at Columbia Univ. (1952–53), the Mannes College of Music (1952–57), and at the Univ. of Calif. at Los Angeles (from 1957), where he was a prof. (from 1968). **WORKS: OPERAS:** *The Passion of Oedipus* (1965; Los Angeles, Nov. 8, 1968); *The Black Bacchants* (1982). ORCH.: *Symphonic Allegro* (1951); *Collage* (1967–68); Piano Concerto (1969). CHAMBER: String Quartet (1958); Duo concertante for Violin and Piano (1967); *Barma,* septet for Flute or Piccolo, Piano, Clarinet, Violin, Cello, Double Bass, and Percussion (1968); *Switched-on Ashanti* for Flute or Piccolo and Tape (1973); also piano pieces, including a Sonata No. 1 (1954); songs.

Traxel, Josef, German tenor; b. Mainz, Sept. 29, 1916; d. Stuttgart, Oct. 8, 1975. He studied at the Hochschule für Musik in Darmstadt; then made his debut as Don Ottavio in Mainz in 1942; in 1946 he joined the Nuremberg Opera; from 1952 he was a member of the Württemberg State Theater in Stuttgart; later taught at the Hochschule für Musik there. He also sang at Salzburg, Bayreuth, Berlin, Vienna, and Munich; toured North America as well. His opera repertoire ranged from Mozart to Wagner; he was also a concert singer.

Trebelli, Zélia (real name, **Gloria Caroline Gillebert**), noted French mezzo-soprano; b. Paris, 1838; d. Étretat, Aug. 18, 1892. She took up the study of voice at 16 with Wartel; in 1859 made her operatic debut as Rosina in *Il Barbiere di Siviglia* in Madrid; sang at the Berlin Royal Opera in 1860 and at the Théâtre-Italien in Paris in 1861. On May 6, 1862, she made her 1st appearance in London in *Lucrezia Borgia* at Her Majesty's Theatre, remaining a London favorite for a quarter of a century. She sang Siebel in *Faust* (June 11, 1863), Taven in *Mireille* (July 5, 1864), and Preziosilla in *La forza del destino* (June 22, 1867) at their London premieres; appeared at Drury Lane (1868–70), where she sang Frederick in the London premiere of *Mignon* (July 5, 1870); sang at Covent Garden (1868–71; 1881–82; 1888). She toured the U.S. with Mapleson's company in 1878; on Oct. 26, 1883, she made her Metropolitan Opera debut in N.Y. as Azucena, remaining on the company's roster until 1884. She retired from the operatic stage in 1888. Her husband was the tenor Alessandro Bettini.
BIBL.: M. de Mensiaux, *T.: A Biographical Sketch* (London, 1890).

Treger, Charles, American violinist, teacher, and administrator; b. Detroit, May 13, 1935. He studied with William Engels (1944–52), Szymon Goldberg, Ivan Galamian, and William Kroll; made his debut as a soloist in the Wieniawski 2nd Violin Concerto when he was 11; after winning the Wieniawski Competition in Warsaw in 1962, he toured Europe as soloist with the Pittsburgh Sym. Orch. (1964); in 1969 was a founding member of the Chamber Music Soc. of Lincoln Center, with which he remained active until 1973; from 1978 he toured widely with André Watts. He became a visiting prof. at the Hartt School of Music in Hartford, Conn., in 1972, and also gave master classes; in 1984 he was named president and director of the Meadowmount School in Westport, Conn. Treger has won accolades for his championship of neglected works from the violin repertoire.

Tregian, Francis, English musician; b. 1574; d. London, 1619. He was a recusant, and fled England to escape persecution; was attached to Catholic dignitaries in Douai and in Rome. Returning to England to settle his father's estate, he was convicted in 1609, remaining in prison until his death. His significance for English music lies in the fact that he was the scribe of the *Fitzwilliam Virginal Book* (ed. by J. Fuller Maitland and W. Squire, London and Leipzig, 1894–99) and of 2 MSS containing more than 2,000 motets, madrigals, etc., some of them of his own composition.
BIBL.: E. Cole, "In Search of F. T.," *Music & Letters* (Jan. 1952); P. Willetts, "T.'s Part-books," *Musical Times*, CIV (1963).

Treharne, Bryceson, English-American music editor and composer; b. Merthyr Tydfil, Wales, May 30, 1879; d. N.Y., Feb. 4, 1948. He studied at the Royal College of Music in London, under Parry, Stanford, and Davies. In 1901 he went to Australia; was a prof. at the Univ. of Adelaide; returning to Europe in 1911, he lived in Paris, Milan, Vienna, and Munich; at the outbreak of World War I, he was interned in Ruhleben. There he wrote nearly 200 songs and other works; an exchange of prisoners of war enabled him to return to England. In 1917 he settled in America; was music ed. for the Boston Music Co. and Willis Music Co. (1928–47). Among his songs are *Ozymandias, The Fair Circassian, A Lover's Prayer, The Night, Dreams, Love's Tribute,* and *Renunciation.*

Treigle, Norman, remarkable American bass-baritone; b. New Orleans, March 6, 1927; d. there, Feb. 16, 1975. He sang in a church choir as a child; upon graduation from high school in 1943, he served in the navy. After two years in service, he returned to New Orleans and studied voice with Elizabeth Wood; made his debut in 1947 with the New Orleans Opera as Lodovico in Verdi's *Otello.* He then joined the N.Y. City Opera, making his debut there on March 28, 1953, as Colline in *La Bohème;* he remained with the co. for 20 years, establishing himself as a favorite with the public. Among his most successful roles were Figaro in Mozart's *Le nozze di Figaro,* Don Giovanni, Méphistophélès, and Boris Godunov; he also sang in modern operas, including the leading parts in the world premieres of 3 operas by Carlisle Floyd: *The Passion of Jonathan Wade* (N.Y., Oct. 11, 1962), *The Sojourner and Mollie Sinclair* (Raleigh, N.C., Dec. 2, 1963), and *Markheim* (New Orleans, March 31, 1966). Treigle's other parts in contemporary operas were the title role in Dallapiccola's *The Prisoner* and that of the grandfather in Copland's *The Tender Land.* His untimely death, from an overdose of sleeping pills, deprived the American musical theater of one of its finest talents.

Treitler, Leo, German-born American musicologist; b. Dortmund, Jan. 26, 1931. He emigrated to the U.S. and became a naturalized citizen in 1946; studied at the Univ. of Chicago (B.A., 1950; M.A., 1957); after training in composition from Blacher at the Berlin Hochschule für Musik (1957–58), he pursued studies in musicology at Princeton Univ. (M.F.A., 1960; Ph.D., 1966, with the diss. *The Aquitanian Repertories of Sacred Monody in the 11th and 12th Centuries*). He taught briefly at Princeton Univ. (1960–61) and more extensively at the Univ. of Chicago (1962–66) and Brandeis Univ. (1966–75). In 1974 he became a prof. at the State Univ. of N.Y. at Stony Brook, and in 1987 a Distinguished Prof. at the City Univ. of N.Y. Graduate Center. His valuable articles on the music of the Middle Ages and early Renaissance have appeared in many scholarly journals. He publ. *Music and the Historical Imagination* (1989).

Tremblay, George (Amedée), Canadian-born American pianist, teacher, and composer; b. Ottawa, Jan. 14, 1911; d. Tijuana, Mexico, July 14, 1982. He studied music with his father, a church organist; in 1919 he was taken to the U.S.; eventually settled in Los Angeles; there he met Schoenberg (1936) and became his ardent disciple and friend. In 1939 he became a naturalized U.S. citizen. He adopted the method of composition with 12-tones, which he diversified considerably, expounding his theoretical ideas in a book, *The Definitive Cycle of the 12-Tone Row and its Application in all Fields of Composition, including the Computer* (1974). He became an esteemed teacher; among his students were André Previn, Quincy Jones, and Johnny Mandel, as well as numerous successful composers for television and motion pictures.
WORKS: ORCH.: *Chaparral Symphony* (1938); *Sym. in One Movement* (1949); *Sym. No. 2* (1952); *Prelude, Aria, Fugue and Postlude* for Symphonic Band (1967); *Sym. No. 3* (1973); *The Phoenix: A Dance Symphony* (1982). **CHAMBER:** Wind Sextet (1968); 2 wind quintets (1940, 1950); 4 string quartets (1936–63); Piano Quartet (1958); Quartet for Oboe, Clarinet, Bassoon, and Viola (1964); Piano Trio (1959); String Trio (1964); Duo for Viola and Piano (1966); Double-bass Sonata (1967); 3 piano sonatas; other piano works.

Tremblay, Gilles, Canadian composer; b. Arvida, Quebec, Sept. 6, 1932. He had private lessons with Jocelyne Binet, Edmond Trudel, and Gabriel Cusson; also received training in piano from Germaine Malépart at the Montreal Cons. (1949–54; premier prix, 1953) and took private composition lessons with Claude Champagne; then entered the Paris Cons., where he studied analysis with Messiaen (premier prix, 1957), piano and composition with Loriod, and Ondes Martenot with Martenot (Première Médaille, 1958); also obtained a license in counterpoint from the École Normale Supérieure de Musique (1958); worked with the Groupe de Recherches Musicales at the ORTF in Paris (1959), and attended the Darmstadt summer courses in new music given by Boulez and Pousseur (1960). In subsequent years he was active as a composer, teacher, and lecturer in Canada. He follows the modern French method of composition and uses graphic notation in his scores.

WORKS: *Double Quintet* for Winds (1950); *Cantique de durées* for Orch. (1960; Paris, March 24, 1963); *Champs I* for Piano and 2 Percussionists (1965; rev. 1969); *Kéboka* for Vocal Soloists, Ondes Martenot, and Percussion (1965; Montreal, Feb. 25, 1966); *Sonorisation du Pavillon du Québec*, 24-track stereophonic piece (Expo '67, Montreal, 1967); *Souffles: Champs II* for 2 Flutes, Oboe, Clarinet, Horn, 2 Trumpets, 2 Trombones, Double Bass, Piano, and 2 Percussion (Montreal, March 21, 1968); *Vers: Champs III* for 2 Flutes, Clarinet, Horn, Trumpet, 3 Violins, Double Bass, and 3 Percussion (Stratford, Ontario, Aug. 2, 1969); *. . . le sifflement des vents porteurs de l'amour* for Flute, Percussion, and 4 Microphones (Ottawa, March 1, 1971); *Solstices (ou Les Jours et les saisons tournent)* for Flute, Clarinet, Horn, Double Bass, and 2 Percussion (1971; Montreal, May 17, 1972); *Jeux de Solstices* for Violin, Flute, Clarinet, Trumpet, and Orch. (Ottawa, April 23, 1974); *Oralléluiants* for Soprano, Flute, Bass Clarinet, Horn, 3 Double Basses, 2 or 3 Percussion, and Amplification (Toronto, Feb. 8, 1975); *Fleuves* for Orch. (1976; Montreal, May 3, 1977); *Vers le soleil* for Orch. (Paris, March 11, 1978); *Compostelle I* for Orch. (Paris, Nov. 30, 1978); *DZEI (voies de feu)* for Soprano, Flute, Bass Clarinet, Piano, and Percussion (Vancouver, April 12, 1981); *Envoi*, concerto for Piano and 15 Instruments (Montreal, Feb. 17, 1983); *Triojubilus (à Raphael)* for Flute, Harp, and Cowbells (1985); *Les Vêpres de la Vierge* for Soprano, Chorus, and 13 Instruments (Abbaye de Sylvanes, France, Aug. 20, 1986); *Un 9* for Mime, 2 Trumpets, and 2 Percussion (Montreal, April 9, 1987); *Katadrone: Contrecri* for Orch. (Montreal, Oct. 19, 1988); *Cèdres en voiles* for Cello (1989).

Trento, Vittorio, Italian composer; b. Venice, 1761; d. probably in Lisbon, 1833. He was a pupil of Bertoni at the Cons. dei Mendicanti in Venice; produced several ballets at Venice, followed by a number of cantatas, farces, and comic operas; returned to Venice to serve as maestro al cembalo at the Teatro La Fenice. He served as maestro concertatore of the Italian Opera in Amsterdam (from 1806); then took up a similar post in Lisbon in 1809. His most popular stage work was the opera buffa *Quanti casi in un sol giorno, ossia Gli assassini* (Venice, 1801), which was also given in London, as *Roberto l'assassino* (Feb. 3, 1807). Other operas include *Teresa vedova* (Venice, Jan. 13, 1802), *Ines de Castro* (Livorno, Nov. 9, 1803), *Ifigenia in Aulide* (Naples, Nov. 4, 1804), *Andromeda* (Naples, May 30, 1805), and *Le Gelosie villane* (Florence, Nov. 2, 1825). He also wrote 6 cantatas, some sacred vocal pieces, 6 string quartets, and 2 duets for 2 Violins.

Treptow, Günther (Otto Walther), German tenor; b. Berlin, Oct. 22, 1907; d. there, March 28, 1981. He studied at the Berlin Hochschule für Musik; made his debut in 1936 at the Deutsches Opernhaus in Berlin as the Italian Tenor in *Der Rosenkavalier*. Although placed on the forbidden list of non-Aryans by the Nazis, he continued to sing in Berlin until 1942, when he joined the Bavarian State Opera in Munich. After the Nazi collapse, he again sang in Berlin at the Städtische Oper (1945–50) and at the Vienna State Opera (1947–55); appeared as Siegmund in 1951 and 1952 at the Bayreuth Festival and as Siegfried at London's Covent Garden in 1953. He made his Metropolitan Opera debut in N.Y. as Siegmund in *Die Walküre* on Feb. 1, 1951; remained on its roster until the close of that season; continued to sing in Europe until his retirement in 1961. In 1971 he was made a Kammersänger.

Tretyakov, Viktor (Viktorovich), noted Russian violinist; b. Krasnoyarsk, Oct. 17, 1946. He studied at the Irkutsk Music School as a child, stoutly braving the Siberian cold; then moved to a more temperate climate in Moscow, where he studied at the Central Music School with Yury Yankelevich (from 1959), continuing with him at the Cons. (graduated, 1970) and as a postgraduate student. In 1966 he won the Tchaikovsky Compe-

tition, which automatically lifted him to the upper layers of the violinistic firmament, with applause-rich tours in Russia and later the enviable European and American engagements. A typical product of the Russian school of violin playing, Tretyakov combines the expected virtuosity in technical resources with a diffuse lyricism touched with melancholy in the Romantic repertoire.

Treu, Daniel Gottlob, German composer; b. Stuttgart, 1695; d. Breslau, Aug. 7, 1749. He learned to sing and to play the violin and keyboard as a child, and also received training in composition from Johann Kusser; about 1716 he went to Venice to pursue training with Vivaldi and Biffi. In 1725 he became Kapellmeister to an Italian opera troupe in Breslau, where he brought out 4 of his own operas: *Astaro* (1725), *Caio Martio Coriolano* (1726), *Ulisse e Telemacco* (1726), and *Don Chisciotte* (1727). In 1727 he went to Prague, where he served several families of the nobility as Kapellmeister, instrumentalist, and composer; also was active at the Viennese and Silesian courts, and in Breslau. In 1740 he was made Kapellmeister to the court of Karl Schaffgotsch of Hirschberg in Silesia; he eventually settled in Breslau. Among his other works were violin concertos, serenatas, wind partitas, sonatas, sacred music, and arias, most of which are lost.

Tréville, Yvonne de (real name, **Edyth La Gierse**), American soprano; b. Galveston, Tex. (of a French father and an American mother), Aug. 25, 1881; d. N.Y., Jan. 25, 1954. She made her debut in N.Y. as Marguérite (1898); then went to Paris, where she studied with Madame Marchesi; appeared at the Opéra-Comique as Lakmé (June 20, 1902); sang in Madrid, Brussels, Vienna, Budapest, Cairo, and in Russia; from 1913, gave concert tours in the U.S. and sang in light operas. Her voice had a compass of 3 full octaves, reaching high G.

Trial, family of French musicians and actors:

(1) Jean-Claude Trial, violinist and composer; b. Avignon, Dec. 13, 1732; d. Paris, June 23, 1771. A child prodigy, he began playing violin and composing for the instrument at an early age; then settled in Paris as 1st violinist in the Opéra-Comique orch.; after serving as 2nd violinist in the private orch. of Prince Conti, he was made its director; was co-director (with Pierre Berton) of the Paris Opéra (1767–69).

WORKS: STAGE: *Renaud d'Ast*, opéra comique (Fontainebleau, Oct. 12, 1765; in collaboration with P. Vachon); *Silvie*, opéra-ballet (Fontainebleau, Oct. 17, 1765; in collaboration with P. Berton); *Escope à Cythère*, comédie (Paris, Dec. 15, 1766; in collaboration with P. Vachon); *Thénois, ou Le Toucher*, pastorale héroïque (Fontainebleau, Oct. 11, 1767; in collaboration with P. Berton and L. Granier); *La Fête de Flore*, pastorale héroïque (Fontainebleau, Nov. 15, 1770); *La Chercheuse d'esprit*, comédie (1771); *Linus*, opera (unfinished; in collaboration with P. Berton and A. Dauvergne); also overtures, divertissements, violin pieces, cantatas, and ariettes.

(2) Antoine Trial, tenor and actor, brother of the preceding; b. Avignon, 1737; d. (suicide) Paris, Feb. 5, 1795. He received his education at the maîtrise at Avignon Cathedral; went to Paris and became a member of the Prince of Conti's theater troupe; made his public debut in Paris as Bastien in Philidor's *Le Sorcier* at the Comédie-Italienne (July 4, 1764); became well known for his portrayal of peasants and simpletons. He was a champion of Robespierre and played a prominent role in the period of the Reign of Terror; after Robespierre's downfall in 1794, he lost his following on the stage and took his own life by poison. His wife was the soprano and actress **Marie-Jeanne** (née Milon) **Trial** (b. Paris, Aug. 1, 1746; d. Versailles, Feb. 13, 1818); after vocal training, she made her debut at the Théâtre-Italien in Paris under the name Félicité Mandeville in 1766; following her 1st husband's death, she married Trial and became a popular favorite on the Parisian stage; poor health led to her retirement in 1786. She was particularly esteemed for her performances in works by Grétry and Monsigny. Their son, **Armand-Emmanuel Trial** (*fils*) (b. Paris, March 1, 1771; d. there, Sept. 9, 1803), was a pianist and composer; he began composing for the Comédie-Italienne when he was 17; was director of singing at the Théâtre-Lyrique (from 1797); his dissolute ways led to an early demise. His works, all 1st performed in Paris, included *Julien et Colette, ou La Milice,* comédie (March 3, 1788); *Adélaide et Mirval, ou La Vengeance paternelle* (June 6, 1791); *Les Deux Petits aveugles,* opéra comique (July 28, 1792); *Cécile et Julien, ou Le Siège de Lille,* comédie (Nov. 21, 1792); *Le Congrés des rois,* opera (Feb. 26, 1793; in collaboration with others); and *La Cause et les effets, ou Le Reveil du peuple,* opéra comique (Aug. 17, 1793).

Trifunović, Vitomir, Serbian composer; b. Bukovica, Nov. 4, 1916. He studied composition with Slavenski and Živković at the Belgrade Academy of Music; became an ed. for new music at Radio Belgrade in 1959. His early music is Romantic, but later he acquired a thoroughly modern sound.

Works: Piano Sonatina (1956); Violin Sonata (1958); 2 string quartets (1959, 1973); *Šumadija,* suite for Chamber Orch. (1960); *Lamentoso* for String Orch. (1961); *Heroic Overture* (1962); *Toccata* for Orch. (1963); *Simfonijska slika* (Symphonic Picture; 1964); *Folklorni triptih* (Folklore Triptychon) for Orch. (1961); *Symphonic Dance* (1968); *Synthesen 4* for Orch. (1969); cantata, *Vidici* (The Horizons; 1971); *Antinomije* for Orch. (1972); *Asocijacije* (Associations) for Orch. (1973); arrangements of folk music.

Trimble, Lester (Albert), American music critic, teacher, and composer; b. Bangor, Wis., Aug. 29, 1920; d. N.Y., Dec. 31, 1986. He began violin studies in Milwaukee when he was 9; later studied with Lopatnikoff and Dorian at the Carnegie Inst. of Technology in Pittsburgh (B.F.A., 1948; M.F.A.); also studied with Milhaud and Copland at the Berkshire Music Center at Tanglewood, and then with Boulanger, Milhaud, and Honegger in Paris (1950–52). He began writing music criticism for the *Pittsburgh Post-Gazette* while in school; then was a music critic for the *N.Y. Herald-Tribune* (1952–62), the *Nation* (1957–62), the *Washington Evening Star* (1963–68), and *Stereo Review* (1968–74); also was managing ed. of *Musical America* (1960–61). He was composer-in-residence of the N.Y. Phil. (1967–68) and at the Wolf Trap Farm Park (1973). He was prof. of composition at the Univ. of Maryland (1963–68) and taught at N.Y.'s Juilliard School (from 1971).

Works: dramatic: *Boccaccio's Nightingale,* opera (1958–62; rev. 1983); *Little Clay Cart,* incidental music for Oboe and Percussion (1953); *The Tragical History of Dr. Faustus,* incidental music for 5 Woodwinds and Percussion (1954). **orch.:** 3 syms.: No. 1 (1951); No. 2 (1968); No. 3, *The Tricentennial* (1984–85; Troy, N.Y., Sept. 26, 1986); Concerto for Wind and Strings (1954); *Closing Piece* (1957; rev. as *Sonic Landscape,* 1967); 5 *Episodes* (1961–62; also for Piano); *Notturno* for Strings (1967; arranged from his String Quartet No. 2); Duo Concertante for 2 Violins and Orch. (1968); *Panels I* for 11 Instruments (1969–70), *II* for 13 Instruments (1971–72), and *IV* for 16 Instruments (1973–74; orig. a ballet); *Panels for Orchestra* (1976; rev. 1983); Violin Concerto (1976–81); works for Band. **chamber:** 2 string quartets (1949, 1955); Woodwind Serenade (1952); Double Concerto for Instrumental Ensemble (1964); *Panels V* for String Quartet (1974–75), *VI: Quadraphonics* for Percussion Quartet (1974–75), and *VII: Serenade* for Oboe, Clarinet, Horn, Harpsichord, Violin, Viola, Cello, and Percussion (1975); also choruses; song cycles; solo songs; film scores; electronic pieces.

Trimpin, (Gerhard), German-born inventor, practitioner, and builder of soundsculpture and computerized acoustical instruments; b. Istein bei Lörrach, Basel, Nov. 26, 1951. Professionally he is known by only his surname. He had an ordinary musical training, with an emphasis on playing wind instruments, but recurrent lip infections forced him to abandon such labial practices; he then studied electronic engineering. In 1979 he received a degree in social pedagogy; later was an instructor at the Sweelinck Cons. in Amsterdam (1985–87). He designed 4 *Bowed Cymbals* for Ton de Leeuw's *Resonances* (1987). He also designed a percussive installation of 96 suspended Dutch wooden shoes for the 1986 New Music Festival

in Middelburg; in 1987 designed a similar installation, *Floating Klompen,* at the Jan van Eyck Art Academy in Maastricht. He also collaborated with Conlon Nancarrow on keyboard techniques in Mexico City (1988). He originated his own composition entitled *Circumference* for specially adapted instruments (1989). In 1979 he set up in Seattle a Faustian-looking workshop, a laboratory filled with synchronously and anachronously activated sound objects. In 1989 he participated in the "Composer-to-Composer" symposium in Telluride, Colo., and in 1990 was artist-in-residence at the Banff Art Center. When not engaged in musical endeavors, Trimpin periodically engages in one of his other specialties, fishing. He proved surprisingly apt at catching a lot of salmon on their journey upstream to their place of birth—a talent that paid well when he was out of work.

Tristano, "Lennie" (Leonard Joseph), famous American jazz pianist and teacher; b. Chicago, March 19, 1919; d. N.Y., Nov. 18, 1978. He became blind in childhood but did not allow this handicap to deflect him from a study of music; he attended the American Cons. of Music in Chicago (B.Mus., 1943); after performing in Chicago clubs, he settled in N.Y. in 1946; attracted wide notice with his own sextet in 1947; ran his own jazz school (1951–56) and then taught privately; also made occasional appearances as a performer, touring Europe in 1965 and the U.S. in 1968. He was a master at piano improvisations.

Bibl.: J. McKinney, *The Pedagogy of L. T.* (diss., Fairleigh Dickinson Univ., 1978); L. Feather, "Piano Giants of Jazz: L. T.," *Contemporary Keyboard,* VI/1 (1980).

Tritonius, Petrus (real name, **Peter Treybenreif**), esteemed Austrian composer; b. Bozen, c.1465; d. probably in Hall, Tirol, c.1525. After studies at the Univ. of Vienna (1486), he matriculated at the Univ. of Ingolstadt (1497); it was about this time that he took the name Petrus Tritonius and became associated with the humanist Conradus Celtis. He then was active as a Latin teacher in the Tirol; after taking a doctorate at the Univ. of Padua (1502), he went to Vienna as a teacher; then served as director of the Lateinschule in Bozen (1508–12); later was active in Halle and Schwaz am Inn. He composed a distinguished set of Horatian odes, *Melopoiae sive harmoniae tetracenticae super XXII genera carminum Heroicorum Elegiacorum Lyricorum et ecclesiasticorum hymnorum* (Augsburg, 1507; 2nd ed., 1507; 3rd ed., 1532; 4th ed., 1551), which exercised influence on German composers in the 16th century.

Tritto, Giacomo (Domenico Mario Antonio Pasquale Giuseppe), Italian composer and teacher; b. Altamura, April 2, 1733; d. Naples, Sept. 16, 1824. He studied with Cafaro at the Cons. della Pietà de' Turchini in Naples; became maestrino there and Cafaro's assistant; was made maestro straordinario in 1785, secondo maestro in 1793, and primo maestro in 1799. In 1804 he was appointed maestro of the royal chamber. Bellini, Spontini, Mercadante, Meyerbeer, and Conti were his pupils. He wrote over 50 operas, both comic and serious; many were produced in various Neapolitan theaters, and others in Rome, Madrid, Vienna, and Venice; however, they were generally undistinguished. He also composed much sacred music. He publ. *Partimenti e regole generali per conoscere qual numerica dar si deve ai vari movimenti del basso* (Milan, 1821) and *Scuola di contrappunto, ossia Teoria musicale* (Milan, 1823).

Bibl.: F. Florimo, *La scuola musicale di Napoli ed i suoi conservatorii,* III (Naples, 1882); G. de Napoli, "G. T.," *La Lettura* (Oct. 1924); idem, *La triade melodrammatica altamurana: G. T., Vincenzo Lavigna, Saverio Mercandante* (Milan, 1931).

Trneček, Hanuš, Bohemian harpist, pianist, pedagogue, and composer; b. Prague, May 16, 1858; d. there, March 28, 1914. He studied at the Prague Cons.; was harpist in the Schwerin Court Orch. (1882–88); then taught harp and piano at the Prague Cons. He wrote some fine works for solo harp and didactic piano pieces which were widely known.

Works: operas: *Der Geigenmacher von Cremona* (Schwerin, April 16, 1886); *Amaranta* (1884–89; Prague, Nov. 16, 1890); *Andrea Crini* (1898; Prague, Feb. 2, 1900). ORCH.: 3 syms.; 2 suites; 2 violin concertos; Piano Concerto; Clarinet Concerto; Flute Concerto. CHAMBER: 2 piano quintets; Piano Quartet; pieces for Violin, Cello, and Harp; Violin Sonata; solo harp pieces; much piano music, including over 50 études.

Trojahn, Manfred, German composer; b. Cremlingen, near Braunschweig, Oct. 22, 1949. He studied flute in Braunschweig (1966–70); then studied at the Hochschule für Musik in Hamburg (1970–78); also took private lessons in composition with Diether de la Motte (1970–73). His music is neo-Baroque in form and programmatic in content; his songs are expressionistic in their chromatic Angst.

WORKS: ORCH.: 3 syms.: No. 1, *Makramee* (1973); No. 2 (Donaueschingen, Oct. 22, 1978); No. 3 (1982–83; Berlin, April 19, 1985); *Notturni trasognati* for Alto Flute and Orch. (London, June 13, 1977); *Conduct,* 2nd version, for Strings and Percussion (1978; Gelsenkirchen, May 14, 1979; 1st version is for Organ Solo); *Abschied,* fragment (1978; Düsseldorf, Oct. 18, 1979); Flute Concerto (1977–83; Berlin, Sept. 14, 1983); *Berceuse* (1980); *Erstes See-Bild* (1979–80; U.S. premiere, N.Y., Feb. 24, 1983); *. . . une campagne noire de soleil,* 7 ballet scenes (1986); *Variationen* (1987); *L'autunno, Sonata per gli amici* (1987); *Cinq épigraphes* (1987); *Processions* (1987); *La nuit* (1988). VOCAL: *Risse des Himmels,* 4 songs for Soprano, Flute, and Guitar (1968–74); *Architectura Caelestis* for 8 Female Voices and Orch. (1974–76); *. . . stiller Gefährt der Nacht,* chamber music after a poem by Klopstock, for Soprano, Flute, Cello, Percussion, and Celesta (1978); *Elegía del tiempo final* for Tenor and 7 Instruments (1981–82); *Zweites See-Bild,* subtitled *Schatten von Kähnen,* after a poem by Georg Haym, for Mezzo-soprano and Orch. (1981); Requiem (1983–85; Braunschweig, Nov. 10, 1985). CHAMBER: *Les Couleurs de la pluie* for 5 Flutes and Alto Flute (1972); *Kammerkonzert* for 8 Instruments (1973); *2 Brief Pieces* for String Quartet (1973); 3 string quartets: No. 1 (1976); No. 2, with Clarinet and Mezzo-soprano (1979–80); No. 3 (1983); *Fantasia* for Guitar (1979); Violin Sonata (1982); Cello Sonata (1983); *Solares* for Piano and String Quartet (1985); *Preludes* for Piano (1985).

Trojan, Václav, Czech composer; b. Pilsen, April 24, 1907; d. Prague, July 5, 1983. He studied composition with Křička and Alois Hába, and conducting with Ostrčil and Dědeček at the Prague Cons., graduating in 1929. He dedicated himself mainly to light music for the theater; many of his pieces are humorous in intent.

WORKS: 2 string quintets (1928, 1929); Wind Quintet on folk themes (1935); children's opera, *Kolotoč* (The Merry-go-round; 1936–40; Ostrava, 1960); *Pohádky* (Fairy Tales) for Accordion and Orch. (1959); *Sinfonietta armoniosa* for Chamber Orch. (1971); *Capricious Variations* for Trombone, Saxophone, and Orch. (1971); "stage poem" with dance, *The Golden Gate* (1973; Prague, Feb. 17, 1974); *4 Caricatures (and One Extra)* for Wind Orch., Percussion, and Piano (1974); Concertino for Trumpet and Chamber Orch. (1977); *Divertimento* for Wind Quintet (1977); *Noneto Favoloso* for Wind Quintet and String Quartet (1977); *Sen noci svátojanské* (A Midsummer Night's Dream), ballet-pantomime after Shakespeare (1982); film music.

Trombetti (real name, **Cavallari**), **Ascanio,** Italian cornett player and composer; b. Bologna (baptized), Nov. 27, 1544; d. (murdered) there, Sept. 20 or 21, 1590. He made appearances as a cornett player in the cappella musicale at S. Petronio (from 1560), where he held a regular position (from 1573); also was maestro di cappella at the church of S. Giovanni in Monte (1583–89). He became intimate with the wife of a book dealer whose husband took his revenge by killing him. Trombetti was an especially skillful composer of secular vocal works, which included *Il primo libro delle napolitane* for 3 Voices (Venice, 1573), *Il primo libro di madrigali* for 5 Voices (Venice, 1583), *Il primo libro di madrigali* for 4 Voices (Venice, 1586), and *Musica fatta sopra le conclusioni di legge difese dall'Illustre Sig. Alessandro Viustini piacentino* (Bologna, 1587); also other

works in contemporary collections. Among his sacred works is *Il primo libro de motetti accomodati per cantare e far concerti a 5–8, 10, 12* (Venice, 1589).

Trombly, Preston (Andrew), American composer; b. Hartford, Conn., Dec. 30, 1945. He studied composition with Whittenberg at the Univ. of Conn. (B.M., 1968), with Arel and Davidovsky at Yale Univ. (M.M.A., 1972), and with Crumb at the Berkshire Music Center at Tanglewood; also had some instruction in conducting from Bernstein and Barzin; then devoted himself to teaching and composing.

WORKS: ORCH.: *Set for Jazz Orchestra* (1968); *Doubles* (1970); *Music for the Theatre* (1972); Chamber Concerto for Piano and 11 Instruments (1975). CHAMBER: Woodwind Quintet (1968); *Opera/Septima* for Flute, Oboe, Bass Clarinet, Trumpet, Violin, Viola, and Cello (1969–70); *Music* for Violin, Viola, and Cello (1970); *In memoriam: Igor Stravinsky* for Woodwind Quartet, Viola, and Double Bass (1972); *Trio in 3 Movements* for Flute, Double Bass, and Percussion (1973); *Trio da camera* for Flute, Cello, and Piano (1975); *The Windmills of Paris* for Flute, Clarinet, Violin, Cello, and Piano (1976); *The Bridge: 3 Pieces after Hart Crane* for Clarinet, Saxophone, Cello, and Piano (1979); String Quartet (1979); *Time of the Supple Iris* for Viola, Double Bass, Oboe or English Horn, Bass Clarinet, and Percussion (1980); *Aurora Quartet* for Oboe, Violin, Cello, and Harpsichord (1983–84). WITH TAPE: *Kinetics III* for Flute (1971); *G.H.M.T.S.* for Flute, Clarinet, Double Bass, and Vibraphone (1971–72); *Fantasy* for Cello (1974); *Toccata* for Trombone (1974); *The Trumpets of Solitude* for Flute, Clarinet, Violin, Cello, and Piano (1982).

Tromboncino, Bartolomeo, important Italian composer; b. in or near Verona, c.1470; d. in or near Venice, c.1535. He was active in Mantua until 1489, when he went to Florence; in 1494 he returned to Mantua, where he was active at the court; also traveled to other courts. His association with the Mantuan court was a stormy one, even though he was held in high esteem there; he fled the court in 1495 and went to Venice, but returned that same year. When he discovered his wife entertaining a lover in 1499, he murdered her; he appears, however, to have been pardoned at his trial. In 1501 he left Mantua again and made his way to Ferrara, where he was in the service of Lucrezia Borgia until 1508. He remained in Ferrara until at least 1513; in 1521 he went to Venice. Tromboncino was one of the leading composers of secular music of his era, producing over 150 frottolas. He also wrote some sacred music, including Lamentations and laude.

Tromlitz, Johann Georg, German flutist, teacher, instrument designer, and composer; b. Reinsdorf über Artern, Nov. 8, 1725; d. Leipzig, Feb. 4, 1805. He began his training in Gera before settling in Leipzig, where he took courses in law at the Univ. and earned the title of Imperial Public Notary; was 1st flutist in Hiller's Grosses Konzert (from 1754); also toured as a virtuoso; about 1775 he gave up public appearances and devoted himself to teaching and working to improve the flute. His extant compositions comprise 3 *concerts* for Flute and String Quartet, and several sonatas for Keyboard, Cello, and Flute or Violin.

WRITINGS: *Kurze Abhandlung vom Flötenspielen* (Leipzig, 1786); *Ausführlicher und gründlicher Unterricht die Flöte zu spielen* (Leipzig, 1791); *Über die Flöten mit mehrern Klappen* (Leipzig, 1800); the 2 preceding were later publ. as *Flötenschule.*

BIBL.: F. Demmler, *J.G. T.* (diss., Free Univ. of Berlin, 1961); P. Bate, *The Flute* (London, 1969); T. Warner, "T.'s Flute Treatise: A Neglected Source of Eighteenth-century Performance Practice," *A Musical Offering: Essays in Honor of Martin Bernstein* (N.Y., 1977).

Trotère (real name, **Trotter**), **Henry,** English song composer; b. London, Dec. 14, 1855; d. there, April 10, 1912. Some of his songs that enjoyed success were *Once for All, Léonore, Ever dear, Asthore, The Deathless Army,* and *Love can wait.*

Troyanos, Tatiana, brilliant American mezzo-soprano; b. N.Y., Sept. 12, 1938. She received her musical training at the Juilliard School of Music in N.Y. and from Hans Heinz; made her operatic debut as Hippolyta in *A Midsummer Night's Dream* at the N.Y. City Opera on April 25, 1963. She was a member of the Hamburg State Opera (1965–75), where she created the role of Jeanne in *The Devils of Louden* (1969). In 1969 she sang at Covent Garden in London; in 1971 she was engaged at the Paris Opéra; that same year she appeared as Ariodante in the 1st operatic production at the Kennedy Center in Washington, D.C. On March 8, 1976, she made a memorable Metropolitan Opera debut in N.Y. as Octavian in *Der Rosenkavalier;* in subsequent seasons she became one of the company's leading members. Among her outstanding roles are Cherubino, Dorabella, Carmen, Adalgisa, Kundry, Poppea, the Composer, and Charlotte.

Truax, Barry, Canadian composer; b. Chatham, Ontario, May 10, 1947. He studied physics and mathematics at Queen's Univ., Kingston (B.S., 1969); became interested in electronic sounds and pursued training with Cortland Hultberg at the Univ. of British Columbia (M.M., 1971); completed his studies with O. Laske and G. Koenig at the Inst. of Sonology in Utrecht. In 1973 he became associated with R. Murray Schafer through the World Soundscape Project in Vancouver; was director of the Sonic Research Studio and assistant prof. in the dept. of communication at Simon Fraser Univ. (1976–83), where he subsequently was associate prof.; also was associate prof. in the Centre for the Arts. He publ. *Handbook for Acoustic Ecology* (1978) and *Acoustic Communication* (1985).

Works: dramatic: *The Little Prince* for Narrator, Vocal Soloists, and Tape, after Saint-Exupéry (1971); *Gilgamesh* for Voices, Narrator, Chorus, Sopranino Recorder, Oboe, Dancers, and Tape (1972–74). **with tape:** *Hexameron* for Flute, Clarinet, Horn, Viola, and Piano (1970); *Children* for Soprano (1970); *From the Steppenwolf* for 12 Singers (1970); *Sonic Landscape No. 1* for Horn (1970), *No. 2* for Flute and Piano (1971), and *No. 4* for Organ (1977); *Nautilus* for Percussion (1976); *Aerial* for Horn (1979); *East Wind* for Amplified Recorder (1981); *Letter to My Grandmother* for Voice (1981); *Nightwatch* for Marimba (1982); *Étude* for Cello (1983–84); *Tongues of Angels* for Oboe d'Amore and English Horn (1988); also works for computer graphic slides and tape, including *Divan* (1985) and *Wings of Nike* (1987); solo tape pieces; vocal works; piano pieces.

Trudić, Božidar, Serbian composer; b. Smederevska Palanka, March 24, 1911. He studied with Slavenski; became a teacher in Sarajevo. His music is inspired by Serbian folk songs, but the harmonic treatment is often modernistic. Among his works are a cantata, *1804* (Sarajevo, Dec. 26, 1956); Violin Concerto (1951); Cello Concerto (1952); 2 syms. (1946, 1957); choruses and songs.

Truhn, Friedrich Hieronymus, German composer and writer on music; b. Elbing, Nov. 14, 1811; d. Berlin, April 30, 1886. He studied with Dehn, Klein, and Mendelssohn; wrote for the Leipzig *Neue Zeitschrift für Musik;* lived chiefly in Berlin, where he founded and conducted the Neue Liedertafel.

Works: Marionette opera, *Der baierische Hiesel* (Berlin, 1832); operetta, *Der vierjährige Posten* (1833); comic opera, *Trilby* (Berlin, May 22, 1835); melodrama, *Kleopatra* (Berlin, 1853).

Truinet. See Nuitter.

Trunk, Richard, German pianist, conductor, music critic, and composer; b. Tauberbischofsheim, Baden, Feb. 10, 1879; d. Herrsching-am-Ammersee, June 2, 1968. He studied with Iwan Knorr at the Hoch Cons. in Frankfurt am Main (1894–95) and with Rheinberger at the Munich Academy of Music (1896–99). He was then active as a choral conductor and music critic in Munich; went to Cologne in 1925 as director of the Rheinische Hochschule für Musik and as a prof. at the Staatliche Hochschule für Musik; also was active as a choral conductor; from 1934 to 1945, was president of the Munich Academy of Music and also director of the Lehrergesangverein (1934–

39). He was a prolific composer of choral music; also wrote a singspiel, *Herzdame* (Munich, 1917), as well as orch. pieces and chamber music; also over 200 lieder.

Bibl.: A. Ott, *R. T.: Leben und Werk* (Munich, 1964).

Trutovsky, Vasili (Fyodorovich), Russian composer and folk-song collector; b. Ivanovskaya Sloboda, c.1740; d. St. Petersburg, 1810. He was the son of an Orthodox priest; was a court singer and player on the *gusli* during the reigns of Elizabeth, Peter III, and Catherine II. His historic achievement was the compilation of the 1st comprehensive collection of Russian folk songs, in 4 fascicles (1776, 1778, 1779, 1795). He also was the 1st in Russia to publ. piano pieces; the earlier publications of Russian piano music were anonymous. His *Chanson russe variée* for Harpsichord or Piano (St. Petersburg, 1780) was ed. by A. Drozdov and T. Trofimov (Moscow, 1946).

Trythall, (Harry) Gil(bert), American composer and teacher, brother of **Richard Trythall;** b. Knoxville, Tenn., Oct. 28, 1930. He studied theory and composition with David Van Vactor at the Univ. of Tennessee (B.A., 1951), composition with Wallingford Riegger at Northwestern Univ. (M.Mus., 1952), and composition with Robert Palmer and musicology with Donald Grout at Cornell Univ. (D.M.A., 1960). He was assistant prof. at Knox College in Galesburg, Ill. (1960–64); after serving as prof. of theory and composition (1964–75) and chairman of the music school (1973–75) at George Peabody College for Teachers in Nashville, he was prof. of music (from 1975) and dean of the creative arts center (1975–81) at West Virginia Univ. in Morgantown. He publ. *Principles and Practices of Electronic Music* (N.Y., 1974).

Works: operas: *The Music Lesson,* opera buffa (1960); *The Terminal Opera* (1982; rev. 1987). **orch.:** *A Solemn Chant* for String Orch. (1955); Sym. No. 1 (1958; rev. 1963); Harp Concerto (1963); *Dionysia* (1964); *Chroma I* (1970); *Cindy the Synthe (Minnie the Moog)* for Synthesizer and Strings (1975). **chamber:** Flute Sonata (1964); *A Vacuum Soprano* for Brass Quintet and Tape (1966); *Entropy* for Brass, Harp, Celesta, Piano, and Tape (1967); *Parallax* for 4 to 40 Brass, Tape, Audience, and Slide Projection (1968); *Echospace* for Brass and Tape (1973); piano pieces; organ works. **vocal:** *In the Presence* for Chorus and Tape (1969); *Spanish Songs* for Soprano and Synthesizer (1986–87); Mass in English and Spanish for Congregation, Organ, and Descant (1988); also electronic, mixed-media, and film music.

Trythall, Richard, American pianist and composer, brother of **(Harry) Gil(bert) Trythall;** b. Knoxville, Tenn., July 25, 1939. He studied with David Van Vactor at the Univ. of Tennessee (B.M., 1961) and with Roger Sessions, Earl Kim, and Edward Cone at Princeton Univ. (M.F.A., 1963); then continued his training at the Berlin Hochschule für Musik on a Fulbright fellowship (1963–64); held a Guggenheim fellowship (1967–68). He settled in Rome, where he became a teacher at St. Stephen's School in 1966 and music liaison at the American Academy in 1975. As a pianist, Trythall is a determined champion of modern music and has performed scores ranging from Ives to Stockhausen.

Works: orch.: Sym. (1961); *Composition* for Piano and Orch. (1965); *Penelope's Monologue* for Soprano and Orch. (1966); *Costruzione* (1967); *Continuums* (1968). **chamber:** Duets for Treble Instruments (1958); Suite for Harpsichord and Tape (1973); *Variations on a Theme by Haydn* for Woodwind Quintet and Tape (1976); *Salute to the '50s* for Percussionist and Tape (1977); *Bolero* for 4 Percussion (1979); piano pieces; tape works, including *Study No. 1* (1967) and *Omaggio a Jerry Lee Lewis* (1975); vocal works, including *4 Songs* for Soprano and Piano (1962).

Tschirch, (Friedrich) Wilhelm, German choral conductor and composer; b. Lichtenau, June 8, 1818; d. Gera, Jan. 6, 1892. He was a pupil at the Royal Inst. for Church Music, Berlin; was music director at Liegnitz (1843–52) and then court conductor at Gera. By invitation of German-American choral societies he visited the U.S. in 1869, and produced many of his celebrated men's choruses at N.Y., Philadelphia, Baltimore, Washington, D.C., and Chicago. He publ. salon pieces for piano under the pseudonym Alexander Czersky.

Tschudi or **Shudi, Burkhard.** See **Broadwood & Sons.**

Tsfasman, Alexander, Russian jazz bandleader; b. Alexandrovsk, Ukraine, Dec. 14, 1906; d. Moscow, Feb. 20, 1971. He studied piano with Felix Blumenfeld at the Moscow Cons. In 1926 he organized a jazz band in Moscow, and from 1939 to 1946 was music director of the All-Union Radio Jazz Band; he toured with it all over Russia. He also composed a Concerto for Piano and Jazz Band, and numerous popular songs.

Tsintsadze, Sulkhan, Russian composer and cellist; b. Gori, Aug. 23, 1925. He studied cello and composition at the Moscow Cons.; in 1963 joined the faculty of the Tbilisi Cons. In his music he emphasizes ethnic elements, presenting them in congenial modal harmonies. In 1966 he joined the Communist party.
WORKS: STAGE: OPERAS: *The Golden Fleece* (1953); *The Hermit* (1972). **BALLETS:** *The Treasure of the Blue Mountain* (1956); *The Demon,* after Lermontov's poem (1961). **ORCH.:** *Georgian Rhapsody* for Violin and Orch. (1955); 2 violin concertos (1947, 1968); 2 cello concertos (1947, 1964); 2 piano concertos (1949, 1968); 3 suites for String Orch. (1948, 1950, 1955); 4 syms. (1952, 1963, 1969, 1979). **CHAMBER:** 9 string quartets (1947–78). **PIANO:** *24 Preludes* (1980); also an oratorio, *Immortality,* for the centenary of Lenin's birth (1970).

Tsontakis, George, American composer; b. N.Y., Oct. 24, 1951. He studied at the Juilliard School in N.Y. (1978–86); attended a seminar given by Stockhausen in Rome (1981) and also took private lessons with Sessions (1974–79). He was an assistant to the electronic faculty at the Juilliard School (1978) and an assistant prof. at the Brooklyn College Cons. of Music (1986–87). In 1987 he received the Koussevitzky Foundation orchestral commission.
WORKS: ORCH.: *5 Sighs and a Fantasy* (N.Y., Oct. 20, 1984); *Fantasia Habanera* (Baltimore, May 28, 1986); *Overture Vera* (1988); *To the Sowers of the Seed* (Aspen, Colo., Aug. 18, 1989). **CHAMBER:** 4 string quartets: No. 1, *The Mother's Hymn,* with Mezzo-soprano (1980); No. 2, *Emerson* (N.Y., April 29, 1984); No. 3, *Coraggio* (Aspen, Colo., July 26, 1986); No. 4, *Beneath the Tenderness of Thy Heart* (N.Y., Jan. 17, 1989); *3 Sighs, 3* variations for Violin (Haywood, Calif., Sept. 25, 1981); *Preludio ed Fantasia* for Cello, Brass Quintet, Piano, and Timpani (N.Y., May 22, 1983); *Birdwind Quintet* for Wind Quintet (Aspen, Colo., July 10, 1983); Brass Quintet (N.Y., April 18, 1984); *The Past, The Passion* for 14–15 Players (N.Y., March 4, 1987); *Mercurial Etudes* for Flute (N.Y., Dec. 7, 1988); *3 Mood Sketches* for Wind Quintet (Leningrad, Nov. 22, 1989); *Heartsounds,* quintet for Piano and Strings (Cambridge, Mass., April 20, 1990). **VOCAL: SACRED:** *Scenes from the Apocalypse* for Vocal Soloists, Actor, Chorus, and Orch. (1978); *The Epistle of James,* Chapter 1 for Reader, Chorus, and Orch. (1980); *5 Choral Sketches on "Is Aghios"* (One, Holy) for Chorus, with Clarinet obbligato (N.Y., May 22, 1984); *Saviors* for Soprano, Chorus, and Orch. (N.Y., May 11, 1985); *Byzantium Kanon* for Chorus and Brass Quintet (N.Y., June 1, 1986); *3 Byzantine Hymns* for Chorus and Brass Quintet (1988); *Stabat Mater* for Soprano, Chorus, and Orch. (N.Y., May 19, 1990). **SECULAR:** *Erotokritos,* oratorio for Chorus and Orch. (N.Y., May 15, 1982); *Galway Kinnell Songs* for Mezzo-soprano, Piano, and String Quartet (N.Y., Feb. 4, 1987).

Tsoupaki, Calliope, Greek pianist and composer; b. Piraeus, May 27, 1963. She studied piano, harmony, counterpoint, and fugue in Athens; then entered the composition class of Yannis Ionnithis at the Nikos Skalkottas Cons. (1985); in 1988 she settled in The Hague, where she continued her studies with Louis Andriessen and with Gilus van Bergeyk and Dick Raaijmakers (electronic composition) at the Royal Cons.; also attended summer courses with Xenakis (1985), Messiaen (1987), and Boulez (1988) at Darmstadt.
WORKS: *Eclipse* for Orch. (1986); *Earinon* for 8 Horns and

Percussion (1986); *Krystallina Ymenea* for Chamber Ensemble (1986); *Touch of a Silent Echo* for Oboe, Viola, Cello, Percussion, and Piano (1987); *Silver Moments* for 2 Pianos and 2 Percussion Players (1987); *Nocturnal Sounds . . . and the Ivy Leafs Are Trembling* for Cello and Piano (1988); *Music for Saxophone Quartet* (1989); *Your Thought* for Voice, Tape, and Lighting (1989); *Visions of the Night* for Amplified Ensemble (1989); *Paraklitikon* for Vocal Ensemble (1990); *When I Was 27* for Amplified Viola and Contrabass (1990); also numerous solo pieces, including *Orfikon* for Viola (1986), *Mania* for Amplified Violin (1988), and *Greek Dance* for Piano (1990).

Tsouyopoulos, Georges, Greek composer; b. Athens, Oct. 11, 1930. He received his early training in Athens and Milan; then went to Zürich to study with Hindemith. In 1962 he settled in Munich. His early compositions are neo-Classical in style; later he adopted serial methods, determinedly pursuing the goal of structural indeterminacy.
WORKS: *Sinfonietta da camera* for 8 Instruments (1955); *Serenata* for Soprano, Flute, Guitar, and Viola (1957); *2 madrigali* for Soprano and Orch. (1957); *3 frammenti* for Chorus and Orch. (1958); *3 toccatas* for Piano (1958, 1959, 1965); *Music for Percussion* (1959); 2 string quartets; vocal pieces.

Tsuji, Shōichi, Japanese musicologist; b. Gifu, Dec. 20, 1895; d. Tokyo, April 21, 1987. He took a degree in psychology at Tokyo Univ. (1920); studied composition and conducting with Ryūtarō Hirota, violin with Shin Kusakawa, and gagaku with Yoshiisa Oku. He taught at St. Paul's Univ., Tokyo (1922–65); lectured at Tokyo Univ., the Tokyo National Univ. of Fine Arts and Music, and Kyūshū Univ. In 1968 he became a prof. at Kunitachi Music College. Tsuji, the 1st important Japanese scholar to specialize in Western music, introduced musicology to Japan. He specialized in J.S. Bach and Protestant church music, and wrote biographies of Bach, Mozart, and Schubert. He was one of the founders of the Japanese Musicological Soc.; served as its president (1964–70). After his death, St. Paul's Univ. instituted the annual Tsuji Shōichi Award for achievement in the enhancement of Christian music studies and/or performance.

Tsukatani, Akihirô, Japanese composer; b. Tokyo, March 16, 1919. He graduated in law from Tokyo Univ. in 1941 and became a prof. in the history of economics there; concurrently he took lessons in music theory from Saburo Moroi. In 1949, with Yoritsuné Matsudaira, he organized the Shin Sakkyokuka Kyokai (New Composers' Association); taught music at Tokyo Univ.
WORKS: 3 operas: *Pongo,* based on a Japanese Noh drama (1965); *Ajatasatru* (1966); *Kakitsubata* (Tokyo, May 24, 1967); a musical, *Fairy's Cap,* for Chorus, Piano, and Percussion (Tokyo, Dec. 9, 1968); *Saiten* (Festival), symphonic suite (1950); *Mythology of Today,* ballet suite (1956); *Suite* for Percussion and String Orch. (1960); Piano Concerto (1961); *Japan Festival Dance Music* for Chamber Orch. (1969); Sonata for Flute, Cello, and Piano (1949); Clarinet Sonata (1952); *Suite* for Horn, Trumpet, Trombone, and Timpani (1959); *Fu 1* and *2* for Flute (1970); *3 Worlds* for Flute (1971–72); *2 Movements* for Cello (1972); *Fantasia* for Violin, Piano, and Tam-tam (1973); *Oracle* for Nonet (1983); *Composition* for Oboe and Piano (1984); *Images* for Ondes Martenot, Flute, Oboe, and String Quartet (1987); *2 Compositions* for Oboe (1988); choruses; songs.

Tsvetanov, Tsvetan, Bulgarian composer and teacher; b. Sofia, Nov. 6, 1931; d. Paris, April 4, 1982. He studied composition with P. Hadzhiev and P. Vladigerov at the Bulgarian State Cons. in Sofia (graduated, 1956); in 1958 he joined its faculty, becoming a prof. in composition and harmony in 1976; also was its rector (1976–80); served as secretary of the Union of Bulgarian Composers (1969–75; 1976–80).
WORKS: BALLET: *Orpheus and Rodopa* (1960; also an orch. suite). **ORCH.:** Sinfonietta (1956); *The Great Beginning,* symphonic poem for Narrator and Orch. (1961–63); 4 syms.: No. 1 (1965); No. 2 (1968); No. 3, *1923* (1972); No. 4 for Chamber Orch. (1975); *Overture* (1968); Concertino for Piano and Cham-

ber Orch. (1970); *Overture of Joy* (1971); *Festive Concerto* (1974); Symphonic Variations (1976); *Back to the Feat,* symphonic poem for Narrator and String Orch. (1977). **CHAMBER:** Variations for String Quartet (1953); Violin Sonata (1955); Piano Sonata (1961); Cello Sonata (1973). **VOCAL:** *The Staircase,* ballad for Alto, Men's Chorus, and Orch. (1966); *Ballad of Botev's Kiss,* poem for Chorus and Orch. (1973); *Immortality,* oratorio (1981); also incidental music for plays, film scores, songs, vocal works for amateurs, folk-song transcriptions, etc.

Tua, Teresina (actually, **Maria Felicità**), Italian violinist; b. Turin, May 22, 1867; d. Rome, Oct. 29, 1955. She studied with Massart at the Paris Cons., where she took the 1st prize in 1880; toured the Continent with brilliant success; made her English debut at the Crystal Palace in London, May 5, 1883; appeared in America (1887). In 1889 she married Count Franchi-Verney della Valetta, and withdrew from the concert stage till the autumn of 1895, when she set out on a successful European tour, including Russia, where her accompanist and joint artist was Rachmaninoff. Franchi died in 1911; in 1913 she married Emilio Quadrio. She taught at the Milan Cons. from 1915 to 1924, and then at the Accademia di Santa Cecilia in Rome; subsequently abandoned her career, and entered the Convento dell'Adorazione in Rome as Sister Maria di Gesù.

Tubb, Carrie (actually, **Caroline Elizabeth**), English soprano; b. London, May 17, 1876; d. there, Sept. 20, 1976, at the age of 100. She studied at the Guildhall School of Music in London; began her career singing in a vocal quartet during her student days; after winning notice as an oratorio singer, she appeared at Covent Garden and at His Majesty's Theatre in London (1910); however, she soon abandoned opera and pursued a career as a concert artist until her retirement in 1930; in the latter year she became a prof. at the Guildhall School of Music, where she taught for almost 30 years. She excelled both in Mozart arias and in concert excerpts from Wagner and Verdi. At the zenith of her career, her singing was described in glowing superlatives by such otherwise sober auditors as Eric Blom. As her voice betrayed the inexorable signs of senescence, she applied herself to teaching, following G.B. Shaw's dictum, "Who can, do; who cannot, teach."

Tubb, Ernest (Dale), American country-music singer, guitarist, and songwriter; b. near Crisp, Tex., Feb. 9, 1914; d. Nashville, Tenn., Sept. 6, 1984. Following in the path of Jimmie Rodgers, he became a leading figure in the development of the "western swing" or "honky-tonk" style of country-western music; his recording of *Walking the Floor over You* in 1941 established his reputation; from 1942 he made regular appearances on the "Grand Ole Opry" radio program in Nashville. In 1965 he was elected to the Country Music Hall of Fame.
   BIBL.: N. Barthel, *E. T.: The Original E. T.* (Roland, Okla., 1984).

Tubin, Eduard, Estonian-born Swedish composer and conductor; b. Kallaste, near Tartu, June 18, 1905; d. Stockholm, Nov. 17, 1982. He studied with A. Kapp at the Tartu Cons. and later with Kodály in Budapest. From 1931 to 1944 he conducted the Vanemuine Theater Orch. in Tartu; in 1944 he settled in Stockholm. In 1961 he became a naturalized Swedish citizen; in 1982 he was elected to the Royal Swedish Academy of Music. He was at work on his 11th Sym. at the time of his death.
   WORKS: STAGE: Operas: *Barbara von Tisenhusen* (Tallinn, Dec. 4, 1969); *Prosten från Reigi* (The Priest from Reigi; 1971). **BALLET:** *Skratten* (Laughter; 1939–41). **ORCH.:** 10 syms.: No. 1 (1934); No. 2, *Legendary* (1937); No. 3 (1942; Tallinn, Feb. 26, 1943); No. 4, *Lyrical* (1943; Tallinn, April 16, 1944; rev. 1978; Bergen, Nov. 5, 1981); No. 5 (1946); No. 6 (1954); No. 7 (1958); No. 8 (1966); No. 9, *Sinfonia semplice* (1969; Stockholm, Nov. 20, 1971); No. 10 (1973); *Estonian Dance Suite* for Orch. (1938); 2 violin concertos (1942, 1945); *Concertino* for Piano and Orch. (1944–46); Double-bass Concerto (1948); Balalaika Concerto (1964). **CHAMBER:** 2 violin sonatas (1936, 1949); Saxophone Sonata (1951); Solo Violin Sonata

(1962); Viola Sonata (1965); *Capriccio* for Violin and Piano (1971); 10 preludes for Piano (1928–76); Flute Sonata (1979); *Suite on Estonian Dance Tunes* for Solo Violin (1979); *Quartet on Estonian Motifs* for String Quartet (1979). **VOCAL:** 5 *Kosjalaulud* for Baritone and Orch. (1975); *Ylermi,* ballad for Baritone and Orch. (1935; rev. 1977); *Requiem for Fallen Soldiers* for Alto, Male Chorus, Solo Trumpet, Percussion, and Organ (1979).

Tucci, Gabriella, noted Italian soprano; b. Rome, Aug. 4, 1929. She studied at the Accademia di Santa Cecilia in Rome, and then with Leonardo Filoni, who became her husband. In 1951 she won the international singing competition in Spoleto; after appearances in provincial Italian opera houses, she sang at La Scala in Milan and at the Rome Opera. On Sept. 25, 1959, she made her American debut as Madeleine in *Andrea Chénier* at the San Francisco Opera; her Metropolitan Opera debut followed in N.Y. on Oct. 29, 1960, as Cio-Cio-San in *Madama Butterfly.* She continued to sing at the Metropolitan with increasing success; especially noted were her appearances as Desdemona (March 10, 1963), Marguerite in Gounod's *Faust* (Sept. 27, 1965), and Mimi in *La Bohème* (April 16, 1966). Her other roles were Violetta, Aida, Tosca, Gilda in *Rigoletto,* and Liù in *Turandot.* Her European career was equally successful; she sang at Covent Garden in London, at San Carlo in Naples, at the Vienna State Opera, at the Deutsche Oper in Berlin, at the Bavarian State Opera in Munich, at the Bolshoi Theatre in Moscow, at the Teatro Colón in Buenos Aires, and in Japan. She taught at the Indiana Univ. School of Music in Bloomington (from 1983).

Tucker (originally, **Abuza**), **Sophie,** popular American entertainer; b. in Russia, Jan. 13, 1884; d. N.Y., Feb. 9, 1966. She was taken to the U.S. in infancy; began her career as a singer in her father's restaurant in Hartford, Conn.; then sang in burlesque, vaudeville, and English music halls; gained fame during the World War I era, and remained a popular entertainer for some 60 years; she continued her professional appearances in nightclubs, in films, and on radio and television. She was well known for her rendition of *Some of These Days,* which became her theme song.

Tucker, Richard (real name, **Reuben Ticker**), brilliant American tenor; b. N.Y., Aug. 28, 1913; d. Kalamazoo, Mich., Jan. 8, 1975. He sang in a synagogue choir in N.Y. as a child; studied voice with Paul Althouse; subsequently sang on the radio. His 1st public appearance in opera was as Alfredo in *La Traviata* in 1943 with the Salmaggi Co. in N.Y. On Jan. 25, 1945, he made his Metropolitan Opera debut in N.Y. as Enzo in *La Gioconda;* he remained on its roster until his death, specializing in the Italian repertoire. In 1947 he made his European debut at the Verona Arena as Enzo (Maria Callas made her Italian debut as Gioconda in the same performance); he also sang at Covent Garden in London, at La Scala in Milan, in Vienna, and in other major music centers abroad. He died while on a concert tour. He was the brother-in-law of the American tenor **Jan Peerce.**
   BIBL.: J. Drake, *R. T.: a Biography* (N.Y., 1984).

Tuckerman, Samuel Parkman, American organist and composer; b. Boston, Feb. 11, 1819; d. Newport, R.I., June 30, 1890. He was a pupil of Carl Zeuner in Boston; later studied in Europe. After serving as organist and choirmaster at St. Paul's Church in Boston (1840–49), he studied in London, where he received the Lambeth Mus.D. in 1851, and then in Rome, where he obtained a diploma from the Accademia di Santa Cecilia in 1852. He then returned to his duties at St. Paul's; after another English sojourn (1856–50), he went to N.Y. as organist at Trinity Church in 1864. He wrote various anthems and services; publ. in Boston the following works: *Episcopal Harp* (1844); with H. Oliver and S. Bancroft, *National Lyre* (1848); also *A Collection of Cathedral Chants* (1858) and an ed. of Edward Hodge's *Trinity Collection of Church Music* (1864).

Tuckey, William, English-American singer, singing teacher, and composer; b. Somerset, 1708; d. Philadelphia, Sept. 14,

1781. He claimed to have been a vicar-choral at Bristol Cathedral before going to N.Y. in 1753, where he was active as a singer and singing teacher until 1773; also conducted what was probably the 1st American performance of Handel's *Messiah* (Jan. 16, 1770; overture and 16 numbers). About 1773 he settled in Philadelphia, where he was made clerk at St. Peter's Church in 1778. He wrote several hymn tunes.

BIBL.: O. Sonneck, *Early Concert-Life in America (1731–1800)* (Leipzig, 1907); A. Aaron, "W. T., a Choirmaster in Colonial New York," *Musical Quarterly* (Jan. 1978).

Tuckwell, Barry (Emmanuel), noted Australian horn player and conductor; b. Melbourne, March 5, 1931. He was taught piano by his father and violin by his older brother; was a chorister at St. Andrew's Cathedral in Sydney, and also acted as an organist there. At age 13 he began studying the horn with Alan Mann at the Sydney Cons.; making rapid progress, he played in the Sydney Sym. Orch. (1947–50). He then went to England, where he received valuable advice on horn technique from Dennis Brain; he also gathered some ideas about horn sound from listening to recordings by Tommy Dorsey. He filled positions as assistant 1st horn with the Hallé Orch. in Manchester (1951–53), with the Scottish National Orch. (1953–54), and, as 1st horn, with the Bournemouth Sym. Orch. (1954–55); then served for 13 years (1955–68) as 1st horn player with the London Sym. Orch. He subsequently launched a solo career, achieving recognition as one of the foremost virtuosos on the instrument. In the academic field, he compiled a horn method and ed. horn literature. Several modern composers wrote special works for him: Thea Musgrave (a Concerto that requires the horn to play quarter-tones); Richard Rodney Bennett (*Actaeon* for Horn and Orch.); Iain Hamilton (*Voyage* for Horn and Orch.); Alun Hoddinott (Concerto); and Don Banks (Concerto). He also pursued a career as a conductor, making guest appearances in Australia, Europe, and the U.S. He was conductor of the Tasmanian Sym. Orch. (1980–83); was music director of the newly-founded Maryland Sym. Orch. in Hagerstown (from 1982). In 1965 he was made an Officer of the Order of the British Empire.

BIBL.: W. Sargeant, "Profiles: Something I Could Do," *New Yorker* (March 14, 1977).

Tudor, David (Eugene), American pianist and composer; b. Philadelphia, Jan. 20, 1926. At the age of 11, he encountered one of Messiaen's organ compositions, an occasion marking the beginning of his devotion to the music of his time. He studied piano with Josef Marin and Irma Wolpe Rademacher, organ and theory with H. William Hawke, and composition and analysis with Stefan Wolpe. His role as a pioneer performer of new music was established as early as 1950, when he gave the U.S. premiere of Boulez's 2nd Piano Sonata (N.Y., Dec. 17, 1950). He also began a close association with John Cage, whose works he propagated in the U.S., Europe, and Japan. Tudor evolved imaginative and virtuosic solutions to the challenges of avant-garde works through a rigorous preparation process, distilling compositions that incorporated some degree of indeterminacy into more conventional notation for performance through the refining apparatus of measurements, calculations, conversion tables, and intricate computations. A special technique he applied in performing 5 *Piano Pieces for David Tudor* by Sylvano Bussotti was to put on thick leather gloves for tone-clusters. After mastering the problems unique to avant-garde music, Tudor moved gradually into another pioneer territory, live electronic music. In 1953 he became affiliated with the Merce Cunningham Dance Co., for which he produced numerous works, including *RainForest I* (1968), *Toneburst* (1974), *Forest Speech* (1976), *Weatherings* (1978), *Phonemes* (1981), *Sextet for 7* (1982), *Fragments* (1984), *Webwork* (1987), *5 Stone Wind* (with Cage and Takehisa Kosugi; 1988), and *Virtual Focus* (1990). He was also a member of the summer faculty of Black Mountain College (1951–53), and taught courses in piano and new music performance at the Internationale Ferienkurse für Neue Musik at Darmstadt (1956, 1958, 1959, 1961). He gave courses in live electronic music at the

State Univ. of N.Y. at Buffalo (1965–66), the Univ. of Calif. at Davis (1967), Mills College in Oakland, Calif. (1967–68), and the National Inst. of Design in Ahmedabad, India (1969). In 1968 he was selected as one of 4 Core Artists for the design and construction of the Pepsico Pavilion at Expo '70 in Osaka. Some of his biographers claim for him a direct descent, through a morganatic line, from Henry Tudor (Henry VII), and/or from one of the decapitated lovers of the beheaded Queen Anne Boleyn. Since Henry VII himself dabbled about in "aleatorick musick," Tudor's own preoccupation with tonal indeterminacy could be construed by people of easy imagination as a recessive royal trait.

WORKS: *Fluorescent Sound* (Stockholm, Sept. 13, 1964); *Bandoneon!* for Factorial Bandoneon, idempotentially multiplied ad infinitum (1966); *Reunion* (with John Cage, Lowell Cross, Marcel and Teeny Duchamp, and Gordon Mumma; 1968); *Pepsi Bird, Pepscillator,* and *Anima Pepsi* (1970); *Untitled* (1972); *Melodics* (1972); *RainForest III* (1972); *RainForest IV* (1973); *Microphone (1–9)* (1973); *Laser Bird* and *Laser Rock* (1973); *Photocell Action* (with light composition by Anthony Martin; 1974); *Island Eye Island Ear,* sound and fog environment (with Fujiko Nakaya; 1974–78); *Pulsars* (1976); *Pulsars 2* (1978); *Likeness to Voices/Dialects* (1982); *Sea Tails* (with film by Molly Davies and underwater kites by Jackie Matisse; 1983); *Hedgehog* (1985); *Tailing Dream* (with video by Jackie Matisse; 1985); *Electronics W/Talking Shrimp* (1986); *9 Lines, Reflected* (1986); *For "Bye, Bye, Kipling"* (with Jackie Matisse; 1986); *Line & Cluster* (1986); *Web for J.C., Web for J.C. II,* and *Electronic Web* (1987); *Volatils with Sonic Reflections* (with aluminum kites by Jackie Matisse; 1988).

Tudoran, Ionel, Rumanian tenor; b. Baragtii de Vede, June 24, 1913. He studied at the Iaşi Cons.; made his debut as Roland in Ziehrer's *Landstreicher* in 1936 in Iaşi; then sang with the Cluj Opera (1937–48) and the Bucharest Opera (1948–63); also made guest appearances in Prague, Leipzig, Berlin, Dresden, Moscow, and other music centers. He retired in 1963 and taught voice at the Bucharest Cons. His finest roles were Don José, Faust, and Cavaradossi.

Tudway, Thomas, English organist, music transcriber, and composer; b. c.1650; d. Cambridge, Nov. 23, 1726. He was a chorister at the Chapel Royal; served as organist at King's College, Cambridge (1670–1706; 1707–26); also was master of the choristers there (1670–80) and later was Univ. organist and organist at Pembroke College. In 1681 he took the Mus. B. degree at Cambridge; in 1705 the Univ. resuscitated the title of prof. of music for him and granted him the Mus.D. degree. He composed services, motets, and anthems; his *Collection of Services and Anthems used in the Church of England from the Reformation to the Restoration of King Charles II,* in 6 MS vols., is in the British Museum.

BIBL.: E. Turnbull, "T. T. and the Harleian Collection," *Journal of the American Musicological Society,* VII (1955).

Tufts, John, American minister and pioneer compiler of church music; b. Medford, Mass., Feb. 26, 1689; d. Amesbury, Mass., Aug. 17, 1750. He graduated from Harvard Univ. in 1708; was ordained a minister at Newbury, Mass., in 1714, where he then served at the Second Church until 1738; then settled in Amesbury as a shopkeeper. In 1721 he publ. in Boston *A Very Plain and Easy Introduction to the Art of Singing Psalm Tunes*; in this book, letters instead of notes were used on the staff; it was very popular (at least 11 eds. publ. up to 1774; reprint of the 5th ed. of 1726, Philadelphia, 1954).

BIBL.: F. Metcalf, *American Writers and Compilers of Sacred Music* (N.Y., 1925); C. Shipton, "J. T.," *Sibley's Harvard Graduates,* V (Boston, 1937); I. Lowens, "J. T.' Introduction to the Singing of Psalm-Tunes (1721–1744): The First American Music Textbook," *Journal of Research in Music Education,* 2 (1954).

Tufts, John Wheeler, American organist and teacher; b. Dover, N.H., May 12, 1825; d. Camden, Maine, March 18, 1908. He went to Germany in 1846; studied in Frankfurt am Main and then in Leipzig, where his teachers were Moscheles in piano and Hauptmann in theory. He returned to America in 1848 and organized in Bangor, Maine, a choral society which he conducted for several years; he then served as church organist in Portland, Maine, and in Boston (c.1880–95). He wrote many songs and hymn tunes, and brought out a series of school-music works, notably the *Normal Music Course* (1885–98).

Tuksar, Stanislav, Croatian musicologist; b. Gornji Kraljevec, July 27, 1945. He studied philosophy and English at the Univ. of Zagreb; then cello with R. Matz and musicology with I. Supicić at the Zagreb Cons.; subsequently studied with E. Weber in Paris (1974–76). He was a researcher at the Zagreb Inst. of Musicology and taught at the Cons.; received the Humboldt scholarship from the Institut für Musikforschung in Berlin (1986). He wrote numerous articles about esthetics, philosophy, and terminology of music of the 16th to 18th centuries and about the musical archives in Croatia. He publ. a book on Croatian music theorists of the Renaissance, *Hrvatski renesansni teoreticari glazbe* (Zagreb, 1978; Eng. tr., 1980). He also wrote music criticism and tr. several books by Zofia Lissa and Erich Fromm into Croatian.

Tulindberg, Erik (Eriksson), Finnish composer; b. Lillkyro, Feb. 22, 1761; d. Åbo, Sept. 1, 1814. He studied academic disciplines at the Åbo Academy, obtaining the degree of Magister Philosophiae in 1782; was subsequently a municipal functionary. Music was his avocation; he learned to play the violin; owned a large library, including works of Mozart, Haydn, and Boccherini; in 1797 he was elected a member of the Royal Swedish Academy of Music. He wrote a Violin Concerto and 6 string quartets in the traditional style of the Viennese School.

Tully, Alice, American mezzo-soprano, soprano, and music patroness; b. Corning, N.Y., Sept. 11, 1902. A scion of a family of wealth, she studied voice in Paris with Jean Périer and Miguel Fontecha, where she made her concert debut with the Pasdeloup Orch. in 1927. Returning to the U.S., she gave a song recital in N.Y. in 1936, and received critical praise for her interpretation of French songs. She eventually gave up her artistic ambition and devoted herself to various philanthropic endeavors. Her major gift was to Lincoln Center in N.Y., for the construction of a chamber music hall; it was dedicated as Alice Tully Hall in 1969. She also helped to organize the Chamber Music Society of Lincoln Center. She received the National Medal of Arts in 1985.

Tulou, Jean-Louis, prominent French flutist, pedagogue, and composer; b. Paris, Sept. 12, 1786; d. Nantes, July 23, 1865. He was only 10 when he entered the Paris Cons., receiving the 2nd prix in 1799 and the premier prix in 1801. He launched his career in 1804; joined the orch. of the Paris Opéra in 1813, resigning in 1822, but resumed the position in 1826 (with the title of "première flûte solo"); in 1829 was appointed prof. of flute at the Cons.; retired from both positions in 1856. He performed on the old-fashioned flute, and obstinately opposed the introduction of Böhm's improved instrument into the Cons. With J. Nonon, he pursued a partnership as a flute manufacturer from 1831 to 1853; then continued to make flutes under his own name. He wrote 5 flute concertos; *airs variés* for flute with orch.; a Trio for 3 Flutes; flute duos; many solo pieces for flute. He also publ. *Méthode de flûte* (Mainz, c.1835; modern ed., Kassel, 1965).

Tuma, Franz (actually, **František Ignác Antonín Tůma**), Czech viola da gambist, theorbist, and composer; b. Kostelec, Oct. 2, 1704; d. Vienna, Jan. 30, 1774. He began music studies with his father, a Kostelec organist; after serving as a chorister at the Minorite church of St. James in Prague under B. Cernohorsky, he went to Vienna; by 1722 he was a vice-Kapellmeister; by 1731 he was Compositor and Capellen-Meister to Count Franz Ferdinand Kinsky, the High Chancellor of Bohemia, who made it possible for him to receive counterpoint lessons from Fux; was Kapellmeister to the dowager Empress Elisabeth (1741–50), and thereafter remained active at the court as a

viola da gambist, theorbist, and composer; about 1768 he went to the Premonstratensian monastery in Geras, but returned to Vienna shortly before his death. He was praised as both an instrumentalist and a composer by his contemporaries. Among his works are some 60 masses, 3 Magnificats, a Te Deum, 29 vespers and Psalms, 25 motets, offertories, and graduals, 20 litanies, 13 Marian antiphons, 8 hymns, 13 sinfonias, 18 partitas for Strings, 16 sonatas, and a Fugue for Organ. Several of his instrumental works have been ed. in Musica Antiqua Bohemica, LXVII (1965) and LXIX (1967).

BIBL.: F. Laurencin, "Franz Tuma," *Neue Zeitschrift für Musik*, XXXI (1864); O. Ball, *Franz Tuma* (diss., Univ. of Vienna, 1901); J. Bušek, "F. Tůma," *Hudební vychova*, XIII (Prague, 1932); E. Toldra, "F. Tůma," *Cyril*, LX (Prague, 1934); A. Peschek, *Die Messen von Franz Tuma* (diss., Univ. of Vienna, 1956; includes thematic catalogue and list of MS sources).

Tunder, Franz, celebrated German organist and composer; b. Bannesdorf, near Burg, Fehmarn, 1614; d. Lübeck, Nov. 5, 1667. From 1632 to 1641 he was court organist at Gottorp, where he studied with J. Heckelauer, a pupil of Frescobaldi; in 1641 he became organist of the Marienkirche in Lübeck, being succeeded at his death by his son-in-law, **Dietrich Buxtehude.** In addition to his regular duties as organist there, he founded a series of evening concerts (Abendmusiken) for the performance of organ works by himself and other German composers and vocal pieces by Italian composers. His extant works comprise 17 vocal pieces, 14 organ works, and a Sinfonia. See M. Seiffert, ed., *Franz Tunder: Kantaten und Chorwerke*, Denkmäler Deutscher Tonkunst, III (1900), idem, ed., *Franz Tunder: Vier Praeludien*, Organum, IV/6 (Leipzig, 1925), R. Walter, ed., *Franz Tunder: Sämtliche Choralbearbeitungen* (Mainz, 1959), J. Golos and A. Sutkowski, eds., *Keyboard Music from Polish Manuscripts: Organ Chorales by Heinrich Scheidemann and Franz Tunder*, Corpus of Early Keyboard Music, X (1967), and K. Beckmann, ed., *Franz Tunder: Sämtliche Orgelwerke* (Wiesbaden, 1974).

BIBL.: W. Stahl, "F. T. und Dietrich Buxtehude," *Archiv für Musikwissenschaft*, VIII (1926; also publ. separately in Leipzig, 1926); J. Hennings, "T.iana," *Lübeckische Blätter*, 75, no. 53 (1934); K. Gudewill, *F. T. und die nordelbingische Musikkultur seiner Zeit* (Lübeck, 1967); G. Sharp, "F. T.: 1614–1667," *Musical Times*, CVIII (1967); J. Roche, "Rovetta and T.: An Interesting Example of Plagiarism," *Early Music*, III (1975).

Tunley, David (Evatt), respected Australian musicologist and composer; b. Sydney, May 3, 1930. He studied at the New South Wales State Conservatorium of Music in Sydney (diploma, 1950), at Trinity College, London (diploma, 1950), at the Univ. of Durham (B.Mus., 1958; M.Mus., 1963), with Nadia Boulanger in Paris (1964–65), and at the Univ. of Western Australia (D.Litt., 1970, with the diss. *The Eighteenth Century Secular French Cantata*; publ. in London, 1974). In 1958 he joined the faculty of the Univ. of Western Australia, where he served as a prof. (from 1979) and as head of the music dept. (from 1985). In 1980–81 he was national president of the Musicological Soc. of Australia. In 1987 he was made a member of the Order of Australia. He contributed articles to various learned journals, and also to *The New Grove Dictionary of Music and Musicians* (1980). Among his compositions are *Wedding Masque* for Soloists, Women's Choir, and Orch. (1961; rev. 1970); Concerto for Clarinet and Strings (1966); *Inflorescence* for Choir, Clarinet, and Timpani (1978); and *Elegy—in memoriam Salek Minc* for Chamber Ensemble (1986). His books include *Australian Composition in the 20th Century* (ed., with F. Callaway; Melbourne, 1980), *Couperin* (London, 1982), and *Harmony in Action* (London, 1984).

Tupkov, Dimiter, Bulgarian composer; b. Sofia, July 12, 1929. He studied with Goleminov at the Bulgarian State Cons. in Sofia, graduating in 1956; then joined its faculty.

WORKS: Flute Concerto (1955); *The Story of Belassitsa Mountain,* overture (1956); 3 *Children's Sinfoniettas* (1961, 1968, 1975); Concerto for Orch. (1969); *Rhapsodic Diverti-*

mento for Orch. (1970); Harp Concerto (1971); 6 *Bagatelles* for Orch. (1972); *September Overture* (1974); *Peace Cantata* (1975); 2 string quartets (1956, 1958); choral songs; folk-song arrangements.

Turchaninov, Piotr (Ivanovich), Russian composer; b. Kiev, Dec. 1, 1779; d. St. Petersburg, March 28, 1856. He studied music with Sarti when the latter was at the St. Petersburg court; was ordained a priest in 1803; from 1827, taught singing at the imperial court chapel; from 1831 to 1841, was archpriest at various churches. His masterly arrangements and harmonizations of old liturgical melodies of the Russian Church were ed. by Kastalsky (Moscow, 1906). His autobiography was publ. in St. Petersburg in 1863.

BIBL.: A. Preobrazhensky, *The Archpriest P.I. T.* (St. Petersburg, 1910); V. Lebedev, *P.I. T.* (Tambov, 1910).

Turchi, Guido, Italian composer and teacher; b. Rome, Nov. 10, 1916. He studied piano and composition with Dobici, Ferdinandi, and Bustini at the Rome Cons. (diplomas, 1940) and pursued graduate training with Pizzetti at the Accademia di Santa Cecilia in Rome (diploma, 1945). He taught at the Rome Cons. (1941–67; again from 1972); was artistic director of the Accademia Filarmonica in Rome (1963–66); served as director of the Parma and Florence cons. (1967–72); was artistic director of the Teatro Comunale in Bologna (1968–70) and at the Accademia di Santa Cecilia in Rome (from 1970). In his early music, Turchi followed Pizzetti's style of Italian Baroque, with Romantic and impressionistic extensions; he then changed his idiom toward a more robust and accentuated type of music-making, influenced mainly by a study of the works of Béla Bartók. Turchi's Concerto for String Orch. is dedicated to Bartók's memory.

WORKS: Trio for Flute, Clarinet, and Viola (1945); *Invettiva* for Small Chorus and 2 Pianos (1946); Concerto for String Orch. (Venice, Sept. 8, 1948); *Piccolo concerto notturno* for Orch. (1950); opera, *Il buon soldato Svejk* (Milan, April 6, 1962); *3 metamorfosi* for Orch. (1970); *Dedalo,* ballet (Florence, 1972); *Dedica* for Flute (1972); also choral works, songs, incidental music to plays, film scores, etc.

BIBL.: F. d'Amico, "G. T.," *Tempo,* No. 21 (1951).

Tureck, Rosalyn, eminent American pianist, harpsichordist, and clavichordist; b. Chicago, Dec. 14, 1914. She studied piano in Chicago with Sophia Brilliant-Liven (1925–29), Jan Chiapusso (1929–31), and Gavin Williamson (1931–32); then went to N.Y., where she studied with Olga Samaroff at the Juilliard School of Music, graduating in 1935. In her concert career she dedicated herself mainly to Bach. In 1947 she made her 1st European tour; subsequently gave concerts in South America, South Africa, and Israel. She made some appearances as a conductor from 1956; however, she concentrated her activities on the keyboard, making appearances as a harpsichordist and a clavichordist (from 1960) as well as a pianist. In 1971 she made a world tour. She held teaching posts at the Philadelphia Cons. of Music (1935–42), Juilliard School of Music (1943–55), and Univ. of Calif., San Diego (1966–72). In 1966 she founded the International Bach Inst. and in 1981 the Tureck Bach Inst. She received honorary doctorates from Roosevelt Univ. in 1968 and the Univ. of Oxford in 1977. In order to demonstrate the universal applicability of Bach's keyboard techniques, she played Bach on the Moog synthesizer; in 1971 she gave a concert announced as "Bach and Rock." She publ. *An Introduction to the Performance of Bach* (3 vols., London, 1959–60; also publ. in Japanese, 1966, and Spanish, 1972).

Turina (y Perez), Joaquín, prominent Spanish composer; b. Seville, Dec. 9, 1882; d. Madrid, Jan. 14, 1949. He studied with local teachers; then entered the Madrid Cons. as a pupil of Tragó (piano). In 1905 he went to Paris, where he studied composition with d'Indy at the Schola Cantorum and piano with Moszkowski. At the urging of Albéniz, he turned to Spanish folk music for inspiration. Returning to Madrid in 1914, he produced 2 symphonic works in a characteristic Spanish

style: *La procesión del rocío* and *Sinfonía sevillana,* combining Romantic and impressionist elements in an individual manner; the same effective combination is found in his chamber music of Spanish inspiration (*Escena andaluza, La oración del torero,* etc.) and his piano music (*Sonata romántica, Mujeres españolas,* etc.); he also wrote operas and incidental music for the theater. In 1930 he was appointed a prof. of composition at the Madrid Cons.; also founded the general music commission of the Ministry of Education, serving as its commissioner in 1941.

WORKS: STAGE: *La sulamita* (opera; c.1900); *Fea y con gracia* (zarzuela; 1904); *Margot* (lyric comedy; Madrid, Oct. 10, 1914); *Navidad* (incidental music; Madrid, 1916); *La adúltera penitente* (incidental music; Barcelona, 1917); *Jardín de oriente* (opera; Madrid, March 6, 1923); *La anunciación* (comedia; Madrid, 1924). **ORCH.:** *La procesión del rocío,* symphonic poem (Madrid, March 30, 1913); *Evangelio,* symphonic poem (Madrid, April 8, 1915); *3 danzas fantásticas* (1920); *Sinfonía sevillana* (San Sebastian, Sept. 11, 1920); *Rítmos,* choreographic fantasy (Barcelona, Oct. 25, 1928); *Rapsodia sinfónica* for Piano and String Orch. (Madrid, March 11, 1933). **CHAMBER:** Piano Quintet (1907); String Quartet (1911); *Escena andaluza* for Viola, String Quartet, and Piano (1912); *La oración del torero* for String Quartet (1925); 2 piano trios (1926, 1933); 2 violin sonatas (1929, 1934); Piano Quartet (1931); *Serenata* for String Quartet (1935); *Círculo* for Violin, Cello, and Piano (1936); *Las nueve Musas* (9 pieces for Various Instruments; 1945). **PIANO:** *Sevilla, suite pintoresca* (1909); *Sonata romántica* (1909); *Coins de Séville,* suite (1911); *3 danzas andaluzas* (1912); *Album de viaje* (1916); *Mujeres españolas* (2 sets; 1917, 1932); *Cuentos de España,* 2 sets of 7 pieces each (1918, 1928); *Niñerías,* 2 sets of children's pieces (1919, 1931); *Sanlúcar de Barrameda* (1922); *El Cristo de la Calavera* (1924); *Jardines de Andalucía,* suite (1924); *La venta de los gatos* (1925); *El Barrio de Santa Cruz* (1925); *La leyenda de la Giralda,* suite (1927); *2 danzas sobre temas populares españoles* (1927); *Verbena madrileña,* 5 pieces (1927); *Mallorca,* suite (1928); *Evocaciones,* 3 pieces (1929); *Recuerdos de la antigua España,* 4 pieces (1929); *Viaje marítimo,* suite (1930); *Ciclo pianístico: Tocata y fuga, Partita, Pieza romántica, El castillo de Almodóvar* (1930–31); *Miniaturas,* 8 pieces (1930); *Danzas gitanas,* 2 sets of 5 pieces each (1930, 1934); *Tarjetas postales* (1931); *Sonata fantasía* (1930); *Radio Madrid,* suite (1931); *Jardín de niños,* 8 pieces (1931); *El circo,* 6 pieces (1932); *Silhuetas,* 5 pieces (1932); *En la zapatería,* 7 pieces (1933); *Fantasía italiana* (1933); *Trilogía: El poema infinito* (1933); *Ofrenda* (1934); *Hipócrates* (1934); *Rincones de Sanlúcar* (1933); *Bailete, suite de danzas del siglo XIX* (1933); *Preludios* (1933); *Fantasía sobre cinco notas* (1934); *Concierto sin orquesta* (1935); *En el cortijo,* 4 pieces (1936–40); *Prelude* for Organ (1914); *Musette* for Organ (1915). **GUITAR:** *Sevillana* (1923); *Fandanguillo* (1926); *Ráfaga* (1930); *Sonata* (1932); *Homenaje a Tárrega,* 2 pieces (1935). **SONGS:** *Rima* (1911); *Poema en forma de canciones* (1918); *3 arias* (1923); *Canto a Sevilla,* cycle (1927); *2 canciones* (1927); *Corazón de mujer* (1927); *Tríptico* (1929); *3 sonetos* (1930); *3 poemas* (1933); *Homenaje a Lope de Vega* (1935).

WRITINGS: *Enciclopedia abreviada de la música* (Madrid, 1917); *Tratado de composición* (Madrid, 1946).

BIBL.: F. Sopeña, *J. T.* (Madrid, 1943; 2nd ed., rev., 1956); W. Dean, "J. T.," *Chesterian* (April 1949); L. Powell, *The Piano Music of J. T.* (diss., Univ. of North Carolina, 1974); idem, "The Influence of Dance Rhythms on the Piano Music of J. T.," *Music Review,* XXXVII (1976).

Turini, Gregorio, prominent Italian singer and instrumentalist; b. Brescia, c.1560; d. Prague, c.1600. He was a pupil of Giovanni Contino in Brescia; entered the service of Emperor Rudolf II in Prague as a singer and cornett player in 1582, and was held in great esteem there; later was active as a trumpeter and drummer as well. He publ. *Cantiones admondum devotae cum aliquot psalmis Davidicis* for 4 Equal Voices (Venice, 1589; 15 ed. in K. Proske, *Musica Divina,* II and III, Regensburg, 1854–59), *Neue liebliche teutsche Lieder, nach Art der welschen Villanellen* for 4 Voices (Nuremberg, 1590), and *Il-*

primo libro de canzonette for 4 Voices (Nuremberg, 1597). His son, **Francesco Turini** (b. Prague, c.1589; d. Brescia, 1656), was an esteemed organist, teacher, and composer; studied with his father; was only 12 when he was made court organist; Emperor Rudolf made it possible for him to pursue training in organ, singing, and composition in Venice and Rome; after returning to Prague, he resumed his court post; went to Italy about 1612; was organist at Brescia Cathedral (1620–56).

Turini, Ronald (Walter), Canadian pianist; b. Montreal, Sept. 30, 1934. He studied at the Quebec Cons.; subsequently took private lesseons with Isabelle Vengerova and Vladimir Horowitz in N.Y. He toured Europe as a soloist with the Montreal Sym. Orch. in 1962; subsequently appeared with many other leading orchs. and as a recitalist in the major music centers.

Türk, Daniel Gottlob, eminent German organist, pedagogue, music theorist, and composer; b. Claussnitz, near Chemnitz, Aug. 10, 1750; d. Halle, Aug. 26, 1813. He was the son of Daniel Türcke, an instrumentalist in the service of Count Schönburg. He received music lessons from his father and studied wind instruments with his father's fellow musicians; then received instruction in harmony and counterpoint from G.A. Homilius at the Dresden Kreuzschule; subsequently entered the Univ. of Leipzig in 1772, but also pursued music training with J.A. Hiller, in whose "popular concerts" he served as 1st violinist; also studied clavichord with J.W. Hässler. In 1774 he settled in Halle, where he became Kantor at the Ulrichskirche and a teacher at the Lutheran Gymnasium; in 1779 he was named director of music at the Univ., where he taught theory and composition; left his Gymnasium post in 1787 to become organist and music director of the city's principal church, the Marktkirche (Liebfrauenkirche); was given an honorary doctorate at the Univ. in 1808, and that same year was promoted to prof. of music there. As the leading Halle musician of his day, he played an energetic role in its concert life as both a performer and an organizer. He was held in the highest esteem by his contemporaries. Among his compositions are various vocal works and keyboard pieces.
BIBL.: J. Lippert, *Verzeichniss der musikalischen und andern Bücher, so wie auch der gedruckten und geschriebenen Musikalien des seligen Professor der Musik und Universitäts-Musikdirektor Dr. T., welche. . .versteigert werden sollen* (Halle, 1816); G. Hedler, *D.G. T. (1750–1813)* (diss., Univ. of Leipzig, 1936); B. Grahmann, ed., *D.G. T.: der Begründer der hallischen Händeltradition* (Wolfenbüttel and Berlin, 1938); D. Raessler, "T., touch and slurring: finding a rationale," *Early Music* (Feb. 1989).

Turnage, Mark-Anthony, English composer; b. Essex, June 10, 1960. He studied with Oliver Knussen in the junior dept. of the Royal College of Music in London (1974–78), continuing his training there as a senior student under John Lambert (diploma, 1982); then received instruction from Gunther Schuller and Hans Werner Henze at the Berkshire Music Center at Tanglewood (1983). He was named composer-in-association with the City of Birmingham Sym. Orch. for 1989 to 1992.
WORKS: *And Still a Softer Morning* for Flute, Vibraphone, Harp, and Cello (1978–83; Montepulciano, July 31, 1984); *Let Us Sleep Now* for Chamber Orch. (1979–82; Shape, June 14, 1983); *Night Dances* for Orch. (1980–81; London, Feb. 1, 1982); *Kind of Blue: In Memoriam, Thelonious Monk* for Orch. (London, March 21, 1982); *After Dark* for Wind and String Quintets (London, April 13, 1983); *Lament for a Hanging Man* for Soprano and Ensemble (1983; Durham, Feb. 4, 1984); *Ekaya: Elegy in Memory of Marvin Gaye* for Orch. (1984; Greenwich, March 29, 1985); *On All Fours* for Chamber Ensemble (1985; London, Feb. 4, 1986); *1 Hand in Brooklyn Heights* for 16 Mixed Voices (1986; Bath, June 3, 1986); *Beating About the Bush* for Mezzo-soprano and Chamber Ensemble (London, June 14, 1987); *Release* for 8 Players (1987); *Greek,* opera

(Munich, June 17, 1988); *3 Screaming Popes* for Orch. (Birmingham, Oct. 5, 1989).
BIBL.: S. Pettitt, "M.-A. T. and 'Greek,'" *Musical Times* (Aug. 1988).

Turner, Dame Eva, distinguished English soprano; b. Oldham, March 10, 1892; d. London, June 16, 1990. She was a pupil of Dan Roothan in Bristol; Giglia Levy, Edgardo Levy, and Mary Wilson at the Royal Academy of Music in London; and Albert Richards Broad. In 1916 she made her operatic debut as a Page in *Tannhäuser* with the Carl Rosa Opera Co., with which she sang until 1924; sang with the company at London's Covent Garden in 1920. In 1924 she made her 1st appearance at Milan's La Scala as Freia in *Das Rheingold;* then toured Germany with an Italian opera company in 1925. She sang Turandot in Brescia in 1926; appeared at Covent Garden (1928–30; 1933; 1935–39; 1947–48); was a guest artist in other European music centers, in Chicago, and in South America. She taught at the Univ. of Oklahoma (1950–59) and then at the Royal Academy of Music. In 1962 she was made a Dame Commander of the Order of the British Empire. Her other esteemed roles included Agatha, Amelia, Santuzza, Aida, Isolde, Sieglinde, and Cio-cio-san.
BIBL.: T. English, "E. T.," *Opera,* i/6 (1950); J. Richards, "E. T.," *Record Collector,* XI (1957); I. Cook, "This Is E. T.," *Opera News* (Nov. 28, 1959).

Turner, Godfrey, English composer; b. Manchester, March 27, 1913; d. (suicide) N.Y., Dec. 7, 1948. He studied with E.J. Dent at Cambridge Univ. (musicology) and with Nadia Boulanger (composition) in Paris. He went to the U.S. in 1936; taught at the San Francisco Cons. (1938–43); was music ed. for Boosey & Hawkes, N.Y. (1944–46); then secretary of the American Music Center, N.Y. (1946–48).
WORKS: *Trinity Concerto* for Chamber Orch.; Viola Concerto; *Sonata concertante* for Piano and String Orch.; *Fanfare, Chorale and Finale* for Brass; *Saraband and Tango; Gregorian Overture* (Columbus, Ohio, Dec. 2, 1947; winner of the B.M., Inc., contest).

Turner, Ike, black American soul and rock musician; b. Clarksdale, Miss., Nov. 5, 1931. He played piano and guitar as a child; while still in school he formed a group called the Kings of Rhythm, which gained success with their recording of *Rocket 88* (1951), with the allusion to the 88 keys of the piano keyboard; the record was one of the 1st in the rock'n'roll manner. He then went to St. Louis with the group, where he took on the singer Anna Mae Bullock in 1956; they were married in 1958 and toured as the Ike and Tina Turner Revue with a female dance-and-vocal trio called the Ikettes. In 1971 they won a Grammy Award for their recording of *Proud Mary.* Their partnership, both on and off the stage, came to an end in 1976; they were divorced in 1978.

Turner, Joe, black American jazz pianist; b. Baltimore, Nov. 3, 1907; d. Paris, July 21, 1990. As a child, he studied piano with his mother; later took lessons with Frank Johnson and cultivated a method that became known as "stride" pianism. He worked with several bands, including those of Benny Carter and Louis Armstrong.

Turner, Joseph Vernon "Big Joe", black American blues singer; b. Kansas City, Mo., May 18, 1911; d. Englewood, Calif., Nov. 24, 1985. He 1st worked as a singing bartender in local nightclubs; then became associated with the pianist Pete Johnson; in 1938 they appeared at Carnegie Hall in N.Y. After moving to Calif., he sang with Duke Ellington's band; in 1945 he and Pete Johnson began appearing at their own club in Los Angeles; he later made tours in the U.S. and Europe. His *Shake, Rattle, and Roll* (1954) became famous as a result of the rock craze which swept the nation in the 1950s.

Turner, Robert (Comrie), Canadian composer; b. Montreal, June 6, 1920. He studied with Champagne at McGill Univ. in Montreal, graduating in 1943; with Herbert Howells and Gordon Jacob at the Royal College of Music in London (1947–48), with Messiaen at the Berkshire Music Center in Tanglewood (1949), and with Roy Harris at the George Peabody College for Teachers in Nashville, Tenn. (M.M., 1950); then completed his training at McGill Univ. (Mus.D., 1953). From 1952 to 1968 he was a music producer for the CBC in Vancouver; taught at the Acadia Univ. in Wolfville, Nova Scotia (1968–69) and was prof. of theory and composition at the Univ. of Manitoba (1969–85).

WORKS: OPERAS: *The Brideship* (Vancouver, Dec. 12, 1967); *Vile Shadows* (1983; rev. 1986); also incidental music for radio and television. ORCH.: *Canzona* (1950); Concerto for Chamber Orch. (1950); *Sinfonia* for Small Orch. (1953); *Opening Night*, theater overture (1955); *Lyric Interlude* (1956); *A Children's Overture* (1958); *The Pemberton Valley*, suite from the film score (1958); Sym. for String Orch. (Montreal, March 27, 1961); *3 Episodes* (1963; Toronto, Feb. 27, 1966); 2-piano Concerto (1971); *Eidolons*, 12 images for Chamber Orch. (Vancouver, Sept. 12, 1972); Chamber Concerto for Bassoon and 17 Instruments (1973); *Capriccio concertante* for Cello, Piano, and Orch. (1975); *From a Different Country (Homage to Gabrieli)* for Solo Brass Quintet and Chamber Orch. (1976); *Symphony in One Movement ("Gift from the Sea")* (1983; Winnipeg, Dec. 5, 1986); *Encounters I-IX* (1985); *Playhouse Music* (1986); Viola Concerto (1987; Montreal, May 24, 1988); *Shades of Autumn* (1987). CHAMBER: 3 string quartets (1949, 1954, 1975); Oboe Sonatina (1956); *Variations and Toccata* for Wind and String Quintets (1959); *Mobile* for Chorus and 7 Percussionists (1960); *Serenade* for Wind Quintet (1960); *4 Fragments* for Brass Quintet (1961); *Fantasia* for Organ, Brass Quintet, and Timpani (1962); *The Phoenix and the Turtle* for Mezzo-soprano and 8 Instruments (1964); *Suite in Homage to Melville* for Soprano, Contralto, Viola, and Piano (1966); *Diversities* for Violin, Bassoon, and Piano (1967); Piano Trio (1969); *Nostalgia* for Soprano Saxophone and Piano (1972); *Lament for Linos* for Reciter, Flute, Clarinet, and Piano (1978); *Shadow Pieces I* for Flute, Bassoon, Violin, Cello, and Piano (1981); also piano pieces, including *Sonata lyrica* (1955; rev. 1963) and *Vestiges* (1987); also *6 Voluntaries* for Organ (1959).

Turner, Tina (real name, **Anna Mae Bullock**), pulsating black American soul and rock singer and actress; b. Brownsville, Tenn., Nov. 26, 1939. She joined Ike Turner and his band, the Kings of Rhythm, in St. Louis in 1956; the 2 were married in 1958, and toured the chitlin' circuit as the Ike and Tina Turner Revue, accompanied by a female dance-and-vocal trio named the Ikettes. Their 1st successful recording was *A Fool in Love* (1960); she made an explosive impact as a sexually provocative singer, belting out such numbers as *I've Been Lovin' You Too Long* and *River Deep, Mountain High* (1966). A 1969 tour of the U.S. with the Rolling Stones catapulted the Revue onto center stage; they won a Grammy Award for their recording of *Proud Mary* in 1971. While continuing to make appearances with her husband, she also made the solo albums *Let Me Touch Your Hand* (1972) and *Tina Turns the Country On* (1974). In 1975 she appeared as the Acid Queen in the rock-opera film *Tommy*, and that same year brought out the album *Acid Queen*. Having loved her husband too long, she left him in 1976 and obtained a divorce in 1978. She then pursued a solo career as a raunch-and-roll songstress, producing the tremendously successful album *Private Dancer* in 1984; that same year she won 4 Grammy Awards, with *What's Love Got to Do with It?* being honored as best song and best record of the year. In 1985 she starred in the film *Mad Max beyond Thunderdome*. With K. Loder, she publ. the book *I, Tina: My Life Story* (N.Y., 1986).

BIBL.: L. Fissinger, *T. T.* (N.Y., 1985); B. Mills, *Tina* (N.Y., 1985); D. Mabery, *T. T.* (Minneapolis, 1986).

Turner, William, English singer and composer; b. Oxford, 1651; d. London, Jan. 13, 1740. He received training in music as a chorister under Edward Lowe at Christ Church, Oxford; then was a chorister at the Chapel Royal, where he collaborated with Blow and Humfrey on "The Club Anthem" *I will always give thanks;* in 1666 he was placed in charge of Henry Cooke. He was master of the choristers at Lincoln Cathedral (1667–

69); in 1669 he became a Gentleman of the Chapel Royal, where he remained until his death. In 1672 he became a member of the King's Private Musick; in 1683 he was made a vicar-choral at St. Paul's Cathedral; in 1699 he became a lay vicar in the choir at Westminster Abbey. In 1696 he received the Mus.D. degree from the Univ. of Cambridge. He was buried in Westminster Abbey. He particularly distinguished himself as a composer for the church, producing more than 40 anthems, 3 services, a motet, hymns, and chants. Among his secular works are 2 odes, a cantata, many songs, a few pieces for theater productions, and 3 keyboard works.

Turner, W(alter) J(ames Redfern), Australian poet and writer on music; b. Shanghai, Oct. 13, 1889; d. London, Nov. 18, 1946. He studied with his father (who was organist of St. Paul's Cathedral, Melbourne, Australia) and privately in Dresden, Munich, and Vienna. He settled in London, where he was music critic for the *New Statesman* (1916–40); also was drama critic of the *London Mercury* (1919–23) and literary ed. of the *Daily Herald* (1920–23) and *The Spectator* (from 1942).

WRITINGS (all publ. in London): *Music and Life* (1922); *Variations on the Theme of Music* (1924); *Orpheus, or The Music of the Future* (1926); *Beethoven: The Search for Reality* (1927; new ed., 1933); *Musical Meanderings* (1928); *Music: A Short History* (1932; 2nd ed., 1949); *Facing the Music: Reflections of a Music Critic* (1933); *Wagner* (1933); *Berlioz: The Man and His Work* (1934; 2nd ed., rev., 1939); *Music: An Introduction to Its Nature and Appreciation* (1936); *Mozart: The Man and His Works* (1938; 2nd ed., rev., 1965, by C. Raeburn); *English Music* (1941); *English Ballet* (1944).

Turnhout, Gérard de (van), Flemish composer; b. Turnhout, c.1520; d. Madrid, Sept. 15, 1580. He began his career at Antwerp Cathedral and at the church of St. Gommaire of Lierre, where he was made maître de chapelle in 1559; took Holy Orders; was made music master of the Confrérie de la Vierge at Antwerp Cathedral in 1562, and then maître de chant there in 1563; in 1571 he was named maestro de capilla to the court of Philip II of Spain in Madrid. He publ. *Sacrarum ac aliarum cantionum trium vocum* (Louvain, 1569); his Missa *O Maria vernans rosa* for 5 Voices was included in *Praestantissimorum divinae musices auctorum missae decem* (Louvain, 1570), 3 Latin works and 10 chansons in *Liber musicus* (Louvain, 1571), 4 Dutch songs in *Een duytsch Musyck Boeck* (Louvain, 1572; ed. by F. Van Duyse, Vereeniging voor Nederlandsche Muziekgeschiedenis, XXVI, 1903), 4 French sacred works and other pieces in *Premier livre du meslange des pseaumes et cantiques* (Geneva, 1577), and a French sacred work and other pieces in *Second livre du meslange des pseaumes et catiques* (Geneva, 1577); see L. Wagner, ed., *Gérard de Turnhout, Sacred and Secular Songs for Three Voices* (Madison, Wis., 1970). His brother, **Jan-Jacob van (Jean-Jacque de) Turnhout** (b. probably in Brussels, c.1545; d. probably there, after 1618), was also a composer; was maître de chapelle at St. Rombaut in Mechelen (1577–80?); was maître de chapelle to Alexander Farnese, governor general of the Low Countries, by 1586; in 1611 he served with Géry Ghersem as maître de chapelle for the funeral of Archduchess Margaret of Austria. He publ. *Il primo libro di madrigali* for 6 Voices (Antwerp, 1589) and *Sacrarum cantionum* for 5 to 6 and 8 Voices . . . *liber primus* (Douai, 1594).

BIBL.: L. de Burbure, "Le Nom de famille de Jean de Turnhout, compositeur de musique du XVIᵉ siècle," *Bulletin de l'Académie royale de Belgique*, XLVI (1878); G. van Doorslaer, "Jean van Turnhout, compositeur, maître de chapelle à Malines et à Bruxelles (1545?-après 1618)," *Musica Sacra*, XLII (Mechelen, 1935).

Turnovský, Martin, Czech conductor; b. Prague, Sept. 29, 1928. He studied conducting with Karel Ančerl at the Prague Academy of Music, and later with Szell. In 1958 he won 1st prize at the Besançon competition; then was chief conductor of the Brno State Phil. (1959–63) and the Plzeň Radio Sym. Orch. (1963–66). He subsequently served as Generalmusikdirektor of the Dresden State Opera and Orch. (1966–68). In 1968 he made his U.S. debut as guest conductor with the Cleveland Orch. After the period of political turmoil in Czechoslovakia in 1968, he went to Vienna; in 1975–80 he served as music director of the Norwegian Opera in Oslo; in 1979 he became chief conductor of the City Theater in Bonn; also shared the chief conductorship of the Beethovenhalle Orch. there with Jan Krenz; resigned his posts in 1983.

Turok, Paul (Harris), American composer and music critic; b. N.Y., Dec. 3, 1929. He studied composition at Queens College with Karol Rathaus (B.A., 1950); then at the Univ. of Calif., Berkeley, with Roger Sessions (M.A., 1951) and at the Juilliard School of Music with Bernard Wagenaar (1951–53); later studied at Baruch College (M.S., 1986). He was a lecturer on music at the City College of N.Y. (1960–63) and was a visiting prof. at Williams College in Williamstown, Mass. (1963–64); then wrote music criticism for the N.Y. Herald-Tribune (1964–65), the Music Journal (1964–80), Ovation (1980–89), and Fanfare (from 1980). As a composer, he follows the principle of stylistic freedom and technical precision, without doctrinaire adherence to any circumscribed modernistic modus operandi.
Works: stage: operas: Scene: Domestic, chamber opera (1955; Aspen, Colo., Aug. 2, 1973); Richard III (1975); A Secular Masque (1979). **ballet:** Youngest Brother (N.Y., Jan. 23, 1953). **orch.:** Violin Concerto (1953); Symphony in 2 Movements (1955); Lyric Variations for Oboe and Strings (1971; Louisville, March 9, 1973); A Scott Joplin Overture (Cleveland, June 19, 1973); A Sousa Overture (1975; Philadelphia, May 13, 1976); Ragtime Caprice for Piano and Orch. (1976); Threnody for String Orch. (1979); Canzona concertante No. 1 for English Horn and Orch. (1980); Ultima Thule (1981); Canzona concertante No. 2 for Trombone and Orch. (1982). **chamber:** Variations on a Theme by Schoenberg for String Quartet (1952); String Trio (1954); 3 string quartets (1955, 1969, 1980); Wind Quintet (1960); Brass Quintet (1971); Clarinet Trio (1974); Quintet for English Horn and String Quartet (1981); piano pieces; also choruses; songs.

Turpin, Edmund Hart, English organist and composer; b. Nottingham, May 4, 1835; d. London, Oct. 25, 1907. He was a pupil of Hullah and Pauer in London, where he settled in 1857; he served as organist of various churches; wrote the oratorios St. John the Baptist and Hezekiah; hymn tunes; many works for organ. He was ed. of the Musical Standard (from 1880) and for a time also of the Musical World.
Bibl.: C. Pearce, A Biographical Sketch of E.H. T. (London, 1911).

Turski, Zbigniew, Polish composer; b. Konstancin, near Warsaw, July 28, 1908; d. Warsaw, Jan. 7, 1979. He studied composition with Rytel and conducting with Bierdiajew at the Warsaw Cons.; was music producer of the Polish Radio in Warsaw (1936–39); conducted the Baltic Phil. in Gdansk (1945–46); in 1957 he established himself in Warsaw. He wrote in an advanced harmonic idiom, influenced by French modernism. All of his early music MSS were lost during World War II.
Works: Micro-opera, Rozmowki (Chats; 1966; Warsaw, 1967); dance scores, including the ballet Tytania i osiol (Titania and the Donkey; 1966); Sinfonia da camera (1947); Sym. No. 2, Sinfonia Olimpica (1948); 2 violin concertos (1951, 1959); Sym. No. 3 (1953); Little Overture (1955); 2 cantatas, Ziemia (1952) and Vistula River (1953); L'Ombre, nocturne for Tenor, Chorus, and Percussion (1967); Canti de nativitate patriae for Tenor, Bass, Chorus, and Orch. (1969); Regno Ejukori, triptych for Bass and Orch. (Wroclaw, Sept. 2, 1974); String Quartet No. 2 (1951); miscellaneous piano pieces; songs; music for the theater, films, and radio.

Tusler, Robert Leon, American musicologist; b. Stoughton, Wis., April 1, 1920. He studied piano and organ at Friends' Univ., Wichita, Kans. (B.M., 1947); musicology at the Univ. of Calif., Los Angeles (M.A., 1952); then at the Univ. of Utrecht, the Netherlands (1956–58). In 1958 he joined the music faculty of the Univ. of Calif., Los Angeles; retired in 1983. He wrote

The Style of J.S. Bach's Chorale Preludes (Berkeley, Calif., 1956) and The Organ Music of Jan Pieterszoon Sweelinck (Bilthoven, 1958).

Tuthill, Burnet Corwin, American composer and conductor; b. N.Y., Nov. 16, 1888; d. Knoxville, Tenn., Jan. 18, 1982. His father, William Burnet Tuthill, was the architect of Carnegie Hall. He studied at Columbia Univ. (B.A., 1909; M.A., 1910) and the Cincinnati College of Music (M.M., 1935). He conducted the Columbia Univ. Orch. (1909–13). In 1919 he organized the Society for Publication of American Music, which continued to function for nearly half a century, and which publ. about 85 works by American composers; also was executive secretary of the National Assoc. of Schools of Music in Cincinnati (1924–59). After serving as general manager of the Cincinnati College of Music (1922–30), he was head of the music dept. at Southwestern Univ. in Memphis (1935–59); also was conductor of the Memphis Sym. Orch. (1938–46) and head of the fine arts dept. of Shrivenham American Univ. in England (1945). He began to compose rather late in life, but compensated for this delay by increasing productivity in subsequent years. His autobiography was publ. as Recollections of a Musical Life, 1900–74 (Memphis, 1974).
Works: orch.: Bethlehem, pastorale (Interlochen, Mich., July 22, 1934); Laurentia, symphonic poem (Rochester, N.Y., Oct. 30, 1936); Come 7, rhapsody (1935; St. Louis, Feb. 19, 1944); Sym. (1940); several instrumental concertos for: Clarinet (1949); Double Bass (1962); Saxophone (1965); Trombone (1967); Tuba (1975); numerous pieces with a multiplicity of clarinets; Flute Sonata; Oboe Sonata; Trumpet Sonata; Saxophone Sonata; a plethora of sacred choruses.
Bibl.: J. Raines, B.C. T.: His Life and Music (diss., Michigan State Univ., 1979).

Tuukkanen, Kalervo, Finnish conductor and composer; b. Mikkeli, Oct. 14, 1909; d. Helsinki, July 12, 1979. He studied composition with Leevi Madetoja and theory with Krohn in Helsinki; subsequently conducted local orchs. and choirs; from 1967 to 1969, was a visiting prof. of music at the Chinese Univ. of Hong Kong. He wrote 6 syms. (1944, 1949, 1952, 1958, 1961, 1978); 2 violin concertos (1943, 1956); a Cello Concerto (1946); a Sinfonietta (1948); Man and the Elements for Soprano, Chorus, and Orch. (1949); an opera, Indumati (1962); Youth Cantata (1963); and A Chorale Echo for Flute and Piano (1967). He also publ. a monograph on the life and works of Leevi Madetoja (Helsinki, 1947).

Tuxen, Erik (Oluf), Danish conductor; b. Mannheim (of Danish parents), July 4, 1902; d. Copenhagen, Aug. 28, 1957. In 1916 he moved to Denmark; studied architecture and music in Copenhagen; continued his studies in Paris, Vienna, and Berlin; conducted the Danish State Radio Sym. Orch. from 1936 until his death; made guest appearances in the U.S. (1950–51), presenting a concert of Scandinavian music at Carnegie Hall (April 2, 1951); in the summer of 1954 he conducted in South America.

Tveitt, (Nils) Geirr, Norwegian pianist, teacher, music critic, and composer; b. Hardanger, Oct. 19, 1908; d. Oslo, Feb. 1, 1981. He studied at the Leipzig Cons. with Grabner, in Vienna, and with Schmitt, Honegger, and Bigot in Paris. He toured Europe as a pianist; settled in Oslo as a teacher and music critic. He made a profound study of Norwegian folk instruments, which he employed in his own compositions. He publ. Tonalitätstheorie des parallelen Leittonsystems (Oslo, 1937; traces the origin of church modes back to old Norwegian scale forms).
Works: stage: operas: Nordvest—Sud—Nordaust—Nord (1939); Dragaredokko (1940); Roald Amundsen; Stevleik, chamber opera; Jeppe (1964; Bergen, June 10, 1966; rev. 1968). **ballets:** Baldurs draumar (Dreams of Baldur; Berlin, 1935); Birgingu (Oslo, 1939); Husguden (The Household Deity; Bergen, 1956); also incidental music to the play Jonsoknatt, for Small Orch. (Oslo, 1936). **orch.:** 6 piano concertos: No. 1 (1930); No. 2 (Vienna, 1933); No. 3, Hommage à Brahms (Ber-

gen, 1947); No. 4, *Northern Lights* (Paris, 1947); No. 5 (Paris, 1954); No. 6 (1960); Concerto for String Quartet and Orch. (Oslo, 1933); *Variations* for 2 Pianos and Orch. (Oslo, 1937); *8 Dances* (Paris, 1939); Violin Concerto (Oslo, 1939); 2 harp concertos; 2 concertos for Hardanger Fiddle (Bergen, 1956); *100 Folk Tunes from Hardanger*, originally for Piano, then arr. in 5 orch. suites; 4 syms.; *Skaldaspillirs kvad: Håkonarmål* for Soloists, Chorus, and Orch. (Bergen, 1962). **CHAMBER:** Quartet for 4 Violins (Oslo, 1935); 2 string quartets; 3 string sextets (No. 3, Oslo, 1934); *8 Arabian Melodies* for Flute, Celesta, and Percussion (Oslo, 1962); fully 29 piano sonatas.

Twardowski, Romuald, Polish pianist and composer; b. Vilnius, June 17, 1930. He studied composition and piano with Juzeliunas at the Vilnius Cons. (1952–57); after further training with Woytowicz at the Warsaw Cons. (1957–60), he studied medieval polyphony and Gregorian chant with Boulanger in Paris (1963).

WORKS: OPERAS: *Cyrano de Bergerac* (1962; Bytom, July 6, 1963); a "morality," *Tragedyja albo rzecz o Janie i Herodzie* (Tragedy, or Story of John and Herod; 1965; Lodz, April 24, 1969); *Lord Jim* (1972–73); radio opera, *Upadek ojca Suryna* (The Fall of Father Surin; 1968; scenic version, Krakow, 1969); *Maria Stuart* (1978); *Story of St. Katherine* (1981; Warsaw, Dec. 14, 1985). **BALLETS:** *The Naked Prince* (1960; Warsaw, 1964); *The Magician's Statues* (1963; Wroclaw, 1971). **ORCH.:** *3 Sketches* for Strings (1955); Piano Concerto (1956); Concerto (1957); *Suita w dawnym stylu* (Suite in Old Style) (1957); *Mala symfonia konzertująca* (Little Symphony Concertante) for Piano, Strings, and Percussion (1958); *Antifone* for 3 Orch. Groups (1961); *Nomopedia*, 5 movements (1962); *Ode 64* (1964); *The St. Mary Triptych*, 3 scenes and dances for String Orch. (1973); *Prelude, Toccata and Chorale* (1973); *Study in A* (1974; Warsaw, Sept. 21, 1976); *2 Landscapes* (1975); *Capriccio in Blue* (*George Gershwin in memoriam*) for Violin and Orch. (1979); *Little Concerto* for Piano and Instrumental Group (1980); Piano Concerto (1984); *Spanish Fantasia* for Violin and Orch. (1985); *3 Frescoes* (1986); *Symphonic Variations on a Theme by Gershwin* for Solo Percussion and Orch. (1986). **VOCAL:** Cantata, *Pieśń o Bialym Domu* (Song about the White House) for Tenor, Chorus, 2 Pianos, and Percussion (1959); *Cantus antiqui* for Soprano, Harpsichord, Piano, and Percussion (1962); *Trittico fiorentino: I, 3 studi secondo Giotto* for Chamber Orch. (1966), *II, Sonetti di Petrarca* for Tenor Solo and 2 Choruses a cappella (1965), and *III, Impressioni fiorentini* for 4 Instrumental Choruses (1967); *Mala liturgia prawoslawna* (Little Orthodox Liturgy) for Vocal Ensemble and 3 Instrumental Groups (1969); *Oda do mlodości* (Ode to Youth) for Narrator, Chorus, and Orch. (1969); *3 sonnets d'adieux* for Bass-baritone, Piano, Strings, and Percussion (1971); *Polish Landscape*, 3 songs for Bass-baritone and Orch. (1975). **CHAMBER:** *Burlesque* for Wind Quintet (1984); *Allegro rustico* for Oboe and Piano (1986); Trio for Violin, Cello, and Piano (1987); *Lithuanian Variations* for Wind Quintet (1988). **PIANO:** *Little Sonata* (1958); *Toccata* for 2 Pianos (1974); *Improvisations and Toccata* for 2 Pianos (1974).

Tweedy, Donald (Nichols), American composer; b. Danbury, Conn., April 23, 1890; d. there, July 21, 1948. He was educated at Harvard Univ. (B.A., 1912; M.A., 1917), where his teachers were William Heilman, E.B. Hill, and Walter Spalding; later studied in Europe and with Goetschius in N.Y. He taught at Vassar College (1914–16), the Eastman School of Music (1923–27), Hamilton College (1937–38), and Texas Christian Univ. (1945–46). He publ. a *Manual of Harmonic Technic Based on the Practice of J.S. Bach* (1928).

WORKS: Ballet, *Alice in Wonderland* (1935); *L'Allegro*, symphonic study (Rochester, N.Y., May 1, 1925); *3 Dances* for Orch. (1925); *Williamsburg*, suite for Orch. (1941); Viola Sonata (1916); Violin Sonata (1920); Cello Sonata (1930); piano pieces.

Twitty, Conway (real name, **Harold Lloyd Jenkins**), American country–music and pop singer and songwriter; b. Friars Point, Miss., Sept. 1, 1933. After completing his army service,

he launched his career as a rock musician, appearing with his own group in nightclubs. By 1958 he attained a high position on the blues, rock, and country charts, and maintained his high scoring with a succession of hits. In 1982 he founded Twitty City and Music Village USA in Hendersonville, Tenn.

BIBL.: W. Cross and M. Kosser, *The C. T. Story: An Authorized Biography* (Garden City, N.Y., 1986).

Tye, Christopher, English organist and composer; b. c.1505; d. c.1572. In 1536 he received his Mus.B. from Cambridge; in 1537 he was made lay clerk at King's College there; in 1543 he became Magister choristarum at Ely Cathedral; in 1545 he received the D.Mus. degree from the Univ. of Cambridge. After becoming a deacon and a priest in 1560, he left his position at Ely Cathedral in 1561; held livings at Doddington-cum-Marche in the Isle of Ely (from 1561), and at Wilbraham Parva (1564–67) and Newton-cum-capella (1564–70). His son–in–law was **Robert White** or **Whyte**. He described himself as a gentleman of the King's Chapel on the title page of his only publ. work, *The Actes of the Apostles, translated into Englyshe metre to synge and also to play upon the Lute* (London, 1553; it includes the 1st 14 chapters of the Acts). The hymn tunes *Windsor* and *Winchester Old* are adaptations from this collection. Tye was an important composer of English church music; he left masses, services, motets, and anthems. The following eds. of his works have been publ.: R. Weidner, *Christopher Tye: The Instrumental Music* (New Haven, Conn., 1967); J. Satterfield, *Christopher Tye: The Latin Church Music* (Madison, Wis., 1972); J. Morehen, *Christopher Tye: The English Sacred Music* in Early English Church Music, XIX (1977).

BIBL.: R. Weidner, "The Instrumental Music of C. T." *Journal of the American Musicological Society*, XVII (1964); J. Langdon, "T. and His Church Music," *Musical Times*, CXIII (1972); N. Davison, "T.'s Mass 'Euge bone,' " *Musical Times* (Nov. 1980).

Tyes, John, English organist and composer who flourished in the early 15th century. A Gloria for 2 Voices and One Instrument and a Sanctus for 4 Voices are among the works included in the *Old Hall Manuscripts*.

Tyler, James (Henry), American lutenist, and cittern and viol player; b. Hartford, Conn., Aug. 3, 1940. He studied at the Hartt School of Music in Hartford; also took lessons with Joseph Iadone. He made his debut in 1962 with the N.Y. Pro Musica; later went to Germany, where he specialized in performances on early Renaissance instruments; was a member of the Studio der frühen Musik in Munich. He went to England in 1969, where he joined the Early Music Consort of London and Musica Reservata; also served as co-director of the Consort of Musicke with Anthony Rooley. In 1974 he became a member of the Julian Bream Consort. In 1976 he organized The London Early Music Group, devoted principally to performing works of the 16th and 17th centuries. A versatile musician, he also gave concerts of ragtime music with his own quintet, the New Excelsior Talking Machine. In 1986 he became prof. of music and director of the early music program at the Univ. of Southern Calif. in Los Angeles. He wrote *The Early Guitar* (London, 1980) and *The Early Mandolin* (with P. Sparks; Oxford, 1989).

Tyner, (Alfred) McCoy, black American jazz pianist and composer; b. Philadelphia, Dec. 11, 1938. He studied piano; in 1960 he joined John Coltrane's jazz group; in 1965 he formed his own trio, with which he toured in the U.S., in Europe, and in Japan.

BIBL.: L. Feather, "Piano Giants of Jazz: M. T.," *Contemporary Keyboard*, IV/8 (1978); B. Doerschuk, "M. T.," ibid., VII/8 (1981).

Typp, W., English singer and composer who flourished in the early 15th century. An Agnus Dei, 2 Credos, and 4 Sanctus settings by him are found among the *Old Hall Manuscripts*.

Tyranny, "Blue" Gene (real name, **Robert Nathan Sheff**), American keyboardist and composer; b. San Antonio, Jan. 1, 1945. He studied piano and composition privately (1957–62), winning a BMI Student Composers award for his *Piano So-*

nata on Expanding Thoughts (1961). He was active in the ONCE Group in Ann Arbor (1962–68), helping to establish its reputation for mixed-media and cross-cultural performance; also taught keyboard and jazz composition at Mills College in Oakland, Calif. (1971–81). He made numerous recordings, and performed with Laurie Anderson and Peter Gordon; collaborated on Robert Ashley's *Perfect Lives (Private Parts)* (1976–83); also wrote scores for dance, theater, film, and video. A 1975 fire destroyed about half of his early scores, many of which he is reconstructing. Tyranny is an important proponent of integrating jazz and rock elements into concert music; the range of imagination and genre evidenced by his catalog is remarkable.

WORKS: PROCEDURAL SCORES: *The Interior Distance* (1960; realized for 7 Instruments or Voices, 1990); *How to Make Music from the Sounds of Your Daily Life* (1967; realized on Tape as *Country Boy Country Dog*); *How to Do It* (1973; intentionally incomplete); *Archaeo-Acoustics (The Shining Net)* (1977); *PALS/Action at a Distance* (1977); *The Telekinesis Tape* (1977); *Taking Out the Garbage* (1977); *The Intermediary* (1981; realized for Piano, Tape, and Computer); *The More He Sings, The More He Cries, The Better He Feels . . . Tango* (1984; realized for Tape and Piano; orchestrated, 1985); *A Letter from Home* (1986; orig. for Voice and Electronics, 1976); *Somewhere in Arizona, 1970* (1987); *Extreme Realizations Just Before Sunset (Mobile)* (1987; realized for Tape and Piano). **OTHER:** *Music for 3 Begins* for Tapes and Audio Engineer (1958); *4 Chorales* for Keyboard and Electronic Sampling (1958); *How Things That Can't Exist May Exist*, 20–odd theater and street pieces (1958–76); *Ballad/The Road and Other Lines* for 1 to 40 Instruments or Voices (1960); *Meditation/The Reference Moves, The Form Remains*, graphic score (1962; orchestrated, 1963); *Diotima*, graphic score with Tape (1963); *Home Movie* for Film, Tape, and Rock Band (1963); *Just Walk On In*, theater work (1965); *Closed Transmission* for Tape (1966); *The Bust* for Any Kind of Band (1967); *The CBCD Transforms*, electronic codes for acoustic performance (1968–71); *Live and Let Live* for Video and Live Electronics (1972); *Remembering* for Voice and Electronics (1974); *A Letter from Home* for Voice and Electronics (1976; recomposed as procedural score, 1986); *No Job, No Warm, No Nothing*, songs with Electronics (1976); *David Kopay (Portrait)* for Instruments (1976); *Harvey Milk (Portrait)* for Tape (1978); *The White Night Riot* for Tape and Movement (1979); *The Country Boy Country Dog Concert* for Improvisors and Electronics (1980; arranged as *The Country Boy Country Dog Variations* for Soloist[s] and Orch.); *The World's Greatest Piano Player* for Electric Keyboard (1981); *The Song of the Street of the Singing Chicken* for Keyboard (1981); *A Rendition of Stardust* for Tape (1982); *Choral Ode 3* for Voice and Electronics (1987); *The Forecaster* for Orch. and Electronics (1988–89); *Nocturne with and without Memory* for 1 to 3 Pianos (1988–89); *The Great Seal (Transmigration)* for Piano Duo (1990); *My Language Is Me (Millennium)* for Voice and Electronics (1990); *Vocal Responses during Transformation* for Voices and Live Electronics (1990); songs.

Tyrwhitt-Wilson, Sir Gerald Hugh, Baronet. See **Berners, Lord.**

Tyson, Alan (Walker), English musicologist; b. Glasgow, Oct. 27, 1926. He was educated at Magdalen College, Oxford; studied litterae humaniores there (1947–51); in 1952 was elected a fellow of All Souls College, Oxford; later pursued training in psychoanalysis and medicine (qualified, 1965). In 1971 he became a senior research fellow at All Souls College. He has made extensive textual and bibliographical studies of the period 1770–1850; particularly noteworthy are his contributions to the study of Beethoven.

WRITINGS: *The Authentic English Editions of Beethoven* (London, 1963); with O. Neighbour, *English Music Publishers' Plate Numbers in the First Half of the Nineteenth Century* (London, 1965); *Thematic Catalogue of the Works of Muzio Clementi* (Tutzing, 1967); ed., *Beethoven Studies* (N.Y., 1974), *Beethoven Studies 2* (London, 1977), *Beethoven Studies 3* (London, 1982); *Mozart: Studies of the Autograph Scores* (Cambridge, Mass., 1987).

Tzipine, Georges, French conductor; b. Paris, June 22, 1907. He studied violin at the Paris Cons., winning a premier prix; made his debut as a violinist with the Paris Radio (1926); then pursued training in harmony, counterpoint, and conducting. In 1931 he began his career as a conductor with the Paris Radio; after further studies with Marc de Rance and Reynaldo Hahn, he appeared as a guest conductor with various Paris orchs. and toured France as a ballet conductor. He was music director of the Cannes Casino (1945–49); then toured Europe and North and South America as a guest conductor. After serving as music director of the Melbourne Sym. Orch. (1961–65), he taught conducting at the Paris Cons. (from 1966).

Tzybin, Vladimir, Russian flutist, teacher, and composer; b. Ivanovo-Voznesensk, 1877; d. Moscow, May 31, 1949. He played the flute in the orch. of the Bolshoi Theater in Moscow from 1896 to 1907 and from 1921 to 1929. From 1907 to 1920 he was 1st flutist at the Imperial Opera of St. Petersburg. He composed 2 operas: *Flengo* (1918) and *Tale of the Dead Princess and 7 Heroes* (1947); publ. several collections of flute pieces. He was esteemed as a pedagogue.

U

Uber, family of German musicians:

(1) Christian Benjamin Uber, lawyer, glass-harmonica player, and composer; b. Breslau, Sept. 20, 1746; d. there, 1812. He was educated in Halle and Breslau, becoming a civil servant in the latter city in 1772; although an amateur musician, he excelled as a performer on the glass harmonica at concerts he gave in his own home. He wrote a comic opera, *Clarissa oder Das unbekannte Dienstmädchen* (1772); 2 cantatas and other vocal pieces; and much chamber music. He had 2 sons who became professional musicians:

(2) Christian Friedrich Hermann Uber, violinist, conductor, and composer; b. Breslau, April 22, 1781; d. Dresden, March 2, 1822. After training with his father, he engaged in law studies in Halle; receiving encouragement from D.G. Türk, he decided to pursue a career in music. In 1804 he accompanied Prince Radziwill to Berlin, where he entered the service of Prince Louis Ferdinand; then was a violinist in Braunschweig. He was director of the Kassel Opera (1808–14); after conducting in Mainz (1814–16), he went to Dresden as director of the Seconda company; after a sojourn in Leipzig as a teacher, lecturer, and writer on music, he returned to Dresden in 1818 to serve as Kantor at the Kreuzschule and music director of the Kreuzkirche. He composed 2 operas, *Der frohe Tag* (Mainz, 1815) and *Les Marins;* a melodrama, *Der Taucher;* an intermezzo, *Der falsche Werber* (Kassel, 1808); incidental music to plays; the oratorio *Die letzten Worte des Erlösers* (1822); also some cantatas, violin concertos, and songs.

(3) Alexander Uber, cellist and composer; b. Breslau, 1783; d. Carolath, Silesia, 1824. He received initial training from his father in Breslau, where he later studied violin with J.

Janetzek, cello with J. Jäger, and theory with J.I. Schnabel; following tours as a virtuoso, he settled as Kapellmeister to the Prince of Schönaich-Carolath. He wrote several overtures, a Cello Concerto, (2) *Air varié* for Flute and Orch., Variations for Cello and Orch., 16 Variations for Cello and Orch., choruses and other vocal pieces, and various chamber works.

Uberti (real name, **Hubert), Antonio,** celebrated Italian castrato soprano, known as "Il Porporino," after his teacher Porpora; b. Verona (of German parents), 1697; d. Berlin, Jan. 20, 1783. He was Porpora's favorite pupil. In 1741 he entered the service of Frederick the Great in Berlin. He was greatly renowned in Germany for his singing of Italian operas. He was the teacher of Gertrud Mara.

Uccellini, Marco, significant Italian composer; b. c.1603; d. Forlimpopoli, near Forlì, Sept. 10, 1680. He was educated in Assisi; then went to Modena, where he became head of instrumental music at the Este court in 1641 and maestro di cappella at the Cathedral in 1647; subsequently was maestro di cappella at the Farnese court in Parma (1665–80). Most of his works for the stage are not extant, but his concertos are preserved and give evidence of excellent knowledge of technique in writing for the violin and other string instruments.

WORKS: OPERA: *Gli eventi di Filandro ad Edessa* (Parma, 1675). **BALLETS:** *Le navi d'Enea* (Parma, 1673) and *Il Giove d'Elide fulminato* (Parma, 1677). **OTHER** (all publ. in Venice unless otherwise given): *Sonate, sinfonie et correnti, a 2–4,* with Basso Continuo, *libro II* (1639); *Sonate, arie et correnti, a 2, 3,* with Basso Continuo (1642); *Sonate, correnti et arie, a 1–3,* with Basso Continuo, op. 4 (1645; 2 sonatas, 3 correnti,

and 3 arias ed. by L. Torchi in *L'arte musicale in Italia*, VII, Milan, 1907); *Sonate, over canzoni* for Violin and Basso Continuo, op. 5 (1649); *Salmi* for 1 and 3 to 5 Voices and Basso Continuo, *concertante parte con instrumenti e parte senza, con Letanie della beata virgine* for 5 Voices and Basso Continuo, op. 6 (1654); *Ozio regio: Compositioni armoniche sopra il violino e diversi altri strumenti* for 1 to 6 Voices and Basso Continuo, *libro VII* (abridged ed., 1660; not extant; 2nd ed. as *Sonate sopra il violini*, Antwerp, 1668); *Sinfonici concerti brevi e facili, a 1–4*, op. 9 (1667); *Sinfonie boscareccie* for Violin, Basso Continuo, and 2 Violins ad libitum, op. 8 (Antwerp, 1669).
BIBL.: W. Newman, *The Sonata in the Baroque Era* (Chapel Hill, 1959; 4th ed., rev., 1983).

Uchida, Mitsuko, talented Japanese pianist; b. Tokyo, Dec. 20, 1948. She began training in childhood in her native city, and at the age of 12 became a pupil of Richard Hauser at the Vienna Academy of Music. In 1968 she won the Beethoven Competition, and in 1970 received 2nd prize at the Chopin Competition in Warsaw. In 1982 she won particular notice in London and Tokyo for her performances of the complete piano sonatas of Mozart; during the 1985–86 season, she appeared as soloist-conductor in all the piano concertos of Mozart with the English Chamber Orch. in London. On Feb. 15, 1987, she made her N.Y. recital debut. Her repertoire includes, in addition to the classics, works by Debussy, Schoenberg, and Bartók.
BIBL.: D. Stearns, "M. U.: Mozart and Beyond," *Ovation* (Oct. 1988).

Udbye, Martin Andreas, distinguished Norwegian organist and composer; b. Trondheim, June 18, 1820; d. there, Jan. 10, 1889. He studied organ with Carl Becker and composition with Hauptmann at the Leipzig Cons. (1851–52); pursued further studies in Berlin, Leipzig, Dresden, Vienna, and London (1858–59). From 1844 to 1869 he served as organist at the Hospitalskirken in Trondheim, and after 1869 was organist at the church of Our Lady there. He was regarded as one of the finest Norwegian composers of his era; he wrote the 1st Norwegian opera, *Fredkulla* (The Peacemaker; 1858). His other works include the operettas *Hr. Perrichons reise* (1861), *Hjemve* (Homesickness; 1862; Christiania, April 8, 1864), and *Junkeren og flubergrosen* (The Squire and the Rose of Fluberg; 1867; Christiania, Jan. 7, 1872); the orch. sketch *Lumpasivagabundus* (1861); Fantasy for Violin and Orch. (1866); the cantatas *Sonatorrek* (The Loss of a Son; 1872) and *Islaendinger i Norge* (1873); also choral pieces, 3 string quartets (1851–55), 20 piano trios, and 100 organ preludes.

Ugalde, Delphine (née **Beaucé**), French soprano; b. Paris, Dec. 3, 1829; d. there, July 19, 1910. She received her first instruction in singing from her mother, an actress; subsequently studied with Moreau-Sainti; made her debut in Paris in 1848 as Angèle in Auber's *Domino noir*; in 1866, assumed the management of the Bouffes-Parisiens, taking leading roles in Offenbach's operettas; in 1867 she appeared in her own operetta, *La Halte au moulin*. She retired in 1871, and settled down as a successful vocal teacher.

Ugarte, Floro M(anuel), Argentine composer; b. Buenos Aires, Sept. 15, 1884; d. there, June 11, 1975. He studied in Buenos Aires, and at the Paris Cons. under Fourdrain, with whom he collaborated in writing the ballet *Sigolene*. He returned to Argentina in 1913; in 1924, became a prof. at the National Cons. in Buenos Aires; was general director of the Teatro Colón, founder-president of the National Music Society, prof. at the Escuela Superior de Bellas Artes at La Plata Univ., and director of the Buenos Aires Municipal Cons.
WORKS: Operatic fairy tale, *Saika* (1918; Buenos Aires, July 21, 1920). ORCH.: *Entre las montañas*, symphonic suite (1922); *De mi tierra*, 2 symphonic suites (1923, 1934); *La rebelión del agua*, symphonic poem (1931; Buenos Aires, Oct. 16, 1935); *Piri*, choreographic poem (1944); Sym. in A (1946; Buenos Aires, May 13, 1952); *Vidala* (1948); *Preludio* (1949); *Tango* (Buenos Aires, Sept. 5, 1951); Violin Concerto (1963); Piano

Quartet (1921); Sonata for Violin or Cello and Piano (1928); String Quartet (1935); piano pieces; songs.

Ughi, Uto, talented Italian violinist; b. Busto Arsizio, near Milan, Jan. 21, 1944. A child prodigy, he commenced musical training when he was 4 and made his formal debut at 7 in a recital at Milan's Teatro Lirico; pursued studies at the Conservatorio di Santa Cecilia in Rome; also received lessons from Enesco (1954). In 1959 he made an extensive tour of Europe; after performing in Australia (1963), he made his U.S. debut in N.Y. on Feb. 27, 1967; subsequently toured worldwide. In 1977 he was made a member of the Accademia di Santa Cecilia in Milan. In 1979 he organized the "Hommage to Venice" festival to raise funds for restoring the city's art treasures. His instrument is the "Van Houten–Kreutzer" Stradivarius, which dates from 1701. His repertoire includes, besides the classics, a wide selection of modern concertos for the violin.

Ugolina da Orvieto (Ugolino di Francesco Urbevetano), Italian music theorist and composer; b. probably in Orvieto, c.1380; d. Ferrara, 1457. He was active in the chapter at Forlì Cathedral by 1411; was made a canon in 1415 and archdeacon in 1425 at S. Croce there, as well as rector at S. Antonio di Rivaldini. As a leading figure in the Guelph faction, he was compelled to leave Forlì in the wake of the success of the Ghibelline faction in 1430; settled in Ferrara, where he was archpresbyter at the Cathedral from about 1437 until 1448. He wrote the treatise *Declaratio musice discipline* (modern critical ed. by A. Seay, 3 vols., Corpus Scriptorum Musicae, 1959–62).
BIBL.: U. Kornmüller, "Die Musiklehre des Ugolino von Orvieto," *Kirchenmusikalisches Jahrbuch*, X (1895); A. Seay, "Ugolino of Orvieto, Theorist and Composer," *Musica Disciplina*, IX (1955); A. Hughes, "Ugolino: The Monochord and Musica Ficta," ibid., XXIII (1969).

Ugolini, Vincenzo, Italian composer; b. Perugia, c.1580; d. Rome, May 6, 1638. He was a pupil of G.B. Nanino from 1592 to 1594 at the choir school of S. Luigi dei Francesi, Rome; was a bass there from 1600; from 1603 to 1609 he was maestro di cappella at S. Maria Maggiore there; from 1610 to 1614, was at Benevento Cathedral. Returning to Rome, he was director of music to Cardinal Arrigoni (from 1614); from 1616 to 1620, was maestro di cappella at S. Luigi dei Francesi and from 1620 to 1626 at the Cappella Giulia at St. Peter's; in 1631 he resumed his former post at S. Luigi dei Francesi, retaining it until his death. He was the teacher of Benevoli. A notable representative of Palestrina's school, he publ. 4 books of motets for 1 to 4 Voices (1616–19), 1 book of Psalms for 8 Voices and Basso Continuo (1628), 1 book of Psalms and motets for 2 Voices and Basso Continuo (1630), 2 books of madrigals for 5 Voices (1630), etc.; also other works in contemporary collections.
BIBL.: V. Raeli, *Da V. U. ad Orazio Benevoli nella cappella della Basilica Liberiana (1603–1646)* (Rome, 1920).

Uhde, Hermann, noted German bass-baritone; b. Bremen, July 20, 1914; d. (during a performance) Copenhagen, Oct. 10, 1965. He studied at Philipp Kraus's opera school in Bremen, making his operatic debut there as Titurel in *Parsifal* in 1936; appeared in Freiburg and then sang with the Bavarian State Opera in Munich (1940–43) and with the German Opera at The Hague (1943–44). He subsequently was engaged at Hannover (1947–48), Hamburg (1948–50), Vienna (1950–51), Munich (1951–56), Stuttgart (1956–57), and again in Vienna (1957–61). He made his American debut at the Metropolitan Opera in N.Y. as Telramund in *Lohengrin* on Nov. 18, 1955; was on its roster until 1957, then again from 1958 to 1961 and in 1963–64. He was particularly acclaimed for his performances in Wagnerian roles.

Uhl, Alfred, Austrian composer and pedagogue; b. Vienna, June 5, 1909. He studied composition with Franz Schmidt at the Vienna Academy of Music (diploma, 1932); then in 1940–41, during World War II, was in the Austrian army, where he was severely wounded. In 1943 he became a composition teacher at the Vienna Academy of Music; also served as president of the Austrian copyright society (1970–75). In 1980 he was awarded the Austrian Badge of Honor for Science and Arts. His music is patterned after Classical forms, with emphasis on contrapuntal clarity.

WORKS: STAGE: *Katzenmusik*, ballet-opera (1957); *Der Mysteriöse Herr X*, opera, after Lingen (1962–65; Vienna, June 8, 1966). **ORCH.:** *Konzertante Sinfonie* for Clarinet and Orch. (1943; Vienna, Nov. 5, 1944); *4 Capricen* (1944–45); *Introduktion und Variationen über eine Melodie aus dem 16. Jahrhundert* for String Orch. (1947; Salzburg Festival, 1948); *Sonata graziosa* (1947); *Rondeau*, dance variations, after Molière (1948); *Concerto a ballo* (1966; N.Y., Oct. 9, 1967); *Sinfonietta* (1978; Vienna, May 31, 1979); Concerto for 2 Oboes, 2 Horns, and Strings (Murcia, Spain, April 21, 1984). **VOCAL:** *Gilgamesh*, oratorio (1954–56; rev. 1967–68; Vienna, June 13, 1969); *Wer einsam ist, der hat es gut*, cantata (1960; rev. 1963; Linz, Jan. 27, 1964); *Festlicher Auftrakt* for Chorus, Organ, and Orch. (1970); choruses; songs. **CHAMBER:** Divertimento for 3 Clarinets and Bass Clarinet (1943); *Eine vergnügliche Musik* for 8 Winds (1944); String Quartet No. 1 (1945–46; rev. 1969); *Jubiläumsquartett* for String Quartet (1961); *Sonata classica* (1968); *Commedia musicale* for Clarinet, Viola, and Piano (1982).

BIBL.: A. Witeschnik, *A. U.: Eine biographische Studie* (Vienna, 1966).

Uhl, Fritz, Austrian tenor; b. Vienna, April 2, 1928. He studied at the Vienna Academy of Music; made his operatic debut in Graz (1950); sang there in 1952–53. He then sang in Oberhausen (1954–56) and Wuppertal; in 1958 he joined the Bavarian State Opera in Munich; in 1961, became a member of the Vienna State Opera; also made regular appearances at Bayreuth, Salzburg, Covent Garden in London, and the San Francisco Opera. He distinguished himself primarily in Wagnerian roles.

Uhlig, Theodor, German violinist, writer on music, and composer; b. Wurzen, near Leipzig, Feb. 15, 1822; d. Dresden, Jan. 3, 1853. He studied violin with Schneider in Dessau (1837–40), and in 1841 became a violinist in the Dresden Court Orch. He was one of the most devoted friends and admirers of Wagner; prepared the vocal score of *Lohengrin*. His death at the age of 30 was lamented. Of his 84 works (syms., chamber music, theater pieces, etc.) only a Violin Concerto and some piano pieces and songs were publ. His articles are of some importance; they were publ. as *Musikalische Schriften* by L. Frankenstein (Regensburg, 1913).

BIBL.: M. Ahrend, *T. U., Der früh verstorbene Wagnerianer* (Bayreuth, 1904).

Ujfalussy, József, eminent Hungarian musicologist; b. Debrecen, Feb. 13, 1920. He received training in piano and composition at the Debrecen Music School, and in the classics at the Univ. of Debrecen (Ph.D., 1944, with a diss. on Homer's epics); then studied composition with Veress, conducting with Ferencsik, musicology with Szabolcsi and Bartha, and folk music with Kodály at the Budapest Academy of Music (1946–49). He became a member (1948) and served as head of the music dept. (1951–55) of the Ministry of Culture; then was prof. of esthetics and theory at the Budapest Academy of Music (from 1955). In 1961 he became associated with the Bartók Archives (the Inst. of Musicology from 1969) of the Hungarian Academy of Sciences; in 1973 he was made a corresponding member of the latter, where he was president of the musicological commission and director of the Inst. of Musicology (from 1973). In 1961 he received the Erkel Prize and in 1966 the Kossuth Prize.

WRITINGS: He edited *Bartók-breviárium* (Bartók Breviary; Budapest, 1958; 2nd ed., rev., 1974; letters, writings, and documents); *Achille-Claude Debussy* (Budapest, 1959); *A valóság zenei képe* (The Musical Image of Reality; Budapest, 1962); *Bartók Béla* (Budapest, 1965; 2nd ed., enl., 1970; Eng. tr., 1971); *Az esztétika alapjai és a zene* (The Bases of Esthetics and Music; Budapest, 1968); *Farkas Ferenc* (Budapest, 1969);

ed. *A Liszt Ferenc zenemüvészeti föiskola 100 eve* (100 Years of the Franz Liszt Academy of Music; Budapest, 1977).

Ujj, Béla, Hungarian composer of operettas; b. Vienna, July 2, 1873; d. there, Feb. 1, 1942. He lost his sight in childhood, but studied music and composed a number of successful operettas which were produced in Vienna: *Der Herr Professor* (Dec. 4, 1903); *Kaisermanöver* (March 4, 1905); *Die kleine Prinzessin* (May 5, 1907); *Drei Stunden Leben* (Nov. 1, 1909); *Chanteclee* (Oct. 25, 1910); *Der Türmer von St. Stephan* (Sept. 13, 1912); *Teresita* (June 27, 1914); *Der Müller und sein Kind* (Oct. 30, 1917).

Ulbrich, Maximilian, Austrian civil servant and composer; b. Vienna, c.1741; d. there, Sept. 14, 1814. He was a student at the Jesuit seminary in Vienna; received training in harmony and composition from G.C. Wagenseil and in organ and sacred music from J.G. Reutter; he was a civil servant from 1770 to 1804, and concurrently appeared as a bass singer, cellist, and pianist in chamber music concerts at the court.

WORKS: 2 operas: *Frühling und Liebe* (Vienna, 1778) and *Der blaue Schmetterling* (Vienna, April 2, 1782); operetta, *Schnitterfreude* (Vienna, 1785); sacred music, including the oratorio *Die Israeliten in der Wüste* (1779), a Mass, a Te Deum, a Salve Regina, and 6 motets; 4 syms.; Piano Concerto; chamber music.

Ulfrstad, Marius Moaritz, Norwegian composer; b. Borgund, Sept. 11, 1890; d. Oslo, Oct. 29, 1968. He studied piano and composition at the Christiania Cons. (graduated, 1910); continued his training in Berlin, with Pizzetti in Florence, Respighi in Rome, and Ravel in Paris. He settled in Christiania, where he founded his own music school (1921); was music critic of the *Morgenposten* (1922–40) and the *Aftenposten* (1945–47).

WORKS: ORCH.: 5 syms. (1921–44); 2 violin concertos (1923, 1935); Piano Concerto (1935); several suites, most inspired by the geography of Norway, Iceland, and Greenland (*Stavern og Sörlands, Islandia, Arctic, Norvegia, Grönlandia, Svalbardia, Möre og Romsdal, Oslo, Norwegian Middleage*, etc.). **CANTATAS:** *Aere der evige forar i livet* (1932); *Arnljot Gelline* (1932); *Heilag Olav* (1933); *Lex imperator* (1935); *Gnisten* (1935); also some chamber music; incidental music; about 250 choral pieces; nearly 1,000 songs, including arrangements of folk songs.

Ulfung, Ragnar (Sigurd), Norwegian tenor; b. Oslo, Feb. 28, 1927. He studied at the Oslo Cons. and in Milan; in 1951 he made his stage debut in Menotti's *The Consul* in Stockholm, where he joined the Royal Opera in 1958. He appeared in the premiere there of Blomdahl's *Aniara* in 1960; that same year he sang with the company at London's Covent Garden. In 1967 he made his U.S. debut with the San Francisco Opera; sang at the Hamburg State Opera in 1969. In 1972 he created the title role in Maxwell Davies's *Taverner* at Covent Garden. On Dec. 12, 1972, he made his Metropolitan Opera debut in N.Y. as Mime.

Ullmann, Viktor, Austrian composer; b. Teschen, Jan. 1, 1898; d. probably in Auschwitz, Oct. 1944. He studied composition with Schoenberg in Vienna (c.1918–21) and quarter-tone composition at the Prague Cons. (1935–37); was active as an accompanist and conductor at the New German Theater in Prague. He wrote music in the expressionistic manner, without renouncing latent tonality. In 1942 he was arrested by the Nazis and sent to the concentration camp in Theresienstadt; there he composed a one-act opera, *Der Kaiser von Atlantis*, depicting a tyrannical monarch who outlaws death but later begs for its return to relieve humanity from the horrors of life. The MS was preserved, and the work was performed for the first time in Amsterdam on Dec. 16, 1975.

WORKS: OPERAS: *Peer Gynt*; *Der Sturz des Antichrists*; *Der Kaiser von Atlantis oder die Tod-Verweigerung* (1943; Amsterdam, Dec. 16, 1975). **ORCH.:** 5 Variations and Double Fugue on a Piano Piece of Arnold Schoenberg (1929); Concerto for Orch.; Piano Concerto (1940); *Don Quixote*, overture (1944; piano score only). **CHAMBER:** 3 string quartets, including No.

3 (1943); Octet for Piano, Winds, and Strings; Sonata for Quarter-tone Clarinet and Piano; Sonata for Violin and Piano; also choral works; songs; piano pieces, including 7 sonatas.

Ulrich, Homer, American musicologist; b. Chicago, March 27, 1906. He studied bassoon and cello at the Chicago Musical College, and played these instruments in various orchs.; was bassoonist with the Chicago Sym. Orch. (1929–35); received his M.A. at the Univ. of Chicago with the thesis *The Penitential Psalms of Lasso* (1939). He was head of the music dept. of Monticello College (1935–38); then taught at the Univ. of Texas (associate prof., 1939; prof., 1951); also played bassoon with the San Antonio Sym. Orch. In 1953 he was appointed head of the music dept. of the Univ. of Maryland; retired in 1972. He publ. *Chamber Music* (N.Y., 1948; 2nd ed., 1966); *Education of a Concert-Goer* (N.Y., 1949); *Symphonic Music* (N.Y., 1952); *Famous Women Singers* (N.Y., 1953); *Music: A Design for Listening* (N.Y., 1957; 3rd ed., 1970); *A History of Music and Musical Style* (with Paul Pisk; N.Y., 1963); *A Survey of Choral Music* (N.Y., 1973).

Ulrich, Hugo, German composer; b. Oppeln, Silesia, Nov. 26, 1827; d. Berlin, May 23, 1872. After studying in Breslau, he went to Berlin in 1846 and took lessons from Dehn; taught at the Stern Cons. (1859–63); otherwise earned his living by working for publishers. He wrote 3 syms., of which the 2nd, *Symphonie triomphale,* won a prize of 1,500 francs offered by the Brussels Academy in 1853. Other works include a Piano Trio, Cello Sonata, String Quartet, piano pieces, and songs. He made excellent arrangements of Beethoven's syms. for piano, 4-hands.

Ulybyshev, Alexander Dmitrievich. See Oulibishev, Alexander Dmitrievich.

Um Kalthoum (actually, **Fatma el-Zahraa Ibrahim**), Egyptian singer; b. Tamay az-Zahirah, 1898; d. Cairo, Feb. 3, 1975. During a career of more than 50 years, she was one of the most famous singers in the Arab world; she was particularly renowned for her renditions of nationalistic, religious, and sentimental songs, which resulted in her being dubbed the "Star of the East" and the "Nightingale of the Nile." Her death precipitated widespread mourning in Egypt and other Arab countries.

Umlauf, Carl Ignaz Franz, noted Austrian zither player, teacher, and composer; b. Baden, near Vienna, Sept. 19, 1824; d. Vienna, Feb. 25, 1902. He studied violin with Jansa and theory with Sechter; made regular tours of Europe as a virtuoso (from 1844); held the title of Hofmusikus at the Austrian court. With the zither manufacturer Anton Kiendl, he developed the Viennese zither. He publ. the standard method, *Neue vollständige theoretisch-praktische Zitherschule* (Vienna, 1859); also brought out *Salon-Album für Zitherspieler* (18 vols.), which includes his own works and transcriptions.

Umlauf, Ignaz, Austrian violist, conductor, and composer, father of **Michael Umlauf;** b. Vienna, 1746; d. Meidling, near Vienna, June 8, 1796. By 1772 he was 4th violist in the Vienna court orch.; by 1775 he was principal violist in the German Theater orch. there, where he was made Kapellmeister in 1778; by 1782 he was deputy court Kapellmeister under Salieri. He was a highly popular composer of singspiels; inaugurated the season of the German singspiels at the Burg Theater (Feb. 17, 1778) with his piece *Die Bergknappen* (ed. by R. Haas in Denkmäler der Tonkunst in Österreich, XXXVI, Jg. XVIII/1, 1911). His other singspiels, all first performed in Vienna, were: *Die Insul der Liebe* (1772?); *Die Apotheke* (June 20, 1778); *Die schöne Schusterin oder Die pücefarbenen Schuhe* (June 22, 1779); *Das Irrlicht oder Endlich fand er sie* (Jan. 17, 1782); *Welche ist die beste Nation?* (Dec. 13, 1782); *Die glücklichen Jäger* (Feb. 17, 1786); *Der Ring der Liebe oder Zemirens und Azors Ehestand* (Dec. 3, 1786). *Zu Steffan sprach im Traume,* an aria from *Das Irrlicht,* enjoyed great popularity; Eberl wrote a set of variations on it which was misattributed to Mozart. He also wrote a Piano Concerto, a Concerto for 2 Pianos, some chamber music, and sacred vocal pieces.

BIBL.: L. Skrbensky, "Drei deutsche Tonkünstler: Christian Umlauflt, I. U., Michael Umlaufl," *Mitteilungen zur Geschichte der Familien Umlauff,* II (Prague, 1926).

Umlauf, Michael, Austrian violinist, conductor, and composer, son of **Ignaz Umlauf;** b. Vienna, Aug. 9, 1781; d. Baden, near Vienna, June 20, 1842. He joined the Vienna court orch. as a violinist at an early age; conducted at court theaters from about 1809 to 1825; from 1840 he served as music director of the 2 court theaters. He assisted Beethoven in conducting the 9th Sym. and other works (actually led the performances, with Beethoven indicating the initial tempos). Umlauf had some success as a composer of ballets, the most successful being *Paul und Rosette oder Die Winzer* (Vienna, March 5, 1806). Other works include the singspiel *Der Grenadier* (July 8, 1812), and the ballets *Amors Rache* (Oct. 18, 1804) and *Das eigensinnige Landmädchen* (April 9, 1810); he also composed a few sacred vocal works and piano pieces.

BIBL.: L. Skrbensky, "Drei deutsche Tonkünstler: Christian Umlauflt, Ignaz Umlauf, M. U.," *Mitteilungen zur Geschichte der Familien Umlauff,* II (Prague, 1926).

Underwood, James, American composer; b. Richmond, Calif., March 4, 1951. He played the trumpet as a youth; then studied composition with Robert Basart at Calif. State Univ. in Hayward (1969–75; M.A., 1975) and with Frederick Fox at Indiana Univ. (1978–82; D.A., 1982). His music is prudently modernistic, with atonal and polytonal divagations from modal harmonic structures within a general Baroque framework; there is an element of neo-Handelian humor in some of his compositions.

WORKS: ORCH.: *Variations on B-A-C-H* (Hayward, Calif., June 8, 1973); *The Orchestral Noises of October Nights* (1980–81; Bloomington, Ind., March 31, 1982). **VOCAL:** *The Road* for Chorus and Orch. (Richmond, Calif., June 11, 1969); *Requiem* for Male Voice and Orch. (1970); *Dynamisms* for Soprano and Orch. (Hayward, May 2, 1975); *Arms and the Boy* for Soprano, Narrator, Flute, Bass Clarinet, Trumpet, 2 Violins, Viola, Piano, and 5 Percussionists (1979); *To Eros* for Soprano, Violin, Viola, Piano, and Percussion (1980); *After Dinner with Al Capone* for Soprano and Trumpet (1981); *Remembrance* for Soprano, Flute, Clarinet, Violin, Cello, Piano, and Percussion (1982). **CHAMBER:** *Lament* for Clarinet (1970); *Textures I* for 5 Instruments (1971); *Textures II* for Flute (1979); *Textures III* for 2 Cellos (1972); *Loomings* for Double String Quartet and Bass (1979); *4 Jurassic Scenes* for Trombone, Bass Trombone, and 3 Percussionists (1980); *Nightwork* for 8 Instruments (1981); *Brave New Zoos* for String Quartet (1982); *Reactions* for Piccolo (1982); *Green County Purple* for Bassoon (1983); *Cadenzas* for Alto Trombone, String Quartet, Piano, and Percussion (1983); *Deluge* for Brass Quintet (1983).

Ung, Chinary, Cambodian-born American composer; b. Prey Lovea, Nov. 24, 1942. He left his homeland in 1964 and settled in the U.S., where he studied clarinet at the Manhattan School of Music and received composition lessons from Chou Wen-Chung in N.Y. He then devoted himself to composing and teaching, serving on the faculty of Arizona State Univ. in Tempe. In 1989 he received the prestigious Grawemeyer Award. His compositions include *Mohori* for Mezzo-soprano and Chamber Ensemble, *Anicca* and *Inner Voices* for Chamber Orch., *Khse Buon* for Cello, and *Tall Wind* for Soprano, Flute, Oboe, Guitar, and Cello, to a text by e.e. cummings and requiring 5 scores for performance.

Unger, Caroline, famous Hungarian contralto; b. Stuhlweissenburg, Oct. 28, 1803; d. near Florence, March 23, 1877. She studied piano as a child, and then received singing lessons from Joseph Mazotti and Ugo Bassi; then studied voice with Aloysia Weber, J.M. Vogl, and in Milan with D. Roncini. In 1824 she made her operatic debut in Vienna as Dorabella in *Così fan tutte.* Beethoven chose her to sing the contralto part in the 1st performance of his 9th Sym. (May 7, 1824); long afterward, she recounted that she turned Beethoven around that he might see the applause, which he could no longer hear. She went to Italy, where she changed the spelling of her name to Ungher, to secure proper pronunciation in Italian. Several Italian composers (Donizetti, Bellini, Mercadante) wrote operas especially for her. In 1833 she appeared in Paris. In 1839 she was engaged to be married to the poet Lenau, but the engagement soon was broken; in 1841 she married the French writer François Sabatier (1818–91) and retired from the stage. She publ. an album of 46 songs, under the title *Lieder, Mélodies et Stornelli.*

BIBL.: "K. U.," *Dresdener Abendzeitung* (March 1, 1826); "K. U. in Padua," *Allgemeine Theaterzeitung,* XXV, Nos. 174–176 (Vienna, 1832); *Trionfi melodrammatici di Carolina U. in Vienna* (Vienna, 1839); O. Hartwig, "F. Sabatier und K. Sabatier-U.," *Deutsche Rundschau* (May 1897); F. Margit Polgár, *U.-Sabatier* (Budapest, 1941).

Unger, Georg, famous German tenor; b. Leipzig, March 6, 1837; d. there, Feb. 2, 1887. He was originally a student of theology; made his operatic debut in Leipzig at the age of 30. Hans Richter heard him in Mannheim and recommended him to Wagner for the role of Siegfried, which he created at the Bayreuth Festival (1876); after appearing in London in a series of Wagner concerts in 1877, he went that year to Leipzig, where he sang with the Opera until 1881. He was the 1st Wagnerian Heldentenor.

Unger, Gerhard, German tenor; b. Bad Salzungen, Nov. 26, 1916. He received his musical education at the Berlin Hochschule für Musik; began his career as a concert singer. In 1947 he sang opera in Weimar; from 1949 to 1961, was a member of the (East) Berlin State Opera; then sang in Stuttgart (1961–63), at the Hamburg State Opera (1963–66), and at the Vienna State Opera (1966–70); also made guest appearances at the Bayreuth Festival, at La Scala in Milan, and at the Chicago Lyric Opera. Among his finest roles were David, Mime, Pedrillo, and Jaquino; also sang a large concert repertory.

Unger, Heinz, German-Canadian conductor; b. Berlin, Dec. 14, 1895; d. Toronto, Feb. 25, 1965. He studied in Berlin and Munich; was active as a choral conductor in Berlin until the advent of the Nazi regime in 1933; then was conductor of the Leningrad Radio Orch. (1934–36). After a sojourn in England, he settled in Toronto in 1948; that same year, he founded the York Concert Society, which he conducted in many works by Mahler. He publ. an account of his conducting experiences in Russia under the title *Hammer, Sickle and Baton* (London, 1939).

Unger, (Gustav) Hermann, German composer and writer on music; b. Kamenz, Oct. 26, 1886; d. Cologne, Dec. 31, 1958. He studied classical philology in Freiburg, Leipzig, and Munich (graduated, 1910, with a work on Greek poetry); also took a course in musicology in Munich with Edgar Istel and Joseph Haas; subsequently went to Meiningen, where he took lessons with Max Reger (1910–13). He settled in Cologne, where he taught at the Cons. (1919–25) and Univ. (1922–45); also was prof. at the Staatliche Hochschule für Musik (1925–47) and director of the Rheinische Musikschule (from 1934).

WORKS: Operas: *Der Zauberhandschuh* (1927) and *Richmodis von Aducht* (1928); Christmas fairy tale, *Die Geschichten vom Weihnachtsbaum* (1943); 2 syms.; several symphonic poems; much chamber music; choral works; song cycles; piano suites.

WRITINGS: *Max Reger* (Munich, 1921); *Musikalisches Laienbrevier* (Munich, 1921); *Das Volk und seine Musik* (Hamburg, 1922); *Musikgeschichte in Selbstzeugnissen* (Munich, 1928); *Musikanten gestern und heute* (Siegen, 1935); *Anton Bruckner und seine 7. Sinfonie* (Bonn, 1944); *Harmonielehre* (Frankfurt am Main, 1946); *Die musikalische Widmung* (Munich, 1958).

Unger, (Ernst) Max, German musicologist, conductor, and painter; b. Taura, Saxony, May 28, 1883; d. Zürich, Dec. 1, 1959. He studied at the Leipzig Cons., and also attended Riemann's lectures at the Univ. of Leipzig (Ph.D., 1911, with the diss. *Muzio Clementis Leben;* publ. in Langensalza, 1914).

He was conductor of the Vereinigte Leipziger Schauspielhauser in 1906; then was conductor of the Leipzig Madrigal Society (1912–14) and ed. of the *Neue Zeitschrift für Musik* (1919–20); after living in Zürich (1932–40), he went to Italy; returned to Germany after World War II. He devoted his research mainly to Beethoven; publ. about 150 papers dealing with various aspects of Beethoven's life and works; among his books are *Mendelssohn-Bartholdys Beziehungen zu England* (Langensalza, 1909); *Auf Spuren von Beethovens unsterblicher Geliebten* (Langensalza, 1911); *Beethoven über eine Gesamtausgabe seiner Werke* (Bonn, 1920); *Ludwig van Beethoven und seine Verleger S.A. Steiner und Tobias Haslinger in Wien, Ad. Mart. Schlesinger in Berlin* (Berlin and Vienna, 1921); *Beethovens Handschrift* (Bonn, 1926); *Ein Faustopernplan Beethovens und Goethes* (Regensburg, 1952); he also ed. the catalogue of the Bodmer Beethoven collection in Zürich, under the title *Eine schweizer Beethovensammlung: Katalog* (Zurich, 1939).

Uninsky, Alexander, Russian-American pianist; b. Kiev, Feb. 2, 1910; d. Dallas, Dec. 19, 1972. He studied at the Kiev Cons.; in 1932 he won the first prize at the International Chopin Contest in Warsaw; after a concert tour in Europe, he went to the U.S. in 1943, and gave recitals; he excelled as a performer of Chopin's music. In 1955 he was appointed prof. of piano at the Royal Cons. of Music of Toronto; then held a similar position at Southern Methodist Univ. in Dallas.

Uppman, Theodor, American baritone; b. San Jose, Calif., Jan. 12, 1920. He studied at the Curtis Inst. of Music in Philadelphia (1939–41); attended the opera workshops at Stanford Univ. (1941–42) and the Univ. of Southern Calif. (1948–50). In 1951 he created the title role in Benjamin Britten's opera *Billy Budd* at Covent Garden in London. On Nov. 27, 1953, he made his Metropolitan Opera debut in N.Y. as Pelléas, and in 1955 joined the company's roster. He taught at the Mannes College of Music in N.Y. (from 1977); also gave master classes at the Britten-Pears School for Advanced Musical Studies in Aldeburgh (from 1985).

Upshaw, Dawn, American soprano; b. Nashville, Tenn., July 17, 1960. She studied at Illinois Wesleyan Univ. (B.A., 1982) and then pursued vocal training with Ellen Faull at the Manhattan School of Music in N.Y. (M.A., 1984); she also attended courses given by Jan DeGaetani at the Aspen (Colo.) Music School. In 1984 she won the Young Concert Artists auditions and entered the Metropolitan Opera's young artists development program. She was co-winner of the Naumburg Competition in N.Y. (1985). After appearing in minor roles at the Metropolitan Opera in N.Y., she displayed her vocal gifts in such major roles as Donizetti's Adina and Mozart's Despina in 1988. She also pursued a notably successful career as a soloist with major orchs. and as a recitalist. Her remarkable concert repertoire ranges from early music to the most intimidating of avant-garde scores.

Upton, George P(utnam), American writer on music; b. Roxbury, Mass., Oct. 25, 1834; d. Chicago, May 19, 1919. He studied at Brown Univ., graduating in 1854; then was music critic of the *Chicago Tribune* (1863–81), where he was its assoc. ed. (1872–1905).

WRITINGS (all publ. in Chicago unless otherwise given): *Woman in Music* (Boston, 1880; 2nd ed., rev. and enlarged, 1886); *The Standard Operas* (1886; rev. and enlarged by F. Borowski, 1928); *The Standard Oratorios* (1887; 12th ed., 1909); *The Standard Cantatas* (1888; 7th ed., 1899); *The Standard Symphonies* (1889); *Musical Pastels* (1902); *The Standard Light Operas* (1902); ed. *Theodore Thomas: A Musical Autobiography* (1905); with G. Kelley, *Edouard Remenyi: Musician, Littérateur and Man* (1906); *Musical Memories: My Recollections of Celebrities of the Half Century, 1850-1900* (1908); *The Standard Concert Guide* (1908; 3rd ed., rev. and enlarged by F. Borowski, 1930); *Standard Concert Repertory* (1909); *Standard Musical Biographies* (1910); *The Song* (1915); *In Music's Land* (1920).

BIBL.: M. Feldman, *G.P. U.: Journalist, Music Critic and Mentor in Early Chicago* (diss., Univ. of Minnesota, 1983).

Upton, William Treat, American pianist, organist, teacher, and musicologist; b. Tallmadge, Ohio, Dec. 17, 1870; d. Adelphi, Md., Jan. 19, 1961. He was educated at the Oberlin Cons. of Music (B.A., 1896; Mus.B., 1904; M.A., 1924); also studied piano with Leschetizky in Vienna (1896–98) and with Josef Lhévinne in Berlin (1913–14). He taught piano at the Oberlin Cons. of Music (1894–1936); also was organist at the Calvary Prebyterian Church in Oberlin (until 1918).
WRITINGS: *Art-Song in America* (Boston, 1930; supplement, 1938); *Anthony Philip Heinrich: A 19th-Century Composer in America* (N.Y., 1939); ed. O. Sonneck's *Bibliography of Early Secular American Music* (2nd ed., rev., 1945); *The Musical Works of William Henry Fry in the Collection of the Library company of Philadelphia* (Philadelphia, 1946); *William Henry Fry, American Journalist and Composer-Critic* (N.Y., 1954).

Urbach, Otto, German pianist, teacher, and composer; b. Eisenach, Feb. 6, 1871; d. Dresden, Dec. 14, 1927. He studied with Iwan Knorr and Humperdinck in Frankfurt am Main, with Draeseke in Dresden, and with Klindworth in Berlin. In 1898 he was appointed a prof. of piano at the Dresden Cons. He wrote an opera, *Der Müller von Sans-Souci* (Frankfurt am Main, 1896); an overture, *Bergfahrt*; String Quartet; Septet for Wind Instruments; piano pieces; many songs.

Urban, Heinrich, German violinist, pedagogue, and composer; b. Berlin, Aug. 27, 1837; d. there, Nov. 24, 1901. He studied with Ries (violin), Laub, and others in Berlin; was a professional violinist; wrote much symphonic and chamber music; in 1881, became a prof. at Kullak's Academy in Berlin. He acquired fame as a theory teacher; among his pupils was Paderewski. His works include a concert overture, *Scheherazade*; a sym., *Frühling*; Violin Concerto; many violin pieces; songs. His brother, **Friedrich Julius Urban** (b. Berlin, Dec. 23, 1838; d. there, July 17, 1918), was a singing teacher and composer.

Urbanner, Erich, Austrian composer, teacher, and conductor; b. Innsbruck, March 26, 1936. He studied composition with Karl Schiske and Hanns Jelinek, piano with Grete Hinterhofer, and conducting with Hans Swarowsky at the Vienna Academy of Music (1955–61); also attended the summer courses in new music in Darmstadt given by Fortner, Stockhausen, and Maderna. He taught at the Vienna Academy of Music (from 1961) and at the Vienna Hochschule für Musik (from 1969); also was active as a conductor (from 1968). He won various prizes, including the City of Vienna Förderungspreis (1962), the City of Innsbruck prize (1980), the Würdigungspreis for music given by the Austrian Ministry of Education and Art (1982), and the City of Vienna prize (1984).
WORKS: STAGE: *Der Gluckerich, oder Tugend und Tadel der Nützlichkeit,* musical burlesque (1963; Vienna, May 27, 1965); *Ninive, oder Das leben geth Weiter,* opera (1987; Innsbruck, Sept. 24, 1988). **ORCH.:** *Prolog* (1957; Innsbruck, May 11, 1958); *Intrada* for Chamber Orch. (1957); Piano Concerto (1958; Innsbruck, June 1959); Flute Concerto (1959; Innsbruck, June 4, 1964); Sym. (1963; Vienna, April 5, 1964); *Dialoge* for Piano and Orch. (1965; Vienna, April 2, 1967); Concerto for Oboe and String Orch. (1966; Innsbruck, June 9, 1968); Violin Concerto (1971; Innsbruck, Oct. 19, 1972); *Concerto "Wolfgang Amadeus"* for 2 Orchs., 3 Trombones, and Celesta (1972; Salzburg, Jan. 20, 1973); Double-bass Concerto (1973; Innsbruck, Nov. 26, 1974); *Sinfonietta 79* for Chamber Orch. (1979; Innsbruck, April 30, 1980); Cello Concerto (1981; Innsbruck, May 2, 1982); *Sinfonia concertante* for Chamber Orch. (1982; Vienna, March 12, 1983); Double Concerto for Flute, Clarinet, and Orch. (Salzburg, Aug. 8, 1984). **CHAMBER:** 3 string quartets (1956, 1957, 1972); *Étude* for Wind Quintet (1965); *Improvisation III* for Chamber Ensemble (1969); Sextet for Flute, Oboe, Bassoon, Violin, Cello, and Harpsichord (1973); *Takes* for Piano Trio (1977); *Quartetto concertato* for String Quartet and 6 String Duos (1978); *6 Phan-tasten und 2 Schlagzeuger* for 2 Pianos, Celesta, Harpsichord, Organ, Harmonium, and Percussion (1980); *Nonett 1981* for Flute, Clarinet, Trombone, Guitar, Piano, Violin, Cello, and Double Bass (1981);

Emotionen for Saxophone Quartet (1984); keyboard works. **VOCAL:** *Missa Benedicite Gentes* for 4 Solo Voices, Choir, and Organ (1958); *Lateinisches Requiem* for Soprano, Alto, Tenor, Baritone, Choir, and Orch. (1982–83; Innsbruck, Feb. 20, 1985); *Àchte Tyroller Lieder* for Soprano, Tenor, and Chamber Ensemble (1985; Innsbruck, April 5, 1986); songs.

Urfey, Thomas d', English playwright and poet; b. Exeter, 1653; d. London, Feb. 26, 1723. He produced about 30 plays, the songs in some of which were set to music by Purcell (e.g. *The Comical History of Don Quixote,* in 3 parts, 1694–96). He ingratiated himself into the circle of Charles II by his talent for singing his poems, adapted to popular airs of his time. Between 1683 and 1710 he publ. several collections of airs with music, and in 1719 he ed. *Songs Compleat, Pleasant and Divertive* (5 vols., his own songs assembled in vols. 1 and 2); this was reissued the same year under the better-known title *Wit and Mirth: or Pills to Purge Melancholy* (a 6th vol. was added in 1720), and the whole was reprinted and ed. by C. Day (N.Y., 1959).
BIBL.: C. Day, *The Songs of T. D'U.* (Cambridge, Mass., 1933).

Urhan, Chrétien, French violist, violinist, organist, and composer of German descent; b. Montjoie, near Aachen, Feb. 16, 1790; d. Paris, Nov. 2, 1845. He taught himself to play various instruments; settled in Paris, where he studied composition with Le Sueur; became a member of the Opéra orch. in 1814, where he was made 1st violinist in 1823 and soloist in 1836; also appeared as a violist with it. In 1827 he became organist at St. Vincent and in 1828 concertmaster of the Société des Concerts du Conservatoire; also played in chamber-music concerts. In the Cons. Concerts he employed a 5-stringed violin (*violon-alto*, with the tuning c-g-d^1-a^1-e^2), producing charming effects. He composed a cantata, *Les champs de repos*, 2 string quintets, piano pieces, and songs.
BIBL.: A. Förster, "C. U.: ein sonderausgeprägter Kunstfürst und Heilskämpfer," *Studien und Mitteilungen,* XXV (1904), XXVI (1905), and XXVII (1906); P. Garnault, "C. U. (1790-1845)," *Revue de Musicologie,* XI (1930).

Uriarte, Eustaquio de, Spanish musicologist; b. Durango, Nov. 2, 1863; d. Motrico, Sept. 17, 1900. In 1878 he entered the Augustinian Order at Valladolid and in 1888 went to the monastery of Silos, near Burgos, devoting himself to the study and restoration of Gregorian chant; was a promoter of the Asociación Isidoriana de la Reforma de la Música Religiosa. His fundamental work was the *Tratado teórico-prático de canto gregoriano, según la verdadera tradición* (Madrid, 1891). A selection of his newspaper articles and addresses were ed. by L. Villalba as *Estética y crítica musical del padre Uriarte* (Barcelona, 1904).

Uribe-Holguín, Guillermo, eminent Colombian composer and pedagogue; b. Bogotá, March 17, 1880; d. there, June 26, 1971. He studied violin with Figueroa at the Bogotá Academy of Music (1890) and with Narciso Garay; taught at the Academy (1905–7). In 1907 he went to Paris, where he studied with Vincent d'Indy at the Schola Cantorum; then took violin lessons with César Thomson and Emile Chaumont in Brussels. He returned to Colombia in 1910 and became director of the newly reorganized National Cons. in Bogotá; resigned in 1935 and devoted his time to the family coffee plantation. He continued to compose and conduct, and was again director of the Cons. from 1942 to 1947. In 1910 he married the pianist Lucía Gutiérrez. His music bears the imprint of the modern French style, but its thematic material is related to native musical resources; particularly remarkable are his *Trozos en el sentimiento popular* for Piano, of which he wrote about 350; they are stylizations of Colombian melorhythms in a brilliant pianistic setting. He publ. an autobiography, *Vida de un músico colombiano* (Bogotá, 1941).
WORKS: OPERA: *Furatena.* **ORCH.** (all 1st perf. in Bogotá): *Sinfonia del terruño* (Oct. 20, 1924); *3 danzas* (May 27, 1927); *Marcha festiva* (Aug. 20, 1928); *Serenata* (Oct. 29, 1928); *Car-*

navalesca (July 8, 1929); *Cantares* (Sept. 2, 1929); *Villanesca* (Sept. 1, 1930); *Bajo su ventana* (Oct. 20, 1930); *Suite típica* (Nov. 21, 1932); *Concierto a la manera antigua* for Piano and Orch. (Oct. 15, 1939); *Bochica* (April 12, 1940); 11 syms. (1910–50); *Conquistadores* (April 3, 1959); 2 violin concertos; Viola Concerto. **CHAMBER:** 10 string quartets; 2 piano trios; 7 violin sonatas; Cello Sonata; Viola Sonata; Piano Quartet; 2 piano quintets; choruses; sacred works; numerous song cycles.

BIBL.: F. Lange, "G. U.-H.," *Boletín Latino-Americano de Musica,* IV (Bogotá, 1938); G. Guillermo Rendón, "Maestros de la música: G. U.H. (1880-1971)," *Música,* No. 51 (Havana, 1975).

Urich, Jean, composer and publisher; b. Trinidad, Sept. 9, 1849; d. London, Dec. 14, 1939. He studied in Paris with Lenepveu (1868), and in London with Gounod (1871–74). In 1890 he founded the Edition Paul Dupont in Paris, and ed. *Le Figaro Musical.*

WORKS: OPERAS: *L'Orage* (Brussels, 1879); *Flora Macdonald* (Bologna, 1885); *Le Pilote* (Monte Carlo, 1890); *Le Carillon* (Aix-les-Bains, 1895); *Hermann und Dorothea* (Berlin, 1899); *La Cigale et la fourmi* (in Eng. as *The Cicada,* London, 1912); *Tsing-Tau* (London, 1914).

Urio, Francesco Antonio, Italian composer; b. Milan, c.1631; d. there, c.1719. He became a Franciscan friar; served as maestro di cappella at Spoleto Cathedral (1679), in Urbino (1681–83), in Assisi, in Genoa, at the Basilica de' Santi Dodici Apostoli in Rome (1690), at I Frari in Venice (1697), and at S. Francesco in Milan (1715–19). He publ. *Motetti di concerto a 2, 3, e 4 voci con violini e senza,* op. 1 (Rome, 1690); *Salmi concertati a 3 voci con violini,* op. 2 (Bologna, 1697); also composed several oratorios and a Te Deum, from which Handel "borrowed" numerous themes, chiefly for his *Dettingen Te Deum,* and also for his *Saul* and *Israel in Egypt.* Urio's Te Deum was publ. by Chrysander in Denkmäler der Tonkunst (Vol. V, Bergedorf, near Hamburg, 1871; later publ. as Supplement 2 of Handel's complete works).

BIBL.: E. Prout, "U.'s 'Te Deum' and Handel's Use Thereof," *Monthly Musical Record* (Nov. 1871); S. Taylor, *The Indebtedness of Handel to Works by Other Composers* (Cambridge, 1906); P. Robinson, *Handel and His Orbit* (London, 1908); idem, "Handel, or U., Stradella and Erba," *Music & Letters,* XVI (1935).

Urlus, Jacques (Jacobus), noted Dutch tenor; b. Hergenrath, near Aachen, Jan. 9, 1867; d. Noordwijk, June 6, 1935. When he was 10, his parents moved to Tilburg, the Netherlands, where he received instruction from an uncle who was a choral conductor; he later studied singing with Anton Averkamp, Hugo Nolthenius, and Cornelie van Zanten. He was a member of the Dutch National Opera (1894–99) and of the Leipzig Opera (1900–1914), where he excelled as a Wagnerian. In 1910 he made his London debut at Covent Garden as Tristan, a role he repeated for his U.S. debut in Boston on Feb. 12, 1912, and for his Metropolitan Opera debut in N.Y. on Feb. 8, 1913. He remained on the roster of the Metropolitan Opera until 1917, and in subsequent years toured in Europe and the U.S. His other distinguished roles included Parsifal, Tamino, Otello, and Don José. He publ. *Mijn Loopbaan* (My Career; Amsterdam, 1930).

BIBL.: O. Spengler, *J. U.* (N.Y., 1917); L. Riemens, "J. U.," *Gramophone,* XV (1938; with discography).

Urreda, Johannes, eminent composer who flourished in the 2nd half of the 15th century. He may have been of Flemish birth; whatever the case, he pursued his career in Spain. In 1476 he became a singer in the chapel of García Alvarez de Toledo, the 1st Duke of Alva; by 1477 he was in the service of King Ferdinand V as master of the court chapel. His works were widely disseminated in Spain, Italy, and France. Among the most celebrated were the hymn *Pange lingua* for 4 Voices and the cancion *Nunca fue pena mayor* for 3 Voices; both were borrowed by subsequent composers. A few other sacred and secular vocal works are extant.

BIBL.: Duke of Alva, "Disquisiciones acerca del cantor flamenco Juan de Wrede," *Boletin de la Real Academmia de la*

Historia, LXXV (1919); H. Anglès, "El 'Pange lingua' de J. de U, maestro de capilla del Rey Fernando el Católico," *Anuario Musical,* VII (1952).

Urreta, Alicia, Mexican pianist and composer; b. Veracruz, Oct. 12, 1935; d. Mexico City, Dec. 20, 1986. She studied piano with Joaquin Amparán and harmony with Rodolfo Halffter in Mexico City (1948–54); then engaged in teaching. Among her works are a radio opera, *Romance de Doña Balada* (Mexico City, 1972); *De natura mortis* for Voice, Instruments, and Tape (1972); several scores of *musique concrète.*

Urrutia-Blondel, Jorge, Chilean composer; b. La Serena, Sept. 17, 1903; d. Santiago, July 5, 1981. He studied with Pedro Humberto Allende and Domingo Santa Cruz; in 1928, traveled to Europe, where he took lessons with Koechlin, Dukas, and Nadia Boulanger in Paris, and with Hindemith and Hans Mersmann in Berlin. Returning to Chile, he was appointed prof. of harmony at the Cons. in Santiago (1931). His early works followed along nationalist lines but he later turned to post-impressionism and neo-classicism. He wrote many articles on contemporary music and folk music in his homeland; with S. Claro, he publ. the study *Historia de la música en Chile* (Santiago, 1973).

WORKS: Ballet: *La guitarra del diablo* (Santiago, Nov. 27, 1942; 2 sym. suites., 1942); *Música para un Cuento de Antaño* for Orch. (1948); Piano Concerto (1950); Piano Trio (1933); Concertino for Harp and Guitar (1943); String Quartet (1944); Violin Sonata (1954); several choruses; song cycles on Chilean motifs; piano pieces.

Urso, Camilla, esteemed French-American violinist; b. Nantes, June 13, 1842; d. N.Y., Jan. 20, 1902. Her father was an Italian musician and her mother a Portuguese singer. A child prodigy, she entered the Paris Cons. when she was 7, becoming the 1st girl ever accorded that distinction; she was a pupil there of Lambert Massart, winning 1st prizes in all subjects. On Oct. 29, 1852, she made her U.S. debut in N.Y.; appeared with Marietta Alboni, toured widely with the Germania Musical Soc., and gave concerts with Henriette Sontag. After withdrawing from public life (1855–63), she resumed her career with major tours of the U.S. and Europe; also toured Australia (1879, 1894) and South Africa (1895). In 1895 she retired and settled in N.Y. as a teacher.

BIBL.: C. Barnard, *C.: A Tale of a Violin, Being the Artist Life of C. U.* (Boston, 1874); S. Kagan, "C. U.: A Nineteenth-Century Violinist's View," *Signs,* II (1977).

Urspruch, Anton, German pianist, teacher, and composer; b. Frankfurt am Main, Feb. 17, 1850; d. there, Jan. 7, 1907. He had lessons with Raff and Liszt; subsequently taught at the Hoch Cons. in Frankfurt. He wrote several operas, including *Das Unmöglichste von Allem,* after Lope de Vega's comedy *El mayor imposible* (Karlsruhe, Nov. 5, 1897); also a Sym.; Piano Concerto; Piano Quintet; Piano Trio; Violin Sonata; Cello Sonata; many piano pieces.

Ursprung, Otto, learned German musicologist; b. Günzlhofen, Jan. 16, 1879; d. Schöndorf-am-Ammersee, Sept. 14, 1960. He studied philosophy and theology at the Univ. of Munich (1899–1904) and was ordained as a Catholic priest; returned to the Univ. of Munich (Ph.D., 1911, with the diss. *Jacobus de Kerle: sein Leben und seine Werke (1531/32–91);* publ. in Munich, 1913); held the title of honorary prof. of music history there (1932–49). He was an authority on Catholic church music and the musical history of Munich.

WRITINGS: *Restauration und Palestrina-Renaissance in der katholischen Kirchenmusik der letzten zwei Jahrhunderte* (Augsburg, 1924); *Münchens musikalische Vergangenheit* (Munich, 1927); *Die katholische Kirchenmusik* (Potsdam, 1931).

Ursuleac, Viorica, noted Rumanian soprano; b. Cernăuţi, March 26, 1894; d. Ehrwald, Tirol, Oct. 22, 1985. She studied in Vienna with Franz Steiner and Philip Forstén and in Berlin with Lilli Lehmann; made her debut as Charlotte in Massenet's *Werther* in Agram in 1922; then sang in Cernăuţi (1923–24) and with the Vienna Volksoper (1924–26). In 1926 she joined the Frankfurt Opera, and then pursued a distinguished career as a member of the Vienna State Opera (1930–34), the Berlin State Opera (1935–37), and the Bavarian State Opera in Munich (1937–44). Richard Strauss held her in the highest esteem; in his operas she created the roles of Arabella (1933), Maria in *Der Friedenstag* (1938), the Countess in *Capriccio* (1942), and Danae in *Die Liebe der Danae* (public dress rehearsal, 1944). She was also highly successful in the operas of Mozart, Wagner, and Verdi. She was married to **Clemens Krauss,** with whom she often appeared in concert. After his death in 1954, she settled in Ehrwald. With R. Schlötterer, she wrote *Singen für Richard Strauss: Erinnerungen und Dokumente* (Vienna, 1986).

Usandizaga, José María, Basque composer; b. San Sebastián, March 31, 1887; d. there, Oct. 5, 1915. Encouraged by Planté and d'Indy, he entered the Paris Schola Cantorum when he was 14; studied piano with Grovlez and counterpoint with Tricon. In 1906 he returned to his native city and associated himself with the Basque musical movement, to which he gave a great impetus with the production of his stage work *Mendi mendiyan* (High in the Mountains; 1909–10; San Sebastián, 1911); then followed his drama lírico *Las golondrinas* (The Swallows; 1913; Madrid, Feb. 5, 1914; rev. as an opera by his brother, R. Usandizaga, Barcelona, 1929), which obtained excellent success; his last stage work was the drama lírico *La llama* (The Flame; 1915; completed by R. Usandizaga, San Sebastián, 1918). He also wrote several orch. works, including a Suite (1904), a symphonic poem, *Dans la mer* (1904), *Ouverture symphonique sur un thème de plain-chant* (1904–5), and band pieces; choral music; songs; folksong arrangements; a String Quartet; works for violin or cello and piano; piano pieces; organ music. His death from tuberculosis at the age of 28 was deeply lamented by Spanish musicians.

BIBL.: L. Villalba Muñoz, *Últimos músicos españoles: J.M. U.* (Madrid, 1918); J. de Arozamena, *J.M. U. y la bella época donostiarra* (San Sebastian, 1969).

Usiglio, Emilio, Italian conductor and composer; b. Parma, Jan. 8, 1841; d. Milan, July 7, 1910. He studied in Pisa and Florence; pursued a successful career as an opera conductor until a wayward lifestyle and abuse of alcohol took its toll. In his last years, he conducted in provincial opera houses before retiring to Milan with his wife, the singer Clementina Brusa.

WORKS: OPERAS: *La Locandiera* (Turin, Sept. 5, 1861); *L'eredità in Corsica* (Milan, June 17, 1864); *Le Educande di Sorrento* (Florence, May 1, 1868); *La scommessa* (Florence, July 6, 1870); *Le Donne curiose* (Madrid, Feb. 11, 1879); *Le nozze in prigione* (Milan, March 23, 1881); several ballets; chamber music.

Usmanbaş, Ilhan, Turkish composer; b. Constantinople, Sept. 28, 1921. He studied cello as a child; then studied composition and piano at the Ankara State Cons.; in 1948 he was appointed to its faculty. In 1952 he traveled in the U.S.; had further training from Dallapiccola at the Berkshire Music Center in Tanglewood; visited the U.S. again in 1958. His early compositions followed the ethnic patterns of Turkish folk songs, but after his travels in the U.S. he gradually adopted serial techniques, with occasional aleatory episodes.

WORKS: ORCH.: Violin Concerto (1946); Sym. (1948); Sym. for Strings (Ankara, April 20, 1950); *Music for String Orch., Percussion, Piano, and Narrator* (1950); *Mortuary* for Narrator, Chorus, and Orch. (1952–53); *On 3 Paintings of Salvador Dali* for Strings (1953); *Japanese Music* for Women's Chorus and Orch. (1956); *Un Coup de des* for Chorus and Orch. (1959); *Gölgeler* (Shadows; 1964); *Bursting Sinfonietta* (1968); *Music for a Ballet* (1969); *Symphonic Movement* (1972); *Little Night Music* (1972). **CHAMBER:** String Quartet (1947); Clarinet Quintet (1949); Oboe Sonata (1949); Trumpet Sonata (1949); *Music with a Poem* for Mezzo-soprano, Flute, Clarinet, Bassoon, and 2 Violins (1958); *A Jump into Space* for Violin and 4 Instruments (1966); *String Quartet '70* (1970); piano pieces.

Uspensky, Victor Alexandrovich, Russian composer and ethnomusicologist; b. Kaluga, Aug. 31, 1879; d. Tashkent, Oct.

9, 1949. He was brought up in Central Asia, where his father held a government post; attended the composition classes of Liadov at the St. Petersburg Cons.; graduated in 1913. In 1918 he went to Tashkent; from 1932 to 1948, was active with the Musical Folklore Division of Uzbekistan, and did valuable research work in native folklore; he also worked on the restoration of Uzbek musical instruments; from these authentic materials he fashioned an Uzbek opera, *Farhad and Shirin,* produced in Tashkent on Feb. 26, 1936. Other works include *Turkmenian Capriccio* for Orch. (1945); *Uzbek Rhapsody* for Orch. (1946); several choral works; piano pieces; songs. He collaborated with Victor Belaiev on a scholarly treatise, *Turkmenian Music* (Moscow, 1928).

BIBL.: J. Pekker, *V.A. U.* (Moscow, 1953; 2nd ed., 1958).

Ussachevsky, Vladimir (Alexis), innovative Russian-born American composer; b. Hailar, Manchuria, Nov. 3, 1911; d. N.Y., Jan. 2, 1990. His parents settled in Manchuria shortly after the Russo-Japanese War of 1905, at the time when Russian culture was still a powerful social factor there. His father was an officer of the Russian army, and his mother was a professional pianist. In 1930 he went to the U.S. and settled in Calif., where he took private piano lessons with Clarence Mader; from 1931 to 1933 he attended Pasadena Junior College; in 1933 he received a scholarship to study at Pomona College (B.A., 1935). He then enrolled in the Eastman School of Music in Rochester, N.Y., in the classes of Howard Hanson, Bernard Rogers, and Edward Royce in composition (M.M., 1936; Ph.D., 1939); he also had some instruction with Burrill Phillips. In 1942, as an American citizen, Ussachevsky was drafted into the U.S. Army; thanks to his fluency in Russian, his knowledge of English and French, and a certain ability to communicate in rudimentary Chinese, he was engaged in the Intelligence Division; subsequently he served as a research analyst at the War Dept. in Washington, D.C. He then pursued postdoctoral work with Luening at Columbia Univ., joining its faculty in 1947; was prof. of music (1964–80). At various times he taught at other institutions, including several years as composer-in-residence at the Univ. of Utah (from 1970) and was a faculty member there (1980–85). His early works were influenced by Russian church music, in the tradition of Tchaikovsky and Rachmaninoff. A distinct change in his career as a composer came in 1951, when he became interested in the resources of electronic music; to this period belong his works *Transposition, Reverberation, Experiment, Composition* and *Underwater Valse,* which make use of electronic sound. On Oct. 28, 1952, Stokowski conducted in N.Y. the first performance of Ussachevsky's *Sonic Contours,* in which a piano part was metamorphosed with the aid of various sonorific devices, superimposed on each other. About that time he began a fruitful partnership with Otto Luening; with him he composed *Incantation for Tape Recorder,* which was broadcast in 1953. Luening and Ussachevsky then conceived the idea of combining electronic tape sounds with conventional instruments played by human musicians; the result was *Rhapsodic Variations,* first performed in N.Y. on March 20, 1954. The work anticipated by a few months the composition of the important score *Déserts* by Varèse, which effectively combined electronic sound with other instruments. The next work by Ussachevsky and Luening was *A Poem in Cycles and Bells* for Tape Recorder and Orch., first performed by the Los Angeles Phil. on Nov. 22, 1954. On March 31, 1960, Leonard Bernstein conducted the N.Y. Phil. in the commissioned work by Ussachevsky and Luening entitled *Concerted Piece for Tape Recorder and Orchestra.* On Jan. 12, 1956, Ussachevsky and Luening provided taped background for Shakespeare's *King Lear,* produced by Orson Welles, at the N.Y. City Center, and for Margaret Webster's production of *Back to Methuselah* for the N.Y. Theater Guild in 1958. They also provided the electronic score for the documentary *The Incredible Voyage,* broadcast over the CBS Television network on Oct. 13, 1965. Among works that Ussachevsky wrote for electronic sound without partnership were *A Piece for Tape Recorder* (1956), *Studies in Sound, Plus* (1959), and *The Cre-*

ation (1960). In 1968 Ussachevsky began experimenting with the synthesizer, with the aid of a computer. One of the works resulting from these experiments was *Conflict* (1971); it is intended to represent the mystical struggle between 2 ancient deities. In 1959 Ussachevsky was one of the founders of the Columbia-Princeton Electronic Music Center; was active as a lecturer at various exhibitions of electronic sounds; traveled also to Russia and in China to present his music. He held 2 Guggenheim fellowships, in 1957 and in 1960. In 1973 Ussachevsky was elected to membership in the National Inst. of Arts and Letters.

WORKS: TAPE: *Transposition, Reverberation, Experiment, Composition* (1951–52); *Sonic Contours* (N.Y., Oct. 28, 1952); *Underwater Valse* (1952); *Piece for Tape Recorder* (1956); *Metamorphoses* (1957); *Improvisation on 4711* (1958); *Linear Contrasts* (1958); *Studies in Sound, Plus* (1959); *Wireless Fantasy: De Forrest Murmurs* (1960); *Of Wood and Brass* (1964–65); *Suite from Music for Films* (1967); *Piece for Computer* (1968); *2 Sketches for Computer Piece No. 2* (1971); *Conflict*, electronic scene from *Creation* (1973–75). WITH TAPE: *3 Scenes from Creation: Prologue "Enumu Elish"* for 2 Choruses and Tape, *Interlude* for Soprano, Mezzo-soprano, and Tape (1960; rev. 1973), and *Epilogue "Spell of Creation"* for Soprano and Chorus (1971); *Creation Prologue* for 4 Choruses and Tape (1960–61); *Scenes from No Exit* for Speaker and Tape (1963); *Colloquy* for Solo Instruments, Orch. and Tape (Salt Lake City, Feb. 20, 1976); *Two Experiments* for Electronic Valve Instrument and Tape (1979; in collaboration with N. Steiner); *Celebration 1980* for Electronic Valve Instrument, String Orch., and Tape (N.Y., April 1980); *Pentagram* for Oboe and Tape (BBC, London, Nov. 1980); *Celebration 1981* for Electronic Valve Instrument, 6 Winds, Strings, and Tape (N.Y., Oct. 30, 1981; rev. as *Divertimento* for Electronic Valve Instrument, 3 Winds, 3 Brass, Strings, Percussion, and Tape, 1980–81); *Dialogues and Contrasts* for Brass Quintet and Tape (N.Y., Feb. 12, 1984). INCIDENTAL MUSIC FOR TAPE: *To Catch a Thief* (sound effects for the film; 1954); *Mathematics* (television score; 1957); *The Boy who Saw Through* (film; 1959); *No Exit* (film; 1962); *Line of Apogee* (film; 1967); *Mourning Becomes Electra* (sound effects for the opera by M. Levy; 1967); *The Cannibals* (play; 1969); *2 Images for the Computer Piece* (film; 1969); *Duck, Duck* (film; 1970); *We* (radio play; 1970). FILM SCORE: *Circle of Fire* (1940). ORCH.: *Theme and Variations* (1936); *Piece* for Flute and Chamber Orch. (1947); *Miniatures for a Curious Child* (1950); *Intermezzo* for Piano and Orch. (1952); *Dances and Fanfares for a Festive Occasion* (1980). CHAMBER: *2 Dances* for Flute and Piano (1948); *4 Studies* for Clarinet and Electronic Valve Instrument (1979); *Suite for Trombone Choir* (1980); *Triskelion* for Oboe and Piano (1982); *Nouvelette pour Bourges* for Electronic Valve Instrument and Piano (1983); piano pieces. VOCAL: *Jubilee Cantata* for Baritone, Reader, Chorus, and Orch. (1937–38); *Psalm XXIV* for Chorus and Organ, or Organ and 5 Brass, or 7 Brass (1948); *2 Autumn Songs on Rilke's Text* for Soprano and Piano (1952); *Missa Brevis* for Soprano, Chorus, and Brass (1972). WITH OTTO LUENING: *Incantation* for Tape (1953); *Rhapsodic Variations* for Orch. and Tape (1953–54; N.Y., March 20, 1954); *A Poem in Cycles and Bells* for Orch. and Tape (Los Angeles, Nov. 22, 1954); *Of Identity*, ballet for Tape (1954); *Carlsbad Caverns*, television score for Tape (1955); *King Lear*, incidental music (3 versions, 1956); *Back to Methuselah*, incidental music for Tape (1958); *Concerted Piece* for Orch. and Tape (N.Y., March 31, 1960); *Incredible Voyage*, television score for Tape (1968; also with Shields and Smiley).

Ustvolskaya, Galina (Ivanovna), Russian composer; b. Petrograd, July 17, 1919. She was a student of Shostakovich at the Leningrad Cons., graduating in 1947; subsequently was on its faculty. Her early music was marked by a Romantic Russian manner; later she progressed toward greater melodic diversity and harmonic complexity; in some of her chamber music she boldly applied serial procedures. Although her compositions were never officially condemned, they were accused of being difficult to understand, "narrow-minded," and "obstinate."

WORKS: *Concerto for Piano, String Orchestra, and Kettledrums* (1946); 6 piano sonatas (1947, 1949, 1952, 1957, 1986, 1988); *Trio* for Clarinet, Violin, and Piano (1949); *Octet* for 2 Oboes, 4 Violins, Timpani, and Piano (1949–50); *Violin Sonata* (1952); *First Symphony* for 2 Boy's Voices and Orch. (1955); *Grand Duet* for Cello and Piano (1959); *Duet* for Violin and Piano (1964); *Composition No. 1—Dona nobis pacem* for Piccolo, Tuba, and Piano (1970–71); *Composition No. 2—Dies irae* for 8 Double Basses, Percussion, and Piano (1972–73); *Composition No. 3—Benedictus qui venit* for 4 Flutes, 4 Bassoons, and Piano (1974–75); *Second Symphony—True and Eternal Bliss* for Voice and Orch. (1979); *Third Symphony—Jesus Messiah, Save Us!* for Soloist and Orch. (1983); *Fourth Symphony—Prayer* for Trumpet, Tom-Tom, Piano, and Alto (1985–87); *Fifth Symphony* for Oboe, Trumpet, Tuba, Violin, and Percussion (1989–90).

Utendal, Alexander, Netherlandish composer; b. c.1535; d. Innsbruck, May 7, 1581. He entered the service of the Habsburgs at an early age; became an alto in the court choir of the emperor's son, Archduke Ferdinand, in Prague in 1564. He followed his patron to Innsbruck when the latter became governor of the Tirol in 1566; was deputy Kapellmeister in the court chapel from about 1572 until his death.

WORKS (all publ. in Nuremberg): 7 *psalmi poenitentiales* (1570); *Sacrarum cantionum* for 5 Voices (1571); *Sacrae cantiones* for 6 and More Voices (1573); 3 *missae* for 5 to 6 Voices (1573); *Fröliche neue teutsche und frantzösiche Lieder* for 4 to 5 and More Voices (1574); *Liber 3 sacrarum cantionum* for 5 to 6 Voices (1577); *Responsoria* (1586); other works in contemporary collections and MSS.

BIBL.: O. Kade, "Nachtrag zu A. Utenthal oder Utendal," *Monatshefte für Musikgeschichte*, VIII (1876); J. Lechthaler, *Die kirchenmusikalischen Werke von A. U.* (diss., Univ. of Vienna, 1919).

Uttini, Francesco Antonio Baldassare, Italian composer and conductor; b. Bologna, 1723; d. Stockholm, Oct. 25, 1795. He studied with Padre Martini, Perti, and Sandoni. In 1743 he became a member of the Accademia dei Filarmonici in Bologna. He first appeared as a singer and conductor with Mingotti's operatic touring group (c. 1752); in 1755, went to Stockholm as conductor of an Italian opera company; was named Master of the King's Music in 1767, and also was principal conductor at the Royal Opera until his retirement in 1788. Historically he is important as the composer of the earliest operas on Swedish texts; the 1st, *Thetis och Pelée*, was written for the inauguration of the new Royal Opera in Stockholm (Jan. 18, 1773); another opera to a Swedish libretto, tr. from the French, was *Aline, Drotning uti Golconda* (Aline, Queen of Golconda), produced at the Royal Opera on Jan. 11, 1776. Of Uttini's Italian operas, the best is *Il Re pastore* (Stockholm, July 24, 1755). A great admirer of Gluck, he brought out many of that composer's works in Stockholm. He also wrote 3 sinfonie, the oratorios *La Giuditta* (Bologna, 1742) and *La passione di Gesù* (Stockholm, 1776), several cantatas, 6 sonatas for Harpsichord (Stockholm, 1756), and 6 Sonatas for 2 Violins and Bass (London, 1768).

BIBL.: E. Sundström, "F.A. U. och Adolf Fredriks italienska operatrupp," *Svensk Tidskrift för Musikforskning*, 13 (1931).

Utyosov, Leonid, Russian jazz composer; b. Odessa, March 21, 1895; d. Moscow, March 10, 1982. He played violin as a child; after the Revolution, he performed as an actor and entertainer in various cabarets, often combining different functions, including acrobatics. In 1920 he organized the first Soviet jazz group, which he named Tea Jazz, with allusion to the song "Tea for Two" by Youmans, which was immensely popular in Russia at the time; subsequently he created various brief musical comedies such as *Jazz on the Turning Point* (1930). He also performed numerous popular Russian songs and revived old army and navy ballads. He publ. a brief biographical book, *Thanks, Heart* (Moscow, 1976).

V

Vaccai, Nicola, Italian composer and singing teacher; b. Tolentino, March 15, 1790; d. Pesaro, Aug. 5, 1848. He went to Rome as a youth and took lessons in counterpoint with Jannaconi; then studied with Paisiello in Naples (from 1812). He was a singing teacher in Venice (1818–21), Trieste (1821–23), and in Frohsdorf, near Wiener Neustadt (1822). He taught in Paris (1830) and in England (1830–33) before returning to Italy; later became vice censore at the Milan Cons., assuming the post of censore in 1838; in 1844 he retired to Pesaro. Although he found little success as a composer for the theater, he won distinction as a singing teacher; his *Metodo pratico di canto italiano per camera diviso in 15 lezioni, ossiano Solfeggi progressivi ed elementari sopra parole di Metastasio* (London, 1832) became a standard work in its field. Among his operas were *Pietro il Grande, ossia Un geloso all tortura* (Parma, Jan. 17, 1824), *La Pastorella feudataria* (Turin, Sept. 18, 1824), and *Giulietta e Romeo,* after Shakespeare (Milan, Oct. 31, 1825), the last scene of which was often used in performances of Bellini's *I Capuletti e i Montecchi.* He also composed much vocal music, including sacred works, cantatas, and over 100 chamber pieces.

BIBL.: G. Vaccai, *La vita di N. V. scritta dal figlio Giulio con prefazione del professore A. Biaggi* (Bologna, 1882).

Vacek, Miloš, Czech composer; b. Horní Roveň, June 20, 1928. He studied organ at the Prague Cons. (1943–47); then took a course in composition with Řídký and Pícha at the Prague Academy of Arts and Music (1947–51); devoted himself totally to composition from 1954.

WORKS: OPERAS: *Jan Želivský* (1953–56; rev. 1974); *Bratr Žak* (Brother Jacques; 1976–78); *Romance pro křídlovku* (Romance for Bugle-horn; 1980–81); *Kocour Mikeš* (Mikeš the Tom Cat; 1981–82). **BALLETS:** *Komediantská pohádka* (The Comedian's Fairytale; 1957–58); *Vítr ve vlasech* (Wind in the Hair; 1960–61); *Posledni pampeliška* (The Last Dandelion; 1963–64); *Milá sedmi loupežníků* (The Mistress of Seven Robbers; 1966); *Meteor* (1966); *Šťastná sedma* (Lucky Sevens; 1966). **MUSICALS:** *Noc je můj den* (The Night Is My Day), blues-drama about the life of Bessie Smith (1962; Frankfurt am Main, March 15, 1964); *Cisařovy nové šaty* (The Emperor's New Clothes; 1962); *Madame Sans Gêne* (1968); *Vítr z Alabamy* (Wind from Alabama; 1970). **ORCH.:** Sinfonietta (1951); *Jarní suita* (Spring Suite) for Flute, Clarinet, Horn or English Horn, and Strings (1963); *Serenáda* for Strings (1965); *Symfonie Májová* (May Sym.; 1974); *Poéma o padlých hrdinech* (Poem of Fallen Heroes) for Alto and Orch. (1974); *Olympijský oheň* (Olympic Flame), symphonic poem (1975); *Mé Kamenici nad Lipou* (To My Kamenici nad Lipou), suite (1979); *Svědomí světa* (World's Conscience), symphonic poem to commemorate the 40th anniversary of the razing of Lidice and Ležáky (1981). **CHAMBER:** *Suite* for Cello and Piano (1947); Violin Sonatina (1949); String Quartet (1949); *Divertimento* for Violin, Cello, Guitar, and Bass Clarinet (1965); *Šumavské metamorfózy* (Šumava Metamorphoses), quintet for Flute, Oboe, Violin, Viola, and Cello (1971); *Lovecká suita* (Hunting Suite) for 4 Horns (1973); *Bukolická suita* (Bucolic Suite) for 4 Trombones (1977); also works for Piano, including *Sonata drammatica* (1972) and *Zatoulané listy z milostného deníčku* (Sheets from a Love Diary Gone Astray; 1972; also for Chamber Orch.); cantatas; choruses; songs; organ works, including *Dramatic Prelude* (1958) and *Organum Pragense* (1969).

Vach, Ferdinand, Moravian choral conductor and composer; b. Jažlovice, Feb. 25, 1860; d. Brno, Feb. 16, 1939. He studied at the Organ School in Prague; in 1886, was appointed conductor of the "Moravian" choir at Kroměříž; also taught singing at the Pedagogium there, and from among his pupils formed in 1903 the Moravian Teachers' Choir, with which he toured in Germany, Russia, and England (1919). In 1905 he became a prof. at the Teachers' School in Brno; he composed choruses, cantatas, and church music.

Vachon, Pierre, French violinist and composer; b. Arles, June 1731; d. Berlin, Oct. 7, 1803. He studied with Chiabrano in Paris from 1751; first appeared at the Concert Spirituel on Dec. 24, 1756, as soloist in his own concerto; was 1st violinist in the orch. of the Prince de Conti (from 1761). In 1772 he gave concerts in London and then returned to Paris; by 1775 he was again in London, where he remained for some 10 years. He then went to Germany, and became concertmaster of the royal orch. in Berlin in 1788; was pensioned in 1798.
WORKS: STAGE: *Renaud d'Ast,* comédie (Fontainebleau, Oct. 12, 1765; in collaboration with J.-C. Trial); *Ésope à Cythère,* comédie (Paris, Dec. 15, 1766; in collaboration with J.-C. Trial); *Les Femmes et le secret,* comédie (Paris, Nov. 9, 1767); *Hippomène et Atalante,* ballet héroïque (Paris, Aug. 8, 1769); *Sara, ou La Fermière écossaise,* comédie (Paris, May 8, 1773). **ORCH.:** *6 symphonies à 4 parties* with Horns ad libitum (Paris, 1761); other syms.; at least 2 violin concertos. **CHAMBER:** String quartets: 6 as op. 6 (Paris, c.1773); 6 as op. 7, book 2 (Paris, 1773; also publ. as *6 Quartettos,* London, c.1776); 6 as op. 9, book 3 (Paris, 1774); 6 as op. 5 (London, c.1775); 6 as op. 6 (London, 1776); *6 quatuors concertans,* op. 11 (Paris, 1782); *3 Quartettos* (London, n.d.); 6 sonates for Violin and Bass, op. 1 (Paris, 1760); 6 sonates for Violin and Bass, op. 3 (Paris, 1769; also publ. as *6 soli,* London, c.1769); 6 trios for 2 Violins and Bass, op. 4 (Paris, c.1772); 6 trios for 2 Violins and Cello, op. 5 (Paris, c.1772); 6 trios for 2 Violins and Basso Continuo, op. 4 (London, c.1775); *6 Easy Duettos* for 2 Violins, op. 5 (London, c.1775); other pieces in contemporary collections.

Vačkář, family of Czech composers:
(1) Václav Vačkář; b. Prague, Aug. 12, 1881; d. there, Feb. 4, 1954. He received training in military music in Przemyśl, Poland (1895–98), then was active as a conductor and orch. player in various locales before playing in the Czech Phil. (1913–19), the Vinohrad Opera Orch. (1919–20), and the Šak Phil. (1920–21); after composition studies with Říhovský and Křička (1920–22), he devoted himself to composing, writing on music, and administrative work. He was awarded the Smetana Prize of Prague in 1952. He wrote *Lidová nauka o harmonii* (Popular Treatise on Harmony; Prague, 1942) and with D. Vačkář, *Instrumentace symfonického orchestra a hudby dechové* (Instrumentation for the Symphony Orchestra and Wind Music; Prague, 1954). Of his more than 300 works, about half are in a popular or light vein, including numerous marches and waltzes. He also wrote several symphonic poems, a Clarinet Concertino, 4 string quartets, choral pieces, and songs.
(2) Dalibor Cyril Vačkář, son of the preceding; b. Korčula, Yugoslavia, Sept. 19, 1906; d. Prague, Oct. 21, 1984. He studied violin with Reissig and composition with Šín at the Prague Cons. (1923–29); also attended master classes of Hoffmann and Suk (1929–31). From 1934 to 1945 he played violin in the Prague Radio Orch.; after working as a film dramatist (1945–47), he devoted himself mainly to composition; also wrote music criticism, poetry, and plays. He used the pseudonyms Pip Faltys, Peter Filip, Tomáš Martin, and Karel Raymond for his light music. With his father, he wrote *Instrumentace symfonického orchestru a hudby dechové* (Instrumentation for the Symphony Orchestra and Wind Music; Prague, 1954).
WORKS: BALLETS: *Švanda dudák* (Svanda the Bagpiper; 1950–53; Prague Radio, April 7, 1954) and *Sen noci svatojanské* (A Midsummer Night's Dream), after Shakespeare (1955–57).

ORCH.: *Overture* (1929); 2 violin concertos (1931, 1958); 5 syms.: No. 1, *Optimistická* (Optimistic; 1941); No. 2, *Země vyvolená* (The Chosen Land), with Contralto and Chorus (1947); No. 3, *Smoking Symphony* (1947–48; orchestration of his *Smoking Sonata* for Piano; the curious subtitle, symbolizing fire and smoke in the life of men from antiquity to the present day, is in Eng. only); No. 4, *O míru* (Of Peace; 1949–50); No. 5, *Pro juventute* (1978–82); *Symphonic Scherzo* (1945); Sinfonietta for Strings, Horn, Timpani, and Piano (1947); *Czech Concerto* for Piano and Orch. (1952); *Prelude and Metamorphoses* (1953); *Furiant-Fantasie* for Chamber Orch. (1960); *Concerto da camera* for Bassoon and Chamber String Orch. (1962); *Charakteristikon,* concerto for Trombone and Orch. (1965); *Legenda o člověku* (Legend of Men), concerto for Harpsichord, Winds, and Percussion (1966); Clarinet Concerto (1966); *Prelude* for Chamber String Orch. (1966); *Concerto grosso* for Soprano Saxophone, Accordion, Guitar, and Orch. (1967); *In fide, spe et caritate,* concerto for Organ, Winds, and Percussion (1969); *Appellatio,* with Female Chorus (1970; Prague, Oct. 20, 1977); *Příběh o pěti kapitolách* (5-Chapter Story), music for Clarinet, Strings, and Percussion (1971); *Musica concertante* (1973); Sinfonietta No. 2, *Jubilee* (1984).
CHAMBER: *Trio giocoso* for Piano Trio (1929); Violin Sonata (1930); String Quartet (1931–32); *Jaro 38,* Piano Trio (1938); *Monolog* for Violin (1940); Quartet for Piano, Oboe, Clarinet, and Bassoon (1948); *Quintetto giocoso* for Wind Instruments (1950; music from the ballet *Švanda dudák*); *Suite giocoso* for Piano Trio (1960); *Dialogue* for Violin (1961); *3 Studies* for Harpsichord (1961); *Dedication,* sonata for Violin and Piano (1961; each movement dedicated to Vačkář's teachers: Reissig, Šín, Hoffmann, and Suk); Concerto for String Quartet (1962); Concerto for Trumpet, Piano, and Percussion (1963); *Pianoforte cantante,* 5 lyric reminiscences for Piano, Double Bass, and Percussion (1968); *Partita* for Trumpet (1968); *Milieu d'enfant* for 5 Percussion Groups (1970); *Intimní hudba* (Private Music) for Violin and Piano (1972); *Furiant-fantasie* for Piano Trio (1974); *Verses* for Flute and Guitar (1975); *Symposium* for Brass Quintet (1976); *Oboe concertante* for Oboe, Clarinet, Bass Clarinet, Horn, String Quartet, Percussion, and Piano (1977); *Monograms,* 4 poems for String Quartet (1979; transcribed from the piano work); *Portraits* for Wind Quintet (1980; transcribed from the piano work); *Juniores,* 4 movements for String Quartet (1981; transcribed from the piano work); *Extempore,* piano quartet (1983).
PIANO: *Smoking Sonata* (1936); *Extempore,* 6 pieces (1937); *Piano Fantasy,* on a theme from Schubert's *The Arch* (1962); *Perspektivy* (1971); *3 Etudes* (1977); *Monograms* (1978); *Portraits* (1980); *Juniores* (1981).
(3) Tomáš Vačkář, son of the preceding; b. Prague, July 31, 1945; d. (suicide) there, May 2, 1963. He was a gifted composer, but chose to end his life shortly after his graduation from the Prague Cons. at the age of 18. His works, all written between July 1960 and April 1963, include *Sonatina furore* for Piano; *Concerto recitativo* for Flute, String Orch., and Piano; *Tři dopisy dívkam* (3 Letters to a Girl), after a poem by an anonymous Czech student, for Voice and Piano or Winds and Percussion; *Teen-agers,* piano sonata; *Metamorfózy na tema japonske ukolebavky* (Metamorphoses on the Theme of a Japanese Lullaby) for Orch.; *Scherzo melancolico* for Orch.; *Skicář Tomáše Vačkáře* (Tomáš Vačkář's Sketchbook), 10 pieces for Piano; a *Requiem* remained unfinished.

Vadé, Jean-Joseph, French poet, dramatist, and composer; b. Ham, Picardy, Jan. 17, 1719; d. Paris, July 4, 1757. He was taken to Paris by his family when he was 5; was made contrôleur du vingtième arrondissement (a tax-collecting position) in Soissons in 1739; after serving in this capacity in Laon and Rouen, he was made secretary to the Duke of Agenois in Paris in 1743. He began writing for the Comédie-Française in Paris in 1749, scoring success with his 1st opéra comique, *La Fileuse* (1752); subsequently brought out other works there. He was awarded a pension by Louis XV (1751). His importance rests upon his creation of the genre poissard, or fish-market style, which permeates his opéras comiques and chansons. **WORKS: OPÉRAS COMIQUES** (all 1st perf. in Paris): *La Fileuse* (March 8, 1752); *Le Poirier* (Aug. 7, 1752); *Le Bouquet du roi* (Aug. 24, 1752; in collaboration with J. Fleury and Lattaignant); *Le Suffisant, ou Le Petit Maître dupé* (March 12, 1753); *Le Rien* (April 10, 1753); *Le Trompeur trompé, ou La Rencontre imprévue* (Feb. 18, 1754); *Il était temps* (June 28, 1754); *La Fontaine de jouvence* (Sept. 17, 1754; in collaboration with Noverre); *La Nouvelle Bastienne* (Sept. 17, 1754; in collaboration with L. Anseaume); *Compliment de clôture* (Oct. 6, 1754); *Les Troyennes en Champagne* (Feb. 1, 1755); *Jérôme et Fanchonette, ou La Pastorale de la grenouillère* (Feb. 18, 1755); *Compliment de clôture* (April 6, 1755); *Le Confidant heureux* (July 31, 1755); *Folette, ou L'Enfant gâté* (Sept. 6, 1755); *Nicaise* (Feb. 7, 1756); *Les Raccoleurs* (March 11, 1756); *L'Impromptu du cœur* (Feb. 8, 1757); *Compliment pour la clôture de l'Opéra-Comique* (April 3, 1757); *Le Mauvais plaisant, ou Le Drôle de corps* (Aug. 17, 1757); also *La Folle raisonnable* (not perf.).

Vaet, Jacobus, Flemish composer; b. Courtrai or Harelbeke, c.1529; d. Vienna, Jan. 8, 1567. He was a choirboy in the Church of Notre Dame at Courtrai (1543–46); after his voice changed, he received a scholarship from the church, and entered the Univ. of Louvain in 1547; in 1550 he was a tenor in the Flemish Chapel of Charles V; by Jan. 1, 1554, he was listed as Kapellmeister of the chapel of Maximilian, then the nominal King of Bohemia. His position was enhanced when his patron became Emperor Maximilian II. Vaet's music exhibits a great variety of techniques, ranging in style from those of Josquin des Prez to those of Lassus. The formative influence, however, is mainly that of Nicolas Gombert, with a characteristic florid imitation in contrapuntal parts.

WORKS: 9 masses; 8 Magnificats; motets: *Modulationes, liber I* for 5 Voices (Venice, 1562); *Modulationes, liber II* for 5 to 6 Voices (Venice, 1562); *Qui operatus est Petro* for 6 Voices (Venice, 1560); other motets publ. in contemporary collections; 8 Salve Reginas; 8 hymns; several other pieces, including 3 chansons. See M. Steinhardt, ed., *Jacobus Vaet: Sämtliche Werke,* Denkmäler der Tonkunst in Österreich, XCVIII (1961), C (1962), CIII–CIV (1963), CVIII–CIX (1964), CXIII–CXIV (1965), CXVI (1967), and CXVIII (1968).

BIBL.: M. Steinhardt, *J. V. and His Motets* (East Lansing, Mich., 1951); idem, "The Hymns of J. V.," *Journal of the American Musicological Society* (Fall 1956); idem, "Addenda to the Biography of J. V.," *The Commonwealth of Music, in Honor of Curt Sachs* (N.Y., 1965); idem, "The Missa 'Si me tenes': A Problem of Authorship," *Aspects of Medieval and Renaissance Music: A Birthday Offering to Gustave Reese* (N.Y., 1966); W. Pass, "J. V.s und Georg Prenners Vertonungen des 'Salve regina' in Joanellus' Sammelwerk von 1568," *De ratione in musica: Festschrift Erich Schenck* (Kassel, 1975).

Vainberg, Moisei, Polish-born Russian composer; b. Warsaw, Dec. 8, 1919. He studied piano with Turczynski at the Warsaw Cons., graduating in 1939; then studied composition with Zolotarev at the Minsk Cons.; in 1943 he settled in Moscow. In his music he follows the precepts of socialist realism in its ethnic aspects; according to the subject, he makes use of Jewish, Polish, Moldavian, or Armenian folk melos, in tasteful harmonic arrangements devoid of abrasive dissonances.

WORKS: OPERAS: *The Sword of Uzbekistan* (1942); *The Woman Passenger* (1968); *Love of D'Artagnan,* after Alexandre Dumas (1972). **BALLETS:** *Battle for the Fatherland* (1942); *The Golden Key* (1955); *The White Chrysanthemum* (1958); *Requiem* (1967). **CANTATAS:** *On This Day Lenin Was Born* for Chorus and Orch. (1970); *Hiroshima Haikus* (1966); *The Diary of Love* (1965). **ORCH.:** 16 syms.: No. 1 (1942); No. 2 for String Orch. (1946); No. 3 (1949); No. 4 (1957); No. 5 (1962); No. 6, with Boys' Chorus (1963); No. 7 for Strings and Harpsichord (1964); No. 8, *The Flowers of Poland,* for Tenor, Chorus, and Orch. (1964); No. 9, *Surviving Pages,* for Reader, Chorus, and Orch. (1967); No. 10 for String Orch. (1968); No. 11, *Triumphant Symphony,* for Chorus and Orch., dedicated to Lenin's centennial (1969); No. 12 (1976; Moscow, Oct. 13, 1979);

No. 13 (1976); No. 14 (1977; Moscow, Oct. 8, 1980); No. 15, with Chorus, "I have faith in this earth" (1977; Moscow, April 12, 1979); No. 16 (1981; Moscow, Oct. 19, 1982); 2 sinfoniettas (1948, 1960); *Moldavian Rhapsody* (Moscow, Nov. 30, 1949); *Slavic Rhapsody* (1950); Cello Concerto (1956); Violin Concerto (1960); Flute Concerto (1961); Trumpet Concerto (1967); Clarinet Concerto (1970). **CHAMBER:** 12 string quartets (1937–70); Piano Quintet (1944); Piano Trio (1945); String Trio (1951); 20 sonatas and 2 sonatinas for Various Instruments, with Piano; 24 preludes for Cello Solo; 23 preludes for Piano; also songs.

Vajda, János, Hungarian composer; b. Miskolc, Oct. 8, 1949. He received training in choral conducting from István Párkai and in composition from Emil Petrovics at the Budapest Academy of Music (graduated, 1975); after serving as répétiteur with the Hungarian Radio and Television Choir (1974–79), he completed his composition studies at the Sweelinck Cons. in Amsterdam (1979–80). From 1981 he taught at the Budapest Academy of Music.

WORKS: OPERAS: *Barabbás* (1976–77); *Mario és a varázsló* (Mario and the Magician; 1983–85). **BALLETS:** *Az igazság pillanata* (The Moment of Truth; 1981); *Don Juan árnyéka rajtunk* (Don Juan's Shadow Is Cast on Us; 1981); *Izzó planéták* (Glowing Planets; 1983); *Jön a cirkusz* (Circus Is Coming; 1984). **ORCH.:** *Holland anziksz* (Picture Postcard from Holland) for Chamber Ensemble (1979); *Búcsú* (Farewell; 1978–80); *Pentaton, in memoriam R.M.* for Chamber Ensemble (1983). **CHAMBER:** *Gregorián ének* (Gregorian Chant) for Cimbalom (1974); *Két teszt* (2 Tests) for Mezzo-soprano, Flute, Clarinet, and Bassoon (1975); *De angelis* for Wind Quintet and Tape (1978); *All That Music* for 2 Cimbaloms (1981); *Just for You* for Cello (1984); *Mozi-zene* (Movie Music) for Piano and String Trio (1986); *Just for You No. 2* for Violin (1987); *Változatok* (Variations) for Piano (1987). **CHORAL:** *Tenebrae factae sunt* (1972); *Fekete gloria* (Black Halo; 1977); *Stabat Mater* for 2 Female Soloists, Female Choir, and Chamber Ensemble (1978); *Ave Maris Stella* (1979); Cantata No. 1 for Chamber Choir, Wind Quintet, String Quintet, and Celesta (1981); *Tristis est anima mea* (1982); *Via crucis* for Choir, 8 Winds, and Organ (1983); *Alleluja* (1983); *Kolinda* (1984); *Karácsonyi kantáta* (Christmas Cantata) for 2 Child Soloists, Choir, Children's Choir, and Orch. (1984–86); *Rapszódia* (1987–88).

Valcárcel, Edgar, Peruvian composer and pianist, nephew of **Teodoro Valcárcel;** b. Puno, Dec. 4, 1932. He studied composition with Andrés Sas at the Lima Cons.; then went to N.Y., where he studied with Donald Lybbert at Hunter College; subsequently traveled to Buenos Aires, where he took composition lessons with Alberto Ginastera; also had sessions with Olivier Messiaen in Paris, and with Riccardo Malipiero, Bruno Maderna, and Luigi Dallapiccola in Italy; furthermore, he joined the Electronic Music Center of Columbia and Princeton Univs. and worked with Vladimir Ussachevsky; held 2 Guggenheim Foundation grants (1966, 1968). He was prof. of composition at the Lima Cons. (from 1965). In his compositions he adopted an extremely advanced idiom that combined serial and aleatory principles, leaving to the performer the choice to use or not to use given thematic materials.

WORKS: ORCH.: Concerto for Clarinet and Strings (Lima, March 6, 1966); *Quenua* (Lima, Aug. 18, 1965); *Aleaciones* (Lima, May 5, 1967); Piano Concerto (Lima, Aug. 8, 1968); *Checán II* (Lima, June 5, 1970); *Ma'karabotasaq hachana* (1971); *Sajra* (1974). **CHAMBER:** 2 string quartets (1962, 1963); *Espectros I* for Flute, Viola, and Piano (1964); *Espectros II* for Horn, Cello, and Piano (1968); *Dicotomías III* for 12 Instruments (Mexico City, Nov. 20, 1966); *Fisiones* for 10 Instruments (1967); *Hiwana uru* for 11 Instruments (1967); Trio for Amplified Violin, Trombone, and Clarinet (1968); *Poema* for Amplified Violin, Voice, Piano, and Percussion (1969); *Checán I* for 6 Instruments (1969); *Checán III* for 19 Instruments (1971); *Montage 59* for String Quartet, Clarinet, Piano, and Lights (1971); *Espectros III* for Oboe, Violin, and Piano (1974); *Checán V* for Strings (1974). **PIANO:** *Dicotomías I* and *II* (1966);

2 sonatas (1963, 1972). ELECTRONIC: *Antaras* for Flute, Percussion, and Electronic Sounds (1968); various multimedia pieces with chorus, electronic sounds, and lights; also several choruses a cappella.

Valcárcel, Teodoro, Peruvian composer, uncle of **Edgar Valcárcel;** b. Puno, Oct. 17, 1900; d. Lima, March 20, 1942. He studied at the Milan Cons. (1914–16) and with Felipe Pedrell in Barcelona. In 1928 he won the National Prize for Peruvian composers, and was awarded a gold medal from the municipality of Lima for his studies in Peruvian folk music. In 1929 he went to Europe once more; presented a concert of his works in Paris (April 12, 1930). In 1931 he settled in Lima. He was of pure Indian origin; as a native of the highlands, he was able to collect Indian songs unpolluted by urban influences. He publ. *30 cantos de alma vernacular; 4 canciones incaicas; 25 romances de costa y sierra peruana; 180 melodias del folklore.* Among his original works are the ballets (with singing) *Suray-Surita* and *Ckori Kancha;* 2 symphonic suites (both 1939); *En las ruinas del Templo del Sol,* tone poem (1940); *Concierto indio* for Violin and Orch. (1940); *3 ensayos* for an ensemble of Native Instruments; *Fiestas andinas* for Piano; *Suite autóctona* for Violin and Piano; songs. A catalogue of his works was publ. by R. Holzmann in *Boletín Bibliográfico de la Universidad nacional mayor de San Marcos,* XII (1942).
BIBL.: R. Holzmann, "Ensayo analítico de la obra musical del compositor peruano T. V.," *Revista Eco Musical* (Buenos Aires, 1943).

Valdengo, Giuseppe, Italian baritone; b. Turin, May 24, 1914. He studied cello at the Turin Cons., and also played the oboe; then decided to cultivate his voice, and took singing lessons with Michele Accoriutti. In 1936 he made his operatic debut as Figaro in *Il Barbiere di Siviglia* in Parma; in 1939, was engaged to sing at La Scala in Milan. On Sept. 19, 1946, he made his N.Y. City Opera debut as Sharpless, remaining on its roster until 1948. On Dec. 19, 1947, he made his Metropolitan Opera debut in N.Y. as Tonio; continued on the company's roster until 1954; was also chosen by Toscanini to sing the roles of Amonasro, Renato, Iago, and Falstaff with the NBC Sym. Orch. He made guest appearances in London, Paris, Vienna, and South America. He also acted the part of Antonio Scotti in the film *The Great Caruso.* His association with Toscanini is related in his *Ho cantato con Toscanini* (Como, 1962).

Valderrábano, Enrique Enriquez de. See Enriquez de Valderrábano, Enrique.

Valderrama, Carlos, Peruvian composer; b. Trujillo, Sept. 4, 1887; d. Lima, Aug. 1, 1950. He studied engineering at Cornell Univ., then decided to devote himself to music; made his debut as a pianist at Carnegie Hall in N.Y. (Feb. 22, 1920). He wrote many piano pieces on old Inca themes, in a salon style (several of them publ.), and some ballet music.

Valdrighi, Count Luigi Francesco, Italian music scholar; b. Modena, July 30, 1827; d. there, April 20, 1899. He was curator of the music archives of the Estense Library. He acquired an extensive collection of musical instruments of the 15th to 19th centuries, which was later partly sold and partly given to the Modena Museum. He publ. numerous valuable monographs on the music and musicians of Modena; among his theoretical writings the most important was *Nomocheliurgografia antica e moderna* (1884; 2 supplements, 1888, 1894). With G. Ferrari-Moreni, he completed a chronicle of theater life in Modena, *Cronistoria dei teatri di Modena* (1873).
BIBL.: E. Zoccoli, *Il Conte L.F. V.* (Modena, 1899).

Válek, Jiří, remarkable Czech composer; b. Prague, May 28, 1923. He studied composition at the Prague Cons. and then at its Master's School with Řídký; also studied at the Univ. of Prague (Ph.D., 1952). He was secretary of the Guild of Czech Composers (1949–52) and ed.-in-chief of children's musical programming at the Czech Radio in Prague (1952–55), of the editorial division of the Central House of the Czech Army (1955–59), and of Panton, the publishing house of the

Guild (1959–73); was an instructor in music theory at the Prague Cons.
WORKS: OPERAS: *Opuštěná* (The Deserted Woman), chamber opera (1980); *Hamlet Our Contemporary* (1979–84). **ORCH.:** 14 programmatic syms.: No. 1, *Rok 1948* (The Year 1948) for Trumpet, Piano, and Orch. (1948); No. 2, *Klasická* (Classic) for 2 Flutes, 2 Clarinets, Chamber String Orch., and Piano (1957); No. 3, *Romantická,* for Soprano Saxophone, Tenor Saxophone, and Orch. (1962); No. 4, *Dialogy s vnitřním hlasem* (Dialogues with an Inner Voice), to Shakespearean texts, for Contralto, Baritone, Large Wind Orch., Percussion, and Piano (1967); No. 5, *Guernica,* after the Picasso painting (1968); No. 6, *Ekpyrosis,* reflecting philosophical ideals of Heraclitus, for Flute, String Orch., Percussion, and Piano (1968–69); No. 7, *Pompejské fresky* (Pompeian Frescoes) for Chamber Orch., Piano, and Percussion (1969–70); No. 8, *Hic sunt homines!,* on the theme of a novella by Stefan Zweig, for Soprano and Orch. (1970–71); No. 9, *Renesanční* (Renaissance), triple concerto for Violin, Viola, Cello, and String Orch. (1971); No. 10, *Barokní* (Baroque), to commemorate the 300th anniversary of the death of the Czech Baroque painter Karel Škréta and the 150th anniversary of the birth of Smetana, double concerto for Violin, Piano, and Orch. (1973); No. 11, *Revoluční* (Revolutionary), to commemorate the 30th anniversary of Czech liberation, for Piano Trio, Wind Quintet, and Orch. (1974); No. 12, *Shakespearean,* double concerto for Violin, Viola, and Chamber String Orch. (1976); No. 13, *Gotická,* for Chorus and Orch. (1978); No. 14, *Trionphale,* for 2 Pianos and Orch. (1983); Sinfonietta (1944); *The Dam,* symphonic poem (1959); *Reflections on a Summer Lake,* dance suite (1972); *Beyond the Bounds of Tomorrow,* ceremonial march (1972); *La portenza della Primavera,* 5 dithyrambs for Soprano and Orch. (1972); *Hymnus slunce* (Hymn to the Sun), violin concerto (1975); Concerto for 2 Flutes and Chamber Orch. (1975); *Shakespearean Fresques* for Violin, Viola, and Orch. (1976); *Concerto giocoso* for Flute, Marimba, Harp, and Orch. (1978); *Festive Fresque* (1979); Cello Concerto: *Maestoso* (1981); English Horn Concerto (1985). **CHAMBER:** 4 string quartets (1943; 1945; *The Rumburk Uprising,* 1960; *Quattrocento,* 1972–73); 2 violin sonatas (1944, 1960); 2 viola sonatas (1948, 1961); *Serenade* for 9 Winds and Piano (1959); *Eroica,* sonata for Trumpet or Clarinet and Piano (1960); *Concerto-notturno* for Violin, Viola, and Cello (1967); *Shakespeare Variations* for Nonet (1967); Flute Sonata (1969); *Nenie* for Violin or Cello (1969); Concerto for Flute, Oboe, Violin, Viola, Cello, and Harpsichord (1970); *Villa dei Misteri,* 11 fresques for Violin and Piano (1971); *Aesop* for Children's Choir, Narrator, Ballet, Flute, 2 Clarinets, Bassoon, and Percussion (1972); *Objevování dne* (Coming of the Day), 2nd concerto for 6 Instruments (1979); *4 Profiles from Shakespeare,* concerto for Oboe and Bassoon (1979); *Concertante Meditations* for Clarinet, Violin, Viola, and Cello (1980); 3 piano sonatas (*The Year 1942,* 1942; 1961; 1970); songs.

Valen, (Olav) Fartein, noted Norwegian composer; b. Stavanger, Aug. 25, 1887; d. Haugesund, Dec. 14, 1952. His father was a missionary in Madagascar, and Valen spent his early childhood there; when he was 6 the family returned to Stavanger, and he received piano lessons from Jeannette Mohr and others; taught himself theory. In 1906 he entered the Univ. of Christiania as a student of language and literature; he soon devoted himself entirely to music, pursuing his training in theory with Elling at the Christiania Cons., graduating as an organist in 1909; then received instruction in composition from Bruch, in theory and composition from Karl Leopold Wolf, and in piano from Heschberg at the Berlin Hochschule für Musik (1909–11). From 1916 to 1924 he lived on his family's farm in Valevåg; he then was active in Oslo, where he held the post of inspector of the Norwegian Music Collection at the library of the Univ. (1927–36). In 1935 he received the Norwegian State Salary of Art (a government life pension). His early music reflects the influence of Brahms, but later he developed a sui generis method of composition which he termed "atonal polyphony," completely free from traditional tonal relationships but strongly cohesive in contrapuntal fabric and greatly varied in rhythm; his first work in which he made use of this technique was a Piano Trio written in 1924. He never adopted an explicit 12-tone method of composition, but a parallelism with Schoenberg's music is observable. Valen stood apart from all nationalist developments in Oslo, yet his music attracted attention in modern circles; a Valen Society was formed in Norway in 1949, and in England in 1952, shortly before his death.

WORKS: ORCH.: 5 syms.: No. 1 (1937–39; Bergen, Feb. 2, 1956); No. 2 (1941–44; Oslo, March 28, 1957); No. 3 (1944–46; Oslo, April 13, 1951); No. 4 (1947–49; Malmö, Oct. 16, 1956); No. 5 (1951–52; unfinished); *Pastorale* (1929–30); *Sonetto di Michelangelo* (1932); *Nenia* (1932); *Cantico di ringraziamento* (Song of Thanksgiving; 1932–33); *An die Hoffnung* (To Hope, after Keats's poem; 1933); *Epithalamion* (1933); *Le Cimetière marin* (Graveyard by the Sea; 1933–34); *La isla de las calmas* (The Silent Island; 1934); *Ode til Ensomheten* (Ode to Solitude; 1939); Violin Concerto (1940; Oslo, Oct. 24, 1947); Concerto for Piano and Chamber Orch. (1949–51; Oslo, Jan. 15, 1953). **SOPRANO AND ORCH.:** *Ave Maria* (1917–21); *3 Gedichte von Goethe* (1925–27); *Mignon,* 2 songs after Goethe (1920–27); *2 chinesische Gedichte* (1925–27); *Dearest Thou Now, O Soul,* after Whitman (1920–28); *La noche oscura del alma* (The Dark Night of the Soul), after St. John of the Cross (1939). **CHAMBER:** Violin Sonata (1916); Piano Trio (1917–24); 2 string quartets (1928–29; 1930–31); *Serenade* for Wind Quintet (1946–47). **PIANO:** *Legend* (1907); 2 sonatas: No. 1 (1912) and No. 2, *The Hound of Heaven,* after the poem by Francis Thompson (1940–41); *4 Pieces* (1934–35); *Variations* (1935–36); *Gavotte and Musette* (1936); *Prelude and Fugue* (1937); *2 Preludes* (1937); *Intermezzo* (1939–40). **ORGAN:** *Prelude and Fugue* (1939) and *Pastoral* (1939). He also wrote songs and motets.

BIBL.: O. Gurvin, *F. V., En banebryter i nyere norsk musikk* (F. V., a Pioneer in Norwegian Music; Oslo, 1962); B. Kortsen, *Studies of Form in F. V.'s Music* (Oslo, 1962); idem, *Melodic Structure and Thematic Unity in F. V.'s Music* (2 vols., Glasgow, 1963); idem, *F. V., Life and Music* (3 vols., Oslo, 1965); Anonymous, *Komponisten F. V. 1887–1952* (Oslo, 1976); P. Rapoport, *Opus Est: Six Composers from Northern Europe* (London, 1978).

Valencia, Antonio María, Colombian pianist and composer; b. Cali, Nov. 10, 1902; d. there, July 22, 1952. He studied at the Schola Cantorum in Paris (from 1923) with d'Indy, Pierné, Le Flem, and others; returning to Colombia in 1930, he was founder-director of the Cali Conservatorio y Escuela de Bellas Artes (1933–37; 1938–52); also was director of the Bogotá Cons. (1937–38).

WORKS: *Chirimía y bambuco sotareño* for Orch. (1942); *Egloga incaica* for Flute, Oboe, Clarinet, and Bassoon (1935); *Emociones caucanas* for Piano, Violin, and Cello (1938); numerous pieces for piano solo, inspired by native melorhythms (*8 ritmos y cantos suramericanos, Sonatina boyacense,* etc.); Requiem (1943); other church music; choruses and songs.

BIBL.: A. Tovar, *A.M. V., artista integral* (Cali, 1958).

Valente, Antonio, blind Italian organist and composer who flourished in the 2nd half of the 16th century, known as "il Cieco" ("the blind man"). He became blind as a child; was organist at Sant'Angelo a Nido in Naples (1565–80). His 1st publication, *Intavolatura de cimbalo: Recercate, fantasie et canzoni francese desminuite con alcuni tenori balli et varie sorti de contraponti . . .* (Naples, 1575), is in Spanish keyboard tablature and contains early keyboard fantasias, written out in detail; his 2nd book, *Versi spirituali sopra tutte le note, con diversi canoni spartiti per suonar negli organi, messe, vespere et altri offici divini* (Naples, 1580), represents an early type of keyboard partitura; I. Fuser ed. *Antonio Valente: Versi spirituali per organo* (Padua, 1958).

BIBL.: N. Caravaglios, "Una nuova *Intavolatura de cimbalo* di A. V. Cieco," *Rivista Musicale Italiana,* XXIII (1916); J. Burns, *Neapolitan Keyboard Music from V. to Frescobaldi* (diss.,

Harvard Univ., 1953; includes an ed. of the *Intavolatura de cimbalo*); idem, "A. V., Neapolitan Keyboard Primitive," *Journal of the American Musicological Society,* XII (1959).

Valente, Benita, distinguished American soprano; b. Delano, Calif., Oct. 19, 1934. She began serious musical training with Chester Hayden at Delano High School; at 16 she became a private pupil of Lotte Lehmann, and at 17 received a scholarship to continue her studies with Lehmann at the Music Academy of the West in Santa Barbara; in 1955 she won a scholarship to the Curtis Inst. of Music in Philadelphia, where she studied with Martial Singher. Upon graduation in 1960, she made her formal debut in a Marlboro (Vt.) Festival concert. On Oct. 8, 1960, she made her N.Y. concert debut at the New School for Social Research. After winning the Metropolitan Opera Auditions in 1960, she pursued further studies with Margaret Harshaw. She then sang with the Freiburg Opera, making her debut there as Pamina in 1962; after appearances with the Nuremberg Opera (1966), she returned to the U.S. and established herself as a versatile recitalist, soloist with orchs., and opera singer. Her interpretation of Pamina was especially well received, and it was in that role that she made her long-awaited Metropolitan Opera debut in N.Y. on Sept. 22, 1973. She won praise for her performances in operas by Monteverdi, Handel, Verdi, Puccini, and Britten. Her extensive recital and concert repertoire ranges from Schubert to Ginastera.

BIBL.: *Current Biography* (March 1988).

Valente, Giorgio. See **Vitalis, George.**

Valente, Vincenzo, Italian composer; b. Corigliano Calabro, Feb. 21, 1855; d. Naples, Sept. 6, 1921. At the age of 15 he wrote a song, *Ntuniella,* which became popular; he continued writing Neapolitan songs of great appeal (*Basta ca po', Comme te voglio amà!, Canzone cafona, Mugliera comme fa, Ninuccia, Tiempe felice, L'acqua,* etc.), about 400 songs in all. He also brought out operettas: *I Granatieri* (Turin, Oct. 26, 1889); *La Sposa di Charolles* (Rome, March 3, 1894); *Rolandino* (Turin, Oct. 15, 1897); *L'usignuolo* (Naples, May 10, 1899); *Lena* (Foggia, Jan. 1, 1918); *L'Avvocato Trafichetti* (Naples, May 24, 1919); *Nèmesi* (posthumous, Naples, July 23, 1923). His son, **Nicola Valente** (b. Naples, Aug. 28, 1881; d. there, Sept. 16, 1946), was also a composer of Neapolitan songs and light operas.

Valenti, Fernando, noted American harpsichordist and teacher; b. N.Y., Dec. 4, 1926; d. Red Bank, N.J., Sept. 6, 1990. He studied piano with José Iturbi; then attended Yale Univ., where he took instruction in harpsichord with Ralph Kirkpatrick. He made his N.Y. recital debut in 1950. In 1951 he was appointed prof. of harpsichord at the Juilliard School of Music in N.Y.; also taught at various other academic institutions. He publ. the book *The Harpsichord: A Dialogue for Beginners* (1982). His performances of the music of Domenico Scarlatti were highly praised.

Valentin, Erich, distinguished German musicologist; b. Strasbourg, Nov. 27, 1906. He studied music with Courvoisier and Röhr in Munich; took courses in musicology with Sandberger at the Univ. of Munich, where he received his Ph.D. in 1928 with the dissertation *Die Entwicklung der Tokkata im 17. und 18. Jahrhundert* (publ. in Munich, 1930). From 1929 to 1935 he taught at the Staatliches Privatmusiklehrer-Seminar in Magdeburg; from 1939 to 1945 he was director of the Zentralinstitut für Mozartforschung. He taught at the Nordwestdeutsche Hochschule für Musik in Munich from 1953, where he was a prof. from 1955 and its director (1964–72). From 1950 to 1955 he was ed.-in-chief of the *Zeitschrift für Musik,* and from 1955–59 co-ed. of the *Neue Zeitschrift für Musik.* He became ed.-in-chief of *Acta Mozartiana* in 1954. In addition to his many articles for music journals, he also prepared eds. of works by Mozart, Telemann, and others.

WRITINGS: *Georg Philipp Telemann* (Burg, 1931; 3rd ed., 1952); *Richard Wagner* (Regensburg, 1937); *Dichtung und Oper: Eine Untersuchung zum Stilproblem der Oper* (Leipzig,

1938); *Hans Pfitzner* (Regensburg, 1939); *Wege zu Mozart* (Regensburg, 1941; 4th ed., 1950); *Beethoven* (Salzburg, 1942; Eng. ed., N.Y., 1958); *W.A. Mozart: Wesen und Wandlung* (Hamelin, 1948); *Kleine Bilder grosser Meister* (Mainz, 1952); *Handbuch der Chormusik* (Regensburg, 1953–74); *Handbuch der Instrumentenkunde* (Regensburg, 1954; 6th ed., 1974); *Der früheste Mozart* (Munich, 1956); *Beethoven* (pictorial bibliography; Munich, 1957); *Die Tokkata*, in *Das Musikwerk*, XVII (1958); *Mozart* (pictorial bibliography; Munich, 1959); *Musica domestica: Über Wesen und Geschichte der Hausmusik* (Trossingen, 1959); *Telemann in seiner Zeit* (Hamburg, 1960); *Handbuch der Schulmusik* (Regensburg, 1962); *Die goldene Spur: Mozart in der Dichtung Hermann Hesses* (Augsburg, 1965); *Die evangelische Kirchenmusik* (with F. Hofmann; Regensburg, 1967); *Handbuch des Musikunterrichts* (with W. Gebhardt and W. Vetter; Regensburg, 1970); *Die schönsten Beethoven-Briefe* (Munich, 1973).
BIBL.: G. Weiss, ed., *E. V. zum 70. Geburtstag* (Regensburg, 1976).

Valentini-Terrani, Lucia, Italian mezzo-soprano; b. Padua, Aug. 28, 1948. She studied in Padua; made her operatic debut in the title role of Rossini's *La Cenerentola* in Brescia (1969); then sang in various Italian opera houses. She made her Metropolitan Opera debut in N.Y. as Isabella in *L'Italiana in Algeri* on Nov. 16, 1974; also sang in Paris, Moscow, London, Vienna, Munich, Stuttgart, and Dresden. She became well known for her roles in Italian operas, most especially those by Rossini and Verdi.

Valentini, Giovanni, Italian composer; b. Venice, 1582; d. Vienna, April 29, 1649. He was a pupil of Giovanni Gabrieli. He was organist to King Sigismund III at the Polish court; from 1614, was chamber organist to the Archduke Ferdinand at Graz, becoming court organist at Vienna when Ferdinand ascended the throne in 1619; by 1626 he was Imperial Kapellmeister.
WORKS (all publ. in Venice unless otherwise given): *Canzoni, libro primo* for 3, 5 to 6, and 8 Voices (1609); *Motetti* for 4 to 6 Voices (1611); *Secondo libro de madrigali* for 4 to 5 and 8 to 11 Voices and Basso Continuo (1616); *Missae concertatae* for 4, 6, and 8 Voices and Basso Continuo (1617); *Salmi, hinni, Magnificat, antifone, falsibordone et motetti* for 1 to 4 Voices and Basso Continuo (1618); *Musiche concertate* for 6 to 10 Voices and Basso Continuo (1619); *Musica di camera, libro quarto* for 1 to 6 Voices and Basso Continuo (1621); *Missae quatuor* for 8 to 12 Voices with Basso Continuo ad libitum (1621); *Messa, Magnificat et Jubilate Deo*, 7 choruses with Trumpet (Vienna, 1621); *Musiche* for 2 Voices (1622); *Il quinto libro de madrigali* for 3 to 6 Voices and Basso Continuo (1625); *Sacri concerti* for 2 to 5 Voices and Basso Continuo (1625); various other works in contemporary collections.

Valentini, Giuseppe, Italian violinist and composer; b. Florence, c.1680; d. after 1759. He was at Rome in 1700; was in the service of Prince Francesco Maria Ruspoli as a violinist, c.1708–13; may then have been at Bologna in the service of the Prince di Caserta; from 1735, was at the grand-ducal court of Florence. His violin technique was highly developed (some compositions call for the 6th position).
WORKS: OPERAS: *La finta rapita* (Cisterna, 1714; in collaboration with N. Romaldi and G. Cesarini); *La costanza in amore* (Cisterna, 1715). **ORATORIOS AND CANTATAS:** *La superbia punita in Absalone* (Rome, 1705); *Oratorio per l'assunzione della beata vergine* (Rome, 1730); *Cantata da recitarsi nel palazzo apostolico la notte del santissimo natale* (Rome, 1733); *Cantata per la natività della beata vergine* (Rome, 1746); *Nell'amoroso foco*, cantata for Soprano, 2 Violins, and Basso Continuo. **INSTRUMENTAL** (all publ. in Rome unless otherwise given): (12) *Sinfonie* for 2 Violins, Cello, and Bass (1701); (7) *Bizzarrie per camera* for 2 Violins and Violone or Harpsichord (1703); (12) *Fantasie musicali* for 2 Violins and Violone or Harpsichord (1706); (7) *Idee per camera* for Violin and Violone or Harpsichord (1706–7); (12) *Villeggiature armoniche* for 2 Violins and Cello or Basso Continuo (1707); *Rime varie* (not extant); (12) *Concerti*

grossi for 2 or 4 Violins, Viola, and Cello Concertino or 2 Violins and Bass (Bologna, 1710); (12) *Allettamenti per camera* for Violin and Cello or Harpsichord (1714); *X concerti* for 2 Violins and Bass Concertino and 2 Violins, Viola, and Bass (Amsterdam, 1724); several concertos in contemporary collections.
BIBL.: W. Newman, *The Sonata in the Baroque Era* (Chapel Hill, 1959; 4th ed., rev., 1983).

Valentini, Pier (Pietro) Francesco, Italian music theorist, poet, and composer; b. Rome, c.1570; d. there, 1654. He was a pupil of G.B. Nanino. Although he called himself an amateur musician, he especially distinguished himself as a music theorist.
WORKS (all publ. in Rome): **SACRED VOCAL:** *Canone sopra le parole del Salve Regina, "Illos tuos misericordes oculos ad nos converte," con le resolutioni a 2, 3, 4 e 5 voci* (1629; a canon with over 2,000 possible resolutions; the theme is in Kircher's *Musurgia*, I); *In animas purgatorii: canon 4 compositus subjectis* for 20 Voices (1645); *Motetti, libro primo* for Voice, Instruments, and Basso Continuo (1654); *Motetti, libro secondo* for Voice, Instruments, and Basso Continuo (1654); *Motetti e concerti, libro primo* for 2 to 4 Voices and Basso Continuo (1654); *Letanie e concerti* for 2 to 4 Voices, Violin, Cornetto, Theorbo or Lute, and Basso Continuo (1654); *Motetti per le processioni del Corpus Domini, della beata vergine, e della settimana santa, libro primo* for 4 to 5 Voices (1655); *Motetti per processioni diversi, libro primo* (1655); other works in MS. **SECULAR VOCAL:** *Madrigali, musica e parole del Signor . . . Valentini . . . libro primo* for 5 Voices and Basso Continuo ad libitum (1654); *Madrigali . . . libro secondo* for 5 Voices and Basso Continuo ad libitum (1654); *Canzonette et arie, musica e parole del Signor . . . Valentini . . . libro primo* for 1 to 2 Voices and Basso Continuo (1657); *Canzonette et arie . . . libro secondo* for 1 to 2 Voices and Basso Continuo (1657); other works in MS.
BIBL.: L. Kurz, *Die Tonartenlehre des römischen Theoretikers und Komponisten P.F. V.* (diss., Univ. of Kassel, 1937).

Valentino, Henri-Justin-Armand-Joseph, French conductor; b. Lille, Oct. 14, 1785; d. Versailles, Jan. 20, 1865. He began his career as a theater conductor when he was only 14; after working in Rouen, he settled in Paris. About 1820 he became 2nd conductor at the Opéra, where he shared the duties of 1st conductor with Habeneck (1824–30); then was chief conductor of the Opéra-Comique (1831–36). After a sojourn in Chantilly (1836–37), he returned to Paris and conducted his own "Concerts Valentino" until 1841; then retired to Versailles.

Valerius, Adrianus (Adriaan, Adriaen), Dutch lawyer, historian, poet, and musician; b. probably in Middelburg, c.1575; d. Veere, Zeeland, Jan. 27, 1625. He settled in Veere as a notary in 1606; later became sheriff and served as dean of the chamber of rhetoric. He wrote *Neder-landtsche gedenck-clanck* (Haarlem, 1626), a history of the Dutch and Spanish wars from 1555 to 1625; it includes 76 popular songs with accompaniments in French tablature for 1 or more 7-stringed lutes and 4-stringed citterns. P.J. Meertens, N.B. Tenhaeff, and A. Komter-Kuipers edited a complete ed. of the text with melodies but without the tablatures (Amsterdam, 1942); K. Bernet Kampers and C. Lelij edited the song texts and tunes as *De liederen uit Valerius' Nederlandtsche gedenck-clanck* (Rotterdam, 1941).
BIBL.: J. Enschedé, "De Wilhelmus-melodie in de Gedenck-Clanck van V.," *Tijdschrift van de Vereeniging voor Nederlandsche Muziekgeschiedenis*, 5 (1897).

Valkare, Gunnar, Swedish organist, teacher, and composer; b. Norrköping, April 25, 1943. He studied piano with Stina Sundell, organ with Alf Linder, and composition with Ingvar Lidholm at the Stockholm Musikhögskolan (1963–69); was active as an organist and teacher (1964–79); served as resident composer in Gislaved (1973) and Kalmar (1977–78). His music is militantly aggressive in its tonal, atonal, and polytonal assault on the most cherished notions of harmonious sweetness.
WORKS: *4 Cardiograms* for Solo Singers, Chorus, and Instru-

ments in varying combinations (1965–66); *A Study in the Story of Human Stupidity* for Orch. (Århus, Feb. 5, 1968); *Nomo* for 7 Narrators, 6 Winds, and Tape (1967); church drama, *Eld för ett altare* (Fire from an Altar; 1968); *Kanske en pastoral om det får tina upp* (Perhaps a Pastorale If It Will Thaw) for Percussion, Piano, and Strings (1968); musical-dramatic dance, *A Play about the Medieval Värend and the Dacke Feud*, for Winds, Violin, Nickelharp, and Xylophone (1971); *Från mitt rosa badkar* (From My Rosy Bathtub) for Orch., Pop Group, and Chorus (1971); *Det ringer i mitt öra* (There Is a Ringing in My Ears) for Voices and Instruments (1972); *Tahuantisuyos ekonomi* for Chorus, Winds, and Strings (1974); *Mellan berg och hav, mellan himmel och jard* (Between the Mountains and the Ocean, Between the Sky and the Earth), play on Chinese history, for Singer, Actor, and Instrumental Ensemble (1975); *Stages* for 6 Musicians (1976); *Variationer och tema* for 4 Clarinets (1978); *Gesellen* for Chorus and Organ (1979); *Blöpark* for Wind Orch. and Percussion (1982); Concerto for Treble Recorder and Chamber Orch. (1983); *Flight of the Mechanical Heart* for Flute, Guitar, and Harpsichord (1984); Sym. (1986; Norrköping, Nov. 12, 1987); *Kinema* for Orch. (1988); *Örnen och ugglan: En inidansk saga* for Solo Voices and Instrumental Accompaniment (1988).

Vallas, Léon, distinguished French musicologist; b. Roanne, Loire, May 17, 1879; d. Lyons, May 9, 1956. After studying medicine in Lyons, he pursued his musicological training at the Univ. there (Ph.D., 1908). In 1902 he became music critic of *Tout Lyon*; in 1903, founded the *Revue Musicale de Lyon*, which became the *Revue Française de Musique* in 1912 and the *Nouvelle Revue Musicale* in 1920; also wrote for the *Progrès de Lyon* (1919–54). With G. Witkowski, he founded a schola cantorum in Lyons in 1902; taught music theory at the Univ. (1908–11) and the Cons. (1912) there, and later at the Sorbonne in Paris (1928–30). He was president of the Société Française de Musicologie (1937–43) and artistic director of Radiodiffusion de Lyon (1938–41).

WRITINGS: *Georges Migot* (Paris, n.d.); *Debussy, 1862–1918* (Paris, 1926); *Les Idées de Claude Debussy, musicien français* (Paris, 1927; 2nd ed., 1932; Eng. tr., 1929, as *The Theories of Claude Debussy*); *Claude Debussy et son temps* (Paris, 1932; 2nd ed., 1958; Eng. tr., 1933, as *Claude Debussy: His Life and Works*); *Achille-Claude Debussy* (Paris, 1944); *Vincent d'Indy* (2 vols., Paris, 1946, 1949); *César Franck* (London, 1951; in French, 1955, as *La Véritable Histoire de César Franck*).

BIBL.: N. Dufourcq, "L. V.," *Revue de Musicologie*, XXXVIII (1956).

Valle de Paz, Edgardo del. See **Del Valle de Paz, Edgardo.**

Vallee, Rudy (real name, **Hubert Prior Vallée**), American singer, saxophonist, bandleader, and actor; b. Island Pond, Vt., July 28, 1901; d. Los Angeles, July 3, 1986. He studied clarinet and saxophone in his youth; his admiration for the saxophonist Rudy Wiedoeft prompted him to adopt Rudy as his own 1st name. He was educated at the Univ. of Maine and at Yale Univ. (B.A., 1927); concurrently performed in nightclubs and vaudeville. In 1928 he gained fame when his band was engaged at N.Y.'s Heigh-Ho Club. His nasal-crooned rendition of *My Time Is Your Time*, a popular favorite, became his theme song. He struck a responsive chord with such numbers as *The Whiffenpoof Song* and *I'm Just a Vagabond Lover*. From 1929 to 1939 he was one of the leading performers on radio; starred in his own variety show; also appeared in many forgettable films. He made a remarkable comeback when he starred in the hit Broadway musical *How to Succeed in Business without Really Trying* (1961), a title that aptly described his own lucrative career in show business; he also appeared in its film version (1967). He publ. 3 autobiographical books: *Vagabond Dreams Come True* (N.Y., 1930), *My Time Is Your Time* (with G. McKean; N.Y., 1962), and *Let the Chips Fall* (Harrisburg, Pa., 1975). He tried to persuade municipal authorities to name the street on which he lived after him, but without success.

BIBL.: L. Kiner, *The R. V. Discography* (Westport, Conn., 1985).

Vallerand, Jean, Canadian composer, music critic, teacher, and administrator; b. Montreal, Dec. 24, 1915. He received violin lessons from Lucien Sicotte (1921–36); also studied at the Collège Ste.-Marie de Montréal (B.A., 1935), and was a composition pupil of Claude Champagne (1935–42); also obtained a diploma in journalism (1938) and a licence ès lettres (1939) from the Univ. of Montreal. He ed. *Quartier Latin* (1937–39); then wrote music criticism for *Le Canada* (1941–46), *Montréal-Matin* (1948–49), *Le Devoir* (1952–61), *Nouveau Journal* (1961–62), and *La Presse* (1962–66). He served as titular prof. in the music faculty of the Univ. of Montreal (1951–66), and as ed. of the French music broadcasts of Radio Canada (1964–66); was director general of the Quebec Ministry of Cultural Affairs (1970–73) and of the Quebec Province Cons. (1971–78). In 1967 he was awarded the Centenary Medal of Canada, and in 1975 received an honorary doctorate from the Univ. of Ottawa. In addition to his many reviews and articles in journals, he publ. the books *Introduction à la musique* (Montreal, 1949) and *La Musique et les tout-petits* (Montreal, 1950). He wrote music in a neo-Romantic manner; in his later compositions he experimented with serial techniques.

WORKS: OPERA: *Le Magicien* (Orford, Quebec, Sept. 2, 1961, with piano; Montreal, May 30, 1962, with orch.). **ORCH.:** *Le Diable dans le beffroi*, symphonic poem (1939; Montreal, April 24, 1942); *Nocturne* (1944); *Prélude* (1946); *Réverbérations contradictoires* (1960; Montreal, Feb. 26, 1961); *Cordes en mouvement* for String Orch. (Montreal, March 27, 1961); *Étude concertante* for Violin and Orch. (1968; Montreal, June 1969). **CHAMBER:** Violin Sonata (Montreal, Nov. 9, 1950; also for Violin and Orch., 1951); String Quartet (Radio Canada, Feb. 28, 1955). **VOCAL:** *Les Roses à la mer* for Voice and Piano (1939; also for Voice and String Orch.); *Notre-Dame de la Couronne* and *Notre-Dame du Pain*, cantatas for Tenor, Chorus, and Orch. (1946); *Quatre mélodies sur des poèmes de St. Denys Garneau* for Voice and Piano (1954).

Valleria (real name, **Schoening**), **Alwina,** noted American soprano; b. Baltimore, Oct. 12, 1848; d. Nice, Feb. 17, 1925. She went to London and entered the Royal Academy of Music in 1867, where she studied piano with W.H. Holmes and voice with Wallworth; after further studies with Arditi, she made her formal debut in a London concert on June 2, 1871. On Oct. 23, 1871, she made her operatic debut with the Italian Opera in St. Petersburg in *Linda di Chamounix;* after appearances in Germany and Italy, she returned to London and sang at the Drury Lane Theatre (1873–75), Her Majesty's Theatre (1877–78), and Covent Garden (1879–82). On Oct. 22, 1879, she made her U.S. debut as Marguerite in N.Y. with Mapleson's company; after appearances with the Carl Rosa company in England (1882–83), she returned to the U.S. and made her Metropolitan Opera debut in N.Y. as Leonora in *Il Trovatore* on Oct. 26, 1883, remaining on its roster for the season; then pursued her career in England until retiring in 1886.

Valle-Riestra, José María, Peruvian composer; b. Lima, Nov. 9, 1859; d. there, Jan. 25, 1925. He studied as a child in London; after his return to Lima, he continued his musical education without a teacher; as a mature musician, he went to Paris for further studies with André Gédalge (1895–97). When the Academia Nacional de Música was organized in Lima, he was appointed a prof. there. In his compositions, it was his aim to contribute toward the establishment of a national school by the employment of old Inca melodies. His opera *Ollanta* (Lima, Dec. 26, 1900) was a successful dramatization of an Inca subject. His other 2 operas on Inca themes were *Las rosas de Jamaica* and *Atahualpa*. He also wrote *Misa de Requiem* for Chorus and Orch.; *En Oriente* for Orch.; *Elegía* for String Orch.; choruses a cappella; songs.

Vallet or **Valet, Nicolas,** eminent French-born Netherlandish lutenist and composer; b. probably in Corbény, Ile-de-France, c.1583; d. probably in Amsterdam, after 1642. He apparently received his musical training in his homeland; was in Amsterdam by 1614. He was greatly esteemed as a performer and composer; also was active as a teacher.

Works (all publ. in Amsterdam): *21 Psalmen Davids* for Voice and Lute (1615; 2nd ed., 1619, as *XXI pseaumes de David*); *Secretum musarum* for Lute (1615; 2nd ed., 1618, as *Le Secret des Muses: Paradisus musicus testudinis*); *Het tweede boeck van de* (30) *luyt-tablatuer* for 1 and 4 Lutes (1616; 2nd ed., 1619, as *Le Second Livre de tablature de luth, intitulé Le Secret des Muses*); *Bruylofts-gesang* for 5 Voices (1619); *Regia pietas, hoc est* (150) *Psalmi Davidici* for Lute (1620); *Apollinis süsse Leyr, das ist . . . Pavannen, Galliarden, Balletten, Bransles, Couranten . . . fransösiche Stück . . . engelsche Stück* for Viola and Basso Continuo (1642); *Le Mont Parnasse . . . contenant plusiers pavannes, galliardes, ballets, bransles, courantes, fantasies, et batailles, a 5, 6* (c.1644); several lute pieces in MS collections. A. Souris edited *Œuvres de Nicolas Vallet pour luth seul: Le Secret des Muses, livres I, II* (1970).

Bibl.: (J.) Boers, "Valet," *Bouwsteenen: Jaarboek der Vereeniging voor Nederlandsche muziekgeschiedenis*, II (1872–74); M. Rollin, "Étude biographique," *Œuvres de N. Vallet pour luth seul: Le Secret des Muses, livres I, II* (1970).

Valletti, Cesare, Italian tenor; b. Rome, Dec. 18, 1922. He studied with Tito Schipa; made his debut in Bari as Alfredo; then sang throughout Italy. In 1950 he appeared with the visiting La Scala company at London's Covent Garden as Fenton; in 1953 he made his U.S. debut as Werther at the San Francisco Opera. On Dec. 10, 1953, he made his Metropolitan Opera debut in N.Y.; remained on the company's roster until 1960. He retired from the operatic stage in 1968. His repertoire ranged from Mozart to the Italian bel canto roles.

Vallotti, Francesco Antonio, Italian music theorist and composer; b. Vercelli, June 11, 1697; d. Padua, Jan. 10, 1780. A Franciscan monk, he was a pupil of Donati in Milan and in Padua, where he settled; became 3rd organist at the basilica of S. Antonio in 1723, where he subsequently was its maestro di cappella from 1730 until his death. As a composer, he greatly distinguished himself as a contrapuntist. He composed much sacred vocal music, including masses, Psalms, hymns, antiphons, and other pieces; also wrote 30 fugues for various instruments. He wrote various treatises, which remain in MS. Also publ. *Della scienza teorica e pratica della moderna musica,* book 1 (Padua, 1779; books 2–4 ed. by G. Zanon and B. Rizzi as *Trattato della moderna musica,* Padua, 1950).

Bibl.: L. Sabbatini, *Notizie sopra la vita e le opere del rev. P.F.A. V.* (Padua, 1780); O. Wessely, "Johann Joseph Fux und F.A. V.," *Jahresgabe der J.J. Fux-Gesellschaft 1966* (Graz, 1967).

Valvasensi, Lazaro, Italian organist and composer; b. Valvasone, near Udine (baptized), June 20, 1585; d. there, June 26, 1661. In 1622 he was an organist at Murano Cathedral (Venice); in 1626, choirmaster at Tolmezzo Cathedral (Udine); from 1634 to 1640, was an organist at Valvasone; later was apostolic protonotary and canon in Caorle.

Works (all publ. in Venice): *Brevi concerti ecclesiastici alla romana* for Voice and Harpsichord (1620); *Letanie della B. V.* for 5 Voices (1622); *Compieta concertata* for 4 Voices and Basso Continuo (1626); *Secondo giardino d'amorosi fiori* for Voice and Basso Continuo (1634); *Messe concertate* for 2 to 4 Voices and Basso Continuo (1636); *Salmi concertati* for 2 Voices and Basso Continuo (1640).

Bibl.: V. Formentini and L. Stella, "L. V.: Musicista di Valvasone," *Itinerari,* XXVI/3 (1974).

Valverde, Joaquín, Spanish composer; b. Badajoz, Feb. 27, 1846; d. Madrid, March 17, 1910. He played the flute in bands from the age of 13; then studied at the Cons. of Madrid; his sym., *Batylo,* won a prize of the Sociedad Fomento de las Artes (1871). He wrote some 30 zarzuelas, some in collaboration with others; his most celebrated was *La gran vía* (Madrid, July 2, 1886; in collaboration with Chueca); it contains the march *Cádiz,* which became immensely popular. He publ. the book *La flauta: Su historia su estudio* (Madrid, 1886). His son, **Quinto (Joaquín) Valverde Sanjuán** (b. Madrid, Jan. 2, 1875; d. Mexico City, Nov. 4, 1918), was also a composer;

he studied with his father and with Irache; wrote some 250 light pieces for the theater; his zarzuela *El gran capitán* was especially successful. He died during a tour which he undertook as conductor of a light opera company.

Van Aerde, Raymond (Joseph Justin), Belgian musicologist; b. Mechelen, June 4, 1876; d. there, March 16, 1944. He was a librarian and a lecturer on music history at the Mechelen Cons.

Writings (all publ. in Mechelen): *Notice sur la vie et les oeuvres de Cipriano de Rore* (1909); *Ménestrels communaux et instrumentistes à Malines de 1311 à 1790* (1911); *Les Tuerlinckx, luthiers à Malines* (1914); *Musicalia; Documents pour servir à l'histoire de la musique à Malines* (2 vols., 1925–30); *Les Ancêtres flamands de Beethoven* (1928).

Van Allan, Richard (real name, **Alan Philip Jones**), English bass; b. Clipstone, Nottinghamshire, May 28, 1935. He studied at the Worcester College of Education, and received vocal training from David Franklin at the Birmingham School of Music; joined the Glyndebourne Festival Chorus in 1964; made his operatic debut there in 1966. From 1969 he sang at the Sadler's Wells Opera Co., and from 1971 at Covent Garden, making his 1st appearance there as the Mandarin in *Turandot*. In 1976 he sang the role of Baron Ochs at the San Diego Opera. He served as director of the National Opera Studio from 1986. Among his best roles are Osmin, Don Giovanni, Leporello, Mozart's Figaro, the Grand Inquisitor, Philip II, and Verdi's Banquo.

van Appledorn, Mary Jeanne, American composer, pianist, and teacher; b. Holland, Mich., Oct. 2, 1927. She studied piano with Cecile Staub Genhart (B.Mus., 1948), theory (M.Mus., 1950), and composition with Bernard Rogers and Alan Hovhaness at the Eastman School of Music in Rochester, N.Y., where she received her Ph.D. in 1966 with the dissertation *A Stylistic Study of Claude Debussy's Opera, Pelléas et Mélisande*; pursued postdoctoral studies at the Mass. Inst. of Technology (1982). She served as prof. and as chairman of the theory and composition dept. in the music school at Texas Technical Univ. in Lubbock (1950–87); also made appearances as a pianist.

Works: ballet: *Set of 7* (N.Y., May 10, 1988). **orch.:** *Concerto brevis* for Piano and Orch. (1954); *A Choreographic Overture* for Concert Band (1957); Concerto for Trumpet and Band (1960); *Passacaglia and Chorale* (1973); *Cacophony* for Wind Ensemble, Percussion, and Toys (1980); *Lux: Legend of Sankta Lucia* for Symphonic Band, Harp, Percussion Ensemble, and Handbells (1981). **chamber:** *Cellano Rhapsody* for Cello and Piano (1948); *Burlesca* for Piano, Brass, and Percussion (1951); *Matrices* for Saxophone and Piano (1979); *Liquid Gold* for Saxophone and Piano (1982); *4 Duos* for Alto Saxophones (1985); *4 Duos* for Viola and Cello (1986); *Sonic Mutation* for Harp (1986); Sonatine for Clarinet and Piano (N.Y., Oct. 17, 1988); *Cornucopia* for Trumpet (1988); also various piano pieces and vocal works.

Van Beinum, Eduard. See **Beinum, Eduard van.**

Van Bree, Joannes. See **Bree, Jean Bernard van.**

Vancea, Zeno (Octavian), outstanding Rumanian composer and musicologist; b. Bocşa-Vasiova, Oct. 21, 1900. He studied at the Cluj Cons. (1919–21); then took lessons in composition with Ernst Kanitz in Vienna. Returning to Rumania, he taught at conservatories in Tîrgu-Mureş (1926–40; director, 1946–48), Timişoara (1940–45), and Bucharest (1949–73). He was the ed. of the important Rumanian monthly *Muzica* (1953–64). Vancea belongs to the national school of Rumanian composers; in his music he makes use of folk-song patterns without direct quotations. Harmonically, he adopts many procedures of cosmopolitan modern music while cautiously avoiding abrasive sonorities.

Writings: *Istoria muzicii româneşti* (Bucharest, 1953); *Creaţia muzicală românească, secolele XIX–XX* (Rumanian Musical Compositions of the XIX–XX Centuries; Bucharest, 1968); *Studii şi eseuri muzicale* (Musical Studies and Essays; Bucharest, 1974).

Works: stage: *Priculiciul* (The Werewolf), ballet-pantomime (1933; Bucharest, April 30, 1943; rev. 1957). ORCH.: *Rapsodia bănăteană No. 1* (1926); *Scoarte*, suite for Chamber Orch. (1928); *2 Grotesque Dances* (1937); *Simfonieta I* (1948); *O zi de vară* (On a Summer Day), suite (Bucharest, Sept. 23, 1951); *Triptic simfonic: Preambul, Intermezzo, Marş* (1958; Bucharest, May 10, 1959); *Burlesca* (1959); *Concerto for Orchestra* (1961; Bucharest, May 10, 1962); *5 Piese* (Pieces) for String Orch. (1964; Rumanian TV, Feb. 4, 1965); *Prolog simfonic* (Bucharest, March 9, 1974); *Elegie* for String Orch. (Tîrgu-Mureş, June 10, 1977). CHAMBER: *Cvartet bizantin* (Byzantine Quartet; 1931); 8 string quartets (1934, 1953, 1957, 1965, 1970, 1970, 1978, 1980); String Trio (1981). VOCAL: *Requiem* for Soprano, Alto, Tenor, Bass, Choir, and Orch. (1941); *Cîntecul păcii* (Song of Peace) for Soprano, Choir, and Orch. (1961); 5 songs for Tenor and Orch. (Tîrgu-Mureş, Sept. 25, 1977); choruses; solo songs with piano.

Van Dam, José (real name, **Joseph Van Damme**), outstanding Belgian bass-baritone; b. Brussels, Aug. 25, 1940. He began to study piano and solfège at 11; commenced vocal studies at 13, and then entered the Brussels Cons. at 17, graduating with 1st prizes in voice and opera performance at 18; subsequently captured 1st prizes in vocal competitions in Liège, Paris, Toulouse, and Geneva. After making his operatic debut as Don Basilio in *Il Barbiere di Siviglia* in Liège, he gained experience as a member of the Opéra and the Opéra-Comique in Paris (1961–65) and of the Geneva Opera (1965–67). In 1967 he joined the Berlin Deutsche Oper, where he established himself as one of its principal artists via such roles as Figaro, Leporello, Don Alfonso, Caspar, and Escamillo. While continuing to sing in Berlin, he pursued a notable international career. In 1973 he made his 1st appearance at London's Covent Garden as Escamillo, a role he also chose for his Metropolitan Opera debut in N.Y. on Nov. 21, 1975. He was chosen to create the title role in Messiaen's opera *Saint François d'Assise* at the Paris Opéra on Nov. 28, 1983, thereby adding further luster to his reputation. During the 1985–86 season, he appeared as Hans Sachs at the Chicago Lyric Opera. Among his other esteemed roles are Don Giovanni, Verdi's Attila, the Dutchman, Golaud, and Wozzeck. He has also won renown as a concert artist, making appearances with the foremost orchs. of Europe and the U.S.

Van Delden, Lex. See **Delden, Lex van.**

Van de Moortel, Arie, Belgian composer and violist; b. Laeken, July 17, 1918; d. Brussels, May 1, 1976. He studied at the Royal Cons. in Brussels and in Ghent; made his debut as a violist in 1938 in the "Trio of the Court of Belgium"; taught chamber music at the Brussels Cons. (1946–76), and was director of the music academy at Anderlecht (1957–76).

WORKS: *Silly Symphony*; Trio for Oboe, Clarinet, and Bassoon (1939; rev. 1954); Concerto for Orch.; *Toccata* for Piano; Viola Sonata; *Nocturne* for Clarinet, Saxophone, Cello, and Piano; Sonata for Solo Harp (1955); *Capriccio* for Carillon (1957); *Danse d'Espagne* for Harp; *Improvisation on a Choral Theme* for Flute and Piano (1967); Sonata for Flute Solo (1968); Violin Sonatina (1969); *Rondo-pastorale*, in memoriam E. Ysaÿe, for Violin and Piano (1970); *Sonata ostinato* for Violin and Organ (1974).

Van den Boorn-Coclet, Henriette, Belgian composer; b. Liège, Jan. 15, 1866; d. there, March 6, 1945. She studied with Radoux and Dupuis at the Liège Cons., and subsequently taught harmony there. Her compositions attracted considerable attention. She wrote a Sym.; a symphonic poem, *Le Renouveau; Sérénade* for Cello and Piano; various piano pieces (*Mazurka, Caprice*, etc.); songs.

Van den Borren, Charles (-Jean-Eugène), eminent Belgian musicologist; b. Ixelles, near Brussels, Nov. 17, 1874; d. Brussels, Jan. 14, 1966. He received training in music history from Kufferath and in harmony, counterpoint, and fugue with E. Closson. He was a barrister in the court of appeals until 1905; was music critic of *L'Indépendance Belge* (1909–14); then taught at the Brussels Institut des Hautes Études Musicales

et Dramatiques and at the Free Univ., where he later was prof. of music history (1926–45); also was librarian at the Royal Cons. in Brussels (1919–40) and a lecturer in musicology at the Univ. of Liège (1927–44). He served as 1st chairman of the Société de Musicologie Belge (1946); in 1939, was elected a member of the Académie Royale de Belgique, Classe des Beaux-Arts, serving as its president in 1953. **Safford Cape** was his son-in-law.

WRITINGS: *L'Œuvre dramatique de César Franck, Hulda et Ghiselle* (Brussels, 1907); *Les Origines de la musique de clavecin en Angleterre* (Brussels, 1912; Eng. tr., 1914, as *The Sources of Keyboard Music in England); Les Musiciens belges en Angleterre à l'époque de la Renaissance* (Brussels, 1913); *Les Débuts de la musique à Venise* (Brussels, 1914); *Origine et développement de l'art polyphonique vocal du XVIᵉ siècle* (Brussels, 1920); *Orlando de Lassus* (Paris, 1920); *Le Manuscrit musical M.222 C.22 de la Bibliothèque de Strasbourg* (1924); *Guillaume Dufay: Son importance dans l'évolution de la musique au XVᵉ siècle* (Brussels, 1926); *Études sur le quinzième siècle musical* (1941); *Peter Benoît* (1942); *Roland de Lassus* (1943); *Geschiedenis van de muziek in de Nederlanden* (2 vols., 1948, 1951); *César Franck* (Brussels, 1949); with E. Closson, *La musique en Belgique du Moyen-Âge à nos jours* (Brussels, 1950).

EDITIONS: with G. van Doorslaer, *Philippe de Monte: Opera omnia* (Bruges and Düsseldorf, 1927–39); *Polyphonia sacra: A Continental Miscellany of the Fifteenth Century* (Burnham, Buckinghamshire, 1932; 2nd ed., rev., 1962).

BIBL.: *Hommage à C. V.d. B. à l'occasion du centenaire de sa naissance* (Brussels, 1974).

Van den Eeden, Jean-Baptiste. See **Eeden, Jean-Baptiste van den.**

Van der Horst, Anthon. See **Horst, Anthon van der.**

Van der Linden, Cornelis, Dutch conductor and composer; b. Dordrecht, Aug. 24, 1839; d. Amsterdam, May 29, 1918. He studied with Kwast (piano) and F. Böhme (theory); after sojourns in Belgium, Paris, and Germany, he conducted various choral organizations; from 1875, also led sym. concerts; was conductor of the newly established Nederlandsche Oper in Amsterdam (1888–94); produced 2 of his own operas there: *Catharina en Lambert* (Nov. 24, 1888) and *Leiden ontzet* (The Relief of Leiden; April 1, 1893); also wrote 7 overtures and many choral works.

Vandermaesbrugge, Max, Belgian composer; b. Couillet, June 14, 1933. He studied with Moulaert, Souris, Stehman, Louel, and Absil at the Royal Cons. in Brussels (1951–60); taught piano and solfeggio at the music academies in Anderlecht (1955–62), Josse-ten-Noode (1958–62), and de Forest (1959–62), and at Etterbeek (1963–66). In 1966 he was appointed to the faculty of the Brussels Cons.; in 1972 he succeeded Defossez as inspector of Belgian music schools.

WORKS: *Drum Follies*, variations for 10 Percussionists (1961); *Caprice* for Violin and Piano (1961); *4 fables de Florian* for Soprano, Contralto, and Baritone (1961); *Miniature Variations* for Guitar (1962); Duo for Flute and Viola (1962); *En petits caractères* for 2 Trumpets and Piano obbligato (1963); Quartet for 4 Clarinets (1965); *Tema e Variazioni* for Carillon (1967); *Divertimento* for Flute and Strings (1969); *Hiver*, symphonic poem (1970); *4 instantanés* for Flute and Guitar (1972); *Sinfonia* for Strings (1972); *Saxofolies* for Saxophone Septet (1974); *Intrada e Scherzando* for Trumpet and Piano (1978).

Vandernoot, André, Belgian conductor; b. Brussels, June 2, 1927. He studied at the Brussels Cons.; later took courses at the Vienna Academy of Music. In 1958 he was appointed first conductor of the Royal Flemish Opera in Antwerp; from 1959 to 1973 he served as music director of the Théâtre Royal de la Monnaie in Brussels. In 1974–75 he was music director of the Orch. National de Belgique in Brussels; in 1976, was named 1st guest conductor of the Antwerp Phil. In 1978–79 he was music director of the Noordhollands Phil. in Haarlem and then of the Brabants Orch. (1979–89).

Van der Slice, John, American composer, ethnomusicologist, and teacher; b. Ann Arbor, Feb. 19, 1940. He studied at the Univ. of Calif., Berkeley (B.A., 1964), with Russell, McKay, and Dahl at the Univ. of Hawaii (M.A. in ethnomusicology; M.M., 1973), and at the Univ. of Illinois, Urbana (Ph.D., 1980, with a diss. on Ligeti's *Atmosphères*). He taught at the Univ. of Hawaii at Hilo and served in an administrative position at the Univ. of Hawaii at Honolulu; then joined the faculty of the Univ. of Miami. His musical tastes range from the medieval period to the contemporary era, and also include jazz and non-Western musics; he studied performance traditions of the Japanese koto, the Korean kayakeum, and the bonang panerus member of the Javanese gamelan. His compositional language involves both pitch set permutation and a subtle implication of tonal hierarchy.
    WORKS: *Jo-ha-kyu* for Orch. (1977–79); *Pulse/Impulse* for Percussion (1983); Trio for Clarinet, Viola, and Marimba (1984); *Doodle Music* for Piccolo and Percussion (1985); Piano Trio (1986); *Animistic Study* for Double Bass (1986); *Time Shadows* for 11 Instruments (1987); *Fantasia* for Orch. (1988).

Van der Straeten, Edmond, Belgian music historian; b. Audenarde, Dec. 3, 1826; d. there, Nov. 26, 1895. He studied philosophy in Ghent; went to Brussels in 1857 as secretary to Fétis, with whom he studied counterpoint. He held a lifelong position at the Royal Library, and rarely left Belgium; was active as a music critic (1859–72); wrote an opera, *Le Proscrit.* His reputation rests upon his scholarly publications, dealing with music in the Low Countries. He publ. a monumental work of reference, *La Musique au Pays-Bas avant le XIXe siècle* (8 vols., 1867–88); other writings are: *Coup d'œil sur la musique actuelle à Audenarde* (1851); *Notice sur Charles-Félix de Hollande* (1854); *Notice sur les carillons d'Audenarde* (1855); *Recherches sur la musique à Audenarde avant le XIXe siècle* (1856); *Examen des chants populaires des Flamands de France, publiés par E. de Coussemaker* (1858); *J.-F.-J. Janssens* (1866); *Wagner; Verslag aan den heer minister van binnenlandsche Zaaken* (1871); *Le Théâtre villageois en Flandre* (2 vols., 1874, 1880); *Les Musiciens belges en Italie* (1875); *Voltaire musicien* (1878); *Les Ballets des rois en Flandre; Xylographie, musique, coutumes, etc.* (1892); *Charles V musicien* (1894); *Les Willems, luthiers gantois du XVIIe siècle* (1896; with C. Snoeck).

Van der Stucken, Frank (Valentin), American conductor and composer; b. Fredericksburg, Texas, Oct. 15, 1858; d. Hamburg, Aug. 16, 1929. In 1866 he was taken by his parents to Antwerp, where he studied with Peter Benoit at the Cons.; then with Reinecke in Leipzig (1877–79); in 1881 he became conductor at the Breslau Stadttheater. In 1884 he became Leopold Damrosch's successor as conductor of the Arion Soc., a men's chorus in N.Y.; he soon acquired a reputation as an advocate of American music; conducted MacDowell's Piano Concerto with the composer as soloist, as well as works by Chadwick, Foote, and Paine at the Paris Exposition (July 12, 1889). After serving as conductor of the North American Sangerbund in Newark (1891) and N.Y. (1894), he was the 1st permanent conductor of the Cincinnati Sym. Orch. (1895–1907); also was dean of the Cincinnati College of Music (1896–1901); served as music director of the Cincinnati May Festival (1906–12), returning there in 1923 and once again serving as its music director in 1925 and 1927. He lived mostly in Europe from 1907. In 1898 he was elected to the National Inst. of Arts and Letters and in 1929 to the American Academy of Arts and Letters. He composed a few orch. works, choral music, numerous songs, and piano pieces.

Van der Velden, Renier, Belgian composer; b. Antwerp, Jan. 14, 1910. He studied in Brussels with Jan Broeckx, Karel Candael, and Joseph Jongen; in 1945, was appointed program director of the French services of Belgian Radio in Antwerp. In 1970 he became a member of the Royal Flemish Academy of Arts, Letters, and Sciences.
    WORKS: BALLETS: *Indruk aan Zee* for Small Orch. (1930); *Provinciestad 1900* (1937); *L'Enlèvement de Proserpine* (1947);

Les Amours de torero (1948); *De zakdoekjes* (1947); *Dulle Griet* (1949; rev. 1967); *Les Ancêtres* (1949); *Arlequinade* (1950); *Judith* for 2 Pianos and Percussion (1951; orch. version, 1953); *De Triomf van de dood* (1963); *Oostendse maskers* (1965); *Ballet Music* for 20 Winds and Piano (1972); *Impression maritime* for Small Orch. (1930); *Divertimento* for String Orch. (1938); *Hommage à Ravel,* symphonic suite (1938); Trumpet Concerto (1940); Oboe Concerto (1941); Sinfonietta for String Orch. (1942); 2 suites for Orch. (1945, 1955); Concertino for Clarinet, Bassoon, Piano, and String Orch. (1949); *Kamermuziek* for Viola and Chamber Ensemble (1956); Violin Concerto (1958); Concertino for Viola and Chamber Orch. (1964); Concertino for Flute and Strings (1965); *Beweging* for Orch. (1968); *Étude* for 11 Instruments (1969); Concertino for Piano and Strings (1971); *Hulde aan Janáček* (Homage to Janáček), 3 short pieces for Flute, Oboe, and String Orch. (1973); *Landschappen* for Chamber Orch. (1976); *Nocturne voor beeldhouwer Mark Macken* for String Orch. (1979); 2 concertos for Wind Quintet (1939, 1955); *Adagio and Finale* for String Trio (1940); Trio for Oboe, Clarinet, and Bassoon (1943); Sextet for Wind Quintet and Piano (1948); *Divertimento* for Oboe, Clarinet, and Bassoon (1957); Concertino for Brass Quintet and 2 Pianos (1965); *Fantaisie* for 4 Clarinets (1967); 2 *Dialogues* for Clarinet and Piano (1971); *Arlequinade* for Flute (1980); *Nocturne* for Flute, Guitar, and Cello (1980); 2 suites for Piano (1937, 1944); *Beweging* for 2 Pianos (1965); songs, among them 8 *poèmes de Karel van de Woestijne* for High Voice and Piano (1946; orchestrated 1951).

Van de Vate, Nancy, American composer; b. Plainfield, N.J., Dec. 30, 1930. She studied piano at the Eastman School of Music in Rochester, N.Y., Wellesley College (A.B., 1952), and with Bruce Simonds at Yale Univ.; then concentrated on composition at the Univ. of Mississippi (M.M., 1958) and later at Florida State Univ. (D.M., 1968). She taught at Memphis State Univ. (1964–66), the Univ. of Tennessee (1967), Knoxville College (1968–69; 1971–72), Maryville College (1973–74), the Univ. of Hawaii (1975–76), and Hawaii Loa College (1977–80). She was secretary and then president of the Southeast Composers League (1965–73; 1973–75); in 1975 she founded the International League of Women Composers, and served as chairperson until 1982, when she moved to Indonesia; from 1985 she lived in Vienna. Her music—highly charged and dissonantly colored by way of influences as varied as Prokofiev, Shostakovich, Penderecki, Crumb, and Varèse—has won international awards.
    WORKS: STAGE: *A Night in the Royal Ontario Museum,* theater piece for Soprano and Tape (1983; Washington, D.C., April 13, 1984); *The Saga of Cocaine Lil,* theater piece for Mezzo-soprano, 4 Singers, and Percussion (1986; Frankfurt am Main, April 20, 1988). **ORCH.:** *Adagio* (1957); *Variations* for Chamber Orch. (1958); Piano Concerto (1968); *Concertpiece* for Cello and Small Orch. (1975–76; rev. 1978); *Dark Nebulae* (1981; Columbus, Ohio, Jan. 29, 1983); *Gema Jawa* for String Orch. (1984); *Journeys* (1981–84); *Distant Worlds* for Violin and Orch. (1985; Krakow, June 20, 1987); Violin Concerto No. 1 (1985–86; Pittsburgh, Kans., Nov. 15, 1987); *Chernobyl* (1987); *Pura Besakih* (1987); *Krakow Concerto* for Percussion and Orch. (1988; Krakow, Nov. 28, 1989); *Katyn* for Chorus and Orch. (Krakow, Nov. 28, 1989; dedicated to the victims of the Katyn Forest massacre). **CHAMBER AND VOCAL:** *Short Suite* for Brass Quintet (1960); Wind Quartet (1964); String Quartet No. 1 (1969); Clarinet Sonata (1970); *An American Essay,* after Whitman, for Chorus, Piano, and Percussion (Knoxville, May 16, 1972); 3 *Sound Pieces* for Brass and Percussion (1973); String Trio (1974); Quintet for Flute, Violin, Clarinet, Cello, and Piano (1975); *Letter to a Friend's Loneliness* for Soprano and String Quartet (1976); *Cantata for Women's Voices* for Women's Chorus and 7 Instrumentalists (1979); Trio for Bassoon, Percussion, and Piano (1980); Piano Trio (1983); *Music for MW2* for Flute, Cello, Piano, 4-hands, and Percussion (1985); *Teufelstanz* for 6 Percussionists (1988); 7 *Fantasy Pieces* for Violin and Piano (1989); choruses; songs.

KEYBOARD: 2 piano sonatas (1978, 1983); *9 Preludes* for Piano (1978); Sonata for Harpsichord (1982); *Fantasy* for Harpsichord (1982); *Contrasts* for 2 Pianos, 6-hands (1984); *12 Pieces on 1 to 12 Notes* for Piano (1986).

Van de Woestijne, David, Belgian composer; b. Llanidloes, Wales, Feb. 18, 1915; d. Brussels, May 18, 1979. He was the son of the painter Gustav van de Woestijne and the nephew of the Flemish poet Karel van de Woestijne. After studies in harmony and counterpoint with Désiré Defauw and Paul Gilson, he took lessons with Oscar Esplá. Van de Woestijne's music reflects the trends of cosmopolitan modernism, gravitating toward neo-Baroque techniques.

WORKS: OPERAS: *Le Débat de la folie et de l'amour,* opera-ballet (1959); *De zoemende musikant,* television opera (1967); *Graal 68 ou L'Impromptu de Gand* (Ghent, 1968). **ORCH.:** Double Concerto for Piano, Cello, and Orch. (1935); *Fantasia* for Oboe and Orch. (1936); Piano Concerto (1938); *Ballade* for Piano and Orch. (1940); Concerto for Violin and 12 Solo Instruments (1945); *Sérénades* for Piano, 12 Wind Instruments, Double Bass, and Percussion (1946; Copenhagen, June 2, 1947); Sym. (1958); Sym. in 1 Movement (1965); *Concertino da camera* for Flute, Oboe, and Strings (1967); *Aswoendag* (Ash Wednesday) for Narrator, Soli, Chorus, and Orch. (1971); Concerto for 2 Pianos (1972); Concerto for String Quartet, 14 Wind Instruments, and Double Bass (1974); *Hommage à Purcell* for Harpsichord and Strings (1974); *Eénentwintig* for Piano, 19 Winds, and Double Bass (1976). **VOCAL:** 2 cantatas: *La Belle Cordière* for Soprano and Orch. (1954) and *Les Aéronautes* for Soli, Chorus, Speaking Chorus, and Orch. (1963). **CHAMBER:** *Divertimento* for Oboe, Clarinet, and Bassoon (1942); Quintet for Flute, Oboe, Violin, Viola, and Cello (1953); Violin Sonata (1956); *Variations* for 7 Instruments (1965); *Sarabande* for 2 Guitars (1965); *Devant une sculpture* for 12 Instruments (1969); String Quartet (1970); *Notturno* for Flute and Piano (1976); *Music* for Tuba or Saxhorn, and Piano (1976); *Minuetto capriccioso* for Trumpet and Piano (1976); *Toccata* for Piano (1935); Piano Sonatina (1945); 2-Piano Sonata (1955); songs.

Van Dieren, Bernard. See **Dieren, Bernard van.**

Van Doorslaer, Georges, Belgian musicologist; b. Mechelen, Sept. 27, 1864; d. there, Jan. 16, 1940. He was a physician by profession, but studied music as an avocation; wrote the valuable treatises *Herry Bredemers, 1472–1522* (Antwerp, 1915); *De Toonkunstenaars der familie Vredeman* (Antwerp, 1920); *La Vie et les œuvres de Philippe de Monte* (Brussels, 1921); *Rinaldo del Mel* (Antwerp, 1922); also ed. 8 vols. in the collected edition of works by Philippe de Monte.

Van Dresser, Marcia, American soprano; b. Memphis, Tenn., Dec. 4, 1877; d. London, July 11, 1937. She studied in Chicago and N.Y.; sang minor parts at the Metropolitan Opera (1903–4); after further study in Germany, she made her European debut in Dresden (1907); was a member of the Dessau Opera (1908–10) and the Frankfurt Opera (1911–14); gave a recital in N.Y. (March 22, 1915); sang with the Chicago Opera (1915–17).

Van Durme, Jef, Belgian composer; b. Kemzeke-Waas, May 7, 1907; d. Brussels, Jan. 28, 1965. He studied at the Royal Flemish Cons. in Antwerp with Flor Alpaerts; in 1931 he went to Vienna, where he took lessons in advanced composition with Alban Berg.

WORKS: Operas: *Remous,* after Weterings (Brussels, 1936); *The Death of a Salesman,* after Arthur Miller (1954–55); also *King Lear* (1955–57), *Anthony and Cleopatra* (1957–59), and *Richard III* (1960–61), all after Shakespeare; 2 ballets: *De dageraad* (1932–33; Antwerp, 1934) and *Orestes* (1934–35); suite for Orch. (1936–40); 2 symphonic poems: *Hamlet* (1929) and *Beatrice* (1930); oratorio, *De 14 stonden* (1931); 6 syms.: No. 1 (1934); No. 2 (1938–39); No. 3 (1945–46); No. 4 (1950–51); No. 5 (1952); No. 6 (1953); 2 *Elegies* for Orch. (1933, 1938); *Poème héroïque* (1935); *Breughel Symphony* (1935–42); 2 *Sinfonie da camera* (1937, 1949); 3 *Ballads* for Orch.: No. 1, *In memoriam Alban Berg* (1938); No. 2 (1947–48); No. 3

(1961); 2 piano concertos (1943, 1946); *Symphonic Prologue* (1944–45); Violin Concerto (1946–47); 3 suites for Orch. (1947; 1948–60; 1962); *Van Gogh Suite* for Orch. (1954); Sinfonietta for Strings (1962); 3 violin sonatas (1928, 1938, 1947); Sextet for Piano and Wind Quintet (1930); 5 string quartets (1932–33; 1937; 1945–48; 1948–53; 1953); Piano Quartet (1934); 2 piano sonatas (1946, 1952–53); 4 piano trios (1928, 1929, 1942, 1949); Cello Sonata (1952); Wind Quintet (1951–52); piano pieces; 21 songs, 2 with orch.

Van Dyck, Ernest (Marie Hubert), distinguished Belgian tenor; b. Antwerp, April 2, 1861; d. Berlaer-lez-Lierre, Aug. 31, 1923. He studied law; was a journalist in Paris, where he studied voice with Saint-Yves Bax. He sang at the Lamoureux concerts (from 1883); made his operatic debut in *Lohengrin* (May 3, 1887). After further training with Julius Kniese, he appeared at the Bayreuth Festival as Parsifal in 1888, a role he sang there regularly until 1912; also appeared as Lohengrin there in 1894; from 1888 to 1900 he was a member of the Vienna Court Opera; on May 19, 1891, he made his London debut at Covent Garden, returning there in 1897, 1898, and 1901; made his 1st appearance at the Paris Opéra as Lohengrin on Sept. 16, 1891, which role he also sang at his debut at the Théâtre Royal de la Monnaie in Brussels on April 28, 1894. He made his U.S. debut as Tannhäuser in Chicago (Nov. 9, 1898); made his 1st appearance at the Metropolitan Opera in N.Y. in the same role (Nov. 29, 1898), and remained with the company until 1902. In 1907 he served as manager of the German Opera season at Covent Garden, where he also sang Tristan and Siegmund; in 1908 he sang Siegfried in *Götterdämmerung* and in 1914 Parsifal at the Paris Opéra. He taught voice in Paris and later in Brussels. He was equally at home in Wagnerian roles and the French repertoire.

Vaness, Carol (Theresa), talented American soprano; b. San Diego, July 27, 1952. She grew up in Pomona, where she took piano lessons; while attending a parochial girls' school, she sang in its choir, then studied English and piano at Calif. State Polytechnic College before concentrating on music at Calif. State Univ. in Northridge (M.A., 1976), where her vocal instructor was David Scott. After serving an apprenticeship at the San Francisco Opera, she made her N.Y. City Opera debut as Vitellia in *La clemenza di Tito* on Oct. 25, 1979, and continued to appear there until 1983, when she scored a major success as Handel's Alcina. On Jan. 9, 1981, she made her European debut as Vitellia in Bordeaux; made her 1st appearance at the Glyndebourne Festival in 1982 as Donna Anna in *Don Giovanni,* a role she subsequently sang to much acclaim throughout Europe. On Feb. 14, 1984, she made her Metropolitan Opera debut in N.Y. as Armida in Handel's *Rinaldo,* and continued to sing there in later seasons; also appeared with other U.S. opera houses and toured as a concert artist. Her other roles include Dalila in Handel's *Samson,* Electra in *Idomeneo,* Fiordiligi, the Countess in *Le nozze di Figaro,* Rosina, Violetta, Gilda, Nedda, and Mimi.

BIBL.: B. Paolucci, "C. V.," *Ovation* (April 1986); *Current Biography* (Sept. 1986).

Van Gilse, Jan. See **Gilse, Jan van.**

Van Hagen, Peter Albrecht, Sr., Dutch-American musician; b. in the Netherlands, 1755; d. Boston, Aug. 20, 1803. After marrying **Elizabeth Joanetta Catherine van Hagen** (b. probably in Amsterdam, 1750; d. Suffolk County, Mass., c.1809), he went with her to Charleston, S.C., in 1774; by 1789 they were in N.Y., where they were active as performers, teachers, and concert managers; promoted their own "Old City Concerts" series; settled in Boston in 1796, taking the name Von Hagen. He was active as a music dealer and publisher; also directed a theater orch., and served as organist at King's Chapel (1798–1803). His son, **Peter Albrecht Von Hagen, Jr.** (b. probably in Charleston, S.C., c.1779; d. Boston, Sept. 12, 1837), was a violinist, organist, violist, and composer; in 1810 he was made organist at Trinity Church in Boston; later conducted bands in South Boston and in Fort Eustis, Va.;

his later years were plagued by alcoholism. All the members of the family composed; the authorship of many of the works of the father and son is in dispute; their output includes overtures, marches for piano, and songs. Elizabeth composed 2 piano concertos, a Piano Sonata, and *The Country Maid*, a set of keyboard variations.

BIBL.: O. Sonneck, *Early Concert-Life in America* (1731–1800) (Leipzig, 1907); H. Johnson, *Musical Interludes in Boston 1795–1830* (N.Y., 1942); R. Wolfe, *Early American Music Engraving and Printing* (Urbana, Ill., 1980).

Vanhal (also **van Hal, Vanhall, Wanhal,** etc.), **Johan Baptist (Jan Křtitel),** noted Czech composer and teacher; b. Nové Nechanice, Bohemia, May 12, 1739; d. Vienna, Aug. 20, 1813. He was born into a bonded peasant family; began his musical training as a teacher and organist in Maršov, and then studied organ with the cantor A. Erban in Nové Nechanice. In 1757 he became organist in Opocno; in 1759 he was named choirmaster in Hnevceves. After he won the favor of Countess Schaffgotsch, his patron took him to Vienna about 1761, and he was able to further his training under Dittersdorf. He obtained his release from bondage, and then traveled in Italy (1769–71) before returning to Vienna. Although stricken with mental illness, he recovered and devoted his energies to teaching and composing. He was a prolific composer; some 700 works are extant. Vanhal was a particularly significant composer of syms. in the early Classical style. His keyboard sonatas are also notable. His output includes works for both professional and amateur performers. He publ. the pedagogical vol. *Anfangsgründe des Generalbasses* (Vienna, 1817).

WORKS: OPERAS: *Il Demofoonte* (Rome, 1770); *Il trionfo di Clelia* (Rome, 1770). **ORCH.:** About 73 syms. (c.1767–85); several concertos for Harpsichord or Piano; other concertos for Violin, Cello, Viola, Flute, Bassoon, Clarinet, and Double Bass; marches, dances, etc.; 6 string quintets; over 75 string quartets; more than 100 string trios; many other chamber pieces, including keyboard trios, string duos, keyboard duos, and solo keyboard works of various descriptions; about 60 masses, more than 60 motets, a Stabat Mater, a Te Deum, a Passion oratorio, and other sacred works; many secular songs.

BIBL.: J. Bušek, *Jansa, Kalivoda, V.* (Prague, 1926); P. Bryan, *The Symphonies of J. V.* (diss., Univ. of Michigan, 1955); N. Dlouhá-Mikotová, *Klavírní koncerty J.K. V.a* (J.K. V.'s Keyboard Concertos; diss., Univ. of Prague, 1958); A. Borková, *Stylová charakteristika klavírních sonát J.K. V.a* (Stylistic Characteristics of J.K. V.'s Keyboard Sonatas; diss., Univ. of Brno, 1967).

Van Heusen, Jimmy (real name, **Edward Chester Babcock**), American composer of popular music; b. Syracuse, N.Y., Jan. 26, 1913. He studied singing with Howard Lyman, then worked as a composer at Harlem's Cotton Club and as a pianist and song plugger for Tin Pan Alley music publishers before scoring his 1st success as a songwriter with *It's the Dreamer in Me* (1938; in collaboration with Jimmy Dorsey). In 1939 he began working with the lyricist Johnny Burke, with whom he wrote songs for 16 of Bing Crosby's films, including the popular *Swingin' on a Star* from *Going My Way* (1944), which captured an Academy Award; they also ran their own music publishing company (from 1944). He then worked with Sammy Cahn (1955–69), with whom he wrote such songs as *Love and Marriage* (1955) for the television version of Thornton Wilder's *Our Town, All the Way* for the film *The Joker Is Wild* (1957), *High Hopes* for the film *A Hole in the Head* (1959), and *Call Me Irresponsible* for the film *Papa's Delicate Condition* (1963), all of which won Academy Awards.

Van Hoogstraten, Willem. See **Hoogstraten, Willem van.**

Van Hoose, Ellison, American tenor; b. Murfreesboro, Tenn., Aug. 18, 1868; d. Houston, March 24, 1936. He studied with Luckstone in N.Y., Jean de Reszke in Paris, and in Rome and London. He made his operatic debut with the Damrosch Opera Co. in Philadelphia as Tannhäuser (Dec. 11, 1897); toured with Melba in the U.S. (1903–5) and with Sembrich (1906–7); toured in Europe (1908–10); was a member of the

Chicago Opera Co. (1911–12); then devoted himself mainly to oratorio singing.

Van Katwijk, Paul. See **Katwijk, Paul van.**

Van Lier, Bertus, Dutch composer; b. Utrecht, Sept. 10, 1906; d. Roden, Feb. 14, 1972. He studied composition with Willem Pijper in Amsterdam and conducting with Scherchen in Strasbourg; settled in Utrecht as a conductor, composer, and music critic. He taught at the Rotterdam Cons. (1945–60) and thereafter worked in the dept. of art history at the Univ. of Groningen. His early compositions are modeled on Pijper's "germ-cell" theory, to which he imparted a literary symbolism. He publ. a number of essays on music under the title *Buiten de maastreep* (Beyond the Bar Line; Amsterdam, 1948) and *Rhythme en metrum* (Groningen, 1967).

WORKS: Ballet, *Katharsis* (1945; concert version, Utrecht, Nov. 29, 1950); 3 syms. (1928; 1930–31, rev. 1946; 1938–39); Concertino for Cello and Chamber Orch. (1933); *De dijk* (The Dike) for Narrator and Chamber Orch. (1937); *Canticum* for Female Chorus, 2 Flutes, Piano, 4-hands, and Strings (1939); *O Netherlands, Pay Attention*, cantata for Chorus, Timpani, and Strings (1945); *Het Hooglied* (The Song of Songs) for Soloists, Chorus, and Small Orch. (1949; in Dutch and Eng.); Bassoon Concerto (1950); *Symfonia* for 2 String Orchs., Double Wind Quintet, and Timpani (1954); *Cantate voor Kerstmis* (Christmas Cantata) for Chorus and Orch. (1955); *Divertimento facile* for Orch. (1957); *Concertante Music* for Violin, Oboe, and Orch. (1959); *5 Mei: Zij* (5th of May: They), oratorio (Radio Hilversum, May 5, 1963); *Intrada reale e Sinfonia festiva* for Orch. (1964); *Variaties en thema* for Orch. (1967; Bergen, Jan. 17, 1968); String Quartet (1929); Solo Violin Sonata (1931); *Small Suite* for Violin and Piano (1935); *3 Old Persian Quatrains* for Soprano, Bass Flute, Oboe d'Amore, and Piano (1956); incidental music for Sophocles' *Ajax* (1932) and *Antigone* (1952); piano pieces; choruses.

Van Lier, Jacques, Dutch cellist; b. The Hague, April 24, 1875; d. Worthing, England, Feb. 25, 1951. He studied cello with Hartog in The Hague and with Eberle in Rotterdam; joined the Berlin Phil. in 1897; from 1899 to 1915, was an instructor of cello at the Klindworth-Scharwenka Cons. in Berlin. He was cellist in the Holländisches Trio with J. van Veen (violin) and Coenraad Bos (piano); the trio enjoyed a European reputation (1900–7); in 1915 he settled in The Hague; went to England in 1939. He publ. *Violoncellbogentechnik* and *Moderne Violoncelltechnik der linken und der rechten Hand*; also ed. about 400 classical pieces for cello.

Van Maldeghem, Robert Julien. See **Maldeghem, Robert Julien van.**

Van Maldere, Pierre. See **Maldere, Pierre van.**

Vanni-Marcoux. See **Marcoux, Vanni.**

Vannuccini, Luigi, noted Italian singing master; b. Fojano, Dec. 4, 1828; d. Montecatini, Aug. 14, 1911. He studied at the Florence Cons.; became an opera conductor (1848); then turned to the study of the piano, and appeared as a concert pianist with excellent success; finally settled in Florence, devoted himself exclusively to vocal training, and acquired fame as a singing master. He publ. some songs and piano pieces.

BIBL.: L. Neretti, "L. V.," *Musica d'Oggi* (1931).

Van Otterloo, Willem. See **Otterloo, Willem van.**

Van Raalte, Albert. See **Raalte, Albert van.**

Van Rooy, Anton(ius Maria Josephus), celebrated Dutch bass-baritone; b. Rotterdam, Jan. 1, 1870; d. Munich, Nov. 28, 1932. He studied voice with Julius Stockhausen in Frankfurt am Main; in 1897 he made his 1st appearance at the Bayreuth Festival as Wotan, a role he sang there each season until 1902; also appeared there as Hans Sachs in 1899 and as the Dutchman in 1901 and 1902. From 1898 to 1913 he sang at London's Covent Garden. On Dec. 14, 1898, he made his U.S. debut as Wotan in *Die Walküre* at the Metropolitan Opera in N.Y., remaining on its roster until 1908, except for

1900–1901. In 1908 he was engaged as a regular member of the Frankfurt Opera, retiring in 1913. He was particularly distinguished in Wagnerian roles, but also was noted for his interpretations of Escamillo, Valentin, and Don Fernando in *Fidelio*. He also distinguished himself as a lieder artist.

Van Slyck, Nicholas, American pianist, conductor, music educator, and composer; b. Philadelphia, Oct. 25, 1922; d. Boston, July 3, 1983. He studied piano with George Reeves, conducting with Henry Swoboda, and composition with Walter Piston at Harvard Univ., where he obtained his M.A. He was founder and conductor of the Dedham (Mass.) Chorus in 1954 and also led the Quincy (Mass.) Orch. (1962–67); served as director of the South End Music Center of Boston (1950–62) and of the Longy School of Music (1962–76). In 1976 he organized the New School of Music in Cambridge, Mass. His music is pragmatic in its form and destination, while the technical structure is catholic, ranging from triadic to dodecaphonic. He compiled a piano anthology, *Looking Forward* (1981).

Works: *Variations* for Piano and Orch. (1947); 2 divertimenti for Chamber Orch. (1947, 1948); Sonatina for Clarinet and String Orch. (1948); Piano Concerto No. 2 (1957); 2 *Symphonic Paraphrases* (1960, 1966); *Legend of Sleepy Hollow* for Chamber Orch. (1963); 2 clarinet sonatas (1947, 1958); 2 cello sonatas (1954, 1968); 4 violin sonatas (1956–65); Flute Sonata (1957); Quartet for Clarinet, Violin, Cello, and Piano (1959); Octet for Flute, Clarinet, Horn, Violin, Viola, Cello, Timpani, and Piano (1962); 6 piano sonatas (1947–59); 6 piano sonatinas (1956–68); numerous piano pieces, choruses, and songs.

Van Tieghem, David, American composer and percussionist; b. Washington, D.C., April 21, 1955. He studied in N.Y. with Justin DiCioccio at the High School of Music and Art, and also attended the Manhattan School of Music (1973–76), where he studied with Paul Price. In 1977 he created a solo percussion theater piece using found objects and sophisticated technology; he has since performed variations on this work throughout the U.S. and Europe as *Message Received . . . Proceed Accordingly* or *A Man and His Toys*. He performed with Steve Reich and Musicians (1975–80), and recorded with Laurie Anderson, Robert Ashley, and Brian Eno; also created scores for films, performance works, and dance pieces. In 1989 he wrote the music for and performed the lead role in the theater piece *The Ghost Writer*. His interesting variations on dance and percussion textures have led to his widespread popularity in the N.Y. commercial and avant-garde music communities. Other works include *These Things Happen* (1984), *Safety in Numbers* (1987), and *Strange Cargo* (1989).

Van Vactor, David, American flutist, conductor, teacher, and composer; b. Plymouth, Ind., May 8, 1906. He enrolled in the premedical classes at Northwestern Univ. (1924–27); then changed to the music school there, studying flute with Arthur Kitti and theory with Arne Oldberg, Felix Borowski, and Albert Noelte (B.M., 1928; M.M., 1935); also studied flute with Josef Niedermayr and composition with Franz Schmidt at the Vienna Academy of Music (1928–29), and then flute with Marcel Moyse at the Paris Cons. and composition with Dukas at the École Normale de Musique. Returning to the U.S., he was engaged as a flutist in the Chicago Sym. Orch. (1931–43); also was an assistant conductor of the Chicago Civic Orch. (1933–34) and a teacher of theory at Northwestern Univ., where he was conductor of its sym. and chamber orchs. (1935–39). From 1943 to 1945 he was assistant conductor of the Kansas City Phil., where he also was a flutist; was founder-conductor of the Kansas City Allied Arts Orch. (1945–47); concurrently was head of the theory and composition dept. at the Kansas City Cons. From 1947 to 1972 he was conductor of the Knoxville Sym. Orch.; in 1947 he organized the fine arts dept. at the Univ. of Tennessee, where he was a prof. until 1976. In 1941 he toured as a flutist with the North American Woodwind Quintet and in 1945, 1946, and 1964 as a conductor in South America under the auspices of the U.S. State Dept. He held Fulbright and Guggenheim fellowships in 1957–58. In 1976 he was honored with the title of Composer

Laureate of the State of Tennessee. He publ. *Every Child May Hear* (1960). As a composer, Van Vactor adheres mainly to basic tonalities, but he enhances them with ingeniously contrived melodic gargoyles, creating a simulation of atonality. The rhythmic vivacity of his inventive writing creates a cheerful, hedonistic atmosphere.

Works: orch.: *Chaconne* for String Orch. (Rochester, N.Y., May 17, 1928); 5 *Small Pieces for Large Orchestra* (Ravinia Park, Ill., July 5, 1931); *The Masque of the Red Death*, after Edgar Allan Poe (1932); Flute Concerto (Chicago, Feb. 26, 1933); *Passacaglia and Fugue* (Chicago, Jan. 28, 1934); *Concerto grosso* for 3 Flutes, Harp, and Orch. (Chicago, April 4, 1935); *Overture to a Comedy* No. 1 (Chicago, June 20, 1937); *Overture to a Comedy* No. 2 (Indianapolis, March 14, 1941); *Symphonic Suite* (Ravinia Park, Ill., July 21, 1938); 8 syms.: No. 1 in D (1936–37; N.Y., Jan. 19, 1939, composer conducting; awarded prize of $1,000 in the American Composers Contest sponsored by the N.Y. Phil.); No. 2, *Music for the Marines* (1943; Indianapolis, March 27, 1943; programmed as a suite, not a sym.); No. 3 (1958; Pittsburgh, April 3, 1959; perf. and recorded as No. 2); No. 4, *Walden*, for Chorus and Orch., to texts from Thoreau's *Walden* (1970–71; 1st complete perf., Maryville, Tenn., May 9, 1971; listed as Sym. No. 3 at its premiere); No. 5 (1976; Knoxville, Tenn., March 11, 1976); No. 6 for Orch. or Band (1980; for Orch., Knoxville, Nov. 19, 1981; for Band, Muncie, Ind., April 13, 1983); No. 7 (1983); No. 8 (1984); 5 *Bagatelles* for Strings (Chicago, Feb. 7, 1938); Viola Concerto (Ravinia Park, July 13, 1940); *Variazioni Solenne* (1941; 1st perf. under the title *Gothic Impressions* by the Chicago Sym. Orch., Feb. 26, 1942); *Pastorale and Dance* for Flute and Strings (1947); Violin Concerto (Knoxville, April 10, 1951); *Fantasia, Chaconne and Allegro* (Louisville, Feb. 20, 1957); *Suite* for Trumpet and Small Orch. (1962); *Suite on Chilean Folk Tunes* (1963); *Passacaglia, Chorale and Scamper* for Band (1964); *Sinfonia breve* (1964; Santiago, Chile, Sept. 3, 1965); *Sarabande and Variations* for Brass Quintet and Strings (1968; Knoxville, May 4, 1969); *Requiescat* for Strings (Knoxville, Oct. 17, 1970); *Andante and Allegro* for Saxophone and Strings (1972); *Set of 5* for Wind Instruments and Percussion (1973); *Nostalgia* for Band (1975); *Prelude and Fugue* for Strings (1975); *Fanfare and Chorale* for Band (1977); *The Elements* for Band (Knoxville, May 22, 1979).

vocal: *Credo* for Chorus and Orch (1941); Cantata for 3 Treble Voices and Orch. (1947); *The New Light*, Christmas cantata (1954); *Christmas Songs for Young People* for Chorus and Orch. (1961); *A Song of Mankind*, 1st part of a 7-part cantata (Indianapolis, Sept. 26, 1971); *Processional "Veni Immanuel"* for Chorus and Orch. (1974); *Brethren We Have Met to Worship* for Chorus and Orch. (1975); *Episodes—Jesus Christ* for Chorus and Orch. (Knoxville, May 2, 1977); *Processional* for Chorus, Wind Instruments, and Percussion (Knoxville, Dec. 1, 1979).

chamber: Quintet for 2 Violins, Viola, Cello, and Flute (1932); *Suite* for 2 Flutes (1934); *Divertimento* for Wind Quintet (1936); 2 string quartets (1940, 1949); Piano Trio (1942); Flute Sonatina (1949); *Duettino* for Violin and Cello (1952); Wind Quintet (1959); *Children of the Stars*, 6 pieces for Violin and Piano (1960); 5 *Etudes* for Trumpet (1963); Octet for Brass (1963); *Economy Band* No. 1 for Trumpet, Trombone, and Percussion (1966); *Economy Band* No. 2 for Horn, Tuba, and Percussion (1969); *Music for Woodwinds* (1966–67); 4 *Etudes* for Wind Instruments and Percussion (1968); Tuba Quartet (1971); Suite for 12 Solo Trombones (1972); 5 *Songs* for Flute and Guitar (1974).

Van Vechten, Carl, American novelist and writer on music; b. Cedar Rapids, Iowa, June 17, 1880; d. N.Y., Dec. 21, 1964. He graduated from the Univ. of Chicago (1903); was music critic of the *N.Y. Times* (1906–7; 1910–13); was its Paris correspondent in 1908–9. From 1931 he occupied himself with photography, and took a great number of pictures of musicians; his collection of photographs is at Fiske Univ. in Nashville. He publ. *5 Old English Ditties* (1904). His books on music are *Music after the Great War* (1915); *Music and Bad Manners* (1916); *Interpreters and Interpretations* (1917); *The Music of Spain* (1918); *Red: Papers on Musical Subjects* (1925).

BIBL.: E. Lueders, *C. V. V. and the Twenties* (Albuquerque, 1955).

Van Vleck, Jacob, Moravian minister, violinist, and organist; b. N.Y., 1751; d. Bethlehem, Pa., July 3, 1831. He was director of the Young Ladies' Seminary at Bethlehem from 1790 to 1800; was consecrated a bishop in 1815. He was the 1st American-born Moravian to be active as a composer.

BIBL.: A. Rau and H. David, *A Catalogue of Music by American Moravians* (Bethlehem, 1938); H. David, "Background for Bethlehem: Moravian Music in Pennsylvania," *Magazine of Art* (April 1939); idem, "Musical Life in the Pennsylvania Settlements of the *Unitas Fratrum*," *Transactions of the Moravian Historical Society* (1942; reprinted as Moravian Music Foundation Publication No. 6, Winston-Salem, N.C., 1959); J. Falconer, "The Second Berlin Song School in America," *Musical Quarterly* (July 1973).

Van Westerhout, Nicola (Niccolò), Italian pianist and composer of Dutch descent; b. Mola di Bari, Dec. 17, 1857; d. Naples, Aug. 21, 1898. He was a pupil of Nicola d'Arienzo, De Giosa, and Lauro Rossi at the Naples Cons. and of Antonio Tari at the Univ. of Naples; then pursued a fine career as a pianist. He taught harmony at the Naples Cons. (1897–98).

WORKS: OPERAS: *Una notte a Venezia* (rev. as *Cimbelino*, Rome, April 7, 1892); *Fortunio* (Milan, May 16, 1895); *Doña Flor* (Mola di Bari, April 18, 1896, on the opening of the Teatro Van Westerhout, named after him); *Colomba* (Naples, March 27, 1923); *Tilde* (not perf.). **ORCH.:** 3 syms., No. 3 unfinished; Serenata; Overture to Shakespeare's *Julius Caesar*; Violin Concerto; also chamber music; many piano pieces of considerable merit; songs.

BIBL.: A. Giovane, "Nicola van W.," *Musicisti e cantanti della terra di Bari* (Bari, 1968).

Van Wyk, Arnold. See **Wyk, Arnold van.**

Van Zandt, Marie, American soprano; b. N.Y., Oct. 8, 1858; d. Cannes, Dec. 31, 1919. She studied with her mother, the well-known American soprano **Jennie van Zandt,** and with Lamperti; made her operatic debut as Zerlina in Turin (Jan. 1879); her 1st appearance in London followed later that year as Amina at Her Majesty's Theatre; she then sang with notable success at the Paris Opéra-Comique (1880–85). She made her U.S. debut as Amina in Chicago on Nov. 13, 1891, which role she sang at her Metropolitan Opera debut in N.Y. on Dec. 21, 1891, where she sang for 1 season. She continued to tour as a guest artist until her marriage in 1898. Delibes wrote the role of Lakmé for her, and she created it at the Opéra-Comique on April 14, 1883. Among her other roles were Cherubino, Dinorah, and Mignon.

Van Zanten, Cornelie, famous Dutch soprano and pedagogue; b. Dordrecht, Aug. 2, 1855; d. The Hague, Jan. 10, 1946. She studied with K. Schneider at the Cologne Cons., and in Milan with Lamperti, who developed her original contralto into a coloratura soprano voice. She made her operatic debut in Turin in 1875 as Leonora in *La Favorite;* sang in Breslau (1880–82) and Kassel (1882–83); then in Amsterdam (from 1884); also toured in the U.S. in 1886–87 as a member of the National Opera Co. under the directorship of Theodore Thomas; then appeared in special performances of *Der Ring des Nibelungen* in Russia. She taught at the Amsterdam Cons. (1895–1903); subsequently lived in Berlin, highly esteemed as a singing teacher; eventually settled in The Hague. Her most distinguished roles were Orfeo, Fidès, Ortrud, Azucena, and Amneris. She publ. songs to German and Dutch texts; with C. Poser, brought out *Leitfaden zum Kunstgesang* (Berlin, 1903).

BIBL.: J. Hofstra, "C. v.Z.," *Mens en Melodie,* 1 (1946).

Varady, Julia, Rumanian-born German soprano; b. Oradea, Sept. 1, 1941. She was educated at the Cluj Cons. and at the Bucharest Cons.; sang at the Cluj Opera (1960–70), then was a member of the Frankfurt Opera (1970–72) and the Bavarian State Opera in Munich (from 1972); she also appeared in Hamburg, Vienna, Berlin, Paris, Edinburgh, and other operatic centers. In 1974 she married **Dietrich Fischer-Dieskau.** Among her roles are Fiordiligi, Donna Elvira, Giorgetta, Alcestis, Madama Butterfly, and Arabella.

Vardi, Emanuel, outstanding Israeli-American violist; b. Jerusalem, April 21, 1917. He began to study the viola in his youth; also studied painting at the Florence Academy of Fine Arts. In 1940 he went to the U.S., and soon established himself as an outstanding virtuoso in the limited field of viola literature. He arranged works by Bach, Frescobaldi, Tartini, Paganini, and Chopin for viola; also commissioned works for the viola from Michael Colgrass, Alan Hovhaness, Alan Shulman, and others. For variety's sake, he made an incursion into the conducting arena; was music director of the South Dakota Sym. Orch. (1978–82). In his leisure time he painted. In 1951 he won the International Prize of Rapallo, and had 1-man exhibits in N.Y., South Dakota, and Italy.

Varèse, Edgard (Victor Achille Charles), remarkable French-born American composer, who introduced a totally original principle of organizing the materials and forms of sound, profoundly influencing the direction of new music; b. Paris, Dec. 22, 1883; d. N.Y., Nov. 6, 1965. The original spelling of his first Christian name was Edgard, but most of his works were first publ. under the name **Edgar;** about 1940 he chose to return to the legal spelling. He spent his early childhood in Paris and in Burgundy, and began to compose early in life. In 1892 his parents went to Turin; his paternal grandfather was Italian; his other grandparents were French. He took private lessons in composition with Giovanni Bolzoni, who taught him gratis. Varèse gained some performing experience by playing percussion in the school orch. He stayed there until 1903; then went to Paris. In 1904 he entered the Schola Cantorum, where he studied composition, counterpoint, and fugue with Albert Roussel, preclassical music with Charles Bordes, and conducting with Vincent d'Indy; then entered the composition class of Charles-Marie Widor at the Cons. in 1905. In 1907 he received the "bourse artistique" offered by the City of Paris; at that time he founded and conducted the chorus of the Université Populaire and organized concerts at the Château du Peuple. He became associated with musicians and artists of the avant-garde; also met Debussy, who showed interest in his career. In 1907 he married a young actress, Suzanne Bing; they had a daughter. Together they went to Berlin, at that time the center of new music that offered opportunities to Varèse. The marriage was not successful, and they separated in 1913. Romain Rolland gave to Varèse a letter of recommendation for Richard Strauss, who in turn showed interest in Varèse's music. He was also instrumental in arranging a performance of Varèse's symphonic poem *Bourgogne,* which was performed in Berlin on Dec. 15, 1910. But the greatest experience for Varèse in Berlin was his meeting and friendship with Busoni. Varèse greatly admired Busoni's book on new music esthetics, and was profoundly influenced by Busoni's views. He composed industriously, mostly for orch.; the most ambitious of these works was a symphonic poem, *Gargantua,* but it was never completed. Other works were *Souvenirs, Prélude à la fin d'un jour, Cycles du Nord,* and an incomplete opera, *Oedipus und die Sphinx,* to the text by Hofmannsthal. All these works, in manuscript, were lost under somewhat mysterious circumstances, and Varèse himself destroyed the score of *Bourgogne* later in life. A hostile reception that he encountered from Berlin critics for *Bourgogne* upset Varèse, who expressed his unhappiness in a letter to Debussy. However, Debussy responded with a friendly letter of encouragement, advising Varèse not to pay too much attention to critics. As early as 1913, Varèse began an earnest quest for new musical resources; upon his return to Paris, he worked on related problems with the Italian musical futurist Luigi Russolo, although he disapproved of the attempt to find a way to new music through the medium of instrumental noises. He was briefly called to the French army at the outbreak of the First World War, but was discharged because of a chronic lung ailment. In 1915 he went to N.Y. There he met the young American writer Louise Norton; they set up a household together; in 1921, when she obtained her own divorce from a previous marriage, they were married. As in Paris and Berlin, Varèse had chronic financial difficulties in America; the royalties from his few publ. works were minimal; in order to supplement his earnings he accepted a job as a piano salesman, which was repulsive to him. He also appeared in a minor role in a John Barrymore silent film in 1918. Some welcome aid came from the wealthy artist Gertrude Vanderbilt, who sent him monthly allowances for a certain length of time. Varèse also had an opportunity to appear as a conductor. As the U.S. neared the entrance into war against Germany, there was a demand for French conductors to replace the German music directors who had held the monopoly on American orchs. On April 1, 1917, Varèse conducted in N.Y. the Requiem Mass of Berlioz. On March 17, 1918, he conducted a concert of the Cincinnati Sym. Orch. in a program of French and Russian music; he also included an excerpt from *Lohengrin,* thus defying the general ban on German music. However, he apparently lacked that indefinable quality that makes a conductor, and he was forced to cancel further concerts with the Cincinnati Sym. Orch. Eager to promote the cause of modern music, he organized a sym. orch. in N.Y. with the specific purpose of giving performances of new and unusual music; it presented its first concert on April 11, 1919. In 1922 he organized with Carlos Salzedo the International Composers' Guild, which gave its inaugural concert in N.Y. on Dec. 17, 1922. In 1926 he founded, in association with a few progressive musicians, the Pan American Society, dedicated to the promotion of music of the Americas. He intensified his study of the nature of sound, working with the acoustician Harvey Fletcher (1926–36), and with the Russian electrical engineer Leon Theremin, then resident in the U.S. These studies led him to the formulation of the concept of "organized sound," in which the sonorous elements in themselves determined the progress of composition; this process eliminated conventional thematic development; yet the firm cohesion of musical ideas made Varèse's music all the more solid, while the distinction between consonances and dissonances became no longer of basic validity. The resulting product was unique in modern music; characteristically, Varèse attached to his works titles from the field of mathematics or physics, such as *Intégrales, Hyperprism* (a projection of a prism into the 4th dimension), *Ionisation, Density 21.5* (the specific weight of platinum), etc., while the score of his large orch. work *Arcana* derived its inspiration from the cosmology of Paracelsus. An important development was Varèse's application of electronic music in his *Déserts* and, much more extensively, in his *Poème électronique,* commissioned for the Brussels World Exposition in 1958. He wrote relatively few works in small forms, and none for piano solo. The unfamiliarity of Varèse's idiom and the tremendous difficulty of his orch. works militated against frequent performances. Among conductors, only Leopold Stokowski was bold enough to put Varèse's formidable scores *Amériques* and *Arcana* on his programs with the Philadelphia Orch.; they evoked yelps of derision and outbursts of righteous indignation from the public and the press. Ironically, it was left to a mere beginner, Nicolas Slonimsky, to be the 1st to perform and record Varèse's unique masterpiece, *Ionisation.* An extraordinary reversal of attitudes toward Varèse's music, owing perhaps to the general advance of musical intelligence and the emergence of young music critics, took place within Varèse's lifetime, resulting in a spectacular increase of interest in his works and the number of their performances; also, musicians themselves learned to overcome the rhythmic difficulties presented in Varèse's scores. Thus Varèse lived to witness this long-delayed recognition of his music as a major stimulus of modern art; his name joined those of Stravinsky, Ives, Schoenberg, and Webern among the great masters of 20th-century music. Recognition came also from an unexpected field when scientists working on the atom bomb at Oak Ridge in 1940

played Slonimsky's recording of *Ionisation* for relaxation and stimulation in their work. In 1955 he was elected to membership in the National Inst. of Arts and Letters and in 1962 in the Royal Swedish Academy. He became a naturalized U.S. citizen in 1926. Like Schoenberg, Varèse refused to regard himself as a revolutionary in music; indeed, he professed great admiration for his remote predecessors, particularly those of the Notre Dame school, representing the flowering of the Ars Antiqua. On the centennial of his birth in 1983, festivals of his music were staged in Strasbourg, Paris, Rome, Washington, D.C., N.Y., and Los Angeles. In 1981, Frank Zappa, the leader of the modern school of rock music and a sincere admirer of Varèse's music, staged in N.Y. at his own expense a concert of Varèse's works; he presented a similar concert in San Francisco in 1982.

WORKS: *Un Grand Sommeil noir* for Voice and Piano (1906); *Amériques* for Orch. (1918–21; Philadelphia, April 9, 1926, L. Stokowski conducting; rev. 1927; Paris, May 30, 1929, G. Poulet conducting); *Dedications,* later renamed *Offrandes* for Soprano and Chamber Orch. (1921; N.Y., April 23, 1922, N. Koshetz soloist, C. Salzedo conducting); *Hyperprism* for 9 Wind Instruments and 18 Percussion Devices (N.Y., March 4, 1923, composer conducting); *Octandre* for Flute, Oboe, Clarinet, Bassoon, Horn, Trombone, and Double Bass (1923; N.Y., Jan. 13, 1924, R. Schmitz conducting); *Intégrales* for 11 Instruments and 4 Percussion (N.Y., March 1, 1925, L. Stokowski conducting); *Arcana* for Orch. (1925–27; Philadelphia, April 8, 1927, L. Stokowski conducting; rev. 1960); *Ionisation* for 13 Percussionists (using instruments of indefinite pitch), Piano, and 2 Sirens (1929–31; N.Y., March 6, 1933, N. Slonimsky conducting); *Ecuatorial* for Bass, 4 Trumpets, 4 Trombones, Piano, Organ, Percussion, and Thereminovox (1932–34; N.Y., April 15, 1934, C. Baromeo soloist, N. Slonimsky conducting; also for Men's Chorus, 2 Ondes Martenot, and Orch.); *Density 21.5* for Flute (N.Y., Feb. 16, 1936; G. Barrère, soloist, on his platinum flute of specific gravity 21.5); *Étude pour Espace* for Mixed Chorus, 2 Pianos, and Percussion (N.Y., Feb. 23, 1947, composer conducting); *Déserts* for Wind Instruments, Percussion, and 3 Interpolations of Electronic Sound (1950–54; Paris, Dec. 2, 1954, H. Scherchen conducting); *La Procession de Vergès,* tape for the film *Around and About Joan Miró* (1955); *Poème électronique* for More Than 400 Spatially Distributed Loudspeakers (1957–58; Brussels Exposition, May 2, 1958); *Nocturnal* for Soprano, Bass Chorus, and Chamber Orch. (N.Y., May 1, 1961, R. Craft conducting; unfinished; completed from notes and sketches by Chou Wen-Chung).

WRITINGS: L. Hirbour, ed., *Écrits* (Paris, 1983).

BIBL.: H. Cowell, "The Music of E. V.," *Modern Music,* V/ 2 (1928; reprint in H. Cowell, ed., *American Composers on American Music,* Stanford, Calif., 1933); J. Klaren, *E. V., Pioneer of New Music in America* (Boston, 1928); M. Wilkinson, "An Introduction to the Music of E. V.," *The Score,* No. 19 (1957); G. Schuller, "Conversation with V.," *Perspectives of New Music,* III/2 (1965); Chou Wen-Chung, "V: A Sketch of the Man and His Music," *Musical Quarterly,* LII (1966); F. Quellette, *E. V.* (Paris, 1966; Eng. tr., 1968); L. Varèse, *V.: A Looking Glass Diary* (N.Y., 1972); O. Vivier, *V.* (Paris, 1973); J.-J. Nattiez, *Essai d'analyse distributionelle de 'Densité 21.5' de V.* (Montreal, 1975; Eng. tr. by A. Barry in *Music Analysis,* I, 1982); G. Wehmeyer, *E. V.* (Regensburg, 1977); S. Van Solkema, ed., *The New Worlds of E. V.: Symposium* (Brooklyn, 1979); A. Carpentier, *V. vivant* (Paris, 1982); M. Bredel, *E. V.* (Paris, 1984); J. Bernard, *The Music of E. V.* (New Haven, Conn., 1987); P. Griffiths, "The Mystery of E. V.," *Musical Times* (Sept. 1987).

Varesi, Felice, noted French-Italian baritone; b. Calais, 1813; d. Milan, March 13, 1889. He made his debut in Donizetti's *Furioso all'isola di San Domingo* in Varese in 1834; then sang throughout Italy; made guest appearances at Vienna's Kärnthnertortheater (1842–47), where he created the role of Antonio in Donizetti's *Linda di Chamounix* (May 19, 1842); was chosen to create the title roles in Verdi's *Macbeth* (Florence, March

14, 1847) and *Rigoletto* (Venice, March 11, 1851), and Germont *père* in *La Traviata* (Venice, March 6, 1853). On April 19, 1864, he made his London debut as Rigoletto at Her Majesty's Theatre. His wife was the soprano **Cecilia Boccabadati** (b. c.1825; d. Florence, 1906); their daughter, **Elena Boccabadati-Varesi** (b. Florence, c.1854; d. Chicago, June 15, 1920), was also a soprano; made her London debut as Gilda at Drury Lane (April 17, 1875); after appearing throughout Europe, she settled in Chicago, where she taught voice from 1888; her finest role was Lucia; was also admired for her portrayals of Zerlina and Amina.

Varga, Ovidiu, Rumanian composer; b. Pascani, Oct. 5, 1913. He studied violin and composition in Işai; subsequently became a prof. at the Bucharest Cons. He excels in vocal music; has written several cantatas on patriotic subjects; an oratorio; many Mass songs; songs for voice and piano; Concerto for String Orch. and Percussion (1957); String Quartet No. 1 (1960) and other instrumental works.

Varga, Tibor, Hungarian-born English violinist, conductor, and pedagogue; b. Györ, July 4, 1921. He took courses in philosophy at the Univ. of Budapest (1939–43), and studied violin with Hubay at the Budapest Academy of Music and with Flesch at the Berlin Hochschule für Musik (1931–38). He made his debut when he was 10; pursued an active concert career from the age of 12. In 1949 he became prof. of violin at the North-West German Academy of Music in Detmold, where he founded his own chamber orch. in 1954; he settled in 1955 in Switzerland, where he organized his own festival in Sion in 1964. His repertoire is extensive, although he has become best known for his advocacy of contemporary works.

Vargas, Pedro, Mexican tenor; b. San Miguel de Allende, April 29, 1904; d. Mexico City, Oct. 30, 1989. He tried to become a bullfighter, but failed miserably; then turned to medical study, succeeding even less than as a torero. After vocal studies at the National Cons. of Music, he made his operatic debut as Turiddu in *Cavalleria rusticana* (1928); finally found his true vocation as a popularizer of Mexican ballads. He sang for U.S. presidents and appeared on the stage with Frank Sinatra; also appeared in dozens of Mexican films. With Augustín Lara, he popularized the bolero and the pasodoble; his rendition of *Fleur-de-lis* was celebrated throughout Latin America in the 1930s.

Varkonyi, Béla, Hungarian composer and pianist; b. Budapest, July 5, 1878; d. N.Y., Jan. 25, 1947. He studied with Hans Koessler and István Thomán at the Royal Academy of Music in Budapest (Ph.D. in law and M.M. in music, 1902). After winning the Robert Volkmann Competition twice and receiving the Hungarian national scholarship, he studied in London and Paris; returned in 1907 to Budapest, where he taught at the Royal Academy of Music. At the outbreak of World War I in 1914, he joined the Hungarian army; was captured by the Russians, and spent 3 years as a prisoner of war; he continued to compose, but his MSS were destroyed when the Danish Consulate was burned. After the war, he emigrated to the U.S. (1923); taught at Breneau College, Georgia (until 1928), and Centenary College in Tennessee (1928–30); then settled in N.Y., where he was active as a teacher and composer. Varkonyi is reported to have had a fantastic memory; he was able to recount more than 40 years of his life by day and date; S. Rath devotes a chapter to it in his book *Hungarian Curiosities* (1955).

WORKS: Piano Concerto in E minor (Budapest, 1902); Overture in D minor (Budapest, 1902); *Dobozy,* symphonic poem (Budapest, 1903); Symphonic Ballad (Budapest, 1907); *Captive Woman,* melodrama (Budapest, 1911); *Spring Night,* melodrama (Budapest, 1912); Sym. in C minor (1913); Piano Trio in F major, op. 17 (N.Y., Nov. 24, 1918); Scherzo for String Quartet (N.Y., Nov. 24, 1918); also *Fantastic Scenes* for Orch., op. 43; *Leda,* op. 42 (also *Leda Fantasy,* op. 42a); *Hungarian Chorus Rhapsody*; 100 songs; many piano works.

Varlamov, Alexander Egorovich, Russian composer of Moldavian descent; b. Moscow, Nov. 27, 1801; d. St. Petersburg,

Oct. 27, 1848. At the age of 10 he entered the Imperial Chapel at St. Petersburg, where his fine voice attracted the attention of Bortiansky, the director, who then became his teacher; after Varlamov's voice broke in 1818, he left the choir and went to The Hague in 1819 as director of the choir at the Russian ambassadorial chapel; in 1823 he returned to St. Petersburg as singing teacher at the Drama School, which post he held until 1826; after teaching the young solo singers in the court chapel choir (1829–31), he served as Kapellmeister of the Moscow imperial theaters (1832–43); he returned in 1845 to St. Petersburg, where he gave private singing lessons. He composed 2 ballets, incidental music to 17 plays, and piano pieces, but became best known as a song composer. In addition to the songs he wrote for plays, he wrote 138 solo songs and 31 songs for vocal ensembles; also made arrangements of over 50 folk melodies. A complete edition of his works was ed. by F. Stellovsky as *Polnoye sobraniye sochineniy* (12 vols., St. Petersburg, 1861–64). He publ. *Polnaya shkola peniya* (Complete School of Singing; Moscow, 1840; 2nd ed., 1953).
    BIBL.: N. Listova, *A. V.* (Moscow, 1968).

Várnai, Péter P(ál), Hungarian writer on music; b. Budapest, July 10, 1922. He studied composition with Szervánszky and conducting with Ferencsik at the Budapest Cons.; worked for the Hungarian Radio (1945–50) and was active as a conductor (1951–54). He then devoted himself to music research and criticism; was an ed. of Editio Musica in Budapest (1956–82). In addition to his writings on contemporary Hungarian music and musicians, he also wrote authoritatively on Verdi.
    WRITINGS (all publ. in Budapest): *Goldmark Károly* (1956); *A lengyel zene története* (History of Polish Music; 1959); *Heinrich Schütz* (1959); *Tardos Béla* (1966); *Maros Rudolf* (1967); *Székely Mihály* (1967); *Rösler Endre* (1969); *Oratóriumok könyve* (Book of Oratorios; 1972); *Operalexikon* (1975); *Verdi Magyarországon* (Verdi in Hungary; 1975); *Verdi-operakalauz* (Verdi's Operas; 1978); *Beszélgetések Ligeti György-gyel* (In Conversation with György Ligeti; 1979; Eng. tr., 1983).

Varnay, Astrid (Ibolyka Maria), noted Swedish-born American soprano and mezzo-soprano; b. Stockholm (of Austro-Hungarian parents), April 25, 1918. Her parents were professional singers; she was taken to the U.S. in 1920, and began vocal studies with her mother; then studied with Paul Althouse, and with the conductor Hermann Weigert (1890–1955), whom she married in 1944. She made her debut as Sieglinde at the Metropolitan Opera in N.Y. (Dec. 6, 1941), substituting for Lotte Lehmann without rehearsal; appeared at the Metropolitan until 1956, and again from 1974 to 1976; her last performance there was in 1979. From 1962 she sang mezzo-soprano roles, appearing as Strauss's Herodias and Clytemnestra and as Begbick in Weill's *Aufstieg und Fall der Stadt Mahagonny*; however, she was best known for such Wagnerian roles as Isolde, Kundry, Senta, and Brünnhilde.
    BIBL.: B. Wessling, *A. V.* (Bremen, 1965).

Varney, Louis, French composer and conductor, son of **Pierre Joseph Alphonse Varney;** b. New Orleans, La., May 30, 1844; d. Paris, Aug. 20, 1908. He was taken to Paris at the age of 7; studied with his father, then began his career as a conductor at the Théâtre de l'Athénée, where he also brought out several stage works; from 1880 to 1905 he produced some 40 operettas, the best known of which is *Les Mousquetaires au couvent* (Paris, March 16, 1880). Other operettas include *La Femme de Narcisse* (April 14, 1892), *La Fiancée de Thylda* (Jan. 26, 1900), and *Mademoiselle George* (Dec. 2, 1900), all of which were first performed in Paris.

Varney, Pierre Joseph Alphonse, French composer and conductor, father of **Louis Varney;** b. Paris, Dec. 1, 1811; d. there, Feb. 7, 1879. He studied with Reicha at the Paris Cons.; was active as a theater conductor in Belgium, the Netherlands, and France. From 1840 to 1850 he was director of the French Opera Co. in New Orleans, where he married Jeanne Aimée Andry. The family returned to Paris in 1851. Varney set to music a poem by Rouget de Lisle, *Mourir pour la patrie*, which became popular during the Paris revolution of 1848.

Varro, Marie-Aimée, French pianist; b. Brunoy, Feb. 18, 1915; d. Neuchâtel, Sept. 14, 1971. She studied piano at the Paris Cons., obtaining the Premier Prix; subsequently worked with Robert Casadesus and Alfred Cortot; she completed her advanced studies with Emil von Sauer in Vienna, who gave her indications for authentic interpretation of Liszt's piano works, which he had received from Liszt himself. She specialized in the works of the great Romantic composers, particularly Schumann, Chopin, Liszt, and Brahms. She gave recitals in Europe and America; also appeared as a soloist with major orchs.

Varviso, Silvio, Swiss conductor; b. Zürich, Feb. 26, 1924. He studied piano at the Zürich Cons. and conducting in Vienna with Clemens Krauss. In 1944 he made his debut at St. Gallen, conducting *Die Zauberflöte*, and remained at the theater there until 1950; then conducted at the Basel Stadttheater, where he later served as its music director (1956–62); also made guest appearances in Berlin and Paris in 1958, and then made his U.S. debut with the San Francisco Opera in 1959. On Nov. 26, 1961, he made his Metropolitan Opera debut in N.Y.; remained on its roster until 1966, and returned there in 1968–69 and in 1982–83. In 1962 he made his British debut at the Glyndebourne Festival; later that year he made his 1st appearance at London's Covent Garden; in 1969 he made his Bayreuth Festival debut with *Der fliegende Holländer*. From 1965 to 1972 he was chief conductor of the Royal Theater in Stockholm; after serving as Generalmusikdirektor at the Württemberg State Theater in Stuttgart (1972–80), he was chief conductor of the Paris Opéra (1980–86).

Varvoglis, Mario, Greek composer; b. Brussels, Dec. 22, 1885; d. Athens, July 30, 1967. He studied at the Paris Cons. with Leroux, and later at the Schola Cantorum with d'Indy. Returning to Athens, he taught at the Cons. (1920–24) and at the Hellenic Cons. (from 1924), where he was co-director in 1947; served as president of the League of Greek Composers (from 1957). His output was strongly influenced by d'Indy, Fauré, and Ravel.

WORKS: OPERAS: *Aya Varvara* (1912; only fragments extant); *Tó apóyeme tís agápis* (The Afternoon of Love; 1935; Athens, June 10, 1944); incidental music to 6 Greek dramas. **ORCH.:** *Tó panigyri,* tone poem (1906–9); *Suite pastorale* for Strings (1912; also for String Quartet); *Sainte-Barbara,* symphonic prelude (1912); *Caprice grec* for Cello and Orch. (1914; also for Cello and Piano); Sym. (c.1919; destroyed); *Dáphnes ke kyparíssia* (Laurels and Cypresses), symphonic study (1950). **CHAMBER:** *Hommage à Cesar Franck* for Violin and Piano (1922); *Meditation of Areti* for String Quartet (1929); *Stochasmós* (Meditation) for String Quartet (1932; rev. for String Orch., 1936); *Laikó poíma* (Folk Poem) for Piano Trio (1943); piano pieces, including 14 for children; also choruses; songs.

Vásáry, Tamás, noted Hungarian-born Swiss pianist and conductor; b. Debrecen, Aug. 11, 1933. He studied piano at the Franz Liszt Academy of Music in Budapest; in 1947, won 1st prize in the Liszt Competition, and later garnered several more prizes. He made his London debut in 1961, and played in N.Y. in 1962. In 1971 he became a naturalized Swiss citizen. He made his conducting debut at the Merton Festival in 1971, and subsequently appeared as a guest conductor throughout Europe and the U.S. With Ivan Fischer, he served as co-conductor of the Northern Sinfonia in Newcastle upon Tyne (1979–82). In 1989 he became principal conductor of the Bournemouth Sinfonietta.

Vasconcellos, Joaquim (António da Fonseca) de, Portuguese lexicographer; b. Oporto, Feb. 10, 1849; d. there, March 1, 1936. From 1865 to 1869 he studied at the Univ. of Coïmbra; from 1871 to 1875, traveled in Germany, France, England, and Spain; from 1883, was a prof. of German at the Lyceum of Oporto, and from 1886, also director of the Museum for Industries and Commerce. He publ. the dictionary *Os musicos portuguezes: Biographia-bibliographia* (1870), containing much new matter and many emendations of old; a monograph, *Luiza Todi: Estudo critico* (1873; 2nd ed., 1929); *Ensajo critico sobre o catalogo de el-Rey D. João IV* (1873); a facsimile ed. of the catalogue of the Royal Library of Lisbon, destroyed by the earthquake of 1755 (1874–76; with index and commentary, 1905); he also contributed to Pougin's supplement to Fétis's *Biographie universelle.*

Vasconcelos, Jorge Croner de, Portuguese composer; b. Lisbon, April 11, 1910; d. there, Dec. 9, 1974. He took piano lessons with Aroldo Silva in Lisbon (1927–31); studied composition with Luís de Freitas Branco at the National Cons. there (1927–34); then went to Paris and had courses with Paul Dukas, Nadia Boulanger, and Roger-Ducasse (1934–37). Returning to Portugal in 1939, he taught composition at the Lisbon Cons.

WORKS: Ballets: *A Faina do mar* (1940) and *Coimbra* (1959); *Melodias sobre antigos textos portugueses* for Voice, Flute, and String Quartet (1937); Piano Quartet (1938); *Partita* for Piano (1961); *A vela vermelha* for Orch. (1962); *Vilancico para a Festa de Santa Cecilia* for Chorus and Orch. (1967).

Vasilenko, Sergei (Nikiforovich), noted Russian conductor, pedagogue, and composer; b. Moscow, March 30, 1872; d. there, March 11, 1956. He studied jurisprudence at Moscow Univ., graduating in 1895; took private music lessons with Gretchaninoff and G. Conus; in 1895, entered the Moscow Cons. in the classes of Taneyev, Ippolitov-Ivanov, and Safonov, graduating in 1901. He also studied ancient Russian chants under the direction of Smolensky. In 1906 he joined the faculty of the Moscow Cons.; subsequently was prof. there (1907–41; 1943–56). From 1907 to 1917 he conducted in Moscow a series of popular sym. concerts in programs of music arranged in a historical sequence. In 1938 he went to Tashkent to help native musicians develop a national school of composition. His music is inspired primarily by the pattern of Russian folk song, but he was also attracted by exotic subjects, particularly those of the East; in his harmonic settings, there is a distinct influence of French Impressionism.

WORKS: OPERAS: *Skazaniye o grade velikom Kitezhe i tikhom ozere Svetoyare* (The Legend of the Great City of Kitezh and the Calm Lake Svetoyar), dramatic cantata (Moscow, March 1, 1902; operatic version, Moscow, March 3, 1903); *Sin solntsa* (Son of the Sun; Moscow, May 23, 1929); *Khristofor Kolumb* (Christopher Columbus; 1933); *Buran* (The Snowstorm; 1938; Tashkent, June 12, 1939; in collaboration with M. Ashrafi); *Suvorov* (1941; Moscow, Feb. 23, 1942). **BALLETS:** *Noyya,* ballet-pantomime (1923); *Iosif prekrasniy* (Joseph the Handsome; Moscow, March 3, 1925); *Lola* (1926; rev. Moscow, June 25, 1943); *Tsigani* (The Gypsies; Leningrad, Nov. 18, 1937); *Akbilyak* (1942; Tashkent, Nov. 7, 1943); *Mirandolina* (1946; Moscow, Jan. 16, 1949). **ORCH.:** 5 syms.: No. 1 (1904; Moscow, Feb. 17, 1907); No. 2 (Moscow, Jan. 7, 1913); No. 3, *Italian,* for Wind Instruments and Russian Folk Instruments (1925); No. 4, *Arctic* (Moscow, April 5, 1933); No. 5 (1938); *Vir* for Bass and Orch. (Kislovodsk, July 6, 1896); *3 Combats,* symphonic poem (1900); *Poème épique,* symphonic poem (Moscow, March 14, 1903); *Sad smerti* (The Garden of Death; Moscow, May 4, 1908); *Hircus nocturnus* (Moscow, Feb. 3, 1909); *Incantation* for Voice and Orch. (1910); Violin Concerto (1910–13); *Au Soleil,* suite (Moscow, 1911); *Valse fantastique* (Moscow, Jan. 16, 1915); *Zodiac,* suite on old French melodies (1914); *Exotic Suite* for Tenor and 12 Instruments (1916); *Chinese Suite* (Leningrad, Oct. 30, 1927); *Hindu Suite* (Moscow, 1927); *Turkmenian Suite* (Moscow, 1931); *Soviet East* (1932); *Uzbek Suite* (1942); Cello Concerto (1944); *Ukraine* (1945); Trumpet Concerto (1945); several works for folk instruments; Concerto for Balalaika and Orch. (1931). **CHAMBER:** 3 string quartets; Piano Trio; Viola Sonata; *Serenade* for Cello and Piano; *Oriental Dance* for Clarinet and Piano (1923); *Japanese Suite* for Wind Instruments, Xylophone, and Piano (1938); *Chinese Sketches* for Woodwind Instruments (1938); Woodwind Quartet on

American themes (1938); Suite for Balalaika and Accordion (1945). Also a number of songs, of which *A Maiden Sang in a Church Choir* (1908) is the best; *10 Russian Folk Songs* for Voice, Oboe, Balalaika, Accordion, and Piano (1929).

WRITINGS: *Stranitsi vospominaniy* (Pages of Reminiscences; Moscow and Leningrad, 1948); *Instrumentovka dlya simfonicheskovo orkestra* (Vol. I, Moscow, 1952; ed. with a supplement by Y. Fortunatov, Moscow, 1959); T. Livanova, ed., *Vospominaniya* (Memoirs; Moscow, 1979).

BIBL.: V. Belaiev, *S.N. V.* (Moscow, 1927); G. Polianovsky, *S.N. V.* (Moscow, 1947); idem, *S.N. V.: Zhizn i tvorchestvo* (S.N.V.: Life and Work; Moscow, 1964).

Vasiliev-Buglay, Dmitri, Russian composer; b. Moscow, Aug. 9, 1888; d. there, Oct. 15, 1956. He studied with Kastalsky at the Moscow Synod Seminary (1898–1906); after the Revolution, he became an active member of RAPM (Russian Assoc. of Proletarian Musicians), postulating the necessity of creating music for the needs of the class-conscious, socialist proletariat, and also joined the Union of Revolutionary Composers and Musical Workers. He was one of the pioneers of mass Soviet songs; wrote patriotic ballads and many choruses to revolutionary texts. He also composed the opera *Fatherland's Call*, to promote self-discipline on collective farms.

BIBL.: D. Lokshin, *D. V.-B.* (Moscow, 1958).

Vasquez (Vázquez), Juan, eminent Spanish composer; b. Badajoz, c.1510; d. probably in Seville, c.1560. He was a singer at Badajoz Cathedral by 1530, becoming sochantre in 1535; became a singer at Palencia Cathedral in 1539. After serving as maestro de capilla at the provincial cathedral in Badajoz (1545–50), he went to Seville and entered the service of Don Antonio de Zuñiga, a nobleman, in 1551. He was greatly admired as a composer of secular music, but also distinguished himself as a composer of sacred works. Vihuela intabulations of several of his secular works were publ. by Valderrábano in 1547 and by Pisador in 1552.

WORKS: SECULAR: (26) *Villancicos i canciones* for 3 to 5 Voices (Osuna, 1551); *Recopilación de* (67) *sonetos y villancicos* for 4 to 5 Voices (Seville, 1560; ed. in Monumentos de la Música Española, IV, 1946). **SACRED:** *Agenda defunctorum* for 4 Voices (Seville, 1556; ed. by S. Rubio, Madrid, 1975).

BIBL.: E. Russell, *Villancicos and Other Secular Polyphonic Music of J. V.: A Courtly Tradition in Spain's Siglo del Oro* (diss., Univ. of Southern Calif., 1970); idem, "The Patrons of J. V.: A Biographical Contribution," *Analecta Musicologica,* XXVI (1972); C. Solis, "J. V. en la Catedral de Badajoz," *Revista de Estudios Extremenos,* I/1 (1974); F. Pedraja Muñoz, ed., *J. V., polifonista pacense del siglo XVI* (Badajoz, 1974).

Vasseur, Léon (Félix Augustin Joseph), French organist, conductor, and composer; b. Bapaume, Pas-de-Calais, May 28, 1844; d. Paris, July 25, 1917. He studied at the École Niedermeyer in Paris; in 1870, became organist of the Versailles Cathedral; after a few years, he turned to composing light music; also conducted theater orchs. He wrote about 30 operettas, but his most successful one was *La Timbale d'argent* (Paris, April 9, 1872). Other operettas include *Le Voyage de Suzette* (Paris, 1890), *Au premier hussard* (Paris, Aug. 6, 1896), and *La Souris blanche* (Paris, Nov. 9, 1897; in collaboration with de Thuisy). He also publ. sacred music: *L'Office divin* (a collection of masses, offertories, antiphons, etc.); *20 motets des grands maîtres;* a method for organ or harmonium (Paris, 1867); transcriptions for harmonium and piano.

Vatielli, Francesco, Italian musicologist; b. Pesaro, Dec. 31, 1876; d. Portogruaro, Dec. 12, 1946. He studied in Bologna at the Univ. (arts degree, 1895) and with Mascagni and Antonio Cicognani at the Liceo Musicale; from 1905 to 1906, was an instructor of music history at the Liceo Musicale in Bologna; then was director of its library until 1945; he also was prof. of music history at the Univ. (from 1908). He was co-founder of the Associazione dei Musicologisti Italiani; also ed. various music journals. He wrote incidental music for several plays; also piano pieces and songs. Among his important writings were *La civiltà musicale di moda: ragionamenti di Petronio*

Isaurico (Turin, 1913; 2nd ed., 1924, as *Ragionamenti e fantasie musicali di Petronio Isaurico*), *Arte e vita musicale a Bologna* (Bologna, 1927), and *Il Principe di Venosa e Leonora d'Este* (Milan, 1941).; also ed. *Antiche cantate d'amore* (Bologna, 1907–20); *A. Banchieri: Musiche corali,* CMI, I–III (1919); *Antiche cantate bolognesi* (Bologna, 1919); *F. Azzaiolo: Villotte del fiore* (Bologna, 1921), and *Madrigali di Carlo Gesualdo, principe de Venosa,* PIISM, Monumenta, II (1942).

BIBL.: A. Della Corte, "F. V.," *Rivista Musicale Italiana* (April–Sept. 1947); F. Ghisi, "F. V.," *Die Musikforschung,* II (1949).

Vaucorbeil, Auguste-Emmanuel, French composer; b. Rouen, Dec. 15, 1821; d. Paris, Nov. 2, 1884. He studied with Marmontel and Cherubini at the Paris Cons.; joined its faculty as prof. of vocal ensemble (1871); became government commissioner of state theaters (1872); was named Inspector General for the Arts (1878); was appointed director of the Paris Opéra (1879). He wrote the operas *La Bataille d'amour* (Paris, April 13, 1863) and *Mahomet* (not perf.), as well as the lyric scene *La Mort de Diane* (Paris, 1870).

Vaughan, Denis (Edward), Australian conductor and music scholar; b. Melbourne, June 6, 1926. He studied at Wesley College, Melbourne (1939–42), and at the Univ. of Melbourne (Mus.B., 1947), then went to London, where he studied organ with G. Thalben-Ball and double bass with E. Cruft at the Royal College of Music (1947–50); also studied organ with A. Marchal in Paris. He played double bass in the Royal Phil. in London (1950–54); in 1953 he made his debut as a conductor in London; served as Beecham's assistant (1954–57), and was founder-conductor of the Beecham Choral Soc.; also toured in Europe as an organist, harpsichordist, and clavichordist. He made a special study of the autograph scores versus the printed eds. of the operas of Verdi and Puccini, discovering myriad discrepancies in the latter; proceeded to agitate for published corrected eds. of these works. From 1981 to 1984 he was music director of the State Opera of South Australia.

Vaughan, Sarah (Lois), black American jazz and popular singer and pianist; b. Newark, N.J., March 27, 1924; d. Los Angeles, April 3, 1990. She began to study music as a child; after winning an amateur singing contest at Harlem's Apollo Theater in N.Y. in 1942, she joined the Earl Hines band in the dual role of singer and pianist; then played and sang with the bands of Billy Eckstine (1944–45) and John Kirby (1945–46); subsequently pursued a successful solo career as a jazz and pop singer, appearing on radio, television, and recordings. A versatile musician, she also ventured to appear as a soloist with sym. orchs.

BIBL.: R. Leydi, *S. V.* (Milan, 1961).

Vaughan Williams, Ralph, great English composer who created the gloriously self-consistent English style of composition, deeply rooted in native folk songs, yet unmistakably participant of modern ways in harmony, counterpoint, and instrumentation; b. Down Ampney, Gloucestershire, Oct. 12, 1872; d. London, Aug. 26, 1958. His father, a clergyman, died when Vaughan Williams was a child; the family then moved to the residence of his maternal grandfather at Leith Hill Place, Surrey. There he began to study piano and violin; in 1887 he entered Charterhouse School in London and played violin and viola in the school orch. From 1890 to 1892 he studied harmony with F.E. Gladstone, theory of composition with Parry, and organ with Parratt at the Royal College of Music in London; then enrolled at Trinity College, Cambridge, where he took courses in composition with Charles Wood and in organ with Alan Gray, obtaining his Mus.B. in 1894 and his B.A. in 1895; he subsequently returned to the Royal College of Music, studying with Stanford. In 1897 he went to Berlin for further instruction with Max Bruch; in 1901 he took his Mus.D. at Cambridge. Dissatisfied with his academic studies, he decided, in 1908, to seek advice in Paris from Ravel in order to acquire the technique of modern orchestration that emphasized color. In the meantime, he became active as a collector of English folk songs; in 1904 he joined the Folk Song Society; in 1905 he became conductor of the Leith Hill Festival in Dorking, a position that he held, off and on, until his old age. In 1906 he composed his *3 Norfolk Rhapsodies*, which reveal the ultimate techniques and manners of his national style; he discarded the 2nd and 3rd of the set as not satisfactory in reflecting the subject. In 1903 he began work on a choral sym. inspired by Walt Whitman's poetry and entitled *A Sea Symphony;* he completed it in 1909; there followed in 1910 *Fantasia on a Theme of Thomas Tallis*, scored for string quartet and double string orch.; in it Vaughan Williams evoked the song style of an early English composer. After this brief work, he engaged in a grandiose score, entitled *A London Symphony* and intended as a musical glorification of the great capital city. However, he emphatically denied that the score was to be a representation of London life. He even suggested that it might be more aptly entitled *Symphony by a Londoner*, which would explain the immediately recognizable quotations of the street song *Sweet Lavender* and of the Westminster chimes in the score; indeed, Vaughan Williams declared that the work must be judged as a piece of absolute or abstract music. Yet prosaically minded commentators insisted that *A London Symphony* realistically depicted in its 4 movements the scenes of London at twilight, the hubbub of Bloomsbury, a Saturday-evening reverie, and, in conclusion, the serene flow of the Thames River. Concurrently with *A London Symphony*, he wrote the ballad opera *Hugh the Drover*, set in England in the year 1812, and reflecting the solitary struggle of the English against Napoleon.

At the outbreak of World War I in 1914, Vaughan Williams enlisted in the British army, and served in Salonika and in France as an officer in the artillery. After the Armistice, he was from 1919 to 1939 a prof. of composition at the Royal College of Music in London; from 1920 to 1928 he also conducted the London Bach Choir. In 1921 he completed *A Pastoral Symphony*, the music of which reflects the contemplative aspect of his inspiration; an interesting innovation in this score is the use of a wordless vocal solo in the last movement. In 1922 he visited the U.S. and conducted the *Pastoral Symphony* at the Norfolk (Conn.) Festival; in 1932 he returned to the U.S. to lecture at Bryn Mawr College. In 1930 he was awarded the Gold Medal of the Royal Phil. Society of London; in 1935 he received the Order of Merit from King George V. In 1930 he wrote a masque, *Job*, based on Blake's *Illustrations of the Book of Job*, which was first performed in a concert version in 1930 and was then presented on the stage in London on July 5, 1931. His 4th Sym., in F minor, written between 1931 and 1935 and first performed by the BBC Sym. Orch. in London on April 10, 1935, presents an extraordinary deviation from his accustomed solid style of composition. Here he experimented with dissonant harmonies in conflicting tonalities, bristling with angular rhythms. A peripheral work was *Fantasia on Greensleeves*, arranged for harp, strings, and optional flutes; this was the composer's tribute to his fascination with English folk songs; he had used it in his opera *Sir John in Love*, after Shakespeare's *The Merry Wives of Windsor*, performed in London in 1929. He always professed great admiration for Sibelius; indeed, there was a harmonious kinship between the 2 great contemporary nationalist composers; there was also the peculiar circumstance that in his 4th Sym. Sibelius ventured into the domain of modernism, as did Vaughan Williams in his own 4th Sym., and both were taken to task by astounded critics for such musical philandering. Vaughan Williams dedicated his 5th Sym., in D major, composed between 1938 and 1943, to Sibelius as a token of his admiration. In the 6th Sym., in E minor, written during the years 1944 to 1947, Vaughan Williams returned to the erstwhile serenity of his inspiration, but the sym. has its turbulent moments and an episode of folksy dancing exhilaration. Vaughan Williams was 80 years old when he completed his challenging *Sinfonia antartica*, scored for soprano, women's chorus, and orch.; the music was an expansion of the background score he wrote for a motion picture on the expedition of Sir Robert Scott to the South Pole in 1912. Here the music is almost geographic in its literal representation of the regions that Scott had explored; it may well be compared in its realism with the *Alpine Symphony* of Richard Strauss. In *Sinfonia antartica* Vaughan Williams inserted, in addition to a large orch., several keyboard instruments and a wind machine. To make the reference clear, he used in the epilogue of the work the actual quotations from Scott's journal. Numerically, *Sinfonia antartica* was his 7th; it was first performed in Manchester on Jan. 14, 1953. In the 8th Sym. he once more returned to the ideal of absolute music; the work is conceived in the form of a neo-Classical suite, but, faithful to the spirit of the times, he included in the score the modern instruments, such as vibraphone and xylophone, as well as the sempiternal gongs and bells. His last sym. bore the fateful number 9, which had for many composers the sense of the ultimate, since it was the numeral of Beethoven's last sym. In this work Vaughan Williams, at the ancient age of 85, still asserted himself as a composer of the modern age; for the first time, he used a trio of saxophones, with a pointed caveat that they should not behave "like demented cats," but rather remain their romantic selves. Anticipating the inevitable, he added after the last bar of the score the Italian word "niente." The 9th Sym. was first performed in London on April 2, 1958; Vaughan Williams died later in the same year. It should be mentioned as a testimony to his extraordinary vitality that after the death of his 1st wife, he married, on Feb. 7, 1953 (at the age of 80), the poet and writer Ursula Wood, and in the following year he once more paid a visit to the U.S. on a lecture tour to several American univs.

Summarizing the esthetic and technical aspects of the style of composition of Vaughan Williams, there is a distinctly modern treatment of harmonic writing, with massive agglomeration of chordal sonorities; parallel triadic progressions are especially favored. There seems to be no intention of adopting any particular method of composition; rather, there is a great variety of procedures integrated into a distinctively personal and thoroughly English style, nationalistic but not isolationist. Vaughan Williams was particularly adept at exploring the modern ways of modal counterpoint, with tonality freely shifting between major and minor triadic entities; this procedure astutely evokes sweetly archaic usages in modern applications; thus Vaughan Williams combines the modalities of the Tudor era with the sparkling polytonalities of the modern age.

WORKS: OPERAS: *Hugh the Drover*, ballad opera (1911–14; London, July 14, 1924); *The Shepherds of the Delectable Mountains*, a "pastoral episode" after Bunyan's *The Pilgrim's Progress* (1921–22; London, July 11, 1922); *Sir John in Love*, after Shakespeare's *The Merry Wives of Windsor* (1925–29; London, March 21, 1929); *Riders to the Sea*, after the drama by John Millington Synge (1925–32; London, Dec. 1, 1937); *The Poisoned Kiss*, a "romantic extravaganza" (1927–29; Cambridge, May 12, 1936; rev. 1934–37 and 1956–57); *The Pilgrim's Progress*, a "morality" (includes material from the earlier opera *The Shepherds of the Delectable Mountains*; 1925–36, 1944–51; Covent Garden, London, April 26, 1951).

BALLETS: *Old King Cole* (1923; Cambridge, June 5, 1923); *On Christmas Night*, masque (1925–26; Chicago, Dec. 26, 1926); *Job, a Masque for Dancing* (1927–30; concert perf., Norwich, Oct. 23, 1930; stage perf., London, July 5, 1931).

INCIDENTAL MUSIC: To Ben Jonson's *Pan's Anniversary* (1905; Stratford-upon-Avon, April 24, 1905); to Aristophanes's *The Wasps* (1909; Cambridge, Nov. 26, 1909); film music: *49th Parallel* (1940–41); *The People's Land* (1941–42); *Coastal Command* (1942); *The Story of a Flemish Farm* (1943; suite for Orch. from it, London, July 31, 1945); *Stricken Peninsula* (1944); *The Loves of Joanna Godden* (1946); *Scott of the Antarctic* (1947–48; material taken from it incorporated in the *Sinfonia antartica*); *Dim Little Island* (1949); *Bitter Springs* (1950); *The England of Elizabeth* (1955); *The Vision of William Blake* (1957); also unpubl. music for a radio serial, *The Mayor of Casterbridge*, after Thomas Hardy (1950).

VOCAL: *Willow Wood* for Baritone, Women's Chorus, and Orch., after Dante Gabriel Rossetti (1903; Liverpool Festival,

Sept. 25, 1909); *Songs of Travel* for Voice and Piano, to texts by Robert Louis Stevenson (1904; London, Dec. 2, 1904); *Toward the Unknown Region* for Chorus and Orch., after Walt Whitman (1905–7; Leeds Festival, Oct. 10, 1907; rev. 1918); *A Sea Symphony* (Sym. No. 1) for Soprano, Baritone, Chorus, and Orch., after Walt Whitman (1906–9; Leeds Festival, Oct. 12, 1910, composer conducting); *On Wenlock Edge,* song cycle for Tenor, Piano, and String Quartet ad libitum, to poems from A.E. Housman's *A Shropshire Lad* (1909; London, Nov. 15, 1909); *5 Mystical Songs* for Baritone, Optional Chorus, and Orch. (1911; Worcester Cathedral, Sept. 14, 1911); *Fantasia on Christmas Carols* for Baritone, Chorus, and Orch. (1912; Hereford Festival, Sept. 12, 1912); *4 Hymns* for Tenor and Piano, with Viola obbligato (1914; Cardiff, May 26, 1920); Mass in G minor (1920–21; Birmingham, Dec. 6, 1922); *Flos Campi,* suite for Viola, Wordless Mixed Chorus, and Small Orch. (1925; London, Oct. 19, 1925); *Sancta civitas* for Tenor, Baritone, Chorus, and Orch. (1923–25; Oxford, May 7, 1926); *Te Deum* for Mixed Chorus and Organ (1928; Canterbury Cathedral, Dec. 4, 1928); *Benedicite* for Soprano, Chorus, and Orch. (1929; Dorking, May 2, 1930); *The Hundredth Psalm* for Mixed Chorus and Orch. (1929; Dorking, April 29, 1930); *3 Choral Hymns* for Baritone, Mixed Chorus, and Orch. (1930; Dorking, April 30, 1930); *In Windsor Forest,* cantata for Mixed Chorus and Orch., adapted from the opera *Sir John in Love* (1931; Windsor, Nov. 9, 1931); *Magnificat* for Contralto, Women's Chorus, and Orch. (1932; Worcester Cathedral, Sept. 8, 1932); *5 Tudor Portraits* for Mezzo-soprano, Baritone, Chorus, and Orch. (1935; Norwich Festival, Sept. 25, 1936); *Dona nobis pacem* for Soprano, Baritone, Chorus, and Orch. (1936; Huddersfield, Oct. 2, 1936); *Festival Te Deum* (1937); *Flourish for a Coronation* (1937; London, April 1, 1937); *Serenade to Music* for 16 Solo Voices and Orch. (1938; London, Oct. 5, 1938); *The Bridal Day,* masque based on Edmund Spenser's *Epithalamion* (1938–39; rev. 1952–53; BBC television, London, June 5, 1953, in celebration of the coronation of Elizabeth II; rev. as the cantata *Epithalamion,* London, Sept. 30, 1957); *Thanksgiving for Victory* for Soprano, Speaker, Chorus, and Orch. (1944; BBC broadcast, London, May 13, 1945); *An Oxford Elegy* for Speaker, Chorus, and Orch., to words by Matthew Arnold (1949; Dorking, Nov. 20, 1949); *Folk Songs of the 4 Seasons,* cantata on traditional folk songs, for Women's Voices and Orch. (1949; London, June 15, 1950); *The Sons of Light* for Children's Chorus (1951; London, May 6, 1951); *Hodie* (This Day), Christmas cantata for Soprano, Tenor, Baritone, Chorus, and Orch. (1953–54; Worcester, Sept. 8, 1954); *A Vision of Aeroplanes,* motet for Chorus and Organ, on a text from Ezekiel, Chapter 1 (1955; St. Michael's, Cornhill, London, June 4, 1956); *10 Blake Songs* for Tenor and Oboe (1958; BBC, London, Oct. 8, 1958); other songs to words by English poets; arrangements of English folk songs; hymn tunes; carols.

ORCH.: *Serenade* for Small Orch. (1898); *Bucolic Suite* (1902; Bournemouth, March 10, 1902); *2 Impressions: Harnham Down* and *Boldrewood* (1902; London, Nov. 12, 1907); *3 Norfolk Rhapsodies* (1906; No. 1, in E minor, London, Aug. 23, 1906; No. 2, Cardiff Festival, Sept. 27, 1907; No. 3, not perf.; Nos. 2 and 3 withdrawn by the composer); *In the Fen Country,* symphonic impression (1904 and subsequent revs.; London, Feb. 22, 1909, Beecham conducting); *The Wasps,* Aristophanic suite (1909; London, July 23, 1912, composer conducting); *Fantasia on a Theme by Thomas Tallis* for String Quartet and Double String Orch. (1910; Gloucester Festival, Sept. 6, 1910, composer conducting; rev. 1923); *A London Symphony* (Sym. No. 2; 1911–14; London, March 27, 1914; rev. version, London, May 4, 1920); *The Lark Ascending,* romance for Violin and Orch. (1914–20; London, June 14, 1921); *A Pastoral Symphony* (Sym. No. 3; 1916–21; London, Jan. 26, 1922); Concerto in D minor for Violin and Strings, *Concerto accademico* (1924–25; London, Nov. 6, 1925); Piano Concerto in C major (1926–31; London, Feb. 1, 1933; also rev. for 2 Pianos and Orch., 1946); *Fantasia on Sussex Folk-Tunes* for Cello and Orch. (1930; London, March 13, 1930; Casals, soloist; Barbirolli conducting); *Prelude and Fugue in C minor* (1930; Hereford, Sept.

12, 1930); Suite for Viola and Small Orch. (1934; London, Nov. 12, 1934); *Fantasia on Greensleeves* (arr. from the opera *Sir John in Love* by Greaves, 1934); Sym. No. 4, in F minor (1931–35; London, April 10, 1935, Boult conducting); *5 Variants of "Dives and Lazarus"* for String Orch. and Harp, commissioned by the British Council for the N.Y. World's Fair (1939; N.Y., June 10, 1939); *Serenade to Music* (orch. version of 1938 original, 1940; London, Feb. 10, 1940); Sym. No. 5, in D major (1938–43; London, June 24, 1943, composer conducting); Concerto in A minor for Oboe and Strings (1943–44; Liverpool, Sept. 30, 1944); Sym. No. 6, in E minor (1944–47; London, April 21, 1948, Boult conducting); Partita for Double String Orch. (orch. version of Double Trio for String Sextet, 1946–48; BBC, London, March 20, 1948); Concerto Grosso for String Orch. (1950; London, Nov. 18, 1950, Boult conducting); *Romance* in D-flat major for Harmonica, Strings, and Piano (1951; N.Y., May 3, 1952); *Sinfonia antartica* (Sym. No. 7; 1949–52; Manchester, Jan. 14, 1953, Barbirolli conducting); Concerto in F minor for Tuba and Orch. (1954; London, June 14, 1954); Sym. No. 8, in D minor (1953–55; Manchester, May 2, 1956, Barbirolli conducting); *Flourish for Glorious John* (for Barbirolli; 1957; Manchester, Oct. 16, 1957, Barbirolli conducting); Sym. No. 9, in E minor (1956–58; London, April 2, 1958, Sargent conducting).

CHAMBER: String Quartet in C minor (1898; June 30, 1904); Quintet in D major for Clarinet, Horn, Violin, Cello, and Piano (June 5, 1900); Piano Quintet in C minor for Piano, Violin, Viola, Cello, and Double Bass (London, Dec. 14, 1905); String Quartet in G minor (No. 1; London, Nov. 8, 1909); Phantasy Quintet for 2 Violins, 2 Violas, and Cello (1912; London, March 23, 1914); *6 studies in English folk song* for Cello and Piano (London, June 4, 1926); Double Trio for String Sextet (London, Jan. 21, 1939); String Quartet No. 2, in A minor (1942–44; London, Oct. 12, 1944); Violin Sonata in A minor (BBC, London, Oct. 12, 1954); also some short piano pieces; Introduction and Fugue for 2 Pianos (1946); organ pieces.

WRITINGS: *The English Hymnal* (1906; 2nd ed., 1933); *Songs of Praise* (with M. Shaw; 1925; 2nd ed., 1931); *The Oxford Book of Carols* (with P. Dearmer and M. Shaw; 1928); lectures and articles, reprinted in *National Music and Other Essays* (London, 1963); R. Palmer ed. *Folk Songs Collected by Ralph Vaughan Williams* (London, 1983).

BIBL.: A.H. Fox Strangways, "R. V.W.," *Music & Letters,* I (1920); H. Colles, "The Music of V.W.," *Chesterian,* XXI (1922); H. Howells, "V.W.'s 'Pastoral Symphony,' " *Music & Letters,* III (1922); A. Dickinson, *An Introduction to the Music of R. V.W.* (London, 1928); H. Ould, "The Songs of R. V.W.," *English Review,* XLVI (1928); F. Toye, "Studies in English Music: V.W. and the Folk Music Movement," *Listener,* V (1931); E. Rubbra, "V.W., Some Technical Characteristics," *Monthly Musical Record,* LXIV (1934); idem, "The Later V.W.," *Music & Letters,* XVIII (1937); S. Goddard, "The Operas of V.W.," *Listener,* XX (1938); W. Kimmel, "V.W.'s Choice of Words," *Music & Letters,* XIX (1938); idem, "V.W.'s Melodic Style," *Musical Quarterly* (Oct. 1941); H. Foss, "V.W.'s Symphonic Manner," *Listener,* XXVII (1942); idem, *R. V.W.* (London, 1950); A. Hutchings, "V.W. and the Tudor Tradition," *Listener,* XLV (1951); E. Payne, *The Folksong Element in the Music of V.W.* (diss., Univ. of Liverpool, 1953); R. Taylor, "V.W. and English National Music," *Cambridge Journal,* VI (1953); P. Young, *V.W.* (London, 1953); F. Howes, *The Music of R. V.W.* (London, 1954); E. Payne, "V.W. and Folksong," *Music Review,* XV (1954); J. Bergsagel, *The National Aspects of the Music of R. V.W.* (diss., Cornell Univ., 1957); S. Pakenham, *R. V.W.: A Discovery of His Music* (London, 1957); J. Warrack, "V.W. and Opera," *Opera,* IX (1958); D. Brown, "V.W.'s Symphonies: Some Judgments Reviewed," *Monthly Musical Record,* XC (1960); J. Day, *V. W.* (London, 1961; 2nd ed., rev., 1975); P. Willetts, "The R. V.W. Collection," *British Museum Quarterly,* XXIV (1961); A. Dickinson, "The V.W. Manuscripts," *Music Review,* XXIII (1962); idem, *V.W.* (London, 1963); M. Kennedy, *The Works of R. V.W.* (London, 1964; 2nd ed., rev., 1980); H. Ottaway, "VW-5—A New Analysis,"

Musical Times, CV (1964); E. Schwartz, *The Symphonies of R. V.W.* (Amherst, 1964); U. Vaughan Williams, *R. V.W.: A Biography* (London, 1964); H. Ottaway, *V.W.* (London, 1966); P. Starbuck, *R. V.W., O.M., 1872–1958: A Bibliography of His Literary Writings and Criticism of His Musical Works* (diss., Library Assoc., 1967); M. Hurd, *V.W.* (London, 1970); J. Lunn and U. Vaughan Williams, *R. V.W.: A Pictorial Biography* (London, 1971); U. Vaughan Williams, "V.W. and Opera," *Composer*, XLI (1971); R. Douglas, *Working with R. V.W.* (London, 1972); H. Ottaway, *V.W. Symphonies* (London, 1972); U. Vaughan Williams, "The VW Centenary," *Musical Times*, CXIII (1972); M. Kennedy, "The Unknown V.W.," *Proceedings of the Royal Musical Association*, XCIX (1972–73); A. Frogley, "V.W. and Thomas Hardy: 'Tess' and the Slow Movement of the Ninth Symphony," *Music & Letters* (Jan. 1987); U. Vaughan Williams, *R. V.W.: A Biography of R. V.W.* (Oxford, 1988); N. Butterworth, *R. V.W.: A Guide to Research* (N.Y., 1989); W. Mellers, *V.W. and the Vision of Albion* (1989).

Vautor, Thomas, English composer; b. c.1590; place and date of death unknown. He was in the service of the Villiers family; was admitted B.Mus. of Oxford through Lincoln College (1616). He publ. *The First Set, beeing Songs of Divers Ayres and Natures, of Five and Sixe Parts, Apt for Vyols and Voyces* (London, 1619–20; ed. in The English Madrigalists, XXXIV, 1958). **BIBL.:** E. Fellowes, *The English Madrigal Composers* (Oxford, 1921; 2nd ed., 1948).

Vázsonyi, Bálint, distinguished Hungarian-American pianist; b. Budapest, March 7, 1936. He entered the Franz Liszt Academy of Music in Budapest as a youth; made his debut as a pianist at 12. He left Hungary in the midst of political turmoil in 1956; then continued his training at the Vienna Academy of Music (1957–58); eventually went to America, where he continued his studies with Ernst von Dohnányi. In 1977 he made a transcontinental tour of the U.S.; served on the faculty of the Indiana Univ. School of Music in Bloomington (1978–84). In 1983 he founded Telemusic, a film and video music production company. One of his signal feats of pianofortitude was his performance, on 2 consecutive days, of all 32 piano sonatas of Beethoven in chronological order (N.Y., Oct. 31 and Nov. 1, 1976); he repeated this cycle in Boston and London shortly afterward. He is the author of the standard biography of Dohnányi (Budapest, 1971). His pianism is marked by a transcendental virtuosity of technique coupled with the mellow lyricism typical of traditional Hungarian pianism, and particularly effective in the music of Liszt.

Vazzana, Anthony, American composer and educator; b. Troy, N.Y., Nov. 4, 1922. He was of a musical family; his father played the mandolin. He studied piano with George H. Pickering; attended the State Univ. of N.Y. College at Potsdam; in 1943 he was inducted into the U.S. Air Force, where he arranged and conducted suitable music in concert bands. He resumed his musical studies after his discharge, and in 1946 enrolled at the Berkshire Summer Music School at Tanglewood, where his instructors were Irving Fine, Robert Shaw, Stanley Chapple, Leonard Bernstein, and Hugh Ross. In 1948 he enrolled at the Univ. of Southern Calif. in Los Angeles in the classes of Halsey Stevens, Ingolf Dahl, and Ernest Kanitz; received his M.M. in 1948. Subsequently he divided his time between composing and teaching; was successively on the faculty of Calif. State Univ. at Long Beach and at Los Angeles, Champlain College, and Danbury (Conn.) State College. In 1959 he received the degree of doctor in composition at the Univ. of Southern Calif., and in 1959 joined the faculty of its School of Music. In his teaching he resolutely promoted advanced techniques in composition; wrote a set of books on music theory, *Projects in Musicianship* (4 vols., 1965–68). In his compositions, he pursued a logical evolutionary line, beginning with neo-Classical formations and continuing with progressive harmonic and contrapuntal complications, in which dissonances are ultimately emancipated and rhythms become increasingly asymmetrical, all this aided and abetted by elo-

quent pregnant pauses separating brief melodic ejaculations. Special effects, such as whipping and scourging the bodies of musical instruments with taps and kicks, soundlessly blowing through the embouchure of a wind instrument, such as a horn, and the like, add to the quaquaversal quality of sonorism in his works. **WORKS:** Sonata for Clarinet, Horn, and Piano (1947); String Quartet (1948); Woodwind Quintet (1948); Suite for Viola and Piano (1948); Quartet for Violin, Viola, Cello, and Piano (1949); *Andante and Allegro* for Orch. (1949); Sonata for Violin and Piano (1958); *Symphonic Allegro* for Orch. (1958); *Harlequin Suite* for Orch. (1959); Sonata for Piano (1962); *Songs of Life and Nature* for Voice and Piano (1962); *Music for 2 Flutes* (1962); Suite for Strings (1963); Sym. No. 1 (1963); *Spectra* for Band (1965); *Fantasia concertante* for Cello and Piano (1970); *Incontri* for Violin and Piano (1971); *Partite sopra victimae paschali laudes* for Wind Orch. (1976); *Tre monodie* for Trombone (1976); *Cambi* for Tuba and Percussion (1977); *Trinakie* for Orch. (1977); *Disegni* for Piano (1978); *Montaggi* for 4 Tubas (1978); *Studi* for Saxophone (1979); *Buccina* for Horn and Piano (1979); *Partita* for Euphonium, Piano, and Percussion (1980); *Concerto a tre* for Clarinet, Double Bass, and Instrumental Ensemble (1981); *Varianti* for Orch. (1982); *Coriolano* for Viola and Horn (1982).

Veasey, Josephine, English mezzo-soprano and teacher; b. Peckham, July 10, 1930. She studied with Audrey Langford in London; in 1949 she joined the chorus at London's Covent Garden; made her Covent Garden debut as the Shepherd Boy in *Tannhäuser* in 1955, and later appeared as Waltraute, Fricka, Brangäne, Berlioz's Dido, Dorabella, etc.; she created the role of the Emperor in Henze's *We Come to the River* (1976). On Nov. 22, 1968, she made her Metropolitan Opera debut in N.Y. as Fricka; also made guest appearances throughout Europe and in South America; likewise sang in concerts. In 1982 she retired from the operatic stage and became active as a teacher; taught at the Royal Academy of Music (from 1983), and was a voice consultant to the English National Opera (from 1985).

Vecchi, Horatio (actually, **Orazio Tiberio**), significant Italian composer; b. Modena (baptized), Dec. 6, 1550; d. there, Feb. 19, 1605. He received ecclesiastical training from the Benedictines of S. Pietro in Modena; studied music in Modena with the Servite monk Salvatore Essenga; later took Holy Orders. He was maestro di cappella at Salò Cathedral (1581–84); in 1584 he became maestro di cappella at Modena Cathedral, where he adopted the rendering of Horatio for his 1st name; within a short time he accepted the post of maestro di cappella in Reggio Emilia, and then became canon at Correggio Cathedral in 1586; was made archdeacon in 1591. In 1593 he returned to Modena Cathedral as maestro di cappella, and was elevated to mansionario in 1596; also served in the brotherhood of the Annunciation at the churches of S. Maria and S. Pietro. In 1598 he was named maestro di corte by Duke Cesare d'Este. In 1604 he was dismissed from his duties at the Cathedral for disregarding the bishop's admonition to cease directing music at the Cathedral convent. He was greatly admired in his day for his 6 books of *Canzonette*. His lasting fame is due above all to his "commedia harmonica" *L'Amfiparnasso*, performed at Modena in 1594 and printed at Venice in 1597; this is a kind of musical farce written not in the monodic style of Peri's *Dafne* but in madrigal style, with all the text sung by several voices (i.e., a chorus a 4–5); it has been called a "madrigal opera," but it was not intended for the theater and stood entirely apart from the path that opera was to take. It was ed. in Publikationen Älterer Praktischer und Theoretischer Musikwerke, XXVI, 1902; in Capolavori Polifonici del Secolo XVI, V (Rome, 1953); and in Early Musical Masterworks (Chapel Hill, 1977). Another important secular work was his *Dialoghi da cantarsi et concertarsi con ogni sorte di stromenti* for 7 to 8 Voices (1608); other works appeared in contemporary collections; some of his works were later included in 19th- and 20th-century collections. He also publ. in Venice a number of sacred works, including *Lamentationes cum 4 paribus vocibus* (1587) and *Hymni qui per totum annum in Ecclesia Romana concinuntur* for 4 Voices (1604).

BIBL.: A. Catellani, *Della vita e delle opere di O. V.* (Milan, 1858); E. Dent, "The *Amfiparnasso* of O. V.," *Monthly Musical Record* (1906); idem, "Notes on the *Amfiparnasso* of O. V.," *Sammelbände der Internationalen Musik-Gesellschaft,* XXII (1910–11); L. Frati, "Un capitolo autobiografico di O. V.," *Rivista Musicale Italiana,* XXII (1915); J. Hol, *H. V. als weltlicher Komponist* (diss., Univ. of Basel, 1917); idem, "H. V. et l'évolution créatrice," in *Scheurleer-Festschrift* (1925); G. Roncaglia, "Il luogo e la data di nascita di O. V.," *Rassegna Musicale* (April 1929); J. Hol, "H. V.," *Rivista Musicale Italiana,* XXXVII (1930); idem, *H. V.s weltliche Werke* (Strasbourg, 1934); C. Perinello, "*L'Amfiparnasso,* commedia harmonica d'H. V.," *Rivista Musicale Italiana,* XLI (1937); G. Roncaglia, "O. V. precursore drammatico ed umorista," ibid., LI (1949); A. Lualdi, "O. V.," ibid. (1950); G. Roncaglia, "Gli elementi precursori del melodramma nell'opera di O. V.: Attuazioni e limiti," ibid. (1953); L. Ronga, "Lettura storica dell'*Amfiparnasso* di O. V.," *Rassegna Musicale* (1953); J. Rodgers, *The Madrigals of O. V.* (diss., Univ. of Calif., Los Angeles, 1954); *Commemorazione di O. V. nel 350° anniversario della morte* (Modena, 1955); W. Martin, *The Convito musicale of O. V.* (diss., Oxford Univ., 1964); R. Rüegge, *O. V.s geistliche Werke* (Bern, 1967); W. Kirkendale, "Francheschina, Girometta, and Their Companions in a Madrigal *a diversi linguaggi* by Luca Marenzio and O. V.," *Acta Musicologica,* XLIV (1972).

Vecchi, Orfeo, distinguished Italian composer; b. probably in Milan, c.1550; d. there before April 1604. He became a priest; was maestro di cappella of the royal and ducal church of S. Maria della Scala in Milan from about 1590 until his death. He was an outstanding polyphonist.

WORKS (all publ. in Milan unless otherwise given): *Missarum liber primus* for 5 Voices (1588); *Missa, psalmi ad Vesperas dominicales, Magnificat et psalmorum modulationes* (1590); *Psalmi integri in totius anni solemnitatibus, 2 Magnificat, 4 antiphonae ad B.V.M.* for 5 Voices and Basso Continuo (1596); *Missarum liber primus* for 4 Voices and Basso Continuo (1597); *Missarum liber secundus, Missa pro defunctis, sacrae cantiones* for 5 Voices (1598); *Motectorum liber secundus* for 5 Voices and Basso Continuo (1598); *Motectorum liber tertius* for 6 Voices (1598); *Falsi bordoni figurati sopra gli otto toni ecclesiastici, Magnificat, Te Deum laudamus, hinni, antifone, Letanie* for 3 to 5 and 8 Voices (1600); *Hymni totius anni . . . cum antiphonis et Litaniis B.V.M.* for 5 Voices (1600); *In septem Regii Prophetae psalmos, liber quartus* for 6 Voices (1601); *Psalmi in totius anni solemnitatibus, 2 Magnificat* for 5 Voices (1601); *Missarum liber tertius* for 5 Voices (1602); *La donna vestita di sole . . . 21 madrigali* (1602); *Magnificat liber primus* for 5 Voices (1603); *Motectorum liber primus* for 4 Voices (1603); *Cantiones sacrae* for 6 Voices (Antwerp, 1608); other works in contemporary collections.

BIBL.: F. Haberl, "O. V.," *Kirchenmusikalisches Jahrbuch,* XXII (1907); A. Einstein, "Un libro di canzoni spirituali di O. V.," *La Bibliofilia,* XL (1938).

Vécsey, Jenö, Hungarian musicologist and composer; b. Felsöcéce, July 19, 1909; d. Budapest, Sept. 18, 1966. He studied composition with Kodály at the Budapest Academy of Music (diploma, 1935); took courses in chemistry and biology at the Univ. of Budapest (graduated, 1941), and completed his musical training in Vienna (1941–42); joined the staff of the National Széchényi Library in Budapest in 1942, where he was head of its music dept. from 1945 until his death. He made valuable contributions to the historical and bibliographical music literature preserved there; initiated and directed editorial work on the Musica Rinata series (1963–66); did preparatory work on the new Haydn Collected Edition. He publ. *Joseph Haydn müvei az Országos Széchényi könyvtár zenei gyüjteményében* (Joseph Haydn's Compositions in the Music Collection of the National Széchényi Library; Budapest, 1959; Eng. tr., 1960).

WORKS: BALLET: *Kele diák* (Scholar Kele; 1943). **ORCH.:**

Divertimento (1939–40); *Rhapsody* (1940–41); *Intermezzi* for Strings (1942); *2 Symphonic Dances* (1945; from *Kele diák*); *Boldogkő vara* (Boldogkő Castle), symphonic poem (1951; rev. as *Praeludium, notturno és scherzo,* 1958); Piano Concertino (1953); Double-bass Concertino (1954); *Szimfonikus concerto Krúdy Gyula emlékére* (Symphonic Concerto in Memory of Gyula Krúdy; 1958). **CHAMBER:** String Quartet (1942); String Sextet (1956); *Bagatelles* for 2 Pianos (1962); songs.

Vedernikov, Alexander, Russian bass; b. Mokino, Dec. 23, 1927. He studied voice at the Moscow Cons., graduating in 1955; won 1st prize at the International Schumann Competition in Berlin in 1956 and, in the same year, 1st prize at the Soviet competition for performing songs by Soviet composers. In 1957 he made his debut at the Bolshoi Theater in Moscow. In 1961 he entered the La Scala Opera School of Milan as an aspirant; subsequently toured as a concert singer in France, Italy, England, Austria, and Canada. He was particularly noted for his performances of the Russian repertoire; his portrayal of Boris Godunov in Mussorgsky's opera approached Chaliapin's in its grandeur. He also distinguished himself in the Italian buffo roles, such as Don Basilio in Rossini's *Il Barbiere di Siviglia.* In 1964 he joined the Communist Party of the U.S.S.R.

Veerhoff, Carlos, Argentine-German composer; b. Buenos Aires, June 3, 1926. He studied in Berlin with Grabner (1943–44); returned to Argentina and taught at Tucumán National Univ. He moved permanently to Germany in 1951; was an assistant to Fricsay in Berlin (1951–52), and studied with Boris Blacher at the Hochschule für Musik there (1952); then settled in Munich.

WORKS: STAGE: 2 operas: *Targusis* (1958) and *Die goldene Maske* (1968); chamber opera, *Der Grune* (1972); mini-opera, *Es gibt doch Zebrastreifen* (Ulm, Jan. 20, 1972); 2 ballets: *Pavane royale* (1953) and *El porquerizo del ray* (Buenos Aires, 1963). **ORCH.:** *Prólogo sinfónico* (1951); *Symphonic Movement* (1952); 4 syms.: No. 1, *Panta rhei* (Everything Flows; the philosophic apothegm of Heraclitus; 1953); No. 2, in 1 movement (1956); No. 3, *Spirales* (1966; rev. 1969); No. 4 (1974); *Mirages* (1961); *Akróasis* for 24 Winds and Percussion (1966); *Textur* for String Orch. (1969; rev. 1971); *Torso* (Lübeck, Jan. 14, 1974); *Sinotrauc* (Munich, Jan. 19, 1973). **VOCAL:** *Gesänge auf dem Wege* for Baritone and Orch. (1964); *Ut omnes unum sint,* chamber cantata (1967). **CHAMBER:** 2 string quartets (1951, 1974); 2 wind quintets (1958, 1969); Solo Violin Sonata (1954); *Dialogues* for Saxophone and Piano (1967).

Vega, Aurelio de la, Cuban-born American composer, teacher, and writer on music; b. Havana, Nov. 28, 1925. He studied in Havana at De La Salle College (B.A. in humanities, 1944), with Frederick Kramer (theory, composition, and orchestration, 1942–46), and at the Univ. (doctorate in diplomacy, 1947). In 1947 he went to the U.S., and served as cultural attaché at the Cuban Consulate in Los Angeles; there he took composition lessons with Ernst Toch. Returning to Cuba, he was dean of the Music School at the Univ. of Oriente in Santiago de Cuba (1953–59); in 1959 he settled in California, and taught at the San Fernando Valley State College (later Calif. State Univ., Northridge); became a naturalized U.S. citizen in 1966. He publ. the books *Arnold Schönberg and the Atonalists* (1947), *The Negative Emotion* (1950), and *The New Romanticism* (1951). In his early works he cultivated Cuban melorhythms, but later adopted increasingly radical modernistic methods of composition with fantastically reticulated, circumvoluted, and in some instances palindromic, contrapuntal schemes, graphically notated in optically proportioned note values, so that the linear extant of a bar is invariant in relation to the aggregate of rhythmic units contained therein, reaching its heroic ultima ratio in a work entitled *Olep ed Arudamot* (backward reading of a Spanish idiom meaning "pulling your leg"); the visual impression of the score itself is that of an abstract expressionist painting. Sonorifically, he avails himself of a great variety of acoustical materials, electronic and humanoid, including the whirring sound of shuffling feet by string players.

WORKS: Piano Trio (1949); *Soliloquio* for Viola and Piano (1950); *Obertura a una Farsa seria* (Havana, April 28, 1951); *Leyenda del Ariel Criollo* for Cello and Piano (1953); *Elegía* for Strings (London, Nov. 16, 1954); String Quartet (1957); Wind Quintet (1959); Trio for Flute, Oboe, and Clarinet (1960); *Sinfonía en 4 partes* (Washington, D.C., April 30, 1961); *Structures* for Piano and String Quartet (1962); *Coordinates* for Magnetic Tape (1963); *Analigus* for Orch. (1966); *Intrata* for Orch. (Los Angeles, May 12, 1972); *Olep ed Arudamot* (1974); *Septicilium* for Clarinet and Instrumental Ensemble (1975); *Inflorescence* for Soprano, Bass Clarinet, and Tape (Los Angeles, Oct. 25, 1976); *The Infinite Square* for any combination of any Instruments and/or Voices (Los Angeles, Sept. 24, 1977); *Adiós* for Orch. (Los Angeles, April 20, 1978; Mehta conducting); *Undici colori* for Bassoon, Stamping Right Foot, and Slide Projections (1981; Los Angeles, Jan. 25, 1982); *Galandiacoa* for Clarinet and Guitar (1982); *Tropimapal* for 9 Instruments (1983); *Asonante* for Soprano and 7 Instruments (1985); *Whispers and Chants*, song cycle (Santa Ana, Calif., Jan. 10, 1988); *Two Songs* for Soprano, Bass Clarinet, and Piano (Bern, May 24, 1988); *Odissea* for Orch. (Los Angeles, Nov. 10, 1988); *Metamorphoses* for Wind Ensemble (Los Angeles, April 19, 1989); piano music; songs.

BIBL.: R. Erin, "Cuban Elements in the Music of A. d.l.V.," *Latin American Music Review,* V/l (1984).

Vega, Carlos, Argentine writer on music; b. Cañuelas, near Buenos Aires, April 14, 1898; d. Buenos Aires, Feb. 10, 1966. He studied at the Univ. of Buenos Aires (philosophy and literature); subsequently devoted himself mainly to folklore research in music. In 1933 he was placed in charge of the folklore division of the literature faculty at the Univ. of Buenos Aires. He traveled throughout the rural regions of Argentina and other South American countries to collect materials on folk songs and folk dances, using a phonograph to record them; devised a special choreographic notation. His many books are basic sources for the study of Argentine folk music.

WRITINGS (all publ. in Buenos Aires): *La música de un códice colonial del siglo XVII* (1931); *Danzas y canciones argentinas* (1936); *La música popular argentina: Canciones y danzas criollas* (1941); *Panorama de la música popular argentina* (1944); *Los instrumentos musicales de la Argentina* (1946); *Danzas argentinas* (1962); *Las canciones folklóricas argentinas* (1964); *Lectura y notación de la música* (1965).

Vega, Suzanne, American songwriter, singer, and guitarist; b. Santa Monica, Calif., July 11, 1960. She was reared in N.Y., where she attended the High School of Music and Art and later received a degree in English literature from Barnard College. In the early 1980s she joined the Greenwich Village folk-music scene, becoming a devotee of Nichiren Buddhism. Her 1st album, *Suzanne Vega* (1985), attracted notice for its cool, sophisticated lyrics and hypnotically repetitive melodies. Other albums include *Live in London* (1986) and *Solitude Standing* (1987); also a music video, *Live at the Royal Albert Hall* (1987).

Végh, Sándor (Alexandre), Hungarian-born French violinist, conductor, and pedagogue; b. Klausenburg, May 17, 1912. He was a pupil of Zsolt, Waldbauer, and Weiner at the Budapest Academy of Music; then studied violin with Hubay and composition with Kodály. He was a member of the Hungarian Trio (1931–33) and the Hungarian Quartet (1934–40); also made appearances as a soloist (from 1934). In 1940 he founded the Végh Quartet, which remained active until 1980. From 1941 to 1946 he was a prof. at the Budapest Academy of Music; he subsequently emigrated to France, becoming a naturalized citizen in 1953. From 1953 to 1969 he was active at the Prades Festivals; also taught master classes in various European locales. From 1968 to 1971 he conducted the Orchestre du Chambre Sándor Végh; he taught at the Salzburg Mozarteum (from 1971), where he was conductor of its Camerata Academica (from 1978).

Veinus, Abraham, American musicologist; b. N.Y., Feb. 12, 1916. He studied at the City College of N.Y. (B.A., 1936), Cornell Univ. (M.A., 1937), and Columbia Univ. (1946–48); was prof. of musicology and fine arts at Syracuse Univ. (from 1948). He wrote *The Concerto* (1944; 2nd ed., rev. 1964); *The Victor Book of Concertos* (1948); *The Pocket Book of Great Operas* (with Henry Simon, 1949); *Understanding Music: Style, Structure and History* (with W. Fleming, N.Y., 1958).

Veit, Wenzel Heinrich (actually, **Václav Jindřich**), Bohemian composer; b. Řepnice, near Leitmeritz, Jan. 19, 1806; d. Leitmeritz, Feb. 15, 1864. He studied organ and piano; took courses in law and philosophy at the Univ. of Prague; was active as a private music teacher while pursuing a legal career. He was briefly music director in Aachen (1841), but then decided to devote himself fully to composition. He helped to advance the cause of the Romantic movement in music in his homeland.

WORKS: ORCH.: Overture (1842); Violin Concertino (1844); Sym. in E minor (1859). **CHAMBER:** 3 quintets for 2 Violins, Viola, and 2 Cellos (1835); 2 quintets for 2 Violins, 2 Violas, and Cello (1837, 1851); 4 string quartets (1836, 1838, 1839, 1840); Piano Trio (1860); *Les Adieux* for Cello and Piano (c.1845); piano pieces. **VOCAL:** *Hymnus* (1840); Mass in D major (1858); Te Deum (1863); *Böhmens bester Bergsegen,* cantata (1845); part-songs for men's voices; solo songs.

Vejvanovský, Pavel Josef, distinguished Moravian trumpeter and composer; b. Hukvaldy or Hlucin, c.1633; d. Kroměříž (buried), Sept. 24, 1693. He was educated at the Opava Jesuit College; entered the service of E. Castelle, an administrator at the court of the Prince-Bishop of Olmütz, Leopold Wilhelm, as a trumpeter in 1661; then was made principal trumpeter and Kapellmeister to the new Prince-Bishop, Karl Liechtenstein-Kastelkorn, in 1664; later served as his Hof- and Feld-trompeter. His masterful writing for the trumpet and the cornett is found in both his instrumental and his vocal works. Among his output are 14 masses, offertories, motets, vespers, litanies, antiphons, a number of sonatas in which the trumpet is prominent, balletti, Intrada, and Serenadas. See J. Pohanska, ed., *Pavel Josef Vejvanovský: Serenate e sonate per orchestra,* Musica Antiqua Bohemica, XXXVI (1950), and *Pavel Josef Vejvanovský: Composizioni per orchestra,* ibid., XLVII–XLIX (1960–61).

Velasco-Llanos, Santiago, Colombian composer; b. Cali, Jan. 28, 1915. He studied in Cali with Antonio María Valencia, and later with Domingo Santa Cruz and Pedro Humberto Allende in Santiago, Chile; then was director of the Cali Cons.

WORKS: *Sinfonia breve* (1947); *Sinfonietta* (1966); *Bambuco jocoso* for Orch. (1967); 2 string quartets; piano pieces; choruses; songs.

Velasco Maidana, José María, Bolivian composer and conductor; b. Sucre, July 4, 1899. He studied violin in Buenos Aires; subsequently taught music history at the National Cons. of La Paz. In 1937 he conducted some of his works in Buenos Aires, and in 1938, in Berlin; in 1943 he toured in South America and Mexico. His ballet *Amerindia,* on a subject from pre-Columbian history, was produced in Berlin (Dec. 6, 1938). He conducted the 1st performance of his symphonic works with the La Paz Sym. Orch., of which he was the conductor: *Cory Wara* (Oct. 6, 1941); *Los hijos del sol* (Feb. 6, 1942); *Vida de cóndores* (March 14, 1942); *Los huacos* (April 22, 1942); *Los khusillos* and *Cuento brujo* (April 11, 1943).

Velázquez, Higinio, Mexican violinist and composer; b. Guadalajara, Jan. 11, 1926. He studied composition with Bernal Jiménez and Rodolfo Halffter; was a violinist in the National Sym. Orch.; in 1969, became violinist in the string quartet of the National Inst. of Fine Arts.

WORKS: *Vivencias* for Orch. (1958); *Cacique,* overture (1958); "sinfonia breve," *Juárez* (1961); *Revolución,* symphonic poem (1969); *Elegía* for Oboe and Piano (1969); *Estructuas* for Piano (1969); Sonatina for Cello Solo (1970); String Quartet (1970); *Andante atonal* for Strings (1971).

Velimirović, Miloš, eminent Serbian-American music scholar; b. Belgrade, Dec. 10, 1922. He studied violin and piano at the Belgrade Academy of Music with Petar Stojanovic; in 1943, was sent to a forced labor camp by the German occupation authorities; after the liberation, he studied Byzantine art at the Univ. of Belgrade, graduating in 1951; simultaneously took composition lessons with Mihovil Logar at the Belgrade Academy of Music; in 1952 he emigrated to the U.S.; studied at Harvard Univ., obtaining his M.A. in 1953 and his Ph.D. in 1957 with the dissertation *Byzantine Elements in Early Slavic Chant* (publ. in an enlarged ed., 1960, in Monumenta Musicae Byzantinae, *Subsidiae,* IV, 1960); also took a course in Byzantine music with Egon Wellesz at Dumbarton Oaks in Washington, D.C. (1954). He was on the faculty of Yale Univ. (1957–69) and the Univ. of Wisconsin (1969–73); in 1973, was appointed a prof. of music at the Univ. of Virginia in Charlottesville; served as chairman of the music dept. there (1974–77). A linguist, he has contributed a number of scholarly articles to various publications, mainly on subjects connected with liturgical music in Byzantium and in the Slavic countries. He was general ed. of Collegium Musicum (1958–73) and associate ed. (jointly with Egon Wellesz) of *Studies in Eastern Chant* (4 vols., London, 1966–78); wrote articles on Russian and Slavic church music for *The New Grove Dictionary of Music and Musicians* (1980).

Velluti, Giovanni Battista, famous Italian castrato soprano; b. Montolmo, Ancona, Jan. 28, 1781; d. Sambruson di Dolo, Venice, Jan. 22, 1861. He studied with Mattei in Bologna and with Calpi in Ravenna; in 1801 he made his debut in Forlì, then sang in Naples in the premieres of Guglielmi's *Asteria e Teseo* and Andreozzi's *Pirano e Tisbe*. From 1805 to 1808 he was in Rome, where he appeared in the premiere of Nicolini's *Traiano in Dacio*; his La Scala debut in Milan followed in that composer's *Coriolano* (Dec. 26, 1808). After appearances in Venice (1810) and Turin (1811), he sang in Vienna (1812); also appeared in Munich, where he was named Bavarian court singer. He sang in the premiere of Rossini's *Aureliano in Palmira* in Milan (Dec. 26, 1813), and then toured throughout Italy; also made appearances in Germany and Russia. On March 7, 1824, he created the role of Armando in Meyerbeer's *Il Crociato in Egitto* in Venice; chose that same role for his London debut on June 3, 1825, at the King's Theatre, where he continued to sing until 1826; made his farewell to London in 1829. Velluti was the last great castrato of the age.
BIBL.: A. Heriot, *The Castrati in Opera* (London, 1956).

Venegas de Henestrosa, Luis, Spanish organist and composer; b. Henestrosa, Burgon, c.1510; d. Toledo, c.1557. He was in the service of Cardinal Juan Tavera in Toledo (c.1534–45); also was a priest in Hontova (1543). He publ. the oldest known Spanish book of organ music, *Libro de cifra nueva para tecla, harpa y vihuela* (Alcalá de Henares, 1557; ed. by H. Anglès, Monumentos de la Música Española, II, 1944); it contains organ pieces by Palero, P. Vila, Soto, Venegas himself, et al.; also pieces for vihuela, transcriptions of sacred works by Morales, Josquin, Soto, et al., and solo songs with instrumental accompaniment. The book is written in Spanish organ tablature.
BIBL.: J. Moll Roqueta, "Músicos de la corte del Cardenal Juan Tavera (1542–1545): L. V.d.H.," *Anuario Musical,* VI (1951); J. Ward, "The Editorial Methods of V.d.H.," *Musica Disciplina,* VI (1952).

Vengerova, Isabelle (actually, **Isabella Afanasievna**), distinguished Russian-born pianist and pedagogue; b. Minsk, March 1, 1877; d. N.Y., Feb. 7, 1956. She studied at the Vienna Cons. with Joseph Dachs, and privately with Leschetizky; then with Anna Essipova in St. Petersburg. In 1906 she was appointed an instructor at the St. Petersburg Cons.; in 1910 she became a prof. there, remaining on its faculty until 1920. She made tours in Russia and Europe (1920–23); then went to the U.S. in 1923; made her American debut with the Detroit Sym. Orch. (Feb. 8, 1925) in Schumann's Piano Concerto.

She became a prof. at the Curtis Inst. of Music in Philadelphia when it was founded in 1924; in 1950 she received an honorary doctor's degree there. Among her piano pupils at the Curtis Inst. were Leonard Bernstein, Samuel Barber, and Lukas Foss. She also taught privately in N.Y. Her nephew was **Nicolas Slonimsky.**
BIBL.: N. Slonimsky, " 'Musique': Reminiscences of a Vanished World and a Great Teacher," *Piano Teacher,* VI/1 (1963); E. Flissler, "The Venerable V.: Magician of Pianoforte," *Music Journal,* XXIII/3 (1965); R. Schick, *The V. System of Piano Playing* (University Park, Pa., 1982); N. Slonimsky, *Perfect Pitch: A Life Story* (Oxford and N.Y., 1988).

Vento, Ivo de, organist and composer; b. 1544; d. Munich, 1575. He was a choirboy at the Bavarian Hofkapelle in Munich (1556–59), then studied organ with Claudio Merulo in Venice (1560); within a few years, he returned to Munich to serve as 3rd organist at the Hofkapelle. After holding the post of choirmaster at the Landshut court (1568–69), he resumed his duties in Munich, where he sometimes served as sole organist. He became best known for his lieder, which influenced such composers as Lechner and Hassler.
WORKS (all publ. in Munich): SACRED VOCAL: *Latinae cantiones, quas vulgo moteta vocant* for 4 Voices (1569); *Latinae cantiones, quas vulgo moteta vocant* for 5 Voices (1570); *Liber motetorum* for 4 Voices (1571); *Mutetae aliquot sacrae* for 4 Voices (1571); also 3 masses for 4 to 6 Voices in MS. SECULAR VOCAL: *Neue teutsche Liedlein* for 5 Voices (1569); *Neue teutsche Lieder* for 4 to 6 Voices (1570); *Neue teutsche Lieder* for 4 Voices, *samt zweien Dialogen* (1570); *Neue teutsche Lieder* for 3 Voices (1572); *Schöne auserlesene neue teutsche Lieder* for 4 Voices (1572); *Teutsche Lieder* for 5 Voices, *samt einem Dialogo* for 8 Voices (1573); *5 motetae, 2 madrigalia, (2) gallicae cantiones . . . et 4 germanicae* for 5 and 8 to 9 Voices (1575); other madrigals in contemporary collections.
BIBL.: K. Huber, *I. d.V. (ca. 1540–1575)* (Lindenberg im Allgäu, 1918).

Ventura, Ray(mond), French jazz bandleader; b. Paris, April 16, 1908; d. Palma, Majorca, Spain, March 29, 1979. He founded the Collegiate Five in 1925, which later was expanded to include additional musicians to form the Collegians; after the jazz violinist Stéphane Grapelli joined the band, it became popular in France. During World War II, he led it on tours in South America. After the war, he returned to France; then became director of a film co. The renditions by the Collegians of Paul Misraki's *Fantastique* (1932) and *Tout va très bien, Madame la marquise* (1935) were famous.

Venuti, "Joe" (Giuseppe), Italian-born American jazz violinist; b. Lecco, April 4, 1898; d. Seattle, Aug. 14, 1978. He was taken to the U.S. as a child, and reared in Philadelphia. There he received a thorough classical training on the violin, but after meeting the jazz guitarist Eddie Lang, he turned to popular music. After playing with Paul Whiteman, he formed his own band in 1935, and led it until 1943; then went to the West Coast, where he became a studio musician in Hollywood. His great merit was to make the theretofore-suspect violin a respectable instrument among the plebs of California.

Venzano, Luigi, Italian cellist, teacher, and composer; b. Genoa, 1814; d. there, Jan. 26, 1878. He played cello at the Carlo Felice Theater in Genoa, and taught at the Cons. there; publ. many songs, including *Valzer cantabile*; also composed an operetta, *La notte dei schiaffi* (Genoa, April 25, 1873), and a ballet, *Benvenuto Cellini* (Milan, Aug. 24, 1861); publ. piano pieces and singing exercises.

Veprik, Alexander (Moiseievich), Russian composer and musicologist; b. Balta, near Odessa, June 23, 1899; d. Moscow, Oct. 13, 1958. While still a young boy he went to Leipzig, where he took piano lessons with Karl Wendling; then pursued training in composition with Zhitomirsky at the Petrograd Cons. (1918–21) and with Miaskovsky at the Moscow Cons. (1921–23), where he subsequently taught orchestration (1923–43). He was associated with the Jewish cultural movement in Russia, and composed several works in the traditional ethnic manner of Jewish cantillations. In his harmonic and formal treatment, he followed the "orientalistic" tradition of the Russian national school.

WORKS: OPERAS: *Toktogul*, on Kirghiz motifs (1938–39; Frunze, 1940); *Toktogul* (1949; in collaboration with A. Maldibaiev). **ORCH.:** 2 syms. (1931, 1938); *Traurnaya pesnya* (Sad Song; 1932); *Pesnya likovaniya* (Peace Song; 1935); *Pastorale* (1946; rev. 1958); 2 *poems* (1957); *Improvizatsiya* (1958). **CANTATAS:** *Proklyatiye fashizmu* (Fascism Be Cursed; 1944); *Narod-geroy* (The People-The Hero; 1955). **CHAMBER:** Rhapsody for Viola and Piano (1926); piano pieces, including 3 sonatas (1922, 1924, 1928); also songs; film music.

WRITINGS: *O metodakh prepodavaniya instrumentovki: K voprosu o klassovoy obuslovlennosti orkestrovovo pisma* (Methods of Instrument Teaching: On the Question of the Classification of Orchestral Writing; Moscow, 1931); *Traktovka instrumenov orkestra* (The Treatment of Orchestral Instruments; Moscow, 1948; 2nd ed., 1961).

BIBL.: V. Bogdanov-Berezovsky, *A.M. V.* (Moscow and Leningrad, 1964).

Veracini, Antonio, esteemed Italian violinist, teacher, and composer, uncle of **Francesco Maria Veracini;** b. Florence, Jan. 17, 1659; d. there, Oct. 26, 1733. His father, **Francesco di Niccolo,** was a gifted violinist; he most likely received his initial training from him, and appeared with him as a youth. Antonio Veracini was in the service of Grand Duchess Vittoria of Tuscany (1682–94); served as maestro di cappella at the church of S. Michele (from 1700) and also was active at other Florentine churches; in 1708 he took over his father's music school, where he was mentor to his nephew. His extant works are (10) *Sonate a tre* for 2 Violins, Violone or Archlute, and Basso Continuo, op. 1 (Florence, 1692), (10) *Sonate da camera* for Violin, op. 2 (Modena, c.1694), and (10) *Sonate da camera a due* for Violin, Violone or Archlute, and Basso Continuo, op. 3 (Modena, 1696).

Veracini, Francesco Maria, noted Italian violinist and composer, nephew of **Antonio Veracini;** b. Florence, Feb. 1, 1690; d. there, Oct. 31, 1768. He studied violin with his uncle, with whom he appeared in concerts in Florence; also received instruction from Giovanni Maria Casini and Francesco Feroci, and from G.A. Bernabei in Germany (1715). In 1711 he went to Venice, where he appeared as a soloist at the Christmas masses at San Marco; in 1714 he gave a series of benefit concerts in London, and in 1716 entered the private service of the Elector of Saxony; in 1717 he went to Dresden and entered the court service. In 1723 he returned to Florence, where he was active as a performer and composer of sacred works; also gave private concerts. In 1733 he returned to London, where he played for the Opera of the Nobility, a rival to Handel's opera company; also composed operas during his London years. In 1745 he returned to Italy, where from 1755 until his death he was maestro di cappella for the Vallambrosian fathers at the church of S. Pancrazio in Florence; he also held that position for the Teatini fathers at the church of S. Michele agl'Antinori there (from 1758). He acquired a reputation as an eccentric, and some considered him mad. Be that as it may, he was esteemed as a violinist and composer.

WORKS: VOCAL: Operas (all 1st perf. in London): *Adriano in Siria* (Nov. 26, 1735); *La clemenza di Tito* (April 12, 1737); *Partenio* (March 14, 1738); *Rosalinda* (Jan. 31, 1744); 8 oratorios, all of which are lost; a few sacred works, all of which are lost; some cantatas and songs. **INSTRUMENTAL:** (12) *Sonate* for Violin or Recorder and Basso Continuo (1716; ed. by W. Kolneder, Leipzig, 1959–61); (12) *Sonate* for Violin and Basso Continuo, op. 1 (Dresden, 1721; ed. by W. Kolneder, Leipzig, 1958–59); (12) *Sonate accademiche* for Violin and Basso Continuo, op. 2 (London and Florence, 1744; ed. by F. Bar, Kassel, 1959–); (12) *Dissertazioni . . . sopra l'opera quinta del Corelli* (n.d.; ed. by W. Kolneder, Mainz, 1961); 15 sonatas in MS; 3 concertos in contemporary collections; 2 concertos and an overture in MS.

BIBL.: J. Mattheson, *Critica musica*, I (Hamburg, 1722); A. Naldo, "Un trattato inedito e ignoto di F.M. V.," *Rivista Musicale Italiana*, XLII (1938); A. Damerini, "Elogio dell' asino e monte di Stradella in un trattato di F.M. V.," *La Scala* (March 1956); H. Smith, *F.M. V.'s Il trionfo della pratica musicale* (diss., Indiana Univ., 1963); M. Clarke, *The Violin Sonatas of F.M. V.: Some Aspects of Italian Late Baroque Instrumental Style Exemplified* (diss., Univ. of North Carolina, 1967); F. Ricci, "Appunti per una biografia di F.M. V. nel bicentenario della morte (1690–1768)," *Annuario dell' Accademia nazionale di Santa Cecilia* (1968); J. Hill, *The Life and Works of F.M. V.* (diss., Harvard Univ., 1972; rev., Ann Arbor, 1979); M. White, "The Life of F.M. V.," *Music & Letters*, LIII (1972); J. Hill, "V. in Italy," *Music & Letters*, LVI (1975); idem, "The Anti-galant Attitude of F.M. V.," *Studies in Musicology in Honor of Otto E. Albrecht* (Kassel, 1977, and Clifton, N.J., 1980); B. Schwarz, *Great Masters of the Violin* (N.Y., 1983).

Verbesselt, August, Belgian flutist and composer; b. Klein-Willebroek, Oct. 22, 1919. He studied at the Antwerp Cons.; from 1942, was flutist in the orch. of the Antwerp Royal Flemish Opera.

WORKS: ORCH.: Flute Concerto (1952); *Diagrams* for Chamber Orch. (1972); *Universum* for 2 Orchs. and Tape (1975); *Strukturen* (1981); Clarinet Concerto (1983); Piano Concerto (1986); Oboe Concerto (1986); Concerto for Clarinet Quartet and Chamber Orch. (1986); *Pax* for Chamber Orch. (1986); *Sluierdans* for Harmony Orch. (1988); *Oase* for Chamber Orch. (1988); Chamber Concerto for Bass Clarinet and Strings (1988); ballet music. **CHAMBER:** *Hexatone-Synthèse* for Flute, Oboe, Clarinet, Cello, and Harp (1964); *3 Monologhi* for Flute (1981); *Tre movimenti* for Clarinet (1982); *Conversazione* for Oboe and Piano (1982); *Introduzione ed Allegro* for Saxophone and Piano (1982); *Iberia* for Flute and Guitar (1982); *12 Concert Studies* for Flute (1984); *Due dialoghi* for Bassoon and Piano (1984); *Iskato*, trio for Oboe, Clarinet, and Bassoon (1985); 2 clarinet quartets (both 1985); *Per flauto* for Flute (1986); *Per violino* for Violin (1987); *Metropolis* for Flute and Piano (1987); some vocal pieces.

Verbrugghen, Henri, Belgian violinist and conductor; b. Brussels, Aug. 1, 1873; d. Northfield, Minn., Nov. 12, 1934. He studied with Hubay and Ysaÿe at the Brussels Cons.; in 1893, was engaged as a violinist in the Scottish Orch. in Glasgow; then was concertmaster in various orchs. in Wales; also conducted summer concerts there while retaining his position in Glasgow. In 1915 he went to Australia, where he was director of the State Conservatorium and conductor of its orch. in Sydney; also was conductor of the New South Wales State Orch.; then was conductor of the Minneapolis Sym. Orch. (1923–31).

Vercoe, Barry, New Zealand-born American composer and computer-music specialist; b. Wellington, July 24, 1937. He was educated at the Univ. of Auckland (Mus.B. in composition, 1959; B.A. in mathematics, 1962) and the Univ. of Michigan (A.Mus.D., 1968). After completing postdoctoral research at Princeton Univ. (1968–70), he served as U.S. adviser to the UNESCO Joint European Studies Committee on Technology and Arts (1977–78); also was resident composer/researcher at IRCAM (1983–84), where he developed "cpmusic," a system for synchronizing computer-processed sound with live instruments by computer tracking of performers in real time. He was a visiting lecturer at the Yale Univ. School of Music (1970–71); then joined the faculty at the Mass. Inst. of Technology, first as an associate prof. in its dept. of humanities (1971–85) and then as a prof. in its dept. of media arts and sciences (from 1985). His work in psychoacoustic and computer music research has been supported by sizable grants from the National Science Foundation (1976; 1987–89), the N.E.A. (1978–82), and the John D. and Catherine T. MacArthur Foundation (1981), among others. He held a Guggenheim fellowship (1982–83). His developments in the field of computer audio systems include "Music–11" (1976; in 1984, rewritten to "Csound"), for fast digital processing of audio on PDP–11 minicomputers, and "MUSIC 360" (1969), a programming language used for processing sound on large IBM machines. He is married to **Elizabeth Vercoe.**

Works: *Digressions* for Band, 2 Choirs, Computer, and Orch. (1968); *Synthesism* for Computer (1970); *Synapse* for Viola and Computer (1976); *Synapse II* for Flute and 4X Processor (1984).

Vercoe, Elizabeth, American composer; b. Washington, D.C., April 23, 1941. She was educated at Wellesley College (B.A., 1962), the Univ. of Michigan (M.M., 1963), and Boston Univ. (D.M.A., 1978); taught at Westminster Choir College in Princeton, N.J. (1969–71), and Framingham (Mass.) State College (1973–74). She was composer-in-residence at the Cité Internationale des Arts in Paris and the Charles Ives Center for American Music; in 1988, participated in the U.S./U.S.S.R. Young Composers' Exchange. She wrote a variety of articles actively promoting the cause of women's music; was a founding member of the Mass. Chapter of American Women Composers (1984) and a board member of the International League of Women Composers; co-directed the Women's Music Festival/85 in Boston. She is married to **Barry Vercoe.**

Works: *Children's Caprice* for Orch. (1963); *Herstory I* for Soprano, Piano, and Vibraphone (1975; to texts by American women poets); Concerto for Violin and Orch. (1977); *Herstory II: 13 Japanese Lyrics* for Soprano, Piano, and Percussion (1979; to texts by medieval Japanese women poets); *Irreveries from Sappho* for Women's Chorus and Piano (1981); *Fantavia* for Flute and Percussion (1982); *Suite française* for Violin (1983); *Despite our Differences No. 1* for Violin, Cello, and Piano (1984); *9 Epigrams from Poor Richard* for Voice and Tape (1986); *Herstory III: Jehanne de Lorraine*, staged monodrama for Voice and Piano (1986; to texts by Villon, Shaw, Twain, and others); *Despite our Differences No. 2* for Piano and Chamber Orch. (1988).

Verdelot, Philippe, noted French composer; b. Verdelot, Les Loges, Seine-et-Marne, c.1470–80; d. before 1552. He made his way to northern Italy; by 1522 he was in Florence, where he served as maestro di cappella at the Baptisterium S. Giovanni (1523–25) and at the Cathedral (1523–27); also was in Rome (1523–24). With the siege of Florence (1529–30), Verdelot disappears from the pages of history. His extant works include 2 masses, one known as *Philomena*, a *Magnificat sexti toni*, some 58 motets, numerous madrigals, including some publ. in *Madrigali a cinque, libro primo* (Venice, c.1535), and 4 chansons. His madrigals and motets were widely disseminated in the 16th century. A number of works attributed to him are of doubtful authenticity. The *Opera omnia*, ed. by A.-M. Bragard in Corpus Mensurabilis Musicae, began publication in 1966.

Bibl.: A.-M. Bragard, "V. en Italie," *Revue Belge de Musicologie*, XI (1957); D. Hersh, *P. V. and the Early Madrigal* (diss., Univ. of Calif., Berkeley, 1963); A.-M. Bragard, *Étude bio-bibliographique sur P. V., musicien français de la Renaissance* (Brussels, 1964); N. Böker-Heil, *Die Motetten von P. V.* (Cologne, 1967).

Verdi, Giuseppe (Fortunino Francesco), great Italian opera composer whose genius for dramatic, lyric, and tragic stage music has made him the perennial favorite of a multitude of opera enthusiasts; b. Le Roncole, near Busseto, Duchy of Parma, Oct. 9, 1813; d. Milan, Jan. 27, 1901. His father kept a tavern, and street singing gave Verdi his early appreciation of music produced by natural means. A *magister parvulorum*, one Pietro Baistrocchi, a church organist, noticed his love of musical sound and took him on as a pupil. When Baistrocchi died, Verdi, still a small child, took over some of his duties at the keyboard. His father sent him to Busseto for further musical training; there he began his academic studies and also took music lessons with Ferdinando Provesi, the director of the municipal music school. At the age of 18 he became a resident in the home of Antonio Barezzi, a local merchant and patron of music; Barezzi supplied him with enough funds so that he could go to Milan for serious study. Surprisingly

enough, in view of Verdi's future greatness, he failed to pass an entrance examination to the Milan Cons.; the registrar, Francesco Basili, reported that Verdi's piano technique was inadequate and that in composition he lacked technical knowledge. Verdi then turned to Vincenzo Lavigna, an excellent musician, for private lessons, and worked industriously to master counterpoint, canon, and fugue. In 1834 he applied for the post of maestro di musica in Busseto, and after passing his examination received the desired appointment. On May 4, 1836, he married a daughter of his patron Barezzi; it was a love marriage, but tragedy intervened when their 2 infant children died, and his wife succumbed on June 18, 1840. Verdi deeply mourned his bereavement, but he found solace in music. In 1838 he completed his first opera, *Oberto, conte di San Bonifacio*. In 1839 he moved to Milan. He submitted the score of *Oberto* to the directorship of La Scala; it was accepted for a performance, which took place on Nov. 17, 1839, with satisfactory success. He was now under contract to write more operas for that renowned theater. His comic opera *Un giorno di regno* was performed at La Scala in 1840, but it did not succeed at pleasing the public. Somewhat downhearted at this reverse, Verdi began composition of an opera, *Nabucodonosor*, on the biblical subject (the title was later abbreviated to *Nabucco*). It was staged at La Scala on March 9, 1842, scoring considerable success. Giuseppina Strepponi created the leading female role of Abigaille. *Nabucco* was followed by another successful opera on a historic subject, *I Lombardi alla prima Crociata*, produced at La Scala on Feb. 11, 1843. The next opera was *Ernani*, after Victor Hugo's drama on the life of a revolutionary outlaw; the subject suited the rise of national spirit, and its production in Venice on March 9, 1844, won great acclaim. Not so popular were Verdi's succeeding operas, *I due Foscari* (1844), *Giovanna d'Arco* (1845), *Alzira* (1845), and *Attila* (1846). On March 14, 1847, Verdi produced in Florence his 1st Shakespearean opera, *Macbeth*. In the same year he received a commission to write an opera for London; the result was *I Masnadieri*, based on Schiller's drama *Die Räuber*. It was produced at Her Majesty's Theatre in London on July 22, 1847, with Jenny Lind taking the leading female role. A commission from Paris followed; for it Verdi revised his opera *I Lombardi alla prima Crociata* in a French version, renamed *Jérusalem*; it was produced at the Paris Opéra on Nov. 26, 1847; the Italian production followed at La Scala on Dec. 26, 1850. This was one of the several operas by him and other Italian composers where mistaken identity was the chief dramatic device propelling the action. During his stay in Paris for the performance of *Jérusalem*, he renewed his acquaintance with Giuseppina Strepponi; after several years of cohabitation, their union was legalized in a private ceremony in Savoy on Aug. 29, 1859. In 1848 he produced his opera *Il Corsaro*, after Byron's poem *The Corsair*. There followed *La battaglia di Legnano*, celebrating the defeat of the armies of Barbarossa by the Lombards in 1176. Its premiere took place in Rome on Jan. 27, 1849, but Verdi was forced to change names and places so as not to offend the central European powers that dominated Italy. The subsequent operas *Luisa Miller* (1849), after Schiller's drama *Kabale und Liebe*, and *Stiffelio* (1850) were not successful. Verdi's great triumph came in 1851 with the production of *Rigoletto*, fashioned after Victor Hugo's drama *Le Roi s'amuse*; it was performed for the 1st time at the Teatro La Fenice in Venice on March 11, 1851, and brought Verdi lasting fame; it entered the repertoire of every opera house around the globe. The aria of the libidinous Duke, *La donna è mobile*, became one of the most popular operatic tunes sung, or ground on the barrel organ, throughout Europe. This success was followed by an even greater acclaim with the production in 1853 of *Il Trovatore* (Rome, Jan. 19, 1853) and *La Traviata* (Venice, March 6, 1853); both captivated world audiences without diminution of their melodramatic effect on succeeding generations in Europe and America, and this despite the absurdity of the action represented on the stage. *Il Trovatore* resorts to the common device of unrecognized identities of close relatives, while *La Traviata* strains credulity when the eponymous soprano sings enchantingly and long despite her struggle with terminal consumption. The character of Traviata was based on the story of a real person, as depicted in the drama *La Dame aux camélias* by Alexandre Dumas *fils*. The Italian title is untranslatable, *Traviata* being the feminine passive voice of the verb meaning "to lead astray," and it would have to be rendered, in English, by the construction "a woman who has been led astray." Another commission coming from Paris resulted in Verdi's first French opera, *Les Vêpres siciliennes*, after a libretto by Scribe to Donizetti's unfinished opera *Le Duc d'Albe*; the action deals with the medieval slaughter of the French occupation army in Sicily by local patriots. Despite the offensiveness of the subject to French patriots, the opera was given successfully in Paris on June 13, 1855. His next opera, *Simone Boccanegra*, was produced at the Teatro La Fenice in Venice on March 12, 1857. This was followed by *Un ballo in maschera*, which made history. The original libretto was written by Scribe for Auber's opera *Gustave III*, dealing with the assassination of King Gustave III of Sweden in 1792. But the censors would not have any regicide shown on the stage, and Verdi was compelled to transfer the scene of action from Sweden to Massachusetts. Ridiculous as it was, Gustave III became Governor Riccardo of Boston; the opera was produced in this politically sterilized version in Rome on Feb. 17, 1859. Attempts were made later to restore the original libretto and to return the action to Sweden, but audiences resented the change of the familiar version. Unexpectedly, Verdi became a factor in the political struggle for the independence of Italy; the symbol of the nationalist movement was the name of Vittorio Emanuele, the future king of Italy. Demonstrators painted the name of Verdi in capital letters, separated by punctuation, on fences and walls of Italian towns (V.E.R.D.I., the initials of Vittorio Emanuele, Re D'Italia), and the cry "Viva Verdi!" became "Viva Vittorio Emanuele Re D'Italia!" In 1861 he received a commission to write an opera for the Imperial Opera of St. Petersburg, Russia; he selected the mystic subject *La forza del destino*. The premiere took place in St. Petersburg on Nov. 22, 1862, and Verdi made a special trip to attend. He then wrote an opera to a French text, *Don Carlos*, after Schiller's famous drama. It was first heard at the Paris Opéra on March 11, 1867, with numerous cuts; they were not restored in the score until a century had elapsed after the initial production. In June 1870 he received a contract to write a new work for the opera in Cairo, Egypt, where *Rigoletto* had already been performed a year before. The terms were most advantageous, with a guarantee of 150,000 francs for the Egyptian rights alone. The opera, based on life in ancient Egypt, was *Aida*; the original libretto was in French; Antonio Ghislanzoni prepared the Italian text. It had its premiere in Cairo on Christmas Eve of 1871, with great éclat. A special boat was equipped to carry officials and journalists from Italy to Cairo for the occasion, but Verdi stubbornly refused to join the caravan despite persuasion by a number of influential Italian musicians and statesmen; he declared that a composer's job was to supply the music, not to attend performances. The success of *Aida* exceeded all expectations; the production was hailed as a world event, and the work itself became one of the most famous in opera history.

After Rossini's death, in 1868, Verdi conceived the idea of honoring his memory by a collective composition of a Requiem, to which several Italian composers would contribute a movement each, Verdi reserving the last section, *Libera me*, for himself. He completed the score in 1869, but it was never performed in its original form. The death of the famous Italian poet Alessandro Manzoni in 1873 led him to write his great *Messa da Requiem*, which became known simply as the "Manzoni" Requiem, and he incorporated in it the section originally composed for Rossini. The *Messa da Requiem* received its premiere on the 1st anniversary of Manzoni's death, on May 22, 1874, in Milan. There was some criticism of the Requiem as being too operatic for a religious work, but it remained in musical annals as a masterpiece. After a lapse of some 13 years of rural retirement, Verdi turned once more to Shake-

speare; the result this time was *Otello;* the libretto was by Arrigo Boito, a master poet who rendered Shakespeare's lines into Italian with extraordinary felicity. It received its premiere at La Scala on Feb. 5, 1887. Verdi was 79 years old when he wrote yet another Shakespearean opera, *Falstaff*, also to a libretto by Boito; in his libretto Boito used materials from *The Merry Wives of Windsor* and *Henry IV*. *Falstaff* was performed for the 1st time at La Scala on Feb. 9, 1893. The score reveals Verdi's genius for subtle comedy coupled with melodic invention of the highest order. His last composition was a group of sacred choruses, an *Ave Maria*, *Laudi alla Vergine Maria*, *Stabat Mater*, and *Te Deum*, publ. in 1898 as *4 pezzi sacri;* in the *Ave Maria*, Verdi made use of the so-called scala enigmatica (C, D-flat, E, F-sharp, G-sharp, A-sharp, B, and C).

Innumerable honors were bestowed upon Verdi. In 1864 he was elected to membership in the Académie des Beaux Arts in Paris, where he filled the vacancy made by the death of Meyerbeer. In 1875 he was nominated a senator to the Italian Parliament. Following the premiere of *Falstaff*, the King of Italy wished to make him "Marchese di Busseto," but he declined the honor. After the death of his 2nd wife, on Nov. 14, 1897, he founded in Milan the Casa di Riposo per Musicisti, a home for aged musicians; for its maintenance, he set aside 2,500,000 lire. On Jan. 21, 1901, Verdi suffered an apoplectic attack; he died 6 days later at the age of 87.

Historic evaluation of Verdi's music changed several times after his death. The musical atmosphere was heavily Wagnerian; admiration for Wagner produced a denigration of Verdi as a purveyor of "barrel-organ" music. Then the winds of musical opinion reversed their direction; sophisticated modern composers, music historians, and academic theoreticians discovered unexpected attractions in the flowing Verdian melodies, easily modulating harmonies, and stimulating symmetric rhythms; a theory was even advanced that the appeal of Verdi's music lies in its adaptability to modernistic elaboration and contrapuntal variegations. By natural transvaluation of opposites, Wagnerianism went into eclipse after it reached the limit of complexity. The slogan "Viva Verdi!" assumed, paradoxically, an esthetic meaning. Scholarly research into Verdi's biography greatly increased. The Istituto di Studi Verdiani was founded in Parma in 1959. An American Inst. for Verdi Studies was founded in 1976 with its archive at N.Y. Univ.; it publ. a newsletter.

WORKS: OPERAS: In the literature on Verdi, mention is sometimes made of 2 early operatic attempts, *Lord Hamilton* and *Rocester;* however, nothing definitive has ever been established concerning these 2 works. The accepted list of his operas is as follows: *Oberto, conte di San Bonifacio* (1837–38; La Scala, Milan, Nov. 17, 1839; libretto rev. by Graffigna and given as *I Bonifazi ed i Salinguerra* in Venice in 1842); *Un giorno di regno* (later known as *Il finto Stanislao*), melodramma giocoso (1840; La Scala, Milan, Sept. 5, 1840); *Nabucodonosor* (later known as *Nabucco*), dramma lirico (1841; La Scala, Milan, March 9, 1842); *I Lombardi alla prima Crociata*, dramma lirico (1842; La Scala, Milan, Feb. 11, 1843; rev. version, with a French libretto by Royer and Vaëz, given as *Jérusalem* at the Paris Opéra, Nov. 26, 1847); *Ernani*, dramma lirico (1843; Teatro La Fenice, Venice, March 9, 1844); *I due Foscari*, tragedia lirica (1844; Teatro Argentina, Rome, Nov. 3, 1844); *Giovanna d'Arco*, dramma lirico (1844; La Scala, Milan, Feb. 15, 1845); *Alzira*, tragedia lirica (1845; Teatro San Carlo, Naples, Aug. 12, 1845); *Attila*, dramma lirico (1845–46; Teatro La Fenice, Venice, March 17, 1846); *Macbeth* (1846–47; Teatro alla Pergola, Florence, March 14, 1847; rev. version, with a French tr. by Nuittier and Beaumont of the Italian libretto, Théâtre-Lyrique, Paris, April 21, 1865); *I Masnadieri* (1846–47; Her Majesty's Theatre, London, July 22, 1847); *Il Corsaro* (1847–48; Teatro Grande, Trieste, Oct. 25, 1848); *La battaglia di Legnano*, tragedia lirica (1848; Teatro Argentina, Rome, Jan. 27, 1849); *Luisa Miller*, melodramma tragico (1849; Teatro San Carlo, Naples, Dec. 8, 1849); *Stiffelio* (1850; Teatro Grande, Trieste, Nov. 16, 1850; later rev. as *Aroldo*); *Rigoletto*, melodramma (1850–51; Teatro La Fenice, Venice, March 11,

1851); *Il Trovatore*, dramma (1851–52; Teatro Apollo, Rome, Jan. 19, 1853; rev. 1857); *La Traviata* (1853; Teatro La Fenice, Venice, March 6, 1853); *Les Vêpres siciliennes* (1854; Opéra, Paris, June 13, 1855); *Simone Boccanegra* (1856–57; Teatro La Fenice, Venice, March 12, 1857; rev. 1880–81; La Scala, Milan, March 24, 1881); *Aroldo* (revision of *Stiffelio*; 1856–57; Teatro Nuovo, Rimini, Aug. 16, 1857); *Un ballo in maschera*, melodramma (1857–58; Teatro Apollo, Rome, Feb. 17, 1859); *La forza del destino* (1861; Imperial Theater, St. Petersburg, Nov. 22, 1862; rev. version, La Scala, Milan, Feb. 27, 1869); *Don Carlos* (1866; Opéra, Paris, March 11, 1867; rev. version, 1883–84, with Italian libretto by Lauzières and Zanardini, La Scala, Milan, Jan. 10, 1884); *Aida* (1870–71; Opera House, Cairo, Dec. 24, 1871); *Otello*, dramma lirico (1884–86; La Scala, Milan, Feb. 5, 1887); *Falstaff*, commedia lirica (1889–93; La Scala, Milan, Feb. 9, 1893).

OTHER WORKS: *Inno popolare* for Men's Voices and Piano (1848); *Inno delle Nazioni* for Solo Voice, Mixed Chorus, and Orch. (1862; London, May 24, 1862; composed for the London Exhibition); *Libera me* for Soprano, Mixed Chorus, and Orch. (1868–69; composed for the *Rossini Requiem*, and later incorporated in the *Messa da Requiem*); String Quartet in E minor (1873); *Messa da Requiem* for Soprano, Alto, Tenor, Bass, Mixed Chorus, and Orch., the "Manzoni" Requiem (1873–74; San Marco, Milan, May 22, 1874); *Ave Maria* for Soprano and Strings (1880); *Pater noster* for 5-part Chorus a cappella (1880); *4 pezzi sacri: Ave Maria* for Chorus a cappella (1888–89), *Stabat Mater* for Chorus and Orch. (1895–97), *Laudi alla Vergine Maria* for Female Chorus a cappella (1888–89), and *Te Deum* for Soprano, Double Mixed Chorus, and Orch. (1895–97). Songs: 6 *romanze* (1838; *Non t'accostare all'urna; More, Elisa, lo stanco poeta; In solitaria stanza; Nell'orro di notte oscura; Perduta ho la pace; Deh, pietoso, oh Addolorata*); *Notturno* for Soprano, Tenor, Bass, and Piano, with Flute obbligato (1839); *L'Esule* (1839); *La seduzione* (1839); *Chi i bei di m'adduce ancora* (1842); 6 *romanze* (1845; *Il tramonto* [2 versions]; *La Zingara; Ad una stella; Lo Spazzacamino; Il mistero; Brindisi*); *Il Poveretto* (1847); *Suona la tromba* (1848); *L'Abandonnée* (1849); *Barcarola* (1850); *La preghiera del poeta* (1858); *Il brigidino* (1863); *Tu dici che non m'ami* (1869); *Cupo è il sepolcro mutolo* (1873); *Pietà, Signor* (1894). Also a *Tantum ergo* for Tenor and Orch. (1836?); *Romanza senza parole* for Piano (1865); Waltz for Piano.

BIBL.: COLLECTED WORKS, SOURCE MATERIAL: There is still no complete critical ed. of Verdi's works, but Ricordi and the Univ. of Chicago Press are preparing a definitive ed. Important sources include the following: C. Vanbianchi, *Nel I° centenario di G. V., 1813–1913: Saggio di bibliografia verdiana* (Milan, 1913); C. Hopkinson, "Bibliographical Problems Concerned with V. and His Publishers," *I° congresso internazionale di studi verdiani: Venezia 1966*; D. Lawton, "Per una bibliografia ragionata verdiana," ibid.; M. Pavarani, "Per una bibliografia e documentazione verdiana," ibid.; O. Strunk, "Verdiana alla Biblioteca del Congresso," ibid.; G. Tintori, "Bibliografia verdiana in Russia," ibid.; D. Kämpfer, "Das deutsche V.-Schriften: Hauptlinien der Interpretation," *Analecta Musicologica*, no. 11 (1972); D. Lawton and D. Rosen, "V.'s Non-Definitive Revisions: The Early Operas," *3° congresso internazionale di studi verdiani: Milano 1972*; C. Hopkinson, *A Bibliography of the Works of G. V., 1813–1901* (2 vols., N.Y., 1973 and 1978); M. Chusid, *A Catalog of V.'s Operas* (Hackensack, N.J., 1974); M. Mila, *La giovinezza di V.* (Turin, 1974); E. Surian, "Lo stato attuale degli studi verdiani: Appunti e bibliografia ragionata," *Rivista Italiana di Musicologia*, XII (1977); D. Rosen, "Recent V. Literature: A Survey," *Musical Times* (June 1983); D. Rosen and A. Porter, eds., *V.'s Macbeth: A Sourcebook* (Cambridge, 1984).

BIOGRAPHICAL: G. Monaldi, *V. e le sue opere* (Florence, 1878); A. Pougin, *G. V.: Vita aneddotica* (Milan, 1881; in French, Paris, 1886; in Eng., N.Y., 1887); E. Hanslick, "G. V. Zur Geschichte seines Lebens, inbesondere seiner Jugendzeit," in *Suite* (Vienna, 1884); L. Parodi, *G. V.* (Genoa, 1895); Prince de Valori, *V. et son œuvre* (Paris, 1895); F. Crowest, *V.: Man*

and Musician (London, 1897); G. Cavarretta, *V.: Il genio, la vita, le opere* (Palermo, 1899); G. Monaldi, *V.* (Turin, 1899; Ger. tr. as *G. V. und seine Werke*, Stuttgart, 1898, publ. before the Italian original; 4th Italian ed., 1951); C. Perinello, *G. V.* (Berlin, 1900); M. Basso, *G. V.: La sua vita, le sue opere, la sua morte* (Milan, 1901); O. Boni, *V.: L'Uomo, le opere, l'artista* (Parma, 1901; 2nd ed., 1913); E. Checchi, *G. V.* (Florence, 1901); N. Marini, *G. V.* (Rome, 1901); E. Colonna, *G. V. nella vita e nelle opere* (Palermo, 1902); F. Garibaldi, *G. V. nella vita e nell'arte* (Florence, 1904); L. Sorge, *G. V.: Uomo, artista, patriota* (Lanciano, 1904); P. Voss, *G. V.: Ein Lebensbild* (Diessen, 1904); G. Bragagnolo and E. Bettazzi, *La vita di G. V. narrata al popolo* (Milan, 1905); A. Visetti, *V.* (London, 1905); A. d'Angeli, *G. V.* (Bologna, 1910; 2nd ed., 1912); C. Bellaigue, *V.: Biographie critique* (Paris, 1912; Italian tr., Milan, 1913); M. Chop, *V.* (Leipzig, 1913); M. Lottici, *Bio-bibliografia di G. V.* (Parma, 1913); A. Mackenzie, *V.* (N.Y., 1913); G. Monaldi, *Il Maestro della rivoluzione italiana* (Milan, 1913); A. Righetti, *G. V.: Vita aneddotica* (Rome, 1913); A. Neisser, *G. V.* (Leipzig, 1914); G. Roncaglia, *G. V.* (Naples, 1914); A. Weissmann, *V.* (Berlin, 1922); A. Bonaventura, *G. V.* (Paris, 1923); F. Werfel, *V., Roman der Oper* (a biographical novel; Berlin, 1924; Eng. tr., N.Y., 1925); G. Monaldi, *V. anedottico* (Turin, 1926); E. Gascó Contell, *V.: Su vida y sus obras* (Paris, 1927); F. Ridella, *V.* (Genoa, 1928); F. Bonavia, *V.* (London, 1930; 2nd ed., 1947); C. Gatti, *V.* (Milan, 1931; 2nd ed., 1951; Eng. tr. as *V.: The Man and His Music*, N.Y., 1955); F. Toye, *G. V.: His Life and Works* (London, 1931); H. Gerigk, *G. V.* (Potsdam, 1932); R. de Rensis, *Franco Faccio e V.* (Milan, 1934); R. Manganella, *V.* (Milan, 1936); L. d'Ambra, *G. V.* (Milan, 1937); D. Hussey, *V.* (London, 1940; 5th ed., 1973); F. Botti, *G. V.* (Rome, 1941); G. Roncaglia, *G. V.* (Florence, 1941); K. Holl, *V.* (Vienna, 1942); U. Zoppi, *Angelo Mariani, G. V. e Teresa Stolz* (Milan, 1947); D. Humphreys, *V., Force of Destiny* (N.Y., 1948); F. Törnblom, *V.* (Stockholm, 1948); G. Cenzato, *Itinerari verdiani* (Parma, 1949; 2nd ed., Milan, 1955); A. Cherbuliez, *G. V.* (Zürich, 1949); A. Oberdorfer, *G. V.* (Verona, 1949); L. Orsini, *G. V.* (Turin, 1949); F. Abbiati, ed., *G. V.* (Milan, 1951); L. Gianoli, *V.* (Brescia, 1951); G. Monaldi, *V., La vita, le opere* (Milan, 1951); E. Radius, *V. vivo* (Milan, 1951); G. Stefani, *V. e Trieste* (Trieste, 1951); idem, *G. V.* (a collection of articles; Siena, 1951); F. Botti, *V. e l'ospedale di Villanova d'Arda* (Parma, 1952); G. Mondini, *Nel cinquantennio della morte di G. V.* (Cremona, 1952); T. Ybarra, *V., Miracle Man of Opera* (N.Y., 1955); M. Mila, *G. V.* (Bari, 1958); P. Petit, *V.* (Paris, 1958); V. Sheean, *Orpheus at Eighty* (N.Y., 1958); F. Abbiati, *G. V.* (4 vols., Milan, 1959); F. Walker, *The Man V.* (contains new material on Verdi; N.Y., 1962); G. Martin, *V.: His Music, Life and Times* (N.Y., 1963; 3rd ed., rev., 1983); M. Matz, "The V. Family of Sant'Agata and Roncole: Legend and Truth," *I° congresso internazionale di studi verdiani: Venezia 1966*; idem, "V.: The Roots of the Tree," *V.: Bollettino dell'Istituto di Studi Verdiani*, III (1969–73); J. Wechsberg, *V.* (N.Y., 1974); W. Weaver, ed., *V.: A Documentary Study* (N.Y. and London, 1977); G. Mendelsohn, "V. the Man and V. the Dramatist," *19th Century Music* (Nov. 1978; March 1979); G. Marchesi, *G. V., l'uomo, il genio, l'artista* (Rozzano, 1982); G. Tintori, *Invito all'ascolto di G. V.* (Milan, 1983); M. Conati, ed., and R. Stokes, tr., *Interviews and Encounters with V.* (London, 1984); J. Budden, *V.* (London, 1985); C. Osborne, *V.: A Life in the Theatre* (N.Y., 1987).

CRITICAL, ANALYTICAL: A. Basevi, *Studio sulle opere di G. V.* (Florence, 1859); G. Bertrand, *Les Nationalités musicales étudiées dans le drame lyrique. Verdisme et Wagnérisme* (Paris, 1872); E. Hanslick, "V.," in *Die moderne Oper* (Berlin, 1875; several subsequent eds.); B. Roosevelt, *V., Milan and Otello* (Milan, 1887); V. Maurel, *A propos de la mise-en-scène du drame lyrique "Otello"* (Rome, 1888); L. Destranges, *L'Evolution musicale chez V.: Aïda, Otello, Falstaff* (Paris, 1895); C. Abate, *Wagner e V. Studio critico-musicale* (Mistretta, 1896); P. Bellezza, *Manzoni e V., i due grandi* (Rome, 1901); A. Soffredini, *Le opere di G. V.: Studio critico-analitico* (Milan, 1901); G. Tebaldini, *Da Rossini a V.* (Naples, 1901); J. Huneker,

Overtones (N.Y., 1904); F. Flamini, *Pagine di critica e d'arte* (contains a study on the operas of Verdi; Livorno, 1905); J. Hadden, *The Operas of V.* (London, 1910); K. Regensburger, *Über den "Trovador" des García Gutiérrez, die Quelle von V.s "Il Trovatore"* (Berlin, 1911); C. Vanbianchi, *Saggio di bibliografia verdiana* (Milan, 1913); G. Roncaglia, *G. V.: L'ascensione dell'arte sua* (Naples, 1914); A. St. John-Brenon, "G. V.," ibid. (Jan. 1916); E. Istel, "The 'Othello' of V. and Shakespeare," *Musical Quarterly* (July 1916); E. Istel, "A Genetic Study of the Aïda Libretto," ibid. (Jan. 1917); P. Berl, *Die Opern V.s in ihrer Instrumentation* (diss., Univ. of Vienna, 1931); A. Maecklenburg, "V. and Manzoni," *Musical Quarterly* (April 1931); G. Menghini, *G. V. e il melodramma italiano* (Rimini, 1931); M. Mila, *Il melodramma di V.* (Bari, 1933); A. Parente, *Il problema della critica verdiana* (Turin, 1933); L. Unterholzner, *G. V.s Operntypus* (Hannover, 1933); R. Gallusser, *V.s Frauengestalten* (diss., Univ. of Zürich, 1936); G. Engler, *V.s Anschauung vom Wesen der Oper* (diss., Univ. of Breslau, 1938); J. Loschelder, *Das Todesproblem in V.s Opernschaffen* (Cologne, 1938); G. Roncaglia, *L'ascensione creatrice di G. V.* (Florence, 1940); G. Mule and G. Nataletti, V., *Studi e memorie* (Rome, 1941); M. Rinaldi, *V. critico* (Rome, 1951); C. Gatti, *Revisioni e rivalutazioni verdiane* (Turin, 1952); E. Cone, "The Stature of *Falstaff*: Technique and Content in V.'s Last Opera," *Center*, I (1954); F. Travis, *V.'s Orchestration* (Zürich, 1956); G. Roncaglia, *Galleria verdiana: Studi e figure* (Milan, 1959); M. Mila, *Il melodramma di V.* (Milan, 1960); W. Herrmann, Jr., *Religion in the Operas of G. V.* (diss., Columbia Univ., 1963); P. Pingagli, *Romanticismo di V.* (Florence, 1967); W. Dean, "V.'s *Otello*: A Shakespearian Masterpiece," *Shakespeare Survey*, XXI (1968); S. Hughes, *Famous V. Operas* (London, 1968); C. Osborne, *The Complete Operas of V.* (London, 1969); G. Baldini, *Abitare la battaglia: La storia di G. V.* (Milan, 1970); A. Porter, "The Making of Don Carlos," *Proceedings of the Royal Musical Association*, XCVIII (1971–72); W. Osthoff, "Die beiden Fassungen von V.s *Macbeth*," *Archiv für Musikwissenschaft*, XXIX (1972); J. Budden, "The Two *Traviatas*," *Proceedings of the Royal Musical Association*, XCIX (1972–73); idem, *The Operas of V.* (a valuable study; 3 vols., London, 1973–81); A. Geck, *"Aida," die Oper: Schriftenreiche über musikalische Bühnenwerke* (Berlin, 1973); D. Lawton, *Tonality and Drama in V.'s Early Operas* (diss., Univ. of Calif., Berkeley, 1973); V. Godefroy, *The Dramatic Genius of V.: Studies of Selected Operas* (2 vols., London, 1975 and 1977); D. Rosen, *The Genesis of V.'s Requiem* (diss., Univ. of Calif., Berkeley, 1976); F. Noske, *The Signifier and the Signified: Studies in the Operas of Mozart and V.* (The Hague, 1977); H. Busch, *V.'s Aida: The History of an Opera in Letters and Documents* (Minneapolis, 1978); W. Weaver and M. Chusid, eds., *The V. Companion* (N.Y., 1979); D. Kimbell, *V. in the Age of Italian Romanticism* (Cambridge, 1981); R. Parker, *Studies in Early V. (1832–1844): New Information and Perspectives on the Milanese Musical Milieu and the Operas from Oberto to Ernani* (diss., King's College, London, 1981); H. Gál, *G. V. und die Oper* (Frankfurt, 1982); A. Duault, *V., la musique et la drame* (Paris, 1986); S. Corse, *Opera and the Uses of Language: Mozart, V., and Britten* (London and Toronto, 1987); J. Hepokoski, *G. V.: Otello* (Cambridge, 1987); J.-F. Labie, *Le cas V.* (Paris, 1987); H. Busch, *V.'s Otello and Simon Boccanegra in Letters and Documents* (Oxford, 1988); M. Engelhardt, *Die Chöre in der frühen Opern G. V.s* (Tutzing, 1988); A. Sopart, *G. V.s "Simon Boccanegra" (1857 and 1881): Eine musikalisch-dramaturgische Analyse* (Laaber, 1988); G. Martin, *Aspects of V.* (London, 1989).

CORRESPONDENCE, ICONOGRAPHY: I. Pizzi, *Ricordi verdiani inediti* (Turin, 1901); T. Costantini, *Sei lettere di V. a Giovanni Bottesini* (relating to the production of *Aïda* in Cairo; Trieste, 1908); G. Cesari and A. Luzio, *G. V.: I copialettere pubblicati e illustrati* (Leipzig, 1913; Eng. tr. in an abr. ed. by C. Osborne as *Letters of G. V.*, 1971); G. Monaldi, *Saggio di iconografia verdiana* (Bergamo, 1913); J.-G. Prod'homme, "Unpublished Letters from V. to Camille Du Locle (1866–76)," *Musical Quarterly* (Jan. 1921); A. Martinelli, *G. V.: Raggi e Penombre. Le*

ultime lettere (Trieste, 1926); F. Werfel and P. Stefan, *Das Bildnis G. V.s* (Vienna, 1926; Eng. tr. in an enlarged ed. as *V., The Man in His Letters*, N.Y., 1942); G. Morazzoni, *Lettere inedite di G. V.* (Milan, 1929); A. Alberti, *V. intimo: Carteggio di G. V. con il conte Opprandino Arrivabene (1861–1866)* (Verona, 1931); L. Garibaldi, *G. V. nelle lettere di Emanuele Muzio ad Antonio Barezzi* (Milan, 1931); A. Luzio, *Carteggi verdiani* (Rome; vols. I–II, 1935; vols. III–IV, 1947); H. Schultz, *G. V., 1813–1901: Sein Leben in Bildern* (Leipzig, 1938); C. Gatti, *V. nelle immagini* (Milan, 1941); C. Graziani, *G. V.: Autobiografia dalle lettere* (censored ed., Milan, 1941; complete ed., 1951, under Graziani's real name, Aldo Oberdorfer); F. Walker, "Verdian Forgeries," *Music Review*, XIX (1958) and XX (1959); J. Klein, "Verdian Forgeries: A Summing-up," ibid., XX (1959); H. Kuehner, *G. V. in Selbstzeugnissen und Bilddokumenten* (Reinbek bei Hamburg, 1961); R. Petzoldt, *G. V., 1813–1901: Sein Leben in Bildern* (Leipzig, 1961).

Verdonck, Cornelis, Flemish composer; b. Turnhout, 1563; d. Antwerp, July 5, 1625. He commenced his training as a chorister in the court chapel of Philip II in Madrid; after studies with Séverin Cornet in Antwerp, he returned to Madrid, and sang at the royal chapel (1584–98); then pursued his career in his homeland. He was a fine composer of chansons and madrigals.

WORKS: SACRED VOCAL: *Ave gratia plena* for 4 Voices (Antwerp, 1584); *Magnificat* for 5 Voices (Antwerp, 1585); also 4 motets in contemporary collections. **CHANSONS:** *Poésies françaises de divers autheurs mises en musique par C. Verdonck,* (15) *à 5 parties avec une chanson à 10* (Antwerp, 1599); also 13 chansons in contemporary collections. **MADRIGALS:** *Madrigali novamente posti in luce* for 6 Voices (Antwerp, 1603); also 21 madrigals in contemporary collections.

BIBL.: M. Seiffert, "C. V.," *Tijdschrift van de Vereniging voor Nederlandse Muziekgeschiedenis*, V/3 (1897); P. Bergmans, *La Biographie du compositeur Corneille V.* (Brussels, 1919).

Vere (real name, **Wood de Vere), Clémentine Duchene de,** French soprano; b. Paris, Dec. 12, 1864; d. Mount Vernon, N.Y., Jan. 19, 1954. Her father was a Belgian nobleman; her mother, an English lady. Her musical education was completed under the instruction of Mme. Albertini-Baucardé in Florence, where she made her début at the age of 16 as Marguerite de Valois in *Les Huguenots*. On Feb. 2, 1896, she made her American debut at the Metropolitan Opera, N.Y., as Marguerite in Gounod's *Faust*; she remained on its roster until 1897; was again at the Metropolitan from 1898 to 1900; her other roles with it were Violetta, Gilda, and Lucia. In 1892 she married the conductor Romualdo Sapio; taught voice from 1914. Her voice was a brilliant high soprano; she excelled in coloratura.

Vered, Ilana, Israeli pianist; b. Tel Aviv, Dec. 6, 1939. Her mother was a concert pianist and her father was a violinist; she took piano lessons as a child with her mother; at 13, won an Israeli government grant to continue her studies at the Paris Cons.; subsequently took lessons with Rosina Lhévinne and Nadia Reisenberg at the Juilliard School of Music in N.Y. In 1969 she received a grant from the Martha Baird Rockefeller Foundation for a major tour of Europe; subsequently made regular tours there and in the U.S.

Vereen, Ben(jamin Augustus), black American entertainer; b. Miami, Oct. 10, 1946. He studied at the High School of Performing Arts in N.Y., the Dance Theater of Harlem, and the Pentacostal Theological Seminary. He began his career as a singer with the Brooklyn group Sensational Twilights; made his professional debut in 1965 in Langston Hughes's play *The Prodigal Son*; subsequently he was active mainly as a nightclub singer.

Veremans, Renaat, Belgian composer; b. Lierre, March 2, 1894; d. Antwerp, June 5, 1969. He studied at the Lemmens Inst. in Mechelen and at the Antwerp Cons. with Auguste De Boeck; was awarded the Premier Prix in organ and piano in 1914; from 1921 to 1944 he served as director of the Flemish

Opera in Antwerp; for 31 years, taught at the Antwerp Cons. In his music he follows the Romantic tradition of the Belgian-Flemish school of composition.

Works: 4 operas: *Beatrijs* (1928); *Anna-Marie* (Antwerp, Feb. 22, 1938); *Bietje* (1954); *Lanceloot en Sanderien* (Antwerp, Sept. 13, 1968); 2 operettas: *The Strange Adventure* and *The Mill of Sans Souci*; 2 oratorios: *The XIV Stations of the Cross* and *The 5 Joyful Mysteries*; *Groenendal Cantata*; 3 syms. (1959, 1961, 1968); Trumpet Concerto (1960); Concerto for Flute and Chamber Orch. (1962); Concerto for Oboe and Small Orch. (1964); Horn Concerto (1965); symphonic poems: *Morgendeschemer (Dawn)*; *Night and the Awakening of Day beside the River Nete*; *Sylvan Scenes*; chamber music; choruses; many songs.

Veress, Sándor, eminent Hungarian-born Swiss composer; b. Kolozsvár, Feb. 1, 1907. He studied piano with his mother; received instruction in piano from Bartók and in composition from Kodály at the Royal Academy of Music in Budapest (1923–27); obtained his teacher's diploma (1932); also took lessons with Lajtha at the Hungarian Ethnographical Museum (1929–33). He worked with Bartók on the folklore collection at the Academy of Sciences in Budapest (1937–40); subsequently taught at the Academy of Music in Budapest (1943–48). In 1949 he went to Switzerland, where he received an appointment as guest prof. on folk music at the Univ. of Bern; then taught at the Bern Cons. from 1950 to 1977; also was active as a guest lecturer in the U.S. and elsewhere; taught musicology at the Univ. of Bern (1968–77). In 1975 he became a naturalized Swiss citizen.

Works: STAGE: Children's opera: *Hangjegyek lázadása* (Revolt of the Musical Notes; 1931); ballets: *Csodafurulya* (The Miraculous Pipe; 1937; Rome, 1941); *Térszili Katicza* (Katica from Térszil; 1942–43; Stockholm, Feb. 16, 1949). **ORCH.:** *Divertimento* for Small Orch. (1935); *Partita* for Small Orch. (1936); Violin Concerto (1937–39; Zürich, Jan. 9, 1951); *Csürdöngölő* (Hungarian Barn Dance; 1938); 2 syms: No. 1 (1940); No. 2, *Sinfonia minneapolitana* (1952; Minneapolis, March 12, 1954); *4 danze transilvane* for String Orch. (1944–49); *Sirató ének* [Threnody] *in memoriam Béla Bartók* (1945); *Előjáték egy tragédiahoz* (Prelude to a Tragedy; 1947); *Drámai változatok* (Dramatic Variations; 1947); *Republica*, overture (1948); *Hommage à Paul Klee*, fantasia for 2 Pianos and String Orch. (1951; Bern, Jan. 22, 1952); Concerto for Piano, Strings, and Percussion (1952; Baden-Baden, Jan. 19, 1954); Sonata (Brussels, July 8, 1952); Concerto for String Quartet and Orch. (1960–61; Basel, Jan. 25, 1962); *Passacaglia concertante* for Oboe and Strings (Lucerne, Aug. 31, 1961); *Variations on a Theme by Zoltán Kodály* (1962); *Elegie* for Baritone, String Orch., and Harp (1964); *Expovare* for Flute, Oboe, and Strings (1964); *Musica concertante* for 12 Strings (1965–66); Clarinet Concerto (1981–82); *Orbis tonorum* for Chamber Orch. (1986); *Concerto Tilinko* for Flute and Orch. (1988–89); Concerto for 2 Trombones and Orch. (1989). **CHAMBER:** 2 string quartets (1931; 1936–37); Sonata for Solo Violin (1935); 2nd Sonata for Violin and Piano (1939); Trio for Violin, Viola, and Cello (1954); Trio for Piano, Violin, and Cello (1963); Sonata for Solo Cello (1967); Wind Quintet (1968); *Introduzione e Coda* for Clarinet, Violin, and Cello (1972); Trio for Baryton, Viola, and Cello (1985); *Stories and Fairy Tales* for 2 Percussionists (1987); piano pieces, including *Fingerlarks*, 88 pieces (1946); also various choral works; songs. **Writings:** With L. Lajtha, *Népdal, népzenegyűjés* (Folk Song, Folk Music Collecting; Budapest, 1936); *Béla Bartók, the Man and the Artist* (London, 1948); *La raccolta della musica popolare ungherese* (Rome, 1949). **Bibl.:** A. Traub, *S. V.: Festschrift zum 80. Geburtstag* (Berlin, 1986).

Veretti, Antonio, Italian composer; b. Verona, Feb. 20, 1900; d. Rome, July 13, 1978. He studied in Verona and with Mattioli and Alfano at the Liceo Musicale of Bologna, graduating in 1921. He founded his own Cons. Musicale della Gioventù Italiana in Rome, teaching there until 1943; was director of the Cons. G. Rossini in Pesaro (1950–52) and of the Cons. of Cagliari in Sardinia (1953–55); from 1956 to 1970 he was director of the L. Cherubini Cons. in Florence. His music follows the traditional lines of Italian modernism, but in some of his later works he experimented with serial techniques.

Works: 2 operas: *Il Medico volante* (1928) and *Il Favorito del re* (La Scala, Milan, March 17, 1932; rev. as the opera-ballet, *Burlesca*, Rome, Jan. 29, 1955); 2 ballets: *Il galante tiratore* (The Gallant Killer; San Remo, Feb. 11, 1933) and *Una favola di Andersen* (A Fable by Andersen; Venice, Sept. 15, 1934); choreographic musical mystery, *I sette peccati* (La Scala, April 24, 1956); 2 oratorios: *Il cantico dei cantici* (Bologna, 1922) and *Il Figliuol prodigo* (Rome, Nov. 21, 1942); *Sinfonia italiana* (Liège, Sept. 4, 1930); *Suite* for Orch. (1934); *Morte e deificazione di Dafni* for Voice and 11 Instruments (Venice Festival, Sept. 8, 1937); *Sinfonia epica* (1938); *Divertimento* for Harpsichord and 6 Instruments (1939); *Sinfonia sacra* for Male Voices and Orch. (1946; Rome, April 1947); Piano Concerto (Venice, Sept. 9, 1950); *4 poesie di Giorgio Vigolo* for Voice, and Orch. or Piano (1950; orch. version, Torino, Feb. 17, 1956); *Ouverture della campana* (RAI, Nov. 10, 1951); *Fantasie* for Clarinet, and Orch. or Piano (1959); Concertino for Flute, and Chamber Orch. or Piano (1959); *Duo strumentale* for Violin and Piano (1925); Cello Sonata (1926); Piano Trio (1927); Violin Sonata (1952); *Elegie in Friulano* for Voice, Violin, Clarinet, and Guitar (1963); music for films. **Bibl.:** N. Costarelli, "Musicisti del nostro tempo: A. V.," *Rassegna Musicale* (Jan.–March 1955).

Verevka, Grigori, Ukrainian composer; b. Bereznia, Chernigov district, Dec. 25, 1895; d. Kiev, Oct. 21, 1964. He was a boy chorister in Chernigov; then studied at the Kiev Inst. of Music and Drama; became engaged in choral conducting. He wrote a number of choruses which entered the general repertoire; made choral arrangements of nearly 100 revolutionary songs.

Vergnet, Edmond-Alphonse-Jean, French tenor; b. Montpellier, July 4, 1850; d. Nice, Feb. 25, 1904. He first played violin in the orch. of the Théâtre-Lyrique in Paris; then studied voice in Paris; made his debut at the Paris Opéra in 1874, continuing as a member there until 1893; also made guest appearances at La Scala in Milan, Covent Garden in London (1881–82), and in the U.S. (1885–86). Among the roles he created were Jean in Massenet's *Hérodiade* and Admeto in Catalani's *Dejanice*; his other roles were Faust, Radames, and Lohengrin.

Verheyden, Edward, Belgian composer; b. Antwerp, Oct. 8, 1878; d. there, April 10, 1959. He studied violin in Antwerp and Brussels; then turned to composition. He wrote the operas *Heibieke* (1908) and *De Geest* (1924); symphonic works; lieder and choruses.

Verhulst, Johannes (actually, **Josephus Hermanus**), Dutch conductor and composer; b. The Hague, March 19, 1816; d. there, Jan. 17, 1891. He studied in The Hague and Cologne; in 1838, went to Leipzig, where he became friendly with Schumann; was engaged as conductor of the Euterpe concerts (until 1842); then returned to The Hague. He was conductor of the renowned Diligentia concerts at The Hague from 1860 until 1886; also conducted in Amsterdam and Rotterdam. He wrote a Sym. (1841), 4 overtures, much choral music, 2 string quartets, piano pieces, and songs. **Bibl.:** J. van Riemsdijk, *J.J.H. V.* (Haarlem, 1886).

Vermeulen, Matthijs, remarkable Dutch composer and music critic; b. Helmond, Feb. 8, 1888; d. Laren, July 26, 1967. Principally self-taught, he traveled in 1905 to Amsterdam, where he received musical guidance from Daniël le Lange and Alphons Diepenbrock; in 1907 he began to write music criticism for Dutch and French publications, and continued his journalistic activities until 1956. In 1921 Vermeulen went to France; returned to the Netherlands in 1947, when he became music ed. of *De Groene Amsterdammer*. He entertained a strong belief in the mystical powers of music; in order to enhance the universality of melodic, rhythmic, and contrapuntal elements, he introduced in his compositions a unifying set of *cantus firmi* against a diversified network of interdependent melodies of an atonal character; it was not until the last years of his life that his works began to attract serious attention for their originality and purely musical qualities.

WORKS: ORCH.: 7 syms.: No. 1, *Symphonia Carminum* (1912–14; Arnhem, March 12, 1919; 1st professional perf., Amsterdam, May 5, 1964); No. 2, *Prélude à la nouvelle journée* (1919–20; first perf. as an identified work, Amsterdam, July 5, 1956; had won 5th prize at the Queen Elisabeth Composition Competition in Brussels in 1953, and was performed anonymously on Dec. 9); No. 3, *Thrène et Péan* (1921–22; Amsterdam, May 24, 1939); No. 4, *Les Victoires* (1940–41; Rotterdam, Sept. 30, 1949); No. 5, *Les Lendemains Chantants* (1941–45; Amsterdam, Oct. 12, 1949); No. 6, *Les Minutes heureuses* (1956–58; Utrecht, Nov. 25, 1959); No. 7, *Dithyrambes pour les temps à venir* (1963–65; Amsterdam, April 2, 1967); *Passacaille et Cortège* (1930; concert fragments from his music for the open-air play *The Flying Dutchman*); *Symphonic Prolog* (1930). **OTHER WORKS:** Songs: *The Soldier*, after Rupert Brooke (1916); *On ne passe pas* (1917); *Les Filles du roi d'Espagne* (1917); *La Veille* (1917; orch. 1929); *3 Salutations à Notre-Dame* (1942); *Le Balcon* (1943); *3 Chants d'amour* (1962); 2 cello sonatas (1918, 1938); String Trio (1924); Violin Sonata (1925); String Quartet (1960–61).

WRITINGS: *De twee muzieken* (The Two Musics; 2 vols., Leyden, 1918); "Klankbord" (Sound Board) and "De eene grondtoon" (The One Key Note) in *De vrije bladen* (Amsterdam, 1929 and 1932); *Het avontuur van den geest* (The Adventure of the Spirit; Amsterdam, 1947); *Princiepen der Europese Muziek* (Principles of European Music; Amsterdam, 1948); *De Muziek, Dat Wonder* (Music, A Miracle; The Hague, 1958).

BIBL.: W. Paap, "De Componist M. V.," *Mens en Melodie* (Nov. 1949); E. Vermeulen, "M. V.," *Sonorum Speculum*, 28 (1966); W. Paap, "In Memoriam M. V.," *Mens en Melodie* (Sept. 1967); R. de Leeuw, "M. V.," *Sonorum Speculum*, 52 (1973); J. Bernlef, " 'I've Never Felt the Need of a System,' " and O. Ketting, "Prelude as Postlude," *Key Notes*, 3 (1976); P. Rapoport, *Opus Est: Six Composers from Northern Europe* (London, 1978).

Verne (real name, **Wurm**), family of English pianists, all sisters. They adopted the name Verne in 1893. **Mathilde Verne** (b. Southampton, May 25, 1865; d. London, June 4, 1936) studied with her parents, and then became a pupil of Clara Schumann in Frankfurt; was very successful in England; from 1907 to 1936, gave concerts of chamber music in London; was a renowned teacher. **Alice Verne Bredt** (b. Southampton, Aug. 9, 1868; d. London, April 12, 1958) was best known as a piano teacher; she also composed pedagogical works. **Adela Verne** (b. Southampton, Feb. 27, 1877; d. London, Feb. 5, 1952) studied with her sisters, and later took lessons from Paderewski in Switzerland; returning to London, she developed a successful career, and became extremely popular as a concert player in England; also made tours in the U.S.

BIBL.: M. Verne, *Chords of Remembrance* (London, 1936).

Verneuil, Raoul de, Peruvian composer; b. Lima, April 9, 1899. He studied in Paris with André Bloch, and lived there for many years; returned to Lima in 1940, after a brief sojourn in N.Y. His works include *Danza Peruana* for Orch.; *Inca Legend* for Voice and 8 Instruments; *Rítmos del Sol* for 12-part Chorus; piano pieces.

Vernon, Ashley. See Manschinger, Kurt.

Verrall, John (Weedon), American composer and teacher; b. Britt, Iowa, June 17, 1908. He studied piano and composition with Donald Ferguson; then attended classes at the Royal College of Music in London with R.O. Morris, and took lessons with Kodály in Budapest. Returning to the U.S., he studied at the Minneapolis College of Music and Hamline Univ. (B.A., 1932); received further training at the Berkshire Music Center at Tanglewood, with Roy Harris, and with Fredrik Jacobi;

held a Guggenheim fellowship (1947). He held teaching positions at Hamline Univ. (1934–42), at Mount Holyoke College (1942–46), and at the Univ. of Washington in Seattle (1948–73).

WORKS: OPERAS: *The Cowherd and the Sky Maiden*, after a Chinese legend (1951; Seattle, Jan. 17, 1952); *The Wedding Knell*, after Hawthorne (Seattle, Dec. 5, 1952); *3 Blind Mice* (Seattle, May 22, 1955). **ORCH.:** 3 syms: No. 1 (1939; Minneapolis, Jan. 16, 1940); No. 2 (1948); No. 3 (1968); Violin Concerto (1946); *Symphony for Young Orchestras* (1948); *The Dark Night of St. John* for Chamber Orch. (1949); *Sinfonia festiva* for Band (1954); Piano Concerto (1960); Viola Concerto (1968); *Radiant Bridge* (1976); *Rhapsody* for Horn and Strings (1979). **CHAMBER:** 2 viola sonatas (1939, 1963); Piano Quintet (1953); 7 string quartets (1941, 1942, 1948, 1949, 1952, 1956, 1961); 2 serenades for Wind Quintet (1944, 1950); *Nocturne* for Bass Clarinet and Piano (1956); Septet for Winds (1966); Nonet for Wind Quintet and String Quartet (1966); Flute Sonata (1972); *Eusebius Remembered* for Horn and Piano (1976); *Invocation to Eos* for Horn and Piano (1983); Sonata for 2 Pianos (1984); also choruses; songs; carillon pieces; band arrangements.

WRITINGS: *Elements of Harmony* (n.p., 1937); with S. Moseley, *Form and Meaning in the Arts* (N.Y., 1958); *Fugue and Invention in Theory and Practice* (Palo Alto, Calif., 1966); *Basic Theory of Scales, Modes and Intervals* (Palo Alto, Calif., 1969).

BIBL.: J. Beale, "The Music of J. V.," *American Composers Alliance Bulletin*, VII/4 (1958).

Verrett, Shirley, noted black American mezzo-soprano, later soprano; b. New Orleans, May 31, 1931. Her father, a choirmaster at the Seventh-Day Adventist church in New Orleans, gave her rudimentary instruction in singing. Later she moved to California and took voice lessons with John Charles Thomas and Lotte Lehmann. In 1955 she won the Marian Anderson Award and a scholarship at the Juilliard School of Music in N.Y., where she became a student of Marion Székely-Freschl; while still a student, she appeared as soloist in Falla's *El amor brujo* under Stokowski, and made her operatic debut as Britten's Lucretia in Yellow Springs, Ohio (1957). In 1962 she scored a major success as Carmen at the Festival of Two Worlds at Spoleto, Italy. In 1963 she made a tour of the Soviet Union, and sang Carmen at the Bolshoi Theater in Moscow. In 1966 she made her debut at Milan's La Scala and at London's Covent Garden. On Sept. 21, 1968, she made her debut at the Metropolitan Opera in N.Y., again as Carmen. On Oct. 22, 1973, she undertook 2 parts, those of Dido and Cassandra, in *Les Troyens* of Berlioz, produced at the Metropolitan. She won distinction in mezzo-soprano roles, and later as a soprano; thus she sang the title role in Bellini's *Norma*, a soprano, and also the role of mezzo-soprano Adalgisa in the same opera. Her other roles included Tosca, Azucena, Amneris, and Dalila. She also showed her ability to cope with the difficult parts in modern operas, such as Bartók's *Bluebeard's Castle*. Her voice is of a remarkably flexible quality, encompassing lyric and dramatic parts with equal expressiveness and technical proficiency. Her concert repertory ranges from Schubert to Rorem, and also includes spirituals.

BIBL.: W. Sargeant, "Profiles: S. V.," *New Yorker* (April 14, 1975).

Verstovsky, Alexei (Nikolaievich), important Russian composer; b. on the family estate of Seliverstovo, Tambov district, March 1, 1799; d. Moscow, Nov. 17, 1862. He was taken as a child to Ufa; at the age of 17, was sent to St. Petersburg, where he entered the Inst. of Transport Engineers; took piano lessons with Johann Heinrich Miller, Daniel Steibelt, and John Field; studied violin with Ludwig Maurer and voice with Tarquini. He became a member of the flourishing literary and artistic milieu in St. Petersburg; among his friends was Pushkin. In 1823 he went to Moscow; in 1825 he was named inspector of its theater; then was director of all of its theaters (1842–60). Almost all of his compositions for the stage followed the French model, with long scenes of speech accompanied on the keyboard; his 1st effort was couplets for the vaudeville, *Les perroquets de la mère Philippe* (1819); he also composed popular songs and couplets for various other vaudevilles and stage pieces. He contributed a great deal to the progress of operatic art in Russia, but his music lacked distinction and inventive power; with the advent of Glinka and Dargomyzhsky on the Russian operatic scene, Verstovsky's productions receded into insignificance.

WORKS: OPERAS (all 1st perf. in Moscow): *Pan Twardowski* (June 5, 1828); *Vadim, ili Probuzhdeniye dvendtsati spyashchikh dev* (Vadim, or The Awakening of the Twelve Sleeping Maidens; Dec. 7, 1832); *Askoldova nogila* (Askold's Grave; Sept. 27, 1835); *Tosko po rodine* (Longing for the Homeland; Sept. 2, 1839); *Churova Dolina, ili Son nayavu* (Chur Valley, or The Waking Dream; Aug. 28, 1841); *Gromoboy* (Feb. 5, 1858); also incidental music, songs for dramas, couplets, romances for vaudevilles, choruses, solo songs, orch. music, and piano pieces.

BIBL.: B. Dobrohotov, *A.N. V.* (Moscow, 1949); G Abraham, "The Operas of A. V.," *19th Century Music* (April 1984).

Vesque von Püttlingen, Johann, Austrian composer; b. Opole, Poland, July 23, 1803; d. Vienna, Oct. 29, 1883. He studied law in Vienna, and became a councillor of state; at the same time he studied with Moscheles (piano) and Sechter (theory), and made his mark as a composer of operas, under the pseudonym J. Hoven. He also publ. a book on musical copyright, *Das musikalische Autorrecht* (Vienna, 1864).

WORKS: OPERAS (all 1st perf. in Vienna unless otherwise given): *Turandot* (Oct. 3, 1838); *Johanna d'Arc* (Dec. 30, 1840); *Liebeszauber* (1845); *Ein Abenteuer Carls des Zweiten* (Jan. 12, 1850); *Der lustige Rat* (Weimar, April 12, 1852); also orch. music, 2 masses, 3 string quartets, some 300 songs, and piano pieces.

BIBL.: E. Hanslick, "V. v.P.," *Musikalisches Skizzenbuch* (Berlin, 1888); H. Schultz, *J.V. v.P.* (Regensburg, 1930); H. Ibl, *Studien zu J.v. v.P.s Leben und Opernschaffen* (diss., Univ. of Vienna, 1950).

Vetter, Michael, German composer and performer; b. Obertsdorf, Allgäu, Sept. 18, 1943. He studied philosophy and theology (1964–69), then became known as a recorder player, specializing in ancient and contemporary works. He was associated with Stockhausen's circle, and performed in *Alphabet pour Liège* (1972). His notated compositions are almost exclusively graphic. His recordings of the 1980s include *Overtones, Tambura Preludes,* and *Pro-Vocationes,* all scored for voice and tambura; the voice uses a multiphonic technique similar to Buddhist chant, supported by the dense overtones of the tambura in an improvisational structure. He publ. a textbook, *Il flauto dolce e acerbo* (Celle, 1964–69).

WORKS: *Figurationen III* for Any Instrument (1965); *Orzismus* for Audience, Players, and Projections (1969); *Sonnenuntergang* for Electric Guitar, Electric Recorder, Trumpet, and Percussion (1971).

Vetter, Walther, distinguished German musicologist; b. Berlin, May 10, 1891; d. there, April 1, 1967. He studied at the Leipzig Cons.; subsequently took a course in musicology with Hermann Abert at the Univ. of Halle, where he received his Ph.D. in 1920 with the diss. *Die Arie bei Gluck;* he completed his Habilitation at the Univ. of Breslau with his *Das frühdeutsche Lied* in 1927 (publ. in Münster, 1928). He taught at the univs. of Halle, Hamburg, Breslau, and Greifswald before joining the Univ. of Poznań in 1941; from 1946 to 1958 he was a prof. at Humboldt Univ. in Berlin, and also served as director of its Inst. of Musicology. From 1948 to 1961 he was co-ed. of *Die Musikforschung;* from 1956 to 1966 he was ed. of the *Deutsches Jahrbuch für Musikwissenschaft.*

WRITINGS: *Der humanistische Bildungsgedanke in Musik und Musikwissenschaft* (Langensalza, 1928); *Franz Schubert* (Potsdam, 1934); *Antike Musik* (Munich, 1935); *J.S. Bach: Leben und Werk* (Leipzig, 1938); *Beethoven und die militärpolitischen Ereignisse seiner Zeit* (Poznan, 1943); *Der Kapellmeister Bach: Versuch einer Deutung Bachs auf Grund seines*

Wirkens als Kapellmeister in Köthen (Potsdam, 1950); *Der Klassiker Schubert* (2 vols., Leipzig, 1953); *Mythos—Melos—Musica: Ausgewählte Aufsätze zur Musikgeschichte* (a collection of articles; 2 vols., Leipzig, 1957 and 1961); *Christoph Willibald Gluck* (Leipzig, 1964).

BIBL.: *Musa—mens—musici: Im Gedenken an W. V.* (Leipzig, 1969).

Veyron-Lacroix, Robert, noted French pianist and harpsichordist; b. Paris, Dec. 13, 1922; d. there, April 2, 1991. He studied piano at the Paris Cons. with Yves Nat and Samuel-Rousseau. After a series of successful recitals as pianist and harpsichordist, he toured as accompanist to Jean-Pierre Rampal. He also was a noted teacher; conducted seminars at the Schola Cantorum in Paris (1956); then was appointed to the piano faculty at the Paris Cons. (1967). He publ. *Recherches de musique ancienne* (Paris, 1955).

Viadana (real name, **Grossi**), **Lodovico,** esteemed Italian composer and teacher; b. Viadana, near Parma, c.1560; d. Gualtieri, near Parma, May 2, 1627. He adopted the name Viadana when he entered the order of the Minor Observants; was maestro di cappella at Mantua Cathedral (c.1594–97). After a sojourn in Rome, he was maestro di cappella at the convent of S. Luca in Cremona in 1602; then held that post at Concordia Cathedral (1608–9) and at Fano Cathedral (1610–12); served as diffinitor of his order for Bologna province (1614–17); after a sojourn in Busseto, he settled in the convent of S. Andrea in Gualtieri. He was formerly accredited with the invention of the basso continuo (thoroughbass), but Peri's *Euridice* (publ. 1600) has a figured bass in certain numbers, as does Banchieri's *Concerti ecclesiastici* (publ. 1595), whereas Viadana's *Cento concerti con il basso continuo* did not appear until 1602 (Venice). However, he was the 1st to write church concertos with so few parts that the organ continuo was employed as a necessary harmonic support. A prolific composer, he publ. numerous masses, Psalms, Magnificats, Lamentations, motets, etc. C. Gallico brought out *Opere di Lodovico Viadana* in Monumenti Musicali Mantovani (Kassel, 1964–).

BIBL.: A. Parazzi, *Della vita e delle opere musicali di L. Grossi-V. inventore del basso continuo nel secolo XVI* (Milan, 1877); F. Haberl, "L. Grossi da V.: Eine bio-bibliographische Studie," *Kirchenmusikalisches Jahrbuch,* IV (1889); F. Pratella, "V. e la sinfonia," *Il Pensiero Musicale* (Sept.–Nov. 1922); C. Gallico, "L'arte dei *Cento concerti ecclesiastici* di L. V.," *Quaderni della Rassegna Musicale,* III (1965).

Vianesi, Auguste-Charles-Léonard-François, Italian-born French conductor; b. Livorno, Nov. 2, 1837; d. N.Y., Nov. 4, 1908. After studying in Italy, he went to Paris in 1857; then became conductor at Drury Lane in London; in 1858–59 he was a conductor in N.Y.; after appearances in Moscow and St. Petersburg, he conducted the Italian, French, and German repertories at London's Covent Garden (1870–80); in 1887, became principal conductor at the Grand Opéra in Paris. He conducted the performance of *Faust* at the opening night of the Metropolitan Opera House in N.Y. (Oct. 22, 1883), and was on its staff throughout its first season; also conducted during the season of 1891–92; then remained in N.Y. as a vocal teacher.

Vianna (Viana), Fructuoso (Frutuoso de Lima), Brazilian pianist, teacher, and composer; b. Itajubá, Oct. 6, 1896; d. Rio de Janeiro, April 22, 1976. He studied music with his father, a municipal judge, who composed polkas and waltzes. In 1917 he entered the Rio de Janeiro Cons., and studied piano with Oswald and harmony with Gouveia and França; in 1923 he went to Europe, where he pursued piano training with Hanschild in Berlin, De Greef in Brussels, and Selva in Paris, where he also studied the Dalcroze method of eurhythmics. Returning to Brazil, he was active as a teacher; was prof. of piano at the Belo Horizonte Cons. (1929–30) and the São Paulo Cons. (1930–38), and prof. of choral singing at the National Technical School in Rio de Janeiro (from 1942); also was prof. of piano at Bennet College. His works are based on native Brazilian melorhythms pleasurably seasoned with acrid dissonances, achieving a certain *trompe-l'oreille* euphony. His musical output consists mainly of piano pieces and songs of such nature; among them are numerous "valsas" (European waltzes in a Brazilian dressing), "toadas" (melodious romances), and "tanguinhos" (little tangos *à la brésilienne*). They are all perfumed with impressionistic overtones.

Vianna da Motta, José, esteemed Portuguese pianist and pedagogue; b. Isle St. Thomas, Portuguese Africa, April 22, 1868; d. Lisbon, May 31, 1948. His family returned to Lisbon when he was a year old; he studied with local teachers; gave his 1st concert at the age of 13; then studied piano in Berlin with X. Scharwenka and composition with P. Scharwenka. In 1885 he went to Weimar, where he became a pupil of Liszt; also took lessons with Hans von Bülow in Frankfurt (1887). He then undertook a series of concert tours throughout Europe (1887–88), the U.S. (1892–93; 1899), and South America (1902). He was in Berlin until 1915; then became director of the Geneva Cons. In 1919 he was appointed director of the Lisbon Cons., retiring in 1938. At the height of his career, he was greatly esteemed as a fine interpreter of Bach and Beethoven. He was also the author of many articles in German, French, and Portuguese; wrote *Studien bei Bülow* (1896); *Betrachtungen über Franz Liszt* (1898); *Die Entwicklung des Klavierkonzerts* (as a program book to Busoni's concerts); essays on Alkan; critical articles in the *Kunstwart, Klavierlehrer, Bayreuther Blätter*, etc. He was a prolific composer; among his works are *Die Lusiaden* for Orch. and Chorus; Sym.; String Quartet; many piano pieces, in some of which (e.g., the 5 *Portuguese Rhapsodies* and the Portuguese dance *Vito*) he employs folk themes with striking effect. In 1951 the Vianna da Motta International Piano Competition was founded in Lisbon in his memory.

BIBL.: F. Lopes Graça, *V. d.M.: Subsidios para una biographia* (Lisbon, 1949).

Viardot-García, (Michelle Fedinande) Pauline, celebrated French mezzo-soprano and pedagogue of Spanish descent, daughter of **Manuel del Popolo García** and sister of **Maria Malibran;** b. Paris, July 18, 1821; d. there, May 18, 1910. She commenced vocal training with her mother; then received lessons in piano from Meysenberg and Liszt and in composition from Reicha. Her concert debut was in Brussels in 1837; her stage debut was in London, May 9, 1839, as Desdemona in Rossini's *Otello;* she was then engaged by Louis Viardot, director of the Théâter-Italien in Paris, where she scored a notable success in her debut as Desdemona on Oct. 8, 1839; sang there until her marriage to Viardot in 1840; he then accompanied her on long tours throughout Europe. In 1843 she made her 1st appearances in Russia, where she won distinction singing in both Italian and Russian; in subsequent years she championed the cause of Russian music. She created the role of Fidès in Meyerbeer's *Le Prophète* at the Paris Opéra in 1849, and that of Sapho in Gounod's opera in 1851; after another succession of tours, she took the role of Orphée in Berlioz's revival of Gluck's opera at the Théâtre-Lyrique in Paris (1859), singing the part for 150 nights to crowded houses. She retired in 1863. Her *École classique de chant* was publ. in Paris in 1861. In 1871 she settled in Paris, and devoted herself to teaching and composing. Through her efforts, the music of Gounod, Massenet, and Fauré was given wide hearing. She was one of the great dramatic singers of her era, excelling particularly in the works of Gluck, Meyerbeer, and Halévy. Among her compositions are some operettas and numerous songs; she also prepared vocal transcriptions of some of Chopin's mazurkas. Two of her children were musicians: **Louise (Pauline Marie) Héritte** (b. Paris, Dec. 14, 1841; d. Heidelberg, Jan. 17, 1918) was a contralto, teacher, and composer; devoted herself mainly to teaching in St. Petersburg, Frankfurt am Main, Berlin, and Heidelberg; publ. *Memories and Adventures* (London, 1913); composed a comic opera, *Lindoro* (Weimar, 1879), a cantata, *Das Bacchusfest* (Stockholm, 1880), a String Quartet, and many songs. **Paul (Louis Joachim)** (b.

Courtavenel, July 20, 1857; d. Algiers, Dec. 11, 1941) was a violinist, conductor, and composer; studied with Léonard; conducted at the Paris Opéra; wrote the books *Histoire de la musique* (Paris, 1905), *Rapport officiel (mission artistique de 1907) sur la musique en Scandinavie* (Paris, 1908), and *Souvenirs d'un artiste* (Paris, 1910); composed 2 violin sonatas and a Piano Trio.

BIBL.: La Mara, *P. V.-G.* (Leipzig, 1882); L. Torrigi, *P. V.-G.: Sa biographie, ses compositions, son enseignement* (Geneva, 1901); C. Kaminski, *Lettres à Mlle. V. d'Ivan Tourgéneff* (Paris, 1907); L. Héritte-Viardot, *Memories and Adventures* (London, 1913; tr. from original German MS; also in French, Paris, 1923); "P. V.-G. to J. Rietz. Letters of Friendship," *Musical Quarterly* (July 1915–Jan. 1916); T. Marix-Spite, "Gounod and His First Interpreter, P. V.," *Musical Quarterly* (April, July 1945); A. Rachmanowa (pseud.), *Die Liebe eines Lebens: Iwan Turgenjew und P. V.* (Frauenfeld, 1952); A. FitzLyon, *The Price of Genius: A Life of P. V.* (London, 1964).

Vicentino, Nicola, noted Italian music theorist and composer; b. Vicenza, 1511; d. Rome, 1575 or 1576. He was a pupil of Willaert in Venice; then became maestro and music master to Cardinal Ippolito d'Este in Ferrara and in Rome. In 1563–64 he was maestro di cappella at Vicenza Cathedral; by 1570 he was in Milan as rector of St. Thomas; he died during the plague of 1575–76. His book of madrigals for 5 voices (Venice, 1546), an attempt to revive the chromatic and enharmonic genera of the Greeks, led to an academic controversy with the learned Portuguese musician Lusitano; defeated, Vicentino publ. a theoretical treatise, *L'antica musica ridotta alla moderna prattica* (Rome, 1555; 2nd ed., 1557), which contains a description of his invention, an instrument called the archicembalo (having 6 keyboards, with separate strings and keys for distinguishing the ancient genera-diatonic, chromatic, and enharmonic). It was followed by his treatise *Descrizione dell'arciorgano* (Venice, 1561; annotated Eng. tr. by H. Kaufmann, *Journal of Music Theory*, V, 1961). He also invented and described (1561) an "archiorgano." In chromatic composition he was followed by Cipriano de Rore and Gesualdo. His work paved the way for the monodic style, and the eventual disuse of the church modes. H. Kaufmann brought out the modern ed. *Nicola Vicentino: Opera omnia* in Corpus Mensurabilis Musicae, XXVI (1963).

WORKS: *Madrigali* for 5 Voices, *libro primo* (Venice, 1546); *Moteta* for 5 Voices, *liber quartus* (Milan, 1571); *Madrigali* for 5 Voices, *libro quinto* (Milan, 1572); also pieces in contemporary collections.

BIBL.: H. Zenck, "N. V.s 'L'antica musica' (1555)," *Theodor Kroyer: Festschrift zum sechzigsten Geburtstage* (Regensburg, 1933); H. Kaufmann, "The Motets of N. V.," *Musica Disciplina*, XV (1961); idem, "V. and the Greek Genera," *Journal of the American Musicological Society*," XVI (1963).

Vickers, Jon(athan Stewart), eminent Canadian tenor; b. Prince Albert, Saskatchewan, Oct. 29, 1926. He sang in church choirs as a boy; engaged in a mercantile career to earn a living, and served as a manager in Canadian Woolworth stores; then was employed as a purchasing agent for the Hudson's Bay Co., and moved to Winnipeg. He won a scholarship at the Royal Cons. of Music of Toronto, where he studied voice with George Lambert; made his operatic debut in 1952 at the Toronto Opera Festival as the Duke in *Rigoletto*. In 1957 he sang Riccardo at Covent Garden in London; in 1958 he appeared as Siegmund in *Die Walküre* at the Bayreuth Festival; in 1959 he sang at the Vienna State Opera; on Jan. 17, 1960, he made his debut at the Metropolitan Opera in N.Y. as Canio in *Pagliacci*. He is particularly renowned as the Heldentenor in Wagner's operas. In 1969 he was made a Companion of Honour of the Order of Canada.

Victoria, Tomás Luis de, great Spanish organist and composer; b. Avila, 1548; d. Madrid, Aug. 20, 1611. He was a choirboy at Avila Cathedral. In 1565 he went to Rome, and to prepare himself for the priesthood entered the Jesuit Collegium Germanicum; his teacher may have been Palestrina, who from 1566 to 1571 was music master at the Roman Seminary, at this time amalgamated with the Collegium Germanicum. Victoria was about the same age as Palestrina's 2 sons, Rodolfo and Angelo, who were students at the Roman Seminary; the Italian master is known to have befriended his young Spanish colleague, and when Palestrina left the Seminary in 1571, it was Victoria who succeeded him as maestro there. In 1569 Victoria had left the Collegium Germanicum to become singer and organist in the Church of Sta. Maria di Montserrato, posts he held until 1564; from this time on he also officiated frequently at musical ceremonies in the Church of S. Giaccomo degli Spagnuoli. He taught music at the Collegium Germanicum from 1571, becoming its maestro di cappella in 1573; it moved to the Palazzo di S. Apollinaire in 1574 and to the adjoining church in 1576, where he remained as maestro di cappella until 1577. In Aug. 1575 he was ordained a priest; in Jan. of that year he had received a benefice at León from the Pope, and in 1579 he was granted another benefice at Zamora, neither requiring residence. In 1577 he joined the Congregazione dei Preti dell'Oratorio; served as chaplain at the Church of S. Girolamo della Carità from 1578 until 1585; this was the church where St. Philip Neri held his famous religious meetings, which led to the founding of the Congregation of the Oratory in 1575. Though Victoria was not a member of the Oratory, he must have taken some part in its important musical activities, living as he did for 5 years under the same roof with its founder (St. Philip left S. Girolamo in 1583); he is known to have been on terms of the closest friendship with Juvenal Ancina, a priest of the Oratory who wrote texts for many of the "Laudi spirituali" sung at the meetings of the Congregation. He served as chaplain to the King's sister, the Dowager Empress Maria, at the Monasterio de las Descalzas in Madrid from at least 1587 until her death in 1603; also was maestro of its convent choir until 1604, and then was its organist until his death. His last work, a Requiem Mass for the Empress Maria, regarded as his masterpiece, was publ. in 1605.

Beginning with a vol. of motets in 1572, dedicated to his chief patron, Cardinal Otto Truchsess, Bishop of Augsburg, most of Victoria's works were printed in Italy, in sumptuous eds., showing that he had the backing of wealthy patrons. A vol. of masses, Magnificats, motets, and other church music publ. at Madrid in 1600 is of special interest because it makes provision for an organ accompaniment.

A man of deep religious sentiment, Victoria expresses in his music all the ardor and exaltation of Spanish mysticism. He is generally regarded as a leading representative of the Roman School, but it should be remembered that, before the appearance of Palestrina, this school was already profoundly marked by Hispanic influences through the work of Morales, Guerrero, Escobedo, and other Spanish composers resident in Rome. Thus Victoria inherited at least as much from his own countrymen as from Palestrina, and in its dramatic intensity, its rhythmic variety, its tragic grandeur and spiritual fervor, his music is thoroughly personal and thoroughly Spanish.

WORKS (all publ. in Rome unless otherwise given): (33) *Motecta* for 4 to 6 and 8 Voices (Venice, 1572); *Liber primus: qui missas, psalmos, Magnificat . . . aliaque complectitur* for 4 to 6 and 8 Voices (Venice, 1576); *Cantica beatae virginis vulgo Magnificat, una cum 4 antiphonis beatae virginis per annum* for 4 to 5 and 8 Voices (1581); (32) *Hymni totius anni secundum sanctae romanae ecclesiae consuetudinem* for 4 Voices, *una cum 4 psalmis, pro praecipuis festivitatibus* for 8 Voices (1581; 2nd ed., 1600); (9) *Missarum libri duo* for 4 to 6 Voices (1583); (53) *Motecta* for 4 to 6, 8, and 12 Voices (1583; 2nd ed., 1589; 3rd ed., rev. 1603); (37) *Motecta festorum totius anni cum communi sanctorum* for 4 to 6 and 8 Voices (1585); (37) *Officium Hebdomadae Sanctae* for 3 to 6 Voices (1585); (7) *Missae, una cum antiphonis Asperrges, et Vidi aquam totius anni: liber secundus* for 4 to 6 and 8 Voices (1592); (32) *Missae, Magnificat, motecta, psalmi et alia quam plurima* for 3 to 4, 8 to 9, and 12 Voices (Madrid, 1600); *Officium defunctorum: in obitu et obsequiis sacrae imperatricis*

for 6 Voices (Madrid, 1605). See F. Pedrell, ed., *Tomás Luis de Victoria: Opera omnia* (8 vols., Leipzig, 1902–13) and H. Anglès, ed., *Tomás Luis de Victoria: Opera omnia, Monumentos de la Música Española*, XXV, XXVI, XXX, and XXXI (1965–68).

BIBL.: F. Haberl, "T.L. d.V.: Eine bio-bibliographische Studie," *Kirchenmusikalisches Jahrbuch*, XI (1896); H. Collet, V. (Paris, 1914); F. Pedrell, *T.L. d.V. Abulense* (Valencia, 1918); W. Hirschl, *The Styles of V. and Palestrina: A Comparative Study, with Special Reference to Dissonance Treatment* (diss., Univ. of Calif., Berkeley, 1933); E. Young, *The Contrapuntal Practices of V.* (diss., Univ. of Rochester, N.Y., 1942); H. von May, *Die Kompositions-Technik T.L. d.V.s* (Bern, 1943); N. Saxton, *The Masses of V.* (diss., Westminster Choir College, Princeton, N.J., 1951); R. Stevenson, *Spanish Cathedral Music in the Golden Age* (Berkeley and Los Angeles, 1961); T. Rive, *An Investigation into Harmonic and Cadential Procedures in the Works of T.L. d.V., 1548–1611* (diss., Univ. of Auckland, 1963); R. Stevenson, "Estudio biográfico y estilístico de T.L. d.V.," *Revista Musical Chilena*, No. 20 (1966); J. Kriewald, *The Contrapuntal and Harmonic Style of T.L. d.V.* (diss., Univ. of Wisconsin, 1968); J. Soler, V. (Barcelona, 1983).

Victory, Gerard (real name, **Alan Loraine**), Irish composer; b. Dublin, Dec. 24, 1921. He studied in Dublin at Univ. College (arts degree) and at the Univ. (B.Mus.); then was active with RTE (Irish Radio and Television) from 1948, serving as its director of music from 1967 to 1982. His compositions are imbued with the broad pentatonic melos of Irish folk music; but in some of his instrumental works of a later period he began to apply serial structures.

WORKS: STAGE: OPERAS: *An fear a phós balbhán* (Dublin, April 6, 1953); *Iomrall Aithne* (1956); *The Music Hath Mischief* (1964; Dublin, Dec. 2, 1968); *Chatterton* (1968–70); *Eloise and Abelard* (1972). **OPERETTAS:** *Nita* (1944); *Once upon a Moon* (1949). **BALLET:** *The Enchanted Garden* (1950). **ORCH.:** 2 piano concertos (1954, 1972); *The Midnight Court* (1959); 2 syms.: No. 1, *Short Symphony* (1961); No. 2, *Il Ricorso* (1977); *5 Mantras* (1963); *Homage to Petrarch* for String Orch. (1969); *4 Tableaux* (1969); *Cyrano de Bergerac*, overture (1970); *Miroirs* for Chamber Orch. (1970); Concerto for Harp and Chamber Orch. (1971); *Jonathan Swift*, symphonic portrait (1971); *Tetragon* for Oboe and Orch. (1971); *Capriccio* for Violin and Orch. (1975); *Barocco Suite* (1978); *9 Variations on the Cravate* (1978); Cello Concerto (1978); *3 Irish Pictures* (1979–80); *6 Epiphanies on the Author*, in memory of Joyce (Dublin, Feb. 5, 1982). **CHAMBER:** Wind Quintet (1957); String Quartet (1963); *Rodomontade* for Woodwind Quintet (1964); *Sémantiques* for Flute and Piano (1967); Piano Quintet (1971). **VOCAL:** *The River of Heaven*, cantata for Choir and Orch. (1965); *Kriegslieder* for Tenor, Choir, Trumpet, and Percussion (1966); *Voyelles* for Soprano, Flute, Percussion, and String Orch. (1966); *The Passionate Pilgrim*, song cycle (1969); *4 Idylls from Theocritus* for 4 Voices (1971).

Vidal, Louis-Antoine, French writer on music; b. Rouen, July 10, 1820; d. Paris, Jan. 7, 1891. He studied cello with Franchomme; made a specialty of research on string instruments; publ. a valuable survey, *Les Instruments à archet, les faiseurs, les joueurs d'instruments, leur histoire sur le continent européen, suivie d'un catalogue général de la musique de chambre* (3 vols., Paris, 1876–78); sections of this work were publ. separately as *Les Vieilles Corporations de Paris* (1878) and *La Lutherie et les luthiers* (1889).

Vidal, Paul (Antonin), noted French conductor, pedagogue, and composer; b. Toulouse, June 16, 1863; d. Paris, April 9, 1931. He studied at the Paris Cons., and in 1883 won the Prix de Rome with his cantata *Le Gladiateur*; in 1889 he joined the staff of the Paris Opéra as assistant choral director; later became chief conductor there (1906). He taught elementary courses at the Paris Cons. from 1894 until 1909, when he was appointed a prof. of composition. He was music director of the Opéra-Comique from 1914 to 1919. His brother, **Joseph Bernard Vidal** (b. Toulouse, Nov. 15, 1859; d. Paris, Dec.

18, 1924), was a conductor and composer; made a name for himself as a composer of operettas.

WORKS: STAGE: *Eros*, fantaisie lyrique (Paris, April 22, 1892); *L'Amour dans les enfers* (1892); *Guernica*, drame lyrique (Paris, June 7, 1895); *La Burgonde*, opera (Paris, Dec. 23, 1898); *Ramsès*, drame (Paris, June 27, 1900). **BALLETS:** *La Maladetta* (Paris, Feb. 24, 1893); *Fête russe* (Paris, Oct. 24, 1893); *L'Impératrice* (1903); *Zino-Zina* (1908); *Ballet de Terpsichore* (1909); also pantomimes, incidental music to plays, a few orch. pieces, choral works, chamber music, songs, and piano pieces.

BIBL.: A. Hoérée, "Nécrologie: Hommage à P. V.," *Revue Musicale* XII (1931).

Viderø, Finn, noted Danish organist, pedagogue, and composer; b. Fuglebjerg, Aug. 15, 1906; d. Copenhagen, March 13, 1987. He went to Copenhagen and studied at the Cons. (graduated, 1926), then pursued musicological training at the Univ. (M.A., 1929); was active as a church organist there, holding appointments at the German-French Reformed (1928), Jaegersborg (1940), Trinitas (1947), and St. Andreas (1971) churches; also toured as a recitalist. He taught music theory (1935–45) and organ and harpsichord (1949–74) at the Univ. of Copenhagen; was a visiting prof. at Yale Univ. (1959–60) and North Texas State Univ. (1967–68); also gave master classes. He wrote valuable articles on 16th- and 17th-century performing practice and ed. vols. of organ music, hymn tunes, choral pieces, and folk songs; also publ. *Orgelskole* (with O. Ring; 1933; 2nd ed., 1963). He composed choral works, organ music, piano pieces, and songs.

Vidu, Ion, Rumanian choral conductor and composer; b. Mînerău, Dec. 14, 1863; d. Lugoj, Feb. 7, 1931. He studied in Iaşi; became a choral conductor in Lugoj. He wrote a great number of choruses in a distinct native style, but harmonized his melodies according to German models; many of his arrangements have become repertoire pieces in Rumania.

BIBL.: V. Cosma, *Un maestru al muzicii corale: I. V.* (Bucharest, 1965).

Vierdanck, Johann, German organist and composer; b. c.1605; d. (buried) Stralsund, April 1, 1646. He was a chorister at the Dresden Hofkapelle, where he received training in composition, violin, and cornett; was sent to Vienna in 1628 for further study; was organist at the Marienkirche in Stralsund (1635–46). Among his works are *Erster Theil geistlicher Concerten* for 2 to 4 Voices and Basso Continuo (Greifswald, 1641) and *Erster Theil newer Pavanen Gagliarden, Balletten und Correnten* for 2 Violins and Basso Continuo (Greifswald, 1637).

BIBL.: G. Weiss, *J. V. (ca. 1605–1646): Sein Leben und sein Werk* (diss., Univ. of Marburg, 1956).

Vierk, Lois V, American composer; b. Hammond, Ind., Aug. 4, 1951. (The middle V is without punctuation; it is derived from Von Vierek, the old version of her family name, traditionally abbreviated without a period.) She studied composition privately with Druckman and Leonard Stein and at the Calif. Inst. of the Arts with Mel Powell and Subotnick (M.F.A., 1978); also studied gagaku with Suenobu Togi in Los Angeles (1971–78), and ryuteki (a transverse flute) in Tokyo with Sukeyasu Shiba (1982–84). She produced radio programs of world music for KPFK-FM in Los Angeles; collaborated with choreographer Anita Feldman to create a unified approach to tap dance and sound. In 1989 she formed LVV, an ensemble devoted to the performance of her music, which was featured on the "Lois V Vierk Special" on WNYC-FM in N.Y. Her minimalistic music is often microtonal and monochromatic, involving numerous similar instruments live or on tape; they typically reach an intense, gradual climax consisting of sensually overlapping textures. Her most frequently played work, *Go Guitars* for 5 Electric Guitars (1981), makes use in its title of the Japanese character for "5," transcribed as "go." Other works include *Dark Bourn* for 4 Bassoons and 4 Cellos (1985), *Manhattan Cascade* for 4 Accordions (1985), and *Hexie Mountain Torrent*

for Flute, Clarinet, Bassoon, Saxophones, Synthesizer, and Percussion (1987).

Vierling, Georg, German organist and composer; b. Frankenthal, Bavaria, Sept. 5, 1820; d. Wiesbaden, May 1, 1901. He was a pupil of his father, the organist **Jacob Vierling** (1796–1867); then studied composition with A.B. Marx in Berlin. He occupied various posts as an organist and choral conductor in the German provinces; settled in Berlin, where he founded and conducted the Bach-Verein. His works include the secular cantatas *Der Raub der Sabinerinne, Alarichs Tod,* and *Constantin;* the choral works (with Orch.) *Hero und Leander* and *Zur Weinlese;* a Sym.; several overtures (*Maria Stuart, Die Hexe, Im Frühling,* etc.); *Capriccio* for Piano and Orch.; *Phantasiestück* for Cello and Piano; 2 string quartets; Piano Trio; a number of piano pieces (*Valse-Caprice,* 2 impromptus, etc.); songs.

Vierling, Johann Gottfried, German organist and composer; b. Metzels, near Meiningen, Jan. 25, 1750; d. Schmalkalden, Nov. 22, 1813. His teachers included Kirnberger in Berlin, whom he succeeded in Schmalkalden in 1773. He publ. *Versuch einer Anleitung zum Präludieren für Ungeübtere mit Beispielen* (Leipzig, 1794) and *Allgemeiner fasslicher Unterricht im Generalbass mit Rücksicht auf den jetzt herrschenden Geschmack in der Composition durch treffende Beispiele erläutert* (Leipzig, 1805–7). His compositions include about 160 cantatas, some lieder, 2 syms., some chamber music, and many organ pieces.

BIBL.: K. Paulke, "J.G. V. 1750–1813," *Archiv für Musikwissenschaft,* IV (1922).

Vierne, Louis, eminent French organist, pedagogue, and composer; b. Poitiers, Oct. 8, 1870; d. (while playing his 1,750th recital at Notre-Dame) Paris, June 2, 1937. He was born blind but gained limited sight through an operation in 1877. He showed musical talent at an early age, and studied at the Institution Nationale des Jeunes Aveugles in Paris (1881–88); received organ lessons from Franck, then was a pupil of Widor at the Paris Cons. (1890–93), winning a premier prix in organ (1894). In 1892 he became Widor's assistant at St.-Sulpice, and in 1900 was appointed organist at Notre-Dame, where he remained until his death. He taught organ at the Paris Cons. (1894–1911) and at the Schola Cantorum (from 1911); among his pupils were Nadia Boulanger and Marcel Dupré. In 1927 he made a 4-month North American concert tour. His 6 organ syms. are principal works of the genre.

WORKS: ORCH.: Sym. (1907–8; Paris, Jan. 26, 1919); *Les djinns,* symphonic poem (1919); *Marche triomphale pour le centenaire de Napoléon* for Brass, Timpani, and Organ (1921); *Poème* for Piano and Orch. (1926); *Symphonic Piece* for Organ and Orch. (1926; arranged from the 1st 3 organ syms.). **CHAMBER:** String Quartet (n.d.); Sonata for Violin and Piano (1906); Sonata for Cello and Piano (1910); Piano Quintet (1917); *Soirs étrangers* for Cello and Piano (1928). **VOCAL:** *Messe solonnelle* for 4 Voices and 2 Organs (1900); *Praxinoé,* symphonic legend for Soloists, Chorus, and Orch. (1903–6); *Psyché* for Voice and Orch. (1914); *Les Angélus* for Voice and Organ or Orch. (1930); *Ballade du désespéré* for Tenor and Piano or Orch. (1931); songs. **ORGAN:** 6 syms. (1898–99; 1902–3; 1911; 1914; 1923–24; 1930); *Allegretto* (1894); *Messe basse* (1912); 24 *pièces en style libre* (1913–14); *Pièces de fantaisie* (4 books, 1926–27); *Triptyche* (1929–31); *Messe basse pour les défunts* (1934); also several piano pieces.

BIBL.: *In Memoriam L. V.* (Paris, 1939); B. Gavoty, *L. V., La Vie et l'œuvre* (Paris, 1943); S. Cantrell, "L. V.: His Life and Works" and "V.'s Six Symphonies: Textual Corrections," *American Organist* (Nov. 1980); I. Simrock, "L. V. and the 24 Pièces de Fantaisie,'" *Musical Times* (Aug. 1989).

Vieru, Anatol, distinguished Rumanian composer and musicologist; b. Iaşi, June 8, 1926. He studied harmony with Paul Constantinescu, orchestration with Theodor Rogalski, composition with Leon Klepper, and conducting with Constantin Silvestri at the Bucharest Cons. (1946–51); continued his composition studies with Aram Khachaturian at the Moscow Cons. (1951–54); received his doctorate in musicology from the Cluj Cons. (1978). He was a conductor at the Bucharest National Theater (1947–50); was ed. of the journal *Muzica* (1950–51); then taught at the Bucharest Cons. (from 1955); also lectured abroad. He wrote various articles on music; publ. the study *Cartea modurilor* (The Book of Modes; Bucharest, 1980). He was awarded numerous prizes, including the State Prize (1949), the Georges Enesco Prize of the Rumanian Academy (1967), prizes of the Union of Composers and Musicologists (1975, 1977, 1979), and the Herder Prize (1986). From his earliest years he composed music in a relatively advanced idiom, without losing contact with the characteristic melo-rhythmic patterns of Rumanian folk songs. Interesting in this respect is his oratorio *Miorita* (1957), after a Rumanian folk tale, in which he applies serial procedures to folklike materials. His Concerto for Cello and Orch. (1962), written in an original manner combining neo-Baroque and impressionistic traits, brought him international attention when it received 1st prize in a 1962 Geneva competition.

WORKS: OPERAS: *Iona* (Jonah; 1972–76; Bucharest, Oct. 31, 1976); *Praznicul Calicilor* (The Feast of the Cadgers; 1978–81); *Telegrame, Temã şi Variatiuni* (Telegrams, Theme and Variations; 1982–83; Bucharest, Nov. 8, 1983). **ORCH.:** 5 syms.: No. 1, *Ode to Silence* (1967; Bucharest, March 26, 1968); No. 2 (1973; West Berlin, March 21, 1974); No. 3 (1976–78; Bucharest, March 1979); No. 4 (1982; Cluj, May 15, 1983); No. 5 for Choir and Orch. (1984–85; Bucharest, Jan. 30, 1986); *Suite in Ancient Style* for String Orch. (1945); Concerto (1955); Flute Concerto (1958); Cello Concerto (1962); Sym. for Mezzo-soprano and 15 Instrumentalists (1962); *Jocuri* (Games) for Piano and Orch. (1963); Violin Concerto (1964); *Museum Music* for Harpsichord and 12 Strings (1968) *Clepsydra I* (Water Clock) for Trumpet and Orch. (1968); *Ecran* (Screen; 1970); Clarinet Concerto (1975); Concerto for Violin, Cello, and Orch. (1979); *Scoica* (Shell) for 15 Strings (1981); *Narration II* for Saxophone(s) and Orch. (Nice, Feb. 9, 1986). **CHAMBER:** 6 string quartets (1955, 1956, 1973, 1980, 1982, 1986); Quintet for Clarinet and Strings (1957); Sonata for Solo Cello (1963); *Trepte ale tacerii* (Steps of Silence) for String Quartet and Percussion Player (1966; Washington, D.C., Jan. 12, 1968; as a ballet, N.Y., Nov. 13, 1968); *Sita lui Eratostene* (Eratosthenes's Sieve) for Clarinet, Violin, Viola, Cello, and Piano (1969); Piano Sonata (1976); *Double Duos* for Alto Saxophone or Bass Clarinet and Vibraphone or Marimbaphone (1983); Sonata for Violin and Cello (1984–85); *Millefolium* for 4 Flutes (1986). **VOCAL:** *Miorita* (The Ewe), oratorio (1957); *Cantata anilor luminã* (Cantata of the Luminous Years; Bucharest, June 18, 1960); *Muzica pentru Bacovia si Labis* (Music for Bacovia and Labis), 3 cycles for Voice and Piano with Instrumental Interludes (1959–63); *Clepsydra II* for Choir, Orch., Panpipe, and Cimbalom (1971); *Patru unghiuri din care am vazut Florenţa* (4 Angles to See Florence) for Soprano, Piano or Harpsichord, and Percussion (1973); *Comorile din stafida* (The Treasures from the Raisin) for Children's Choir and Chamber Orch. (1982); choruses; also electronic music; film scores.

BIBL.: F. Popovici, "A. V.," *Muzica*, no. 4 (1981).

Vietinghoff-Scheel, Boris, Baron, Russian composer; b. in Latvia, 1829; d. St. Petersburg, Sept. 25, 1901. He was a student of Henselt and Dargomyzhsky in St. Petersburg. Three of his operas were produced in St. Petersburg: *Mazeppa* (May 17, 1859), *Tamara* (May 2, 1886), and *Don Juan de Tenorio* (Nov. 2, 1888); 2 other operas, *Mary Stuart* and *Heliodora*, were not produced. He also wrote a *Fantastic Overture* (1859; Liszt commented with interest on the use of the whole-tone scale in the finale). Vietinghoff publ. a book of memoirs, *World Celebrities* (St. Petersburg, 1899).

Vieuille, Félix, French bass; b. Saugéon, Oct. 15, 1872; d. there, Feb. 28, 1953. He was a member of the Opéra-Comique from 1898 to 1928; created the role of Arkel in Debussy's *Pelléas et Mélisande* (1902); also appeared with the Manhattan Opera in N.Y. (1908–9).

Vieuxtemps, Henri, celebrated Belgian violinist and composer; b. Verviers, Feb. 17, 1820; d. Mustapha, Algiers, June 6, 1881. His 1st teacher was his father, an amateur musician; continued his training with Lecloux-Dejonc. At age 6 he made his debut in Verviers; after performing in Liège in 1827, he gave several concerts in Brussels in 1828, where he attracted the notice of Bériot, who accepted him as a pupil; Vieuxtemps studied with Bériot until 1831. In 1833 his father took him on a concert tour of Germany; he continued his studies in Vienna, where he received lessons in counterpoint from Sechter. On March 16, 1834, he performed as soloist in the Beethoven Violin Concerto in Vienna, scoring a notable success. On June 2, 1834, he made his British debut with the Phil. Society of London. After training in composition from Reicha in Paris (1835–36), he set out on his 1st tour of Europe (1837). During his constant travels, he composed violin concertos and other violin works which became part of the standard repertoire, and which he performed in Europe to the greatest acclaim. He made his 1st American tour in 1843–44. In 1846 he was engaged as a prof. at the St. Petersburg Cons., and remained in Russia for 5 seasons; his influence on Russian concert life and violin composition was considerable. In 1853 he recommenced his concert tours in Europe; paid 2 more visits to America, in 1857–58 (with Thalberg) and in 1870–71 (with Christine Nilsson). He was a prof. of violin at the Brussels Cons. (1871–73); a stroke of paralysis, affecting his left side, forced him to end all his concert activities, but he continued to teach privately. He went to Algiers for rest, and died there; one of his most prominent pupils, Jenö Hubay, was with him at his death. In 1844 Vieuxtemps married the pianist **Josephine Eder** (b. Vienna, Dec. 15, 1815; d. Celle-St. Cloud, June 29, 1868). With Bériot, Vieuxtemps stood at the head of the French school of violin playing; contemporary accounts speak of the extraordinary precision of his technique and of his perfect ability to sustain a flowing melody; the expression "le roi du violon" was often applied to him in the press. He had 2 brothers who were musicians: **(Jean-Joseph-) Lucien Vieuxtemps** (b. Verviers, July 5, 1828; d. Brussels, Jan. 1901), was a pianist and teacher; studied with Edouard Wolff in Paris; made his debut at a concert given by his elder brother in Brussels (March 19, 1845); devoted himself mainly to teaching there; also wrote a few piano pieces. **(Jules-Joseph-) Ernest Vieuxtemps** (b. Brussels, March 18, 1832; d. Belfast, March 20, 1896), was a cellist; appeared with his elder brother in London (1855); was solo cellist in the Italian Opera Orch. there before going to Manchester as principal cellist of the Hallé Orch. (1858).

WORKS: ORCH.: 7 violin concertos: No. 1 in E major, op. 10 (1840); No. 2 in F-sharp minor, op. 19 (1836); No. 3 in A minor, op. 25 (1844); No. 4 in D minor, op. 31 (c.1850); No. 5 in A minor, op. 37, *Grétry* (1861); No. 6 in G major, op. 47 (Paris, 1883); No. 7 in A minor, op. 49 (Paris, 1883). **VIOLIN AND ORCH. OR PIANO:** *Hommage à Paganini*, op. 9 (Leipzig, c.1845); *Fantaisie-caprice*, op. 11 (Mainz, 1845); *Norma*, fantasia on the G string, op. 18 (Leipzig, c.1845); *Fantasia appassionata*, op. 35 (Leipzig, c.1860); *Ballade and Polonaise*, op. 38 (Leipzig, c.1860); 2 cello concertos (Paris, 1877, c.1883); *Duo brillant* for Violin, Cello, and Orch., op. 39 (Paris, c.1864); Overture and Belgian national anthem for Chorus and Orch., op. 41 (Mainz, 1863). **CHAMBER:** 3 string quartets (1871, 1884, 1884); Piano Trio on themes from Meyerbeer's *L'Africaine* (Paris, n.d.); *Elègie* for Viola or Cello and Piano, op. 30 (c.1854); Viola Sonata, op. 36 (1863); *Allegro and Scherzo* for Viola and Piano, op. 60 (1884); numerous works for Violin and Piano.

BIBL.: L. Escudier, *Mes Souvenirs: Les Virtuoses* (Paris, 1868); M. Kufferath, *H. V.* (Brussels, 1882); J. Radoux, *V., Sa vie, ses œuvres* (Liège, 1891; Eng. tr., 1983); P. Bergmans, *H. V.* (Turnhout, 1920); B. Schwarz, *Great Masters of the Violin* (N.Y., 1983).

Viganò, Salvatore, Italian composer and choreographer; b. Naples, March 25, 1769; d. Milan, Aug. 10, 1821. He was the son and pupil of a dancer; studied music with **Luigi Boc-**

cherini, who was his uncle; began his career as a dancer at Rome in 1783, and also produced there an opera buffa, *La Vedova scoperta;* in 1789 he went to Madrid, where he married the celebrated ballerina María Medina; they subsequently toured as dancers; won particular distinction in Vienna in 1793. After separating from his wife, he served as ballet-master in Vienna (1799–1803). Beethoven wrote the music for Viganò's "heroic ballet" *Die Geschöpfe des Prometheus* (Vienna, March 28, 1801), in which Viganò danced the leading male role. After producing ballets in several Italian cities, he was active at Milan's La Scala (1811–21)

BIBL.: C. von Ayrenhoff, *Über die theatratischen Tänze und die Ballettmeister Noverre, Muzzarelli, und V.* (Vienna, 1794); C. Ritorni, *Commentarii della vita e delle opere coreodrammatiche di S. V.* (Milan, 1838); H. Prunières, "S. V.," *Revue Musicale,* III/1 (1921); A. Levinson, *Meister des Balletts: Stendhal und V.: Eine Seite aus der Geschichte der Romantik* (Potsdam, 1923).

Viglione-Borghese, Domenico, Italian baritone; b. Mondovi, July 3, 1877; d. Milan, Oct. 26, 1957. He studied in Milan and Pesaro; made his debut as the Herald in *Lohengrin* in Lodi in 1899, and continued to sing in provincial Italian opera companies; then gave up singing in 1901, and went to the U.S., where he earned his living as a railroad worker in San Francisco. There he met Caruso, who recommended him to the impresario Scognamillo, who engaged him for a South American tour (1905–6); subsequently pursued his career in Italy, retiring in 1940. He sang some 40 roles, the best known being Jack Rance in Puccini's *La Fanciulla del West,* which he first sang in Brescia in 1911 and for the last time in Rome in 1940.

Vignas, Francisco, noted Spanish tenor; b. Moya, near Barcelona, March 27, 1863; d. Barcelona, July 14, 1933. He studied at the Barcelona Cons., and later in Paris. He made his debut in Barcelona in 1888 as Lohengrin; then sang in Italian opera houses; made his first appearance in London in 1893 at the Shaftesbury Theatre. On Nov. 29, 1893, he made his Metropolitan Opera debut in N.Y. as Turiddu; after only 1 season there, he returned to Europe.

Vila, Pedro Alberto, Spanish organist and composer; b. 1517; d. Barcelona, Nov. 16, 1582. He was organist and canon at Barcelona Cathedral; was one of the few Spanish composers who cultivated the madrigal; publ. *Odarum quas vulgo Madrigales appellamus* (Barcelona, 1561) with texts in Spanish, Catalan, Italian, and French; some of his organ works are found in the tablature book of Venegas de Henestrosa. His nephew Luis Ferrán Vila succeeded him as organist at Barcelona Cathedral.

BIBL.: F. Pedrell, *Càtalech de la Biblioteca Musical de la Diputació de Barcelona* (1908–9); S. Kastner, *Contribución al estudio de la música española y portuguesa* (Lisbon, 1941).

Vilback, (Alfonse Charles) Renaud de, French organist and composer; b. Montpellier, June 3, 1829; d. Paris, March 19, 1884. He studied piano with Lemoine, organ with Benoist, and composition with Halévy at the Paris Cons., winning the Grand Prix de Rome at the age of 15. In 1856 he became organist at St.-Eugène, Paris; remained there until 1871. He wrote 2 operas: *Au clair de lune* (Paris, Sept. 4, 1857) and *Almanzor* (Paris, April 16, 1858); also orch. pieces, piano works in salon style, and transcriptions.

Vilboa (Villebois), Konstantin, Russian composer of French origin; b. St. Petersburg, May 29, 1817; d. Warsaw, July 16, 1882. He studied in a military school, and was sent by the government to collect folk songs in the country; also directed various choirs in military establishments. In 1876 he went to Warsaw as a functionary in the ministry of war. His opera *Natasha, or The Volga Brigands* was produced in Moscow on Nov. 12, 1861. Two other operas, *Taras Bulba* (after Gogol) and *Tziganka* (The Gypsy), remain unperformed.

Vilhar, Franz, Croatian composer; b. Senožeče, Jan. 5, 1852; d. Zagreb, March 4, 1928. He studied music with Skuherský

in Prague; after serving as an organist in various churches, he settled in Zagreb, in 1891, as choirmaster at St. Mark's. He composed a Croatian opera, *Smiljana* (Zagreb, Jan. 31, 1897); *Croatian Dances* for Orch.; a number of choruses that were popular for a time.

Villa, Ricardo, Spanish composer and conductor; b. Madrid, Oct. 23, 1873; d. there, April 10, 1935. He studied at the Madrid Cons.; was founder-conductor of the Madrid municipal band (from 1909). He wrote the operas *El Cristo de la Vega* and *Raimundo Lulio;* a number of pieces for band in the Spanish vein: *La visión de Fray Martín, Impresiones sinfónicas,* and also *Cantos regionales asturianos; Rapsodía asturiana* for Violin and Orch.; *Fantasía española* for Piano and Orch.; light music.

Villalba Muñoz, Padre Luis, Spanish musicologist and composer; b. Valladolid, Sept. 22, 1872; d. Madrid, Jan. 8, 1921. He entered the Augustinian order at the age of 14; was maestro de capilla at the monastery of the Escorial (1898–1916); also taught history and other subjects; ed. the review *La Ciudad de Dios* (1898–1916), to which he contributed valuable essays on Spanish music; also founded the *Biblioteca sacro* (1911); then was organist at S. Sebastian in Madrid and ed. of the *Ilustración Española y Americana.* He publ. the valuable *Antología de organistas clásicos españoles* (Madrid, 1914; 2nd ed., 1971, by S. Rubio) and *Diez canciones españolas de los siglos XV y XVI, traducidas y transcritas para piano y canto* (Madrid, n.d.); wrote monographs on Pedrell, Granados, and Usandizaga, and *Ultimos músicos españoles del siglo XIX* (Madrid, 1914); composed organ works; sacred choruses; chamber music.

Villa-Lobos, Heitor, remarkable Brazilian composer of great originality and unique ability to recreate native melodic and rhythmic elements in large instrumental and choral forms; b. Rio de Janeiro, March 5, 1887; d. there, Nov. 17, 1959. He studied music with his father, a writer and amateur cello player; after his father's death in 1899, Villa-Lobos earned a living by playing the cello in cafés and restaurants; also studied cello with Benno Niederberger. From 1905 to 1912 he traveled in Brazil in order to collect authentic folk songs. In 1907 he entered the National Inst. of Music in Rio de Janeiro, where he studied with Frederico Nascimento, Angelo França, and Francisco Braga. In 1912 he undertook an expedition into the interior of Brazil, where he gathered a rich collection of Indian songs. On Nov. 13, 1915, he presented in Rio de Janeiro a concert of his compositions, creating a sensation by the exuberance of his music and the radical character of his technical idiom. He met the pianist Artur Rubinstein, who became his ardent admirer; for him Villa-Lobos composed a transcendentally difficult *Rudepoema.* In 1923 Villa-Lobos went to Paris on a Brazilian government grant; upon returning to Brazil in 1930, he was active in São Paulo and then in Rio de Janeiro in music education; founded a Cons. under the sponsorship of the Ministry of Education in 1942. He introduced bold innovations into the national program of music education, with an emphasis on the cultural resources of Brazil; compiled a *Guia pratico,* containing choral arrangements of folk songs of Brazil and other nations; organized the "orpheonic concentrations" of schoolchildren, whom he trained to sing according to his own cheironomic method of solfeggio. In 1944 he made his 1st tour of the U.S., and conducted his works in Los Angeles, Boston, and N.Y. in 1945. In 1945 he established in Rio de Janeiro the Brazilian Academy of Music, serving as its president from 1947 until his death. He made frequent visits to the U.S. and France during the last 15 years of his life.

Villa-Lobos was one of the most original composers of the 20th century. He lacked formal academic training, but far from hampering his development, this deficiency liberated him from pedantic restrictions, so that he evolved an idiosyncratic technique of composition, curiously eclectic, but all the better suited to his musical esthetics. An ardent Brazilian nationalist, he resolved from his earliest attempts in composition to use authentic Brazilian song materials as the source of his inspiration; yet he avoided using actual quotations from popular songs; rather, he wrote melodies which are authentic in their melodic and rhythmic content. In his desire to relate Brazilian folk resources to universal values, he composed a series of extraordinary works, *Bachianas brasileiras*, in which Brazilian melorhythms are treated in Bachian counterpoint. He also composed a number of works under the generic title *Chôros*, a popular Brazilian dance form, marked by incisive rhythm and a balladlike melody. An experimenter by nature, Villa-Lobos devised a graphic method of composition, using geometrical contours of drawings and photographs as outlines for the melody; in this manner he wrote *The New York Skyline*, using a photograph for guidance. Villa-Lobos wrote operas, ballets, syms., chamber music, choruses, piano pieces, songs; the total number of his compositions is in excess of 2,000.

WORKS: OPERAS: *Izaht* (1912–14; rev. 1932; concert premiere, Rio de Janeiro, April 6, 1940; stage premiere, Rio de Janeiro, Dec. 13, 1958); *Magdalena* (1947; Los Angeles, July 26, 1948); *Yerma* (1953–56; Santa Fe, Aug. 12, 1971); *A menina das nuvens* (1957–58; Rio de Janeiro, Nov. 29, 1960); others left unfinished.

BALLETS: (many converted from symphonic poems): *Uirapuru* (1917; Buenos Aires, May 25, 1935; rev. 1948); *Possessão* (1929); *Pedra Bonita* (1933); *Dança da terra* (1939; Rio de Janeiro, Sept. 7, 1943); *Rudá* (1951); *Gênesis* (1954; as a symphonic poem, Rio de Janeiro, 1969); *Emperor Jones* (1955; Ellenville, N.Y., July 12, 1956).

9 BACHIANAS BRASILEIRAS: No. 1 for 8 Cellos (Rio de Janeiro, Sept. 12, 1932); No. 2 for Chamber Orch. (1933); No. 3 for Piano and Orch. (1934); No. 4 for Piano (1930–40; orchestrated, N.Y., June 6, 1942); No. 5 for Voice and 8 Cellos (1938; Rio de Janeiro, March 25, 1939); No. 6 for Flute and Bassoon (1938); No. 7 for Orch. (1942; Rio de Janeiro, March 13, 1944); No. 8 for Orch. (1944; Rome, Aug. 6, 1947); No. 9 for Chorus a cappella or String Orch. (1944).

15 CHÔROS: No. 1 for Guitar (1920); No. 2 for Flute and Clarinet (1921); No. 3 for Male Chorus and 7 Wind Instruments (1925); No. 4 for 3 Horns and Trombone (1926); No. 5, *Alma brasileira*, for Piano (1926); No. 6 for Orch. (1926; Rio de Janeiro, July 15, 1942); No. 7 for Flute, Oboe, Clarinet, Saxophone, Bassoon, Violin, and Cello (1924); No. 8 for Large Orch. and 2 Pianos (1925; Paris, Oct. 24, 1927); No. 9 for Orch. (1929; Rio de Janeiro, July 15, 1942); No. 10, *Rasga o Coração*, for Chorus and Orch. (1925; Rio de Janeiro, Dec. 15, 1926); No. 11 for Piano and Orch. (1928; Rio de Janeiro, July 15, 1942); No. 12 for Orch. (1929; Cambridge, Mass., Feb. 21, 1945); No. 13 for 2 Orch. and Band (1929); No. 14 for Orch., Band, and Chorus (1928); also a supernumerary *Chôros bis* for Violin and Cello (1928).

OTHER ORCH.: 12 syms.: No. 1, *Imprevisto* (1916; Rio de Janeiro, Aug. 30, 1920); No. 2, *Ascenção* (1917); No. 3, *Guerra* (Rio de Janeiro, July 30, 1919); No. 4, *Vitória* (1920); No. 5, *Paz* (1921); No. 6, *Montanhas do Brasil* (1944); No. 7, *Odisséia da paz* (1945; London, March 27, 1949); No. 8 (1950; Philadelphia, Jan. 14, 1955); No. 9 (1951; Caracas, May 16, 1966); No. 10, *Sume Pater Patrium*, for Soloists, Chorus, and Orch. (1952; Paris, April 4, 1957); No. 11 (1955; Boston, March 2, 1956); No. 12 (1957; Washington, D.C., April 20, 1958). Also, *Dansas africanas* (1914; Paris, April 5, 1928); 2 cello concertos: No. 1, *Grand Concerto* (1915), and No. 2 (1953; N.Y., Feb. 5, 1955); 2 sinfoniettas (1916, 1947); *Amazonas* (1917; Paris, May 30, 1929); *Fantasy of Mixed Movements* for Violin and Orch. (Rio de Janeiro, Dec. 15, 1922); *Momoprecoce* for Piano and Orch. (Amsterdam, 1929); *Caixinha de Boâs Festas* (Rio de Janeiro, Dec. 8, 1932); *Ciranda das sete notes* for Bassoon and String Orch. (1933); 3 of 4 suites titled *Descobrimento do Brasil* (1937; No. 4 is an oratorio); *The New York Skyline* (1939); *Rudepoema* (orch. version of the piano work of that name; Rio de Janeiro, July 15, 1942); *Madona*, tone poem (1945; Rio de Janeiro, Oct. 8, 1946); 5 piano concertos (1945; 1948; 1952–57; 1952; 1954); *Fantasia* for Cello and Orch. (1945); *Fantasia* for Soprano Saxophone, String Orch., and 2 Horns (1948); *Erosion, or The Origin of the Amazon River*

(Louisville, Ky., Nov. 7, 1951); Guitar Concerto (1951); Harp Concerto (1953; Philadelphia, Jan. 14, 1955); *Odyssey of a Race*, symphonic poem written for Israel (1953; Haifa, May 30, 1954); *Dawn in a Tropical Forest* (1953; Louisville, Jan. 23, 1954); Harmonica Concerto (1955; Jerusalem, Oct. 27, 1959); *Izi*, symphonic poem (1957).

OTHER CHAMBER: 17 string quartets (1915, 1915, 1916, 1917, 1931, 1938, 1942, 1944, 1945, 1946, 1948, 1950, 1952, 1953, 1954, 1955, 1958); 3 piano trios (1911, 1916, 1918); *Quinteto duplo de cordas* (1912); 4 *Sonatas-Fantasia* for Violin and Piano (1912, 1914, 1915, 1918); 2 cello sonatas (1915, 1916); Piano Quintet (1916); *Mystic Sextet* for Flute, Clarinet, Saxophone, Celesta, Harp, and Guitar (1917); Trio for Oboe, Clarinet, and Bassoon (1921); Woodwind Quartet (1928); *Quintet in the Form of a Chôros* for Flute, Oboe, Clarinet, Bassoon, and English Horn (1928; rev. 1953, replacing English Horn with French Horn); String Trio (1946); *Duo* for Violin and Viola (1946); *Fantasia concertante* for Piano, Clarinet, and Bassoon (1953); *Duo* for Oboe and Bassoon (1957); Quintet for Flute, Harp, Violin, Viola, and Cello (1957); *Fantasia concertante* for Cello Ensemble (N.Y., Dec. 10, 1958).

OTHER VOCAL: CHORUS: *Crianças* (1908); *Vidapura*, oratorio for Chorus, Orch., and Organ (1918; Rio de Janeiro, Nov. 11, 1922); *Hinos aos artistas* for Chorus and Orch. (1919); Quartet for Harp, Celesta, Flute, Saxophone, and Women's Voices (1921); Nonetto for Flute, Oboe, Clarinet, Saxophone, Bassoon, Harp, Celesta, Percussion, and Chorus (1923); *Cantiga da Roda* for Women's Chorus and Orch. (1925); *Na Bah a tem* (1925); *Canção da Terra* (1925); *Missa São Sebastião* (1937); Suite No. 4 of *Descobrimento do Brasil* for Orch. and Chorus (1937); *Mandu-Carará*, cantata profana for Chorus and Orch. (1940; N.Y., Jan. 23, 1948; also a ballet); *Bendita sabedoria* (Blessed Wisdom; 1958); *Magnificat-Alleluia* for Boy Contralto, Chorus, Organ, and Orch. (Rio de Janeiro, Nov. 8, 1958; by request of Pope Pius XII); etc. **SONGS:** *Confidencia* (1908); *Noite de Luar* (1912); *Mal secreto* (1913); *Fleur fanée* (1913); *Il nome di Maria* (1915); *Sertão no Estio* (1919); *Canções típicas brasileiras* (10 numbers; 1919); *Historiettes* (6 numbers; 1920); *Epigrammes ironiques et sentimentales* (8 numbers; 1921); *Suite* for Voice and Violin (1923); *Poème de l'Enfant et de sa Mère* for Voice, Flute, Clarinet, and Cello (1923); *Serestas* (suite of 14 numbers; one of his best song cycles; 1925); *3 poemas indígenas* (1926); *Suite sugestiva* for Voice and Orch. (1929); *Modinhas e canções* (2 albums; 1933, 1943); *Poem of Itabira* for Alto and Orch. (1941; Rio de Janeiro, Dec. 30, 1946); *Canção das aguas claras* for Voice and Orch. (1956).

OTHER PIANO: *Valsa romantica* (1908); *Brinquedo de Roda* (6 pieces; 1912); *Primeira suite infantil* (5 pieces; 1912); *Segunda suite infantil* (4 pieces; 1913); *Danças africanas* (1915); *Prole do Bebé*, Suite No. 1 (8 pieces, including the popular *Polichinello*; 1918); *Fábulas características* (3 pieces; 1914–18); *Historia da Carochinha* (4 pieces; 1919); *Carnaval das crianças brasileiras* (8 pieces; 1919); *Lenda do Caboclo* (1920); *Dança infernal* (1920); *Prole do Bebé*, Suite No. 2 (9 pieces; 1921); *Sul América* (1925); *Cirandinhas* (12 pieces; 1925); *Rudepoema* (1921–26); *Cirandas* (16 pieces; 1926); *Alma brasileira* (*Chôros* No. 5; 1926); *Prole do Bebé*, Suite No. 3 (9 pieces; 1929); *Lembrança do Sertão* (1930); *Caixinha de música quebrada* (1931); *Ciclo brasileiro* (4 pieces; 1936); *As Três Marías* (3 pieces; 1939; very popular); *Poema singelo* (1942); *Homenagem a Chopin* (1949).

BIBL.: F. Lange, "V.-L., un pedagogo creador," *Boletín Latino-Americano de Música*, I (Montevideo, 1935); B. Marx, "Brazilian Portrait," *Modern Music* (Oct.–Nov. 1939); special issue of *Musica Viva*, I (Rio de Janeiro, 1940–41); N. Slonimsky, *Music of Latin America* (N.Y., 1945); O. Fernandez, "A Contribuição Harmonica de V.-L. para a Música Brasileira," *Boletín Latino-Americano de Música* (Rio de Janeiro, 1946); L. Peppercorn, "The History of V.-L.' Birth-Date," *Monthly Musical Record* (July–Aug. 1948); Vasco Mariz, *H. V.-L., Compositor brasileiro* (Rio de Janeiro, 1948; 5th ed., rev. and augmented, 1977; Eng. tr., 1970); C. de Paula Barros, *O Romance de V.-L.* (Rio de Janeiro, 1951); *Homenagem a V.- L.* (Rio de Janeiro, 1960); C. Maul, *A glória escandaloso de H. V.-L.* (Rio de Janeiro, 1960; a scurrilous "exposé," unconvincingly accusing Villa-Lobos of plagiarism); M. Beaufils, *V.-L., Musicien et poete du Brésil* (Rio de Janeiro, 1967); E. Nogueria França, *V.-L.: Síntese crítica e biográfica* (Rio de Janeiro, 1970; 2nd ed., 1973); L. Guimarães, *V.-L. visto da plateia e na intimidade (1912–1935)* (Rio de Janeiro, 1972); L. Peppercorn, *H. V.-L.: Leben und Werk des Brasilianischen Komponisten* (Zürich, 1972); F. Pereira da Silva, *V.-L.* (Rio de Janeiro, 1974); V. Mariz, *H. V.-L., compositor brasileiro* (Rio de Janeiro, 1983); T. Santos, *H. V.-L. and the Guitar* (Bank, County Cork, 1985); P. Carvalho, *V.-L.: Do crepúsculo à alvorada* (Rio de Janeiro, 1987); M. Claret, ed., *O Pensamento vivo de H. V.-L.* (São Paulo, 1987); M. Machado, *H. V.-L.: Tradição e renovacão na música brasileira* (Rio de Janeiro, 1987); A. Schic, *V.-L.: Souvenirs de l'indien blanc* (Arles and Paris, 1987); E. Stornio, *V.-L.* (Madrid, 1987); D. Appleby, *H. V.-L.: A Bio-bibliography* (N.Y., 1988).

Villar, Rogelio del, Spanish musicologist, teacher, and composer; b. León, Nov. 13, 1875; d. Madrid, Nov. 4, 1937. He studied at the Madrid Cons., where he later taught (1919–36); was ed. of the *Revista Musical Hispano-Americana* (ceased publication in 1917).

WORKS: ORCH.: *Suite romántica* (1907); *Las hilanderas* (1915); *Escenas populares* (1917); *Egloga* (1919); also 3 string quartets; piano pieces; songs.

WRITINGS: *Músicos españoles* (1918); *Soliloquios de un músico español* (1923); *La armonia en la música contemporánea* (1927); etc.

Villoing, Alexander, notable Russian pianist and teacher, uncle of **Vasili Villoing;** b. Moscow, March 12, 1804; d. there, Sept. 2, 1878. He was born of a French émigré family; studied piano with John Field in Moscow; taught piano there (1830–62); enjoyed a reputation as one of the best pedagogues in Russia. Anton and Nikolai Rubinstein were among his pupils; he traveled with them in Europe. His *Ecole pratique du piano* (St. Petersburg, 1863) was accepted by the St. Petersburg Cons. as a teaching guide. He publ. a book of piano exercises, which he called *Exercises for the Rubinstein Brothers.*

Villoing, Vasili, Russian pianist, violinist, conductor, teacher, and composer, nephew of **Alexander Villoing;** b. Moscow, Oct. 28, 1850; d. Nizhny-Novgorod, Sept. 15, 1922. He studied piano with his uncle and violin with Ferdinand Laub at the Moscow Cons. He then moved to Nizhny-Novgorod, where he organized a music school and conducted a local orch. founded by him. Among his piano students were Dobrowen and Liapunov. He composed 3 operas, 4 string quartets, and a number of piano pieces and songs.

Villoteau, Guillaume-André, French music scholar; b. Bellême, Orne, Sept. 6, 1759; d. Tours, April 27, 1839. He attended the maîtrise at Le Mans Cathedral, and studied philosophy at the Sorbonne in Paris; entered the priesthood and joined the maîtrise at Notre Dame in 1789, but with the coming of the Revolution the maîtrise was suppressed, and he joined the Opéra chorus. He was a member of the scientific commission that accompanied Napoleon to Egypt (1798–1800), and he made a special study of oriental music. He contributed 4 essays to E. Jomard, ed., *La Description de l'Egypte* (20 vols., Paris, 1809–22; 2nd ed., 1821–30); they were publ. separately and in *Recueil de tous les mémoires sur la musique des egyptens et des orientaux* (1846). He also publ. "Mémoire sur la possibilité et l'utilité d'une théorie exacte des principes naturels de la musique" (1807), an introduction to his *Recherches sur l'analogie de la musique avec les arts qui ont pour object l'imitation du langage* (2 vols., 1807).

Viña (Manteola), Facundo de la, Spanish composer; b. Gijon, Feb. 21, 1876; d. Madrid, Nov. 19, 1952. He studied at the Madrid Cons. and in Paris; his music reflects the character of Asturian regional folklore. He composed the operas *Almas muertas; La princesa flor de roble; La espigadora* (Barcelona, 1927); the symphonic poems *Canto de trilla; Sierra de Gredos; Covadonga; Por tierras de Castilla.*

Vinay, Ramón, Chilean baritone, later tenor; b. Chillán (of French and Italian parents), Aug. 31, 1912. He was a pupil of José Pierson in Mexico City, where he made his debut as Alfonso in *La favorite* (1931); after appearances in baritone roles, he pursued further training and turned to the tenor repertory, making his 2nd debut as Don José in Mexico City in 1943; chose that same role for his N.Y. debut in 1945. On Feb. 22, 1946, he made his Metropolitan Opera debut in N.Y. as Don José; remained on its roster until 1958, and sang there again from 1959 to 1962 and in 1965–66. He also appeared in Europe, opening the 1947–48 season at Milan's La Scala in his most famous role, Othello; sang at the Bayreuth Festivals (1952–57) and regularly at London's Covent Garden (1953–60). From 1969 to 1971 he was artistic director of the Santiago Opera. Among his other roles were Bartolo, Iago, Falstaff, Scarpia, Telramund, Parsifal, Tristan, Siegfried, and Tannhäuser.

Vincent, Alexandre-Joseph Hydulphe, French music theorist; b. Hesdin, Pas-de-Calais, Nov. 20, 1797; d. Paris, Nov. 26, 1868. An investigator of ancient Greek and Latin music, he advanced the idea that the Greeks used chorus (harmony); he similarly sought to revive the employment of the intervals smaller than a half-tone that were described in Greek theory. On these subjects he publ. a great number of essays, some of which were reprinted in pamphlet form. Especially important is his *Notice sur divers manuscrits grecs relatifs à la musique* (1847).

Vincent (real name, **Winzenhörlein**), **Heinrich Joseph,** German tenor, singing teacher, music theorist, and composer; b. Teilheim, near Würzburg, Feb. 23, 1819; d. Vienna, May 19, 1901. He studied law, and also sang in theaters in Vienna (1847), Halle, and Würzburg; eventually settled in Vienna as a singing teacher. He composed 2 operas, *Die Bettlerin* (Halle, 1864) and *König Murat* (Würzburg, 1870); also operettas and popular songs. He followed the tenets of the Chroma Society in championing the harmonic system based on the functional equality of the 12 notes of the chromatic scale; publ. the studies *Kein Generalbass mehr* (1860), *Die Einheit in der Tonwelt* (1862), *Die Neuklaviatur* (1874), *Die Zwölfzahl in der Tonwelt* (1885), and *Eine neue Tonschrift* (1900), and articles on the chromatic keyboard and notation.

Vincent, John, American composer and teacher; b. Birmingham, Ala., May 17, 1902; d. Santa Monica, Calif., Jan. 21, 1977. He studied flute with Georges Laurent at the New England Cons. of Music in Boston (1922–26), and composition there with Converse and Chadwick (1926–27); then took courses at the George Peabody College in Nashville (M.A., 1933) and at Harvard Univ., where his principal teacher was Walter Piston (1933–35); then went to Paris, where he studied at the École Normale de Musique (1935–37), and took private lessons with Nadia Boulanger; received his Ph.D. from Cornell Univ. in 1942. He was in charge of music in the El Paso (Tex.) public schools (1927–30); taught at George Peabody College in Nashville (1930–33), at Western Kentucky Teachers College (1937–46), and at the Univ. of Calif., Los Angeles (1946–69). After his death, the John Vincent Archive was established at UCLA. In his music he evolved a tonal idiom which he termed "paratonality"; fugal elements are particularly strong in his instrumental compositions. He publ. the books *Music for Sight Reading* (N.Y., 1940); *More Music for Sight Reading* (N.Y., 1941); *The Diatonic Modes in Modern Music* (N.Y., 1951; 2nd ed., rev., 1974).

WORKS: Opera, *Primeval Void* (1969); ballet, *3 Jacks* (1942; rev. 1954; rev. as an orch. suite, 1954; rev. as *The House That Jack Built* for Narrator and Orch., 1957); *Nude Descending a Staircase* for String Orch. (1948; arr. for Xylophone and Piano, or Strings, 1974); Sym. in D (Louisville, Feb. 5, 1952; rev. ver., Philadelphia, April 12, 1957); *Symphonic Poem after Descartes* (Philadelphia, March 20, 1959; his most significant work, with the motto of Descartes, "Cogito ergo sum," suggested by the thematic rhythm on the kettledrums); *La Jolla Concerto* for Chamber Orch. (La Jolla, Calif., July 19, 1959); *Consort* for Piano and String Orch. (1960; arr. as Sym. No. 2 for Strings, 1976); *Benjamin Franklin Suite* for Orch. and Glass Harmonica (based on the string quartet attributed to Benjamin Franklin; Philadelphia, March 24, 1963); *Rondo-Rhapsody* (Washington, D.C., May 9, 1965); *The Phoenix, Fabulous Bird,* symphonic poem (Phoenix, Ariz., Feb. 21, 1966); 2 string quartets (1936, 1967); *Stabat Mater* for Male Chorus and Soprano Solo (1969); *Mary at Calvary* for Chorus and Organ (1972); choruses (*O God, Our Help in Ages Past; Cindy Gal; Glory to God; Behold the Star;* etc.); *Baroque Album,* 16 Baroque works transcribed for String Orch., with Piano (1972).

BIBL.: C. Parker, *J. V. (1902–1977): An Alabama Composer's Odyssey* (diss., Univ. of Calif., Los Angeles, 1981).

Vinci, Leonardo, noted Italian composer; b. Strongoli, c.1690; d. Naples, May 27, 1730. He studied at the Cons. dei Poveri di Gesù Cristo in Naples, where he was a pupil of Gaetano Greco. In 1719 he served as maestro di cappella to the Prince of Sansevero; was provicemaestro at the Royal Chapel in Naples from 1725 until his death; in 1728 he was also maestro di cappella at the Cons. dei Poveri di Gesù Cristo. He was highly esteemed by his contemporaries as a composer for the theater. He produced a number of opera serie, including *Silla dittatore* (Naples, Oct. 19, 1723); *L'Astianatte* (Naples, 1725); *La caduta dei Decemviri* (Naples, Oct. 1, 1727); *Artaserse* (Rome, Feb. 4, 1730); also many commedie musicali; an oratorio, *Le glorie del Ss. Rosario;* 6 chamber cantatas; etc.

BIBL.: E. Dent, "Notes on L. V.," *Musical Antiquary* (July 1913); A. Della Corte, *L'opera comica italiana nel 1700,* vol. I (Bari, 1923); A. Cametti, "L. V. e i suoi drammi in musica al Teatro delle Dame 1724–30," *Musica d'Oggi* (Oct. 1924); U. Prota-Giurleo, *Nicola Logroscino* (Naples, 1927; appendix, "La morte di V."); K. Geiringer, "Ein Geburtstagkantate von P. Metastasio und L. V.," *Archiv für Musikwissenschaft,* IX (1926–27); G. Silvestri Silva, *Illustri musici calabresi: L. V.* (Genoa, 1935).

Vinci, Pietro, distinguished Italian composer and teacher; b. Nicosia, Sicily, c.1535; d. there or in Piazza Armerina, c.June 15, 1584. After living in various areas of Italy, he served as maestro di cappella at the Basilica of S. Maria Maggiore in Bergamo (1568–80); then returned to Sicily in 1581. He was distinguished as a madrigalist. Among his pupils were Paolo Caracciolo and Antonio Il Verso. He composed masses, other sacred works, 12 books of madrigals (1561–84), and ricercares. A complete ed. of his works was publ. in Musiche Rinascimentali Siciliane (1971–).

BIBL.: F. Mompellio, *P. V. madrigalista siciliano* (Milan, 1937).

Vincze, Imre, Hungarian composer; b. Kocs, Sept. 26, 1926; d. Budapest, May 3, 1969. He studied with Szabó at the Budapest Academy of Music; taught there (from 1951); won the Erkel Prize in 1952 and 1956. He wrote 3 syms. (1951, 1953, 1963); *Felicitation,* overture (1954); *Movimento sinfonico* (1957); *Aforismo* for Orch. (1959); Concertino for Orch. (1961); *Rapsodia concertante* for Piano and Orch. (1966); 4 string quartets (1954, 1958, 1961, 1965); Violin Sonata (1956); *Divertimento* for Wind Quintet (1962); Bassoon Sonata (1964); *Fantasy and Fugue* for Organ (1960); choral works; film music.

Viñes, Ricardo, Spanish pianist; b. Lérida, Feb. 5, 1875; d. Barcelona, April 29, 1943. He studied in Barcelona with Juan Pujol; settled in Paris in 1887, where he studied piano with Bériot (premier prix, 1894), composition with Godard, and harmony with Lavignac at the Cons. In 1895 he gave his first concert in Paris, and established himself in later years as an ardent propagandist of new French and Spanish music; he possessed particular affinity with the composers of the modern French school, and performed their works in a colorful and imaginative manner. He gave concerts in London, Berlin, and other music centers, but lived most of his life in Paris; contributed articles on Spanish music to publications in France and Spain.

BIBL.: E. Brody, "V. in Paris: New Light on Twentieth-century Performance Practice," *A Musical Offering: Essays in Honor of Martin Bernstein* (N.Y., 1977).

Vinogradsky, Alexander, Russian conductor and composer; b. Kiev, Aug. 5, 1855; d. there, Oct. 17, 1912. He studied at the St. Petersburg Cons.; in 1888, became conductor of the sym. concerts of the Imperial Russian Music Society in Kiev; also conducted in Paris, Vienna, and Berlin. He wrote 2 syms.; a symphonic fantasy, *En Bourgogne;* a symphonic poem, *La Nonne;* a number of minor pieces.

Vinson, Eddie "Cleanhead," black American jazz alto saxophonist and blues singer; b. Houston, Dec. 18, 1917; d. Los Angeles, July 2, 1988. He learned to play the alto saxophone in his youth; after performing in the South and the Midwest, he went to N.Y., where he played in Cootie Williams's band (1942–45); then led his own group. In 1969 he toured Europe with Hootie McShann. He made his home in Los Angeles, but made frequent appearances in U.S. and European jazz and blues centers. Vinson derived his nickname from his clean-shaven pate. He was one of the finest exponents of bebop saxophone artistry of his generation.

Viola, Alfonso. See **Dalla Viola, Alfonso.**

Viola, Francesco. See **Dalla Viola, Francesco.**

Viola, P. Anselm, Catalan composer; b. Teruel, July 1738; d. Montserrat, Jan. 25, 1798. He was a monk at Montserrat; wrote much instrumental music of surprising excellence in a fine Baroque style. His Concerto for 2 Oboes, 2 Horns, Violins, and Cellos obbligato is included in D. Pujol, ed., *Música instrumental* (Vol. II, Montserrat, 1936).

Viole, Rudolf, German pianist and composer; b. Schochwitz, Mansfeld, May 10, 1825; d. Berlin, Dec. 7, 1867. He was a pupil of R. Hentschel in Weissenfels and of Liszt, who recommended his compositions and ed. his 100 études. He was active in Berlin as a piano teacher and writer on music. Viole wrote mostly for piano, including 11 sonatas, a *Caprice héroïque,* a Ballade, a Polonaise, etc.

Viotta, Henri(cus Anastasius), Dutch conductor and music scholar, son of **Johannes Josephus Viotta;** b. Amsterdam, July 16, 1848; d. Montreux, Feb. 17, 1933. He studied with his father and with R. Hol in Amsterdam; pursued training in piano with W. Bargiel and F. Breuning, in violin with O. von Königslöw, in cello with H. Schmitt, and in composition with F. Hiller at the Cologne Cons.; completed his education by studying law at the Univ. of Leiden (doctorate, 1877, with a diss. on musical copyright). He became a conductor of various musical groups in Amsterdam, including the Wagnervereeniging (1883–1919); was director of The Hague Cons. (1896–1917); also was founder-director of the Residentie Orch. in The Hague (1903–17). He publ. *Lexicon der toonkunst* (3 vols., 1881–85) and the *Handboek der muziekgeschiedenis* (1916). In 1920 he went to live in Switzerland.

Viotta, Johannes Josephus, Dutch physician and composer of Italian descent, father of **Henri(cus Anastasius) Viotta;** b. Amsterdam, Jan. 14, 1814; d. there, Feb. 6, 1859. He was autodidact in music; studied medicine at the Univ. of Leiden (wrote a diss. on the health of the human voice, 1837). He was active as a physician in Amsterdam; also served as president of the Vereeniging tot Bevordring der Toonkunst (1844, 1848, 1852, 1854), being répétiteur of its chapter's chorus and a champion of the music of Mendelssohn, Schumann, Gade, et al. As a composer, he became well known for his school songs and folk-song arrangements; he also wrote syms., choral works, and piano pieces.

Viotti, Giovanni Battista, famous Italian violinist and composer; b. Fontanetto da Po, May 12, 1755; d. London, March 3, 1824. His father, a blacksmith, was an amateur musician; taught him music, and bought a small violin for him to practice on. At the age of 11 Viotti was sent to Turin, where he gained the favor of Alfonso del Pozzo, Prince della Cisterna, who oversaw his education. After lessons with Antonio Celoniat, Viotti became a pupil of Pugnani in 1770. In 1775 he became a member of the last desk of 1st violins in the orch. of the Royal Chapel in Naples. In 1780 he and Pugnani launched a major concert tour, performing in Switzerland, Dresden, Berlin, Warsaw, and St. Petersburg. By 1782 Viotta was in Paris on his own, where he first appeared at the Concert Spirituel (March 17). He immediately established himself as the premier violin virtuoso of the day, and gave regular concerts there until 1783. In 1784 he entered the service of Marie Antoinette in Versailles; also acted as concertmaster of the orch. of Prince Rohan-Guéménée. Thanks to the patronage of the Court of Provence, he opened the Théâtre de Monsieur in Paris in 1788, which became the Théâtre Feydeau in 1791. During his tenure there, he staged major works from the Italian and French repertories, including those of his close friend Cherubini. In 1792 he fled the revolution-wracked city of Paris for London, where he made his debut at Salomon's Hanover Square Concert on Feb. 7, 1793; was the featured violinist of Salomon's concerts until 1795; also was acting manager of the Italian opera at the King's Theatre (1794–95); in 1795, became music director of the new Opera Concerts and in 1797, concertmaster and director of the orch. at the King's Theatre. In 1798 he was ordered by the British government to leave England on suspicion of Jacobin sympathies. After living in Schenfeldt, near Hamburg (1798–99), he was back in London by 1801; was engaged mainly in a wine business, although he later helped to found the Phil. Society and appeared in some of its chamber-music programs. In 1818 his wine business failed, and he returned to Paris, where he became director of the Opéra in 1819; he resigned in 1821; served as its nominal director until 1822, then abandoned music altogether, and returned to London in 1823.

Viotti's role in the history of instrumental music, in both performance and composition, was very important. He elevated performing standards from mere entertainment to artistic presentation, and may be regarded as one of the chief creators of modern violin playing. He was the 1st to write violin concertos in a consciously formulated sonata form, with the solo part and the orch. accompaniment utilizing the full resources of instrumental sonority more abundantly than ever before in violin concertos. He publ. 29 violin concertos (of which No. 22, in A minor, is a great favorite); 10 piano concertos (some of which are transcriptions of violin concertos); 2 *symphonies concertantes* for 2 Violins, Strings, Oboes, and Horns; 21 string quartets; 21 string trios; various duos for 2 Violins; 6 serenades for 2 Violins; several duos for 2 Cellos; 3 divertissements for Violin Unaccompanied; 12 sonatas for Violin and Piano; etc. His song known as *La polacca de Viotti* (used in Paisiello's *La Serva padrona*, 1794) acquired great popularity. For the rectification of Viotti's birth date (heretofore given as May 23, 1753), see *Stampa di Torino* of Sept. 29, 1935, which publ. for the 1st time the text of his birth certificate; an infant brother of Viotti was born in 1753; their Christian names were identical (the brother having died before the birth of the future musician), which led to confusion; the bicentennial of Viotti was widely celebrated in the wrong year (1953). C. White ed. a thematic catalogue of his works (N.Y., 1985).

BIBL.: A. d'Eymar, *Anecdotes sur V., précédées de quelques réflexions sur l'expression en musique* (Paris, 1792); F. Fayolle, *Notices sur Corelli et V.* (Paris, 1810); P. Baillot, *Notice sur J.B. V.* (Paris, 1825); E. Miel, *Notice historique sur J.B. V.* (Paris, 1827); A. Pougin, *V. et l'école moderne de violon* (Paris, 1888); H. de Curzon, "Quelques souvenirs de V.," *Le Ménestrel* (April 1924); L. de La Laurencie, "Les Débuts de V. comme directeur de l'Opéra en 1819," *Revue de Musicologie* (Aug. 1924); idem, *L'École française de violon de Lully à V.* (Paris, 1922–25); M. Pincherle, "Le méthode de violon de J.B. V.," *Feuillets d'histoire du violon* (Paris, 1927); R. Giazotto, *G.B. V.* (Milan, 1956); C. White, *G.B. V. and his Violin Concertos* (diss., Princeton Univ., 1957); ibid, "Did V. Write Any Original Piano Concertos?," *Journal of the American Musicological Society*, XXII (1969); V. Milton, *An Analysis of Selected Violin Concertos of G.B. V. Within the Context of the Violin Concerto in France of the Late Eighteenth and Early Nineteenth Centuries* (diss., American Cons. of Music, 1986).

Virdung, Sebastian, German music theorist and composer; b. Amberg, Jan. 19 or 20, c.1465; place and date of death unknown. He was educated at the Univ. of Heidelberg; also studied with Johannes von Soest at the chapel of the Palatine court in Heidelberg, where he was an alto and Kapellmeister. After being ordained, he also served as chaplain. He was a singer at the Württemberg court chapel in Stuttgart (1506–7); then was 1 of the 9 succentors at Konstanz Cathedral (1507–8). He wrote a work of importance for the history of musical instruments: *Musica getutscht und auszgezogen durch Sebastianum Virdung, Priesters von Amberg, und alles Gesang ausz den Noten in die Tabulaturen diser benannten dryer Instrumenten, der Orgeln, der Lauten und der Flöten transferieren zu lernen kurtzlich gemacht* (Basel, 1511; facsimile reprint in Eitner's Publikationen Älterer Praktischer und Theoretischer Musikwerke, vol. 11, 1882; also by L. Schrade, Kassel, 1931, and by K. Niemöller, Kassel, 1970). Virdung's method was violently attacked by Arnolt Schlick in his *Tabulatur etlicher Lobgesänge* (1512). Four of Virdung's songs are in Schöffer's *Teutsche Lieder mit 4 Stimmen* (1513).

BIBL.: B. Wallner, "S. V. von Amberg: Beiträge zu seiner Lebensgeschichte," *Kirchenmusikalisches Jahrbuch*, XXIV (1911); E. Ripin, "A reevaluation of V.'s *Musica getutscht*," *Journal of the American Musicological Society* (Summer 1976).

Virizlay, Mihály, Hungarian-born American cellist, teacher, and composer; b. Budapest, Nov. 2, 1931. He began violin studies at an early age with his father; after receiving instruction in cello from Janos Starker, he studied with Miklós Zsambolski and Edi Banda (cello) and Pál Járdanyi and Kodály (composition) at the Budapest Academy of Music (graduated, 1955). In 1957 he emigrated to the U.S., and became a naturalized U.S. citizen (1962); after playing in the Dallas Sym. Orch., he was assistant principal cellist of the Pittsburgh Sym. Orch. (1960–62) and then principal cellist of the Baltimore Sym. Orch. (from 1962); also pursued a career as an orch. soloist, recitalist, and chamber music artist, making appearances on both sides of the Atlantic. He taught at the Peabody Cons. of Music in Baltimore (from 1963), and also held master classes throughout the U.S. He was distinguished for his performances of contemporary music.

WORKS: *The Emperor's New Clothes,* orch. suite (1964); Trombone Concerto (Baltimore, Nov. 2, 1985); Cello Concerto (1985; Baltimore, Feb. 12, 1987); *Ének* (Song) for Cello and Piano (1955); Sonata for Solo Cello (1972); Rhapsody for Cello and Piano (1973); Piano Sonata (1981); Grand Duo for 2 Flutes (1985).

Viscarra Monje, Humberto, Bolivian composer; b. Sorata, March 30, 1898; d. La Paz, Sept. 2, 1971. He studied at the National Cons. of Bolivia in La Paz; then went to Europe, and studied piano and composition in Italy and France. Returning to La Paz, he served as director of the Cons. (1930–32; 1950–68). He composed some attractive piano pieces based on Bolivian motifs.

Visconti (di Modrone), Count Luchino, prominent Italian film, theater, and opera director; b. Milan, Nov. 2, 1906; d. Rome, March 17, 1976. After World War II, he assumed a leading position among film directors, producing motion pictures notable for their realism. In 1954 he enlarged the scope of his work to include opera, his 1st production being Spontini's *Le vestale* at Milan's La Scala with Maria Callas; his 1st production outside his homeland was *Don Carlos* at London's Covent Garden in 1958; that same year his *Macbeth* opened the Spoleto Festival, where he maintained a close association in subsequent seasons. His opera productions were impressive, particularly for his ability to complement the dramatic qualities of the music with the action on stage to effect a total theatrical experience.

BIBL.: M. Estève, ed., *L. V.: L'Histoire et l'esthétique* (Paris, 1963).

Visée, Robert de, French guitarist, theorbo and viol player, singer, and composer; b. c.1650; d. c.1725. About 1680 he became a chamber musician to Louis XIV; was guitar teacher to the King from 1695, a position he held officially from 1719; also sang in the royal chapel from 1709.

Works: *Livre de guittarre dédié au roy* (Paris, 1682); *Livre de pièces pour la guittarre* (Paris, 1686); *Pièces de théorbe et de luth mises en partition dessus et basse* (Paris, 1732); other works in contemporary collections. His guitar works have been ed. by R. Strizich (Paris, 1971).

Bibl.: O. Chilesotti, "Notes sur le guitariste R. d.V.," *Sammelbände der Internationalen Musik-Gesellschaft*, IX (1907–8); M. Rollin, "Les Tombeaux de R. d.V.," *Bulletin de la Société d'Étude du XVIIᵉ Siècle*, XXXIV (1957).

Visetti, Alberto Antonio, Italian singing teacher, conductor, and composer; b. Salona, May 13, 1846; d. London, July 10, 1928. He studied at the Milan Cons.; first appeared as a pianist; went to Paris, where he was appointed a chamber musician to Empress Eugénie. After the fall of the Empire in France, he settled in London, where he taught singing; also conducted the Bath Phil. Society (1878–90). He publ. *History of the Art of Singing* and *Verdi* (1905); the score of his opera *Les Trois Mousquetaires* was lost during the siege of Paris (1871). He also wrote a cantata, *The Desert and the Praise of Song;* and a waltz-song for Adelina Patti, *La Diva.*

Vishnevskaya, Galina (Pavlovna), prominent Russian soprano; b. Leningrad, Oct. 25, 1926. After vocal studies with Vera Garina in Leningrad, she sang in operetta; in 1952 she joined the operatic staff of the Bolshoi Theater in Moscow; there her roles were Violetta, Tosca, Madama Butterfly, and an entire repertoire of soprano parts in Russian operas. In 1955 she married **Mstislav Rostropovich,** with whom she frequently appeared in concert. She made her debut at the Metropolitan Opera in N.Y. on Nov. 6, 1961, as Aida. Owing to the recurrent differences that developed between Rostropovich and the cultural authorities of the Soviet Union (Rostropovich had sheltered the dissident writer Solzhenitsyn in his summer house), they left Russia in 1974; settled in the U.S., when Rostropovich was appointed music director of the National Sym. Orch. in Washington, D.C., in 1977. In March 1978, both he and Vishnevskaya, as "ideological renegades," were stripped of their Soviet citizenship by a decree of the Soviet government. Her autobiography was publ. as *Galina: A Russian Story* (N.Y., 1984). After Gorbachev's rise to power in her homeland, her Soviet citizenship was restored in 1990.

Viski, János, Hungarian composer; b. Kolozsvár, June 10, 1906; d. Budapest, Jan. 16, 1961. He studied violin at an early age; then took lessons in composition from Kodály at the Budapest Academy of Music (1927–32). From 1942 until his death he was a prof. of composition at the Budapest Academy of Music; won the Erkel Prize in 1954 and the Kossuth Prize in 1956. Most of his music is permeated with Hungarian melorhythms, and is set in classical forms.

Works: *Symphonic Suite* (1935); *2 Hungarian Dances* for Orch. (1938); *Enigma,* symphonic poem (1939–40); Violin Concerto (1947); Piano Concerto (1953); Cello Concerto (1955); *Az irisórai szarvas* (The Deer of Irisóra) for Baritone and Orch. (1958); String Trio (1930, lost); *Epitaph for Anton Webern* for Piano (1960); choral works; songs.

Vitali, Filippo, Italian composer; b. Florence, c.1590; d. probably there, after April 1, 1653. In 1631 he became a singer in the Pontifical Choir in Rome; also was a priest in the service of Cardinal Francesco Barberini and Cardinal Antonio Barberini. In 1642 he returned to Florence as maestro di cappella of the grand ducal chapel of S. Lorenzo; in 1648–49, was also maestro di cappella at S. Maria Maggiore in Bergamo. His "favola in musica" *L'Aretusa,* performed on Feb. 8, 1620, at the home of Monsignor Corsini, is regarded as the 1st attempt at opera in Rome (publ. there, 1620). In 1622 he composed 6 intermedi for the comedy *La finta mora* by J. Cicognini,

performed at the palace of Cardinal de' Medici in Florence (publ. there, 1623). He was highly esteemed by his contemporaries for his mastery of polyphony; his most significant works are the cycle of 34 hymns set to Latin texts and publ. in the *Brevarium romanum* (1632); also composed other sacred and secular works.

Bibl.: J. Pruett, *The Works of F. V.* (diss., Univ. of North Carolina, 1962).

Vitali, Giovanni Battista, significant Italian composer; b. Bologna, Feb. 18, 1632; d. there, Oct. 12, 1692. He became a singer and violoncino player (cellist) at S. Petronio in Bologna, where he was a pupil of Cazzati, its maestro di cappella; by 1666 a member of the Accademia Filarmonica of Bologna by 1666. After serving as maestro di cappella at S. Rosario in Bologna (1673–74), he was made 1 of the 2 vicemaestri di cappella to Duke Francesco II at the Este court in Modena; was his maestro di cappella from 1684 to 1686 before reverting to vicemaestro in 1686. Vitali was a leading figure in the development of the Baroque sonata, most particularly of the trio sonata. He publ. the influential pedagogical work *Artificii musicali,* op. 13 (Modena, 1689).

Works: INSTRUMENTAL: *Correnti, e balletti da camera* for 2 Violins and Basso Continuo, op. 1 (Bologna, 1666); *Sonate* for 2 Violins and Basso Continuo (organ), op. 2 (Bologna, 1667); *Balletti, correnti alla francese, gagliarde, e brando per ballare* for 4 Instruments, op. 3 (Bologna, 1679); *Balletti, correnti, gighe, allemande, e sarabande* for Violin, Violone or Spinet, and 2 Violins ad libitum, op. 4 (Bologna, 1668); *Sonate* for 2 to 5 Instruments, op. 5 (Bologna, 1669); *Varie partite del passemezo, ciaccona, capricii, e passagalii* for 2 Violins and Violone or Spinet, op. 7 (Modena, 1682); *Balletti, correnti, e capricci per camera* for 2 Violins and Basso Continuo, op. 9 (Venice, 1684); *Varie sonate alla francese, e all'italgiana* for 6 Instruments, op. 11 (Modena, 1684); *Balli in stile francese* for 5 Instruments, op. 12 (Modena, 1685); *Artificii musicali ne qualli se contengono canoni in diverse maniere, contrapunti dopii, inventioni curiose, capritii, e sonate,* op. 13 (Modena, 1689; ed. by L. Rood and G. Smith, Smith College Music Archives, XIV, 1959); T. Vitali, ed., *Sonate da camera* for 2 Violins and Violone, op. 14 (Modena, 1692). He also wrote 6 oratorios, including *L'ambitione debellata overo La caduta di Monmuth* (Modena, 1686) and *Il Giono* (Modena, 1689), 10 cantatas, *Salmi concerti* for 2 to 5 Instruments, op. 6 (Bologna, 1677), and *Hinni sacri per tutto l'anno* for Voice and 5 Instruments, op. 10 (Modena, 1684).

Bibl.: G. Roncaglia, *La cappella musicale del duomo di Modena* (Florence, 1957); A. Damerini, "La sonata di G.B. V.," *Musicisti lombardi ed emiliani,* XV (Chigiana, 1958); W. Newman, *The Sonata in the Baroque Era* (Chapel Hill, 1959; 4th ed., rev., 1983); J. Suess, *G.B. V. and the "Sonata da chiesa"* (diss., Yale Univ., 1963).

Vitalini, Alberico, Italian conductor and composer; b. Rome, July 18, 1921. He studied at the Santa Cecilia Cons. in Rome, obtaining diplomas in violin (1940), viola (1942), composition (1944), and conducting (1945). He subsequently became active mainly as a conductor; in 1950, was appointed director of musical programs of Radio Vaticana; in 1973, was nominated a member of the Accademia Internazionale de Propaganda Culturale. He specializes in sacred choral music.

Works: *Fantasia* for Piano and Orch. (1949; Rome, 1969); *Assisi* for Chorus and Orch. (1949; Rome, 1967); *Le sette parole di Cristo* for Baritone and String Orch. (Rome, 1952); *Magnificat* for Soprano, Chorus, and Orch. (1954; Rome, 1957); *Tiberiade* for Small Orch. (1955); *Canti in italiano,* for a new liturgy in the Italian language (1965–71).

Vitalis, George, Greek composer and conductor; b. Athens, Jan. 9, 1895; d. there, April 27, 1959. He studied with Armani in Milan; conducted light opera in Athens (1923–36); went to the U.S. in 1945; settled in N.Y. He composed the operas *Perseus and Andromeda, The Return of the Gods,* and *Golfo* (concert perf., N.Y., Jan. 1, 1949); *Greek Fantasy* for Orch.

(Athens, Nov. 11, 1945); light orch. pieces under the pseudonym **Giorgio Valente.**

Vītoliņš, Jēkab, Latvian musicologist; b. Bākšani, Aug. 5, 1898. He studied composition with Jāzeps Vītols at the Latvian Cons. in Riga (1920–24); later took lessons in conducting with Emil Cooper, and took courses in music history at the Univ. of Vienna (1929, 1931); then attended the Sorbonne in Paris (1936–37). He received a *kandidat* degree from the Univ. of Leningrad (1956) and a doctorate there for his work on Latvian folk music (1961). He was a dramaturge at the Latvian National Opera (1925–29), ed. of the journal *Mūzikas apskats* (1932–39), and senior research fellow at the Inst. of Ethnography and Folklore of the Latvian Academy of Sciences. He taught at the College of Education in Riga (1922–38) and at the Latvian Cons. (1938–44; 1946–61), becoming a prof. in 1941. He was dismissed from his post at the Cons. in 1961 for publishing a collection of reviews by Jānis Zālītis (1884–1943), the anti-Soviet Latvian composer and music critic. His numerous books and articles, mostly in Latvian or Russian, are concerned principally with Latvian folk music.

Vitry, Philippe de, famous French music theorist, composer, poet, and churchman, also known as **Philippus de Vitriaco;** b. Vitry, Champagne, Oct. 31, 1291; d. Meaux, June 9, 1361. There are 6 towns in Champagne named Vitry, and it is not known in which of these Vitry was born; was educated at the Sorbonne in Paris, where he later was magister artium; was ordained a deacon early in life, and from 1323 held several benefices; was canon of Soissons and archbishop of Brie. He became a clerk of the royal household in Paris, and about 1346 was made counselor of the court of requests ("maître des requêtes"); from 1346 to 1350 he was also in the service of Duke Jean of Normandy (heir to the throne), with whom he took part in the siege of Aiguillon (1346); when Duke Jean became king in 1350, he sent Vitry to Avignon on a mission to Pope Clement VI, who on Jan. 3, 1351, appointed him bishop of Meaux. Vitry was known as a poet and a composer, but his enduring fame rests on his *Ars nova*, a treatise expounding a new theory of mensural notation, particularly important for its development of the principle of binary rhythm; it also gives the most complete account of the various uses to which colored notes were put. Of the 4 treatises attributed to Vitry in Coussemaker's *Scriptores*, III, only the last 10 of the 24 chapters of *Ars nova* (publ., with corrections, in *Musica Disciplina*, 1956) are now considered authentic. Most of Vitry's works are lost; L. Schrade ed. 12 of his motets as *The Works of Philippe de Vitry*, Polyphonic Music of the Fourteenth Century, I (Monaco, 1956); another motet, with tenor only, is also extant.
BIBL.: A. Coville, "P. d.V., Notes biographiques," *Romania* (Oct. 1933); L. Schrade, "P. d.V.: Some New Discoveries," *Musical Quarterly* (July 1956).

Vittadini, Franco, Italian composer; b. Pavia, April 9, 1884; d. there, Nov. 30, 1948. He studied at the Milan Cons.; after serving as organist and maestro di cappella in Varese, he returned to Pavia, where he was founder-director of the Istituto Musicale (1924–48).
WORKS: OPERAS: *Il mare di Tiberiade* (c.1912–14); *Anima allegra* (1918–19; Rome, April 15, 1921); *Nazareth* (Pavia, May 28, 1925); *La Sagredo* (Milan, April 26, 1930); *Caracciolo* (Rome, Feb. 7, 1938); *Fiammetta e l'avvaro* (1942; Brescia, 1951); pastoral triptych, *Il natale di Gesù* (Bari, Dec. 20, 1933). **BALLETS:** *Vecchia Milano* (Milan, 1928); *Fiordisole* (Milan, Feb. 14, 1935); *La Taglioni* (Milan, 1945); also film music. **ORCH.:** *Armonie della notte* (1923); *Scherzo* (1931); *Poemetto romantico* for Strings (1938); also various sacred vocal works, including *L'agonia del Redentore* (1933), many masses, and numerous motets; chamber music; organ pieces; piano music; songs.
BIBL.: A. Baratti, *Vita del musicista F. V.* (Milan, 1955).

Vittori, Loreto, prominent Italian castrato soprano and composer; b. Spoleto (baptized), Sept. 5, 1600; d. Rome, April 23, 1670. After serving as a chorister at Spoleto Cathedral (1614–17), he went to Rome to pursue his musical training; about

1618 he proceeded to Florence, where he continued his studies and began his operatic career in 1619. Returning to Rome, he was in the service of Cardinal Lodovico Ludovisi (1621–32); also sang in the papal choir (1622–47), where he was camerlengo (1642–44); likewise was in the service of Cardinal Antonio Barberini (1637–42). About 1623 he was created Cavaliere della Milizia di Gesù Cristo by Pope Urban VIII; in 1643 he entered the priesthood. He composed both sacred and secular dramatic works, but the music to most of these is lost; his fine pastoral opera, *La Galatea* (Rome, 1639), is extant. He was also a poet; publ. *Dialoghi sacri, e morali* (Rome, 1652) and *La Troja rapita* (Macerata, 1662).
BIBL.: C. Rau, *L. V.: Beiträge zur historisch-kritischen Würdigung seines Lebens, Wirkens und Schaffens* (Munich, 1916); L. Fausti, "Un autobiografia poetica di L. V.," *Atti dell'Accademia Spoletina, 1920–22* (Spoleto, 1922); B. Antolini, "La carriera di cantante e compositore di L. V.," *Studi Musicale*, VII (1978).

Vivaldi, Antonio (Lucio), greatly renowned Italian composer; b. Venice, March 4, 1678; d. Vienna, July 28, 1741. He was the son of **Giovanni Battista Vivaldi** (b. Brescia, c.1655; d. Venice, May 14, 1736), a violinist who entered the orch. at San Marco in Venice in 1685 under the surname of Rossi, remaining there until 1729; was also director of instrumental music at the Mendicanti (1689–93). The younger Vivaldi was trained for the priesthood at S. Geminiano and at S. Giovanni in Oleo, taking the tonsure on Sept. 18, 1693, and Holy Orders on March 23, 1703. Because of his red hair he was called "il prete rosso" ("the red priest"). In 1703 he became maestro di violino at the Pio Ospedale della Pietà, where he remained until 1709; during this period, his 1st publ. works appeared. In 1711 he resumed his duties at the Pietà, and was named its maestro de' concerti in 1716. In 1711 his set of 12 concerti known as *L'estro armonico*, op. 3, appeared in print in Amsterdam; it proved to be the most important music publication of the 1st half of the 18th century. His 1st known opera, *Ottone in Villa*, was given in Vicenza in May 1713, and soon thereafter he became active as a composer and impresario in Venice. From 1718 to 1720 he was active in Mantua, where the Habsburg governor Prince Philipp of Hessen-Darmstadt made him maestro di cappella la (or di) camera, a title he retained even after leaving Mantua. In subsequent years he traveled widely in Italy, bringing out his operas in various music centers. However, he retained his association with the Pietà. About 1725 he became associated with the contralto Anna Giraud (or Girò), one of his voice students; her sister, Paolina, also became a constant companion of the composer, leading to speculation by his contemporaries that the 2 sisters were his mistresses, a contention he denied. His *La cetra*, op. 9 (2 books, Amsterdam, 1727), was dedicated to the Austrian Emperor Charles VI. From 1735 to 1738 he once more served as maestro di cappella at the Pietà. He also was named maestro di cappella to Francis Stephen, Duke of Lorraine (later the Emperor Francis I), in 1735. In 1738 he visited Amsterdam, where he took charge of the musical performances for the centennial celebration of the Schouwburg theater. Returning to Venice, he found little favor with the theatergoing public; as a result, he set out for Austria in 1740, arriving in Vienna in June 1741, but dying a month later. Although he had received large sums of money in his day, he died in poverty and was given a pauper's burial at the Spettaler Gottesacher (Hospital Burial Ground).

Vivaldi's greatness lies mainly in his superb instrumental works, most notably some 500 concertos, in which he displayed an extraordinary mastery of ritornello form and of orchestration. More than 230 of his concertos are for solo violin and strings, and another 120 or so are for other solo instrument and strings. In some 60 concerti ripieni (string concertos *sans* solo instrument), he honed a style akin to operatic sinfonias. He also wrote about 90 sonatas. Only 21 of his operas are extant, some missing 1 or more acts. He also composed various sacred vocal works.

WORKS: OPERAS: *Ottone in Villa* (Vicenza, May 1713); *Orlando finto pazzo* (Venice, 1714); *Nerone fatto Cesare* (Venice, Carnival 1715); *La costanza trionfante degl'amori e de gl'odii* (Venice, Carnival 1716); *Arsilda Regina di Ponto* (Venice, 1716); *L'incoronazione di Dario* (Venice, Carnival 1717); *Tieteberga* (Venice, 1717); *Scanderbeg* (Florence, June 22, 1718); *Armida al campo d'Egitto* (Venice, Carnival 1718); *Teuzzone* (Mantua, Carnival 1719); *Tito Manlio* (Mantua, Carnival 1719); *La Candace o siano Li veri amici* (Mantua, Carnival 1720); *La verità in cimento* (Venice, 1720); *Tito Manlio*, pasticcio (Rome, 1720; in collaboration with G. Boni and C. Giorgio); *Filippo Re di Macedonia* (Venice, Carnival 1721; in collaboration with G. Boneveni); *La Silvia* (Milan, Aug. 26, 1721); *Ercole su'l Termodonte* (Rome, Jan. 23, 1723); *Giustino* (Rome, Carnival 1724); *La virtù trionfante dell'amore e dell'odio overo Il Tigrane* (Rome, Carnival 1724; in collaboration with B. Micheli and N. Romaldi); *L'inganno trionfante in amore* (Venice, 1725); *Cunegonda* (Venice, Carnival 1726); *La Fede tradita e vendicata* (Venice, Carnival 1726); *Dorilla in Tempe* (Venice, 1726); *Ipermestra* (Florence, Carnival 1727); *Siroe, Re di Persia* (Reggio, May 1727); *Farnace* (Venice, 1727); *Orlando (furioso)* (Venice, 1727); *Rosilena ed Oronta* (Venice, Jan. 17, 1728); *L'Atenaide o sia Gli affetti generosi* (Florence, Dec. 29, 1728); *Argippo* (Prague, 1730); *Alvilda, Regina de' Goti* (Prague, 1731); *La fida ninfa* (Verona, Jan. 6, 1732; rev. as *Il giorno felice*); *Semiramide* (Mantua, Carnival 1732); *Motezuma* (Venice, 1733); *L'Olimpiade* (Venice, Carnival 1734); *Griselda* (Venice, May 1735); *Aristide* (Venice, May 1735); *Bajazet* or *Tamerlano* (Venice, Carnival 1735; based on music by other composers); *Ginevra, Principessa di Scozia* (Florence, Jan. 1736); *Didone* (London, April 1737); *Catone in Utica* (Verona, May 1737); *Il giorno felice* (Vienna, 1737); *Rosmira (fedele)* (Venice, Carnival 1738; based on music by other composers); *L'oracolo in Messenia* (Venice, Carnival 1738); *Feraspe* (Venice, 1739). **SERENATAS:** *Le gare del dovere* for 5 Voices (Rovigo, 1708); *Dall'eccelsa mia Reggia* (1725); *Questa, Eurilla gentil* for 4 Voices (Mantua, July 31, 1726); *L'unione della Pace e di Marte* for 3 Voices (Venice, 1727); *La Sena festeggiante* for 3 Voices (1726); *Il Mopso* (Venice, c.1738); *Le gare della Giustizia e della Pace*; *Mio cor povero cor* for 3 Voices; 31 solo cantatas with Basso Continuo; 9 solo cantatas with Instrument(s) and Basso Continuo. **ORATORIOS:** *La vittoria navale* (Vicenza, 1713); *Moyses Deus Pharaonis* (Venice, 1714); *Juditha triumphans devicta Holofernes barbarie* (Venice, 1716); *L'adorazione delli tre re magi* (Milan, 1722); other sacred vocal works include 7 masses or Mass sections, Psalms, hymns, antiphons, motets, etc. **CONCERTOS AND SINFONIAS** (all publ. in Amsterdam): *L'estro armonico*, op. 3 (2 books, 1711); *La stravaganza*, op. 4 (2 books, c.1714); *VI concerti a 5 stromenti*, op. 6 (1716–17); *Concerti a 5 stromenti*, op. 7 (2 books, c.1716–17); *Il cimento dell'armonia e dell'inventione*, op. 8 (2 books, 1725); *La cetra*, op. 9 (2 books, 1727); *VI concerti*, op. 10 (c.1728); *6 concerti*, op. 11 (1729); *6 concerti*, op. 12 (1729). **SONATAS:** *Suonate da camera a 3* for 2 Violins and Violone or Harpsichord, op. 1 (Venice, 1705); *Sonate* for Violin and Harpsichord (Venice, 1709; publ. as op. 2, Amsterdam, 1712–13); *VI sonate* for Violin or 2 Violins and Basso Continuo, op. 5 (Amsterdam, 1716); *VI sonates* for Cello and Basso Continuo (Paris, 1740).

BIBL.: COLLECTED EDITIONS, SOURCE MATERIAL: G.F. Malipiero et al., eds., *Le opere di A. V.* (Rome, 1947–72). A new critical ed. commenced publication in Milan in 1982 under the auspices of the Istituto Italiano Antonio Vivaldi. P. Ryom edited *Verzeichnis der Werke A. V.s: Kleine Ausgabe* (Leipzig, 1974; 2nd ed., 1979) and *Repertoire des œuvres d'A. V.* (vol. I, Copenhagen, 1986). See also M. Rinaldi, *Catalogo numerico tematico delle composizioni di A. V.* (Rome, 1945); M. Pincherle, *Inventaire thématique* (Paris, 1948; in II of *A. V. et la musique instrumentale*); A. Fanna, *A. V.: Catalogo numerico-tematico delle opere strumentali* (Milan, 1968; rev. ed., 1986); K. Heller, *Die deutsche Überlieferung der Instrumentalwerke V.s* (Leipzig, 1971); N. Ohmura, *A Reference Concordance Table of V.'s Instrumental Works* (Tokyo, 1972); P. Ryom, *A. V.: Table de concordances des œuvres* (Copenhagen, 1973); idem, *Les Manuscrits de V.* (Copenhagen, 1977); M. Talbot, *A. V.: A Guide to Research* (N.Y., 1988).

BIOGRAPHICAL, ANALYTICAL: *A. V.: Note e documenti sulla vita e sulle opere*, Chigiana, I (1939); M. Abbado, *A. V.* (Turin, 1942); M. Rinaldi, *A. V.* (Milan, 1943); M. Pincherle, *A. V. et la musique instrumentale* (Paris, 1948); W. Newman, "The Sonatas of Albinoni and V.," *Journal of the American Musicological Society*, V (1952); W. Kolneder, *Aufführungspraxis bei V.* (Leipzig, 1955; 2nd ed., 1973); M. Pincherle, *V.* (Paris, 1955; Eng. tr., 1958); R. Eller, *V.s Konzertform* (diss., Univ. of Leipzig, 1956); G. Malipiero, *A. V., il prete rosso* (Milan, 1958); H. Rarig, *The Instrumental Sonatas of A. V.* (diss., Univ. of Michigan, 1958); L. Rowell, *4 Operas of A. V.* (diss., Univ. of Rochester, 1958); W. Kolneder, *Die Solokonzertform bei V.* (Strasbourg and Baden-Baden, 1961); R. Giazotto, *V.* (Milan, 1965); W. Kolneder, *A. V.: Leben und Werk* (Wiesbaden, 1965; Eng. tr., 1970); R. de Candé, *V.* (Paris, 1967); M. Dunham, *The Secular Cantatas of A. V. in the Foà Collection* (diss., Univ. of Michigan, 1969); *V.ana* (Brussels, 1969); R. Giazotto, *A. V.* (Turin, 1973); W. Kolneder, *Melodietypen bei V.* (Berg am Irchel and Zürich, 1973); F. Degrada and M. Muraro, eds., *A. V. da Venezia all'Europa* (Milan, 1978); M. Talbot, *V.* (London, 1978; 2nd ed., 1984); W. Kolneder, *A. V.: Dokumente seines Lebens und Schaffens* (Wilhelmshaven, 1979); E. Cross, *The Late Operas of A. V., 1727–1738* (Ann Arbor, 1980); A. Bellini, B. Brizi, and M. Pensa, *I libretti V.ana: Recensione e collazione dei testimoni a stampa* (Florence, 1982); K. Heller, *Concerto ripieno und Sinfonia bei V.* (diss., Univ. of Rostock, 1982); R.-C. Travers, *La Maladie de V.* (Poitiers, 1982); M. Collins and E. Kirk, eds., *Opera and V.* (Austin, Tex., 1984); M. Talbot, "V. and Rome: Observations and Hypotheses," *Journal of the Royal Musical Association*, 113/1 (1988).

Vivell, Cölestin (actually, **Max**), German music scholar and churchman; b. Wolfach, Oct. 21, 1846; d. Seckau, Austria, March 10, 1923. Having completed his univ. studies, he joined the order of Benedictines at Beuron; from 1883, lived in the monastery at Seckau. **WRITINGS:** *Erklärung der vatikanischen Choralschrift nebst Proben aus dem Kyriale* (Graz, 1906); *Vom Musiktraktate Gregors des Grossen: Eine Untersuchung über Gregors Autorschaft und über den Inhalt der Schrift* (Leipzig, 1911); *Initia tractatuum musices: Ex codicibus editorium collegit et ordine alphabetico disposuit* (Graz, 1912); ed. *Commentarius anonymus in Micrologum Guidonis Aretini* (Vienna, 1917); ed. *Frutolfi Breviarium de musica et Tonarius* (Vienna, 1919).

Vives, Amadeo, Spanish composer; b. Collbató, near Barcelona, Nov. 18, 1871; d. Madrid, Dec. 1, 1932. He was a pupil of Ribera and then of Felipe Pedrell in Barcelona; with L. Millet, founded the famous choral society Orfeó Català (1891). In his first opera, *Artus* (Barcelona, 1895), he made use of Catalonian folk songs. Subsequently he moved to Madrid, where he produced his comic opera *Don Lucas del Cigarral* (Feb. 18, 1899); his opera *Euda d'Uriach*, originally to a Catalan libretto, was brought out in Italian at Barcelona (Oct. 24, 1900). Then followed his most popular opera, *Maruxa* (Madrid, May 28, 1914); other operas are *Balada de Carnaval* (Madrid, July 5, 1919) and *Doña Francisquita* (Madrid, Oct. 17, 1923). The style of his stage productions shared qualities of the French light opera and the Spanish zarzuela; he wrote nearly 100 of these; also composed songs and piano pieces; publ. a book of essays, *Sofia* (Madrid, 1923).
BIBL.: A. Sagardía, *A. V.: Vida y obra* (Madrid, 1971).

Vivier, Albert-Joseph, Belgian music theorist and composer; b. Huy, Dec. 15, 1816; d. Brussels, Jan. 3, 1903. He studied with Fétis at the Brussels Cons.; wrote an interesting *Traité complet d'harmonie* (1862; many later eds.), in which he explained secondary chords as accidental formations through incorporation of auxiliary notes; he also wrote essays on acoustics (*Des vrais rapports des sons musicaux*, *Eléments d'acoustique musicale*, etc.). His opera *Spadillo le tavernier* was produced in Brussels on May 22, 1857.

Vivier, Claude, Canadian composer; b. Montreal, April 14, 1948; d. (found strangled to death, by parties unknown, in his apartment), Paris, March 7, 1983. He studied music with Tremblay at the Montreal Cons. (1967–70); then took courses in electronic music with Koening at the Inst. of Sonology at the Univ. of Utrecht; also attended classes in electronic composition given by Stockhausen in Cologne. In 1976 he traveled in the Orient to study non-European musical cultures. He was in Paris on a Canada Council Grant to compose an opera on the death of Tchaikovsky, to be titled *Crois-tu en l'immortalité de l'âme?*, at the time of his murder.

WORKS: Chamber opera, *Copernicus (Rituel de mort)* for Soloists, Instruments, and Tape (1979; Montreal, May 8, 1980); String Quartet (1969); *Prolifération* for Ondes Martenot, Piano, and Percussion (1969; rev. 1975); *Hiérophanie* for Soprano and Chamber Ensemble (1970); *Deva et Asura* for Chamber Ensemble (1972); *Désintégration* for 2 Pianos, 4 Violins, and 2 Violas (1972); *O! Kosmos* for a cappella Chorus (1974); *Lettura di Dante* for Soprano and Ensemble (1974); *Liebesgedichte* for Vocal Quartet and Instruments (1975); *Piece* for Bassoon and Piano (1975); *Pour violon et clarinette* (1975); *Siddhartha* for Orch. (1976); *Orion* for Orch. (1979); *Zipangu* for String Orch. (1980); *Bouchara (Chanson d'amour)* for Soprano and 11 Instruments (1982).

Vivier, Eugène (-Léon), French horn player, composer, and writer on music; b. Brioude, Haute-Loire, Dec. 4, 1817; d. Nice, Feb. 24, 1900. He learned to play violin and was a member of the orch. of the Grand Théâtre in Lyons; went to Paris in 1843, where he received some lessons in horn playing from Gallay; then played in theater orchs. and in the orch. at the Opéra, eventually becoming a favorite at the court; also toured Europe. After the establishment of the republic, he retired to Nice. An eccentric, he prided himself on his ability to play 2 notes simultaneously on his instrument, through clever overblowing. He publ. a number of pamphlets on music and the theater, and also an autobiography (largely fictitious), *La Vie et les aventures d'un corniste* (Paris, 1900). Among his compositions are several romances.

Vix, Geneviève, French soprano; b. Nantes, Dec. 31, 1879; d. Paris, Aug. 25, 1939. She studied at the Paris Cons.; won 1st prize for opera (1908); sang at the Paris Opéra, in Madrid, and in Buenos Aires; made her American debut with the Chicago Opera Co. as Manon in Massenet's opera (Dec. 1, 1917); married Prince Cyril Naryshkin in N.Y. (Feb. 9, 1918). She possessed a fine lyric voice, and was also adept as an actress.

Vlad, Roman, Rumanian-born Italian composer and writer on music; b. Cernăuţi, Dec. 29, 1919. He was a pupil at the Cernăuţi Cons.; in 1938, went to Rome, where he continued his training at the Univ., and studied piano with Casella at the Accademia di Santa Cecilia. He was active as a pianist and lecturer; served as artistic director of the Accademia Filarmonia in Rome, the Maggio Musicale Fiorentino and the Teatro Comunale in Florence, and the RAI sym. orch. in Turin. He taught at the Perugia Cons. (from 1968). He was co-ed. of the *Enciclopedia dello spettacolo* (1958–62) and of the *Nuova Rivista Musicale Italiana* (from 1967). In 1943 he adopted the 12-tone method of composition.

WORKS: OPERAS: *Storia di una mamma* (Venice, Oct. 5, 1951); *Il dottore di vetro*, radio opera (RAI, Turin, Feb. 23, 1959; 1st stage perf., Berlin, 1961); *La fantarca*, television opera (1967). **BALLETS:** *La strada sul caffè* (1942–43; also an orch. suite); *La dama delle camelie* (Rome, Nov. 20, 1945; rev. 1956; also an orch. suite); *Masques ostendais* (Spoleto, June 12, 1959; rev. 1960); *Die Wiederkehr* (Cologne, 1962; rev. as *Ricercare*, Rome, 1968); *Il gabbiano* (Siena, 1968); various other dramatic works, including incidental music and film scores. **ORCH.:** *Sinfonietta* (1941); Suite (1941); *Sinfonia all'antica* (Venice, Sept. 8, 1948); *Variazioni concertanti su una serie di 12 note dal Don Giovanni di Mozart* for Piano and Orch. (Venice, Sept. 18, 1955); *Musica per archi* (1955–57); *Musica concertata* for Harp and Orch. (Turin, April 24,

1958); *Ode super Chrysea Phorminx* for Guitar and Orch. (1964); *Divertimento sinfonico* (1965–67). **CHAMBER:** Divertimento for 11 Instruments (1948); String Quartet (1955–57); Serenata for 12 Instruments (1959); *Improvvisazione su di una melodia* for Clarinet and Piano (1970); *Il magico flauto di Severino* for Flute and Piano (1971); various piano pieces, including *Studi dodecafonici* (1943; rev. 1957) and *Sognando il sogno: Variazioni su una variazione* (1971). **CHORAL:** Cantata No. 1: *Dove sei, Elohim?* for Chorus and Orch. (1940–42); Cantata No. 2: *De profundis* for Chorus and Orch. (1942–46); Cantata No. 3: *Le ciel est vide* for Chorus and Orch. (1952–53); *Letture di Michelangelo* (1964; rev. as *Cadenze michelangiolesche* for Tenor or Soprano and Orch., 1967); *La vespa di Toti* for Boy's Voices and Instruments (1975–76); also various solo works.

WRITINGS: *Modernità e tradizione nella musica contemporanea* (Turin, 1955); with A. Piovesan and R. Craft, *Le musiche religiose di Igor Strawinsky* (Venice, 1956); *Luigi Dallapiccola* (Milan, 1957); *Storia della dodecafonia* (Milan, 1958); *Strawinsky* (Turin, 1958; Eng. tr., 1960; 3rd ed., rev., 1979).

Vladigerov, Alexander, Bulgarian conductor and composer, son of **Pantcho Vladigerov**; b. Sofia, Aug. 4, 1933. He studied composition with his father and conducting with Simeonov at the Bulgarian State Cons. in Sofia, graduating in 1956; also took conducting courses in Kiev with Rakhlin. He was conductor of the orch. in Ruse; then was engaged as conductor for Bulgarian Radio and Television.

WORKS: Children's operetta, *Little Red Riding Hood* (1969); 2 musicals: *The Jolly Town Musicians* (1971) and *The Wolf and the 7 Kids* (1973); *Youth March* for Orch. (1948); *Rondo concertante* for Violin and Orch. (1955); *Rumanian Dance* for Orch. (1960); piano pieces.

Vladigerov, Pantcho, prominent Bulgarian composer, father of **Alexander Vladigerov;** b. Zürich, March 13, 1899, in a geminal parturition; d. Sofia, Sept. 8, 1978. Distrustful of Bulgarian puerperal skill, his mother sped from Shumen to Zürich as soon as she learned that she was going to have a plural birth. Pantcho's non-identical twin brother, Luben, a violinist, was born 16 hours earlier than Pantcho, on the previous day, March 12, 1899. Vladigerov studied piano and theory with local teachers in Sofia (1910–12); then went to Berlin, where he took lessons in composition with Paul Juon and Georg Schumann, and piano with Leonid Kreutzer at the Akademie der Künste; then served as conductor and composer of the Max Reinhardt Theater (1921–32); subsequently was a reader (1932–38) and a prof. of piano and composition (1938–72) at the Bulgarian State Cons. of Music in Sofia. His music is rooted in Bulgarian folk songs, artfully combining the peculiar melodic and rhythmic patterns of native material with stark modern harmonies; the method is similar to that of Béla Bartók.

WORKS: STAGE: *Tsar Kaloyan*, opera (1935–36; Sofia, April 20, 1936); *Legenda za ezeroto* (Legend of the Lake), ballet (1946; Sofia, Nov. 11, 1962). **ORCH.:** 2 suites (1947, 1953); 5 piano concertos (1918, 1930, 1937, 1953, 1963); *Legend* (1919); *3 Impressions* (1920; orchestration of 3 of his *10 Impressions* for Piano); 2 violin concertos (1921, 1968); *Burlesk Suite* for Violin and Orch. (1922); *Scandinavian Suite* (1924); *Bulgarian Suite* (1927); *Vardar*, Bulgarian rhapsody (1927; orchestration of his earlier violin and piano piece); 7 *Bulgarian Symphonic Dances* (1931); 2 overtures: *Zemja* (1933) and *The 9th of September* (1949); 2 syms.: No. 1 (1939) and No. 2, *Majska* (May) for String Orch. (1949); *Concert Fantasy* for Cello and Orch. (1941); 4 *Rumanian Symphonic Dances* (1942); *Improvisation and Toccata* (1942; orchestration of the final 2 pieces of his piano cycle *Episodes*); 2 *Rumanian Symphonic Sketches* (1943); *Prelude and Balkan Dance* (1950); *Evreyska poema* (Jewish Poem) (1951); *Song of Peace*, dramatic poem (1956); 7 *Pieces* for String Orch. (1969–70; orchestration of pieces taken from 3 different piano cycles). **CHAMBER:** Violin Sonata (1914); Piano Trio (1916). **VIOLIN AND PIANO:** 2 *Improvisations* (1919); 4 *Pieces* (1920); *Vardar* (1922); 2 *Bulgarian Paraphrases* (1925); 2 *Pieces* (1926); String Quartet (1940); several piano cycles, many of which are also scored for chamber orch.: *4 Pieces* (1915); *11 Variations* (1916); *10 Impressions* (1920); *4 Pieces* (1920); *3 Pieces* (1922); *6 Exotic Preludes* (1924); *Classical and Romantic*, 7 pieces (1931); *Bulgarian Songs and Dances* (1932); *Sonatina concertante* (1934); *Shumen*, 6 miniatures (1934); *5 Episodes* (1941); *Aquarelles* (1942); *3 Pictures* (1950); *Suite*, 5 pieces (1954); *3 Pieces* (1957); *3 Concert Pieces* (1959); *5 Novelettes* (1965); *5 Pieces* (1965); orchestration of Dinicu's *Hora staccato*.

BIBL.: E. Pavlov, *P. V.: A Monograph* (Sofia, 1961).

Vlasov, Vladimir (Alexandrovich), Russian conductor, ethnomusicologist, and composer; b. Moscow, Jan. 7, 1903; d. there, Sept. 7, 1986. He studied violin at the Moscow Cons.; was active as a teacher. In 1936 he traveled to Frunze, Kirghizia, where he diligently went about collecting authentic songs of the natives. In collaboration with Vladimir Fere, similarly intentioned, he wrote a number of operas based on Kirghiz national melorhythms supplied by local musicians. These operas include: *Altin kiz* (The Golden Girl; Frunze, May 1, 1937); *Aychurek* (Moon Beauty; Frunze, May 1, 1942); *Za schastye naroda* (For the People's Happiness; Frunze, May 1, 1941); *Sin naroda* (A Son of His People; Frunze, Nov. 8, 1947); *Na beregakh Issikh-kulya* (On the Shores of Lake Issik; Frunze, Feb. 1, 1951); *Vedma* (The Witch; 1961); etc. He also composed 2 operettas and several ballets. Among his other works are 2 cello concertos, 3 string quartets, a Suite for Folk Instruments (1955), and more than 1,000 songs.

BIBL.: V. Vinogradov, *A. Maldibayev, V. V., V. Fere* (Moscow, 1958).

Vlijmen, Jan van, Dutch composer; b. Rotterdam, Oct. 11, 1935. He studied composition with Kees van Baaren. Upon completion of his musical education, he was director of the Amersfoort Music School (1961–65); was a lecturer in theory at the Utrecht Cons. (1965–67); became deputy director of the Royal Cons. of Music at The Hague in 1967, and, upon Baaren's death, became its director in 1971.

WORKS: OPERAS: *Reconstructie*, an anti-U.S. work (1968–69; Holland Festival, June 29, 1969; in collaboration with Louis Andriessen, Reinbert de Leeuw, Misha Mengelberg, and Peter Schat); *Axel* (1975–77; Holland Festival, Scheveningen, June 10, 1977; in collaboration with Reinbert de Leeuw); String Quartet (1955); *Morgensternlieder* for Mezzo-soprano and Piano (1958); 2 wind quintets (1958, 1972); *Construzione* for 2 Pianos (1959); *Serie* for 6 Instruments (1960); *Gruppi* for 20 Instruments in 4 groups, and Percussion (1961–62; rev. 1980); *Mythos* for Mezzo-soprano and 9 Instruments (1962); *Spostamenti* for Orch. (1963); *Serenata I* for 12 Instruments and Percussion (1963–64; rev. 1967); *Serenata II* for Flute and 4 Instrumental Groups (Amsterdam, Sept. 10, 1965); *Sonata* for Piano and 3 Instrumental Groups (1966); *Dialogue* for Clarinet and Piano (1966); *Per diciasette* for 17 Winds (1967); *Interpolations* for Orch. and Electronic Sound (Rotterdam, Nov. 24, 1968; rev. 1981); *Ommagio a Gesualdo* for Violin and 6 Instrumental Groups (Amsterdam, April 9, 1971); *4 Songs* for Mezzo-soprano and Orch. (1975); *Quaterni* for Orch. (1979); *Trimurti* for String Quartet (1980; rev. 1981); *Solo II* for Clarinet (1986).

Vockerodt, Gottfried, German writer on music; b. Mühlhausen, Thuringia, Sept. 24, 1665; d. Gotha, Oct. 10, 1727. He was educated at the Univ. of Jena (M.A., 1685); then taught classical languages there. After serving as Konrektor at the Halle Gymnasium (1689–93), he settled in Gotha as a teacher at the Fürstenschule, becoming its director in 1694. It was his opinion that excessive enjoyment of music injures the intellect, and that Caligula, Claudius, and Nero became totally depraved through their passion for music. He advocated these ideas in a number of publs., including *Illustri Gymnasii Gothani summons patronos . . . ad publicas orationes, De falsa mentium intemperatarum medicina* (Gotha, 1696); *Missbrauch der freyen Künste, insonderheit der Music, nebenst abgenöthigter Erörterung der Frage: was nach D. Luthers und andere evangelischen Theologorum und Politicorum Meinung von Opern und Comodien zu halten sey?* (Frankfurt am Main, 1697);

Wiederholtes Zeugnüs der Wahrheit gegen die verderbte Music und Schauspiele, Opern, Comödien und dergleichen Eitelkeiten, welche die heutige Welt vor unschuldige Mitteldinge will gehalten wissen (Frankfurt am Main and Leipzig, 1698).

Vockner, Josef, Austrian organist, composer, and teacher; b. Ebensee, March 18, 1842; d. Vienna, Sept. 11, 1906. He was a pupil of Bruckner; became a prof. of organ at the Vienna Cons. He composed an oratorio, *Das jüngste Gericht;* Cello Sonata; Piano Quartet; fugues and other pieces for organ; songs.

Vodušek, Valens, Slovenian ethnomusicologist and conductor; b. Ljubljana, Jan. 29, 1912. He studied at the Univ. of Ljubljana (L.L.D., 1938) and took courses in piano and conducting at the Ljubljana State Cons. (1930–36); was self-taught in musicology and ethnomusicology. He became head of the music section at the Ministry of Culture in Slovenia (1946–51), then joined the Inst. for Ethnomusicology in Ljubljana. He was director of the Ljubljana Opera (1951–55), returning to the Inst. as director until 1972, when it combined with the Inst. of Ethnology of the Slovene Academy of Sciences and Arts; at that time he became head of its ethnomusicology dept. He conducted the Ljubljana Radio Choir (1946–51; renamed the Slovene Phil. Choir in 1948), and was artistic director of the Slovene Octet (1956–72). Vodušek instigated systematic fieldwork and classification in Slovene ethnic music.

Vogel, Adolf, German bass-baritone; b. Munich, Aug. 18, 1897; d. Vienna, Dec. 20, 1969. He studied voice with Anna Bahr-Mildenburg and J. Kiechle; made his operatic debut as Daland in Klagenfurt (1923); was a member of the Bavarian State Opera in Munich from 1930 to 1937; made his U.S. debut at the Metropolitan Opera in N.Y. as Alberich (Dec. 3, 1937); remained on its roster until 1939; then taught voice at the Vienna Academy of Music (from 1940). He became best known for his buffo roles.

Vogel, Charles Louis Adolphe, French violinist and composer, grandson of **Johann Christoph Vogel;** b. Lille, May 17, 1808; d. Paris, Sept. 11, 1892. He studied in Lille and then at the Paris Cons. with A. Kreutzer (violin) and Reicha (theory). After winning popularity with his song *Les Trois Couleurs* during the July Revolution (1830), he brought out a series of successful operas: *Le Podestat* (Paris, Dec. 16, 1831); *Le Siège de Leyde* (The Hague, March 14, 1847); *La Moissonneuse* (Paris, Sept. 3, 1853); *Rompons* (Paris, Sept. 21, 1857); *Le Nid de Cigognes* (Baden-Baden, Sept. 1858); *Gredin de Pigoche* (Paris, Oct. 19, 1866); *La Filleule du roi* (Brussels, April 1875). He also wrote syms., chamber music, sacred works, songs, and piano pieces.

Vogel, (Johannes) Emil (Eduard Bernhard), German musicologist; b. Wriezen an der Oder, Jan. 21, 1859; d. Nikolassee, near Berlin, June 18, 1908. He studied at Greifswald and Berlin; in 1893 he organized the Peters Music Library in Leipzig, serving as its librarian (1895–1901); also was founder-ed. of the *Jahrbuch der Musikbibliothek Peters.* He publ. the catalogue *Die Handschriften nebst den älteren Druckwerken der Musikabteilung der herzoglichen Bibliothek zu Wolfenbüttel* (1890) and *Bibliothek der gedruckten weltlichen Vokalmusik Italiens aus den Jahren 1500 bis 1700* (1892; new ed., completely rev. by Alfred Einstein, publ. in *Notes,* June 1945–Sept. 1948; another ed. by F. Lesure and C. Sartoi, eds., *Il nuovo Vogel: Bibliografia della musica italiana vocale profana pubblicata dal 1500–1700,* Geneva, 1977).

Vogel, Friedrich Wilhelm Ferdinand, German organist, teacher, and composer; b. Havelberg, Prussia, Sept. 9, 1807; d. Bergen, Norway, July 20, 1892. He studied with Birnbach in Berlin; made tours as an organ virtuoso; taught at Hamburg (1838–41) and Copenhagen (1845–52); then settled in Bergen, where he founded an organ school. He publ. a number of works for organ, including 60 chorale-preludes, 10 postludes, and 2 preludes and fugues; also chamber music; overtures; choruses.

Vogel, Jaroslav, Czech conductor and composer; b. Pilsen, Jan. 11, 1894; d. Prague, Feb. 2, 1970. He studied violin with

Ševčík and composition with Novák in Prague; after taking courses in Munich (1910–12) and at the Paris Schola Cantorum with d'Indy (1912–13), he completed his training with Novák at the Prague Cons. (graduated, 1919). He was a conductor at the Pilsen Opera (1914–15) and in Ostrava (1919–23); after conducting in Prague (1923–27), he was chief conductor of the Ostrava Opera (1927–43); then conducted at the Prague National Theater (1949–58), and was chief conductor of the Brno State Phil. (1959–62). In 1964 he was made an Artist of Merit by the Czech government. As a conductor, he championed the music of Smetana, Janáček, and Novák. He publ. (in German) the useful study *Leoš Janáček: Sein Leben und Werk* (Prague, 1958; abridged Eng. tr., 1962; Czech original, 1963). He composed the operas *Maréja* (Olomouc, 1923), *Meister Georg* or *Mistr Jíra* (Prague, 1926), *Jovana* (Ostrava, 1939), and *Hiawatha* (Ostrava, 1974), orch. pieces, and chamber music.

Vogel, Johann Christoph, German composer, grandfather of **Charles Louis Adolphe Vogel;** b. Nuremberg (baptized), March 18, 1756; d. Paris, June 27, 1788. He was a pupil of Riepel at Regensburg; went to Paris in 1776 and was in the service of the Duke of Montmorency; later was in the service of the Count of Valentinois. He wrote 2 operas in Gluck's style: *La Toison d'or* (Paris, Sept. 5, 1786) and *Démophon,* which he completed shortly before his untimely death at the age of 32, and which was produced posthumously (Paris, Sept. 22, 1789). He also composed an oratorio, *Jepthe* (1781), 3 syms., several simphonies concertantes, a Violin Concerto (1782), 3 flute concertos, 2 oboe concertos, some 6 clarinet concertos, a Bassoon Concerto (1782), and much chamber music.

BIBL.: A. Bickel, *J.C. V.: Der grosse Nürnberger Komponist zwischen Gluck und Mozart (1756–1788)* (Nuremberg, 1956).

Vogel, Wladimir (Rudolfovich), significant German-Russian-born Swiss composer; b. Moscow (of a German father and a Russian mother), Feb. 29, 1896; d. Zürich, June 19, 1984. He began composing in his youth. At the outbreak of World War I (1914), he was interned in Russia as an enemy alien; after the Armistice in 1918, he went to Berlin, where he studied with Heinz Tiessen (1919–21) and with Busoni (1921–24). He was greatly influenced by both Busoni and Schoenberg. From 1929 to 1933 Vogel taught at the Klindworth-Scharwenka Cons. in Berlin; with the advent to power of the Nazi government, Vogel, although not a Jew, chose to leave Germany. He worked in Strasbourg and Brussels with Hermann Scherchen on various problems of musical techniques; then went to Switzerland, and in 1954 became a Swiss citizen. Vogel's idiom of composition underwent several changes throughout the years. A convinced believer in the mystical power of music, he felt great affinity with Scriabin's mystical ideas and techniques; he built his melodies along the upper overtones of the harmonic series, and his harmonies on a massive superimposition of perfect fourths and tritones. Gradually he approached the method of composition in 12 tones as promulgated by Schoenberg, while Busoni's precepts of neo-Classical structures governed Vogel's own works as far as formal design was concerned; many of his polyphonic compositions adhered to the Classical harmonic structures in 4 parts, which he maintained even in choral pieces using the *Sprechstimme.* Serialist procedures are adumbrated in Vogel's music through the astute organization of melodic and rhythmic elements.

WORKS: ORCH.: *Sinfonia fugata* (1924); *4 Studies: Ritmica funèbre, Ritmica scherzosa, Ostinato perpetuo,* and *Ritmica ostinata* (1930–32); *Rallye* (1932); *Tripartita* (1934; Geneva, Nov. 21, 1935); Violin Concerto (1937); *Passacaglia* (1946); *Sept aspects d'une série de douze sons* (1949–50); *Spiegelungen* (1952; Frankfurt am Main, June 26, 1953); Cello Concerto (1954; Zürich, Nov. 27, 1956); *Interludio lirico* (1954); *Preludio, Interludio lirico, Postludio* (1954); *Hörformen I* (1967) and *II* (1967–69); *Cantique en forme d'un canon à quatre voix* (1969); *Abschied* for String Orch. (1973); *Meloformen* for String Orch. (1974); *Hommage* for String Orch. (1974). **CHAMBER:** *La Ticinella* for Flute, Oboe, Clarinet, Saxophone, and Bassoon

(1941); *12 variétudes* for Flute, Clarinet, Violin, and Cello (1942); *Inspiré par Jean Arp* for Violin, Flute, Clarinet, and Cello (1965); *Analogien,* "Hörformen" for String Quartet (1973); *Monophonie* for Violin (1974); *Für Flöte, Oboe, Klarinette, und Fagott* (1974); *Poème* for Cello (1974); *Terzett* for Flute, Clarinet, and Bassoon (1975). **PIANO:** *Nature vivante,* 6 expressionistic pieces (1917–21); *Einsames Getröpfel und Gewuchsel* (1921; rev. 1968); *Dai tempi più remoti,* 3 pieces (1922–31; rev. 1968); *Etude-Toccata* (1926); *Epitaffio per Alban Berg* (1936); *Klavier-eigene Interpretationsstudie einer varierten Zwölftonfolge* (1972); *4 Versionen einer Zwölftonfolge* (1972); *Musik* for Wind Quartet and Strings (1975). **VOCAL:** Oratorio, *Thyl Claes (Till Eulenspiegel)* in 2 parts: *Oppression* (1938; Geneva, 1943) and *Liberation* (1943–45; Geneva, 1947); orch. suite, Palermo, April 26, 1949); *Wagadus Untergang durch die Eitelkeit,* cantata for 3 Soloists, Mixed Chorus, Speaking Chorus, and 5 Saxophones (1930); *An die Jugend der Welt* for Chorus and Chamber Orch. (1954); *Goethe-Aphorismen* for Soprano and Strings (Venice, Sept. 1955); *Eine Gotthardkantate* for Baritone and Strings (1956); *Jona ging doch nach Ninive* for Baritone, Speaking Soloists and Chorus, Mixed Chorus, and Orch. (1958); *Meditazione su Amadeo Modigliani* for 4 Soloists, Narrator, Chorus, and Orch. (Lugano, March 31, 1962); *Die Flucht,* dramatic oratorio (1963–64; Zürich, Nov. 8, 1966); *Schritte* for Alto and Orch. (1968); *Gli Spaziali* for Speakers, Vocalists, and Orch., to words from the writings of Leonardo da Vinci, *Autour de la lune* by Jules Verne, and utterances of the American astronauts (1969–71).

BIBL.: H. Oesch, *W. V.: Sein Weg zu einer neuen musikalischen Wirklichkeit* (Bern, 1967); W. Labhart, *W. V.: Konturen eines Mitbegründes der Neuen Musik* (Zürich, 1982).

Vogeleis, Martin, Alsatian music scholar; b. Erstein, June 5, 1861; d. Sélestat, Aug. 11, 1930. He studied for the priesthood, and was ordained in 1885; taught music at the Episcopalian Seminary in Zillesheim (1886–91); then was chaplain and choirmaster in Grafenstaden (1891–96); was pastor in Behlenheim (1896–1906); from 1908, was pastor in Schlettstadt (Sélestat). He made a special study of music in Alsace; publ. *Quellen und Bausteine zu einer Geschichte der Musik und des Theaters im Elsass 500–1800* (Strasbourg, 1911).

BIBL.: M. Metz, "Histoire de la musique en Alsace d'après les travaux de M. V.," *La musique en Alsace hier et aujourd'hui* (Strasbourg, 1970).

Vogelweide, Walther von der, famous German Minnesinger and poet; b. c.1170; d. probably in Würzburg, c.1230. He learned his craft as a singer and poet in Austria; from about 1190 to 1198 he was active in Vienna, where he was associated with the court. He led a wandering life, and visited various European courts, finally entering the service of Friedrich of Sicily (later Emperor Friedrich II), who gave him a fief in Würzburg about 1220. Many of his poems are extant; however, only 1 complete original melody by him is preserved, the so-called *Palästinalied.* For text eds. of his works, see K. Lachmann, *Die Gedichte Walthers von der Vogelweide* (Berlin, 1827; 10th ed., rev., 1936, by C. von Kraus; 13th ed., 1965, by H. Kuhn); W. Wilmanns, ed., *Walther von der Vogelweide* (Halle, 1869; 4th ed., rev., 1916–24, by V. Michels); H. Paul, ed., *Walther von der Vogelweide: Gedichte* (Halle, 1882; 6th ed., rev., 1943, by A. Leitzmann; 9th ed., 1959, by H. Kuhn); F. Maurer, ed., *Die Lieder Walthers von der Vogelweide, unter Beifügung erhaltener und erschlossener Melodien,* Altdeutsche Textbibliothek, XLIII (Tübingen, 1956; 2nd ed., rev., 1965); for his music, see E. Jammers, ed., *Ausgewählte Melodien des Minnesangs* (Tübingen, 1963); H. Moser and J. Müller-Blattau, eds., *Deutsche Lieder des Mittelalters* (Stuttgart, 1968); R. Taylor, ed., *The Art of the Minnesinger* (Cardiff, 1968).

BIBL.: C. von Kraus, *W. v.d.V.: Untersuchungen* (Berlin, 1935); J. Huisman, *Neue Wege zur dichterischen und musikalischen Technik W.s v.d.V.* (Utrecht, 1950); K. Klein, *Zur Spruchdichtung und Heimatfrage W.s v.d.V.* (Innsbruck, 1952); D. Kralik, *Die Elegie W.s v.d.V.* (Vienna, 1952); K. Halbach, *W. v.d.V.* (Stuttgart, 1965; 2nd ed., rev., 1968); F. Scheibe,

W. v.d.V., Troubadour of the Middle Ages: His Life and Reputation in the English Speaking Countries (N.Y., 1969); M. Scholz, *Bibliographie zu W. v.d.V.* (Berlin, 1969).

Vogl, Heinrich, famous German tenor; b. Au, near Munich, Jan. 15, 1845; d. Munich, April 21, 1900. He studied music with Franz Lachner; made a successful debut as Max in *Der Freischütz* at the Munich Court Opera (Nov. 5, 1865), and remained on its roster until his death. He succeeded Schnorr von Carolsfeld as the model Tristan in Wagner's opera, and was for years considered the greatest interpreter of that role. He created the roles of Loge in *Das Rheingold* (Sept. 22, 1869) and of Siegmund in *Die Walküre* (June 26, 1870); sang Loge in the 1st complete *Ring* cycle at the Bayreuth Festival (1876). He also appeared as Siegfried in the 1st Munich mountings of *Siegfried* and *Götterdammerung* (1878), Loge and Siegmund in the 1st Berlin *Ring* cycle (1881), and Loge and Siegfried in the 1st London *Ring* cycle (1882). In 1882 he toured in Europe with Angelo Neumann's Wagner Co.; in 1886 he sang Tristan and Parsifal in Bayreuth; on Jan. 1, 1890, he made his debut at the Metropolitan Opera in N.Y. as Lohengrin, where he appeared later in the season as Tannhäuser, Loge, both Siegfrieds, and Siegmund. On April 17, 1900, just 4 days before his death, he appeared as Canio in his last role in Munich. He was also a composer; wrote an opera, *Der Fremdling,* in which he sang the leading role (Munich, May 7, 1899). In 1868 he married the German soprano **Therese Thoma** (b. Tutzing, Nov. 12, 1845; d. Munich, Sept. 29, 1921); was a member of the Munich Court Opera (1866–92), where she appeared as Isolde opposite her husband's Tristan (1869), Wellgunde in the premiere of *Das Rheingold* (1869), and Sieglinde in the premiere of *Die Walküre* (June 26, 1870); appeared as Brünnhilde in the 1st complete *Ring* cycles in Munich (1878) and London (1882); gave her farewell appearance as Isolde in Munich (Oct. 9, 1892).

BIBL.: H. von der Pfordten, *H. V.: Zur Erinnerung und zum Vermächtnis* (Munich, 1900); K. Pottgiesser, "H. V.," *Allgemeine Musikzeitung* (May 4, 1900); R. Wünnenberg, *Das Sangerehepaar H. und T. V.: Ein Beitrag zur Operngeschichte des 19. Jahrhunderts* (Tutzing, 1982).

Vogl, Johann Michael, Austrian baritone and composer; b. Ennsdorf, near Steyr, Aug. 10, 1768; d. Vienna, Nov. 19, 1840. He was orphaned at an early age; his vocal gifts were admired by the parish church choirmaster, who gave him his 1st music lessons. While studying languages and philosophy at the Kremsmünster Gymnasium, he was befriended by his fellow pupil, Franz Xaver Süssmayr; in 1786 he went to Vienna to study law at the Univ. After briefly practicing law, he joined Süssmayr's German opera company, making his debut at the Hofoper on May 1, 1795; was chosen to sing the role of Pizarro in the revised version of Beethoven's *Fidelio* in 1814. In 1817 he met Schubert, who became his close friend and whose lieder he subsequently championed; he also created the leading role in Schubert's opera *Die Zwillingsbrüder* (1820). Vogl wrote 3 masses, an offertory, and a number of songs.

BIBL.: A. Stadler, "Nekrolog auf J.M. V.," *Warte an der Donau* (Nov. 30, 1840); A. Weiss, *Der Schubertsänger J.M. V.* (Vienna, 1915); S. Loewy, "Der erste, der ein Schubertlied sang," *Neues Wiener Tagblatt* (Nov. 26, 1928); A. Liess, *J.M. V.: Hofoperist und Schubertsänger* (Graz and Cologne, 1954).

Vogler, Georg Joseph, noted German pianist, organist, pedagogue, music theorist, and composer, known as **Abbé** or **Abt Vogler;** b. Pleichach, near Würzburg, June 15, 1749; d. Darmstadt, May 6, 1814. His father was a violinist and instrument maker at the court of the Prince-Bishop of Würzburg. After studying humanities at the Univ. of Würzburg (magisterium, 1766), he received training in law there (1766–67) and in theology in Bamberg (1767–70). In 1771 he went to Mannheim as almoner at the court of Carl Theodor, the Elector Palatine; by 1772 he was court chaplain there; with the assistance of the elector, he pursued his musical training in Italy (1773–

75); was active in Bologna, Padua, Venice, and Rome, his principal mentors being Padres Martini and Francesco Antonio Vallotti; while in Rome, Pope Pius VI made him a chamberlain, a prothonotary, and a Knight of the Order of the Golden Spur. In 1775 he returned to Mannheim as spiritual counselor and Vice-Kapellmeister to his patron; founded the Mannheimer Tonschule for teaching his own method of composition. In 1780 he was in Paris, where he submitted a paper to the Académie Royale des Sciences, *Essai de diriger le goût des amateurs de musique,* an explanation of his system of teaching (publ. in Paris, 1782); in Paris he also produced his opera *La Kermesse* (1783), which was a fiasco; that same year he visited London, where his method won the approbation of the Royal Soc. After serving as 1st Kapellmeister at the Electoral Court in Munich (1784–86), he became Kapellmeister and teacher to the Crown Prince at the Swedish court in Stockholm in 1786; also traveled extensively in Europe, and in 1792–93 visited North Africa. Following the conclusion of his contract in Stockholm in 1794, he once again traveled in Europe, during which time he was active as both a performer and a teacher. In 1807 he was made Hofkapellmeister and privy councillor for ecclesiastical affairs at the Hessen-Darmstadt court; founded a Tonschule there, where Weber and Meyerbeer were his pupils. Vogler established himself as a leading keyboard virtuoso, teacher, and music theorist. He was a distinguished master of keyboard improvisation. While in Amsterdam in 1789, he completed construction of a portable organ, the "orchestrion," which he promoted in succeeding years during his various concert tours. His writings proved influential, but his compositions, which included stage works, syms., piano concertos, and chamber works, failed to make an impact and are now completely forgotten.

WRITINGS: *Tonwissenschaft und Tonsetzkunst* (Mannheim, 1776); *Stimmbildungskunst* (Mannheim, 1776); *Kuhrpfälzische Tonschule* (Mannheim, 1778); *Betrachtungen der Mannheimer Tonschule,* I–III (Mannheim, 1778–81); *Entwurf eines neuen Wörterbuchs für die Tonschule* (Frankfurt am Main, 1780); *Essai propre à diriger le goût de ceux qui ne sont pas musiciens* (Paris, 1782); *Verbesserung der Forkel's chen Veränderungen über das englische Volkslied God Save the King* (Frankfurt am Main, 1793); *Erste musikalische Preisausteilung für das Jahr 1791 nebst 40 Kupfertafeln* (Frankfurt am Main, 1794); *Inledning til harmoniens kännedom* (Stockholm, 1794); *Claverschola med 44 graverade tabeller* (Stockholm, 1798); *Organistschola med 8 graverade tabeller* (Stockholm, 1798–99); *Lection til choral eleven* (Stockholm, 1799–1800); *Choral-System* (Copenhagen, 1800); *Data zur Akustik* (Leipzig, 1801); *Handbuch zur Harmonielehre und für den Generalbass* (Prague, 1802); *Zergliederung der 32 Orgelpräludien* (Munich, 1806); *Über die harmonische Akustik* (Offenbach, 1807); *Zergliederung der musikalischen Bearbeitung der Busspsalmen* (Munich, 1807); *Grundliche Anleitung zum Clavirstimmen* (Stuttgart, 1807); *Utile dulci: Belehrende musikalische Herausgaben,* I (Munich, 1808); *Über Sprach- und Gesangsautomaten* (Frankfurt am Main, 1810); *System für den Fugenbau* (Offenbach, c.1818); *Über Choral- und Kirchengesange* (Munich, 1813).

BIBL.: J. Fröhlich, *Biographie des grossen Tonkünstlers Abt G.J. V.* (Würzburg, 1845); H. Künzel, *Abt V.* (Darmstadt, 1867); E. Pasqué, *Abt V. als Tonkünstler, Lehrer und Priester* (Darmstadt, 1884); K. von Schafhäutl, *Abt G.J. V., Sein Leben, sein Charakter und musikalisches System* (Augsburg, 1888); M. Brenet, "L'Abbé V. à Paris," *Archives Historiques Artistiques et Littéraires* (Feb. 1891); J. Simon, *Abt V.s kompositorisches Wirken* (Berlin, 1904); E. Rupp, *Abbé V. als Mensch, Musiker, und Orgelbautheoretiker* (Ludwigsburg, 1922); P. Vretland, *Abbé V. in Stockholm* (Würzburg, 1924); idem, *Abbé V.* (1933); H. Schweiger, *Abbé G.J. V.s Orgellehre* (diss., Univ. of Vienna, 1938); idem, "Abt V.," *Musical Quarterly* (April 1939); H. Kreitz, *Abbe G.J. V. als Musiktheoretiker* (diss., Univ. of Saarbrücken, 1957); D. Britton, *Abbe G.J. V.: His Life and His Theories on Organ Design* (diss., Univ. of Rochester, 1973); F. and M. Grave, *In Praise of Harmony: The Teachings of Abbé G.J. V.* (Lincoln, Nebr., 1987).

Vogrich, Max (Wilhelm Karl), pianist and composer; b. Hermannstadt, Transylvania, Jan. 24, 1852; d. N.Y., June 10, 1916. He gave a piano concert at the age of 7; then studied at the Leipzig Cons. with Reinecke and Moscheles; traveled as a pianist in Europe, South America, and the U.S.; also toured Australia. In 1886 he settled in N.Y.; then lived in Weimar (1902–8), and in London until 1914, returning to N.Y. at the outbreak of World War I. He wrote several operas to his own librettos: *Vanda* (Florence, 1875); *King Arthur* (Leipzig, Nov. 26, 1893); *Der Buddha* (Weimar, 1904); etc.; an oratorio, *The Captivity* (1884); 2 syms.; Piano Concerto; several pieces for violin, including a Violin Concerto subtitled *E pur si muove* (1913); 12 concert studies for Piano; *Album of Ancient and Modern Dances* for Piano; anthems; songs. He ed. the complete piano works of Schumann, Clementi's *Gradus ad Parnassum* (in progressive order), and other collections.

Vogt, Augustus Stephen, Canadian choral conductor; b. Washington, Ontario, Aug. 14, 1861; d. Toronto, Sept. 17, 1926. He studied at the New England Cons. of Music in Boston, and then at the Leipzig Cons. with Reinecke and Jadassohn. In 1888 he settled in Toronto; founded and conducted the Mendelssohn Choir (1894–97; 1900–17); toured with it in the U.S.; was principal of the Toronto Cons. (1913–26). He was an important figure in music education in Canada; publ. choral works: *The Sea, Crossing the Bar, An Indian Lullaby, The Lord's Prayer,* etc.; *Standard Anthem Book* (1894); *Modern Pianoforte Technique* (1900).
BIBL.: A. Bridle, "V., A Great Chorus Master," *Year Book of Canadian Art* (1913).

Vogt, Gustave, noted French oboist, pedagogue, and composer; b. Strasbourg, March 18, 1781; d. Paris, May 30, 1870. He was taken to Paris at an early age; enrolled in 1798 at the Cons., where he was a pupil of A. Sallantin (premier prix, 1799) and then of Rey. In 1798 he became 2nd oboist in the orch. of the Théâtre Montansier; in 1801 he joined the orch. of the Théâtre de l'Ambigu-Comique, and shortly afterward was made 1st oboist in the orch. of the Théâtre-Italien. He served as 1st oboist in Napoleon's private orch. (1804–14), the orch. of the Opéra (1812–34), the orch. at the Théâtre Feydeau (1814), and Louis XVIII's orch. (1814; 1819–30). In 1828 he became a founding member and 1st oboist of the Société des Concerts du Conservatoire, where he played until 1844. He was a prof. at the Cons. (1816–53). He publ. *Solfège à l'usage des écoles primaires* (Kolmar, 1862); also wrote a *Méthode de hautbois.* Among his compositions are 5 oboe concertos, 4 oboe concertinos, various other virtuoso works for oboe and orch., an English Horn Concerto, serenades for wind band, marches, some chamber music, including several works utilizing oboe, various solo oboe pieces, piano music, and a few vocal scores.
BIBL.: B. Friedland, "G. V.'s Souvenir Album of Music Autographs," *Notes,* XXXI (1974–75).

Vogt, Hans, German composer; b. Danzig, May 14, 1911. He attended a master class in composition at the Prussian Academy of Arts (1929–34), and took courses in piano, cello, conducting, and music education at the Akademie für Kirchen- und Schulmusik (1930–34) in Berlin. After serving as director of opera in Detmold (1935–38) and as municipal music director in Stralsund (1938–44), he was prof. of composition at the Mannheim Hochschule für Musik (from 1949); also taught at the Univ. of Mannheim. He wrote the book *Neue Musik seit 1945* (Stuttgart, 1972).
WORKS: OPERAS: *Die Stadt hinter dem Strom* (North German Radio, Hamburg, 1953); *Athenerkomödie* (Mannheim, 1964). **ORCH.:** 2 concertos for Orch. (1950, rev. 1953; 1961); *Rhythmic Suite* for Strings (1952); Piano Concerto (1955); Cello Concerto (1968); *Divertimenti concertanti* for Piano and Orch. (1969); *Azioni sinfoniche* (1972); Violin Concerto (1981); *Dona nobis pacem,* sym. (1986). **CHAMBER:** Trio for Flute, Viola, and Harp (1951); Quintet for Flute, Oboe, Bassoon, Violin, and Harpsichord (1958); *Trio-Dialoge* for Piano Trio (1960); Sonata for Flute and Piano (1960); 4 string quartets (1961–82); String Quintet (1967); String Trio (1970); *Elemente für eine Sonate* for Cello and Piano (1973); Sonata for Violin and Piano (1986); piano pieces. **VOCAL:** *De profundis* for Chorus (1951); *Historie der Verkundigung,* chamber oratorio (1954); *Masken* for Soprano and Orch. (1956); *4 English Sons* for Soprano and 5 Instruments (1958); *Poems of Herman Moon's London Hourbook* for 4 Solo Voices and Piano (1960); *Passionsmusik* for Tenor, Chorus, and Percussion (1963); *Sine nomine* for Tenor, Chorus, and Orch. (1965); *Requiem* for Soprano, Bass, and Percussion (1970); *3 Pieces on Texts by W.H. Auden* for Chorus (1972–73); *Historie vom Propheten Jona,* chamber oratorio for Alto, Tenor, Chorus, and 6 Instruments (1979).
BIBL.: H. Renner, "H. V.," *Musica,* XI (1957); W. Steger, "Vom Eigenwert der Musik: H. V.," ibid., XXV (1971).

Vogt, Johann, German pianist and composer; b. Gross-Tinz, near Liegnitz, Jan. 17, 1823; d. Eberswalde, July 31, 1888. He studied in Berlin and Breslau; taught piano in St. Petersburg (1850–55); subsequently lived in Dresden and in Berlin; visited N.Y. (1871–73). He wrote a Piano Trio, String Quintet, many salon pieces for piano (in all, over 150 opus numbers).

Voicu, Ion, Rumanian violinist and conductor; b. Bucharest, Oct. 8, 1925. He enrolled at the Bucharest Cons. at 13 as a violin pupil of George Enacovici; after making his debut on the Bucharest Radio in 1940, he continued his training with Enesco (1945); then studied with A. Yampolsky and D. Oistrakh at the Moscow Cons. (1955–57). In 1969 he founded a chamber orch. in Bucharest; toured widely with this ensemble in succeeding years. From 1971 to 1982 he was music director of the Georges Enesco Phil. in Bucharest.

Voigt, Henriette (née **Kunze**), German pianist; b. Leipzig, Nov. 24, 1808; d. there, Oct. 15, 1839. She studied with Ludwig Berger; married the merchant Karl Voigt, whose house was the rendezvous of many of the most eminent musicians of the time. Schumann dedicated to her the Piano Sonata in G minor (op. 22).
BIBL.: "Acht Briefe und ein Faksimile von F. Mendelssohn-Bartholdy" (Leipzig, 1871; Eng. tr. in *Macmillan's Magazine,* June 1871); J. Gensel, *Schumanns Briefwechsel mit Henriette Voigt* (Leipzig, 1892); idem, *Aus Rochlitzens Briefen an Henriette Voigt* (Leipzig, 1906).

Voigt, Johann Georg Hermann, German organist and composer; b. Osterwieck, May 14, 1769; d. Leipzig, Feb. 24, 1811. He served for many years as organist at the Thomaskirche in Leipzig; publ. chamber music and piano pieces.

Voisin, Roger (Louis), distinguished French-born American trumpeter and teacher; b. Angers, June 26, 1918. He was taken to Boston as a child by his family; became a naturalized U.S. citizen in 1932; studied initially with his father, a member of the Boston Sym. Orch., then with Georges Mager (1933) and Marcel LaFosse (1934). In 1935 he became 3rd trumpeter in the Boston Sym. Orch.; after serving as its 1st trumpeter (1949–67), he was again 3rd trumpeter from 1967 until his retirement in 1973. He taught at the Berkshire Music Center, the New England Cons. of Music, and Boston Univ.

Volbach, Fritz, German choral conductor, music scholar, and composer; b. Wipperfürth, near Cologne, Dec. 17, 1861; d. Wiesbaden, Nov. 30, 1940. He studied at the Cologne Cons. with Hiller, Jensen, and Seiss, and in Berlin with Taubert and Löschhorn; completed his education at the Univ. of Bonn (Ph.D., 1899, with the diss. *Die Praxis der Händel-Aufführung*). In 1892 he was appointed conductor of the Liedertafel and the Damengesangverein in Mainz; after serving as music director at the Univ. of Tübingen (1907–18), he went to Münster as prof. at the Univ. and as conductor of the city orch.; retired to Wiesbaden in 1930. A versatile musician, he had command of almost every orch. instrument.
WORKS: Opera: *Die Kunst zu lieben* (1910). Symphonic poems: *Ostern* (1895); *Es waren zwei Königskinder* (1901); *Alt-Heidelberg, du feine* (1904); Sym. (1909); numerous choral works; lieder; Piano Quintet (1912); piano pieces.
WRITINGS: *Lehrbuch der Begleitung des gregorianischen*

Gesangs (Berlin, 1888); *G.F. Händel* (Berlin, 1898; 2nd ed., 1907); *Beethoven: Die Zeit des Klassizismus* (Munich, 1905; 2nd ed., 1929); *Die deutsche Musik im 19. Jahrhundert* (Kempten, 1909); *Das moderne Orchester in seiner Entwicklung* (Leipzig, 1910; 2nd ed., 1919); *Die Instrumente des Orchesters* (Leipzig, 1913; 2nd ed., 1921); *Erläuterwungen zu den Klavier-Sonaten Beethovens* (Cologne, 1919; 3rd ed., 1924); *Handbuch der Musikwissenschaften* (2 vols., Münster, 1926, 1930); *Die Kunst der Sprache* (Mainz, 1929); *Der Chormeister* (Mainz, 1931); *Erlebtes und Erstrebtes* (autobiography; Mainz, 1956). **BIBL.:** J. Hagemann, *F. V.*, Monographien Moderner Musiker, III (Leipzig, 1909); G. Schwake, *F. V.s Werke* (Münster, 1921); K. Hortschansky, ed. *F. V., 1861–1940: Komponist, Dirigent und Musikwissenschaftler* (Hagen, 1987).

Volckmar, Wilhelm (Adam Valentin), German organist, teacher, and composer; b. Hersfeld, Dec. 26, 1812; d. Homberg, near Kassel, Aug. 27, 1887. He received his training from his father. In 1835 he settled at Homberg, where he taught music and played organ; toured extensively as an organ virtuoso. In 1846 he received an honorary doctorate; was made a prof. in 1868. He publ. an *Orgelschule* (Leipzig, 1863) and other books; ed. various organ works; his own compositions total nearly 700 works, including organ syms., concertos, 36 sonatas, and liturgical pieces, as well as many orch. and vocal works. **BIBL.:** H. Gehrig, *W. V.* (Homberg, 1888).

Volek, Jaroslav, prominent Czech musicologist and esthetician; b. Trenčín, July 15, 1923. He studied composition at the Prague Cons. (1941–46) and then attended the master classes of Šín, Hába, and Řídký (1946–48); took courses in musicology and esthetics at the Univ. of Bratislava (Ph.D., 1952, with the diss. *Teoretické základy harmonie z hladiska vedeckej filozófie* [The Theoretical Bases of Harmony from the Viewpoint of Scientific Philosophy]; publ. in Bratislava, 1954) and at the Univ. of Prague (C.Sc., 1958, with the diss. *O specifičnosti předmětu uměleckého odrazu skutečnosti* [Specific Quality in the Artistic Reflection of Reality]; publ. in L. Tondl et al., *Otázky teorie poznání*, Prague, 1957; D.Sc., 1968, with the diss. *Základy obecné teorie umění* [The Bases of General Art Theory]; publ. in Prague, 1968). He was a lecturer (1952–57), reader (1957–68), and prof. (from 1968) at the Univ. of Prague; also was active as a music critic and served as ed. of the journal *Estetika* (1969–71). He played a significant role in the development of Marxist music criticism. **WRITINGS** (all publ. in Prague): *Novodobé harmonické systémy* (Contemporary Harmonic Systems; 1961); *Kotázkám předmětu a metod estetiky a obecné teori umění* (The Subject and Methods of Esthetics and the General Theory of Art; 1963); *Die Frage der Zahl der Funktion in der traditionellen Harmonik* (1968); *Kapitoly z dějin estetiky* (Chapters from the History of Esthetics; 1969); *K antropologické problematice estetiky a obecné teorie umění* (Anthropological Problems in the Esthetics and General History of Art; 1970).

Völker, Franz, gifted German tenor; b. Neu-Isenburg, March 31, 1899; d. Darmstadt, Dec. 5, 1965. He studied in Frankfurt; made his debut at the Frankfurt Opera as Florestan in 1926; continued on its roster until 1935; also sang at the Vienna State Opera (1931–36; 1939–40; 1949–50), the Berlin State Opera (1933–43), and the Bavarian State Opera in Munich (1936–37; 1945–52); he made guest appearances at Covent Garden in London, and in Salzburg and Bayreuth; after his retirement in 1952, he taught voice in Neu-Isenburg; was a prof. at the Stuttgart Hochschule für Musik from 1958. Among his finest roles were Parsifal, Lohengrin, Siegmund, Florestan, the Emperor in *Die Frau ohne Schatten*, Othello, and Max in *Der Freischütz.*

Volkert, Franz (Joseph), Austrian organist, conductor, and composer, b. Heimersdorf, Bohemia, Feb. 2, 1767; d. Vienna, March 22, 1845. He was active as an organist in Vienna; from c.1814 until 1824 he was deputy Kapellmeister at the Leopoldstadt Theater. He produced over 100 comic operas, singspiels,

melodramas, farces, etc., many of which were popular; also church music, chamber music, and organ pieces.

Volkmann, (Friedrich) Robert, significant German composer; b. Lommatzsch, April 6, 1815; d. Budapest, Oct. 29, 1883. He studied organ and piano with his father, a cantor; at 17, entered the Freiberg Gymnasium and studied music with Anacker; in 1836 he went to Leipzig as a student of C.F. Becker; was greatly encouraged by Schumann. After teaching music in Prague (1839–41), he settled in Budapest, where he spent the rest of his life, except for 4 years (1854–58) in Vienna. In 1875 he was appointed a prof. at the National Academy of Music in Budapest. His music was regarded very highly in his lifetime, but after his death it faded into oblivion. **WORKS:** 2 syms.; 3 serenades for Strings; 4 overtures; Cello Concerto; 6 string quartets; 2 piano trios; *Konzertstück* for Piano and Orch.; *Chant du Troubadour* for Violin and Piano; *Allegretto capriccioso* for Violin and Piano; 2 violin sonatas; *Romanze* for Cello and Piano; *Capriccio* for Cello and Piano; *Schlummerlied* for Harp, Clarinet, and Horn (also arranged for Piano, Viola, and Cello; his last completed work); many works for Solo Piano, including *Phantasiebilder; Dithyrambe und Toccate; Souvenir de Maróth; Nocturne;* Sonata in C minor; *Buch der Lieder; Deutsche Tanzweisen; Cavatine und Barcarole; Visegrád;* 4 marches; *Wanderskizzen; Fantasie; Intermezzo; Variations* on a theme of Handel; *Lieder der Grossmutter;* 3 *Improvisations; Am Grab des Grafen Széchenyi; Ballade und Scherzetto;* transcriptions of songs by Mozart and Schubert; works for Piano, 4-hands, including *Musikalisches Bilderbuch; Ungarische Skizzen; Die Tageszeiten;* 3 marches; *Rondino und Marsch-Caprice;* transcriptions of his other works; also vocal works, including 2 masses for Male Chorus; 5 sacred songs for Mixed Chorus; offertories; Christmas carol of the 12th century; old German hymn for Double Male Chorus; 6 duets on old German poems; *An die Nacht* for Alto Solo with Orch.; dramatic scene for Soprano and Orch., *Sappho; Kirchenarie* for Bass, Flute, and Strings; *Weihnacht* for Female Chorus; *Im Wiesengrün* for Mixed Chorus; etc. **BIBL.:** B. Vogel, *R. V.* (Leipzig, 1875); H. Volkmann, *R. V. Sein Leben und seine Werke* (Leipzig, 1903; abr. ed., 1915; 2nd ed., rev., 1922); C. Preiss, *R. V. Kritische Beiträge zu seinem Schaffen* (Graz, 1912); V. von Herzfeld, "R. V.," *Musical Quarterly* (July 1915); H. Volkmann, ed., *Briefe von R. V.* (Leipzig, 1917); idem, *Thematisches Verzeichnis der Werke von R. V.* (Dresden, 1937); T. Brawley, *The Instrumental Works of R. V.* (diss., Northwestern Univ., 1975).

Volkonsky, Andrei (Mikhailovich), Russian harpsichordist, conductor, and composer; b. Geneva (of Russian parents of princely nobility), Feb. 14, 1933. He was 11 when he began piano studies with Auber at the Geneva Cons.; received training in composition from Boulanger in Paris (1945–47), and also continued his piano study with Dinu Lipatti; then went to Russia and pursued his training at the Tambov Music School; completed his training in composition with Shaporin at the Moscow Cons. (1950–54). In 1955 he was a co-founder, with Barshai, of the Moscow Chamber Orch.; then devoted himself to harpsichord playing; in 1964 he organized in Moscow the concert group Madrigal, with which he gave annual series of highly successful concerts in the Soviet Union, East Germany, and Czechoslovakia. His early works were set in evocative impressionistic colors, in the manner of the French modern school, but soon he deployed a serial technique of composition analogous to Schoenberg's method of composition with 12 tones outside traditional tonality. He was outspoken in his criticism of the direction that Soviet music was taking, and he entirely rejected the official tenets of socialist realism. This attitude, and the nature of his own music, resulted in the cancellation of performances of his works; he was expelled from the Union of Soviet Composers, and could no longer give concerts. In 1973 he returned to Switzerland. **WORKS:** Cantatas: *Rus* (Russia), after Gogol (1952), and *The Image of the World* (Moscow, May 8, 1953); Concerto for Orch. (Moscow, June 10, 1954); *Capriccio* for Orch.; Piano Quintet

(1954); String Quartet (1955); Piano Sonata (1956); *Musica stricta* for Piano (1956); 2 *Japanese Songs* for Chorus, Electronic Sound, and Percussion (1957); *Music* for 12 Instruments (1957); *Serenade to an Insect* for Chamber Orch. (1959); *Suite des miroirs* for Soprano, Organ, Guitar, Violin, Flute, and Percussion (1960); Viola Sonata (1960); *The Lament of Shaza* for Soprano and Small Orch. (1961; Moscow, May 12, 1965); *Jeux à trois* for Flute, Violin, and Harpsichord (1962); *Concerto itinérant* for Soprano, Violin, Percussion, and 26 Instruments (1967); *Réplique* for Small Orch. (1969); *Les Mailles du temps* for 3 Instrumental Groups (1969); some music for plays.

Volkov, Feodor (Grigorievich), Russian musician; b. Kostroma, Feb. 19, 1729; d. St. Petersburg, April 14, 1763. He studied in Yaroslavl and Moscow (1741–48); returning to Yaroslavl, he organized a public theater in 1750. In 1754 he entered a military school in St. Petersburg; in 1759 he was sent to Moscow, where he was in charge of the spectacles accompanying the coronation of Catherine II (1763); also was director of the Russian Theater in St. Petersburg (from 1761). Volkov was an able practical musician, even though he totally lacked professional training. His supposed authorship of the comic opera *Taniusha, ili Schastilvagya vstrecha* (Taniusha, or A Happy Encounter; St. Petersburg, Dec. 20, 1756) is extremely doubtful; in fact, the existence of such an opera has never been proved. Volkov's role in the early history of the Russian musical stage is confined to his activities as an organizer.
BIBL.: M. Luchansky, *F. V.* (Moscow, 1937).

Vollenweider, Andreas, popular Swiss composer and instrumentalist; b. Zürich, Oct. 4, 1953. His father was the organist Hans Vollenweider; the family home was frequented by artists and musicians. He studied guitar, flute, and other instruments before settling on the harp, which he modified and amplified in developing his own technique; played concerts and made recordings with the ensemble Poetry and Music. His 1st solo recording was *Eine art Suite* (1979); it was followed by the debut concert of Andreas Vollenweider and Friends at the 1981 Montreux Jazz Festival. His ensuing recordings were highly successful, marketed under jazz, pop, and classical categories, and considered among the most engaging of New Age recordings. His 1st U.S. tour was in 1984; that same year he directed the video *Pace verde*. In 1989 he produced another video, *Pearls and Tears*. His titles reflect his mystical roots; the music itself involves a delicate mix of electric and acoustic timbres in lively, syncopated textures. Other noteworthy recordings include . . . *Behind the Gardens—Behind the Wall—Under the Tree* . . . (1981), *Caverna Magica* (. . . *Under the Tree—In the Cave* . . .) (1983), *White Winds* (1985), *Down to the Moon* (1986), and *Dancing with the Lion* (1989).

Vollerthun, Georg, German composer; b. Fürstenau, Sept. 29, 1876; d. Strausberg, near Berlin, Sept. 15, 1945. He studied with Tappert, Radecke, and Gernsheim; was a theater conductor in Prague, Berlin, Barmen, and Mainz (1899–1905); went to Berlin as a music critic and teacher in 1910; from 1922, lived mostly in Strausberg.
WORKS: Operas: *Veeda* (Kassel, 1916); *Island-Saga* (Munich, Jan. 17, 1925); *Der Freikorporal* (Hannover, Nov. 10, 1931); *Das königliche Opfer* (Hannover, 1942); *Alt-Danzig Suite* for Orch. (1938); cantatas and other vocal works; many German songs.
BIBL.: E. Krieger, *G: V.* (Berlin, 1942).

Voloshinov, Victor, Russian composer and teacher; b. Kiev, Oct. 17, 1905; d. Leningrad, Oct. 22, 1960. He studied composition with Scherbatchev at the Leningrad Cons.; later became a prof. there. He wrote the operas *Glory* (1939) and *Stronger Than Death* (1942); several symphonic suites on Central Asian themes; chamber music; songs; incidental music for the theater. He enjoyed great renown as a pedagogue; many Soviet composers were his students.

Volpe, Arnold (David), Russian-born American conductor and composer; b. Kovno, Lithuania, July 9, 1869; d. Miami, Fla., Feb. 2, 1940. He studied violin with Leopold Auer at the St. Petersburg Cons. (1887–91), and composition there

with Soloviev (1893–97). In 1898 he emigrated to America, settling in N.Y.; in 1902, founded the Young Men's Sym. Orch. of N.Y., which he conducted until 1919; also conducted the Volpe Sym. Orch. (1904–14). In 1918–19 he conducted the summer concerts at the Lewisohn Stadium in N.Y.; then moved to Washington, D.C., where he was music director of the Washington, D.C., Community Opera (1919–22); subsequently was director of the Kansas City Cons. (1922–25); in 1926 he went to Florida, where he organized the Univ. of Miami Sym. Orch. He composed orch. works, chamber music, solo instrumental pieces, and songs.
BIBL.: M. Volpe (his widow), *A. V.: Bridge between Two Musical Worlds* (Coral Gables, Fla., 1950).

Vomáčka, Boleslav, Czech composer; b. Mladá Boleslav, June 28, 1887; d. Prague, March 1, 1965. He studied law at the Charles Univ. in Prague (LL.D., 1913); studied organ (1906–9), composition (with Novák; 1909–10), and singing (with Krummer) at the Prague Cons; was in the service of the Labor Ministry in Prague (1919–50); wrote music criticism in several newspapers there; was ed. of *Listy Hudební Matice* (1922–35). In 1955 he was made an Artist of Merit by the Czech government. He publ. *Josef Suk* (Prague, 1922), *Stanislav Suda* (Prague, 1933), and *Sukova sborová tvorba* (Suk's Choral Works; Prague, 1935). He began to compose early in life; developed a strong national style of composition.
WORKS: OPERAS: *Vodník* (The Water Spirit; 1934–37; Prague, Dec. 17, 1937); *Boleslav I* (1953–55; Prague, March 8, 1957); *Čekanky* (Waiting for a Husband; 1939; 1956–57). CANTATAS: *Romance Svatojirská* (Romance of St. George; 1920, 1943); *Živí mrtvým* (To the Dead; 1927–28; Prague, Feb. 24, 1929); *Strážce majáku* (The Keeper of the Lighthouse; 1931–33); *Prapor míru nad Duklou* (The Banner of Peace Over Duklou; 1951); *Bojka partyzánka* (The Partisan Struggle; 1952); many choral works; sets of songs. ORCH.: *Ciaconna* (1910); Sym. (1945); *Dukla*, overture (1948); *Fanfáry míru* (Fanfares of Peace) for Trumpet and Orch. (1960). CHAMBER: Violin Sonata (1912); Duo for Violin and Cello (1925–27); Sonatina for 2 Violins (1936; also for Violin and Viola and as *Kvartetino* for String Quartet, 1941); Nonet for Wind Instruments (1957); String Quartet (1959); 2 piano sonatas (1917; *Sonata quasi fantasia*, 1942); piano pieces.
BIBL.: H. Doležil, *B. V.* (Prague, 1941).

Von Blon, Franz, German composer and conductor; b. Berlin, July 16, 1861; d. there, Oct. 21, 1945. He studied in Berlin at the Stern Cons.; was active as a conductor in Warsaw and Berlin; wrote several operettas (*Sub rosa*, *Die Amazone*, *Die tolle Prinzess*, etc.) and much light music for piano; also a number of military marches, of which one, *Unter dem Siegesbanner*, became extremely popular.

Vonk, Hans, Dutch conductor; b. Amsterdam, June 18, 1942. He studied law at the Univ. of Amsterdam; took courses in piano, conducting, and composition at the Amsterdam Cons., then studied conducting with Scherchen and Ferrara. From 1966 to 1973 he was conductor of the Netherlands National Ballet; also was assistant conductor of the Concertgebouw Orch. in Amsterdam. In 1974 he made his U.S. debut as a guest conductor with the San Francisco Sym. Orch. He was conductor of the Netherlands Radio Phil. in Hilversum (1973–79); also was associate conductor of the Royal Phil. in London (1976–79). He served as chief conductor of the Netherlands Opera in Amsterdam (1976–85) and of the Residentie Orch. in The Hague (1980–85). He appeared regularly as a guest conductor with the Dresden State Orch. and Opera from 1980; was permanent conductor (1984–85) and chief conductor (1985–91) of the Dresden State Opera, and also chief conductor of the Dresden State Orch. (1985–91). In 1991 he became chief conductor of the Cologne Radio Sym. Orch.

Von Stade, Frederica, remarkable American mezzo-soprano; b. Somerville, N.J., June 1, 1945. She was educated at the Norton Academy in Conn.; after an apprenticeship at the Long Wharf Theater in New Haven, she studied with Sebastian

Engelberg, Paul Berl, and Otto Guth at the Mannes College of Music in N.Y. Although she reached only the semi-finals of the Metropolitan Opera Auditions in 1969, she attracted the attention of Rudolf Bing, its general manager, who arranged for her debut with the company in N.Y. as the 3rd boy in *Die Zauberflöte* on Jan. 11, 1970; she gradually took on more important roles there before going to Europe, where she gave an arresting portrayal of Cherubino at the opera house at the palace of Versailles in 1974. In 1974 she sang Nina in the premiere of Pasatieri's *The Seagull* at the Houston Grand Opera. In 1975 she made her debut at London's Covent Garden as Rosina; subsequently attained extraordinary success in lyric mezzo-soprano roles with the world's major opera houses and also pursued an extensive concert career, appearing regularly with the Chamber Music Soc. of Lincoln Center. In 1988 she sang the role of Tina in the premiere of Argento's *The Aspern Papers* at the Dallas Lyric Opera, and in 1990 appeared in recital in N.Y.'s Carnegie Hall. Her memorable roles include Dorabella, Idamante, Adalgisa in *Norma*, Charlotte in *Werther*, Mélisande, Octavian, and Malcolm in *La Donna del lago*. She has also proved successful as a crossover artist, especially in Broadway musical recordings.

BIBL.: H. Saal, "'The Prima Donna Next Door': F. v.S.," *Ovation* (May 1983); S. Shirakawa, "F. v.S.," ibid. (Nov. 1988).

Von Tilzer (real name, **Gumm**), **Harry**, American composer of popular songs; b. Detroit, July 8, 1872; d. N.Y., Jan. 10, 1946. He assumed his mother's maiden name, Tilzer, and intercalated the nobiliary particle Von. Though autodidact in music, he wrote many songs that attained great popularity. After selling his songs for paltry sums, in 1905 he opened his own publishing company, which was the 1st to publish works by Irving Berlin and George Gershwin. Among his more than 8,000 songs, of which more than 2,000 were published, are *My Old New Hampshire Home* (1898), *A Bird in a Gilded Cage* (1900), *Down on the Farm* (1905), *That Mansion of Aching Hearts* (sequel to *A Bird* . . . , 1905), *I Want a Girl Just Like the Girl That Married Dear Old Dad* (1911), and *And the Green Grass Grew All Around* (1912). He had 4 brothers, each of whom also assumed the name Von Tilzer and was active in music. The most successful was **Albert Von Tilzer** (b. Indianapolis, March 29, 1878; d. Los Angeles, Oct. 1, 1956), whose songs include *That's What the Daisy Said* (1903), *Take Me Out to the Ball Game* (a perennial favorite; 1908), *Put Your Arms Around Me, Honey* (1910), and *I'll Be with You in Apple Blossom Time* (1920).

Voorhees, Donald, American conductor; b. Guthville, Pa., July 26, 1903; d. Cape May Court House, N.J., Jan. 10, 1989. He joined the Lyric Theatre orch. in Allentown, Pa., as a pianist at age 12, becoming its conductor when he was 15; at 17 he made his 1st appearance as a conductor on Broadway with the musical revue *Broadway Brevities of 1920*; subsequently conducted various Broadway shows. He also was active as a conductor on radio from 1925; in 1940 he became music director of the highly successful network radio show the "Bell Telephone Hour," for which he composed its signature theme, the *Bell Waltz*; after the show moved to television in 1959, he remained as its music director until its last telecast in 1968.

Voormolen, Alexander (Nicolas), Dutch composer; b. Rotterdam, March 3, 1895; d. The Hague, Nov. 12, 1980. He was a scion of a family of municipal functionaries in the Netherlands, and on his mother's side was a descendant of Claude Rameau, a brother of Jean-Philippe Rameau. He entered the Utrecht School of Music, where he studied with Johan Wagenaar and Willam Petri; he began to compose as a very young man; from his earliest steps he experienced a strong influence of French Impressionism; he went to Paris in 1916, where he was befriended by Ravel, whose influence became decisive. In 1923 he settled in The Hague; after serving as a music critic of the *Nieuwe Rotterdamsche Courant*, he was librarian of The Hague Cons. (1938–55). In his early idiom Voormolen affected richly extended harmonies, and followed Ravel's exam-

ple in writing works in neo-Baroque forms, marked by gentle symmetric melodies. His compositions later followed along neo-Classical lines. His works were initially successful in his homeland, but eventually fell into desuetude. His last years of life were unhappy.

WORKS: 4 ballets: *Le Roi Grenouille* (1916; withdrawn); *Baron Hop*, in 2 suites (1923–24, 1931); *Diana* (1935–36); *Spiegel-Suite* for Small Orch., to Langendijk's play (1943). ORCH.: *De drei ruitertjes* (The 3 Little Horsemen), variations on a Dutch song (1927); *Een Zomerlied* (1928); Oboe Concerto (1938); *Sinfonia* (1939); *Kleine Haagsche Suite* for Small Orch. (1939); *Pastorale* for Oboe and String Orch. (1940); Cello Concerto (1941); *Arethuza*, symphonic myth after the Dutch novelist L. Couperus (1947; Amsterdam, Nov. 11, 1948); *La Sirène* for Solo Saxophone and Orch. (1949); Concerto for 2 Harpsichords or Pianos and Orch. (1950); *Sinfonia concertante* for Clarinet, Horn, and String Orch. (1951); *Eline*, nocturne (1957; orchestrated and enl. version of the 1951 piano piece); *Chaconne en Fuga* (1958). CHAMBER: 2 violin sonatas (1917, 1934); Suite for Cello and Piano (1917); Piano Trio (1918); *Suite* for Harpsichord (1921); *Divertissement* for Cello and Piano (1922); 2 string quartets (1939, 1942); Viola Sonata (1935). PIANO: *Valse triste* (1914); *Suite* No. 1 (1914–16); *Falbalas* (1915); *Eléphants* (1919); *Tableaux des Pays Bas*, in 2 series (1919–20, 1924); *Scène et danse érotique* (1920); *Le Souper clandestin* (1921); *Sonnet* (1922); *Livre des enfants*, in 2 series (1923, 1925); *Berceuse* (1924); Sonata (1944); *Eline*, nocturne (1951). VOCAL: *Beatrijs*, melodrama for Narrator and Piano (1921); 3 *Gedichten* for Voice and Orch. (1932); *Een nieuwe Lente op Holland's erf* for Voice and Orch. (1936); *Herinneringen aan Holland* (Memories of Holland) for Baritone, Bass Clarinet, and Strings (1966); *Stanzas of Charles II* for Baritone, Flute, English Horn, Celesta, Percussion, and Strings (1966); cantata; *Amsterdam* (1967); *From: The Recollection* for Medium Voice, String Orch., and Celesta (1970); *Ex minimis patet ipse Deus*, hymn for Middle Voice, Strings, and Celesta (1971; exists in many alternate versions); *Ave Maria* for Chorus, Harp, and String Orch. (1973; exists in many alternate versions); songs and choruses to Dutch, German, and French texts.

BIBL.: E. Reeser, "A. V.," *Sonorum Speculum*, 22–23 (1965); P.-J. Wagemans, "A. V.," *Key Notes* (1982/1).

Voorn, Joop (Josephus Hermanus Maria), Dutch composer; b. The Hague, Oct. 16, 1932. He studied at the Brabant Cons., and then taught there (from 1969).

WORKS: *Cyclus* for Organ (1967); *Psalm CXIV In Exitu* for Soprano, Children's Chorus, and Orch. (1968); *Ludi ed Interludi* for Piano (1969); 2 string quartets (No. 2, 1970; rev. 1980); *Nakupenda*, trio for Flute, Violin, and Viola (1971); *Soft Music for Angela* for Flute (1973); *Immobile: Music for Tutankhamun* for Orch. (1973; Brabant, Dec. 2, 1975); *Sucevita chorals* for 2 Oboes, 2 Clarinets, Bass Clarinet, and Bassoon (1974); Trio for Oboe, Clarinet, and Bassoon (1974); *Petit concert de printemps* for Flute and Strings (1975; Brabant, April 25, 1976); *Prelude and Fugue*, Quintet for Piano, Oboe, Clarinet, Horn, and Bassoon (1975–76); *Speaking of Siva* for Chorus and Chamber Orch. (1977); 3 *Studies* for English Horn (1979); Sym. for Wind Orch. (1981); Sonata for Saxophone and Piano (1984); *Schrijdende* for Organ, Oboe, Clarinet, Horn, and Bassoon (1985); Serenade for Bassoon and Piano (1985–86).

Vopelius, Gottfried, German composer; b. Herwigsdorf, near Zittau, Jan. 28, 1635; d. Leipzig, Feb. 3, 1715. He studied at the Univ. of Leipzig; was made collaborator ultimus at the St. Nikolai school in Leipzig in 1671; was made Kantor there and at the Nikolaikirche in 1676. He publ. the valuable collection *Neu Leipziger Gesangbuch, von den schönsten und besten Liedern verfasset . . . mit 4. 5. bis 6. stimmen, deren Melodeyen Theils aus Johann Herman Scheins Cantional, und Andern guten Autoribus zusammen getragen, theils aber selbsten componiret* (Leipzig, 1682), which includes over 400 works, among them 3 by Vopelius.

BIBL.: J. Grimm, *Das "Neu Leipziger Gesangbuch" des*

G. V. (*Leipzig, 1682*): *Untersuchungen zur Klärung seiner geschichtlichen Stellung* (Berlin, 1969).

Voříšek, Ján Vaclav. See **Woržischek (Voříšek), Johann Hugo (Jan Václav).**

Vorlová, Sláva (actually, **Miroslava Johnova**), Czech composer; b. Náchod, March 15, 1894; d. Prague, Aug. 24, 1973. She studied piano with her mother; received training in voice at the Vienna Academy of Music; took private lessons in composition with V. Novák and in piano with V. Štěpán in Prague. After passing her state examinations in piano and singing (1918), she continued her piano studies with Maxián and her composition studies with Řídký, completing her training with the latter at the Prague Cons. master classes (graduated, 1948). She became interested in writing music for instruments rarely used for solo performances; wrote one of the few concertos for bass clarinet. Her music is tinted with impressionistic colors.

WORKS: 4 operas: *Zlaté ptáče* (The Golden Birds; 1949–50); *Rozmarýnka* (Rosemary; 1952; Kladno, 1955); *Náchodská kasace* (The Náchod Cassation; 1955); *Dva světy* (2 Worlds; 1958). ORCH.: *Fantasy* for Cello and Orch. (1940); *Symphony JM*, dedicated to Jan Masaryk (1947–48); *Songs of Gondwana*, symphonic epos with Soloists and Chorus (1948–49); *Božena Němcová*, suite (1950–51); Oboe Concerto (1952); *3 Bohemian Dances* (1952–53); Trumpet Concerto (1953); Viola Concerto (1954); Clarinet Concerto (1957); *Memento* (1957); *Thuringian Dances* (1957); Flute Concerto (1959); Concerto for Bass Clarinet and Strings (1961); *Kybernetic Studies* (1962); Concerto for Oboe, Harp, and Orch. (1963); *Dedications* (1965); *Bhukhar* (Fever Birds) (1965); Concerto for Double Bass and Strings (1968). CHAMBER: *Correlations* for Bass Clarinet, Piano, and Strings (1968); *Polarization* for Harp, Wind Orch., and Percussion (1970); *Emergence* for Violin and Orch. (1973; Prague, March 24, 1974); String Quartet (1939); Nonet (1944); *Melodious Variations* for String Quartet (1950); *Puzzles* for 2 Pianos (1953); *Miniatures* for Bass Clarinet and Piano (1962); *Dessins tetraharpes* for 4 Harps (1963); 2 *African Fables* for Narrator, Alto Flute, and Percussion (1964); *Variations on a Theme by Handel* for Bass Clarinet and Piano (1965); *6 pro 5* for Brass Quintet (1967); *Immanence* for Bass Clarinet, Piano, and Percussion (1970); *Brief Considerations* for Soprano, Alto, and Piano (1971); songs.

Voss, Charles, German pianist and composer; b. Schmarsow, Sept. 20, 1815; d. Verona, Aug. 29, 1882. He studied in Berlin, but made his career in Paris, where he went in 1846; enjoyed great success in Paris society as a pianist and composer; publ. a great number of salon pieces, transcriptions, paraphrases, etc.; also wrote piano concertos and études. His 1st Piano Concerto, in F minor, was praised by Mendelssohn.

Voss, Friedrich, German composer, b. Halberstadt, Dec. 12, 1930. He studied composition and piano at the (West) Berlin Hochschule für Musik (1949–54), then devoted himself to composition, winning the Munich Chamber Orch. competition (1955), the Stuttgart Music Prize (1960), the (West) Berlin Art Prize (1961), the Düsseldorf Robert Schumann Prize (1962), the Villa Massimo Award (1964, 1977), and the Mannheim Johann Wenzel Stamitz Prize (1985).

WORKS: BALLET: *Die Nachtigall und die Rose*, after Oscar Wilde (1961; Oberhausen, Jan. 5, 1962). ORCH.: *Concerto da camera* for Strings (1953); Symphonic Suite (1954; Berlin, July 9, 1958); 4 syms.: No. 1 (1958–59; Berlin, March 23, 1960); No. 2 (1962–63; Bonn, March 7, 1966); No. 3 (1966–67; Berlin, Nov. 12, 1969); No. 4 (1972–76); 2 violin concertos: No. 1 (1962; Brussels, May 28, 1966); No. 2 (1985–87); *Hamlet Overture* (1968–69); *Dithryrambus über ein Motiv von Beethoven* (1969); *Metamorphosis* (1978–79; Tokyo, June 10, 1980); also choral pieces; chamber works, including 3 string quartets.

Vossius, Isaac, Netherlands scholar; b. Leiden, 1618; d. Windsor, England, Feb. 21, 1689. He was educated at the Univ. of Leiden; after traveling in England, France, and Italy (1641–46), he taught at the court of Queen Christina of Sweden (1649–54); was active in The Hague from 1655 before settling in England in 1670; that same year he was made a doctor of civil law by Oxford Univ.; became canon of St. George's Chapel, Windsor, in 1673. In addition to his writings on non-musical subjects, he wrote the important treatise *De poematum cantus et viribus rythmi* (London, 1673), which influenced such composers as Bach, Kuhnau, and Mattheson.

BIBL.: W. Serauky, "Die Affekten-Metrik des I. V. in ihrem Einfluss auf Joh. Kuhnau and Joh. Seb. Bach," *Festschrift Max Schneider* (Leipzig, 1955); H. Davies, "Dryden and V.: A Reconsideration," *Journal of the Warburg and Courtauld Institutes*, XXIX (1966).

Vostřák, Zbyněk, Czech composer and conductor; b. Prague, June 10, 1920; d. Strakonice, Aug. 4, 1985. He studied composition privately with Rudolf Karel (1938–43); attended the conducting classes of Pavel Dědeček at the Prague Cons. In 1963 he became conductor of the Prague chamber ensemble Musica Viva Pragensis; worked in an electronic music studio in Prague. His music evolved from the Central European type of modernism; later he annexed serial techniques, electronic sound, and aleatory practices.

WORKS: OPERAS: *Rohovín čtverrohý* (The 4-horned Rohovin; 1947–48; Olomouc, 1949); *Kutnohorští havíři* (The King's Master of the Mint; 1951–53; Prague, 1955); *Pražské nokturno* (A Prague Nocturne; 1957–58; Ustí-on-the-Elbe, 1960); *Rozbitý džbán* (The Broken Jug; 1960–61; Prague, 1963); 5 ballets: *The Primrose* (1944–45); *Filosofská historie* (A Story of Students of Philosophy; 1949); *Viktorka* (Little Victoria; 1950); *Sněhurka* (Snow White; 1955); *Veselí vodníci* (Jolly Water Sprites; 1978–79). ORCH.: *Prague Overture* (1941); *Zrození měsíce* (The Birth of the Moon) for Chamber Orch. (Prague, March 8, 1967); *Kyvadlo času* (The Pendulum of Time) for Cello, 4 Instrumental Groups, and Electric Organ (1966–67; Donaueschingen, Oct. 19, 1968); *Metahudba* (Metamusic) (1968; Prague, March 2, 1970); *Tajemství elipsy* (The Secret of Ellipsis) (1970; Prague, March 5, 1971); *Parable* for Orch. and Tape (1976–77); *Kapesní vesmír* (The Pocket Universe) for Flute, Dulcimer, and Strings (1980–81); *The Cathedral* (1982); *The Crystals* for English Horn, Strings, and Percussion (1983); Piano Concerto (1984). CHAMBER: *Elements* for String Quartet (1964); *Synchronia* for 6 Instruments (1965); *Trigonum* for Violin, Oboe, and Piano (1965); *Kosmogonia* for String Quartet (1968); *Sextant* for Wind Quintet (1969); *Fair Play* for Harpsichord and 6 Instruments (1978); String Quartet No. 4 (1979); *The Secret of the Rose* for Organ, Brass Quintet, and Percussion (1985); also tape pieces; piano works.

Votapek, Ralph, American pianist and teacher; b. Milwaukee, March 20, 1939. He studied at Northwestern Univ. (B.A., 1960), with Gui Mombaerts and Robert Goldsand at the Manhattan School of Music in N.Y. (M.M., 1961), and with Rosina Lhévinne at the Juilliard School of Music in N.Y. (1961–62). He won the Van Cliburn International Competition for pianists in 1962, and then embarked on a concert career. He taught at Michigan State Univ. in East Lansing (from 1968).

Votto, Antonino, Italian conductor; b. Piacenza, Oct. 30, 1896; d. Milan, Sept. 9, 1985. He studied piano with Longo and composition with De Nardis at the Cons. di Musica S. Pietro a Majella in Naples; made his debut as a concert pianist in Trieste in 1919. From 1919 to 1921 he taught piano at the Cons. di Musica G. Verdi in Trieste. In 1921 he became a conductor at the Teatro Colón in Buenos Aires; in 1923 he made his 1st appearance at Milan's La Scala conducting *Manon Lescaut*; then was a répétiteur and assistant conductor there under Toscanini until 1929. He subsequently made guest conducting appearances throughout Italy, Europe, and South America. From 1948 to 1970 he was a regular conductor at La Scala, during which period he led performances in major productions with Callas and other famous singers; also conducted at the Chicago Lyric Opera (1960–61; 1970). He was on the faculty of the Milan Cons. (1941–67).

Vranken, Jaap, Dutch organist, teacher, and composer; b. Utrecht, April 16, 1897; d. The Hague, April 20, 1956. He was the son of the organist **Joseph Vranken** (1870–1948), with whom he studied organ and theory. From 1916 to 1918 he was in the U.S., studying with Percy Goetschius. He returned to the Netherlands in 1920, and was appointed organist at the church of St. Anthonius in The Hague; acquired a fine reputation as a teacher. He composed mostly sacred music; also instrumental music in Classical style; publ. a manual on counterpoint (1948).

Vredenburg, Max, Dutch composer; b. Brussels (of Dutch parents), Jan. 16, 1904; d. Laren, the Netherlands, Aug. 9, 1976. He was taken to the Netherlands as a child and received an elementary musical education there; in 1926, went to Paris and studied at the École Normale de Musique with Paul Dukas; was a music correspondent for the *Nieuwe Rotterdamsche courant* (1936–40); fled to Java in 1941, where he was interned by the Japanese (1942–45), but was allowed to organize concerts with his fellow internee, Szymond Goldberg; after his liberation, he settled in Amsterdam; was director of the Dutch section of the Fédération Internationale des Jeunesses Musicales (1953–69); also was founder-director of the National Youth Orch. (1957–76). He wrote the book *Langs de vijf Lijnen* (1947).
WORKS: *Au pays des vendanges*, wind quintet (1951); Oboe Concerto (1951); *Akiba* for Mezzo-soprano and Chamber Orch. (1951); *Du printemps* for Mezzo-soprano and Chamber Orch. (1952); *Lamento* for Viola and Piano (1953); *Suite dansante* for Youth Orch. (1956); *Horizons hollandaises* for Orch. (1959); Trio for Oboe, Clarinet, and Bassoon (1965); piano pieces; many songs.

Vretblad, Viktor Patrik, Swedish organist, musicologist, and composer; b. Svartnäs, April 5, 1876; d. Stockholm, Jan. 15, 1953. He made his livelihood as a post office official (1900–1940). He served as organist of Stockholm's French Reformed Church (1900–1907) and of St. Oskar's (1906–43); likewise as music critic for several journals. He composed some instrumental and vocal music.
WRITINGS (all publ. in Stockholm): *Johan Helmich Roman 1694–1758: Svenska musikens fader* (1914); *Konsertlivet i Stockholm under 1700–talet* (1918); *Andreas Hallén* (1918); *Den tjeckiscka tonkonsten* (1930); *Polen i musikhistorien* (1938).

Vreuls, Victor (Jean Léonard), Belgian composer; b. Verviers, Feb. 4, 1876; d. Brussels, July 27, 1944. He studied at the Cons. in Verviers; later took harmony lessons with Sylvain Dupuis and counterpoint with J.T. Radoux at the Cons. in Liège. He then went to Paris, where he took a course with d'Indy at the Schola Cantorum; from 1906 to 1926, was director of the Luxembourg Cons.; in 1925 he was elected to membership in the Belgian Royal Academy. His major works were written in an expansive Romantic style.
WORKS: 2 operas: *Olivier le simple* (1909–11; Brussels, March 9, 1922) and *Un Songe d'une nuit d'été*, after Shakespeare (1923–24; Brussels, Dec. 17, 1925); ballet, *Le Loup-garou* (The Werewolf; 1935; Ghent, 1937); 3 symphonic poems: *Cortège héroïque* (1894); *Jour de fête* (1904); *Werther* (1907); Sym. with Solo Violin (1899); 2 *Poèmes* for Cello and Orch. (1900, 1930); *Elégie* for Flute and Chamber Orch. (1917); *Morceau de concert* for Trumpet and Orch. (1917); *Fantaisie* for Horn and Orch. (1918); *Romance* and *Caprice* for Violin and Chamber Orch. (both 1924); *Suite de danses* for Orch. (1939); *Ouverture pour un drame* (1940); Piano Quartet (1894); Piano Trio (1896); 2 violin sonatas (1899, 1919); String Quartet (1918); Cello Sonata (1922); choruses; songs.
BIBL.: L. Samuel, "Notice sur V. V.," *Annuaire de l'Académie Royale de Belgique*, CXXIII (1957).

Vriend, Jan, Dutch composer; b. Sijbekarspel, Nov. 10, 1938. He studied piano and music theory with Ton de Leeuw at the Amsterdam Cons.; attended a course in electronic music given by G.M. Koenig at the Inst. of Sonology at Utrecht Univ. (1966–67) and a series of lectures on "formalization in music" given by Xenakis at the Schola Cantorum in Paris (1968). He taught theory and conducted ensembles for contemporary

music at the Utrecht Cons. (1968–69). He builds his musical thematics on the theories of Xenakis, involving probabilities and stochastic teleologies.
WORKS: *4 12-Tone Studies* for Piano (1960); *Pour le flûte* for Flute (1961); String Quartet (1962–63); *Paroesie for 10 Instruments* (1963); *Mater-Muziek* for 65 Performers and Electronic Sound (1966); *Diamant*, "a symphony for the Earth," for Orch. (1964–67); *Transformation (On the Way to Halleluja)* for Chorus and Orch. (1965–67); *Huantan* for Organ and 28 Wind Instruments in 4 Groups (1967–68); *Introitus (Hommage to Ton de Leeuw)* for Chorus, 6 Clarinets, 2 Bass Clarinets, and 4 Trombones (1969); *Bau* for Small Orch. (1970); *Elements of Logic* for Wind Orch. (in collaboration with Jos Kunst, 1972; Scheveningen, Feb. 25, 1973); *Kri* for Chorus and Chamber Ensemble (1975); *Heterostase* for Flute, Bass Clarinet, and Piano (1981); *Toque, por la tierra vacia* for 2 Guitars (1981); *Vectorial*, "a monument for J.S. Bach" for Oboe, Clarinet, Bassoon, 2 Trumpets, Piano, and Harp (1983); *Gravity's Dance* for Piano (1984); *Jets d'orgue* for Organ (1985); *Wu Li* for Cello (1986).

Vrieslander, Otto, German composer and writer on music; b. Münster, July 18, 1880; d. Tegna, Switzerland, Dec. 16, 1950. After attending the Cologne Cons., he went to Munich in 1904; in 1911–12 he was in Vienna, where he studied with Heinrich Schenker, becoming one of his disciples. In 1929 he settled in Switzerland. He wrote the highly expressive song cycles *Lieder aus des Knaben Wunderhorn* and *Pierrot lunaire*. He wrote the valuable study *Carl Philipp Emanuel Bach* (Munich, 1923), and also wrote articles on and prepared eds. of his music.

Vronsky, Vitya (actually, **Victoria),** Russian-American pianist; b. Evpatoria, Crimea, Aug. 22, 1909. She studied at the Kiev Cons.; then with Petri and Schnabel in Berlin, and with Cortot in Paris. She married the pianist **Victor Babin** on Aug. 31, 1933; went to the U.S. in 1937; toured widely with Babin in duo-piano recitals.

Vroons, Frans (actually, **Franciscus**), Dutch tenor; b. Amsterdam, April 28, 1911; d. 's-Hertogenbosch, June 1, 1983. He studied in Amsterdam and Paris; made his operatic debut as Pelléas in 1937; in 1945 he became the principal tenor at the Netherlands Opera in Amsterdam, where he sang for 2 decades; also was its co-director (1956–71). In 1948 he made his 1st appearance at London's Covent Garden as Don José and in 1951 in San Francisco as Massenet's Des Grieux; taught voice in Amsterdam (from 1971). His other roles included Florestan, Tamino, Hoffmann, and Peter Grimes.

Vroye, Thédore-Joseph. See **Devroye, Thédore-Joseph.**

Vuataz, Roger, Swiss organist, conductor, and composer; b. Geneva, Jan. 4, 1898; d. Chêne-Bougeries, Aug. 2, 1988. He studied with Otto Barblan and Jaques-Dalcroze at the Geneva Cons.; was a church organist in Geneva (1917–73) and a music critic there (1940–60); was director of music programming at Radio Geneva (1942–63); taught at the Geneva Cons. (1962–69); conducted choruses.
WORKS: STAGE: Opera-buffa, *Monsieur Jabot* (Geneva, Nov. 28, 1958); 3 ballets: *Le Rhône* for Chorus and Orch. (1929); *Poème méditerranéen pour un ballet* for Orch. (1938–50); *Solitude* for Orch. (1962); radiophonic pieces; *Genève ouverte au ciel*, "évocation lyrique" in 5 pictures for Tenor, Narrator, 3 Choruses, Orch., and Organ (1941); 2 oratorios: *Abraham* (1927; rev. 1936) and *Jésus* (1949). ORCH.: *Suite symphonique* (1925); *8 poèmes d'Orient* for Soprano and Orch. (1925); *Triptych* (1929–42); *Images de Grèce*, sym. (1938–39); *Nocturne and Dance* for Trumpet and Orch. (1940); Violin Concerto (1948); *Epopée antique*, 2 suites (1947–51); Piano Concerto (1964); *Images poétiques et pathétiques* for Cello and Orch. (1977). CHAMBER: Cello Sonata (1928); 2 suites for Ondes Martenot (1930); *Musique* for Wind Quintet (1937–61); *Destin*, "symphonie à trois" for Saxophone, Harp, and Percussion (1954); Flute Sonata (1948–54); String Quartet (1970); *Nocturnes* for Cello (1974); piano pieces.

Vučković, Vojislav, Serbian conductor, musicologist, and composer; b. Pirot, Oct. 18, 1910; d. (murdered by the German police) Belgrade, Dec. 25, 1942. He went to Prague and studied composition with Karel and conducting with Malko at the Cons., becoming a pupil in Suk's master class in composition there in 1943; he also took courses in musicology at the Univ. of Prague (Ph.D., 1934). He then returned to Belgrade, where he was active as a conductor, lecturer, broadcaster, and writer on music; also taught at the Stanković Music School. He publ. pamphlets on the materialistic interpretation of music in the light of Marxist dialectics. He was in the resistance movement during the German occupation of his homeland, but was hunted down and murdered. His collected essays were publ. as *Studije, eseji, kritike* (Belgrade, 1968). After a period of composition in the expressionistic manner (including the application of quarter-tones), he abruptly changed his style out of ideological considerations and embraced programmatic realism.
WORKS: ORCH.: Overture for Chamber Orch. (1933); 3 syms.: No. 1 (1933); No. 2 (1942; unfinished; orchestrated by P. Osghian); No. 3: *Heroic Oratorio* for Soloists, Chorus, and Orch. (1942; unfinished; orchestrated by A. Obradović; Cetinje, Sept. 5, 1951); *Zaveštanje Modesta Musorgskog* (Modest Mussorgsky's Legacy; 1940); *Ozareni put* (The Radiant Road), symphonic poem (1940); *Vesnik bure* (The Harbinger of the Storm), symphonic poem (1941); *Burevesnik* (Stormy Petrel), symphonic poem (1942; Belgrade, Dec. 25, 1944). Also a ballet, *Čovek koji je ukrao sunce* (The Man Who Stole the Sun; 1940); chamber music; choral works; songs.
BIBL.: V. V.: *Umetnik i borac* (Belgrade, 1968).

Vuillaume, Jean-Baptiste, celebrated French violin maker; b. Mirecourt, Oct. 7, 1798; d. Paris, March 19, 1875. He came from a family of violin makers, and learned the trade from his father, **Claude Vuillaume** (1772–1834). At 19 he went to Paris and worked with Chanot until 1821, and from 1821 to 1825 for Lété, with whom he then entered into partnership. After Lété's retirement in 1828, Vuillaume worked alone, and put his own name on several instruments which he had constructed with the greatest care and fine craftsmanship; but he was unable to overcome the general distrust of the native product, and began manufacturing imitations of Italian instruments. After long and patient labor he placed a "Stradivarius" violin on the market for 300 francs; it bore the master's label and possessed a full, sonorous tone; he also built a cello priced at 500 francs. The sight of a Duiffoprugcar viola da gamba inspired him with the idea of further imitations, hence the hundreds of "Duiffoprugcar" violins and cellos with their quaint shape, carved scrolls, inlays, and the motto "viva fui in sylvis, etc." By dint of indefatigable research and experiments, Vuillaume carried the construction of these various instruments to the highest perfection. His own inventions were numerous: in 1849 the huge "Octobasse," a double bass 4 meters in length, 3-stringed (CC–GG–C), with a special lever-mechanism to aid the left hand (an "octobasse" is in the Museum of the Paris Cons.); in 1855 a viola, which he called the "contre-alto," with greater strength of tone, but clumsy to play; in 1867 a kind of mute, the "pédale sourdine"; also a machine for manufacturing gut strings of perfectly equal thickness. He also formulated the laws governing the tapering of the stick of the Tourte bow. His brother, **Nicolas-François Vuillaume** (b. May 21, 1802; d. Jan. 16, 1876), was also a violin maker; after receiving his training from Jean-Baptiste, he was active in Brussels (1842–76). A nephew, **Sébastien Vuillaume** (b. June 18, 1835; d. Nov. 17, 1875), was also a violin maker.
BIBL.: R. Millant, *J.-B. V., Sa vie et son œuvre* (London, 1972; in French, Eng., and Ger.).

Vuillermoz, Emile, French music critic; b. Lyons, May 23, 1878; d. Paris, March 2, 1960. He studied organ and piano in Lyons, and composition at the Paris Cons. with Fauré. He was one of the organizers of the Société Musicale Indépendante (1909), and ed. the *Revue Musicale S. I. M.* (from 1911); eventually became music critic of the daily *L'Excelsior,* and also contributed articles to *Le Temps.* Among his publications are *Musiques d'aujourd'hui* (Paris, 1923), *La Vie amoureuse de Chopin* (Paris, 1927), *Histoire de la musique* (Paris, 1949; rev. ed., 1973, by J. Lonchampt), *Claude Debussy* (Geneva, 1957; 2nd ed., 1962), and *Gabriel Fauré* (Paris, 1960).

Vuillermoz, Jean, French composer; b. Monte Carlo, Dec. 29, 1906; d. (killed while on patrol duty in the last hours before the Franco-German armistice), Lobsonn, Alsace, June 21, 1940. He studied with Busser and Rabaud at the Paris Cons.; received the 2nd Prix de Rome for his cantata *Le Pardon* (1932).
WORKS: *Triptique* for Orch. (Paris, May 31, 1932); Concerto for Horn and Orch. (Paris, March 11, 1934); ballet, *Veglione* (1937); Cello Concerto; *Promenade zoologique* for Chamber Orch.; Piano Trio; String Trio.

Vukdragović, Mihailo, Serbian conductor, pedagogue, and composer; b. Okučani, Nov. 8, 1900; d. Belgrade, March 14, 1986. He was a pupil in composition of Milojević at the Belgrade School of Music; then studied composition with Jirák and Novák and conducting with Talich at the Prague Cons. (graduated, 1927); subsequently was active as a choral, operatic, and sym. conductor in Zagreb and Belgrade. He was prof. and director of the Stanković School of Music, prof. of conducting (1940–73) and rector (1947–52) of the Belgrade Academy of Music, and also of the Belgrade Academy of the Arts (1957–59); was made a corresponding member (1950) and a full member (1961) of the Serbian Academy. He wrote several works in an impressionistic style before embracing the esthetics of socialist realism.
WORKS: ORCH.: *Simfonijska meditacija* (1938); *Put u pobedu* (Road to Victory), symphonic poem (1944; Belgrade, Oct. 19, 1945); *Besmirtna mladost* (Immortal Youth), symphonic suite (1948). **VOCAL:** *Vezilja slobode* (The Embroidress of Freedom), cantata (1947; Belgrade, Jan. 5, 1948); *Svetli groboiv* (Illustrious Tombs), cantata (1954); *Vokalna lirika* for Voice and Orch. (1955); *Srbija* (Serbia), cantata (Nis, July 6, 1961); choruses; also 2 string quartets (1925, 1944); theater music; film scores; folk-song arrangements.

Vulpius (real name, **Fuchs**), **Melchior,** German composer, writer on music, and schoolmaster; b. Wasungen, near Meiningen, c.1570; d. Weimar (buried), Aug. 7, 1615. He studied with Johann Steuerlein at the Wasungen Lateinschule. In 1589 he became a supernumerary teacher of Latin at the Schleusingen Lateinschule, finally attaining a permanent teaching post in 1592; then was municipal Kantor and a teacher at the Weimar Lateinschule (1596–1615). He was a prolific composer of sacred music; his Protestant hymn tunes became widely known in Germany during his lifetime. He wrote the theoretical vol. *Musicae compendium latino germanicum M. Heinrici Fabri . . . aliquantulum variatum ac dispositum, cum facili brevique de modis tractatu* (1608).
WORKS: SACRED VOCAL (all publ. in Jena unless otherwise given): *Pars prima cantionum sacrarum* for 6 to 8 and More Voices (1602; ed. by M. Ehrhorn, Kassel, 1968); *Pars secunda selectissimarum cantionum sacrarum* for 6 to 8 and More Voices (1603); *Kirchen Gesend und geistliche Lieder . . . mehrerntheils auff zwey oder dreyerley art . . . contrapunctsweise* for 4 to 5 Voices (Leipzig, 1604; 2nd ed., enlarged, 1609 as *Ein schön geistlich Gesangbuch*); *Canticum Beatissimae Virginis Mariae* for 4 to 6 and More Voices (1605); *Opusculum novum selectissimarum cantionum sacrarum* for 4 to 8 Voices (Erfurt, 1610); *Erster Theil deutscher sontäglicher evangelischer Sprüche von Advent bis auff Trinitatis* for 4 Voices (1612; ed. by H. Nitsche and H. Stern, Stuttgart, 1960); *Das Leiden und Sterben . . . Jesu Christi, aus dem heiligen Evangelisten Matthäo* for 4 and More Voices (Erfurt, 1613; ed. by K. Ziebler, Kassel, 1934); *Der ander Theil deutscher sontäglicher evangelischer Sprüche von Trinitatis bis auff Advent* for 4 and More Voices (1614; ed. by H. Nitsche and

H. Stern, Stuttgart, 1960); some other vols. are not extant.
BIBL.: H. Eggebrecht, *M. V.* (diss., Univ. of Jena, 1949).

Vycpálek, Ladislav, eminent Czech composer; b. Prague, Feb. 23, 1882; d. there, Jan. 9, 1969. He received training in voice, violin, and piano in his youth; studied Czech and German at the Univ. of Prague (Ph.D., 1906, with a diss. on legends in Czech literature concerning the youth of Mary and Jesus); took composition lessons with Novák (1908–12). In 1907 he joined the staff of the Univ. of Prague library, where he later was founder-director of its music section (1922–42); also was active as a violinist in the amateur quartet led by Josef Pick (1909–39); in 1936 he served as artistic director of the National Theater. In 1924 he became a member of the Czech Academy; was chairman of its music section (1950–51). In 1957 he was made an Artist of Merit and in 1967 a National Artist by the Czech government. He greatly distinguished himself as a composer of vocal music; among his finest scores is the *Kantáta o posledních věcech člověka* (Cantata on the Last Things of Man; 1920–22).

WORKS: ORCH.: *Vzhůru srdce* (Lift Up Your Hearts), 2 variation fantasias on hymns from Hus's day (1950). **CHAMBER:** String Quartet (1909); Sonata "Chvála houslí" (Praise to the Violin) for Violin, Mezzo-soprano, and Piano (1927–28); Suite for Viola (1929); Suite for Violin (1930); Sonatina for Violin and Piano (1947); solo piano pieces, including *Cestou* (On the Way), 5 pieces (1911–14), and *Doma* (Home), a suite (1959). **VOCAL:** *Kantáta o posledních věcech člověka* (Cantata on the Last Things of Man) for Soprano, Baritone, Chorus, and Orch. (1920–22); *Blashoslavený ten člověk* (Blessed Is This Man), cantata for Soprano, Baritone, Chorus, and Orch. (1933); *České requiem "Smrt a spaseni"* (Czech Requiem "Death and Redemption") for Soprano, Alto, Baritone, Chorus, and Orch. (1940); choruses; songs; folk-song arrangements.

BIBL.: J. Smolka, *L. V.: Tvůrči vývoj* (L. V.: Creative Evolution; Prague, 1960); M. Svobodova and H. Krupka, *Národní umělec L. V.* (Prague, 1973).

Vysloužil, Jiří, distinguished Czech musicologist; b. Košice, May 11, 1924. He studied musicology with Jan Racek and Bohumír Štědroň, philosophy with Arnošt Bláha and Mirko Novák, and history with Josef Macůrek at the Univ. of Brno (Ph.D, 1949, with the diss. *Problémy a metody hudebního lidopisu* [Problems and Methods of Music Ethnography]; C.Sc., 1959, with the diss. *Leoš Janáček a lidova piseň* [Leoš Janáček and Folk Song]; D.Sc., 1974, with the diss. *Alois Hába*; publ. in Prague, 1974). He worked at the Dept. for Ethnography and Folklore in Brno until 1952; after serving as a lecturer and vice-dean at the Brno Academy (1952–61), in 1961 he joined the faculty of the Univ. of Brno, where he became a prof. in 1973. He served as head of the editorial board of the complete critical ed. of the works of Janáček, which commenced publication in Prague in 1978. He publ. *Hudobníci 20. storočia* (Musicians of the 20th Century; Bratislava, 1964; 2nd ed., 1981), *Leoš Janáček* (Brno, 1978), and *Leoš Janáček: Für Sie porträtiert von Jiří Vysloužil* (Leipzig, 1981).

Vyvyan, Jennifer (Brigit), English soprano; b. Broadstairs, Kent, March 13, 1925; d. London, April 5, 1974. She studied piano and voice at the Royal Academy of Music in London (1941–43), then voice with Roy Henderson; made her debut as Jenny Diver in *The Beggar's Opera* with the English Opera Group (1947). After further vocal training with Fernando Carpi in Switzerland (1950), she won 1st prize in the Geneva international competition (1951). She gained success with her portrayal of Constanze at London's Sadler's Wells Opera Co. (1952); then created the role of Penelope Rich in Britten's *Gloriana* at London's Covent Garden (1953). She made guest appearances at the Glyndebourne Festivals, and in Milan, Rome, Vienna, and Paris. She appeared in many contemporary operas, and was closely associated with those of Britten; created the Governess in his *Turn of the Screw* (1954), Tytania in *A Midsummer Night's Dream* (1960), and Miss Julian in *Owen Wingrave* (1971).

W

Waart, Edo (actually, **Eduard) de,** noted Dutch conductor; b. Amsterdam, June 1, 1941. He was a member of a musical family; his father sang in the chorus of the Netherlands Opera. He first studied the piano; at 13 he took up the oboe; at 16 he entered the Amsterdam Muzieklyceum, where he studied oboe and later cello (graduated, 1962); during the summer of 1960 he attended the conducting classes in Salzburg given by Dean Dixon. He played oboe in the Amsterdam Phil. (1962–63) and then joined the Concertgebouw Orch.; also studied conducting with Franco Ferrara in Hilversum, where he made his debut as a conductor with the Netherlands Radio Phil. in 1964. He went to the U.S. in 1964 and was one of the winners in the Mitropoulos Competition in N.Y.; in 1965–66 he was assistant conductor with the N.Y. Phil. Upon his return to Amsterdam in 1966, he was appointed assistant conductor of the Concertgebouw Orch., and accompanied it on a tour of the U.S. in 1967. He also organized the Netherlands Wind Ensemble, with which he established his reputation through extensive tours. In 1967 he became a guest conductor of the Rotterdam Phil.; from 1973 to 1979, served as its chief conductor. He toured with it in England in 1970 and 1974; in the U.S. in 1971, 1975, and 1977; and in Germany and Austria in 1976. In 1971, 1972, and 1975 he was a guest conductor of the Santa Fe Opera in New Mexico; in 1975 he also conducted opera in Houston. In 1976 he conducted at Covent Garden in London. On Feb. 27, 1974, he made a successful debut with the San Francisco Sym. In 1975 he was made its principal guest conductor and in 1977 its music director. In 1986 he became music director of the Minnesota Orch. in Minneapolis, and in 1988 was named artistic director of the Dutch Radio Phil. Orch. in Hilversum. De Waart represents the modern generation of symphonic and operatic conductors; his objective approach to interpretation, combined with his regard for stylistic propriety and avoidance of ostentatious conductorial display, makes his performances of the traditional and contemporary repertory particularly appealing. He is tall, athletic-looking, and boasts a rich crown of hair; these attributes, topologically speaking, help him dominate the orch.

Waart, Hendrikus Aloysius Petrus de, Dutch composer and organist; b. Amsterdam, June 28, 1863; d. Voorburg, near The Hague, April 2, 1931. He studied in The Hague; then taught piano and organ at the Cons. there; wrote 3 syms., numerous choral works, a String Trio, piano works, and songs.

Wachs, Paul Étienne Victor, French organist and composer; b. Paris, Sept. 19, 1851; d. St. Mandé, July 6, 1915. He studied with César Franck and Victor Massé at the Paris Cons., and won 1st prize for organ playing; subsequently was engaged as a church organist in Paris. He wrote works for organ, chamber music, etc., but achieved his most signal success as a composer of attractive salon pieces for piano (*Pluie d'étoiles, Le Collier de perles, Les Doigts,* etc.); also well known are his *Pastorale* and *Hosanna* for Organ.

Wachsmann, Klaus P(hilipp), noted German ethnomusicologist; b. Berlin, March 8, 1907; d. Tisbury, Wiltshire, July 17, 1984. He received training in musicology with Blume and Schering and in comparative musicology with Hornbostel and Sachs at the Univ. of Berlin (1930–32); after further studies with Fellerer at the Univ. of Fribourg in Switzerland (Ph.D., 1935, with the diss. *Untersuchungen zum vorgregorianischen*

Gesang; publ. in Regensburg, 1935), he pursued linguistic studies at the London School of Oriental and African Studies. He then was active in Uganda, where he was made curator of the Uganda Museum in Kampala in 1948; after serving as scientific officer in charge of ethnological collections at the Wellcome Foundation in London (1958–63), he taught in the music dept. and Inst. of Ethnomusicology at the Univ. of Calif. at Los Angeles (1963–68); then was prof. in the school of music and dept. of linguistics at Northwestern Univ. in Evanston, Ill. (from 1968). He was an authority on African music, specializing in organology and tribal music of Uganda; his years spent outside of academic circles made him an independent and imaginative thinker about music in its relation to culture and philosophy. C. Seeger ed. *Essays for a Humanist: An Offering to Klaus Wachsmann* (N.Y., 1977).

WRITINGS: *Folk Musicians in Uganda* (Kampala, 1956); ed. *An International Catalogue of Published Records of Folk Music* (London, 1960); ed. *A Select Bibliography of Music in Africa* (London, 1965); ed. *Essays on Music and History in Africa* (Evanston, Ill., 1971).

Wachtel, Theodor, famous German tenor; b. Hamburg, March 10, 1823; d. Frankfurt am Main, Nov. 14, 1893. The son of a livery-stable keeper, he carried on the business from the age of 17, after his father's death. When his voice was discovered, he was sent to Hamburg for study, and soon appeared in opera; made his operatic debut in Hamburg (March 12, 1849); made his debut at London's Covent Garden as Edgardo (June 7, 1862), and sang at the Berlin Royal Opera (1862–79); also toured the U.S. (1871–72; 1875–76). His voice was a powerful and brilliant lyric tenor; the role in which he made himself famous was that of the postilion in Adam's *Le Postillon de Longjumeau*, which he sang more than 1,000 times; also was successful as Manrico, John of Leyden, and Pollione.

Wachtmeister, Axel Raoul, Count, Swedish composer; b. London (son of the Swedish ambassador there), April 2, 1865; d. Paris, Dec. 12, 1947. He studied music with Gédalge and d'Indy. He lived mostly in Paris, going to Sweden in the summers; spent some time in the U.S.; his cantata *Sappho* was performed in N.Y. in 1917. He also wrote 2 syms.; a symphonic poem, *Le Récit de l'horloge; Hymne à la lune* for Baritone, Chorus, and Orch. (Cincinnati, 1933); *Suite romantique* for Piano; songs.

Wade, Joseph Augustine, Irish composer; b. Dublin, 1796; d. London, July 15, 1845. He went to London in 1821, and established himself as a highly successful composer of popular ballads; his song *Meet me by moonlight alone* (1826) enjoyed great vogue, as did his vocal duet *I've wandered in dreams.* He also wrote the comic operas *The Two Houses of Granada* (London, Oct. 31, 1826) and *The Convent Belles* (London, July 8, 1833; in collaboration with W. Hawes), and an operetta, *The Pupil of Da Vinci* (London, Nov. 30, 1839).

Wadsworth, Charles (William), American pianist and harpsichordist; b. Barnesville, Ga., May 21, 1929. He studied piano with Rosalyn Tureck and conducting with Jean Morel at the Juilliard School of Music in N.Y. (B.S., 1951; M.S., 1952); also studied the French song repertoire with Pierre Bernac in Paris and German lieder with Meinhard von Zallinger in Munich. In 1960 Gian Carlo Menotti invited him to organize the Chamber Music Concerts at the Festival of Two Worlds in Spoleto, Italy; he was its director and pianist for 20 years. In 1969 he helped to found the Chamber Music Society of Lincoln Center in N.Y., and was its artistic director until 1989; in 1977 he also created the chamber music series for the Charleston, S.C., Spoleto Festival U.S.A. In addition to numerous appearances as a pianist and harpsichordist with various ensembles, he also appeared in performances with such noted musicians as Dietrich Fischer-Dieskau, Beverly Sills, Hermann Prey, and Shirley Verrett.

Waechter, Eberhard, Austrian baritone and operatic administrator; b. Vienna, July 9, 1929. He studied piano and music theory at the Univ. of Vienna and at the Academy of Music there (1950–53); took private voice lessons with Elisabeth Rado; in 1953 he made his debut as Silvio at the Vienna Volksoper; in 1955 he became a member of the Vienna State Opera; subsequently made guest appearances at Bayreuth, Salzburg, Covent Garden in London, and La Scala in Milan. On Jan. 25, 1961, he made his debut at the Metropolitan Opera in N.Y. as Wolfram in *Tannhäuser.* In 1963 he was named an Austrian Kammersänger. After retiring from the operatic stage, he became director of the Vienna Volksoper in 1987; in 1991, became director of the Vienna State Opera as well. He was particularly distinguished in lyric baritone parts, among them Count Almaviva, Don Giovanni, and Wolfram; he also sang the role of Orest in *Elektra* by Richard Strauss.

Waefelghem, Louis van, Belgian violinist, violist, viola d'amorist, pedagogue, and composer; b. Bruges, Jan. 13, 1840; d. Paris, June 19, 1908. He studied violin at the Brussels Cons. with Meerts (1857–60); became concertmaster of the Budapest Opera orch.; settled in Paris in 1863, where he studied the viola, becoming a member of the Opéra orch. in 1868; later was prof. of viola at the Cons. In 1871 he played in the opera orch. at Her Majesty's Theatre and in the concerts at the Musical Union in London. He was a member of the Lamoureux Orch. in Paris (1881–95). With Grillet, Diémer, and Delsart he founded the Société des Instruments Anciens in Paris (1895), where he played the viola d'amore; composed and arranged a number of pieces for that instrument.

BIBL.: E. van der Straeten, "L. v.W.," *The Strad,* XIX (1908).

Waelput, Hendrik, Belgian conductor and composer; b. Ghent, Oct. 26, 1845; d. there, July 8, 1885. He studied at the Brussels Cons.; won the Prix de Rome for his cantata *Het woud* (The Forest; 1867). He was assistant director of the Bruges music school (1869–71); conducted theater orchs. at The Hague, Dijon, Douai, Fécamp, and Lille (1872–76). From 1876 to 1879 he was conductor of the Ghent Theater; in 1879, was appointed prof. of harmony at the Antwerp Cons.; became director of the Ghent Opera in 1884. He wrote 3 operas: *La Ferme du diable* (Ghent, 1865), *Berken de diamantslijper* (1868), and *Stella* (Brussels, March 14, 1881); 5 syms.; 4 overtures; Flute Concerto; several cantatas, including *Het woud* (1867), *Memlingcantate* (1871), and *De pacificatier van Gent* (1876); part-songs; solo songs; chamber music; piano pieces.

BIBL.: E. Callaert, *Levensschets van H. W.* (Ghent, 1886); E. De Vynck, *Henry W.* (diss., Univ. of Brussels, 1935).

Waelrant, Hubert, Flemish singer, teacher, music editor, and composer; b. between Nov. 20, 1516, and Nov. 19, 1517; d. Antwerp, Nov. 19, 1595. He was active mainly in Antwerp, where he began his career as a tenor soloist at the Cathedral (1544–45); taught music in a school operated by his landlord, Gregorius de Coninck (1553–56). From 1554 to about 1566 he served as music ed. for the printer Jean de Laet, who was a fine composer of motets. He has been credited with abandoning the old system of solmization by hexachords and introducing a new system of the 7 tone-names, *bo ce di ga lo ma ni* (hence called "bocedization"; also "voces Belgicae").

WORKS (all publ. in Antwerp unless otherwise given): (15) *Sacrarum cantionum . . . liber sextus* for 5 to 6 Voices (1556?); several other motets in contemporary collections; metrical Psalms: 9 in various contemporary collections; chansons: *Il primo libro de madrigali et* [11] *canzoni francezi* for 5 Voices (1558); other chansons in contemporary collections; madrigals: *Il primo libro de* [9] *madrigali et canzoni francezi* for 5 Voices (1558); other madrigals in contemporary collections; napolitane: *Le* [30] *canzoni napolitane* for 4 Voices (Venice, 1565); other napolitane in contemporary collections.

BIBL.: G. Becker, *H. W. et ses psaumes: Notice biographique et bibliographique* (Paris, 1881); H. Slenk, "The Music School of H. W.," *Journal of the American Musicological Society,* XXI (1968); R. Weaver, *The Motets of H. W. (c.1517–1595)* (diss., Syracuse Univ., 1971).

Waesberghe, Jos(eph Maria Antonius Franciscus) Smits van. See **Smits van Waesberghe, Jos(eph Maria Antonius Franciscus).**

Wagemans, Peter Jan, Dutch composer; b. The Hague, Sept. 7, 1952. He studied organ, composition (with Vlijmen), and music theory. He composed a Sym. (1972); *Overture* (1972); Wind Quintet (1973); Saxophone Quartet (1975); *Music I for Winds and Timpani* (1975); *Music II for Strings, 3 Trumpets, 3 Trombones, and Percussion* (1976; Baden-Baden, Oct. 20, 1979); *From "De zangen van Maldoror"* for Orch. (1976); *Alla marcia* for Tuba and 12 Instrumentalists (1977); *3 Dances* for Orch. (1978); String Quartet (1980; rev. 1981); *Romance* for Violin and Orch. (1981); *Muziek III: Europa na de regen* for Soloists, Choir, and Orch. (1984); *Fragmenten* for 7 Instruments (1984); *Klang* for Orch. (1985–86); *Great Expectations* for Violin and Piano (1986).

Wagenaar, Bernard, Dutch-born American violinist, conductor, teacher, and composer, son of **Johan Wagenaar;** b. Arnhem, July 18, 1894; d. York, Maine, May 19, 1971. He studied music with his father; violin with Gerard Veerman in Utrecht. In 1920 he settled in the U.S.; became a naturalized citizen in 1927; was a violinist in the N.Y. Phil. (1921–23). He joined the Inst. of Musical Art in N.Y., and remained with it when it became the Juilliard School of Music (1925–68). He was made an Officer of the Order of Oranje-Nassau of the Netherlands. His output followed along neo-Classical lines.
  WORKS: *Pieces of 8,* chamber opera (1943; N.Y., May 9, 1944); Sym. No. 1 (1926; N.Y., Oct. 7, 1928); Divertimento No. 1 (1927; Detroit, Nov. 28, 1929); Sinfonietta (1929; N.Y., Jan. 16, 1930); Sym. No. 2 (1930; N.Y., Nov. 10, 1932); Sym. No. 3 (1936; N.Y., Jan. 23, 1937); Triple Concerto for Flute, Harp, Cello, and Orch. (1935; N.Y., May 20, 1941); Violin Concerto (1940); Sym. No. 4 (1946; Boston, Dec. 16, 1949); Divertimento No. 2 (1952); *5 Tableaux* for Cello and Orch. (1952); *3 Songs from the Chinese* for Soprano, Flute, Harp, and Piano (1921); Violin Sonata (1925); 4 string quartets (1926, 1932, 1936, 1960); Piano Sonata (1928); Concertino for 8 Instruments (1942); songs.
  BIBL.: D. Fuller, "B. W.," *Modern Music* (May 1944).

Wagenaar, Johan, distinguished Dutch organist, choral conductor, pedagogue, and composer, father of **Bernard Wagenaar;** b. Utrecht, Nov. 1, 1862; d. The Hague, June 17, 1941. He studied with Richard Hol in Utrecht (1875–85) and with H. von Herzogenberg in Berlin (1889); from 1887 to 1904 he was director of the Utrecht Music School; also was organist at the Cathedral (1887–1919). From 1919 to 1936 he was director of the Royal Cons. in The Hague.
  WORKS: OPERAS: *De Doge van Venetie* (1901; Utrecht, 1904); *De Cid* (1915; Utrecht, 1916); *Jupiter Amans,* burlesque opera (Scheveningen, 1925). **ORCH.:** Symphonic poems: *Levenszomer* (1901); *Saul en David* (1906); *Elverhoi* (1939); overtures: *Koning Jan* (1889); *Cyrano de Bergerac* (1905); *De getemde feeks* (1906); *Driekoningenavond* (1927); *De philosofische prinses* (1931); also numerous choral works; songs; organ pieces.
  BIBL.: Special issue of *De Muziek* (1932).

Wagenseil, Georg Christoph, Austrian composer and music theorist; b. Vienna, Jan. 29, 1715; d. there, March 1, 1777. He studied with J.J. Fux; was the music teacher of the Empress Maria Theresa and her children; in 1739 was appointed court composer; remained in the Imperial service until his death. He wrote many operas in Italian.
  WORKS: Operas (all 1st perf. in Vienna): *La generosità trionfante* (1745); *Ariodante* (May 14, 1746); *La clemenza di Tito* (Oct. 15, 1746); *Alexander der Grosse in Indien* (July 7, 1748); *Il Siroe* (Oct. 4, 1748); *L'Olimpiade* (May 13, 1749); *Andromeda* (March 30, 1750); *Antigone* (May 13, 1750); *Armida placato* (Aug. 28, 1750); *Euridice* (July 26, 1750); *Le Cacciatrici amanti* (Laxenburg, June 1755); *Demetrio* (1760); also 3 oratorios; 30 syms.; 27 harpsichord concertos; organ works. Two syms. and a Trio Sonata are in Denkmäler der Tonkunst in Österreich,

31 (15.ii); a Divertimento was ed. by Blume. Wagenseil publ. the following: *Suavis, artificiose elaboratus concentus musicus, continens: 6 selectas parthias ad clavicembalum compositas* (1740); *18 Divertimenti di cembalo,* opp. 1–3; Divertimento for 2 Harpsichords; 2 divertimentos for Harpsichord, 2 Violins, and Cello, op. 5; 10 syms. for Harpsichord, 2 Violins, and Cello, opp. 4, 7, 8; 6 violin sonatas, with Harpsichord, op. 6.
  BIBL.: K. Horwitz, *W. als Symphoniker* (diss., Univ. of Vienna, 1906); W. Vetter, "G.C. W., Ein Vorläufer Glucks," *Zeitschrift für Musikwissenschaft,* VIII (1926); idem, "Der Opernkomponist G.C. W. und sein Verhältnis zu Mozart und Gluck," *Hermann Abert-Gedenkschrift* (Halle, 1928); J. Pelikant, *Die Klavier-Werke W.s* (Vienna, 1926); G. Hausswald, "Der Divertimento-Begriff bei G.C. W.," *Archiv für Musikwissenschaft,* IX (1952); J. Kucaba, *The Symphonies of G.C. W.* (diss., Boston Univ., 1967); H. Scholz-Michelitsch, *G.C. W. als Klavierkomponist: Eine Studie zu seinen zyklischen Soloklavierwerken* (diss., Univ. of Vienna, 1967).

Wagenseil, Johann Christoph, German scholar; b. Nuremberg, Nov. 26, 1633; d. Altdorf, Oct. 9, 1708. He traveled throughout Europe in the capacity of a Hofmeister (traveling companion to young patricians); was made prof. of public and canon law, history, and oriental languages at the Civic Univ. of Nuremberg in Altdorf in 1649, where he later served as rector, dean of law, and librarian; received a doctor of laws degree from the Univ. of Orléans. He publ. an important book, *De Sacri Rom. Imperii Libera Civitate Noribergensi Commentatio* (Altdorf, 1697), with a 140-page supplement (in German), *Buch von der Meister-Singer holdseligen Kunst: Anfang, Fortübung, Nutzbarkeiten und Lehr-Sätz,* containing poems and melodies by Frauenlob, Mügling, Marner, and Regenbogen; this section was the main literary source that Wagner used in *Die Meistersinger von Nürnberg.*
  BIBL.: H. Thompson, *Wagner & W.: A Source of Wagner's Opera "Die Meistersinger"* (London, 1927); H. Zohn and M. Davis, "J.C. W., Polymath," *Monatshefte für Deutschen Unterricht: Journal Devoted to the Study of the German Language and Literature,* XLVI (1954).

Waghalter, Ignatz, conductor and composer; b. Warsaw, March 15, 1882; d. N.Y., April 7, 1949. He studied in Berlin, where he later was conductor of the Komische Oper (1907–11); then conducted in Essen (1911–12), and at the Deutsches Opernhaus in Berlin-Charlottenburg. In 1925 he succeeded Stransky as conductor of the State Sym. Orch. in N.Y. (for one season only); then returned to Berlin; in 1933 he went to Prague, and in 1934 to Vienna. He settled in N.Y. in 1938.
  WORKS: OPERAS: *Der Teufelsweg* (Berlin, 1911); *Mandragola* (Berlin, Jan. 23, 1914; N.Y., March 4, 1925); *Jugend* (Berlin, 1917); *Der späte Gast* (Berlin, 1922); *Sataniel* (Berlin, 1923); operettas: *Der Weiberkrieg* and *Wem gehört Helena?;* Violin Concerto; Violin Sonata; String Quartet; piano pieces.
  BIBL.: H. Leichtentritt, *I. W.* (N.Y., 1924).

Wagner, Cosima, wife of **Richard Wagner,** daughter of **Franz Liszt** and the Countess Marie d'Agoult; b. Bellagio, on Lake Como, Dec. 24, 1837; d. Bayreuth, April 1, 1930. She received an excellent education in Paris; married **Hans von Bülow** on Aug. 18, 1857; there were 2 daughters of this marriage, Blandine and Daniela; the 3rd daughter, Isolde, was Wagner's child, as was the 4th, Eva, and the son, Siegfried. A divorce followed on July 18, 1870; the marriage to Wagner took place in a few weeks, on Aug. 25, 1870. A woman of high intelligence, practical sense, and imperious character, Cosima Wagner emerged after Wagner's death as a powerful personage in all affairs regarding the continuance of the Bayreuth Festivals, as well as the complex matters pertaining to the rights of performance of Wagner's works all over the world. She publ. her reminiscences of Liszt: *Franz Liszt, Ein Gedenkblatt von seiner Tochter* (Munich, 2nd ed., 1911). Her diaries were ed. by M. Gregor-Dellin and D. Mack as *Cosima Wagner: Die Tagebücher, 1869–1877* (2 vols., Munich, 1976–77; Eng. tr. by G. Skelton as *Cosima Wagner's Diaries,* 2 vols., N.Y., 1977 and 1980).

BIBL.: M. Strauss, *Wie ich Frau C. W. sehe* (Magdeburg, 1912); W. Siegfried, *Frau C. W.* (Stuttgart, 1930); M. von Waldberg, *C. W.s Briefe an ihre Tochter Daniela von Bülow, 1866–85* (Stuttgart, 1933); P. Pretzsch, *C. W. und H.S. Chamberlain im Briefwechsel, 1888–1908* (Leipzig, 1934); L. Scalero, *C. W.* (Zürich, 1934); *Briefwechsel zwischen C. W. und Fürst Ernst zu Hohenlohe-Langenburg* (Stuttgart, 1937); M. von Millenkovich (M. Morold), *C. W., Ein Lebensbild* (Leipzig, 1937); E. Thierbach, ed., *Die Briefe C. W.s an Friedrich Nietzsche* (Weimar, 1938–40); A. Sojoloff, *C. W., Extraordinary Daughter of Franz Liszt* (N.Y., 1969); D. Mack, ed., *C. W.: Das zweite Leben: Briefe und Aufzeichnungen, 1883–1930* (Munich, 1980); G. Marek, *C. W.* (N.Y., 1981); G. Skelton, *Richard and C. Wagner: Biography of a Marriage* (London, 1982).

Wagner, Georg Gottfried, German violinist and composer; b. Mühlberg, April 5, 1698; d. Plauen, March 23, 1756. He studied with Kuhnau at the Thomasschule in Leipzig (1712–18); studied at the Univ. of Leipzig (1718–26); was a violinist in Bach's orch., and was recommended by Bach for the post of cantor at Plauen, which he held from 1726 to his death. He wrote numerous sacred works and instrumental compositions; his motet *Lob und Ehre* was misattributed to Bach by Breitkopf & Härtel (publ. 1819 as BWV anh.162).

BIBL.: B. Hammerschmidt, *G.G. W.* (Chemnitz, 1912); H.-J. Schulze, "Johann Sebastian Bach und G.G. W.—Neue Dokumente," *Bach-Studien,* V (1975).

Wagner, Gerrit Anthonie Alexander, Dutch conductor and composer; b. Amsterdam, March 8, 1862; d. Antwerp, Nov. 24, 1892. He studied with Brandts-Buys in Amsterdam and with Benoit and Blockx in Antwerp; became a choral conductor there. He wrote an oratorio, *Babylonische gevangenschap;* a symphonic poem, *Zusterengelen;* much choral music; his promising career was terminated by an early death.

Wagner, J(osef) F(ranz), Austrian bandmaster and composer; b. Vienna, March 20, 1856; d. there, June 5, 1908. He was a popular leader of military bands in Vienna; produced the operetta *Der Herzbub* (Vienna, Feb. 7, 1895), which had little success, but achieved fame as the composer of the Austrian march *Unter dem Doppeladler* (1893), which became a semi-official march of the Austro-Hungarian Empire.

Wagner, Johanna, German soprano; b. Lohnde, near Hannover, Oct. 13, 1826; d. Würzburg, Oct. 16, 1894. She was a natural daughter of Lieutenant Bock von Wülfingen of Hannover, and was adopted by Richard Wagner's brother, Albert; was thus regarded as Wagner's niece. Of a precocious talent, she acted on the stage as a small child; through Wagner she obtained a position at the Dresden Opera when she was 17; produced an excellent impression as Agathe in *Der Freischütz,* and was engaged as a regular member. She studied the part of Elisabeth in *Tannhäuser* with Wagner, and sang it in the premiere of the opera on Oct. 19, 1845, when she was barely 19 years old. In 1846 she went to Paris for further study with Pauline Viardot-García (1846–48); then was engaged at the Hamburg Opera (1849) and finally at the Court Opera in Berlin (1850–61). In 1856 she made her London debut at Her Majesty's Theatre. In 1859 she married the district judge Alfred Jachmann. After 1862 she acted mainly on the dramatic stage, reappearing in opera at the Bayreuth Festival in 1876 in the parts of Schwertleite and the 1st Norn in the 1st complete mounting of the *Ring* cycle. She taught at the Royal Music School in Munich (1882–84); then taught privately.

BIBL.: J. Kapp and H. Jachmann, *Richard Wagner und seine erste "Elisabeth," J. J.-W.* (Berlin, 1927; in Eng. as *Wagner and His First Elisabeth,* London, 1944).

Wagner, Joseph Frederick, American composer and conductor; b. Springfield, Mass., Jan. 9, 1900; d. Los Angeles, Oct. 12, 1974. He was educated at the Technical High School in Providence and studied piano and organ privately; then entered the New England Cons., where he studied composition with Frederick Converse (diploma, 1923); later took lessons in composition with Alfredo Casella in Boston in 1927, and

took courses at Boston Univ. (B.M., 1932); in 1934–35 he studied composition with Nadia Boulanger and conducting with Pierre Monteux in Paris, and also conducting with Felix Weingartner in Basel. He was assistant director of music in Boston public schools (1923–44); taught at Boston Univ. (1929–40), Hunter College in N.Y. (1945–56), and Brooklyn College (1945–47). In 1925 he organized the Boston Civic Sym. Orch., which he conducted until 1944; subsequently was conductor of the Duluth Sym. Orch. (1947–50) and of the Orquesta Sinfónica Nacional de Costa Rica in San José (1950–54); was also a guest conductor in Helsinki, Stockholm, Washington, D.C., and Buffalo. In 1960 he settled in Hollywood; in 1961 was appointed a prof. at Pepperdine College in Los Angeles. His music is distinguished by excellent craftsmanship; it is set in a fairly advanced idiom, with bitonality as a frequent resource in his later works. Shortly before his death he completed the score of *Tribute to America* (Sym. No. 4) for Chorus, Soprano Solo, Narrator, and Orch., planned for the bicentennial year 1976, but never performed. Indeed, most performances of Wagner's orch. works were conducted by himself. Wistfully, he kept a file of rejection slips from conductors, arranged in alphabetical order, from A to Z (from Abravanel to Zipper). A memorial brochure, *Joseph Wagner: A Retrospective of a Composer-Conductor,* ed. by Lance Bowling, with an introductory article, "Joseph Wagner: The Most Undiscovered among American Composers," by N. Slonimsky, was publ. in Lomita, Calif., in 1976. He publ. 2 useful books: *Orchestration: A Practical Handbook* (N.Y., 1958) and *Band Scoring* (N.Y., 1960).

WORKS: Opera, *New England Sampler* (Los Angeles, Feb. 26, 1965); ballets: *The Birthday of the Infanta* (1935) and *Hudson River Legend* (1941; Boston, March 1, 1944); *Miniature Concerto* for Piano and Orch. (1919; Providence, June 11, 1920; rev. as *Concerto in G Minor;* New Brunswick, N.J., Aug. 3, 1930); *Rhapsody* for Piano, Clarinet, and Strings (1925); Sym. No. 1 (Rochester, N.Y., Oct. 19, 1944); Sym. No. 2 (1945; Wilmington, Del., March 1, 1960); Sym. No. 3 (1951); Sym. No. 4, *Tribute to America* (1974); Violin Concerto (1955); Sinfonietta No. 1 (1931); Sinfonietta No. 2 for String Orch. (1941); *Pastoral Costarricense* (1958); *Merlin and Sir Boss,* symphonic tale for Concert Band, after Mark Twain's *A Connecticut Yankee* (1963); Concerto for Organ, Brass, and Percussion (1963); Harp Concerto (1964); Violin Sonata (1941); *Introduction and Scherzo* for Bassoon and Piano (1951); *Patterns of Contrast* for Wind Quartet (1959); *Fantasy Sonata* for Harp Solo (1963); *Preludes and Toccata* for Harp, Violin, and Cello (1964); *Fantasy and Fugue* for Woodwind Quartet (1968); *Sonata of Sonnets* for Voice and Piano (1961); *12 Concert Preludes* for Organ (1974); for Piano: *Radio City Snapshots* (1945) and *Sonata with Differences* (1952); *David Jazz* for Men's Chorus, with Piano (1934); for Chorus: *Under Freedom's Flag* (1940) and *Ballad of Brotherhood* (1947); *Missa sacra* for Chorus, Mezzo-soprano, and Orch. (1952); *American Ballad* for Chorus a cappella (1963).

Wagner, Karl Jakob, German oboist, conductor, and composer; b. Darmstadt, Feb. 22, 1772; d. there, Nov. 24, 1822. He was apprenticed to the Darmstadt Hofkapelle when he was 16, becoming a member of its orch. as violinist and horn player at 18; studied theory with Abbé Vogler. In 1800 he was named master of military music; after touring as a concert artist, he was active in Paris (1805–11); then returned to Darmstadt as Hofkapellmeister (1811–20). He wrote 4 operas for Darmstadt: *Der Zahnarzt* (1803), *Pygmalion* (1809), *Siuph und Nitetis* (1811), and *Chimene* (1821); also incidental music to plays, orch. works, chamber music, vocal works, and piano pieces.

Wagner, Peter (Joseph), eminent German musicologist; b. Kürenz, near Trier, Aug. 19, 1865; d. Fribourg, Switzerland, Oct. 17, 1931. He studied at the Univ. of Strasbourg; received his Ph.D. in 1890 with the dissertation. *Palestrina als weltlicher Komponist* (publ. as "Das Madrigal und Palestrina," *Vierteljahrsschrift für Musikwissenschaft,* VIII, 1892); studied further in Berlin under Bellermann and Spitta; in 1893 he was appointed an instructor at the Univ. of Fribourg in Switzerland; subsequently was a prof. (1902–21) and rector (1920–31). In 1901 he established its Académie Grégorienne for theoretical and practical study of plainsong, in which field he was an eminent authority. He was a member of the Papal Commission for the *Editio Vaticana* of the Roman Gradual (1904), and was made a Papal Chamberlain.

WRITINGS: *Einführung in die gregorianischen Melodien: Ein Handbuch der Choralwissenschaft* (vol. I, Fribourg, 1895; 3rd ed., 1911; Eng. tr., 1907; vol. II, Leipzig, 1905; 2nd ed., 1912; vol. III, Leipzig, 1921); *Elemente des gregorianischen Gesanges zur Einführung in die vatikanische Choralausgabe* (Regensburg, 1909); *Geschichte der Messe I: bis 1600* (Leipzig, 1913); *Einführung in die katholische Kirchenmusik: Vorträge gehalten an der Universität Freiburg in der Schweiz für Theologen und andere Freunde kirchlicher Musik* (Düsseldorf, 1919).

BIBL.: K. Weinmann, ed., *Festschrift P. W. zum 60. Geburtstag* (Leipzig, 1926).

Wagner, (Wilhelm) Richard, great German composer whose operas, written to his own librettos, have radically transformed the concept of stage music, postulating the inherent equality of drama and symphonic accompaniment, and establishing the uninterrupted continuity of the action; b. Leipzig, May 22, 1813; d. Venice, Feb. 13, 1883. The antecedents of his family, and his own origin, are open to controversy. His father was a police registrar in Leipzig who died when Wagner was only 6 months old; his mother, Johanna (Rosine), née Pätz, was the daughter of a baker in Weissenfels; it is possible also that she was an illegitimate offspring of Prince Friedrich Ferdinand Constantin of Weimar. Eight months after her husband's death, Johanna Wagner married, on Aug. 28, 1814, the actor Ludwig Geyer. This hasty marriage generated speculation that Geyer may have been Wagner's real father; Wagner himself entertained this possibility, pointing out the similarity of his and Geyer's prominent noses; in the end he abandoned this surmise. The problem of Wagner's origin arose with renewed force after the triumph of the Nazi party in Germany, as Hitler's adoration of Wagner was put in jeopardy by suspicions that Geyer might have been Jewish and that if Wagner was indeed his natural son then he himself was tainted by Semitic blood. The phantom of Wagner's possible contamination with Jewish hemoglobin struck horror into the hearts of good Nazi biologists and archivists; they delved anxiously into Geyer's own ancestry, and much to the relief of Goebbels and other Nazi intellectuals, it was found that Geyer, like Wagner's nominal father, was the purest of Aryans; Wagner's possible illegitimate birth was of no concern to the racial tenets of the Nazi *Weltanschauung*.

Geyer was a member of the Court Theater in Dresden, and the family moved there in 1814. Geyer died on Sept. 30, 1821; in 1822 Wagner entered the Dresden Kreuzschule, where he remained a pupil until 1827. Carl Maria von Weber often visited the Geyer home; these visits exercised a beneficial influence on him in his formative years. In 1825 he began to take piano lessons from a local musician named Humann, and also studied violin with Robert Sipp. Wagner showed strong literary inclinations, and under the spell of Shakespeare, wrote a tragedy, *Leubald*. In 1827 he moved with his mother back to Leipzig, where his uncle Adolf Wagner gave him guidance in his classical reading. In 1828 he was enrolled in the Nikolaischule; while in school, he had lessons in harmony with Christian Gottlieb Müller, a violinist in the theater orch. In June 1830 he entered the Thomasschule, where he began to compose; he wrote a String Quartet and some piano music; his *Overture in B-flat major* was performed at the Leipzig Theater on Dec. 24, 1830, under the direction of the famous musician Heinrich Dorn. Now determined to dedicate himself entirely to music, he became a student of Theodor Weinlig, cantor of the Thomaskirche, from whom he received a thorough training in counterpoint and composition. His 1st publ. work was a Piano Sonata in B-flat major, to which he assigned the opus number 1; it

was brought out by the prestigious publishing house of Breitkopf & Härtel in 1832. He then wrote an overture to *König Enzio*, which was performed at the Leipzig Theater on Feb. 17, 1832; it was followed by an Overture in C major, which was presented at a Gewandhaus concert on April 30, 1832. Wagner's 1st major orch. work, a Sym. in C major, was performed at a Prague Cons. concert in Nov. 1832; on Jan. 10, 1833, it was played by the Gewandhaus Orch. in Leipzig; he was 19 years old at the time. In 1832 he wrote an opera, *Die Hochzeit*, after J.G. Büsching's *Ritterzeit und Ritterwesen;* an introduction, a septet, and a chorus from this work are extant. Early in 1833 he began work on *Die Feen*, to a libretto after Carlo Gozzi's *La Donna serpente.* Upon completion of *Die Feen* in Jan. 1834, he offered the score to the Leipzig Theater, but it was rejected. In June 1834 he began to sketch out a new opera, *Das Liebesverbot*, after Shakespeare's play *Measure for Measure.* In July 1834 he obtained the position of music director with Heinrich Bethmann's theater company, based in Magdeburg; he made his debut in Bad Lauschstadt, conducting Mozart's *Don Giovanni.* On March 29, 1836, he led in Magdeburg the premiere of his opera *Das Liebesverbot*, presented under the title *Die Novize von Palermo.* Bethmann's company soon went out of business; Wagner, who was by that time deeply involved with Christine Wilhelmine ("Minna") Planer, an actress with the company, followed her to Königsberg, where they were married on Nov. 24, 1836. In Königsberg he composed the overture *Rule Britannia;* on April 1, 1837, he was appointed music director of the Königsberg town theater. His marital affairs suffered a setback when Minna left him for a rich businessman by the name of Dietrich. In Aug. 1837 he went to Riga as music director of the theater there; coincidentally, Minna's sister was engaged as a singer at the same theater; Minna soon joined her, and became reconciled with Wagner. In Riga Wagner worked on his new opera, *Rienzi, der letzte der Tribunen*, after a popular novel by Bulwer-Lytton.

In March 1839 he lost his position in Riga; he and Minna, burdened by debts, left town to seek their fortune elsewhere. In their passage by sea from Pillau they encountered a fierce storm, and the ship was forced to drop anchor in the Norwegian fjord of Sandwike. They made their way to London, and then set out for Boulogne; there Wagner met Meyerbeer, who gave him a letter of recommendation to the director of the Paris Opéra. He arrived in Paris with Minna in Sept. 1839, and remained there until 1842. He was forced to eke out a meager subsistence by making piano arrangements of operas and writing occasional articles for the *Gazette Musicale.* In Jan. 1840 he completed his Overture to *Faust* (later rev. as *Eine Faust-Ouvertüre*). Soon he found himself in dire financial straits; he owed money that he could not repay, and on Oct. 28, 1840, he was confined in debtors' prison; he was released on Nov. 17, 1840. The conditions of his containment were light, and he was able to leave prison on certain days. In the meantime he had completed the libretto for *Der fliegende Holländer;* he submitted it to the director of the Paris Opéra, but the director had already asked Paul Foucher to prepare a libretto on the same subject. The director was willing, however, to buy Wagner's scenario for 500 French francs; Wagner accepted the offer (July 2, 1841). Louis Dietsch brought out his treatment of the subject in his opera *Le Vaisseau fantôme* (Paris Opéra, Nov. 9, 1842).

In 1842 Wagner received the welcome news from Dresden that his opera *Rienzi* had been accepted for production; it was staged there on Oct. 20, 1842, with considerable success. *Der fliegende Holländer* was also accepted by Dresden, and Wagner conducted its first performance there on Jan. 2, 1843. On Feb. 2 of that year, he was named 2nd Hofkapellmeister in Dresden, where he conducted a large repertoire of Classical operas, among them *Don Giovanni, Le nozze di Figaro, Die Zauberflöte, Fidelio,* and *Der Freischütz.* In 1846 he conducted a memorable performance in Dresden of Beethoven's 9th Sym. In Dresden he led the prestigious choral society Liedertafel, for which he wrote several works, including the "biblical scene" *Das Liebesmahl der Apostel.* He was also preoccupied during those years in working on the score and music for *Tannhäuser*, completing it on April 13, 1845. He conducted its first performance in Dresden on Oct. 19, 1845. He subsequently revised the score, which was staged to better advantage there on Aug. 1, 1847. Concurrently, he began work on *Lohengrin*, which he completed on April 28, 1848. Wagner's efforts to have his works publ. failed, leaving him again in debt. Without waiting for further performances of his operas that had already been presented to the public, he drew up the first prose outline of *Der Nibelungen-Mythus als Entwurf zu einem Drama*, the prototype of the epic *Ring* cycle; in Nov. 1848 he began work on the poem for *Siegfrieds Tod*. At that time he joined the revolutionary Vaterlandsverein, and was drawn into active participation in the movement, culminating in an open uprising in May 1849. An order was issued for his arrest, and he had to leave Dresden; he made his way to Weimar, where he found a cordial reception from Liszt; he then proceeded to Vienna, where a Prof. Widmann lent him his own passport so that Wagner could cross the border of Saxony on his way to Zürich; there he made his home in July 1849; Minna joined him there a few months later. Shortly before leaving Dresden he had sketched 2 dramas, *Jesus von Nazareth* and *Achilleus*; both remained unfinished. In Zürich he wrote a number of essays expounding his philosophy of art: *Die Kunst und die Revolution* (1849), *Das Kunstwerk der Zukunft* (1849), *Kunst und Klima* (1850), *Oper und Drama* (1851; rev. 1868), and *Eine Mitteilung an meine Freunde* (1851). The ideas expressed in *Das Kunstwerk der Zukunft* gave rise to the description of Wagner's operas as "music of the future" by his opponents; they were also described as *Gesamtkunstwerk*, "total artwork," by his admirers. He rejected both descriptions as distortions of his real views. He was equally opposed to the term "music drama," which nevertheless became an accepted definition for all of his operas.

In Feb. 1850 Wagner was again in Paris; there he fell in love with Jessie Laussot, the wife of a wine merchant; however, she eventually left Wagner, and he returned to Minna in Zürich. On Aug. 28, 1850, Liszt conducted the successful premiere of *Lohengrin* in Weimar. In 1851 he wrote the verse text of *Der junge Siegfried*, and prose sketches for *Das Rheingold* and *Die Walküre*. In June 1852 he finished the text of *Die Walküre* and of *Das Rheingold;* he completed the entire libretto of *Der Ring des Nibelungen* on Dec. 15, 1852, and it was privately printed in 1853. In Nov. 1853 he began composition of the music for *Das Rheingold*, completing the full score on Sept. 26, 1854. In June 1854 he commenced work on the music of *Die Walküre*, which he finished on March 20, 1856. In 1854 he became friendly with a wealthy Zürich merchant, Otto Wesendonck, and his wife, Mathilde. Wesendonck was willing to give Wagner a substantial loan, to be repaid out of his performance rights. The situation became complicated when Wagner developed an affection for Mathilde, which in all probability remained Platonic. But he set to music 5 lyric poems written by Mathilde herself; the album was publ. as the *Wesendonk-Lieder* in 1857. In 1855 he conducted a series of 8 concerts with the Phil. Society of London (March 12–June 25). His performances were greatly praised by English musicians, and he had the honor of meeting Queen Victoria, who invited him to her loge at the intermission of his 7th concert. In June 1856 he made substantial revisions in the last dramas of *Der Ring des Nibelungen*, changing their titles to *Siegfried* and *Götterdämmerung*. Throughout these years he was preoccupied with writing a new opera, *Tristan und Isolde*, permeated with the dual feelings of love and death. In April 1857 he prepared the first sketch of *Parzival* (later titled *Parsifal*). In 1858 he moved to Venice, where he completed the full score of the 2nd act of *Tristan und Isolde*. The Dresden authorities, acting through their Austrian confederates and still determined to bring Wagner to trial as a revolutionary, pressured Venice to expel him from its territory. Once more Wagner took refuge in Switzerland; he decided to stay in Lucerne; while there he completed the score of *Tristan und Isolde*, on Aug. 6, 1859.

In Sept. 1859 he moved to Paris, where Minna joined him. In 1860 he conducted 3 concerts of his music at the Théâtre-Italien. Napoleon III became interested in his work, and in March 1860 ordered the director of the Paris Opéra to produce Wagner's opera *Tannhäuser;* after considerable work, revisions, and a tr. into French, it was given at the Opéra on March 13, 1861. It proved to be a fiasco, and Wagner withdrew the opera after 3 performances. For some reason the Jockey Club of Paris led a vehement protest against him; the critics also joined in this opposition, mainly because the French audiences were not accustomed to the mystically romantic, heavily Germanic operatic music. Invectives hurled against him by the Paris press make extraordinary reading; the comparison of Wagner's music with the sound produced by a domestic cat walking down the keyboard of the piano was one of the favorite critical devices. The French caricaturists exercised their wit by picturing him in the act of hammering a poor listener's ear. A Wagner "Schimpflexikon" was compiled by Wilhelm Tappert and publ. in 1877 in the hope of putting Wagner's detractors to shame, but they would not be pacified; the amount of black bile poured on him even after he had attained the stature of celebrity is incredible for its grossness and vulgarity. Hanslick used his great literary gift and a flair for a striking simile to damn him as a purveyor of cacophony. Oscar Wilde added his measure of wit. "I like Wagner's music better than anybody's," he remarked in *The Picture of Dorian Gray*. "It is so loud that one can talk the whole time without people hearing what one says." In an amazing turnabout, Nietzsche, a worshipful admirer of Wagner, publ. a venomous denunciation of his erstwhile idol in *Der Fall Wagner*, in which he vesuviated in a sulfuric eruption of righteous wrath; Wagner made music itself sick, he proclaimed; but at the time Nietzsche himself was already on the borderline of madness.

Politically, Wagner's prospects began to improve; on July 22, 1860, he was informed of a partial amnesty by the Saxon authorities. In Aug. 1860 he visited Baden-Baden, in his 1st visit to Germany in 11 years. Finally, on March 18, 1862, he was granted a total amnesty, which allowed him access to Saxony. In Nov. 1861 Wesendonck had invited Wagner to Venice; free from political persecution, he could now go there without fear. While in Venice he returned to a scenario he had prepared in Marienbad in 1845 for a comic opera, *Die Meistersinger von Nürnberg*. In Feb. 1862 he moved to Biebrich, where he began composing the score for *Die Meistersinger*. Minna, after a brief period of reconciliation with Wagner, left him, settling in Dresden, where she died in 1866. In order to repair his financial situation, he accepted a number of concert appearances, traveling as an orch. conductor to Vienna, Prague, St. Petersburg, Moscow, and other cities (1862–63). In 1862 he gave in Vienna a private reading of *Die Meistersinger*. It is said that the formidable Vienna critic Hanslick was angered when he found out that Wagner had caricatured him in the part of Beckmesser in *Die Meistersinger* (the original name of the character was Hans Lick), and he let out his discomfiture in further attacks on Wagner.

Wagner's fortunes changed spectacularly in 1864 when young King Ludwig II of Bavaria ascended the throne and invited him to Munich with the promise of unlimited help in carrying out his various projects. In return, Wagner composed the *Huldigungsmarsch*, which he dedicated to his royal patron. The publ. correspondence between Wagner and the King is extraordinary in its display of mutual admiration, gratitude, and affection; still, difficulties soon developed when the Bavarian Cabinet told Ludwig that his lavish support of Wagner's projects threatened the Bavarian economy. Ludwig was forced to advise him to leave Munich. Wagner took this advice as an order, and late in 1865 he went to Switzerland. A very serious difficulty arose also in Wagner's emotional life, when he became intimately involved with Liszt's daughter Cosima, wife of Hans von Bülow, the famous conductor and an impassioned proponent of Wagner's music. On April 10, 1865, Cosima Bülow gave birth to Wagner's daughter, whom he named Isolde after the heroine of his opera that Bülow was preparing for performance in Munich. Its premiere took place with great acclaim on June 10, 1865, 2 months after the birth of Isolde, with Bülow conducting. During the summer of 1865 he prepared the prose sketch of *Parzival*, and began to dictate his autobiography, *Mein Leben*, to Cosima. In Jan. 1866 he resumed the composition of *Die Meistersinger*; he settled in a villa in Tribschen, on Lake Lucerne, where Cosima joined him permanently in Nov. 1868. He completed the full score of *Die Meistersinger* on Oct. 24, 1867. On June 21, 1868, Bülow conducted its premiere in Munich in the presence of King Ludwig, who sat in the royal box with Wagner. A son, significantly named Siegfried, was born to Cosima and Wagner on June 6, 1869. On Sept. 22, 1869, *Das Rheingold* was produced in Munich. On June 26, 1870, *Die Walküre* was staged there. On July 18, 1870, Cosima and Bülow were divorced, and on Aug. 25, 1870, Wagner and Cosima were married in Lucerne. In Dec. 1870 Wagner wrote the *Siegfried Idyll*, based on the themes from his opera; it was performed in their villa in Bayreuth on Christmas morning, the day after Cosima's birthday, as a surprise for her. In 1871 he wrote the *Kaisermarsch* to mark the victorious conclusion of the Franco-German War; he conducted it in the presence of Kaiser Wilhelm I at a concert in the Royal Opera House in Berlin on May 5, 1871.

On May 12 of that year, while in Leipzig, Wagner made public his plans for realizing his cherished dream of building his own theater in Bayreuth for the production of the entire cycle of *Der Ring des Nibelungen*. In Dec. 1871 the Bayreuth town council offered him a site for a proposed Festspielhaus; on May 22, 1872, the cornerstone was laid; Wagner commemorated the event by conducting a performance of Beethoven's 9th Sym. (this was his 59th birthday). In 1873 Wagner began to build his own home in Bayreuth, which he called "Wahnfried," i.e., "Free from Delusion." In order to complete the building of the Festspielhaus, he appealed to King Ludwig for additional funds. Ludwig gave him 100,000 talers for this purpose. Now the dream of Wagner's life was realized. Between June and Aug. 1876 *Der Ring des Nibelungen* went through 3 rehearsals; King Ludwig attended the final dress rehearsals; the official premiere of the cycle took place on Aug. 13, 14, 16, and 17, 1876, under the direction of Hans Richter. Kaiser Wilhelm I made a special journey from Berlin to attend the performances of *Das Rheingold* and *Die Walküre*. In all, 3 complete productions of the *Ring* cycle were given between Aug. 13 and Aug. 30, 1876. Ludwig was faithful to the end to Wagner, whom he called "my divine friend." In his castle Neuschwanstein he installed architectural representations of scenes from Wagner's operas. Soon Ludwig's mental deterioration became obvious to everyone, and he was committed to an asylum. There, on June 13, 1883, he overpowered the psychiatrist escorting him on a walk and dragged him to his death in the Starnberg Lake, drowning himself as well. Ludwig survived Wagner by 4 months.

The spectacles in Bayreuth attracted music-lovers and notables from all over the world. Even those who were not partial to Wagner's ideas or appreciative of his music went to Bayreuth out of curiosity. Tchaikovsky was one such skeptical visitor. Despite world success and fame, Wagner still labored under financial difficulties. He even addressed a letter to an American dentist practicing in Dresden (who also treated Wagner's teeth) in which he tried to interest him in arranging Wagner's permanent transfer to the U.S. He voiced disillusionment in his future prospects in Germany, and said he would be willing to settle in America provided a sum of $1 million would be guaranteed to him by American bankers, and a comfortable estate for him and his family could be found in a climatically clement part of the country. Nothing came of this particular proposal. He did establish an American connection when he wrote, for a fee of $5,000, a *Grosser Festmarsch* for the observance of the U.S. centennial in 1876, dedicated to the "beautiful young ladies of America." In the middle of all this, Wagner became infatuated with Judith Gautier; their affair lasted for about 2 years (1876–78). He completed the full score of *Parsifal* (as it was now called) on Jan. 13, 1882, in Palermo. It was

performed for the 1st time at the Bayreuth Festival on July 26, 1882, followed by 15 subsequent performances. At the final performance, on Aug. 29, 1882, Wagner stepped to the podium in the last act and conducted the work to its close; this was his last appearance as a conductor. He went to Venice in Sept. 1882 for a period of rest (he had angina pectoris). Early in the afternoon of Feb. 13, 1883, he suffered a massive heart attack, and died in Cosima's presence. His body was interred in a vault in the garden of his Wahnfried villa in Bayreuth.

Wagner's role in music history is immense. Not only did he create works of great beauty and tremendous brilliance, but he generated an entirely new concept of the art of music, exercising an influence on generations of composers all over the globe. Richard Strauss extended Wagner's grandiose vision to symphonic music, fashioning the form of a tone poem that uses leading motifs and vivid programmatic description of the scenes portrayed in his music. Even Rimsky-Korsakov, far as he stood from Wagner's ideas of musical composition, reflected the spirit of *Parsifal* in his own religious opera, *The Legend of the City of Kitezh*. Schoenberg's 1st significant work, *Verklärte Nacht*, is Wagnerian in its color. Lesser composers, unable to escape Wagner's magic domination, attempted to follow him literally by writing trilogies and tetralogies on a parallel plan with his *Ring*; a pathetic example is the career of August Bungert, who wrote 2 operatic cycles using Homer's epics as the source of his libretti. Wagner's reform of opera was incomparably more far-reaching in aim, import, and effect than that of Gluck, whose main purpose was to counteract the arbitrary predominance of the singers; this goal Wagner accomplished through insistence upon the dramatic truth of his music. When he rejected traditional opera, he did so in the conviction that such an artificial form could not serve as a basis for true dramatic expression. In its place he gave the world a new form and new techniques. So revolutionary was Wagner's art that conductors and singers had to undergo special training in the new style of interpretation in order to perform his works. Thus he became the founder of interpretative conducting and of a new school of dramatic singing, so that such terms as "Wagnerian tenor" and "Wagnerian soprano" became a part of the musical vocabulary.

In his many essays and declarations Wagner condemns the illogical plan of Italian opera and French grand opera. To quote his own words, "The mistake in the art-form of the opera consists in this, that a means of expression (music) was made the end, and the end to be expressed (the drama) was made a means." The choice of subjects assumes utmost importance in Wagner's esthetics. He wrote: "The subject treated by the word-tone poet [*Worttondichter*] is entirely human, freed from all convention and from everything historically formal." The new artwork creates its own artistic form; continuous thematic development of basic motifs becomes a fundamental procedure for the logical cohesion of the drama; these highly individualized generating motifs, appearing singly, in bold relief, or subtly varied and intertwined with other motifs, present the ever-changing soul states of the characters of the drama, and form the connecting links for the dramatic situations of the total artwork, in a form of musical declamation that Wagner described as "Sprechsingen." Characters in Wagner's stage works become themselves symbols of such soul states, so that even mythical gods, magic-workers, heroic horses, and speaking birds become expressions of eternal verities, illuminating the human behavior. It is for this reason that Wagner selected in most of his operas figures that reflect philosophical ideas. Yet, this very solemnity of Wagner's great images on the stage bore the seeds of their own destruction in a world governed by different esthetic principles. Thus it came to pass that the Wagnerian domination of the musical stage suddenly lost its power with changes in human society and esthetic codes. Spectators and listeners were no longer interested in solving artistic puzzles on the stage. A demand for human simplicity arose against Wagnerian heroic complexity. The public at large found greater enjoyment in the realistic nonsense of Verdi's romantic operas than in the unreality of symbolic truth in Wagner's operas. By the 2nd quarter of the 20th century, few if any composers tried to imitate Wagner; all at once his grandeur and animation became an unnatural and asphyxiating constraint.

In the domain of melody, harmony, and orchestration, Wagner's art was as revolutionary as was his total artwork on the stage. He introduced the idea of an endless melody, a continuous flow of diatonic and chromatic tones; the tonality became fluid and uncertain, producing an impression of unattainability, so that the listener accustomed to Classical modulatory schemes could not easily feel the direction toward the tonic; the Prelude to *Tristan und Isolde* is a classic example of such fluidity of harmonic elements. The use of long unresolved dominant-ninth-chords and the dramatic tremolos of diminished-seventh-chords contributed to this state of musical uncertainty, which disturbed the critics and the audiences alike. But Wagnerian harmony also became the foundation of the new method of composition that adopted a free flow of modulatory progressions. Without Wagner the chromatic idioms of the 20th century could not exist. In orchestration, too, Wagner introduced great innovations; he created new instruments, such as the so-called "Wagner tuba," and he increased his demands on the virtuosity of individual orch. players. The vertiginous flight of the bassoon to the high E in the Overture to *Tannhäuser* could not have been attempted before the advent of Wagner.

Wagner became the target of political contention during World War I when audiences in the Allied countries associated his sonorous works with German imperialism. An even greater obstacle to further performances of Wagner's music arose with the rise of Hitler. Hitler ordered the slaughter of millions of Jews; he was an enthusiastic admirer of Wagner, who himself entertained anti-Semitic notions; *ergo*, Wagner was guilty by association of mass murder. Can art be separated from politics, particularly when politics become murderous? Jewish musicians in Tel Aviv refused to play the Prelude to *Tristan und Isolde* when it was put on the program of a sym. concert under Zubin Mehta, and booed him for his intention to inflict Wagner on Wagner's philosophical victims.

Several periodicals dealing with Wagner were publ. in Germany and elsewhere; Wagner himself began issuing *Bayreuther Blätter* in 1878 as an aid to understanding his operas; this journal continued publication until 1938. Remarkably enough, a French periodical, *Revue Wagnérienne*, began appearing in 1885, at a time when French composers realized the tremendous power of Wagnerian esthetics; it was publ. sporadically for a number of years. A Wagner Society in London publ., from 1888 to 1895, a quarterly journal entitled, significantly, *The Meister.*

WORKS: OPERAS AND MUSIC DRAMAS: *Die Hochzeit* (1832–33; partly destroyed; introduction, septet, and chorus perf. at the Neues Theater, Leipzig, Feb. 13, 1938); *Die Feen*, romantische Oper (1833–34; Königliches Hof- und Nationaltheater, Munich, June 29, 1888, Fischer conducting); *Das Liebesverbot, oder Die Novize von Palermo*, grosse komische Oper (1834–35; Magdeburg, March 29, 1836, composer conducting); *Rienzi, der Letzte der Tribunen*, grosse tragische Oper (1837–40; Königliches Hoftheater, Dresden, Oct. 20, 1842, Reissiger conducting; rev. 1843); *Der fliegende Holländer*, romantische Oper (1841; Königliches Hoftheater, Dresden, Jan. 2, 1843, composer conducting; reorchestrated in 1846, then rev. in 1852 and 1860); *Tannhäuser und der Sängerkrieg auf Wartburg*, grosse romantische Oper (first titled *Der Venusberg; "Dresden"* version, 1842–45; Königliches Hoftheater, Dresden, Oct. 19, 1845, composer conducting; rev. 1845–47; "Paris" version, a rev. version with additions and a French tr., 1860–61; Opéra, Paris, March 13, 1861, Dietsch conducting; final version, with a German tr. of the French revision and additions, 1865; Königliches Hof- und Nationaltheater, Munich, March 5, 1865); *Lohengrin*, romantische Oper (1845–48; Hoftheater, Weimar, Aug. 28, 1850, Liszt conducting); *Tristan und Isolde* (1856–59; Königliches Hof- und Nationaltheater, Munich, June 10,

1865, Bülow conducting); *Die Meistersinger von Nürnberg* (1st sketch, 1845; 1861–67; Königliches Hof- und Nationaltheater, Munich, June 21, 1868, Bülow conducting); *Der Ring des Nibelungen*, Bühnenfestspiel für drei Tage und einen Vorabend (1st prose outline as *Der Nibelungen-Mythus als Entwurf zu einem Drama*, 1848; Vorabend: *Das Rheingold*, 1851–54; Königliches Hof- und Nationaltheater, Munich, Sept. 22, 1869, Wüllner conducting; erster Tag: *Die Walküre*, 1851–56; Königliches Hof- und Nationaltheater, Munich, June 26, 1870, Wüllner conducting; zweiter Tag: *Siegfried*, first titled *Der junge Siegfried;* 1851–52, 1857, 1864–65, and 1869; Festspielhaus, Bayreuth, Aug. 16, 1876, Richter conducting; dritter Tag: *Götterdämmerung*, first titled *Siegfrieds Tod;* 1848–52 and 1869–74; Festspielhaus, Bayreuth, Aug. 17, 1876, Richter conducting; 1st complete perf. of the *Ring* cycle, Festspielhaus, Bayreuth, Aug. 13, 14, 16, and 17, 1876, Richter conducting); *Parsifal*, Bühnenweihfestspiel (first titled *Parzival;* first sketch, 1857; 1865 and 1877–82; Festspielhaus, Bayreuth, July 26, 1882, Levi conducting).

ORCH.: Overture in B-flat major, the *Paukenschlag-Ouvertüre* (Leipzig, Dec. 24, 1830; not extant); Overture to Schiller's *Die Braut von Messina* (1830; not extant); Overture in C major (1830; not extant); Overture in D minor (Leipzig, Dec. 25, 1831); Overture in E-flat major (1831; not extant); Overture to Raupach's *König Enzio*, in E minor (Leipzig, Feb. 17, 1832); Overture in C major (Leipzig, April 30, 1832); Sym. in C major (Prague, Nov. 1832); Sym. in E major (1834; fragment); Overture to Apel's *Columbus*, in E-flat major (Magdeburg, Feb. 16, 1835); Overture *Polonia*, in C major (begun 1832, finished 1836); Overture *Rule Britannia*, in D major (1837); music for Singer's *Die letzte Heidenverschwörung in Preussen* (1837; fragment); Overture to Goethe's *Faust* (1840; reorchestrated 1843–44; Dresden, July 22, 1844; rev. and reorchestrated as *Eine Faust-Ouvertüre*, 1855; Zürich, Jan. 23, 1855); *Trauermusik* for Wind Instruments, after motifs from Weber's *Euryanthe* (Dresden, Dec. 14, 1844, for the reburial ceremony of Weber's remains); *Träume* for Violin and Small Orch. (Zürich, Dec. 23, 1857); *Huldigungsmarsch* (1st version, for Military Band, Munich, Oct. 5, 1864; 2nd version, for Large Orch., completed by Raff); *Siegfried Idyll* for Small Orch. (Tribschen, Dec. 25, 1870); *Kaisermarsch* (Berlin, May 5, 1871); *Grosser Festmarsch zur Eröffnung der hundertjährigen Gedenkfeier der Unabhängigkeitserklärung der vereinigten Staaten von Nord-Amerika* (also known as *The American Centennial March;* Philadelphia, May 10, 1876). Also a projected orch. work in E minor (1830?; fragment); a scene for a pastoral play after Goethe's *Laune der Verliebten* (1830?); *Entreacte tragique* No. 1, in D major (1832?; fragment); *Entreacte tragique* No. 2, in C minor (1832?; sketch).

CHORAL: *Neujahrs-Kantate* for Mixed Chorus, and Orch. (Magdeburg, Dec. 31, 1834; arranged with a new text by Peter Cornelius as *Künstlerweihe*, and produced at Bayreuth on Wagner's 60th birthday, May 22, 1873); *Nicolai Volkshymne* for Tenor or Soprano, Mixed Chorus, and Orch. (Riga, Nov. 21, 1837); *Descendons, descendons* for Mixed Chorus, for *La Descente de la courtille* (1840); *Weihegruss zur feierlichen Enthüllung des Denkmals Königs Friedrich August I* ("des Gerechten") von Sachsen (Der Tag erscheint) for Men's Chorus a cappella (1843; as *Gesang zur Enthüllung des Denkmals Sr. Maj. des hochseligen Königs Friedrich August des Gerechten am 7. Juni 1843* for Men's Chorus and Brass; for the unveiling of the statue of King Friedrich August of Saxony, Dresden, June 7, 1843); *Das Liebesmahl der Apostel*, biblical scene for Men's Chorus and Orch. (Dresden, July 6, 1843); *Gruss seiner Treuen an Friedrich August den Geliebten* (*Im treuen Sachsenland*) for Men's Chorus a cappella (Dresden, Aug. 12, 1843; for the return from England of King Friedrich August of Saxony); *Hebt an den Sang* (*An Webers Grabe*) for Men's Chorus a cappella (Dresden, Dec. 15, 1844; for the reburial ceremony of Weber's remains); *Wahlspruch für die deutsche Feuerwehr* (*Treue sei unsre Zier*) (1869); *Kinderkatechismus zu Kosels Geburtstag* for 4 High Voices (1873; orchestrated 1874). Also a scene and aria for Soprano and Orch. (1832; not extant);

"Doch jetzt wohin ich blicke," aria for Tenor and Orch. for Marschner's opera *Der Vampyr* (1833); aria for Bass and Orch. for Weigl's opera *Die Schweizerfamilie* (1837; not extant); "Sanfte Wehmut will sich regen," aria for Bass and Orch. for Blum's singspiel *Marie, Max und Michel* (Riga, Sept. 1, 1837); "Norma il prédesse," aria for Bass, Male Chorus, and Orch. for Bellini's opera *Norma* (1839).

PIANO: Sonata in D minor (1829; not extant); Sonata in F minor (1829; not extant); *Doppelfuge* (1831?; 103 bars, with corrections in Weinlig's hand); Sonata in B-flat major, for 4-hands (1831; not extant); Sonata in B-flat major, op. 1 (1831); *Fantasie* in F-sharp minor, op. 3 (1831); *Polonaise* in D major (1831–32); *Polonaise* in D major, for 4-hands, op. 2 (1832?); Sonata in A major, op. 4 (1832); *Albumblatt* (*Lied ohne Worte*) in E major (1840); Polka in G major (1853); *Eine Sonate für das Album von Frau M*[athilde].*W*[esendonck]. in A-flat major (1853); *Züricher Vielliebchen: Walzer, Polka oder sonst was* in E-flat major (1854); *Albumblatt, In das Album der Fürstin M*[etternich]. in C major (1861); *Ankunft bei den schwarzen Schwänen* (*Albumblatt* for Countess Pourtalès) in A-flat major (1861); *Albumblatt für Frau Betty Schott* in E-flat major (1875).

SONGS: *Sieben Kompositionen zu Goethes Faust,* op. 5: 1, *Lied der Soldaten* (*Burgen mit hohen Mauern*); 2, *Bauern unter der Linde* (*Der Schäfter putzte sich zum Tanz*); 3, *Branders Lied* (*Es war eine Ratt im Kellernest*); 4, *Lied des Mephistopheles* (*Es war einmal ein König*); 5, *Lied des Mephistopheles* (*Was machst du mir vor Liebchens Tür*); 6, *Gretchen am Spinnrade* (*Meine Ruh ist hin*); 7, *Melodram Gretchens* (*Ach neige, du Schmerzenreiche*) (1831; rev. 1832); *Glockentöne* (1832; not extant); *Carnevalslied* from *Das Liebesverbot* (1835–36); *Der Tannenbaum* (1838); *Tout n'est qu'images fugitives* (1839); *3 mélodies*: 1, *Dors, mon enfant*; 2, *Mignonne*; 3, *L'Attente* (1839); *Adieux de Marie Stuart* (1840); *Les Deux Grenadiers,* to the poem by Heine (1840); *Gruss seiner Treuen an Friedrich August den Geliebten* (*Im treuen Sachsenland*) (a version for Baritone; 1844); *5 Gedichte für eine Frauenstimme* (*Wesendonk-Lieder*): 1, *Der Engel* (1857); 2, *Stehe still* (1858); 3, *Im Treibhaus* (1858); 4, *Schmerzen* (1857); 5, *Träume* (1857); *Scherzlied für Louis Kraft* (1871); also *Extase* (1839; fragment) and *La Tombe dit à la rose* (1839; fragment).

ARRANGEMENTS AND EDITIONS: Piano score of Beethoven's 9th Sym. (1830; unpubl.); Piano score of J. Haydn's Sym. No. 103, in E-flat major (1831–32; not extant); Aria from Bellini's *Il Pirata,* as orchestrated from the piano score for use in *La Straniera* (1833); arrangement of vocal score for Donizetti's *La Favorite* (1840) and *L'elisir d'amore* (1840); arrangement of vocal score for Halévy's *La Reine de Chypre* (1841) and *Le Guitarrero* (1841); new tr. and new close to the overture of Gluck's *Iphigénie en Aulide* (1846–47; Dresden, Feb. 22, 1847); Palestrina's *Stabat Mater,* with indications for performance (Dresden, March 8, 1848); Mozart's *Don Giovanni,* version of dialogues and recitatives and, in parts, new tr. (Zürich, Nov. 8, 1850; not extant).

WRITINGS: Wagner devoted a large amount of his enormous productive activity to writing. Besides the dramatic works he set to music, he also wrote the following: *Leubald. Ein Trauerspiel* (1826–28); *Die hohe Braut, oder Bianca und Giuseppe,* 4-act tragic opera (prose scenario, 1836 and 1842; music composed by Johann Kittl and produced as *Bianca und Giuseppe, oder Die Franzosen vor Nizza* in Prague, 1848); *Männerlist grösser als Frauenlist, oder Die glückliche Bärenfamilie,* 2-act comic opera (libretto, 1837; some music completed); *Eine Pilgerfahrt zu Beethoven,* novella (1840); *Ein Ende in Paris,* novella (1841); *Ein glücklicher Abend,* novella (1841); *Die Sarazenin,* 3-act opera (prose scenario, 1841–42; verse text, 1843); *Die Bergwerke zu Falun,* 3-act opera (prose scenario for an unwritten libretto, 1841–42); *Friedrich I.,* play (prose scenario, 1846 and 1848); *Alexander der Grosse,* sketch for a play (184?; not extant); *Jesus von Nazareth,* play (prose scenario, 1849); *Achilleus,* sketch for a play (1849–50; fragments only); *Wieland der Schmied,* 3-act opera (prose scenario, 1850); *Die Sieger,* opera (prose sketch, 1856); *Luther* or *Luthers Hochzeit,* sketch for a play (1868); *Lustspiel in 1 Akt* (draft, 1868); *Eine*

Kapitulation: Lustspiel in antiker Manier, poem (1870).

Wagner expounded his theories on music, politics, philosophy, religion, etc., in numerous essays; among the most important are *Über deutsches Musikwesen* (1840); *Die Kunst und die Revolution* (1849); *Das Kunstwerk der Zukunft* (1849); *Kunst und Klima* (1850); *Oper und Drama* (1851; rev. 1868); *Eine Mitteilung an meine Freunde* (1851); *Über Staat und Religion* (1864); *Über das Dirigieren* (1869); *Beethoven* (1870); *Über die Anwendung der Musik auf das Drama* (1879); and *Religion und Kunst* (1880). The 1st ed. of his collected writings, *R. Wagner: Gesammelte Schriften und Dichtungen* (9 vols., Leipzig, 1871–73; vol. 10, 1883), was prepared by Wagner himself; W.A. Ellis ed. and tr. it into Eng. as *Richard Wagner's Prose Works* (8 vols., London, 1892–99). H. von Wolzogen and R. Sternfeld ed. the 5th ed. of the German original as *Sämtliche Schriften und Dichtungen,* adding vols. XI and XII (Leipzig, 1911); they also prepared the 6th ed., adding vols. XIII–XVI (Leipzig, 1914).

Wagner's important autobiography, *Mein Leben,* in 4 parts, was privately publ.; parts 1–3, bringing the narrative down to Aug. 1861, were publ. between 1870 and 1875; part 4, covering the years from 1861 to 1864, was publ. in 1881; these were limited eds., being distributed only among his friends; the entire work was finally publ. in an abridged ed. in Munich in 1911 (Eng. tr. as *My Life,* London and N.Y., 1911); the suppressed passages were first publ. in *Die Musik,* XXII (1929–30), and then were tr. into Eng. in E. Newman's *Fact and Fiction about Wagner* (London, 1931); a definitive ed., based on the original MS, was publ. in Munich in 1963, ed. by M. Gregor-Dellin.

Another important source is Wagner's diary-notebook, the so-called *Brown Book,* in which he made entries between 1865 and 1882; it was ed. by J. Bergfeld as *Richard Wagner: Das Braune Buch: Tagebuchaufzeichnungen, 1865–1882* (Zürich, 1975; Eng. tr. by G. Bird as *The Diary of Richard Wagner, 1865–1882; The Brown Book,* London, 1980). See also the diaries of Cosima Wagner; they have been ed. by M. Gregor-Dellin and D. Mack as *Cosima Wagner: Die Tagebücher, 1869–1877* (2 vols., Munich, 1976–77; Eng. tr. by G. Skelton as *Cosima Wagner's Diaries,* 2 vols., N.Y., 1977 and 1980).

BIBL.: COLLECTED EDITIONS, SOURCE MATERIAL: The 1st collected ed. of his works, *R. W.s Werke,* was ed. by M. Balling (10 vols., Leipzig, 1912–29); the Bayerische Akademie der Schönen Künste of Munich is now publishing a new critical ed., the *Gesamtausgabe der Werke R. W.s,* under the editorship of C. Dahlhaus et al. (Mainz, 1970–   ).

E. Kastner prepared a *W.-Catalog: Chronologisches Verzeichniss der von und über R. W. erschienenen Schriften, Musikwerke* (Offenbach, 1878). J. Deathridge, M. Geck, and E. Voss have ed. an exhaustive *Verzeichnis der musikalischen Werke R. W.s und ihrer Quellen* (Mainz, 1983).

Other sources include the following: N. Oesterlein, *Katalog einer R. W.-Bibliothek: Nach den vorliegenden Originalien zu einem authentischen Nachschlagebuch durch die gesammte insbesondere deutsche W.-Litteratur bearbeitet und veröffentlicht* (describes the treasures of the W.-Museum and contains an extensive bibliography of books and articles publ. about the composer during his life [10,181 titles]; 4 vols., Leipzig, 1882, 1886, 1891, and 1895); C. Glasenapp and H. von Stein, *W.-Lexikon. Hauptbegriffe der Kunst und Weltanschauung W.s in wörtlichen Ausführungen aus seinen Schriften zusammengestellt* (Stuttgart, 1883); C. Glasenapp, *W.-Enzyklopädie. Haupterscheinungen der Kunst- und Kulturgeschichte im Lichte der Anschauung W.s in wörtlichen Ausführungen aus seinen Schriften dargestellt* (2 vols., Leipzig, 1891); E. Kastner, *Verzeichnis der ersten Aufführungen von R. W.s dramatischen Werken* (Vienna, 1896; 2nd ed., Leipzig, 1899); H. Silège, *Bibliographie wagnérienne française* (Paris, 1902); P. Pabst, *Verzeichnis von R. W.s Werken, Schriften und Dichtungen, deren hauptsächlichsten Bearbeitungen, sowie von besonders interessanter Litteratur, Abbildungen, Büsten und Kunstblättern, den Meister und seine Schöpfungen betreffend* (Leipzig, 1905); L. Frankenstein, *Bibliographie der auf R. W. bezüglichen*

Literatur für die Jahre 1907–11 (Berlin, 1912); M. Burrell, *Catalogue of the Burrell Collection of W. Documents, Letters and Other Biographical Material* (London, 1929); O. Strobel, *Genie am Werk: R. W.s Schaffen und Wirken im Spiegel eigenhandschriftlicher Urkunden: Führer durch die einmalige Ausstellung einer umfassenden Auswahl von Schätzen aus dem Archiv des Hauses Wahnfried* (Bayreuth, 1933; rev. ed., 1934); E. Terry, *A R. W. Dictionary* (N.Y., 1939); O. Strobel, "R.-W.-Forschungsstätte und Archiv des Hauses Wahnfried," *Das Bayerland*, LII (1942); H. Barth, ed., *Internationale W.-Bibliographie: 1945–55* (Bayreuth, 1956; also for 1956–60, publ. 1961, and for 1961–66, publ. 1968); C. von Westernhagen, *R. W.s Dresdener Bibliothek, 1842–1849: Neue Dokumente zur Geschichte seines Schaffens* (Wiesbaden, 1966); H. Kirchmeyer, *Das zeitgenössische W.-Bild* (3 vols., Regensburg; vol. I, *W. in Dresden*, publ. 1972; vol. II, *Dokumente, 1842–45*, publ. 1967; vol. III, *Dokumente, 1846–50*, publ. 1968); H.-M. Plesske, *R. W. in der Dichtung: Bibliographie deutschsprachiger Veröffentlichungen* (Bayreuth, 1971); W. Schuler, *Der Bayreuther Kreis von seiner Entstehung bis zum Ausgang der wilhelminischen Ära: Wagnerkult und Kulturreform im Geiste völkischer Weltanschauung* (Münster, 1971); H. Klein, *Erst- und Frühdrucke der Textbücher von R. W.: Bibliographie* (Tutzing, 1979); J. Deathridge, "Cataloguing W.," *Musical Times* (Feb. 1983); H. Klein, *Erstdrucke der musikalischen Werke von R. W.* (Tutzing, 1983); H.-J. Bauer, *R. W. Lexikon* (Bergisch Gladbach, 1988).

YEARBOOKS AND OTHER PUBLICATIONS: *Bayreuther Blätter* (founded by Wagner; Chemnitz, later Bayreuth, 1878–1938); *La Revue Wagnérienne* (Paris, 1885–88); *R.-W.-Jahrbuch* (Stuttgart, 1886); *The Meister* (quarterly journal of the British Wagner Society, London, 1888–95); *Bayreuth. Handbuch für Festspielbesucher* (Bayreuth, 1894–1930); *Bayreuther Festspielführer* (also issued under other titles; Bayreuth, 1901–39); L. Frankenstein, ed., *R.-W.-Jahrbuch* (5 vols., Berlin, 1906, 1907, 1908, 1912, and 1913); O. Strobel, ed., *Neue W.-Forschungen. Veröffentlichungen der R.-W.-Forschungsstätte Bayreuth* (Karlsruhe, 1943); *Das Bayreuther Festspielbuch* (Bayreuth, 1950–51); *"Bayreuth"-Jahreshefte* (Bayreuth, 1954–   ); *Tribschener Blätter* (publ. by the Zeitschrift der Schweizerischen Richard-Wagner-Gesellschaft of Lucerne, 1956–   ); *W.* (publ. by the Wagner Society of London, 1971–   ).

CORRESPONDENCE: Almost all of the collections of his letters to 1912 were republ. by Breitkopf & Härtel as *R. W.s Briefe in Originalausgaben* (17 vols., Leipzig, 1912); a number of the letters appear in mutilated form (portions expressing political and religious views being suppressed); an early attempt to bring out an unmutilated ed. was begun by J. Kapp and E. Kastner, *R. W.s Gesammelte Briefe (1830–50)* (2 vols., Leipzig, 1914); however, this ed. was never completed; see also the following: J.-G. Prod'homme, "W. and the Paris Opéra: Unpublished Letters (February–March, 1861)," *Musical Quarterly* (April 1915); E. Kloss, *Briefe an Hans von Bülow* (Jena, 1916); S. von Hausegger, ed., *R. W.s Briefe an Frau Julie Ritter* (Munich, 1920); L. Karpath, ed., *R. W.: Briefe an Hans Richter* (Berlin, 1924); W. Altmann, *R. W.s Briefe, ausgewählt und erläutert* (2 vols., Leipzig, 1925; Eng. tr., London, 1927); W. Lippert, *R. W.s Verbannung und Rückkehr, 1849–62* (Dresden, 1927; Eng. tr. as *W. in Exile*, London, 1930); R. Sternfeld, *R. W. Aufsätze und Briefe des Meisters aus Paris* (Grossenwörden, 1927); H. Scholz, ed., *R. W. an Mathilde Maier (1862–1878)* (Leipzig, 1930); E. Lenrow, ed. and tr., *The Letters of R. W. to Anton Pusinelli* (N.Y., 1932); J. Tiersot, *Lettres françaises de R. W.* (Paris, 1935); K. Geiringer, "W. and Brahms, with Unpublished Letters," *Musical Quarterly* (April 1936); W. Schuh, ed. and tr., *Die Briefe R. W.s an Judith Gautier* (Zürich, 1936; enl. ed., with French original, as *R. et Cosima W.: Lettres à Judith Gautier*, ed. by L. Guichard, 1964); O. Strobel, ed., *König Ludwig II. und R. W.: Briefwechsel, mit vielen anderen Urkunden* (5 vols., Karlsruhe, 1936–39); A. Holde, "Four Unknown Letters of R. W.," *Musical Quarterly* (April 1941); J. Burk, ed., *Letters of R. W. The Burrell Collection* (N.Y., 1950; German ed., Frankfurt, 1953); G. Strobel and W. Wolf, eds., *R. W.: Sämtliche Briefe* (a projected complete ed. in 15 vols.; Leipzig, 1967–   ); S. Spencer and B. Millington, trs. and eds., *Selected Letters of R. W.* (London, 1987).

BIOGRAPHICAL: C. Cabrol, *R. W.* (Paris, 1861); A. de Gasperini, *La Nouvelle Allemagne musicale: R. W.* (Paris, 1866); F. Hueffer, *R. W.* (London, 1872; 3rd ed., 1912); F. Filippi, *R. W.* (Leipzig, 1876); C. Glasenapp, *R. W.s Leben und Wirken* (2 vols., Leipzig, 1876–77; 3rd ed., rev. and enl., as *Das Leben R. W.s*, 6 vols., Leipzig, 1894–1911; Eng. tr. by W. Ellis as *Life of R. W.*, 6 vols., London, 1900–8; vols. I–III based on Glasenapp; reprinted N.Y., 1977, with new introduction by G. Buelow; 5th Ger. ed., rev., 1910–23); P. Lindau, *R. W.* (Paris, 1885); A. Jullien, *R. W.: Sa vie et ses œuvres* (Paris, 1886; Eng. tr., Boston, 1892); G. Kobbé, *W.'s Life and Works* (2 vols., N.Y., 1890); H. Finck, *W. and His Works* (2 vols., N.Y., 1893; 5th ed., 1898); H. Chamberlain, *R. W.* (Munich, 1896; Eng. tr., London, 1897; 9th Ger. ed., 1936); M. Burrell, compiler, *R. W.: Life and Works from 1813 to 1834* (London, 1898); W.J. Henderson, *R. W., His Life and His Dramas* (N.Y., 1901; rev. ed., 1923); R. Bürkner, *R. W.: Sein Leben und seine Werke* (Jena, 1906; 6th ed., 1911); M. Koch, *R. W.* (3 vols., Berlin, 1907, 1913, and 1918); J. Kapp, *R. W.* (Berlin, 1910; numerous reprints); F. Pfohl, *R. W.: Sein Leben und Schaffen* (Berlin, 1911; 4th ed., Bielefeld, 1924); E. Newman, *W. as Man and Artist* (London, 1914; 2nd ed., rev., 1924); L. Barthou, *La Vie amoureuse de R. W.* (Paris, 1925; in Eng. as *The Prodigious Lover*, N.Y., 1927); H. Lichtenberger, *W.* (Paris, 1925); W. Wallace, *W. as He Lived* (London, 1925; new ed., 1933); V. d'Indy, *R. W. et son influence sur l'art musical français* (Paris, 1930); M. Morold (pen name of Max von Millenkovitch, *W.s Kampf und Sieg, dargestellt in seinen Beziehungen zu Wien* (Zürich, 1930; 2nd ed., 1950); H. Reisiger, *Unruhiges Gestirn; Die Jugend R. W.s* (Leipzig, 1930; in Eng. as *Restless Star*, N.Y., 1932); G. de Pourtalès, *W.: Histoire d'un artiste* (Paris; Eng. tr., N.Y., 1932; 2nd French ed., enl., 1942); P. Lalo, *R. W.* (Paris, 1933); E. Newman, *The Life of R. W.* (4 vols., N.Y., 1933, 1937, 1941, and 1946); A. Spring, *R. W.s Weg und Wirken* (Stuttgart, 1933); W. Turner, *W.* (London, 1933); M. Fehr, *R. W.s Schweizer Zeit* (2 vols., Aarau, 1934–53); W. Hadow, *R. W.* (London, 1934); R. Jacobs, *W.* (London, 1935; 3rd ed., 1947); H. Malherbe, *R. W. Révolutionnaire* (Paris, 1938); E. Kretzschmar, *R. W.: Sein Leben in Selbstzeugnissen, Briefen und Berichten* (Berlin, 1939); O. Strobel, *Neue Urkunden zur Lebensgeschichte R. W.s, 1864–1882* (a supplement to his ed. of *König Ludwig II. und R. W.: Briefwechsel*; Karlsruhe, 1939; see **CORRESPONDENCE**); M. von Millenkovitch, *Dreigestirn: W., Liszt, Bülow* (Leipzig, 1941); W. Reich, *R. W., Leben, Fühlen, Schaffen* (Olten, 1948); K. Ipser, *R. W. in Italien* (Salzburg, 1951); L. Strecker, *R. W. als Verlagsgefährte: Eine Darstellung mit Briefen und Dokumenten* (Mainz, 1951); T. Adorno, *Versuch über W.* (Berlin, 1952); P. Loos, *R. W., Vollendung und Tragik der deutschen Romantik* (Munich, 1952); O. Strobel, *R. W.: Leben und Schaffen: Eine Zeittafel* (Bayreuth, 1952); Z. von Kraft, *R. W.: Ein dramatisches Leben* (Munich, 1953); R. Dumesnil, *R. W.* (Paris, 1954); H. Mayer, *R. W.s geistige Entwicklung* (Düsseldorf and Hamburg, 1954); C. von Westernhagen, *R. W.: Sein Werk, sein Wesen, seine Welt* (Zürich, 1956); W. Vordtriede, "R. W.s 'Tod in Venedig,'" *Euphorion*, LII (1958–59); H. Mayer, *R. W. in Selbstzeugnissen und Bilddokumenten* (Reinbek bei Hamburg, 1959; Eng. tr., 1972); O. Daube, *R. W.: "Ich schreibe keine Symphonien mehr": R. W.s Lehrjahre nach den erhaltenen Dokumenten* (Cologne, 1960); R. Gutman, *R. W.: The Man, His Mind and His Music* (London, 1968); C. von Westernhagen, *W.* (2 vols., Zürich, 1968; 2nd ed., rev. and enl., 1978; Eng. tr., Cambridge, 1978); M. Gregor-Martin, *W.-Chronik: Daten zu Leben* (Munich, 1972; 2nd rev. ed., 1983); H. Barth, D. Mack, and E. Voss, eds., *W.: Sein Leben und seine Welt in zeitgenössischen Bildern und Texten* (Vienna, 1975; Eng. tr. as *W.: A Documentary Study*, London, 1975); R. Taylor, *R. W.: His Life, Art and Thought* (London, 1979); D. Watson, *R. W.: A Biography* (N.Y. and London, 1979); M. Gregor-Dellin, *R. W.: Sein Leben, sein Werk, sein Jahrhundert* (Munich, 1980; in Eng. as *R. W.: His Life, His Work, His Century*, London, 1983); D. Watson,

R. W. (N.Y., 1981); G. Skelton, *R. and Cosima W.: A Biography of a Marriage* (London, 1982); M. van Amerongen, *W.: A Case History* (London, 1983); M. Kahane and N. Wild, *W. et la France* (Paris, 1983); E. Voss, compiler, *R. W.: Dokumentarbiographie* (Munich and Mainz, 1983); B. Millington, *W.* (London, 1984); J. Katz, *The Darker Side of Genius: R. W.'s Anti-Semitism* (Hanover, N.H. and London, 1986); R. Sabor, *The Real W.* (London, 1987); W. Beck, *R. W.: Neue Dokumente zur Biographie. Die Spiritualität im Drama seines Lebens* (Tutzing, 1988).

PERSONAL REMINISCENCES: H. von Wolzogen, *Erinnerungen an R. W.* (Leipzig, 1883; Eng. tr., Bayreuth, 1894); A. Schilling, *Aus R. W.s Jugendzeit* (Berlin, 1898; reminiscences of Wagner's stepsister Cäcilie Avenarius); E. Schuré, *Souvenirs sur R. W.* (Paris, 1900; Ger. tr., Leipzig, 1900); E. von Possart, *Die Separat-Vorstellungen vor König Ludwig II. Erinnerungen* (Munich, 1901); L. Schemann, *Meine Erinnerungen an R. W.* (Stuttgart, 1902); G. Kietz, *R. W. in den Jahren 1842–49 und 1873–75* (Dresden, 1905); A. Kohut, *Der Meister von Bayreuth* (Berlin, 1905); E. Michotte, *Souvenirs: La Visite de R. W. à Rossini (Paris, 1860): Détails inédites et commentaires* (Paris, 1906; Eng. tr. by H. Weinstock, Chicago, 1968); A. Gobineau, *Ein Erinnerungsbild aus Wahnfried* (Stuttgart, 1907); A. Neumann, *Erinnerungen an R. W.* (Leipzig, 1907; Eng. tr., N.Y., 1908); H. Schmidt and U. Hartmann, *R. W. in Bayreuth. Erinnerungen* (Leipzig, 1910); S. Wagner, *Erinnerungen* (Stuttgart, 1923; extended ed., privately printed, 1935); J. Gautier, *Auprès de R. W.; Souvenirs (1861–1883)* (Paris, 1943).

RELATIONS WITH CONTEMPORARIES: J. Craemer, *König Ludwig II. und R. W.* (Munich, 1901); F. Gerard, *Romance of King Ludwig II of Bavaria. His Relation with R. W.* (London, 1901); S. Röckel, *Ludwig II. und R. W. in den Jahren 1864–65* (Munich, 1903; 2nd ed., 1913); J. Kapp, *R. W. und Franz Liszt. Eine Freundschaft* (Berlin, 1908); H. Bélart, *Friedrich Nietzsches Freundschaftstragödie mit R. W.* (Dresden, 1912) and *R. W.s Liebestragödie mit Mathilde Wesendonck* (Dresden, 1912); J. Kapp, *R. W. und die Frauen* (Berlin, 1912; new rev. ed., 1951; in Eng. as *The Women in W.'s Life*, N.Y., 1931); E. Förster-Nietzsche, *W. und Nietzsche zur Zeit ihrer Freundschaft* (Munich, 1915; Eng. tr. as *The Nietzsche-Wagner Correspondence*, N.Y., 1921); C. Sarti, *W. and Nietzsche* (N.Y., 1915); E. Schuré, *Femmes inspiratrices* (Paris, 1930); M. Herwegh, *Au banquet des dieux: F. Liszt, R. W. et ses amis* (Paris, 1931); L. Barthou, "R. W. et Judith Gautier," *Revue de Paris* (1932); P.G. Dippel, *Nietzsche und W.* (Berne, 1934); D. Fischer-Dieskau, *W. und Nietzsche* (Stuttgart, 1974; Eng. tr., N.Y., 1976); E. Werner, "Jews Around R. and Cosima W.," *Musical Quarterly*, no. 2 (1985).

CRITICAL, ANALYTICAL: Liszt's essays on *Tannhäuser* (1849), *Lohengrin* (1850), *Der fliegende Holländer* (1854), and *Das Rheingold* (1855) are in vol. III, 2, of his *Gesammelte Schriften* (Leipzig, 1899); F. Hinrichs, *R. W. und die neuere Musik: Eine kritische Skizze* (Halle, 1854); F. Müller, *R. W. und das Musik-Drama* (Leipzig, 1861); L. Nohl, *Gluck und W. über die Entwicklung des Musikdramas* (Munich, 1870); F. Nietzsche, *Die Geburt der Tragödie aus dem Geiste der Musik* (Leipzig, 1872; Eng. tr. by W. Kaufmann as *The Birth of Tragedy out of the Spirit of Music* in *The Basic Writings of Nietzsche*, N.Y., 1968); E. Dannreuther, *R. W. His Tendencies and Theories* (London, 1873); F. Hueffer, *R. W. and the Music of the Future* (London, 1874); E. Schuré, *Le Drame musical: I. La Musique et la poésie dans leur développement historique. II. W. Son œuvre et son idée* (Paris, 1875; 3rd ed., augmented, 1894); L. Nohl, *Das moderne Musikdrama* (Vienna, 1884); G. Kobbé, *R. W.s "Tristan und Isolde"* (N.Y., 1886); W. Ellis, *R. W. as Poet, Musician and Mystic* (London, 1887); F. Nietzsche, *Der Fall W.* (Leipzig, 1888; Eng. tr. by W. Kaufmann as *The Case of W.* in *The Basic Writings of Nietzsche*, N.Y., 1968); idem, *Nietzsche contra W.* (Leipzig, 1888; Eng. tr. by W. Kaufmann in *The Portable Nietzsche*, N.Y., 1954); H. von Wolzogen, *Wagneriana: Gesammelte Aufsätze über R. W.s Werke vom Ring bis zum Gral* (Bayreuth, 1888); M. Kufferath, *Parsifal de R. W.: Légende, drame, partition* (Paris, 1890; Eng.

tr., 1904); L. Torchi, *Riccardo W.: Studio critico* (Bologna, 1890); H. Krehbiel, *Studies in the Wagnerian Drama* (N.Y., 1891); M. Kufferath, *Le Théâtre de W. de Tannhäuser à Parsifal. Essais de critique littéraire, esthétique et musicale* (6 vols., Paris, 1891–98); A. Smolian, *The Themes of "Tannhäuser"* (London, 1891); H. Chamberlain, *Das Drama R. W.s: Eine Anregung* (Leipzig, 1892; 5th ed., 1913; Eng. tr., London, 1915); M. Kufferath, *Guide thématique et analyse de Tristan et Iseult* (Paris, 1894); A. Lavignac, *Le Voyage artistique à Bayreuth* (Paris, 1897; many subsequent printings; Eng. tr. as *The Music-Dramas of R. W.*, N.Y., 1898; new ed., 1932); G. Servières, *R. W. jugé en France* (Paris, 1897); G.B. Shaw, *The Perfect Wagnerite* (London, 1898; 4th ed., 1923; also in vol. 17 of the complete works, 1932); J. Tiersot, *Études sur les Maîtres-Chanteurs de Nuremberg, de R. W.* (Paris, 1899); A. Smolian, *R. W.'s Bühnenfestspiel Der Ring des Nibelungen: Ein Vademecum* (Berlin, 1901); F. Muncker, "R. W.s Operntext 'Die Hochzeit,'" *Die Musik*, I (1901–2); A. Seidl, *Wagneriana* (2 vols., Berlin, 1901–2); G. Adler, *R. W.: Vorlesungen gehalten an der Universität zu Wien* (Vienna and Munich, 1904; 2nd ed., 1922); G. Kobbé, *W.'s Music Dramas Analyzed* (N.Y., 1904); H. Abert, "Gedanken zu R. W.s 'Die Meistersinger von Nürnberg,'" *Die Musik*, IV (1904–5); W. Golther, "Zur Entstehung von R. W.s Tristan," ibid., V (1905–6); K. Mey, "Über R. W.s Huldigungschor an König Friedrich August II. von Sachsen 1844," ibid.; W. Dry, *Erläuterungen zur R. W.s Tondramen* (2 vols., Leipzig, 1906–7); K. Mey, "R. W.s Webertrauermarsch," *Die Musik*, VI (1906–7); W. Golther, *Tristan und Isolde in den Dichtungen des Mittelalters und der neuen Zeit* (Leipzig, 1907); S. Hamer, *The Story of "The Ring"* (N.Y., 1907); M. Burckhardt, *Führer durch R. W.s Musikdramen* (Berlin, 1909); E. Istel, *Das Kunstwerk R. W.s* (Leipzig, 1910; 2nd ed., 1919); E. Kloss, *R. W. über die "Meistersinger von Nürnberg": Aussprüche des Meisters über sein Werk* (Leipzig, 1910); W. Krienetz, *R. W.s "Feen"* (Munich, 1910); A. Altmann, "Zur Geschichte der Entstehung und Veröffentlichung von W.s 'Der Ring des Nibelungen,'" *Allgemeine Musik-Zeitung*, XXXVIII (1911); A. Heuss, "Die Grundlagen der Parsifal-Dichtung," *Die Musik*, XII (1912–13); E. Lindner, *R. W. über "Parsifal": Aussprüche des Meisters über sein Werk* (Leipzig, 1913); idem, *R. W. über "Tannhäuser": Aussprüche des Meisters über sein Werk* (Leipzig, 1914); A. Seidl, *Neue Wagneriana: Gesammelte Aufsätze und Studien* (Regensburg, 1914); H. von Wolzogen, *R. W. über den "Fliegenden Holländer": Die Entstehung, Gestaltung und Darstellung des Werkes aus den Schriften und Briefen des Meisters zusammengestellt* (Leipzig, 1914); A. Halm, *Von Grenzen und Ländern der Musik* (Munich, 1916); E. Kurth, *Romantische Harmonik und ihre Krise in W.s "Tristan"* (Berlin, 1920; 2nd ed., 1923); H. von Waltershausen, *Das Siegfried-Idyll, oder Die Rückkehr zur Natur* (Munich, 1920); L. Windsperger, *Das Buch der Motive und Themen aus sämtlichen Opern und Musikdramen R. W.s* (for piano, with explanatory text; Mainz, 1921); F. Zademack, *Die Meistersinger von Nürnberg: R. W.s Dichtung und ihre Quellen* (Berlin, 1921); W. Wilmshurst, *Parsifal* (London, 1922); R. Sternfeld, "Die erste Fassung von W.s Faust-Ouvertüre," *Die Musik*, XV (1922–23); P. Bekker, *R. W.: Das Leben im Werke* (Stuttgart, 1924; Eng. tr., London, 1931); A. Cœuroy, *La Walkyrie de R. W.* (Paris, 1924); O. Strobel, *R. W. über sein Schaffen: Ein Beitrag zur "Künstlerästhetik"* (Munich, 1924); H. Wiessner, *Der Stabreimvers in R. W.s "Ring des Nibelungen"* (Berlin, 1924); A. Himonet, *Lohengrin de R. W.* (Paris, 1925); L. Leroy, *W.'s Music Drama of the Ring* (London, 1925); C. Winn, *The Mastersingers of W.* (London, 1925); A. Dickinson, *The Musical Design of "The Ring"* (London, 1926); W. Hapke, *Die musikalische Darstellung der Gebärde in R. W.s Ring des Nibelungen* (Leipzig, 1927); A. Buesst, *R. W., The Nibelung's Ring* (London, 1932; 2nd ed., 1952); O. Strobel, "Zur Entstehungsgeschichte der Götterdämmerung: Unbekannte Dokumente," *Die Musik*, XXV (1932–33); W. Engelsmann, *W.s klingendes Universum* (Potsdam, 1933); J. Kapp, *Das Liebesverbot, Entstehung und Schicksale des Werkes von R. W.* (Berlin, 1933); idem, *W. und die Berliner Oper* (Berlin, 1933); T. Mann, "Leiden und

Grösse R. W.s," *Neue Rundschau*, XLIV (1933; Eng. tr. by H. Lowe-Porter in *Thomas Mann: Past Masters and Other Papers*, N.Y., 1933); R. Grisson, *Beiträge zur Auslegung von R. W.'s "Ring des Nibelungen"* (Leipzig, 1934); H. Nathan, *Das Rezitativ der Frühopern R. W.s: Ein Beitrag zur Stilistik des Opernrezitativs in der ersten Hälfte des 19. Jahrhunderts* (diss., Univ. of Berlin, 1934); A. Bahr-Mildenburg, *Tristan und Isolde: Darstellung der Werke R. W.s aus dem Geiste der Dichtung und Musik: Vollständige Regiebearbeitung sämtlicher Partien mit Notenbeispielen* (Leipzig, 1936); L. Gilman, *W.'s Operas* (N.Y., 1937); V. d'Indy, *Introduction à l'étude de Parsifal de W.* (Paris, 1937); T. Mann, "R. W. and the *Ring*" (lecture, Univ. of Zürich, 1937; publ. in *Essays of Three Decades*, N.Y., 1947); R. Schuster, *R. W. und die Welt der Oper* (Munich, 1937); E. Borrelli, *Estetica wagneriana* (Florence, 1940); E. Hutcheson, *A Musical Guide to the R. W. Ring of the Nibelung* (N.Y., 1940); J. Barzun, *Darwin, Marx, W.; Critique of a Heritage* (Boston, 1941; rev. ed., 1958); S. Luciani, *Il Tristano e Isolda di R. W.* (Florence, 1942); G. Gavazzeni, *Il Siegfried di R. W.* (Florence, 1944); M. Doisy, *L'Œuvre de R. W. du Vaisseau fantôme à Parsifal* (Brussels, 1945); M. Beaufils, *W. et le wagnérisme* (Paris, 1947); K. Overhoff, *R. W.s Tristan Partitur; Eine musikalisch-philosophische Deutung* (Bayreuth, 1948); E. Newman, *W. Nights* (London, 1949; American ed. as *The W. Operas*, N.Y., 1949); K. Overhoff, *R. W.s Parsifal* (Lindau in Bodensee, 1951); T. Adorno, *Versuch über W.* (Berlin and Frankfurt, 1952); W. Hess, " 'Die Meistersinger von Nürnberg': Ihr dichterisch-musikalische Gesamtform," *Zeitschrift für Musik*, 113 (1952); P. Jacob, *Taten der Musik; R. W. und sein Werk* (Regensburg, 1952); P. Loos, *R. W.: Vollendung und Tragik der deutschen Romantik* (Bern and Munich, 1952); H. Engel, "Versuche einer Sinndeutung von R. W.s 'Ring des Nibelungen,' " *Die Musikforschung*, X (1957); H. Blümer, *Über den Tonarten-Charakter bei R. W.* (diss., Univ. of Munich, 1958); V. Levi, *Tristano e Isotta di Riccardo W.* (Venice, 1958); E. Lippman, "The Aesthetic Theories of R. W.," *Musical Quarterly* (April 1958); W. Serauky, "Die Todesverkündigungsszene in R. W.s *Walküre* als musikalisch-geistige Achse des Werkes," *Die Musikforschung*, XII (1959); J. Stein, *R. W. and the Synthesis of the Arts* (Detroit, 1960); H. von Stein, *Dichtung und Musik im Werk R. W.s* (Berlin, 1962); M. Vogel, *Der Tristan-Akkord und die Krise der modernen Harmonie-Lehre* (Düsseldorf, 1962); C. von Westernhagen, *Vom Holländer zum Parsifal: Neue W. Studien* (Freiburg, 1962); J. Bergfeld, *W.s Werk und unsere Zeit* (Berlin and Wunsiedel, 1963); R. Donington, *W.s "Ring" and Its Symbols: The Music and the Myth* (London, 1963; 3rd ed., rev. and enl., 1974); H. Engel, "Über R. W.s Oper *Das Liebesverbot*," in *Festschrift Friedrich Blume* (Kassel, 1963); H. Gál, *R. W.: Versuch einer Würdigung* (Frankfurt, 1963; Eng. tr., 1976); G. Knepler, "R. W.s musikalische Gestaltungsprinzipien," *Beiträge zur Musikwissenschaft*, V (1963); J. Mainka, "Sonatenform, Leitmotiv und Charakterbegleitung," ibid.; H. Scharschuch, *Gesamtanalyse der Harmonik von R. W.s Musikdrama "Tristan und Isolde": Unter spezifischer Berücksichtigung der Sequenztechnik des Tristanstiles* (Regensburg, 1963); H. Truscott, "W.'s Tristan and the Twentieth Century," *Music Review*, XXIV (1963); C. von Westernhagen, "Die Kompositions-Skizze zu 'Siegfrieds Tod' aus dem Jahre 1850," *Neue Zeitschrift für Musik*, 124 (1963); E. Zuckerman, *The First Hundred Years of W.'s "Tristan"* (N.Y. and London, 1964); H. Mayer, *Anmerkungen zu W.* (Frankfurt, 1966); W. Mitchell, "The Tristan Prelude: Techniques and Structure," *Music Forum*, I (1967); W. White, *An Introduction to the Life and Works of R. W.* (Englewood Cliffs, N.J., 1967); K. Overhoff, *Die Musikdramen R. W.s: Eine thematisch-musikalische Interpretation* (Salzburg, 1968); R. Bailey, *The Genesis of Tristan und Isolde, and a Study of W.'s Sketches and Drafts for the First Act* (diss., Princeton Univ., 1969); R. Raphael, *R. W.* (N.Y., 1969); C. Dahlhaus, ed., *Das Drama R. W.s als musikalisches Kunstwerk* (Regensburg, 1970); idem, *Die Bedeutung des Gestischen in W.s Musikdramen* (Munich, 1970); E. Voss, *Studien zur Instrumentation R. W.s* (Regensburg, 1970); D. Coren, *A Study of R. W.s "Siegfried"* (diss., Univ. of Calif., Berkeley, 1971); C. Dahlhaus, *Die Musikdramen R. W.s* (Velber, 1971; Eng. tr. as *R. W.'s Music Dramas*, Cambridge,

1979); idem, *W.s Konzeption des musikalischen Dramas* (Regensburg, 1971); A. Sommer, *Die Komplikationen des musikalischen Rhythmus in den Bühnenwerken R. W.s* (Giebing, 1971); R. Bailey, "The Evolution of W.'s Compositional Procedure after Lohengrin," *International Musicological Society Congress Report*, XI (Copenhagen, 1972); W. Breig, *Studien zur Entstehungsgeschichte von W.s "Ring des Nibelungen"* (diss., Univ. of Freiburg, 1973); C. von Westernhagen, *Die Entstehung des "Ring," dargestellt an den Kompositionsskizzen R. W.s* (Zürich, 1973; Eng. tr. as *The Forging of the "Ring,"* Cambridge, 1976); J. Deathridge, "The Nomenclature of W.'s Sketches," *Proceedings of the Royal Musical Association*, CI (1974–75); R. Jackson, "*Leitmotive* and Form in the *Tristan* Prelude," *Music Review*, XXXVI (1975); K. Kropfinger, *W. und Beethoven: Untersuchungen zur Beethoven-Rezeption R. W.s* (Regensburg, 1975); J. Culshaw, *Reflections on W.'s Ring* (N.Y., 1976); P. Machlin, *The Flying Dutchman: Sketches, Revisions and Analysis* (diss., Univ. of Calif., Berkeley, 1976); H.-J. Bauer, *W.s Parsifal: Kriterien der Kompositionstechnik* (Munich, 1977); J. Deathridge, *W.'s Rienzi: A Reappraisal Based on a Study of the Sketches and Drafts* (Oxford, 1977); E. Voss, *R. W. und die Instrumentalmusik: W.s symphonischer Ehrgeiz* (Wilhelmshaven, 1977); J. Di Gaetani, *Penetrating W.'s Ring: An Anthology* (Cranbury, N.J., 1978); F. Oberkogler, *R. W.: Vom Ring zum Gral; Wiedergewinnung seines Werkes aus Musik und Mythos* (Stuttgart, 1978); P. Wapnewski, *Der traurige Gott: R. W. in seinen Helden* (Munich, 1978); P. Burbridge and R. Sutton, eds., *The W. Companion* (N.Y., 1979); D. Cooke, *I Saw the World End: A Study of W.'s Ring* (London, 1979); L. Rather, *The Dream of Self-Destruction: W.'s Ring and the Modern World* (Baton Rouge, La., 1979); A. Blyth, *W.'s Ring: An Introduction* (London, 1980); L. Beckett, *R. W.: Parsifal* (Cambridge, 1981); M. Ewans, *W. and Aeschylus: The Ring and the Oresteia* (London, 1982); C. Dahlhaus, "W.'s 'A Communication to My Friends': Reminiscence and Adaptation," *Musical Times* (Feb. 1983); N. Benvenga, *Kingdom on the Rhine: History, Myth and Legend on W.'s Ring* (Harwich, 1983); J. Deathridge, "Rienzi . . . A Few of the Facts," *Musical Times* (Sept. 1983); A. Aberbach, *The Ideas of R. W.* (Lanham, 1984); S. Fay and R. Wood, *The Ring: An Anatomy of an Opera* (London, 1984); B. Millington, " 'The Flying Dutchman', 'Le vaisseau fantôme' and Other Nautical Yarns," *Musical Times* (March 1986); A. Ingenhoff, *Drama oder Epos? R. W.s Gattungstheorie des musikalischen Dramas* (Tübingen, 1987); M. McKnight, "W. and the New York Press, 1855–76," *American Music* (Summer 1987); H.-M. Palm, *R. W.s 'Lohengrin': Studien zur Sprachbehandlung* (Munich, 1987); L. Shaw, N. Cirillo, and M. Miller, eds., *W. in Retrospect: A Centennial Reappraisal* (Amsterdam, 1987); J. Webster, "To Understand Verdi and W. We Must Understand Mozart," *19th Century Music* (Fall 1987); W. Darcy, "Everything That Is, Ends!: The Genesis and Meaning of the Erda Episode in 'Das Rheingold,' " *Musical Times* (Sept. 1988); A. Groos, "W.'s 'Tristan und Isolde': In Defence of the Libretto," *Music & Letters* (Oct. 1988); D. White, *The Turning Wheel: A Study of Contracts and Oaths in W.'s 'Ring'* (Selinsgrove, N.Y., 1988); R. Donington, "The Search for Redemption in W.," *Musical Times* (Jan. 1989).

WAGNER'S ART IN RELATION TO ESTHETICS, PHILOSOPHY, AND RELIGION: F. von Hausegger, *R. W. und Schopenhauer* (Leipzig, 1878; 2nd ed., 1897); J. Freson, *Essais de philosophie et de l'art: L'Esthétique de R. W.* (2 vols., Paris, 1893); M. Hébert, *Le Sentiment religieux dans l'œuvre de R. W.* (Paris, 1894); R. Louis, *Die Weltanschauung R. W.s* (Leipzig, 1898); D. Irvine, *Parsifal and W.'s Christianity* (London, 1899); M. Kufferath, *Musiciens et philosophes: Tolstoy, Schopenhauer, Nietzsche, W.* (Paris, 1899); P. Moos, *R. W. als Ästhetiker* (Berlin, 1906); R. Richter, *Kunst und Philosophie bei R. W.* (Leipzig, 1906); H. Bélart, *F. Nietzsche und R. W.: Ihre persönlichen Beziehungen, Kunst- und Weltanschauungen* (Berlin, 1907); G. Robert, *Philosophie et drame. Essai d'une explication des drames wagnériens* (Paris, 1907); O. Schmiedel, *R. W.s religiöse Weltan-*

schauung (Tübingen, 1907); W. Vollert, *R. W.s Stellung zur christlichen Religion* (Wismar, 1907); L. Dauriac, *Le Musicien-poète R. W. Étude de psychologie musicale* (Paris, 1908); G. Braschowanoff, *Von Olympia nach Bayreuth* (2 vols., Leipzig, 1911–12); F. Gross, *Die Wiedergeburt des Sehers* (Zürich, 1927); A. Drews, *Ideengehalt von W.s dramatischen Dichtungen* (Leipzig, 1931); G. Wooley, *R. W. et le symbolisme français* (Paris, 1931); F. Gross, *Der Mythos W.s* (Vienna, 1932); G. Frommel, *Der Geist der Antike bei R. W.* (Berlin, 1933); I. Wyzewska, *La Revue Wagnérienne; Essai sur l'interprétation esthétique de W. en France* (Paris, 1934); K. Karzer, *R. W. der Revolutionär gegen das 19. Jahrhundert* (1934); W. Engelsmann, *Erlösung dem Erlöser: R. W.s religiöse Weltgestalt* (Leipzig, 1936); M. Boucher, *Les Idées politiques de W.* (Paris, 1948; in Eng., N.Y., 1950); K. Overhoff, *R. W.s germanisch-christlicher Mythos* (Dinkelsbühl, 1955); B. Magee, *Aspects of W.* (London, 1968; rev. ed., 1972); M. Gregor-Dellin, *R. W.: Die Revolution als Oper* (Munich, 1973); R. Hollinrake, *Nietzsche, W. and the Philosophy of Pessimism* (London, 1982).

WAGNER'S ART IN RELATION TO THEORY AND TECHNIQUE: C. Kistler, *Harmonielehre* (Heilbronn, 1879; 2nd ed., greatly augmented, 1903; based on Wagner's harmonic innovations); K. Mayrberger, *Die Harmonik R. W.s* (Chemnitz, 1883); S. Jadassohn, *Melodik und Harmonik bei R. W.* (Berlin, 1899); E. Thomas, *Die Instrumentation der "Meistersinger" von R. W.* (2 vols., Mannheim, 1899; 2nd ed., Leipzig, 1907); G. Capellen, *Ist das System Simon Sechters ein geeigneter Ausgangspunkt für die theoretische Wagnerforschung?* (Leipzig, 1902); E. Poirée, *Le Discours musical, son principe, ses formes expressives, spécialement d'après la partition des "Maîtres-Chanteurs" de R. W.* (Paris, 1902); E. Ergo, *Über R. W.s Harmonik und Melodik* (Leipzig, 1914); E. Kurth, *Romantische Harmonik und ihre Krise in W.s "Tristan"* (Bern and Leipzig, 1920; 2nd ed., Berlin, 1923); A. Lorenze, *Das Geheimnis der Form bei R. W.* (4 vols., Berlin: I, *Der Ring*, 1924; II, *Tristan*, 1926; III, *Meistersinger*, 1930; IV, *Parsifal*, 1933).

WAGNER AND BAYREUTH: F. Nietzsche, *W. in Bayreuth* (Chemnitz, 1876; in vol. I of *Nietzsches Werke*, Leipzig, 1895; new ed., 1931; Eng. tr. in complete works, Edinburgh, 1910–14); H. von Wolzogen, *Grundlage und Aufgabe des Allgem. Patronalvereins zur Pflege und Erhaltung der Bühnenfestspiele in Bayreuth* (Chemnitz, 1877); K. Heckel, *Die Bühnenfestspiele in Bayreuth* (Leipzig, 1891); H. Porges, *Die Bühnenproben zu den Festspielen des Jahren 1876* (Leipzig, 1896); F. Weingartner, *Bayreuth, 1876–96* (Berlin, 1896; 2nd ed., 1904); H. Chamberlain, *Die ersten 20 Jahre der Bayreuther Bühnenfestspiele* (Bayreuth, 1896); E. Kloss, *Zwanzig Jahre Bayreuth* (Berlin, 1896; Eng. tr., London, 1896); A. Prüfer, *Die Bühnenfestspiele in Bayreuth* (Leipzig, 1899; 2nd ed., 1909, as *Das Werk von Bayreuth*; new ed., 1921, as *Tannhäuser und der Sängerkrieg auf der Wartburg*); F. Hofmann, *Bayreuth und seine Kunstdenkmale* (Munich, 1902); W. Golther, *Bayreuth* (Berlin, 1904); R. Sternfeld, *R. W. und die Bayreuth Bühnenfestspiele* (2 vols., Berlin, 1906; new ed., 1927); M. Conrad, *W.s Geist und Kunst in Bayreuth* (Munich, 1906); K. Glazenapp, *Bayreuther Briefe von R. W.* (Berlin, 1907; abridged Eng. tr. as *The Story of Bayreuth as Told in the Bayreuth Letters of R. W.*, Boston, 1912); A. Prüfer, *R. W. in Bayreuth* (Leipzig, 1910); H. von Wolzogen, *Heinrich von Steins Briefwechsel mit H. von Wolzogen. Ein Beitrag zur Geschichte des Bayreuther Gedankens* (Leipzig, 1910); H. Bahr and A. Bahr-Mildenburg, *Bayreuth und das W.-Theater* (Leipzig, 1910; 2nd ed., 1912; Eng. tr., London, 1921); R. Du Moulin-Eckart, *Wahnfried* (Leipzig, 1925); P. Bülow, *R. W. und sein Werk von Bayreuth* (Frankfurt, 1927); F. Klose, *Bayreuth. Eindrücke und Erlebnisse* (Regensburg, 1929); O. Bie, *R. W. und Bayreuth* (Leipzig, 1931); J. Kneise, *Der Kampf zweier Welten um das Bayreuther Erbe* (Kassel, 1931); L. Reichwein, *Bayreuth* (Bielefeld and Leipzig, 1934); H. Brand, *Aus R. W.s Leben in Bayreuth* (Munich, 1935); S. Rützow, *R. W. und Bayreuth* (Munich, 1943; 2nd ed., 1953); J. Bertram, *Der Seher von Bayreuth* (Berlin, 1943); E. Ebermayer, *Magisches Bayreuth, Legende und Wirklichkeit* (Stuttgart, 1951); W. Wagner, ed., *R. W. und das neue Bayreuth*

(Munich, 1962); G. Skelton, *W. at Bayreuth: Experiment and Tradition* (London, 1965; rev. ed., 1976); P. Turing, *New Bayreuth* (London, 1969; rev. ed., 1971); H. Barth, ed., *Der Festspielhügel: 100 Jahre Bayreuther Festspiele in einer repräsentativen Dokumentation* (Bayreuth, 1973; 2nd ed., 1976); L. Lucas, *Die Festspiel-Idee R. W.s* (Regensburg, 1973); M. Karbaum, *Studien zur Geschichte der Bayreuther Festspiele: 1876–1976* (Regensburg, 1976); R. Hartford, ed., *Bayreuth: The Early Years* (London, 1980); B. Wessling, ed., *Bayreuth im Dritten Reich: R. W.s politische Erben: Eine Dokumentation* (Weinheim, 1983).

WAGNER'S LITERARY SOURCES: F. Schultz, *Das neue Deutschland. Seine alten Heldensagen und R. W.* (Leipzig, 1888); E. Meinck, *Die sagenwissenschaftlichen Grundlagen der Nibelungendichtung W.s* (Berlin, 1892); J. Weston, *The Legends of the Wagnerian Drama* (London, 1896; new ed., 1903); A. Bowen, *The Sources and Text of W.'s "Die Meistersinger von Nürnberg"* (Munich, 1897); J. Nover, *Die Tannhäusersage und ihre poetische Gestaltung* (Hamburg, 1897); E. Wechsler, *Die Sage vom hl. Gral in ihrer Entwicklung bis auf R. W.s "Parsifal"* (Halle, 1898); J. Nover, *Die Lohengrinsage und ihre poetische Gestaltung* (Hamburg, 1899); H. von der Pfordten, *Handlung und Dichtung der Bühnenwerke R. W.s nach ihren Grundlagen in Sage und Geschichte* (Berlin, 1900; 4th ed., 1908); W. Golther, *Die sagengeschichtlichen Grundlagen der Ringdichtung R. W.s* (Berlin, 1902); S. Valot, *Les Héros de R. W. Etudes sur les origines indoeuropéennes des légendes wagnériennes* (Paris, 1903); W. Sawyer, *Teutonic Legends in the Nibelungenlied and the Nibelungen Ring* (Philadelphia, 1904); W. Golther, *Tristan und Isolde in den Dichtungen des Mittelalters und der neuen Zeit* (Leipzig, 1907); R. von Kralik, *Die Gralssage* (Ravensburg, 1907); E. Elster, *Tannhäuser in Geschichte, Sage und Dichtung* (Bromberg, 1908); L. von Schroeder, *Die Wurzeln der Sage vom hl. Gral* (Vienna, 1910); F. Strich, *Die Mythologie in der deutschen Litteratur von Klopstock bis W.* (2 vols., Halle, 1910); W. Golther, *Zur deutschen Sage und Dichtung* (Leipzig, 1911); O. Rank, *Die Lohengrinsage* (Vienna, 1911); W. Golther, *Parsifal und der Gral in deutscher Sage des Mittelalters und der Neuzeit* (Leipzig, 1913); A. Bonilla y San Martin, *Las leyendas de W. en la literatura española* (Madrid, 1913); G. Brownell, *The Wagnerian Romances* (N.Y., 1925); H. Thompson, *W. and Wagenseil: A Source of W.'s Opera "Die Meistersinger"* (London, 1927); M. Unger, "The Cradle of the Parsifal Legend," *Musical Quarterly* (July 1932); A. Salazar, "Parsifal in Romantic Lands," ibid. (Jan. 1939); R. Rayner, *Wagner and "Die Meistersinger"* (Oxford, 1940); H. Hirsch, *R. W. und das deutsche Mittelalter* (Vienna, 1944).

CHARACTERS: C. Maude, *W.'s Heroes* (London, 1896) and *W.'s Heroines* (London, 1896); H. von Wolzogen, *R. W.s Heldengestalten erläutert* (Hannover, 1896); A. Höfler, *Wotan, Eine Studie zum "Ring des Nibelungen"* (Vienna, 1897); H. Bélart, *Taschenbuch der Wagnerkünstlerin. W.s Frauengestalten in gesangdramatischer Beziehung* (Leipzig, 1898); E. Destranges, *Les Femmes dans l'œuvre de R. W.* (Paris, 1899); F. Schwabe, *Die Frauengestalten W.s als Typen des "Ewig-weiblichen"* (Munich, 1902); H. Materna, *R. W.s Frauengestalten* (Leipzig, 1904); W. Broesel, *Evchen Pogner* (Berlin, 1906); H. Güntert, *Kundry* (Heidelberg, 1928).

WAGNER AS WRITER: H. von Wolzogen, *Die Sprache in R. W.s Dichtungen* (Leipzig, 1878); J. Gautier, *R. W. et son œuvre poétique* (Paris, 1882); B. Vogel, *W. als Dichter. Ein Überblick seines poetischen Schaffens* (Leipzig, 1889); A. Ernst, *L'Art de W.: L'Œuvre poétique* (Paris, 1893); H. Lichtenberger, *R. W., poète et penseur* (Paris, 1898; new ed., 1931; Ger. tr., Dresden, 1899 [augmented ed., 1913]); O. Lüning, *R. W. als Dichter und Denker* (Zürich, 1900); W. Golther, *W. als Dichter* (Berlin, 1904; Eng. tr., London, 1905); R. Weltrich, *R. W.s "Tristan und Isolde" als Dichtung. Nebst einigen allgemeinen Bemerkungen über W.s Kunst* (Berlin, 1904); E. Meinck, *Fr. Hebbels und R. W.s Nibelungen-Trilogien* (Leipzig, 1905); J. Schuler, *The Language of R. W.'s "Ring des Nibelungen"* (Lancaster, Pa., 1910); K. Reichelt, *R. W. und die englische Literatur* (Leipzig, 1912); E. von Schrenck, *R. W. als Dichter*

(Munich, 1913); P. Bülow, *Die Jugendschriften R. W.s* (Leipzig, 1917); W. Ramann, *Der dichterische Stil R. W.s* (Leipzig, 1929); O. Strobel, *Skizzen und Entwürfe zur Ring-Dichtung* (Munich, 1930); H. Galli, *W. und die deutsche Klassik* (Berne, 1936); H. Garten, *W. the Dramatist* (London, 1977).

ICONOGRAPHY: J. Grand-Carteret, *R. W. en caricatures* (Paris, 1892); E. Fuchs and E. Kreowski, *R. W. in der Karikatur* (Berlin, 1907; 6th ed., 1913); A. Vanselow, *R. W.s photographische Bildnisse* (Munich, 1908); E. Engel, *R. W.s Leben und Werke im Bilde* (2 vols., Vienna, 1913; new ed., Leipzig, 1922); J. Kapp, *R. W. Sein Leben, sein Werk, seine Welt in 260 Bildern* (Berlin, 1933); P. Bülow, *R. W. Sein Leben in Bildern* (Leipzig, 1936); R. Bory, *R. W. Sein Leben und sein Werk in Bildern* (Leipzig, 1938); M. Geck, *Die Bildnisse R. W.s* (Munich, 1970); W.-S. Wagner, *Die Geschichte unserer Familie in Bildern* (Munich, 1976); Eng. tr. as *The W. Family Albums*, London, 1976).

MISCELLANEOUS: C. Baudelaire, *R. W. et Tannhäuser à Paris* (Paris, 1861); W. Tappert, *Wagner-Lexikon. Wörterbuch der Unhöflichkeit* (Leipzig, 1877; new aug. ed. as *R. W. im Spiegel der Kritik*, 1903; an interesting collection of adverse and abusive comments); *Über Schicksale und Bestimmung des W.-Museums* (Leipzig, 1892); E. Kloss, *Das W.-Museum in Eisenach*, in *Ein W.-Lesebuch* (Leipzig, 1904); K. Grunsky, *R. W. und die Juden* (Munich, 1921); W. Lange, *R. W. und seine Vaterstadt, Leipzig* (Leipzig, 1921); J. Marnold, *Le Cas W.: La Musique pendant la guerre* (Paris, 1920); *W. et la France*, special issue of the *Revue Musicale* (Oct. 1923); P. Stefan, *Die Feindschaft gegen W.* (Regensburg, 1918); E. Newman, *Fact and Fiction about W.* (N.Y., 1931); E. Stemplinger, *W. in Munich* (Munich, 1933); W. Golther, *R. W. Leben und Werke in urkundlichen Zeugnissen, Briefen, Schriften, Berichten* (Ebenhausen, near Munich, 1936); W. Lange, *R. W.s Sippe*, with genealogical table (Leipzig, 1938); L. Weinhold, *Handschriften von R. W. in Leipzig* (Leipzig, 1938); O. Daube, *Humor bei R. W.* (Gütersloh, 1944); L. Stein, *The Racial Thinking of R. W.* (N.Y., 1950); L. Strecker, *R. W. als Verlagsgefährte* (Mainz, 1951); R. Holloway, *Debussy and W.* (London, 1979); F. Glass, *The Fertilizing Seed: W.'s Concept of the Poetic Intent* (Ann Arbor, Mich., 1983); P. Winters, "W.: Writing the Wrongs," *New Criterion* (Feb. 1983); P. Hodson, *Who's Who in W.: An A-to-Z Look at his Life and Work* (N.Y., 1984); D. Large and W. Weber, eds., *W.ism in European Culture and Politics* (N.Y., 1984).

Wagner, Roger (Francis), French-born American choral conductor; b. Le Puy, Jan. 16, 1914. He was brought to the U.S. as a child; after studying for the priesthood in Santa Barbara, he returned to France to study organ with Marcel Dupré; he settled in Los Angeles in 1937 and became organist and choirmaster at St. Joseph's; also took courses in philosophy and French literature at the Univ. of Calif. in Los Angeles, and at the Univ. of Southern Calif. He studied conducting with Otto Klemperer and Bruno Walter, and orchestration with Lucien Caillet. In 1946 he founded the Roger Wagner Chorale, and toured extensively with it in the U.S., Canada, and Latin America. He was also founder-conductor of the Los Angeles Master Chorale and Sinfonia Orch. (1965–85). He was head of the dept. of music at Marymount College in Los Angeles (1951–66); also taught at the Univ. of Calif. from 1959 to 1981. He was knighted by Pope Paul VI in 1966.

Wagner, Siegfried (Helferich Richard), German conductor and composer, son of **(Wilhelm) Richard** and **Cosima Wagner;** b. Triebschen, June 6, 1869; d. Bayreuth, Aug. 4, 1930. His parents were married on Aug. 25, 1870, and Siegfried was thus legitimated. Richard Wagner named the *Siegfried Idyll* for him, and it was performed in Wagner's house in Triebschen on Christmas Day, 1870. He studied with Humperdinck in Frankfurt am Main and then pursued training as an architect in Berlin and Karlsruhe; during his tenure as an assistant in Bayreuth (1892–96), he studied with his mother, Hans Richter, and Julius Kniese. From 1896 he was a regular conductor in Bayreuth, where he was general director of the Festival productions from 1906. On Sept. 21, 1915, he married Winifred Williams, an adopted daughter of Karl Klindworth.

In 1923–24 he visited the U.S. in order to raise funds for the reopening of the Bayreuth Festspielhaus, which had been closed during the course of World War I. He conducted from memory, and left-handed. In his career as a composer, he was greatly handicapped by inevitable comparisons with his father. His memoirs were publ. in Stuttgart in 1923.

WORKS: OPERAS: *Der Bärenhäuter* (1898; Munich, Jan. 22, 1899); *Herzog Wildfang* (Munich, March 14, 1901); *Der Kobold* (1903; Hamburg, Jan. 29, 1904); *Bruder Lustig* (Hamburg, Oct. 13, 1905); *Sternengebot* (1907; Hamburg, Jan. 21, 1908); *Banadietrich* (1909; Karlsruhe, Jan. 23, 1910); *Schwarzschwanenreich* (1911; Karlsruhe, Dec. 6, 1917); *Sonnenflammen* (1914; Darmstadt, Oct. 30, 1918); *Der Heidenkönig* (1914; Cologne, Dec. 16, 1933); *Der Friedensengel* (1915; Karlsruhe, March 4, 1926); *An allem ist Hütchen Schuld* (1916; Stuttgart, Dec. 6, 1917); *Der Schmied von Marienburg* (1920; Rostock, Dec. 16, 1923); *Wahnopfer* (1928; unfinished). ORCH.: *Sehnsucht*, symphonic poem (1895); *Konzertstück* for Flute and Orch. (1914); Violin Concerto (1915); *Und wenn die Welt voll Teufel wär!*, scherzo (1923); *Glück*, symphonic poem (1924); Sym. in C major (1925); *Das Märchen von dicken fetten Pfannkucken* for Baritone and Orch. (1913); *Der Fahnenschwur* for Men's Chorus, Orch., and Organ (1915); *Wer liebt uns* for Men's Chorus and Woodwinds (1924); also chamber music.

BIBL.: L. Karpeth, *S. W. als Mensch und Künstler* (Leipzig, 1902); C. Glasenapp, *S. W.* (Berlin, 1906); idem, *S. W. und seine Kunst* (Leipzig, 1911; essays on the operas; new series, 1913, as *Schwarzschwanenreich*; 2nd new series, ed. by P. Pretzsch, 1919, as *Sonnenflammen*); P. Pretzsch, *Die Kunst S. W.s* (Leipzig, 1919); O. Daube, *S. W. und sein Werk* (Bayreuth, 1925); *Festschrift zu S. W.s 60. Geburtstag* (Bayreuth, 1929); H. Rebois, *Lettres de S. W.* (Paris, 1933); O. Daube, *S. W. und die Märchenoper* (Leipzig, 1936); F. Starsen, *Erinnerungen an S. W.* (Detmold, 1942); Z. von Kraft, *Der Sohn: S. W.s Leben und Umwelt* (Graz, 1963); P. Pachl, *S. W.s musikdramatisches Schaffen* (Tutzing, 1979).

Wagner, Sieglinde, Austrian contralto; b. Linz, April 21, 1921. She received her musical training in Linz; then took vocal lessons in Munich with Luise Willer and Carl Hartmann. After making her debut in Linz in 1943, she sang at the Vienna State Opera (1947–52); in 1952 she joined the Berlin City Opera; also sang in Rome, Milan, Amsterdam, Salzburg, and Bayreuth; made many concert appearances as well.

Wagner, (Adolf) Wieland (Gottfried), German opera producer and stage designer, son of **Siegfried (Helferich Richard)** and brother of **Wolfgang (Manfred Martin) Wagner;** b. Bayreuth, Jan. 5, 1917; d. Munich, Oct. 16, 1966. He received his general education in Munich, and devoted himself to the problem of modernizing the productions of Wagner's operas. With his brother, Wolfgang Wagner, he served as co-director of the Bayreuth Festivals from 1951 to 1966. Abandoning the luxuriant scenery of 19th-century opera, he emphasized the symbolic meaning of Wagner's music dramas, eschewing realistic effects, such as machinery propelling the Rhine maidens through the wavy gauze of the river, or the bright paper flames of the burning Valhalla. He even introduced Freudian sexual overtones, as in his production of *Tristan und Isolde*, where a phallic pillar was conspicuously placed on the stage.

BIBL.: W. Panofsky, *W. W.* (Bremen, 1964); C. Lust, *W. W. et la survie du théâtre lyrique* (Lausanne, 1969); W. Schäfer, *W. W.: Persönlichkeit und Leistung* (Tübingen, 1970); G. Skelton, *W. W.: The Positive Sceptic* (London, 1971).

Wagner, Wolfgang (Manfred Martin), German opera producer, son of **Siegfried (Helferich Richard)** and brother of **(Adolf) Wieland (Gottfried) Wagner;** b. Bayreuth, Aug. 30, 1919. He studied music privately in Bayreuth; then worked in various capacities at the Bayreuth Festivals and the Berlin State Opera. With his brother, Wieland Wagner, he was co-director of the Bayreuth Festivals from 1951 to 1966; after his brother's death in 1966, he was its sole director. Like his brother, he departed radically from the traditional staging of the Wagner operas, and introduced a psychoanalytic and surrealist *mise en scène*, often with suggestive phallic and other sexual symbols in the décor.

Wagner-Régeny, Rudolf, Rumanian-born German composer, pedagogue, pianist, and clavichordist; b. Szász-Régen, Transylvania, Aug. 28, 1903; d. Berlin, Sept. 18, 1969. He entered the Leipzig Cons. as a piano pupil of Robert Teichmüller in 1919; in 1920 he enrolled at the Berlin Hochschule für Musik as a student in conducting of Rudolf Krasselt and Siegfried Ochs, in orchestration of Emil Reznicek, and in theory and composition of Friedrich Koch and Franz Schreker. He first gained notice as a composer with his theater pieces for Essen; in 1930 he became a naturalized German citizen, and with the rise of the Nazis was promoted by a faction of the party as a composer of the future; however, the success of his opera *Der Günstling* (Dresden, Feb. 20, 1935) was followed by his supporters' doubts regarding his subsequent output, ending in a scandal with his opera *Johanna Balk* at the Vienna State Opera (April 4, 1941). In 1942 he was drafted into the German army; after the close of World War II, he settled in East Germany; was director of the Rostock Hochschule für Musik (1947–50); then was a prof. of composition at the (East) Berlin Hochschule für Musik and at the Academy of Arts. After composing works along traditional lines, he adopted his own 12-note serial technique in 1950.

Works: OPERAS: *Sganarelle oder Der Schein trügt* (1923; Essen, March 1929); *Moschopulos* (Gera, Dec. 1, 1928); *Der nackte König* (1928; Gera, Dec. 1, 1930); *Der Günstling oder Die letzten Tage des grossen Herrn Fabiano* (1932–34; Dresden, Feb. 20, 1935); *Die Bürger von Calais* (1936–38; Berlin, Jan. 28, 1939); *Johanna Balk* (1938–40; Vienna, April 4, 1941); *Das Bergwerk zu Falun* (1958–60; Salzburg, Aug. 16, 1961). *BALLETS: Moritat* (1928; Essen, March 1929); *Der zerbrochene Krug* (Berlin, 1937). Other stage works include *Esau und Jacob*, biblical scene for 4 Soloists, Speaker, and String Orch. (1929; Gera, 1930); *La Sainte Courtisane* for 4 Speakers and Chamber Orch. (Dessau, 1930); *Die Fabel vom seligen Schlachtermeister* (1931–32; Dresden, May 23, 1964); *Persische Episode* (1940–50; Rostock, March 27, 1963); *Prometheus,* scene oratorio (1957–58; Kassel, Sept. 12, 1959); incidental music to 7 plays. ORCH.: *Orchestermusik mit Klavier* (Piano Concerto; 1935); *Mythologische Figurinen* (1951; Salzburg, June 21, 1952); *3 Orchestersätze* (1952); *Einleitung und Ode* (1967); *8 Kommentare zu einer Weise des Guillaume Machauts* for Chamber Orch. (1968). CHAMBER: *Kleine Gemeinschaftsmusik* for 6 Instruments (1929); *Spinettmusik* (1934); String Quartet (1948); *Introduction et communication à mon ange gardien* for String Trio (1951); *Divertimento* for 3 Winds and Percussion (1954); piano pieces. VOCAL: *Cantica Davidi regis* for Boys' Chorus, Bass Chorus, and Chamber Orch. (1954); *Genesis* for Alto, Chorus, and Small Orch. (1955–56); *An die Sonne,* cantata for Alto and Orch. (1967–68); *Hermann-Hesse-Gesänge* for Baritone and Small Orch. (1968–69); many songs with piano. **BIBL.:** A. Burgartz, *R. W.-R.* (Berlin, 1935); T. Müller-Medek, ed., *R. W.-R.: Begegnungen, biographische Aufzeichnungen, Tagebücher und sein Briefwechsel mit Caspar Neher* (Berlin, 1968).

Wagoner, Porter, American country-music singer, guitarist, and songwriter; b. West Plains, Mo., Aug. 12, 1927. He was forced to drop out of grade school to help his father on the family farm; at the same time he took up the guitar, and secured a spot singing and playing on a local radio station; subsequently he toured as a country-music entertainer, and scored major hits with his renditions of such country staples as *The Green, Green Grass of Home* (1965) and *The Cold Hard Facts of Life* (1967). With Dolly Parton, his featured television partner from 1967 to 1974, he won success with such numbers as *We'll Get Ahead Someday* (1968) and *Please Don't Stop Loving Me* (1974).

Wahlberg, Rune, Swedish pianist, conductor, and composer; b. Gävle, March 15, 1910. He studied in Stockholm (1928–35) and Leipzig (1936–37); was active as a conductor; and toured as a pianist.

Works: OPERA: *En Saga* (1952). ORCH.: Piano Concerto (1938); *Meditation* for Violin and Orch. (1941); 7 syms.: No. 1 (1941); No. 2 (1945); No. 3 (1951; Toronto, March 6, 1961); No. 4 (1959; Hofors, March 13, 1960); No. 5, *Havet,* for Men's Chorus and Orch. (1979); No. 6, *Episoder* (1980); No. 7, *Jordesång* (1981); *Nordic Suite* (1943); *Afrodite,* suite (1944); *Preludium, Larghetto and Fugue* (1952); *Nordland* for Male Chorus and Orch. (1957); Violin Concerto (1958); *Concerto barocco* for Violin and String Orch. (1960); Cello Concerto (1961); Bass-clarinet Concerto (1961); *Concert Suite* for Strings (1961); Violin Concertino (1963); *Florez och blanzeflor* for Male Chorus and Orch. (1963); *Concert Fantasy* for Piano and Orch. (1967); *Havsfyren* for Male Chorus and Orch. (1971); *Lantlig Suite* for String Orch. (1977); *Canzone* for Violin and Orch. (1980); *Jubileumsspel* (1980); 3 symphonic poems (1982); *Fantasia concertante* for 2 Violas and Orch. (1985). CHAMBER: Violin Sonata (1959); *Prisma* for Saxophone Quartet (1961); *Helgdagsvisa* for 4 Violins (1971); String Quartet (1972); *Concerto fantastico* for Percussion (1973); *Lyric Fantasy* for Violin and Piano (1975); Trio for Violin, Cello, and Piano (1977); *Två lyriska poem* for Piano Trio (1982); *Preludium och fuga* for String Quartet (1985); *Notturno* for Flute and Piano (1988).

Wailly, (Louis Auguste) Paul (Warnier) de, French composer; b. Amiens, May 16, 1854; d. Paris, June 18, 1933. He was a pupil of César Franck, and in his works showed himself a follower of Franck's precepts. He wrote 3 syms.; a dramatic oratorio, *L'Apôtre* (1924); *26 pièces* for Harmonium; publ. *La Vie et l'âme de César Franck* (Paris, 1922). **BIBL.:** A. Laurent, *P. d.W.: L'Artiste, l'œuvre* (Paris, 1933); idem, *P. d.W.: Le Compositeur, l'artiste* (Eu, 1940).

Waissel (Waisselius), Matthäus, German lutenist and intabulator; b. Bartenstein, East Prussia, c.1537; d. probably in Königsberg, 1602. He matriculated at the Univ. of Königsberg (1561); received lute training during tours in Germany and Italy (1565–70). He was Rektor of the school in Schippenbeil, East Prussia (1573–74), then parish priest in Langheim, near Rastenburg (1574–87). **Works** (all publ. in Frankfurt an der Oder): *Tablatura continens insignes et selectissimas quasque cantiones, testudini aptatas* for Lute (1573); *Tabulatura allerley künstlicher Preammbulen, auserlesener deudtscher und polnischer Tentze* for Lute (1591); *Lautenbuch, darinnen von der Tabulatur und Application der Lauten gründlicher und voller Unterricht* for Lute (1592); *Tabulatura guter gemeiner deudtscher Tentze* for 1 to 2 Lutes (1592).

Waits, Tom, American songwriter and performer; b. Pomona, Calif., Dec. 7, 1949. He began his career playing in Los Angeles clubs as a singer, pianist, and guitarist, sometimes with his group, Nocturnal Emissions. After being signed by Frank Zappa's manager in 1972, he produced his 1st record album, *Closing Time* (1973). He slowly rose from cultdom to stardom through such songs as *Shiver Me Timbers, Diamonds on My Windshield,* and *The Piano Has Been Drinking.* He made a number of recordings for the Asylum label; with *Swordfishtrombones* (1983), he expanded his accompaniment to include a broad spectrum of exotic instruments. He wrote the score for Francis Ford Coppola's film *One from the Heart* (1982), and later made the concert movie *Big Time* (1988). He also collaborated with his wife, Kathleen Brennan, on the stage show *Frank's Wild Years* (1987), which includes the pastiches *Temptation* and *Innocent When You Dream.* Among the artists who have performed his music are Bette Midler, Crystal Gayle, Bruce Springsteen, and the Manhattan Transfer; he also made frequent appearances as a film and stage actor. Waits is a jazz songwriter who regards the beatniks of the 1950s as his primary inspiration; his imaginative lyrics are full of slang and focus on the sad flotsam of cheap bars and motels. He accompanies his gravelly voice with rough instruments or electronics, but always with sensitive musicianship and ironic pathos. Among his other albums are *Nighthawks at the Diner* (1975), *Heartattack and Vine* (1980), and *Rain Dogs* (1985).

Wakasugi, Hiroshi, Japanese conductor; b. Tokyo, May 31, 1935. He studied conducting with Hideo Saito and Nobori Kaneko; in 1967 he was awarded a prize by the Japanese Ministry of Culture. In 1975 he became conductor of the Kyoto Sym. Orch. From 1977 to 1983 he was chief conductor of the Cologne Radio Sym. Orch.; also was Generalmusikdirektor of the Deutsche Oper am Rhein in Düsseldorf (1982–87). In 1981 he made his U.S. debut as a guest conductor of the Boston Sym. Orch. He was chief conductor of the Tonhalle Orch. in Zürich (from 1985) and the Tokyo Metropolitan Sym. Orch. (from 1987).

Walaciński, Adam, Polish composer; b. Krakow, Sept. 18, 1928. He studied violin with E. Umińska at the Krakow Cons. (1947–52); had private composition lessons with S. Kisielewski (1953–55) and with Boguslaw Schäffer; was a violinist in the Krakow Radio Orch. (1948–56). In 1972 he was appointed instructor at the Krakow Cons. He was a member of the avantgarde Grupa Krakowska.

WORKS: *Composition "Alfa"* for Orch. (1958); String Quartet (1959); *Modifications* for Viola and Piano (1960); *Rotazioni* for Piano (1961); *Intrada* for 7 Players (1962); *Canto tricolore* for Flute, Violin, and Vibraphone (1962); *Horizons* for Chamber Orch. (1962); *Sekwencje* for Concertante Flute and Orch. (1963); *Liryka sprzed zaśniecia (A Lyric before Falling Asleep)* for Soprano, Flute, and 2 Pianos (1963); *Concerto da camera* for Violin and String Orch. (1964; rev. 1967); *Fogli volanti,* optically notated composition for String Trio (1965); *Canzona* for Cello, Piano, and Tape (1966); *Epigrams* for Chamber Ensemble (1967); *Dichromia* for Flute and Piano (1967); *Refrains et réflexions* for Orch. (1969); *Notturno 70* for 24 Strings, 3 Flutes, and Percussion (1970); *Allaloa,* optically notated composition for electronically transformed Piano (1970); *Torso* for Orch. (1971; Krakow, Jan. 21, 1972); *On peut écouter* for Flute, Oboe, and Bassoon (1971); *Divertimento interrotto* for 13 Players (1974); *Mirophonies* for Soprano, Actor, Clarinet, Viola, Cello, Harp, and Percussion (1974); *Ballada* for Flute and Piano (1986); *Little Autumn Music* for Oboe, Violin, Viola, and Cello (1986); *Drama e burla* for Orch. (Warsaw, Oct. 21, 1988).

Walcha, (Arthur Emil) Helmut, noted German organist and pedagogue; b. Leipzig, Oct. 27, 1907. He lost his eyesight in his youth, but courageously persevered in his musical studies; studied organ with Ramin at the Leipzig Cons. (1922–27); in 1924 he made his debut in Leipzig. He then served as assistant organist at the Thomaskirche there (1926–29). In 1929 he settled in Frankfurt as a church organist; in 1933 he joined the faculty of the Frankfurt Cons.; in 1938 he was named prof. at the Hochschule für Musik there. He retired from his professorship in 1972 but continued to give organ recitals. He was honored with a Festschrift for his 70th birthday (Frankfurt, 1978).

Walcker, Eberhard Friedrich, German organ builder; b. Cannstadt, near Stuttgart, July 3, 1794; d. Ludwigsburg, Oct. 2, 1872. Trained in the workshops of his father, **Johann Eberhard Walcker** (1756–1843), a skilled organ builder, he set up for himself in Ludwigsburg in 1820 and won great renown by his excellent work and numerous inventions. After his death, the business passed to his 5 sons: **Heinrich** (b. Oct. 10, 1828; d. Kirchheim, Nov. 24, 1903), **Friedrich** (b. Sept. 17, 1829; d. Dec. 6, 1895), **Karl** (b. March 6, 1845; d. Stuttgart, May 19, 1908), **Paul** (b. May 31, 1846; d. 1928), and **Eberhard** (b. April 8, 1850; d. 1927). In 1916 **Oscar Walcker** (son of Friedrich; b. Ludwigsburg, Jan. 1, 1869; d. there, Nov. 4, 1948) became head of the firm; it was merged with W. Sauer of Frankfurt in 1910, and then with Ziegler of Steinsfurt in 1932. His reminiscences, *Erinnerungen eines Orgelbaumeisters,* were publ. in Kassel in 1948. In 1948 his grandson, **Werner Walcker-Mayer** (b. Ludwigsburg, Feb. 1, 1923), took charge of the firm; its headquarters were moved to Murrhardt in 1975. Among the firm's finest instruments are those in Ulm Cathedral (1841–56; 3 manuals, 100 stops), Festival Hall, Boston (1863; 4 manuals, 89 stops), St. Stephen's, Mulhouse (1865; 3 manuals, 61 stops), Riga Cathedral (1881; 4 manuals, 122 stops),

the Petrikirche, Hamburg (1884; 3 manuals, 60 stops), the old Gewandhaus, Leipzig (1884; 3 manuals, 54 stops), St. Stephen's Cathedral, Vienna (1886; 3 manuals, 90 stops), St. Michaelis, Hamburg (1909–12; 15 manuals, 163 stops), City Hall, Stockholm (1924–25; 4 manuals, 115 stops), Kongresshalle, Nuremberg (1936; 5 manuals, 220 stops), Stuttgart Radio (1951; 4 manuals, 72 stops), and the Stiftskirche, Stuttgart (1958; 4 manuals, 84 stops).

BIBL.: H. Walcker, *Das Geschlecht der W. in sechs Jahrhunderten* (Belser, 1925; 2nd ed., 1940); J. Fischer, *Das Orgelbauergeschlecht W. in Ludwigsburg* (Kassel, 1966).

Wald, Max, American composer and teacher; b. Litchfield, Ill., July 14, 1889; d. Dowagiac, Mich., Aug. 14, 1954. After studying in Chicago, he was active as a theater conductor; went to Paris in 1922 to study with Vincent d'Indy, and remained in Europe until 1936; then became chairman of the theory dept. of the Chicago Musical College. His symphonic poem *The Dancer Dead* won 2nd prize in the NBC competition in 1932, and was broadcast from N.Y. on May 1, 1932. His other works include *Retrospectives* for Orch. (Chicago, Jan. 15, 1926); *Comedy Overture* (1937); *In Praise of Pageantry* for Orch. (Chicago, Oct. 31, 1946); *October Moonlight,* song cycle for Soprano, String Quartet, Flute, Clarinet, and Piano (1937); 2 piano sonatas; other piano music; also an opera, *Mirandolina* (1936), and a light opera, *Gay Little World* (1942).

Waldman, Frederic, Austrian-born American conductor; b. Vienna, April 17, 1903. He studied conducting with Szell; made his way to N.Y. in 1941; taught at the Juilliard School of Music, where he served as director of its Opera Theater. In 1961 he organized the Musica Aeterna Orch. and Chorus, with which he gave many concerts of rarely performed music.

Waldmann, Maria, Austrian mezzo-soprano; b. Vienna, 1842; d. Ferrara, Nov. 6, 1920. She studied in Vienna with Passy-Cornet and in Milan with Lamperti; made her debut as Pierotto in *Linda di Chamounix* in Pressburg in 1865; then sang in Wiesbaden, Amsterdam, Trieste, and Moscow (with the Italian Opera, 1869–70), at La Scala in Milan (1871–72), and in Cairo (1873–76). She retired in 1876. Verdi admired her singing, and he chose her for the premiere of his Requiem.

Waldrop, Gideon W(illiam), American music educator, conductor, and composer; b. Haskell County, Tex., Sept. 2, 1919. He studied at Baylor Univ. (B.M., 1940) and took courses in composition with Bernard Rogers and Howard Hanson at the Eastman School of Music in Rochester, N.Y. (M.M., 1941; Ph.D., 1952). He was conductor of the Waco-Baylor Sym. Orch. (1939–51); also was associate prof. at Baylor Univ. (1946–51). He served as ed. of the *Musical Courier* (1953–58) and as music consultant to the Ford Foundation (1958–61). He was assistant to the president (1961–63) and then dean (1963–85) of the Juilliard School in N.Y.; then was president of the Manhattan School of Music (1986–88).

WORKS: Orch.: *From the Southwest,* suite (1948); Sym. No. 1 (1951); *Pressures* for String Orch. (1955); *Prelude and Fugue* (1962); *Songs of the Southwest* for Baritone and Chamber Orch. (1982); chamber music; choral pieces; songs.

Waldstein, Ferdinand Ernst Joseph Gabriel, Count von Waldstein und Wartenberg zu Dux, German-Bohemian amateur musician; b. Duchov, Bohemia, March 24, 1762; d. Vienna, Aug. 29, 1823. In 1787 he began his novitiate in the Teutonic Order in Ellingen, transferring to the electoral court in Bonn in 1788, where he received his order; became acquainted with Beethoven, and on several occasions aided him materially, pretending that the sums were extra allowances from the Elector; after Beethoven's departure for Vienna, Waldstein introduced him in the circles of the aristocracy there; from 1795 he traveled widely, first in the military and later in diplomatic service. By 1812 his relations with Beethoven had cooled. In 1816 he declared bankruptcy and eventually died in poverty. Beethoven wrote a set of variations in C for piano, 4-hands, on a theme of Waldstein (publ. 1794), and later (1805) dedicated to him the great Sonata in C, op. 53.

Waldstein also planned the *Ritter-Ballet* (1791), to which Beethoven wrote the music (score publ. 1872). Waldstein composed a Sym. in D major (ed. in Denkmäler Rheinischer Musik, I, Düsseldorf, 1951).

BIBL.: J. Heer, *Der Graf von W. und sein Verhältnis zu Beethoven* (Leipzig, 1933).

Waldteufel (original family surname, **Lévy**), **(Charles-) Émile,** famous French conductor and composer of light music; b. Strasbourg, Dec. 9, 1837; d. Paris, Feb. 12, 1915. His father, Louis (1801–84), and his brother, Léon (1832–84), were violinists and dance composers, and his mother was a pianist. In 1842 the family went to Paris, where he studied piano with his mother and then with Joseph Heyberger; subsequently was an auditor in L.-A. Marmontel's class at the Paris Cons., where he became a pupil of A. Laurent in 1853, but left before completing his courses. He became a piano tester for the manufacturer Scholtus; also taught piano and played in soirées; when he had time, he composed dance music for Paris salons. In 1865 he became court pianist to the Empress Eugénie and in 1866 conductor of the state balls. His 1st waltz, *Joies et peines,* which he publ. at his own expense in 1859, was an immediate success, and he became known in Paris high society. In 1867 he publ. another successful waltz, with the German title *Vergissmeinnicht.* Then followed a series of waltzes that established his fame as a French counterpart to Johann Strauss, Jr.: *Manola* (1873), *Mon Rêve* (1877), *Pomone* (1877), *Toujours ou jamais* (1877), *Les Sirènes* (1878), *Très jolie* (1878), *Pluie de diamants* (1879), *Dolorès* (1880), and the most famous of them, *Les Patineurs* (1882). His dance music symbolized the "gai Paris" of his time as fittingly as the music of Johann Strauss reflected the gaiety of old Vienna. Waldteufel lived most of his life in Paris, but he also filled conducting engagements abroad, visiting London in 1885 and Berlin in 1889.

BIBL.: A. Lamb, *E. W. (1837–1915): The Parisian Waltz King* (Littlehampton, 1979); J.- P. Zeder, *Les W. et la valse française* (Strasbourg, 1980); A. Lamb, "The W.s," *Musical Times* (Oct. 1982).

Walker, Alan, English musicologist; b. Scunthorpe, April 6, 1930. He was educated at the Guildhall School of Music in London (ARCM, 1949) and at the Univ. of Durham (B.Mus., 1956; D.Mus., 1965); also studied with Hans Keller (1958–60). He was prof. of harmony and counterpoint at the Guildhall School of Music (1958–60); after serving as a producer for the BBC music division (1961–71), he was chairman of the music dept. and a prof. at McMaster Univ. in Hamilton, Ontario (from 1971).

WRITINGS: (all publ. in London): *A Study in Musical Analysis* (1962); *An Anatomy of Musical Criticism* (1966); ed., *Frédéric Chopin: Profiles of the Man and the Musician* (1966; 2nd ed., rev. and enl., 1978); ed., *Franz Liszt: The Man and His Music* (1970; 2nd ed., rev., 1976); *Liszt* (1971); ed., *Robert Schumann: The Man and His Music* (1972; 2nd ed., rev., 1976); *Schumann* (1976); *Franz Liszt: Vol. I, The Virtuoso Years, 1811–1847* (1983; rev. 1987); *Franz Liszt: Vol. II, The Weimar Years, 1848–1861* (1989).

Walker, Edyth, American mezzo-soprano; b. Hopewell, N.Y., March 27, 1867; d. N.Y., Feb. 19, 1950. She studied singing with Aglaja Orgeni at the Dresden Cons.; made her debut as Fidès in *Le Prophète* at the Berlin Royal Opera on Nov. 11, 1894. She was a member of the Vienna Court Opera (1895–1903); made her debut at London's Covent Garden as Amneris in 1900. She made her U.S. debut at the Metropolitan Opera in N.Y. (Nov. 30, 1903), remaining on its roster until 1906, singing soprano as well as mezzo-soprano roles; also sang both mezzo-soprano and soprano roles at the Hamburg Opera (1903–12); was the 1st London Electra (1910). After singing at the Bayreuth and Munich Festivals (1912–17), she turned to private teaching; was on the faculty of the American Cons. in Fontainebleau (1933–36) before settling in N.Y.

Walker, Ernest, English pianist, teacher, writer on music, and composer; b. Bombay, India, July 15, 1870; d. Oxford,

Feb. 21, 1949. He was educated at Balliol College, Oxford (D.Mus., 1898); was director of music there (1901–25). He publ. the valuable compendium *A History of Music in England* (Oxford, 1907; 2nd ed., 1924; 3rd ed., rev. by J. Westrup, 1952); a monograph on Beethoven in the Music of the Masters series (1905). His collection of essays, *Free Thought and the Musician,* was publ. in 1946. Among his compositions are *Fantasia-Variations on a Norfolk Folksong* for Small Orch. (1930; also for Piano Duet), *Fantasia* for String Quartet (1905), *Variations on a Theme of Joachim* for Violin and Piano (1918), and a Sonata for Cello and Piano (1914).

BIBL.: M. Deneke, *E. W.* (London, 1951).

Walker, Frank, English musicologist; b. Gosport, Hampshire, June 10, 1907; d. (suicide) Tring, Feb. 25?, 1962. He studied telegraphy; in 1926, went to Rio de Janeiro as a representative of the Western Telegraph Co. From 1931 to 1943 he was in London; in 1944–45 he was in Naples, and later in Vienna, before returning to London. He contributed valuable articles on the composers of the Neapolitan School; wrote the books *Hugo Wolf: A Biography* (London, 1951; 2nd ed., 1968) and *The Man Verdi* (London, 1962).

Walker, George (Theophilus), black American pianist, teacher, and composer; b. Washington, D.C., June 27, 1922. He studied at the Oberlin College Cons. of Music (M.B., 1941); then entered the Curtis Inst. of Music in Philadelphia, where he studied piano with Rudolf Serkin, composition with Rosario Scalero and Gian Carlo Menotti, and chamber music with Gregor Piatigorsky and William Primrose (Artist Diploma, 1945); also took piano lessons with Robert Casadesus in Fontainebleau in France (diploma, 1947); obtained his D.M.A. from the Eastman School of Music in Rochester, N.Y., in 1957. In 1957 he received a Fulbright fellowship for travel to Paris, where he took courses in composition with Nadia Boulanger. In 1945 he made his debut as a pianist, and subsequently appeared throughout the U.S. and abroad; was also active as a teacher; held appointments at Dillard Univ. in New Orleans (1953), The New School for Social Research in N.Y., the Dalcroze School of Music (1961), Smith College (1961–68), and the Univ. of Colorado (1968). In 1969 he was appointed a prof. at Rutgers, the State Univ. of New Jersey; was chairman of the composition dept. there in 1974; in 1975, was also named Distinguished Prof. at the Univ. of Delaware and adjunct prof. at the Peabody Inst. in Baltimore. In 1969 he received a Guggenheim fellowship; also held 2 Rockefeller fellowships for study in Italy (1971, 1975). In 1982 he was made a member of the American Academy and Inst. of Arts and Letters. In his music he maintains a median modern line with an infusion of black folk idioms.

WORKS: ORCH.: Trombone Concerto (1957; also for Trombone and Piano); *Address* (1959; Mons, Oct. 22, 1971); Sym. (1961); *Antiphonys* for Chamber Orch. (1968; also for Strings); *Variations* (1971); *Spirituals* (1974); Piano Concerto (1975); *Dialogues* for Cello and Orch. (1975–76); *Mass* for Soloists, Chorus, and Orch. (1976); *Overture: In Praise of Folly* (1980); Cello Concerto (N.Y., Jan. 14, 1982); *An Eastman Overture* (Washington, D.C., Jan. 15, 1983); *Serenata* for Chamber Orch. (1983); *Sinfonia* (1984); Violin Concerto (1984). **CHAMBER:** 2 string quartets (1946; 1967; rev. 1968); Cello Sonata (1957); 2 violin sonatas (1959, 1979); *Perimeters* for Clarinet and Piano (1966); *Music for 3* for Violin, Cello, and Piano (1970); *5 Fancies* for Clarinet and Piano, 4-hands (1974); *Music (Sacred and Profane)* for Brass (1975); 4 piano sonatas (1953, 1957, 1975, 1985); other piano pieces; numerous vocal works, including *3 Lyrics* for Chorus (1958) and *Mass* for Soprano, Alto, Tenor, Baritone, Chorus, and Orch. (1978); choruses; songs.

Walker, Robert, English composer; b. Northampton, March 18, 1946. He was a chorister at St. Matthew's Church in Northampton and a choral and then organ scholar at Jesus College, Cambridge (1965–68; M.A., 1968). After serving as an organist and schoolmaster in Lincolnshire, he devoted himself to composing, teaching, and broadcasting.

WORKS: ORCH.: *Pavan* for Violin and Orch. (Eltham Palace,

June 26, 1975); *At Bignor Hill* (Lisbon, April 9, 1979); Chamber Sym. No. 1 (1981; Greenwich, June 15, 1982); *Variations on a Theme of Elgar* (Chichester, July 13, 1982); *Charms and Exultations of Trumpets* (1985; Salisbury, April 2, 1986); Sym. No. 1 (Exeter, May 26, 1987). CHAMBER: String Quartet No. 1 (1982); *Gonfalons* for 4 Trumpets, 4 Trombones, Organ, and Optional Unison Choir (1983); Piano Quintet (1984); *Serenade* for Flute, Harp, Violin, Viola, and Cello (1987); piano pieces, including *Five Capriccios, Set 1* (1982) and *Set 2* (1985); *Passacaglia* for 2 Pianos (1984). VOCAL: *Requiem* for Tenor, Choir, and Orch. (1976); *Canticle of the Rose* for Soprano, Baritone, Choir, and Orch. (1980); *The Sun Used to Shine* for Tenor, Harp, and String Orch. (1983); *Magnificat and Nunc Dimittis* for Choir and Organ (1985); *Missa Brevis* for Choir and Organ (1985); *Singer by the Yellow River* for Soprano, Flute, and Harp (1985); *Jubilate* for Choir and Brass Quintet (1987); *English Parody Mass* for Choir and Organ (1988); also various unaccompanied vocal pieces.

Walker, Sarah, English mezzo-soprano; b. Cheltenham, March 11, 1943. She studied violin at the Royal College of Music in London before turning to voice; made her operatic debut as Monteverdi's Ottavia with the Kent Opera (1970). She sang with the Sadler's Wells Opera Co. in London (from 1972), continuing with it when it became the English National Opera (1974); made her Covent Garden debut as Charlotte in 1979; also gave recitals throughout Europe and North America.

Wallace, (William) Vincent, Irish violinist, organist, and composer; b. Waterford, March 11, 1812; d. Château de Bagen, Haute-Garonne, France, Oct. 12, 1865. The son of a bandmaster, Wallace was brought up in a musical atmosphere. He was 13 when the family moved to Dublin, and soon entered a professional career, playing violin in theater orchs. and organ in churches. One of his earliest compositions was *The Harp in the Air*, which later became famous when he incorporated it into his opera *Maritana*. In 1831 he married Isabella Kelly. He applied himself to the study of violin, and subsequently was able to give successful concerts. With his wife he traveled in Australia, South America, Mexico, and the U.S. Returning to Europe in 1844, he toured Germany; in 1845 he was in London, where he produced his opera *Maritana* (Drury Lane, Nov. 15, 1845), which obtained excellent success; it was followed by another opera, *Matilda of Hungary* (Drury Lane, Feb. 2, 1847), which was a failure. About 1850 he "married" the American pianist Hélène Stoepel, declaring his 1st marriage invalid; she made appearances as Mrs. Wallace from 1851. From 1850 to 1853 he visited South and North America. His other operas include *Lurline* (1847; Covent Garden, Feb. 23, 1860), *The Maid of Zürich* (unpubl.), *The Amber Witch* (Haymarket, Feb. 28, 1861), *Love's Triumph* (Covent Garden, Nov. 3, 1862), and *The Desert Flower* (Covent Garden, Oct. 12, 1863); he also wrote the opera *Estrella* (unfinished), the operettas *Gulnare* and *Olga*, the cantata *Maypole*, a Violin Concerto, and numerous piano pieces.
BIBL.: A. Pougin, *W.V. W., Étude biographique et critique* (Paris, 1866); W.H.G. Flood, *W.V. W.: A Memoir* (Waterford, 1912); J. Klein, "V. W. (1812–65): A Reassessment," *Opera*, XVI (1965).

Wallace, William, Scottish composer and music educator; b. Greenock, July 3, 1860; d. Malmesbury, Wiltshire, Dec. 16, 1940. The son of a surgeon, he studied medicine at Glasgow Univ. (M.D., 1888); specialized in ophthalmology in Vienna, and was employed in the Royal Army Medical Corps during World War I; was 29 when he took up musical studies, pursuing his training at the Royal Academy of Music in London. He devoted much of his energy to the protection of the rights of British composers; served on the Composers' Copyright Committee of the Society of British Authors; also taught at the Royal Academy of Music.
WORKS: Symphonic poems: *The Passing of Beatrice* (1892); *Amboss oder Hammer*, after Goethe (1896); *Sister Helen* (1899); *To the New Century* (1901); *William Wallace* (for the 6th cen-

tenary of the death of the national hero of Scotland, and namesake of the composer; 1905); *François Villon* (1909); a sym., *The Creation* (1899); suites for Orch.: *The Lady from the Sea*, after Ibsen (1892), and *Pelléas and Mélisande*, after Maeterlinck (1900); overture, *In Praise of Scottish Poesie* (1894); *The Massacre of the Macpherson*, burlesque cantata; song cycles: *Freebooter Songs* (with Orch.; his most famous work); *Lords of the Sea; Jacobite Songs*.
WRITINGS: *The Threshold of Music: An Inquiry into the Development of the Musical Sense* (1908); *The Musical Faculty: Its Origins and Processes* (1914); *Richard Wagner as He Lived* (1925); *Liszt, Wagner and the Princess* (1927).

Wallaschek, Richard, Austrian music theorist; b. Brünn, Nov. 16, 1860; d. Vienna, April 24, 1917. He studied law and philosophy in Vienna, Heidelberg, Tübingen, and Bern; from 1890 to 1895, was in London, engaged in research work. He taught at the Univ. of Vienna (from 1896), where he was named extraordinary prof. (1908) and honorary prof. (1911); also taught at the Cons. of the Gesellschaft der Musikfreunde (1900–1902).
WRITINGS: *Ästhetik der Tonkunst* (Stuttgart, 1886); *Primitive Music: An Inquiry into the Origin and Development of Music, Song, Instruments, Dances and Pantomimes of Savage Races* (London, 1893; 2nd ed., enl., 1903, as *Anfänge der Tonkunst*); *Geschichte der Wiener Hofoper* (Vienna, 1907–8); *Psychologische Ästhetik* (Vienna, 1930).
BIBL.: R. Lach, "Zur Erinnerung an R. W.," *Zeitschrift für Ästhetik*, XII (Vienna, 1917).

Wallat, Hans, German conductor; b. Berlin, Oct. 18, 1929. He was educated at the Schwerin Cons.; then conducted in several provincial German music centers. He was music director in Cottbus (1956–58) and 1st conductor of the Leipzig Opera (1958–61); then conducted in Stuttgart (1961–64) and at the Deutsche Oper in West Berlin (1964–65). He was Generalmusikdirektor at the Bremen Opera (1965–70); made appearances as a guest conductor with various opera houses and orchs. in Europe; on Oct. 7, 1971, he made his Metropolitan Opera debut in N.Y. conducting *Fidelio*. He was Generalmusikdirektor in Mannheim (1970–80), Dortmund (1980–85), and of the Deutsche Oper am Rhein in Düsseldorf (from 1987).

Wallberg, Heinz, German conductor; b. Herringen-Hamm, March 16, 1923. He studied at the Dortmund Cons. and the Cologne Hochschule für Musik; after pursuing a career as a trumpeter and violinist, he turned to conducting; was Generalmusikdirektor in Wiesbaden (1961–74) and chief conductor of the Vienna Niederösterreichisches Tonkünstler-Orch. (1964–75); subsequently was Generalmusikdirektor in Essen (1975–86) and chief conductor of the Munich Radio Orch. (1975–82).

Wallek-Walewski, Boleslaw, Polish conductor, pedagogue, and composer; b. Lemberg. Jan. 23, 1885; d. Krakow, April 9, 1944. He studied theory and composition with Soltys and Niewiadomski and piano with Maliszowa and Zelinger in Lemberg; then continued his training with Zeleński and Szopski at the Krakow Cons.; completed his studies with Riemann and Prüfer in Leipzig. He became a prof. (1910) and director (1913) of the Krakow Cons.; was founder-conductor of his own choral society, and also appeared as an operatic and sym. conductor. His compositions follow along Romantic lines.
WORKS: OPERAS: *Pan Twardowski* (1911; Krakow, 1915); *Dola* (Lot; Krakow, 1919); *Pomsta Jontkowa* (1926); *Legenda o królewnie Wandzie* (The Legend of the King's Daughter Wanda; 1936); symphonic poems: *Pawel i Gawel* (1908) and *Zygmunt August i Barbara* (1912); oratorios; cantatas; songs.
BIBL.: A. Kopyciński, "B. W.-W. 1885–1944," *Ruch Muzyczny*, no. 3 (1945).

Wallenstein, Alfred, American cellist and conductor; b. Chicago, Oct. 7, 1898; d. N.Y., Feb. 8, 1983. His parents were of German and Austrian extraction; Wallenstein believed that he was a direct descendant of Albrecht von Wallenstein, the illustrious leader during the Thirty Years' War. The family moved to Los Angeles in 1905; Wallenstein took cello lessons with the mother of Ferde Grofé; as a young boy he played in hotels and movie theaters; also gave public recitals advertised as "the wonder-boy cellist." He played with the San Francisco Sym. Orch. (1916–17); subsequently toured in South America with the troupe of Anna Pavlova, being featured as cello soloist to accompany her famous portrayal of the dying swan. In 1919 he became a member of the Los Angeles Phil.; in 1920 he studied cello with Julius Klengel in Leipzig. He was a cellist in the Chicago Sym. Orch. (1922–29), and also appeared with it as a soloist; from 1927 to 1929 he was head of the cello dept. of the Chicago Musical College. In 1929 Toscanini engaged him as 1st cellist with the N.Y. Phil.; it was Toscanini who urged Wallenstein to try his hand at conducting; he began his conducting career by leading classical programs over the radio. In 1933 he formed the Wallenstein Sinfonietta, giving regular Sunday broadcasts; an important feature was a series of performances of Bach's cantatas. He also programmed numerous premieres of works by contemporary composers. After Toscanini resigned as music director of the N.Y. Phil. in 1936, Wallenstein also left his job as 1st cellist of the orch., and devoted himself exclusively to radio performances and guest conducting. In 1943 he was named conductor of the Los Angeles Phil.; was also director of the Hollywood Bowl (1952–56). In 1956 he made a tour of the Orient with the Los Angeles Phil. under the auspices of the State Dept.; after this tour he resigned as its conductor; subsequently made appearances as a guest conductor. In 1968 he joined the faculty of the Juilliard School of Music in N.Y. as instructor in conducting. In 1979, at the age of 81, he made his last public appearance as a conductor, leading the Juilliard School Orch. in N.Y. Wallenstein never pretended to be a glamorous virtuoso of the baton, but he was a master builder of orch. organizations; more in praise than in dispraise, he was described as a "vertical" conductor who offered dispassionate rather than impassioned interpretations; but no one doubted his selfless devotion to music and musicians.

Wallenstein, Martin, German pianist and composer; b. Frankfurt am Main, July 22, 1843; d. there, Nov. 29, 1896. He studied with Dreyschock in Prague, and with Hauptmann and Rietz in Leipzig; made many successful tours as a pianist. His opera, *Das Testament*, was produced at Frankfurt in 1870; he also wrote a Piano Concerto; many piano studies and characteristic pieces.

Waller, "Fats" (Thomas Wright), noted black American jazz pianist, organist, singer, bandleader, and composer; b. N.Y., May 21, 1904; d. Kansas City, Mo., Dec. 15, 1943. As a child he had private piano instruction and studied violin and double bass in school, but his most significant early lessons came from the player piano and nickelodeon pianists whom he studiously imitated; at 14 he was playing organ professionally in a Harlem theater; at 16 he received piano training from Russell Brooks and James P. Johnson; he claimed that he later had some lessons from Leopold Godowsky and studied composition with Carl Bohm at the Juilliard School of Music. In 1922 he began to make recordings and in 1923 made his 1st appearance on the radio; subsequently made frequent broadcasts as a singer and pianist. On Feb. 27, 1928, he made his debut at N.Y.'s Carnegie Hall as a piano soloist. With the lyricist Any Razaf, he composed most of the music for the all-black Broadway musical *Keep Shufflin'* (1928), and then collaborated on the shows *Load of Coal* and *Hot Chocolates* (1929), which includes the song *Ain't Misbehavin'*. He worked with Ted Lewis (1930), Jack Teagarden (1931), and Billy Banks's Rhythmakers (1932) before organizing his own band, Fats Waller and his Rhythm, in 1934; was active on the West Coast and appeared in the Hollywood films *Hooray for Love* and *King of Burlesque* (both 1935). In 1938 he toured Europe, and again in 1939; in 1943 he appeared in the Hollywood film *Stormy Weather* leading an all-star band. As a jazz pianist, he was considered a leading exponent of "stride piano," playing with a delicacy and lightness of touch that belied his consider-

able bulk of almost 300 pounds. Much of his popularity was due to his skills as an entertainer; he was especially effective in improvising lyrics to deflate the sentimentality of popular songs. A musical tribute to Waller, the revue *Ain't Misbehavin'*, was one of the great successes of the N.Y. theater season in 1978.

BIBL.: J. Davies, *The Music of T. "F." W.* (London, 1953); E. Kirkeby, D. Scheidt, and S. Traill, *Ain't Misbehavin': The Story of F. W.* (N.Y., 1966); M. Berger, "F. W.: The Outside Insider," *Journal of Jazz Studies,* i/1 (1973); J. Vance, *F. W.: His Life and Times* (Chicago, 1977); M. Waller (his son) and A. Calabrese, *F. W.* (N.Y., 1977); W. Balliett, "Jazz: F.," *New Yorker* (April 10, 1978); idem, *Jelly Roll, Jabbo and F.* (N.Y., 1983); P. Machlin, *Stride: The Music of F. W.* (Boston, 1985); A. Shipton, *F. W.: His Life & Times* (N.Y., 1988).

Wallerstein, Anton, German violinist and composer; b. Dresden, Sept. 28, 1813; d. Geneva, March 26, 1892. He played in public as a child; joined the Dresden Court Orch. (1829–32) and later was Konzertmeister in Hannover (1832–41); then toured as a soloist. He wrote a number of popular dance compositions, of which about 300 were publ.; also violin pieces and songs.

Wallerstein, Lothar, Bohemian-born American pianist and conductor; b. Prague, Nov. 6, 1882; d. New Orleans, Nov. 13, 1949. He studied art and music in Prague and Munich; also attended the Geneva Cons., where he later taught piano; after serving as accompanist at the Dresden Court Opera (1909), he was conductor and stage director in Posen (1910–14), Breslau (1918–22), Duisberg (1922–24), and Frankfurt (1924–26); was producer at the Vienna State Opera (1927–38); conducted at La Scala in Milan (1929). He went to the U.S. in 1941; was a producer at the Metropolitan Opera in N.Y. (1941–46). In 1945 he became a naturalized American citizen.

BIBL.: A. Berger, *Über die Spielleitung der Oper. Betrachtungen zur musikalischen Dramaturgie Dr. L. W.s* (Graz, 1928).

Wallfisch, Raphael, English cellist and teacher; b. London, June 15, 1953. He commenced cello playing at age 8; studied with Amaryllis Fleming in London (1966–69), Amadeo Baldovino in Rome (1969), Derek Simpson at the Royal Academy of Music in London (1969–72), and with Gregor Piatigorsky in Los Angeles (1972–74); won 1st prize in the Gaspar Cassadó competition in Florence in 1977. He made his formal debut as soloist in the Schumann Cello Concerto with the English Chamber Orch. in London in 1974; subsequently appeared as a soloist with major orchs. on both sides of the Atlantic, and also gave recitals and played in chamber music settings. In 1980 he became a prof. at the Guildhall School of Music in London. His repertoire includes some 60 concertos, ranging from early scores to contemporary works, as well as numerous solo and chamber music pieces.

Walliser, Christoph Thomas, important Alsatian composer; b. Strasbourg, April 17, 1568; d. there, April 26, 1648. After attending the Protestant Gymnasium in Strasbourg, he pursued his training in the liberal arts and sciences in Bohemia, Hungary, Italy, Switzerland, and Germany; upon his return to Strasbourg in 1598, he was made musicus ordinarius at the Gymnasium; also was active at the Thomaskirche (from 1600). With the coming of the Thirty Years' War, he lost his post at the Gymnasium (1634) and spent his last years in poverty. He was the foremost Alsatian composer of his time, excelling particularly in music for the church.

WORKS (all publ. in Strasbourg unless otherwise given): *Teutsche Psalmen* for 5 Voices (Nuremberg, 1602); *Hexastichon* for 6 Voices (Liegnitz, 1610); *Choris musici . . . in Andromeda Tragoedia* for 3 to 6 Voices (1612); *In festum nativitatis Domini* for 5 Voices (1613); *Ecclesiodiae* for 4 to 6 Voices (1614); *Te Deum laudamus* for 6 Voices (1617); *Ecclesiodiae novae* for 4 to 7 Voices (1625); *Herrn Wilhelmus Salusten von Bartas Triumph des Glaubens* for 5 Voices (1627); *Chorus musicus . . . D. Leopoldo Austria Archduci* for 3 Voices (1628); *Fons Israelis* for 8 Voices (1641); also motets in contemporary collections, and madrigals.

BIBL.: A. Bähre, "C.T. W.," *Festschrift zur Feier des 350-jährigen Bestehens des protestantischen Gymnasiums zu Strassburg* (Strasbourg, 1888); U. Klein, *C.T. W. (1568–1648): Ein Beitrag zur Musikgeschichte Strassburgs* (diss., Univ. of Texas, 1964).

Wallnöfer, Adolf, Austrian tenor and composer; b. Vienna, April 26, 1854; d. Munich, June 9, 1946. He studied singing with Rokitansky; composition with Krenn and Dessoff. He began his career as a baritone, but developed his voice into a tenor in 1880; joined Neumann's Wagner troupe in 1881; then sang in Bremen and at the German Opera in Prague (1885–95); from 1896 to 1898, appeared in the U.S.; then toured in Russia (1899); in 1906 he was engaged at the Vienna Court Opera; in 1908 he went to Munich. He composed an opera, *Eddystone* (Prague, 1889); several works for solo voice, chorus, and orch. (*Die Grenzen der Menschheit, Gersprenz, Hymne an die Erde,* etc.); piano pieces; numerous songs and ballads, a selection of which was publ. in 5 vols. He publ. *Resonanztonlehre* (1911).

Walmisley, Thomas Attwood, English organist, teacher, and composer, son of **Thomas Forbes Walmisley;** b. London, Jan. 21, 1814; d. Hastings, Jan. 17, 1856. He studied composition with his godfather, Thomas Attwood; at 16 he became organist at Croydon Parish Church; in 1833 he received the combined organistships of Trinity and St. John's Colleges, Cambridge, obtaining his Mus.B. from the former that same year. He matriculated at Corpus Christi College (1834); while still an undergraduate, he was appointed prof. of music in 1836; received the B.A. degree and became a full member of Trinity College in 1838; took his M.A. in 1841 and his Mus.D. in 1848. Walmisley distinguished himself as an organist and teacher; as a composer, he is best known for his Evening Service in D minor (c.1855). His other works include anthems, part-songs, solo songs, some orch. works, and several chamber music pieces. His father ed. *T.A. Walmisley: Cathedral Music, a Collection of Services and Anthems* (London, 1875).

BIBL.: J. Bumpus, "T.A. W.," *Musical News,* VI (1894; rev. in *A History of English Cathedral Music,* London, 1908); N. Temperley, "T.A. W.'s Secular Music," *Musical Times,* XCVII (1956).

Walmisley, Thomas Forbes, English organist, teacher, and composer, father of **Thomas Attwood Walmisley;** b. London, May 22, 1783; d. there, July 23, 1866. He was a chorister at Westminster Abbey; studied with John Spencer and Thomas Attwood; was active as a teacher of piano and singing (from 1803); was organist at the Female Orphan Asylum (1810–14) and at St. Martin-in-the-Fields (1814–54). He was a popular composer of glees; publ. 3 sets containing 6 glees each; also *A Collection of Glees, Trios, Rounds and Canons* (1826); several single glees and songs.

Walsh, John, English music seller, publisher, and instrument maker; b. c.1666; d. London, March 13, 1736. From about 1690 he had his business at the sign of the "Golden Harp and Hoboy" in the Strand in London; in 1692 he was appointed "musical instrument maker in ordinary to His Majesty." He developed a flourishing trade, and achieved great renown; in England he was unquestionably the foremost publisher of music in his time. In 1711 he publ. Handel's *Rinaldo,* and the firm became Handel's principal publisher. He was succeeded by his son about 1730, also named **John Walsh** (b. London, Dec. 23, 1709; d. there, Jan. 15, 1766), who maintained the firm's high standards; was also made instrument maker to the King in 1731.

BIBL.: F. Kidson, "Handel's Publisher, J. W., His Successors and Contemporaries," *Musical Quarterly,* VI (1920); W. Smith, "J. W., Music Publisher: The First Twenty-Five Years," *The Library,* 5th series, i/1 (1946); idem, *A Bibliography of the Musical Works published by J. W. during the Years 1695–1720* (London, 1948); J. Walsh, *A Catalogue of Music Published by J. W. and his Successors* (London, 1953); W. Smith and C.

Humphries, *A Bibliography of the Musical Works published by the Firm of J. W., 1721–1766* (London, 1968).

Walter, Arnold (Maria), Moravian-born Canadian composer; b. Hannsdorf, Aug. 30, 1902; d. Toronto, Oct. 6, 1973. He received a doctorate in law from the Univ. of Prague in 1926; then studied music in Berlin with H. Albert, J. Wolf, and Curt Sachs; emigrated to Canada in 1937 and taught at the Upper Canada College in Toronto until 1943; was director of the Toronto Cons. Senior School (1945–52) and director of the music faculty of the Univ. of Toronto (1952–68); among his numerous honors was the title of Officer of the Order of Canada (1972). He publ. *Music and the Common Understanding* (Saskatoon, 1966) and ed. *Aspects of Music in Canada* (Toronto, 1969). He turned to composition rather late in life; most of his music is Romantic in its sources of inspiration.

WORKS: Cello Sonatina (1940); Violin Sonata (1940); Piano Trio (1940); *Sacred Songs* for Soprano and String Trio (1941); Sym. in G minor (1942; Toronto, Feb. 1, 1944); *Toccata* for Piano (1947); *For the Fallen,* cantata (1949); Piano Sonata (1950); Concerto for Orch. (1958); *Legend* for Piano (1962); electronic pieces.

Walter, Bruno (full name, **Bruno Walter Schlesinger**), eminent German-born American conductor; b. Berlin, Sept. 15, 1876; d. Beverly Hills, Calif., Feb. 17, 1962. He entered the Stern Cons. in Berlin at age 8, where he studied with H. Ehrlich, L. Bussler, and R. Radecke. At age 9 he performed in public as a pianist but at 13 decided to pursue his interest in conducting. In 1893 he became a coach at the Cologne Opera, where he made his conducting debut with Lortzing's *Waffenschmied;* in the following year he was engaged as assistant conductor at the Hamburg Stadttheater, under Gustav Mahler; this contact was decisive in his career, and he became in subsequent years an ardent champion of Mahler's music; conducted the premieres of the posthumous Sym. No. 9 and *Das Lied von der Erde.* During the 1896–97 season, Walter was engaged as 2nd conductor at the Stadttheater in Breslau; then became principal conductor in Pressburg, and in 1898 at Riga, where he conducted for 2 seasons. In 1900 he received the important engagement of conductor at the Berlin Royal Opera under a 5-year contract; however, he left this post in 1901 when he received an offer from Mahler to become his assistant at the Vienna Court Opera. He established himself as an efficient opera conductor; also conducted in England (first appearance, March 3, 1909, with the Royal Phil. Society in London). He remained at the Vienna Court Opera after the death of Mahler; on Jan. 1, 1913, he became Royal Bavarian Generalmusikdirektor in Munich; under his guidance, the Munich Opera enjoyed brilliant performances, particularly of Mozart's works. Seeking greater freedom for his artistic activities, he left Munich in 1922, and gave numerous performances as a guest conductor with European orchs.; conducted the series "Bruno Walter Concerts" with the Berlin Phil. from 1921 to 1933; from 1925 he also conducted summer concerts of the Salzburg Festival; his performances of Mozart's music there set a standard. He also appeared as pianist in Mozart's chamber works. On Feb. 15, 1923, he made his American debut with the N.Y. Sym. Society, and appeared with it again in 1924 and 1925. From 1925 to 1929 he was conductor of the Städtische Oper in Berlin-Charlottenburg; in 1929 he succeeded Furtwängler as conductor of the Gewandhaus Orch. in Leipzig, but continued to give special concerts in Berlin. On Jan. 14, 1932, he was guest conductor of the N.Y. Phil., acting also as soloist in a Mozart piano concerto; was reengaged during the next 3 seasons as associate conductor with Toscanini. He was also a guest conductor in Philadelphia, Washington, D.C., and Baltimore. With the advent of the Nazi regime in Germany in 1933, his engagement with the Gewandhaus Orch. was canceled, and he was also prevented from continuing his orch. concerts in Berlin. He filled several engagements with the Concertgebouw in Amsterdam, and also conducted in Salzburg. In 1936 he was engaged as music director of the Vienna State Opera; this was terminated with the Nazi annexation of Austria in 1938. Walter, with his family, then went to France, where he was granted French citizenship. After the outbreak of World War II in 1939, he sailed for America, establishing his residence in California, and eventually became a naturalized American citizen. He was guest conductor with the NBC Sym. Orch. (1939); also conducted many performances of the Metropolitan Opera in N.Y. (debut in *Fidelio* on Feb. 14, 1941). From 1947 to 1949 he was conductor and musical adviser of the N.Y. Phil.; returned regularly as guest conductor until 1960; also conducted in Europe (1949–60), giving his farewell performance in Vienna with the Vienna Phil. in 1960.

Walter achieved the reputation of a perfect classicist among contemporary conductors; his interpretations of the masterpieces of the Vienna School were particularly notable. He is acknowledged to have been a foremost conductor of Mahler's syms. His own compositions include 2 syms.; *Siegesfahrt* for Solo Voices, Chorus, and Orch.; String Quartet; Piano Quintet; Piano Trio; several albums of songs. He publ. the books *Von den moralischen Kräften der Musik* (Vienna, 1935); *Gustav Mahler* (Vienna, 1936; 2nd ed., 1957; Eng. tr., 1927; 2nd ed., 1941); *Theme and Variations: An Autobiography* (N.Y., 1946; Ger. original, 1947); *Von der Musik und vom Musizieren* (Frankfurt am Main, 1957; Eng. tr., 1961); L. Walter-Lindt, ed., *Briefe 1894–1962* (Frankfurt am Main, 1970).

BIBL.: M. Komorn-Rebhan, *Was wir von B. W. lernten* (Vienna, 1913); P. Stefan, *B. W.* (Vienna, 1936); T. Mann, "To B. W. on His 70th Birthday," *Musical Quarterly* (Oct. 1946); B. Gavoty, *B. W.* (Geneva, 1956); H. Schonberg, *The Great Conductors* (N.Y., 1967).

Walter, David Edgar, American composer and bass-baritone; b. Boston, Feb. 2, 1953. He studied composition at the Juilliard School of Music in N.Y. with David Diamond, Otto Luening, and Vincent Persichetti (B.M. in composition, 1975); continued study with Edward Richer and Calvin Hampton (1976–78) and at Boston Univ. with David del Tredici, Joyce Mekeel, and John Thow (1978–81). He also studied voice at Rutgers Univ. with John Powell (1970–75) and at Trenton State College with Oren Brown, Lois Bove, and Shirley Meier (M.A., 1978); finally enrolled in the Boston Cons. and the New England Cons. of Music, where he took voice lessons with Janet Wheeler. In subsequent years he appeared as a bass-baritone at Trinity Church in Boston and Resurrection and Calvary Church in N.Y. He also wrote vocal music for church performances in which he himself took part as soloist. In his compositions he follows the ideal of unmitigated accessibility to the public and practical convenience for the performer.

WORKS: *Passion According to St. Mark* for 13 Soloists, Chorus, Flute, and Organ; *A Lavender Requiem* for Soprano, Chorus, Strings, and Timpani; *Scrooge, the Great Liberator*, ballet; *Scaramouche et Pulcinella*, ballet; *The Balcony*, opera for 3 Singers and Pianos; *Five Choral Preludes* for Organ; *The Book of the Hanging Fruit Flies* for Piano, 5-Fingers; *Antithesis of Kevin* for String Quartet; Harpsichord Sonata; Flute Octet; numerous organ pieces and choruses.

Walter, Fried, German composer; b. Ottendorf-Okrilla, near Dresden, Dec. 19, 1907. He studied in Dresden; filled various posts as opera coach and conductor in Germany; in 1949, became chief of the light music dept. at Berlin Radio.

WORKS: Operas: *Königin Elizabeth* (Stockholm, Nov. 24, 1939); *Andreas Wolfius* (Berlin, Dec. 19, 1940); *Dorfmusik* (Wiesbaden, Nov. 1, 1943); dance drama, *Kleopatra* (Prague, 1943); dance fairy tale, *Der Pfeil* (Berlin, Dec. 22, 1946); *Kleine Sinfonie* (1942); numerous dramatic ballads; chamber music; songs.

Walter, Georg A., German tenor, pedagogue, and composer; b. Hoboken, N.J. (of German parents), Nov. 13, 1875; d. Berlin, Sept. 13, 1952. He studied singing in Milan, Dresden, Berlin, and London; composition with Wilhelm Berger in Berlin; made a career as a singer, particularly distinguishing himself in the works of Bach and Handel. He was a prof. at the Stuttgart Hochschule für Musik (1925–34); then settled in Berlin as a

vocal teacher; his most celebrated student was Dietrich Fischer-Dieskau. He brought out new eds. of works by the sons of Bach, Schütz, et al.

Walter (also, **Walther** or **Walderth**), **(Johann) Ignaz (Joseph),** German tenor and composer; b. Radonitz, Bohemia, Aug. 31, 1755; d. Regensburg, Feb. 22, 1822. After training from the organist Ignaz Neudörfl, he entered the Univ. of Vienna in 1773; also received instruction in singing and composition from Starzer. He sang at Vienna's Nationaltheater (1780–82); was in Prague (1782–84) and in Riga (1784–86), where he married the soprano Juliane Browne Roberts (1759–1835); they appeared at the combined Frankfurt and Mainz theaters (from 1786), serving as court singers (from 1789); they also appeared with Grossmann's company in Hannover and Bremen in 1792, where Walter was named opera director; in 1804 he became director of the new Regensburg theater. He composed some 20 singspiels, ballet music, incidental music to plays, orch. works, chamber music, 4 cantatas, and some arias.

Walter or **Walther** (real name, **Blanckenmüller**), **Johann(es),** German composer and poet; b. Kahla, Thuringia, 1496; d. Torgau, March 25, 1570. He was adopted by a townsman in Kahla and pursued his career under the name Johann Walter; studied at the Univ. of Leipzig from 1521 to 1525; during this time he entered the chapel of the Elector Friedrich the Wise of Saxony as a bass (the Elector divided his residence between Altenburg, Torgau, and Weimar). In 1524, at Wittenberg, he publ. the *Geystliches gesangk Buchleyn* for 3 to 5 Voices, the first Protestant singing book. In 1525 he was summoned to Wittenburg by Luther to assist in the composition and regulation of the German Mass. Shortly after the death of the Elector Friedrich (1525), his chapel was disbanded, and Walter became cantor of the Municipal Latin-School in Torgau and director of the Stadtkantorei (community choir) there (1526–48). In 1548 he was called upon by the new Elector of Saxony, Moritz, to organize the court chapel in Dresden, and remained there as Kapellmeister until 1554, when he retired to Torgau on a pension.

WORKS: *Cantio septem vocum in laudem Dei omnipotentis et Evangelii ejus* (Wittenberg, 1544); *Ein schöner geistlicher und Christlicher Berckreyen. . .Herzlich tut mich erfrewen* (Wittenberg, 1552); *Magnificat octo tonorum* for 4 to 6 Voices (Jena, 1557); *Ein newes Christliches Lied* for 4 Voices (Wittenberg, 1561); *Das Christlich Kinderlied D. Martini Lutheri Erhalt uns Herr* for 6 Voices (Wittenberg, 1566); various other works, including Magnificat settings, passion music, motets, and fugues. See O. Schröder, ed., *Johann Walter: Sämtliche Werke* (6 vols., Kassel, 1953–73).

WRITINGS: *Lob und Preis der löblichen Kunst Musica* (Wittenberg, 1538; ed. by W. Gurlitt, Kassel, 1938); *Lob und Preis der himmlischen Kunst Musica* (Wittenberg, 1564).

BIBL.: H. Holstein, "Der Lieder- und Tondichter Johann Walther," *Archiv für Literaturgeschichte*, XII (1884); A. Aber, *Die Pflege der Musik unter den Wettinern und wettinischen Ernestinern* (Bückeburg and Leipzig, 1921); W. Gurlitt, "Johannes Walter und die Musik der Reformationszeit," *Luther-Jahrbuch*, XV (1933); O. Michaelis, *Johann Walter (1496–1570), der Musiker-Dichter in Luthers Gefolgschaft* (Leipzig and Hamburg, 1939); C. Gerhardt, *Die Torgauer Walter-Handschriften; Eine Studie zur Quellenkunde der Musikgeschichte der deutschen Reformationszeit* (Kassel, 1949); J. Stalmann, *Johann Walters Cantiones latinae* (diss., Univ. of Tübingen, 1960).

Walter, Karl, German organist, campanologist, and composer; b. Cransberg, Oct. 27, 1862; d. Montabaur, Dec. 4, 1929. He studied at the Montabaur Seminary, where he became an instructor in 1893; in 1899, was appointed diocesan inspector for the building of organs and bells; in 1903, became an instructor of church music at the Limburg Seminary. He wrote organ music and sacred works; publ. several manuals on organ building, and on the construction of bells, a field in which he was an authority. His publications are *Kleine Orgelbaulehre* (1904); *Orgelbegleitung zu den Melodien des Gesangbuchs für das Bis-*

tum Limburg (1907; 2nd ed., 1911); *Glockenkunde* (1913); *Kleine Glockenkunde* (1916).

Walter, Thomas, American clergyman and tunebook compiler; b. Roxbury, Mass., Dec. 13, 1696; d. there, Jan. 10, 1725. He was the son of a clergyman, and a nephew of Cotton Mather; was educated at Harvard College (M.A., 1713); on Oct. 29, 1718, he was ordained at the First Church of Roxbury; was assistant pastor to his father at Roxbury. With the aim of correcting what he described as "an horrid medley of confused and disorderly sounds" prevailing in the singing in New England churches, he publ. *The Grounds and Rules of Musick Explained; or, an Introduction to the Art of Singing by Note; Fitted to the Meanest Capacities* (Boston, 1721; 8 eds. up to 1764). It was the 2nd singing book to be publ. in America, following that of John Tufts. He also publ. *The Sweet Psalmist of Israel* (1722).

BIBL.: F. Metcalf, *American Writers and Compilers of Sacred Music* (N.Y., 1925); E. Pierce, "The Rise and Fall of the 'Fugue-Tune' in America," *Musical Quarterly* (April 1930); M. Jones, "Bibliographical Notes on T. W.'s 'Grounds and Rules of Musick Explained,'" *Proceedings of the American Antiquarian Society* (Oct. 1932; also reprinted separately, Worcester, Mass., 1933); C. Shipton, "T. W.," *Sibley's Harvard Graduates,* VI (Boston, 1942).

Waltershausen, H(ermann) W(olfgang Sartorius), Freiherr von, German composer, writer on music, and teacher; b. Göttingen, Oct. 12, 1882; d. Munich, Aug. 13, 1954. He began his music studies with M.J. Erb in Strasbourg; although he lost his right arm and leg in an accident when he was 10, he learned to play the piano and conduct with his left hand. He settled in Munich in 1901, where he studied composition with Thuille and piano with Schmid-Lindner; also studied music history with Sandberger at the Univ. of Munich. In 1917 he established there a seminar for operatic dramaturgy, the Praktisches Seminar für Fortgeschrittene Musikstudierende; was a prof. and assistant director of the Munich Akademie der Tonkunst (1920–22), then director (1922–33); later founded his own Seminar für Privatmusiklehrer, which became the Waltershausen-Seminar in 1948. In his music he adopted a neo-Romantic style, rather advanced in harmonic treatment. **WORKS:** Operas: *Else Klapperzehen* (Dresden, May 15, 1909); *Oberst Chabert* (Frankfurt, Jan. 18, 1912); *Richardis,* dramatic mystery (Karlsruhe, Nov. 14, 1915); *Die Rauensteiner Hochzeit* (Karlsruhe, 1919); *Die Gräfin von Tolosa* (1934; Bavarian Radio, Munich, 1958); *Apokalyptische Symphonie* (1924); symphonic poem, *Hero und Leander* (1925); *Krippenmusik* for Chamber Orch. and Harpsichord Obbligato (1926); *Orchesterpartita über 3 Kirchenlieder* (1928); String Quartet (1910); songs; piano pieces, including studies and transcriptions for left hand alone. **WRITINGS:** *Der Freischütz: Ein Versuch über die musikalische Romantik* (Munich, 1920); *Richard Strauss: Ein Versuch* (Munich, 1921); *Musik, Dramaturgie, Erziehung* (collected essays; Munich, 1926); *Dirigentenerziehung* (Leipzig, 1929); *Die Kunst des Dirigierens* (Berlin, 1942; 2nd ed., 1954). **BIBL.:** K.-R. Danler and R. Mader, *H.W. v.W.* (Tutzing, 1984).

Walther, Johann Gottfried, eminent German organist, music scholar, pedagogue, and composer; b. Erfurt, Sept. 18, 1684; d. Weimar, March 23, 1748. He studied organ in Erfurt with Johann Bernhard Bach and Johann Andreas Kretschmar; became organist of the Thomaskirche there in 1702 and concurrently studied philosophy and law briefly at the Univ. of Erfurt. He studied composition with Johann Heinrich Buttstett; after travel in Germany, he continued his studies with Wilhelm Hieronymus Pachelbel in Nuremberg (1706), then became organist of the church of St. Peter and St. Paul in Weimar (1707), a post he held for the rest of his life; also served as music master at the ducal court and was made Hofmusicus of the ducal Court Orch. in 1721. Walther assembled a valuable library of music and books on music, which prompted him to pursue diligent musical research. This culminated in his great *Musicalisches Lexicon* (1732), the 1st music dictionary to encompass biographies of musicians of the past and present, musical terms, and bibliographies. He also left in MS the important treatise *Praecepta der musicalischen Composition* (1708), which was not publ. until the 20th century. He composed much sacred vocal music, but only one work, *Kyrie, Christe, Kyrie eleison über Wo Gott zum Haus nicht giebt sein Gunst,* has survived. However, over 100 chorale preludes for organ are extant. These place him next to J.S. Bach—his distant relation and lifelong friend—as a master of the genre. He also prepared valuable MS copies of works by other composers, many of which remain the only known sources. For his organ music, see M. Seiffert, ed., *J.G. Walther: Gesammelte Werke für Orgel,* in Denkmäler Deutscher Tonkunst, XXVI–XXVII (1906; this ed. includes some works now known not to be by Walther); other works for keyboard are also extant.

WRITINGS: *Praecepta der musicalischen Composition* (1708; ed. by P. Benary, Leipzig, 1960); *Alte und neue musicalische Bibliothek* (Weimar and Erfurt, 1728; only entries under A publ. as a preliminary to the following); *Musicalisches Lexicon, oder Musicalische Bibliothec* (Leipzig, 1732; facsimile, with bibliographical notes, ed. by R. Schaal, Kassel, 1953). **BIBL.:** H. Gehrmann, "J.G. W. als Theoretiker," *Vierteljahrsschrift für Musikwissenschaft,* VII (1891); H. Egel, *J.G. W.s Leben und Werke* (diss., Univ. of Leipzig, 1904); O. Brodde, *J.G. W.: Leben und Werk* (Kassel, 1937); H. Eggebrecht, "W.s Musikalisches Lexikon in seinen terminologischen Partien," *Acta Musicologica,* XXIX (1957); G. Barber, "J.G. W. (1684–1748): A Tercentenary Tribute," *Musical Times* (Dec. 1984); K. Beckmann and H.-J. Schulze, eds., *J.G. W.: Briefe* (Leipzig, 1987).

Walther, Johann Jakob, noted German violinist and composer; b. Witterda, near Erfurt, c.1650; d. Mainz, Nov. 2, 1717. After a period in Florence (c.1670–73), he returned to Germany to accept the appointment of primo violinista da camera at the Electoral Court of Saxony in Dresden (from Jan. 1, 1674); remained there until at least 1681, when he became clerk and Italian secretary in charge of the correspondence with Rome at the Electoral Court in Mainz; was designated a Doctor in 1693. **WORKS:** *Scherzi da violino solo con il basso continuo per l'organo o cembalo accompagnabile anche con una viola o leuto* (Frankfurt and Leipzig, 1676; 2nd ed., 1687; reprinted in Das Erbe Deutscher Musik, 1st series, XVII, 1941); *Hortulus chelicus uni violino duabus, tribus et quatuor subinde chordis simul sonantibus harmonice modulanti* (Mainz, 1688; 2nd ed., 1694, as *Wohlgepflanzter Violinischer Lustgarten;* 3 works ed. in the Saslav diss. listed below). **BIBL.:** G. Beckmann, *Das Violinspiel in Deutschland* (Berlin and Leipzig, 1918–21); A. Moser, *Geschichte des Violinspiels* (Berlin, 1923; 2nd ed., rev., 1966–67); F. Gothel, "J.J. W.," *Das Musikleben,* III (1950); W. Newman, *The Sonata in the Baroque Era* (Chapel Hill, N.C., 1959; 4th ed., rev., 1983); D. Boyden, *The History of Violin Playing from Its Origins to 1761* (London, 1965); I. Saslav, *Three Works from J.J. W.'s "Hortulus chelicus"* (diss., Indiana Univ., 1969); B. Schwarz, *Great Masters of the Violin* (N.Y., 1983).

Walther von der Vogelweide. See **Vogelweide, Walther von der.**

Walthew, Richard Henry, English composer, conductor, and pedagogue; b. London, Nov. 4, 1872; d. East Preston, Sussex, Nov. 14, 1951. He studied with Parry at the Royal College of Music (1890–94); after a directorship of the Passmore Edwards Settlement Place (1900–1904), he was appointed instructor of the opera class at the Guildhall School of Music; in 1907 became a prof. of music at Queen's College; also conducted provincial orchs. His works include 2 operettas: *The Enchanted Island* (London, May 8, 1900) and *The Gardeners* (London, Feb. 12, 1906); cantatas: *Ode to a Nightingale* and *The Pied Piper of Hamelin;* Piano Concerto; Piano Quintet; Piano Quartet; 2 piano trios; Violin Sonata; vocal quartets, with piano;

songs. He was the author of *The Development of Chamber Music* (1909).

Bibl.: K. Leech, "R.H. W.," *Musical Opinion* (Jan. 1952).

Walton, Sir William (Turner), eminent English composer; b. Oldham, Lancashire, March 29, 1902; d. Ischia, Italy, March 8, 1983. Both his parents were professional singers, and Walton himself had a fine singing voice as a youth; he entered the Cathedral Choir School at Christ Church, Oxford, and began to compose choral pieces for performance. Sir Hugh Allen, organist of New College, advised him to develop his interest in composition, and sponsored his admission to Christ Church at an early age; however, he never graduated, and instead began to write unconventional music in the manner that was fashionable in the 1920s. His talent manifested itself in a string quartet he wrote at the age of 17, which was accepted for performance for the 1st festival of the ISCM in 1923. In London he formed a congenial association with the Sitwell family of quintessential cognoscenti and literati who combined a patrician sense of artistic superiority with a benign attitude toward the social plebs; they also provided Walton with residence at their manor in Chelsea, where he lived off and on for some 15 years. Fascinated by Edith Sitwell's oxymoronic verse, Walton set it to music bristling with novel jazzy effects in brisk, irregular rhythms and modern harmonies; Walton was only 19 when he wrote it. Under the title *Façade*, it was first performed in London in 1923, with Edith Sitwell herself delivering her doggerel with a megaphone; as expected, the show provoked an outburst of feigned indignation in the press and undisguised delight among the young in spirit. But Walton did not pursue the path of facile hedonism so fashionable at the time; he soon demonstrated his ability to write music in a Classical manner in his fetching concert overture *Portsmouth Point*, first performed in Zürich in 1926, and later in the comedy-overture *Scapino*. His biblical oratorio *Belshazzar's Feast*, written in 1931, reveals a deep emotional stream and nobility of design that places Walton directly in line from Handel and Elgar among English masters. His symphonic works show him as an inheritor of the grand Romantic tradition; his concertos for violin, for viola, and for cello demonstrate an adroitness in effective instrumental writing. Walton was a modernist in his acceptance of the new musical resources, but he never deviated from fundamental tonality and formal clarity of design. Above all, his music was profoundly national, unmistakably British in its inspiration and content. Quite appropriately, he was asked to contribute to two royal occasions: he wrote *Crown Imperial March* for the coronation of King George VI in 1937 and *Orb and Sceptre* for that of Queen Elizabeth II in 1953. He received an honorary doctorate from Oxford Univ. in 1942; was knighted in 1951. He spent the last years of his life on the island of Ischia off Naples with his Argentine-born wife, Susana Gil Passo.

Works: stage: Opera, *Troilus and Cressida,* after Chaucer (London, Dec. 3, 1954); *The Bear,* "an extravaganza" in one act, after a comedy by Chekhov (Aldeburgh Festival, June 3, 1967); *Façade,* "an entertainment" for Declamation, Flute, Clarinet, Saxophone, Trumpet, Cello, and Percussion, to texts in blank verse by Edith Sitwell (first perf. privately at the Sitwell home in London, Jan. 24, 1922; 1st public perf., London, June 12, 1923; rev. 1942); *The Wise Virgins,* ballet arr. from 6 pieces by Bach (London, April 24, 1940); *The Quest,* ballet (1943).

orch.: *Portsmouth Point,* concert overture (Zürich, June 22, 1926); *Siesta* (1926); *Sinfonia concertante* for Piano and Orch. (London, Jan. 5, 1928); Viola Concerto (London, Oct. 3, 1929, Paul Hindemith, soloist; rev. version, London, Jan. 18, 1962); Sym. No. 1 (London, Nov. 6, 1935); *Crown Imperial,* coronation march for King George VI (Westminster Abbey, London, May 12, 1937); 2 orch. suites from *Façade*: No. 1 (Siena, Sept. 14, 1928) and No. 2 (N.Y., March 30, 1938); Violin Concerto (Cleveland, Dec. 7, 1939; Jascha Heifetz, soloist); *Scapino,* comedy-overture (Chicago, April 3, 1941); *Spitfire: Prelude and Fugue,* glorifying the famous British combat

plane (1942); *Orb and Sceptre,* coronation march for Elizabeth II (Westminster Abbey, London, June 2, 1953); *Johannesburg Festival Overture* (Johannesburg, Sept. 25, 1956); Cello Concerto (Boston, Jan. 25, 1957; Piatigorsky, soloist); *Partita* (Cleveland, Jan. 30, 1958); *Fanfare* for the Queen's entrance at the NATO Parliamentary Conference (London, June 5, 1959); Sym. No. 2 (Edinburgh, Sept. 2, 1960); *Variations on a Theme by Hindemith* (London, March 8, 1963); *Capriccio Burlesco* (N.Y., Dec. 7, 1968); *Improvisations on an Impromptu of Britten* (San Francisco, Jan. 14, 1970); Sonata for String Orch. (1972; orch. of the 1947 String Quartet); *Varii Capricci* (London, May 4, 1976; orchestration of the 5 *Bagatelles* for Guitar); *Prologo e Fantasia* (London, Feb. 20, 1982).

vocal: *Belshazzar's Feast,* oratorio for Baritone, Chorus, and Orch. (Leeds Festival, Oct. 8, 1931); *In Honour of the City of London* for Chorus and Orch. (Leeds Festival, 1937); *Te Deum* for the coronation of Queen Elizabeth II (London, June 2, 1953); *Gloria* for Soloists, Mixed Chorus, and Orch. (Liverpool, Nov. 24, 1961); *A Song for the Lord Mayor's Table* for Soprano and Piano (London, July 18, 1962); *The Twelve* for Chorus and Organ (Oxford, May 16, 1965); *Missa Brevis* for Double Mixed Chorus and Organ (Coventry, April 10, 1966); *Cantico del Sole* for Chorus a cappella (1974).

chamber: Piano Quartet (1918; rev. 1974); String Quartet (1922; London, July 5, 1923); *Toccata* for Violin and Piano (1923); String Quartet (1947); Violin Sonata (1949); 5 *Bagatelles* for Guitar (1972).

film music: *Escape Me Never* (1934); *As You Like It* (1936); *Stolen Life* (1939); *Major Barbara* (1941); *Henry V* (1944); *Hamlet* (1947); *Richard III* (1954); etc.; several suites have been drawn from these scores.

Bibl.: H. Foss, "W. W.," *Musical Quarterly* (Oct. 1940); F. Howes, *The Music of W. W.* (2 vols.; London, 1942 and 1943; new amplified ed., 1965); E. Evans, "W. W.," *Musical Times* (1944); K. Avery, "W. W.," *Music & Letters* (Jan. 1947); S. Craggs, *W. W.: A Thematic Catalogue of His Musical Works* (London, 1977); A. Poulton, *Sir W. W.: A Discography* (London, 1980); B. Northcott, "In Search of W.," *Musical Times* (March 1982); N. Tierney, *W. W.: His Life and Music* (London, 1984); S. Walton, *W. W.: Behind the Facade* (Oxford, 1988).

Waltz, Gustavus, German bass; place and date of birth unknown; d. London, c.1759. His 1st recorded appearance was at the Little Haymarket Theatre in London in Lampe's *Amelia* (March 13, 1732); he then sang in the pirated ed. of Handel's *Acis and Galatea* there (May 17, 1732); subsequently appeared in various London theaters. After accompanying Handel to Oxford in 1733, where he appeared in several of his works, he returned to London as a member of Handel's company until 1736; created the roles of Minos in *Arianna in Creta* (Jan. 26, 1734), Mars in *Il Parnasso in festa* (April 13, 1734), the King of Scotland in *Ariodante* (Jan. 8, 1735), Melisso in *Alcina* (April 16, 1736), and Nicandro in *Atalanta* (May 12, 1736); also sang in various oratorio performances. He was subsequently active as a singer in light English theater pieces; however, he continued to make some concert appearances; sang in performances of Handel's *Messiah* at the Foundling Hospital (1754, 1758, 1759). He is mentioned in the reported acrid comment of Handel on Gluck: "He knows no more of counterpoint than my cook, Waltz."

Bibl.: W. Smith, "G. W.: Was He Handel's Cook?," in *Concerning Handel* (London, 1948).

Walzel, Leopold Matthias, Austrian composer; b. Vienna, Nov. 29, 1902; d. there, June 9, 1970. A lawyer by profession, he also studied music at the Univ. of Vienna; composed 5 syms.; an opera, *Salamis;* Piano Quartet; Octet; 2 quintets; several song cycles.

Wambach, Emile, Belgian composer; b. Arlon, Luxembourg, Nov. 26, 1854; d. Antwerp, May 6, 1924. He studied with Benoit, Mertens, and Callaerts at the Antwerp Cons.; in 1913, became its director. He wrote music in the National Flemish style, following the model of Benoit. He wrote the Flemish opera *Nathans Parabel;* 4 oratorios: *Mozes op den Nijl* (1881);

Yolande (1884); *Blancefloer* (1889); *Jeanne d'Arc* (1909); choral works; piano pieces; songs.

BIBL.: L. Vocht, "Levensbericht over E. W.," *Annuaire of the Académie Royale de Belgique,* 118 (1952; with a list of works).

Wand, Günter, distinguished German conductor; b. Elberfeld, Jan. 7, 1912. He studied in Wuppertal; attended the Univ. of Cologne and took courses in composition with Philipp Jarnach and in piano with Paul Baumgartner at the Cologne Cons. and Hochschule für Musik; received instruction in conducting from Franz von Hoesslin at the Munich Academy of Music. After working as a répétiteur and conductor in Wuppertal and other provincial music centers, he became chief conductor in Detmold. He was conductor at the Cologne Opera (1939–44), then of the Salzburg Mozarteum Orch. (1944–45). In 1946 he was appointed Generalmusikdirektor of Cologne, being responsible for both orch. and operatic performances; in 1947 he was named conductor of the Gürzenich Orch. there, a post he retained until 1974; also was prof. of conducting at the Cologne Hochschule für Musik (from 1948). He appeared as a guest conductor throughout Europe and also in Japan. After leaving Cologne, he conducted in Bern. He subsequently served as chief conductor of the North German Radio Sym. Orch. in Hamburg (1982–91); also was a principal guest conductor of the BBC Sym. Orch. in London and later of the (West) Berlin Radio Sym. Orch. (1989–90). On Jan. 19, 1989, he made his belated U.S. debut at the age of 77 as a guest conductor with the Chicago Sym. Orch. A conductor in the revered Austro-German tradition, he acquired a fine reputation as an interpreter of Mozart, Beethoven, Brahms, and most especially Bruckner; also did much to foster contemporary music.

BIBL.: F. Berger, *G. W.: Gürzenichkapellmeister 1947–1974* (Cologne, 1974).

Wangemann, Otto, German organist, teacher, and composer; b. Loitz-on-the-Peene, Jan. 9, 1848; d. Berlin, Feb. 25, 1914. He studied with F. Kiel in Berlin; in 1886 settled there as a church organist and singing teacher. He publ. *Grundriss der Musik-Geschichte* (1878); *Geschichte der Orgel* (1897; 3rd ed., 1887); *Geschichte des Oratoriums* (1880); also singing manuals for schools; *Weihnachtsmusik* for Solo Voices, Chorus, and Orch.; school songs; piano pieces.

Wangenheim, Volker, German conductor; b. Berlin, July 1, 1928. He studied piano, oboe, violin, composition, and conducting at the Hochschule für Musik in Berlin; later played oboe with several Berlin ensembles. He was founder-principal conductor of the Berlin Mozart Orch. (1950–59); also conducted at the Mecklenburg State Theater in Schwerin (1951–52) and with the Berlin Academic Orch. (1954–57). He was music director (1957–63) and then Generalmusikdirektor (1963–78) in Bonn, where he served as principal conductor of the Beethovenhalle Orch., the Phil. Choir, and the Bonn Beethoven Festivals; also was co-founder and artistic director of the German National Youth Orch. (1969–84). He appeared as a guest conductor in Germany and abroad from 1954. In 1972 he became a prof. at the Cologne Hochschule für Musik.

WORKS: *Sinfonietta concertante* (1963); *Concerto for Strings* (1964); *Sinfonia notturna* (1965); *Klangspiel I* for Strings (1971) and *II* for Chamber Ensemble (1973); *Psalm 123* for Choir (1973); *Nicodemus Iesum nocte visitat: Canticum secundum Ioannem* for Choir (1980); various folksongs for choir.

Wangermée, Robert, distinguished Belgian musicologist; b. Lodelinsart, Sept. 21, 1920. He received training in music from J. Absil; pursued musicological studies at the Free Univ. of Brussels (Ph.D., 1946, with the diss. *Le Goût musical en France au XIXᵉ siècle*); then was on its faculty as a lecturer (1948–62), reader (1962–65), and prof. (from 1975); also was active with the Belgian Radio and Television (from 1946), serving as its director of music (1953–60) and as director-general of its French-language broadcasts (1960–84).

WRITINGS (all publ. in Brussels): *Jean-Sébastien Bach* (1944); *Ludwig van Beethoven* (1945); *Les Maîtres de chant des XVIIᵉ et XVIIIᵉ siècles à la collégiale des SS. Michel et Gudale, à Bruxelles* (1950); *François-Joseph Fétis, musicologue et compositeur* (1951); *La Musique belge contemporaine* (1959); *La Musique flamande dans la société des XVᵉ et XVIᵉ siècles* (1965; Eng. tr., 1965); *La Musique en Wallonie et à Bruxelles* (2 vols., 1980–82).

BIBL.: H. Vanhulst and M. Haine, eds., *Musique et Société: Hommages à R. W.* (Brussels, 1988).

Wanless, John, English organist and composer; place and date of birth unknown; d. York (buried), Feb. 2, 1712. He was organist at the Lincoln Cathedral between 1616 and 1625; only a few of his church works are extant, among them an anthem, *Plead thou my cause.* His son, **Thomas Wanless** (d. 1721), was organist of York Minster from 1691 to 1695. He publ. a psalter, *The Metre Psalm-tunes,* in 4 parts (London, 1702); composed *York Litany.*

Wannenmacher (Latinized as **Vannius**), **Johannes,** important German composer; b. probably in Neuenburg am Rhein, c.1485; d. Bern, 1551. He was choirmaster at the Vincentius-Stift in Bern (1510–13); went to Fribourg as choirmaster at St. Nikolaus in 1513; there he became choirmaster at the new college foundation in 1515; later was removed from his post, arrested, tried, and finally exiled. He served as magistrate's clerk in Interlaken from 1531. He was one of the leading composers in Switzerland in his era. His extant works number 26, including both sacred and secular vocal pieces. Several of his works appeared in contemporary collections.

BIBL.: W. Schuh, "J. W., Musiker und Landschreiber," *Schweizerische Musikzeitung/Revue Musicale Suisse,* LXXI (1930); A. Geering, *Die Vokalmusik in der Schweiz zur Zeit der Reformation: Leben und Werke von Bartholomäus Frank, J. W., Cosmas Alder* (Aarau, 1933).

Ward, David, Scottish bass; b. Dumbarton, July 3, 1922; d. Dunedin, July 16, 1983. He studied with Clive Carey at the Royal College of Music in London; later had voice training with Hans Hotter in Munich. In 1953 he made his operatic debut at the Sadler's Wells Opera in London; in 1960 he joined the Royal Opera, Covent Garden. He was equally proficient in dramatic, heroic, and buffo roles. In 1972 he was made a Commander of the Order of the British Empire.

Ward, John, English composer; b. Canterbury (baptized), Sept. 8, 1571; d. before Aug. 31, 1638. He settled in London and entered the employ of the office of the Remembrancer of the Exchequer, where he eventually attained the rank of Attorney; also served as household musician to Sir Henry Fanshawe and his family. He dedicated *The First Set of [25] English Madrigals to 3, 4, 5 and 6 Parts apt both for Viols and Voyces, with a Mourning Song in Memory of Prince Henry* (London, 1613; ed. in The English Madrigalists, XIX, 2nd ed., 1968) to Fanshawe. His other works include 2 sacred services, 22 verse anthems (ed. in Early English Church Music, XI, 1970), and various instrumental pieces, including 42 fantasias for viols.

BIBL.: E. Fellowes, *The English Madrigal Composers* (Oxford, 1921; 2nd ed., 1948); M. Strover, *The Fantasias and In Nomines of J. W.* (diss., Oxford Univ., 1957); M. Forster, *The Sacred Music of J. W.* (diss., Univ. of Durham, 1971).

Ward, John M(ilton), American musicologist; b. Oakland, Calif., July 6, 1917. He studied at San Francisco State College (B.A., 1941), the Univ. of Washington (M.M., 1942), with Milhaud (composition, 1943–44), and at N.Y. Univ. (Ph.D., 1953, with the diss. *The Vihuela de Mano and Its Music (1536–1576)*; taught at Michigan State Univ. (1947–53), the Univ. of Illinois (1953–55), and at Harvard Univ. (1955–85). He ed. *The Dublin Virginal Manuscript,* Wellesley Edition, III (1954; 2nd ed., rev. and aug., 1964; new ed., 1983); also contributed numerous essays and specialized articles to various scholarly music magazines.

BIBL.: A. Shapiro, ed., *Music and Context: Essays for J.M. W.* (1985).

Ward, Robert (Eugene), American composer and teacher; b. Cleveland, Sept. 13, 1917. He studied with Rogers, Royce,

and Hanson at the Eastman School of Music in Rochester, N.Y. (B.Mus., 1939) and with Jacobi at the Juilliard Graduate School in N.Y. (certificate, 1946); also studied conducting with Stoessel and Schenkman and received some training in composition from Copland. He taught at Columbia Univ. (1946–48) and at the Juilliard School of Music (1946–56); also was music director of the 3rd Street Music Settlement (1952–55); then was vice-president and managing ed. of the Galaxy Music Corp. (1956–67). After serving as president of the North Carolina School of the Arts in Winston-Salem (1967–74), where he continued as a teacher of composition until 1979, he held the chair of Mary Duke Biddle Prof. of Music at Duke Univ. (from 1979). In 1950, 1952, and 1966 he held Guggenheim fellowships; in 1962 he won the Pulitzer Prize in Music and the N.Y. Music Critics' Circle Award for his opera *The Crucible*. In 1972 he was elected a member of the National Inst. of Arts and Letters. He evolved an effective idiom, modern but not aggressively so; composed a number of dramatic and compact stage works on American subjects. **WORKS: OPERAS:** *He Who Gets Slapped* (1955; N.Y., May 17, 1956; rev. 1973); *The Crucible* (N.Y., Oct. 26, 1961); *The Lady from Colorado* (Central City, Colo., July 3, 1961); *Claudia Legare* (1973; Minneapolis, April 14, 1978); *Minutes till Midnight* (1978–82; Miami, June 4, 1982); *Abelard and Heloise* (1981). **ORCH.:** *Slow Music* (1938); *Ode* (1939); 5 syms.: No. 1 (N.Y., May 10, 1941); No. 2 (1947; Washington, D.C., Jan. 25, 1948); No. 3 (Washington, D.C., March 31, 1950); No. 4 (1958); No. 5, *Canticles of America*, for Soprano, Baritone, Narrator, Chorus, and Orch., after Whitman and Longfellow (1976); *Jubilation Overture* (Los Angeles, Nov. 21, 1946); *Concert Piece* (1947–48); *Concert Music* (1948); *Night Music* for Small Orch. (1949); *Jonathan and the Gingery Snare* for Narrator, Small Orch., and Percussion (N.Y., Feb. 4, 1950); *Fantasia* for Brass Choir and Timpani (1953); *Euphony* (1954); *Divertimento* (1960); *Night Fantasy* for Band (1962); *Invocation and Toccata* (1963); *Antiphony for Winds* for Woodwinds and Percussion (1968); Piano Concerto (1968); *Sonic Structure* (1981); *Dialogues* for Violin, Cello, and Orch. (1983; arr. for Piano Trio, 1984); Saxophone Concerto (1984); several chamber music pieces, including a Violin Sonata (1950), String Quartet No. 1 (1966), *Raleigh Divertimento* for Wind Quintet (1986), and piano pieces. **VOCAL:** *Fatal Interview* for Soprano and Orch. (1937); *Sacred Songs for Pantheists* for Soprano and Orch. (1951); *Earth Shall Be Fair*, cantata for Soprano, Chorus, Children's Chorus, Organ, and Orch. (1960); *Let the Word Go Forth* for Chorus and Instruments (1965); *Sweet Freedom Songs*, cantata for Bass, Narrator, Chorus, and Orch. (1965); songs.
BIBL.: S. Fleming, "R. W.," *High Fidelity/Musical America*, XXXII/5 (1982); K. Kreitner, *R. W.: A Bio-Bibliography* (Westport, Conn., 1988).

Ward, Samuel Augustus, American composer and dealer in musical instruments; b. Newark, N.J., Dec. 28, 1848; d. there, Sept. 28, 1903. He was the author of the famous hymn *Materna*, first publ. in the *Parish Choir* (Boston, 1888) to the words of "O Mother dear, Jerusalem." Eventually, his hymn tune was combined with the words of the poem *America, the Beautiful*, written by Katherine Lee Bates in 1893, and became one of the most widely sung patriotic American anthems.

Ward-Steinman, David, American composer, teacher, and pianist; b. Alexandria, La., Nov. 6, 1936. He studied at Florida State Univ. (B.Mus., 1957); also received training from Riegger (1954), Milhaud at the Aspen (Colo.) Music School (1956), and Babbitt and Copland at the Berkshire Music Center, Tanglewood (1957); after further studies at the Univ. of Illinois (M.M., 1958), he pursued private training with Boulanger in Paris (1958–59); then returned to the Univ. of Illinois to complete his education (D.M.A., 1961). In 1961 he became a faculty member and composer-in-residence at San Diego State Univ., where he served as prof. of music (from 1968); also was the Ford Foundation composer-in-residence of the Tampa Bay area in Florida (1970–72) and the Fulbright Senior Scholar at Victo-

rian College of the Arts and La Trobe Univ. in Melbourne, Australia (1989–90). With S. Ward-Steinman, he publ. *Comparative Anthology of Musical Forms* (2 vols., Belmont, Calif., 1976); also publ. *Toward a Comparative Structural Theory of the Arts* (San Diego, 1989).
WORKS: BALLETS: *Wester Orpheus* (1964); *These 3* (1966). **STAGE:** *Rituals* for Dancers and Musicians (1971); *Tamar*, multimedia music drama (1970–77). **ORCH.:** *Concert Overture* (1957); Sym. (1959); Concerto Grosso for Combo and Chamber Orch. (1960); Concerto No. 2 for Chamber Orch. (1962); *Prelude and Toccata* (1962); Cello Concerto (1966); *Antares* for Synthesizer or Tape, Gospel Choir ad libitum, and Orch. (1971); *Arcturus* for Synthesizer and Orch. (1972); *Bishop's Gambit* (1979); *Moiré* for Piano and Chamber Ensemble (1983); *Olympics Overture* (1984); *Chroma*, concerto for Multiple Keyboards, Percussion, and Chamber Orch. (1985); *Elegy for Astronauts* (1986); *Winging It* for Chamber Orch. (1986). **BAND OR WINDS:** *Jazz Tangents* for Band (1967); *Rāga* for Winds (1972); *Scorpio* for Band or Winds (1976). **CHAMBER:** Quintet No. 1 for Brass (1958–59); *Montage* for Woodwind Quintet (1968); *Putney 3* for Woodwind Quintet, Prepared Piano, and Synthesizer or Tape (1971); *The Tracker* for Clarinet, Fortified Piano, and Tape (1976); *Brancusi's Brass Beds*, Quintet No. 2 (1977); Toccata for Synthesizer and Slide Projectors (1978; rev. 1982); *Quintessence* for Woodwind Quintet, Brass Quintet, and Percussion (1985); *Gemini*, 3 pieces for 2 Guitars (1988). **PIANO:** Sonata (1956–57); *Improvisations on Children's Songs* (1967); *3 Lyric Preludes* (1968); *Elegy for Martin Luther King* (1969); *Latter-Day Lullabies* (1972); Sonata for Fortified Piano (1972); *What's Left* for Piano, Left Hand (1987). **VOCAL:** *Psalms of Rejoicing* for Chorus (1961); *The Song of Moses* for Narrator, 4 Solo Voices, Chorus, and Orch. or Piano (1964); *Fragments from Sappho* for Soprano, Flute, Clarinet, and Piano (1965); *The Tale of Issoumbochi* for Narrator, Soprano, and Chamber Ensemble (1968); *And in These Times*, Christmas cantata for Narrator, Soloists, Chorus, Cello obbligato, and Wind Ensemble (1979–81); *Children's Corner Revisited*, songs for Medium Voice and Piano (1985).

Ware, Harriet, American pianist and composer; b. Waupun, Wis., Aug. 26, 1877; d. N.Y., Feb. 9, 1962. She received her musical instruction from her father, a professional musician and choral conductor; then studied piano with William Mason in N.Y. and Sigismund Stojowski in Paris, and composition with Hugo Kaun in Berlin. Her *Women's Triumphal March* was made the national song of the Federation of Women's Clubs in 1927; her symphonic poem *The Artisan* was given by the N.Y. Sym. Orch. in 1929. Some of her songs (*Boat Song, Joy of the Morning, The Call of Radha, Stars, Sunlight Waltz Song*, etc.) achieved considerable popularity. She also wrote the choral cycles *Trees* and *Undine;* an operetta, *Waltz for 3;* piano pieces.

Warfield, Sandra, American mezzo-soprano; b. Kansas City, Mo., Aug. 6, 1929. She studied voice in Kansas City, and later in Milan; returning to the U.S., she won 1st prize in the Metropolitan Opera Auditions of the Air, which led to her debut in N.Y. on Nov. 20, 1953, as a peasant girl in *Le nozze di Figaro;* later she sang more important roles at the Metropolitan, and also appeared with other American opera houses, and in Europe. Married to the noted American tenor **James McCracken,** she sang numerous concert duos with him. Among her most successful operatic roles are Dalila in *Samson et Dalila*, Amneris in *Aida*, and Carmen. With her husband, she publ. the autobiographical *A Star in the Family* (N.Y., 1971).

Warfield, William (Caesar), black American baritone and teacher; b. West Helena, Ark., Jan. 22, 1920. He studied at the Eastman School of Music in Rochester, N.Y., graduating in 1942; sang in opera and musical comedy; gave his 1st N.Y. song recital on March 19, 1950, with excellent critical acclaim. He subsequently toured Europe in the role of Porgy in the production of Gershwin's *Porgy and Bess*. He married the soprano **Leontyne Price** in 1952 (divorced, 1972). In 1974 he was appointed a prof. of music at the Univ. of Illinois.

Waring, Fred(eric Malcolm), famous American conductor of popular music and inventor of sundry kitchen appliances; b. Tyrone, Pa., June 9, 1900; d. Danville, Pa., July 29, 1984. He learned music at his mother's knee, and a sense of moral rectitude was inculcated in him by his father, a banker who gave speeches at spiritual revivals and temperance meetings. He took up the banjo at 16, and organized a quartet that he called The Banjazzatra. He studied engineering and architecture at Pa. State Univ.; he retained his love for gadgets throughout his musical career, and in 1937 patented the Waring Blendor, for whipping food or drinks to a foam; another invention was a traveling iron. He acquired fame with his own band, The Pennsylvanians, which played on national tours at concert halls, hotels, and college campuses; the group was particularly successful on radio programs sponsored by tobacco companies and the Ford Motor Co. His repertoire consisted of wholesome American songs, many of them composed by himself. Among his soloists on special programs were Bing Crosby, Hoagy Carmichael, Irving Berlin, and Frank Sinatra. Waring had a natural streak for publicity; he once bet that he could lead a bull into a Fifth Avenue china shop, and succeeded, without breaking a single piece of crockery. He was a friend of President Dwight Eisenhower. In 1983 President Ronald Reagan awarded him the Congressional Gold Medal. He continued to lead youth choral groups, giving a concert at Pa. State Univ. a day before he suffered a stroke, and 2 days before his death.

Warlich, Reinhold von, German baritone; b. St. Petersburg, May 24, 1877; d. N.Y., Nov. 10, 1939. His father was an opera conductor active in St. Petersburg; studied at the Hamburg Cons., in Florence, and in Cologne. He toured in Europe as a singer of German lieder, and was especially distinguished as an interpreter of Schubert, whose song cycles he gave in their entirety. He lived for some time in Canada; later was a singing teacher in Paris and London; made concert tours in the U.S. from 1909, eventually settling in N.Y.

Warlock, Peter. See Heseltine, Philip (Arnold).

Warner, Harry Waldo, English violist and composer; b. Northampton, Jan. 4, 1874; d. London, June 1, 1945. He studied violin with Alfred Gibson and theory with R. Orlando Morgan at the Guildhall School of Music in London; was engaged as violist in the London String Quartet (1907–28). In 1921 he received the Elizabeth Sprague Coolidge prize for a piano trio, and a Cobbett prize for another piano trio. He also wrote several other attractive pieces for string quartet; one of them, arr. for string orch., was performed in London on Sept. 22, 1928, under the title *Suite in the Olden Style.*

Warnots, Henri, Belgian tenor, teacher, and composer; b. Brussels, July 11, 1832; d. Saint-Josse-ten-Noode, Feb. 27, 1893. He studied at the Brussels Cons.; made his debut in Liège (1856); then sang in Paris and Strasbourg. In 1867 he became a prof. at the Brussels Cons. In 1870, established a music school in Saint-Josse-ten-Noode, where he remained until his death. His operetta, *Une heure de mariage,* was produced in Strasbourg on Jan. 24, 1865.

Warrack, Guy (Douglas Hamilton), Scottish conductor and composer, father of **John (Hamilton) Warrack;** b. Edinburgh, Feb. 8, 1900; d. Englefield Green, Feb. 12, 1986. He studied at Oxford Univ. and received training in conducting from Boult and in composition from Vaughan Williams at the Royal College of Music in London, where he subsequently taught (1925–35); in 1925 he made his conducting debut in London. After conducting the BBC Scottish Orch. in Glasgow (1936–45), he returned to London to serve as music director of the Sadler's Wells Royal Ballet (1948–51). He publ. the book *Sherlock Holmes and Music* (1947) and wrote articles for many journals. Among his compositions are a Sym. and a number of documentary film scores, including the official coronation film for Queen Elizabeth II, *A Queen Is Crowned* (1953).

Warrack, John (Hamilton), English writer on music, son of **Guy (Douglas Hamilton) Warrack;** b. London, Feb. 9, 1928. He studied at Winchester College; then took up oboe and composition at the Royal College of Music in London; subsequently played oboe in several ensembles. In 1953 he became music ed. of the Oxford Univ. Press; in 1954 he joined the staff of the *Daily Telegraph,* where he was a music critic; then was chief music critic of the *Sunday Telegraph* (1961–72); served as director of the Leeds Festival (1977–83); was a lecturer at Oxford Univ. (from 1983). He contributed numerous articles and reviews to *Opera* and *Gramophone.* His biography of Weber is the standard modern source.

WRITINGS: *Six Great Composers* (London, 1958); co-ed. (with H. Rosenthal), *The Concise Oxford Dictionary of Opera* (London, 1964; 2nd ed., rev., 1979); *Carl Maria von Weber* (London, 1968; also in Ger., 1972; 2nd ed., rev., London, 1976); *Tchaikovsky: Symphonies and Concertos* (London, 1969; 2nd ed., rev., 1974); *Tchaikovsky* (London, 1973); *Tchaikovsky: Ballet Music* (London, 1978).

Warren, Elinor Remick, American pianist and composer; b. Los Angeles, Feb. 23, 1900; d. there, April 27, 1991. She studied piano as a small child with Kathryn Cocke, taking up composition studies at 14; her 1st works were publ. while she was still in high school. After attending Mills College, she studied with Olga Steeb, Paolo Gallico, Frank La Forge, and Clarence Dickinson in N.Y.; much later received training from Nadia Boulanger in Paris (1959). She was mainly active as a piano accompanist to such singers as Bori and Tibbett.

WORKS: ORCH.: *The Fountain* (1942); Suite (1955; rev. 1958); *The Crystal Lake* (1958); *Along the Western Shore: Dark Hills, Nocturne, Sea Rhapsody* (1963); *Intermezzo* (1970); Sym. in 1 Movement (1971). **CHAMBER:** Woodwind Quintet; various piano pieces; also several sacred choral pieces; secular choral works and numerous solo songs.

BIBL.: V. Bortin, *E.R. W.: Her Life and her Music* (Metuchen, N.J., 1987).

Warren, George William, American organist and composer, father of **Richard Henry Warren;** b. Albany, N.Y., Aug. 17, 1828; d. N.Y., March 17, 1902. He was self-taught; held positions as a church organist in Albany (1846–60), Brooklyn (1860–70), and at St. Thomas in N.Y. (1870–1900). He publ. *Warren's Hymns and Tunes, as Sung at St. Thomas Church* (1888); also wrote salon piano music; his "Marche di Bravura," *The Andes,* was the rage of the salons in 1862–63, especially in a 2-piano arrangement made by Louis Moreau Gottschalk. He is remembered chiefly for his tune *National Hymn,* to which *God of Our Fathers* is sung.

Warren, Harry (real name, **Salvatore Guaragna**), American composer of popular songs; b. Brooklyn, Dec. 24, 1893; d. Los Angeles, Sept. 22, 1981. He was the 11th child in a proliferating but impoverished Italian family; his father was a boot maker who, like most Brooklyn-born Italians, also loved music. Warren dropped out of high school to play drums with a touring carnival co.; with the money earned, he bought himself a ramshackle old piano and became engaged as a movie pianist for the silent screen. Endowed with a God-given gift of melody, he turned out, without benefit of academic training, a slew of irresistible tunes, some of which became perennial favorites. His early hits were *Rose of the Rio Grande, Back Home in Pasadena,* and *So This Is Venice* (Venice, Calif., that is). In 1932 Salvatore Guaragna, now advantageously transfigured into Harry Warren, moved to the center of musical glamour, Hollywood, and unleashed an avalanche of hits for films. Among his greatest songs were *42nd Street* (1933), *You Must Have Been a Beautiful Baby* (1938), *Jeepers Creepers* (1938), *Chattanooga Choo-Choo* (1941), and *On the Atchison, Topeka and the Santa Fe* (1946).

BIBL.: T. Thomas, *H. W. and the Hollywood Musical* (Secaucus, N.J., 1975; with complete list of works).

Warren, Leonard, outstanding American baritone; b. N.Y., April 21, 1911; d. there, March 4, 1960, on the stage of the

Metropolitan Opera House while singing the role of Don Carlo during a performance of *La forza del destino*. The original family name was Warenoff; it was Americanized as Warren when his Russian father settled in the U.S. He was first employed in his father's fur business in N.Y.; in 1935 he joined the chorus of Radio City Music Hall; he also studied voice with Sidney Dietch and Giuseppe De Luca. In 1938 he won the Metropolitan Opera Auditions of the Air and was granted a stipend to study in Italy, where he took voice lessons with Pais and Piccozi. Returning to America, he made his debut at the Metropolitan Opera in excerpts from *La Traviata* and *Pagliacci* during a concert in N.Y. on Nov. 27, 1938; his formal operatic debut took place there on Jan. 13, 1939, when he sang Paolo in *Simon Boccanegra*. He quickly advanced in the favor of the public, eventually assuming a leading place among the noted baritones of his time. He also sang in San Francisco, Chicago, Canada, and South America. He appeared at La Scala in Milan in 1953; in 1958 he made a highly successful tour of the Soviet Union. His last complete performance at the Metropolitan Opera was as Simon Boccanegra on March 1, 1960, 3 days before his tragic death. He was particularly acclaimed as one of the foremost interpreters of the great Verdi baritone roles; he also sang the parts of Tonio in *Pagliacci*, Escamillo in *Carmen*, and Scarpia in *Tosca*. He collapsed while singing the aria "Urna fatale dal mio destino," underlining the tragic irony of the words, and died of a cerebral hemorrhage backstage. He was reputed to be a person of an intractable character, who always tried to impose his will on stage designers, managers, and even conductors, in matters of production, direction, and tempi. He caused pain, a colleague said, but he had a great voice.

Warren, Raymond (Henry Charles), English composer; b. Weston-Super-Mare, Nov. 7, 1928. He studied with Robin Orr at Cambridge Univ. (1949–52) and later took lessons with Michael Tippett and Lennox Berkeley; received his Mus.B. (1952), M.A. (1955), and Mus.D. (1967) at Cambridge Univ.; taught at the Univ. of Belfast (1955–72); in 1972, was appointed prof. of music at Bristol Univ.

WORKS: *The Lady of Ephesus*, chamber opera (Belfast, Feb. 16, 1959); *Finn and the Black Hag*, children's opera (Belfast, Dec. 11, 1959); *Graduation Ode*, comic opera (Belfast, Nov. 20, 1963); 3 children's church operas: *Let My People Go* (Liverpool, March 22, 1972), *St. Patrick* (Liverpool, May 3, 1979), and *In the Beginning* (Clifton, July 22, 1982); 2 oratorios: *The Passion* (Belfast, Dec. 11, 1959) and *Continuing Cities* (Bristol, April 22, 1989); *Nocturne* for Orch. (1964); 2 syms. (1965, 1969); Violin Concerto (1966); *Seaside Sketches*, orch. suite (1968); *Wexford Bells*, orch. suite (1970); 3 string quartets (1965, 1975, 1977); *Duo concertante* for Cello and Piano (1972); *Burnt Norton Sketches* for Piano Trio (1985); *Exchanges* for Oboe and Piano (1986); 2 piano sonatas (1952, 1977); song cycles, solo songs, choral pieces, etc.

Warren, Richard Henry, American organist and composer, son of **George William Warren;** b. Albany, N.Y., Sept. 17, 1859; d. South Chatham, Mass., Dec. 3, 1933. He studied with his father, then pursued his training in Europe (1880–86), where his principal mentor was Widor. He was organist and choirmaster in various churches in N.Y.; in 1886, founded the Church Choral Society, which he conducted until 1895 and again from 1903 to 1907, producing many important works, including the American premieres of choral compositions by Dvořák, Liszt, Gounod, Saint-Saëns, et al. Horatio Parker wrote his *Hora Novissima* for this society, and Warren brought it out on May 3, 1893. Among Warren's own compositions are the operettas: *Igala* (1880); *All on a Summer's Day* (1882); *Magnolia* (1886); *The Rightful Heir* (1899); a "romantic opera," *Phyllis* (N.Y., May 7, 1900); a cantata, *Ticonderoga* (1894); services; anthems; songs.

Warren, Samuel Prowse, American organist and composer; b. Montreal, Feb. 18, 1841; d. N.Y., Oct. 7, 1915. He studied organ with Haupt, piano with Gustav Schumann, and theory

with Wieprecht in Berlin. After filling various positions in N.Y. churches, he inaugurated a series of organ recitals, which were greatly appreciated and created for him a reputation as one of the foremost concert organists in the U.S. He publ. many organ pieces and songs; also made excellent transcriptions for organ of works by Weber, Beethoven, Schumann, and Wagner.

BIBL.: P. Jennings, "The Art of S.P. W.," *Musical America*, XXIII/11 (1916).

Wartel, Pierre-François, noted French tenor and teacher; b. Versailles, April 3, 1806; d. Paris, Aug. 3, 1882. In 1825 he entered the Paris Cons. as a pupil of Halévy, but soon thereafter began studies with Choron at the Institut de la Musique Religieuse; in 1828 he returned to the Paris Cons. to pursue vocal training with Davide Banderali and Adolphe Nourrit (premier prix in singing, 1829). He was a member of the Paris Opéra (1831–46); also made successful concert tours to Berlin, Prague, and Vienna; with Nourrit, he helped create an appreciation of Schubert's lieder in France via his song recitals. He was mainly active as a singing teacher from 1842; his most prominent pupils were Christine Nilsson and Zélia Trebelli. His wife, **Atale Thérèse Annette Wartel** (née **Adrien;** b. Paris, July 2, 1814; d. there, Nov. 6, 1865), was a talented pianist; studied at the Paris Cons.; after serving as an accompanist there, she was a prof. of piano (1831–38); composed piano studies and other pieces.

Warwick(e), (Marie) Dionne, black American pop and soul singer; b. East Orange, N.J., Dec. 12, 1941. She studied voice at the Hartt College of Music in Hartford, Conn., but soon left and plunged herself into her natural environment as a born singer of popular songs. Her decision was wise, for she made a hit with audiences. She made her 1st appearance with the Drinkard Singers, a gospel group managed by her mother; toured with the Gospelaires, a trio formed with her sister and cousin. In 1960 she met Burt Bacharach and Hal David in N.Y., who subsequently wrote most of her hit songs, including *Anyone Who Had a Heart* (1963), *Walk On By* (1964), *I Say a Little Prayer* (1967), *Do You Know the Way to San Jose?* (1968), and *I'll Never Fall in Love Again* (1969). In 1979 she brought out the album *Dionne*, which included the hit single *I'll Never Love This Way Again*.

Washburn, Robert, American composer and music educator; b. Bouckville, N.Y., July 11, 1928. He studied music education at the Crane School of Music at the State Univ. of N.Y. College at Potsdam (B.S., 1949; M.S., 1955) and composition at the Eastman School of Music in Rochester, N.Y. (Ph.D., 1960); continued his study of composition with Milhaud at the Aspen (Colo.) Music School (1963) and with Nadia Boulanger in Paris (1964). He taught at the Crane School of Music (from 1954), where he served as its dean (1982–85); held fellowships from the Ford Foundation (1959–60) and the MacDowell Colony (1963); also an N.E.A. grant (1981) and a Fulbright fellowship (1985). He has written many effective works for college and high school groups.

WORKS: ORCH.: Sym. No. 1 (1959; 1st movement extracted as *Festive Overture* (1962); *St. Lawrence Overture* (1962); *Passacaglia and Fugue* for Strings (1963); *Sinfonietta* for Strings (1965); *Serenade* for Strings (1966); *Song and Dance* for Strings (1967); *North Country Sketch* (1969); *Excursion* (1970); *Elegy* (1974); *Overture: Mid-America* (1976). **BAND:** *Ode* (1955); *Burlesk* (1956); *Pageantry* (1962); Sym. (1963); *Partita* (1964); *Suite* (1967); *Ceremonial Music* (1968); *Intrada, Chorale, and Toccata* (1970); *Prelude and Paragrams* (1972); *Trigon* (1975); *Impressions of Cairo* (1978); *Olympic March* (1979); *Kilimanjaro* (1981); *Equinox* (1983); *Pageant Royale* (1988). **CHAMBER:** *Suite* for Wind Quintet (1960); String Quartet (1963); Woodwind Quintet (1967); Brass Quintet (1970); *Pent-agons* for Percussion (1973); Trio for Piano and Strings (1984); piano pieces; also numerous choral works, including *3 Shakespearean Love Songs* for Men's Voices (1967); *Spring Cantata* (1975); *3 Thoughts from Thoreau* (1980).

Washington, Dinah (real name, **Ruth Lee Jones**), black American singer of blues and popular music; b. Tuscaloosa, Ala., Aug. 8?, 1924; d. (as a result of an overdose of drugs) Detroit, Dec. 14, 1963. She went to Chicago; won an amateur singing contest at the age of 15; made local appearances before singing in Lionel Hampton's band (1943–46); she soon established herself as a major rhythm and blues artist with such songs as "Blow Top Blues" and "Evil Gal Blues." She was best known for her renditions of "What a Difference a Day Makes," "Homeward Bound," "Stormy Weather," and "September in the Rain."
　　BIBL.: J. Haskins, *Queen of the Blues: A Biography of D. W.* (N.Y., 1987).

Wasielewski, Wilhelm Joseph von, eminent German violinist, conductor, and music scholar; b. Gross-Leesen, near Danzig, June 17, 1822; d. Sondershausen, Dec. 13, 1896. He studied with Mendelssohn, Hauptmann, and David at the Leipzig Cons. (1843–46). He played in the Gewandhaus Orch. (until 1850); went to Düsseldorf, where he was concertmaster under Schumann (1850–52); then was choral conductor in Bonn (1852–55); in 1855 he settled in Dresden as a writer, in which capacity he greatly distinguished himself. In 1869 he became town music director in Bonn, remaining in that position until 1884, when he went to Sondershausen, where he settled as a teacher of music history at the Cons.
　　WRITINGS: *Robert Schumann* (Dresden, 1858; 2nd ed., rev. and augmented, 1906 by Waldemar von Wasielewski; Eng. tr., 1871); *Die Violine und ihre Meister* (Leipzig, 1869; 3rd ed., augmented, 1893; 5th ed., rev., 1910 by Waldemar von Wasielewski; 8th ed., 1927); *Die Violine im XVII. Jahrhundert und die Anfänge der Instrumentalkomposition* (Bonn, 1874); *Geschichte der Instrumental-Musik im XVI. Jahrhundert* (Berlin, 1878); *Schumanniana* (Bonn, 1883); *Ludwig van Beethoven* (Berlin, 1888); *Das Violoncell und seine Geschichte* (Leipzig, 1889; 3rd ed., rev. and augmented, 1925, by Waldemar von Wasielewski; Eng. tr., 1894); *Carl Reinecke* (Leipzig, 1892); *Aus 70 Jahren: Lebenserinnerungen* (Stuttgart, 1897).
　　BIBL.: R. Federhofer-Königs, *W.J. v.W. (1822–1896) im Spiegel seiner Korrespondenz* (Tutzing, 1975).

Wasitodiningrat, K.R.T. (**Kanjeng Raden Tumengung,** a title of honorary royal status), important Indonesian composer and performer; b. Yogyakarta, Java, March 17, 1909. (His former names are Wasitolodoro, Tjokrowasito, and Wasitodipuro; he is frequently known as Ki Wasitodiningrat, Ki being an honorific for artistic achievement.) He was born in the Pakualaman Palace, one of 3 principal courts of central Java, where his father was director of musical activities. Wasitodiningrat studied dance from the age of 6, graduating from the SMA National High School in 1922. He became music director of the Yogyakarta radio station MAVRO in 1934, and remained there through the Japanese occupation, when the station was called Jogja Hosokjoku. In 1945 the station became RRI (Radio Republik Indonesia); he served as director there again in 1951. Between 1951 and 1970 he taught dance at the Konservatori Tari and the Academy Tari, both in Yogyakarta, and music at the Academy Karawitan in Surakarta; he also founded and directed the Wasitodipuro Center for Vocal Studies in Yogyakarta. In 1953 he toured Asia, North America, and Europe; in 1961 he became associated with the new dance/theater form *sendratari,* later becoming music director for P.L.T. Bagong Kussudiardjo's troupe. He succeeded his father as director of the Pakualaman gamelan in 1962. In 1971 he joined the faculty of the Calif. Inst. of the Arts as master of Javanese gamelan; taught workshops at both the Los Angeles and Berkeley campuses of the Univ. of Calif. Wasitodiningrat is a leading performer and composer of central Javanese music; the Pakualaman gamelan's recordings are considered exemplary; 1 is included in the 40 minutes of music installed in the spacecraft *Voyager,* intended to represent our planet's music to outsiders. His numerous awards include a gold medal from the Indonesian government honoring his devotion to Javanese music.

He frequently performs with his daughter, Nanik, and her Balinese husband, **Nyoman Wenten.**

Wassenaer, Count Unico Wilhelm van, Dutch government official and talented amateur composer; b. Twickel, Nov. 2, 1692; d. The Hague, Nov. 9, 1766. He received his education in Leiden and assumed control of the family estate in 1717; later held government posts and served as the United Provinces ambassador abroad. His *6 Concerti armonici,* publ. anonymously in 1740, were attributed to Pergolesi and then to Ricciotti before being confirmed as the work of Wassenaer.
　　BIBL.: A. Dunning, *Count U.W. v.W. (1692–1766); A Master Unmasked; or, The Pergolesi-Ricciotti Puzzle Solved* (Buren, 1980).

Wassermann, Heinrich Joseph, German conductor and composer; b. Schwarzbach, near Fulda, April 3, 1791; d. Riehen, near Basel, Sept. 3, 1838. He was a pupil of Spohr; became an orch. conductor in Switzerland. He wrote a *Thème original varié* for String Quartet; Quartet for Flute, Violin, Viola, and Cello; *Air varié* for Bassoon and String Orch.; *Divertissement* (on the Tyrolian "Alma Lied") for Violin and Orch.; a number of orch. dances; pieces for guitar.

Watanabe, Akeo, Japanese conductor; b. Tokyo, June 5, 1919; d. there, June 22, 1990. He studied piano and violin as a youth; received training in conducting from Joseph Rosenstock at the Tokyo Academy of Music and from Jean Morel at the Juilliard School of Music in N.Y. In 1945 he made his conducting debut with the Tokyo Sym. Orch.; was conductor of the Tokyo Phil. (1948–54); served as founder-conductor of the Japan Phil. in Tokyo (1956–68); was conductor of the Tokyo Metropolitan Sym. Orch. (1972–78); also appeared as guest conductor in the U.S. and Europe. He served again as conductor of the Japan Phil. (1978–83), then was music director of the Hiroshima Sym. Orch. (from 1988).

Waters, Edward N(eighbor), American musicologist; b. Leavenworth, Kans., July 23, 1906; d. Mitchellville, Md., July 27, 1991. He studied piano and theory at the Eastman School of Music in Rochester, N.Y. (B.M., 1927; M.M. in musicology, 1928). In 1931 he joined the staff of the Music Division of the Library of Congress in Washington, D.C.; from 1972 to 1976 served as chief of the Music Division; was president of the Music Library Assoc. (1941–46); was program annotator for the National Sym. Orch. in Washington (1934–43); was ed. of *Notes* (1963–66); also wrote many articles and book reviews for professional journals. The Cleveland Inst. of Music conferred upon him the honorary degree of D.Mus. (1973). He wrote a definitive biography of Victor Herbert (N.Y., 1955).

Waters, Ethel (née **Howard**), prominent black American singer and actress; b. Chester, Pa., Oct. 31, 1896 (the fruit of a knife-point rape, when her mother was 12½ years old); d. Chatsworth, Calif., Sept. 1, 1977. After a disastrous marriage at the age of 13, she worked as a laundress in Philadelphia. When her ability as a natural singer was discovered, she began her career as a singer of "coon" songs; eventually developed a following with her personal renditions of popular songs and jazz numbers. She also developed a notably successful career as an actress; appeared in Irving Berlin's *As Thousands Cheer* (1933), Dorothy and Dubose Heyward's *Mamba's Daughters* (1939), Vernon Duke's *Cabin in the Sky* (1940), and Carson McCullers's *The Member of the Wedding* (1950); later toured as a singer with the evangelist Billy Graham (1960–75). With C. Samuels, she publ. the autobiographical vols. *His Eye is on the Sparrow* (Garden City, N.Y., 1951) and *To Me It's Wonderful* (N.Y., 1972).

Waters, Muddy (real name, **McKinley Morganfield**), black American blues singer, top exponent of the Mississippi Delta Blues style; b. Rolling Fork, Miss., April 4, 1915; d. Westmont, Ill., April 30, 1983. His parents were separated, and he was reared by his maternal grandmother on a plantation near Clarksdale, Miss.; she called him "Muddy" because of his childhood habit of playing in the mud; his playmates called him "Waters," and he accepted the nickname "Muddy Waters" when he began to sing and play the guitar. In 1941, Alan Lomax and John Work recorded his singing for the Library of Congress; this encouraged him to try his luck in commercial recording. In 1943 he moved to Chicago, where he made his first successes; indeed, he soon earned the sobriquet "King of Chicago Blues." Fortunately for him, his followers, and jazz historians, he totally lacked any vocal training and was forced to develop his own unrestricted lexicon of sounds, ranging from soft trembling moans to a ferocious animal-like roar. To make his mode of delivery even more physically stunning, he used electric amplification on his guitar, and soon assembled a band that hit an all-time decibel record. He played electric blues in England in 1958, which struck holy terror into the ears and hearts of sissified British folk-song experts, but he recruited to his cause the young enthusiasts, among them Mick Jagger; in fact, Jagger and his friends named their famous band The Rolling Stones after Waters's early hit song *Rollin' Stone*; the rock journal *Rolling Stone* also owed its name to Muddy's song; Bob Dylan created his own rock tune *Like a Rolling Stone* as an unconscious tribute to him. He died peacefully, in his sleep.

BIBL.: P. Oliver, *M. W.* (Bexhill-on-Sea, 1964); J. Rooney, *Bossmen: Bill Monroe and M. W.* (N.Y., 1971).

Watkinson, Carolyn, English mezzo-soprano; b. Preston, March 19, 1949. She studied at the Royal Manchester College of Music; then pursued a fine career as a concert artist in a repertoire ranging from early music to the 20th century; also sang opera in Brussels, Spoleto, Salzburg, Milan, and Glyndebourne. Her operatic repertoire includes such roles as Poppea, Ariodante, Cherubino, and Cenerentola.

Watson (real name, **McLamore**), **Claire,** American soprano; b. N.Y., Feb. 3, 1924; d. Utting, Germany, July 16, 1986. She studied voice in N.Y. with Elisabeth Schumann and Sergius Kagen; received further training in Vienna. She made her operatic debut as Desdemona in Graz in 1951; was a member of the Frankfurt Opera (1956–58) and the Bavarian State Opera in Munich from 1958 until her farewell as the Marschallin in 1976. She made guest appearances at the Salzburg Festival and with opera houses in London, Vienna, Milan, Rome, Chicago, and San Francisco.

Watters, Lu(cius Carl), American jazz trumpeter and bandleader; b. Santa Cruz, Calif., Dec. 19, 1911. He learned to play the trumpet and later appeared with his own swing band; in 1940 he organized in San Francisco the Yerba Buena Jazz Band, which sparked the revival of the New Orleans and Chicago jazz styles; he quit the music business in 1957. He composed the jazz numbers *Big Bear Stomp* and *Emperor Norton's Hunch*, and the piano rag *The Villain*.

Watts, André, brilliant American pianist; b. Nuremberg, June 20, 1946. He was born in a U.S. Army camp to a black American soldier and a Hungarian woman. His mother gave him his earliest piano lessons. After the family moved to the U.S., he studied with Genia Robiner, Doris Bawden, and Clement Petrillo at the Philadelphia Musical Academy. At the age of 9 he made his 1st public appearance playing the Haydn Concerto in D major at a children's concert of the Philadelphia Orch. His parents were divorced in 1962, but his mother continued to guide his studies. At 14 he played César Franck's *Symphonic Variations* with the Philadelphia Orch.; at 16 he became an instant celebrity when he played Liszt's 1st Piano Concerto at one of the televised Young People's Concerts with the N.Y. Phil., conducted by Leonard Bernstein, on Jan. 15, 1963. His youth and the fact that he was partly black contributed to his success, but it was the grand and poetic manner of his virtuosity that conquered the usually skeptical press. Still, he insisted on completing his academic education. In 1969 he joined the class of Leon Fleisher at the Peabody Cons. of Music in Baltimore, obtaining his Artist's Diploma in 1972. In the meantime he developed an international career. He made his European debut as soloist with the London Sym. Orch. on June 12, 1966; then played with the Concertgebouw Orch.

in Amsterdam. On Oct. 26, 1966, he played his first solo recital in N.Y., inviting comparisons in the press with the great piano virtuosos of the past. In 1967 he was soloist with the Los Angeles Phil. under Zubin Mehta on a tour of Europe and Asia. On his 21st birthday he played the 2nd Piano Concerto of Brahms with the Berlin Phil. In 1970 he revisited his place of birth and played a solo recital with a success that was made all the more sensational because he was a native son, albeit not of the native race. He also became a favorite at important political occasions; he played at President Richard Nixon's inaugural concert at Constitution Hall in 1969, at the coronation of the Shah of Iran, and at a festive celebration of the President of the Congo. In 1973 he toured Russia. On Nov. 28, 1976, he played a solo recital on live network television. He was also the subject of a film documentary. In 1973 he received an honorary doctorate from Yale Univ.; in 1975 he was given another honorary doctorate by Albright College. He celebrated the 25th anniversary of his debut with the N.Y. Phil. as soloist under Zubin Mehta in the Liszt 1st Concerto, the Beethoven 2nd Concerto, and the Rachmaninoff 2nd Concerto in a concert telecast live on PBS (Jan. 13, 1988); he received the Avery Fisher Prize (1988).

Watts, Helen (Josephine), Welsh contralto; b. Milford Haven, Dec. 7, 1927. She was educated at the Royal Academy of Music in London; made her debut in a Promenade Concert in London in 1955; in 1958, sang with the Handel Opera Society at the Camden Festival; later appeared with the English Opera Group and at Covent Garden in London. She made her U.S. debut in a concert with the N.Y. Phil. in 1966. In 1978 she was made a Commander of the Order of the British Empire.

Watts, John (Everett), American composer and synthesizer player; b. Cleveland, Tenn., July 16, 1930; d. N.Y., July 1, 1982. He was educated at the Univ. of Tennessee (B.A., 1949), the Univ. of Colorado (M.M., 1953), the Univ. of Illinois (1955–56), Cornell Univ. (1958–60), and the Univ. of Calif. at Los Angeles (1961–62); among his mentors were David Van Vactor, Cecil Effinger, Burrill Phillips, Robert Palmer, and Roy Harris. He was founder-director of the Composers Theatre in N.Y. (1964–82), which presented a vast number of works by American composers; taught at the New School for Social Research in N.Y. (from 1967), where he was founder-director of its electronic music program (from 1969); made many appearances as a virtuoso on the ARP synthesizer.

WORKS: INSTRUMENTAL AND/OR VOCAL: Piano Sonata (1958; rev. 1960); *Signals* for Soprano and Orch. (1970); *Piano for Te* for Piano, 13 Players, and Tape (1973); *Laugharne* for Soprano, Tape, and Orch. (1974); *Mots d'heures: Gousses, Rames* for Voices and Tape (1974); *Piano for Te Tutti* for Piano and Tape (1975); *Maxi-concerto* (1976); *Canonades* for String Orch. (1978); *Keepsakes* for Tape and Orch. (1978); *Le Match de Boxe* (1978); *Barbro Variations* for Piano 4-hands (1979); *Easy Songs for Lazy Singers* (1981). ELECTRONIC: *WARP* for Brass Quintet, Synthesizer, and Tape (1971); *Elegy to Chimney: in memoriam* for Trumpet, Synthesizer, and Tape (1972); *MAS* (1976); *Entectics* for Tape and Synthesizer (1978); *Processional* for Tape and 10 Trumpets (1978); *A Little Night Music* (1979); *Timespace* for Tape (1979); *Ach!* for Tape and Optional Synthesizer (1980). DANCE SCORES: *Study for Solo Figure/Film* (1968); *Perimeters* (1969); *Glass and Shadows* (1971); *Laura's Dance* (1971); *Margins* (1972); *Still Life* (1972); *Locrian* (1973); *Songandance* (1973); *BUD* (1975) (1975); *Heirlooms* (1977); *#SS* (1977); *UPS* (1977); *Entries* (1978); *GO* (1978); *Night Remembrance* (1979); also film scores and conceptual art.

Watts, Wintter (Haynes), American composer; b. Cincinnati, March 14, 1884; d. N.Y., Nov. 1, 1962. He studied at the Inst. of Musical Art in N.Y. He received the American Prix de Rome, which enabled him to study at the American Academy in Rome (1923–25). He lived for some time in Europe, returning to N.Y. in 1931. Among his larger works are a *Bridal Overture* (1916) and an orch. suite, *Etchings* (1922), but he is chiefly known as a composer of fine songs: *Wings of Night,*

Joy, With the Tide, Wild Tears, Alone; a cycle of 9 songs to poems by Sara Teasdale, *Vignettes of Italy*; etc.

Watzke, Rudolf, German bass; b. Niemes, April 5, 1892; d. Wuppertal, Dec. 18, 1972. He studied voice in Reichenberg, Bayreuth, and Berlin; from 1924 to 1928, was a member of the Berlin State Opera. From 1928 he devoted himself mainly to oratorio performances; also taught at the Dortmund Cons. (1956–69).

Waxman (real name, **Wachsmann), Franz,** German-American composer and conductor; b. Königshütte, Dec. 24, 1906; d. Los Angeles, Feb. 24, 1967. He studied in Dresden and Berlin; went to the U.S. in 1934 and settled in Hollywood, where he took lessons with Arnold Schoenberg; became a successful composer for films; his musical score for *Sunset Boulevard* won the Academy Award for 1950; also was active as a conductor; was founder-conductor of the Los Angeles Music Festival (1947–67). His other film scores included *Magnificent Obsession* (1935), *Captains Courageous* (1937), *The Philadelphia Story* (1940), *Sunset Boulevard* (1950), *Stalag 17* (1953), *Sayonara* (1957), and *Sunrise at Campobello* (1960); he also composed the orch. works *Athaneal the Trumpeter*, overture (1945), a Trumpet Concerto (1946), *Carmen Fantasy* for Violin and Orch., after Bizet (1947), Sinfonietta for Strings and Timpani (1955), *Goyana* for Piano and Strings (1960), and a Cello Concerto; also some vocal pieces, including *Joshua*, an oratorio for Narrator, Solo Voices, Chorus, and Orch. (Dallas, May 23, 1959).

Wayditch, Gabriel (real name, **Baron Gabriel Wajditch Verbovac von Dönhoff**), Hungarian-American composer; b. Budapest, Dec. 28, 1888; d. N.Y., July 28, 1969. He studied piano with Emil von Sauer and composition with Hans Koessler at the Budapest Academy of Music. In 1907 he emigrated to the U.S. He wrote 14 lengthy operas to his own libretti in Hungarian, dealing mostly with oriental or religious subjects; of these only one, *Horus*, was performed in his lifetime, at his own expense (Philadelphia, Jan. 5, 1939). His longest opera, *The Heretics*, takes 8 hours to perform; the shortest, *The Caliph's Magician*, in one act, takes 2 hours. The other operas are *Opium Dreams, Buddha, Jesus before Herod, Maria Magdalena, Maria Tesztver, Nereida, Sahara, The Catacombs, Anthony of Padua, The Venus Dwellers, Neptune's Daughter.*

Weatherford, Teddy, black American jazz pianist and bandleader; b. Bluefield, W.Va., Oct. 11, 1903; d. Calcutta, India, April 25, 1945. He learned to play the piano in New Orleans; then worked in Chicago; in 1926 he became a member of Jack Carter's Orch. and accompanied it on a tour to the Orient; he decided to remain there, and led his own bands in Singapore, Manila, and Shanghai; eventually settled in Calcutta, where he led his own band at the city's Grand Hotel.

Weathers, Felicia, black American soprano; b. St. Louis, Aug. 13, 1937. She took vocal lessons at the Indiana Univ. School of Music in Bloomington with St. Leger, Kullman, and Manski; then went to Europe; made her operatic debut in Zürich in 1961. In 1963 she sang at the Hamburg State Opera and subsequently became a regular member (1966–70). In 1965 she made her Metropolitan Opera debut in N.Y.; also sang at Covent Garden in London in 1970.

Weaver, Powell, American pianist, organist, and composer; b. Clearfield, Pa., June 10, 1890; d. Oakland, Calif., Dec. 22, 1951. He studied organ with Dethier, piano with Caroline Beebe, and composition with Goetschius at the Inst. of Musical Art in N.Y. (1909–12); after further organ studies with Pietro Yon in N.Y., he went to Rome to study organ with Remigio Renzi and later received training in composition with Respighi (1924–25). He was active as an organist at Kansas City's Grand Ave. Temple (1912–37) and the First Baptist Church (1937–51); was engaged as accompanist to prominent singers; also gave organ recitals. From 1937 to 1945 he was head of the music dept. at Ottawa Univ. in Kansas City.

Works: *As We Like It*, comic opera pastiche (1922). **Orch.:** *Plantation Overture* (1925); *The Little Faun* (1925; Boston,

April 14, 1929); *The Vagabond*, symphonic poem (Minneapolis, March 6, 1931); *Dance of the Sand-Dune Cranes* for Piano and Orch. (1941). **Chamber:** Piano Quintet (1936); String Quartet (1937); Violin Sonata (1945); piano pieces; organ music; much vocal music.

Bibl.: M. Schwartz, *P. W.: His Life and Contributions to Organ Music in Kansas City* (diss., Univ. of Missouri, 1976).

Webb, Charles H(aizlip, Jr.), American pianist, organist, conductor, and music educator; b. Dallas, Feb. 14, 1933. He was educated at Southern Methodist Univ. (A.B. and M.Mus., 1955) and Indiana Univ. (D.Mus., 1964); joined the faculty of Indiana Univ. as an instructor in piano (1958); became an assistant prof. of music in 1964 and an associate prof. in 1967. He was named assistant dean of the School of Music in 1964, associate dean in 1969, and dean in 1973. He toured the U.S. with the pianist Wallace Hornibrook in duo-recitals; also toured as a concert organist. He served as organist at the 1st Methodist Church in Bloomington, Ind. (from 1961) and as conductor of the Indianapolis Symphonic Choir (1967–81). In 1967 he was appointed commissioner of the Indiana Arts Commission. In 1983 he was named a member of the Indiana Academy.

Webb, "Chick" (William Henry), black American jazz drummer and bandleader; b. Baltimore, Feb. 10, 1909; d. there, June 16, 1939. He was stricken with tuberculosis of the spine, which left him a hunchback; took up the drums as a youngster; then played in the Jazzola Orch.; moving to N.Y., he led his own band there, scoring a success at the Savoy Ballroom. In 1935 he introduced Ella Fitzgerald, and she subsequently toured with his group.

Bibl.: D. Baker, "C. W. 1928–1939," *Micography*, no. 31 (1974).

Webb, Frank Rush, American organist and bandmaster; b. Covington, Ind., Oct. 8, 1851; d. Baltimore, Oct. 20, 1934. He studied at the New England Cons. of Music in Boston; then was a church organist in Indianapolis and a piano teacher in Ohio; from 1883 to 1910 he was director of the School of Music in the Virginia Female Inst. in Staunton, Va.; from 1883 to 1892, also bandmaster of the Stonewall Brigade Band. He publ. nearly 200 pieces for military band; also much salon music for piano, amounting to 108 opus numbers; church music; songs.

Bibl.: M. Brice, *The Stonewall Brigade Band* (Verona, Va., 1967).

Webb, George James, English-American organist, conductor, music educator, editor, and composer; b. Rushmore Lodge, near Salisbury, June 24, 1803; d. Orange, N.J., Oct. 7, 1887. He was a pupil of Alexander Lucas in Salisbury; then was an organist in Falmouth. He settled in Boston in 1830; served as organist of the Old South Church; was a founder of the Boston Academy of Music in 1836, and president of the Handel and Haydn Society in 1840; was active as a conductor with both of these groups, as well as with the Musical Fund Society. In 1870 he settled in Orange, N.J., but continued musical activities in N.Y. as a teacher. Although he composed a number of hymn tunes, only one remains known today: *Goodwin*, first written to secular words and subsequently known as *Webb* ("Stand up, stand up for Jesus"). With L. Mason, he ed. *The Musical Library* (1835–36) and with T. Hayward, *The Musical Cabinet* (1841–42). He also brought out the following eds., all publ. in Boston unless otherwise given: *Scripture Worship* (1834); *The Massachusetts Collection of Psalmody* (1840); *The American Glee Book* (1841); with L. Mason, *The Psaltery* (1845), *The National Psalmist* (1848), *Cantica laudis* (N.Y., 1850), and *The Melodist* (N.Y., 1850); *Cantica ecclesiastica* (1859).

Bibl.: F. Metcalf, *American Writers and Compilers of Sacred Music* (N.Y., 1925).

Webbe, Samuel, foremost English composer of glees; b. probably in London, 1740; d. there, May 15, 1816. He was apprenticed to a carpenter when he was 11, but also studied music on his own; was a music copyist while studying with the organ-

Webber–Weber

ist Barbandt. His canon *O that I had wings* won a prize of the Noblemen's and Gentlemen's Catch Club in 1766, and he subsequently carried off 26 other prizes from then until 1792. He became organist of the Portuguese and Sardinian chapels in 1776, and remained active at the latter until about 1813. He was made librarian of the Glee Club at its foundation in 1787; his glee *Glorious Apollo* was the opening glee at every one of its meetings during its existence; he also served as secretary of the Catch Club from 1794 until his death. Although he was most famous in his day for his glees, he also wrote music for the Roman Catholic liturgy; his antiphon *O salutaris hostia* (1782) is his best-known work today, being the hymn tune *Melcombe,* generally used for Keble's hymn *New every morning is the love;* he also wrote music for the Anglican service. His son, also named **Samuel Webbe** (b. London, c.1770; d. there, Nov. 25, 1843), was an organist and composer; he studied with his father and then held various posts as an organist; wrote the music for an operatic farce, *The Speechless Wife* (Covent Garden, London, May 22, 1794); composed numerous glees, catches, and songs; music for the Roman Catholic liturgy; 4 harp sonatas; much piano music.

WORKS: SECULAR VOCAL: 8 books of catches, canons, and glees for 3 to 6 Voices (London, c.1764–95); *A Collection of Vocal Music* for 2 to 5 Voices (London, 1795; with his son); *6 Original Glees* (London, 1840; ed. by his son); various other works in anthologies of the 18th and 19th centuries. **LATIN SACRED VOCAL:** *An Essay on the Church Plain Chant* (London, 1782); *A Collection of Sacred Music as Used in the Chapel of the King of Sardinia* (London, c.1785); *A Collection of Masses with Accompaniment for the Organ* (London, 1792); *A Collection of Motetts or Antiphons* (London, 1792). **ENGLISH SACRED VOCAL:** *8 Anthems in Score for the Use of Cathedrals and Country Choirs* (London, 1794); *12 Anthems* (London, c.1798); *A Collection of Original Psalm Tunes* for 3 to 4 Voices (London, c.1805; with his son). **INSTRUMENTAL:** 6 sonatas for Piano or Harpsichord (London, c.1780); organ music.

BIBL.: J. Knapp, "S. W. and the Glee," *Music & Letters,* XXXIII (1952).

Webber, Andrew Lloyd. See **Lloyd Webber, Andrew.**

Webber, Julian Lloyd. See **Lloyd Webber, Julian.**

Weber, Alain, French composer; b. Château-Thierry, Dec. 8, 1930. He studied at the Paris Cons. with Tony Aubin and Messiaen; received the Premier Grand Prix de Rome in 1952; taught at the Paris Cons. (from 1957). His music is hedonistic in its lucid harmony and kinetic rhythmic dash.

WORKS: Ballet, *Le Petit Jeu* (Paris, 1953); chamber operas, *La Voie unique* (1958) and *La Rivière perdue* (1982); Horn Concerto (1954); *Suite pour une pièce vue* for Orch. (1954); *Symphonie* (1957); symphonic poem, *Midjaay* (1963); Trumpet Concerto (1965); *Strophes* for Trumpet, Strings, and Percussion (1966); *Strophes* for Trumpet and Orch. (1966); *Commentaires concertantes* for Flute and Orch. (1967); *Syllepse* for Chamber Orch. (1970); *Cantus* for Harp and Instrumental Ensemble (1984); Wind Quintet (1954); Woodwind Trio (1959); Sonata for Oboe and Harp (1960); *Variants* for 2 Pianos and Percussion (1964); *Palindromes* for Bassoon and Piano (1967); Violin Sonata (1968); *Synecdoque* for Oboe (1968); *Solipsisme* for String Quartet, Piano, and Percussion (1968); Piano Trio (1972); *Projections* for 5 Percussion (1972); *Koleda* for Celtic Harp (1973); *Mutances* for Clarinet and Instruments (1985–88); *Quasi Sonatina* for Guitar (1987); *Climax* for Piano (1988).

Weber, Ben (actually, **William Jennings Bryan**), American composer; b. St. Louis, July 23, 1916; d. N.Y., May 9, 1979. He studied medicine at the Univ. of Illinois; then entered De Paul Univ. in Chicago, where he studied voice, piano, and music theory. In composition he was practically self-taught, but he was attracted to the method of composition with 12 tones after meeting Schoenberg; paradoxically, he retained the firm tonal foundation of his melodic and contrapuntal structures. He moved to N.Y., where he held various positions in the recording industry; also taught composition privately. In 1959 he was elected president of the American

Composers Alliance. He received 2 Guggenheim fellowships (1950, 1953), an award and citation from the National Inst. of Arts and Letters (1960), and the 1st Phoebe Ketchum Thorne Music Fund Award (1965–68). In 1971 he was elected a member of the National Inst. of Arts and Letters. He left a memoir, *How I Took 63 Years to Commit Suicide* (1979; excerpts in the *Brooklyn Literary Review,* II, 1981).

WORKS: ORCH.: *Symphony on Poems of William Blake* for Baritone and Chamber Orch. (1950; N.Y., Oct. 28, 1952); Violin Concerto (1954); *Prelude and Passacaglia* (1954; Louisville, Jan. 1, 1955); *Rapsodie concertante* for Viola and Small Orch. (1957); Piano Concerto (1961); *Dramatic Piece* for Violin and Orch. (1970); *Sinfonia Clarion* for Small Orch. (1973; N.Y., Feb. 16, 1974). **CHAMBER:** 2 violin sonatas (1939; 1942, rev. 1943); 3 string quartets (1941, 1951, 1959, unfinished); Concerto for Piano, Cello, and Wind Quintet (1950); *Colloquy* for Brass Septet (1955); Serenade for String Quartet and Double Bass (1956); *Prelude and Nocturne* for Flute, Celesta, and Cello (1965); *Consort of Winds* for Wind Quintet (1974); *Capriccio* for Cello and Piano (1977); piano pieces; songs.

Weber, Bernhard Anselm, German pianist, conductor, and composer; b. Mannheim, April 18, 1764; d. Berlin, March 23, 1821. He commenced keyboard training with Vogler in 1773; after studying singing with Holzbauer and theory with Einberger, he returned to Vogler to study composition in 1775. He took courses in theology and law at the Univ. of Heidelberg in 1781; then traveled as a performer on the Xänorphica, a keyboard instrument invented by Rölling. In 1787 he became music director of Grossmann's opera troupe in Hannover, touring with it in 1790 in Holland, Germany, and Scandinavia. After a sojourn in Stockholm, he performed in Hamburg. In 1792 he was named joint music director (with Bernhard Wessely) of Berlin's Nationaltheater; in 1796 became its 1st music director, and in 1803 was elevated to the post of Kapellmeister; he retained his title when the German and Italian theaters merged in 1811. During his Berlin tenure, he championed the music of Gluck; conducted his *Iphigénie en Tauride* on Feb. 24, 1795. Weber distinguished himself as a pianist and conductor. Although he was a prolific composer, only a few songs from his stage works retained their popularity; his incidental music to Schiller's drama *Wilhelm Tell* (1804), however, was long admired.

BIBL.: H. Fischer, *B.A. W.* (diss., Univ. of Berlin, 1923).

Weber, Bernhard Christian, German organist and composer; b. Wolferschwenda, Dec. 1, 1712; d. Tennstedt, Feb. 5, 1758. He settled in Tennstedt as town organist in 1732. Inspired by Bach's example, and at the instigation of Bach's pupil G.H. Noah, Weber composed for organ a work containing 24 preludes and fugues in all keys, entitled *Das wohltemperierte Clavier* (1743).

Weber, Carl Maria (Friedrich Ernst) von, celebrated German composer, pianist, and conductor; b. Eutin, Oldenburg, Nov. 18, 1786; d. London, June 5, 1826. His father, Franz Anton von Weber (1734?–1812), was an army officer and a good musical amateur who played the violin and served as Kapellmeister in Eutin. It was his fondest wish that Carl Maria would follow in the footsteps of Mozart as a child prodigy (Constanze Weber, Mozart's wife, was his niece, thus making Carl Maria a 1st cousin of Mozart by marriage). Carl Maria's mother was a singer of some ability; she died when he was 11. Franz Anton led a wandering life as music director of his own theater company, taking his family with him on his tours. Although this mode of life interfered with his regular education, it gave him practical knowledge of the stage, and stimulated his imagination as a dramatic composer. Weber's 1st teachers were his father and his half-brother Fritz, a pupil of Haydn; at Hildburghausen, where he found himself with his father's company in 1796, he also received piano instruction from J.P. Heuschkel. The next year he was in Salzburg, where he attracted the attention of Michael Haydn, who taught him counterpoint; he composed a set of *6 Fughetten* there, which were publ. in 1798. As his peregrinations continued, he was taught singing by Valesi (J.B. Wallishauser) and composition by J.N. Kalcher in Munich (1798–1800). At the age of 12, he wrote an opera, *Die Macht der Liebe und des Weins*; it was never performed and the MS has not survived. Through a meeting with Aloys Senefelder, the inventor of lithography, he became interested in engraving; he became Senefelder's apprentice, acquiring considerable skill in the method; he engraved his own 6 *Variations on an Original Theme* for Piano (Munich, 1800). His father became interested in the business possibilities of lithography, and set up a workshop with him in Freiberg; however, the venture failed, and the young Carl Maria turned again to music. He composed a 2-act comic opera, *Das Waldmädchen*, in 1800; it was premiered in Freiberg on Nov. 24, 1800, 6 days after his 14th birthday; performances followed in Chemnitz (Dec. 5, 1800) and Vienna (Dec. 4, 1804). In 1801 the family was once more in Salzburg, where he studied further with Michael Haydn; wrote another opera, *Peter Schmoll und seine Nachbarn* (1801–2). He gave a concert in Hamburg in Oct. 1802, and the family then proceeded to Augsburg; they remained there from Dec. 1802 until settling in Vienna in Sept. 1803; there Weber continued his studies with Abbé Vogler, at whose recommendation he secured the post of conductor of the Breslau Opera in 1804. He resigned this post in 1806 after his attempts at operatic reform caused dissension. In 1806 he became honorary Intendant to Duke Eugen of Württemberg-Öls at Schloss Carlsruhe in Upper Silesia; much of his time was devoted to composition there. In 1807 he was engaged as private secretary to Duke Ludwig in Stuttgart, and also gave music lessons to his children. This employment was abruptly terminated when Weber became innocently involved in a scheme of securing a ducal appointment for a rich man's son in order to exempt him from military service, and accepted a loan of money. This was a common practice at the Stuttgart court, but as a result of the disclosure of Weber's involvement, he was arrested (Feb. 9, 1810) and kept in prison for 16 days. This matter, along with several others, was settled to his advantage, only to find him the target of his many creditors, who had him rearrested on Feb. 17. Finally, agreeing to pay off his debts as swiftly as possible, he was released and then banished by King Friedrich. He then went to Mannheim, where he made appearances as a pianist. He next went to Darmstadt, where he rejoined his former teacher, Vogler, for whom he wrote the introduction to his teacher's ed. of 12 Bach chorales. On Sept. 16, 1810, Weber's opera *Silvana* was successfully premiered in Frankfurt; the title role was sung by Caroline Brandt, who later became a member of the Prague Opera; Weber and Brandt were married in Prague on Nov. 4, 1817. Weber left Darmstadt in Feb. 1811 for Munich, where he composed several important orch. works, including the Clarinet Concertino, the 2 clarinet concertos, and the Bassoon Concerto. His clarinet pieces were written for the noted virtuoso Heinrich Bärmann. Weber's 1-act singspiel, *Abu Hassan*, was successfully given in Munich on June 4, 1811. From Aug. to Dec. 1811, Weber and Bärmann gave concerts in Switzerland; after appearing in Prague in Dec. 1811, they went to Leipzig in Jan. 1812, and then on to Weimar and Dresden. On March 15, 1812, they gave a concert in Berlin, which was attended by King Friedrich Wilhelm III. On Dec. 17, 1812, Weber was soloist at the premiere of his 2nd Piano Concerto in Gotha. Upon his return to Prague in Jan. 1813, he was informed that he was to be the director of the German Opera there. He was given extensive authority, and traveled to Vienna to engage singers and also secured the services of Franz Clement as concertmaster. During his tenure, Weber presented a distinguished repertoire, which included Beethoven's *Fidelio;* however, when his reforms encountered determined opposition, he submitted his resignation (1816). On Dec. 14, 1816, he was appointed Musikdirektor of the German Opera in Dresden by King Friedrich August III. He opened his 1st season on Jan. 30, 1817; that same year he was named Königlich Kapellmeister, and began to make sweeping reforms. About this time he approached Friedrich Kind, a Dresden lawyer and writer, and suggested to him the idea of preparing a libretto on a

Romantic German subject for his next opera. They agreed on *Der Freischütz*, a fairy tale from the *Gespensterbuch*, a collection of ghost stories by J.A. Apel and F. Laun. The composition of this work, which was to prove his masterpiece, occupied him for 3 years; the score was completed on May 13, 1820, and 2 weeks later Weber began work on the incidental music to Wolff's *Preciosa*, a play in 4 acts with spoken dialogue; it was produced in Berlin on March 14, 1821. A comic opera, *Die drei Pintos*, which Weber started at about the same time, was left unfinished. After some revisions, *Der Freischütz* was accepted for performance at the opening of Berlin's Neues Schauspielhaus. There arose an undercurrent of rivalry with Spontini, director of the Berlin Opera, a highly influential figure in operatic circles and at court. Spontini considered himself the guardian of the Italian-French tradition in opposition to the new German Romantic movement in music. Weber conducted the triumphant premiere of *Der Freischütz* on June 18, 1821; the work's success surpassed all expectations and the cause of new Romantic art was won; *Der Freischütz* was soon staged by all the major opera houses of Europe. In English, it was given first in London, on July 22, 1824; translations into other languages followed. Weber's next opera was *Euryanthe*, produced in Vienna on Oct. 25, 1823, with only moderate success. Meanwhile, Weber's health was affected by incipient tuberculosis and he was compelled to spend part of 1824 in Marienbad for a cure. He recovered sufficiently to begin the composition of *Oberon*, a commission from London's Covent Garden. The English libretto was prepared by J.R. Planché, based on a translation of C.M. Wieland's verse-romance of the same name. Once more illness interrupted Weber's progress on his work; he spent part of the summer of 1825 in Ems to prepare himself for the journey to England. He set out for London in Feb. 1826, a dying man. On his arrival, he was housed with Sir George Smart, the conductor of the Phil. Society of London. Weber threw himself into his work, presiding over 16 rehearsals for *Oberon*. On April 12, 1826, he conducted its premiere at Covent Garden, obtaining a tremendous success. Despite his greatly weakened condition, he conducted 11 more performances of the score, and also participated in various London concerts, playing for the last time a week before his death. He was found dead in his room on the morning of June 5, 1826. He was buried in London. His remains were removed to Dresden in 1844. On Dec. 14, 1844, they were taken to the Catholic cemetery in Dresden to the accompaniment of funeral music arranged from motifs from *Euryanthe* for wind instruments as prepared and conducted by Wagner. The next day, Weber's remains were interred as Wagner delivered an oration and conducted a chorus in his specially composed *An Webers Grabe*.

Weber's role in music history is epoch-making; in his operas, particularly in *Der Freischütz*, he opened the era of musical Romanticism, in decisive opposition to the established Italianate style. The highly dramatic and poetic portrayal of a German fairy tale, with its aura of supernatural mystery, appealed to the public, whose imagination had been stirred by the emergent Romantic literature of the period. Weber's melodic genius and mastery of the craft of composition made it possible for him to break with tradition and to start on a new path, at a critical time when individualism and nationalism began to emerge as sources of creative artistry. His instrumental works, too, possessed a new quality that signalized the transition from Classical to Romantic music. For piano he wrote pieces of extraordinary brilliance, introducing some novel elements in chord writing and passage work. He was himself an excellent pianist; his large hands gave him an unusual command of the keyboard (he could stretch the interval of a twelfth). Weber's influence on the development of German music was very great. The evolutionary link to Wagner's music drama is evident in the coloring of the orch. parts in Weber's operas and in the adumbration of the principle of leading motifs. Finally, he was one of the 1st outstanding interpretative conducting podium figures.

WORKS: In the list of Weber's works that follows, his compositions are identified by the J. numbers established by F. Jähns in his *Carl Maria von Weber in seinen Werken: Chronologisch-thematisches Verzeichniss seiner sämmtlichen Compositionen* (Berlin, 1871).

WORKS: OPERAS: *Die Macht der Liebe und des Weins*, J. Anh. 6 (singspiel, 1798; not perf.; not extant); *Das Waldmädchen*, J. Anh. 1 (Romantic comic opera, 1800; Freiberg, Nov. 24, 1800; only fragments extant); *Peter Schmoll und seine Nachbarn*, J.8 (1801–2; Augsburg, March 1803?; music not extant, dialogue lost); *Rübezahl*, J.44–46 (1804–5; unfinished; only 3 numbers extant); *Silvana*, J.87 (Romantic opera, 1808–10; Frankfurt, Sept. 16, 1810, composer conducting); *Abu Hassan*, J.106 (singspiel, 1810–11; Munich, June 4, 1811, composer conducting); *Der Freischütz*, J.277 (Romantic opera, 1817–21; Berlin, June 18, 1821, composer conducting); *Die drei Pintos*, J. Anh. 5 (comic opera, begun in 1820; unfinished; rev. by the composer's grandson, Carl von Weber, and Gustav Mahler; extant music completed by adding other works by the composer, with scoring by Mahler; Leipzig, Jan. 20, 1888, Mahler conducting); *Euryanthe*, J.291 (grand heroic Romantic opera, 1822–23; Vienna, Oct. 25, 1823, composer conducting); *Oberon, or The Elf King's Oath*, J.306 (Romantic opera, 1825–26; London, April 12, 1826, composer conducting).

OTHER WORKS FOR THE THEATER: Overture and 6 numbers for Schiller's tr. of Gozzi's *Turandot, Prinzessin von China*, J.75 (Stuttgart, Sept. 1809); Rondo alla polacca for Tenor for Haydn's pasticchio *Der Freibrief*, J.77 (1809); Duet for Soprano and Tenor for Haydn's *Der Freibrief*, J.78 (1809); 4 songs for Voice and Guitar (one with Male Chorus) for Kotzebue's *Der arme Minnesinger*, J.110–13 (1811); Scena ed aria for Soprano for Méhul's opera *Héléna*, J.178 (1815); 2 songs for Baritone and for Soprano and Bass for Fischer's singspiel *Der travestirte Aeneas*, J.183–84 (1815); 2 songs for Baritone and for Tenor for Gubitz's festspiel *Lieb' und Versöhnen*, J.186–87 (1815); Ballade for Baritone and Harp for Reinbeck's *Gordon und Montrose*, J.189 (1815); Arietta for Soprano for Huber's and Kauer's *Das Sternenmädchen im Maidlinger Walde*, J.194 (1816; text not extant); Romance for Voice and Guitar for Castelli's *Diana von Poitiers*, J.195 (1816); 10 numbers and 1 song for Unaccompanied Mezzo-soprano for Müllner's *König Yngurd*, J.214 (Dresden, April 14, 1817); 6 numbers for Moreto's *Donna Diana*, J.220 (1817); Song for Solo Voices and Chorus for Kind's *Der Weinberg an der Elbe*, J.222 (1817); Romance for Voice and Guitar for Kind's *Das Nachtlager von Granada*, J.223 (1818); 2-part song for Tenor and Bass for Holbein's *Die drei Wahrzeichen*, J.225 (1818); Dance and song for Tenor and Chorus for Hell's *Das Haus Anglade*, J.227 (1818; may not be by Weber); 8 numbers for Gehe's *Heinrich IV, König von Frankreich*, J.237 (Dresden, June 6, 1818); Scena ed aria for Soprano for Cherubini's opera *Lodoïska*, J.239 (1818); Chorus for 2 Sopranos and Bass for Grillparzer's *Sappho*, J.240 (1818); Song for Voice and Piano or Guitar for Kind's *Der Abend am Waldbrunnen*, J.243 (1818); 4 vocal numbers, march, and melodrama for Rublack's *Leib' um Liebe*, J.246 (1818); Agnus Dei for 2 Sopranos, Alto, and Wind Instruments for Blankensee's *Carlo*, J.273 (1820); 4 harp numbers for Houwald's *Der Leuchtturm*, J.276 (Dresden, April 26, 1820); Overture and 11 numbers to Wolff's *Preciosa*, J.279 (Berlin, March 14, 1821); Song for 2 Sopranos, Alto, Chorus, and Guitar for Shakespeare's *The Merchant of Venice*, J.280 (1821); one instrumental number (from the adagio of the Sym. No. 1 in C major, J.50) and 5 choruses for Robert's *Den Sachsensohn vermählet heute*, J.289 (1822); Arioso and recitative for Bass and Soprano for Spontini's opera *Olympie*, J.305 (1825).

CONCERT ARIAS: "Il momento s'avvicina," recitative and rondo for Soprano and Orch., J.93 (1810); "Misera me!," scena ed aria for Soprano and Orch. for *Atalia* J.121 (1811); "Qual altro attendi," scena ed aria for Tenor, Chorus, and Orch., J.126 (1812); "Signor, se padre sei," scena ed aria for Tenor, Choruses, and Orch. for *Ines de Castro*, J.142 (1812); "Non paventar mia vita," scena ed aria for Soprano and Orch. for *Ines de Castro*, J.181 (1815).

MASSES: Mass in E-flat major for Soprano, Alto, Tenor, Bass,

Choir, Organ, and Orch., J. Anh. 8 (1802); Mass in E-flat major for Soprano, Alto, Tenor, Bass, Choir, and Orch., J.224, "Missa Sancta No. 1" (1817–18); Offertory, "Gloria et honore," for Soprano, Choir, and Orch., for the Missa Sancta No. 1, J.226 (1818); Offertory, "In die solemnitatis," for Soprano, Choir, and Orch., for the Missa Sancta No. 2, J.250 (1818); Mass in G major for Soli, Choir, and Orch., J.251, "Missa Sancta No. 2" or "Jubelmesse" (1818–19).

CANTATAS: *Der erste Ton* for Reciter and Orch., with closing chorus, J.58 (1808; rev. 1810); *In seiner Ordnung schafft der Herr*, hymn for Soli, Chorus, and Orch., J.154 (1812); *Kampf und Sieg* for Soli, Chorus, and Orch., J.190 (concerning the battle of Waterloo; 1815); *L'Accoglienza* for 3 Sopranos, Tenor, 2 Basses, Chorus, and Orch., J.221 (1817); *Jubel-Cantate* for Soli, Chorus, and Orch., J.224 (1818); *Du, bekränzend unsre Laren* for 2 Sopranos, Alto, Tenor, Bass, Chorus, Piano, and Flute, J.283 (1821); *Wo nehm ich Blumen her* for Soprano, Tenor, Bass, and Piano, J.290 (1823); also many other choral works and part songs, including *Trauer-Musik* for Baritone, Choir, and 10 Wind Instruments, J.116 (1811); *Das Turnierbankett* for 2 Tenors, Bass, and 2 Male Choirs, J.132 (1812); *Schwäbisches Tanzlied* for Soprano, 2 Tenors, 2 Basses, and Piano, J.135 (1812); *Kriegs-Eid* for Unison Male Voices and 7 Instruments, J.139 (1812); *Leyer und Schwert*, 6 songs for 4 Male Voices, J.168–73 (1814); *Natur und Liebe* for 2 Sopranos, 2 Tenors, 2 Basses, and Piano, J.241 (1818); also canons for 3 or 4 Voices; more than 80 songs; 6 vocal duets; *Zehn schottische Nationalgesänge*, arrangements for Voice with accompaniments for Flute, Violin, Cello, and Piano, J.295–304 (1825).

ORCH.: *Romanza Siciliana* in G minor for Flute and Orch., J.47 (1805); Horn Concertino in E minor, J.188 (1806; not extant; 2nd ver., 1815); 6 Variations on "A Schüsserl und a Reind'rl" in C major for Viola and Orch., J.49 (1806); Sym. No. 1 in C major, J.50 (1807); Sym. No. 2 in C major, J.51 (1807); *Grande Ouverture à plusiers instruments*, J.54 (rev. overture to *Peter Schmoll und seine Nachbarn*, J.8; 1807); *Grand Pot-Pourri* for Cello and Orch., J.64 (1808); *Andante e Rondo Ungarese* in C minor for Viola and Orch., J.79 (1809); Variations in F major for Cello and Orch., J.94 (1810); Piano Concerto No. 1 in C Major, J.98 (1810); Clarinet Concertino in E-flat major, J.109 (1811); Clarinet Concerto No. 1 in F minor, J.114 (1811); *Adagio und Rondo* in F Major for Harmonichord and Orch., J.115 (1811); Clarinet Concerto No. 2 in E-flat major, J.118 (1811); Bassoon Concerto in F major, J.127 (1811; 1st confirmed perf., Prague, Feb. 19, 1813; rev. 1822); *Der Beherrscher der Geister*, overture, J.122 (rev. of the lost *Rübezahl* overture; 1811); Piano Concerto No. 2 in E-flat major, J.155 (Gotha, Dec. 17, 1812, composer soloist); *Andante e Rondo Ungarese* in C minor for Bassoon and Orch., J.158 (rev. of J.79; 1813); *Deutscher (Original-Walzer)* in D major, J.185 (orch. arr. of a song in Fischer's singspiel, *Der travestirte Aeneas*, J.183–84; 1815); *Tedesco* in D major, J.191 (1816); *Jubel-Ouvertüre* in E major, J.245 (1818); *Konzertstück* in F minor for Piano and Orch., J.282 (1821).

WIND INSTRUMENTS: *Tusch* for 20 Trumpets, J.47a (1806); Waltz for Flute, 2 Clarinets, 2 Horns, Trumpet, and 2 Bassoons, J.149 (1812); *Marcia vivace* for 10 Trumpets, J.288 (1822); March for Wind Band, J.307 (also arr. for Soloists, Chorus, and Orch.; rev. of No. 5 of *Six Petites Pièces Faciles*, J.13; 1826).

PIANO: *Sechs Fughetten*, J.1–6 (1798); *Six Variations on an Original Theme*, J.7 (1800); *Douze Allemandes*, J.15–26 (1801); *Sechs Ecossaisen*, J.29–34 (1802); *Huit variations sur l'air de ballet de Castor et Pollux* from Vogler's opera, J.40 (1804); *Six variations sur l'air de Naga "Woher mag dies wohl kommen?"* from Vogler's opera *Samori*, with Violin and Cello ad libitum, J.43 (1804); *Sept variations sur l'air "Vien quà, Dorina bella"* by Bianchi, J.53 (1807); *Theme original varié* (7 variations), J.55 (1808); *Momento capriccioso* in B-flat major, J.56 (1808); *Grande Polonaise* in E-flat major, J.59 (1808); Piano Sonata No. 1 in C major, J.138 (1812); 7 variations on "A peine au sortir de l'enfance" from Méhul's opera *Joseph*, J.141

(1812); *Sechs Favorit-Walzer der Kaiserin von Frankreich, Ma-Rie Louise,* J.143–48 (1812); *Air russe* ("Schöne Minka") (9 variations), J.179 (1815); Piano Sonata No. 2 in A-flat major, J.199 (1816); Piano Sonata No. 3 in D minor, J.206 (1816); *Sieben Variationen über ein Zigeunerlied,* J.219 (1817); *Rondo brillante* ("La gaité") in E-flat major, J.252 (1819); *Aufforderung zum Tanze: Rondo brillant* in D-flat major, J.260 (1819); *Polacca brillante* "L'hilarite") in E major, J.268 (1819); Piano Sonata No. 4 in E minor, J.287 (1822). PIANO DUET: *Six petites pièces faciles,* J.9–14 (1801); *Six pièces,* J.81–86 (1809); *Huit pièces,* J.236, 242, 248, 253–54, 264–66 (1818–19).

CHAMBER: *Neuf variations sur un air norvégien* for Violin and Piano, J.61 (1808); Piano Quartet in B-flat major, J.76 (1809); *Six sonates progressives* for Violin and Piano, J.99–104 (1810); *Melody* in F major for Clarinet, J.119 (1811); *Seven Variations on a Theme from Silvana* for Clarinet and Piano, J.128 (1811); Clarinet Quintet in B-flat major, J.182 (1815); *Grand Duo Concertant* for Piano and Clarinet, J.204 (1815–16); *Divertimento assai facile* for Guitar and Piano, J.207 (1816); Trio for Flute, Cello, and Piano, J.259 (1819).

WRITINGS: Weber's critical writings on music are valuable. He also left an autobiographical sketch, an unfinished novel, poems, etc. Editions of his writings include T. Hell, ed., *Hinterlassene Schriften von C.M. v.W.* (3 vols., Dresden and Leipzig, 1828; 2nd ed., 1850); G. Kaiser, ed., *Sämtliche Schriften von C.M. v.W.: Kritische Ausgabe* (Berlin and Leipzig, 1908); W. Altmann, ed., *W.s ausgewählte Schriften* (Regensburg, 1928); K. Laux, ed., *C.M. v.W.: Kunstansichten* (Leipzig, 1969; 2nd ed., 1975); J. Warrack, ed., and M. Cooper, tr., *C.M. v.W.: Writings on Music* (Cambridge, 1982).

BIBL.: COLLECTED WORKS, SOURCE MATERIAL: There is no complete ed. of Weber's works. A projected collected ed., *C.M. v.W.: Musikalische Werke: Erste kritische Gesamtausgabe,* under the general editorship of H.J. Moser, was abandoned with the outbreak of World War II; only 3 vols. were publ. (Vol. II/1, Augsburg, 1926; Vol. II/2, Augsburg, 1928; Vol. II/3, Braunschweig, 1939). Previously unpubl. works are found in L. Hirschberg, ed., *Reliquienschrein des Meisters C.M. v.W.* (Berlin, 1927). The standard thematic catalogue was prepared by F. Jähns, *C.M. v.W in seinen Werken: Chronologisch-thematisches Verzeichniss seiner sämmtlichen Compositionen* (Berlin, 1871). See also the vols. by H. Dunnebeil, *C.M. v.W.: Verzeichnis seiner Kompositionen* (Berlin, 1942; 2nd ed., 1947) and *Schrifttum über C.M. v.W.* (Berlin, 1947; 4th ed., 1957); and D. and A. Henderson, *C.M. v.W.: A Guide to Research* (N.Y., 1989).

CORRESPONDENCE: C. von Weber (grandson of the composer), ed., *Reise-Briefe von C.M. v.W. an seine Gattin Carolina* (Leipzig, 1886); E. Rudorff, *Briefe von C.M. v.W. an Hinrich Lichtenstein* (Braunschweig, 1900); G. Kaiser, ed., *W.s Briefe an den Grafen Karl von Brühl* (Leipzig, 1911); L. Hirschberg, ed., *Siebenundsiebzig bisher ungedruckte Briefe C.M. v.W.s* (Hildburghausen, 1926); G. Kinsky, "Ungedruckte Briefe C.M. v.W.s," *Zeitschrift für Musik* (1926); W. Virneisel, "Aus dem Berliner Freundeskreise W.s," in G. Hausswald, ed., *C.M. v.W.: eine Gedenkschrift* (Dresden, 1951); H. Worbs, ed., *C.M. v.W. Briefe* (Frankfurt, 1982).

BIOGRAPHICAL: W. Neumann, *W.: eine Biographie* (Kassel, 1855); M. von Weber (son of the composer), *C.M. v.W.: ein Lebensbild* (3 vols., Leipzig, 1864–66; abr. Eng. tr. by J. Simpson as *W.: The Life of an Artist,* 2 vols., London, 1865; 2nd Ger. ed., abr., by R. Pechel, Berlin, 1912); F. Jähns, *C.M. v.W.: eine Lebensskizze nach authentischen Quellen* (Leipzig, 1873); J. Benedict, *W.* (London and N.Y., 1881; 5th ed., 1899); L. Nohl, *W.* (Leipzig, 1883); A. Reissmann, *W., Sein Leben und seine Werke* (Berlin, 1886); H. Gehrmann, *C.M. v.W.* (Berlin, 1899); G. Servières, *W.* (Paris, 1906; new ed., 1925); H. von der Pfordten, *W.* (Leipzig, 1919); A. Cœuroy, *W.* (Paris, 1925; 2nd ed., 1953); E. Kroll, *C.M. v.W.* (Potsdam, 1934); W. Saunders, *W.* (London and N.Y., 1940); L. and R. Stebbins, *Enchanted Wanderer: The Life of C.M. v.W.* (N.Y., 1940); H. Moser, *C.M. v.W.: Leben und Werk* (Leipzig, 1941; 2nd ed., 1955); P. Raabe, *Wege zu W.* (Regensburg, 1942); W. Zentner,

C.M. v.W.: Sein Leben und sein Schaffen (Olten, 1952); H. Schnoor, *W.: Gestalt und Schöpfung* (Dresden, 1953); F. Grüniger, *C.M. v.W.: Leben und Werk* (Freiburg im Breisgau, 1954); K. Laux, *C.M. v.W.* (Leipzig, 1966; 2nd ed., 1986); J. Warrack, *C.M. v.W.* (N.Y. and London, 1968; 2nd ed., 1976); D. Härtwig, *C.M. v.W.* (Leipzig, 1986); K. Höcker, *Oberons Horn: das Leben von C.M. v.W.* (Berlin, 1986); H. Hoffmann, *C.M. v.W.: Biographie eines realistichen Romantikers* (Düsseldorf, 1986).

WEBER AND HIS CONTEMPORARIES: J. Lobe, "Gespräche mit C.M. v.W.," *Fliegende Blätter für Musik,* I (Leipzig, 1855; reprinted in his *Consonanzen und Dissonanzen,* Leipzig, 1869); M. Runze, *Loewe und W.," Loewe Redivivus* (Berlin, 1888); H. Krüger, *Pseudoromantik, Friedrich Kind und der Dresdener Liederkreis* (Leipzig, 1904); H. and C. Cox, eds., *Leaves from the Journals of Sir George Smart* (London, 1907); K. Huschke, "W.s Beziehungen zu Ludwig von Beethoven und Franz Schubert," *Deutsche Revue* (May–June 1919); E. Kroll, "E.T.A. Hoffmann und W.," *Neue Musik-Zeitung,* XLIII (1921); K. Huschke, "Spohr und W.," *Allgemeine Musik-Zeitung* (1934); E. Kroll, "Beethoven und W.," *Neues Beethoven-Jahrbuch* (1935); L. Schmidt, "Zeitgenössische Nachrichten über C.M. v.W.," *Die Musik,* XXXIII (1940–41).

CRITICAL, ANALYTICAL: H. von Chezy, "C.M. v.W.s Euryanthe: ein Beitrag zur Geschichte der deutschen Oper," *Neue Zeitschrift für Musik,* XIII (1840); F. Kind, *Freischütz-Buch* (Leipzig, 1843); R. Wagner: articles on W. in his *Gesammelte Schriften und Dichtungen* (Vol. I, Leipzig, 1871; Eng. tr. by W. Ashton Ellis as *The Prose Works of Richard Wagner,* Vol. VII, London, 1898); A. Jullien, *W. à Paris en 1826* (Paris, 1877); G. Kaiser, *Beiträge zu einer Charakteristik W.s als Musikschriftsteller* (Leipzig, 1910); G. Servières, *Le "Freischütz"* de W. (Paris, 1913); W. Georgii, *C.M. v.W. als Klavierkomponist* (diss., Univ. of Halle, 1914); E. Dent, "A W. Centenary," *Music & Letters* (July 1921); E. Hasselberg, ed., *Der Freischütz: Friedrich Kinds Operndichtung und ihre Quellen* (Berlin, 1921); M. Degen, *Die Lieder von C.M. v.W.* (Freiburg, 1923); A. Cœuroy, "Le Problème d'Euryanthe," *Le Correspondent* (Oct. 25, 1923); idem, "W. as Writer," *Musical Quarterly* (Jan. 1925); E. Reiter, *W.s künstlerische Persönlichkeit aus seinen Schriften* (Leipzig, 1926); H. Abert, "W. und sein Freischütz," *Jahrbuch der Musikbibliothek Peters 1926* (reprinted in his *Gesammelte Schriften und Vorträge,* Halle, 1929); J.-G. Prod'homme, "The Works of W. in France," *Musical Quarterly* (July 1928); A. Sandt, *W.s Opern in ihrer Instrumentation* (Frankfurt, 1932); G. Kinsky, "Was Mendelssohn Indebted to W.?," *Musical Quarterly* (April 1933); G. Abraham, "W. as Novelist and Critic," ibid. (Jan. 1934); P. Listl, *C.M. v.W. als Ouvertürenkomponist* (diss., Univ. of Würzburg, 1936); A. Einstein, "C.M. v.W.," *Music & Letters* (Jan. 1937); H. Schnoor, *W. auf dem Welttheater; Ein Freischützbuch* (Dresden, 1942; 4th ed., 1963); P. Kirby, "W.'s Operas in London, 1824–26," *Musical Quarterly* (July 1946); G. Jones, *Backgrounds and Themes of the Operas of C.M. v.W.* (diss., Cornell Univ., 1972); idem, "W.'s 'Secondary Worlds': the Later Operas of C.M. v.W.," *International Review of the Aesthetics and Sociology of Music,* VII (1976); R. Langley, "W. and the Piano," *Musical Times* (Nov. 1986).

MISCELLANEOUS: R. Haas, "Ein Notizen-Buch C.M. v.W.s aus Prag," *Der Merker,* VII (1916); A. Maecklenburg, "Der Fall Spontini-W.," *Zeitschrift für Musikwissenschaft,* VI (1923–24); F. Rapp, *Ein unbekanntes Bildnis W.s* (Stuttgart, 1937); G. Hausswald, ed., *C.M. v.W.: eine Gedenkschrift* (Dresden, 1951).

Weber, Fridolin, German singer and violinist, uncle of **Carl Maria (Friedrich Ernst) von Weber;** b. Zell, Wiesental, 1733; d. Vienna, Oct. 23, 1779. He served in the Mannheim electoral chapel. He had 4 daughters:

(1) (Maria) Josepha Weber, soprano; b. Zell, c.1759; d. Vienna, Dec. 29, 1819. After appearances in provincial music centers, she settled in Vienna in 1788; that same year she married the violinist Franz de Paula Hofer (1755–96), one of Mozart's friends; her 2nd husband was the bass and actor (Friedrich) Sebastian Mayer (1773–1835), the creator of the role of Pizarro in Beethoven's *Fidelio*. She was one of the leading singers in Vienna, being closely associated with Schikaneder's Theater auf der Wieden from 1790; she retired from the stage in 1805. Mozart wrote the aria *Schon lacht der holde Frühling*, K. 580, for her, as well as the role of the Queen of the Night in his opera *Die Zauberflöte*; nevertheless, he disparaged her character in a letter of Dec. 15, 1781.

(2) (Maria) Aloysia (Louise Antonia) Weber, soprano; b. c.1760; d. Salzburg, June 8, 1839. She studied voice with Mozart while he was in Mannheim (1777–78); he fell in love with her, but she left him; after singing in Munich (1778–79), she went to Vienna as a member of the German opera (1779–82) and the Italian opera (1782–92). She married the court actor and painter Joseph Lange (1751–1831) in 1780; she left him in 1795 to pursue a concert career. Mozart wrote a number of concert arias for her, as well as the role of Madame Herz in his *Der Schauspieldirektor*.

(3) (Maria) Constanze (Constantia) (Caecilia Josepha Johanna Aloisia) Weber, soprano; b. Zell, Jan. 4, 1762; d. Salzburg, March 6, 1842. She was the wife of **Wolfgang Amadeus Mozart.**

(4) (Maria) Sophie Weber, soprano; b. Zell, Oct. 1763; d. Salzburg, Oct. 26, 1846. She married the tenor and composer **Jakob Haibel** in 1807. She was with Mozart during the last hours of his life, and related her account of his death to her brother-in-law, **Georg Nikolaus Nissen,** who wrote a biography of Mozart.

Weber, Friedrich Dionys (actually, **Bedrich Diviš**), Bohemian pedagogue, writer on music, and composer; b. Velichov, near Carlsbad, Oct. 9, 1766; d. Prague, Dec. 25, 1842. He began his musical studies with F. Beier in Velichov; after studies at the Doupov Gymnasium and courses in theology, philosophy, and law in Prague, he completed his musical training with Abbé Vogler; also met Mozart. He devoted himself mainly to pedagogy; was one of the founders of the Prague Cons., which he served as its 1st director from 1811 until his death; also was director of the Prague Organ School (1839–42). Among his extant works are the opera *König der Genien* (Prague, June 1, 1800), the cantata *Böhmens Errettung* (Prague, April 22, 1797), various dance pieces for orch., 3 quartets for 4 horns, 3 sextets for 6 horns, and a number of piano pieces.

WRITINGS (all publ. in Prague): *Das Konservatorium der Musik zu Prag* (1817); *Allgemeine theoretisch-praktische Vorschule der Musik* (1828); *Lehrbuch der Harmonielehre und des Generalbasses* (1830–34); *Vollständige Theorie der Musik* (1840); *Allgemeine musikalische Zeichenlehre* (2nd ed., 1841); *Harmonielehre* (2nd ed., 1841); *Notenbeispiele zu F.D. Webers Vorschule der Musik* (1843); *Theoretisch-praktisches Lehrbuch der Tonsetzkunst* (2nd ed., 1843).

Weber, Georg Viktor, German ecclesiastic and choral conductor; b. Ober-Erlenbach, Feb. 25, 1838; d. Mainz, Sept. 24, 1911. He took Holy Orders in 1863; in 1866, was appointed music director and organist at the Mainz Cathedral, where he presented fine concerts of a cappella music of the 15th and 16th centuries with his excellent choir; was also an expert on organ building.

WRITINGS: *Manuale cantus ecclesiastici juxta ritum S. Rom. ecclesiae* (1878; 2nd ed., 1897); *Orgelbuch zum Mainzer Diocesan-Gesangbuch* (1880; 3rd ed., 1896); *Über Orgeldispositionen* (1890); *Die Verbesserung der "Medicaea"* (1901).

Weber, (Jacob) Gottfried, eminent German music theorist and composer; b. Freinsheim, near Mannheim, March 1, 1779; d. Kreuznach, Sept. 21, 1839. He studied law at Heidelberg and Göttingen, and filled positions as judge in Mannheim (1802), Mainz (1814), and Darmstadt (1818); was appointed General State Prosecutor of Hesse in 1832. He was an excellent amateur pianist and also played the flute and the cello; in 1806, founded a musical society called "Conservatorium" in Mannheim; in 1824, began the magazine *Caecilia,* and ed. it until his death. He made a thorough study of the theoretical works of Marpurg, Kirnberger, Abbé Vogler, and others, and

then brought out his important treatise *Versuch einer geordneten Theorie der Tonsetzkunst* (3 vols., 1817–21; 2nd ed. in 4 vols., 1824; 3rd ed. in 4 vols., 1830–32), in which he introduced the now widely accepted symbols for designating the major keys with capital letters and minor keys with small letters, Roman figures for degrees of the scale, etc. It was publ. in Eng. in Boston (1846) and London (1851). His other writings include *Über chronometrische Tempobezeichnung* (Mainz, 1817), *Allgemeine Musiklehre zum Selbstunterricht für Lehrer und Lernende* (Darmstadt, 1822; 3rd ed., 1831), *Ergebnisse der bisherigen Forschungen über die Echtheit des Mozart'schen Requiems* (Mainz, 1826), *Weitere Ergebnisse der weiteren Forschungen über die Echtheit des Mozart'schen Requiems* (Mainz, 1827), and *Generalbasslehre zum Selbstunterricht* (Mainz, 1833). He composed 2 masses, a requiem mass, a Te Deum, and other sacred works, some chamber music, and songs.

Weber, Gustav, Swiss organist, conductor, and composer; b. Münchenbuchsee, Oct. 30, 1845; d. Zürich, June 12, 1887. He studied at the Leipzig Cons. (1861), with V. Lachner in Mannheim (1865), and with Tausig in Berlin (1869–70); his symphonic poem *Zur Iliade* was presented by Liszt at the Beethoven Centennial Festival in 1870. In 1872 he settled in Zürich as a church organist, teacher at the Cons., and choral conductor; was ed. of the *Schweizerische Musikzeitung* (1876–83). His compositions are in the Romantic tradition; among his output are orch. works, piano pieces, and much vocal music. He contributed articles to various publs. and wrote the study *Heinrich Zwingli: Seine Stellung zur Musik und seine Lieder* (Zürich, 1884).

BIBL.: A. Schneider, *G. W.* (Zürich, 1888); A. Steiner, *G. W.* (Zürich, 1910).

Weber, Joseph Miroslav, Czech violinist and composer; b. Prague, Nov. 9, 1854; d. Munich, Jan. 1, 1906. He was taught by his father, and played violin in public as a child; then studied at the Prague Cons. He subsequently occupied posts as concertmaster in Sondershausen (1873–75) and Darmstadt (1875–83), and then assistant Kapellmeister (1883–89) and 1st Kapellmeister (1889–93) in Wiesbaden. He joined the Court Opera in Munich in 1894 and became its concertmaster in 1901.

WORKS: *Der selige Herr Vetter,* comic opera (Wiesbaden, 1894); *Die neue Mamsell,* operetta (Munich, Nov. 21, 1896); *Die Rheinnixe,* ballet (Wiesbaden, May 31, 1884); Violin Concerto (1898); 2 orch. suites; Septet for Clarinet, Bassoon, 2 Horns, Violin, Viola, and Cello, *Aus meinem Leben* (1899); 2 string quartets; choral pieces.

Weber, Ludwig, eminent Austrian bass; b. Vienna, July 29, 1899; d. there, Dec. 9, 1974. He studied with Alfred Boruttau in Vienna; made his debut there at the Volksoper as Fiorello in 1920; then sang in Barmen-Elberfeld (1925–27), Düsseldorf (1927–30), and Cologne (1930–33). After singing at the Bavarian State Opera in Munich (1933–45), he was one of the principal members of the Vienna State Opera (1945–60); also appeared at London's Covent Garden (1936–39; 1947; 1950–51) and at the Bayreuth Festivals (1951–60). He was a prof. at the Salzburg Mozarteum (from 1961). He was one of the foremost Wagnerian bass singers of his time, excelling particularly as Daland, Gurnemanz, and Hagen; he also distinguished himself in such roles as Rocco, Kaspar, Baron Ochs, Méphistophélès, and Wozzeck.

Weber, Margrit, Swiss pianist; b. Ebnat-Kappel, Feb. 24, 1924. She studied organ with Heinrich Funk in Zürich; then received training in piano from Max Egger and Walter Lang at the Cons. there. She was employed as an organist at the age of 15; then devoted herself chiefly to the piano. She toured Europe, presenting many new works; also played in the U.S. and Canada. She was the soloist in the 1st performances of piano concertos by Martinů and Alexander Tcherepnin, and of Stravinsky's *Movements* for Piano and Orch., which she performed under Stravinsky's direction in N.Y., on Jan. 10, 1960.

Weber, Wilhelm, German choral conductor and composer; b. Bruchsal, Nov. 16, 1859; d. Augsburg, Oct. 14, 1918. After studying at the Stuttgart Cons., he went to Augsburg, where he taught at the Hochschule für Musik from 1884, becoming its director in 1905. From 1892 he was conductor of the Oratorienverein, notable for its numerous German premieres of works by foreign composers; he also conducted at various festivals in Germany. He publ. 2 books of *Landsknechtslieder* and other songs; choruses; piano pieces. He was the author of *Beethovens Missa solemnis* (1897; 2nd ed., 1903) and *Händels Oratorien, übersetzt und bearbeitet von F. Chrysander* (3 vols., 1898, 1900, 1902).

Webern, Anton (Friedrich Wilhelm) von, remarkable Austrian composer (he removed the nobiliary particle "von" in 1918 when such distinctions were outlawed in Austria); b. Vienna, Dec. 3, 1883; d. (accidentally shot and killed by an American soldier) Mittersill, Sept. 15, 1945. He received his first instruction in music from his mother, an amateur pianist; then studied piano, cello, and theory with Edwin Komauer in Klagenfurt; also played cello in the orch. there. In 1902 he entered the Univ. of Vienna, where he studied harmony with Graedener and counterpoint with Navratil; also attended classes in musicology with Guido Adler; received his Ph.D. in 1906 with a dissertation on Heinrich Isaac's *Choralis Constantinus II.* In 1904 he began private studies in composition with Arnold Schoenberg, whose ardent disciple he became; Alban Berg also studied with Schoenberg; together, Schoenberg, Berg, and Webern laid the foundations of what became known as the 2nd Viennese School of composition. The unifying element was the adoption of Schoenberg's method of composition with 12 tones related only to one another. Malevolent opponents referred to Schoenberg, Berg, and Webern as a Vienna Trinity, with Schoenberg as God the Father, Berg as God the Son, and Webern as the Holy Ghost; the last appellation was supposed to describe the phantomlike substance of some of Webern's works. From 1908 to 1914 Webern was active as a conductor in Vienna and in Germany; in 1915–16 he served in the army; in 1917–18, was conductor at the Deutsches Theater in Prague. In 1918 he settled in Mödling, near Vienna, where he taught composition privately; from 1918 to 1922 he supervised the programs of the Verein für Musikalische Privataufführungen (Society for Private Musical Performances), organized in Vienna by Schoenberg with the intention of promoting modern music without being exposed to reactionary opposition (music critics were not admitted to these performances). Webern was conductor of the Schubertbund (1921–22) and the Mödling Male Chorus (1921–26); he also led the Vienna Workers' Sym. concerts (1922–34) and the Vienna Workers' Chorus (1923–34), both sponsored by the Social Democratic Party. From 1927 to 1938 he was a conductor on the Austrian Radio; furthermore, he conducted guest engagements in Germany, Switzerland, and Spain; from 1929, made several visits to England, where he was a guest conductor with the BBC Sym. Orch. For the most part, however, he devoted himself to composition, private teaching, and lecturing. After Hitler came to power in Germany in 1933, Webern's music was banned as a manifestation of "cultural Bolshevism" and "degenerate art." His position became more difficult after the Anschluss in 1938, for his works could no longer be publ.; he eked out an existence by teaching a few private pupils and making piano arrangements of musical scores by others for Universal Edition. After his son was killed in an air bombardment of a train in Feb. 1945, he and his wife fled from Vienna to Mittersill, near Salzburg, to stay with his married daughters and grandchildren. His life ended tragically on the evening of Sept. 15, 1945, when he was shot and killed by an American soldier after stepping outside his son-in-law's residence (for a full account, see H. Moldenhauer, *The Death of Anton Webern: A Drama in Documents,* N.Y., 1961).

Webern left relatively few works, and most of them are of short duration (the 4th of his 5 Pieces for Orch., op. 10, scored for clarinet, trumpet, trombone, mandolin, celesta, harp, drum,

violin, and viola, takes only 19 seconds to play), but in his music he achieves the utmost subtilization of expressive means. He adopted the 12-tone method of composition almost immediately after its definitive formulation by Schoenberg (1924), and extended the principle of nonrepetition of notes to tone colors, so that in some of his works (e.g., Sym., op. 21) solo instruments are rarely allowed to play 2 successive thematic notes. Dynamic marks are similarly diversified. Typically, each 12-tone row is divided into symmetric sections of 2, 4, or 6 members, which enter mutually into intricate but invariably logical canonic imitations. Inversions and augmentations are inherent features; melodically and harmonically, the intervals of the major seventh and minor ninth are stressed; single motifs are brief, and stand out as individual particles or lyric ejaculations. The impact of these works on the general public and on the critics was disconcerting, and upon occasion led to violent demonstrations; however, the extraordinary skill and novelty of technique made this music endure beyond the fashions of the times; performances of Webern's works multiplied after his death, and began to influence increasingly larger groups of modern musicians; Stravinsky acknowledged the use of Webern's methods in his latest works; jazz composers have professed to follow Webern's ideas of tone color; analytical treatises have been publ. in several languages. The International Webern Festival celebrated the centennial of his birth in Dec. 1983 in Vienna.

Works: Orch.: *Im Sommerwind,* idyll for Large Orch. (1904; Seattle, May 25, 1962, Ormandy conducting); *Passacaglia,* op. 1 (1908; Vienna, Nov. 4, 1908, composer conducting); *6 Orchestral Pieces,* op. 6 (1909; Vienna, March 31, 1913, Schoenberg conducting; rev. 1928; Berlin, Jan. 27, 1929); *5 Orchestral Pieces,* op. 10 (1911–13; Zürich, June 22, 1926, composer conducting); *5 Orchestral Pieces,* op. posthumous (1913; Cologne, Jan. 13, 1969); Sym. for Chamber Ensemble, op. 21 (1928; N.Y., Dec. 18, 1929); 5 Movements for String Quartet, op. 5, arr. for String Orch. (1928–29; Philadelphia, March 26, 1930); *Variations,* op. 30 (1940; Winterthur, March 3, 1943). **Vocal:** *Entflieht auf leichten Kähnen,* op. 2, for Unaccompanied Chorus (1908; Furstenfeld, April 10, 1927); 2 songs to words by Goethe, op. 19, for Chorus, Celesta, Guitar, Violin, Clarinet, and Bass Clarinet (1926); *Das Augenlicht,* op. 26, for Chorus and Orch. (1935; London, June 17, 1938); *1st Cantata* for Soprano, Mixed Chorus, and Orch. (1938–39; London, July 12, 1946); *2nd Cantata* for Soprano, Bass, Mixed Chorus, and Orch. (1941–43; Brussels, June 23, 1950); 2 sets of 5 songs for Voice and Piano, to poems by Stefan George, opp. 3 and 4 (1908–9); 2 songs for Voice and Instrumental Ensemble, on poems by Rilke, op. 8 (1910; rev. 1921 and 1925); 4 songs for Voice and Piano, op. 12 (1915–17); 4 songs for Voice and Orch., op. 13 (1914–18); 6 songs for Voice and Instruments, on poems by Georg Trakl, op. 14 (1919–21; Donaueschingen, July 20, 1924); *5 Sacred Songs* for Voice and Instruments, op. 15 (1917–22; Vienna, Oct. 9, 1924, composer conducting); *5 Canons* on Latin texts for Voice, Clarinet, and Bass Clarinet, op. 16 (1923–24; N.Y., May 8, 1951); *3 Traditional Rhymes* for Voice and Instruments, op. 17 (1924–25; N.Y., March 16, 1952); 3 songs for Voice, Clarinet, and Guitar, op. 18 (1925; Los Angeles, Feb. 8, 1954); 3 songs for Voice and Piano, op. 23 (1933–34); 3 songs for Voice and Piano, op. 25 (1934). **Chamber:** String Quartet, in one movement (1905; Seattle, May 26, 1962); Piano Quintet, in one movement (Vienna, Nov. 7, 1907); 5 Movements for String Quartet (1909; Vienna, Feb. 8, 1910); 4 pieces for Violin and Piano, op. 7 (1910; rev. 1914); 6 bagatelles for String Quartet, op. 9 (1911–13; Donaueschingen, July 19, 1924); *3 Little Pieces* for Cello and Piano, op. 11 (1914; Mainz, Dec. 2, 1924); String Trio, op. 20 (1926–27; Vienna, Jan. 16, 1928); Quartet for Violin, Clarinet, Tenor Saxophone, and Piano, op. 22 (1930; Vienna, April 13, 1931); Concerto for 9 Instruments, op. 24 (1934; Prague, Sept. 4, 1935); String Quartet, op. 28 (1936–38; Pittsfield, Mass., Sept. 22, 1938); Variations for Piano (1936; Vienna, Oct. 26, 1937); arrangements for Chamber Orch. of Schoenberg's Chamber Sym., op. 9 (1923), Schubert's *Deutsche Tänze* (1931), and

Bach's Ricercare *a 6* from *Das musikalische Opfer* (London, April 25, 1935, composer conducting).

WRITINGS: W. Reich ed. *Der Weg zur neuen Musik* (Vienna, 1933; new ed., 1960; Eng. tr., 1963) and *Anton Webern: Weg und Gestalt: Selbstzeugnisse und Worte der Freunde* (Zürich, 1961).

BIBL.: "W. zum 50. Geburtstag," special issue of the magazine *23*, no. 14 (Vienna, 1934); R. Leibowitz, *Schoenberg et son école* (Paris, 1947; Eng. tr., 1949); L. Rognoni, *Espressionismo e dodecafonia* (Turin, 1954; 2nd ed., rev., 1966, as *La scuola musicale di Vienna*); "A. W.: Dokumente, Bekenntnis, Erkenntnisse, Analysen," *Die Reihe*, no. 2 (1955; Eng. tr. in *Die Reihe*, 1958); W. Kolneder, *A. W.: Einführung in Werk und Stil* (Rodenkirchen, 1961; Eng. tr., 1968); H. Moldenhauer, *The Death of A. W.: A Drama in Documents* (N.Y., 1961); G. Perle, *Serial Composition and Atonality: An Introduction to the Music of Schoenberg, Berg and W.* (Berkeley, 1962; 5th ed., rev., 1982); H. Moldenhauer and D. Irvine, eds., *A. v. W.: Perspectives* (Seattle, 1966); F. Wildgans, *A. W.* (London, 1966); *A. v.W.: Sketches (1926–1945)* (facsimile reproductions from W.'s sketchbooks, with commentary by E. Krenek and foreword by H. Moldenhauer, N.Y., 1968); R. Ringger, *A. W.s Klavierlieder* (Zürich, 1968); L. Somfai, *A. W.* (Budapest, 1968); C. Rostand, *A. W.: L'Homme et son œuvre* (Paris, 1969); H. Deppert, *Studien zur Kompositionstechnik im instrumentalen Spätwerk A. W.s* (Darmstadt, 1972); W. Stroh, *A. v.W.*; *Historische Legitimation* (Göppingen, 1973); F. Döhl, *W.s Beitrag zur Stilwende der neuen Musik* (Munich, 1976); H. and R. Moldenhauer, *A. v.W.: Chronicle of His Life and Work* (N.Y., 1978); R. Schulz, *Über das Verhältnis von Konstruktion und Ausdruck in den Werken A. W.s* (Munich, 1982); E. Hilmar, ed., *A. W. 1883–1983: Eine Festschrift zum hundertsten Geburtstag* (Vienna, 1983); A. Whittall, "W. and Atonality: The Path from the Old Aesthetic," *Musical Times* (Dec. 1983); Z. Roman, *A. v.W.: An Annotated Bibliography* (Detroit, 1983); J. Straus, "Recompositions by Schoenberg, Stravinsky, and W.," *Musical Quarterly*, no. 3 (1986); E. Jensen, "W. and Giovanni Segantini's *Trittico della natura*," *Musical Times* (Jan. 1989).

Webster, Beveridge, respected American pianist and teacher; b. Pittsburgh, May 13, 1908. He studied music with his father, who was director of the Pittsburgh Cons. of Music; at the age of 13, he was sent to Paris to study with Isidor Philipp at the Cons.; graduated in 1926, winning the premier prix for piano. He gave concerts in Europe; returned to the U.S. in 1934, and developed a successful concert career, appearing with major orchs.; also continued to give concerts in Europe. In 1946 he was appointed prof. of piano at the Juilliard School of Music in N.Y.; gave a piano recital at the Juilliard Theater on his 70th birthday, in May 1978; on Nov. 11, 1984, he celebrated the 50th anniversary of his U.S. debut with a recital in N.Y. In addition to works from the 18th and 19th centuries, he won particular distinction for his insightful performances of Debussy, Ravel, and contemporary American composers.

Webster, Sir David (Lumsden), Scottish operatic administrator; b. Dundee, July 3, 1903; d. London, May 11, 1971. He was educated at the Univ. of Liverpool; then commenced a commercial career while pursuing his various interests in the arts; from 1940 to 1945, was chairman of the Liverpool Phil. Society. In 1945 he became general administrator of the Covent Garden Opera Trust; in this capacity he helped to launch the careers of many famous singers, among them Jon Vickers and Joan Sutherland. He was knighted in 1961 and was made a Knight Commander of the Royal Victorian Order in 1970. An account of his career by M. Haltrecht, under the title *The Reluctant Showman*, was publ. in 1975.

Wecker, Georg Kaspar, German organist, teacher, and composer; b. Nuremberg (baptized), April 2, 1632; d. there, April 20, 1695. He studied organ with Erasmus Kindermann, and in 1651 obtained a position as church organist in Nuremberg; his last appointment was at the Sebaldkirche there (1686–95). He also was a respected teacher; Johann Krieger and Pa-

chelbel were among his pupils. His extant works comprise 5 cantatas, 37 sacred and 1 secular song, and a keyboard fugue.

Weckerlin, Jean-Baptiste-Théodore, eminent French music scholar and composer; b. Guebwiller, Alsace, Nov. 9, 1821; d. Trottberg, near Guebwiller, May 20, 1910. He ran away from home and settled in Paris in 1843; entered the Paris Cons. in 1844, where he studied with Ponchard (singing) and Halévy (composition). He wrote a heroic sym., *Roland*, for Soloists, Chorus, and Orch. (1847) while still a student; after graduating in 1849, he took part with Seghers in the direction of the Société Sainte-Cécile (1850–55), which brought out some of his works. He achieved his 1st success with the 1-act comic opera, *L'Organiste dans l'embarras* (Théâtre-Lyrique, 1853). It was followed by 2 comic operas in Alsatian dialect, *Die drifach Hochzitt im Bäsethal* (Colmar, 1863) and *D'r verhäxt' Herbst* (Colmar, 1879), and the 1-act opera *Après Fontenoy* (Théâtre-Lyrique, 1877). In 1863 he became librarian and archivist of the Société des Compositeurs de Musique. He became assistant librarian (1869) and librarian (1876) of the Paris Cons., retiring in 1909. He won distinction as a composer of grand choral works; also wrote 12 stage works, orch. music, chamber music, hundreds of songs, and many piano pieces. He ed. various early French stage works and many folksong collections.

WRITINGS: All publ. in Paris: *Opuscules sur la chanson populaire et sur la musique* (1874); *Musiciana* (1877); *Bibliothèque du Conservatoire national de musique et de déclamation: catalogue bibliographique . . . de la Reserve* (1885); *La chanson populaire* (1886); *Nouveau musiciana* (1890); *Dernier musiciana* (1899).

BIBL.: H. Expert, *Catalogue de la bibliothèque musicale de M. J.B. W.* (Paris, 1908).

Weckmann, Matthias, distinguished German organist and composer; b. Niederdorla, near Mühlhausen, Thuringia, c.1619; d. Hamburg, Feb. 24, 1674. He was the son of a clergyman and organist; was a chorister in the Dresden court chapel, where he was a pupil of Heinrich Schütz. In 1633 he was sent to Hamburg for further study with Reinken, Jakob Praetorius, and H. Scheidemann, by whom he was trained in the organ method of Sweelinck. In 1637 he became organist at the Dresden electoral chapel; in 1642 he was made director of the court chapel in Nyköbing, Denmark; then resumed his Dresden post in 1647, where he became a friend of J.J. Froberger; in 1655 he went to Hamburg as organist at the Jacobikirche, and founded in 1660, with Christoph Bernhard, the Collegium Musicum, a concert society for the performance of new works (it was discontinued after Weckmann's death). Among his extant works are 13 accompanied vocal compositions, 9 songs, 9 sonatas a 4, 2 sonatas a 3, and a few keyboard pieces. See M. Seiffert, ed., Denkmäler Deutscher Tonkunst, VI (1901), and *Matthias Weckmann: Vierzehn Praeludien, Fugen und Toccaten*, Organum, 4th series, III (Leipzig, 1925); also G. Ilgner, ed., *Matthias Weckmann: Gesammelte Werke*, Das Erbe Deutscher Musik, 2nd series, IV (1942).

BIBL.: M. Seiffert, "M. W. und das Collegium Musicum in Hamburg," *Sammelbände der Internationalen Musik-Gesellschaft*, II (1900–1901); G. Ilgner, *M. W. Sein Leben und seine Werke* (Wolfenbüttel and Berlin, 1939); G. Sharp, "M. W., 1619–74," *Musical Times*, CXV (1974).

Weelkes, Thomas, important English organist and composer; b. c.1575; d. London, Nov. 30, 1623. He was organist at Winchester Cathedral (1598–1601?), then organist and informator choristarum at Chichester Cathedral; held both positions until his drunkenness led to his dismissal in 1617; again served erratically as organist from 1622. In 1602 he was granted the degree of B.Mus. at New College, Oxford. Weelkes was one of the great English madrigalists, possessing remarkable power in melodic characterization of text; he occasionally used chromatic progressions in harmony that were well in advance of his time. He wrote a considerable amount of church music and instrumental works.

WORKS: 10 services; many anthems (see D. Brown, W. Collins, and P. le Huray, eds., *Thomas Weelkes: Collected Anthems*, Musica Britannica, XXIII, 1966; 2nd ed., rev., 1975); *Madrigals to 3. 4. 5. & 6. Voyces* (London, 1597; ed. by E. Fellowes; 2nd ed., rev., 1967, by T. Dart, The English Madrigalists, IX); *Balletts and Madrigals to Five Voyces, with One to 6. Voyces* (London, 1598; ed. by E. Fellowes; 2nd ed., rev., 1968, by T. Dart, The English Madrigalists, X); *Madrigals of 5. and 6. Parts, apt for the Viols and Voices* (London, 1600; ed. by E. Fellowes; 2nd ed., rev., 1968, by T. Dart, The English Madrigalists, XI, XII); *Ayeres or Phantasticke Spirites for Three Voices* (London, 1608; ed. by E. Fellowes; 2nd ed., rev., 1965, by T. Dart, The English Madrigalists, XIII); 4 keyboard pieces; several works for Viols.

BIBL.: E. Fellowes, "T. W.," *Proceedings of the Musical Association*, XLII (1915–16); idem, *The English Madrigal Composers* (Oxford, 1921; 2nd ed., 1948); G. Holst, "The Tercentenary of Byrd and W.," *Proceedings of the Musical Association*, XLIX (1922–23); D. Arnold, "T. W. and the Madrigal," *Music & Letters*, XXXI (1950); C. Welch, *Two Cathedral Organists, T. W. (1601–1623) and Thomas Kelway (1720–1744)* (Chichester, 1957); W. Collins, *The Anthems of T. W.* (diss., Univ. of Michigan, 1960); D. Morse, *Word-painting and Symbolism in the Secular Choral Works by T. W.*, Tudor Composer (diss., N. Y. Univ., 1961); W. Ford, "Chichester Cathedral and T. W.," *Sussex Archaeological Collections*, C (1962); W. Collins, "Recent Discoveries concerning the Biography of T. W.," *Music & Letters*, XLIV (1963); D. Brown, "The Anthems of T. W.," *Proceedings of the Royal Musical Association*, XCI (1964–65); idem, "T. W.," *Recorder and Music Magazine*, II (1967); idem, *T. W.: A Biographical and Critical Study* (London, 1969); P. Brett, "The Two Musical Personalities of T. W.," *Music & Letters*, LIII (1972); T. McCann, "The Death of T. W. in 1623," ibid., LV (1974); G. Philipps, "Patronage in the Career of T. W.," *Musical Quarterly* (Jan. 1976).

Weerbeke (also **Weerbecke, Werbecke, Werbeke, Werbeck**), **Gaspar van,** significant Netherlandish composer; b. Oudenaarde, c.1445; d. after 1517. By 1471 he was active at the Sforza court in Milan; was in Flanders and Burgundy in 1472–73 to recruit singers for the court choir of Duke Galeazzo Maria Sforza, whom he served as vice-abbate of the cantori de camera. After serving as a member of the papal choir (1471–92), he was again active in Milan at the court of Duke Ludovico Sforza, "il Moro"; also held benefices in the Utrecht and Thérouanne dioceses and was associated with the court choir of Philip the Fair, Archduke of Austria and Duke of Burgundy. From 1500 to 1509 he was again a member of the papal choir; however, he was referred to as "Cantor capellae papalis" as late as 1514; in 1517 he was listed as canonicus of the church of S. Maria ad Gradus in Mainz. Weerbeke was an outstanding composer of liturgical and non-liturgical sacred music. His extant works include 8 mass ordinaries, 2 credos, 22 motet cycles, and 21 other motets. Five chansons attributed to him remain doubtful. See A. Smijers, ed., *Van Ockeghem tot Sweelinck* (Amsterdam, 1949–56) and G. Tintori, *Gaspar van Weerbeke: Messe e mottetti*, Archivum Musices Metropolitanum Mediolanense, XI (Milan, 1963).

BIBL.: G. Croll, *Das Motettenwerk G. v.W.* (diss., Univ. of Göttingen, 1954); E. Fiedler, "Heinrich Finck, G. v.W. und die Göttin Venus," *Renaissance-Studien: Helmuth Osthoff zum 80. Geburtstag* (Tutzing, 1977).

Wegeler, Franz Gerhard, German physician and music amateur; b. Bonn, Aug. 22, 1765; d. Coblenz, May 7, 1848. He was a practicing physician in Bonn and Coblenz, and knew Beethoven as a youth. With Ries, he publ. *Biographische Notizen über Ludwig van Beethoven* (1838; supplement, 1845; reprinted by A. Kalischer, 1906).

BIBL.: S. Ley, ed., *Beethoven als Freund der Familie W.* (Bonn, 1927).

Wegelius, Martin, eminent Finnish composer and pedagogue; b. Helsinki, Nov. 10, 1846; d. there, March 22, 1906. He studied philosophy, taking his master's degree in 1869; studied music with Rudolf Bibl in Vienna (1870–71), with Richter, Reinecke, and Jadassohn in Leipzig (1871–73), and with Rheinberger in Munich (1877–78). In 1882 he was appointed director of the newly founded Helsinki Cons., holding this post until his death. Under his guidance, the institution became one of the finest schools in Europe, with excellent teachers. Sibelius was one of the pupils of Wegelius; others were Järnefelt, Melartin, and Palmgren. Wegelius emphasized the cultivation of national Finnish music, and thus was mainly responsible for the magnificent development of Finland as a musical nation.

WORKS: Overture, *Daniel Hjort* (1872); *Divertissement à la hongroise* (1880); *Rondo quasi fantasia* for Piano and Orch. (1872); *Mignon*, 6 songs with Orch., after Goethe's *Westöstlicher Diwan* (1875); Christmas Cantata (1877); festival cantata, *The 6th of May* (1878); Violin Sonata; piano pieces; songs.

WRITINGS: *Lärobok i allmän musiklära och analys* (Textbook of General Music Theory and Analysis; 2 vols., Helsinki, 1888–89); *Hufvuddragen af denn västerländska musikens historia* (Outlines of the History of Western Music; 3 vols., Helsinki, 1891–93); *Kurs i homofons sats* (Course in Homophonic Composition; 2 vols., Helsinki, 1897–1905).

BIBL.: K. Flodin, *M. W.* (in Swedish, Stockholm, 1916; in Finnish, Helsinki, 1922); O. Andersson, ed., *M. W.: konstnärsbrev* (M.W.: Letters; 2 vols., Helsinki, 1918–19).

Wehle, Gerhard Fürchtegott, German musicologist and composer; b. Paramaribo, Dutch Guiana, Oct. 11, 1884; d. Berlin, Oct. 15, 1973. He studied in Germany, and settled in Berlin (1907); he was active primarily as a music critic and pedagogue; taught improvisation and other subjects; publ. *Die Kunst der Improvisation* (2 vols., Münster, 1925–26); *Die Orgel-Improvisation* (Leipzig, 1932; both titles reissued in 3 vols., Hamburg, 1950–53); *Neue Wege im Kompositions-Unterricht* (2 vols., Hamburg, 1955); *Die höhere Kompositionstechnik* (2 vols., Hamburg, n.d.). Among his musical works are 26 symphonic cantatas; 3 syms.; much chamber music. He was also a successful novelist.

Wehle, Karl, Bohemian pianist and composer; b. Prague, March 17, 1825; d. Paris, June 3, 1883. Trained for a mercantile career, he abandoned it for music; studied piano with Moscheles at Leipzig and Kullak in Berlin; made extended tours to Asia, Africa, America, and Australia, but resided chiefly in Paris. He publ. a number of brilliant compositions for piano, among them *Sérénade napolitaine, Allegro à la hongroise, 3 tarentelles, 2 impromptus, Berceuse javanaise, Marche cosaque, Fête bohémienne, Un Songe à Vaucluse.*

Wehrli, Werner, Swiss composer; b. Aarau, Jan. 8, 1892; d. Lucerne, June 27, 1944. He studied at the Zürich Cons. with Hegar and in Frankfurt with Knorr; wrote a number of "festival operas" in a Romantic vein; cantatas; chamber music. His oratorio *Wallfahrt* (1939) enjoyed a modicum of success. His opera *Das heisse Eisen*, after Hans Sachs, was produced in Bern on Dec. 11, 1918.

BIBL.: W. Müller von Kulm, "W. W.," *Schweizerische Musikzeitung*, LXXXIV (1944); G. Leuenberger, "W. W.," ibid., XCII (1952).

Weidemann, Friedrich, German baritone; b. Ratzeburg, Jan. 1, 1871; d. Vienna, Jan. 30, 1919. He studied with Vilmar in Hamburg and Muschler in Berlin; made his debut in 1896 in Brieg; then sang in Essen (1897–98), Hamburg (1898–1901), and Riga (1901–3). In 1903 he joined the Vienna Court Opera, where he remained until his death. He was highly regarded for his performances in operas by Wagner and Richard Strauss.

Weidig, Adolf, German-American music teacher and composer; b. Hamburg, Nov. 28, 1867; d. Hinsdale, Ill., Sept. 23, 1931. He studied at the Hamburg Cons. with Bargheer (violin) and later with Hugo Riemann (theory); then in Munich with Rheinberger (composition). In 1892 he settled in Chicago; played the violin in the Chicago Orch. (1892–96); in 1898 he joined the faculty of the American Cons. of Music; conducted his own works in Chicago, Minneapolis, and also in Germany. He was greatly esteemed as a teacher; publ. *Harmonic Material* *and Its Uses* (1923); composed 2 syms.; a symphonic poem, *Semiramis; 3 Episoden* for Orch.; String Quintet; 3 string quartets; Piano Trio; songs.

Weidinger, Anton, Austrian trumpeter; b. Vienna, June 9, 1767; d. there, Sept. 20, 1852. He was trained in Vienna; after service in regimental bands, he became a member of the Vienna Court Orch. in 1792; later mastered the keyed trumpet and gave many concerts in Vienna. In 1803 he toured Germany, France, and England as a virtuoso. Haydn wrote his Trumpet Concerto for him.

BIBL.: R. Heuberger, "A. W.," *Die Musik,* VII (1907–8).

Weidt, Lucie, German-born Austrian soprano; b. Troppau, Silesia, c.1876; d. Vienna, July 28, 1940. She studied with her father, and then with Rosa Papier in Vienna; made her operatic debut in Leipzig in 1900; in 1902 she made her 1st appearance at the Vienna Opera as Elisabeth, remaining on its roster until 1927. She sang in Munich from 1908 to 1910. On Nov. 18, 1910, she made her 1st American appearance, as Brünnhilde in *Die Walküre,* at the Metropolitan Opera in N.Y.; after a season there, she sang in Italy. In 1909 she married Baron Joseph von Urmenyi. Her voice was of unusual attractiveness and power, enabling her to perform Wagnerian parts with distinction.

Weigel, Eugene (Herbert), American composer, violist, organist, and teacher; b. Cleveland, Oct. 11, 1910. He studied composition with Arthur Shepherd at Western Reserve Univ. and violin with Maurice Hewitt at the Cleveland Inst. of Music (1930–32); later had composition lessons with Hindemith at Yale Univ. (B.M., 1946) and viola lessons with Hugo Kortschak. He was active as an organist and choirmaster (1929–41); also was a founding member of the Walden String Quartet (1930–35). While at Yale Univ., he served as music director of its Thomas More Chapel and played viola in the New Haven (Conn.) Sym. Orch.; appeared in various ensembles, including one in N.Y. with Hindemith on the viola d'amore in a performance of Bach's *St. John Passion.* In 1946–47, he was again a member of the Walden String Quartet during its residency at Cornell Univ.; played in the 1st performances of Schoenberg's String Trio and Ives's 2nd String Quartet; continued to play with the quartet at the Univ. of Illinois (1947–57), where he also taught composition and experimental music theory. In 1954–55 he held a Guggenheim fellowship. In 1955 he became composer-in-residence at Montana State Univ. in Missoula, which was renamed the Univ. of Montana that same year; remained there until 1972. He also was a founder-member of the Montana String Quartet (1957–72). In 1972 he retired to Vancouver Island, Canada; conducted the Malespina Chorus and was prof. emeritus at Malespina College (1974–76). In later years he devoted much time to writing poetry, preparing his memoirs, and pursuing an avid interest in architecture.

WORKS: OPERAS: *The Lion Makers* (1953); *The Mountain Child* (1959). **ORCH.:** *Sonata* for Strings (1948); *Festival Fanfare* (1948); *Prairie Symphony* (1952); *Concerto festivo* for Flute, Harpsichord, and Strings (Berlin Festival, 1959); *Fantasy and Fugue* for Concert Band (1967). **CHAMBER:** Clarinet Quintet (1946); Woodwind Quintet (1949); Trombone Quartet (1953); *Maine Sketches* for Horn and Piano (1954); Duo for Clarinet and Bassoon (1955); piano pieces; also vocal works, including *Fall of the Leaf* for Baritone and String Quartet (1938) and *Prayer for Peace* for Chorus, Brass, and Percussion (1961); songs.

Weigl, family of Austrian musicians:

(1) Joseph (Franz) Weigl, cellist; b. in Bavaria, May 19, 1740; d. Vienna, Jan. 25, 1820. Upon the recommendation of Haydn, he was made a cellist at the Eisenstadt court in 1761; married (Anna Maria) Josepha Scheffstoss, a former singer at the court, in 1764. In 1769 he was named 1st cellist of the Italian Opera orch. at the Kärnthnertortheater in Vienna; in 1792 he became a member of the Hofkapelle.

(2) Joseph Weigl, composer and conductor, son of the preceding; b. Eisenstadt, March 28, 1766; d. Vienna, Feb. 3, 1846. He was taken to Vienna in 1769; trained with Sebastian Witzig

(singing and thoroughbass) in 1775; soon became a pupil of Albrechtsberger, with whom he remained until 1782. At age 16 he wrote his 1st opera, *Die unnütze Vorsicht,* for a marionette theater, winning the esteem of Gluck and Salieri. At 19 he became a pupil in composition of Salieri, who secured a position for him in the Court Theater; he was deputy Kapellmeister by 1790; in 1792 he was made Kapellmeister and composer. From 1827 to 1838 he was Vice-Kapellmeister at the court, retiring from public life in 1839. His 1st notable success as a composer for the theater came with his opera *La Principessa d'Amalfi* (Vienna, Jan. 10, 1794), which Haydn described as a masterpiece (in a letter to Weigl after the perf.); it was followed by *Das Waisenhaus* (Vienna, Oct. 4, 1808) and *Die Schweizerfamilie* (Vienna, March 14, 1809; produced in Paris, Feb. 6, 1827, as *Emmeline, ou La Famille suisse*); it was staged in opera houses all over Europe until about 1900, when it disappeared from the repertoire. His ballets also won a wide hearing.

WORKS: OPERAS (all 1st perf. in Vienna unless otherwise given): *Die unnütze Vorsicht oder Die betrogene Arglist* (Feb. 23, 1783); *Il Pazzo per forza* (Nov. 14, 1788); *La caffettiera bizzarra* (Sept. 15, 1790); *Der Strassensammler (Lumpensammler) oder Ein gutes Herz ziert jeden Stand,* comic opera (Oct. 13, 1792); *La Principessa d'Amalfi,* comic opera (Jan. 10, 1794); *Das Petermännchen* (part 1, April 8, 1794; part 2, April ?, 1794); *Giulietta e Pierotto* (Oct. 16, 1794); *I solitari,* opera seria (March 15, 1797); *L'amor marinaro ossia Il Corsaro* (Oct. 15, 1797); *Das Dorf im Gebirge,* singspiel (April 17, 1798); *L'accademia del maestro Cisolfaut* (Oct. 14, 1798); *L'uniforme,* heroic-comic opera (1800); *Die Herrenhuterin,* singspiel (Nov. 26, 1804; in collaboration with I. Umlauf and F. Devienne); *Vestas Feuer,* heroic opera (Aug. 7, 1805); *Il Principe invisibile* (Oct. 4, 1806); *Kaiser Hadrian* (May 21, 1807); *Ostade oder Adrian von Ostade* (Oct. 3, 1807); *Cleopatra* (Milan, Dec. 19, 1807); *Il Rivale di se stesso* (Milan, April 18, 1808); *Das Waisenhaus,* singspiel (Oct. 4, 1808); *Die Schweizerfamilie,* singspiel (March 14, 1809); *Die Verwandlungen,* operetta (Berlin, Feb. 1810); *Der Einsiedler auf den Alpen* (June 13, 1810); *Franciska von Foix,* heroic-comic opera (Feb. 7, 1812); *Der Bergsturz,* singspiel (Dec. 19, 1813); *Die Jugend (Jugendjahre) Peter des Grossen* (Dec. 10, 1814); *L'imboscata* (Milan, Nov. 8, 1815); *Margaritta d'Anjou ossia L'Orfano d'Inghilterra,* melodramma eroi-comico (Milan, July 26, 1816); *Die Nachtigall und der Rabe* (April 20, 1818); *Daniel in der Löwengrube oder Baals Sturz,* heroic opera (April 13, 1820); *König Waldemar oder Die dänischen Fischer,* singspiel (May 11, 1821); *Edmund und Caroline* (Oct. 21, 1821); *Die eiserne Pforte,* grand opera (Feb. 27, 1823); also ballets; incidental music used in several plays; many cantatas; songs; masses; the oratorio *La passione di Gesù Cristo* (1804); instrumental works.

(3) Thaddäus Weigl, conductor, music publisher, and composer, brother of the preceding; b. April 8, 1776; d. Vienna, Feb. 29, 1844. He studied theory with Albrechtsberger; was employed in the Court Theater's music publishing house from 1795. He organized his own publishing concern in 1803; also was Vice-Kapellmeister to his brother, becoming a composer at the Court Theater in 1806; his publishing business ended in bankruptcy in 1831. He wrote 5 operettas and 15 ballets.

BIBL.: E. Fulter, "Beethoven and W.," *Schweizerische Musikzeitung/Revue Musicale Suisse,* LXVIII (1928); F. Grasberger, *J. W. (1766–1846): Leben und Werk mit besonderer Berücksichtigung der Kirchenmusik* (diss., Univ. of Vienna, 1938); H. Hausner, "J. W. . . . Daten aus seinem Leben und Schaffen," *Mitteilungen der Internationalen Stiftung Mozarteum,* XIV/3–4 (1966); R. Angermüller, "Zwei Selstbiographien von J. W. (1766–1846)," *Deutsches Jahrbuch der Musikwissenschaft,* XVI (1973).

Weigl, Bruno, Czech writer on music and composer; b. Brünn, June 16, 1881; d. there (Brno), Sept. 25, 1938. He publ. several useful teaching manuals: *Die Geschichte des Walzers, nebst einem Anhang über die moderne Operette* (Langensalza, 1910); *Handbuch der Violoncell-Literatur* (Vienna, 1911; rev. ed.,

1929); *Harmonielehre* (2 vols., Mainz, 1925); composed a comic opera, *Mandragola* (Brünn, 1912); song cycles; organ works.

Weigl, Karl, Austrian-born American composer, husband of **Valery (Vally) Weigl;** b. Vienna, Feb. 6, 1881; d. N.Y., Aug. 11, 1949. He studied piano with Door and music theory with Fuchs at the Cons. of the Gesellschaft der Musikfreunde in Vienna (graduated, 1902); then took composition lessons with Zemlinsky; attended courses in musicology at the Univ. of Vienna with Adler (Ph.D., 1903). From 1918 to 1928 he was on the faculty of the New Vienna Cons.; from 1930 to 1938, taught music theory at the Univ. of Vienna. After the Anschluss in 1938, he emigrated to N.Y.; became a naturalized U.S. citizen in 1943. He was respected both in Austria and in America as a composer, and a concerted effort was made to promote his music, but with little success. His 5th Sym., *Apocalyptic* (1945), was performed posthumously by Leopold Stokowski with the American Sym. Orch. (N.Y., Oct. 27, 1968). He wrote 6 syms.: No. 1 (1908); No. 2 (1922); No. 3 (1931); No. 4 (1936); No. 5 (1945); No. 6 (1947); several overtures; Violin Concerto (1928); 8 string quartets; String Sextet; 2 violin sonatas; numerous choruses; piano pieces; songs.

Weigl, Valery (Vally), Austrian-born American composer and music therapist, wife of **Karl Weigl;** b. Vienna, Sept. 11, 1894; d. N.Y., Dec. 25, 1982. She studied music in Vienna with her husband. She taught music in Vienna and Salzburg (1921–38); after the Anschluss she and her husband went to America, where she obtained employment as music adviser with the American Theater Wing in N.Y. (1947–58); from 1954 to 1964 she gave courses in music therapy at the N.Y. Medical College and wrote therapy programs for UNESCO. She was an energetic peace activist, and served as a co-founder of the Friends' Arts for World Unity Committee. With equal energy, she promoted her husband's compositions, which were little appreciated and seldom played.
    WORKS: *New England Suite* for Clarinet, Cello, and Piano (1955); *Nature Moods* for Soprano, Clarinet, and Violin (1960); *Mood Sketches* for Wind Quintet (1964); *Peace Is a Shelter* for Chorus, Soloist, and Piano (1970); cantata, *The People Yes* (1976).

Weikert, Ralf, Austrian conductor; b. St. Florian, Nov. 10, 1940. He studied at the Bruckner Cons. in Linz; then took a course in conducting with Hans Swarowsky at the Vienna Academy of Music. In 1965 he won 1st prize in the Nicolai Malko Conducting Competition in Copenhagen. In 1966 he became conductor of the City Theater in Bonn; then was chief conductor there (1968–77). In 1977 he was appointed deputy Generalmusikdirektor of the Frankfurt Opera; also conducted opera with the Hamburg State Opera, the Deutsche Oper in Berlin, the Vienna State Opera, and the Zürich Opera. In 1981 he was named chief conductor of the Salzburg Mozarteum Orch. and music director of the Landestheater in Salzburg. He was music director of the Zürich Opera from 1984.

Weikl, Bernhard, Austrian baritone; b. Vienna, July 29, 1942. He studied at the Mainz Cons. (1962–65) and at the Hochschule für Musik in Hannover (1965–67). From 1968 to 1970 he sang at the Opera in Hannover. In 1973 he became a member of the Hamburg State Opera. He also was a guest artist at the Bayreuth Festivals (1973–75). In 1975 he made his Covent Garden debut in London as Rossini's Figaro. On Dec. 22, 1977, he made his 1st appearance at the Metropolitan Opera in N.Y. as Wolfram, later returning there to sing such roles as Amfortas, Mandryka, and Beethoven's Don Fernando.

Weil, Hermann, German baritone; b. Karlsruhe, May 29, 1876; d. (of a heart attack, while fishing in Blue Mountain Lake, N.Y.) July 6, 1949. He studied voice with Adolf Dippel in Frankfurt; made his debut as Wolfram in *Tannhäuser* at Freiburg, Baden, on Sept. 8, 1901; then sang in Vienna, Brussels, Amsterdam, Milan, and London; participated in the Bayreuth Festivals (1909–12). On Nov. 17, 1911, he made a successful debut as Kurvenal in *Tristan und Isolde*, at the Metropolitan Opera in N.Y. In 1917 he returned to Germany.

He sang at the Vienna State Opera (1920–23), toured the U.S. with the German Opera Co. (1923–24), and appeared at the Bayreuth Festival (1924–25); in 1939 he settled in N.Y. as a vocal teacher. The extensive range of his voice, spanning 3 full octaves, enabled him to undertake bass parts as well as those in the baritone compass. He had about 100 roles in his repertoire, excelling in Wagnerian operas.

Weill, Kurt (Julian), remarkable German-born American composer; b. Dessau, March 2, 1900; d. N.Y., April 3, 1950. He was a private pupil of Albert Bing in Dessau (1915–18); in 1918–19, studied at the Berlin Hochschule für Musik with Humperdinck (composition), Friedrich Koch (counterpoint), and Krasselt (conducting). He was then engaged as an opera coach in Dessau and was also theater conductor at Lüdenscheid. In 1920 he moved to Berlin and became a student of Busoni at the Prussian Academy of Arts (1920–23); also studied with Jarnach there (1921–23). His 1st major work, the Sym. No. 1, *Berliner Sinfonie,* was composed in 1921. However, it was not performed in his lifetime; indeed, its MS was not recovered until 1955, and it was finally premiered by the North German Radio Sym. Orch. in Hamburg in 1958. Under the impact of new trends in the musical theater, Weill proceeded to write short satirical operas in a sharp modernistic manner: *Der Protagonist* (1924–25) and *Royal Palace* (1925–26). There followed a striking "songspiel" (a hybrid term of English and German words), *Mahagonny,* to a libretto by Bertolt Brecht, savagely satirizing the American primacy of money (1927); it was remodeled and was presented as the 3-act opera *Aufstieg und Fall der Stadt Mahagonny* (1929). Weill's greatest hit in this genre came with a modernistic version of Gay's *The Beggar's Opera,* to a pungent libretto by Brecht; under the title *Die Dreigroschenoper* (1928), it was staged all over Germany, and was also produced in translation throughout Europe. Marc Blitzstein later made a new libretto for the opera, versified in a modern American style, which was produced as *The Threepenny Opera,* the exact translation of the German title. Its hit number, *Mack the Knife,* became tremendously successful. After the Nazi ascent to power in Germany, Weill and his wife, the actress and singer **Lotte Lenya,** who appeared in many of his musical plays, went to Paris in 1934. They settled in the U.S. in 1935; Weill became a naturalized American citizen in 1943. Quickly absorbing the modes and fashions of American popular music, he re-created, with astonishing facility, and felicity, the typical form and content of American musicals; this stylistic transition was facilitated by the fact that in his European productions he had already absorbed elements of American popular songs and jazz rhythms. His highly developed assimilative faculty enabled him to combine this Americanized idiom with the advanced techniques of modern music (atonality, polytonality, polyrhythms) and present the product in a pleasing, and yet sophisticated and challenging, manner. But for all his success in American-produced scores, the great majority of his European works remained to be produced in America only posthumously.
    WORKS: THEATER: *Zaubernacht,* ballet (Berlin, Nov. 18, 1922); *Der Protagonist,* opera (1924–25; Dresden, March 27, 1926); *Royal Palace,* ballet-opera (1925–26; Berlin, March 2, 1927; original orchestration not extant; reconstructed as a ballet by Gunther Schuller and Noam Sheriff, San Francisco, Oct. 5, 1968); *Na und?,* opera (1926–27; not perf.; not extant); *Der Zar lässt sich photographieren,* opera (1927; Leipzig, Feb. 18, 1928; U.S. premiere as *The Shah Has Himself Photographed,* N.Y., Oct. 27, 1949); *Mahagonny,* "songspiel" (Baden-Baden, July 17, 1927; remodeled as a 3-act opera, *Aufstieg und Fall der Stadt Mahagonny,* 1927–29; Leipzig, March 9, 1930; U.S. premiere, N.Y., April 28, 1970); *Happy End,* comedy (Berlin, Sept. 2, 1929; professional U.S. premiere, New Haven, Conn., April 6, 1972); *Der Jasager,* school opera (Berlin radio, June 23, 1930; U.S. premiere as *The One Who Sang Yes,* N.Y., April 25, 1933); *Die Bürgschaft,* opera (1930–31; Berlin, March 10, 1932); *Der Silbersee,* musical play (1932–33; simultaneous premiere in Leipzig, Erfurt, and Magdeburg, Feb. 18, 1933; U.S.

premiere as *Silverlake*, slightly abr. and with the addition of his 1927 incidental music to Strindberg's play *Gustav III*, N.Y., March 20, 1980); *Die sieben Todsünden der Kleinbürger*, ballet (Paris, June 7, 1933; U.S. premiere, N.Y., Dec. 4, 1958); *Der Kuhnhandel*, operetta (1934; Düsseldorf, March 22, 1990; rev. as a musical comedy, *A Kingdom for a Cow*, London, June 28, 1935); *Der Weg der Verheissung*, biblical drama (1934–35; not perf.; rev. by L. Lewisohn as *The Eternal Road*, 1935–36; N.Y., Jan. 7, 1937); *Johnny Johnson*, musical fable (N.Y., Nov. 19, 1936); *Davy Crockett*, musical play (1938; unfinished); *Knickerbocker Holiday*, operetta (Hartford, Conn., Sept. 26, 1938; contains the popular *September Song*; *Railroads on Parade*, historical pageant (1938–39; N.Y. World's Fair, April 30, 1939); *The Ballad of Magna Carta*, scenic cantata (1939; CBS, Feb. 4, 1940); *Ulysses Africanus*, musical play (1939; unfinished); *Lady in the Dark*, musical play (1940; N.Y., Jan. 23, 1941); *One Touch of Venus*, musical comedy (N.Y., Oct. 7, 1943; *The Firebrand of Florence*, operetta (1944; N.Y., March 22, 1945); *Street Scene*, opera (1946; N.Y., Jan. 9, 1947); *Down in the Valley*, folk opera (1945–48; Indiana Univ., Bloomington, July 15, 1948); *Love Life*, vaudeville (1947; N.Y., Oct. 7, 1948); *Lost in the Stars*, musical tragedy (after Alan Paton's *Cry, the Beloved Country*; N.Y., Oct. 30, 1949); *Huckleberry Finn*, musical (1950; unfinished).

ORCH.: Symphonic Poem (1920?; not extant); Sym. (1920; not extant); Sym. No. 1, *Berliner Sinfonie* (1921; score recovered in 1955 and premiered by the North German Radio Sym. Orch., Hamburg, Jan. 17, 1958; U.S. premiere, Greenwich, Conn., Oct. 21, 1978); Sym. No. 2, *Pariser Symphonie* (1933; Amsterdam, Oct. 11, 1934; U.S. premiere as *3 Night Scenes*, N.Y., Dec. 13, 1934); Divertimento (1922); *Sinfonia sacra* or *Fantasia, Passacaglia, und Hymnus* (1922); *Quodlibet*, suite from *Zaubernacht* (1923; Coburg, Feb. 6, 1926; U.S. premiere, N.Y., Feb. 24, 1963); Concerto for Violin, Woodwinds, Double Bass, and Percussion (1924; Paris, June 11, 1925; U.S. premiere, Cincinnati, March 28, 1930); *Berlin im Licht* for Military Band (1928); *Kleine Dreigroschenmusik* for Winds, concert suite from *Die Dreigroschenoper* (1929).

VOCAL: *Sulamith*, cantata for Soprano, Women's Chorus, and Orch. (1920; not extant); *Psalm VIII* for 8 Voices (1921; partly lost); *Recordare* for Choir and Children's Chorus (1923); *Das Studenbuch*, 6 songs for Tenor or Soprano and Orch. (1924; partly lost); *Der neue Orpheus*, cantata for Soprano, Violin, and Orch. (1925; Berlin, March 2, 1927; U.S. premiere, New Haven, Conn., Oct. 5, 1972); *Vom Tod im Wald*, ballad for Bass and 10 Wind Instruments (Berlin, Nov. 23, 1927; U.S. premiere, N.Y., March 7, 1977); *Das Berliner Requiem*, cantata for Tenor, Baritone, Bass, Chorus, and 15 Instruments (1928; Frankfurt Radio, May 22, 1929; U.S. premiere, Cincinnati, April 3, 1970); *Der Lindberghflug*, cantata after a radio score for Tenor, Baritone, Chorus, and Orch. (with Hindemith; Baden-Baden, July 28, 1929; rescored by Weill as totally his own work, Berlin, Dec. 5, 1929; rev. 1930 as *Der Flug des Lindberghs* and then later retitled *Der Ozeanflug*, without Lindbergh's name, as a gesture of protest against Lindbergh's militant neutrality toward Nazi Germany); *Zu Potsdam unter den Eichen* for Men's Voices (1929); *Song of the Railroads* (1938); *4 American Songs* (1939); *Kiddush* for Tenor, Chorus, and Organ (1946).

CHAMBER: 2 movements for String Quartet: *Allegro deciso* and *Andantino* (n.d.; N.Y., March 7, 1977); String Quartet in B minor (1919); Cello Sonata (1920; U.S. premiere, Philadelphia, May 4, 1979); String Quartet No. 1 (1923; U.S. premiere, Yale Univ., May 13, 1971).

FILM SCORES: *You and Me* (1937–38); *The River Is Blue* (1937–38; discarded); *Where Do We Go from Here?* (1943–44); *Salute to France* (1944). He also wrote a number of other scores for the theater and radio, many of which are not extant; likewise many songs.

BIBL.: V. Thomson, "Most Melodious Tears," *Modern Music*, XI (1933); H. Heinsheimer, "K. W.," *Tomorrow* (March 1948); H. Strobel, "Erinnerung an K. W.," *Melos* (May 1950); D. Drew, "Topicality and the Universal: The Strange Case of W.'s *Die Bürgschaft*," *Music & Letters* (July 1958); H. Kotschenreuther, K. W. (Berlin, 1962); J. Waterhouse, "W.'s Debt to Busoni," *Musical Times*, CV (1964); K. Kowalke, *K. W. in Europe* (Ann Arbor, 1979); R. Sanders, *The Days Grow Short: The Life and Music of K. W.* (N.Y., 1980); D. Jarman, *K. W.: an Illustrated Biography* (Bloomington, Ind., 1982); J. Schebera, *K. W.: Leben und Werk* (Leipzig, 1983); K. Kowalke, ed., *A New Orpheus: Essays on K. W.* (New Haven, 1986); S. Cook, *Opera During the Weimar Republic: The Zeitopern of Ernst Krenek, K. W., and Paul Hindemith* (Ann Arbor, 1987); D. Drew, *K. W.: A Handbook* (Berkeley, 1987); idem, "K. W.: Doubtful and Chimerical Works," *Musical Times* (Oct. 1987); J. Schebera, *K. W. 1900–1950. Eine Biographie in Texten, Bildern und Dokumenten* (Leipzig, 1990).

Weinberg, Jacob, Russian-American pianist, teacher, and composer; b. Odessa, July 7, 1879; d. N.Y., Nov. 2, 1956. He studied at the Moscow Cons. with Igumnov (piano) and with Taneyev and Ippolitov-Ivanov (composition); was a private pupil of Leschetizky in Vienna (1910–11); taught piano at the Odessa Cons. (1915–21); after living in Palestine (1921–26), he emigrated to the U.S.; taught piano at Hunter College and the N.Y. College of Music. He composed an opera on a modern Hebrew subject, *Hechalutz (The Pioneers)*; fragments were performed in Jerusalem, in Hebrew, on April 4, 1925; the complete opera was performed in N.Y. on Nov. 25, 1934, under the title *The Pioneers of Israel*, in English; he also wrote the oratorios *Isaiah* (1948) and *The Life of Moses* (1952); *The Gettysburg Address*, ode for Chorus and Orch. (N.Y., 1936); *Sabbath Liturgy* for Baritone, Chorus, and Organ; Piano Concerto; Piano Trio; String Quartet; Violin Sonata; contributed essays on Russian music to the *Musical Quarterly* and other periodicals.

Weinberger, Jaromir, notable Czech composer; b. Prague, Jan. 8, 1896; d. (suicide by overdose of sedative drugs) St. Petersburg, Fla., Aug. 8, 1967. He studied with Křička and Hoffmeister at the Prague Cons., then briefly with Max Reger in Leipzig. In 1922 he visited the U.S., and taught for a semester at the Ithaca Cons. in N.Y. Returning to Europe, he was active as a teacher in Bratislava, Prague, and Vienna; lived mostly in Prague until 1937; in 1939 he settled permanently in the U.S., living in St. Petersburg. He achieved sudden fame with the production of his opera in a popular Bohemian style, *Švanda dudák* (Schwanda the Bagpiper), at the National Theater in Prague on April 27, 1927. Its success was immediate, and performances followed all over Europe in several languages; it was produced in German (as *Schwanda der Dudelsackpfeifer*) at the Metropolitan Opera in N.Y. on Nov. 7, 1931; the *Polka and Fugue* from this opera has become a popular number in the orch. repertoire.

WORKS: OPERAS: *Kocourkov* (c.1926); *Švanda dudák* (Schwanda the Bagpiper; Prague, April 27, 1927); *Die geliebte Stimme* (Munich, Feb. 28, 1931); *Lidé z Pokerflatu* (The Outcasts of Poker Flat; Brno, Nov. 19, 1932); *Valdštejn* (Vienna, Nov. 18, 1937). **OPERETTAS:** *Frühlingssturme* (Berlin, 1933); *Apropo co dela Andula* (n.d.); *Na ruzich ustlano* (Bed of Roses; Prague, 1934); *Cisar pan na tresnich* (n.d.). **ORCH.:** *Overture to a Marionette Play* (1916); *Under the Spreading Chestnut Tree* for Piano and Orch. (N.Y., Oct. 12, 1939; rev. 1941); *The Bird's Opera*, overture (1940; Detroit, Nov. 13, 1941); *Song of the High Seas* (N.Y., Nov. 9, 1940); *The Lincoln Symphony* (Cincinnati, Oct. 17, 1941); *Czech Rhapsody* (Washington, D.C., Nov. 5, 1941); *Préludes religieux et profanes* (1953); *A Waltz Overture* (1960). Also many works for violin and Piano; vocal works, including *Ecclesiastes* for Soprano, Baritone, Chorus, Organ, and Bells (1945); many Czech songs.

BIBL.: D. Kushner, "J. W. (1896–1967): From Bohemia to America," *American Music* (Fall 1988).

Weiner, Lazar, Russian-American pianist, conductor, and composer, father of **Yehudi Wyner;** b. Cherkassy, near Kiev, Oct. 27, 1897; d. N.Y., Jan. 10, 1982. He emigrated to America in 1914, and became associated with numerous Jewish artistic activities in N.Y.; also took private lessons in composition with

Robert Russell Bennett, Frederick Jacobi, and Joseph Schillinger. From 1929 to 1975 he was music director of the Central Synagogue in N.Y.; conducted classes in the Yiddish art song at Hebrew Union College, the Jewish Theological Seminary, and the 92nd Street Y; served as music director of the WABC weekly radio program "The Message of Israel" (1934–69).

Works: Opera: *The Golem* (1956; White Plains, N.Y., Jan. 13, 1957); 5 ballets; 7 cantatas, including *Man of the World* (1939), *To Thee, America* (1943), *The Legend of Toil* (1945), *The Last Judgement* (1966), and *Amos* (1970); over 100 liturgical works; more than 150 songs, many to Yiddish texts; some orch. and chamber music.

Bibl.: M. Edelman, "In memoriam: L. W. (1897–1982)," *Musica judaica*, IV (1981–82).

Weiner, Léo, outstanding Hungarian composer and pedagogue; b. Budapest, April 16, 1885; d. there, Sept. 13, 1960. He was a pupil of Hans Koessler at the Budapest Academy of Music (1901–6), winning several prizes for excellence; in 1906 he won the Franz-Josef-Jubiläumspreis, which enabled him to study further in Austria, Germany, and France. Returning to Budapest, he became a teacher at the Academy of Music (1908); was named prof. of composition in 1912 and then of chamber music in 1920; although he was granted a pension in 1949, he continued to teach there as prof. emeritus until his death. He won the Coolidge Prize in 1922 for his 2nd String Quartet, the Kossuth Prize in 1950, and became an Eminent Artist of the Hungarian People's Republic in 1953. He publ. a number of didactic vols. on musical form, analytical harmony, and forms of instrumental music (1910–55). In his compositions he adopted a characteristic Hungarian style within the framework of Romantic forms.

Works: opera: *A gondolás* (The Gondolier; in collaboration with A. Szirmai; not extant); incidental music to Vörösmarty's play *Csongor és Tünde* (1913; Budapest, Dec. 6, 1916; as a ballet, Budapest, Nov. 8, 1930; orch. suite, 1937). ORCH.: *Scherzo* (1905; not extant); *Serenade* for Small Orch. (Budapest, Oct. 22, 1906); *Farsang* (Carnival) for Small Orch. (1907); Piano Concertino (1923); *Katonásdi* (Toy Soldiers; 1924); *Suite* (1931); 5 divertimenti: Nos. 1 and 2 for Strings (1934, 1938) and Nos. 3–5 for Orch. (1949, 1951, 1951); *Pastorale, phantaisie et fugue* for Strings (1934); *Ballata* for Clarinet and Orch. (1949); *Romanze* for Cello, Harp, and Strings (1949); *Változatok egy magyar népdal fölött* (Variations on a Hungarian Folksong; 1949); 2 violin concertos (1950, 1957; both arr. from the 2 violin sonatas, 1911, 1918); *Preludio, notturno e scherzo diabolico* for Orch. (1950); *Toldi*, symphonic poem (1952; 2 suites, 1954–55); *Passacaglia* (1955). CHAMBER: 3 string quartets (1906; 1921; 1938, *Pastorale, phantaisie et fugue*); String Trio (1908); 2 violin sonatas (1911, 1918; both arr. as violin concertos, 1950, 1957); *Romanze* for Cello and Piano (1921); *Peregi verbunk* (Pereg Recruiting Dance) for Violin or Viola or Clarinet and Piano (1951; arr. for Wind Quintet and String Quintet, 1957); a number of piano pieces; cadenzas for Beethoven's piano concertos Nos. 1–4 (Milan, 1950); many orch. arrangements of works by Bach, Berlioz, Liszt, Schubert, and Bartók.

Bibl.: G. Gál, *W. L. életüve* (L. W.'s Life-work; Budapest, 1959).

Weingartner, (Paul) Felix, Edler von Münzberg, illustrious Austrian conductor; b. Zara, Dalmatia, June 2, 1863; d. Winterthur, May 7, 1942. After his father's death in 1868, his mother took him to Graz, where he studied music with W.A. Rémy. He publ. some piano pieces when he was 16 years old; Brahms recommended him for a stipend that enabled him to take music courses with Reinecke, Jadassohn, and Paul at the Leipzig Cons. (1881–83). He received the Mozart Prize at his graduation; he was introduced to Liszt, who recommended Weingartner's opera *Sakuntala* for production in Weimar (March 23, 1884), a signal honor for a young man not yet 21 years old. While progressing rapidly as a composer, Weingartner launched a brilliant career as a conductor, which was to become his prime vocation. He conducted in Königsberg (1884–85), Danzig (1885–87), Hamburg (1887–

89), and Mannheim (1889–91). In 1891 he was engaged as court conductor in Berlin, where he led the Royal Opera until 1898 and the royal orch. concerts until 1907; also conducted the Kaim Orch. in Munich (1898–1905). His reputation as a fine musician was enhanced by his appearances as an ensemble player in the Weingartner Trio, with himself as pianist, Rettich as violinist, and Warnke as cellist. In 1908 he succeeded Mahler as music director of the Vienna Court Opera, and conducted there until 1911. From 1912 to 1914 he conducted the Municipal Opera in Hamburg; from 1914 to 1918 was in charge of the Darmstadt Orch. He was subsequently music director at the Vienna Volksoper (1919–24), and conducted the Vienna Phil. (1908–27); in 1927 he was appointed director of the Basel Cons.; was guest conductor at the Vienna State Opera during the season 1934–35; served as director in 1935–36, and continued guest appearances until 1938. In the interim he had engagements as guest conductor with major European orchs.; made his American debut with the N.Y. Phil. on Feb. 12, 1904, and later conducted the N.Y. Sym. Society (Jan.–March 1906). He appeared with the Boston Opera Co. on Feb. 12, 1912, conducting *Tristan und Isolde;* he and his 3rd wife, the mezzo-soprano **Lucille Marcel,** were engaged for a season with the Boston Opera Co. in 1913. (His 1st wife was Marie Juillerat, whom he married in 1891; his 2nd wife was the Baroness Feodora von Dreifus, whom he married in 1903). He made his debut at Covent Garden in London in 1939, conducting *Parsifal.* He eventually settled in Interlaken, where he established a summer conducting school. Weingartner was a competent music editor; he was on the editorial board for the complete works of Berlioz (1899) and of Haydn (1907). Despite the pressure of his activities as a conductor, he found time for composition. In addition to his 1st opera, *Sakuntala,* he wrote the operas *Malawika* (Munich, 1886); *Genesius* (Berlin, Nov. 15, 1892); *Orestes,* a trilogy (Leipzig, Feb. 15, 1902); *Kain und Abel* (Darmstadt, May 17, 1914); *Dame Kobold* (Darmstadt, Feb. 23, 1916); *Die Dorfschule* (Vienna, May 13, 1920); *Meister Andrea* (Vienna, May 13, 1920); *Der Apostat* (not perf.). He also composed 7 syms. (1899–1937); various other orch. works, including pieces for Voice and Orch. and Chorus and Orch.; songs; much chamber music, including 5 string quartets, 2 sonatas for Violin and Piano, and piano pieces. He made arrangements of Beethoven's "Hammerklavier" Sonata, op. 106, and of Weber's *Aufforderung zum Tanz.* He was an excellent writer on musical subjects. Among his publs. are: *Die Lehre von der Wiedergeburt und das musikalische Drama* (1895); *Über das Dirigieren* (1896; 5th ed., 1913; a fundamental essay on conducting); *Bayreuth 1876–1896* (1897; 2nd ed., 1904); *Die Symphonie nach Beethoven* (1897; 4th ed., 1901; in Eng., 1904; new tr. as *The Symphony since Beethoven,* 1926); *Ratschläge für Aufführung der Sinfonien Beethovens* (1906; 3rd ed., 1928; in Eng., London, 1907); *Akkorde: gesammelte Aufsätze von Felix Weingartner* (1912); a polemical pamphlet, *Erlebnisse eines kgl. Kapellmeisters in Berlin* (1912; an attack upon the Berlin intendancy; a rebuttal was publ. by A. Wolff in *Der Fall Weingartner,* 1912); *Ratschläge für Aufführung der Sinfonien Schuberts und Schumanns* (1918); *Ratschläge für Aufführung der Sinfonien Mozarts* (1923); *Lebenserinnerungen* (vol. I, 1923; vol. II, 1929; Eng. version as *Buffets and Rewards: A Musician's Reminiscences,* London, 1937); *Unwirkliches und Wirkliches* (1936).

Bibl.: E. Krause, *F. W. als schaffender Künstler* (Berlin, 1904); P. Riesenfeld, *F. W. Ein kritischer Versuch* (Breslau, 1906); W. Hutschenruyter, *Levensschets en portret van F. W.* (Haarlem, 1906); J. Lustig, *F. W. Persönlichkeiten* (Berlin, 1908); P. Raabe, "F. W.," *Die Musik* (Jan. 1908); F. Günther, *F. W.* (1917); W. Jacob, *F. W.* (Wiesbaden, 1933); *Festschrift für Dr. F. W. zu seinem siebzigsten Geburtstag* (Basel, 1933); H. Schonberg, *The Great Conductors* (N.Y., 1967); C. Dyment, *F. W.: Recollections and Recordings* (Rickmansworth, 1975).

Weinlig, Christian Ehregott, German organist and composer, uncle of **(Christian) Theodor Weinlig;** b. Dresden, Sept. 30, 1743; d. there, March 14, 1813. He studied with

Homilius at the Dresden Kreuzschule; in 1767 he was organist at the Evangelical Church in Leipzig; in 1773, at Thorn; in 1780, accompanist at the Italian Opera in Dresden, and organist at the Frauenkirche; in 1785, succeeded his teacher, Homilius, as Kantor of the Kreuzschule. He publ. sonatas for piano, with flute and cello; brought out several oratorios; also light theater pieces.

Weinlig, (Christian) Theodor, noted German music theorist and teacher, nephew of **Christian Ehregott Weinlig;** b. Dresden, July 25, 1780; d. Leipzig, March 7, 1842. After a period of study with his uncle (1804–6), he became a pupil of Stanislao Mattei in Bologna. He was Kantor of the Dresden Kreuzschule (1814–17) and of the Leipzig Thomasschule (from 1823). He enjoyed high repute as a teacher of theory and composition; Richard Wagner was his pupil. His own works include a *Deutsches Magnificat* for Soli, Chorus, and Orch.; vocalises; publ. a manual, *Theoretisch-praktische Anleitung zur Fuge, für den Selbstunterricht* (Dresden, 1845; 2nd ed., 1852).
  BIBL.: A. Kurz, *Geschichte der Familie W. von 1580 bis 1850* (Bonn, 1912); R. Roch, *C.T. W., der Lehrer Richard Wagners* (diss., Univ. of Leipzig, 1917).

Weinmann, Karl, eminent German musicologist; b. Vohenstrauss, Upper Palatinate, Dec. 22, 1873; d. Pielenhofen, near Regensburg, Sept. 26, 1929. He was a pupil of Haberl and Haller at the Kirchenmusikschule in Regensburg, in Berlin, and in Innsbruck; after further study with Peter Wagner at the Univ. of Freiburg, he obtained the degree of Ph.D. there (1905) with the dissertation *Das Hymnarium Parisiense;* later obtained a doctorate in theology at the Kirchenmusikschule in Regensburg (1917). After his ordination to the priesthood, he became a prof. at the Kirchenmusikschule in Regensburg; in 1910, succeeded Haberl as its director. He was ed. of the *Kirchenmusikalisches Jahrbuch* (1909–11), *Musica Sacra* (from 1911), and *Cäcilienvereinsorgan* (from 1926). He ed. for Pustet (after the *Editio vaticana*) *Römisches Gradualbuch* (1909; 4th ed., 1928); *Graduale* (1910); *Kyriale* (1911); *Totenoffizium* (1912; 2nd ed., 1928); *Graduale parvum* (1913); *Römisches Vesperbuch mit Psalmenbuch* (1915); *Karwochenbuch* (1924); *Feier der heiligen Karwoche* (1925); *Sonntagsvesper und Komplet* (2nd ed., 1928). He was also ed. of the collection *Kirchenmusik,* for which he wrote *Geschichte der Kirchenmusik* (1906; 4th ed., 1925; Eng. tr., 1910; also tr. into French, Italian, Polish, and Hungarian), and monographs on Leonhard Paminger (1907) and Carl Proske (1909). Other writings include *Palestrinas Geburtsjahr* (Regensburg, 1915); *Stille Nacht, heilige Nacht: Die Geschichte des Liedes zu seinem 100. Geburtstag* (1918; 2nd ed., 1920); *Das Konzil von Trent und die Kirchenmusik* (1919).

Weinrich, Carl, eminent American organist and teacher; b. Paterson, N.J., July 2, 1904; d. Princeton, N.J., May 13, 1991. After graduation from N.Y. Univ. (B.A., 1927), he studied at the Curtis Inst. of Music in Philadelphia (1927–30); also studied organ privately with Lynnwood Farnam and Marcel Dupré, and piano with Abram Chasins. In 1930 he became the successor of Lynnwood Farnam as organist at the Holy Communion Church in N.Y.; taught at Westminster Choir College in Princeton, N.J. (1934–40), Wellesley College (1936–46), and at Columbia Univ. (1942–52); also was director of music at Princeton Univ. Chapel (1943–73); toured extensively as a recitalist.

Weinstock, Herbert, American writer on music; b. Milwaukee, Nov. 16, 1905; d. N.Y., Oct. 21, 1971. He was educated in his native town; later took courses at the Univ. of Chicago. He was active in N.Y. as a music ed. for the publisher Alfred A. Knopf.
  WRITINGS: All publ. in N.Y.: With W. Brockway, *Men of Music* (1939; 2nd ed., rev. and enl., 1950); with Brockway, *The Opera: A History of its Creation and Performance* (1941; 2nd ed., 1962, as *The World of Opera*); *Tchaikovsky* (1943); *Handel* (1946; 2nd ed., 1959; also in German); *Chopin: The Man and His Music* (1949; 2nd ed., 1959); *Music As an Art* (1953; 2nd ed., 1966, as *What Music Is*); *Donizetti and the*

World of Opera in Italy, Paris and Vienna in the First Half of the Nineteenth Century (1963); *Rossini: a Biography* (1968); *Vincenzo Bellini: His Life and Operas* (N.Y., 1971).

Weinwurm, Rudolf, Austrian choral conductor and composer; b. Schaidldorf-on-the-Thaja, April 3, 1835; d. Vienna, May 26, 1911. He was trained musically as a chorister in the Imperial Chapel in Vienna; conducted the Vienna Singakademie (from 1864) and the Männergesangverein (from 1866); in 1880 he became music director of the Univ. of Vienna. He publ. the manuals *Allgemeine Musiklehre* (1870); *Musikalische Lehrmittel* (1873); *Methodik des Gesangunterrichts* (1876); composed a *Deutsches Requiem* for Male Chorus a cappella, and one for Female Chorus, with Organ; also other church music.
  BIBL.: P. Altmann, *R. W., 1835–1911* (Vienna, 1985).

Weinzierl, Max, Ritter von, Austrian conductor and composer; b. Bergstadtl, Bohemia, Sept. 16, 1841; d. Mödling, near Vienna, July 10, 1898. He served as conductor at various theaters in Vienna; from 1882 he was chorus master of the Männergesangverein. He wrote the operas *Don Quixote* (Vienna, Feb. 15, 1879; with L. Roth); *Die weiblichen Jäger* (Vienna, May 5, 1880); *Moclemos* (Vienna, June 5, 1880); *Fioretta* (Prague, 1886); *Page Fritz* (Prague, 1889); *Der Schwiegerpapa* (Berlin, 1893); oratorio, *Hiob* (Vienna, 1870); choral works, with Orch.: *Nachtgruss, Liedesweihe, Gesang der Nixen, Die Sphinx, Der Zigeuner, Donausage, Hubertus,* etc.; many male choruses a cappella.

Weinzweig, John (Jacob), Canadian composer; b. Toronto, March 11, 1913. He learned to play mandolin, piano, tuba, and double bass; then took lessons in orchestration with MacMillan, in counterpoint and fugue with Willan, and in harmony with Leo Smith at the Univ. of Toronto (B.Mus., 1937); continued his study in composition with Bernard Rogers at the Eastman School of Music in Rochester, N.Y. (M. Mus., 1938). He taught at the Toronto Cons. (1939–43; 1945–60) and at the Univ. of Toronto (1952–78). On Feb. 3, 1951, he organized the Canadian League of Composers and was its first president. In 1974 he was made an Officer of the Order of Canada.
  WORKS: Ballet, *Red Ear of Corn* (Toronto, March 3, 1949). **ORCH.:** *Legend* (1937); *The Enchanted Hill* (1938); *Suite* (1938); *Spectre* for String Orch. and Timpani (1938); *A Tale of Tamotu* for Bassoon and Orch. (1939); *Sym.* (1940); *Rhapsody* (1941); *Interlude in an Artist's Life* for String Orch. (1943); *Our Canada* (1943); *Divertimento No. 1* for Flute and String Orch. (Vancouver, Dec. 29, 1946); *Divertimento No. 2* for Oboe and String Orch. (Toronto, April 30, 1948); *Divertimento No. 3* for Bassoon and String Orch. (Toronto, May 5, 1961); *Divertimento No. 5* for Trumpet, Trombone, and Wind Ensemble (Pittsburgh, June 9, 1961; numbered out of chronological order); *Divertimento No. 4* for Clarinet, and String Orch. or String Quintet (Vancouver, Sept. 19, 1968); *Divertimento No. 6* for Saxophone and String Orch. (Toronto, Aug. 21, 1972); *Divertimento No. 7* for Horn and String Orch. (1979); *Divertimento No. 8* for Tuba and Orch. (1980); *Divertimento No. 9* (1982); *Edge of the World,* symphonic poem (1946); *Round Dance* for Small Orch. (1950; version for Full Orch., 1977); *Violin Concerto* (Toronto, May 30, 1955); *Wine of Peace,* 3 songs for Soprano and Orch. (1957); *Symphonic Ode* (1958); *Piano Concerto* (Toronto, Dec. 15, 1966); *Concerto for Harp and Chamber Orch.* (Toronto, April 30, 1967); *Dummiyah* (Silence; Toronto, July 4, 1969). **CHAMBER:** 3 string quartets (1937, 1946, 1962); *Violin Sonata* (1941); cello sonata, *Israel* (1949); *Wind Quintet* (1964); *Clarinet Quartet* (1965); *Around the Stage in 25 Minutes during Which a Variety of Instruments Are Struck!* for Percussionist (*Trialogue* for Soprano, Flute, and Piano (1971); *Riffs* for Flute (1974); *Pieces of 5,* brass quintet (1976); *Contrasts* for Guitar (1976); *Refrains* for Double Bass and Piano (1977); *15 Pieces* for Harp (1983). **KEYBOARD:** 2 suites for Piano (1939, 1950); *Piano Sonata* (1950); *Impromptus* for Piano (1973); *Improvisation on an Indian Tune* for Organ (1942). **VOCAL:** Choruses; *Private Collection,* 8 songs for Soprano and Piano (1975).

Weir, Gillian (Constance), outstanding New Zealand organist and harpsichordist; b. Martinsborough, Jan. 17, 1941. She studied with Ralph Downes at the Royal College of Music in London (1962–65), then pursued private training with Anton Heiller, Marie-Claire Alain, and Nadia Boulanger (1965–66); won the St. Albans International Organ Competition in 1964; in 1965 she made her debut at London's Royal Festival Hall; subsequently appeared throughout the world as a recitalist on both the organ and the harpsichord. In 1982 she was featured in the television film "Toccata: Two Weeks in the Life of Gillian Weir." In 1984 she gave a recital at N.Y.'s Alice Tully Hall on an organ designed by her husband. She maintains a catholic repertory; has given the premiere performances of many works written for her, including William Mathias's Organ Concerto (London, Sept. 12, 1984).

Weir, Judith, Scottish composer; b. Aberdeen, May 11, 1954. She studied in London with John Tavener; after instruction in computer music from Barry Vercoe at the Mass. Inst. of Technology (1973), she studied with Robin Holloway at King's College, Cambridge (1973–76); also received instruction from Schuller and Messiaen at the Berkshire Music Center at Tanglewood (1975). She taught at the Univ. of Glasgow (1979–82); then held a creative arts fellowship at Trinity College, Cambridge (1983–85).
Works: stage: operas: *The Black Spider* (1984; Canterbury, March 6, 1985); *A Night at the Chinese Opera* (Cheltenham, July 8, 1987). **music drama:** *The Consolations of Scholarship* (Durham, May 5, 1985). **orch.:** *Isti mirant stella* (Orkney, June 23, 1981); *Ballad* (Glasgow, Sept. 17, 1981); *The Ride over Lake Constance* (London, March 12, 1984); *Variation on "Summer is icumen in"* (Snape, June 13, 1987). **chamber:** *Out of the Air* for Flute, Oboe, Clarinet, Horn, and Bassoon (1975); *Hans the Hedgehog* for Speaker, 2 Oboes, Bassoon, and Harpsichord (1978); *King Harald Sails to Byzantium* for 6 Players (1979); *Several Concertos* for Flute, Cello, and Piano (1980); *Thread!* for Narrator and 8 Players (1981); *Spij dobrze (Pleasant Dreams)* for Double Bass and Tape (1983); *A Serbian Cabaret* for Violin, Viola, Cello, and Piano, with some spoken recitation by the instrumentalists (1984); *Airs from Another Planet* for 6 Players (1986); *Gentle Violence* for Piccolo and Guitar (1987); keyboard pieces. **vocal:** *Black Birdsong* for Baritone, Flute, Oboe, Violin, and Cello (1977); *King Harald's Saga*, "grand opera" for Solo Soprano (1979); *Scotch Minstrelsy* for Tenor or Soprano and Piano (1982); *Ascending into Heaven* for Choir and Organ (1983); *Illuminare, Jerusalem (Jerusalem, Rejos for Joy)* for Choir and Organ (1985).
Bibl.: J. Weir, "A Note on a Chinese Opera," *Musical Times* (July 1987).

Weis, (Carl) Flemming, Danish composer and organist; b. Copenhagen, April 15, 1898; d. there, Sept. 30, 1981. He studied organ and theory with Gustav Helsted at the Royal Danish Cons. in Copenhagen (1916–20); then took courses in organ with Karl Straube and in theory and composition with Paul Graener at the Leipzig Hochschule für Musik (graduated, 1923). He served as organist of the St. Anna Church in Copenhagen (1929–68); was a member of the board of the Society for Contemporary Music (1926–56; president, 1942–56) and a member of the board of the Danish Society of Composers (president, 1963–75). His music follows the traditions of the Danish School; under the influence of Carl Nielsen, he wrote a number of symphonic pieces imbued with Romantic fervor and gentle humor.
Works: *Praeludium og Intermezzo* for Oboe and Strings (1933); *Concertino* for Clarinet and Strings (1935); *Symphonic Overture* (1938); *In temporis vernalis* for Orch. (1945; Copenhagen, Jan. 14, 1948); *Introduction grave* for Piano and Orch. (1941); 2 syms. (1942, 1948); *Det forjoettede land* (The Promised Land) for Chorus and Orch. (Copenhagen, Nov. 8, 1949); *Musikantiski ouverture* (1949); *Sinfonia proverbiorum* for Chorus and Orch. (Copenhagen, June 21, 1959); *Concertino* for Strings (1960); *Femdelt form III* (Quintuple Form) for Orch. (Randers, Feb. 5, 1963); *Sine nomine* for Orch. (Copenhagen,

March 18, 1973); *Chaconne* for Orch. (1974); 4 string quartets (1922, 1925, 1937, 1977); *Music* for 3 Woodwinds (1928); Clarinet Sonata (1931); Violin Sonata (1932–41); *Serenade uden reelle hensigter* (Serenade without Serious Intentions) for Wind Quintet (1938); Sonatina for Flute, Violin, and Cello (1942); *Diverterende musik* (Diverting Music) for Flute, Violin, Viola, and Cello (1943); Oboe Sonata (1946); *Variations* for Wind Quintet (1946); Flute Sonata (1956); *Fantasia seria* for String Quartet (1956); 5 *Epigrams* for String Quartet (1960); *Femdelt form II* for String Quintet (1962); *Rhapsodic Suite* for Violin (1966); *Static Situations* for String Quartet (1970); *3 søstre* (3 Sisters) for Cello (1973); 3 *Mobiles* for Flute, Violin, Viola, and Cello (1974); 3 *Aspects* for Guitar (1975); 3 *Japanese Bird Cries* for Soprano, Viola, and Guitar (1976); *Dialogues* for Flute and Guitar (1977). For Piano: *Suite in B* (1945–46); Sonatina (1949); 12 *Monologues* (1958); *Femdelt Form I* (1961); *Limitations I* (1965); *Limitations II* (1968). For Organ: Concertino (1957); *Coeli enarrant* for Soprano and Organ (1955–56); choruses; songs; anthems.

Weis, Karel, Czech writer on music, ethnomusicologist, and composer; b. Prague, Feb. 13, 1862; d. there, April 4, 1944. He studied violin at the Prague Cons.; also organ with Skuherský and composition with Fibich at the Organ School in Prague; subsequently filled various posts as organist and conductor in Prague and other cities. He devoted much of his time to collecting Bohemian folk songs, and publ. them in 15 vols. (1928–41).
Works: Operas: *Viola*, after Shakespeare's *Twelfth Night* (Prague, Jan. 17, 1892; rev. as *Blíženci* [The Twins], Prague, Feb. 28, 1917); *Der polnische Jude* (Prague, March 3, 1901); *Die Dorfmusikanten* (Prague, Jan. 1, 1905); *Der Revisor*, after Gogol (1907); *Utok na mlýn*, after Zola's *L'Attaque du moulin* (Prague, March 29, 1912); *Lešetínský kovář* (The Blacksmith of Lešetín; Prague, June 6, 1920); *Bojarská nevěsta* (The Boyar's Bride; Prague, Feb. 18, 1943); other works include *Helios a Selene*, symphonic poem; Sym. in C minor; choral pieces; songs; piano works.
Bibl.: L. Firkušný, *K. W.* (Prague, 1949).

Weisberg, Arthur, American bassoonist and conductor; b. N.Y., April 4, 1931. He attended the Juilliard School of Music in N.Y., where he studied bassoon with Simon Kovar and conducting with Jean Morel. He played bassoon with the Houston, Baltimore, and Cleveland orchs.; from 1956 to 1970, was bassoonist with the N.Y. Woodwind Quintet. In 1960 he formed the Contemporary Chamber Ensemble, with which he travels widely in Europe and America. He held teaching posts at the Juilliard School of Music (1960–68), at the State Univ. of N.Y. at Stony Brook (1971–89), and at Yale Univ. (1975–89). In 1987–88 he was chief conductor of the Iceland Sym. Orch. in Reykjavík. He publ. the book *The Art of Wind Playing* (1973).

Weisgall, Hugo (David), distinguished Moravian-born American composer and pedagogue; b. Eibenschütz, Oct. 13, 1912. He emigrated with his family to the U.S. and became a naturalized citizen in 1926. He studied at the Peabody Cons. of Music in Baltimore (1927–32); subsequently had composition lessons with Sessions at various times between 1932 and 1941; also was a pupil of Reiner (conducting diploma, 1938) and Scalero (composition diploma, 1939) at the Curtis Inst. of Music in Philadelphia, and pursued academic studies at Johns Hopkins Univ. (Ph.D., 1940, with a diss. on primitivism in 17th-century German poetry). After military service in World War II, he was active as a conductor, singer, teacher, and composer. He was founder-conductor of the Chamber Society of Baltimore (1948) and the Hilltop Opera Co. (1952); was director of the Baltimore Inst. of Musical Arts (1949–51); taught at Johns Hopkins Univ. (1951–57); was made chairman of the faculty of the Cantors' Inst. at the Jewish Theological Center in N.Y. in 1952. He taught at the Juilliard School of Music (1957–70) and at Queens College of the City Univ. of N.Y. (from 1961). He served as president of the American Music Center (1963–73); in 1966 he was composer-in-residence at the American Academy in Rome. He held 3 Guggenheim fellowships and received many prizes and commissions; in 1975 he was elected to membership in the National Inst. of Arts and Letters, and in 1990 became president of the American Academy and Inst. of Arts and Letters. His music constitutes the paragon of enlightened but inoffensive modernism; he is a master of all musical idioms, and bungler of none. His intentions in each of his works never fail in the execution; for this reason his music enjoys numerous performances, which are usually accepted with pleasure by the audiences, if not by the majority of important music critics.

WORKS: STAGE: OPERAS: *Night* (1932); *Lillith* (1934); *The Tenor* (1948–50; Baltimore, Feb. 1, 1952); *The Stronger* (Lutherville, Md., Aug. 9, 1952); *6 Characters in Search of an Author* (1953–56; N.Y., April 26, 1959); *Purgatory* (1958; Washington, D.C., Feb. 17, 1961); *The Gardens of Adonis* (1959; rev. 1977–81); *Athaliah* (1960–63; N.Y., Feb. 17, 1964); *9 Rivers from Jordan* (1964–68; N.Y., Oct. 9, 1968); *Jennie, or The Hundred Nights* (1975–76; N.Y., April 22, 1976). **BALLETS:** *Quest* (Baltimore, May 17, 1938; suite, N.Y., March 21, 1942); *Art Appreciation* (Baltimore, 1938); *One Thing Is Certain* (Baltimore, Feb. 25, 1939); *Outpost* (1947). **ORCH.:** *Overture in F* (London, July 29, 1943); *Appearances and Entrances* (1960); *Proclamation* (1960); *Prospect* (1983); *Tekiator* (1985). **CHAMBER:** Piano Sonata (1931); *Chorale Prelude* for Organ (1938); *Variations* for Piano (1939); *Graven Images,* chamber pieces for Various Instruments (1964–); Piano Sonata (1982); *Arioso and Burlesca* for Cello and Piano (1984); *Tangents* for Flute and Marimba (1985); also many vocal works, including *Hymn* for Chorus and Orch. (1941), *Soldier Songs* for Baritone and Orch. (1944–46; N.Y., April 26, 1954; rev. 1965; Baltimore, March 30, 1966), and *A Garden Eastward,* cantata for High Voice and Orch. (1952; Baltimore, Jan. 31, 1953); also songs.

Weisgarber, Elliot, American composer; b. Pittsfield, Mass., Dec. 5, 1919. He studied with Bernard Rogers and Howard Hanson at the Eastman School of Music in Rochester, N.Y. (1939–43); then had lessons with Nadia Boulanger in Paris (1952–53) and with Halsey Stevens in Los Angeles (1958–59). From 1966 to 1969 he was in Japan, where he studied koto and other indigenous instruments. He taught at the Women's College of the Univ. of North Carolina (1944–60) and at the Univ. of British Columbia in Vancouver (1960–84).

WORKS: Sonata for Flute, Clarinet, and Piano (1953); *Divertimento* for String Trio (1956); *Divertimento* for Horn, Viola, and Piano (1959); *Sinfonia pastorale* (1961); *Sinfonia concertante* for Oboe, 2 Horns, and Strings (1962); Flute Sonata (1963); *Suite* for Viola and Piano (1964); Sonata for Solo Cello (1965); *Kyōto Landscapes: Lyrical Evocations,* for Voice and Orch. (1973); *Night* for Baritone, Chorus, and Strings (1973; rev. 1982); *Autumnal Music* for English Horn and String Orch. (1973); *Musica serena* for Orch. (1974); *Netori: A Fantasia* for Saxophone and Orch. (1974); *A Pacific Trilogy* for Orch. (1974); Violin Concerto (1974; rev. 1985); *A Northumbrian Elegy* for Orch. (1977); 6 string quartets; Wind Quintet (1978); 3 syms., including No. 3 (1983); Quintet for Clarinet, 2 Violins, Viola, and Cello (1988); many vocal works, including *Canticle* for Chorus, Horn, and Strings (1978) and *10 Japanese Folk Songs* (1981).

Weismann, Julius, German pianist, conductor, and composer; b. Freiburg im Breisgau, Dec. 26, 1879; d. Singen am Hohentweil, Dec. 22, 1950. He began piano lessons at 9 with Seyffart; later studied composition with Rheinberger in Munich (1892); received advanced piano training from Dimmler in Freiburg im Breisgau (1893), and took courses at the Univ. of Lausanne; also studied composition with Bussmeyer, von Herzogenberg in Berlin (1898–99), and Thuille in Munich (1899–1902). He was active as a pianist and conductor in Freiburg im Breisgau from 1906, where he founded (with E. Doflein) the Musikseminar in 1930, subsequently serving as a teacher of harmony and as director of the piano master class; after retiring in 1939, he devoted himself fully to composition. He received the Beethoven Prize (1930), the Bach Prize of Leipzig (1939), and the Ehrenbürgerrecht of Freiburg im Breis-

gau (1939); was made an honorary prof. by the government (1936) and by the state of Baden (1950). The Julius Weismann Archive was founded in his memory in Duisburg in 1954.

WORKS: STAGE: OPERAS: *Schwanenweiss* (1919–20; Duisburg, Sept. 29, 1923); *Ein Traumspiel* (1922–24; Duisburg, 1925); *Leonce und Lena* (Mannheim, 1924); *Regina del lago* (Karlsruhe, 1928); *Die Gespenstersonate* (1929–30; Munich, Dec. 19, 1930); *Die pfiffige Magd* (1937–38; Leipzig, Feb. 11, 1939). **BALLETS:** *Tanzphantasie* (1910; orchestrated from the piano piece); *Die Landsknechte: Totentanz* (1936); *Sinfonisches Spiel* (1937). **ORCH.:** 3 piano concertos (1909–10, rev. 1936; 1941–42; 1942–48); 4 violin concertos (1910–11; 1929; 1942; 1943); *Suite* for Piano and Orch. (1927); Concerto for Flute, Clarinet, Bassoon, Trumpet, Timpani, and Strings (1930); Horn Concerto (1935); Cello Concerto (1941–43); 2 syms. (1940, 1940); *Theme, Variations and Fugue* for Trautonium and Orch. (1943; also for Violin and Piano); *Musik* for Bassoon and Orch. (1947). **CHAMBER:** 13 string quartets (1905; 1907; 1910; *Fantastischer Reigen,* 1913; 1914; 1922; 1918–22; 1929; *Fugue,* 1931; 1932; 1940; 1943–45; 1947); Piano Quintet (1902); 3 piano trios (1908–9; 1916; 1921); Trio for Flute, Clarinet, and Bassoon (1942); 4 sonatas for Violin and Piano (1909; 1917; 1917, arranged for Clarinet and Piano, 1941; 1921); Sonata for Flute and Piano (1941); *Sonatina concertante* for Cello and Piano (1941; also for Cello and Chamber Orch.); *Theme, Variations and Fugue* for Violin and Piano (1943; also for Trautonium and Orch.); Sonata for Viola (1945); various other chamber works; piano pieces. **CHORAL WITH ORCH.:** *Macht hoch die Tür,* Christmas cantata for Soprano, Chorus, and Orch. (1912); *Psalm XC* for Baritone, Chorus, and Orch. (1912); *Der Wächterruf* for Soprano, Baritone, Chorus, and Orch. (1947–50); various men's and women's choruses; solo songs.

BIBL.: F. Herzfeld, *J. W. und seine Generation* (Duisburg, 1965).

Weismann, Wilhelm, German composer; b. Alfdorf, Sept. 20, 1900; d. Leipzig, May 14, 1980. He studied at the Stuttgart Cons. with Schlegel and Lang (1919–21) and at the Leipzig Cons. with Ludwig and Karg-Elert (1921–23). From 1946 to 1955 he was on the faculty of the Hochschule für Musik in Leipzig; served as ed. for the C.F. Peters Publishing firm in Leipzig (1929–65), while continuing his teaching at the Hochschule für Musik (rejoined in 1961). He wrote a number of choral works, both secular and sacred; also composed several collections of madrigals, as well as solo cantatas. He supervised a complete edition of madrigals by Gesualdo.

Weiss, family of German musicians:

(1) Johann Jacob Weiss, lutenist and composer; b. c.1662; d. Mannheim, Jan. 30, 1754. He was active in Breslau from about 1686; around 1708 he was made court lutenist of the Palatine chapel in Düsseldorf, following it to Heidelberg in 1718 and to Mannheim in 1720.

(2) Silvius Leopold Weiss, lutenist and composer, son of the preceding; b. Breslau, Oct. 12, 1686; d. Dresden, Oct. 16, 1750. He most likely was a pupil of his father; was in the service of Count Carl Philipp of the Palatinate in Breslau by 1706; then was in Italy with Alexander Sobiesky, Prince of Poland (1708–14). In 1715 he entered the service of the Hessen-Kassel court, and shortly thereafter went to Düsseldorf; in 1717 he joined the chapel of the Saxon court in Dresden, where his status was formalized in 1718. He also traveled as a virtuoso, appearing in Prague (1717), London (1718), Vienna (1718–19), Munich (1722), Berlin (1728), and Leipzig (1739), where he visited J.S. Bach. Weiss was one of the foremost performers on and composers for the lute. His extant works number almost 600, the largest corpus of solo lute works by any composer in history. D. Smith ed. his complete works (Frankfurt am Main, 1980–). His son, **Johann Adolf Faustinus Weiss** (b. Dresden, April 15, 1741; d. there, Jan. 21, 1814), was also a lutenist and composer; served as chamber lutenist at the Dresden court from 1763 until his death; also traveled widely; composed a number of lute pieces and some guitar music.

BIBL.: K. Prusik, *Kompositionen des Lautenisten S.L. W.* (diss., Univ. of Vienna, 1924); W. Mason, *The Lute Music of S.L. W.* (diss., Univ. of North Carolina, 1949); D. Smith, *The Late Sonatas of S.L. W.* (diss., Stanford Univ., 1977).

(3) Johann Sigismund Weiss, lutenist, viola da gambist, violinist, and composer, brother of the preceding; b. probably in Breslau, c.1689; d. Mannheim, April 12, 1737. He most likely studied with his father; became a lutenist at the Palatine chapel in Düsseldorf about 1708, following it to Heidelberg in 1718 and to Mannheim in 1720; in 1732 he was named director of instrumental music there, and later served as Konzertmeister and theorbo player. As a composer, he was one of the finest representatives of the early Mannheim school.

Weiss, Adolph, American composer and bassoonist; b. Baltimore, Sept. 12, 1891; d. Van Nuys, Calif., Feb. 21, 1971. He studied piano, violin, and bassoon; at the age of 16, was engaged as 1st bassoonist of the Russian Sym. Orch. of N.Y.; then joined the N.Y. Phil. (1909) and the N.Y. Sym. Orch. (1910); he studied composition with Cornelius Rybner at Columbia Univ. In 1916 he joined the Chicago Sym. Orch. as bassoonist; studied theory with Adolf Weidig and Theodore Ötterstrom in Chicago; then was bassoonist with the Eastman Theatre Orch. in Rochester, N.Y. (from 1921). In 1926 he went to Berlin and became the 1st American student of Schoenberg, whose influence was decisive in the formation of his musical style. Returning to the U.S., he played in the San Francisco Sym. Orch. (from 1936), the MGM Studios orch. (from 1938), and the Los Angeles Phil. (from 1951). He held a Guggenheim fellowship (1931); received a National Inst. of Arts and Letters award in 1955.

WORKS: *Fantasie* for Piano (1918); *I segreti* for Orch. (1922; Rochester, N.Y., May 1, 1925); 3 string quartets (1925, 1926, 1932); Chamber Sym. for 10 Instruments (1927); *12 Preludes* for Piano (1927); *American Life,* "Scherzoso Jazzoso" for Orch. (N.Y., Feb. 21, 1930); *Sonata da camera* for Flute and Viola (1929); *7 Songs* for Soprano and String Quartet (1928); *The Libation Bearers,* choreographic cantata for Soloists, Chorus, and Orch. (1930); Quintet for Flute, Oboe, Clarinet, Bassoon, and Horn (1931); Piano Sonata (1932); *Theme and Variations* for Orch. (1933); *Suite* for Orch. (1938); *Petite suite* for Flute, Clarinet, and Bassoon (1939); Violin Sonata (1941); *Passacaglia* for Horn and Viola (1942); *10 Pieces* for Low Instrument and Orch. (1943); *Ode to the West Wind* for Baritone, Viola, and Piano (1945); *Protest* for 2 Pianos (1945); Sextet for Flute, Oboe, Clarinet, Bassoon, Horn, and Piano (1947); Trio for Clarinet, Viola, and Cello (1948); Concerto for Bassoon and String Quartet (1949); *Pulse of the Sea,* étude for Piano (1950); Concerto for Trumpet and Orch. (1952); Trio for Flute, Violin, and Piano (1955); *5 Fantasies* for Violin and Piano (1956); *Tone Poem* for Brass and Percussion (1957); *Rhapsody* for 4 French Horns (1957); *Vade mecum* for Wind Instruments (1958).

BIBL.: W. Riegger, "A. W. and Colin McPhee," in H. Cowell, ed., *American Composers on American Music* (Stanford, Calif., 1933); W. George, *A. W.* (diss., Univ. of Iowa, 1971); B. Kopp, *The Twelve-tone Techniques of A. W.* (diss., Northwestern Univ., 1981).

Weiss, Franz, Austrian violist and composer; b. Silesia, Jan. 18, 1778; d. Vienna, Jan. 25, 1830. When Prince Razumovsky formed his string quartet in Vienna (1808), Weiss was engaged as violist, with Schuppanzigh as 1st violin, Prince Razumovsky as 2nd violin, and Linke as cellist. Weiss composed some orch. pieces and chamber music.

Weissberg, Yulia (Lazarevna), Russian composer; b. Orenburg, Jan. 6, 1880; d. Leningrad, March 1, 1942. She studied piano with Rimsky-Korsakov and instrumentation with Glazunov at the St. Petersburg Cons. (1903–5) and continued her musical training with Humperdinck and Reger in Germany (1907–12); was a co-ed. of the journal *Muzykalny Sovremennik* (1915–17) and choral director of the Young Workers' Cons. (1921–23). She married **Andrei Rimsky-Korsakov.**

WORKS: Operas: *Mermaid,* after Andersen (1923); *Gülnara*

(1935); *The Dead Princess* (1937); 2 children's operas: *Little Rabbit's House* (1935) and *Geese and Swans* (1937); *The 12* for Chorus and Orch. (Leningrad, May 12, 1926); symphonic poem, *In the Night* (1929); *Sailor's Dance* for Orch. (1936); several song cycles; children's choruses; solo songs; folksong arrangements.

Weisse, Hans, Austrian music theorist and composer; b. Vienna, March 31, 1892; d. N.Y., Feb. 10, 1940. He studied with Schenker and became an exponent of his theory. In 1931 he went to the U.S. and gave courses in theory at the Mannes Music School in N.Y. He wrote mostly chamber music: 3 string quartets (1920–36); String Sextet (1924); Quintet for Clarinet and Strings (1928); Octet for Strings and Winds (1929); Concerto for Flute, Oboe, and Harpsichord (1937); *Choral Partita* for Strings and Winds (1938).

Weissenbäck, (Franz) Andreas, Austrian choral conductor and composer; b. St. Lorenzen, Styria, Nov. 26, 1880; d. Vienna, March 14, 1960. He studied in Graz; in 1899, entered the monastery at Klosterneuburg, near Vienna; became a Catholic priest in 1904; then took up musicology under Guido Adler at the Univ. of Vienna (Ph.D., 1912); was for many years choirmaster at Klosterneuburg. He publ. *Sacra musica,* a lexicon of Catholic church music (1937); contributed valuable papers to various publs., particularly on Gregorian chant; also was an expert on church bells. He composed a German Mass for Male Chorus; publ. many sacred works; also a Mass for Mixed Chorus and 7 Wind Instruments, including 2 Saxophones.

Weissenberg, Alexis (Sigismond), noted Bulgarian-born French pianist; b. Sofia, July 26, 1929. He studied piano at a very early age with his mother, and then pursued his training with Pantcho Vladigerov; during the German occupation of his homeland, he and his mother were briefly confined in a concentration camp but then were allowed to emigrate to Palestine; in 1945 he made his 1st appearance as a soloist with an orch. there. In 1946 he went to N.Y. to study at the Juilliard School of Music; his principal mentor was Olga Samaroff, but he also received instruction from Artur Schnabel and Wanda Landowska. In 1947 he won the Leventritt Competition, which led to his U.S. debut that same year with George Szell and the N.Y. Phil.; after touring extensively, he settled in France in 1956, became a naturalized citizen, and withdrew from public appearances for a decade in which he devoted himself to further study and teaching. In 1966 he resumed his career and subsequently toured all over the world.

Weissenborn, Günther (Albert Friedrich), German pianist and conductor; b. Coburg, June 2, 1911. He studied at the Hochschule für Musik in Berlin; was an organist and choir director in Berlin (1934–37). He was then a conductor in Halle (1937–42), Hannover (1944), and Göttingen (1945–47) before returning to Hannover as conductor of the Hausegger Chamber Orch. Apart from his activities as a conductor, Weissenborn earned a fine reputation as a piano accompanist in lieder recitals.

Weissensee, Friedrich, distinguished German composer; b. Schwerstedt, Thuringia, c.1560; d. Altenweddingen, near Magdeburg, 1622. He became Rektor of the grammar school in Gebesee, near Erfurt, in 1590; about 1596 he was made Kantor at the grammar school in Magdeburg; in 1602 he became a clergyman in Altenweddingen. He was one of the finest German composers of Protestant church music of his era.

WORKS (all publ. in Magdeburg): *Evangelisch Sprüche auf die vornehmsten Fest-Tage* for 5 Voices (1595); *Hochzeit-Lied aus den Sprüchwörten Salomonis am 31. Capitel . . . dem . . . Peters Rathmann* for 6 Voices (1599); *Hochzeitlicher Ehren Dantz, auff das adelige Beylager des . . . Wolffgang Spitznasen zu Magdeburgk Domherrn* for 6 Voices (1600); *Opus melicum methodicum et plane novum, singulis diebus . . . et festis accomodatas* for 4 to 10 and 12 Voices (1602); *Geistliche Braut und Hochzeit Gesang, zu Ehren . . . Georgio Schultzen* for 6 Voices (1611); *Sponsis novellis* for 8 Voices (1619); *Geistlich Braut und Hochzeitlied, ex Cant. Cant. Cantic. Cap. 5 und 7 ad 9* for 6 Voices (n.d.); various other works in contemporary collections.

BIBL.: B. Engelke, *F. W. und sein Opus melicum* (diss., Univ. of Kiel, 1927).

Weissheimer, Wendelin, German conductor and composer; b. Osthofen, Alsace, Feb. 26, 1838; d. Nuremberg, June 16, 1910. He studied at the Leipzig Cons., and later took lessons in composition with Liszt at Weimar. He served as Kapellmeister in Mainz (1858, 1861, and later years), Würzburg (1866–68), Strasbourg (1873–78), and other cities; eventually settled in Nuremberg in 1900. As a composer, he followed the Wagnerian vogue; wrote 2 operas, *Theodor Körner* (Munich, May 28, 1872) and *Meister Martin und seine Gesellen* (Karlsruhe, April 14, 1879); also a Sym.; 18 songs to words by Goethe; 5 *geistliche Sonette* for Voice, Flute, Oboe, Clarinet, and Harmonium. His book of reminiscences, *Erlebnisse mit Richard Wagner, Franz Liszt und vielen anderen Zeitgenossen, nebst deren Briefen* (Stuttgart, 1898), quotes many letters from Wagner, with whom he maintained a friendship.

Weissmann, John (actually, **János Schützer**), Hungarianborn English writer on music; b. Budapest, July 10, 1910; d. London, March 23, 1980. He studied at the Budapest Cons.; was a répétiteur at the Budapest Opera (1932) and the Municipal Theater (1932–34). Following studies with Dukas in Paris (1934–35), he was assistant conductor at the Budapest Municipal Theater (1935–37). In 1937 he settled in London, where he attended Sir Henry Wood's conducting classes at the Royal Academy of Music (1937–40); also pursued academic studies at the Univ. He was mainly active as a writer; also was director of the London branch of Vox Records (1953–60).

WRITINGS: *Gottfredo Petrassi* (Milan, 1957); *Béla Bartók and His String Quartets* (Hamburg, 1962).

Weitzmann, Carl Friedrich, noted German music theorist, writer on music, and composer; b. Berlin, Aug. 10, 1808; d. there, Nov. 7, 1880. He studied violin with Henning and theory with Klein; later, at Kassel, was a pupil of Spohr and Hauptmann. He was concertmaster in Riga (1832–34), Reval (1834–36), and St. Petersburg (1836–46). After sojourns in Paris and London (1846–48), he settled in Berlin as a teacher of composition. He was an ardent disciple and friend of Wagner and Liszt; among his posthumous papers was found the original MS of a double fugue for piano by Wagner, with corrections in the handwriting of Weinlig (Wagner's teacher). The piece was publ. by E. Istel in *Die Musik* (July 1912). Weitzmann was an original thinker in his harmonic theories; made an investigation of the modulatory functions of the whole-tone scale, and interested Liszt in its use. He composed a 4th variation to Liszt's *Todtentanz.* A full exposition of his theories is found in a book by his American pupil E.M. Bowman, *K.F. Weitzmann's Manual of Musical Theory* (N.Y., 1877). Weitzmann's theoretical works include *Der übermässige Dreiklang* (1853); *Geschichte der Septimen-Akkordes* (1854); *Der verminderte Septimen-Akkord* (1854); *Geschichte der griechischen Musik* (1855); *Harmoniesystem* (1860); *Die neue Harmonielehre im Streit mit der alten* (1861); *Geschichte des Klavierspiels und der Klavierlitteratur* (1863, as Part III of the Lebert-Stark piano method; 2nd ed., 1879, printed separately, with an added *Geschichte des Klaviers;* in Eng., N.Y., 1894, with a biographical sketch by Otto Lessmann; 3rd German ed., Leipzig, 1899, as *Geschichte der Klaviermusik,* ed. by Max Seiffert, with a supplement, *Geschichte des Klaviers,* by Otto Fleischer); *Der letzte der Virtuosen* (on Tausig; 1868); many essays in various musical periodicals. As a composer, he followed the fashionable Romantic trends; wrote the operas *Räuberliebe* (1834), *Walpurgisnacht* (1835), and *Lorbeer und Bettelstab* (1836), which he brought out in Reval; 3 books of *Valses nobles* for Piano; *Preludes and Modulations* for Piano, 2 parts, "Classic" and "Romantic"; also wrote 2 books of ingenious canonic *Rätsel* for piano, 4-hands, and 2 books of *Kontrapunkt-Studien* for piano.

Welcher, Dan, American bassoonist and composer; b. Rochester, N.Y., March 2, 1948. He studied in N.Y. with Washburn,

Adler, and Benson at the Eastman School of Music in Rochester (1965–69) and with Ulehla at the Manhattan School of Music (M.M., 1972). He was a bassoonist with the Rochester (N.Y.) Phil. (1968–69), the U.S. Military Academy at West Point, N.Y. (1969–72), the Louisville Orch. (1972–78), and the Aspen (Colo.) Chamber Sym. (from 1976). He taught composition at the Univ. of Louisville (1972–78) and at the Univ. of Texas in Austin (from 1978); also served as assistant conductor of the Austin Sym. Orch. In 1976 he became a member of the artist faculty of the Aspen (Colo.) Music Festival. In 1990 he was appointed composer-in-residence of the Honolulu Sym. Orch.

WORKS: OPERA: *Della's Gift,* after O. Henry (Austin, Tex., Feb. 1987). **ORCH.:** *5 Tactical Experiences* for Winds and Percussion (1970); *Episodes* (1971); Flute Concerto (1973); *Concerto da Camera* for Bassoon and Chamber Orch. (1972–75); *Dervishes: Ritual Dance Scene* (1976); *The Visions of Merlin* (Sunriver, Oreg., Aug. 23, 1980); *Arches: An Impression* for Concert Band or Wind Ensemble (1985); *Prairie Light: 3 Texas Watercolors of Georgia O'Keeffe* (Sherman, Tex., March 1, 1986); *The Yellowstone Fires* for Wind Ensemble (Austin, Tex., Feb. 23, 1988); Clarinet Concerto (1989). **CHAMBER:** 2 wind quintets; *Black Riders,* after Crane, for Soprano and 4 Instruments (1972); Piano Trio (1976); Partita for Horn, Violin, and Piano (1980); Clarinet Quintet (1983); *Evening Scenes,* after Agee, for Tenor and 6 Instruments (1985); *Hauntings* for Tuba Ensemble (1986); String Quartet No. 1 (1987); *Chameleon Music* for Percussion Ensemble (1988); piano works, including *High Tech Etudes* (1988).

Weldon, George, English conductor; b. Chichester, June 5, 1906; d. Cape Town, South Africa, Aug. 16, 1963. He studied at the Royal College of Music in London with Malcolm Sargent; conducted various provincial orchs.; traveled as a guest conductor in North Africa, Turkey, and Yugoslavia. He was conductor of the City of Birmingham Sym. Orch. (1943–51); was 2nd conductor of the Hallé Orch. in Manchester under Barbirolli (from 1952); also conducted the Sadler's Wells Royal Ballet in London (1955–56).

Weldon, Georgina (née **Thomas**), English soprano; b. London, May 24, 1837; d. Brighton, Jan. 11, 1914. She took up singing after her marriage to Capt. Weldon in 1860, and did not appear in public until 1870. She organized an orphan asylum for the purpose of musical education, and also dabbled in music publishing. Special interest attaches to her because of her romantic friendship with Gounod, who during his London sojourn (1870–75) lived at her residence, and whom she assisted in training the Gounod Choir. She translated his autobiography (which goes only as far as 1859) into English (1875). Their relationship deteriorated, leading to a legal entanglement in connection with her claims regarding the copyright of Gounod's choral works; she wrote acrimonious letters to the press, defending her stand. She also publ. some songs of her own (to French texts) and the didactic manuals *Hints for Pronunciation in Singing* (1872) and *Musical Reform* (1875).

Welin, Karl-Erik (Vilhelm), Swedish organist, pianist, and composer; b. Genarp, May 31, 1934. He studied organ with Alf Linden at the Stockholm Musikhögskolan (1956–61); took composition lessons with Gunnar Bucht (1958–60) and Lidholm (1960–64); attended summer seminars in new music at Darmstadt (1960–62), working with David Tudor on avant-garde techniques. In 1958 he joined the experimental group "Fylkingen" in Stockholm. As a composer, he followed in his youthful works the fashionable impressionistic trends, mostly in miniature forms, in colorful and unusual instrumental groupings. He created a sensation at his piano recital at the Stockholm Musikhögskolan on March 6, 1964, when he exploded a pyrotechnic device lodged in the frame of the piano and then proceeded to saw off the piano legs with an electrically powered handsaw, accidentally cutting himself so seriously that he had to undergo surgery.

WORKS: *4 Chinese Poems* for Chorus (1956); *Sermo modulatus* for Flute and Clarinet (1959); *Renovations* for Soprano,

Flute, Violin, Mandolin, Celesta, and Percussion (1960); *Cantata* for Children's Chorus, Violin, Flute, and Harpsichord (1960); *Manzit* for Clarinet, Trombone, Violin, Piano, and Percussion (1962); *Esservecchia* for Electric Guitar, Horn, Trombone, and Piano (1963); *Warum nicht?* for Flute, Violin, Cello, Xylophone, Vibraphone, and Tam-tam (1964); *Pereo* for 36 Strings (1964); *Kazimir* for 4 Flutes (1965); *Visoka 12* for 2 Flutes, 2 Violins, and 2 Cellos (1965); *Etwas für . . .* for Wind Quintet (1966); a children's television opera, *Dummerjöns* (Tom Fool), after H.C. Andersen (1966–67); *Eigentlich nicht*, 2nd string quartet (1967); *Copelius*, ballet of concrete music (1968); *Ondine*, theater music (1968); *Vindarnas grotta* (Cave of the Winds), television ballet (Stockholm Television, March 30, 1969); *Glazba* for 3 Flutes, Bassoon, and Soprano (1968); *Ben fatto* for a Solo Instrument or an infinite number of Instruments (1968); *PC-132* for String Quartet (1970); *A New Map of Hell* for Chorus (1971); *Recidivans*, 3rd string quartet (1972); *Aver la forza di . . .* for Chorus and String Orch. (1972); opera, *Drottning Jag* (Queen Ego; 1972; Stockholm, Feb. 17, 1973); *Harmonies* for Clarinet, Trombone, Cello, and Piano (1972); *Pagabile* for Chamber Ensemble (1972); *Residuo*, 4th string quartet (1974); *Ett svenskt rekviem* for Soli, Chorus, and Orch. (1976); *Eurytmi* for Piano Quartet (1979); String Quartet No. 6 (1982); *L'Aveu* for Soloists, Chorus, and Orch. (1982–83); String Quartet No. 7 (1984); Sym. No. 1 (1985–86; Malmö, Oct. 22, 1987); String Quartet No. 8 (1986–87); *EssAEG* for 2 Pianos and Electronics (1988).

Welitsch (real name, **Veličkova**), **Ljuba,** remarkable Bulgarian-born Austrian soprano; b. Borissovo, July 10, 1913. She studied violin as a child; after attending the Sofia Cons. and the Univ. of Sofia, she studied voice with Lierhammer in Vienna. In 1936 she made her operatic debut at the Sofia Opera; after singing in Graz (1937–40), Hamburg (1942–43), and Munich (1943–46), she joined the Vienna State Opera, having sung there previously at the 80th birthday celebration for Richard Strauss on June 11, 1944, as Salome, which became her most celebrated role. She made her London debut with the visiting Vienna State Opera as Donna Anna in *Don Giovanni* on Sept. 20, 1947, a role she repeated in 1948 at the Glyndebourne Festival. On Feb. 4, 1949, she made her Metropolitan Opera debut in N.Y. as Salome, remaining on the company's roster until 1952; she sang at London's Covent Garden in 1953. In subsequent years she appeared in character roles in Vienna; returned to the Metropolitan Opera in 1972 in a speaking role in *La Fille du régiment.* Among her other notable roles were Aida, Musetta, Minnie, Rosalinde, Jenůfa, and Tosca.

Welk, Lawrence, popular American bandleader and accordionist; b. Strasburg, N.Dak., March 11, 1903. He began playing accordion in German-speaking areas of his native state as a youth; then performed with his own combos, gaining success as a self-described purveyor of "champagne music"; after touring and making numerous radio appearances, he launched his own television program in Los Angeles in 1951; it subsequently was featured on network television (1955–71). He owed his popularity to his skillful selection of programs containing a varied mixture of semi-classical pieces, western American ballads, and Slavic folk-dance tunes. His use of an accordion section in his arrangements, steadfast rhythmic beat, and sentimentalized tempi imparted to his renditions a rudimentary sound quality that made him a favorite with undiscriminating audiences. He publ. (with some outside help) an autobiography, *Wunnerful, Wunnerful!* (N.Y., 1971), radiating euphoria, and a sequel: *Ah-one, ah-two: Life with My Musical Family* (N.Y., 1974).

Wellek, Albert, eminent Austrian musicologist and psychologist; b. Vienna, Oct. 16, 1904; d. Mainz, Aug. 27, 1972. He studied composition and conducting at the Prague Cons. (graduated, 1926) and music history, literature, and philosophy at the Univ. of Prague; was a student of Adler, Lach, Ficker, and Wellesz at the Univ. of Vienna (Ph.D., 1928, with the diss. *Doppelempfinden und Programmusik*); then studied psy-

chology in Vienna and at the Univ. of Leipzig; in 1938 he completed his Habilitation at the Univ. of Munich with his *Typologie der Musikbegabung im deutschen Volke: Grundlegung einer psychologischen Theorie der Musik und Musikgeschichte* (publ. in Munich, 1939; 2nd ed., 1970). He became an assistant lecturer and then lecturer at the Univ. of Leipzig Inst. of Psychology in 1938; in 1942 he was made acting prof. of psychology at the Univ. of Halle; after serving as prof. of psychology and educational science at the Univ. of Breslau (1943–46), he founded the Univ. of Mainz Inst. of Psychology in 1946, remaining there until his death. Wellek was the foremost music psychologist of his time, being an authority on the theory of hearing.

WRITINGS: *Das absolute Gehör und seine Typen* (Leipzig, 1938; 2nd ed., 1970); *Das Problem des seelischen Seins: Die Strukturtheorie Felix Kruegers: Deutung und Kritik* (Leipzig, 1941; 2nd ed., 1953); *Die Polarität im Aufbau des Charakters: System der konkreten Charakterkunde* (Bern and Munich, 1950; 3rd ed., 1966); *Die Wiederherstellung der Seelenwissenschaft im Lebenswerk Felix Kruegers: Längsschnitt durch ein halbes Jahrhundert der Psychologie* (Hamburg, 1950; 2nd ed., 1968); *Ganzheitspsychologie und Strukturtheorie* (Bern, 1955; 2nd ed., 1969); ed. *20. Kongress der Deutschen Gesellschaft für Psychologie: Berlin 1955; Der Rückfall in die Methodenkrise der Psychologie und ihre Überwindung* (Göttingen, 1959; 2nd ed., 1970); *Musikpsychologie und Musikästhetik: Grundriss der systematischen Musikwissenschaft* (Frankfurt am Main, 1963); *Psychologie* (Berlin and Munich, 1963; 3rd ed., 1971); *Melancholie in der Musik* (Hamburg, 1969); *Witz-Lyrik-Sprache* (Bern and Munich, 1970).

BIBL.: *Archiv für die Gesamt Psychologie,* CXVI (1964; includes Festschrift for Wellek's 60th birthday).

Weller, Walter, Austrian conductor; b. Vienna, Nov. 30, 1939. He was educated at the Vienna Academy of Music, where he studied violin and attended classes in conducting held by Karl Böhm. In 1956 he became a violinist in the Vienna Phil.; was one of its concertmasters from 1964 to 1969. In 1958 he founded the noted Weller Quartet, which subsequently toured with great success in Europe, North America, and Asia. He made his debut as a conductor in 1966; became a regular conductor of both the Vienna State Opera and Volksoper in 1969; was Generalmusikdirektor in Duisburg (1971–72); also conducted the Niederösterreiches Tonkünstler-Orch. in Vienna (1975–78). In 1977 he was named principal conductor and musical adviser of the Royal Liverpool Phil. In 1980 he became principal conductor of the Royal Phil. Orch. of London, which post he held until 1985; then served as its principal guest conductor.

Wellesz, Egon (Joseph), eminent Austrian-born English composer, musicologist, and pedagogue; b. Vienna, Oct. 21, 1885; d. Oxford, Nov. 9, 1974. He studied harmony with Carl Frühling and then was a pupil in musicology with Guido Adler at the Univ. of Vienna (graduated, 1908); also received private instruction from Schoenberg. From 1911 to 1915 he taught music history at the Neues Cons. in Vienna; in 1913 he was engaged as a lecturer on musicology at the Univ. of Vienna, and was a prof. there from 1930 to 1938, when the annexation of Austria by Nazi Germany compelled him to leave. He went to England in 1938; joined the music dept. of the Univ. of Oxford, which in 1932 had conferred upon him the degree of Mus.Doc. (*honoris causa*). In 1943 he became a lecturer in music history at the Univ. of Oxford; in 1946 he was appointed to the editorial board of the *New Oxford History of Music*, to which he then contributed, and was Univ. Reader in Byzantine music at Oxford (1948–56); received the Prize of the City of Vienna in 1953; was president of the Univ. of Oxford Byzantine Society (1955–66); in 1957, was made a Commander of the Order of the British Empire and was awarded the Grande Médaille d'Argent of the City of Paris. In 1961 he was awarded the Austrian Great State prize. A scholar and a musician of extraordinary capacities, Wellesz distinguished himself as a composer of highly complex musical scores, and as an authority on Byzantine music.

WORKS: OPERAS: *Die Prinzessin Girnara* (1919–20; Hannover, May 15, 1921; rev. ver., Mannheim, Sept. 2, 1928); *Alkestis* (1922–23; Mannheim, March 20, 1924); *Opferung des Gefangenen* (1924–25; Cologne, April 10, 1926); *Scherz, List und Rache* (1926–27; Stuttgart, March 1, 1928); *Die Bakchantinnen* (1929–30; Vienna, June 20, 1931); *Incognita* (Oxford, Dec. 5, 1951). **BALLETS:** *Das Wunder der Diana* (1915; Mannheim, March 20, 1924); *Persisches Ballett* (1920; Donaueschingen, 1924); *Achilles auf Skyros* (1921; Stuttgart, March 4, 1926); *Die Nächtlichen* (1923; Berlin, Nov. 20, 1924). **ORCH.:** 9 syms.: No. 1, in C (1945); No. 2, in E-flat (1948); No. 3, in A (1951); No. 4, *Symphonia Austriaca*, in G (1953); No. 5 (1956; Düsseldorf, Feb. 20, 1958); No. 6 (1965; Nuremberg, June 1, 1966); No. 7 (1968); No. 8 (1971; Vienna, Nov. 22, 1972); *Vorfrühling*, symphonic poem (1912); *Suite for Violin and Chamber Orch.* (1924); Piano Concerto (1934); *Prosperos Beschwörungen*, after Shakespeare's *The Tempest* (1936–38; Vienna, Feb. 19, 1938); Violin Concerto (1961; Vienna, Jan. 19, 1962); *Music for String Orch.* (1964); *Divertimento* for Chamber Orch. (1969); *Symphonischer Epilog* (1969). **VOCAL:** *Gebete der Mädchen zur Maria* for Soprano, Chorus, and Orch. (1909); *Mitte des Lebens*, cantata (1932); *Amor timido*, cantata for Soprano and Orch. (1935); *5 Sonnets by Elizabeth Barrett Browning* for Soprano and String Quartet (1935); *Lied der Welt* for Soprano and Orch. (1937); *Leben, Traum und Tod* for Contralto and Orch. (1937); *Short Mass* for Chorus and Small Orch. (1937); *The Leaden Echo and the Golden Echo*, after Hopkins, for Soprano, Violin, Clarinet, Cello, and Piano (1944); *4 Songs of Return* for Soprano and Small Orch. (1961); *Duineser Elegie* for Soprano, Chorus, and Chamber Ensemble (1963); *Ode to Music* for Baritone and Chamber Orch. (1964); *Vision* for Soprano and Orch. (1966); *Mirabile Mysterium*, Christmas cantata (1967); *Canticum Sapientiae* for Baritone, Chorus, and Orch. (1968; Graz, Oct. 25, 1969). **CHAMBER:** 9 string quartets (1912, 1917, 1918, 1920, 1944, 1947, 1948, 1957, 1966); *Geistiges Lied* for Piano Trio (1918); Sonata for Solo Cello (1921); *2 Pieces* for Clarinet and Piano (1922); Sonata for Solo Violin (1924); *Suite for Violin and Piano* (1937); *Little Suite* for Flute (1937); Octet for Clarinet, Horn, Bassoon, and String Quintet (1948–49); *Suite for Wind Quintet* (1954); *Suite in 3 movements* for Bassoon (1956); Clarinet Quintet (1959); *2 string trios* (1962, 1969); *5 Miniatures* for Violin and Piano (1965); *Music for String Quartet* (1968); String Quintet (1970). **PIANO:** *3 Piano Pieces* (1912); *Epigramme* (1913); *5 Dance Pieces* (1927); *Triptych* (1966); *Studies in Grey* (1969). **ORGAN:** *Partita* (1966).

WRITINGS: *Arnold Schönberg* (Vienna, 1921; Eng. tr., 1924); *Byzantinische Kirchenmusik* (Breslau, 1927); *Eastern Elements in Western Chant: Studies in the Early History of Ecclesiastical Music*, Monumenta Musicae Byzantinae, subsidia, II (1947; 2nd ed., 1967); *A History of Byzantine Music and Hymnography* (Oxford, 1949; 3rd ed., rev., 1963); *Essays on Opera* (London, 1950); *The Origin of Schoenberg's 12-tone System* (Washington, D.C., 1958); *Byzantinische Musik*, Das Musikwerk, I (1959; Eng. tr., 1959); *Die Hymnen der alten Kirche*, Basiliensis de musica orationes, I (Kassel, 1962); *J.J. Fux* (London, 1965); also ed. *Ancient and Oriental Music*, Vol. I, *The New Oxford History of Music* (Oxford, 1957); ed., with M. Velimirović, *Studies in Eastern Chant*, I–III (London, 1966–71); ed. with F. Sternfeld, *The Age of Enlightenment (1745–1790)*, Vol. VII, *The New Oxford History of Music* (Oxford, 1973).

BIBL.: O. Beer, "E. W. und die Oper," *Die Musik* (Sept. 1931); H. Redlich, "E. W.," *Musical Quarterly* (Jan. 1940); R. Reti, "E. W., Musician and Scholar," ibid., (Jan. 1956); R. Schollum, *E. W.* (Vienna, 1964); C. Benser, *E. W. (1885–1974): Chronicle of a Twentieth-Century Musician* (N.Y., 1985).

Wells, Kitty (real name, **Muriel Ellen Deason**), American country-music singer and songwriter; b. Nashville, Tenn., Aug. 30, 1919. She sang gospel tunes in local churches while a child; then appeared with John and Jack and the Tennessee Mountain Boys; in 1952 she joined the "Grand Ole Opry," where she reigned as the "queen of country music" for more than a decade. In 1976 she was elected to the Country Music Hall of Fame.

Welser-Möst (real name, **Möst**), **Franz**, Austrian conductor; b. Linz, Aug. 16, 1960. He studied at the Munich Hochschule für Musik; after becoming a finalist in the Karajan conducting competition in 1979, he served as principal conductor of the Austrian Youth Orch. In 1985 he was named music director of the Winterthur and Norrköping sym. orchs. He made a successful British debut as a guest conductor with the London Phil. in 1986, and subsequently led it on a tour of Europe. In 1989 he made his U.S. debut as a guest conductor with the St. Louis Sym. Orch. In 1990 he was named principal conductor of the London Phil.

BIBL.: D. Henry, "F. W.-M.," *Musical America* (March 1991).

Welsh, Thomas, English bass, teacher, and composer; b. Wells, c.1780; d. Brighton, Jan. 24, 1848. He was a grandson of Thomas Linley, Sr. He became a chorister at Wells Cathedral, and a pupil of J.B. Cramer and Baumgarten. He made his opera debut in London at the age of 12; after his voice changed, he became a bass, and sang in oratorio. He was particularly distinguished as a vocal teacher; publ. *Vocal Instructor, or the Art of Singing Exemplified in 15 Lessons leading to 40 Progressive Exercises* (London, 1825). His wife and pupil, **Mary Anne** (née **Wilson**; 1802–67), whom he married in 1827, was a noted soprano who made her debut at Drury Lane on Jan. 18, 1821, in Arne's *Artaxerxes*. He composed several theater pieces, including *The Green-eyed Monster, or How to Get your Money* (operatic farce; London, Oct. 14, 1811); also piano sonatas; glees, duets, and part-songs.

Welte, Michael, German manufacturer of musical instruments; b. Unterkirnach, Black Forest, Sept. 29, 1807; d. Freiburg im Breisgau, Jan. 17, 1880. Having served an apprenticeship with Josef Blessing, a maker of musical clocks, he established himself at Voehrenbach (1832); exhibited his first "orchestrion" at Karlsruhe in 1849; later took his sons (**Emil, Berthold,** and **Michael, Jr.**) into partnership. His instruments obtained first prizes at London (1862), Paris (1867), Munich (1885), Vienna (1892), Chicago (1893), St. Louis (1904), Leipzig (1909), and Turin (1911); in 1872 the factory was removed to Freiburg im Breisgau. His oldest son, **Emil Welte** (b. Voehrenbach, April 20, 1841; d. Norwich, Conn., Oct. 25, 1923), established a branch in N.Y. (1865); he improved the then newly invented paper roll (taking the place of the earlier wooden cylinders), and was the first to use it, in connection with a pneumatic action, in a large orchestrion built for Theiss's Alhambra Court (N.Y.). A son of Berthold Welte, **Edwin** (b. Freiburg im Breisgau, 1875; d. there, Jan. 4, 1958), applied the paper roll to the piano, creating in 1904 the "Welte-Mignon Reproducing Piano," which could control pedaling and gradations of touch, a definite improvement on the ordinary player-piano, which could produce only pitches. Josef Hoffmann, Paderewski, and Wanda Landowska made rolls for it. The application of the same principle to the organ resulted in the invention of the "Philharmonic Organ" (1912). The firm ceased to exist in 1954.

Welting, Ruth, American soprano; b. Memphis, Tenn., May 11, 1949. She studied voice in N.Y. with Daniel Ferro, in Rome with Luigi Ricci, and in Paris with Jeanne Reiss; made her operatic debut at the N.Y. City Opera in 1970 as Blondchen in Mozart's *Die Entführung aus dem Serail*; also sang with opera companies in Houston, San Antonio, Dallas, Santa Fe, and San Francisco. She made her Metropolitan Opera debut in N.Y. on March 20, 1976, as Zerbinetta in *Ariadne auf Naxos*.

Wendel, Eugen, Rumanian composer; b. Valea-Rea, Dec. 18, 1934. He studied with Vancea, Olah, and Stroe at the Bucharest Cons. (1959–65); worked as a sound engineer with the Rumanian recording firm Electrecord.

Works: Concerto for Orch. (1964); *Symphonic Meditations* (1965); *Gravitations* for Orch. (1968); *Transmutations* for Orch. (1969); *Resonances* for Orch. (1972); Violin Sonata (1963); String Quartet (1964); *Interferences* for Violin, Viola, Cello, Clarinet, and Piano (1966); *Fusion* for Clarinet, Piano, and Tape (1968); *Rêve*, music for 8 Instrumentalists (1969; also a version for Clarinet, Violin, Viola, Cello, and Piano); *Genèse* for Piano Quartet (1972); *Verso* for Oboe (1973); Piano Sonata (1966); choruses; songs.

Wendland, Waldemar, German composer; b. Liegnitz, May 10, 1873; d. Zeitz, Aug. 15, 1947. He studied for a short time with Humperdinck while acting as an assistant conductor at the Frankfurt Opera; then settled in Berlin. He wrote the operas *Das kluge Felleisen* (Madgeburg, 1909); *Das vergessene Ich* (Berlin, 1911); *Der Schneider von Malta* (Leipzig, 1818); *Peter Sukoff* (Basel, 1921); *Die vier Temperamente* (Freiburg, 1927); *Koreanisches Märchen* (Altenburg, May 11, 1946); several ballets; orch. works; chamber music; about 200 songs.

Wendling, family of German musicians of Alsatian descent: **(1) Johann Baptist Wendling,** flutist and composer; b. Rappoltsweiler, Alsace, June 17, 1723; d. Munich, Nov. 27, 1797. He was a flutist in Zweibrücken (1747–50), where he gave lessons to Duke Christian IV; was active in Mannheim as an instructor to the elector, Carl Theodor, and as a member of the Court Orch. In 1752 he married Dorothea Spurni, who often traveled with him on concert tours; among the cities he visited were Paris (played at the Concert Spirituel with Christian IV, 1762, and with Mozart, 1778), London (1771), and Vienna (1776). In 1778 he went with the Mannheim court to Munich, although he spent most of his later years in Mannheim. He composed 9 flute concertos, 9 quartets, 36 trios, and various other works. Mozart orchestrated 1 of his flute concertos (K. 284e).
(2) Dorothea (née Spurni) **Wendling,** singer, wife of **Johann Baptist Wendling;** b. Stuttgart, March 21, 1736; d. Munich, Aug. 20, 1811. In 1752 she joined the Mannheim court as a singer; by 1760 she was its principal member; when the court moved to Munich in 1778, she elected to remain in Mannheim, where she was active mainly as a teacher from 1790. She was held in great repute by her contemporaries; Mozart composed the role of Ilia in *Idomeneo* and the concert aria K. 486a/295a for her.
(3) Elisabeth Augusta Wendling, singer, daughter of **Johann Baptist** and **Dorothea** (née Spurni) **Wendling;** b. Mannheim, Oct. 4, 1752; d. Munich, Feb. 18, 1794. She first sang at the Mannheim Court Opera on Nov. 4, 1769, with her mother and her aunt; appeared in Zweibrücken in 1772; was a guest artist in Munich (from 1784). Mozart wrote the 2 French ariettas K. 307 and K. 308 for her.
(4) Franz (Anton) Wendling, violinist, brother of **Johann Baptist Wendling;** b. Rappoltsweiler, Oct. 21, 1729; d. Munich, May 16, 1786. In 1755 he became a violinist and in 1774 1st violinist in the Mannheim Court Orch.; went with it to Munich in 1778, where he also appeared as a ballet conductor. In 1764 he married Elisabeth Augusta Sarselli.
(5) Elisabeth Augusta (née Sarselli) **Wendling,** singer, wife of **Franz (Anton) Wendling;** b. Mannheim, Feb. 20, 1746; d. Munich, Jan. 10, 1786. In 1762 she became a court musician in Mannheim; in 1776 she was named 3rd soprano; in 1778 she went with the court to Munich. She was greatly admired by her contemporaries; Mozart wrote the role of Electra in *Idomeneo* for her.
(6) Dorothea Wendling, singer, daughter of **Franz (Anton)** and **Elisabeth Augusta** (née Sarselli) **Wendling;** b. Mannheim, Jan. 27, 1767; d. Munich, May 19, 1839. She was a pupil of her aunt, **Dorothea** (née Spurni) **Wendling,** in Mannheim; in 1778 she made her debut in Munich; sang mainly in Mannheim before devoting herself to teaching.
(7) (Johann) Karl Wendling, violinist and conductor, nephew of **Johann Baptist Wendling;** b. Zweibrücken, March 30, 1750; d. Mannheim, Nov. 10, 1834. He was a violinist in the Mannheim Court Orch. (from 1765); after the Court

Orch. moved to Munich in 1778, he remained in Mannheim and was a violinist in the new National Theater there; was active as a conductor there from about 1782.

Wendling, Karl, German pianist and teacher; b. Frankenthal, Nov. 14, 1857; d. Leipzig, June 20, 1918. He studied at the Leipzig Cons.; made a specialty of the Jankó keyboard, on which he became highly proficient; also taught piano at the Leipzig Cons.; publ. *Meisterwerke aus der Etüden-Literatur* (4 books, in progressive order).

Wendt, Ernst Adolf, German pianist, teacher, and composer; b. Schwiebus, Prussia, Jan. 6, 1806; d. Neuwied, Feb. 5, 1850. He was a pupil of Zelter in Berlin; then became an instructor at the Teacher's Seminary there. He publ. variations for piano and orch.; Piano Trio; 4-hand Piano Sonata; a collection of his organ pieces was publ. by Karl Becker as *Wendt Album.*

Wendt, Larry, American organic chemist and experimenter in text-sound composition; b. Napa, Calif., April 5, 1946. His musical creations are experimental and can be classified as laboratory products in sound. His identifiable musical creations exist only on tape, their titles indicating his interest in science. Among his works are *Music from the Time Curve Poems, Volume IX* (1978) and *Metropolitan Fractalizations* (1978), an anthology that includes *Plastics I Have Known.*

Wenkel, Ortrun, German mezzo-soprano; b. Buttstädt, Oct. 25, 1942. She studied at the Franz Liszt Hochschule für Musik in Weimar, and at the Frankfurt Hochschule für Musik with Paul Lohmann and Elsa Cavelti; made her operatic debut as Gluck's *Orpheus* in Heidelberg in 1971; then sang in Stuttgart, Munich, Cologne, Bayreuth, Geneva, and in the U.S.

Wenkoff, Spas, Bulgarian tenor; b. Tirnovo, Sept. 23, 1928. He received his musical training in Sofia and Dresden. After his operatic debut in Tirnovo in 1954, he undertook a number of guest engagements in Russia (1962–65), Dobeln (1965–68), Magdeburg (1968–71), and Halle (1971–75). In 1976 he joined the Berlin State Opera. He distinguished himself mainly in lyric tenor parts.

Wennerberg, Gunnar, Swedish writer, politician, and composer, uncle of **Sara (Margarete Eugenia Euphrosyne) Wennerberg-Reuter;** b. Lidköping, Oct. 2, 1817; d. Läckö, Aug. 22, 1901. He studied at the Univ. of Uppsala (Ph.D., 1845), and entered the Swedish Parliament in 1876. Although he was autodidact as a composer, he found a following as a composer of vocal music; became best known for his works for men's voices, most notably *Hor oss, Svea!* (1853); publ. a popular collection of vocal duets for men's voices and piano as *Gluntarne* (1849–51) and 55 of the *Psalms* for solo voice or voices, chorus, and piano (1861–86). He attempted to write several major works, including a *Stabat mater* and a series of oratorios on the life of Christ, but only 2 of the latter were completed. His literary works were publ. in 4 vols. (1881–85).
Bibl.: S. Almquist, *Om G. W.: Hans tid och hans gärning* (Stockholm, 1917); C. Hennerberg, *Förteckning över G. W.s Tonverk* (Stockholm, 1918); G. Jeanson, *G. W. som Musiker* (Stockholm, 1929).

Wenten, Nyoman, Indonesian musician and dancer; b. Sading, near Denpasar, Bali, June 15, 1945. He studied dance and music from an early age with his grandfather; continued studies at the National Cons. of Music and Dance in Bali, the Traditional Music Cons. in Surakarta (1962–65), and the National Music and Dance Academy in Yogyakarta (B.F.A., 1970); taught at the latter institutions as well as the Dance Cons. in Yogyakarta (1964–70). He received an M.F.A. from the Calif. Inst. of the Arts (1974); taught there (from 1971) and also gave workshops at both the Los Angeles and Berkeley campuses of the Univ. of Calif. He is director of the Music, Dance, and Language Program for the Indonesian consulate in Los Angeles. He has toured in Asia, North America, and Europe (from 1964); appeared at the Los Angeles Olympic Arts Festival (1984) and the International Festival of Arts in

Mexico (1985). He is a remarkable performer in both Balinese and Javanese dance and music; he frequently performs with his wife, Nanik, and her father, **K.R.T. Wasitodiningrat.**

Wenzel, Ernst Ferdinand, German pianist and teacher; b. Walddorf, near Löbau, Jan. 25, 1808; d. Bad Kösen, Aug. 16, 1880. A student of philosophy at the Univ. of Leipzig, he also had private piano lessons with Friedrich Wieck, became a friend of his fellow-pupil Schumann, and was a frequent contributor to the *Neue Zeitschrift für Musik* during Schumann's editorship (until 1844). He was also a close friend of Mendelssohn; taught piano at the Leipzig Cons. from its foundation in 1843 until his death; the majority of the English-speaking students there were in his classes, or had private instruction from him.

Wenzel, Leopold, Italian violinist, conductor, and composer; b. Naples, Jan. 23, 1847; d. Asnières, near Paris, Aug. 21, 1925. He studied at the Cons. S. Pietro a Majella in Naples, but left it at the age of 13, traveling as a violinist in Greece, Turkey, and Egypt, eventually going to Paris as a theater conductor. From 1889 to 1914 he was in London, conducting at the Empire Theatre and the Gaiety Theatre. He wrote about 20 ballets, the most successful being *Dream of Wealth, Katrina,* and *The Girl I Left Behind Me;* operettas: *Le Chevalier Mignon* (Paris, 1884) and *L'Élève du Conservatoire* (Paris, 1894); many songs.

Wenzinger, August, prominent Swiss cellist, viola da gambist, conductor, teacher, and music editor; b. Basel, Nov. 14, 1905. He received his basic training at the Basel Cons.; then went to Germany and studied cello with Paul Grümmer and music theory with Philipp Jarnach at the Hochschule für Musik in Cologne; also took private cello lessons with Emanuel Feuermann in Berlin. He subsequently served as 1st cellist in the Bremen City Orch. (1929–34) and the Basel Allgemeine Musikgesellschaft (1936–70). He became interested in reviving the classical Baroque repertoire on original instruments, and acquired facility on the viola da gamba; conducted early music with the Capella Coloniensis of the West German Radio in Cologne (1954–58) and later led performances of Baroque operas in Hannover (1958–66). He taught at the Schola Cantorum Basiliensis (from 1933); founded its viola da gamba trio in 1968. He ed. Bach's unaccompanied cello suites and several Baroque operas; publ. exercises for the viola da gamba, *Gambenübung* (2 vols., 1935, 1938) and *Gambenfibel* (with Marianne Majer, 1943).

Werba, Erik, eminent Austrian pianist, composer, and writer on music; b. Baden, near Vienna, May 23, 1918. He studied piano with Oskar Dachs and composition with Joseph Marx at the Vienna Academy of Music and musicology with Lach, Wellesz, and Schenk at the Univ. of Vienna (1936–40). He was active as a music critic for various newspapers (1945–65); also was on the staff of the *Österreichische Musikzeitschrift* (from 1952). In 1949 he commenced touring throughout Europe as an accompanist to leading singers of the day; also was a prof. of song and oratorio at the Vienna Academy of Music (from 1949). In addition to numerous articles, he publ. *Joseph Marx* (Vienna, 1964), *Hugo Wolf oder der zornige Romantiker* (Vienna, 1971), *Erich Marckhl* (Vienna, 1972), and *Hugo Wolf und seine Lieder* (Vienna, 1984). He composed a singspiel, *Trauben für die Kaiserin* (Vienna, 1949); several song cycles and chamber music pieces, among them *Sonata notturna* for Bassoon and Piano (1972).

Werckmeister, Andreas, eminent German organist, organ examiner, music theorist, and composer; b. Benneckenstein, Thuringia, Nov. 30, 1645; d. Halberstadt, Oct. 26, 1706. He studied organ with his uncle, Christian Werckmeister, organist in Bennungen, near Sangerhausen; after studies at the Nordhausen Gymnasium (1660–62), he continued his training at the Quedlinburg Gymnasium, where another of his uncles, Victor Werckmeister, served as Kantor. He was organist in Hasselfelde, near Blankenburg (1664–74); after serving as organist and notary in Elbingerode (1674–75), he went to Qued-

linburg as organist of the collegiate church of St. Servatius and of the court of the abbess and Countess of Palatine, Anna Sophia I; also was named organist of the Wipertikirche in 1677; in 1696 he settled in Halberstadt as organist of the Martinikirche. Werckmeister was highly influential as a music theorist; his exposition of number symbolism in music and its theological basis remains invaluable. Among his compositions are *Musikalische Privatlust* for Violin and Basso Continuo (Quedlinburg, 1689) and various organ pieces.

WRITINGS: *Orgel-Probe, oder Kurtze Beschreibung, wie und welcher Gestalt man die Orgel-Wercke von den Orgelmachern annehmen, probiren, untersuchen und den Kirchen liefern könne und solle* (Frankfurt am Main and Leipzig, 1681; 2nd ed., 1698, as *Erweiterte und verbesserte Orgel-Probe;* 5th ed., 1783; Eng. tr. by G. Krapf, 1976); *Musicae mathematicae Hodegus curiosus, oder Richtiger musicalischer Weg-Weiser* (Frankfurt am Main and Leipzig, 1686; 2nd ed., 1687); *Musicalische Temperatur, oder Deutlicher und warer mathematischer Unterricht, wie man durch Anweisung des Monochordi ein Clavier, sonderlich die Orgel-Wercke, Positive, Regale, Spinetten und dergleichen wol temperirt stimmen könne* (Frankfurt am Main and Leipzig, c.1686–87; not extant; 2nd ed., 1691); *Der edlen Music-Kunst Würde, Gebrauch und Missbrauch, so wohl aus der heiligen Schrift als auch aus etlich alten und neubewährten reinen Kirchen-Lehrern* (Frankfurt am Main and Leipzig, 1691); *Hypomnemata musica, oder Musicalisches Memorial, welches bestehet in kurtzer Erinnerung dessen, so bisshero unter guten Freunden discurs-weise, insonderheit von der Composition und Temperatur möchte vorgangen seyn* (Quedlinburg, 1697); *Die nothwendigsten Anmerckungen und Regeln, wie der Bassus continuus oder General-Bass wol könne tractiret werden* (Aschersleben, 1698; 2nd ed., 1715); *Cribrum musicum, oder Musicalisches Sieb, darinnen einige Mängel eines halb gelehrten Componisten vorgestellet und das Böse von dem Guten gleichsam ausgesiebet und abgesondert worden* (Quedlinburg and Leipzig, 1700); *Harmonologia musica, oder Kurtze Anleitung zur musicalischen Composition* (Frankfurt am Main and Leipzig, 1702); *J.N.J. Organum Gruningense redivivum, oder Kurtze Beschreibung des in der Grüningischen Schlos-Kirchen berühmten Orgel-Wercks* (Quedlinburg and Aschersleben, 1705); *Musicalische Paradoxal-Discourse, oder Ungemeine Vorstellungen, wie die Musica einen hohen und göttlichen Ursprung habe* (Quedlinburg, 1707).

BIBL.: J. Götzen, *Der Welt-berühmte Musicus und Organista wurde bey trauriger Leich-Bestellung des Weyland edlen und Kunst-Hocherfahrnen Herr Andeae W.s* (Halberstadt, 1707); W. Serauky, "A. W. als Musiktheoretiker," *Festschrift Max Schneider zum 60. Geburtstag* (Halle, 1935); R. Dammann, "Zur Musiklehre des A. W.," *Archiv für Musikwissenschaft,* XI (1954); *W.-Kolloquium (1985)* (in German and Eng., Michaelstein/Blankenburg, 1986).

Werder, Felix, German-born Australian composer and music critic; b. Berlin, Feb. 22, 1922. He acquired early music training from his father, a cantor and composer of liturgical music; also learned to play piano, viola, and clarinet; among his teachers were Boas Bischofswerder and Arno Nadel. His family emigrated to England in 1934 to escape Nazi persecution; then went to Australia in 1941. Werder taught music at high schools in Melbourne, and was a music critic for the Melbourne newspaper the *Age* (1960–77). He wrote 500 works, but discarded about 60% of them; his musical idiom was determined by the cross-currents of European modernism, with a gradual increase in the forcefulness of his resources; these include electronics.

WORKS: STAGE: OPERAS: *Kisses for a Quid* (1960); *The General* (1966); *Agamemnon* (1967); *The Affair* (1969); *Private,* television opera (1969); *The Vicious Square* (1971); *The Conversion* (1973); *Banker,* music theater (1973). **BALLETS:** *En passant* (1964); *La belle dame sans merci* (1973); *Quantum* (1973). **ORCH.:** 5 syms.: No. 1 (1948–51; withdrawn); No. 2 (1959); No. 3, *The Laocoön* (1965); No. 4 (1970); No. 5 (1971); Flute Concerto (1954); Piano Concerto (1955); 2 violin concertos

(1956, 1966); *Brand*, symphonic poem (1956); *Sinfonia in Italian Style* (1957); *La Primavera*, symphonic poem (1957); *Abstraction* (1958); *Hexastrophe* (1961); *Monostrophe* (1961); Clarinet Concerto (1962); Viola Concerto (1963); *Konzert Musik for 10 Solo Instruments and Orch.* (1964); *Dramaturgie* (1966); *Morgen Rot* for Violin and Chamber Orch. (1968); *Strettophone* (1968); *Tower Concerto* (1968); *After Watteau* for Violin and Orch. (1968); *Sound Canvas* (1969); *Klang Bilder* (1969); *Triple Measure* (1970); *Don Giovanni Retired*, epilogue (1971); *Prom Gothic* for Organ and Orch. (1972); *Sans souci*, flute concerto (1974); *Brandenburgisches Konzert* for Strings (1974). VOCAL: Oratorio, *Francis Bacon Essays* (1971); an anti-Vietnam War cantata, *Radics Piece* (1967); songs. CHAMBER: 12 string quartets, including Nos. 1–3 (withdrawn) and Nos. 4–9 (1955, 1956, 1962, 1965, 1966, 1968); 3 violin sonatas (1947, 1958, 1963); Piano Quartet (1954); *3-Part Fantasias* for String Trio (1955); Cello Sonata (1956); 3 piano trios (1958, 1963, 1969); Quintet for Clarinet, Horn, and String Trio (1959); Flute Sonata (1960); Clarinet Sonata (1960); Horn Sonata (1960); Sonata for Wind Quintet (1961); Septet for Flute, Clarinet, Horn, and Strings (1963); Piano Quintet (1963); Solo Violin Sonata (1965); *Apostrophe* for Wind Quintet (1965); Quintet for Clarinet and String Quartet (1965); *Satyricon* for 6 Horns (1967); Sonata for Cello Solo (1968); *Strophe* for Violin (1968); Trio for Harp, Bass Clarinet, and Percussion (1969); *Activity* for Piano and Percussion (1969); *Triphony* for Flute, Guitar, and Bongos (1969); *Faggotiana* for Bassoon and String Trio (1970); *Tetract* for Viola, Oboe, and 2 Percussionists (1970); *Divertimento* for Guitar and String Quartet (1970); Wind Quartet (1971); *Percussion Play* for Percussion (1971). KEYBOARD: 4 piano sonatas (1942, 1953, 1968, 1970); 2-piano Sonata (1960); Harpsichord Sonata (1963); *Toccata* for Organ (1971).

Werle, Lars Johan, Swedish composer; b. Gävle, June 23, 1926. He studied with Sven-Erik Bäck (composition) and Carl-Allan Moberg (musicology) at Uppsala Univ. (1948–51); held positions at the Swedish Radio (1958–70) and as an instructor at the National School of Music Drama in Stockholm. In his music he employs an amiably modern idiom, stimulating to the untutored ear while retaining the specific gravity of triadic tonal constructions. His theater operas have been received with smiling approbation.

WORKS: OPERAS: *Drömmen om Thérèse* (The Dream of Thérèse), with Electronic Sound, after Zola's short story *Pour une nuit d'amour* (Stockholm, May 26, 1964); *Resan* (The Voyage), after a novel by J.P. Jersild, containing film-projection (Hamburg, March 2, 1969); *Tintomara*, after C.J.L. Almquist's novel *The Queen's Jewels* (Stockholm, Jan. 18, 1973); television opera, *En saga om sinnen* (Swedish Television, June 21, 1971); *Kvinnogräl* (Göteborg, Oct. 18, 1986); *Lionardo* (1985–88; Stockholm, March 31, 1988); *Medusan och djävulen* (Medusa and the Devil), lyrical mystery play (1973); *Animalen*, musical (Göteborg, May 19, 1979); *En midsommarnattsdröm*, musical after Shakespeare (1984; Malmö, Feb. 8, 1985); *Gudars skymning eller När kärleken blev blind . . .*, cabaret (1985). BALLETS: *Zodiak* (1966; Stockholm, Feb. 12, 1967); *Är gryningen redan här* (Göteborg, Sept. 5, 1980). ORCH.: *Sinfonia da camera* (1960); *Summer Music 1965* for Strings and Piano (1965); *Vaggsång för jorden* (1977). CHAMBER: *Pentagram* for String Quartet (1959–60); *Attitudes* for Piano (1965); *Variété* for String Quartet (1971). VOCAL: *Canzone 126 di Francesco Petrarca* for Chorus (1967); *Nautical Preludes* for Chorus (1970); *Chants for Dark Hours* for Mezzo-soprano, Flute, Guitar, and Percussion (1972); *Flower Power* for 6 or More Voices and Instruments (1974); *Trees*, 4 poems for Baritone and Chorus, after e.e. cummings (1979).

Wermann, Friedrich Oskar, German organist, conductor, and composer; b. Neichen, near Trebsen, April 30, 1840; d. Oberloschwitz, near Dresden, Nov. 22, 1906. He was a pupil of Friedrich Wieck (piano); later of Reinecke, Hauptmann, and Richter at the Leipzig Cons. He occupied various positions as an organist in Alsace, before settling in Dresden (1868) as a teacher and church organist; also conducted the Lehrerge-

sangverein there. He composed a Christmas fairy tale, *Die Wunderglocke;* a symphonic poem, *König Witichis;* several overtures; a *Reformationskantate;* a *Passionskantate;* 2 masses; several Psalms for double chorus a cappella; numerous organ works; études for piano; part-songs.

Werner, Arno, German organist and musicologist; b. Prittitz, Weissenfels, Nov. 22, 1865; d. Bitterfeld, Feb. 15, 1955. He studied at the Royal Inst. for Church-Music in Berlin (1889–90); in 1890, became municipal organist at Bitterfeld; in 1894 was appointed music teacher at the Gymnasium there, retiring in 1931; he continued his activities as a musicologist until his death; contributed articles to *Die Musik in Geschichte und Gegenwart* (1953).

WRITINGS: *Samuel und Gottfried Scheidt* (1900); *Geschichte der Kantorei-Gesellschaften im Gebiete des Kurfürstentums Sachsen* (1902); *Die Kantorei zu Bitterfeld* (1903); *Städtische und fürstliche Musikpflege in Weissenfels* (1911); *Städtische und fürstliche Musikpflege in Zeitz* (1922); *Zur Geschichte der Kantorei in Zörbig* (1927); *Musikpflege in Stadt und Kreis Bitterfeld* (1931); *Vier Jahrhunderte im Dienste der Kirchenmusik. Geschichte der Kantoren, Organisten und Stadtpfeifer seit der Reformation* (1932); *Der deutsche Kantor* (1933); *Freie Musikgemeinschaften im mitteldeutschen Raum* (1940).

Werner, Eric, Austrian-American musicologist; b. Lundenberg, near Vienna, Aug. 1, 1901; d. N.Y., July 28, 1988. He studied composition with Kornauth in Vienna, and with Schrecker and Busoni in Berlin; also took courses at the Univs. of Graz, Vienna, Prague, Berlin, Göttingen, and Strasbourg; received his Ph.D. in 1928 from the Univ. of Strasbourg; held teaching positions at the Saarbrücken Cons. (1926–33) and the Breslau Jewish Theological Seminary (1935–38). In 1938 he settled in the U.S.; was a prof. at the Hebrew Union College (later merged with the Jewish Inst. of Religion in N.Y.) in Cincinnati (1939–67); then was chairman of the musicology dept. at the Univ. of Tel Aviv (1967–72). He was an authority on Jewish and early Christian music.

WRITINGS: *In the Choir Loft: A Manual for Organists and Choir Directors in American Synagogues* (N.Y., 1957); *The Sacred Bridge: Liturgical Parallels in Synagogue and Early Church* (2 vols., N.Y., 1959, 1984); *Hebrew Music* (Cologne, 1961); *From Generation to Generation: Studies on Jewish Musical Tradition* (N.Y., 1962); *Mendelssohn: A New Image of the Composer and His Age* (N.Y., 1963); *A Voice Still Heard: The Sacred Songs of the Ashkenazic Jews* (Philadelphia, 1976). BIBL.: J. Cohen, *Bibliography of the Publications of E. W.* (Tel Aviv, 1968).

Werner, Gregor Joseph, Austrian organist and composer; b. Ybbs an der Donau, Jan. 28, 1693; d. Eisenstadt, Burgenland, March 3, 1766. In 1728 he was appointed Kapellmeister to Prince Esterházy at Eisenstadt; in 1761 Haydn was named Vice-Kapellmeister, and succeeded him after his death. Werner wrote a number of works, including 26 masses, 18 oratorios, and many instrumental pieces. Haydn had great respect for him, and arranged his fugues for string quartet. BIBL.: H. Dopf, *Die Messenkompositionen G.J. W.s* (diss., Univ. of Innsbruck, 1956); C. Warner, *A Study of Selected Works of G.J. W.* (diss., Catholic Univ. of America, 1965).

Werner, Heinrich, German composer; b. Kirchohmfeld, Oct. 2, 1800; d. Braunschweig, May 3, 1833. His song *Haidenröslein* became a perennial favorite in Germany; he also publ. male quartets and light piano music. BIBL.: P. Egert, *Festschrift zur Einweihung des Denkmals für den Komponisten H. W. in Kirchohmfeld* (1910); F. Mecke, *H. W.* (diss., Univ. of Bonn, 1913).

Werner, Johann Gottlob, German organist, teacher, and composer; b. Grossenhain, 1777; d. Chemnitz, July 19, 1822. After holding minor positions as an organist in provincial towns, he was appointed cathedral organist and music director at Merseburg, but died 3 years later. He publ. organ methods that were much in use: *Orgelschule* (1805; Part II as *Lehrbuch, das Orgelwerk . . . kennen . . . zu lernen*, 1823; both often republ.); *Musikalisches ABC* for beginners on the piano (1806; often republ.); *Choralbuch zum holländischen Psalm-und Gesangbuch* (1814); *Choralbuch zu den neuern sächsischen Gesangbüchern* (Leipzig); *Versuch einer kurzen und deutlichen Darstellung der Harmonielehre* (2 parts, 1818, 1819); many chorale preludes; 40 organ pieces for beginners; etc.

Wernick, Richard (Frank), American composer; b. Boston, Jan. 16, 1934. He studied composition with Irving Fine, Harold Shapero, and Arthur Berger at Brandeis Univ. (B.A., 1955) and with Leon Kirchner at Mills College in Oakland, Calif. (M.A., 1957); also took lessons in composition with Ernst Toch, Boris Blacher, and Aaron Copland and in conducting with Leonard Bernstein and Seymour Lipkin at the Berkshire Music Center, Tanglewood (1954, 1955). He composed much music for the theater, films, and television between 1953 and 1962; was music director and composer-in-residence of the Royal Winnipeg Ballet of Canada (1957–58). He taught at the State Univ. of N.Y. at Buffalo (1964–65) and at the Univ. of Chicago (1965–68). In 1968 he joined the faculty of the Univ. of Pa.; was made a prof. of music there in 1977. In 1976 he received a Guggenheim fellowship. He was awarded the Pulitzer Prize in Music in 1977 for his *Visions of Terror and Wonder*. In his early compositions he integrated the techniques of all his teachers, but ultimately fashioned an individual style of his own.

Works: Trio for Violin, Clarinet, and Cello (1961); *Hexagrams* for Chamber Orch. (1962); String Quartet No. 1 (1963); *Music* for Viola d'Amore (1964); *Stretti* for Clarinet, Violin, Viola, and Guitar (1965); *Lyrics from IXI* for Soprano, Vibraphone-marimba, and Contrabass, after e.e. cummings (1966); *Aevia* for Orch. (1966); *Haiku of Bashō* for Soprano, Flute, Clarinet, Violin, Contrabass, 2 Percussion Instruments, Piano, and Tape (1968); *Moonsongs from the Japanese* for Soprano and 2 prerecorded tracks of Soprano Voice (1969); *A Prayer for Jerusalem* for Mezzo-soprano and Percussion (1971); *Kaddish Requiem*, a "secular service for the victims of Indo-China" for Mezzo-soprano, Chamber Ensemble, and Tape (1971); String Quartet No. 2 (1972–73); *Songs of Remembrance* for Shawm, English Horn, Oboe, and Mezzo-soprano (1973); *Visions of Terror and Wonder* for Mezzo-soprano and Orch., to texts from the Bible and the Koran, in Hebrew, Arabic, and Greek (Aspen (Colo.) Music Festival, July 19, 1976); *Contemplations of the Tenth Muse, Books I–II* for Soprano (1977, 1979); *Introits and Canons* for Chamber Ensemble (1977); "And on the Seventh Day—," sacred service for Cantor and Percussion Players (1979); *A Poison Tree* for Flute, Clarinet, Violin, Cello, Piano, and Soprano (1979); Concerto for Cello and 10 Players (1979); *Formula: P--- ----m* for Chamber Ensemble (1981); Piano Sonata (1982); Sonata for Cello and Piano, *Portraits of Antiquity* (1982); *The Oracle of Shimon Bar Yochai* for Cello, Piano, and Soprano (1982); Concerto for Violin and Orch. (1984; Philadelphia, Jan. 17, 1986; 1st prize, Kennedy Center Friedheim Award, 1986); Concerto for Viola and Orch. (1986; Annandale-on-Hudson, N.Y., May 8, 1987); *Musica Ptolemeica* for Brass Quintet (1986); *Oracle II* (1987); Sym. No. 1 (1987); String Quartet No. 3 (1988); Concerto for Piano and Orch. (1989).

Werrecore (also **Vercore, Verecore, Verrechore, Werrekoren**), **Matthias Hermann,** composer; b. probably in Vercore or Warcoing, Hainaut, date unknown; d. after 1574. He most likely was of Flemish birth; however, the records of Milan Cathedral reveal that his father, Eligio, was from Milan. In 1522 he became maestro di cappella at Milan Cathedral; in 1550 Oliviero di Phalansis was named his temporary successor, followed by Simon Boyleau in 1557–58. Werrecore was mistakenly identified with Matthäus Le Maistre by Fétis and Kade; research by Haberl, Elsa Bienenfeld, and Cecie Stainer demonstrated the fallacy of this assumption. He composed the famous *Bataglia taliana* for 4 Voices, which celebrated the defeat of France at the Battle of Pavia in 1525 (publ. with the German title *Die Schlacht vor Pavia* in Schmeltzl's collection *Guter seltzamer . . . teutscher Gesang*, Nuremberg, 1544; ed. in

Denkmäler der Tonkunst in Österreich, XXXVII, Jg. XVIII/2, 1911; reprint as *La bataglia taliana . . . con alcune villote*, Venice, 1549; 2nd ed., enl., 1552). He also composed 20 *Cantum . . . liber primus* for 5 Voices (Milan, 1555) and a few motets.

Bibl.: F. Haberl, "Matthius Herman Werrecorensis: Eine bibliographischkritische Studie," *Monatshefte für Musikgeschichte*, III (1871).

Werrenrath, Reinald, American baritone; b. Brooklyn, Aug. 7, 1883; d. Plattsburg, N.Y., Sept. 12, 1953. He was a pupil of his father, a tenor; then studied with David Bispham and Herbert Witherspoon. He began his career as a concert singer; also in oratorio; made his operatic debut on Feb. 19, 1919, at the Metropolitan Opera in N.Y., as Silvio in *Pagliacci*, and remained with the company until 1921; then devoted himself to teaching and concert singing; appeared in public for the last time at Carnegie Hall in N.Y. on Oct. 23, 1952. He ed. *Modern Scandinavian Songs* (2 vols.; Boston, 1925–26).

Wert, Giaches (or **Jaches**) **de,** eminent Flemish composer; b. probably in Weert, near Antwerp, between May 6 and Aug. 18, 1535; d. Mantua, May 6, 1596. He was taken to Italy in childhood to serve as a chorister at the court of Maria di Cordona, Marchese della Padulla, in Avellino, near Naples; by 1558 he was in the service of Count Alfonso Gonzaga in Novellara; in 1565 he was appointed maestro di cappella at the ducal chapel of S. Barbara in Mantua, which was to remain the center of his activities for the remainder of his life. Wert's early years in Mantua were made difficult by the enmity of his fellow members of the cappella, most especially Agostino Bonvicino, who had hoped to become maestro di cappella; while he failed to attain this post, he did succeed in pursuing an adulterous relationship with Wert's wife. Wert himself later had an affair with Tarquinia Molza, a niece of Francesco Maria Molza, a fine poet and musician in Ferrara. In 1580 Wert received Mantuan citizenship. In 1582–83 and again in 1585 Gastoldi was called upon to serve as maestro di cappella during bouts of ill health by Wert; in 1592 he was formally appointed Wert's successor, although Wert remained active at the court until his death. Wert was greatly esteemed by contemporary musicians; Palestrina praised him, and he was also mentioned favorably by Thomas Morley, Artusi, G.B. Doni, and Monteverdi. Wert was distinguished as both a madrigalist and a composer of sacred works.

Works (all 1st publ. in Venice): SECULAR: *Il primo libro de madrigali* for 5 Voices (1558); *Il primo libro de madrigali* for 4 Voices (1561); *Madrigali del fiore, libro primo* for 5 Voices (1561); *Madrigali del fiore, libro secondo* for 5 Voices (1561); *Il terzo libro de madrigali* for 5 Voices (1563); *Il secondo libro de madrigali, nuovamente con nuova giunta ristampati* for 5 Voices (1564); *Il quarto libro de madrigali* for 5 Voices (1567); *Il quinto libro de madrigali* for 5 Voices (1571); *Il sesto libro de madrigali* for 5 Voices (1577); *Il settimo libro de madrigali* for 5 Voices (1581); *L'ottavo libro de madrigali* for 5 Voices (1586); *Il nono libro de madrigali* for 5 Voices (1581); *Il primo libro delle canzonette, villanelle* for 5 Voices (1589); *Il decimo libro de madrigali* for 5 Voices (1591); *L'undecimo libro de madrigali* for 5 Voices (1595); *Il duodecimo libro de madrigali* for 4 to 7 Voices (1608); other works in contemporary collections. SACRED: *Motectorum liber primus* for 5 Voices (1566); *Il secondo libro de motetti* for 5 Voices (1581); *Modulationum liber primus* for 6 Voices (1581); other works in contemporary collections. INSTRUMENTAL: Fantasias, *a 4*. See C. MacClintock and M. Bernstein, eds., *G. d.W.: Collected Works*, Corpus Mensurabilis Musicae, XXIV (1961–).

Bibl.: C. MacClintock, *The Five-part Madrigals of G. d.W.* (diss., Indiana Univ., 1955); M. Bernstein, *The Sacred Vocal Music of G. d.W.* (diss., Univ. of North Carolina, 1964); C. MacClintock, *G. d.W. (1535–1596): Life and Works*, Musicological Studies and Documents, XVII (1966); idem, "New Light on G. d.W.," *Aspects of Medieval and Renaissance Music: A Birthday Offering to Gustave Reese* (N.Y., 1966); A. Newcomb,

"Form and Fantasy in W.'s Instrumental Polyphony," *Studi Musicali*, VII (1978).

Wesembeek, Léon-Philippe-Marie Burbure de. See **Burbure de Wesembeek, Léon-Philippe-Marie.**

Wesendonck, Mathilde (née **Luckemeyer**), German poet, friend of Wagner; b. Elberfeld, Dec. 23, 1828; d. Traunblick, near Altmünster on the Traunsee, Austria, Aug. 31, 1902. Her 1st meeting with Wagner took place in Zürich, early in 1852, and soon developed into a deep friendship. She wrote the famous *Fünf Gedichte* (*Der Engel, Stehe still, Träume, Schmerzen, Im Treibhaus*), which Wagner set to music as studies for *Tristan und Isolde*. On May 19, 1848, she married **Otto Wesendonck** (b. March 16, 1815; d. Berlin, Nov. 18, 1896); in 1857 he gave Wagner the use of a beautiful house on his estate on Lake Zürich, where the first act of *Tristan und Isolde* was written, and the 2nd act sketched.
BIBL.: A. Heintz, "Meine Erinnerungen" (reminiscences of M. W.), *Allgemeine Musikzeitung* (Feb. 14, 1896); idem, ed., *Briefe Richard Wagners an Otto Wesendonk* (Charlottenburg, 1898; 2nd ed., augmented, 1905 by W. Golther; Eng. tr., 1911); idem, ed., *Richard Wagner an M. W.: Tagebuchblätter und Briefe 1853–1871* (Leipzig, 1904; 30th ed., rev., 1906; Eng. tr., 1905); H. Bélart, *Richard Wagners Liebestragödie mit M. W.* (Dresden, 1912); J. Kapp, ed., *Richard Wagner an M. und Otto W.* (Leipzig, 1915; 2nd ed., 1936); E.H. Müller von Asow, ed., *Johannes Brahms und M. W.; Ein Briefwechsel* (Vienna, 1943); J. Bergfeld, *Otto und M. W.s Bedeutung für das Leben und Schaffen Richard Wagners* (Bayreuth, 1968).

Wesley, prominent English family:
(1) John Wesley, clergyman and a founder of Methodism, brother of **Charles Wesley;** b. Epworth, Lincolnshire, June 17, 1703; d. London, March 2, 1791. He was educated at Christ Church, Oxford (graduated, 1724); in 1728 he became a priest. With his brother Charles and 2 others, he helped to found the Methodist movement; in 1735 he went to the U.S. with his brother to do missionary work, and publ. his 1st *Collection of Psalms and Hymns* (Charlestown, 1737). Returning to England, he spread the doctrine of Methodism and became famous as a preacher and writer. He has been called "the father of Methodist hymnology."
BIBL.: R. Green, *Works of J. and Charles W.* (London, 1896); J. Lightwood, *Methodist Music in the 18th Century* (London, 1927); J. Nuelsen, *J. W. und das deutsche Kirchenlied* (Bremen, 1938); E. Routley, *The Musical W.s* (London, 1968).
(2) Charles Wesley, clergyman, a founder of Methodism, and hymn writer, brother of **John Wesley;** b. Epworth, Lincolnshire, Dec. 18, 1707; d. London, March 29, 1788. He was educated at Christ Church, Oxford; with his brother and 2 others, he helped to organize the Methodist movement. In 1735 he followed his brother to the U.S. as a missionary but soon returned to England, where he later became associated with the Church of England. During his years as a Methodist, he acquired a notable reputation as a hymn writer; among his most celebrated hymns are *Hark, the Herald Angels Sing, Christ the Lord Is Risen Today,* and *Love Divine, All Loves Excelling.*
BIBL.: R. Green, *Works of John and C. W.* (London, 1896); J. Lightwood, *Methodist Music in the 18th Century* (London, 1927); E. Routley, *The Musical W.s* (London, 1968).
(3) Charles Wesley, organist and composer, nephew of **John** and **Charles** and brother of **Samuel Wesley;** b. Bristol, Dec. 11, 1757; d. London, May 23, 1834. He was a pupil of Kelway and Boyce in London; then held various positions as a church organist. He publ. in London 6 string quartets (c.1776), 6 concertos for Organ or Harpsichord and Orch. (c.1781), *Concerto grosso in 7 parts* (c.1782), *Variations on God Save the King* for Piano (c.1799), 6 voluntaries for Organ (1812), and a Piano Sonata (c.1820); his vocal works include the cantata *Caractacus* (1791), 15 anthems, 6 hymns, and various songs.
BIBL.: E. Routley, *The Musical W.s* (London, 1968).
(4) Samuel Wesley, organist and composer, nephew of **John** and **Charles Wesley** and brother of the preceding; b. Bristol,

Feb. 24, 1766; d. London, Oct. 11, 1837. When he was 6 he commenced music studies with the Bristol organist David Williams, and he began to compose at the age of 8; learned to play the violin as well as the organ. He composed the oratorio *Ruth* when he was only 8; publ. 8 sonatas for keyboard at 12. He soon acquired a fine reputation as an organist, while composing prolifically. In 1787 he suffered a skull injury in a fall into a building excavation, which impaired him emotionally for the remainder of his life. He was married to Charlotte Martin in 1793, but they separated in 1795; some years later he became intimate with his housekeeper, Sarah Suter; the burden of supporting his children by both Martin and Suter exacerbated his condition. In order to make ends meet, he played in concerts, appeared as an organist and conductor, gave lectures, and taught. In his last years he wrote a number of hymns. Wesley was a notable composer of Latin church music; he also wrote for the Anglican church. He composed much instrumental music, his masterpiece being the Sym. in B-flat major (1802). He also wrote an autobiography (c.1836).
WORKS: 5 masses and about 55 other Latin sacred works; the oratorios *Ruth* (1774) and *The Death of Abel* (1779); services and anthems; hymn tunes; sacred songs; secular choruses, part-songs, glees, duets, and solo songs; 5 overtures (1775, 1778, 1780, 1813, c.1834); 4 syms. (1784, 1784, c.1790, 1802); 2 harpsichord concertos (both c.1774); 4 organ concertos (1787, 1800, c.1811, c.1815); 8 violin concertos (1779, 1781, c.1782, 1782, c.1782, 1783, 1785, c.1812); Sinfonia obbligato (1781); 3 string quartets (1779; 1779–80; c.1800); several trios and sonatas; numerous works for Organ and other Solo Keyboard Instruments.
BIBL.: Anonymous, "Professional Memoranda of the Late Mr. S. W.'s Life," *Musical World*, VII (1837); W. Winters, *An Account of the Remarkable Musical Talents of Several Members of the W. Family* (London, 1874); E. Wesley (his daughter), *Letters of S. W. to Mr. Jacobs Relating to the Introduction in This Country of the Works of Bach* (London, 1875; 2nd ed., 1878); G. Stevenson, *Memorials of the W. Family* (London, 1876); J. Lightwood, *S. W., Musician: The Story of His Life* (London, 1937); E. Routley, *The Musical W.s* (London, 1968); H. Ambrose, *The Anglican Anthems and Roman Catholic Motets of S. W.* (1766–1837) (diss., Boston Univ., 1969); J. Schwarz, Jr., *The Orchestral Music of S. W.* (diss., Univ. of Maryland, 1971); J. Marsh, *The Latin Church Music of S. W.* (diss., Univ. of York, 1975); L. Ritchey, "The Untimely Death of S. W.; or, The Perils of Plagiarism," *Music & Letters*, LX (1979).
(5) Samuel Sebastian Wesley, organist and composer, illegitimate son of the preceding; b. London, Aug. 14, 1810; d. Gloucester, April 19, 1876. When he was 10 he was elected a chorister of the Chapel Royal; also sang at St. Paul's Cathedral. He received training in organ and composition from his father; from age 16 he was organist in various London churches, including St. James's Chapel (from 1826), St. Giles (1829–32), St. John (1829–31), and Hampton Parish Church (1831–32); then was organist at Hereford Cathedral (1832–35), Exeter Cathedral (1835–41), Leeds Parish Church (1842–49), Winchester Cathedral (1849–65), Winchester College (1850–65), and Gloucester Cathedral (1865–76). He received the degrees of B.Mus. and D.Mus. at Oxford (1839). He won great renown as an organist, excelling at improvisation. As a composer, he became best known for his Anglican cathedral music.
WORKS: 13 pieces of service music; 38 anthems, including such well-known examples as *Ascribe unto the Lord, Blessed Be the God and the Father, Let Us Lift Up Our Heart, The Wilderness and the Solitary Place, Thou Wilt Keep Him in Perfect Peace,* and *Wash Me Thoroughly;* secular choruses, part-songs, glees, and songs; Sym. (c.1832); ballet music; Overture in C (c.1827); organ music; piano pieces.
COLLECTIONS AND EDITIONS: *The Psalter . . . with Chants* (Leeds, 1843); *A Selection of Psalms and Hymns* (London, 1864); *The European Psalmist* (London, 1872); *The Welburn Appendix of Original Hymns and Tunes* (London, 1875).
WRITINGS: *A Few Words on Cathedral Music* (London, 1849); *Reply to the Inquiries of the Cathedral Commissioners*

Relative to the Improvement in the Music of Divine Worship in Cathedrals (London, 1854).
BIBL.: G. Stevenson, *Memorials of the W. Family* (London, 1876); G. Spink, "S.S. W.: A Biography," *Musical Times*, LXXVIII (1937); E. Routley, *The Musical W.s* (London, 1968); W. Shaw, "The Achievement of S.S. W.," *Musical Times*, CXVII (1976); P. Chappell, *Dr. S.S. W.* (Great Wakering, 1977).

Wessel, Mark, American composer and teacher; b. Coldwater, Mich., March 26, 1894; d. Beverly Hills, Mich., May 2, 1973. He studied at Northwestern Univ. (M.M., 1918); then had instruction with Schoenberg in Vienna (1922). Returning to America, he was active primarily as a teacher. He wrote a Sym. (1932); 2 piano concertos; *Plains and Mountains* for Piano and String Quartet (1937); Sextet for Piano and 5 Wind Instruments; 2 cello sonatas; piano pieces.

Wessely, Othmar, Austrian musicologist; b. Linz, Oct. 31, 1922. He was educated at the Bruckner Cons. in Linz, the Vienna Academy of Music, and the Univ. of Vienna (Ph.D., 1947, with the diss. *Anton Bruckner in Linz*; Habilitationsschrift, 1959, with his *Arnold von Bruck: Leben und Umwelt*). From 1950 to 1963 he was a member of the faculty of the Univ. of Vienna; after teaching at the Univ. of Graz (1963–71), he returned to the Univ. of Vienna in 1971 as prof. of musicology.
WRITINGS: *Musik in Oberösterreich* (Linz, 1951); *Die Musikinstrumentensammlung des Oberösterreichischen Landesmuseums* (Linz, 1952); *Johann Joseph Fux und Johann Mattheson* (Graz, 1966); ed. *Ernst Ludwig Gerber: Historisch-biographisches Lexikon der Tonkünstler (1790–1792) und Neues historisch-biographisches Lexikon der Tonkünstler (1812–1814)* (4 vols., Graz, 1966–77); *Johann Joseph Fux und Francesco Antonio Vallotti* (Graz, 1967); *Pietro Pariatis Libretto zu Johann Joseph Fuxens "Costanza e fortezza"* (Graz, 1969); *Johann Joseph Fux: Persönlichkeit, Umwelt, Nachwelt* (Graz, 1979).

Wessman, Harri (Kristian), Finnish composer; b. Helsinki, March 29, 1949. He learned to play the cello and double bass in his youth; took courses in musicology and languages at the Univ. of Helsinki (1967–73) and also studied composition privately with Joonas Kokkonen, continuing under his tutelage at the Sibelius Academy in Helsinki (1973–78). His works are lyrical and melodic.
WORKS: STAGE: *Onnen arvoitus* (The Riddle of Happiness), play for Children's Chorus, Recorder, and Percussion (1986); *Päivikki*, ballet (1987). **ORCH.:** *Serenade* for Trumpet and String Orch. (1976); *Sarja jousiorkesterille musiiksta Eha Lättemäen runoihin* (Suite for String Orch. from the Music to Poems by Eha Lättemäe; 1978); *Prinsessa joka nukkui sata vuotta* (The Princess Who Slept a Hundred Years) for Trumpet or Soprano and String Orch. (1981); *Concertino No. 1* for Piano and String Orch. (1982); *Loitsunpuhallus* for Wind Orch. (1984); *Koraalialkusoitto* (Choral Overture; 1984); *Serenade* for Piano and String Orch. (1985); *Tango tan-tan-tan* (1985); *Väinämöinen* (1985); *Trumpet Concerto* (1987). **CHAMBER:** *Musiikkia uruille* (Music for Organ; 1987); Sonata for Violin and Piano (1978); Sonata No. 2 for Cello and Piano (1979); *Syksyn sävyinen fantasia* (Autumnal Fantasia) for Cello and Piano (1980); 2 intermezzi for Piano (1980, 1981); Trio for Accordion, Flute, and Guitar (1981); *Je chante la beauté de la solitude* for Accordion (1982); *Prelude and Sicilienne* for Violin, Cello, and Piano (1983); Piano Quartet (1985); *Es sangen drei Engel* for Oboe and Organ (1986); Accordion Sonata (1986); *Teema ja muunnelmia vaskiyhtyeelle* (Theme and Variations for Brass Ensemble; 1986–87). **VOCAL:** *Lauluja tuimista linnuista* for Choir and Piano (1977); *Kolme laulua V.A. Koskenniemen runoihin* (3 Songs to Poems by V.A. Koskenniemi) for Choir (1979); *Kaksi laulua sekakuorolle Marianna Kalliolan runoihin* (2 Songs for Mixed Choir to Poems by Marianna Kalliola; 1980); *Vaggvisa, Det viner på fjällen* for Children's Choir (1982); *Nelja laulua Lauri Pohjanpään runoihin* (4 Songs to Poems by Lauri Pohjanpää) for Children's Choir (1983); *Ligg ej och dra dig!* for Men's Choir (1984); *Det blir kyligt* for Men's Choir (1985).

West, Dottie, American country-music singer; b. McMinnville, Tenn., Oct. 11, 1932. After receiving an A.B. degree from Tennessee Tech., she launched her career as a singer and songwriter; with her 1st husband, Bill West, she wrote the hit *Here Comes My Baby*, and soon after, she became a regular performer at the Grand Ole Opry in Nashville; she also toured widely and made recordings.

West, John Ebenezer, English organist and composer; b. London, Dec. 7, 1863; d. there, Feb. 28, 1929. He was a nephew of **Ebenezer Prout,** and studied with him at the Royal Academy of Music in London; was organist and choirmaster at various London churches (1884–1902); in 1884, was appointed to the editorial staff of Novello & Co. He wrote 2 cantatas, *The Healing of the Canaanite's Daughter* (1882) and *Seed-time and Harvest* (1892); several church services and anthems; an orch. march, *Victoria, Our Queen*; organ music; publ. *Cathedral Organists* (London, 1899; new ed., 1921).

Westbrook, William Joseph, English organist and composer; b. London, Jan. 1, 1831; d. Sydenham, March 24, 1894. He studied with R. Temple; was organist at St. Bartholomew's, Bethnal Green (1848–51) and at St. Bartholomew's, Sydenham (1851–94); received his Mus.B. in 1876 and his Mus.D. in 1878 from Cambridge. He was a founder-ed. of the *Musical Standard* (1862–70); wrote an oratorio, *Jesus*; a cantata, *The Lord Is My Shepherd*; services; anthems; part-songs; sonatas and voluntaries for organ; transcriptions for organ; several textbooks on the organ; etc.

Westenburg, Richard, American conductor; b. Minneapolis, April 26, 1932. He studied at Lawrence Univ. (B.Mus., 1954) and at the Univ. of Minnesota (M.A., 1956); then went to Paris, where he studied with Nadia Boulanger and Pierre Cochereau (1959–60); subsequently did postgraduate work at the Theological Seminary School of Sacred Music in N.Y. (1960–66). From 1956 to 1960 he taught music at the Univ. of Montana; then served as director of music at the First Unitarian Church in Worcester, Mass. (1960–62). In 1964 he went to N.Y., where he was engaged as organist and choirmaster of the Central Presbyterian Church, holding this position until 1974. In 1968 he founded Musica Sacra and became its music director; also served as music director of the Collegiate Chorale (1973–79). He was conductor-in-residence at the Cathedral Church of St. John the Divine (1974–86) and music director there (1976–83). He served as head of the choral dept. of the Juilliard School in N.Y. from 1977 to 1989; was appointed visiting prof. at Rutgers, the State Univ. of New Jersey, in 1986; became music director at the Fifth Avenue Presbyterian Church in 1990.

Westerberg, Stig (Evald Börje), Swedish conductor; b. Malmö, Nov. 26, 1918. He studied at the Stockholm Musikhögskolan (1937–42) and with Kletzki in Paris. He was a répétiteur at Stockholm's Royal Theater (1943–46), and then conducted at the Oscarsteatern; after conducting the Gävleborg Sym. Orch. (1949–53), he returned to Stockholm as a conductor at the Royal Theater; in 1957 he became chief conductor of the Swedish Radio Sym. Orch.; taught conducting at the Musikhögskolan from 1969, becoming a prof. there in 1971. From 1978 to 1985 he was chief conductor of the Malmö Sym. Orch. He became well known for his performances of both traditional and contemporary Swedish scores.

Westergaard, Peter (Talbot), American composer and pedagogue; b. Champaign, Ill., May 28, 1931. He studied composition at Harvard Univ. with Walter Piston (A.B., 1953); then had fruitful sessions with Sessions at Princeton Univ. (M.F.A., 1956). In 1956 he went to Germany, where he studied with Fortner in Detmold. Returning to the U.S., he joined the music faculty of Columbia Univ. in N.Y. (1958–66); then was at Amherst College (1967–68); in 1968, became associate prof. at Princeton Univ.; prof. in 1971; was chairman of the music dept. (1974–78; 1983–86). He publ. *An Introduction to Tonal Theory* (N.Y., 1975). In his music he explores the possibility of total organization of tones, rhythms, and other elements of composition.

WORKS: STAGE: *CHAMBER OPERAS: Charivari* (1953); *Mr. and Mrs. Discobbolos* (1966). *OPERA: The Tempest* (1988). **ORCH.:** *Symphonic Movement* (1954); *5 Movements for Small Orch.* (1958); *Noises, Sounds, and Sweet Airs* for Chamber Orch. (1968); *Tuckets and Sennets* for Band (1969). **CHAMBER:** String Quartet (1957); Quartet for Violin, Vibraphone, Clarinet, and Cello (1960); Trio for Flute, Cello, and Piano (1962); *Variations for 6 Players* for Flute, Clarinet, Percussion, Piano, Violin, and Cello (1963); *Divertimento on Discobbolic Fragments* for Flute and Piano (1967); *Moto perpetuo* for Flute, Oboe, Clarinet, Bassoon, Trumpet, and Horn (1976). **VOCAL:** *Cantata I: The Plot Against the Giant* for Women's Chorus, Clarinet, Cello, and Harp (1956); *Cantata II: A Refusal to Mourn the Death, by Fire, of a Child in London* for Bass and 10 Instruments (1958); *Cantata III: Leda and the Swan* for Mezzo-soprano, Vibraphone, Marimba, and Viola (1961); *Ode* for Soprano and 5 Instruments (1989).

Westergaard, Svend, Danish composer and pedagogue; b. Copenhagen, Oct. 8, 1922. He studied composition with Høffding, Hjelmborg, and Jersild at the Royal Danish Cons. of Music in Copenhagen; began teaching there in 1951; was a prof. of theory from 1967; also its director (1967–71). He publ. the study *Harmonilaere* (Copenhagen, 1961).

WORKS: *Elegy* for Strings (1949); *Pezzo sinfonico* (1950); Oboe Concerto (1950); 2 syms.: No. 1, *Sinfonia* (1955), and No. 2, *Sinfonia da camera* (1968); *L'Homme armé,* canzona for 16 Instruments (1959; rev. for Orch., 1970); *Capriccio* for Violin and String Orch. (1960); *Variazioni sinfoniche* (Danish Radio, June 12, 1960); Cello Concerto (1961; Århus, Oct. 22, 1962; rev. 1973); *Pezzo concertante* for Orch. (Danish Radio, Aug. 19, 1965); *Sinfonia da camera* (Copenhagen, March 24, 1969); *Varianti sinfoniche* for Winds and Percussion (1972); 2 wind quintets (1948, 1949); *Tema con variazioni* for Clarinet Quintet (1949); String Quartet (1968); Sonata for Solo Flute (1971).

Westerhout, Nicolà (Niccolò) van. See **Van Westerhout, Nicolà (Niccolò).**

Westerlinck, Wilfried, Belgian composer; b. Louvain, Oct. 3, 1945. He studied harmony with Legley at the Brussels Cons., and conducting with Sternefeld and musical analysis with Verbesselt at the Antwerp Cons.; was a producer with the Belgian Radio and Television (from 1968).

WORKS: Clarinet Quartet (1966); *Epigrammen* for String Trio (1968); *Metamorfose* for Orch. (1971); *Maclou* for Horn (1975); *Elegie van de zee en van de liefde* for Orch. (1975); *Canto I* for Guitar (1976); *Aquarel* for Flute (1977); *Landschappen I* for Wind Quintet (1977); String Quartet (1978); *Landschappen II* for String Orch. (1979); *"S"* for Trombone and Tape (1972–80); *Landschappen III* for Quintet (1980); *Landschappen IV* for Flute, Harp, and String Trio (1981); *Canto II* for Cello (1982); *Canto III* for Harp (1982); *Landschappen V* (1983); *Epitaphe* for String Quartet (1983); 3 piano sonatas (1983, 1985, 1986); *Variations on a Theme by Paganini* for Piano (1985); Sinfonietta for Chamber Ensemble (1986).

Westlake, Frederick, English pianist, teacher, and composer; b. Romsey, Hampshire, Feb. 25, 1840; d. London, Feb. 12, 1898. He studied at the Royal Academy of Music in London with W. Macfarren (piano) and G.A. Macfarren (harmony); in 1862, was appointed to the faculty as a piano teacher. He wrote several masses, hymns, piano pieces, and a collection of part-songs, *Lyra Studentium.*

Westmorland, 11th Earl of. See **Burghersh, Lord John Fane, 11th Earl of Westmorland.**

Westphal, Rudolf (Georg Hermann), notable German music scholar; b. Oberkirchen, July 3, 1826; d. Stadthagen, July 10, 1892. He was a student of classical philology in Marburg; taught at the Univ. of Breslau (1858–62) and at the Moscow lyceum (1875–80); subsequently lived in Leipzig, Bückeburg, and Stadthagen. He wrote numerous learned papers on Greek music, and maintained that the Greeks employed polyphony, a theory that he himself eventually abandoned as untenable.

WRITINGS: With A. Rossbach, *Metrik der griechischen Dramatiker und Lyriker* (3 vols., 1854–63; 3rd ed. as *Theorie der musischen Künste der Hellenen,* 1885–89); *Die Fragmente und Lehrsätze der griechischen Rhythmiker* (1861); *System der antiken Rhythmik* (1865); *Geschichte der alten und mittelalterlichen Musik* (1865; unfinished; includes *Plutarch über die Musik,* 1864); *Theorie der neuhochdeutschen Metrik* (1870; 2nd ed., 1877); *Elemente des musikalischen Rhythmus mit besonderer Rücksicht auf unsre Opernmusik* (1872); *Allgemeine Theorie der musikalischen Rhythmik seit J.Seb. Bach* (1880); *Die Musik des griechischen Altertums* (1883); *Allgemeine Metrik der indo-germanischen und semitischen Völker auf Grundlage der vergleichenden Sprachwissenschaft* (1892; with addendum by R. Kruse, *Der griechische Hexameter in der deutschen Nachdichtung*); *Aristoxenos von Tarent: Metrik und Rhythmik des klassischen Hellenentums* (2 vols., 1883–93).

Westrup, Sir Jack (Allan), eminent English musicologist; b. London, July 26, 1904; d. Headley, Hampshire, April 21, 1975. He received his education at Dulwich College, London (1917–22), and at Balliol College, Oxford (B.A. and B.Mus., 1926; M.A., 1929). He was an assistant classics master at Dulwich College (1928–34); then was a music critic for the *Daily Telegraph* (1934–39); also was ed. of the *Monthly Musical Record* (1933–45). He was actively engaged in musical education. He gave classes at the Royal Academy of Music in London (1938–40); then was lecturer in music at King's College, Newcastle upon Tyne (1941–44), the Univ. of Birmingham (1944–47), and Wadham College, Oxford (1947–71). In 1946 he received an honorary degree of D.Mus. at Oxford Univ. In 1947 he was named chairman of the editorial board of *The New Oxford History of Music.* In 1959 he succeeded Eric Blom as ed. of *Music & Letters.* From 1958 to 1963 he was president of the Royal Musical Association. He was also active as a conductor; he conducted the Oxford Opera Club (1947–62), the Oxford Univ. Orch. (1954–63), and the Oxford Bach Choir and Oxford Orch. Society (1970–71). He was knighted in 1961. He prepared major revisions of Walker's *A History of Music in England* (Oxford, 3rd ed., 1952) and of Fellowes's *English Cathedral Music* (London, 5th ed., 1969); he also supervised rev. eds. of Blom's *Everyman's Dictionary of Music* (4th ed., 1962; 5th ed., 1971). He was co-ed., with F. Harrison, of the *Collins Music Encyclopedia* (London, 1959; American ed. as *The New College Encyclopedia of Music,* N.Y., 1960).

WRITINGS: All publ. in London unless otherwise given: *Purcell* (1937; 4th ed., rev., 1980); *Handel* (1938); *Liszt* (1940); *Sharps and Flats* (1940); *British Music* (1943; 3rd ed., 1949); *The Meaning of Musical History* (1946); *An Introduction to Musical History* (1955); *Music: Its Past and Its Present* (Washington, D.C., 1964); *Bach Cantatas* (1966); *Schubert Chamber Music* (1969); *Musical Interpretation* (1971).

BIBL.: F. Sternfeld et al., eds., *Essays on Opera and English Music in Honour of Sir J. W.* (Oxford, 1975).

Wettergren, Gertrud (née **Pålson**), Swedish contralto; b. Eslöv, Feb. 17, 1897. She studied at the Stockholm Cons., and later in London; made her operatic debut as Cherubino at the Royal Opera in Stockholm in 1922, and remained on its roster for 30 years. On Dec. 20, 1935, she appeared at the Metropolitan Opera in N.Y. as Amneris in *Aida;* sang there until 1938; also sang with the Chicago Opera (1936–38) and at London's Covent Garden (1936, 1939). In 1925 she married Erik Wettergren, director of the National Museum of Stockholm. Among her most esteemed roles were Venus, Fricka, Brangäne, Dalila, Carmen, Mignon, Marfa, and Herodias; she also sang in many Swedish operas.

Wetz, Richard, German composer, conductor, and teacher; b. Gleiwitz, Feb. 26, 1875; d. Erfurt, Jan. 16, 1935. He studied with R. Hofmann in Leipzig and Thuille in Munich (1899–1900); also attended the Univ. of Munich. He was a theater conductor in Stralsund and Barmen; in 1906 he settled in Erfurt as conductor of the Musikverein and the Singakademie; also taught at the Weimar Hochschule für Musik (from 1916).

His output was greatly influenced by Bruckner. A Richard Wetz-Gesellschaft was founded in Gleiwitz in 1943 to promote his music.

Works: *Das ewige Feuer,* opera (Düsseldorf, March 19, 1907); *Kleistouvertüre* for Orch.; 2 violin concertos; 3 syms.; also various choral works, including a *Requiem* for Baritone, Chorus, and Orch. and the *Weihnachtsoratorio* for Soprano, Baritone, Chorus, and Orch.; lieder; some chamber music, including 2 string quartets.

Writings: *Anton Bruckner* (Leipzig, 1922); *Franz Liszt* (Leipzig, 1925); *Beethoven* (Erfurt, 1927; 2nd ed., 1933).

Bibl.: G. Armin, *Die Lieder von R. W.* (Leipzig, 1911); E. Schellenberg, *R. W.* (Leipzig, 1911; 2nd ed., 1914); H. Polack, *R. W. Sein Werk* (Leipzig, 1935).

Wetzel, Justus Hermann, German composer and musicologist; b. Kyritz, March 11, 1879; d. Überlingen (Bodensee), Dec. 6, 1973. He studied natural sciences, philosophy, and art history in Berlin, Munich, and Marburg (Ph.D., 1901); then studied composition with Schrader and Taubert. He taught at the Riemann Cons. in Stettin (1905–7); settled in Berlin in 1910; taught at the Academy for Church and School Music (from 1926; became a prof. in 1935). He composed about 400 songs; choral works; chamber music; piano pieces; ed. and arr. several collections of German songs.

Bibl.: F. Welter, *J.H. W.* (Berlin, 1931; with list of works).

Wetzler, Hermann (Hans), American organist, conductor, and composer; b. Frankfurt am Main (of American parents), Sept. 8, 1870; d. N.Y., May 29, 1943. He was taken to the U.S. as a child, but in 1882 returned to Germany, where he studied at the Hoch Cons. in Frankfurt am Main and studied with Clara Schumann (piano), Iwan Knorr (counterpoint), and Humperdinck (instrumentation). In 1892 he went to N.Y., where he was organist at Old Trinity Church (1897–1901); in 1903 he established the Wetzler Sym. Concerts, which had considerable success; Richard Strauss conducted a series of 4 concerts of his own works with the Wetzler group (Feb.–March, 1904), including the world premiere of the *Sinfonia domestica*. In 1905 he returned to Germany and conducted in various German cities and throughout Europe. In 1940 he returned to the U.S. He publ. *Wege zur Musik* (Leipzig, 1938).

Works: OPERA: *Die baskische Venus* (Leipzig, Nov. 18, 1928; the *Symphonic Dance in the Basque Style* was extracted from this score as a concert piece); incidental music to Shakespeare's *As You Like It* (1917). ORCH.: *Symphonic Fantasy* (1922); *Visionen* (1923); *Assisi,* legend (1924); *Symphonie concertante* for Violin and Orch. (1932); also some chamber music, including a String Quartet (1937); much vocal music, including a *Magnificat* for Soprano, Boys' or Women's Chorus, and Organ (1936), choruses, and songs.

Weweler, August, German composer; b. Reike, Oct. 20, 1868; d. Detmold, Dec. 8, 1952. He studied at the Leipzig Cons. with Jadassohn and others; in 1898, settled in Detmold as a teacher. He composed the operas *Dornröschen* (Kassel, 1903) and *Der grobe Märker* (Detmold, 1908); the oratorio *Die Sintflut* (Detmold, 1914); a ballet, *Des Malers Traumbild;* male choruses; piano pieces. He publ. *Ave Musica! Das Wesen der Tonkunst und die modernen Bestrebungen* (1913; 2nd ed., 1919).

Weymarn, Pavel, Russian writer on music and composer; b. St. Petersburg, 1857; d. Narva, Sept. 22, 1905. He studied piano and theory at the St. Petersburg Cons.; from 1888 to 1890, ed. the music periodical *Bayan;* publ. monographs on Napravnik (1889) and Cui (1897); was music critic for several Russian newspapers. He composed a String Quartet, piano pieces, and songs.

Weyrauch, August Heinrich von, German composer; b. Riga, April 30, 1788; place and date of death unknown. In 1824 he publ. (under his own name) a song, *Nach Osten* (words by Wetzel). About 1840 an anonymous Paris publisher reprinted it, with Schubert's name on the title page, as *Adieu* (French words by Bélanger); a piano transcription of it, also crediting the authorship to Schubert, was publ. by Döhler in

Germany (1843); Schlesinger of Berlin reprinted the song, with a German tr. of the French text, as Schubert's in 1845; since then it has been reprinted many times as Schubert's by European and American publishers.

Weyse, Christoph Ernst Friedrich, eminent Danish pianist, organist, pedagogue, and composer of German descent; b. Altona, March 5, 1774; d. Copenhagen, Oct. 8, 1842. He studied with his grandfather, a cantor in Altona; in 1789 he went to Copenhagen, where he studied with J.A.P. Schulz; he remained there the rest of his life. After establishing his reputation as a pianist, he devoted himself to the organ; was deputy organist (1792–94) and principal organist (1794–1805) at the Reformed Church; served as principal organist at the Cathedral from 1805 until his death, winning great renown as a master of improvisation. In 1816 he was named titular prof. at the Univ. and was awarded an honorary doctorate in 1842, the year of his death. In 1819 he was appointed court composer. Through the court conductor Kunzen, he became interested in a movement for the establishment of a national school of Danish opera, for which his works (together with those of Kuhlau) effectively prepared the way. He remains best known for his fine songs. He also wrote some effective piano music, including the *Allegri di bravura* and *Études.*

Works: OPERAS (all 1st perf. in Copenhagen): *Sovedrikken* (The Sleeping Potion; April 21, 1809); *Faruk* (Jan. 30, 1812); *Ludlams hule* (Ludlam's Cave; Jan. 30, 1816); *Floribella* (Jan. 29, 1825); *Et eventyr i Rosenborg Have* (An Adventure in Rosenborg Gardens; May 26, 1827); *Festen på Kenilworth* (Jan. 6, 1836); incidental music to Shakespeare's *Macbeth* (1817) and J. Ewald's *Balders død* (The Death of Baldur; 1832); 7 syms. (1795–99); *Miserere* for Double Chorus and Orch. (1818); various cantatas (1818–22); Sonata for 2 Bassoons (c.1798); various piano works, including (6) *Allegri di bravura* (Berlin, 1796); (8) *Études* (1837), and many waltzes, impromptus, and écossaises; 32 organ preludes; the folk-song collection *Halvtresindstyve gamle kaempeviser* (1840–42); numerous songs, many of which were publ. as *Romancer og sange* (1852–60).

Bibl.: C. Thrane, "C.E.F. W.," *Danske komponister* (Copenhagen, 1875); A. Berggreen, *C.E.F. W.s biographie* (Copenhagen, 1876); W. Behrend, "W. und Kuhlau," *Die Musik,* III/3 (1903–4); J. Larsen, *W.s sange* (Copenhagen, 1942); C. Hatting, *W.s kantater* (diss., Univ. of Copenhagen, 1955).

Whear, Paul William, American composer; b. Auburn, Ind., Nov. 13, 1925. He studied engineering at Marquette Univ. (B.N.S.), DePauw Univ. (B.A.), and Case Western Reserve Univ. (Ph.D.); then made a 180° turn toward the art of music; attended classes of Gardner Read at Boston Univ. and of Wayne Barlow at the Eastman School of Music in Rochester, N.Y. From 1960 to 1969 Whear served as chairman of the music dept. at Doane College; in 1969 he was appointed a prof. of music and chairman of the theory and composition dept. at Marshall Univ. He wrote 4 syms.; Sym. No. 2 (1971) is subtitled *The Bridge;* Sym. No. 3 (1975), *The Galleries;* Sym. No. 4 is for Band (1979). He also wrote overtures, chamber music, and choral works.

Whettam, Graham (Dudley), English composer; b. Swindon, Sept. 7, 1927. He received guidance from Eric Fenby but otherwise was an autodidact as a musician; devoted himself principally to composition and the cause of copyright protection; served as chairman of the Composers' Guild of Great Britain (1971; 1983–86), and subsequently was its copyright consultant. He withdrew most of his compositions written prior to 1959. Whettam has revealed a fine command of orch. writing. His works have been widely performed in England and on the Continent.

Works: ORCH.: 2 clarinet concertos: No. 1 (Bournemouth, Nov. 5, 1959); No. 2 (1982; Warwick, Jan. 8, 1983); *Introduction and Scherzo impetuoso* (1960); *Variations* for Oboe, Bassoon, and Strings (1961); *Sinfonia contra timore* (1962; Birmingham, Feb. 25, 1965); Cello Concerto (1962; Manchester, Dec. 1981); *Sinfonietta stravagante* (1964); *Sinfonia concertante* (Newcastle upon Tyne, Oct. 1966); *The Masque of the*

Red Death, 2 dance scenes (1968); *Sinfonia intrepida* (1976; Liverpool, Jan. 18, 1977); *Sinfonia drammatica* (Jena, March 15, 1978); *Hymnos* for String Orch. (1978; adapted from the String Quartet No. 2); *Concerto conciso* for String Orch. (Stratford-upon-Avon, Aug. 21, 1981); *An English Suite* (1984); *Symphonic Prelude* (1985); *Ballade* for Violin and Orch. (1988). **BRASS BAND:** *Partita* (1975); *Invocation* (1977). **CHAMBER:** *Prelude, Allegro and Postlude* for Flute, Oboe, and Piano (1955); 2 sonatas for Solo Violin (1957, rev. 1987; 1972); *Fantasy* for 10 Winds (1960; rev. 1979); 2 oboe quartets (1960, 1973); *Music for Brass* for 3 Trumpets and 3 Trombones (1964); 3 string quartets: No. 1 (1967); No. 2, *Hymnos* (1978); No. 3 (1980); Sextet for Flute, Oboe, Clarinet, Bassoon, Horn, and Piano (1970); *Duo declamando* for Horn and Piano (1972); Trio for Oboe, Clarinet, and Bassoon (1975); Trio for Horn, Violin, and Piano (1976); Concerto for 10 Winds (1979); *Quintetto concertato* for Flute, Oboe, Clarinet, Bassoon, and Horn (1979); *Serenade* for Viola or Clarinet and Guitar (1981); *Suite* for Timpani (1982); *Percussion Partita* for 6 Players (1985); Quartet for 4 Horns (1986); *Canticles* for Horn Quartet and Organ (1987). **PIANO:** *Prelude, Scherzo, and Elegy* (1964; rev. 1986); *Prelude and Scherzo impetuoso* (1967); *Night Music* (1969). **ORGAN:** *Partita* (1962); *Triptych* (1966). **CHORAL:** *The Wounded Surgeon Plies the Steel* (1959); *Magnificat and Nunc dimittis* for Chorus and Organ (1961); *Missa brevis* for Chorus and Organ (1963); *Mary Modyr Cum and Se* for Chorus and Organ (1963); *Do Not Go Gentle into That Good Night* for 5 Solo Voices or 5-part Chorus (1965); *Celebration* for Contralto, Chorus, Organ, Orch., Brass Band, and Audience Unisono (1975); *On the Beach at Night* (1979); *Consecration* for Chorus, Organ, Brass, and Percussion (1982); *A Mass for Canterbury* (1986); songs.

White, Andrew (Nathanial, III), black American saxophonist; b. Washington, D.C., Sept. 6, 1942. He studied saxophone as a child and later took lessons in oboe and music theory at Howard Univ. in Washington, D.C. (graduated, 1964). After further study at Dartmouth College in Hanover, N.H., and at the Paris Cons., he was engaged as principal oboist in the American Ballet Theatre orch. in N.Y. (1968–72). He veered away from classical music and played bass guitar for Stevie Wonder and other popular musicians (1969–73); also made transcriptions of solo performances by the great jazzmen John Coltrane, Eric Dolphy, and Charlie Parker. In 1976 he arranged the music for and performed in the big-band tribute to Coltrane at the Newport Jazz Festival. He then focused on jazz, playing alto and soprano saxophone as a sideman to Elvin Jones and Beaver Harris. He publ. 2 books relating his experiences in the music business: *Hey Kid! Wanna Buy a Record? A Treatise on Self Production in the Music Business* (Washington, D.C., 1982) and *Andrew's X-rated Band Stories* (Washington, D.C., 1984).
BIBL.: D. McGinty, "Conversation with A. W., 'Keeper of the Trane,'" *Black Perspective in Music*, XII/1 (1984).

White, Clarence Cameron, black American violinist and composer; b. Clarksville, Tenn., Aug. 10, 1880; d. N.Y., June 30, 1960. He studied at the Oberlin Cons. (1896–1901), with Samuel Coleridge-Taylor in London (1906; 1908–10), and with Raoul Laparra in Paris (1930–32). He taught at various institutions while pursuing a concert career; was director of music at the Hampton (Va.) Inst. (1932–35). In 1919 he helped to organize the National Association of Negro Musicians. He won the Bispham Medal for his opera *Ouanga* (1932) and the Benjamin Award for his *Elegy* for Orch. (1954). His major works were written in a neo-Romantic style with occasional infusions of Negro folk melos.
WORKS: OPERAS: *Ouanga* (concert perf., Chicago, Nov. 1932; stage perf., South Bend, Ind., June 10, 1949); *Carnival Romance* (1952). **BALLET:** *A Night in Sans Souci* (1929); incidental music to J. Matheus's *Tambour* (1929). **ORCH.:** Sym.; *Kutamba Rhapsody* (1942); *Elegy* (1954); *Dance Rhapsody* (1955); *Poeme* (1955). **CHAMBER:** *Bandana Sketches*, violin suite (1918); *From the Cotton Fields*, violin suite (1920); 2

string quartets (1931, 1931); *Legende d'Afrique* for Cello and Piano (1955); keyboard pieces; also vocal works, including *Heritage* for Soprano, Tenor, Chorus, and Orch. (1959); songs; numerous arrangements of spirituals, including *40 Negro Spirituals* (1927) and *Traditional Negro Spirituals* (1940).
BIBL.: L. Simms, "C. C. W.: Violinist, Composer, Teacher," *Negro History Bulletin*, XLIII (1980); V. Edwards and M. Mark, "In Retrospect: C.C. W.," *Black Perspective in Music*, IX (1981); W. Shirley, ed., "Letters of C.C. W. in the Collections of the Music Division of the Library of Congress," ibid., X (1982).

White, Donald H(oward), American composer and pedagogue; b. Narberth, Pa., Feb. 28, 1921. He studied music education at Temple Univ. in Philadelphia (B.S., 1942) and composition with Persichetti at the Philadelphia Cons. (1946) and with Bernard Rogers and Howard Hanson at the Eastman School of Music in Rochester, N.Y. (M.M., 1947; Ph.D., 1952). In 1947 he joined the faculty of DePauw Univ. in Greencastle, Ind., where he was chairman of composition and theory studies (1948–81), a prof. (1959–81), and director of the school of music (1974–78); was chairman of the music dept. at Central Washington Univ. in Ellensburg, Wash. (1981–90).
WORKS: ORCH.: *Sagan*, overture (1946); *Kennebec Suite* (1947); Overture (1951); Cello Concerto (1952); *Divertimento No. 2* for Strings (1968). **BAND:** *Ambrosian Hymn Variants* (1963); *Terpsimetrics* (1968); Concertino for Timpani, Winds, and Percussion (1973); *Lyric Suite* for Euphonium and Wind Ensemble (1978); *Bagatelles* (1989). **CHAMBER:** Sonata for Trumpet and Piano (1946); *3 to 5* for Woodwind Quintet (1964); *Serenade No. 3* for Brass Quintet (1965); Sonata for Trombone and Piano (1966); Sonata for Tuba and Piano (1978); Quintet for Brass (1980). **VOCAL:** *Song of Mankind* for Soloists, Chorus, and Orch. (1970); *From the Navajo Children* for Chorus and Wind Ensemble (1978); also works for Chorus a cappella.

White, Eric Walter, English writer on music and administrator; b. Bristol, Sept. 10, 1905; d. London, Sept. 13, 1985. He attended Clifton College, Bristol, and studied English at Balliol College, Oxford (1924–27). After working as a translator for the League of Nations in Geneva (1929–33), he was employed by the National Council for Social Service in London (1935–42); in 1942 he became assistant secretary of the Council for the Encouragement of Music and the Arts, which became the Arts Council of Great Britain in 1946; he retired in 1971. He publ. valuable studies on Stravinsky and an invaluable register of English opera premieres.
WRITINGS (all publ. in London): *Stravinsky's Sacrifice to Apollo* (1930); *Stravinsky: A Critical Survey* (1947); *Benjamin Britten: A Sketch of His Life and Works* (1948; 3rd ed., enl., 1970 as *Benjamin Britten: His Life and Operas*); *The Rise of English Opera* (1951); *Stravinsky: The Composer and His Works* (1966; 2nd ed., rev., 1979); *A History of English Opera* (1983); *A Register of First Performances of English Operas and Semi-Operas from the 16th Century to 1980* (1983).

White, Felix Harold, English composer; b. London, April 27, 1884; d. there, Jan. 31, 1945. He was born into a Jewish family originally named Weiss. He was mostly self-taught, except for some piano lessons from his mother. He was a keyboard player in the London Phil. Orch. (1933–35); concurrently was on the staff at Covent Garden. He devoted himself mainly to composition; also was active as a writer on music; publ. a *Dictionary of Musical Terms*; wrote short biographical monographs on noted musicians; ed. the piano works of Scriabin.
WORKS: ORCH.: *Shylock*, overture (London, Sept. 1907); Polonaise in B minor (1908); *Astarte Syriaca*, tone poem after D.G. Rossetti (1909; London, Jan. 1911); *Meditation* (1911; Bournemouth, 1923); Suite (1913); *Impressions of England*, suite (London, 1918); *The Deserted Village*, tone poem (1923); Nocturne (1936); Overture in F major (1937). **CHAMBER:** Romance in D major for Cello and Piano (London, 1907); Cello Sonata (1910); *Dawn*, study for 12 Cellos (1922); Trio for Oboe or Violin, Viola, and Piano, a setting of Andrew Marvell's *The Nymph's Complaint for the Death of Her Fawn* (1922; Carnegie

Award); *4 Proverbs* for Flute, Oboe, Violin, Viola, and Cello (1925; Carnegie Award); *Orison* for 4 Cellos (1937); also choral works; 60 part-songs; about 250 songs; 80 piano pieces.

BIBL.: S. Craggs, "F. W.: A Centenary Note," *Musical Times* (April 1984).

White, John, American organist, teacher, and composer; b. West Springfield, Mass., March 12, 1855; d. Bad Nauheim, Germany, July 18, 1902. He studied organ with Dudley Buck in N.Y. (1861–63) and Karl Haupt in Berlin, and composition with Rheinberger in Munich (1883–87). He was organist at St. Francis Xavier Church (1880–83) and at the Church of the Ascension in N.Y. (1887–96); then went back to Germany. He wrote a *Missa solemnis* (1889), a *Requiem* (1902), a *Libera me* (1902), and many other sacred works.

White, John (Reeves), American musicologist and conductor; b. Houston, Miss., May 2, 1924; d. N.Y., July 12, 1984. He studied at the Cincinnati Cons. (1941–43); also took courses at the Paris Cons. (1945); obtained his M.A. at Colorado College in 1948, and his Ph.D. at Indiana Univ. in 1952; also received the degree of Dr. of Natural Philosophy at the Inst. of Neurophenomenology in Amherst, Mass. (1975). He held teaching posts at Colorado College (1947–52), the Univ. of Richmond (1953–61), and Indiana Univ. (1961–66 and 1970–71); in 1971, was appointed to the faculty of Hunter College. From 1966 to 1970 he conducted the N.Y. Pro Musica; produced reconstructions of several medieval and Renaissance dramatic works; ed. *The Keyboard Tablature of Johannes of Lublin* (6 vols., 1964–67), *François Dandrieu: Harpsichord Music* (1965), and *Michelangelo Rossi: Complete Keyboard Works* (1967). With J. Dos Passos and H. Fitzgerald, he ed. *The Arts between the Wars: A Symposium* (1964).

White, Maude Valérie, English composer; b. Dieppe, France (of English parents), June 23, 1855; d. London, Nov. 2, 1937. She studied with W.S. Rockstro in Torquay and Oliver May in London; then was a pupil of G.A. Macfarren at the Royal Academy of Music in London (1876–79), where she became the 1st woman to win the Mendelssohn Scholarship (1879). She continued her studies with R. Fuchs in Vienna (1883). She traveled extensively through Europe and South America; lived in London, and for some years in Florence. She was best known as a composer of songs. She publ. her memoirs, *Friends and Memories* (London, 1914), and *My Indian Summer* (London, 1932).

WORKS: *The Enchanted Heart,* ballet (1912–13); incidental music; *Agnus Dei* for Chorus and Orch. (1879); about 200 songs to Eng., Ger., French, and Italian texts; vocal duets; *Naissance d'amour* for Cello and Piano (1893); many piano pieces.

White, Michael, American composer; b. Chicago, March 6, 1931. He studied at the Chicago Musical College and at the Juilliard School of Music in N.Y. with Peter Mennin. In 1963 he received a Guggenheim fellowship. He taught at the Oberlin (Ohio) Cons. (1964–66), the Philadelphia College of Performing Arts (1966–79), and the Juilliard School in N.Y. (from 1979). Among his works are several operas, including *Metamorphosis* (1968); *Opposites* for Wind Ensemble (1970); *Passion According to a Cynic* (1971); Violin Concerto (1979); Double Concerto for Violin, Viola, and Orch. (1981); *The 3 Muses* for Harpsichord (1984); *Museum Pieces* for Flute and Guitar (1987); Sonata for Solo Viola (1988); other chamber pieces; guitar music; choruses; song cycles.

White, Paul, American violinist, composer, and conductor; b. Bangor, Maine, Aug. 22, 1895; d. Henrietta, near Rochester, N.Y., May 31, 1973. He studied theory at the New England Cons. of Music in Boston; then took violin lessons with Eugène Ysaÿe in Cincinnati; also studied conducting with Eugene Goossens in Rochester, N.Y. In 1929 he was appointed associate conductor of the Rochester Civic Orch. He composed *Pagan Festival Overture* (Rochester, N.Y., April 28, 1936); *Andante and Rondo* for Cello and Orch. (1945); *5 Miniatures* for Piano,

including the popular *Mosquito Dance;* various pieces of chamber music.

White, Robert, American tenor; b. N.Y., Oct. 27, 1936. He was the son of Joseph White, the "Silver Masked Tenor" of the early radio era in N.Y. He began his career with appearances on Fred Allen's radio program when he was 9; after studying music at Hunter College, he continued his training with Nadia Boulanger and Gérard Souzay in France; then completed his studies at the Juilliard School of Music in N.Y. (M.S., 1968), where he found a mentor in Beverley Peck Johnson. He sang with the N.Y. Pro Musica and appeared with various American opera companies before becoming successful as a concert singer. His repertoire ranges from the Baroque to Irish ballads. He sang in a "Homage to John McCormack" at N.Y.'s Alice Tully Hall during the 1985–86 season.

BIBL.: H. Kupferberg, "R. W.: America Reclaims Its Irish Tenor," *Ovation* (Oct. 1985).

White (or **Whyte**), **Robert,** English composer; b. c.1538; d. London, Nov. 1574. He was a chorister and subsequently one of the cantores at Trinity College, Cambridge; obtained his Mus.B. from Cambridge (1560). In 1562 he was made Master of the Choristers at Ely Cathedral, a post formerly held by his father-in-law, **Christopher Tye;** he left his post in 1566 and by 1567 was Master of the Choristers at Chester Cathedral; in 1569 he assumed that post at Westminster Abbey, being formally confirmed in 1570. He died of the plague. While not as gifted a composer as Tye, he was nevertheless highly influential. His finest works are 2 sets of Lamentations; he was also one of the 1st English composers to write fantasias. See P. Buck et al., eds., *Robert White,* Tudor Church Music, V (1926), and I. Spector, ed., *Robert White: The Instrumental Music,* Recent Researches in the Music of the Renaissance, XII (1972).

BIBL.: I. Spector, "The Music of R. W.," *The Consort,* XXIII (1966); F. Hudson, "R. W. and His Contemporaries: Early Elisabethan Music and Drama," *Festschrift für Ernst Hermann Meyer* (Leipzig, 1973); D. Mateer, *A Comparative Study and Critical Transcription of the Latin Sacred Music of R. W.* (diss., Queen's Univ., Belfast, 1976).

White, Ruth, American composer; b. Pittsburgh, Sept. 1, 1925. She studied composition with Lopatnikoff (B.F.A., 1948; M.F.A., 1949) and received training in piano at the Mellon Inst. in Pittsburgh; then studied at the Univ. of Calif. at Los Angeles (1951–54) and had private composition lessons with Antheil (1952–54). She specialized in teaching music to children and wrote much didactic music. Her other music followed along conventional lines until she took up electronic composition in 1964.

WORKS: *Pinions,* opera (1967); film and television music; Suite for Orch. (1949); *Shofar Symphony* (1965); various chamber music pieces; piano pieces. **VOCAL:** *Palestinean Song Cycle* for Voice, Bassoon, Piano, and Percussion (1949); *Songs from the Japanese Poets* for Voice and Piano (1949); *Settings for Lullabies from 'round the World* for Tenor, Soprano, Piano, Cello, and Horn (1955); *Garden of Delights* for Soprano and Electronics (1971); about 150 songs for children. **ELECTRONIC:** *7 Trumps from the Tarot Cards* (1967); *Flowers of Evil* (1969); *Short Circuits* (1970); pedagogical pieces.

White, William, English composer; b. c.1585; d. c.1665. He served as one of the singing-men at Westminster. He is known to have composed fantasies and anthems; some of the works attributed to him may be by Matthew White or other composers named White.

White, William C., American bandmaster and march composer; b. Centerville, Utah, Sept. 29, 1881; d. Tenafly, N.J., Sept. 30, 1964. He studied violin at the New England Cons. of Music in Boston and at the Inst. of Musical Art in N.Y., graduating in 1914. He was a member of the 10th U.S. Coast Artillery Band (1907–12) and led the Mecca Temple Band (1919–20) and the Almes Temple Band in Washington, D.C. (1921–28); then served as principal of the Army Music School on Governors Island. He composed several marches, among them the popular *American Doughboy; publ. A History of Military Music in America* (1943); *Military Band Arranging; Tone Building and Intonation Studies for Military Bands.*

Whitehead, Alfred (Ernest), English-born Canadian organist, choirmaster, teacher, and composer; b. Peterborough, July 10, 1887; d. Amherst, Nova Scotia, April 1, 1974. He was a pupil of Haydn Keeton and C.C. Francis of Peterborough Cathedral, and then of A. Eaglefield Hull. In 1912 he emigrated to Canada, and in 1913 became the 1st fellow by examination of the Canadian Guild (later College) of Organists; in 1916 he obtained his B.Mus. at the Univ. of Toronto and in 1922 his D.Mus. at McGill Univ. in Montreal; in 1924 he became a fellow of the Royal College of Organists and winner of the Lafontaine Prize. He was organist and choirmaster at St. Andrew's Presbyterian Church in Truro, Nova Scotia (1912–15); then was organist and choirmaster at St. Peter's Anglican Church in Sherbrooke, Quebec (1915–22), and at Christ Church Cathedral in Montreal (1922–47); also taught organ, theory, and composition at the McGill Cons. (1922–30). After serving as head of the music dept. at Mt. Allison Univ. (1947–53), he was organist and choirmaster at Trinity United Church in Amherst (1953–71). He was president of the Canadian College of Organists (1930–31; 1935–37); was honorary vice-president (1971–73) and honorary president (1973–74) of the Royal Canadian College of Organists. He wrote a number of distinguished sacred works, excelling as a composer of motets and anthems. He was also a painter and philatelist.

Whitehill, Clarence (Eugene), American baritone, later bass-baritone; b. Parnell, Iowa, Nov. 5, 1871; d. N.Y., Dec. 18, 1932. He studied with L.A. Phelps in Chicago; earned his living as a clerk in an express office, and also sang in churches; then went to Paris in 1896, where he studied with Giraudet and Sbriglia; made his operatic debut on Oct. 31, 1898, at the Théâtre de la Monnaie in Brussels; was the 1st American male singer to be engaged at the Opéra-Comique in Paris (1899); then was a member of Henry Savage's Grand English Opera Co. at the Metropolitan Opera in N.Y. in 1900; went for further study to Stockhausen in Frankfurt am Main, and from there to Bayreuth, where he studied the entire Wagnerian repertoire with Cosima Wagner; after engagements in Germany, he was a member of the Cologne Opera (1903–8), the Metropolitan Opera (1909–10), the Chicago Opera (1911–14; 1915–17), and again the Metropolitan (1914–32).

Whitehouse, William Edward, esteemed English cellist and pedagogue; b. London, May 20, 1859; d. there, Jan. 12, 1935. He studied at the Royal Academy of Music in London; joined its faculty after graduation. From 1889 until 1904 he was cellist in the London Trio with Achille Simonetti (violin) and Amina Goodwin (piano), with whom he toured all over Europe. He was greatly esteemed as a teacher; among his pupils were Felix Salmond and Beatrice Harrison. He wrote a number of attractive cello pieces (*Allegro perpetuo, Remembrance, Serenade,* etc.) and ed. several cello works of the 18th century. He publ. a memoir, *Recollections of a Violoncellist* (London, 1930).

White Lafitte, José (Silvestre de los Dolores), noted Cuban violinist, teacher, and composer; b. Matanzas, Jan. 17, 1836; d. Paris, March 15, 1918. He went to Paris as a youth; studied violin with Alard at the Paris Cons., obtaining 1st prize in 1856. After playing 1st violin in a quintet and giving concerts (1857–58), he was active in Cuba; was again in Paris (1861–74), where he secured his reputation as a virtuoso and chamber music artist; also toured in Europe and South America, later becoming court violinist to the emperor Dom Pedro II of Brazil. In 1889 he settled in Paris, where he later taught a master class at the Cons. He composed a Violin Concerto, a String Quartet, pieces for violin and piano, and some church music.

Whiteman, Paul, celebrated American conductor of popular music; b. Denver, Colo., March 28, 1890; d. Doylestown, Pa., Dec. 29, 1967. He played viola in the Denver Sym. Orch.

and later in the San Francisco People's Sym. Orch.; in 1917–18, was conductor of a 40-piece band in the U.S. Navy. He then formed a hotel orch. in Santa Barbara, Calif., and began to develop a style of playing known as "symphonic jazz," which soon made him famous. On Feb. 12, 1924, he gave a concert in Aeolian Hall in N.Y., at which he introduced Gershwin's *Rhapsody in Blue,* written for his orch., with Gershwin himself as soloist. In 1926 he made a tour in Europe. While not himself a jazz musician, he was popularly known as the "King of Jazz," and frequently featured at his concerts such notables of the jazz world as Bix Beiderbecke, Frank Trumbauer, and Benny Goodman; Bing Crosby achieved his early fame as a member of Paul Whiteman's Rhythm Boys. Whiteman established the Whiteman Awards, made annually for "symphonic jazz" compositions written by Americans. He publ. the books *Jazz* (with M. McBride; N.Y., 1926), *How to Be a Bandleader* (with L. Lieber; N.Y., 1941), and *Records for the Millions* (N.Y., 1948).
    BIBL.: C. Johnson, *P. W.: A Chronology* (Williamstown, N.J., 1977); T. DeLong, *Pops: P. W., the King of Jazz* (Piscataway, N.J., 1983).

Whithorne (real name, **Whittern**), **Emerson,** American composer; b. Cleveland, Sept. 6, 1884; d. Lyme, Conn., March 25, 1958. He had his name legally changed in 1918 to Whithorne (the original family name of his paternal grandfather). He studied in Cleveland with J.H. Rogers; embarked on a musical career at the age of 15, and appeared as a pianist on the Chautauqua circuit for 2 seasons. In 1904 he went to Vienna and took piano lessons with Leschetizky and theory and composition lessons with Robert Fuchs; from 1905 to 1907 he was a piano pupil of Artur Schnabel. In 1907 he married **Ethel Leginska,** acting as her impresaria in Germany until 1909; they were separated in 1912, and divorced in 1916. Between 1907 and 1915, Whithorne lived mainly in London; he studied Chinese and Japanese music from materials in the British Museum, and wrote several pieces based on oriental tunes (*Adventures of a Samurai;* settings for *The Yellow Jacket; The Typhoon*). Returning to America, he became ed. for the Art Publication Society of St. Louis (1915–20); then settled in N.Y. and devoted himself entirely to composition; was an active member of the League of Composers in N.Y. In his music he assumed a militantly modernistic attitude; wrote several pieces in the fashionable "machine music" style.
    WORKS: ORCH.: *The Rain* (Detroit, Feb. 22, 1913); *The Aeroplane* (1920; Birmingham, England, Jan. 30, 1926; arr. from the piano piece); *Saturday's Child* for Mezzo-soprano, Tenor, and Small Orch. (N.Y., March 13, 1926); *New York Days and Nights* (1923; Philadelphia, July 30, 1926; originally for Piano); *Poem* for Piano and Orch. (Chicago, Feb. 4, 1927); *Fata Morgana,* symphonic poem (N.Y., Oct. 11, 1928); incidental music to Eugene O'Neill's *Marco Millions* (1928); Sym. No. 1 (1929; Cincinnati, Jan. 12, 1934); *The Dream Pedlar,* symphonic poem (Los Angeles, Jan. 15, 1931); Violin Concerto (Chicago, Nov. 12, 1931); *Fandango* (N.Y., April 19, 1932); *Moon Trail,* symphonic poem (Boston, Dec. 15, 1933); Sym. No. 2 (1935; Cincinnati, March 19, 1937); *Sierra Morena* (N.Y., May 7, 1938); Piano Quintet (N.Y., Dec. 19, 1926); other chamber music; piano pieces; songs.
    BIBL.: J. Howard, *E. W.* (N.Y., 1929); R. Hammond, "E. W.," *Modern Music,* VIII/2 (1931).

Whiting, Arthur Battelle, American pianist, teacher, and composer, nephew of **George E(lbridge) Whiting;** b. Cambridge, Mass., June 20, 1861; d. Beverly, Mass., July 20, 1936. He studied in Boston with Sherwood (piano), Maas (harmony), and Chadwick (composition). In 1883 he went to Munich and took courses at the Cons. with Rheinberger (until 1885). Returning to the U.S., he stayed in Boston until 1895, then settled in N.Y.; from 1907, gave educational chamber music concerts at Yale, Harvard, Princeton, and Columbia Univs.; in 1911 he inaugurated a series of concerts of early music, playing the harpsichord, other artists being Constance Edson (violin), Georges Barrère (flute), and Paul Kéfer (viola da gamba).
    WORKS: *Concert Overture* (Boston, Feb. 5, 1886); Piano Con-

certo (Boston, Nov. 16, 1888, composer soloist); *Fantasie* for Piano and Orch. (Boston, March 5, 1897, composer soloist); *Suite* for Strings and 4 Horns (Boston, March 13, 1891); *The Golden Cage*, dance pageant (1926); Piano Quintet; String Quartet; Piano Trio; Violin Sonata; many piano pieces, including *6 Bagatelles*, *Suite moderne*, and *3 Characteristic Waltzes*; also *Melodious Technical Studies*; *Pianoforte Pedal Studies* (with text in Eng. and Ger.); musical settings from the *Rubáiyát of Omar Khayyám* for Baritone; anthems; songs; etc.

BIBL.: D. Mason, "A. W.," *Musical Quarterly* (Jan. 1937); idem, *Music in My Time* (N.Y., 1938).

Whiting, George E(lbridge), American organist, pedagogue, and composer, uncle of **Arthur Battelle Whiting**; b. Holliston, Mass., Sept. 14, 1840; d. Cambridge, Mass., Oct. 14, 1923. He began to study at age 5 with his brother Amos, a church organist, and played in public at the age of 13; at 17 he became organist of the North Congregational Church at Hartford; studied with George W. Morgan in N.Y.; then went to England, where he became a pupil of W.T. Best of Liverpool (1863). Returning to America, he became organist at St. Joseph's in Albany, N.Y., where the famous soprano Emma Albani sang in his choir. He then moved to Boston, where he was organist at King's Chapel (1869–74); in 1874 he went to Berlin and studied harmony with Haupt and orchestration with Radecke. Settling finally in Boston, he taught the organ at the New England Cons. of Music (until 1879, and again from 1883 to 1897). In the interim he was a teacher at the Cincinnati College of Music (1879–83). He was renowned as a teacher; publ. *The Organist* (Boston, 1870) and *The First 6 Months on the Organ* (1871). He also wrote many sacred works: 2 masses; Vesper Services; a *Te Deum*; the secular cantatas *The Tale of the Viking*; *Dream Pictures*; *March of the Monks of Bangor*; *Midnight*; *Henry of Navarre*; the one-act opera *Lenora*, to an Italian libretto (1893); a Sym.; a Piano Concerto; an overture to Tennyson's *The Princess*; a Suite for Cello and Orch.; piano pieces; songs; etc.

Whiting, Richard, American composer of popular music; b. Peoria, Ill., Nov. 12, 1891; d. Beverly Hills, Feb. 10, 1938. He learned to play piano and picked up music theory on his own; was manager of the Detroit branch of the Remick music publishing firm (1912–19), which brought out his 1st songs; then went to N.Y., where he wrote songs for the revue *Toot Sweet* (1919) and *George White's Scandals of 1919*; eventually settled in California and composed for films. Among his most successful songs were *It's Tulip Time in Holland* (1915), *Till We Meet Again* (1918), *Japanese Sandman* (1920), *Ain't We Got Fun?* (1921), *Sleepy Time Gal* (1925), *Breezin' Along with the Breeze* (1926), and *I Can't Escape from You* (1937). His daughter, **Margaret Whiting** (b. Detroit, July 22, 1924), was a popular singer.

Whitmer, T(homas) Carl, American organist, teacher, and composer; b. Altoona, Pa., June 24, 1873; d. Poughkeepsie, N.Y., May 30, 1959. He studied piano with C. Jarvis, organ with S.P. Warren, and composition with W.W. Gilchrist. He was director of the School of Music, Stephens College, Columbia, Mo. (1899–1909); director of music at the Pa. College for Women in Pittsburgh (1909–16); organist and choirmaster of the Sixth Presbyterian Church in Pittsburgh (1916–32); then taught privately at Dramamount, his farm near Newburgh, N.Y. He publ. *The Way of My Heart and Mind* (Pittsburgh, 1920) and *The Art of Improvisation: A Handbook of Principles and Methods* (N.Y., 1934; rev. ed., 1941).

WORKS: *Poem of Life* for Piano and Orch. (1914); *A Syrian Night*, ballet suite for Orch. (Philadelphia Orch., Pittsburgh, Feb. 17, 1919); *When God Laughed* for Chorus a cappella (1932); *Radiations over a 13th Century Theme* for String Orch. (1935); *Supper at Emmaus*, choral suite (Pittsburgh, Feb. 21, 1939); cantata, *Chant Me the Poem That Comes from the Soul of America*, after Walt Whitman (Pittsburgh, Feb. 19, 1942); one-act opera, *Oh, Isabel* (1951); chamber music; piano pieces; songs.

BIBL.: H. Gaul, "One Man—and a Lot of Imagination,"

American Organist, XIV (1931); T. Buhrman, "T.C. W.: Royally Celebrated in Pittsburgh," ibid., XXVII (1944).

Whitney, John, American experimental filmmaker, computer-graphics artist, and Pythagorean-inspired speculative theorist of the analogies between musical and visual arts; b. Pasadena, Calif., April 8, 1917. He is a pioneer in 20th-century motion graphics, having invented cinema techniques in the 1940s that became an established part of the repertoire of special effects later used in film titles and television. His interest in the complementarity of visual and aural arts began with a series of experimental films made with his brother James, including the silent *24 Variations* (1939–40) and the series of *5 Film Exercises* (1943–44), which made use of synthesized pendulum music. With the development of computer graphics, he produced a number of what are now classic pieces, utilizing the music of a variety of composers; these include *Permutations* (1968; re-ed., 1979; with Indian tabla music by Balachandra), *Matrix I* (1971; with music adapted from sonatas by Antonio Soler) and *III* (1972; with music from Terry Riley's *Rainbow in Curved Air*), and *Arabesque* (1975; with improvised music by Manoocheher Sadeghi). In the 1980s, advanced computer technology enabled him to compose both music and graphics; he produced a number of compositions inspired by Native American subjects, including *Hopi, Navajo, Chaco, Mimbres Star* (inspired by 1 of literally thousands of 8th- through 10th-century plates discovered in 1989 in Mimbres, N.Mex.), and *Black Elk*. These and many other computer-generated aural/ visual compositions exemplify his ideas about the inherent complementarity of music and visual art, with the harmonic motion evident in tonal music made visible in the charge and release of tensional visual forces. His work has been supported by IBM; he also received NEA grants and a Guggenheim fellowship (1947–48). After retiring from his teaching position in the art dept. of the Univ. of Calif. at Los Angeles in 1986, he devoted himself to producing aural/visual compositions in his studio in Pacific Palisades, Calif. He publ. *Digital Harmony: On the Complementarity of Music and Visual Art* (Peterborough, N.H., 1980); see also his "Writing on Water—Action Painting with Music," *Media Arts Journal* (Spring–Summer 1990).

Whitney, Myron (William), esteemed American bass; b. Ashby, Mass., Sept. 5, 1836; d. Sandwich, Mass., Sept. 19, 1910. He was a pupil of E.H. Frost in Boston; made his debut there at the Tremont Temple as a soloist in Handel's *Messiah* (Dec. 25, 1858); sang throughout New England during the next 10 years and then pursued training with Vannucini in Florence and Randegger in London. He sang regularly in opera as well as oratorio in the U.S. from 1873; toured with the Theodore Thomas Orch. (1878–82) and appeared frequently with the Boston Ideal Opera Co. (1879–1900); also was a member of the American Opera Co. (1885–86). He was generally considered the leading American oratorio artist of his day. His son, **Myron Whitney, Jr.** (1872–1954), a baritone, traveled as joint artist with Melba and Nordica; taught singing at the New England Cons. of Music in Boston.

Whitney, Robert (Sutton), American conductor; b. Newcastle upon Tyne, England (of an American father and an English mother), July 9, 1904; d. Louisville, Ky., Nov. 22, 1986. He studied with Leo Sowerby in Chicago; took lessons in conducting with Eric De Lamarter there. In 1937 he was engaged as conductor of the Louisville Phil. (later renamed the Louisville Orch.), a post he held until 1967. A munificent grant from the Rockefeller Foundation enabled the Louisville Orch. to commission works from American and foreign composers, each to be paid a set fee of $1,000; the project proved highly successful, and the orch. was able to give 1st performances of works by Honegger, Milhaud, Malipiero, Petrassi, Krenek, Dallapiccola, Toch, Chávez, Villa-Lobos, Ginastera, Schuman, Virgil Thomson, Cowell, Piston, Sessions, Antheil, Creston, Mennin, and others; it recorded some 200 contemporary symphonic works on Louisville Orch. Records. From 1956 to 1972 he was dean of the Univ. of Louisville School of Music; also taught conducting at the Univ. of Cincinnati College-Cons. of Music (1967–70). He composed a *Concerto Grosso* (1934); Sym. in E minor (1936); *Sospiri di Roma* for Chorus and Orch. (1941); Concertino (1960).

BIBL.: H. Stoddard, "R. W. and the Louisville Orchestra," *International Musician,* LV/10 (1957); F. Woolsey, "W. and His Louisville Orchestra," *Music Magazine/Musical Courier,* CLXIII/12 (1961).

Whittaker, Howard, American composer and music educator; b. Lakewood, Ohio, Dec. 19, 1922. He studied with Herbert Elwell in Cleveland; in 1948, was appointed director of the Cleveland Music School Settlement. In most of his works he applies modified serial procedures, but refuses to abandon tonality. Among his compositions are a Piano Concerto, *2 Murals* for Orch. (Cleveland, March 31, 1960), chamber music, organ pieces, and songs.

Whittaker, W(illiam) G(illies), respected English choral conductor, pedagogue, and composer; b. Newcastle upon Tyne, July 23, 1876; d. Orkney Islands, July 5, 1944. He studied science at Armstrong College, Univ. of Durham, and also received training in organ and singing before joining its faculty in 1898; was the 1st Gardiner Prof. of Music at the Univ. of Glasgow (1929–38) and was principal of the Royal Scottish Academy of Music in Glasgow (1929–41); also was active as a choral conductor; conducted various choral societies in Newcastle and London. He became well known as a Bach conductor and scholar; ed. various instrumental works of the 17th and 18th centuries. He composed *A Lykewake Dirge* and *The Celestial Sphere* for Chorus and Orch.; Psalm CXXXIX; *Among the Northumbrian Hills,* piano quintet; piano pieces; songs; prepared folk-song arrangements.

WRITINGS: *Fugitive Notes on Certain Cantatas and the Motets of J.S. Bach* (London, 1924); *Class Singing* (London, 1925; 2nd ed., 1930); *Collected Essays* (Oxford, 1940); *The Cantatas of J.S. Bach, Sacred and Secular* (London, 1959).

BIBL.: H. Foss, "W.G. W.," *Music Bulletin,* VI (1924).

Whittal, Arnold (Morgan), English musicologist; b. Shrewsbury, Nov. 11, 1935. He took courses at Emmanuel College, Cambridge (B.A., 1959), completing his training at the Univ. there (Ph.D., 1964, with the diss. *La Querelle des Bouffons*); then taught at the Univ. of Nottingham (1964–69), Univ. College, Cardiff (1969–75), and King's College, London (from 1976).

WRITINGS: *Schoenberg Chamber Music* (London, 1972); *Music since the First World War* (London, 1977; 3rd ed., 1988); *Britten and Tippett: Studies in Themes and Techniques* (Cambridge, 1982); *Romantic Music: A Concise History from Schubert to Sibelius* (London, 1987); with J. Dunsby, *Music Analysis in Theory and Practice* (New Haven, Conn., 1988).

Whittall, Gertrude Clarke, American patroness of music and literature; b. Bellevue, Nebr., Oct. 7, 1867; d. Washington, D.C., June 29, 1965. Her maiden name was **Clarke;** she married Matthew John Whittall on June 4, 1906. In 1935 she donated to the Library of Congress in Washington, D.C., a quartet of Stradivari instruments—2 violins (including the famous "Betts"), a viola, and a cello—together with 4 Tourte bows; she added another Stradivari violin (the "Ward") and another Tourte bow in 1937. In 1936 she established an endowment fund in the Library of Congress to provide public concerts at which these instruments would be used, and in 1938 the Whittall Pavilion was built in the library to house them and to serve other purposes in the musical life of the library. In subsequent years, she continued to add to her gifts to the library on behalf of both music and literature; one series enabled the Whittall Foundation to acquire many valuable autograph MSS of composers from Bach to Schoenberg, and in particular the finest single group of Brahms MSS gathered anywhere in the world.

BIBL.: W. Orcutt, *The Stradivari Memorial at Washington* (Washington, D.C., 1938); E. Waters, *Autograph Musical Scores in the W. Foundation Collection* (Washington, D.C., 1951).

Whittenberg, Charles, American composer; b. St. Louis, July 6, 1927; d. Hartford, Conn., Aug. 22, 1984. He studied with Burrill Phillips and Bernard Rogers at the Eastman School of Music in Rochester, N.Y. (B.A., 1948); in 1962, became affiliated with the Columbia-Princeton Electronic Music Center and taught at Bennington (Vt.) College; ed. the *American Composers Alliance Bulletin* (1961–63). After teaching at the Center of Liberal Studies in Washington, D.C. (1965), he was associate prof. at the Univ. of Connecticut in Storrs (1967–77), where he became director of Contemporary Music Projects. He received Guggenheim fellowships in 1963 and 1964, and the prize of the American Academy in Rome (1965–66). He was especially adept at writing music for brass instruments.

WORKS: *Dialogue and Aria* for Flute and Piano (1956); *Study* for Cello and Tape (1960); *Structures* for 2 Pianos (1961); *Fantasy* for Wind Quintet (1961); *Electronic Study II* for Double Bass and Tape (1961); *Triptych* for Brass Quintet (1962); *Event* for Chamber Orch. and tape (1963; N.Y., April 28, 1964); Chamber Concerto for Violin and 7 Instrumentalists (1963); *Duo-Divertimento* for Flute and Double Bass (1963); Variations for 9 Players (1964; rev. 1970); 2 string quartets (1965; 1974–75); *Polyphony* for Trumpet (1965); *3 Compositions* for Piano (1967; rev. 1969); Sextet (1967); *Games of 5* for Wind Quintet (1968); *Iambi* for 2 Oboes (1968; rev. 1972); Concerto for Brass Quintet (1968–69); *In Memoriam Benjamin Britten* for Percussion (1977).

Whythorne, Thomas, English lutenist, teacher, and composer; b. Ilminster, 1528; d. London, July 31(?), 1596. He attended Magdalen College School, Oxford, and matriculated at Magdalen College; then was a servant and scholar to John Heyward, during which time he took up the virginals and lute and learned to write English verse; subsequently was in the service of the Duchess of Northumberland. After traveling on the Continent (c.1553–55), he returned to England; was in the service of various patrons. In 1571 he was named master of music at the chapel of Archbishop Parker. His *Songes for Three, Fower and Five Voyces* (London, 1571) were the 1st in that genre to be publ. in England; later brought out *Duos, or Songs for Two Voices* (London, 1590). His autobiography (c.1576), discovered in 1955, was publ. in Oxford in 1961 in his original phonetic spelling, and reprinted in modern spelling in 1963, ed. by J.M. Osborn.

BIBL.: P. Warlock, *T. W.: An Unknown Elizabethan Composer* (London, 1925); J. Jobling, *A Critical Study and Partial Transcription of the Two Published Collections of T. W.* (diss., Univ. of Sheffield, 1978).

Wich, Günther, German conductor; b. Bamberg, May 23, 1928. He studied flute with Gustav Scheck in Freiburg im Breisgau (1948–52); in 1952 he made his conducting debut there, serving as chief conductor of its Opera until 1959; then was conductor of the Graz Opera (1959–61); later was Generalmusikdirektor in Hannover (1961–65) and at the Deutsche Oper am Rhein in Düsseldorf (1965–80). In 1982 he joined the faculty of the Würzburg Hochschule für Musik.

Wickham, Florence, American contralto and composer; b. Beaver, Pa., 1880; d. N.Y., Oct. 20, 1962. She studied in Philadelphia; then was a pupil of Franz Emerich in Berlin; also studied with Mathilde Mallinger. In 1902 she made her operatic debut as Meyerbeer's Fidès in Wiesbaden; after appearances in Schwerin and Munich, she sang the role of Kundry in *Parsifal* in Henry W. Savage's touring opera troupe in America (1904–5). In 1908 she appeared in Wagnerian roles at London's Covent Garden. On Nov. 17, 1909, she made her Metropolitan Opera debut in N.Y. as Verdi's Emilia; remained on its roster until 1912, then sang in concerts and devoted herself to composition. She wrote the operettas *Rosalynd* (1938) and *The Legend of Hex Mountain* (1957), as well as a number of songs.

Wicks, (Edward) Allan, English organist and choirmaster; b. Harden, Yorkshire, June 6, 1923. He studied organ with Thomas Armstrong at Christ Church, Oxford; also was made a Fellow of the Royal College of Organists. He was assistant organist at York Minster (1947–54); after serving as organist and choirmaster at Manchester Cathedral (1954–61), he distinguished himself in those capacities at Canterbury Cathedral (1961–88); also toured as a recitalist in England, Europe, and the U.S. In 1974 he was awarded a D.Mus. by the Archbishop of Canterbury and in 1985 was given an honorary D.Mus. by the Univ. of Kent; in 1988 he was made a Commander of the Order of the British Empire. His repertoire is exhaustive, ranging from early music to modern English compositions.

Widerkehr (also **Wiederkehr** or **Viderkehr**), **Jacques (-Christian-Michel),** Alsatian composer and cellist; b. Strasbourg, April 18, 1759; d. Paris, April 1823. He studied with F.X. Richter and Dumonchau in Strasbourg; settled about 1783 in Paris, where he was active as a cellist. He became well known as a composer of symphonies concertantes for wind instruments. He also wrote an opera, *Oreste;* Revolutionary hymns; and much chamber music, including 2 sonatas for Piano with Violin and Bass Accompaniment, 6 *Duo concertants* for 2 Violins or Cellos (Paris, c.1794), 3 *quatuors concertants* for String Quartet (Paris, 1797), 3 *quatuors* (Paris, c.1803), 1er *quintetto* for 2 Violins, 2 Violas, and Cello (Paris, c.1808), 3 duos for Piano and Violin or Oboe or Clarinet (Paris, c.1817), 4 *quatuors* (Paris, c.1819), and 3 trios for Flute, Horn, and Bassoon (Paris, c.1820). He has often been confused with the trombonist, teacher, and composer Philippe Widerkehr, who was active in Paris (1793–1816) and who may have been his brother.

Widmann, Erasmus, distinguished German organist, instrumentalist, teacher, and composer; b. Schwäbisch Hall (baptized), Sept. 15, 1572; d. Rothenburg ob der Tauber, Oct. 31, 1634. While attending the Schwäbisch Hall Lateinschule, he learned to play the organ, harpsichord, lute, viol, flute, trombone, and zither; then pursued his education at the Univ. of Tübingen (B.A., 1590). By 1595 he was organist in Eisenerz, Styria; then was organist in Graz (1596–98). He subsequently returned to Schwäbisch Hall as Kantor. From 1602 to 1613 he was Präzeptor and organist at the Weickersheim court. In 1613 he went to Rothenburg ob der Tauber as Präzeptor and Kantor; in 1614 he also became organist at the Jacobskirche there. His last years were made miserable by the 30 Years' War. His wife and daughter died of the plague, which also claimed him. He was a significant composer of instrumental and vocal music, both sacred and secular. A selected edition of his works was ed. by G. Reichert in Das Erbe Deutscher Musik, Sonderreihe, III (1955).

WRITINGS: *Musicae praecepta latino-germanica in usum studiosae juventutis* (Rothenburg ob der Tauber, 1614).

BIBL.: E. Schmidt, *Zur Geschichte des Gottesdienstes und der Kirchenmusik in Rothenburg ob der Tauber* (Rothenburg ob der Tauber, 1905); Graf zu Eulenberg, *E. W.s Leben und Werke* (Munich, 1907); G. Reichert, *E. W.: Leben, Wirken und Werke eines württembergisch-fränkischen Musikers* (Stuttgart, 1951).

Widmann, Joseph Viktor, Swiss writer and journalist; b. Nennowitz, Moravia, Feb. 20, 1842; d. Bern, Nov. 6, 1911. He was educated in Basel, Heidelberg, and Jena; was taken to Switzerland as a child; became engaged in the literary profession; was well known as a dramatist; from 1880 he was literary ed. of the *Berner Bund;* he also wrote librettos. He was a friend of Brahms, and publ. *Johannes Brahms in Erinnerungen* (Berlin, 1898; new ed. by W. Reich, Basel, 1947).

BIBL.: E. and M. Widmann, *J.V. W.* (2 vols., 1922, 1924); M. Waser, *J.V. W.* (Leipzig, 1927).

Widor, Charles-Marie (-Jean-Albert), distinguished French organist, pedagogue, and composer; b. Lyons, Feb. 21, 1844; d. Paris, March 12, 1937. His father, an Alsatian of Hungarian descent, was organist at the church of St.-François in Lyons and was active as an organ builder. Widor was a skillful improviser on the organ while still a boy, and became organist at the Lyons lycée when he was 11. After studies with Fétis (composition) and Lemmens (organ) in Brussels,

he became organist at St.-François in Lyons (1860), and gained high repute via provincial concerts. In 1870–71 he held a provisional appointment as organist at St.-Sulpice in Paris, where he served as organist from 1871 until 1934. On April 19, 1934, he played his *Pièce mystique* there, composed at age 90. Around 1880 he began writing music criticism under the pen name "Aulétès" for the daily *L'Estafette.* In 1890 he became prof. of organ and in 1896 prof. of composition at the Paris Cons. In 1910 he was elected a member of the Académie des Beaux-Arts, of which he became permanent secretary in 1913. He had many distinguished pupils, including Albert Schweitzer, with whom he collaborated in editing the 1st 5 vols. of an 8-vol. ed. of J.S. Bach's organ works (N.Y., 1912–14). As a composer, he wrote copiously in many forms but is best known for his organ music, especially his 10 "symphonies" (suites). A master organ virtuoso, he won great renown for his performances of Bach and for his inspired improvisations.

WORKS: STAGE (all 1st perf. in Paris): *Maître Ambros,* opera (May 6, 1886); *Les Pêcheurs de Saint-Jean,* opera (Dec. 26, 1905); *Nerto,* opera (Oct. 27, 1924); *La Korrigane,* ballet (Dec. 1, 1880); *Jeanne d'Arc,* ballet-pantomime (1890); incidental music to *Conte d'avril* (Sept. 22, 1885) and to *Les Jacobites* (Nov. 21, 1885). ORCH.: Syms.: No. 1 (c.1870); No. 2 (1886); No. 3 for Organ and Orch. (1895); *Sinfonia sacra* for Organ and Orch. (1908); *Symphonie antique* for Organ and Orch. (1911); 2 piano concertos (1876, 1906); Cello Concerto (1882); *La Nuit de Walpurgis,* symphonic poem for Chorus and Orch. (c.1887; London, April 19, 1888); *Fantaisie* for Piano and Orch. (1889); *Ouverture espagnole* (1898); *Choral et variations* for Harp and Orch. (1900). CHAMBER: 2 piano quintets (c.1890, 1896); Piano Quartet (1891); Piano Trio (1875); *Sérénade* for Piano, Flute, Violin, Cello, and Harmonium (c.1883); *4 pièces* for Piano, Violin, and Cello (1890); *Suite* for Flute and Piano (1898); *Soirs d'Alsace* for Piano, Violin, and Cello (1908); *Introduction et rondo* for Clarinet and Piano (1898); *3 pièces* for Oboe and Piano (1909); *Suite* for Cello and Piano (1912); *Suite florentine* for Piano and Flute or Violin (1920). PIANO: *Variations de concert sur un thème original* (1867); *6 morceaux de salon* (1872); *6 valses caractéristiques* (1877); *12 feuillets d'album* (1877); *La Barque* (1877); *La Corricolo* (1877); *Suite polonaise* (c.1885); *Suite* (c.1887); *Conte d'automne* (1904); *Suite écossaise* (c.1905). ORGAN: 10 syms.: Nos. 1–4 (1876); Nos. 5–8 (c.1880); *Symphonie gothique* (1895); *Symphonie romaine* (1900); *Suite latine* (1927); *3 nouvelles pièces* (1934); *Pièce mystique* (c.1934); 8 sonatas; also many vocal works, both sacred and secular, with instrumental and orch. accompaniment.

WRITINGS (all publ. in Paris): *Technique de l'orchestre moderne* (1904; 5th ed., rev. and enl., 1925; Eng. tr., 1906; 2nd ed., rev., 1946); *Notice sur la vie et les œuvres de Camille Saint-Saëns* (1922); *Initiation musicale* (1923); *Académie des Beaux-Arts: Fondations, portraits de Massenet à Paladilhe* (1927); *L'Orgue moderne: La Décadence dans la facture contemporaine* (1928).

BIBL.: H. Reynaud, *L'Œuvre de C.-M. W.* (Lyons, 1900); J. Rupp, *C.-M. W. und sein Werk* (Bremen, 1912); L. Vierne, "C.-M. W.," *Les Amis de l'Orgue,* nos. 30–31 (1937); G. Bret, "Les Symphonies pour orgue de C.-M. W.," ibid. (Sept. 1938); I. Philipp, "C.-M. W.: A Portrait," *Musical Quarterly* (April 1944); J. Handschin, "C.-M. W.," *Gedenkschrift Jacques Handschin* (Bern and Stuttgart, 1957); E. Marhefka, "W.s Orgelkompositionen," *Musik und Kirche,* XXIX (1959); A. Thomson, *The Life and Times of C.-M. W., 1844–1937* (Oxford, 1988).

Wiechowicz, Stanislaw, Polish composer and pedagogue; b. Kroszyce, Nov. 27, 1893; d. Krakow, May 12, 1963. He studied successively in Krakow, Dresden, St. Petersburg, and Paris; taught at the Poznań Cons. (1921–39); from 1945 to his death, taught at the State College of Music in Krakow.

WORKS: ORCH.: *Babie lato* (Martinmas Summer), symphonic poem (1922); *Chmiel* (The Hopvine), symphonic scherzo (1926); *Ulegalki* (The Wild Pears), symphonic portraits (1944); *Kasia* (Kate), folk suite for 2 Clarinets and Strings

(1946); *Koncert staromiejski* (Old Town Concerto) for Strings (1954). **VOCAL:** *Pastoralki*, Christmas cantata for Voice, Chorus, and Percussion (1929); *Kantata romantyczna* for Soprano, Chorus, and Orch. (1930); *Kantata zniwna* (Harvest Cantata) for Chorus (1948); *A czemuześ nie przyjechal?* (Why Did You Not Come?), rustic scene for Chorus and Orch. (1948); *List do Marc Chagalla* (Letter to Marc Chagall), dramatic rhapsody for 2 Solo Voices, Male Speaker, Female Speaker, Chorus, and Orch. (1961); *Zstąp, golębico* (O Dove, Descend), cantata for Soprano, Chorus, and Orch. (1962–63); many other vocal works; numerous folk-song arrangements.

BIBL.: S. Kisielewski, "S. W. 1893–1963," *Ruch muzyczny*, no. 12 (1963).

Wieck, family of German musicians:
(1) (Johann Gottlob) Friedrich Wieck, music pedagogue; b. Pretzsch, near Torgau, Aug. 18, 1785; d. Loschwitz, near Dresden, Oct. 6, 1873. After studying music with P.-J. Milchmeyer in Torgau, he pursued training in theology at the Univ. of Wittenberg; then was active as a private tutor. In 1816 he went to Leipzig as a music teacher; in 1818 he founded a piano factory and a circulating music library, but eventually devoted himself entirely to pedagogy; in 1843 Mendelssohn offered him a professorship in piano at the newly organized Leipzig Cons., which he declined; in 1844 he settled in Dresden. In 1871 he helped to establish the Wieck-Stiftung to assist musically gifted youths. He married Marianne Tromlitz in 1816; after their divorce in 1824, she married his old friend Adolf Bargiel; the product of this marriage was Woldemar Bargiel. In 1828 Wieck married Clementine Fechner. He won great distinction as a pedagogue. Among his pupils were his daughters **Clara** and **Marie,** his son **Alwin,** Hans von Bülow, Fritz Spindler, Isidor Seiss, and Gustav Merkel. He was also Robert Schumann's teacher, but bitterly opposed Schumann's marriage to his daughter Clara. He publ. *Klavier und Gesang* (Leipzig, 1853; 3rd ed., augmented, 1878; Eng. tr., 1878) and *Musikalische Bauernspruche* (Dresden, 1871; 2nd ed., 1876); also publ. studies and dances for piano, songs, and singing exercises; ed. piano pieces. For a biography of his daughter Clara, see **Schumann, Clara (Josephine)** (née **Wieck**). Biographies of his other children are as follows:
(2) Alwin Wieck, violinist, pianist, and teacher; b. Leipzig, Aug. 27, 1821; d. Dresden, Oct. 21, 1885. He studied piano with his father and violin with David; after playing violin in the St. Petersburg Italian Opera orch. (1849–59), he settled in Dresden as a music teacher. He publ. *Materialen zu Friedrich Wiecks Pianoforte-Methodik* (Berlin, 1875) and *Vademecum perpetuum für den ersten Pianoforte-Unterricht nach Fr. Wiecks Methode* (Leipzig, c.1875); also wrote piano music.
(3) Marie Wieck, pianist and teacher; b. Leipzig, Jan. 17, 1832; d. Dresden, Nov. 2, 1916. She studied with her father; at the age of 11, made her debut at a concert given by her half sister, Clara Schumann; was appointed court pianist to the Prince of Hohenzollern in 1858; after tours of Germany, England, and Scandinavia, she settled in Dresden as a teacher of piano and singing. Her last public appearance was with the Dresden Phil. in Nov. 1915, playing the Schumann Concerto. She publ. piano pieces and songs; ed. her father's *Pianoforte-Studien*; wrote *Aus dem Kreise Wieck-Schumann* (1912; 2nd ed., augmented, 1914).

BIBL.: A. von Meichsner, *F. W. und seine beiden Töchter Clara Schumann, geb. Wieck, und Marie Wieck* (Leipzig, 1875); A. Kohut, *F. W.: Ein Lebens- und Künsterbild* (Dresden, 1888); V. Joss, *F. W. und sein Verhältnis zu Robert Schumann* (Leipzig, 1900); idem, *Der Musikpädagoge F. W. und seine Familie* (Dresden, 1902); M. Wieck, *Aus dem Kreise W.-Schumann* (Dresden, 1912; 2nd ed., 1914); T. Müller-Reuter, "F. W.," *Bilder und Klänge des Friedens* (Leipzig, 1919); K. Walch-Schumann, *F. W.: Briefe aus den Jahren 1830–1838* (Cologne, 1968).

Wiedebein, Gottlob, German organist, conductor, and composer; b. Eilenstadt, July 27, 1779; d. Braunschweig, April 17, 1854. After studying in Braunschweig with his uncle and J. Schwanenberger, he was active as a teacher until being made principal conductor of the court orch. (1816) and opera (1818); was compelled by ill health to give up his posts in 1832. He enjoyed a great reputation; Schumann sought his advice. He wrote some excellent lieder. Among his other works are an overture, the oratorio *Die Befreiung Deutschlands* (c.1822), various cantatas and motets, piano pieces, and organ music.

BIBL.: F. Jansen, "Briefwechsel Beethovens und Schumanns mit Cplm. G. W.," *Neue Zeitschrift für Musik*, LXXVI (1880); P. Merbach, "Aus vergangenen Tagen: Briefe von Poissl, Bader, Lindpaintner und Spohr an G. W.," ibid., Jg.78 (1911); idem, "Aus den Briefschaften G. W.s," *Jahrbuch des Geschichtsverein für das Herzogtum Braunschweig*, XI (1912); E. Anderson, ed., *The Letters of Beethoven* (London, 1961).

Wiedemann, Ernst Johann, German organist, conductor, teacher, and composer; b. Hohengiersdorf, Silesia, March 28, 1797; d. Potsdam, Dec. 7, 1873. From 1818 to 1852 he was organist of the Roman Catholic Church in Berlin; founded and conducted 2 singing societies there; composed a Te Deum for Soli, Chorus, and Orch.; masses; motets; hymns.

Wiegand, (Josef Anton) Heinrich, German bass; b. Fränkisch-Crumbach in the Odenwald, Sept. 9, 1842; d. Frankfurt am Main, May 28, 1899. He studied voice privately in Paris; became a member of the opera at Zürich in 1870; then sang in Cologne, and from 1873 to 1877 was the leading bass at the Frankfurt Opera. In 1877 he toured America with the Adams-Pappenheim troupe; was in Leipzig (1878–82); sang at the Vienna Court Opera (1882–84); then was engaged at Hamburg. He also appeared in the *Ring* cycle in Berlin (1881) and London (1882).

Wiel, Taddeo, Italian musicologist and composer; b. Oderzo, Treviso, Sept. 24, 1849; d. Venice, Feb. 17, 1920. He studied in Venice; was assistant librarian of the Venice Biblioteca Marciana. He composed some vocal music and piano pieces, and prepared librettos, but his importance rests upon his work as a musicologist.

WRITINGS: All publ. in Venice: *I codici musicali contariniani del secolo XVII nella R. Biblioteca di San Marco in Venezia* (1888); *Benedetto Marcello: un prologo e un sonetto satirico* (1894); *I teatri musicali veneziani del settecento: Catalogo delle opere in musica rappresentate nel secolo XVIII in Venezia* (1897).

BIBL.: R. Strohm, "T. W. und die venezianische Opernbibliographie," *Deutsches Jahrbuch der Musikwissenschaft*, XVIII (1973–77).

Wielhorsky, Count Mikhail, Russian patron of the arts and composer of Polish descent; b. Volhynia, Nov. 11, 1788; d. Moscow, Sept. 9, 1856. His principal mentor in music was Martín y Soler; he learned to play the violin and piano, and began composing at 13. After studying counterpoint in Riga, he completed his studies with Cherubini in Paris (1808). In 1810 he went to St. Petersburg, where his home became the gathering place of many eminent musicians; in 1816 he went to live at his estate in the Kursk province, where he maintained a private concert. After living in Moscow (1823–26) and again in St. Petersburg (1826–56), he spent his last days at his estate near Moscow. His brother, **Count Matvei Wielhorsky** (b. St. Petersburg, April 26, 1794; d. Nice, March 3, 1866), was also a patron of the arts as well as a cellist; he studied cello with Adolph Meinhardt and Bernard Romberg; toured throughout Russia and in Europe. He lived with his brother in St. Petersburg (1826–56), where he helped to organize the city's branch of the Russian Musical Soc. in 1859. A distant relative, Joseph Wielhorsky (1817–92), was also a musician; wrote piano pieces and songs.

WORKS: *Tsigane* (The Gypsies), opera (1838); 3 syms. (1822, 1822, n.d.); 2 overtures (1822, 1836); *Air varié* for Cello and Orch.; *Theme varié*; String Quartet; String Quintet; piano pieces; many choral works and songs.

Wiéner, Jean, French pianist and composer of Austrian parentage; b. Paris, March 19, 1896; d. there, June 8, 1982. He studied with Gédalge at the Paris Cons. From 1920 to 1924 he presented the Concerts Jean Wiéner, devoted to the energetic propaganda of new music; he presented several world premieres of works by modern French composers; also performed pieces by Schoenberg, Berg, and Webern. He was the first Frenchman to proclaim jazz as a legitimate art form; also teamed with Clément Doucet in duo-piano recitals, in programs stretching from Mozart to jazz. His compositions reflect his ecumenical convictions, as exemplified in such works as *Concerto franco-américain* for Clarinet and Strings (1923) and a desegregationist operetta, *Olive chez les nègres* (1926). He also wrote an Accordion Concerto (1957) and a Concerto for 2 Guitars (1966), but he became famous mainly for his idiosyncratic film music.

Wiener, Otto, Austrian baritone; b. Vienna, Feb. 13, 1913. He was educated in Vienna; made his concert debut in 1939 and his operatic debut in 1953 as Simon Boccanegra in Graz. He sang in Düsseldorf, Frankfurt, Stuttgart, and Berlin. In 1957 he became a member of the Vienna State Opera; from 1960 to 1970 he sang at the Bavarian State Opera in Munich; later filled engagements as a guest artist in various European music centers. On Oct. 18, 1962, he made his Metropolitan Opera debut in N.Y. as Hans Sachs. His other important roles included the Dutchman, Gunther, and Wotan.

Wieniawski, Adam Tadeusz, Polish composer, nephew of **Henryk** and **Józef Wieniawski;** b. Warsaw, Nov. 27, 1879; d. Bydgoszcz, April 21, 1950. He studied in Warsaw with H. Melcer-Szczawiński and Z. Noskowski; then in Berlin with Bargiel, and in Paris with d'Indy, Fauré, and Gédalge. He fought in the French army during World War I; returned to Warsaw in 1918 as a teacher at the Chopin School of Music; was appointed its director in 1928.

WORKS: OPERAS: *Megaïe* (1910; Warsaw, Dec. 28, 1912); *Zofka*, comic opera (1923); *Wyzwolony* (The Freed Man; Warsaw, July 5, 1928); *Król Kochanek* (The King as Paramour), musical comedy (Warsaw, March 19, 1931). BALLETS: *Lalita* (1922) and *Aktea w Jerozolimie* (Actea in Jerusalem; Warsaw, June 4, 1927); also orch. pieces, including *Bajeczki* (Tittletattle), sinfonietta, and 8 symphonic poems; chamber music; piano pieces; folk-song arrangements.

Wieniawski, Henryk (also known as **Henri**), famous Polish violinist, teacher, and composer, brother of **Józef** and uncle of **Adam Tadeusz Wieniawski;** b. Lublin, July 10, 1835; d. Moscow, March 31, 1880. His mother, Regina Wolff-Wieniawska, was a talented pianist; he began training with Jan Hornziel and Stanisław Serwaczyński in Warsaw; upon the advice of his mother's brother, **Edouard Wolff,** who lived in France, she took Henryk to Paris, where he entered the Cons. at the age of 8, first in Clavel's class, and the following year, in the advanced class of Massart. At the age of 11 he graduated with 1st prize in violin, an unprecedented event in the annals of the Paris Cons. After further private studies with Massart (1846–48), he made his Paris debut on Jan. 30, 1848, in a concert accompanied by his brother at the piano; gave his 1st concert in St. Petersburg on March 31, 1848, and played 4 more concerts there; then played in Finland and the Baltic provinces; after several successful appearances in Warsaw, he returned in 1849 to Paris, where he studied composition with Hippolyte Collet at the Cons., graduating with an "accessit" prize in 1850. From 1851 to 1853 he gave about 200 concerts in Russia with his brother. He also devoted much time to composition, and by age 18 had composed and publ. his virtuoso 1st Violin Concerto, which he played with extraordinary success in Leipzig that same year. In 1858 he appeared with Anton Rubinstein in Paris and in 1859 in the Beethoven Quartet Society concerts in London, where he appeared as a violist as well as a violinist. In 1860 he went to St. Petersburg and was named solo violinist to the Czar, and also concertmaster of the orch. and 1st violinist of the string quartet of the Russian Musical Soc.; likewise served as prof. of violin at the newly founded Cons. (1862–68). He continued to compose and introduced his greatly esteemed 2nd Violin

Concerto in St. Petersburg on Nov. 27, 1862, with Rubinstein conducting. In 1872 he went on a tour of the U.S. with Rubinstein; one of the featured works was Beethoven's *Kreutzer Sonata*, which they performed about 70 times. When Rubinstein returned to Europe, Wieniawski continued his American tour, which included California. He returned to Europe in 1874, gave several concerts with Rubinstein in Paris, and in the same year succeeded Vieuxtemps as prof. of violin at the Brussels Cons., resigning in 1877 owing to an increasingly grave heart condition; he suffered an attack during a concert in Berlin on Nov. 11, 1878, but still agreed to play several concerts in Russia; made his farewell appearance in Odessa in April 1879. His last months were spent in Moscow, where he was taken to the home of Madame von Meck, Tchaikovsky's patroness, in Feb. 1880. He was married to Isobel Hampton, an Englishwoman; their youngest daughter, Irene, wrote music under the pen name Poldowski. Wieniawski was undoubtedly one of the greatest violinists of the 19th century; he possessed a virtuoso technique and an extraordinary range of dynamics. He was equally distinguished as a chamber music player. As a composer, he remains best known today for his 2 violin concertos and an outstanding set of études. He also composed numerous other orch. works as well as pieces for solo or 2 violins. A complete ed. of his works commenced publication in Krakow in 1962.

BIBL.: A. Desfossez, *Henri W.: Esquisse* (The Hague, 1856); J. Reiss, *Henryk W.* (Warsaw, 1931; 2nd ed., 1970); I. Yampolsky, *G. Vinyavsky* (Moscow, 1955); V. Grigoriev, *G. Vinyavsky* (Moscow, 1966); W. Dulęba, *Henryk W.* (Krakow, 1967); B. Schwarz, *Great Masters of the Violin* (N.Y., 1983); W. Grigoriew, *Henryk W.: Zycie i twórczość* (Warsaw, 1986).

Wieniawski, Józef, distinguished Polish pianist, pedagogue, and composer, brother of **Henryk** and uncle of **Adam Tadeusz Wieniawski;** b. Lublin, May 23, 1837; d. Brussels, Nov. 11, 1912. He studied piano with Synek in Lublin, and at age 10 entered the Paris Cons., where he received lessons in piano from Zimmerman, Marmontel, and Alkan and in composition from LeCouppey (graduated, 1850). He toured Russia with his brother (1851–53), then was awarded a scholarship from the Czar for study with Liszt in Weimar (1855–56); received training in theory from A.B. Marx in Berlin (1856–58). He taught piano at the Russian Musical Soc. in Moscow (1864–65), then taught piano for 1 term at the Moscow Cons. before resuming private teaching. In 1875–76 he was director of the Warsaw Musical Soc., with which he appeared as a chamber music artist and as a choral conductor; then was prof. of piano at the Brussels Cons. (1878–1912).

WORKS: ORCH.: Sym.; Piano Concerto; *Fantasia* for 2 Pianos and Orch.; *Suite romantique; Guillaume de Paciturne,* overture. CHAMBER: Violin Sonata; Cello Sonata; String Quartet; Piano Trio. SOLO PIANO: 5 waltzes; 2 tarantellas; 3 fantasias; 2 barcarolles; 4 polonaises; Sonata; 9 mazurkas; 2 études de concert; 24 études; also vocal music.

BIBL.: J. Delcroix, *Joseph W.: Notices biographiques et anecdotiques* (Brussels, 1908).

Wieprecht, Friedrich Wilhelm, German trombonist and inventor; b. Aschersleben, Aug. 8, 1802; d. Berlin, Aug. 4, 1872. He studied in Dresden and Leipzig, where he was already famous as a trombonist. He invented the bass tuba (1835, with the instrument maker Moritz); the bathyphon, a contrabass clarinet (1839, with Skorra); the "piangendo" on brass instruments with pistons; and an improved contrabass bassoon; his claim of priority over Sax, in the invention of the saxhorns, remains moot.

BIBL.: A. Kalkbrenner, *W. W., Direktor: Sein Leben und Wirken nebst einem Auszug seiner Schriften* (Berlin, 1882).

Wier, Albert Ernest, American music editor; b. Chelsea, Mass., July 22, 1879; d. N.Y., Sept. 8, 1945. He studied music at the New England Cons. of Music in Boston and at Harvard Univ.; from 1900, was music ed. for various publ. firms in N.Y.; ed. many collections and arrangements; devised the "arrow signal" system, in which arrows and other markings are added to orch. scores to identify the main themes; used the system in numerous collections; ed. *The Macmillan Encyclopedia of Music and Musicians* (1938; withdrawn from circulation owing to an excessive number of demonstrable errors) and other reference works of questionable scholarship.

Wiesengrund-Adorno, Theodor. See **Adorno, Theodor.**

Wieslander, (Axel Otto) Ingvar, Swedish composer and conductor; b. Jönköping, May 19, 1917; d. Malmö, April 29, 1963. He studied at the Royal Academy of Music in Stockholm; also took lessons in composition from S.-E. Svensson in Uppsala. He was music director of the Sundbyberg Orch. Society (1944–47); then music director (1949–60) and choirmaster (1960–63) of the Malmö Municipal Theater. His music followed the eclectic modalities of Scandinavian Romanticism; but he was not averse to circumspect experimentation in modernistic modalities, including a mitigated dodecaphonic scheme, while steadfastly maintaining the framework of Baroque forms.

WORKS: 2 chamber operas: *Fröknarna i parken* (1953) and *Skålknallen* (1958; Malmö, Feb. 7, 1959); 2 ballets: *Nordisk saga* (1950) and *Skymningslekar* (1954); 6 syms.: Sym. in D (1951); *Sinfonia piccola* (1953); *Sinfonia notturna* (1954); *Sinfonia seria* (1956); *Sinfonia da camera* (1962); *Sinfonia ecloga,* with Solo Soprano (1962); *Overtura giocosa* (1957); Concerto for String Orch. (1961); *Förspel (Intrada seria)* for Orch. (1961); *Mutazioni* for 2 Pianos and Orch. (Malmö, Nov. 27, 1962); 5 string quartets (1948; 1949, rev. 1954; 1957; 1958; 1961); choruses; songs.

Wigglesworth, Frank, American composer and teacher; b. Boston, March 3, 1918. He was educated at Columbia Univ. (B.S., 1940) and Converse College, Spartanburg, S.C. (M.Mus., 1942), his principal mentors being Ernest White, Luening, and Cowell; also studied with Varèse (1948–51). He taught at Converse College (1941–42), Greenwich House, N.Y. (1946–47), Columbia Univ. and Barnard College (1947–51), and Queens College of the City Univ. of N.Y. (1955–56); in 1954 he joined the faculty of the New School for Social Research in N.Y., where he was chairman of the music dept. (from 1965); also taught at the Dalcroze School in N.Y. (from 1959) and at the City Univ. of N.Y. (1970–76). From 1951 to 1954 he was a fellow and in 1969–70 composer-in-residence at the American Academy in Rome; held MacDowell Colony fellowships in 1965 and 1972; in 1985 he was composer-in-residence at Bennington College's Chamber Music Conference and Composers' Forum of the East. He is a great-nephew of **Elizabeth Sprague Coolidge**. His output reflects a fine command of orch., instrumental, and vocal writing; he makes use of both tonal and atonal techniques.

WORKS: STAGE: *Young Goodman Brown,* ballet (1951); *Between the Atoms and the Stars,* musical play (1959); *Ballet for Esther Brooks,* ballet (1961); *The Willowdale Handcar,* opera (1969); incidental music to Shakespeare's *Hamlet* (1960). **ORCH.:** *New England Concerto* for Violin and Strings (1941); *Music* for Strings (1946); *Fantasia* for Strings (1947); *3 Movements* for Strings (1949); *Summer Scenes* (1951); *Telesis* (1951); Concertino for Piano and Strings (1953); 3 syms. (1953, 1958, 1960); *Concert Piece* (1954); Concertino for Viola and Orch. (1965); *3 Portraits* for Strings (1970); *Music* for Strings (1981); *Aurora* (1983); *Sea Winds* (1984). **CHAMBER:** Trio for Flute, Banjo, and Harp (1942); *Serenade* for Flute, Viola, and Guitar (1954); Brass Quintet (1958); Harpsichord Sonata (1960); Viola Sonata (1965); String Trio (1972); Woodwind Quintet (1975); *4 Winds* for Horn, 2 Trumpets, and Trombone (1978); Brass Quintet (1980); Viola Sonata (1980); *After Summer Music* for Flute, Viola, and Guitar (1983); *Honeysuckle* for Viola (1984); piano pieces. **VOCAL:** *Isaiah* for Chorus and Orch. (1942); *Sleep Becalmed* for Chorus and Orch. (1950); *Super flumina Babilonis* for Chorus (1965); *Psalm CXLVIII* for Chorus, 3 Flutes, and 3 Trombones (1973); *Duets,* song cycle for Mezzo-soprano and Clarinet (1977–78); various masses, anthems, and solo songs.

Wihan, Hans (actually, **Hanuš**), noted Czech cellist and pedagogue; b. Politz, near Braunau, Bohemia, June 5, 1855; d. Prague, May 1, 1920. He studied at the Prague Cons. with František Hegenbarth; while still a young man, he taught cello at the Salzburg Mozarteum; completed his studies with C. Davidov. He played in orchs. in Nice, Prague, Berlin, Sondershausen, and Munich; in 1888 he succeeded Hegenbarth as prof. of cello and chamber music at the Prague Cons. In 1891 he formed the Bohemian String Quartet, selecting his four most talented pupils (Karel Hoffmann, Josef Suk, Oscar Nedbal, and Otto Berger); after Berger's retirement in 1897, owing to ill health, Wihan himself took his place as cellist (until 1914); also toured widely as a soloist in Europe. In 1919 he resumed his position at the Prague Cons. Dvořák wrote his Cello Concerto for Wihan; however, the 2 had a falling out and the 1st performance was given by Leo Stern; Strauss wrote his E-flat major Sonata for him.

Wihtol (Vitols), Joseph (actually, **Jāzeps**), eminent Latvian composer and pedagogue; b. Volmar, July 26, 1863; d. Lübeck, April 24, 1948. He studied at the St. Petersburg Cons. (1880–86) with Rimsky-Korsakov; after graduation, was engaged as an instructor there; succeeded Rimsky-Korsakov in 1908 as prof. of composition; among his students were Prokofiev and Miaskovsky. He was also music critic for the German daily *St. Petersburger Zeitung* (1897–1914). In 1918 he left St. Petersburg; was director of the Latvian Opera in Riga (from 1918); in 1919, founded the National Cons. there, serving as its rector from 1919 to 1935 and again from 1937 to 1944; many Latvian composers were his students. As the Soviet armies approached Riga (1944), Wihtol went to Germany, remaining there until his death. His autobiography and collection of writings appeared in 1944. He composed the 1st Latvian sym. In his music he followed the harmonic practices of the Russian school, but often employed Latvian folk-song patterns.

WORKS: Sym. (St. Petersburg, Dec. 17, 1887); *La Fête Ligho,* symphonic tableau (1890); *Beverinas dziedonis* (The Bard of Beverin) for Chorus and Orch. (1891); *Ouverture dramatique* (1895); *Gaismas pils* (The Castle of Light) for Chorus and Orch. (1899); *Upe un cilvēka dzive* (River and Human Life) for Chorus (1903); *Spriditis,* Latvian fairy tale for Orch. (1908); cantatas: *Song* (1908) and *Aurora Borealis* (1914); arrangements of 200 Latvian songs for voice and piano and for piano solo (2 books; 1906, 1919); many Latvian choral ballads; String Quartet (1899); *10 chants populaires lettons,* "miniature paraphrases" for Piano; songs.

BIBL.: O. Gravitis, *Jāzeps Vītols un latviešu tautas dziesma* (Jāzeps Vitols and Latvian Folk Song; Riga, 1958).

Wijdeveld, Wolfgang, Dutch pianist, teacher, music critic, and composer; b. The Hague, May 9, 1910; d. Laren, Dec. 12, 1985. He was the son of the noted Dutch architect Hendricus Wijdeveld. He studied piano with Willem Andriessen, theory with Sem Dresden, and violin with Kint at the Amsterdam Cons.; also took private lessons in composition with Willem Pijper. He was director of the Zwolle Cons. (1940–46); taught piano at the Utrecht Cons. (1946–76); was music critic for the Amsterdam newspaper *Het Vrije Volk* (1956–68). He toured the U.S. in 1939 with the Yvonne Georgi Ballet as a pianist and composer; gave concerts and seminars at 15 North American univs. (1962–63).

WORKS: *Psalm 150* for Chorus and Orch. (1950); *Concertstük* for Wind Quintet and Strings (1952); *Matrooslied* for Chorus and Small Orch. (1966); Wind Quintet (1934); Trio for Flute, Oboe, and Bassoon (1958); Concerto for Guitar and String Trio (1960); Sonata for 2 Violins and Piano (1952); Violin Sonata (1948); *Sonatine simple* for Violin and Piano (1952); *Introduction and Caprice* for Violin and Piano (1956); Flute Sonatina (1948); *Snarenspel* for Guitar and Piano (1958); Sonatina for Accordion (1963); 3 piano sonatas: No. 1 (1940), No. 2 (1956), and No. 3, *For Americans* (1963); 2 piano sonatinas (1946, 1953); *Escapades* for Piano (1944–45); *Kermesse,* ballet music for 2 Pianos (1935); *Notebooks I–IV* for Piano (1968–69); *Notebook V* for Harpsichord (1968); *Introduction* *and Gigue* for Organ (1949); *3 Songs*, after Walt Whitman, for 2 Voices, Violin, Viola, Clarinet, and Piano (1949); other songs.

Wijk, Arnold(us Christian Vlok) van. See **Wyk, Arnold(us Christian Vlok) van.**

Wiklund, Adolf, Swedish pianist, conductor, and composer; b. Långserud, June 5, 1879; d. Stockholm, April 2, 1950. He studied with J. Lindegren (composition) and R. Andersson (piano) at the Stockholm Cons.; was granted a state fellowship for study abroad; took lessons with James Kwast in Berlin (piano); returning to Sweden in 1911, he became 2nd conductor of the Stockholm Royal Theater; then led the Stockholm Court Orch. (1911–24) and the Concert Soc. Orch. (1925–38); was also a guest conductor in Europe. His works reveal a Romantic bent with later infusions of Impressionism. He composed a Sym. (1923); 2 piano concertos (1906, rev. 1935; 1917); *Konsertstycke* for Piano and Orch. (1902); a symphonic poem, *Sommarnatt och soluppgång* (1918); *Little Suite* for Orch. (1928); *3 Pieces* for String Orch. (1924); Violin Sonata (1906); several albums of lyric pieces for piano; songs.

Wikmanson, Johan, Swedish organist and composer; b. Stockholm, Dec. 28, 1753; d. there, Jan. 10, 1800. He was trained as an engineer, but also had lessons in thoroughbass and piano from H.P. Johnsen; also studied composition with Abbé Vogler and J.M. Kraus. He served as organist at the Dutch Reformed Church (1772–81) and at the Storkyrkan Cathedral (1781–1800); in 1788 he was elected a member of the Royal Academy of Music, where he was made director of education in 1796 and a teacher of harmony and theory in 1797. His output reveals the influence of Kraus, Haydn, and C.P.E. Bach. Among his compositions are music for various stage pieces; *Menuetto allegro* for Orch.; 3 string quartets (publ. in Stockholm, 1801; ed. in Monumenta Musicae Svecicae, II, 1970); a Zither Sonata; numerous keyboard works, including 2 piano sonatas; a cantata, *Häckingen;* and some 30 songs.
BIBL.: C.-G. Mörner, *J. W. und de Brüder Silverstolpe* (diss., Univ. of Uppsala, 1952).

Wilbye, John, important English composer; b. Diss, Norfolk (baptized), March 7, 1574; d. Colchester, c.Sept. 1638. By 1598 he was a musician at Hengrave Hall, the home of Sir Thomas Kytson, near Bury St. Edmunds. After the death of Lady Kytson (1628), he settled in Colchester, where he spent his last years with her daughter, Lady Rivers. During his years at Hengrave, he acquired considerable wealth. He was a master of the madrigal; his *Second Set of Madrigals* (1609) constitutes the most significant collection of English madrigals.
WORKS: *The First Set of English Madrigals* for 3 to 6 Voices (London, 1598; ed. by E. Fellowes, The English Madrigalists; 2nd ed., rev., 1966, by T. Dart); *The Second Set of Madrigals* for 3 to 6 Voices, *Apt both for Voyals and Voyces* (London, 1609; ed. by E. Fellowes, The English Madrigalists; 2nd ed., rev., 1966, by T. Dart); also a few sacred vocal pieces and instrumental works.
BIBL.: E. Fellowes, "J. W.," *Proceedings of the Musical Association,* XLI (1914–15); idem, *The English Madrigal Composers* (Oxford, 1921; 2nd ed., 1948); H. Heurich, *J. W. in seinen Madrigalen: Studien zu einem Bilde seiner Persönlichkeit* (Augsburg, 1931); R. Collet, "J. W.: Some Aspects of His Music," *Score,* no. 4 (1951); D. Brown, *J. W.* (London, 1974).

Wilckens, Friedrich, Austrian pianist and composer; b. Liezen, April 13, 1899; d. Munich, July 27, 1986. He studied piano with Lalewicz in Vienna and composition with Schreker there and in Berlin (1916–20); toured widely as a ballet pianist. He wrote the ballets *Himmel und Erde* and *Schwingender Tempel;* also film scores and piano pieces.

Wild, Earl, greatly talented American pianist; b. Pittsburgh, Nov. 26, 1915. He was a child prodigy; blessed with absolute pitch, he could read music and play piano by age 6; when he was 12, he became a student of Selmar Jansen; also pursued training at the Carnegie Inst. of Technology (graduated, 1934). While still a teenager, he played on KDKA Radio in Pittsburgh

and in the Pittsburgh Sym. Orch. After appearing as a soloist with the NBC Orch. in N.Y. in 1934, he settled there; pursued further training with Egon Petri, and later with Paul Doguereau and Volya Lincoln. In 1937 he became the staff pianist of Toscanini's NBC Sym. Orch. He was the 1st American pianist to give a recital on U.S. television, in 1939. In 1942 he appeared as soloist in Gershwin's *Rhapsody in Blue* with Toscanini and the NBC Sym. Orch. He made his N.Y. recital debut at Town Hall on Oct. 30, 1944. From 1944 to 1968 he worked as a staff pianist, conductor, and composer for ABC while continuing to make occasional appearances as a soloist with orchs. and as a recitalist. After leaving ABC, he pursued a brilliant international career as a virtuoso par excellence; also served as artistic director of the Concert Soloists of Wolf Trap, a chamber ensemble (1978–81). He devoted part of his time to teaching; was on the faculties of Pennsylvania State Univ. (1965–68), the Juilliard School in N.Y. (1977–87), the Manhattan School of Music (1982–84), and Ohio State Univ. (from 1987). Among his compositions are the Easter oratorio *Revelations* (1962), a ballet, incidental music, orch. pieces, and a number of transcendentally resonant piano transcriptions of vocal and orch. works. A phenomenal technician of the keyboard, he won particular renown for his brilliant performances of the Romantic repertoire. In addition to works by such masters as Liszt and Chopin, he sought out and performed rarely heard works of the past. He also performed contemporary music, becoming especially esteemed for his idiomatic interpretations of Gershwin. Among the scores he commissioned and introduced to the public were concertos by Paul Creston (1949) and Marvin David Levy (1970).
BIBL.: H. Schonberg, *The Great Pianists* (N.Y., 1963; 2nd ed., rev., 1987); *Current Biography* (July 1988).

Wildberger, Jacques, Swiss composer and teacher; b. Basel, Jan. 3, 1922. He studied piano and theory at the Basel Cons., and took lessons in composition with Wladimir Vogel (1948–52); taught at the Karlsruhe Staatliche Hochschule für Musik (1959–66); in 1967 he was appointed a lecturer in harmony and instrumentation at the Basel Academy of Music. In his music he observes the formal traditions of the Baroque, but develops a highly intricate system of interrelated tones, intervals, and rhythms, resulting in a sui generis serial system, with a total emancipation of dissonances.
WORKS: Quartet for Flute, Clarinet, Violin, and Cello (1952); *Tre mutazioni* for Chamber Orch. (1953); Trio for Oboe, Clarinet, and Bassoon (1953); *Vom Kommen und Gehen des Menschen,* cantata (1954); *Concertrum* for Harpsichord (1956); *Ihr meint, das Leben sei kurz,* cantata for Chorus and 10 Instruments (1957); *Intensio—Centrum—Remissio* for Orch. (1958); *Zeitebenen* for 8 Instruments (1958); *Musik* for 22 Solo Strings (1960); *Épitaphe pour Évariste Galois,* "documented action" commemorating a mathematical genius killed in a duel at the age of 20, for Narrator, Soprano, Baritone, Speaking Chorus, Tape, and Orch. (1962; Basel, May 20, 1964); Oboe Concerto (1963); *In My End Is My Beginning,* cantata after T.S. Eliot, for Soprano, Tenor, and Chamber Orch. (1964); *Mouvements* for Orch. (1964); Quartet for Flute, Oboe, Harp, and Piano (1967); *La notte,* trittico for Tape, Mezzo-soprano, and 5 Instruments (1967); *Contratempi* for Flute and 4 Orch. Groups (1970); *Double Refrain* for Flute, English Horn, Guitar, and Tape (1972); *Die Stimme, die alte, schwächer werdende Stimme* for Soprano, Cello, Tape, and Orch. (1974); *Tod und Verklärung* for Baritone and Chamber Orch. (1977); *An die Hoffnung* for Soprano, Narrator, and Orch. (1979); *Live-electronic Mixed Pickles* for Live Electronics and 15 Instruments (1979); *Konzertante Szenen* for Saxophone and Orch. (1981); *Canto* for Orch. (1982).

Wildbrunn (real name, **Wehrenpfennig**), **Helene,** Austrian soprano; b. Vienna, April 8, 1882; d. there, April 10, 1972. She studied with Rosa Papier in Vienna; made her debut as a contralto at the Vienna Volksoper in 1906; then sang in Dortmund (1907–14); she began singing soprano roles in 1914, when she joined the Stuttgart Opera, where she remained until 1918; sang in Berlin at the State Opera (1916–25) and the Deutsche Oper (1926–29); was a principal member of the Vienna State Opera (1919–32); made guest appearances at Covent Garden in London, La Scala in Milan, and the Teatro Colón in Buenos Aires. After her retirement in 1932, she taught voice at the Vienna Academy of Music (until 1950). Among her finest roles were Kundry, Brünnhilde, Fricka, Isolde, Donna Anna, and Leonore.

Wilder, Alec (actually, **Alexander Lafayette Chew**), remarkably gifted American composer, distinguished in both popular and serious music; b. Rochester, N.Y., Feb. 16, 1907; d. Gainesville, Fla., Dec. 22, 1980. He studied composition at the Eastman School of Music in Rochester with Herbert Inch and Edward Royce; then moved to N.Y., where he entered the world of popular music; he also wrote excellent prose. His popular songs were performed by Frank Sinatra, Judy Garland, and other celebrated singers; his band pieces were in the repertoire of Benny Goodman and Jimmy Dorsey. He excelled in the genre of short operas scored for a limited ensemble of singers and instruments and suitable for performance in schools, while most of his serious compositions, especially his chamber music, are set in an affably melodious, hedonistic, and altogether ingratiating manner. He publ. a useful critical compilation, *American Popular Song: The Great Innovators* (N.Y., 1972), which included analyses of the songs of Jerome Kern, Vincent Youmans, George Gershwin, Cole Porter, and others. He also publ. the vol. *Letters I Never Mailed* (1975).
WORKS: STAGE: *The Lowland Sea,* folk drama (Montclair, N.J., May 8, 1952); *Cumberland Fair,* a jamboree (Montclair, May 22, 1953); *Sunday Excursion,* musical comedy (Interlochen, Mich., July 18, 1953); *Miss Chicken Little* (CBS-TV, Dec. 27, 1953; stage production, Piermont, N.Y., Aug. 29, 1958); 3 operas: *Kittiwake Island* (Interlochen, Aug. 7, 1954); *The Long Way* (Nyack, N.Y., June 3, 1955); *The Impossible Forest* (Westport, Conn., July 13, 1958); *The Truth about Windmills,* chamber opera (Rochester, N.Y., Oct. 14, 1973); *The Tattooed Countess,* chamber opera (1974); *The Opening,* comic opera (1975); 3 children's operas: *The Churkendoose; Rachetty Pachetty House; Herman Ermine in Rabbit Town;* ballet, *Juke Box* (1942). **ORCH.:** *8 Songs* for Voice and Orch. (Rochester, N.Y., June 8, 1928); *Symphonic Piece* (Rochester, N.Y., June 3, 1929); *Suite* for Clarinet and Strings (1947); Concerto for Oboe and Strings (1950); *Beginner's Luck* for Wind Ensemble (1953); 2 concertos for Horn and Chamber Orch. (1954, 1960); 4 works entitled *An Entertainment* (1961–71): No. 1 for Wind Ensemble; No. 2 for Orch.; No. 3 for Wind Ensemble; No. 4 for Horn and Chamber Orch.; 2 concertos for Trumpet and Wind Ensemble; Concerto for Tuba and Wind Ensemble; *Suite* for Horn and Strings (1965); *Suite* for Saxophone and Strings (1965); Concerto for Saxophone and Chamber Orch. (1967); *Air* for Horn and Wind Ensemble (1968); Concerto for Euphonium and Wind Ensemble (1971). **CHAMBER:** Nonet for Brass (1969); 10 wind quintets (1953–72); 4 brass quintets; quintets, quartets, trios, duets (many called *Suites*) for numerous wind and brass instruments; 2 flute sonatas (1958, 1962); Clarinet Sonata (1963); 3 bassoon sonatas (1964, 1968, 1973); Saxophone Sonata (1960); 3 horn sonatas (1954, 1957, 1965); sonatas for Viola, Cello, String Bass, Oboe, English Horn, Trumpet, Trombone, Bass Trombone, Euphonium, and Tuba; piano pieces (Sonata; *12 Mosaics; A Debutante's Diary; Neurotic Goldfish; Walking Home in the Spring;* etc.). **VOCAL:** *Children's Plea for Peace* for Narrator, Chorus, and Orch. (1969); many songs; also a series of instrumental pieces with satirical words.
BIBL.: W. Balliett, "The President of the Derrière-garde," *New Yorker* (July 9, 1973); *A. W. and His Friends* (Boston, 1974).

Wilder, Philip van, Flemish-born English lutenist and composer; b. c.1500; d. London, Feb. 24, 1553. He entered the service of King Henry VIII of England about 1520; later took charge of the King's private music and taught lute to Princess Mary. He was held in high esteem at the court as both a lutenist and a composer; wrote both sacred and secular vocal music and instrumental pieces.
BIBL.: D. Humphreys, "P. v.W.: A Study of His Work and Its Sources," *Soundings,* IX (1979–80).

Wilder, (Jérôme Albert) Victor (van), Belgian writer on music; b. Wetteren, near Ghent, Aug. 21, 1835; d. Paris, Sept. 8, 1892. He studied philosophy and law at the Univ. of Ghent and music at the Artevelde Cons.; settled in Paris about 1861, where he was active as a music critic. He became a champion of Wagner and tr. into French all of his operas from *Lohengrin* forward; also tr. into French countless other works by German and Italian composers; wrote librettos. He publ. *Mozart, L'Homme et l'artiste* (Paris, 1880; Eng. tr., 1908) and *Beethoven: Sa vie et ses œuvre* (Paris, 1883).

Wilderer, Johann Hugo von, German composer; b. in Bavaria, 1670 or 1671; d. Mannheim (buried), June 7, 1724. He studied with Legrenzi in Venice; by 1692 he was court organist at the St. Andreas church in Düsseldorf; by 1696 he was vice-Kapellmeister at the court there, being elevated to Kapellmeister in 1703; after a new elector came upon the scene in 1716, the courts of Düsseldorf and Innsbruck were joined in Heidelberg and then in Mannheim (1720), during which time Wilderer remained in his position. His importance rests upon his role in fostering the development of German opera and of what became known as the Mannheim school of composition. He wrote 11 operas, 2 oratorios, 4 cantatas, and some sacred works.

Wildgans, Friedrich, Austrian composer; b. Vienna, June 5, 1913; d. Mödling, near Vienna, Nov. 7, 1965. He studied with J. Marx; taught at the Salzburg Mozarteum (1934–36). In 1936 he became a clarinetist in the Vienna State Opera orch.; owing to his opposition to the Nazis, he lost his position in 1939 and remained suspect until the destruction of the Third Reich. He then was a teacher (1945–47; 1950–57) and a prof. (1957–65) at the Vienna Academy of Music. In 1946 he married Ilona Steingruber. He publ. *Entwicklung der Musik in Österreich im 20. Jahrhundert* (Vienna, 1950) and *Anton Webern* (London, 1966). He wrote in all genres, in an ultramodern style, eventually adopting the 12-tone technique.
WORKS: STAGE: *Der Baum der Erkenntniss,* opera (1932); *Der Diktator,* operetta (1933); music for theater, films, and radio. **ORCH.:** 2 concertos for Clarinet and Small Orch. (1933, 1948); *Sinfonia austriaca* (1934); *Laienmusik* (1941); also chamber music, choruses, and piano pieces, including 2 sonatas (1926, 1929).

Wilding-White, Raymond, American composer; b. Caterham, Surrey, England, Oct. 9, 1922. He studied at the Juilliard School of Music in N.Y. (1947–49) and at the New England Cons. of Music in Boston (B.M., 1951; M.M., 1953); spent the summers of 1949, 1950, and 1951 at the Berkshire Music Center at Tanglewood studying with Ibert, Dallapiccola, and Copland; completed his training with Gardner Read at Boston Univ. (D.M.A., 1962). He was a producer-director for WGBH radio and television in Boston (1951–56); held the Kulas Chair of Music at the Case Inst. of Technology in Cleveland (1961–67); in 1967, was appointed to the faculty of De Paul Univ. in Chicago, where he founded a multimedia ensemble, The Loop Group; was a prof. there (from 1979).
WORKS: Ballet, *The Trees,* for Wind Quartet, Brass, Percussion, and Piano (1949); chamber opera, *The Tub,* for Soloists and Piano (1952); *The Selfish Giant,* fable for television (1952; Cleveland, 1965); *The Lonesome Valley,* ballet for Organ and Percussion (1960); opera, *Yerma* (1962); *Monday Morning at the Gargoyle Works,* "action-piece" for 5 Performers (1968); Piano Concerto (1949); *Even Now,* variations for Baritone and Orch. (1954); Concertante for Violin, Horn, and Strings (1963); *Bandmusic* for Concert Band (1966); *Haiku* for Soprano, Tenor, and Instruments (1967); *Whatzit No. 4* (for Louis Lane) for Orch. and Tape (1969); 10 other *Whatzits,* mostly for a particular solo performer, usually accompanied by tape (1967–75); String Quartet (1948); Piano Sonata (1950); Violin Sonata

(1956); *Variations* for Chamber Organ and String Trio (1959); *Paraphernalia*, regalia of madrigalia from Pound, for Chorus, Trumpet, Oboe, Clarinet, Violin, and Harpsichord (1959); *For Mallets* for Percussion Ensemble (1962); *5 Fragments* for Jazz Ensemble (1966); *Movement* for String Quartet (1973); songs; a cappella works; electronic pieces.

Wilhelm, Carl Friedrich, German pianist, conductor, and composer; b. Schmalkalden, Sept. 5, 1815; d. there, Aug. 26, 1873. He studied piano with Aloys Schmitt and theory with Johann André in Frankfurt am Main. He was active as a pianist; was conductor of the Krefeld Liedertafel (from 1841) and the Singverein (from 1849); in 1865 he returned to Schmalkalden. He composed many men's choruses, among them *Die Wacht am Rhein*, which became a national song of the Germans; it was first performed by the Liedertafel on June 11, 1854, and first publ. in the *Chorliedersammlung* of Erk and Greef (Essen, 1854). In 1860 he received the title of Royal Prussian Music Director; in 1871 he was granted a pension of 3,000 marks.
BIBL.: K. Gollmick, *C.F. W.* (Frankfurt, 1848); W. Buchner, *C.F. W.* (Leipzig, 1874); G. Rogati, *C. W. der Komponist der "Wacht am Rhein"* (Hamburg, 1932).

Wilhelmj, August (Emil Daniel Ferdinand Viktor), famous German violinist; b. Usingen, Sept. 21, 1845; d. London, Jan. 22, 1908. He received his earliest instruction in music from his mother, who was an amateur pianist; then studied violin with Konrad Fischer, court musician at Wiesbaden in 1849; made his 1st appearance there as a child prodigy on Jan. 8, 1854. In 1861, at the recommendation of Liszt, he was sent to the Leipzig Cons., where he studied with David (violin) and with Hauptmann and Richter (harmony and composition); in 1864 he went to Frankfurt for an additional course with Raff; in 1865 he began his concert career, touring Switzerland; then played in the Netherlands and England (1866); France and Italy (1867); Russia, Switzerland, France, and Belgium (1869); England, Scotland, and Ireland (1869–70); then traveled through the Netherlands, Scandinavia, Germany, and Austria (1871–74); to England (1875–77) and to America (1878); made a tour of the world to South America, Australia, and Asia (1878–82). In 1876 he was concertmaster of the Bayreuth Festival orch. For several years he lived chiefly at Biebrich am Rhein, where he established (with R. Niemann) a master school for violin playing. In 1886 he moved to Blasewitz, near Dresden; in 1894 he was appointed prof. of violin at the Guildhall School of Music in London. His 1st wife, whom he married in 1866, was Baroness Liphardt, a niece of David; in 1895 he married the pianist Mariella Mausch. He made a famous arrangement of Bach's air from the orch. *Suite* in D major that became known as the *Air on the G String* (Bach's original bore no such specification); also arranged Wagner's *Träume* for violin and orch.; wrote a cadenza to Beethoven's Violin Concerto; further composed, for Violin and Orch., 2 *Konzertstücke* (No. 2, *In memoriam*), *Alla polacca*, and Theme and Variations (after 2 caprices of Paganini); *Romanze* for Piano; songs. With James Brown he publ. *A Modern School for the Violin* (6 parts).
BIBL.: E. Frassinesi, *A. W. Violinista. Memorie* (Mirandola, 1913); H. Morgan-Browne, "An Approximation to the Truth about A. W.," *Music & Letters,* III (1922); E. Wagner, *Der Geigerkönig A. W.* (Homburg, 1928); B. Schwarz, *Great Masters of the Violin* (N.Y., 1983).

Wilhem (real name, **Bocquillon**), **Guillaume-Louis,** French music educator; b. Paris, Dec. 18, 1781; d. there, April 26, 1842. The son of an army officer, he himself entered active service at the age of 12; but from 1795–1801, studied at the school of Liancourt, and then for 2 years in the Paris Cons. He taught music in the military school of Saint-Cyr, and in 1810 was appointed a teacher of music at the Lycée Napoléon (later the Collège Henri IV), occupying this position until his death. The system of *enseignement mutuel* (mutual instruction), which had been introduced into the popular schools of France, attracted Wilhem's attention; in 1815 he began to apply it in music teaching, and met with such marked success

that in 1819 he was chosen to organize a system of music instruction for the primary schools in Paris; he was appointed singing teacher to the Polytechnique in 1820, and director of the Normal School of Music. In 1833 he conceived the idea of instituting regular reunions of the pupils in one grand chorus, to which he gave the name of Orphéon. In 1835 he was made director-general of music instruction in all the primary schools of Paris, and was created a Chevalier of the Legion of Honor. Besides his school classes, he formed classes of adults, chiefly workingmen, in which the success of his system was equally conspicuous, and which later, under the name of Orphéons, included several popular singing societies. He publ. numerous songs and choruses; also a collection of a cappella choruses, *Orphéon,* in 5 (later 10) vols.; and 4 textbooks.
BIBL.: E. Niboyet, *Notice historique sur la vie et les ouvrages de G.L. B. W.* (Paris, 1843); J. La Fage, *Notice sur B.-W.* (Paris, 1845).

Wilkes, Josué Teófilo, Argentine composer and musicologist; b. Buenos Aires, Jan. 8, 1883; d. there, Jan. 10, 1968. He studied with Alberto Williams; in 1908, went to Europe for further study; took some lessons from Liapunov in St. Petersburg, and also at the Schola Cantorum in Paris; returned to Argentina in 1914; for many years taught music in primary schools in Buenos Aires; later was a teacher of music history at the Universidad del Litoral in Santa Fé (1948–56). He made a special study of Gregorian chant; also transcribed and harmonized old colonial songs; composed 3 operas: *Nuite persane* (1916–20), *Por el cetro y la corona,* Byzantine tragedy after *Bajazet* of Racine (1924), and *El horóscopo,* after Calderón (1926–27); secular oratorio, *La cautiva* (1930); symphonic trilogy, *Humahuaca* (1911–14); String Octet; other chamber music; songs; *50 canciones populares cuyanas* (arranged and harmonized); *Cancionero musical rioplatense* (Argentine dances). With I. Guerrero Cárpena, he publ. *Formas musicales rioplatenses: cifras, estilas y milongas—su génesis hispánica* (Buenos Aires, 1946).

Wilkomirska, Maria, Polish pianist, daughter of **Alfred Wilkomirski;** b. Moscow, April 3, 1904. She studied at the Moscow Cons. with Briusova and Yavorsky; in 1920 she went to Warsaw and continued her studies with Turczyński. She subsequently taught piano in Kalisz, Gdansk, and Lodz; in 1951 she became a prof. at the Warsaw Music School. With her brother, the cellist **Kazimierz Wilkomirski,** and her sister, the violinist **Wanda Wilkomirska,** she organized a trio that toured widely.

Wilkomirska, Wanda, Polish violinist, daughter of **Alfred Wilkomirski;** b. Warsaw, Jan. 11, 1929. She studied violin with her father, and later with Irene Dubiska in Warsaw and with Zathureczky in Budapest. She won a prize at the international violin competition in Geneva in 1946 and similar prizes in Budapest in 1948 and in Poznan in 1953. In 1960 she went to Paris and took lessons with Henryk Szeryng. With her brother, the cellist **Kazimierz Wilkomirski,** and her sister, the pianist **Maria Wilkomirska,** she formed a trio that toured widely.

Wilkomirski, Alfred, Polish violinist and pedagogue, father of **Kazimierz Wilkomirski** and of **Maria** and **Wanda Wilkomirska;** b. Asov, Russia, Jan. 3, 1873; d. Lodz, July 31, 1950. He studied with Hřimaly at the Moscow Cons.; taught violin in Kalisz (1920–26) and in Lodz (1929–39; 1945–50).

Wilkomirski, Kazimierz, Polish cellist, conductor, composer, and pedagogue, son of **Alfred Wilkomirski;** b. Moscow, Sept. 1, 1900. He studied cello and conducting at the Moscow Cons.; then took courses in composition with Statkowski and in conducting with Mlynarski at the Warsaw Cons. (diploma, 1929); later studied conducting with Scherchen in Switzerland (1932–34). From 1934 to 1939 he served as director of the Gdansk Cons. and also conducted the Gdansk Opera. The Nazi assault on Poland forced Wilkomirski to interrupt his musical activities. After the liberation, he was rector of the Lodz Cons. (1945–47), and later served as a pedagogue at the conservatories of

Zopport (1952–57), Wroclaw (1958–65), and Warsaw (from 1963); also was chief conductor of the Wroclaw Opera (1957–62). His works are attractively eclectic and Romantically imitative; the best of them are his cello pieces, including several concertos, a method of cello playing, and 12 études. His autobiography, *Wospomnenia*, was publ. in 1971. With his sisters, the pianist **Maria** and the violinist **Wanda Wilkomirska**, he formed a trio that achieved notable success in tours in Europe and the Orient.

Willaert, Adrian, important Flemish composer and pedagogue; b. Bruges or Roulaers, c.1490; d. Venice, Dec. 7, 1562. He enrolled as a law student at the Univ. of Paris; then devoted himself to music; studied composition with Jean Mouton, a musician in the Royal Chapel. In 1515 he entered the service of Cardinal Ippolito I d'Este of Ferrara; he accompanied the cardinal, who was Archbishop of Esztergom, to Hungary in 1517; the cardinal died in 1520, and Willaert entered the service of Duke Alfonso I d'Este of Ferrara (1522); subsequently was in the service of Cardinal Ippolito II d'Este, the Archbishop of Milan (1525–27). On Dec. 12, 1527, he was appointed maestro di cappella of San Marco in Venice; with the exception of 2 visits to Flanders (1542 and 1556–57), he remained in Venice for the rest of his life, as a composer and teacher. Among his famous pupils were Zarlino, Cipriano de Rore, Andrea Gabrieli, and Costanzo Porta. Willaert was justly regarded as a founder of the great Venetian school of composition; the style of writing for 2 antiphonal choirs (prompted by the twin opposed organs of San Marco) was principally initiated by him. He was one of the greatest masters of the madrigal and of the instrumental ricercare; he also wrote motets, chansons, Psalms, and masses.

WORKS: *Liber quinque missarum* (Venice, 1536); *Hymnorum musica* (Venice, 1542); *I sacri e santi salmi che si cantano a Vespro e Compieta . . .* for 4 Voices (Venice, 1555; augmented ed., 1571); *Motecta . . . liber primus* for 4 Voices (Venice, 1539; augmented ed., 1545); *Mottetti . . . libro secundo* for 4 Voices (Venice, 1539; augmented ed., 1545); *Motecta . . . liber primus* for 5 Voices (Venice, 1539); *Il primo libro di motetti* for 6 Voices (Venice, 1542); *Musica nova* (Venice, 1559); *Livre de meslanges . . . 26 chansons* (Paris, 1560); *Cincquiesme livre de chansons* for 3 Voices (Paris, 1560); *Musica nova* (Venice, 1559); *Madrigali* for 4 Voices (Venice, 1563); *9 ricercares a 3* (1551; ed. by H. Zenck, Mainz and Leipzig, 1933). For the complete works, see H. Zenck and W. Gerstenberg, eds., *Adrian Willaert: Opera omnia,* in the Corpus Mensurabilis Musicae series, iii/1 (Rome, 1950–77).

BIBL.: E. Gregoir, *A. W.* (Brussels, 1869); E. Hertzmann, *A. W. in der weltlichen Vokalmusik seiner Zeit* (Leipzig, 1931); R. Lenaerts, "Notes sur A. W.," *Bulletin de l'Institut Historique Belge de Rome,* XV (1935); idem, "La Chapelle de Saint-Marc à Venise sous A. W.," *Bulletin de l'Institut Historique Belge de Rome,* XIX (1938); J. Levitan, "A. W.'s Famous *Duo Quidnam ebrietas,*" *Tijdschrift van de Vereniging voor Nederlandse Muziekgeschiedenis,* XV/3 (1938) and XV/4 (1939); R. Lenaerts, "Voor de biographie van A. W.," *Hommage à Charles van den Borren: Mélanges* (Antwerp, 1945); A. Carapetyan, "The Musica Nova of A. W.," *Journal of Renaissance and Baroque Music,* I (1946–47); A. Einstein, *The Italian Madrigal* (Princeton, N.J., 1949); E. Lowinsky, "A. W.'s Chromatic Duo Re-examined," *Tijdschrift van de Vereniging voor Nederlandse Muziekgeschiedenis,* XVIII/1 (1956); H. Beck, "A. W.s Messen," *Archiv für Musikwissenschaft,* XVII (1960); A. Carver, "The Psalms of W. and His North Italian Contemporaries," *Acta Musicologica,* XLVII (1975); I. Bossuyt, *A. W., ca. 1490–1562: Leven en werk: Stijl en genres* (Leuven, 1985); G. Ongaro, *The Chapel of St. Mark's at the Time of A. W. (1527–1562); A Documentary study* (diss., Univ. of North Carolina, 1986).

Willan, Healey, eminent English-born Canadian composer, organist, and music educator; b. Balham, Surrey, Oct. 12, 1880; d. Toronto, Feb. 16, 1968. He began his musical training at St. Saviour's Choir School in Eastbourne (1888–95); later studied with Hoyte and was made a Fellow of the Royal College

of Organists (1899). He was an organist and choirmaster in and around London; then went to Toronto in 1913 as head of the theory dept. at the Cons. and as organist at St. Paul's; he was vice-principal there (1920–36). In 1914 he was appointed a lecturer and examiner at the Univ. of Toronto; in 1937, a prof. of music; he retired in 1950; was also the univ. organist (1932–64) and precentor of St. Mary Magdalene Church in Toronto from 1921 until his death; was founder and conductor of the Tudor Singers (1934–39). In 1956 he was awarded the historic Lambeth Doctorate by the Archbishop of Canterbury, and in 1967 was the 1st musician to become a Companion of the Order of Canada. He was greatly esteemed as a pedagogue.

WORKS: 2 radio operas, *Transit through Fire* (1941–42; Canadian Radio, March 8, 1942) and *Deirdre* (1943–45; Canadian Radio, April 20, 1946; rev. 1962 and 1965; first stage perf., Toronto, 1965); historical pageant, *Brébeuf and His Brethren* (CBC Radio, Sept. 26, 1943); several ballad-operas; 2 syms.: No. 1 (Toronto, Oct. 8, 1936) and No. 2 (1941; rev. 1948; Toronto, May 18, 1950); Piano Concerto (Montreal, Aug. 24, 1944; rev. 1949); *Agincourt Song* for Chorus and Small Orch. (1929); *Overture to an Unwritten Comedy* (1951); several ceremonial pieces, including *Coronation March* for Orch. (1937), *Te Deum Laudamus* for Chorus and Small Orch. (1937), *Coronation Suite* for Chorus and Orch. (1952), *Royal Salute* for Orch. (1959), and *Centennial March* for Orch. (1967); *Royce Hall Suite* for Symphonic Band (1949); 2 violin sonatas (1920, 1923); several character pieces for piano; organ works, among the most noteworthy being *Introduction, Passacaglia and Fugue* (1916; his major work in the genre), *Epithalamium* (1948), *Epithalame* (1957), *A Fugal Trilogy* (1958), *Passacaglia and Fugue No. 2* (1959), and *Andante, Fugue, and Chorale* (1965); carols and hymn tunes; church services; motets a cappella; anthems with organ accompaniment; many other choral works; songs; arrangements of Canadian and British songs; school manuals. A catalogue of Willan's works was publ. by G. Bryant (Ottawa, 1972).

BIBL.: G. Bryant, "Choral Works of H. W.," *The American Organist* (Oct. 1980); N. Johnson, "H. W. 1880–1968" and "Organ Works of H. W.," ibid.; F. Clarke, *H. W.: Life and Music* (Toronto, 1983).

Willcocks, Sir David (Valentine), English organist, conductor, and music educator; b. Newquay, Dec. 30, 1919. He was educated at Clifton College, the Royal College of Music, and King's College, Cambridge; served in the British army; after World War II, he was organist at Salisbury Cathedral (1947–50) and Worcester Cathedral (1950–57); then at King's College, Cambridge (1957–73); also held the posts of univ. lecturer (1957–74) and univ. organist (1958–74) at Cambridge; concurrently he led the City of Birmingham Choir (1950–57) and was conductor of the Cambridge Univ. Musical Soc. (1958–73). In 1960 he became music director of the Bach Choir; in 1974 he also assumed the post of director of the Royal College of Music in London, remaining there until 1984. He was made a Commander of the Order of the British Empire in 1971; was knighted in 1977. He served as general ed. of the Church Music series of the Oxford Univ. Press.

Willent-Bordogni, Jean-Baptiste-Joseph, French bassoonist, teacher, and composer; b. Douai, Dec. 8, 1809; d. Paris, May 11, 1852. He studied with Delcambre at the Paris Cons.; played the bassoon in the orch. of the Théâtre-Italien in Paris; married the daughter of the singing teacher Bordogni (1834) and added her name to his; taught at the Brussels Cons.; in 1848, was appointed to the faculty of the Paris Cons. He wrote a number of works for the bassoon, and publ. a method for it; also brought out 2 operas in Brussels: *Le Moine* (1844) and *Van Dyck* (1845).

Williams, Alberto, prolific Argentine composer; b. Buenos Aires, Nov. 23, 1862; d. there, June 17, 1952. He was the grandson of an Englishman; his maternal grandfather, Amancio Alcorta, was one of Argentina's early composers. Williams studied piano with Mathías, harmony with Durand, counterpoint with Godard, and composition with Franck and Bériot on a scholarship at the Paris Cons. He returned to Argentina in 1889; founded the Alberto Williams Cons. in 1893; also organized branches of the Cons. in provincial towns of Argentina, numbering more than 100; founded a music publ. firm, La Quena (also a music magazine of that name). He was the most prolific composer of Argentina; 112 opus numbers were publ. by La Quena. The greatest influence in his music was that of Franck, but modernistic usages are found in Williams's application of whole-tone scales, parallel chord progressions, etc. In many of his works he used characteristic melorhythms of Argentina; composed a number of piano pieces in Argentine song and dance forms (milongas, gatos, cielitos, etc.).

WORKS: 9 syms., all 1st perf. in Buenos Aires: No. 1 (Nov. 25, 1907); No. 2, *La bruja de las montañas* (Sept. 9, 1910); No. 3, *La Selva sagrada* (Dec. 8, 1934); No. 4, *El Ataja-Caminos* (Dec. 15, 1935); No. 5, *El corazón de la muñeca* (Nov. 29, 1936); No. 6, *La muerte del cometa* (Nov. 26, 1937); No. 7, *Eterno reposo* (Nov. 26, 1937); several suites of Argentine dances; 3 violin sonatas (1905, 1906, 1907); Cello Sonata (1906); Piano Trio (1907); a great number of piano albums, the last of which was *En el parque* (1952). He also publ. numerous didactic works and several books of poetry.

BIBL.: Z. Lacoigne, *A. W.; Músico argentino* (Buenos Aires, 1942); *Homenajes a A. W.* (Buenos Aires, 1942); N. Slonimsky, "A. W.: Father of Argentinian Music," *Musical America* (Jan. 10, 1942); V. Risolía, *A. W., Curriculum vitae* (Buenos Aires, 1944).

Williams, Andy (Andrew), American singer of popular music; b. Wall Lake, Iowa, Dec. 3, 1930. With 3 of his brothers, he formed the Williams Brothers Quartet and sang on the radio in Des Moines, Chicago, Cincinnati, and Los Angeles; Kay Thompson later joined the group; they toured together until 1953; he then began a solo career as a vocalist; made numerous concert appearances, as well as films, television stints, and recordings.

Williams, Camilla, black American soprano and teacher; b. Danville, Va., Oct. 18, 1922. She studied at Virginia State College (B.S., 1941) and with Marion Szekely-Freschl, Hubert Giesen, Sergius Kagen, and Leo Taubman in Philadelphia; won the Marian Anderson Award twice (1943, 1944), as well as the Philadelphia Orch. Youth Award (1944). On May 15, 1946, she made her operatic debut at the N.Y. City Opera as Madama Butterfly, remaining on its roster until 1954; also toured widely as a concert artist. She taught at Brooklyn College of the City Univ. of N.Y. (1970–73) and at the Indiana Univ. School of Music in Bloomington (from 1977).

Williams, Clifton, American bandmaster and composer; b. Traskwood, Ark., March 26, 1923; d. South Miami, Fla., Feb. 12, 1976. He studied at Louisiana State Univ. (B.M., 1947) and with Bernard Rogers and Howard Hanson at the Eastman School of Music in Rochester, N.Y. (M.M., 1948). He played horn with the sym. orchs. of San Antonio and New Orleans; was on the staff of the music dept. at the Univ. of Texas in Austin (1949–66); then at the Univ. of Miami (1966–76). He composed band music, including the phenomenally popular *Sinfonians*. His other band pieces include *Trail Scenes; Trilogy Suite; Concertino* for Percussion and Band; 3 symphonic dances; *Fanfare and Allegro; Dedicatory Overture; Dramatic Essay: The Ramparts; The Patriots* (commissioned by NORAD); *Songs of Heritage; Academic Procession; Castle Gap March; Strategic Air Command.*

Williams, "Cootie" (Charles Melvin), black American jazz trumpeter and bandleader; b. Mobile, Ala., July 24, 1908; d. N.Y., Sept. 15, 1985. He took trumpet lessons with Charles Lipskin; made his way to N.Y. and joined groups led by Chick Webb and Fletcher Henderson. From 1929 to 1940 he was a member of Duke Ellington's band; after working with Benny Goodman (1940–41), he led his own groups until rejoining Ellington's band in 1962; he left in 1975 but continued to perform until 1983. He was one of the leading jazz trumpeters of his era.

Williams, Grace (Mary), Welsh composer; b. Barry, Glamorganshire, Feb. 19, 1906; d. there, Feb. 10, 1977. Her father led the local boys' chorus and played the piano in a home trio, with Grace on the violin and her brother on the cello. In 1923 she entered the music dept. of the Univ. of Wales in Cardiff, in the composition class of David Evans. Upon graduation in 1926, she enrolled at the Royal College of Music in London. There she was accepted as a student of Vaughan Williams, who had the greatest influence on her career as a composer, both in idiom and form; she also took classes with Gordon Jacob. She subsequently received the Octavia Traveling Scholarship and went to Vienna to take lessons with Egon Wellesz (1930–31). She did not espouse the atonal technique of the 2nd Viennese School, but her distinctly diatonic harmony with strong tertian underpinning was artfully embroidered with nicely hung deciduous chromatics of a decidedly nontonal origin. She marked May 10, 1951, in her diary as a "day of destruction," when she burned all her MSS unworthy of preservation. Among her practical occupations were teaching school and writing educational scripts for the BBC. She was particularly active in her advancement of Welsh music.

WORKS: STAGE: *Theseus and Ariadne,* ballet (1935); *The Parlour,* opera (1961). ORCH.: 2 syms. (1943; 1956, rev. 1975); *Sinfonia concertante* for Piano and Orch. (1941); *Sea Sketches* for Strings (1944); Violin Concerto (1950); Trumpet Concerto (1963); *Castell Caernarfon,* for the investiture of the Prince of Wales (1969). CHAMBER: Sextet for Oboe, Trumpet, Violin, Viola, Cello, and Piano (1931); *Suite* for 9 Instruments (1934); also numerous choruses and songs.

BIBL.: M. Boyd, *G. W.* (Cardiff, 1980).

Williams, (Hiram) Hank, seeded American country-music singer, guitarist, and songwriter; b. Georgiana, Ala., Sept. 17, 1923; d. Oak Hill, Va., Jan. 1, 1953. He sang church hymns and learned to play the organ at a very early age; then took guitar lessons from a black street singer. At 12 he won a prize in an amateur contest in Montgomery singing his own song, *W.P.A. Blues.* At 14 he formed his own band, Hank Williams and His Drifting Cowboys. In 1946 he went to Nashville; in 1949 he joined the famous "Grand Ole Opry" there, and made an instant success with his rendition of *Lovesick Blues;* its disk sold over a million copies. In 1950 he put out several recordings of his own songs, *Long Gone Lonesome Blues, I Just Don't Like This Kind of Livin', Why Don't You Love Me?,* and *Moanin' the Blues,* which sold prodigiously. His subsequent releases, also magically successful, were *Hey, Good Lookin', Your Cheatin' Heart, Move It On Over, Cold, Cold Heart,* and *Jambalaya (On the Bayou),* but the nemesis of so many country singers—drugs, alcohol, women in excess—and a cardiac disorder killed him before he reached the age of 30. His son, **(Randall) Hank Williams, Jr.** (b. Shreveport, La., May 26, 1949), was also a successful country-western singer, guitarist, and songwriter; his career was also hampered by alcohol and drug problems; in 1975 he sustained severe injuries while mountain climbing, but eventually resumed his career. A television show on his life, *Living Proof,* was produced in 1983.

BIBL.: G. Koon, *H. W.: A Bio-Bibliography in Popular Culture* (Westport, Conn., 1983).

Williams, John (Christopher), remarkable Australian guitarist; b. Melbourne, April 24, 1941. He first studied with his father, the guitarist Leonard Williams; when he was 14 he performed in London, then took guitar lessons with Segovia at the Accademia Chigiana in Siena (1957–59). In 1962 he made a tour of the Soviet Union; also played in America and Japan. In addition to classical music, he includes in his programs pieces of pop music and jazz; this egalitarian versatility makes him a favorite with untutored youth in England and America.

Williams, John (Towner), enormously successful American composer and conductor; b. N.Y., Feb. 8, 1932. He grew up in a musical atmosphere; his father was a film studio musician. He began to take piano lessons; later he learned to play trombone, trumpet, and clarinet. In 1948 the family moved to Los

Angeles, where he studied orchestration with Robert van Epps at Los Angeles City College and composition privately with Mario Castelnuovo-Tedesco; he also took piano lessons with Rosina Lhévinne at the Juilliard School of Music in N.Y. He began his career as a composer, arranger, and conductor for films and television; wrote the film scores, rich in sounding brass and tinkling cymbals, for *Close Encounters of the Third Kind, Superman, The Empire Strikes Back, Raiders of the Lost Ark, E.T., The Extraterrestrial,* and *Return of the Jedi.* He won Academy Awards for *Fiddler on the Roof* (1971), *Jaws* (1975), and *Star Wars* (1977). The record albums for these background scores sold into the millions. He also wrote 2 syms., a Violin Concerto, a Flute Concerto, an *Essay for Strings,* and a number of chamber music pieces. In 1980 he was chosen conductor of the Boston Pops Orch., succeeding the late Arthur Fiedler, who had held that post for almost 50 years; Williams declared openly that no one could hope to equal Fiedler in charisma and showmanship, not to mention Fiedler's splendiferous aureole of white hair (as contrasted with his successor's alopecia), but he said he would try his darndest to bridge the gap. He largely succeeded, and diversified his appeal to Boston Pops audiences by playing selections from his own sparkling film scores.

BIBL.: R. Dyer, "J. W.," *Ovation* (June 1983).

Williams, John Gerrard, English composer; b. London, Dec. 10, 1888; d. Oxted, Surrey, March 7, 1947. He was an architect by profession, but took some lessons in music from Richard Walthew. He wrote a ballad opera, *Kate, the Cabin-Boy* (London, 1924); 2 operettas; a ballet, *The Wings of Horus* (1928); *3 Miniatures* and *Elegiac Rhapsody* for Orch.; 2 string quartets; many songs and part-songs.

Williams, John M., American pianist and pedagogue; b. on a plantation in Washington County, Tex., Jan. 1, 1884; d. Los Angeles, Dec. 6, 1974. He studied in N.Y. and Chicago; from 1913, lectured on musical pedagogy to music teachers in the U.S., Canada, England, and Scotland. His teaching material has had worldwide distribution. Some 10 million copies of his various piano books have been sold.

Williams, Joseph, English music publisher. He was the son of Lucy Williams, who established a printing shop in London in 1808. Joseph (1819–83) continued the business; was succeeded in 1883 by his son, **Joseph Benjamin Williams** (1847–1923), who publ. some of his own pieces under the nom de plume of Florian Pascal; the business was incorporated as Joseph Williams, Ltd., in 1900. His successor was his son, **Florian Williams** (1879–1973); the firm was sold in 1961. Its catalogue was extensive, ranging from Elizabethan music to such composers as Elgar, Vaughan Williams, Ireland, and Bax.

BIBL.: F. Williams, "After Forty Years. Recollections of a Music Publisher," *Musical Opinion* (Feb.–Dec. 1940).

Williams, Mary Lou (real name, **Mary Elfrieda Scruggs**), black American jazz pianist, composer, and arranger; b. Atlanta, May 8, 1910; d. Durham, N.C., May 28, 1981. She began her career as a pianist in Kansas City with Andy Kirk's band; in 1931 she became pianist and arranger for Kirk's Twelve Clouds of Joy band, and provided him with such songs as *Walkin' & Swingin', Twinklin', Cloudy,* and *Little Joe from Chicago;* she then worked with Duke Ellington, Benny Goodman, and others. In 1945 she composed the bebop hit *In the Land of Oo-Bla-Dee* for Dizzy Gillespie; she also wrote *The Zodiac Suite,* which was performed by the N.Y. Phil. After becoming a Roman Catholic, she composed a number of religious works, including *St. Martin de Porres* and 3 masses; her mass *Music for Peace* became popularly known as "Mary Lou's Mass." In 1977 she was named artist-in-residence at Duke Univ. in Durham. She was one of the leading figures in the jazz field for almost 60 years.

Williams, Ralph Vaughan. See **Vaughan Williams, Ralph.**

Williams, Spencer, American composer of popular music; b. New Orleans, Oct. 14, 1889; d. N.Y., July 14, 1965. He

played piano in nightclubs in New Orleans, Chicago, and N.Y.; wrote songs in the slow rhythmic manner of the New Orleans blues. In 1932 he went to Europe for a prolonged stay; lived in Paris (where he was accompanist for Josephine Baker), London, and Stockholm; returned to the U.S. in 1957. His most famous song is *Basin Street Blues* (1928); he wrote many blues and other songs: *Tishomingo Blues* (1917), *Arkansas Blues, Mississippi Blues, Royal Garden Blues;* his *Mahogany Hall Stomp* became a perennial favorite.

Williamson, Cris, American vocalist and songwriter; b. Deadwood, S.Dak., Feb. 15, 1947. She wrote her 1st song at the age of 16, making several recordings on the Avanti label in Wyoming before she was 18. She studied academic subjects at the Univ. of Denver (B.A., 1969), then signed with Olivia Records of Oakland, Calif., a recording company specializing in women's music; she produced *The Changer and the Changed* (1975), one of the widest-selling independently issued records ever made. Her Carnegie Hall appearance in N.Y. on Nov. 26, 1982, with Meg Christian, led to the album *Meg/Chris at Carnegie Hall* (1983). She publ. 2 song collections and wrote much music for theater, film, and television, most notably *Don't Lose Heart* for Jane Chambers's lesbian drama *Last Summer at Bluefish Cove.* With Christian and Holly Near, Williamson is among the most important figures in the women's music movement that began in Berkeley in the 1970s. Her music is characteristically influenced by folk, country, and pop styles, with emphasis on ballad and communal dance. Her passionate lyrics express an ecstatic, transcendental sensuality. Among her finest recordings are *Strange Paradise* (1978), *Lumière* (1982; a children's record that won the Parents' Choice Award), and *Country Blessed* (1989; with Teresa Trull).

Williamson, John Finley, American choral conductor; b. Canton, Ohio, June 23, 1887; d. Toledo, Ohio, May 28, 1964. He studied at Otterbein College in Westerville, Ohio (graduated, 1911); then studied singing with Herbert Wilbur Greene, Herbert Witherspoon, and David Bispham in N.Y. and organ with Karl Straube in Leipzig. He became minister of music at the Westminster Presbyterian Church in Dayton, Ohio, where he founded a choir in 1920; in 1926 he founded the Westminster Choir School there; in 1929 he moved it to Ithaca, N.Y., and in 1932 to Princeton, N.J., where it later became Westminster Choir College; was its president until 1958. He led its choir on many tours of the U.S. and took it on 4 world tours; ed. the Westminster Series of choral music.

BIBL.: D. Wehr, *J.F. W. (1887–1964): His Life and Contribution to Choral Music* (diss., Miami Univ., Oxford, Ohio, 1971).

Williamson, Malcolm (Benjamin Graham Christopher), Australian composer; b. Sydney, Nov. 21, 1931. He studied composition with Eugene Goossens at the Sydney Cons. (1944–50); in 1953 he went to London, where he took lessons with Elisabeth Lutyens and Erwin Stein (until 1957); learned to play the organ and was employed as a church organist in England; visited the U.S. in 1970, and was composer-in-residence at Westminster Choir College in Princeton, N.J., for an academic season; then returned to England. In 1975 he became Master of the Queen's Musick; in 1976, was made a Commander of the Order of the British Empire; in 1977, was elected president of the Royal Phil. Orch.

WORKS: STAGE: OPERAS: *Our Man in Havana,* after Graham Greene's novel (London, July 2, 1963); *The English Eccentrics,* chamber opera (Aldeburgh Festival, June 11, 1964); *The Happy Prince,* children's opera after Oscar Wilde (Farnham, May 22, 1965); *Julius Caesar Jones,* children's opera for Children's Voices and 3 Adults (London, Jan. 4, 1966); *The Violins of St. Jacques* (London, Nov. 29, 1966); *Dunstan and the Devil* (Cookham, May 19, 1967); *The Growing Castle,* chamber opera, after Strindberg's *Dream Play* (Dynevor Festival, Aug. 13, 1968); *Lucky-Peter's Journey,* after Strindberg's fairy-tale play (London, Dec. 18, 1969); *The Stone Wall* (London, Sept. 18, 1971); *Genesis* (1971; London, April 23, 1973); *The Red Sea* (Dartington, April 14, 1972); *The Death of Cuchulain* (1972); *The Winter Star* (1972); choral operatic sequence *The Brilliant* *and the Dark*, for Women's Voices and Orch. (1969); 3 cassations for Audience, and Orch. or Piano: *The Moonrakers* (1967; Brighton, April 22, 1967); *Knights in Shining Armour* (1968; Brighton, April 19, 1968); *The Snow Wolf* (Brighton, April 30, 1968). **BALLETS:** *The Display*, dance sym. in 4 movements (Adelaide Festival, March 14, 1964); *Sun into Darkness* (London, April 13, 1966); *Perisynthyon* (1974). **ORCH.:** Sym. No. 1, *Elevamini* (1956–57); *Santiago de Espada*, overture (1958); 3 piano concertos (1958; with String Orch., 1960; 1961); Organ Concerto (1961); *Sinfonietta concertante* for 3 Trumpets, Piano, and Strings (1959–61); Violin Concerto (Bath, England, June 15, 1965; Yehudi Menuhin, soloist); Sinfonietta (1965); *Concerto Grosso* for Orch. (London, Aug. 28, 1965); *Symphonic Variations* (Edinburgh, Sept. 9, 1965); Sym. No. 2 (Bristol, Oct. 29, 1969); *Epitaphs for Edith Sitwell* for Strings (1969; originally for Organ, 1965); Concerto for 2 Pianos and Strings (1972); *The Icy Mirror* for Soloists, Chorus, and Orch. (Cheltenham Festival, July 9, 1972); *Ode to Music* for Chorus, Echo Chorus, and Orch. (London, Feb. 3, 1973); *Hammarskjöld Portrait* for Soprano and Strings (London, July 30, 1974); Sym. No. 4 (1977); Sym. No. 5, *Aquero* (1980); *Lament* for Violin and String Orch. (1980); Sym. No. 7 (1984). **CHAMBER:** *Variations* for Cello and Piano (1964); Concerto for 2 Pianos (8-hands) and Wind Quintet (1965); *Serenade* for Flute, Piano, and String Trio (1967); Piano Quintet (1967–68); Piano Trio (1976). **KEYBOARD:** 2 piano sonatas (1958; rev. 1971–72); 5 *Preludes* for Piano (1966); 2-piano Sonata (1967); Sym. for Organ (1960). **VOCAL:** *Symphony for Voices* for Chorus a cappella (1962); *The Icy Mirror*, cantata (Sym. No. 3) for Soprano, Mezzo-soprano, 2 Baritones, Chorus, and Orch. (1972); *Ode to Music* for Children's Voices and Orch. (1973); *Canticle of Fire* for Solo Voices, Chorus, and Organ (1973); *Mass of Christ the King* for Chorus and Orch. (1977); various choruses, sacred pieces, hymns, and carols.

Willis, Henry, English organ builder; b. London, April 27, 1821; d. there, Feb. 11, 1901. As a youth he worked for John Gray (later Gray & Davidson), and while yet an apprentice, invented the special manual and pedal couplers that he later used in his own instruments; from 1842 to 1845 he worked for Evans at Cheltenham, and in 1848 established his own business in London. He rebuilt the organ in the Gloucester Cathedral; exhibited a large organ at the Crystal Palace in 1851, which won the Council Medal and was installed in the Winchester Cathedral; he subsequently was commissioned to build the great organ in St. George's Hall in Liverpool (1855). In 1878 he took his sons Vincent and Henry into partnership, adopting the firm name of Henry Willis & Sons; he became generally known as "Father Willis." Willis himself regarded the organ in St. Paul's, which he built in 1891, as his masterpiece (77 speaking stops, 19 couplers). After the founder's death in 1901, his son Henry Willis became the head of the business, and soon took his son, also named Henry Willis, into partnership. They built the organ in the Liverpool Cathedral (167 speaking stops, 48 couplers) from 1912 to 1914; this organ was the largest in the world at the time.
BIBL.: W. Summer, *Father H. W.* (London, 1955).

Willis, Richard Storrs, American composer and writer on music; b. Boston, Feb. 10, 1819; d. Detroit, May 7, 1900. He was a brother of the poet Nathaniel Parker Willis; studied at Yale Univ., where he was president of the Beethoven Society (1837), for which he wrote choruses and instrumental pieces; then studied theory with Schnyder von Wartensee in Frankfurt and with Hauptmann in Leipzig. He ed. the periodical *Musical World* (1852–60); brought out the collections *Church Chorals and Choir Studies* (N.Y., 1850) and *Our Church Music* (N.Y., 1856); also composed student songs and patriotic hymns, later collected as *Waif of Song* and publ. in Paris (1876).

Willis Music Co., American music publishers. The business was founded by Charles H. Willis at Cincinnati in 1899, in association with his son William H. Willis. The firm became known as W.H. Willis & Co.; after the absorption of G.B. Jennings & Co. in 1910 it was incorporated as the Willis Music Co. On July 1, 1919, the business was acquired by Gustave Schirmer of N.Y. The company specialized in educational publications.

Willman, Allan (Arthur), American composer and pianist; b. Hinckley, Ill., May 11, 1909. He studied at the Chicago Musical College (M.M., 1930); then took lessons with Nadia Boulanger and Thomas de Hartmann in Paris (1935–36). In 1936 he joined the faculty of the Univ. of Wyoming. His works include *Idyl* for Orch. (1930); *Solitude* for Orch. (1930; Boston, April 20, 1936); *A Ballade of the Night* for Voice and String Quartet (1936); numerous piano pieces and songs.

Willmers, Rudolf, Danish pianist and composer; b. Copenhagen, Oct. 31, 1821; d. Vienna, Aug. 24, 1878. His father, a Danish agriculturist, sent him to Germany at the age of 13 to study science, but Willmers turned to music; took lessons with Hummel for 2 years and with Friedrich Schneider for a year; became a concert pianist and toured successfully in Germany and Austria; was much acclaimed in Paris and London (1846–47); in 1866, settled in Vienna. His technical specialty was the performance of "chains of trills," for which he was famous. He wrote a number of brilliant piano solos: 6 *études*; *Sérénade érotique* (for the left hand); *Sehnsucht am Meere*; *Un Jour d'été en Norvège*; 2 *études de concert* (*La pompa di festa* and *La danza delle Baccanti*); *Sonata héroïque*; *Tarantella giocosa*; *La Sylphide*; *Trillerketten*; *Aus der Geisterwelt*, tremolo-caprice; *Allegro symphonique*; he also composed some chamber music.
BIBL.: T. de L***, "Notice sur la vie et les travaux artistiques de R. W.," *Archives des Hommes du Jour* (April 1847; also publ. separately).

Willner, Arthur, pianist and composer; b. Teplice, Czechoslovakia, March 5, 1881; d. London, April 7, 1959. He studied at the Leipzig Cons. and in Munich. From 1904 to 1924 he taught at the Stern Cons. in Berlin; from 1924 to 1938 he lived in Vienna; in 1938 settled in London. His works include a Sym.; Cello Concerto; Piano Concerto; 5 string quartets; 4 violin sonatas; 3 sonatas for violin and piano; 4 piano sonatas and several character pieces; choral works; organ works; songs.

Wills, Arthur, English organist, teacher, and composer; b. Coventry, Sept. 19, 1926. He was educated at the College of St. Nicholas in Canterbury and at the Univ. of Durham (D.Mus.); was assistant organist (1949–58) and organist (1958–90) at Ely Cathedral. He taught organ, theory, and composition at the Royal Academy of Music in London (from 1964).
WORKS: Sym. (1957); Concerto for Organ, Timpani, and Strings (1971); sacred choral works, including *Missa eliensis* (1959); *Jubilate Deo* (1965); *Te Deum* (1967); *An English Requiem* for Soprano, Baritone, Chorus, and Orch. (1971); services, anthems, motets, etc.; songs, including *The Dark Lady*: 8 *Shakespeare Sonnets* for Baritone and Piano (1986); *Sacrae symphoniae: Veni Creator Spiritus* for Double Wind Quintet (1987); organ pieces, including a Sonata and *Sinfonia eliensis* (1976), as well as a transcription of Mussorgsky's *Pictures at an Exhibition*; guitar pieces, including a Sonata (1972), *Moods and Diversions* (1975), and *Concerto lirico* for Guitar Quartet (1987); also *Sonata 1984* for Piano (1984).
BIBL.: M. Musgrave, "A. W. at 60," *Musical Times* (Sept. 1986).

Wills, Bob (James Robert), American country-music singer, fiddler, bandleader, and songwriter; b. near Kosse, Tex., March 6, 1905; d. Fort Worth, May 13, 1975. He first took up the mandolin, then began to play the fiddle; through his association with local black musicians, he learned blues and jazz as well. In 1928 he organized his own group, the Wills Fiddle Band; subsequently he appeared on radio and made many recordings. After settling in Tulsa, Okla. (1934), he became a fixture on station KVOO with his Texas Playboys band. From 1942 he was active with the group on the West Coast; also appeared in films. He gained popularity with his composition *San Antonio Rose*; he was elected to the Country Music Hall of Fame in 1968.

BIBL.: J. Latham, *The Life of B. W.: The King of Western Swing* (1974; 2nd ed., rev., 1987); C. Townsend, *San Antonio Rose: The Life and Music of B. W.* (Urbana, Ill., 1976).

Willson, (Robert Reiniger) Meredith, American composer of coruscating Americanistic musicals, and a fine flutist; b. Mason City, Iowa, May 18, 1902; d. Santa Monica, Calif., June 15, 1984. He learned to play the flute as a child, then went to N.Y. and studied at the Damrosch Inst. (1919–22) and received instruction in flute from Georges Barrère (1920–29); also studied with H. Hadley (1923–24) and Julius Gold (1921–23). He was 1st flutist in Sousa's band (1921–23) and a member of the N.Y. Phil. (1924–29); then became a musical director for various radio shows. For the 30th anniversary of the San Francisco earthquake he wrote a Sym., which he conducted in its 1st performance (San Francisco, April 19, 1936). His 2nd Sym. was first played by the Los Angeles Phil. on April 4, 1940. His other symphonic works include *The Jervis Bay; Symphonic Variations on an American Theme;* and *O.O. McIntyre Suite.* He also wrote many band pieces and a choral work, *Anthem of the Atomic Age.* However, he devoted himself mainly to the composition of popular music, in which he revealed a triple talent as a performer, writer, and composer. He appeared as a comedian on a radio program, "The Big Show," in which he engaged in a comic colloquy with Tallulah Bankhead, closing with an inspirational hymn, *May the Good Lord Bless and Keep You,* which became very popular as an anthem. Willson achieved his triumph with his musical revue *The Music Man,* for which he wrote the book, the lyrics, and the music. It opened on Broadway on Dec. 19, 1957, and became an immediate success, thanks to the satirical and yet somehow patriotic subject, dealing with a traveling salesman of band uniforms and instruments who sells them to hick-town suckers; and to the sparkling score, containing the hit chorus *76 Trombones.* His subsequent musicals were *The Unsinkable Molly Brown,* produced on Broadway on Nov. 3, 1960, for which he wrote the musical score, and *Here's Love,* produced on Broadway on Oct. 3, 1963, an adaptation of the film *Miracle on 34th Street. The Music Man* and *The Unsinkable Molly Brown* were made into films. Willson was also active as an arranger and orchestrator in Hollywood; he helped Charlie Chaplin in arranging the score for his anti-Hitler, anti-Mussolini film, *The Great Dictator* (1940). He publ. the autobiographical books *And There I Stood with My Piccolo* (N.Y., 1948), *Eggs I Have Laid* (N.Y., 1955), and *But He Doesn't Know the Territory* (descriptive of the origin of *The Music Man;* N.Y., 1959).

Willy. Pen name of **Gauthier-Villars, Henri.**

Wilm, (Peter) Nicolai von, German pianist, conductor, and composer; b. Riga, March 4, 1834; d. Wiesbaden, Feb. 20, 1911. He studied with Plaidy, Becker, and Richter at the Leipzig Cons.; in 1857–58, was in Riga as a theater conductor, and in 1860 proceeded to St. Petersburg, where he was an instructor at the Nikolaievsky Inst. until 1875; he subsequently lived in Dresden (1875–78) and then Wiesbaden. A highly prolific composer (more than 250 scores), he is best known through his chamber music; wrote a String Sextet, String Quartet, Piano Trio, Cello Sonata, 2 violin sonatas, Sonata for Violin and Harp; numerous pieces for piano solo: *Kleine Suite; Herbstfrüchte; Im russischen Dorf; Stimmungen; Dorf und Waldidyllen; Musikalisches Dekameron;* etc.; for Piano, 4-hands: *Eine Nordlandfahrt; Reisebilder aus Schlesien; Musikalische Federzeichnungen; Kalendarium;* etc.; also variations and other pieces for 2 pianos; men's choruses; songs.

Wilms, Jan Willem (actually, **Johann Wilhelm**), German-born Dutch pianist, organist, flutist, teacher, and composer; b. Witzhelden, near Solingen, March 30, 1772; d. Amsterdam, July 19, 1847. He received his early musical training from his father and elder brother. In 1791 he settled in Amsterdam as a pianist, flutist, and teacher; later was organist of the United Baptist Church (1823–46). He composed 2 piano concertos, 2 flute concertos, 2 string quartets, 2 piano trios, 3 violin sonatas, 2 flute sonatas, a Clarinet Concerto; also 3 syms. He was

the author of the Dutch national song *Wien Neerlands bloed door d'aderen vloeit* (1815).

BIBL.: E. Klusen, *J.W. W. und das Amsterdamer Musikleben (1772–1847)* (Buren, 1975).

Wilsing, Daniel Friedrich Eduard, German composer; b. Hörde, near Dortmund, Oct. 21, 1809; d. Berlin, May 2, 1893. He was an organist in Wesel from 1829 to 1834; then moved to Berlin. He composed an oratorio in 2 parts, *Jesus Christus* (produced in Bonn in 1889, by Wilsing's pupil Arnold Mendelssohn); a *De profundis a* 16, which won the gold medal for art at Berlin; piano sonatas; songs.

Wilson, Brian (Douglas), American singer, composer, and producer; b. Hawthorne, Calif., June 20, 1942. He twanged the string bass and banged the keyboard. In 1961 he got together with his similarly endowed brothers, **Dennis Wilson,** who beat the drums (b. Hawthorne, Dec. 4, 1944; drowned while surfing at Marina del Rey, Dec. 28, 1983), and **Carl Wilson** (b. Hawthorne, Dec. 21, 1946) and, in company with their 1st cousin, **Mike Love** (b. Los Angeles, March 15, 1941), and their mutual friend Al Jardine (b. Los Angeles, Sept. 3, 1942), organized a band named The Beach Boys, devoted to the celebration of surfing, fast cars, and long-legged California girls. Their adoration of these ingredients of California's lifestyle was reflected in their songs with such fetching titles as *Surfin' USA, Surfer Girl, Little Deuce Coupe, Surfin' Safari, Be True to Your School, Help Me Rhonda,* and such reiterative chants as *Fun, Fun, Fun,* and *Dance, Dance, Dance.* Overdoing things, Brian Wilson suffered a nervous breakdown and a serious attack of aphasia, ailments that he commemorated in something called *Death Sounds.* Without waiting for Brian Wilson to come back to reality, The Beach Boys issued a monumental single recording called *Good Vibrations,* which hit the ears of teeny-boppers with a multidecibel roar and, figuratively speaking, drove them into the sea a horde of mythical lemmings. A physiological reaction to this frenzy turned The Beach Boys toward the mystical world of Transcendental Meditation, as Mike Love led them to worship at the feet of a luxuriantly bearded Indian guru; but they soon returned to their commercially profitable recording work (75 million of their records were estimated to have been sold) and once more deployed their contented large bodies on the white sand beaches of California until tragedy struck on Dec. 28, 1983, when Dennis Wilson dived off their boat and never surfaced alive. By special dispensation (which involved an intercession from President Ronald Reagan, an admirer of The Beach Boys), Dennis Wilson was allowed at his widow's request to be buried bodily at sea, without preliminary cremation, circumventing the California law banning such burials, but it was specified that this should take place at more than 3 miles from the shore and at no less than 100 fathoms below the surface of the sea. In 1988 Brian Wilson made his solo debut with the album *Love and Mercy.*

BIBL.: *Current Biography* (July 1988).

Wilson, Charles M., Canadian composer; b. Toronto, May 8, 1931. He attended the Univ. of Toronto (D.Mus., 1954); studied composition with Lukas Foss (1950) and Carlos Chávez (1951) at the Berkshire Music Center at Tanglewood; also studied conducting there with Leonard Bernstein. From 1962 to 1970 he was head of the music dept. at Guelph Collegiate Vocational Inst. His music is contrapuntally dense and dissonant, but the formal element is preserved in Baroque structures.

WORKS: 2 operas: *Heloïse and Abelard* (Toronto, Sept. 8, 1973) and *Kamouraska* (1975); church opera, *The Summoning of Everyman* (Halifax, April 6, 1973); children's opera, *The Selfish Giant* (Toronto, Dec. 20, 1973); 3 string quartets (1950, 1968, 1975); Sym. in A (1954); *Sonata da chiesa* for Oboe and Strings (1960); String Trio (1963); *The Angels of the Earth,* oratorio (1966; Guelph, June 19, 1967); *En Guise d'Orphée* for Baritone and String Orch. (1968); *Phrases from Orpheus,* mixed-media score for Chorus and Dancers (Guelph Spring, Ontario, May 10, 1971); *Concerto 5x4x3* for String Quintet,

Woodwind Quartet, and Brass Trio (1970); *Sinfonia* for Double Orch. (Toronto, March 3, 1973); *Image out of Season* for Chorus and Brass Quintet (1973); *Christo paremus canticum* for Chorus and Orch. (Hamilton, Dec. 2, 1973); *Symphonic Perspectives: Kingsmere* (Ottawa, Oct. 4, 1974); *Missa brevis* for Chorus and Organ (1975).

Wilson, Domingo Santa Cruz. See **Santa Cruz Wilson, Domingo.**

Wilson, Grenville Dean, American composer; b. Plymouth, Conn., Jan. 26, 1833; d. Nyack, N.Y., Sept. 20, 1897. He was taught piano by his mother; then studied theory with A.W. Johnson in Boston; some of his piano pieces were publ. before he was 10 years old. In 1871 he became head of the music dept. of the Rockland Inst. in Nyack; in 1877 he organized the Nyack Sym. Soc. He publ. 178 pieces, chiefly for piano, some of which were popular (*The Shepherd-boy, Wayside Chapel, Chapel in the Mountains, Moonlight on the Hudson, Voix du matin,* etc.).

Wilson, Jackie, top-seeded black American rock-and-roll singer; b. Detroit, June 9, 1934; d. Mount Holly, N.J., Jan. 21, 1984. He was trained as a boxer but, yielding to his mother's pleas, he turned to the relatively less hazardous pursuit of rock singing. In 1953 he joined Billy Ward and the Dominoes, a rhythm-and-blues group, as its lead singer. In 1957 he launched a successful solo career. He made discs for the Motown Record Co. in Detroit; his recording of *Lonely Teardrops* topped the popularity charts in its category in 1959, selling more than a million copies. Among his other hits were *Am I the Man* and *Higher and Higher.* A bit of scandal touched him in 1961 when he was shot in a N.Y. hotel by a scorned female groupie; he was not badly hurt. As a performer, Wilson exercised a mesmeric force over his audience; his voice was almost operatic in its range; he emulated coloratura effects with his explosions of blues chromatics. All this was abruptly ended when he suffered a massive heart attack on stage on Sept. 29, 1975, in Cherry Hill, N.J., resulting in an irreversible coma. He lingered for several years while a court battle for his estate raged between his estranged wife and a son by a previous marriage. The wife won the litigation.

BIBL.: *Rolling Stone* (March 15, 1984).

Wilson, John, English lutenist, singer, and composer; b. Faversham, Kent, April 5, 1595; d. London, Feb. 22, 1674. He was musically gifted; at the age of 19, wrote music for *The Maske of Flowers.* According to some indications, he participated as a singer in a production of Shakespeare's *Much Ado about Nothing* (as Jacke Wilson). In 1635 he was made one of the King's Musicians; was in favor with Charles I, whom he followed to Oxford during the civil war in 1644, and was made a D.Mus. by Oxford Univ. on March 10, 1644; he was "Musick Professor" there from 1656 until 1661. Upon the Restoration he resumed his post at court, and on Oct. 22, 1662, became the successor of Henry Lawes as a Gentleman of the Chapel Royal. He publ. *Psalterium Carolinum: The Devotions of His Sacred Majestie* for 3 Voices and Basso Continuo (London, 1657) and *Cheerfull Ayres or Ballads. . .* for 3 Voices and Basso Continuo (Oxford, 1660); also numerous songs in contemporary collections.

BIBL.: E. Rimbault, *Who was "J. W.," the Singer of Shakespeare's Stage?* (London, 1846); E. Hart, "Caroline Lyrics and Contemporary Song-Books," *Library* (June 1953); V. Duckles, "The 'Curious' Art of J. W.: An Introduction to his Songs and Lute Music," *Journal of the American Musicological Society* (Summer 1954); H. Henderson, *The Vocal Music of J. W.* (diss., Univ. of North Carolina, 1962); M. Hobbs, "J. W.'s Literary Sources," *Lute Society Journal,* XVII (1975); P. Walls, "New Light on Songs by William Lawes and J. W.," *Music & Letters,* LVII (1976).

Wilson, Nancy (Sue), black American singer of popular music; b. Chillicothe, Ohio, Feb. 20, 1937. She sang in a church choir; commenced a professional career at 16 with appearances in local nightclubs; in 1959 she met Cannonball Adderley, who was instrumental in launching her on a career as a vocalist; she made numerous tours, singing jazz, soul, pop, and blues numbers, and received an honorary doctorate in music from an Ohio college.

Wilson, Olly (Woodrow), black American composer; b. St. Louis, Sept. 7, 1937. He was educated at Washington Univ. in St. Louis (B.M., 1959), at the Univ. of Illinois (Mus.M., 1960), and at the Univ. of Iowa, where his teachers were Robert Sykes, Robert Kelley, and Phillip Bezanson (Ph.D., 1964). In 1971–72 he traveled in West Africa to study indigenous music; then devoted himself to teaching and composition; was on the faculty of Florida A. & M. Univ. (1960–62 and 1964–65) and the Oberlin Cons. (1965–70); then was a prof. at the Univ. of Calif. at Berkeley (from 1970). In 1971 and 1977 he held Guggenheim fellowships; in 1977–78 he was a visiting artist at the American Academy in Rome.

WORKS: *Prelude and Line Study* for Woodwind Quartet (1959); Trio for Flute, Cello, and Piano (1959); String Quartet (1960); *Wry Fragments* for Tenor and Percussion (1961); Violin Sonata (1961); *Dance Suite* for Wind Ensemble (1962); *Soliloquy* for Bass Viol (1962); Sextet (1963); *3 Movements* for Orch. (1964); *Piece for 4* for Flute, Trumpet, Double Bass, and Piano (1966); *In Memoriam Martin Luther King, Jr.,* for Chorus and Electronic Sound (1968); *Voices* for Orch. (1970); *The 18 Hands of Jerome Harris,* electronic ballet (1971); *Akwan* for Piano, Electronic Piano, and Orch. (1972); *Black Martyrs,* electronic composition (1972); *Spirit Song* for Soprano, Chorus, and Orch. (1973); *Sometimes* for Tenor and Tape (1976); Piano Trio (1977); *Reflections* for Orch. (1978); *Trilogy* for Orch. (1979–80); *Lumina* for Orch. (1981); *Sinfonia* for Orch. (1983–84); *No More* for Tenor, Flute, Clarinet, Violin, Cello, Harp, Piano, and Percussion (1985).

Wilson, Philip, English singer and music editor; b. Hove, Sussex, Nov. 29, 1886; d. London, July 26, 1924. After studying singing in London, he went to Australia in 1913 as a vocal teacher at the Sydney Cons.; returning to England in 1920, he gave historical recitals, especially of Elizabethan songs. With Peter Warlock (Philip Heseltine), he ed. *English Ayres, Elizabethan and Jacobean* and *Chromatic Tunes of 1606;* also ed. *The Musical Proverbs* (London, 1924), from the "Lekingfelde" MS.

Wilson, Ransom, outstanding American flutist; b. Tuscaloosa, Ala., Oct. 25, 1951. He studied with Philip Dunigan at the North Carolina School of the Arts; also profited from advice given by Jean-Pierre Rampal. He made a European tour with the Juilliard Chamber Orch. under Peter Maag, and soon established himself as a brilliant virtuoso. In 1980 he founded and served as conductor-soloist with his own ensemble, Solisti New York; also appeared as guest conductor with other ensembles; served as principal guest conductor of the Flint (Mich.) Sym. Orch. (from 1987). His repertoire is catholic, covering all periods and styles; he also commissioned special works for the flute, and arranged music for use in his concerts.

BIBL.: A Kozinn, "R. W.," *Ovation* (Aug. 1984).

Wilson, Richard (Edward), American composer, pianist, and teacher; b. Cleveland, May 15, 1941. He studied cello, piano, theory, and composition in Cleveland; in 1959, entered Harvard Univ., where he took courses in music with Randall Thompson, G. Wallace Woodworth, and Robert Moevs (A.B., 1963, magna cum laude); he subsequently attended classes at Rutgers Univ. (M.A., 1966); also studied piano with Leonard Shure in N.Y. (1960) and with Friedrich Wührer in Munich (1963). In 1966 he joined the faculty of Vassar College; was made a prof. in 1976; from 1979 to 1982, served as chairman of the music dept. there, and again from 1985 to 1988. In 1986 he received the Walter Hinrichsen Award of the American Academy and Inst. of Arts and Letters; in 1988 he was awarded the Cleveland Arts Prize.

WORKS: *Suite for 5 Players* (1963); Trio for Oboe, Violin, and Cello (1964); *Fantasy and Variations* for Chamber Ensemble (1965); String Quartet No. 1 (1968); Quartet for 2 Flutes,

Double Bass, and Harpsichord (1969); *Initiation* for Orch. (1970); Wind Quintet (1974); String Quartet No. 2 (1977); *Serenade: Variations on a Simple March* for Clarinet, Viola, and Double Bass (1978); *Sour Flowers: 8 Piano Pieces in the Form of an Herbal* (1979); *Deux pas de trois: Pavane and Tango* for Flute, Oboe, and Harpsichord (1979); Concerto for Violin and Chamber Orch. (1979); *Figuration* for Clarinet, Cello, and Piano (1981); *Gnomics* for Flute, Oboe, and Clarinet (1981); String Quartet No. 3 (1982); Suite for Wind Instruments (1983); Concerto for Bassoon and Chamber Orch. (1983); Sym. No. 1 (1984); *Flutations* for Flute (1985); *Intercalations* for Piano (1986); Sym. No. 2 (1986); *Jubilation* for Wind Ensemble (1987); *Silhouette* for Orch. (1988); *Contentions* for Chamber Ensemble (1988); *Suite* for Small Orch. (1988); *Articulations* for Orch. (1989); Sonata for Violin and Piano (1989).

Wilson, Teddy (Theodore Shaw), noted black American jazz pianist; b. Austin, Tex., Nov. 24, 1912; d. New Britain, Conn., July 31, 1986. He studied piano, violin, clarinet, and oboe; attended Talladega College in Alabama for a year as a music student, then played in Lawrence "Speed" Webb's band in Detroit (1929–31) and in Milton Senior's band in Toledo (1931). He then worked in Chicago with Louis Armstrong, Jimmie Noone, and others before going to N.Y. (1934); after performing with Benny Goodman (1935–39), he was active mainly with his own groups; appeared again with Goodman on his Russian tour (1962); later played at N.Y.'s Carnegie Hall (1980). He was one of the most highly regarded pianists of the swing era, being especially praised for his contrapuntal style and his imaginative improvisations.

Wimberger, Gerhard, Austrian composer; b. Vienna, Aug. 30, 1923. He studied composition with J.N. David and conducting with C. Krauss at the Salzburg Mozarteum; taught there (from 1953). In 1967 he received the Austrian State Prize.
    WORKS: STAGE: *König für einen Tag,* ballet (1950–51); *Schaubundengeschichte,* opera (1952–53; Mannheim, 1954); *Der Handschuh,* chamber ballet (Frankfurt, 1955); *La Battaglia oder Der rote Federbusch,* comic opera (Schwetzingen, 1960); *Hero und Leander,* dance drama (Wiesbaden, 1963); *Lebensregeln,* "catechism with music" (1970–72; Munich, Aug. 27, 1972); *Paradou,* opera (1985); *Fürst von Salzburg-Wolf Dietrich,* scenic chronicle (Salzburg, 1987). **ORCH.:** *Divertimento* for String Orch. (1954); Concerto for Piano and Chamber Orch. (1955); *Étude dramatique* (1961); *Risonanze* for 3 Orch. Groups (1965–66; Berlin, Jan. 31, 1968); *Multiplay* for 23 Players (1972–73); *Motus* (1976); *Programm* (1978); *Ausstrahlungen W.A. Mozart'scher Themen* (1978); Concerto for 2 Pianos and Orch. (1981); *Nachtmusik Trauermusik Finalmusik* (1988); *Vagabondage* for Big Band (1988). **CHAMBER:** Sonata for 2 Pianos (1950); *Stories* for Winds and Percussion (1962); String Quartet (1978); *Phantasie* for 8 Players (1982). **VOCAL:** *Kantate vom Sport* (1953); *Heiratspostkantate* for Chorus, Harpsichord, and Double Bass (1957); *Ars amatoria,* cantata for Soprano, Baritone, Chorus, Combo, and Chamber Orch. (1967); *Memento vivere: Gesänge vom Tod* for Mezzo-soprano, Baritone, 3 Narrators, Chorus, and Orch. (1973–74); *Wir hören zu atmen nicht auf,* song cycle for Female Voice and Piano (1988).

Winant, William, American percussionist; b. N.Y., Feb. 11, 1953. His mother was the well-known casting director Ethel Winant; his father, H.M. Wynant, an actor. He was educated at N.Y. Univ. (B.F.A., 1977) and Mills College in Oakland, Calif. (M.F.A., 1982). In 1983 he became a visiting lecturer at the Univ. of Calif. at Santa Cruz, and in 1984 joined the percussion faculty at the Univ. of Calif. at Berkeley; also was principal percussionist of the Cabrillo Music Festival (from 1984) and of the San Francisco Contemporary Chamber Players (from 1988). A leading avant-garde percussionist, Winant has given 1st performances of works by such composers as Frederic Rzewski, Daniel Lentz, Somei Satoh, and Morton Feldman. In 1984 he formed (with David Abel, violin, and Julie Steinberg, piano) the Abel-Steinberg-Winant Trio, with which he toured widely and recorded; he also performed with Room (with Larry Ochs and Chris Brown) and with the live electro-acoustic ensemble Challenge (with Anthony Braxton and David Rosenboom).

Winbeck, Heinz, German composer; b. Piflas, Feb. 11, 1946. He studied piano and composition at the Richard Strauss Cons. in Munich (1964–66) and composition with Genzmer and Bialas at the Hochschule für Musik there (1967–73); was a theater composer in Ingolstadt and Wunsiedel (1974–78). From 1980 he lectured at the Hochschule für Musik in Munich. His compositions are often influenced by literature and are personal reflections in a modern, neo-Impressionistic style.
    WORKS: ORCH.: *Sonoscillent* for Cello and String Orch. (1971); *Entgegengesang* for Chamber Orch. (1973; Stuttgart, June 16, 1974); *Lenau-Fantasien* for Cello and Chamber Orch. (1979); *Denk ich an Haydn,* 3 fragments (1981–82; Remscheid, March 31, 1982); 3 syms.: No. 1, *Tu Solus* (1982–83; rev. 1985; Munich, April 19, 1985); No. 2, *Pegasusartefakt* (1984); No. 3, *Grodek* (Munich, Nov. 25, 1988). **CHAMBER:** *In Memoriam Paul Celan* for Soprano, Flute, Piano, and Percussion (1970); *Sie tanzt,* after Sachs, for Baritone and Chamber Ensemble (1971); Music for Wind Quintet (1971); *Espaces* for 4 Percussionists, Piano, and Flute (1971–72); *Nocturnes I* for Chamber Ensemble (1972) and *II, Nacht mein Augentrost,* for Chorus, 5 Flutes, 2 Guitars, Bandolon, Organ, and 5 Percussionists (1973); *Poco a poco* for Piano and String Trio (1974); *Chansons à temps* for Female Voices and 13 Instruments (1976); 3 string quartets: No. 1, *Tempi capricciosi* (1979), No. 2, *Tempi notturni* (1979), and No. 3, *Jagdquartett* (1984); *Blick in den Strom,* string quintet (1981).

Wincenc, Carol, talented American flutist and teacher; b. Buffalo, June 29, 1949. She studied in Italy with Severino Gazzelloni, taking courses at the Accademia Chigiana in Siena (1966–67) and at the Accademia di Santa Cecilia in Rome (1967–68); was a pupil of Robert Willoughby at the Oberlin Cons. (1967–69), of Harold Bennett at the Manhattan School of Music in N.Y. (B.Mus., 1971), and of Arthur Lora at the Juilliard School in N.Y. (M.M., 1972). She was 1st flutist in the National Orchestral Assoc. in N.Y. (1970–71), the Aspen (Colo.) Festival Chamber Orch. (1970–72), and the St. Paul (Minn.) Chamber Orch. (1972–77). After winning the Concert Artist's Guild Award, she made her recital debut at N.Y.'s Carnegie Recital Hall in 1972; won 1st prize at the Naumburg Competition in 1978. In subsequent years she appeared as a soloist with many of the major world orchs., as a recitalist and as a chamber music player; was founder–artistic director of the International Flute Festival in St. Paul, Minn. (1985–87). She taught at the Manhattan School of Music (1980–86), the Indiana Univ. School of Music (from 1986), and the Juilliard School (from 1988). She won particular distinction for her promotion of contemporary music; commissioned and premiered various works for flute, including pieces by Lukas Foss, Joan Tower, Giya Kancheli, and Henryk Gorecki.

Windgassen, Wolfgang (Fritz Hermann), distinguished German tenor; b. Annemasse, Haute Savoie, June 26, 1914; d. Stuttgart, Sept. 8, 1974. He received his early vocal training from his father, **Fritz Windgassen** (b. Hamburg, Feb. 9, 1883; d. Murnau, April 17, 1963), who was a leading tenor at the Stuttgart Opera; then continued his studies at the Stuttgart Cons. with Maria Ranzow and Alfons Fischer. He made his operatic debut in Pforzheim in 1941 as Alvaro in *La forza del destino;* after military service in the German army, he joined the Stuttgart Opera in 1945, remaining on its roster until 1972. From 1951 to 1970 he appeared at the Bayreuth Festivals, where he was a leading Heldentenor. He made his Metropolitan Opera debut in N.Y. on Jan. 22, 1957, as Siegmund. He sang regularly at Convent Garden from 1955 to 1966. He was especially successful in Wagnerian roles, as Tannhäuser, Tristan, Parsifal, Siegfried, and Lohengrin; he also appeared as Radames in *Aida* and Don José in *Carmen.*
    BIBL.: B. Wessling, *W. W.* (Bremen, 1967).

Winding, August (Henrik), Danish pianist and composer; b. Taaro, March 24, 1835; d. Copenhagen, June 16, 1899.

He studied with Gade; was appointed a prof. at the Copenhagen Cons. in 1867; from 1891 until his death, was its director. He composed a Sym.; *Nordische Ouvertüre;* Piano Concerto; cadenzas to Beethoven's piano concertos and to many of Mozart's; String Sextet; Piano Quartet; 2 violin sonatas; many piano pieces (3 *Fantasiestücke, Reisebilder, Ländliche Szenen, Studien und Stimmungen, Idyllen und Legenden, Albumblätter,* etc.); songs.

Winding, Kai (Chresten), Danish-born American jazz trombonist and composer; b. Århus, May 18, 1922; d. Yonkers, N.Y., May 6, 1983. He was taken to the U.S. in 1934; took up the trombone while in high school; then served in the U.S. Coast Guard. Following his discharge, he played with Benny Goodman (1945–46) and Stan Kenton (1947); was a member of J.J. Johnson's quintet (1954–56); then led his own septet. As a trombone player, he excelled in bop.

Windingstad, Ole, Norwegian-American conductor and composer; b. Sandefjord, May 18, 1886; d. Kingston, N.Y., June 3, 1959. He graduated from the Oslo Cons. in 1902; then studied at the Leipzig Cons.; settled in N.Y. in 1913, and established the Scandinavian Sym. Orch., which he conducted until 1929; also conducted the Brooklyn Sym. Orch. (1930–32), the Knickerbocker Sym. Orch. in Albany, N.Y. (1937–39), the New Orleans Sym. Orch. (1940–44), the Albany Sym. Orch. (1945–48), and the Dutchess County (N.Y.) Phil. (1945–59). In 1929 he was decorated with the Norwegian Order of Saint Olaf. He composed a Sym. (1913); a cantata, *The Skald of Norway* (1929); *The Tides* for Orch. (Albany, Feb. 13, 1938, composer conducting); many minor pieces.

Windt, Herbert, German composer; b. Senftenberg, Sept. 15, 1894; d. Deisenhofen, Nov. 22, 1965. He studied piano as a child; then took courses in music theory with Klatte and Schreker in Berlin. In 1923 he obtained the Mendelssohn Prize; in 1936, was awarded the Olympic Prize for his work *Marathon 1936.*
WORKS: *Andromache,* opera (Berlin, March 16, 1932); cantata, *Flug zum Niederwald* (1935); chamber sym., *Andante religioso,* for Voice and 35 Instruments (1921); numerous film scores.

Winham, Godfrey, English-American composer and computer specialist; b. London, Dec. 11, 1934; d. Princeton, N.J., April 26, 1975. He studied composition and piano at the Royal Academy of Music in London; in 1954 went to the U.S., where he took courses at Princeton Univ. (A.B., 1956; M.F.A., 1958); received his Ph.D. degree there with the dissertation *Composition with Arrays* (1965); then joined the staff as a lecturer on electronic music and computer composition. In 1969 he worked on the computerized synthesis of music and speech. Apart from his programmed compositions on a computer, he wrote 2 string quartets, *The Habit of Perfection* for Voice and String Quartet, and several piano pieces. He married **Bethany Beardslee** in 1956.

Winkelmann, Hermann, notable German tenor; b. Braunschweig, March 8, 1849; d. Vienna, Jan. 18, 1912. He started out as a piano maker, but became interested in singing; studied voice in Paris and with Koch in Hannover; made his operatic debut in *Il Trovatore* in Sondershausen (1875), and then sang in Altenburg, Darmstadt, and Leipzig. In 1878 he joined the Hamburg Opera, and appeared with the company during its visit to London in 1882 at Drury Lane under Richter's direction in Wagnerian roles. His success induced Richter to recommend him to Wagner, who chose him to create the role of Parsifal at Bayreuth (July 26, 1882). From 1883 to 1906, when he retired on a pension, he was one of the brightest stars of the Vienna Court Opera, where one of his most brilliant achievements was the performance of the role of Tristan (with Materna as Isolde) in the Vienna premiere (Oct. 4, 1883). In 1884 he sang in the U.S. at the Wagner festivals given by Theodore Thomas in N.Y., Boston, Philadelphia, Cincinnati, and Chicago.

Winkler, Alexander (Gustav Adolfovich), Russian composer and pianist; b. Kharkov, March 3, 1865; d. Besançon,

France, Aug. 6, 1935. He studied piano with Slatin at the Music Inst. of the Russian Music Soc. (graduated, 1889), then with Duvernoy in Paris and Leschetizky in Vienna, where he also studied composition with Navrátil. Returning to Russia, he was a piano teacher in his native city (1890–96); then was a prof. at the St. Petersburg Cons. (1907–24); among his students was Prokofiev. In 1924 he emigrated to France and became a prof. at the Besançon Cons. He composed an overture, *En Bretagne* (1908); orch. variations on a Russian folk song (1912) and on a Finnish folk song (1913); *Dernier printemps* for Cello and Orch. (1935); 3 string quartets (1892, 1901, 1909); Piano Quintet (1899); Viola Sonata (1902); other chamber pieces; piano pieces; songs.

Winkler, Peter K(enton), American composer; b. Los Angeles, Jan. 26, 1943. He studied with Seymour Shifrin, David Lewin, and Andrew Imbrie at the Univ. of Calif. at Berkeley (B.A., 1964) and with Earl Kim, Milton Babbitt, and Edward T. Cone at Princeton Univ. (M.F.A., 1967). He taught at the State Univ. of N.Y. at Stony Brook (from 1971) and was a visiting faculty member of Evergreen State College in Olympia, Wash. (1989–90). In 1978 he held a MacDowell Colony fellowship.
WORKS: Musical theater pieces and incidental music for plays, radio, and television. ORCH.: *Praise of Silence* for Soprano, Chorus, Renaissance Ensemble, and Tape (1969); Sym. (1971–78). CHAMBER: String Quartet (1965–67); *Clarinet Bouquet: 4 Concert Rags* for Clarinet, Piano, and Bassoon (1976–80); *Recitativo e Terzetto* for Oboe, Clarinet, and Bassoon (1980); *No Condition is Permanent* for Flute, Clarinet, Violin, Cello, Piano, and Percussion (1980–89).

Winner, Septimus, American composer of popular music; b. Philadelphia, May 11, 1827; d. there, Nov. 22, 1902. He learned to play the violin; married at the age of 20 and opened a music store in Philadelphia, where he began giving lessons on the violin, guitar, and banjo. In 1854 he wrote his best-known song, *Listen to the Mocking Bird* (based on a melody originated by his black errand boy, "Whistling Dick" Milburn), selling the copyright for $5; in his lifetime the song sold 20 million copies. In 1862 he wrote *Give Us Back Our Old Commander: Little Mac, the People's Pride,* voicing a widespread sentiment for the return of General McClellan; the song was regarded as subversive and Winner was arraigned, but soon released; later the song, slightly altered, was used for Grant's presidential campaign. Winner also wrote the song *Whispering Hope,* which became extremely popular. He was a pioneer in bringing music to the masses; wrote over 200 vols. of music, including many instructive works, for 23 different instruments, and made about 2,000 arrangements for violin and piano. He used the pen name Alice Hawthorne (in honor of his mother, Mary Ann Hawthorne) for many of his songs, including *Listen to the Mocking Bird.*
BIBL.: C. Claghorn, *The Mocking Bird: The Life and Diary of Its Author, Sep. W.* (Philadelphia, 1937).

Winograd, Arthur, American cellist and conductor; b. N.Y., April 22, 1920. He studied at the New England Cons. of Music in Boston (1937–40) and at the Curtis Inst. of Music in Philadelphia (1940–41); played the cello in the Boston Sym. Orch. (1940–41) and in the NBC Sym. Orch. (1942–43); then was a member of the Juilliard String Quartet and the faculty of the Juilliard School of Music (1946–55). He was active as a conductor for MGM Records (1954–58) and Audio Fidelity Records (1958–60); then was music director of the Birmingham (Ala.) Sym. Orch. (1960–64) and the Hartford (Conn.) Sym. Orch. (1964–85).

Winter, Paul, American composer and instrumentalist; b. Altoona, Pa., Aug. 31, 1939. He was in the 3rd generation of a family of professional musicians; his great-aunts and -uncles belonged to the vaudeville troupe that introduced the saxophone to the U.S. He began playing drums at the age of 5, piano at 6, and clarinet at 8; by the time he was 12 he had discovered bebop, chosen the saxophone as his primary instrument, and formed his 1st band. He studied English composition at Northwestern Univ. (B.A., 1961) while frequenting jazz clubs in Chicago; in 1961 he formed with fellow students the Paul Winter Sextet, which was subsequently sent abroad on a State Dept. cultural exchange program (1962); before disbanding in 1965, the group had released 7 recordings. Winter moved to Connecticut and in 1967 formed the stylistically eclectic Paul Winter Consort, which released 4 highly successful recordings before disbanding in 1972; the group was reformed in 1977 with a more consistent style that integrated natural sounds with gentle, improvisatory music. In 1980 Winter founded Living Music Records, whose name suggests his strong environmental and humanistic concerns. Many of his concerts and recordings take place in unusual locations or for the benefit of social causes; he is an artist-in-residence at the Cathedral of St. John the Divine in N.Y. His compositions combine jazz, folk, ethnic, and classical elements in a style that has been a prototype for New Age music. Among his noteworthy recordings are *Icarus* (1972), *Common Ground* (1977), and *Earth: Voices of a Planet* (1990).

Winter, Peter (von), German composer; b. Mannheim (baptized), Aug. 28, 1754; d. Munich, Oct. 17, 1825. He was a violinist in the Electoral orch. at the age of 10; was given permanent employment there in 1776; studied with Abbé Vogler; went with the court to Munich in 1778 and became director of the Court Orch.; in 1787 he was named court Vice-Kapellmeister and in 1798 court Kapellmeister. In 1814 he received a title of nobility from the court for his long service. In Munich he brought out a number of operas, of which the most important are *Helena und Paris* (Feb. 5, 1782), *Der Bettelstudent oder Das Donnerwetter* (Feb. 2, 1785), *Der Sturm* (1798), *Marie von Montalban* (Jan. 28, 1800), and *Colmal* (Sept. 15, 1809). Frequent leaves of absence from Munich enabled him to travel; in Venice he produced his operas *Catone in Utica* (1791), *I sacrifizi di Creta ossia Arianna e Teseo* (Feb. 13, 1792), *I Fratelli rivali* (Nov. 1793), and *Belisa ossia La fedeltà riconosciuta* (Feb. 5, 1794). In Prague he produced the opera *Ogus ossia Il trionfo del bel sesso* (1795). In Vienna he brought out *Das unterbrochene Opferfest* (June 14, 1796; his most successful opera; produced all over Europe), *Babylons Pyramiden* (Oct. 25, 1797), and *Das Labirint oder Der Kampf mit den Elementen* (June 12, 1798); in Paris he produced his only French opera, *Tamerlan* (Sept. 14, 1802); in London, the Italian operas *La grotta di Calipso* (May 31, 1803), *Il trionfo dell'amor fraterno* (March 22, 1804), *Il ratto di Proserpina* (May 3, 1804), and *Zaira* (Jan. 29, 1805); in Milan, *Maometto II* (Jan. 28, 1817), *I due Valdomiri* (Dec. 26, 1817), and *Etelinda* (March 23, 1818). He also wrote several ballets; oratorios and sacred cantatas for the Munich court chapel; 28 masses and a vast amount of other church music; 4 syms. (including the grand choral sym. *Die Schlacht*, 1814); overtures; Violin Concerto; Flute Concerto; Bassoon Concerto; 2 oboe concertos; other concerted works; much chamber music, including 12 divertimentos for 2 Violins, Viola, and Cello and a Divertimento for 2 Violins, Viola, Cello, and 2 Horns, 6 string quartets, 3 quintets, 2 sextets, a Septet, an Octet, sonatas, etc. He publ. *Vollständige Singschule* (Mainz, 1825; 2nd ed., 1874). **BIBL.:** J. Arnold, *P. W.* (Erfurt, 1810); W. Neumann, *P. W.* (Kassel, 1856); V. Frensdorf, *P. W. als Opernkomponist* (diss., Univ. of Munich, 1908); L. Kuckuk, *P. W. als deutscher Opernkomponist* (diss., Univ. of Heidelberg, 1923); E. Loeffler, *P. W. als Kirchenmusiker* (diss., Univ. of Frankfurt, 1929).

Winterberger, Alexander, German pianist, teacher, music critic, and composer; b. Weimar, Aug. 14, 1834; d. Leipzig, Sept. 23, 1914. He studied at the Leipzig Cons. (1848) and with Liszt. In 1869, he became piano prof. at the St. Petersburg Cons.; he returned to Leipzig in 1872 and remained there as a teacher and music critic. He publ. some piano pieces: *Alinen-Tänze* (waltzes, mazurkas, minuets, etc.), *Concert-Etude, Valse-Caprice, Concert-Adagio*; songs; German and Slavonic duets. **BIBL.:** O. Foerster, *A. W.: Seine Werke, sein Leben* (Hannover, 1905; with a list of works).

Winterfeld, Carl (Georg Vivigens) von, German writer on music; b. Berlin, Jan. 28, 1784; d. there, Feb. 19, 1852. He studied law at the Univ. of Halle; then occupied juridical positions in Breslau and Berlin. He collected a valuable library of early music, which he donated to the Library of Berlin. **WRITINGS:** *Johannes Pierluigi von Palestrina* (1832); *Johannes Gabrieli und sein Zeitalter* (3 vols., 1834); *Über K. Fr. Chr. Faschs geistliche Gesangswerke* (1839); *Dr. Martin Luthers deutsche geistliche Lieder* (1840); *Der evangelische Kirchengesang und sein Verhältnis zur Kunst des Tonsatzes* (3 vols., 1843–47); *Über Herstellung des Gemeinde- und Chorgesangs in der evangelischen Kirche* (1848); *Zur Geschichte heiliger Tonkunst* (2 parts; 1850, 1852); *Musiktreiben und Musikempfindungen im 16. und 17. Jahrhundert* (1851); *Alceste von Lulli, Händel und Gluck* (1851); *Allegorisch-poetische Festopern am Kaiserlichen Hofe zu Wien in der letzten Hälfte des 17. Jahrhunderts* (1852). **BIBL.:** A. Prüfer, ed., *Briefwechsel zwischen C. v.W. und Eduard Krüger* (Leipzig, 1898); B. Stockmann, *C. v.W.* (diss., Univ. of Kiel, 1958).

Winter-Hjelm, Otto, Norwegian organist, music critic, and composer; b. Christiania, Oct. 8, 1837; d. there (Oslo), May 3, 1931. He studied with H. Kjerulf in Christiania, at the Leipzig Cons. (1857–58), and with Kullak and Wüerst in Berlin. With Grieg, he organized the 1st Norwegian music academy in 1867; was organist in the Trefoldighetskirke in Christiania from 1874 till 1921; wrote music criticism in the *Aftenposten* (1887–1913). He publ. *Af Kristiania teaterliv i den seneste tid* (essays; Christiania, 1875). **WORKS:** Sym. No. 1 (Christiania, Sept. 27, 1862); Sym. No. 2 (1862; Christiania, March 18, 1916); many choruses for Men's Voices; ed. *50 Melodier til Hauges og Landstads Salmebøger* and *50 Salmemelodier* for Piano; also church music.

Winternitz, Emanuel, Austrian-American musicologist and museum curator; b. Vienna, Aug. 4, 1898; d. N.Y., Aug. 22, 1983. He served in the Austrian army in World War I; after the Armistice, studied jurisprudence at the Univ. of Vienna (LL.D., 1922); then was engaged as a corporate lawyer in Vienna (1929–38). After the Anschluss in 1938, he emigrated to the U.S., where he devoted himself mainly to lecturing on art; served as Peripatetic Professor for the Carnegie Foundation. In 1942 he was appointed keeper of musical instruments at the Metropolitan Museum in N.Y.; in 1949, was named curator of the Crosby Brown Collection of Musical Instruments of All Nations at the Metropolitan. He also administered the André Mertens Galleries for Musical Instruments (1971–73). In 1973 he became curator emeritus of the Metropolitan. Among his principal endeavors was musical iconography; he publ. a valuable reference work, *Musical Autographs from Monteverdi to Hindemith* (2 vols., Princeton, N.J., 1955); other books were *Keyboard Instruments in the Metropolitan Museum of Art* (N.Y., 1961); *Die schönsten Musikinstrumente des Abendlandes* (Munich, 1966; in Eng. as *Musical Instruments of the Western World*, N.Y., 1967); *Gaudenzio Ferrari, his School, and the Early History of the Violin* (Milan, 1967); *Musical Instruments and their Symbolism in Western Art* (N.Y., 1967; 2nd ed., 1979); *Leonardo da Vinci as a Musician* (New Haven, Conn., 1982).

Wintzer, Richard, German composer; b. Nauendorf, near Halle, March 9, 1866; d. Berlin, Aug. 14, 1952. He studied painting, and also music (with Bargiel); lived mostly in Berlin, and was active as a painter, composer, and music critic. He wrote 2 operas, *Die Willis* (1895) and *Marienkind* (1905); *Auf hohen Bergen* for Baritone, Chorus, and Orch.; some fine songs (*Ernste Gesänge, Kinderlieder, Sturmlieder*); piano pieces. He also publ. *Menschen von anderem Schlage* (1912) and an autobiography. **BIBL.:** H. Killer, "R. W., Ein Leben zwischen den Künsten," *Musik* (March 1941).

Winwood, Stevie, English pop singer and songwriter; b. Birmingham, May 12, 1948. He learned to play guitar, keyboard instruments, and string bass; joined The Spencer Davis Group and composed, in part, its hits *Gimme Some Lovin'* and *I'm a Man.* He soon formed his own band, called Traffic, with which he toured America in 1968. The personnel of Traffic changed with eponymous rapidity, with the titles of their record albums reflecting their loss of direction: *Last Exit, Traffic, Heavy Traffic,* and *On the Road.* Winwood found the right turn on his rocking freeway with his solo album *Arc of a Diver,* which received a platinum award.

Wiora, Walter, renowned German musicologist; b. Kattowitz, Dec. 30, 1906. He studied in Berlin at the Hochschule für Musik (1925–27) and received training in musicology from Abert, Blume, Hornbostel, Sachs, Schering, and Schünemann; continued his studies with Gurlitt at the Univ. of Freiburg (Ph.D., 1937, with the diss. *Die Variantenbildung im Volkslied: Ein Beitrag zur systematischen Musikwissenschaft*); completed his Habilitation there in 1941 with his *Die Herkunft der Melodien in Kretschmers und Zuccalmaglios Sammlung* (publ. in an enl. ed. as *Die rheinisch-bergischen Melodien bei Zuccalmaglio und Brahms,* Bad Godesberg, 1953). He was an assistant at the Deutsches Volksliedarchiv in Freiburg (1936–41); after serving as a reader in musicology at the Univ. of Posen, he returned to Freiburg and was archivist at the Deutsches Volksliedarchiv (1946–58); then was prof. of musicology at the Univ. of Kiel (1958–64) and at the Univ. of Saarbrücken (1964–72). His principal achievement was his advocacy of a system of "essential research" in musicology that utilizes both traditional and contemporary principles.

WRITINGS: *Die deutsche Volksliedweise und der Osten* (Wolfenbüttel and Berlin, 1940); *Zur Frühgeschichte der Musik in den Alpenländern* (Basel, 1949); *Das echte Volkslied* (Heidelberg, 1950); *Europäische Volksmusik und abendländische Tonkunst* (Kassel, 1957); *Die geschichtliche Sonderstellung der abendländischen Musik* (Mainz, 1959); *Die vier Weltalter der Musik* (Stuttgart, 1961; Eng. tr., 1965, as *The Four Ages of Music*); *Komponist und Mitwelt* (Kassel, 1964); ed. *Die Ausbreitung des Historismus über die Musik* (Regensburg, 1969); *Das deutsche Lied: Zur Geschichte und Ästhetik einer musikalischen Gattung* (Wolfenbüttel and Zürich, 1971); *Historische und systematische Musikwissenschaft* (Tutzing, 1972); *Ergebnisse und Aufgaben vergleichender Musikforschung* (Darmstadt, 1975); *Das musikalische Kunstwerk* (Tutzing, 1983).

BIBL.: L. Finscher and C.-H. Mahling, eds., *Festschrift für W. W.* (Kassel, 1967); C.-H. Mahling, ed., *Beiträge zu einer musikalischen Gattung: W. W. zum 70. Geburtstag* (Tutzing, 1979).

Wirén, Dag (Ivar), prominent Swedish composer; b. Striberg, Oct. 15, 1905; d. Danderyd, April 19, 1986. He studied at the Stockholm Cons. with Oskar Lindberg and Ernest Ellberg (1926–31); then in Paris with Leonid Sabaneyev (1932–34). He returned to Sweden in 1934, and was music critic for the *Svenska Morgonbladet* (1938–46); was vice-president of the Soc. of Swedish Composers (1947–63). His early music was influenced by Scandinavian Romanticism; later he adopted a more sober and more cosmopolitan neo-Classicism, stressing the symmetry of formal structure; in his thematic procedures he adopted the method of systematic intervallic metamorphosis rather than development and variation. He ceased composing in 1972.

WORKS: *Oscarbalen* (Oscarian Ball, 1949); television ballet, *Den elaka drottningen* (The Wicked Queen, 1960; Swedish television, Nov. 22, 1961); 2 radio operettas, *Blått, gult, rött* (1940; inspired by Churchill's famous speech containing the phrase "Blood, sweat, tears") and *Den glada patiensen* (1941); 2 concert overtures (1931, 1940); 5 syms.: No. 1 (1932); No. 2 (1939); No. 3 (1943–44); No. 4 (1951–52); No. 5 (1964; Stockholm, Dec. 5, 1964); *Sinfonietta* for Orch. (1933–34); Cello Concerto (1936); *Serenade* for Strings (1937); *Little Suite* for Orch. (1941); *Romantic Suite* for Orch. (1945); Violin Concerto (1945–46); Piano Concerto (1947–50); *Divertimento* for Orch. (1954–57); *Triptyk* for Orch. (1958); *Music* for Strings (1966–67; Stockholm, Jan. 12, 1968); Flute Concertino (1972);

5 string quartets (1930; 1935; 1941–45; 1952–53; 1969–70); *Theme and Variations* for Piano (1933); 2 piano trios (1933, 1961); Violin Sonatina (1939); 5 *Ironic Miniatures* for Piano (1942–45); Piano Sonatina (1950); Quartet for Flute, Oboe, Clarinet, and Cello (1956); 5 *Improvisations* for Piano (1959); *Little Serenade* for Guitar (1964); Wind Quintet (1971); *Little Piano Suite* (1971); incidental music for many plays and films; songs.

BIBL.: L. Hedwall, "D. W.," *Musikrevy,* IX (1954; Eng. tr. in *Music in Sweden: Musikrevy International,* 1954).

Wirth, Emanuel, Bohemian violinist; b. Luditz, Oct. 18, 1842; d. Berlin, Jan. 5, 1923. He was a pupil of Kittl at the Prague Cons.; then taught at the Cons. of Rotterdam, and was concertmaster of the local orch.; succeeded Rappoldi as viola player in the Joachim String Quartet, in Berlin; subsequently formed his own trio, with R. Hausmann (cello) and H. Barth (piano), presenting numerous concerts in Germany.

Wirth, Helmut (Richard Adolf Friedrich Karl), German musicologist and composer; b. Kiel, Oct. 10, 1912. He studied composition with R. Oppel; then took courses in musicology with Fritz Stein and Blume at the Univ. of Kiel (Ph.D., 1937, with the diss. *Joseph Haydn als Dramatiker*; publ. in Wolfenbüttel and Berlin, 1940); from 1936 he was active with the Hamburg Radio; also was lecturer at the Schleswig-Holstein Academy of Music in Lübeck (1952–72). He was a founder-member of the Haydn Inst. of Cologne, and edited works for the complete ed. of Haydn's works. He publ. the study *Max Reger* (Hamburg, 1973). Among his compositions are orch. pieces, chamber music, piano pieces, and songs.

Wise, Michael, English organist and composer; b. probably in Salisbury, c.1647; d. there (killed in a dispute with the night watch), Aug. 24, 1687. He was a chorister at the Chapel Royal (1660–63); after serving as lay clerk at St. George's Chapel in Windsor and at Eton College (1666–68), he was organist and instructor of the choristers at Salisbury Cathedral (from 1668); in 1676 he also was made a Gentleman of the Chapel Royal; in 1687 he was appointed almoner and master of the choristers at St. Paul's Cathedral. His extant works comprise some 31 anthems, 4 services, songs, and catches.

BIBL.: M. Smith, "The Church Music of M. W.," *Musical Times,* CXIV (1973).

Wishart, Peter (Charles Arthur), English composer; b. Crowborough, June 25, 1921; d. Frome, Aug. 14, 1984. He received training in composition from Hely-Hutchinson at the Univ. of Birmingham (1938–41) and from Boulanger in Paris (1947–48); taught at the Univ. of Birmingham (1950–59), the Guildhall School of Music in London (from 1961), King's College, London (1972–77), and the Univ. of Reading (1977–84). He publ. the books *Harmony* (London, 1956) and *Key to Music* (London, 1971).

WORKS: STAGE: Operas: *2 in the Bush* (1956); *The Captive* (1960); *The Clandestine Marriage* (1971); *Clytemnestra* (1973); ballets; incidental music. **ORCH.:** 2 syms. (1953, 1973); 2 violin concertos (1951, 1968); *Aubade* for Flute and Strings (1955); *Concerto piccolo* (1955); *Concerto for Orchestra* (1957); Concerto for Piano and Small Orch. (1958); *Divisions* (1965); 5 *Pieces* for Strings (1967). **CHAMBER:** 2 cassations for Violin and Viola (1948, 1950); Sonata for Piano Duet (1949); 2 string quartets (1951, 1954); *Cantilena* for 4 Cellos (1957); *Profane Concerto* for Flute, Oboe, and Harpsichord (1962). Also organ music; much vocal music, both sacred and secular.

Wislocki, Stanislaw, Polish conductor and composer; b. Rzeszów, July 7, 1921. He studied in Lwow and Timişoara; conducted the Poznań Phil. (1947–58); served as chief conductor of the Polish Radio National Sym. Orch. in Katowice (1977–81) and of the Buenos Aires Phil. (1981). He composed a Sym. (1944); 4 *Poems* for Tenor and Chamber Orch. (1944); *Symphonic Nocturne* (1947); Piano Concerto (1948–49); *Symphonic Ballad* (1950); *Symfonia tańcu* (Symphony on Dancing, 1952); Sonata for Violin and Piano (1942); Piano Quartet (1943); piano pieces.

Wissmer, Pierre, Swiss-born French composer; b. Geneva, Oct. 30, 1915. He studied with Roger-Ducasse at the Paris Cons. and with Daniel-Lesur at the Schola Cantorum; also studied conducting with Munch at the École Normale de Musique. After living in Switzerland (1939–49), he settled in France and became a naturalized citizen in 1958; taught composition and orchestration at the Schola Cantorum in Paris, where he was named honorary director in 1963; was director of the École Nationale de Musique in Le Mans (1969–81). From 1973 to 1986 he was prof. of composition and orchestration at the Geneva Cons. He writes affable and pleasingly dissonant music in a natural contrapuntal idiom that is never congested by polyphonic superfluities.

WORKS: Radio opera, *Marion ou La Belle au tricorne* (1945; Geneva, Radio Suisse Romande, April 16, 1947); comic opera, *Capitaine Bruno* (Geneva, Nov. 9, 1952); opéra bouffe, *Léonidas ou La Cruauté mentale* (Paris, Sept. 12, 1958); ballet, *Le Beau Dimanche* (1939; Geneva, March 20, 1944); *Alerte, puis 211* (Geneva, 1964); *Christina et les chimères* (French Television, 1967); *Naïades* for Narrator, Soli, Chorus, and Orch. (Geneva, Jan. 21, 1942); *Le Quatrième Mage*, oratorio (Paris, Oct. 14, 1969); 6 syms. (1938, 1951, 1955, 1962, 1969, 1977); *Divertissement sur un choral* for 11 Instruments (Geneva, Dec. 8, 1939); *Mouvement* for String Orch. (Geneva, Feb. 1, 1940); symphonic suite, *Antoine et Cléopâtre* (Geneva, Oct. 2, 1946); overture, *La Mandrellina* (Geneva, April 16, 1952); 3 string quartets (1937, 1949, 1972); *Sérénade* for Oboe, Clarinet, and Bassoon (1938); Sonatina for Clarinet and Piano (1941); Sonatina for Violin and Piano (1946); Piano Sonata (1949); *Concerto valcrosiano* for Orch. (1966); 3 piano concertos (1937, 1948, 1972); 2 violin concertos (1944, 1954); Guitar Concerto (1957); Clarinet Concerto (1960); Trumpet Concerto (1961); Oboe Concerto (1963); *Concertino-Crosière* for Flute, String Orch., and Piano (1966); *Symphonietta concertante* for Flute, Harp, and Orch. (1982); Wind Quintet (1966); *Quadrige* for Flute, Violin, Cello, and Piano (1961); *Cantique en l'ounour dou grand santlouis, rei de franco et patroun de vaucros de cuers* for Chorus, with Piano or Organ (1971); songs; choruses.

Wiszniewski, Zbigniew, Polish composer; b. Lwow, July 30, 1922. He studied composition with Sikorski at the Cons. in Lodz (1948–52); taught at the Warsaw Cons. (1954); from 1957 to 1962 he was director of the Experimental Studio of the Polish Radio in Warsaw. In 1979 he joined the faculty of the Warsaw Academy of Music.

WORKS: 3 radio operas: *Neffru* (1958–59; Warsaw, 1959); *Tak jakby* (As If, 1968–70; Warsaw, 1970); *Paternoster* (Warsaw, 1972); 2 ballets: *Obywatel walc* (1955) and *Ad hominem* (1962); 2 oratorios: *Genesis* (1967–68) and *Brothers* (1970–72); 2 cantatas: *Aubade* (1960) and *Sichel versäumter Stunden* (1971). **ORCH.:** *3 pezzi della tradizione* for 3-part Chorus and Orch. (1964); Oboe Concerto (1951); Sym. (1954); Concerto for Clarinet and String Orch. (1968–70); Violin Concerto (1987); Double Concerto (1989). **CHAMBER:** 2 string quartets (1954, 1957); Trio for Oboe, Harp, and Viola (1963); Solo Violin Sonata (1963); *Kammermusik I* for Oboe, Oboe d'Amore, English Horn, and Bassoon (1965), *II* (1966), and *IV, Little Symphony,* for 10 Instruments (1972–73); Quartet for Flute, Horn, Piano, and Double Bass (1972); *Pezzo concertante* for Flute and 3 Percussionists (1975); Sonata for Solo Cello (1977); Quartet for 4 Violins (1982); Quintet for Oboe, Bassoon, Violin, Viola, and Cello (1984); Trio for Oboe, Clarinet, and Bassoon (1988); piano pieces.

Wit, Antoni, Polish conductor; b. Krakow, Feb. 7, 1944. He was educated in his native city, taking courses in conducting at the State College of Music (graduated, 1967) and in law at the Jagiellonian Univ. (graduated, 1969); won 2nd prize in the Karajan Competition in Berlin (1971) and completed his conducting studies at the Berkshire Music Center, Tanglewood (1973). He was assistant conductor of the National Phil. in Warsaw (1967–70); then conducted the Poznan State Phil. (1970–72) and the Pomeranian Phil. in Bydgoszcz (1974–77). After serving as artistic director of the Polish Radio and Televi-

sion Sym. Orch. in Krakow (1977–83), he held that title with the Polish Radio and Television National Sym. Orch. in Katowice (from 1983); also toured widely as a guest conductor.

Wit, Paul de, Dutch violist; b. Maastricht, Jan. 4, 1852; d. Leipzig, Dec. 10, 1925. He studied cello in Maastricht before taking up the viola; in 1879 he settled in Leipzig and in 1880 founded the *Zeitschrift für Instrumentenbau;* opened a museum of early instruments in 1886, but sold his collections to the Berlin Hochschule für Musik in 1888 and 1891; he then made a 3rd collection, which he sold in 1906 to Heyer of Cologne. Wit was a fine player on the viola da gamba, as well as a violist. He publ. *Geigenzettel alter Meister vom 16. bis zur Mitte des 19. Jahrhunderts* (1902; 2nd ed., 1910); *Weltadressbuch der gesammten Musikinstrumenten-Industrie* (1903; 8th ed., 1912); *Kurz-gefaszter Katalog aller im musikhistorischen Museums von Paul de Wie vorhandenen Musik-Instrumente* (1903).

BIBL.: P. Daehne, "P. d.W.s Leben und Wirken," *Zeitschrift für Instrumentenbau,* XLIV (1926).

Witherspoon, Herbert, American bass; b. Buffalo, N.Y., July 21, 1873; d. N.Y., May 10, 1935. He studied composition with Horatio Parker and voice with Gustav Stoeckel at Yale Univ. (graduated, 1895); then was a pupil of MacDowell in N.Y. He then studied singing with Bouhy in Paris, Henry Wood in London, and G.B. Lamperti in Berlin. Returning to America, he made his operatic debut as Ramfis in *Aida* with Savage's Castle Square Opera Co. in N.Y. in 1898. On Nov. 26, 1908, he made his Metropolitan Opera debut in N.Y. as Titurel in *Parsifal;* remained on its roster until 1916, where he distinguished himself in such roles as Sarastro, King Marke, Pogner, the Landgrave, and Gurnemanz. In 1922 he founded the American Academy of Teachers of Singing, subsequently serving as its 1st president; in 1925, became president of the Chicago Musical College, and in 1931, president of the Cincinnati Cons. of Music; in 1933 he returned to N.Y., and in May 1935, was chosen to succeed Gatti-Casazza as general manager of the Metropolitan Opera, but he died of a heart attack after only a month in his post. He publ. *Singing: A Treatise for Teachers and Students* (N.Y., 1925), and *36 Lessons in Singing for Teacher and Student* (Chicago, 1930).

Witkowski, Georges-Martin, French conductor, pedagogue, and composer; b. Mostaganem, Algeria (of a French father and a Polish mother), Jan. 6, 1867; d. Lyons, Aug. 12, 1943. He was educated at the military school of St.-Cyr; studied composition with d'Indy at the Paris Schola Cantorum (1894–97); later left for the army and settled in Lyons, where he founded the Société des Grands Concerts in 1905 for the production of oratorios. In 1924 he was appointed director of the Lyons Cons., retiring in 1941.

WORKS: Opera, *La Princesse lointaine,* after Rostand (1928–32; Paris, March 26, 1934); 2 syms. (1900, 1910); *Poème de la maison* for Solo Voices, Chorus, and Orch. (Lyons, Jan. 25, 1919); *Mon lac* for Piano and Orch. (Lyons, Nov. 20, 1921); for Voice and Orch.: *4 poèmes du cœur innombrable* (1925), *3 poèmes de Ronsard* (1935), *Paysage rêvé* (1937); *Introduction et Danse* for Violin and Orch. (Paris, Oct. 10, 1937); Piano Quintet (1897); String Quartet (1902); Violin Sonata (1907).

BIBL.: M. Boucher, "G.-M. W.," *Revue Musicale* (March 1926).

Witt, Franz Xaver, German composer of church music; b. Walderbach, Feb. 9, 1834; d. Landshut, Dec. 2, 1888. He studied with Proske and Schrems in Regensburg; took Holy Orders in 1856. In 1866 he established and ed. *Fliegende Blätter für katholische Kirchenmusik* and in 1868 *Musica Sacra;* in 1869 he founded the Allgemeiner Deutscher Cäcilienverein for the improvement of Catholic church music, which, while opposing the introduction of orch. instruments into the church, helped to arouse interest in the great masterpieces of church music. In 1880 he founded the Scuola Gregoriana in Rome. In his own early masses, Witt employed the orch. Besides numerous masses, he publ. 2 Requiems, many litanies, offertories, motets, and hymns (55 opus numbers); also some secular men's choruses; was the author of *Der Zustand der katholischen Kirchenmusik zunächst in Altbayern* (1865), *Über das Dirigieren katholischer Kirchenmusik* (1870), *Gestatten die liturgischen Gesetze beim Hochamt deutsch zu singen?* (1873; 2nd ed., 1886), and *Das königliche bayerische Cultusministerium, die bayerische Abgeordneten-Kammer und der Cäcilien-Verein* (1886); his articles are collected in a centennial vol., *Ausgewählte Anfsätze zur Kirchenmusik* (Cologne, 1934).

BIBL.: A. Walter, *Dr. F. W.: Gründer und erster Generalpräses des Cäcilienvereins: Ein Lebensbild* (Regensburg, 1889; 2nd ed., 1906); K. Fellerer, "Grundlagen und Anfänge der Kirchenmusikalischen Organisation F.X. W.s," *Kirchenmusikalisches Jahrbuch*, LV (1971).

Witt, Friedrich, German violinist and composer; b. Hallenbergstetten, Württemberg, Nov. 8, 1770; d. Würzburg, Jan. 3, 1836. At the age of 19, he was engaged as violinist in the orch. of Prince von Oettingen; from 1802 he was Kapellmeister at Würzburg, at first to the Prince-Bishop, then to the Grand Duke, and finally to the city. It was Witt who composed the so-called Jena Sym., misattributed to Beethoven (see H.C. Robbins Landon's article in the *Music Review* for May 1957). Other works by Witt include the historical opera *Palma* (Frankfurt, 1804); the comic opera *Das Fischerweib* (Würzburg, 1806); the oratorios *Der leidende Heiland* (Würzburg, 1802) and *Die Auferstehung Jesu*; masses and cantatas; 9 syms.; music for wind band; 7 concertos and sinfonie concertanti; Flute Concerto; Quintetto for Piano and Strings or Winds; Septet for String Quartet and Winds; etc.

Wittassek, Johann Nepomuk August, Bohemian pianist and composer; b. Hořín, March 23, 1770; d. Prague, Dec. 7, 1839. The son of a schoolmaster, he received a good education; took music lessons with F.X. Dušek and J.A. Koželuch in Prague; succeeded Koželuch in 1814 as music director at the Prague Cathedral; was appointed director of the School for Organists in Prague in 1830. He wrote an opera, *David*, brought out in Prague; 4 piano concertos; concertos for violin, for clarinet, and for bassoon; 6 string quartets; 4 violin sonatas; much church music.

Wittgenstein, Count Friedrich Ernst. See **Sayn-Wittgenstein-Berleburg, Count Friedrich Ernst.**

Wittgenstein, Paul, Austrian-born American pianist; b. Vienna, Nov. 5, 1887; d. Manhasset, Long Island, N.Y., March 3, 1961. He was of a musical family; studied piano with Malvine Brée and Theodor Leschetizky and theory with Josef Labor; made his 1st public appearance as a pianist in 1913 in Vienna. He lost his right arm in World War I, at the Russian front; was a prisoner of war in Omsk, Siberia; was repatriated in 1916. He then developed an extraordinary technique for left hand alone, and performed a concerto specially composed for him by his teacher, Labor. He subsequently commissioned left-hand piano concertos from Richard Strauss, Ravel, Prokofiev, Korngold, Benjamin Britten, and other composers, of which he gave the world premieres (except the Prokofiev concerto, which he found unsuitable). He appeared in the major musical centers in Europe; toured America in 1934; in 1938, settled in N.Y.; became a naturalized U.S. citizen in 1946. He taught privately in N.Y. (1938–60); also at the Ralph Wolfe Cons. in New Rochelle (1938–43), and at Manhattanville College of the Sacred Heart (1940–45). John Barchilon's novel *The Crown Prince* (1984) is based on his career. He was a brother of the famous philosopher Ludwig Wittgenstein.

Wittich, Marie, German soprano; b. Giessen, May 27, 1868; d. Dresden, Aug. 4, 1931. She studied with Otto-Ubridz in Würzburg; made her debut as Azucena at the age of 14 in Magdeburg in 1882; then sang in Düsseldorf, Basel, and Schwerin; in 1889 she became a member of the Dresden Court Opera, remaining on its roster until 1914; while there, she was chosen by Richard Strauss to create the role of Salome in 1905; she also made guest appearances at Covent Garden in London (1905–6) and in Bayreuth (1901–10).

Wittinger, Robert, Austrian-born German composer; b. Knittelfeld, April 10, 1945. He grew up in Budapest, where he studied with Zsolt Durkó; then studied in Warsaw (1964), received training in electronic music in Munich (1965), and attended the summer courses in new music in Darmstadt (1965–68); subsequently was active at the Villa Massimo in Rome on a scholarship (1972–73). His technique of composition is sonoristic, with sound blocks forming thematic groups, while the continuity is achieved by Baroque formulas; the titles of his pieces are indicative of their construction (Dissociations, Concentrations, Compensations, Irreversibilities, Divergences, Montage, Tendencies, Tensions, Symmetrical Structures, etc.).

WORKS: ORCH.: 3 syms.: No. 1 (1962–63; rev. 1976); No. 2, with Women's Chorus (1978–80); No. 3, *Funèbre* (1982); *Dissoziazioni* (1964); *Consonante* for English Horn and Orch. (1965); *Espressioni*, ballet music (1966); *Concentrazione* (1966); *Compensazioni* for Small Orch. (1967); *Irreversibilitazione* for Cello and Orch. (1967); *Om* (1968); *Divergenti* (West Berlin, Oct. 4, 1970); *Sinfonia* for String Orch. (1970); *Costellazioni* (Stuttgart, Sept. 25, 1971); *Montaggio*, concerto No. 1 for Small Orch. (1972); *Relazioni* for 7 Soloists and Orch. (West Berlin, April 11, 1972); Concerto for Oboe, Harp, and String Orch. (1972); *Concerto Polemica* (1975); *Concerto Lirico* (1977); *Concerto Entusiastico* (1977); 2-Piano Concerto (1981); Concerto Grosso (1983); *Intreccio*, sinfonietta (1985); *Maldoror-Requiem* for Chorus and Orch. (1984–86); Violin Concerto (1988). **CHAMBER:** 4 string quartets (1964, 1966, 1970, 1977); *Concentrazioni*, wind quintet (1965); *Itrospezioni* for Bassoon (1967); *Tendenze* for Piano, Cello, and Percussion (1970); *Tensioni*, wind quintet (1970); *Tolleranza* for Oboe, Celesta, and Percussion (1970); 6 *Strutture simmetriche*, each for a different Solo Instrument (1970); *Catalizzazioni* for 24 Vocalists and 7 Instrumentalists (1972); *Sillogismo* for Violin and Percussion (1974); *Dialoghi e scherzino* for 2 Pianos (1985).

Wittrisch, Marcel, German tenor; b. Antwerp, Oct. 1, 1901; d. Stuttgart, June 3, 1955. He studied at the Munich and Leipzig conservatories; made his debut as Konrad in *Hans Heiling* in Halle in 1925; then sang in Braunschweig (1927–29); in 1929 he became a member of the Berlin State Opera, where he sang leading roles until 1943; also made guest appearances at Covent Garden in London (1931) and at Bayreuth (1937); in 1950 he joined the Stuttgart Opera, where he remained until his death. In addition to his operatic career, he gained wide renown as a concert singer.

Wixell, Ingvar, Swedish baritone; b. Luleå, May 7, 1931. He was educated at the Stockholm Musikhögskolan; made his concert debut in 1952 in Gävle; in 1955 he made his operatic debut as Papageno at the Royal Theater in Stockholm, where he subsequently was a member of the company from 1956; appeared as Handel's Ruggiero with the company during its visit to London's Covent Garden in 1960. He joined the Deutsche Oper in West Berlin in 1967; that same year he made his U.S. debut as Belcore in Chicago. He made regular appearances at Covent Garden from 1970 and at the Bayreuth Festivals from 1971. On Jan. 29, 1973, he made his debut at the Metropolitan Opera in N.Y. as Rigoletto.

Woehl, Waldemar, German music teacher and composer; b. Lipine, near Bethuen, Prussia, Aug. 31, 1902. He studied with his father, and later in Berlin at the Akademie für Kirchen- und Schulmusik with Max Seiffert, Thiel, and Jöde; taught at the Folkwangschule in Essen; during World War II, led the Musikschule für Jugend und Volk in Villach, Austria; eventually settled in Soyen, Bavaria, as a teacher and flute maker; started a movement for the restoration of vertical flutes (recorders). He publ. *Melodielehre* (Leipzig, 1929); *Klavierbuch für den Anfang* (Berlin, 1932); *Das Bach-Buch für Klavierspieler* (Berlin, 1932); *Musik für Blockflöten* (4 vols.; Hannover, 1930–34); a method, *Blockflötenschule* (1930); *Kurze Spielanweisung für das Scheitholz* (1951); composed numerous pieces for the recorder and for ensembles of recorders; ed. much 18th-century chamber music.

Wohl, Yehuda, German-born Israeli composer; b. Berlin, March 5, 1904; d. Tel Aviv, July 12, 1988. He went to Palestine in 1933 and had private studies with Ben-Haim in Tel Aviv; taught until 1972. Under the pseudonym Yehuda Bentow, he wrote popular songs in the ethnic style.

WORKS: 2 radio operas: *Hagadér* (1947) and *The Circle* (1976). ORCH.: 3 syms. (1944, 1946, 1954); *Rondo patetico* for String Orch. (1950); *Miriam-Danze* (1955); *Discussione* for Piano and Orch. (1956); *An Arch Smile* for Narrator and Orch. (1959); *Fata morgana* (1960); *Canto capricioso* (1967); *With Mixed Feelings* for Piano, Percussion, and String Orch. (1970); *Light and Shadow* (1972); *Those Were the Days* (1973); *Festival Overture* (1979). CHAMBER: *Quartetto appassionato* for String Quartet (1949); *Duo sensible* for Violin and Piano (1951); *Tagore-Songs* for 2 Voices, Piano, and Flute (1955); *Diary* for Flute, Oboe, Clarinet, and Bassoon (1961); *Associations* for Chamber Ensemble (1966); *Hagashot* (Encounters) for Chamber Ensemble (1968); *Atmosphere* for Organ and Tape (1970); *Trigon* for Piano Trio (1971); *Faces* for Brass Ensemble and Percussion (1973); many piano pieces.

Wohlfahrt, Franz, German piano pedagogue, son of **Heinrich Wohlfahrt;** b. Frauenpriesnitz, March 7, 1833; d. Gohlis, Feb. 14, 1884. He taught at Leipzig; publ. many piano studies, some of which were long standard exercises.

Wohlfahrt, Heinrich, German piano pedagogue, father of **Franz Wohlfahrt;** b. Kössnitz, near Apolda, Dec. 16, 1797; d. Connewitz, near Leipzig, May 9, 1883. He studied with Häser at Weimar; was a cantor and tutor in Thuringian towns; taught at Jena and (from 1867) Leipzig. He publ. both didactic books and compositions.

Woikowski-Biedau, Viktor Hugo von, German composer; b. Nieder-Arnsdorf, near Schweidnitz, Sept. 2, 1866; d. Berlin, Jan. 1, 1935. He studied music with Wilhelm Berger in Berlin; was employed in the government statistics bureau.

WORKS: Operas: *Helga* (Wiesbaden, 1904); *Der lange Kerl* (Berlin, 1906); *Das Nothemd* (Dessau, 1913); 3 melodramas: *Jung Olaf; Der Todspieler; Die Mette von Marienburg;* 4 ballads for Baritone and Orch.: *Die Jüdin von Worms; Der Triumph des Lebens; Rahab, die Jerichonitin; Jan van Jühren; Aus einem Menschenleben* for Violin and Piano; song cycles (*Frühlingslieder; Lebensträume; Schiffslieder; Königslieder; Pagen-Balladen; Osterzauber; Des Sultans Gesetz;* etc.).

Woldemar, Michel, French violinist and composer; b. Orléans, June 17, 1750; d. Clermont-Ferrand, Dec. 19, 1815. He studied with Lolli and Mestrino; after teaching violin in Paris, he served as music director of a group of strolling players; eventually settled in Clermont-Ferrand as maître de chapelle at the Cathedral. By adding a 5th string (*c*) to the violin, he obtained an instrument that he called "violon-alto," because it included the viola range, and for which he wrote a concerto. He also publ. 3 violin concertos, a String Quartet, duos for 2 violins and for violin and viola; *Sonates fantomagiques* for 2 violins and for violin and viola; *Sonates fantomagiques* (*L'Ombre de Lolli, de Mestrino, de Pugnani, de Tartini*); 12 grand solos; *6 rêves ou Caprices; Caprices ou Etudes; Le Nouveau Labyrinth pour violon,* followed by studies in double stops; *Le Nouvel Art de l'archet; Etude élémentaire de l'archet moderne;* variations on *Les Folies d'Espagne,* etc.; methods for violin, viola, and clarinet; also a system of musical stenography (*Tableau mélotachigraphique*) and a method of musical correspondence (*Notographie*).

Wöldike, Mogens, Danish organist and conductor; b. Copenhagen, July 5, 1897; d. there, Oct. 20, 1988. He studied at the Univ. of Copenhagen and with Carl Nielsen; was organist and choirmaster in several Copenhagen churches. In 1924 he founded the Copenhagen Boys' Choir; was organist at Christiansborg Palace church (from 1931) and at Copenhagen Cathedral (1959–72); appeared as a conductor with the Danish Radio Sym. Orch. in Copenhagen regularly from 1937 to 1967; also toured extensively as a guest conductor in Europe. With his

son-in-law, **Jens Peter Larsen,** he ed. the hymnbook of the Danish Church; publ. 2 vols. of organ music (Copenhagen, 1943, 1960).

Wolf, Ernst Wilhelm, German composer; b. Grossenbehringen, near Gotha (baptized), Feb. 25, 1735; d. Weimar (buried), Dec. 1, 1792. After studies at the Eisenach and Gotha Gymnasien, he entered the Univ. of Jena (1755), where he was made director of the collegium musicum. He was active in Naumburg as a music teacher before becoming music tutor to the sons of Duchess Anna Amalia in Weimar; later was named court Konzertmeister (1761), organist (1763), and Kapellmeister (1772) there. He publ. *Auch eine Reise aber nur eine kleine Musik in den Monaten Junius, Julius und August 1782 zum Vergnügen angestellt und auf Verlangen beschrieben* (Weimar, 1784), *Vorbericht als eine Anleitung zum guten Vortrag beim Klavier-Spielen* (Leipzig, 1785), and *Musikalischer Unterricht für Liebhaber und diejenigen, welche die Musik treiben und lehren wollen* (Dresden, 1788).

WORKS: STAGE (all 1st perf. in Weimar): *Das Gärtnermädchen,* comic opera (1769); *Das Rosenfest,* operetta (1772); *Die Dorfdeputierten,* comic opera (1772); *Die treuen Köhler,* operetta (1772); *Der Abend im Walde,* comic opera (1773); *Das grosse Los,* comic opera (1774); *Ehrlichkeit und Liebe,* Schauspiel (1776); *Le Monde de la lune,* comic opera (n.d.); *Alceste,* opera (1780); 10 others not extant. ORCH.: Various syms. (partitas); about 25 concertos for Harpsichord or Piano. CHAMBER: 6 string quartets; 2 quintets; 6 sonatas for Piano, Violin, and Cello; over 55 sonatas for Piano or Harpsichord. VOCAL: 9 cantatas; 5 oratorios; a sacred concerto; sacred choruses and songs; secular cantatas and songs.

BIBL.: J. Brockt, *E.W. W.: Leben und Werke* (diss., Univ. of Breslau, 1927); E. Böhme, "E.W. W., der Weimarische Hofkapellmeister der Goethezeit," *Zeitschrift für Musikwissenschaft,* XV (1932–33).

Wolf, Hugo (Filipp Jakob), famous Austrian composer, one of the greatest masters of the German lied; b. Windischgraz, Styria, March 13, 1860; d. Vienna, Feb. 22, 1903. His father, Philipp Wolf (1828–87), was a gifted musician from whom Hugo received piano and violin lessons at a very early age; he later played 2nd violin in the family orch. While attending the village primary school (1865–69), he studied piano and theory with Sebastian Weixler. In 1870 he was sent to the Graz regional secondary school, but left after a single semester and in 1871 entered the St. Paul Benedictine Abbey in Carinthia, where he played violin, organ, and piano; in 1873 he was transferred to the Marburg secondary school and remained devoted to musical pursuits; in 1875 he went to Vienna, where he became a pupil at the Cons.; studied piano with Wilhelm Schenner and harmony and composition with Robert Fuchs and later with Franz Krenn. When Wagner visited Vienna in 1875, Wolf went to see him, bringing along some of his compositions; the fact that Wagner received him at all, and even said a few words of encouragement, gave Wolf great impetus toward further composition. But he was incapable of submitting himself to academic discipline, and soon difficulties arose between him and the Cons. authorities. He openly expressed his dissatisfaction with the teaching, which led to his expulsion for lack of discipline in 1877. He then returned to his native town, but after a few months at home decided to go to Vienna again; there he managed to support himself by giving music lessons to children in the homes of friends. By that time he was composing diligently, writing songs to texts by his favorite poets— Goethe, Lenau, Heine. It was also about that time that the 1st signs of a syphilitic infection became manifest. An unhappy encounter with Brahms in 1879, who advised him to study counterpoint before attempting to compose, embittered him, and he became determined to follow his own musical inclinations without seeking further advice. That same year he met Melanie (née Lang) Köchert, whose husband, Heinrich Köchert, was the Vienna court jeweller. By 1884 she had become Wolf's mistress and a great inspiration in his creative work. After serving a brief and acrimonious tenure as 2nd conductor in Salzburg in 1881, he returned to Vienna in 1882 and in 1883 became music critic of the weekly *Wiener Salonblatt.* He took this opportunity to indulge his professional frustration by attacking those not sympathetic to new trends in music; he poured invective of extraordinary virulence on Brahms, thus antagonizing the influential Hanslick and other admirers of Brahms. But he also formed a coterie of staunch friends, who had faith in his ability. Yet he was singularly unsuccessful in his repeated attempts to secure performances for his works. He submitted a string quartet to the celebrated Rosé Quartet, but it was rejected. Finally, Hans Richter accepted for the Vienna Phil. Wolf's symphonic poem *Penthesilea,* but the public performance was a fiasco, and Wolf even accused Richter of deliberately sabotaging the work; later he reorchestrated the score, eliminating certain crudities of the early version. In 1887 he resigned as music critic of the *Wiener Salonblatt* and devoted himself entirely to composition. He became convinced that he was creating the greatest masterpieces of song since Schubert and Schumann, and stated his conviction in plain terms in his letters. In historical perspective, his self-appraisal has proved remarkably accurate, but psychologists may well wonder whether Wolf was not consciously trying to give himself the needed encouragement by what must have seemed to him a wild exaggeration. However, a favorable turn in his fortunes soon came. On March 2, 1888, Rosa Papier became the 1st artist to sing one of Wolf's songs in public. On March 23, 1888, Wolf himself played and sang several of his songs at a meeting of the Vienna Wagner-Verein; on Dec. 15, 1888, he made his public debut as accompanist in his songs to the tenor Ferdinand Jäger, which proved the 1st of many highly successful recitals by both artists. Soon Wolf's name became known in Germany; he presented concerts of his own works in Berlin, Darmstadt, Mannheim, and other musical centers. He completed the first part of his great cycle of 22 songs, *Italienisches Liederbuch,* in 1891, and composed the 2nd part (24 songs) in 5 weeks, in the spring of 1896. While Wolf could compose songs with a facility and degree of excellence that were truly astounding, he labored painfully on his orch. works. His early sym. was never completed, nor was a violin concerto; the work on *Penthesilea* took him a disproportionately long time. In 1895 he undertook the composition of his opera, *Der Corregidor,* to the famous tale by Alarcón, *El sombrero de tres picos,* and, working feverishly, completed the vocal score with piano accompaniment in a few months. The orchestration took him a much longer time. *Der Corregidor* had its premiere in Mannheim on June 7, 1896; while initially a success, the opera failed to find wide appeal and was soon dropped from the repertoire. Wolf subsequently revised the score, and in its new version *Der Corregidor* was brought out in Strasbourg on April 29, 1898. He never completed his 2nd opera, *Manuel Venegas* (also after Alarcón); fragments were presented in concert in Mannheim on March 1, 1903. In the meantime, his fame grew. A Hugo Wolf–Verein was organized at Berlin in 1896, and did excellent work in furthering performances of Wolf's songs in Germany. Even more effective was the Hugo Wolf-Verein in Vienna, founded by Michel Haberlandt on April 22, 1897 (disbanded in 1906). As appreciation of Wolf's remarkable gifts as a master of lied began to find recognition abroad, tragedy struck. By early 1897, he was a very ill man, both mentally and physically. According to Wolf, Mahler promised to use his position as director of the Vienna Court Opera to mount a production of *Der Corregidor.* When the production failed to materialize, Wolf's mental condition disintegrated. He declared to friends that Mahler had been relieved of his post, and that he, Wolf, had been appointed in his stead. On Sept. 20, 1897, Wolf was placed in a private mental institution; after a favorable remission, he was discharged (Jan. 24, 1898), and traveled in Italy and Austria. After his return to Vienna, symptoms of mental derangement manifested themselves in even greater degree. In Oct. 1898 he attempted suicide by throwing himself into the Traunsee in Traunkirchen, but was saved and placed in the Lower Austrian provincial asylum in Vienna. (A parallel with Schumann's case forcibly suggests

itself.) He remained in confinement, gradually lapsing into complete irrationality. He died at the age of 42, and was buried near the graves of Schubert and Beethoven in Vienna's Central Cemetery; a monument was unveiled on Oct. 20, 1904. His mistress plunged to her death from the 4th-floor window of her home in Vienna on March 21, 1906.

Wolf's significance in music history rests on his songs, about 300 in number, many of them publ. posthumously. The sobriquet "the Wagner of the lied" may well be justified in regard to involved contrapuntal texture and chromatic harmony, for Wolf accepted the Wagnerian idiom through natural affinity as well as by clear choice. The elaboration of the accompaniment, and the incorporation of the vocal line into the contrapuntal scheme of the whole, are Wagnerian traits. But with these external similarities, Wolf's dependence on Wagner's models ceases. In his intimate penetration of the poetic spirit of the text, Wolf appears a legitimate successor to Schubert and Schumann. Wolf's songs are symphonic poems in miniature, artistically designed and admirably arranged for voice and piano, the combination in which he was a master.

WORKS: OPERAS: *König Alboin* (1876–77; fragment); *Der Corregidor* (1895; Mannheim, June 7, 1896); *Manuel Venegas* (1897; fragments perf. in concert, Mannheim, March 1, 1903). **INCIDENTAL MUSIC:** to Kleist's *Prinz Friedrich von Homburg* (1884; unfinished); Ibsen's *Das Fest auf Solhaug* (Vienna, Nov. 21, 1891).

ORCH.: Violin Concerto (1875; unfinished); Sym. in B-flat major (1876–77; unfinished; Scherzo and Finale completed; scored by H. Schultz and publ. in Leipzig and Vienna, 1940); Sym. in G Minor (1877; unfinished); Sym. in F minor (1879; not extant); *The Corsair,* overture (1877–78; not extant); *Penthesilea,* symphonic poem (1883–85); *Italienische Serenade* for Small Orch. (1892; arrangement of the *Serenade* for String Quartet); *Dritte Italienische Serenade* (1897; unfinished); *Trantella* on *Funiculi, funiculà* (1897; fragment).

CHAMBER: String Quartet in D major (1876; unfinished); Piano Quintet (1876; fragment; not extant); Violin Sonata in G minor (1877; fragment); String Quartet in D minor (1878–84); *Intermezzo* in E-flat major for String Quartet (1886); *Serenade* for String Quartet (1887; arr. for Small Orch. as *Italienische Serenade,* 1892); *Serenade* (1889; fragment).

PIANO: Sonata in E-flat major/D major (1875; unfinished); *Variations* in G major (1875); *Variations* in E major/A major (c.1875; fragment); Sonata in D major (1875; unfinished); Sonata in G major (1876; unfinished); *Fantasia* in B-flat major (1876; unfinished); *March* in E-flat major for 4-hands (1876); Sonata in G minor (1876; unfinished); *Rondo capriccioso* (1876); *Wellenspiel* in D major (1877; unfinished; not extant); *Verlegenheit* in A minor (1877; fragment); *Humoreske* in G minor (1877); *Schlummerlied* in G major (1878); *Scherz und Spiel* in G major (1878); *Fantasie über Lortzings Zar und Zimmermann* (c.1878; not extant); *Reiseblätter nach Gedichten von Lenau* (c.1878–79; not extant); *Paraphrase über Die Meistersinger von Nürnberg von Richard Wagner* in G major (c.1880); *Paraphrase über Die Walküre von Richard Wagner* in E minor (c.1880); *Canons* in C major (c.1882).

CHORAL: *Die Stimme des Kindes* for Voices and Piano (1876); *Im stillen Friedhof* for Voices and Piano (1876); *Im Sommer* for Men's Voices (1876); *Geistesgruss* for Men's Voices (1876); *Mailied* for Men's Voices (1876); *Wanderers Nachtlied* for Men's Voices (1876; not extant); *Die schöne Nacht* for Men's Voices (1876; not extant); *Fröhliche Fahrt* for Voices (1876); *Mailied* for Men's Voices (1876; fragment); *Grablied* for Voices (1876); *An Himmelshohn die Sterne gehn* for Voices (c.1876); *Die Stunden verrauschen* for Solo Voices, Mixed Voices, and Orch. (1878; unfinished); *Sechs geistliche Lieder* for Voices (all 1881; rev. by E. Thomas, 1903); *Wahlspruch* for Men's Voices (c.1883; not extant); *Christnacht* for Solo Voices, Mixed Voices, and Orch. (1886–89; rev. by M. Reger and F. Foll, 1903); *Elfenlied* for Soprano, Women's Voices, and Orch. (1889–91).

SONGS: 12 *Lieder aus der Jugendzeit* (1888); *Lieder nach verschiedenen Dichtern,* 31 songs (1877–97); *Gedichte von Mörike,* 53 songs (1888); *Gedichte von Eichendorff,* 20 songs (1886–

88); *Gedichte von Goethe*, 51 songs (1888–89); *Spanisches Liederbuch*, 44 songs after Geibel and Heyse (1889–90); *Italienisches Liederbuch*, 46 songs after Heyse, in 2 parts: 22 songs (1890–91), 24 songs (1896). 20 of the songs were orchestrated by Wolf; others by Max Reger. 40 previously unpubl. songs, mostly of the earliest period, were publ. in Leipzig in 1936, in 4 vols., as *Nachgelassene Werke*, ed. by R. Haas and H. Schultz.

A complete ed. of his works, ed. by H. Jancik et al., began publ. in Vienna in 1960.

WRITINGS: R. Batka and H. Werner, eds., *Hugo Wolf: Musikalische Kritiken* (Leipzig, 1911; Eng. tr., 1979).

BIBL.: CORRESPONDENCE: E. Hellmer, ed., *H. W.: Briefe an Emil Kauffmann* (Berlin, 1903); M. Haberlandt, ed., *H. W.: Brief an Hugo Faisst* (Stuttgart, 1904); H. Werner, ed., *H. W.: Briefe an Oskar Grohe* (Berlin, 1905); E. Hellmer, ed., *H. W.: Familienbriefe* (Leipzig, 1912); H. Werner, ed., *H. W.: Briefe an Rosa Mayreder, mit einem Nachwort der Dichtetrin des "Corregidors"* (Vienna, 1921); idem, *H. W.: Briefe an Henriette Lang, nebst den briefen an deren Gatten, Prof. Joseph Freiherr von Schey* (Regensburg, 1922); H. Nonveiller, ed., *H. W.: Briefe an Heinrich Potpeschnigg* (Stuttgart, 1923); K. Geiringer, "H. W. and Frida von Lipperheide: Some Unpublished Letters," *Musical Times*, LXXVII (1936); F. Grasberger, ed., *H. W.: Briefe an Melanie Kochert* (Tutzing, 1964); R. Schaal, ed., "Ungedruckte Briefe von H. W.," *Deutsches Jahrbuch der Musikwissenschaft*, XIII (1968); E. Werba, "Briefe H. W.s an seine Schwester Adrienne," *Österreichische Musikzeitschrift*, XXVII (1972); E. Hilmar and W. Obermaier, eds., *Briefe an Frieda Zerny* (Vienna, 1978).

MEMOIRS: H. Haberlandt, *H. W.: Erinnerungen und Gedanken* (Leipzig, 1903; 2nd ed., enl., 1911); H. Werner, *H. W. in Maierling: eine Idyll* (Leipzig, 1913); E. Hellmer, *H. W.: Erlebtes und Erlauschtes* (Vienna, 1921); H. Werner, *Der H. W.-Verein in Wien* (Regensburg, 1921); idem, *Gustav Schur: Erinnerungen an H. W., nebst H. W.s Briefen an Gustav Schur* (Regensburg, 1922); idem, *H. W. in Perchtoldsdorf* (Regensburg, 1924); R. Kukula, *Erinnerungen eines Bibliothekars* (Weimar, 1925); H. Werner, *H. W. und der Wiener Akademische Wagner-Verein* (Regensburg, 1927); F. Eckstein, *Alte unnennbare Tage* (Vienna, 1936); M. Klinckerfuss, *Aufklänge aus versunkener Zeit* (Urach, 1947).

BIOGRAPHICAL: E. Decsey, *H. W.* (Berlin and Leipzig, 1903–6); E. Schmitz, *H. W.* (Leipzig, 1906); E. Newman, *H. W.* (London, 1907); M. Morold, *H. W.* (Leipzig, 1912); E. Decsey, *H. W.: das Leben und das Lied* (Berlin, 1919; 2nd ed., 1921); K. Grunsky, *H. W.* (Leipzig, 1928); W. and B. Leibbrand, "H. W. und seiner Geisteskrankheit," *Die medizinische Welt*, XVII (1930); B. Benevisti–Viterbi, *H. W.* (Rome, 1931); H. Hécaen, *Mani et inspiration musicale: le cas H. W.* (Bourdeaux, 1934); H. Schouten, *H. W.: mens en componist* (Amsterdam, 1935); A. Ehrmann, *H. W.: Sein Leben in Bildern* (Leipzig, 1937); R. Litterscheid, *H. W.* (Potsdam, 1939); M. Hattingberg-Graedener, *H. W.: vom Wesen und Werk des grössten Liedschöpfers* (Vienna and Leipzig, 1941; 2nd ed., rev., 1953); K. Eickemeyer, *Der Verlauf der Paralyse H. W.s* (diss., Univ. of Jena, 1945); A. Orel, *H. W.* (Vienna, 1947); F. Walker, *H. W.: A Biography* (London, 1951; 2nd ed., enl., 1968); N. Loeser, *H. W.* (Antwerp, 1955); D. Lindner, *H. W.* (Vienna, 1960); E. Werba, *H. W. oder der zornige Romantiker* (Vienna, 1971); K. Honolka, *H. W.: sein Leben, sein Werk, seine Zeit* (Stuttgart, 1988).

CRITICAL, ANALYTICAL: *Gesammelte Aufsätze über H. W.* (Berlin, 1898–1900); special issue of *Die Musik*, II (1902–3); P. Müller, *H. W.* (Berlin, 1904); K. Heckel, *H. W. in seinem Verhältnis zu Richard Wagner* (Munich, 1905); K. Grunsky, *H. W.-Fest in Stuttgart: Festschrift* (Gutenberg, 1906); F. Austin, "The Songs of H. W.," *Proceedings of the Musical Association*, XXXVIII (1911–12); W. Salomon, *H. W. als Liederkomponist* (diss., Univ. of Frankfurt am Main, 1925); K. Varges, *Der Musikkritiker H. W.* (Magdeburg, 1934); G. Bieri, *Die Lieder von H. W.* (Bern, 1935); A. Breitenseher, *Der Gesangstechnik in den Liedern H. W.s* (diss., Univ. of Vienna, 1938);

F. Walker, "The History of W.'s *Italian Serenade*," *Music Review*, VIII (1947); special issue of *Österreichische Musikzeitschrift*, VIII (1953); U. Sennhenn, *H. W.s Spanisches und Italienisches Liederbuch* (diss., Univ. of Frankfurt am Main, 1955); E. Sams, *The Songs of H. W.* (London, 1961; 2nd ed., rev. and enl., 1981); R. Egger, *Die Deklamationsrhythmik H. W.s in historischer Sicht* (Tutzing, 1963); M. Shott, *H. W.'s Music Criticism* (diss., Indiana Univ., 1964); C. Rostand, *H. W.* (Paris, 1967); P. Boylan, *The Lieder of H. W.* (diss., Univ. of Michigan, 1968); B. Campbell, *The Solo Sacred Lieder of H. W.* (diss., Columbia Univ., 1969); special issue of *Österreichische Musikzeitschrift*, XXVIII (1973); M. Carner, *H. W. Songs* (London, 1982); E. Werba, *H. W. und seine Lieder* (Vienna, 1984); D. Stein, *H. W.'s Lieder and Extensions of Tonality* (Ann Arbor, Mich., 1985); J. Haywood, *The Musical Language of H. W.* (Ilfracombe, 1986); D. Ossenkop, *H. W.: A Guide to Research* (Westport, Conn., 1988).

Wolf, Johannes, eminent German musicologist; b. Berlin, April 17, 1869; d. Munich, May 25, 1947. He studied at the Hochschule für Musik in Berlin; took courses in musicology at the Univ. of Berlin with Philipp Spitta and Heinrich Bellermann, and then with Riemann at the Univ. of Leipzig, where he received his Ph.D. in 1893 with the dissertation *Ein anonymer Musiktraktat des 11. bis 12. Jahrhunderts*; he completed his Habilitation at the Univ. of Berlin with his *Florenz in der Musikgeschichte des 14. Jahrhunderts* in 1902, and then taught the history of early music and church music there; also was on the faculty of the Berlin Akademie für Kirchen- und Schulmusik from 1908 to 1927. He was appointed director of the early music collection of the Prussian Library in Berlin in 1915; from 1927 to 1934 he was director of its entire music collection. He was a leading authority on medieval and Renaissance music; his writings on the history of notation are especially important. He ed. a complete edition of the works of Obrecht (Leipzig, 1908–21); for Denkmäler Deutscher Tonkunst, he selected vocal works of J.R. Ahle (vol. V, 1901) and G. Rhau's *Newe deudsche geistliche Gesenge für die gemeinen Schulen* (vol. XXXIV, 1908); for Denkmäler der Tonkunst in Österreich, he ed. H. Isaac's secular works (vols. XXVIII, Jg.XIV/1, 1907, and XXXIII, Jg.XVI/1, 1909); also ed. *Der Squarcialupi-Codex aus dem Nachlass herausgegeben von H. Albrecht* (Lippstadt, 1955).

WRITINGS: *Geschichte der Mensuralnotation von 1250 bis 1460 nach den theoretischen und praktischen Quellen* (Leipzig, 1904); *Handbuch der Notationskunde* (very valuable; 2 parts, Leipzig, 1913, 1919); *Musikalische Schrifttafeln* (Leipzig, 1922–23; 2nd ed., 1927); *Die Tonschriften* (Breslau, 1924); *Geschichte der Musik in allgemeinverständlicher Form* (3 vols., Leipzig, 1925–29).

BIBL.: W. Lott, H. Osthoff, and W. Wolffheim, eds., *Musikwissenschaftliche Beiträge: Festschrift für J. W. zu seinem 60. Geburtstag* (Berlin, 1929); O. Gombosi, "J. W.," *Musical Quarterly* (April 1948); O. Kinkeldey, "J. W.," *Journal of the American Musicological Society* (Spring 1948).

Wolf, Ludwig, German pianist, violinist, and composer; b. Frankfurt am Main, 1804; d. Vienna, Aug. 6, 1859. He studied composition with Seyfried; was skillful both as a pianist and violinist; composed 3 string quartets; a Piano Quartet; 4 string trios; many other works in MS.

Wolf, Wilhelm, German pianist and teacher; b. Breslau, April 22, 1838; d. Berlin, Jan. 8, 1913. He studied with Theodor Kullak; in 1881, established himself in Berlin as a teacher; contributed to musical periodicals; wrote *Musik-Ästhetik in kurzer und gemeinfasslicher Darstellung* (2 vols., 1895, 1906); a collection of essays appeared as *Gesammelte musikästhetische Aufsätze* (1894).

Wolfe, Jacques (Leon), Rumanian-American pianist, teacher, and composer; b. Botoshan, April 29, 1896; d. Bradenton, Fla., June 22, 1973. He was taken to the U.S. as a child; studied music in N.Y. at the Inst. of Musical Art with Goetschius, Robinson, and Friskin (graduated, 1915). During World

War I, he was a clarinetist in the 50th Infantry Band; then taught music in N.Y. public schools and was active as a pianist; in 1947 he settled in Miami, where he became well known as a photographer. Many of his songs are in the manner of spirituals; some of them acquired popularity (*De Glory Road, Gwine to Hebb'n, Halleluja Rhythm, Short'nin' Bread*, etc.); he also wrote *Betsy's Boy, The Hand-Organ Man, Sailormen, British Children's Prayer;* numerous choral works; piano pieces.

Wolfe, Stanley, American music educator and composer; b. N.Y., Feb. 7, 1924. After service in the U.S. Army during World War II, he enrolled at the Juilliard School of Music in N.Y., studying composition with William Bergsma, Vincent Persichetti, and Peter Mennin (B.S., 1952; M.S., 1955); then joined its faculty; in 1963, was appointed director of the Juilliard Extension Division.
WORKS: *Adagio* for Woodwind Quintet (1948); Sym. No. 1 (1954); Sym. No. 2 (1955); *3 Profiles* for Piano (1955); *Lincoln Square Overture* (1957); Sym. No. 3 (Albuquerque, Nov. 18, 1959); Sym. No. 4 (Albuquerque, Dec. 7, 1966); *Variations* for Orch. (1967); Sym. No. 5 (N.Y., April 2, 1971).

Wolfes, Felix, German-American pianist, conductor, and composer; b. Hannover, Sept. 2, 1892; d. Boston, March 28, 1971. He studied at the Leipzig Cons. with Max Reger (theory) and R. Teichmüller (piano); later in Strasbourg with Pfitzner (composition); made his conducting debut in Breslau in 1923; conducted opera at Breslau, Essen (1924–31), and Dortmund (until 1933); then went to France. In 1936–37 he conducted the Monte Carlo Opera; in 1938, went to the U.S., and was appointed assistant conductor at the Metropolitan Opera in N.Y.; subsequently joined the faculty of the New England Cons. of Music in Boston. He publ. 5 vols. of songs (1962).

Wolff, Albert (Louis), noted French conductor and composer; b. Paris (of Dutch parents), Jan. 19, 1884; d. there, Feb. 20, 1970. He studied with Leroux, Gédalge, and Vidal at the Paris Cons.; began his career as a pianist in Parisian cabarets; from 1906 to 1910, was organist at St. Thomas Aquinas. In 1908 he became a member of the staff of the Opéra-Comique; after serving as its chorus master, he made his conducting debut there, leading the premiere of Laparra's *La Jota*, on April 26, 1911. From 1919 to 1921 he was conductor of the French repertoire at the Metropolitan Opera in N.Y.; conducted the world premiere of his opera *L'Oiseau bleu* there on Dec. 27, 1919. Upon his return to Paris in 1921, he was appointed Messager's successor as music director of the Opéra-Comique until 1924; in 1925 he became 2nd conductor of the Concerts Pasdeloup, and then was principal conductor from 1934 to 1940; also was conductor of the Concerts Lamoureux from 1928 to 1934. He toured South America from 1940 to 1945; then returned to Paris, where he was director-general of the Opéra-Comique in 1945–46; thereafter he continued to conduct occasionally there; also at the Paris Opéra from 1949; in addition, he made appearances as a sym. conductor. He particularly distinguished himself as a champion of French music of his era; he conducted the premieres of Debussy's *La Boîte à joujoux,* Ravel's *L'Enfant et les sortilèges,* Roussel's Sym. No. 4, and Poulenc's *Les Mamelles de Tirésias.*
WORKS: OPERAS: *Soeur Béatrice* (1911; Nice, 1948); *Le marchand de masques* (Nice, 1914); *L'oiseau bleu* (N.Y., Dec. 27, 1919). **ORCH.:** *La randonnée de l'âme défunte,* symphonic poem (1926); Flute Concerto (1943); Sym. (1951); also *Requiem* for Soloists, Chorus, and Orch. (1939); chamber music; vocal pieces; film music.
BIBL.: S. Wolff, "A. W., doyen de l'Opéra-Comique," *Guide du Concert et du Disque* (Oct. 3, 1958).

Wolff, Auguste (Désiré Bernard), French pianist and piano manufacturer; b. Paris, May 3, 1821; d. there, Feb. 3, 1887. He studied piano with Zimmerman at the Paris Cons. and composition with Halévy; after a few years of teaching, he joined the firm of the piano maker Camille Pleyel in 1852, succeeding him as head in 1855; the firm then became known as Pleyel-Wolff & Cie.

Wolff, Beverly, American mezzo-soprano; b. Atlanta, Nov. 6, 1928. She learned to play the trumpet and then played in the Atlanta Sym. Orch.; subsequently received vocal training from Sidney Dietch and Vera McIntyre at the Academy of Vocal Arts in Philadelphia. In 1952 she won the Philadelphia Youth Auditions and made her formal debut with Ormandy and the Philadelphia Orch.; also appeared as Dinah in the television premiere of Bernstein's *Trouble in Tahiti.* On April 6, 1958, she made her N.Y. City Opera debut as Dinah, and subsequently sang there regularly until 1971; also was a guest artist with various other opera companies in the U.S. and abroad.

Wolff, Christian, French-born American composer and teacher; b. Nice, March 8, 1934. He went to the U.S. in 1941 and became a naturalized citizen in 1946. He studied piano with Grete Sultan (1949–51) and composition with John Cage (1950–51); then pursued training in classical languages at Harvard Univ. (B.A., 1955); after studying Italian literature and classics at the Univ. of Florence (1955–56), he returned to Harvard (Ph.D. in comparative literature, 1963). From 1962 to 1970 he taught classics at Harvard; in 1971 he joined the faculty of Dartmouth College to teach classics, comparative literature, and music; was made prof. of music and of classics in 1978; also was a guest lecturer at various institutions of higher learning; contributed articles on literature and music to many publications. He evolved a curiously static method of composition, using drastically restricted numbers of pitches. His only structural resources became arithmetical progressions of rhythmic values and the expressive use of rests. He used 3 different pitches in his Duo for Violin and Piano; 4 different pitches in the Trio for Flute, Cello, and Trumpet (1951); 9 in a piano piece called *For Piano I.* Beginning in 1957 he introduced into his works various degrees of free choice; sometimes the players are required to react to the musical activities of their partners according to spontaneous and unanticipated cues.
WORKS: Trio for Flute, Trumpet, and Cello (1951); *Summer* for String Quartet (1961); *For 5 or 10 Players* for Any Instruments (1962); *In Between Pieces* for 3 Players Using Any Sound Sources (1963); *For 1, 2 or 3 People* for Any Sound-producing Means (1964); Septet for Any 7 Players and Conductor (1964); *Pairs* for Any 2, 4, 6, or 8 Players (1968); *Prose Collection* for Variable Numbers of Players, Found and Constructed Materials, Instruments, and Voices (1968–71); *Lines* for String Quartet (1972); *Changing the System* for 8 or More Instruments, Voices, and Percussion (1972–73); *Wobbly Music* for Chorus, Keyboard, Guitars, and at Least 2 Melody Instruments (1975–76); *Braverman Music* for Chamber Ensemble (1978); *Rock About, Instrumental, Starving to Death on a Government Claim* for Violin and Viola (1979–80); *Isn't This a Time* for Any Saxophone or Multiple Reeds (1982); *Peace March 1* for Flute (1983–84); *Peace March 2* for Flute, Clarinet, Cello, Percussion, and Piano (1984); *Peace March 3* for Flute, Cello, and Percussion (1984).

Wolff, Christoph (Johannes), eminent German musicologist; b. Solingen, May 24, 1940. He studied church music at the Berlin Hochschule für Musik and in Freiburg im Breisgau; took courses in musicology at the Univs. of Berlin and Erlangen; obtained his Ph.D. in 1966 from the latter (diss., *Der stile antico in der Musik Johann Sebastian Bachs: Studien zu Bachs Spätwerk,* publ. in Wiesbaden, 1968). He taught at the Univ. of Erlangen (1965–69); also at the Univ. of Toronto (1968–70); then at Columbia Univ. (1970–76). In 1976 he became a prof. of music at Harvard Univ. He has written extensively on the history of music from the 15th to the 20th century, particularly on Bach and Mozart. He has distinguished himself by innovative research into formative elements in Bach's works. He became ed. of the *Bach-Jahrbuch* in 1974; ed. vols. of the *Neue Bach-Ausgabe* (V/2, *Goldberg Variations;* 14 Canons; VIII/1, *Musical Offering;* Canons); the *Neue Mozart-Ausgabe* (V/15, 2–3, *Piano Concertos*), and the *Hindemith-Gesamtausgabe* (opera *Cardillac,* op. 39). He wrote the major portion of the article on the Bach family for *The New Grove Dictionary of Music and Musicians* (1980); also ed. *The String Quartets of Haydn, Mozart, and Beethoven: Studies of the Autograph Manuscripts* (Cambridge, Mass., 1980) and with H.-J. Schulze, *Bach Compendium: Analytisch-bibliographisches Repertorium der Werke Johann Sebastian Bachs* (5 vols., Leipzig and Dresden, 1985–). In 1984 he discovered 33 unknown organ chorales by Bach in the Neumeister Collection of the music library at Yale Univ.; they were publ. in 1985. In 1978 he was awarded the Dent Medal of the Royal Musical Association of London and in 1982 he was elected a Fellow of the American Academy of Arts and Sciences.

Wolff, Edouard, Polish pianist, teacher, and composer; b. Warsaw, Sept. 15, 1816; d. Paris, Oct. 16, 1880. He studied in Warsaw with Zawadski (piano) and Elsner (composition); then was a piano pupil of Würfel in Vienna. In 1835 he settled in Paris, and became an esteemed teacher; he was a friend of Chopin, and imitated him in his piano music. He publ. 350 opus numbers for piano, among them several albums of études; a waltz, *La Favorite*; *Chansons polonaises originales*; *Tarentelle*; *Chansons bacchiques*; a Piano Concerto; also 30 celebrated duos for piano and violin with Bériot, and 8 more with Vieuxtemps. His sister, **Regina Wolff,** a pianist, was the mother of the violinist **Henryk Wieniawski.**

Wolff, Erich, Austrian pianist and composer; b. Vienna, Dec. 3, 1874; d. (on a concert tour) N.Y., March 20, 1913. He studied in Vienna with Anton Door (piano); lived in Vienna, and (from 1906) in Berlin; became well known as an excellent accompanist of singers. A vol. of 60 of his German songs was publ. posthumously, eliciting great praise. He also wrote a Violin Concerto and some chamber music.

Wolff, Fritz, German tenor; b. Munich, Oct. 28, 1894; d. there, Jan. 18, 1957. He studied with Heinrich König in Würzburg; made his debut as Loge in 1925 at the Bayreuth Festival, where he continued to make appearances until 1941; also sang in Hagen and Chemnitz. In 1930 he joined the Berlin State Opera, remaining on its roster until 1943; also made guest appearances at Covent Garden in London (1929–33; 1937–38), and in Vienna, Paris, Chicago, and Cleveland. From 1950 he was a prof. at the Hochschule für Musik in Munich. His finest roles included Parsifal and Lohengrin.

Wolff, Hellmuth Christian, German musicologist and composer; b. Zürich, May 23, 1906; d. Leipzig, July 1, 1988. He studied musicology at the Univ. of Berlin with Abert, Schering, Blume, and Sachs (Ph.D., 1932, with the diss. *Die Venezianische Oper in der zweiten Hälfte des 17. Jahrhunderts*; publ. in Berlin, 1937; 2nd ed., 1975). He completed his Habilitation at the Univ. of Kiel in 1942 with *Die Barockoper in Hamburg 1678–1738* (publ. in Wolfenbüttel, 1957); from 1954 to 1971 he was a prof. of musicology at the Univ. of Leipzig; beginning in 1956 he devoted a great deal of his time to painting, and exhibited in Leipzig and other German cities.
    WORKS: STAGE: OPERAS: *Der kleine und der grosse Klaus* (1931; rev. 1940); *Die törichten Wünsche* (1942–43); *Der Tod des Orpheus* (1947); *Ich lass' mich scheiden* (1950). **BALLET:** *Moresca* (1969). **SCENIC ORATORIO:** *Esther* (1945); incidental music. **ORCH.:** *3 Werke* for Chamber Orch. (1932); *Concerto* (1933); Concerto for Oboe and Chamber Orch. (1933); *Heitere Musik über ostinate Rhythmen* (1938); Suite (1940); *Inferno 1944* (1946); Serenade for Strings (1946); Concerto for Piano and Strings (1947); Violin Concerto (1948); *Sinfonia da missa* (1949); Double Bass Concerto (1968); *Händel Suite* (1970); *Paul Klee Suite* (1973); also chamber music; piano pieces; songs.
    WRITINGS: *Agrippina, eine italienische Jugendoper von G.Fr. Händel* (Wolfenbüttel and Berlin, 1943); *Die Musik der alten Niederländer (15. und 16. Jahrhundert)* (Leipzig, 1956); *Die Händel-Oper auf der modernen Bühne* (Leipzig, 1957); *Oper: Szene und Darstellung von 1600 bis 1900* (Leipzig, 1968); *Die Oper* (3 vols., Cologne, 1971–72; also in Eng.); *Ordnung und Gestalt: die Musik von 1900 bis 1950* (Bonn, 1977).

Wolff, Hugh (MacPherson), American conductor; b. Paris (of American parents), Oct. 21, 1953. He was taken to the U.S. by his family when he was 10; studied piano with Fleisher and Shure and composition with Crumb; then received instruction in composition from Kirchner at Harvard Univ. (B.A., 1975). After studying composition with Messiaen, piano with Sancan, and conducting with Bruck at the Paris Cons., he completed his training with Fleisher at the Peabody Inst. in Baltimore (M.M. in piano, 1977; M.M. in conducting, 1978). He was Exxon/Arts Endowment Conductor (1979–82) and associate conductor (1982–85) of the National Sym. Orch. in Washington, D.C.; also was music director of the Northeastern Pennsylvania Phil. (1981–86); likewise appeared as a guest conductor throughout the U.S.; made his European debut with the London Phil. (1983). In 1985 he became the 1st co-recipient (with Kent Nagano) of the Affiliated Artists' Seaver Conducting Award. He was music director of the New Jersey Sym. Orch. (1985–92). In 1986 he made his N.Y. City Opera debut conducting *Le nozze di Figaro*. From 1988 to 1991 he was principal conductor of the St. Paul (Minn.) Chamber Orch., then became its music director in 1991.
    BIBL.: H. Kupferberg, "H. W.," *Musical America* (Sept. 1987).

Wolff, Max, Austrian operetta composer; b. Moravia, Feb. 1840; d. Vienna, March 23, 1886. He studied music with Marx and Dessoff; became a successful composer of operettas, of which the following were produced in Vienna: *Die Pilger* (Sept. 6, 1872); *Die Porträt-Dame* (March 1, 1877); *Césarine* (Dec. 13, 1878).

Wolf-Ferrari (real name, **Wolf**), **Ermanno,** famous Italian opera composer; b. Venice, Jan. 12, 1876; d. there, Jan. 21, 1948. His father was a well-known painter of German descent and his mother was Italian; about 1895 he added his mother's maiden name to his surname. He began piano study as a small child but also evinced a talent for art; after studying at the Accademia di Belle Arti in Rome (1891–92), he went to Munich to continue his training but then turned to music and studied counterpoint with Rheinberger at the Akademie der Tonkunst (1892–95). In 1899 he returned to Venice, where his oratorio *La Sulamite* was successfully performed. This was followed by the production of his 1st major opera, *Cenerentola* (1900), which initially proved a failure; however, its revised version for Bremen (1902) was well received and established his reputation as a composer for the theater. From 1903 to 1909 he was director of the Liceo Benedetto Marcello in Venice; then devoted himself mainly to composition; later was prof. of composition at the Salzburg Mozarteum (1939–45). He obtained his 1st unqualified success with the production of the comic opera *Le donne curiose* (Munich, 1903); the next opera, *I quattro rusteghi* (Munich, 1906), was also well received; there followed his little masterpiece, *Il segreto di Susanna* (Munich, 1909), a one-act opera buffa in the style of the Italian *verismo* (Susanna's secret being not infidelity, as her husband suspected, but indulgence in surreptitious smoking). Turning toward grand opera, he wrote *I gioielli della Madonna*; it was brought out at Berlin in 1911, and soon became a repertoire piece everywhere; he continued to compose, but his later operas failed to match the appeal of his early creations.
    WORKS: OPERAS: *Cenerentola* (Venice, Feb. 22, 1900; rev. version as *Aschenbrödel*, Bremen, Jan. 31, 1902); *Le Donne curiose* (1902–3; in German as *Die neugierigen Frauen*, Munich, Nov. 27, 1903; in Italian, N.Y., Jan. 3, 1912); *I quattro rusteghi* (in German as *Die vier Grobiane*, Munich, March 19, 1906); *Il segreto di Susanna* (in German as *Susannens Geheimnis*, Munich, Dec. 4, 1909; in Italian, N.Y., March 14, 1911); *I gioielli della Madonna* (in German as *Der Schmuck der Madonna*, Berlin, Dec. 23, 1911; in Italian, Chicago, Jan. 16, 1912; in Eng. as *The Jewels of the Madonna*, N.Y., Oct. 14, 1913); *L'amore medico* (in German as *Der Liebhaber als Arzt*, Dresden, Dec. 4, 1913; in Italian, N.Y., March 25, 1914); *Gli Amanti sposi* (c.1916; Venice, Feb. 19, 1925); *Das Himmelskleid* (c.1917–25; Munich, April 21, 1927; in Italian as *La*

veste di cielo); *Sly, ovvero La leggenda del dormiente risvegliato* (Milan, Dec. 29, 1927); *La vedova scaltra* (Rome, March 5, 1931); *Il campiello* (Milan, Feb. 11, 1936); *La dama boba* (Milan, Feb. 1, 1939); *Gli dei a Tebe* (in German as *Der Kuckuck in Theben*, Hannover, June 5, 1943); also an ed. of Mozart's *Idomeneo* (Munich, June 15, 1931). ORCH.: *Serenade* for Strings (c.1893); *Kammersymphonie* (1901); *Idillio-concertino* for Oboe, 2 Horns, and Strings (1933); *Suite-concertino* for Bassoon, 2 Horns, and Strings (1933); *Suite veneziano* for Small Orch. (1936); *Divertimento* (1937); *Arabeschi* (1940); Violin Concerto (1946); *Symphonia brevis* (1947). CHAMBER: String Quintet (1894); 3 violin sonatas (1895, 1901, c.1940); 2 piano trios (c.1897, 1900); Piano Quintet (1900); String Quartet (1940); *Introduzione e balletto* for Violin and Cello (1946); piano pieces. VOCAL: *La Sulamite*, canto biblico (1889); *Talitha kumi*, oratorio (1900); *La vita nuova*, cantata (1901; Munich, Feb. 21, 1903); *La passione* for Chorus (1939; also for Voice and Piano, 1940); other large and small choral works. BIBL.: H. Teibler, *E. W.-F.* (Leipzig, 1906); E. Stahl, ed., *E. W.-F.* (Salzburg, 1936); R. de Rensis, *E. W.-F., La sua vita d'artista* (Milan, 1937); A. Grisson, *E. W.-F.: autorisierte Lebensbeschreibung* (Regensburg, 1941; 2nd ed., enl., 1958); R. de Rensis and G. Vannini, *In memoria di E. W.-F.* (Siena, 1948); W. Pfannkuch, *Das Opernschaffen E. W.-F.s* (diss., Univ. of Kiel, 1952); A. Suder, ed., *E. W.-F.* (Tutzing, 1986).

Wölfl (Woelfl, Wölffl), Joseph, Austrian pianist and composer; b. Salzburg, Dec. 24, 1773; d. London, May 21, 1812. He was a pupil of Leopold Mozart and Michael Haydn while serving as a chorister at the Salzburg Cathedral (1783–86); was then in Vienna (1790–92) and Warsaw (1793); again in Vienna from 1795; was considered Beethoven's rival as a pianist; in 1798 he married the actress Therese Klemm. Traveling through Germany, he gave numerous concerts as a pianist, reaching Paris in 1801; produced 2 French operas and was acclaimed as a piano virtuoso. In 1805 he went to London, and almost immediately established himself in the public's favor as a pianist and teacher. He was, however, of an eccentric disposition, and became involved in all sorts of trouble. He died in obscurity at the age of 38. In his professional life, he emphasized the sensational element; gave fanciful titles to his works; named one of his piano sonatas *Ne plus ultra*, and claimed that it was the most difficult piece ever written.
WORKS: STAGE: OPERAS: *Der Höllenberg* (Vienna, Nov. 21, 1795); *Das schöne Milchmädchen, oder der Guckkasten* (Vienna, Jan. 5, 1797); *Der Kopf ohne Mann* (Vienna, Dec. 3, 1798); *Das trojanische Pferd* (Vienna, 1797); *L'Amour romanesque* (Paris, 1804); *Fernando, ou Les Maures* (Paris, 1805). BALLETS: *La Surprise de Diane* (London, Sept. 21, 1805); *Alzire* (London, Jan. 27, 1807). ORCH.: 7 piano concertos, including *Le Calme* and *Grand concerto*; other publ. compositions are 2 syms.; 12 string quartets; 6 piano trios; 2 trios for 2 Clarinets and Bassoon; numerous sonatas; many sets of variations for Keyboard; a *Méthode de piano* (with 100 studies); sonatas for 4-hands; waltzes, polonaises, rondos, fantasias, etc.; songs. Some of his piano pieces were publ. in monthly issues, under the title *The Harmonic Budget* (London, 1810). BIBL.: R. Duval, "Un Rival de Beethoven: J. Woelfl," *Rivista Musicale Italiana*, V (1898; also publ. separately, Turin, 1898); R. Baum, *J. Wölfl: Leben, Klavierwerke, Klavierkammermusik und Klavierkonzerte* (Kassel, 1928).

Wolfram, Joseph Maria, Bohemian composer; b. Dobrzan, July 21, 1789; d. Teplitz, Sept. 30, 1839. He studied with J.A. Koželuch in Prague; moved to Vienna as a music teacher; then became a government official at Theusing, and mayor of Teplitz (1824). He brought out several successful operas: *Maja und Alpino* (Prague, May 24, 1826); *Der Bergmönch* (Dresden, March 14, 1830); *Das Schloss Candra* (Dresden, Dec. 1, 1832); a *Missa nuptialis* and some piano pieces and songs by him were publ.

Wolfrum, Philipp, German conductor, musicologist, and composer; b. Schwarzenbach-am-Wald, Dec. 17, 1854; d. Sa-

maden, May 8, 1919. He was a pupil of Rheinberger and Wüllner in Munich; received his Ph.D. at Leipzig Univ. in 1890 with the dissertation *Die Entstehung und erste Entwickelung des deutschen evangelischen Kirchenliedes in musikalischer Beziehung*. After serving as a music teacher in a Bamberg seminary (1879–84), he was named director of music at Heidelberg Univ., where he was made a prof. in 1898; he was also founder-conductor of the noted Heidelberg Bachverein (from 1885), with which he championed the music of Bach; he also furthered the cause of Bruckner and Reger. His brother, **Karl Wolfrum** (b. Schwarzenbach-am-Wald, Aug. 14, 1856; d. Neustadt-an-der-Aisch, May 27, 1937), was a pedagogue and composer. WRITINGS: *Joh. Seb. Bach* (2 vols., 1906; 2nd ed. of vol. 1, 1910); *Die evangelische Kirchenmusik: Ihr Stand und ihre Weiterentwicklung* (1914); *Luther und Bach* (1917); *Luther und die Musik* (1918). WORKS: *Festliche Ouvertüre; Das grosse Halleluja*, ode for Chorus and Orch. (1886); *Ein Weihnachtsmysterium*, Christmas play, for Chorus and Orch. (1899); Piano Quartet; String Quartet; Piano Trio; Cello Sonata; 3 organ sonatas; he also ed. *Der evangelische Kirchenchor* (collection of 44 hymns) and *Pfälzisches Melodienbuch*. BIBL.: K. Hasse, "P. W.," *Zeitschrift für Musikwissenschaft* (1919).

Wolfurt, Kurt von, German composer; b. Lettin, Sept. 7, 1880; d. Munich, Feb. 25, 1957. He studied science at the Univs. of Dorpat, Leipzig, and Munich; then took lessons in composition with Reger and in piano with Krause in Munich. He eventually went to Berlin as a teacher at the municipal cons. (1936–45); later taught in Göttingen (1945–49) and in Johannesburg (1949–52). He publ. monographs on Mussorgsky (Stuttgart, 1927) and Tchaikovsky (Zürich, 1951). Among his works is the opera *Dame Kobold* (Kassel, March 14, 1940); also *Gesang des Meeres*, symphonic poem; Concerto grosso for Chamber Orch. (1931); Piano Concerto (1933); *Serenade* for Orch. (1936); chamber music; vocal works; etc. BIBL.: Special issue of *Zeitschrift für Musik* (Oct. 1940).

Wolkenstein, Oswald von, South Tirolean Minnesänger; b. Schöneck in Pustertal, c.1377; d. Merano, Aug. 2, 1445. He led an adventurous life, traveling through Russia, Persia, Greece, Spain, France, Italy (with King Ruprecht in 1401), etc. For several years (from 1415) he was in the service of King (later Emperor) Sigismund, whom he accompanied to the Council of Constance. The musical settings that he devised for his poems are notable for their genuine melodic quality; some of them are in 2-part and 3-part counterpoint; there are also examples of canonic imitation. For his output, see J. Schatz and O. Keller, eds., *Oswald von Wolkenstein: Geistliche und weltliche Lieder, ein- und mehrstimmig*, Denkmäler der Tonkunst in Österreich, XVIII, Jg.IX (1902), K. Klein, W. Weiss, N. Wolf, and W. Salmen, eds., *Die Lieder Oswalds von Wolkenstein* (Tübingen, 1962; 2nd ed., rev., 1975 by H. Moser, N.R. Wolf, and N. Wolf), B. Wachinger, ed. and tr., *Oswald von Wolkenstein: eine Auswahl aus seinen Liedern* (Ebenhausen, 1964), H. Moser and U. Müller, eds., *Oswald von Wolkenstein: Abbildungen zur Überlieferung, I: Die Innsbrucker Wolkenstein-Handschrift* (Göppingen, 1972), and U. Müller and F. Spechter, eds., *Oswald von Wolkenstein: Handschrift A in Abbildung* (Stuttgart, 1974). BIBL.: W. Marold, *Kommentar zu den Liedern O.s v.W.* (diss., Univ. of Göttingen, 1926); H. Lowenstein, *Wort und Ton bei O. v.W.* (Königsberg, 1932); W. Salmen, "Werdegang und Lebensfülle des O. v.W.," *Musica Disciplina*, VII (1953); E. Timm, *Die Überlieferung der Lieder O.s v.W.* (Lübeck and Hamburg, 1972); I. Pelnar, *Die mehrstimmigen Lieder O.s v.W.* (diss., Univ. of Munich, 1977); A. Schwob, *O. v.W.: eine Biographie* (Bolzano, 1977).

Wollanck, (Johann Ernst) Friedrich, German composer; b. Berlin, Nov. 3, 1781; d. there, Sept. 6, 1831. He studied with J.A. Gürlich and C.F.C. Fasch; was a lawyer and held a government position as counselor of the city court in Berlin.

His works include an opera, *Der Alpenhirten* (Berlin, Feb. 19, 1811); a "Liederspiel," *Thibaut von Lowis;* 2 masses; a Requiem and other church music; more than 100 songs; 33 part-songs; 3 string quartets; 2 string sextets; other chamber music; piano sonatas.

Wolle, John Frederick, American choral conductor and organist; b. Bethlehem, Pa., April 4, 1863; d. there, Jan. 12, 1933. He studied with Rheinberger in Munich (1884–85); served as organist at the Moravian Church in Bethlehem (1885–1905); in 1900 he inaugurated the Bach Choir in Bethlehem, which became famous for its fine performances.
    Bibl.: R. Walters, *The Bethlehem Bach Choir* (Boston, 1918); M.A. DeWolfe Howe, "Venite in Bethlehem," *Musical Quarterly* (April 1942).

Wolle, Peter, Moravian minister, bishop, and composer; b. New Herrnhut, St. Thomas, West Indies, Jan. 5, 1792; d. Bethlehem, Pa., Nov. 14, 1871. He was consecrated to the episcopacy on Sept. 26, 1845. He left several compositions; ed. the *Moravian Tune Book* (1836).

Wollenhaupt, Hermann Adolf, German pianist and composer; b. Schkeuditz, near Leipzig, Sept. 27, 1827; d. N.Y., Sept. 18, 1863. He studied in Leipzig with Julius Knorr (piano) and Moritz Hauptmann (composition). In 1845 he settled in N.Y.; made a reputation as a concert pianist and teacher. He wrote about 100 brilliant piano pieces, among them *Galop di bravura, Valses styriennes, Improvisation, Nocturne,* and *Scherzo brillante;* he also made numerous transcriptions and arrangements.

Wolpe, Stefan, significant German-American composer and pedagogue; b. Berlin, Aug. 25, 1902; d. N.Y., April 4, 1972. He studied music theory with Paul Juon and Franz Schreker at the Berlin Hochschule für Musik (1919–24). After graduation, he became associated with choral and theatrical groups in Berlin, promoting social causes; composed songs on revolutionary themes. With the advent of the anti-Semitic Nazi regime in 1933, he went to Vienna, where he took lessons with Anton von Webern; then traveled to Palestine in 1934; taught at the Jerusalem Cons. In 1938 he emigrated to the U.S., where he devoted himself mainly to teaching; was on the faculty of the Settlement Music School in Philadelphia (1939–42); at the Philadelphia Academy of Music (1949–52); at Black Mountain College, N.C. (1952–56); and at Long Island Univ. (1957–68). He also taught privately. Among his students were Elmer Bernstein, Ezra Laderman, Ralph Shapey, David Tudor, and Morton Feldman. He was married successively to Ola Okuniewska, a painter, in 1927, to Irma Schoenberg (1902–84), a Rumanian pianist, in 1934, and to Hilda Morley, a poet, in 1948. In 1966 he was elected a member of the National Inst. of Arts and Letters. He contributed numerous articles to German and American music magazines. In his style of composition, he attempted to reconcile the contradictions of triadic tonality (which he cultivated during his early period of writing "proletarian" music), atonality without procrustean dodecaphony, and serialism of contrasts obtained by intervallic contraction and expansion, metrical alteration, and dynamic variegation; superadded to these were explorations of Jewish cantillation and infatuation with jazz. Remarkably enough, the very copiousness of these resources contributed to a clearly identifiable idiom.
    Works: operas: *Schöne Geschichten* (1927–29); *Zeus und Elida* (1928); *Cantata about Sport* (1952); *Street Music* for Baritone, Speaker, and 5 Instruments (1963–68); Cantata to texts by Hölderlin, Herodotus, and Robert Creeley (1963–68); incidental music: *Da liegt Hund begraben* (1932); *The Good Woman of Setzuan,* to a play by Bertolt Brecht (1953); *The Exception and the Rule,* to a play by Bertolt Brecht (1960). **orch.:** *Passacaglia* (1937); *The Man from Midian,* ballet suite (1942); Sym. (1955–56; rev. 1964); *Chamber Piece No. 1* for 14 Players (1964); *Chamber Piece No. 2* for 14 Players (1965–66). **chamber:** *Duo in Hexachord* for Oboe and Clarinet (1936); Oboe Sonata (1941); Violin Sonata (1949); Quartet for Trum-

pet, Saxophone, Percussion, and Piano (1950); Oboe Quartet (1955); Quintet with Voice for Baritone, Clarinet, Horn, Cello, Harp, and Piano (1956–57); Trio for Flute, Cello, and Piano (1964); *From Here on Farther* for Clarinet, Bass Clarinet, Violin, and Piano (1969); String Quartet (1969); *Piece* for Trumpet and 7 Instruments (1971). **piano:** *March and Variations* for 2 Pianos (1933); *4 Studies on Basic Rows* (1935–36); *Toccata* (1941); *Enactments* for 3 Pianos (1950–53); *Broken Sequences* (1969); songs.
    Bibl.: M. Bauer, "S. W.," *Modern Music,* XVII (1940); H. Sucoff, *Catalogue and Evaluation of the Work of S. W.* (N.Y., 1969); M. Babbitt, E. Carter, L. Stempel, and C. Wuorinen, "In Memoriam S. W.," *Perspectives of New Music,* XI/1 (1972); A. Clarkson, "The Works of S. W.: A Brief Catalogue," *Notes* (June 1985).

Wolpert, Franz Alfons, German composer and music theorist; b. Wiesentheid, Oct. 11, 1917; d. there, Aug. 7, 1978. He sang in the Cathedral choir in Regensburg, and studied there at a Catholic church music school; took lessons in composition with Wolf-Ferrari at the Salzburg Mozarteum (1939–41), where he subsequently taught (1941–44); was a teacher in Salem, Lake Constance (from 1950). He publ. the useful vol. *Neue Harmonik: die Lehre von den Akkordtypen* (Regensburg, 1952; 2nd ed., rev. and enl., 1972). His compositions include a comic opera, *Der eingebildete Kranke* (1975), a ballet, *Der goldene Schuh* (1956); *Banchetto musicale No. 1* for Violin and Chamber Orch. (1952) and *No. 2* for Piano and Orch. (1953), and several chamber and choral works; also organ and piano pieces and over 50 lieder.

Wolstenholme, William, blind English organist and composer; b. Blackburn, Lancashire, Feb. 24, 1865; d. London, July 23, 1931. He entered the College for Blind Sons of Gentlemen in Worcester at the age of 9; studied with Done, the Cathedral organist there; received a Mus.Bac. from Oxford Univ. in 1887; subsequently filled various posts as a church organist in Blackburn, and (from 1902) in London.
    Works: *Lord Ullin's Daughter,* cantata; *Sir Humphrey Gilbert,* ballad for Women's Voices; *To Take the Air,* madrigal; *Suite* in F for String Orch.; about 100 compositions for Organ; Wind Quintet; Piano Quartet; 2 string quartets; Piano Trio; Violin Sonata; piano pieces; songs and part-songs.
    Bibl.: F. Wood, "W. W.," *Musical Times* (1931).

Wolzogen, (Karl August) Alfred, Freiherr von, German writer on music, father of **Ernst** and **Hans (Paul), Freiherr von Wolzogen;** b. Frankfurt am Main, May 27, 1823; d. San Remo, Jan. 14, 1883. From 1868 he was Intendant of the Court Theater at Schwerin. He was the author of *Über Theater und Musik* (Breslau, 1860); *Über die szenische Darstellung von Mozarts "Don Giovanni"* (1860); *Wilhelmine Schröder-Devrient* (Leipzig, 1863); new German versions of Mozart's *Don Giovanni* and *Schauspieldirektor;* also articles in periodicals.

Wolzogen, Ernst, Freiherr von, German poet and writer, son of **(Karl August) Alfred, Freiherr von Wolzogen** and half brother of **Hans (Paul), Freiherr von Wolzogen;** b. Breslau, April 23, 1855; d. Munich, July 30, 1934. He studied at the univs. of Strasbourg and Leipzig. In 1901 he established in Berlin (with O.J. Bierbaum and F. Wedekind) the Überbrettl, a kind of artistic cabaret for the production of dramatic pieces, pantomimes, poems with recitation and music, etc., most of them reflecting or satirizing contemporary German life; Oskar Straus provided most of the music, and Schoenberg contributed some of the numbers; 2 journals, *Das moderne Brettl* and *Bühne und Brettl,* were publ. for a year or so to promote the ideas of the enterprise, but the cabaret closed after 2 sensationally successful seasons. Wolzogen publ. 2 books dealing with music: *Der Kraftmayr* (1897; humorous novel with Liszt as the central figure; Eng. tr. as *Florian Mayr,* 1914) and *Ansichten und Aussichten* (1908; essays). His wife, Elsa Laura (née Seeman von Mangern), became known as a singer, making a specialty of songs with lute accompaniment; with her husband she made a tour of the U.S. (1910–11); publ. 7 vols. of folk songs with lute accompaniment (*Meine Lieder zur Laute*).

Bibl.: A. Hertwig, *E. v.W. "Überbrettl" in Wort und Bild* (Berlin, 1901).

Wolzogen, Hans (Paul), Freiherr von, German writer on music, son of **(Karl August) Alfred, Freiherr von Wolzogen** and half brother of **Ernst, Freiherr von Wolzogen;** b. Potsdam, Nov. 13, 1848; d. Bayreuth, June 2, 1938. He studied philosophy and comparative philology in Berlin (1868–71); then devoted himself to literature; in 1878, at Wagner's invitation, he became ed. of the *Bayreuther Blätter* and lived in Bayreuth most of his life. He popularized the term "leitmotif," first used by F.W. Jähns, in his "Motive in Wagners *Götterdämmerung*," publ. in the *Musikalisches Wochenblatt* in 1887 (Wagner's preferred term was "Grundthema").

Writings: *Der Nibelungenmythos in Sage und Literatur* (1876; 3rd ed., 1890); *Thematischer Lietfaden durch die Musik von R. Wagners Festspiel "Der Ring des Nibelungen"* (1876; 4th ed. as *Erläuterungen zu R. Wagners Nibelungendrama,* 1878); *Die Tragödie in Bayreuth und ihr Satyrspiel* (1876; 5th ed., 1881); *Poetische Lautsymbolik. Psychische Wirkungen der Sprachlaute aus R. Wagners "Ring des Nibelungen"* (1876; 3rd ed., 1897); *Grundlage und Aufgabe des allgemeinen Patronatvereins zur Pflege und Erhaltung der Bühnenfestspiele in Bayreuth* (1877); *Die Sprache in Wagners Dichtungen* (1877; 2nd ed., 1881); *R. Wagners Tristan und Isolde* (1880); *Unsre Zeit und unsre Kunst* (1881); *Was ist Stil? was will Wagner?* (1881); *Die Religion des Mitleidens* (1882); *Parsifal. Ein thematischer Leitfaden* (1882; 21st printing, 1914); *R. Wagners Heldengestalten erläutert* (2nd ed., 1886); *Wagneriana* (1888); *R. Wagner und die Tierwelt; auch eine Biographie* (1890; 3rd ed., 1910); *Wagners Lebensbericht* (1884; the original work of "The Work and Mission of My Life," publ. 1879 in the *North American Review,* under Wagner's name); *Erinnerungen an R. Wagner* (1883); *Die Idealisierung des Theaters* (1885); *Grossmeister deutscher Musik* (1897); *Musikalisch-dramatische Parallelen* (1906); *E.T.A. Hoffmann und R. Wagner* (1906); *Aus R. Wagners Geisteswelt* (1908); *Kunst und Kirche* (1913); *E.T.A. Hoffmann, Der deutsche Geisterseher* (1922); *Lebensbilder* (autobiographical; 1923); *Wagner und seine Werke* (1924); *Wohltäterin Musik* (1925); *Musik und Theater* (1929).

Wonder, Stevie (real name, **Steveland Judkins Hardaway**), phenomenally successful black American soul singer, keyboardist, and songwriter; b. Saginaw, Mich., May 13, 1950. He was blind from birth; learned to play the drums and piano; improvised his 1st song, *Lonely Boy,* at the age of 10, and at 12 composed *Fingertips,* which became a hit. He signed with Berry Gordy (Motown Records) in 1961. Possessed by that indefinable gift of song, he rapidly advanced in the rosters of popular success; the shows at which he sings, accompanying himself at the piano, have become great money-makers. Among his early pop hits are *Living for the City, You Are the Sunshine of My Life, My Cherie Amour, I Was Made to Love Her,* and *Uptight.* In his nearly 30-year career, his music has evolved with the times and thus his popularity has never waned; won 16 Grammy awards. In the 1970s and 1980s he produced such enduring ballads as *Isn't She Lovely, Part-Time Lover,* and *I Just Called to Say I Love You.* He devoted much time, energy, and money to social causes; added his voice to a campaign against drunk driving and donated to AIDS and cancer research; contributed to USA for Africa's charity record, *We Are the World* (1985).

Bibl.: C. Elsner, *S. W.* (N.Y., 1977); J. Peish, *S. W.* (N.Y., 1984); J. Swenson, *S. W.* (London, 1986).

Wood, Charles, Irish pedagogue and composer, brother of **William G. Wood;** b. Armagh, June 15, 1866; d. Cambridge, England, July 12, 1926. He studied at the Royal College of Music in London, and subsequently taught harmony there; received his Mus.Doc. degree from Cambridge in 1894; was a univ. lecturer in harmony and counterpoint there from 1897, succeeding Stanford as prof. of music in 1924. He wrote 6

string quartets (mostly in an Irish manner); vocal works with Orch.: *Ode on Time* (1898), *Dirge for 2 Veterans* (1901), *Song of the Tempest* (1902), *Ballad of Dundee* (1904); a comic opera, *Pickwick Papers* (London, 1922); church music; ed. a collection of Irish folk songs (1897).

Wood, David Duffle, blind American organist, teacher, and composer; b. Pittsburgh, March 2, 1838; d. Philadelphia, March 27, 1910. Having lost his eyesight in an accident at the age of 3, he was educated at the Pa. Inst. for the Blind; from 1858 till his death he was an instructor of music there. He was a fine organist; wrote anthems and songs. He publ. *A Dictionary of Musical Terms, for the Use of the Blind* (Philadelphia, 1869).

Wood, Haydn, English violinist and composer; b. Slaithwaite, March 25, 1882; d. London, March 11, 1959. He entered the Royal College of Music in London at 15; studied there with Fernández Arbós (violin) and Stanford (composition); later studied with César Thomson in Brussels. His works include a Piano Concerto, a Violin Concerto, 8 overtures, 8 rhapsodies for band, 18 orch. studies, 31 entr'actes for orch., 12 violin solos, 2 flute pieces, 3 accordion solos, and about 200 songs.

Wood, Sir Henry J(oseph), eminent English conductor; b. London, March 3, 1869; d. Hitchin, Hertfordshire, Aug. 19, 1944. Of musical parentage, he was taught to play the piano by his mother; he participated in family musicales from the age of 6; was equally precocious on the organ; at the age of 10 he often acted as a deputy organist, and gave organ recitals at the Fisheries Exhibition (1883) and at the Inventions Exhibition (1885). In 1886 he entered the Royal Academy of Music in London, where his teachers were Prout, Steggall, Macfarren, and Garcia; he won 4 medals. In 1888 he brought out some of his songs; then composed light operas and cantatas. But soon his ambition crystallized in the direction of conducting; after making his debut in 1888, he was active with various theater companies. On Aug. 10, 1895, he began his 1st series of Promenade Concerts (the famous "Proms") in Queen's Hall, London, with an orch. of about 80 members. Their success was so conspicuous that a new series of concerts was inaugurated on Jan. 30, 1897, under Wood's direction, and flourished from the beginning. In 1899 he founded the Nottingham Orch.; also was conductor of the Wolverhampton Festival Choral Society (1900), the Sheffield Festival (1902–11), and the Norwich Festival (1908). In 1904 he was a guest conductor of the N.Y. Phil. He was married to Olga Urusova, a Russian noblewoman, and became greatly interested in Russian music, which he performed frequently at his concerts. He adopted a Russian pseudonym, Paul Klenovsky, for his compositions and arrangements, and supplied an imaginary biography of his alter ego for use in program notes. His wife died in 1909, and Wood married Muriel Greatorex in 1911. In 1921 he received the Gold Medal of the Royal Phil. Soc. He was made a Companion of Honour in 1944. In 1918 he was offered the conductorship of the Boston Sym. Orch. as successor to Muck, but declined. In 1923 he was appointed prof. of conducting and orch. playing at the Royal Academy of Music. Wood continued to conduct the Promenade Concerts almost to the end of his life, presenting the last concert on July 28, 1944. Among his popular arrangements were Chopin's *Marche Funèbre,* some works by Bach, and the *Trumpet Voluntary* (mistakenly attributed to Purcell, but actually by Jeremiah Clarke). He publ. *The Gentle Art of Singing* (4 vols.; 1927–28) and *About Conducting* (London, 1945), and ed. the *Handbook of Miniature Orchestral and Chamber Music Scores* (1937); wrote an autobiography, *My Life and Music* (London, 1938). A commemorative postage stamp with his portrait was issued by the Post Office of Great Britain on Sept. 1, 1980.

Bibl.: R. Newmarch, *H.J. W.* (London, 1904); T. Russell et al., eds., *Homage to Sir H. W.: A World Symposium* (London, 1944); W. Thompson et al., *Sir H. W.: Fifty Years of the Proms* (London, 1944); J. Wood, *The Last Years of H.J. W.* (London, 1954); R. Pound, *Sir H. W.: A Biography* (London, 1969); A. Orga, *The Proms* (London, 1974); D. Cox, *The H. W. Proms*

(London, 1980); D. Lambourn, "H. W. and Schoenberg," *Musical Times* (Aug. 1987).

Wood, Hugh (Bradshaw), English composer; b. Parbold, near Wigan, Lancashire, June 27, 1932. He studied modern history at Oxford and received private training in harmony and counterpoint from Lloyd Webber (from 1954); then studied theory and composition with Anthony Milner, Iain Hamilton, and Mátyás Seiber in London (1957–60); taught at Morley College in London (1958–67) and at the Royal Academy of Music (1962–65); was composer-in-residence at the Univ. of Glasgow (1966–70); from 1971 to 1973 he was a lecturer at the Univ. of Liverpool; in 1976 was appointed a lecturer at the Univ. of Cambridge.

WORKS: *Variations* for Viola and Piano (1957–59); *4 Songs* for Mezzo-soprano, Clarinet, Violin, and Cello (1959–61); Trio for Flute, Viola, and Piano (1961); 3 string quartets (1962, 1970, 1978); *3 Pieces* for Piano (1960–63); *Scenes from "Comus,"* after Milton, for Soprano, Tenor, and Orch. (1962–65; London, Aug. 2, 1965); Quintet for Clarinet, Horn, Violin, Cello, and Piano (1967); Cello Concerto (1965–69; London, Aug. 26, 1969); Chamber Concerto (1970–71; London, Nov. 27, 1971); Violin Concerto (1970–72; Liverpool, Sept. 19, 1972); *Song Cycle to Poems of Neruda* for High Voice and Chamber Orch. (1973; London, Feb. 18, 1974); Sym. (1979–82); Piano Trio (1984).

Wood, Joseph, American composer; b. Pittsburgh, May 12, 1915. He studied with Bernard Wagenaar at the Juilliard School of Music in N.Y., graduating in 1949, and with Otto Luening at Columbia Univ. (M.A., 1950). In 1950 he was appointed prof. in composition at the Oberlin Cons. of Music in Ohio; he retired in 1985. His music is couched in a modern Romantic vein; upon occasion he applies serial techniques.

WORKS: Opera, *The Mother* (1945); 4 syms. (1939, 1952, 1958, 1983); Piano Trio (1937); Viola Sonata (1938); 3 string quartets (1942, 1965, 1975); Violin Sonata (1947); Piano Quintet (1956); *Divertimento* for Piano and Chamber Orch. (1959); Violin Concerto (1961); *The Progression*, ballet-cantata (1968); Concerto for Chamber Orch. (1973–74); *Te Deum* for Chorus and Orch. (1982); incidental music; choruses; songs; piano pieces.

Wood, Mary Knight, American pianist and composer; b. Easthampton, Mass., April 7, 1857; d. Florence, Dec. 20, 1944. She studied in Boston with B.J. Lang and in N.Y. with Huss; married A.B. Mason and settled in Florence. She publ. about 30 songs, among them "Ashes of Roses," "In Harbor," and "Poppies."

Wood, Thomas, English composer and author; b. Chorley, Lancashire, Nov. 28, 1892; d. Bures, Essex, Nov. 19, 1950. He was educated at Exeter College, Oxford; then studied at the Royal Academy of Music in London with Stanford (composition) and Herbert Fryer (piano); subsequently took his D.Mus. at Oxford Univ. (1920). He was music director at Tonbridge School (1920–24); lecturer and precentor at Exeter College (1924–28). His extensive travels took him to the Far East and the Arctic; his familiarity with the sea was reflected in many of his compositions (for Chorus and Orch.), such as *40 Singing Seamen* (1925), *Master Mariners* (1927), *Merchantmen* (1934), and in *A Seaman's Overture* (for Orch., 1927). He ed. vol. II of the *Oxford Song Book* (1928; 3rd ed., 1937). His books include *Music and Boyhood* (1925) and the autobiographical *True Thomas* (1936); he also publ. *Cobbers* (on his Australian tour of 1930–32), which became highly popular in England, and a sequel to it, *Cobbers Campaigning* (1940).

BIBL.: N. Coghill, "T. W.," *Music & Letters* (April 1951).

Wood, William G., Irish organist and composer, brother of **Charles Wood;** b. Armagh, Jan. 16, 1859; d. London, Sept. 25, 1895. He studied at the Royal Academy of Music in London; from 1886 till his death he was organist and music master at the Highgate Grammar School. He composed some fine organ music (3 canons, a Sonata, *Fantasia and Fugue, Introduction and Allegro, Minuet and Trio,* etc.).

Woodbury, Arthur N(eum), American composer, bassoonist, saxophonist, and teacher; b. Kimball, Nebr., June 20, 1930. He studied composition with William Billingsley at the Univ. of Idaho (B.S., 1951; M.M., 1955); after private composition lessons with Robert Morton in San Francisco (1956–57), he pursued postgraduate composition studies with Imbrie at the Univ. of Calif. at Berkeley (1957–58); later studied computer music at Stanford Univ. (1970). He pursued a vigorous career as a performer, both as a member of various orchs. and as a soloist; from 1963 to 1972 he taught at the Univ. of Calif. at Davis. From 1967 to 1972 he served as ed. of the avant-garde journal *Source*; in 1972 he joined the faculty of the Univ. of South Florida in Tampa, where he was a prof. from 1987. His early works are written in a traditional modern idiom; later he branched out as a composer of experimental music, making use of electronics and aleatory techniques.

WORKS: Woodwind Quartet (1955); Sym. (1958); *Introduction and Allegro* for Band (1965); *Autobiography: Patricia Belle* for Soprano, Live Electronics, and Amplified Instruments (1968); *Recall*, theater piece for Actor, Tape, and Live Electronics (1969); *Remembrances*, trio for Violin, Alto Saxophone, and Vibraphone (1969); *Velox*, computer piece (1970); *WernerVonBraunasaurus Rex* for Electronic Piano, Guitar, and Moog Synthesizer (1979); *Jazz Fugue* for Saxophone Quartet and Accompaniment (1980); *Diversions* for Piano (1980–83); *Passacaglia, Interlude, and Canon* for Organ (1981; also for Concert Band, 1984); *Tocata española* for Marimba or Percussion and Cello (1983); *No More Jim Beam, Please* for Jazz Quartet (1985); *Learnin' the Blues* for Jazz Quintet (1986); *Wild Nights* for Voice and Piano (1988); *Variations on a Cadenza* for Flute and Percussion (1989).

Woodbury (real name, **Woodberry**), **Isaac Baker,** American composer, organist, teacher, editor, and writer on music; b. Beverly, Mass., Oct. 23, 1819; d. Columbia, S.C., Oct. 26, 1858. Originally a blacksmith, he began training in music with Lowell Mason in Boston in 1832 and later studied in London and Paris (1838–39); returning to Boston, he pursued a varied career; with his cousin Benjamin F. Baker, he organized the National Musical Convention, a teacher training school. In 1849 he went to N.Y.; was organist at Rutgers Street Church (1850–51); served as ed. of the *American Monthly Musical Review* (1850–53) and the *New York Musical Pioneer* (1855–58). His prolific output includes some 700 compositions and publs., among them 16 collections and eds., 3 oratorios, a musical drama, over 400 hymn tunes, several songs, piano pieces, and 8 pedagogical vols.

BIBL.: J. Higginson, "I.B. W. (1819–1858)," *The Hymn*, XX (1969); R. Copeland, *The Life and Works of I.B. W. (1819–1858)* (diss., Univ. of Cincinnati, 1974).

Woodman, (Raymond) Huntington, American organist and composer; b. Brooklyn, Jan. 18, 1861; d. there, Dec. 25, 1943. He studied piano with his father; theory with Dudley Buck (1881–85); then went to Paris, where he took lessons in organ playing from César Franck (1888). He filled various posts as a church organist and teacher in N.Y.; also taught theory and conducted a choral society in Brooklyn. He publ. about 150 compositions, among them anthems, organ pieces, piano pieces (*Romance, The Brook, Spring Song, 3 Album-Leaves,* etc.), and songs, of which *A Birthday* was especially successful.

Woodward, Roger (Robert), Australian pianist; b. Sydney, Dec. 20, 1942. He studied piano with Alexander Sverjensky in Sydney; then obtained a Polish government scholarship and went to Warsaw, where he took lessons with Zbigniew Drzwiecki. He won 1st prize in the Chopin Competition in 1968, an auspicious award that propelled him on an international career. In 1971 he settled in London, where he gained renown among international avant-garde composers by repeatedly performing works by such uncompromising celebrants of quaquaversal modern idioms as Takemitsu, Barraqué, Stockhausen, and Birtwistle; faithful to his antecedents, he also placed on his programs works of Australian composers such as Boyd, Meale, and Sculthorpe. He participated in several

American concerts of contemporary music, including a marathon series presented in Los Angeles. In 1985 he played the complete works of Chopin in a series of 16 concerts. In 1986 he was soloist in the 1st performance of Xenakis's *Keqrops* with Zubin Mehta and the N.Y. Phil. In 1980 he was made an Officer of the Order of the British Empire.

Woodworth, G(eorge) Wallace, American choral conductor, organist, and music educator; b. Boston, Nov. 6, 1902; d. Cambridge, Mass., July 18, 1969. He was educated at Harvard Univ. (B.A., 1924; M.A., 1926); also studied conducting with Malcolm Sargent at the Royal College of Music in London (1927–28). In 1924 he joined the staff of the music dept. at Harvard, and was engaged as conductor of the Radcliffe Choral Soc.; also led the Pierian Sodality Orch. of Harvard Univ. (1928–32) and the Harvard Glee Club (1933–38). In 1940 he was appointed organist and choirmaster for the Harvard Univ. Chapel. He was made James Edward Ditson Professor of Music at Harvard in 1954. He conducted the Harvard-Radcliffe Chorus on its transcontinental U.S. tour in 1954, and took the Harvard Glee Club on its European tour in 1956. He retired in 1969. He publ. *The World of Music* (Cambridge, Mass., 1964).
BIBL.: L. Berman, ed., *Words and Music: The Composer's View: A Medley of Problems and Solutions in Honor of G.W. W.* (Cambridge, 1972).

Wooldridge, David (Humphry Michael), English composer, conductor, and writer on music, grandson of **H(arry) E(llis) Wooldridge;** b. Deal, Kent, Aug. 24, 1927. He was the godson of Rachmaninoff, from whom he received some friendly piano lessons at the age of 4. He began studying the violin at 6; at 16, made his conducting debut; in 1952 he graduated from the Univ. of London, summa cum laude; was then apprenticed to Clemens Krauss at the Vienna State Opera; in 1954–55 he was on the roster of the Bavarian State Opera in Munich. After guest appearances in the U.S., he was music director of the Lebanese National Orch. in Beirut (1961–65); conducted the Cape Town Sym. Orch. (1965–67); again was in the U.S. as a visiting univ. lecturer and also as a conductor. He publ. the books *Conductor's World* (N.Y., 1970) and *From the Steeples and Mountains,* a biography of Charles Ives (N.Y., 1974).
WORKS: Viola Concerto (1949); ballet, *Les Parapluies* (1956); Cello Concerto (1957); ballet, *Octet* (1958); *Suite Libanaise* (1962); *4 Armenian Dances* (1964); *Partita* for Small Orch. (1967); *Partita* for Large Orch. (1968); ballet, *Movements* (1970); symphonic poem, *The Legend of Lillanonah* (1975); opera, *The Duchess of Amalfi* (1978); incidental music; film scores.

Wooldridge, H(arry) E(llis), English musicologist, grandfather of **David (Humphry Michael) Wooldridge;** b. Winchester, March 28, 1845; d. London, Feb. 13, 1917. While studying at Trinity College, Oxford (1860–64), he became deeply interested in painting and music; entered the Royal Academy of Fine Arts in 1865, at the same time beginning his research regarding early music in the libraries of Oxford and London; from 1895 until his death, he was Slade Prof. of Fine Arts at Oxford Univ.
WRITINGS: *The English Metrical Psalter* (1890); *The Polyphonic Period,* vols. I and II of the *Oxford History of Music* (1901, 1905; 2nd ed., rev. by P. Buck, 1929–32); radically rev. Chappell's *Popular Music of the Olden Times,* and publ. it as *Old English Popular Music* (2 vols., 1893); ed. *Early English Harmony* (2 vols., 1897, 1913); *The Yattendon Hymnal* (1899; with R. Bridges).

Woolf, Benjamin Edward, English-American composer and music critic; b. London, Feb. 16, 1836; d. Boston, Feb. 7, 1901. He was taken to America as a child; studied organ with W.R. Bristow in N.Y.; in 1870, settled in Boston, where he wrote on music and drama in the *Boston Globe* and the *Boston Herald.* He composed the "operatic comedietta" *Lawn Tennis, or Djakh and Djill* (Boston, 1880); comic opera, *Pounce &*

Co. (Boston, 1883); operetta, *Westward Ho!* (Boston, Dec. 31, 1894); also some chamber music and piano pieces.

Woollen, (Charles) Russell, American composer and keyboard player; b. Hartford, Conn., Jan. 7, 1923. He studied for the priesthood; attended the Pius X School of Liturgical Music in N.Y.; in 1948 studied Gregorian chant at the Benedictine Abbey at Solesmes. He was ordained a priest of the Hartford Diocese, in 1947; was released by his bishop in 1964, and was married twice (1971, 1977). He received his B.A. from St. Mary's Univ. in Baltimore (1944); an M.A. in Romance languages from the Catholic Univ. of America in Washington, D.C. (1948); he had private lessons in piano and organ; studied composition with Franz Wasner of the Trapp Family Singers, with Nicolas Nabokov at the Peabody Cons. in Baltimore (1949–51), with Nadia Boulanger in Paris (1951), and with Walter Piston at Harvard Univ. (1953–55). He was a member of the music faculty of the Catholic Univ. (1948–62) and of Howard Univ. (1969–74); from 1956 to 1980 he was staff keyboard player with the National Sym. Orch. in Washington, D.C.; then was organist at Arlington (Va.) Unitarian Church (from 1982).
WORKS: Opera, *The Decorator* (N.Y., May 24, 1959); Sym. No. 1 (1957–58); Sym. No. 2 (1978); Piano Quartet (1952); Quartet for Flute and Strings (1953); Woodwind Quintet (1955); Piano Trio (1957); *Suite* for Flute and Strings (1966; rev. 1979); Trio for Flute, Oboe, and Harpsichord (1967); *Fantasy* for Flute and Harpsichord (1968); Sonata for Trombone and Piano (1972); Quartet for Woodwinds (1975); *2 Pieces* for Piano and Orch. (1975–76); 16 masses; numerous choral works; 40 duets on *Au clair de la lune* for Recorders.

Woollett, Henri (Henry) Edouard, French composer; b. Le Havre (of English parents), Aug. 13, 1864; d. there, Oct. 9, 1936. He studied in Paris with Pugno (piano) and Massenet (composition); returning to Le Havre, he established himself as a teacher; among his students were André Caplet and Honegger. His music is of a lyrical nature, in the manner of Massenet. He publ. *Petit traité de prosodie* (Paris, 1903) and *Histoire de la musique depuis l'antiquité jusqu'à nos jours* (4 vols., Paris, 1909–25).
WORKS: *La Rose de Sharon,* "poème lyrique" for Orch. (1895); *Konzertstück* for Cello and Orch. (1911); String Quartet (1929); 2 violin sonatas (1908, 1922); Viola Sonata; Flute Sonata; Cello Sonata; many piano pieces in a Romantic vein (*Nocturnes et pastorales, Pièces intimes, A travers la vie, Au jardin de France, Préludes et valses*); many attractive songs.

Worbs, Hans Christoph, German music scholar; b. Guben, Jan. 13, 1927. He studied at the Humboldt Univ. in Berlin (degrees, 1952 and 1958); subsequently settled in Hamburg, where he was active as a music critic and writer.
WRITINGS: *Der Schlager: Bestandsaufnahme, Analyse, Dokumentation* (Bremen, 1963); *Welterfolge der modernen Oper* (Berlin, 1967); *Felix Mendelssohn-Bartholdy* (Reinbek, 1967); *Modest Mussorgsky* (Reinbek, 1976); *Albert Lortzing* (Reinbek, 1980); *Das Dampfkonzert: Musik und Musikleben des 19. Jahrhunderts in der Karikatur* (Wilhelmshaven, 1981).

Wordsworth, William (Brocklesby), English composer; b. London, Dec. 17, 1908; d. Kingussie, Scotland, March 10, 1988. He was descended from the brother of the poet William Wordsworth. He studied with his father; then with George Oldroyd (1921–31), and later with Tovey at the Univ. of Edinburgh (1934–36). In 1950 he won 1st prize in the Edinburgh International Festival Soc. competition with his 2nd Sym. In 1959 he served as president of the Composers' Guild of Great Britain. His music is marked by a certain austerity in the deployment of thematic materials.
WORKS: ORCH.: *Sinfonia* for Strings (1936); *3 Pastoral Sketches* (1937); *Theme and Variations* (1941); 8 syms. (1944–86); Piano Concerto (1946); *Divertimento* (1954); Violin Concerto (1955); Sinfonietta for Small Orch. (1957); *Variations on a Scottish Theme* for Small Orch. (1962); Cello Concerto (1963); *A Highland Overture* (1964); *Jubilation* (1965); *Con-*

flict, overture (1968); *Sinfonia semplice* for Amateur String Orch. (1969); *Valediction* (1969); *A Pattern of Love* for Low Voice and String Orch. (1969–70); *Spring Festival Overture* (1970); *Confluence*, symphonic variations (1975); *Elegy for Frieda* for String Orch. (1982). VOCAL: *The Houseless Dead*, after D.H. Lawrence, for Baritone, Chorus, and Orch. (1939); oratorio, *Dies Domini* (1942–44); *Lucifer Yields* for Soloists, Chorus, and Orch. (1949); *A Vision* for Women's Chorus and Strings (1950); *A Song of Praise* for Chorus and Orch. (1956); dramatic cantata, *The Two Brigs* (1971); *The Solitary Reaper* for Soprano, Piano, and Clarinet (1973). CHAMBER: 6 string quartets (1943–64); 2 cello sonatas (1937, 1959); 2 violin sonatas (1944, 1967); String Trio (1945); Piano Quartet (1948); Piano Trio (1949); Oboe Quartet (1949); Clarinet Quintet (1952); Wind Trio (1953); Piano Quintet (1959); Sonata for Solo Cello (1961); *Symposium* for Violin, Strings, Piano, and Percussion (1972); *Conversation Piece* for Violin and Guitar (1983); solo piano pieces, including a Sonata (1939); songs.

Work, Henry Clay, American composer of popular songs; b. Middletown, Conn., Oct. 1, 1832; d. Hartford, June 8, 1884. He was a printer by trade; was entirely self-taught in music; his 1st success was *We Are Coming, Sister Mary* (1853); other well-known songs were *Kingdom Coming* (1862), *Come Home, Father* (1864), *Wake, Nicodemus!* (1864), *Marching through Georgia* (1865), and *Grandfather's Clock* (1876). A complete edition of his songs was ed. by B. Work (N.Y., 1884).
BIBL.: R. Hill, "The Mysterious Chord of H.C. W.," *Notes* (March–June 1953).

Workman, William, American baritone; b. Valdosta, Ga., Feb. 4, 1940. He studied with Martial Singher at the Curtis Inst. of Music in Philadelphia and at the Music Academy of the West in Santa Barbara, Calif.; then went to Europe and took voice lessons with Hedwig Schilling in Hamburg; made his operatic debut with the Hamburg State Opera in 1965. In 1972 he became a member of the Frankfurt Opera; also made guest appearances in Stuttgart, Strasbourg, Paris, and Vienna. In 1984 he appeared at London's Covent Garden.

Wormser, André (Alphonse-Toussaint), French composer; b. Paris, Nov. 1, 1851; d. there, Nov. 4, 1926. He studied at the Paris Cons. with Marmontel (piano) and Bazin (theory); won 1st prize for piano in 1872, and the Grand Prix de Rome in 1875 with the cantata *Clytemnestre*. His most successful work was the pantomime, or "wordless opera," *L'Enfant prodigue* (Paris, June 14, 1890); he also composed other stage works; orch. works; men's choruses; songs; piano pieces.

Wörner, Karl(heinz) H(einrich), German musicologist; b. Waldorf, near Heidelberg, Jan. 6, 1910; d. Heiligenkirchen, near Detmold, Aug. 11, 1969. He studied at the Berlin Hochschule für Musik and took courses in musicology with Schünemann, Schering, Blume, Hornbostel, and Sachs at the Univ. of Berlin (Ph.D., 1931, with the diss. *Beiträge zur Geschichte des Leitmotivs in der Oper*). He was music critic of the *Berliner Zeitung am Mittag* (1933–34); then (1935–40) opera conductor at Stettin, Magdeburg, and Frankfurt. He was in the German army during World War II; in 1944, was taken prisoner of war by the U.S. Army and spent 2 years in an American internment camp. After his release, he taught at the Heidelberg Hochschule für Musik (1946–54). From 1954 to 1958 he was on the staff of B. Schotts Söhne (Mainz); in 1958, joined the faculty of the Folkwangschule in Essen; from 1961, taught at the North-West Germany Academy of Music in Detmold.
WORKS: *Mendelssohn-Bartholdy* (Wiesbaden, 1947); *Musik der Gegenwart: Geschichte des neuen Musik* (Mainz, 1949); *Robert Schumann* (Zürich, 1949); *Musiker-Worte* (Baden-Baden, 1949); *Geschichte der Musik* (Göttingen, 1954; 6th ed., Aug., 1975; in Eng., 1973); *Neue Musik in der Entscheidung* (Mainz, 1954); *Gotteswort und Magie: Die Oper "Moses und Aron" von Arnold Schönberg* (Heidelberg, 1959; aug. Eng. tr., 1963); *Karlheinz Stockhausen: Werk und Wollen 1950–1962* (Rodenkirchen, 1963; aug. Eng. tr., 1973); *Das Zeitalter der*

thematischen Prozesse in der Geschichte der Musik (Regensburg, 1969); *Die Musik in der Geistesgeschichte: Studien zur Situation der Jahre um 1910* (Bonn, 1970).

Woronoff, Wladimir, Russian-born Belgian composer; b. St. Petersburg, Jan. 5, 1903; d. Brussels, April 21, 1980. He studied violin as a child; left Russia after the Revolution and settled in Belgium in 1922; took lessons in composition with André Souris in Brussels. In 1954 he destroyed most of his early works, including the ballet *Le Masque de la mort rouge, Suite de Bruxelles* for Orch., and *Concert lyrique* for Piano and Orch.; he revised most of his remaining scores. His catalogue of extant works after this self-auto-da-fé can boast of the following: *La Foule* for Bass, Chorus, and Orch. (1934; rev. 1965); *Annas et le Lépreux* for Low Voice and Piano (1946); *Les 12*, 3 fragments from the poem by Alexander Blok, for Low Voice, and Orch. or Piano (1921–63); *Strophes concertantes* for Piano and Orch. (1964); *Lueur tournante* for Narrator and Orch. (1967); *Tripartita* for Viola and Chamber Orch. (1970); *Vallées* for 2 Pianos (1971).

Worp, Johannes, Dutch organist, composer, and arranger; b. Broek, Dec. 24, 1821; d. Groningen, April 21, 1891. He studied in Amsterdam, where he was active as a church organist; then went to Leipzig, where he took a course with Moscheles; returning to the Netherlands, he became organist at Groningen. He publ. valuable organ works and methods, which have gone through numerous eds.: *De melodieën der evangelische gezangen* for Organ, Piano, and Chorus; *De melodieën der Psalmen en lof- en bedezangen* for Organ, Piano, and Chorus (20th printing, 1947); the manual *Algemeene muziekleer* (13th printing, 1932; rev. by S. Dresden); *Kleine muziekleer* for schools; *Eerste en tweede zangboekje* for schools; *De zingende kinderwereld* (songs for children; many eds.); *Volksliedjes uit het land der liefde;* etc.

Woržischek (Voříšek), Johann Hugo (Jan Václav), esteemed Bohemian composer, pianist, and organist; b. Wamberg, May 11, 1791; d. Vienna, Nov. 19, 1825. He began his music studies with his father; while still a child, he toured Bohemia as a keyboard prodigy; after training in law and esthetics at the Univ. of Prague (1810–13), he completed his law studies in Vienna, and also studied composition with Tomaschek in Prague. In 1813 he settled in Vienna, where he was employed in the civil service while making appearances as a keyboard artist; also received piano lessons from Hummel. From 1818 until his death he was conductor of the Gesellschaft der Musikfreunde; also served as assistant court organist (1822–23) and as principal court organist (from 1823). He was a friend of Schubert, and also knew Beethoven. He composed a Sym.; choral works with Orch.; a Piano Concerto; etc.; of more interest are his piano pieces, especially the *Rhapsodies* (1818) and *Impromptus* (1822), because Schubert was strongly influenced by them. A Piano Sonata in B minor (1820) shows kinship with Beethoven.
BIBL.: A. Simpson, "A Profile of Jan Václav Voříšek," *Proceedings of the Royal Musical Association*, XCVII (1970–71).

Wöss, Josef Venantius von, Austrian editor and composer; b. Cattaro, Dalmatia, June 13, 1863; d. Vienna, Oct. 22, 1943. He received his 1st musical instruction from his mother and an uncle; studied theory at the Vienna Cons. with Franz Krenn. He was an ed. for Universal Edition (1908–31) and also ed. the journal *Musica Divina* (1913–34).
WRITINGS: *Deutsche Meister des Liedes* (Vienna, 1910); *Gustav Mahler, Das Lied von der Erde: thematische Analyse* (Leipzig, 1912); *Die Modulation* (Vienna, 1921).
WORKS: OPERAS: *Lenzlüge* (Elberfeld, 1905); *Flaviennes Abenteuer* (Breslau, 1910); *Carmilhan* (n.d.); *Serenade* for Orch.; *Sakuntala*, overture; sacred music; various secular vocal works, including choruses and about 150 lieder; chamber works, including a Violin Sonata, String Quartet, Piano Sextet, and organ music.

Wöss, Kurt, Austrian conductor; b. Linz, May 2, 1914; d. Dresden (while rehearsing the Dresden Phil.), Dec. 4, 1987.

He studied conducting with Felix Weingartner in Vienna, and also pursued musicological studies at the Univ. of Vienna with Haas, Lach, Orel, and Wellesz; taught an orch. class at the Vienna Academy of Music (1938–40). He conducted the Niederösterreichisches Tonkünstler-Orch. in Vienna (1948–51) and the Nippon Phil. in Tokyo (1951–54). From 1956 to 1959 he was principal conductor of the Victorian Sym. Orch. in Melbourne and of the Australian National Opera; in 1961 he returned to Linz, where he was chief conductor of the Bruckner Orch. until 1976; also conducted again in Tokyo. He publ. *Ratschläge zur Aufführung der Symphonien Anton Bruckners* (Linz, 1974).

Wotquenne (-Plattel), Alfred (Camille), Belgian musicologist; b. Lobbes, Jan. 25, 1867; d. Antibes, France, Sept. 25, 1939. He studied at the Royal Cons. in Brussels with Brassin (piano), Mailly (organ; premier prix, 1888), and Dupont and Gevaert (theory); from 1894 to 1896 he was deputy secretary and librarian and from 1896 to 1918 secretary and librarian there. He settled in Antibes as a singing teacher and organist, and subsequently was made maître de chapelle at its cathedral (1921). He prepared a card catalogue of 18,000 Italian "cantate da camera" of the 18th century; ed. *Chansons italiennes de la fin du XVIe siècle* (canzonette a 4); continued the collections begun by Gevaert, *Répertoire classique du chant français* and *Répertoire français de l'ancien chant classique;* and ed. a new collection, *Répertoire Wotquenne* (4 vols. publ.); also ed. violin sonatas of Tartini, Veracini, and others; composed much sacred music. The MSS of several important bibliographies in his collection were bought by the Library of Congress in Washington, D.C., in 1929; these comprise *Répertoire des textes publiés par les éditeurs parisiens Ballard; Histoire musicale et chronologique du Théâtre de la Foire depuis 1680 jusqu'à 1762; Histoire du nouveau Théâtre-Italien à Paris (1718–1762);* etc. A large part of his private music library was also bought by the Library of Congress.

WRITINGS: *Catalogue de la bibliothèque du Conservatoire Royal de Musique de Bruxelles* (vol. I, 1894; with a supplement, *Libretti d'opéras et d'oratorios italiens du XVIIe siècle*, 1901; II, 1902; III, 1908; IV, 1912; V, 1914); *Étude bibliographique sur les oeuvres de Baldassare Galuppi* (1899; 2nd ed., augmented, 1902 as *Baldassare Galuppi: étude bibliographique sur ses œuvres dramatiques); Thematisches Verzeichnis der Werke von Chr.W. v. Gluck* (1904); *Alphabetisches Verzeichnis der Stücke in Versen aus den dramatischer Werken von Zeno, Metastasio und Goldoni* (1905); *Thematisches Verzeichnis der Werke von Carl Philipp Emanuel Bach* (1905); *Étude bibliographique sur le compositeur napolitain Luigi Rossi* (1909; with thematic catalogue).

Wouters, (François) Adolphe, Belgian organist and composer; b. Brussels, May 28, 1849; d. there, April 16, 1924. He studied at the Brussels Cons.; then taught piano there (1871–1920); from 1868 he was also organist at Notre-Dame-de-Finistère and maître de chapelle at Saint-Nicolas. He composed church music, men's choruses, technical studies and transcriptions for piano, etc.

Woyrsch, Felix von, German organist, conductor, and composer; b. Troppau, Silesia, Oct. 8, 1860; d. Altona-Hamburg, March 20, 1944. He studied with E. Chevallier in Hamburg, but was chiefly self-taught. In 1887 he settled in Altona as conductor of the Allgemeine Liedertafel; from 1893, led the Kirchenchor, then Singakademie (from 1895), and finally the municipal sym. concerts and Volkskonzerte (from 1903); from 1895 to 1903 he was organist of the Friedenskirche; then of the Johanniskirche until 1926; retired from public life in 1937.

WORKS: OPERAS: *Der Pfarrer von Meudon* (Hamburg, 1886); *Der Weiberkrieg* (Hamburg, 1890); *Wikingerfahrt* (Nuremberg, 1896); *Faust* (n.d.). **ORCH.:** Symphonic prologue to Dante's *Divina Commedia* (1892); *Skaldische Rhapsodie* for Violin and Orch. (c.1904); 6 syms. (1908, 1914, 1921, c.1921, 1927, c.1933); *3 Böcklin-Phantasien* (1910); *Hamlet*, overture (1913). **VOCAL:** various choral works, including *Die Geburt Jesu* (c.1885), *Der Vandalen Auszug* (c.1890), and *Da Jesus auf Erden*

ging (c.1915). **CHAMBER:** 5 string quartets (1909; 1916; 1918; 1926; c.1938–40); Piano Trio (1924); String Sextet (1926); Piano Quintet (1927); piano pieces; organ music.

BIBL.: F. Pfohl, *F. W.* (Leipzig, 1934).

Woytowicz, Boleslaw, Polish pianist and composer; b. Dunajowce, Podolia, Dec. 5, 1899; d. Katowice, July 11, 1980. He studied piano with Michalowski and composition with Wielhorski, Szopski, and Maliszewski in Warsaw; then went to Paris, where he took lessons in composition with Nadia Boulanger (1929–32). In 1945 he was appointed a prof. of piano and composition at the Katowice Cons., and in 1963 a prof. of composition at the Krakow Cons.

WORKS: *Kolysanka* (Cradle Song) for Soprano, Flute, Clarinet, Bassoon, and Harp (1931); 2 string quartets (1932, 1953); Piano Concerto (1932); *Zalobny poema* (Funeral Poem) for Orch. (1935); ballet, *Powrót*; 3 syms.: No. 1 (1938), No. 2 (1945; Krakow, Sept. 27, 1946), and No. 3, *Concertante*, for Piano and Orch. (1963); *Kantata na pochwale pracy* (Cantata in Praise of Labor; 1948); *12 Etudes* for Piano (1948); *Symphonic Sketches* for Orch. (1949); cantata, *Prorok* (The Prophet; 1950); Flute Sonata (1952); *Lamento* for Soprano, Piano, and Clarinet (1960); *10 Etudes* for Piano (1960); *Little Piano Sonata* (1974).

Wrangel, Baron Vasili, Russian composer; b. St. Petersburg, June 25, 1862; d. there, March 10, 1901. A functionary at the Ministry of Home Affairs, he was a musician by avocation; took several courses at the St. Petersburg Cons. His songs, many of which were publ., attracted singers by their artless melodic quality, and enjoyed some popularity for a time; he also wrote a ballet, *The Mikado's Daughter* (St. Petersburg, Nov. 9, 1897).

Wranitzky, Anton, Bohemian violinist, pedagogue, and composer, brother of **Paul Wranitzky;** b. Neureisch, Moravia, June 13, 1761; d. Vienna, Aug. 6, 1820. He studied violin with his brother; then had composition lessons in Vienna with Albrechtsberger, Haydn, and Mozart. In 1783 he became choirmaster at the chapel of the Theresianisch-Savoyische Akademie in Vienna; in 1790 he entered the service of Prince Lobkowitz, becoming his Kapellmeister in 1797; from 1807 he was also director of the orch. of the Court Theater and from 1814 director of the orch. of the Theater an der Wien. His students included Mayseder and Schuppanzigh. His large output includes 15 syms., overtures, 15 violin concertos, a concerto for 2 violins, 2 concertos for violin and cello, a concerto for 2 violins and cello, a concerto for 2 violas, serenatas, notturnos, dances, marches, etc.; also much chamber music, including string quartets, sextets, quintets, and trios, as well as various sonatas and keyboard pieces; vocal works, including masses and other sacred pieces, and various secular choruses, songs, etc.

Wranitzky, Paul, distinguished Bohemian violinist, conductor, and composer, brother of **Anton Wranitzky;** b. Neureisch, Moravia, Dec. 30, 1756; d. Vienna, Sept. 26, 1808. After studying in Moravia, he went in 1776 to Vienna, where he was a pupil of Joseph Martin Kraus ahd Haydn. Around 1785 he was named music director to Count Johann Nepomuk Esterházy; from about 1790 he served as director of the orchs. at the Court Theaters in Vienna. His opera *Oberon, König der Elfen* was given with excellent success in Vienna on Nov. 7, 1789; other operas and singspiels produced by him in Vienna were *Rudolf von Felseck* (Oct. 6, 1792); *Merkur, der Heurat-Stifter* (Feb. 21, 1793); *Das Fest der Lazzaroni* (Feb. 4, 1794); *Die gute Mutter* (May 11, 1795); *Johanna von Montfaucon* (Jan. 25, 1799); *Der Schreiner* (July 18, 1799); *Das Mitgefühl* (April 21, 1804); *Die Erkenntlichkeit* (July 22, 1805). He also produced several successful ballets; wrote incidental music to plays; composed a great deal of instrumental music, including 51 syms.; 5 concertos for various instruments with orch.; various quintets; over 80 string quartets; quartets for flute and strings; piano quartets; string trios; keyboard sonatas; vocal works.

BIBL.: J. Pešková, *Vranického Oberon a jeho vliv na rozvoj singspielu* (W.'s *Oberon* and Its Influence on the Development of the Singspiel; diss., Univ. of Prague, 1955); M. Vyšínová, *Ke komorní tvorbě Pavla Vranického* (P. W.'s Chamber Works; diss., Univ. of Prague, 1969).

Wrightson, Herbert James, English-American composer and teacher; b. Sunderland, Dec. 20, 1869; d. West Lebanon, N.Y., Dec. 24, 1949. He studied at the Leipzig Cons. with Jadassohn and Reinecke. In 1897 he settled in the U.S.; taught in Philadelphia, Chicago, etc. His works include a Sym.; organ pieces; piano pieces; 2 melodramas; 144 songs, of which nearly 100 were publ. His hymns are included in various hymnals. He publ. *Elements of the Theory of Music* (Boston, 1921).

Wuensch, Gerhard, Austrian-born Canadian composer; b. Vienna, Dec. 23, 1925. He received his Ph.D. from the Univ. of Vienna in 1950, and an artist's diploma in composition and piano from the Academy of Music in Vienna in 1952; studied music theory with Paul Pisk at the Univ. of Texas (1954–56). He then taught at Butler Univ. in Indianapolis (1956–62), the Univ. of Toronto (1963–69), and the Univ. of Calgary (1969–73); in 1973, was appointed to the faculty of the Univ. of Western Ontario in London, Ontario. He writes in an affable modernistic vein in neo-Classical forms.

WORKS: Ballet, *Labyrinth* (1957); musical comedy, *Il pomo d'oro* (1958); *Nocturne* for Orch. (1956); *Variations on a Dorian Hexachord* for Orch. (1959); *Caribbean Rhapsody* for Sym. Band (1959); Sym. No. 1 (1959); Piano Concerto (1961); *Ballad* for Trumpet and Orch. (1962); *Symphonia sacra* for Soloists, Chorus, Brass, and Percussion (1965); Sym. for Brass and Percussion (1967); Concerto for Piano and Chamber Orch. (1971); *Scherzo* for Piano and Wind Ensemble (1971); *6 Guises* for Narrator, Winds, and Percussion (1972); Bassoon Concerto (1976); Organ Concerto (1979); Concerto for 2 Pianos and Orch. (1981); *Serenade for a Summer Evening* for Orch. (1986); *Variations and Fugue on a Mozartian Theme* for Band (1986); Trio for Clarinet, Bassoon, and Piano (1948); 2 string quartets (1955, 1963); *Mosaic* for Brass Quartet (1959); *Ricercare* for 8 Horns and Organ (1963); 2 wind quintets (1963, 1967); Horn Sonata (1964); *Music for 7 Brasses* (1966); Trumpet Sonata (1966); Sextet for Horns (1966); *Music in 4 Dimensions* for Brass, Harp, and Percussion (1970); Piano Trio (1971); *Prelude, Aria and Fugue* for Accordion and String Quartet (1971); *Saxophone Sonata* (1971); *Concerto grosso* for Accordion and Strings (1978); *6 Songs* for Voice, Flute, and Accordion (1970); *Laus sapientiae*, cantata (1978); *3 Episodes from St. John* for Soloists, Chorus, and Organ (1987); piano pieces; choruses.

Wüerst, Richard (Ferdinand), German composer, music critic, and teacher; b. Berlin, Feb. 22, 1824; d. there, Oct. 9, 1881. He studied violin with Ferdinand David at the Leipzig Cons., where he also took lessons with Mendelssohn. He then taught at Kullak's Neue Akademie der Tonkunst in Berlin. As music critic for the *Berliner Fremdenblatt*, he exercised considerable influence; publ. *Leitfaden der Elementartheorie der Musik* (1867; Eng. tr. as *Elementary Theory of Music and Treatment of Chords*, Boston, 1893). As a composer, he was a follower of Mendelssohn.

WORKS: OPERAS: *Der Rotmantel* (Berlin, 1848); *Vineta* (Pressburg, Dec. 21, 1862); *Eine Künstlerreise* (with Winterfeld; Berlin, 1868); *Faublas* (Berlin, 1873); *A-ing-fo-hi* (Berlin, Jan. 28, 1878); *Die Offiziere der Kaiserin* (Berlin, 1878); cantata, *Der Wasserneck*; 3 syms.; *Ein Märchen*, symphonic fantasy; *Variations sur une chanson nègre de Kentucky* for Orch. (on Stephen Foster's *My Old Kentucky Home*); *Sous le balcon*, serenade for String Orch. with Cello Obbligato; *Russische Suite* for String Orch. with Violin Obbligato; *Tanz der Mücken, Fliegen und Käfer,* orch. scherzo; Piano Trio; Cello Sonata; 3 string quartets; various violin pieces; songs; vocal duets and terzets.

Wührer, Friedrich (Anton Franz), distinguished Austrian pianist and pedagogue; b. Vienna, June 29, 1900; d. Mannheim,

Dec. 27, 1975. He studied piano with Franz Schmidt, theory and composition with Joseph Marx, and conducting with Ferdinand Löwe at the Vienna Academy of Music (1915–20); also studied law and musicology at the Univ. of Vienna. From 1923 he made regular tours of Europe. He taught at the Vienna Academy of Music (1922–32), at the Hochschule für Musik in Mannheim (1934–36), in Kiel (1936–39), in Vienna (1939–45), at the Salzburg Mozarteum (1948–51), in Mannheim (1952–57), and in Munich (1957–68). He publ. *Meisterwerke der Klaviermusik* (Wilhelmshaven, 1966). His performances of the Classical and Romantic repertoires were highly regarded. He also championed the cause of 20th-century composers, ranging from Schoenberg to Prokofiev.

Wüllner, Franz, important German pianist, conductor, and composer, father of **Ludwig Wüllner;** b. Münster, Jan. 28, 1832; d. Braunfels-an-der-Lahn, Sept. 7, 1902. He studied with Schindler in Münster and Frankfurt (1846–50). From 1850 to 1854 he was active as a concert artist; was a teacher at the Munich music school (1856–58); then was music director in Aachen (1858–64). He returned to Munich in 1864, where he became court music director of the church choir; then taught at the music school (from 1867); also conducted at the Court Opera. Under unfavorable conditions (against Wagner's wishes), he prepared and conducted the 1st perf. of *Das Rheingold* (Sept. 22, 1869) and *Die Walküre* (June 26, 1870); his success led to his appointment as principal conductor there in 1871. In 1877 he became court conductor at Dresden, and also director of the Cons.; in 1882 Schuch was promoted to take his place; thereafter Wüllner was one of the conductors of the Berlin Phil. for the 1882–1885 seasons; became conductor of the Gurzenich Concerts in Cologne in 1884, and director of the Cologne Cons., later becoming also municipal music director, posts he held until his death. He was highly regarded as a choral composer; publ. the valuable book of vocal exercises *Chorübungen der Münchener Musikschule* (3 vols., Munich, 1876; new ed. by R. Stephani, 1953–54; Eng. tr., 1882). He was a friend of Brahms.

WORKS: Vocal with Orch.: *Die Flucht der heiligen Familie; Heinrich der Finkler; Deutscher Siegesgesang; Lied und Leben; Psalm 98; Psalm 127;* church music; songs.

BIBL.: E. Prieger, *F. W.: ein Nachruf* (Bonn, 1902); O. Klauwell, *Studien und Erinnerungen* (Langensalza, 1906); E. Wolff, ed., *Johannes Brahms im Briefwechsel mit F. W.* (Berlin, 1922; with a list of works); J. Wüllner, "Johannes Brahms in seiner Lebensfreundschaft mit F. W.," *Die Musik* (March 1942); D. Kämper, *F. W.: Leben, Wirken und kompositorisches Schaffen* (Cologne, 1963); idem, ed., *Richard Strauss und F. W. im Briefwechsel* (Cologne, 1963).

Wüllner, Ludwig, distinguished German singer, son of **Franz Wüllner;** b. Münster, Aug. 19, 1858; d. Kiel, March 19, 1938. He studied Germanic philology at the Univs. of Munich, Berlin, and Strasbourg; taught Germanic philology at the Akademie in Münster (1884–87), and sang occasionally in concert; his musical training began only in 1887, when he took a course of study at the Cologne Cons. A 2nd change of vocation brought him to the Meiningen Court Theater, where he appeared as an actor of heroic parts in the spoken drama (1889–95); he became friendly with Brahms, who commended his singing of German folk songs. In 1895 he gave song recitals in Berlin with such acclaim that he decided to devote himself mainly to lieder. He then made tours of all Europe, arousing tremendous enthusiasm; his 1st recital in N.Y. (Nov. 15, 1908) was a sensational success, and he followed it by an extensive tour of the U.S. and then another (1909–10). His peculiar distinction was his ability to give an actor's impersonation of the character of each song, introducing an element of drama on the concert stage.

BIBL.: F. Ludwig, *L. W.: Sein Leben und seine Kunst* (Leipzig, 1931).

Wunderer, Alexander, Austrian oboist, composer, and teacher; b. Vienna, April 11, 1877; d. Zinkenbach, near St. Gilgen (Salzkammergut), Dec. 29, 1955. He taught the oboe and other wind instruments at the Vienna Academy of Music (1919–37) and oboe at the Salzburg Mozarteum (from 1945); wrote chamber music; was co-author of a book on orchestration.

Wunderlich, Fritz (actually, **Friedrich Karl Otto**), noted German tenor; b. Kusel, Sept. 26 1930; d. Heidelberg, Sept. 17, 1966. He received his musical education at the Freiburg Hochschule für Musik; then sang opera in Stuttgart (1955–58), Frankfurt (1958–60), and Munich (from 1960); in 1965 he appeared as Don Ottavio at London's Covent Garden. While still a young man, he gained a fine reputation as a lyric tenor; his performances of Mozart roles were especially acclaimed for their expressive power. His untimely death (in a domestic accident) deprived the opera stage of one of its finest artists.

Wunderlich, Heinz, noted German organist, choral conductor, and pedagogue; b. Leipzig, April 25, 1919. He studied organ with K. Straube in Leipzig (1935–41); then composition and conducting with J.N. David. He held several organ and choral conducting posts (1943–58); taught at the Halle Staatliche Hochschule für Musik (1947–58); was Kirchenmusikdirektor at St. Jacobi in Hamburg (1958–82), where his concerts of choral music by the German masters and of the organ works of M. Reger, as well as his restoration of the famous Arp Schnitger organ, received great acclaim; he toured the U.S. with his choir (1978). As prof. of organ at the Hamburg Hochschule für Musik (from 1974), he attracted students from many countries.

Wunsch, Hermann, German composer; b. Neuss, Aug. 9, 1884; d. Berlin, Dec. 21, 1954. He studied in Düsseldorf and Cologne, and later at the Hochschule für Musik in Berlin, where he subsequently taught, becoming a prof. in 1945. He composed 6 syms., of which the 5th won the Schubert Memorial Prize (German section) of the Columbia Phonograph Co. contest (Schubert Centennial, 1928). Other works include the chamber operas *Bianca* (Weimar, May 22, 1927), *Don Juans Sohn* (Weimar, 1928), and *Franzosenzeit* (Schwerin, 1933); 2 masses; *Südpolkantate* for Chorus and Orch.; *Helden* for Chorus and Orch. (Berlin, 1941); 3 violin concertos; Concerto for Piano and Small Orch.; *Kleine Lustspielsuite* for Orch.; *Fest auf Monbijou,* suite for Chamber Orch.; *Erntelied,* sym. with a concluding chorus.

Wünsch, Walther, Austrian ethnomusicologist; b. Gablonz an der Niesse, July 23, 1908. He studied with Becking at the German Univ. in Prague (Ph.D., 1932, with the diss. *Die Geigentechnik der jugoslawischen Guslaren;* publ. in Brno, 1934); completed his Habilitation in 1960 at the Univ. of Graz. After working at the musicological inst. of the Pestalozzi Academy in Prague (1932–35), he was active at the Inst. for Acoustics in Berlin (1935–38); from 1945 he was active as a chamber music player and taught at the Steiermarkischen Landeskonservatorium; in 1960 he joined the faculty of the Inst. for Music Ethnology at the Graz Hochschule für Musik, where he became a prof. in 1968. He publ. several important studies on ethnomusicology, including *Heldensänger in Südosteuropa* (Leipzig, 1937).

Wuorinen, Charles, American composer; b. N.Y., June 9, 1938. His family roots originated in Finland; his father was a prof. of history at Columbia Univ.; the environment at home was highly intellectual. Wuorinen received a fine academic training; he began to play piano and to compose, so they say, at the incredible age of 5. He then took lessons in music theory with Beeson and Ussachevsky. He received the Young Composers Award from the N.Y. Phil. when he was 16 years old. At 18 he wrote his earliest orch. work, *Into the Organ Pipes and Steeples.* At the age of 21 he composed, in quick succession, 3 full-fledged syms. In 1956 he entered Columbia Univ. as a student of Otto Luening; received his B.A. in 1961 and his M.A. in 1963. In 1964 he was appointed an instructor in music at Columbia, and taught there until 1971, when he resigned in a flurry of angry controversy, vesuviating in sulfuric wrath and ire about the refusal of the faculty to grant him tenure. He then taught at the Manhattan School of Music (1972–79).

In 1968 and 1972 he held Guggenheim fellowships. In 1969 he received a commission from Nonesuch Records for a work using synthesized sound, titled *Time's Encomium;* it was awarded the Pulitzer Prize in Music in 1970, an unprecedented honor for a work written expressly for a recording; later he rearranged it for a regular orch. In 1985 he was made a member of the American Academy and Inst. of Arts and Letters. From 1985 to 1987 he served as composer-in-residence of the San Francisco Sym. From his very 1st essays in free composition, Wuorinen asserted himself as a true representative of the modernistic 2nd half of the 20th century. His techniques derived from Stravinsky's early period, when stark primitivism gave way to austere linear counterpoint; an even greater affinity in Wuorinen's music is with the agglutinative formations of unrelated thematic statements as practiced by Varèse; a more literal dependence connects Wuorinen's works with the dodecaphonic method of composition as promulgated by Schoenberg. These modalities and relationships coalesce in Wuorinen's writing into a sui generis complex subdivided into melodic, harmonic, and contrapuntal units that build a definitive formal structure. The foundation of his method of composition is serialism, in which pitch, time, and rhythmic divisions relate to one another in a "time point system," which lends itself to unlimited tonal and temporal arrangements, combinations, and permutations. Enormously prolific, Wuorinen finds it possible to explore the entire vocabulary of serial composition. Most of his works are instrumental, but he also wrote an opera entitled *The W. of Babylon* (alluding to the apocalyptic Babylonian whore), a work he prefers to describe as a "baroque burlesque." Its *dramatis personae* include a libidinous assortment of lascivious French noble and ignoble men and women of the immoral 17th century, spouting lewd declarations and performing lecherous acts. As a helpful glossary to his music, Wuorinen publ. a manual, *Simple Composition* (N.Y., 1979).

WORKS: STAGE: Masque, *The Politics of Harmony* (1967); opera, *The W. of Babylon* (partial perf., N.Y., Dec. 15, 1975; 1st complete perf., San Francisco, Jan. 20, 1989). **ORCH.:** 3 syms. (1958, 1959, 1959); 4 *concertante* for Solo Instruments and Orch. (1957–59); *Concertone* for Brass Quintet and Orch. (1960); *Evolutio transcripta* (1961); *Orchestral and Electronic Exchanges* for Orch. and Tape (1965); Piano Concerto No. 1 (1966); *Contrafactum* (1969); Concerto for Amplified Violin and Orch. (Tanglewood, Aug. 4, 1972); Piano Concerto No. 2 for Amplified Piano and Orch. (N.Y. Phil., Dec. 6, 1974, composer soloist); *A Reliquary for Igor Stravinsky* (Ojai [Calif.] Festival, May 30, 1975); *Tashi Concerto* for 4 Instruments and Orch. (Cleveland, Oct. 13, 1976); *Percussion Symphony* (1976; Somerset, N.J., Jan. 26, 1978); *Two-Part Symphony* (N.Y., Dec. 11, 1978); *"ng. c."* (1980); *Bamboula Squared* (N.Y., June 4, 1984); *Movers and Shakers* (Cleveland, Dec. 13, 1984); *Rhapsody* for Violin and Orch. (San Francisco, Jan. 16, 1985); *Crossfire* (Baltimore, May 9, 1985). **CHAMBER:** *Triptych* for Violin, Viola, and Percussion (1957); *Alternating Currents* for Chamber Ensemble (1957); *Dr. Faustus Lights the Lights* for Narrator and Instruments (1957); 3 *Pieces* for String Quartet (1958); *Spectrum* for Violin, Brass Quintet, and Piano (1958); *Trio concertante* (1959); *Musica duarum partum ecclesiastica* for Brass Quintet, Piano, Organ, and Timpani (1959); Flute Sonata (1960); *Turetzky Pieces* for Flute, Clarinet, and Double Bass (1960); *Tiento sobre cabeza* for 7 Instruments (1961); Octet for Flute, Clarinet, Horn, Trombone, Violin, Cello, Double Bass, and Piano (1962); Chamber Concerto for Cello and 10 Players (1963); *Composition* for Violin and 10 Instruments (1964); Chamber Concerto for Flute and 10 Players (1964); *Janissary Music* for Percussion (1966); *Harpsichord Division* for Harpsichord (1966); *John Bull: Salve Regina Versus Septem* for Chamber Ensemble (1966); Duo for Violin and Piano (1966–67); String Trio (1968); *Ringing Changes* for Percussion Ensemble (1970); Chamber Concerto for Tuba, 12 Wind Instruments, and 12 Drums (1970); *Canzona* for 12 Instruments (1971); Harp Variations for Harp, Violin, Viola, and Cello (1972); Bassoon Variations for Bassoon, Harp, and Timpani (1972); Violin Variations (1972); *On Alligators* for 8 Instruments (1972); *Speculum speculi* for Flute, Oboe, Bass Clarinet, Double Bass, Piano, and Percussion (1972); *Grand Union* for Cello and Drums (1973); *Arabia felix* for Flute, Bassoon, Violin, Electric Guitar, Vibraphone, and Piano (1973); Fantasia for Violin and Piano (1974); *Hyperion* for 12 Instruments (1976); *The Winds* for 8 Instruments (1977); *Fast Fantasy* for Cello (1977); *Archangel* for Bass Trombone and String Quartet (1977); Wind Quintet (1977); 6 Pieces for Violin and Piano (1977); *Ancestors* for Chamber Ensemble (1978); *Joan's* for Chamber Ensemble (1980); *Archaeopteryx* for Bass Trombone (1980); Trio for Double Bass, Bass Trombone, and Tuba (1981); Horn Trio (1981); *Winds of Parnassus* for Wind and Brass Ensemble (1984); String Quartet No. 3 (1987); Sonata for Violin and Piano (Washington, D.C., Nov. 25, 1988). VOCAL: *Madrigali spirituale* for Tenor, Baritone, 2 Oboes, 2 Violins, Cello, and Double Bass (1960); *Symphonia sacra* for Tenor, Baritone, Bass, 2 Oboes, 2 Violins, Double Bass, and Organ (1961); *The Prayer of Jonah* for Voices and String Quintet (1962); *Super salutem* for Male Voices and Instruments (1964); *A Message to Denmark Hill* for Baritone, Flute, Cello, and Piano (1970); *A Song to the Lute in Musicke* for Soprano and Piano (1970); *Mannheim, 87.87.87* for Unison Chorus and Organ (1973); *An Anthem for Epiphany* for Chorus, Organ, and Trumpet (1974); *6 Songs* for 2 Voices, Violin, and Piano (1977); *The Celestial Sphere*, sacred oratorio for Chorus and Orch. (1979; Augustana College, April 25, 1981). ELECTRONIC: *Consort from Instruments and Voices* for Magnetic Tape (1961); *Time's Encomium* for synthesized sound and processed synthesized sound (1969; received the Pulitzer Prize in Music in 1970).

Würfel, Wenzel Wilhelm (actually, **Václav Vilem**), Bohemian pianist, conductor, teacher, and composer; b. Plánany, near Kolín, May 6, 1790; d. Vienna, March 23, 1832. He made tours as a pianist while still a child; then was a pupil of Tomaschek in Prague. In 1815 he went to Warsaw as prof. of organ and thoroughbass at the Cons.; Chopin was one of his students. After conducting at the Kärnthnertortheater in Vienna (1824–26), he toured as a pianist. His opera *Rübezahl* was first performed in Prague on Oct. 7, 1824, with excellent success, and enjoyed popularity for some years; he also wrote the opera *Der Rotmantel* (1826) and many piano pieces in a bravura style; also pedagogical pieces for keyboard.

Wurlitzer, family of German-American instrument dealers and makers:

(Franz) Rudolph Wurlitzer (b. Schoneck, Saxony, Jan. 31, 1831; d. Cincinnati, Jan. 14, 1914) emigrated to the U.S. in 1853; after settling in Cincinnati, he became active as an instrument dealer; with his brother Anton, he organized Rudolph Wurlitzer & Bro. in 1872; the business became the Rudolph Wurlitzer Co. in 1890, with Rudolph serving as president (1890–1912) and as chairman (1912–14). In 1889 his eldest son, **Howard Eugene Wurlitzer** (b. Cincinnati, Sept. 5, 1871; d. N.Y., Oct. 30, 1928), joined the firm; through his efforts, the company became highly successful; he served as its president (1912–27) and chairman (1927–28). Rudolph's 2nd son, **Rudolph Henry Wurlitzer** (b. Cincinnati, Dec. 30, 1873; d. there, May 27, 1948), studied in Cincinnati and then went to Berlin in 1891 to study violin with Emanuel Wirth, the history of musical instruments with Oskar Fleischer, and acoustics with Hermann von Helmholtz; he also studied with the violin authority August Riechers; upon his return to Cincinnati in 1894, he joined the firm as a director, and then held the posts of secretary and treasurer (1899–1912), vice-president (1912–27), president (1927–32), and chairman (1932–42). Rudolph's 3rd son, **Farny Reginald Wurlitzer** (b. Cincinnati, Dec. 7, 1883; d. North Tonawanda, N.Y., May 6, 1972), studied at the Cincinnati Technical School before pursuing his education in Germany as an apprentice to various instrument makers (1901–4); he then returned to Cincinnati to join the firm and became head of the automatic musical instrument dept. in 1907; in 1909 he became head of the Rudolph Wurlitzer Manufacturing Co. in North Tonawanda, which commenced

making coin-operated phonographs in 1933; he was president (1932–41) and chairman (1941–66) of the firm. Rudolph Henry's son, **Rembert Wurlitzer** (b. Cincinnati, March 27, 1904; d. N.Y., Oct. 21, 1963), studied at Princeton Univ.; he then received training in violin making from Amédée Dieudonné in Mirecourt and worked with Alfred Hill in London; after returning to Cincinnati, he was made a vice-president of the company; in 1937 he became head of the company's violin dept. in N.Y., which he made an independent firm in 1949; the company won great distinction and remained active until 1974. The Wurlitzer firm brought out the Wurlitzer Hope-Jones Unit Orch. (later known as "the Mighty Wurlitzer," a theater organ, in 1910; their jukeboxes were manufactured between 1933 and 1974; in 1935 they began making a console upright spinet piano; from 1947 they manufactured electronic organs.

BIBL.: J. Fairfield, *W. World of Music: 100 Years of Musical Achievement* (Chicago, 1956); J. Landon, *Behold the Mighty W.* (Westport, Conn., 1983).

Wurm, Marie, noted English pianist; b. Southampton, May 18, 1860; d. Munich, Jan. 21, 1938. She studied piano with Raff and Clara Schumann in Germany; returning to England, she took theory lessons with Stanford and Arthur Sullivan. She was quite successful as a concert pianist in England and Germany; in 1925 she settled in Munich. Her avocation was conducting; she organized a women's orch. in Berlin, and conducted its inaugural concert on Oct. 10, 1899, arousing considerable curiosity. She also was an ambitious composer. Her sisters, **Adela Wurm** and **Mathilda Wurm**, who made their careers in England, changed their last name to **Verne** in order to exorcise the vermicular sound of the original German family name, as pronounced in English.

WORKS: Opera, *Die Mitschuldigen* (Leipzig, 1923); Piano Concerto; String Quartet; Violin Sonata; Cello Sonata; Piano Sonata; numerous piano pieces (*Valse de concert, Barcarolle, Sylph Dance, Suite,* gavottes, mazurkas, etc.); publ. *Das ABC der Musik* and *Praktische Vorschule zur Caland-Lehre.*

Würtzler, Aristid von, Hungarian-born American harpist and composer; b. Budapest, Sept. 20, 1930. He attended the Franz Liszt Academy of Music in Budapest (1951–56), where he studied harp with Miklós Rékai and composition with Kodály. He left Hungary during the 1956 uprising and emigrated to the U.S., where he became 1st harpist with the Detroit Sym. Orch. (1957) and the N.Y. Phil. (1958–62). He subsequently served as head of the harp dept. of the Hartt College of Music in Hartford, Conn. (1963–70). In 1970 he accepted teaching positions at N.Y. Univ. and Hofstra Univ.; founded the N.Y. Harp Ensemble, for which he commissioned works from contemporary composers, including Ligeti, Stockhausen, Hovhaness, Bernstein, Serly, Saygun, and Takemitsu. In 1981 he gave master classes in China, the 1st of their kind.

Wyk, Arnold(us Christian Vlok) van, South African composer, pianist, and teacher; b. Calvinia, Cape Province, April 26, 1916; d. Cape Town, May 27, 1983. He studied at Stellenbosch Univ., near Cape Town (1936–38); then went to London, where he studied with Theodore Holland (composition) and Harold Craxton (piano) at the Royal Academy of Music (1938–43). From 1939 to 1944 he worked with the British Broadcasting Corp.; went back to South Africa in 1946; taught there at the Univ. of Cape Town (1949–61); in 1961, joined the faculty of Stellenbosch Univ.; retired in 1978; he also made many appearances as a pianist.

WORKS: ORCH.: 2 syms.: No. 1 (1941–43); No. 2, *Sinfonia ricercata* (Cape Town, March 13, 1952); *Southern Cross* (1943); *Rhapsody* (Cape Town, March 4, 1952); *Aubade* for Small Orch. (1955); *Primavera* (1960); *Maskerade* (1962–64); *Gebede by jaargetye in die Boland* (1966). CHAMBER: 5 *Elegies* for String Quartet (1940–41); String Quartet No. 1 (1946); *Duo concertante* for Viola and Piano (1962); *Music for 13 Players* (1969); various piano pieces; also choral works and songs.

Wykes, Robert (Arthur), American flutist, teacher, and composer; b. Aliquippa, Pa., May 19, 1926. He studied composition with Phillips and Barlow at the Eastman School of Music in Rochester, N.Y. (B.M. and M.M., 1949); played flute in the Toledo Sym. Orch. while teaching at Bowling Green State Univ. (1950–52); then taught at the Univ. of Illinois (1952–55). In 1955 he joined the faculty of Washington Univ. in St. Louis, where he was a prof. (1965–88); also was a flutist with the St. Louis Sym. Orch. (1963–67) and the Studio for New Music in St. Louis (1966–69).

WORKS: STAGE: *The Prankster*, chamber opera (1951; Bowling Green, Ohio, Jan. 12, 1952). ORCH.: *Divertimento* for Small Orch. (1949); *Density III* (1959; St. Louis, Jan. 8, 1960); Concertino for Flute, Oboe, Piano, and Strings (1963); *Wave Forms and Pulses* (University City, Mo., May 2, 1964); *Horizons* (1964); *The Shape of Time* (St. Louis, April 1, 1965); *In Common Cause* for Strings, Trumpet, English Horn, and Percussion (1966); *Toward Time's Receding* (St. Louis, April 7, 1972); *A Shadow of Silence I* (1972); *Western Wyndes* for Symphonic Band (Barrington, Ill., May 21, 1974); *A Lyric Symphony* (St. Louis, May 10, 1980); *Paris: 2nd Symphony* (St. Louis, Sept. 27, 1981). CHAMBER: Flute Sonata (1955); String Sextet (1958); Piano Quintet (1959); *Points and Excursions* for Brass Quintet (1962); *Man against Machine* for Chamber Group (1966); *Cheirality* for String Quartet (1970); *3 Concert Études* for Flute (1989); piano and organ pieces. VOCAL: *Letter to an Alto Man* for Chorus, Harp, Piano, Percussion, Soloist, and Orch. (1966–67; St. Louis, May 19, 1967); *The Adequate Earth* for 2 Male Narrators, Baritone, 3 Choruses, and Orch., after Donald Finkel's poems about Antarctica (1975–76; St. Louis, Feb. 5, 1976); other vocal works; music for documentary films, including *Robert Kennedy Remembered* (Academy Award, 1969), *Monument to the Dream, John F. Kennedy 1917–1963*, and *The Eye of Jefferson*.

Wylde, Henry, English conductor, composer, and music educator; b. Bushey, Hertfordshire, May 22, 1822; d. London, March 13, 1890. He was the son of Henry Wylde, a London organist and composer of glees. He studied piano with Moscheles; then with Cipriani Potter at the Royal Academy of Music in London. In 1852 he founded in London the New Phil. Society, and conducted its concerts in cooperation with Spohr until 1858, when he took complete charge of its concerts (until 1879). In 1861 he founded the London Academy of Music; supervised the building of St. George's Hall (1867) to house it. In 1863 he became a prof. of music there, retaining this post until his death. He publ. *The Science of Music* (1865); *Music in Its Art-Mysteries* (1867); *Modern Counterpoint in Major Keys* (1873); *Occult Principles of Music* (1881); *Music as an Educator* (1882); *The Evolution of the Beautiful in Sound* (1888). Among his works are *Paradise Lost*, oratorio after Milton (London, May 11, 1853), a Piano Concerto (London, April 14, 1852), songs, and piano pieces.

Wyner, Susan Davenny, American soprano, wife of **Yehudi Wyner;** b. New Haven, Conn., Oct. 17, 1943. She was educated at Cornell Univ., graduating summa cum laude in music and English literature in 1965; then pursued vocal studies with Herta Glaz (1969–75). She received a Fulbright scholarship and a grant from the Ford Foundation; also won the Walter W. Naumberg Prize. In 1972 she made her Carnegie Recital Hall debut in N.Y.; in 1974 she made her orch. debut as a soloist with the Boston Sym. Orch. On Oct. 23, 1977, she made her 1st appearance at the N.Y. City Opera as Monteverdi's Poppaea. On Oct. 8, 1981, she made her Metropolitan Opera debut in N.Y. as Woglinde in *Das Rheingold*. An exceptionally intelligent singer, she became equally successful as a performer of music in all historic idioms, from early Renaissance works to the most intransigent ultramodern scores.

Wyner (real name, **Weiner**), **Yehudi,** Canadian-born American composer, pianist, conductor, and teacher, son of **Lazar Weiner** and husband of **Susan Davenny Wyner;** b. Calgary, June 1, 1929. He followed his parents to the U.S.; enrolled in the Juilliard School of Music in N.Y., graduating in 1946; then entered Yale Univ., where his principal teacher was Richard Donovan (A.B., 1950; B.Mus., 1951; M.Mus., 1953); he

also acquired an M.A. degree from Harvard Univ. in 1952, where he studied with Walter Piston. From 1953 to 1956 he worked at the American Academy in Rome, then was active in N.Y. as a conductor and keyboard player; later performed with the Bach Aria Group. From 1963 to 1977 he taught at Yale Univ., where he was chairman of the music dept. (1969–73); from 1976 he was a teacher and performer at the Berkshire Music Center in Tanglewood; also was prof. of music at the State Univ. of N.Y. at Purchase from 1978 to 1990, where he was dean of the music division (1978–82). In 1987–88 he was a visiting prof. at Brandeis Univ., and in 1989 was made prof. of composition there. In 1958–59 and 1977–78 he held Guggenheim fellowships. His music is expressively vigesimosecular in its structural sobriety and melorhythmic aggressiveness; his serial techniques, anchored in tritones and major sevenths, are mitigated by a certain combinatorial harmoniousness; formally, his works followed along neo-Classical lines but eventually developed more contemporary forms.

WORKS: Incidental music to R. Lowell's *The Old Glory* (1964) and I. Singer's *The Mirror* (1972–73). ORCH.: *Da camera* for Piano and Orch. (1967). CHAMBER: *Dance Variations* for Wind Quintet, Trumpet, Trombone, and Cello (1953; rev. 1959); *Serenade* for Flute, Trumpet, Horn, Trombone, Viola, Cello, and Piano (1958); *Passover Offering* for Flute, Clarinet, Trombone, and Cello (1959); *De novo* for Cello and Small Ensemble (1971); *2 Romances* for Piano Quartet (1980); *Tanz and Maissele* for Violin, Cello, Clarinet, and Piano (1981); *Passage I* for Small Ensemble (1983); String Quartet (1984–85); *Composition* for Viola and Piano (1986); piano and organ pieces. VOCAL: *Canto cantabile* for Soprano and Band (1972); *Intermedio*, lyric ballet for Soprano and Strings (1974); *On This Most Voluptuous Night*, song cycle for Soprano and 7 Instruments (1982); *Leonardo Vincitore* for 2 Sopranos, String Bass, and Piano for Leonard Bernstein's 70th Birthday (1988).

Wynette, Tammy (real name, **Wynette Pugh**), American country-music singer; b. Red Bay, Ala., May 5, 1942. She taught herself to play the piano and guitar; after holding various jobs, including a position as a beauty operator, she decided to seek fame and fortune in Nashville, Tenn., as a singer of country music; in 1969 she joined the "Grand Ole Opry." She struck a responsive chord with such songs as *Your Good Girl's Gonna Go Bad, Bedtime Story*, and *Let's Get Together*; her hit recording of *Stand by Your Man* also served as the title of her autobiography (written with J. Dew; N.Y., 1979). She was married to the country-music star **George Jones** (1969–75).

Wyschnegradsky, Ivan (Alexandrovich), Russian composer, master of microtonal music; b. St. Petersburg, May 16, 1893; d. Paris, Sept. 29, 1979. He studied composition with Nikolai Sokoloff at the St. Petersburg Cons.; in 1920 he settled in Paris. He devoted virtually his entire musical career to the exploration and creative realization of music in quarter-tones and other microtonal intervals; had a quarter-tone piano constructed for him; also publ. a guide, *Manuel d'harmonie à quarts de ton* (Paris, 1932). On Nov. 10, 1945, he presented in Paris a concert of his music, at which he conducted the 1st performance of his *Cosmos* for 4 Pianos, with each pair tuned at quarter-tones. Bruce Mather took interest in Wyschnegradsky's music and gave a concert of his works at McGill Univ. in Montreal that included 3 world premieres (Feb. 10, 1977). But with the exception of these rare concerts, Wyschnegradsky remains a figure of legend; few performances of his music are ever given in Europe or North America. He regarded his *La Journée de l'existence* for Narrator, ad libitum Chorus, and Orch. (to his own text; 1916–17; rev. 1927 and 1940) as his germinal work, opening the path to microtonal harmony; he dated this "awakening to ultrachromaticism" as having occurred on Nov. 7, 1918. At his death he left sketches for a short opera in 5 scenes, *L'Éternel Étranger*, begun in 1939 but never completed. Also unfinished was the ambitious *Polyphonie spatiale*.

OTHER WORKS (all in quarter-tones unless otherwise given): *Chant douloureux et étude* for Violin and Piano (1918); *7 Varia-*

tions on the Note C for 2 Pianos (1918–20; perf. in 1945 as *5 Variations;* then 2 more were added); *Chant funèbre* for Strings and 2 Harps (1922); *Chant nocturne* for Violin and 2 Pianos (1923; rev. 1972); 2 string quartets (1924, 1931–32); *2 Choruses* for Voices and 4 Pianos (1926); *Prélude et fugue sur un chant de l'Evangile rouge* for String Quartet (1927); *Prélude et Danse* for 2 Pianos (1928); *Ainsi parlait Zarathoustra* (Thus Spake Zarathustra) for Orch. (1929–30; arr. for 4 Pianos, 1936); *2 études de concert* for Piano (1931; arr. for 2 Pianos, 1936); *Etude en forme de scherzo* for 2 Pianos (1932); *Prélude et Fugue* for 2 Pianos (1933); *24 préludes* for 2 Pianos (1934; rev. 1958–60); 4 *Fragments symphoniques* for 4 Pianos (1934, final version, 1968; 1937; 1946; 1956); *Le Mot* for Soprano and Piano (1935; half-tones); *Linnite,* pantomime for 3 Female Voices and 4 Pianos (1937); *Acte chorégraphique* for Bass-baritone, Chorus, and 4 Pianos (1938–40; rev. 1958–59); *Cosmos* for 4 Pianos (1940; suppressed); *Prélude et Fugue* for 3 Pianos (1945); *2 Fugues* for 2 Pianos (1951); *5 variations sans thème et conclusion* for Orch. (1951–52); *Sonate en un mouvement* for Viola and 2 Pianos (1956; suppressed); *Transparences I and II* for Ondes Martenot and 2 Pianos (1956, 1963); *Arc-en-ciel* for 6 Pianos (1956); *Etude sur le carré magique sonore* for Piano (1956; based on the "magic square" principle of cyclical structure, written in a tempered scale without quarter-tones); *Etude tricesimoprimal* for Fokker-organ (1959; for the Dutch physicist Adriaan Fokker's 31-tone organ); *Composition* for String Quartet (1960); *2 pièces* for Microtonal Piano (1960); *Etude sur les mouvements rotatoires* for 4 Pianos (1961; orchestrated 1964); *2 Compositions:* No. 1 for 3 Pianos and No. 2 for 2 Pianos (1962); *Prélude et étude* for Microtonal Piano (1966); *Intégrations* for 2 Pianos (1967); *Symphonie en un mouvement* for Orch. (1969); *Dialogues à trois* for 3 Pianos (1973–74; sixth-tones). **BIBL.:** C. Ballif, ed., "I. W., L'Ultrachromatisme, et les espaces non octaviants," *La Revue Musicale,* nos. 290–291 (1972–73).

Wyss, Niklaus, Swiss conductor; b. Zürich, Nov. 5, 1936. He studied piano and violin in Zürich; conducting in Brussels and Rome. He toured extensively as a guest conductor with various opera companies and orchs.; conducted many contemporary scores.

Wyttenbach, Jürg, Swiss pianist and composer; b. Bern, Dec. 2, 1935. He studied piano and theory with Fischer and Veress at the Bern Cons.; after further training from Lefébure and Calvet at the Paris Cons. (1955–57), he completed his piano studies with Karl Engel (1958–59). He taught piano at the Biel Cons. (1959–67); was a prof. of piano at the Bern Cons. (1962–66); was at the Basel Academy of Music from 1967. His music pursues the median line of European modernism, marked by a strong rhythmic pulse, dissonant counterpoint, and atonal diversions, without falling into the bottomless pit of dodecaphony. **WORKS:** 4 works of "instrumental theater": *Execution ajournée I–III* (1969–70) and *Kunststücke, die Zeit totzuschlagen* (Tricks to Kill Time; 1972); Piano Concerto (1959; rev. 1973); Sonata for Solo Oboe (1961); *3 Movements* for Oboe, Harp, and Piano (1962); ballet, *Der Gefesselte* (Heidelberg, 1962); *Divisions* for Piano and 9 Solo Strings (1964); *De Metalli* for Baritone and Orch. (1964–65); *Anrufungen und Ausbruch* for 28 Woodwinds and Brass (1966); *Nachspiel* for 2 Pianos (1966); *Paraphrase* for a Narrator, a Flutist, and a Pianist (1967–68); *Conteste* for Chamber Orch. (1969); *3 Pieces* for Piano (1969); *Ad libitum* for 1 or 2 Flutes (1969); madrigal comedy, *Chansons ricochets* (1981).

Wyzewa (Wyzewski), Théodore (Teodor) de, noted Polish-born French musicologist; b. Kalushin, Russian Poland, Sept. 12, 1862; d. Paris, April 7, 1917. In 1869 his parents settled in France; he was educated in Beauvais, Paris, and at the Univ. of Nancy (licence-ès-lettres, 1882). In 1884 he founded in Paris, with Edouard Dujardin, the *Revue Wagnérienne,* which, until it ceased publication in 1888, did much to advance the cause of Wagner in France. Wyzewa's importance as a musicologist rests upon his research concerning the life and work of Mozart, about whom he publ. new facts in "Recherches sur la jeunesse de Mozart," in the *Revue des Deux Mondes* (1904–5), and in *Wolfgang Amédée Mozart. Sa vie musicale et son œuvre, de l'enfance à la pleine maturité* (with G. de Saint-Foix; 2 vols., Paris, 1912; 3 more vols. added by Saint-Foix in 1937, 1940, and 1946). Wyzewa also wrote *Beethoven et Wagner* (Paris, 1898; new ed., 1914); ed. 20 piano sonatas of Clementi with a biographical notice (vol. I, Paris, 1917; vol. II, by H. Expert). **BIBL.:** P. Delsemme, *Teodor de Wyzewa et le cosmopolitisme littéraire en France à l'époque du symbolisme* (Brussels, 1967); N. di Girolamo, *Teodor de Wyzewa: dal simbolismo ad tradizionalismo 1885–87* (Bologna, 1969).

X

Xanrof (real name, **Fourneaux**), **Léon,** French composer of popular music; b. Paris, Dec. 9, 1867; d. there, May 17, 1953. Xanrof is an anagram of *fornax*, the Latin equivalent of *fourneau*. He was a lawyer by profession; from 1890, produced light stage pieces in the Paris theaters; the chansonnette *Le Fiacre*, which he wrote for Yvette Guilbert, achieved great popularity. He also contributed music criticism to various Paris newspapers.

Xenakis, Iannis, eminent Greek-born French composer and music theorist; b. Brăila, Rumania (of Greek parents), May 29, 1922. At the age of 10 he was taken by his family to Greece, where he began to study engineering, but he became involved in the Greek resistance movement against the Nazi occupation forces; was wounded in a skirmish in 1945, and lost sight in one eye. Shortly after he was captured, but managed to escape to the U.S. In 1947 he went to Paris and later became a naturalized French citizen; studied architecture with Le Corbusier and became his assistant (1948–60); during the same period, he took lessons in composition with Honegger and Milhaud at the École Normale de Musique in Paris and with Messiaen at the Paris Cons. (1950–53). He aided Le Corbusier in the design of the Philips Pavillion at the 1958 World's Fair in Brussels; met Varèse, who was then working on his *Poème électronique* for the exhibit, and received from him some stimulating advice on the creative potentialities of the electronic medium. During his entire career, Xenakis strove to connect mathematical concepts with the organization of a musical composition, using the theory of sets, symbolic logic, and probabilistic calculus; he promulgated the stochastic

method, which is teleologically directed and deterministic, as distinct from a purely aleatory handling of data. He publ. a comprehensive vol. dealing with these procedures, *Musiques formelles* (Paris, 1963; in Eng., N.Y., 1971). He was founder and director of the Centre d'Études Mathématiques et Automatiques Musicales in Paris in 1966, and founder and director of the Center for Mathematical and Automated Music at Indiana Univ. in the U.S., where he served on the faculty from 1967 to 1972. His influence on the development of advanced composition in Europe and America is considerable; several composers adopted his theories and imitated the scientific-sounding titles of some of his compositions. Xenakis uses Greek words for the titles of virtually all of his works to stress the philosophical derivation of modern science and modern arts from classical Greek concepts; in some cases he uses computer symbols for titles.

WORKS: *Metastasis* for 61 Instruments (1953–54; Donaueschingen, Oct. 15, 1955); *Pithoprakta* for 50 Instruments (1955–56; Munich, March 8, 1957); *Achorripsis* for 21 Instruments (1956–57; Brussels, July 20, 1958); *Diamorphoses* for Tape (1957); *Concret PH* for Tape (1957); *Analogiques A & B* for 9 Strings and Tape (1959); *Syrmos* for 18 Strings (1959); *Duel,* musical game for 2 "antagonistic" Conductors and 2 Orchs. playing different material, mathematically based on game theory, with the audience determining the winning orch. (1959; Radio Hilversum, Oct. 1971); *Orient-Occident* for Tape (1960); *Herma* for Piano (1960–61); *ST/48-1,240162* (1956–62; ST = stochastic; 48 = number of players; 1 = 1st work for this contingent; 240162 = 24 January 1962, date on which the work, derived from earlier sketches, was finally calculated by the IBM 7090 electronic computer in Paris as programmed probabilistically by Xenakis); *ST/10-1,080262* (1956–62; ST = stochastic; 10 = number of players; 1 = 1st work of this contingent; 080262 = 8 February 1962, date on which this work was finally electronically calculated; a version of this work for String Quartet is entitled *ST/4*); *Morsima-Amorsima* (Morsima = that which comes by Fate; Amorsima = that which does not come by Fate) for Violin, Cello, Double Bass, and Piano (1956–62); *Atrées* for 10 Players (1956–62; written in homage to Blaise Pascal and calculated by the 7090 computer, with some license); *Stratégie*, musical game for 2 Conductors and 2 Orchs. (1959–62; Venice Festival, April 23, 1963; Bruno Maderna's orch. won over that of Konstantin Simonovic); *Bohor I and II* for Tape (1962, 1975); *Polla ta dhina* (Many Are the Wonders) for Children's Choir and Small Orch., to a text from Sophocles's *Antigone* (1962); *Eonta* (neuter plural of the present participle of the verb "to be" in the Ionian dialect, the title being in Cypriot syllabic characters of Creto-Mycenean origin) for Piano, 2 Trumpets, and 3 Tenor Trombones (1963–64); *Hiketides*, stage music for 50 Women's Voices, 10 Instruments, and Percussion, after Aeschylus (1964); *Akrata* (Pure) for 16 Wind Instruments (1964–65; Oxford, June 28, 1966); *Terretektorh* for 88 Players scattered among the audience (1965–66; Royan Festival, April 3, 1966); *Oresteia*, incidental music for Aeschylus's tragedy, for Chorus and Chamber Orch. (1965–66; also a concert suite); *Nomos Alpha* (Law Alpha) for Cello (1966); *Polytope de Montréal*, light-and-sound spectacle for the Montreal EXPO '67, for 4 Small, Identical Orchs. (1967); *Nuits* for 12 Mixed Voices a cappella (1967); *Medea*, stage music for Male Chorus and Instrumental Ensemble (1967); *Nomos Gamma* for 98 Players scattered among the audience (1967–68; Royan Festival, April 3, 1969); *Kraanerg*, ballet music for Tape and Orch. (1968–69; Ottawa, June 2, 1969); *Anaktoria* for 8 Instruments (1969); *Persephassa* for 6 Percussionists scattered among the audience (1969); *Synaphai* for 1 or 2 Pianos, and Orch. (1969); *Hibiki-Hana-Ma*, 12-channel electroacoustic music distributed kinematically over 800 loudspeakers, for the Osaka EXPO '70 (1969–70; also a 4-channel version); *Charisma* for Clarinet and Cello (1971); *Aroura* for 12 Strings (1971); *Persepolis*, light-and-sound spectacle with 8- or 4-channel electroacoustic music (1971); *Antikhthon*, ballet music for Orch. (1971; Bonn, Sept. 21, 1974); *Linaia-Agon* for Horn, Tenor Trombone, and Tuba (1972); *Mikka* for Violin (1972); *Polytope de Cluny*, version of *Polytope de Montréal*,

for 4-channel Tape (1972); *Eridanos* for 8 Brasses and 10 String Instruments or their multiples (La Rochelle Festival, 1973); *Evryali* for Piano (1973); *Cendrées* for Chorus and Orch. (Lisbon, June 18, 1974); *Erikhthon* for Piano and Orch. (Paris, May 1974); *Gmeeoorh* for Organ (1974); *Noomena* for Orch. (Paris, Oct. 16, 1974); *Empreintes* for Orch. (La Rochelle Festival, June 29, 1975); *Phlegra* for 11 Instruments (1975; London, Jan. 28, 1976); *Psappha* for Percussion (1975); *N'shima* for 2 Horns, 2 Trombones, Cello, and 2 Mezzo-sopranos (1975); *Theraps* for Double Bass (1975–76); *Khoaï* for Harpsichord (1976); *Retours—Windungen* for 12 Cellists (Bonn, Dec. 20, 1976); *Dmaathen* for Oboe and Percussion (1976); *Epeï* for English Horn, Clarinet, Trumpet, 2 Tenor Trombones, and Double Bass (1976); *Mikka S* for Violin (1976); *Akanthos* for 9 Players (1977); *Kottos* for Cello (1977); *Hélène* for Mezzo-soprano, Female Chorus, and 2 Clarinets (1977); *Diatope* for 4- or 8-track Tapes (1977); *Ais* for Baritone, Percussion, and Orch.; *Palimpsest* for Piano and Percussion (1979); *Embellie* for Viola (1981); *Nekuia* for Chorus and Orch. (1981); *Mists* for Piano (1981); *Serment Orkos* for Chorus (1981); *Pour les baleines* for String Orch. (1982); *Pour la paix* for Narrator, Chorus, and Band (1982); *Shaar* for String Orch. (1983); *Chant des soleils* for Chorus, Children's Chorus, Winds, and Percussion (1983); *Khal Perr* for Wind Quintet and Percussion (1983); *Tetras* for String Quartet (1983); *Lichens I* for Orch. (1984; London, May 30, 1986); *Thallein* for 14 Instrumentalists (1984); *Alax* for 3 Instrumental Ensembles (Cologne, Sept. 15, 1985); *Idmen A* for Chorus and 4 Percussionists (1985); *Keqrops* for Piano and Orch. (N.Y., Nov. 13, 1986); *Akea* for String Quartet and Piano (1987); *Jalons* for Orch. (1988); *Tracées* for Orch. (1988).

BIBL.: M. Bois, *I. X.: The Man and His Music: A Conversation with the Composer and a Description of His Works* (Westport, Conn., 1980); N. Matossian, *I. X.* (Paris, 1981; Eng. tr., 1986); E. Restagno, ed., *X.* (Turin, 1988).

Xyndas, Spyridon, Greek composer; b. Corfu, June 8, 1812; d. Athens, Nov. 12, 1896. He studied in Italy; composed many attractive popular Greek songs; several operas to Italian librettos (*Il Conte Giuliano, I due pretendenti*, etc.); also *The Parliamentary Candidate* (Athens, March 1888), which was probably the first opera with a Greek text. He became blind toward the end of his life.

Y

Yamada, Kōsaku (Kôsçak), eminent Japanese conductor and composer; b. Tokyo, June 9, 1886; d. there, Dec. 29, 1965. He studied vocal music with Tamaki Shibata and cello and theory with Werkmeister at the Tokyo Imperial Academy of Music (1904–8); then composition with Bruch and Karl Leopold Wolf at the Berlin Hochschule für Musik (1908–13). He founded the Tokyo Phil. Orch. in 1915; appeared as a guest conductor with the N.Y. Phil. in 1918 in a program of Japanese music, including some of his own works; conducted in Russia in 1930 and 1933, and then throughout Europe in 1937. His compositions follow in the German Romantic tradition of Wagner and Strauss, with impressionistic overtones. Although most of his MSS were destroyed during the Allied air raid on Tokyo on May 25, 1945, several works have been restored from extant orch. parts.

WORKS: OPERAS: *Ochitaru tennyo* (The Depraved Heavenly Maiden; 1912; Tokyo, Dec. 3, 1929); *Alladine et Palomides* (1913); *Ayame* (The Sweet Flag; Théâtre Pigalle, Paris, 1931); *Kurofune* (The Black Ships; 1939); *Yoake* (The Dawn; 1939; Tokyo, Nov. 28, 1940); *Hsiang Fei* (1946–47; Tokyo, May 1954). **CANTATAS**: *Bonno-Koru* (Tokyo, Oct. 9, 1932) and *Tairiku no reimei* (The Dawn of the Orient; Tokyo, July 7, 1941). **ORCH.**: Sym., *Kachidoki to heiwa* (The Shout of Victory and Peace; 1912; Tokyo, Dec. 6, 1914); *Meiji shōka* (Ode to the Meiji) for Chorus and Orch. (1921; Tokyo, April 26, 1925); *Shōwa sanka* (Homage to Shōwa), symphonic poem (1938; Tokyo, May 13, 1939); *Kamikaze*, symphonic poem (1944); also chamber music; nearly 1,000 choral pieces and songs.

Yamaguchi, Motohumi, Japanese instrumentalist and composer; b. Tokyo, Nov. 7, 1954. After cello studies at Masashino Music Univ., he became the main flute and shamisen player for Kodo, a highly disciplined performing ensemble founded in 1971 by Tagayasu Den, a scholar of traditional Japanese arts, under the name Ondekoza ("demon drummers"); under the direction of a new leader, Kawauchi, the group was renamed Kodo (translating to both "heartbeat" and "children of the drum," referring to the taiko that is so central to its performances). Kodo has given choreographed performances throughout Asia, the Americas, and Europe; in 1988 the ensemble held its 1st annual Earth Celebration on Sado Island, attracting performers from all over the world. Yamaguchi joined Kodo on Jan. 14, 1980, and is considered one of its most important members; among his compositions for the group are *Hae* for Koto, Japanese Drum, and Caribbean Drum (1982), *Tjanang Sari* for Percussion, after Balinese gamelan (1987), and *Kariuta* for 2 Shinobue (Japanese flutes) (1989). Other members of the ensemble include Leonard Eto (b. N.Y., March 5, 1963) and Yoshiaki Oi (b. Tokyo, March 28, 1951). Among Kodo's many celebrated recordings are *Kodo* (1981), *Kodo, Heartbeat Drummers of Japan* (1985), and *Blessing of the Earth* (1989).

Yamash'ta, Stomu (real name, **Tsutomu Yamashita**), Japanese percussionist and composer; b. Kyoto, March 10, 1947. He was trained in music by his father; played piano in his infancy, and drums at puberty; in early adolescence became a timpanist for the Kyoto Phil. and Osaka Phil.; also worked in several film studios in Tokyo; at the same time he was active in sports; won the speed skating championship of Japan for his age group. At 16 he went to London for further study; later went to the U.S. as a scholarship student at the Interlochen Arts Academy; continued his musical education in Boston, N.Y., and Chicago. Returning to Japan, he gave solo performances as a percussionist; developed a phenomenal degree of equilibristic prestidigitation, synchronously manipulating a plethora of drums and a congregation of oriental bells and gongs while rotating 360° from the center of a circle to reach the prescribed percussionable objects. As a composer, he cultivates a manner of controlled improvisation marked by constantly shifting meters. In 1970 he formed the Red Buddha Theater (an ensemble of 36 actors, musicians, and dancers), for which he composed 2 musical pageants, *Man from the East* (1971) and *Rain Mountain* (1973). Other works include a ballet, *Fox* (1968); *Hito* for any 3 Instruments (1970); *Prisms for Percussion* (1970); *Red Buddha* for Chamber Ensemble (1971); percussion scores for some 77 Japanese films, as well as for Ken Russell's *The Devils* (with Peter Maxwell Davies, 1971) and Robert Altman's *Images* (1972).

Yampolsky, Abram (Ilyich), distinguished Russian violin pedagogue, uncle of **Izrail (Markovich) Yampolsky;** b. Ekaterinoslav, Oct. 11, 1890; d. Moscow, Aug. 17, 1956. He studied violin with Korguyev at the St. Petersburg Cons. (graduated, 1913); also received instruction in composition from Sokolov, Wihtol, and Steinberg. After teaching at the Ekaterinoslav music school (1913–20), he settled in Moscow, where he was concertmaster of the conductorless ensemble Persymfans (1922–32); was also prof. (1926–56) and chairman of the violin dept. (1936–56) at the Moscow Cons.; was made a Doctor of Arts (1940). He was teacher and adviser to a number of prominent Soviet violinists, among them Kogan, Elizaveta Gilels, Grach, Zhuk, and Sitkovetsky.

Yampolsky, Izrail (Markovich), Russian musicologist and lexicographer, nephew of **Abram (Ilyich) Yampolsky;** b. Kiev, Nov. 21, 1905; d. Moscow, Sept. 20, 1976. He studied violin with his uncle, then entered the Moscow Cons., where he took courses in advanced music theory with Miaskovsky and Glière; he subsequently taught violin at the Music Academy in Moscow (1931–58); gave lectures in music history there; also taught at the Cons. (1934–49). A fine and diligent research scholar, he publ. a number of excellent monographs dealing mainly with violin and violinists: *Foundations of Violin Fingering* (Moscow, 1933; 3rd expanded ed., 1955; in Eng., London, 1967); *Henryk Wieniawski* (Moscow, 1955); *Enescu* (Moscow, 1956; also in Rumanian, Bucharest, 1959); *Music of Yugoslavia* (Moscow, 1958); *Paganini* (Moscow, 1961; 2nd ed., 1968); *David Oistrakh* (Moscow, 1964); *Fritz Kreisler* (1975). He was co-ed., with Boris Steinpress, of the 1-vol. reference work *Encyclopedic Music Dictionary* (Moscow, 1959; rev. 1966). He was acting ed.-in-chief of the 1st 3 vols. of the 5-vol. *Musical Encyclopedia* (Moscow, 1973, 1974, 1976).

Yancey, "Jimmy" (James Edward), black American jazz pianist; b. Chicago, c.1894; d. there, Sept. 17, 1951. He was a singer and dancer in a vaudeville act as a child; then taught himself to play the piano and appeared in Chicago clubs. In 1925 he gave up his stage career and worked as a groundskeeper at Comiskey Park. With the revival of boogie-woogie, he returned to playing jazz piano, and became quite a figure in jazz circles.

Yankelevich, Yuri, Russian violinist and pedagogue; b. Basel, March 7, 1909; d. Moscow, Sept. 12, 1973. He studied with Anisim Berlin in Omsk, Johannes Nalbandian at the Petrograd Cons., and A. Yampolsky at the Moscow Cons. (graduated, 1932); then taught there, becoming a prof. in 1961. Among his outstanding students were V. Spivakov and V. Tretyakov.

Yankovich, Al(fred), American musical parodist and accordionist; b. Lynwood, Calif., Oct. 23, 1959. He studied at the Calif. Polytechnic Inst. at San Luis Obispo (B.S. in architecture, 1980); as an undergraduate he worked at the college radio station, ultimately acquiring his own weekly show and the nickname "Weird Al." He used the men's room across the hall from the station to record his 1st parody, *My Bologna* (1980), which abruptly became a national hit syndicated by the "Dr. Demento" radio show. More parodies followed, including *I Love Rocky Road* and *Another One Rides the Bus*, and were incorporated into his 1st album (1983). In addition to making numerous music videos, Yankovich has hosted television shows and scored film projects, including *Naked Gun* (1988) and *UHF* (1989). His elaborate parodies employ remarkably imitative abilities as a vocalist and arranger; his bizarre lyrics and neat timings sometimes improve on the original. Among his most popular recordings are *Weird Al Yankovich* (1983), *Dare to Be Stupid* (1984), and *Even Worse* (1988). With T. Insana, he publ. *The Authorized Al: The Amazing and Somewhat Made-Up Story of a Rock and Roll Legend* (Chicago, 1985).

Yannatos, James, American composer and conductor; b. N.Y., March 13, 1929. He studied composition and conducting with Bernstein, Steinberg, Boulanger, Milhaud, Dallapiccola, Hindemith, Bezanson, Weisgall, Quincy Porter, and Bacon; received degrees from Yale Univ. (B.M., 1951; M.M., 1952) and the Univ. of Iowa (Ph.D., 1960). In 1964 he was appointed to the music faculty of Harvard Univ. He worked with youth orchs. and choral groups and conducted chamber orchs. in Hanover, N.H.; Saratoga, N.Y.; and Banff, Canada. Among his works are 2 ballets: *Oedipus* (1960) and *A Suite for Orpheus and Eurydice* (1980); an opera, *The Rocket's Red Glare* (1971); *Sounds of Desolation and Joy* for Solo Voice (1978); many choral works, pieces for chamber orch., and didactic works for children. He publ. *Explorations in Musical Materials* (1978).

Yannay, Yehuda, Rumanian-born Israeli-American composer; b. Timişoara, May 26, 1937. He went to Israel in 1951, and studied composition with Boscovich (1959–64); received a Fulbright travel grant and went to the U.S., where he studied composition with Arthur Berger and Harold Shapero at Brandeis Univ. (M.F.A., 1966); attended summer classes of Gunther Schuller at the Berkshire Music Center in Tanglewood (1965); later studied composition at the Univ. of Illinois, Urbana (1968–70). In 1970 he joined the faculty of the Univ. of Wisconsin at Milwaukee; organized there a group called the Music from Almost Yesterday Ensemble. He received his Ph.D. in 1974 from the Univ. of Illinois, Urbana. Yannay's extensive output follows along post-modern lines with distinct personal modes of expression.

WORKS: MEDIA AND THEATRICAL: *Coheleth*, environmental piece (1970); *Bug Piece* with live insect notation for Any Instrumental and/or Vocal Group (1972; also for Dancers); *Autopiano or Piano Minus Pianist* for Actor (1976); *All Our Women*, musical theater/chamber opera (1981). **FILMS:** *Houdini's Ninth* (1973) and *Jidyll* (1988). **ORCH.:** *Mirkamim* (Textures of Sound) (1967–68); 5 Songs for Tenor and Orch. (1976–77); 7 *Late Spring Pieces* (1980); 3 *Jazz Moods* (1982). **CHAMBER:** *Mutatis mutandis* for Oboe, Clarinet, Trumpet, Horn, Viola, and Contrabassoon (1968); *Per se* for Violin and 7 Instruments (1969); *preFIX-FIX-sufFIX* for Bassoon, Horn, and Cello (1971); *At the End of the Parade* for Baritone and 6 Players (1974); Trio for Clarinet, Cello, and Piano (1982); 9 *Branches of the Olive Tree* for Recorders, Bass Clarinet, Guitar, and Percussion (1984); *M. My Dear* for Jazz Violin, Guitar, and Double Bass (1985); *Celan Ensembles* for Tenor and Ensemble (1986–). **SOLO:** *Music for Piano* (1962); *Permutations* for Percussion (1964); *Statement* for Flute (1964); *Continuum* for Piano (1964); 7 *Late Spring Pieces* for Piano (1973); *Im Silberwald* for Trombone, Tuned Glasses, and Tape (1983); *Between the Raindrops* for Guitar (1984). **CHORAL:** *Dawn and Departure* for 9 Singers or Chamber Choir and Flute, Clarinet, Cello, Piano, and Percussion (1970–72); *Tombeau de Satie* for Choir and Organ (1979); *Le campane di Leopardi* for Choir, Organ, and Tuned Glasses (1979). **COLLABORATIVE:** 3 *Visions of the Age* for Digital Synthesizers and Instruments (with J. Welstead and J. Thome; 1985).

Yansons, Arvid, Latvian conductor, father of **Mariss Jansons;** b. Leipaja, Oct. 24, 1914; d. Manchester, England, Nov. 21, 1984. He studied violin at the Leipaja Cons. (1929–35), then took courses in violin, conducting, and composition at the Riga Cons. (1940–44). In 1944 he made his conducting debut in Riga; in 1948 he was made associate conductor of the Leningrad Phil.; also appeared as a guest conductor throughout the Soviet Union, Europe, Australia, and Japan. From 1965 he made regular guest conducting appearances with the Hallé Orch. in Manchester; also served as head of the conducting class at the Leningrad Cons. (from 1972).

Yardumian, Richard, American composer; b. Philadelphia (of Armenian parents), April 5, 1917; d. Bryn Athyn, Pa., Aug. 15, 1985. He studied harmony with William Happich, counterpoint with H. Alexander Matthews, and piano with George Boyle (1939–41); later attended Monteux's conducting school in Hancock, Maine (summer 1947), and received additional musical training from Thomson in N.Y. (1953). His compositions reflect the spirit of Armenian folk songs and religious melodies. A number of his works were first performed by the Philadelphia Orch.

WORKS: ORCH.: *Armenian Suite* (1937–54; Philadelphia, March 5, 1954); Symphonic Suite (1939); *3 Pictographs of an Ancient Kingdom* (1941); *Desolate City* (1943–44; Philadelphia, April 6, 1945); Violin Concerto (1949; Philadelphia, March 30, 1950; rev. 1960); 2 syms.: No. 1 (1950; rev., Philadelphia, Dec. 1, 1961); No. 2, *Psalms*, for Mezzo-soprano or Baritone and Orch. (1947–64; Philadelphia, Nov. 13, 1964); *Epigram: William M. Kincaid* for Flute and Strings (1951; also for Flute and String Quartet); *Passacaglia, Recitatives and Fugue*, piano concerto (1957; Philadelphia, Jan. 3, 1958); *Veni sancte Spiritus*, chorale prelude for Chamber Orch. (1958); *Num komm der heiden Heiland*, chorale prelude (1978; arr. from an organ piece). **CHAMBER:** Flute Quintet (1951; arr. for Flute and Strings); *Cantus animae et cordis* for String Quartet (1955; arr. for Strings, 1955). **PIANO:** *3 Preludes: Wind* (1938), *Sea* (1936), and *Sky* (1944; orchestrated 1945); *Dance* (1942); *Chromatic Sonata* (1946); *Prelude and Chorale* (1946); organ pieces. **VOCAL:** *Create in Me a Clean Heart* for Mezzo-soprano or Baritone and Chorus (1962); *Magnificat* for Women's Voices (1965); *Come Creator Spirit*, mass for Mezzo-soprano or Baritone, Chorus, Congregation, and Orch. or Organ (1965–66; N.Y., March 31, 1967); *The Story of Abraham*, oratorio for Soloists, Chorus, Orch., and Film (1968–71; rev. 1973); *Narek: Der Asdvadz* for Mezzo-soprano, Horn, and Harp (1983); *Hrashapar* for Chorus, Organ, and Orch. (1984); about 100 chorales for Chorus (1944–85).

Yarrow, Peter, American folksinger, of the singing trio Peter, Paul and Mary; b. N.Y., May 31, 1938. A serious musician, he went to Cornell Univ. to study psychology. He sang at the Newport Folk Festival in 1960; then got together with two other folk singers, Paul Stookey (b. Birmingham, Mich., Nov. 30, 1937) and Mary Travers (b. Louisville, Nov. 7, 1937), and launched a trio using only their first names and specializing in folksy and unambiguously wholesome songs dedicated to the improvement of humanity and of America by non-violent means. They aligned themselves with such social singers as Pete Seeger and Bob Dylan. By himself, Yarrow recorded the solipsistic songs *Peter* and *That's Enough for Me*. Together they sang Pete Seeger's nostalgic numbers *Where Have All the Flowers Gone*, *Puff, the Magic Dragon*, and *Song Will Rise*. They were most successful singing other people's songs in folk style, among them *Blowin' in the Wind*, *I Dig Rock-and-Roll Music*, and *Leaving on a Jet Plane*.

Yarustovsky, Boris (Mikhailovich), Russian musicologist; b. Moscow, May 14, 1911; d. there, July 12, 1978. He studied music history and theory at the Moscow Cons., graduating in 1937; also obtained the degree of Doctor of Arts in 1952 with the dissertation *Some Problems of the Dramaturgy of Classical Russian Operas.* He publ. *Tchaikovsky, Life and Works* (Moscow, 1940); *Operatic Dramaturgy of Tchaikovsky* (Moscow, 1947); *Music of the New World* (Moscow, 1964); *Igor Stravinsky: A Short Study of His Life and Works* (Moscow, 1966; 2nd ed., 1969); *Essays on the Dramaturgy of 20th-Century Opera* (Moscow, 1971).

Yashirō, Akio, Japanese composer; b. Tokyo, Sept. 10, 1929; d. Yokohama, April 9, 1976. He studied piano with Leonid Kreutzer and composition with Hashimoto, Ifukube, and Ikenouchi at the Tokyo Geijutsu Daigaku, graduating in 1949; then went to Paris, where he studied composition with Noël Gallon at the Paris Cons. (1951–54), and took private lessons with Nadia Boulanger and Messiaen. Returning to Japan, he joined the faculty of the Tokyo Geijutsu Daigaku (1956) and the Tōhō Gakuen School of Music (1958).

WORKS: String Quartet (1954–55); Sonata for 2 Flutes and Piano (1957–58); Sym. (Tokyo, June 9, 1958); Cello Concerto (Tokyo, June 24, 1960); Piano Sonata (1960); Piano Concerto (Tokyo, Nov. 5, 1967); *Ouverture de fête* for Brass Ensemble (14th Winter Olympic Games, Sapporo, Feb. 3, 1972).

Yasser, Joseph, Polish-born Russian-American organist, conductor, and musicologist; b. Lodz, April 16, 1893; d. N.Y., Sept. 6, 1981. He studied at the Moscow Cons., graduating in 1917 as an organist; after several years of teaching organ in Moscow and Siberia, he reached Shanghai in 1921, and conducted a choral society there; subsequently emigrated to the U.S. (1923); served as organist at Temple Rodeph Sholom in N.Y. (1929–60); held various positions in American musicological groups. His most important contribution to music theory was *A Theory of Evolving Tonality* (N.Y., 1932), in which he proffered an ingenious hypothesis as to the origin of the pentatonic and heptatonic scales, and, operating by inductive reasoning, suggested that the ultimate Western scale would contain 19 degrees. He contributed several articles to *Musical Quarterly* (April and July 1937 and July 1938) dealing with quartal harmony, which were publ. in a separate ed. (N.Y., 1938).

Yates, Peter B., Canadian-American writer on music; b. Toronto, Nov. 30, 1909; d. N.Y., Feb. 25, 1976. He studied at Princeton Univ. (B.A., 1931); married the pianist Frances Mullen in 1933. From 1937 to 1962 he was a functionary at the Calif. Dept. of Employment in Los Angeles, but this bureaucratic occupation did not preclude his activities as a musical catalyst. In 1939 he inaugurated on the rooftop of his house in the Silver Lake district of Los Angeles a chamber concert series which was to become an important cultural enterprise in subcultural California, under the name Evenings on the Roof; he served as coordinator of these concerts from 1939 to 1954, when they were moved to a larger auditorium in downtown Los Angeles and became known as the Monday Evening Concerts. In 1968 he was appointed chairman of the music dept. at the State Univ. of N.Y. at Buffalo. He publ. *An Amateur at the Keyboard* (N.Y., 1964), *Twentieth-Century Music* (N.Y., 1967), and a collection of poems.

Yavorsky, Boleslav (Leopoldovich), Russian pianist and music theorist; b. Kharkov, June 22, 1877; d. Saratov, Nov. 26, 1942. He studied piano and composition with Taneyev in Moscow; in 1906, founded a People's Cons. there. From 1915 to 1919 he taught at the Kiev Cons.; then went to Moscow. His theory of aural gravitation as the determining factor of the formation of modes is embodied in his publications *Structure of Musical Speech* (Moscow, 1908) and *Exercises in Schematic Formation of Modal Rhythm* (Moscow, 1915), and in several monographs. He was also active in the field of general musical education, and his methods influenced Soviet practice in pedagogy. Vol. 1 of the collected ed. of his articles and letters was publ. in Moscow in 1964.

Yepes, Narciso, Spanish guitarist; b. Lorca, Nov. 14, 1927. He was educated at the Valencia Cons.; made his debut with the Orquesta Nacional in Madrid in 1947; then launched an international career, appearing in the U.S., South America, and Japan. He also wrote music for films and prepared various transcriptions for guitar.

Yeston, Maury, American composer and music theorist; b. Jersey City, N.J., Oct. 23, 1945. He studied at Yale Univ. with Waite and Forte (B.A., 1967; Ph.D., 1974), subsequently joining the composition faculty there and becoming director of the BMI Musical Theater Workshop in N.Y. His 1st major stage work was the Broadway musical *Nine* (1982), based on Fellini's movie *8½*, which won Tony and Drama Desk awards;

it includes opulent recollections of Baroque and Romantic styles, continuing the operatic trend in musical theater established by Stephen Sondheim and Andrew Lloyd Webber. He also wrote incidental music for Caryl Churchill's play *Cloud Nine* and for *Nukata*, a musical written in Japanese and premiered in Tokyo. His theoretical writings are sophisticated; his *Stratification of Musical Rhythm* (New Haven, 1975), elucidates one of the only plausible theories on rhythmic structure yet proposed. He also ed. *Readings in Schenker Analysis* (New Haven, 1977). Among his compositions are a Concerto for Cello and Orchestra (1977), *Goya, a Life in Song* (1987), and another musical, *Grand Hotel* (1989).

Yo-Yo Ma. See Ma, Yo-Yo.

Yoffe, Shlomo, Polish-born Israeli composer; b. Warsaw, May 19, 1909. He studied in Poland and Czechoslovakia; went to Palestine in 1930; studied with Partos and Boscovich at the music academies of Jerusalem and Tel Aviv; was director of the Studio for Music Education for Gilboa and Bet-Shean (1953–73).

    WORKS: *Ruth,* symphonic suite (1954); 3 syms. (1955, 1957, 1958); Violin Concerto (1956); *Views of the Emek,* symphonic suite (1958); *Symphonic Poem on Jewish Themes* (1959); *Divertimento* for Orch. (1959); Cello Concertino (1959); Oboe Concerto (1960); Concerto for Strings (1961); *3 Pieces* for Horn and Strings (1966); *Fantasia concertante* for Brass Quartet and Orch. (1968); *Beit-Alfa,* symphonic poem (1972); *Introduction, Dance and Finale* for Chamber Orch. (1972); *Sobu Zion,* overture (1973); *5 Sketches of Old Jerusalem* for Chamber Orch. (1973); *Fantasy* for Oboe and Chamber Orch. (1975); 6 cantatas: *Alilot Hagilboa* (1954); *Erez Hanegev* (1955); *Alu* (1958); *Shaalu Shelom Yerushalayim* (1967); *Religious Cantata* (1969); *Psalm CXX* (1974); Quartet for 2 Flutes, Cello, and Piano (1957); 2 string quartets (1961, 1969); *Fantasy* for String Quartet (1966); *Chamber Concerto* for Violin and 10 Players (1966); *Affettuoso* for 2 Flutes (1966); Brass Quartet (1967); *Musica concertante* for Clarinet and 3 Percussionists (1973); *4 Miniatures* for Wind Quintet (1973); *Etude* for 13 Players (1974); *Serenata* for Wind Quintet (1975); *5 Songs* for Soprano and 13 Players (1975); *Nonetto,* fantasy for Strings (1976); *What Name Shall I Call?* for Soprano and Chamber Orch. (1975); *Rising Night after Night,* cantata (1977); Sinfonietta for Chamber Ensemble (1977); *The Beautiful City* for Orch. (1978); *Psalm 125* for Narrator and Orch. (1978); Concerto for Vibraphone and Strings (1979); *Landscapes* for Orch. (1981); *Depressed Story* for Clarinet and String Quartet (1983); *A Prayer of the Afflicted,* cantata (1983); *Israel Sketches* for Orch. (1984); Quintet for Horn and String Quartet (1986).

Yon, Pietro Alessandro, Italian-born American organist, composer, and teacher; b. Settimo Vittone, Aug. 8, 1886; d. Huntington, Long Island, N.Y., Nov. 22, 1943. He studied with Fumagalli at the Milan Cons.; then at the Turin Cons. (1901–4), and at the Accademia di Santa Cecilia in Rome with Remigio Renzi (organ) and Sgambati (piano), graduating in 1905; subsequently served as organist at St. Peter's in Rome (1905–7). In 1907 he emigrated to the U.S.; from 1907 to 1919, and again from 1921 to 1926, was organist at St. Francis-Xavier's in N.Y.; then was appointed organist of St. Patrick's Cathedral in N.Y., a post he held until his death. He became a naturalized U.S. citizen in 1921. He was greatly esteemed as an organist and teacher; composed numerous organ pieces, of which *Gesù Bambino* (1917) became popular and was publ. in various instrumental and vocal arrangements; he also wrote an oratorio, *The Triumph of St. Patrick* (N.Y., April 29, 1934); several masses and other religious services. A novel based on his life, *The Heavens Heard Him,* written by V.B. Hammann and M.C. Yon, was publ. in N.Y. in 1963.

Yonge (also **Young, Younge**), **Nicholas,** English singer and music editor; b. Lewes; d. London (buried), Oct. 23, 1619. He was a chorister at St. Paul's Cathedral. He translated and arranged a number of Italian madrigals, which he publ. in 2 books under the general title *Musica transalpina* (1588, 1597).

    BIBL.: A. Einstein, "The Elizabethan Madrigal and 'Musica transalpina,'" *Music & Letters,* XXV (1944); D. Scott, *A Transcription and Detailed Study of "Musica transalpina"* (diss., Univ. of London, 1968); idem, "N. Y. and His Transalpine Music," *Musical Times,* CXVI (1975).

Yoshida, Tsunezō, Japanese ethnomusicologist; b. Kohama, Fukui prefecture, Feb. 3, 1872; d. Kyoto, May 16, 1957. After graduating from the Tokyo School of Music (1897), he taught at training colleges in Fukui (1897–1903) and Kyoto (1903–35). In 1920 he began studying Buddhist music in collaboration with Dōnin Taki (1890–1943), a priest of the Tendai sect and a performer of Buddhist chant, with whom he produced several books and transcription anthologies on Buddhist chant, beginning with *Kada ongaku ron* (On the Music of Gātha; 1934). Yoshida founded a research inst. on Buddhist music at Enryaku-ji (the headquarters of the Tendai sect) in 1950. He received a number of honors during his lifetime, including the Medal of Honor with Purple Ribbon (1955).

Yossifov, Alexander, Bulgarian composer; b. Sofia, Aug. 12, 1940. He studied composition with Vladigerov and conducting with Iliev at the Bulgarian State Cons. in Sofia, graduating in 1966.

    WORKS: Opera, *Back to the Beginning;* 3 ballets: *Wings of Friendship* (1969); *The Woman Partisan* (1969); *Student's Farewell Ball* (1969); 2 oratorios: *Homeland* (1966) and *The Great White Road* (1969); 5 nationalist cantatas: *Revolution,* overture (1964); 2 symphonic tales: *The Wolf and the 7 Kids* (1966) and *Little Red Riding Hood* (1969); 4 syms.: No. 1, *Sinfonietta* (1966); No. 2 (1970); No. 3, *Bulgarian Blood,* for Bass and Orch. (1973); No. 4 (1974); Concerto for 2 Pianos, String Orch., and Percussion (1970); Piano Concerto (1971–72); *Festive Overture* (1974).

Yost, Michel, famous French clarinetist and composer; b. Paris, 1754; d. there, July 5, 1786. He studied with Beer; wrote 14 clarinet concertos; 30 quartets for Clarinet and Strings; 8 books of duos for clarinets; *Airs variés* for Clarinet, with Viola and Bass.

Youdin, Mikhail, Russian composer; b. St. Petersburg, Sept. 29, 1893; d. Kazan, Feb. 8, 1948. He studied at the St. Petersburg Cons., graduating in 1923; joined its staff as an instructor in 1926. He went to Kazan in 1942, and taught at the Cons. there until his death.

    WORKS: Opera, *Farida* (1943); cantata, *Song of Spring and Joy* (Leningrad, Nov. 25, 1936); *Heroic Oratorio* (1937); *Poem 1926* for Orch. (Leningrad, March 30, 1927); other symphonic pieces; 2 string quartets; Piano Sonata; Organ Toccata; choruses; songs; arrangements of folk songs.

Youll, Henry, English composer who flourished c.1600. He publ. *Canzonets to three voyces* (London, 1608; ed. in The English Madrigalists, XXVIII, 1968).

Youmans, Vincent (Millie), American composer of popular music; b. N.Y., Sept. 27, 1898; d. Denver, April 5, 1946. He took piano lessons as a child, but was apprenticed by his father to enter the business world; he served as a messenger in a Wall Street bank; then enlisted in the U.S. Navy; also played the piano in a Navy band; wrote a song, *Hallelujah,* which was picked up by John Philip Sousa, who performed it with his own bands; later it was incorporated by Youmans in his musical *Hit the Deck.* After World War I, Youmans earned a living as a song plugger for publishers in N.Y. He produced 2 musical comedies, *2 Little Girls in Blue* (May 3, 1921) and *The Wildflower* (Feb. 7, 1923); both were moderately successful, but he achieved fame with his next production, *No, No, Nanette;* it opened in Detroit on April 21, 1924; was next staged in Chicago on May 5, 1924, and after a 49-week run there, moved to London, where it was produced on March 11, 1925; it finally reached Broadway on Sept. 16, 1925, and proved to be one of the most beguiling and enduring American musicals; its hit song, *Tea for Two,* became a perennial favorite all over the world (Shostakovich arranged it in 1927 for a salon orch.

under the title *Tahiti Trot*). There followed several other successful musicals: *A Night Out* (1925), *Oh, Please!* (1926), *Hit the Deck!* (1927), *Rainbow* (1928), *Great Day* (1929), and *Through the Years* (1932). In 1933 Youmans went to Hollywood to complete his score for the film *Flying Down to Rio*. Because of an increasingly aggravated tubercular condition, he retired to Denver in the hope of recuperation in its then-unpolluted environment, and remained there until his death. Among his songs the following were hits: *Bambalina; I Want to Be Happy; Hallelujah; Sometimes I'm Happy; Great Day; Without a Song; Time on My Hands; Through the Years; Oh, Me, Oh, My, Oh, You; Carioca; Orchids in the Moonlight; Drums in My Heart; More Than You Know; Rise 'n' Shine*.

BIBL.: D. Dunn, *The Making of No, No, Nanette* (Secaucus, N.J., 1972); G. Boardman, *Days to Be Happy, Years to Be Sad: The Life and Music of V. Y.* (N.Y., 1982).

Young-Uck Kim. See **Kim, Young-Uck.**

Young (real name, **Youngs**), **(Basil) Alexander,** English tenor; b. London, Oct. 18, 1920. He was a pupil of Steffan Pollmann at the Royal College of Music in London; sang with the BBC and Glyndebourne choruses (1948–49); in 1950 he made his operatic debut as Scaramuccio in *Ariadne auf Naxos* at the Edinburgh Festival; sang regularly at London's Covent Garden (1955–70); also appeared with other English opera companies and in the U.S., and toured widely as a concert artist. From 1973 to 1986 he was head of the school of vocal studies at the Royal Northern College of Music in Manchester; was founder-conductor of the Jubilate Choir of Manchester (1977). His operatic repertory ranged from Monteverdi to Stravinsky; he was particularly admired for his performances of Handel's music.

Young, Cecilia, English soprano; b. London, 1711; d. there, Oct. 6, 1789. She studied with Geminiani; made her 1st public appearance at a benefit concert at the Drury Lane Theatre on March 4, 1730; in 1735 was engaged by Handel for his opera company; married **T.A. Arne** on March 15, 1737; went with him to Dublin in 1742, and sang in his works presented there (*Comus, Judgment of Paris, Alfred,* etc.).

Young, Douglas, English composer and pianist; b. London, July 18, 1947. He studied at the Royal College of Music with Anthony Milner (composition) and Anthony Hopkins (piano), obtaining his B.Mus. in 1969; in 1970 he made his debut as a pianist at the Royal Festival Hall in London. He was founder-director of the Dreamtiger ensemble (from 1975).

WORKS: BALLETS: *Pasiphae* (1969); *Charlotte Brontë-Portrait* (1973–74); *Ludwig, Fragmente eines Rätsels* (Munich, June 14, 1986). **ORCH.:** Sinfonietta (1968–70); Piano Concertino (1972–74); *3 Regions from Terrain* (1974); *Sea Change* (1976); *Circus Band Et Al (after Ives)* (1977); *Virages-Region I,* cello concerto (1978); *William Booth Enters Heaven (after Ives)* (1980); *Rain, Steam, and Speed* (1981); *Lament on the Destruction of Forests* (1986). **CHAMBER:** *Essay* for String Quartet (1971); *Compasses* for Clarinet and String Trio (1972–77); *Croquis et Agaceries (after Satie)* for Flute, Cello, and Piano (1976); *10 préludes de la porte héroique du Ciel* for Cello and Piano (1977); *Trajet/inter/lignes* for Flute (1978–80); *Fantomes* for String Trio (1980–81); *Sports et Divertissement (after Satie)* for Narrator, Clarinet, String Trio, and Piano (1981); *Arabesque brève* for Cello (1982); *String Trio 1985* for Violin, Viola, and Cello (1983–85); piano pieces. **VOCAL:** *The Listeners,* cantata for Narrator, Soprano, Women's Voices, and Chamber Orch. (1967); *Vers d'un voyage vers l'hiver* for 12 Solo Voices (1975–77); *Journey between 2 Worlds* for Chorus, Rock Group, Steel Band, and Orch. (1979); *Songs of Exile* for Countertenor or Contralto and Lute (1984).

Young, Faron, American singer of country and popular music; b. Shreveport, La., Feb. 25, 1932. He took up the guitar; after attending Centenary College for a time, he began his career as a singer of country music on the "Louisiana Hayride" program. He served in the Korean War; after his discharge he joined the Grand Ole Opry in Nashville, Tenn.; also appeared

in films and on television. His hits included *Hello Walls* (1957) and *It's Four in the Morning* (1971).

Young, La Monte (Thornton), American composer of the extreme avant-garde; b. Bern, Idaho, Oct. 14, 1935. He studied clarinet and saxophone with William Green in Los Angeles (1951–54); also attended Los Angeles City College (1953–56) and studied counterpoint and composition privately with Leonard Stein (1955–56); was a pupil of Robert Stevenson at the Univ. of Calif. at Los Angeles (B.A., 1958); pursued further training with Seymour Shifrin and Andrew Imbrie at the Univ. of Calif. at Berkeley (1958–60) and attended the summer courses in new music in Darmstadt; subsequently studied electronic music with Richard Maxfield at the New School for Social Research in N.Y. (1960–61). In 1963 he married the artist and illustrator Marian Zazeela with whom he subsequently gave audio-visual performances in a series of "Sound/Light Environments" in Europe and America. In 1970 he visited India to study Eastern philosophy and train himself physically, mentally, and vocally for cosmic awareness, gradually arriving at the realization that any human, subhuman, or inhuman activity constitutes art; in his *Composition 1990* he starts a fire on the stage while releasing captive butterflies in the hall. In his attempt to overcome terrestrial limitations, he has decreed for himself a circadian period of 26 hours. He achieves timelessness by declaring, "This piece of music may play without stopping for thousands of years." Several of his works consist solely of imperious commands: "Push the piano to the wall; push it through the wall; keep pushing," or, more succinctly, "Urinate." He ed. *An Anthology of Chance Operations, Concept Art, Anti-Art,* etc. (N.Y., 1963; 2nd ed., rev., 1970), which, with his own *Compositions 1960,* had primary influence on concept art and the Fluxus movement; his own contribution to it was a line drawn in India ink on a 3 × 5 filing card. He has contributed extensively to the study of just intonation and to the development of tuning systems based on the set of rational numbers which make up the components of his periodic composite sound waveform environments. He received a Guggenheim fellowship and a grant from the N.E.A. Among his ascertainable works are 5 *Little Pieces* for String Quartet (1956); *For Brass* (1957); *For Guitar* (1958); *Trio for Strings* (1958); *Poem for Tables, Chairs, and Benches* (moving furniture about; Univ. of Calif., Berkeley, Jan. 5, 1960); *Arabic Numeral (any Integer)* for Gong or Piano (1960); *Studies in the Bowed Disc* for Gong (1963); *The Well-Tuned Piano* (1964); *The Tortoise Droning Selected Pitches from the Holy Numbers of the 2 Black Tigers, the Green Tiger, and the Hermit* (N.Y., Oct. 30, 1964); *The Tortoise Recalling the Drone of the Holy Numbers as They Were Revealed in the Dreams of the Whirlwind and the Obsidian Gong, Illuminated by the Sawmill, the Green Sawtooth Ocelot, and the High-Tension Line Stepdown Transformer* (N.Y., Dec. 12, 1964); *Map of 49's Dream of Two Systems of 11 Sets of Galactic Intervals Ornamental Lightyears Tracery* for Voices, Various Instruments, and Sine Wave Drones (Pasadena, Calif., Jan. 28, 1968); and *The Subsequent Dreams of China* (1980). Also an arbitrary number of pieces of "conceptual" music and tape recordings of his own monophonous vocalizing achieved by both inspiration and expiration so that the vocal line is maintained indefinitely; various physical exercises with or without audible sounds. His *Selected Writings* were publ. in Munich in 1969.

BIBL.: R. Palmer, "A Father Figure for the Avant-garde," *The Atlantic* (May 1981).

Young, Lester (Willis) "Pres" or **"Prez,"** remarkable black American jazz tenor saxophonist; b. Woodville, Miss., Aug. 27, 1909; d. N.Y., March 15, 1959. He studied trumpet, alto sax, violin, and drums with his father; then played in his family's band; turning to the tenor saxophone at 19, he began performing with various groups in the Midwest; was a member of Count Basie's band (1934; 1936–40; 1943–44). While serving in the U.S. Army, he was court-martialed for using drugs; upon his release in 1945, he resumed his career which was plagued by his abuse of alcohol. All the same, he continued to perform until shortly before his death. He made recordings with various jazz notables, including Billie Holiday, who dubbed him "Pres" (a contraction of "The President") for his outstanding abilities. One of the great jazz saxophonists, he influenced numerous successors through his sinuous tone quality and improvised solos.

BIBL.: J. McDonough, *L. Y.* (Chicago, 1980); D. Gelly, *L. Y.* (N.Y., 1984); L. Porter, *L. Y.* (Boston, 1985); F. Büchmann-Møller, *You Just Fight for Your Life: The Story of L. Y.* (Westport, Conn., 1990).

Young, Neil, Canadian-born folk-rock singer, instrumentalist, and composer; b. Toronto, Nov. 12, 1945. He learned to play the banjo and guitar in his youth; moving to Los Angeles in 1966, he formed the Buffalo Springfield band, which produced Young's hits *Broken Arrow* and *I Am a Child.* In 1969 he joined with David Crosby, Stephen Stills, and Graham Nash at the Woodstock Festival, later scoring a hit with their album *Déjà Vu.* Eventually he espoused a solo career, making the albums *Everybody Knows This Is Nowhere* (1969), *After the Goldrush* (with the backup group Crazy Horse; 1970), *Harvest* (1972), *Tonight's the Night* (1975), *Rust Never Sleeps* (1979), *Rector* (1981), and *Old Ways* (1985). In his songs he created an effective conglomeration of folk, country music, and hard rock; among his best are *Southern Man, Cowgirl in the Sand, Heart of Gold, Country Girl, Helpless,* and the surrealistic *Vampire Blues.*

Young, Percy M(arshall), English writer on music; b. Northwich, Cheshire, May 17, 1912. He studied English, music, and history as an organ scholar at Selwyn College, Cambridge (B.A., 1933; Mus.B., 1934), then went to Dublin, where he graduated from Trinity College (Mus.D., 1937); upon his return to England, he took courses with C.B. Rootham and E.J. Dent in Cambridge; subsequently occupied various teaching posts; from 1944 to 1966, was director of music at the College of Technology in Wolverhampton. He publ. a number of arrangements of early English songs, and also composed some vocal pieces and a Fugal Concerto for 2 Pianos and Strings (1954); he is known principally for his scholarly biographical studies and essays.

WRITINGS (all publ. in London): *Samuel Pepys' Music Book* (1942); *Handel* (1947; 3rd ed., rev., 1979); *The Oratorios of Handel* (1953); *Messiah: A Study in Interpretation* (1951); *A Critical Dictionary of Composers and Their Music* (1954; U.S. ed. as *Biographical Dictionary of Composers*); *Elgar, O.M.: A Study of a Musician* (1955; 2nd ed., 1973); ed. *Letters of Edward Elgar and Other Writings* (1956); *Tragic Muse: The Life and Works of Robert Schumann* (1957; 2nd ed., rev., 1961); *The Choral Tradition: An Historical and Analytical Survey from the 16th Century to the Present Day* (1962; 2nd ed., rev., 1982); *Zoltán Kodály* (1964); ed. *Letters to Nimrod from Edward Elgar* (1965); *A History of British Music* (1967); *Keyboard Musicians of the World* (1967); ed. *Elgar: A Future for English Music and Other Lectures* (1968); *Debussy* (1969); *The Bachs, 1500–1850* (1970); *Sir Arthur Sullivan* (1971); *A Concise History of Music* (1974); *Beethoven: A Victorian Tribute* (1976); *Alice Elgar: Enigma of a Victorian Lady* (1977); *George Grove* (1980); *Mozart* (1987).

Young, Polly (Mary), English soprano; b. London, c.1745; d. there, Sept. 20, 1799. She lived in Dublin with her aunt, the soprano **Cecilia Young** (Mrs. T.A. Arne), and made her debut as a singer upon her return to London in 1762. In 1766 she married the composer **François-Hippolyte Barthélemon;** their daughter, Cecilia Maria (Mrs. Henslowe), was a talented musician.

Young, Victor, American pianist and composer; b. Bristol, Tenn., April 9, 1889; d. Ossining, N.Y., Sept. 2, 1968. He studied piano with Isidor Philipp in Paris; toured in England and the U.S. as accompanist to prominent singers; held various teaching positions; was music director in Thomas A. Edison's Experimental Laboratory in West Orange, N.J., conducting tonal tests and making piano recordings under Edison's personal supervision (1919–27). He wrote the musical score for one of the earliest sound motion pictures, *In Old California;* composed some 300 film scores altogether; also wrote, for orch., *Scherzetto, Jeep, In the Great Smokies, Charm Assembly Line Ballet,* etc.; piano pieces (including *Under a Spanish Moon*); songs (*Gossip, Cuckoo Clock,* etc.).

Young, Victor, American violinist, conductor, and composer of popular music; b. Chicago, Aug. 8, 1900; d. Palm Springs, Calif., Nov. 10, 1956. As a youth he was sent to Poland, where he studied violin at the Warsaw Cons., and made his debut with the Warsaw Phil. in 1917. He returned to Chicago in 1920, and made his U.S. debut there in 1921; after working as a theater musician (1922–29), he was active on the radio; was music director of Brunswick Records (1931–35) before settling in Hollywood as conductor of his own orch. and as a composer for films, radio, and television. Some of his songs became famous (*Sweet Sue, Street of Dreams, Can't We Talk It Over, My Romance, Ghost of a Chance, Love Letters, Golden Earrings, Stella by Starlight, My Foolish Heart, Song of Delilah,* etc.). Shortly before his death, he completed the musical score for the motion picture *Around the World in 80 Days* (1956).

Young, William, English viol player and composer; place and date of birth unknown; d. Innsbruck, April 23, 1662. By at least 1652 he was in the service of the Archduke Ferdinand Karl in Innsbruck; accompanied the archduke on sojourns to Italy. Another William Young, who was a violinist in the royal music of Charles II in London (1660–71), may have been his son. The elder Young was a distinguished composer of music for the viol; his publ. works comprise *Almain and Sarabande* for Lyra-viol (1651), and 11 *Sonate a 3, 4, 5 voci con alcune allemand, correnti e balletti à 3* (Innsbruck, 1653; 11 sonatas and 4 suites ed. in 1930); various other instrumental works remain in MS.

BIBL.: W. Whittaker, *The Concerted Music of W. Y.* (Oxford, 1931); idem, "W. Y.," *Collected Essays* (Oxford, 1940).

Youssoupoff, Prince Nikolai Borisovich, Russian musical dilettante and writer on music; b. St. Petersburg, 1827; d. Baden-Baden, Aug. 3, 1891. He studied violin with Vieuxtemps, and was an eager collector of violin literature; had a private orch. in his palace in St. Petersburg, but lived abroad for many years. He composed a programmatic sym., *Gonzalvo de Córdova,* with Violin obbligato; *Concerto symphonique* for Violin and Orch.; several pieces for violin and piano (*Féeries de la scène, Hallucination, Chant d'amour, Plainte, Saltimbanques,* etc.); publ. an interesting book on violin making, *Luthomonographie, historique et raisonnée: Essai sur l'histoire du violon et sur les ouvrages des anciens luthiers célèbres du temps de la Renaissance, par un amateur* (Frankfurt, 1862), and *Musique sacrée suivie d'un choix de morceaux de chants d'église* (Paris, 1862, as vol. I of a projected *Histoire de la musique en Russie;* contains a valuable study of Russian neumes and examples of traditional chants). Themes from Youssoupoff's *Ballet d'Espagne* were used by Bériot for a group of 6 violin duets.

Yradier (Iradier), Sebastián de, Spanish song composer; b. Sauciego, Alava, Jan. 20, 1809; d. Vitoria, Dec. 6, 1865. He composed theater music; after 1851, became singing master to the Empress Eugénie in Paris; for some time he lived in Cuba. He publ. a number of melodious songs in a Spanish manner; one of them, *El arreglito,* subtitled *Chanson havanaise,* was used by Bizet for the famous Habanera in *Carmen;* Bizet retained the key and the pattern of the accompaniment, making minor changes in the melody to adjust it to French words. Yradier's other songs that became famous are *La paloma* and *Ay Chiquita!* In Paris he publ. 2 collections, *Echo d'Espagne* (8 songs) and *Fleurs d'Espagne* (25 songs).

BIBL.: E. Istel, *Bizet und "Carmen"* (Stuttgart, 1927); J. Tiersot, "Bizet and Spanish Music," *Musical Quarterly* (Oct. 1927).

Yriarte (Iriarte), Tomás de, Spanish poet and musician; b. Puerto de la Cruz de Orotava, Tenerife, Canary Islands, Sept. 18, 1750; d. Santa María, near Cádiz, Sept. 17, 1791. He studied in Madrid; was secretary at the Chancellery of State in Madrid and chief archivist at the Ministry of War. His literary works include a long didactic poem, *La música*

(Madrid, 1779; Eng. tr., 1807). He composed tonadillas and some vocal and instrumental music.

BIBL.: E. Cotarelo y Mori, *I. y su época* (Madrid, 1897); J. Subirá, *El compositor I. y el cultivo español del melólogo* (2 vols., Madrid, 1949–50); R. Cox, *T. d.I.* (N.Y., 1972).

Ysaÿe, Eugène (-Auguste), famous Belgian violinist, conductor, and composer, brother of **Théophile Ysaÿe;** b. Liège, July 16, 1858; d. Brussels, May 12, 1931. At the age of 4 he began to study violin with his father, a theater conductor; at the age of 7 he was enrolled at the Liège Cons. as a pupil of Désiré Heynberg, winning 2nd prize in 1867; in 1869 he left the Cons. in a dispute with his mentor, but was readmitted in 1872 as a pupil of Rodolphe Massart, winning 1st prize in 1873 and the silver medal in 1874; then continued his training on a scholarship at the Brussels Cons. with Wieniawski; later completed his studies with Vieuxtemps in Paris (1876–79). In 1879 he became concertmaster of Bilse's orch. in Berlin; appeared as a soloist at Pauline Lucca's concerts in Cologne and Aachen; in Germany he met Anton Rubinstein, who took him to Russia, where he spent 2 winters; he also toured in Norway. In 1883 he settled in Paris, where he met César Franck, Vincent d'Indy, et al., and gave successful concerts; he formed a duo with the pianist Raoul Pugno, and started a long series of concerts with him, establishing a new standard of excellence. On Sept. 26, 1886, he married Louise Bourdeau; Franck dedicated his Violin Sonata to them as a wedding present; Ysaÿe's interpretation of this work made it famous. In 1886 he was named a prof. at the Brussels Cons. (resigned in 1898); in 1886 he also organized the Ysaÿe Quartet (with Crickboom, Léon Van Hout, and Joseph Jacob); Debussy dedicated his String Quartet to Ysaÿe's group, which gave it its 1st performance at the Société Nationale in Paris on Dec. 29, 1893. In 1889 Ysaÿe made successful appearances in England; on Nov. 16, 1894, he made his American debut, playing the Beethoven Violin Concerto with the N.Y. Phil., and creating a sensation by his virtuosity. He revisited America many times, with undiminished acclaim. He began his career as a conductor in 1894, and established in Brussels his own orch., the Société des Concerts Ysaÿe. When the Germans invaded Belgium in 1914, he fled to London, where he remained during World War I. On April 5, 1918, he made his American debut as a conductor with the Cincinnati Sym. Orch., and also led the Cincinnati May Festival in that year. His success was so great that he was offered a permanent position as conductor of the Cincinnati Sym. Orch., which he held from 1918 to 1922. He then returned to Belgium and resumed leadership of the Société des Concerts Ysaÿe. After the death of his 1st wife, he married, on July 9, 1927, an American pupil, Jeannette Dincin.

Ysaÿe's style of playing is best described as heroic; but his art was equally convincing in the expression of moods of exquisite delicacy and tenderness; his frequent employment of "tempo rubato" produced an effect of elasticity without distorting the melodic line. His works include 8 violin concertos; 6 sonatas for Solo Violin; *Poème nocturne* for Violin, Cello, and Strings; *Les Harmonies du soir* for String Quartet and String Orch.; *Divertimento* for Violin and Orch.; *Méditation* for Cello and String Orch.; *Chant d'hiver* for Violin and Chamber Orch.; *Trio de concert* for 2 Violins, Viola, and Orch.; *Amitié* for 2 Violins and Orch. At the age of 70 he began the composition of an opera in the Walloon language, *Piér li Houïeu* (Peter the Miner), which was produced in Liège on March 4, 1931, in the presence of the composer, who was brought to the theater in an invalid's chair, suffering from the extreme ravages of diabetes, which had necessitated the amputation of his left foot. He began the composition of a 2nd Walloon opera, *L'Avierge di Piér* (La Vierge de Pierre), but had no time to complete it. In 1937 Queen Elisabeth of Belgium inaugurated the annual Prix International Eugène Ysaÿe in Brussels; the 1st winner was the Russian violinist David Oistrakh.

BIBL.: M. Pincherle, *Feuillets d'histoire du violon* (Paris, 1927); J. Quitin, *E. Y.: Étude biographique et critique* (Brussels, 1938); E. Christen, *Y.* (Geneva, 1946; 2nd ed., 1947); A. Ysaÿe and B. Ratcliffe, *Y.: His Life, Work and Influence* (London, 1947); A. Ysaÿe, *E. Y.: Sa vie d'après les documents receuillis par son fils* (Brussels, 1948; a considerably altered version of the preceding; Eng. tr. as *Y., By His Son Antoine,* Buckinghamshire, 1980); A. Ysaÿe, *E. Y., 1858–1931* (Brussels, 1972); B. Schwarz, *Great Masters of the Violin* (N.Y., 1983).

Ysaÿe, Théophile, Belgian pianist and composer, brother of **Eugène (-Auguste) Ysaÿe;** b. Verviers, March 22, 1865; d. Nice, March 24, 1918. He was a pupil at the Liège Cons. (1876–80); then studied at the Kullak Academy in Berlin (from 1881), and took lessons from César Franck in Paris (1885); returning to Belgium, he became director of the Académie de Musique in Brussels; was noted as a fine ensemble player, and gave sonata recitals with his brother; during the latter's absence on tours, he also conducted the Société des Concerts Ysaÿe in Brussels. After the invasion of Belgium in 1914, he went with his brother to London; fearful of the Zeppelin air raids on London, he went to Nice, where he remained until his death. He was a prolific composer; his brother conducted a concert of Théophile's works in Brussels, on Nov. 6, 1904, including the premieres of his Sym. in F major and the symphonic poem *Le Cygne*. Other works are: Piano Concerto; symphonic poems (*Les Abeilles, La Forêt et l'oiseau*); *Fantaisie sur un thème populaire wallon* for Orch.; Piano Quintet; piano pieces; a Requiem.

Yttrehus, Rolv (Berger), American composer; b. Duluth, March 12, 1926. He studied at the Univ. of Minnesota in Duluth (B.S. in music, 1950), and then was a student of Finney at the Univ. of Michigan (M.M., 1953); went to Europe, where he took lessons with Brustad in Oslo (1953–54) and Boulanger in Paris (1954–55); upon his return home, he had satisfying sessions with Sessions (1957–60) at Princeton Univ.; then went to Rome and had instruction in advanced composition with Petrassi at the Accademia di Santa Cecilia (1960–62). Back in the U.S., he taught at the Univ. of Missouri (1963–68), Purdue Univ. (1968–69), the Univ. of Wisconsin in Oshkosh (1969–77), and Rutgers, the State Univ. of N.J. (from 1977). He ditched the scores written in the first 35 years of his life as deciduous juvenilia; in his later works he cultivated distributive serialism, in which each note, each interval, and each rhythmic unit stands in an esoteric but surmisable relationship with other individual note groups.

WORKS: *6 Haiku* for Soprano, Flute, Cello, and Harp (1959); *Music for Winds, Percussion, and Viola* (1961); *Expressioni* for Orch. (1962); Sextet for Horn, Trumpet, Violin, Double Bass, Piano, and Percussion (1964–70; rev. 1974); *Music for Winds, Percussion, Cello, and Voices* (1969); *Angstwagen* for Soprano and Percussion (1971; rev. 1981); Quintet for Flute, Violin, Clarinet, Cello, and Piano (1973); *Gradus ad Parnassum* for Soprano and Chamber Orch., after Nietzsche and Fux (1974–79); Sonata for Percussion and Piano (1983; rev. 1988); *Explorations* for Piano (1985); Sonata for Cello and Piano (1988); *Raritan Variation* for Piano (1989).

Yuasa, Joji, Japanese composer; b. Koriyama, Aug. 12, 1929. He was a medical student at Keio Univ.; studied composition in the "experimental workshop" in Tokyo (1951–57). In 1968 he received a Japan Society Fellowship for a lecture tour throughout the U.S. and Europe. In 1969 he was one of the organizers of the Crosstalk Festival of Japanese and American multimedia works in Tokyo and Osaka; was a member of the "tranSonic" composers' group, in association with Ichiyanagi, Matsudaira, Takemitsu, and others. From 1976 to 1978 he was a visiting composer and lecturer in Germany, and then in Canada in 1981; from 1982 he taught at the Univ. of Calif., San Diego. In his productions he adopts the most advanced multimedia techniques.

WORKS: *Projection* for 7 Players (1955); *Cosmos Haptic* for Piano (1957); *Projection Topologic* for Piano (1959); *Aoi no Ue*, musique concrète (1961); *Interpenetration* for 2 Flutes (1963); *Projection Esemplastic* for Electronic Media (1964);

Kansoku for Voices (1965); *Projection* for Cello and Piano (1967); *Projection* for several Kotos and Orch. (1967); *Projection* for Electric Guitars (1968); *Projection* for String Quartet (1970); *Triplicity* for Double Bass (1970); *Questions* for Chorus (1971); *On the Keyboard* for Piano (1971); *Interposiplaytion I* for Flute, Piano, and Percussion (1972) and *II* for Flute, Harp, and Percussion (1973); *Chronoplastic* for Orch. (1972; Tokyo, Nov. 15, 1972); *Territory* for Marimba, Flute, Clarinet, Percussion, and Double Bass (1974); *Time of Orchestral Time* for Orch. (1976); *Requiem* for Orch. (1980); *Scenes from Basho* for Orch. (1980); *A Perspective* for Orch. (1983); *Towards the Midnight Sun* for Computer Generated Tape and Amplified Piano (1984); *Revealed Time* for Viola and Orch. (1986); *9 Levels by Ze-ami* for Orch. and 4-Channel Tape (1988); *Mutterings* for Soprano and 7 Instruments (1988).

Yudina, Maria, eminent Russian pianist and pedagogue; b. Nevel, near Vitebsk, Sept. 9, 1899; d. Moscow, Nov. 19, 1970. She took piano lessons in Vitebsk with Frieda Teitelbaum-Levinson; then enrolled at the Petrograd Cons., where she studied piano with Anna Essipoff, Vladimir Drozdov, and Leonid Nikolayev, music theory with Maximilian Steinberg and J. Wihtol, and score reading with N. Tcherepnin and Emil Cooper. In 1921 she joined the piano faculty of the Petrograd Cons., holding this position until 1930. From 1932 to 1934 she taught at the Tiflis Cons. From 1936–51 she was a prof. at the Moscow Cons., and from 1944 to 1960 taught piano and chamber music performance at the Gnessin Inst. in Moscow. Among her students was Andrei Balanchivadze. Yudina began her career as a pianist in 1921; gave her last concert in Moscow on May 18, 1969. She also was a guest artist in East Germany (1950) and in Poland (1954). She publ. memoirs and reminiscences of famous composers she had met in Russia. Yudina enjoyed great renown as an intellectual musician capable of presenting the works she performed with a grand line, both didactic and inspired. But rather than accepting the traditional interpretation of classical music, she introduced a strong personal element differing from accepted norms, so that her performances of works by Bach, Mozart, Beethoven, and Brahms were revelations to some listeners, and abominations to the old school of pianism. Yudina was also an ardent champion of modern music, placing on her programs compositions by such masters of new techniques as Stravinsky, Schoenberg, Berg, Webern, and Bartók at a time when their works were not acceptable in Russia. She also played piano pieces by Soviet composers, particularly Prokofiev and Shostakovich. She gave numerous concerts of chamber music.
BIBL.: M. Y.: *Articles, Reminiscences, Materials* (Moscow, 1978).

Yun, Isang, important Korean-born German composer; b. Tongyong, Sept. 17, 1917. He studied Western music in Korea (1935–37) and in Japan (1941–43). During World War II, he was active in the anti-Japanese underground; in 1943 he was imprisoned, and then spent the rest of the war in hiding until the liberation in 1945. He became a music teacher in Tongyong in 1946, and later taught in Pusan; in 1953 he became a prof. of composition at the Univ. of Seoul; then studied with Revel at the Paris Cons. (1956–57) and with Blacher, Rufer, and Schwarz-Schilling at the Berlin Hochschule für Musik (1958–59); also attended the summer courses in new music in Darmstadt. He settled permanently in Berlin, where he produced several successful theatrical works, marked by a fine expressionistic and coloristic quality, and written in an idiom of euphonious dissonance. His career was dramatically interrupted when, on June 17, 1967, he and his wife were brutally abducted from West Berlin by secret police agents of South Korea, and forced to board a plane for Seoul, where they were brought to trial for sedition; he was sentenced to life imprisonment; his wife was given 3 years in jail. This act of lawlessness perpetrated on the territory of another country prompted an indignant protest by the government of West Germany, which threatened to cut off its substantial economic aid to South Korea; 23 celebrated musicians, including Igor Stravinsky, is-

sued a vigorous letter of protest. As a result of this moral and material pressure, South Korea released Yun and his wife after nearly 2 years of detention, and they returned to Germany. In 1970 he was appointed lecturer in composition at the Berlin Hochschule für Musik, being made a prof. there in 1973. In 1971 he became a naturalized German citizen.
WORKS: OPERAS: *Der Traum des Liu-Tung* (Berlin, Sept. 25, 1965); *Die Witwe des Schmetterlings* (completed by him in his Seoul prison cell and produced in absentia in Bonn on Dec. 9, 1967; Eng. version as *Butterfly Widow*, Northwestern Univ., Evanston, Ill., Feb. 27, 1970); *Träume* (an amalgam of the previous 2 operas, Nuremberg, Feb. 23, 1969); *Geisterliebe* (1969–70; Kiel, June 20, 1971); *Sim Tjong* (1971–72; Munich, Aug. 1, 1972). **ORCH.:** *Symphonische Szene* (1960); *Bara* (1960); *Colloides sonores* for String Orch. (1961); *Fluktuationen* (1964; Berlin, Feb. 10, 1965); *Réak* (Donaueschingen, Oct. 23, 1966); *Dimensionen* (Nuremberg, Oct. 22, 1971); *Konzertante Figuren* for Small Orch. (1972; Hamburg, Nov. 30, 1973); *Ouvertüre* (1973–74); Cello Concerto (Royan, March 25, 1976); Concerto for Flute and Small Orch. (1977); Double Concerto for Oboe, Harp, and Small Orch. (1977); *Muak* (1978); *Teile Dich, Nacht* for Soprano and Orch. (1980); 2 violin concertos (1981, 1986); Clarinet Concerto (1981); *Exemplum: "In memoriam Kwangju"* (1981); 5 syms.: No. 1 (1983); No. 2 (1984); No. 3 (Saarbrücken, Sept. 22, 1985); No. 4 (1986); No. 5 for Baritone and Orch. (Berlin, Sept. 17, 1987); *Gong-Hu* for Harp and Strings (1984); Double Concerto for Oboe, Cello, and String Orch. (1987). **VOCAL:** *Om mani padme hum*, cycle for Soprano, Baritone, Chorus, and Orch. (1964; Hannover, Jan. 30, 1965); *Namo* for 3 Sopranos and Orch. (Berlin, May 4, 1971); *Der weise Mann*, cantata after P. Salomo, for Baritone, Chorus, and Small Orch. (1977). **CHAMBER:** *Musik* for 7 Instruments (1959); String Quartet No. 3 (1959; Nos. 1 and 2 were withdrawn); *Loyang* for Chamber Ensemble (1962); *Gasa* for Violin and Piano (1963); *Garak* for Flute and Piano (1963); *Nore* for Cello and Piano (1964); *Riul* for Clarinet and Piano (1968); *Images* for Flute, Oboe, Violin, and Cello (1968); *Glissées* for Cello (1970); *Piri* for Oboe (1971); *Gagok* for Guitar, Percussion, and Voice (1972); Trio for Flute, Oboe, and Violin (1972–73); *Memory* for Mezzo-soprano, Baritone, Narrator, and Percussion (1974); *Etüden* for Flute (1974); *Harmonia* for 13 or 16 Winds, Harp, and Percussion (1974); *An der Schwelle*, 2 sonnets for Baritone, Female Chorus, Organ, and Instruments (1975); *Rondell* for Oboe, Clarinet, and Bassoon (1975); Piano Trio (1972–75); *Pièce concertante* for Chamber Ensemble (1976); Duo for Viola and Piano (1976); *Königliches Thema* for Violin (1976); Sonata for Oboe, Harp, and Viola or Cello (1979); Concertino for Accordion and String Quartet (1983); Quintet for Clarinet and String Quartet (1984); *Mugung-Dong*, invocation for Winds, Percussion, and Double Bass (1986); *Rencontre* for Clarinet, Harp, and Cello (1986); Quartet for 4 Flutes (1986); Quintet for Flute and String Quartet (1986); *Distanzen* for Winds and String Quartet (1988). **KEYBOARD:** 5 *Pieces* for Piano (1959); *Shao Yang Yin* for Harpsichord (1966); *Tuyaux sonores* for Organ (1967); *Fragment* for Organ (1975); *Interludium A* for Piano (1982).
BIBL.: H.-W. Heister and W.-W. Sparrer, eds., *Der Komponist I. Y.* (Munich, 1987).

Yuon, Paul. See **Juon, Paul.**

Yurgenson, Peter. See **Jurgenson, Pyotr.**

Yussupov, Prince Nikolai Borisovich. See **Youssoupoff, Prince Nikolai Borisovich.**

Yvain, Maurice, French composer of musical comedies; b. Paris, Feb. 12, 1891; d. there, July 28, 1965. Among his successful productions are *Ta bouche* (1922), *Pas sur la bouche* (1925), *Bouche à bouche* (1936), and film scores (*Rien qu'un baiser; J'ai tant d'amour;* etc.). He also produced a ballet, *Blanche neige* (Paris Opéra, Nov. 14, 1951).

Yzac, Heinrich. See **Isaac, Heinrich.**

Z

Zabaleta, Nicanor, eminent Spanish harpist; b. San Sebastian, Jan. 7, 1907. He began his training in San Sebastian; after further studies in Madrid, he went to Paris to study harp with Marcel Tournier and composition with Eugene Cools; then toured extensively in Europe, South America, and the U.S. He is noted for his efforts to increase the number of works available for the harp, both by bringing to light neglected compositions of early composers, and by prompting modern composers to write music for the harp.

Zabalza y Olaso, Don Dámaso, Spanish composer and pianist; b. Irurita, Navarra, Dec. 11, 1833; d. Madrid, Feb. 25, 1894. He studied with Mariano García; in 1858 settled in Madrid as a piano teacher at the National Cons. He publ. a number of piano pieces, many of which became very popular; also piano studies that were used at the Paris Cons., in Italy, and in Spain.

Zabel, Albert Heinrich, German harpist, teacher, and composer; b. Berlin, Feb. 22, 1834; d. St. Petersburg, Feb. 16, 1910. He studied at the Inst. für Kirchenmusik in Berlin; toured Germany, Russia, England, and America with Gungl's band (1845–48); then was solo harpist in the orch. of the Berlin Royal Opera (1848–51). In 1855 he became solo harpist of the orch. of the St. Petersburg Imperial Ballet, a post he held until his death; also was made a teacher (1862), prof. (1879), and honorary distinguished prof. (1904) of harp at the St. Petersburg Cons. He composed a Harp Concerto and numerous short pieces for the harp (*Elégie fantastique, Légende, Marguérite au rouet, Am Springbrunnen, Chanson du pêcheur, Warum?, Murmure de cascade,* etc.); publ. a harp method (Leipzig,

1900; in Ger., French, and Eng.) and a pamphlet, *Ein Wort an die Herren Komponisten über die praktische Werwendung der Harfe im Orchester* (Leipzig, 1894; also in Russian).

Zabrack, Harold, American pianist and composer; b. St. Louis, June 30, 1928. He studied piano with Rudolph Ganz at the Chicago Musical College (M.M., 1951); composition with Nadia Boulanger at Fontainebleau. From 1955 to 1957 he held a Fulbright grant for travel in Europe; gave concerts in West Germany. Returning to St. Louis, he became active as a concert pianist and teacher; in 1974 he left St. Louis to teach at Westminster Choir College. He publ. *Creative Musical Encounters* (N.Y., 1978).

WORKS: *Piano Variations* (1959); 2 duets for Viola and Oboe (1961); Piano Sonata (1964); Piano Concerto No. 1 (St. Louis, April 5, 1964, composer soloist); Piano Concerto No. 2 (1965); *Symphonic Variations* for Piano and Orch.

Zaccaria, Nicola (Angelo), Greek bass; b. Piraeus, March 9, 1923. He was educated at the Royal Cons. in Athens; made his debut at the Athens Opera in 1949 as Raymond in *Lucia di Lammermoor*. In 1953 he won at the international singing competition sponsored by La Scala in Milan, where he made his 1st appearance as Sparafucile that same year; also made appearances in Rome, Verona, and Florence; subsequently he had engagements at the Vienna State Opera; in Berlin, Cologne, and London; and at the Edinburgh and Salzburg festivals. In addition to opera, he was successful in solo recitals.

Zacconi, Lodovico (Giulio Cesare), Italian music theorist; b. Pesaro, June 11, 1555; d. Fiorenzuola di Focara, near Pesaro, March 23, 1627. He became an Augustinian novice in Pesaro in 1568, where he was a subdeacon by 1573 and received training in organ; in 1575 he became a priest. In 1577 he entered the Augustinian convent of S. Stefano in Venice, where he sang in the convent choir under I. Baccusi; also studied counterpoint with A. Gabrieli. He pursued literary studies in Pavia, where he became cursorato in 1583; then studied theology in Padua. In 1585 he began preaching in Boara Polesine, near Rovigo, but later that year became a singer to Archduke Karl of Austria in Graz. In 1590 he entered the service of Duke Wilhelm V of Bavaria. In 1596 he resumed his service in the Augustinian order as a preacher and administrator in Italy and Crete, and as a prior in Pesaro; he retired in 1612. His chief work, *Prattica di musica utile et necessaria si al compositore per comporre i canti suoi regolatamente, si anco al cantore* (Venice, 1592) and *Prattica di musica seconda parte* (Venice, 1622), contains treatises on mensural theory and counterpoint, detailed descriptions of contemporary musical instruments, and explanations for executing the ornaments in vocal polyphonic music. He also wrote 4 books of *Canoni musicali,* with comments and solutions (publ. by F. Vatielli, Pesaro, 1905); most of his other music is lost. He also prepared a MS autobiography (1626).

Bibl.: F. Chrysander, "L. Z. als Lehrer des Kunstgesanges," *Vierteljahrsschrift für Musikwissenschaft,* VII (1891), IX (1893), and X (1894); H. Kretzschmar, "L. Z.s Leben auf Grund seiner Autobiographie," *Jahrbuch der Musikbibliothek Peters 1910;* F. Vatielli, *Di L. Z.: Notizie su la vita e le opere* (Pesaro, 1912); G. Singer, *L. Z.'s Treatment of the "Suitability and Classification of All Musical Instruments" in the "Prattica di musica" of 1592* (diss., Univ. of Southern Calif., 1968); G. Gruber, *L. Z. als Musiktheoretiker* (Habilitationsschrift, Univ. of Vienna, 1972).

Zach, Jan, Czech composer and organist; b. Czellakowitz, Nov. 13, 1699; d. Ellwangen, May 24, 1773. He went to Prague in 1724, and became a violinist at St. Gallus and St. Martin; also studied organ and composition with B. Czernohorsky; served as organist at St. Martin and later at the monastic church of the Merciful Brethren and the Minorite chapel of St. Ann; after serving as court Kapellmeister in Mainz (1745–56), he traveled widely as a performer. He composed both sacred and instrumental works, including a fine Requiem in C minor, a *Stabat Mater,* a *Missa solemnis,* sinfonias, partitas, concertos, and keyboard works.

Bibl.: K. Komma, *Johann Z. und die tschechischen Musiker im deutschen Umbruch des 18. Jahrhundert* (Kassel, 1938); A. Ollig, *Die Orgelmusik Johann Z.s* (diss., Univ. of Mainz, 1954).

Zach, Max (Wilhelm), Austrian conductor; b. Lemberg, Aug. 31, 1864; d. St. Louis, Feb. 3, 1921. He studied violin with Grün, harmony with Fuchs, and composition with Krenn at the Vienna Cons. (1880–86). In 1886 he emigrated to the U.S., and played 1st viola in the Boston Sym. Orch. until 1907; also was violist in the Adamowski Quartet (1889–1906). He conducted the Boston Pops (1895–1902; 1905–7) and the St. Louis Sym. Orch. (1907–21).

Zacharewitsch, Michael, Russian-born English violinist and composer; b. Ostrov, Aug. 26, 1879; d. London, Dec. 20, 1953. He studied with Ševčik in Prague, and later with Ysaÿe in Brussels. He went to London in 1903, and became a British subject in 1915; toured Australia, New Zealand, and South Africa. He wrote *The New Art of Violin Playing* (1934), and composed *Dunkirk* (1945) for Violin and Orch., as well as violin exercises.

Zacharias, Christian, German pianist; b. Tamshedpur, India (of German parents), April 27, 1950. He was taken to Germany, where he studied with Irene Slavin in Karlsruhe; he completed his studies with Vlado Perlemuter in Paris; won several prizes, including the Ravel Prize in the European Broadcasting Union Competition (1975). He made his London debut in 1976 and his U.S. debut as soloist with the Boston Sym. Orch. in 1979; subsequently toured in Europe.

Zachow (Zachau), Friedrich Wilhelm, distinguished German organist, pedagogue, and composer; b. Leipzig, probably on Nov. 13, 1663; d. Halle, Aug. 7, 1712. His maternal grandfather and father were Stadtpfeifer; he received training in organ and as a Stadtpfeifer; in 1676 he went with his family to Eilenburg, where he most likely studied with Johann Hildebrand. From 1684 until his death he was organist at the Marienkirche in Halle, where he also led the noted musical performances every 3rd Sunday. Zachow was one of the leading composers of church cantatas and keyboard works of his day. He also was a noted teacher, numbering Handel among his pupils. For his works, see G. Körner, ed., *F.W. Z.: Gesammtausgabe seiner sämmtlichen Orgelcompositionen* (Erfurt and Leipzig, c.1850); M. Seiffert, ed., *F.W. Z: Gesammelte Werke,* Denkmäler Deutscher Tonkunst, XXI–XXII (1905); A. Adrio, ed., *F.W. Z.: Choralvorspiele für Orgel* (Berlin, 1952); and H. Lohmann, ed., *F.W. Z: Gesammelte Werke für Tasteninstrumente* (Wiesbaden, 1966).

Bibl.: A. Heuss, "F.W. Z. als dramatischer Kantatenkomponist," *Zeitschrift der Internationalen Musik-Gesellschaft,* X (1908–9); A. Wicke, *Die Kantaten F.W. Z.s in ihrer geschichtlichen Stellung* (diss., Humboldt Univ., Berlin, 1956); G. Thomas, *F.W. Z.* (Regensburg, 1966).

Zádor, Dezsö, Hungarian baritone; b. Horna Krupa, March 8, 1873; d. Berlin, April 24, 1931. He studied in Budapest and Vienna; made his debut as Almaviva in 1898 in Czernowitz; then sang in Elberfeld (1898–1901) and Prague (1901–6); was subsequently a member of the Komische Oper in Berlin (1906–11). In 1911 he joined the Dresden Court Opera, singing there until 1916; then went to the Budapest Opera (1916–19); was later a member of the Berlin Städtische Oper (1920–24). He made guest appearances at Covent Garden in London and in Paris, Milan, and Chicago. During the last years of his career, he sang bass roles.

Zador, Eugene (real name, **Jenő Zádor**), Hungarian-American composer; b. Bátaszék, Nov. 5, 1894; d. Los Angeles, April 4, 1977. He studied music with a local teacher; in 1911, enrolled in the Vienna Cons., and studied composition with Richard Heuberger. From 1912 to 1914 he was in Leipzig, where he took a course with Max Reger; also attended classes in musicology with Hermann Abert and Arnold Schering; continued musicological studies with Fritz Volbach at the Univ. of Münster (Ph.D., 1921, with the diss. *Wesen und Form der symphonischen Dichtung von Liszt bis Strauss*). He settled in Vienna, and taught at the Neues Konservatorium there. Following the Anschluss of Austria by the Nazi regime in 1938, Zádor emigrated to the U.S.; he settled in Hollywood, where he became successful and prosperous as an orchestrator of film scores; made some 120 orchs. in all; at the same time he continued to compose music in every conceivable genre. Zádor was a master of musical sciences, excelling in euphonious modern harmonies, and an expert weaver of contrapuntal voices; his colorful writing for instruments was exemplary. He possessed a special skill in handling Hungarian folk motifs in variation form; in this, he followed the tradition of Liszt. During his European period, he composed some fashionable "machine music," as demonstrated with particular effect in his *Sinfonia tecnica.*

Works: operas: *Diana* (Budapest, Dec. 22, 1923); *A holtak szigete* (The Island of the Dead; Budapest, March 29, 1928); *Revisor* (The Inspector General; 1928; rev. and reorchestrated, Los Angeles, June 11, 1971); *X-mal Rembrandt* (referring to the multiple copies of Rembrandt's self-portraits; Gera, May 24, 1930); *Asra* (Budapest, Feb. 15, 1936); *Christoph Columbus* (N.Y., Oct. 8, 1939); *The Virgin and the Fawn* (Los Angeles, Oct. 24, 1964); *The Magic Chair* (Baton Rouge, La., May 14, 1966); *The Scarlet Mill* (N.Y., Oct. 26, 1968); *Yehu, a Christmas Legend* (1974). **ballet:** *Maschinenmensch* (1934).

orch.: Symphonic poem, *Bánk bán* (1918); 4 syms.: No. 1, *Romantische Symphonie* (1922); No. 2, *Sinfonia tecnica* (Paris, May 26, 1932); No. 3, *Tanzsymphonie* (Budapest, Feb. 8, 1937); No. 4, *Children's Symphony* (1941); *Variations on* *a Hungarian Folk Song* (Vienna, Feb. 9, 1927; his most successful work of this type); *Rondo* (Vienna, 1934); *Hungarian Caprice* (Budapest, Feb. 1, 1935); *Pastorale and Tarantella* (Chicago, Feb. 5, 1942); *Biblical Triptych* (Chicago, Dec. 9, 1943); *Elegie and Dance* (Philadelphia, March 12, 1954); *Divertimento* for Strings (1955); *Fugue-Fantasia* (1958); *Rhapsody* (Los Angeles, Feb. 5, 1961); *Christmas Overture* (1961); *The Remarkable Adventure of Henry Bold* for Narrator and Orch. (Beverly Hills, Calif., Oct. 24, 1963); *Variations on a Merry Theme* (1963; Birmingham, Ala., Jan. 12, 1965); *5 Contrasts for Orchestra* (Philadelphia, Jan. 8, 1965); Trombone Concerto (Rochester, Mich., July 20, 1967); *Rhapsody* for Cimbalom and Orch. (Los Angeles, Nov. 2, 1969); *Studies* (Detroit, Nov. 12, 1970); *Fantasia hungarica* for Double Bass and Orch. (1970); Accordion Concerto (1971); *Hungarian Scherzo* (1975); Concerto for Oboe and Strings (1975). **CHAMBER:** *Chamber Concerto* for Strings, 2 Horns, and Piano (1930); Piano Quintet (1933); *Suite* for Brass (1961); *Suite for 8 Celli* (1966); *Suite* for Woodwind Quintet (1972); Brass Quintet (1973); piano pieces. **VOCAL:** *Cantata tecnica* (1961); *Scherzo domestico* for Chorus (1961); *The Judgement*, oratorio (1974); *Cain*, melodrama for Baritone, Chorus, and Orch. (1976); songs. **BIBL.:** L. Zador, *E. Z.: A Catalogue of His Works* (San Diego, Calif., 1978).

Zadora, Michael (actually, **Michal**), American pianist and composer; b. N.Y. (of Polish parents), June 14, 1882; d. there, June 30, 1946. He studied with his father; then at the Paris Cons. (1899), and later with Leschetizky and Busoni. He taught a master class at the Lemberg Cons. (1911–12); then at the Inst. of Musical Art in N.Y. (1913–14). He transcribed for piano several organ and violin works by Buxtehude and Bach; also composed piano pieces, songs, etc.

Zafred, Mario, Italian composer and conductor; b. Trieste, Feb. 21, 1922; d. Rome, May 22, 1987. He studied with Pizzetti at the Accademia di Santa Cecilia in Rome; was music critic of *Unità* (1949–56) and *Giustizia* (1956–63); then conducted opera in Trieste and in Rome; served as artistic director of the Rome Opera (1968–74). In conformity with his political philosophy of communism, he renounced the modernistic trends of his musical environment, and wrote music in an idiom accessible to the common people. **WORKS: OPERAS:** *Amleto* (Rome, 1961) and *Wallenstein* (Rome, 1965); 7 syms. (1943, 1944, 1949, 1950, 1954, 1958, 1970); *Sinfonia breve* for String Orch. (1955); Flute Concerto (1951); Violin Concerto (1953); Triple Concerto for Violin, Cello, Piano, and Orch. (1954); Harp Concerto (1956); Viola Concerto (1957); Cello Concerto (1958); Piano Concerto (1960); Concerto for 2 Pianos and Orch. (1961); *Metamorfosi* for Orch. (1964); Concerto for Strings (1969); String Sextet (1967); Wind Quintet (1952); 4 string quartets (1941, 1947, 1948, 1953); 3 piano trios (1942, 1945, 1954); 4 piano sonatas (1941, 1943, 1950, 1960); numerous choruses and solo songs.

Zagiba, Franz, eminent Austrian musicologist; b. Rosenau, Oct. 20, 1912; d. Vienna, Aug. 12, 1977. He studied musicology with Dobroslav Orel and received training in Hungarian and Slavonic studies at the Univ. of Bratislava (Ph.D., 1937, with the diss. *Denkmäler der Musik in den Franziskanerklöstern in der Ostslovakei*; publ. in Prague, 1940, as *Hudobné pamiatky františkánskych kláštorov na východnom Slovensku*); completed his Habilitation in 1944 at the Univ. of Vienna with his *Geschichte der slowakischen Musik* (publ. in Bratislava, 1943, as *Dejiny slovenskj hudby od najstarších čias až do reformácie*). After serving as director of the musicological inst. of the Bratislava Academy of Sciences, he joined the faculty of the Univ. of Vienna in 1944, where he became a full prof. in 1972; in 1952 he founded the International Chopin Society. His learned writings ranged from pre-medieval to 20th-century music. **WRITINGS:** *Literárny a hudobný život v Rožňave v 18. a 19. storoči* (Literary and Musical Life in Roznava in the 18th and 19th Centuries; Košice, 1947); *Tvorba sovietskych komponistov*

(The Music of Soviet Composers; Bratislava, 1947); *Chopin und Wien* (Vienna, 1951); *Tschaikowskij: Leben und Werk* (Vienna, 1953); *Die ältesten musikalischen Denkmäler zu Ehren des hl. Leopold: Ein Beitrag zur Choralpflege in Österreich am Ausgang des Mittelalters* (Vienna, 1954); *Johann L. Bella (1843–1936) und das Wiener Musikleben* (Vienna, 1955); *Das Geistesleben der Slaven im frühen Mittelalter: Die Anfänge des slavischen Schrifttums aus dem Gebiete des östlichen Mitteleuropa vom 8. bis 10. Jahrhundert* (Vienna, 1971); *Musikgeschichte Mitteleuropas von den Anfängen bis zum Ende des 10. Jahrhunderts* (Vienna, 1976).

Zagortsev, Vladimir, Russian composer; b. Kiev, Oct. 27, 1944. He studied composition with Boris Lyatoshinsky and Andrei Shtogarenko at the Kiev Cons. Upon graduation, he joined a group of Soviet avant-garde composers who were active in Kiev and who followed the Western techniques. Zagortsev set for himself the task of organizing the elements of pitch, rhythm, dynamics, and tone color in a total serial procedure, but he never abandoned the ethnic resources of Ukrainian folk songs, which remain the thematic source of many of his works, even those written in an extreme modern style. **WORKS:** *Priskazki*, vocal cycle on Ukrainian folk texts (1963); Violin Sonata (1964); String Quartet (1964); *Obyomi* (Sizes) for 5 Instruments (1965); *Gradations* for Chamber Group (1966); *Games* for Chamber Orch. (1967–68); Sym. No. 1 (1968); *Music for 4 Strings* No. 1 (1968); Sonata for Strings, Piano, and Percussion (1969); *Rhythms* for Piano (1969–70); Sym. No. 2 for Soprano, Tenor, and Orch., on Ukrainian folk texts (1976–78); Oboe Sonata (1978); *Music for 4 Strings* No. 2 (1978); *A Day in Pereyaslavl* for Soloists, Chorus, and Orch., on Ukrainian folk texts (1978–79); *In the Children's Room*, cantata on Russian folk texts (1978–79).

Zagrosek, Lothar, German conductor; b. Waging, Nov. 13, 1942. He studied in Munich and at the Essen Folkwangschule; was a pupil of Swarowsky in Vienna, and also received guidance from Karajan and Maderna. He began his career as a conductor in Kiel. In 1977 he became Generalmusikdirektor in Krefeld/Mönchengladbach; also made frequent guest conducting appearances with the London Sinfonietta (from 1978). In 1982 he became chief conductor of the Austrian Radio Sym. Orch. in Vienna; also was music director of the Paris Opéra for a season (1986–87) and principal guest conductor of the BBC Sym. Orch. in London (from 1988). In 1990 he was named chief conductor of the Leipzig City Theater.

Zagwijn, Henri, Dutch composer; b. Nieuwer-Amstel, July 17, 1878; d. The Hague, Oct. 23, 1954. He had no formal education in music, but followed the trends of Impressionism and wrote music in the modern French style. In 1916 he was appointed a teacher at the Rotterdam School of Music; in 1918, founded (with Sem Dresden) the Society of Modern Composers in the Netherlands. From 1931 he was a teacher at the Rotterdam Cons. He was a follower of Rudolf Steiner's anthroposophic movement, and publ. *De muziek in het licht der anthroposophie* (Rotterdam, 1925); also publ. a biography of Debussy (The Hague, 1940). **WORKS:** *Auferstehung*, overture (1918); 2 *concertantes* for Piano and Orch. (1939, 1946); Harp Concerto (1948); String Sextet (1932); Quintet for Flute, Violin, Viola, Cello, and Harp (1937); Trio for Flute, Oboe, and Clarinet (1944); Trio for Violin, Viola, and Cello (1946); Quintet for Flute, Oboe, Clarinet, Horn, and Bassoon (1948); Trio for Flute, Oboe, and Clarinet (1949); 2 string quartets; several albums of piano pieces; choral works; a number of songs; *Musik zur Eurhythmie* (6 books of piano pieces for eurhythmic exercises). **BIBL.:** W. Paap, "H. Z.," *Mens en Melodie* (Sept. 1948; Nov. 1954).

Zahn, Johannes, German composer and music scholar; b. Eschenbach, Aug. 1, 1817; d. Neudettelsau, Feb. 17, 1895. He was a student of theology at the Univ. of Erlangen (1837–41); was director of the teachers' seminary at Altdorf (1854–88). In 1875 he founded the periodical *Siona*, devoted to liturgy and church music. He publ. a valuable work, *Die Melodien der deutschen evangelischen Kirchenlieder, aus den Quellen geschöpft und mitgetheilt* (6 vols., Gütersloh, 1889–93), a compilation of some 9,000 melodies; also various other eds. and publications.

Bibl.: K. Ameln, "J. Z.s Bedeutung für die Erneuerung des evangelischen Kirchenliedes," *Musik und Kirche*, XXIV (1954).

Zajc, Ivan. See **Zaytz, Giovanni von.**

Zajíček, Jeronym, Czech-born American composer; b. Krásné Březno, Nov. 10, 1926. He studied musicology at the Charles Univ. in Prague (1946–49); then served as program director of the Czech section of Radio Free Europe in Munich (1950–52). He emigrated to the U.S. in 1952; studied composition with K. Jirák at Roosevelt Univ. in Chicago (1955–58) and later with Paul Pisk (1959–60). In 1964 he was appointed an instructor in composition and conducting at the Chicago City College. He became a naturalized American citizen in 1957. His music mirrors the lyrical traditions of his Czech heritage.

Works: Variations for Piano (1956–57); Piano Trio (1957); Clarinet Sonata (1957); Sinfonietta (1958); Violin Sonata (1961); String Quartet (1962–63); Concertino for Flute and String Orch. (1963–64; Chicago, Feb. 26, 1967); *Intrada and Processionale* for Brass, Timpani, and Organ (1970); Cello Sonata (1975); songs.

Zak, Yakov (Izrailevich), Russian pianist and teacher; b. Odessa, Nov. 20, 1913; d. Moscow, June 28, 1976. He studied with Starkova at the Odessa Cons., graduating in 1932; then was a student of Neuhaus at the Moscow Cons., graduating in 1935. At the International Competition for pianists in Warsaw in 1937 he received 1st prize and a special award of a posthumous mask of Chopin for his performance of a Chopin mazurka. He joined the faculty of the Moscow Cons. in 1935; became head of the piano dept. there in 1965. As a concert pianist, Zak toured all over Europe. He played in the U.S. in 1965 and 1967, and was acclaimed for his Soviet-like virtuosity. In 1966 he was made a People's Artist of the U.S.S.R.

Zakharov, Vladimir, Russian composer of songs; b. Bogodukhov, Oct. 18, 1901; d. Moscow, July 13, 1956. He studied at the Rostov Cons.; after 1932, devoted himself mainly to the composition of mass songs, derived from the polyphonic essence of Russian folk music and employing asymmetric meters. Of these songs, 2 *Falcons* and *Who Can Tell?* attained immense popularity in Russia. He received several prizes, and was awarded the Order of Lenin.

Zallinger, Meinhard von, Austrian conductor; b. Vienna, Feb. 25, 1897; d. Salzburg, Sept. 24, 1990. He studied piano and conducting at the Salzburg Mozarteum; also took music courses at the Univ. of Innsbruck. He conducted at the Mozarteum (1920–22); then was on the staff of the Bavarian State Opera in Munich (1926–29) and the Cologne Opera (1929–35). He returned to the Bavarian State Opera in 1935, conducting there until 1944; was then made Generalmusikdirektor in Duisburg. In 1947 he became director of the Mozarteum Orch.; also held the same office at the Salzburg Landestheater. He was music director in Graz (1949–50), of the Vienna Volksoper (1950–53), and the Komische Oper in East Berlin (1953–56). He served again as a conductor at the Bavarian State Opera (1956–73); was concurrently director of the summer academy at the Mozarteum (1956–68).

Zamara, Antonio, Italian harpist, pedagogue, and composer; b. Milan, June 13, 1829; d. Hietzing, near Vienna, Nov. 11, 1901. He studied with Sechter at the Vienna Cons.; was solo harpist in the orch. of the Vienna Court Opera (from 1842); also was prof. of harp at the Vienna Cons. He publ. *Harfenschule* (4 books); a number of pieces for Harp Solo (*Barcarolle, La Rêveuse, Chant du berceau, L'Absence, Marche des Croates,* etc.); also pieces for Harp and Cello (*Elégie, L'addio,* etc.) and transcriptions of operatic airs for 2 harps.

Zamboni, Luigi, noted Italian bass; b. Bologna, 1767; d. Florence, Feb. 28, 1837. He made his debut in 1791 in Ravenna

in *Fanatico in Berlina* by Cimarosa; then sang throughout Italy, establishing himself as one of the finest interpreters of buffo roles of his time; 1816 he created the role of Figaro in Rossini's *Il Barbiere di Siviglia.* He retired from the stage in 1825.

Zandonai, Riccardo, Italian composer; b. Sacco di Rovereto, Trentino, May 30, 1883; d. Pesaro, June 5, 1944. He was a pupil of Gianferrari at Rovereto (1893–98); then studied with Mascagni at the Liceo Rossini in Pesaro. He graduated in 1902; for his final examination he composed a symphonic poem for Solo Voices, Chorus, and Orch., *Il ritorno di Odisseo.* He then turned to opera, which remained his favored genre throughout his career. His 1st opera was *La coppa del re* (c.1906), which was never performed. After writing the children's opera *L'uccelino d'oro* (Sacco di Rovereto, 1907), he won notable success with his 3rd opera, *Il grillo del focolare,* after Dickens's *The Cricket on the Hearth* (Turin, Nov. 28, 1908). With his next opera, *Conchita,* after the novel *La Femme et le pantin* by Pierre Louÿs (Milan, Oct. 14, 1911), he established himself as an important Italian composer; the title role was created by the soprano Tarquinia Tarquini, whom Zandonai married in 1917. *Conchita* received its American premiere in San Francisco on Sept. 28, 1912; as *La Femme et le pantin* it was given at the Opéra-Comique in Paris on March 11, 1929. Zandonai's reputation was enhanced by subsequent works, notably *Francesca da Rimini,* after Gabriele d'Annunzio (Turin, Feb. 19, 1914; Metropolitan Opera, N.Y., Dec. 22, 1916), but a previous opera, *Melenis* (Milan, Nov. 13, 1912), was unsuccessful. During World War I, Zandonai participated in the political agitation for the return of former Italian provinces; he wrote a student hymn calling for the redemption of Trieste (1915). His other operas were: *La via della finestra* (Pesaro, July 27, 1919; rev. version, Trieste, Jan. 18, 1923); *Giulietta e Romeo* (Rome, Feb. 14, 1922); *I Cavalieri di Ekebù* (Milan, March 7, 1925); *Giuliano* (Naples, Feb. 4, 1928); *Una partita* (Milan, Jan. 19, 1933); *La farsa amorosa,* after Alarcón's *El sombrero de tres picos* (Rome, Feb. 22, 1933); *Il bacio* (1940–44; unfinished). Among his orch. works were *Serenata medioevale* for Cello, Harp, 2 Horns, and Strings (1909); *Terra nativa,* 2 suites: *Primavera in Val di Sole* (1914–15) and *Autunno fra i monti* (*Patria lontana*) (1917–18); *Concerto romantico* for Violin and Orch. (1919); *Ballata eroica* (1929); *Fra gli alberghi delle Dolomiti* (1929); *Quadri di Segantini* (1930–31); *Il flauto notturno* for Flute and Small Orch. (1934); *Concerto andaluso* for Cello and Small Orch. (1934); *Colombina* overture (1935); *Rapsodia trentina* (1936); *Biancaneve* (1940); works for band; *Messa da Requiem* for Chorus (1915) and various other choral works; several vocal works with orch.; some chamber music. In 1939 he was appointed director of the Liceo Rossini in Pesaro, remaining there for the rest of his life.

Bibl.: "R. Z.," *Bollettino Bibliografico Musicali,* VI/12 (Milan, 1931); V. Bonajuti Tarquini, *R. Z. nel ricordo dei suoi intimi* (Milan, 1951); G. Barblan, R. Mariani, et al., *A R. Z.* (Trento, 1952); B. Cagnoli, *R. Z.* (Trento, 1978); R. Chiesa, ed., *R. Z.* (Milan, 1984); A. Bassi, *R. Z.* (Milan, 1989).

Zandt, Marie Van. See **Van Zandt, Marie.**

Zanella, Amilcare, Italian composer, pianist, and conductor; b. Monticelli d'Ongina, Piacenza, Sept. 26, 1873; d. Pesaro, Jan. 9, 1949. He studied with Andreotti in Cremona, then with Bottesini at the Parma Cons., graduating in 1891. In 1892 he went to South America as a pianist and opera conductor; returning to Italy in 1901, he organized his own orch., giving sym. concerts in the principal Italian cities and introducing his own works. He then was director of the Parma Cons. (1903–5) and the Liceo Rossini in Pesaro (1905–39); also served as pianist of the Trio di Pesaro (1927–49).

Works: **operas:** *Aura* (Pesaro, Aug. 27, 1910); *La Sulamita* (Piacenza, Feb. 11, 1926); *Il Revisore,* after Gogol (1938; Trieste, Feb. 20, 1940). **orch.:** *Concerto sinfonico* for Piano and Orch. (1897–98); *Fede,* symphonic poem (1901); 2 syms.: No. 1 (1901); No. 2, *Sinfonia fantastica* (1919); *Fantasia e grande fugato sinfonico* for Piano and Orch. (1902); *Vita,* symphonic poem (1907); *Fantasia sinfonica* (1918); *Edgar Poe,* symphonic impression (c.1921); *Poemetto* for Violin and Orch. (1922); *Elegia e momento frenetico* for Keyed Xylophone and Strings (1923). **CHAMBER:** 2 piano trios (1899, 1928); Brass Quintet (n.d.); Nonet (1906); 2 string quartets (1918, 1924); Piano Quintet (1917); Sonata for Violin and Piano (1917); Sonata for Cello and Piano (1917); various piano pieces; vocal works, including *Messa di Requiem* for 3 Men's Voices and Organ (1915).

BIBL.: *A. Z., artista, uomo, educatore,* a compendium (Ferrara, 1932); A. Dioli and M. Nobili, *La vita e l'arte di A. Z.* (Bergamo, 1941).

Zanelli (Morales), Renato, esteemed Chilean baritone, later tenor; b. Valparaiso, April 1, 1892; d. Santiago, March 25, 1935. After studies in Neuchâtel and Turin, he pursued a business career in his homeland; his voice was discovered by Angelo Querez, who became his mentor in Santiago; made his debut as a baritone there as Valentine in 1916. On Nov. 19, 1919, he appeared for the 1st time with the Metropolitan Opera in N.Y. as Amonasro; he remained on its roster until 1923; then went to Milan, where he resumed vocal studies; made his debut as a tenor in the role of Raoul at the Teatro San Carlo in Naples in 1924; subsequently appeared in Rome, in London (Covent Garden, 1928–30), at La Scala in Milan (1920–32), and at the Teatro Colón in Buenos Aires. He won great distinction with his portrayals of Othello, Lohengrin, and Tristan.

Zanettini, Antonio. See Gianettini, Antonio.

Zang, Johann Heinrich, German organist and composer; b. Zella St. Blasii, near Gotha, April 13, 1733; d. Würzburg, Aug. 18, 1811. He is said to have been a pupil of Bach in Leipzig (1748–49); received training from J.K. Heller in Coburg; then was in government service in Banz, and served as organist at Hohenstein Castle, near Coburg; was Kantor in Walsdorf, near Bamberg (1751–52) and then in Mainstockheim. His compositions are not extant; ed. the collection *Die singende Muse am Mayn* (1776); publ. *Vollkomne Buttner- oder Kuferlehre* (1796) and a sequel, *Der vollkommene Orgelmacher oder lehre von der Orgel und Windprobe* (1798), the latter appearing as the 2nd part of his *Des Kunst- und Handwerksbuchs.*

Zanger (Zangerus), Johannes, Austrian theologian and musician; b. Innsbruck, 1517; d. Braunschweig, April 5, 1587. He was a pupil of Heinrich Finck, Arnold von Bruck, and others in Vienna, where he also studied at the Univ.; then studied in Prague, and took courses in law at the Univ. of Cologne; finally studied theology at the Univ. of Wittenberg, where he also taught music; in 1545 he settled in Braunschweig, and held various church and school positions. He publ. *Practicae musicae praecepta* (Leipzig, 1554).

BIBL.: H.J. Moser, "J. Z.'s *Praecepta," Musica Disciplina,* V (1951); O. Wessely, "Beiträge zur Lebensgeschichte von J. Z.," *Kongressbericht: Wien Mozartjahr 1956.*

Zangius (Zange), Nikolaus, German organist and composer; b. c.1570; d. Berlin, c.1618. He was a chamber musician in Braunschweig (1597); went to Danzig as deputy Kapellmeister (1599), and soon became Kapellmeister at the Marienkirche; left at the outbreak of the plague in 1602; was active in the imperial court in Prague until 1605; returned to Danzig in 1607, but soon went to Stettin; finally returned to his court post in Prague in 1610. He was active in Berlin as Kapellmeister to the Elector of Brandenburg from 1612. He was a distinguished composer of secular and sacred ensemble songs. For his works, see H. Sachs and A. Pfalz, *Nikolaus Zangius: Geistliche und weltliche Gesange,* Denkmäler der Tonkunst in Österreich, LXXXVII (1951).

BIBL.: J. Sachs, *N. Zanges weltliche Lieder* (diss., Univ. of Vienna, 1934).

Zanten, Cornelie Van. See Van Zanten, Cornelie.

Zappa, Frank (Francis Vincent), seeded American rock artist; b. Baltimore, Dec. 21, 1940, of Italian descent (Zappa means "hoe" in Italian). The family moved to California. From his school days he played guitar and organized groups with weird names such as The Omens and Captain Glasspack and His Magic Mufflers. In 1960 he composed the sound track for the film *The World's Greatest Sinner,* and in 1963 he wrote another sound track, *Run Home Slow.* In 1965 he joined the rhythm-and-blues band The Soul Giants; he soon took it under his own aegis and thought up for it the surrealist logo *The Mothers of Invention.* His recording of it, and another album, *Freak Out!,* became underground hits; along with *We're Only in It for the Money* and *Cruising with Ruben and The Jets,* these works constituted the earliest "concept" albums, touching every nerve in a gradually decivilized California life-style— rebellious, anarchistic, incomprehensible, and yet tantalizing. The band became a mixed-media celebration of total artistic, political, and social opposition to the Establishment, the ingredients of their final album, *Mothermania.* Moving farther afield, Zappa produced a video-movie, *200 Motels,* glorifying itinerant sex activities. He became a cult figure, and as such suffered the penalty of violent adulation. Playing in London in 1971, he was painfully injured when a besotted fan pushed him off the stage. Similar assaults forced Zappa to hire an athletic bodyguard for protection. In 1982 his planned appearance in Palermo, Sicily, the birthplace of his parents, had to be cancelled because the mob rioted in anticipation of the event. He deliberately confronted the most cherished social and emotional sentiments by putting on such songs as *Broken Hearts Are for Assholes,* and his release *Jewish Princess* offended, mistakenly, the sensitivity of American Jews. His production *Joe's Garage* contained Zappa's favorite scatological materials, and he went on analyzing and ridiculing urinary functions in such numbers as *Why Does It Hurt When I Pee.* He managed to upset the members of his own faith in the number titled *Catholic Girls.* His *Hot Rats,* a jazz-rock release, included the famous *Willie the Pimp,* and exploited the natural revulsion to unclean animals. In 1980 he produced the film *Baby Snakes,* which shocked even the most impervious senses. He declared in an interview that classical music is only "for old ladies and faggots." But he astounded the musical community when he proclaimed his total adoration of the music of Edgar Varèse and gave a lecture on Varèse in N.Y. Somehow, without formal study, he managed to absorb the essence of Varèse's difficult music. This process led Zappa to produce truly astonishing full orch. scores reveling in artful dissonant counterpoint, *Bob in Dacron and Sad Jane* and *Mo' 'n Herb's Vacation,* and the cataclysmic *Penis Dimension* for chorus, soloists, and orch., with a text so anatomically precise that it could not be performed for any English-speaking audience.

An accounting of Zappa's scatological and sexological proclivities stands in remarkable contrast to his unimpeachable private life and total abstention from alcohol and narcotic drugs. An unexpected reflection of Zappa's own popularity was the emergence of his adolescent daughter, curiously named Moon Unit, as a voice-over speaker on his hit *Valley Girls,* in which she used the vocabulary of growing womanhood of the San Fernando Valley near Los Angeles, with such locutions as "Grody to the Max" (repellent) and "Barfs Me Out" (disgusting). His son, Dweezil Zappa, is also a musician; his 1st album, *Havin' a Bad Day,* was modestly successful. In 1985 Zappa became an outspoken opponent of the activities of the PMRC (Parents Music Resource Center), an organization comprised largely of wives of U.S. Senators who accused the recording industry of exposing the youth of America to "sex, violence, and the glorification of drugs and alcohol." Their demands to the RIAA (Recording Industry Association of America) included the labeling of record albums to indicate lyric content. Zappa voiced his opinions in no uncertain terms, first in an open letter published in *Cashbox,* and then in one direct to President Reagan; finally, on Sept. 19, 1985, he appeared at the 1st of a series of highly publicized hearings involving the Senate Commerce, Technology and Transporation Committee, the PMRC, and the RIAA, where he delivered a statement to Congress which began "The PMRC proposal is an ill-conceived piece of nonsense which fails to deliver any real benefits to children, infringes the civil liberties of people who are not children and promises to keep the courts busy for years, dealing with the interpretational and enforcemental problems inherent in the proposal's design." Audio excerpts from these hearings can be heard, in original and Synclavier-manipulated forms, on his album *Zappa Meets The Mothers of Prevention*. Other recent recordings which make extensive use of the Synclavier include *Francesco Zappa* and *Jazz From Hell*. With P. Occhiogrosso, he publ. an unrestrained autobiographical vol., *The Real Frank Zappa Book* (N.Y., London, Toronto, Sydney, and Tokyo, 1988), rich in undeleted scatalogical expletives.

BIBL.: N. Obermanns, *Z.log* (Los Angeles, 1981); J. Aikin and B. Doerschuk, "F. Z.: Sample This!," *Keyboard* (Feb. 1987).

Zarate, Eliodoro Ortíz de, Chilean composer; b. Valparaiso, Dec. 29, 1865; d. Santiago, June 27, 1953. He studied in his native city, and at the Milan Cons., graduating in 1888. Returning to Chile, he brought out his opera (to his own libretto in Italian), *La Fioraia di Lugano* (Santiago, Nov. 1, 1895), which was one of the earliest operas, if not the 1st, by a Chilean composer to be produced in Santiago.

Zarębski (Zarembski), Juliusz, Polish pianist and composer; b. Zhitomir, Feb. 28, 1854; d. there, Sept. 15, 1885. He studied piano with Dachs and composition with Krenn at the Vienna Cons., graduating with gold medals in both in 1872, attended classes at the St. Petersburg Cons. (1873), and completed his training with Liszt in Rome (1874); toured as a virtuoso from 1874, and was prof. of piano at the Brussels Cons. (from 1880). He wrote a distinguished Piano Quintet and several effective piano pieces.

BIBL.: T. Strumillo, *J. Z.* (Krakow, 1954).

Zaremba, Nikolai (Ivanovich), Russian composer and pedagogue; b. near Vitebsk, June 15, 1821; d. St. Petersburg, April 8, 1879. He studied piano and cello; then went to Berlin, where he took lessons with Adolf Marx; also attended the Univ. of St. Petersburg. In 1854 he became director of the choral society at the Lutheran church of St. Peter and St. Paul in St. Petersburg; became a teacher of harmony and composition at the St. Petersburg branch of the Russian Musical Society in 1859. When the St. Petersburg Cons. was founded in 1862, he was engaged as a teacher of composition; from 1867 to 1871 he was its director. He was the 1st to teach music theory using Russian terminology rather than the prevalent German nomenclature; among his students was Tchaikovsky. In his musical views Zaremba was extremely conservative; he was also apt to connect harmony rules with religious notions (such as piety being expressed by major keys, and sin and corruption by minor keys). Mussorgsky ridiculed Zaremba in his satirical piece *Rayok*, in which he illustrated Zaremba's Classical tastes by a mock quotation from Handel.

Zarinš, Margeris, Latvian composer; b. Jaunpiebalga, May 24, 1910. He studied composition in Riga with Wihtol at the Latvian Cons. (1929–33); also took lessons in piano and organ. From 1940 to 1950 he was director of music of the Latvian Art Theater. From 1956 to 1968 he was secretary-general of the Union of Latvian Composers. In his works he stylizes the elements of Latvian folk songs; he is particularly successful in his operas on contemporary subjects, often with a satirical tilt. In his *Opera uz lankuma* (Opera in the Town Square; 1970), he attempted to revive the early Soviet attempts to bring theatrical spectacles into the streets.

WORKS: OPERAS: *Kungs un spēlmanitis* (The King and the Little Musician; 1939); *Uz jauno krastu* (To New Shores; 1955); *Zalās dzirnavas* (The Green Mill; 1958); *Nabaqu opera* (Beggar's Opera; 1964); *Sveta Mauricija brinumdarbs* (Miracle of St. Mauritius; 1964); *Opera uz lankuma* (Opera in the Town Square; 1970); oratorios: *Valmieras varoni* (The Heroes of Valmiera; 1950); *Mahagoni* (Mahagonny), a propaganda work denouncing the Western colonial policies in Africa (1965); Piano Concerto (1937); *Greek Vases* for Piano and Orch. (1946; rev.

1960); numerous choruses based on Latvian folk songs; film music.

BIBL.: L. Krasinska, *M. Z.* (Riga, 1960).

Zarlino, Gioseffo (Gioseffe), important Italian music theorist and composer; b. Chioggia, probably Jan. 31, 1517; d. Venice, Feb. 4, 1590. He received his academic training from the Franciscans; his teacher in music was Francesco Maria Delfico. In 1532 he received the 1st tonsure, in 1537 took minor orders, and in 1539 was made a deacon. He was active as a singer (1536) and organist (1539–40) at Chioggia Cathedral. After his ordination, he was elected capellano and mansionario of the Scuola di S. Francesco in Chioggia in 1540. In 1541 he went to Venice to continue his musical training with Willaert; on July 5, 1565, he succeeded his fellow pupil Cipriano de Rore as maestro di cappella at San Marco, holding this position until his death; also was chaplain of S. Severo (from 1565) and a canon of the Chioggia Cathedral chapter (from 1583). His students included G.M. Artusi, Girolamo Diruta, Vincenzo Galilei, and Claudio Merulo. Zarlino's historical significance rests upon his theoretical works, particularly his *Le istitutioni harmoniche* (1558), in which he treats the major and minor thirds as inversions within a fifth, and consequently, the major and minor triads as mutual mirror reflections of component intervals, thus anticipating the modern dualism of Rameau, Tartini, Hauptmann, and Riemann; he also gives lucid and practical demonstrations of double counterpoint and canon, illustrated by numerous musical examples; while adhering to the system of 12 modes, he places the Ionian rather than the Dorian mode at the head of the list, thus pointing toward the emergence of the major scale as the preponderant mode; he gives 10 rules for proper syllabification of the text in musical settings. His *Dimostrationi harmoniche* (1571) was publ. in the form of 5 dialogues between Willaert and his disciples and friends. Zarlino's theories were attacked, with a violence uncommon even for the polemical spirit of the age, by Vincenzo Galilei, his former pupil, in *Dialogo della musica antica e della moderna* (Florence, 1581) and *Discorso intorno alle opere di Gioseffo Zarlino* (Florence, 1589). In reply to the 1st of Galilei's books, Zarlino publ. *Sopplimenti musicali* (1588). In the latter, he suggests equal temperament for the tuning of the lute. As a composer, Zarlino was an accomplished craftsman; he wrote both sacred and secular works.

WRITINGS: *Le istitutioni harmoniche* (Venice, 1558; 3rd ed., rev., 1573; Eng. tr. of part 3 by G. Marco and C. Palisca, 1968, as *The Art of Counterpoint*); *Dimostrationi harmoniche* (Venice, 1571; 2nd ed., 1573); *Sopplimenti musicali* (Venice, 1588); also *De tutte l'opere del r.m.G. Zarlino* (4 vols., 1588–89; contains the 3 preceding vols. with a 4th vol. of non-musical writings).

BIBL.: G. Artusi, *Impresa del molto Rev. M.Gioseffo Z. da Chioggia. . .dichiarata* (Bologna, 1604); G. Ravagnan, *Elogio di Giuseppe Z. e di Cristoforo Sabbadino* (Venice, 1819); F. Caffi, *Della vita e delle opere del prete Gioseffo Z.* (Venice, 1856); V. Bellemo, *Giuseppe Z.: memoria* (Chioggia, 1884); H. Riemann, *Geschichte der Musiktheorie im IX.–XIX. Jahrhundert* (Berlin, 2nd ed., 1921; Eng. tr., 1962); F. Högler, "Bemerkungen zu Z.s Theorie," *Zeitschrift für Musikwissenschaft*, IX (1926–27); H. Zenck, "Z.'s 'Istitutioni harmoniche' als Quelle zur Musikanschauung der italienischen Renaissance," ibid., XII (1929–30); R. Flury, *Gioseffo Z. als Komponist* (Winterthur, 1962); J. Haar, "Z.'s Definition of Fugue and Imitation," *Journal of the American Musicological Society*, XXIV (1971); K. Berger, *Musica Ficta: Theories of Accidental Inflections in Vocal Polyphony from Marchetto da Padova to G. Z.* (Cambridge, 1987); R. Airoldi, *La teoria del temperamento nell'età di G. Z.* (Cremona, 1989).

Zarotus, Antonio, Italian music printer, active in Milan. He printed a *Missale Romanum* dated April 26, 1476, in which he used for the 1st time movable type for the music (the type is in Gothic style). This incunabulum was publ. 6 months earlier than the Missale of Ulrich Han, at one time considered the earliest specimen of music printed from movable type.

BIBL.: O. Kinkeldey, "Music and Music Printing in Incunabula," *Papers of the Bibliographic Society of America* (1932).

Zarth (also **Czard, Czarth, Szarth, Tzarth, Zardt**), **Georg,** Bohemian violinist and composer; b. Hochtann, near Deutschbrod, April 8, 1708; d. probably in Mannheim, after 1778. He first studied with Lukas Lorenz in Deutschbrod; then received training in violin from F. Trimmer and J. Rosetter and in flute from Biarelli in Vienna; there he became a friend of Franz Benda, with whom he remained professionally associated for some 20 years. In 1729 he went to Poland; about 1731 he entered the service of the royal chapel in Warsaw. In 1733 he became a musician in the Dresden Court Orch.; in 1734 he entered the service of the Crown Prince (later Friedrich II the Great of Prussia) in Ruppin; moved with his patron to Rheinsberg in 1736, and then to Berlin in 1740 when Friedrich became King. Zarth went in 1757–58 to Mannheim, where he was a member of the Court Orch. until 1778. He publ. 6 *sonates* for Violin and Basso Continuo, op. 2 (Paris, c.1750; not extant); several sonatas and trios are in MS.

Zarzycki, Alexander, Polish pianist and composer; b. Lemberg, Feb. 21, 1834; d. Warsaw, Nov. 1, 1895. He studied piano with Rudolf Viole in Berlin and composition with N. Reber and K. Reinecke in Paris; began his career in his homeland in 1856 and subsequently gave brilliant concerts in Germany, Austria, and England. He was director of the Warsaw Music Society (1871–75). From 1879 to 1888 he was director of the Warsaw Music Inst. He wrote effective piano pieces (nocturnes, mazurkas, waltzes, etc.); also a Piano Concerto; *Grande Polonaise* for Piano, with Orch.; *Introduction et Cracovienne* for Violin and Orch.; *Suite polonaise* for Orch.; *Mazourka* in G major for Violin, with Orch. (very popular); also 2 albums of songs.

Zaslaw, Neal (Alexander), American musicologist; b. N.Y., June 28, 1939. He studied at Harvard Univ. (B.A., 1961); then took flute lessons at the Juilliard School of Music (M.S., 1963); subsequently studied musicology with Paul Henry Lang at Columbia Univ. (M.A., 1965; Ph.D., 1970, with the diss. *Materials for the Life and Works of Jean-Marie Leclair l'Aîné*). He taught at City College of the City Univ. of N.Y. (1968–70); in 1970 he joined the faculty of Cornell Univ. He was ed.-in-chief of *Current Musicology* (1967–70); publ. the vols. *Edward A. MacDowell* (N.Y., 1964) and *Mozart's Symphonies: Context, Performance Practice, Reception* (Oxford, 1990).

Zavertal, Ladislaw (Joseph Philip Paul; actually, **Josef Filip Pavel),** Czech-born English conductor and composer; b. Milan, Sept. 29, 1849; d. Cadenabbia, Jan. 29, 1942. He was the son of the conductor and composer **Wenceslaw (Václav) Hugo Zavrtal** (b. Polepy, Aug. 31, 1821; d. Leitmeritz, Sept. 8, 1899) and nephew of the conductor and composer **Josef Rudolf Zavrtal** (b. Polepy, Nov. 5, 1819; d. Leitmeritz, May 3, 1893). He began his musical training with his father and his mother, the soprano Carlotta Maironi da Ponte; then studied violin with Tosti at the Naples Cons. His 1st opera, *Tita,* was orchestrated by his father and premiered in Treviso (May 29, 1870); in 1871 he went to Milan as music director of the Teatro Milanese. That same year he went to Glasgow, where he conducted various orch. groups; in 1881 he became bandmaster of the Royal Artillery Band at Woolwich; then was active in London, where he conducted concerts at St. James's Hall and Queen's Hall (1889–95) and Sunday concerts at the Royal Albert Hall (1895–1905); in 1896 he became a British subject; in 1906 he retired to Italy.
    WORKS: OPERAS: *Tita* (Treviso, May 29, 1870; orchestrated by his father; rev. 1880 as *Adriana, ovvero Il burratinaro di Venezia*); *I tre perucchi* (Milan, 1871); *La sura palmira sposa* (Milan, 1872); *Una notte a Firenze* (1872–73; in Czech as *Noc ve Florence,* Prague, March 20, 1880); *A Lesson in Magic* (1880; Woolwich, April 27, 1883; rev. as *Love's Magic,* 1889; Woolwich, Feb. 18, 1890); *Mirra* (1882–83; in Czech, Prague, Nov. 7, 1886). **ORCH.:** 2 syms. (1878–84; 1884); 3 overtures:

Garibaldi (1882; not extant; reconstructed as *Sinfonia patriottica,* 1918); *Loyal Hearts* (1897); *Slavonic Overture* (1898); *Chanson arabe* (1882); *Al fresco* for Strings (1884); *Virtute et valore,* march; also band pieces; Piano Quintet (1877); Piano Quartet (c.1877); choral works.
    BIBL.: "Un ambrosiano" (pseudonym of G. Bampo), *Del maestro di musica milanese Ladislao Z.* (Milan, 1904); A. Faraone, *Il Commendatore Ladislao Z.* (Treviso, 1929); H. Farmer, *Ladislao Z.: His Life and Work* (London, 1949); idem, *Cavaliere Z. and the Royal Artillery Band* (London, 1951).

Zaytz, Giovanni von (real name, **Ivan Zajc**), Croatian composer; b. Fiume, Aug. 3, 1831; d. Zagreb, Dec. 16, 1914. He was trained by his father, a bandmaster in the Austrian army; then at the Milan Cons. with Stefano Ronchetti-Monteviti, Lauro Rossi, and Alberto Mazzucato (1850–55). Returning to Fiume, he conducted the municipal band; then was a theater conductor in Vienna (1862–70). Upon entering professional life, he changed his name to Giovanni von Zaytz. In 1870 he settled in Zagreb; was conductor of the Zagreb Opera (1870–89) and director of the Cons. there (until 1908). He composed about 1,200 works of all descriptions (among them 20 operas), and was the author of the 1st Croatian national opera, *Nikola Šubrič Zrinski* (Zagreb, Nov. 4, 1876). He also wrote several Italian operas, of which *Amelia, ossia Il Bandito* (Fiume, April 14, 1860) enjoyed considerable popularity. Other operas and operettas (all first perf. in Vienna) are: *Mannschaft an Bord* (Dec. 15, 1863); *Fitzliputzli* (Nov. 5, 1864); *Die Lazzaroni vom Stanzel* (May 4, 1865); *Die Hexe von Boissy* (April 24, 1866); *Nachtschwärmer* (Nov. 10, 1866); *Das Rendezvous in der Schweiz* (April 3, 1867); *Das Gaugericht* (Sept. 14, 1867); *Nach Mekka* (Jan. 11, 1868); *Somnambula* (Jan. 21, 1868); *Schützen von Einst und Jetzt* (July 25, 1868); *Meister Puff* (May 22, 1869); *Der gefangene Amor* (Sept. 12, 1874). In addition, he wrote incidental music for 22 plays; 60 cantatas; 250 choral works, sacred and secular; 40 overtures; symphonic poems; more than 200 songs; chamber music; numerous piano pieces.
    BIBL.: A. Goglia, *Ivan pl. Zajc* (Zagreb, 1932); H. Pettan, *Ivan Zajc* (Zagreb, 1971).

Zbar, Michel, French composer; b. Clermont-Ferrand, April 24, 1942. He studied at the Paris Cons. with Olivier Messiaen and Tony Aubin, graduating in 1967; also worked with Pierre Schaeffer at the Groupe de Recherches Musicales of Paris Radio. In 1968 he won the competition for the Prix de Rome with his *Tragédie d'Hamlet.* Other works include *Tropismes* for Violin and Orch. (1969); *Incandescences* for Soprano, Speaker, and Orch. (1970); *Swingle Novae* for the Swingle Singers, Chorus, and 5 Instrumental Groups (1970); *Apex II* for Chamber Orch. (1971); *Negative—Positive* for Ondes Martenot, Electric Guitar, and Percussion (Orléans, March 23, 1973).

Zbinden, Julien-François, Swiss composer; b. Rolle, Nov. 11, 1917. He studied at the Lausanne Cons. (1934–38); also received training in piano in Geneva from Décosterd (1930–35) and Panthés (1940–45), and in counterpoint and orchestration in Neuchâtel from Gerber (1941–45). After playing in jazz orchs., he became a pianist and assistant director of Radio Lausanne in 1947; in 1956 he joined the Service Musical of Radio-Television Suisse Romande.
    WORKS: OPERA: *Fait divers* (1960); farce-ballet, *La Pantoufle,* for 5 Soloists and 2 Pianos (1958); 4 "pièces radiophoniques": *Microbus 666* (1955), *Le Petit Garçon de l'autobus* (1958), *Esperanto* (1961), and *Ethiopiques* (1971–72); Piano Concerto (1944); Concertino for Trumpet, String, and Timpani (1946); *Divertissement* for Double Bass and Orch. (1948); *Concerto da camera* for Piano and String Orch. (1950–51); 2 sym. (1953, 1951–57); *Fantaisie* for Flute and Chamber Orch. (1954); *Suite française* for String Orch. (1954); *Rhapsodie* for Violin and Orch. (1956); *Jazzific 59–16* for Jazz Group and Strings (1958); *Ballade* for Bassoon and Orch. (1961); *Concerto breve* for Cello and Orch. (1962); Violin Concerto (1962–64); *Orchalau-Concerto* for Orch. (1962); *Lémanic 70,* overture (1970); Concerto

for Orch. (1977); *Terra Dei*, oratorio (1966–67); *Monophrases* for Chorus, 2 Pianos, and 6 Percussionists (1970); *Jardins*, suite for Baritone, Soprano, and Orch. (1974); Septet (1947); String Trio (1949); Trio for Trumpet, Horn, and Trombone (1949); Violin Sonata (1950); *3 Pieces* for 4 Horns (1953); *Partita* for Violin and Cello (1954); *Prelude, Fugue and Postlude* for Trumpet and Piano (1963); Capriccio for Flute, English Horn, Bassoon, Violin, and Harpsichord (1968); *Sonate en Trio* for 2 Viole da Gamba and Harpsichord (1969); *Dialogue* for Trumpet and Organ (1972–73); *Introduction and Scherzo-Valse* for Flute and Harp (1974).

Bibl.: H. Jaccard, *Initiation à la musique contemporaine. Trois compositeurs vaudois: Raffaele d'Alessandro, Constantin Regamey, J.-F. Z.* (Lausanne, 1955).

Zeani (real name, **Zahan**), **Virginia**, Rumanian soprano; b. Solovastru, Oct. 21, 1928. She studied in Bucharest with Lipkowska and with Pertile in Milan; made her debut as Violetta in Bologna in 1948; then sang in London (1953), in Rome, at La Scala in Milan (1956), and at Covent Garden in London (1959). She made her Metropolitan Opera debut in N.Y. as Violetta on Nov. 12, 1966. In 1980 she joined the faculty of the Indiana Univ. School of Music in Bloomington. She married **Nicola Rossi-Lemeni** in 1958. Among her finest roles were Lucia, Elvira, Maria di Rohan, Desdemona, Aida, Leonora, and Tosca.

Zecchi, Adone, Italian composer and conductor; b. Bologna, July 23, 1904. He studied composition with Franco Alfano at the Liceo Musicale in Bologna, graduating in 1926; in 1930 he established the Orch. Bolognese de Camera, and also organized the choral group Corale Euridice, which he led from 1927 to 1943; in 1942 he was appointed to the faculty of the Bologna Cons.; he became its director in 1961. In his compositions he follows the path of Italian neo-Classicism, but applies dodecaphonic formulas in some of his music. He publ. a number of manuals on choral conducting, including the reference work *Il coro nella storia e dizionario dei nomi e dei termini* (Bologna, 1960) and *Il direttore di coro* (Milan, 1965). In collaboration with R. Allorto he brought out *Educazione musicale* (Milan, 1962); *Canti natalizi di altri paesi* (Milan, 1965); *Canti natalizi italiani* (Milan, 1965); *Canti della vecchia America* (Milan, 1966); and *Il mondo della musica* (Milan, 1969).

Works: *Partita* for Orch. (1933); *Toccata, Ricercare e Finale* for Orch. (1941); *2 astrazioni in forma di fuga* for Small Ensemble (Copenhagen, June 2, 1947); *Requiem* for Chorus and Orch. (1946); *Caleidofonia* for Violin, Piano, and Orch. (1963); *Trattenimento musicale* for 11 groups of String Instruments (1969).

Zecchi, Carlo, Italian pianist and conductor; b. Rome, July 8, 1903; d. Salzburg, Aug. 31, 1984. He studied at the Liceo and Cons. in Rome, where he received instruction in piano from Bajardi and in composition from Bustini, Refice, and Setaccioli; continued his training with Schnabel and Busoni in Berlin, where he made his debut as a pianist at the age of 17; subsequently toured throughout Europe and the U.S. until giving up his solo career in 1939 to tour in duo recitals with the cellist Enrico Mainardi; also studied conducting with H. Münch and Guarnieri; from 1947 he pursued a successful career as a guest conductor; taught at the Accademia di Santa Cecilia in Rome and also gave summer master classes in Salzburg.

Zech, Frederick, Jr., American pianist and composer; b. Philadelphia, May 10, 1858; d. San Francisco, Oct. 25, 1926. After preliminary training as a pianist in San Francisco he went to Berlin, where he studied at Kullak's Music School (1878–82); returning to San Francisco, he held classes in advanced piano playing; also was director-conductor of his own sym. concerts (1902–3).

Works: OPERAS: *La Paloma, or The Cruise of the Excelsior* (San Francisco, 1896); *Wa-Kin-Yon, or The Passing of the Red Man* (San Francisco, 1914). ORCH.: 5 syms. (c.1883–93); 4 piano concertos (1881–96); 5 symphonic poems (1892–1906); Cello Concerto (1907); Violin Concerto (n.d.). CHAMBER: 3 vio-

lin sonatas (1895–99); 2 string quartets (1897–1902); Piano Quintet (1903); Flute Sonata (1906); Piano Trio (n.d.); also various choruses and songs.

Zechberger, Günther, Austrian conductor and composer; b. Zams, Tirol, April 24, 1951. He studied guitar at the Innsbruck Cons. (1968–74) and music theory at the Univ. of Innsbruck (1974–80); received instruction in conducting from Eric Ericson and Witold Rowicki and in composition from Günther Andergassen and Boguslaw Schaeffer; was founder-conductor of the Tiroler Ensemble für Neue Musik (from 1984).

Works: 2 pieces for Flute, Oboe, Clarinet, and String Quartet (1972–73); Trio for Clarinet, English Horn, and Bassoon (1972–73); Trio for Violins (1975); *Das neue Preislied* for Women's Chorus and Speaker (1975); *O crux ave* for Double Mixed Chorus (1978); *Schlus stück* for Mixed Chorus and Orch. (1979); *Mass* for Mixed Chorus and Orch. (1979); Trombone Quartet (1980); *Stabat Mater* for Mixed Chorus (1981); *Impromptus I-Choral-Impromptus II* for Guitar (1981); *Im Nebel* for Mezzo-soprano and Orch., after Hermann Hesse (1982); *Study* for 12 Strings (1982–83); Sextet for 3 Guitars and 3 Metronomes (1982–83); *Kanon* for 2 Tape Recorders, Musicians, and Audience (1983); *Hendekagon* for 26 Instruments (1983–84); *Tieferschüttert* for Mezzo-soprano, Trombone, and Guitar (1984); String Quartet (1984–85); *Choros* for 5 Musicians (1985); *Stabat Mater II* for Alto, Mixed Chorus, Recorder, Flute, Alto Saxophone, Trombone, Guitar, Violin, and Double Bass (1985–88); *Kammermusik* for Conductor and 5 Musicians (1986); *Dear Mr. J.* (1987); *Interview* for Tape Recorder (1987); Guitar Concerto (1988); Duet for Guitars (1988).

Zechlin, Ruth, German composer and harpsichordist; b. Grosshartmannsdorf, near Freiberg, June 22, 1926. She studied composition with Johann Nepomuk David and Wilhelm Weismann at the Hochschule für Musik in Leipzig, and keyboard playing with Karl Straube, Günther Ramin, and Rudolf Fischer (1943–49). In 1950 she became a lecturer in composition at the Hochschule für Musik in East Berlin; in 1975 she was made a member of the Akademie der Künste in East Berlin. She gave concerts as a harpsichord player; concurrently composed music in all genres; her style of composition follows linear principles with a contrapuntal ornamentation in a quasi-impressionistic vein.

Works: STAGE: Opera for actors, *Reineke Fuchs* (1967); *An Aphrodite*, scenic chamber music for Alto, Baritone, 2 Pantomimists, and 7 Instrumentalists (1976); opera, *Die Salamandrin und die Bildsäule* (1989). ORCH.: *Musik I* (1957) and *II* (1980); *Music for Chamber Orchestra* (1961); Violin Concerto (1963); Suite for Strings (1964); 3 syms. (1965, 1966, 1971); *Amor und Psyche* for Harpsichord and Chamber Orch. (1966); 2 chamber syms. (1967, 1973); *Polyphone Meditationen* for String Orch. (1968); *Thema mit 5 Veränderungen* (1969); *Dynamische Studien* for Chamber Ensemble (1971); *Emotionen* (1971); Piano Concerto (1974); 3 organ concertos (1974; 1975; *Prager Orgelkonzert*, 1980); *Kristalle* for Harpsichord and Strings (1975); *Dionysos und Apollo* for Flute, Strings, and Percussion (1976); *Farbspiele*, after Paul Dessau (1977); *Vita Nova* (1978); *Briefe* (1978); *Szenen*, homage to Shakespeare, for Flute, Oboe, English Horn, Trumpet, and Strings (1978); *Situationen* (1980); *Metamorphosen* (1982); *Kristallisationen* (1987). CHAMBER: Flute Sonatina (1955); Trio for Oboe, Viola, and Cello (1957); 6 string quartets (1959, 1965, 1970, 1971, 1971, 1977); *Stationen* for Wind Quintet and Keyboard Instruments (1972); *17 Kommentare*, inspired by Van Gogh, for String Quartet (1973); *Kammermusik zu Kleists "Marquise von O"* for Oboe, Cello, and Percussion (1974); *Harfentrio* for Flute, Viola, and Harp (1978); *Reflexionen* for 14 Solo Strings (1979); *Beschwörungen* for Percussionist (1980); *Katharsis* for Oboe, Cello, and Percussion (1981); *Erwartungen* for Flute and Bassoon (1984); *Konstellationen* for 10 Wind Instruments (1985); *Synthese* for Organ and Percussion (1986). VOCAL: *Lidice Kantate* for Baritone, Chorus, and Chamber Orch. (1958); *Wenn der Wacholder blüht*, oratorio (1960); *Ode* *an die Luft,* to texts by Neruda, for Mezzo-soprano and Orch. (1962); *Keuner Geschichten,* after Brecht, for Voice and Chamber Ensemble (1966); *Gedanken der Liebe* for Chorus and Orch. (1970); *Canzoni alla Notte,* after Quasimodo, for Baritone and Orch. (1974; Leipzig, Oct. 14, 1976); *Das Hohelied* for Tenor and Orch. (1979); *Hommage à Bach* for Chorus (1985); *Varianten zu Michelangelo* for Mezzo-soprano and Cello (1987); choruses; songs. PIANO: *Suite* (1953); Sonatina (1955); *Kleine Klaviermusik* (1959); *4 Inventionen* (1968); *Konstellationen* (1974); *Stücke für Palucca* (1976). HARPSICHORD: *Toccata und Passacaglia* (1962); *Kontrapunkte* (1970); *Epitaph* (1973); *Hommage à Bettina von Arnim* (1984). ORGAN: *5 Visionen* (1969); *Wandlungen* (1972); *Spektrum* (1973); *Orpheus* (1975).

Zeckwer, Camille, American pianist, teacher, and composer, son of **Richard Zeckwer;** b. Philadelphia, June 26, 1875; d. Southampton, N.Y., Aug. 7, 1924. He was educated by his father, and had the good fortune to take composition lessons in N.Y. with Dvořák (1893–95); then went to Berlin and studied with Philipp Scharwenka; returning to Philadelphia, he was active mainly as a teacher. Like his father, he composed a number of unnecessary orch. and other pieces; his symphonic poem *Sohrab and Rustum* (1915) was performed in Philadelphia on Feb. 4, 1916; he performed his Piano Concerto (1897) thrice with the Philadelphia Orch. (1899, 1904, and 1914); wrote an opera, *Jane and Janetta,* but could not secure a production for it. He also composed another symphonic poem, *Jade Butterflies* (Chicago, March 30, 1922), chamber music, piano pieces, and songs.

Zeckwer, Richard, German-American pianist, teacher, and composer, father of **Camille Zeckwer;** b. Stendal, April 30, 1850; d. Philadelphia, Dec. 30, 1922. He studied piano with Moscheles, and theory with Hauptmann, Richter, and Reinecke at the Leipzig Cons. In 1870 he emigrated to the U.S., and settled in Philadelphia as a piano teacher and church organist. He composed a couple of unnecessary concert overtures and a number of perishable songs; publ. *A Scientific Investigation of Piano-Touch* (1902).

Zedda, Alberto, Italian conductor and musicologist; b. Milan, Jan. 2, 1928. He studied organ with Galliera, conducting with Votto and Giulini, and composition with Fait at the Milan Cons.; in 1956, made his debut as a conductor in Milan. He subsequently went to the U.S., where he taught at the Cincinnati College of Music (1957–59). Returning to Europe, he conducted at the Deutsche Oper in West Berlin (1961–63); then conducted at the N.Y. City Opera. With Philip Gossett, he served as co-ed. of the complete works of Rossini.

Zednik, Heinz, Austrian tenor; b. Vienna, Feb. 21, 1940. He studied voice in Vienna; made his operatic debut in Graz in 1963. He then joined the Vienna State Opera in 1965, and also appeared in Munich, Paris, Nice, and Moscow. From 1970 to 1980 he sang at the Bayreuth Festivals, where he appeared as Loge and Mime in the centennial production of the *Ring* cycle. In 1980 he was made an Austrian Kammersänger.

Zeerleder, Niklaus, Swiss cleric and music theorist; b. Bern, July 5, 1628; d. Kirchberg, July 5, 1691. He was a cantor in Bern, and later in Kirchberg. He publ. a singing instruction book, *Musica figuralis oder Kurtze Gründliche Underweysung der Sing Kunst* (Bern, 1658).

Zeffirelli, Franco (real name, **Gian Franco Corsi**), prominent Italian opera director and designer; b. Florence, Feb. 12, 1923. He began his career as an actor, and then became an assistant to Visconti; his 1st production was *La Cenerentola* at Milan's La Scala (1953). In 1958 he mounted *La Traviata* in Dallas, and in 1959 *Lucia di Lammermoor* at London's Covent Garden, where he later produced *Falstaff* (1961), *Alcina* and *Don Giovanni* (1962), and *Tosca.* He also worked at the Metropolitan Opera in N.Y., where he was chosen to produce Barber's *Antony and Cleopatra* as the opening work at the new house at Lincoln Center in 1966. In later years he devoted himself to operatic film productions, winning particular acclaim for his filming of *La Traviata* (1983) and *Otello* (1986);

he also brought out the film biography *The Young Toscanini* (1988).

Zehnder, Max, Swiss composer; b. Turgi, Canton Aargau, Nov. 17, 1901; d. St. Gallen, July 16, 1972. He studied with Wenz, Lang, Andreae, Vogler, and Laquai at the Zürich Cons. (1923–26); was on the faculty of the Rorschach Training College in Canton St. Gallen (1931–68), where he also conducted its orch. His compositions devloped from a late-Romantic to a neo-Classical style; among them are String Quartet (1928); *Präludium und Chaconne* for Strings (1941); 2 Cantatas (1947, 1960); *In memoriam* for Strings and Organ (1965); *Mouvements* for Strings (1970); various choruses; songs.

Zeidman, Boris, Russian composer and pedagogue; b. St. Petersburg, Feb. 10, 1908; d. Tashkent, Dec. 30, 1981. He studied composition at the Leningrad Cons. with Maximilian Steinberg, graduating in 1931; then taught music in various schools in Russia, Azerbaijan, and Uzbekistan. He performed an important educational service in these regions, formerly deficient in music culture, as teacher and adviser.

WORKS: OPERAS: *The People's Wrath* (Baku, Dec. 28, 1941); *Son of the Regiment* (Baku, Feb. 23, 1955); *Zainab and Omon* (1958); *The Russians* (1970); BALLETS: *The Gold Key* (1955); *The Dragon and the Sun* (1964). ORCH.: 2 piano concertos (1931, 1935); Viola Concerto (1938); Bassoon Concerto (1938); Cello Concerto (1948); *Songs of Struggle* (1966); Violin Concerto (1968); *Days of Spring* (1971). Also chamber music; songs; teaching collections.

Zeinally, Assaf, Azerbaijani composer; b. Derbent, April 5, 1909; d. Baku, Oct. 27, 1932. He studied cello and trumpet at the Baku Cons., graduating in 1931, but died a year later, at the age of 23. He was a highly promising musician; his particular merit was the attempt to compose music in classical forms on folk themes; in this manner he wrote several violin pieces, a Children's Suite for Piano, and many songs to words by native poets.

BIBL.: Kh. Melikov, *A. Z.* (Baku, 1956; 2nd ed., 1969).

Zeisl, Eric(h), Austrian-born American composer; b. Vienna, May 18, 1905; d. Los Angeles, Feb. 18, 1959. A son of prosperous parents who owned a coffeehouse, he entered the Vienna Academy of Music at 14; was a pupil of Richard Stöhr, Joseph Marx, and Hugo Kauder; publ. his 1st songs at 16. In 1934 he won the Austrian State Prize for his *Requiem concertante.* After the seizure of Austria by the Nazis in 1938, he fled to Paris, and at the outbreak of World War II in 1939, went to the U.S.: in 1941 he settled in Los Angeles; in 1945 he became an American citizen. He taught at the Southern Calif. School of Music; from 1949 until his death he was on the staff at Los Angeles City College. Increasingly conscious in exile of his Jewish heritage, he selected biblical themes for his stage works; death interrupted the composition of his major work, the music drama *Job;* Hebraic cantillation is basic to this period. His style of composition reflects the late Romantic school of Vienna, imbued with poetic melancholy, with relief provided by eruptions of dancing optimism. He was at his best in his song cycles.

WORKS: STAGE: *Die Fahrt ins Wunderland,* children's opera (Vienna, 1934); *Leonce und Lena,* singspiel (1937; Los Angeles, 1952); *Job,* opera (1939–41; 1957–59; unfinished); *Pierrot in der Flasche,* ballet (Vienna Radio, 1935); *Uranium 235,* ballet (1946); *Naboth's Vineyard,* ballet (1953); *Jacob und Rachel,* ballet (1954). ORCH.: *Kleine Symphonie* (Vienna Radio, May 30, 1937); *Passacaglia-Fantasie* (Vienna, Nov. 4, 1937); *November,* suite for Chamber Orch. (N.Y., Jan. 25, 1941); *Cossack Dance* (from the unfinished opera *Job,* Los Angeles, Aug. 18, 1946); *Return of Ulysses,* suite for Chamber Orch. (Chicago, Nov. 17, 1948); *Variations and Fugue on Christmas Carols* (1950); Piano Concerto (1951); *Concerto grosso* for Cello and Orch. (1956). CHAMBER: Trio for Flute, Viola, and Harp (1956); Violin Sonata (1950); Viola Sonata (1950); Cello Sonata (1951). VOCAL: *Requiem ebraico* (1945); *Mondbilder* for Baritone and Orch. (1928); choruses; the song cycles *Kinderlieder* for Soprano; *6 Lieder* for Baritone.

BIBL.: M. Cole and B. Barclay, *Armseelchen: The Life and Music of E. Z.* (Westport, Conn., 1984).

Zeisler, Fannie Bloomfield (née **Blumenfeld**), noted Austrian-American pianist; b. Bielitz, Austrian Silesia, July 16, 1863; d. Chicago, Aug. 20, 1927. Her original name was changed when the family settled in Chicago in 1868. Her 1st teachers there were Carl Wolfsohn and Bernhard Ziehn. She made her concert debut in Chicago on Feb. 26, 1875; went to Vienna, where she studied with Leschetizky (1878–83). From 1883 until 1893 she played annually in the U.S.; in 1893 she made a tour of Germany and Austria, which established her reputation as one of the best women pianists; other European tours followed in 1894–95, 1898, 1902–3, 1911–12, and 1914. She then returned to Chicago; made her farewell appearance there on Feb. 25, 1925, in a special concert to mark her golden jubilee. On Oct. 18, 1885, she married Sigmund Zeisler, a Chicago lawyer.

Zeitlin, Zvi, Yugoslav-American violinist and pedagogue; b. Dubrovnik, Feb. 21, 1923. He studied at the Hebrew Univ. in Jerusalem; then was a violin student of Sascha Jacobson, Louis Persinger, and Ivan Galamian at the Juilliard School of Music in N.Y. In 1940 he made his professional debut as soloist with the Palestine Orch.; in 1951 he made his N.Y. debut. He subsequently appeared as a soloist with many orchs., and also gave recitals. In 1967 he joined the faculty of the Eastman School of Music in Rochester, N.Y. He was noted for his intelligent performances of modern violin works.

Zelenka, István, Hungarian composer; b. Budapest, July 30, 1936. He studied at the Budapest Academy of Music and later with Schiske and Jelinek at the Vienna Academy of Music (1956–62); then settled in Switzerland. His works, all in an experimental style, with the application of serial and electronic techniques, include a chamber opera, *Ein Zwischenspiel* (1960); *Conversionen* for 3 String Quartets, Piano, Harmonium, and Harpsichord (1961); *Décors* for Chamber Orch. (1962); *Biais* for Chamber Orch., spatially and serially divided into 3 autochthonic groups (1963); *Hommage à Joan Miró* for Orch. (1965); *Dictionnaire* for Orch. (1967); *A propos Fafner* for Orch. (1971).

Zelenka, Jan Dismas (Lukáš), distinguished Bohemian composer; b. Lounovice, Oct. 16, 1679; d. Dresden, Dec. 22, 1745. He is believed to have studied theory at the Jesuit College Clementinum in Prague; then was in the service of Count Hartig in Prague (1709–10). In 1710 he became a double-bass player in the Dresden Court Orch.; while traveling with the orch., he pursued studies with Fux in Vienna (1715) and with Lotti in Venice (1716); after another sojourn in Vienna (1717–19), he resumed his duties in Dresden, where he later became assistant to the ailing Kapellmeister Heinischen. Upon the latter's death in 1733, J.A. Hasse was named his successor, and the disappointed Zelenka had to wait until 1735 before he received recognition as Kirchen-compositeur. Zelenka was admired by Bach and Telemann. He wrote a large body of sacred vocal music, including the oratorios *Il serpente di bronzo* (1730), *Gesù al Calvario* (1735), and *I Penitenti al sepolchro del Redentore* (1736); the cantatas *Immisit Dominus* (1709), *Attendite et videte* (1712), and *Deus Dux* (1716); several masses and mass movements; 2 Magnificats; and various motets, Psalms, antiphons, hymns, and other pieces. His festival opera, *Sub olea pacis et palma virtutis conspicua Orbi regia Bohemia corona* or *Melodrama de Sancto Wenceslao*, was premiered in Prague on Nov. 12, 1723. Among his instrumental works are 6 sonate for 2 Oboes and Bass, Simphonie *a 8* (Prague, 1723), *Hipocondrie a 7* (Prague, 1723), Concerto *a 8*, and an Overture (Prague, 1723). **BIBL.:** N. Schulzt, *J.D. Z.* (diss., Univ. of Berlin, 1944); W. Reich, *Zwei Z.-Stücken* (Dresden, 1987).

Zeleński, Wladislaw, Polish composer and pedagogue; b. Grodkowice, near Krakow, July 6, 1837; d. Krakow, Jan. 23, 1921. He studied violin with Wojciechowski; then received training in piano from Germasz and in composition from Mirecki in Krakow (1854–59); in 1859 he entered the Jagiellonian Univ. in Prague as a philosophy student (Ph.D., 1862), and pursued training in piano with Dreyschock and in organ and counterpoint with J. Kreiči. After further studies with N.H. Reber at the Paris Cons. (1866), he completed his musical training with Damcke (1868–70). He taught at the Warsaw Music Inst. (1872–81), where he also was music director of the music society. In 1881 he organized the Krakow Cons., and remained its director until his death; he also taught piano and theory there. As a pedagogue, he enjoyed a very high reputation; among his pupils were Stojowski, Opienski, and Szopski. **WORKS: OPERAS:** *Konrad Wallenrod* (Lemberg, Feb. 26, 1885); *Goplana* (Krakow, July 23, 1896); *Janek* (Lemberg, Oct. 4, 1900); *Stara baśń* (Lemberg, March 14, 1907). **ORCH.:** 2 syms. (1871, 1913); 3 overtures (1857; *W Tatrach* [In the Tatras], 1871–72; *Echa lesne* [Echoes of the Woods], n.d.); Piano Concerto (n.d.). **CHAMBER:** 4 string quartets; String Sextet; Piano Trio; 2 violin sonatas; Piano Quartet; numerous piano pieces, including 3 sonatas; also sacred and secular choral works; about 100 solo songs. **BIBL.:** F. Szopski, *W. Z.* (Warsaw, 1928); Z. Jachimecki, *W. Z.; Zycie i twórczość, 1837–1921* (Krakow, 1952).

Železný, Lubomír, Czech composer; b. Ostrava, March 16, 1925; d. Prague, Sept. 27, 1979. He studied composition with Karel Janeček at the Prague Cons. (1945–48) and with Bořkovec at the Prague Academy of Musical Arts (1948–50). He worked in the music dept. of Prague Radio; was chairman of the Union of Czech Composers and Concert Artists (1972–79). **WORKS:** 2 *Gavottes* for Orch. (1954); 2 violin concertos (1958–59; 1974–75); 2 syms.: No. 1 for Large Orch. (1961–62) and No. 2 for Small Orch. (1970); Concerto for Flute, Strings, and Piano (1966); Cello Concerto (1968); *Concertant Music* for Viola, Strings, and Piano (1969); *Festive March* for Orch. (1971); *Brigand Songs* for Tenor and Orch. (1958); Flute Sonata (1943); Trio for Flute, Viola, and Cello (1946); 2 violin sonatas (1948, 1971); Quartet for Flute, Violin, Viola, and Cello (1948); 2 string quartets (1959–60, 1968); Piano Trio (1966); Quintet for 2 Violins, Clarinet, Viola, and Cello (1969); Wind Quintet (1970); choruses; songs.

Zelinka, Jan Evangelista, Czech composer; b. Prague, Jan. 13, 1893; d. there, June 30, 1969. He studied music with his father, the organist and composer, **Jan Evangelista Zelinka** (1856–1935), and later with J.B. Foerster, Suk, Novák, and Ostrčil. **WORKS: OPERAS:** *Dceruška hostinského* (The Tavern-keeper's Little Daughter; 1921; Prague, Feb. 24, 1925); *Devátá louka* (The 9th Meadow; 1929; Prague, Sept. 19, 1931); *Odchod dona Quijota* (Departure of Don Quixote; 1936); *Paličatý švec* (The Stubborn Cobbler; 1940; Prague, March 28, 1944); *Meluzína* (The Wailing Wind; 1947; Plzeň, April 15, 1950); radio opera, *Námluvy bez konce* (Endless Wooing; Czech Radio, Jan. 27, 1950); *Masopustní noc* (Shrovetide Night; 1956); *Lásky žal i smích,* after Goldoni (Love's Woe and Laughter; 1958); *Škola pro ženy,* after Molière (School for Wives; 1959); *Blouznivé jaro* (A Fanciful Spring; 1960); satirical opera, *Dřevěný kůň* (The Wooden Horse; 1962–63); ballet-pantomime, *Skleněná panna* (The Glass Doll; 1927; Prague, July 2, 1928); scenic melodrama, *Srdce na prázdninách* (Heart on a Fishhook; 1932; Brno, Jan. 28, 1938). **ORCH.:** *Overture to a Renaissance Comedy* (1919); *Pariz—Glotton,* overture burlesque (1931); *Weekend,* suite (1939); *Sinfonia rustica* (1956); *A Slovak Summer* (1959); *Musichetta primaverale* for Chamber Orch. (1962); *Satiricon,* suite (1964). Also numerous cantatas; much chamber music, including 2 nonets: *Capriccio* (1937) and *Cassation* (1943); *Late Summer,* piano trio (1949); *Sonata leggera* for Saxophone and Piano (1962); Piano Sonata (1926); organ pieces; songs and incidental music.

Zeljenka, Ilja, Slovak composer; b. Bratislava, Dec. 21, 1932. He studied composition with Cikker, piano with Macudzinski, and esthetics with Ferenczy at the Bratislava Academy of Music and Dramatic Arts (1951–56). He was dramaturge of the Slovak Phil. in Bratislava (1957–61) and lecturer for Bratislava Radio (1961–68); in 1961 he and Ivan Statdrucker established at the Czech Radio in Bratislava the 1st electronic music studio in Czechoslovakia. After a period of infatuation with hedonistic simplicity laced with permissible discords, he turned toward modern sonorism, including electronics.

WORKS: *Suite* for Small Orch. (1952); 2 piano quintets (1953, 1959); 3 syms. (1954; for String Orch., 1960; 1975); *Dramatic Overture* (1955); *Bagatelles* for Piano (1955); *Ballad* for Chorus and Orch. (1957); 2 piano sonatas (1958, 1975); *Oswieczym*, melodrama on the tragedy of the infamous Nazi concentration camp, for 2 Narrators, 2 Choruses, and Orch. (1960; Bratislava, April 29, 1965); 7 *Compositional Studies* for Chamber Ensemble (1962); ballet, *Cosmos* (1962–63); 3 string quartets (1963, 1976, 1979); *Štruktúry* (Structures) for Orch. (1964); *Metamorphoses XV*, after Ovid, for Speaker and 9 Instruments (1964); *Polymetric Quartet* for 4 Piano Parts (1965); *Hudba* (Music) for Chorus and Orch. (1965); Piano Concerto (1966); *Zaklínadlá* (Incantations) for Chorus and Orch. (1967); *Hry* (Games), musical dada for 13 Singers playing Bells and Drums (1968); *Musica polymetrica* for 4 String Quartets (1970); *Meditation* for Orch. (1971); Violin Concerto (1974); Piano Trio (1975); *Elegy* for Chamber Orch. (1975); *Music* for Piano and Strings (1976); Wind Quintet, with Percussion (1977); *Ballet Symphony* (1978); *The Word*, cantata (1980); Piano Concerto No. 2, *Transformations* (1982); Clarinet Concerto (1984); *Talks* for Cello and Chamber Orch. (1984; Bratislava, Sept. 28, 1985); Piano Sonata No. 3 (1985); *Music* for Orch. (1988).

Zelle, Friedrich, German musicologist; b. Berlin, Jan. 24, 1845; d. there, Sept. 10, 1927. He studied piano with Kullak and composition with Geyer and Bellermann; taught at the Humboldt Akademie in Berlin (1875–92) and later was director of the Berlin Realschule (1893–1915). He ed. Hassler's *Lustgarten* (1887), J.W. Franck's *Choral-kantate* (1890), and Keiser's opera *Jodelet* (1892); also Passions by Sebastiani and Theile for Denkmäler Deutscher Tonkunst, 17.

WRITINGS: *Beiträge zur Geschichte der ältesten deutschen Oper:* I, *J.W. Franck* (1889), II, *Joh. Theile und N.A. Strungk* (1891), III, *J.Ph. Förtsch* (1893); *Die Singweisen der ältesten evangelischen Lieder* (1899, 1900); *Theorie der Musik* (1880); *Das erste evangelische Choralbuch* [Osiander, 1586] (1913); *Das älteste lutherische Hausgesangbuch* [the so-called *Färbefass-Enchiridion* of 1524] (1903); *Ballettstücke aus Keiserschen Opern* (1890).

Zeller, Carl (Johann Adam), Austrian composer of operettas; b. St. Peter-in-der-Au, June 19, 1842; d. Baden, near Vienna, Aug. 17, 1898. He learned to sing and play various instruments in his youth; at age 11 he became a member of the boy's choir at the Vienna court chapel; pursued training in law at the Univ. of Vienna and the Univ. of Graz (Dr.Jur., 1869) and in composition from Simon Sechter in Vienna; after practicing law, he was an official in the Austrian Ministry of Education and Culture (from 1873). Although following music only as an avocation, he became one of the most popular operetta composers of the day, winning extraordinary success with his *Der Vogelhändler* (Vienna, Jan. 10, 1891) and *Der Obersteiger* (Vienna, Jan. 5, 1894). Other successful operettas (all produced in Vienna) were *Joconda* (March 18, 1876), *Die Carbonari* (Nov. 27, 1880), *Der Vagabund* (Oct. 30, 1886), and *Der Kellermeister* (Dec. 21, 1901).

BIBL.: C.W. Zeller, *Mein Vater C. Z.* (St. Pölten, 1942).

Zellner, Julius, Austrian pianist and composer; b. Vienna, May 18, 1832; d. Mürzzuschlag, July 28, 1900. He was first engaged in a mercantile career, but abandoned it for music; became successful in Vienna as a teacher and composer.

WORKS: 2 syms.; *Melusine*, symphonic suite; Piano Concerto; Piano Quartet; 3 piano trios; 2 cello sonatas; 2 violin sonatas; piano pieces (*Adagio und Allegro appassionato; 2 kleine*

Suiten; 2 Sonatinen; etc.); piano pieces, 4-hands (3 *deutsche Tänze,* etc.); a puppet play, *Wasserkaspar.*

Zellner, Leopold Alexander, Austrian organist and music editor; b. Agram, Sept. 23, 1823; d. Vienna, Nov. 24, 1894. He studied with his father, organist of the Agram Cathedral; at 15 he became a church organist; taught music in Vienna; founded and ed. the *Blätter für Theater, Musik und bildende Kunst* (1855–68). In 1868 he became a prof. of harmony at the Vienna Cons.; wrote a method for the harmonium, and made improvements in its mechanism; publ. instructive pieces; composed choruses and chamber music. His lectures were publ. as *Vorträge über Akustik* (2 vols., 1892) and *Vorträge über Orgelbau* (1893).

Zelter, Carl Friedrich, eminent German composer and teacher; b. Berlin, Dec. 11, 1758; d. there, May 15, 1832. The son of a mason, he was brought up in the same trade, but his musical inclinations soon asserted themselves; began training in piano and violin at 17; from 1779 he was a part-time violinist in the Doebbelin Theater orch. in Berlin; was a pupil of C.F.C. Fasch (1784–86). In 1786 he brought out a funeral cantata on the death of Frederick the Great; in 1791 he joined the Singverein (later Singakademie) conducted by Fasch, often acting as his deputy, and succeeding him in 1800. He was elected associate ("Assessor") of the Royal Academy of the Arts in Berlin in 1806; became a prof. in 1809. In 1807 he organized a Ripienschule for orch. practice; in 1809 he founded in Berlin the Liedertafel, a pioneer men's choral society which became famous; similar organizations were subsequently formed throughout Germany, and later in America. Zelter composed about 100 men's choruses for the Liedertafel. In 1822 he founded the Royal Inst. for Church Music in Berlin, of which he was director until his death (the Inst. was later reorganized as the Akademie für Kirchen- und Schulmusik). His students included Mendelssohn, Meyerbeer, Loewe, and Nicolai. Goethe greatly admired Zelter's musical settings of his poems, preferring them to Schubert's and Beethoven's; this predilection led to their friendship, which was reflected in a voluminous correspondence, *Briefwechsel zwischen Goethe und Zelter* (ed. in 6 vols. by F.W. Riemer, Berlin, 1833–34; ed. in 3 vols. by L. Geiger, Leipzig, 1906; ed. in 4 vols. by M. Hecker, Leipzig, 1913; Eng. tr. by A.D. Coleridge, London, 1887). His songs are historically important, since they form a link between old ballad types and the new art of the lied, which found its flowering in Schubert and Schumann. Zelter's settings of Goethe's *König von Thule* and of *Es ist ein Schuss gefallen* became extremely popular. He publ. a biography of Fasch (Berlin, 1801). Zelter's autobiography was first publ. under the title *C.F. Zelter. Eine Lebensbeschreibung nach autobiographischen Manuscripten,* ed. by W. Rintel; then as *C.F. Zelter. Darstellungen seines Lebens* (Weimar, 1931).

WORKS: Viola Concerto (1779); various keyboard pieces; much vocal music, including sacred and secular choral works; Lieder: *12 Lieder am Klavier zu singen* (Berlin and Leipzig, 1796); *12 Lieder am Klavier zu singen* (Berlin, 1801); *Sammlung kleiner Balladen und Lieder* (Hamburg, c.1802); *Sämmtliche Lieder, Balladen und Romanzen* (4 vols., Berlin, 1810–13); *Neue Liedersammlung* (Zürich and Berlin, 1821); *6 deutsche Lieder* for Bass and Piano (Berlin, c.1826); *6 deutsche Lieder* for Alto and Piano (Berlin, c.1827); *Täfellieder für 4 Männerstimmen* (Berlin, n.d.); *10 Lieder für Männerstimmen* (Berlin, c.1831); *Liedertafel-Gesänge* (6 vols.); etc.

BIBL.: W. Bornemann, *Die Z.sche Liedertafel in Berlin* (Berlin, 1851); L. Sieber, *C.F. Z. und der deutsche Männergesang* (Basel, 1862); G. Kruse, *Z.* (Leipzig, 1915; 2nd ed., 1921); A. Morgenroth, *C.F. Z.* (diss., Univ. of Berlin, 1922); J.-W. Schottländer, "Z.s Beziehungen zu den Komponisten seiner Zeit," *Jahrbuch der Sammlung Kippenberg,* VIII (1930); H. Moser, "C.F. Z. und das Lied," *Jahrbuch der Musikbibliothek Peters 1932;* G. Schünemann, *C.F. Z., der Begründer der preussischen Musikpflege* (Berlin, 1932); G. Wittmann, *Das klavierbegleitete Sololied K.F. Z.s* (diss., Univ. of Giessen, 1936); G. Schünemann, *C.F. Z.: Der Mensch und sein Werk* (Berlin, 1937); S.

Holtzmann, ed., *C.F. Z. im Spiegel seines Briefwechsel mit Goethe* (Weimar, 1957); W. Reich, ed., *C.F. Z., Selbstdarstellung* (Zürich, 1958); K. Taubert, *C.F. Z.: Ein Leben durch das Handwerk für die Musik* (Berlin, 1958); M. Victor, *C.F. Z. und seine Freundschaft mit Goethe* (Berlin and Weimar, 1958); R. Barr, *C.F. Z.: A Study of the Lied in Berlin during the Late 18th and Early 19th Centuries* (diss., Univ. of Wisconsin, 1968).

Zeltser, Mark, talented Russian-born American pianist; b. Kishinev, April 8, 1947. He began piano lessons with his mother as a small child, and at the age of 9 was a soloist with the Kishinev Phil.; then studied with Flier at the Moscow Cons., graduating in 1971; he won a prize at the Marguerite Long-Jacques Thibaud Competition in Paris, and at the Busoni Competition in Italy; in 1976 he emigrated to the U.S., making his home in N.Y.; in 1977, played at the Salzburg Festival; subsequently was soloist in a series of concerts with Karajan and the Berlin Phil.; also played with the N.Y. Phil., Boston Sym., Cleveland Orch., Chicago Sym., and Philadelphia Orch., and made tours in recitals in Asia, Africa, and Australia.

Zemlinsky, Alexander von, important Austrian composer and conductor of partly Jewish parentage (he removed the nobiliary particle "von" in 1918 when such distinctions were outlawed in Austria); b. Vienna, Oct. 14, 1871; d. Larchmont, N.Y., March 15, 1942. At the Vienna Cons. he studied piano with Door (1887–90) and composition with Krenn, Robert Fuchs, and J.N. Fuchs (1890–92). In 1893 he joined the Vienna Tonkünstlerverein; in 1895 he became connected with the orch. society Polyhymnia, and met Schoenberg, whom he advised on the technical aspects of chamber music; Schoenberg always had the highest regard for Zemlinsky as a composer and lamented the lack of appreciation for Zemlinsky's music. There was also a personal bond between them; in 1901 Schoenberg married Zemlinsky's sister Mathilde. Zemlinsky's 1st opera, *Sarema,* to a libretto by his own father, was produced in Munich on Oct. 10, 1897; Schoenberg made a Klavierauszug of it. Zemlinsky also entered into contact with Mahler, music director of the Vienna Court Opera, who accepted Zemlinsky's opera *Es war einmal* for performance; Mahler conducted its premiere at the Court Opera on Jan. 22, 1900, and it became Zemlinsky's most popular production. From 1900 to 1906 Zemlinsky served as conductor of the Karlstheater in Vienna; in 1903 he conducted at the Theater an der Wien; in 1904 he was named chief conductor of the Volksoper; in 1910 he orchestrated and conducted the ballet *Der Schneemann* by the greatly talented 11-year-old *wunderkind* Erich Korngold. About that time, he and Schoenberg organized in Vienna the Union of Creative Musicians, which performed his tone poem *Die Seejungfrau.* In 1911 Zemlinsky moved to Prague, where he became conductor at the German Opera, and also taught conducting and composition at the German Academy of Music (from 1920). In 1927 he moved to Berlin, where he obtained the appointment of assistant conductor at the Kroll Opera, with Otto Klemperer as chief conductor and music director. When the Nazis came to power in Germany in 1933, he returned to Vienna, and also filled engagements as guest conductor in Russia and elsewhere. After the Anschluss of 1938 he emigrated to America. As a composer, Zemlinsky followed the post-Romantic trends of Mahler and Richard Strauss. He was greatly admired but his works were seldom performed, despite the efforts of Schoenberg and his associates to revive his music. How strongly he influenced his younger contemporaries is illustrated by the fact that Alban Berg quoted some of Zemlinsky's music from the *Lyric Symphony* in his own *Lyrische Suite.*

WORKS: STAGE: OPERAS: *Sarema* (1894–95; Munich, Oct. 10, 1897); *Es war einmal* (1897–99; Vienna, Jan. 22, 1900); *Der Traumgörge* (1903–6; Nuremberg, Oct. 11, 1980); *Kleider machen Leute* (1908; Vienna, Dec. 2, 1910; rev. 1921); *Eine florentinische Tragödie,* after Oscar Wilde (1915–16; Stuttgart, Jan. 30, 1917); *Der Zwerg,* after Oscar Wilde's *The Birthday of the Infanta* (1920–21; Cologne, May 28, 1922); *Der Kreidekreis* (1930–32; Zürich, Oct. 14, 1933); *König Kandaules* (1935–

36; unfinished; completed only in short score); 5 other unfinished operas: *Malwa,* based on Maxim Gorki's short story (1902/1912–13); *Herrn Arnes Schatz* (1917); *Raphael,* based on Balzac's *La Peau de chagrin* (1918); *Vitalis* (1926); *Circe* (1939–41). Ballets: *Das gläserne Herz,* after Hofmannsthal (1901) and *Cymbeline,* incidental music to Shakespeare's play (1914). Also a "mimodrama," *Ein Lichtstrahl* (1903). **ORCH.:** Sym. No. 1 (1892); Sym. No. 2 (1897; Vienna, March 5, 1899); *Die Seejungfrau,* tone poem after Andersen (1903); *Lyrische Symphonie* in 7 sections, after Rabindranath Tagore, for Soprano, Baritone, and Orch. (1922–23; Prague, June 4, 1924); Sinfonietta (1934); overture, *Der Ring des Ofterdingen* (1894–95). **CHAMBER:** *Ländliche Tänze* for Piano (1891); Serenade in A (1892); Suite in A for Violin and Piano (1892); String Quartet (1895); Trio for Clarinet (or Viola), Cello, and Piano (1895); *Fantasien über Gedichte von Richard Dehmel* for Piano (1898); 4 string quartets: No. 1 (1895; Vienna, Dec. 2, 1896); No. 2 (1913–15); No. 3 (1924); No. 4 (1936). **VOCAL:** *Waldgespräch* for Soprano, 2 Horns, Harp, and Strings (1895–96); *Der alte Garten* and *Die Reisen,* to poems by Eichendorff, for Voice and Orch. (1895) *Früglingsbegräbnis* for Chorus, Soloists, and Orch. (1896; Vienna, Feb. 11, 1900); *Frühlingsglaube* for Chorus and Strings (1896); 3 Psalms for Chorus and Orch.: No. 83 (1900); No. 23 (1910); No. 13 (1935); *Maeterlinck Lieder,* 6 songs for Medium Voice and Orch. (1910–13); *Symphonische Gesänge* for Voice and Orch. (1929); 4 vols. of lieder to texts by Heyse and Liliencron (1894–97); also songs to words by Dehmel, Jacobsen, Bierbaum, Morgenstern, Ammann, Heine, George, Kalidasa, Maeterlinck, Goethe, Beer-Hofmann, Baudelaire, and Hofmannsthal (1898–1913; 1929–36).

BIBL.: Special issue of *Der Auftakt,* 1 (Prague, 1921); L. Oncley, "The Works of A. Z.: A Chronological List," *Notes* (Dec. 1977); H. Weber, *A. Z.: Eine Studie* (Vienna, 1977); A. Clayton, "Z.'s One-act Operas," *Musical Times* (Aug. 1983).

Zenatello, Giovanni, Italian tenor; b. Verona, Feb. 22, 1876; d. N.Y., Feb. 11, 1949. He was originally trained as a baritone by Zannoni and Moretti in Verona; made his official debut as such in Belluno in 1898 as Silvio in *Pagliacci;* sang in minor opera companies in Italy; then went to Naples, where he sang the tenor role of Canio in 1899; sang the role of Pinkerton in the 1st performance of Puccini's *Madama Butterfly* (La Scala, Milan, Feb. 17, 1904); in 1905 he sang at Covent Garden, London; on Nov. 4, 1907, made his American debut in N.Y. as Enzo Grimaldo in Ponchielli's *La Gioconda.* From 1909 to 1912, and again in 1913–14, he was the leading tenor of the Boston Opera Co.; during the season of 1912–13 he sang with the Chicago Opera Co; also traveled with various touring opera companies in South America, Spain, and Russia. He eventually settled in N.Y. as a singing teacher, maintaining a studio with his wife, the contralto **Maria Gay,** whom he married in 1913. Together, they trained many famous singers, among them Lily Pons and Nino Martini. He retired from the stage in 1928.

Zenck, Hermann, German musicologist; b. Karlsruhe, March 19, 1898; d. Freiburg im Breisgau, Dec. 2, 1950. He studied with Ordenstein at the Karlsruhe Cons.; pursued training in musicology with Sandberger at the Univ. of Munich and with Kroyer at the Univs. of Heidelberg and Leipzig (Ph.D., 1924; Habilitation, 1929). He became assistant at the Inst. for Musicology in Leipzig, where he also taught at the Cons. In 1932 he joined the faculty of the Univ. of Göttingen; in 1942 went to Freiburg im Breisgau as a prof. at the Univ. there. He ed. the periodical *Musik und Volk;* was ed. of works by Willaert (2 vols., 1937; vol. 3, 1950) and Sixtus Dietrich (1942); also ed. the *Megalynodia* of Praetorius (1934); Johann Schultz's *Musikalischer Lustgarten* (1937); Handel's Italian cantatas, etc. He publ. *Marienklage und Osterspiel des Wolfenbüttler Codex* (Hamburg, 1927).

Zender, (Johannes Wolfgang) Hans, German conductor and composer; b. Wiesbaden, Nov. 22, 1936. He studied at the Frankfurt Hochschule für Musik (1956–59), then received instruction in composition from Fortner at the Freiburg im Breisgau Hochschule für Musik (1959–63); was concurrently a conductor at the city theater; also studied composition with Zimmermann in Rome (1963). He was chief conductor of the Bonn City Theater (1964–68), Generalmusikdirektor in Kiel (1969–71), and chief conductor of the Saarland Radio Sym. Orch. in Saarbrücken (1971–84). Having been a guest conductor at the Hamburg State Opera from 1977, he subsequently served as its Generalmusikdirektor (1984–87); concurrently held that title with the Hamburg State Phil. as well; then conducted the Netherlands Radio Chamber Orch. in Hilversum (from 1987).

WORKS: OPERA: *Stephen Climax*, opera (Frankfurt, June 15, 1986). **ORCH.:** *3 Songs* for Soprano and Orch., after Eichendorff (1964); *Les Sirènes chantent quand la raison s'endort* for Soprano and Instruments (1966); *Canto II* for Soprano, Choir, and Orch. (1967); *Canto III* for Soprano, Tenor, Baritone, and Instruments (1968); *Schachspiel* for 2 Orch. Groups (1969); *Canto IV* for 16 Voices and 16 Instruments (1969–72); *Zeitströme* for Orch. (1974); *Lo-Shu III* for Flute and 24 Instruments (1978); *5 Haiku* for Flute and Strings (1982); *Dialog mit Haydn* for 3 Orch. Groups (1982); *Die Wüste hat zwölf Ding* for Voices and Orch. (1985). **CHAMBER:** *Vexilla Regis* for Soprano, Flute, Trombone, Wind, Kettledrum, and Organ (1964); Quartet for Flute, Cello, Piano, and Percussion (1964); *Canto I* for Various Players (1965); *Bremen Wodu*, electronic study (1967); *Canto V* for Voices (1972–74); *Litanei* for 3 Cellos (1976); *Lo-Shu II* for Flute, "Mondschrift" (1978); *Hölderlin Lesen* for String Quartet and Speaker ad libitum (1979); *Cantata* for Alto, Flute, Cello, and Harpsichord (1980).

Zenger, Max, German composer and conductor; b. Munich, Feb. 2, 1837; d. there, Nov. 18, 1911. He studied in Munich and Leipzig; in 1860 became a theater conductor in Regensburg; in 1869, music director of the Munich Court Opera; then was court conductor at Karlsruhe (1872–78); conductor of the Munich Oratorio Society (1878–85) and other choral societies in Munich. He wrote *Entstehung und Entwicklung der Instrumentalmusik* (Langensalza, 1906) and *Geschichte der Münchener Oper* (ed. by T. Kroyer, 1923).

WORKS: OPERAS: *Die Foscari* (Munich, 1863); *Ruy Blas* (Mannheim, 1868); *Wieland der Schmied* (Munich, 1880; rev. 1894); *Eros und Psyche* (Munich, 1901); oratorio, *Kain*, after Byron (Munich, 1867); secular cantata, *Die Heinzelmännchen*; 2 ballets for King Ludwig II of Bavaria, *Venus und Adonis* and *Les Plaisirs de l'île enchantée* (1881); 2 Gretchen scenes from *Faust* for Soprano and Small Orch.; 2 *Konzertstücke* for Mixed Chorus and String Orch.; *Altgriechisches Liederspiel* for Soprano, Chorus, and Orch.; *Die Kraniche des Ibikus*, melodrama with Orch.; *Die deutsche Flotte* for Men's Chorus and Orch.; Sym.; *Tragische Ouvertüre*; *Adagio concertante* for Cello and Orch.; Piano Trio; Cello Sonata; choruses; piano pieces; songs.

Zeno, Apostolo, famous Italian opera librettist; b. Venice, Dec. 11, 1668; d. there, Nov. 11, 1750. In 1710 he founded the *Giornale dei Letterati d'Italia*; in 1718 he was appointed court poet at Vienna; returned to Venice in 1729. The total number of librettos written by him (some in collaboration with Pietro Pariati) is 71; they were collected and ed. by Gasparo Gozzi as *Poesie drammatiche di Apostolo Zeno* (10 vols., Venice, 1744; reprinted in 11 vols., Orléans, 1785–86). A man of great knowledge and culture, he was also an ardent numismatist; his large collection of coins was exhibited at Vienna in 1955.

BIBL.: M. Fehr, *A. Z. und seine Reform des Operntexts* (diss., Univ. of Zürich, 1912); R. Giazotto, "A. Z., Pietro Metastasio e la critica del settecento," *Rivista Musicale Italiana*, XLVIII (1946), XLIX (1947), L (1948), and LI (1949); R. Freeman, *Opera Without Drama: Currents of Change in Italian Opera, 1675–1725, and the Roles Played therein by Z., Caldara, and Others* (diss., Princeton Univ., 1967).

Zepler, Bogumil, German composer; b. Breslau, May 6, 1858; d. Krummhübel im Riesengebirge, Aug. 17, 1918. He studied architecture in Berlin, then medicine at the Univ. of Breslau (M.D., 1884); later began the study of music with H. Urban in Berlin; he attracted attention in 1891 with *Cavalleria Bero-*

lina, a parody on Mascagni's *Cavalleria rusticana;* wrote stage music for Ernst von Wolzogen's artistic cabaret, "Überbrettl" (1901–2); also wrote a parody on Strauss's *Salome.* He further composed the comic operas *Der Brautmarkt zu Hira* (Berlin, 1892), *Der Vicomte von Letorières* (Hamburg, 1899), *Die Bäder von Lucca* (Berlin, 1905), *Monsieur Bonaparte* (Leipzig, 1911); several operettas (*Diogenes, Pick und Pocket, Die Liebesfestung,* etc.); a serious 1-act opera, *Nacht* (Bern, 1901); 2 pantomimes: *Die Galgenfrist* and *Die Geisterbraut;* songs (*Rokokolieder,* etc.).

Zerrahn, Carl, German-American conductor; b. Malchow, Mecklenburg, July 28, 1826; d. Milton, Mass., Dec. 29, 1909. He studied in Rostock, Hannover, and Berlin; after the revolutionary events of 1848, he emigrated to the U.S. and settled in Boston. He played the flute in the Germania Orch.; then became a professional conductor. For 42 years (1854–96) he led the concerts of the Handel and Haydn Society in Boston, and also conducted the Boston Phil. (1855–63) and the Harvard Musical Assoc. (1865–82). He was music director, from 1866 to 1897, of the prestigious music festivals in Worcester, Mass., and choral director for the famous Peace Jubilee Concerts in Boston in 1869 and 1872, leading the huge choruses assembled on these occasions. From 1867 to 1898 he taught theory and singing at the New England Cons. of Music in Boston.

Zeuner, Charles (actually, **Heinrich Christoph**), German-American organist; b. Eisleben, Saxony, Sept. 20, 1795; d. (suicide) Philadelphia, Nov. 7, 1857. He studied in Weimar with Hummel and with Michael Gottard Fischer in Erfurt. About 1830 he settled in Boston, where he became organist at the Park St. Church; was also organist of the Handel and Haydn Society (1830–37), and briefly its president (1838–39). He then went to Philadelphia, where he served as a church organist. He composed one of the earliest American oratorios, *The Feast of Tabernacles* (1832; Boston, May 3, 1837); publ. *Church Music, Consisting of New and Original Anthems, Motets and Chants* (1831); *The American Harp* (1832); *The Ancient Lyre*, a book of hymn tunes (1833 and several later eds.); *Organ Voluntaries* (1840); contributed to Lowell Mason's *Lyra Sacra* (1832); some of his compositions are also included in *The Psaltery,* ed. by Mason and Webb (1845).

BIBL.: W. Biggers, *The Choral Music of C. Z. (1795–1857), German-American Composer, with a Performance Edition of Representative Works* (diss., Univ. of Iowa, 1976).

Zeuner, Karl Traugott, German pianist and composer; b. Dresden, April 28, 1775; d. Paris, Jan. 24, 1841. He studied with Türk in Halle and Clementi in St. Petersburg; gave concerts and taught in Paris, Vienna, St. Petersburg, and Dresden. He composed 2 piano concertos; 3 string quartets; *Variations on a Russian Theme* for Piano, Violin, and Cello; polonaises, fantasias, etc., for piano; these pieces were much in vogue in his time.

Žganec, Vinko, Croatian ethnomusicologist; b. Vratišinci, Jan. 22, 1890; d. Zagreb, Dec. 12, 1976. He studied law at the Univ. of Zagreb (doctorate, 1919); then became interested in song collecting; traveled in the countryside gathering native melodies; publ. several albums of harmonizations of these songs and numerous articles in Croatian, German, and American music journals dealing with specific aspects of Croatian songs; in his analyses of their structure he applied modern methods of ethnomusicology. He was a lecturer on folk music at the Zagreb Academy of Music (1949–68).

Zhelobinsky, Valeri (Viktorovich), Russian composer; b. Tambov, Jan. 27, 1913; d. Leningrad, Aug. 13, 1946. He received elementary musical training in Tambov; then entered the Leningrad Cons. as a student of Vladimir Shcherbachev (1928–32). He gave piano recitals, playing his own compositions; taught at the Tambov Music School; then returned to Leningrad. During his brief span of life, he composed several operas in a fine Romantic manner, as well as syms. and chamber music.

WORKS: OPERAS: *Kamarinsky muzhik* (Leningrad, Sept. 15, 1933); *Her Saint's Day* (Leningrad, Feb. 22, 1935); *Mother,* after Maxim Gorky (Leningrad, Dec. 30, 1938); operetta, *The Last Ball* (Leningrad, March 30, 1939); 6 syms.: No. 1 (1930); No. 2, *To the Memory of Revolutionary Victims* (1932); No. 3, *Dramatic Symphony* (Moscow, Dec. 17, 1939); No. 4 (Moscow, May 30, 1943); No. 5 (1944); No. 6 (1946); 3 piano concertos (1933, 1934, 1939); Violin Concerto (1934); *Romantic Poem* for Violin and Orch. (1939); 24 *Preludes* for Piano; 2 children's albums for piano; film music.

Zhiganov, Nazib, Russian composer of Tatar heritage; b. Uralsk, Jan. 15, 1911; d. Kazan, June 2, 1988. He was brought up in an orphan asylum; was educated in a music school in Kazan; went to Moscow, where he studied in a technological school; then took courses with Litinsky at the Moscow Cons., graduating in 1938. In 1945 he was appointed director and prof. of the newly founded Cons. of Kazan. In his music he set for himself the task of creating a new national Tatar school of composition, following the harmonic and instrumental precepts of the Russian national school; wrote several successful operas, syms., and symphonic suites on Tatar themes.

WORKS: OPERAS (all 1st perf. in Kazan): *Katchkyn* (June 17, 1939); *Irek* (Liberty; Feb. 24, 1940); *Altyntchetch* (The Golden-haired; July 12, 1941); *Ildar* (Nov. 7, 1942); *Tulyak* (July 27, 1945); *Namus* (Honor; June 25, 1950); ballet, *Zugra* (Kazan, May 17, 1946); 2 *Legends* (1970); cantata, *My Republic* (1960); operatic monologue, *Dzhalil* (1950); 4 syms. (1937, 1968, 1971, 1973); several suites on Tatar themes; chamber music; piano pieces; songs.

BIBL.: Y. Girshman, *N. Z.* (Moscow, 1957).

Zhitomirsky, Alexander, Russian composer and pedagogue; b. Kherson, May 23, 1881; d. Leningrad, Dec. 16, 1937. He took violin lessons in Odessa and in Vienna; also studied piano. Returning to Russia, he entered the St. Petersburg Cons. as a student of Rimsky-Korsakov, Liadov, and Glazunov, graduating in 1910; from 1915 to 1937 he was on its faculty, as an instructor in composition and orchestration. In his compositions he followed the style and manner of the Russian national school; he wrote a Violin Concerto (1937); String Quartet (1923); a number of songs and choruses.

Zhivotov, Alexei, Russian composer; b. Kazan, Nov. 14, 1904; d. Leningrad, Aug. 27, 1964. He studied at the Leningrad Cons. with Vladimir Shcherbachev, graduating in 1930. During the siege of Leningrad by the Nazis (1941–42), he remained in the city and was awarded a medal for valor. Most of his music is set in a lyrical-dramatic vein; he also wrote patriotic songs and choruses.

WORKS: ORCH.: *Dance Suite* (1935); *Romantic Poem* (1940); *Heroic Poem* (1946); *Theater Suite* (1949). VOCAL: *The West*, song cycle with Orch. (1932); *Lyric Etudes* (1934); *Spring* (1942); *Happiness* (1943); *Songs of Leningrad* (1944); also film music.

Zhuk, Isaak, Russian violinist; b. Poltava, Dec. 16, 1902; d. Moscow, April 4, 1973. He studied with I. Goldberg in Poltava, where he made his debut (1917); then with S. Korguyev at the Leningrad Cons. (1924) and A. Yampolsky at the Moscow Cons. (1925–30). He organized the Bolshoi Quartet and was one of its members (1931–68); was concertmaster of the U.S.S.R. Sym. Orch. (1952–69). His son, **Valentin Zhuk** (b. Moscow, June 28, 1934), is a talented violinist; he studied with Yampolsky, and received prizes in various international competitions, including the Tchaikovsky (Moscow, 6th, 1958), Paganini (Genoa, 2nd, 1963), and Long-Thibaud (Paris, 2nd, 1960); he was concertmaster of the Moscow Phil. (from 1970).

Zhukovsky, Herman, Ukrainian composer; b. Radzivilovo, Volynya, Nov. 13, 1913; d. Kiev, March 15, 1976. He studied piano and composition at the Kiev Cons., graduating in 1941; from 1951 to 1958 he taught music theory there. He wrote operas, ballets, symphonic music, and other works in the approved style of socialist realism, using authentic Ukrainian song patterns for his materials, but a crisis supervened in his steady progress when his opera *From the Bottom of My Heart* (Moscow, Jan. 16, 1951) was viciously attacked by the cultural authorities of the Soviet government for alleged ideological and musical aberrations; he revised the score, and the new version was approved. His other operas are *Marina* (Kiev, March 12, 1939); *The First Spring* (1960); *Contrasts of Centuries*, operatic trilogy (1967); monodrama for Baritone, *A Soldier's Wife* (1968); ballets: *Rostislava* (1955); *Forest Song* (Moscow, May 1, 1961); political cantatas: *Oath of the World Youth* (1951); *My Fatherland* (1949); several orch. suites; chamber music; film scores.

Ziani, Marco Antonio, Italian composer, nephew of **Pietro Andrea Ziani;** b. Venice, c.1653; d. Vienna, Jan. 22, 1715. In 1686 he was named maestro di cappella at S. Barbara in Mantua; in 1700 he became Vice-Hofkapellmeister at the Vienna court; in 1712 he was elevated to Hofkapellmeister. He composed 45 operas and serenades, of which the following were produced in Vienna: *Il Giordano pio* (July 26, 1700); *Gli ossequi della notte* (July 22, 1701); *Il Temistocle* (June 9, 1701); *La fuga dell'invidia* (Nov. 15, 1701); *Il Romolo* (June 9, 1702); *Cajo Popilio* (June 9, 1704); *L'Ercole vincitore dell'invidia* (March 19, 1706); *Il Meleagro* (Aug. 16, 1706); *Chilonida* (April 21, 1709); *Il Campidoglio ricuperato* (July 26, 1709); *L'Atenaide* (with Negri, Caldara, and F. Conti; Nov. 19, 1714). He also composed church music.

Ziani, Pietro Andrea, Italian organist and composer, uncle of **Marco Antonio Ziani;** b. Venice, c.1616; d. Naples, Feb. 12, 1684. He took holy orders in 1640; was a canon regular and organist at S. Salvatore in Venice; from 1657 to 1659 he served as maestro di cappella at S. Maria Maggiore in Bergamo; in 1662 he became Vice-Kapellmeister to the Dowager Empress Eleonora in Vienna. In 1669 he succeeded Cavalli as 1st organist at San Marco in Venice; went to Naples in 1677; was named a teacher at the Cons. S. Onofrio there; also became honorary organist at the Naples court, where he was made maestro di cappella in 1680; was pensioned in 1684. He wrote 23 operas, including *Le fortune di Rodope, e di Damira* (Venice, Carnival 1657), *L'Antigona delusa da Alceste* (Venice, Jan. 15, 1660), *La congiura del vizio contra la virtù* (Vienna, Nov. 15, 1663), and *La Circe* (Vienna, June 9, 1665); sonatas for 3, 4, 5, or 6 instruments (1691); church music; etc.

Zich, Jaroslav, Czech musicologist and composer, son of **Otakar Zich;** b. Prague, Jan. 17, 1912. He studied with his father and with J.B. Foerster (1928–31); went to the Charles Univ. in Prague, obtaining a Ph.D. in 1936; then devoted himself to administrative work and program directing at Prague Radio; in 1952 was appointed to the faculty at the Academy of Musical Arts in Prague.

WORKS: *Letmý host* (The Temporary Guest), cycle of songs with Orch. (1932); Duo for Violin and Cello (1932); String Quartet (1932); *Romance helgolandská*, melodrama with Orch. (1934); *U muziky* (At the Dance), 9 dances on folk motifs for Octet (1940); *Rhapsody* for Cello and Orch. (1956); Wind Quintet (1965).

Zich, Otakar, Czech composer and musicologist, father of **Jaroslav Zich;** b: Králové Městec, March 25, 1879; d. Ouběnice, near Benešov, July 9, 1934. He studied mathematics at the Univ. of Prague (Ph.D., 1901); also received training in musicology from Otakar Hostinský and in composition from Stecker (1897–1901); completed his Habilitation at the Univ. of Prague in 1911. After teaching in a secondary school in Domažlice (from 1901), he was made prof. of philosophy at the Univ. of Brno in 1919; from 1924 he was prof. of esthetics at the Univ. of Prague.

WRITINGS: *Smetanova Hubička* (Smetana's The Kiss; Prague, 1911); *Hector Berlioz a jeho Episoda ze života umělcova* (Hector Berlioz and His Episode from the Life of an Artist; Prague, 1914); *České lidové tance s proměnlivým taktem* (Czech Folkdances with a Changing Beat; Prague, 1917); *Symfonické básně Smetanovy* (Smetana's Symphonic Poems; Prague, 1924; 2nd ed., 1949); *Estetika dramatického uměni* (Esthetics of Dramatic Art; Prague, 1931).

WORKS: OPERAS: *Malířský nápad* (Painter's Whim; 1908;

Prague, March 11, 1910); *Vina* (Guilt; 1911–15; Prague, March 14, 1922); *Preciézky,* after Molière's *Les Précieuses ridicules* (1924; Prague, May 11, 1926); also cantatas, song cycles, part-songs, etc. He compiled *Vojenský spěvník československý* (unaccompanied melodies; Prague, 1922).

BIBL.: J. Hutter, *O. Z. a jeho "Vina"* (Prague, 1922); J. Burjanek, *O. Z.: Studie k vývoji českého muzikologického myšleni v prvni třetine našeho stoleti* (O.Z.: A Study of the Development of Czech Musicological Thought in the First Third of This Century; Prague, 1966).

Zichy, Géza, Count Vasony-Keö, Hungarian left-hand pianist and composer; b. Sztára Castle, July 22, 1849; d. Budapest, Jan. 14, 1924. He studied with Volkmann and Liszt. At the age of 14 he lost his right arm in a hunting accident, and, refusing to give up music, developed his left-hand technique to the point of virtuosity; also made arrangements for left hand. On several occasions he played in public with Liszt an arrangement of the *Rákóczy March* for 3 hands. From 1875 to 1918 he was president of the National Cons. in Budapest; was also Intendant of the National Theater and Opera there (1890–94). He composed operas, produced at Budapest: *A vár története* (Castle Story; May 16, 1888); *Alár* (April 11, 1896); *Roland mester* (Jan. 10, 1899); a dramatic trilogy on the life of Rákóczi: *Nemo* (March 30, 1905), *Rákóczi Ferenz* (Jan. 30, 1909), and *Rodostó* (March 20, 1912); ballet, *Gemma* (Prague, 1903); cantata, *Dolores* (1889); Piano Concerto (1902); Piano Sonata; studies and piano pieces for the left hand alone; songs; etc. He publ. an autobiography, *Aus meinem Leben* (German ed., 3 vols., 1911–20).

Ziehn, Bernhard, noted German-American music theorist and teacher; b. Erfurt, Jan. 20, 1845; d. Chicago, Sept. 8, 1912. He studied in Erfurt; was a schoolteacher in Mühlhausen; in 1868 he emigrated to the U.S.; taught German, mathematics, and music theory at the German Lutheran School in Chicago (1868–71); subsequently became a private music teacher, and established himself as a theorist. His "enharmonic law," built on the principle of functional equality of chords, is an original contribution to the theory of harmony.

WRITINGS: *System der Übungen für Clavierspieler* (1881); *Ein Lehrgang für den ersten Clavierunterricht* (1881); *Harmonie- und Modulationslehre* (1887; 2nd ed., 1909; completely recast and publ. in Eng. as *Manual of Harmony: Theoretical and Practical,* 1907); *Five- and Six-Part Harmonies* (1911); *Canonical Studies; A New Technic in Composition* (1912; in both Eng. and German); *Gesammelte Aufsätze zur Geschichte und Theorie der Musik* (Chicago, 1927).

BIBL.: W. Sargeant, "B. Z., Precursor," *Musical Quarterly* (April 1933); H.J. Moser, *B. Z.: Der deutsch-amerikanische Musiktheoretiker* (Bayreuth, 1950).

Ziehrer, Carl Michael, Austrian bandleader and composer; b. Vienna, May 2, 1843; d. there, Nov. 14, 1922. Entirely self-taught in music, he organized in 1863 a dance orch., with which he made tours of Austria and Germany, introducing his own pieces; with an enlarged orch. (50 players), he established a regular series of popular concerts in Vienna, which met with great success; in 1908 he was appointed music director of the court balls. He wrote nearly 600 marches and dances for orch. (some very popular: *Meeresleuchten, Evatöchter, Donauwalzer, Alt-Wien, Ziehrereien,* etc.), and produced in Vienna a number of operettas: *Wiener Kinder* (Feb. 19, 1881); *Mahomeds Paradies* (Feb. 26, 1866); *König Jerôme* (Nov. 28, 1878); *Ein Deutschmeister* (Nov. 30, 1888); *Der schöne Rigo* (May 24, 1898); *Die Landstreicher,* his best work (July 29, 1899); *Die drei Wünsche* (March 9, 1901); *Der Fremdenführer* (Oct. 11, 1902); *Der Schätzmeister* (Dec. 10, 1904); *Fesche Geister* (July 7, 1905); *Am Lido* (Aug. 31, 1907); *Ein tolles Mädel* (Nov. 8, 1907); *Der Liebeswalzer* (Oct. 24, 1908); *Die Gaukler* (Sept. 6, 1909); *Herr und Frau Biedermeier* (Oct. 5, 1910); *In 50 Jahren* (Jan. 7, 1911); *Fürst Casimir* (Sept. 13, 1913); *Der Husarengeneral* (Oct. 3, 1913); *Das dumme Herz* (Feb. 27, 1914); *Die verliebte Eskadron* (July 11, 1920).

BIBL.: M. Schönherr, *C.M. Z.* (Vienna, 1973); idem, *C.M. Z.: Sein Werk, sein Leben, seine Zeit* (Vienna, 1975).

Zielinski, Jaroslaw de, Polish-American pianist and composer; b. Lubycza Królewska, Galicia, March 31, 1844; d. Santa Barbara, Calif., July 25, 1922. He studied piano with Mikuli in Lemberg and Schulhoff in Vienna; took part in the Polish uprising against Russia in 1863; was severely wounded; went to the U.S. in 1864, enlisted in a Mass. regiment, and served to the end of the Civil War; subsequently was active as a pianist and teacher in N.Y., Detroit, and Buffalo; eventually settled in California, where he founded the Zielinski Trio Club. He publ. some graceful piano music (*Prelude, At the Spring, Gavotte, Minuet, Bourrée, Dreams,* mazurkas, etc.).

Zilcher, Hermann (Karl Josef), German composer; b. Frankfurt am Main, Aug. 18, 1881; d. Würzburg, Jan. 1, 1948. He studied piano with his father, Paul Zilcher, a music teacher; later at the Hoch Cons. in Frankfurt with Kwast (piano), and Knorr and B. Scholz (composition). From 1901 to 1905 he was in Berlin as a concert pianist and teacher; from 1905 to 1908, taught piano at the Hoch Cons.; from 1908 to 1920, was a prof. at the Akademie der Tonkunst in Munich; from 1920, was director of the Würzburg Cons. and conductor of the sym. concerts there; retired from the Cons. in 1944. He toured as a pianist; also in the U.S. (1905, with Franz von Vecsey).

WORKS: Incidental music for Shakespearean plays: *As You Like It* (1917), *The Winter's Tale* (1919), *The Taming of the Shrew* (1926), and *A Comedy of Errors* (1934); operas: *Fitzebutze* (1903) and *Doktor Eisenbart* (Mannheim, 1922); *Liebesmesser,* oratorio (Strasbourg, 1913); 5 syms. (No. 5, 1947; Hamburg, Feb. 11, 1948); Double Concerto for 2 Violins and Orch.; Violin Concerto; Piano Concerto; chamber music; many piano pieces; about 150 songs; etc.

BIBL.: W. Altmann, *H. Z.* (Leipzig, 1907); H. Oppenheim, *H. Z.* (Munich, 1921).

Zillig, Winfried (Petrus Ignatius), German conductor and composer; b. Würzburg, April 1, 1905; d. Hamburg, Dec. 17, 1963. He studied at the Würzburg Cons. and with Schoenberg in Vienna (1925–26) and in his master classes at the Prussian Academy of Arts in Berlin (1926–28). After working as répétiteur in Oldenburg (1928–32), he conducted in Düsseldorf (1932–37); was music director of the Essen Opera (1937–40), the Poznán Opera (1940–43), and the Düsseldorf Opera (1946–47); then was chief conductor of the Hesse Radio in Frankfurt (1947–51). He was director of the music division of the North German Radio in Hamburg from 1959 to 1963.

WORKS: OPERAS: *Rosse* (Düsseldorf, Feb. 11, 1933); *Das Opfer* (Hamburg, Nov. 12, 1937); *Die Windsbraut* (Leipzig, May 12, 1941); *Troilus und Cressida* (1949; rev. 1963); *Bauernpassion,* television opera (1955); *Die Verlobung in St. Domingo,* radio opera (1956); *Das Verlöbnis* (1962; Linz, Nov. 23, 1963); incidental music. **ORCH.:** *Choralkonzert* (1924); Overture (1928); Concerto for Orch. (1930); Concerto for Cello and Wind Orch. (1934; rev. 1952); Concerto in One Movement (1948); Violin Concerto (1955); *Fantasia, Passacaglia, and Fugue on the Meistersinger Chorale* (1963); other orch. works; choral and solo vocal works; chamber music.

WRITINGS: *Variationen über neue Musik* (Munich, 1959; 2nd ed., 1963, as *Die neue Musik: Linien und Porträts; Von Wagner bis Strauss* (Munich, 1966).

Ziloti, Alexander. See **Siloti, Alexander.**

Zimbalist, Efrem (Alexandrovich), eminent Russian-born American violinist and pedagogue; b. Rostov-on-the-Don, April 21, 1889; d. Reno, Nev., Feb. 22, 1985. He studied violin with his father, an orch. musician; from 1901 to 1907 he was a pupil of Leopold Auer at the St. Petersburg Cons., graduating with the gold medal. He made a highly successful European appearance as a soloist in the Brahms Concerto in Berlin, Nov. 7, 1907. In 1911 he emigrated to the U.S.; made his American debut with the Boston Sym. Orch. on Oct. 27, 1911, playing the first American performance of Glazunov's Violin

Concerto. In 1914 he married the singer **Alma Gluck,** who died in 1938; his 2nd wife, whom he married in 1943, was Mary Louise Curtis Bok, founder of the Curtis Inst. of Music in Philadelphia; in 1928 he joined its faculty; was its director from 1941 to 1968. After Mrs. Zimbalist's death in 1970, he moved to Reno, Nev., to live with his daughter. His son, Efrem Zimbalist, Jr., is a well-known actor. Zimbalist was also a composer. He wrote the opera *Landara* (Philadelphia, April 6, 1956); a musical comedy, *Honeydew* (N.Y., 1920); *Slavonic Dances* for Violin and Orch. (1911); *American Rhapsody* for Orch. (Chicago, March 3, 1936; rev. version, Philadelphia, Feb. 5, 1943); *Portrait of an Artist,* symphonic poem (Philadelphia, Dec. 7, 1945); Violin Concerto (1947); Cello Concerto (1969); String Quartet; Violin Sonata; *Concert Phantasy on Le Coq d'or* for Violin and Piano; *Sarasateana* for Violin and Piano; songs; etc. He publ. *One Hour's Daily Exercise* for the violin.

BIBL.: B. Schwarz, *Great Masters of the Violin* (N.Y., 1983).

Zimerman, Krystian, outstanding Polish pianist; b. Zabrze, Dec. 5, 1956. He commenced piano lessons at age 5 with his father; when he was 7 he became a pupil of Andrzej Jasiński, with whom he later studied at the Katowice Cons. In 1975 he won 1st prize in the Chopin Competition in Warsaw; then played with great success in Munich, Paris, London, and Vienna. In 1976 he was a soloist with the Berlin Phil. He made his 1st American appearance in 1978, and subsequently toured throughout the world to great critical acclaim. His performances of the Romantic repertory are remarkable for their discerning spontaneity.

BIBL.: K. Monson, "A Compelling Communicator: K. Z.," *Ovation* (April 1987); H. Robinson, "K. Z.," *Musical America* (May 1987).

Zimmer, Friedrich, German composer, son of **Friedrich August Zimmer;** b. Gardelegen, Sept. 22, 1855; d. Giessen, Dec. 5, 1919. He studied theology; publ. several collections of Lutheran hymns; composed choruses and songs for children. He was greatly esteemed as an educator.

BIBL.: W. Stölten, *F. Z., Ein deutscher Volkserzieher* (Berlin, 1933).

Zimmer, Friedrich August, German organist and music educator, father of **Friedrich Zimmer;** b. Herrengosserstädt, Thuringia, Feb. 26, 1826; d. Berlin, Feb. 8, 1899. He studied in Weissenfels; then devoted himself principally to teaching. He publ. the manuals *Elementarmusiklehre, Violin-Schule,* and *Die Orgel.*

Zimmer, Ján, significant Slovak composer; b. Ružomberok, May 16, 1926. He studied piano, organ, and composition with Suchoň at the Bratislava Cons. (graduated, 1948), with Farkas at the Budapest Academy of Music (1948–49), and in Salzburg (1949); taught theory and piano at the Bratislava Cons. (1948–52). An accomplished pianist, he limits himself to the performance of his own compositions, either at solo concerts or with orchs.

WORKS: 7 piano sonatas (1948, 1961, 1965, 1971, 1978, 1980, 1988); 2 *Tatras Suites* for Piano (1951–52, 1956); Concerto for Solo Piano (1956); 2 *Pieces* for 2 Pianos, 8-hands (1969); 2 *by Piano* for Piano, 4-hands (1973); 7 piano concertos: No. 1 (1949; Bratislava, March 14, 1950); No. 2 (1952); No. 3 (1958; Bratislava, Jan. 14, 1960); No. 4 (1960; Bratislava, Oct. 11, 1962); No. 5, for left hand alone (1964; Bratislava, June 3, 1965); No. 6 (1972); Concerto for 2 Pianos and Orch. (1967; Bratislava, Nov. 3, 1968); No. 7 (1985); *Concerto grosso* for 2 Pianos, 2 String Orchs., and Percussion (1950–51); *Rhapsody* for Piano and Orch. (1954); Concertino for Piano and Strings (1955; Prague, Feb. 17, 1957); *Small Fantasy* for Piano and Orch. (1960); 12 syms.: No. 1 (1955; Bratislava, Dec. 2, 1956); No. 2 (1957–58); No. 3 (1959); No. 4, for Soprano, Tenor, Mixed Chorus, and Orch. (1959; Bratislava, Feb. 2, 1961); No. 5 (1961; Bratislava, March 3, 1963); No. 6, *Improvisata* (1964–65); No. 7 (1966; Bratislava, March 4, 1967); No. 8 (1971); No. 9 (1973); No. 10 for Chamber Orch. (1976);

No. 11 (1981); No. 12 for Orch. and Tape (1986); Piano Quintet (1949–50); *Magnificat,* cantata (1951); *The Peace* for Male Choir and Orch. (1954); Violin Concerto (1953; Bratislava, May 4, 1956); *Insurrection,* cantata (1954); Concerto for Organ, Strings, and Percussion (1957; Bratislava, Dec. 5, 1957); *Ahasver,* opera (1957; unfinished); *Suite* for Violin and Piano (1957); Solo Violin Sonata (1958); *Fantasy and Toccata* for Organ (1958); *Strečno,* symphonic poem (1958); 3 string quartets (1960, 1984, 1987); *The Dove of Peace,* small cantata (1960); Concerto for Solo Organ (1960); *Concerto da camera* for Oboe and Strings (1962); *Oedipus Rex,* opera (1963–64); *The Dead Do Not Return,* oratorio (1968); *French Suite* for Chamber Orch. (1968); Organ Sonata (1970); *Héraklés,* opera (1972); *Concerto polyphonico* for Organ and Orch. (1986); Concerto for Viola and Chamber Orch. (1989); songs; music for films.

Zimmerman, Franklin B(ershir), American musicologist; b. Wauneta, Kans., June 20, 1923. He was educated at the Univ. of Southern Calif. in Los Angeles (B.A., 1949; M.A., 1952; Ph.D., 1958, with the diss. *Purcell's Musical Heritage: A Study of Musical Styles in 17th-century England*) and at Oxford Univ. (B.Litt., 1956). He taught at the State Univ. of N.Y. in Potsdam (1958–59) and at the Univ. of Southern Calif. (1959–64); then was prof. of music at Dartmouth College (1964–67), the Univ. of Kentucky (1967–68), and the Univ. of Pa. (from 1968). He devoted much time to the study of English Baroque music, particularly the life and works of Purcell.

WRITINGS: *Henry Purcell, 1659–1695: An Analytical Catalogue of His Music* (London, 1963); *Henry Purcell, 1659–1695: His Life and Times* (London, 1967; 2nd ed., rev., 1983); *Henry Purcell, 1659–1694: Melodic and Intervallic Indexes to His Complete Works* (Philadelphia, 1975); *Henry Purcell: A Guide to Research* (N.Y., 1988).

Zimmerman, Pierre-Joseph-Guillaume, famous French piano teacher and composer; b. Paris, March 19, 1785; d. there, Oct. 29, 1853. The son of a Paris piano maker, he entered the Paris Cons. in 1798, studying under Boieldieu, Rey, Catel, and Cherubini; won 1st prize for piano in 1800, and for harmony in 1802; became a prof. of piano at the Cons. in 1816, and was pensioned in 1848. Among his many pupils were Alkan, Marmontel, Lacombe, Ambroise Thomas, and César Franck. His chief work is the *Encyclopédie du pianiste,* a complete method for piano, part III of which is a treatise on harmony and counterpoint.

WORKS: Opera, *L'Enlèvement* (Paris, Oct. 26, 1830); 2 piano concertos; Piano Sonata; 24 études; etc.

BIBL.: J. Labat, *Z. et l'Ecole française de piano* (Paris, 1865).

Zimmermann, Agnes (Marie Jacobina), German-English pianist and composer; b. Cologne, July 5, 1845; d. London, Nov. 14, 1925. As a young girl she went to England, and at 9 became a student of Cipriani Potter and Charles Steggall at the Royal Academy of Music in London, where she later studied with Ernst Pauer (piano) and G. Macfarren (composition). She made her debut at the Crystal Palace on Dec. 5, 1863; toured England with excellent success; was praised for her fine renditions of classical works. She ed. the sonatas of Mozart and Beethoven and the complete piano works of Schumann (for Novello). She was also a competent composer; wrote a Piano Trio; 3 violin sonatas; a Cello Sonata; and many playable piano pieces.

BIBL.: Lady Arbuthnot, "In Memoriam A. Z.," *Musical Times* (1926).

Zimmermann, Anton, Austrian composer; b. Pressburg, 1741; d. there, Oct. 16, 1781. He was organist at St. Martin's Church in Pressburg; in 1776 he was named Kapellmeister and court composer to Count Joseph Batthyany, the Archibishop (later cardinal) of Hungary.

WORKS: STAGE: *Narcisse et Pierre* (singspiel; Pressburg, 1772; not extant); *Andromeda und Perseus* (melodrama; Vienna, April 23, 1781); *Zelmor und Ermide* (melodrama; n.d.). **ORCH.:** About 25 syms. (serenatas); concertos; also much chamber music, including various nocturnes, cassations, 12 string quintets, 6 string quartets, sonatas, etc.; much sacred music.

Zimmermann, Bernd (actually, **Bernhard**) **Alois,** important German composer; b. Bliesheim, near Cologne, March 20, 1918; d. (suicide) Königsdorf, Aug. 10, 1970. He studied at the Cologne Hochschule für Musik and at the Univs. of Cologne and Bonn until he was drafted for military service during World War II; after his discharge, he became a pupil of Lemacher and Jarnach (1942); later attended the summer courses in new music of Fortner and Leibowitz in Darmstadt (1948–50). He taught theory at the Univ. of Cologne (1950–52) and at the Cologne Hochschule für Musik (1957–70). Plagued by failing eyesight and obsessed with notions of death, he reflected these moods in his own music of the final period; his *Requiem für einen jungen Dichter* was written to texts by various poets, all of whom committed suicide; he killed himself shortly after the completion of this morbid score. His idiom of composition is mainly expressionistic, with a melodic line of anguished chromaticism which does not preclude the observance of strict formal structures in his instrumental works. While in his lifetime he was primarily known to limited music circles in Germany, the significance of his music began to be realized after his death.

WORKS: *Alagoana* (*Caprichos brasileiros*), ballet (1940–43; 1947–50; Essen, Dec. 17, 1955; ballet suite, Hamburg, Nov. 21, 1953); *Lob der Torheit,* burlesque cantata after Goethe (1948; Cologne, May 25, 1948); Concerto for String Orch. (1948; rescoring of a discarded string trio of 1942–43); Violin Sonata (1949); Violin Concerto (1949–50; Baden-Baden, Dec. 10, 1950; an orchestration and rev. of the Violin Sonata); *Rheinische Kirmestänze* for 13 Winds (1950; rev. 1962); Solo Violin Sonata (1951); Sym. in 1 movement (1947–52; rev. 1953; Brussels, Nov. 20, 1953); *Enchiridion,* small piece for Piano (1949–52); Concerto for Oboe and Small Orch. (1952; Donaueschingen Festival, Oct. 1952); *Kontraste,* music for an imaginary ballet, for Orch. (1953; orch. suite, Hamburg, 1953; ballet, Bielefeld, April 24, 1954); *Nobody Knows de Trouble I See,* concerto for Trumpet and Orch. (1954; Hamburg, Oct. 11, 1955); Solo Viola Sonata (1955); *Konfigurationen,* 8 pieces for Piano (1954–56); *Perspektiven,* music for an imaginary ballet, for 2 Pianos (1955; ballet version, Düsseldorf, June 2, 1957); *Canto di speranza,* cantata for Cello and Small Orch. (1952–57; Baden-Baden Radio, July 28, 1958); *Omnia tempus habent,* cantata for Soprano and 17 Instruments (1957); *Impromptu* for Orch. (1958); *Vocal Symphony* for 5 Soloists and Orch. (1959; scenes from the opera *Die Soldaten*); *Die Soldaten,* opera in 4 acts after J.M.R. Lenz (1958–60; rev. 1963–64; Cologne, Feb. 15, 1965); Solo Cello Sonata (1959–60); *Dialoge,* concerto for 2 Pianos and Orch., in homage to Debussy (1960; rev. 1965; original version, Cologne Radio, Dec. 5, 1960); *Présence,* "ballet blanc" in 5 scenes for Piano Trio (1961; Darmstadt, Sept. 8, 1961); *Antiphonen* for Viola and 25 Instrumentalists, some of whom speak a text drawn from Joyce, Dante, Dostoyevsky, Camus, and Novalis (1961; Zürich, 1966); *5 capricci di G. Frescobaldi,* "La Frescobalda," for 3 Recorders, Oboe d'Amore, 3 Viole da Gamba, Lute, 3 Trumpets, and 3 Trombones (1962); *Tempus loquendi,* "pezzi ellittici" for Flauto Grande, Flute in G, and Bass Flute, for 1 Performer (1963); *Monologe* for 2 Pianos (1960–64; version of *Dialoge*); Concerto for Cello and Orch., in the form of a "pas de trois" (1965–66; concert version, Strasbourg, April 8, 1968; ballet version, Wuppertal, May 12, 1968); *Tratto I* and *II* for Tape (in the form of a choreographic study, 1966; 1968); *Musique pour les soupers du Roi Ubu,* "ballet noir" in 7 parts and an entrée, for Orch. (1966; Düsseldorf, 1968); *Intercomunicazione* for Cello and Piano (1967); *Ode to Eleutheria* in the form of death dances from music for the radio play *Die Befristeten* for Jazz Quintet (1967); *Photoptosis,* prelude for Orch. (1968; Gelsenkirchen, Feb. 19, 1969); *Requiem für einen jungen Dichter,* "lingual" for Narrator, Soprano, and Baritone Soloists, 3 Choruses, Tape, Orch., and Jazz Combo, and Organ, to texts drawn

from various poems, articles, and news reports (1967–69; Düsseldorf, Dec. 11, 1969); 4 short *Studies* for Cello (1970); *Stille und Umkehr,* sketch for Orch. (1970; Nuremberg, March 19, 1971); *Ich wandte mich und sah an alles Unrecht das geschah unter der Sonne,* "ecclesiastical action" for 2 Narrators, Bass, and Orch. (1970; Kiel, Sept. 2, 1972).

WRITINGS: *Intervall und Zeit: Aufsätze und Schriften zum Werk* (Mainz, 1974).

BIBL.: W. Konold, ed., *B.A. Z.: Dokumente und Interpretationen* (Cologne, 1986); idem, *B.A. Z.:Der Komponist und sein Werk* (Cologne, 1986).

Zimmermann, Frank Peter, German violinist; b. Duisburg, Feb. 27, 1965. As a child he took violin lessons with his mother, making his public debut with the Duisburg Sym. Orch. at 10; then studied with W. Gradow at the Essen Folkwang-Musikhochschule and with H. Krebbers at the Robert-Schumann-Institut of the Düsseldorf Hochschule für Musik. In 1979 he appeared at the Lucerne Festival; made his British debut as soloist with the Royal Phil. at the Portsmouth Festival in 1981; toured the Soviet Union in 1984. In the same year, he made his U.S. debut as soloist with the Pittsburgh Sym. Orch., and thenceforth continued his successful career.

Zimmermann, Louis, Dutch violinist and composer; b. Groningen, July 19, 1873; d. Amsterdam, March 6, 1954. He studied at the Leipzig Cons. with Hans Sitt and Carl Reinecke; also with Eugène Ysaÿe in Brussels. He was a member of the Concertgebouw Orch. in Amsterdam (1899–1904); taught violin at the Royal College of Music in London (1904–9); then rejoined the Concertgebouw as its concertmaster, retiring in 1940. He wrote numerous violin pieces; also cadenzas for the violin concertos by Beethoven and Brahms.

Zimmermann, Udo, German composer; b. Dresden, Oct. 6, 1943. He studied composition with J.P. Thilman at the Hochschule für Musik in Dresden (1962–68); from 1968 to 1970, attended the master classes in composition of Günter Kochan at the Akademie der Künste in East Berlin. From 1970 to 1985 he was composer and producer at the Dresden State Opera; in 1974 he founded the Studio of New Music in Dresden. In 1978 he became a prof. of composition at the Dresden Hochschule für Musik, and in 1982 was appointed prof. of the experimental music theater there. In 1986 he became director of the Dresden Center for Contemporary Music. His music follows the median course of restrained ultramodernism, with a democratically equal treatment of formerly disallowed dissonances.

WORKS: OPERAS: *Die weisse Rose* (Dresden, 1967); *Die zweite Entscheidung* (Magdeburg, 1970); *Levins Mühle* (1972–73; Dresden, March 27, 1973); *Der Schuhu und die fliegende Prinzessin* (1975); *Die wundersame Schustersfrau* (1978–82); *Die weisse Rose* (a different work from his 1st opera of the same title; Hamburg, Feb. 27, 1986); *Die Sündflut* (Cologne, 1988). **ORCH.:** *Dramatische Impression auf den Tod von J.F. Kennedy* for Cello and Orch. (1966; originally written immediately after Kennedy's assassination in 1963, for Cello and Piano); *Musik für Streicher* (1967); *Sieh, meine Augen,* reflections for Chamber Orch. (1970); *Mutazioni* (1972; Dresden, Oct. 26, 1973); *Sinfonia come un grande lamento,* in memory of Federico García Lorca (1977); *Songerie* for Chamber Orch. in memory of Karl Böhm (1982); Piano Concerto (Leipzig, April 19, 1987); Horn Concerto (1987); *Nouveau divertissement,* viola concerto (1988). **VOCAL:** *5 Songs,* after Borchert, for Baritone and Orch. (1964); *L'Homme,* cantata (1969; Dresden, Sept. 22, 1972); *Der Mensch,* cantata for Soprano and 13 Instrumentalists (1969); *Ein Zeuge der Liebe besingt den Tod* for Soprano and Chamber Orch. (1971; Frankfurt, March 11, 1973); *Psalm der Nacht,* after Sachs, for 17-voice Female Choir, Percussion, and Organ (1973); *Ode an das Leben,* to texts by Neruda and Carus, for Mezzo-soprano, 3 Choruses, and Orch. (1974); *Hymnus an die Sonne,* after Kleist, for Soprano, Flute, and Harpsichord (1976); *Pax questuosa* for 5 Soloists, 3 Choirs, and Orch. (1980). **CHAMBER:** *Movimenti caratteristici* for Cello (1965); *Sonetti amorosi* for Contralto,

Flute, and String Quartet (1967); *Choreographien nach Edgar Degas* for 21 Instrumentalists (1974).

BIBL.: F. Hennenberg, *U. Z., für Sie portratiert* (Leipzig, 1983).

Zimmermann, Walter, German composer; b. Schwabach, April 15, 1949. He studied piano, violin, and oboe, and began to compose at the age of 12. He was a pianist in the "arsnova-ensemble" of Nuremberg (1968–70) while studying composition with Werner Heider and with Otto Laske at the Institut voor Sonologie in Utrecht. Subsequently he attended the Ethnological Center Jaap Kunst in Amsterdam (1970–73). He went to the U.S. to study computer music in 1974, and spent 2 years performing and absorbing new ethnic styles. He returned in 1977 to Germany, where he opened the Beginner Studio in a former factory in Cologne, specializing in concerts of novel music. He also lectured at the Darmstadt summer courses (1982) and at the Liège Cons. (from 1982). His compositions include a number of short works scored for varied ensembles, and grouped under quite general titles.

WORKS: *Lokale Musik,* 15 works for Various Forces (1977–81); *Über die Dörfer,* dramatic song for Soprano, Chorus, and Orch. (1985–86); *Fragmente der Liebe* for Saxophone, Clarinet, Soprano, and String Quartet (1987).

Zinck, Bendix (actually, **Benedikt**) **Friedrich,** German instrumentalist and composer, brother of **Hardenack Otto Conrad Zinck;** b. Husum, Holstein (baptized), March 8, 1743; d. Ludwigslust, Mecklenburg, June 23, 1801. He studied violin, harpsichord, and organ with his father, the town musician Bendix Friedrich Zinck; was a violinist in the Ludwigslust Hofkapelle (1767–1801); also toured as a violinist and keyboard artist in Europe. In 1781 he married the court singer Charlotte Nussbaum (1760–1817). Among his works are 15 syms., vocal pieces, and chamber music.

Zinck, Hardenack Otto Conrad, German instrumentalist, singer, teacher, and composer, brother of **Bendix (Benedikt) Friedrich Zinck;** b. Husum, Holstein, July 2, 1746; d. Copenhagen, Feb. 15, 1832. He began his training with his father, the town musician Bendix Friedrich Zinck, and later studied with C.P.E. Bach in Hamburg. In 1777 he became 1st flutist and chamber musician in the Ludwigslust Hofkapelle; in 1787 he was named Singmeister (1st accompanist) in the Copenhagen Hofkapelle; also was active as a church organist and teacher in Copenhagen, where he founded a Singakademie (1800). He produced an opera to a Danish text, *Selim og Mirza* (Copenhagen, Feb. 1, 1790); also composed several oratorios and cantatas, lieder, instrumental music, etc.; publ. *Die nördliche Harfe, ein Versuch in Fragmenten und Skizzen über Musik und ihre Anwendung im Norden* (Copenhagen, 1801; on Scandinavian music) and *Vorlesungen über Musik und ihre nützlichste Anwendung* (Copenhagen, 1813).

Zingarelli, Nicola Antonio, Italian composer and pedagogue; b. Naples, April 4, 1752; d. Torre del Greco, near Naples, May 5, 1837. He studied at the Cons. S. Maria di Loreto in Naples with Fenaroli, Speranza, Anfossi, and Sacchini. His 1st stage work, *I quattro pazzi,* was performed at the Cons. in 1768. After finishing school in 1772, he earned his living as a violin teacher. He spent much time traveling throughout Italy, supervising the production of his operas. In 1793 he was appointed maestro di cappella at the Cathedral of Milan; in 1794, at the Santa Casa in Loreto; in 1804, at the Sistine Chapel in the Vatican. In 1811, for refusing to conduct a Te Deum to celebrate the birthday of Napoleon's son, the "King of Rome," he was imprisoned at Civitavecchia, and later transported to Paris by order of Napoleon, who set him at liberty and liberally paid him for a Mass written in Paris. As Fioravanti had meanwhile become maestro di cappella at St. Peter's, Zingarelli went to Naples, and in 1813 became director of the royal Collegio di Musica; in 1816 he succeeded Paisiello as maestro di cappella at the Naples Cathedral. He was renowned as a teacher; Bellini, Mercadante, Carlo Conti, Lauro Rossi, Morlacchi, and Sir Michael Costa were his students. His operas,

interpreted by the finest singers of the time (Catalani, Crescentini, Grassini, Marchesi, and Rubinelli), were highly successful. His facility was such that he was able to write an opera in a week. He wrote 37 operas in all.

WORKS: OPERAS (all 1st perf. at La Scala in Milan): *Alsinda* (Feb. 22, 1785); *Ifigenia in Aulide* (Jan. 27, 1787); *La morte de Cesare* (Dec. 26, 1790); *Pirro, re d'Epiro* (Dec. 26, 1791); *Il mercato di Monfregoso* (Sept. 22, 1792); *La secchia rapita* (Sept. 7, 1793); *Artaserse* (Dec. 26, 1793); *Giulietta e Romeo,* after Shakespeare (Jan. 30, 1796; his best-known work; staged all over Europe, and also in N.Y., with considerable success, but disappeared from the repertoire after Zingarelli's death); *Meleagro* (Jan. 1798); *Il ritratto* (Oct. 12, 1799); *Clitennestra* (Dec. 26, 1800); *Il bevitore fortunato* (Nov. 1803); other operas: *I quattro pazzi* (Naples, 1768); *Montezuma* (Naples, Aug. 13, 1781); *Ricimero* (Venice, May 5, 1785); *Armida* (Rome, Carnival 1786); *Antigono* (Mantua, April 13, 1786); *Artaserse* (Trieste, March 19, 1789); *Antigone* (Paris, April 30, 1790); *Pharamond* (1790); *Annibale in Torino* (Turin, Carnival 1792); *Atalanta* (Turin, Carnival 1792); *L'oracolo sannita* (Turin, Carnival 1792); *La Rossana* (Genoa, Carnival 1793); *Apelle* (Venice, Nov. 18, 1793; rev. as *Apelle e Campaspe,* Bologna, 1795); *Gerusalemme distrutta* (Florence, 1794); *Alzira* (Florence, Sept. 7, 1794); *Quinto Fabio·* (Livorno, 1794); *Il conte di Saldagna* (Venice, Dec. 26, 1794); *Gli Orazi e i Curiazi* (Naples, Nov. 4, 1795); *Andromeda* (Venice, 1796); *La morte di Mitridate* (Venice, May 27, 1797); *Ines de Castro* (Milan, Oct. 11, 1798); *Carolina e Mexicow* (Venice, Carnival 1798); *I veri amici repubblicani* (Turin, Dec. 26, 1798); *Il ratto delle Sabine* (Venice, Dec. 26, 1799); *Edipo a Colono* (Venice, Dec. 26, 1802); *La notte dell'amicizia* (Venice, Carnival 1802); *Il ritorno di Serse* (Modena, July 16, 1808); *Baldovino* (Rome, Feb. 11, 1811); *Berenice, regina d'Armenia* (Rome, Nov. 12, 1811); *Malvina* (Naples, Carnival 1829; in collaboration with M. Costa). **ORATORIOS:** *Pimmalione* (Naples, 1779); *Ero* (Milan, 1786); *Telemaco* (Milan, 1787); *Il trionfo di David* (Naples, 1788); *Francesca da Rimini* (Rome, 1804); *Tancredi al sepolcro di Clorinda* (Naples, 1805); *La fuga in Egitto* (Naples, 1837); a vast amount of church music; the Cons. di Loreto contains 541 MSS by Zingarelli, in a collection known as "Annuale di Zingarelli" (or "Annuale di Loreto"), including a series of masses for every day in the year; a 4-part *Miserere* "alla Palestrina" (1827); 73 Magnificats, 28 Stabat Maters, 21 Credos, many Te Deums, motets, hymns, etc.; also syms., solfeggi, arias, organ sonatas, some chamber music.

BIBL.: R. Liberatore, *Necrologia di N. Z.* (Naples, 1837); A. Schmid, *Joseph Haydn und N. Z.* (Vienna, 1847); S. di Giacomo, "Il fiero Z.," *Musica d'Oggi* (June 1923); P. Dotto, "N. Z.," ibid. (July 1941); R. Longyear, "The Symphonies of N. Z.," *Analecta Musicologica,* No. 19 (1979).

Zingel, Rudolf Ewald, German organist and composer; b. Liegnitz, Sept. 5, 1876; d. there, Feb. 20, 1944. He studied at the Hochschule für Musik in Berlin; then was active as a church organist and choral conductor in Berlin and in Frankfurt an der Oder. He wrote 2 operas, *Margot* (Frankfurt an der Oder, 1902) and *Persepolis* (Rostock, 1909); an operetta, *Liebeszauber* (Stralsund, 1908); symphonic poem, *Freudvoll und liedvoll;* secular oratorio, *Der wilde Jäger;* several sacred cantatas for men's chorus and string orch.; numerous piano pieces and songs.

Zinkeisen, Konrad Ludwig Dietrich, German violinist and composer; b. Hannover, June 3, 1779; d. Braunschweig, Nov. 28, 1838. He was trained by his father, and by Rode at Wolfenbüttel; played first violin under Forkel at the Academic Concerts in Göttingen; in 1819 he was appointed a chamber musician in the Braunschweig court orch. He wrote 6 violin concertos, 4 orch. overtures, 3 string quartets; concertos for oboe, for clarinet, for basset horn, and for bassoon; and various other pieces for solo instruments with orch.; music for military band; choral works.

Zinman, David (Joel), talented American conductor; b. N.Y., July 9, 1936. He studied violin at the Oberlin Cons. (B.M.,

1958), and composition at the Univ. of Minnesota (M.A., 1963); took lessons in conducting at the Berkshire Music Center at Tanglewood, and with Pierre Monteux at his summer school in Maine; from 1961 to 1964 he was Monteux's assistant. After a successful engagement as guest conductor with the Nederlands Kamerorkest, he served as its conductor from 1965 to 1977. In 1972 he was appointed music adviser to the Rochester (N.Y.) Phil.; then was its music director (1974–85); also served as chief conductor of the Rotterdam Phil. (1979–82). He was principal guest conductor (1983–85) and then music director (from 1985) of the Baltimore Sym. Orch. He appeared as a guest conductor with various orchs. in North America and Europe, becoming well known for his performances of the Classical and Romantic repertory.

Zinnen, Jean-Antoine, Luxembourg composer; b. Neuenbourg, April 25, 1827; d. Neuilly-sur-Seine, May 16, 1898. He was the composer of the National Hymn of Luxembourg (1864); wrote several operettas. In 1881 he went to Paris. After his death, his remains were taken to Luxembourg. A postage stamp in his honor was issued in 1950.

Zipoli, Domenico, Italian composer and organist; b. Prato, Oct. 16, 1688; d. Santa Catalina, near Córdoba, Argentina, Jan. 2, 1726. He studied in Florence, then with A. Scarlatti in Naples, L.F. Vannucci in Bologna, and B. Pasquini in Rome, where he became organist at the Jesuit Church in 1715. His oratorios *Sant' Antonio di Padova* (1712) and *Santa Caterina, vergine, e martire* (1714) were presented in Rome. In 1716 he publ. *Sonate d'intavolatura per organo e cimbalo.* He joined the Jesuit order at Seville in 1716; in 1717, went to South America, where he became organist of the Jesuit church in Córdoba, Argentina. Walsh of London reprinted parts of the *Sonate d'intavolatura* under the titles *Six Suits of Italian Lessons for the Harpsichord* and *Third Collection of Toccatas, Vollentarys and Fugues.*

Bibl.: L. Ayestarán, *D. Z., el gran compositor y organista romano del 1700 en el Rio de La Plata* (Montevideo, 1941; radically rev. and amplified, Montevideo, 1962); A. Salazar, "El Caso de D. Z.," *Nuestra Musica* (Mexico, May 1946); V. de Rubertis, "Dove e quando nacque e morì D. Z.," *Rivista Musicale Italiana* (April–June 1951); S. Erickson-Bloch, *The Keyboard Music of D. Z.* (diss., Cornell Univ., 1975).

Zipp, Friedrich, German composer, organist, and pedagogue; b. Frankfurt am Main, June 20, 1914. He studied at the Hoch Cons. in Frankfurt (1933–34) and in Berlin at the Univ. and at the Staatliche Hoschule für Musik, where his composition teacher was Knab; in 1947 he became a teacher and in 1962 a prof. at the Staatliche Hochschule für Musik in Frankfurt; also was active as an organist. He composed *Musik* for Orch. (1936); *Sinfonietta* for Youth Orch. (1958); *Kirchensuite* for String Orch. (1962); String Quartet (1943); *Au clair de la lune* for Oboe and Piano (1963); numerous choral pieces and songs. He publ. *Vom Wesen der Musik* (Heidelberg, 1974).

Zítek, Otakar, Czech music critic and composer; b. Prague, Nov. 5, 1892; d. Bratislava, April 28, 1955. He studied composition with Novák at the Prague Cons. and musicology with Guido Adler and Grädener at the Univ. of Vienna. Upon graduation he wrote music criticism for the *Hudební Revue* and the *Lidové Noviny* in Prague; gave lectures on opera at the Prague Cons.; then was administrator at the National Theater in Brno (1921–29); taught at the Brno Cons. (1931–39). From 1939 to 1941 he was in the Buchenwald concentration camp, but was released, and worked as a theater director in Plzeň (1941–43); supervised opera theaters in Prague and Brno (1946–49). He composed the operas *Vznesene srdce* (The Exalted Heart; 1918) and *Pád Petra Králence* (The Downfall of Peter Králence; Brno, March 23, 1923); a ballet after Wilde's *Birthday of the Infanta* (Pilsen, 1942); *Město,* symphonic poem (1925); songs; etc. He publ. *O novou zpěvohru* (On New Opera; Prague, 1920).

Ziv, Mikhail, Russian composer; b. Moscow, May 25, 1921. He studied at the Moscow Cons. with Kabalevsky; graduated in 1947. As a composer, Ziv devoted himself mainly to the musical theater; wrote the comic operas *Son of a King's Minister* (1973) and *Gentlemen Artists* (1980); several fairy tales for children; 3 syms. (1946, 1960, 1968); 2 sinfoniettas (1958, 1962); 2 string quartets (1945, 1955); Piano Quintet (1947); many choruses, piano pieces, and songs; film music.

Živković, Milenko, Serbian composer; b. Belgrade, May 25, 1901; d. there, June 29, 1964. He studied at the Stanković Music School in Belgrade and graduated in law from the Univ. of Belgrade (1924); then studied composition with Grabner at the Leipzig Cons. (1925–29) and d'Indy at the Paris Schola Cantorum (1929–31). Returning to Belgrade, he was director of the Stanković Music School (1937–47); taught at the Academy of Music (1945–64); was rector and prof. of composition there (1952–60). A follower of the national school of composition, he wrote music permeated with ethnic Balkan melorhythms. His works include: *Symphonic Prologue* (Belgrade, April 16, 1935); *Zelena godina* (Green Year), folk ballet scenes for Orch. (Belgrade, April 27, 1937); several suites of Yugoslav dances for piano, and numerous choruses.

Zmeskall, Nikolaus (Paul), Edler von Domanovecz, Hungarian diplomat and musical amateur; b. Lestine (baptized), Nov. 20), 1759; d. Vienna, June 23, 1833. He served as secretary of the Hungarian Chancellery in Vienna (1784–1825), and was a close friend of Beethoven, who dedicated to him the String Quartet, op. 95. Zmeskall was also a composer in his own right; he wrote 16 string quartets and other instrumental music.

Bibl.: A. Sandberger, *Beethovens Freund Z. als Komponist* (Munich, 1924); C. Pidoll, *Verklungenes Spiel: Erinnerungen des Herrn N. Z.* (Innsbruck, 1949).

Znosko-Borovsky, Alexander, Russian composer; b. Kiev, Feb. 27, 1908; d. there, March 8, 1983. He studied violin and composition at the Kiev Cons.; then was active as a composer for films (1931–41). In 1941 he left Kiev, threatened by the Nazi invasion, and went to Ashkhabad, Turkmenia; was instrumental in promoting indigenous music culture there; several of his works are based on Turkmenian themes.

Works: Ballet, *Akpamyk* (Ashkhabad, April 14, 1945); cantata, *Our Victory* (Kiev, May 8, 1946); 3 syms. (1958, 1960, 1967); symphonic poem, *Kiev* (Kiev, March 9, 1949); Violin Concerto (Kiev, Dec. 17, 1955); symphonic poem, *At the Mausoleum* (1960); String Quartet on Ukrainian themes (1937); String Quartet on Turkmenian themes (1942); Sonata for Unaccompanied Violin (1950); *Scherzo* for 3 Trombones (1938); various pieces for different instruments.

Zoeller, Carli (Karl), German-English violist, bandmaster, and composer; b. Berlin, March 26, 1840; d. London, July 13, 1889. He studied violin with Hubert Ries, harmony with W. Gärich, and counterpoint with A.E. Grell at the Berlin Cons.; after traveling in Germany with various opera troupes as a violinist, he went to London, settling there in 1873; in 1879, he became bandmaster of the 7th (Queen's Own) Hussars. In England he often performed on the viola d'amore; publ. *The Viola d'Amour, Its Origin and History, and Art of Playing It.* He composed an operetta, *The Missing Heir,* and a serious music drama, *Mary Stuart of Fotheringay;* a Violin Concerto; songs.

Zoellner, Joseph, Sr., American violinist; b. Brooklyn, Feb. 2, 1862; d. Los Angeles, Jan. 24, 1950. He studied violin; traveled to Europe, with a prolonged stay in Brussels (1907–12), where he organized, with his 2 sons and a daughter, the Zoellner Quartet. From 1912 to 1922, they lived in N.Y.; in 1922 Zoellner founded with his children the Zoellner Cons. of Music in Los Angeles.

Zoghby, Linda, American soprano; b. Mobile, Ala., Aug. 17, 1949. She studied voice with Elena Nikolaidi at Florida State Univ.; made her professional debut at the Grant Park Festival in Chicago in 1973; subsequently sang opera in N.Y., Washington, D.C., Dallas, Santa Fe, Houston, and New Orleans. She received a critical accolade on Jan. 19, 1982, when she substituted on short notice for Teresa Stratas and sang the role of

Mimi in the Zeffirelli production of *La Bohème* at the Metropolitan Opera in N.Y. Her other roles include Pamina, Donna Elvira, and Marguerite in *Faust*.

Zoilo, Annibale, Italian composer; b. Rome, c.1537; d. Loreto, 1592. He was maestro di cappella at San Luigi dei Francesi from 1561 to 1566; at San Giovanni in Laterano from Jan. 1568 to June 1570. In 1570 he became a singer in the Papal Choir in Rome, remaining there until he left due to ill health in 1577; then was in the service of Cardinal Sirleto. After serving as maestro di cappella at Todi Cathedral (1581–84), he held that post at the Santa Casa in Loreto (from 1584). In 1577 he and Palestrina were entrusted with the revision of the Roman Gradual (*Editio Medicaea*). He composed both sacred and secular vocal works; publ. *Libro secondo de madrigali* for 4 to 5 Voices (Rome, 1563); other madrigals were publ. in contemporary collections.

BIBL.: R. Casimiri, "A. Z. (1540?–1592) e la sua famiglia: Nuovi documenti biografici," *Note d'Archivio* (Jan.–April 1940); H. Lincoln, *A. Z.: The Life and Works of a Sixteenth-century Italian Composer* (diss., Northwestern Univ., 1951).

Zöller, Karlheinz, German flutist; b. Höhr-Grenzhausen, Aug. 24, 1928. He was educated at the Frankfurt Hochschule für Musik and the Northwest German Music Academy in Detmold; in 1947 he won 1st prize in the German radio competition in Frankfurt; then was active as a recitalist and chamber player; was 1st flutist with the Berlin Phil. (1960–69). After a series of concert appearances in Europe and America, he rejoined the Berlin Phil. in 1977.

Zöllner, Carl Friedrich, German choral conductor and composer, father of **Heinrich Zöllner;** b. Mittelhausen, March 17, 1800; d. Leipzig, Sept. 25, 1860. He studied at the Thomasschule in Leipzig; became a vocal instructor, and began writing male choruses; in 1833 he founded in Leipzig a "Liedertafel" known as the Zöllner-Verein, a male choral society modeled after Zelter's Berlin organization; after Zöllner's death, several choral societies were united to form the Zöllner-Bund. Zöllner was one of the most successful German composers of partsongs for male choruses; he also wrote for mixed chorus, and songs with piano accompaniment.

BIBL.: R. Hänsch, *Der Liedermeister C.F. Z.* (Dresden, 1927).

Zöllner, Heinrich, German organist and composer; b. Öls, Silesia, May 5, 1792; d. Wandsbeck, near Hamburg, July 2, 1836. He toured Germany as an organist; in 1833, settled in Hamburg. He wrote an opera, *Kunz von Kauffungen* (Vienna, March 27, 1826); a melodrama, *Ein Uhr;* publ. masses, motets, Psalms, part-songs, organ pieces, a Piano Sonata, piano pieces, etc.

Zöllner, Heinrich, German composer and conductor, son of **Carl Friedrich Zöllner;** b. Leipzig, July 4, 1854; d. Freiburg im Breisgau, May 4, 1941. He studied at the Leipzig Cons., where his teachers were Reinecke, Jadassohn, Richter, and Wenzel (1875–77); then went to Tartu, where he was music director at the Univ.; in 1885 he went to Cologne, where he taught at the Cons. and conducted choruses. In 1890 he was engaged to lead the Deutscher Liederkranz in N.Y.; in 1898 he returned to Germany; from 1902 to 1907 he taught composition at the Leipzig Cons.; from 1907 to 1914 he was conductor at the Flemish Opera in Antwerp; subsequently settled in Freiburg.

WORKS: He wrote 10 operas, of which the following were produced: *Frithjof* (Cologne, 1884); *Die lustigen Chinesinnen* (Cologne, 1886); *Faust* (Munich, Oct. 19, 1887); *Matteo Falcone* (N.Y., 1894); *Der Überfall* (Dresden, Sept. 7, 1895); *Die versunkene Glocke* (Berlin, July 8, 1899; his best opera); *Der Schützenkönig* (Leipzig, 1903); *Zigeuner* (Stuttgart, 1912); the musical comedy *Das hölzerne Schwert* (Kassel, 1897); a great number of choral works with orch.; also 5 syms. and some chamber music.

BIBL.: E. Segnitz, "H. Z.," *20 Biographien zeitgenössischer Tonsetzer* (Leipzig, 1907).

Zolotarev, Vasili (Andreievich), eminent Russian composer and pedagogue; b. Taganrog, March 7, 1872; d. Moscow, May 25, 1964. He studied violin and music theory at the Imperial Court Chapel in St. Petersburg; from 1893 to 1897 he took composition lessons with Balakirev; then entered the St. Petersburg Cons. in the class of Rimsky-Korsakov, graduating in 1900; received the Rubinstein Prize for his cantata *Paradise and Peri.* He was instructor of violin at the Court Chapel (1897–1900); teacher of composition at the Rostov Music School (1906–8), the Moscow Cons. (1908–18), the Ekaterinodar Cons. (1918–24), the Odessa Cons. (1924–26), the Kiev Musico-Dramatic Inst. (1926–31), the Sverdlovsk Music School (1931–33), and the Minsk Cons. (1933–41). In 1955 he was awarded the Order of Lenin. Several well-known Soviet composers were his pupils, among them Polovinkin, Dankevich, and Vainberg. In his music Zolotarev continued the line of the Russian national school of composition, based on broad diatonic melos, mellifluous euphonious harmonies, and, in his operas, a resonant flow of choral singing. He publ. a manual on the fugue (Moscow, 1932; 3rd ed., 1965).

WORKS: Operas: *The Decembrists* (Moscow, Dec. 27, 1925) and *Ak-Gul*, on Uzbek themes (1942); ballet, *Lake Prince* (Minsk, Jan. 15, 1949); 7 syms.: No. 1 (1902); No. 2 (1905); No. 3 (1935); No. 4 (1936); No. 5 (1942); No. 6 (1943); No. 7 (1962); overture, *Fête villageoise; Rhapsodie hébraïque* for Orch.; symphonic suites: *Moldavian Suite* (1926); *Uzbek Suite* (1931); *Tadzhik Suite* (1932); *Belorussian Suite* (1936); Cello Concerto (1943); 6 string quartets (1899, 1902, 1907, 1912, 1916, 1945); Piano Quintet (1904); String Quintet (1904); Piano Trio (1905); Violin Sonata (1922); 2 piano sonatas (1903, 1919); many songs.

BIBL.: V. Zolotarev, *Reminiscences about My Great Pupils, Friends and Colleagues* (Moscow, 1957); S. Nisievich, *V.A. Z.* (Moscow, 1964).

Zoltán, Aladár, Rumanian composer; b. Mărtinis-Harghita, May 31, 1929; d. Tîrgu-Mureş, July 9, 1978. He studied with Jodál and Demian at the Cluj Cons. (1946–53); in 1960 he was appointed secretary of the Tîrgu-Mureş branch of the Union of Rumanian Composers, and in 1965 was elected director of the Tîrgu-Mureş Phil.

WORKS: STAGE: In Hungarian, *Biborkáne Iánya* (The Marriage; 1962); in Rumanian, *Poarta de sur* (1963); in French, *Coutumes d'hiver* (1969) and *Les "Marieurs" de Bihor* (1971); 4 cantatas; 5 *Lyrical Songs* for Tenor and Orch. (1963); *Divertissement* for 2 Clarinets and Strings (1952); 2 syms. (1961, 1971); *Dansuri de pe Mureş* for Orch. (1968); *Suite piccola* for Orch. (1970); *Introduction and Allegro* for Orch. (1974–77); *Nonet* (1953); Bassoon Sonata (1955); String Quartet (1965); *Suite piccola* for Piano (1964–69); choruses; songs.

Zopff, Hermann, German music critic and composer; b. Glogau, June 1, 1826; d. Leipzig, July 12, 1883. He studied agriculture, then music with A.B. Marx and T. Kullak at the Stern Cons. in Berlin, where he later taught theory; founded an "Opernakademie" and an "Orchesterverein" in Berlin; in 1864 he settled in Leipzig as co-ed. of the *Neue Zeitschrift für Musik*, becoming ed.-in-chief in 1868. He publ. *Ratschläge für angehende Dirigenten* (1861; 3rd ed., 1922), *Grundzüge einer Theorie der Oper* (Leipzig, 1868), and *Die Behandlung guter und schlechter Stimme im gesunden un kranken Zustande* (1878). His compositions include a symphonic poem, *Wilhelm Tell; 3 Idyllen* for Small Orch.; *Gesangsstück* for Cello and Orch.; *Asträa, oder Das Evangelium der Tat* for Solo Voices, Chorus, and Orch.; piano pieces; male choruses; songs. His 2 operas, *Makkabäus* and *Mohammed*, were publ. but not produced.

Zoras, Leonidas, Greek composer and conductor; b. Sparta, March 8, 1905; d. Athens, Dec. 22, 1987. He studied law at the Univ. of Athens; at the same time took conducting lessons with Mitropoulos, and studied composition with Kalomiris, Lavrangas, and Riadis. From 1926 to 1938 he taught music theory at the Odeon Music School in Athens; then studied conducting with Gmeindl, Schmalstich, and F. Stein and composition with Blacher, Grabner, and Hoffer at the Berlin Hochschule für

Musik (1938–40). After conducting at the Greek National Opera (1948–58), he returned to Berlin as a conductor at the Deutsche Opera and RIAS (1958–68). He was director of the Athens National Cons. from 1968. He wrote an opera, *Elektra* (1969); the ballet *Violanto* (1931); *Night Song* for Cello Solo and Chamber Orch. (1927); *Legend* for Orch. (1936); Sym. (1947); Concertino for Violin and 11 Woodwind Instruments (1950); String Quartet (1969); Violin Sonata (1950); numerous piano pieces, choruses, and songs.

Zorn, John, innovative American composer and instrumentalist; b. N.Y., Sept. 2, 1953. He plays saxophone, keyboards, duck calls, and other semi-demi-musical instruments in dense, loud aural canvases that have been compared to the works of Jackson Pollock (and also to an elephant trapped in barbed wire). After a brief college "stint" in St. Louis and world travels, he became an active contributor to the downtown music scene in N.Y.; performed with various avant-garde and rock musicians, including pianist Wayne Horvitz, drummer David Moss, and the Kronos Quartet. His *The Big Gundown* (1986) uses the music of film composer Ennio Morricone (b. 1928) as material to be freely distorted and reworked. His major recordings include *Archery* (1981), *Cobra* (group improvisation; 1986), *A Classic Guide to Strategy, Vol. I* (solo with tape), *News for Lulu* for Trio (1987), and *Spillane* (1988).

Zorzor, Ştefan, Rumanian composer; b. Oradea, April 4, 1932. He studied with Chirescu, Negrea, I. Dumitrescu, Ciortea, Andricu, Olah, and Mendelsohn at the Bucharest Cons. (1951–52; 1956–61); then occupied teaching positions in Bucharest.

WORKS: *Ţara mea* (My Country), cantata for Female Chorus and Small Orch. (1956); Piano Sonata (1959); 3 string quartets (1960, 1962, 1968); Violin Sonata (1963); Concerto for Orch. (1965); *Nocturne* for Orch. (1966); Wind Quintet (1968); *Heteroquintet* for Flute, Violin, Cello, Piano, and Percussion (1969); *Circulara*, experimental music for 5 Different Instruments (1969); *Pièces diverses* for Piano (1967–72); choruses.

Zottmayr, Georg, distinguished German bass; b. Munich, Jan. 24, 1869; d. Dresden, Dec. 11, 1941. He studied in Munich; began his career primarily as a concert singer. In 1906 he made his operatic debut with the Vienna Court Opera; later was a member of the German Theater in Prague (1908–10). In 1910 he joined the Dresden Court (later State) Opera, where he enjoyed a career of great distinction. He was considered one of the outstanding Wagnerians of his time; among his famous roles were King Marke, Hunding, Gurnemanz, Pogner, and Daland.

Zouhar, Zdeněk, Czech composer; b. Kotvrdovice, Feb. 8, 1927. He studied with Jan Kunc (1948–50) and A. Moyzes (1950–51) in Bratislava; also studied composition with Schaefer at the Brno Academy of Music, and completed his education at the Univ. of Brno (Ph.D., 1962). He was head of the music dept. of the Brno Univ. library (1953–61); in 1962, was appointed to the faculty of the Janáček Music Academy in Brno. In his music he makes multifarious use of modern techniques, including a fairly orthodox dodecaphony.

WORKS: *Spring Suite* for 3 Violins (1949); *Prelude and Epilogue* for Cello (1949); *Aulularia*, suite for Chamber Ensemble (1956); *Partita* for Organ (1956); *Prelude* for 2 Pianos (1957); *Midnight Mass* for Soloists, Chorus, Orch., and Organ (1957); *151*, music for Wind Quintet (1958); *Sportovní stránky* (Sports Pages), suite for Orch. (1959); Trio for Flute, Clarinet, and Bass Clarinet (1961); *3 Studies* for 4 Horns (1963); *Divertimento* for 4 Winds and Percussion (1965); *Variations* for Oboe and Piano (1965); *Music for Strings* (1966); 2 string quartets (1966, 1972); *Symphonic Triptych* (1967; Brno Radio, Nov. 29, 1967); *Music for Wind Quintet* (1968); *Triple Concerto* for Clarinet, Trumpet, Trombone, and Orch. (1970); chamber radio opera, *Metamorphosis* (1971).

Zschocher, Johann, noted German piano pedagogue; b. Leipzig, May 16, 1821. d. there, Jan. 6, 1897. He was a pupil of Iwan Knorr, T. Kullak, Henselt, and Liszt. In 1846 he founded the Zschocher'sches Musik-Inst. in Leipzig, which became a flourishing music school.

Zsolt, Nándor, Hungarian violinist, conductor, and composer; b. Esztergom, May 12, 1887; d. Budapest, June 24, 1936. He studied violin with Hubay and composition with Koessler at the Budapest Academy of Music; in 1908–9, was concertmaster of the Queen's Hall Orch. in London, and also active as a chamber-music player until being interned as an enemy alien in 1914; returned to Budapest in 1919 as prof. of violin at the Academy of Music; in 1930 he founded the Budapest Chamber Orch.; from 1934 he was conductor of the Debrecen Phil. He wrote a Sym. (1918), a Violin Concerto (1906), a Piano Quintet (1908), various pieces for violin and piano, and songs.

BIBL.: C. Scott, "N. Z.," *Monthly Musical Record* (1915).

Zubiaurre (y Urionabarrenechea), Valentí, Spanish composer; b. Villa de Garay, Feb. 13, 1837; d. Madrid, Jan. 13, 1914. He was a chorister at Bilbao; at the age of 16 he undertook a voyage to South America; he returned to Spain in 1866, and took music lessons with Hilarión Eslava at the Madrid Cons. He wrote a considerable number of sacred works; then turned to opera; received 1st national prize with his opera *Fernando el Emplazado* (Madrid, May 12, 1871). In 1875 he was named 2nd maestro at the Royal Chapel in Madrid, and in 1878 succeeded Eslava as 1st maestro; in the same year he was appointed a prof. at the Madrid Cons. His 2nd opera, *Ledia*, was produced with considerable success in Madrid, on April 22, 1877. He also composed several zarzuelas; a Sym.; a potpourri of Basque folk songs; choruses.

Zucca, Mana. See **Mana-Zucca.**

Zuccalmaglio, Anton Wilhelm Florentin von, German collector of folk songs and writer on music; b. Waldbröl, April 12, 1803; d. Nachrodt, near Grüna, Westphalia, March 23, 1869. The son of a physician who was a musical amateur, he learned music at home; pursued academic studies in Mulheim am Rhein, Cologne, and the Univ. of Heidelberg; contributed to the *Neue Zeitschrift für Musik* during Schumann's editorship, under the pseudonyms Wilhelm von Waldbrühl and Dorfküster Wedel; publ. 2 collections of folk songs, in 1829 and 1836 (with E. Baumstark); then brought out (with A. Kretzschmer) the important compilation *Deutsche Volkslieder mit ihren Originalweisen* (2 vols., 1838, 1840; reprint, Hildesheim, 1969). However, these songs are only partly authentic; a few melodies were composed by Zuccalmaglio himself; others were combined from various sources; the texts were frequently rearranged. Brahms made use of the collection for his arrangements of German folk songs.

BIBL.: M. Friedlaender, "Z. und das Volkslied," *Jahrbuch der Bibliothek Peters* (1918); W. Wiora, "Die Herkunft der Melodien in Kretzschmers und Z.s Sammlung," *Jahrbuch für Volksliedforschung* (1941; rev. and publ. as *Die rheinisch-bergischen Melodien bei Z. und Brahms*, Bad Godesberg, 1953).

Zuckerkandl, Victor, Austrian musicologist and esthetician; b. Vienna, July 2, 1896; d. Locarno, April 25, 1965. He studied at the Univ. of Vienna (Ph.D., 1927); conducted in Vienna and in other cities; also was a music critic for Berlin newspapers (1927–33) and taught music theory and appreciation courses in Vienna (1934–38). He went to the U.S. to teach at Wellesley College (1940–42); during World War II, he worked as a machinist in a Boston defense plant (1942–44). He then taught music theory at the New School for Social Research in N.Y. (1946–48). A grant from the American Philosophical Soc. enabled him to develop a course for non-musicians on the nature and significance of tonal music; after he joined the faculty of St. John's College in 1948, this course was adopted as a general requirement. He retired to Ascona in 1964, lecturing at the Jung Inst. and the Eranos Conference in Zürich before his death. His books represent a synthesis of music theory (mostly following Schenker's analytic theories; music cognition; and intellectual metaphysics); they include *Sound and Symbol: Music and the External World* (1956), *The Sense of Music* (1959), and *Man the Musician* (1973).

Zuckert, Leon, Russian-born Canadian composer; b. Poltava, May 4, 1904. He emigrated to Canada in 1929; played viola in several orchs. in Canada and the U.S.; was principal violinist and assistant conductor of the Halifax Sym. Orch. (1963–65; 1967–69). He is autodidactic as a composer.

WORKS: *My Canadian Travels* for Orch. (1938); 2 syms. (1948–50; 1959–62); *Quetico,* symphonic suite (1957); *Oriental Romance* for Small Orch. (1960); *Dniepr,* cantata (1961); *Song in Brass* for Voice, Viola, and Orch. without Woodwinds (1964); *Divertimento Orientale* for Oboe and String Orch. (1965); *2 Moods in 1* for String Orch. (1968); *My Paintings* for String Orch. (1969); *Impressions of Teneriffe,* symphonic suite (1970); *Fantasia on Ukrainian Themes* for Orch. (1973); *In the Gleam of Northern Lights,* choreographic oratorio (1974); *2 Spanish Meditations* for Orch. or Piano (1975); 3 string quartets (1965, 1971, 1972); *Little Prince in Montreal* for Wind Quintet (1968); *Psychedelic Suite* for Brass Quintet (1968); *Short Suite* for Trumpet or Clarinet or Viola, and Piano (1974); *Suite* for Solo Bassoon (1975); Concerto for Bassoon and String Orch. (1976); *Elegy* for Orch. (1977).

Zuelli, Guglielmo, Italian composer; b. Reggio Emilia, Oct. 20, 1859; d. Milan, Oct. 8, 1941. He studied with A. Busi and L. Mancinelli in Bologna; after teaching and conducting in various provincial towns, he was director of the Palermo Cons. (1894–1911), the Parma Cons. (1911–29), and the Liceo Musicale of Alessandria, Piedmont (1929–33). He publ. *Gioacchino Rossini: Pagine segrete* (Bologna, 1922).

WORKS: Opera, *La Fata del Nord* (Milan, May 4, 1884; Sonzogno prize); opera-ballet, *Il Profeta di Korassan; Inno alla notte* for Solo Voices, Chorus, and Orch.; 2 syms.; *Un saluto al mare,* symphonic suite (its 3rd movement, *Festa delle sirene,* became extremely popular as a separate piece); *Il canto del Coaro Romagnuolo* for Orch.; String Quartet; minor pieces for strings; fugues for organ; songs; etc.

Zukerman, Eugenia (née Rich); American flutist; b. Cambridge, Mass., Sept. 25, 1944. She studied flute with Julius Baker at the Juilliard School of Music in N.Y. (1964–66). In 1970 she won the Young Concert Artists Audition, which resulted in her formal recital debut at Town Hall in N.Y. in 1971; subsequently appeared as a soloist with orchs., as a recitalist, and as a chamber music player. From 1968 to 1985 she was married to **Pinchas Zukerman,** with whom she often appeared in concerts. She contributed various articles on music to newspapers and journals and appeared as a commentator on music on television; authored a novel deceptively titled *Deceptive Cadence* (1980).

Zukerman, Pinchas, outstanding Israeli violinist, violist, and conductor; b. Tel Aviv, July 16, 1948. He began to study music with his father, taking up the violin at age 6; he then enrolled at the Cons. in Tel Aviv, where he studied with Ilona Feher. With the encouragement of Isaac Stern and Pablo Casals, he became a scholarship student at the Juilliard School of Music in N.Y., where he studied with Ivan Galamian (1961–67). In 1967 he shared 1st prize in the Leventritt Competition in N.Y. with Kyung-Wha Chung, and then launched a brilliant career as a soloist with the major American and European orchs. He also appeared as both violinist and violist in recitals with Isaac Stern and Itzhak Perlman. He subsequently devoted part of his time to conducting, appearing as a guest conductor with the N.Y. Phil., Philadelphia Orch., Boston Sym. Orch., Los Angeles Phil., and many others. From 1980 to 1987 he was music director of the St. Paul (Minn.) Chamber Orch. He was married to **Eugenia Zukerman** from 1968 to 1985; then married the American actress Tuesday Weld. His performances as a violinist are distinguished by their innate emotional élan and modern virtuoso technique.

BIBL.: B. Schwarz, *Great Masters of the Violin* (N.Y., 1983); J. von Rhein, "Z. in St. Paul: A Musical and Personal Metamorphosis," *Ovation* (Dec. 1985).

Zukofsky, Paul, remarkable American violinist and talented conductor; b. N.Y., Oct. 22, 1943. Reared in an acutely intellec-

tual environment (his father was a poet who experimented in highly complex verbal forms), he began playing the violin at the age of 4 on a quarter-size instrument; when he was 7 he began lessons with Ivan Galamian; was soloist with the New Haven (Conn.) Sym. Orch. at the age of 8, and made his Carnegie Hall recital debut in N.Y. when he was 13. At 16 he entered the Juilliard School of Music. From his earliest years he was fascinated by ultramodern music and developed maximal celerity, dexterity, and alacrity in manipulating special techniques, in effect transforming the violin into a multimedia instrument beyond its normal capacities. In 1969 he inaugurated in N.Y. a concert series, Music for the Twentieth Century Violin, performing works often requiring acrobatic coordination. His repertoire includes all 4 violin sonatas by Charles Ives, the violin concertos by William Schuman and Roger Sessions, *Capriccio* by Penderecki, the solo violin works of John Cage, etc. As a violin instructor, he held the post of Creative Associate at the Buffalo Center of the Creative and Performing Arts; also taught at the Berkshire Music Center in Tanglewood and at the New England Cons. of Music. In later years he became active as a conductor; served as conductor of the Contemporary Chamber Ensemble at the Juilliard School (from 1984), and also was director of chamber music activities there (1987–89). In 1970 his father publ. a novel, *Little,* dealing with the trials and triumphs of a violin *wunderkind.*

Zumpe, Herman, German conductor and composer; b. Oppach, April 9, 1850; d. Munich, Sept. 4, 1903. He studied in Bautzen and Leipzig. In 1872 he joined Wagner at Bayreuth, aiding in the preparation of the performances of *Der Ring des Nibelungen;* then conducted opera in Salzburg, Würzburg, Madgeburg, Frankfurt, and Hamburg. After some years spent in teaching and composing, he was appointed court conductor in Stuttgart in 1891; in 1895, was called to Munich to become conductor of the Kaim Orch.; then was court conductor in Schwerin (1897–1900); returned to Munich in 1900 as Generalmusikdirektor.

WORKS: Opera, *Anahna* (Berlin, 1881); operettas: *Farinelli* (Hamburg, 1886); *Karin* (Hamburg, 1888); *Polnische Wirtschaft* (Hamburg, 1889); overtures; songs. Two operas were performed posthumously: *Sawitri* (completed by Rössler; Schwerin, Sept. 8, 1907) and *Das Gespenst von Horodin* (Hamburg, 1910). Other works include a Sym. (1868), 2 string quartets (1871, 1891), piano pieces, and many vocal works.

BIBL.: E. von Possart et al., *H. Z.: Persönliche Erinnerungen nebst Mitteilungen aus seinen Tagebuchblättern und Briefen* (Munich, 1905).

Zumsteeg, Johann Rudolf, German composer and conductor; b. Sachsenflur, Odenwald, Jan. 10, 1760; d. Stuttgart, Jan. 27, 1802. As a pupil at the Carlsschule (near Stuttgart), he was a classmate of Schiller. He studied cello with Eberhard Malterre and cello and composition with Agostino Poli in Stuttgart; in 1781 he became solo cellist in the Court Orch. there; served as music master at the Carlsschule (1785–94); in 1791 he was made director of German music at the Stuttgart Court Theater, and in 1793 he succeeded Poli as court Konzertmeister, where he championed the works of Mozart. He produced 8 operas at Stuttgart, of which the best was *Die Geisterinsel,* after Shakespeare's *The Tempest* (Nov. 7, 1798); his other stage works included *Zalaor* (March 2, 1787), *Tamira* (June 13, 1788), *Das Pfauenfest* (Feb. 24, 1801), and *Ebondocani* (Dec. 8, 1803). He also wrote a Sym., 2 overtures, 10 cello concertos, 2 flute concertos, a Concerto for 2 Flutes, chamber music, and choral works, including some 30 cantatas. But it is chiefly as the precursor of Loewe and Schubert in the composition of art songs that he is historically important; he wrote 20 ballades for Solo Voice with Piano Accompaniment, including settings for Schiller's *Maria Stuart,* Bürger's *Lenore,* Goethe's *Colma,* etc.

BIBL.: I. Arnold, *J.R. Z.: Seine kurze Biographie* (Erfurt, 1810; with a list of works); L. Landshoff, *J.R. Z. (1760–1802): Ein Beitrag zur Geschichte des Liedes und der Ballade* (diss., Univ. of Berlin, 1902); A. Sandberger, "J.R. Z. und Franz Schubert," *Ausgewahlte Aufsätze zur Musikgeschichte,* I (Munich, 1921); F. Szymichowski, *J.R. Z. als Komponist von Balladen und Monodien* (Stuttgart, 1932); G. Maier, *Die Lieder J.R. Z.s und ihr Verhältnis zu Schubert* (Göppingen, 1971).

Zundel, John, German organist and hymn writer; b. Hochdorf, Dec. 10, 1815; d. Cannstadt, July 1882. He was an organist and bandmaster in St. Petersburg; in 1847, went to America, where he became organist at the Central Methodist Episcopal Church in N.Y. He went back to Germany in 1877. In America he ed. the *Monthly Choir and Organ Journal;* was also one of the compilers, in association with Henry Ward Beecher, of the *Plymouth Collection* (1855). He wrote the celebrated hymn *Love Divine,* also known as *Beecher* or *Zundel;* it is included in *Zundel's Christian Heart Songs* (1870).

Zupko, Ramon, American composer; b. Pittsburgh, Nov. 14, 1932. He studied composition with Persichetti and piano with Gordon Stanley at the Juilliard School of Music in N.Y. (M.S., 1957); pursued his training on a Fulbright scholarship with Schiske at the Vienna Academy of Music (1958–59); subsequently studied electronic music at Columbia Univ. and with Koenig at the Univ. of Utrecht. He taught theory, and was director of the electronic music studio at the Chicago Musical College of Roosevelt Univ. (1967–71); in 1971 he joined the faculty of Western Michigan Univ. in Kalamazoo, where he served as a prof. of composition and as director of its electronic music studio and new music ensemble. His highly advanced compositions, beginning in 1965, are the only ones for which he encourages performance.

WORKS: *Elegy* for String Orch. (1957); *Ballade* for Orch. (1957); *Introduction and Bagatelle* for 10 Instruments (1957); ballet, *The Lottery* (1957); Piano Trio (1958); Piano Sonata (1959–60); *Prologue, Aria and Dance* for Horn and String Orch. (1961); *Variations* for Orch. (1961); *This Is the Garden* for Chorus, Strings, Solo Winds, and Percussion (1962); Violin Concerto (1962; winner of 1st prize in the 1965 City of Trieste International Composition Contest); ballet, *Gilgamesh* (1963); *Centroids* for Orch. (1963); *Reflexions* for 8 Instruments (1964); *La Guerre* for Soprano, Piano, Vibraphone, Clarinet, and 2 Percussion Groups (1965); *Conversions* for Wind Band and Percussion (1966); *Translucents* for String Orch. (1967); *Tangents* for 18 Brasses (1967); multimedia score, *3rd Planet from the Sun,* for Dancers, Tape, Musicians, Film, and Slides (1969–70); *Emulations* for Piano and Synthesizer (1969); *Radiants* for Orch. (1971); *Trichromes* for Winds, Percussion, and Tape (1973); *Masques* for Piano and Brass Quintet (1973); *Fixations* for Piano, Violin, Cello, and Tape (1974); Bicentennial multimedia musical theater, *Proud Music of the Storm,* for Orch., 2 Bands, Chorus, Dancers, Films, Slides, and Tape, with costumes and sets (1975–76; Western Michigan Univ., Kalamazoo, Dec. 4, 1976); *Fluxus I* for Tape (1977); *Windsongs,* concerto for Piano and Orch. (1979); *Noosphere* for String Quartet (1980); *Life Dances* for Orch. (1981); *Canti terrae* for Orch. (1982); *Earth and Sky,* sym. for Band (1984); *Blue Roots,* sym. (1986); *Chorale* for Brass Quintet (1989); pieces for Symphonic Band; choruses.

Zur Mühlen, Raimund von, German tenor and pedagogue; b. Livonia, Nov. 10, 1854; d. Steyning, Sussex, Dec. 9, 1931. He began his training at the Berlin Hochschule für Musik; then studied with Stockhausen in Frankfurt and Bussine in Paris; then took a special course with Clara Schumann, who instructed him in the interpretation of songs by Schumann and Schubert; this gave him the foundation of his career. He had his greatest success in England, where he lived from 1905 until his death. It was he who introduced into London the "song recital" (*Liederabend;* programs devoted exclusively to songs). He was also a fine teacher. **BIBL.:** D. von Zur Mühlen, *Der Sänger R. v.Z.M.* (Hannover, 1969).

Zur Nieden, Albrecht, German choral conductor and composer; b. Emmerich, March 6, 1819; d. Duisburg, April 14, 1873. He studied theology in Bonn, and music with F.

Schneider at Dessau. In 1850 he settled in Duisburg as a choral conductor. He wrote the "lyrico-dramatic song" *Die Sage von der Martinswand* for Solo Voices, Chorus, and Orch., and 2 more works of a similar nature, *Der blinde König* and *Das Grab im Busento;* also a *Deutscher Marsch* for Piano, 4-hands; songs.

Zuschneid, Karl, German choral conductor and composer; b. Oberglogau, Silesia, May 29, 1854; d. Weimar, Aug. 1, 1926. He studied piano and composition at the Stuttgart Cons.; occupied various posts as a choral conductor and teacher in Göttingen (1879–89), Minden (1889–97), and Erfurt (1897–1907); was director of the Hochschule für Musik in Mannheim; retired in 1917. He publ. *Theoretisch-praktische Klavierschule* and *Methodischer Leitfaden für den Klavierunterricht* (2nd ed., Berlin, 1947).

WORKS: Chorus and Orch.: *Hermann der Befreier; Lenzfahrt; Sängergebet; Deutschlands Erwachen; Die Zollern und das Reich; Unter den Sternen;* men's choruses; *Konzertstück* for Violin and Orch.; piano pieces; songs.

Zuth, Josef, Austrian guitarist and musicologist; b. Fischern, near Karlsbad, Nov. 24, 1879; d. Vienna, Aug. 30, 1932. He began to study music late in life; studied guitar with R. Batka; attended classes in musicology under Adler and Koczirz at the Univ. of Vienna (Ph.D., 1919, with the diss. *Simon Molitor und die wiener Gitarristik*). He taught guitar at the Volksschule Urania in Vienna (from 1919) and ed. (from 1921) the *Zeitschrift für die Gitarre* (in 1927 the title was changed to *Musik im Haus*); ed. many works for the guitar; publ. several guitar manuals: *R. Batkas Vorschule des Gitarren- und Lautenspiels* (1919); *Das künstlerische Gitarrenspiel* (1920); *Die Gitarre, Spezialstudien auf theoretischer Grundlage* (6 parts; 1920); *F. Carullis Gitarrenschule* (10 parts; 1921); *Volkstümliche Gitarrenschule* (1922); *Handbuch der Laute und Gitarre* (Vienna, 1926–28).

Zverev, Nikolai, noted Russian piano pedagogue; b. Volokalamsk, 1832; d. Moscow, Oct. 12, 1893. He was a student of Alexander Dubuc in Moscow and Henselt in St. Petersburg; also took harmony lessons with Tchaikovsky. He established in Moscow a music boarding school for young pianists; among these inmates were Rachmaninoff and Siloti. Scriabin also took piano lessons with Zverev, although he did not lodge in his music school. From 1870 to his death, Zverev taught piano at the Moscow Cons. Zverev was highly esteemed as a pedagogue, and was one of the most prominent representatives of the Russian pianistic method, which emphasized songful melody and freedom of hand movement.

Zvonař, Joseph Leopold, Czech organist, composer, and teacher; b. Kublov, near Prague, Jan. 22, 1824; d. Prague, Nov. 23, 1865. He studied at the Prague School for Organists, and taught there from 1844; also served as a church organist. He publ. the 1st treatise on harmony in the Czech language; contributed articles on Czech music to various publications; publ. a valuable collection of choral arrangements of national songs, *Hudební památky české* (4 vols., 1862–64); composed *Der Ritt zum Elfenstein* for Solo Voices, Chorus, and Orch.; a Requiem; piano pieces (*Impromptu, Loreley,* etc.); men's choruses; songs. His opera *Záboj* remains unperformed.

Zweers, Bernard, Dutch composer; b. Amsterdam, May 18, 1854; d. there, Dec. 9, 1924. He studied at the Amsterdam Cons., and later in Leipzig with Jadassohn; returning to the Netherlands, he became a prof. of theory at the Amsterdam Cons. (1895). He wrote 3 syms.; *Kroningscantate* for Soprano, Tenor, Chorus, and Orch.; *St. Nicolaasfeest,* children's cantata; *Kosmos* (Psalm 104) for Chorus and Orch.; *Ons Hollandsch* for Men's Chorus and Orch.; church music; songs. **BIBL.:** H. Rutters, "B. Z.," *Mens en Melodie* (Dec. 1949).

Zweig, Fritz, Bohemian-American conductor; b. Olmütz, Sept. 8, 1893; d. Los Angeles, Feb. 28, 1984. He studied theory with Schoenberg in Vienna; in 1913, was appointed choral coach at the Mannheim National Theater; in 1919, became assistant conductor at Barmen-Elberfeld; in 1923, became a conductor at the Volksoper in Berlin; and in 1927 was appointed to the conducting staff of the Städtische Oper in Berlin. With the usurpation of power by the Nazis in 1933, Zweig went to Prague, where he conducted at the German Theater from 1934 to 1938. When Prague, too, was captured by the Nazis, he went to Paris; after the fall of France in 1940, he emigrated to America. In 1947 he settled in Hollywood as a private music teacher.

Zwilich, Ellen Taaffe, remarkable American composer; b. Miami, April 30, 1939. She studied composition with John Boda and violin with Richard Burgin at Florida State Univ. (B.M., 1956; M.M., 1962); then moved to N.Y., where she continued her violin studies with Ivan Galamian. After playing in the American Sym. Orch. there (1965–72), she enrolled at the Juilliard School in N.Y., and had semi-weekly sessions with Roger Sessions and Elliott Carter; she was the 1st woman to receive a D.M.A. in composition from that school (1975). In 1983 she received the Pulitzer prize in music for her Sym. No. 1 (originally titled *3 Movements for Orchestra*), first performed in N.Y. on May 5, 1982. There are not many composers in the modern world who possess the lucky combination of writing music of substance and at the same time exercising an immediate appeal to mixed audiences. Ravel was one, and so, in a quite different way, were Bartók and Prokofiev. Zwilich offers this happy combination of purely technical excellence and a distinct power of communication, while a poetic element pervades the melody, harmony, and counterpoint of her creations. This combination of qualities explains the frequency and variety of prizes awarded her from various sources: the Elizabeth Sprague Coolidge Chamber Music Prize; a gold medal at the 26th Annual International Composition Competition in Vercelli, Italy; N.E.A. grants; a Guggenheim fellowship (1980–81); the Ernst von Dohnányi Citation; and an award from the American Academy and Inst. of Arts and Letters (1984). Conductors in America, Europe, and Japan are also eager to program her works. Commissions are galore, and festivals of her works of various forms and sizes are not lacking. At his concert with the N.Y. Phil. in Leningrad during his 1988 tour of Russia, Zubin Mehta presented the world premiere of her *Symbolon*—symbolically, on a "white night" (June 1) of the ci-devant capital of the former Russian empire.

WORKS: STAGE: *Tanzspiel*, ballet (1987; N.Y., April 27, 1988). **ORCH.:** *Symposium* (1973; N.Y., Jan. 31, 1975); *Passages* for Soprano and Orch. (1982; also for Soprano, Flute, Clarinet, Violin, Viola, Cello, Piano, and Percussion, 1981); Sym. No. 1 (originally entitled *3 Movements for Orchestra*; N.Y., May 5, 1982; won the Pulitzer prize in music in 1983); *Prologue and Variations* for String Orch. (1983); *Celebrations* (Indianapolis, Oct. 12, 1984); *Concerto grosso 1985* (1985); Sym. No. 2, *Cello Symphony* (San Francisco, Nov. 13, 1985); Piano Concerto (Detroit, June 26, 1986); *Images* for 2 Pianos and Orch. (1987); *Symbolon* (Leningrad, June 1, 1988); Trombone Concerto (1988; Chicago, Feb. 2, 1989); Sym. for Winds (Tallahassee, Fla., March 3, 1989); Flute Concerto (1990); Oboe Concerto (Cleveland, Jan. 17, 1991). **CHAMBER:** *Sonata in 3 Movements* for Violin and Piano (1973–74); String Quartet (1974; Boston, Oct. 31, 1975); *Clarino Quartet* for 4 Trumpets or Clarinets (1977); *Chamber Symphony* for Flute, Clarinet, Violin, Viola, Cello, and Piano (Boston, Nov. 30, 1979); String Trio (1982); *Divertimento* for Flute, Clarinet, Violin, and Cello (1983); *Intrada* for Flute, Clarinet, Violin, Cello, and Piano (1983); Double Quartet for Strings (N.Y., Oct. 21, 1984); Chamber Concerto for Trumpet and 5 Players (1984; Pittsburgh,

May 6, 1985); Piano Trio (1987); *Praeludium* for Organ (Philadelphia, May 1, 1988); Clarinet Quintet (1990). **VOCAL:** *Einsame Nacht*, song cycle for Baritone and Piano, after Hesse (1971); *Im Nebel* for Contralto and Piano, after Hesse (1972); *Trompeten (Trumpets)* for Soprano and Piano, after Georg Trakl (1974); *Emlékezet* for Soprano and Piano, after Sándor Petöfi (1978); *Passages* for Soprano, Flute, Clarinet, Violin, Viola, Cello, Piano, and Percussion (1981; also for Soprano and Orch., 1982).

BIBL.: *Current Biography* (Jan. 1986); P. Moor, "E.T. Z.," *Musical America* (March 1989).

Zwintscher, Bruno, German pianist and pedagogue; b. Ziegenhain, May 15, 1838; d. Oberlössnitz, near Dresden, March 4, 1905. He studied piano with Julius Otto in Dresden and with Moscheles in Leipzig; also took lessons with Plaidy. He subsequently taught piano at the Leipzig Cons. (1875–96); then settled in Dresden, where he became a successful piano teacher. He publ. the manual *Klavier-Technik*, which became extremely successful; it was also publ. in Eng. under the title *Technical Exercises Systematically*. He further publ. *Musikalische Verzierungen*, which contains practical exercises and theoretical notations pertaining to the proper performance of ornamentation.

Zwyssig, Alberich (actually, **Joseph),** Swiss composer; b. Bauen, Nov. 17, 1808; d. Mehrerau, Nov. 18, 1854. He entered the order of the Cistercians in 1826, giving up his real name, **Joseph,** for the monastic name Alberich; he was Kapellmeister in the monasteries of Wettingen, Zug, Wurmbach, and (shortly before his death) Mehrerau. His *Schweizer Psalm* for Men's Chorus a cappella (1841) attained great popularity, and in 1961 it was named as a *pro tempore* national anthem of Switzerland. He further composed many sacred and secular choruses, and church music with organ accompaniment.

BIBL.: B. Widmann, *A. Z. als Komponist* (Bregenz, 1905); H. Meng, *A. Z., 1808–1854; Gedenkschrift* (Wettingen, 1954).

Zykan, Otto M., Austrian pianist and composer; b. Vienna, April 29, 1935. He studied piano and composition at the Vienna Academy of Music; in 1958 won 1st prize at the Darmstadt Competition for young pianists, and started on a successful concert career, specializing in modern music. His own compositions reveal a strong influence of Anton von Webern, but he does not exclude tonal, and even triadic, combinations, and accepts formal periodicity in structure.

WORKS: Sonata for Cello and Piano (1958); String Quartet (1958); Piano Concerto (1958); *Kryptomnemie* for Winds, Percussion, and Piano (1963); *Kammermusik* for Chamber Ensemble (1965); *Schön der Reihe nach,* ballet (1966); *Kurze Anweisung* for Orch. (1969); *Miles Smiles,* chamber music (1970); *Lehrstück am Beispiel Schönbergs,* music theater (1974); *Symphonie der heilen Welt,* scenic concerto (1977); Trio for Violin (1977); *Ausgesucht Freundliches,* concerto for 2 Soloists, Chorus, and Orch. (1979); *Kunst kommt von Gönnon,* opera (1980); Cello Concerto (1982); *Auszählreim,* opera (1986).

Zylis-Gara, Teresa, Polish soprano; b. Landvarov, Jan. 23, 1935. She studied voice in Lodz; in 1956 she made her debut as Halka in Katowice; after singing in various Polish music centers, she appeared in Oberhausen, Dortmund, Düsseldorf, Vienna, and Salzburg. On Dec. 17, 1968, she made her Metropolitan Opera debut in N.Y. as Elvira in *Don Giovanni;* she sang there in subsequent seasons with much success; also made appearances as a concert artist. Among her finest roles were Poppea, Fiordiligi, Anna Bolena, and the Marschallin.

Photo by James Arkatov